# NAVE'S STUDY BIBLE

Revised and Expanded Edition

KING JAMES VERSION

BROADMAN PRESS
Nashville, Tennessee

ISBN: 0-8054-1135-6

Item Number: 4211-35

*Printed in the United States of America*

# Preface

Many twentieth-century Christians still maintain that the Authorized (or King James) Version of the Bible is the best all-around English version of the Bible. The Authorized Version is beautiful not only from a literary viewpoint, but also from a perspective that attaches importance to the reverent handling of God's inerrant Word on the part of the translators. The editors and publisher of this *Revised and Expanded Edition* of the famous *Nave's Study Bible* believe that in the King James Version we have a heritage worth preserving.

To promote intensive and thorough study of God's Word, several valuable features have been added to the original edition: a Glossary of words peculiar to the King James Version, Doctrinal Outlines with Scriptural Indexes, an Old Testament-New Testament Cross Reference Index, a comprehensive Geographical Gazeteer, and the latest full-color Hammond maps. The addition of these helpful study aids helps to make this new edition one of the most useable King James study Bibles ever published.

Thorough acquaintance with the many features of this edition *of Nave's Study Bible* will aid you in your in-depth study of God's Word. This can be achieved by studying the contents page, the Helpful Hints section, and the introductory statements that precede many of the new features.

# Contents

# Principal Features

(New features are indicated by color.)

- The King James (Authorized) Version.
- Alternate translations: American Revised Version and/or English Revised Version.
- Pronunciation aids for difficult words, placed in the Scriptural text.
- Chapter summaries at the beginning of each chapter.
- More than 80,000 topical notes in the margins.
- Marginal notes connecting related verses in both the Old and New Testaments.
- Footnotes which exhaustively cover all Scriptural subjects.
- Index to all footnotes combined with a concordance.
- Outline and Index on The Sovereignty of God.
- Outline and Index on The Trinity and the Covenant of Grace.
- Old Testament-New Testament Cross Reference Index.
- Glossary of Archaic Words and Phrases.
- Tables of Weights and Measures.
- Revised chronology.
- Geographical Gazetteer.
- Atlas of Bible maps.

# Helpful Hints

## ALTERNATE TRANSLATIONS

Where the translation in one of the Revised Versions differs essentially from that of the King James (Authorized) Version, the alternate reading is noted in the margin. You will be alerted to an alternate translation by a small superior numeral preceding the word or phrase ([1]), directing you to the alternate reading in the margin. If the American Revised Version agrees with the English Revised Version, the word or phrase will simply be preceded by the letters *R.V.* Where the American Revised Version differs from the English Revised Version, the American Committee's rendering is given preference. In such cases the reading in the margin is preceded by the abbreviation *Am. R.V.*

In certain instances where the alternate reading in the Revised Versions was especially helpful in clarifying the text, it is not preceded by any abbreviation, but simply by the word *Or.*

When the Revised Versions omit a verse or an essential part of a verse in the King James Version, this fact is noted in the margin, but the subjects in such omitted passages are footnoted as usual, without regard to such omission.

## ABBREVIATIONS, PUNCTUATION, AND PRONUNCIATION

Immediately following these Helpful Hints is a one-page chart of easily interpreted abbreviations, punctuation style and a pronunciation key. Knowing the location of the pronunciation guide (p. xii) will enable you to turn to it quickly when you come to a name in the Bible that is difficult to pronounce.

## MARGINAL NOTES

More than eighty thousand subject annotations are printed in the margins, opposite the passages from which they were gleaned. The subject listings and the

a system of chain references that relate a passage of the Bible concerned with a certain subject to every other passage dealing with the same subject.

Consulting the first verse in the Bible will help you to understand and use this valuable feature of the *Nave's Study Bible.* First, note the superior lowercase letters preceding each of the following words: [a]*beginning,* [b]*God,* [c]*created,* [d]*heaven,* and [e]*earth.* The superior letters direct you to five topics or subjects in the margin opposite Genesis 1:1; (a) Time; (b) God, creator; (c) Creation, beginning of; (d) Heavens, physical; (e) Earth, created. Following each of these entries in the margin is a Scripture reference directing you to another verse or passage in the Bible concerned with the same subject, and also an extensive footnote listing many additional passages. For another example you may want to consult Matthew 5:3. In that verse you will find seven superior letters, each referring you to a subject in the margin and its accompanying Scripture reference that, in turn, will refer you to another Bible verse concerned with the same subject and a footnote.

The marginal notes not only serve as chain references, but frequently also as a very brief commentary.

In addition to the subject annotations in the margins you will find notes referring to verses connecting them to related verse in both the Old and New Testaments.

## FOOTNOTES

All footnotes in the *Nave's Study Bible* concern the subjects developed in the marginal notes. Each footnote appears on a page where the subject is prominent in a Scriptural passage on that page. An asterisk (*), a dagger (†), or another typographic symbol in the Scripture text will direct you to the footnote. Obviously, some subjects are discussed many places in Scripture, but for practical reasons the footnote concerning that subject appears only once. However, you can always determine where a subject is discussed in a footnote by consulting the marginal notes. If you prefer to make a topical study of a particular subject in the Bible, you can consult the Index to Footnotes and Concordance (pp. 1717-1797), where all footnotes are indexed by subject.

The footnotes in the *Nave's Study Bible* are not only a system of cross references, but also a condensation, in outline form, of the subject of that footnote. Thus, each footnote is a terse but thorough analysis of the subject under discussion.

## MESSIANIC PASSAGES

Scripture passages that are clearly Messianic in character have been annotated under the term *Jesus* rather than *Messiah.* This was done for two reasons: (1) The Messiah is foreshadowed first in the promise that the seed of the woman shall bruise the serpent's head, the Messiah triumphing over the power of evil. He is later foreshadowed in the types of atoning animal sacrifices as the Savior of His people from their sins. These are dominant themes that identify *Jesus as Savior.* The term *Messiah* does not express this idea. (2) The Messianic idea of the Old Testament in the promise to David and his seed, and also the prophecies of the glorious kingdom of Israel, foreshadowed a king. In these passages the logical annotation would be *Messiah*, but to avoid confusion one name, *Jesus*, was used.

Under this name are grouped all Scripture passages relating to both Savior and triumphant Lord.

When studying Messianic passages in the Bible, the new Index of Old Testament and New Testament Cross References (pp. 1855-1874) will be of great help. Complete instructions for the use of this appendix precede the index itself (pp. 1855-1856).

## INDEX TO FOOTNOTES WITH CONCORDANCE

This combined index and concordance (pp. 1717-1797) can be a valuable tool for the serious Bible student. The subjects of all footnotes are listed alphabetically and the page reference for each is given. Also listed in this appendix are all the key words in the Bible, along with the brief contextual setting, and book, chapter, and verse references.

## DOCTRINAL OUTLINES AND INDEXES

Two new appendices are unique to this study Bible. They are "The Sovereignty of God: The Master Theme of Holy Scripture" (pp. 1799-1819) and "The Holy Trinity and the Covenant of Grace" (pp. 1821-1853). Each is a thorough doctrinal outline with thousands of Scripture references. Following each outline is a complete index of all Scriptural passages cited in this outline. Every Bible passage cited in these outlines is marked with the letter *S* ([s]) or *T* ([T]) in the Bible text itself. Since these symbols appear throughout the Bible, you are urged to become fully acquainted with this new feature. Full instructions precede each of these outlines and indexes.

## OLD TESTAMENT-NEW TESTAMENT CROSS REFERENCE INDEX

This new appendix is a complete list of all New Testament quotations from and allusion to the Old Testament. They are cross referenced for even greater usefulness. Again, every passage cited in this index is identified in the actual text of the Bible with the letter *Q* ([Q]). As with the doctrinal outlines and indexes, you are urged to turn to read the instructions which precede this helpful supplement (pp. 1855-56). Your study of Scripture will pay rich dividends if you take the time to understand these new features of the *Nave's Study Bible.*

## GLOSSARY

The editors of this *Revised and Expanded Edition* of *Nave's Study Bible* have compiled the most thorough glossary on the Authorized Version ever to be published (pp. 1875-1929). Included are archaic words and phrases, archaic spellings, seldom-used words and phrases, and words with precise theological denotation. Each of these words is identified in the Bible text by the letter *G* ([G]). Frequent consultation of this appendix will be of immense aid in mastering the vocabulary and language of the King James (Authorized) Version. Preceding this glossary is a helpful introduction (p. 1875).

## TABLES OF WEIGHTS AND MEASURES

Up-to-date equivalents of Bible terms are given in these charts (pp. 1931-1934).

## CHRONOLOGY

The chronological notes in the margins of this *Revised and Expanded Edition* have been revised. A complete explanation is given on pages 1935-36.

## GEOGRAPHICAL GAZETTEER AND ATLAS

Entirely new to this edition of *Nave's Study Bible* is a Geographical Gazetteer listing and identifying almost 1300 geographical names occuring in the Bible and on the maps included in a new atlas of surface configuration maps (pp. 1937-2002). To identify any city, river, etc. named in the Bible, turn to the Geographical Gazetteer and there you will find a brief description of its location and importance in Bible history. By means of a map number and grid numbers, this entry will also direct you to an exact location on one or more of the maps in the atlas.

# Abbreviations, Punctuation,
and
# Pronunciation Guide

## ABBREVIATIONS

A .D.—Anno Domini.
B. C.—Before Christ.
A. V.—Authorized Version.
R. V.—Revised Version.
Am. R. V.—American Revised Version.
Eng. R. V.—English Revised Version.

## PUNCTUATION OF REFERENCES

Colons (:) separate chapter numbers from verse numbers, as, for instance, Gen. 1:1.
Semi-colons (;) separate chapters from chapters, as, for instance, Gen. 1:1; 2:1; 10:6.
Commas (,) separate verses from verses, as, for instance, Gen. 1:1, 2, 6, 10.

## PRONUNCIATION

### BROAD, OBTUSE, AND OBSCURE SOUNDS

â as in câre, Âr′a-răt.
ä " ärm, Tär′sus.
ȧ " ȧst, Ā-bī′ȧ.
a̤ " a̤ll, Cla̤u′dȧ.
ẽ (*obtuse*) as in fẽrn, Dẽr′bē̇.
ĩ (*obtuse*) as in vĩrgin, Ĩr.
ô " ôrb, Hôr.
û (*obtuse*) " ûrn, Hûr.
u̧ " ru̧de, Lu̧′bĭm.
ụ " rụb, Ā′nụb.

### CONSONANT SOUNDS

ç (*soft*) as in çite, Çȳ′prus.
c (*hard*) is not marked.
ġ (*soft*) as in ġem, Ġĕn′tīle.
ḡ (*hard*) as in ḡet, Ḡĭb′e-on.
ş (*z*) as in muşe, Mō′şeş.
x̣ (*gs*) as in ex̣ample, Ăl-ĕx̣-ăn′dẽr.

### LONG, INTERMEDIATE, AND SHORT SOUNDS

ā as in āge, Ā′bĕl.
ȧ " ȧbout, Ȧ-bī′jah.
ă " băt, Ăd′dŏn.
ē " mēte, Ē′lī.
ė " ėvent, Bė-rī′ah.
ĕ " mĕt, Hĕth

ī as in vīne, Ȧ-hī′am.
ı̇ " ı̇dea, İ-du̧-mē′ȧ.
ĭ " fĭn, Mĭd′ĭ-an.
ō " ōld, Gō′shen.
ȯ " ȯbey, Gȯ-lī′ath.
ŏ " ŏdd, Hĕz′rŏn.

ū as in ūse, Jū′dah.
ŭ " ŭp, Ŭz-zī′ah.
ȳ " stȳle, Tȳ′rus.
y̆ " pity̆, Sy̆r′ĭ-ȧ.

# Books of the Bible

## THE BOOKS OF THE OLD TESTAMENT



## THE BOOKS OF THE NEW TESTAMENT

THE

# OLD TESTAMENT

(KING JAMES VERSION, WITH ELABORATE MARGINAL READINGS FROM THE AMERICAN REVISED VERSION)

## WITH MARGINAL NOTES AND FOOTNOTES

THE FIRST BOOK OF MOSES,

CALLED

# GENESIS

## CHAPTER 1

*The creation of heaven and earth, 3 of the light, 6 and of the firmament. 9 The earth separated from the waters, 11 and made fruitful. 14 The creation of the sun, moon, and stars, 20 of fish and fowl, 24 of beasts and cattle, 26 and of man, in the image of God. 29 Also the appointment of food.*

IN[S T] the [a]beginning [b]God [c]cre-
ated the [d]heaven and the
[e]earth.[T Q]
2 And the [e]earth was without
form, and void;[G] and *darkness
*was* upon the face of the deep.
And the [f]Spirit of [b]God [1]moved
upon the face of the [g]waters.[T]
3 ¶ And [b]God said, Let there
be †light: and there was light.[Q T]
4 And God saw the light, that *it*
*was* good: and [b]God divided the
light from the *darkness.
5 And God called the †light
‡Day, and the *darkness he
called ‖Night. And the evening
and the morning were the first
‡,[a]day.
6 ¶[Q] And [b]God said, Let there
be a [2,] §firmament[G] in the midst of
the [g]waters, and let it divide the
waters from the waters.
7 And [b]God made the §firma-
ment, and divided the [g]waters
which *were* under the firmament
from the waters which *were*
above the firmament: and it was
so.
8 And [b]God called the §firma-
ment Heaven. And the evening
and the morning were the second
‡,[a]day.
9 ¶ And [b]God said, Let the
[g]waters under the heaven be
gathered together unto [h]one
place, and let the dry [i]*land* appear: and it was so.[Q]
10 And [b]God called the dry
[i]*land* [e]Earth; and the gathering
together of the [g]waters called he
[h]Seas: and God saw that [j]*it was*
good.
11 And [b]God said, Let the
[e]earth [k]bring forth [l]grass,[G] the
herb yielding [m]seed, *and* the fruit
tree yielding fruit [n]after[G] his kind,
whose seed *is* in itself, upon the
earth: and it was so.[Q]
12 And the [e]earth [k]brought
forth [l]grass,[G] *and* herb[G] yielding

**1**
*a* *Time*, Rev. 10:6.
*b* *God, creator*, Gen. 2:2.
*c* *Creation, beginning of*, Mark 13:19.
*d* *Heavens, physical*, Psa. 8:3.
*e* *Earth, created by God*, Prov. 8:23.

**2**
*f* *Holy Spirit*, Acts 1:2.
*g* *Water*, 1 Kin. 17:10.
1 *Or*, was brooding upon

**6**
2 *Heb.* expanse

**9**
*h* *Sea*, Jer. 5:22.
*i* *Land*, Ruth 4:3.

**10**
*j* *Works, of God*, Psa. 40:5.

**11**
*k* *Propagation*, Gen. 8:17.
*l* *Grass*, Isa. 40:7.
*m* *Seed*, Lev. 19:19.
*n* *Nature, laws of, uniform in operation*, Jas. 3:12.

---

***DARKNESS.** *Over the face of the earth*, Gen. 1:2; Job 38:9; Jer. 4:23. *Called* NIGHT, Gen. 1:5. *God creates*, Isa. 45:7. *Miraculous: In Egypt*, Ex. 10:21, 22; Psa. 105:28; *at the crucifixion*, Matt. 27:45; Mark 15:33; Luke 23:44.

**Figurative:** *Of judgments*, Prov. 20:20; Isa. 8:22; 13:10; Jer. 4:28; 13:16; Lam. 3:2; Ezek. 32:7,8; Joel 2:2, 10; Amos 4:13; 5:18, 20; 8:9; Mic. 7:8; Matt. 24:29; Mark 13:24; Rev. 8:12; 9:2. *Of abode of the lost*, Matt. 8:12; 22:13; 25:30. *Of powers of evil*, Luke 22:53; Eph. 6:12; Col. 1:13; 1 Thess. 5:5. *Of the divine inscrutability*, 2 Sam. 22:10, 12; Psa. 18:9, 11; 97:2.

*Of spiritual blindness*, Isa. 9:2; 42:16; 50:10; Matt. 4:16; 6:22, 23; Luke 1:79; John 1:5; 3:19, 21; 8:12; 11:9, 10; 12:35; Acts 26:18; Rom. 1:21; 13:12, 13; 1 Cor. 4:5; 2 Cor. 4:6; 6:14; Eph. 5:8, 11; 1 Thess. 5:4, 5; 1 Pet. 2:9; 1 John 1:5–7; 2:8–11.

**Symbolical of Divine Inscrutability:** *On Mt. Sinai*, Ex. 19:16; 20:21; Deut. 4:11; 5:22; Heb. 12:18. *In the Sanctuary*, 1 Kin. 8:12; 2 Chr. 6:1.

†**LIGHT.** *Created*, Gen. 1:3–5; Psa. 74:16; Isa. 45:7; 2 Cor. 4:6. *Miraculous*, Ex. 13:21; Deut. 1:33; Matt. 17:2; Mark 9:3; Luke 9:29; Acts 9:3; 12;7; 26:13.

See footnote, LIGHT, *Figurative*, Matt. 5:14.

‡**DAY.** *A creative period*, Gen. 1:5, 8, 13, 19, 23, 31; 2:2. *Prophetic period*, Dan. 8:14, 26; 12:11, 12; Rev. 9:15; 11:3; 12:6. *Divided into twelve hours*, John 11:9. *Six working days ordained*, Ex. 20:9; Ezek. 46:1. *Sixth day of the week called preparation day*, Mark 15:42; John 19:14, 31, 42. *First day of the week called the Lord's day*, Rev. 1:10. *Day's journey, eighteen or twenty miles*, Ex. 3:18; 1 Kin. 19:4; Jonah 3:4. *Sabbath day's journey, probably about 1,000 yards*, Acts 1:12.

**Figurative:** *Times of adversity called Day of the Lord*, Isa. 2:12; 13:6, 9; 34:8; Jer. 46:10; Lam. 2:22; Ezek. 30:3; Amos 5:18; Joel 2:1; Obad. 15; Zeph. 1:8,18; 2:2, 3; Zech. 14:1. *Of spiritual illumination*, Prov. 4:18; 1 Thess. 5:8.

‖**NIGHT,** Gen. 1:5, 16, 18; Psa. 19:2; 139:11. *Divided into watches*, Ex. 14:24; Judg. 7:19; 1 Sam. 11:11; Psa. 63:6; 119:148; Lam. 2:19; Matt. 14:25; Luke 12:38. *Divided into hours*, Acts 23:23.

*Meditation in*, Psa. 1:2; 77:6; 119:148. *Worship in*, Psa. 134:1. *None in heaven*, Rev. 21:25; 22:5.

**Figurative:** *Of the passing of opportunity*, John 9:4. *Of spiritual ignorance*, Rom. 13:12. *Of the state of the wicked*, 1 Thess. 5:5.

§ **FIRMAMENT.** *The expanse above the earth*, Gen. 1:6–8, 14–17, 20; Psa. 19:1; Dan. 12:3.

14
o *Sun*, Josh. 10:12.
p *Moon*, Song. 6:10.
q *Token*, Psa. 86: 17.
r *Seasons*, Dan. 2: 21.
s *Year*, Lev. 25:29.

16
t *Stars*, Judg. 5:20.

20
u *Fish, creation of*, Matt. 17:27.
v *Birds, creation of*, Eccl. 12:4.
3 *Or*, swarm with swarms of living creatures,
4 *Heb*. on the face of the expanse of the heaven.

21
w R. V. Sea Monster, see footnote, *Dragon*, Deut. 32:33.

22
x *Benedictions*, Deut. 21:5.

[m]seed [n]after his kind, and the
tree yielding fruit, whose seed
*was* in itself, after his kind: and
[b]God saw that *it was* good.
13 And the evening and the
morning were the third [‡]day.
14 ¶ And [b]God said, Let there
be [o,p]lights in the [§]firmament of
the heaven to divide the [‡]day
from the [‖]night; and let them be
for [q]signs, and for [r]seasons, and
for days, and [s]years:
15 And let them be for lights in
the [§]firmament of the heaven to
give [†]light upon the [e]earth: and
it was so.
16 And [b]God made two great
lights; the [o]greater light to rule
the [‡]day, and the [p]lesser[C] light to
rule the [‖]night: *he made* the
[t]stars also.
17 And [b]God set them in the
[§]firmament of the heaven to give
light upon the [e]earth.
18 And to rule over the [‡]day
and over the [‖]night, and to divide the [†]light from the *darkness: and [b]God saw that [j]*it was*
good.
19 And the evening and the
morning were the fourth [‡]day.
20 And [b]God said, Let the [g]wa-
ters [3,k]bring forth abundantly
the moving [u]creature that hath
life,[C] and [v]fowl *that* may fly above
the earth [4]in the open [§]firma-
ment of heaven.
21 And [b]God created great
[w]whales, and every living creature that moveth, which the [g]wa-
ters [k]brought forth abundantly,
[n]after their kind, and every
winged [v]fowl after his kind: and
God saw that [j]*it was* good.
22 And [b]God [x]blessed them,
saying, [k]Be fruitful, and multiply, and fill the [g]waters in the
[h]seas, and let [v]fowl multiply in
the earth.
23 And the evening and the
morning were the fifth [‡]day.
24 ¶ And God said, Let the
[e]earth [k]bring forth the living
creature [n]after his kind, [y]cattle,
and [z]creeping thing, and beast of
the earth after his kind: and it
was so.
25 And [b]God made the [y]beast
of the earth [n]after his kind, and
cattle after their kind, and every
thing that [z]creepeth upon the
earth after his kind: and God
saw that [a]*it was* good.
26 ¶ And [b]God said, Let us
make [c,d]man in our [e]image, after
our likeness: and let [f]them have
dominion over the [g]fish of the
sea, and over the [h]fowl of the air,
and over the [i]cattle, and over all
the [j]earth, and over every
[k]creeping thing that creepeth
upon the earth. [T] [Q]
27 So [b]God created [c,d]man in
his *own* [e]image, in the image of
God created he him; [l]male and
[m]female created he them. [S] [Q]
28 And [n]God [o]blessed them,
and God said unto them, [p]Be
fruitful, and multiply, and replenish[C] the earth, and subdue it:
and have [f]dominion over the
[g]fish of the [q]sea, and over the
[h]fowl of the air, and over every
living thing that moveth upon
the [j]earth.
29 ¶[S] And God said, Behold,
[r,s]I have given you every herb
bearing seed, which *is* upon the
face of all the earth, and every
tree, in the which *is* the fruit
of a tree yielding seed; to you it
shall be for [t]meat.[C] [Q]
30 And to every [i]beast of the
earth, and to every [h]fowl of the
air, and to every [k]thing that
creepeth upon the earth, wherein
*there is* [5,u]life,[C] [r,s]I *have given*
every green herb for [t]meat:[C] and
it was so.[S]
31 And God saw [a]every thing
that [b]he had made, and, behold,
[v]*it was* very good. And the evening and the morning were the
sixth [‡]day. [T] [Q]

v.26—4045 BC
See footnote, *Time*, Rev. 10:6.

24
y *Animals, Jer.* 27:5.
z *Creeping Things*, Rom. 1:23.

25
a *Works, of God*, Psa. 40:5.

26
b *God, creator*, Gen. 2:2.
c *Man, creation of*, Job 4:17.
d *Adam*, Gen. 2:19.
e *Image, figurative*, 1 Cor. 11:7.
f *Man, dominion of*, Job 4:17.
g *Fish*, Matt. 17:27.
h *Birds*, Eccl. 12:4.
i *Animals*, Jer. 27:5.
j *Earth*, Prov. 8:23.
k *Creeping Things*, Rom. 1:23.

27
l Matt. 19:4; Mark 10:6.
m *Women*, Prov. 31: 10.

28
n *God, love of*, Gen. 2:2.
o *Benedictions, by God upon man*, Deut. 21:5.
p *Propagation, enjoined*, Gen. 8:17.
q *Sea*, Jer. 5:22.

29
r *God, providence of*, Gen. 2:2.
s *Temporal Blessings, from God*, Psa. 103:2.
t *Food, from God*, Psa. 136:25.

30
u *Life*, Eccl. 8:15.
5 *Heb*. a living soul,

31
v *Works, of God*, Psa. 40:5.

v.1–4045 BC
See footnote, *Time*, Rev. 10:6.

**1**

*a* *Heavens, physical, creation of*, Psa. 8:3.
*b* *Earth, creation of*, Prov. 8:23.
*c* *Creation*, Mark 13: 19.

**2**

*d* *Seven, days*, Gen. 7:2.
*e* *Day, creative period*, Gen. 1:5.
*f* Heb. 4:4.
*g* *Anthropomorphisms*, Gen. 11:5.
*h* *Sabbath, a rest period*, Ex. 16:23.

## CHAPTER 2

*The first sabbath. 8 The garden of Eden. 17 Eating of the fruit of the tree of knowledge forbidden. 19 The creatures named. 22 The making of woman, and institution of marriage.*

THUS [T] the [a]heavens and the
[b]earth were [c]finished, and
all the host of them.
2 And on the [d]seventh [e]day
*God ended his work which he
had [c]made; and [f]he [g]rested on
the [h]seventh day from all his
work which he had made. [Q]
3 And *God [i]blessed the [h]sev-
enth day, and [j]sanctified [C] it: because that in it he had [g]rested
from all his work which God
created [G] and made. [Q]
4 ¶ These *are* the generations of
the [a]heavens and of the [b]earth
when they were created, in the
day that the LORD *God made [S]
the earth and the heavens.
5 And every plant of the field before it was in the earth, and every

v.3–4045 BC
See footnote, *Time*, Rev. 10:6.

**3**

*i* *Benedictions*, Deut. 21.5.
*j* *Sabbath, holy*, **Ex. 16:23.**

---

***GOD. Appearances of:** *To Adam*, Gen. 3:8-21. *To Abraham*, Gen. 17:1; 18:2-33. *To Jacob, at Peniel*, Gen. 32:30; *at Bethel*, Gen. 35:7,9. *To Moses, in the burning bush*, Ex. 3:2; Deut. 33:16; Mark 12:26; Luke 20:37; Acts 7:30; *at Sinai*, Ex. 19:16-24; 24:10; 33:18-23. *To Moses and Joshua*, Deut. 31:14, 15. *To princes of Israel, at Sinai*, Ex. 24:9-11. *To Gideon*, Judg. 6:11-24. *To Solomon*, 1 Kin. 3:5; 9:2; 11:9; 2 Chr. 1:7-12; 7:12-22. *To Isaiah*, Isa. 6:1-5. *To Ezekiel*, Ezek. 1:26-28.

**Condescension of,** Psa. 113:5, 6.

MANIFESTED: *In reasoning with Noah*, Gen. 6:11-13; *with Moses*, Ex. 4:2-17; *with sinners*, Isa. 1:18-20. *In entering into covenant with Abraham*, Gen. 15:1-21; 18:1-22. *In indulging Abraham's intercession for Sodom*, Gen. 18:2-33. *In indulging Moses's prayer to behold his glory*, Ex. 33:18-23. *In indulging Gideon's tests*, Judg. 6:36-40. *In his care of man*, Psa. 8:4-6; 144:3. *In redemption*, John 3:16; Rom. 5:8; Heb. 6:17, 18.

**Creator,** Psa. 148:3-5; Prov. 16:4; Isa. 45:7; 66:2; Jer. 51:19; Amos 4:13; Mark 13:19; Acts 7:50; Rom. 1:20; 1 Cor. 11:12; Heb. 2:10; 3:4; Rev. 4:11.

*Of the earth*, Gen. 1:1, 2, 9, 10; 2:1-4; Ex. 20:11; 1 Sam. 2:8; 2 Kin. 19:15; Neh. 9:6; Job 38:4,7-10; Psa. 24:1,2; 89:11; 90:2; 95:5; 102:25; 104:2, 3, 5, 6, 24, 30; 119:90; 121:2; 124:8; 136:5-9; 146:5, 6; Prov. 3:19; 8:26-29; Isa. 37:16; 40:28; 42:5; 44:24; 45:12, 18; 48:13; 51:13, 16; Jer. 10:12; 27:5; 32:17; 51:15; Jonah 1:9; Acts 4:24; 14:15; 17:24, 25; Rev. 10:6; 14:7.

*Of the heavens*, Gen. 1:1, 6-8; 2:1-4; Ex. 20:11; 2 Kin. 19:15; 1 Chr. 16:26; Neh. 9:6; Job 9:8,9; 37:16, 18; Psa. 8:3; 19:1, 4; 96:5; 102:25; 104:2, 3, 5, 6, 24, 30; 121:2; 124:8; 136:5; 146:5, 6; Prov. 3:19; 8:26-28; Isa. 37:16; 42:5; 44:24; 45:18; Jer. 32:17; Amos 5:8; Acts 4:24; 14:15; Rev. 10:6; 14:7.

*Of the sun, moon and stars*, Gen. 1:14-19; Psa. 136:7-9.

*Of the seas*, Gen. 1:9,10; Ex. 20:11; Neh. 9:6; Psa. 95:5; 146:5,6; Prov. 8:26-29; Jonah 1:9; Acts 4:24; 14:15; Rev. 10:6; 14:7.

*Of vegetation*, Gen. 1:11, 12.

*Of animals*, Gen. 1:20-25; Job 12:7-9; Jer. 27:5.

*Of man*, Gen. 1:26-28; 2:7; 5:1, 2; 9:6; Ex. 4:11; Deut. 4:32; 32:6, 15, 18; Job 10:3, 8, 9, 11, 12; 31:15; 33:4; 34:19; Psa. 94:9; 95:6; 100:3; 119:73; 149:2; Prov. 20:12; 22:2; Eccl. 7:29; 12:1; Isa. 17:7; 42:5; 43:1, 7, 15; 44:2, 24; 45:12; 51:13; 64:8; Jer. 27:5; Zech. 12:1; Mal. 2:10; Mark 10:6; Acts 17:24-29; 1 Cor. 12:18, 24, 25; Heb. 12:9; 1 Pet. 4:19.

*Through Christ*, Rom. 11:36; 1 Cor. 8:6; Eph. 3:9; Heb. 1:1,2. See footnote, JESUS, *Creator*, Matt. 1:21. *By his word*, Psa. 33:6, 7, 9; 2 Cor. 4:6; Heb. 11:3; 2 Pet. 3:5. *By his will*, Rev. 4:11.

**Dissertations on:** *His works and providence*, Job 5:8-20. *The administration of his government*, Job 9:2-35; 10:1-22. *His sovereignty*, Job 12:7-20; 26:1-14. *His providence and grace*, Job 33:4-30; Psa. 107. *His righteousness*, Job 34: 10-30; 35:1-16; Nah. 1:2-9. *His majesty and justice*, Job 36; 37. *His majesty and works*, Psa. 104;105.

**Dwells with the righteous,** Ex. 25:8; 29:45; Lev. 26:11,12; 1 Kin. 6:13; Ezek. 37:26,27; 2 Cor. 6:16; Rev. 21:3.

**Eternity of,** Gen. 21:33; Ex. 3:15; 15:18; Deut. 32:40; 33:27; 1 Chr. 16:36; 29:10; Neh. 9:5; Job 36:26; Psa. 9:7; 41:13; 90:1, 2, 4; 92:8; 93:2; 102:12, 24-27; 145:13; 146:10; Isa. 40:28; 44:6; 57:15; 63:16; Jer. 10:10; Lam. 5:19; Dan. 4:3, 34; Hab. 1:12; Rom. 1:20; 16:26; Eph. 3:21; 1 Tim. 1:17; 6:15, 16; 2 Pet. 3:8; Rev. 4:8-10; 11:17.

**Faithfulness of,** Gen. 9:16; 28:15; Lev. 26:44, 45; Deut. 4:31; Judg. 2:1; 1 Sam. 12:22; Isa. 42:16; 44:21; 49:7, 14-16; Jer. 29:10; 31:36, 37; 32:40; 33:14, 20, 21, 25, 26; Ezek. 16:60; Hos. 2:19, 20; Rom. 3:3, 4; Heb. 6:10, 13-19.

*Confidence in*, Num. 23:19; Deut. 32:4; 2 Sam. 7:28; 1 Chr. 28:20; Neh. 1:5; Psa. 36:5; 40:10; 89:1, 2, 5, 8, 14, 24, 28, 33, 34; 92:1, 2, 15; 94:14; 105:8, 42; 111:5, 7-9; 119:90, 91; 132:11; 25:1; Lam. 3:23; Dan. 9:4; Mic. 7:20; 1 Cor. 1:9; 10:13; 2 Cor. 1:18-20; 1 Thess. 5:24; 2 Thess. 3:3; 2 Tim. 2:13, 19; Tit. 1:2; Heb. 10:23; 11:11; 1 Pet. 4:19; 2 Pet. 3:9; 1 John 1:9.

EXEMPLIFIED, Gen. 21:1; 24:27; Ex. 2:24; 6:4, 5; Deut. 7:8, 9; 9:5; Josh. 21:45; 23:14; 1 Kin. 8:15, 20, 23, 24, 56; 2 Kin. 8:19; 13:23; 2 Chr. 6:4-15; 21:7; Neh. 1:5; 9:7, 8; Psa. 98:3; Hag. 2:5; Luke 1:54, 55, 68-70, 72, 73; Acts 13:32, 33; Heb. 6:10, 13-19.

**Fatherhood of:** *Taught in the Old Testament*, Ex. 4:22; Deut. 14:1; 32:5, 6; 2 Sam. 7:14; 1 Chr. 28:6; 29:10; Psa. 68:5; 89:26; Isa. 1:2; 9:6; 63:16; 64:8; Jer. 3:19; Hos. 1:10; 11:1.

*Taught by Jesus*, Matt. 5:45; 6:4, 8, 9; 7:11; 10:20, 29, 32, 33; 11:25-27; 12:50; 13:43; 15:13; 16:17, 27; 18:10, 14, 19; 20:23; 26:29, 39; Mark 8:38; 11:25; 13:32; Luke 2:49; 10:21, 22; 11:2, 13; 22:29; 23:46; 24:49; John 1:14, 18; 2:16; 4:21, 23; 5:17-23, 36, 37, 43; 6:27, 32, 44-46; 8:19, 27, 38, 41, 42, 49; 10:15, 29, 30, 32, 33, 36-38; 12:26-28, 50; 13:1, 3; 14:2, 6-13, 16, 20, 21, 23, 24, 26, 31; 15:8-10, 16, 23, 24, 26; 16:3, 10, 15, 23, 25-28; 17:1, 5, 11, 21, 24; 20:17, 21.

*Taught by the apostles*, Acts 1:4; 2:33; Rom. 1:3, 4, 7 (with 1 Cor. 1:3; Gal. 1:3; Eph. 1:2; 6:23; Phil. 1:2; Col. 1:2; 1 Thess. 1:1; 2 Thess. 1:2; 1 Tim. 1:2; 2 Tim. 1:2; Tit. 1:4); 8:14-16; 1 Cor. 8:6; 15:24; 2 Cor. 1:3; 6:18; Gal. 1:1, 4; 4:4-7; Eph. 1:3, 17; 2:18; 3:14; 4:6; 5:20; Col. 1:3, 12; 3:17; 1 Thess. 1:1, 3; 3:11, 13; 2 Thess. 1:1, 2; 2:16; Heb. 1:5, 6; 12:9; Jas. 1:17, 27; 3:9; 1 Pet. 1:2, 3, 17; 1 John 1:2; 2:1, 13, 15, 22-24; 3:1; 4:14; 2 John 3, 4, 9; Jude 1; Rev. 1:5, 6; 3:5; 14:1.

See footnote, SPIRITUAL ADOPTION, Rom. 8:15.

**Foreknowledge of,** Acts 15:18. *Of contingencies*, 1 Sam. 23:10-12. *Of future events*, Isa. 42:9; 44:7; 45:11; 46:9, 10; 48:5, 6; Jer. 1:5; Dan. 2:28, 29; Acts 2:23. *Of human needs*, Matt. 6:8. *Of the day of judgment*, Matt. 24:36; Mark 13:32. *Of the redeemed*, Rom. 8:29; 11:2; 1 Pet. 1:2.

**Glory of,** Psa. 24:8-10; 57:5, 11; 72:18, 19; Isa. 40:5; Phil. 1:11.

*Described*, Ezek. 1:26-28; Hab. 3:3-6. *Transcendent*, Psa. 113:4. *Shall endure forever*, Psa. 104:31.

*Ascribed by angels*, Luke 2:14. *To be ascribed by men*, Psa. 29:2; Rom. 11:36.

MANIFESTED: *In the burning bush*, Ex. 3:2. *In Mount Sinai*, Ex. 19:18 (with Ex. 20:18, 19; Deut. 4:11, 12, 33, 36; 5:5, 24, 25); Ex. 24:10, 17; 33:18-23; 34:5, 29-35; Heb. 12:18-21. *In the tabernacle*, Ex. 40:34, 35. *In the heavens*, 2 Sam. 22:10-15; Psa. 18:9-14; 19:1. *In his sovereignty*, Psa. 97:2-6; 145:5, 11, 12; Isa. 6:1-5; 24:23; Jude 24, 25. *In the church*, Isa. 35:2; 60:1, 2, 19-21; 61:3; 62:3; Eph. 3:21. *In Christ*, John 13:31, 32; 14:13; 17:1. *To Ezekiel*, Ezek. 3:12, 23; 8:4. *To Stephen*, Acts 7:35.

**Goodness of,** Ex. 33:19; Deut. 30:9; Psa. 25: 8-10; 31:19; 33:5; 36:7; 86:5; 100:5; 106:1; 119:68; Nah. 1:7; Matt. 5:45; Acts 14:17; Jas. 1:17.

*Enduring*, Psa. 52:1. *Leads to repentance*, Rom. 2:4.

*Gratefully acknowledged*, 1 Chr. 16:34; 2 Chr. 5:13; 7:3; Psa. 68:19; 107:8, 9, 43; 118:29; 135:3; 136:1; 145:7, 9; Isa. 63:7.

MANIFESTED: *In gracious providences*, Matt. 7:11. *To the righteous*, Psa. 31:19; Lam. 3:25; Rom. 11:22. *To the wicked*, Luke 6:35.

**Guidance of,** Gen. 12:1; 24:27; Psa. 23:2, 3; 48:14; 73:24; Prov. 3:6; Jer. 3:4; 32:19; Luke 1:79; John 10:3, 4. *By pillars of cloud and fire*, Ex. 13:21; Neh. 9:19. *By his presence*, Ex. 15:13; 33:13-15; Deut. 32:10, 12; Psa. 78:52; 80:1; 107:7. *By the ark of the covenant*, Num. 10:33. *By his counsel*, 2 Sam. 22:29; Psa. 5:8; 25:9; Isa. 48:17. *By his Spirit*, John 16:13. *Prayed for*, Psa. 25:5; 27:11; 31:3; 61:2. *Promised*, Psa. 32:8; Isa. 40: 11; 42:16; 58:11.

**Holiness of,** Josh. 24:19; 1 Sam. 6:20; 1 Chr. 16:10; **Job 6:10; 15:15; 25:5; Psa. 11:7; 22:3; 36:6; 47:8; 60:6;**

v.5—4045 BC
See footnote, *Time*, Rev. 10:6.

5
k *Meteorology*, Matt. 16:2.
l *Agriculture*, Gen. 3:23.

7
m *Man, creation of*, Job 4:17.
n *Breath, of life*, Gen. 7:15.
o Job 33:4.
p *Life, breath of*, Eccl. 8:15.
q 1 Cor. 15:45.

8
r *Eden*, Isa. 51:3.

herb of the field before it grew: for
the LORD God had not caused it
to [k]rain upon the earth, and *there*
*was* not a man to [l]till the ground.
6 But there went up a [k]mist
from the earth, and watered the
whole face[G] of the ground.
7 And the LORD *God formed
[m]man *of* the dust of the
ground, and breathed into his
nostrils the [n,o]breath of [p]life;
and man [q]became a living soul.[TQ G S]
8 ¶ And the LORD *God plant-
ed a garden eastward in [r]Ē′dĕn;
and there he put the man
whom he had formed.[Q]
9[Q] And out of the ground made
the LORD *God to grow every
tree that is pleasant to the sight,
and good for food; the [s,t]tree of
[p]life also in the midst of the
garden, and the tree of [u]knowl-
edge of good and evil.
10 And a river went out of
[r]Ē′dĕn to water the garden; and
from thence it was parted, and
became into four heads.[Q]
11 The name of the first *is* Pī′-

v.8—4045 BC
See footnote, *Time*, Rev. 10:6.

9
s *Tree, of life*, Rev. 22:14.
t *Symbols and Similitudes*, Heb. 9:9.
u *Knowledge*, Luke 11:52.

89:35; 98:1; 105:3; 111:9; 119:142; 145:17; Prov. 9:10; Isa. 5:16; 6:3; 29:19, 23; 41:14; 43:14, 15; 45:19; 47:4; 49:7; 52:10; 57:15; Ezek. 36:21, 22; 39:7, 25; Dan. 4:8; Hos. 11:9; Hab. 1:12, 13; Luke 1:49; John 17:11; Rom. 1:23; 1 John 2:20; Rev. 4:8; 6:10; 15:4.

*Incomparable*, Ex. 15:11; 1 Sam. 2:2; Job 4:17-19. *Without iniquity*, Deut. 32:4; 2 Chr. 19:7; Job 34:10; 36:23; Psa. 92:15; Jer. 2:5; Lam. 3:38; Matt. 19:17; Mark 10:18; Luke 18:19; Jas. 1:13.

*A reason for man's holiness*, Lev. 11:44; 19:2; 20:26; 21:8; 2 Chr. 19:7; Matt. 5:48; 1 Pet. 1:15, 16. *A reason for thanksgiving*, Psa. 30:4; 99:3, 5, 9; Isa. 12:6. *A reason for reverent approach to God*, Ex. 3:5; Josh. 5:15.

*Light, figurative of*, 1 John 1:5.

See footnote, SIN, *separates from God*, Rom. 5:12. See GOD, *Perfections of*, below; *Righteousness of*, below.

**Immanence of,** Acts 17:27, 28.

**Immutable,** Num. 23:19, 20; 1 Sam. 15:29; Psa. 102:27; Isa. 40:28; Jas. 1:17.

*In purpose*, Job 23:13; Psa. 33:11; Prov. 19:21; Eccl. 3:14; 7:13; Isa. 31:2; Heb. 6:17, 18. *In faithfulness*, Psa. 119:89-91. *In mercy*, Isa. 59:1; Hos. 13:14; Mal. 3:6; Rom. 11:29.

**Impartial,** Deut. 10:17. *Despiseth none*, Job 36:5. *No respecter of persons*, 2 Chr. 19:7; Job 34:19; 37:24; Acts 10:34, 35; Rom. 2:6, 11; Eph. 6:8, 9; Col. 3:25; 1 Pet. 1:17.

**Incomprehensible,** Job 15:8; 37:1-24; Isa. 40:12-31; 55:8, 9; Matt. 11:27; 1 Cor. 2:16.

**Infinite,** 1 Kin. 8:27; 2 Chr. 2:6; 6:1, 18; Psa. 147:5; Jer. 23:24.

**Invisible,** Ex. 20:21; 33:20; Deut. 4:11, 12, 15; 5:22; 1 Kin. 8:12 (with 2 Chr. 6:1); Job 9:11; 23:8, 9; Psa. 18:11; 97:2; John 1:18; 5:37; 6:46; Rom. 1:20; Col. 1:13-15; 1 Tim. 1:17; 6:16; Heb. 11:27; 1 John 4:12.

**Jealous,** Ex. 20:5, 7; 34:14; Deut. 4:24; 5:9, 11; 6:15; 29:20; 32:16, 21; Josh. 24:19; 2 Chr. 16:7-10; Isa. 30:1, 2; Ezek. 23:25; 36:5; 39:25; Joel 2:18, Nah. 1:2; Zech. 1:14; 1 Cor. 10:22.

**Judge,** Gen. 16:5; Judg. 11:27; 1 Sam. 2:3, 10; 24:12, 15; 1 Chr. 16:33; Job 21:22; Psa. 11:4, 5; 26:1, 2; 35:24; 43:1; 50:4, 6; 58:11; 75:7; 76:8, 9; 82:8; 94:1, 2; 135:14; Prov. 16:2; 29:26; Eccl. 3:17; 11:9; 12:14; Isa. 3:13, 14; 28:17, 21; 30:18, 27; 33:22; Jer. 32:19; Dan. 7:9, 10; Nah. 1:3; Mal. 3:5; Acts 17:31; 1 Cor. 5:13; Heb. 10:30, 31; 12:22, 23; Rev. 6:16, 17; 11:18; 16:5; 18:8.

*Just*, Gen. 18:21, 25; Num. 16:22; Deut. 32:4; Neh. 9:33; Job. 4:17; 8:3; 34:10-12; Psa. 7:9, 11; 9:4, 7, 8; 67:4; 96:10, 13; 98:9; Isa. 26:7; 45:21; Jer. 32:19; Rom. 2:2, 5-16; 3:4-6, 26; 11:22, 23; Eph. 6:8, 9; 1 Pet. 1:17; Rev. 19:2.

*Incorruptible*, Deut. 10:17; 2 Chr. 19:7; Job 8:3; 34:19.

**Justice of,** Deut. 32:4; 2 Sam. 22:25; 1 Kin. 8:32; Job 31:13-15; Psa. 51:4; 62:12; 89:14; 97:2; 145:17; Prov. 21:2, 3; 24:12; Isa. 61:8; Jer. 9:24; 11:20; 20:12; 32:19; 50:7; Ezek. 14:23; 18:25, 29, 30; 33:7-19; Dan. 9:7, 14; Nah. 1:3, 6; Zeph. 3:5; Acts 17:31; Rom. 2:2, 5-16; Heb. 6:10; 1 Pet. 1:17; 2 Pet. 2:9; 1 John 1:9; Jude 6; Rev. 11:18; 15:3.

**Knowledge of,** Gen. 6:5; 1 Sam. 2:3; Job 12:13, 22; 21:22; 22:13, 14; 26:6; 28:23, 24; 36:4, 5; 37:16; Psa. 147:4, 5; Prov. 3:19, 20; Isa. 40:13, 14, 26-28; 46:9, 10; Matt. 24:36; Mark 13:32; Rom. 11:33, 34; 1 Cor. 1:25; 1 John 1:5.

*Of man's state and condition*, Gen. 16:13; Ex. 3:7; Deut. 2:7; 2 Kin 19:27; 2 Chr. 16:9; Job 23:10; 31:4; 34:21, 25; Psa. 1:6; 11:4; 33:13-15; 37:18; 38:9; 66:7; 69:19; 103:14; 119:168; 139:1-4, 6, 12, 14-16; 142:3; Prov. 5:21; 15:3, 11; Isa. 29:15, 16; 37:28; 66:18; Jer. 23:24; 32:19; Amos 9:2-4; Matt. 10:29, 30; 1 Cor. 8:3.

*Of man's heart*, Gen. 20:6; Deut. 31:21; 1 Sam. 16:7; 2 Sam. 7:20; 1 Kin. 8:39; 1 Chr. 28:9; 29:17; 2 Chr. 6:30; Job 11:11; Psa. 7:9; 44:21; 94:9-11; Prov. 15:11; 16:2; 17:3; 21:2; 24:12; Jer. 11:20; 16:17; 17:10; 20:12; Ezek. 11:5; Amos 4:13; Matt. 6:4, 8, 18, 32; Luke 16:15; Acts 1:24; 15:8; 1 Cor. 3:20; 1 Thess. 2:4; Heb. 4:13; 1 John 3:20. See FOREKNOWLEDGE OF, above; WISDOM OF, below.

**Light,** Dan. 2:22; Jas. 1:17; 1 John 1:5.

**Longsuffering of,** Gen. 6:3; 15:16; Ex. 34:6; Num. 14:18; Psa. 86:15; 103:8-10; Isa. 5:1-4; 30:18; 48:9, 11; 57:16; Jer. 7:13, 23-25; 9:24; Ezek. 20:17; Joel 2:13; Hab. 1:2-4; Matt. 21:33-41; Mark 12:1-9; Luke 20:9-16; Acts 14:16; Rom. 3:25; 15:5; 1 Pet. 3:20.

*Abused*, Neh. 9:28-31; Prov. 1:24-27; 29:1; Eccl. 8:11; Isa. 5:1-4; Jer. 7:13, 23-25; Matt. 24:48-51; Luke 13:6-9. See MERCY OF, below.

MANIFESTED: *In deferring judgments*, Mic. 7:18; Luke 13:6-9; Acts 17:20; Rom. 9:22, 23; 2 Pet. 3:9, 15. *In giving time for repentance*, Jer. 11:7; Matt. 23:37; Luke 13:34; Rom. 2:4.

**Love of,** Deut. 4:37; 7:7, 8, 13; 10:15, 18; 23:5; 33:3, 12; 2 Sam. 12:24; Job 7:17; Psa. 42:8; 47:4; 69:16; Hos. 11:1; Mal. 1:2; 2 Cor. 13:11, 14; 1 John 3:1; 4:12, 16, 19; Jude 21.

*Everlasting*, 2 Chr. 20:21; Jer. 31:3. *Better than life*, Psa. 63:3.

*For the wicked*, Matt. 18:12-14; Luke 15:4-7, 11-27; Rom. 5:8; Eph. 2:4, 5. *For the righteous*, Psa. 103:13; 146:8; Prov. 15:9; John 14:21, 23; 16:27; 17:10, 23, 26; Rom. 1:7; 9:13; 11:28; 2 Thess. 2:16. *For the cheerful giver*, 2 Cor. 9:7.

EXEMPLIFIED, Ex. 19:4-6; Lev. 20:24, 26; Deut. 32:9-12; 2 Sam. 7:23, 24; Psa. 48:9, 14; Isa. 43:1-4; 49:13-16; 54:5, 6, 10; 62:4, 5; 63:7-9; 66:13; Jer. 3:14, 15; Ezek. 16:8; Hos. 2:19, 20, 23; Zech. 2:8.

*In forgiveness of sins*, Isa. 38:17; Tit. 3:4, 5. *In the gift of his Son*, John 3:16; 1 John 4:8-10. *In chastisements*, Heb. 12:6.

**Mercy of,** Ex. 20:2, 6 (with Deut. 5:10); Ex. 33:19; Deut. 4:31; 7:9; 1 Kin. 8:23; 2 Chr. 30:9; Ezra 9:9; Psa. 18:50; 25:6, 8; 31:7; 32:10; 36:5; 57:10; 62:12; 69:16; 98:3; 108:4; 111:4; 116:5; 117:2; 119:64, 156; 138:2; 146:7, 8; Isa. 60:10; Jer. 9:24; 31:20; 32:18; Dan. 9:4; Hos. 2:23; Zech. 10:6; Luke 6:36; Acts 17:30; Rom. 9:15; 11:32; 15:9; 2 Cor. 1:3; Heb. 4:16; 1 Pet. 1:3; 2 Pet. 3:9.

*Everlasting*, 1 Chr. 16:34, 41; 2 Chr. 5:13; 7:3, 6, 14; Ezra 3:11; Psa. 89:1, 2, 28; 100:5; 103:17; 106:1; 107:1; 118:1-4, 29; 136:1-26.

MANIFESTED: *In withholding punishment*, Gen. 8:21; 18:26, 30-32; Ex. 32:14; Num. 16:48; 2 Sam. 24:14, 16; 2 Kin. 13:23; Ezra 9:13; Job 11:6; Isa. 12:1; 54:9; Ezek. 16:6, 42, 63; 20:17; Hos. 11:8, 9; Joel 2:13, 18; Jonah 4:2, 10, 11; Mal. 3:6. *In rescuing from destruction*, Gen. 19:16; Num. 21:8; Judg. 2:18; 2 Kin. 14:26, 27; Neh. 1:10; 9:17-20, 27-31. *In leading his people*, Ex. 15:13. *In comforting the afflicted*, 2 Cor. 12:9. *In hearing prayer*, Ex. 22:27; Heb. 4:16. *In solicitude for sinners*, Deut. 5:29; 32:29; Judg. 10:16; 2 Chr. 36:15; Isa. 65:2, 8; Jer. 2:9; 7:25; Ezek. 18:23, 31, 32; 33:11; Matt. 18:12-14; Luke 15:4-7; 1 Tim. 2:4, 6. *In forbearance toward sinners*, 2 Chr. 24:18, 19; Psa. 145:8, 9; Lam. 3:22, 23, 31-33; Dan. 4:22-27; Nah. 1-3. *In granting forgiveness*, Ex. 34:6, 7; Num. 14:18-20; 2 Sam. 12:13; 2 Chr. 7:14; Job 33:14-30; Psa. 32:1, 2, 5; 65:3; 78:38, 39; 85:2, 3; 86:5, 13, 15; 99:8; 103:3, 8-14; 130:3,

v.11–4045 BC

11
*v Gold,* Ezek. 7:19.

12
*w* Num. 11:7.
*x Onyx,* Ezek. 28: 13.
1 *Or,* beryl.

13
*y Ethiopia,* Isa. 18:1.

14
2 *That is,* Tigris:
*z* Dan. 10:4.

son: that *is* it which compasseth
the whole land of Hăv′i-lah,
where *there is* [v]gold.
12 And the [v]gold of that land *is*
good: there *is* [w]bdellium and
the [1,x]onyx stone.
13 And the name of the second
river *is* Gī′hon: the same *is* it
that compasseth the whole land
of [y]Ē-thĭ-ō′pĭ-ȧ.
14 And the name of the third
river *is* [2,z]Hĭd′de-kĕl: that *is* it
which goeth toward the east of
[a]Ăs-sȳr′ĭ-ȧ. And the fourth
river *is* [b]Eū-phrā′tēs̱.
15 And the LORD *God took
the [c]man, and [d]put him into
the garden of [e]Ē′dĕn to [f]dress[c] it
and to keep it.
16 And the LORD *God commanded the [c]man, saying, Of
every tree of the garden thou
mayest freely eat:
17 But of the [g]tree of the
knowledge of good and evil,
[h]thou shalt not eat of it: for in

v.14–4045 BC

*a Assyria,* Gen. 25: 18.
*b Euphrates,* Gen. 15:18.

15
*c Man,* Job 4:17.
*d Probation,* vs. 15-17; Rom. 5:4.
*e Eden,* Isa. 51:3.
*f Agriculture,* Gen. 3:23.

17
*g Tree, of knowledge,* Rev. 22:14.
*h Statute fixing the penalty for disobedience,* Deut. 8:2.

---

4, 7, 8; Prov. 16:6; 28:13; Isa. 55:7-9; Jer. 3:12, 22; 31:20, 34; 33:8, 11; 36:3; 50:20; Ezek. 36:25; Dan. 9:9; Hos. 14:4; Mic. 7:18, 19; Matt. 6:14; 18:23-27; Luke 1:50, 77, 78; Acts 3:19; 26:18; Rom. 10:12, 13; 2 Cor. 5:19; Eph. 1:6-8; 2:4-7; 1 Tim. 1:13; Tit. 3:5; Heb. 8:12; 1 John 1:9.

SYMBOLIZED: *In the mercy-seat,* Ex. 25:17.

**Name of:** *Proclaimed,* Ex. 6:3; 15:3; 34:5, 14; Psa. 83:18. *To be reverenced,* Ex. 20:7; Deut. 5:11; 28:58; Psa. 111:9; Mic. 4:5; 1 Tim. 6:1. *To be praised,* Psa. 34:3; 72:17. *Not to be profaned,* Ex. 20:7; Lev. 18:21; 19:12; 20:3; 21:6; 22:2, 32; Deut. 5:11; Psa. 139:20; Prov. 30:9; Isa. 52:5; Rom. 2:24; Rev. 16:9. *Profaned,* Psa. 139:20.

**Omnipotent,** Gen. 17:1; 18:14; Job 42:2; Acts 26:8; Rev. 19:6; 21:22. See POWER OF, below.

**Omnipresent,** Gen. 28:16; 1 Kin. 8:27; 2 Chr. 2:6; Acts 7:48, 49; Psa. 139:3, 5, 7-10; Jer. 23:23, 24; Acts 17: 24, 27, 28.

See PRESENCE OF, below.

**Omniscient,** see KNOWLEDGE OF, above; WISDOM OF, below.

**Perfection of,** Deut. 32:4; 2 Sam. 22:31; Psa. 18:30; Matt. 5:48; Rom. 12:2; Jas. 1:17; 1 John 1:5; Rev. 15:3. See HOLINESS OF, above; RIGHTEOUSNESS OF, below.

**Power of,** Ex. 9:16; 15:6, 7, 11, 12; Num. 11:23; Deut. 7:21; 11:2; Job 37:23 (with vs. 1-22); Psa. 21:13; 29:3-9; 62:11; 68:34, 35; 74:13, 15; 77:14, 16, 18; 78:12-51; 79:11; 89:8, 13; 93:1, 4; 105:26-41; 106:8; 111:6; 135:6, 8-12; 147:5, 16-18; Isa. 26:4; 40:12, 22, 24, 26, 28; 51:10, 15; 63:12; Jer. 5:22; 27:5; 32:17, 27; Dan. 2:20; Matt. 19:26 (with Mark 10:27; Luke 18:27); 22:29; Mark 14:36; Luke 1:49, 51; 1 Cor. 6:14; Rev. 19:1.

*Supreme,* Deut. 32:39; Josh. 4:24; 1 Sam. 2:6, 7; 14:6; 1 Chr. 29:11, 12; 2 Chr. 14:11; 25:8, 9; Job 5:9; 23:13, 14; 26:7-14; 36:5, 22, 27-33; 38:8, 11; 40:9; 42:2; Psa. 104:7, 9, 29, 30, 32; Dan. 4:35.

*Irresistible,* Deut. 32:39 (with Job 10:7); 1 Sam. 2:10; 2 Chr. 20:6; Job 9:4-7, 10, 12, 13, 19; 11:10; 12:14-16; 14:20; 41:10, 11; Psa. 66:3, 7; 76:7; Isa. 14:24, 27; 31:3; 43:13, 16, 17; 46:10, 11; 50:2, 3; Nah. 1:3-6. *Incomparable,* Deut. 3:24; Job 40:9; Psa. 89:8. *Omnipotent,* Gen. 18:14; Jer. 32:27; Matt. 19:26. *Everlasting,* Rom. 1:20.

*Creation by,* Jer. 10:12. *The resurrection of Christ by,* 1 Cor. 6:14; 2 Cor. 13:4; *of saints by,* 1 Cor. 6:14.

*Manifested in behalf of saints,* Deut. 33:26, 27; 2 Chr. 16:9; Ezra 8:22; Neh. 1:10; Jer. 20:11; Dan. 3:17.

*Manifested in his works,* Deut. 3:24; Psa. 33:9; 107:25, 29; 114:7, 8; Prov. 30:4; Isa. 48:13; Jer. 10:12, 13; 51:15; Rom. 1:20. See OMNIPOTENT, above.

**Presence of,** Gen. 16:13; 28:16; Ex. 20:24; 29:42, 43; 30:6; 33:14; Deut. 4:34-36, 39; 1 Kin. 8:27; Psa. 139:3, 5, 7-10; Isa. 57:15; 66:1; Jer. 23:23, 24; 32:18, 19; Jonah 1:3, 4; Acts 17:24, 27, 28; 1 Cor. 12:6.

*Manifested on the mercy-seat,* see footnote, SHEKINAH, Lev. 16:2.

**Preserver,** Neh. 9:6; Job 33:18; Psa. 3:3; 12:7; 17:7; 68:6; 73:23; Isa. 27:3; 49:8; Jer. 2:6; Dan. 5:23; Matt. 10: 29-31; Luke 12:6, 7; 21:18; John 17:11, 15; 1 Pet. 3:12, 13; 2 Pet. 2:9.

*Of the righteous,* Gen. 15:1; 28:15; 49:24, 25; Ex. 8:22, 23; 9:26; 11:7; 12:13, 17, 23; 15:2, 13, 16, 17; 19:4; 23:20-31; Deut. 1:30, 31; 32:10; 33:12, 25-28; Josh. 23:10; 1 Sam. 2:9; 2 Sam. 22:1-51; 2 Chr. 16:9; Job 1:10; 5:11, 18-24; 10:12; Psa. 9:9; 18:14; 23:1-6; 31:20, 23; 32:6, 8; 34:7, 15, 17, 19-22; 37:17, 23, 24, 28, 32, 33; 41:1-3; 46:1, 7; 50:15; 84:11; 91:1, 3, 4, 7, 9, 10, 14, 15; 102:19, 20; 103:2-5; 107:9, 10, 13; 116:6; 118:13; 121:3, 4, 7, 8; 125:1-3; 145:14, 19, 20; 146:7, 8; Prov. 2:7, 8; 10:3, 30; Isa. 25:4; 30:21, 26; 33:16; 40:11, 29, 31; 42:16; 43:2; 46:3, 4; 52:12; 58:11; 63:9; Jer. 31:9, 10, 28; Ezek. 11:16; 34:11-16, 22, 31; Dan. 3:27, 28; Joel 2:18; Zech. 2:5, 8; Matt. 4:6; 1 Cor. 10: 13; 2 Tim. 4:18; 2 Thess. 3:3; Jas. 4:15.

HIS PRESERVING CARE EXEMPLIFIED: *To Noah and his family, at the time of the flood,* Gen. 6:8, 13-21; 7; 8:1, 15, 16. *To Abraham and Sarah, in Egypt,* Gen. 12:17; *in Gerar,* Gen. 20:3. *To Lot, when Sodom was destroyed,* Gen. 19. *To Hagar, when Abraham cast her out,* Gen. 21:17, 19. *To Jacob, when he fled from home,* Gen. 35:3; *when he fled from Laban, his father-in-law,* Gen. 31:24, 29; *when he met Esau,* Gen. 33:3-10; *as he journeyed in the land of Canaan,* Gen. 35:3. *To Joseph, in Egypt,* Gen. 39:2, 21. *To Moses, in his infancy,* Ex. 2:1-10.

To the Israelites: *In bringing about their deliverance from bondage,* Ex. 1:9-12; 2:23-25; 3:7-9. *In exempting the land of Goshen from the plague of flies,* Ex. 8:22. *In preserving their cattle from the plague of murrain,* Ex. 9:4-7. *In exempting the land of Goshen from the plague of darkness,* Ex. 10:21-23. *In saving the firstborn, when the plague of death destroyed the firstborn of Egypt,* Ex. 12:13, 23. *In deliverance from Egypt,* Ex. 13:3, 17-22; 14; 19:4; Lev. 26:13; *in the wilderness,* Ex. 40:36-38; Num. 9:17-23; 10:33; 22:12; 23:8; Deut. 1:31; 23:5; 26:7-9. *In victories under Joshua, over the Canaanites* Josh. chaps. 6–11; 24:11-13; *under Othniel,* Judg. 3:9-11; *under Ehud,* Judg. 3:15-30; *under Shamgar,* Judg. 3:31; *under Deborah,* Judg. 4:5; *under Gideon,* Judg. 7; 8:1-23; *under Jephthah,* Judg. 11:29-40; *under David,* 1 Sam. 17:45-49; *under Ahab,* 1 Kin. 20. *In delivering the kingdom of Israel from Syria,* 2 Sam. 8. *In delivering Israel by Jeroboam II,* 2 Kin. 14:26, 27; *by Abijah,* 2 Chr. 13:4-18. *In delivering from the oppressions of the king of Syria,* 2 Kin. 13:2-5.

To the kingdom of Judah: *In delivering from Egypt,* 2 Chr. 12:2-12; *from the Ethiopian host,* 2 Chr. 14:11-14. *In giving peace with other nations,* 2 Chr. 17. *In delivering them from the army of the Assyrians,* 2 Kin. 19.

*To David,* 1 Sam. 17:32, 45-47; 2 Sam. 7; 1 Chr. 11:13, 14. *To Hezekiah,* 2 Kin. 19; Job 1:9-12; 2:6. *To Jeremiah and Baruch,* Jer. 36:26. *To Daniel and the three Hebrew captives,* Dan. 2:18-23; 3:27, 28; 6. *To Jonah,* Jonah 1:17. *To the wise men of the east,* Matt. 2:12. *To Jesus and his parents,* Matt. 2:13, 19-22. *To Peter,* Acts 12:3-17. *To Paul and Silas,* Acts 16:26-39. *To Paul,* Acts 27:24; 28:5, 6 (with Mark 16:18). See PROVIDENCE OF, below. See footnote, POOR, *God's care of,* Prov. 21:13.

**Providence of,** Gen. 24:7, 40-50, 56; 26:24; Lev. 26: 4-6, 10; Deut. 8:18; 11:12-15; 15:4-6; 32:11-14; 1 Sam. 2:6-9; 1 Kin. 11:14-40; 1 Chr. 29:14, 16; Psa. 23:1-6; 34:7, 9, 10; 71:6, 7, 15; 107: 1-43; 127:1-5; 136:5-25; 144: 12-15; 147:8, 9, 13, 14; Prov. 16:33; Eccl. 2:24; 3:13; 5:19; Isa. 46:4; 51:2; 55:10; Ezek. 36:28-38; Joel 2:18-26; Matt. 5:45; Rom. 8:28; Jas. 4:15.

*In providing for temporal necessities,* Gen. 1:29, 30; 2:16; 8:22; 9:1-3; 28:20, 21; 48:15, 16; 49:24, 25; Ex. 16:15; Lev. 25:20-22; Deut. 2:7; 7:13-15; 8:4; 10:18; 28:2-13; 29:5; Ruth 1:6; Neh. 9:24, 25; Job 5:8-11; 22:18, 25; Psa. 36:6, 7; 37:3, 19, 22, 25, 34; 65:9-13; 67:6; 85:12; 104:10-15; 111:5; 136:25; 145:15, 16; Isa. 43:20; 48:21; Jer. 5:24; 27:6; Hos. 2:8; Jonah 4:6; Zech. 10:1; Matt. 6:26, 30-33; 10:29-31; Luke 12:6, 7, 24-28; 22:35; John 6:31; Acts 14:17; 2 Cor. 9:10.

*In sending prosperity,* Psa. 75:7; 127:1, 2; Isa. 48:14, 15; 54:16, 17; Ezek. 29:19, 20. *In sending adversity,* 1 Sam. 2:6-9; 2 Sam. 17:14; Psa. 75:7; Eccl. 3:10. *In saving from adversity,* Gen. 7:1; Ex. 9:26; 15:26; 23:25, 26; Psa. 103:3-5; 116:1-15; 118:5, 6, 13, 14; 146:7-9; Dan. 6:20-22.

*In delivering from enemies,* Gen. 14:20; Ex. 3:17; 6:7; 14:29, 30; 23:22; 34:24; Deut. 20:4; 23:14; 30:4, 20; 31:3,

v.17—4045 BC

*i Sin, punishment of,* Rom. 5:12.
*j Wicked, punishment of,* Psa. 73:3.
*k Punishment, design of,* Lev. 26: 41.
*l Death, penalty,* Num. 23: 10.
**18**
*m Wife,* Prov. 5:18.
**19**
*n Ground,* Gen. 3: 19.

the day that thou [i]eatest thereof
[j]thou shalt surely [k,l]die.[G Q]
18 ¶ And the LORD *God said,
*It is* not good that the [†,c]man
should be alone; I will make him
an [m]help meet[c] for him. [Q]
19 And out of the [n]ground the
LORD *God formed every [o]beast
of the field, and every [p]fowl of
the air; and [q]brought *them* unto
[3,†]Ăd'ăm to see what he would
call them: and whatsoever [3]Ăd'-
ăm called every living creature,
that *was* the name thereof.
20 And [3,†]Ăd'ăm gave names
to all [o]cattle, and to the [p]fowl of
the air, and to every [o]beast of the
field; but for [3]Ăd'ăm there was

v.19—4045 BC

*o Animals,* Jer. 27:5.
*p Birds,* Eccl. 12:4
*q Anthropomorphisms, attributing ordinary actions to God,* Gen. 11:5.
3 R. V. the man

**8**; 2 Kings 20:6; 2 Chr. 20:3-30; 32:8; Ezra 8:22, 23; Psa. 18:17, 27; 44:1-3; 61:3; 78:52-55; 97:10; 105:14-45 (with Acts 7:34-36); 124:1-8; Prov. 16:7. *In thwarting evil purpose,* Gen. 50:20 (with Gen. 45:5-7; Psa. 105:17; Acts 7:9, 10); Ex. 14:4; Num. 23:7, 8, 23 (with Num. 22:12-18; 24:10-13); Ezra 5:5; Neh. 6:16; Esth. 7:10 (with 6:1-12; 9:25); Job 5:12, 13 (with Isa. 8:9, 10); Psa. 33:10; Acts 5:38, 39. *In turning curse into blessing,* Deut. 23:4, 5; Phil. 1:12, 19. *In exalting the lowly,* 2 Sam. 7:8, 9; 1 Chr. 17:7, 8; Psa. 68:6; 113:7, 8. *In leading men to repentance,* **Amos** 4:7-12. *In punishing evil-doers,* Deut. 2:30; Josh. 10:10, 11, 19; 11:20; Judg. 9:23, 24; 1 Chr. 5:26; Isa. **41:2, 4.**

*In punishing rulers,* Dan. 5:18, 22. *In punishing nations,* Deut. 9:4, 5; Job 12:23; Ezek. 29:19, 20. *In ordaining instruments of chastisement,* Isa. 13:3-5. *In using the heathen to execute his purpose,* Ezra 6:22; Isa. 44:28; 45:1-6, 13.

*In fulfilling prophecy,* 1 Kin. 12:15; 2 Chr. 10:15; 36:22, 23; Ezra 1:1; Acts 3:17, 18.

*In nature,* Job 12:7-20; 37:6-24; 38:25-27, 41; 39:5, 6; Psa. 104:16-19, 24-30; 135:7; Jer. 10:13; 51:16; 14:22; 31:35.

INSTANCES OF: *Saving Noah,* Gen. 7:1; 2 Pet. 2:5. *The call of Abraham,* Gen. 12:1. *Protecting Abraham, Sarah, and Abimelech,* Gen. 20:3-6. *Deliverance of Lot,* Gen. 19. *Care of Isaac,* Gen. 26:2, 3; *of Jacob,* Gen. 31:7. *The mission of Joseph,* Gen. 37: 5-10; 39:2, 3, 21, 23; 45:7, 8; 50:20; Psa. 105:17-22. *Warning Pharaoh of famine,* Gen. 41. *Delivering the Israelites,* Ex. 3:8; 11:3; 13:18; Acts 7:34-36. *The pillar of cloud,* Ex. 13:21; 14:19, 20. *Dividing the Red Sea,* Ex. 14:21. *Delaying and destroying Pharaoh,* Ex. 14:25-30. *Purifying the waters of Marah,* Ex. 15:25. *Supplying manna and quail,* Ex. 16:13-15; Num. 11:31, 32. *Supplying water at Meribah,* Num. 20:7-11; Neh. 9:10-25. *Protection of homes while at feasts,* Ex. 34:24. *In the conquest of Canaan,* Psa. 44:2, 3. *Saving David's army,* 2 Sam. 5:23-25. *The revolt of the ten tribes,* 1 Kin. 12:15, 24; 2 Chr. 10:15. *Fighting the battles of Israel,* 2 Chr. 13:12, 18; 14:9-14; 16:7-9; 20:15; 17, 22, 23; 32:21, 22. *Restoring Manasseh after his conversion,* 2 Chr. 33:12, 13. *Feeding Elijah and the widow,* 1 Kin. 17; 19:1-8. *In prospering Hezekiah,* 2 Kin. 18:6, 7; 2 Chr. 32:29; *and Asa,* 2 Chr. 14:6,7; *and Jehoshaphat,* 2 Chr. 17:3, 5:20: 30; *and Uzziah,* 2 Chr. 26:5-15; *and Jotham,* 2 Chr. 27:6; *and Job,* Job 1:10; 42:10, 12; *and Daniel,* Dan. 1:9. *In turning the heart of the king of Assyria to favor the Jews,* Ezra 6:22. *In rescuing Jeremiah,* Lam. 3:52-58 (with Jer. 38:6-13). *Restoration of the Jews,* 2 Chr. 36:22, 23; Ezra 1:1. *Rescuing the Jews from Haman's plot,* the Book of Esther. *Rebuilding the walls of Jerusalem,* Neh. 6:16. *Warning Joseph in dreams,* Matt. 1:20; 2:13, 19, 20; *and the wise men of the east,* Matt. 2:12, 13. *Deliverance of Paul,* 2 Cor. 1:10. *Restoring Epaphroditus,* Phil. 2:27. *Banishment of John to Patmos,* Rev. 1:9.

MYSTERIOUS AND MISINTERPRETED: *The silence of God,* Job 33: 13. *The adversity of the righteous,* Eccl. 7:15; 8:14. *The prosperity of the wicked,* Job 12:6; 21:7; 24:1; Psa. 73:2-5, 12-17; Eccl. 7:15; 8:14; Jer. 12:1, 2; Mal. 3:14, 15. *Likeness in the lot of the righteous and the wicked,* Eccl. 9:2, 11. *Permitting the violence of the wicked toward the righteous,* Job 24:1-12; Hab. 1:2, 3, 11, 13, 14.

**Righteousness of,** Gen. 18:25; Judg. 5:11; Psa. 7:9; 72:1; 88:12; 89:16; 119:40; 143:1; Isa. 41:10; 56:1; Jer. 4:2; 9:24; Mic. 7:9; Acts 17:31;

*Ascribed by men,* Ex. 9:27; Ezra 9;15; Job 36:3; Psa. 5:8; 48:10; 71:15, 19; 89:14; 97:2; 116:5; 145:7, 17; Jer. 12:1; Dan. 9:7, 14; 2 Tim. 4:8. *Ascribed by Jesus,* John 17:25. *Ascribed by the angel,* Rev. 16:5. *Revealed in the heavens,* Psa. 50:6. *Revealed in the gospel,* Rom. 1:17; 3:4-6, 21, 22; 10:3, 4; 2 Pet. 1:1.

*Endureth forever,* Psa. 119:142, 144; Isa. 51:8. See HOLINESS OF, PERFECTION OF, above.

**Saviour,** Ex. 6:6, 7; Psa. 3:8; 18:30; 28:8; 31:5; 33:18, 19; 34:22; 37:39, 40; 74:12; 76:8, 9; 85:9; 96:2; 98:2, 3; 111:9; 118:14; 121:7; 149:4; Isa. 26:1; 33:22; 35:4; 43:3, 11, 12, 14; 45:15, 17, 21, 22; 46:12, 13; 49:25; 50:2; 59:1; 60:16; 63:8, 16; Jer. 3:23; 14:8; 33:6; Ezek. 37:23; Hos. 1:7; 13:4; Joel 3:16; Jonah 2:9; Luke 1:68; John 3:16, 17; Rom. 8:30-32; 1 Tim. 2:3, 4; 4:10; Tit. 1:2, 3; 2:10, 11; 3:4, 5; 1 John 4:9, 10.

*Called Redeemer,* Psa. 19:14; Isa. 41:14; 47:4; 48:17; Jer. 50:34; *salvation,* Psa. 27:1; 62:1, 2, 6, 7; Isa. 12:2; *God of salvation,* Psa. 25:5; 65:5; 68:19, 20; 88:1; *rock of salvation,* Deut. 32:15, 31; *shield,* Deut. 33:29.

*From national adversity,* Ex. 15:2; Isa. 25:4, 9; 52:3, 9,10. *From sin,* Job. 33:24, 27-30; Isa. 44:22-24; Rom. 1:16; *through Christ,* 2 Tim. 1:9.

**Self-Existent:** *Hath life in himself,* John 5:26. *Is the I am that I am,* Ex. 3:14. *Is the first and the last,* Isa. 44:6. *Is the living God,* Jer. 10:10. *Liveth forever,* Deut. 32:40. *Needeth nothing,* Acts 17:24, 25.

**Sovereign,** Ex. 20:3; Job. 25:2; 33:13; 41:11; Psa. 44:4; 47:8; 59:13; 74:12; 82:1, 8; 83:18; 93:1, 2; 95:3-5; 96:10; 97:1, 5, 9; 98:6; 99:1; 103:19; 105:7; 113:4; 115:3, 16; 136:2, 3; Isa. 24:23; 33:22; 40:22, 23; 43:15; 44:6; 52:7; 66:1; Lam. 3:37; Mic. 4:7, 13; Mal. 1:14; John 10:29; 19:11; Acts 7:49; Rom. 9:19; 11:36; Eph. 4:6; 1 Tim. 6:15, 16; Heb. 1:3; Jas. 4:12; Rev. 4:11; 19:6.

*Of heaven,* 2 Chr. 20:6. *Of earth,* Ex. 9:29; Josh. 3:11; Psa. 24:1, 10; 47:2, 7, 8; 50:10-12; Isa. 54:5; Jer. 10:10; 1 Cor. 10:26. *Of heaven and earth,* Gen. 14:18-20, 22; 24:3; Ex. 19:5; Deut. 4:39; 10:14, 17; Josh. 2:11; 2 Kin. 19:15; 1 Chr. 29:11, 12; Neh. 9:6; Psa. 89:11; 135:5, 6; Matt. 6:10; 11:25; Luke 10:21; Acts 17:24-26; Rev. 11:4, 13, 17.

*Of the spirits of all flesh,* Num. 27:16; Deut. 32:39; Job 12:9, 10, 16, 17; Psa. 22:28, 29; Eccl. 9:1; Isa. 45:23; Jer. 18:1-23; Ezek. 18:4; Rom. 14:11.

*In human affairs,* Psa. 75:6, 7; Jer. 27:5-7; 32:27, 28; Ezek. 16:50; 17:24; Dan. 2:20, 21, 47; 4:3, 17, 25, 34, 35, 37; 5:18, 26-28.

*Everlasting,* Ex. 15:18; Psa. 10:16; 29:10; 66:7; 145:11-13; 146:10; Lam. 5:19; Dan. 6:26.

**Spirit,** John 4:24; Acts 17:29.

See footnote, HOLY SPIRIT, Acts 1:2.

**Teacher,** Job 36:22; Psa. 94:10, 12; 119:135, 171; Isa. 28:26; 54:13; John 6:45; 1 Thess. 4:9.

**Truth,** Gen. 24:27; Ex. 34:6; Num. 23:19; 1 Sam. 15: 29; Psa.25:10; 31:5; 33:4; 43:3; 57:3, 10; 71:22; 86:11, 15; 89:14; 108:4; 132:11; 138:2; Isa. 25:1; 65:16; Dan. 4:37; John 8:26; Rom. 3:4, 7; Tit. 1:2; Rev. 6:10; 15:3.

*Endureth to all generations,* Psa. 117:2; 146:6.

**Ubiquitous.** See OMNIPRESENT, above.

**Unity of,** Deut. 6:4; Isa. 42:8. *Taught by Jesus,* Mark 12:29, 32; John 17:3; *by St. Paul,* 1 Cor. 8:4, 6; Gal. 3:20; Eph. 4:6; 1 Tim. 2:5.

*Disbelieved in by Syrians,* 1 Kin. 20:28.

*Believed in by devils,* Jas. 2:19.

**Unsearchable,** Deut. 29:29; Job 5:8, 9; 9:10; 11:7-9; 26:9, 14; 36:26; 37:5, 23; Psa. 77:19; 139:6; 145:3; Prov. 30:4; Eccl. 3:11; 11:5; Isa. 40:28; 45:15; 55:8, 9; Rom. 11:33, 34; 1 Cor. 2:10, 11, 16.

SYMBOLIZED: *By darkness,* Ex. 20:21; Deut. 4:11; 5:22; 1 Kin. 8:12; Psa. 18:11; 97:2. *By the cloud upon the mercy-seat,* Lev. 16:2.

*Name of, secret,* Judg. 13:18. *Dwells in thick darkness,* 1 Kin. 8:12; Psa. 97:2. *Known only to Christ, and to those to whom Christ reveals him,* Matt. 11:27.

See footnote, MYSTERIES, Mark 4:11.

**Wisdom of,** Ezra 7:25; Job 9:4; 12:13, 16; Isa. 31:2; Dan. 2:20-22, 28; Rom. 11:33; 16:27; 1 Cor. 1:24, 25.

*Infinite,* Psa. 147:5. *Manifold,* Eph. 3:10. *Ascribed, by angels,* Rev. 7:12.

*Works made in,* Psa. 104:24; 136:5; Prov. 3:19, 20; Jer. 10:12.

See KNOWLEDGE OF, above.

**† ADAM.** *Creation of,* Gen. 1:26-28; 2:7; 1 Cor. 15:45; 1 Tim. 2:13. *History of, before he sinned,* Gen. 1:26-30; 2:16-25. *Temptation and sin of,* Gen. 3; Job 31:33; Isa. 43:27; Hos. 6:7; Rom. 5:14-21; 1 Tim. 2:14. *Subsequent history of,* Gen. 3:20-24; *Children of,* Gen. 4:1, 2, 25; 5:3, 4. *Age of, at death,* Gen. 5:1-5. *Brought sin into the world,* 1 Cor. 15:22.

*Type of Christ,* Rom. 5:14.

not found an [m]help meet[C] for him.

21[Q]And the LORD God caused a deep sleep to fall upon [3]Ăd′ăm, and he slept: and he took one of his ribs, and closed up the flesh instead thereof:[S]

22 And the rib, which the LORD God had taken from man, [4]made he a [r,s]woman, and brought her unto the man.[Q S]

23 And Ăd′ăm said, This *is* now bone of my bones, and flesh of my flesh: she shall be called [r]Woman[C], because she was taken out of Man.[C Q]

24 [t]Therefore shall a [u]man leave his [v]father and his [w]mother, and shall cleave unto his [m]wife: and they shall be [x]one flesh.[Q]

25 And they were both naked, the man and his [m]wife, and were [y]not ashamed.[T]

## CHAPTER 3

*The serpent deceives Eve. 6 Man's fall. 9 God arraigns them. 14 The serpent is cursed. 15 The promised seed. 16 The punishment of mankind. 21 Their first clothing. 23 They are driven out of paradise.*

NOW[T] the [a,b]serpent was more [c]subtil than any beast of the field which the LORD God had made. And he [d,e]said unto the [f]woman, Yea, hath God said, Ye shall not eat of every tree of the garden?[Q]

2 And the [f]woman said unto the [a,b]serpent, We may eat of the fruit of the trees of the garden:

3 But of the fruit of the [g,h]tree which *is* in the midst of the garden, God hath said, [i]Ye shall not eat of it, neither shall ye touch it, lest ye die.

4 And the [a,b]serpent [j]said unto the [f]woman, [d,k]Ye shall not surely die:[Q]

5 [d,k]For God doth know that in the day ye eat thereof, then your eyes shall be opened, and ye shall be as [1]gods, [l]knowing *good and evil.

6 [m]And when the [f]woman saw that the [g]tree *was* [n]good for food, and that it *was* pleasant to the eyes, and a tree [2]to be [o,p]desired to make *one* [q]*wise*, †she [r]took of the fruit thereof, and did eat, and [d]gave also unto her [s]husband with her; and †he did eat.[Q]

7 [t]And the eyes of them both were opened, and they [u]knew that they *were* naked; and they sewed [v]fig leaves together, and made themselves [3,w]aprons.

8 And they heard the [4,x]voice of the LORD God walking in the garden in the [5]cool of the day: and [6,s]Ăd′ăm and his [f]wife [u,y]hid themselves from the presence of the LORD [z]God amongst the trees of the garden.

9 And the LORD God called unto [6,a]Ăd′ăm, and said unto him, Where *art* thou?

10 And [a]he said, I heard thy voice in the garden, and I was [b,c]afraid, because I *was* naked; and I hid myself.

11 And he said, Who told thee that thou *wast* naked? †,[d]Hast thou eaten of the tree, whereof I commanded thee that thou shouldest not eat?

12 And the man [e,f]said, [g]The [h]woman whom thou gavest *to be* with me, she gave me of the tree, and I †did eat.

13 And the LORD God said unto the [h]woman, What *is* this *that* thou hast done? And the woman [g]said, The [i,j]serpent beguiled me, and I †did eat.[Q]

14 And the LORD God said unto the [i,j]serpent, Because thou hast done this, thou *art* [k]cursed

---

v.20—4045 BC
See footnote, *Time*, Rev. 10:6.

**22**
r *Women, creation of*, Prov. 31:10.
s *Eve*, Gen. 3:20.
4 *Heb.* builded he into

**24**
t *Commandments, enjoining fidelity in wedlock*, Deut. 8:2.
u *Husband, relation of, to wife*, Num. 30:6.
v *Father*, Psa. 27:10.
w *Mother*, 1 Kin. 2:20.
x *Marriage, unity of husband and wife in*, Gen. 34:9.

**25**
y *Innocency*, Psa. 26:6.

**1**
a *Serpent, subtlety of*, Num. 21:6.
b *Satan, symbolized*, Matt. 4:10.
c *Craftiness, instances of*, Psa. 83:3.
d *Influence, evil, instances of*, 1 Cor. 7:14.
e *Temptation, sources of*, vs. 1-15; Luke 11:4.
f *Woman, fall of, and curse upon*, vs. 1-16; Prov. 31:10.

**3**
g *Tree, of knowledge*, Rev. 22:14.
h *Symbols and Similitudes*, Heb. 9:9.
i *Probation*, Rom. 5:4.

**4**
j *Presumption, instances of*, Psa. 19:13.
k *Falsehood, instances of*, Job 21:34.

v.5—4045 BC

**5**
l *Knowledge*, Luke 11:52.
1 R. V. God,

**6**
m *Unbelief, instances of*, Heb. 3:12.
n *Appetite, an occasion of temptation*, Prov. 23:2.
o *Ambition, instances of*, Hab. 2:5.
p *Covetousness, instances of*, Isa. 57:17.
q *Wisdom, worldly*, Prov. 2:2.
r *Disobedience to God, instances of*, Eph. 5:6.
s *Adam, temptation and sin of*, Gen. 2:19.
2 *Or*, desirable to look upon

**7**
t *Innocency, contrasted with guilt*, Psa. 26:6.
u *Conscience, guilty, instances of*, Acts 23:1.
v *Fig Tree, leaves of*, Luke 13:6.
w *Dress*, Zech. 3:4.
3 *Or*, girdles.

**8**
x *Anthropomorphisms, voice attributed to God*, Gen. 11:5.
y *Conviction of sin, instances of*, John 16:8.
z *God, appearances of*, Gen. 2:2.
4 *Or*, sound
5 *Heb.* wind
6 R.V. the man

**9**
a *Adam*, Gen. 2:19.

**10**
b *Fear of God*, Acts 9:31.
c *Sin, fruits of*, Rom. 5:12.

**11**
d *Sin, known to God*, Rom. 5:12.

**12**
e *Cowardice, instances of*, Lev. 26:36.
f *Excuses, for disobedience*, Luke 14:18.
g *Responsibility, attempts to shift*, Ezek. 18:20.
h *Woman*, Prov. 31:10.

**13**
i *Serpent*, Num. 21:6.
j *Satan, symbolized*, Matt. 4:10.

**14**
k *Curse*, Judg. 5:23

---

*** GOOD AND EVIL.** *Choice between, by Adam and Eve*, Gen. 3. *Exhortation to choose between*, Josh. 24:15. *Subjective conflict between*, Rom. 7:9-25.

**† FALL OF MAN.** *By transgression of commandments*, Gen. 2:16, 17; 3:1-3, 6, 11, 12; Job 31:33; Isa. 43:27; Hos. 6:7. *Through deception of Satan*, Gen. 3:4, 5, 13; 2 Cor. 11:3; 1 Tim. 2:14. *Through evil desire*, Gen. 3:6.

**Consequences of:** *Knowledge of nakedness*, Gen. 3:7; *of guilt*, Gen. 3:8-10. *Cursing of serpent*, Gen. 3:14, 15; *of the ground*, Gen. 3:17, 18. *Multiplying of sorrow*, Gen

v.14—4045 BC
See footnote, *Time*, Rev. 10:8.

*l Judgments*, Ex. 6:6.

15
*m Malice*, Eph. 4: 31.
*n Jesus, prophecies concerning coming of*, Matt. 1: 21.
*o Promises, of victory of Messiah over Satan*, 2 Cor. 1:20.
7 Or, lie in wait for

16
*p Wicked, punishment of*, vs.16-19; Psa. 73:3.
*q Sin, punishment of*, vs. 16-19; Rom. 5:12.
*r Adversity, a dispensation of God*, Psa. 10:6.
*s Birth*, Psa. 48:6.
*t Children*, Mark 10:14.
*u Husband*, Num. 30:6.
*v Family, government of*, 1 Chr. 13:14.
*w Wife*, Prov. 5:18.

17
*x Disobedience, instances of*, Eph. 5:6.
8 R. V. toil

18
*y Thorn*, Hos. 2:6.
*z Thistle*, Hos. 10:8.

19
*a Curse*, Judg. 5: 23.
*b Labor*, Luke 10:7.
*c Death, as a judgment*, Num. 23:10.
*d Dust*, Eccl. 3:20.
*e Corruption*, Job 17:14.

20
*f Adam*, Gen. 2:19.
*g Wife*, Prov. 5:18.
*h Race, unity of*, Acts 17:26.

above all cattle, and above every
beast of the field; [l]upon thy belly
shalt thou go, and dust shalt
thou eat all the days of thy life:
15 And I will put [m]enmity between
[i,j]thee and the [h]woman,
and between thy seed and her
[n]seed; [o]it shall [7]bruise thy head,
and thou shalt [7]bruise his heel.
16 Unto the [p]woman he said,
[l,q]I will greatly multiply thy
[r]sorrow, and thy conception; in
sorrow thou shalt [s]bring forth
[t]children; and thy desire *shall be*
to thy [u]husband, and [v]he shall
rule over [w]thee.
17 And unto [p]Ăd'ăm he said,
Because thou hast hearkened
unto the voice of thy [w]wife, and
[†,x]hast eaten of the tree, of
which I commanded thee, saying,
Thou shalt not eat of it:
[k,l]cursed *is* the [‡]ground for thy
sake; in [8]sorrow shalt thou eat
*of* it all the days of thy life:
18 [l,y]Thorns also and [z]thistles
shall it bring forth to thee; and
thou shalt eat the herb of the
field;
19 [a]In the [‖,b]sweat of thy face
shalt thou eat bread, till thou
[c]return unto the [‡]ground; for
out of it wast thou taken: for
[d]dust thou *art*, and [e]unto dust
shalt thou return.
20 And [f]Ăd'ăm called his
[g]wife's name [§]Ēve; because she
was the mother of [h]all living.
21 Unto [f]Ăd'ăm also and to his
wife did the LORD God make
[i]coats of skins, and clothed them.
22 ¶ And the LORD [j]God said,
Behold, the [f]man is become as
one of us, to [k]know *good and
evil: and now, lest he put forth
his hand, and take also of the
[l]tree of [m]life, and eat, and [n]live
for ever:
23 Therefore the LORD God
[o]sent him forth from the garden
of [p]Ē'dĕn, to [+]till the [‡]ground
from whence he was taken.
24 So he drove out the [f]man;
and he placed at the east of the
garden of [p]Ē'dĕn [q]Chĕr'u-bĭmṣ,
and [9]a flaming sword which
turned every way, to keep the
way of the [l,r]tree of life.

## CHAPTER 4

*The birth, occupation, and religion of Cain and Abel. 3 Their offerings unto the Lord. 8 The murder of Abel. 11 The curse of Cain. 17 His son Enoch, and the first city. 19 Lamech and his two wives. 25 The birth of Seth, 26 and Enos.*

AND [a]Ăd'ăm knew [b]Ēve his
wife; and she conceived,
and bare *Cāin, and said, I have
gotten a [c]man from the LORD.
2 And [b]she again bare his
brother [†]Ā'bĕl. And Ā'bĕl was a
[d]keeper of sheep, but *Cāin was
a [e]tiller of the ground.
3 And in process of time it came
to pass, that *Cāin brought of
the fruit of the ground an [f]offering
unto the LORD.
4 And [†]Ā'bĕl, he also brought
of the [f]firstlings of his flock and

v.21—4045 BC

21
*i Dress*, Zech. 3:4.

22
*j God*, Gen. 2:2.
*k Knowledge, of good and evil*, Luke 11:52.
*l Tree, of life*, Rev. 22:14.
*m Life, tree of*, Eccl. 8:15.
*n Immortality*, 1 Cor. 15:54

23
*o Banishment*, Ezra 7:26.
*p Eden*, Isa. 51:3.

24
*q Cherubim*, Ex. 37:7.
*r Symbols and Similitudes*, Heb.9:9.
9 R. V. the flame of a

1
*a Adam*, vs. 12,25; Gen. 2:19.
*b Eve, children of*, Gen. 3:20
*c Children, the gift of God*, Mark 10:14.

2
*d Shepherd, instances of*, Jer. 31:10.
*e Agriculture*, Gen. 3:23.

3
*f Offerings*, Lev. 6:17.

3:16-19. *Death, physical*, Gen. 3:19; Rom. 5:12, 14; 1 Cor. 15:21, 22; *spiritual*, Rom. 5:12, 14, 18, 19, 21. See footnote, DEPRAVITY OF MAN, Job. 15:14.

‡ **GROUND.** *Man made from*, Gen. 2:7; 3:19, 23; Job 4: 19; 33:6. *Animals from*, Gen.2:19. *Vegetables from*, Gen. 2:9. *Cursed*, Gen. 3:17; 5:29.

‖ **SWEAT**, Gen. 3:19. *An offense in the sanctuary*, Ezek. 44:18. *As of blood*, Luke 22:44.

§ **EVE** (*life*). *Creation of*, Gen. 1:27; 2:21-24; 1 Tim. 2:13. *Named by Adam*, Gen. 2:23; 3:20. *Beguiled by Satan*, Gen. 3; 2 Cor. 11:3; 1 Tim. 2:14. *Clothed with fig leaves*, Gen. 3:7; *with skins*, Gen. 3:21. *Curse denounced against*, Gen. 3:16. *Messiah promised to*, Gen. 3:15. *Children of*, Gen. 4:1, 2, 25; 5:3, 4.

+**AGRICULTURE**, Isa. 28:24-28; 2 Cor. 9:6; Gal. 6:7. *Divinely instituted*, Gen. 2:5, 15; 3:19, 23. *God to be acknowledged in*, Jer. 5:24; Hos. 2:8. *Requires wisdom*, Isa. 28:26; *diligence*, Prov. 27:23-27; Eccl. 11:6; *patience*, Jas. 5:7; *toil*, 2 Tim. 2:6.

*Seedtime and harvest guaranteed*, Gen. 8:22. *Irrigation used in*, Deut. 11:10. *Implements used in*, 1 Sam. 13:19-21. *Practiced by Cain*, Gen. 4:2; *by Noah*, Gen. 9:20; *by Elisha*, 1 Kin. 19:19; *by David*, 1 Chr. 27:26-31; *by Uzziah*, 2 Chr. 26:10; *by Solomon*, Eccl. 2:4-6.

**Laws Concerning:** *As to trespass*, Ex. 22:5; Deut. 23: 24, 25; *damages*, Ex. 22:6; *Sabbath observance*, Ex. 20:10 23:12; 34.21; Matt. 12:1; *the Sabbatic year*, Ex. 23:10, 11; Lev. 25:2-7; *the Jubilee*, Lev. 25:8-28; *the feasts*, Ex. 34:22; *gleanings*, Lev 19:9, 10; Deut. 24:19-21; *first fruits*, Prov. 3:9, 10; *planting of orchards*, Lev. 19:23-25; *hybridizing*, Lev. 19:19; Deut. 22:10. *Planters of new vineyards exempt from military service*, Deut. 20:6.

**Figurative**, Jer. 4:3; 12:13; Matt. 13:3-8, 19-30, 36-43; Luke 8:5-15.

* **CAIN** (*a lance*). *Son of Adam*, Gen. 4:1. *Jealousy and crime of*, Gen. 4:3-15; Heb. 11:4; 1 John 3:12; Jude 11. *Sojourns in the land of Nod*, Gen. 4:16. *Children and descendants of*, Gen. 4:17, 18.

† **ABEL** (*a breath*). Son of Adam. *History of*, Gen. 4:1-15, 25. *References to the death of*, Matt. 23:35; Luke 11:51; Heb. 11:4; 12:24; 1 John 3:12.

of the fat thereof. And the LORD had respect unto [†]Ā′bĕl and to his [1,g]offering:[Q]

5 But unto [*]Cāin and to his [h]offering he had not respect. And Cāin was very [i,j,k]wroth,[C] and his [l]countenance[C] fell.

6 And the LORD said unto [*]Cāin, Why art thou [i]wroth[C]? and why is thy [l]countenance[C] fallen[C]?

7 If thou doest well, [1,m]shalt thou not be accepted? and if thou doest not well, sin lieth at the door. And unto thee [2]*shall be* his desire, and thou shalt rule over him.

8 And [*]Cāin talked with [†]Ā′bĕl his brother: and it came to pass, when they were in the field, that Cāin [n]rose up against Ā′bĕl his brother, and [‡,o]slew him.[Q]

9 And the LORD said unto [*]Cāin, Where *is* [†]Ā′bĕl thy brother? And he [p,q]said, I know not: [r,s]*Am* I my brother's keeper?

10 And he said, What hast thou done? [t]the voice of thy brother's blood crieth unto me from the ground.[Q]

11 And [u]now *art* thou [v]cursed from the earth, which hath opened her mouth to receive thy brother's blood from thy hand;

12 [u]When thou [e]tillest[C] the ground, it shall not henceforth yield unto thee her strength; [w]a fugitive and a [3]vagabond[C] shalt thou be in the earth.

13 And [*]Cāin said unto the LORD, [4,x]My punishment *is* greater [5]than I can bear.

14 [y]Behold, thou hast [z]driven me out this day from the face of the earth; and from thy face shall I be hid; and [a]I shall be a fugitive and a [3]vagabond in the earth; and it shall come to pass, *that* every one that findeth me shall [b]slay me.

15 And the LORD said unto him, Therefore [b]whosoever slayeth [*]Cāin, vengeance shall be taken on him sevenfold. And the LORD set a mark upon Cāin, lest any finding him should kill him.

16 ¶ And [*]Cāin went out from the presence of the LORD, and dwelt in the land of Nŏd, on the east of [c]Ē′dĕn.

17 And [*]Cāin knew his wife; and she conceived, and bare Ē′nŏch: and he builded a [d]city, and called the name of the city, after the name of his son, Ē′nŏch.

18 And [e]unto Ē′nŏch was born Ī′răd: and Ī′răd begat Mē-hū′-ja-el: and Mē-hū′ja-el begat Mē-thu̥′sa-el: and Mē-thu̥′sa-el begat Lā′mech.

19 ¶ And Lā′mech [f]took unto him two wives: the name of the one *was* Ā′dah, and the name of the other Zĭl′lah.

20 And Ā′dah bare[C] Jā′bal: he was the father of such as dwell in [g]tents, and *of such as have* cattle.[C]

21 And his brother's name *was* [h]Jū′bal: he was the [i]father of all such as [j]handle the [k,l]harp[C] and [6]organ.[C]

22 And Zĭl′lah, she also bare Tu̥′bal-cāin, [7]an [m,n]instructer[C] of every artificer[C] in [8,o]brass[C] and [p]iron: and the sister of Tu̥′bal-cāin *was* Nā′a-mah.

23 And Lā′mech said unto his [f]wives, Ā′dah and Zĭl′lah, Hear my voice; ye wives of Lā′mech, hearken unto my speech: for I have [q]slain a man [9]to my wounding, and a young man [10]to my hurt.

24 If [*]Cāin shall be [b]avenged sevenfold, truly Lā′mech seventy and sevenfold.

25 ¶ And[Q] [r]Ăd′ăm knew his wife again; and she bare a son, and

4
g *Jesus, typified in offerings,* Matt. 1:21.

5
h *Worship, of the wicked, rejected,* Gen. 22:5.
i *Anger, instances of,* Psa. 37:8.
j *Envy,* Prov. 14:13.
k *Jealousy, instances of,* vs. 6, 8; Psa. 78:58.
l *Countenance,* Prov. 15:13.

7
m *Judgment, according to opportunity and works,* 1 Pet. 1:17.
1 *Or,* shall it not be lifted up?
2 *Or,* is its desire, but thou shouldst rule over it.

8
n *Malice,* Eph. 4:31.
o *Homicide, felonious,* vs. 9-12; Deut. 5:17.

9
p *Falsehood, instances of,* Job 21:34.
q *Sin, fruits of,* vs. 9-14; Rom. 5:12.
r *Sarcasm, instances of,* Judg. 10:14.
s *Selfishness,* 2 Tim. 3:2.

10
t *Sin, known to God,* Rom. 5:12.

11
u *Judgments, on Cain,* vs. 11-15; Ex. 6:6.
v *Curse,* Judg. 5:23.

12
w *Punishment, no escape from,* Lev. 26:41.
3 R. V. wanderer

13
x *Despondency, instances of,* Eccl. 2:20.
4 *Or,* mine iniquity
5 *Or,* than can be forgiven.

14
y *Murmuring, instances of,* Num. 14:2.
z *Banishment,* Ezra 7:26.

a *Despondency, instances of,* Eccl. 2:20.
b *Avenger of Blood,* Deut. 19:6.

See footnote, *Time,* Rev. 10:6.

16
c *Eden,* Isa. 51:3.

17
d *Cities,* Num. 35:8.

18
e *Genealogy,* vs. 16-22; 1 Chr. 5:1.

19
f *Polygamy,* Deut. 17:17.

20
g *Tent,* Gen. 13:5.

21
h *Artisans,* 1 Chr. 29:5.
i *Invention,* 2 Chr. 26:15.
j *Art,* 2 Chr. 16:14.
k *Harp,* Dan. 3:10.
l *Music, instruments of,* 2 Chr. 5:13.

22
m *Master Workman, instances of,* 1 Cor. 3:10.
n *Brazier,* 2 Tim. 4:14.
o *Brass,* Job 28:2.
p *Iron,* Prov. 27:17.
6 R. V. pipe.
7 R. V. the forger of every cutting instrument of
8 *Or,* copper

23
q *Homicide, felonious,* Deut. 5; 17.
9 R. V. for wounding me,
10 R. V. for bruising me.

v.25–3916 BC

25
r *Adam,* Gen. 2:19.

‡**FRATRICIDE.** INSTANCES OF: *By Cain,* Gen. 4:8. *By Abimelech,* Judg. 9:5. *By Absalom,* 2 Sam. 13:28, 29. *By Solomon,* 1 Kin. 2:23-25. *By Jehoram,* 2 Chr. 21:4. See footnote, HOMICIDE, Deut. 5:17.

v.26–3811 BC
See footnote, *Time,* Rev. 10:6.

called his name ‖Sĕth: For God,
*said she,* hath appointed me another seed instead of Ā′bĕl,
whom Cāin slew.

26
*s* *Enos,* 1 Chr. 1:1.
*t* *Worship,* Gen. 22:5.

26 And to ‖Sĕth, to him also
there was born a son; and he
called his name [s]Ē′nos: then began men to [t]call upon the name
of the LORD.

## CHAPTER 5

*The genealogy, age, and death of the patriarchs from Adam to Noah. 24 The godliness and translation of Enoch.*

v.1–4045 BC

1
*a* *Book,* Num. 5:23.
*b* *Genealogy,* vs. 1-32; 1 Chr. 5:1.
*c* *Adam,* Gen. 2:19.
*d* *God, creator,* Gen. 2:2.
*e* *Man, created,* Job 4:17.
*f* *Image, figurative,* 1 Cor. 11:7.

THIS [S,T] *is* the [a]book of the [b]gen-
erations of [c]Ă′dăm. In the
day that [d]God created [e]man, in
the [f]likeness of God made he him; [Q]

2
*g* Mark 10:6.

2 [g]Male and female created he
them; and blessed them, and
called their name [c]Ăd′ăm, in the
day when they were created. [S T Q]

3
*h* *Heredity,* Ezek. 18:2.
*i* *Seth,* Gen. 4:25.

3 ¶ And [c]Ăd′ăm lived an hundred and thirty years, and begat
*a son* in his [h]own likeness, after
his image; and called his name
[i]Sĕth: [Q]
4 And the days of [c]Ăd′ăm after
he had begotten [i]Sĕth were
eight hundred years: and he begat sons and daughters:

v.3–3916 BC

5
*j* *Longevity,* Psa. 91:16.

5 And all the days that [c]Ăd′ăm
lived were [j]nine hundred and
thirty years: and he died.

v.6–3811 BC

6
*k* *Enos,* 1 Chr. 1:1.

6 And [i]Sĕth lived an hundred
and five years, and begat [k]Ē′nos:
7 And [i]Sĕth lived after he begat [G] [k]Ē′nos eight hundred and
seven years, and begat sons and
daughters:
8 And all the days of [i]Sĕth were
[j]nine hundred and twelve years:
and he died.

v.9–3721 BC

9 ¶ And [k]Ē′nos lived ninety
years, and begat *Cā-ī′nan:
10 And [k]Ē′nos lived after he
begat *Cā-ī′nan eight hundred
and fifteen years, and begat sons
and daughters:
11 And all the days of [k]Ē′nos
were [j]nine hundred and five
years: and he died.

v.12–3651 BC

12 ¶ And *Cā-ī′nan lived seventy years, and begat †Mā-hā′-
la-lē-el:
13 And *Cā-ī′nan lived after he
begat †Mā-hā′la-lē-el eight hundred and forty years, and begat
sons and daughters:
14 And all the days of *Cā-ī′-
nan were [j]nine hundred and ten
years: and he died.

v.15–3586 BC

15 ¶ And †Mā-hā′la-lē-el lived
sixty and five years, and begat
‡Jā′red:
16 And †Mā-hā′la-lē-el lived
after he begat ‡Jā′red eight hundred and thirty years, and begat
sons and daughters:
17 And all the days of †Mā-
hā′la-lē-el were [j]eight hundred
ninety and five years: and he died.

v.18–3424 BC

18 ¶ And ‡Jā′red lived an hundred sixty and two years, and he
begat ‖Ē′nŏch:
19 And ‡Jā′red lived after he
begat ‖Ē′nŏch eight hundred
years, and begat sons and
daughters:
20 And all the days of ‡Jā′red
were [j]nine hundred sixty and
two years: and he died.

v.21–3359 BC

21
*l* 1 Chr. 1:3; Luke 3:37.

21 ¶ And ‖Ē′noch lived sixty
and five years, and begat [l]Mĕ-
thụ′se-lah:

22
*m* *Fellowship, with God,* 1 Cor. 1:9.

22 And ‖Ē′nŏch §,[m]walked with
God after he begat [l]Mĕ-thụ′se-
lah three hundred years, and begat sons and daughters:
23 And all the days of ‖Ē′nŏch
were [j]three hundred sixty and
five years:
24 And ‖Ē′nŏch §,[m]walked

‖**SETH** (*compensation*). *Son of Adam,* Gen. 4:25, 26; 5:3, 8; 1 Chr. 1:1; Luke 3:38. *Children of,* Gen. 4:26; 5:6, 7. *Age of, at death,* Gen. 5:8.

***CAINAN,** called also KENAN. *Son of Enos,* Gen. 5:9-14; 1 Chr. 1-2; Luke 3:37.

†**MAHALALEEL** (*praise of God*). *Son of Cainan,* Gen. 5:12-17; 1 Chr. 1:2; Luke 3:37.

‡**JARED.** *A descendant of Seth,* Gen. 5:15, 16, 18, 19, 20; 1 Chr. 1:2; Luke 3:37.

‖**ENOCH.** *Father of Methuselah,* Gen. 5:21; 1 Chr. 1:3; Luke 3:37. *Preached to the Antediluvians,* Jude 14, 15. *Translation of,* Gen. 5:18-24; Heb. 11:5.

§ **WALKING. Figurative:** *With God,* Gen. 5:22, 24; 6:9; 17:1. *In Christ,* Col. 2:6. *By the Spirit,* Gal. 5:16. *In love,* Eph. 5:2. *In the light,* 1 John 1:7. *By faith,* 2 Cor. 5:7. *Worthily of the Lord,* Col. 1:10.

See footnotes: COMMUNION WITH GOD, 2 Cor. 13:14; FELLOWSHIP WITH GOD, 1 Cor. 1:9.

v.25–3172 BC

24
n Heb. 11:5.
o *Death, exemption from,* Num. 23:10.
p *Immortality, implied in the translation of Enoch,* 1 Cor. 15:54.
q *Translation,* Heb. 11:5.

v.28–2990 BC

29
r *Children, a blessing,* Mark 10:14.
s *Ground, cursed,* Gen. 3:19.
1 *Or,* which cometh from the ground

v 31–2395 BC

32
t *Shem,* Gen. 6:10.
u *Japheth,* Gen. 7:13.
v.32–2490 BC

with God: and [n]he [o]*was* not: for
God [p,q]took him.[Q]
25 ¶ And [l]Mē-thu̇'se-lah lived
an hundred eighty and seven
years, and begat +Lā'mech:
26 And [l]Mē-thu̇'se-lah lived after he begat+ Lā'mech seven hundred eighty and two years, and
begat sons and daughters:
27 And all the days of [l]Mē-
thu̇'se-lah were [j]nine hundred
sixty and nine years: and he died.
28 ¶ And +Lā'mech lived an
hundred eighty and two years,
and begat a son:
29 And he called his name
☉Nō'ah, saying, [r]This *same* shall
comfort us concerning our work
and toil of our hands, [1]because of
the [s]ground which the LORD
hath cursed.[Q]
30 And +Lā'mech lived after he
begat ☉Nō'ah five hundred ninety and five years, and begat sons
and daughters:
31 And all the days of +Lā'-
mech were [j]seven hundred seventy and seven years: and he
died.
32 ¶ And ☉Nō'ah was five hundred years old: and Nō'ah begat
[t]Shĕm, ▲Hăm, and [u]Jāpheth.[Q]

## CHAPTER 6

*The wickedness of the world, which provoked God's wrath, and caused the flood. 8 Noah finds grace. 14 The order, form, and use of the ark.*

AND[Q] it came to pass, when
*men began to multiply on
the face of the earth, and daughters were born unto them,
2 That the sons of God saw
the daughters of men that they
*were* fair; and they [a]took them
wives of all which they chose.
3 And the [b]LORD said, [c]My
spirit shall not always strive[G] with
[d]man, for that he also *is* flesh:
yet his days shall be [e]an hundred and twenty years.[T]
4 There were giants in the
earth in those days; and also
after that, when the sons of God
came in unto the daughters of
men, and they bare children to
them, the same *became* mighty
men which *were* of old, men of
renown.
5 ¶[Q] And [f]God saw that the
[g]wickedness of *,[h]man *was* great
in the earth, and *that* every
†imagination[G] of the thoughts of
his [i]heart *was* only evil continually.[S T]
6 [j]And it [k,l]repented the
[m]LORD that he had made [h]man
on the earth, and it grieved him
at his heart.
7 And the LORD said, I will
[n,o]destroy [p]man whom I have
created from the face of the
earth; both man, and [q]beast, and
the [r]creeping thing, and the
fowls of the air; for [k]it repenteth
me that I have made them.[T]
8[T] But [s]Nō'ah found [t]grace in
the eyes of the LORD.[S]
9 ¶ These[Q] *are* the [u]generations
of [s]Nō'ah: Nō'ah was a just man
*and* [1,v]perfect in his generations,
*and* Nō'ah [w,x]walked with God.[T]
10 And [s]Nō'ah begat three
sons, ‡Shĕm, [y]Hăm, and [z]Jă'-
pheth.

2
a *Marriage,* Gen. 34:9.
3
b *God, long-suffering of,* Gen. 2:2.
c *Holy Spirit, withdrawn,* Acts 1:2.
d *Wicked, Spirit of God withdrawn from,* Psa. 73:3.
e *Longevity,* Psa. 91:16.
v.3–2510 BC
5
f *God, knowledge of,* Gen. 2:2.
g *Depravity,* Job 15:14.
h *Reprobates,* 1 Cor. 9:27.
i *Heart, known to God,* Psa. 44:21.
6
j *Sin, repugnant to God,* Rom. 5:12.
k *Anthropomorphisms, repentance attributed to God,* Gen. 11:5.
l *Repentance, attributed to God,* Mark 1:4.
m *God, creator,* Gen. 2:2.
7
n *Judgments,* Ex. 6:6.
o *Death, a judgment,* Num. 23:10.
p *Wicked, punishment of,* Psa. 73:3.
q *Animals, under the curse,* Jer. 27:5.
r *Creeping Things,* Rom. 1:23.
8
s *Noah,* Gen. 5:29.
t *Grace of God,* Rom. 4:16.
9
u *Genealogy,* 1 Chr. 5:1.
v *Perfection, attributed to Noah,* Heb. 6:1.
w *Walking, with God,* Gen. 5:22.
x *Fellowship, with God,* 1 Cor. 1:9.
1 *Or,* blameless
10
y *Ham,* Gen. 5:32.
z *Japheth,* Gen. 7:13.

---

**+ LAMECH.** *Son of Methuselah, and father of Noah, lived* 777 *years,* Gen. 5:25-31; 1 Chr. 1:3. *Ancestor of Jesus,* Luke 3:36.

**☉ NOAH** (*rest, quiet*). *Son of Lamech,* Gen. 5:28, 29. *Builds an ark and saves his family from the flood,* Gen. 6:14-22; 7:8; Matt. 24:38, 39; Luke 17:26, 27; Heb. 11:7; 1 Pet. 3:20; 2 Pet. 2:5. *Builds an altar and offers sacrifices,* Gen. 8:20, 21. *Receives the covenant from God that no flood should again visit the earth; the rainbow instituted as a token of the covenant,* Gen. 8:20-22; 9:9-17. *Intoxication of, and his curse upon Canaan,* Gen. 9:20-27. *His blessing upon Shem and Japheth,* Gen. 9:26, 27. *Dies at the age of nine hundred and fifty years,* Gen. 9:28, 29. *Character of,* Gen. 7:1; Ezek. 14:14, 20.

**▲ HAM.** *Son of Noah,* Gen. 5:32; 9:18, 24; 1 Chr. 1:4. *Provokes his father's wrath and his descendants are cursed.* Gen. 9:20-27. *His children,* Gen. 10:6-20; 1 Chr. 1:8-16.

*** ANTEDILUVIANS.** *Worship God,* Gen. 4:3, 4, 26. *Occupations of,* Gen. 4:2, 3, 20-22. *Arts of,* Gen. 4:2, 3, 20-22; 6:14-22. *Longevity of,* Gen. 5:3-32. *Giants among,* Gen. 6:4. *Enoch prophesies to,* Jude 14,15. *Noah preaches to,* 2 Pet. 2:5. *Christ preaches to,* 1 Pet. 3:19, 20. *Wickedness of,* Gen. 6:5-7. *Destruction of,* Gen. 6:13, 17; 7:1, 21-23; Job 22:15-17; Matt. 24:37-39. Luke 17:26, 27; 2 Pet. 2:5.

**† EVIL IMAGINATION,** Gen. 6:5; 8:21. *Known to God,* 1 Chr. 28:9. *Abomination to God,* Prov. 6:16-18. *Lustful,* Matt. 5:28; 15:19; Mark 7:21; Rom. 1:21. *War against,* 2 Cor. 10:3, 5.

**‡ SHEM.** *Son of Noah,* Gen 5:32; 6:10. *Preserved in the ark,* Gen. 7:13; 9:18; 1 Chr. 1:4. *His filial conduct,* Gen. 9:23-27. *Blessed by Noah,* Gen. 9:26, 27. *In the lineage of Jesus,* Luke 3:36. *Descendants of,* Gen. 10:1, 21-31; 11:10-29; 1 Chr. 1:17-54.

11
a *Depravity*, Job 15:14.

13
b *God*, Gen. 2:2.
c *Revelation, to Noah*, vs. 14-22; 2 Cor. 12:1.
d *Noah*, Gen. 5:29.
e *Wicked, punishment of*, Psa. 73.

14
f *Carpentry*, vs. 14-16; 2 Kin. 12:11.
g *Pitch*, Isa. 34:9.

15
h *Cubit*, Ex. 36:9.

16
i *Window*, Josh. 2:15.
2 R. V. light

17
j *Breath, of life*, Gen. 7:15.
k *Death, penalty*, Num. 23:10.

11 The earth also was [a]corrupt before God, and the earth was filled with violence.

12 And God looked upon the earth, and, behold, it was [a]corrupt; for all flesh had corrupted his way upon the earth.[Q]

13 [Q] And [b]God [c]said unto [d]Nō'ah, The end of all flesh is come before me; for the earth is filled with violence through them; and, behold, I will [e]destroy them with the earth.

14 [f]Make [d]thee an ‖ark[G] of gopher wood; rooms shalt thou make in the ark, and shalt pitch it within and without with [g]pitch.

15 And this *is the fashion*[G] which thou shalt make it *of*: The length of the ‖ark *shall* be three hundred [h]cubits,[G] the breadth of it fifty cubits,[G] and the height of it thirty cubits.[G]

16 A [2,i]window shalt thou make to the ‖ark, and in a [h]cubit shalt thou finish it above; and the door of the ark shalt thou set in the side thereof; *with* lower, second, and third *stories* shalt thou make it.

17 And, behold, [b]I, even I, do bring a §flood of waters upon the earth, to [e]destroy all flesh, wherein *is* the [j]breath of life, from under heaven; *and* every thing that *is* in the earth shall [k]die.

18 But with [d,l]thee will [m]I establish my [n]covenant; and thou shalt come into the ‖ark, thou, and thy [o]sons, and thy wife, and thy sons' wives with thee.

19 And of every [p]living thing of all flesh, two of every *sort* shalt thou bring into the ‖ark, to keep *them* alive with thee; they shall be male and female.

20 Of fowls after their kind, and of cattle after their kind, of every creeping thing of the earth after his kind, two of every *sort* shall come unto thee, to keep *them* alive.

21 And take [d]thou unto thee of all [q]food that is eaten, and thou shalt gather *it* to thee; and it shall be for food for thee, and for [p]them.

22 Thus [r]did [d]Nō'ah; according to all that God commanded him, so did he.[Q]

## CHAPTER 7

*Noah, with his family, and the living creatures, enter into the ark. 17 The beginning, increase, and continuance of the flood. 21 All flesh destroyed.*

AND the [a]LORD said unto [b]Nō'ah, [c]Come thou and [d]all thy house into the [e]ark; for thee have I seen righteous before me in this generation.[Q]

2 Of every clean [f]beast thou shalt take to thee by *sevens,

18
l *Parents, covenant benefits of*, 2 Cor. 12:14.
m *God, faithfulness of*, Gen. 2:2.
n *Covenant, of God with men*, Deut. 29:1.
o *Children, share benefits of covenant privileges*, Mark 10:14.

19
p *Animals*, Jer. 27:5.

21
q *Food*, Psa. 136: 25.

22
r *Obedience, instances of*, Heb. 5:8.

v.1-2390 BC

1
a *God, preserver, exemplified*, Gen. 2:2.
b *Noah*, Gen. 5:29.
c *Temporal Blessings, from God*, Psa. 103:2.
d *Children, of the righteous, blessed of God*, Mark 10: 14.
e *Ark, Noah's*, Gen. 6:14.

2
f *Animals*, Jer. 27:5.

‖ **ARK**, Noah's. *Directions for building of*, Gen. 6:14-16. *Noah and family preserved in*, Gen. 6:18; 7; 8; Matt. 24:38; Heb. 11:7; 1 Pet. 3:20. *Animals saved in*, Gen. 6:19, 20; 7:1-16; 8:16-19.

§ **FLOOD**, the deluge. *Foretold*, Gen. 6:13, 17. *History of*, Gen. chaps. 6-8. *References to*, Job 22:16; Psa. 90:5; Matt. 24:38, 39; Luke 17:26, 27; Heb. 11:7; 1 Pet. 3:20; 2 Pet. 2:5; 3:6. *The promise that it should not recur*, Gen. 8:20, 21; 9:8-17; Isa. 54:9.

See footnote, METEOROLOGY, Matt. 16:2.

* **SEVEN.** Interesting facts concerning the number, which by many is believed to be mystical.

**Seven Days:** *Week consists of*, Gen. 2:3; Ex. 20:11; Deut. 5:13, 14. *Noah in the ark before the flood*, Gen. 7:4, 10; *remains in the ark after sending forth the dove*, Gen. 8:10, 12. *Mourning for Jacob lasted*, Gen. 50:10; *of Job*, Job 2:13. *The plague of bloody waters in Egypt lasted*, Ex. 7:25. *The passover lasted*, Ex. 12:15. *The feast of tabernacles lasted*, Lev. 23:34, 42. *The Israelites compassed Jericho*, Josh. 6:4. *Saul directed by Samuel to tarry at Gilgal, awaiting the prophet's command*, 1 Sam. 10:8; 13:8. *The elders of Jabesh-gilead ask for a truce of*, 1 Sam. 11:3. *Consecration of priests and altars lasted*, Ex. 29:30, 35. Ezek. 43:25, 26. *Defilements lasted*, Lev. 12:2; 13:4. *Fasts of*, 1 Sam. 31:13. *The firstborn of flocks and sheep shall remain with mother, before being offered*, Ex. 22:30. *Dedication of the temple lasted double*, 1 Kin. 8:65. *Ezekiel sits by the river Chebar in astonishment*, Ezek. 3:15. *The feast of Ahasuerus continued*, Esth. 1:5. *Paul tarries at Tyre*, Acts 21:4; *at Puteoli*, Acts 28:14.

**Seven Weeks:** *The period between the passover and the pentecost*, Lev. 23:15. *In Daniel's vision concerning the coming of the Messiah*, Dan. 9:25. *Ten times*, Dan. 9:24.

**Seven Months:** *Holy convocations in the seventh month*, Lev. 23:24-44; Num. 29; Ezek. 45:25.

**Seven Years:** *Jacob serves for each of his wives*, Gen. 29:15-30. *Of plenty and famine in Egypt*, Gen. 41. *Of famine in Canaan*, 2 Kin. 8:1. *Insanity of Nebuchadnezzar*, Dan. 4: 32. *Seven times, the period between the jubilees*, Lev. 25:8.

**Miscellany of Sevens:** *Of clean beasts taken into the ark*, Gen. 7:2. *Abraham gives Abimelech seven lambs*, Gen. 21:28-30. *Seven kine and seven ears of corn in Pharaoh's vision*, Gen. 41:26-27. *Rams and bullocks to the number of, required in sacrifices*, Lev. 23:18; Num. 23: 1; 29:32; 1 Chr. 15:26; 2 Chr. 29:21; Job 42:8; Ezek. 45:23. *Blood sprinkled seven times*, Lev. 4:6; 14:7. *Oil sprinkled seven times*, Lev. 14:16. *The Israelites compassed Jericho seven times, on the seventh day sounding seven trumpets*, Josh. 6:4. *Elisha's servant looked seven times for appearance of rain*, 1 Kin. 18:43. *Naaman required to*

v.2–2390 BC
See footnote, *Time*, Rev. 10:6.

3
*g Birds*, Eccl. 12:4.

4
*h Rain*, 2 Sam. 1:21.
*i Meteorology*, Matt. 16:2.
*j Forty*, Jonah 3:4.
*k Judgments, on the Antediluvians*, Ex. 6:6.

5
*l Obedience, instances of*, Heb. 5:8.

6
*m Flood*, Gen. 6:17.

11
*n Month*, Ex. 12:2.

the male and his female: and of
beasts that *are* not clean by two,
the male and his female.
3 Of [g]fowls also of the air by
*sevens, the male and the female;
to keep seed[C] alive upon the face
of all the earth.
4 For yet *seven days, and I will
cause it to [h,i]rain upon the earth
[j]forty days and forty nights; and
every living substance[C] that I
have made will I [k]destroy from
off the face of the earth.
5 And [b]Nō′ah [l]did according
unto all that the LORD commanded him.
6 And [b]Nō′ah *was* six hundred
years old when the [m]flood of waters was upon the earth.
7 And [b]Nō′ah went in, and his
sons, and his wife, and his sons'
wives with him, into the [e]ark, because of the waters of the [m]flood.[Q]
8 Of clean [f]beasts, and of
beasts that *are* not clean, and of
[g]fowls, and of every thing that
creepeth upon the earth.
9 There went in two and two
unto [b]Nō′ah into the [e]ark, the
male and the female, as God had
commanded Nō′ah.
10 And it came to pass after
*seven days, that the waters of
the[Q] [m]flood were upon the earth.
11 In the six hundredth year of
[b]Nō′ah's life, in the second
[n]month, the seventeenth day of
the month, the same day were
all the fountains of the great
deep broken up, and the windows of heaven were opened.
12 And the [h,i]rain was upon the
earth [j]forty days and forty
nights.
13 In the selfsame[C] day entered
[b]Nō′ah, and [o]Shĕm, and [p]Hăm,
and †Jā′pheth, the sons of
Nō′ah, and Nō′ah's wife, and
the three wives of his sons with
them, into the [e]ark;
14 They, and every [f]beast after
his kind, and all the cattle after
their kind, and every creeping
thing that creepeth upon the
earth after his kind, and every
[g]fowl after his kind, every bird
of every sort.
15 And they went in unto
[b]Nō′ah into the [e]ark, two and
two of all flesh, wherein *is* the
‡breath of life.
16 And they that went in, went
in male and female of all flesh,
as God had commanded him:
and the LORD shut him in.
17 And the [m]flood was [j]forty
days upon the earth; and the waters increased, and bare[C] up the
[e]ark, and it was lift up above
the earth.
18 And the waters prevailed,
and were increased greatly upon
the earth; and the [e]ark went upon the face of the waters.
19 And the waters prevailed exceedingly upon the earth; and all
the high [1]hills, that *were* under
the whole heaven, were covered.
20 Fifteen [q]cubits upward did
the waters prevail; and the
mountains were covered.
21 And all flesh [k,r]died that
moved upon the earth, both of
fowl, and of cattle, and of beast,

v.12–2390 BC
See footnote *Time*, Rev. 10:6.

13
*o Shem*, Gen. 6:10.
*p Ham*, Gen. 5:32.

19
1 R. V. mountains.

20
*q Cubit*, Ex. 36:9.

21
*r Death, penalty*, Num. 23:10.

*wash in Jordan seven times*, 2 Kin. 5:10. *Seven steps in the temple seen in Ezekiel's vision*, Ezek. 40:22, 26. *The heat of Nebuchadnezzar's furnace intensified sevenfold*, Dan. 3:19. *The light of the sun intensified sevenfold*, Isa. 30:26. *The threatened sevenfold punishment of Israel*, Lev. 26:18-21. *Silver purified seven times*, Psa. 12:6. *Worshiping seven times a day*, Psa. 119:164. *Seven chamberlains at the court of Ahasuerus*, Esth. 1:10. *Seven princes*, Esth. 1:14. *Seven counsellors at the court of Artaxerxes*. Ezra 7:14. *Seven maidens given to Esther*, Esth. 2:9. *Figurative of many sons*, Ruth 4:15; 1 Sam. 2:5; Jer. 15:9. *Seven magi*, Prov. 26:16. *Seven women shall seek polygamous marriage*, Isa. 4:1. *Seven shepherds to be sent forth against Assyria*, Mic. 5:5, 6. *Seven lamps and pipes*, Zech. 4:2. *Seven deacons in the apostolic church*, Acts 6:3. *Seven churches in Asia*, Rev. 1:4, 20. *Seven seals*, Rev. 5:1. *Seven thunders*, Rev. 10:3. *Seven heads and seven crowns*, Rev. 12:3; 13:1; 17:9. *Seven kings*, Rev. 17:10. *Seven stars*, Amos. 5:8; Rev. 1:16, 20; 3:1. *Seven spirits*, Rev. 1:4; 3:1; 4:5; 5:6. *Seven eyes of the Lord*, Zech. 3:9; 4:10; Rev. 5:6. *Seven golden candlesticks*, Rev. 1:12. *Seven angels with seven trumpets*, Rev. 8:2. *Seven plagues*, Rev. 15:1. *Seven horns and seven eyes*, Rev. 5:6. *Seven angels with seven plagues*, Rev. 15:6. *Seven golden vials*, Rev. 15:7. *Scarlet colored beast having seven heads*, Rev. 17:3, 7.

† **JAPHETH.** *Son of Noah*, Gen. 5:32; 6:10; 9:18, 10:21. *His life preserved at the time of the flood*, Gen. 7:13; 9:18. *Prudence of, on the occasion of Noah's drunkenness*, Gen. 9:23, 27. *Descendants of*, Gen. 10:2-5; 1 Chr. 1:5-7.

‡ **BREATH.** *Of life*, Gen. 2:7; 7:22; Acts 17:25. *Of God*, 2 Sam. 22:16; Job 4:9; 33:4; 37:10; Psa. 18:15; 33:6; Isa. 30:33.
**Figurative**, Ezek. 37:9.

and of every [2]creeping thing that creepeth upon the earth, and every [s]man:[Q]

22 All in whose nostrils *was* the [‡]breath of life, of all that *was* in the dry *land*, [k,r]died.

23 And every living substance[G] was [k]destroyed which was upon the face of the ground, both [s]man, and [f]cattle, and the creeping things, and the [g]fowl of the heaven; and they were destroyed from the earth: and [b]Nō'ah only remained *alive*, and they that *were* with him in the [e]ark.

24 And the [m]waters prevailed upon the earth an hundred and fifty days.[Q]

## CHAPTER 8

*The waters assuage. 4 The ark rests on Ararat. 7 The raven and the dove. 15 Noah, being commanded, 18 goeth forth out of the ark. 20 He builds an altar, and offers sacrifice, 21 which God accepts, and promises to curse the earth no more.*

AND [a]God [b]remembered [c]Nō'ah, and every living thing, and all the cattle that *was* with him in the [d]ark: and God made a [e]wind to pass over the [f]earth, and the [g]waters assuaged[G];

2 The fountains also of the deep and the windows of heaven were stopped, and the [h]rain from heaven was restrained;

3 And the waters returned from off the [f]earth continually: and after the end of the hundred and fifty days the waters were abated.

4 And the [d]ark rested in the seventh [i]month, on the seventeenth day of the month, upon the mountains of *Âr'a-răt.

5 And the [g]waters decreased continually until the tenth [i]month: in the tenth *month*, on the first *day* of the month, were the tops of the mountains seen.

6 ¶ And it came to pass at the end of [j]forty days, that [c]Nō'ah opened the [k]window of the [d]ark which he had made:

7 And he sent forth a [l]raven, which went forth to and fro, until the [g]waters were dried up from off the [f]earth.

8 Also he sent forth a [†]dove from him, to see if the [g]waters were abated from off the face of the ground;

9 But the [†]dove found no rest for the sole of her foot, and she returned unto him into the [d]ark, for the waters *were* on the face[G] of the whole earth: then he put forth his hand, and took her, and pulled her in unto him into the ark.

10 And he stayed[G] yet other [m]seven days; and again he sent forth the [†]dove out of the [d]ark;

11 And the [†]dove came in to him in the evening; and, lo, in her mouth *was* an [n]olive leaf pluckt off: so Nō'ah knew that the waters were abated from off the [f]earth.

12 And he stayed yet other [m]seven days; and sent forth the [†]dove; which returned not again unto him any more.

13 ¶ And it came to pass in the six hundredth and first year, in the first [i]*month*, the first *day* of the month, the [g]waters were dried up from off the earth: and [c]Nō'ah removed the covering of the [d]ark, and looked, and, behold, the face of the [o]ground was dry.

14 And in the second [i]month,

**v.21–2390 BC**
See footnote, *Time*, Rev. 10:6.

s *Antediluvians, destruction of*, Gen. 6:1.
2 *Or*, swarming thing that swarmeth

**1**
a *God, His preserving care, exemplified*, Gen. 2:2.
b *Anthropomorphisms, attributing memory to God*, Gen. 11:5.
c *Noah*, vs. 1-22; Gen. 5:29.
d *Ark, Noah's*, vs. 1-22; Gen. 6:14.
e *Meteorology, phenomena of*, vs. 1-22; Matt. 16:2.
f *Earth*, Prov. 8:23.
g *Flood*, vs. 1-22; Gen. 6:17.

**2**
h *Meteorology*, Matt. 16:2.

**4**
i *Time*, Rev. 10:6.

**v.5–2390 BC**
See footnote, *Time*, Rev. 10:6.

**6**
j *Forty, days*, Jonah 3:4.
k *Window*, Josh. 2:15.

**7**
l *Raven*, Job. 38:41.

**10**
m *Seven, days*, Gen. 7:2.

**11**
n *Olive*, Deut. 6:11.

**v.13–2389 BC**

**13**
o *Ground*, Gen. 3:19.

***ARARAT** (*sacred* or *holy land*). *A district of Armenia*, Jer. 51:27. *Ark rested in mountains of*, Gen. 8:4. *Assassins of Sennacherib took refuge in*, 2 Kin. 19:37; Isa.37: 38.

†**DOVE.** *Sent out from the ark by Noah*, Gen. 8:8-12. *Moaning of*, Isa. 38:14; 59:11; Nah. 2:7. *Domesticated*, Isa. 60:8. *Nests of*, Jer. 48:28. *Typical of gentleness*, Matt. 10:16. *Sacrificial uses of*, Gen. 15:9.
**Prescribed for Offerings:** *Purification of women*, Lev. 12:6, 8; Luke 2: 24; *of Nazarites*, Num. 6:10; *of lepers*, Lev. 14:22.
*Burnt offering of*, Lev. 1:14-17. *Trespass offering of, for the impecunious*, Lev. 5:7-10: 12:8. *Sin offering of, for defilement*, Num. 6:10.
*Market for, in the temple*, Matt. 21:12; John 2:14.
*Holy Spirit descends upon Jesus in similitude of*, Matt. 3:16; Luke 3:22; John 1:32.

**v.14–2389 BC**
See footnote, *Time*, Rev. 10:6.

on the seven and twentieth day of
the month, was the [l]earth dried.
15 ¶ And [a]God spake unto
Nō'ah, saying,
16 Go forth of the [d]ark, thou,
and thy wife, and thy sons, and
thy sons' wives with thee.
17 Bring forth with thee every
living thing that *is* with thee, of
all flesh, *both* of fowl, and of cattle, and of every creeping thing
that creepeth upon the earth;
that they may [‡]breed abundantly in the earth, and be fruitful,
and multiply upon the earth.
18 And Nō'ah went forth, and
his sons, and his wife, and his
sons' wives with him:[Q]
19 Every beast, every creeping
thing, and every fowl, *and* whatsoever creepeth upon the earth,
after their kinds, went forth out
of the ark.
20 ¶ And Nō'ah builded an
[‖]altar unto the LORD; and took
of every clean [p]beast, and of
every clean [q]fowl, and [r]offered
burnt [s,t]offerings on the altar.
21 And the LORD smelled a
[u]sweet savour; and the [v]LORD
said in his heart, [w,x]I will not
again [y]curse the [o]ground any
more for man's sake; for the
[z]imagination of man's [a]heart *is*
[b]evil from his youth; neither will
I again smite any more every
thing living, as I have done.[S T Q]
22 [c,d,e]While the earth remaineth, [f]seedtime and [g]harvest, and
cold and heat, and [h]summer and
[§]winter, and [i]day and [j]night
shall not cease.[S T]

## CHAPTER 9

*God blesses Noah. 4 Murder and the eating of blood are forbidden. 8 God's covenant, 13 signified by the rainbow. 18 Noah replenishes the world, 20 plants a vineyard, 21 is drunken, and mocked by Ham. 25 He curses Canaan, 26 blesses Shem and Japheth, 29 and dies.*

AND [S] [a]God [b]blessed [c]Nō'ah
and his sons, and said unto
them, [d,e]Be fruitful, and multiply, and replenish[G] the earth.
2 [f,g]And the fear of [h]you and
the dread of you shall be upon
every [i]beast of the earth, and upon every [j]fowl of the air, upon all
that moveth *upon* the earth, and
upon all the [k]fishes of the sea; into your hand are they delivered.
3 Every moving thing that liveth shall be [l]meat[G] for you; even
as the green herb have [a]I given
you all things.[S Q]
4 [m]But flesh with the life thereof, *which is* the [*]blood thereof,
shall ye not eat.[Q]
5 And surely your [*,n,o,p]blood
of your lives will I require; at
the hand of every beast will I require it, and at the hand of man;

**20**
*p* *Animals, offered in sacrifice*, Jer. 27:5.
*q* *Birds*, Eccl. 12:4.
*r* *Thankfulness, to God, instances of*, Acts 24:3.
*s* *Offerings, burnt*, Lev. 6:17.
*t* *Jesus, typified in offerings*, Matt. 1:21.

**21**
*u* *Worship, acceptable to God*, Gen. 22:5.
*v* *God, mercy of*, Gen. 2: 2.
*w* *Promises, of God's favor*, 2 Cor. 1:20.
*x* *Covenant, of God with men*, Deut. 29:1.
*y* *Curse*, Judg. 5: 23.
*z* *Evil Imagination*, Gen. 6:5.

*a* *Heart, the unregenerate*, Psa. 44: 21.
*b* *Depravity*, Job 15:14.

**v.21–23[illegible]9 BC**

**22**
*c* *Temporal Blessings, from God*, Psa. 103:2.
*d* *God, providence of*, Gen. 2:2.
*e* *Promise, of stability of nature's laws*, 2 Cor. 1:20.
*f* *Agriculture, facts about*, Gen. 3:23.
*g* *Harvests*, Ex. 34: 21.
*h* *Summer*, Isa. 28:4.
*i* *Day*, Gen. 1:5.
*j* *Night*, Gen. 1:5.

**1**
*a* *God, providence of*, vs. 1–3; Gen. 2:2.
*b* *Benedictions, by God upon Noah*, Deut. 21:5.
*c* *Noah*, Gen. 5:29.
*d* *Commandment, enjoining propagation of children*, Deut. 8:2.
*e* *Propagation, of species, enjoined*, Gen. 8:17.

**2**
*f* *Temporal Blessings, from God*, Psa. 103:2.
*g* *Commandment, ordaining man's supremacy over the animal kingdom*, Deut. 8:2.
*h* *Man, dominion of*, Job 4:17.
*i* *Animals*, Jer. 27:5.
*j* *Birds*, Eccl. 12:4.
*k* *Fish, appointed for food*, Matt. 17:27.

**3**
*l* *Food, from God*, Psa. 136:25.

**4**
*m* *Commandment, forbidding eating blood*, Deut. 8:2.

**5**
*n* *Judgments*, Ex. 6:6.
*o* *Death, penalty*, Num. 23:10.
*p* *Homicide, punishment of*, Deut. 5:17.

‡ **PROPAGATION.** *Of species, enjoined*, Gen. 1:11, 12, 21–25, 28; 8:17; 9:1, 7.

‖**ALTAR. Of burnt Offerings:** *Built by Noah*, Gen. 8:20; *by Abraham*, Gen. 12:7, 8; 13:4, 18; 22:9; *by Isaac*, Gen. 26:25; *by Jacob*, Gen. 33:20; 35:1-7; *by Moses*, Ex. 17:15; 24:4; *by Balak*, Num. 23:1, 14, 29; *by Joshua*, Deut. 27:4-7; Josh. 8:30-32: *by Reubenites, Gadites, and half tribe of Manasseh*, Josh. 22:10, 34; *by Gideon*, Judg. 6:26, 27; *by Samuel*, 1 Sam. 7:17; *by Saul*, 1 Sam. 14:35; *by David*, 2 Sam. 24:18, 19, 25; *by Elijah*, 1 Kin. 18:31, 32.

*Used in idolatrous worship*, Judg. 6:25; 1 Kin. 12:32; 16:32; 18:26; 2 Kin. 16:10; 23:12, 15; Isa. 27:9; 65:3; Hos. 8:11; Acts 17:23.

*Mosaic commandments prescribing the construction of*, Ex. 20:24-26; Deut. 27:5-7; Josh. 8:30, 31. See Ezek. 43: 13.

*Called* BRAZEN ALTAR, Ex. 39:39; 1 Kin. 8:64; 2 Kin. 16:14, 15; 2 Chr. 1:5, 6; ALTAR OF GOD, Psa. 43:4; ALTAR OF THE LORD, Mal. 2:13.

IN THE TABERNACLE: *Pattern of*, Ex. 27:1-8. *Constructed by Bezaleel*, Ex. 38:1–7, with 37:1. *Located before the door of the tabernacle*, Ex, 40:6, 29; Lev. 4:18. *Furniture of*, Ex. 27:3-7; 38:3-7; 1 Sam. 2:13, 14. *Horns of*, Ex. 27:2.

*How sanctified*, Ex. 29:36, 37, 44; 30:26-28; 40:10; Lev. 8:10, 11; Num. 7. See Ezek. 43:18-27. *Sanctified everything that touched it*, Ex. 29:37; 30:29; Matt. 23:18, 19. *Fire on, not permitted to go out*, Lev. 6:9-13. *A place of refuge*, Ex. 21:14; 1 Kin. 1:50; 2:28.

IN SOLOMON'S TEMPLE: *Description of*, 2 Chr. 4:1. *Renewed by Asa*, 2 Chr. 15:8. *Removed by Ahaz, and one of idolatrous fashion substituted*, 2 Kin. 16:14-17. *Cleansed by Hezekiah*, 2 Chr. 29:18-24. *Repaired by Manasseh*, 2 Chr. 33:16. *Furniture of, taken to Babylon*, 2 Kin. 25:14.

IN SECOND TEMPLE, Ezra 3:1-6.

EZEKIEL'S VISION OF, Ezek. 43:13-27.

**Altar of Incense,** see footnote, ALTAR OF INCENSE, Ex. 30:1.

§ **WINTER.** *Annual return of, shall never cease*, Gen. 8:22. *Plowing in, in Canaan*, Prov. 20:4. *Rainy season in, in Canaan*, Song 2:11. *Shipping suspended in, on the Mediterranean Sea*, Acts 27:12; 28:11. *Paul remains one, at Nicopolis*, Tit. 3:12. *Summer and winter houses*, Jer. 36:32; Amos 3:15.

See footnote, METEOROLOGY, Matt. 16:2.

* **BLOOD.** *Is the life*, Gen. 9:4; Lev. 17: 11, 14; 19:16; Deut. 12:23; Matt. 27:4, 24. *Forbidden to be used as food*, Gen. 9:4; Lev. 3:17; 7:26, 27; 17:10-14; 19:26; Deut. 12:16, 23; 15:23; 1 Sam. 14:34; Ezek. 33:25; Acts 15:20, 29; 21:25. *Eaten with food*, 1 Sam. 14:33.

*Plague of*, Ex. 7:17–25; Psa. 78:44; 105:29.

See footnotes: BLOOD OF THE COVENANT, Ex. 24:8; BLOOD, *Sacrifical*, Heb. 9:19.

**Figurative:** *Of victories*, Psa. 58:10. *Of oppression and cruelty*, Hab. 2:12. *Of destruction*, Ezek. 35:6. *Of guilt*, Lev. 20:9, 11, 13, 16; 2 Sam. 1:16; Ezek. 18:13. *Of judgments*, Ezek. 16:38; Rev. 16:6.

v.5–2389 BC

5

*q* *Brother*, Prov. 18: 24.
*r* *Avenger of Blood*, Deut. 19:6.
*s* *Punishment, death penalty*, Lev. 26:41.

6

*t* *Commandments, enjoining punishment of murder*, Deut. 8:2.
*u* *Image, figurative*, 1 Cor. 11:7.
*v* *God, creator*, Gen. 2:2.
*w* *Man, created in image of God*, Job 4:17.

8

*x* *God, preserver*, Gen. 2:2.

9

*y* *Covenant, of God with men*, Deut. 29:1.

10

*z* *Animals, God's care of*, Jer. 27:5.

11

*a* *God, preserver*, Gen. 2:2.
*b* *Promises, against the recurrence of a universal flood*, 2 Cor. 1:20.
*c* *Covenant, of God with men*, Deut. 29:1.
*d* *Rain*, 2 Sam. 1: 21.
*e* *Flood*, Gen. 6:17.

12

*f* *Token*, Psa. 86: 17.
*g* *Symbols and Similitudes*, Heb. 9:9.

15

*h* *God, faithfulness of*, Gen. 2:2.

at the hand of every man's
[q,r]brother will I [s]require the life
of man.
6 [t]Whoso sheddeth man's
*blood, by [r]man shall his [s]blood
be shed: for in the [u]image of
[v]God made he [w]man.[S Q]
7 And you, [d,e]be ye fruitful, and
multiply; bring forth abundantly
in the earth, and multiply
therein.
8 ¶ And [x]God spake unto
Nō'ah, and to his sons with
him, saying,
9 [T]And I, behold, [x]I establish
my [y]covenant with you, and
with your seed after you:
10 [y]And with every [z]living
creature that *is* with you, of the
fowl, of the cattle, and of every
beast of the earth with you;
from all that go out of the ark,
to every beast of the earth.
11 And [a,b]I will establish my
[c]covenant with you; neither shall
all flesh be cut off any more by
the [d]waters of a [e]flood; neither
shall there any more be a flood
to destroy the earth.
12 And [a]God said, This *is* the
[f,g]token of the [c]covenant[C] which I
make between me and you and
every living creature that *is* with
you, for perpetual generations:
13 I do set my [†,g]bow in the
cloud, and it shall be for a [f]token
of a [c]covenant between me and
the earth.
14 And it shall come to pass,
when I bring a cloud over the
earth, that the [†,g]bow[C] shall be
seen in the cloud:
15 And [h]I will remember my
[c]covenant, which *is* between me
and you and every living creature of all flesh; and the waters
shall no more become a [e]flood to
destroy all flesh.
16 And the [†]bow shall be in the
cloud; and [b]I will look upon it,
that [a]I may [i]remember the everlasting [c]covenant between God
and every living creature of all
flesh that *is* upon the earth.
17 And God said unto [j]Nō'ah,
[†]This *is* the [f]token of the [c]cove-
nant, which [a]I have established
between me and all flesh that *is*
upon the earth.[T]
18 ¶ And the sons of [r]Nō'ah,
that went forth of the [k]ark, were
[l]Shĕm, and [m]Hăm, and [n]Jā'-
pheth: and Hăm *is* the father of
[‡]Cā'năan.
19 These *are* the three sons of
[j]Nō'ah: and of them was the
whole earth overspread.
20 ¶ And [j]Nō'ah began *to be* an
husbandman,[G] and he [o]planted a
[p]vineyard:
21 And [j]he drank of the [q]wine,
and was [r]drunken; and he was
uncovered within his [s]tent.
22 And [m]Hăm, the father of
[‡]Cā'năan, saw the nakedness of
his father, and told his two
brethren without.[C]
23 And [l]Shĕm and [n]Jā'pheth
took a garment, and laid *it* upon
both their shoulders, and went
backward, and covered the nakedness of their father; and
[t]their faces *were* backward, and
they saw not their father's nakedness.
24 And [j]Nō'ah awoke from his
[q,r]wine, and knew what his
[1,m]younger son had done unto
him.
25 And he said, [u]Cursed *be*
[‡,v]Cā'năan; a servant of servants shall he be unto his brethren.
26 And [j,w]he said, Blessed *be*
the LORD God of [l]Shĕm; and
[‡]Cā'năan shall be his servant.
27 [w]God shall enlarge [n]Jā'-
pheth, and he shall dwell in the
tents of [l]Shĕm; and [‡]Cā'năan
shall be his servant.

v.16–2389 BC
See footnote, *Time*, Rev. 10:6.

16

*i* *Anthropomorphisms, memory attributed to God*, Gen. 11:5.

17

*j* *Noah*, Gen. 5:29.

18

*k* *Ark*, Gen. 6:14.
*l* *Shem*, Gen. 6:10.
*m* *Ham*, Gen. 5:32.
*n* *Japheth*, Gen. 7: 13.

20

*o* *Agriculture*, Gen. 3:23.
*p* *Grape*, Lev. 25:5.

21

*q* *Wine*, Prov. 23: 31.
*r* *Drunkenness*, Luke 21:34.
*s* *Tent*, Gen. 13:5.

23

*t* *Children, good*, Mark 10:14.

24

1 R.V. youngest

25

*u* *Curse*, Judg. 5: 23.
*v* *Children, wicked*, Mark 10:14.

26

*w* *Parents, blessings of*, 2 Cor. 12:14.

† **RAINBOW**, Ezek. 1:28. *A token that the earth shall no more be destroyed by flood*, Gen. 9:8-16. SYMBOLICAL, Rev. 4:3; 10:1.

‡ **CANAAN** (*submissive*). *Son of Ham*, Gen. 9:18, 22, 25-27; 10:6; 1 Chr. 1:8. *Descendants of*, Gen. 10:15-20; 1 Chr. 1:13-16.

28 And Nō′ah lived after the
flood three hundred and fifty
years.
29 And all the days of Nō′ah
were [x]nine hundred and fifty
years: and he died.

## CHAPTER 10

*The generations of Noah. 2 The sons of Japheth. 6 The sons of Ham. 8 Nimrod the first monarch. 21 The sons of Shem.*

NOW these *are* the [a]genera-
tions of the sons of [b]Nō′ah,
[c]Shĕm, [d]Hăm, and [e]Jā′pheth:
and unto them were sons born
after the [f]flood.
2 [g]The sons of [e]Jā′pheth; [g]Gō′-
mēr, and [h]Mā′gŏg, and [i]Măd′-
a-ī, and [j]Jā′văn, and *Tu′bal,
and [k]Mē′shech, and [k]Tī′ras.
3 And the sons of [g]Gō′mēr;
†Ăsh′ke-năz, and [l]Rī′phăth, and
[m]Tō-gär′mah.
4 And the sons of [j]Jā′văn;
‡Ē-lī′shah, and [n]Tär′shish, [o]Kĭt′-
tim, and [p]Dō′da-nim.
5 By these were the isles of the
[1]Gĕn′tīleṣ [q]divided in their
lands; every one after his
[r]tongue, after their families, in
their nations.
6 ¶ [a]And the sons of [d]Hăm;
[s]Cŭsh, and [t]Mĭz′ra-ĭm, and
[u]Phŭt, and [v]Cā′năan.
7 [a]And the sons of [s]Cŭsh; [w]Sē′-
bȧ, and [w]Hăv′i-lah, and [w]Săb′-
tah, and [w]Rā′a-mah, and [w]Săb′-
te-chah: and the sons of Rā′a-
mah; [w]Shē′bȧ, and [w]Dē′dan.
8 And [s]Cŭsh begat [x]Nĭm′rŏd:
he began to be a mighty one in
the earth.
9 He was a mighty [y]hunter before the LORD: wherefore it is
said, Even as [x]Nĭm′rŏd the
mighty hunter before the LORD.
10 And the beginning of his
kingdom was [z]Bā′bel, and
Ē′rĕch, and Ăc′căd, and [a]Căl′-
neh, in the land of Shī′när.
11 Out of that land [2]went forth
Ăs′shur, and builded [b]Nĭn′e-
veh, and the city Rē-hō′both,
and Cā′lah,
12 And Rē′sen between [b]Nĭn′e-
veh and Cā′lah: the same *is* a
great city.
13 And [c]Mĭz′ra-ĭm begat [d]Lụ′-
dim, and [d]Ăn′a-mĭm, and [d]Lē′-
hȧ-bĭm, and [d]Năph′tu-hĭm,
14 And [e]Păth-rụ′sim, and
[e]Căs′lụ-hĭm, out of whom
came [f]Phĭ-lĭs′tim, and [g]Căph′-
tŏ-rĭm.
15 ¶ And [h]Cā′năan begat [i]Sī′-
dŏn his firstborn, and [i]Hĕth,
16 And the [j]Jĕb′u-sīte, and the
[k]Ăm′ôr-īte, and the [l]Gĭr′ga-sīte,
17 And the ‖Hī′vīte, and the
[m]Ärk′īte, and the [m]Sĭn′īte,
18 And the §Är′vad-īte, and the
[n]Zĕm′a-rīte, and the [o]Hā′math-
īte: and afterward were the families of the [p]Cā′năan-ītes spread
abroad.
19 And the border of the [p]Cā′-
năan-ītes was from [q]Sī′dŏn, as
thou comest to [r]Gē′rär, unto
+Gā′zȧ; as thou goest, unto
[s]Sŏd′om, and [t]Gō-mŏr′rah, and
[u]Ăd′mah, and [v]Ze-bō′im, even
unto Lā′shȧ.
20 These *are* the sons of [w]Hăm,
after their families, after their
[x]tongues, in their countries, *and*
in their nations.
21 ¶ Unto [y]Shĕm also, the fa-

29 *x Longevity,* Psa. 91:16.
v.29–2119 BC
1 *a Genealogy,* vs. 1–32; 1 Chr. 5:1.
*b Noah,* Gen. 5:29.
*c Shem,* Gen. 6:10.
*d Ham,* Gen. 5:32.
*e Japheth,* Gen. 7:13.
*f Flood,* Gen. 6:17.
2 *g* 1 Chr. 1:5, 6.
*h Magog,* 1 Chr. 1:5.
*i* 1 Chr. 1:5.
*j* 1 Chr. 1:5, 7.
*k* 1 Chr. 1:5.
3 *l* 1 Chr. 1:6.
*m Togarmah,* Ezek. 27:14.
4 *n* 1 Chr. 1:7.
*o Chittim,* Dan. 11:30.
*p* Or, *Rodanim,* 1 Chr. 1:7.
5 1 R.V. nations
*q Dispersion,* Gen. 11:8.
*r Language,* Dan. 3:29.
6 *s* 1 Chr. 1:8–10.
*t* 1 Chr. 1:8–11.
*u* 1 Chr. 1:8.
*v Canaan,* Gen. 9:18.
7 *w* 1 Chr. 1:9.
8 *x Nimrod,* 1 Chr. 1:10.
9 *y Hunting,* Gen. 27:5.

10 *z Babylon, empire of,* Ezra 5:12.
*a Calneh,* Amos 6:2.
11 2 R. V. he went forth into Assyria,
*b Nineveh,* Jonah 1:2.
13 *c* 1 Chr. 1:8, 11.
*d* 1 Chr. 1:11.
14 *e* 1 Chr. 1:12.
*f Philistines,* Gen. 26:14.
*g Caphtorim,* Deut. 2:23.
15 *h Canaan,* Gen. 9:18.
*i* 1 Chr. 1:13.
16 *j Jebusites,* Deut. 7:1.
*k Amorites,* Gen. 14:13.
*l Girgashites,* Neh. 9:8.
17 *m* 1 Chr. 1:15.
18 *n* 1 Chr. 1:16.
*o Hamath,* 1 Chr. 18:3.
*p Canaanites,* Ex. 23:28.
19 *q Zidon,* Ezek. 28:21.
*r Gerar,* Gen. 20:1.
*s Sodom,* Gen. 13:10.
*t Gomorrah,* Gen. 13:10.
*u Admah,* Deut. 29:23.
*v Zeboim,* Hos. 11:8.
20 *w Ham,* Gen. 5:32.
*x Language,* Dan. 3:29.
21 *y Shem,* Gen. 6:10.

***TUBAL** (*a flowing forth*). *Son of Japheth,* Gen. 10:2; 1 Chr. 1:5. *Descendants of, become a nation,* Isa. 66:19; Ezek. 27:13; 32:26; 38:2, 3; 39:1.

†**ASHKENAZ.** *Son of Gomer,* Gen. 10:3; 1 Chr. 1:6. *Descendants of,* Jer. 51:27.

‡**ELISHAH.** *A descendant of Noah,* Gen. 10:4; 1 Chr. 1:7. *Islands of the Mediterranean bear the name of,* Ezek. 27:7.

‖**HIVITES.** *A tribe of Canaanites,* Gen. 10:17; 1 Chr. 1:15. *Shechemites and Gibeonites were families of,* Gen. 34:2; Josh. 9:7; 11:19. *Esau takes a wife of the,* Gen. 36:2. *Dwelling place of,* Josh. 11:3; Judg. 3:3; 2 Sam. 24:7. *Their land given to the Israelites,* Ex. 23:23, 28; Deut. 20:17; Judg. 3:5. *Conquered by Joshua,* Josh. 9:1; 12:8; 24:11. *Pay tribute to Solomon,* 1 Kin. 9:20, 21; 2 Chr. 8:7, 8.

§**ARVADITES.** *Descendants of Canaan,* Gen. 10:18; 1 Chr. 1:16; Ezek. 27:8, 11.

+**GAZA.** *One of the border cities of the Canaanites,* Gen. 10:19. *A city of the Avim and Anakim,* Deut. 2:23; Josh. 11:22. *A city of the Philistines,* Josh. 13:3; Jer. 25:20; Acts 8:26–39. *Allotted to Judah,* Josh. 15:47; Judg. 1:18. *A temple of Dagon situated at,* Judg. 16:21, 23. *Samson dies at,* Judg. 16:21–31. *On the western boundary of the kingdom of Israel in the time of Solomon,* 1 Kin. 4:24. *Smitten by Pharaoh,* Jer. 47:1. *Prophecies relating to,* Amos 1:6, 7; Zeph. 2:4; Zech. 9:5.

ther of all the children of ○Ē′bĕr, the brother of [z]Jā′pheth the elder, even to him were *children* born.

22 [a]The children of [b]Shĕm; Ē′lăm, and [c]Ăs′shụr, and ▲Är-phăx′ad, and [c]Lŭd, and [c]Ā′ram.

23 And the children of [c]Ā′ram; [c]Ŭz, and [c]Hŭl, and Gē′thĕr, and Măsh.

24 And ▲Är-phăx′ad begat[C] ●Sā′lah; and Sā′lah begat ○Ē′bĕr.

25 And unto ○Ē′bĕr were born two sons: the name of one *was* **Pē′lĕg; for in his days was the [d]earth divided; and his brother's name *was* [e]Jŏk′tan.

26 And [e]Jŏk′tan begat [f]Ăl-mō′-dăd, and [f]Shē′leph, and [f]Hā-zar-mā′veth, and [f]Jē′räh,

27 And [g]Hă-dō′ram, and [g]Ū′zal, and [g]Dĭk′lah,

28 And [h]Ō′bal, and [i]Ă-bĭm′-a-el, and [i]Shē′bȧ,

29 And [j]Ō′phīr, and [j]Hăv′i-lah, and [j]Jō′băb: all these *were* the sons of [e]Jŏk′tan.

30 And their dwelling was from Mē′shȧ, as thou goest unto Sē′-phar a mount of the east.

31 These *are* the sons of [b]Shĕm, after their families, after their [k]tongues, in[C] their lands, after their nations.

32 These *are* the families of the sons of [l]Nō′ah, after their generations, in their nations: and by these were the nations [m]divided in the [d]earth after the [n]flood.

*z Japheth,* Gen. 7:13.

22
*a Genealogy,* 1 Chr. 5:1.
*b Shem,* Gen. 6:10.
*c* 1 Chr. 1:17.

25
*d Earth, early divisions of,* Prov. 8:23.
*e* 1 Chr. 1:19, 20. 23.

26
*f* 1 Chr. 1:20.

27
*g* 1 Chr. 1:21.

28
*h* Or, *Ebal,* 1 Chr. 1:22.
*i* 1 Chr. 1:22.

29
*j* 1 Chr. 1:23.

31
*k Language,* Dan. 3:29.

32
*l Noah,* Gen. 5:29.
*m Dispersion,* Gen. 11:8.
*n Flood,* Gen. 6:17.

## CHAPTER 11

*One language in the world. 3 The building of Babel. 6 The confusion of tongues. 10 The generations of Shem. 27 The generations of Terah the father of Abram. 31 Terah goes from Ur to Haran.*

AND the whole earth was of one [a]language, and of one speech.

2 And it came to pass, as they journeyed from the east, that they found a plain in the land of [b]Shī′när; and they dwelt there.

3 And they said one to another, Go[C] to, let us [c]make *brick, and burn them thoroughly. And they had brick for stone, and †slime[C] had they for [d]morter.

4 And they said, Go to,[C] [e]let us build us a city and a [f]tower, whose top *may reach* unto heaven; and let us [g]make us a name, lest we be scattered abroad upon the face of the whole earth.

5 And the LORD came down to ‡see the city and the [f]tower, which the children of men builded.

6 And the LORD said, Behold, the people *is* one, and they have all one [a]language; and this they begin to do: and now nothing will be restrained[C] from them, which they [g]have imagined to do.

7[S] Go[G] to, let us go down, and there [h]confound their language, that they may not understand one another's speech.[T]

8 So the LORD ‖scattered them abroad from thence upon the

1
*a Language, unity of.* Dan. 3:29.

2
*b Babylon,* Ezra 5:12.

3
*c Art, brickmaking,* 2 Chr. 16:14.
*d Mortar,* Lev. 14. 42.

4
*e False Confidence, instances of,* Psa. 30:6.
*f Tower, of Babel.* 2 Chr. 26:9.
*g Ambition, instances of,* Hab. 2:5.

7
*h Language, confusion of,* Dan. 3:29.

○**EBER.** *The probable founder of the Hebrew race,* Gen. 10:21–25; 11:14, 16, 17; 1 Chr. 1:18, 19, 25; Luke 3:35. *Prophecy concerning,* Num. 24:24.

▲**ARPHAXAD.** *Son of Shem,* Gen. 11:10–13; 1 Chr. 1:17, 18, 24; Luke 3:36.

●**SALAH.** *Son of Arphaxad,* Gen. 11:12–15; 1 Chr. 1:18, 24. *Ancestor of Joseph,* Luke 3:35.

****PELEG** (*division*). *Son of Eber,* Gen. 11:16–19; 1 Chr. 1:19, 25; Luke 3:35.

***BRICK.** USED IN BUILDING: *Babel,* Gen. 11:3; *cities in Egypt,* Ex. 1:11, 14; *houses,* Isa. 9:10; *altars,* Isa. 65:3. *Made by Israelites,* Ex. 5:7–19; 2 Sam. 12:31; Jer. 43:9; Nah. 3:14.

†**BITUMEN.** *An inflammable substance,* Isa. 34:9. *Abounded in the valley of the Dead Sea,* Gen. 14:10. *Used at Babel,* Gen. 11:3; *in the ark of Moses,* Ex. 2:3.

‡**ANTHROPOMORPHISMS,** figures of speech, which attribute human forms, acts, and affections to God. *Representing God as repenting,* Gen. 6:6, 7; Ex. 32:14; Judg. 2:18; 1 Sam. 15:35; 2 Sam. 24:16; 1 Chr. 21:15; Psa. 106:45; Jer. 26:19; Amos 7:3; Jonah 3:10; *as being grieved,* Gen. 6:6; *as being vexed,* Isa. 63:10; *as being jealous,* see footnote, JEALOUSY, Psa. 78:58; *as being angry,* Ex. 22:24; Num. 11:1, 10, 33; 12:9, see footnote, ANGER, OF GOD, 2 Kin. 13:3; *as being amazed,* Isa. 59:16; 63:5; *as reasoning,* Isa. 1:18; *as having memory,* Gen. 9:16; Isa. 43:26; *as having an understanding,* Psa. 147:5; *as having a will,* Rom. 9:19; *as taking an oath,* Isa. 62:8; Heb. 6:17; 7:21, 28; *as laughing,* Psa. 2:4; 37:13; *as walking,* Gen. 3:8; Lev. 26:12; *as standing,* Gen. 28:13; *as resting,* Gen. 2:2, 3; Ex. 20:11; *as sleeping,* Psa. 44:23; 78:65; *as seeing,* Gen. 9:16; 11:5, Ex 3:4, 7; Psa. 94:9; Hab. 1:13; 1 Pet. 3:12; *as hearing,* Psa. 31:2; 94:9; 1 Pet. 3:12; *as talking,* Gen. 22:12, 35:12, 13; *as soliloquizing,* Gen. 11:7.

*For various additional anthropomorphic expressions and terms,* see footnotes: FIGURATIVE, *under* ARM, Psa. 89:13; EAR, Lev. 8:23; EYE, Matt. 6:22; HAND, Ezra 10:19, etc.

‖**DISPERSION.** *Of the descendants of Noah,* Gen. 10:

face of all the earth: and they
left off to build the city.
9 Therefore is the name of it
called [b]Bā′bel; because the
LORD [h]did there confound the
language of all the earth: and
from thence did the LORD ‖scat-
ter them abroad upon the face
of all the earth. [s]
10 ¶ These *are* the [i]generations
of [j]Shĕm: Shĕm *was* an hundred
years old, and begat [k]Är-phăx′-
ad two years after the [l]flood:
11 And Shĕm lived after he begat Är-phăx′ad [m]five hundred
years, and begat sons and
daughters.
12 And [k]Är-phăx′ad lived five
and thirty years, and begat
[n]Sā′lah:
13 And Är-phăx′ad lived after
he begat Sā′lah [m]four hundred
and three years, and begat sons
and daughters.
14 And [n]Sā′lah lived thirty
years, and begat [o]Ē′bĕr:
15 And [n]Sā′lah lived after he
begat [o]Ē′bĕr [m]four hundred and
three years, and begat sons and
daughters.
16 And [o]Ē′bĕr lived four and
thirty years, and begat [p]Pē′lĕg:
17 And [o]Ē′bĕr lived after he begat [p]Pē′lĕg [m]four hundred and
thirty years, and begat sons and
daughters.
18 And [p]Pē′lĕg lived thirty
years, and begat §Rē′u:
19 And [p]Pē′lĕg lived after he
begat §Rē′u [m]two hundred and
nine years, and begat sons and
daughters.

20 And §Rē′u lived two and
thirty years, and begat +Sē′-
rug:
21 And §Rē′u lived after he begat +Sē′rug [m]two hundred and
seven years, and begat sons and
daughters.
22 And +Sē′rug lived thirty
years, and begat ○Nā′hôr:
23 And +Sē′rug lived after he
begat ○Nā′hôr [m]two hundred
years, and begat sons and
daughters.
24 And ○Nā′hôr lived nine and
twenty years, and begat
▲Tē′rah:
25 And ○Nā′hôr lived after he
begat ▲Tē′rah [m]an hundred and
nineteen years, and begat sons
and daughters.
26 And ▲Tē′rah lived seventy
years, and begat [q]Ā′brăm, [r]Nā′-
hôr, and Hā′ran.
27 ¶ Now these *are* the generations of ▲Tē′rah: Tē′rah begat
[q]Ā′brăm, [r]Nā′hôr, and Hā′ran;
and Hā′ran begat •Lŏt.
28 And Hā′ran died before his
father Tē′rah in the land of his
nativity, in **Ûr of the [s]Chăl′-
dees.
29 And [q]Ā′brăm and [r]Nā′hôr
[t,u]took them wives: the name of
Ā′brăm's wife *was* [v]Sā′rāi; and
the name of Nā′hôr's wife,
††Mĭl′cah, the daughter of Hā′-
ran, the father of Mĭl′cah, and
the father of Ĭs′cah.
30 But [v]Sā′rāi was [w]barren;
she *had* no child.
31 And ▲Tē′rah took [q]Ā′brăm
his son, and •Lŏt the son of

10
i *Genealogy*, vs. 10–32; 1 Chr. 5:1.
j *Shem*, Gen. 6:10.
k *Arphaxad*, Gen. 10:22.
l *Flood*, Gen. 6:17.
v.10–2467 BC
11
m *Longevity*, Psa. 91.16.
v.12–2353 BC
12
n *Salah*, Gen. 10:24.
v.14–2323 BC
14
o *Eber*, Gen. 10:21
v.16–2289 BC
16
p *Peleg*, Gen. 10:25
v.18–2259 BC

v.20–2227 BC See footnote, *Time*, Rev. 10:6.
v.22–2197 BC
v.24–2168 BC
v.26–2098 BC
26
q *Abraham*, Gen 17:5.
r *Nahor*, Gen. 22:20.
28
s *Chaldea*, Ezek. 11:24.
29
t *Marriage*, Gen. 34:9.
u *Incest*, Lev. 18:6.
v *Sarah*, Gen. 17.15.
30
w *Barrenness*, Deut. 7:14.

*after building the tower of Babel*, Gen. 11:1-9; Deut. 32:8. *Of the Jews*, John 7:35; *foretold*, Lev. 26:33; Deut. 28:64; Jer. 16:15; 24:9; Ezek. 12:15. See footnotes: ISRAEL, *prophecies of dispersion of*, Ex. 2:22; JUDAH, *prophecies of dispersion of*, 2 Chr. 11:17.

§ **REU** (*friend*). *Son of Peleg, and ancestor of Abraham*, 1 Chr. 1:25; Luke 3:35.

\+ **SERUG.** *An ancestor of Abraham*, Gen. 11:20-23; 1 Chr. 1:26. *In the lineage of Jesus*, Luke 3:35.

○ **NAHOR.** *Grandfather of Abraham*, Gen. 11:22-25; 1 Chr. 1:26. *In the lineage of Jesus*, Luke 3:34.

▲ **TERAH.** *Father of Abraham*, Gen. 11:24-32. *Was an idolater*, Josh. 24:2. *In the lineage of Jesus*, Luke 3:34.

• **LOT.** *The son of Haran*, Gen. 11:27. *Accompanies Terah from Ur to Haran*, Gen. 11:31. *Migrates with Abraham to Canaan*, Gen. 12:4. *Accompanies Abraham to Egypt; returns to Bethel*, Gen. 13:1-3. *Rich in flocks, and herds, and servants; separates from Abraham, and locates in Sodom*, Gen. 13:5-14. *Taken captive by Chedorlaomer; rescued by Abraham*, Gen. 14:1-16. *Dwelt in Sodom*, Gen. 13:12. *Providentially saved from destruction in Sodom*, Gen. 19; Luke 17:28, 29. *Righteous*, 2 Pet. 2:7, 8. *Disobediently protests against going to the mountains, and chooses Zoar*, Gen. 19:17-22. *His wife disobediently longs after Sodom, and becomes a pillar of salt*, Gen. 19:26; Luke 17:32. *Commits incest with his daughters*, Gen. 19:30-38. *Descendants of*, see footnotes: AMMONITES, Deut. 2:20; MOABITES, Gen. 19:37.

** **UR** (*light*). *Abraham's native place*, Gen. 11:27, 28. *Abraham leaves*, Gen. 11:31; 15:7; Neh. 9:7.

†† **MILCAH** (*advice*). *Wife of Nahor, and mother of Bethuel*, Gen. 11:29; 22:20-23; 24:15, 24, 47.

Hā′ran his son's son, and [v]Sā′-
rāi his daughter in law, his son
Ā′brăm's wife; and they went
forth with them from Ûr of
the Chăl′deeș, to go into the
land of [x]Cā′năan; and they came
unto ‡‡Hā′ran, and dwelt there.
32 And the days of Tē′rah
were two hundred and five
years: and Tē′rah [y]died in
‡‡Hā′ran.

## CHAPTER 12

*God calls Abram, and blesses him. 3 A promise of Messiah. 4 Abram departeth with Lot from Haran. 6 He journeys through the land of Canaan, 7 which is promised him in a vision. 10 He is driven by a famine into Egypt. 11 Fear makes him feign his wife to be his sister. 14 Pharaoh, having taken her from him, is compelled by plagues to restore her.*

NOW [T]the LORD had said
unto [a]Ā′brăm, [b,c,d]Get
thee out of thy country, and
from thy kindred, and from thy
father's house, unto a [e]land that
[f]I will shew thee: [Q]
2 And [g]I will make of [a,h]thee a
great nation, and I will [i]bless
thee, and make thy name great;
and thou shalt be a blessing:
3 And [g]I will bless them that
bless thee, and curse him that
curseth thee: and *,[j]in [a]thee
shall [k]all [l]families of the earth
be blessed.[T Q]
4 So [a]Ā′brăm [m,n]departed, as
the LORD had spoken unto him;
and [o]Lŏt went with him: and
Ā′brăm *was* seventy and five
years old when he departed out
of [p]Hā′ran.
5 And [a]Ā′brăm took [q]Sā′rāi
his wife, and [o]Lŏt his brother's
son, and all their substance[G] that
they had gathered, and the souls[G]
that they had gotten in [p]Hā′ran;
and they went forth to go into
the land of [e]Cā′năan: and into
the land of Cā′năan they came.[Q]
6 ¶ And [a]Ā′brăm passed
through the land unto the place
of Sī′chem, unto the [1]plain of
[r]Mō′reh. And the [s]Cā′năan-īte
*was* then in the land.
7 And the LORD appeared unto
[a]Ā′brăm, and said, Unto thy
[t,u]seed will I give this [e]land: and
there [v]builded he an [w,x]altar unto the LORD, who appeared unto
him.[T Q]
8 And [a]he removed from thence
unto a mountain on the east of
[y]Bĕth′el, and pitched his tent,

31
*x* *Canaan, land of,* Gen. 37:1.

v.32–1963 BC

32
*y* *Death,* Num. 23: 10.

1
*a* *Abraham,* Gen. 17:5.
*b* *Call, personal, to special duty,* vs. 1-3; Phil. 3:14.
*c* *Faith, trial of, instances of,* Mark 11:22.
*d* Acts 7:3.
*e* *Canaan, land of,* Gen. 37:1.
*f* *God, guide,* Gen. 2:2.

2
*g* *Covenant, of God with men,* Deut. 29:1.
*h* *Promotion, instances of,* Psa. 75:6.
*i* *Temporal Blessings, from God,* Psa. 103:2.

v.3–1963 BC

3
*j* *Jesus, prophecies of the coming of,* Matt. 1:21.
*k* *Gentiles, prophecies of conversion of,* Acts 10:45.
*l* *Nations blessed in Abraham,* Gen. 18:18.

4
*m* *Obedience, instances of,* Heb. 5:8.
*n* *Faith,* Mark 11: 22.
*o* *Lot,* Gen. 11:27.
*p* *Haran,* Gen. 11: 31.

5
*q* *Sarah,* Gen. 17: 15.

6
*r* Deut. 11:30.
*s* *Canaanites.* Ex. 23:28.
1 R. V. oak

7
*t* *Israel, prophecies concerning,* Ex. 4:22.
*u* *Children, share covenant with parents,* Mark 10:14.
*v* *Thankfulness, of man to God,* Acts 24:3.
*w* *Altar,* Gen. 8:20.
*x* *Family Worship,* 1 Sam 1:19.

8
*y* *Bethel,* Josh. 18:13.

‡‡ **HARAN,** called also CHARRAN. *A city in Mesopotamia to which Terah and Abraham migrated,* Gen. 11:31; Acts 7:2, 4. *Death of Terah at,* Gen. 11:32. *Abraham leaves, by divine command,* Gen. 12:1-5. *Jacob flees to,* Gen. 27:43; 28:7, 10; 29; *returns from, with Rachel and Leah,* Gen. 31:17-21. *Conquest of, by king of Assyria,* 2 Kin. 19:12; Isa. 37:12. *Merchants of,* Ezek. 27:23. *Idolatry in,* Josh. 24:2, 14; Isa. 37:12.

* **PROPHECIES Concerning Jesus, the Messiah, and their Fulfillment.** Many of the prophetic scriptures, which are commonly described as Messianic, find their fulfillment, according to the common view among Christian interpreters, in JESUS, the *Saviour;* such as, the prophetic announcement of the victor over Satan described as "the seed of the woman," Gen. 3:15, and the promise to Abraham "In thy seed shall all the nations of the earth be blessed," Gen. 22:18. Other Messianic scriptures relate to the Messiah as *the Sovereign of a Universal Kingdom,* as in the promise to David that his throne should be established forever, 2 Sam. 7:16, and the prophecy in Psa. 2:8, 9, of all nations coming into the Messiah's kingdom. In the Old Testament prophecies this universal king is the promised *Messiah;* in the New Testament he is the *Christ,* both being identical with *Jesus,* Matt. 1:21. Without attempting to keep up a distinction between Jesus, the *Saviour,* and the Messiah, or Christ, the *King,* the following scriptures are assembled:

Gen. 12:3; 18:18; 22:18, *with* Acts 3:25; Gal. 3:8.
Gen. 17:7, 19; 22:16, 17, *with* Luke 1:55, 72–74.
Deut. 18:15, 18, *with* Acts 3:22, 23; 7:37.
Psa. 2:1, 2, *with* Acts 4:25, 26.
Psa. 2.7, *with* Acts 13:33; Heb. 1:5; 5:5.
Psa. 16:8–11, *with* Acts 2:25–28, 31.
Psa. 16:10, *with* Acts 13:35.
Psa. 22:1, *with* Matt. 27:46; Mark 15:34.
Psa. 22:18, *with* Mark 15:24; Luke 23:34; John 19:24.
Psa. 22:22, *with* Heb. 2:12.
Psa. 41:9, *with* John 13:18; Acts 1:16.
Psa. 45:6, 7, *with* Heb. 1:8, 9.
Psa. 68:18, *with* Eph. 4:8-10.
Psa. 69:21, *with* Matt. 27:48; Mark 15:36; Luke 23:36; John 19:28, 29.
Psa. 78:2, *with* Matt. 13:35.
Psa. 110:1, *with* Matt. 22:44; Mark 12:36; Luke 20:42; Acts 2:34, 35; Heb. 1:13.
Psa. 110:4, *with* Heb. 5:6.
Psa. 118:22, 23, *with* Matt. 21:42; Mark 12:10, 11; Luke 20:17; Acts 4:11.
Psa. 118:25, 26, *with* Matt. 21:9; Mark 11:9; John 12:13.
Psa. 132:11, 17, *with* Luke 1:69; Acts 2:30.
Isa. 7:14, *with* Matt. 1:23.
Isa. 9:1, 2, *with* Matt. 4:15, 16.
Isa. 9:7, *with* Dan. 7:14, 27, *with* Luke 1:32, 33.
Isa. 11:10, *with* Rom. 15:12.
Isa. 28:16, *with* Rom. 9:33; 1 Pet. 2:6.
Isa. 40:3–5, *with* Matt. 3:3; Mark 1:3; Luke 3:4–6.
Isa. 42:1–4, *with* Matt. 12:17–21.
Isa. 49:6, *with* Luke 2:32; Acts 13:47, 48; 26:23.
Isa. 53:1, *with* John 12:38; Rom. 10:16.
Isa. 53:3–6, *with* Acts 26:22, 23.
Isa. 53:4–6, 11, *with* 1 Pet. 2:24, 25.
Isa. 53:4, *with* Matt. 8:17.
Isa. 53:9, *with* 1 Pet. 2:22.
Isa. 53:12, *with* Luke 22:37.
Isa. 55:3, *with* Acts 13:34.
Isa. 59:20, 21, *with* Rom. 11:26, 27.
Jer. 31:31–34, *with* Heb. 8:8–12; 10:16, 17.
Mic. 5:2, *with* Matt. 2:5, 6; John 7:42.
Hab. 1:5, *with* Acts 13:40, 41.
Zech. 9:9, *with* Matt. 21:4, 5; John 12:14, 15.
Zech. 11:13, *with* Matt. 27:9, 10.
Zech. 12:10, *with* John 19:37.
Zech. 13:7, *with* Matt. 26:31, 56; Mark 14:27, 50
Mal. 3:1, *with* Matt. 11:10; Mark 1:2; Luke 7:27.
See footnote, JESUS, *Prophecies concerning; kingdom of, prophecies concerning,* Matt. 1:21.

v.8–1963 BC
See footnote, *Time,* Rev. 10:6.

*z* Gen. 13:3.

*a* *Altar,* Gen. 8:20.
*b* *Worship,* Gen. 22:5.

9
*c* *Abraham,* Gen. 17:5.

10
*d* *Famine,* 2 Kin. 8:1.
*e* *Egypt,* Gen. 41:8.

11
*f* *Sarah,* Gen. 17:15.
*g* *Wife,* Prov. 5:18.
*h* *Beauty, instances of,* Prov. 6:25.

12
*i* *Egyptians,* Gen. 50:3.
*j* *Cowardice, instances of,* Lev. 26:36.
*k* *Doubting, exemplified,* Rom. 14:23.

13
*l* *Deception, instances of,* Josh. 9:4.
*m* *Temptation, yielding to, instances of,* Luke 11:4.
*n* Gen. 20:13.
*o* *Falsehood, instances of,* Job. 21:34.
*p* *Marriage, consanguineous,* Gen. 34:9.

15
*q* Psa. 105:14.

16
*r* *Hospitality, instances of,* Rom. 12:13.
*s* *Sheep,* Deut. 32:14.
*t* *Ass,* 2 Chr. 28:15.
*u* *Camel,* 1 Sam. 30:17.

17
*v* *God, preserver, exemplified,* Gen. 2:2.
*w* *Judgments,* Ex. 6:6.

*having* Bĕth′el on the west, and
[z]Hā′ī on the east: and there he
builded an [a]altar unto the
LORD, and [b]called[c] upon the
name of the LORD.
9 And [c]Ā′brăm journeyed, going on still toward the south.
10 ¶ And there was a [d]famine
in the land: and [c]Ā′brăm went
down into [e]Ē′ġy̆pt to sojourn
there; for the famine *was*
grievous[c] in the land.
11 And it came to pass, when
he was come near to enter into
[e]Ē′ġy̆pt, that he said unto [f]Sā′rāi
his [g]wife, Behold now, I know
that thou *art* a [h]fair woman to
look upon:
12 Therefore it shall come to
pass, when the [i]Ē′ġy̆p-tianș shall
see [f]thee, that they shall say,
This *is* his [g]wife: and [j,k]they will
kill me, but they will save thee
alive.
13 [l,m,n]Say, I pray thee, [o]thou
*art* my [p]sister: that it may be
well with me for thy sake; and
my soul shall live because of
thee.
14 ¶ And it came to pass, that,
when [c]Ā′brăm was come into
[e]Ē′ġy̆pt, the [i]Ē-ġy̆p′tianș beheld
the [f]woman that she *was* very
[h]fair.
15 The princes also of [q]Phā′-
raōh saw her, and commended
her before Phā′raōh: and the
woman was taken into Phā′-
raōh's house.
16 And he [r]entreated[c] Ā′brăm
well for her sake: and he had
[s]sheep, and oxen, and he [t]asses,
and menservants, and maidservants, and she asses, and [u]camels.
17 And the [v]LORD [w]plagued
[q]Phā′raōh and his house with
great plagues because of [f]Sā′rāi
Ā′brăm's wife.
18 And [q]Phā′raōh called
Ā′brăm, and said, [x,y]What *is*
this *that* thou hast done unto
me? [z]why didst thou not tell me
that she *was* thy [a]wife?
19 Why [b]saidst thou, [c]She *is*
my sister? [z]so I might have taken her to me to [a]wife: [d]now
therefore behold thy wife, [e]take
*her,* and go thy way.
20 And Phā′raōh [d,e]com-
manded *his* men concerning
him: and they sent him away,
and his [a]wife, and all that he
had.

## CHAPTER 13

*Abraham and Lot return out of Egypt. 7 Because of the disagreement between their herdmen, they part asunder. 10 Lot goes to wicked Sodom. 14 God renews the promise to Abram. 18 He removes to Hebron, and there builds an altar.*

AND [a]Ā′brăm went up out
of [b]Ē′ġy̆pt, he, and his
wife, and all that he had, and
[c]Lŏt with him, into the south.
2 And [a]Ā′brăm *was* very [d]rich
in cattle, in [e]silver, and in [f]gold.
3 And he went on his journeys
from the south even to [g]Bĕth′el
unto the place where his tent
had been at the beginning, between Bĕth′el and [h]Hā′ī;
4 Unto the place of the [i]altar,
which he had made there at the
first: and there [a]Ā′brăm [j,k]called
on the name of the LORD.
5 ¶ And [c]Lŏt also, which went
with Ā′brăm, had flocks, and
herds, and *tents.
6 And the land was not able to
bear[c] them, that they might dwell
together: for their substance was
great, so that they could not
dwell together.
7 And there was a [l]strife
between the [m]herdmen of
[a]Ā′brăm's cattle[c] and the herdmen of [c]Lŏt's cattle: and the
[n]Cā′năan-īte and the [o]Pĕr′ĭz-zīte
dwelled then in the land.
8 And [a]Ā′brăm said unto [c]Lŏt,

18
*x* *Conscience, faithful, instances of,* Acts 23:1.
*y* *Temptation, leading into, instances of,* Luke 11:4.
*z* *Ignorance, sins of,* Acts 3:17.

*a* *Wife,* Prov. 5:18.

19
*b* *Deception, instances of,* Josh. 9:4.
*c* *Falsehood, instances of,* Job 21:34.
*d* *Rulers, righteous,* Ex. 18:21.
*e* *Integrity,* Job 2:3.

1
*a* *Abraham,* Gen. 17:5.
*b* *Egypt,* Gen. 41:8.
*c* *Lot,* Gen. 11:27.

2
*d* *Rich, instances of,* James 5:1.
*e* *Silver,* 1 Chr. 28:14.
*f* *Gold,* Ezek. 7:19.

3
*g* *Bethel,* Josh. 18:13.
*h* Gen. 12:8.

4
*i* *Altar,* Gen. 8:20.
*j* *Thankfulness, to God, instances of,* Acts 24:3.
*k* *Family Worship,* 1 Sam. 1:19.

7
*l* *Strife, instances of,* Prov. 20:3
*m* *Servant, wicked and unfaithful,* Jer. 2:14.
*n* *Canaanites,* Ex. 23:28.
*o* *Perizzites,* Gen. 15:20.

* **TENT.** *Used for dwelling,* Gen. 4:20; *by Noah,* Gen. 9:21; *by Abraham,* Gen. 12:8; 13:18; 18:1; *by Lot,* Gen. 13:5; *by Moses,* Ex. 18:7; *by children of Israel,* Num. 24:5, 6; 2 Sam. 20:1; 1 Kin. 12:16; *by the Midianites,* Judg. 6:5; *by Cushites,* Hab. 3:7; *by Arabians,* Isa. 13:20; *by shepherds,* Isa. 38:12; Jer. 6:3. *Women had tents apart from men,* Gen. 24:67; 31:33. *Used for cattle,* 2 Chr. 14:15. *Manufacture of,* Acts 18:3.
*Used as a place of worship,* see footnote, **TABERNACLE,** Ex. 27:9.

8
*p Meekness, instances of,* Psa. 45:4.
*q Social Peace, instances of,* Jer. 29:7.
*r Fraternity,* Zech. 11:14.
9
*s Unselfishness, instances of,* 1 Cor. 10:24.
*t Love, of man for man,* 1 John 4:7.
*u Self-denial, instances of,* Mark 8:34.
10
*v Jordan, plain of,* Gen. 32:10.
*w Zoar,* Deut. 34:3.
12
*x Canaan,* Gen. 37:1.
1 R. V. as far as
13
*y Wicked, described,* Psa. 73:3.
15
*z Land, gift from God,* Ruth 4:3.

---

*a Abraham, God's covenant with,* Gen. 17:5.
*b Covenant, of God with men,* Deut. 29:1.
*c Children, share benefits of covenant with parents,* Mark 10:14.
*d Israel, prophecies concerning,* Ex. 4:22.

[p,q]Let there be no [l]strife, I pray thee, between me and thee, and between my [m]herdmen and thy herdmen; for we *be* [r]brethren.[C]

9 [s]*Is* not the whole land before thee? separate thyself, I pray thee, from me: [t]if *thou wilt take* the left hand, [u]then I will go to the right; or if *thou depart* to the right hand, then I will go to the left.

10 And Lŏt lifted up his eyes, and beheld all the plain of [v]Jôr′dan, that it *was* well watered everywhere, before the LORD destroyed †Sŏd′om and ‡Gŏ-mŏr′rah, *even* as the garden of the LORD, like the land of Ē′ġy̆pt, as thou comest unto [w]Zō′ar.

11 Then Lŏt chose him all the plain of [v]Jôr′dan; and Lŏt journeyed east: and they separated themselves the one from the other.

12 [a]Ā′brăm dwelled in the land of [x]Cā′năan, and Lŏt dwelled in the cities of the plain, and pitched *his* tent [1]toward †Sŏd′om.

13 But the men of †Sŏd′om *were* [y]wicked and sinners before the LORD exceedingly.

14 ¶ And the LORD said unto [a]Ā′brăm, after that Lŏt was separated from him, Lift up now thine eyes, and look from the [x]place where thou art northward, and southward, and eastward, and westward:

15 For all the [z]land which thou seest, to [a]thee will [b]I give it, and to thy [c,d]seed for ever.[Q]

16 And [b]I will make thy [c,d]seed[C] as the dust of the earth: so that if a man can number the dust of the earth, *then* shall thy seed also be numbered.

17 Arise, walk through the [e,f]land in the length of it and in the breadth of it; [b]for I will give it unto thee.

18 Then Ā′brăm removed *his* tent, and came and dwelt [2]in the plain of ‖Măm′rē, which *is* in [g]Hē′bron, and built there an [h]altar unto the LORD.

## CHAPTER 14

*The battle of four kings against five. 12 Lot is taken prisoner. 14 Abram rescues him. 18 Melchizedek blesses Abram. 20 Abram gives him tithes. 22 The rest of the spoils, his partners having had their portions, he restores to the king of Sodom.*

AND it came to pass in the days of Ăm′ra-phĕl king of [a]Shī′när, Ā′rĭ-ŏch king of Ĕl′-la-sär, Chĕd-or-lā′o-mēr king of [b]Ē′lăm, and Tī′dal king of nations;

2 *That these* made [c]war with Be′rȧ king of [d]Sŏd′om, and with Bīr′shȧ king of [e]Gŏ-mŏr′rah, Shī′năb king of [f]Ăd′mah, and Shĕm-ē′ber king of [g]Ze-bōi′im, and the king of Bē′lȧ, which is [h]Zō′ar.

3 All these were joined together in the vale of Sĭd′dim, which is the *salt sea.

4 Twelve years they served Chĕd-or-lā′o-mēr, and in the thirteenth year they rebelled.

5 And in the fourteenth year came Chĕd-or-lā′o-mēr, and the kings that *were* with him, and smote[C] the †Rĕph′a-ĭms in Ăsh′-

17
*e Land, title to, from God,* Ruth 4:3.
*f Canaan,* Gen. 37:1.
18
*g Hebron,* Gen. 23:2.
*h Altar,* Gen. 8:20.
2 R.V. by the oaks
1
*a* Or, *Babylon, empire of,* Ezra 5:12.
*b Elam,* Isa. 11:11.
2
*c War,* Judg. 3:2.
*d Sodom,* Gen. 13:10.
*e Gomorrah,* Gen. 13:10.
*f Admah,* Deut. 29:23.
*g Zeboim,* Hos. 11:8.
*h Zoar,* Deut. 34:3.

. 1913?

† **SODOM.** *Situated in the plain of the Jordan,* Gen. 13:10. *The southeastern limit of the Canaanites,* Gen. 10:19. *Lot dwells at,* Gen. 13:12. *King of, joins other kings of the nations resisting the invasion of Chedorlaomer,* Gen. 14:1-12. *Wickedness of the inhabitants of,* Gen. 13:13; 19:4-13; Deut. 32:32; Isa. 3:9; Jer. 23:14; Lam. 4:6; Ezek. 16:46, 48, 49; Jude 7. *Abraham's intercession for,* Gen. 18:16-33. *Destroyed on account of the wickedness of the people,* Gen. 19:1-29; Deut. 29:23; Isa. 13:19; Jer. 20:16; 49:18; 50:40; Lam. 4:6; Ezek. 16:48-50; Amos 4:11; Zeph. 2:9; Matt. 10:15; Luke 17:29; Rom. 9:29; 2 Pet. 2:6, 7; Jude 7.

**Figurative:** *Of wickedness,* Deut. 23:17; 32:32; Isa. 1:10; Ezek. 16:46-56.

§ **GOMORRAH.** *One of the cities of the plain of the Jordan,* Gen. 19:19; 13:10. *Its king defeated by Chedorlaomer,* Gen. 14:2, 8, 11. *Wickedness of,* Gen. 18:20. *Destroyed,* Gen. 19:24-28; Deut. 29:23; 32:32; Isa. 1:9; 13:19; Jer. 23:14; 49:18; 50:40; Amos 4:11; Zeph. 2:9; Matt. 10:15; Rom. 9:29; 2 Pet 2:6; Jude 7.

‖ **MAMRE,** a part of, or perhaps identical with, or perhaps an ancient name of, Hebron. *Abraham, resides in,* Gen. 13:18; 14:13; *entertains three angels at, and is promised a son,* Gen. 18:1-15. *Isaac dwell in,* Gen. 35:27.

* **DEAD SEA,** lies southeast of Jerusalem. *Called* SALT SEA, Gen. 14:3; Num. 34:12; Deut. 3:17; Josh. 3:16; SEA OF THE PLAIN, Deut. 4:49; 2 Kin. 14:25; EASTERN SEA, Joel 2:20; Zech. 14:8.
*Prophecy concerning,* Ezek. 47:7-10, 18.

† **REPHAIM,** an ancient people of great stature. *In*

5
i *Zamzummims*, Deut. 2:20, 21.
j Deut. 2:10, 11.
6
k *Seir*, Deut. 1:2.
7
l *Amalekites*, Num. 13:29.
m Or, *Engedi*, 2 Chr. 20: 2.
9
R. V. against
2 R. V. against the
10
n *Bitumen*, Gen. 11:3.
11
o *Spoils*, 1 Chr. 26: 27.
12
p *Captive*, 1 Sam. 30:3.
q *Lot*, Gen. 11:27.
r *Abraham*, Gen. 17:5.
13
s *Hebrew*, Gen. 40: 15.
3 R.V. by the oaks

tĕ-rŏth Kär-nā′im, and the [i]Zū′-
zims̤ in Hăm, and the [j]Ē′mims̤
in Shā′veh Kĭr-ĭ-a-thā′im.
6 And the Hō′rītes in their
mount [k]Sē′ïr, unto[G] Ĕl-pā′ran,
which *is* by the wilderness.
7 And they returned, and came
to Ĕn-mĭsh′pat, which *is* ‡Kā′-
desh, and smote[G] all the country
of the [l]Ăm′a-lĕk-ītes, and also
the ‖Ăm′ôr-ītes, that dwelt in
[m]Hăz′e-zon-tā′mar.
8 And there went out the king
of [d]Sŏd′om, and the king of
[e]Gō-mŏr′rah, and the king of
[f]Ăd′mah, and the king of [g]Ze-
bō̆i′im, and the king of Bē′lȧ
(the same *is* [h]Zō′ar;) and they
joined [c]battle with them in the
vale[G] of Sĭd′dim:
9 [1]With Chĕd-or-lā′o-mĕr the
king of [b]Ē′lăm, and with Tī′dal
king of nations, and Ăm′ra-phĕl
king of [a]Shī′när, and Ā′rĭ-ŏch
king of Ĕl′la-sär; four kings
[2]with five.
10 And the vale[G] of Sĭd′dim *was*
*full of* [n]slimepits; and the kings
of [d]Sŏd′om and [e]Gō-mŏr′rah
fled, and fell there; and they that
remained fled to the mountain.
11 And they took all the [o]goods
of [d]Sŏd′om and [e]Gō-mŏr′rah,
and all their victuals[G], and went
their way.
12 And they took [p,q]Lŏt,
[r]Ā′brăm's brother's son, who
dwelt in [d]Sŏd′om, and his
[o]goods, and departed.
13 ¶ And there came one that
had escaped, and told [r]Ā′brăm
the [s]Hē′brew; for he dwelt [3]in
the plain of Măm′rē the ‖Ăm′-
ôr-īte, brother of Ĕsh′cŏl, and
brother of Ā′nēr: and these *were*
[t]confederate with Ā′brăm.[T]
14 And [u,v]when [r]Ā′brăm heard
that his [w]brother was taken
[p]captive, he armed his trained
[x]*servants*, born in his own house,
three hundred and eighteen, and
pursued *them* unto [y]Dăn.[G]
15 And he [z]divided himself
against them, he and his [a]serv-
ants, by night, and smote them,
and pursued them unto Hō′bah,
which *is* on the [4]left hand of
[b]Dȧ-măs′cus.
16 And he brought back all the
goods[G], and also brought again
his [c]brother [d]Lŏt, and his goods,
and the women also, and the
people.
17 ¶ [Q]And the king of [e]Sŏd′om
went out to meet [f]him after his
return from the slaughter of
Chĕd-or-lā′o-mĕr, and of the
kings that *were* with him, at the
valley of Shā′veh, which *is* the
[g]king's dale.
18[T] And §Mĕl-chĭz′e-dĕk [h]king
of [i]Sā′lem [j]brought forth bread
and [k]wine: and he *was* the
[l,m]priest of the most high [n]God.
19[Q] And §he [o]blessed him, and
said, Blessed *be* [f]Ā′brăm of the
most high [n]God, [5]possessor of
heaven and earth:[T]
20 And [p,q]blessed be the most
high [r]God, which hath delivered
thine enemies into thy hand.
And [s]he gave him [6,t]tithes of all.[Q]
21 And the [h]king of [e]Sŏd′om
said unto [f]Ā′brăm, Give me the
persons, and [u,v]take the goods
thyself.

t *Alliances, political*, Josh. 9:15.
14
u *Love, of man for man, instances of*, 1 John 4:7.
v *Friendship, instances of*, Prov. 22:24.
w *Brother*, Prov. 18: 24.
x *Servant*, Jer. 2: 14.
y *Dan, city of*, Judg. 18:29.
15
z *Strategy, in war*, Judg. 7:16.

a *Servant*, Jer. 2:14.
b *Damascus*, Isa. 8:4.
4 *Or*, north
16
c *Brother*, Prov. 18: 24.
d *Lot*, Gen. 11:27.
17
e *Sodom*, Gen. 13: 10.
f *Abraham*, Gen. 17:5.
g *King's Dale*, 2 Sam. 18:18.
18
h *Rulers*, Ex. 18: 21.
i *Jerusalem*, Judg. 19:10.
j *Hospitality, instances of*, Rom. 12:13.
k *Wine*, Prov. 23: 31.
l *Priest, antemosaic*, Lev. 1:5.
m *Jesus, priesthood of, typified*, Matt. 1:21.
n *God, sovereign*, Gen. 2:2.
19
o *Benediction, instances of*, Deut. 21.5.
5 *Or*, maker
20
p *Praise*, Psa. 150.1.
q *Thankfulness, to God*, Acts 24:3.
r *God, providence of*, Gen. 2:2.
s Heb. 7:4.
t *Tithes*, Num. 18: 24.
6 R. V. a tenth
21
u *Liberality, instances of*, 1 Tim. 6:18.
v *Unselfishness, instances of*, 1 Cor 10:24.

*Palestine*. Gen. 15:20; Deut. 2:11, 20; 3:11, 13; Josh. 12: 4; 13:12; 17:15.

‡ **KADESH,** *called also* KADESH-BARNEA, Deut. 1:19. *A city on the southern boundary of Palestine*, Josh. 15:3. *Smitten by Chedorlaomer*, Gen. 14:7. *Abraham dwells by the wells near*, Gen. 20:1 (with 14:7; 16:14). *Israel encamps at*, Num. 12:16; 13:26; 20:1; 33:36; Deut. 1:19, 46. *Canaanites defeated at*, Josh. 10:14.

‖ **AMORITES** (*mountaineers*). *Descendants of Canaan*, Gen. 10:15, 16; 1 Chr. 1:13, 14. *Were giants*, Amos 2:9. *Smitten by Chedorlaomer and rescued by Abraham*, Gen. 14. *Chiefs of*, Josh. 13:21. *Wickedness of*, Gen. 15:16; 2 Kin. 21:11; Ezra 9:1. *Idolatry of*, Judg. 6:10; 11:23, 24; 1 Kin. 21:26. *Judgments denounced against*, Ex. 23:23, 24; 33:2; 34:10, 11; Deut. 20:17, 18. *Hornets sent among*, Josh. 24: 12. *Not exterminated*, Judg. 1:34-36; 3:1-3, 5-8; 1 Sam. 7:14; 2 Sam. 21:2; 1 Kin. 9:20, 21; 2 Chr. 8:7. *Intermarry with Jews*, Ezra 9:1, 2; 10:18-44. *Kings of*, Josh. 10:3-26; 13:21.

**Territory of,** Gen. 14:7; Num. 13:29; 21:13. Deut. 1:4, 7, 19; 3:8, 9; Josh. 5:1; 10:5; 12:2, 3; Judg. 1:35, 36; 11:22. *Given to descendants of Abraham*, Gen. 15:21; 48:22; Deut. 1:20; 2:26-36; 7:1; Josh. 3:10; Judg. 11:23; Amos 2:10. *Allotted to Reuben, Gad, and Manasseh*, Num. 32:33-42; Josh. 13:15-21. *Conquest of*, Num. 21:21-30; Josh. 10:11; Judg. 1:34-36; 11:21, 22.

§ **MELCHIZEDEK** (*king of righteousness*). *King of Salem*, Gen. 14:18-20. *Abraham gave tithes to*, Gen. 14:20; Heb. 7:4. *A priest, and type of Christ*, Psa. 110:4; Heb. 5:6, 10; 6:20; 7:1-21.

22 And Ā'brăm said to the
king of [e]Sŏd'om, I have [w]lift[G] up
mine [x]hand unto the LORD, the
most high [n]God, the possessor
of heaven and earth,[Q]
23 That I will not *take* from a
thread even to a shoelatchet,[G] and
that I will not take any thing
that *is* thine, [y]lest thou shouldest say, I have made Ā'brăm
rich:
24 Save only that which the
young men have eaten, and the
portion of the men which went
with me, Ā'nēr, Ĕsh'cŏl, and
Măm'rē; let them take their
portion.

## CHAPTER 15

*God encourages Abram. 2 Abram complains for want of an heir. 4 God promises him a son, and a numerous seed. 6 Abraham is justified by faith. 7 Canaan is promised again, and confirmed by a sign, 12 and a vision.*

AFTER these things the
word of the LORD came
unto [a,b]Ā'brăm in a [c]vision, saying, Fear not, Ā'brăm: [d,e,f]I *am*
thy [g]shield, *and* thy exceeding
great reward.[S T]
2 And [a]Ā'brăm [h]said, Lord
GOD, [i]what wilt thou give me,
seeing I go[G] childless, and [1]the
steward[G] of my house *is* this [j]Ĕ-li-
ē'zēr of [k]Dă-măs'cus?
3 And [a]Ā'brăm said, Behold, to
me thou hast given no seed: and,
lo, one[G] born in my house is mine
*,[l]heir.
4 And, behold, the word of the
LORD *came* unto him, saying,
This shall not be thine *heir;
but [e,m]he that shall come forth
out of thine own bowels[G] shall be
thine heir.
5 And he brought him forth
abroad, and said, Look now toward heaven, and tell[G] the stars,
if thou be able to number them:
and he said unto him, So shall
thy [n,o]seed be.[Q]
6 And he †believed in the
LORD; and he [p]counted it to him
for [q]righteousness.[S T Q]
7 And he said unto him, [d]I *am*
the LORD that brought thee out
of [r]Ûr of the [s]Chăl'dees, to give
thee this [t]land to inherit it.
8 And he [u]said, Lord GOD,
[v,w]whereby shall I know that I
shall inherit it?
9 And he said unto him, Take
me an [x]heifer of three years old,
and a she [y]goat of three years
old, and a ram of three years old,
and a [z]turtledove, and a young
‡pigeon.
10 And he took unto him [a]all
these, and divided them in the
midst, and laid each piece one
against another: but the birds
divided he not.
11 And when the fowls came
down upon the carcases,
[b]Ā'brăm drove them away.
12 And when the sun was going
down, a deep [c]sleep fell upon
[b]Ā'brăm; and, lo, an horror of
great darkness fell upon him.
13[Q] And he said unto [b]Ā'brăm,
Know of a surety [d]that thy [e]seed
shall be a stranger[G] in a [f]land
*that is* not their's, and shall serve
them; and they shall afflict them
[g]four hundred years;
14 And also that [h]nation, whom
[e]they shall serve, will I [i]judge:
and afterward shall they come
out with great substance.[T Q]
15 And [b]thou shalt [j]go to thy
fathers in peace; thou shalt be
buried in a good [k]old age.
16 [l]But in the fourth genera-

**22**
w *Oath, a solemn qualification,* Num. 5:19.
x *Hand, lifted in solemnizing an oath,* Ezra 10:19.

**23**
y *Prudence, instances of,* 2 Chr. 2:12.

**1**
a *Abraham,* Gen. 17:5.
b *Righteous, promises to,* Psa. 64:10.
c *Vision,* Acts 9:10.
d *God, preserver,* Gen. 2:2.
e *Covenant, of God with men,* Deut. 29:1.
f *Promises, to the righteous, of divine protection,* 2 Cor. 1:20.
g *Shield, figurative,* 1 Kin. 14:27.

**2**
h *Prayer,* Acts 6:4.
i *Blessings, temporal, prayer for, instances of,* Psa. 103:2.
j Gen. 24.
k *Damascus,* Isa. 8:4.
1 R. V. he that shall be possessor

**3**
l *Inheritance,* Num. 27:7.

**4**
m *Children, in answer to prayer,* Mark 10:14.

**5**
n *Descendants of Abraham,* Gen. 22:17.
o *Israel, prophecies concerning,* Ex. 4:22.

**6**
p *Grace of God,* Rom. 4:16.
q *Righteousness,* Psa. 15:2.

**7**
r *Ur,* Gen. 11:28.
s *Chaldea,* Ezek. 11:24.
t *Land, title to, from God,* Ruth 4:3.

**8**
u *Doubting, of Abram,* Rom. 14:23.
v *Faith, strengthened by miracles,* vs. 8–18; Mark 11:22.
w *Miracles,* vs. 8–18; Luke 23:8.

**9**
x *Heifer,* Num. 19:2.
y *Goat,* Deut. 14:4.
z *Dove,* Gen. 8:8.

**10**
a *Offering, burnt,* Lev. 6:17.

**11**
b *Abraham,* Gen. 17:5.

**12**
c *Sleep,* Psa. 127:2.

**13**
d Acts 7:6, 7.
e *Israel, prophecies concerning,* Ex. 4:22.
f *Egypt, prophecies about,* Gen. 41:8.
g Gal. 3:17.

**14**
h *Egyptians,* Gen. 50:3.
i *Judgments,* Ex. 6:6.

**15**
j *Death, described,* Num. 23:10.
k *Old Age,* Isa. 46:4.

**16**
l *God, long suffering of,* Gen. 2:2.

* **HEIR,** Eccl. 2:18, 19. *Children of concubines as well as of wives are,* Gen. 15:3; 21:10; 25:5, 6; Gal. 4:30. *Mosaic law relating to inheritance of,* Num. 27:8–11; 36:1–8; Josh. 17:3–6; *prescribing right of, to redeem alienated land,* Lev. 25:25; Ruth 4:1–12; *prescribing right of to inherit slaves,* Lev. 25:45, 46; *prescribing right of, firstborn son to have double portion,* Deut. 21:15–17.
*Minor, under guardians,* Gal. 4:1, 2.
See footnote, INHERITANCE, Num. 27:7.

**Figurative:** *Of spiritual adoption,* Rom. 8:14–17; Gal. 3:29; 4:6, 7; Tit. 3:7; Jas. 2:5.
See footnote, SPIRITUAL ADOPTION, Rom. 8:15.

† **FAITH.** *Reckoned for righteousness,* Rom. 4:3; Gal. 3:6; Jas. 2:23. See footnote, FAITH, Mark 11:22.

‡ **PIGEON.** *Used as sacrifice,* Lev. 1:14; 5:7; 12:8; 14:22; Luke 2:24.
See footnote, DOVE, Gen. 8:8

m *Amorites,* Gen. 14:13.
n *Probation,* Rom. 5:4.

17
o *Sun,* Josh. 10:12.
p *Miracles,* Luke 23:8.
q *Fire,* Ex. 12:8.

18
r *Covenant, of God with men,* Deut. 29:1.
s *Canaan, land of, promised to Abraham and his seed,* Gen. 37:1.

19
t *Kenites,* 1 Sam. 15:6.

20
u *Hittite,* Judg. 1: 26.
v *Rephaim,* Gen. 14:5.

21
w *Canaanites,* Ex. 23:28.
x *Girgashites,* Neh. 9:8.
y *Jebusites,* Deut. 7:1.

1
a *Sarah,* Gen. 17: 15.
b *Abraham,* Gen. 17:5.
c *Servant,* Jer. 2:14.

2
d *Barrenness, a reproach,* Deut. 7: 14.

v.3–1953 BC

tion they shall come hither again: for the iniquity of the [m]Ăm′ôr-ītes [n]*is* not yet full. [Q]

17 And it came to pass, that, when the [o]sun went down, and it was dark, [p]behold a smoking [q]furnace, and a burning lamp[C] that passed between those [a]pieces.

18 In the same day the LORD made a [r]covenant[C] with [b]Ā′brăm, saying, Unto thy seed have I given this [s]land, from the river of ‖Ē′ġy̆pt unto the great river, the river §Eū-phrā′tēṣ: [T Q]

19 The [t]Kĕn′ītes, and the Kĕn′ĭz-zītes, and the Kăd′mon-ītes,

20 And the [u]Hĭt′tītes, and the +Pĕr′ĭz-zītes, and the [v]Rĕph′a-ĭmṣ,

21 And the [m]Ăm′ôr-ītes, and the [w]Cā′năan-ītes, and the [x]Gĭr′ga-shītes, and the [y]Jĕb′u-sītes.

## CHAPTER 16

*Sarai gives Hagar to Abram; 6 who fleeing from her mistress, 7 is sent back by an angel. 15 Ishmael is born.*

NOW [a]Sā′rāi [b]Ā′brăm's wife bare him no children; and she had an [c]handmaid,[C] an Ē-ġy̆p′tian, whose name *was* *Hā′gar. [Q]

2 And [a]Sā′rāi said unto [b]Ā′brăm, Behold now, the LORD hath [d]restrained me from bearing: I pray thee, go[C] in unto my *,[c]maid; it may be that I may obtain children by her. And Ā′brăm hearkened to the voice of Sā′rāi.

3 And [a]Sā′rāi [b]Ā′brăm's wife took *Hā′gar her [c]maid the Ē-ġy̆p′tian, after Ā′brăm had dwelt ten years in the land of Cā′năan, and [e]gave her to her husband Ā′brăm to be his [f]wife.

4 And he went in unto *Hā′gar, and she conceived: and when she saw that she had conceived, her mistress was [g]despised in her eyes.

5 [h]And [a]Sā′rāi said unto [b]Ā′brăm, [i,j,k]My wrong *be* upon thee: I have given my [c]maid into thy bosom; and when she saw that she had conceived, I was despised in her eyes: the [l]LORD judge between me and thee. [Q]

6 But [b]Ā·brăm said unto [a]Sā′rāi, Behold, thy [c]maid *is* in thy hand; do to her as it pleaseth thee. And when [m]Sā′rāi [n,o]dealt hardly with her, she fled from her face.

7 ¶ [T]And the [p]angel of the LORD [q]found *her by a fountain of water in the wilderness, by the fountain in the way to [r]Shûr. [S]

8 And he said, *Hā′gar, Sā′rāi's [c]maid, whence camest thou? and whither wilt thou go? And she said, I flee from the face of my mistress Sā′rāi.

9 And the [p]angel of the LORD said unto *,[c]her, Return to thy mistress, and submit thyself under her hands.

10 And the [p]angel of the LORD said unto *her, I will multiply thy seed exceedingly, that it shall not be numbered for multitude.

11 And the [p]angel of the LORD said unto *her, Behold, thou *art* with child, and shalt bear a son,

v.3–1953 BC

3
e *Concubinage,* 2 Sam. 21:11.
f *Polygamy,* Deut. 17:17.

4
g *Hatred,* Prov. 15: 17.

5
h *Family, infelicity in, instances of,* 1 Chr. 13:14.
i *Responsibility, attempt to shift,* Ezek. 18:20.
j *Envy, instances of,* Prov. 14:30.
k *Jealousy, instances of,* Psa. 78:58.
l *God, judge,* Gen. 2:2.

6
m *Master, unjust,* Col. 4:1.
n *Cruelty, instances of,* Psa. 27:12.
o *Oppression, instances of,* Eccl. 5:8.

7
p *Angel,* Heb. 1:13.
q *Affliction, consolation in,* vs. 7–13; Psa. 34:19.
r *Shur,* 1 Sam. 15:7.

‖ **EGYPT, Brook of.** *A small stream flowing into the Mediterranean Sea; the western boundary of the land promised to the children of Israel,* Num. 34:5; Josh. 13:3; 15:4, 47; 1 Kin. 8:65; 2 Kin. 24:7; 2 Chr. 7:8; Isa. 27:12; Ezek. 47:19; 48:28.

§ **EUPHRATES.** *A river in the garden of Eden,* Gen. 2:14. *The eastern limit of the kingdom of Israel,* Gen. 15:18; Ex. 23:31; Deut. 1:7; 11:24; Josh. 1:4; 2 Sam. 8:3; 1 Kin. 4:21; 1 Chr. 5:9; 18:3. *Pharaoh-nechoh, king of Egypt, made conquest to,* 2 Kin. 24:7; Jer. 46:2–10. *On the banks of, Jeremiah symbolically buries his girdle,* Jer. 13:1–7. *Roll containing the prophecies against Babylon cast into,* Jer. 51: 59–64.

SYMBOLICAL: *The inundations of, of the extension of the empire of Assyria,* Isa. 8:6–8. *In the symbolisms of the Apocalypse,* Rev. 9:14; 16:12.

+ **PERIZZITES** (*villagers*). *One of the seven nations in the land of Canaan,* Gen. 13:7. *Territory of, given to Abraham,* Gen. 15:20; Ex. 3:8; 23:23 *Doomed to destruction,* Deut. 20:17. *Not all destroyed; Israelites marry among,* Judg. 3:5–7; Ezra 9:1, 2. See footnote, CANAANITES, Ex. 23:28.

* **HAGAR,** a servant of Abraham and handmaid of Sarah. *Given by Sarah to Abraham to be his wife,* Gen. 16. *Descendants of,* Gen. 25:12–15; 1 Chr. 5:10, 19–22; Psa. 83:6.

**Figurative,** Gal. 4:24, 25.

v.16–1952 BC
See footnote, *Time*, Rev. 10:6.

and shalt call his name †Ĭsh′-
ma-el; because the LORD hath
heard thy [q]affliction.[T Q]
12 And †he will be [1]a wild
man; his hand *will be* against
every man, and every man's
hand against him; and he shall
dwell in the [2]presence of all his
brethren.
13 And she called the name of
the LORD that spake unto her,
[s]Thou [3,t]God seest me: for she
said, Have I also here looked
after him that seeth me?[S]
14 Wherefore the well was
called ‡Bē′er-la-hāi′roi; behold, *it is* between [u]Kā′desh and
Bē′red.
15 And Hā′gar bare [b]Ā′brăm
a son: and Ā′brăm called his
son's name, which Hā′gar bare,
†Ĭsh′ma-el.
16 And [b]Ā′brăm *was* fourscore
and six years old, when Hā′gar
bare †Ĭsh′ma-el to Ā′brăm.

12
1 R. V. as a wild ass among men;
2 *Or*, over against *or*, to the east of

13
*s* *Faith, instances of*, Mark 11:22.
*t* *God, knowledge of*, Gen. 2:2.
3 R. V. art a God that seeth:

14
*u* *Kadesh*, Gen. 14:7.

v.1–1939 BC

## CHAPTER 17

*God renews the covenant. 5 The name of Abram is changed in token of a greater blessing. 10 Circumcision is instituted. 15 The name of Sarai is changed, and she blessed. 16 Isaac is promised. 23 Abraham and Ishmael are circumcised.*

AND [T]when *Ā′brăm was
ninety years old and nine,
the LORD appeared to Ā′brăm,
and said unto him, I *am* the Almighty [a]God; [b]walk before me,
and be thou [c,d]perfect.[G S]
2 And I will make my [e]cove-
nant between me and thee, and
will multiply thee exceedingly.
3 And *Ā′brăm [f,g]fell on his
face: and God [h]talked with him,
saying,
4 As for me, behold, my [e]cove-
nant *is* with thee, and thou shalt
be a father of many nations.[T]
5 Neither shall thy [i]name any
more be called Ā′brăm, but thy
name shall be *Ā′bră-hăm; for
a father of many [j]nations have
I made thee.[Q]
6 And I will make thee exceeding fruitful, and I will make [l]na-
tions of thee, and [k]kings shall
come out of thee.
7 [T]And I will establish my [e]cove-
nant[G] between me and thee and
thy [l,m]seed after thee in their
generations for an everlasting
covenant, to be a [n]God unto
thee, and to thy seed after thee.[Q]
8 And I will give unto *thee,
and to thy seed after thee, the
land wherein thou art a stranger,[C]
all the land of [o]Cā′năan, for an
everlasting possession; and I will
be their God.[Q]
9 ¶ And God said unto *Ā′bră-
hăm, Thou shalt [p]keep my
[e]covenant therefore, thou, and
thy seed after thee in their
generations.
10 This[Q] *is* my [e]covenant, which
ye shall [p]keep, between me and

1
*a* *God, omnipotent*, Gen. 2:2.
*b* *Walking, with God, instances of*. Gen. 5:22.
*c* *Perfection*, Heb. 6:1.
*d* *Holiness, enjoined*, Ex. 39:30.

v.2–1939 BC

2
*e* *Covenant, of God with men*, Deut. 29:1.

3
*f* *Worship*, Gen. 22:5.
*g* *Reverence*, Lev. 19:30.
*h* *Communion, with God*, 2 Cor. 13:14.

5
*i* *Name*, Prov. 22:1.
*j* *Descendants of Abraham*, Gen. 22:17.

6
*k* *Rulers*, Ex. 18:21.

7
*l* *Israel, prophecies concerning*, Ex. 4:22.
*m* *Children of righteous, blessed*, Mark 10:14.
*n* *God, love of*, Gen. 2:2.

8
*o* *Canaan, land of, promised to Abraham and his seed*, Gen. 37:1.

9
*p* *Obedience, enjoined*, Heb. 5:8.

† **ISHMAEL** (*whom God hears*). *Son of Abraham*, Gen. 16:11, 15, 16; 1 Chr. 1:28. *Prayer of Abraham for*, Gen. 17:18, 20. *Circumcised*, Gen. 17:23–26. *Mocks Isaac*, Gen. 21:9; Gal. 4:29. *Sent away by Abraham*, Gen. 21:6–21. *Blessed of God*, Gen. 21:20. *With Isaac buries his father*, Gen. 25:9. *Children of*, Gen. 25:12–18; 1 Chr. 1:29–31. *Daughter of, marries Esau*, Gen. 28:9; 36:2, 3. *Death of*, Gen. 25:17, 18. *Prophecies concerning*, Gen. 16:11, 12; 17:20; 21:12, 13, 18.

‡ **BEER-LAHAI-ROI** (*well of the living one that sees me*), a well near Kadesh, called also LAHAIROI. *Hagar fled to*, Gen. 16:7–14. *Isaac dwells at*, Gen. 24:62; 25:11.

* **ABRAHAM** (*father of a multitude*), called also ABRAM. *Son of Terah*, Gen. 11:26, 27. *Marries Sarah*, Gen. 11:29. *Dwells in Ur, but removes to Haran*, Gen. 11:31; Josh. 24:2; Neh. 9:7; Acts 7:4; *to Canaan*, Gen. 12:4–6; Acts 7:4.

*Divine call of*, Gen. 12:1–3; Josh. 24:3; Neh. 9:7; Isa. 15:2; Acts 7:2, 3; Heb. 11:8. *Canaan given to*, Gen. 12:1, 7; 15:7–21; Josh. 1:6; Psa. 105:8–11; Ezek. 33:24. *Dwells in Bethel*, Gen. 12:8. *Sojourns in Egypt*, Gen. 12:10–20; 26:1. *Returns to Canaan*, Gen. 13:1–5. *Deferring to Lot, chooses Hebron*, Gen. 13:6–12; 14:13; 35:27.

*Defeats Chedorlaomer*, Gen. 14:5–24; Heb. 7:1. *Is blessed by Melchizedek*, Gen. 14:18–20; Heb. 7:1–10.

*God's covenant with, to become a great nation*, Gen. 13:14–17; 15; 17:1–22; 22:17, 18, with Acts 3:25; Ex. 32:13; Deut. 1:10; 1 Kin. 3:8; Psa. 105:9, 10; Mic. 7:20; Luke 1:73; Rom. 4:13, 17; Gal. 3:6–18, 29; Heb. 6:13, 14;11: 12. *Called* ABRAHAM, Gen. 17:5; Neh. 9:7. *Circumcision of*, Gen. 17:10–14, 23–27. *Angels appear to*, Gen. 18:1–16; 22:11, 15. *His questions about the destruction of the righteous and wicked in Sodom*, Gen. 18:23–32. *Witnesses the destruction of Sodom*, Gen. 19:27, 28. *Ishmael born to*, Gen. 16:3, 15. *Dwells in Gerar; deceives Abimelech concerning Sarah, his wife*, Gen. 20; 21:22–34. *Isaac born to*, Gen. 21:2, 3; Gal. 4:22–30. *Sends Hagar and Ishmael away*, Gen. 21:10–14; Gal. 4:22–30.

*Trial of his faith in the offering of Isaac*, Gen. 22:1–19; Heb. 11:17; Jas. 2:21. *Sarah, his wife, dies*, Gen. 23:1, 2. *He purchases a place for her burial, and buries her in a cave*, Gen. 23:3–20. *Marries Keturah*, Gen. 25:1. *Provides a wife for Isaac*, Gen. 24.

*Children of*, Gen. 16:15; 21:2, 3; 25:1–4; 1 Chr. 1:28–34. *Testament of*, Gen. 25:5, 6. *Wealth of*, Gen. 13:2; 24:35; *Age of, at different periods*, Gen. 12:4; 16:16; 21:5; 25:7. *Death of*, Gen. 15:15; 25:8–10. *In Paradise*, Matt. 8:11; Luke 13:28; 16:22–31.

*Friend of God*, 2 Chr. 20:7; Isa. 41:8; Jas. 2:23. *Piety of*, Gen. 12:7, 8; 13:4, 18; 18:19; 20:7; 21:33; 22:3–13; 26:5; 2 Chr. 20:7; Neh. 9:7, 8; Isa. 41:8; Rom. 4:16–18; Jas. 2:23. *Faith of*, Gen. 15:6; Rom. 4:1–22; Gal. 3:6–9; Heb. 11:

v.10–1939 BC
See footnote, *Time*, Rev. 10:6.

11
q *Symbols and Similitudes*, Heb. 9:9.
r *Token*, Psa. 86:17.

12
s *Family, religion in*, 1 Chr. 13:14.
t *Servant, homeborn*, Jer. 2:14.
u *Money*, Jer. 32:9.

14
v *Disfellowship*, Num. 15:31.
w *Church, rules of discipline in*, Matt. 16:18.

15
x *God*, Gen. 2:2.

16
y *Children, gift of God*, Mark 10:14.

17
z *Doubting*, Rom. 14:23.

you and thy seed after thee; Every man child among you shall be †circumcised.

11 And ye shall †,[q]circumcise the flesh of your foreskin; and it shall be a [r]token of the [e]covenant betwixt me and you.[T] [Q]

12 [s]And he that is eight days old shall be †circumcised among you, every man child in your generations, [t]he that is born in the house, or bought with [u]money of any stranger, which *is* not of thy seed. [Q]

13 [t]He[T] that is born in thy house, and he that is bought with thy [u]money, must needs[C] be †circumcised: and my [e]covenant shall be in your flesh for an everlasting covenant.[Q]

14 And the uncircumcised man child whose flesh of his foreskin is not circumcised, that soul shall be [v,w]cut off from his people; he hath broken my [e]covenant.[T]

15 ¶ And [x]God said unto *Ā′bră-hăm, As for Sā′rāi thy wife, thou shalt not call her name Sā′rāi, but ‡Sā′rah *shall* her name *be*.

16 And I will bless ‡her, and give thee a [y]son also of her: yea, I will bless her, and she shall be *a mother* of nations; kings of people shall be of her.

17 Then *Ā′bră-hăm fell upon his face, and laughed, and [z]said in his heart, Shall *a child* be born unto him that is an hundred years old? and shall ‡Sā′rah, that is ninety years old, bear? [Q]

18 And *,[a]Ā′bră-hăm said unto God, O that [b,c]Ĭsh′ma-el might live before thee!

19 [T]And God said, ‡Sā′rah thy wife shall bear thee a son indeed; and thou shalt call his name [d]Ī′ṣaac: and I will establish my [e]covenant with him for an everlasting covenant, *and* with his [f,g]seed after him. [Q]

20 And as for [c]Ĭsh′ma-el, I have [h]heard thee: Behold, I have blessed him, and will make him fruitful, and will multiply him exceedingly; twelve princes shall he beget, and I will make him a great nation.

21 But my [e]covenant will I establish with [d]Ī′ṣaac, which ‡Sā′rah shall bear unto thee at this set[C] time in the next year. [T]

22 And he left off talking with him, and [i]God went up from *Ā′bră-hăm.

23 ¶ [j]And *Ā′bră-hăm took [c]Ĭsh′ma-el his son, and all that were born in his house, and all that were bought with his money, every [k]male among the men of Ā′bră-hăm's house; and †circumcised[C] the flesh of their foreskin in the selfsame day, as [i]God had said unto him.

24 And *Ā′bră-hăm *was* ninety years old and nine, when he was †circumcised in the flesh of his foreskin.

v.17–1939 BC

18
a *Parents*, 2 Cor. 12:14.
b *Children, prayer for*, Mark. 10:14.
c *Ishmael*, Gen. 16:11.

19
d *Isaac*, Gen. 21:3.
e *Covenant, of God with men*, Deut. 29:1.
f *Jesus, prophecies of the coming of*, Matt. 1:21.
g *Prophecies, of the Messiah*, Gen. 12:3.

20
h *Prayer, answered*, Acts 6:4.

22
i *God*, Gen. 2:2.

23
j *Obedience, instances of*, Heb. 5:8.
k *Servant*, Jer. 2 14.

8-10, 17–19; Jas. 2:21–24. *Unselfishness of*, Gen. 13:9; 21:25–30. *Independence of, in character*, Gen. 14:23; 23:6–16. *Ancestors of, idolatrous*, Josh. 24·2. *How regarded by his descendants*, Matt. 3:9; Luke 13:16, 28; 19:9; John 8:33–40, 52–59. *Ancestor of Jesus*, Matt. 1:1;Luke 3:23–34.

† **CIRCUMCISION.** *Institution of*, Gen. 17:10–14; Lev. 12:3; John 7:22; Acts 7:8; Rom. 4:11. *A seal of righteousness*, Rom. 2:25–29, 4:11. *Performed on all males on the eighth day*, Gen. 17:12, 13; Lev. 12:3; Luke 1:59; 2:21; Acts 7:8; Phil. 3:5. *Child named at the time of*, Gen. 21:3, 4; Luke 1:59; 2:21. *Rite of, observed on the Sabbath*, John 7:23. *A prerequisite of the privileges of the passover*, Ex. 12:48. *Neglect of, punished*, Gen. 17:14; Ex. 4:24. *Neglected*, Josh. 5:7. *Covenant promises of*, Gen. 17:4–14; Acts 7:8; Rom. 3:1; 4:11; Gal. 5:3. *Necessity of, falsely taught by Judaizing Christians*, Acts 15:1. *Paul's argument against the continuance of*, Rom. 2:25, 28; Gal. 6:12–15. *Characterized by Peter as a yoke*, Acts 15:10. *Abrogated*, Acts 15:5–29; Rom. 3:30; 4:9–11; 1 Cor. 7:18, 19; Gal. 2: 3, 4; 5:2–11; 6:12; Eph. 2:11, 15; Col. 2:11; 3:11.

**Instances of:** *Abraham*, Gen. 17:23–27. *Isaac*, Gen. 21:3, 4; Acts 7:8. *Schechemites*, Gen. 34:24. *Gershom*, Ex. 4:25. *Israelites at Gilgal*, Josh. 5:2–9. *John the Baptist*, Luke 1:59. *Jesus*, Luke 2:21. *Paul*, Phil. 3:5. *Timothy*, Acts 16:3.

**Figurative,** Ex. 6:12; Deut. 10:16; 30:6; Jer. 4:4; 6:10; 9:26; Rom. 2:29; 15:8; Phil. 3:3; Col. 2:11; 3:11.

*A designation of the Jews*, Acts 10:45; 11:2; Rom. 2:30; Gal. 2:9; Eph. 2:11; Col. 4:11; Tit. 1:10; *of Christians*, Phil. 3:3.

‡ **SARAH** (*princess*). *Wife of Abraham*, Gen. 11:29–31; 12:5. *Abraham's half sister;* Gen. 12:19; 20:12. *Abraham represents her as being his sister, she is taken by Pharaoh to be his wife, but is returned to Abraham*, Gen. 12:10–20; *Abimelech, king of Gerar, takes her; she is restored to Abraham by means of a dream*, Gen. 20:1–14. *Is sterile*, Gen. 11:30; 16:1. *Gives her maid, Hagar, to Abraham as a wife*, Gen. 16:1–3. *Her jealousy of Hagar*, Gen. 16:4–6; 21:9–14. *Her miraculous conception of Isaac*, Gen. 17:15–21; 18:9–15; Rom. 9:9. *Name changed from Sarai to Sarah*, Gen. 17:15. *Gives birth to Isaac*, Gen. 21:2, 3, 6–8. *Death and burial of*, Gen. 23; 25:10. *Character of*, Heb. 11:11; 1 Pet. 3:5, 6.

v.25–1939 BC
See footnote, *Time,* Rev. 10:6.

25 And Ĭsh′ma-el his son *was*
thirteen years old, when he was
circumcised in the flesh of his
foreskin.
26 In the selfsame day was
Ā′brā-hăm circumcised, and
Ĭsh′ma-el his son.
27 And all the men of his
house, born in the house, and
bought with money of the stranger, were circumcised with him.

## CHAPTER 18

*The Lord appears unto Abraham. 2 He entertains three strangers. 9 Sarah is reproved for laughing at God's promise. 17 The destruction of Sodom is revealed to Abraham, 23 who makes intercession for the men thereof.*

AND the [a]LORD appeared
unto [b]him [1]in the plains
of [c]Măm′rē: and he sat in the
[d]tent door in the heat of the day;
2 And he lift up his eyes and
looked, and, lo, three [e,f]men
stood by him: and when he saw
*them,* he ran to meet them from
the [d]tent door, and [*,g]bowed
himself toward the ground,
3 And said, My Lord, if now I
have found favour in thy sight,
[h]pass not away, I pray thee,
from thy servant:
4 Let a little water, I pray you,
be fetched, and [i]wash your feet,
and rest yourselves under the
tree:
5 [h]And I will fetch a morsel of
[j]bread, and comfort ye your
hearts; after that ye shall pass
on: for therefore are ye come to
your servant. And [f]they said, So
do, as thou hast said.
6 And [b]Ā′brā-hăm hastened into the tent unto [k,l,m]Sā′rah, and
said, Make ready quickly three
[n]measures of fine meal, knead *it,*
and make [j]cakes [2]upon the
hearth.
7 And [b]Ā′brā-hăm ran unto
the herd, and fetcht a calf tender
and good, and gave *it* unto [3]a
young man; and he hasted to
dress it.
8 And he took [†]butter, and
[o]milk, and the calf which he had
dressed, and set *it* before them;
and he stood by them under the
tree, and they did [‡]eat.
9 ¶ And they said unto [b]him,
Where *is* [k]Sā′rah thy [m]wife?
And he said, Behold, in the
[d]tent.
10 And he said, I will certainly
return unto thee according to
the time of life; and, lo, [k]Sā′rah
thy [m]wife shall have a [p]son. And
Sā′rah heard *it* in the [d]tent door,
which *was* behind him.
11 Now [b]Ā′brā-hăm and [k]Sā′-
rah *were* old *and* well stricken in
age; *and* it ceased to be with Sā′-
rah after the [q]manner of women.
12 Therefore [k]Sā′rah [r]laughed
within herself, saying, [s]After I
am waxed old shall I have pleasure, my [b,t]lord being old also?
13 And the [u]LORD said unto
[b]Ā′brā-hăm, Wherefore did
[k]Sā′rah laugh, saying, Shall I of
a surety bear a child, which am
old?
14 Is any thing too hard for the
[v]LORD? At the time appointed
I will return unto thee, according to the time of life, and Sā′rah
[w]shall have a son.
15 Then [k]Sā′rah [x,y]denied,
saying, I laughed not; for she
was afraid. And he said, Nay;
but thou didst laugh.
16 ¶ And the men rose up
from thence, and looked toward
[z]Sŏd′om: and [a]Ā′brā-hăm went
with them to bring them on the
way.

1
a *God, appearance of,* Gen. 2:2.
b *Abraham,* Gen. 17:5.
c *Mamre,* vs. 1–15; Gen. 13:18.
d *Tent,* Gen. 13:5.
1 R.V. by the oaks
2
e *Angel, appearance of,* Heb. 1:13.
f *Guest,* Zeph. 1:7.
g *Salutations,* Luke 1:44.
3
h *Hospitality, instances of,* Rom. 12:13.
4
i *Ablution,* Judg. 19:21.
5
j *Bread,* Ezek. 4:13.
6
k *Sarah,* Gen. 17:15.
l *Women, duties of,* Prov. 31:10.
m *Wife,* Prov. 5:18.
n *Measure, dry,* Deut. 25:15.
2 R. V. omits *upon the hearth.*

v.7–1939 BC
See footnote, *Time,* Rev. 10:6.
7
3 R.V. the servant;
8
o *Milk,* Job 10:10.
10
p *Isaac,* Gen. 21:3.
11
q *Menstruation,* Ezek. 18:6.
12
r *Derision, instances of,* Job 30:1.
s *Doubting,* Rom. 14:23.
t 1 Pet. 3:6.
13
u *God, knowledge of,* Gen. 2:2.
14
v *God, omnipotent,* Gen. 2:2.
w *Miracles,* Luke 23:8.
15
x *Falsehood, instances of,* Job 21:34.
y *Temptation, yielding to,* Luke 11:4.
z *Sodom,* Gen. 13:10.
16
a *Abraham,* Gen. 17:5.

* **MANNERS.** *Obeisance to strangers,* Gen. 18:2; 19:1. *Standing while guests eat,* Gen. 18:8. *Standing in presence of superiors,* Gen. 31:35; Job 29:8; *of the aged,* Lev. 19:32. *Rules for guests,* Prov. 23:1, 2; Luke 14:8–10; 1 Cor. 10:27. *Jews forbidden to associate with heathen,* Acts 10:28; 11:3; Gal. 2:12. *Evangelists required not to salute on highway,* Luke 10:4; compare 2 Kin. 4:29.

See footnote, SALUTATIONS, Luke 1:44.

† **BUTTER,** Deut. 32:14; Judg. 5:25; 2 Sam. 17:29; Job 20:17; Isa. 7:15, 22. *Made by churning,* Prov. 30:33.

‡ **EATING.** *The host acting as waiter,* Gen. 18:8. *Favored guests served an extra portion,* Gen. 43:34. *Table used in,* Judg. 1:7. *Reclining on couches,* Amos 6:4, 7; Luke 7:37, 38; John 13:25. *Ablutions before,* Matt. 15:2.

See footnotes: FEASTS, Mark 12:39; FOOD, Psa. 139:25; GLUTTONY, Prov. 30:22.

v.17–1939 BC

17
[b] *Anthropomorphisms,* Gen. 11:5.

18
[c] *Jesus, prophecies of the coming of,* Matt. 1:21.

19
[d] *Parents, duty of,* 2 Cor. 12:14
[e] *Master, good,* Col. 4:1.
[f] *Family, government of,* 1 Chr. 13:14.
[g] *Obedience,* Heb. 5:8.

20
[h] *God, judge,* Gen. 2:2.
[i] *Sodom,* Gen. 13:10.
[j] *Gomorrah,* Gen. 13:10.
[k] *Nation, punishment of,* vs. 20–32; Isa. 2:4.
[l] *Wicked, described,* Psa. 73:3.
[m] *Sin, punishment of,* vs. 20–32; Rom. 5:12.

22
[n] *Angel,* Heb. 1:13.

23
[o] *Boldness, of the righteous,* Phil. 1:20.
[p] *Communion, with God,* 2 Cor. 13:14.
[q] *Intercession, instances of,* Jer. 27:18.

25
[r] *God, righteousness of,* Gen. 2:2.

26
[s] *God, mercy of,* vs. 26–32; Gen. 2:2.
[t] *Prayer, answered, instances of,* Acts 6:4.
[u] *Intercession, influence of the righteous,* Jer. 27:18

17 And the LORD said, Shall I [b]hide from [a]Ā′bră-hăm that thing which I do;

18 Seeing that [a]Ā′bră-hăm shall surely become a great[C] and mighty nation, and [c]all the ‖nations of the earth shall be blessed in him?[Q]

19 For I know [a]him, that [d,e]he will command his children and his [f]household after him, and they shall [g]keep the way of the LORD, to do justice and judgment; that the LORD may bring upon Ā′bră-hăm that which he hath spoken of him.

20[Q] And the [h]LORD said, Because the cry of [i]Sŏd′om and [j]Gŏ-mŏr′rah is great, and because [k,l]their [m]sin is very grievous;

21 I will go down now, and [b]see whether [l]they have done altogether according to the cry of it, which is come unto me; and if not, I will know.[Q]

22 And the [n]men turned their faces from thence, and went toward [i]Sŏd′om: but [a]Ā′bră-hăm stood yet before the LORD.

23 ¶ And [a]Ā′bră-hăm [o]drew near, and [p,q]said, Wilt thou also [k]destroy the righteous with the wicked?

24 [o]Peradventure[C] there be fifty righteous within the city: [q]wilt thou also destroy and not spare the place for the fifty righteous that *are* therein?

25 [o,q]That be far from thee to do after this manner, to slay the righteous with the wicked: and that the righteous should be as the wicked, that be far from thee: Shall not the [h]Judge of all the earth [r]do right?[S T Q]

26[S] And the LORD said, If I find in [i]Sŏd′om fifty righteous within the city, then [s,t]I will spare all the place for their [u]sakes.

27 And [a]Ā′bră-hăm answered and [v]said, Behold now, [w]I have taken upon me to speak unto the Lord, [x,y]which *am but* dust and ashes;

28 [v]Peradventure[C] there shall lack five of the fifty righteous: [q]wilt thou destroy all the city for *lack of* five? And he said, [s,t,u]If I find there forty and five, I will not destroy *it*.[Q]

29 And he [v]spake unto him yet again, and said, Peradventure[C] there shall be forty found there. And he said, [s,t]I will not do *it* for forty's [u]sake.

30 And he [v]said *unto him,* [x]Oh let not the Lord be angry, and I will speak: Peradventure[C] there shall thirty be found there. And he said, [s,t,u]I will not do *it,* if I find thirty there.

31 And he [v,w]said, Behold now, I have taken upon me to speak unto the Lord: Peradventure[C] there shall be twenty found there. And he said, [s,t]I will not destroy *it* for twenty's [u]sake.

32 And he [v,x]said, Oh let not the Lord be angry, and I will speak yet but this once: Peradventure[C] ten shall be found there. And he said, [s,t]I will not destroy *it* for ten's [u]sake.[S]

33 And the LORD went his way, as soon as he had left[C] [p]communing[C] with [a]Ā′bră-hăm: and Ā′bră-hăm returned unto his place.[T]

## CHAPTER 19

*Lot entertaineth two angels. 4 The Sodomites are stricken with blindness. 12 Lot is commanded to flee for safety to the mountain. 18 He is permitted to go into Zoar. 24 Sodom and Gomorrah are destroyed. 26 Lot's wife becomes a pillar of salt. 30 Lot dwells in a cave. 31 The origin of Moab and Ammon.*

AND[Q] there came two [a]angels to [b]Sŏd′om at even; and [c]Lŏt sat in the [d]gate of Sŏd′om: and Lŏt seeing *them* [e]rose up to meet them; and he [f]bowed

v.27–1939 BC

27
[v] *Prayer, importunity in,* Acts 6:4.
[w] *Presumption, instances of,* Psa. 19:13.
[x] *Humility, exemplified,* Prov. 22:4.
[y] *Man, insignificance of,* Job 4:17.

1
[a] *Angel, appearances of,* Heb. 1:13.
[b] *Sodom,* Gen. 13:10.
[c] *Lot,* Gen. 11:27.
[d] *Gates, open square at,* Deut. 3:5.
[e] *Salutations,* Luke 1:44.
[f] *Manners,* Gen. 18:2.

‖ **NATIONS BLESSED IN ABRAHAM,** Gen. 12:23; 18:18; 22:18; 26:4; Acts 3:25; Gal. 3:8. See footnote, NATION, Isa. 2:4.

v.1–1939 BC
See footnote, *Time*, Rev. 10:6.

2
*g Hospitality, instances of*, Rom. 12:13.
*h Guests*, Zeph. 1:7.
*i Ablutions*, Judg. 19:21.

3
*j Feasts*, Mark 12:39.
*k Bread*, Ezek. 4:13.

5
*Lasciviousness, instances of*, 1 Pet. 4:3.
*m Sodomy*, vs. 5–8; Lev. 18:22.

9
*n Obduracy*, Prov. 29:1.

himself with his face toward the ground;

2 And [c]he said, Behold now, my lords, [g]turn in, I pray [h]you, into your servant's house, and tarry all night, and [i]wash your feet, and ye shall *rise up early, and go on your ways. And they said, Nay; but we will abide in the street all night.

3 And [c]he [g]pressed upon them greatly; and they turned in unto him, and entered into his house; and he made them a [j]feast, and did bake unleavened [k]bread, and they did eat.

4 ¶ But before [a]they lay down, the men of the city, *even* the men of [b]Sŏd'om, compassed the house round, both old and young, all the people from every quarter:

5 And they called unto [c]Lŏt, and said unto him, [l]Where *are* the men which came in to thee this night? bring them out unto us, that we may [m]know them.

6 And [c]Lŏt went out at the door unto them, and shut the door after him,

7 And said, I pray you, ‡brethren, do not so wickedly.

8 Behold now, I have two daughters which have not known man; let me, I pray you, bring them out unto you, and do ye to them as *is* good in your eyes: only unto [h]these men do nothing; for therefore came they [g]under the shadow of my roof.

9 And they said, Stand back. And they said *again*, This one *fellow* came in to sojourn, and he will needs be a judge: now will we deal worse with thee, than with them. And they [n]pressed sore upon the man, *even* [c]Lŏt, and came near to break the door.

10 But the [a]men put forth their hand, and pulled Lŏt into the house to them, and shut to the door.

11 And [a]they smote the ‡men that *were* at the door of the house with [o,p]blindness, both small and great: so that they wearied themselves to find the door.

12 ¶ [q]And the [a]men said unto [c]Lŏt, Hast thou here any besides? †son in law, and thy [r]sons, and thy daughters, and whatsoever thou hast in the city, bring *them* out of this place:

13 For we will [s]destroy this place, because the [t]cry of [u]them is waxen great before the face of the LORD; and the LORD hath sent us to destroy it.

14 And [c]Lŏt went out, and spake unto his †sons in law, which married his daughters, and said, Up, get you out of [v]this place; for the LORD will [s]destroy this city. But he seemed as one that mocked unto his [w]sons in law.

15 ¶ And when the morning arose, then the [a]angels hastened [c]Lŏt, saying, Arise, take thy wife, and thy two daughters, which are here; lest thou be consumed in the [1,t]iniquity of the city.

16 And while he lingered, the [a]men laid hold upon his hand, and upon the hand of his wife, and upon the hand of his two [r]daughters; the [x]LORD being merciful unto him: and they brought him forth, and set him without the city.

17 And it came to pass, when they had brought them forth abroad, that [a]he said, Escape

v.9–1939 BC
See footnote, *Time*, Rev. 10:6.

11
*o Blindness*, 2 Kin. 6:18.
*p Miracles*, Luke 23:8.

12
*q God, preserver*. Gen. 2:2.
*r Children, of righteous, blessed*, Mark 10:14.

13
*s Judgments*, Ex. 6:6.
*t Sin, punishment of*, Rom. 5:12.
*u Reprobates*, 1 Cor. 9:27.

14
*v Evil Company*, Prov. 13:20.
*w Children, wicked, instances of*, Mark 10:14.

15
1 *Or*, punishment

16
*x God, mercy of*, Gen. 2:2.

* **RISING. Early:** *For prayer*, Mark 1:35. *For religious instruction*, Acts 5:21. *Practiced by the diligent*, Prov. 31:15; *by drunkards*, Isa. 5:11.

INSTANCES OF: *Lot*, Gen. 19:23. *Abraham*, Gen. 19:27; 21:14; 22:3. *Isaac*, Gen. 26:31. *Abimelech*, Gen. 20:8. *Jacob*, Gen. 28:18; 32:31. *Laban*, Gen. 31:55. *Moses*, Ex. 8:20; 9:13; 34:4. *Joshua*, Josh. 3:1; 6:12, 15; 7:16. *Gideon*, Judg. 6:38. *Elkanah*, 1 Sam. 1:19. *Samuel*, 1 Sam. 15:12. *David*, 1 Sam. 17:20. *Mary*, Mark 16:2; Luke 24:1. *Apostles*, Acts 5:21.

See footnote, INDUSTRY, 1 Kin. 11:28.

**Late:** *By sluggards*, Prov. 6:9–11; 24:33, 34.

See footnotes: IDLENESS, Eccl. 10:18; LAZINESS, Prov. 19:15.

† **SON-IN-LAW.** Wicked, Gen. 19:14. UNJUST, *Jacob*, Gen. 30:37–42. FAITHFUL, *Peter*, Mark 1:29, 30; Luke 4:38.

v.17–1939 BC
See footnote, *Time*, Rev. 10:6.

for thy life; look not behind
thee, neither stay thou in all the
plain; escape to the mountain,
lest thou be [s,t]consumed.[Q]
18 And Lŏt said unto them,
Oh, not so, my Lord:[T]
19 [T]Behold now, thy servant
hath found grace in thy sight,
and thou hast magnified [x]thy
mercy, which [q]thou hast shewed
unto me in saving my life; and I
cannot escape to the mountain,
lest some evil take[G] me, and I die:
20 Behold now, this [y]city *is*
near to flee unto, and it *is* a little
one: Oh, let me escape thither,
(*is* it not a little one?) and my
soul[G] shall live.
21 And he said unto him, See, I
have accepted[G] thee concerning
this thing also, that I will not
overthrow this city, for the
which thou [z]hast spoken.
22 Haste thee, escape thither;
for I cannot do any thing till
thou be come thither. Therefore
the name of the city was called
[a]Zō'ar.[T]
23 The sun was risen upon the
earth when [b]Lŏt entered into
[a]Zō'ar.
24 Then[Q] the LORD [c,d,e]rained
upon [f]Sŏd'om and upon [g]Gŏ-
mŏr'rah [h]brimstone and [i]fire
from the LORD out of heaven:[T]
25 And he [c]overthrew those
cities, and all the plain, and all
the ‡inhabitants of the cities,
and that which grew upon the
ground.[Q]
26 But his [j]wife [k]looked back
from behind him, and she became a [l]pillar of [m]salt.[Q]
27 And [n]Ā'bră-hăm *gat[G] up
early in the morning to the place
where he stood before the LORD:
28 And he looked toward [f]Sŏd'-
om and [g]Gŏ-mŏr'rah, and toward all the land of the plain,
and beheld, and, lo, the smoke
of the country went up as the
smoke of a furnace.[Q]
29 ¶ And it came to pass, when
God [c]destroyed the cities of the
plain, that [o]God [p,q]remembered
[n]Ā'bră-hăm, and sent [b]Lŏt out
of the midst of the overthrow,
when he overthrew the cities in
the which Lŏt dwelt.
30 ¶ And [b]Lŏt went up out of
[a]Zō'ar, and dwelt in the mountain, and his two daughters with
him; for he [r]feared to dwell in
Zō'ar: and he dwelt in a cave,
he and his two daughters.
31 And the [s]firstborn said unto
the younger, Our father *is* old,
and *there is* not a man in the
earth to [t]come in unto us after
the manner of all the earth:
32 Come, let [s]us make our father drink [u]wine, and we will
[t,v]lie with him, that we may preserve seed of our father.
33 And [s]they made their [b]fa-
ther drink [u]wine that night: and
the firstborn went in, and [v]lay
with her father; and [w]he perceived not when she lay down
nor when she arose.
34 And it came to pass on the
morrow[G], that the [s]firstborn said
unto the younger, Behold, I [v]lay
yesternight with my father: let
us make him [w]drink [u]wine this
night also; and go thou in, *and*
lie with him, that we may preserve seed of our father.
35 And [s]they made their [b]father
[w]drink [u]wine that night also:
and the younger arose, and [v]lay
with him; and he perceived not
when she lay down, nor when
she arose.
36 Thus were both the [s]daugh-
ters of [b]Lŏt with child by their
father.
37 And the firstborn bare a

20
*y* *Zoar*, Deut. 34:3.

21
*z* *Intercession, of man with God*, Jer. 27:18.

22
*a* *Zoar*, Deut. 34:3.

23
*b* *Lot*, Gen. 11:27.

24
*c* *Judgments*, Ex. 6:6.
*d* *Miracles*, Luke 23:8.
*e* *Meteorology, phenomena*, Matt. 16:2.
*f* *Sodom*, Gen. 13:10.
*g* *Gomorrah*, Gen. 13:10.
*h* *Brimstone*, Deut. 29:23.
*i* *Fire, miracles connected with*, Ex. 12:8.

26
*j* *Women, wicked, instances of*, Prov. 31:10.
*k* *Disobedience, instances of*, Eph. 5:6.
*l* *Pillar, of salt*, Gen. 28:18.
*m* *Salt, pillar of*, 2 Kin. 2:20.

27
*n* *Abraham*, Gen. 17:5.

v.28–1939 BC
See footnote, *Time*, Rev. 10:6.

29
*o* *God, mercy of*, Gen. 2:2.
*p* *Anthropomorphisms, memory attributed to God*, Gen. 11:5.
*q* *Intercession, influence of the righteous*, Jer. 27:18.

30
*r* *Doubting, exemplified*, Rom. 14:23.

31
*s* *Children, wicked, instances of*, Mark 10:14.
*t* *Lasciviousness*, 1 Pet. 4:3.

32
*u* *Wine, intoxication from, instances of*, Prov. 23:31.
*v* *Incest*, Lev. 18:6.

33
*w* *Drunkenness, instances of*, Luke 21:34.

‡ **SODOMITES**, inhabitants of Sodom. *Wickedness of*, Gen. 19:4-14. *Destroyed by fire as a judgment*, Gen. 19:24, 25. *To be judged according to opportunity*, Matt. 10:15; 11:24; Luke 10:12.

**Those who practiced sodomy as a religious rite**, Deut. 23:17; 1 Kin. 14:24; 15:12; 22:46; 2 Kin. 23:7; Hos 4:14.
See footnote, SODOMY, Lev. 18:22.

37

x *Bastard, instances of,* Deut. 23:2.

38

y *Ammonites, descendants of Ammon,* Deut. 2:20.

v.1–1939 BC

1

a *Abraham,* Gen. 17:5.

b *Kadesh,* Gen. 14:7.

c *Shur,* 1 Sam. 15:7.

2

d *Cowardice, instances of,* Lev. 26:36.

e *Deception, instances of,* Josh. 9:4.

f *Sarah,* Gen. 17:15.

g Gen. 21:22–32.

3

h *God, providence of,* Gen. 2:2.

i *Dream, instances of,* Dan. 1:17.

j *Marriage,* Gen. 34:9.

4

k *God, righteousness of,* Gen. 2:2.

l *Nation, involved in sins of rulers,* Isa. 2:4.

5

m *Integrity, instances of,* Job 2:3.

6

n *God, knowledge of,* Gen. 2:2.

o *Grace, of God,* Rom. 4:16.

[x]son, and called his name Mō′-
ab: the same *is* the father of the
‖Mō′ab-ītes unto this day.
38 And the younger, she also
bare a [x]son, and called his name
Bĕn-ăm′mī: the same *is* the father of the [y]children of Ăm′-
mŏn unto this day.

## CHAPTER 20

*Abraham sojourneth at Gerar, 2 and denies his wife. 3 Abimelech taking her is reproved in a dream. 9 He rebukes Abraham, 14 restores Sarah, 16 and reproves her. 17 At the intercession of Abraham, he is healed.*

AND [a]Ā′bra-hăm journeyed
from thence toward the
south country, and dwelled between [b]Ka′desh and [c]Shûr, and
sojourned in *Ḡe′rär.
2 And [a]Ā′brā-hăm [d,e]said of
[f]Sā′rah his wife, She *is* my sister: and [g]Ā-bĭm′e-lĕch king of
Ḡē′rär sent, and took Sā′rah.
3 But [h]God came to [g]Ā-bĭm′e-
lĕch in a [i]dream by night, and
said to him, Behold, thou *art but*
a dead man, for the [f]woman
which thou hast taken; for she *is*
a man's [j]wife.
4 But [g]Ā-bĭm′e-lĕch had not
come near her: and he said,
[k]Lord, wilt thou slay also a
righteous [l]nation?
5 [e]Said he not unto me, She *is*
my sister? and she, even she herself said, He *is* my brother: in
the [m]integrity of my heart and
innocency of my hands have I
done this.
6 And God said unto him in a
[i]dream, Yea, [n]I know that thou
didst this in the [m]integrity of thy
heart; for I also [o]withheld thee
from sinning against me: therefore suffered[G] I thee not to touch
her.
7 Now therefore restore the
[a]man *his* [j]wife; for he *is* a
prophet, and he shall [p,q]pray for
thee, and thou shalt live: and [r]if
thou restore *her* not, know thou
that thou shalt surely die, thou,
and all that *are* thine.
8 Therefore [g]Ā-bĭm′e-lĕch [s]rose
early in the morning, and called
all his servants, and told all these
things in their ears: and the men
were sore[G] afraid.
9 Then [g]Ā-bĭm′e-lĕch called
[a]Ā′brā-hăm, and said unto him,
[t]What hast thou done unto us?
and what have I offended thee,
that thou hast brought on me
and on my [l]kingdom a great sin?
thou hast done deeds unto me
that ought not to be done.
10 And [g]Ā-bĭm′e-lĕch said unto
[a]Ā′brā-hăm, What sawest[G] thou,
that thou hast done this thing?
11 And [a]Ā′brā-hăm said, [u]be-
cause I [v]thought, Surely the
[w]fear of God *is* not in this place;
and they will slay me for my
[x]wife's sake.
12 And yet indeed *she is* my sister; she *is* the daughter of my father, but not the daughter of my
mother; and she [y]became my
wife.
13 And it came to pass, when
[h]God caused me to wander from
my father's house, that I [d]said
unto her, This *is* thy kindness
which thou shalt shew unto me;
at every place whither we shall
come, [e,z]say of me, He *is* my
brother.[T]
14 And [a]Ā-bĭm′e-lĕch took
sheep, and oxen, and menservants, and womenservants, and
[†,b]gave *them* unto [c]Ā′brā-hăm,
and restored him Sā′rah his wife.

v.7–1939 BC

7

p *Prayer, intercessory,* Acts 6:4.

q *Intercession, of man with God,* Jer. 27:18.

r *Adultery, penalties for,* Lev. 20:10.

8

s *Rising, early, instances of,* Gen. 19:2.

9

t *Temptation, leading into,* Luke 11:4.

11

u *Excuses,* Luke 14:18.

v *Doubting, of Abraham,* Rom. 14:23.

w *Fear of God, restraining,* Acts 9:31.

x *Wife,* Prov. 5:18.

12

y *Incest, instances of,* Lev. 18:6.

13

z Gen. 12:13.

14

a *Abimelech,* Gen. 21:22–32.

b *Good for evil, instances of,* Luke 6:27.

c *Abraham,* Gen. 17:5.

‖ **MOABITES.** *Descendants of Lot through his son Moab,* Gen. 19:37. *Called the people of Chemosh,* Num. 21:29. *Children of Israel commanded not to distress,* Deut. 2:9. *Refuse passage of Jephthah's army through their territory,* Judg. 11:17, 18. *Balak was king of,* Num. 22:4; Josh. 24:9; Judg. 11:25; Mic. 6:5; *calls for Baalam to curse Israel,* Num. 22; 23; 24; Josh. 24:9; Mic. 6:5. *Idolatry of,* Judg. 10:6; 1 Kin. 11:7. *Human sacrifices offered by,* 2 Kin. 3:27. *Are a snare to the Israelites,* Num. 25:1–3; Ruth 1:4; 1 Kin. 11:1; 1 Chr. 8:8; Ezra 9:1, 2; Neh. 13:23. *Land of, not given to the Israelites as a possession,* Deut. 2:9, 29. *David takes refuge among, from Saul,* 1 Sam. 22:3, 4. *David conquers,* 2 Sam. 8:2; 18:2, 11. *Paid tribute to king of Israel,* 2 Kin. 3:4. *Israelites had war with,* 2 Kin. 3:5–27; 13:20; 24:2; 2 Chr. 20. *Prophecies concerning judgments upon,* Isa. 15; 16; Jer. 48; Ezek. 25:8 11.

* **GERAR.** *A city of the Philistines,* Gen. 10:19. *Abimelech, king of,* Gen. 20:1, 2; 26:1 8. *Visited by Abraham,* Gen. 20:1; *by Isaac,* Gen 26:1; 2 Chr. 14:13, 14.

† **GENEROSITY. Instances of:** *Hittites to Abraham,*

v.15–1939 BC

15
*d Hospitality,* Rom. 12:13.

16
*e Sarah,* Gen. 17: 15.
*f Silver,* 1 Chr. 28: 14.
1 R. V. it is for thee
2 R.V. (marg.) in respect of all men thou art righted:

17
*g Intercession, of man with God,* Jer. 27:18.
*h Prayer, answered,* Acts 6:4.
*i Healing, the Lord the healer,* Acts 4:22.
*j Miracles,* Luke 23:8.

18
*k Barrenness,* Deut. 7:14.
*l Judgments,* Ex. 6:6.

15 And [a]Ā-bĭm′e-lĕch said,
†,[b]Behold, my land *is* before
thee: [d]dwell where it pleaseth
thee.
16 And unto [e]Sā′rah he said,
Behold, I have given thy [c]broth-
er a thousand *pieces* of [f]silver:
behold, [1]he *is* to thee a covering
of the eyes, unto all that *are* with
thee, and [2]with all *other*: thus
she was reproved.
17 So [c]Ā′brā-hăm [g,h]prayed unto God: and God [i,j]healed
Ā-bĭm′e-lĕch, and his wife, and
his maidservants; and they bare
*children.*
18 For the LORD had fast[G]
[k,l]closed up all the wombs of the
house of Ā-bĭm′e-lĕch, because
of Sā′rah Ā′brā-hăm's wife.

## CHAPTER 21

*Isaac is born. 4 He is circumcised. 6 Sarah's joy. 9 Hagar and Ishmael are cast forth. 15 Hagar in distress. 17 The angel comforts her. 22 Abimelech's covenant with Abraham at Beer-sheba.*

1
*a God, faithfulness of,* Gen. 2:2.
*b Sarah,* Gen. 17: 15.

v.2–1938 BC

2
*c Miracles,* Luke 23:8.
*d Abraham,* Gen. 17:5.
*e Children, in answer to prayer,* Mark 10:14.

4
*f Circumcision, instances of,* Gen. 17:10.
*g Obedience, instances of,* Heb. 5:8.

AND the [a]LORD visited [b]Sā′-
rah as he had said, and
the LORD did unto Sā′rah as
he had spoken.[S]
2 For [b]Sā′rah *,[c]conceived, and
bare [d]Ā′brā-hăm a [e]son in his
old age, at the set[G] time of which
[a]God had spoken to him.[Q]
3 And [d]Ā′brā-hăm called the
name of his son that was born
unto him, whom [b]Sā′rah bare to
him, †Ī′ṣaac.[Q]
4 And [d]Ā′brā-hăm [f]circumcised
his son Ī′ṣaac being eight days
old, [g]as God had commanded
him.[Q]
5 And [d]Ā′brā-hăm was an hundred years old, when his son
†Ī′ṣaac was born unto him.
6 And [b]Sā′rah [h]said, God hath
made me to laugh, *so that* all that
hear will laugh with me.
7 And [b]she [h]said, Who would
have said unto Ā′brā-hăm, that
Sā′rah should have given children suck? for I have born *him*
a son in his old age.
8 And the child grew, and was
[i]weaned: and [d]Ā′brā-hăm made
a great [j]feast the *same* day that
†Ī′ṣaac was weaned.
9 ¶ [k,l]And [b]Sā′rah saw the [m]son
of [n]Hā′gar the Ē-ġўp′tian,
which she had born unto [d]Ā′brā-
hăm, [o]mocking.[Q]
10 [p]Wherefore she said unto
[d]Ā′brā-hăm, [q,r]Cast out this
[s]bondwoman and her [m]son: for
[k,t]the son of this bondwoman
shall not be [u,v]heir with my son,
*even* with †Ī′ṣaac.[Q]
11 And the thing was very
grievous[G] in Ā′brā-hăm's sight
because of his [m]son.
12 And [w]God said unto Ā′brā-
hăm, [x]Let it not be grievous in
thy sight because of the [m]lad,
and because of thy [n,s]bond-
woman; in all that Sā′rah hath
said unto thee, hearken unto her
voice; for [y,z]in †Ī′ṣaac shall thy
seed be called.[S Q]
13 And also of the [a]son of the
bondwoman [b]will I make a nation, because he *is* thy [c,d]seed.[G]
14 And [e]Ā′brā-hăm [f]rose up
early in the morning, and took
bread, and a ‡bottle[G] of water,
and gave *it* unto [g]Hā′gar, put-

v.5–1938 BC

6
*h Thankfulness, to God,* Acts 24:3.

8
*i Children, weaning of,* Mark 10: 14.
*j Feasts,* Mark 12: 39.

9
*k Malice, instances of,* Eph. 4:31.
*l Polygamy, evil effects of,* Deut. 17: 17.
*m Ishmael,* Gen. 16: 11.
*n Hagar,* Gen. 16:1.
*o Mocking,* 1 Kin. 18:27.

v.8–1933 BC

10
*p Family, infelicity in, instances of,* 1 Chr. 13:14.
*q* Gal. 4:30.
*r Cruelty, instances of,* Psa. 27:12.
*s Servant,* Jer. 2: 14.
*t Envy, instances of,* Prov. 14:30.
*u Heir,* Gen. 15:3.
*v Inheritance,* Num. 27:7.

12
*w God,* Gen. 2:2.
*x Affliction, consolation in,* Psa. 34:19.
*y* Rom. 9:7; Heb. 11:18.
*z Foreordination,* Rom. 8:30.

13
*a Ishmael,* Gen. 16: 11.
*b Foreordination,* Rom. 8:30.
*c Children, share benefits of covenant with parents,* Mark 10:14.
*d Children, of righteous, blessed,* Mark 10:14.

14
*e Abraham,* Gen. 17:5.
*f Rising, early, instances of,* Gen. 19:2.
*g Hagar,* Gen. 16:1.

Gen. 23:6, 11. *Abimelech to Abraham,* Gen. 20:14. *Joseph to his father and brethren,* Gen. 43:11, 12; 45:22, 23; 47:11, 12. *David to Mephibosheth,* 2 Sam. 9:7.
See footnote, LIBERALITY, 1 Tim. 6:18.

*** CONCEPTION, Miraculous.** INSTANCES OF: *Sarah,* Heb. 11:11. *Rebekah,* Gen. 25:21. *Rachel,* Gen. 30:22. *Manoah's wife,* Judg. 13:3–24. *Hannah,* 1 Sam. 1:19, 20. *Elisabeth,* Luke 1:24, 25, 36, 37, 58. *Mary, by the Holy Spirit,* Matt. 1:18, 20; Luke 1:31–35.

**† ISAAC** *(laughter). Miraculous son of Abraham,* Gen. 17:15–19; 18:1–15; 21:1–8; Josh. 24:3; 1 Chr. 1:28; Gal. 4:28; Heb. 11:11. *Offered in sacrifice by his father,* Gen. 22:1–19; Heb. 11:17; Jas. 2:21. *Is provided a wife from among his kindred,* Gen. 24; 25:20. *Abrahamic covenant confirmed in,* Gen. 26:2–5; Josh. 1:6; 1 Chr. 16:15–18; Psa. 105:9. *Dwells in the south country at the well Lahai-roi,* Gen. 24:62; 25:11. *Buries his father,* Gen. 25:9. *Esau and Jacob born to,* Gen. 25:19–26; Josh. 24:4; 1 Chr. 1:34. *Dwells in Gerar,* Gen. 26:1–18. *Prospers,* Gen. 26:12–14. *Possesses large flocks and herds,* Gen. 26:14. *Digs wells, and is defrauded of them by the herdsmen of Abimelech,* Gen. 26: 15–21. *Removes to Beer-sheba,* Gen. 26:22–33. *Grieved at marriage of Esau,* Gen. 26:35. *Last blessing on his sons,* Gen. 27:16–40; Heb. 11:20. *Death and burial of,* Gen. 35: 27–29; 49:31. *His filial obedience,* Gen. 22:9. *His peaceableness,* Gen. 26:14–22. *His devoutness,* Gen. 24:63; 25:21; 26:25. *Prophecies concerning,* Gen. 17:16–21; 18:10–14; 21:12; Ex. 32:13. *Ancestor of Jesus,* Matt. 1:2; Luke 3:34.

**‡ BOTTLE.** *Made of skins,* Josh. 9:4, 13; Job 32:19; Psa. 119:83; Matt. 9:17; Mark 2:22; Luke 5:37, 38; *of clay,* Isa. 30:14; Jer. 19:1, 10; 48:12. *Used as a lachrymatory,* Psa. 56:8.

v.14–1933 BC
See footnote, *Time*, Rev. 10:6.

*h* *Beer-sheba, wilderness of*, Judg. 20:1.

15
*i* *Despondency, instances of*, Eccl. 2:20.

16
*i* *Parents, affection of*, 2 Cor. 12:14.

17
*k* *God, providence of*, Gen. 2:2.
*l* *Adversity, consolation in*, Psa. 10:6.

20
*m* *Grace, of God*, Rom. 4:16.

21
*n* *Marriage, parents contract for children*, Gen. 34:9.
*o* *Egypt*, Gen. 41:8.

22
*p* Gen. 20.
*q* Gen. 26:26.
*r* *Captain*, Num. 31:48.
*s* *Diplomacy, instances of*, 2 Kin. 16:7.
*t* *Temporal Blessings, from God*, Psa. 103:2.

23
*u* *Alliances, political, ratification of*, Josh. 9:15.
*v* *Oath*, Num. 5:19.

ting *it* on her shoulder, and the
[a]child, and sent her away: and
she departed, and wandered in
the wilderness of [h]Bē'er-shē'bȧ.
15 [i]And the water was spent[C] in
the bottle,[G] and she cast the
[a]child under one of the shrubs.
16 [i]And she went, and sat her
down over[C] against *him* a good
way off, as it were a bowshot:
for [j]she said, Let me not see the
death of the child. And she sat
over[C] against *him*, and lift[C] up her
voice, and wept.
17 And [k]God heard the voice of
the lad; and the angel of God
called to [g]Hā'gar out of heaven,
and said unto her, What aileth
thee, Hā'gar? [l]fear not; for God
hath heard the voice of the lad
where he *is*.[T]
18 [l]Arise, lift up the [a]lad, and
hold[C] him in thine hand; [b]for I
will make [c,d]him a great nation.
19 And God opened her eyes,
and she saw a ‖well of water;
and she went, and filled the
‡bottle[C] with water, and gave the
[a]lad drink.[S]
20 And [m]God was with the
[a]lad; and he grew, and dwelt in
the wilderness, and became an
§archer.
21 And he dwelt in the wilderness of ✝Pā'ran: and his mother
took him a [n]wife out of the land
of [o]Ē'ġȳpt.
22 ¶ And it came to pass at
that time, that [p]Ȧ-bĭm'e-lĕch
and [q]Phī'chol the chief [r]captain
of his host[G] spake unto [e]Ā'bră-
hăm, [s]saying, [m,t]God *is* with
thee in all that thou doest:
23 [u]Now therefore [v]swear unto
me here by God that thou wilt
not deal falsely with me, nor
with my son, nor with my son's
son: *but* according to the kindness that I have done unto thee,
thou shalt do unto me, and to
the land wherein thou hast sojourned.
24 And Ā'bră-hăm said, I will
[v]swear.
25 And Ā'bră-hăm reproved
[p]Ȧ-bĭm'e-lĕch because of a
‖,[w]well of water, which Ȧ-bĭm'e-
lĕch's [x]servants had [y]violently
[z]taken away.
26 And [a]Ȧ-bĭm'e-lĕch said, I
wot[C] not who hath done this
thing: neither didst thou tell me,
neither yet heard I *of it*, but to
day.
27 And [b]Ā'bră-hăm took [c]sheep
and oxen, and gave them unto
[a]Ȧ-bĭm'e-lĕch; and both of them
made a [d]covenant.
28 And [b]Ā'bră-hăm set [e]seven
ewe lambs of the flock by themselves.
29 And [a]Ȧ-bĭm'e-lĕch said unto
[b]Ā'bră-hăm, What *mean* these
[e]seven ewe lambs which thou
hast set by themselves?
30 And [b]he said, For *these* [e]sev-
en ewe lambs shalt [a]thou take of
my hand, that they may be a
[c]witness unto me, that I have
digged[C] this ‖well.
31 Wherefore he called that
place [f]Bē'er-shē'bȧ; because
there they [g]sware both of them.
32 Thus they made a [d]covenant
at [f]Bē'er-shē'bȧ: then [a]Ȧ-bĭm'e-
lĕch rose up, and [h]Phī'chol the
chief [i]captain of his host, and
they returned into the land of
the [j]Phĭ-lĭs'tīneṣ.
33 ¶ And [b]Ā'bră-hăm planted

v.23–1933 BC
See footnote, *Time*, Rev. 10:6.

25
*w* *Property, in real estate, rights in, violated*, Lev. 27:15.
*x* *Servant, wicked and unfaithful*, Jer. 2:14.
*y* *Strife, instances of*, Prov. 20:3.
*z* *Dishonesty*, Ezek. 22:13.

26
*a* Gen. 20.

27
*b* *Abraham*, Gen. 17:5.
*c* *Token, present*, Psa. 86:17.
*d* *Covenant, of man with men*, Deut. 29:1.

28
*e* *Seven, miscellany of*, Gen. 7:2.

31
*f* *Beer-sheba*, Judg. 20:1.
*g* *Oath*, Num. 5:19.

32
*h* Gen. 26:26.
*i* *Captain*, Num. 31:48.
*j* *Philistines*, Gen. 26:14.

‖ **WELLS.** *Of Jacob*, John 4:6. *Of Uzziah*, 2 Chr. 26:10. *At Haran*, Gen. 24:16.
**The occasion of feuds:** *Between Abraham and Abimelech*, Gen. 21:25–30. *Between Isaac and Abimelech*, Gen. 26:15–22, 32, 33.
**Figurative:** *Of salvation*, Isa. 12:3; John 4:14.

§ **ARCHERY.** *Practiced by Ishmael*, Gen. 21:20; *by Esau*, Gen. 27:3; *by Jonathan*, 1 Sam. 20:20, 36, 37; *by sons of Ulam*, 1 Chr. 8:40; *by Philistines*, 1 Sam. 31:1–3; 1 Chr. 10:3; *by people of Kedar*, Isa. 21:17; *by Syrians*, 1 Kin. 22:31–34; *by Israelites*, 2 Sam. 1:18; 1 Chr. 5:18; 12:2; 2 Chr. 14:8; 26:14; Neh. 4:13; Zech. 9:13; *by Lydians*, Jer. 46:9.
*In war*, Gen. 49:23; Judg. 5:11; 1 Sam. 31:3; 2 Chr. 17:17; Isa. 22:3; Jer. 4:29; 51:3.
See footnotes: ARROW, 1 Sam. 20:20; BOW, 2 Sam. 1:18.

✝ **PARAN** (*a place of caves*). *Desert or wilderness of*, Gen. 21:21; Num. 10:12; 12:16; 13:3, 26; Deut. 1:1. *Mountains of*, Deut. 33:2; Hab. 3:3. *Israelites encamp in*, Num. 12:16. *David takes refuge in*, 1 Sam. 25:1. *Hadad flees to*, 1 Kin. 11:17, 18.

33
k *Worship*, Gen. 22:5.
l *God, eternity of*, Gen. 2:2.

1
a *God*, Gen. 2:2.
b *Temptation, a test*, Luke 11:4.
c *Abraham*, Gen. 17:5.
d *Communion, with God, instances of*, 2 Cor. 13:14.
1 R. V. did prove
2
e *Faith, trial of*, Mark 11:22.
f *Isaac*, Gen. 21:3.
g 2 Chr. 3:1.
h *Human Sacrifices*, vs. 1–19; Deut. 12:31.
i *Offerings, burnt*, Lev. 6:17.
j *Mountain*, Mic. 7:12.
k *High Places*, 1 Kin. 3:2.
3
l *Obedience, instances of*, Heb. 5:8.
m *Rising, early, instances of*, Gen. 19:2.
n *Ass*, 2 Chr. 28:15.
o *Young Men*, Prov. 1:4.

a grove in [f]Bē′er-shē′bȧ, and
[k]called there on the name of the
LORD, the [l]everlasting[G] God.[S]
34 And Ā′brā-hăm sojourned
in the Phĭ-lĭs′tĭneș′ land many
days.

## CHAPTER 22

*Abraham commanded to offer Isaac.* 3 *He gives proof of his faith and obedience.* 11 *The Angel stays him.* 13 *A ram is sacrificed instead of Isaac.* 14 *The place is called Jehovah-jireh.* 15 *Abraham is blessed again.* 20 *The generation of Nahor unto Rebekah.*

AND[Q] it came to pass after
these things, that [a]God
did [1,b]tempt[G] [c]Ā′brā-hăm, and
[d]said unto him, Ā′brā-hăm: and
he said, Behold, *here* I *am*.
2 And he said, [e]Take now thy
son, thine only *son* [f]Ī′ṣaac,
whom thou lovest, and get thee
into the land of [g]Mō-rī′ah; and
offer [h]him there for a burnt [i]of-
fering upon one of the [j,k]moun-
tains which I will tell thee of.[Q]
3 And [c,l]Ā′brā-hăm [m]rose up
early in the morning, and saddled his [n]ass, and took two of
his [o]young men with him, and
[f]Ī′ṣaac his son, and clave[G] the
wood for the burnt [i]offering, and
rose up, and went unto the place
of which God had told him.
4 Then on the third day [c]Ā′brā-
hăm lifted up his eyes, and saw
the place afar off.
5 And [c]Ā′brā-hăm said unto his
[o]young men, Abide ye here with
the [n]ass; and I and the [f]lad will
go yonder and *worship, and
come again to you.

6 And [c,l]Ā′brā-hăm took the
wood of the burnt [i]offering, and
laid *it* upon [f]Ī′ṣaac his son; and
he took the fire in his hand, and
a †knife; and they went both of
them together.
7 And [f]Ī′ṣaac spake unto
[c]Ā′brā-hăm his father, and said,
My father: and he said, Here *am*
I, my son. And he said, Behold
the fire and the wood: but where
*is* the [p]lamb for a burnt
[i]offering?
8 And Ā′brā-hăm [q]said, My
son, God will provide himself
a lamb for a burnt [i]offering: so
they went both of them together.[Q]
9 And they came to the [g]place
which God had told him of; and
[c]Ā′brā-hăm built an [r]altar there,
and laid the wood in order, and
[l]bound [f]Ī′ṣaac his son, and [s]laid
[h]him on the altar upon the wood.[Q]
10 And [c,l]Ā′brā-hăm stretched
forth his hand, and took the
†knife to slay his [f,h]son.[Q]
11 [T]And the [t]angel of the LORD
called unto him out of heaven,
and said, Ā′brā-hăm, Ā′brā-
hăm: and he said, Here *am* I.
12 And [t]he said, Lay not thine
hand upon the [f]lad, neither do
thou anything unto him: for
now I know that thou [u]fearest
God, seeing [l]thou hast [v]not withheld thy son, thine only *son*
from me.
13 And [c]Ā′brā-hăm lifted up
his eyes, and looked, and behold
behind *him* a [w]ram[G] caught in a

7
p *Lamb*, Num. 7:15.
8
q *Faith, instances of*, Mark 11:22.
9
r *Altar*, Gen. 8:20.
s *Consecration, instances of*, Lev. 7:37.
11
t *Angel*, Heb. 1:13.
12
u *Fear of God*, Acts 9:31.
v *Self-denial*, Mark 8:34.
13
w *Sheep*, Deut. 32:14.

* **WORSHIP**, Gen. 4:26. *To be rendered to God only*, Ex. 20:3; Deut. 6:13; Matt. 4:10; Luke 4:8; Acts 10:25, 26, 14:11, 15; Col. 2:18; Rev. 19:10; 22:8. *Not needed by God*, Acts 17:24, 25. *Acceptable to God*, Gen. 4:4; 8:20, 21. *Divine presence in*, Ex. 29:42, 43; Num. 17:4; 2 Chr. 5:13, 14; Matt. 18:20; Acts 2:1-4. *Of angels, forbidden*, Rev. 19:10; 22:8, 9. *Sanctuary instituted for*, Ex. 25:8, 22; 29:43; 40:34, 35. *Summons to*, Psa. 95:6; Isa. 2:3; Mic. 4:2.
*Enjoined*, Gen. 35:1; Ex. 23:17, 18; 34:23; Deut. 12:5–7, 11, 12; 16:6–8; 31:11–13; 33:19; 2 Kin. 17:36; 1 Chr. 16:29; Psa. 29:2; 76:11; 96:8, 9; 97:7; 99:5; Isa. 12:5, 6; 49:13; 52:9; Joel 2:15–17; Nah. 1:15; Zech. 14:16–18; Matt. 8:4; Mark 1:44; Luke 4:8; 5:14; 1 Tim. 2:8; Heb. 10:25; Rev. 14:7; 19:10.
*With music*, 2 Chr. 5:13, 14; Ezra 3:10, 11; Psa. 100:1, 2; 126:1–3; Isa. 30:29; 38:20. *Rendering praise*, Psa. 22:22; 138:2; 149:1; *thanksgiving*, Psa. 35:18; 100:4; 116:17.
*In spirit and in truth*, John 4:23, 24; 1 Cor. 14:15; Phil. 3:3. *Renews strength*, Isa. 40:31. *Loved by God's people*, Psa. 27:4; 84:1–4, 10; Zech. 8:21.
*Preparation for*, Ex. 19:10–13, 21–24; 20:24, 25; 30:19–21; Lev. 10:3; Psa. 26:6; Isa. 56:6, 7; Zeph. 3:18; Mal. 3:3, 4. *Proprieties in*, Eccl. 5:1, 2; 1 Cor. 11:13, 20–22; 14:2-19. *Reverence in*, Ex. 3:5; 19:10–12, 21–24; 24:1, 2; Eccl. 5:1; Hab. 2:20.
*Private*, Matt. 6:6; 14:23; Luke 6:12.
*At night*, Isa. 30:29, Acts 16:25. *In the temple*, Jer. 26:2; Luke 18:10; 24:53; Acts 3:1. *In private homes*, Acts 1:13, 14; 5:42; 12:12; 20:7-9; Rom. 16:5; 1 Cor. 16:19; Col. 4:15; Phile. 2. *Anywhere*, John 4:21–24. *To become universal*, Isa. 45:23; Rom. 14:11; Phil. 2:10.
*Of hypocrites, repugnant to God*, Isa. 1:11–15; 29:13–16; Hos. 6:6; Amos 5:21–24. *Of the wicked, rejected*, Gen. 4:5, 7.
**Family**, Deut. 16:11, 14. *Of Abraham*, Gen. 12:7, 8; 13:4, 18. *Of Jacob*, Gen. 35:2, 3. *Of Job*, Job 1:5. *Of the Philippian jailer*, Acts 16:34.
**National**, Deut. 16:11; 31:11–13.
See footnotes: PRAISE, Psa. 150:1; PRAYER, Acts 6:4.

† **KNIFE**, an edged tool. *Used by Abraham in offering Isaac*, Gen. 22:6. *Of the temple, returned from Babylon*,

thicket by his horns: and Ā′bră-
hăm went and took the ram,
and offered him up for a burnt
[x]offering [y]in the stead[C] of his
son.
14 And Ā′bră-hăm called the
name of that place [2]Jĕ-hō′vah-
jī′reh: as it is said *to* this day,
In the mount of the LORD it
shall be [3]seen.
15 ¶ [T]And the [t]angel of the
LORD called unto Ā′bră-hăm
out of heaven the second time.
16 [Q]And said, [z]By myself have I
[a, b]sworn, saith the LORD, for
[c]because thou hast done this
thing, and hast [d]not withheld
thy [e]son, thine only *son*:
17 [c]That[Q] in blessing I will [f]bless
[g]thee, and in multiplying I will
multiply thy [‡, h]seed as the stars
of the heaven, and as the sand
which *is* upon the sea shore; and
thy [i]seed shall possess the gate
of his enemies;[S]
18 And in thy [j]seed shall all the
[k, l]nations of the earth be
blessed; because thou hast
[m]obeyed my voice. [T Q]
19 So [n]Ā′bră-hăm returned unto his young men, and they rose
up and went together to [o]Bē′er-
shē′bȧ; and Ā′bră-hăm dwelt at
Bē′er-shē′bȧ.
20 ¶ And it came to pass after
these things, that it was told
[n]Ā′bră-hăm, saying, Behold,
[p]Mĭl′cah, she hath also born
children unto thy brother
[‖]Nā′hôr:
21 [q]Hŭz his firstborn, and Bŭz
his brother, and Kĕ-mū′el the
father of Ā′ram,
22 [q]And Chē′sed, and Hā′zō,
and Pĭl′dăsh, and Jĭd′laph, and
[r]Bĕth-ụ′el.
23 [q]And [r]Bĕth-ụ′el begat [s]Rĕ-
bĕk′ah: these eight [p]Mĭl′cah did
bear to [‖]Nā′hôr, [n]Ā′bră-hăm's
brother.
24 [q]And his [t]concubine,[C] whose
name *was* Reụ′mah, she bare also Tē′bah, and Gā′hăm, and
Thā′hăsh, and Mā′a-chah.

## CHAPTER 23

*The age and death of Sarah. 3 The purchase of Machpelah, 19 where Sarah was buried.*

AND [a]Sā′rah was [b]an hundred and seven and twen-
ty years old: *these were* the
years of the life of Sā′rah.
2 And Sā′rah [c]died in Kĭr′jăth-
är′bȧ; the same *is* *Hē′bron in
the land of [d]Cā′năan: and
[e]Ā′bră-hăm came to [f, g]mourn
for Sā′rah, and to [h]weep for her.
3 ¶ And [e]Ā′bră-hăm stood up
from before his dead, and spake
unto the [i]sons of Hĕth, saying,
4 I *am* a stranger and a sojourner with you: give me a possession of a †buryingplace with
you, that I may [j]bury my dead
out of my sight.[Q]
5 And the [i]children of Hĕth

*x Jesus, typified in offerings,* Matt. 1:21.
*y Substitution,* Lev. 1:4.

**14**
2 *That is,* Jehovah will see, *or,* provide:
3 R. V. provided.

**16**
*z* Heb. 6:13.

*a Oath, attributed to God,* Num. 5:19.
*b Covenant, of God with man,* Deut. 29:1.
*c Afflictions, benefits of, illustrated,* Psa. 34:19.
*d Self-denial,* Mark 8:34.
*e Isaac,* Gen. 21:3.

**17**
*f Temporal Blessings, from God,* Psa. 103:2.
*g Righteous, promises to,* Psa. 64:10.
*h Children, gift of God,* Mark 10:14.
*i Israel, prophecies concerning,* Ex. 4:22.

**18**
*j Jesus, prophecies concerning,* Matt. 1:21.
*k Nations to be blessed in Abraham,* Gen. 18:18.
*l Gentiles, prophecies concerning conversion of,* Acts 10:45.
*m Obedience,* Heb. 5:8.

**19**
*n Abraham,* Gen. 17:5.
*o Beer-sheba,* Judg. 20:1.

**20**
*p Milcah,* Gen. 11:29.

**21**
*q Genealogy,* vs. 20–24; 1 Chr. 5:1.

**22**
*r Bethuel,* Gen. 24:15.

**23**
*s Rebekah,* Gen. 24:15.

**24**
*t Concubinage,* 2 Sam. 21:11.

**1**
*a Sarah,* Gen. 17:15
*b Longevity,* Psa. 91:16.

v.2–1920 BC

**2**
*c Death,* Num. 23:10.
*d Canaan,* Gen. 37:1.
*e Abraham,* Gen. 17.5.
*f Mourning,* Lam. 2:5.
*g Bereavement,* Hos. 9:12.
*h Weeping,* Ezra 3:13.

**3**
*i Hittites,* Judg. 1:26.

**4**
*j Burial,* Acts 8:2.

Ezra 1:9. *Used for sharpening pens,* Jer. 36:23. *Self-flagellation with, in idolatrous worship,* 1 Kin. 18:28.

‡ **DESCENDANTS OF ABRAHAM,** Gen. 15:5; Ex. 32:13; Acts 3:25; 1 Chr. 27:23; Rom. 4:17, 18; Heb. 6:14; 11:12. See footnote, ABRAHAM, Gen. 17:5.

‖ **NAHOR.** *Brother of Abraham,* Gen. 11:26; Josh. 24:2. *Marriage and descendants of,* Gen. 11:27, 29; 22:20–24; 24:15, 24, 47.

* **HEBRON,** a city of Judah, S. of Jerusalem. *When built,* Num. 13:22. *Fortified,* 2 Chr. 11:10. *Called* KIRIATH-ARBA, Gen. 23:2; Gen. 35:27; Josh. 15:13. *Abraham dwells and Sarah dies at,* Gen. 23:2. *Isaac dwells at,* Gen. 35:27. *Jacob dwells at,* Gen. 37:14. *Hoham, king of, confederated with other kings of the Canaanites against Joshua,* Josh. 10:3–39. *Children of Anakim dwell at,* Num. 13:22; Josh. 11:21. *Conquest of, by Caleb,* Josh. 14:6–15; Judge. 1:10, 20. *A city of refuge,* Josh. 20:7; 21:11, 13. *David crowned king of Judah at,* 2 Sam. 2:1–11; 3; 1 Chr. 11:1–3 *of Israel,* at, 2 Sam. 5:1–5. *The burial place of Sarah,* Gen. 23:2; *of Abner,* 2 Sam. 3:32; *of Ish-bosheth,* 2 Sam. 4:12. *The conspirators against Ish-bosheth hanged at,* 2 Sam. 4:12. *Absalom made king at,* 2 Sam. 15:9, 10. *Jews of the Babylonian captivity dwell at,* Neh. 11:25.

*Pool of,* 2 Sam. 4:12.

† **BURYING PLACES.** *Bought by Abraham,* Gen. 23; 25:9; *by the chief priests with the money returned by Judas,* Acts 1:18; with Matt. 27:5–10. *Prepared by Jacob,* Gen. 50:5; *by Asa,* 2 Chr. 16:14; *by Joseph,* Matt. 27:60. *On hills,* Josh. 24:33; 2 Kin. 23:16. *In valleys,* Jer. 7:32.

*Family,* Gen. 47:30; 49:29; Acts 7:16. *Of kings,* 1 Kin. 2:10; 2 Chr. 32:33. *Of kings, a place of honor,* 2 Chr. 21:20; 24:16, 25. *For poor and strangers,* Jer. 26:23; Matt. 27:7.

TOMBS: *In houses,* 1 Sam. 25:1; 1 Kin. 2:34; 2 Chr. 33:20. *In gardens,* 2 Kin. 21:18, 16; John 19:41. *In caves,* Gen. 23:9; Gen. 49:29; 50:13; John 11:38. *Under trees, Deborah's,* Gen. 35:8; *King Saul's,* 1 Sam. 31:13.

SEPULCHRES: *Closed with stones,* Matt. 27:60, 66; Mark 15:46; 16:3, 4; Luke 2:2: John 11:38; 20:1. *Sealed,* Matt. 27:64, 66. *Marked with pillars, Rachel's,* Gen. 35:20; *the prophets,* 2 Kin. 23:17. *Painted and garnished,* Matt. 23:27, 29. *Demoniacs dwell in,* Matt. 8:28. *Any who touched, were unclean,* Num. 19:16, 18; Isa. 65:4. *Refused to the dead,* Rev. 11:9. *Robbed,* Jer. 8:1.

See footnote, CREMATION, Josh. 7:25.

**Figurative,** Isa. 22:16.

v.5–1920 BC
See footnote, *Time*, Rev. 10:6.

6
*k Generosity, instances of*, Gen. 20:14.
*l Kindness*, Acts 28:2.

7
*m Salutations*, Luke 1:44.

8
*n Zohar*, Gen. 25:9.

9
*o Cave, burial place*, Judg. 6:2.
*p Land, bought and sold*, Ruth 4:3.
*q Money*, Jer. 32:9.

10
*r Gates*, Deut. 3:5.

11
*s Witness, to transfer of land*, Num. 35:30.

answered [e]Ā′brā-hăm, saying
unto him,
6 Hear us, my lord: thou *art* a
mighty prince among us: [k]in the
choice of our †sepulchres [j]bury
thy dead; [l]none of us shall withhold from thee his sepulchre, but
that thou mayest bury thy dead.
7 And [e]Ā′brā-hăm stood up,
and [m]bowed himself to the people of the land, *even* to the [i]chil-
dren of Hĕth.
8 And he communed[c] with
them, saying, If it be in your
mind that I should [j]bury my
dead out of my sight; hear me,
and intreat for me to ‡Ē′phron
the son of [n]Zō′här,
9 That he may give me the
[o,p]cave of ‖Măch-pē′lah, which
he hath, which *is* in the end of
his field; for as much [q]money as
it is worth he shall give it me for
a possession of a †buryingplace
amongst you.
10 And ‡Ē′phron dwelt among
the [i]children of Hĕth: and
Ē′phron the Hĭt′tīte answered
[e]Ā′brā-hăm in the audience[c] of
the children of Hĕth, *even* of all
that went in at the [r]gate of his
city, saying,
11 Nay, my lord, hear me: [l]the
[p]field give I thee, and the [o]cave
that *is* therein, I give it thee; [s]in
the presence of the sons of my
people give I it thee: bury thy
dead.
12 And Ā′brā-hăm [m]bowed
down himself before the people
of the land.
13 And he spake unto ‡Ē′phron
in the audience[c] of the people of
the land, saying, But if thou *wilt*
*give it*, I pray thee, hear me: I
will give thee [q]money for the
[p]field; take *it* of me, and I will
bury my dead there.
14 And ‡Ē′phron answered
[e]Ā′brā-hăm, saying unto him,

15 My lord, hearken unto me:
the [p]land *is worth* four hundred
[t]shekels[c] of [u]silver; what *is* that
betwixt me and thee? bury
therefore thy dead.
16[Q] And Ā′brā-hăm hearkened
unto ‡Ē′phron; and Ā′brā-hăm
weighed to Ē′phron the [u]silver,
which he had named in the audience[c] of the sons of Hĕth, four
hundred shekels of silver, current [q]*money* with the [v]mer-
chant.
17 And the [w]field of ‡Ē′phron,
which *was* in ‖Măch-pē′lah,
which *was* before [x]Măm′rē, the
field, and the cave which *was*
therein, and all the trees that
*were* in the field, that *were* in all
the borders round about, were
[y]made sure[Q]
18 Unto Ā′brā-hăm for a
[w]possession in the [s]presence of
the [i]children of Hĕth, before all
that went in at the [r]gate of his
city.
19 And after this, Ā′brā-hăm
[j]buried Sā′rah his wife in the
[o]cave of the field of ‖Măch-pē′-
lah before [x]Măm′rē: the same *is*
*Hē′bron in the land of Cā′-
năan.
20 And the field, and the [o]cave
that *is* therein, were [y]made sure[c]
unto Ā′brā-hăm for a [w]posses-
sion of a †buryingplace by the
[i]sons of Hĕth.

## CHAPTER 24

*Abraham sends his servant to get a wife for his son Isaac.* 15 *Rebekah meets him,* 25 *and invites him home.* 29 *Laban entertains him.* 34 *The servant tells his errand,* 50 *and obtains Rebekah.* 62 *Isaac meets her.*

AND [a]Ā′brā-hăm was [b]old,
*and* well stricken[c] in age:
and the LORD had [c]blessed
Ā′brā-hăm in all things.
2 And Ā′brā-hăm said unto his
eldest [d,e]servant of his house,
that ruled over all that he had,

v.15–1920 BC

15
*t Shekel*, Ex. 30:13.
*u Silver*, 1 Chr. 28:14.

16
*v Merchant*, Neh. 3:32.

17
*w Property, real estate*, Lev. 27:15.
*x Mamre*, Gen. 13:18.
*y Contracts, ratified*, Matt. 20:2.

v.1–1898 BC

1
*a Abraham*, Gen 17:5.
*b Old Age*, Isa. 46:4.
*c Temporal Blessings, from God*, Psa. 103:2.

2
*d Servant, good, instances of*, Jer. 2:14.
*e Eliezer*, Gen. 15:2.

‡ **EPHRON**, son of Zohar, the Hittite. *Sells to Abraham the field containing the cave Machpelah*, Gen. 23:8–20; 25:8–10; 49:29, 30; 50:13.

‖ **MACHPELAH.** *The burying place of Sarah and Abraham, Isaac, Rebekah, Leah, and Jacob*, Gen. 23:9, 17–20; 25:9; 49:30, 31; 50:13; Acts. 7:16.

v.2–1898 BC
See footnote, *Time*, Rev. 10:6.

3
*f* *Oath*, Num. 5:19.
*g* *God, sovereign*, Gen. 2:2.
*h* *Marriage*, Gen. 34:9.
*i* *Wife*, Prov. 5:18.
*j* *Canaanites*, Ex. 23:28.

4
*k* *Isaac*, Gen. 21.3.

7
*l* *God, providence of*, Gen. 2:2.
*m* *Canaan, promised to Abraham*, Gen. 37:1.
*n* *Faith, instances of*, Mark 11:22.
*o* *Angels, functions of*, Heb. 1:13.

10
*p* *Camel*, 1 Sam. 30:17.

Put, I pray thee, thy hand under
my thigh:
3 And I will make [d,e]thee
[f]swear by the LORD, the [g]God of
heaven, and the God of the
earth, that thou shalt not [h]take
a [i]wife unto my son of the
daughters of the [j]Cā′năan-ītes,
among whom I dwell:
4 But [d,e]thou shalt go unto
my country, and to my kindred,
and take a [i]wife unto my son
[k]Ī′ṣaac.
5 And the [d,e]servant said unto
him, Peradventure[C] the woman
will not be willing to follow me
unto this land: must I needs
bring thy [k]son again unto the
land from whence thou camest?
6 And [a]Ā′brā-hăm said unto
him, Beware thou that thou
bring not my [k]son thither again.
7 The LORD [l]God of heaven
which took me from my father's
house, and from the land of my
kindred, and which spake unto
me, and that [f]sware unto me,
saying, Unto thy seed will I give
this [m]land; [n]he shall send his
[o]angel before thee, and thou
shalt [h]take a [i]wife unto my son
from thence.[S T Q]
8 And if the woman will not be
willing to follow thee, then thou
shalt be clear[C] from this my
[f]oath: only bring not my son
thither again.
9 And the [d,e]servant put his
hand under the thigh of [a]Ā′brā-
hăm his master,[G] and [f]sware to
him concerning that matter.
10 ¶ And the [d,e]servant took
ten [p]camels of the camels of his
master, and departed; for all the
goods[G] of his master *were* in his
hand: and he arose, and went to
*Mĕs-o-pŏ-tā′mĭ-ȧ, unto the city
of [q]Nā′hôr.
11 And he made his [p]camels to
kneel down without[C] the city by a
well of water at the time of the
evening, *even* the time that
[r]women go out to draw *water*.
12 And [d]he [s]said, O LORD God
of my master [a]Ā′brā-hăm, I pray
thee, [t]send me good speed[C] this
day, and [u]shew kindness unto
my master Ā′brā-hăm.
13 [s]Behold, I stand *here* by the
well of water; and the [r]daugh-
ters of the men of the city come
out to draw water.
14 And [s,v]let it come to pass,
that the damsel to whom I shall
say, Let down thy pitcher, I pray
thee, that I may drink; and she
shall say, Drink, and I will give
thy camels drink also: *let the
same be* she *that* thou hast appointed for thy servant [k]Ī′ṣaac;
and thereby shall I know that
thou hast shewed kindness unto
my master.
15 ¶ And it came to pass, before [d]he had done[C] speaking, that,
behold, †Rė-bĕk′ah came out,
who was born to ‡Bĕth-ụ̈′el, son
of [w]Mĭl′cah, the wife of [x]Nā′hôr,
Ā′brā-hăm's brother, with her
pitcher upon her shoulder.
16 And the †damsel *was* very
[y]fair to look upon, a virgin, neither had any man known her:
and she went down to the well,
and filled her pitcher, and came
up.
17 And the [d]servant ran to meet
†her, and said, Let me, I pray
thee, drink a little water of thy
pitcher.
18 And †she said, Drink, my
lord: and she hasted, and let

v.10–1898 BC
See footnote, *Time*, Rev. 10:6.
*q* *Nahor*, Gen. 11:22.

11
*r* *Women*, Prov. 31:10.

12
*s* *Prayer, exemplified*, Acts 6:4.
*t* *Temporal Blessings, prayer for*, Psa. 103:2.
*u* *Intercession, instances of*, Jer. 27:18.

14
*v* *Prayer, token asked in*, Acts 6:4.

15
*w* *Milcah*, Gen. 11:29.
*x* *Nahor*, Gen. 22:20.

16
*y* *Beauty, instances of*, Prov. 6:25.

* **MESOPOTAMIA** (*in the midst of rivers*). The country between the Tigris and the Euphrates. *Called* PADAN-ARAM, Gen. 25:20; 28:2, 5–7; 31:1–8. *Abraham a native of*, Acts 7:2. *Nahor dwelt in*, Gen. 24:10. *People who dwelt in, called Syrians*, Gen. 25:20. *Jacob goes to*, Gen. 29:1. *Balaam from*, Deut. 23:4. *The children of Israel subjected to, eight years under the judgments of God*, Judg. 3:8; *delivered from, by Othniel*, Judg. 3:9, 10. *Chariots hired from, by the Ammonites*, 1 Chr. 19:6, 7. *People of, present at Pentecost*, Acts 2:9.

† **REBEKAH.** *Daughter of Bethuel, grandniece of Abraham*, Gen. 22:20–23. *Becomes Isaac's wife*, Gen. 24:15–67; 25:20. *Mother of Esau and Jacob*, Gen. 25:21–28. *Passes as Isaac's sister*, Gen. 26:6–11. *Displeased with Esau's wives*, Gen. 26:34, 35. *Prompts Jacob to deceive Isaac*, Gen. 27:5–29. *Sends Jacob to Laban*, Gen. 27:42–46. *Burial place of*, Gen. 49:31. *Called* REBECCA, Rom. 9:10.

‡ **BETHUEL** (*man of God*). *Son of Nahor, father of Rebekah*, Gen. 22:22, 23; 24:15, 24; 25:20; 28:2, 5.

v.18–1898 BC
See footnote, *Time*, Rev. 10:6.

19
z *Animals, kindness to*, Jer. 27:5.

21
a *Eliezer*, Gen. 15:2

22
b *Shekel*, Ex. 30:13.
c *Gold*, Ezek. 7:19.
1 *Or*, ring

24
d *Milcah*, Gen. 11:29.
e *Nahor*, Gen. 22:20.

25
f *Hospitality*, Rom. 12:13.

26
g *Prayer, postures in*, Acts 6:4.
h *Worship*, Gen. 22:5.

27
i *Thankfulness, to God, instances of*, Acts 24:3.
j *God, faithfulness of*, Gen. 2:2.
k *Abraham*, Gen. 17:5.
l *God, mercy of*, Gen. 2:2.
m *God, truth*, Gen. 2:2.
n *God, guide*, Gen. 2:2.

29
o *Laban*, Gen. 28:5.

down her pitcher upon her hand,
and gave him drink.
19 And when †she had done[c]
giving him drink, she said, I will
draw *water* for thy [z]camels also,
until they have done drinking.
20 And †she hasted, and emptied her pitcher into the trough,
and ran again unto the well to
draw *water*, and drew for all his
[z]camels.
21 And the [a]man wondering at
her held his peace, to wit[c] whether the LORD had made his journey prosperous or not.
22 And it came to pass, as the
camels had done[c] drinking, that
the [a]man took a golden [1]earring
of half a [b]shekel weight, and two
‖bracelets for her hands[c] of ten
*shekels* weight of [c]gold;
23 And said, Whose daughter
*art* thou? tell me, I pray thee: is
there room *in* thy father's house
for us to lodge[c] in?
24 And she said unto him, †I
*am* the daughter of ‡Běth-ū'el
the son of [d]Mĭl'cah, which she
bare unto [e]Nā'hôr.
25 †She said moreover unto
him, [f]We have both straw and
provender[c] enough, and room to
lodge in.
26 And the [a]man [g]bowed down
his head, and [h]worshipped the
LORD.
27 And he [i]said, Blessed *be* the
[j]LORD God of my master
[k]Ā'brā-hăm, who hath not left
destitute my master of [l]his mercy
and [m]his truth: I *being* in the
way, the [n]LORD led me to the
house of my master's brethren.
28 And the †damsel[c] ran, and
told *them of* her mother's house
these things.
29 ¶ And †Rĕ-bĕk'ah had a
brother, and his name *was* [o]Lā'-
ban: and Lā'ban ran out unto
the man, unto the well.
30 And it came to pass, when
[o]he saw the earring and ‖brace-
lets upon his sister's hands[c], and
when he heard the words of †Rĕ-
bĕk'ah his sister, saying, Thus
spake the [a]man unto me; that he
came unto the man; and, behold, he stood by the [p]camels at
the well.
31 And he said, [f]Come in, [q]thou
blessed of the LORD; wherefore
standest thou without[c]? for I
have prepared the house, and
room for the [p]camels.
32 And the man came into the
house: and he ungirded his
[p]camels, and gave §straw and
provender[c] for the camels, and
water to [r]wash his feet, and the
men's feet that *were* with him.
33 And there was set *meat*[c] before him to eat: but he said, [s]I
will not eat, until I have told
mine errand. And [o]he said,
Speak on.
34 And he said, I *am* [k]Ā'brā-
hăm's [t]servant.
35 And the LORD hath [u]blessed
my [k]master greatly; and he is become great: and he hath given
him flocks, and herds, and [v]sil-
ver, and [w]gold, and menservants,
and maidservants, and [p]camels,
and [x]asses.
36 And [y]Sā'rah my master's
[z]wife bare a [a]son to my master
when she was old: and unto him
hath he given [b]all that he
hath.
37 And my [c]master made me
[d]swear, saying, [e]Thou shalt not
take a [f]wife to my [a]son of the
daughters of the [g]Cā'năan-ītes,
in whose land I dwell:
38 But thou shalt go unto my
father's house, and to my kindred[c], and take a [f]wife unto my
[a]son.

v.29–1898 BC
See footnote, *Time*, Rev. 10:6.

30
p *Camel*, 1 Sam. 30:17.

31
q *Salutations*, Luke 1:44.

32
r *Ablution*, Judg. 19:21.

33
s *Faithfulness, instances of*, Luke 16:10.

34
t *Servant*, Jer. 2:14.

35
u *Temporal Blessings, from God*. Psa. 103:2.
v *Silver*, 1 Chr. 28:14.
w *Gold*, Ezek. 7:19.
x *Ass*, 2 Chr. 28:15.

36
y *Sarah*, Gen. 17:15.
z *Wife*, Prov. 5:18.

a *Isaac*, Gen. 21:3.
b *Inheritance*, Num. 27:7.

37
c *Abraham*, Gen. 17:5.
d *Oath*, Num. 5:19.
e *Miscegenation, forbidden*, Josh. 23:12.
f *Wife*, Prov. 5:18.
g *Canaanites*, Ex. 23:28.

‖ **BRACELET.** *Present of*, Gen. 24:22. *Worn by women*, Gen. 24:30; Isa. 3:19. *Dedicated to the tabernacle*, Num. 31:50. *Taken as spoils*, Num. 31:50; 2 Sam. 1:10. **Figurative**, Ezek. 16:11.

§ **STRAW.** *Used for provender*, Gen. 24:32; Isa. 65:25; *for brick*, Ex. 5:7.

v.39–1898 BC

39
h *Eliezer*, Gen. 15:2.

40
i *Faith, instances of*, Mark, 11:22.
j *God, providence of*, Gen. 2:2.
k *Walking, with God*, Gen. 5:22.
l *Angel*, Heb. 1:13.
m *Temporal Blessings, from God*, Psa. 103:2.

41
n *Oath*, Num. 5:19.

42
o *Temporal Blessings, prayer for*, Psa. 103:2.

45
p *Prayer, answered*, Acts 6:4.

46
q *Animals, kindness to*, Jer. 27:5.

47
r *Nahor*, Gen. 22:20.
s *Milcah*, Gen. 11:29.

39 And [h]I said unto my [c]master, Peradventure[G] the woman will not follow me.

40 And [c]he [i]said unto me, The [j]LORD, before whom I [k]walk, will send his [l]angel with thee, and [m]prosper thy way; and thou shalt take a [f]wife for my [a]son of my kindred, and of my father's house:[S T]

41 Then shalt thou be clear[G] from *this* my [n]oath[G], when thou comest to my kindred: and if they give not thee *one*, thou shalt be clear from my oath.

42 And I came this day unto the well, and [o]said, O LORD God of my master [c]Ā'brā-hăm, if now thou do [m]prosper my way which I go:

43 Behold, I stand by the well of water; and it shall come to pass, that when the virgin cometh forth to draw *water*, and I say to her, Give me, I pray thee, a little water of thy pitcher to drink;

44 And she say to me, Both drink thou, and I will also draw for thy camels: *let* the same *be* the woman whom the LORD hath appointed out for my master's [a]son.

45 And before I had done[G] [p]speaking in mine heart, behold, [†]Rē-bĕk'ah came forth with her pitcher on her shoulder; and she went down unto the well, and drew *water*: and I said unto her, Let me drink, I pray thee.

46 And [†]she made haste, and let down her pitcher from her *shoulder*, and said, Drink, and I will give thy [q]camels drink also: so I drank, and she made the camels drink also.

47 And I asked her, and said, Whose daughter *art* thou? And she said, The daughter of [‡]Bĕth-u'el, [r]Nā'hôr's son, whom [s]Mĭl'cah bare unto him: and I put the [1,t]earring upon her [2]face, and the [‖]bracelets upon her hands.[G]

48 And I bowed down my head, and [u]worshipped the LORD, and blessed the LORD God of my master [c]Ā'brā-hăm, which had [v]led me in the right way to take my master's brother's daughter unto his son.

49 And now if ye will deal kindly and truly with my master, tell me: and if not, tell me; that I may turn[G] to the right hand, or to the left.

50 Then [w]Lā'ban and [‡]Bĕth-u'el answered and [i]said, The thing proceedeth from the LORD: [x]we cannot speak unto thee bad or good.

51 Behold, [†]Rē-bĕk'ah *is* before thee, take *her*, and go, and let her be thy master's son's wife, as the LORD hath spoken.

52 And it came to pass, that, when Ā'brā-hăm's [h,y]servant heard their words, he worshipped the LORD, [z]*bowing himself* to the earth.

53 And the [a,b]servant brought forth [+]jewels of [c]silver, and jewels of [d]gold, and raiment, and gave [e]*them* to [†,f]Rē-bĕk'ah: he gave also to her brother and to her mother precious things.

54 And they did eat and drink, [b]he and the men that *were* with him, and tarried all night; and they rose up in the morning, and he said, [g]Send me away unto my [h]master.

55 And her [i]brother and her mother said, Let the [†]damsel abide with us *a few* days, at the least ten; after that she shall go.

56 And [b]he said unto them, Hinder me not, seeing the [j]LORD hath [k]prospered my way; send me away that I may go to my [h]master.

v.47–1898 BC

t *Presents*, Gen. 32:13.
2 R. V. nose.

48
u *Worship*, Gen. 22:5.
v *God, guide*, Gen. 2:2.

50
w *Laban*, Gen. 28:5.
x *Obedience, instances of*, Heb. 5:8.

52
y *Servant*, Jer. 2:14.
z *Prayer, postures in*, Acts 6:4.

53
a *Servant*, Jer. 2:14.
b *Eliezer*, Gen. 15:2.
c *Silver*, 1 Chr. 28:14.
d *Gold*, Ezek. 7:19.
e *Presents*, Gen. 32:13.
f *Bride*, Isa. 49:18.

54
g *Faithfulness, instances of*, Luke 16:10.
h *Abraham*, Gen. 17:5.

55
i *Laban*, Gen. 28:5.

56
j *God, providence of*, Gen. 2:2.
k *Temporal Blessings, from God*, Psa. 103:2.

**+ JEWEL.** *Betrothal presents of*, Gen. 24:53. *Borrowed from Egyptians by Israelites*, Ex. 3:22; 11:2; 12:35. *Dedicated to the tabernacle*, Ex. 35:22; Num. 31:50-52. *Discarded by penitents*, Gen. 35:4; Ex. 33:4-6; Isa. 3:18-21. *Tokens of love*, Ezek. 16:11-13. *Worn by men*, Ezek. 23:42. **Figurative**, Prov. 20:15; **Mal. 3:17.**

v.57–1898 BC
See footnote, *Time*, Rev. 10:6.

57 And they said, We will call the †damsel, and enquire[c] at her mouth.

58 And they called †Rĕ-bĕk'ah, and said unto her, Wilt thou go with this [b]man? And she said, I will go.

59 And they sent away [†,l]Rĕ-bĕk'ah their sister, and her [l,m]nurse, and [h]Ā'bră-hăm's [a,b]servant, and his men.

60 And they [n]blessed †Rĕ-bĕk'ah, and said unto her, Thou *art* our sister, [o]be thou *the mother* of thousands of [3]millions, and let thy seed[c] possess[c] the gate of those which hate them.

61 ¶ And †Rĕ-bĕk'ah arose, and her damsels, and they rode upon the [p]camels, and followed the [b]man: and the [a]servant took Rĕ-bĕk'ah, and went his way.

62 And [q]Ī'ṣaac came from the way of the well [r]Lă-hāi'-roi; for he dwelt in the south country.

63 And [q]Ī'ṣaac went out to [s]meditate in the field at the eventide[c]: and he lifted up his eyes, and saw, and, behold, the [p]camels *were* coming.

64 And †Rĕ-bĕk'ah lifted up her eyes, and when she saw [q]Ī'ṣaac, she lighted[c] off the [p]camel.

65 For she *had* said unto the [a]servant, What man *is* this that walketh in the field to meet us? And the servant *had* said, It *is* my [q]master: therefore [t]she took a ⊙vail, and covered herself.

66 And the [a,b]servant told [q]Ī'ṣaac all things that he had done.

67 And [q]Ī'ṣaac brought her into his mother [u]Sā'rah's [v]tent, and took †Rĕ-bĕk'ah, and she became his [w]wife; and [x]he loved her: and Ī'ṣaac was comforted after his mother's *death*.

**59**
l Gen. 35:8.
m *Nurse*, 2 Chr. 22:11.

**60**
n *Benedictions, instances of*, Deut. 21:5.
o *Temporal Blessings, prayer for*, Psa. 103:2.
3 R. V. ten thousands.

**61**
p *Camels*, 1 Sam. 30:17.

**62**
q *Isaac*, Gen. 21:3.
r Or, *Beer-lahai-roi*, Gen. 16:14.

**63**
s *Meditation, instances of*, Psa. 49:3.

**65**
t *Women, veiled*, Prov. 31:10.

**67**
u *Sarah*, Gen. 17:15.
v *Tent*, Gen. 13:5.
w *Wife*, Prov. 5:18.
x *Husband, faithful*, Num. 30:6.

## CHAPTER 25

*The sons of Abraham by Keturah. 5 Abraham divides his goods. 7 His age, and death. 9 His burial. 12 The generations of Ishmael. 17 Ishmael's age, and death. 21 Isaac prays for Rebekah. 24 The birth of Esau and Jacob. 27 Their difference of character. 29 Esau sells his birthright.*

B.C. 1853?
See footnote, *Time*, Rev. 10:6.

THEN again [a]Ā'bră-hăm took a wife, and her name *was* [b]Kĕ-tū'rah.

2 [c]And she bare him [b]Zĭm'ran, and [b]Jŏk'shan, and [b]Mē'dan, and [d]Mĭd'ĭ-an, and [b]Ĭsh'băk and [b]Shụ'ah.

3 And [b]Jŏk'shan begat [b]Shē'bȧ, and [b]Dē'dan. And the sons of Dē'dan were Ăs-shụ'rim, and Lĕ-tụ'shim, and Lĕ-ŭm'mim.

4 And the sons of [d]Mĭd'ĭ-an; *Ē'phah, and [e]Ē'phĕr, and [f]Hā'nŏch, and [e]Ā-bī'dah, and [e]Ĕl'da-ah. All these *were* the children of [b]Kĕ-tū'rah.

5 And [a]Ā'bră-hăm [g]gave [h]all that he had unto [i,j]Ī'ṣaac.

6 But unto the sons of the [k]concubines, which [a]Ā'bră-hăm had, Ā'bră-hăm [g]gave gifts, and sent them away from [j]Ī'ṣaac his son, while he yet lived, eastward, unto the east country.

7 And these *are* the days of the years of [a]Ā'bră-hăm's life which he lived, [l]an hundred threescore[c] and fifteen [m]years.

8 Then Ā'bră-hăm gave up the ghost[c], and [n]died in a good old age, an old man, and full *of years;* and was gathered[c] to his people.

9 And his sons [j]Ī'ṣaac and [o]Ĭsh'ma-el buried him in the [p,q]cave of [r]Măch-pē'lah, in the field of [s]Ē'phron the son of [t]Zō'hăr the Hĭt'tīte, which *is* before Măm'rē;

10 The [u]field which [a]Ā'bră-hăm purchased of the [v]sons of Hĕth: there was Ā'bră-hăm buried, and [w]Sā'rah his wife.

11 And it came to pass after the

**1**
a *Abraham*, Gen 17:5.
b 1 Chr. 1:32.

**2**
c *Genealogy*, vs. 1–4, 12–16; 1 Chr. 5:1.
d 1 Chr. 1:32, 33.

**4**
e 1 Chr. 1:33.
f Or, *Henoch*, 1 Chr. 1:33.

**5**
g *Will*, Heb. 9:16.
h *Inheritance*, Num. 27:7.
i *Heir*, Gen. 15:3.
j *Isaac*, Gen. 21:3.

**6**
k *Concubinage*, 2 Sam. 21:11.

v.8–1863 BC

**7**
l *Longevity*, Psa. 91:16.
m *Year, age computed by*, Lev. 25:29.

**8**
n *Death*, Num. 23:10.

**9**
o *Ishmael*, Gen. 16:11.
p *Cave*, Judg. 6:2.
q *Burying Places*, Gen. 23:4.
r *Machpelah*, Gen. 23:9.
s *Ephron*, Gen. 23:8.
t Gen. 23:8.

**10**
u *Land, bought and sold*, Ruth 4:3.
v *Hittites*, Judg. 1:26.
w *Sarah*, Gen. 17:15.

⊙ **VEIL.** *Worn by Rebekah*, Gen. 24:65; *by Tamar*, Gen. 38:14, 19; *by Moses, to screen his face when he descended from Mount Sinai*, Ex. 34:33, 35; 2 Cor. 3:13–16.

See footnote, DRESS, Zech. 3:4.

* **EPHAH.** *A son of Midian*, Gen. 25:4; 1 Chr. 1:33; Isa. 60:6.

v.11–1863 BC
See footnote, *Time*, Rev. 10:6.

11
*x Beer-lahai-roi*, Gen. 16:14.

12
*y Hagar*, Gen.16:1.

13
*z* 1 Chr. 1:29.

14
*a* 1 Chr. 1:30.

15
*b* Or, *Hadad*, 1 Chr. 1:30.
*c* 1 Chr. 1:31.

16
*d Ishmael*, Gen. 16:11.
1 R. V. encampments;

v.17–1815 BC

17
*e Longevity*, Psa. 91:16.
*f Death, called giving up the ghost*, Num. 23:10.

18
*g Ishmaelite*, Gen. 39:1.
*h* 1 Sam. 15:7.
*i Shur*, 1 Sam. 15:7.
*j Egypt*, Gen.41:8.
2 R. V. abode.

19
*k Genealogy*, 1 Chr. 5:1.
*l Isaac*, Gen. 21:3.
*m Abraham*, Gen. 17:5.

death of Ā′bră-hăm, that God
blessed his son [l]Ī′ṣaac; and
Ī′ṣaac dwelt by the well [x]Lȧ-
hāi′-roi.
12 ¶ Now these *are* the generations of [o]Ĭsh′ma-el, Ā′bră-hăm's
son, whom [y]Hā′gar the Ē-ġy̆p′-
tian, [w]Sā′rah's handmaid, bare
unto Ā′bră-hăm:
13 And these *are* the names of
the sons of [o]Ĭsh′ma-el, by their
names, according to their generations: the firstborn of Ĭsh′-
ma-el, †Nĕ-bā′joth; and [z]Kē′-
där, and [z]Ăd′bĕ-el, and [z]Mĭb′-
sam,
14 And [a]Mĭsh′mȧ, and ‡Du′-
mah, and [a]Măs′sȧ,
15 [b]Hā′där, and [a]Tē′mȧ, [c]Jē′-
tŭr, [c]Nā′phish, and [c]Kĕd′e-mah:
16 These *are* the sons of [d]Ĭsh′-
ma-el, and these *are* their names,
by their towns, and by their
[1]castles[G]; twelve princes according to their nations.
17 And these *are* the years of
the life of [d]Ĭsh′ma-el, [e]an hundred and thirty and seven years:
and he [f]gave up the ghost[G] and
died; and was gathered unto
his people.
18 And [g]they dwelt from [h]Hăv′-
i-lah unto [i]Shûr, that *is* before
[j]Ē′ġy̆pt, as thou goest toward
‖Ăs-sy̆r′ĭ-ȧ: *and* he [2]died in the
presence of all his brethren.
19 ¶ And [k]these *are* the generations of [l]Ī′ṣaac, [m]Ā′bră-hăm's
son: Ā′bră-hăm begat Ī′ṣaac:
20 And [l]Ī′ṣaac was forty years
old when he took [n]Rĕ-bĕk′ah to
wife, the daughter of [o]Bĕth-u′el
the [p]Sy̆r′ĭ-an of [q]Pā′dan-ā′ram,
the sister to [r]Lā′ban the [3]Sy̆r′ĭ-an.
21 And [l]Ī′ṣaac [s]intreated the
LORD for his wife, because she
*was* [t]barren: and the LORD [u]was
intreated[G] of him, and Rĕ-bĕk′ah
his wife [v,w,x]conceived.[S Q]
22 And the children struggled
together within her; and she
said, If *it be* so, why *am* I thus?
And she went to inquire[G] of the
LORD.[Q]
23 [u]And the LORD said unto
her, [y,z]Two nations *are* in thy
womb, and two manner of people shall be separated from thy
bowels[G]; and *the one* people shall
be stronger than *the other* people;
and [a]the elder shall serve the
younger.[T Q]
24 And when her days to be delivered were fulfilled, behold,
*there were* [b]twins in her womb.
25 And the first came out [4]red,
all over like an hairy garment;
and they called his name §Ē′sau.
26 And after that came his
brother out, and his hand took
hold on §Ē′sau's heel; and his
name was called [c]Jā′cob: and
Ī′ṣaac *was* threescore years old
when she bare them.[Q]
27 And the boys grew[G]: and
§Ē′sau was a cunning [d]hunter, a
man of the field; and [c]Jā′cob *was*
a plain man, dwelling in [e]tents.
28 [f,g]And [h]Ī′ṣaac loved §Ē′sau,
because he did eat of *his* veni-

v.20–1898 BC

20
*n Rebekah*, Gen.24:15.
*o Bethuel*, Gen. 24:15.
*p Syria*, 2 Kin. 6:23.
*q Padan-aram*, Gen. 28:2.
*r Laban*, Gen.28:5.
3 *Heb.* Aramean

21
*s Temporal Blessings, prayer for*, Psa. 103:2.
*t Barrenness*, Deut. 7:14.
*u Prayer, answered, instances of*, Acts 6:4.
*v Children, in answer to prayer*, Mark 10:14.
*w Conception, miraculous*, Gen. 21:2.
*x Miracles*, Luke 23:8.

23
*y Edomites, prophecies concerning*, 2 Kin. 8:21.
*z Israel, prophecies concerning*, Ex. 4:22.
*a* Rom. 9:12.

24
*b Twins*, Gen. 38:27–30.

25
4 *Or*, ruddy.
v.24–1878 BC

26
*c Jacob*, Gen. 27:11.

27
*d Hunting*, Gen. 27:5.
*e Tent*, Gen. 13:5.

28
*f Parents, partiality of*, 2 Cor. 12.14.
*g Partiality*, 1 Tim: 5:21.
*h Isaac*, Gen. 21:3.

† **NEBAJOTH.** *Son of Ishmael*, Gen. 25:13; 28:9; 36:3; 1 Chr. 1:29. *Prophecies concerning*, Isa. 60:7.

‡ **DUMAH** (*silence*). *Son of Ishmael*, Gen. 25:14; 1 Chr 1:30; Isa. 21:11, 12.

‖ **ASSYRIA** (*a plain*). *An empire founded by Nimrod*, Gen. 10:8–12; Mic. 5:6. *It extended from east of the Tigris*, Gen. 2:14; 10:11; *possibly to Egypt*, Gen. 25:18. *Its armies invade the land of Israel under Pul*, 2 Kin. 15:19, 20; 1 Chr. 5:26; *under Tiglath*, 2 Kin. 15:29; 1 Chr. 5:6, 26; *under Shalmaneser*, 2 Kin. 17:3–6, 24–27; 18:9–12; Jer. 50:17; *under Sennacherib*, 2 Kin. 18:13–37; 19; 2 Chr. 32; Isa. 36; 37.

*Army of, destroyed by the angel of the Lord*, 2 Kin. 19:35; Isa. 37:36. *Alliances with, sought by Judah and Israel*, Hos. 5:13. *Israelites subject to*, Lam. 5:6. *Israelites carried captive into*, 2 Kin. 17:3–23. *Jews carried captive into*, 2 Kin. 24; 25; 2 Chr. 36:5–21. *Invaded by Pharaoh-nechoh*, 2 Kin. 23:29.

*Commerce of*, Ezek. 27:23. *Productiveness of*, Isa. 36:17. *Prophecies concerning*, Isa. 7:17–25; 8:4–8; 10:5–34; 14:24–28; 19:23–25; 20; 30:27–33; 31:8, 9; 37:21–35; Jer. 1:15; Ezek. 31; Jonah 3:1–4; Nah. 1; 2; 3; Zeph. 2:13–15; Zech. 10:11.

*Prophecies of captivity of Israelites in*, Hos. 9:3; 11:5, 11.

§ **ESAU** (*hairy*). Elder of twin sons born to Isaac and Rebekah. *Birth of*, Gen. 25:19–26; 1 Chr. 1:34; Rom. 9:11–13. *Hairy*, Gen. 25:25; 27:11, 23. *Called* EDOM, Gen. 36:1, 8. *A hunter*, Gen. 25:27; 27:3. *Beloved by Isaac*, Gen. 25:28. *Isaac's blessing of*, Gen. 27:39, 40; Heb. 11:20; 12:17. *Sells his birthright for a mess of pottage*, Gen. 25:29–34; Heb. 12:16. *Hated of God*, Mal. 1:3; Rom. 9:13. *Marries a Hittite*, Gen. 26:34. *His marriage a grief to Isaac and Rebekah*, Gen. 26:34, 35; 27:46; 28:8. *Polygamy of*, Gen. 26:34; 28:9; 36:2, 3. *Is defrauded of his father's blessing by Jacob*, Gen. 27. *Meets Jacob on the return of the latter from Haran*, Gen. 33:1–17. *With Jacob, buries his father*, Gen. 35:29. *Descendants of*, Gen. 36; 1 Chr. 1:35–57. *Enmity of descendants of, toward descendants of Jacob*, Obad. 10–14. *Ancestor of Edomites*, Jer. 49:8. *Mount of Edom, called* MOUNT OF ESAU, Obad. 8, 9, 18, 19, 21. *His name used to denote his descendants and their country*, Deut.

son[G]: but [i]Rē-bĕk'ah loved [c]Jā'-
cob.
29 And [c]Jā'cob sod[G] pottage[G]:
and [§]Ē'sa̤u came from the field,
and he *was* [j,k]faint:
30 And [§]Ē'sa̤u said to [c]Jā'cob,
Feed me, I pray thee, with that
same red *pottage*[G]; for I *am*
[j,k]faint: therefore was his name
called Ē'dom.
31 And [c]Jā'cob said,[l,m] Sell me
this day [n]thy [o]birthright.
32 And [§,n]Ē'sa̤u said, [j,k]Be-
hold, I *am* at the point to die:
and what profit shall this [o]birth-
right do to me?
33 And [c]Jā'cob said, [p]Swear to
me this day; and he sware unto
him: and [q]he sold his [o]birthright
unto Jā'cob.[Q]
34 Then [c]Jā'cob gave [§]Ē'sa̤u
bread and pottage of [+]lentiles;
and he did eat and drink, and
rose up, and went his way: thus
Ē'sa̤u despised *his* [o]birthright.

## CHAPTER 26

*Isaac because of famine goes to Gerar. 2 God instructs and blesses him. 7 He is reproved by Abimelech for denying his wife. 12 He grows rich. 18 He digs the wells Esek, Sitnah, and Rehoboth. 26 Abimelech makes a covenant with him at Beer-sheba. 34 Esau's wives.*

AND there was a [a]famine in
the land, beside the first
famine that was in the days
of [b]Ā'brā-hăm. And [c]Ī'sa̤ac
went unto Ă-bĭm'e-lĕch king of
the *Phĭ-lĭs'tĭne̤s unto [d]Gē'rär.
2[T] And the [e]LORD appeared unto him, and said, Go not down
into [f]Ē'ġypt; dwell in the [g]land
which I shall tell thee of:
3 [h]Sojourn in this [g]land, and [e]I
will be with thee, and will bless
thee; for unto thee, and unto thy
[i,j]seed, I will give all these countries, and I will [1]perform the
[k,l]oath which I sware unto
Ā'brā-hăm thy father;[Q]
4 And [e]I will make [m]thy [i,j]seed[G]
to multiply as the [n]stars of heav-
en, and will [o]give unto thy seed
all these [g]countries; and in thy
[p]seed shall all the [q]nations of the
earth be blessed;[S T Q]
5 Because that [b]Ā'brā-hăm
[h]obeyed my voice, and kept my
charge, my commandments, my
statutes, and my laws.
6 ¶ And [c]Ī'sa̤ac dwelt in
[d]Gē'rär:
7 And the men of the place
asked [c]*him* of his [r]wife; and [s]he
[t,u,v]said, She *is* my sister: for he
[w]feared to say, *She is* my wife;
lest, *said he,* the men of the place
should kill me for [x]Rē-bĕk'ah;
because she *was* [y]fair[G] to look
upon.
8 And it came to pass, when he
had been there a long time, that
Ă-bĭm'e-lĕch king of the *Phĭ-
lĭs'tĭne̤s looked out at a [z]window,
and saw, and, behold, Ī'sa̤ac
*was* sporting[G] with [x]Rē-bĕk'ah
his wife.
9 And Ă-bĭm'e-lĕch called
[a]Ī'sa̤ac, and said, Behold, of a
surety[G] [b]she *is* thy [c]wife: and
how [d,e]saidst thou, She *is* my
sister? And Ī'sa̤ac said unto
him, [f]Because I said, Lest I die
for her.
10 And [g,h]Ă-bĭm'e-lĕch said,
What *is* this thou hast done unto
us? one of the people might
lightly[G] have lien[G] with thy [c]wife,
and thou shouldest have brought
guiltiness upon us.
11 And Ă-bĭm'e-lĕch [h]charged
all *his* people, saying, He that
toucheth this [a]man or his [c]wife
shall surely be [i]put to death.
12 Then [a]Ī'sa̤ac [j]sowed in that
land, and received[G] in the same
year an hundredfold: and the
LORD [k]blessed him.
13 And the [a]man waxed[G] great,
and went[G] forward, and grew until he became very great:
14 For he had [l]possession of

---

i *Rebekah,* Gen. 24: 15.

**29**

j *Appetite,* Prov. 23:2.

k *Hunger,* Neh. 9: 15.

**31**

l *Covetousness, instances of,* Isa. 57:17.

m *Craftiness, instances of,* Psa. 83:3.

n *Firstborn, birthright of,* Zech. 12: 10.

o *Birthright,* 2 Chr. 21:3.

**33**

p *Oath, a solemn qualification,* Num. 5:19.

q Heb. 12:16.

**1**

a *Famine, instances of,* 2 Kin. 8:1.

b *Abraham,* Gen. 17:5.

c *Isaac,* Gen. 21:3.

d *Gerar,* Gen. 20:1.

**2**

e *God, providence of,* Gen. 2:2.

f *Egypt,* Gen. 41:8.

g *Canaan,* Gen. 37:1.

**3**

h *Obedience, rewards of,* Heb. 5:8.

i *Children, of the righteous, blessed of God,* Mark 10:14.

j *Israel, prophecies concerning,* Ex. 4:22.

k *Covenant, of God with men,* Deut. 29:1.

l *Oath, attributed to God,* Num. 5: 19.

1 R. V. establish

**4**

m *Righteous, promises to,* Psa. 64: 10.

n *Stars,* Judg. 5: 20.

o *Temporal Blessings, from God,* Psa. 103:2.

p *Jesus, prophecies concerning,* Matt. 1:21.

q *Nations to be blessed in Abraham,* Gen. 18: 18.

**7**

r *Wife,* Prov. 5:18.

s *Doubting, exemplified,* Rom. 14: 23.

t *Temptation, yielding to,* Luke 11:4.

u *Falsehood, instances of,* Job 21:34.

v *Deception, instances of,* Josh. 9:4.

w *Cowardice, instances of,* Lev. 26:36.

x *Rebekah,* Gen. 24. 15.

y *Beauty,* Prov. 6: 25.

**8**

z *Window,* Josh. 2: 15.

**9**

a *Isaac,* Gen. 21:3.

b *Rebekah,* Gen. 24: 15.

c *Wife,* Prov. 5:18.

d *Falsehood, instances of,* Job 21:34.

e *Deception, instances of,* Josh. 9:4.

f *Cowardice, instances of,* Lev. 26:36.

**10**

g *Conscience, faithful, instances of,* Acts 23:1.

h *Integrity, instances of,* Job 2:3.

**11**

i *Adultery, penalties for,* Lev. 20: 10.

**12**

j *Agriculture,* Gen. 3:23.

k *Temporal Blessings, from God,* Psa. 103:2.

**14**

l *Rich,* Jas. 5:1.

---

2:5; Jer. 49:8, 10; Obad. 6. *Mt. Seir given to,* Deut. 2:5, 12, 22; Josh. 24:4. *Prophecies concerning,* Obad. 18.

**+ LENTILES,** Gen. 25:34; 2 Sam. 17:28; 23:11; Ezek. 4:9.

m *Envy, instances of,* Prov. 14:30.

15

n *Wells,* Gen. 21: 19.

o *Servant,* Jer. 2: 14.

p *Abraham,* Gen. 17:5.

17

q *Gerar,* Gen. 20:1.

18

r *Property, real estate,* Lev. 27:15.

20

s *Strife, instances of,* Prov. 20:3.

2 *That is,* Contention;

21

3 *That is,* Enmity.

22

t *Meekness, instances of,* Psa. 45:4.

u *Thankfulness, to God, instances of,* Acts 24:3.

4 *That is,* Broad places;

flocks, and possession of herds, and great store of servants: and the *Phĭ-lĭs′tĭneṣ [m]envied him.

15 For all the [n]wells which his father's [o]servants had digged in the days of [p]Ā′bră-hăm his father, the *Phĭ-lĭs′tĭneṣ had stopped them, and filled them with earth.

16 And Ă-bĭm′e-lĕch said unto [a]Ī′ṣaac, Go from us; for thou art much mightier than we.

17 ¶ And [a]Ī′ṣaac departed thence, and pitched his tent in the valley of [q]Gē′rär, and dwelt there.

18 And Ī′ṣaac digged again the [n, r]wells of water, which they had digged in the days of [p]Ā′bră-hăm his father; for the *Phĭ-lĭs′tĭneṣ had stopped them after the death of Ā′bră-hăm: and he called their names after the names by which his father had called them.

19 And [a]Ī′ṣaac's [o]servants digged in the valley, and found there a [n]well of springing water.

20 And the herdmen of [q]Gē′rär did [s]strive with Ī′ṣaac's herdmen, saying, The water *is* ours: and he called the name of the well [2]Ē′sĕk; because they strove with him.

21 And they digged another [n]well, and [s]strove for that also: and he called the name of it [3]Sĭt′nah.

22 And [a, t]he removed from thence, and digged another [n]well; and for that they [s]strove not: and he called the name of it [4]Rē-hō′both; and he [u]said, For now the LORD hath made room for us, and we shall be fruitful in the land.

23 And he went up from thence to [v]Bē′er-shē′bȧ.

24 And the LORD appeared unto him the same night, and said, I *am* the God of Ā′bră-hăm thy father: [w]fear not, for [x]I *am* with [y]thee, and will bless thee, and multiply thy seed for my servant Ā′bră-hăm's sake.

25 And he builded an [z]altar there, and [a]called upon the name of the LORD, and pitched his [b]tent there: and there [c]Ī′ṣaac's [d]servants digged a [e]well.

26 ¶ Then Ă-bĭm′e-lĕch went to [c]him from [f]Gē′rär, and Ă-hŭz′zath one of his friends, and [g]Phī′chol the chief captain of his army

27 And [c]Ī′ṣaac said unto them, Wherefore come ye to me, seeing ye [h]hate me, and have sent me away from you?

28 And they [i]said, We saw certainly that the LORD was with thee: and we said, Let there be now an [j]oath betwixt us, *even* betwixt us and thee, and let us make a [k, l]covenant with thee;

29 [m]That thou wilt do us no hurt, as we have not touched thee, and as we have done unto thee nothing but good, and have sent thee away in peace: thou *art* now the blessed of the LORD.

30 [m]And [c]he [n]made them a [o]feast, and they did eat and drink.

31 And they [p]rose up betimes in the morning, and [j]sware one to another: and Ī′ṣaac sent them away, and they departed from him in [m]peace.

32 And it came to pass the same day, that [c]Ī′ṣaac's [d]servants came, and told him con-

23

v *Beer-sheba,* Judg. 20:1.

24

w *Adversity, consolation in,* Psa. 10:6.

x *God, providence of,* Gen. 2:2.

y *Righteous, promises to,* Psa. 64: 10.

25

z *Altar,* Gen. 8:20.

a *Worship,* Gen. 22:5.

b *Tent,* Gen. 13:5.

c *Isaac,* Gen. 21:3.

d *Servant,* Jer. 2: 14.

e *Well,* Gen. 21:19.

26

f *Gerar,* Gen. 20:1.

g Gen. 21:22, 23.

27

h *Hatred,* Prov. 15: 17.

28

i *Diplomacy, instances of,* 2 Kin. 16:7.

j *Oath,* Num. 5:19.

k *Covenant, of men with men,* Deut. 29:1.

l *Alliances,* Josh. 9:15.

29

m *Social Peace, instances of,* Jer. 29:7.

30

n *Hospitality, instances of,* Rom. 12:13.

o *Feasts,* Mark 12: 39.

31

p *Rising, early, instances of,* Gen. 19:2

* **PHILISTINES** (*strangers, sojourners*). *Descendants of Mizraim,* Gen. 10:14; 1 Chr. 1:12. *Idolatry of,* Judg. 10:6; 1 Sam. 5:1-7. *Territory of,* Ex. 13:17; 23:31; Deut. 2:23; Josh. 13:3; 15:47. *Lords of,* Josh. 13:3; Judg. 3:3; 16:5, 30; 1 Sam. 5:8, 11; 6:4, 12; 7:7; 29:2, 6, 7.
Kings of: *Abimelech I,* Gen. 20; *Abimelech II,* Gen. 26; *Achish,* 1 Sam. 21:10-15; 27:2-12; 28:1, 2; 29.
*Suffered to remain in Canaan,* Judg. 3:1-4. *Shamgar slays six hundred with an ox goad,* Judg. 3:31.
*For their history during Samson's leadership of Israel,* see Judg. 13; 14; 15; 16. *Defeat the Israelites: take the ark; suffer plagues, and return the ark,* 1 Sam. 4; 5; 6. *Army of,* 1 Sam. 13:5. *Defeated by Samuel,* 1 Sam. 7; *by Saul and Jonathan,* 1 Sam. 13; 14. *Their champion, Goliath, slain by David,* 1 Sam. 17. *David slays two hundred,* 1 Sam. 18:22-30. *David finds refuge among,* 1 Sam. 27. *Defeat the Israelites,* 1 Sam. 31; 1 Chr. 10:1. *Defeated by David,* 2 Sam. 5:17-25; 23:9 10; 1 Chr. 14:8-16. *Pay tribute to Jehoshaphat,* 2 Chr. 17:11. *Defeated by Hezekiah,* 2 Kin. 18:8. *Prophecies against,* Isa. 9:11, 12; 14:29-31;

33
q *Beer-sheba*, Judg. 20:1.

v.34–1838 BC

34
r *Esau*, Gen. 25:25.
s *Polygamy*, Deut. 17:17.
t *Miscegenation*, Josh. 23:12.
u *Hittites*, Judg. 1:26.
v Gen. 36:2.

35
w *Rebekah*, Gen. 24:15.
5 *Heb.* bitterness of spirit

1
a *Isaac*, Gen. 21:3.
b *Blindness, instances of*, 2 Kin. 6:18.
c *Esau*, Gen. 25:25.

2
d *Death*, Num. 23:10.

3
e *Archery*, Gen. 21:20.
f Isa. 22:6.

cerning the well which they had
digged, and said unto him, We
have found water.
33 And he called it Shē′bah:
therefore the name of the city *is*
[q]Bē′er-shē′bȧ unto this day.
34 And [r]Ē′sạu was forty years
old when he [s,t]took to wife Jū′-
dĭth the daughter of Bė-ē′rī the
[u]Hĭt′tīte, and Băsh′e-măth the
daughter of [v]Ē′lŏn the Hĭt′tīte:
35 Which were [5]a grief of mind
unto Ī′ṣaac and [w]Rė-bĕk′ah.

## CHAPTER 27

*Isaac sends Esau for venison. 6 Jacob, instructed by Rebekah, 15 obtains the blessing. 34 Esau complains, and by importunity obtains a blessing. 41 He threatens Jacob's life. 43 Rebekah sends Jacob to Laban.*

AND it came to pass, that
when [a]Ī′ṣaac was old,
and his eyes were dim, so
that he could [b]not see, he called
[c]Ē′sạu his eldest son, and said
unto him, My son: and he said
unto him, Behold, *here am* I.
2 And he said, Behold now, I
am old, I know not the day of
my [d]death:
3 Now therefore take, I pray
thee, thy [e]weapons, thy [f]quiver
and thy bow, and go out to the
field, and *take me *some* venison[c];
4 And make me savoury meat,[c]
such as I love, and bring *it* to
me, that I may eat; that [g]my
soul may bless thee before I die.
5 And [h]Rė-bĕk′ah heard when
[a]Ī′ṣaac spake to [c]Ē′sạu his son.
And Ē′sạu went to the field to
*hunt *for* venison, *and* to bring
*it*.
6 ¶ And [h,i]Rė-bĕk′ah spake unto †Jā′cob her son, saying, Behold, I heard thy father speak
unto [c]Ē′sạu thy brother, saying,
7 Bring me venison and make
me savoury meat,[c] that [a]I may
eat, and [g]bless thee before the
LORD before my death.
8 [j,k]Now therefore, [l]my †son,
obey my voice according to that
which I command thee.
9 Go now to the flock, and
fetch me from thence two good
kids of the [m]goats, and [l]I will
make them savoury [n]meat[c] for
thy father, such as he loveth:
10 [j,k]And †thou shalt bring *it*
to thy [a]father, that he may eat,
and [i]that [g]he may bless thee
before his [d]death.
11 And †Jā′cob said to [h]Rė-
bĕk′ah his mother, Behold,
[c]Ē′sạu my brother *is* a hairy
man, and I *am* a smooth man;[c]
12 My [a]father peradventure[c]
will feel me, and I shall seem to
him as a [1]deceiver; and I shall

4
g *Parents, blessings of*, 2 Cor. 12:14.

5
h *Rebekah*, Gen. 24:15.

6
i *Partiality*, vs. 7–17; 1 Tim. 5:21.

8
j *Craftiness, instances of*, vs. 9–29; Psa. 83:3.
k *Temptation, leading others into*, vs. 9–17; Luke 11:4.
l *Woman, wicked*, vs. 9–17; Prov. 31:10.

9
m *Goat*, Deut. 14:4.
n *Food, prepared by women*, Psa. 136:25.

12
1 *Or*, mocker;

Jer. 25:17–20; 47; Ezek. 25:15–17; Amos 1:6–8; Zeph. 2:4–7; Zech. 9:5–7.

***HUNTING.** *By Nimrod*, Gen. 10:9. *By Ishmael*, Gen. 21:20. *By Esau*, Gen. 25:27; 27:3, 5, 30, 33. *Fowling*, 1 Sam. 26:20; Psa. 140:5; 141:9, 10; Prov. 1:17; Eccl. 9:12; Lam. 3:52; Amos. 3:5. *Authorized in the Mosaic law*, Lev. 17:13.

**Figurative,** Jer. 16:16.

† **JACOB.** *The supplanter*, Gen. 27:36 (with Gen. 25:33). *Son of Isaac, and twin brother of Esau*, Gen. 25:24–26; Josh. 24:4; 1 Chr. 1:34; Hos. 12:3; Acts 7:8. *Ancestor of Jesus*, Matt. 1:2; Luke 3:34. *Given in answer to prayer*, Gen. 25:21. *Obtains Esau's birthright for a mess of pottage*, Gen. 25:29–34; Heb. 12:16. *Fraudulently obtains his father's blessing*, Gen. 27:1–29; Heb. 11:20. *Esau seeks to slay*, Gen. 27:41–46.

*Escapes to Padan-aram*, Gen. 28:1–5; Hos. 12:12. *His vision of the ladder*, Gen. 28:10–22; Hos. 12:4. *God confirms the covenant of Abraham to*, Gen. 28:13–22; 35:9–15; Josh. 1:6; 1 Chr. 16:13–18.

*Sojourns in Haran with his uncle, Laban*, Gen. 29; 30; Hos. 12:12. *Serves fourteen years for Leah and Rachel*. Gen. 29:15–30; Hos. 12:12. *Sharp practice of, with the flocks and herds of Laban*, Gen. 30:32–43; Hos. 12:7. *Dissatisfied with Laban's treatment and returns to the land of Canaan*, Gen. 31. *Meets angels of God on the journey and calls the place Mahanaim*, Gen. 32:1, 2. *Dreads to meet Esau; sends him presents*, Gen. 32:3–23. *Wrestles with an angel*, Gen. 32:24–29; Hos. 12:4.

*Name of, changed to Israel*, Gen. 32:28; 35:10, 1 Kin. 18:31; 2 Kin. 17:34. *Reconciliation of, with Esau*, Gen. 33:4.

*Journeys to Succoth*, Gen. 33:17; *to Shechem, where he purchases a parcel of ground from Hamor, and erects an altar*, Gen. 33:18–20; Josh. 24:32; John 4:5. *His daughter, Dinah, humbled*, Gen. 34. *Returns to Bethel, where he builds an altar, and erects and dedicates a pillar*, Gen. 35:1–7. *Deborah, Rebekah's nurse, dies, and is buried at Bethel*, Gen. 35:8.

*Journeys to Ephrath; Benjamin is born to; Rachel dies, and is buried*, Gen. 35:16–19; 48:7. *Erects a monument at Rachel's grave*, Gen. 35:20. *The incest of his son, Reuben, and his concubine, Bilhah*, Gen. 35:22. *List of the names of his twelve sons*, Gen. 35:21–26. *Returns to Kiriath-arba, the city of his father*, Gen. 35:27. *With Esau buries his father*, Gen. 35:29. *Dwells in the land of Canaan*, Gen. 37:1.

*His partiality for his son, Joseph, and the consequent jealousy of his other sons*, Gen. 37:3, 4. *Joseph's prophetic dream concerning*, Gen. 37:9–11. *His grief over the loss of Joseph*, Gen. 37:34, 35. *Sends into Egypt to buy corn*, Gen. 42:1, 2; 43:1–14; Acts 7:12. *His grief over the detention of Simeon, and the demand for Benjamin to be taken into Egypt*, Gen. 42:36. *His love for Benjamin*, Gen. 43:14; 44:29. *Hears that Joseph still lives*, Gen. 45:26–28.

*Removes to Egypt*, Gen. 46:1–7; 47:28; Deut. 26:5; 1 Sam. 12:8; Psa. 105:23; Acts 7:14, 15. *List of his children and grandchildren who went down into Egypt*, Gen. 46:8–27. *Meets Joseph*, Gen. 46:28–34. *Pharaoh receives him, and is blessed by Jacob*, Gen. 47:1–10. *The land of Goshen as-*

12
*o* *Curse, parental,* Judg. 5:23.

13
*p* *Penalty, vicariously assumed,* 1 Sam. 25:24.

17
*q* **Bread,** **Ezek. 4:13.**

19
*r* *Falsehood, instances of,* Job 21:34.
*s* *Dishonesty, instances of,* Ezek. 22:13.
*t* *Deception, instances of,* Josh. 9:4.
*u* *Firstborn,* Zech. 12:10.

20
2 R. V. sent me good speed.

bring a [o]curse upon me, and not a [g]blessing.

13 And his [h,l]mother said unto him, [p]Upon me *be* thy [o]curse, my son: only obey my voice, and go fetch me *them*.

14 And [†]he went, and fetched, and brought *them* to his mother: and his [h,l]mother made savoury [n]meat,[C] such as his father loved.

15 And [h,l]Rĕ-bĕk'ah took goodly[C] raiment[C] of her eldest son [c]Ē'sa̤u, which *were* with her in the house, and put them upon [†]Jā'cob her younger son:

16 And [h,l]she put the skins of the kids of the [m]goats upon his hands, and upon the smooth of his neck:

17 And she [k]gave the savoury [n]meat[C] and the [q]bread, which she had prepared into the hand of her son [†]Jā'cob.

18 ¶ And [†]he came unto his [a]father, and said, My father: and he said, Here *am* I; who *art* thou, my son?

19 And [†]Jā'cob [r,s,t]said unto his father, I *am* Ē'sa̤u thy [u]firstborn; I have done according as thou badest me: arise, I pray thee, sit and eat of my venison, that [g]thy soul may bless me.

20 And [a]Ī'ṣaac said unto his [†]son, How *is it* that thou hast found *it* so quickly, my son? And he [r,s,t]said, Because the LORD thy God [2]brought *it* to me.

21 And [a]Ī'ṣaac said unto [†]Jā'cob, Come near, I pray thee, that I may feel thee, my son, whether thou *be* my very[C] son Ē'sa̤u or not.

22 And [†]Jā'cob went near unto Ī'ṣaac his father; and he felt him, and said, The voice *is* Jā'cob's voice, but the hands *are* the hands of Ē'sa̤u.

23 And he discerned[C] him not, because his hands were hairy, as his brother Ē'sa̤u's hands: so [g]he [v]blessed him.

24 And he said, *Art* thou my very son Ē'sa̤u? And [†]he [r,s,t]said, I *am*.

25 And he said, Bring *it* near to me, and I will eat of my son's venison, [g]that my soul may bless thee. And he brought *it* near to him, and he did eat: and he brought him [w]wine, and he drank.

26 And his [x]father Ī'ṣaac said unto him, Come near now, and [y]kiss me, my son.

27 [Q]And he came near, and [y]kissed him: and he smelled the smell of his raiment,[C] and [g]blessed [†]him, and said, See, the smell of my son *is* as the smell of a field which the LORD hath blessed:

28 Therefore [v,z]God give [a]thee of the [b]dew of heaven, and the [c]fatness of the earth, and plenty of corn[C] and wine:

29 [d]Let people serve [a]thee, and nations bow down to thee: be lord over thy brethren, and let thy mother's sons bow down to thee: [e]cursed *be* every one that curseth thee, and blessed *be* he that blesseth thee.[Q]

30 ¶ [Q]And it came to pass, as soon as [f]Ī'ṣaac had made an end of [g]blessing [†]Jā'cob, and Jā'cob was yet scarce[C] gone out from the presence of Ī'ṣaac his father, that [h]Ē'sa̤u his brother came in from his *hunting.

31 And he also had made savoury meat,[C] and brought it unto his father, and said unto his fa-

23
*v* *Benedictions,* Deut. 21:5.

25
*w* **Wine,** **Prov. 23: 31.**

26
*x* *Parents, affection exemplified,* 2 Cor. 12:14.
*y* *Kiss,* Ruth 1:14.

28
*z* *Prayer, intercessory,* Acts 6:4.

*a* *Israel, prophecies concerning,* Ex. 4:22.
*b* *Dew, figurative,* Dan. 4:15.
*c* *Temporal Blessings, from God,* Psa. 103:2.

29
*d* *Prayer, intercessory,* Acts 6:4.
*e* *Prayer, imprecatory,* Acts 6:4.

30
*f* *Isaac,* Gen. 21:3.
*g* *Parents, blessings of,* 2 Cor. 12:14.
*h* *Esau,* Gen. 25: 25.

*signed to,* Gen. 47:6, 11, 12, 27. *Dwells in Egypt seventeen years,* Gen. 47:28. *Exacts a promise from Joseph to bury him with his fathers,* Gen. 47:29–31. *His benediction upon Joseph and his two sons,* Gen. 48:15–22; Heb. 11:21. *Gives the land of the Amorites to Joseph,* Gen. 48:22; John 4:5.

*His final prophetic benedictions upon his sons,* Gen. 49: **3–27.** *Charges his sons to bury him in the field of Machpelah,* Gen. 49:29. **30.** *Death of,* Gen. 49:**33.** *Body of, embalmed,* Gen. 50:2. *Forty days' mourning for,* **Gen.** 50:3. *Burial of,* **Gen. 47**:29–31; 49:29, 30; 50:4–13.

*Descendants of,* Gen. 29:31–35; 30:1–24; 35:18, 22–26; 46:8–27; Ex. 1:1–5; 1 Chr. chapters 2–9. *His wealth,* Gen. 36:6, **7.** *Well of,* John 4:6–13. *Prophecies concerning him and his descendants,* Gen. 25:23; 27:28, **29**; **28**:10–15; 31:3; 35:9–13; 46:3; Deut. 1:8; Psa. 105:10, **11.**

ther, Let my father arise, and
eat of his son's venison, that [g]thy
soul may bless me.
32 And Ī'ṣaac his father said
unto him, Who *art* thou? And
he said, I *am* thy son, thy [i]first-
born [h]Ē'sa̤u.
33 And [f]Ī'ṣaac trembled very
exceedingly, and said, Who?
where *is* he that hath taken[c] venison, and brought *it* me, and I
have eaten of all before thou
camest, and have [g]blessed him?
yea, *and* he shall be blessed.
34 And when [h]Ē'sa̤u heard the
words of his father, he cried with
a great and exceeding bitter cry,
and said unto his father, [g]Bless
me, *even* me also, O my father.
35 And he said, Thy †brother
came with [3,j,k]subtilty, and hath
taken away thy [g]blessing.
36 And he said, Is not he rightly named †Jā'cob? for he hath
supplanted me these two times:
he took away [i]my [l]birthright;
and, behold, now he hath taken
away my blessing. And he said,
Hast thou not reserved a [g]bless-
ing for me?
37 And [f]Ī'ṣaac answered and
said unto [h]Ē'sa̤u, Behold, [q]I
have made him thy lord, and all
his brethren have I given to him
for servants; and with corn[c] and
wine have I sustained him: and
what shall I do now unto thee,
my son?
38 And [h]Ē'sa̤u said unto his
[f]father, Hast [g]thou but one blessing, my father? bless me, *even*
me also, O my father. And Ē'sa̤u
lifted up his voice, and [m]wept.
39[Q] And [f]Ī'ṣaac his father answered and said unto him, [g]Be-
hold, thy dwelling shall be the
fatness of the earth, and of the
[b]dew of heaven from above:
40 And [n]by thy [o]sword shalt
thou live, and shalt serve thy
brother; and it shall come to pass
when thou shalt [4]have the dominion, that thou shalt [5]break
his yoke from off thy neck.[Q]
41 ¶ And [h]Ē'sa̤u [p]hated †Jā'-
cob because of the [g]blessing
wherewith his father blessed
him: and Ē'sa̤u said in his heart,
The days of [q]mourning for my
father are at hand; then will I
[r,s]slay my brother Jā'cob.
42 And these words of [h]Ē'sa̤u
her [i]elder son were told to [t]Rē-
běk'ah: and she sent and called
†Jā'cob her younger son, and
said unto him, Behold, thy
brother Ē'sa̤u, as touching[c] thee,
doth comfort himself, [s]*purposing* to [r]kill thee.
43 Now therefore, my son, obey
my voice; and arise, flee thou to
[u]Lā'ban my brother to [v]Hā'ran;
44 And tarry with him a few
days, until thy [h]brother's [w]fury
turn away:
45 Until thy [h]brother's [w]anger
turn away from †thee, and he
forget *that* which thou hast done
to him: then [t]I will send, and
fetch thee from thence: why
should I be deprived also of you
both in one day?
46 And [t]Rē-běk'ah said to
[f]Ī'ṣaac, [x]I am weary of my life
because of the [y]daughters of
Hěth: if †Jā'cob take a [z]wife of
the daughters of Hěth, such as
these *which are* of the daughters
of the land, what good shall my
life do me?

## CHAPTER 28

*Isaac blesses Jacob, and sends him to Padan-aram. 6 Esau marries the daughter of Ishmael. 10 The vision of Jacob's ladder. 18 The stone of Bethel. 20 Jacob's vow.*

AND [a]Ī'ṣaac called [b]Jā'cob,
and [c,d]blessed him, and
charged[c] him, and said unto
him, Thou shalt not [e]take a
[f]wife of the [g]daughters of
Cā'năan.
2 Arise, go to *Pā'dan-ā'ram,

32
*i* *Firstborn*, Zech. 12:10.

35
*j* *Falsehood*, Job 21:34.
*k* *Craftiness, instances of*, Psa. 83:3.
3 R. V. guile,

36
*l* *Birthright*, 2 Chr. 21:3.

38
*m* *Weeping*, Ezra 3:13.

40
*n* *Edomites, prophecies concerning*, 2 Kin. 8:21.
*o* *Sword, figurative*, 1 Chr. 21:5.

v.40–1801 BC
4 R. V. break loose,
5 R. V. shake

41
*p* *Hatred*, Prov. 15:17.
*q* *Mourning*, Lam. 2:5.
*r* *Homicide*, Deut. 5:17.
*s* *Malice, instances of*, Eph. 4:31.

42
*t* *Rebekah*, Gen. 24:15.

43
*u* *Laban*, Gen. 28:5.
*v* *Haran*, Gen. 11:31.

44
*w* *Anger*, Psa. 37:8.

46
*x* Gen. 26:34, 35.
*y* *Hittites*, Judg. 1:26.
*z* *Wife*, Prov. 5:18.

1
*a* *Isaac*, Gen. 21:3.
*b* *Jacob*, Gen. 27:11.
*c* *Benedictions, instances of*, Deut. 21:5.
*d* *Parents, blessing of*, 2 Cor. 12:14.
*e* *Miscegenation*, Josh. 23:12.
*f* *Wife*, Prov. 5:18.
*g* *Canaanites*. Ex. 23:28.

*** PADAN-ARAM** (*the plain of Aram*). Gen. 25:20; 28: 2, 5, 6, 7; 31:18; 33:18; 35:9, 26; 46:15.

v.2-1801 BC
See footnote, *Time*, Rev. 10:6.

**2**
*h* *Bethuel*, Gen. 24:15.
*i* *Rebekah*, Gen. 24:15.
*j* *Marriage, consanguineous*, Gen. 34:9.

**3**
*k* *Temporal Blessings, prayer for*, Psa. 103:2.
*l* *Children, gift of God*, Mark 10:14.

**4**
*m* *Covenant, of God with men*, Deut. 29:1.
*n* *Abraham*, Gen. 17:5.
*o* *Canaan, promised to Abraham*, Gen. 37:1.

**5**
*p* *Esau*, Gen. 25:25.
1 *Heb.* Aramean,

**9**
*q* *Ishmael*, Gen. 16:11.
*r* *Polygamy*, Deut. 17:17.
*s* Or, *Bashemath*, Gen. 36:3, 4, 10, 13, 17.
*t* Or, *Nebaioth*, Gen. 25:13.

**10**
*u* *Beer-sheba*, Judg. 20:1.
*v* *Haran*, Gen. 11:31.

**11**
*w* *Bethel*, Josh. 18:13.

to the house of [h]Bĕth-ụ'el thy [i]mother's father; and [j]take thee a [j]wife from thence of the daughters of †Lā'ban thy mother's brother.

3 And [d,k]God Almighty bless thee, and make thee [l]fruitful, and multiply thee, that thou mayest be a multitude of people;

4 [k]And give thee the [m]blessing[G] of [n]Ā'bră-hăm, to thee, and to thy seed with thee; that thou mayest inherit the [o]land wherein thou art a stranger[G] which God gave unto Ā'bră-hăm.[T]

5 And Ī'ṣaac sent away Jā'cob: and he went to *Pā'dan-ā'ram unto †Lā'ban, son of [h]Bĕth-ụ'el the [1]Sȳr-ĭ'an, the brother of [i]Rē-bĕk'ah, Jā'cob's and [p]Ē'sạu's mother.

6 ¶ When [p]Ē'sạu saw that [a]Ī'ṣaac had [d]blessed [b]Jā'cob, and sent him away to *Pā'dan-ā'ram, to take him a [j]wife from thence; and that as he blessed him he gave him a charge, saying, Thou shalt not take a wife of the [g]daughters of Cā'năan;

7 And that [b]Jā'cob obeyed his father and his mother, and was gone to *Pā'dan-ā'ram;

8 And [p]Ē'sạu seeing that the [g]daughters of Cā'năan pleased not [a]Ī'ṣaac his father;

9 Then went [p]Ē'sạu unto [q]Ĭsh'ma-el, and [r]took unto the wives which he had [s]Mā'ha-lăth the daughter of Ĭsh'ma-el Ā'bră-hăm's son, the sister of [t]Nĕ-bā'joth, to be his wife.

10 ¶ And Jā'cob went out from [u]Bē'er-shē'bȧ, and went toward [v]Hā'ran.

11 [T]And [b]he lighted[G] upon a certain [w]place, and tarried there all night, because the sun was set; and he took of the stones of that place, and put *them for* his pillows, and lay down in that place to sleep.

12 And [b]he [x,y]dreamed, and behold a ladder set up on the earth, and the top of it reached to heaven: and behold the [z]angels of God ascending and descending on it.[Q]

13 And, behold, the LORD [a]stood above it, and [b]said, I *am* the LORD God of [c]Ā'bră-hăm thy father, and the God of [d]Ī'ṣaac: the [e]land whereon thou liest, to [f]thee will I [g]give it, and to thy seed;

14 And thy [h]seed[G] shall be as the dust of the earth, and thou shalt spread abroad to the west, and to the east, and to the north, and to the south: and in thee and in thy [i]seed shall all the [j]families of the earth be blessed.

15 And, behold, I *am* with [k]thee, and will [l]keep[G] thee in all *places* whither thou goest, and will bring thee again into this [j]land; for [m]I will not leave thee, until I have done *that* which I have spoken to thee of.[S] [Q]

16 ¶ And [d]Jā'cob awaked out of his sleep, and he said, Surely the [n]LORD is in[S] this place; and I knew *it* not.

17 And he was [G][o]afraid, and said, How dreadful *is* this place! this *is* none other but the house of God, and this *is* the [p]gate of heaven.

18 And [d]Jā'cob [q]rose up early in the morning, and took the [r]stone that he had put *for* his pillows, and set it up *for* a ‡pillar, and [s]poured [t]oil upon the top of it.

19 And he called the name of

v.11-1801 BC
See footnote, *Time*, Rev. 10:6.

**12**
*x* *Dream, instances of*, Dan. 1:17.
*y* *Vision*, Acts 9:10.
*z* *Angel, appearances of*, Heb. 1:13.

**13**
*a* *Anthropomorphisms, standing attributed to God*, Gen. 11:5.
*b* *Communion, with God, instances of*, 2 Cor. 13:14.
*c* *Abraham*, Gen. 17:5.
*d* *Isaac*, Gen. 21:3.
*e* *Canaan, promised to Abraham and his seed*, Gen. 37:1.
*f* *Jacob*, Gen. 27:11.
*g* *Covenant, of God with men, instances of*, Deut. 29:1.

**14**
*h* *Israel, prophecies concerning*, Ex. 4:22.
*i* *Jesus, prophecies concerning*, Matt. 1:21.
*j* *Nations, blessed in Abraham*, Gen. 18:18.

**15**
*k* *Righteous, promises to*, Psa. 64:10.
*l* *God, preserver*, Gen. 2:2.
*m* *God, faithfulness of*, Gen. 2:2.

**16**
*n* *God, presence of*, Gen. 2:2.

**17**
*o* *Fear, of God, instances of*, Acts 9:31.
*p* *Gates, figurative*, Deut. 3:5.

**18**
*q* *Rising, early, instances of*, Gen. 19:2.
*r* *Stones, memorial*, Ex. 24:12.
*s* *Anointing, in consecration*, Lev. 8:12.
*t* *Oil, anointing*, Deut. 12:17.

† **LABAN** (*white*). *Son of Bethuel*, Gen. 28:5. *Brother of Rebekah*, Gen. 22:23; 24:15, 29. *Receives the servant of Abraham*, Gen. 24:29–33. *Receives Jacob, and gives him his daughters in marriage*, Gen. 29:12–30. *Jacob becomes his servant*, Gen. 29:15–20, 27; 30:27–43. *Outwitted by Jacob*, Gen. 30:37–43; 31:1–21. *Pursues Jacob, overtakes him at Mount Gilead, and covenants with him*, Gen. 31:22–55.

‡ **PILLAR.** *For screen at tabernacle door*, Ex. 26:37; 36:38. *Of the tabernacle*, Ex. 27:10–12, 14–17; 36:36, 38; 38:10–12, 14, 19; 39:33; Num. 3:36, 37; 4:31, 32; *overlaid with gold*, Ex. 36:36. *Of the court of the tabernacle*, Ex. 27:9–17; 38:9–20; Num. 3:37. *Of Solomon's temple*, 1 Kin. 7:13–22; 2 Kin. 25:16, 17. *Broken and carried to Babylon*, 2 Kin. 25:13; Jer. 52:17, 20, 21. *Of Solomon's palaces*, 1 Kin. 7:2, 6. *To mark graves*, Gen. 35:20. *Pillar of salt, Lot's wife*

v.19–1801 BC
See footnote, *Time*, Rev. 10:6.

19
*u Bethel*, Josh. 18:13.

20
*v Vows, instances of*, Num. 30:2.
*w Covenant, of man with God*, Deut. 29:1.
*x Consecration, conditional*, Lev. 7:37.
*y God, providence of*, Gen. 2:2.
*z Temporal Blessings, from God*, Psa. 103:2.

that place [u]Bĕth′el: but the
name of that city *was called* Lŭz
at the first.
20[s] And [d]Jā′cob vowed a
[v,w]vow,[c] saying, [x]If [y]God will be
with me, and will keep me in
this way that I go, and will give
me [z]bread to eat, and raiment
to put on,
21 So that I come again to my
father's house in peace; [v,x]then
shall the LORD be my God:[s]
22 And this [a]stone, which I
have set *for* a [‡]pillar, shall be
God's house: and of [b]all that
thou shalt give me I will surely
[c]give the [d]tenth unto thee.[T]

22
*a Stones, memorial*, Ex. 24:12.
*b Temporal Blessings, from God*, Psa. 103:2.
*c Liberality, instances of*, 1 Tim. 6:18.
*d Tithes*, Num. 18:24.

## CHAPTER 29

*Jacob comes to the well of Haran. 9 He meets Rachel; 13 and is entertained by Laban. 18 He covenants for Rachel, 23 but is deceived with Leah. 28 He marries Rachel also, and serves for her seven years more. 32 Leah bears Reuben, 33 Simeon, 34 Levi, 35 and Judah.*

1
*a Jacob*, Gen. 27:11.

THEN [a]Jā′cob went on his
journey, and came into the
land of the people of the east.
2 And he looked, and behold a
[b]well in the field, and, lo, there
*were* three flocks of [c]sheep lying
by it; for out of that well [d]they
watered the flocks: and a great
stone *was* upon the well's mouth.
3 And thither were all the
flocks gathered: and [d]they rolled
the stone from the [b]well's mouth,
and watered the [c]sheep, and put
the stone again upon the well's
mouth in his place.
4 And [a]Jā′cob said unto them,
My brethren, whence *be* ye?
And they said, Of [e]Hā′ran *are*
we.
5 And he said unto them, Know
ye [f]Lā′ban the son of [g]Nā′hôr?
and they said, We know *him*.

2
*b Wells*, Gen. 21:19.
*c Sheep*, Deut. 32:14.
*d Shepherd*, Jer.31:10.

4
*e Haran*, Gen. 11:31.

5
*f Laban*, Gen.28:5.
*g Nahor*, Gen. 22:20.

6 And [a]he said unto them, *Is*
*he* well? And they said, *He is*
well: and, behold, *Rā′chel his
daughter cometh with the
sheep.
7 And [a]he said, Lo, *it is* yet
high day, neither *is it* time that
the cattle should be gathered together:
water ye the [c]sheep, and
go *and* feed *them*.
8 And they said, We cannot,
until all the flocks be gathered
together, and *till* they roll the
stone from the [b]well's mouth;
then we water the sheep.
9 ¶ And while he yet spake with
them, *Rā′chel came with her
father's sheep: for [h]she kept
them.
10 And it came to pass, when
[a]Jā′cob saw *Rā′chel the daughter
of [f]Lā′ban his [i]mother's
brother, and the sheep of Lā′ban
his mother's brother, that Jā′cob
went near, and rolled the stone
from the well's mouth, and watered
the flock of Lā′ban his
mother's brother.
11 And [a]Jā′cob [j]kissed *Rā′chel,
and lifted up his voice, and
wept.
12 And [a]Jā′cob told *Rā′chel
that he *was* her [f]father's brother,
and that he *was* [i]Rĕ-bĕk′ah's
son: and she ran and told her
father.
13 And it came to pass, when
[f]Lā′ban heard the tidings of
[a]Jā′cob his [i]sister's son, that he
ran to meet him, and embraced
him, and [j]kissed him, and
[k]brought him to his house. And
he told Lā′ban all these things.
14 And [f]Lā′ban said to him,
Surely thou *art* my bone[c] and my

v.6–1801 BC
See footnote, *Time*, Rev. 10:6.

9
*h Women, tend flocks*, Prov. 31:10.

10
*i Rebekah*, Gen.24:15.

11
*j Kiss*, Ruth 1:14.

13
*k Hospitality, instances of*, Rom. 12:13.

*turned to*, Gen. 19:26; Luke 17:32. *As a boundary*, Josh. 15:6; 18:17; *a waymark*, 1 Sam. 20:19; Jer. 31:21; *a landmark*, 2 Sam. 20:8; 1 Kin. 1:9. *Prophecy of one in Egypt*, Isa. 19:19. *Monuments of idolatry, to be destroyed*, Deut. 12:3.

MONUMENTS ERECTED TO COMMEMORATE EVENTS: *By Jacob, his vision of angels*, Gen. 28:18; 31:13; 35:14; *his covenant with Laban*, Gen. 31:45. *By Moses, the covenant between Jehovah and Israel*, Ex. 24:4. *By Joshua, the passing over Jordan*, Josh. 4:1–9 (with Deut. 27:2–6); *at Mount Ebal*, Josh. 8:30; *at Shechem*, Josh. 24:25–27; Judg. 9:6. *By Samuel, the discomfiture of the Philistines*, 1 Sam. 7:12. *By Absalom, to keep his name in remembrance*, 2 Sam. 18:18.

**Figurative**, Rev. 3:12.

* **RACHEL**, daughter of Laban and wife of Jacob. *Meets Jacob at the well*, Gen. 29:9–12. *Jacob serves Laban fourteen years to secure her for his wife*, Gen. 29:15–30. *Sterility of*, Gen. 29:31. *Her grief in consequence of her sterility; gives her maid to Jacob in order to secure children in her own name*, Gen. 30:1–8, 15, 22–34. *Later fecundity of; becomes the mother of Joseph*, Gen. 30:22–25; *of Benjamin*, Gen. 35:16–18, 24. *Steals the household images of her father*, Gen. 31:4, 14–19, 33–35. *Builder of the house of Israel*, Ruth 4:11. *Her death and burial*, Gen. 35:18–20; 48:7; 1 Sam. 10:2.

v.14–1801 BC
See footnote, *Time*, Rev. 10:6.

**14**
*l Month*, Ex. 12:2.

**15**
*m Hired Servant*, Lev. 25.40.
*n Wages*, Gen. 31:7.

**17**
*o Beauty, instances of*, Prov. 6:25.

**18**
*p Seven, years*, Gen. 7:2.
*q Marriage, wives obtained by purchase*, Gen. 34:9.

**19**
*r Contracts*, Matt. 20:2.

v.21–1794 BC

**21**
*s Father-in-law*, Judg. 19:3.
*t Marriage, consanguineous*, Gen. 34:9.
*u Wife*, Prov. 5:18.

**22**
*v Feast*, Mark 12: 39.

**23**
*w Dishonesty, instances of*, Ezek. 22:13.
*x Deception*, Josh. 9:4.

**24**
*y Bride*, Isa. 49:18.
*z Servant, given as dowry*, Jer. 2:14.

**25**
*a Jacob*, Gen. 27: 11.
*b Laban*, Gen. 28:5.

flesh. And he abode with him
the space of a [l]month.
15 ¶ And Lā′ban said unto
[a]Jā′cob, Because thou *art* my
brother, shouldest thou therefore serve me for nought[c]? tell
me, what *shall* [m]thy[n] wages *be*?
16 And Lā′ban had two
daughters: the name of the elder
*was* †Lē′ah, and the name of the
younger *was* *Rā′chel.
17 †Lē′ah *was* tender eyed[c]; but
*Rā′chel was [o]beautiful and well
favoured[c].
18 And [a]Jā′cob loved *Rā′-
chel; and said, I will [m]serve thee
[p]seven years [q]for Rā′chel thy
younger daughter.
19 And Lā′ban said, *It is* better that I [r]give her to thee than
that I should give her to another
man: abide with me.
20 And [a]Jā′cob served [p]seven
years [q]for *Rā′chel; and they
seemed unto him *but* a few days,
for the love he had to her.
21 ¶ And [a]Jā′cob said unto
[s]Lā′ban, Give *me* my [t,u]wife,
for my days are fulfilled, that I
may go in unto her.
22 And Lā′ban gathered together all the men of the place,
and made a [v]feast.
23 And it came to pass in the
evening, that he [w,x]took †Lē′ah
his daughter, and [t]brought her
to him; and he went in unto her.
24 And Lā′ban gave unto his
daughter [†,y]Lē′ah ‡Zĭl′pah his
[z]maid *for* an handmaid.
25 And it came to pass, that in
the morning, behold, it *was*
†Lē′ah: and [a]he said to [b]Lā′ban,
What *is* this thou hast done unto
me? did not I serve with thee for
*Rā′chel? wherefore then hast
thou [c]beguiled me?
26 And [b]Lā′ban said, It must
not be so done in our country, to
give the younger before the
[d]firstborn.
27 Fulfil her week, and we will
[e]give thee this also for the service
which thou shalt serve with me
yet [f]seven other years.
28 And [a]Jā′cob did so, and fulfilled her week: and he gave him
*Rā′chel his daughter to [g]wife
also.
29 And [b]Lā′ban gave to [*,h]Rā′-
chel his daughter ‖Bĭl′hah his
[i]handmaid to be her maid.
30 And he [j]went in also unto
*Rā′chel, and he loved also Rā′-
chel[k]more than †Lē′ah, and served with him yet [f]seven other years.
31 ¶ And when the LORD saw
that †Lē′ah *was* [l,m]hated, he
opened[c] her womb: but *Rā′chel
*was* [n]barren.
32 And †Lē′ah conceived, and
bare a son, and she called his
name [o]Reu′ben: for she [p]said,
Surely the LORD hath looked
upon my affliction; now therefore my husband will love me.
33 And she conceived again,
and bare a son; and [p]said, Because the LORD hath heard that
I *was* hated, he hath therefore
given me this [q]*son* also: and she
called his name §Sĭm′e-on.
34 And she conceived again,
and bare a son; and said, Now
this time will my husband be
joined unto me, because I have
born him three sons: therefore
was his name called +Lē′vī.

.25–1794 BC
See footnote, *Time*, Rev. 10:6.

*c Deception*, Josh. 9:4.

**26**
*d Firstborn*, Zech. 12:10.

**27**
*e Marriage, wives obtained by purchase*, Gen. 34:9.
*f Seven, years*, Gen. 7:2.

**28**
*g Wife*, Prov. 5:18.

**29**
*h Bride*, Isa. 49:18.
*i Servant, given as dowry*, Jer. 2:14.

**30**
*j Polygamy, evil effects of*, vs. 30–34; Deut. 17:17.
*k Partiality*, 1 Tim. 5:21.

**31**
*l Hatred*, Prov. 15: 17.
*m Family, infelicity in*, 1 Chr. 13:14.
*n Barrenness, a reproach*, Deut. 7: 14.

**32**
*o Reuben*, Gen. 35: 22.
*p Thankfulness to God, instances of*, Acts 24:3.

**33**
*q Children, the gift of God*, Mark 10: 14.

† **LEAH** (*weary*). *Daughter of Laban*, Gen. 29:16. *Married to Jacob*, Gen. 29:23–26. *Children of*, Gen. 29: 31–35; 30:9–13, 17–21. *Flees with Jacob*, Gen. 31:4, 14, 17; 33:2–7. *Builder of the house of Israel*, Ruth 4:11.

‡ **ZILPAH.** *Leah's handmaid*, Gen. 29:24. *Mother of Gad and Asher by Jacob*, Gen. 30:9–13; 35:26; 37:2; 46:16, 17, 18.

‖ **BILHAH.** *Rachel's servant, bears children by Jacob*, Gen. 29:29; 30:3, 4; 37:2. *Mother of Dan and Naphtali*, Gen. 30:1–8; 35:25; 46:23–25; 1 Chr. 7:13. *Reuben's incest with*, Gen. 35:22; 49:4.

§ **SIMEON.** *Son of Jacob*, Gen. 29:33; 35:23; Ex. 1:1, 2; 1 Chr. 2:1. *With Levi avenges upon the Shechemites the seduction of Dinah*, Gen. 34; 49:5–7. *Jacob's denunciation of*, Gen. 34:30; 49:5–7. *Goes down into Egypt to buy corn; is bound by Joseph, and detained*, Gen. 42:24, 36; 43:23. *His sons*, Gen. 46:10; Ex. 6:15; 1 Chr. 4:24. *Descendants of*, Num. 26:12–14; 1 Chr. 4:24–27.

See footnote, SIMEON *tribe of*, Num. 2:12.

+ **LEVI.** *Son of Jacob*, Gen. 29:34; 35:23; 1 Chr. 2:1. *Avenges the seduction of Dinah*, Gen. 34; 49:5–7. *Jacob's prophecy regarding*, Gen. 49:5–7. *His age at death*, Ex. 6:16. *Descendants of, made ministers of religion*, see footnote, LEVITES, Deut. 10:8.

35 And she conceived again,
and bare a son: and she [p]said,
Now will I praise the LORD:
therefore she called his name
[r]Jū′dah; and left[C] bearing.[Q]

## CHAPTER 30

*Rachel gives Bilhah her maid unto Jacob. 5 She bears Dan and Naphtali. 9 Leah gives Zilpah her maid, who bears Gad and Asher. 17 Leah bears Issachar, Zebulun, and Dinah. 22 Rachel bears Joseph. 25 Jacob desires to depart. 27 Laban stays him on a new covenant. 37 Jacob's policy whereby he became rich.*

AND [a,b]when [c]Rā′chel saw
that she [d]bare [e]Jā′cob no
children, Rā′chel [f]envied her
sister; and said unto Jā′cob,
Give me children, or else I
die.
2 And [e]Jā′cob's [g]anger was kindled against [c]Rā′chel: and he
said, *Am* I in God's stead,[C] who
hath [d]withheld from thee the
[h]fruit of the womb?
3 And [c]she said, Behold my
[i]maid [j]Bĭl′hah, go in unto her;
and she shall bear upon my
knees, that I may also have
children by her.
4 And she gave him [j]Bĭl′hah
her [i]handmaid to [b,k]wife: and
Jā′cob went in unto her.
5 And [j]Bĭl′hah conceived, and
bare [e]Jā′cob a son.
6 And [c]Rā′chel [l]said, God hath
judged me, and hath also heard
my voice, and hath given me a
[h]son: therefore called she his
name *Dăn.
7 And [j]Bĭl′hah [c]Rā′chel's
[i]maid conceived again, and bare
[e]Jā′cob a second son.
8 And [c]Rā′chel said, With
great †wrestlings have I wres-
tled with my sister, and I have
prevailed: and she called his
name ‡Năph′ta-lī.
9 When [m]Lē′ah saw that she
had left[C] bearing, she took [n]Zĭl′-
pah her [i]maid, and gave her
Jā′cob to [b,k]wife.
10 And [n]Zĭl′pah [m]Lē′ah's [i]maid
bare [e]Jā′cob a son.
11 And [m]Lē′ah said, A troop
cometh: and she called his name
‖Găd.
12 And [n]Zĭl′pah [m]Lē′ah's [i]maid
bare [e]Jā′cob a second son.
13 And [m]Lē′ah said, Happy am
I, for the daughters will call me
blessed: and she called his name
§Āsh′ēr.
14 ¶ And [o]Reu′ben went in the
days of wheat harvest, and
found [p]mandrakes[C] in the field,
and brought them unto his
mother [m]Lē′ah. Then [c]Rā′chel
said to Lē′ah, Give me, I pray
thee, of thy son's mandrakes.[C]
15 [a,b]And [m]she said unto her,
*Is it* a small matter that thou
hast taken my [q]husband? and
wouldest thou take away my
son's [p]mandrakes also? And
[c]Rā′chel said, Therefore he shall
lie with thee to night for thy
son's mandrakes.
16 And [e]Jā′cob came out of the
field in the evening, and [m]Lē′ah
went out to meet him, and said,
Thou must come in unto me;
for surely I have hired thee with
my son's [p]mandrakes. And he
lay with her that night.
17 And [r]God hearkened unto
Lē′ah, and she conceived, and
bare Jā′cob the fifth [s]son.
18 And [m]Lē′ah said, [r]God hath
given me my hire, because I
have given my maiden to my

**35**
*r* *Judah,* Gen. 37:26.

**1**
*a* *Family, infelicity in, instances of,* vs. 1–23; 1 Chr. 13:14.
*b* *Polygamy, evil effects of,* vs. 1–23; Deut. 17:17.
*c* *Rachel,* Gen. 29:6.
*d* *Barrenness, a reproach,* Deut. 7:14.
*e* *Jacob,* Gen. 27:11.
*f* *Envy, instances of,* Prov. 14:30.

**2**
*g* *Anger,* Psa. 37:8.
*h* *Children, the gift of God,* Mark 10:14.

**3**
*i* *Servant,* Jer. 2:14.
*j* *Bilhah,* Gen. 29:29.

**4**
*k* *Concubinage,* 2 Sam. 21:11.

**6**
*l* *Thankfulness to God, instances of,* Acts 24:3.

**9**
*m* *Leah,* Gen. 29:16.
*n* *Zilpah,* Gen. 29:24.

**14**
*o* *Reuben,* Gen. 35:22.
*p* Song 7:13.

**15**
*q* *Husband,* Num. 30:6.

**17**
*r* *God, goodness of,* Gen. 2:2.
*s* *Children, in answer to prayer,* Mark 10:14.

* **DAN** (*a judge*). *Son of Jacob and Bilhah,* Gen. 35:25. *Descendants of,* Gen. 46:23; Num. 26:42, 43. *Blessed of Jacob,* Gen. 49:16, 17.

**Tribe of:** *Census of,* Num. 1:39; 26:42, 43. *Position of, in journey and camp, during the exodus,* Num. 2:25, 31; 10:25. *Blessed by Moses,* Deut. 33:22. *Inheritance of, according to the allotment of Joshua,* Josh. 19:40–47; *of Ezekiel,* Ezek. 48:1. *Fail to conquer the Amorites,* Judg. 1:34, 35. *Conquests by,* Josh. 19:47; Judg. 18:27–29. *Deborah upbraids, for cowardice,* Judg. 5:17. *Idolatry of,* Judg. 18.

† **WRESTLING. Figurative,** Gen. 30:8; 32:24, 25; Eph. 6:12.

‡ **NAPHTALI** (*my wrestling*). *Son of Jacob and Bilhah,* Gen. 30:7; 35:25. *Jacob blesses,* Gen. 49:21. *Sons of,* Gen. 46:24; 1 Chr. 7:13.

‖ **GAD** (*fortune*). *Jacob's seventh son,* Gen. 35:26; Ex. 1:4. *Children of,* Gen. 46:16; Num. 26:15–18. *Prophecy concerning,* Gen. 49:19.

§ **ASHER** (*happy*). *Son of Jacob, by Zilpah,* Gen. 35:26; Ex. 1:4; 1 Chr. 2:2. *Prophecy concerning,* Gen. 49:20.

[q]husband: and she called his
name +Ĭs'sa-char.
19 And [m]Lē'ah conceived
again, and bare [e]Jā'cob the
sixth son.
20 And [m]Lē'ah said, [r]God hath
endued[G] me *with* a good dowry;
now will my [q]husband dwell
with me, because I have born
him six sons: and she called his
name ©Zĕb'u-lŭn.
21 And afterwards she bare a
daughter, and called her name
[t]Dī'nah.
22 ¶ And [r]God remembered
[c]Rā'chel, and God [u]hearkened to
her, and opened her womb.[S]
23 And she conceived, and bare
a [s]son; and said, [r,u]God hath
taken away my [d]reproach:[Q]
24 And she called his name
[v]Jō'ṣeph; and said, [w]The LORD
shall add to me another son.
25 ¶ And it came to pass, when
Rā'chel had born [v]Jō'ṣeph, that
Jā'cob said unto [x]Lā'ban, Send
me away, that I may go unto
mine own place, and to my
country.
26 Give *me* my [y]wives and my
children, for whom [z]I have
served thee, and let me go: for
thou knowest my service which
I have done thee.
27 And [a]Lā'ban said unto [b]him,
I pray[G] thee, if I have found favour in thine eyes, *tarry*: *for* I
have learned by experience that
the LORD hath [c,d]blessed me for
thy sake.
28 And he said, Appoint[G] me
[e]thy [f]wages, and [g]I will give *it*.
29 And [b]he said unto [a]him,
Thou knowest how I have
[e]served thee, and how thy cattle
was with me.
30 For *it was* little which thou
hadst before I *came*, and it is
*now* [d]increased unto a multitude;
and the LORD hath [c]blessed thee
since my coming: and now when
shall [h,i]I provide for mine own
[j]house also?
31 And [a]he said, What shall I
give [e]thee? And [b]Jā'cob said,
Thou shalt not give me any
thing: if thou wilt do this thing
for me, I will again feed *and*
keep thy flock.
32 [b]I will pass through all thy
flock to day, removing from
thence [1]all the speckled and
spotted cattle, and all the brown
cattle among the [k]sheep, and the
spotted and speckled among the
[l]goats: and *of such* shall be my
[f]hire.
33 So shall [b]my righteousness[G]
answer for me in time to come,
when it shall come for my [f]hire
before thy face: every one that *is*
not speckled and spotted among
the [l]goats, and [2]brown among
the [k]sheep, that shall be counted
stolen with me.
34 And [a]Lā'ban said, Behold, I
would it might be according to
thy word.
35 And he removed that day
the he goats that were ringstraked[G] and spotted, and all the
she goats that were speckled and
spotted, *and* every one that had
*some* white in it, and all the
[2]brown among the sheep, and
gave *them* into the hand of his
sons.
36 And he set three days' journey betwixt himself and [b]Jā'cob:
and Jā'cob fed the rest of [a]Lā'-
ban's flocks.
37 ¶ [m,n,o]And [b]Jā'cob took him
rods of green [3,p]poplar, and of
the [4]hazel and chestnut tree; and
[5]pilled[G] white strakes[G] in them,
and made the white appear
which *was* in the rods.
38 And he set the rods which he

21
t Gen. 34.

v.23–1787 BC
22
u *Prayer, answered, instances of*, Acts 6:4.

24
v *Joseph*, Gen. 33:2.
w *Children, the gift of God*, Mark 10:14.

25
x *Laban*, Gen. 28:5.

26
y *Wife*, Prov. 5:18.
z *Hired Servant*, Lev. 25:40.

27
a *Laban*, Gen. 28:5.
b *Jacob*, Gen. 27:11.
c *Temporal Blessings, from God*, Psa. 103:2.
d *Prosperity*, Eccl. 7:14.

28
e *Hired Servant*, Lev. 25:40.
f *Wages*, Gen. 31:7.
g *Contracts*, Matt. 20:2.

30
h *Father, duty of*, Psa. 27:10.
i *Husband, duty of*, Num. 30:6.
j *Family, husband should provide for*, 1 Chr. 13:14.

32
k *Sheep*, Deut. 32:14.
l *Goats*, Deut. 14:4.
1 R. V. every speckled and spotted one, and every black one

33
2 R. V. black

37
m *Covetousness, instances of*, Isa. 57:17.
n *Dishonesty*, vs. 37–42; Ezek. 22:13.
o *Contracts, violated*, vs. 37–43; Matt. 20:2.
p Hos. 4:13.
3 *Or*, storax tree,
4 R.V. almond and of the plane tree;

*Descendants of*, Gen. 46:17; Num. 26:44–47. See footnote, ASHER, *tribe of*, Num. 1:40.
+ **ISSACHAR** (*a hire*). *Son of Jacob*, Gen. 30:18; Ex. 1:3; 1 Chr. 2:1. *Jacob's prophetic benedictions upon*, Gen. 49:14, 15. See footnote, ISSACHAR, *tribe of*, Num. 1:28.
© **ZEBULUN** (*dwelling*). *Son of Jacob and Leah*, Gen. 35:23; 46:14; Ex. 1:3; 1 Chr. 2:1. *Prophecy concerning*, Gen. 49:13. *Descendants of*, Gen. 46:14; Num. 26:26, 27.

38
[q] *Animals, breeding of,* Jer. 27:5.
5 R. V. peeled

40
6 R. V. flock.

43
[r] *Servant,* Jer. 2:14.
[s] *Camel,* 1 Sam. 30:17.
[t] *Ass, domesticated,* 2 Chr. 28:15.
7 R.V. large flocks,

had [5]pilled before the flocks in the gutters in the watering troughs when the flocks came to drink, that [q]they should conceive when they came to drink.

39 And the flocks [q]conceived before the rods, and brought forth cattle ringstraked, speckled, and spotted.

40 And [b]Jā′cob did separate the lambs, and set the faces of the flocks toward the ringstraked, and all the [2]brown in the flock of [a]Lā′ban; and he put his own flocks by themselves, and put them not unto Lā′ban's [6]cattle.

41 And it came to pass, whensoever the stronger [6]cattle did [q]conceive, that [b]Jā′cob laid the rods before the eyes of the [6]cattle in the gutters, that they might conceive among the rods.

42 But when the [6]cattle were feeble, he [n]put *them* not in: so the feebler were [a]Lā′ban's, [m]and the stronger [b]Jā′cob's.

43 And the [b]man increased exceedingly, and had [7]much cattle, and [r]maidservants, and menservants, and [s]camels, and [t]asses.

## CHAPTER 31

*Jacob departs secretly from Laban. 19 Rachel steals her father's images. 22 Laban pursues after Jacob. 26 and complains of the wrong. 34 Rachel's policy to hide the images. 36 Jacob's complaint of Laban. 43 The covenant of Laban and Jacob at Galeed.*

v.1–1781 BC
1
[a] *Laban,* Gen. 28:5.
[b] *Jacob,* Gen. 27:11.
[c] *Envy, instances of,* Prov. 14:30.
1 *Or,* wealth.

2
[d] *Countenance,* Prov. 15:13.

AND he heard the words of [a]Lā′ban's sons, saying, [b]Jā′cob hath taken away all that *was* our father's; and [c]of *that* which *was* our father's hath he gotten all this [1]glory.

2 And [b]Jā′cob beheld the [d]countenance of [a]Lā′ban, and, behold, it *was* not toward him as before.

3 And the LORD said unto [b]Jā′cob, Return unto the land of thy fathers, and to thy kindred; and [e]I will be with thee.

4 And [b]Jā′cob sent and called [f]Rā′chel and [g]Lē′ah to the field unto his flock,

5 And said unto them, I see your father's [d]countenance, that it *is* not toward me as before; but the [e]God of my father hath been with me.

6 And ye know that with all my power [h]I have served your father.

7 And your [a,i,j]father hath deceived me, and [k,l]changed my *wages ten times; but God suffered him not to hurt me.

8 If he said thus, The speckled shall be thy *wages; then all the [2]cattle bare speckled: and if he said thus, The ringstraked shall be thy hire; then bare all the cattle ringstraked.

9 Thus God hath taken away the cattle of your [a,i,j]father, and given *them* to me.

10 And it came to pass at the time that the [2]cattle [m]conceived, that I lifted up mine eyes, and saw in a [n]dream, and, behold, the [3]rams which leaped upon the [2]cattle *were* ringstraked, speckled, and grisled.

11 And the [o]angel of God spake unto me in a dream, *saying,* [b]Jā′cob: and I said, Here *am* I.

12 And he said, Lift up now thine eyes, and see, all the [3]rams which leap upon the [2]cattle *are* ringstraked, speckled, and grisled: for I have seen all that [a]Lā′ban doeth unto thee.

13 I *am* the God of [p]Běth′el, where thou [q]anointedst the [r]pillar, *and* where thou vowedst a [s]vow unto me: now arise, get thee out from this land, and return unto the land of thy kindred.

v.3–1781 BC
3
[e] *God, preserver,* Gen. 2:2.
4
[f] *Rachel,* Gen. 29:6.
[g] *Leah,* Gen. 29:16.

6
[h] *Hired Servant,* Lev. 25:40.
7
[i] *Father-in-law,* Judg. 19:3
[j] *Master, unjust,* Col. 4:1.
[k] *Contracts violated,* Matt. 20:2.
[l] *Covetousness, instances of,* Isa. 57:17.
8
2 R. V. flock

10
[m] *Animals, breeding of,* Jer. 27:5.
[n] *Dream, instances of,* Dan. 1:17.
3 R. V. he-goats

11
[o] *Angel, appearances of,* Heb. 1:13.

13
[p] *Bethel,* Josh. 18:13.
[q] *Anointing, in consecration,* Lev. 8:12.
[r] *Pillar,* Gen. 28:18.
[s] *Vows,* Num 30:2.

* **WAGES.** *Of Jacob,* Gen. 29:15-30; 30:28-34; 31:7, 41. *Laborer entitled to,* Deut. 25:4; Matt. 10:10; Luke 10:7; Rom. 4:4. *Must be just,* Col. 4:1. *Must be paid promptly,* Lev. 19:13; Deut. 24:15. *Withholding of, denounced,* Jer. 22:13; Mal. 3:5; Jas. 5:4. *Wasting of, denounced,* Hag. 1:6. *Contentment with, enjoined,* Luke 3:14. *Parable concerning,* Matt. 20:1-15.
**Figurative,** Rom. 6:23.

v.14–1781 BC
See footnote, *Time*, Rev. 10:6.

14
*t Wife, loyal*, Prov. 5:18.
*u Inheritance*, Num. 27:7.

15
*v Money*, Jer. 32:9.

16
*w Riches*, Eccl. 4:8.

17
*x Camel*, 1 Sam. 30:17.

18
*y Padan-aram*, Gen. 28:2.
*z Isaac*, Gen. 21:3.

---

*a Canaan*, Gen. 37: 1.

19
*b Laban*, Gen. 28:5.
*c Sheep*, Deut. 32: 14.
*d Rachel*, Gen. 29:6.
*e Women, wicked*, Prov. 31:10.
*f Theft, instances of*, Mark 7:22.
*g Teraphim, idol*, Judg. 17:5.
*h Idolatry*, 1 Sam. 15:23.

20
*i Jacob*, Gen. 27:11.

21
*j Euphrates*, Gen. 15:18.
*k Gilead, a mountain*, Song 4:1.

24
*l God, preserver*, Gen. 2:2.
*m Dream, instances of*, Dan. 1:17.

25
*n Tent*, Gen. 13:5.

14 And [t,t]Rā′chel and [g,t]Lē′ah answered and said unto him, *Is there* yet any portion or [u]inheritance for us in our father's house?

15 Are we not counted of him strangers? for he hath sold us, and hath quite devoured also our [v]money.

16 For all the [w]riches which God hath taken from our father, that *is* our's, and our children's: now then, whatsoever God hath said unto thee, do.

17 ¶ Then Jā′cob rose up, and set his sons and his wives upon [x]camels;

18 And he carried away all his cattle, and all his goods which he had gotten, the cattle of his getting, which he had gotten in [y]Pā′dan-ā′ram, for to go to [z]Ī′ṣaac his father in the land of [a]Cā′năan.

19 And [b]Lā′ban went to shear his [c]sheep: and [d,e]Rā′chel had [f]stolen the [g,h]images[G] that *were* her father's.

20 And [i]Jā′cob stole away unawares to [b]Lā′ban the Sy̆r′ĭ-an, in that he told him not that he fled.

21 So he fled with all that he had; and he rose up, and passed over the [j]river, and set his face *toward* the mount [k]Gĭl′e-ăd.

22 And it was told [b]Lā′ban on the third day that [i]Jā′cob was fled.

23 And he took his brethren with him, and pursued after him seven days' journey; and they overtook him in the mount [k]Gĭl′e-ăd.

24 And [l]God came to [b]Lā′ban the Sy̆r′ĭ-an in a [m]dream by night, and said unto him, Take heed that thou speak not to [i]Jā′cob either good or bad.

25 ¶ Then [b]Lā′ban overtook [i]Jā′cob.[G] Now Jā′cob had pitched[G] his [n]tent in the mount: and Lā′ban with his brethren pitched in the mount of [k]Gĭl′e-ăd.

26 And [b]Lā′ban said to [i]Jā′cob, What hast thou done, that thou hast stolen away unawares to me, and carried away my daughters, as captives *taken* with the sword?

27 Wherefore didst thou flee away secretly, and steal away from me; and didst not tell me, that I might have sent thee away with mirth, and with [o]songs, with tabret,[G] and with [p]harp?

28 And hast not suffered[G] me to [q]kiss my sons and my daughters? thou hast now done foolishly in *so* doing.

29 It is in the power[G] of my hand to do you hurt: [r]but the God of your father spake unto me yesternight, saying, Take thou heed that thou speak not to [i]Jā′cob either good or bad.

30 And now, *though* thou wouldest needs[G] be gone, because thou sore[G] longedst after thy father's house, *yet* wherefore hast thou [f]stolen my [g,h]gods?

31 And [i]Jā′cob answered and said to [b]Lā′ban, Because I was [s]afraid: for I said, Peradventure[G] thou wouldest take by force thy daughters from me.

32 With whomsoever thou findest thy [g,h]gods, let him not live: before our brethren discern thou what *is* thine with me, and take *it* to thee. For [i]Jā′cob knew not that [d]Rā′chel had [f]stolen them.

33 And [b]Lā′ban went into [i]Jā′cob's [n]tent, and into [t,u]Lē′ah's tent, and into the two [v]maidservants' tents; but he found *them* not. Then went he out of Lē′ah's tent, and entered into Rā′chel's tent.

34 Now [d]Rā′chel had taken the [g,h]images, and put them in the [w]camel's furniture,[G] and sat upon

v.25–1781 BC
See footnote, *Time*, Rev. 10:6.

27
*o Music*, 2 Chr. 5: 13.
*p Harp*, Dan. 3:10.

28
*q Kiss*, Ruth 1:14.

29
*r Obedience, to God, exemplified*, Heb. 5:8.

31
*s Cowardice, instances of*, Lev. 26:36.

33
*t Leah*, Gen. 29:16.
*u Women, had separate apartments* Prov. 31:10.
*v Servant*, Jer. 2: 14.

34
*w Camel*, 1 Sam. 30:17.

v.34–1781 BC
See footnote, *Time*, Rev. 10:6.

**35**
*x Manners*, Gen. 18:2.
*y Menstruation*, Ezek. 18:6.

**36**
*z Anger*, 37:8.Psa.

*a Strife, instances of*, Prov. 30.3.
*b Laban*, Gen.28:5.

**37**
*c Arbitration, instances of*, 1 Kin. 3:16.

**38**
*d Jacob*, Gen. 27:11.
*e Shepherd*, Jer. 31:10.

**39**
*f Oppression, instances of*, Eccl. 5:8.

**41**
*g Wife, bought*, Prov. 5:18.
*h Marriage*, Gen. 34:9.

**42**
*i Temporal Blessings, from God*, Psa. 103:2.
*j God, preserver*, Gen. 2:2.
*k Adversity, consolation in*, Psa. 10:6.

them. And [b]Lā′ban searched all the [n]tent, but found *them* not.

35 And she said to her father; Let it not displease my lord that I can not [x]rise up before thee, for the [y]custom of women *is* upon me. And he searched, but found not the [g,h]images.

36 ¶ And [i]Jā′cob was [z]wroth,[G] and [a]chode[G] with [b]Lā′ban: and Jā′cob answered and said to Lā′ban, What *is* my trespass[G]? what *is* my sin, that thou hast so hotly pursued after me?

37 Whereas thou hast searched all my stuff,[G] what hast thou found of all thy household stuff[G]? set *it* here before my brethren and thy brethren, that they may [c]judge betwixt us both.

38 This twenty years *have* [d,e]I *been* with thee; thy ewes and thy she goats have not cast their young, and the rams of thy flock have I not eaten.

39 That which was torn *of beasts* I brought not unto thee; I bare the loss of it; of my hand [f]didst thou require it, *whether* stolen by day, or stolen by night.

40 *Thus* I was; in the day the †drought consumed me, and the frost by night; and my sleep departed from mine eyes.

41 Thus have [d]I been twenty years in thy house; I served thee fourteen years [g,h]for thy two daughters, and six years for thy [2]cattle: and thou hast changed my *wages ten times.

42 [i]Except the [j]God of my father, the God of Ā′brā-hăm, and the fear[G] of Ī′ṣaac, had been with me, surely thou hadst sent me away now empty. God hath seen mine [k]affliction and the labour of my hands, and rebuked *thee* yesternight.

43 ¶ And [b]Lā′ban answered and said unto [d]Jā′cob, *These* daughters *are* my daughters, and *these* [l]children *are* my children, and *these* [2]cattle *are* my [2]cattle, and all that thou seest *is* mine: and what can I do this day unto these my daughters, or unto their children which they have born?

44 Now therefore come thou, let us make a [m]covenant, I and thou; and let it be for a witness between me and thee.

45 And [d]Jā′cob took a [n]stone, and set it up *for* a [o]pillar.

46 And [d]Jā′cob said unto his brethren, Gather [n]stones; and they took stones, and made an heap: and they did [p]eat there upon the heap.

47 And [b]Lā′ban called it [4]Jē′-gar-sā-hȧ-dū′thȧ: but [d]Jā′cob called it [4]Găl′e-ĕd.

48 And [b]Lā′ban said, This heap *is* a witness between me and thee this day. Therefore was the name of it called [4]Găl′e-ĕd;

49 And ‡Mĭz′pah; for he said, The LORD watch between me and thee, when we are absent one from another.

50 If thou shalt afflict my daughters, or if thou shalt take *other* wives beside my daughters, no man *is* with us; see, God *is* witness betwixt me and thee.

51 And [b]Lā′ban said to [d]Jā′cob, Behold this heap, and behold *this* [o]pillar, which I have cast betwixt me and thee;

52 This heap *be* witness, and *this* [o]pillar *be* witness, that I will not pass over this heap to thee, and that thou shalt not pass over this heap and this pillar unto me, for harm.

53 The [q]God of Ā′brā-hăm, and the God of Nā′hôr, the [5]God of their father, judge betwixt us.

v.43–1781 BC
See footnote, *Time*, Rev. 10:6.

**43**
*l Children*, Mark 10:14.

**44**
*m Covenant, of men with men*, Deut. 29:1.

**45**
*n Stones, memorial*, Ex. 24:12.
*o Pillar*, Gen. 28:18.

**46**
*p Feasts*, Mark 12:39.

**47**
4 *That is*, the heap of witness:

**53**
*q God, judge*, Gen. 2:2.
5 R. V. (marg.) gods

† **DROUGHT,** 1 Kin. chapters 17, 18; Jer. 14:1-6. *Sent by God as a judgment*, Deut. 28:23, 24; 1 Kin. 8:35; 2 Chr. 6:26; 7:13. **Figurative**, Psa. 32:4; Isa. 44:3.

‡ **MIZPAH** (*watch-tower*). *In Gilead*, Gen. 31:49. *Possibly identical with city of Gad in Gilead*, Judg. 10:17; 11:11, 29, 34.

v.53–1781 BC

r *Oath, a solemn qualification,* Num. 5:19.

54

s *Worship,* Gen. 22:5.

t *Offerings, burnt,* Lev. 6:17.

u *High Places,* 1 Kin. 3:2.

55

v *Rising, early,* Gen. 19:2.

w *Kiss, of affection,* Ruth 1:14.

x *Parents, blessing of,* 2 Cor. 12:14.

1

a *Jacob,* Gen. 27:11.

b *Angel,* Heb. 1:13.

3

c *Prudence, instances of,* 2 Chr. 2:12.

d *Esau,* Gen. 25:25.

e *Seir,* Deut. 1:2.

f *Edom,* Obad. 1.

4

g *Laban,* Gen. 28:5.

5

h *Ass,* 2 Chr. 28:15.

i *Servant,* Jer. 2:14.

And Jā'cob [r]sware[G] by the fear[G]
of his father Ī'ṣaac.
54 Then [d]Jā'cob [s]offered [t]sac-
rifice[G] upon the [u]mount, and
called his brethren to eat bread:
and they did eat bread, and tarried all night in the mount.
55 And [v]early in the morning
[b]Lā'ban rose up, and [w]kissed
his sons and his daughters, and
[x]blessed them: and Lā'ban departed, and returned unto his
place.

## CHAPTER 32

*Jacob's vision at Mahanaim. 3 His message to Esau. 6 He is afraid of Esau's coming. 9 He prays for deliverance. 13 He sends a present to Esau. 24 He wrestles with an angel at Peniel, where he is called Israel. 31 He halts upon his thigh.*

AND [a]Jā'cob went on his
way, and the [b]angels[G] of
God met him.
2 And when [a]Jā'cob saw [b]them,
he said, This *is* God's host: and
he called the name of that place
*Mā-hă-nā'im.
3 And [a]Jā'cob [c]sent messengers
before him to [d]Ē'sau his brother
unto the land of [e]Sē'ïr, the country of [f]Ē'dom.
4 And he commanded them,
saying, [c]Thus shall ye speak unto my lord [d]Ē'sau; Thy servant
[a]Jā'cob saith thus, I have sojourned with [g]Lā'ban, and
stayed there until now:
5 And I have oxen, and [h]asses,
flocks, and [i]menservants, and
womenservants: and I have sent
to tell my lord, that I may find
grace in thy sight.
6 ¶ And the messengers returned to [a]Jā'cob, saying, We
came to thy brother [d]Ē'sau, and
also he cometh to meet thee, and
four hundred men with him.
7 Then [a]Jā'cob was greatly
afraid and distressed: and [c]he
divided the people that *was* with
him, and the flocks, and herds,
and the camels, into two bands;
8 [c]And said, If [d]Ē'sau come to
the one company, and smite[G] it,
then the other company which is
left shall escape.
9 ¶ And [a]Jā'cob [j]said, O God of
my father Ā'bră-hăm, and God of
my father Ī'ṣaac, the LORD which
saidst unto me, Return unto thy
country, and to thy kindred, and
I will deal[G] well with thee:
10 [j,k]I am [l]not worthy of the
least of all the [m,n]mercies, and of
all the [o]truth, which thou hast
shewed unto thy servant; for
with my staff I passed over this
†Jôr'dan; and now I am become
two bands.[G S]
11 [j]Deliver me, I pray thee,
from the hand of my brother,
from the hand of [d]Ē'sau: for I
fear him, lest he will come and
smite me, *and* the mother with
the children.
12 And [p]thou saidst, I will surely
do thee good, and make thy [q]seed
as the sand of the sea, which cannot be numbered for multitude.[G Q]
13 ¶ And [a]he lodged there that
same night; and [c]took of that
which came to his hand a ‡pres-
ent for [d]Ē'sau his brother;

v.6–1781 BC
See footnote, *Time,* Rev. 10:6.

9

j *Prayer, exemplified,* vs. 9–12; Acts 6:4.

10

k *Thankfulness, exemplified,* Acts 24:3.

l *Humility, exemplified,* Prov. 22:4.

m *God, mercy of,* Gen. 2:2.

n *Temporal Blessings, from God,* Psa. 103:2.

o *God, truth,* Gen. 2:2.

12

p *Prayer, pleas offered in,* Acts 6:4.

q *Israel, prophecies concerning,* Ex. 4:22.

* **MAHANAIM** (*two hosts or companies*). *The place where Jacob had the vision of angels,* Gen. 32:2. *The town of, allotted to Gad,* Josh. 13:26, 30. *Given to sons of Merari,* 1 Chr. 6:80. *One of the Levitical cities,* Josh. 21:38. *Ishbosheth establishes himself at, when made king over Israel,* 2 Sam. 2:8–12. *David lodges at, at the time of Absalom's rebellion,* 2 Sam. 17:27–29; 1 Kin. 2:8.

† **JORDAN,** a river in Palestine. *Empties into the Dead Sea,* Josh. 15:5. *Fords of,* Gen. 32:10; Josh. 2:7; Judg. 3:28; 7:24; 8:4; 10:9; 12:5, 6; 2 Sam. 2:29; 17:22, 24; 19:15, 31; 1 Chr. 19:17. *Swelling of, at harvest time,* Josh. 3:15; Jer. 12:5; *and in the early spring,* 1 Chr. 12:15. *The waters of, miraculously separated for the passage of the Israelites,* Josh. 3:4; 5:1; Psa. 114:3; *of Elijah,* 2 Kin. 2:6–8; *of Elisha,* 2 Kin. 2:14. *Crossed by a ferryboat,* 2 Sam. 19:18. *Naaman washes in, for the healing of his leprosy,* 2 Kin. 5:10–14. *John the Baptist, baptizes in,* Matt. 3:6; Mark 1:5; John 1:28; *baptizes Jesus in.* Matt. 3:13; Mark 1:9.

**Plain of,** Gen. 13:10–12. *Israelites camped in,* Num. 21:1; 26:3, 63. *Solomon's foundry in,* 1 Kin. 7:46; 2 Chr. 4:17.

‡ **PRESENTS.** *To Abraham, by Abimelech,* Gen. 20:14. *To Rebekah,* Gen. 24:22. *To Esau,* Gen. 32:13–15. *By Joseph to his brethren,* Gen. 45:22; *to his father,* Gen. 45:23. *To Saul by Jesse,* 1 Sam. 16:20. *To prophets,* 1 Kin. 14:3; 2 Kin. 4:42. *To those in adversity,* Job 42:10, 11. *Kings to kings,* 2 Sam. 8:10; 1 Kin. 10:10, 13; 15:18, 19; 2 Kin. 20:12.

*On memorial days,* Neh. 8:10, 12; Esth. 9:19, 22; Rev. 11:10. *Betrothal,* Gen. 24:53. *Marriage,* Esth. 2:18. *Propitiatory,* Gen. 32:20; 33:8–11; 1 Sam. 25:27–35; Prov. 21:14. *To confirm covenants,* Gen. 21:28–30; 1 Sam. 18:3, 4. *To obtain favor,* 1 Sam. 25:27; Prov. 17:8; 18:16. *Rewards of service,* Dan. 5:7.

*To corrupt courts, forbidden,* Ex. 23:8; Deut. 16:19; 27:25; Isa. 5:23.

See footnote, BRIBERY, 1 Sam. 8:3.

v.14–1781 BC

14
r *Goat*, Deut. 14:4.
s *Sheep*, Deut. 32:14.

15
t *Milk*, Job 10:10.
u *Camel*, 1 Sam. 30:17.
v *Ass, domesticated*, 2 Chr. 28:15.

14 Two hundred she [r]goats, and twenty he goats, two hundred [s]ewes, and twenty rams,

15 Thirty [t]milch[C] [u]camels with their colts, forty kine[C], and ten bulls, twenty she [v]asses, and ten foals.

16 And [a]he delivered *them* into the hand of his [i]servants, every drove by themselves; and said unto his servants, Pass over before me, and put a space betwixt drove and drove.

17 And he commanded the foremost, saying, When [d]Ē'sau my brother meeteth thee, and asketh thee, saying, Whose *art* thou? and whither goest thou? and whose *are* these before thee?

18 [c]Then thou shalt say, *They be* thy servant [a]Jā'cob's; it *is* a [‡]present sent unto my lord [d]Ē'sau: and, behold, also he *is* behind us.

19 And so commanded he the second, and the third, and all that followed the droves, saying, On[C] this manner shall ye speak unto [d]Ē'sau, when ye find him.

20 And say ye moreover, Behold, thy servant [a]Jā'cob *is* behind us. For he said, [c]I will appease him with the [‡]present that goeth before me, and afterward I will see his face; peradventure[C] he will accept[C] of[C] me.

21 So went the [‡]present over before him: and himself lodged that night in the company.[C]

22 And he rose up that night, and took his two wives, and his two [i]womenservants, and his eleven sons, and passed over the ford [w]Jăb'bŏk.

22
w *Jabbok*, Num. 21:24.

23 And he took them, and sent them over the brook, and sent over that he had.

24 ¶ [T]And Jā'cob was left alone; and there [x]wrestled a man with him until the breaking of the day.

24
x *Wrestling, figurative*, Gen. 30:8.

25 And when he saw that he prevailed not against him, he touched the hollow of his thigh; and the hollow of Jā'cob's thigh was [1]out of joint, as he [x]wrestled with him.

26 And he said, Let me go, for the day breaketh. And he [y]said, [z]I will not let thee go, except thou bless me.

27 And he said unto him, What *is* thy [a]name? And he said, [b]Jā'cob.

28 And he said, Thy [a]name shall be called no more [b]Jā'cob, but ‖Iș'ra-el: for [2]as a prince hast thou [c]power with God and with men, and hast prevailed.

29 And [b]Jā'cob asked *him*, and said, Tell *me*, I pray thee, thy name. And he said, Wherefore *is* it *that* thou dost ask after my name?[S] And he [d]blessed him there.

30 And [b]Jā'cob called the name of the place [e]Pē-nī'el: for I have seen [f]God face to face, and my life is preserved.[T]

31 And as he passed over [e]Pē-nū'el the sun rose upon him, and he halted[C] upon his thigh.

32 Therefore the children of Iș'ra-el eat not *of* the sinew [3]which shrank, which *is* upon the hollow of the thigh, unto this day: because he touched the hollow of [b]Jā'cob's thigh in the sinew [3]that shrank.

v.25–1781 BC
See footnote, *Time*, Rev. 10:6.

25
1 R. V. strained,

26
y *Prayer, importunity in*, Acts 6:4.
z *Perseverance, instances of*, Eph. 6:18.

27
a *Name*, Prov. 22:1.
b *Jacob*, Gen. 27:11.

28
c *Spiritual Power*, Luke 24:49.
2 R. V. thou hast striven

29
d *Regeneration, instances of*, Titus 3:5.

30
e Or, *Penuel* (*the face of God*), Judg. 8:8, 9, 17; 1 Kin. 12:25.
f *God, appearances of*, Gen. 2:2.

32
3 R. V. of the hip

## CHAPTER 33

*The kindness of Jacob and Esau at their meeting. 17 Jacob comes to Succoth. 18 At Shalem he buys a field, and builds an altar called El-elohe-Israel.*

AND [a]Jā'cob lifted up his eyes, and looked, and, behold, [b]Ē'sau came, and with him four hundred men. And he divided the children unto [c]Lē'ah, and unto [d]Rā'chel, and unto the two [e]handmaids.

2 And he put the [e]handmaids

1
a *Jacob*, Gen. 27:11.
b *Esau*, Gen. 25:25.
c *Leah*, Gen. 29:16.
d *Rachel*, Gen. 29:6.
e *Servant*, Jer. 2:14.

‖ **ISRAEL** (*he who striveth with God*, or, *God striveth*). *A name given to Jacob*, Gen. 32:24-32; 35:10; 2 Kin. 17:34.

v.2–1781 BC
See footnote, *Time*, Rev. 10:6.

2
f *Partiality*, 1 Tim. 5:21.

3
g *Salutations*, Luke 1:44.

4
h *Brother, reconciled*, Prov. 18:24.
i *Forgiveness, instances of*, Matt. 18:21.
j *Reconciliation, between man and man*, 2 Cor. 5:18.
k *Kiss*, Ruth 1:14.
l *Weeping, instances of*, Ezra 3:13.

5
m *Children, gift of God*. Mark 10:14.

8
n *Presents, flocks and herds*, Gen. 32:13.
o *Conscience, accusing, instances of*, Acts 23:1.

9
p *Contentment, instances of*, 1 Tim. 6:6.

10
q *Flattery, instances of*, Prov. 6:24.

and their children foremost, and
[c]Lē'ah and her children after,
[f]and [d]Rā'chel and *Jō'ṣeph
hindermost.[G]
3 And he passed over before
them, and [g]bowed himself to the
ground seven times, until he
came near to his brother.
4 And [b,h]Ē'sa̤u ran to meet him,
and [i,j]embraced him, and fell on
his neck, and [k]kissed him: and
they [l]wept.
5 And he lifted up his eyes, and
saw the women and the children;
and said, Who *are* those with
thee? And he said, The [m]chil-
dren which God hath graciously
given thy servant.
6 Then the [e]handmaidens
came near, they and their
children, and they [g]bowed
themselves.
7 And [c]Lē'ah also with her children came near, and [g]bowed
themselves: and after came *Jō'-
ṣeph near and [d]Rā'chel, and
they [g]bowed themselves.
8 And [b]he said, What *meanest*
thou by all this drove which I
met? And [a]he said, [n,o]*These are*
to find grace in the sight of my
lord.
9 And [b]Ē'sa̤u said, [p]I have
enough, my brother; keep that
thou hast unto thyself.
10 And [a]Jā'cob said, Nay, I
pray thee, if now I have found
grace in thy sight, then receive
my [n]present at my hand: [q]for
therefore I have seen thy face,
as though I had seen the face of
God, and thou wast pleased
with me.
11 Take, I pray thee, my
[1,n]blessing that is brought to
thee; because God hath [r]dealt
graciously with me, and because
I have enough. And he urged
him, and he took *it*.
12 And he said, Let us take our
journey, and let us go, and I will
go before thee.
13 And [a]he said unto [b]him, My
lord knoweth that the children
*are* tender,[G] and the flocks and
herds with young *are* with me:
and [s]if men should overdrive
them one day, all the flock will
die.
14 Let my lord, I pray thee,
pass over before his servant: and
I will lead on softly, according
as the cattle that goeth before me
and the children be able to endure, until I come unto my lord
unto [t]Sē'ïr.
15 And [b]Ē'sa̤u said, Let me
now leave with thee *some* of the
folk that *are* with me. And [a]he
said, What needeth it? let me
find grace in the sight of my lord.
16 ¶ So [b]Ē'sa̤u returned that
day on his way unto [t]Sē'ïr.
17 And [a]Jā'cob journeyed to
[u]Sŭc'coth, and built him an
house, and made [v]booths[G] for his
cattle: therefore the name of the
place is called Sŭc'coth.
18 ¶ And Jā'cob came to Shā'-
lem, a city of [w]Shē'chem, which
*is* in the land of [x]Cā'năan, when
he came from [y]Pādan-ā'ram;

v.10–1731 BC
See footnote, *Time*, Rev. 10:6.

11
r *Prosperity, from God*, Eccl. 7:14.
1 R. V. gift

13
s *Animals, kindness to*, Jer. 27:5.

14
t *Seir*, Deut. 1:2.

17
u *Succoth*, Judg. 8:5.
v *Booth*, Lev. 23:42.

18
w *Shechem*, Josh. 20:7.
x *Canaan*, Gen. 37:1.
y *Padan-aram*, Gen. 28:2.

* **JOSEPH** (*increase*). *Son of Jacob*, Gen. 30:24. *Personal appearance of*, Gen. 39:6. *His father's favorite child*, Gen. 33:2; 37:3, 4, 35; 48:22; 1 Chr. 5:2; John 4:5. *His father's partiality for, excites the jealousy of his brethren*, Gen. 37:4, 11,18 28; Psa. 105:17; Acts 7:9. *His prophetic dreams of his fortunes in Egypt*, Gen. 37:5-11. *Sold into Egypt*, Gen. 37:27, 28; Psa. 105:17. *Is falsely reported to his father as killed by wild beasts*, Gen. 37:29-35. *Is bought by Potiphar, an officer of Pharaoh*, Gen. 37:36. *Is prospered of God*, Gen. 39:2-5, 21, 23. *Is falsely accused, and cast into prison; is delivered by the friendship of another prisoner*, Gen. 39; 40; 41; Psa. 105:18. *Is an interpreter of dreams: of the two prisoners*, Gen. 40:5-23; *of Pharaoh*, Gen. 41:1-37. *His name is changed to Zaphnath-paaneah, which signifies a revealer of secrets*, Gen. 41:45. *Is promoted to authority next to Pharaoh at thirty years of age*, Gen. 41:37-46; Psa. 105:19 22. *Takes to wife the daughter of the priest of On*, Gen. 41:45. *Provides against the years of famine*, Gen. 41:46-57. *Sells the stores of food to the people of Egypt, exacting of them all their money, flocks and herds, lands and lives*, Gen. 47:13 26. *Exempts the priests from the exactions*, Gen. 47:22, 26.

*His father sends down into Egypt to buy corn*, Gen. 42; 43; 44. *Reveals himself to his brethren; sends for his father; provides the land of Goshen for his people; and sustains them during the famine*, Gen. 45; 46; 47:1-12; Acts 7:13, 14. *His two sons*, Gen. 41:50-52. See footnotes: EPHRAIM, Gen. 41:52; MANASSEH, Gen. 46:20. *Mourns the death of his father*, Gen. 50:1 14. *Exacts a pledge from his brethren to convey his remains to Canaan*, Gen. 50:24, 25; Heb. 11:22 (with Ex. 13:19; Josh. 24:32; Acts 7:16). *Death of*, Gen. 50:22-26.

*Kindness of heart*, Gen. 40:7, 8. *His integrity*, Gen. 39, 7 12; *humility*, Gen. 41:16; 45:7-9; *wisdom*, Gen. 41:33-57 *piety*, Gen. 41:51, 52; *faith*, Gen. 45:5-8. *Was a prophet*, Gen. 41:38, 39; 50:25; Ex. 13:19. *God's providence with* Gen. 39:2 5; Psa. 105:17-22. *His sons conjointly called* JOSEPH, Deut. 33:13-17. *Descendants of*, Gen. 46:20 Num. 26:28-37.

v.18–1781 BC
See footnote, *Time,* Rev. 10:6.

19
z *Land,* Ruth 4:3.

a *Hamor,* Gen. 34:18.
b *Shechem,* Gen. 34:2.
c *Money,* Jer. 32:9.

20
d *Altar,* Gen. 8:20.
3 *That is,* God, the God of Israel.

and pitched his tent before the
city.
19 And he bought a parcel[C] of a
[z]field, where he had spread his
tent, at the hand of the children
of [a]Hā′mor, [b]Shē′chem's father,
for an hundred pieces of [c]money.[Q]
20 And he erected there an [d]al-
tar, and called it [3]Ĕl-e-lō′hĕ-
Iṣ′ra-el.

## CHAPTER 34

*Dinah is defiled by Shechem. 4 He sues to marry her. 13 The sons of Jacob offer the condition of circumcision to the Shechemites. 20 Hamor and Shechem persuade them to accept it. 25 The sons of Jacob upon that advantage slay them, 27 and spoil their city. 30 Jacob reproves Simeon and Levi.*

1
a Gen. 30:21.
b *Leah,* Gen. 29:16.
c *Jacob,* Gen. 27:11.

2
d *Hivites,* Gen. 10:17.
e *Seduction, instances of,* Deut. 22:23.
f *Adultery, instances of,* Lev. 20:10.
1 R. V. humbled

3
2 *Heb.* to the heart of the damsel.

4
g *Wife,* Prov. 5:18.

AND [a]Dī′nah the daughter
of [b]Lē′ah, which she bare
unto [c]Jā′cob, went out to see
the daughters of the land.
2 And when *Shē′chem the son
of ‖Hā′mor the [d]Hī′vīte, prince
of the country, saw her, he took
her, and [e, f]lay with her, and [1]de-
filed her.
3 And his soul clave[C] unto [a]Dī′-
nah the daughter of [c]Jā′cob, and
*he loved the damsel, and spake
[2]kindly unto the damsel.
4 And *Shē′chem spake unto
his father Hā′mor, saying, Get
me this damsel[C] to [g, †]wife.
5 And [c]Jā′cob heard that he
had defiled [a]Dī′nah his daughter: now his sons were with his
cattle in the field: and Jā′cob
[h]held his peace until they were
come.
6 ¶ And Hā′mor the father of
*Shē′chem went out unto [c]Jā′-
cob to commune[C] with him.
7 And the sons of Jā′cob came
out of the field when they heard
*it*: and the men were grieved,
and they were very [i]wroth,[C] because he had wrought folly[C] in
Iṣ′ra-el in [e, f]lying with Jā′cob's
daughter; which thing ought not
to be done.
8 And Hā′mor communed[C]
with them, saying, The soul of
my son *Shē′chem longeth for
your daughter: I pray you give
[j]her him to [g, †]wife.
9 And make ye †marriages with
us, *and* give your daughters
unto us, and take our daughters
unto you.
10 And ye shall dwell with us:
and the land shall be before you;
dwell and trade ye therein, and
get you possessions therein.
11 And *Shē′chem said unto
her father and unto her brethren, Let me find grace in your
eyes, and what ye shall say unto
me I will give.

5
h *Prudence, instances of,* 2 Chr. 2:12.

7
i *Anger, instances of,* Psa. 37:8.

8
j *Women, could not marry without consent of parents,* Prov. 31:10.

* **SHECHEM,** son of Hamor. *Seduces Jacob's daughter, slain by Jacob's sons,* Gen. 33:19; 34; Josh. 24:32; Judg. 9:28.

† **MARRIAGE.** *Divine institution of,* Gen. 2:18, 20–24; Matt. 19:4–6; Mark 10:7, 8; 1 Cor. 6:16; Eph. 5:31. *Based on law of nature,* 1 Cor. 11:11, 12 (with Gen. 2:18). *Unity of husband and wife in,* Gen. 2:23, 24; Matt. 19:5, 6; Mark 10:2–10; 1 Cor. 6:16; Eph. 5:31, 33. *Commended,* Prov. 18:22; Heb. 13:4. *Obligations under, inferior to duty to God,* Deut. 13:6–10; Matt. 19:29; Luke 14:26. *Indissoluble except for adultery,* Mal. 2:13–16; Matt. 5:31, 32; Mark 10:11, 12; Luke 16:18; Rom. 7:1–3; 1 Cor. 7:39, 40. *Dissolved by death,* Rom. 7:1–3. *Enjoined on exiled Jews,* Jer. 29:6. *Enjoined for sake of chastity,* 1 Cor. 7:1–7. *None in the resurrection state,* Matt. 22:29, 30; Mark 12:24, 25. *Levirate* (the brother required to marry a brother's widow), Gen. 38:8, 11; Deut. 25:5–10; Ruth 4:5; Matt. 22:24–27; Mark 12:19–23; Luke 20:28–33.

Mosaic laws concerning: *Of priests.* Lev. 21:1, 7, 13–15. *Of captives,* Deut. 21:10–14. *Of divorced persons,* Deut. 24:1–5. *Within tribes,* Num. 36:8. *Incestuous, forbidden,* Lev. 18:6–18 (with Deut. 22:30); 20:14, 17, 19–21; Mark 6:17, 18.

*Among antediluvians,* Gen. 6:2. *Among relatives, Abraham and Sarah,* Gen. 11:29; 12:13; 20:2, 9–16; *Isaac and Rebekah,* Gen. 24:3, 4, 67; *Jacob and his wives,* Gen. 28:2; 29:15–30.

Parents contract for their children: *Hagar selects a wife for Ishmael,* Gen. 21:21. *Abraham for Isaac,* Gen. 24. *Laban arranges for his daughters' marriage,* Gen. 29. *Samson asks his parents to procure him a wife,* Judg. 14:2. *Parents' consent required in the Mosaic law,* Ex. 22:17. *Presents given to parents to secure their favor,* Gen. 24:53; 34:12; 1 Sam. 18:25. *Nuptial feasts,* Gen. 29:22; Judg. 14:12; Esth. 2:18; Matt. 22:11, 12. *Jesus present at,* John 2:1–5. *Ceremony attested by witnesses,* Ruth 4:1–11; Isa. 8:1–3. *Bridegroom exempt one year from military duty,* Deut. 24:5. *Bridal ornaments,* Isa. 49:18; Jer. 2:32. *Bridal presents,* Gen. 24:53. *Herald preceded the bridegroom,* Matt. 25:6. *Wedding robes adorned with jewels,* Isa. 61:10. *Festivities attending,* Jer. 7:34; 16:9; 25:10; Rev. 18:23.

*Wives obtained by purchase,* Gen. 29:20, 27–29; 31:41; Ruth 4:10; 2 Sam. 3:14; Hos. 3:2; 12:12; *by kidnapping,* Judg. 21:21–23. *Given by Kings,* 1 Sam. 17:25; 18:17, 27. *Daughters given in, as rewards of valor,* Judg. 1:12; 1 Sam. 17:25; 18:27.

*Wives taken by edict,* Esth. 2:2–4, 8–14.

*Wives among the Israelites must be Israelites,* Ex. 34:16; Deut. 7:3, 4; Ezra 9:1, 2, 12; Neh. 10:30; 13:26, 27; Mal. 2:11. *Betrothal a quasi-marriage,* Matt. 1:18; Luke 1:27. *Discouraged among the Corinthians,* 1 Cor. 7:8, 9, 25–40 (with v. 1). *Celibacy deplored,* Judg. 11:38; Isa. 4:1. *Unhappiness in,* Prov. 21:9, 19.

*Of widows,* Rom. 7:1–3; 1 Cor. 7:39, 40; 1 Tim. 5:14. *Of ministers,* Lev. 21:7, 8, 13, 14; Ezek. 44:22; 1 Cor. 9:5; 1 Tim. 3:2, 12. *Prophecies concerning the forbidding of,* 1 Tim. 4:1, 3.

**Figurative,** Isa. 54:5; 62:4, 5; Jer. 3:14; 31:32; Ezek. 16:8; Hos. 2:19, 20; Eph. 5:23–32; Rev. 19:7–9. *Parables of,* Matt. 22:2–10; 25:1–10; Mark 2:19, 20; John 3:29; 2 Cor. 11:2.

See footnotes: BRIDE, Isa. 49:18; BRIDEGROOM, Isa. 61:10; DIVORCE, Matt. 19:7; HUSBAND, Num. 30:6; **WIFE,** Prov. 5:18.

12 Ask me never so much ‡dowry and gift, and I will give according as ye shall say unto me: but give me the [a,i]damsel to [g]†wife.

13 And the sons of [c]Jā′cob answered *Shē′chem and ‖Hā′mor his father [k]deceitfully, and said, because he had defiled [a]Dī′nah their sister:

14 And they said unto them, We cannot do this thing, to give our sister to one that is uncircumcised; for that *were* a reproach unto us:

15 But in this will we consent unto you: [k]If ye will be as we *be*, that every male of you be [l]circumcised;

16 [k,m]Then will we give our daughters unto you, and we will take your daughters to us, and we will dwell with you, and we will become one people.

17 But if ye will not hearken unto us, to be [l]circumcised; then will we take our daughter, and we will be gone.

18 And their words pleased ‖Hā′mor, and *Shē′chem Hā′mor's son.

19 And the young man deferred not to do the thing, because he had delight in [c]Jā′cob's [a]daughter: and he *was* more honourable than all the house of his father.

20 And ‖Hā′mor and *Shē′chem his son came unto the [n]gate of their city, and communed with the men of their city, saying,

21 These men *are* peaceable with us; therefore let them dwell in the land, and trade therein; for the land, behold, *it is* large enough for them; let us †take their daughters to us for wives, and let us give them our daughters.

22 Only herein will the men consent unto us for to dwell with us, to be one people, if every male among us be [l]circumcised, as they *are* circumcised.

23 *Shall* not their cattle and their substance and every beast of their's *be* our's? only let us consent unto them, and they will dwell with us.

24 And unto ‖Hā′mor and unto *Shē′chem his son hearkened all that went out of the [n]gate of his city; and every male was [l]circumcised, all that went out of the gate of his city.

25 ¶ And it came to pass on the third day, when they were sore, that two of the sons of [c]Jā′cob, [o]Sĭm′e-on and [p]Lē′vī, Dī′nah's brethren, took each man his [q]sword, and came upon the city [3]boldly, and [r,s]slew all the males.

26 And they [r,s]slew ‖Hā′mor and *Shē′chem his son with the edge of the [q]sword, and took Dī′nah out of Shē′chem's house, and went out.

27 The sons of Jā′cob came upon the slain, and [t]spoiled the city, because they had [e,i]defiled their sister.

28 They took their [t]sheep, and their oxen, and their asses, and that which *was* in the city, and that which *was* in the field.

29 And all their wealth, and all their little ones, and their wives took they captive, and [t]spoiled even all that *was* in the house.

30 And [c]Jā′cob said to [o]Sĭm′e-on and [p]Lē′vī, Ye have troubled me to make me to stink among the inhabitants of the land, among the [u]Cā′năan-ītes and the [v]Pĕr′ĭz-zītes: and I *being* few in number, they shall gather themselves together against me, and slay me; and I shall be destroyed, I and my house.

31 And they said, Should he

13 *k Deception, instances of*, Josh. 9:4.

15 *l Circumcision*, Gen. 17:10.

16 *m Covenant, of men with men*, Deut. 29:1.

20 *n Gates*, Deut. 3:5.

25 *o Simeon*, Gen. 29:33.
*p Levi*, Gen. 29:34.
*q Sword*, 1 Chr. 21:5.
*r Homicide, instances of felonious*, Deut. 5:17.
*s Revenge, instances of*, Ezek. 25:15.
3 R. V. unawares.

27 *t Spoils*, 1 Chr. 26:27.

30 *u Canaanites*, Ex. 23:28.
*v Perizzites*, Gen. 15:20.

‡ **DOWRY.** *Sum paid to parents for a daughter taken as wife.* Gen. 34:12; Ex. 22:16, 17; 1 Sam. 18:25.
‖ **HAMOR,** father of Shechem. *Jacob buys ground from children of*, Gen. 33:19; Josh. 24:32; Judg. 9:28. (In Acts 7:16, this purchase is attributed to Abraham.) *Murdered by the sons of Jacob*, Gen. 34:26; 49:6.

deal with our sister as with an harlot?

## CHAPTER 35

*God sends Jacob to Bethel. 2 Jacob puts away the strange gods from his household. 6 He builds an altar at Bethel. 8 Deborah dies. 9 God blesses Jacob at Bethel. 16 Rachel travails with Benjamin, and dies in the way to Bethlehem. 23 The sons of Jacob. 27 Jacob comes to Isaac at Hebron. 28 The age, death, and burial of Isaac.*

AND God said unto [a]Jā'cob, Arise, go up to [b]Bĕth'el, and dwell there: and [c,d]make there an [e]altar unto God, that appeared unto thee when thou fleddest from the face of [f]Ē'sau thy brother.

2 Then [a]Jā'cob said unto his household, and to all that *were* with him, [g]Put away the strange[c] [h]gods that *are* among you, and [1,i,j]be clean, and change your garments:

3 And let [k]us arise, and go up to [b]Bĕth'el; and [l]I will make there an [e]altar unto God, [m]who answered me in the day of my distress, and was with me in the way which I went.

4 And they gave unto [a]Jā'cob all the strange[c] [h]gods which *were* in their hand, and *all their* [n,o]earrings which *were* in their ears; and Jā'cob hid them under the [2,*]oak which *was* by [p]Shē'chem.

5 And they journeyed: and the terror of God was upon the cities that *were* round about them, and they did not pursue after the sons of [a]Jā'cob.

6 ¶ So [a]Jā'cob came to Lŭz, which *is* in the land of [q]Cā'năan, that *is*, [b]Bĕth'el, he, and all the people that *were* with him.[T]

7 And he built there an [e]altar, and called the place [3]Ĕl-bĕth'-el: because there God appeared unto him, when he fled from the face of his brother.

8 But [r]Dĕb'o-rah [s]Rē-bĕk'ah's [t]nurse died, and she was buried beneath [b]Bĕth'el [u]under an [*]oak: and the name of it was called [4]Ăl'lŏn-băch'ụth.

9 ¶ And [v]God appeared unto [a]Jā'cob again, when he came out of [w]Pā'dan-ā'ram, and [x]blessed him.

10 And God said unto him, Thy [y]name *is* Jā'cob: thy name shall not be called any more Jā'-cob, but [z]Ĭs'ra-el shall be thy name: and he called his name Ĭs'ra-el.

11 And God said unto him, I *am* [5,a]God Almighty: be fruitful and multiply; a [b]nation and a company of nations shall be of thee, and kings shall come out of thy loins[c];

12 And the [c]land which I gave [d]Ā'bră-hăm and [e]Ī'ṣaac, to thee I will give it, and to thy seed after thee will I give the land.[Q]

13 And God went up from him in the place where he [f]talked with him.

14 And [g]Jā'cob set up a [h]pillar in the place where he talked with him, *even* a pillar of stone: and he poured a drink [i]offering thereon, and he [j]poured [k]oil thereon.

15 And [g]Jā'cob called the name of the place where God [f]spake with him, [l]Bĕth'el.

16 ¶ And they journeyed from [l]Bĕth'el; and there was but a little way to come to [m]Ĕph'răth: and [n]Rā'chel travailed[c], and she had hard labour.

17 And it came to pass, when [n]she was in hard labour, that the [†]midwife said unto her, Fear not; thou shalt have this son also.

18 And it came to pass, as [n]her soul was in departing, (for she [o]died) that she called his name [6]Bĕnō'nī: but his father called him [‡]Bĕn'ja-mĭn.

19 And [n]Rā'chel [o]died, and

**1**
a *Jacob*, Gen. 27:11.
b *Bethel*, Josh. 18:13.
c *Commandments, enjoining worship*, Deut. 8:2.
d *Worship, enjoined*, Gen. 22:5.
e *Altar*, Gen. 8:20.
f *Esau*, Gen. 25:25.

**2**
g *Idolatry, denounced*, 1 Sam. 15:23.
h *Teraphim, idol*, Judg. 17:5.
i *Holiness, enjoined*, Ex. 39:30.
j *Purification*, Num. 19:19.
1 R. V. purify yourselves,

**3**
k *Family Worship*, 1 Sam. 1:19.
l *Thankfulness, to God*, Acts 24:3.
m *God, preserver*, Gen. 2:2.

**4**
n *Earring*, Prov. 25:12.
o *Jewels*, Gen. 24:53.
p *Shechem*, Josh. 20:7.
2 *Or*, terebinth

**6**
q *Canaan*, Gen. 37:1.

**7**
3 *That is*, the God of Bethel:

**8**
r Gen. 24:59.
s *Rebekah*, Gen. 24:15.
t *Nurse*, 2 Chr. 22:11.
u *Burying Places*, Gen. 23:4.
4 *That is*, the oak of weeping.

**9**
v *God, appearance of*, Gen. 2:2.
w *Padan-aram*, Gen. 28:2.
x *Temporal Blessings, from God*, Psa. 103:2.

**10**
y *Name*, Prov. 22:1.
z *Israel*, Gen. 32:28.

**11**
a *God, omnipotent*, Gen. 2:2.
b *Israel, prophecies concerning*, Ex. 4:22.
5 *Heb.* El Shaddai:

**12**
c *Canaan*, Gen. 37:1.
d *Abraham*, Gen. 17:5.
e *Isaac*, Gen. 21:3.

**13**
f *Communion, with God*, 2 Cor. 13:14.

**14**
g *Jacob*, Gen. 27:11.
h *Pillar*, Gen. 28:18.
i *Offerings, drink*, Lev. 6:17.
j *Anointing, in consecration*, Lev. 8:12.
k *Oil*, Deut. 12:17.

**15**
l *Bethel*, Josh. 18:13.

**16**
m Or, *Bethlehem*, Gen. 48:7.
n *Rachel*, Gen. 29:6.

**18**
o *Death*, Num. 23:10.
6 *That is*, the son of my sorrow:

* **OAK**, a tree. *Grew in Palestine*, Gen. 35:4. *Absalom hung in the boughs of*, 2 Sam. 18:9, 14. *Deborah buried under*, Gen. 35:8. *Oars made of*, Ezek. 27:6. **Figurative**, Amos 2:9.

† **MIDWIFERY**, Gen. 35:17; Ex. 1:15-21; Ezek. 16:4.
‡ **BENJAMIN** (*son of the right hand*). *Son of Jacob by Rachel*, Gen. 35:18, 24; 46:19. *Taken into Egypt*, Gen. chapters 42-45. *Prophecy concerning*, Gen. 49:27. *De-*

was [p]buried in the way to Ĕph'-
răth, which *is* [m]Bĕth'lĕ-hĕm.
20 And Jā'cob set a [h]pillar
upon her grave: that *is* the pillar
of [n]Rā'chel's grave unto this day.
21 ¶ And Ī̤s'ra-el journeyed,
and spread his [q]tent beyond the
[r]tower of [s]Ē'där.
22 And it came to pass, when
Ī̤s'ra-el dwelt in that land, that
‖Reu̇'ben went and [t]lay with
[u]Bĭl'hah his father's [v]concubine:
and Ī̤s'ra-el heard *it*. Now the
sons of Jā'cob were twelve:
23 [w]The sons of [x]Lē'ah; ‖Reu̇'-
ben, Jā'cob's [y]firstborn, and
[z]Sĭm'e-on, and [a]Lē'vī, and [b]Jū'-
dah, and [c]Ĭs'sa-char, and [d]Zĕb'-
u-lŭn:
24 [e]The sons of [f]Rā'chel; [g]Jō'-
s̤eph, and ‡Bĕn'ja-mĭn:
25 [ε]And the sons of [h]Bĭl'hah,
[f]Rā'chel's [i]handmaid; [j]Dăn, and
[k]Năph'ta-lī:
26 And the sons of [l]Zĭl'pah,
[m]Lē'ah's [i]handmaid; [n]Găd, and
[o]Āsh'ēr: these *are* the sons of
[p]Jā'cob, which were born to him
in [q]Pā'dan-ā'ram.
27 ¶ And [p]Jā'cob came unto
[r]Ī's̤aac his father unto [s]Măm'rē,
unto the city of Är'bah, which *is*
[t]Hē'bron, where [u]Ā'bră-hăm
and Ī's̤aac sojourned.[Q]
28 And the days of [r]Ī's̤aac were
[v]an hundred and fourscore years.
29 And [r]Ī's̤aac [w]gave up the
ghost,[C] and died, and was gathered unto his people, *being* [v]old
and full of days: and his sons
[x]Ē's̤au and [p]Jā'cob [y]buried him.

## CHAPTER 36

*Esau's family in Canaan. 6 He removes to Mount Seir. 9 His descendants in Seir. 20 The sons and dukes of Seir. 31 The kings of Edom. 40 The dukes that descended of Esau.*

NOW these *are* the [a]genera-
tions of [b]Ē's̤au, who *is* Ē'dom.
2 [b]Ē's̤au took his [c]wives of the
[d]daughters of Cā'năan; Ā'dah
the daughter of [e]Ē'lŏn the [f]Hĭt'-
tīte, and Ā-hŏl-i-bā'mah the
daughter of Ā'nah the daughter
of Zĭb'e-on the [g]Hī'vīte;
3 And [h]Băsh'e-măth [i]Ĭsh'ma-
el's daughter, sister of [j]Nē-bā'-
joth.
4 And Ā'dah bare to [b]Ē's̤au
[k]Ĕl'i-phăz; and [h]Băsh'e-măth
bare [l]Reu̇'el;
5 And Ā-hŏl-i-bā'mah bare
[k]Jē'ŭsh, and [k]Jā-ā'lam, and
Kō'rah: these *are* the sons of
[b]Ē's̤au, which were born unto
him in the land of [m]Cā'năan.
6 And [b]Ē's̤au took his [c]wives,
and his sons, and his daughters,
and all the persons of his house,
and his cattle, and all his beasts,
and all his substance, which he
had got in the land of [m]Cā'năan;
and went into the country from
the face of his brother [n]Jā'cob.
7 For their riches were more
than that they might dwell together; and the land wherein
they were strangers could not
bear them because of their
cattle.
8 Thus dwelt Ē's̤au in mount
[o]Sē'īr: Ē's̤au *is* Ē'dom.
9 ¶ And these *are* the [a]genera-
tions of [b]Ē's̤au the father of the
[p]Ē'dom-ītes in mount [o]Sē'īr:
10 [a]These *are* the names of
Ē's̤au's sons; [k]Ĕl'i-phăz the son
of Ā'dah the wife of Ē's̤au,
[l]Reu̇'el the son of [h]Băsh'e-măth
the wife of Ē's̤au.
11 And [a]the sons of [k]Ĕl'i-phăz
were [q]Tē'man, [r]Ō'mar, [s]Zē'phō,
and [r]Gā'tam, and [r]Kē'năz.
12 And Tĭm'na was [t]concubine
to [k]Ĕl'i-phăz Ē's̤au's son; and
she bare to Ĕl'i-phăz [r]Ăm'a-lĕk:
these *were* the sons of Ā'dah
Ē's̤au's wife.
13 And these *are* the sons of

19
p *Burial*, Acts 8:2.
21
q *Tent*, Gen. 13:5.
r *Tower*, 2 Chr. 26:9.
s Mic. 4:8 (marg.)
22
*Incest, instances of*, Lev. 18:6.
u *Bilhah*, Gen. 29:29.
v *Concubinage*, 2 Sam. 21:11.
23
w *Genealogy*, vs. 23–26; 1 Chr. 5:1.
x *Leah*, Gen. 29:16.
y *Firstborn*, Zech. 12:10.
z *Simeon*, Gen. 29:33.
a *Levi*, Gen. 29:34.
b *Judah*, Gen. 37:26.
c *Issachar*, Gen. 30:18.
d *Zebulun*, Gen. 30:20.
24
e *Genealogy*, 1 Chr. 5:1.
f *Rachel*, Gen. 29:6.
g *Joseph*, Gen. 33:2.
25
h *Bilhah*, Gen. 29:29.
i *Servant*, Jer. 2:14.
j *Dan*, Gen. 30:6.
k *Naphtali*, Gen. 30:8.
26
l *Zilpah*, Gen. 29:24.
m *Leah*, Gen. 29:16.
n *Gad*, Gen. 30:11.
o *Asher*, Gen. 30:13.
p *Jacob*, Gen. 27:11.
q *Padan-aram*, Gen. 28:2.
27
r *Isaac*, Gen. 21:3.
s *Mamre*, Gen. 13:18.
t *Hebron*, Gen. 23:2.
u *Abraham*, Gen. 17:5.
28
v *Longevity, instances of*, Psa. 91:16.
v.29–1758 BC
29
w *Death, described*, Num. 23:10.
x *Esau*, Gen. 25:25.
y *Burial*, Acts 8:2.
1
a *Genealogy, of Esau*, vs. 1–43; 1 Chr. 5:1.
b *Esau*, Gen. 25:25.
c *Polygamy*, Deut. 17:17.

d *Canaanites*, Ex. 23:28.
e Gen. 26:34.
f *Hittites*, Judg. 1:26.
g *Hivites*, Gen. 10:17.
3
h Or, *Mahalath*, Gen. 28:9.
i *Ishmael*, Gen. 16:11.
j Gen. 25:13.
4
k 1 Chr. 1:35.
l 1 Chr. 1.35, 37.
5
m *Canaan*, Gen. 37:1.
6
n *Jacob*, Gen. 27:11.
8
o *Seir*, Deut. 1:2.
9
p *Edomites*, 2 Kin. 8:21.
11
q 1 Chr. 1:36, 53.
r 1 Chr. 1:36.
s Or, *Zephi*, 1 Chr. 1:36.
12
t *Concubinage*, 2 Sam. 21:11.

scendants of, Gen 46:21: Num. 26:38–41: 1 Chr. 7:6–12. TRIBE OF, see footnote, BENJAMIN, *Tribe of*, Num. 1:37.
‖ **REUBEN.** *Son of Jacob*, Gen. 29:32; 1 Chr. 2:1. *Brings mandrakes to his mother*, Gen. 30:14. *Commits incest with one of his father's concubines, and, in consequence, forfeits the birthright*, Gen. 35:22; 49:4, 1 Chr. 5:1. *Adroitly*

13
u 1 Chr. 1:37.

16
v Edom, Obad. 1.

20
w 1 Chr. 1:38.
x 1 Chr 1:38, 39.
y 1 Chr. 1:38, 40.
z 1 Chr. 1:38, 42.

22
a 1 Chr. 1:38, 39.

[l]Reu̥'el; [u]Nā'hăth, and [u]Zē'rah, [u]Shăm'mah, and [u]Mĭz'zah: these were the sons of [h]Băsh'e-măth [b]Ē'sau̥'s wife.

14 And [a]these were the sons of Ȧ-hŏl-i-bā'mah, the daughter of Ā'nah the daughter of Zĭb'e-on, [b]Ē'sau̥'s wife: and she bare to Ē'sau̥ [k]Jē'ŭsh, and [k]Jȧ-ā'lam, and Kō'rah.

15 ¶ These *were* *dukes[G] of the sons of Ē'sau̥: the sons of [k]Ĕl'i-phăz the firstborn *son* of Ē'sau̥; duke[G] [q]Tē'man, duke [r]Ō'mar, duke[G] [s]Zē'phō, duke [r]Kē'năz,

16 Duke Kō'rah, duke [r]Gā'tam, *and* duke [r]Ăm'a-lĕk: these *are* the dukes *that came* of [k]Ĕl'i-phăz in the land of [v]Ē'dom; these *were* the sons of Ā'dah.

17 And these *are* the sons of [l]Reu̥'el Ē'sau̥'s son; duke [u]Nā'hăth, duke [u]Zē'rah, duke [u]Shăm'mah, duke [u]Mĭz'zah: these *are* the *dukes *that came* of Reu̥'el in the land of [v]Ē'dom; these *are* the sons of [h]Băsh'e-măth [b]Ē'sau̥'s wife.

18 And these *are* the sons of Ȧ-hŏl-i-bā'mah [b]Ē'sau̥'s wife; duke [k]Jē'ŭsh, duke [k]Jȧ-ā'lam, duke Kō'rah: these *were* the *dukes *that came* of Ȧ-hŏl-i-bā'mah the daughter of Ā'nah, Ē'sau̥'s wife.

19 These *are* the sons of [b]Ē'sau̥, who *is* Ē'dom, and these *are* their *dukes.

20 ¶ These *are* the sons of [w]Sē'ĭr the Hō'rīte, who inhabited the land; [x]Lō'tan, and [y]Shō'bal, and [y]Zĭb'e-on, and [w]Ā'nah,

21 And [w]Dī'shon, and [z]Ē'zĕr, and [w]Dī'shan: these *are* the dukes of the Hō'rītes, the children of [w]Sē'ĭr in the land of [v]Ē'dom.

22 And the children of [a]Lō'tan were [b]Hō'rī and [c]Hē'mam; and Lō'tan's sister *was* [b]Tĭm'nȧ.

23 And the children of [d]Shō'bal *were* these; [e]Ăl'van, and [f]Măn'a-hăth, and [f]Ē'bal, [g]Shē'phō, and [f]Ō'nam.

24 And these *are* the children of [d]Zĭb'e-on; both [h]Ā'jah, and [i]Ā'nah: this *was that* Ā'nah that found the [1]mules in the wilderness, as he fed the asses of Zĭb'e-on his father.

25 And the children of [i]Ā'nah *were* these; [j]Dī'shon, and Ȧ-hŏl-i-bā'mah the daughter of Ā'nah.

26 And these *are* the children of [j]Dī'shon; [k]Hĕm'dan, and [j]Ĕsh'ban, and [j]Ĭth'ran, and [j]Chē'ran.

27 The children of [l]Ē'zĕr *are* these; [m]Bĭl'han, and [m]Zā'a-văn, and [n]Ā'kăn.

28 The children of [o]Dī'shan *are* these; [p]Ŭz, and [p]Ā'răn.

29 These *are* the *dukes *that came* of the Hō'rītes; duke Lō'tan, duke [d]Shō'bal, duke [d]Zĭb'e-on, duke[G] [o]Ā'nah,

30 Duke[G] [o]Dī'shon, duke [o]Ē'zĕr, duke[G] [o]Dī'shan: these *are* the dukes[G] *that came* of Hō'rī, among their dukes in the land of Sē'ĭr.

31 ¶ And these *are* the [q]kings that reigned in the land of [r]Ē'dom, before there reigned any king over the children of [s]Ĭs̤'ra-el.

32 And [t]Bē'lȧ the son of [u]Bē'or reigned in Ē'dom: and the name of his city *was* [u]Dĭn'ha-bah.

33 And [t]Bē'lȧ died, and [v]Jō'băb the son of [w]Zē'rah of †Bŏz'rah reigned in his stead.

34 And [v]Jō'băb died, and [x]Hū'sham of the land of Tĕm'a-nī reigned in his stead.

35 And [x]Hū'sham died, and [y]Hā'dăd the son of Bē'dăd, who smote [z]Mĭd'ī-an in the field of [a]Mō'ab, reigned in his stead:

b 1 Chr. 1:39.
c Or, *Homam*, 1 Chr. 1:39.

23
d 1 Chr. 1:38, 40.
e Or, *Alian*, 1 Chr. 1:40.
f 1 Chr. 1:40.
g Or, *Shephi*, 1 Chr. 1:40.

24
h Or, *Aiah*, 1 Chr. 1:40
i 1 Chr. 1:40, 41.
1 R. V. hot springs

25
j 1 Chr. 1:41.

26
k Or, *Amram*. 1 Chr. 1:41.

27
l 1 Chr. 1:38, 42.
m 1 Chr. 1:42.
n Or, *Jaakan*, Deut. 10:6; or, *Jakan*, 1 Chr. 1:42.

28
o 1 Chr. 1:38.
p 1 Chr. 1:42.

31
q *Rulers*, Ex. 18:21.
r *Edom*, Obad. 1.
s *Israel*, Ex. 4:22.

32
t 1 Chr. 1:43, 44.
u 1 Chr. 1:43.

33
v 1 Chr. 1:44, 45.
w 1 Chr. 1:44.

34
x 1 Chr. 1:45, 46.

35
y 1 Chr. 1:46.
z *Midianites*, Gen. 37:28.
a *Moab*, Num. 26:3.

*seeks to save Joseph from the conspiracy of his brothers*, Gen. 37:21-30; 42:22. *Offers to become surety for Benjamin*, Gen. 42:37. *Jacob's prophetic benediction upon*, Gen. 49:3, 4. *His children*, Gen. 46.9; Ex. 6:14; 1 Chr. 5:3-6; Num. 16:1. TRIBE OF, see footnote, REUBENITES, *Tribe of*, Josh. 22:1

* **DUKE.** *Title of the princes, of Edom*, Gen. 36:15-43; Ex. 15:15; 1 Chr. 1:51-54; *of the Midianites*, Josh. 13:21.
† **BOZRAH** (*fortress*). *A city of Edom*, Gen. 36:33; 1 Chr. 1:44. *Sheep of*, Mic. 2:12. *Prophecies concerning*, Isa. 34:6; 63:1; Jer. 49:13, 22; Amos. 1:12.

and the name of his city *was*
[b]Ā′vĭth.
36 And [b]Hā′dăd died, and
[c]Săm′lah of [d]Măs′re-kah reigned
in his stead.
37 And [c]Săm′lah died, and
[e]Sa̤ul of [f]Rē-hō′both *by* the
river reigned in his stead.
38 And [e]Sa̤ul died, and [g]Bā′al-
hā′nan the son of [h]Ăch′bôr
reigned in his stead.
39 And [g]Bā′al-hā′nan the son
of [h]Ăch′bôr died, and [i]Hā′där
reigned in his stead: and the
name of his city *was* [j]Pā′u; and
his wife's name *was* [k]Mĕ-hĕt′a-
bĕl, the daughter of [k]Mā′tred,
the daughter of [k]Mĕz′a-hăb.
40 ¶ And these *are* the names of
the dukes[C] *that came* of [l]Ē′sa̤u,
according to their families, after
their places, by their names;
duke [m]Tĭm′nah, duke [n]Ăl′vah,
duke [m]Jē′theth,
41 Duke[C] Ā-hŏl-i-bā′mah, duke[C]
[o]Ē′lah, duke[C] [o]Pī′non,
42 Duke[C] [p]Kē′năz, duke[C] [p]Tē′-
man, duke[C] [p]Mĭb′zär,
43 Duke[C] [q]Măg′dĭ-el, duke[C]
[q]Ī′ram: these *be* the dukes[C] of
Ē′dom, according to their habitations in the land of their possession: he *is* [l]Ē′sa̤u the father of
the [r]Ē′dom-ītes.

## CHAPTER 37

*Joseph is hated of his brethren. 5 His two dreams. 13 Jacob sends him to visit his brethren. 18 His brethren conspire to slay him. 21 Reuben saves him. 26 They sell him to the Ishmaelites. 31 His father, deceived by the bloody coat, mourns for him. 36 He is sold to Potiphar in Egypt.*

AND [a]Jā′cob dwelt in the
land wherein his father
was a stranger,[C] in the land
of *Cā′năan.

b 1 Chr. 1:46.
**36**
c 1 Chr. 1:47, 48.
d 1 Chr. 1:47.
**37**
e Or, *Shaul*, 1 Chr. 1:48, 49.
f 1 Chr. 1:48, 49.
**38**
g 1 Chr. 1:49, 50.
h 1 Chr. 1:49.
i Or, *Hadad*, 1 Chr. 1:50.
j Or, *Pai*, 1 Chr. 1:50.
k 1 Chr. 1:50.
**40**
l *Esau*, Gen. 25:25.
m 1 Chr. 1:51.
n Or, *Aliah*, 1 Chr. 1:51.
**41**
o 1 Chr. 1:52.
**42**
p 1 Chr. 1:53.
**43**
q 1 Chr. 1:54.
r *Edomites*, 2 Kin. 8:21.

**v.1–1770 BC**
See footnote, *Time*, Rev. 10:6.
**1**
a *Jacob*, Gen. 27:11.

2 These *are* the generations of
[a]Jā′cob. [b]Jō′s̤eph, *being* seventeen years old, was feeding the
flock with his brethren; and the
lad *was* with the sons of [c]Bĭl′-
hah, and with the sons of [d]Zĭl′-
pah, his father's [e]wives: and Jō′-
s̤eph [f]brought unto his father
their evil report.
3 Now [a,g]Ĭs̤′ra-el loved [b]Jō′-
s̤eph [h]more than all his [i]children,
because he *was* the son of his old
age: and he made him [1]a coat of
*many* colours.
4 And when his brethren saw
that their [a,g]father loved him
[h,i]more than all his brethren,
they [j,k,l]hated him, and could
not speak peaceably unto him.
5 ¶ And [b]Jō′s̤eph dreamed a
[m]dream, and he told *it* his brethren: and they [j]hated him yet the
more.
6 And he said unto them, Hear,
I pray you, this [m]dream which I
have dreamed:
7 For, behold, we *were* binding
sheaves in the field, and, lo, my
sheaf arose, and also stood upright; and, behold, your sheaves
stood round about, and made
obeisance[C] to my sheaf.
8 And his brethren said to him,
Shalt thou indeed reign over us?
or shalt thou indeed have dominion over us? And they
[j,k,l]hated him yet the more for
his [m]dreams, and for his
words.
9 And he dreamed yet another
[m]dream, and told it his brethren,
and said, Behold, I have
dreamed a dream more; and,
behold, the [n]sun and the [o]moon

**v.2–1770 BC**
See footnote, *Time*, Rev. 10:6.
**2**
b *Joseph*, Gen. 33:2.
c *Bilhah*, Gen. 29:29.
d *Zilpah*, Gen. 29:24.
e *Concubinage*, 2 Sam. 21:11.
f *Talebearing*, Prov. 11:13.
**3**
g *Parents, partiality of*, 2 Cor. 12:14.
h *Partiality*, 1 Tim. 5:21.
i *Children, partiality of parents among*, Mark 10:14.
1 *Or*, a long garment with sleeves.
**4**
j *Hatred*, Prov. 15:17.
k *Jealousy, instances of*, Psa. 78:58.
l *Envy, instances of*, Prov. 14:30.
**5**
m *Dream, instances of*, Dan. 1:17.
**9**
n *Sun*, Josh. 10:12.
o *Moon*, Song 6:10.

***CANAAN** (*lowland*). **Land of**, Gen. 11:31; 17:8; 23:2. *Called* THE SANCTUARY, Ex. 15:17; LAND OF ISRAEL, 1 Sam. 13:19; LAND OF THE HEBREWS, Gen. 40:15; LAND OF THE JEWS, Acts 10:39; LAND OF PROMISE, Heb. 11:9; HOLY LAND, Zech. 2:12; JEHOVAH'S LAND, Hos. 9:3; IMMANUEL'S LAND, Isa. 8:8; BEULAH, Isa. 62:4.

*Promised to Abraham and his seed*, Gen. 12:1-7; 13:14-17; 15:7, 18-21; 17:8; 22:17; 24:7; 28:4; 35:12; Deut. 12:9, 10; 34:4; Psa. 105:10, 11; 15:11: 12;23; Ezek. 23:40; 47:14; Acts 7:5; Gal. 3:16. *Promise renewed to Isaac*, Gen. 26:3; *to Jacob*, Gen. 28:13; 35:12; Psa. 105:10, 11. *Given to the Israelites*, Ex. 3:8; 6:4, 8; 13:5, 11; Lev. 20:24. Psa. 135:11, 12. Extent of: *According to the promise*, Gen. 15:18; Ex. 23:31; Deut. 11:24; Josh. 1:4; 15:1; *after the conquest by Joshua*, Josh. 12:1-8; *in Solomon's time*, 1 Kin. 4:21, 24; 2 Chr. 7:8; 9:26. *Prophecy concerning, after the restoration of Israel*, Ezek. 47:13-20.

*Fertility of*, Deut. 8:7-9; 11:10-15. *Fruitfulness of, flowing with milk and honey*, Ex. 3:8, 17; 13:5; 33:3; Lev. 20:24; Num. 13:27; 14:7, 8; Deut. 26:9, 15; Jer. 2:7; 11:5; 32:22; Ezek. 20:6.

Products of: *Fruits*, Deut. 8:8; Jer. 40: 10, 12. *Mineral*, Deut. 8:9. *Exports of*, Ezek. 27:17.

*Famines in*, Gen. 12:10; 26:1; 47:13; Ruth 1:1; 2 Sam. 21:1; 1 Kin. 17.

*Spies sent into, by Moses*, Num. 13:17-29. *Conquest of*

v.9–1770 BC
See footnote, *Time*, Rev. 10:6.

*p Stars*, Judg.5:20.

10
*q Salutations*, Luke 1:44.

12
*r Shechem*, Josh. 20:7.

14
*s Hebron, Jacob dwells at*, Gen. 23:2.

17
*t* 2 Kin. 6:13–19.

18
*u Conspiracy, instances of*, 1 Kin. 16:9.

and the eleven [p]stars made obeisance to me.
10 And he told *it* to his father,
and to his brethren: and his father rebuked him, and said unto
him, What *is* this [m]dream that
thou hast dreamed? Shall I and
thy mother and thy brethren indeed come to [q]bow down ourselves to thee to the earth?
11 And his brethren [k,l]envied
him; but his [a,g]father observed
the saying.
12 ¶ And his brethren went to
feed their father's flock in [r]Shē'-
chem.
13 And [a]Īṣ'ra-el said unto [b]Jō'-
ṣeph, Do not thy brethren feed
*the flock* in [r]Shē'chem? come,
and I will send thee unto them.
And he said to him, Here *am I*.
14 And he said to him, Go, I
pray thee, see whether it be well
with thy brethren, and well with
the flocks: and bring me word
again. So he sent him out of the
vale of [s]Hē'bron, and he came to
[r]Shē'chem.
15 And a certain man found
him, and, behold, *he was* wandering in the field: and the man
asked him, saying, What seekest
thou?
16 And he said, I seek my
brethren: tell me, I pray thee,
where they feed *their flocks*.
17 And the man said, They are
departed hence; for I heard
them say, Let us go to [t]Dō'than.
And [b]Jō'ṣeph went after his
brethren and found them in
Dō'than.
18 ¶ And when they saw him
afar off, even before he came
near unto them, they [u,j,k,l]con-
spired against him to slay him.

19 And they said one to another, Behold, this dreamer
cometh.
20 [u]Come now therefore, and
[j,k,l]let us slay him, and cast him
into some pit, and we will [v]say,
Some evil beast hath devoured
him: and we shall see what will
become of his [m]dreams.
21 And [w,x]Reu̇'ben heard *it*,
and he delivered him out of their
hands; and [y]said, Let us not
kill him.
22 And [w,x]Reu̇'ben [y]said unto
them, Shed no blood, *but* cast
him into this pit that *is* in the
wilderness, and lay no hand upon him; that he might rid him
out of their hands, to deliver him
to his father again.
23 ¶ And it came to pass, when
Jō'ṣeph was come unto his
brethren, that they stript Jō'-
ṣeph out of his coat, *his* coat of
*many* colours that *was* on him;
24 And they took him, and
[z]cast him into a pit: and the pit
*was* empty, *there was* no water
in it.
25 And they sat down to eat
bread: and they lifted up their
eyes and looked, and, behold, a
company of [a]Ĭsh'me-el-ītes came
from [b]Gĭl'e-ăd with their [c]cam-
els bearing [d,e]spicery and †balm
and [f]myrrh, [g]going to carry *it*
down to [h]Ē'ġy̌pt.
26 And ‡Jū'dah [i]said unto his
brethren, What profit *is it* if we
slay our [j,k]brother, and conceal
his blood?
27 [i]Come, and let us sell him to
the [a]Ĭsh'me-el-ītes, and let not
our hand be upon him; for he *is*
our [j,k]brother *and* our flesh.
And his brethren [2]were content.

v.19–1770 BC
See footnote, *Time*, Rev. 10:6.

20
*v Falsehood, instances of*, Job 21:34.

21
*w Reuben*, Gen. 35:22.
*x Brother*, Prov.18:24.
*y Intercession, of man with man, instances of*, Jer. 27:18.

24
*z Cruelty, instances of*, Psa. 27:12.

25
*a Ishmaelites*, Gen. 39:1.
*b Gilead*, Deut. 3:13.
*c Camel*, 1 Sam. 30:17.
*d Spices*, 1 Kin. 10:2.
*e Imports*, 1 Kin. 10:11.
*f Myrrh*, Ex. 30:23.
*g Commerce*, 1 Kin. 10:15.
*h Egypt*, Gen. 41:8.

26
*i Intercession, of man with man*, Jer. 27:18.
*j Brother*, Prov.18:24.
*k Joseph*, Gen. 33:2.

27
2 R. V. hearkened unto him.

*by the Israelites*, Num. 21:21–35; Deut. 3:3–6; Josh. chapters 6–12; Psa. 44:1–3. *Divided by lot among the twelve tribes and families*, Num. 26:55, 56; 33:54; 34:13; *by Joshua, Eleazar and a prince from each tribe*, Num. 34:16–29; Josh. chapters 14–19. *Divided into twelve provinces by Solomon*, 1 Kin. 4:7–19. *Into two kingdoms, Judah and Israel*, 1 Kin. 11:29:36; 12:16–21. *Roman provinces of*, Luke 3:1; John 4:3, 4.

† **BALM**, *a medicinal balsam*, Gen. 37:25; 43:11; Jer. 8:22; 46:11; 51:8; Ezek. 27:17.

‡ **JUDAH** (*praise*). *Son of Jacob*, Gen. 35:23. *Intercedes for Joseph's life, and proposes that they sell him to the Ishmaelites*, Gen. 37:26, 27. *Takes two wives*, Gen. 38:1–6. *Dwells at Chezib*, Gen. 38:5. *His incest with his daughter-in-law*, Gen. 38:12–26. *Goes down into Egypt for corn*, Gen. 43:1–10; 44:14–34; 46:28. *Is accorded the leadership of primogeniture forfeited by Reuben*, 1 Chr. 5:1, 2; 28:4; Psa. 60:7. *Prophetic benediction of his father upon*, Gen. 49:8–12. *Ancestor of Jesus*, Matt. 1:2, 3; Luke 3:33; Rev.5:5. TRIBE OF, see footnote, JUDAH, *Tribe of*, Num. 10:14.

v.28–1770 BC
See footnote. *Time*, Rev. 10:6.

28
*l Servant, bought and sold*, Jer. 2:14.
*m Silver*, 1 Chr. 28:14.

29
*n Reuben*, Gen. 35:22.
*o Rending, of garments*, 2 Chr. 34:27.
*p Mourning*, Lam. 2:5.

31
*q Deception, instances of*, Josh. 9:4.
3 R. V. he-goat.

32
*r Jacob*, Gen. 27:11.
*s Falsehood, instances of*, Job 21:34.
*t Hypocrisy, instances of*, Jas. 3:17.

34
*u Sackcloth*, Isa. 15:3.
*v Bereavement, instances of*, Hos. 9:12.

35
*w Weeping, instances of*, Ezra 3:13.
4 *Heb.* Sheol

36
*x* Gen. 39:1.
*y Captain*, Num. 31:48.
5 *Heb.* chief of the executioners.

28 Then there passed by +Mĭd′-ĭ-an-ītes merchantmen; and they drew and lifted up [i,k]Jō′ṣeph out of the pit, and [l]sold Jō′ṣeph to the Ĭsh′me-el-ītes for twenty *pieces* of [m]silver: and they brought Jō′ṣeph into [h]Ē′ġy̆pt.[Q]

29 ¶ And [n]Reu̦′ben returned unto the pit; and, behold, [i,k]Jō′ṣeph *was* not in the pit; and he [o,p]rent[C] his clothes.

30 And [n]he returned unto his brethren, and said, The [i,k]child[C] *is* not; and I, whither shall I go?

31 ¶ And [q]they took [k]Jō′ṣeph's coat, and killed a [3]kid of the goats, and dipped the coat in the blood;

32 And [q]they sent the coat of *many* colours, and they brought *it* to their [r]father; and [s,t]said, This have we found: know now whether it *be* thy son's coat or no.[C]

33 And he knew it, and said, *It is* my son's coat; an evil beast hath devoured him; [k]Jō′ṣeph is without doubt rent[C] in pieces.

34 And [r]Jā′cob [o]rent[C] his clothes, and put [u]sackcloth[C] upon his loins, and [p,v]mourned for his son many days.

35 And all his sons and all his daughters rose up to comfort him; but he refused to be comforted; and he said, For I will go down into the [4]grave[C] unto my son [p,v]mourning. Thus his father [w]wept for him.

36 And the +Mĭd′ĭ-an-ītes [l]sold [k]him into [h]Ē′ġy̆pt unto [x]Pŏt′ĭ-phar, an officer of ⊙Phā′raŏh's, *and* [5,y]captain of the guard.

## CHAPTER 38

*Judah begets Er, Onan, and Shelah. 6 Er marries Tamar. 8 The trespass of Onan. 11 Tamar waits for Shelah. 13 She deceives Judah. 27 She bears twins, Pharez and Zarah.*

AND it came to pass at that time, that [a]Jū′dah went down from his brethren, and turned in to a certain Ă-dŭl′-lam-īte, whose name *was* Hī′rah.

2 And [a]Jū′dah saw there a daughter of a certain [b]Cā′năan-īte, whose name *was* [c]Shu̦′ah; and he took her, and [d]went in unto her.

3 And she conceived, and bare a son; and he called his name *Ēr.

4 And she conceived again, and bare a son; and she called his name §Ō′nan.

5 And she yet again conceived, and bare a son; and called his name †Shē′lah: and he was at ‡Chē′zĭb, when she bare him.

6 And [a]Jū′dah took a wife for *Ēr his [e]firstborn, whose name *was* ‖Tā′mar.

7 And *Ēr, [a]Jū′dah's [e]firstborn, was wicked in the sight of the LORD; and the LORD [f]slew[C] him.

8 And [a]Jū′dah said unto §Ō′nan, Go in unto thy brother's wife, and [g]marry her, and raise up seed to thy brother.[Q]

9 And §Ō′nan knew that the seed should not be his; and it came to pass, when he went in unto his brother's wife, that he spilled *it* on the ground, lest that he should give seed to his brother.

10 And the thing which §he did

1
*a Judah*, Gen. 37:26.

2
*b Canaanites*, Ex. 23:28.
*c Shuah*, 1 Chr. 2:3.
*d Adultery*, Lev. 20:10.

6
*e Firstborn*, Zech. 12:10.

7
*f Judgments*, Ex. 6:6.

8
*g Marriage, levirate*, Gen. 34:9.

+ **MIDIANITES.** *Descendants of Midian, son of Abraham by Keturah*, Gen. 25:1, 2, 4; 1 Chr. 1:32, 33. *Called* ISHMAELITES, Gen. 37:25, 28; Judg. 8:24. *Were merchantmen*, Gen. 37:28. *Buy Joseph and sell him to Potiphar*, Gen. 37:28, 36. *Defeated by the Israelites under Phinehas, five of their kings slain; the women taken captives; cities burned; and rich spoils taken*, Num. 31. *Defeated by Gideon*, Judg. chapters 6–8. *Owned multitudes of camels, and dromedaries, and large quantities of gold*, Isa. 60:6. *A snare to the Israelites*, Num. 25:16–18. *Prophecies concerning*, Isa. 60:6; Hab. 3:7.

⊙ **PHARAOH.** *King of Egypt in the days of Joseph*, Gen. 39:1. *His dream and its interpretation*, Gen. 41:1–32. *Exalts Joseph to be premier*, Gen. 41:37–44. *His hospitality to Israel*, Gen. 47:5–10. *Permits Joseph to accompany the remains of his father to Canaan*, Gen. 50:4–6.

* **ER.** *Son of Judah*, Gen. 38:3, 6, 7; 46:12; Num. 26:19; 1 Chr. 2:3.

† **SHELAH.** *Son of Judah*, Gen. 38:5, 11, 14, 26; 46:12; Num. 26:20; 1 Chr. 2:3; 4:21.

‡ **CHEZIB.** *Birthplace of Shelah*, Gen. 38:5, *probably identical with* CHOZEBA, 1 Chr. 4:22, *and* ACHZIB, Josh. 15:44.

‖ **TAMAR** (*palm tree*). *Wife of the son of Judah*, Gen. 38:6-24; Ruth 4:12; 1 Chr. 2:4. *Ancestor of Jesus*, Matt. 1:3.

§ **ONAN**, son of Judah. *Slain for his refusal to raise seed to his brother*, Gen. 38:4, 8–10; 46:12; Num. 26:19; 1 Chr. 2:3.

displeased the LORD: wherefore
he [j]slew him also.
11 Then said [a]Jū'dah to ‖Tā'-
mar his daughter in law, Remain
a widow at thy father's house,
till †Shē'lah my son be grown:
for he said, Lest peradventure[c] he
die also, as his brethren *did*.
And Tā'mar went and dwelt in
her father's house.
12 ¶ And in process of time the
daughter of [c]Shṳ'ah [a]Jū'dah's
wife died; and Jū'dah was comforted, and went up unto his
sheepshearers to Tĭm'nath, he
and his friend Hī'rah the Ă-dŭl'-
lam-īte.
13 And it was told ‖Tā'mar,
saying, Behold thy [a]father in law
goeth up to Tĭm'nath to shear
his [h]sheep.
14 And ‖,[i]she put her [j]widow's
[k]garments off from her, and covered her with a [l]vail, and
wrapped herself, and sat in [1]an
open place, which *is* by the way
to Tĭm'nath; for she saw that
†Shē'lah was grown, and she
was not given unto him to wife.
15 When [a]Jū'dah saw her, he
thought her *to be* an [m]harlot; because she had covered her face.
16 And [a]he turned unto her by
the way, and said, Go[c] to, I pray
thee, [n]let me come in unto thee;
(for he knew not that she *was* his
daughter in law.) And ‖she
said, What wilt thou give me,
that thou mayest come in unto
me?
17 And he said, I will send *thee*
a kid from the flock. And she
said, Wilt thou give *me* a
[o]pledge, till thou send *it*?
18 And he said, What [o]pledge
shall I give thee? And she said,
Thy [p]signet[c], and thy bracelets,
and thy staff that *is* in thine
hand. And he gave *it* her, and
[n,q]came in unto her, and she
conceived by him.

13
*h Sheep*, Deut. 32: 14.

14
*i Women, wicked*, Prov. 31:10.
*j Widow*, 2 Sam. 14:5.
*k Mourning, dress*, Lam. 2:5.
*l Veil*, Gen. 24:65.
1 R. V. the gate of Enaim,

15
*m Harlot*, Prov. 7: 10.
*n Lasciviousness, instances of*, 1 Pet. 4:3.

17
*o Pledge*, Deut. 24: 10–13.

18
*p Seal*, 1 Kin. 21:8.
*q Incest, instances of*, Lev. 18:6.

19 And ‖she arose, and went
away, and laid by her [l]vail from
her, and put on the [k]garments of
her [j]widowhood.
20 And [a]Jū'dah sent the kid by
the hand of his friend the Ă-dŭl'-
lam-īte, to receive *his* [o]pledge
from the woman's hand: but he
found her not.
21 Then he asked the men of
that place, saying, Where *is* the
[m]harlot, that *was* openly[c] by the
way side? And they said, There
was no harlot in this *place*.
22 And he returned to [a]Jū'dah,
and said, I cannot find her; and
also the men of the place said,
*that* there was no [m]harlot in this
*place*.
23 And [a]Jū'dah said, Let her
take *it* to her, lest we be shamed:
behold, I sent this kid, and thou
hast not found her.
24 ¶ And it came to pass about
three months after, that it was
told [a]Jū'dah, saying, ‖Tā'mar
thy daughter in law hath [d]played
the [m]harlot; and also, behold,
she *is* with child by whoredom[c].
And [r]Jū'dah said, Bring her
forth, and [s]let her be [t,u]burnt.
25 When ‖she *was* brought
forth, she sent to her father in
law, saying, By the man, whose
these *are*, *am* I with child: and
she said, Discern, I pray thee,
whose *are* these, the [p]signet, and
[2]bracelets, and staff.
26 And [a]Jū'dah acknowledged
*them*, and [v]said, She hath been
more righteous than I; because
that I gave her not to †Shē'lah
my son. And he knew her again
no more.
27 ¶ And it came to pass in the
time of her travail[c], that, behold,
[w]twins *were* in her womb.
28 And it came to pass, when
she travailed[c], that *the one* put
out *his* hand: and the [x]midwife
took and bound upon his hand a

24
*r Rulers, patriarchal*, Ex. 18:21.
*s Adultery, penalties for*, Lev. 20: 10.
*t Punishment, death*, Lev. 26: 41.
*u Death, penalty*, Num. 23:10.

25
2 R. V. the cords,

26
*v Conscience, guilty* Acts 23:1.

27
*w* Gen. 25:24–26.

28
*x Midwife*, Gen. 35:17.

scarlet thread, saying, This came
out first.
29[Q] And it came to pass, as he
drew back his hand, that, behold, his brother came out: and
she said, How hast thou broken
forth? *this* breach *be* upon thee:
therefore his name was called
+Phā′rĕz.
30 And afterward came out his
brother, that had the scarlet
thread upon his hand: and his
name was called ©Zā′rah.[Q]

## CHAPTER 39

*Joseph, advanced in Potiphar's house, 7 resists his mistress's temptation. 13 He is falsely accused, 20 and cast into prison. 21 God is with him.*

AND [a]Jō′ṣeph was brought
down to [b]Ē′ġy̆pt; and [c]Pŏt′-
ĭ-phar, an officer of [d]Phạ′-
raōh, captain of the guard,
an Ė-ġy̆p′tian, bought him of
the hands of the *Ĭsh′me-el-ītes,
which had brought him down
thither.
2[Q] And the [e,f]LORD was with
[a]Jō′ṣeph, and he was a prosperous man; and [g]he was in the
house of his [c]master the Ė-ġy̆p′-
tian.
3 And his [c]master saw that the
[e,f]LORD *was* with him, and that
the LORD made all that he did
to [h]prosper in his hand.[Q]
4 And [a]Jō′ṣeph found grace in
his sight, and [g]he served him:
and he [i]made him overseer over
his house, and all *that* he had he
put into his hand.
5 And it came to pass from the
time *that* he had [i]made him overseer in his house, and over all
that he had, that the [e]LORD
blessed the Ė-ġy̆p′tian's house
[j]for Jō′ṣeph's sake; and the
[h]blessing of the LORD was upon

v.1–1770 BC
See footnote, *Time*, Rev. 10:6.

1
*a* *Joseph*, Gen. 33:2.
*b* *Egypt*, Gen. 41:8.
*c* Gen. 37:36.
*d* *Pharaoh*, Gen. 37:36.

2
*e* *God, providence of*, Gen. 2:2.
*f* *God, dwells with the righteous*, 1 Kin. 6:13.
*g* *Servant, good, instances of*, Jer. 2:14.

3
*h* *Temporal Blessings, from God*, Psa. 103:2.

4
*i* *Civil Service, appointment in, on account of merit*, Dan. 1:5.

5
*j* *Intercession, intercessional influence of the righteous*, Jer. 27:18.

all that he had in the house, and
in the field.
6 And he left all that he had in
[a]Jō′ṣeph's hand; and he knew not
ought[C] he had, save the bread[C]
which he did eat. And Jō′ṣeph
was *a* [k]goodly[C] *person*, and well
favoured.[C]
7 ¶ And it came to pass after
these things, that his [c]master's
[l,m]wife cast her eyes upon [a]Jō′-
ṣeph; and she [n]said, Lie with me.
8 But [o]he [p,q,r,s]refused, and
said unto his master's wife, Behold, my master [1]wotteth[C] not
what *is* with me in the house,
and he hath committed all that
he hath to my hand;
9 *There is* none greater in this
house than I; neither hath he
kept back any thing from me
but thee, because thou *art* his
wife: [t]how then can I do this
great wickedness, and sin
against God?
10 And it came to pass, as
[l,m]she spake to [a]Jō′ṣeph day by
day, that he [q,r,u]hearkened not
unto her, to lie by her, *or* to be
with her.
11 And it came to pass about
this time, that *Jo′seph* went into
the house to do his business; and
*there was* none of the men of the
house there within.
12 And [l,m]she caught him by
his garment, saying, [n]Lie with
me: and [r,s,u]he left his garment
in her hand, and fled, and got
him out.
13 And it came to pass, when
she saw that he had left his garment in her hand, and was fled
forth,
14 That [m]she called unto the
men of her house, and spake unto them, [v]saying, See, he hath

v.5–1770 BC
See footnote, *Time*, Rev. 10:6.

6
*k* *Beauty, instances of*, Prov. 6:25.

7
*l* *Wife, unfaithful*, Prov. 5:18.
*m* *Women, wicked*, Prov. 31:10.
*n* *Temptation*, Luke 11:4.

8
*o* *Sin, repugnant to the righteous*, Rom. 5:12.
*p* *Chastity, instances of*, Job 31:1.
*q* *Character, firmness in, instances of*, 1 Phil. 2:15.
*r* *Integrity, instances of*, Job 2:3.
*s* *Decision, instances of*, Isa. 50:7.
1 R. V. knoweth

9
*t* *Conscience, faithful*, Acts 23:1.

10
*u* *Temptation, resistance to*, Luke 11:4.

14
*v* *Malice, instances of*, Eph. 4:31.

+ **PHAREZ** (*breach*). *A twin son of Judah by Tamar*, Gen. 38:29; 1 Chr. 2:4. *Children of*, Gen. 46:12; Num. 26:20, 21; 1 Chr. 2:5; 9:4; *return from the captivity, where he is called* PEREZ, Neh. 11:4, 6. *In the lineage of Jesus*, Matt. 1:3; Luke 3:33.

© **ZARAH,** *called also* ZERAH *and* ZARA. *A twin son of Judah by Tamar*, Gen. 38:30; 46:12; Num. 26:20; 1 Chr. 2:4, 6; 9:6; Neh. 11:24; Matt. 1:3.

* **ISHMAELITES.** *Descendants of Ishmael*, Gen. 25:12–18. *Called also* HAGARITES, *and in* R.V. HAGRITES, 1 Chr. 5:10, 19–22; *and* HAGARINES, Psa. 83:6. *Merchants of, buy*

**v.14–1770 BC**
See footnote, *Time*, Rev. 10:6.

*w Hebrew*, Gen. 40:15.
*x Falsehood, instances of*, Job 21:34.
*y Slander, instances of*, Prov. 10:18.
*z False Accusation*, 2 Tim. 3:3.

brought in an [w]Hē'brew unto
us to mock us; [x,y,z]he came in
unto me to lie with me, and I
cried with a loud voice:
15 [x,y,z]And it came to pass,
when he heard that I lifted up
my voice and cried, that he left
his garment with me, and fled,
and got him out.
16 And she laid up his garment
by her, until his lord came home.
17 And [m]she spake unto him
according to these words, saying,
[x,y,z]The [w]Hē'brew servant,
which thou hast brought unto
us, came in unto me to mock me:
18 [x,y,z]And it came to pass, as
I lifted up my voice and cried,
that he left his garment with me,
and fled out.
19 And it came to pass, when
his [a]master heard the words of
his [b]wife, which she spake unto
him, saying, After this manner
did thy servant to me; that his
[c]wrath[C] was kindled.
20 And [d]Jō'ṣeph's master took
him, and [e,f]put him into the
†prison, a place where the king's
[g,h]prisoners *were* bound: and he
was there in the prison.[Q]
21 But the [i,j]LORD was with
[d]Jō'ṣeph, and shewed him [2]mer-
cy, and gave him favour in the
sight of the keeper of the †prison.[Q]
22 And the keeper of the
†prison committed to [d]Jō'ṣeph's
hand all the [g,h]prisoners that
*were* in the prison; and whatsoever they did there, he was the
doer[C] *of it*.
23 The keeper of the †prison
looked not to any thing *that was*
under his hand; because the
[i,j]LORD was with him, and *that*
which he did, the [k]LORD made
*it* to [l]prosper.

**19**
*a* Gen. 37:36.
*b Wife*, Prov. 5:18.
*c Anger*, Psa. 37:8.

**20**
*d Joseph*, Gen. 33:2.
*e Imprisonment*, Acts 12:4.
*f Punishment, of minor offenses*, Lev. 26:41.
*g Prisoners*, Psa. 79:11.
*h Criminals*, Matt. 27:15.

**21**
*i God, preserver*, Gen. 2:2.
*j God, dwells with the righteous*, 1 Kin. 6:13.
2 R. V. kindness,

**23**
*k God, providence of*, Gen. 2:2.
*l Temporal Blessings*, Psa. 103:2.

## CHAPTER 40

*The butler and baker of Pharaoh in prison. 4 Joseph has charge of them. 5 He interprets their dreams, 20 which come to pass according to his interpretation. 23 The ingratitude of the butler.*

AND it came to pass after
these things, *that* the [a]but-
ler of the king of [b]Ē'ġy̆pt and
*his* [c,d]baker had offended their
lord[C] the king of Ē'ġy̆pt.
2 And [e]Phā'raōh was [f]wroth[C]
against two *of* his officers,
against the chief of the [a]butlers
and against the chief of the
[c]bakers.
3 And he [g]put [h]them in ward[C] in
the house of the captain of the
guard, into the [i]prison, the place
where [j]Jō'ṣeph *was* bound[C].
4 And the captain of the guard
charged [j]Jō'ṣeph with [a,c]them,
and he served them: and they
continued a season[C] in [i]ward.
5 ¶ And they dreamed a
[k]dream both of them, each man
his dream in one night, each
man according to the interpretation of his dream, the [a]butler
and the [c]baker of the king of
[b]Ē'ġy̆pt, which *were* bound in
the prison.
6 And [j]Jō'ṣeph came in unto
them in the morning, and looked
upon them, and, behold, they
*were* [l]sad.
7 And he asked [e]Phā'raōh's
officers that *were* with him in the
ward[C] of his lord's house, saying,
Wherefore [l]look ye *so* sadly to
day?
8 And they said unto him, We
have dreamed a [k]dream, and
*there is* no *interpreter of it.
And [j]Jō'ṣeph said unto them,
*Do* not interpretations *belong* to
God? tell me *them*, I pray you.
9 And the chief [a]butler told his

**v.1–1759 BC**
See footnote, *Time*, Rev. 10:6.

**1**
*a Cupbearer*, 1 Kin. 10:5.
*b Egypt*, Gen. 41:8.
*c Baker*, 1 Sam. 8:13.
*d Art*, 2 Cor. 16:14.

**2**
*e Pharaoh*, vs. 2-23; Gen. 37:36.
*f Angry*, Psa. 37:8.

**3**
*g Punishment, of minor offences*, Lev. 26:41.
*h Prisoners*, Psa. 79:11.
*i Prison*, Gen. 39:20.
*j Joseph*, Gen. 33:2.

**v.5–1759 BC**
See footnote, *Time*, Rev. 10:6.

**5**
*k Dream, instances of*, Dan. 1:17.

**6**
*l Countenance, sad*, Prov. 15:13.

---

*Joseph*, Gen. 37:25-36; 39:1. *Called* MIDIANITES, Gen. 37:28, 36; Judg. 8:24, 26. *Enemies to Israel*, Psa. 83:6.
See footnote, ISHMAEL, Gen. 16:11.

† **PRISON**, Gen. 39:20; 42:16-19; Lev. 24:12; Num. 15:34; Ezra 7:26; Jer. 52:11; Luke 23:19; Acts 4:3; 12:4, 5. *Public ward of*, Acts 5:18. *Cells of*, Acts 16:24. *Court of*, Jer. 33:1. *Dungeon in*, Jer. 38:6· Lam. 3:53

**Figurative**, 1 Pet. 3:19.
See footnotes: IMPRISONMENT, Acts 12:4; PRISONERS, Psa. 79:11.

* **INTERPRETER.** *Of dreams*, Gen. 41:15-36; Dan. 2:18-30. *Of languages*, Gen. 42:23; 2 Chr. 32:31. *In Christian churches*, 1 Cor. 12:10, 30; 14:5, 13, 26-28.
**Figurative**, Job 33:23.

v.9–1759 BC
See footnote. *Time,* Rev 10.6.

[k]dream to [j]Jō'ṣeph, and said to
him, In my dream, behold, a
vine *was* before me;
10 And in the vine *were* three
branches: and it *was* as though
it budded, *and* her blossoms shot
forth; and the clusters thereof
brought forth ripe grapes:
11 And [e]Phā'raōh's cup *was* in
my hand: and [a]I took the grapes,
and pressed them into Phā'-
raōh's cup, and I gave the cup
into Phā'raōh's hand.
12 And [j]Jō'ṣeph said unto him,
This *is* the *interpretation of it:
The three branches *are* three
days:
13 Yet within three days shall
[e]Phā'raōh lift up thine head, and
restore thee unto thy place: and
thou shalt deliver Phā'raōh's cup
into his hand, after the former
manner when thou wast his
[a]butler.
14 But think on me when it
shall be well with thee, and shew
kindness I pray thee, unto me,
and [m]make mention of me unto
Phā'raōh, and bring me out of
this house:
15 For indeed [j]I was stolen
away out of the [n]land of the
†Hē'brews: and here also [o]have
I done nothing that [p]they should
put me into the dungeon.
16 When the chief [c]baker saw
that the *interpretation was
good, he said unto [j]Jō'ṣeph, I
also *was* in my [k]dream, and, behold, [1]*I had* three white [q]bas-
kets on my head:
17 And in the uppermost [q]bas-
ket *there was* of all manner of
bakemeats[c] for Phā'raōh; and the
[r]birds did eat them out of the
basket upon my head.
18 And [j]Jō'ṣeph answered and
said, This *is* the *interpretation
thereof: The three [q]baskets *are*
three days:
19 Yet within three days shall
[e]Phā'raōh lift up thy head from
off thee, and shall [s,t]hang thee
on a tree; and the [r]birds shall eat
thy flesh from off thee.
20 ¶ And it came to pass the
third day, *which was* Phā'raōh's
‡birthday, that he made a [u]feast
unto all his servants: and he
lifted up the head of the chief
butler and of the chief baker
among his servants.
21 And he restored the chief
butler unto his butlership
again; and he gave the cup unto
Phā'raōh's hand:
22 But he [s,t,v]hanged the chief
baker: as [j]Jō'ṣeph had *interpreted to them.
23 Yet did not the chief [w]butler
remember [j]Jō'ṣeph, but [x]forgat
him.

## CHAPTER 41

*Pharaoh's two dreams. 25 Joseph interprets them. 33 He gives Pharaoh counsel. 38 Joseph is advanced. 50 The birth of Manasseh and Ephraim. 53 The famine begins.*

AND it came to pass at the
end of two full years, that
[a]Phā'raōh [b]dreamed: and, behold, he stood by the [1]river.
2 And, behold, there came up
out of the river [c]seven well favoured[c] kine[c] and fatfleshed; and
they fed in a meadow.
3 And, behold, [c]seven other
kine[c] came up after them out of
the river, ill favoured[c] and lean-
fleshed; and stood by the *other*
kine upon the brink of the river.
4 And the ill favoured and lean-
fleshed kine[c] did eat up the [c]seven
well favoured and fat kine. So
[a]Phā'raōh awoke.
5 And he slept and [b]dreamed
the second time: and, behold,

14
*m* *Intercession, of man with man,* Jer. 27:18.

15
*n* *Canaan, land of.* Gen. 37:1.
*o* *Integrity,* Job 2:3.
*p* *Rulers, wicked, instances of,* Ex. 18:21.

16
*q* *Basket,* Ex. 29:3.
1 R. V. three baskets of white bread

17
*r* *Birds,* Eccl. 12:4.

v.18–1759 BC
See footnote. *Time,* Rev. 10:6.

19
*s* *Hanging.* Josh. 8:29.
*t* *Punishment, death penalty,* Lev. 26 41.

20
*u* *Feasts,* Mark 12: 39.

22
*v* *Death, penalty,* Num. 23:10.

23
*w* *Friends, false, instances of,* Ex. 33:11.
*x* *Ingratitude, of man to man.* Rom. 1:21.

v.1–1757 BC
See footnote. *Time,* Rev. 10:6.

1
*a* *Pharaoh,* Gen 37:36.
*b* *Dream, revelations by,* Dan 1. 17.
1 *That is,* the Nile.

2
*c* *Seven,* Gen. 7:2.

† **HEBREW.** *A word supposed to be a corruption of the name Eber, who was an ancestor of Abraham,* Gen. 10:24; 11:14-26. *Applied to Abraham,* Gen. 14:13; *and his descendants,* Gen. 39:14; 40:15; 43:32; Ex. 2:6; Deut. 15:12; 1 Sam. 4:9; 29:3; Jonah 1:9; Acts 6:1; 2 Cor. 11:22; Phil. 3:5. *Used to denote the language of the Jews,* John 5:2; 19:20; Acts 21:40; 22:2; 26:14; Rev. 9:11. See footnote, JEWS, Neh. 4:2.

‡ **BIRTHDAY.** *Celebrated by feasts,* Gen. 40:20; Matt. 14:6. *Day of death better than,* Eccl. 7:1. *Cursed,* Job 3; Jer. 20:14, 18.

v.5–1757 BC
See footnote, *Time*, Rev. 10:6.

seven ears of [d]corn[C]came up upon one stalk, [2]rank[C]and good.
6 And, behold, seven thin ears
and blasted[C]with the east [e]wind
sprung up after them.
7 And the [c]seven thin ears devoured the seven [2]rank[C]and full
ears. And [a]Phā′raōh awoke,
and, behold, *it was* a [b]dream.
8 And it came to pass in the
morning that his spirit was troubled; and he sent and called for
all the [3,f,g]magicians of *Ē′ġy̆pt,
and all the wise men thereof:
and Phā′raōh told them his
dream; but *there was* none that
could interpret them unto Phā′-
raōh.
9 ¶ Then [h]spake the chief [i]but-
ler unto [a]Phā′raōh, saying, [j]I do
remember my faults this day:
10 [a]Phā′raōh was [k]wroth[C]with
his servants, and [l]put me in
ward[C] in the captain of the
guard's house, *both* me and the
chief baker:
11 And we dreamed a [b]dream
in one night, I and he; we
dreamed each man according
to the interpretation of his
dream.
12 [h]And *there was* there with
us a young man, an [m]Hē′brew,
[n]servant to the captain of the
guard; and we told him, and he
[o]interpreted to us our dreams; to
each man according to his dream
he did interpret.
13 [h]And it came to pass, as he
interpreted to us, so it was; me
he restored unto mine office, and
him he [p,q]hanged.
14 ¶ Then [a]Phā′raōh sent and
called [r]Jō′ṣeph, and they
brought him hastily out of the

5
d *Corn*, Psa. 65:13.
2 *Heb.* fat

6
e *Meteorology*, Matt. 16:2.

8
f *Magician*, Ex. 7:11.
g *Sorcery*, Isa. 47:9.
3 *Or*, sacred scribes

9
h *Intercession, of man with man, instances of*, Jer. 27:18.
i *Cupbearer*, 1 Kin. 10:5.
j *Conscience, guilty*, Acts 23:1.

10
k *Anger*, Psa. 37:8.
l *Punishment, of minor offenses*, Lev. 26:41.

12
m *Hebrew*, Gen. 40:15.
n *Servant*, Jer. 2:14.
o *Interpreter, of dreams*, Gen. 40:8.

13
p *Punishment, death penalty*, Lev. 26:41.
q *Hanging*, Josh. 8:29

14
r *Joseph*, Gen. 33:2.

[s]dungeon: and he shaved *himself*, and changed his raiment,
and came in unto Phā′raōh.
15 And [a]Phā′raōh said unto
[r]Jō′ṣeph, I have dreamed a
[b]dream, and *there is* none that
can [o]interpret it: and I have
heard say of thee, *that* thou canst
understand a dream to interpret it.
16 And [r]Jō′ṣeph answered
[a]Phā′raōh, saying, [t]*It is* not in
me: God shall give Phā′raōh an
answer of peace.
17 And [a]Phā′raōh said unto
[r]Jō′ṣeph, In my [b]dream, behold,
I stood upon the bank of the
river:
18 And, behold, there came up
out of the river [c]seven kine,[C] fatfleshed and well favoured; and
they fed in a meadow:
19 And, behold, [c]seven other
kine[C] came up after them, poor
and very ill favoured and lean-
fleshed, such as I never saw in
all the land of *Ē′ġy̆pt for bad-
ness:
20 And the lean and the ill favoured kine[C] did eat up the first
[c]seven fat kine:
21 And when they had eaten
them up, it could not be known
that they had eaten them; but
they *were* still ill favoured, as at
the beginning. So I awoke.
22 And I saw in my [b]dream,
and, behold,[c]seven ears came up
in one stalk, full and good:
23 And, behold, [c]seven ears,
withered, thin, *and* blasted[C]with
the east wind, sprung up after
them:
24 And the thin ears devoured
the seven good ears: and I told

v.14–1757 BC
See footnote, *Time*, Rev. 10:6.

s *Criminals, in dungeons*, Matt. 27:15.

16
t *Humility, exemplified*, Prov. 22:4.

* **EGYPT.** *The country of, called* RAHAB, Psa. 87:10; LAND OF HAM, Psa. 105:23; 106:22. *Limits of*, Ezek. 29:10. *Fertility of*, Gen. 13:10. *Abraham dwells in*, Gen. 12:10–20; 13:1. *Productions of*, Num. 11:5; Psa. 78:47; Prov. 7:16; Isa. 19:5–9. *Irrigation employed in*, Deut. 11:10. *Imports of*, Gen. 37:25, 36. *Exports of*, Prov. 7:16; Ezek. 27:7; *horses*, 1 Kin. 10:28, 29.
*Famine in*, Gen. 41; Acts 7:11. *Armies of*, Ex. 14:7; Isa. 31:1. *Army of, destroyed in the Red Sea*, Ex. 14:5–31; Josh. 24:6, 7; Isa. 43:17. *Magi of*, Gen. 41:8; Ex. 7:11; 1 Kin. 4:30; Acts 7:22. *Priests of*, Gen. 41:45; 47:22. *Idols of*, Ezek. 20:7, 8. *Overflowed by the Nile*, Amos 8:8; 9:5. *Plagues in*, Ex. 7:19; and chapters 8 to 10 inclusive. *Joseph's captivity in, and subsequent rule over*, see footnote, JOSEPH, Gen. 33:2. *Civil war in*, Isa. 19:2. *The king acquires title to land of*, Gen. 47:18–26. *Israelites in bondage in*, Ex. chapters 1–14. *Joseph takes Jesus to*, Matt. 2:13–20.
*Prophecies against*, Gen. 15:13, 14; Isa. 19; 20:2–6; 45:14; Jer. 9:25, 26; 43:8–13; 44:30; 46; Ezek. chapters 29–32; Hos 8:13; Joel 3:19; Zech. 10:11.
SYMBOLICAL, Rev. 11:8.
See footnote, EGYPTIANS, Gen. 50:3.

v.24–1757 BC
See footnote, *Time,* Rev. 10:6.

*this* unto the [f,g]magicians; but *there was* none that could [o]declare[G] *it* to me.

25 ¶ And [r,o]Jō'ṣeph said unto [a]Phā'raōh, The [b]dream of Phā'raōh *is* one: [u]God hath shewed Phā'raōh what he *is* about to do.

26 The [c]seven good kine[G] *are* seven years; and the seven good ears *are* seven years: the dream *is* one.

27 And the seven thin and ill favoured kine[G] that came up after them *are* seven years; and the seven empty ears blasted[G] with the east [e]wind shall be [c]seven years of [v]famine.

28 This *is* the thing which I have spoken unto [a]Phā'raōh: What [u]God *is* about to do he sheweth unto Phā'raōh.

29 Behold, there come [c]seven years of great plenty throughout all the land of *Ē'ġy̆pt:

30 And there shall arise after them [c]seven years of [v]famine; and all the plenty shall be forgotten in the land of Ē'ġy̆pt; and the famine shall consume the land;

31 And the plenty shall not be known in the land by reason of that [v]famine following; for it *shall be* very grievous.

32 And for that the [b]dream was doubled[G] unto Phā'raōh twice; *it is* because the thing *is* established by [w]God, and [u]God will shortly bring it to pass.

33 [x]Now therefore let Phā'raōh look[G] out a man [y]discreet and wise, and set him over the land of *Ē'ġy̆pt.

34 Let Phā'raōh do *this,* and let him appoint [4]officers[G] over the land, and take up the [z]fifth part of the land of *Ē'ġy̆pt in the seven plenteous years.

35 And let them gather all the food of those good years that come, and lay up corn[G] under the hand of Phā'raōh, and let them keep food in the [a]cities.

36 And that food shall be for store[G] to the land against the [b]seven years of [c]famine, which shall be in the land of *Ē'ġy̆pt; that the land perish not through the famine.

37 ¶ And the thing was good in the eyes of Phā'raōh, and in the eyes of all his servants.

38 And Phā'raōh said unto his servants, Can we find *such a one* as this *is,* a man in whom the [d]Spirit of God *is*?[T]

39 And Phā'raōh said unto [e,f]Jō'ṣeph, Forasmuch as God hath shewed thee all this, *there is* none so discreet and wise as thou *art*:

40 [f,g,h,i]Thou shalt be over my house, and according unto thy word shall all my people be ruled: only in the [j]throne will I be greater than thou.[Q]

41 And Phā'raōh said unto [e]Jō'ṣeph, See, I have [g,i]set [h]thee over all the land of *Ē'ġy̆pt.

42 And Phā'raōh took off his †ring from his hand, and put it upon [e]Jō'ṣeph's hand, and arrayed him in vestures[G] of [5]fine [k]linen, and put a [l]gold [m]chain about his neck;

43 And he made him to ride in the second [n]chariot which he had; and they cried before him, [o]Bow the knee: and he made him *ruler* over all the land of Ē'ġy̆pt.[Q]

44 And Phā'raōh said unto [e]Jō'ṣeph, I *am* Phā'raōh, and without[G] [g,h,i]thee shall no man lift up his hand or foot in all the land of *Ē'ġy̆pt.

45 And Phā'raōh called [e]Jō'ṣeph's name Zăph'nath-pā-a-nē'ah; and he gave him to wife [p]Ăṣ'e-năth the daughter of

---

25
u *God, providence of,* Gen. 2:2.

27
v *Famine,* 2 Kin. 8:1.

32
w *God, sovereign,* Gen. 2:2.

33
x *Prudence,* 2 Chr. 2:12.
y *Rulers, character and qualifications of,* Ex. 18:21.

34
z *Tax,* Neh. 10:32.
4 R. V. overseers

v.35–1757 BC
See footnote, *Time,* Rev. 10:6.

35
a *Cities, treasure,* Num. 35:8.

36
b *Seven, years,* Gen. 7:2.
c *Famine,* 2 Kin. 8:1.

38
d *Holy Spirit, inspiration of,* Acts 1:2.

39
e *Joseph,* Gen. 33:2.
f *Captive, kindness to,* 1 Sam. 30:3.

40
g *Civil Service, appointment in, on account of merit,* Dan. 1:5.
h *Minister, an officer in civil government,* 2 Chr. 9:4.
i *Promotion,* Psa. 75:6.
j *Throne,* 1 Kin. 2:19.

42
k *Linen,* Ezek. 27:16.
l *Gold,* Ezek. 7:19.
m *Chains, ornaments,* Dan. 5:7.
5 *Or,* cotton,

43
n *Chariot,* Josh. 11:4.
o *Salutations,* Luke 41:4

45
p Gen. 46:20.

---

† **RING.** *Of gold,* Num. 31:50. *Worn as a badge of office,* Gen. 41:42. *Given as a token,* Esth. 3:10, 12; 8:2–10. *Offerings of, to the tabernacle,* Ex. 35:22; Num. 31:50.

v.45–175 BC
See footnote, *Time*, Rev. 10:6.

q Gen. 46:20.
r Gen. 46:20.
6 *Or*, prince

[q]Pŏt′ĭ-phē′rah [6]priest of [r]Ŏn. And Jō′ṣeph went out over *all* the land of Ē′ġy̆pt.

46 And [e]Jō′ṣeph *was* thirty years old when he stood before Phā′raōh king of *Ē′ġy̆pt. And Jō′ṣeph went out from the presence of Phā′raōh, and went throughout all the land of Ē′ġy̆pt.[Q]

47 And in the [b]seven plenteous years the earth brought forth by handfuls.

48 And he gathered up all the food of the [b]seven years, which were in the land of *Ē′ġy̆pt, and laid up the food in the [s]cities: the food of the field, which *was* round about every city, laid he up in the same.

48
s *Cities, treasure*, Num. 35:8.

49 And [e]Jō′ṣeph gathered [t]corn[G] as the sand of the sea, very much, until he left[G] numbering; for *it was* without number.

49
t *Corn*, Psa. 65:13.

50 And unto [e]Jō′ṣeph were born two sons before the years of [c]famine came, which [p]Ă̄s′e-năth the daughter of [q]Pŏt′ĭ-phē′rah priest of [r]Ŏn bare unto him.

51 And [e]Jō′ṣeph called the name of the firstborn [u]Mă̄-năs′seh: [v]For God, *said he*, hath made me forget all my toil, and all my father's house.

51
u *Manasseh*, Gen. 46:20.
v *Thankfulness, to God, instances of*, Acts 24:3.

52 And the name of the second called he ‡Ē′phră-ĭm: [v]For [w]God hath caused me to be fruitful in the land of my affliction.

52
w *Temporal Blessings, from God*, Psa. 103:2.

B.C. 1708?
See footnote, *Time*, Rev. 10:6.

53 ¶ And the [b]seven years of plenteousness, that was in the land of Ē′ġy̆pt, were ended.

54[Q] And the [b]seven years of [c]dearth[G] began to come, according as Jō′ṣeph had said: and the dearth was in all lands; but in all the land of Ē′ġy̆pt there was bread.

v.54–1750 BC
See footnote, *Time*, Rev. 10:6.

55 And when all the land of *Ē′ġy̆pt was [c]famished, the people cried to Phā′raōh for bread: and Phā′raōh said unto all the Ē-ġy̆p′tianṣ, Go unto [h]Jō′ṣeph; what he saith to you, do.[Q]

56 And the famine was over all the face of the earth: And [h]Jō′ṣeph opened all the [x]storehouses, and sold unto the Ē-ġy̆p′tianṣ; and the famine waxed[G] sore[G] in the land of Ē′ġy̆pt.

56
x *Storehouses*, 2 Chr. 32:28.

57 And all countries came into *Ē′ġy̆pt to Jō′ṣeph for to buy [t]*corn*[G]; because that the famine was *so* sore[G] in all lands.

## CHAPTER 42

*Jacob sends his ten sons to buy corn in Egypt. 16 They are imprisoned by Joseph as spies; 18 but are set at liberty, on condition that they bring Benjamin. 21 Their remorse on account of Joseph. 24 Simeon is kept as a pledge. 25 They return home with corn, and with their money. 29 Their report to Jacob. 36 Jacob refuses to send Benjamin.*

NOW when [a]Jā′cob saw that there was [b]corn[G] in [c]Ē′ġy̆pt, Jā′cob said unto his sons, Why do ye look one upon another?

1
a *Jacob*, Gen. 27:11.
b *Corn*, Psa. 65:13.
c *Egypt*, Gen. 41:8.

2 And he said, Behold, I have heard that there is [b]corn[G] in [c]Ē′ġy̆pt: get you down thither and buy for us from thence; that we may live, and not die.[Q]

3 ¶ And [d]Jō′ṣeph's ten brethren went down to buy [b]corn[G] in Ē′ġy̆pt.

3
d *Joseph*, Gen. 33:2.

4 But [e]Bĕn′ja-mĭn, [d]Jō′ṣeph's

4
e *Benjamin*, Gen. 35:18.

‡ **EPHRAIM** (*fruitful*). *Second son of Joseph*, Gen. 41:52. *Adopted by Jacob*, Gen. 48:5. *Blessed before Manasseh; prophecies concerning*, Gen. 48:14–20. *Descendants of*, Num. 26:35–37; 1 Chr. 7:20–27. *Mourns for his sons*, 1 Chr. 7:21, 22.

**Tribe of.** *Prophecy concerning*, Gen. 49: 25, 26; Isa. 9:18–21; 11:13; 28:1; Jer. 31; Hos. 5:14; Zech. 9:10; 10:7. *Numbered at Sinai, and in plains of Moab*, Num. 1:32, 33; 26:37. *Place in camp and march*, Num. 2:18, 24; 10:22. *Blessed by Moses*, Deut. 33:13–17.

*Territory allotted to, after the conquest of Canaan*, Josh. 16:5–9; 17:9, 10, 15–18; 1 Chr. 7:28, 29; Ezek. 48:5. *Fail to expel the Canaanites*, Josh. 16:10. *Take Beth-el in battle*, Judg. 1:22–25. *Upbraid Gideon for not summoning them to join the war against the Midianites*, Judg. 8:1. *Join Gideon against the Midianites*, Judg. 7:24, 25. *Their jealousy of Jephthah*, Judg. 12:1; *defeated by him*, Judg. 12:4–6. *Receive Ish-bosheth as king*, 2 Sam. 2:9. *Jeroboam set up a golden calf in Beth-el, a city of*, 1 Kin. 12:29. *Revolt from house of David*, 1 Kin. 12:16, 19; 2 Chr. 10:16. *Some of tribe join Judah under Asa*, 2 Chr. 15:9. *Chastise Ahaz and Judah*, 2 Chr. 28:7. *Join Hezekiah in reinstituting the passover*, 2 Chr. 30:18. *Join in the destruction of idolatrous forms in Jerusalem*, 2 Chr. 31:1. *Submit to the scepter of Josiah*, 2 Chr. 34:1–6. *Worshiped Baal*, Hos. 13:1. *Sin of, remembered by God*, Hos. 13:12. *Reallotment of territory to, by Ezekiel*, Ezek. 48:5.

*Name of, applied to the ten tribes*, 2 Chr. 17:2; 25:6, 7; Isa. 7:8, 9; 11:12, 13; 17:3; Jer. 31:18, 20; Hos. 4:17; 5:3, 5; 6:4, 10; 7:1–16; 8:11; 12:14. *Tribe of, called* JOSEPH, Rev. 7:8.

brother, [f]Jā′cob [g]sent not with his brethren; for he said, Lest peradventure[C] mischief befall him.

5 And the sons of [a]Ĭṣ′ra-el came to buy [b]*corn*[C] among those that came: for the [h]famine was in the land of [i]Cā′năan.[Q]

6 And [d]Jō′ṣeph *was* the governor over the land, *and* he *it was* that sold to all the people of the land: and Jō′ṣeph's brethren came, and [j]bowed down themselves before him *with* their faces to the earth.

7 And [d]Jō′ṣeph saw his brethren, and he knew them, but [k]made himself strange unto them, and spake roughly[C] unto them; and he said unto them, Whence come ye? And they said, From the land of [i]Cā′năan to buy food.

8 And [d]Jō′ṣeph knew his brethren, but they knew not him.

9 And [d]Jō′ṣeph remembered the [l]dreams which he dreamed of them, and said unto them, [m]Ye *are* [n]spies; to see the nakedness[C] of the land ye are come.

10 And they said unto him, Nay, my lord, but to buy [o]food are thy servants come.

11 We *are* all one man's sons; we *are* true *men*, thy servants are no [n]spies.

12 And he [m]said unto them, Nay, but to see the nakedness of the land ye are come.

13 And they said, Thy servants *are* twelve brethren, the sons of one man in the land of [i]Cā′năan; and, behold, the [e]youngest *is* this day with our father, and one *is* not.

14 And [d]Jō′ṣeph said unto them, That *is it* that I spake unto you, [m]saying, Ye *are* [n]spies:

15 Hereby ye shall be proved[C]: By the life of [p]Phā′raōh ye shall not go forth hence, except your [e]youngest brother come hither.

16 Send one of you, and let him fetch your brother, and ye shall be [1]kept in prison, that your words may be proved,[C] whether *there be any* truth in you: or else by the life of [p]Phā′raōh surely ye *are* [n]spies.

17 And he [q]put them all together into [r]ward[C] three days.

18 And [d]Jō′ṣeph said unto them the third day, This do, and live; *for* I [s]fear God:

19 If ye *be* true *men*, let one of your brethren be bound in the house of your [r]prison: go ye, carry [b]corn[C] for the [h]famine of your houses:

20 But bring your [e]youngest brother unto me; so shall your words be verified, and ye shall not die. And they did so.

21 ¶ And [t, u]they said one to another, [v]We *are* verily guilty concerning our brother, in that we saw the anguish of his soul, when he besought us, and we would not hear; therefore is this distress come upon us.

22 And [w]Reu′ben answered them, saying, Spake I not unto you, saying, Do not sin against the child[C]; and ye would not hear? therefore, behold, also his blood is required.

23 And they knew not that [d]Jō′ṣeph understood *them*; for he spake unto them by an [x]interpreter.

24 And he turned himself about from them, and [y]wept; and returned[C] to them again, and communed[C] with them, and took from them [z]Sĭm′e-on, and bound him before their eyes.

25 ¶ Then [a]Jō′ṣeph commanded to fill their sacks with [b]corn,[C] and to restore every man's [c]money into his sack, and to give them provision for the way: and thus did he unto them.

26 And they laded[C] their [d]asses

*f Parents, partiality of,* 2 Cor. 12:14.
*g Partiality,* 1 Tim. 5:21.

5
*h Famine,* 2 Kin. 8:1.
*i Canaan,* Gen. 37:1.

6
*j Salutations,* Luke 1:44.

7
*k Deception, instances of,* Josh. 9:4.

9
*l Dream,* Dan. 1:17.
*m False Accusation, incidents illustrative of,* 2 Tim 3:3
*n Spies,* Josh. 6:23.

10
*o Food* Psa. 136:25.

15
*p Pharaoh,* Gen. 37:36.

16
1 R. V. bound.

17
*q Prisoners,* Psa. 79:11.
*r Prison,* Gen. 39:20.

18
*s Fear of God, instances of,* Acts 9:31.

21
*t Adversity, benefits of, illustrated,* Psa. 10:6.
*u Conscience, guilty, instances of,* Acts 23:1.
*v Conviction, of sin, instances of,* John 16:8.

22
*w Reuben,* Gen. 35:22.

23
*x Interpreter,* Gen. 40:8.

24
*y Weeping, instances of,* Ezra 3:13.
*z Simeon,* Gen. 29:33.

25
*a Joseph,* Gen. 33:2.
*b Corn,* Psa. 65:13.
*c Money,* Jer. 32:9.

26
*d Ass,* 2 Chr. 28:15.

with the [b]corn,[G] and departed
thence.
27 And as one of them opened
his sack to give his ass provender[G]
in the inn,[G] he espied[G] his [c]money;
for, behold, it *was* in his sack's
mouth.
28 And he said unto his brethren, My [c]money is restored; and,
lo,[G] *it is* even in my sack: and
their heart failed *them,* and they
were afraid, saying one to another, [e]What *is* this *that* God
hath done unto us?
29 ¶ And they came unto [f]Jā'-
cob their father unto the land of
[g]Cā'năan, and told him all that
befell unto them; saying,
30 The man, *who is* the [h]lord of
the land, spake roughly[G] to us,
and took us for [i]spies of the
country.
31 And we said unto him, We
*are* true *men*; we are no [i]spies:
32 We *be* twelve brethren, sons
of our father; [a]one *is* not, and
the [j]youngest *is* this day with our
father in the land of [g]Cā'năan.
33 And the man, the [h]lord[G] of
the country, said unto us, Hereby shall I know that ye *are* true
*men*; leave [k]one of your brethren
*here* with me, and take [l]*food for*
the [m]famine of your households,
and be gone:
34 And bring your [j]youngest
brother unto me: then shall I
know that ye *are* no [i]spies, but
*that* ye *are* true *men*: *so* will I deliver you your [k]brother, and ye
shall traffick[G] in the land.
35 And it came to pass as they
emptied their sacks, that, behold, every man's bundle of
[c]money *was* in his sack: and
when *both* they and their father
saw the bundles of money, they
were afraid.
36 And [f]Jā'cob their father said
unto them, Me have ye bereaved
*of my children*: [a]Jō'şeph *is* not,
and [k]Sĭm'e-on *is* not, and ye will

**28**
*e* *Conscience, guilty, instances of,* Acts 23:1.

**29**
*f* *Jacob,* Gen. 27: 11.
*g* *Canaan,* Gen. 37:1.

**30**
*h* *Rulers,* Ex. 18: 21.
*i* *Spies,* Josh. 6:23.

**32**
*j* *Benjamin,* Gen. 35:18.

**33**
*k* *Simeon,* Gen. 29: 33.
*l* *Food,* Psa. 136: 25.
*m* *Famine,* 2 Kin. 8:1.

take [j]Bĕn'ja-mĭn *away*: all these
things are against me.
37 And [n]Reu'ben spake unto
his father, saying, Slay my two
sons, if I bring him not to thee:
deliver him into my hand, and I
will bring him to thee again.
38 And [o]he said, [p]My [j]son shall
not go down with you; for his
brother is dead, and he is left
alone: if mischief[G] befall[G] him by
the way in the which ye go, then
shall ye bring down my gray
hairs with sorrow to the [q]grave.[G]

## CHAPTER 43

*Jacob is hardly persuaded to send Benjamin. 15 Joseph entertains his brethren. 31 He makes them a feast.*

AND the [a]famine *was* sore[G]
in the land.
2 And it came to pass, when
they had eaten up the corn[G]
which they had brought out of
[b]Ē'ġўpt, their [c]father said unto
them, Go again, buy us a little
food.
3 And [d]Jū'dah spake unto him,
saying, The [e]man did solemnly
protest[G] unto us, saying, Ye shall
not see my face, except your
[f]brother *be* with you.
4 If thou wilt send our [f]brother
with us, we will go down and
buy thee food:
5 But if thou wilt not send *him,*
we will not go down: for the
[e]man said unto us, Ye shall not
see my face, except your brother
*be* with you.
6 And [c]Is'ra-el said, Wherefore
dealt ye *so* ill with me, *as* to tell
the man whether ye had yet a
brother?
7 And they said, The [e]man
asked us straitly[G] of our state,
and of our kindred, saying, *Is*
your father yet alive? have ye
*another* brother? and we told
him according to the tenor of
these words: could we certainly
know that he would say, Bring
your [f]brother down?

**37**
*n* *Reuben,* Gen. 35: 22.

**38**
*o* *Parents, partiality of,* 2 Cor. 12: 14.
*p* *Partiality,* 1 Tim. 5:21.
*q* *Sheol,* Mark 9: 43.

**1**
*a* *Famine,* 2 Kin. 8:1.

**2**
*b* *Egypt,* Gen. 41:8.
*c* *Jacob,* Gen. 27: 11.

**3**
*d* *Judah,* Gen. 37: 26.
*e* *Joseph,* Gen. 33:2.
*f* *Benjamin,* Gen. 35:18.

v.8–1748 BC
See footnote, *Time*, Rev. 10:6.

9
1 *Heb.* I shall have sinned against thee forever.

11
g *Presents*, Gen.32: 13.
h *Balm*, Gen. 37: 25.
i *Honey*, Prov. 25: 27.
j *Spices*, 1 Kin. 10:2.
k *Myrrh*, Ex. 30: 23.
2 *That is*, pistachio nuts.

12
l *Money*, Jer. 32:9.
m *Honesty, instances of*, Rom. 13: 13.

14
n *Prayer, in adversity*, Acts 6:4.
o *Adversity, prayer in*, Psa. 10:6.
p *Simeon*, Gen. 29: 33.
q *Parents, affection of, exemplified*, 2 Cor. 12:14.

8 And [d]Jū'dah said unto [c]Ī̤s'ra-el his father, Send the lad with me, and we will arise and go; that we may live, and not die, both we, and thou, *and* also our little ones.

9 I will be surety[c] for him; of my hand shalt thou require him: if I bring him not unto thee, and set him before thee, then [1]let me bear the blame for ever:

10 For except we had lingered, surely now we had returned this second time.

11 And their father [c]Ī̤s'ra-el said unto them, If *it must be* so now, do this; take of the best fruits in the land in your vessels, and carry down the man a [g]present, a little [h]balm[c], and a little [i]honey, [j]spices and [k]myrrh, [2]nuts, and *almonds:

12 And take double [l]money in your hand; and the money that was brought again in the mouth of your sacks, [m]carry *it* again in your hand; peradventure[c] it *was* an oversight:

13 Take also your [f]brother, and arise, go again unto the [e]man:

14 And [n,o]God Almighty give you mercy before the man, that he may send away your [p]other brother, and [f]Běn'ja-mĭn. If [q]I be bereaved *of my children*, I am bereaved.

15 ¶ And the men took that [g]present, and they took double [l]money in their hand, and [f]Běn'ja-mĭn; and rose up, and went down to [b]Ē'ġy̆pt, and stood before [e]Jō'ṣeph.

16 And when [e]Jō'ṣeph saw [f]Běn'ja-mĭn with them, he said to the †ruler of his house, Bring *these* men home, and slay[c], and make ready; for *these* men shall dine with me at noon.

17 And the man did as [e]Jō'ṣeph bade[c]; and the man brought the men into Jō'ṣeph's house.

18 And the men were afraid, because they were brought into [e]Jō'ṣeph's house; and they said, Because of the [l]money that was returned in our sacks at the first time are we brought in; that he may seek occasion against us, and fall upon us, and take us for [r]bondmen[c], and our asses.

19 And they came near to the †steward of Jō'ṣeph's house, and they communed[c] with him at the door of the house.

20 And said, O sir, we came indeed down at the first time to buy [s]food:

21 And it came to pass, when we came to the inn[c], that we opened our sacks, and, behold, *every* man's [l]money *was* in the mouth of his sack, our money in full weight: and we have [m]brought it again in our hand.

22 And other [l]money have we brought down in our hands to buy [s]food: we cannot tell who put our money in our sacks.

23 And [t]he said, Peace *be* to you, fear not: your God, and the God of your father, hath given you [u]treasure in your sacks: I had your money. And he brought [p]Sĭm'e-on out unto them.

24 And the †man brought the men into [e]Jō'ṣeph's house, and gave *them* water, and they [v]washed their [w]feet; and he gave their [x]asses provender[c].

25 And they made ready the [g]present against[c] [e]Jō'ṣeph came at noon: for they heard that they should eat bread there.

26 And when [e]Jō'ṣeph came home, they brought him the

v.17–1748 BC
See footnote, *Time*, Rev. 10:6.

18
r *Servant*, Jer. 2:4.

20
s *Food*, Psa. 136: 25.

23
t *Kindness, instances of*, Acts 28:2.
u *Temporal Blessings, from God*, Psa. 103:2.

24
v *Ablution*, Judg. 19:2.
w *Feet*, 2 Sam. 4:4.
x *Animals, kindness to*, Jer. 27:5.

* **ALMOND**, a tree. *Fruit of*, Gen. 43:11. *Aaron's rod of the*, Num. 17:8. *Bowls of candlestick in the tabernacle fashioned after the blossom of the*, Ex. 25:33, 34; 37:19, 20.
**Figurative use of**, Eccl. 12:5; Jer. 1:11.

† **STEWARD**, Gen. 15:2; 43:19; Gen. 44:4; Luke 8:3. *Faithful, illustrative of the faithful righteous; and the unfaithful, illustrative of the unfaithful righteous*, Luke 12:35–38, 42; 16:1–8. *See the parable of the pounds*, Luke 19:12–27; *of the talents*, Matt. 25:14–30. *Must be faithful*, 1 Cor. 4:1, 2; Tit. 1:7; 1 Pet. 4:10.

v.26–1748 BC
See footnote, *Time*, Rev. 10:6.

26
y *Salutations*, Luke 1:44.

29
z *Prayer, intercessory*, Acts 6:4.

30
a *Joseph*, Gen. 33:2.
b *Bowels, figurative*, 1 Kin. 3:26.
c *Brother*, Prov.18:24.
d *Benjamin*, Gen. 35:18.
e *Weeping, instances of*, Ezra 3:13.

31
f *Ablution*, Judg. 19:2.
g *Hospitality, instances of*, Rom. 12:13.

32
h *Egyptians*, Gen. 50:3.
i *Hebrews*, Gen.40:15.

33
j *Firstborn*, Zech. 12:10.
k *Birthright*, 2 Chr. 21:3.

34
l *Partiality*, 1 Tim. 5:21.
3 *Heb.* drank largely.

[g]present which *was* in their hand into the house, and [y]bowed themselves to him to the earth.

27 And he asked them of *their* welfare, and said, *Is* your father well, the old man of whom ye spake? *Is* he yet alive?

28 And they answered, Thy servant our father *is* in good health, he *is* yet alive. And they bowed down their heads, and made [y]obeisance.

29 And he lifted up his eyes, and saw his brother Bĕn′ja-mĭn, his mother's son, and said, *Is* this your younger brother, of whom ye spake unto me? And he [z]said, God be gracious unto thee, my son.

30 And [a]Jō′seph made haste; for his [b]bowels[C] did yearn[C] upon his [c,d]brother: and he sought *where* to weep; and he entered into *his* chamber, and [e]wept there.

31 And he [f]washed his face, and went out, and refrained[C] himself, and [g]said, Set on bread.

32 And they set on for him by himself, and for them by themselves, and for the [h]Ē-ġy̆p′tians, which did eat with him, by themselves: because the Ē-ġy̆p′tians might not eat bread with the [i]Hē′brews; for that *is* an abomination unto the Ē-ġy̆p′tians.

33 [g]And they sat before him, the [j]firstborn according to his [k]birthright, and the youngest according to his youth: and the men marvelled one at another.

34 [g]And [a,c]he took *and sent* messes unto them from before him: [l]but [d]Bĕn′ja-mĭn's mess[C] was five times so much as any of their's. And they drank, and [3]were merry with him.

## CHAPTER 44

*Joseph's policy to stay his brethren. 14 Judah's humble supplication to Joseph.*

AND [a]he commanded the [b]steward of his house, saying, Fill the men's sacks *with* food, as much as they can carry, and put every man's [c]money in his sack's mouth.

2 And put my *cup, the silver cup, in the sack's mouth of the [d]youngest, and his corn[C] money. And he did according to the word that Jō′seph had spoken.

3 As soon as the morning was light, the men were sent away, they and their [e]asses.

4 *And* when they were gone out of the city, *and* not *yet* far off, [a]Jō′seph said unto his [b]steward, Up, follow after the men; and when thou dost overtake them, say unto them, Wherefore have ye rewarded [f]evil for good?

5 *Is* not this *it* in which my lord drinketh, and whereby indeed he [g]divineth[C]? ye have done evil in so doing.

6 And he overtook them, and he spake unto them these same words.

7 And they said unto him, Wherefore saith my lord these words? God forbid that thy servants should do according to this thing:

8 Behold, the [c]money, which we found in our sacks' mouths, we brought again unto thee out of the land of [h]Cā′năan: how then should we steal out of thy lord's house [i]silver or [j]gold?

9 With whomsoever of thy servants it be found, both let him die, and we also will be my lord's bondmen[C].

10 And he said, Now also *let* it *be* according unto your words: he with whom it is found shall be

v.1–1748 BC
See footnote, *Time*, Rev. 10:6.

1
a *Joseph*, Gen. 33:2.
b *Steward*, Gen.43:19.
c *Money*, Jer. 32:9.

2
d *Benjamin*, Gen. 35:18.

3
e *Ass*, 2 Chr. 28:15.

4
f *Evil, for good*, Psa. 35:12.

5
g *Sorcery*, Isa. 47:9.

8
h *Canaan*, Gen. 37:1.
i *Silver*, 1 Chr. 28:14.
j *Gold*, Ezek. 7:19.

* **CUP**, Gen. 40:11; 2 Sam. 12:3; 1 Kin. 7:26; Matt. 23:25. *Made, of silver*, Gen. 44:2; *of gold*, 1 Chr. 28:17; Jer. 52:19. *Used in the institution of the Lord's Supper*, Matt. 26:27; Mark 14:23; Luke 22:20; 1 Cor. 10:21.

v.10–1748 BC
See footnote, *Time*, Rev. 10:6.

my servant; and ye shall be blameless.

11 Then they speedily took down every man his sack to the ground, and opened every man his sack.

12 And he searched, *and* began at the eldest, and left[G] at the youngest: and the *cup was found in [d]Běn′ja-mĭn's sack.

13 Then [k]they [l]rent[G] their clothes, and laded[G] every man his ass, and returned to the city.

14 And [m]Jū′dah and his brethren came to [a]Jō′ṣeph's house; for he *was* yet there: and they fell before him on the ground.

15 And [a]Jō′ṣeph [n]said unto them, [o]What deed *is* this that ye have done? [1]wot[G] ye not that such a man as I can certainly [g]divine?

16 And [m]Jū′dah said, What shall we say unto my lord? what shall we speak? or how shall we clear ourselves? [p]God hath found out the [q]iniquity of thy servants: behold, we *are* my lord's servants, both we, and *he* also with whom the *cup is found.

17 And he said, God forbid that I should do so: *but* the man in whose hand the *cup is found, he shall be my servant; and as for you, get you up in peace unto your father.

18 ¶ Then [m,r,s]Jū′dah came near unto him, and said, Oh my lord, let thy servant, I pray thee, speak a word in my lord's ears, and let not thine anger burn against thy servant: for thou *art* even as [t]Phā′raōh.

19 My lord asked his servants, saying, Have ye a [u]father, or a brother?

20 And we said unto my lord, We have a [u]father, an old man, and a [d]child of his old age, a little one; and his [a]brother is dead, and he alone is left of his mother, and his father loveth him.

21 And thou saidst unto thy servants, Bring [d]him down unto me, that I may set mine eyes upon him.

22 And we said unto my lord, The [d]lad cannot leave his [u]father: for *if* he should leave his father, *his father* would die.

23 And thou saidst unto thy servants, Except your [d]youngest brother come down with you, ye shall see my face no more.

24 And it came to pass when we came up unto thy servant my [u]father, we told him the words of my lord.

25 And our [u]father said, Go again, *and* buy us a little food.

26 And we said, We cannot go down: if our [d]youngest brother be with us, then will we go down: for we may not see the man's face, except our youngest brother *be* with us.

27 And thy servant my [u]father said unto us, Ye know that my wife bare me two *sons*:

28 And the [a]one went out from me, and I said, Surely he is torn in pieces; and I saw him not since:

29 And if ye take [d]this also from me, and mischief befall him, ye shall bring down my gray hairs with sorrow to the [v]grave.[G]

30 Now therefore when [s]I come[G] to thy servant my [u]father, and the [d]lad *be* not with us; seeing that [2]his life is bound up in the lad's life;

31 It shall come to pass, when [u]he seeth that the [d]lad *is* not *with us*, that he will die: and thy servants shall bring down the gray hairs of thy servant [s]our father with sorrow to the [v]grave.[G]

32 For thy [m,s]servant became [†]surety[G] for the [c]lad unto my

13
k *Mourning*, Lam. 2:5.
l *Rending of Garments, a token of sorrow*, 2 Chr. 34:27.

14
m *Judah*, Gen. 37:26.

15
n *Dissembling, instances of*, Josh. 7:11.
o *False Accusation*, 2 Tim. 3:3.
1 R. V. know

16
p *Conscience, guilty, instances of*, Acts 23:1.
q *Conviction, of sin, instances of*, John 16:8.

18
r *Orator*, vs. 18–44; Acts 24:1.
s *Children, love of, for parents*, vs. 18–34; Mark 10:14.
t *Pharaoh*, Gen. 37:36.

19
u *Jacob*, Gen. 27:11.

v.20–1748 BC
See footnote, *Time*, Rev. 10.6.

29
v *Sheol*, Mark 9:43.

30
2 *Or*, his soul is knit with the lad's soul;

† **SURETY,** Ex. 22:26, 27; Deut. 24:10-13; Prov. 6:1-5; 11:15; 17:18; 20:16; 22:26; 27:13; Ezek. 18:7, 12; 33:15; Amos 2:8.

[u]father, saying, If I bring him
not unto thee, then I shall bear
the blame to my father for ever.
33 Now therefore, [s]I pray
thee,[w, x]let thy servant abide[G] [y]in-
stead of the lad a bondman[G] to
my lord; and let the lad go up
with his brethren.
34 For[s, w]how shall I go up to my
father, and the lad *be* not with
me? lest peradventure[G][s]I see the
evil that shall come on my
father.

## CHAPTER 45

*Joseph makes himself known to his brethren; 5 and comforts them in God's providence. 9 He sends for his father. 16 Pharaoh confirms it. 21 Joseph furnishes them for their journey, and exhorts them to concord. 25 Jacob is revived with the news.*

[a, b]THEN [c]Jō'ṣeph could not
refrain[G] himself before all
them that stood by him; and
he cried, Cause every man to
go out from me. And there
stood no man with him, while
Jō'ṣeph made himself known
unto his [d]brethren.[Q]
2 And he [e]wept aloud: and the
[f]Ē-ġy̆p'tianṣ and the house of
[g]Phā'raōh heard.
3 And [c]Jō'ṣeph said unto his
brethren, I *am* Jō'ṣeph; doth my
father yet live? And [h]his brethren could not answer him; for
they were [i]troubled at his presence.[Q]
4 And [c]Jō'ṣeph said unto his
brethren, [j]Come near to me, I
pray you. And they came near.
And he said, I *am* Jō'ṣeph your
[d]brother, whom ye sold into
[k]Ē'ġy̆pt.[Q]
5 [a, b]Now therefore be not
grieved, nor angry with yourselves, that ye sold me hither:
for [l]God did send me before you
[m]to preserve life.
6 For these two years *hath* the
[n]famine *been* in the land: and yet
*there are* five years, in the which
*there shall* neither *be* earing[G] nor
harvest.
7 [o]And [l]God sent me before you
to preserve you a [1]posterity in
the earth, and to save your lives[S]
by a great deliverance.
8 [a, b, o]So now *it was* not you
*that* sent me hither, but God:
and he hath made me a father to
[g]Phā'raōh, and lord of all his
house, and a ruler throughout
all the land of [k]Ē'ġy̆pt.
9[Q] Haste ye, and go up to [p]my
[q, r]father, and say unto him,
Thus saith thy son [c]Jō'ṣeph,
God hath made me lord of all
[k]Ē'ġy̆pt: come down unto me,
tarry not:
10 And thou shalt dwell in the
land of *Gō'shen, and thou shalt
be near unto me, thou, and thy
children, and thy children's
children, and thy flocks, and
thy herds, and all that thou
hast:
11 And there will [c, p]I nourish
thee; for yet *there are* five years
of [n]famine; lest thou, and thy
household, and all that thou
hast, come to poverty.[Q]
12 And, behold, your eyes see,
and the eyes of my brother
[s]Bĕn'ja-mĭn, that *it is* my mouth
that speaketh unto you.
13 And ye shall tell my [q, r]father
of all my glory in [k]Ē'ġy̆pt, and of
all that ye have seen; and ye
shall haste and bring down my
father hither.
14 And he fell upon his brother
[s]Bĕn'ja-mĭn's neck, and [e]wept;
and Bĕn'ja-mĭn wept upon his
neck.
15 Moreover he [t]kissed all his
brethren, and [e]wept upon them:
and after that his brethren
talked with him.
16 ¶ And the fame[G] thereof was
heard in [g]Phā'raōh's house, saying, [c]Jō'ṣeph's brethren are

v.32–1748 BC
See footnote. *Time,* Rev. 10:6.

33
*w* *Unselfishness, instances of,* 1 Cor. 10:24.
*x* *Renunciation, self,* Luke 5:28.
*y* *Substitution,* Lev. 1:4.

1
*a* *Enemy, forgiveness of,* Prov. 24:17.
*b* *Forgiveness, instances of,* vs. 1-8; Matt. 18:21.
*c* *Joseph,* Gen. 33:2.
*d* *Brother,* Prov. 18:24.

2
*e* *Weeping, instances of,* Ezra 3:13.
*f* *Egyptians,* Gen. 50:3.
*g* *Pharaoh,* Gen. 37:36.

3
*h* *Conviction, of sin, instances of,* John 16:8.
*i* *Conscience,* Acts 23:1.

4
*j* *Good for Evil, returning,* Luke 6:27.
*k* *Egypt,* Gen. 41:8.

5
*l* *God, providence of,* Gen. 2:2.
*m* *Afflictions, benefits of, exemplified,* Psa. 34:19.

v.6–1748 BC
6
*n* *Famine,* 2 Kin. 8:1.

v.6–1748 BC
See footnote. *Time,* Rev. 10:6.

7
*o* *Foreordination, of Joseph's mission,* Rom. 8:30.
1 *Heb.* remnant

9
*p* *Children, good,* Mark 10:14.
*q* *Jacob,* Gen. 27:11.
*r* *Father,* Psa. 27:10.

12
*s* *Benjamin,* Gen. 35:18.

15
*t* *Kiss,* Ruth 1:14.

* **GOSHEN,** a district in Egypt especially adapted to herds and flocks. *Israelites dwelt in,* Gen. 46:28; 47. *Exempted from plagues,* Ex. 8:22; 9:26.

v.16– 1748 BC
See footnote, *Time*, Rev. 10:6.

17
u *Kindness, instances of*, Acts 28:2.
v *Canaan*, Gen. 37:1.

18
w *Hospitality, instances of*, Rom. 12:13.
x *Liberality, instances of*, 1 Tim. 6:18.
y *Fat, figurative*, Lev. 7:24.

19
z Num. 7:3–9.

20
a *Hospitality, instances of*, Rom. 12:13.
b *Liberality, instances of*, 1 Tim. 6:18.
c *Egypt*, Gen. 41:8.

21
d *Jacob*, Gen. 27:11.
e *Joseph*, Gen. 33:2.
f *Wagons*, Num. 7:3–9.
g *Pharaoh*, Gen. 37:36.

22
h *Dress*, Zech. 3:4.
i *Benjamin*, Gen. 35:18.
j *Presents*, Gen. 32:13.
k *Silver*, 1 Chr. 28:14.

24
l *Social Peace, enjoined*, Jer. 29:7.
m *Strife*, Prov. 20:3.

25
n *Canaan*, Gen. 37:1.

26
o *Rulers*, Ex. 18:21.
p *Parents, affection of*, 2 Cor. 12:14.

come: and it pleased Phā'raōh
well, and his servants.[Q]
17 And [g]Phā'raōh said unto
Jō'ṣeph, [u]Say unto thy brethren, This do ye: lade[G] your
beasts, and go, get you unto the
land of [v]Cā'năan;
18[Q] And take your [g]father and
your households, and [w]come unto me: and I will [x]give you the
good of the land of Ē'ġy̆pt, and
ye shall eat the [y]fat[G] of the land.
19 [u]Now thou art commanded,
this do ye; take you [z]wagons out
of the land of Ē'ġy̆pt for your
little ones, and for your wives,
and [w]bring your father, and
come.[Q]
20 Also regard not your stuff[G];
for [a, b]the good of all the land of
[c]Ē'ġy̆pt *is* yours.
21 And the children of [d]Īṣ'ra-el
did so: and [e]Jō'ṣeph gave them
[f]wagons, according to the commandment of [g]Phā'raōh, and
gave them provision for the way.
22 To all of them he gave each
man changes of [h]raiment; but to
[i]Bĕn'ja-mĭn he gave [j]three hundred *pieces* of [k]silver, and five
changes of raiment.
23 And to his [d]father he sent after this *manner*; [j]ten asses laden[G]
with the good things of [c]Ē'ġy̆pt,
and ten she asses laden[G] with
corn[G] and bread and meat[G] for
his father by the way.
24 So he sent his brethren
away, and they departed: and
he said unto them, [l]See that ye
[m]fall[G] not out by the way.
25 And they went up out of
[c]Ē'ġy̆pt, and came into the land
of [n]Cā'năan unto [d]Jā'cob their
father,
26 And told [d]him, saying, [e]Jō'-
ṣeph *is* yet alive, and he *is* [o]gov-
ernor over all the land of
[c]Ē'ġy̆pt. And [d, p]Jā'cob's heart
fainted, for he believed them not.
27 And they told [d]him all the
words of [e]Jō'ṣeph, which he had
said unto them: and when he
saw the [f]wagons which Jō'ṣeph
had sent to carry him, the spirit[G]
of Jā'cob their father revived:
28 And [d]Īṣ'ra-el said, *It is*
enough; [e]Jō'ṣeph my son *is* yet
alive: [p]I will go and see him before I die.

## CHAPTER 46

*Jacob is comforted by God at Beer-sheba. 5 Thence he with his household goes down into Egypt. 8 The number of his family that went into Egypt. 28 Joseph meets Jacob. 31 He instructs his brethren how to answer to Pharaoh.*

AND [a]Īṣ'ra-el took his journey with all that he had,
and came to [b]Bē'er-shē'bȧ, and
[c]offered [d]sacrifices[G] unto the God
of his father Ī'ṣaac.
2 And God spake unto [a]Īṣ'ra-el
in the [e, f]visions of the night, and
said, Jā'cob, Jā'cob. And he
said, Here *am* I.
3 And he said, I *am* God, the
God of thy father: [g]fear not to go
down into [h]Ē'ġy̆pt; for [i]I will
there make of thee a great
nation:
4 [i, j]I will go down with thee into [h]Ē'ġy̆pt; and I will also surely
bring thee up *again*: and [k]Jō'-
seph shall put[G] his hand upon
thine eyes.[S]
5[Q] And [a]Jā'cob rose up from
[b]Bē'er-shē'bȧ: and the sons of
Īṣ'ra-el carried Jā'cob their father, and their little ones, and
their wives, in the wagons which
[l]Phā'raōh had sent to carry him.
6 And they took their cattle,
and their goods, which they had
gotten in the land of [m]Cā'năan,
and came into [h]Ē'ġy̆pt, [a]Jā'cob,
and all his seed[G] with him:[Q]
7 His sons, and his sons' sons
with him, his daughters, and his
sons' daughters, and all his seed
brought he with him into Ē'ġy̆pt.
8 ¶ And these *are* the names of
the children of [n]Īṣ'ra-el, which

v.27–1748 BC
See footnote, *Time*, Rev. 10:6.

1
a *Jacob*, Gen. 27:11.
b *Beer-sheba*, Judg. 20:1.
c *Worship*, Gen. 22:5.
d *Offerings, burnt*, Lev. 6:17.

2
e *Vision*, Acts 9:10.
f *Dream, instances of*, Dan. 1:17.

3
g *Commandments, enjoining confidence in God*, Deut. 8:2.
h *Egypt*, Gen. 41:8.
i *Promises, to the righteous*, 2 Cor. 1:20.

4
j *God, providence of*, Gen. 2:2.
k *Joseph*, Gen. 33:2.

5
l *Pharaoh*, Gen. 37:36.

6
m *Canaan*, Gen. 37:1.

8
n *Israel, descendants of Jacob*, Ex. 4:22.

v.8–1748 BC
See footnote, *Time*, Rev. 10:6.

o *Reuben*, Gen. 35:22.
p *Firstborn*, Zech. 12:10.
9
q Ex. 6:14.
r 1 Chr. 5:3.
s Ex. 6:14.
10
t *Simeon*, Gen. 29:33.
u Ex. 6:15, or, *Nemuel*, Num. 26:12; 1 Chr. 4:24.
v Ex. 6:15.
w Num. 26:12; or, *Jarib*, 1 Chr. 4:24.
x Ex. 6:15, or, *Zerah*, Num. 26:13; 1 Chr. 4:24.
y *Shaul*, Ex. 6:15.
11
z *Levi*, Gen. 29:34.

a *Kohath*, Num. 26:58.
12
b *Judah*, Gen. 37:26.
c *Er*, Gen. 38:3.
d *Onan*, Gen. 38:8.
e Gen. 38:5.
f Gen. 38:29.
g Gen. 38:30.
h *Canaan, land of*, Gen. 37:1.
i 1 Chr. 2:5.
j 1 Chr. 2:5.
13
k *Issachar*, Gen. 30:18.
l Num. 26:23.
m Or, *Pua*, Num. 26:23; or, *Puah*, 1 Chr. 7:1.
n Or, *Jashub*, 1 Chr. 7:1.
o *Shimron*, Num. 26:24; 1 Chr. 7:1.
14
p *Zebulun*, Gen. 30:20.
q Num. 26:26.
r Num. 26:26.
s Num. 26:26.
15
t *Leah*, Gen. 29:16.
u *Jacob*, Gen. 27:11.
v *Padan-aram*, Gen. 28:2.
w Gen. 30:21.
16
x *Gad*, Gen. 30:11.
y Num. 26:15.
z Num. 26:15.

a Num. 26:15.
b Or, *Ozni*, Num. 26:16.
c Num. 26:16.
17
d *Asher*, Gen. 30:13. f Or, *Jimna*, Num. 26:44. f Or, *Isuah*, 1 Chr. 7:30. g Or, *Jesui*, Num. 26:44; 1 Chr. 7:30. h *Beriah*, 1 Chr. 7:30. i *Serah*, Num. 26:46. j Num. 26:45; 1 Chr. 7:31, 32. k Num. 26:45; 1 Chr. 7:31.

came into Ē'ġy̆pt, [a]Jā'cob and
his sons: [o]Reu̧'ben, Jā'cob's
[p]firstborn.
9 And the sons of Reu̧'ben;
[q]Hā'nŏch, and *Phăl'lū, and
[r]Hĕz'rŏn, and [s]Cär'mī.
10 And the sons of [t]Sĭm'e-on;
[u]Jĕ-mū'el, and †Jā'min, and
[v]Ō'hăd, and [w]Jā'chin, and [x]Zō'-
här, and [y]Shā'ul the son of a
Cā'năan-ĭt-ish woman.
11 And the sons of [z]Lē'vī;
‡Gĕr'shŏn, [a]Kō'hăth, and ‖Mĕ-
rā'rī.
12 And the sons of [b]Jū'dah;
[c]Ĕr, and [d]Ō'nan, and [e]Shē'lah,
and [f]Phā'rĕz, and [g]Zā'rah: but
Ĕr and Ō'nan died in the land of
[h]Cā'năan. And the sons of
Pharĕz were [i]Hĕz'rŏn and [j]Hā'-
mŭl.
13 And the sons of [k]Ĭs'sa-char;
[l]Tō'lȧ, and [m]Phū'vah, and [n]Jōb,
and [o]Shĭm'rŏn.
14 And the sons of [p]Zĕb'u-lŭn;
[q]Sē'red, and [r]Ē'lŏn, and [s]Jăh'lĕ-el.
15 These *be* the sons of [t]Lē'ah,
which she bare unto [u]Jā'cob in
[v]Pā'dan-ā'ram, with his daughter [w]Dī'nah: all the souls of his
sons and his daughters *were*
thirty and three.
16 And the sons of [x]Găd;
[y]Zĭph'ĭ-on, and [z]Hăg'gī, [a]Shu̧'-
nī, and [b]Ĕz'bŏn, [c]Ē'rī, and Är'ŏ-
dī, and Ā-rē'lī.
17 And the sons of [d]Ăsh'ēr;
[e]Jĭm'nah, and [f]Ĭsh'u-ah, and
[g]Ĭs'u-ī, and [h]Bĕ-rī'ah, and [i]Sē'-
rah their sister: and the sons of
Bĕ-rī'ah; [j]Hē'ber, and [k]Măl'-
chĭ-el.

18 These *are* the sons of [l]Zĭl'-
pah, whom [m]Lā'ban gave to
[n]Lē'ah his daughter and these
she bare unto [o]Jā'cob, *even* sixteen souls.
19 The sons of [p]Rā'chel [o]Jā'-
cob's wife; [q]Jō'şeph, and [r]Bĕn'-
ja-mĭn.
20 And unto [q]Jō'şeph in the
land of [s]Ē'ġy̆pt were born §Mȧ-
năs'seh and [t]Ē'phră-ĭm, which
[u]Ăs'e-năth the daughter of
[v]Pŏt'ĭ-phē'rah [1]priest of [w]Ŏn
bare unto him.
21 And the sons of [r]Bĕn'ja-mĭn
*were* [x]Bē'lah, and [y]Bē'chēr, and
[z]Ăsh'bĕl, [a]Gē'rȧ, and Nā'a-man,
[b]Ē'hī, and Rŏsh, Mŭp'pim, and
[c]Hŭp'pim, and Ärd.
22 These *are* the sons of [d]Rā'-
chel, which were born to [e]Jā'-
cob: all the souls *were* fourteen.
23 And the sons of [f]Dăn;
[g]Hū'shim.
24 And the sons of [h]Năph'ta-lī;
[i]Jăh'zĕ-el, and [j]Gū'nī, and [k]Jē'-
zĕr, and [l]Shĭl'lem.
25 These *are* the sons of [m]Bĭl'-
hah, which [n]Lā'ban gave unto
[d]Rā'chel his daughter, and she
bare these unto [e]Jā'cob: all the
souls *were* seven.
26 All the souls that came with
[e]Jā'cob into [o]Ē'ġy̆pt, which
came out of his [2]loins, besides
Jā'cob's sons' wives, all the souls
*were* threescore and six;
27 And the sons of [p]Jō'şeph,
which were born him in [o]Ē'ġy̆pt,
*were* two souls: [q]all the souls of
the house of [e]Jā'cob, which
came into Ē'ġy̆pt, *were* threescore and ten.
28 ¶ And he sent [r]Jū'dah be-

v.18–1748 BC
See footnote, *Time*, Rev. 10:6.

18
l *Zilpah*, Gen. 29.24.
m *Laban*, Gen. 28:5.
n *Leah*, Gen. 29:16.
o *Jacob*, Gen. 27:11.
19
p *Rachel*, Gen. 29:6.
q *Joseph*, Gen. 33:2.
r *Benjamin*, Gen. 35:18.
20
s *Egypt*, Gen. 41:8.
t *Ephraim*, Gen. 41:52.
u Gen. 41:45, 50.
v Gen. 41:45, 50.
w Gen. 41:45.
1 Or, prince
21
x *Bela*, Num. 26:38.
y 1 Chr. 7:6, 8.
z Num. 26:38; 1 Chr. 8:1.

a *Gera*, Judg. 3:15.
b Or, *Ehud*, 1 Chr. 8:6.
c 1 Chr. 7:12, 15.
22
d *Rachel*, Gen. 29:6.
e *Jacob*, Gen. 27:11.
23
f *Dan*, Gen. 30:6.
g Or, *Shuham*, Num. 26:42.
24
h *Naphtali*, Gen. 30:8.
i *Jahzeel*, 1 Chr. 7:13.
j Num. 26:48; 1 Chr. 7:13.
k Num. 26:49; 1 Chr. 7:13.
l *Shillem*, Num. 26:49.
m *Bilhah*, Gen. 29:29.
n *Laban*, Gen. 28:5.
26
o *Egypt*, Gen. 41:8.
2 *Heb.* thigh.
27
p *Joseph*, Gen. 33:2.
q *Israel, number of, who went into Egypt*, Ex. 4:22.
28
r *Judah*, Gen. 37:26.

* **PALLU** (*distinguished*). *Son of Reuben*, Gen. 46:9; Ex. 6:14; Num. 26:5, 8; 1 Chr. 5:3.

† **JAMIN** (*right hand*). *Son of Simeon*, Gen. 46:10; Ex. 6:15; Num. 26:12; 1 Chr. 4:24.

‡ **GERSHON** (*stranger*), called also GERSHOM. *Son of Levi*, Gen. 46:11; Ex. 6:16, 17; Num. 3:17–26; 4:22–28, 38; 7:7; 10:17; 26:57; Josh. 21:6; 1 Chr. 6:1, 16, 17, 20, 43, 62, 71; 15:7; 23:6. *Sons of, had charge of the fabrics of the tabernacle*, Num. 3:25, 26; 4:25, 26; *encamped on west side of tabernacle*, Num. 3:23.

See footnote, GERSHONITES, Num. 4:27.

‖ **MERARI.** *The third and youngest son of Levi*, Gen. 46:11. Ex. 6:16; Num. 3:17; 1 Chr. 6:1, 16. *Father of the Merarites*, Num. 26:57.

§ **MANASSEH** (*making to forget*). *Son of Joseph and Asenath*, Gen. 41:50, 51; 46:20. *Adopted by Jacob on his deathbed*, Gen. 48:1, 5–20.

**Tribe of:** Descendants of Joseph. The two sons of Joseph, Ephraim and Manasseh, were reckoned among the primogenitors of the Twelve tribes, taking the places of Joseph and Levi.

*Prophecy concerning*, Gen. 49:25, 26. *Enumeration of*, Num. 1:34, 35; 26:29–34. *Place of, in camp and march*, Num. 2:18, 20; 10:22, 23. *Blessing of Moses on*, Deut. 33:

v.28–1748 BC
See footnote, *Time,* Rev. 10:6.

*s* *Goshen,* Gen. 45:10.
*t* *Israel, dwell in Goshen,* Ex. 4:22.

29
*u* *Children, good, instances of,* Mark 10:14.
*v* *Chariot,* Josh. 11:4.
*w* *Weeping, instances of,* Ezra 3:13.

31
*x* *Wisdom, worldly,* vs. 31–34; Prov. 2:2.
*y* *Prudence,* vs. 31–34; 2 Chr. 2:12.
*z* *Pharaoh,* Gen. 37:36.

*a* *Canaan,* Gen. 37:1.

32
*b* *Shepherd,* Jer. 31:10.

34
*c* *Goshen,* Gen. 45:10.
*d* *Egyptians,* Gen. 50:3.

fore him unto Jō′ṣeph, to direct
his face unto [s]Gō′shen; and [t]they
came into the land of Gō′shen.
29 And [p, u]Jō′ṣeph made ready
his [v]chariot, and went up to meet
Ĭṣ′ra-el his father, to Gō′shen,
and presented himself unto him;
and he fell on his neck, and
[w]wept on his neck a good while.
30 And [e]Ĭṣ′ra-el said unto [p]Jō′-
ṣeph, Now let me die, since I
have seen thy face, because thou
*art* yet alive.
31 And [p]Jō′ṣeph said unto his
brethren, and unto his father's
house, [x, y]I will go up, and shew
[z]Phā′raōh, and say unto him,
My brethren, and my father's
house, which *were* in the land of
[a]Cā′năan, are come unto me;
32 And the men *are* [b]shepherds,
for their trade hath been to feed
cattle; and they have brought
their flocks, and their herds, and
all that they have.
33 And it shall come to pass,
when Phā′raōh shall call you,
and shall say, What *is* your
occupation?
34 That ye shall say, Thy servants' trade hath been about cattle from our youth even until
now, both we, *and* also our fathers: that ye may dwell in the
land of [c]Gō′shen; for every
[b]shepherd *is* an abomination[G] unto the [d]Ē-ġy̆p′tianṣ.

## CHAPTER 47

*Joseph presents five of his brethren, 7 and his father, before Pharaoh. 11 He gives them habitation and maintenance. 13 He obtains all the Egyptians' money, 16 their cattle, 18 and their lands, for Pharaoh. 22 The priests' land was not bought. 23 He lets out the land for a fifth part. 28 Jacob's age. 29 He swears Joseph to bury him with his fathers.*

v.1–1748 BC
See footnote, *Time,* Rev. 10:6.

1
*a* *Joseph,* Gen. 33:2.
*b* *Pharaoh,* Gen. 37:36.
*c* *Jacob,* Gen. 27:11.

THEN [a]Jō′ṣeph came and
told [b]Phā′raōh, and said,
My [c]father and my brethren,
and their flocks, and their herds,
and all that they have, are come
out of the land of [d]Cā′năan;
and, behold, they *are* in the
land of [e]Gō′shen.
2 And he took some of his
brethren, *even* five men, and presented them unto [b]Phā′raōh.
3 And [b]Phā′raōh said unto his
brethren, What *is* your occupation? And they said unto Phā′-
raōh, Thy servants *are* [f]shep-
herds, both we, *and* also our
fathers.
4 They said moreover unto
[b]Phā′raōh, For to sojourn[G] in the
land are we come; for thy servants have no pasture for their
flocks; for the [g]famine *is* sore[G] in
the land of [d]Cā′năan: now therefore, we pray thee, let thy servants dwell in the land of Gō′-
shen.
5 And [b]Phā′raōh spake unto
[a]Jō′ṣeph, saying, Thy father and
thy brethren are come unto
thee:
6 [h]The land of [i]Ē′ġy̆pt *is* before
thee; in the best of the land
make thy father and brethren to
dwell; in the land of [e]Gō′shen
let [j]them dwell: and if thou
knowest *any* [1]men of activity[G]
among them, then make them
rulers over my cattle.
7 And [a]Jō′ṣeph brought in [c]Jā′-
cob his father, and set him before [b]Phā′raōh: and Jā′cob
[k]blessed Phā′raōh.
8 And [b]Phā′raōh said unto
[c]Jā′cob, How old *art* thou?
9 And [c]Jā′cob said unto [b]Phā′-
raōh, The days of the [l]years of
my pilgrimage *are* an hundred
and thirty years: few and evil
have the days of the years of my
[m]life been, and have not attained
unto the [n]days of the years of

v.1–1748 BC
See footnote, *Time,* Rev. 10:6.

*d* *Canaan,* Gen. 37:1.
*e* *Goshen,* Gen. 45:10.

3
*f* *Shepherd,* Jer. 31:10.

4
*g* *Famine,* 2 Kin. 8:1.

6
*h* *Kindness, instances of,* Acts 28:2.
*i* *Egypt,* Gen. 41:8.
*j* *Israel, dwell in Goshen,* Ex. 4:22.
1 R. V. able men

7
*k* *Benedictions, instances of,* Deut. 21:5.

9
*l* *Year,* Lev. 25:29.
*m* *Life, brevity and uncertainty of,* Eccl. 8:15.
*n* *Longevity,* Psa. 91:16.

13–17. *Inheritance of one-half of tribe east of Jordan,* Num. 32:33, 39–42. *One-half of tribe west of Jordan,* Josh. 16:9; 17:5–11. *Cities of, given to Kohathites,* 1 Chr. 6:66–70. *The eastern half assist in the conquest of the country west of the Jordan,* Deut. 3:18–20; Josh. 1:12–15; 4:12, 13. *Join the other eastern tribes in erecting a monument to testify to the unity of all Israel; misunderstood; make satisfactory explanation,* Josh. 22. *Join Gideon in war with Midianites,* Judg. 6:7. *Malcontents of, join David,* 1 Chr. 12:19, 31. *Smitten by Hazael,* 2 Kin. 10:33. *Return from captivity,* 1 Chr. 9:3. *Reallotment of territory to, by Ezekiel,* Ezek. 48:4. *Affiliate with the Jews in the reign of Hezekiah,* 2 Chr. 30. *Incorporated into kingdom of Judah,* 2 Chr. 15:9; 34:6, 7. *In John's vision,* Rev. 7:6.

v.9–1748 BC
See footnote, *Time*, Rev. 10:6.

the life of my fathers in the days of their pilgrimage.[C] [Q]

10 And [c]Jā'cob [k]blessed [b]Phā'raōh, and went out from before Phā'raōh.

11 ¶ And [a.o]Jō'ṣeph *placed his father and his brethren, and gave them a possession in the land of Ē'ġy̆pt, in the best of the land, in the land of †Rȧ-mē'sēs, as Phā'raōh had commanded.

12 And [a.o]Jō'ṣeph nourished his father, and his brethren, and all his father's household, with bread, according to *their* families.

13 ¶ And *there was* no bread in all the land; for the [g]famine *was* very sore,[C] so that the land of [i]Ē'ġy̆pt and *all* the land of [d]Cā'năan fainted by reason of the famine.

14 [p]And [a]Jō'ṣeph gathered up all the [q]money that was found in the land of [i]Ē'ġy̆pt, and in the land of [d]Cā'năan, for the [r]corn[C] which they bought: and Jō'ṣeph brought the money into [b]Phā'raōh's house.

15 And when [q]money failed in the land of [i]Ē'ġy̆pt, and in the land of [d]Cā'năan, all the Ė-ġy̆p'tianṣ came unto Jō'ṣeph, and said, Give us bread: for why should we die in thy presence? for the money faileth.

16 And [a]Jō'ṣeph said, [p]Give your cattle; and I will give you for your cattle, if [q]money fail.

17 And they brought their cattle unto Jō'ṣeph: and Jō'ṣeph gave them bread *in exchange* for [s]horses, and for the flocks, and for the cattle of the herds, and for the [t]asses: and he [2]fed them with bread[C] for all their cattle for that year.

18 When that year was ended, they came unto him the second year and said unto him, We will not hide *it* from my lord, how that our money is spent; [p]my lord also hath our herds of cattle; there is not ought[C] left in the sight of my lord, but our bodies, and our lands:

19 Wherefore shall we die before thine eyes, both we and our land? buy us and our land for bread, and we and our land will be servants unto [b]Phā'raōh: and give *us* seed, that we may live, and not die, that the land be not desolate.

20 And [a]Jō'ṣeph [u]bought all the [v]land of [i]Ē'ġy̆pt for Phā'raōh; for the Ė-ġy̆p'tianṣ sold every man his field, because the [g]famine prevailed over them: so the land became [b]Phā'raōh's.

21 And as for the people, he removed them to [w]cities from *one* end of the borders of Ē'ġy̆pt even to the *other* end thereof.

22 Only the [x]land of the [3]priests bought he not; for the priests had a portion *assigned them* of [b]Phā'raōh, and did eat their portion which Phā'raōh gave them: wherefore they sold not their lands.

23 Then [a]Jō'ṣeph said unto the people, Behold, I have [u]bought you this day and your land for Phā'raōh: lo, *here is* seed for you, and ye shall sow the land.

24 [p]And it shall come to pass in the increase,[C] that ye shall give the [y]fifth *part* unto [b]Phā'raōh, and four parts shall be your own, for seed of the field, and for your food, and for them of your households, and for food for your little ones.

25 And they said, Thou hast saved our lives: let us find grace in the sight of my lord, and we will be Phā'raōh's [z]servants.

26 And Jō'ṣeph made it a law over the land of Ē'ġy̆pt unto this

**11**
o *Children, good, instances of*, Mark 10:14.

**14**
p *Oppression, instances of*, vs. 15–26: Eccl. 5:8.
q *Money*, Jer. 32:9.
r *Corn*, Psa. 65:13.

**17**
s *Horse*, Job 39:19.
t *Ass*, 2 Chr. 28:15.
2 *Heb.* led them as a shepherd

**20**
u *Monopoly*, Isa. 5:8.
v *Land*, Ruth 4:3.

**21**
w *Cities*, Num. 35:8.

**22**
x *Property, exempt from tax*, Lev. 27:15.
3 *Or*, princes

**24**
y *Tax*, Neh. 10:32.

**25**
z *Servant*, Jer. 2:14.

* **NEPOTISM**, official favoritism to relatives. *Of Joseph*, Gen. 47:11, 12. *Of Saul*, 1 Sam. 14:50. *Of David*, 2 Sam. 8:16; 19:13. *Of Nehemiah*, Neh. 7:2.

† **RAMESES** (*son of the sun*). *A district and city in Egypt*, Gen. 47:11; Ex. 12:37; Num. 33:3, 5. *City of, built by the Israelites as a treasure city for Pharaoh*, Ex. 1:11.

day, *that* Phā′raōh should have
the [y]fifth *part*; except the [z]land
of the [3]priests only, *which* became not Phā′raōh's.
27 ¶ And [a]Ĭş′ra-el dwelt in the
land of [b]Ē′ġy̆pt, in the country
of [c]Gō′shen; and they had possessions therein, and grew, and
multiplied exceedingly.
28 And [d]Jā′cob lived in the
land of Ē′ġy̆pt seventeen years:
so the whole age of Jā′cob was
[e]an hundred forty and seven
years.
29 And the time drew nigh that
[d]Ĭş′ra-el must [f]die: and he called
his son [g]Jō′şeph, and said unto
him, If now I have found grace
in thy sight, put, I pray thee, thy
hand under my thigh, and deal
kindly and truly with me; bury
me not, I pray thee, in Ē′ġy̆pt:
30 But I will lie with my fathers, and thou shalt carry me
out of Ē′ġy̆pt, and [h]bury me in
their [i]buryingplace. And he
said, I will do as thou hast said.
31 And he said, Swear unto me.
And he [j]sware unto him. And
Ĭş′ra-el bowed himself upon the
bed's head.

## CHAPTER 48

*Joseph with his sons visits his sick father. 2 Jacob strengthens himself to bless them. 3 He repeats the promise. 5 He takes Ephraim and Manasseh as his own. 7 He tells Joseph of his mother's grave. 8 He blesses Ephraim and Manasseh. 17 He prefers the younger before the elder. 21 He prophesies their return to Canaan.*

AND it came to pass after
these things, that *one* told
[a]Jō′şeph, Behold, thy [b]father
*is* sick: and he took with him
his two sons, [c]Mă-năs′seh and
[d]Ē′phră-ĭm.
2 And *one* told [b]Jā′cob, and
said, Behold, thy son [a]Jō′şeph
cometh unto thee: and Ĭş′ra-el
strengthened himself, and sat
upon the bed.
3 And [b]Jā′cob said unto [a]Jō′-
şeph, God Almighty appeared
unto me at Lŭz in the land of
[e]Cā′năan, and [f]blessed me,
4 And said unto me, Behold, I
will make thee fruitful, and multiply thee, and I will make of
thee a multitude of people; and
will give this land to thy [g]seed
after thee *for* an everlasting
possession.
5 And now thy two sons,
[d]Ē′phră-ĭm and [c]Mă-năs′seh,
which were born unto thee in the
land of [h]Ē′ġy̆pt before I came
unto thee into Ē′ġy̆pt, **are*
mine; as [i]Reu′ben and [j]Sĭm′-
e-on, they shall be mine.
6 And thy issue, which thou [1]be-
gettest after them, shall be thine,
*and* shall be called after the
name of their brethren in their
inheritance.
7 And as for me, when I came
from Pā′dan, [k]Rā′chel died [2]by
me in the land of [e]Cā′năan in the
way, when yet *there was* but a
little way to come unto Ĕph′-
răth: and I [l]buried her there in
the way of Ĕph′răth; the same
*is* †Bĕth′-lĕ-hĕm.
8 And [b]Ĭş′ra-el beheld [a]Jō′-
şeph's sons, and said, Who *are*
these?
9 And Jō′şeph said unto his father, They *are* my [m]sons, whom
God hath given me in this *place*.
And he said, Bring them, I pray
thee, unto me, and I will [n]bless
them.
10 Now the eyes of [b]Ĭş′ra-el were
dim for age, *so that* he could [o]not
see. And he brought them near
unto him; and [p]he [q]kissed them,
and embraced them.

27
*a Israel*, Ex. 4:22.
*b Egypt*, Gen. 41:8.
*c Goshen*, Gen. 45:10.

v.27–1731 BC
See footnote, *Time*, Rev. 10:6.

28
*d Jacob*, Gen. 27:11.
*e Longevity, instances of*, Psa. 91:16.

29
*f Death, preparation for*, Num. 23:10.
*g Joseph*, Gen. 32:2.

30
*h Burial*, Acts 8:2.
*i Burying Places*, Gen. 23:4.

31
*j Oath*, Num. 5:19.

1
*a Joseph*, Gen. 33:2.
*b Jacob*, Gen. 27:11.
*c Manasseh*, Gen. 46:20.
*d Ephraim*, Gen. 41:52.

v.2–1731 BC
See footnote, *Time*, Rev. 10:6.

3
*e Canaan*, Gen. 37:1.
*f Spiritual Blessings, from God*, Eph. 1:3.

4
*g Israel, prophecies concerning*, Ex. 4:22.

5
*h Egypt*, Gen. 41:8.
*i Reuben*, Gen. 35:22.
*j Simeon*, Gen. 29:33.

6
1 *Or*, hast begotten

7
*k Rachel*, Gen. 29:6.
*l Burying Places*, Gen. 23:4.
2 *Or*, to my sorrow

9
*m Children, gift of God*, v. 16; Mark 10:14.
*n Benedictions*, Deut. 21:5.

10
*o Blindness, instances of*, 2 Kin. 6:18.
*p Parents, affection of*, 2 Cor. 12:14.
*q Kiss*, Ruth 1:14.

* **ADOPTION, of Children.** INSTANCES OF: *Of Joseph's sons*, Gen. 48:5, 14, 16, 22. *Of Moses*, Ex. 2:5–10; Acts 7:21; Heb. 11:24. *Of Esther*, Esth. 2:7.
**Spiritual,** see footnote, SPIRITUAL ADOPTION, Rom. 8:15.

† **BETHLEHEM** (*house of bread*). *A city S. W. of Jerusalem*, Judg. 17:7; 19:18. *Called* EPHRATAH, Ruth 4:11; Psa. 132:6; Mic. 5:2; *and* EPHRATH, Gen. 35:16, 19; 48:7; *and* BETH-LEHEM-JUDAH, Judg. 17:7–9; 19:1, 18; Ruth 1:1; 1 Sam. 17:12. *Rachel dies and is buried at*, Gen. 35:16; 48:7. *The city of Boaz*, Ruth 1:1, 19; 2:4; 4. *Taken and held by the Philistines*, 2 Sam. 23:14–16. *Rehoboam converts it into a military stronghold*, 2 Chr. 11:6. *The city of Joseph*, Matt. 2:5, 6; Luke 2:4. *Birthplace of Jesus*, Mic. 5:2; Matt. 2:1–20; Luke 2:4, 15. *Herod slays the children of*, Matt. 2:16–18.

11 And [b]Ĭṣ'ra-el [r]said unto [a]Jō'ṣeph, I had not thought to see thy face: and, lo, God hath shewed me also thy seed.[G]

12 And [a,s]Jō'ṣeph brought them out from between his knees, and he bowed himself with his face to the earth.

13 And [a]Jō'ṣeph took them both, [d]Ē'phră-ĭm in his right hand toward Ĭṣ'ra-el's left hand, and [c]Mă-năs'seh in his left hand toward Ĭṣ'ra-el's right hand, and brought *them* near unto him.

14 And [b]Ĭṣ'ra-el stretched out his right [t]hand, and laid *it* upon [d]Ē'phră-ĭm's head, who *was* the younger, and his left hand upon [c]Mă-năs'seh's head, [3]guiding his hands wittingly;[G] for Mă-năs'seh *was* the [u]firstborn.

15 ¶[T Q] And [v]he blessed Jō'ṣeph, and said, God, before whom my fathers [w]Ā'bră-hăm and [x]I'ṣaac did walk, the [y]God which [z]fed me all my life long unto this day,[S]

16 [a]The [b]Angel which redeemed me from all evil, bless the lads; and let my name be named on them, and the name of my fathers Ā'bră-hăm and I'saac; and let them grow into a multitude in the midst of the earth.[T Q]

17 And when Jō'ṣeph saw that his father laid his right [c]hand upon the head of [d]Ē'phră-ĭm, it displeased him: and he held up his father's hand, to remove it from Ē'phră-ĭm's head unto [e]Mă-năs'seh's head.

18 And Jō'ṣeph said unto his father, Not so, my father: for this *is* the [f,g]firstborn; put thy right hand upon his head.

19 And his father refused, and said, I know *it*, my son, I know *it*: [e]he also shall become a people, and he also shall be great: but truly his younger [d]brother shall be greater than he, and his seed shall become a multitude of nations.

20 And [h]he blessed them that day, saying, [4]In thee shall Ĭṣ'ra-el bless, saying, God make thee as [d]Ē'phră-ĭm and as [e]Mă-năs'seh: and he set Ē'phră-ĭm before Mă-năs'seh.

21 And Ĭṣ'ra-el said unto Jō'ṣeph, Behold, I [i]die: but [j]God shall be with you, and bring you again unto the land of your fathers.

22 Moreover [k]I have given to thee one [l]portion [m]above thy brethren, which I took out of the hand of the [n]Ăm'ôr-ite with my sword and with my bow.[Q]

## CHAPTER 49

*Jacob calls his sons before him. 3 He foretells what will befall them in the last days, and blesses them. 29 His charge concerning his burial. 33 His death.*

AND [a,b]Jā'cob[T] called unto his sons, and said, Gather yourselves together, that I may tell you *that* which shall befall [c]you in the last days.

2 [b]Gather yourselves together, and hear, ye sons of [a]Jā'cob; and hearken unto Ĭṣ'ra-el your father.[T]

3 ¶ [d]Reu̇'ben, thou *art* my [e]firstborn, my might, and the beginning of my strength, the excellency of dignity, and the excellency of power:

4 [1,f,g]Unstable as water, [d]thou shalt not excel; because thou [h,i]wentest up to thy father's bed; then defiledst thou *it*: he went up to my couch.

5 ¶ [j]Sĭm'e-on and [k]Lē'vī *are* brethren; [2]instruments[G] of cruelty *are in* their habitations.

6 O my soul, come not thou into their secret; unto their [l,m]assembly, mine honour, be not thou united: for in their [n]anger they

---

**v.11–1731 BC** See footnote, *Time*, Rev. 10:6.

**11**
r *Thankfulness, exemplified,* Acts 24:3.

**12**
s *Children, good, instances of,* Mark 10:14.

**14**
t *Hand, imposition of,* Ezra 10:19.
u *Firstborn,* Zech. 12:10.
3 *Or,* crossing his hands

**15**
v *Parents, blessings of,* 2 Cor. 12:14.
w *Abraham,* Gen. 17:5.
x *Isaac,* Gen. 21:3.
y *God, providence of,* Gen. 2:2.
z *Food, from God,* Psa. 136:25.

**16**
a *Intercession, of men with God,* Jer. 27:18.
b *God, savior,* Gen. 2.2.

**17**
c *Hand, imposition of,* Ezra 10:19.
d *Ephraim,* Gen. 41:52.
e *Manasseh,* Gen. 46.20.

**18**
f *Firstborn, birthright of,* Zech. 12 10.
g *Birthright,* 2 Chr. 21.3.

**v.19–1731 BC** See footnote, *Time*, Rev. 10:6.

**20**
h *Parents, blessings of,* 2 Cor. 12:14.
4 *Or,* by

**21**
i *Death, scenes of,* Num. 23:10.
j *Faith, instances of,* Mark 11:22.

**22**
k *Parents, partiality of,* 2 Cor. 12: 14.
l *Inheritance,* Num. 27:7.
m *Partiality,* 1 Tim. 5:21.
n *Amorites,* Gen. 14:13.

**1**
a *Jacob,* Gen. 27: 11.
b *Death, preparation for,* vs. 1–33; Num. 23:10.
c *Israel, prophecies concerning,* vs. 1–33; Ex. 4:22.

**3**
d *Reuben,* Gen. 35: 22.
e *Firstborn, birthright of,* Zech. 12: 10.

**4**
f *Character, instability of,* Phil. 2: 15.
g *Instability.* Jas. 1:8.
h *Incest, instances of,* Lev. 18:6.
i *Adultery, instances of,* Lev. 20:10.
1 *Heb.* boiling over as water, thou shalt not have the preeminence;

**5**
j *Simeon,* Gen. 29: 33.
k *Levi,* Gen. 29:34.
2 *Heb.* weapons of violence are their swords.

**6**
l *Company, evil.* Prov. 13:20.
m *Fellowship, with the wicked,* 1 Cor. 1:9.
n *Anger, instances of,* Psa. 37:8.

v.6–1731 BC
See footnote, *Time*, Rev. 10:6.

o *Homicide, felonious*, Deut. 5:17.
3 R. V. houghed an ox.

7
p *Curse, parental*. Judg. 5:23.

8
q *Judah*. Gen. 37:26.
r *Parents blessings of*, 2 Cor. 12:14.
s *Benedictions*, Deut. 21:5.
4 R. V. sons

9
t *Lion, figurative*, Mic. 5:8.
5 R. V. and as a lioness;

10
u *Sceptre, figurative*, Esth. 4:11.
v *Judah, tribe of*. Num. 10:14.
w *Jesus, prophecies concerning*, Matt. 1:21.
x *Gentiles, prophecies concerning*, Acts 10:45.
6 R. V. the ruler's staff
7 *Or*, till he come to Shiloh, having the obedience of the peoples. *Or as otherwise read*, until that which is his shall come, etc.,
8 R. V. obedience

13
y *Sidon*, Ezek. 28:21.
9 *Heb*. beach
10 *Or*, by

14
z *Issachar*, Gen. 30:18.

[o]slew a man, and in their *self-
will they [3]digged[G] down a wall.
7 [p]Cursed *be* their [n]anger, for *it*
*was* fierce; and their wrath,[G] for
it was cruel: I will divide them in
Jā'cob, and scatter them in
Ĭṣ'ra-el.
8 ¶ [q,r,s]Jū'dah, thou *art he*
whom thy brethren shall praise:
thy hand *shall be* in the neck of
thine enemies; thy father's [4]children
shall bow down before thee.
9 [q,r,s]Jū'dah *is* a [t]lion's whelp:
from the prey, my son, thou art
gone up: he stooped down, he
couched[G] as a lion, [5]and as an old
lion; who shall rouse him up?[Q]
10 The [u]sceptre shall not depart
from [v]Jū'dah, nor [6]a lawgiver
from between his feet, [7]until
†,[w]Shī'lōh come; and unto
him *shall* the [8]gathering of the
[x]people *be*.[T Q]
11 Binding his foal unto the
vine, and his ass's colt unto the
choice vine; he washed his garments
in wine, and his clothes in
the blood of grapes:[Q]
12 His eyes *shall be* red with
wine, and his teeth white with
milk.
13 ¶ ‡,[r,s]Zĕb'u-lŭn shall dwell
at the [9]haven of the sea; and he
*shall be* for an [9]haven of ships;
and his border *shall be* [10]unto
[y]Zī'dŏn.
14 ¶ [r,s,z]Ĭs'sa-char *is* a strong
ass couching[G] down between [11]two
burdens:
15 And he saw that [12]rest *was*
good, and the land that *it was*
pleasant: and bowed his shoulder
to bear, and became a servant
[13]unto tribute.[G]
16 ¶ [a,b,c]Dăn shall judge his
people, as one of the tribes of
Ĭṣ'ra-el.
17 [a,b,c]Dăn shall be a [d]serpent
by the way, an ||adder in the
path, that biteth the horse heels,
so that his rider shall fall backward.
18 I have waited for thy salvation,[G]
O LORD.
19 ¶ [b,c,e]Găd, a troop shall
overcome him: but he shall overcome
at the last.
20 ¶ [b,c]Out of [f]Ăsh'ĕr his bread
*shall be* [g]fat, and he shall yield
royal dainties.
21 ¶ [b,c,h]Năph'ta-lī *is* a hind
let loose: he giveth goodly[G] words.
22 ¶ [b,c,i]Jō'ṣeph *is* a fruitful
bough, *even* a fruitful bough by
a well; *whose* branches run over
the wall:
23 The [j]archers have sorely[G]
grieved him, and shot *at him*,
and hated him:
24 [k]But[S] [b,c,i]his [l]bow abode in
strength, and the arms of his
hands were made [14]strong by the
hands of the mighty [15,m]*God* of
[n]Jā'cob; (from thence *is* the

v.14–1731 BC
See footnote, *Time*, Rev. 10:6.

11 R. V. sheepfolds:

15
12 R V. a resting place
13 R.V. under taskwork.

16
a *Dan*, Gen. 30:6.
b *Benedictions, instances of*, Deut. 21:5.
c *Parents, blessings of*, 2 Cor. 12:14.

17
d *Serpent*, Num. 21:6.

19
e *Gad*, Gen. 30:11.

20
f *Asher*, Gen. 30:13.
g *Fat, figurative*, Lev. 7:24.

21
h *Naphtali*, Gen. 30:8.

22
i *Joseph*, Gen. 33:2.

23
j *Archery*, Gen. 21:20.

24
k *Prosperity*, Eccl. 7:14.
l *Bow, figurative*, 2 Sam. 1:18.
m *God, preserver*, Gen. 2:2.
n *Jacob*, Gen. 27:11.
14 *Or*, active
15 R. V. Mighty One

* **SELF-WILL** (*stubbornness*), 1 Sam. 15:23. *Forbidden*, 2 Chr. 30:8; Psa. 75:5. *Proceeds from, unbelief*, 2 Kin. 17:14; *an evil heart*, Jer. 7:24. *Exhibited, in refusing to hearken to God*, Prov. 1:24; *in refusing to hearken to the messengers of God*, 1 Sam. 8:19; Jer. 44:16; Zech. 7:11; *in refusing to walk in the ways of God*, Neh. 9:17; Psa. 78:10; Isa. 42:24; *in refusing to hearken to parents*, Deut. 21:18, 19; *in refusing to receive correction*, Jer. 5:3; 7:28; *in rebelling against God*, Deut. 31:27, Psa. 78:8; *in resisting the Holy Spirit*, Acts 7:51.

*Ministers, should be free from*, Tit. 1:7; *should warn their people against*, Heb. 3:7–12. *Characteristic of the wicked*, Prov. 7:11; 2 Pet. 2:10.

**Exemplified:** *Simeon and Levi*, Gen. 49:6. *Israelites*, Ex. 32:9; Deut. 9:6, 13. *Saul*, 1 Sam. 15:19–23. *Josiah*, 2 Chr. 35:22. *Zedekiah*, 2 Chr. 36:13.

See footnote, OBDURACY, Prov. 29:1.

† **MESSIANIC HOPE,** Matt. 13:17; John 8:56; Acts 9:22; Heb. 11:13; 1 Pet. 1:10–12. *Created, by prophecy*, Gen. 49:10; Num. 24:17; 1 Sam. 1:10; 2 Sam. 7:12, 13; Isa. 9:6, 7; 11:1–9, 33:17; 40:3–5; 55:3–5; 62:10, 11; Jer. 23:5, 6; 33:15–17; Dan. 2:44; 7:13, 14; 9:24–27, Mic. 5:2; Zech. 9:9, Mal. 3:1–3; Acts 13:27; *by the covenant with David to establish his throne forever*, 2 Sam. 7:12–16; 1 Chr. 17:11–14; 22:10; 28:7 (with the Messianic Psalms); *by the Messianic Psalms*, Psa. 2; 21; 22; 45; 72; 87; 89; 96; 110; 132:11, 17, 18. *Confirmed in the vision of Mary*, Luke 1:30–33.

*Exemplified, by the priest, Zacharias*, Luke 1:68–79; *by the prophet, Simeon*, Luke 2:25, 29–32; *by the prophetess, Anna*, Luke 2:36–38; Mark 15:43; *by the wise men of the East*, Matt. 2:1–12; *by John the baptist*, Matt. 11:3; *by the people*, John 7:31, 40–42; 12:34; *by Caiaphas*, Matt. 26:63; Mark 14:61; *by Joseph of Arimathea*, Luke 23:51; Mark 15:43; *by the disciples on the way to Emmaus*, Luke 24:21; *by Paul*, Acts 26:6, 7.

See footnote, JESUS, *prophecies concerning*, Matt. 1:21.

‡ **ZEBULUN, Tribe of.** *Military enrollment of, at Sinai*, Num. 1:30. *Place of, in march and camp*, Num. 2:3, 7; 10:14, 16. *Territory awarded to*, Gen. 49:13; Josh. 19:10–16; Matt. 4:13. *Aboriginal inhabitants of the territory of, not expelled*, Judg. 1:30. *Levitical cities of*, Josh. 21:34, 35; 1 Chr. 6:77. *Benediction of Moses upon*, Deut. 33:18, 19.

*Loyalty of, in resisting the enemies of Israel*, Judg. 4:6, 10; 5:14, 18; *with Gideon against the Midianites*, Judg. 6:35. *Joins David when made king over Israel*, 1 Chr. 12:33, 38–40. *Joins with Hezekiah in renewing the passover*, 2 Chr. 30:11, 18. *Jesus dwelt in the land of*, Matt. 4:15. *Twelve thousand sealed*, Rev. 7:8.

|| **ADDER.** *A venomous serpent*, Gen. 49:17; Psa. 58:4; 91:13; 140:3; Prov. 23:32.

v.24–1731 BC
See footnote, *Time*, Rev. 10:6.

*o* *Shepherd, figurative*, Jer. 31:10.
*p* *Stones, figurative*, Ex. 24:12.

25
*q* *God, providence of*, Gen. 2:2.

26
16 *Or*, that is prince among

27
*r* *Benjamin*, Gen. 35:18.
*s* *Wolf*, Jer. 5:6.

28
*t* *Israel, tribes of*, Ex. 4:22.

29
*u* *Burying Places*, Gen. 23:4.
*v* *Cave*, Judg. 6:2.
*w* *Ephron*, Gen. 23:8.

30
*x* *Machpelah*, Gen. 23:9.
*y* *Mamre*, Gen. 13:18.
*z* *Canaan*, Gen. 37:1.

*a* *Abraham*, Gen. 17:5.

31
*b* *Sarah*, Gen. 17:15.
*c* *Isaac*, Gen. 21:3.
*d* *Rebekah*, Gen. 24:15.

[o]shepherd, the [p]stone of Ĭṣ'-
ra-el:)
25 [b,c]*Even* by the God of [i]thy
father, [q]who shall help thee; and
by the Almighty, who shall bless
thee with [k]blessings of heaven
above, blessings of the deep that
lieth under, blessings of the
breasts, and of the womb:[S]
26 The [b,c]blessings of thy [n]fa-
ther have prevailed above the
blessings of my progenitors unto
the utmost bound of the everlasting hills: they shall be on the
head of [i]Jō'ṣeph, and on the
crown of the head of him [16]that
was separate from his brethren.
27 ¶ [b,c,r]Běn'ja-mĭn shall ravin[G]
*as* a [s]wolf: in the morning he
shall devour the prey, and at
night he shall divide the spoil.
28 ¶ All these *are* the twelve
tribes of [t]Ĭṣ'ra-el: and this *is it*
that their [n]father spake unto
them, and [b,c]blessed them; every
one according to his blessing he
blessed them.
29[Q]And [n]he charged them, and
said unto them, I am to be gathered unto my people: bury me
with my fathers in the [u,v]cave
that *is* in the field of [w]Ē'phron
the Hĭt'tīte,
30 In the [v]cave that *is* in the
field of [x]Măch-pē'lah, which *is*
before [y]Măm'rē, in the land of
[z]Cā'năan, which [a]Ā'brā-hăm
bought with the field of Ē'phron
the Hĭt'tīte for a possession of a
buryingplace.[Q]
31 There they buried [a]Ā'brā-
hăm and [b]Sā'rah his wife; there
they buried [c]Ī'ṣaac and [d]Rĕ-
bĕk'ah his wife; and there I
buried [e]Lē'ah.
32 The purchase of the field
and of the [f]cave that *is* therein
*was* from the [g]children of Hĕth.
33 And when [h]Jā'cob had made
an end of commanding his sons,
he gathered up his feet into the
bed, and [i]yielded up the ghost,[G]
and was gathered unto his
people.[Q]

## CHAPTER 50

*The mourning for Jacob. 4 Joseph gets leave of Pharaoh to go to bury him. 7 The funeral. 15 Joseph assures his brethren of his favor. 22 Joseph's age. 23 He sees the third generation of his sons. 24 He prophesies unto his brethren of their return, 25 and takes an oath of them to carry his bones to Canaan. 26 He dies, and is embalmed.*

AND [a,b,c]Jō'ṣeph fell upon
his [d]father's face, and
[e,f]wept upon him, and [g]kissed
him.
2 And [a]Jō'ṣeph commanded his
servants the [h]physicians to *em-
balm his father: and the physicians embalmed [d]Ĭṣ'ra-el.
3 And [i]forty days were fulfilled
for him; for so are fulfilled the
days of those which are embalmed: and the †Ē-gўp'tianṣ
[f]mourned for him threescore and
ten days.
4 And when the days of his
[f]mourning were past, [a]Jō'ṣeph
spake unto the house of [j]Phā'-
raōh, saying, If now I have
found grace in your eyes, speak,
I pray you, in the ears of Phā'-
raōh, saying,
5 My [d]father made me [k]swear,
saying, Lo, I die: in my [l]grave
which I have [1]digged for me in
the land of [m]Cā'năan, there shalt

v.31–1731 BC
See footnote, *Time*, Rev. 10:6.

*e* *Leah*, Gen. 29:16.

32
*f* *Cave*, Judg. 6:2.
*g* *Hittites*, Judg. 1:26.

33
*h* *Jacob*, Gen. 27:11.
*i* *Death, described*, Num. 23:10.

1
*a* *Joseph*, Gen. 33:2.
*b* *Children, good, instances of*, vs 1-13; Mark 10:14.
*c* *Bereavement, instances of*, Hos. 9:12.
*d* *Jacob*, Gen. 27:11.
*e* *Weeping, instances of*, Ezra 3:13.
*f* *Mourning*, Lam. 2:5.
*g* *Kiss*, Ruth 1:14.

2
*h* *Physician*, 2 Chr. 16:12.

3
*i* *Forty, days*, Jonah 3:4.

4
*j* *Pharaoh*, Gen. 37:36.

5
*k* *Oath*, Num. 5:19.
*l* *Burying Places*, Gen. 23:4.
*m* *Canaan*, Gen. 37:1.
1 *Or*, bought

* **EMBALMING.** *Of Jacob*, Gen. 50:2, 3. *Of Joseph*, Gen. 50:26. *Of Asa*, 2 Chr. 16:14. *Of Jesus*, Mark 15:46; 16:1; Luke 23:56; John 19:39, 40.

† **EGYPTIANS.** *Descendants of Mizraim*, Gen. 10:6, 13, 14. *Wisdom of*, 1 Kin. 4:30. *Hospitality of, to Abraham*, Gen. 12:10-20. *Slaves bought by*, Gen. 37:36. *The art of embalming the dead practiced by*, Gen. 50:2, 3, 26. *Oppress the Israelites*, Ex. chapters 1, 2. *Refuse to release the Israelites*, Ex. chapters 5-10. *Visited by plagues*, Ex. 3:20; chapters 7-12; Deut. 6:22; Neh. 9:10; Psa. 78:43-51; 135:9; Jer. 32:20. *Firstborn of, destroyed*, Ex. 12:29; Num. 8:17; 33:4; Psa. 78:51; 105:36; 135:8; 136:10. *Send the Israelites away*, Ex. 12:29-36. *Pursue Israelites and the army of, destroyed*, Ex. 14:5-30; 15:1-19; Deut. 11:4; Psa. 78:53; 106:11; 136:15; Heb. 11:29.

*Abhorred shepherds*, Gen. 46:34. *Refused to eat with Hebrews*, Gen. 43:32. *Alliances with, forbidden to the Israelites*, Isa. 30:2; 31:1; 36:6; Ezek. 17:15; 29:6. *Eligible to membership in Israelitish congregation in the third generation*, Deut. 23:7, 8.

Invade the land of Israel: *Under Shishak*, 1 Kin. 14:25, 26; 2 Chr. 12:2-9; *under Pharaoh-nechoh*, 2 Kin. 23:29-35; 2 Chr. 35:20-24; 36:3, 4. *Aid the Israelites against the Chaldeans*, Jer. 37:5-11. *Intermarry with the Jews*, 1 Kin. 3:1.

*An enthusiastic Egyptian instigated rebellion against Roman government*, Acts 21:38.

*Prophecies of dispersion and restoration of*, Ezek. 29:12-15; 30:23, 26. *Conversion of, foretold*, Isa. 19:18.

See footnote, EGYPT, Gen. 41:8.

v.5–1731 BC
See footnote, *Time*, Rev. 10:6.

[n] *Burial*, Acts 8:2.

7
[o] *Egypt*, Gen. 41:8.

8
[p] *Goshen*, Gen. 45: 10.

9
[q] *Chariot*, Josh. 11:4.

10
[r] *Jordan*, Gen. 32: 10.
[s] *Seven, days*, Gen. 7:2.

11
[t] *Canaanites*, Ex. 23:28.

13
[u] *Cave*, Judg. 6:2.
[v] *Machpelah*, Gen. 23:9.
[w] *Abraham*, Gen. 17:5.
[x] *Ephron*, Gen. 23:8.
[y] *Mamre*, Gen. 13: 18.

thou bury me. Now therefore let
me go up, I pray thee, and [n]bury
my father, and I will come again.
6 And [j]Phā′raōh said, Go up,
and [n]bury thy father, according
as he made thee [k]swear.
7 ¶ And [a]Jō′ṣeph [m]went up to
[n]bury his father: and with him
went up all the servants of [j]Phā′-
raōh, the elders of his house, and
all the elders of the land of
[o]Ē′ġy̆pt,
8 And all the house of [a]Jō′ṣeph,
and his brethren, and his father's house: only their little
ones, and their flocks, and their
herds, they left in the land of
[p]Gō′shen.
9 And there went up with him
both [q]chariots and horsemen:
and it was a very great company.
10 And they came to the threshing-floor of Ā′tăd, which *is* beyond [r]Jôr′dan, and there they
[l]mourned with a great and very
sore[G] lamentation: and he made
a mourning for his father [s]seven
days.
11 And when the inhabitants of
the land, the [t]Cā′năan-ītes, saw
the [l]mourning in the floor[G] of
Ā′tăd, they said, This *is* a grievous mourning to the Ē-ġy̆p′-
tiaṇs: wherefore the name of
it was called Ā′bel-mĭz′ra-ĭm,
which *is* beyond [r]Jôr′dan.
12 And his [b]sons [n]did unto him
according as he commanded
them:
13 For his sons carried him into
the land of [m]Cā′năan, and [n]bur-
ied him in the [u]cave of the field
of [v]Măch-pē′lah, which [w]Ā′bră-
hăm bought with the field for a
possession of a [l]buryingplace of
[x]Ē′phron the Hĭt′tīte, before
[y]Măm′rē.[Q]
14 And [a]Jō′ṣeph returned into
[o]Ē′ġy̆pt, he, and his brethren,
and all that went up with him to
bury his father, after he had
buried his father.
15 ¶ And when Jō′ṣeph's brethren saw that their father was
dead, [z,a]they said, Jō′ṣeph will
peradventure[G] hate us, and will
certainly requite us all the evil
which we did unto him.
16 And they sent a messenger
unto [b]Jō′ṣeph, saying, Thy [c]fa-
ther did command before he
died, saying,
17 So shall ye say unto [b]Jō′-
ṣeph, [d]Forgive, I pray thee now,
the trespass of thy brethren, and
their sin; for they did unto thee
evil: and now, [e]we pray thee, forgive the trespass of the servants
of the God of thy father. And
Jō′ṣeph [f]wept when they spake
unto him.
18 And his brethren also went
and fell down before his face;
and they said, Behold, we *be* thy
servants.
19 And [b,g]Jō′ṣeph said unto
them, [h,i]Fear not: for *am* I in the
place of God?
20 But as for you, [j]ye thought
evil against me; *but* [k,l]God
meant it unto good, to bring to
pass, as *it is* this day to save
much[G] people alive.[S]
21 [h,i]Now therefore fear ye not:
I will nourish[G] you, and your little
ones. And [g]he comforted them,
and spake [2]kindly unto them.
22 ¶ And [b]Jō′ṣeph dwelt in
[m]Ē′ġy̆pt, he, and his father's
house: and Jō′ṣeph lived an hundred and ten years.
23 And [b]Jō′ṣeph saw [n]Ē′phră-
ĭm's children of the third *generation*: the children also of ‡Mā′chĭr
the son of [o]Mȧ-năs′seh were
brought up upon Jō′ṣeph's knees.
24[Q] And [b]Jō′ṣeph said unto his
brethren, I die: and [k,l]God will
surely visit you, and bring you
out of this land unto the land

v.14–1731 BC
See footnote, *Time*, Rev. 10:6.

15
[z] *Conviction, of sin, instances of*, John 16:8.
[a] *Conscience, guilty*, Acts 23:1.

16
[b] *Joseph*, Gen. 33:2.
[c] *Jacob*, Gen. 27: 11.

17
[d] *Forgiveness, of enemies*, Matt. 18:21.
[e] *Repentance, instances of*, Mark 1:4.
[f] *Weeping*, Ezra 3: 13.

19
[g] *Brother, love of*, Prov. 18:24.
[h] *Kindness, instances of*, Acts 28:2.
[i] *Good for Evil*, vs. 19–21; Luke 6: 27.

20
[j] *Enemy*, Prov. 24: 17.
[k] *God, providence of, instances of*, Gen. 2:2.
[l] *Faith, instances of*, Mark 11:22.

21
2 *Heb.* to their heart.

v.22–1677 BC
See footnote, *Time*, Rev. 10:6.

22
[m] *Egypt*, Gen. 41:8.

23
[n] *Ephraim*, Gen. 44:52.
[o] *Manasseh*, Gen. 46:20.

‡ **MACHIR.** *One of the sons of Manasseh*, Gen. 50:23; 1 Chr. 7:14. *Father of the Machirites*, Num. 26:29, 36:1. *The land of Gilead allotted to*, Num. 32:39, 40; Deut. 3:15; Josh. 13:31. *Certain cities of Bashan given to*, Josh. 13:31; 17:1.

which he [p]sware to [q]Ā'bră-hăm, to [r]Ī'ṣaac, and to [c]Jā'cob.

25 And Jō'ṣeph took an [s]oath of the children of Ĭṣ'ra-el, saying, God will surely visit[G] you, and ye shall carry up my bones from hence.[Q]

26 So [b]Jō'ṣeph [t]died, *being* [u]an hundred and ten years old: and they embalmed him, and he was put in a coffin in Ē'ġy̆pt.

24
p *Covenant, of God with men,* Deut. 29:1.
q *Abraham,* Gen. 17:5.
r *Isaac,* Gen. 21:3.

25 s *Oath,* Num. 5:19.

v.25–1677 BC
See footnote, *Time,* Rev. 10:6.

26
t *Death,* Num. 23:10.
u *Longevity, instances of,* Psa. 91:16.

THE SECOND BOOK OF MOSES,

CALLED

# EXODUS

## CHAPTER 1

*The children of Israel multiply after Joseph's death. 8 The more they are oppressed by a new king, the more they multiply. 15 The midwives fear God, and save the men children alive. 22 Pharaoh commands the male children be cast into the river.*

NOW these *are* the [a]names of the children of [b]Ĭṣ'ra-el, which came into [c]Ē'ġy̆pt; every man and his household came with [d]Jā'cob.

2 [e]Reu̥'ben, [f]Sĭm'e-on, [g]Lē'vī, and [h]Jū'dah,

3 [i]Ĭṣ'sa-char, [j]Zĕb'u-lŭn, and [k]Bĕn'ja-mĭn,

4 [l]Dăn, and [m]Năph'ta-lī, [n]Găd, and [o]Ăsh'ẽr.

5 And all the [b]souls that came out of the loins of [d]Jā'cob were seventy souls: for [p]Jō'ṣeph was in [c]Ē'ġy̆pt *already.*[Q]

6 And [p]Jō'ṣeph died, and all his brethren, and all that generation.[Q]

7[Q] And the children of [q]Ĭṣ'ra-el were fruitful, and increased abundantly, and multiplied, and waxed[G] exceeding mighty; and the land was filled with them.

8 ¶ Now there arose up a new king over [c]Ē'ġy̆pt, [r]which knew not [p]Jō'ṣeph.[Q]

9[Q] And he said unto his people, Behold, the people of the children of [q]Ĭṣ'ra-el *are* [1]more and mightier than we:

10 Come on, let us deal [s]wisely with [q]them; lest they multiply, and it come to pass, that, when there falleth[G] out any war, they join also our enemies, and fight against us, and *so* get them up out of the land.[Q]

11 Therefore they did set over [q]them taskmasters to [t]afflict them with their burdens. And they built for *Phā'raōh †treasure cities, Pī'thom and [u]Ră-ăm'sēṣ.

12 But the more they [t]afflicted [q]them, the more they multiplied and grew. And they were grieved because of the children of Ĭṣ'ra-el.

13 And the [v]Ē-ġy̆p'tianṣ made the children of Ĭṣ'ra-el to serve with rigour:[G]

14 And they made their lives bitter with [t]hard ‡bondage, in [w]morter, and in brick, and in all manner of service in the field: all their service, wherein they made them serve, *was* with rigour.

15 ¶ And the *,[x]king of Ē'ġy̆pt spake to the Hē'brew [y]midwives, of which the name of the one *was* Shĭph'rah, and the name of the other Pū'ah:

16 And [x]he said, When ye do the office of a [y]midwife, to the Hē'brew women, and see *them*

v.1–1748 BC
See footnote, *Time,* Rev. 10:6.

1
a *Genealogy,* 1 Chr. 5:1.
b *Israel, number of, who went into Egypt,* vs. 1–5; Ex. 4:22.
c *Egypt,* Gen. 41:8.
d *Jacob,* Gen. 27:11.

2
e *Reuben,* Gen. 35:22.
f *Simeon,* Gen. 29:33.
g *Levi,* Gen. 29:34.
h *Judah,* Gen. 37:26.

3
i *Issachar,* Gen. 30:18.
j *Zebulun,* Gen. 30:20.
k *Benjamin,* Gen. 35:18.

4
l *Dan,* Gen. 30:6.
m *Naphtali,* Gen. 30:8.
n *Gad,* Gen. 30:11.
o *Asher,* Gen. 30:13.

5
p *Joseph,* Gen. 33:2.

7
q *Israel,* Ex. 4:22.

B.C. 1635?
See footnote, *Time,* Rev. 10:6.

8
r Acts 7:18.

9
1 *Or,* too many and too mighty for us:

10
s *Wisdom, worldly,* Prov. 2:2.

11
t *Oppression, instances of,* Eccl. 5:8.
u *Rameses,* Gen. 47:11.

13
v *Egyptians,* Gen. 50:3.

14
w *Mortar, cement,* Lev. 14:42.

15
x *Rulers, wicked,* Ex. 18:21.
y *Midwifery,* Gen. 35:17.

* **PHARAOH,** king of Egypt in the infancy of Moses. *Imposes hard tasks on Israel,* Ex. 1:8–11. *Decrees the death of all male Hebrew infants,* Ex. 1:16. *Daughter of, adopts Moses,* Ex. 2:5–10 (with Heb. 11:24). *Death of,* Ex. 2:23.

† **TREASURE CITIES.** *Built for the storage of the king's substance,* 1 Kin. 9:19; 2 Chr. 8:4, 6.

‡ **BONDAGE.** *Of Israelites, in Egypt,* Ex. 1:14; 2:23; 6:6; *in Persia,* 2 Kin. 24:10–16; Ezra 2:2; 9:9.

upon the stools; if it *be* a son,
then ye shall ‖kill him: but if it
*be* a daughter, then she shall live.
17 But the [y]midwives [z]feared
God, and [a]did not as the [b]king
of Ē′ġy̆pt commanded them, but
saved the men[C]children alive.
18 And the [b]king of Ē′ġy̆pt
called for the [c]midwives, and
said unto them, Why have ye
done this thing, and have saved
the men[C]children alive? [Q]
19 And the midwives said unto
Phā′raōh, Because the [d]Hē′-
brew women *are* not as the
Ē-ġy̆p′tian women; for they *are*
lively, and are delivered ere[C] the
midwives come in unto them.
20 Therefore [e]God [f]dealt well
with the midwives: and the people multiplied, and waxed[C] very
mighty.
21 And it came to pass, because
the [b]midwives [g]feared God, that
he made them houses.[C]
22 And Phā′raōh charged[C] all
his people, saying, Every [h]son
that is born ye shall ‖cast into
the river, and every daughter ye
shall save alive. [Q]

## CHAPTER 2

*Moses is born, 3 and placed in an ark among the flags of the river. 5 He is found, and brought up by Pharaoh's daughter. 11 He slays an Egyptian. 13 He reproves a Hebrew. 15 He flees into Midian. 21 He marries Zipporah. 22 Gershom is born. 23 God respects the Israelites' cry.*

AND there went a [a]man of
the house of [b]Lē′vī, and
took *to wife* a [c]daughter of Lē′vī.
2 And the [c]woman conceived,
and bare a son: and when she
saw him that [d]he *was a* goodly[C]
*child*, she hid him three months.[Q]
3 And when [e]she could not
longer hide him, she took for
him an ark[C] of *bulrushes, and
daubed it with [f]slime[C] and with
[g]pitch, and put the child therein;
and she laid *it* in the flags[C] by the
river's brink.
4 And his [h]sister stood afar off,
to wit[C] what would be done to him.
5 ¶ And the daughter of [i]Phā′-
raōh came down to [j]wash *herself* at the river; and her maidens
walked along by the river's side;
and when she saw the ark among
the flags, she sent her maid to
fetch it.[Q]
6 And when she had opened *it*,
she saw the child: and, behold,
the babe wept. And she had
[k]compassion on him, and said,
This *is one* of the [l]Hē′brewṣ′
children.
7 Then said his [h]sister to [i]Phā′-
raōh's daughter, Shall I go and
call to thee a [m]nurse of the [l]Hē′-
brew women, that she may nurse
the [n]child for thee?
8 And [i]Phā′raōh's daughter
said to her, Go. And the [h]maid
went and called the child's
[c]mother.
9 And [i]Phā′raōh's daughter
said unto her, Take this [n]child
away, and [m]nurse it for me, and I
will give *thee* thy [o]wages. And
the woman took the child, and
nursed it.
10 And the child grew, and she
brought him unto [i]Phā′raōh's
daughter, and he [p]became her
son. And she called his name
†Mō′ṣeṣ: and she said, Because
I drew him out of the water.[Q]
11 ¶ And it came to pass in
those days, [q]when †Mō′ṣeṣ was
grown, that he went out unto his

17
z *Fear of God, instances of,* Acts 9:31.

a *Integrity, instances of,* Job 2:3.

18
b *Rulers, wicked,* Ex. 18:21.
c *Midwifery,* Gen. 35:17.

19
d *Hebrew,* Gen. 40:15.

20
e *God, providence of,* Gen. 2:2.
f *Righteousness, fruits of,* Psa. 15:2.

21
g *Fear of God, instances of,* Acts 9:31.

22
h *Children, edict to murder,* Mark 10:14.

v.1–1614 BC
See footnote, *Time,* Rev. 10:6.

1
a *Amram,* Ex. 6:18.
b *Levi,* Gen. 29:34.
c *Jochebed,* Ex. 6:20.

2
d Acts 7:20; Heb. 11:23.

3
e *Parents, affection of,* 2 Cor. 12:14.

v.3–1614 BC
See footnote, *Time,* Rev. 10:6.

f *Bitumen,* Gen. 11:3.
g *Pitch,* Isa. 34:9.

4
h *Miriam,* Ex. 15:20.

5
i *Pharaoh,* Ex. 1:11.
j *Ablution,* Judg. 19:21.

6
k *Kindness, instances of,* Acts 28:2.
l *Hebrew,* Gen. 40:15.

7
m *Nurse,* 2 Chr. 22:11.
n *Children, nurse for,* Mark 10:14.

9
o *Wages,* Gen. 31:7.

10
p *Adoption, of children,* Gen. 48:5.

v.10–1574 BC
See footnote, *Time,* Rev. 10:6.

11
q Acts 7:23–28, 35; Heb. 11:24–26.

‖ **INFANTICIDE,** Num. 31:17; Matt. 2:16–18; Acts 7:19.

* **BULRUSH,** *or* papyrus. *Boats of,* Isa. 18:2. *Moses' ark of,* Ex. 2:3. *Called rush,* Job 8:11; Isa. 58:5.

† **MOSES.** *A Levite and son of Amram,* Ex. 2:1–4; 6:20; Num. 26:59; 1 Chr. 23:13. *Hidden three months,* Ex. 2:2; Acts 7:20; Heb. 11:23. *Hidden in an ark,* Ex. 2:3. *Discovered and adopted by the daughter of Pharaoh,* Ex. 2:5–10; Acts 7:21. *Learned in all the wisdom of Egypt,* Acts 7:22. *His loyalty to his race,* Heb. 11:24–26. *Takes the life of an Egyptian; flees from Egypt; finds refuge among the Midianites,* Ex. 2:11–22; Acts 7:24–29. *Joins himself to Jethro, priest of Midian; marries his daughter Zipporah; has two sons,* Ex. 2:15–22; 18:3, 4; 1 Chr. 23:15; Acts 7:29. *Is herdsman for Jethro in the desert of Horeb,* Ex. 3:1. *Has the vision of the burning bush,* Ex. 3:2–6; Acts 7:30–34. *God reveals to him his purpose to deliver the Israelites and bring them into the land of Canaan,* Ex. 3:7–10. *Commissioned as leader of the Israelites,* Ex. 3:10–22; Ex. 4:12; 6:13; Psa. 105:26; Acts 7:34. *Makes excuses,* Ex. 3:11; 4:1, 10, 13; 6:12, 30. *Rod of,* Ex. 4:17, 20; 9:23; 14:16; 17:5, 6; Num. 20:8, 9, 11. *His hand made leprous, and restored,* Ex. 4:6, 7

v.11–1574 BC
See footnote, *Time*, Rev. 10:6.

brethren, and looked on their
burdens: and he spied an
Ē-ġy̆p'tian smiting an [l]Hē'brew,
one of his brethren.
12 And [†]he looked this way
and that way, and [q]when he saw
that *there was* no man, he [r,s]slew
the Ē-ġy̆p'tian, and hid him in
the sand.
13 And [q]when he went out the
second day, behold, two men of
the [l]Hē'brews strove together:
and he said to him that did the
wrong, Wherefore [r]smitest thou
thy fellow?
14 And he said, [q]Who made
thee a prince and a judge over
us? intendest thou to kill me, as
thou killedst the Ē-ġy̆p'tian?
And [†]Mō'ṣeṣ feared, and said,
Surely this thing is known.
15 Now when [i]Phā'raōh heard
this thing, he sought to slay
[†]Mō'ṣeṣ. [t]But Mō'ṣeṣ [u]fled from
the face of Phā'raōh, and dwelt
in the land of [v]Mĭd'ĭ-an: and he
sat down by a well.
16 Now the [w]priest of Mĭd'ĭ-an
had seven daughters: and [x]they
came and drew *water*, and filled
the troughs to water their father's flock.

12
*r Homicide, felonious, instances of*, Deut. 5:17.
*s Rashness, instances of*, 2 Sam. 6:7.

15
*t* Acts 7:29; Heb. 11:27.
*u Fugitives, instances of*, Judg. 12:4.
*v Midianites*, Gen. 37:28.

16
*w Priest, antemosaic*, Lev. 1:5.
*x Women, duties of*, Prov. 31:10.

17 And the [z]shepherds came
and drove them away: but Mō'-
ṣeṣ stood up and [z]helped them,
and watered their flock.
18 And when they came to
[a]Reu'el their father, he said,
How *is it that* ye are come so
soon to day?
19 And they said, An Ē-ġy̆p'-
tian delivered us out of the hand
of the [b]shepherds, and also drew
*water* enough for us, and [c]wa-
tered the flock.
20 And he said unto his daughters, And where *is* he? why *is* it
*that* ye have left the [d]man? [e]call
him, that he may eat bread.
21 And [†]Mō'ṣeṣ was content to
dwell with the [a]man: and he gave
Mō'ṣeṣ [‡]Zĭp-pō'rah his daughter.
22 And she bare *him* a son, and
he called his name [‖]Gēr'shōm:
for he said, I have been [f]a
[d]stranger in a strange land.
23 ¶ And it came to pass in process of time, that the king of
Ē'ġy̆pt died: and the children of
[g]Ĭṣ'ra-el sighed by reason of the
[h,i,j]bondage, and they cried, and
their [k]cry came up unto God by
reason of the bondage.

v.17–1574 BC
See footnote, *Time*, Rev. 10:6.

17
*y Shepherd*, Jer. 31:10.
*z Kindness, instances of*, Acts 28:2.

18
*a* Or, *Jethro*, Ex. 3:1.
*b Shepherd*, Jer. 31:10.
*c Animals, kindness to*, Jer. 27:5.

20
*d Foreigner, kindness to*, Deut. 23:20.
*e Hospitality, instances of*, Rom. 12:13.

22
*f* Acts 7:29.

23
*g Israel*, Ex. 4:22.
*h Bondage*, Ex. 1:14.
*i Adversity, prayer in*, Psa. 10:6.
*j Oppression*, Eccl. 5:8.
*k Prayer, in adversity*, Acts 6:4.

*With his wife and sons leaves Midian to perform his mission*, Ex. 4:18–20. *His controversy with his wife on account of circumcision*, Ex. 4:20–26. *Meets Aaron in the wilderness*, Ex. 4:27, 28.

*With Aaron assembles the leaders of Israel*, Ex. 4:29–31. *With Aaron goes before Pharaoh; in the name of Jehovah demands the liberties of his people*, Ex. 5:1. *Rejected by Pharaoh; hardships of the Israelites increased*, Ex. 5. *People murmur against Moses and Aaron*, Ex. 5:20, 21; 15:24; 16:2, 3; 17:2, 3; Num. 14:2–4; 16:41; 20:2–5; 21:5; Deut. 1:12, 26–28. See footnote, ISRAEL, Ex. 4:22. *Receives comfort and assurance from the Lord*, Ex. 6:1–8. *Renews his appeal to Pharaoh*, Ex. 6:11. *Under divine direction brings plagues upon the land of Egypt*, Ex. chapters 7–12. *Secures the deliverance of the people and leads them out of Egypt*, Ex. 13. *Crosses the Red Sea; Pharaoh and his army are destroyed*, Ex. 14; Psa. 106:8–11; Heb. 11:29. *Composes a song for the children of Israel on their deliverance from Pharaoh*, Ex. 15. *Joined by his family in the wilderness*, Ex. 18:1–12.

*Institutes a system of government*, Ex. 18:13–26; Num. 11:16–30; Deut. 1:9–18. *Receives the law and ordains divers statutes*, see footnote, LAW OF MOSES, Deut. 33:2. *Face of, transfigured*, Ex. 34:29–35; 2 Cor. 3:13. *Sets up the tabernacle*, see footnote, TABERNACLE, Ex. 27:9. *Reproves Aaron, for making the golden calf*, Ex. 32:21; *for irregularity in the offerings*, Lev. 10:16–20. *Receives the second tables of stone*, Ex. 34:1–29. *Jealousy of Aaron and Miriam toward*, Num. 12. *God offers to make him head of a great nation*, Ex. 32:10; Num. 14:12; Deut. 9:14. *Rebellion of Korah, Dathan, and Abiram against*, Num. 16. *Sends twelve spies to view Canaan*, Num. 13:1–3; 32:8; Deut. 1:22–24; Josh. 14:7. *Appoints Joshua as his successor*, Num. 27:22, 23; Deut. 31:7, 8, 14, 23; 34:9.

*Not permitted to enter Canaan, but views the land from Mount Pisgah*, Num. 20:12; 27:12–14; Deut. 1:37; 3:23–29; 32:48–52; 34:1–8. *Death and burial of*, Num. 31:2; Deut. 32:50; 34:1–6. *Body of, disputed over*, Jude 9. *Age of, at various times*, Ex. 7:7; Acts 7:23, 30. *One hundred and twenty years old at death*, Deut. 31:2; 34:7. *Mourning for, thirty days in the plains of Moab*, Deut. 34:8. *His virility*, Deut. 31:2; 34:7.

*Present with Jesus on the mount of transfiguration*, Matt. 17:3, 4; Mark 9:4, 5; Luke 9:30.

*Type of Christ*, Deut. 18:15–18; Acts 3:22; 7:37.

**Benedictions of:** *Upon the people*, Lev. 9:23; Num. 10:35, 36; Deut. 1:11. *Last benediction upon the twelve tribes*, Deut. 33.

**Character of:** *Murmurings of*, Ex. 5:22, 23; Num. 11:10–15. *Impatience of*, Ex. 5:22, 23; 6:12; 32:19; Num. 11:10–15; 16:15; 20:10; 31:14. *Respected and feared*, Ex. 33:8. *Faith of*, Num. 10:29; Deut. 9:1–3; Heb. 11:23–28. Called *the man of God*, Deut. 33:1; Josh. 14:6; 1 Chr. 23:14; 2 Chr. 30:16; Ezra 3:2. *God spake to, as a man to his friend*, Ex. 33:11; Num. 12:8; Deut. 34:10. *Magnified of God*, Ex. 19:9; Num. 14:12–20; Deut. 9:13–29 (with Ex. 32:30). *Magnanimity of, toward Eldad and Medad*, Num. 11:27–29. *Meekness of*, Ex. 14:13, 14; 15:24, 25; 16:2, 3, 7, 8; Num. 12:3; 16:4–11. *Obedience of*, Ex. 7:6; 40:16, 19, 21. *Faithful*, Num. 12:7; Heb. 3:2–5. *Unaspiring*, Num. 14:12–20; Deut. 9:13–29 (with Ex. 32:30).

**Miracles of:** See footnote, MIRACLES, Luke 23:8.

**A Prophet,** Deut. 18:15, 18; 34:10; Hos. 12:13; Acts 7:37, 38.

‡ **ZIPPORAH.** *Wife of Moses*, Ex. 2:16–22 *Reproaches Moses*, Ex. 4:25, 26. *Separates from Moses; is brought again to him by her father*, Ex. 18:2–6. *Miriam and Aaron upbraid Moses concerning*, Num. 12:1.

‖ **GERSHOM.** *Son of Moses*, Ex. 2:22; 18:3; 1 Chr. 23:15, 16; 26:24; Acts 7:29.

**24**
*l* *Anthropomorphisms, hearing and remembering, attributed to God,* Gen. 11:5.
*m* *Prayer, answered,* Acts 6:4.
*n* *God, faithfulness of,* Gen. 2:2.
*o* *Covenant, of God with men,* Lev. 26:44.
*p* *Abraham,* Gen. 17:5.
*q* *Isaac,* Gen. 21:3.
*r* *Jacob,* Gen. 27:11.

**25**
*s* *God, mercy of,* Gen. 2:2.

**v.1–1534 BC**
See footnote, *Time,* Rev. 10:6.

**1**
*a* *Moses,* vs. 1–22; Ex. 2:10.
*b* *Shepherd,* Jer. 31:10.
*c* *Midianites,* Gen. 37:28.
1 R. V. wilderness.

**2**
*d* *Angel,* Ex. 14:19.
*e* *Fire, symbolical,* Ex. 12:8.
*f* *Miracles,* Luke 23:8.

**4**
*g* *Anthropomorphisms,* Gen. 11:5.

**5**
*h* *Reverence, for sacred places,* Lev. 19:30.
*i* *Commandment, enjoining reverence for holy places,* Deut. 8:2.
*j* Acts 7:33.
*k* *Shoe,* Josh. 5:15.

**6**
*l* *Immortality,* 1 Cor. 15:54.

**7**
*m* *God, knowledge of,* Gen. 2:2.
*n* *Adversity, consolations in,* Psa. 10:6.
*o* *Prayer, answered, instances of,* Acts 6:4.

24 And God [l]heard their
[m]groaning, and [n]God remembered his [o]covenant with [p]Ā'brā-
hăm, with [q]Ī'saac, and with
[r]Jā'cob.[S Q]
25 And God looked upon the
children of Ĭs'ra-el, and [s]God
had respect[G] unto *them.*[T]

## CHAPTER 3

*Moses keeps Jethro's flock. 2 God appears to him in a burning bush; 9 and sends him to deliver Israel. 14 The name of God. 15 His message to Israel.*

NOW [a]Mō'ṣeṣ [b]kept the flock
of *Jĕth'rō his father in
law, the priest of [c]Mĭd'ĭan: and
he led the flock to the backside
of the [1]desert, and came to
the mountain of God, *even* to
†Horeb.[Q]
2 [Q]And the [d]angel of the LORD
appeared unto him in a flame of
[e]fire out of the midst of a bush:
and he looked, and, behold, the
‡bush burned with fire, and the
bush [f]*was* not consumed.[S T]
3 And [a]Mō'ṣeṣ said, I will now
turn aside, and see this great
sight, why the bush [f]is not burnt.[Q]
4 And when the LORD [g]saw
that he turned aside to see, God
called unto him out of the midst
of the ‡bush, and said, [a]Mō'ṣeṣ,
Mō'ṣeṣ. And he said, Here *am* I.
5 And he said, [h,i]Draw not nigh[G]
hither[G]: [j]put off thy [k]shoes from
off thy feet, for the place whereon thou standest *is* holy ground.[Q S]
6 [T]Moreover he said, I *am* the
[l]God of thy father, the God of
Ā'brā-hăm, the God of Ī'ṣaac,
and the God of Jā'cob. And
[a]Mō'ṣeṣ hid his face; for he was
afraid to look upon God.[Q]
7 ¶ [Q]And the [m]LORD said, I
have surely seen the [n]affliction of
my people which *are* in Ē'ġȳpt,
and have heard their [o]cry by
reason of their taskmasters; for
I know their sorrows;[S]
8 And [p]I am come down to deliver them out of the hand of the
[q]Ē-ġȳp'tianṣ, and to bring them
up out of that land unto a good
land and a large, unto a land
flowing with [r]milk and [s]honey;
unto the place of the [t]Cā'năan-
ītes, and the [u]Hĭt'tītes, and the
[v]Ăm'ôr-ītes, and the [w]Pĕr'ĭz-
zītes, and the Hī'vītes, and the
[x]Jĕb'u-sītes.
9 Now therefore, behold, the
[o]cry of the children of Ĭṣ'ra-el is
come unto me: and I have also
seen the [y]oppression wherewith
the [q]Ē-ġȳp'tianṣ oppress them.[S]
10 [z]Come now therefore, and I
will send thee unto ‖Phā'raōh,
that thou mayest bring forth my
people the children of Ĭṣ'ra-el
out of Ē'ġȳpt.[T Q]
11 ¶ And [a]Mō'ṣeṣ [b]said unto
God, [c,d]Who *am* I, that I should
go unto ‖Phā'raōh, and [e]that I
should bring forth the children
of Ĭṣ'ra-el out of Ē'ġȳpt?
12 And he said, [f]Certainly I
[g]will be with thee; and this *shall*
*be* a [h]token unto thee, that I have
sent thee: When thou hast
brought forth the people out of
Ē'ġȳpt, ye shall serve God upon
this [i]mountain.[S Q]
13 And [a]Mō'ṣeṣ [b,c]said unto
God, Behold, *when* I come unto
the children of Ĭṣ'ra-el, and shall
say unto them, The God of your
fathers hath sent me unto you;
and they shall say to me, What *is*
his name? what shall I say unto
them?
14 And [j]God [k]said unto [a]Mō'-
ṣeṣ, [2]I[G] AM THAT I[G] AM:
and he [l]said, Thus shalt [m]thou
say unto the children of Ĭṣ'ra-el,
I[G] AM hath sent me unto you.[Q S]

**v.7–1534 BC**
See footnote, *Time,* Rev. 10:6.

**8**
*p* *God, providence of, instances of,* Gen. 2:2.
*q* *Egyptians,* Gen. 50:3.
*r* *Milk, figurative,* Job 10:10.
*s* *Honey, figurative,* Prov. 25:27.
*t* *Canaanites,* Ex. 23:28.
*u* *Hittites,* Judg. 1. 26.
*v* *Amorites,* Gen. 14:13.
*w* *Perizzites,* Gen. 15:20.
*x* *Jebusites,* Deut. 7:1.

**9**
*y* *Oppression,* Eccl. 5:8.

**10**
*z* *Call, to special religious work,* Phil. 3:14.

**11**
*a* *Moses,* Ex. 2:10.
*b* *Excuses,* Luke 14:18.
*c* *Doubting, instances of,* Rom. 14:23.
*d* *Humility,* Prov. 22:4.
*e* *Duty, escape from, sought by Moses,* Eccl. 12:13.

**12**
*f* *Grace of God, instances of,* Rom. 4:16.
*g* *Promise, of divine presence,* 2 Cor. 1:20.
*h* *Token,* Psa. 86:17.
*i* *Mountain,* Mic. 7:12.

**14**
*j* *God, self-existent,* Gen. 2:2.
*k* *Revelation, concerning name of Deity,* 2 Cor. 12:1.
*l* *Inspiration, of prophets,* Job 32:8.
*m* *Prophets, inspiration of,* Isa. 3:2.
2 Or, I am, because I am: *or,* I am **who am:** *or,* **I will be that I** will be:

* **JETHRO,** a priest of Midian. Called RAGUEL and REUEL. *Moses spent forty years of exile with, and married his daughter,* Ex. 2:15–22; 3:1; 4:18; Num. 10:29. *Visits Moses,* Ex. 18.

† **HOREB.** *A range of mountains of which Sinai is chief,* **Ex. 3:1; 17:6; 33:6;** Deut. 1:2, 6, 19; 4:10, 15; 5:2; **9:8; 29:1;** 1 Kin. 8:9; 19:8; 2 Chr. 5:10; **Psa. 106:19;** Mal. 4:4. See footnote, SINAI, Ex. 16:7.

‡ **BURNING BUSH,** Ex. 3:2–5; **Deut. 33:16;** Mark 12:26; Luke 20:37; Acts 7:30–35.

‖ **PHARAOH,** king of Egypt at the time of the Exodus. *Moses intercedes with, for the deliverance of Israel,* Ex. 5:1–4;

v.15–1534 BC
See footnote, *Time*, Rev. 10:6.

15
n *God, eternity of*, Gen. 2:2.

16
o *Government, senatorial*, Isa. 22:21.
p *Senate*, Num. 11:16.

17
q *God, providence of*, Gen. 2:2.
r *Israel, God's promises to*, Ex. 4:22.

18
s *Hebrew*, Gen. 40:15.
t *Day's Journey*, 1 Kin. 19:4.
u *Worship*, Gen. 22:5.

19
v *God, foreknowledge of*, Gen. 2:2.

20
w *Egyptians, visited by plagues*, Gen. 50:3.
x *Miracles, design of*, Luke 23:8.

22
y *Borrowing, instances of*, Ex. 22:14.

15 And God said moreover unto [a]Mō'ṣeṣ, Thus shalt [m]thou say unto the children of Ĭṣ'ra-el, The LORD [l,n]God of your fathers, the God of Ā'bră-hăm, the God of Ī'ṣaac, and the God of Jā'cob, hath sent me unto you: this *is* my name for ever, and this *is* my memorial unto all generations.
16 Go, and gather the [o,p]elders of Ĭṣ'ra-el together, and say unto them The LORD God of your fathers, the God of Ā'bră-hăm, of Ī'ṣaac, and of Jā'cob, appeared unto me, saying, I have surely visited you, and *seen* that which is done to you in Ē'ġўpt:
17 And I have said, [q]I will bring [r]you up out of the affliction of Ē'ġўpt unto the land of the Cā'năan-ītes, and the Hĭt'tītes, and the Ăm'ôr-ītes, and the Pĕr'ĭz-zītes, and the Hī'vītes, and the Jĕb'u-sītes, unto a land flowing with milk and honey.
18 And they shall hearken to thy voice: and [a]thou shalt come, thou and the [p]elders of Ĭṣ'ra-el, unto the king of Ē'ġўpt, and ye shall say unto him, The LORD God of the [s]Hē'brewṣ hath met with us: and now let us go, we beseech thee, three [t]days' journey into the wilderness, that we may [u]sacrifice to the LORD our God.
19 And [v]I am sure that the king of Ē'ġўpt will not let you go, no, not by a mighty hand.
20 And I will stretch out my hand, and smite [w]Ē'ġўpt with all my [x]wonders which I will do in the midst thereof: and after that he will let you go.
21 And I will give this people favour in the sight of the Ē-ġўp'tianṣ: and it shall come to pass, that, when ye go, ye shall not go empty:
22 But every woman shall [y]borrow of her neighbour, and of her that sojourneth in her house, [z]jewels of [a]silver, and jewels of [b]gold, and raiment: and ye shall put *them* upon your sons, and upon your daughters; and ye shall spoil the Ē-ġўp'tianṣ.

## CHAPTER 4

*Moses' rod is turned into a serpent. 6 His hand becomes leprous. 10 He is loath to be sent. 14 Aaron is appointed to assist him. 18 Moses departs from Jethro. 21 God's message to Pharaoh. 24 Zipporah circumcises her son. 27 Aaron is sent to meet Moses. 31 The people believe them.*

AND [a]Mō'ṣeṣ [b]answered and said, [c,d]But, behold, [e]they will [f]not believe me, nor hearken unto my voice: for they will say, The LORD hath not [g]appeared unto thee.
2 And the LORD said unto him, What *is* that in thine hand? And he said, A rod.
3 And he said, Cast it on the ground. And he cast it on the ground, and it [h]became a [i]serpent; and [a]Mō'ṣeṣ fled from before it.
4 And the LORD said unto Mō'ṣeṣ, Put forth thine hand, and take [i]it by the tail. And he put forth his hand, and caught it, and it became a rod in his hand:
5 [j]That they may believe that the LORD God of their fathers, the God of Ā'bră-hăm, the God of Ī'ṣaac, and the God of Jā'cob, hath appeared unto thee.
6 ¶ And the LORD said furthermore unto him, Put now thine hand into thy bosom. And he put his hand into his bosom: and when he took it out, behold, his hand [h]*was* [k]leprous as snow.
7 And he said, Put thine hand into thy bosom again. And he put his hand into his bosom again; and plucked it out of his bosom, and, behold, it was

v.22–1534 BC
See footnote, *Time*, Rev. 10:6.
z *Jewels*, Gen. 24:53.

a *Silver*, 1 Chr. 28:14.
b *Gold*, Ezek. 7:19.

1
a *Moses, makes excuses*, Ex. 2:10.
b *Doubting*, Rom. 14:23.
c *Duty, escape from, sought by Moses*, Eccl. 12:13.
d *Excuses*, Luke 14:18.
e *Israel*, Ex. 4:22.
f *Unbelief*, Heb. 3:12.
g *Call, to special religious duty*, Phil. 3:14.

3
h *Miracles*, Luke 23:8.
i *Serpent*, Num. 21:6.

5
j *Miracles, design of*, Luke 23:8.

6
k *Leprosy*, Lev. 13:2.

7:1–6. *Increased the burdens of Israel*, Ex. 5:6–14. *Refused to let Israel go*, Ex. 7:14. *Is punished by plagues*, Ex. 7:20, 21; 8:6, 17, 24; 9:3, 6, 10, 23–25; 10:13–15, 22, 23; 12:29, 30. *Lets Israel go*, Ex. 12:31–33. *Pursues Israel with his armies*, Ex. 14:8, 9. *Is overthrown in the Red Sea*, Ex. 14:23–28.

v.7–1534 BC
See footnote, *Time*, Rev. 10:6.

turned again as his *other* flesh.[s]
8 And it shall come to pass, if
they will [l]not believe thee, neither hearken to the voice of the
first [h]sign, [i]that they will believe
the voice of the latter sign.
9 And it shall come to pass, if
they will [l]not believe also these
two signs, neither hearken unto
thy voice, that thou shalt take of
the water of the river, and pour
*it* upon the dry *land*: and the water which thou takest out of the
river shall [h]become blood upon
the dry *land*.
10 ¶ [l]And [a]Moses said unto
the LORD, O my Lord, [c,d,m]I *am*
not [1]eloquent, neither heretofore,
nor since thou hast spoken unto
thy servant: but I *am* [n]slow of
speech, and of a slow[C] tongue.
11 And the LORD said unto
him, [o]Who hath made man's
mouth? or who maketh the
*dumb, or [p]deaf, or the seeing,
or the [q]blind? have not [r]I the
LORD?
12 Now therefore go, and [s]I
will be with thy mouth, and
[t,u]teach [v,w]thee what thou shalt
say.
13 [x]And he said, O my Lord,
send, I pray thee, by the hand *of*
*him whom* thou wilt send.
14 And the [y]anger of the LORD
was kindled against Mō'ṣeṣ, and
he said, *Is* not [z]Aăr'on the Lē'vīte thy brother? [a]I know that
he can speak well. And also, behold, he cometh forth to meet
thee: and when he seeth thee, he
will be glad in his heart.

10
*l Faith, trial of,* Mark 11:22.
*m Humility, exemplified,* Prov. 22:4.
*n Stammering,* Isa. 32:4.
1 *Heb.* a man of words,

11
*o Reasoning,* Job 13:6.
*p Deafness,* Matt. 11:5.
*q Blindness,* 2 Kin. 6:18.
*r God, creator, of man,* Gen. 2:2.

12
*s Promise, to the righteous, of divine illumination,* 2 Cor. 1:20.
*t Wisdom, spiritual,* Prov. 2:2.
*u Inspiration,* Job 32:8.
*v Prophets, inspiration of,* Isa. 3:2.
*w Minister, duties of,* Rom. 15:16.

13
*x Disobedience, to God, instances of.* Eph. 5:6.

14
*y Anger, of God,* 2 Kin. 13:3.
*z Aaron,* Ex. 6:20.

*a God, knowledge of,* Gen. 2:2.

15 And [b]thou shalt speak unto
[c]him, and put words in his
mouth: and I will be with thy
mouth, and with his mouth, and
will [d]teach you what ye shall do.
16 And [c]he shall be thy spokesman unto the people: and he
shall be, *even* he shall be to [b]thee
instead[C] of a mouth, and thou
shalt be to him [2]instead of God.
17 And thou shalt take this
†rod in thine hand, wherewith
thou shalt do signs.
18 ¶ And [b]Mō'ṣeṣ went and returned to [e]Jĕth'rō his father in
law, and said unto him, Let me
go, I pray thee, and return
unto my brethren which *are* in
[f]Ē'ġypt, and see whether they be
yet alive. And Jĕth'rō said to
Mō'ṣeṣ, Go in peace.
19 And the LORD said unto
Mō'ṣeṣ in Mĭd'ĭ-an, Go, return
into [f]Ē'ġўpt: for all the men are
dead which sought thy life.[Q]
20 And [b]Mō'ṣeṣ took his wife
and his sons, and set them upon
an ass, and he returned to the
land of [f]Ē'ġўpt: and Mō'ṣeṣ took
the †rod of God in his hand.
21 And the LORD said unto
Mō'ṣeṣ, When thou goest to return into [f]Ē'ġўpt, see that thou
do all those [g]wonders[C] before
[h]Phā'raōh, which I have put in
thine hand: but I will [3]harden his
[i]heart, that he shall not let the
people go.[Q]
22 And thou shalt say unto
[h]Phā'raōh, Thus saith the LORD,
‡Iṣ'ra-el [j]*is* my son, *even* my
[k]firstborn:[S Q]
23 And [l]I say unto thee, Let

v.15–1534 BC
See footnote, *Time*, Rev. 10:6.

15
*b Moses,* Ex. 2:10
*c Aaron,* Ex. 6:20.
*d Inspiration,* Job 32:8.

16
2 R. V. as

18
*e Jethro,* Ex. 3:1.
*f Egypt,* Gen. 41:8.

21
*g Miracles,* Luke 23:8.
*h Pharaoh,* Ex. 3:10.
*i Heart, hardened, instances of,* Psa. 44:21.
3 *Heb.* make strong

22
*j Spiritual Adoption,* Rom. 8:15.
*k Firstborn,* Zech. 12:10.

23
*l God, fatherhood of,* Gen. 2.2.

* **DUMB.** *Stricken of God,* Ex. 4:11; Luke 1:20, 22, 64. *Miraculous healing of, by Jesus,* Matt. 9:32, 33; 12:22; 15:30, 31; Mark 7:37; 9:17, 25, 26.

† **ROD OF MOSES,** Ex. 4:2–4, 17, 20; 9:23; 14:16; 17:5, 6; Num. 20:8, 9, 11.
See footnote, ROD OF AARON, Ex. 7:9.

‡ **ISRAEL.** A name given to the descendants of Jacob, a nation. *Called also* ISRAELITES, *and* HEBREWS, Gen. 43:32; Ex. 1:15; 9:7; 10:3; 21:2; Lev. 23:42; Josh. 13:6; 1 Sam. 4:6; 13:3, 19; 14:11, 21; Phil. 3:5.

TRIBES OF ISRAEL were named after the sons of Jacob. In lists usually the names Levi and Joseph, two sons of Jacob, do not appear. The descendants of Levi were consecrated to the rites of religion, and the two sons of Joseph, Ephraim and Manasseh, were adopted by Jacob in Joseph's stead, Gen. 48:5; Josh. 14:4, and their names appear in the catalogues of tribes instead of those of Levi and Joseph, as follows: ASHER, BENJAMIN, DAN, EPHRAIM, GAD, ISSACHAR, JUDAH, MANASSEH, NAPHTALI, REUBEN, SIMEON, ZEBULUN.

*Names of, seen in John's vision, on the gates of the New Jerusalem,* Rev. 21:12.

*Prophecies concerning,* Gen. 12:7; 17:7, 8; 25:23; 26:4; 27:28, 29, 40; 28:13; 48:19; 49; Deut. 33; Acts 7:5; *the multitude of,* Gen. 13:16; 15:5; 22:17; 26:4; 28:14; 32:12; 48:16; Ex. 32:13; 1 Chr. 27:23; Heb. 11:12; *their captivity in Egypt,* Gen. 15:13, 14; Acts 7:6, 7.

*God's promises to,* Ex. 3:17; 6:4–8; 7:4; Deut. 7:8.

*Were called to be a holy people, separated from the idolatrous nations,* Ex. 19:5, 6; 33:16; Lev. 20:24; Deut. 7:6; 14:2, 21; 26:18; 1 Kin. 8:53; Psa. 135:4. *Taught to be*

v.23–1534 BC
See footnote, *Time*, Rev. 10:6.

m *Firstborn, of Egyptians*, Zech. 12:10.

**25**
n *Zipporah*, Ex. 2:21.
o *Circumcision*, Gen. 17:10.
p *Family, infelicity in, instances of*, 1 Chr. 13:14.
q *Wife*, Prov. 5:18.

**26**
4 R. V. A bridegroom of blood art thou in regard of the circumcision.

**27**
r *God*, Gen. 2:2.
s *Horeb*, Ex. 3:1.
t *Kiss*, Ruth 1:14.

my son go, that he may serve me:
and if thou refuse to let him go,
behold, I will slay thy son, *even*
thy [m]firstborn.
24 ¶ And it came to pass by the
way in the inn, that the LORD
met him, and sought to kill him.
25 Then [n]Zĭp-pō′rah took a
sharp stone, and [o]cut off the
foreskin of her son, and cast *it* at
his feet, and said, [p]Surely a
bloody husband *art* thou to [q]me.
26 So he let him go: then [n]she
said, [4]A bloody[c] husband *thou*
*art*, because of the [o]circumcision.
27 ¶ And the [r]LORD said to
[c]Aâr′on, Go into the wilderness
to meet [b]Mō′ṣeṣ. And he went,
and met him in the [s]mount of
God, and [t]kissed him.
28 And [b]Mō′ṣeṣ told [c]Aâr′on all
the words of the LORD who had
sent him, and all the [o]signs
which he had commanded him.
29 ¶ And [b]Mō′ṣeṣ and [c]Aâr′on
went and gathered together all
the [u]elders of the children of
Ĭṣ′ra-el:
30 And [c]Aâr′on spake all the
words which the LORD had spoken unto [b]Mō′ṣeṣ, and did the
[o]signs in the sight of the people.
31 And the people [v]believed:
and when they heard that the
[w]LORD had visited the children
of Ĭṣ′ra-el, and that he had
looked upon their [x]affliction,
then they [y]bowed their heads
and [z,a]worshipped.

v.29–1534 BC
See footnote, *Time*, Rev. 10:6.

**29**
u *Senate*, Num. 11:16.

**31**
v *Faith, instances of*, Mark 11:22.
w *God, preserver*, Gen. 2:2.
x *Adversity*, Psa. 10:6.
y *Prayer, postures in*, Acts 6:4.
z *Worship*, Gen. 22:5.

a *Thankfulness, to God*, Acts 24:3.

## CHAPTER 5

*Pharaoh chides Moses and Aaron for their message; 5 and increases the Israelites' task. 15 He derides their complaints. 20 They cry out against Moses and Aaron. 22 Moses complains to God.*

AND afterward [a]Mō′ṣeṣ and
[b]Aâr′on went in, and told
[c]Phā′raōh, Thus saith the LORD

**1**
a *Moses*, Ex. 2:10.
b *Aaron*, Ex. 6:20.
c *Pharaoh*, Ex. 3:10.

*holy, by eating none but clean animals*, Lev. 11:1–47; 20:24–26; Deut. 14:1–20; *by being prohibited to wear garments of mixed fabrics, and to sow mixed seeds*, Deut. 22:9–11.

*Divided into families, each of which had a chief*, Num. 25:14; 26; 36:1; Josh. 7:14; 1 Chr. chapters 4–8

*Number of, who went into Egypt*, Gen. 46:8–27; Ex. 1:5; Deut. 10:22; 26:5; Acts 7:14. *Number of, at the time of the exodus*, Ex. 1:7, 20; 12:37, 38 (with Gen. 47:27); Num. 11:21; Deut. 26:5; Psa. 105:24; Acts 7:17. *Number of, fit for military service, when they left Egypt*, Ex. 12:37; *at Sinai, by tribes*, Num. 1:1–50; 2:32, 33; *after the plague*, Num. 26; *when they reached Canaan*, Deut. 1:10; 10:22; *when David numbered Israel*, 2 Sam. 24:1–9; 1 Chr. 21:5, 6; 27:23, 24. *Number of, as recorded in the books of the Kings*, 1 Chr. 9:1 (with chapters 2–9 inclusive); *after the captivity*, Ezra 2:2–64; Neh. 7:7–67; *in John's apocalyptic vision*, Rev. 7:1–8.

*Accompanied by mixed multitude*, Ex. 12:38; Num. 11:4; *of mixed bloods*, Lev. 24:10, 11.

*Dwelt in Goshen*, Gen. 46:28–34; 47:4–10, 27, 28. *Dwelt in Egypt four hundred and thirty years*, Ex. 12:40, 41 (with Gen. 15:13); Acts 7:6; Gal. 3:17. *Were enslaved and oppressed by the Egyptians*, Ex. 1; 2; 5; Acts 7:18–36. *Their groaning heard of God*, Ex. 2:23–25; 6:5. *Moses commissioned as deliverer*, Ex. 3:2–22; 4:1–17. *The land of Egypt plagued on their account*, see footnote, EGYPT, Gen. 41:8. *Exempt from the plagues*, Ex. 8:22, 23; 9:4–6, 26; 10:23; 11:7; 12:13. *Children of, were saved when the firstborn of the Egyptians were slain*, Ex. 12:13, 23.

*Instituted the passover*, Ex. 12:1–28. *Borrowed jewels from the Egyptians*, Ex. 11:2, 3; 12:35, 36; Psa. 105:37. *Urged by the Egyptians to depart*, Ex. 12:31–39.

*Journey from Rameses to Succoth*, Ex. 12:37–39. *Made the journey by night*, Ex. 12:42. *The day of their deliverance to be a memorial*, Ex. 12:42; 13:3–16. *Led of God*, Ex. 13:18, 21, 22. *Providentially cared for*, Deut. 8:3, 4; 29:5, 6; Neh. 9:21; Psa. 105:37. See footnotes: MANNA, Ex. 16:31; PILLAR, *of Cloud and Fire*, Ex. 13:21.

*Journey from Succoth to Etham*, Ex. 13:20; *to Pi-hahiroth*, Ex. 14:2; Num. 33:5–7. *Pursued by the Egyptians*, Ex. 14:5–31. *Passed through the Red Sea*, Ex. 14:19–22; Deut. 11:4; Psa. 66:6; 78:13; 106:9; 136:13, 14. *Order of march*, Num. 2. *Journey to Marah*, Ex. 15:23; Num. 33:8. *Murmur on account of the bitter water*, Ex. 15:23–25; *water sweetened*, Ex. 15:25. *Journey, to Elim*, Ex. 15:27; Num. 33:9; *to the wilderness of Sin*, Ex. 16:1. *For itinerary*, see Num. 33.

*Murmured for food*, Ex. 16:2, 3; Num. 11:4–6; Psa. 78:18; 1 Cor. 10:6; *provided with manna and quails*, Ex. 16:4–36; Num. 11:31–33; Psa. 78:26–29; 105:40. *Murmured for want of water at Rephidim*, Ex. 17:2–7; *water miraculously supplied from the rock at Meribah*, Ex. 17:5–7; Num. 20:1–13; Deut. 8:15; Neh. 9:15; Psa. 78:15; 105:41. *Defeat the Amalekites*, Ex. 17:13.

*Arrive at Sinai*, Ex. 19:1; Num. 33:15. *At the suggestion of Jethro, Moses' father-in-law, they organize a system of government*, Ex. 18:14–27; Deut. 1:9–18. *The message of God to them, requiring that they shall be obedient to his commandments, and as a reward they would be to him a holy nation, and their reply*, Ex. 19:3–8. *Sanctify themselves for receiving the law*, Ex. 19:10–15. *The law delivered to*, Ex. 20; 21; 22; 23; 24:1–4; Lev. chapters 1–25; 27; Deut. chapters 5 and 14–26. *The people receive it, and covenant obedience to it*, Ex. 24:3, 7.

*Idolatry of*, Ex. 32; Deut. 9:12–21. *The anger of the Lord in consequence*, Ex. 32:9–14. *Moses' indignation; breaks the tables of stone; enters the camp; commands the Levites; three thousand slain*, Ex. 32:19–35. *Visited by a plague*, Ex. 32:35. *Obduracy of*, Ex. 33:3; 34:9; Deut. 9:12–29. *God withdraws his presence from*, Ex. 33:1–3. *The mourning of, when God refused to lead them*, Ex. 33:4–10. *Tables containing commandments renewed*, Ex. 34; Deut. 10:1–5.

*Forbidden to marry Canaanites*, Ex. 34:15, 16; Deut. 7:3, 4; Josh. 23:12; Neh. 10:30.

*Pattern for the tabernacle and the appurtenances, and forms of worship to be observed*, Ex. chapters 25–31. *Gifts consecrated for the creation of the tabernacle*, Ex. 35:4–29; 36:1–7; Num. 7. *Taxed for tabernacle*, Ex. 38:26. *The erection of the tabernacle; the manufacture of the appurtenances, including the garments of the priests; and their sanctification*, Ex. 36:8–38; chapters 37–40. *First sacrifice offered by, under the law*, Lev. 8:14–36; 9:8–24. *Second passover observed by*, Num. 9:1–5.

*March out of the wilderness*, Num. 10:11–36. *For itinerary*, see Num. 33. *Order of camp and march*, Num. 2. *Arrive at the border of Canaan*, Num. 12:16.

*Send twelve spies to view the land*, Num. 13; 32:8; Deut. 1:22, 25; Josh. 14:7; *who return with a majority and minority report*, Num. 13:26–33; 14:6–10. *Murmur over the report*, Num. 14:1–5. *The judgment of God upon them in consequence of their unbelief and murmuring*, Num. 14:13–39; 32:11; Deut. 1:34, 35; Psa. 95:11; 106:26; 1 Cor. 10:5, 10; Heb. 3:17, 18; Jude 5. *Reaction, and their purpose to enter the land; are defeated*, Num. 14:40–45; Deut. 1:41–45. *Abide at Kadesh*, Num. 20:1; Deut. 1:46. *Return to the wilderness, where they remain thirty-eight years, and all die except Joshua and Caleb*, Num. 14:20–39.

*Rebellion of Korah, Dathan, and Abiram*, Lev. 10:1, 2. Num. 16:1–40; Deut. 11:6; Psa. 106:17. *Murmur against*

v.1–1534 BC
See footnote, *Time*, Rev. 10:6.

*d* *Israel*, Ex. 4:22.
*e* *Feasts*, Mark 12: 39.

2
*f* *Rulers, wicked*, Ex. 18:21.
*g* *Presumption*, Psa. 19:13.
*h* *Spiritual Blindness*, 2 Cor. 4:4.
*i* *Disobedience, to God, instances of*, Eph. 5:6.

3
*j* *Hebrew*, Gen. 40: 15.
*k* *Worship*, Gen. 22:5.
1 R.V. wilderness.

God of [d]Is̄'ra-el, Let my people
go, that they may hold a [e]feast[G]
unto me in the wilderness.
2 And [c,f]Phā'raōh said, [g]Who
is the LORD that I should obey
his voice to let [d]Israel go? [h]I
know not the LORD, [i]neither
will I let Is̄'ra-el go.
3 And they said, The God of
the [j]Hē'brews̄ hath met with us:
let us go, we pray thee, three
days' journey into the [1]desert,
and [k]sacrifice[G] unto the LORD
our God; lest he fall upon us
with pestilence, or with the
sword.
4 And the [f]king of Ē'gy̆pt said
unto them, Wherefore do ye,
[a]Mō'ṣeṣ and [b]Aâr'on, let[G] the
people from their works? get you
unto your burdens.[G]
5 And [c]Phā'raōh said, Behold,
the people of the land now *are*
many, and ye make them rest
from their burdens.
6 And [c]Phā'raōh [l]commanded
the same day the taskmasters of
the people, and their officers,
saying,
7 [l,m]Ye shall no more give the
[d,n]people [o]straw to make [p]brick,
as heretofore: let them go and
gather straw for themselves.
8 And the tale[G] of the [p]bricks,
which they did make heretofore,
ye shall [l]lay upon [n]them; ye
[m]shall not diminish *ought*[G] thereof: for they *be* idle; therefore
they cry, saying, Let us go *and*
[k]sacrifice to our God.
9 [l,m]Let there more work be
laid upon the men, that they
may labour therein; and let
them not regard vain[G] words.
10 ¶ And the taskmasters of
the people went out, and their
officers, and they spake to the
people, saying, Thus saith
[c,f]Phā'raōh, [l,m]I will not give
you [o]straw.

v.6–1534 BC
See footnote, *Time*, Rev. 10:6.

6
*l* *Oppression*, Eccl. 5:8.

7
*m* *Cruelty, instances of*, Psa. 27:12.
*n* *Servant, cruelty to, instances of*, Jer. 2:14.
*o* *Straw*, Gen. 24: 32.
*p* *Brick*, Gen. 11:3.

*Moses and Aaron; are plagued; fourteen thousand seven hundred die; plague stayed*, Num. 16:41–50.

*Are refused passage through the country of Edom*, Num. 20:14–21. *The death of Aaron*, Num. 20:22, 29; 33:38, 39; Deut. 10:6. *Defeat the Canaanites*, Num. 21:1–3. *Are scourged with serpents*, Num. 21:4–9. *Defeat the Amorites*, Num. 21:21–32; Deut. 2:24–35; *and the king of Bashan*, Num. 21:33–35; Deut. 3:1–17.

*Arrive in the plains of Moab, at the fords of the Jordan*, Num. 22:1; 33:48, 49. *Commit idolatry with the people of Moab*, Num. 25:1–5. *Visited by a plague in consequence; twenty-four thousand die*, Num. 25:6–15; 26:1. *The people numbered for the allotment of the land*, Num. 26. *The daughters of Zelophehad sue for an inheritance*, Num. 27:1–11; Josh. 17:3–6. *Conquest of the Midianites*, Num. 31. *Nations dread*, Deut. 2:25. *Renew the covenant*, Deut. 29. *Joshua appointed leader*, Num. 27:18–23. Deut. 31:23. *Moses dies, and people mourn*, Deut. 34.

*All who were numbered at Sinai perished in the wilderness except Caleb and Joshua*, Num. 26:63, 65; Deut. 2:14–16. *Piety of those who entered Canaan*, Josh. 23:8; Judg. 2:7–10; Jer. 2:2, 3. *Men chosen to allot the lands of Canaan among the tribes and families*, Num. 34:17–29. *Remove from Shittim to Jordan*, Josh. 3:1. *Cross Jordan*, Josh. 4. *Marriage of, with Canaanites*, Judg. 3:5, 6; Ezra chapters 9; 10; Neh. 13:23–30. *Circumcision observed, and passover celebrated*, Josh. 5. *Jericho taken*, Josh. 6. *Ai taken*, Josh. 7 and 8:1–29. *Required to assemble on Mt. Ebal and Mt. Gerizim for the reading of the law*, Deut. 27:1–26; Josh. 8:30–34. *Make a league with the Gibeonites*, Josh. 9. *Defeat the five Amoritish kings*, Josh. 10.

*Conquest of the land*, Josh. 21:43–45 (with Judg. 1). *The land allotted*, Josh. chapters 15–19. *Cities of refuge appointed*, Josh. 20.

*Two and one-half tribes return from the west side of the Jordan; erect a memorial to signify the unity of the tribes; the memorial misunderstood; the controversy which followed; its amicable adjustment*, Josh. 22. *Joshua's exhortation immediately before his death*, Josh. 23. *Covenant renewed; death of Joshua*, Josh. 24; Judg. 2:8, 9. *Religious fidelity during the life of Joshua*, Josh. 24:31; Judg. 2:7.

**Under the Judges:** *Public affairs administered four hundred and fifty years by the judges*, Judg. 2:16–19; Acts 13:20. *The original inhabitants not fully expelled*, Judg. 1:27–36, 3:1–7. *Reproved by an angel for not casting out the original inhabitants*, Judg. 2:1–5. *People turn to idolatry*, Judg. 2:10–23. *Delivered for their idolatry to the king of Mesopotamia during eight years; their repentance and deliverance*, Judg. 3:8–11. *Renew their idolatry, and are put under tribute to the king of Moab during eighteen years; repent and are delivered by Ehud; eighty years of peace follow*, Judg. 3:12–30. *Shamgar resists a foray of the Philistines, and delivers Israel*, Judg. 3:31. *People again do evil; are put under bonds for twenty years to the king of Syria*, Judg. 4:1–3. *Judged by Deborah, a prophetess*, Judg. 4:4, 5. *Defeat Sisera*, Judg. 4:6–24; 5. *Seven years of bondage to the Midianites; delivered by Gideon*, Judg. 6; 7; 8:1–28. *Return to idolatry*, Judg. 8:33, 34. *Abimelech foments an inter-tribal war*, Judg. 9. *Judged, by Tola twenty-three years*, Judg. 10:1, 2; *by Jair twenty-two years*, Judg. 10:3, 4. *People backslide, and are given over to the Philistines for chastisement eighteen years; repent and turn to the Lord; delivered by Jephthah*, Judg. 10:6–18; 11. *Ephraimites go to war against other tribes; defeated by Jephthah*, Judg. 12:1–7. *Judged, by Ibzan seven years*, Judg. 12:8–10; *by Elon ten years*, Judg. 12:11, 12; *by Abdon eight years*, Judg. 12:13–15. *Backslide again and are chastised by the Philistines forty years*, Judg. 13:1. *Judged by Samson twenty years*, Judg. 15:20 (with chapters 13–16). *Scandal of the Bethlehemite's concubine, and the consequent war between the Benjamites and the other tribes*, Judg. chapters 19–21. *Judged by Eli forty years*, 1 Sam. 4:18 (with chapters 1–4). *Smitten by the Philistines at Eben-ezer*, 1 Sam. 4:1, 2, 10, 11. *Demand a king*, 1 Sam. 8:5–20; Acts 13:21.

**Under the kings before the separation into two kingdoms:** *Saul anointed king*, 1 Sam. 10; 11:12–15; 12:13. *Ammonites invade Israel, are defeated*, 1 Sam. 11. *Philistines smitten*, 1 Sam. 14. *Amalekites defeated*, 1 Sam. 15. *David anointed king*, 1 Sam. 16:11–13. *Goliath slain*, 1 Sam. 17. *Israel defeated by the Philistines, and Saul and his sons slain*, 1 Sam. 31.

*David, defeats the Amalekites*, 1 Sam. 30; 2 Sam. 1:1; *made king over Judah*, 2 Sam. 2:4, 11. *Ishbosheth made king*, 2 Sam. 2:8–10.

*The conflict between the two political factions*, 2 Sam. 2:12–32; 3:1.

*David made king over all Israel*, 2 Sam. 5:1–5. *Conquests of David*, 2 Sam. 8. *Absalom's rebellion*, 2 Sam. chapters 15–18.

*Solomon anointed king*, 1 Kin. 1:32–40. *Temple built*, 1 Kin. 6. *Solomon's palace built*, 1 Kin. 7. *Solomon's death*, 1 Kin. 11:41–43.

*Rehoboam's reign before the revolt*, 1 Kin. 12:1–19.

**Israel after the revolt**, see footnote, ISRAEL, *after the revolt*, 1 Kin. 12:1.

**Judah after the revolt**, see footnote, JUDAH, *kingdom of*, 2 Chr. 11:17.

v.11-1534 BC
See footnote, *Time*, Rev. 10:6.

12
[q] *Egypt*, Gen. 41:8.

15
[r] *Petition*, Esth. 5:6.

19
2 *Or*, were set on mischief, when they said.

21
[s] *Murmuring, instances of*, Num. 14:27.
[t] *Evil, for good, instances of*, Psa. 35:12.
[u] *Uncharitableness, instances of*, Matt. 7:1.
[v] *God, providence of, mysterious and misinterpreted*, Gen. 2:2.

11 [l]Go ye, get you [o]straw where ye can find it: yet [m]not ought[C] of your work shall be diminished.

12 So the people were scattered abroad throughout all the land of [q]Ē′ġy̆pt to gather stubble instead of [o]straw.

13 And the taskmasters [m]hasted[C] *them*, saying, Fulfil your works, *your* daily tasks, as when there was [o]straw.

14 And the officers of the children of Ĭs̱′ra-el, which Phā′raōh's taskmasters had s̱et over them, were [*,m]beaten, *and* demanded, Wherefore have ye not fulfilled your task in making [p]brick both yesterday and to day, as heretofore?

15 ¶ Then the officers of the children of Ĭs̱′ra-el came and [r]cried unto Phā′raōh, saying, Wherefore dealest thou thus with thy servants?

16 [r]There is no straw given unto thy servants, and [l,m]they say to us, Make [p]brick: and, behold, thy servants *are* [*]beaten; but the fault *is* in thine own people.

17 But he said, Ye *are* idle, *ye are* idle: therefore ye say, Let us go *and* do [k]sacrifice to the LORD.

18 Go therefore now, *and* work; for there shall no [o]straw be given you, [m]yet shall ye deliver the tale[C] of [p]bricks.

19 And the officers of the children of Ĭs̱′ra-el did see *that* they [2]*were* in evil[C] *case*, after it was said, Ye shall not minish[G] *ought*[G] from your [p]bricks of your daily task.

20 ¶ And they met [a]Mō′s̱es̱ and [b]Aâr′on, who stood in the way, as they came forth from [c]Phā′raōh:

21 And they [s]said unto them, [t,u]The [v]LORD look upon you, and judge; because ye have made our savour[C] to be abhorred[C] in the eyes of Phā′raōh, and in the eyes of his servants, to put a sword in their hand to slay us.[T]

22 And [w,x]Mō′s̱es̱ returned unto the LORD, and said, [v]Lord, wherefore hast thou *so* evil[C] entreated[C] this people? why *is* it *that* thou hast sent me?

23 For since I came to Phā′raōh to speak in thy name, he hath done evil to this people; neither hast thou delivered thy people at all.

## CHAPTER 6

*God renews his promise by his name JEHOVAH. 10 He sends Moses to Pharaoh. 14 The genealogy of Reuben, 15 of Simeon, 16 of Levi, of whom came Moses and Aaron.*

THEN the LORD said unto [a]Mō′s̱es̱, Now shalt thou see what I will do to [b]Phā′raōh: for with a strong hand shall he let [c]them go, and with a strong hand shall he drive them out of his land.[Q]

2 And God spake unto [a]Mō′s̱es̱, and said unto him, I *am* [1]the LORD[G]:

3 And [d]I appeared unto [e]Ā-brā-hăm, unto [f]Ī′s̱aac, and unto [g]Jā′cob, by *the name of* [2]God Almighty, but by my name JĒ-HŌ′VAH was I not known to [c]them.

4[S T] And [h]I have also established my [i]covenant with [c]them, to give them the land of [j]Cā′naăn, the land of their pilgrimage, wherein they [3]were strangers.[G]

5 And I have also heard the [k]groaning of the children of [c]Ĭs̱′ra-el, whom the Ē-ġy̆p′tians̱ keep in [l]bondage; and I have remembered my [i]covenant.[S]

6[S] Wherefore say unto the children of [c]Ĭs̱′ra-el, I *am* [1]the LORD, and [m,n]I will bring you out from under the burdens of the Ē-ġy̆p′tians̱, and I will rid[G]

v.21-1534 BC
See footnote, *Time*, Rev. 10:6.

22
[w] *Doubting, instances of*, Rom. 14:23.
[x] *Murmuring, against God, instances of*, Num. 14:2.

1
[a] *Moses*, Ex. 2:10.
[b] *Pharaoh*, Ex. 3:10.
[c] *Israel*, Ex. 4:22

2
1 R. V. Jehovah:

3
[d] *God, appearance of*, Gen. 2:2.
[e] *Abraham*, Gen. 17:5.
[f] *Isaac*, Gen. 21:3.
[g] *Jacob*, Gen. 27. 11.
2 *Heb.* El Shaddai.

4
[h] *God, faithfulness of*, Gen. 2:2.
[i] *Covenant, of God with men*, Deut. 29:1.
[j] *Canaan*, Gen. 37:1.
3 R. V. sojourned

5
[k] *Prayer, answer to, promised*, Acts 6:4.
[l] *Bondage*, Ex. 1:14.

6
[m] *God, preserver*, Gen. 2:2.
[n] *God, savior*, Gen. 2:2.

***BEATING.** *As a punishment*, Ex. 5:14; Deut. 25:2, 3; Mark 13:9; Acts 5:40; 16:22, 37; 2 Cor. 6:5; 11:25. See footnote, PUNISHMENT, Lev. 26:41.

v.6–1534 BC
See footnote, *Time*, Rev. 10:6.

*o Arm, figurative,* Psa. 89:13.

7
*p God, love of, exemplified,* Gen. 2:2.

8
*q Oath, attributed to God,* Num. 5:19.
*r God, sovereign,* Gen. 2:2.

9
*s Despondency, instances of,* Eccl. 2:20.
*t Affliction,* Psa. 34:19.

11
*u Egypt,* Gen. 41:8.

12
*v Excuses,* Luke 14:18.
*w Doubting, instances of,* Rom. 14:23.
*x Circumcision, figurative,* Gen. 17:10.

13
*y Aaron,* Ex. 6:20.
*z Prophets, inspiration of,* Isa. 3:2.

you out of their [l]bondage, and I[G]
will redeem you with a stretched
out [o]arm, and with great *judgments:[Q]
7 And [p]I will take you to me for
a people, and I will be to you a
God: and ye shall know that I
*am* [1]the LORD your [m,n]God,
which bringeth you out from under the burdens of the Ē-gy̆p′-
tiaṇs.[S]
8 And [m]I will bring you in unto
the [i]land, concerning the which
I did [i,q]swear to give it to [e]Ā′brā-
hăm, to [f]Ī′ṣaac, and to [g]Jā′cob;
and I will give it you for an heritage: [r]I *am* the LORD.[T]
9 ¶ And Mō′ṣeṣ spake so unto
the children of [c]Ĭṣ′ra-el: but they
hearkened not unto Mō′ṣeṣ for
[s]anguish of spirit, and for cruel
[l,t]bondage.
10 And the LORD spake unto
Mō′ṣeṣ, saying,
11 Go in, speak unto [b]Phā′raōh
king of [u]Ē′gy̆pt, that he let the
children of [c]Ĭṣ′ra-el go out of his
land.
12 And Mō′ṣeṣ [v]spake before
the LORD, saying, Behold, the
children of [c]Ĭṣ′ra-el have not
hearkened unto me; [w]how then
shall Phā′raōh hear me, who *am*
of [x]uncircumcised lips?
13 And the LORD spake unto
Mō′ṣeṣ and unto [y]Aăr′on, and
gave [z]them a charge[G] unto the
children of Ĭṣ′ra-el, and unto
Phā′raōh king of Ē′gy̆pt, to
bring the children of Ĭṣ′ra-el out
of the land of Ē′gy̆pt.
14 ¶ [a]These *be* the [b]heads of
their fathers' houses: The sons
of [c]Reu′ben the firstborn of Ĭṣ′-
ra-el; †Hā′nŏch, and [d]Păl′lu,
[e]Hĕz′rŏn, and [f]Cär′mī: these *be*
the [g]families of Reu′ben.
15 And the sons of [h]Sĭm′e-on;
[i]Jē-mū′el, and [j]Jā′min, and
[k]Ō′hăd, and Jā′chin, and [l]Zō′-
här, and ‡Shā′ul the son of a
Cā′năan-ĭt-ish woman: these *are*
the families of Sĭm′e-on.
16 And [a]these *are* the names of
the [m]sons of [n]Lē′vī according to
their generations; [o]Gēr′shŏn,
and [p]Kō′hăth, and [q]Mē-rā′rī:
and the years of the [r]life of Lē′vī
*were* an hundred thirty and
seven years.
17 The sons of [o]Gēr′shŏn;
‖Lĭb′nī, and §Shĭ′mī, according
to their families.
18 And the [s]sons of Kō′hăth;
+Ăm′răm, and [t]Ĭz′här, and
[u]Hē′bron, and [v]Ŭz′zĭ-el: and the
years of the [r]life of [p]Kō′hăth
*were* an hundred thirty and
three years.
19 And the [w]sons of Mē-rā′rī;
[x]Mā′ha-lī and [y]Mū′shī: these
*are* the [m]families of Lē′vī according to their [a]generations.
20 And +Ăm′răm took him

v.13–1534 BC
See footnote, *Time*, Rev. 10:6.

14
*a Genealogy,* 1 Chr. 5:1.
*b Rulers, patriarchal,* Ex. 18:21.
*c Reuben,* Gen. 35:22.
*d* Or, *Phallu,* Gen. 46:9.
*e Hezron,* 1 Chr. 5:3.
*f* Gen. 46:9.
*g Reubenites,* Josh. 22:1.

15
*h Simeon, tribe of,* Num. 2:12.
*i* Gen. 46:10.
*j* Gen. 46:10.
*k* Gen. 46:10.
*l* Gen. 46:10.

16
*m Levites,* Deut. 10:8.
*n Levi,* Gen. 29:34.
*o Gershon,* Gen. 46:11.
*p Kohath,* Num. 26:58.
*q* Gen. 46:11.
*r Longevity,* Psa. 91:16.

v.17–1534 BC
See footnote, *Time*, Rev. 10:6.

18
*s Kohathites,* Num. 3:27.
*t Izhar,* 1 Chr. 6:2.
*u Hebron,* Num. 3:19.
*v Uzziel,* Num. 3:19.

19
*w Merarites,* Num. 26:57.
*x* 1 Chr. 6:19; Ezra 8:18.
*y* 1 Chr. 6:19, 47.

*** JUDGMENTS.** *Misunderstood,* Jer. 16:10; Joel 2:17. *No escape from,* Ex. 20:7; 34:7; Isa. 2:10, 12–19, 21; Ezek. 14:13, 14; Amos 5:16–20; 9:1–4; Matt. 23:33; Heb. 2:1–3; 10:28, 29; 12:25; Rev. 6:16, 17. *Executed by human instrumentality,* Jer. 51:2. *Delayed,* Psa. 50:21.

*Denounced against disobedience,* Lev. 26:14–39; Deut. 28:15–68; 29; 32:19–43; 1 Kin. 9:6, 7.

*Denounced, against Solomon,* 1 Kin. 11:9–14, 23; *against Jeroboam,* 1 Kin. 14:7–15; *against Baasha,* 1 Kin. 16:3, 4; *against Ahab and Jezebel,* 1 Kin. 21:19–24; *against Ahaziah,* 2 Chr. 22:7–9; *against Manasseh,* 2 Chr. 33:11.

**Design of:** *To correct,* Deut. 30:1, 2; 1 Kin. 8:33, 34; 2 Chr. 7:13; Job 5:17; 23:10; 34:31, 32; Psa. 94:12, 13; 107:10–14, 17; Prov. 3:11; Isa. 9:13, 14; 26:9; Jer. 24:5; 30:11; Lam. 1:5, 12; Ezek. 20:37, 43; Hos. 2:6, 7; 5:15; 1 Cor. 11:32; Heb. 12:5–11. *To humble,* 2 Cor. 12:7.

**Instances of:** *On the serpent,* Gen. 3:14, 15. *On Eve,* Gen. 3:16. *On Adam,* Gen. 3:17–19. *On Cain,* Gen. 4:11–15. *On the Antediluvians,* Gen. chapters 6, 7. *On Pharaoh,* Gen. 12:17. *On Sodomites,* Gen. 19:24, 25. *On Egyptians, the plagues and overthrow,* Ex. chapters 7–14. *On Nadab and Abihu,* Lev. 10:1–3. *On Miriam,* Num. 12:1–15. *On Korah, Dathan and Abiram,* Num. 16:1–35.

Upon the Israelites: *For worshiping Aaron's calf,* Ex. 32:35. *For murmuring,* Num. 11:1, 33, 34; 14:22, 23, 32, 35–37; 16:41–50; 21:6; 25:4, 5, 9. *The forty years' wandering, a judgment,* Num. 14:26–39; 26:63–65; Deut. 2:14–17. *Delivered into the hands, of the Assyrians,* 2 Kin. 17:6–41; *of the Chaldeans,* 2 Chr. 36:14–21.

*On the Canaanites,* Lev. 18:25; Deut. 7; 12:29, 30. *On Abimelech,* Judg. 9:52–57. *On Eli's house,* 1 Sam. 2:27–36 (with chapter 4:10–22). *On Uzzah,* 2 Sam. 6:7; 1 Chr. 13:10. *On the prophet of Judah, for disobedience,* 1 Kin. 13:1–24. *On Zimri,* 1 Kin. 16:18, 19. *On Gehazi,* 2 Kin. 5:27. *On Sennacherib,* 2 Kin. 19:35–37. *On Hananiah, the false prophet,* Jer. 28:15, 17.

**† HANOCH.** *Eldest son of Reuben,* Gen. 46:9; Ex. 6:14; Num. 26:5; 1 Chr. 5:3.

**‡ SHAUL.** *Son of Simeon,* Gen. 46:10; Ex. 6:15; Num. 26:13; 1 Chr. 4:24.

**‖ LIBNI.** *Son of Gershon,* Ex. 6:17; Num. 3:18; 1 Chr. 6:17, 20. *Called* LADAN, 1 Chr. 23:7; 26:20, 21. *Descendants called* LIBNITES, Num. 3:21; 26:58.

**§ SHIMI,** called also SHIMEI. *Son of Gershon,* Ex. 6:17; Num. 3:18; 1 Chr. 6:17; 23:7, 10.

**+ AMRAM.** *Father of Moses,* Ex. 2:1, 2; 6:18, 20; Num. 26:58, 59; 1 Chr. 6:3, 18; 23:12, 13. *Head of one of the branches of Levites,* Num. 3:19, 27; 1 Chr. 26:23. *Age of, at death,* Ex. 6:20.

B.C. 1619? See footnote, *Time*, Rev. 10:6.

*z Moses*, Ex. 2:10.

21
*a Korah*, Num. 16:1.

22
*b* Lev. 10:4.
*c Elzaphan*, Lev. 10:4.

B.C. 1530? See footnote, *Time*, Rev. 10:6.

23
*d Amminadab*, Num. 2:3.
*e* Or, *Nahshon*, Num. 7:12.
*f Nadab*, Ex. 24:1.
*g Eleazar*, Num. 3:2.
*h Ithamar*, Ex. 38:21.

24
*i* 1 Chr. 6:22.
*j* 1 Chr. 6:23.

25
*k Phinehas*, Num. 25:7.
*l Genealogy*, 1 Chr. 5:1.
*m Rulers, patriarchal*, Ex. 18:21.
*n Levites*, Deut. 10:8.

26
*o Moses*, Ex. 2:10.
*p Egypt*, Gen. 41:8.
3 R. V. hosts.

v.20–1534 BC See footnote, *Time*, Rev. 10:1.

27
*q Pharaoh*, Ex. 3:10.

⊙Jŏch'e-bĕd his father's sister to
wife[G]; and she bare him ▲Aâr'on
and [z]Mō'ṣeṣ: and the years of
the [r]life of+Ăm'răm *were* an hundred and thirty and seven
years.
21 And the sons of Ī'z'här;
[a]Kō'rah, and Nē'pheg, and
Zĭch'rī.
22 And the sons of Ŭz'zĭ-el;
[b]Mĭsh'a-el, and [c]Ĕl'za-phăn, and
Zĭth'rī.
23 And ▲Aâr'on took him
Ĕ-lĭsh'e-bȧ, daughter of [d]Ăm-
mĭn'a-dăb, sister of [e]Nā-ăsh'on,
to wife[G]; and she bare him [f]Nā'-
dăb, and ●Ȧ-bī'hū, [g]Ē-le-ā'zar,
and [h]Īth'a-mär.
24 And the sons of [a]Kō'rah;
[i]Ăs'sĭr, and [j]Ĕl'kā-nah, and
Ȧ-bī'a-săph: these *are* the families of the Kôr'hītes.
25 And [g]Ē-le-ā'zar ▲Aâr'on's
son took him *one* of the daughters of Pū'tĭ-el to wife[G]; and she
bare him [k]Phĭn'e-has: [l]these *are*
the [m]heads of the fathers of the
[n]Lē'vītes according to their
families.
26 These *are* that ▲Aâr'on and
[o]Mō'ṣeṣ, to whom the LORD
said, Bring out the children of
Ĭṣ'ra-el from the land of [p]Ē'gȳpt
according to their [3]armies.
27 These *are* they which spake
to [q]Phā'raōh king of [p]Ē'gȳpt, to
bring out the children of Ĭṣ'ra-el
from Ē'gȳpt: these *are* that
[o]Mō'ṣeṣ and ▲Aâr'on.
28 ¶ And it came to pass on the
day *when* the LORD spake unto
[o]Mō'ṣeṣ in the land of [p]Ē'gȳpt,
29 That the LORD spake unto
[o]Mō'ṣeṣ, saying, I *am* the LORD:
speak thou unto [q]Phā'raōh king
of Ē'gȳpt all that I say unto thee.
30 And [o]Mō'ṣeṣ [r]said before the
LORD, Behold, I *am* of [s]uncir-
cumcised lips, and [t]how shall
[q]Phā'raōh hearken unto me?

## CHAPTER 7

*Moses is encouraged to go to Pharaoh. 7 His age. 8 His rod is turned into a serpent. 11 The sorcerers do the like. 13 Pharaoh's heart is hardened. 14 God's message to Pharaoh. 19 The river is turned into blood.*

AND the LORD said unto
[a]Mō'ṣeṣ, See, I have made
thee a god to [b,c]Phā'raōh: and
[d]Aâr'on thy brother shall be thy
[e]prophet[G].
2 [a,f]Thou shalt speak all that I
command thee: and [d]Aâr'on thy
brother shall speak unto [b]Phā'-
raōh, that he send the children of
[g]Ĭṣ'ra-el out of his land.
3 And I will harden [b]Phā'raōh's
[h]heart, and [i]multiply my [j]signs
and my wonders in the land of
Ē'gȳpt.[Q]
4 But [b,c]Phā'raōh shall not
hearken unto you, that I may lay
my hand upon Ē'gȳpt, and bring
forth [1]mine armies, *and* my
[g]people the children of Ĭṣ'ra-el,
out of the land of Ē'gȳpt by
great [k]judgments.
5 And the Ē-gȳp'tianṣ [l]shall
know that I *am* the LORD, when
I stretch forth mine hand upon

v.28–1534 BC See footnote, *Time*, Rev. 10:6.

30
*r Duty, escape from, sought by Moses*, Eccl. 12:13.
*s Circumcision, figurative*, Gen. 17:10.
*t Doubting, instances of*, Rom. 14:23.

1
*a Moses*, Ex. 2:10.
*b Pharaoh*, Ex. 3:10.
*c Rulers, wicked*, vs. 1–25; Ex. 18:21.
*d Aaron*, Ex. 6:20.
*e Prophets*, Isa. 3:2.

2
*f Inspiration, of prophets*, Job 32:8.
*g Israel*, Ex. 4:22.

3
*h Heart, hardened*, Psa. 44:21.
*i* Psa. 135:9.
*j Miracles*, Luke 23:8.

4
*k Judgments*, vs. 3–25; Ex. 6:6.
1 R. V. my hosts.

5
*l Miracles, design of*, Luke 23:8.

⊙ **JOCHEBED.** *Mother of Miriam, Aaron, and Moses*, Ex. 6:20; Num. 26:59. *Nurses Moses when he is adopted by Pharaoh's daughter*, Ex. 2:1–9.

▲ **AARON.** *Lineage of*, Ex. 4:14; 6:16–20; Josh. 21:4, 10; 1 Chr. 6:2, 3; 23:13. *Marriage of*, Ex. 6:23. *Children of*, Ex. 6:23, 25; Lev. 10:1; Num. 3:2; 26:60; 1 Chr. 6:3; 24:1, 2; Ezra 7:2–5. *Descendants of*, Ex. 6:23, 25; 1 Chr. 6:3–15, 50–57; 24; Ezra 7:2–5.

*Meets Moses in the wilderness and is made spokesman for Moses*, Ex. 4:14–16, 27–31; 7:1, 2. *Inspiration of*, Ex. 12:1; Lev. 10:8; 11:1; 13:1; 15:1; Num. 2:1; 4:1, 17; 18:1; 19:1; 20:12. *Commissioned as a deliverer of Israel*, Ex. 6:13, 26, 27; Josh. 24:5; 1 Sam. 12:8; Psa. 77:20; 105:26; Mic. 6:4. *Summoned to Sinai with Nadab, Abihu, and seventy elders*, Ex. 19:24; 24:1, 9, 10.

*Priesthood of*, Ex. 28:1; 29:9; Num. 18:1; Psa. 99:6; Heb. 5:4. *Consecration of, to the priesthood*, Ex. 28; 29; Lev. 8. *Enters upon the priestly office*, Lev. 9. *Descendants of, ordained priests forever*, Ex. 28:40–43; 29:9; Num. 3:3; 18:1; 1 Chr. 23:13; 2 Chr. 26:18.

*Judges Israel in the absence of Moses*, Ex. 24:14. *Makes the golden calf*, Ex. 32; Acts 7:40; Deut. 9:20, 21. *Rod of, buds*, Num. 17:8; Heb. 9:4; *is preserved in the ark*, Num. 17:10, 11; Heb. 9:4. *Murmured against, by the people*, Ex. 5:20, 21; 16:2–10; Num. 14:2–4, 10; 16:3, 11, 41; 20:2; Psa. 106:16. *Places pot of manna in the ark*, Ex. 16:34. *With Hur, supports the hands of Moses during battle*, Ex. 17:12. *His benedictions upon the people*, Lev. 9:22; Num. 6:23. *Forbidden to mourn the death of his sons, Nadab and Abihu*, Lev. 10:6. *Intercedes for Miriam*, Num. 12:11, 12. *Stays the plague by priestly intercession*, Num. 16:46–48. *Jealous of Moses*, Num. 12:1. *His presumption, when the rock is smitten*, Num. 20:10–12. *Not permitted to enter Canaan*, Num. 20:12, 23–29. *Various ages of*, Ex. 7:7; Num. 33:38, 39. *Death and burial of*, Num. 20:27, 28; Deut. 10:6; 32:50.

*Character of*, Psa. 106:16.

● **ABIHU.** *Son of Aaron*, Ex. 6:23; Num. 3:2; 1 Chr. 24:1. *Summoned by God to Sinai*, Ex. 24:9. *Called to the priesthood*, Ex. 28:1. *Death of*, Lev. 10:1, 2; Num. 26:61. *Died childless*, Num. 3:4; 1 Chr. 24:2.

v.5–1534 BC
See footnote, *Time*, Rev. 10:6.

m *Nation, punishment of*, vs. 1–25; Isa. 2:4.

6
n *Obedience, instances of*, Heb. 5:8.

7
o *Moses, age of*, Ex. 2:10.

8
p *God*, Gen. 2:2.
q *Inspiration*, Job 32:8.

9
r *Serpent*, Num. 21:6.
2 Any large reptile.

11
s *Sorcery*, Isa. 47:9.

12
t *Miracles, alleged*, Luke 23:8.

13
u *Disobedience to God, instances of*, Eph. 5:6.
3 R. V. Pharaoh's heart was hardened, and

14
v *Obduracy, instances of*, Prov. 29:1.
4 R. V. is stubborn,

15
5 R. V. to meet him;

[m]Ē′ġy̆pt, and bring out the children of Ī̤s′ra-el from among them.

6 And [a]Mō′ṣeṣ and [d]Aâr′on [n]did as the LORD commanded them, so did they.

7 And [o]Mō′ṣeṣ *was* fourscore years old, and [d]Aâr′on fourscore and three years old, when they spake unto [b]Phā′raōh.

8 ¶ And the [p]LORD [q]spake unto [a,f]Mō′ṣeṣ, and unto [d]Aâr′on, saying,

9 When [b]Phā′raōh shall speak unto you, saying, Shew a [j]miracle for you: then thou shalt say unto [d]Aâr′on, Take thy *rod, and cast *it* before Phā′raōh, *and* it shall become a [2,r]serpent.

10 ¶ And [a]Mō′ṣeṣ and [d]Aâr′on went in unto Phā′raōh, and they [n]did so as the LORD had commanded: and Aâr′on cast down his *rod before Phā′raōh, and before his servants, and it [j]became a [2,r]serpent.

11 Then Phā′raōh also called the wise men and the [s]sorcerers:[G] now the †magicians of Ē′ġy̆pt, they also did in like manner with their enchantments.[G Q]

12 For they cast down every man his rod, and they [t]became serpents: but Aâr′on's *rod [j]swallowed up their rods.

13 And [3]he hardened [b]Phā′raōh's [h]heart, that he [u]hearkened not unto them; as the LORD had said.

14 ¶ And the LORD said unto [a]Mō′ṣeṣ, Pha′raōh's [h]heart [4]*is* [v]hardened, he [u]refuseth to let the [g]people go.

15 Get thee unto [b]Phā′raōh in the morning; lo, he goeth out unto the water; and thou shalt stand by the river's brink [5]against[G] he come; and the *rod which was turned to a [r]serpent shalt thou take in thine hand.

16 And thou shalt say unto him, The LORD God of the [w]Hē′brewṣ hath sent me unto thee, saying, Let my people go, that they may serve me in the wilderness: and, behold, hitherto [v]thou wouldest not hear.

17 Thus saith the LORD, In [l]this thou shalt know that I *am* the LORD: behold, I will smite with the *rod that *is* in mine hand upon the waters which *are* in the river, and they shall be turned to [x]blood.[Q]

18 [y]And the fish that *is* in the river shall die, and the river shall stink; and the [z]Ē-gy̆p′tianṣ shall lothe to drink of the water of the river.

19 ¶ And the LORD spake unto [a]Mō′ṣeṣ, Say unto Aâr′on, Take thy *rod, and stretch out thine hand upon the waters of Ē′ġy̆pt, upon their [6]streams, upon their rivers, and upon their ponds, and upon all their pools of water, that they may become blood; and *that* there may be [x]blood throughout all the land of Ē′ġy̆pt, both in *vessels of* wood, and in *vessels of* stone.[Q]

20 [Q]And [a]Mō′ṣeṣ and [d]Aâr′on [n]did so, as the LORD commanded; and he lifted up the *rod, and smote the waters that *were* in the river, in the sight of [b]Phā′raōh, and in the sight of his servants; and all the waters that *were* in the river were turned to [x]blood.

21 [y]And the fish that *was* in the river died; and the river stank, and the Ē-gy̆p′tianṣ could not drink of the water of the river; and there was [x]blood throughout all the land of Ē′ġy̆pt.[Q]

22 And the [†,s]magicians of Ē′ġy̆pt [t]did so with their enchantments: and [b]Phā′raōh's [h]heart was hardened, [u]neither

v.16–1534 BC
See footnote, *Time*, Rev. 10:6.

16
w *Hebrew*, Gen. 40:15.

17
x *Blood, plague of*, Gen. 9:4.

18
y *Plague*. Ex. 11:1.
z *Egyptians, visited by plagues*, Gen. 50:3.

19
6 *Or*, canals.

* **ROD OF AARON**, Ex. 7:9, 10, 12, 15, 19, 20; 8:5, 16, 17; Num. 17:6, 8, 10; Heb. 9:4. See footnote, ROD OF MOSES, Ex. 4:17.

† **MAGICIAN.** *A person who claims to understand and explain mysteries by magic*, Dan. 1:20. *Failed to interpret, Pharaoh's dreams*, Gen. 41:8, 24; *Nebuchadnezzar's*, Dan.

v.22–1534 BC
See footnote, *Time*, Rev. 10:6.

did he hearken unto them; as the LORD had said.[Q]

23 And Phā′raōh turned and went into his house, [v]neither did he set[G] his heart to this also.

24 And all the [z]Ē-ġȳp′tianș digged round about the river for water to drink; for they could not drink of the water of the river.

25 And seven days were fulfilled, after that the LORD had smitten the river.

## CHAPTER 8

*Frogs are sent. 8 Pharaoh asks Moses to entreat the Lord for their removal. 12 Moses' prayer answered. 16 The dust is turned into lice, which the magicians could not do. 20 The swarms of flies. 25 Pharaoh inclines to let the people go, 32 but yet is hardened.*

AND the LORD spake unto [a]Mō′șeș, Go unto [b,c]Phā′raōh, and say unto him, Thus saith the LORD, Let my people go, that they may serve me.

2 And if thou refuse to let *them* go, behold, I [d]will smite[C] all thy borders with *frogs:

3 [e]And the river shall bring forth *frogs abundantly, which shall go up and come into thine house, and into thy bedchamber, and upon thy bed, and into the house of thy servants, and upon thy people, and into thine †ovens, and into thy [f]kneading-troughs:[Q]

4 And the *frogs shall come up both on thee, and upon thy people, and upon all thy servants.[Q]

5 ¶ [S]And the LORD spake unto [a]Mō′șeș, Say unto [g]Aâr′on; Stretch forth thine hand with thy [h]rod over the [1]streams, over the rivers, and over the ponds, and cause frogs to come up upon the land of [i]Ē′ġȳpt.

6 And [g]Aâr′on stretched out his hand over the waters of Ē′ġȳpt; and the *frogs came up, and covered the land of Ē′ġȳpt.[S]

7 And the [j]magicians [k]did so with their [l]enchantments, and brought up *frogs upon the land of [i]Ē′ġȳpt.

8 ¶ Then [b]Phā′raōh [m]called for [a]Mō′șeș and [g]Aâr′on, and said, [n]Intreat the LORD, that he may take away the *frogs from me, and from my people; and I will let the people go, that they may do sacrifice unto the LORD.

9 And [a]Mō′șeș said unto [b]Phā′raōh, Glory over[G] me: when shall I [n]intreat for thee, and for thy servants, and for thy people, to destroy the *frogs from thee and thy houses, *that* they may remain in the river only?

10 And he said, To morrow.[C] And he said, *Be it* according to thy word: that thou mayest know that *there is* none like unto the LORD our God.

11 And the *frogs shall depart from thee, and from thy houses, and from thy servants, and from thy people; they shall remain in the river only.

12 [S]And [a]Mō′șeș and [g]Aâr′on went out from [b]Phā′raōh: and Mō′șeș [o]cried unto the LORD because of the *frogs which he had brought against Phā′raōh.

13 And the LORD [p]did according to the word of Mō′șeș; and the *frogs died out of the houses, out of the villages, and out of the fields.

14 And they gathered them together upon heaps: and the land stank.

15 [q]But when [b]Phā′raōh saw that there was respite, [r,s]he [t]hardened his [u]heart, and [v]hearkened[G] not unto them; as the LORD had said.

16 ¶ And the LORD said unto [a]Mō′șeș, Say unto [g]Aâr′on, Stretch out thy [h]rod, and smite

1
a *Moses*, Ex. 2:10.
b *Pharaoh*, Ex. 3:10.
c *Rulers, wicked*, Ex. 18:21.

2
d *Judgments*, Ex. 6:6.

3
e *Plague*, Ex. 11:1.
f Ex. 12:34; Deut. 28:5, 17.

5
g *Aaron*, Ex. 6:20.
h *Rod of Aaron*, Ex. 7:9.
i *Egyptians, visited by plagues*, Gen. 50:3.
1 *Or*, canals.

v.7–1534 BC
See footnote, *Time*, Rev. 10:6.

7
j *Magician*, Ex. 7:11.
k *Miracles*, Luke 23:8.
l *Sorcery*, Isa. 47:9.

8
m *Afflictions, penitence in*, Psa. 34:19.
n *Intercession, solicited*, Jer. 27:18.

12
o *Intercession, instances of*, Jer. 27:18.

13
p *Intercession, answered*, Jer. 27:18.

15
q *Character, instability of*, Phil. 2:15.
r *Hypocrisy, instances of*, Jas. 3:17.
s *Instability*, Jas. 1:8.
t *Obduracy, instances of*, Prov. 29:1.
u *Heart, hardened, instances of*, Psa. 44:21.
v *Disobedience to God, instances of*, Eph. 5:6.

2:2–13; 4:7. *Wrought apparent miracles*, Ex. 7:11, 12, 22; 8:7, 18. See footnote, SORCERY, Isa. 47:9.

*** FROGS.** *Plague of*, Ex. 8:2–14; Psa. 78:45; 105:30. SYMBOLICAL, Rev. 16:13.

**† OVEN.** *For baking*, Ex. 8:3; Lev. 2:4; 7:9; 11:35; 26:26. See footnote, BREAD, Ezek. 4:13.

**Figurative**, Psa. 21:9; Hos. 7:4, 6, 7; Matt. 6:30; Luke 12:28.

v.16–1534 BC
See footnote. *Time*, Rev. 10:6.

16
w *Lice, plague of*, Psa. 105:31.
x *Plague, of lice*, Ex. 11:1.
2 *Or*, sand flies *or*, fleas

19
y *God, power of*, Gen. 2:2.
z *Adversity, obduracy in*, Job 10:6.

20
a *Moses*, Ex. 2:10.
b *Rising, early*, Gen. 19:2.
c *Pharaoh*, Ex. 3:10.
d *Israel*, Ex. 4:22.

21
e *Judgments*, Ex. 6:6.
f *Flies, plague of*, Eccl. 10:1.
g *Egyptians, visited by plagues*, Gen. 50:3.

22
h *God, preserver*, Gen. 2:2.
i *Goshen*, Gen. 45:10.
j *Miracles, design of*, Luke 23:8.
k *God, sovereign*, Gen. 2:2.

23
3 *Or*, set a sign of deliverance

the dust of the land, that it may become [2,w,x]lice throughout all the land of Ē′ġy̆pt.

17 And they did so; for [g]Aâr′on stretched out his hand with his [h]rod, and smote the dust of the earth, and it [k]became [2,w,x]lice in man, and in beast; all the dust of the land became lice throughout all the land of Ē′ġy̆pt.

18 And the [i]magicians did so with their [l]enchantments to bring forth lice, but they could not: so there were [w,x]lice upon man, and upon beast.

19 Then the magicians said unto Phā′raōh, This *is* the finger of [y]God: and Phā′raōh's [u,z]heart was hardened, and he hearkened not unto them; as the LORD had said.

20 ¶ And the LORD said unto [a]Mō′ṣeṣ, [b]Rise up early in the morning, and stand before [c]Phā′raōh; lo, he cometh forth to the water; and say unto him, Thus saith the LORD, Let my [d]people go, that they may serve me.

21 Else, if thou wilt not let my [d]people go, behold, I [e]will send swarms *of* [f]*flies* upon thee, and upon thy servants, and upon thy people, and into thy houses: and the houses of the [g]Ē-ġy̆p′tianṣ shall be full of swarms *of flies*, and also the ground whereon they *are*.

22 And [h]I will sever in that day the land of [i]Gō′shen, in which my [d]people dwell, that no swarms *of* [f]*flies* shall be there; [j]to the end thou mayest know that [k]I *am* the LORD in the midst of the earth.

23 And I will [3]put a division between my [d]people and thy people: to morrow shall this [f]sign be.

24 And the LORD did so; and there came a grievous swarm *of* [f]*flies* into the house of [c]Phā′raōh, and *into* his servants' houses, and into all the land of Ē′ġy̆pt: the land was [4]corrupted by reason of the swarm *of flies*.

25 ¶ And [c]Phā′raōh called for [a]Mō′ṣeṣ and for [l]Aâr′on, and said, [m]Go ye, [n]sacrifice to your God in the land.

26 And [a]Mō′ṣeṣ said, It is not meet so to do; for we shall sacrifice the abomination of the Ē′ġy̆p′tianṣ to the LORD our God: lo, shall we sacrifice the abomination of the Ē-ġy̆p′tianṣ before their eyes, and will they not stone us?

27 We will go three days' journey into the wilderness, and [n]sacrifice to the LORD our God, as he shall command us.

28 And [c]Phā′raōh said, [m]I will let you go, that ye may [n]sacrifice to the LORD your God in the wilderness; only ye shall not go very far away: [o]intreat for me.

29 And [a]Mō′ṣeṣ said, Behold, I go out from thee, and I will intreat the LORD that the swarms *of* [f]*flies* may depart from [c]Phā′raōh, from his servants, and from his people, to morrow: but let not Phā′raōh deal [p]deceitfully any more in not letting the people go to sacrifice to the LORD.

30 And Mō′ṣeṣ went out from Phā′raōh, and [q]intreated the LORD.

31 And the LORD did according to the [r]word of Mō′ṣeṣ; and he removed the swarms *of flies* from Phā′raōh, from his servants, and from his people; there remained not one.

32 [s]And Phā′raōh [t]hardened his [u]heart at this time also, neither would he let the people go.

## CHAPTER 9

*The murrain of beasts. 8 The plague of boils and blains. 13 The message about the hail. 22 The plague of hail. 27 Pharaoh asks Moses to entreat the Lord, 35 but yet is hardened.*

THEN the LORD said unto [a]Mō′ṣeṣ, Go in unto [b]Phā′-raōh, and tell him, Thus

v.24–1534 BC
See footnote, *Time*, Rev. 10:6.

24
4 *Or*, destroyed

25
l *Aaron*, Ex. 6:20.
m *Affliction, penitence in*, Psa. 34:19.
n *Offerings*, Lev. 6:17.

28
o *Intercession, solicited*, Jer. 27:18.

29
p *Deception*, Josh. 9:4.

30
q *Intercession, exemplified*, Jer. 27:18.

31
r *Intercession, answered*, Jer. 27:18.

32
s *Character, instability of*, Phil. 2:15.
t *Obduracy, instances of*, Prov. 29:1.
u *Heart, hardened*, Psa. 44:21.

1
a *Moses*, Ex. 2:10.
b *Pharaoh*, Ex. 3:10.

v.1–1534 BC
See footnote, *Time*, Rev. 10:6.

c *Hebrew*, Gen. 40:15.
d *Israel*, Ex. 4:22.

3
e *Judgments*, Ex. 6:6.
f *Animals, suffer under divine judgments*, Jer. 27:5.
g *Horse*, Job 39:19.
h *Ass, domesticated*, 2 Chr. 28:15.
i *Camel*, 1 Sam. 30:17.

4
j *God, preserver*, Gen. 2:2.

7
k *Heart, hardened, instances of*, Psa. 44:21.
l *Obduracy, instances of*, Prov. 29:1.
1 R. V. stubborn.

8
m *Aaron*, Ex. 6:20.

9
n *Egyptians, visited by plagues*, Gen. 50:3.

saith the LORD God of the [c]Hē′-
brews, Let my [d]people go, that
they may serve me.
2 For if thou refuse to let *them*
go, and wilt hold them still,
3 [S]Behold, the [e]hand of the
LORD is upon thy [f]cattle which
*is* in the field, upon the [g]horses,
upon the [h]asses, upon the [i]cam-
els, upon the oxen, and upon the
sheep: *there shall be* a very grievous [G]murrain.[G]
4 And the [j]LORD shall sever [G]be-
tween the cattle of [d]Is′ra-el and
the cattle of Ē′ġy̆pt: and there
shall nothing die of all *that is* the
children's of Is′ra-el.
5 And the LORD appointed a
set time, saying, To morrow the
LORD shall do this [e]thing in the
land.
6 And the LORD did that [e]thing
on the morrow,[G] and all the [f]cattle
of Ē′ġy̆pt died: but of the cattle
of the children of [d]Is′ra-el died
not one.
7 And [b]Phā′raōh sent, and, behold, there was not one of the
cattle of the [d]Is′ra-el-ītes dead.
And the heart of Phā′raōh was
[1,k]hardened, and he [l]did not let
the people go.[S]
8 ¶ And the LORD said unto
[b]Mō′ses and unto [m]Aâr′on, Take
to you handfuls of ashes of the
furnace, and let Mō′ses sprinkle
it toward the heaven in the sight
of [b]Phā′raōh.
9 [Q]And it shall become small
dust in all the land of [n]Ē′ġy̆pt,
and shall be a *boil breaking
forth *with* blains[G] upon man, and
upon [f]beast, throughout all the
land of Ē′ġy̆pt.
10 And they took ashes of the
furnace, and stood before [b]Phā′-
raōh; and [a]Mō′ses sprinkled it up
toward heaven; and it became a
*boil breaking forth *with* blains
upon man, and upon beast.[Q]
11 And the [o]magicians could
not stand before [a]Mō′ses because
of the *boils; for the boil was upon the magicians, and upon all
the [n]Ē-ġy̆p′tians.
12 And the LORD hardened the
[k]heart of Phā′raōh, and he
[l]hearkened not unto them; as the
LORD had spoken unto Mō′ses.[Q]
13 ¶ And the LORD said unto
[a]Mō′ses, [p]Rise up early in
the morning, and stand before
[b]Phā′raōh, and say unto him,
Thus saith the LORD God of the
[c]Hē′brews, Let my [d]people go,
that they may serve me.
14 For I will at this time send
all my [q]plagues upon thine heart,
and upon thy servants, and upon
thy people; [r]that thou mayest
know that *there is* none like me
in all the earth.[S]
15 For now I will stretch out
my hand, that I may smite thee
and thy [n]people with [q]pestilence;
and thou shalt be cut off from
the earth.
16 And in very deed [s]for this
[t]*cause* have [u]I [v]raised thee up,
for to shew [2]*in* thee my power;
and that my name may be declared throughout all the earth.[Q][S]
17 As yet [w]exaltest thou thyself
against my [d]people, that thou
wilt not let them go?
18 Behold, to morrow about
this time I will cause it to rain a
very grievous[G] [x]hail, such as hath
not been in Ē′ġy̆pt since the
foundation thereof even until
now.
19 Send therefore now, *and*
gather thy cattle, and all that
thou hast in the field; *for upon*
every man and [f]beast which shall
be found in the field, and shall
not be brought home, the [x]hail
shall come down upon them,
and they shall die.
20 He that [y,z]feared[G] the word

v.11–1534 BC
See footnote, *Time* Rev. 10:6.

11
o *Magician*, Ex. 7:11.

13
p *Rising, early*, Gen. 19:2.

14
q *Plague*, Ex. 11:1.
r *Judgments, design of*, Ex. 6:6.

16
s Rom. 9:17.
t *Suffering, vicarious*, Col. 1:24.
u *God, power of*, Gen. 2:2.
v *Foreordination*, Rom. 8:30.
2 The word *in* is omitted in R. V.

17
w *Self-exaltation, instances of*, Luke 14:11.

18
x *Hail*, Job 38:22.

20
y *Faith, instances of*, Mark 11:22.
z *Fear, of God, instances of*, Acts 9:31.

***BOIL**, a tumor. *Plague, of Egyptians*, Ex. 9:9, 10; Deut. 28:27, 35; *of Philistines*, 1 Sam. 5:6, 9; 6:5. *Of Hezekiah, healed*, 2 Kin. 20:7; Isa. 38:21. *Of Job*, Job 2:7, 8. *Levitical ceremonies prescribed for*, Lev. 13:18–23.

v.20–1534 BC
See footnote, *Time*, Rev. 10:6.

of the LORD among the servants
of Phā′raōh made his servants
and his cattle flee into the
houses:[s]
21 And he that [a]regarded not
the word of the LORD left his
servants and his cattle in the
field.
22 ¶ And the LORD said unto
[b]Mō′ṣeṣ, Stretch forth thine
hand toward heaven, that there
may be [c,d,e]hail in all the land of
Ē′ġy̆pt, upon man, and upon
[f]beast, and upon every herb of
the field, throughout the land of
Ē′ġy̆pt.
23 And [b]Mō′ṣeṣ stretched forth
his [g]rod toward heaven: and the
LORD sent [h]thunder and hail,
and the [i]fire ran along upon the
ground; and the LORD rained
hail upon the land of Ē′ġy̆pt.
24 So there was [c,d]hail, and [i]fire
[3]mingled[G] with the hail, very
grievous, such as there was none
like it in all the land of Ē′ġy̆pt
since it became a nation.[Q]
25 And the [c,d]hail smote
throughout all the land of Ē′ġy̆pt
all that *was* in the field, both
[j]man and [f]beast; and the hail
smote every herb of the field,
and brake every tree of the field.
26 Only in the land of [k]Gō′-
shen, where the children of Ĭṣ′-
ra-el *were*, was there no [c,d]hail.[s]
27 ¶ And [l]Phā′raōh [m]sent, and
called for Mō′ṣeṣ and Aâr′on,
and said unto them, [n,o,p]I have
[q]sinned this time: the [r]LORD *is*
righteous, and I and my people
*are* wicked.
28 [s]Intreat[G] the LORD [4](for *it is*
enough) that there be no *more*
[5]mighty [h]thunderings and [c]hail;
and I will let you go, and ye shall
stay no longer.[Q]
29 And Mō′ṣeṣ said unto him,
As soon as I am gone out of the
city, I will spread abroad my
hands unto the LORD; *and* the
thunder shall cease, neither shall
there be any more hail; [t]that
thou mayest know how that the
earth *is* the [u]LORD's.
30 But as for thee and thy servants, I know that ye [v,w]will not
yet fear the LORD God.
31 And the †flax and the ‡bar-
ley was smitten: for the barley
*was* in the ear, and the flax [6]*was*
bolled.[G]
32 But the [x]wheat and the [y]rie[G]
were not smitten: for they *were*
not grown up.
33 And Mō′ṣeṣ went out of the
city from Phā′raōh, and [z]spread
abroad his hands unto the
LORD: and the [a]thunders and
[b]hail ceased, and the [c]rain was
not poured upon the earth.
34 And when Phā′raōh saw
that the [c]rain and the [b]hail and
the [a]thunders were ceased, [d,e]he
sinned yet more, and [f]hardened
his heart, he and his servants.
35 And the heart of Phā′raōh
was [f]hardened, [g]neither would
he let the children of Ĭṣ′ra-el go;
as the LORD had spoken by
Mō′ṣeṣ.

## CHAPTER 10

*God threatens to send locusts. 7 Pharaoh, moved by his servants, inclines to let the Israelites go. 12 The plague of the locusts. 16 Pharaoh asks Moses to entreat the Lord in his behalf. 21 The plague of darkness. 24 Pharaoh petitions again unto Moses, 27 but yet is hardened.*

AND the LORD said unto
[a]Mō′ṣeṣ, Go in unto
[b]Phā′raōh: for I have hardened
his [c]heart, and the heart of his
servants, that I might shew
these my signs before him:
2 And that [d]thou mayest [e]tell
in the ears of thy [f]son, and of thy
son's son, what things I have

**21**
a *Unbelief*, Heb. 3:12.

**22**
b *Moses*, Ex. 2:10.
c *Hail*, Job 38:22.
d *Plague, of hail*, Ex. 11:1.
e *Meteorology*, Matt. 16:2.
f *Animals, suffer under divine judgments*, Jer. 27:5.

**23**
g *Rod of Moses*, Ex. 4:17.
h *Thunder*, 1 Sam. 7:10.
i *Fire*, Ex. 12:8.

**24**
3 *Or*, flashing continually amidst

**25**
j *Egyptians, visited by plagues*, Gen. 50:3.

**26**
k *Goshen*, Gen. 45:10.

**27**
l *Pharaoh*, Ex. 3:10.
m *Afflictions, penitence in*, Psa. 34:19.
n *Conscience, guilty*, Acts 23:1.
o *Conviction, of sin, instances of*, John 16:8.
p *Repentance, instances of*, Mark 1:4.
q *Sin, confession of*, Rom. 5:12.
r *God, righteousness of*, Gen. 2:2.

**28**
s *Intercession, solicited*, Jer. 27:18.
4 R. V. for there hath been enough of these
5 *Heb.* voices (or thunderings) of God

v.29–1534 BC
See footnote, *Time*, Rev. 10:6.

**29**
t *Miracles, design of*, Luke 23:8.
u *God, sovereign*, Gen. 2:2.

**30**
v *Afflictions, impenitence in, instances of*, Psa. 34:19.
w *Obduracy, instances of*, Psa. 29:1.

**31**
6 *Or*, was in bloom.

**32**
x *Wheat*, Ezra 6:9.
y Isa. 28:25.

**33**
z *Intercession, instances of*, Jer. 27:18.

a *Thunder*, 1 Sam. 7:10.
b *Hail*, Job 38:22.
c *Rain*, 2 Sam. 1:21.

**34**
d *Character, instability of*, Phil. 2:15.
e *Instability*, Jas. 1:8.
f *Heart, hardened instances of*, Psa. 44:21.

**35**
g *Obduracy*, Prov. 29:1.

**1**
a *Moses*, Ex. 2:10.
b *Pharaoh*, Ex. 3:10.
c *Heart, hardened, instances of*, Psa. 44:21.

**2**
d *Parents, duty of*, 2 Cor. 12:14.
e *Instruction, of children*, Prov. 23:23.
f *Children, instruction of*, Mark 10:14.

† **FLAX.** *In Egypt*, Ex. 9:31. *In Palestine*, Josh. 2:6. *Linen made from*, Prov. 31:13; Hos. 2:5, 9. *Robes made of*, Ezek. 40:3.

See footnote, LINEN, Ezek. 27:16.

**Figurative:** *Smoking flax not quenched*, **Isa. 42:3; Matt. 12:20.**

‡ **BARLEY.** *A product, of Egypt*, Ex. 9:31; *of Palestine*, Deut. 8:8; 1 Chr. 11:13; Jer. 41:8. *Fed to horses*, 1 Kin. 4:28. *Used in offerings*, Num. 5:15; Ezek. 45:13. *Traffic in*, 2 Kin. 7:1; 2 Chr. 2:10; Hos. 3:2. *Tribute in*, 2 Chr. 27:5. *Priests estimated value of*, Lev. **27:16.** *Absalom burns Joab's field of*, 2 Sam. 14:30.

*Loaves of*, 2 Kin. 4:42; John 6:9, **13.**

v.2–1534 BC
See footnote. *Time,* Rev. 10:6.

g *Egyptians,* Gen. 50:3.
h *Miracles, design of,* Luke 23:8.

3
i *Aaron,* Ex. 6:20.
j *Hebrew,* Gen. 40:15.
k *Humility,* Prov. 22:4.

4
l *Locusts, plague of,* Neh. 3:17.
m *Plague, of locusts,* Ex. 11:1.
1 R. V. border:

5
n *Hail, plague of,* Job 38:22.

7
o *Intercession, of man with man,* Jer. 27:18.

9
p *Feasts,* Mark 12:39.

wrought in [g]Ē′ġy̆pt, and my [h]signs which I have done among them; that ye may know how that I *am* the LORD.

3 And [a]Mō′ṣeṣ and [i]Aâr′on came in unto [b]Phā′raōh, and said unto him, Thus saith the LORD God of the [j]Hē′brewṣ, How long wilt thou refuse to [k]humble thyself before me? let my people go, that they may serve me.

4 [S]Else, if thou refuse to let my people go, behold, to morrow will I bring the [l,m]locusts into thy [1]coast[G]:

5 And [l,m]they shall cover the face of the earth, that one cannot be able to see the earth: and they shall eat the residue[G] of that which is escaped, which remaineth unto you from the [n]hail, and shall eat every tree which groweth for you out of the field:

6 And [l,m]they shall fill thy houses, and the houses of all thy servants, and the houses of all the [g]Ē-ġy̆p′tianṣ; which neither thy fathers, nor thy fathers' fathers have seen, since the day that they were upon the earth unto this day. And he turned himself, and went out from [b]Phā′raōh.[S]

7 And Phā′raōh's servants said unto him, How long shall this man be a snare unto us? [o]let the men go, that they may serve the LORD their God: knowest thou not yet that Ē′ġy̆pt is destroyed?

8 And [a]Mō′ṣeṣ and [i]Aâr′on were brought again unto [b]Phā′raōh: and he said unto them, Go, serve the LORD your God: *but* who *are* they that shall go?

9 And [a]Mō′ṣeṣ said, We will go with our young and with our old, with our sons and with our daughters, with our flocks and with our herds will we go; for we *must hold* a [p]feast unto the LORD.

10 And he said unto them, Let the LORD be so with you, as I will let you go, and your little ones: look *to it*; for evil *is* before you.

11 Not so: go now ye *that are* men, and serve the LORD; for that ye did desire. And they were [q]driven out from Phā′raōh's presence.

12 ¶ And the LORD said unto [a]Mō′ṣeṣ, Stretch out thine hand over the land of [g]Ē′ġy̆pt for the [l]locusts, that they may come up upon the land of Ē′ġy̆pt, and eat every herb of the land, *even* all that the [n]hail hath left.[Q]

13 [S]And [a]Mō′ṣeṣ stretched forth his [r]rod over the land of [g]Ē′ġy̆pt, and the LORD [s]brought an east [t]wind upon the land all that day, and all *that* night; *and* when it was morning, the east wind brought the [l,m]locusts.

14 And the [l,m]locusts went up over all the land of [g]Ē′ġy̆pt, and rested in all the [1]coasts[G] of Ē′ġy̆pt: very grievous[G] *were they*; before them there were no such locusts as they, neither after them shall be such.

15 For [l,m]they covered the face of the whole earth, so that the land was darkened; and they did eat every herb[G] of the land, and all the fruit of the trees which the [n]hail had left: and there remained not any green thing in the trees, or in the herbs of the field, through all the land of [g]Ē′ġy̆pt.[S] [Q]

16 ¶ Then [b]Phā′raōh called for [a]Mō′ṣeṣ and [i]Aâr′on in haste; and he said, [u,v,w]I have sinned against the LORD your God, and against you.

17 [u,v]Now therefore forgive, I pray thee, my [w]sin only this once, and [x]intreat the LORD your God, that he may take away from me this death only.

18 [S]And [a]he went out from Phā′raōh, and [y]intreated the LORD.

v.10–1534 BC
See footnote *Time,* Rev. 10:6.

11
q *Anger, instances of,* Psa. 37:8.

13
r *Rod of Moses,* Ex. 4:17.
s *Miracles,* Luke 23:8.
t *Meteorology,* Matt. 16:2.

16
u *Conviction, of sin, instances of,* John 16:8.
v *Repentence, instances of,* Mark 1:4.
w *Sin, confession of,* Rom. 5:12.

17
x *Intercession, solicited,* Jer. 27:18.

18
y *Intercession, instances of,* Jer 27:18.

v.19–1534 BC
See footnote, *Time*, Rev. 10:6.

19
z *Wind, miraculous*, Job 37:17.
a *Locusts, plague of*, Nah. 3:17.

20
b *Pharaoh*, Ex. 3:10.
c *Heart, hardened, instances of*, Psa. 44:21.
d *Obduracy, instances of*, Prov. 29:1.
e *Israel*, Ex. 4:22.

21
f *Moses*, Ex. 2:10.
g *Darkness*, Gen. 1:2.
h *Egyptians*, Gen. 50:3.
2 Or, so that men shall grope in darkness.

22
i *Plague, of darkness*, Ex. 11:1.
j *Meteorology*, Matt. 16:2.

25
k *Offerings, burnt*, Lev. 6:17.

19 And the LORD turned a mighty strong west [t,z]wind, which took away the [a]locusts, and cast them into the [§]Red sea; there remained not one locust in all the [1]coasts[G] of Ē′gy̆pt.

20 But the LORD hardened [b]Phā′raōh's [c]heart, so that he [d]would not let the children of [e]Is′ra-el go.

21 ¶ And the LORD said unto [f]Mō′ses, Stretch out thine hand toward heaven, that there may be [g]darkness over the land of [h]Ē′gy̆pt, [2]even darkness *which* may be felt.

22 And [f]Mō′ses stretched forth his hand toward heaven; and there was a thick [g,i,j]darkness in all the land of [h]Ē′gy̆pt three days[Q]:

23 They saw not one another, neither rose any from his place for three days: but all the children of [e]Is′ra-el had light in their dwellings.

24 ¶ And [b]Phā′raōh called unto [f]Mō′ses, and said, Go ye, serve the LORD; only let your flocks and your herds be stayed:[G] let your little ones also go with you.

25 And [f]Mō′ses said, Thou must give us also sacrifices and burnt [k]offerings, that we may sacrifice unto the LORD our God.

26 Our cattle also shall go with us; there shall not an hoof be left behind; for thereof must we take to serve the LORD our God; and we know not with what we must serve the LORD, until we come thither.

27 ¶ But the LORD hardened [b]Phā′raōh's [c]heart, and he [d]would not let them go.

28 [Q]And [b]Phā′raōh said unto him, [l]Get thee from me, take heed to thyself, see my face no more; for in *that* day thou seest my face thou shalt die.

29 And Mō′ses said, [m]Thou hast spoken well, I will see thy face again no more.[Q]

## CHAPTER 11

*God's message to the Israelites to borrow jewels of their neighbors. 4 Moses threatens Pharaoh with the death of the firstborn.*

AND the LORD said unto [a]Mō′ses, Yet will I bring one [*,b]plague *more* upon [c]Phā′raōh, and upon [d]Ē′gy̆pt; [e]afterwards he will let you go hence: when he shall let *you* go, he shall surely thrust you out hence altogether.[S]

2 Speak now in the ears of the [f]people, and let every man [g]borrow[G] of his neighbour, and every woman of her neighbour, [h]jewels of [i]silver, and jewels of [j]gold.

3 And the [k]LORD gave the [f]people favour in the sight of the [d]Ē-gy̆p′tians. Moreover the man [a]Mō′ses *was* very great[G] in the land of [l]Ē′gy̆pt, in the sight of [c]Phā′raōh's servants, and in the sight of the people.

4 ¶ And [a]Mō′ses said, Thus saith the LORD, About midnight will I go out into the midst of [l]Ē′gy̆pt:

5 And all the [m]firstborn in the land of Ē′gy̆pt shall die from the [n]firstborn of Phā′raōh that sitteth upon his throne, even unto the firstborn of the maidservant that *is* behind the [†]mill: and all the firstborn of [1,o]beasts.

6 And there shall be a great cry

v.28–1534 BC
See footnote, *Time*, Rev. 10:6.

28
l *Anger*, Psa. 37:8.

29
m *Reproof, faithfulness in*, Prov. 17:10.

1
a *Moses*, Ex. 2:10.
b *Judgments*, Ex. 6:6.
c *Pharaoh*, Ex. 3:10.
d *Egyptians*, Gen. 50:3.
e *Miracles, design of*, Luke 23:8.

2
f *Israel*, Ex. 4:22.
g *Borrowing, instances of*, Ex. 22:14.
h *Jewels*, Gen. 24:53.
i *Silver*, 1 Chr. 28:14.
j *Gold*, Ezek. 7:19.

3
k *God, providence of, instances of*, Gen. 2:2.
l *Egypt*, Gen. 41:8.

5
m *Firstborn*, Zech. 12:10.
n *Children, involved in sin of parents*, Mark 10:14.
o *Animals, suffer under divine judgments*, Jer. 27:5.
1 That is, domesticated animals.

§ **RED SEA.** *The locusts which devastated Egypt destroyed in*, Ex. 10:19. *Divided*, Ex. 14:21; 15:8; Psa. 74:13; 114:3; Isa. 51:10; 63:12. *Israelites cross; Pharaoh and his army drowned in*, Ex. 14; 15:1, 4, 10, 19; Num. 33:8; Deut. 11:4; Josh. 2:10; 4:23; 24:6, 7; Judg. 11:16; Neh. 9:9–11; Psa. 66:6; 78:13, 53; 106:7–11, 22; 136:13–15; Isa. 43:16, 17; Acts 7:36; 1 Cor. 10:1, 2; Heb. 11:29. *Israelites journey by*, Ex. 14:2, 9; Num. 14:25; 21:4; 33:10, 11; Deut. 1:40; 2:1–3. *Southwest boundary of the promised land*, Ex. 23:31. *Solomon builds ships on*, 1 Kin. 9:26.
*Wilderness of*, Ex. 13:18.

* **PLAGUE.** *As a judgment on the Egyptians*, Psa. 105:26–36; 135:8, 9; Acts 7:36. *The plague, of blood*, Ex. 7:14–25; *of frogs*, Ex. 8:1–15; *of lice*, Ex. 8:16–19; *of flies*, Ex. 8:20–24; *of murrain*, Ex. 9:1–7; *of boils and blains*, Ex. 9:8–12; *of hail*, Ex. 9:18–24; *of locust*, Ex. 10:1–20; *of darkness*, Ex. 10:21–23. *Death of the first born*, Ex. 11:4–7; 12:29, 30.
On the Israelites: *On account of idolatry*, Ex. 32:35; *after eating quail*, Num. 11:33; Psa. 78:27–31; *after refusing to enter the promised land*, Num. 14:36, 37; *after murmuring on account of the destruction of Korah*, Num. 16:41–50; *of serpents*, Num. 21:6; *for the sin of Peor*, Num. 25:4–9; Deut. 4:3; Josh. 22:17; Psa. 106:28–30; *for David's sin in numbering the people*, 2 Sam. 24:10–25; 1 Chr. 21:7–27.
*On the Philistines*, 1 Sam. 6:4, 5.
*Denounced as a judgment*, Lev. 26:21; Deut. 28:21,59. *Foretold*, Rev. 11:6; 15:1, 6–8; 16.

† **MILL.** *Upper and nether stones of*, Deut. 24:6; Isa.

v.6–1534 BC
See footnote, *Time*, Rev. 10:6.

7
*p God, preserver*, Gen. 2:2.

8
*q Anger, instances of*, Psa. 37:8.

9
*r Miracles*, Luke 23:8.

10
*s Aaron*, Ex. 6:20.
*t Heart, hardened, instances of*, Psa. 44:21.

1
*a Inspiration, of prophets*, Job 32:8.
*b Prophets, inspiration of*, Isa. 3:2.
*c Egypt, plagues in*, vs. 1–51; Gen. 41:8.

throughout all the land of [t]Ē'-
ġy̆pt, such as there was none like
it, nor shall be like it any more.
7 But against any of the children of [t]Is̱'ra-el shall not a dog
move his tongue, against man or
beast: that ye may know how
that the [p]LORD doth put a difference between the [d]Ē-ġy̆p'-
tians̱ and [t]Is̱'ra-el.[S]
8 And all these thy servants
shall come down unto me, and
bow down themselves unto me,
saying, Get thee out, and all the
people that follow thee: and after that I will go out. And he
went out from Phā'raōh in a
great [q]anger.
9 And the LORD said unto
[a]Mō'ṣeṣ, [c]Phā'raōh shall not
hearken unto you; that my
[r]wonders[G] may be multiplied in
the land of [t]Ē'ġy̆pt.
10 And [a]Mō'ṣeṣ and [s]Aâr'on
did all these [r]wonders before
Phā'raōh: and the LORD hardened Phā'raōh's [t]heart, so that
he would not let the children of
[t]Is̱'ra-el go out of his land.

## CHAPTER 12

*The beginning of the year is changed.* 3 *The passover is instituted.* 11 *The rite of the passover.* 15 *The seven days of unleavened bread.* 29 *The firstborn are slain.* 31 *The Israelites are driven out of the land.* 37 *They come to Succoth.* 43 *The ordinance of the passover.*

AND[Q] the LORD [a,b]spake unto
Mō'ṣeṣ and Aâr'on in the
land of [c]Ē'ġy̆pt, saying,
2 This *month *shall be* unto
you the beginning of months: it
*shall be* the [d]first month of the
[e]year to you.
3 ¶ [Q]Speak ye unto all the
[f]congregation of Is̱'ra-el, saying, [g]In the tenth *day* of
this month they shall take
to them every man a [1,h,i,j]lamb,
according to the house of
*their* fathers, a lamb for an
house:
4 And if the household be too
little for the lamb, let him and
his neighbour next unto his
house take *it* according to the
number of the souls[G]; every man
according to his eating shall
make your count[G] for the
lamb.
5 Your [h,i,k]lamb shall be [l,m]with-
out [n,o]blemish, a male of the
first year: ye shall take *it* out
from the sheep, or from the
[p]goats:
6 And ye shall keep [h]it up
until the fourteenth day of the
same month: and the whole
assembly of the [f]congregation
of Is̱'ra-el shall [q]kill it [2]in the
evening.[Q]
7 And they shall take of the
[r,s]blood, and strike[G] *it* on the two
side posts and on the [3]upper
door post of the houses, wherein
they shall eat it.
8 [Q]And they shall eat the
flesh in that night, roast with

v.2–1533 BC
See footnote, *Time*, Rev. 10:6.

2
*d Abib, first month of Jewish calendar*, Ex. 13:4.
*e Time*, Rev. 10:6.

3
*f Church, called the congregation*, Matt. 16:18.
*g Passover*, vs. 3–49; Num. 9:5.
*h Lamb*, Num. 7:15.
*i Jesus, typified in the passover lamb*, Matt. 1:21.
*j Symbols and Similitudes, passover*. Heb. 9:9.
1 *Or*, kid,

5
*k Atonement, made by Jesus, typified*, vs. 11–14; Lev. 17:11.
*l Offerings, must be without blemish*, Lev. 6:17.
*m Holiness, typified*, Ex. 39:30.
*n Blemish*, Lev. 14:10.
*o Sin, typified*, Rom. 5:12.
*p Goat, for the paschal feast*, Deut. 14:4.

6
*q Jesus, vicarious death of, typified*, Matt. 1:21.
2 *Heb.* between the two evenings.

7
*r Blood, sacrificial*, vs. 8–23; Heb. 9:19.
*s Jesus, atoning blood of, typified*, Matt. 1:21.
3 R. V. lintel, upon the houses,

47:2; Jer. 25:10. *Used in Egypt*, Ex. 11:5. *Operated, by women*, Matt. 24:41; *by captives*, Judg. 16:21; Lam. 5:13. *Manna ground in*, Num. 11:8. *Sound of, to cease*, Rev. 18:22.

***MONTH.** *Ancient use of*, Gen. 7:11; 8:4. *Twelve months reckoned to a year*, 1 Chr. 27:1–15.

1. **Abib** (*April*). *The Jewish calendar began with*, Ex. 12:2; 13:4; Deut. 16:1. *Passover instituted and celebrated in*, Ex. 12:1–28; 23:15. *Israelites left Egypt in*, Ex. 13:4. *Tabernacle set up in*, Ex. 40:2, 17. *Israelites arrive at Zin in*, Num. 20:1. *Cross Jordan in*, Josh. 4:19. *Jordan overflows in*, 1 Chr. 12:15. *After the captivity called* NISAN, Neh. 2:1; Esth. 3:7.

2. **Zif** (*May*), 1 Kin. 6:1, 37. *Israel numbered in*, Num. 1:1, 18. *Passover to be observed in, by the unclean and others who could not observe it in the first month*, Num. 9:10, 11. *Israel departed from the wilderness of Zin in*, Num. 10:11, 12. *Temple begun in*, 1 Kin. 6:1; 2 Chr. 3:2. *An irregular passover celebrated in*, 2 Chr. 30:1–27. *Rebuilding of the temple begun in*, Ezra 3:8.

3. **Sivan** (*June*), Esth. 8:9. *Asa renews the covenant of himself and people in*, 2 Chr. 15:10.

4. **Tammuz** (*July*). Only the number appears in the Bible. *Jerusalem taken by Nebuchadnezzar in*, Jer. 39:2; 52:6,7.

5. **Ab** (*August*). Only the number mentioned. *Aaron died on the first day of*, Num. 33:38. *Temple destroyed in*, 2 Kin. 25:8–10; Jer. 1:3; 52:12–30. *Jews carried captive to Babylon in*, Jer. 1:3. *Ezra arrived at Jerusalem in*, Ezra 7:8.9.

6. **Elul** (*September*). *Wall of Jerusalem finished in*, Neh. 6:15. *Rebuilding of the temple progressed in*, Hag. 1:14, 15.

7. **Ethanim** (*October*), or TISRI. *The first month in the civil year and the seventh in the ecclesiastical and ancient reckoning*, 1 Kin. 8:2. *Feasts held in*, Lev. 23:24, 27, 34–41; Neh. 8:13–15. *Jubilee proclaimed in*, Lev. 25:9. *Solomon's temple dedicated in*, 1 Kin. 8:2. *Altar rebuilt and offerings renewed in*, Ezra 3:1–6.

8. **Bul** (*November*). *The temple finished in*. 1 Kin. 6:38. *Jeroboam's idolatrous feast in*, 1 Kin. 12:32, 33.

9. **Chisleu** (*December*), Ezra 10:9; Jer. 36:9, 22; Zech. 7:1.

10. **Tebeth** (*January*), Esth. 2:16. *Nebuchadnezzar besieges Jerusalem in*, 2 Kin. 25:1; Jer. 52:4.

11. **Sebat** (*February*), Zech. 1:7.

12. **Adar** (*March*). *Decree to put the Jews to death in*, Esth. 3:12, 13. *Second temple finished in*, Ezra 6:15. *Feast of Purim in*, Esth. 9:1–26.

**Months in prophecy**, Rev. 11:2.

v.8–1533 BC
See footnote, *Time,* Rev. 10:6.

8
*l* *Bitter Herbs,* Num. 9:11.

9
4 R. V. inwards

12
*u* *Firstborn, of Egyptians, slain,* Zech. 12:10.
*v* *Idolatry, objects of,* 1 Sam. 15:23.
*w* *Judgments,* Ex. 6:6.

13
*x* *Token,* Psa. 86:17.
*y* *God, preserver,* vs. 17–23; Gen. 2:2.
*z* *Israel, exempt from the plagues,* Ex. 4:22.

14
*a* *Memorial, passover,* Num. 16:40.
*b* *Passover,* Num. 9:5.
*c* *Ordinance,* Num. 9:14.

15
*d* *Seven, days, passover lasted,* Gen. 7:2.
*e* *Leaven, forbidden at the passover,* Lev. 23:17.

†fire, and unleavened bread;
*and* with [l]bitter *herbs* they shall
eat it.
9 Eat not of [h]it raw, nor sodden[G]
at all with water, but roast *with*
†fire; his head with his legs, and
with the [4]purtenance[G] thereof.
10 And ye shall let nothing of [h]it
remain until the morning; and
that which remaineth of it until
the morning ye shall burn with
†fire.
11 And thus shall ye eat [h]it; *with*
your loins girded, your shoes on
your feet, and your staff in your
hand; and ye shall eat it in haste:
it *is* the LORD's [g]passover.[Q]
12 For I will pass through the
land of [c]Ē'ġy̆pt this night, and
will smite all the [u]firstborn in the
land of Ē'ġy̆pt, both man and
beast; and against all the [v]gods
of Ē'ġy̆pt I will execute [w]judg-
ment: I *am* the LORD.
13 And the [s,r]blood shall be to
you for a [x]token upon the houses
where ye *are*: and when I see the
blood, [y]I will [z]pass over you,
and the plague shall not be upon
you to destroy *you,* when I smite
the land of Ē'ġy̆pt.[S]
14[Q] And this day shall be unto
you for a [a]memorial; and ye shall
keep it a [b]feast[G] to the LORD
throughout your generations; ye
shall keep it a feast by an [c]or-
dinance for ever.
15 ¶ [d]Seven days shall ye eat
unleavened bread; even the first
day ye shall put away [e]leaven[G]
out of your houses: for whosoever eateth leavened bread from
the first day until the seventh
day, that soul[G] shall be [f]cut[G] off
from Ĭs̩'ra-el.[Q]
16 And in the first day *there*
*shall be* an holy convocation[G], and
in the seventh day there shall be
an holy convocation[G] to you; [g]no
manner of work shall be done in
them, save *that* which every man
must eat, that only may be done
of you.[Q]
17 And ye shall observe *the*
[b]*feast of* unleavened bread; for in
this selfsame[G] day have I brought
your [5]armies[G] out of the land of
Ē'ġy̆pt: therefore shall ye observe this day in your generations[G] by an [c]ordinance for ever.[S]
18 In the [h]first **month,* on the
fourteenth day of the month at
even, ye shall eat unleavened
bread, until the one and twentieth day of the month at even.
19 [d]Seven days shall there be no
[e]leaven found in your houses: for
whosoever eateth that which is
leavened, even that soul[G] shall be
[f]cut off from the congregation of
Ĭs̩'ra-el, whether he be a [6,i]stran-
ger,[G] or born in the land.
20 [e]Ye shall eat nothing leavened; in all your habitations
shall ye eat unleavened bread.[Q]
21 ¶ Then[Q] [j]Mō'ṣeṣ called for all
the [k]elders of Ĭs̩'ra-el, and said
unto them, Draw out and take
you a [l]lamb according to your
families, and [m]kill the [b]passover.
22 And ye shall take a bunch of
‡hyssop, and dip *it* in the blood
that *is* in the bason, and strike
the lintel and the two side posts

v.15–1533 BC
See footnote, *Time,* Rev. 10:6.

*f* *Disfellowship,* Num. 15:31.

16
*g* *Rest,* Ex. 23:11.

17
5 R. V. hosts

18
*h* *Abib,* Ex. 13:4.

19
*i* *Foreigner,* Deut. 23:20.
6 R. V. sojourner.

21
*j* *Moses,* Ex. 2:10.
*k* *Senate,* Num. 11:16.
*l* *Jesus, typified in the passover,* Matt. 1:21.
*m* *Jesus, vicarious death of, typified,* Matt. 1:21.

† **FIRE.** *On altar of burnt offering, never to cease burning,* Lev. 6:13. *Not to be kindled on Sabbath,* Ex. 35:3. *Used as a signal in war,* Judg. 20:38, 40; Jer. 6:1. *Furnaces of,* Dan. 3:6. *Children caused to pass through,* 2 Kin. 16:3; 17:17. *Torture by,* Lev. 21:9; Jer. 29:22; Dan. 3.
**Miracles connected with:** *Miraculously consumes Abraham's sacrifice,* Gen. 15:17; *Aaron's,* Lev. 9:24; *David's,* 1 Chr. 21:26; *Elijah's,* 1 Kin. 18:38; *Solomon's, at dedication of the temple,* 2 Chr. 7:1. *The burning bush,* Ex. 3:2. *Display of, in the plagues of Egypt,* Ex. 9:24; *in pillar to guide the children of Israel,* Ex. 13:21, 22; 14:19, 24; 40:38; Num. 9:15–23; *at Elijah's translation,* 2 Kin. 2:11. *Consumes, the conspirators with Korah, Dathan, and Abiram,* Num. 16:35; *the captains and their fifties,* 2 Kin. 1:9–12.
**Figurative:** *Of cleansing,* Isa. 6:6, 7. *Of spiritual power,* Jer. 20:9; Matt. 3:11; Luke 3:16. *Of judgments,* Deut. 4:24; 32:22; Isa. 33:14; Jer. 23:29; Amos 1:4, 7, 10, 12, 14; 2:2; Mal. 3:2; Luke 12:49; Rev. 20:9. *Of the destruction of the wicked,* Matt. 3:12; 13:42, 50; 25:41; Mark 9:43–48; Rev. 9:2; 21:8.
**Everlasting,** Isa. 33:14; Matt. 18:8; 25:41; Mark 9:43–48; Luke 3:37.
**A Symbol:** *Of God's presence,* Gen. 15:17; *in the burning bush,* Ex. 3:2; *on Sinai,* Ex. 19:18. *Tongues of, on the apostles,* Acts 2:3.

‡ **HYSSOP.** *A plant indigenous to western Asia and northern Africa,* 1 Kin. 4:33. *The Israelites used, in sprinkling the blood of the paschal lamb upon the lintels of their doors,* Ex. 12:22; *in sprinkling blood in purifications,* Lev. 14:4, 6, 51, 52; Heb. 9:19. *Used in the sacrifices of separation,* Num. 19:6. *Used in giving vinegar to Jesus on the cross,* John 19:29.
**Figurative:** *Of spiritual cleansing,* Psa. 51:7.

v.22–1533 BC
See footnote, *Time*, Rev. 10:6.

with the blood that *is* in the bason; and none of you shall go out at the [n]door of his house until the morning.

23 For the LORD will pass through to [o]smite the [p]Ē-ġy̆p′tianṣ; and when he seeth the [q]blood upon the lintel, and on the two side posts, the LORD will pass over the [n]door, and will not suffer[G] the destroyer to come in unto your houses to smite [r]*you*.[S]

24[Q] And ye shall observe [b]this thing for an [c]ordinance to thee and to thy sons for ever.

25 And it shall come to pass, when ye be come to the land which the LORD will give you, according as he hath promised, that ye shall keep this [b]service.

26 And it shall come to pass, [s]when your [t]children shall say unto you, What mean ye by this [b]service?

27 That [u]ye shall [v]say, It *is* the sacrifice[G] of the LORD's [b]passover, who passed over the houses of the children of [r]Ĭṣ′ra-el in Ē′ġy̆pt, when he [o]smote the Ē-ġy̆p′tianṣ, and delivered our houses. And the people bowed the head and [w]worshipped.[Q]

28 And the children of Ĭṣ′ra-el went away, and [x]did as the LORD had commanded Mō′ṣeṣ and Aâr′on, so did they.

29 ¶ And it came to pass, that at midnight the LORD [o]smote all the [y,z]firstborn in the land of Ē′ġy̆pt, from the firstborn of [a]Phā′raōh that sat on his throne unto the firstborn of the [b]captive that *was* in the dungeon; and all the firstborn of ‖cattle.[Q]

30 And [a]Phā′raōh rose up in the night, he, and all his servants, and all the Ē-ġy̆p′tianṣ; and there was a great [c]cry in Ē′ġy̆pt; [d]for *there was* not a house where *there was* not one dead.

31 ¶ [e]And [a]he called for [f]Mō′ṣeṣ and [g]Aâr′on by night, and said, Rise up, *and* [h]get you forth from among my people, both ye and the children of [i]Ĭṣ′ra-el; and go, serve the LORD, as ye have said.

32 Also take your flocks and your herds, as ye have said, and [h]be gone; and [j]bless[G] me also.

33 And the [k]Ē-ġy̆p′tianṣ were urgent upon the [i]people, that they might send them out of the land in haste; for they said, We *be* all dead *men*.

34 And the people took their [l]dough before it was [m]leavened, their [n]kneadingtroughs[G] being bound up in their clothes upon their shoulders.

35 And the children of Ĭṣ′ra-el did according to the word of Mō′ṣeṣ; and they [7,o,p]borrowed[G] of the Ē-ġy̆p′tianṣ [q]jewels of [r]silver, and jewels of [s]gold, and [t]raiment:

36 And the LORD gave the [o]people favour in the sight of the [k]Ē-ġy̆p′tianṣ, so that they [8]lent[G] unto them *such things as they required*. And they spoiled the Ē-ġy̆p′tianṣ.

37 ¶ And the children of [u]Ĭṣ′ra-el journeyed from [v]Rā-mē′sēṣ to §Sŭc′coth, about six hundred thousand on foot *that were* men, beside children.

38 And a mixed multitude went up also with them; and flocks, and herds, *even* very much cattle.

39 And they baked unleavened cakes of the [l]dough which they brought forth out of Ē′ġy̆pt, for it was not [m]leavened; because [i]they were thrust out of Ē′ġy̆pt, and could not tarry, neither had

**22**
n *Door, posts of, sprinkled with blood,* Deut. 11:20.

**23**
o *Judgments,* Ex. 6:6.
p *Egyptians,* Gen. 50:3.
q *Jesus, atoning blood of, typified,* Matt. 1:21.
r *Israel, exempt from the plagues,* Ex. 4:22.

**26**
s Deut. 6:20.
t *Children, instruction of,* Mark 10:14.

**27**
u *Parents, duty of, to instruct children in righteousness,* 2 Cor. 12:14.
v *Instruction, of children,* Prov. 23:23.
w *Worship,* Gen. 22:5.

**28**
x *Obedience, instances of,* Heb. 5:8.

**29**
y *Firstborn,* Zech. 12:10.
z *Children, death of, as a judgment upon parents,* Mark 10:14.

a *Pharaoh,* Ex. 3:10.
b *Criminals,* Matt. 27:15.

**30**
c *Mourning,* Lam. 2:5.
d *Bereavement, instances of,* Hos. 9:12.

v.30–1533 BC
See footnote, *Time*, Rev. 10:6.

**31**
e *Miracles, convincing effect of,* Luke 23:8.
f *Moses,* Ex. 2:10.
g *Aaron,* Ex. 6:20.
h *Emancipation,* Deut. 15:12.
i *Israel, urged by Egyptians to depart,* Ex. 4:22.

**32**
j *Intercession, solicited, instances of,* Jer. 27:18.

**33**
k *Egyptians,* Gen. 50:3.

**34**
l *Bread, how prepared,* Ezek. 4:13.
m *Leaven,* Lev. 23:17.
n *Kneading-trough,* Ex. 8:3.

**35**
o *Israel, borrowed jewels from the Egyptians,* Ex. 4:22.
p *Borrowing, instances of,* Ex. 22:14.
q *Jewels,* Gen. 24:53.
r *Silver,* 1 Chr. 28:14.
s *Gold,* Ezek. 7:19.
t *Dress,* Zech. 3:4.
7 R. V. asked

**36**
8 R. V. let them have what they asked.

**37**
u *Israel, number of, fit for military service when they left Egypt,* Ex. 4:22.
v *Rameses,* Gen. 47:11.

‖ **CATTLE.** Used generally in the Bible for domesticated animals of all kinds. Used here in accordance with modern English for animals of the bovine species only.
*Used for sacrifice,* 1 Kin. 8:63. See footnote, OFFERINGS, Lev. 6:17. *Sheltered,* Gen. 33:17. *Stall-fed,* Prov. 15:17. *Gilead adapted to the raising of,* Num. 32:1–4; *and Bashan,* Psa. 22:12; Ezek. 39:18; Amos 4:1.

§ **SUCCOTH.** *First camping place of the Israelites after leaving Rameses,* Ex. 12:37; 13:20; Num. 33:5, 6.

v.39–1533 BC
See footnote, *Time*, Rev. 10:6.

40
w *Israel, dwelt in Egypt* 430 *years,* Ex. 4:22.
x Gal. 3:17.

43
y *Passover,* Num. 9:5.
z *Foreigners, forbidden to eat the passover,* Deut. 23:20.
9 R. V. alien

44
a *Servant,* Jer. 2:14.
b *Money,* Jer. 32:9.
c *Circumcision,* Gen. 17:10.
45
d *Foreigners* Deut. 23:20.
e *Hired Servant,* Lev. 25:40.
46
f *Passover,* Num. 9:5.
g John 19:36.
h *Bones, of passover lamb not to be broken,* Ezek. 37:1.

48
i *Foreigners, religious privileges of,* Deut. 23:20.
j *Naturalization,* Acts 22:28.

they prepared for themselves
any victual.[G]
40 ¶ Now the sojourning[G] of the
children of [w]Is'ra-el, who dwelt
in E'gypt, *was* [x]four hundred
and thirty years.[Q]
41 And it came to pass at the
end of the [x]four hundred and
thirty years, even the selfsame[G]
day it came to pass, that all the
hosts of the LORD went out from
the land of E'gypt.
42 It *is* a night to be much observed[G] unto the LORD for bringing them out from the land of
E'gypt: this *is* that night of the
LORD to be observed of all the
children of Is'ra-el in their
generations.
43 ¶ And the LORD said unto
Mō'ṣeṣ and Aâr'on, This *is* the
ordinance of the [y]passover:
There shall no [9,z]stranger[G] eat
thereof:
44 But every man's [a]servant
that is bought for [b]money, when
thou hast [c]circumcised him, then
shall he eat thereof.
45 A [6,d]foreigner and an [e]hired
servant shall not eat thereof.
46 In one house shall [f]it be eat-
en; thou shalt not carry forth
ought[G] of the flesh abroad out of
the house; [g]neither shall ye
break a [h]bone thereof.[Q]
47 All the congregation of Is'-
ra-el shall keep[G] [f]it.
48 And when a [i]stranger shall
sojourn[G] with thee, and will keep
the [f]passover to the LORD, let all
his males be [c]circumcised, and
then let him come near and keep
it; and [j]he shall be as one that is
born in the land: for no uncircumcised person shall eat thereof.
49 One [+]law shall be to him
that is homeborn, and unto the
[i]stranger that sojourneth[G] among
you.
50 Thus [k]did all the children of
Is'ra-el; as the LORD commanded Mo'ṣeṣ and Aâr'on, so
did they.
51 And it came to pass the selfsame[G] day, *that* the LORD did
bring the children of Is'ra-el out
of the land of E'gypt by their
[10]armies.[Q]

## CHAPTER 13

*The firstborn are to be sanctified to God. 3 The memorial of the passover is commanded. 11 The firstlings of beasts are to be set apart. 17 The Israelites go out of Egypt, and carry Joseph's bones with them. 20 They come to Etham. 21 God guides them by a pillar of a cloud, and a pillar of fire.*

AND the LORD spake unto
[a]Mō'ṣeṣ, saying,
2 [b,c]Sanctify[G] unto me all the
[d]firstborn, whatsoever openeth
the womb among the children of
[e]Is'ra-el, *both* of man and of
beast: it *is* mine.[Q]
3 ¶ And [a]Mō'ṣeṣ said unto the
people, [f]Remember this day, in
which ye came out from [g]E'gypt,
out of the house of bondage; for
by strength of hand the [h]LORD
brought you out from this *place*:
there shall no [i]leavened [j]bread
be eaten.
4 This day came ye out in the
[k]month *A'bib.
5 And it shall be when the
LORD shall bring thee into the
[l]land of the [m]Cā'năan-ītes, and
the [n]Hĭt'tītes, and the [o]Ăm'ôr-
ītes, and the [p]Hī'vītes, and the
[q]Jĕb'u-sītes, which he [r,s]sware
unto thy fathers to give thee, a
land flowing with [t]milk and
[u]honey, that thou shalt keep
[v]this service in this *,[k]month.
6 [w]Seven days thou shalt eat
unleavened bread, and in the
seventh day *shall be* a [v,x]feast[G] to
the LORD.

v.49–1533 BC
See footnote, *Time*, Rev. 10:6.

50
k *Obedience,* Heb. 5:8.

51
10 R. V. hosts.

1
a *Moses, secures the deliverance of Israel,* vs. 1–22; Ex. 2:10.
2
b Luke 2:23.
c *Sanctification,* 1 Pet. 1:2.
d *Firstborn, of man and beast, reserved to God,* Zech. 12:10.
e *Israel,* Ex. 4:22.
3
f *Thankfulness, enjoined,* Acts 24:3.
g *Egypt,* Gen. 41:8.
h *God, providence of,* Gen. 2:2.
i *Leaven,* Lev. 23:17.
j *Bread,* Ezek. 4.13.
4
k *Month,* Ex. 12:2.
5
l *Canaan,* Gen. 37:1.
m *Canaanites,* Ex. 23:28.
n *Hittites,* Judg. 1:26.
o *Amorites,* Gen. 14:13.
p *Hivites,* Gen. 10:17.
q *Jebusites,* Deut. 7:1.
r *Oath,* Num. 5:19.
s *Covenant, of God with men,* Deut. 29:1.
t *Milk, figurative,* Job 10:10.
u *Honey, figurative,* Prov. 25:27.
v *Annual Feasts,* Num. 15. 3.
6
w *Seven, days,* Gen. 7:2.
x *Passover,* Num. 9:5.

**+ LEGISLATION.** *Class, forbidden,* Ex. 12:49; Lev. 24:22; Num. 9:14; 15:15, 16, 29; Gal. 3:28. *Supplemental, concerning Sabbath-breaking,* Num. 15:32–35; *concerning inheritance,* Num. 27:1–11. See footnote, LAW, Deut. 33:2.

* **ABIB** (*April*), called NISAN. *First month in the Jewish calendar,* Ex. 12:2; 13:4. *Passover held in,* Ex. 23:15; Lev. 23:5, 6; Deut. 16:1. *Israelites depart from Egypt in,* Ex. 13:4–10; 23:15; Deut. 16:1. *Tabernacle set up in,* Ex. 40:2, 17. *Israelites, arrive at the wilderness of Zin in,* Num. 20:1; *enter Canaan in,* **Josh. 4:19.** *Jordan overflows in,* **1 Chr. 12:15.**

v.7–1533 BC
See footnote, *Time*, Rev. 10:6.

7
1 R. V. borders.

8
*y* *Parents, duty of*, 2 Cor. 12:14.
*z* *Instruction, of children*, Prov. 23:23.

*a* *Children, instruction of*, Mark 10:1.
*b* *Passover*, Num. 9:5.

9
*c* *Phylactery*, Matt. 23:5.
*d* *Token*, Psa. 86:17.
*e* *Law, of Moses*, Deut. 33:2.
*f* *God, providence of*, Gen. 2:2.

10
*g* *Ordinance*, Num. 9:14.

11
*h* *Israel*, Ex. 4:22.
*i* *Canaan*, Gen. 37:1.
*j* *Oath*, Num. 5:19.
*k* *Covenant, of God with men*, Deut. 29:1.

12
*l* *Memorial, firstborn*, Num. 16:40.
*m* *Firstborn*, Zech. 12:10.
2 R. V. womb,

13
*n* *Ass*, 2 Chr. 28:15.
*o* *Redemption, of property*, Lev. 25:24.
*p* *Lamb*, Num. 7:15.
3 *Or*, kid;

14
*q* *Parents, duty of*, 2 Cor. 12:14.
*r* *Instruction, of children*, Prov. 23:23.
*s* *Egypt*, Gen. 41:8.

15
*t* *Pharaoh*, Ex. 3:10.
*u* *Judgments*, Ex. 6:6.

7 Unleavened [l]bread shall be
eaten [w]seven days; and there
shall no leavened bread be seen
with thee, neither shall there be
[i]leaven seen with thee in all thy
[1]quarters.[Q]
8 And [y]thou shalt [z]shew thy
[a]son in that day, saying, [b]*This
is done* because of that *which* the
LORD did unto me when I came
forth out of Ē′ġy̆pt.
9 And [b]it shall be for a [c,d]sign
unto thee upon thine hand, and
for a memorial between thine
eyes, that the LORD's [e]law may
be in thy mouth: for with a
strong hand hath the [f]LORD
brought thee out of Ē′ġy̆pt.[Q]
10 Thou shalt therefore keep
this [g]ordinance in his season
from year to year.
11 ¶ And it shall be when the
LORD shall bring [h]thee into the
[i]land of the Cā′năan-ītes, as he
[j,k]sware unto thee and to thy fathers, and shall give it thee,
12 That [h]thou shalt set [l]apart
unto the LORD [m]all that openeth
the [2]matrix,[G] and every [m]firstling[G]
that cometh of a beast which
thou hast; the males *shall be* the
LORD's.[Q]
13 And every [m]firstling of an [n]ass
thou shalt [o]redeem with a [3,p]lamb;
and if thou wilt not redeem it,
then thou shalt break his neck:
and all the [m]firstborn of man
among thy children shalt thou
redeem.
14 ¶ And it shall be when thy
[a]son asketh thee in time to come,
saying, What *is* [b]this? that [q]thou
shalt [r]say unto him, By strength
of hand the [f]LORD brought us
out from [s]Ē′ġy̆pt, from the
house of bondage:
15 And it came to pass, when
[t]Phā′raōh would hardly let us
go, that the LORD [u]slew all the
[v]firstborn in the land of [s]Ē′ġy̆pt,
both the firstborn of man, and
the firstborn of beast: therefore I
sacrifice to the LORD all that
openeth the matrix,[G] being
males; but all the [m]firstborn of
my children I [o]redeem.[Q]
16 And it shall be for a [4,d]token
upon thine hand, and for [w]front-
lets[G] between thine eyes: for by
strength of hand the [f]LORD
brought us forth out of
Ē′ġy̆pt.
17 ¶ And it came to pass, when
[t]Phā′raōh had let the people go,
that [f]God led them not *through*
the way of the land of the [x]Phĭ-
lĭs′tīneș, although that *was* near;
for God said, Lest peradventure
the people [y]repent[G] when they
see [z]war, and they return to
Ē′ġy̆pt:
18 But [a]God led the [b]people
about, *through* the way of the
wilderness of the [c]Red sea: and
the children of Ĭș′ra-el went up
[5]harnessed[G] out of the land of
Ē′ġy̆pt.
19 And [d]Mō′șeș took the bones
of [e]Jō′șeph with him: for he had
straitly[G] [f]sworn[G] the children of
[b]Ĭș′ra-el, saying, God will surely
visit[G] you; and ye shall carry
up my bones away hence with
you.[S Q]
20 ¶ And [b]they took their journey from [g]Sŭc′coth, and encamped in [6,h]Ē′tham, in the
edge of the wilderness.
21 [S Q]And the [i]LORD went before
them by day in a [†,j]pillar of a
cloud, to lead them the way; and
by night in a pillar of fire, to give
them light; to go by day and
night:[T]
22 He took not away [†,j]the pillar of the cloud by day, nor the
pillar of fire by night, *from* before the people.[S Q]

v.15–1533 BC
See footnote, *Time*, Rev. 10:6.

*v* *Firstborn, of Egyptians, slain*, Zech. 12:10.

16
*w* Deut. 6:8; 11:18.
4 R. V. sign

17
*x* *Philistines*, Gen. 26:14.
*y* *Cowardice*, Lev. 26:36.
*z* *War*, Judg. 3:2.

18
*a* *God, providence of*, Gen. 2:2.
*b* *Israel*, Ex. 4:22.
*c* *Red Sea*, Ex. 10:19.
5 R. V. armed

19
*d* *Moses*, Ex. 2:10.
*e* *Joseph*, Gen. 33:2.
*f* *Oath*, Num. 5:19.

20
*g* *Succoth*, Ex. 12:37.
*h* *Etham*, Num. 33:6, 7.
6 *Signifying*, boundary of the sea,

21
*i* *God, guide*, Gen. 2:2.
*j* *Symbols and Similitudes*, Heb. 9:9.

† **PILLAR OF CLOUD AND FIRE.** *Symbol of the Lord's presence*, Ex. 13:21 22; 16:10; 19:9, 16; 24:16–18; 33:9, 10; 34:5; Lev. 16:2; Num. 11:25; 12:5, 10; 14:10; 16:19, 42; Deut. 31:15; 1 Kin. 8:10, 11; Matt. 17:5; Luke 9:34, 35; 1 Cor. 10:1.
*A guide to Israel*, Ex. 14:19, 24; 40:36–38; Num. 9:15–23; 10:11, 12, 33–36; Deut. 1:33; Neh. 9:12, 19; Psa. 78:14; 105:39; Isa. 4:5.
*In Isaiah's prophecy*, Isa. 4:5. *In Ezekiel's vision*, Ezek. 10:3, 4, 18; 11:22, 23.

v.1–1533 BC
See footnote, *Time*, Rev. 10:6.

**1**

a *God, his preserving care, exemplified*, vs. 1–31; Gen. 2:2.

b *Inspiration*, Job 32:8.

c *Moses*, Ex. 2:10.

**2**

d *Israel, journey from Succoth*, Ex. 4:22.

e Num. 33:7, 8.

f Num. 33:7, 8.

g *Red Sea*, Ex. 10:19.

h Num. 33:7.

**3**

i *Pharaoh*, Ex. 3:10.

**4**

j *Foreordination*, Rom. 8:30.

k *God, providence of*, Gen. 2:2.

l *Heart, hardened, instances of*, Psa. 44:21.

m *Judgments, on the Egyptians*, Ex. 6:6.

n *Egyptians*, Gen. 50:3.

o *Nation, punishment of*, vs. 4–31; Isa. 2:4.

p *Miracles, design of*, Luke 23:8.

**5**

q *King*, 2 Kin. 3:10.

r *Afflictions, impenitence in, instances of*, Psa. 34:19.

s *Character, instability of*, Phil. 2:15.

t *Instability*, Jas. 1:8.

u *Israel*, Ex. 4:22.

1 R. V. changed toward

**6**

v *Chariot*, Josh. 11:4.

w *Armies*, Deut. 11:4.

**7**

x *Egypt, armies of*, Gen. 41:8.

**9**

y *Egyptians, pursue Israelites*, Gen. 50:3.

z *Horse*, Job 39:19.

a *Pharaoh* Ex. 3:10.

b *Cavalry*, 1 Sam. 13:5.

c *Armies*, Deut. 11:4.

## CHAPTER 14

*God instructs the Israelites in their journey. 5 Pharaoh pursues after them. 10 The Israelites murmur. 13 Moses comforts them. 15 God instructs Moses. 19 The cloud removes behind the camp. 21 The Israelites pass through the Red Sea. 23 The Egyptians pursuing them are drowned.*

AND the [a]LORD [b]spake unto [c]Mō'ṣeṣ, saying,

2 Speak unto the children of [d]Īṣ'ra-el, that they turn and encamp before [e]Pī'-ha-hī'roth, between [f]Mĭg'dol and the [g]sea, over against [h]Bā'al-zē'phon: before it shall ye encamp by the sea.

3 For [i]Phā'raōh will say of the children of [d]Īṣ'ra-el, They *are* entangled in the land, the wilderness hath shut them in.

4 [j]And [k]I will harden [i]Phā'raōh's [l]heart, that he shall follow after them; and [m]I will be honoured upon Phā'raōh, and upon all his host; that the [n,o]Ē-ġy̆p'tianṣ [p]may know that I *am* the LORD. And they did so.

5 ¶ And it was told the [q]king of Ē'ġy̆pt that the people fled: [r]and the [s]heart of [i]Phā'raōh and of his servants was [1,t]turned against the people, and they said, Why have we done this, that we have let [u]Īṣ'ra-el go from serving us?

6 And [i]he made ready his [v]chariot, and took his [w]people with him:

7 And [i]he took six hundred chosen [v]chariots, and all the chariots of [x]Ē'ġy̆pt, and captains over every one of them.

8 And the LORD hardened the [l]heart of [i]Phā'raōh [q]king of Ē'ġy̆pt, and he pursued after the children of [u]Īṣ'ra-el: and the children of Īṣ'ra-el went out with an high hand.

9 But the [y]Ē-ġy̆p'tianṣ pursued after them, all the [z]horses *and* chariots of [a]Phā'raōh, and his [b]horsemen, and his [c]army, and overtook them encamping by the sea, beside [d]Pī'-ha-hī'roth, before [e]Bā'al-zē-phon.

10 ¶ And when [a]Phā'raōh drew nigh, the children of [f]Īṣ'ra-el lifted up their eyes, and, behold, the Ē-ġy̆p'tianṣ marched after them; and they were sore [g,h]afraid: and the children of Īṣ'ra-el [i,j]cried out unto the LORD.

11 And [k,l]they [m]said unto Mō'ṣeṣ, [n]Because *there were* no [o]graves in Ē'ġy̆pt, hast thou taken us away to [p]die in the wilderness? wherefore hast thou dealt thus with us, to carry us forth out of Ē'ġy̆pt?

12 [l,m]*Is* not this the word that we did tell thee in Ē'ġy̆pt, saying, Let us alone, that we may serve the Ē-ġy̆p'tianṣ? For [k]*it had been* better for us to serve the Ē-ġy̆p'tianṣ, than that we should die in the wilderness.

13 ¶ And [q,r]Mō'ṣeṣ said unto the people, [s,t]Fear ye not, stand still, and see the [u]salvation of the [v]LORD, which he will shew to you to day: for the Ē-ġy̆p'tianṣ whom ye have seen to day, ye shall see them again no more for ever.

14 The [v]LORD shall [w]fight for you, and ye shall hold your peace.

15 ¶ And the LORD said unto Mō'ṣeṣ, [x]Wherefore [y,z]criest thou unto me? speak unto the children of Īṣ'ra-el, that they go forward:

16 But lift thou up thy [a]rod, and stretch out thine hand over the [b]sea, and divide it: and the children of Īṣ'ra-el shall go on dry *ground* through the midst of the sea.

17 And I, behold, I will harden the [c]hearts of the [d]Ē-ġy̆p'tianṣ, and they shall follow them: and I will [e]get me honour upon [f]Phā'raōh, and upon all his host, upon his chariots, and upon his horsemen.

v.9–1533 BC
See footnote, *Time*, Rev. 10:6.

d Num. 33:7, 8.

e Num. 33:7.

**10**

f *Israel*, Ex. 4:22.

g *Doubting, of Israelites*, Rom. 14:23.

h *Cowardice*, Lev. 26:36.

i *Adversity, prayer in*, Psa. 10:6.

j *Prayer, in adversity*, Acts 6:4.

**11**

k *Servant, degraded by bondage*, Jer. 2:14.

l *Evil, for good, instances of*, Psa. 35:12.

m *Murmuring, instances of*, Num. 14:27.

n *Sarcasm, instances of*, Judg. 10:14.

o *Burying Places*, Gen. 23:4.

p *Death*, Num. 23:10.

**13**

q *Meekness, exemplified*, Psa. 45:4.

r *Moses, character of*, Ex. 2:10.

s *Adversity, consolations in*, Psa. 10:6.

t *Faith, enjoined, in time of public danger*, Mark 11:22.

u *Salvation*, Acts 16:17.

v *God, providence of*, Gen. 2:2.

**14**

w *War, God in*, Judg. 3:2.

**15**

x *Despondency, instances of*, Eccl. 2:20.

y *Indecision, instances of*, 1 Kin. 18:21.

z *Prayer, rebuked*, Acts 6:4.

**16**

a *Rod of Moses*, Ex. 4:17.

b *Red Sea, divided*, Ex. 10:19.

**17**

c *Heart, hardened*, Psa. 44:21.

d *Egyptians*, Gen. 50:3.

e *Judgments, design of*, Ex. 6:6.

f *Pharaoh*, Ex. 3:10.

18 And the [d]Ė-ġy̆p′tians̩ [g]shall
know[G] that I *am* the LORD, when
I have gotten me honour upon[G]
Phā′raōh, upon his chariots, and
upon his [h]horsemen.[S]
19 ¶ And the *angel[G] of [i]God,
which went before the camp of
Ĭs̩′ra-el, removed and went behind them; and the [j,k]pillar of
the cloud went from before their
face, and stood behind them:[S T]
20[S] And [j]it came between the
camp of the [d]Ė-ġy̆p′tians̩ and
the camp of Ĭs̩′ra-el; and it was
a cloud and darkness *to them,*
but it gave light by night *to these*:
so that the one came not near the
other all the night.
21[Q] And Mō′s̩es̩ stretched out
his hand over the [b]sea; and the
LORD [l]caused the sea to go *back*
by a strong east [m,n]wind all that
night, and made the sea dry
*land,* and the waters were
divided.[S]
22[Q] And the children of [o]Ĭs̩′ra-el
went into the midst of the [b]sea
upon the dry *ground*: and the
waters *were* a wall unto them on
their right hand, and on their
left.[S]
23 ¶[S] And the [d]Ė-ġy̆p′tians̩ pursued, and went in after them to
the midst of the [b]sea, *even* all
Phā′raōh's horses, his chariots,
and his [h]horsemen.
24 And it came to pass, that in
the morning [p,q]watch[G] the LORD
[r]looked unto the host of the
Ė-ġy̆p′tians̩ through the [j]pillar
of fire and of the cloud, and
[2,s]troubled the host of the
Ė-ġy̆p′tians̩.
25 And took off their [t]chariot
wheels, that they drave[G] them
heavily[G]: [u]so that the Ė-ġy̆p′tians
said, Let us flee from the face of
Ĭs̩′ra-el; for the LORD [v]fighteth
for them against the Ė-ġy̆p′-
tians̩.[S]

26[S] And the LORD said unto
Mō′s̩es̩, Stretch out thine hand
over the [b]sea, that the waters
may come again upon the
[d]Ė-ġy̆p′tians̩, upon their chariots, and upon their [h]horsemen.
27 And Mō′s̩es̩ stretched forth
his hand over the [b]sea, and the
sea returned to his strength[G]
when the morning appeared;
and the Ė-ġy̆p′tians̩ fled against
it; and the LORD overthrew the
[w]Ė-ġy̆p′tians̩ in the midst of the
sea.
28 And the waters returned,
and covered the chariots, and
the [h]horsemen, *and* all the [w]host
of Phā′raōh that came into the
sea after them; there remained
not so much as one of them.
29 But the children of [o]Ĭs̩′ra-el
walked upon dry *land* in the
midst of the [b]sea; and the waters
*were* a wall unto them on their
right hand, and on their left.[Q S]
30 Thus the [x]LORD saved Ĭs̩′-
ra-el that day out of the hand of
the Ė-ġy̆p′tians̩; and Ĭs̩′ra-el saw
the Ė-ġy̆p′tians̩ [w]dead upon the
sea shore.[S]
31 And Ĭs̩′ra-el saw that [u]great
work which the LORD did upon
the [w]Ė-ġy̆p′tians̩: and the people
[y]feared[G] the LORD, and [z]believed
the LORD, and his servant
Mō′s̩es̩.[S Q]

## CHAPTER 15

*Moses' song. 22 The people find water. 23 The bitter waters at Marah are sweetened. 27 The people come to Elim where were twelve wells of water.*

[a,b]THEN [c]sang [d]Mō′s̩es̩ and
the children of [e]Ĭs̩′ra-el
this [f]song unto the LORD, and
spake, saying, [g,h]I will [i]sing unto
the LORD, for he hath tri-
umphed gloriously: the horse
and his rider hath he thrown into
the [j]sea.[Q]
2 The [k]LORD *is* my [l]strength

v.18–1533 BC See footnote, *Time,* Rev. 10:6.

**18**
g *Miracles, design of,* Luke 23:8.
h *Cavalry,* 1 Sam. 13:5.

**19**
i *God, providence of,* Gen. 2:2.
j *Pillar, of cloud and fire,* Ex. 13:21.
k *Symbols and Similitudes, of divine presence, pillar of fire,* Heb. 9:9.

**21**
l *Miracles,* Luke 23:8.
m *Wind, miraculous,* Job 37:17.
n *Meteorology,* Matt. 16:2.

**22**
o *Israel, cross the Red Sea,* Ex. 4:22.

**24**
p *Night, divided into watches,* Gen. 1:5.
q *Time, division of,* Rev. 10:6.
r *Anthropomorphisms, vision attributed to God,* Gen. 11:5.
s *Miracles, destruction of Pharaoh's army,* Luke 23:8.
2 R. V. discomfited

**25**
t *Chariot, wheels of, providentially taken off,* Josh. 11:4.
u *Miracles, convincing effect of,* Luke 23:8.
v *War, God in,* Judg. 3:2.

v.26–1533 BC See footnote, *Time,* Rev. 10:6.

**27**
w *Egyptians, destroyed,* Gen. 50:3.

**30**
x *God, preserver,* Gen. 2:2.

**31**
y *Fear of God,* Acts 9:31.
z *Faith,* Mark 11:22.

**1**
a *Faith, instances of,* vs. 1–19; Mark 11:22.
b *Thankfulness, to God,* vs. 1–19; Acts 24:3.
c *Joy, instances of,* Psa. 5:11.
d *Moses, composes song for children of Israel,* vs. 1–27; Ex. 2:10.
e *Israel,* Ex. 4:22.
f *Praise, song of Moses,* vs. 1–21; Psa. 150:1.
g *Poetry, epic,* vs. 1–19; Acts 17:28.
h *War Song,* vs. 1–21; Judg. 5:1.
i Music, vs. 1–21; 2 Chr. 5:13.
j *Red Sea, Pharaoh and army drowned in,* Ex. 10:19.

**2** k *God, preserver,* Gen. 2:2. l *Spiritual Blessings,* Eph. 1:3.

* **ANGEL. One of the Holy Trinity:** Trinitarian authorities interpret the Scriptures cited under this topic as referring to Christ, who, according to this view, was the divine presence in the wilderness. *Called* ANGEL, EX 33:2; Num. 20:16; Acts 7:30, 35; MINE ANGEL, Ex. 23:20 23; 32:34; ANGEL OF GOD, Ex. 14:19; ANGEL OF JE

v.2–1533 BC
See footnote, *Time*, Rev. 10:6.

*m God, savior*, Gen. 2:2.
*n Salvation*, Acts 16:17.
*o Worship*, Gen. 22:5.
3
*p God, name of, proclaimed*, Gen. 2:2.
4
*q Egyptians, destroyed*, Gen. 33:3.
*r Chariots*, Josh. 11:4.
*s Armies*, Deut. 11:4.
*t Death*, Num. 23:10.
6
*u God, power of*, Gen. 2:2.
*v Enemy*, Prov. 24:17.
7
*w Anger, of God*, 2 Kin. 13:3.
8
*x Wind, miraculous*, Job 37:17.
9
*y Spoils, of war*, 1 Chr. 26:27.
10
*z Meteorology*, Matt. 16:2.

---

*a Wind, miraculous*, Job 37:17.
*b Lead*, Ezek. 22:18.
11
*c God, holiness of*, Gen. 2:2.
12
*d Anthropomorphisms, hand attributed to God*, Gen. 11:5.
*e Judgments*, Ex. 6:6.

and song, and [m]he is become my
[n]salvation: he *is* my God, and I
will prepare him an habitation;
my father's God, and I will [o]ex-
alt him.
3 The LORD *is* a man of war:
the [p]LORD *is* his name.
4 [q]Phā'raōh's [r]chariots and his
[s]host hath he cast into the sea:
his chosen captains also are
[t]drowned in the [j]Red sea.
5 The depths have covered
[q]them: they sank into the bottom as a stone.
6 [s]Thy right hand, O LORD, is
become glorious in [u]power: thy
right hand, O LORD, hath
dashed in pieces the [v]enemy.
7 And in the greatness of thine
excellency thou hast overthrown them that rose up
against thee: thou sentest forth
thy [w]wrath, *which* consumed
them as stubble.[s]
8 And with the [x]blast of thy
nostrils the waters were gathered
together, the floods stood upright as an heap, *and* the depths
were congealed in the heart of
the [j]sea.
9 The [v]enemy said, I will pursue, I will overtake, I will divide
the [y]spoil; my lust shall be satisfied upon them; I will draw my
sword, my hand shall destroy
them.
10 Thou didst blow with thy
[z,a]wind, the sea covered them:
they sank as [b]lead in the mighty
waters.
11 Who *is* like unto thee, O
LORD, among the gods? who *is*
like [c]thee, glorious in holiness,
fearful *in* praises, doing wonders?[s Q]
12 Thou stretchedst out thy
right [d]hand, [e]the earth swallowed them.[s]

13 Thou in thy [f]mercy hast [g]led
forth the people *which* thou hast
[h]redeemed: thou hast guided
*them* in thy strength unto thy
holy habitation.[s]
14 The people shall hear, *and*
be [i,j]afraid: sorrow shall take
hold on the inhabitants of
[1,k]Păl-es-tī'nȧ.
15 Then the [l]dukes[G] of [m]Ē'dom
shall be amazed; the mighty
men of [n]Mō'ab, trembling shall
take hold upon them; all the
[o]inhabitants of Cā'năan shall
melt away.
16 F[s]ear and dread shall fall upon them; by the [p]greatness of
thine arm they shall be *as* still as
a stone; till thy people pass over,
O LORD, till the people pass
over, *which* thou hast purchased.
17 Thou shalt bring them in,
and plant them in the mountain
of thine inheritance, *in* the place,
O LORD, *which* thou hast made
for thee to dwell in, *in* the
[q]Sanctuary, O LORD, *which* thy
hands have established.[s]
18 The [r,s]LORD shall reign for
ever and ever.[s Q]
19 For the horse of Phā'raōh
went in with his chariots and
with his [t,u]horsemen into the
[v]sea, and the LORD brought
again the waters of the sea upon
them; but the children of [w]Iș'-
ra-el went on dry *land* in the
midst of the sea.
20 ¶ And *,[x]Mĭr'ĭ-am the
[y]prophetess, the sister of [z]Aâr'-
on, took a †timbrel[G] in her hand
and all the women went out after
her with timbrels and with
[a]dances.
21 And *,[b]Mĭr'ĭ-am answered
them, [c,d,e]Sing ye to the LORD,
for he hath triumphed glorious-

v.13–1533 BC
See footnote, *Time*, Rev. 10:6.

13
*f God, mercy of*, Gen. 2:2.
*g God, guide*, Gen. 2:2.
*h God, preserver*, Gen. 2:2.
14
*i Cowardice*, Lev. 26:36.
*j War, God sends panic in*, Judg. 3:2.
*k Philistines*, Gen. 26:14.
1 R. V. Philistia.
15
*l Duke*, Gen. 36:15.
*m Edomites*, 2 Kin. 8:21.
*n Moabites*, Gen. 19:37.
*o Canaanites*, Ex. 23:28.
16
*p God, power of*, Gen. 2:2.
17
*q Canaan, called the sanctuary*, Gen. 37:1
18
*r God, sovereign*, Gen. 2:2.
*s God, eternity of*, Gen. 2:2.
19
*t Cavalry*, 1 Sam. 13:5.
*u Egyptians, army of, destroyed*, Gen. 50:3.
*v Red Sea, Pharaoh and his army drowned in*, Ex. 10:19.
*w Israel, pass through the Red Sea*, Ex. 4:22.
20
*x Women, as prophets*, Prov. 31:10.
*y Prophetesses*, Judg. 4:4.
*z Aaron*, Ex. 6:20.

---

*a Dancing*, Eccl. 3:4.
21
*b Women, as poets*, Prov. 31:10.
*c Thankfulness, to God*, Acts 24:3.
*d Praise, song of Miriam*, Psa. 150:1.
*e Poetry, epic*, Acts 17:28.

---

HOVAH, Ex. 3:2; Judg. 2:1; ANGEL OF HIS PRESENCE, Isa. 63:9.

* **MIRIAM**, sister of Moses. *Watches over Moses when he is in the ark*, Ex. 2:4–8. *Commissioned with Moses and Aaron*, Mic. 6:4. *Song of, after the destruction of Pharaoh and his army*, Ex. 15:20, 21. *Jealous of Moses; stricken with leprosy; healed on account of the intercession of Moses*, Num. 12; Deut. 24:9. *Dies and is buried at Kadesh*, Num. 20:1.

† **TIMBREL**, an instrument of music of the tambourine sort. *Used, by Miriam*, Ex. 15:20; *by Jephthah's daughter*, Judg. 11:34. *Used in religious service*, 2 Sam. 6:5; 1 Chr. 13:8; Psa. 68:25; 81:2; 149:3; 150:4.
See footnote, MUSIC, *Instruments of*, 2 Chr. 5:13.

v.21–1533 BC
See footnote, *Time*, Rev. 10:6.

*f Horse*, Job 39:19.

22
- *g Moses*, Ex. 2:10.
- *h Israel, journey to Marah*, Ex. 4:22.
- *i Red Sea*, Ex. 10:19.
- *j Shur*, 1 Sam. 15:7.

23
- *k* Num. 33:8, 9.
- 2 *That is*, bitterness.

24
- *l Murmuring*, Num. 14:2.
- *m Evil, for good, instances of*, Psa. 35:12.
- *n Borrowing Trouble, instances of*, Matt. 6:25.

25
- *o Meekness, exemplified*, Psa. 45:4.
- *p Prayer, answered*, Acts 6:4.
- *q God, providence of, instances of*, Gen. 2:2.
- *r Water*, 1 Kin. 17:10.
- *s Miracles*, Luke 23:8.
- *t Law*, Deut. 33:2.
- *u Temptation, a test*, Luke 11:4.
- *v Afflictions, design of*, Psa. 34:19.

26
- *w Blessing, contingent upon obedience*, Deut. 11:26.
- *x Diligence, required in keeping commandments*, Rom. 12:8.
- *y Obedience, reward of*, Heb. 5:8.
- *z Promises, to the obedient, of exemption from afflictions*, 2 Cor. 1:20.

- *a Temporal Blessings, from God*, Psa. 103:2.
- *b God, preserver*, Gen. 2:2.
- *c God, providence of*, Gen. 2:2.
- *d Healing, the Lord the healer*, Acts 4:22. 3 R. V. eyes. **27** *e Israel*, Ex. 4:22.
- *f* Num. 33:9. *g Palm Tree*, Song 7:7. 4 R. V. springs

ly; the [f]horse and his rider hath
he thrown into the sea.
22 ¶ So [g]Mō'ṣeṣ brought [h]Īṣ'-
ra-el from the [i]Red sea, and they
went out into the wilderness of
[j]Shûr; and they went three days
in the wilderness, and found no
water.
23 ¶ And when they came to
[k]Mā'rah, they could not drink of
the waters of Mā'rah, for they
*were* bitter: therefore the name
of it was called [2]Mā'rah.
24 And the people [l,m]mur-
mured against Mō'ṣeṣ, saying,
[n]What shall we drink?
25 And [o]he [p]cried unto the
LORD; and the [q]LORD shewed
him a tree, *which* when he had
cast into the [r]waters, the waters
were [s]made sweet: there he made
for them a [t]statute and an ordinance, and there he [u,v]proved
them.
26 And said, [w]If thou wilt [x]dili-
gently hearken to the voice of the
LORD thy God, and wilt [y]do
that which is right in his [3]sight,
and wilt give ear to his commandments, and keep all his
statutes, [z,a]I will put none of
these ‡diseases upon thee, which
I have brought upon the Ē-ġўp'-
tianṣ: for I *am* the [b,c]LORD that
[d]healeth thee.
27 ¶ And [e]they came to [f]Ē'lim,
where *were* twelve [4]wells of water, and threescore and ten
[g]palm trees: and they encamped
there by the waters.

## CHAPTER 16

*The Israelites come to Sin. 2 They murmur for want of bread. 4 God promises them bread from heaven. 11 Quails are sent. 14 and manna. 16 Directions concerning the manna. 25 None of it found on the sabbath. 32 An omer of it is preserved.*

AND they took their journey
from [a]Ē'lim, and all the
congregation of the children of
[b]Īṣ'ra-el came unto the wilderness of [c]Sĭn, which *is* between
Ē'lim and *Sī'nāi, on the fifteenth day of the second [d]month
after their departing out of the
land of [e]Ē'ġўpt.
2 And the whole congregation
of the children of [f]Īṣ'ra-el
[g,h]murmured against [i]Mō'ṣeṣ
and [j]Aâr'on in the [c]wilderness:
3 [g]And the children of [f]Īṣ'ra-el
[k]said unto them, Would [1]to God
we had died by the hand of the
LORD in the land of Ē'ġўpt,
when we sat by the flesh pots,
*and* when we did eat [l]bread to
the full; for [m,n]ye have brought
us forth into this [c]wilderness, to
kill this whole assembly with
[o]hunger.
4 ¶ Then said the LORD unto
[i]Mō'ṣeṣ, Behold, I will [p]rain
bread from heaven for you; and
the people shall go out and gather a [2]certain rate every day, that
I may [q]prove them, whether they
[r]will walk in my [s]law, or no.
5 And it shall come to pass,
that on the sixth day they shall
prepare *that* which they bring in;
and it shall be twice as much as
they gather daily.
6 And [i]Mō'ṣeṣ and [j]Aâr'on said

v.1–1533 BC
See footnote, *Time*, Rev. 10:6.

1
- *a* Num. 33:9.
- *b Israel, journey to wilderness of Sin*, Ex. 4:22.
- *c Sin, desert of*, Ex. 17:1.
- *d Month*, Ex. 12:2.
- *e Egypt*, Gen. 41:8.

2
- *f Israel, murmurs*, Ex. 4:22.
- *g Murmurings, of Israelites*, Num. 14:2.
- *h Evil, for good, instances of*, Psa. 35:12.
- *i Moses*, Ex. 2:10.
- *j Aaron*, Ex. 6:20.

3
- *k Ingratitude, of man to man*, Rom. 1:21.
- *l Bread*, Ezek. 4:13.
- *m Borrowing Trouble, instances of*, Matt. 6:25.
- *n False Accusation*, 2 Tim. 3:3.
- *o Hunger, a source of temptation*, Neh. 9:15.
- 1 R. V. that we

4
- *p Miracles, design of*, vs. 5, 6; Luke 23:8.
- *q Temptation, a test*, Luke 11:4.
- *r Obedience*, Heb. 5:8.
- *s Law*, Deut. 33:2.
- 2 R. V. day's portion,

‡ **DISEASE.** *Diagnosis of*, Lev. 13:3–59; 14:3. *Sent from God*, Lev. 14:34. As judgments: *Upon David's child*, 2 Sam. 12:15; *upon Gehazi*, 2 Kin. 5:27; *upon Jehoram*, 2 Chr. 21:12–19; *upon Uzziah*, 2 Chr. 26:17–20.

*Of the skin*, Lev. 13:38, 39; Deut. 28:27; Job 7:5. *Of the sexual organs*, Lev. 15; 22:4; Num. 5:2; Deut. 23:10. *Treatment of fractures*, Ezek. 30:21.

*Threatened as judgments*, Lev. 26:16; Deut. 7:15; 28:22, 27, 28, 35, 60; 29:22.

*Physicians employed for*, 2 Chr. 16:12; Matt. 9:12; Mark 5:26. *Remedies used*, Prov. 17:22; Isa. 38:21; Jer. 30:13; 46:11; *poultices*, 2 Kin. 20:7; Isa. 38:21; *ointments*, Isa. 1:6; Jer. 8:22; *emulsions*, Luke 10:34.

**Healing of:** *From God*, Ex. 15:26; 23:25; Deut. 7:15; 2 Chr. 16:12; Psa. 103:3. *By Jesus*, Matt. 4:23, 24; 14:35, 36; Mark 1:31–34; Luke 4:38–40; 6:17, 18; 9:11. *By the twelve*, Matt. 10:1, 8; Luke 9:1, 6. *By the seventy*, Luke 10:9. *By Paul*, Acts 19:12; 28:8, 9. *In answer to prayer, of Hezekiah*, 2 Kin. 20:1–11; Isa. 38:1–8.

*Miraculous healing of, a sign to accompany the preaching of the word*, Mark 16:18; Luke 9:1. See footnote, MIRACLES, Luke 23:8.

See footnote, AFFLICTIONS, Psa. 34:19.

**Figurative,** Isa. 1:6; 3:17; Jer. 30:12; Ezek. 34:4; Matt. 9:12.

* **SINAI,** a mountain in the peninsula between the arms of the Red Sea; called also HOREB. *Children of Israel arrive at, in their wanderings in the wilderness*, Ex. 19:2; Deut. 1:2. *The law delivered to Moses upon*, Ex. 19:3–25; 20; 24:12–18; 32:15, 16; 34:2–4, 28; Lev. 7:38; 25:1; 26:46; 27:34; Num. 3:1; Deut. 4:11, 15; 5:4, 22, 26; 29:1; 33:2; Neh. 9:13; Psa. 68:8, 17; Mal. 4:4; Acts 7:30, 38; Heb. 12:18, 19.

**Figurative,** Gal. 4:24, 25.

See footnote, HOREB, Ex. 3:1.

**Wilderness of:** *Children of Israel, journeyed in*, Num. 10:12; *kept the passover in*, Num. 9:1–5; *numbered in*, Num. 26:64.

v.6–1533 BC
See footnote, *Time*, Rev. 10:6.

*l God, providence of*, Gen. 2.2.

7
*u God, glory of*, Gen. 2.2.
*v Patience, instances of*, Luke 8:15.
*w Meekness, instances of*, Psa. 45:4.

8
*x God, preserver*, Gen. 2.2.
*y Sin, known to God*, Rom. 5:12.
*z Reproof*, Prov. 17.10.

9
*a Moses*, Ex. 2:10.
*b Aaron*, Ex. 6:20.
*c Israel*, Ex. 4:22.
*d Sin, known to God*, Rom. 5:12.
*e Murmuring, of Israelites*, Num. 14:2.

10
*f Sin, wilderness of*, Ex. 17:1.
*g God, glory of*, Gen. 2:2.
*h Pillar, of cloud and fire*, Ex. 13:21.

12
*i Temporal Blessings, from God*, Psa. 103:2.
*j God, longsuffering of*, Gen. 2:2.
*k God, providence of*, Gen. 2:2.

13
*l Dew*, Dan. 4:15.
3 R. V. camp.

unto all the children of Īş'ra-el,
At even, [p]then ye shall know
that the [l]LORD hath brought you
out from the land of Ē'ġȳpt:
7 And in the morning, then ye
shall see the [u]glory of the LORD;
for that he heareth your murmurings against the LORD:
[v.w]and what *are* we, that ye
murmur against us? [Q]
8 And Mō'şeş said, *This shall*
*be*, when the [x]LORD shall give
you in the evening †flesh to eat,
and in the morning bread to the
full; for that the LORD [y]heareth
your murmurings which ye
murmur[G] against him: [w]and what
*are* we? [z]your murmurings *are*
not against us, but against the
LORD.
9 And [a]Mō'şeş spake unto
[b]Aâr'on, Say unto all the congregation of the children of [c]Īş'ra-
el, Come near before the LORD:
for he hath [d]heard your [e]mur-
murings.[G]
10 ¶ And it came to pass, as
[b]Aâr'on spake unto the whole
congregation of the children of
[c]Īş'ra-el, that they looked toward the [f]wilderness, and, behold, the [g]glory of the LORD appeared in the [h]cloud.
11 And the LORD spake unto
[a]Mō'şeş, saying,
12 I have heard the [e]murmur-
ings of the children of [c]Īş'ra-el:
speak unto them, saying, At
even ye shall eat [†,i]flesh, and in
the morning ye shall be filled
with [i]bread; and ye shall
know that I *am* the LORD your
[j,k]God.
13 And it came to pass, that at
even the †quails came up, and
covered the camp: and in the
morning the [l]dew lay round
about the [3]host.[S]
14 And when the [l]dew that lay
was gone up, behold, upon the
face of the wilderness *there lay* a
small round thing, *as* small as
the hoar frost on the ground.[S]
15 And when the children of
[c]Īş'ra-el saw *it*, they said one to
another, [4]It *is* manna[G]: for they
wist[G] not what it *was*. And [a]Mō'-
şeş said unto them, [i]This *is* the
bread which the [k,m]LORD hath
given you to eat.[Q]
16 [S]This *is* the thing which the
LORD hath commanded, Gather
of it every man according to his
eating, an [n]omer[G] for every man,
*according to* the number of your
persons; take ye every man for
*them* which *are* in his [o]tents.
17 And the children of [c]Īş'ra-el
did so, and gathered, some more,
some less.[S]
18 And when they did [n]mete[G] *it*
with an omer, [p]he that gathered much had nothing over,
and he that gathered little had
no lack; they gathered every
man according to his eating.[Q S]
19 And [a]Mō'şeş said, [q]Let no
man leave of it till the morning.
20 [S] Notwithstanding [c]they
[r]hearkened not unto [a]Mō'şeş;
but some of them left of it until
the morning, and it bred [s]worms,
and stank: and Mō'şeş was
[t]wroth[G] with them.[S]
21 And they gathered it every
morning, every man according
to his eating: and when the sun
waxed[G] hot, it melted.
22 ¶ And it came to pass, *that*
on the sixth day they gathered
twice as much bread, two
omers for one *man*: and all the
[u]rulers of the congregation came
and told Mō'şeş.
23 And he said unto them,
This *is that* which the LORD
hath said, To morrow *is* the
[v]rest of the holy ‡sabbath[G] unto
the LORD: [w]bake *that* which ye

v.14–1533 BC
See footnote, *Time*. Rev. 10:6.

15
*m God, preserver*, Gen. 2:2.
4 R. V. What is it?

16
*n Measure, dry*, Deut. 25:15.
*o Tents*, Gen. 13:5.

18
*p* 2 Cor. 8:15.

19
*q Sanitation and Hygiene*, Num. 31:23.

20
*r Disobedience, to God, instances of*, Eph. 5:6.
*s Worm*, Jonah 4:7.
*t Anger*, Psa. 37:8.

22
*u Rulers*, Ex. 18:21.

23
*v Rest, on the Sabbath, enjoined*, Ex. 23:12.
*w Commandment, enjoining preparation for the Sabbath*, Deut. 8:2.

† **QUAIL.** *Miracle of, in the wilderness of Sin*, Ex. 16: 8, 12, 13; *at Kibroth-hattaavah*, Num. 11:31, 32; Psa. 78:27–30; 105:40.

‡ **SABBATH.** *Signifying a rest period*, Gen. 2:2, 3; Lev. 23:25; 26:34, 35. *Holy*, Ex. 16:23; 20:8, 11; 31:14; 35:2; Deut. 5:12; Neh. 9:14; Isa. 58:13, 14; Ezek. 44:24. *A sign,*

v.23–1533 BC
See footnote, *Time*, Rev. 10:6.

24
*x Miracles*, Luke 23:8.

29
*y Commandment, enjoining rest on the Sabbath*, Deut. 8:2.

30
*z Rest*, Ex. 23:12.

31
*a Israel*, Ex. 4:22.
*b* Num. 11:7.
*c Honey*, Prov. 25:27.

32
*d Moses*, Ex. 2:10.

will bake *to day*, and seethe[C] that
ye will seethe; and that which
remaineth over lay up for you to
be kept until the morning.[S]
24[S] And they laid ‖it up till the
morning, as [a]Mō′ṣeṣ bade: and
it [x]did not stink, neither was
there any worm therein.
25 And [a]Mō′ṣeṣ said, Eat that
to day; for to day *is* a ‡sabbath[C]
unto the LORD: to day ye shall
not find ‖it in the field.[S]
26 Six days ye shall gather it; but
on the seventh day, *which is* the
‡sabbath[C], in it there shall be none.
27 ¶ And it came to pass, *that*
there [r]went out *some* of the people on the ‡seventh day for to
gather, and they found none.
28 And the LORD said unto
[a]Mō′ṣeṣ, How long [r]refuse ye to
keep[C] my commandments and
my laws?
29 See, for that the LORD hath
given you the ‡sabbath[C], therefore he giveth you on the sixth
day the bread of two days;
[y]abide ye every man in his place,
let no man go out of his place on
the seventh day.[S]
30 So the people [z]rested on the
‡seventh day.
31 And the house of [a]Ĭṣ′ra-el
called the name thereof ‖Man-
na: and it *was* like [b]coriander
seed, white; and the taste of it
*was* like wafers *made* with
[c]honey.
32 ¶ And [d]Mō′ṣeṣ said, This *is*
the thing which the LORD commandeth, Fill an [e]omer of it to be
kept for your generations; [f,g]that
they may see the bread wherewith [h]I have fed you in the wilderness, when I brought you
forth from the land of [i]Ē′ġy̆pt.
33 And [d]Mō′ṣeṣ said unto
[j]Aâr′on, Take a pot, and put an
[e]omer full of ‖manna therein,[Q]
and lay it up before the LORD,
to be [k]kept for your generations.
34 As the LORD commanded
[d]Mō′ṣeṣ, so [j]Aâr′on laid ‖it up
before the [l]Testimony, to be
kept.
35 And the children of [a]Ĭṣ′ra-el
did eat ‖manna [m]forty years, until they came to a land inhabited;
they did eat manna, until they
came unto the borders of the
land of [n]Cā′năan.[Q]
36 Now an [e]omer *is* the tenth
*part* of an ephah[C].

## CHAPTER 17

*The people murmur for water at Rephidim. 5 God sends them for water to the rock in Horeb. 8 Amalek is overcome by the intercession of Moses' hands. 15 Moses builds the altar Jehovah-nissi.*

AND all the congregation of
the children of [a]Ĭṣ′ra-el
journeyed from the wilderness
of *Sĭn, after their journeys, according to the commandment of
the LORD, and pitched[C] in
†Rĕph′i-dĭm: and *there was* no
[b]water for the people to drink.
2 Wherefore the [a]people [1,c]did

v.32–1533 BC
See footnote, *Time*, Rev. 10:6.

*e Measure, dry*, Deut. 25:15.
*f Instruction, by object lesson*, Prov. 23:23.
*g Thankfulness, enjoined*, Acts 24:3.
*h God, providence of*, Gen. 2:2.
*i Egypt*, Gen. 41:8.

33
*j Aaron*, Ex. 6:20.
*k Memorial*, vs.32–34; Num. 16:40.

34
*l Ark, contents of*, Ex. 25:10.

35
*m Forty, years*, Jonah 3:4.
*n Canaan*, Gen. 37:1.

1
*a Israel*, Ex. 4:22.
*b Water*, 1 Kin. 17:10.

2
*c Ingratitude, of man to man*, Rom. 1:21.
1 R. V. strove

Ex. 31:13, 16, 17; Ezek. 20:12, 13, 16, 20, 21, 24. *The Lord is represented as resting on*, Gen. 2:2, 3; Ex. 31:17; Heb. 4:4.
*Rest on, enjoined*, Ex. 16:28–30; 31:15; 23:12; 34:21; 35:2, 3; Lev. 19:3, 30; 23:1–3; 26:2; Deut. 5:12–15; 2 Chr. 36:21; Jer. 17:21, 22, 24, 25, 27; Luke 23:56. *Rest on, of servants and animals, enjoined*, Ex. 20:10; 23:12; Deut. 5:14. *Labor on, suspended*, Ex. 16:5, 23–30; 20:10; Mark 16:1; Luke 23:56.
*Offerings prescribed for*, Lev. 24:8; Num. 28:9, 10; 1 Chr. 23:31; 2 Chr. 2:4; Ezek. 46:4, 5. *Song for*, Psa. 92:1–15.
*Preparation for*, Ex. 16:5, 22; Matt. 27:62; Mark 15:42; Luke 23:54; John 19:31.
*Worship on*, Ezek. 46:1, 3; Acts 15:21; 16:13; *enjoined*, Ezek. 46:1, 3. *Religious instruction on*, Mark 6:2; Luke 4:16, 31; 6:6; 13:10; Acts 13:14, 27, 42, 44; 15:21; 17:2; 18:4. *Apostles taught on*, Acts 15:14–44; 17:2; 18:4.
*Christ's interpretation of*, Matt. 12:1–8, 10–13; Luke 6:1–10 (with Mark 2:23–28); 13:10–17; 14:1–5; John 7:21–24; 9:14. *Christ is Lord of*, Mark 2:28. *Christ performed miracles on*, Matt. 12:10–13; Mark 3:1–5; Luke 6:1–10; 13.10–17; John 5:5–14; 7:21–24. *Christ taught on*, Mark 1:21, 22; 6:2; Luke 4:16, 31; 6:6; 13:10–17.

*Irksome observance of*, Amos 8:5. *Hypocritical observance of, provokes divine displeasure*, Isa. 1:13; Lam. 2:6; Ezek. 20:12, 13, 16, 21, 24.
*Rewards for observance of*, Isa. 56:2, 4–7; 58:13, 14; Jer. 17:21, 22, 24, 25.
*Profanation of*, Ex. 16:27, 28; Num. 15:32–36; Neh. 10:31; 13:15, 21; Jer. 17:21–23; Ezek. 22:8; 23:38.
**Punishments for violation of:** *Death*, Ex. 35:2; Num. 15:32–36. *Judgments*, Jer. 17:27.

‖ **MANNA,** Ex. 16:4–35; Num. 11:6–10; Deut. 8:3, 16; Josh. 5:12; Neh. 9:15, 20; Psa. 78:24; 105:40; John 6:31, 49, 58. *Preserved in the ark of the testimony*, Ex. 16:33; Heb. 9:4.
**Figurative,** John 6:48–51; 1 Cor. 10:3; Rev. 2:17.

* **SIN,** a wilderness between Elim and Sinai. *Children of Israel, journeyed through*, Ex. 16:1; 17:1; Num. 33:11, 12; *murmur for bread in*, Ex. 16:2. *Manna and quails given in*, Ex. 16:4–36.

† **REPHIDIM,** a camping-place of Israel. *Water brought from rock at; Amalekites join battle with Israel in*, Ex. 17:8–16; 19:2; Num. 33:14, 15.

v.2–1533 BC
See footnote, *Time*, Rev. 10:6.

*d* *Moses*, Ex. 2:10.
*e* *Meekness, instances of*, Psa. 45:4.
*f* *Backsliding, instances of*, Hos. 11:7.
2 R. V. strive

3
*g* *Murmuring, instances of*, Num. 14:2.
*h* *Evil, for good, instances of*, Psa. 35:12.
*i* *Borrowing Trouble, instances of*, Matt. 6:25.
*j* *Egypt*, Gen. 41:8.

4
*k* *Adversity, prayer in*, Psa. 10:6.
*l* *Persecution*, John 15:20.

5
*m* *Prayer, answered, instances of*, vs. 4–6; Acts 6:4.
*n* *Government, Mosaic, the senatorial council*, Isa. 22:21.
*o* *Senate*, Num. 11:16.
*p* *Rod of Moses*, Ex. 4:17.

6
*q* *God, providence of*, Gen. 2:2.
*r* *God, preserver*, Gen. 2:2.
*s* *Horeb*, Ex. 3:1.
*t* *Miracles*, Luke 23:8.
*u* *Temporal Blessings, from God*, Psa. 103:2.

7
*v* *Presumption*, Psa. 19:13.
*w* *Infidelity, of Israel*, 2 Cor. 6:15.
*x* *Doubting*, Rom. 14:23.
3 R. V. striving

8
*y* *Amalekites*, Num. 13:29.
*z* *War*, Judg. 3:2.

*a* *Israel, defeat the Amalekites*, vs. 8–13; Ex. 4:22.

9
*b* *Moses*, Ex. 2:10.
*c* *Joshua*, Josh. 1:1.
*d* *Amalekites*, Num. 13:29.
*e* *Intercession, of man with God*, Jer. 27:18.
*f* *Rod of Moses*, Ex. 4:17.

10
*g* *War*, Judg. 3:2.

chide[G] with [d]Mō′ṣeṣ, and said,
Give us water that we may
drink. And Mō′ṣeṣ said unto
them, [e]Why [2]chide[G] ye with me?
wherefore do ye [f]tempt[G] the
LORD?
3 And the [a]people thirsted there
for [b]water; and the people
[g,h]murmured [c]against [d]Mō′ṣeṣ,
and said, [i]Wherefore *is* this *that*
thou hast brought us up out of
[j]Ē′ġy̆pt, to kill us and our children and our cattle with thirst?
4 And [d]Mō′ṣeṣ [k]cried unto the
LORD, saying, What shall I do
unto this people? they be almost ready to [l]stone me.
5 [S] And the LORD [m]said unto
[d]Mō′ṣeṣ, Go on before the people, and take with thee of the
[n,o]elders of Ĭṣ′ra-el; and thy[G]
[p]rod, wherewith thou smotest
the river, take in thine hand,
and go.
6 Behold, [q,r]I will stand before
thee there upon the rock in [s]Hō′-
reb; and thou shalt smite the
rock, and there [t]shall come [u]wa-
ter out of it, that the people may
drink. And Mō′ṣeṣ did so in the
sight of the [n,o]elders of Ĭṣ′ra-el.[Q]
7 And he called the name of the
place Măs′sah, and ‡Mĕr′i-bah,
because of the [3]chiding[G] of the
children of Ĭṣ′ra-el, and because
they [v]tempted[G] the LORD, [w,x]say-
ing, Is the LORD among us, or
not? [S] [Q]
8 ¶ Then came [y]Ăm′a-lĕk, and
[z]fought with [a]Ĭṣ′ra-el in †Rĕph′-
i-dĭm.
9 And [b]Mō′ṣeṣ said unto
[c]Jŏsh′u-ȧ, Choose us out men,
and go out, fight with [d]Ăm′a-
lĕk: to morrow I will [e]stand on
the top of the hill with the [f]rod
of God in mine hand.[S]
10 So [c]Jŏsh′u-ȧ did as [b]Mō′ṣeṣ
had said to him, and [g]fought
with [d]Ăm′a-lĕk: and Mō′ṣeṣ,
[h]Aâr′on, and [i]Hûr went up to
the top of the hill.
11 And it came to pass, when
[b]Mō′ṣeṣ [j]held up his hand, that
[a,k]Ĭṣ′ra-el prevailed: and when
he let down his hand, [d]Ăm′a-lĕk
prevailed.
12 But [b]Mō′ṣeṣ′ hands *were*
heavy;[G] and they took a stone,
and put *it* under him, and he sat
thereon; and [h]Aâr′on and [i]Hûr
stayed[G] up his hands, the one on
the one side, and the other on
the other side; and [e]his hands
were steady until the going down
of the sun.
13 [a]And [c]Jŏsh′u-ȧ discomfited[G]
[d]Ăm′a-lĕk and his people with
the edge of the [l]sword.
14 And the LORD said unto
[b]Mō′ṣeṣ, Write this *for* a [m]me-
morial in a [n]book, and rehearse
*it* in the ears of [c]Jŏsh′u-ȧ: for I
will utterly [o]put out the remembrance of [p]Ăm′a-lĕk from under
heaven.[S]
15 And Mō′ṣeṣ built an [q,r]altar,
and called the name of it Jĕ-
hō′vah-nĭs′sī:
16 For [s]he said, Because the
LORD hath [t]sworn *that* the
LORD *will have* [g]war with [p]Ăm′-
a-lĕk from generation[G] to generation.[G]

## CHAPTER 18

*Jethro brings to Moses his wife and two sons. 7 Moses entertains him. 13 Jethro's counsel to Moses is heeded. 27 Jethro departs.*

WHEN [a]Jĕth′rō, the [b]priest of
Mĭd′ĭ-an, [c]Mō′ṣeṣ′ [d]father
in law, heard of all that [e]God
had done for Mō′ṣeṣ, and for
[f]Ĭṣ′ra-el his people, *and* that the
LORD had brought Ĭṣ′ra-el out
of [g]Ē′ġy̆pt:
2 Then [a]Jĕth′rō, Mō′ṣeṣ′ [d]fa-
ther in law, took [h]Zĭp-pō′rah,
Mō′ṣeṣ′ wife, after he had sent
her back,
3[Q] And her two [i]sons; of which

v.10–1533 BC
See footnote, *Time*, Rev. 10:6.

*h* *Aaron*, Ex. 6:20.
*i* *Hur*, Ex. 24:14.

11
*j* *Intercession, answered*, Jer. 27:18.
*k* *Prayer, answered*, Acts 6:4.

13
*l* *Sword*, 1 Chr. 21:5.

14
*m* *Memorial*, Num. 16:40.
*n* *Book*, Num. 5:23.
*o* *Judgments*, Ex. 6:6.
*p* *Amalekites, prophecies against*, Num. 13:29.

15
*q* *Altar*, Gen. 8:20.
*r* *Worship*, Gen. 22:5.

16
*s* *Moses, prophecies of*, Ex. 2:10.
*t* *Oath, attributed to God*, Num. 5:19.

1
*a* *Jethro*, Ex. 3:1.
*b* *Priest*, Lev. 1:5.
*c* *Moses*, Ex. 2:10.
*d* *Father-in-law*, Judg. 19:3.
*e* *God, providence of*, Gen. 2:2.
*f* *Israel*, Ex. 4:22.
*g* *Egypt*, Gen. 41:8.

2
*h* *Zipporah*, Ex. 2:21.

3
*i* *Children*, Mark 10:14.

‡ **MERIBAH**, or MASSAH. *Water brought from the rock at*, Ex. 17:1–7; Num. 20:3–13; Deut. 8:15; Neh. 9:15; Psa. 78:15, 16, 20; 105:41; 114:8; Isa. 48:21. *Israelites tempted God at*, Deut. 6:16, Psa. 95:9. *Hearts hardened at*, Psa. 95:8. *Israelites proved at*, Psa. 81:7. *Rock of, typical of Christ*, 1 Cor. 10:4.

v.3–1533 BC
See footnote, *Time*. Rev. 10:6.

*j Gershom*, Ex. 2:22.
*k Foreigner*, Deut. 23:20.
1 R. V. a sojourner

4

*l* 1 Chr. 23:15.
*m Pharaoh*, Ex. 3:10.

5

*n Horeb*, Ex. 3:1.

7

*o Salutations*, Luke 1:44.
*p Kiss*, Ruth 1:14.
*q Tent*, Gen. 13:5.

8

*r Egyptians*, Gen. 50:3.
*s God, goodness of*, Gen. 2:2.

10

*t Thankfulness, to God*, Acts 24:3.

11

*u Faith, instances of*, Mark 11:22.
*v God, sovereign*, Gen. 2:2.
2 R. V. yea.
3 R. V. against them.

12

*w Offerings, burnt*, Lev. 6:17.

the name of the one *was* [j]Gĕr′shŏm; for he said, I have been [1]an [k]alien in a strange[G] land:

4 And the name of the other *was* [l]Ē-li-ē′zēr; for the [e]God of my father, *said he, was* mine help, and delivered me from the sword of [m]Phā′raōh:[Q]

5 And [a]Jĕth′rō, [c]Mō′ṣeṣ′ [d]father in law, came with his [i]sons and his [h]wife unto Mō′ṣeṣ into the wilderness, where he encamped at the [n]mount of God:

6 And [a]he said unto [c]Mō′ṣeṣ, I thy [d]father in law Jĕth′rō am come unto thee, and thy [h]wife, and her two [i]sons with her.

7 And [c]Mō′ṣeṣ went out to meet his [d]father in law, and did [o]obeisance[G], and [p]kissed him; and they asked each other of *their* welfare; and they came into the [q]tent.

8 And [c]Mō′ṣeṣ told his [a]father in law all that the LORD had done unto [m]Phā′raōh and to the [r]Ē-ġȳp′tianṣ for [f]Ĭṣ′ra-el's sake, *and* all the travail[G] that had come upon them by the way, and *how* the [s]LORD delivered them.

9 And [a]Jĕth′rō rejoiced for all the goodness which the [s]LORD had done to [f]Ĭṣ′ra-el, whom he had delivered out of the hand of the [r]Ē-ġȳp′tianṣ.

10 And Jĕth′rō said, [t]Blessed *be* the [s]LORD, who hath delivered you out of the hand of the [r]Ē-ġȳp′tianṣ, and out of the hand of [m]Phā′raōh, who hath delivered the people from under the hand of the Ē-ġȳp′tianṣ.

11 Now I [u]know that the [v]LORD *is* greater than all gods: [2]for in the thing wherein they dealt proudly [3]*he was* above them.[S]

12 And Jĕth′rō, Mō′ṣeṣ′ father in law, took a [w]burnt offering and sacrifices for God: and [x]Aâr′on came, and all the [y,z]elders of Ĭṣ′ra-el, to [a]eat bread[G] with Mō′ṣeṣ′ father in law before God.

13 ¶ And it came to pass on the morrow, that [b,c]Mō′ṣeṣ sat to [d,e]judge the people: and the people stood by Mō′ṣeṣ from the morning unto the evening.

14 And when [b]Mō′ṣeṣ′ [f]father in law saw all that he did to the people, he [g]said, What *is* this thing that thou doest to the people? why sittest thou thyself alone, and all the people stand by thee from morning unto even?

15 And [b]Mō′ṣeṣ said unto his [f]father in law, Because the people come unto me [h]to enquire of God:

16 When they have a [e]matter, they come unto me; and [b,c]I judge [h]between [4]one and another, and I do [i]make *them* know the [j]statutes of God, and his laws.

17 And Mō′ṣeṣ′ [f]father in law said unto him, [g,k]The thing that thou doest *is* not good.

18 [g,k]Thou wilt surely wear away, both thou, and this people that *is* with thee: for this thing *is* too heavy[G] for thee: thou art not able to perform it thyself alone.

19 Hearken now unto my voice, [f]I will give thee [g]counsel, and [l]God shall be with thee: [h,m]Be thou for the people to God-ward, that thou mayest bring the causes[G] unto God:

20 And [b,c]thou shalt [i]teach them ordinances and [j]laws, and shalt shew them the [n]way wherein they must walk, and the [o]work that they must do.

21 Moreover [p]thou shalt provide out of all the people able [q]men, such as [r]fear God, men of [s,t]truth, hating [5,u]covetousness; and place *such* over them, *to be* *rulers of thousands, *and* rulers

v.12–1533 BC
See footnote, *Time*, Rev. 10:6.

*x Aaron*, Ex. 6:20.
*y Government, Mosaic, the senatorial council*, Isa. 22:21.
*z Senate*, Num. 11:16.

*a Feasts*, Mark 12:39.

13

*b Moses*, Ex. 2:10.
*c Judge*, Judg. 2:18.
*d Government, administrative and judicial*, vs. 13–26; Isa. 22:21.
*e Litigation*, Matt. 5:25.

14

*f Jethro*, Ex. 3:1.
*g Counsel*, Prov. 12:15.

15

*h Mediation*, Gal. 3:19.

16

*i Instruction* Prov. 23:23.
*j Law*, Deut. 33:2.
4 R. V. a man and his neighbor,

17

*k Prudence, instances of*, 2 Chr. 2.12.

19

*l Benediction*, Deut. 21:5.
*m Intercession*, Jer. 27:18.

20

*n Way, of holiness*, Isa. 35:8.
*o Works*, 2 Tim 1:9.

21

*p Commandment, enjoining the choice of wise men for rulers*, Deut. 8:2.
*q Judge, character of*, Judg. 2:18.
*r Fear of God, required in rulers*, Acts 9:31.
*s Truth, magistrates should be men of*, John 18:37.
*t Integrity*, Job 2:3.
*u Dishonesty*, Ezek. 22:13.
5 R. V. unjust gain;

* **RULERS.** *Ordained of God*, 2 Chr. 9:8; Rom. 13:1, 2, 4; 1 Pet. 2:14. *Appointed by God*, 1 Sam. 9:15–17; 10:1; 15:17; 16:1, 7, 13; 2 Sam. 7:13–16; 1 Kin. 14:14; 16:1–4; 1 Chr. 28:4, 5; 29:25; Psa. 89:19–37; Dan. 2:21, 37; 5:21; Acts 13:22. *Accountable to God*, 2 Chr. 19:6, 7. *Servants of the people*, 1 Kin. 12:7; 2 Chr. 10:7; Ezek. 34:2–4. *Loyalty to, enjoined*, Ezra 7:26. *Must not be reviled*, Ex. 22:28; 2 Sam. 16:9; 19:21; Eccl. 10:20; Acts 23:5; 2 Pet. 2:10, 11; Jude 8. *Righteous, beloved*, Prov. 29:2, 14. *Incompetent, oppress*

v.21–1533 BC
See footnote, *Time*, Rev. 10:6.

of hundreds, rulers of fifties, and
rulers of tens.
22 And let *,†them [e]judge the
people at all seasons: and it shall
be, *that* every great matter they
shall bring unto [b,c]thee, but
every small matter they shall
judge: [g,k]so shall it be easier for
thyself, and they shall bear *the*
[v]*burden* with thee.
23 [g,k]If thou shalt do this thing,
and God command thee *so*, then
thou shalt be able to endure, and
all this people shall also go to
their place in peace.
24 So [b]Mō'ṣeṣ hearkened to the
voice of his [f]father in law, and
did all that he had said.
25 [d]And [b]Mō'ṣeṣ chose able
[q]men out of all Ĭṣ'ra-el, and
made them heads over the people, *rulers of thousands, rulers
of hundreds, rulers of fifties, and
rulers of tens.
26 And †they judged the people at all seasons: the hard

22
v *Responsibility*, Ezek. 18:10.

v.23–1533 BC
See footnote, *Time*, Rev. 10:6.

---

Prov. 28:16. *Corrupted, by evil counsellors*, Prov. 25:5; *by gifts*, Prov. 29:4; Isa. 1:23; Amos 5:11, 12; Mic. 7:3.

*Should not drink wine*, Prov. 31:4, 5. *Forbidden, to take bribes*, Ex. 23:8; Deut. 16:19; *to respect persons*, Lev. 19:15; Deut. 1:17; 16:19; Prov. 24:23.

*Required to judge justly*, Ex. 18:16, 20, 21; 23:3, 6, 7, 9; Lev. 19:15; 24:22; Deut. 1:16, 17; 25:1; 2 Chr. 9:8; Psa. 82:2–4; Prov. 31:9; Isa. 16:5; 58:6; Jer. 22:2, 3; Zech. 7:9, 10; 8:16. *A terror to evil doers*, Prov. 14:35; Rom. 13:3.

*Mosaic law concerning atonement for sins of*, Lev. 4:22–26.

**Character and Qualifications of**, Num. 27:16, 17; 2 Sam. 23:4; Prov. 20:8, 26, 28. *Diligent*, Rom. 12:8. *Wise*, Gen. 41:33; Deut. 1:13; Psa. 2:10; Prov. 20:26; 28:2. *Merciful*, Isa. 16:5; Zech. 7:9.

*Required, to know the law*, Josh. 1:8; Ezra 7:25; *to fear the Lord*, Psa. 2:11; *to be truthful*, Prov. 17:7; *to be righteous*, Ex. 18:21; Deut. 16:19; 27:19; 2 Sam. 23:3, 4; Prov. 16:10, 12.

**Duties of:** *To rule in righteousness*, Isa. 58:6; Jer. 22:2, 3. *To be judges*, 2 Chr. 9:8. *To judge according to law*, Deut. 17:18, 19; Josh. 1:7, 8. *In judicial functions to make thorough investigation*, Deut. 19:18, 19.

**Righteous.** Instances of: *Pharaoh, in his treatment of Abraham*, Gen. 12:15–20. *Abimelech, in his treatment of Abraham*, Gen. 20; *of Isaac*, Gen. 26:6–11. *Pharaoh, in his treatment of Jacob and his family*, Gen. 47:5, 6; 50:1–6. *Moses, in his administration of the affairs of the children of Israel*, Num. 16:15. *Samuel, in not taking reward for judgment*, 1 Sam. 12:3, 4. *Saul, after the defeat of the Ammonites*, 1 Sam. 11:12, 13. *Solomon, in his judgment between the two women who claimed the same child*, 1 Kin. 3:16–28; *according to the testimony of the queen of Sheba*, 1 Kin. 10:6–9. *Asa, in abolishing sodomy and other abominations of idolatry*, 1 Kin. 15:11–15; 2 Chr. 14:2–5. *Jehoshaphat, in walking in the ways of the Lord*, 1 Kin. 22:41–46; 2 Chr. 17:3–10; 19; 20:3–30. *Hezekiah, in his fear of the Lord*, 2 Kin. 18:3–6; 20:1–11; 2 Chr. 30; 31. *Josiah, in repairing the temple and in other good works*, 2 Kin. 22; 23:1–28; 2 Chr. 34; 35:1–19. *Cyrus, in emancipating the Jews*, Ezra 1. *Darius, in advancing the rebuilding of the temple*, Ezra 6:1–12. *Artaxerxes, in commissioning Ezra to restore the forms of worship at Jerusalem*, Ezra 7. *Nehemiah*, Neh. 2:1–8; 4; 5. *Daniel*, see footnote, Daniel, Dan. 2:16. *King of Nineveh, in repenting, and proclaiming a fast*, Jonah 3:6–9.

**Wicked**, Neh. 9:34–37; Psa. 58:2; 82:2; 94:20, 21; Eccl. 3:16, 17; 5:8; Isa. 5:7; 28:14, 15; Hos. 7:3. *Oppressive*, Ex. 3:9; 1 Sam. 8:10–18; Job 35:9; Prov. 28:15, 16; Amos 4:1; 5:11, 12. *Pervert justice*, Deut. 27:19. *Cause people to mourn*, Prov. 29:2; Eccl. 4:1. *A public calamity*, Eccl. 10:16; Isa. 5:22, 23. *An abomination to God*, Prov. 17:15. *Abhorred by men*, Prov. 24:24; 29:2. *Admonitions to*, Ezek. 34:2–4, 7–10; 45:9. *Denounced*, Ezek. 34:2–4, 7–10; Amos 4:1, 2; Mic. 3:1–3, 9–11; Zeph. 3:3. *Divine judgment upon*, Isa. 3:14, 15; 10:1–3; 30:33; 40:23; Jer. 5:28, 29; Ezek. 21:25, 26; Hos. 5:10; Amos 5:11, 12; Zeph. 1:8.

Instances of: *Pharaoh, oppressing the Israelites*, Ex. chapters 1–11. *Adoni-bezek, torturing seventy kings*, Judg. 1:7. *Abimelech, slaying his seventy brothers*, Judg. 9:1–5. *Samuel's sons, taking bribes*, 1 Sam. 8:1–5. *Saul, sparing Agag and the best of the booty*, 1 Sam. 15:8–35; *in jealous plotting against David*, 1 Sam. 18:8–29; *seeking to slay David*, 1 Sam. 19; *slaying Ahimelech and the priests*, 1 Sam. 22:7–19.

*Hanun, maltreating David's servants*, 2 Sam. 10:4; 1 Chr. 19:4.

*David, causing the death of Uriah*, 2 Sam. 11:14–25; *numbering Israel and Judah*, 1 Chr. 21:1–7. *Solomon, luxurious, and idolatrous*, 1 Kin. 11:1–13; *oppressing the people*, 1 Kin. 12:4 (with 4:7–23). *Rehoboam, making the yoke heavy*, 1 Kin. 12:8–11; 2 Chr. 10:8–15.

*Jeroboam, perverting the true worship*, 1 Kin. 12:26–33; 13:1–5; 14:16; *exalting debased persons to the priesthood*, 1 Kin. 12:31; 13:33; 2 Kin. 17:32; 2 Chr. 11:14, 15. *Abijam, walking in the sins of Rehoboam*, 1 Kin. 15:3. *Nadab, walking in the ways of Jeroboam*, 1 Kin. 15:26. *Baasha, walking in the ways of Jeroboam*, 1 Kin. 15:33, 34. *Asa, imprisoning the seer, and oppressing the people*, 2 Chr. 16:10. *Zimri, walking in the ways of Jeroboam*, 1 Kin. 16:19. *Omri, walking in the ways of Jeroboam*, 1 Kin. 16:25, 26.

*Ahab, serving Baal*, 1 Kin. 16:30–33; 21:25, 26; *confiscating Naboth's vineyard*, 1 Kin. 21. *Jehoram, cleaving to the sins of Jeroboam*, 2 Kin. 3:2, 3. *Hazael, committing rapine*, 2 Kin. 8:12; 10:32; 12:17; 13:3–7. *Jehoram, walking in the ways of the kings of Israel*, 2 Kin. 8:18; 2 Chr. 21:13. *Jehu, departing not from the sins of Jeroboam*, 2 Kin. 10:29. *Jehoahaz, in following the sins of Jeroboam*, 2 Kin. 13:1, 2. *Jehoash, in following the wicked example of Jeroboam*, 2 Kin. 13:10, 11. *Jeroboam II, not departing from the sins of Jeroboam*, 2 Kin. 14:23, 24. *Zachariah, Menahem, Pekahiah, and Pekah, in following the sins of Jeroboam*, 2 Kin. 15:9, 18, 24, 28. *Pekah, in conspiring against and slaying Pekahiah*, 2 Kin. 15:25. *Hoshea, in conspiring against Pekah*, 2 Kin. 15:30, *in permitting Baal-worship*, 2 Kin. 17:1, 2, 7–18. *Ahaz, in burning his children in idolatrous sacrifice*, 2 Kin. 16:3; 2 Chr. 28:2–4. *Manasseh, in committing the abominations of the heathen*, 2 Kin. 21:1–17; 2 Chr. 33:2–7. *Amon, in following the evil example of Manasseh*, 2 Kin. 21:19–22. *Jehoahaz, in following in the ways of his fathers*, 2 Kin. 23:32. *Jehoiakim, in walking in the ways of his fathers*, 2 Kin. 23:37; *and Jehoiachin*, 2 Kin. 24:9. *Zedekiah, in following the evil example of Jehoiakim*, 2 Kin. 24:19; 2 Chr. 36:12, 13; *and persecuting Jeremiah*, Jer. 38:5, 6. *Joash, in slaying Zechariah*, 2 Chr. 24:2, 17–25. *Ahaziah, in doing evil after the house of Ahab*, 2 Chr. 22:1–9. *Amaziah, in worshiping the gods of Seir*, 2 Chr. 25:14. *Uzziah, in invading the priest's office*, 2 Chr. 26:16. *The kings of Judah, in perverting justice*, Isa. 59:14, 15.

*Ahasuerus and Haman, decreeing the death of the Jews*, Esth. 3. *Nebuchadnezzar, commanding to destroy the wise men*, Dan. 2:1–13; *and committing the three Hebrews to the furnace*, Dan. 3:1–23. *Belshazzar, in drunkenness and committing sacrilege*, Dan. 5:22, 23. *Darius, deifying himself*, Dan. 6:7, 9. *The princes, conspiring against Daniel*, Dan. 6:1–9. *The Jews, oppressing their brethren*, Neh. 5:7–9.

*Herod the Great, slaying the children in Bethlehem*, Matt. 2:16–18. *Herod Antipas, beheading John the Baptist*, Matt. 14:1–11; *in craftiness and tyranny*, Luke 13:31, 32; 23:6–15. *Pilate, delivering Jesus for crucifixion*, Matt. 27:11–26; Mark 15:15.

*Chief priests, elders, and all the council, seeking false witness against Jesus*, Matt. 26:59.

*Herod Agrippa, persecuting the church*, Acts 12:1–19. *Ananias, commanding to smite Paul*, Acts 23:2.

**Patriarchal.** Instances of: *Nimrod*, Gen. 10:8–10. *Abraham*, Gen. 14:13–24; 17:6; 21:22–27. *Melchizedek*, Gen. 14:18. *Isaac*, Gen. 26:26–31. *Ishmael*, Gen. 17:20. *Esau, and the dukes of Edom*, Gen. 36:15–43. *Judah*, Gen. 38:24. *Heads of families*, Ex. 6:14.

† **COURT. Civil:** *Justice required of*, Ex. 23:2, 3, 6–8; Deut. 1:16, 17; 25; 27:19; 2 Chr. 19:5–10; Acts 25:16.

*Sentence of, final and obligatory*, Deut. 17:8–12. *Contempt of*, Deut. 17:8–13; Mic. 5:1; Acts 23:1–5.

*Corrupt*, Prov. 17:15; Isa. 1:23; 5:23; 10:1, 2; Mic. 3:11; 7:3; Zeph. 3:3; Matt. 26:59–62; 27:18–26; Mark 14:53, 55–65; 15:10; Acts 4:15–18; 6:11–14; 24:26, 27.

*Accused spoke in his own defense*, Jer. 26:11–16; Mark

v.26–1533 BC
See footnote, *Time*, Rev. 10:6.

[e]causes they brought unto Mō'-
ṣeṣ, but every small matter they
judged themselves.
27 ¶ And Mō'ṣeṣ let his father
in law depart; and he went his
way into his own land.

## CHAPTER 19

*The people come to Sinai. 3 God's message by Moses unto the people from the mount, 8 and their answer in return. 10 The people are to be prepared against the third day. 12 The mountain not to be touched. 16 The presence of God upon the mount.*

IN the[Q] [a]third [b]month, when the
children of [c]Ĭṣ'ra-el were
gone forth out of the land of
[d]Ē'ġy̆pt, the same day came they
*into* the wilderness of [e]Sī'nāi.
2 For they were departed from
[f]Rĕph'i-dĭm, and were come *to*
the desert of [e]Sī'nāi, and had
pitched[G] in the wilderness; and
there [c]Ĭṣ'ra-el camped before
the mount.
3[T] And [g]Mō'ṣeṣ went up unto
God, and the LORD called unto
him out of the [e]mountain, saying, Thus shalt thou say to the
house of Jā'cob, and tell the
children of [c]Ĭṣ'ra-el;
4 [h]Ye have seen what I did unto
the [i]Ē-gy̆p'tianṣ, and *how* [j,k]I
bare you on [l]eagles' wings, and
brought you unto myself.
5 Now therefore, [m]if ye will
[n]obey [o]my voice indeed, and
keep my [p]covenant, [q]then [r]ye
shall be a peculiar[G] treasure unto
me above all people: for all the
[s]earth *is* [t]mine:[Q] [S]
6 And [m]ye shall be unto me a
[u]kingdom of [v]priests, and an
[w]holy nation. [x]These *are* the
words which thou shalt speak
unto the children of Ĭṣ'ra-el.[T] [Q]
7 ¶ And [g]Mō'ṣeṣ came and
called for the [y]elders of the people, and laid before their faces[G]
all these [z]words which the LORD
commanded him.
8 And all the people answered
together, and said, [a]All that the
LORD hath spoken [b]we will
do. And [c]Mō'ṣeṣ returned the
words of the people unto the
LORD.
9 And the LORD said unto
[c]Mō'ṣeṣ, Lo, [d]I come unto thee
in a thick [e,f]cloud, that the people may hear when I speak with
thee, and believe thee for ever.
And Mō'ṣeṣ told the words of the
people unto the LORD.
10 ¶[T]And the LORD said unto
Mō'ṣeṣ, Go unto the people, and
[g]sanctify[G] them to day and to morrow, and let them *,[h]wash their
clothes,
11 And be ready against the
third day: for the third day the
LORD will come down in the
sight of all the people upon
mount [i]Sī'nāi.
12[Q]And thou shalt set bounds
unto the people round about,
saying, [j]Take heed to yourselves,
*that ye* go *not* up into the mount,
or touch the border of it: [k]who-
soever toucheth the mount shall
be surely [l]put to [m]death:
13 [n]There shall not an hand
touch it, but he shall surely be
[o]stoned, or shot through; whether *it be* beast or man, it shall
[l,m]not live: when the [p]trumpet

**1**
a *Time, of exodus*, Rev. 10:6.
b *Month*, Ex. 12:2.
c *Israel, at Mt. Sinai*, Ex. 4:22.
d *Egypt*, Gen. 41:8.
e *Sinai*, Ex. 16:1.
**2**
f *Rephidim*, Ex. 17:1.
**3**
g *Moses*, Ex. 2:10.
**4**
h *Miracles, design of*, Luke 23:8.
i *Egyptians*, Gen. 50:3.
j *God, love of*, Gen. 2:2.
k *God, preserver*, Gen. 2:2.
l *Eagle*, Lev. 11:13.
**5**
m *Blessings, contingent upon obedience*, Deut. 11:26.
n *Obedience*, Heb. 5:8.
o *Government, theocratic*, vs. 3–8; Isa. 22:21.
p *Covenant*, Deut. 29:1.
q *Promise, to the obedient*, 2 Cor. 1:20.
r *Righteous, promises to*, Psa. 64:10.
s *Earth, is the Lord's*, Prov. 8:23.
t *God, sovereign*, Gen. 2:2.
**6**
u 1 Pet. 2:5, 9.
v *Priest, figurative*, Lev. 1:5.
w *Holiness, of the church*, Ex. 39:30.
x *Inspiration*, Job 32:8.

v.6–1533 BC
See footnote, *Time* Rev. 10:6.

**7**
y *Senate*, Num. 11:16.
z *Word of God*, Psa. 119:9.
**8**
a *Theocracy*, Judg. 8:23.
b *Decision, instances of*, Isa. 50:7.
c *Moses*, Ex. 2:10.
**9**
d *God, invisible*, Gen. 2:2.
e *Pillar, of cloud and fire*, Ex. 13:21.
f *Symbols and Similitudes*, Heb. 9:9.
**10**
g *Sanctification*, 1 Pet. 1:2.
h *Purification*, Num. 19:19.
**11**
i *Sinai*, Ex. 16:1.
**12**
j *Fear of God, cultivated*, Acts 9:31.
k Heb. 12:20.
l *Punishment, death penalty*, Lev. 26:41.
m *Death*, Num. 23:10.
**13**
n *Reverence, for God*, Lev. 19:30.
o *Stoning*, 1 Sam. 30:6.
p *Trumpet*, Josh. 6:4.

15:3–5; Acts 4:8–12, 18–20; 5:29–32; 7:1–56; 23:1–7; 26:1–32.
*Held, outside the camp*, Lev. 24:14; *at the tabernacle*, Num. 27:2; *at the gates of cities*, Deut. 21:19; 22:15; 25:7; Josh. 20:4; Ruth 4:1; Zech. 8:16; *under a palm tree*, Judg. 4:5.
*Composition of, and mode of procedure*, Ex. 18:25; Deut. 1:15–17; 17:9; Ruth 4:2–5; 1 Chr. 26:29; 2 Chr. 19:8–11; Mark 14:53, 55–65; 15:1; Luke 22:50–71; John 18:13–28; Acts 5:17–21, 25–28, 34, 38–41.
**Circuit,** 1 Sam. 7:15–17.
**Superior and Inferior,** Ex. 18:21–26; 24:14; Deut. 1:15–17; 17:8–13; 2 Chr. 19:5–10.
**Ecclesiastical,** 1 Chr. 26:29–32; 2 Chr. 19:8–11; Matt. 18:15–18; John 20:23.
*** CEREMONIAL WASHING.** In studying the Mosaic law relating to ablutions, it must be kept in mind that *sin defiles*. To keep this great truth constantly before the Israelites, specific ordinances concerning washings were given to Moses. The purpose was to teach, by this object lesson, that *sin pollutes* the soul, and that only those who were cleansed from their sins could be pure in the sight of the Lord. Heb. 9:10; 10:22.
*Of garments*, Ex. 19:10, 14. *Of priests*, Ex. 29:4; 30:18–21; 40:12, 31, 32; Lev. 8:6; 16:4, 24, 26, 28; Num. 19:7–10, 19; 2 Chr. 4:6. *Of burnt offerings*, Lev. 1:9, 13; 9:14; 2 Chr. 4:6. *Of the hands*, Matt. 15:2; Mark 7:2–5; Luke 11:38. *Of the feet*, 1 Tim. 5:10.
*For defilement*, Lev. 11:24–40. *Of lepers*, Lev. 13:6; 14:9. *Of those having bloody issue*, Lev. 15:5–13. *Of those having eaten, or touched, that which died*, Lev. 11:25, 40; 17:15, 16.
*Traditional forms of, not observed by Jesus*, Luke 11:38, 39. See footnotes: ABLUTION, Judg. 19:21; DEFILEMENT, Lev 5:2; PURIFICATION, Num. 19:19.

soundeth long, they shall come
up to the [i]mount.[Q]
14 ¶ And [c]Mō′ṣeṣ went down
from the [i]mount unto the people,
and [g]sanctified the people; and
they [h]washed their clothes.[S]
15 And he said unto the people,
Be ready against the third day:
[q]come not at[G] *your* wives.
16 ¶[S T]And it came to pass on
the third day in the morning,
that [r]there were [s]thunders, and
[t]lightnings, and a [u]thick [e]cloud
upon the [i]mount, and the voice
of the [p]trumpet exceeding loud;
so that all the people that *was* in
the camp [v]trembled.[Q]
17 And [c]Mō′ṣeṣ brought forth
the people out of the camp to
[w]meet with God; and they stood
at the nether[G] part of the [i]mount.
18 And mount [i]Sī′nāi was altogether on a smoke, because the
[r]LORD descended upon it in
[x]fire: and the smoke thereof ascended as the smoke of a furnace, and [y]the whole mount
[z]quaked[G] greatly.[Q]
19 And when the voice of the
[a]trumpet sounded long, and
waxed[G] louder and louder, [b]Mō′-
ṣeṣ spake, and God answered
him by a [c]voice.
20 And the LORD came down
upon mount [d]Sī′nāi, on the top
of the mount: and the LORD
[c]called Mō′ṣeṣ *up* to the top of
the mount; and Mō′ṣeṣ went up.[Q T S]
21 And the LORD said unto
[b]Mō′ṣeṣ, Go down, [e]charge[G] the
people, lest they break through
unto the LORD to gaze, and
many of them perish.
22 And let the [f]priests also,
which come near to the LORD,
[g,h]sanctify themselves, [e]lest the
LORD break forth upon them.
23 And [b]Mō′ṣeṣ said unto the
LORD, The people cannot come
up to mount [d]Sī′nāi: for thou
chargedst us, saying, Set bounds
about the mount, and sanctify it.
24 And the LORD said unto
him, Away, get thee down, and
[b]thou shalt come up, thou, and
[i]Aâr′on with thee: but [e]let not the
[f]priests and the people break
through to come up unto the
LORD, lest he break forth upon
them.[Q]
25 So [b]Mō′ṣeṣ went down unto
the people, and spake unto them.[T]

## CHAPTER 20

*The ten commandments. 18 The people are afraid. 20 Moses comforts them. 23 Idolatry is forbidden. 25 The manner of building an altar.*

AND[Q] God [a]spake all these
[b,c]words, saying,
2 I *am* the LORD thy [d,e]God,
which have brought thee out of
the land of [f]Ē′gy̆pt, out of the
house of bondage.[T]
3 *,[g,h]Thou[T] shalt have no other
[i]gods before[G] [j]me.
4 *,[i,k]Thou shalt not make unto thee any graven[G] image, or any
likeness *of any thing* that *is* in
heaven above, or that *is* in the
earth beneath, or that *is* in the
water under the earth:
5 *,[k]Thou shalt not [i]bow[G] down
thyself to them, nor serve them:
for [l]I the LORD thy God *am* a
[m,n]jealous God, visiting[G] the [o]in-
iquity of the [p]fathers [q]upon the
[r]children unto the third and
fourth *generation* of [s]them that
[t]hate me;[S Q]
6 [k]And shewing [u,v,w]mercy unto thousands of [x]them that [y]love
me, and [z,a]keep my commandments.[S]
7 *,[b,c]Thou shalt not [d,e]take
the name of the LORD thy God

v.13–1533 BC
See footnote, *Time*, Rev. 10:6.

15
g *Continence*, Matt. 19:12.

16
r *God, glory of*, Gen. 2:2.
s *Thunder*, 1 Sam. 7:10.
t *Lightning*, Job 28:26.
u *Darkness, figurative*, Gen. 1:2.
v *Fear of God*, Acts 9:31.

17
w *Access, to God*, Eph. 3:12.

18
x *Fire, a symbol*, Ex. 12:8.
y Heb. 12:26.
z *Earthquakes, instances of*, Isa. 29:6.

19
a *Trumpet*, Josh. 6:4.
b *Moses*, Ex. 2:10.
c *Anthropomorphisms, voice attributed to God*, Gen. 11:5.

20
d *Sinai*, Ex. 16:1.

21
e *Fear of God, cultivated*, Acts 9:31.

22
f *Priest*, Lev. 1:5.
g *Ministers, character and qualifications of*, Rom. 15:16.
h *Sanctification*, 1 Pet. 1:2.

v.23–1533 BC
See footnote, *Time*, Rev. 10:6.

24
i *Aaron*, Ex. 6:20.

1
a *Revelation, of the law*, vs. 1–26; 2 Cor. 12:1.
b *Law, of Moses, divine authority for*, vs. 1–17; Deut. 33:2.
c *Word of God*, Psa. 119:9.

2
d *God, mercy of*, Gen. 2:2.
e *God, providence of*, Gen. 2:2.
f *Egypt*, Gen. 41:8.

3
g *Commandment, forbidding idolatry*, vs. 4–6; Deut. 8:2.
h Deut. 5:7.
i *Idolatry, forbidden*, 1 Sam. 15:23.
j *God, sovereign*, Gen. 2:2.

4
k Deut. 5:8–10.

5
l *God, jealous*, Gen. 2:2.
m *Anthropomorphisms*, Gen. 11:5.
n *Jealousy*, Psa. 78:58.
o *Sin, consequences of, entailed upon children*, Rom. 5:12.
p *Parents, curses, entailed*, 2 Cor. 12:14.
q *Heredity, results of, judicial*, Ezek. 18:2.
r *Children, involved in sin of parents*, Mark 10:14.
s *Wicked, punishment of*, Psa. 73:3.
t *Hatred*, Prov. 15:17.

6
u *Blessings, contingent upon obedience*, Deut. 11:26.
v *Mercy*, Deut. 5:10. w *Reward, a motive to faithfulness*, Matt. 5:12. x *Parents, covenant benefits of, entailed on children*, 2 Cor. 12:14. y *Love, of man for God*, 1 John 4:19. z *Faithfulness, rewards of*, Luke 16:10.—a *Obedience, rewarded by divine favor*, Heb. 5:8.

7 b *Commandment, against profaning God's name*, Deut. 8:2. c Deut. 5:11. d *Blasphemy, forbidden*, 2 Sam. 12:14. e *Profanation, of God's name, forbidden*, Lev. 22:32.

* **DECALOGUE**, Ex. 20:1–17; Deut. 5:7–21. *Called* WORDS OF THE COVENANT, Ex. 34:28; Deut. 4:13; TABLES OF TESTIMONY, Ex. 31:18; 34:29; 40:20.
See footnote, COMMANDMENTS, Deut. 8:2.
*Written by God*, Ex. 24:12; 31:18; 32:16; Deut. 5:22; 9:10. *Divine authority of*, Ex. 20:1–17; 34:27, 28; Deut. 5:4–22.
*Confirmed, by Jesus*, Matt. 19:18, 19; 22:34–40; Luke 10:25–28; *by Paul*, Rom. 13:8–10.

in vain; for the LORD will not
hold[G] him guiltless that taketh
his name in vain.[Q]
8 *,[f,g]Remember[Q] the [h]sabbath
day, to keep it holy.
9 *,[g,i]Six[Q] days shalt thou [j]la-
bour, and do all thy work:
10 But [k]the seventh day *is* the
[h]sabbath of the LORD thy God:
*in it* thou shalt [l]not do any
work, [m,n]thou, nor thy [o]son, nor
thy daughter, thy [p]manservant,
nor thy maidservant, nor thy
[q]cattle, nor thy [r]stranger that *is*
within thy gates:[Q]
11 For *in* six days the [s]LORD
made [t]heaven and [u]earth, the
sea, and all that in them *is*, and
rested the seventh day: wherefore the LORD blessed the [h]sab-
bath day, and hallowed it.[Q]
12 ¶ *,[v,w,x]Honour[Q] [y]thy [z]father
and thy [z]mother: [a,b]that [c,d]thy
days may be [e]long upon the land
which the LORD thy God giveth
thee.
13 *,[f,g]Thou[Q] shalt [1]not [h]kill.
14 *,[i,j,k]Thou[Q] shalt not commit [l]adultery.
15 *,[m,n]Thou shalt not [o]steal.
16 *,[p,q]Thou shalt not bear
[r]false [s]witness[G] against thy
neighbour.[Q]
17 *,[t,u]Thou shalt not [v]covet
thy neighbour's house, thou
shalt not [w]covet thy neighbour's
[x]wife, nor his manservant, nor
his maidservant, nor his ox, nor
his ass, nor [y]any thing that *is*
thy neighbour's.[T Q]
18 ¶[Q T]And all the people saw
the [z]thunderings, and the [a]light-
nings, and the noise of the
[b]trumpet, and the [c]mountain
smoking: and when the people
saw *it*, they [1,d]removed,[G] and
stood afar off.
19 And they said unto [e]Mō'şeş,
[f]Speak thou with us, and we will
hear: but [d]let not God speak
with us, lest we die.
20 And [e]Mō'şeş said unto the
people, Fear not: for God is
come to prove[G] you, and that his
[d]fear may be before your faces,
that ye [g]sin not.
21 And the people stood afar
off, and [e]Mō'şeş drew near unto
the thick [h,i]darkness where [j]God
*was*.[T S Q]
22 ¶ And the LORD said unto
[e]Mō'şeş, Thus thou shalt say
unto the children of Īş'ra-el, Ye
have seen that I have talked with
you from heaven.
23 [k]Ye shall not make with me
[l]gods of [m]silver, neither shall ye
make unto you gods of [n]gold.
24 [o]An [p]altar of earth thou
shalt make unto me, and shalt
sacrifice thereon thy [q]burnt offerings, and thy [r]peace offerings,
thy sheep, and thine oxen; in all
places where I record[G] my name
[s]I will come unto thee, and [t]I
will bless thee.
25 And if thou wilt make me an
[p]altar of stone, thou shalt not
build it of hewn stone: for if thou
lift up thy tool upon it, thou hast
polluted[G] it.
26 Neither shalt thou go up by
steps unto mine [p]altar, that thy[G]
nakedness be not discovered
thereon.

## CHAPTER 21

*Laws for menservants; 5 for the servant whose ear is bored; 7 for womenservants; 12 for manslaughter; 16 for stealers of men; 17 for cursers of parents; 18 for smiters; 22 for a hurt by chance; 28 for an ox that goreth; 33 and for him that is an occasion of harm.*

NOW [a]these *are* the [b]judg-
ments[G] which thou shalt set
before them.
2 If [c]thou buy an Hē'brew
[d]servant, six years he shall serve:

v.7–1533 BC
See footnote, *Time*, Rev. 10:6.

8
f *Commandment, enjoining keeping the Sabbath holy*, Deut. 8:2.
g Deut. 5:12–14.
h *Sabbath*, Ex. 16:23.

9
i *Commandment, enjoining labor*, Deut. 8:2.
j *Labor, enjoined*, Luke 10:7.

10
k *Commandment, forbidding work on the Sabbath*, Deut. 8:2.
l *Rest, on the Sabbath, enjoined*, Ex. 23:12.
m *Employer, to grant Sabbath rest*, Deut. 24:14.
n *Parents, duty of*, 2 Cor. 12:14.
o *Children*, Mark 10:14.
p *Servant, to have rest on Sabbath*, Jer. 2:14.
q *Animals, kindness to*, Jer. 27:5.
r *Foreigners, required to observe the Sabbath*, Deut. 23:20.

11
s *God, creator*, Gen. 2:2.
t *Heavens, created*, Psa. 8:3.
u *Earth, created*, Prov. 8:23.

12
v *Commandment, enjoining reverence for parents*, Deut. 8:2.
w *Reverence*, Lev. 19:30.
x Deut. 5:16.
y *Children, commandments to*, Mark 10:14.
z *Parents to be revered*, 2 Cor. 12:14.

a *Reward, a motive to honor parents*, Matt. 5:12.
b *Blessings, contingent upon obedience*, Deut. 11:26.
c *Children, promises to*, Mark 10:14.
d *Promises, to children*, 2 Cor. 1:20.
e *Longevity*, Psa. 91:16.

v.18–1533 BC
See footnote, *Time*, Rev. 10:6.

d *Fear of God*, Acts 9:31.
1 R. V. trembled.

19
e *Moses*, Ex. 2:10.
f *Mediation, solicited*, Gal. 3:19.

20
g *Sinlessness*, 1 John 5:18.

21
h *Darkness*, Gen. 1:2.
i *God, incomprehensible*, Gen. 2:2.
j *God, invisible*, Gen. 2:2.

23
k *Commandment, forbidding making idols*, Deut. 8:2.
l *Idol, manufacture of*, 1 Kin. 15:12.
m *Silver*, 1 Chr. 28:14.
n *Gold*, Ezek. 7:19.

24
o *Commandment, enjoining worship*, Deut. 8:2.
p *Altar*, Gen. 8:20.
q *Offerings, burnt*, Lev. 6:17.
r *Offerings, peace*, Lev. 6:17.
s *God, presence of*, Gen. 2:2.
t *Promise, of blessing, to worshipers*, 2 Cor. 1:20.

1
a *Revelation, of the law*, 2 Cor. 12:1.
b *Law, of Moses*, vs. 1–36; Deut. 33:2.

2
c *Israel*, Ex. 4:22.
d *Servant*, Jer. 2:14.

**13** f *Commandment, forbidding murder*, Deut. 8:2. g Deut. 5:17. h *Homicide, felonious*, Deut. 5:17. 1 R. V. do no murder.
**14** i *Commandment, forbidding adultery*, Deut. 8:2. j *Chastity, enjoined*, Job 31:1. k Deut. 5:18. l *Adultery, forbidden*, Lev. 20:10.
**15** m *Commandment, forbidding theft*, Deut. 8:2. n Deut. 5:19. o *Theft, forbidden*, Mark 7:22.
**16** p *Commandment, forbidding false witness*, Deut. 8:2. q Deut. 5:20. r *False Witness, forbidden*, Matt. 19:18. s *Evidence, false, forbidden*, Deut. 17:6.
**17** t *Commandment, forbidding covetousness*, Deut. 8:2. u Deut. 5:21. v *Covetousness, forbidden*, Isa. 57:17. w *Lust, forbidden*, 2 Pet. 1:4. x *Wife*, Prov. 5:18. y *Property*, Lev. 27:15.
**18** z *Thunder*, 1 Sam. 7:10.—a *Lightning*, Job 28:26. b *Trumpet*, Josh. 6:4. c *Sinai*, Ex. 16:1.

v.2–1533 BC
See footnote, *Time*, Rev. 10:6.

[e] *Sabbatic Year*, Lev. 25:2.
[f] *Emancipation, of all Jewish servants*, Deut. 15: 12.
3
[g] *Wife*, Prov. 5: 18.
4
[h] *Property, personal*, Lev. 27:15.
[i] *Servant, home born*, Jer. 2:14.
5
[j] *Family, love for*, 1 Chr. 13:12.
6
[k] *Ear*, Lev. 8:23.
1 R. V. God, and shall
7
[l] *Daughter*, Lev. 12:6.
[m] *Children, sold in marriage*, Mark 10:14.
[n] *Concubinage*, 2 Sam. 21:11.
8
[o] *Betrothal, a quasi marriage*, Deut. 20:7.
[p] *Divorce, Mosaic laws concerning*, Matt. 19:7.
10
[q] *Polygamy*, Deut. 17:17.
11
[r] *Money*, Jer. 32:9.
12
[s] *Commandment, fixing the penalty for murder*, Deut. 8:2.
[t] *Homicide, felonious*, Deut. 5:17.
[u] *Punishment, death penalty*, Lev. 26:41.

and in the [e]seventh he shall go
out [f]free for nothing.[Q]
3 If [d]he came in by himself, he
shall go out by himself: if he
were married, then his [g]wife
shall [f]go out with him.
4 If his master have given [d]him
a [g]wife, and she have born him
sons or daughters; the [h]wife and
her [i]children shall be her master's, and he shall [f]go out by
himself.
5 And if the [d]servant shall
plainly say, I love my master,
my [g,j]wife, and my children; I
will[G] not [f]go out free:
6 Then his master shall bring
[d]him unto [1]the judges[G]; he shall
also bring him to the door, or unto the door post; and his master
shall bore his [k]ear through with
an aul; and he shall serve him
for ever.
7 ¶ And if a man sell his
[l,m]daughter to be a [n]maidserv-
ant, she shall not go out as the
menservants do.
8 If she please not her master,
who hath [o]betrothed her to himself, then shall he let her be [p]re-
deemed: to sell her unto a
strange[G] nation he shall have no
power, seeing he hath dealt deceitfully with her.
9 And if he have [o]betrothed her
unto his son, he shall deal with
her after the manner of [l]daugh-
ters.
10 If he take him another
[g,q]*wife*; her food, her raiment,
and her duty of marriage, shall
he not diminish.
11 And if he do not these three
unto her, then shall she [f]go out
free without [r]money.
12 ¶ [s]He that [t]smiteth a man,
so that he die, shall be surely
[u]put to death.[Q]

13 And if a man [v]lie not in
wait, but God deliver *him* into
his hand; then I will appoint
thee a [w]place whither he shall
flee.
14 But if a man come pre-
sumptuously[G] upon his neighbour, to [t]slay him with guile;
thou shalt take him from mine
[x]altar, [u]that he may die.
15 And [y,z]he that *smiteth his
[a]father, or his [b]mother, shall be
surely [c]put to [d]death.
16 ¶ And [e]he that †,[f]stealeth a
man, and selleth him, or if he be
found in his hand, he shall surely
be [c]put to [d]death.
17 ¶ And [g,h]he that [i]curseth his
[j,k]father, or his mother, shall
surely be [c]put to [f]death.[Q]
18 ¶ And [l]if men strive together, and one *smite another with
a stone, or with *his* fist, and he
die not, but keepeth *his* bed:
19 If he rise again, and walk
abroad upon his staff, then shall
he that smote *him* be quit[G]: only
[l]he shall ‡pay *for* the loss of his
time, and shall cause *him* to be
thoroughly healed.
20 ¶ And [l]if a [m]man [n,o]smite
his [p]servant, or his maid, with a
rod, and he die under his hand;
he shall be surely punished.
21 Notwithstanding, if [p]he continue a day or two, [m]he shall not
be punished: for he *is* his money.
22 ¶ If men strive, and hurt a
woman with child, so that her
fruit[G] ‖depart *from her*, and yet
no mischief[G] follow: [l]he shall be
surely [2,q]punished, according as
the woman's husband will lay
upon him; and he shall ‡pay as
the judges *determine*.
23 And if *any* mischief[G] follow,
then thou shalt give [l,r]life for
life,

v.13–1533 BC
See footnote, *Time*, Rev. 10:6.
13
[v] *Homicide, accidental*, Deut. 5: 17.
[w] *Cities, of refuge*, Num. 35:8.
14
[x] *Altar*, Gen. 8:20.
15
[y] *Commandment, fixing penalty for violent irreverence for parents*, Deut. 8:2.
[z] *Children, wicked*, Mark 10:14.

[a] *Father, to be revered*, Psa. 27:10.
[b] *Mother, dishonoring of, to be punished*, 1 Kin. 2:20.
[c] *Punishment, death penalty*, Lev. 26:41.
[d] *Death, penalty*, Num. 23:10.
16
[e] *Commandment, fixing penalty for manstealing*, Deut. 8:2.
[f] *Theft*, Mark 7:22.
17
[g] *Commandment, fixing penalty for irreverence for parents*, Deut. 8:2.
[h] Matt. 15:4; Mark 7:10.
[i] *Cursing*, Lev. 24: 11.
[j] *Father, cursing of, forbidden*, Psa. 27:10.
[k] *Parents, cursing of, to be punished*, 2 Cor. 12:14.
18
[l] *Commandment, fixing penalty for personal injury*, vs. 19–27; Deut. 8:2.
20
[m] *Master, violent, to be punished*, Col. 4:1.
[n] *Scourging*, Acts 22:24.
[o] *Homicide, felonious*, Deut. 5:17.
[p] *Servant*, Jer. 2:14.
22
[q] *Fine*, Ex. 22:1.
2 R. V. fined,
23
[r] *Retaliation, judicial, ordained in Mosaic law*, Deut. 19:19.

* **ASSAULT AND BATTERY.** *Laws concerning*, Ex. 21:15, 18, 19, 22–27; Deut. 17:8–12; Matt. 5:39; Luke 6:29.
† **KIDNAPPING.** *To be punished*, Ex. 21:16; Deut. 24:7. **Instance of**, Judg. 21:20–23.
‡ **DAMAGES AND COMPENSATION,** Num. 5:5–8. *For assault*, Ex. 21:18, 19, 22. *For personal injury*, Ex. 21:28–34. *For deception*, Lev. 6:1–5. *For slander*, Deut. 22:13–19. *For seduction*, Deut. 22:28, 29. See footnote, FINE, Ex. 22:1.
‖ **ABORTION,** Ex. 21:22–25. *As a judgment*, Hos. 9:14. *Of animals, caused by thunder*, Psa. 29:9.

v.24–1533 BC
See footnote, *Time*, Rev. 10:6.

24
*s* Matt. 5:38.

26
*t Emancipation*, Deut. 15:12.

28
*u Commandment, concerning vicious animals*, Deut. 8:2.
*v Animals*, Jer. 27:5.
*w Property, personal*, vs. 28–36; Lev. 27:15.

29
*x Homicide, felonious*, Deut. 5:17.
*y Commandment, fixing penalty for criminal neglect*, vs. 30–34; Deut. 8:2.

30
*z Restitution*, Ex. 22:3.
3 R. V. ransom,

24 [l,r,s]Eye for eye, tooth for tooth, hand for hand, foot for foot,[Q]

25 [l,r]Burning for burning, wound for wound, stripe for stripe.

26 ¶ And if a [m]man smite the eye of his [p]servant, or the eye of his maid, that it perish; [l]he shall [‡]let him [t]go free for his eye's sake.

27 And if he smite out his manservant's tooth, or his maidservant's tooth; [l]he shall [‡]let him [t]go free for his tooth's sake.

28 ¶ [u]If an [v,w]ox gore a man or a woman, that they die: then the ox shall be surely stoned, and his flesh shall not be eaten; but the owner of the ox *shall be* quit.[G]

29 But [u]if the [v]ox were wont[G] to push with his horn in time past, and it hath been testified to his owner, and he hath not kept him in, but that he hath [x]killed a man or a woman; [y]the ox shall be stoned, and his owner also shall be [c]put to [d]death.

30 If there be laid on him a [3,q]sum of money, then he shall [‡,z]give for the [§]ransom of his life whatsoever is laid upon him.

31 [u]Whether he have gored a son, or have gored a daughter, according to this judgment shall it be done unto him.

32 [u]If the [v,w]ox shall push a [p]manservant or a maidservant; he shall [‡,z]give unto their master [q]thirty shekels[G] of silver, and the [y]ox shall be stoned.[Q]

33 ¶ And [y]if a man shall open a pit, or if a man shall dig a pit, and not cover it, and an [v,w]ox or an ass fall therein;

34 [y]The owner of the pit shall [‡,z]make *it* good, *and* give money unto the owner of them; and the dead *beast* shall be his.

35 ¶ And [u]if one man's [v,w]ox hurt another's, that he die; then they shall sell the live ox, and divide the money of it; and the dead *ox* also they shall divide.

36 Or [u]if it be[G] known that the [v,w]ox hath used to push in time past, and his owner hath not kept him in; he shall surely [‡,z]pay ox for ox; and the dead shall be his own.

## CHAPTER 22

*Laws concerning theft; 5 damage; 7 trespasses; 14 borrowing; 16 fornication; 18 witchcraft; 19 bestiality; 20 idolatry; 21 strangers, widows, and the fatherless; 25 usury; 26 pledges; 28 reverence to magistrates; 29 and the firstfruits.*

IF a man shall [a]steal an ox, or a sheep, and kill it, or sell it; [b]he shall restore [*,c]five oxen for an ox, and four sheep for a sheep.[Q]

2 If a [d]thief be found breaking[G] up, and be smitten that he die, [1]*there shall* no blood *be shed* for him.

3 If the sun be risen upon [d]him, [2]*there shall be* blood *shed* for him; *for* he should make full [†]restitution; if he have nothing, [b]then he shall be [e]sold[G] for his [a]theft.

4 If the [a]theft be certainly found in his hand alive, whether it be ox, or ass, or sheep; he shall [†]restore [*,c]double.

5 ¶ [f,g]If a man shall cause a field or vineyard to be eaten, and shall put in his beast, and shall feed in another man's field; of the best of his own field, and of the best of his own vineyard, shall he make [†]restitution.

6 ¶ If fire break out, and catch in thorns, so that the stacks of

v.34–1533 BC
See footnote, *Time*, Rev. 10:6.

1
*a Theft*, Mark 7:22.
*b Commandment, fixing penalty for theft*, vs. 2–4; Deut. 8:2.
*c Damages and Compensation*, Ex. 21:19.

2
*d Thieves*, Deut. 24:7.
1 R. V. there shall be no bloodguiltiness

3
*e Servant*, Jer. 2:14.
2 R. V. there shall be bloodguiltiness

5
*f Commandment, concerning trespass*, Deut. 8:2.
*g Agriculture, laws concerning*, Gen. 3:23.

§ **RANSOM.** *Of a man's life*, Ex. 21:28–32; 30:12; Job 36:18; Psa. 49:7, 8; Prov. 6:35; 13:8; Hos. 13:14. *Of murderer, prohibited*, Num. 35:31, 32.
**Figurative**, Job 33:24; Isa. 35:10; 51:10; Matt. 20:28; 1 Tim. 2:6. See footnote, REDEMPTION, *of our souls*, Eph. 1:7.

* **FINE**, Num. 5:5–8. *For theft*, Ex. 22:4, 7–9; Prov. 6:30, 31. *For personal injury*, Ex. 21:22, 30. *For sin of ignorance*, Lev. 22:14. *For deception*, Lev. 6:5, 6. See footnote, DAMAGES AND COMPENSATION, Ex. 21:19.

† **RESTITUTION.** *To be made, for injury to life, limb, or property*, Ex. 21:30–36; Lev. 5:16; 6:5; 24:18; *for theft*, Ex. 22:1–4; Prov. 6:30, 31; Ezek. 33:15; *for dishonesty*, Lev 6:2–5; Luke 19:8.
See footnote, DAMAGES AND COMPENSATION, Ex. 21:19.

v.6–1533 BC
See footnote, *Time*, Rev. 10:6.

6
h *Arson*, 2 Sam.14: 30.

7
*Statute, fixing penalty for loss of property held in trust*, vs. 7–13; Deut. 8:2.
j *Neighbor*, Luke 10.29.
k *Money*, Jer. 32:9.

10
l *Property, personal*, Lev. 27:15.

11
m *Oath, a solemn qualification*, Num. 5:19.
n *Witness, qualified by oath*, Num. 35:30.

corn, or the standing corn, or the
field, be consumed *therewith*; he
that [h]kindled the fire shall surely
make †restitution.
7 ¶ [i]If a man shall deliver unto
his [j]neighbour [k]money or stuff
to keep, and it be [a]stolen out of
the man's house; if the [d]thief
be found, let him †,[c]pay *double.
8 [i]If the [d]thief be not found,
then the master of the house
shall [3]be brought unto the judges,
*to see* whether he have put
his hand unto his [j]neighbour's
goods.
9 [f]For all manner of ‡trespass,
*whether it be* for ox, for ass, for
sheep, for raiment, *or* [i]for any
manner of lost thing, which *another*
challengeth to be his, the
cause of both parties shall come
before the [4]judges; *and* whom
the [4]judges shall condemn, he
shall *,[c]pay †double unto his
[j]neighbour.
10 [i]If a man deliver unto his
[j]neighbour an [l]ass, or an ox, or a
sheep, or any beast, to keep; and
it die, or be hurt, or [a]driven
away, no man seeing *it*:
11 [i]*Then* shall an [m]oath of the
LORD be between [n]them both,
that he hath not put his hand unto
his neighbour's [l]goods; and
the owner of it shall accept *thereof*,
and he shall not †make *it*
good.
12 And [i]if [l]it be [a]stolen from
him, he shall make †restitution
unto the owner thereof.
13 If [l]it be torn in pieces, *then*
let him bring it *for* witness, *and*
he shall not make good that
which was torn.
14 ¶ And if a man ‖borrow
[l]*ought* of his neighbour, and it be
hurt, or die, the owner thereof
*being* not with it, [o]he shall surely
†make *it* good.
15 *But* if the owner thereof *be*
with [l]it, he shall not make *it*
good: if it *be* an hired *thing*, it
came for his hire.
16 ¶ And [p]if a man [q]entice a
[r]maid that is not betrothed, and
lie with her, he shall surely [s]endow
her to be his [t]wife.
17 If her father utterly refuse
to give her unto him, [p]he shall
pay money according to the
[s]dowry of [r]virgins.
18 ¶ [u,v]Thou shalt not suffer
a [5,] §,[w]witch to live.
19 ¶ [x]Whosoever lieth with a
beast shall surely be [y]put to
death.
20 ¶ He that [z]sacrificeth unto
*any* god, save unto the LORD
only, he shall be utterly [y]destroyed.
21 ¶ [a]Thou shalt neither vex a
[b]stranger, nor [c]oppress him:
for ye were strangers in the land
of E'gypt.
22 [d]Ye shall not [c]afflict any
[e]widow, or [f]fatherless child.
23 If thou [c]afflict [e,f]them in
any wise, and they [g]cry at all unto
me, [h]I will surely hear their
cry;
24 And my [i]wrath shall wax
hot, and I will [j]kill you with the
sword; and your wives shall be
[e]widows, and your children
fatherless.
25 ¶ If [k]thou [l]lend money to
*any of* my people *that is* [m]poor by
thee, [n]thou shalt not be to him
as [6]an usurer, neither shalt thou
lay upon him +usury.
26 [o]If [k]thou at all take thy

v.14–1533 BC
See footnote, *Time*, Rev. 10:6.

14
o *Statute, fixing penalty for loss of borrowed property*, Deut. 8:2.

16
p *Statute, fixing penalty for seduction*, Deut. 8:2.
q *Seduction*, Deut. 22:23.
r *Virgin*, Isa. 62:5.
s *Dowry*, Gen. 34: 12.
t *Marriage*, Gen. 34:9.

18
u *Statute, fixing penalty for witchcraft*, Deut. 8:2.
v *Punishment, death penalty*, Lev. 26:41.
w *Sorcery*, Isa. 47:9.
5 R. V. sorceress

19
x *Statute, fixing penalty for bestiality*, Deut. 8:2.
y *Punishment, death penalty*, Lev. 26:41.

20
z *Idolatry*, 1 Sam. 15:23.

21
a *Commandment, forbidding oppression, of foreigners*, Deut. 2:8.
b *Foreigners, Israelites forbidden to oppress*, Deut. 23: 20.
c *Injustice, forbidden*, Isa. 26:10.

22
d *Commandment, forbidding oppression, of widows and orphans*, Deut. 8:2.
e *Widow*, 2 Sam. 14:5.
f *Orphan, God the friend of*, Lam. 5:3.

23
g *Prayer, answer to, promised*, Acts 6:4.
h *Promises, to fatherless and widows*, 2 Cor. 1:20.

24
i *Anger, of God*, 2 Kin. 13:3.
j *Judgments*, Ex. 6:6.

25
k *Creditor, laws concerning*, Deut. 15:2.
l *Lending*, Deut. 15:2.
m *Poor, Mosaic laws concerning*, Prov. 21:13. n *Commandment, forbidding exaction of interest, from the poor*, Deut. 8:2. 6 R. V. a creditor.

26 o *Debt, security for*, 1 Sam. 22:2.

‡ **TRESPASS.** Ex. 22:9. *Of an ox*, Ex. 21:28–32, 35, 36. *Of a brother*, Matt. 18:15–18; Luke 17:3,4. *Creditor shall not enter debtor's house to take a pledge*, Deut. 24:10.

‖ **BORROWING.** *Dishonesty in*, Psa. 37:21. *Obligations in*, Ex. 22:14, 15. *Distress from*, Neh. 5:1–5; Prov. 22:7. *Compassion toward debtors, enjoined*, Neh. 5:6–13. *Christ's rule concerning*, Matt. 5:42.

See footnote, BORROWING TROUBLE, Matt. 6:25.

**Instances of:** *Israelites from the Egyptians*, Ex. 3:22; 11:2; 12:35.

§ **WITCHCRAFT**, 1 Sam. 15:23; 2 Kin. 9:22; Nah. 3:4. *Law concerning*, Ex. 22:18; Lev. 19:31; 20:6, 27. *Witch of Endor*, 1 Sam. 28:7–25. *Witches, to be destroyed*, Mic. 5:12; *destroyed*, 1 Sam. 28:3, 9.

See footnote, SORCERY, Isa. 47:9.

+ **INTEREST,** commonly called usury, but not signify-

[m]neighbour's [p]raiment to
[q,r]pledge, thou shalt deliver it
unto him by that the sun goeth
down:
27 For that *is* his covering only,
it *is* his [p]raiment for his skin:
wherein shall he sleep? and it
shall come to pass, when he
[g]crieth unto me, that [s,t]I will
hear; for [u]I *am* gracious.
28 ¶ [v,w,x]Thou shalt not [y,z]re-
vile [4]the gods,[G] [a]nor curse the
[b,c]ruler of thy people.[Q]
29 ¶ [d,e]Thou shalt not [f]delay
[7]*to offer* the first of thy ripe
fruits, and of thy liquors:[G] the
[g]firstborn of thy sons shalt thou
give unto me.
30 [d,e]Likewise shalt thou do
with thine oxen, *and* with thy
sheep: seven days it shall be
with his dam; on the eighth day
thou shalt give it me.
31 ¶ And ye [h]shall be [i]holy[G]
men unto me: [j]neither shall ye
eat *any* [k]flesh *that is* torn of
beasts in the field; ye shall cast
it to the dogs.

## CHAPTER 23

*Of slander and false witness. 3 Of justice. 4 Of charitableness. 10 Of the year of rest. 12 Of the sabbath. 13 Of idolatry. 14 Of the three feasts. 18 Of the blood and the fat of the sacrifice. 20 An Angel is promised, with a blessing, if they obey him.*

[a,b,c]THOU shalt not raise a
[d,e]false report: [f,g,h]put not
thine hand with the wicked to
be an [i]unrighteous witness.
2 [j]Thou shalt not follow a
[k,l]multitude to *do* evil; neither
shalt thou speak in a cause to
[1]decline[G] after many to wrest[G]
*judgment*:
3 [m]Neither shalt [n,o]thou countenance[G] a [p]poor man in his
cause.[G]
4 ¶ If thou[Q] meet thine [q]enemy's
ox or his ass going *astray, [r]thou
shalt surely [s]bring it back to
him again.
5 If thou see the [t,u]ass of him
that [v]hateth thee lying under his
burden, and wouldest forbear to
help him, [r,s]thou shalt surely help
with him.[Q]
6 ¶ [o,w]Thou shalt not wrest[G] the
judgment[G] of thy [p]poor in his
cause.
7 [o,x]Keep thee far from a false
matter; and the innocent and
righteous slay [o]thou not: for I
will not justify the [o,y]wicked.[T]
8 ¶ And [o,z,a]thou shalt take no
[b]gift:[G] for the gift blindeth [2,c]the
wise, and perverteth the [3]words
of the righteous.
9 ¶ Also [d]thou shalt not oppress a [e]stranger:[G] for ye know
the heart of a stranger,[G] seeing ye
were strangers[G] in the land of
[f]Ē'ġȳpt.
10 And [g]six years thou shalt
sow thy [h]land, and shalt gather
in the fruits thereof:
11 But [g]the [i]seventh *year* thou
shalt let [h]it †rest and lie still;
that the [j]poor of thy people may
eat: and what they leave the
beasts of the field shall eat. In
like manner thou shalt deal with
thy vineyard, *and* with thy
oliveyard.
12 [k]Six days thou shalt [l]do thy
[m]work, and on the [n]seventh day
thou shalt †rest: that thine ox
and thine ass may rest, and
the son of thy [o]handmaid,
and the [p]stranger,[G] may be refreshed.
13 And in all *things* that I have
said unto you [4,q]be circumspect:
and make no mention of the

v.26–1533 BC
See footnote, *Time*, Rev. 10:6.

p *Dress*, Zech. 3:4.
q *Surety*, Gen. 44:32.
r *Pawn*, Job 24:3.
27
s *Promise, to the poor*, 2 Cor. 1:20.
t *God, mercy of*, Gen. 2:2.
u *Grace of God*, Rom. 4:16.
28
v *Citizens, duties of*, Luke 15:15.
w *Commandment, against reviling rulers*, Deut. 8:2.
x Acts 23:5.
y *Blasphemy, forbidden*, 2 Sam. 12:14.
z *Speech, evil*, Col. 4:6.
a *Reverence*, Lev. 19:30.
b *Rulers, not to be reviled*, Ex. 18:21.
c *Magistrate*, Ezra 7:25.
29
d *Liberality, enjoined*, 1 Tim. 6:18.
e *Commandment, enjoining liberality, toward the house of God*, Deut. 8:2.
f *Procrastination*, Acts 24:25.
g *Firstborn*, Zech. 12:10.
7 R. V. to offer of the abundance of thy fruits,
31
h *Commandment, enjoining holiness*, Deut. 8:2.
i *Holiness, enjoined*, Ex. 39:30.
j *Sanitation and Hygiene*, Num. 31:23.
k *Food*, Psa. 136:25.

1
a *False Accusation, forbidden*, v. 7; 2 Tim. 3:3.
b *Justice, enjoined*, Deut. 33:21.
c *Injustice, forbidden*, Isa. 26:10.
d *Falsehood, forbidden*, Job 21:34.
e *Slander, forbidden*, Prov. 10:18.
f *Conspiracy, law against*, 1 Kin. 16:9.
g *Commandment, against false testimony, and conspiracy*, Deut. 8:2. h *Evidence, false, forbidden*, Deut. 17:6. i *False Witness, forbidden*, Matt. 19:18. 2 j *Commandment, against popular corruption*, Deut. 8:2. k *Evil Company, forbidden*, Prov. 13:20. l *Mob*, Acts 17:5. 1 R. V. turn aside after a multitude 3 m *Commandment, against unjust prejudice*, Deut. 8:2. n *Rulers, required to judge justly*, Ex. 18:21. o *Court, justice required of*, Ex. 18:26.

v.3–1533 BC
See footnote, *Time*, Rev. 10:6.

p *Poor*, Prov. 21:13.
4
q *Enemy*, Prov. 24:17.
r *Commandment, enjoining kindness to enemies*, Deut. 8:2.
s *Kindness, enjoined*, Acts 28:2.
5
t *Animals, kindness to*, Jer. 27:5.
u *Ass*, 2 Chr. 28:15.
v *Hatred*, Prov. 15:17.
6
w *Commandment, forbidding injustice to the poor*, Deut. 8:2.
7
x *Commandment, enjoining righteousness*, Deut. 8:2.
y *Wicked*, Psa. 73:3.
8
z *Commandment, against bribery*, Deut. 8:2.
a *Rulers, forbidden to take bribes*, Ex. 18:21.
b *Bribery, corrupts conscience*, 1 Sam. 8:3.
c *Conscience*, Acts 23:1.
2 R. V. them that have sight,
3 *Or*, cause
9
d *Commandment, against oppression, of foreigners*, Deut. 8:2.
e *Foreigners, to be treated with justice*, Deut. 23:20.
f *Egypt*, Gen. 41:8.
10
g *Agriculture*, Gen. 3:23.
h *Land*, Ruth 4:3.
11
i *Sabbatic Year*, Lev. 25:2.
j *Poor, Mosaic laws concerning*, Prov. 21:13.
12
k *Commandment, enjoining labor and rest*, Deut. 8.2.
l *Industry, enjoined*, 1 Kin. 11:28.
m *Labor*, Luke 10:7.
n *Sabbath*, Ex. 16:23.
o *Servant, to have rest on the Sabbath*, Jer. 2:14.
p *Foreigner*, Deut. 23:20.
13
q *Watchfulness*, Matt. 24:42.
4 R. V. take ye heed:

ing excessive interest. *Exaction of, from poor Hebrew, forbidden*, Ex. 22:25; Lev. 25:36, 37; Deut. 23:19. *Exaction of, from stranger, authorized*, Deut. 23:20. *Exaction of, unprofitable*, Prov. 28:8. *Exaction of, rebuked*, Neh. 5:1–13; Ezek. 22:12. *Non-exaction of, rewarded*, Psa. 15:5; Ezek. 18:8, 9, 17.

***STRAY.** *Animals straying to be returned*, Ex. 23:4; Deut. 22:1–3. *Instance of animals straying: Kish's*, 1 Sam. 9:3–20; 10:2, 14–16.

**† REST.** *On the Sabbath, enjoined*, Ex. 16:23; 20:10; 23:12; 31:15; 24:21; 35:2; Deut. 5:12, 14. See footnote, SABBATH, Ex. 16:23. *On first and last days of feasts of passover and tabernacles*, Ex. 12:16; Lev. 23:5–8, 39, 40; Num. 28:18, 25; 29:12, 35. *On day of pentecost*, Num. 28:26.

v.13–1533 BC
See footnote, *Time*, Rev. 10:6.

*r Idolatry, forbidden*, 1 Sam. 15: 23.

**14**
*s Annual Feasts*, Num. 15:3.

**15**
*t Passover*, Num. 9:5.
*u Seven*, Gen. 7:2.
*v Abib*, Ex. 13:4.
*w Liberality, enjoined*, 1 Tim. 6:18.

**16**
*x Pentecost, feast of harvest*, Acts 2:1.
*y First Fruits*, Deut. 18:4.
*z Tabernacle, feast of*, Deut. 16:13.

**17**
*a Worship, enjoined*, Gen. 22:5.

**18**
*b Offerings*, Lev. 6: 17.
*c Leaven*, Lev. 23: 17.
*d Fat*, Lev. 7:24.
5 R. V. feast

**19**
*e First Fruits*, Deut. 18:4.
*f Church, called House of the Lord*, 1 Kin. 9:3.
*g Goat*, Deut. 14:4.
*h Milk*, Job 10:10.

**20**
*i God, preserver*, vs. 21–31; Gen. 2:2.
*j Angel*, Ex. 14:19.

**21**
*k Obedience, enjoined*, Heb. 5:8.

**22**
*l Blessings, contingent upon obedience*, Deut. 11:26.
*m Righteous, promises to*, Psa. 64: 10.
*n Obedience, rewarded*, Heb. 5:8.
*o God, providence of*, Gen. 2:2.
*p Promise, to the obedient, of divine care*, 2 Cor. 1:20.

name of other [r]gods, neither let
it be heard out of thy mouth.
14 ¶ Three times thou shalt
keep a [s]feast unto me in the
year.
15 [s]Thou shalt keep the [t]feast
of unleavened bread: (thou
shalt eat unleavened bread [u]sev-
en days, as I commanded thee, in
the time appointed of the month
[v]Ā'bĭb; for in it thou camest out
from [f]Ē'gȳpt: and [w]none shall
appear before me empty:)
16 [s]And the [x]feast of harvest,
the [y]firstfruits of thy labours,
which thou hast sown in the
field: and the [s,z]feast of ingathering, *which is* in the end of the
year, when thou hast gathered in
thy labours out of the field.
17 Three times in the year all
thy males shall [a]appear before
the Lord GOD.
18 Thou shalt not offer the
blood of my [b]sacrifice[G] with [c]leav-
ened bread; neither shall the [d]fat
of my [5]sacrifice[G] remain until the
morning.
19 The first of the [e]firstfruits of
thy land thou shalt bring into the
[f]house of the LORD thy God.
Thou shalt not seethe[G] a [g]kid in
his mother's [h]milk.
20[T] ¶ Behold[Q], [i]I send an [j]Angel
before thee, to keep thee in the
way, and to bring thee into the
place which I have prepared.[S]
21 Beware of him, and [k]obey
his voice, provoke him not; for
he will not pardon your transgressions: for my name *is* in him.[Q]
22 But [l]if [m]thou shalt indeed
[n]obey his voice, and do all that I
speak; then [o,p]I will be an enemy
unto thine enemies, and an adversary unto thine adversaries.[Q S]
23 For mine [j]Angel shall go before thee, and bring thee in
unto the [q]Am'ôr-ītes, and the
[r]Hĭt-tītes, and the [s]Pĕr'ĭz-zītes,
and the ‡Cā'năan-ītes, the [t]Hī'-
vītes, and the [u]Jĕb'u-sītes: and
I will cut[G] them off.[T]
24 Thou shalt not [v]bow down
to their gods, nor serve them,
nor do after their works: but
thou shalt utterly overthrow
them, and [6]quite break down
their images.
25[S] And [w]ye shall serve the
LORD your God, and [o]he shall
[p]bless thy bread, and thy water;
and [x]I will [y]take [z]sickness away
from the midst of thee.
26 ¶ There shall nothing [a]cast
their young, nor be barren, in
thy land: the number of thy days
[b]I will fulfil.[S]
27 [b]I will send my fear before
thee, and will [7]destroy all the
people to whom thou shalt come,
and I will make all thine enemies turn their backs unto thee.
28 And [b]I will send [c]hornets before thee, which shall drive out
the [d]Hī'vīte, the ‡Cā'năan-īte,
and the [e]Hĭt'tīte, from before
thee.
29 [b]I will not drive them out
from before thee in one year;
lest the land become desolate,
and the beast of the field multiply against thee.
30 By little and little [b]I will
drive them out from before thee,
until thou be increased, and inherit the land.
31 And I will set thy bounds[G]

v.22–1533 BC
See footnote, *Time*, Rev. 10:6.

**23**
*q Amorites*, Gen. 14:13.
*r Hittites*, Judg. 1:26.
*s Perizzites*, Gen. 15:20.
*t Hivites*, Gen. 10: 17.
*u Jebusites*, Deut. 7:1.

**24**
*v Idolatry, forbidden*, 1 Sam. 15: 23.
6 R. V. break in pieces their pillars.

**25**
*w Commandment, to serve God*, Deut. 8:2.
*x Promise, to the obedient, of exemption from affliction*, 2 Cor. 1:20.
*y Healing, from God*, Acts 4:22.
*z Disease, healing of, from God*, Ex. 15:26.

**26**
*a Abortion*, Ex. 21: 22.
*b God, providence of*, Gen. 2:2.

**27**
7 R. V. discomfit

**28**
*c Hornet*, Josh. 24: 12.
*d Hivites*, Gen. 10: 17.
*e Hittites*, Judg. 1:26.

*On day of feast of trumpets*, Lev. 23:24, 25; Num. 29:1. *On day of atonement*, Lev. 16:29–31; 23:27, 28; Num. 29:7. *In sabbatic year*, Ex. 23:11; Lev. 25:1–4. *In year of jubilee*, Lev. 25:11, 12.

*Recommended by Jesus*, Mark 6:31, 32 (with Matt. 8:18, 24). *Heavenly*, 2 Thess. 1:7. *Spiritual*, Matt. 11:29; Heb. 4:1–11. See footnote, SPIRITUAL PEACE, Gal. 1:3.

‡ **CANAANITES.** *Eleven nations, descended from Canaan*, Gen. 10:15–19; Deut. 7:1; 1 Chr. 1:13–16. *Territory of*, Gen. 10:19; 12:6; 15:18; Ex. 23:31; Num. 13:29; 34:1–12; Josh. 5:1. *Territory of, given to the Israelites*, Gen. 12:6, 7; 15:18–21; 17:8; Ex. 23:23; Deut. 7:1–3; 32:49; Psa. 135:11, 12.

*Wickedness of*, Gen. 31:13; Lev. 18:25, 27, 28; 20:23. *Israelites warned against wickedness of*, Ex. 23:33; 34:12; Deut. 7:16; Josh. 23:13. *To be expelled from the land*, Ex. 33:2; 34:11. *To be destroyed*, Ex. 23:23, 24; 34:24; Deut. 7:1, 2; 19:1; 31:3–5; Josh. 24:8–13; Psa. 78:55. *Not expelled*, Josh. 17:12–18; Judg. 1:1–33; 3:1–3. *Defeat the Israelites*, Num. 14:45; Judg. 4:1–3. *Defeated, by the Israelites*, Num. 21:1–3; Josh. 11:1–16; Judg. 4:4–24; 5; *by the Egyptians*, 1 Kin. 9:16. *Chariots of*, Josh. 17:16, 18.

*Isaac forbidden by Abraham to take a wife from*, Gen. 28:1. *Israelites forbidden to marry*, Ex. 34:15, 16; Deut. 7:3, 4; Josh. 23:12, 13; 1 Kin. 11:2; Neh. 10:30. *Judah marries a woman of*, Gen. 38:2; 1 Chr. 2:3. *The exile Jews take wives from*, Ezra 9:2.

*Prophecy concerning*, Gen. 9:25–27.

v.31–1533 BC
See footnote, *Time,* Rev. 10:6.

*f* *Red Sea,* Ex. 10:19.
*g* *Philistines,* Gen. 26:14.
*h* *Euphrates,* Gen. 15:18.
*i* *Canaan, extent of,* Gen. 37:1.
8 R. V. wilderness

**32**
*j* *Fellowship, with the wicked, forbidden,* 1 Cor. 1:9.
*k* *Evil Company,* Prov. 13:20.

**33**
*l* *Idolatry,* 1 Sam. 15:23.

from the [f]Red sea even unto the
‖sea of the [g]Phĭ-lĭs′tĭneṣ, and
from the [8]desert unto the [h]river:
for [b]I will deliver the ‡inhabit-
ants of the [i]land into your hand;
and thou shalt drive them out
before thee.
32 [j]Thou shalt make no covenant[G] with [k]them, nor with their
gods.
33 They shall not dwell in thy
land, lest [k]they make thee sin
against me: for if thou [l]serve
their gods, it will surely be a
snare unto thee.

## CHAPTER 24

*Moses is called up into the mountain. 3 The people promise obedience. 4 Moses builds an altar, and twelve pillars. 6 He sprinkles the blood of the covenant. 9 The glory of God appears. 14 Aaron and Hur have the charge of the people. 15 Moses goes into the mountain, where he continues forty days and forty nights.*

**1**
*a* *Moses,* Ex. 2:10.
*b* *Aaron,* vs. 9, 10; Ex. 6:20.
*c* *Abihu,* Ex. 6:23.
*d* *Seventy,* Num. 11:16.
*e* *Government, Mosaic,* Isa. 22:21.
*f* *Senate,* Num. 11:16.
*g* *Worship, enjoined,* Gen. 22:5.

**2**
*h* *Grace of God,* Rom. 4:16.

**3**
*i* *Israel, receive the law, and covenant obedience,* Ex. 4:22.
*j* *Theocracy, established,* Judg. 8:23.
*k* *Word of God,* Psa. 119:9.
*l* *Decision, instances of,* Isa. 50:7.

AND he said unto [a]Mō′ṣeṣ,
Come up unto the LORD,
thou, and [b]Aâr′on, *Nā′dăb,
and [c]Ā-bī′hū, and [d]seventy of
the [e,f]elders of Ĭṣ′ra-el; and
[g]worship ye afar off.
2 And [a]Mō′ṣeṣ alone [h]shall
come near the LORD: but they
shall not come nigh[G]; neither
shall the people go up with him.
3 ¶ And [a]Mō′ṣeṣ came and told
the people all the words of the
LORD, and all the judgments[G]:
and all the [i]people answered
with one voice, and said, [j]All the
[k]words which the LORD hath
said [l]will we do.[Q]
4 And [a]Mō′ṣeṣ wrote all the
[k]words of the LORD, and rose up
early in the morning, and builded an [m]altar under the hill, and
twelve [n]pillars, according to the
twelve tribes of Ĭṣ′ra-el.
5 And he sent [o]young men of
the children of Ĭṣ′ra-el, which offered [p]burnt [q]offerings, and sacrificed [r]peace offerings of oxen
unto the LORD.
6 And [a]Mō′ṣeṣ took half of the
[s,t]blood, and put *it* in basons;
and half of the blood he sprinkled on the [m]altar.
7 And he took the book of the
[u]covenant, and read in the audience[G] of the people: and they said,
[j]All that the LORD hath said
[l]will we do, and be [v]obedient.
8 And [a]Mō′ṣeṣ took the
[s,t]blood, and sprinkled *it* on the
people, and said, Behold the
†blood of the covenant, which
the LORD hath made with you
concerning all these [k]words.[Q]
9 ¶ Then went up [a]Mō′ṣeṣ, and
[b]Aâr′on, *Nā′dăb, and [c]Ā-bī′hū,
and [d]seventy of the [e,f]elders of
Ĭṣ′ra-el:
10 And they [w]saw the [x]God of
Ĭṣ′ra-el: and *there was* under his
feet as it were a paved work of a
[y,z]sapphire stone, and as it were
the body of heaven in *his*
clearness[G].
11 And upon the nobles of the
children of [a]Ĭṣ′ra-el he laid not
his hand: also they saw [b]God,
and did eat and drink.
12 ¶ And the LORD said unto
[c]Mō′ṣeṣ, Come up to me into the
[d]mount, and be there: and I will
give thee [e]tables of ‡stone, and a
[f,g]law, and [h]commandments

v.4–1533 BC
See footnote, *Time,* Rev. 10:6.

**4**
*m* *Altar,* Gen. 8:20.
*n* *Pillar,* Gen. 28:18.

**5**
*o* *Young Men,* Prov. 1:4.
*p* *Offerings, burnt,* Lev. 6:17.
*q* *Jesus, typified in offerings,* Matt. 1:21.
*r* *Offerings, peace,* Lev. 6:17.

**6**
*s* *Blood, sacrificial,* Heb. 9:19.
*t* *Jesus, atoning blood of, typified,* Matt. 1:21.

**7**
*u* *Covenant,* Deut. 29:1.
*v* *Obedience, vows of,* Heb. 5:8.

**10**
*w* *Vision,* Acts 9:10.
*x* *God, appearances of, at Sinai,* Gen. 2:2.
*y* *Sapphire,* Job 28:6.
*z* *Colors, symbolical,* Ezek. 16:6.

**11**
*a* *Israel,* Ex. 4:22.
*b* *God, appearances of,* Gen. 2:2.

**12**
*c* *Moses,* Ex. 2:10.
*d* *Sinai,* Ex. 16:1.
*e* *Table, of testimony,* Ex. 31:18.
*f* *Law, of Moses, divine authority for,* Deut. 33:2.
*g* *Word of God, inspired,* Psa. 119:9.
*h* *Decalogue,* Ex. 20:3.

‖ **MEDITERRANEAN SEA.** *Mentioned in Scripture as, the sea,* Ezra 3:7; *the great sea,* Num. 34:6, 7; Josh. 1:4; 9:1; 15:12, 47; 23:4; Ezek. 47:10, 15, 20; 48:28; *sea of the Philistines,* Ex. 23:31; *the hinder sea,* Deut. 11:24; *the western sea,* Joel 2:20; Zech. 14:8.

* **NADAB.** *Son of Aaron,* Ex. 6:23. *Called to Mount Sinai with Moses and Aaron to worship,* Ex. 24:1, 9. *Set apart to priesthood,* Ex. 28:1, 4, 40–43. *Offers strange fire to God, and is destroyed,* Lev. 10:1, 2; Num. 3:4; 26:61. *Taken out of the camp,* Lev. 10:4, 5. *His father and brothers forbidden to mourn,* Lev. 10:6, 7.

† **BLOOD OF THE COVENANT,** Ex. 24:5–8; Zech. 9:11; Matt. 26:28; Luke 22:20; Heb. 9:18, 19, 22; 10:29; 13:20. See footnotes: BLOOD, *the life,* Gal. 9. 4; BLOOD, *sacrificial,* Heb. 9:19; OFFERINGS, Lev. 6:17.

‡ **STONES.** *Commandments engraved on,* Ex. 24:12; 31:18; 34:1–4; Deut. 4:13; 5:22; 9:9–11; 10:1–3. *The law of Moses written on,* Josh. 8:32. *Houses built of,* Isa. 9:10; Amos 5:11. *Temple built of,* 1 Kin. 5:17, 18; 7:9–12; Matt. 24:2; Luke 19:44; 21:5, 6. *Prepared in the quarries,* 1 Kin. 6:7. *Hewn,* Ex. 34:1; Deut. 10:1; 1 Kin. 5:17; 6:36; 7:9; 2 Kin. 12:12; 22:6; 1 Chr. 22:2; 2 Chr. 34:11; Lam. 3:9. *Sawn,* 1 Kin. 7:9. *Hewers of,* 1 Kin. 5:18; 2 Kin. 12:12; 1 Chr. 22:15. *City walls built of,* Neh. 4:3. *Memorial pillars of,* Gen. 28:18–22; 31:45–52; Josh. 4:2–9, 20–24; 24:26; 1 Sam. 7:12. *Great, as landmarks, of Abel,* 1 Sam. 6:18; *of Ezel,* 1 Sam. 20:19; *of Zoheleth,* 1 Kin. 1:9. *Cast upon accursed ground,* 2 Kin. 3:19, 25. *Used, in building altars,* Josh. 8:31; *for closing sepulchers,* Matt. 27:60; Mark 15:46; 16:3, 4. *Sepulchers hewn in,* Matt. 27:60; Mark 15:46; 16:3. *Idols made of,* Deut. 4:28; 28:36, 64; 29:17; 2 Kin. 19:18; Isa. 37:19; Ezek. 20:32. *Great, in Solomon's temple,* 1 Kin. 5:17, 18; 7:9–12.

v.12–1533 BC
See footnote, *Time*, Rev. 10:6.

i *Instruction, in religion*, Prov. 23:23.

13
j *Joshua*, Josh. 1:1.

14
k *Senate*, Num. 11:16.
l *Government, Mosaic*, Isa. 22:21.
m *Aaron*, Ex. 6:20.
n Ex. 17:10, 12.
o *Court, superior and inferior*, Ex. 18:26.

15
p *Pillar, of cloud and fire*, Ex. 13:21.

16
q *God, glory of*, Gen. 2:2.

18
r *Forty*, Jonah 3:4.

1
a *Inspiration*, Job 32:8.
b *Revelation, of statutes*, vs. 1–40; 2 Cor. 12:1.

2
c *Israel*, Ex. 4:22.
d *Liberality*, 1 Tim. 6:18.

which I have written; that thou mayest [i]teach them.[Q]

13 And [c]Mō′ṣeṣ rose up, and his minister[G] [j]Jŏsh′u-ȧ: and Mō′ṣeṣ went up into the [d]mount of God.

14 And he said unto the [k,l]elders, Tarry ye here for us, until we come again unto you: and, behold, [m]Aâr′on and [n]Hûr *are* with you: if any man have any matters to do, let him come unto [o]them.

15 ¶ And [c]Mō′ṣeṣ went up into the [d]mount, and a [p]cloud covered the mount.

16 And the [q]glory of the LORD abode upon mount [d]Sī′nāi, and the cloud covered it six days: and the seventh day he called unto [c]Mō′ṣeṣ out of the midst of the cloud.

17 And the sight of the [q]glory of the LORD *was* like devouring fire on the top of the [d]mount in the eyes of the children of [a]Ĭṣ′ra-el.[Q]

18 And [c]Mō′ṣeṣ went into the midst of the [p]cloud, and gat[G] him up into the [d]mount: and Mō′ṣeṣ was in the mount [r]forty days and forty nights.

## CHAPTER 25

*What the Israelites must offer for the making of the tabernacle. 10 The form of the ark. 17 The mercy seat with the cherubim. 23 The table, with the furniture thereof. 31 The candlestick, with the instruments thereof.*

AND the[Q] LORD [a,b]spake unto Mō′ṣeṣ, saying,

2 Speak unto the children of [c]Ĭṣ′ra-el, that they bring me an offering: of every man that [d]giveth it willingly with his heart ye shall take my offering.

3 And this *is* the offering which ye shall take of them; [e]gold, and [f]silver, and [g]brass,

4 And [h]blue, and purple, and scarlet, and fine [1]linen, and goats' *hair*,

5 And rams' skins [i]dyed [h]red, and [2,*]badgers' skins, and [3,j]shittim wood,

6 [k]Oil for the light, [l]spices for anointing oil, and for sweet [m]incense,

7 [n]Onyx stones, and [o]stones to be set in the [p]ephod,[G] and in the [q]breastplate.

8 And [r]let them make me a [s,t]sanctuary; that [u]I may dwell among them.

9 According to all that I [a]shew thee, *after* the pattern of the [v]tabernacle, and the pattern of all the [4]instruments[G] thereof, even so shall ye make *it*.

10 ¶ [Q]And they shall make an [†]ark *of* [3,j]shittim wood: two [w]cubits and a half *shall be* the length thereof, and a cubit[G] and a half the breadth thereof, and a cubit and a half the height thereof.

11 And thou shalt overlay [†]it with pure [e]gold, within and without shalt thou overlay it, and shalt make upon it a crown[G] of gold round about.

12 And thou shalt cast four rings of [e]gold for [†]it, and put *them* in the four [5]corners thereof; and two rings *shall be* in the one side of it, and two rings in the other side of it.

v.2–1533 BC
See footnote, *Time*, Rev. 10:6.

3
e *Gold*, Ezek. 7:19.
f *Silver*, 1 Chr. 28:14.
g *Brass*, Job 28:2.

4
h *Colors, symbolical*, Ezek. 16:16.
1 *Or*, cotton,

5
i *Dyeing*, Ex. 26:14.
j *Acacia*, Ex. 26:15.
2 R. V. sealskins.
3 R. V. acacia

6
k *Oil*, Deut. 12:17.
l *Spices*, 1 Kin. 10:2.
m *Incense*, Ex. 37:29.

7
n *Onyx*, Ezek. 28:13.
o *Precious Stones*, Ex. 39:10.
p *Ephod*, Ex. 28:6.
q *Breastplate*, Ex. 28:4.

8
r *Commandment, enjoining building a sanctuary*, Deut. 8:2.
s *Holy of Holies*, Ex. 26:33.
t *Church*, 1 Kin. 9:3.
u *God, dwells with the righteous*, Gen. 2:2.

9
v *Tabernacle, pattern of*, Ex. 27:9.
4 R. V. furniture

10
w *Cubit*, Ex. 36:9.

12
5 R. V. feet

---

*Magnificent, in Herod's temple*, Mark 13:1. *Skill in throwing*, Judg. 20:16; 1 Chr. 12:2.

**Figurative**, Gen. 49:24; Zech. 3:9. *Of temptation, stone of stumbling*, Isa. 8:14; Rom. 9:33; 1 Pet. 2:8.

*Of Christ*, Isa. 28:16; 1 Pet. 2:6; *the true foundation*, Isa. 28:16; Matt. 16:18; Eph. 2:20; *the rock from which flows the water of life*, 1 Cor. 10:4. *Of Christ's rejection, the rejected corner stone*, Psa. 118:22; Matt. 21:42–44; Mark 12:10; Luke 20:17, 18; Acts 4:11; 1 Pet. 2:4. *Of the impenitent heart*, Ezek. 36:26. *Of the witness of the Spirit, the white stone*, Rev. 2:17.

**Symbolical:** *Of the kingdom of Christ*, Dan. 2:34, 45.

***BADGER** (R. V. seal). *Skins of, were used as a covering of the tabernacle*, Ex. 25:5; 26:14; 35:7, 23; 36:19, 39:34; Num. 4:6, 8, 10–12, 25; *were made into shoes*, Ezek. 16:10.

† **ARK.** In the Tabernacle. *Called* ARK, OF THE COVENANT, Num. 10:33; Deut. 31:26; Josh. 4:7; 1 Sam. 4:3; 2 Sam. 15:24; 1 Chr. 15:25; 17:1; Jer. 3:16; Heb. 9:4; OF THE TESTIMONY, Ex. 30:6, Josh. 4:16; OF THE LORD, Josh. 4:11; 1 Sam. 4:6; 6:1; 2 Sam. 6:9; 1 Kin. 8:4; OF GOD, 1 Sam. 3:3; 4:11, 17, 22; 6:3; 14:18; 2 Sam. 6:7; 7:2; 15:25; 1 Chr. 13:12; 15:1, 2, 15, 24; 16:1; OF GOD'S STRENGTH, 2 Chr. 6:41.

*Directions for making*, Ex. 25:10–15; 35:12. *Construction of*, Ex. 37:1–5; Deut. 10:3.

*Sanctification of*, Ex. 30:26. *Holy*, 2 Chr. 8:11; 35:3.

*An oracle of God*, Num. 10:33; 14:44; Josh. 7:6–15; Judg. 20:27, 28; 1 Sam. 4:3, 4, 7; 1 Chr. 13:3; 16:4, 37; 2 Chr. 6:41; Psa. 132:8.

Contents of: *The law*, Ex. 25:16, 21; 40:20; Deut. 10:5; 31:26; 1 Kin. 8:9; 2 Chr. 5:10; *Aaron's rod*, Num. 17:10; Heb. 9:4; *pot of manna*, Ex. 16:33, 34; Heb. 9:4.

*Place of*, Ex. 26:33, 34; 40:21; 1 Sam. 3:3, 2 Sam. 7:2; Heb. 9:2–4.

v.13–1533 BC
See footnote, *Time,* Rev. 10:6.

13 And thou shalt make staves *of* [3,j]shittim wood, and overlay them with [e]gold.

14 And thou shalt put the staves into the rings by the sides of the †ark, that the ark may be borne with them.

15 The staves shall be in the rings of the †ark: they shall not be taken from it.

16 And thou shalt put into the †ark the ‡,[x]testimony which I shall give thee.[Q]

17 ¶ And thou shalt make a ‖,[y,z]mercy seat *of* pure [a]gold: two [b]cubits[G] and a half *shall be* the length thereof, and a cubit and a half the breadth thereof.

18[Q] And thou shalt make two [c]cherubims *of* [a]gold, *of* [d]beaten work shalt thou make them, in the two ends of the ‖mercy seat.

19 And make one cherub on the one end, and the other cherub on the other end: *even* of the ‖mercy seat shall ye make the [c]cherubims on the two ends thereof.

20 And the [c]cherubims shall stretch forth *their* wings on high, covering the mercy seat with their wings, and their faces *shall look* one to another; toward the ‖mercy seat shall the faces of the cherubims be.

21 And thou shalt put the ‖mercy seat above upon the †ark; and in the ark thou shalt put the ‡,[e]testimony that I shall give thee.

22 And [f]there I will meet with [g]thee, and I will [h]commune[G] with thee from above the ‖mercy seat, from between the two [c]cherubims which *are* upon the ark of the ‡testimony, of all *things* which I will [i]give thee in commandment unto the children of Is′ra-el.[Q]

23 ¶ Thou[Q] shalt also make a [j]table *of* [3,k]shittim wood: two [b]cubits *shall be* the length thereof, and a cubit the breadth thereof, and a cubit and a half the height thereof.

24 And thou shalt overlay [j]it with pure [a]gold, and make thereto a crown[G] of gold round about.

25 And thou shalt make unto [j]it a border of an [l,m]hand[G]breadth round about, and thou shalt make a golden crown[G] to the border thereof round about.

26 And thou shalt make for [j]it four rings of [a]gold, and put the rings in the four corners that *are* on the four feet thereof.

27 Over against the border shall the rings be for places of the staves to bear the [j]table.

28 And thou shalt make the staves *of* [3,k]shittim wood, and overlay them with [a]gold, that the [j]table may be borne with them.

29 And thou shalt make the dishes thereof, and [n]spoons thereof, and [6]covers thereof, and §bowls thereof, to [7]cover[G] withal:[G] *of* pure [a]gold shalt thou make them.

30 And thou shalt set upon the

**16**
*x* *Law, of Moses, preserved in ark,* Deut. 33:2.

**17**
*y* *God, mercy of,* Gen. 2:2.
*z* *Symbols, mercy seat, of divine mercy,* v. 22; Heb. 9:9.

*a* *Gold,* Ezek. 7:19.
*b* *Cubit,* Ex. 36:9.

**18**
*c* *Cherubim,* Ex. 37:7.
*d* Num. 8:4.

**21**
*e* *Word of God, inspired,* Psa. 119:9.

**22**
*f* *Shekinah,* Lev. 16:2.

v.22–1533 BC
See footnote, *Time,* Rev. 10:6.

*g* *Prophets, inspiration of,* Isa. 3:2.
*h* *Communion, with God,* 2 Cor. 13:14.
*i* *Inspiration,* Job 32:8.

**23**
*j* *Shewbread, table of,* Ex. 35:13.
*k* *Acacia,* Ex. 26:15.

**25**
*l* *Handbreadth,* 1 Kin. 7:26.
*m* *Measure, linear,* Deut. 25:15.

**29**
*n* *Spoons,* Num. 4:7.
6 R. V. the flagons
7 R. V. pour out

*How prepared for conveyance,* Num. 4:5, 6, 15. *Carried by Kohathites,* Num. 3:30, 31; 4:4, 15; Deut. 10:8; 1 Chr. 15:2, 12, 15. On special occasions carried by priests: *Crossing Jordan,* Josh. 3:6, 14–17; *at siege of Jericho,* Josh. 6:6.
*Taken to battle,* Josh. 6:6–20; 1 Sam. 4:3–22. *Captured by the Philistines,* 1 Sam. 4:10, 11; Psa. 78:61. *Returned by the Philistines,* 1 Sam. 6. *Remains, at the house of Abinadab,* 1 Sam. 7:1, 2; 2 Sam. 6:3, 4; 1 Chr. 13:7; *in the house of Obed-edom,* 2 Sam. 6:10–12; 1 Chr. 13:13, 14. *Transferred to Jerusalem,* 2 Sam. 6: 12–17; 1 Chr. 15:2–28.
*Set up, in Shiloh,* Josh. 18:1; 1 Sam. 4:3, 4; *in Bethel,* Judg. 20:27, 28; *in Jerusalem,* 2 Sam. 6:12–17; 15:24–29; 1 Chr. 6:31; 15; 16:1; 2 Chr. 1:4. *Removed from Jerusalem by Zadok at the time of Absalom's revolt, but returned by command of David,* 2 Sam. 15:24–29. *Transferred to Solomon's temple,* 1 Kin. 8:6–9; 2 Chr. 5:2–9. *Restored to the temple,* 2 Chr. 35:3.
*Prophecy concerning,* Jer. 3:16. *In John's vision,* Rev. 11:19.

‡ **TESTIMONY.** *The commandments revealed to Moses,* Ex. 25:16; Deut. 4:44, 45; 1 Kin. 2:3. *Kept in the ark,* Ex. 25:16, 21. *Engraved on tablets,* Ex. 31:18; 32:15; 38:21. *Mercy seat was over,* Ex. 26:34; 30:6; 40:20. *Ark, called* ARK OF, Ex. 25:22; 26:34; 40:3, 5, 20, 21.
*Tabernacle, called* TABERNACLE OF, Num. 1:50, 53; 9:15, 10:11.

‖ **MERCY SEAT.** *Description of,* Ex. 25:17–22. *Made by Bezaleel,* Ex. 37:1, 6–9. *Placed on the ark of the testimony,* Ex. 26:34; 30:6; 31:7; 40:20; Heb. 9:5. *Materials of, to be a free will offering,* Ex. 35:4–12.
*Sprinkled with blood,* Lev. 16:14, 15. *The shekinah upon,* Ex. 25:22; 30:6, 36; Lev. 16:2; Num. 7:89; 17:4; 1 Sam. 4:4; 2 Sam. 6:2; 1 Chr. 13:6; Psa. 80:1; Psa. 99:1; Isa. 37:16; Heb. 4:16.
*In Solomon's temple,* 1 Chr. 28:11.

§ **BOWL.** *Made of gold, for the tabernacle,* Ex. 25:29; 37:16; *for the temple,* 2 Kin. 25:15; Chr. 28:17. *Made of silver,* Num. 4:7; 7:13, 19, 25, 31, 37, 43, 49, 55, 61, 67, 73, 79, 84.
See footnote, BASIN, 1 Kin. 7:50.
**Figurative,** Eccl. 12:6.

v.6–1533 BC
See footnote, *Time,* Rev. 10:6.

**31**
8 R. V. even its base, and its shaft;

**33**
o *Almond,* Gen.43: 11.

**37**
p *Seven,* Gen. 7:2.
q *Lamp,* Ex. 27: 20.

**38**
r *Snuffers,* 1 Kin. 7:50.
9 Am.R.V. snuffers

table [j]shewbread before me alway.[Q]

31 ¶ And thou shalt make a +candlestick[G] *of* pure [a]gold: *of* beaten work shall the candlestick[G] be made: [8]his shaft, and his branches, his bowls, his knops,[G] and his flowers, shall be of the same.

32 And six branches shall come out of the sides of it; three branches of the +candlestick out of the one side, and three branches of the candlestick[G] out of the other side:

33 Three bowls made like unto [o]almonds, *with* a knop[G] and a flower in one branch; and three bowls made like almonds in the other branch, *with* a knop[G] and a flower: so in the six branches that come out of the +candlestick.[G]

34 And in the +candlestick[G] *shall be* four bowls made like unto [o]almonds, *with* their knops[G] and their flowers.

35 And *there shall be* a knop[G] under two branches of the same, and a knop[G] under two branches of the same, and a knop[G] under two branches of the same, according to the six branches that proceed out of the +candlestick.[G]

36 Their knops[G] and their branches shall be of the same: all of it *shall be* one beaten work *of* pure [a]gold.

37 And thou shalt make the [p]seven [q]lamps thereof: and they shall light the lamps thereof, that they may give light over[G] against it.

38 And the [9,r]tongs thereof, and the snuffdishes thereof, *shall be of* pure [a]gold.

39 *Of* a talent[G] of pure gold shall he make +it, with all these vessels.

40 And [s]look[G] that thou make *them* after their ⊙pattern, which was shewed thee in the [t]mount.[Q]

## CHAPTER 26

*The ten curtains of the tabernacle. 7 The eleven curtains of goats' hair. 14 The covering of rams' skins. 15 The boards of the tabernacle with their sockets and bars. 31 The vail for the ark. 36 The hanging for the door.*

MOREOVER[Q] [a]thou shalt make the [b]tabernacle *with* ten *,[c]curtains *of* fine twined [d]linen, and [e]blue, and [e]purple, and [e]scarlet: [1]*with* [f]cherubims of cunning[G] [g]work shalt thou make them.

2 The length of one *curtain *shall be* eight and twenty [h]cubits,[G] and the breadth of one curtain four cubits[G]: and every one of the curtains shall have one measure.

3 The five *curtains shall be coupled together one to another; and *other* five curtains *shall be* coupled one to another.

4 And thou shalt make loops of [e]blue upon the edge of the one *curtain from the selvedge in the coupling; and likewise shalt thou make in the uttermost edge of *another* curtain, in the coupling of the second.

5 Fifty loops shalt thou make in the one *curtain, and fifty loops shalt thou make in the edge of the curtain that *is* in the coupling of the second; that the loops may take hold one of another.

6 And thou shalt make fifty [2]taches[G] of [i]gold, and couple the *curtains together with the [2]taches[G]: and it shall be one [b]tabernacle.

v.39–1533 BC
See footnote, *Time,* Rev. 10:6.

**40**
s Heb. 8:5.
t *Sinai,* Ex. 16:1.

**1**
a *Revelation, concerning the tabernacle,* vs. 1–37; 2 Cor. 12:1.
b *Tabernacle, description of,* vs. 1–37: Ex. 27:9.
c *Tapestry,* Prov. 7:16.
d *Linen,* Ezek. 27: 16.
e *Colors, symbolical,* Ezek. 16:16.
f *Cherubim,* Ex. 37:7.
g *Embroidery,* Ezek. 26:16.
1 Am. R. V. with cherubim the work of the skillful workman

**2**
h *Cubit* Ex. 36:9.

**6**
i *Gold,* Ezek. 7:19.
2 R. V. clasps

**+ CANDLESTICK. Of the tabernacle:** *Made after divinely revealed pattern,* Ex. 25:31–40; 37:17–24; Num. 8:4. *Place of,* Ex. 26:35; 40:24, 25; Heb. 9:2. *Furniture of,* Ex. 25:38; 37:23; Num. 4:9, 10. *Lamps of, burned every night,* Ex. 27:20, 21; *trimmed every morning,* Ex. 30:7. *Carried by Kohathites,* Num. 4:4, 15. *Called* THE LAMP OF GOD, 1 Sam. 3:3.
**Of the temple:** *Ten branches of,* 1 Kin. 7:49, 50. *Of gold,* 1 Chr. 28:15; 2 Chr. 4:20. *Taken with other spoils to Babylon,* Jer. 52:19.
**Symbolical,** Zech. 4:2, 11; Rev. 1:12, 13, 20; 2:5; 11:3, 4.

**⊙ PATTERN.** *Of the tabernacle, revealed to Moses,* Ex. 25:9, 40; 26:30; 27:8; Heb. 8:5. *Of the temple, revealed to David,* 1 Chr. 28:11–19. *Of altar of incense,* Ex. 30:1–10.

*** CURTAINS.** *For tabernacle,* Ex. 26; 27:9–18; 36: 8–18. *In the palace of Ahasuerus,* Esth. 1:6.
See footnote, TAPESTRY, Prov. 7:16.
**Figurative,** Isa. 40:22; 54:2; Jer. 4:20; 10:20; 49:29.

v.7–1533 BC
See footnote, *Time*, Rev. 10:6.

7
*i* *Goat*, Deut. 14:4.

9
3 R. V. tent.

11
*k* *Brass*, Job 28:2.

14
*l* *Ram*, Ex. 39:34.
*m* *Seal*, Ex. 25:5.
4 R. V. of sealskins above.

15
5 R. V. of acacia

7 ¶ And thou shalt make *curtains *of* [i]goats' *hair* to be a covering upon the tabernacle: eleven curtains shalt thou make.

8 The length of one *curtain *shall be* thirty [h]cubits,[G] and the breadth of one curtain four cubits[G]: and the eleven curtains *shall be all* of one measure.

9 And thou shalt couple five *curtains by themselves, and six curtains by themselves, and shalt double the sixth curtain in the forefront of the [3, b]tabernacle.

10 And thou shalt make fifty loops on the edge of the one curtain *that is* outmost in the coupling, and fifty loops in the edge of the curtain which coupleth the second.

11 And thou shalt make fifty [2]taches of [k]brass, and put the [2]taches[G] into the loops, and couple the [b]tent together, that it may be one.

12 And the remnant that remaineth of the *curtains of the tent, the half curtain that remaineth, shall hang over the backside of the [b]tabernacle.

13 And a [h]cubit[G] on the one side, and a cubit on the other side of that which remaineth in the length of the curtains of the tent, it shall hang over the sides of the [b]tabernacle on this side and on that side, to cover it.

14 And thou shalt make a covering for the [b]tent *of* [l]rams' skins †dyed [e]red, and a covering [4]above *of* [m]badgers' skins.

15 ¶ And thou shalt make boards for the [b]tabernacle [5]*of* ‡shittim wood standing up.

16 Ten [h]cubits[G] *shall be* the length of a board, and a cubit and a half *shall be* the breadth of one board.

17 Two tenons[G] *shall there be* in one board, [6]set in order one against another: thus shalt thou make for all the boards of the [b]tabernacle.

18 And thou shalt make the boards for the [b]tabernacle, twenty boards on the south side southward.

19 And thou shalt make forty sockets of [n]silver under the twenty boards; two sockets under one board for his two tenons, and two sockets under another board for his two tenons.

20 And for the second side of the [b]tabernacle on the north side *there shall be* twenty boards:

21 And their forty sockets *of* [n]silver; two sockets under one board, and two sockets under another board.

22 And for the [7]sides of the [b]tabernacle westward thou shalt make six boards.

23 And two boards shalt thou make for the corners of the [b]tabernacle in the [7]two sides.

24 And they shall be coupled together beneath, and they shall be coupled together above the head of it unto one ring: thus shall it be for them both; they shall be for the two corners.

25 And they shall be eight boards, and their sockets *of* [n]silver, sixteen sockets; two sockets under one board, and two sockets under another board.

26 ¶ And thou shalt make bars [5]*of* ‡shittim wood; five for the boards of the one side of the [b]tabernacle,

27 And five bars for the boards of the other side of the [b]tabernacle, and five bars for the boards of the side of the tabernacle, for the [7]two sides westward.

v.17–1533 BC
See footnote, *Time*, Rev. 10:6.

6 R. V. joined one to another:

19
*n* *Silver*, 1 Chr. 28:14.

22
7 R. V. hinder part

† **DYEING**, Ex. 25:5; 26:14; Isa. 63:1; Ezek. 23:15.
‡ **ACACIA**, A. V. shittah and shittim, a tree, the wood of which is fragrant. *Planted and cultivated*, Isa. 41:19. Articles made of: *The ark of the covenant*, Ex. 25:10; 37:1; Deut. 10:3; *staves of the ark*, Ex. 25:13; 37:4; 38:6; *table of shewbread*, Ex. 37:10; *altar of incense*, Ex. 30:1; 37:25; *boards in the tabernacle*, Ex. 26:15–37; 36:20, 21; *the altar of burnt offerings*, Ex. 38:1, 6.

v.28–1533 BC
See footnote, *Time*, Rev. 10:6.

28 And the middle bar in the midst of the boards shall reach from end to end.

29 And thou shalt overlay the boards with [i]gold, and make their rings *of* gold *for* places for the bars: and thou shalt overlay the bars with gold.

30 And thou shalt rear up the [b]tabernacle according to the [o]fashion thereof which was [p]shewed thee in the [q]mount.[Q]

31 ¶ [Q]And thou shalt make a ‖vail *of* [e]blue, and [e]purple, and [e]scarlet, and fine twined [d]linen of cunning[G] work: with [f]cherubims shall it be made:

32 And thou shalt hang ‖it upon four [r]pillars [5]of ‡shittim *wood* overlaid with [i]gold: their [s]hooks *shall be of* gold, upon the four sockets of [n]silver.

33 And thou shalt hang up the ‖vail under the [2]taches,[G] that thou mayest bring in thither within the vail the [t]ark of the [u]testimony: and the vail shall divide unto you between the §holy *place* and the +most holy.[Q]

34 And thou shalt put the [v]mercy seat upon the [t]ark of the [u]testimony in the +most holy *place*.

35 And thou shalt set the [w]table without[G] the ‖vail, and the [x]candlestick[G] over against the table on the side of the [b]tabernacle toward the south: and thou shalt put the table on the north side.[Q]

36 ¶ And thou shalt make an hanging for the door of the [b]tent, *of* [e]blue, and purple, and scarlet,[G] and fine twined linen, [8]wrought with needlework.

37 And thou shalt make for the hanging five [r]pillars [5]*of* ‡shittim *wood*, and overlay them with [i]gold, *and* their [s]hooks *shall be of* gold: and thou shalt cast five sockets of [y]brass[G] for them.

## CHAPTER 27

*The altar of burnt offering, with the vessels thereof. 9 The court of the tabernacle enclosed with hangings and pillars. 18 The measure of the court. 20 The oil for the lamp.*

AND [a]thou shalt make an [b]altar [1]*of* [c]shittim wood, five [d]cubits long,[G] and five cubits broad; the altar shall be foursquare:[G] and the height thereof *shall be* three cubits.

2 And thou shalt make the horns of [b]it upon the four corners thereof: his horns shall be of the same: and thou shalt overlay it with [e]brass.

3 And thou shalt make his pans to receive his ashes, and his [f]shovels, and his [g]basons, and his *fleshhooks, and his firepans: all the vessels thereof thou shalt make *of* [e]brass.

4 And thou shalt make for [b]it a [h]grate of network *of* [e]brass; and upon the net shalt thou make four brasen[G] rings in the four corners thereof.

5 And thou shalt put it under the [2]compass[G] of the [b]altar beneath, that the net may be even to the midst of the altar.[G]

6 And thou shalt make staves for the [b]altar, staves[G] [1]*of* [c]shittim

**30**
o *Pattern*, Ex. 25:40.
p *Prophets, inspiration of*, Isa. 3:2.
q *Sinai*, Ex. 16:1.

**32**
r *Pillar*, Gen. 28:18.
s *Hooks*, Ex. 36:36.

**33**
t *Ark, place of*, Ex. 25:10.
u *Testimony, the commandments revealed to Moses*, Ex. 25:16.

**34**
v *Mercy Seat*, Ex. 25:17.

**35**
w *Shewbread, table of*, Ex. 35:13.
x *Candlestick*, Ex. 25:31.

v.36–1533 BC
See footnote, *Time*, Rev. 10:6.

**36**
8 R. V. the work of the embroiderer.

**37**
y *Brass*, Job 28:2.

**1**
a *Revelation, of the pattern of the altar*, vs. 1–8; 2 Cor. 12:1.
b *Altar, of burnt offerings*, Gen. 8:20.
c *Acacia*, Ex. 26:15.
d *Cubit*, Ex. 36:9.
1 R. V. of acacia

**2**
e *Brass*, Job 28:2.

**3**
f *Shovel*, Num. 4:14.
g *Basin*, 1 Kin. 7:50.

**4**
h *Grate*, Ex. 38:4,5.

**5**
2 R. V. ledge round

‖ **VAIL.** Hangings used in the tabernacle to divide the holy of holies from the holy place, Ex. 26:31–33; 35:12; 39:34; 40:21. *Called* THE SECOND VEIL, Heb. 9:3. *A type of the humanity of Christ*, Heb. 10:20. *Ordinances prescribing*, Ex. 26:31–33. *Made by Bezaleel and Aholiab*, Ex. 36:35, 36.
**Figurative,** Heb. 6:19.

§ **HOLY PLACE,** in the tabernacle and temple. *Was separated from the most holy place by the vail*, Ex. 26:33.
Contents of: *The altar of incense*, Ex. 30:1–6; 40:5, 26; *the table of shewbread*, Ex. 40:4, 24; Heb. 9:2; *the candlestick*, Ex. 26:35; 40:4, 24; Heb. 9:2.
*Priests ministered in*, Ex. 29:30; 39:1, 41; Heb. 9:6.
*Priests required to eat sin offering in*, Lev. 6:25, 26; 10:17.
See footnote, SANCTUARY, Lev. 4:6.

+ **HOLY OF HOLIES.** *In the tabernacle*, Lev. 4:6. *In the temple*, 1 Kin. 6:16. *Separated from the holy place by the vail*, Ex. 26:33; Heb. 9:3. *Contained mercy seat and ark of the testimony*, Ex. 26:34; 40:20, 21; 1 Kin. 8:6; *the cherubim*, Ex. 25:18–20; 26:34; 37:7–9 (with 26:34); Heb. 9:3–5.
*Divine dwelling place*, Ex. 25:8, 21, 22; Ex. 26:34; Lev. 16:2; Num. 7:89 (with Ex. 26:34). *Entered by the high priest on the day of atonement*, Lev. 16:12, 13 (with Ex. 26:34); Heb. 9:6, 7. *Atonement made for*, Lev. 16:15–17, 33 (with Ex. 26:34).
See footnote, HOLY PLACE, above.
**Figurative,** Ezek. 11:16.
**Symbolical,** Heb. 8:2, 5; 9:8, 12.

* **FLESHHOOK.** *Used in the tabernacle*, Ex. 27:3; 38:3; Num. 4:14; 1 Sam. 2:13, 14. *In the temple, made of gold*, 1 Chr. 28:17; *made of brass*, 2 Chr. 4:16.

v.6–1533 BC
See footnote, *Time*, Rev. 10:6.

wood, and overlay them with brass.

7 And the staves shall be put into the rings, and the staves shall be put upon the two sides of the [b]altar, to bear it.

8 Hollow with boards shalt thou make it: as [i]it was shewed thee in the [j]mount, so shall they make *it*.

9 ¶ And thou shalt make the [k]court of the †tabernacle: for the south side southward *there shall be* [l,m]hangings for the court *of* fine twined [n]linen of an hundred [o]cubits[G] long for one side:

10 And the twenty [p]pillars thereof and their twenty sockets *shall be of* [q]brass[G]; the [r]hooks of the pillars and their fillets[G] *shall be of* [s]silver.

11 And likewise for the north side in length *there shall be* [l,m]hangings of an hundred [o]*cubits* long, and his twenty [p]pillars and their twenty sockets *of* [q]brass[G]; the [r]hooks of the pillars and their fillets[G] *of* [s]silver.

12 And *for* the breadth of the [k]court on the west side *shall be* [l,m]hangings of fifty [o]cubits[G]: their [p]pillars ten, and their sockets ten.

13 And the breadth of the [k]court on the east side eastward *shall be* fifty [o]cubits.

14 The [l,m]hangings of one side *of the gate shall be* fifteen [o]cubits[G]: their [p]pillars three, and their sockets three.

15 And on the other side *shall be* [l,m]hangings fifteen [o]*cubits*: their [p]pillars three, and their sockets three.

16 And for the gate of the [k]court *shall be* an [l,m]hanging of twenty cubits[G], *of* [t]blue, and [t]purple, and [t]scarlet, and fine twined [n]linen, [u]wrought with needlework: *and* their [p]pillars *shall be* four, and their sockets four.

17 All the [p]pillars round about the [k]court *shall be* filleted[G] with [s]silver; their hooks *shall be of* silver, and their sockets *of* [q]brass[G].

18 The length of the [k]court *shall be* an hundred [o]cubits, and the breadth fifty every where, and the height five cubits *of* fine twined [n]linen, and their sockets *of* [q]brass[G].

19 All the [3]vessels of the †tabernacle in all the service thereof, and all the pins thereof, and all the pins of the [k]court, *shall be of* [q]brass.

20 ¶ And thou shalt command the children of [v]Is'ra-el, that they bring thee pure [w]oil olive beaten for the light, to cause the ‡lamp to burn always.

**8**
*i Pattern*, Ex. 25:40.
*j Sinai*, Ex. 16:1.

**9**
*k Court, of tabernacle*, Ex. 38:9.
*l Curtains*, Ex. 26:1.
*m Tapestry*, vs. 9–17; Prov. 7:16.
*n Linen*, Ezek. 27:16.
*o Cubit*, Ex. 36:9.

**10**
*p Pillar*, Gen. 28:18.
*q Brass*, Job 28:2.
*r Hooks*, Ex. 36:36.
*s Silver*, 1 Chr. 28:14.

v.14–1533 BC
See footnote, *Time*, Rev. 10:6.

**16**
*t Colors, symbolical*, Ezek. 16:16.
*u Embroidery*, Ezek. 26:16.

**19**
3 R. V. instruments

**20**
*v Israel*, Ex. 4:22.
*w Oil*, Deut. 12:17.

† **TABERNACLE.** *One existed before Moses received the pattern authorized on Mount Sinai*, Ex. 33:7-11. *The one instituted by Moses was called* TABERNACLE OF TESTIMONY, Ex. 38:21; Num. 1:50; TABERNACLE OF WITNESS, Num. 17:7, 8; 2 Chr. 24:6; TEMPLE OF THE LORD, 1 Sam. 1:9; 3:3; HOUSE OF THE LORD, Josh. 6:24.

*Pattern of, revealed to Moses*, Ex. 25:9; 26:30; 39:32, 42, 43; Acts 7:44; Heb. 8:5. *Materials for, voluntarily offered*, Ex. 25:1-8; 35:4-29; 36:3-7. *Value of the substance contributed for*, Ex. 38:24-31. *Workmen who constructed it were inspired*, Ex. 31:1-11; 35:30-35.

Description of: *Frame of*, Ex. 26:15-30; 36:20-34; *outer covering of*, Ex. 5:5; 26:7-14; 36:14-19; *second covering of*, Ex. 25:5; 26:14; 35:7, 23; 36:19; 39:34; *curtains of*, Ex. 26:1-14, 31-37; 27:9-16; 35:15, 17; 36:8-19, 35, 37; *court of*, Ex. 27:9-17: 38:9-18; 40:8, 33.

*Holy place of*, Ex. 26:31-37; 40:22-26; Heb. 9:2-6, 8. *The most holy place of*, Ex. 26:33-35; 40:20, 21; Heb. 9:3-5, 7, 8.

*Furniture of*, Ex. 25:10-40; 27:1-8, 19; 37; 38:1-8; Ex. 40:1-5, 20-26. See footnotes: ALTAR, Gen. 8:20; ARK, Ex. 25:10; CANDLESTICK, Ex. 25:31; CHERUBIM, Ex. 37:7; LAVER, Ex. 30:18; MERCY SEAT, Ex. 25:17; SHEWBREAD, Ex. 3[illegible]:13.

*Completed*, Ex. 39:32. *Dedicated*, Num. 7. *Sanctified*, Ex. 29:43; 40:9-16; Num. 7:1. *Anointed with holy oil*, Ex. 30:25, 26; Lev. 8:10; Num. 7:1. *Sprinkled with blood*, Lev. 16:15-20; Heb. 9:21, 23. *Filled with the cloud of glory*, Ex. 40:34-38.

*How prepared for removal during the journeyings of the Israelites*, Num. 1:51; 4:5-15. *How, and by whom carried*, Num. 4:5-33; 7:6-9. *Strangers forbidden to enter*, Num. 1:51. *Defilement of, punished*, Lev. 15:31; Num. 19:13, 20. *Israelites worshiped at*, Num. 10:3; 20:6; 25:6; Psa. 27:4. *Offerings brought to*, Lev. 17:4; Num. 31:54; Deut. 12:5, 6, 11-14.

*Duties of the Levites concerning*, see footnote, LEVITES, Deut. 10:8.

*Duties of the priests in relation to*, see footnote, PRIESTS, Lev. 1:5.

*Tribes encamped around, while in the wilderness*, Num. 2. *Carried in front of the children of Israel in the line of march*, Num. 10:33-36; Josh. 3:3-6. *All males required to appear before, three times each year*, Ex. 23:17. *Tabernacle tax*, Ex. 30:11-16.

*The Lord reveals himself at*, Lev. 1:1; Num. 1:1; 7:89; 12:4-10; Deut. 31:14, 15.

*Pitched, at Shiloh*, Josh. 18:1; 19:51; Judg. 18:31; 21:19; 1 Sam. 2:14; 4:3, 4; Jer. 7:12, 14; *at Nob*, 1 Sam. 21:1-6; *at Bethel*, Judg. 20:18, 26, 27; *at Gibeon*, 1 Chr. 21:29; 2 Chr. 1:3. *A duplicate made by David, and pitched on Mount Zion*, 1 Chr. 15:1; 16:1, 2; 2 Chr. 1:4. *Priests were overseers of*, 1 Chr. 24:5. *Solomon offers sacrifice at*, 2 Chr. 1:3-6. *Brought to the temple by Solomon*, 2 Chr. 5:5 (with 1 Kin. 8:1, 4, 5).

*Symbol of spiritual things*, Psa. 15:1; Heb. 8:2, 5; 9:1-12, 24. See footnote, TEMPLE, 1 Kin. 6:17.

‡ **LAMP.** *For the tabernacle*, Ex. 25:31-40; 35:14; 37:17-23; 39:37. *Kept burning at night in the tabernacle, and cared for by priests*, Ex. 27:20, 21; 30:7, 8; Lev. 24:2-4; 1 Sam. 3:3.

v.21–1533 BC
See footnote, *Time*, Rev. 10:6.

21
*x High Priest, duties of*, Lev. 21:10.
*y Priest, duties of*, Lev. 1:5.
4 R. V. tent of meeting

21 In the [4]tabernacle of the
congregation without[G] the vail,
which *is* before the testimony,
[x]Aâr′on and his [y]sons shall order[G] it from evening to morning
before the LORD: *it shall be* a
statute for ever unto their generations on the behalf of the
children of [v]Ĭs′ra-el.[Q]

## CHAPTER 28

*Aaron and his sons are set apart for the priest's office. 2 Holy garments are appointed. 6 The ephod. 15 The breastplate with twelve precious stones. 30 The Urim and Thummim. 31 The robe of the ephod, with pomegranates and bells. 36 The plate of the miter. 39 The embroidered coat. 40 The garments for Aaron's sons.*

1
*a Call, to special religious duty*, Phil. 3:14.
*b Aaron, priesthood of*, vs. 1–43; Ex. 6:20.
*c Minister, call of*, Rom. 15:16.
*d Jesus, priesthood of, typified*, Matt. 1:21.
*e Priest*, Lev. 1:5.
*f Types, of the Messiah*, Heb. 10:1.
*g Nadab*, Ex. 24:1.
*h Abihu*, Ex. 6:23.
*i Eleazar*, Num. 3:2.
*j Ithamar*, Ex. 38:21.

2
*k Holiness, typified*, Ex. 39:30.
*l High Priest, vestments of*, vs. 2–43; Lev. 21:10.

3
*m Inspiration*, Job 32:8.
*n Art*, 2 Cor. 16:14.

4
*o Dress*, Zech. 3:4.
*p Embroidery*, Ezek. 26:16.
*q Girdle*, Prov. 31:24.
1 R. V. coat of chequer work,

AND [a]take thou unto thee
[b,c,d]Aâr′on thy brother,
and his sons with him, from
among the children of Ĭs′ra-el,
that he may minister unto me in
the [e,f]priest's office, *even* Aâr′on,
[g]Nā′dăb and [h]Ā-bī′hū, [i]Ē-le-ā′-
zar and [j]Ĭth′a-mär, Aâr′on's
sons.[Q]

2 And thou shalt make [k]holy[G]
[l]garments for [b]Aâr′on thy brother for glory and for beauty.

3 And thou shalt speak unto all
*that are* wise hearted, whom I
have [m]filled with the *spirit of
wisdom, that they may [n]make
[b]Aâr′on's [l]garments to consecrate him, that he may minister
unto me in the [e]priest's office.[T]

4 And these *are* the [l]garments
which they shall make; a
†breastplate, and an ‖ephod,[G]
and a [o]robe, and a [1,p]broidered
coat, a ‡mitre,[G] and a [q]girdle: and
they shall make [k]holy [l]garments
for Aâr′on thy brother, and his
sons, that he may minister unto
me in the [e]priest's office.

5 And they shall take [r]gold, and
[s]blue, and [s]purple, and [s]scarlet,
and fine [t]linen.

6 ¶ And they shall make the
‖ephod *of* [r]gold, *of* [s]blue, and *of*
[s]purple, *of* [s]scarlet, and fine
twined [t]linen, with [p]cunning[G]
work.

7 ‖It shall have the two shoulderpieces thereof joined at the
two edges thereof; and *so* it shall
be joined together.

8 And the [2]curious[G] [q]girdle of
the ‖ephod, which *is* upon it,
shall be of the same, according
to the work thereof; *even of*
[r]gold, *of* [s]blue, and [s]purple, and
[s]scarlet, and fine twined [t]linen.

9[T] And thou shalt take two
[u]onyx [v]stones, and [w]grave[G] on
them the names of the children
of Ĭs′ra-el:

10 Six of their names on one
[v]stone, and *the other* six names
of the rest on the other stone, according to their birth.

11 With the work of an engraver in stone, *like* the [w]engravings of a [x]signet, shalt thou
engrave the two [v]stones with the
names of the children of Ĭs′ra-el:
thou shalt make them to be set
in ouches[G] of [r]gold.

12 And thou shalt put the two
[v]stones upon the shoulders of the
‖ephod *for* stones of [y]memorial
unto the children of Ĭs′ra-el: and
[b,d,f]Aâr′on shall [z]bear their
names before the LORD upon
his two shoulders for a memorial.[T]

13 And thou shalt make ouches[G]
*of* [a]gold;

14 And two [b]chains *of* pure

v.5–1533 BC
See footnote, *Time*, Rev. 10:6.

5
*r Gold*, Ezek. 7:19.
*s Colors, symbolical*, Ezek. 16:16.
*t Linen*, Ezek. 27:16.

8
2 R. V. cunningly woven band, which is upon it, to gird it on withal,

9
*u Onyx*, Ezek. 28:13.
*v Precious Stones* Ex. 39:10.
*w Engraving*, Ex. 32:4.

11
*x Seal, engraved* 1 Kin. 21:8.

12
*y Memorial*, Num. 16:40.
*z Intercession, of man with God*, Jer. 27:18.

13
*a Gold*, Ezek. 7:19.

14
*b Chains*, Dan. 5:7.

*In the temple*, 1 Kin. 7:49; 2 Chr. 4:20, 21; 13:11. *Carried in processions*, Matt. 25:1–8.
See footnote, CANDLESTICK, Ex. 25:31.
**Figurative:** *Of joy*, Jer. 25:10. *Of life*, Job 18:5, 6; 21:17; Prov. 13:9; 20:20. *Of the word of God*, Psa. 119:105; Prov. 6:23; 2 Pet. 1:19. *Of spiritual illumination*, Matt. 6:22. *Of religious influence*, Matt. 5:15; Mark 4:21; Luke 8:16; 11:33. *Of Christ*, Rev. 21:23.
**Symbolical**, Rev. 4:5; 8:10.

***GENIUS.** *Mechanical, a divine inspiration*, Ex. 28:3; 31:2–11; 35:30–35; 36:1.

†**BREASTPLATE.** *For high priest*, Ex. 25:7. *Directions for the making of*, Ex. 28:15–30. *Made by Bezaleel*, Ex. 39:8, 21. *Free will offering of materials for*, Ex. 35:9, 27. *Worn by Aaron*, Ex. 29:5; Lev. 8:8.

‡**MITER**, Ex. 28:4, 36–39; 29:6; 39:28–31; Lev. 8:9; Ezek. 21:26.

‖**EPHOD**, a sacred vestment worn by the high priest. *Described*, Ex. 25:7; 28:6–14, 31–35. *Making of*, Ex. 39:2–26. *Breastplate attached to*, Ex. 28:22–29. *Worn by Aaron*, Ex. 39:5.
*Used as an oracle*, 1 Sam. 23:9, 12; 30:7, 8.
*An inferior, was worn, by the common priests*, 1 Sam. 22:18; *by Samuel*, 1 Sam. 2:18; *by David*, 2 Sam. 6:14; 1 Chr 15:27. *Called coat*, Ex. 28:40; 29:8; 39:27; 40:14; Lev 8:13; 10:5.

v.14–1533 BC
See footnote, *Time*, Rev. 10:6.

[a]gold at the ends; *of* wreathen work shalt thou make them, and fasten the wreathen[G] chains to the ouches.[G]

15 ¶ And thou shalt make the †breastplate of judgment with cunning[G]work; after the work of the ‖ephod thou shalt make it; *of* [a]gold, *of* [c]blue, and *of* [c]purple, and *of* [c]scarlet, and *of* fine twined [d]linen, shalt thou make it.

16 Foursquare †it shall be *being* doubled;[G] a [e,f]span[G] *shall be* the length thereof, and a span *shall be* the breadth thereof.

17 And thou shalt set in †it settings of [g]stones, *even* four rows of stones: *the first* row *shall be* a §sardius, a [h]topaz, and a [i]carbuncle: *this shall be* the first row.

18 And the second row *shall be* an [j]emerald, a [k]sapphire, and a [l]diamond.

19 And the third row a [3,m]ligure, an +agate, and an [n]amethyst.

20 And the fourth row a [o]beryl, and an [p]onyx, and a [q]jasper: they shall be set in [a]gold in their inclosings.[G]

21 And the [g]stones shall be with the names of the children of Is'ra-el, twelve, according to their names, *like* the [r]engravings of a [s]signet; every one with his name shall they be according to the twelve tribes.[T Q]

22 And thou shalt make upon the †breastplate [b]chains at the ends *of* wreathen[G]work *of* pure [a]gold.

23 And thou shalt make upon the †breastplate two rings of [a]gold, and shall put the two rings on the two ends of the breastplate.

24 And thou shalt put the two wreathen[G] [b]*chains* of gold in the two rings *which are* on the ends of the †breastplate.

25 And *the other* two ends of the two wreathen[G] [b]*chains* thou shalt fasten in the two ouches,[G] and put *them* on the shoulderpieces of the ‖ephod before it.

26 And thou shalt make two rings of [a]gold, and thou shalt put them upon the two ends of the †breastplate in the border thereof, which *is* in the side of the ‖ephod inward.

27 And two *other* rings of [a]gold thou shalt make, and shalt put them on the two sides of the ‖ephod underneath, toward the forepart thereof, over against the *other* coupling thereof, above the curious[G] [t]girdle of the ephod.

28 And they shall bind the †breastplate by the rings thereof unto the rings of the ‖ephod with a lace[G] of blue, that *it* may be above the curious[G] [t]girdle of the ephod, and that the breastplate be not loosed from the ephod.

29 And [u,v,w]Aâr'on shall [x]bear the names of the children of Is'ra-el in the †breastplate of judgment upon his heart, when he goeth in unto the [y]holy *place*; for a [z]memorial before the LORD continually.[T]

30 ¶ And thou shalt put in the †breastplate of judgment the [a]Ū'rim and the Thŭm'mim; and they shall be upon [b]Aâr'on's heart, when he goeth in before the LORD: and [c,d]Aâr'on shall [e]bear[G] the judgment of the children of Is'ra-el upon his heart before the LORD continually.

31 ¶ And thou shalt make the [f]robe of the ‖ephod all *of* [g]blue.

32 And there shall be an hole in the top of it, in the midst thereof:

**15**
*c Colors, symbolical*, Ezek. 16:16.
*d Linen*, Ezek. 27:16.

**16**
*e Span*, Ex. 39:9.
*f Measure, linear*, Deut. 25:15.

**17**
*g Precious Stones*, Ex. 39:10.
*h Topaz*, Ezek. 28:13.
*i Carbuncle, possibly emerald*, Isa. 54:12.

**18**
*j Emerald, possibly carbuncle*, Rev. 4:3.
*k Sapphire*, Job 28:6.
*l Diamond, possibly sardonyx*, Ex. 39:11.

**19**
*m* Ex. 39:12.
*n Amethyst*, Rev. 21:20.
3 R. V. jacinth.

**20**
*o Beryl*, Ezek. 1:16.
*p Onyx*, Ezek. 28:13.
*q Jasper*, Rev. 21:19.

**21**
*r Engraving*, Ex. 32:4.
*s Seal, engraved*, 1 Kin. 21:8.

v.24–1533 BC
See footnote, *Time*, Rev. 10:6.

**27**
*t* **Girdle, Prov. 31:24.**

**29**
*u Aaron*, Ex. 6:20.
*v Types, of the Messiah*, Heb. 10:1.
*w Jesus, priesthood of, typified*, Matt. 1:21.
*x Intercession, of man with God*, Jer. 27:18.
*y Holy Place*, Ex. 26:33.
*z Memorial*, Num. 16:40.

**30**
*a Urim and Thummim*, Lev. 8.8.
*b Aaron*, Ex. 6:20.
*c Jesus, priesthood of, typified*, Matt. 1:21.
*d Types, of the Messiah*, Heb. 10:1.
*e Intercession, of man with God*, Jer. 27:18.

**31**
*f High Priest, vestments of*, Lev. 21:10.
*g Colors, symbolical*, Ezek. 16:16.

*Made by Gideon, became an idolatrous snare to Israel*, Judg. 8:27; 17:5; 18:14, 17, 18, 20.
*Prophecy concerning the absence of, from Israel*, **Hos.** 3:4.

§ **SARDIUS**, possibly ruby, a precious stone. *In the garden of Eden*, Ezek. 28:13. *In the breastplate*, Ex. 28:17; 39:10. *Seen in John's apocalyptic vision of the foundation of the New Jerusalem*, Rev. 21:20.
**Figurative**, Rev. 4:3.

+ **AGATE.** *A precious stone*, Ex. **28:19; Isa. 54:12;** Ezek. 27:16.

v.32–1533 BC
See footnote, *Time,* Rev. 10:6.

32
*h Weaving,* Isa. 38:12.
*i Coat of Mail,* 1 Sam. 17:5.
33
*j Pomegranate,* Num. 13:23.
35
*k Holy Place,* Ex. 26:33.
36
*l Gold,* Ezek. 7:19.
*m Engraving,* Ex. 32:4.
*n Seal, engraved,* 1 Kin. 21:8.
*o Holiness, taught by mottoes,* Ex. 39:30.
*p Legends,* Zech. 14:20.
4 R. V. HOLY TO THE LORD.
39
*q Embroidery,* Ezek. 26:16.
*r Girdle,* Prov. 31:24.
40
*s Priest, vestments of,* Lev. 1:5.
*t Dress,* Zech. 3:4.

it shall have a binding of [h]woven work round about the hole of it, as it were the hole of an [i]habergeon,[c] that it be not rent.

33 And *beneath* upon the hem of it thou shalt make [j]pomegranates *of* [g]blue, and *of* [g]purple, and *of* [g]scarlet, round about the hem thereof; and ⊙bells of gold between them round about:

34 A golden ⊙bell and a [j]pomegranate, a golden bell and a pomegranate, upon the hem of the robe round about.

35 And [i]it shall be upon [b]Aâr′on to minister: and his sound shall be heard when he goeth in unto the [k]holy *place* before the LORD, and when he cometh out, that he die not.

36 ¶ And thou shalt make a plate *of* pure [l]gold, and grave[c] upon it, *like* the [m]engravings of a [n]signet,[c 4,o,p]HOLINESS TO THE LORD.

37 And thou shalt put it on a [g]blue lace,[c] that it may be upon the ‡mitre;[c] upon the forefront of the mitre[c] it shall be.

38 And [i]it shall be upon [b]Aâr′on's forehead, that [c,d]Aâr′on may [e]bear[c] the iniquity of the holy things, which the children of Is′ra-el shall hallow in all their holy gifts; and it shall be always upon his forehead, that they may be accepted before the LORD.

39 ¶ And thou shalt [q]embroider the [i]coat of fine linen, and thou shalt make the ‡mitre *of* fine linen, and thou shalt make the [r]girdle *of* needlework.

40 ¶ And for Aâr′on's sons thou shalt make [s,t]coats, and thou shalt make for them [r]girdles, and ▲bonnets[c] shalt thou make for them, for glory and for beauty.

41 And thou shalt put [i,s]them upon [b]Aâr′on thy brother, and his [s]sons with him; and shalt [u]anoint them, and [v]consecrate them, and [w]sanctify them, that they may minister unto me in the priest's office.

42 And thou shalt make them linen ●,[i,s]breeches to cover their nakedness; from the loins even unto the thighs they shall reach:

43 And [i,s]they shall be upon [b]Aâr′on, and upon his sons, when they come in unto the [5,x]tabernacle of the congregation, or when they come near unto the altar to minister in the [k]holy *place;* that they bear not iniquity, and die: *it shall be* a statute for ever unto him and his seed after him.

## CHAPTER 29

*The sacrifice and ceremonies of consecrating the priests. 38 The continual burnt offering. 45 God's promise to dwell among the children of Israel.*

AND [a]this *is* the thing that thou shalt do unto [b]them to *hallow them, to minister unto me in the priest's office: Take one young ‡bullock, and two rams [c]without [d]blemish,

2 And unleavened bread, and cakes unleavened tempered[c] with [e]oil, and wafers unleavened anointed with oil: *of* wheaten flour shalt thou make them.

3 And thou shalt put them into one †basket, and bring them in the basket, with the ‡bullock and the two rams.

v.40–1533 BC
See footnote, *Time,* Rev. 10:6.

41
*u Anointing,* Lev. 8:12.
*v Ordination, of priests,* Ex. 29:1.
*w Sanctification,* 1 Pet. 1:2.
43
*x Tabernacle,* Ex. 27:9.
5 R. V. tent of meeting,
1
*a Revelation, relating to consecration of the priests,* 2 Cor. 12:1.
*b Priest, consecration of,* vs. 1–9; Lev. 1:5.
*c Holiness, typified,* Ex. 39:30
*d Sin, typified,* Rom. 5:12.
2
*e Oil,* Deut. 12:17.

⊙ **BELL.** *Attached to the hem of the priest's robe,* Ex. 28:33, 34; 39:25, 26. *On horses,* Zech. 14:20.

▲ **TURBAN,** or headtire. *Worn, by priests,* Ex. 28:40; 29:9; 39:28; Lev. 8:13; Ezek. 44:18; *by women,* Isa. 3:20.

● **BREECHES.** *For the priests,* Ex. 28:42; 39:28; Lev. 6:10; 16:4; Ezek. 44:18.

* **ORDINATION.** *Of priests,* Ex. 29:1–9, 19–35; 40:12–16; Lev. 8:6–35; Heb. 7:21. *Of apostles,* Mark 3:14. *Of ministers, the seven deacons,* Acts 6:5, 6; *Paul and Barnabas,* Acts 13:2, 3; *Timothy,* 1 Tim. 4:14.

† **BASKET,** Gen. 40:16, 17; Ex. 29:3, 23, 32; Lev. 8:2, Num. 6:15; Deut. 26:2; 28:5, 17; 2 Kin. 10:7. *Received the fragments after the miracles of the loaves,* Matt. 14:20; 15:37; 16:9, 10; Mark 6:43; 8:8, 19, 20; Luke 9:17; John 6:13. *Paul let down from the wall in,* Acts 9:25; 2 Cor. 11:33.

‡ **BULLOCK,** or ox. **Uses of:** *For food,* Deut. 14:4. *For sacrifice,* Ex. 29:3, 10–14, 36; Lev. 4:1–21; Num. 7:87, 88; 28:11–31; 29; Heb. 9:13; 10:4. *For plowing,* 1 Kin. 19:19; Prov. 14:4; Isa. 32:20; Jer. 31:18. *For treading out corn,* Deut. 25:4. *With wagons,* Num. 7:3–8; 2 Sam. 6:3–6. *To carry burdens,* 1 Chr. 12:40.

v.4–1533 BC
See footnote, *Time*, Rev. 10:6.

**4**
f *Aaron, consecration of, to the priesthood*, vs. 1–35; Ex. 6:20.
g *Tabernacle*, Ex. 27:9.
h *Ceremonial Washing*, Ex. 19:10.
i *Purification*, Num. 19:19.
1 R. V. tent of meeting.

**5**
j *Ephod*, Ex. 28:6.
k *Breastplate*, Ex. 28:4.
l *Girdle*, Prov. 31:24.

**6**
m *Miter*, Ex. 28:4.
2 *Or*, turban

**7**
n *Anointing*, Lev. 8:12.

**9**
o *Turban*, Ex. 28:40.
p *Dress*, Zech. 3:4.
q *Priest, Mosaic, hereditary descent of office*, Lev. 1:5.
3 R. V. bind head-tires

**10**
r *Offerings*, Lev. 6:17.
s *Hand, imposition of*, vs. 15, 19; Ezra 10:19.

**11**
t *Jesus, vicarious death of, typified*, Matt. 1:21.

**12**
u *Blood, sacrificial*, Heb. 9:19.
v *Jesus, atoning blood of, typified*, Matt. 1:21.
w *Altar, of burnt offerings*, Gen. 8:20.

4 *And [b,f]Aâr′on and his [b]sons
thou shalt bring unto the door of
the [1,g]tabernacle[G] of the congregation[G], and shalt [c,h,i]wash them
with water.
5 And thou shalt take the garments, and put upon [b,f]Aâr′on
the coat, and the robe of the
[j]ephod[G], and the ephod[G], and the
[k]breastplate, and gird him with
the curious[G] [l]girdle of the ephod:
6 And thou shalt put the [2,m]mitre[G]
upon [b,f]his head, and put the
holy [‖]crown upon the [2]mitre[G].
7 *Then shalt thou take the
anointing [e]oil, and pour *it* upon
[b,f]his head, and [n]anoint him.
8 And thou shalt bring his [b]sons,
and put coats upon them.
9 And thou shalt gird them
with [l]girdles, Aâr′on and his
sons, and [3]put the [o,p]bonnets[G] on
them: and the [q]priest's office
shall be their's for a perpetual
statute: and thou shalt [*,b,f]con-
secrate Aâr′on and his sons.
10 And thou shalt cause a
[‡,r]bullock to be brought before
the [1,g]tabernacle of the congregation: and [*,b,f]Aâr′on and his
sons shall put their [s]hands upon
the head of the bullock.
11 And thou shalt [t]kill the
[‡,r]bullock before the LORD, *by*
the door of the [1,g]tabernacle of
the congregation.
12 And thou shalt take of the
[u,v]blood of the [‡]bullock, and put
*it* upon the horns of the [w]altar
with thy finger, and pour all the
blood beside the bottom of the
altar.
13 And thou shalt take all the
fat that covereth the inwards,
and the [§]caul[G] *that is* above the
[x]liver, and the two [y]kidneys, and
the fat that *is* upon them, and
burn *them* upon the [w]altar.
14 But the flesh of the [‡]bul-
lock, and his skin, and his dung,
[z]shalt thou burn with fire without[G] the camp: it *is* a [a]sin offering.
15 ¶ Thou shalt also take one
[b]ram; and [c]Aâr′on and his sons
shall put their hands upon the
head of the ram.
16 And thou shalt [d]slay the
[b]ram, and thou shalt take his
[e,f]blood, and sprinkle *it* round
about upon the [g]altar.
17 And thou shalt cut the [b]ram
in pieces, and wash the inwards[G]
of him, and his legs, and put
*them* unto[G] his pieces, and unto
his head.
18 And thou shalt burn the
whole [b]ram upon the [g]altar: it *is*
a [h]burnt offering unto the LORD:
it *is* a sweet[G] savour[G], an offering
made by fire unto the LORD.[Q]
19 And thou shalt take the
other [b,i]ram; *and [c,j]Aâr′on and
his [j]sons shall put their hands
upon the head of the ram.
20 *,[j]Then shalt thou [d]kill the
[b,i]ram, and take of his [k]blood,
and put *it* upon the tip of the
right [l]ear of Aâr′on, and upon
the tip of the right ear of his
sons, and upon the [m]thumb of
their right hand, and upon the
great [n]toe of their right foot, and
sprinkle the blood upon the altar
round about.
21 [j]And thou shalt take of the
blood that *is* upon the [g]altar,
and of the anointing [o]oil, and
sprinkle *it* upon [c]Aâr′on, and
upon his garments, and upon his
sons, and upon the garments of

v.13–1533 BC
See footnote, *Time*, Rev. 10:6.

**13**
x *Liver*, Lev. 3:4.
y *Kidney*, Lev. 3:4.

**14**
z *Sanitation and Hygiene*, Num. 31:23.

a *Offerings, sin*, Lev. 6:17.

**15**
b *Ram*, Ex. 39:34.
c *Aaron, consecration of, to the priesthood*, Ex. 6:20.

**16**
d *Jesus, vicarious death of, typified*, Matt. 1:21.
e *Blood, sacrificial*, Heb. 9:19.
f *Jesus, atoning blood of, typified*, Matt. 1:21.
g *Altar, of burnt offerings*, Gen. 8:20.

**18**
h *Offerings, burnt*, Lev. 6:17.

**19**
i *Offerings, peace* vs. 19–22; Lev. 6:17.
j *Priest, consecration of*, vs. 19–35; Lev. 1:5.

**20**
k *Blood, of peace offering*, Heb. 9:19.
l *Ear*, Lev. 8:23.
m *Thumb*, Lev. 8:23.
n *Toe*, Lev. 14:14.

**21**
o *Oil, sacred*, Deut. 12:17.

**Laws concerning:** *Trespass by*, Ex. 21:28–36. *Theft of*, Ex. 22:1–4, 9. *Rest for*, Ex. 23:12. *Not to be muzzled, when treading grain*, Deut. 25:4; 1 Cor. 9:9; 1 Tim. 5:18. *Not to be yoked with an ass*, Deut. 22:10.
**Brazen:** *Under the molten sea in Solomon's temple*, 1 Kin. 7:25; 2 Chr. 4:4; Jer. 72:20.
**Symbolical**, Ezek. 1:10; Rev. 4:7.

‖ **CROWN.** *Prescribed for priests*, Ex. 29:6; 39:30; Lev. 8:9. *Worn, by kings*, 2 Sam. 1:10; 12:30; 2 Kin. 11:12; Esth. 6:8; Song 3:11; Rev. 6:2; *by queens*, Esth. 1:11; 2:17; 8:15. *Made, of gold*, Psa. 21:3; Zech. 6:11; *of thorns*, Matt. 27:29; Mark 15:17; John 19:25. *Set with gems*, 2 Sam. 12:30; 1 Chr. 20:2; Isa. 62:3; Zech. 9:16. *Given victor in games*, 1 Cor. 9:25; 2 Tim. 2:5.
**Figurative:** *Of gracious visitation*, Isa. 28:5. *Of heavenly reward*, 1 Cor. 9:25; 2 Tim. 4:8; Jas. 1:12; 1 Pet. 5:4; Rev. 2:10; 3:11.
**Symbolical**, Rev. 4:4, 10; 6:2; 9:7; 12:1, 3; 13:1; 14:14; 19:12.

§ **CAUL**, probably the upper lobe of the liver. *Burnt with sacrifice*, Ex. 29:13, 22; Lev. 3:4, 10, 15; 4:9; 7:4; 8:16, 25; 9:10, 19.

his sons with him: and he shall
be *hallowed, and his garments,
and his sons, and his sons' garments with him.
22 Also thou shalt take of the
[b,i]ram the [p]fat and the [4]rump,
and the fat that covereth the inwards, and the §caul[G] *above* the
[q]liver, and the two [r]kidneys, and
the fat that *is* upon them, and
the right [5]shoulder; for it *is* a
ram of *,[j]consecration:
23 And one loaf of [s]bread, and
one cake of oiled bread, and one
[t]wafer out of the †basket of the
unleavened bread that *is* before
the LORD:
24 *And thou shalt put all in
the hands of [c]Aâr′on, and in the
hands of his sons; and shalt
wave[G] them *for* a [u]wave offering
before the LORD.
25 And thou shalt receive them
of their hands, and burn *them*
upon the [g]altar for a [h]burnt offering, for a sweet savour before
the LORD: it *is* an offering made
by fire unto the LORD.
26 And thou shalt take the
breast of the ram of [c]Aâr′on's
[j]consecration, and wave it *for* a
[u]wave offering before the LORD:
and [v]it shall be thy part.
27 And thou shalt sanctify the
breast of the [u]wave offering, and
the [5]shoulder of the [w]heave offering, which is waved, and
which is heaved[G] up, of the ram
of the [j]consecration, *even* of
[v]*that* which *is* for Aâr′on, and of
*that* which *is* for his sons:
28 And [v]it shall be Aâr′on's
and his sons' [6]by a statute[G] for
ever from the children of Ĭs′ra-
el: for it *is* an [w]heave offering:
and it shall be an heave offering
from the children of Ĭs′ra-el of
the sacrifice of their [i]peace offering, *even* their heave offering
unto the LORD.
29 ¶ And the holy [x]garments of
[c]Aâr′on shall be his sons' after
him, to be anointed therein, and
to be *,[j]consecrated in them.
30 *And* that son that is priest in
his stead shall put them on [y]sev-
en days, when he cometh into
the [7]tabernacle of the congregation to minister in the [z]holy
*place*.
31 ¶ And thou shalt take the
[a]ram of the [b]consecration, and
seethe[G] his flesh in the [c]holy place.
32 And *,[d]Aâr′on and his sons
shall eat the [e]flesh of the ram,
and the [f]bread that *is* in the
†basket, *by* the door of the [7]tab-
ernacle of the congregation.
33 *And they shall eat [e]those
things wherewith the [g]atone-
ment was made, to [b]consecrate
*and* to [h]sanctify them: but a
[i]stranger shall not eat *thereof*,
because they *are* holy.[G]
34 And if ought[G] of the flesh of
the [b]consecrations, or of the
[f]bread, remain unto the morning, then [j]thou shalt burn the remainder with fire: it shall not be
eaten, because it *is* holy.
35 *And thus shalt thou do unto [d]Aâr′on, and to his sons, according to all *things* which I
have commanded thee: [k]seven
days shalt thou [b]consecrate
them.
36 And thou shalt offer every
day a ‡bullock *for* a [l]sin [m]offer-
ing for [g]atonement[G]: and thou
shalt cleanse the [n]altar, when
thou hast made an atonement
for it, and thou shalt [o]anoint it,
to [h]sanctify it.
37 [k]Seven days thou shalt make
an [g]atonement for the [n]altar, and
[h]sanctify it; and it shall be an
altar most [p]holy: [q,r]whatsoever
toucheth the altar shall be holy.[Q]
38 ¶ Now this *is that* which
thou shalt [s,t]offer upon the altar;
two [u,v]lambs of the first year day
by day continually.[Q]
39 [s]The one [u,v]lamb thou shalt
[t]offer in the morning; and the

v.21–1533 BC
See footnote, *Time*, Rev. 10:6.

22
p *Fat*, Lev. 7:24.
q *Liver*, Lev. 3:4.
r *Kidney*, Lev. 3:4.
4 R. V. fat tail,
5 R. V. thigh;

23
s *Bread*, Ezek. 4:13.
t *Wafer*, Num. 6:19.

24
u *Offerings, wave*, Lev. 6:17.

26
v *Priest, emoluments of*, vs. 27–34; Lev. 1:5.

27
w *Offerings, heave*, Lev. 6:17.

28
6 R. V. as a due

29
x *High Priest, vestments of*, Lev. 21:10.

v.29–1533 BC
See footnote, *Time*, Rev. 10:6.

30
y *Seven, days*, Gen. 7:2.
z *Holy Place, priests ministered in*, Ex. 26:33.
7 R. V. tent of meeting

31
a *Offerings, peace*, Lev. 6:17.
b *Priest, consecration of*, Lev. 1:5.
c *Holy Place*, Ex. 26:33.

32
d *Aaron*, Ex. 6:20.
e *Priest, emoluments of*, Lev. 1:5.
f *Bread*, Ezek. 4:13.

33
g *Atonement*, Lev. 17:11.
h *Sanctification*, 1 Pet. 1:2.
i *Foreigner, forbidden to eat things offered in sacrifice*, Deut. 23:20.

34
j *Sanitation and Hygiene*, Num. 31:23.

35
k *Seven, days*, Gen. 7:2.

36
l *Offerings, sin*, Lev. 6:17.
m *Jesus, typified in sin offering*, Matt. 1:21.
n *Altar, how sanctified*, Gen. 8:20.
o *Anointing, in consecration*, Lev. 8:12.

37
p *Holiness, typified*, Ex. 39:30.
q Matt. 23:19.
r *Altar, sanctified everything that touched it*, Gen. 8:20.

38
s *Offerings, daily*, vs. 38–42; Lev. 6:17.
t *Offerings, burnt*, Lev. 6:17.
u *Lamb, offering of*, vs. 38–41; Num. 7:15.
v *Jesus, vicarious death of, typified*, vs. 38–42; Matt. 1:21.

v.39–1533 BC
See footnote, *Time*, Rev. 10:6.

**40**
w *Measure, dry*, Deut. 25:15.
x *Measure, liquid*, Deut. 25:15.
y *Oil*, Deut. 12:17.
z *Wine, offered with sacrifices*, Prov. 23:31.

a *Offerings, drink*, Lev. 6:17.
**41**
b *Lamb, offering of*, Num. 7:15.
c *Offerings, meat*, Lev. 6:17.
8 R. V. meal

**42**
d *Offerings, burnt*, Lev. 6:17.
e *Shekinah*, Lev. 16:2.
f *God, presence of*, Gen. 2:2.

**43**
g *Tabernacle, sanctified*, Ex. 27:9.
h *Sanctification, tabernacle sanctified by God's presence*, 1 Pet. 1:2.
9 R. V. the tent

**44**
i *Altar*, Gen. 8:20.
j *Aaron*, Ex. 6:20.
k *Priest*, Lev. 1:5.

**45**
l *God, dwells with the righteous*, Gen. 2:2.
m *Fellowship, with God*, 1 Cor. 1:9.
n *God, love of, exemplified*, Gen. 2:2.

**46**
o *Egypt*, Gen. 41:8.

**1**
a *Revelation, concerning tabernacle furniture and service*, vs. 1–38; 2 Cor. 12:1.
b *Incense*, Ex. 37:29.
c *Acacia*, Ex. 26:15.

other lamb thou shalt offer at
even[G]:
40 And [s]with the one lamb a
[w]tenth[G] deal[G] of flour mingled[G] with
the fourth part of an [+, x]hin of
beaten [y]oil; and the fourth part
of an hin of [z]wine *for* a [a]drink
offering.
41 And the other [b]lamb thou
shalt offer at even[G], and shalt do
thereto according to the [8, c]meat[G]
offering of the morning, and according
to the [a]drink offering
thereof, for a sweet savour, an
offering made by fire unto the
LORD.
42 *This shall be* a continual
[d]burnt offering throughout your
generations *at* the door of the
[7]tabernacle of the congregation
before the LORD: [e]where [f]I will
meet you, to speak there unto
thee.
43 And [e]there [f]I will meet with
the children of Iș'ra-el, and
[9]*the* [g]*tabernacle* shall be [h]sanctified
by my glory.
44 And I will [h]sanctify the
[7, g]tabernacle of the congregation,
and the [i]altar; I will sanctify
also both [j]Aâr'on and his
sons, to minister to me in the
[k]priest's office.
45 And I [l]will [m]dwell among
the children of Is̆'ra-el, and
[n]will be their God.[T]
46 And they shall know that I
*am* the LORD their God, [n]that
brought them forth out of the
land of [o]Ē'ġy̆pt, that [l]I may
dwell among them: I *am* the
LORD their God.

## CHAPTER 30

*The altar of incense. 11 The ransom of souls. 17 The brazen laver. 22 The holy anointing oil. 34 The composition of the perfume.*

AND[Q] [a]thou shalt make an
[*]altar to burn [b]incense
upon: *of* [c]shittim wood shalt
thou make it.
2 A [d]cubit[G] *shall be* the length
thereof, and a cubit the breadth
thereof; foursquare shall [*]it be:
and two cubits[G] *shall be* the height
thereof: the horns thereof *shall
be* of the same.
3 And thou shalt overlay [*]it
with pure [e]gold, the top thereof,
and the sides thereof round
about, and the horns thereof;
and thou shalt make unto it a
crown[G] of gold round about.[Q]
4 And two golden rings shalt
thou make to [*]it under the
crown[G] of it, by the two [1]corners
thereof, upon the two sides of it
shalt thou make *it*; and they
shall be for places for the staves
to bear[G] it withal[G].
5 And thou shalt make the
staves *of* [2, c]shittim wood, and
overlay them with [e]gold.
6 And thou shalt put [*]it before
the vail that *is* by the [f]ark of the
[g]testimony, before the [h]mercy
seat that *is* over the testimony,
[i]where [j]I will meet with thee.[Q]
7 And [k, l]Aâr'on shall burn
thereon sweet [m, n, o]incense every
morning: when he dresseth the
[p]lamps, he shall burn incense
upon it.[Q]
8 And when [k, l]Aâr'on lighteth
the [p]lamps at even[G], he shall burn
[n]incense upon it, a perpetual incense
before the LORD throughout
your generations.[T]
9 Ye shall offer no strange incense
thereon, nor [q]burnt [3]sacrifice,
nor [4, r]meat[G] offering; neither
shall ye pour [s]drink offering
thereon.
10 And [l, t]Aâr'on shall make an
[u]atonement upon the horns of it
once in a year with the [v, w]blood
of the sin offering of atonements:
[x]once in the year shall
he make atonement upon it
throughout your generations: it
*is* most holy unto the LORD.[Q]

v.2–1533 BC
See footnote, *Time*, Rev. 10:6.

**2**
d *Cubit*, Ex. 36:9.

**3**
e *Gold*, Ezek. 7:19.

**4**
1 R. V. ribs

**5**
2 R. V. acacia
**6**
f *Ark, called ark of the testimony*, Ex. 25:10.
g *Testimony*, Ex. 25:16.
h *Mercy Seat*, Ex. 25:17.
i *Shekinah*, Lev. 16:2.
j *God, presence of*, Gen. 2:2.
**7**
k *Aaron*, Ex. 6:20.
l *High Priest, duties of*, Lev. 21:10.
m *Offerings, daily*, Lev. 6:17.
n *Incense, offered morning and evening*, Ex. 37:29.
o *Perfume*, Prov. 27:9.
p *Lamp*, Ex. 27:20.

**9**
q *Offerings, burnt*, Lev. 6:17.
r *Offerings, meat*, Lev. 6:17.
s *Offerings, drink*, Lev. 6:17.
3 R. V. offering,
4 R. V. meal
**10**
t *Jesus, priesthood of, typified*, Matt. 1:21.
u *Atonement*, Lev. 17:11.
v *Blood, of sin offering*, Heb. 9:19.
w *Jesus, atoning blood of, typified*, Matt. 1:21.
x *Day of Atonement*, Lev. 23:27.

**+ HIN.** A measure for liquids, and containing one-sixth or one-seventh of a bath. Jewish authorities disagree as to the exact capacity. *Probably equivalent to about one gallon one quart, or one gallon one and one-half quarts*, Ex. 29:40; Lev. 19:36; 23:13.

*** ALTAR, of incense.** *Called the* GOLDEN ALTAR, EX.

v.11–1533 BC
See footnote, *Time*, Rev. 10:6.

11

*y Revelation, instituting the annual poll tax*, vs. 12–16; 2 Cor. 12:1.

*z Moses*, Ex. 2:10.

12

*a National Religion, supported by taxes*, vs. 12–16; Gal. 1:13.

*b Census, a poll tax, to be levied at*, vs. 12–16; 2 Sam. 24:1.

*c Israel*, Ex. 4:22.

*d Ransom, of a man's life*, Ex. 21:30.

*e Tax, poll*, vs. 11–16; Neh. 10:32.

13

*f Commandment, enjoining liberality to the house of God*, Deut. 8:2.

*g Gerah*, Lev. 27: 25.

15

*h Poor, atonement money of*, Prov. 21:13.

*i Atonement, by money*, vs. 12–16; Lev. 17:11.

16

*j Money, atonement by*, vs. 12–16; Jer. 32:9.

*k Tabernacle, tax for*, vs. 12–16; Ex. 27:9.

5 R. V. tent of meeting;

17

*l Moses*, Ex. 2:10.

18

*m Brass*, Job 28:2.

11 ¶ And the LORD [y]spake unto [z]Mō′ṣeṣ, saying,
12 [a]When thou takest the [b]sum
of the children of [c]Ĭṣ′ra-el after
their number, then shall they
give every man a [d,e]ransom for
his soul unto the LORD, when
thou numberest them; that there
be no plague among them, when
*thou* numberest them.
13 [f]This [c]they shall give, every
one that passeth among them
that are [b]numbered, half a
†shekel[C] after the shekel of the
sanctuary: (a shekel *is* twenty
[g]gerahs[C]:) an half shekel *shall be*
the offering of the LORD.[Q]
14 [f]Every one that passeth
among them that are [b]num-
bered, from twenty years old and
above, shall give an offering unto the LORD.
15 The rich shall not give more,
and the [h]poor shall not give less
than half a †shekel, when *they*
give an offering unto the LORD,
to make an [i]atonement for your
souls.
16 And thou shalt take the
[i]atonement [j]money of the children of [c]Ĭṣ′ra-el, and shalt appoint it for the service of the
[5,k]tabernacle of the congregation; that it may be a memorial
unto the children of Ĭṣ′ra-el before the LORD, to make an
atonement for your souls.
17 ¶ And the LORD spake unto
[l]Mō′ṣeṣ, saying,
18 Thou shalt also make a
‡laver[C] *of* [m]brass[C], and his foot *also*
*of* brass, to wash *withal:* and
thou shalt put it between the
[n]tabernacle of the congregation
and the altar, and thou shalt put
water therein.
19 For [o]Aâr′on and his [o]sons
shall [p]wash their hands and
their feet thereat:
20 When [o]they go into the
[5,n]tabernacle of the congregation, they shall [p]wash with water, that they die not; or when
they come near to the altar to
minister, to [q]burn offering made
by fire unto the LORD:
21 So [o]they shall [p]wash their
hands and their feet, that they
die not: and it shall be a statute
for ever to them, *even* to him and
to his seed[C] throughout their
generations.
22 ¶ Moreover the LORD spake
unto [l]Mō′ṣeṣ, saying,
23 [r]Take thou also unto thee
principal spices, of pure ‖myrrh
five hundred †*shekels*[C], and of
sweet [s]cinnamon half so much,
*even* two hundred and fifty *shekels*[C], and of sweet [t]calamus two
hundred and fifty *shekels*,
24 [r]And of [u]cassia five hundred †*shekels*, after the shekel
of the sanctuary, and of [v]oil an
[w]hin[C]:
25 [r]And thou shalt make it an
[x]oil of holy ointment, an ointment compound[C] after the [y]art of
the [6,z]apothecary: it shall be an
holy anointing oil.
26 And thou shalt [a]anoint [7]the
[b]tabernacle of the congregation

v.18–1533 BC
See footnote, *Time*, Rev. 10:6.

*n Tabernacle*, Ex. 27:9.

19

*o Priest, ablutions of*, Lev. 1:5.

*p Ceremonial Washing*, Ex. 19:10.

20

*q Offerings, burnt*, Lev. 6:17.

23

*r Ointment, sacred, formula for*, Eccl. 7:1.

*s Cinnamon*, Song 4:14.

*t Calamus*, Ezek. 27:19.

24

*u Cassia*, Ezek. 27: 19.

*v Oil, olive*, Deut. 12:17.

*w Measure, liquid*, Deut. 25:15.

25

*x Oil, sacred*, Deut. 12:17.

*y Art*, 2 Chr. 16:14.

*z Apothecary*, Neh. 3:8.

6 R. V. perfumer:

26

*a Anointing*, Lev. 8:12.

*b Tabernacle, anointed with holy oil*, Ex. 27:9.

7 R. V. therewith the tent of meeting,

39:38; Num. 4:11; 2 Chr. 4:19. Described as: *Altar of sweet incense*, Lev. 4:7; *altar before the Lord*, Lev. 16:18.
*Pattern of*, Ex. 30:1–10. *Constructed*, Ex. 37:25–28. *Location of*, Ex. 30:6; 40:5, 26. *A cover made for, of the censers of Korah*, Num. 16:36–40. *Uses of*, Ex. 30:7–10, 26, 27; 40:27; Lev. 4:7, 18; 16:12, 18. *Atonement for*, Lev. 16:18, 33. *How prepared for carrying*, Num. 4:4–15. *Carried by the Kohathites*, Num. 3:27–31. *In Solomon's temple*, 1 Kin. 7:48; 1 Chr. 28:18. *Seen in John's vision*, Rev. 8:3; 9:13. *Used in idolatrous worship*, 1 Kin. 12:33; 13:1.

† **SHEKEL.** *A weight, equal to twenty gerahs*, Ex. 30: 13; Num. 3:47; Ezek. 45:12. *Used to weigh, silver*, Josh. 7:21; Judg. 8:26; 17:2, 3; *gold*, Gen. 24:22; Num. 7:14, 20–86; Josh. 7:21; 1 Kin. 10:16; *spices*, Ex. 30:23; *hair*, 2 Sam. 14:26; *iron*, 1 Sam. 17:7; *myrrh*, Ex. 30:23; *rations*, Ezek. 4:10. *Fractions of, used in currency*, Ex. 30:13; 1 Sam. 9:8; Neh. 10:32. *Fines paid in*, Deut. 22:19, 29. *Fees paid in*, 1 Sam. 9:8. *Sanctuary revenues paid in*, Ex. 30:13; Neh. 10:32; Matt. 17:24–27.

Of different standards: *Of the sanctuary*, Ex. 30:13; *of the king's weight*, 2 Sam. 14:26.
*Corrupted*, Amos 8:5.

‡ **LAVER.** *Directions for making*, Ex. 30:18–20. *Made by Bezaleel*, Ex. 38:8. *Situation of, between tabernacle and brazen altar*, Ex. 40:7, 30. *Sanctified*, Ex. 30:28; 40:11; Lev. 8:11. *Used for washing*, Ex. 40:30–32.
*Brazen, made by Solomon for the temple*, 1 Kin. 7:23–26, 30, 38, 39; 2 Chr. 4:2–14; *altered by Ahaz*, 2 Kin. 16:17; *broken and carried to Babylon by the Chaldeans*, 2 Kin. 25: 13, 16; Jer. 52:17, 20.

‖ **MYRRH,** a fragrant gum. *A product of the land of Canaan*, Song 4:6, 14; 5:1. *One of the compounds in the sacred anointing oil*, Ex. 30:23. *Used as a perfume*, Esth. 2:12; Psa. 45:8; Prov. 7:17; Song 3:6; 5:13. *Brought by wise men as a present to Jesus*, Matt. 2:11. *Traffic in*, Gen. 37:25; 43:11. *Offered to Jesus on the cross*, Mark 15:23. *Used for embalming*, John 19:39.

v.26–1533 BC
See footnote, *Time*, Rev. 10:6.

c *Ark, sanctification of*, Ex.25:10.
27
d *Shewbread, table of*, Ex. 35:13.
e *Candlestick*, Ex. 25:31.
28
f *Altar, how sanctified*, Gen. 8:20.
29
g *Sanctification*, 1 Pet. 1:2.
h *Holiness, typified*, Ex. 39:30.
i *Altar, sanctified every thing that touched it*, Gen. 8:20.
30
j *Aaron*, Ex. 6:20.
k *Priest, consecration of*, Lev. 1:5.
31
l *Israel*, Ex. 4:22.
m *Oil, sacred*, vs. 31–33; Deut. 12:17.
33
n *Foreigner*, Deut. 23:20.
o *Disfellowship*, Num. 15:31.
34
p *Moses*, Ex. 2:10.
q *Spices*, 1 Kin. 10:2.
r *Frankincense*, 1 Chr. 9:29.
35
s *Incense*, vs. 35–38; Ex. 27:29.
t *Perfume*, Prov. 27:9.
u *Apothecary*, Neh. 3:8.
36
v *Tabernacle*, Ex. 27:9.
w *Shekinah*, Lev. 16:2.
x *God, presence of*, Gen. 2:2.

therewith, and the [c]ark of the testimony,

27 And the [d]table and all his vessels, and the [e]candlestick[G] and his vessels,[G] and the *altar of incense,

28 And the [f]altar of burnt offering with all his vessels, and the ‡laver and his foot.

29 And thou shalt [g]sanctify[G] them, that they may be most [h]holy: [i]whatsoever toucheth them shall be holy.

30 And thou shalt [a]anoint [j]Aâr′on and his sons, and consecrate [k]them, that *they* may minister unto me in the priest's office.

31 And thou shalt speak unto the children of [l]Ĭṣ′ra-el, saying, This shall be an [h]holy anointing [m]oil unto me throughout your generations.

32 Upon man's flesh shall [m]it not be poured, neither shall ye make *any other* like it, after the composition of it: it *is* [h]holy, *and* it shall be holy unto you.

33 Whosoever compoundeth[G] *any* like [m]it, or whosoever putteth *any* of it upon a [n]stranger, shall even be [o]cut[G] off from his people.

34 ¶ And the LORD said unto [p]Mō′ṣeṣ, Take unto thee sweet [q]spices, stacte, and onycha, and galbanum; *these* sweet spices with pure [r]frankincense[G]: of each shall there be a like *weight*:

35 And thou shalt make it a [s,t]perfume, a confection[G] after the art of the [6,u]apothecary, tempered[G] together, pure *and* holy:

36 And thou shalt beat *some* of it very small, and put of it before the testimony in the [5,v]tabernacle of the congregation, [w]where [x]I will meet with thee: it shall be unto you most holy.

37 And *as for* the [s,t]perfume which thou shalt make, ye shall not make to yourselves according to the composition thereof: it shall be unto thee holy for the LORD.

38 Whosoever shall make like unto that, to smell thereto, shall even be [o]cut off from his people.

## CHAPTER 31

*Bezaleel and Aholiab are called and qualified for the work of the tabernacle. 13 The observance of the Sabbath is again commanded. 18 Moses receives the two tables.*

AND the LORD spake unto [a]Mō′ṣeṣ, saying,

2 [S]See, I have called by name *Bĕ-zăl′e-el the son of [b]Ū′rī, the son of †Hûr, of the tribe of [c]Jū′dah:

3 And I have filled *,[d]him with the [e]spirit of God, in [f]wisdom, and in understanding, and in knowledge, and in all manner of workmanship,[T]

4 To devise cunning[G] [g]works, to work in [h]gold, and in [i]silver, and in [j]brass,[G]

5 And in [k]cutting of stones, to set *them*, and in [l]carving of timber, to work all manner of workmanship.

6 And I, behold, I have given with him [m]Ă-hō′li-ăb, the son of [n]Ă-hĭs′a-măch, of the tribe of [o]Dăn: and in the hearts of all that are wise hearted I have put [f]wisdom, that they may make all that I have commanded thee,[S]

7 The [1,p]tabernacle of the congregation, and the [q]ark of the testimony, and the [r]mercy seat that *is* thereupon, and all the furniture of the [2]tabernacle,

8 And the [s]table and [3]his furniture, and the pure [t]candlestick[G] with all [3]his furniture, and the [u]altar of incense,

9 And the [v]altar of burnt offering with all [3]his furniture, and the [w]laver and his foot,

10 And the cloths of service,

v.37–1533 BC
See footnote, *Time*, Rev. 10:6.

1
a *Moses*, Ex. 2:10.
2
b *Uri*, Ex. 35:30.
c *Judah, tribe of*, Num. 10:14.
3
d *Master Workman, instances of*, vs. 2–11; 1 Cor. 3:10.
e *Inspiration*, Job 32:8.
f *Wisdom*, Prov. 2:2.
4
g *Art*, 2 Chr. 16:14.
h *Gold*, Ezek. 7:19.
i *Silver*, 1 Chr. 28:14.
j *Brass*, Job 28:2.
5
k *Lapidary*, Ex.35:33.
l *Carving*, Ex. 35:33.
6
m *Aholiab*, Ex. 36:1.
n Ex. 35:34; 38:23.
o *Dan, tribe of*, Gen. 30:6.
7
p *Tabernacle*, Ex. 27:9.
q *Ark*, Ex. 25:10.
r *Mercy Seat*, Ex. 25:17.
1 R. V. tent of meeting,
2 R. V. tent,
8
s *Shewbread, table of*, Ex. 35:13.
t *Candlestick, of the tabernacle*, Ex. 25:31.
u *Altar, of incense*, Ex. 30:1.
3 R. V. its vessels,
9
v *Altar, of burnt offerings*, Gen. 8:20.
w *Laver*, Ex. 30:18.

* **BEZALEEL.** *A divinely inspired mechanic and master workman, who built the tabernacle*, Ex. 31:2; 35:30–35; chapters 36–39; 2 Chr. 1:5.

† **HUR.** *A son of Caleb and grandfather of Bezaleel the inspired artificer*, Ex. 31:2; 35:30; 38:22; 1 Chr. 2:19, 20; 2 Chr. 1:5.

v.10–1533 BC
See footnote. *Time,* Rev. 10:6.

**10**
*x Priest, vestments of,* Lev. 1:5.
*y Aaron,* Ex. 6:20.

**11**
*z Oil, sacred,* Deut. 12:17.

*a Incense,* Ex. 37:29.
*b Holy Place,* Ex. 26:33.

**12**
*c Moses,* Ex. 2:10.

**13**
*d Commandment, enjoining keeping the Sabbath holy,* vs. 14–16; Deut. 8:2.
*e Church, rules of discipline in,* Matt. 16:18.
*f Sabbath, a sign,* Ex. 16:23.
*g Token, the Sabbath,* Psa. 86:17.
*h Sanctification, the Lord the sanctifier,* 1 Pet. 1:2.
*i Spiritual Blessings,* Eph. 1:3.

**14**
*j Sabbath, holy,* Ex. 16:23.
*k Profanation, of the Sabbath,* Lev. 22:32.
*l Punishment, death penalty,* Lev. 26:41.
*m Death, penalty,* Num. 23:10.
*n Commandment, forbidding work on the Sabbath,* Deut. 8:2.
*o Labor,* Luke 10:7.
*p Disfellowship,* Num. 15:31.

**15**
*q Rest, enjoined,* Ex. 23:12.

**16**
*r Israel,* Ex. 4:22.
*s Covenant, of men with God,* Deut. 29:1.

**17**
*t God, creator,* Gen. 2:2.
*u Heavens, physical, creation of,* Psa. 8:3.
*v Earth, created by God,* Prov. 8:23.
*w Anthropomorphisms, resting attributed to God,* Gen. 11:5.

**18**
*x Communion, with God,* 2 Cor. 13:14.
*y Sinai,* Ex. 16:1.
*z Decalogue, written by God,* Ex. 20:3.

and the holy [x]garments for
[y]Aâr′on the priest, and the [x]gar-
ments of his sons, to minister in
the priest's office,
11 And the anointing [z]oil, and
sweet [a]incense for the [b]holy
*place*: according to all that I have
commanded thee shall they do.
12 ¶ And the LORD spake unto
[c]Mō′ṣeṣ, saying,
13 Speak thou also unto the
children of Ĭṣ′ra-el, saying,
[d,e]Verily my [f]sabbaths ye shall
keep[G]: for it *is* a [g]sign between
me and you throughout your
generations; that *ye* may know
that I *am* the LORD that doth
[h,i]sanctify[G] you.
14 [d]Ye shall keep the [j]sabbath
therefore; for it *is* holy unto you:
every one that [k]defileth[G] it shall
surely be [l]put to [m]death: for
[n]whosoever doeth *any* [o]work
therein, that soul[G] shall be [p]cut
off from among his people.
15 Six days may [o]work be done;
but in the seventh *is* the [j]sab-
bath of [q]rest, holy to the LORD:
[n]whosoever doeth *any* work in
the sabbath day, he shall surely
be [l]put to [m]death.
16 Wherefore [d]the children of
[r]Ĭṣ′ra-el shall keep the sabbath,
to observe the sabbath throughout their generations, *for* a perpetual [s]covenant.
17 It *is* a [g]sign between me and
the children of [r]Ĭṣ′ra-el for ever:
for *in* six days the [t]LORD made
[u]heaven and [v]earth, and on the
[j]seventh day he [w]rested, and was
refreshed.
18 ¶ And he gave unto Mō′ṣeṣ,
when he had made an end of
[x]communing[G] with him upon
mount [y]Sī′nāi, two ‡tables of
[z,a]testimony, tables of [b]stone,
written with the finger of God.[Q][T]

*a Word of God, inspiration of,* Psa. 119:9. *b Stones, commandments engraved on,* Ex. 24:12.

## CHAPTER 32

*The people, in absence of Moses, cause Aaron to make a calf. 7 God is angered thereby. 11 At the entreaty of Moses he is appeased. 15 Moses comes down with the tables. 19 He breaks them. 20 He destroys the calf. 22 Aaron's excuse for himself. 25 Moses causes the idolaters to be slain. 30 He prays for the people.*

AND when the [a]people saw
that [b]Mō′ṣeṣ delayed to
come down out of the [c]mount,
[d,e]the people gathered themselves together unto [f]Aâr′on, and
said unto him, Up, [g]make us
[h]gods, which shall go before us;
for *as for* this Mō′ṣeṣ, the man
that brought us up out[G] of the
land of [i]Ē′ġy̆pt, we wot not what
is become of him.[Q]
2 And [f]Aâr′on said unto them,
Break off the golden [j]earrings,
which *are* in the ears of your
[k]wives, of your [l]sons, and of
your daughters, and bring *them*
unto me.
3 And all the [d,e]people brake off
the golden [j]earrings which *were*
in their ears, and brought *them*
unto [f]Aâr′on.
4[Q] And he received *them* at their
hand, and [m]fashioned [n]it with
a *graving[G] tool, after he had
made it a [o]molten [p]calf: and
[d]they said, These *be* thy gods, O
Ĭṣ′ra-el, which brought thee up
out of the land of [i]Ē′ġy̆pt.
5 And when [f]Aâr′on saw *it*, he
built an [q]altar[G] before it; and Aâr′-
on made proclamation, and said,
To morrow *is* a feast to the
LORD.
6 And they [r]rose up early on the
morrow, and [s]offered [t]burnt offerings, and [u]brought [v]peace offerings; and [w]the people sat
down to [x]eat and to drink, and
rose up to play.[G] [Q]
7 ¶ And the LORD said unto
Mō′ṣeṣ, Go, get thee down; for
thy people, which thou brought-

v.1–1533 BC
See footnote. *Time,* Rev. 10:6.

**1**
*a Israel, idolatry of,* Ex. 4:22.
*b Moses,* Ex. 2:10.
*c Sinai,* Ex. 16:1.
*d Backsliding, instances of,* Hos. 11:7.
*e Instability,* Jas. 1:8.
*f Aaron, makes the golden calf,* Ex. 6:20.
*g* Acts 7:40.
*h Idolatry,* 1 Sam. 15:23.
*i Egypt,* Gen. 41:8.

**2**
*j Earring, offering of,* Prov. 25:12.
*k Wife,* Prov. 5:18.
*l Children,* Mark 10:14.

**4**
*m Carving,* Ex. 35:33.
*n Idol, made of gold,* 1 Kin. 15:12.
*o Molding,* 1 Kin. 7:16.
*p Idolatry, objects of,* 1 Sam. 15:23.

**5**
*q Altar,* Gen. 8:20.

**6**
*r Rising, early,* Gen. 19:2.
*s Idolatry, burnt offerings offered in,* 1 Sam. 15:23.
*t Offerings, burnt, offered in idolatrous worship,* Lev. 6:17.
*u Idolatry, peace offerings offered in,* 1 Sam. 15:23.
*v Offerings, peace, offered in idolatrous worship,* Lev. 6:17.
*w* 1 Cor. 10:7.
*x Eating,* Gen. 18:8.

‡ **TABLE.** *Of testimony,* Ex. 31:18; 32:15; 34:29. *The commandments engraved upon,* Ex. 20:3–17; 24:12; Deut. 4:13; 5:4–22; 9:10. *Broken, by Moses in his anger on account of the idolatry of the Israelites,* Ex. 24:12; 31:18; 32:15–19; Deut. 4:13; 9:9–11, 17. *A second set engraved,* Ex. 34:1; Deut. 10:1–4. *Placed in the ark,* Deut. 10:5; 1 Kin. 8:9; Heb. 9:4.

* **ENGRAVING.** *In making idols,* Ex. 32:4. *On the stones set, in the priest's breastplate,* Ex. 28:9–11, 21, 36, 39:8–14; *in the priest's girdle,* Ex. 39:6; *in the priest's crown,* Ex. 39:30.

v.7–1533 BC
See footnote, *Time*, Rev 10:6.

8
*y Character, instability, instances of*, Phil. 2:15.

9
*z Obduracy, instances of*, Prov. 29:1.

10
*a Anger of God*, 2 Kin. 13:3.
*b Judgments*, Ex. 6:6.
*c Moses*, Ex. 2:10.

11
*d Intercession, of man with God*, Jer. 27:18.
*e Israel*, Ex. 4:22.
*f Egypt*, Gen. 41:8.

12
*g Prayer, pleas offered in*, Acts 6:4.
*h Egyptians*, Gen. 50:3.

13
*i Abraham*, Gen. 17:5.
*j Isaac*, Gen. 21:3.
*k Jacob*, Gen. 27:11.
*l Oath*, Num. 5:19.
*m Covenant, of God with men*, Deut. 29:1.
*n Descendants of Abraham*, Gen. 22:17.
*o Heavens, physical*, Psa. 8:3.
*p Canaan, promised to Abraham*, Gen. 37:1.

14
*q God, longsuffering of*, Gen. 2:2.
*r God, mercy of*, Gen. 2:2.
*s Repentance, attributed to God*, Mark 1:4.
*t Anthropomorphisms, attributing repentance to God*, Gen. 11:5.

15
*u Sinai*, Ex. 16:1.
*v Table of Testimony*, Ex. 31:18.
*w Testimony*, Ex. 25:16.
*x Decalogue*, Ex. 20:3.

est out of the land of [i]Ē′ġy̆pt have corrupted *themselves*:

8 They have [d,e,y]turned aside quickly out of the way which I commanded them: they have made them a [o]molten [p]calf, and have [h]worshipped [n]it, and have sacrificed thereunto, and said, These *be* thy gods, O Is̱′ra-el, which have brought thee up out of the land of [i]Ē′ġy̆pt.

9 And the LORD said unto Mō′ṣeṣ, I have seen this people, and, behold, it *is* a [z]stiffnecked[G] people:[Q]

10 Now therefore let me alone, that my [a]wrath may wax[G] hot against them, and that I may [b]consume them: and I will make of [c]thee a great nation.[S]

11 And [c]Mō′ṣeṣ [d]besought the LORD his God, and said, LORD, why doth thy [a]wrath wax[G] hot against thy [e]people, which thou hast brought forth out of the land of [f]Ē′ġy̆pt with great power, and with a mighty hand?

12 [d,g]Wherefore should the [h]Ē-ġy̆p′tianṣ speak, and say, For mischief[G] did he bring them out, to slay them in the mountains, and to consume them from the face of the earth? Turn from thy fierce [a]wrath, and repent of this evil against thy people.

13 [d,g]Remember [i]Ā′bră-hăm, [j]Ī′ṣaac, and [k]Is̱′ra-el, thy servants, to whom thou [l,m]swarest[G] by thine own self, and saidst unto them, I will multiply your [n]seed as the stars of [o]heaven, and all this [p]land that I have spoken of will I give unto your seed, and they shall inherit *it* for ever.[Q]

14 And the [q,r]LORD [s,t]repented of the evil which he thought to do unto his people.

15 ¶ And [c]Mō′ṣeṣ turned, and went down from the[u]mount, and the two [v]tables of the [w,x]testimony *were* in his hand: the tables *were* written on both their sides; on the one side and on the other *were* they written.

16 And the [v]tables *were* the work of God, and the [x,y]writing *was* the writing of God, graven[G] upon the tables.

17 And when [z]Jŏsh′u-ȧ heard the noise of the people as they shouted, he said unto Mō′ṣeṣ, *There is* a noise of war in the camp.

18 And he said, *It is* not the voice of *them that* shout for mastery,[G] neither *is it* the voice of *them that* cry for being overcome: *but* the noise of *them that* sing do I hear.

19 ¶ And it came to pass, as soon as he came nigh[G] unto the camp, that he saw the [a]calf, and the [b]dancing: and [c]Mō′ṣeṣ′ [d]anger waxed[G] hot, and he cast the [e]tables out of his hands, and brake them beneath the [f]mount.

20 And [c,g,h]he took the [a]calf which they had made, and [i]burnt *it* in the fire, and ground *it* to powder, and strawed[G] *it* upon the water, and made the children of Is̱′ra-el drink *of it*.

21 And [c]Mō′ṣeṣ said unto [j]Aâr′on, [g]What did this people unto thee, that thou hast brought so great a sin upon them?

22 And [j]Aâr′on [k,l]said, Let not the anger of my lord wax[G] hot: thou knowest the people, that they *are set* on mischief.

23 [k,l]For they said unto me, Make us gods, which shall go before us: for *as for* this [c]Mō′ṣeṣ, the man that brought us up out of the land of Ē′ġy̆pt, we wot[G] not what is become of him.[Q]

24 And [k,l]I said unto them, Whosoever hath any gold, let them break *it* off. So they gave *it* me: then I cast it into the fire, and there came out this [a]calf.

25 ¶ And when [c]Mō′ṣeṣ saw that the people *were* [1]naked; (for [j]Aâr′on had made them naked

v.15–1533 BC
See footnote, *Time*, Rev. 10:6.

16
*y Law, of Moses, divine authority for*, Deut. 33:2.

17
*z Joshua*, Josh.1:1

19
*a Calf*, Mic. 6:6.
*b Dancing, idolatrous*, Eccl. 3:4.
*c Moses*, Ex. 2:10.
*d Anger, instances of*, Psa. 37:8.
*e Table of Testimony*, Ex. 31:18.
*f Sinai*, Ex. 16:1.

20
*g Reproof, faithfulness in, instances of*, Prov. 17:10.
*h Zeal, instances of*, 2 Cor. 7:11.
*i Iconoclasm*, Num. 33:52.

21
*j Aaron*, Ex. 6:20.

*k Excuses, for disobedience*, Luke 14:18.
*l Responsibility, attempt to shift*, Ezek. 18:20.

25
1 R. V. broken loose; for Aaron had let them loose for a derision among their enemies.

v.25–1533 BC
See footnote, *Time*, Rev. 10:6.

26
*m Levites, religious zeal of*, Deut. 10:8.

27
*n Wicked, punishment of*, Psa. 73:3.

28
2 R. V. sons

30
*o Sin*, Rom. 5:12.
*p Intercession, of man with God*, Jer. 27:18.
*q Atonement*, Lev. 17:11.

31
*r Love, of man for man*, 1 John 4:7.
*s Idolatry*, 1 Sam. 15:23.
*t Idol, made of gold*, 1 Kin. 15:12.

32
*u Sin, forgiveness of*, Rom. 5:12.
*v Prayer, importunity in*, Acts 6:4.
*w Renunciation, of self for others*, Luke 5:11.
*x Book, figurative*, Psa. 139.16.

33
*y Wicked, punishment of*, Psa. 73:3.
*z Sin, punishment of*, Rom. 5:12.

34
*a Canaan*, Gen. 37:1.

unto *their* shame among their enemies:)

26 Then [c]Mō'ṣeṣ stood in the gate of the camp, and said, Who *is* on the LORD's side? *let him come* unto me. And all the sons of [m]Lē'vī gathered themselves together unto him.

27 And [c]he said unto them, Thus saith the LORD God of Iṣ'ra-el, Put every man his sword by his side, and go in and out from gate to gate throughout the camp, and [n]slay every man his brother, and every man his companion, and every man his neighbour.

28 And the [2]children of [m]Lē'vī did according to the word of [c]Mō'ṣeṣ: and there fell of the people that day about three thousand men.

29 For [c]Mō'ṣeṣ had said, Consecrate yourselves to day to the LORD, even every man upon his son, and upon his brother; that he may bestow upon you a blessing this day.

30 ¶ And it came to pass on the morrow, that [c]Mō'ṣeṣ said unto the people, Ye have sinned a great [o]sin: and now I will [p]go up unto the LORD; peradventure I shall make an [q]atonement for your sin.

31 And Mō'ṣeṣ [h,r]returned unto the LORD, and [p]said, Oh, this people have sinned a great [o]sin, and [s]have made them [t]gods of gold.

32 [p]Yet now, if thou wilt [u]forgive their [o]sin—; and [v]if not, [w]blot me, I pray thee, out of thy [x]book which thou hast written.

33 And the LORD said unto Mō'ṣeṣ, [y]Whosoever hath [z]sinned against me, him will I blot out of my [x]book.

34 Therefore now go, lead the people unto [a]*the place* of which I have spoken unto thee: behold, mine[3], [b]Angel shall go before thee: nevertheless in the day when I visit I will visit their [c]sin upon [d]them.

35 And the LORD [e]plagued the [f]people, because they [g]made the [h]calf, which Aâr'on made.

## CHAPTER 33

*The Lord refuses to go, as he had promised, with the people. 4 The people mourn thereat. 7 The tabernacle is removed out of the camp. 9 The Lord talks face to face with Moses. 12 Moses prays for God's presence, 18 and desires to see his glory.*

AND the LORD said unto [a]Mō'ṣeṣ, Depart, *and* go up hence, thou and the people which thou hast brought up out of the land of [b]Ē'ġ̆ypt, unto the [c]land which I [d,e]sware unto [f]Ā'bră-hăm, to [g]Ī'ṣaac, and to [h]Jā'cob, saying, Unto thy seed will I give it:

2 And I will send an [i]angel before thee; and I will drive out the [j]Cā'năan-īte, the [k]Ăm'ôr-īte, and the [l]Hĭt'tīte, and the [m]Pĕr'ĭz-zīte, the [n]Hī'vīte, and the [o]Jĕb'u-sīte:

3 Unto a [c]land flowing with [p]milk and [q]honey: for [r]I will not go up in the midst of thee; for thou *art* a [s]stiffnecked people: lest [t]I [u]consume thee in the way.

4 ¶ And when the [v]people heard these evil tidings, [w]they [x]mourned: and no man did put on him his [y]ornaments.

5 For the LORD had said unto Mō'ṣeṣ, Say unto the children of Iṣ'ra-el, Ye *are* a [s]stiffnecked people: [t]I will come up into the midst of thee in a moment, and [u]consume thee: therefore now put off thy [y]ornaments from thee, that I may know what to do unto thee.

6 And the children of [v]Iṣ'ra-el stripped themselves of their [y]ornaments by the mount [z]Hō'reb.

7 And Mō'ṣeṣ took the [1]taber-

v.34–1533 BC
See footnote, *Time*, Rev. 10:6.

*b Angel*, Ex. 14:19.
*c Sin, punishment of*, Rom. 5.12.
*d Wicked, punishment of*, Psa. 73:3.

34
3 R. V. angel

35
*e Judgments*, Ex. 6:6.
*f Israel, visited by a plague*, Ex. 4:22.
*g Idolatry*, 1 Sam. 15:23.
*h Calf*, Mic. 6:6.

1
*a Moses*, Ex. 2.10.
*b Egypt*, Gen. 41:8.
*c Canaan*, Gen. 37:1.
*d Oath*, Num. 5:19.
*e Covenant, of God with men*, Deut. 29:1.
*f Abraham*, Gen. 17:5.
*g Isaac*, Gen. 21:3.
*h Jacob*, Gen. 27:11.

2
*i Angel, functions of*, Heb. 1:13.
*j Canaanites*, Ex. 23:28.
*k Amorites*, Gen. 14:13.
*l Hittite*, Judg. 1:26.
*m Perizzite*, Gen. 15:20.
*n Hivites*, Gen. 10:17.
*o Jebusite*, Deut. 7:1.

3
*p Milk, figurative*, Job 10:10.
*q Honey, figurative*, Prov. 25:27.
*r Holy Spirit, withdrawn from incorrigible sinners*, Acts 1:2.
*s Obduracy*, Prov 29:1.
*t Anger of God*, 2 Kin. 13:3.
*u Judgments*, Ex. 6:6.

4
*v Israel, mourning of*, Ex. 4:22.
*w Conviction, of sin*, John 16:8.
*x Mourning*, Lam. 2:5.
*y Jewels, discarded by penitents*, Gen. 24:53.

6
*z Horeb*, Ex. 3:1.

7
1 R. V. tent.

v.7–1533 BC
See footnote, *Time*, Rev. 10:6.

*a Tabernacle*, Ex. 27:9.
*b Seekers*, Isa. 55:6.
2 R. V. tent of meeting.

8
*c Moses, character of*, Ex. 2:10.
*d Reverence*, Lev. 19.30.

9
*e Pillar, of cloud and fire*, Ex. 13:21.
*f Communion, with God, instances of*, 2 Cor. 13:14.
*g Prophets, inspiration of*, Isa. 3.2.

10
*h Worship*, Gen. 22:5.

11
*i Joshua*, Josh.1:1.
*j Young Men*, Prov. 1:4.

12
*k Prayer, boldness in, exemplified*, Acts 6:4.
*l Boldness, of the righteous*, vs. 12–18; Phil. 1:20.
*m Grace of God*, Rom. 4:16.

13
*n Prayer, instances of importunity in*, vs. 12–16; Acts 6:4.
*o Guidance, prayer for*, Psa. 48:14.
*p God, guide*, Gen. 2:2.

nacle, and pitched it without[G] the
camp, afar off from the camp,
and called it the [2,a]Tabernacle
of the congregation. And it
came to pass, *that* every one
which [b]sought the LORD went
out unto the [2]tabernacle of the
congregation, which *was* without
the camp.
8 And it came to pass, when
[c]Mō'ṣeṣ went out unto the [1]tab-
ernacle, *that* all the people [d]rose
up, and stood every man *at* his
tent door, and looked after Mō'-
ṣeṣ, until he was gone into the
[1,a]tabernacle.
9 And it came to pass, as Mō'-
ṣeṣ entered into the [1,a]taber-
nacle, the cloudy [e]pillar descended, and stood *at* the door of
the [1]tabernacle, and *the* LORD
[f]talked with [g]Mō'ṣeṣ.
10 And all the people saw the
cloudy [e]pillar stand *at* the [1,a]tab-
ernacle door: and all the people
rose up and [h]worshipped, every
man *in* his tent door.
11 And the LORD spake unto
[g]Mō'ṣeṣ face to face, [j]as a man
speaketh unto his *friend. And
he turned again into the camp:
but his servant [i]Jŏsh'u-ȧ, the
son of Nŭn, a [j]young man, departed not out of the [1,a]taber-
nacle.
12 ¶ And Mō'ṣeṣ [k,l]said unto
the LORD, See, thou sayest unto
me, Bring up this people: and
thou hast not let me know whom
thou wilt send with me. Yet
thou hast said, I know thee by
name, and thou hast also found
[m]grace in my sight.
13 Now therefore, I [k,n]pray
thee, if I have found [m]grace in
thy sight, [o,p]shew me now thy
way, that I may know thee, that
I may find grace in thy sight:
and [q]consider that this nation *is*
thy people.
14 And[T] he said, [r]My [s,t]presence
shall go *with* [u]thee, and I will
give thee rest.[S]
15 And he [k,n]said unto him, [o]If
thy [s]presence go not *with me*,
carry us not up hence.[T]
16 For wherein shall it be
known here that I and thy people have found [m]grace in thy
sight? [o]*is it* not in that [p]thou goest with us? [v]so shall [w]we be
[x]separated, I and thy [y]people,
from all the people that *are* upon
the face of the earth.
17 And the LORD said unto
Mō'ṣeṣ, [z]I will do this thing also
that thou hast spoken: for thou
hast found [a]grace in my sight,[S]
and I know thee by name.
18 And he [b,c]said, I beseech
thee, [d]shew me thy [e]glory.
19 And he said, [f]I will make all
my [g]goodness pass before thee,
and I will proclaim the name of
the LORD before thee; and
[h,i]will be [a]gracious to whom I
will be gracious, and will shew
[j]mercy on whom I will shew
mercy.[S Q]
20 And he said, [k]Thou canst
not see my face: for there shall
no man see me, and live.[S T Q]
21 And the LORD said, Behold,
*there is* a place by me, and thou
shalt stand upon a rock:
22 And it shall come to pass,
while my [e]glory passeth by, that
I will put thee in a clift[C] of the
rock, and will cover thee with
my hand while I pass by:
23 And I will take away mine
hand, and thou shalt see my
back parts: but [k]my face shall
not be seen.

v.13–1533 BC
See footnote, *Time*, Rev. 10:6.

*q Intercession, of man with God*, Jer. 27:18.

14
*r Promises, of guidance to the righteous*, 2 Cor. 1:20.
*s God, presence of*, Gen. 2:2.
*t Fellowship, with God*, 1 Cor. 1:9.
*u Righteous, promises to*, Psa. 64:10.

16
*v Fellowship, with the wicked, avoided*, 1 Cor. 1:9.
*w Righteous, described*, Psa. 64:10.
*x Holiness, typified*, Ex. 39:30.
*y Israel, a separate people*, Ex. 4:22.

17
*z Prayer, answered, instances of*, Acts 6:4.

*a Grace of God*, Rom. 4:16.

18
*b Prayer, boldness in*, Acts 6:4.
*c Prayer, importunity in*, Acts 6:4.
*d Vision*, vs. 18–23; Acts 9:10.
*e God, glory of*, Gen. 2:2.

19
*f Prayer, answered, instances of*, Acts 6:4.
*g God, goodness of*, Gen. 2:2.
*h Foreordination, according to purpose of grace*, Rom. 8:30.
*i* Rom. 9:15.
*j God, mercy of*, Gen. 2:2.

20
*k God, invisible*, Gen. 2:2.

* **FRIENDS**, Prov. 27:6, 9, 10, 14, 17. *Affectionate*, Deut. 13:6; 1 Sam. 18:1; 20:17; John 15:13. *Sympathetic*, Job 2:11; 6:14; Psa. 35:14. *Faithful*, Prov. 17:17; 18:24. *Mercenary*, Prov. 14:20; 19:4, 6.
See footnote, FRIENDSHIP, Prov. 22:24.
**False.** Zech. 13:6; Psa. 41:9, 88:18.
INSTANCES OF: *Pharaoh's butler to Joseph*, Gen. 40:23; *Delilah to Samson*, Judg. 16:4–20; *the Ephraimite's wife*, Judg. 19:1, 2; *Job's friends*, Job 6:15–30, 16:20; 19:13–22; *David to Joab*, 1 Kin. 2:5, 6; *David to Uriah*, 2 Sam. 11; *Ahithophel to David*, 2 Sam. 15:12; *David's friends to David*, Psa. 31:11, 12; 35:11–16, 41:9; 55:12–14, 20, 21; 88:8, 18; *Judas*, Matt. 26:48, 49, Mark 14:43–45, Luke 22:47, 48; Acts 1:16; *Jesus' disciples*, Matt. 26:56, 58; ***Paul's friends***, 2 Tim. 4:16.
See footnote, **HYPOCRISY, Jas. 3:17.**

v.1–1533 BC
See footnote, *Time,* Rev. 10:6.

**1**

a *Revelation, of the law,* vs. 1–35; 2 Cor. 12:1.
b *Moses,* Ex. 2:10.
c *Table, of testimony,* Ex. 31:18.
d *Stones, commandments engraved upon,* Ex. 24:12.
e *Law, of Moses, divine authority for,* vs. 1–4, 27, 28; Deut. 33:2.

**2**

f *Sinai,* Ex. 16:1.

**4**

g *Obedience,* Heb. 5:8.
h *Rising, early,* Gen. 19:2.

**5**

i *Pillar, of cloud and fire,* Ex. 13:21.
j *God, glory of,* Gen. 2:2.
k *God, name of, proclaimed,* Gen. 2:2.

**6**

l *God, mercy of,* Gen. 2:2.
m *God, longsuffering of,* Gen. 2:2.
n *God, goodness of,* Gen. 2:2.
o *God, truth,* Gen. 2:2.
p *Truth, attribute of God,* John 18:37.
1 R. V. a God full of compassion
2 R. V. slow to anger, and plenteous in mercy

**7**

q *Mercy,* Deut. 5:10.
r *Sin, forgiveness of,* Rom. 5:12.
s *God, judge,* Gen. 2:2.
t *Judgments, no escape from,* Ex. 6:6.
u *Punishment,* Lev. 26:41.
v *Sin, consequences of, entailed upon children,* Rom. 5:12.
w *Sin, punishment of,* Rom. 5:12.
x *Wicked, punishment of,* Psa. 73:3.
y *Children, involved in sin of parents,* Mark 10:14.
z *Heredity,* Ezek. 18:2.

**8**

a *Prayer, postures in,* Acts 6:4.

## CHAPTER 34

*The tables are renewed. 5 The name of the LORD proclaimed. 8 Moses entreats God to go with them. 10 God makes a covenant with them, repeating certain duties engraved on the first tables. 28 Moses after forty days in the mount comes down with the tables. 29 His face shines, and he covers it with a veil.*

AND the LORD [a]said unto [b]Mō′ṣeṣ, Hew[G] thee two [c]tables of [d]stone like unto the first: and I will write upon *these* tables the [e]words that were in the first tables, which thou brakest.[Q]

2 And be ready in the morning, and come up in the morning unto mount [f]Sī′nāi, and present thyself there to me in the top of the mount.

3 And no man shall come up with thee, neither let any man be seen throughout all the [f]mount; neither let the flocks nor herds feed before that mount.

4 ¶ And [b]he [g]hewed two [c]tables of stone like unto the first, and Mō′ṣeṣ [h]rose up early in the morning, and went up unto mount [f]Sī′nāi, as the LORD had commanded him, and took in his hand the two tables of stone.

5 And the LORD descended in the [i,j]cloud, and stood with him there, and proclaimed the [k]name of the LORD.

6[T] And the LORD passed by before him, and proclaimed, The LORD, The LORD [1]God, [l]merciful and gracious, [2,m]longsuffering, and abundant in [n]goodness and [o,p]truth,[S Q]

7 Keeping [q]mercy for thousands, [r]forgiving iniquity and transgression and sin, and [s]that will by no means clear[G] *the guilty*; [t,u]visiting the [v,w]iniquity of the [x]fathers upon the [y]children, and [z]upon the children's children, unto the third and to the fourth *generation*.[S T]

8 And Mō′ṣeṣ made haste, and [a]bowed his head toward the earth, and worshipped.

9 And he [b,c]said, If now I have found grace in thy sight, O LORD, let my LORD, I pray thee, go among us; for it *is* a [d,e]stiffnecked [f]people; and pardon our iniquity and our sin, and take us for thine inheritance.

10 ¶ And he said, Behold, I make a [g]covenant[G]: before all thy people I will do marvels, such as have not been done in all the earth, nor in any [h]nation: and all the people among which thou *art* shall see the work of the LORD: for it *is* a terrible[G] thing that I will do with thee.[Q]

11 Observe thou that which I command thee this day: behold, I drive out before thee the [i]Ăm′-ôr-īte, and the [j]Cā′năan-īte, and the [k]Hĭt′tīte, and the [l]Pĕr′ĭz-zīte, and the [m]Hī′vīte, and the [n]Jĕb′u-sīte.

12 [o]Take [p]heed to thyself, lest thou make a [q,r,s]covenant with the [t]inhabitants of the land whither thou goest, lest it be for a [u]snare in the midst of thee:

13 But ye shall destroy their altars, [v]break their [3]images, and cut down their [4]groves[G]:

14 For [w]thou shalt worship no other god: for the [x]LORD, whose name *is* Jealous, *is* a [y]jealous God:[S]

15 [o,p]Lest thou make a [q,r,s]covenant with the [t]inhabitants of the land, and they go[G] a whoring after their gods, and do sacrifice unto their gods, and *one* call thee, and thou eat of his sacrifice;

16 [o,p]And thou [z,a]take of their daughters unto thy sons, and their daughters go a whoring[G] after their gods, and make thy sons go a whoring after their gods.

17 Thou shalt make thee no [b]molten[G] [c]gods.

18 ¶ The [d]feast of unleavened bread shalt thou keep. [e]Seven

v.9–1533 BC
See footnote, *Time,* Rev. 10:6.

**9**

b *Intercession, instances of,* Jer. 27:18.
c *Prayer, intercessory,* Acts 6:4.
d *Obduracy,* Prov. 29:1.
e *Self-will,* Gen. 49:6.
f *Israel, obduracy of,* Ex. 4:22.

**10**

g *Covenant, of God with men,* Deut. 29:1.
h *Nation,* Isa. 2:4.

**11**

i *Amorites,* Gen. 14:13.
j *Canaanites,* Ex. 23:28.
k *Hittites,* Judg. 1:26.
l *Perizzites,* Gen. 15:20.
m *Hivites,* Gen. 10:17.
n *Jebusites,* Deut. 7:1.

**12**

o *Commandment, enjoining watchfulness,* Deut. 8:2.
p *Watchfulness, against evil association, enjoined,* Matt. 24:42.
q *Alliances,* Josh. 9:15.
r *Treaty,* 1 Kin. 5:12.
s *Fellowship, with the wicked forbidden,* 1 Cor. 1:9.
t *Evil Company, forbidden,* Prov. 13:20.
u *Temptation,* Luke 11:4.

**13**

v *Iconoclasm, enjoined,* Num. 33:52.
3 R. V. pillars,
4 R. V. Ashurim:

**14**

w *Idolatry, forbidden,* 1 Sam. 15:23.
x *God, jealous,* Gen. 2:2.
y *Jealousy, attributed to God,* Psa. 78:58.

**16**

z *Miscegenation,* Josh. 23:12.
a *Marriage,* Gen. 34:9.

**17**

b *Molding, of images,* 1 Kin. 7:16.
c *Idol, manufacture of, forbidden,* 1 Kin. 15:12.

**18**

d *Passover, institution of,* Num. 9:5.
e *Seven,* Gen. 7:2.

v.18–1533 BC
See footnote, *Time*, Rev. 10:6.

f *Month*, Ex. 12:2.
g *Abib*, Ex. 13:4.
h *Egypt*, Gen. 41:8.
**19**
i *Firstborn, reserved by God*, Zech. 12:10.
5 R. V. womb
**20**
j *Firstborn, redemption of*, Zech. 12:10.
k *Ass*, 2 Chr. 28:15.
l *Redemption, of property*, Lev. 25:24.
m *Lamb*, Num. 7:15.
n *Commandment, enjoining liberality to the house of God*, Deut. 8:2.
**21**
o *Commandment, enjoining labor and rest*, Deut. 8:2.
p *Labor*, Luke 10:7.
q *Sanitation and Hygiene, rest enjoined*, Num. 31:23.
r *Sabbath*, Ex. 16:23.
s *Rest, on the Sabbath, enjoined*, Ex. 23:12.
t *Agriculture*, Gen. 3:23.
6 R. V. plowing
**22**
u *Pentecost*, Acts 2:1.
v *First Fruits*, Deut. 18:4.
w *Tabernacles, feast of*, Deut. 16:13.
**23**
x *Annual Feasts*, Num. 15:3.
y *Commandment, enjoining public worship*, Deut. 8:2.
**24**
z *Temporal Blessings, from God*, Psa. 103:2.

a *God, providence of*, Gen. 2:2.
b *Canaanites*, Ex. 23:20.
c *Prosperity, from God*, Eccl. 7:14.
d *Worship*, Gen. 22:5.
**25**
e *Jesus, atoning blood of, typified*, Matt. 1:21.
f *Offerings, without leaven*, Lev. 6:17.
g *Leaven*, Lev. 23:17.
**26**

days thou shalt eat unleavened
bread, as I commanded thee, in
the time of the [f]month [g]Ā′bĭb:
for in the month Ā′bĭb thou
camest out from [h]Ē′ġȳpt.
19 [i]All that openeth the [5]ma-
trix[G] *is* mine; and every firstling
among thy cattle, *whether* ox or
sheep, *that is male*.
20 But the [j]firstling of an [k]ass
thou shalt [l]redeem with a [m]lamb:
and if thou redeem *him* not, then
shalt thou break his neck. All
the firstborn of thy sons thou
shalt redeem. And [n]none shall
appear before me empty.
21 ¶ [o]Six days thou shalt
[p]work, but [q]on the [r]seventh day
thou shalt [s]rest: in [6,t]earing[G] time
and in *harvest thou shalt rest.
22 ¶ And thou shalt observe the
[u]feast of weeks, of the [v]first-
fruits of wheat *harvest, and the
[w]feast of ingathering at the
year's end.
23 ¶ [x,y]Thrice[G] in the year shall
all your menchildren appear before the Lord GOD, the God of
Ĭṣ′ra-el.
24 For [z,a]I will cast out the [b]na-
tions before thee, and [c]enlarge
thy borders: neither shall any
man desire thy land, when thou
shalt go up to [d]appear before the
LORD thy God thrice in the year.[S]
25 Thou shalt not offer the
[e]blood of my [f]sacrifice with
[g]leaven; neither shall the sacrifice of the feast of the passover
be left unto the morning.
26 [h]The first of the [i]firstfruits
of thy land thou shalt bring unto
the [j]house of the LORD thy God.
Thou shalt not seethe[G] a [k]kid in
his mother's [l]milk.
27 And the LORD said unto
Mō′ṣeṣ, Write thou these
[m]words: for after[G] the tenor of
these words I have made a [n]cove-
nant[G] with thee and with Ĭṣ′ra-el.
28 And he was there [o]with the
LORD [p]forty days and forty
nights; he [q]did neither eat bread,
nor drink water. And he wrote
upon the [r]tables the words of the
[n]covenant, the ten [s]command-
ments.[Q]
29 ¶ [S Q]And it came to pass, when
[t]Mō′ṣeṣ came down from mount
[u]Sī′nāi with the two [r]tables of
[v]testimony in Mō′ṣeṣ′ hand,
when he came down from the
mount, that Mō′ṣeṣ wist[G] not that
the skin of his [†,w]face [x,y,z]shone
[7]while he talked with him.
30 And when [a]Aâr′on and all
the children of Ĭṣ′ra-el saw
[b]Mō′ṣeṣ, behold, the skin of his
[†,c]face [d]shone; and they were
afraid to come nigh[G] him.[Q]
31 And Mō′ṣeṣ called unto
them; and [a]Aâr′on and all the
[e,f]rulers of the congregation returned unto him: and Mō′ṣeṣ
talked with them.
32 And afterward all the children of Ĭṣ′ra-el came nigh[G]: and
he gave them in commandment
all that the LORD had spoken
with [g]him in mount [h]Sī′nāi.
33 And *till* [b]Mō′ṣeṣ had done
speaking with them, he [i]put a
[j]vail on his face.[Q]
34 But when Mō′ṣeṣ went in before the LORD to speak with him,
he took the [j]vail off, until he came
out. And he came out, and spake
unto the children of Ĭṣ′ra-el *that*
which [g]he was commanded.[Q]
35 And the children of Ĭṣ′ra-el
saw the [†]face of Mō′ṣeṣ, that the
skin of [b]Mō′ṣeṣ′ [c]face [d]shone:
and Mō′ṣeṣ put the [j]vail upon
his face again, until he went in
to speak with him.[S Q]

v.27–1533 BC
See footnote, *Time*, Rev. 10:6.
**27**
m *Word of God, inspiration of*, Psa. 119:9.
n *Covenant, of God with men*, Deut. 29:1.
**28**
o *Communion with God, instances of*, 2 Cor. 13:14.
p *Forty, days, of fasting by Moses*, Jonah 3:4.
q *Fasting, by Moses*, Zech. 8:19.
r *Tables, of testimony*, Ex. 31:18.
s *Decalogue, divine authority for*, Ex. 20:3.
**29**
t *Moses, face of, transfigured*, Ex. 2:10.
u *Sinai*, Ex. 16:1.
v *Law, of Moses, engraved on stone*, Deut. 33:2.
w *Countenance*, Prov. 15:13.
x *Transfiguration, of Moses*, Matt. 17:2.
y *Miracles*, Luke 23:8.
z 2 Cor. 3:7.
7 R. V. by reason of his speaking

**30**
a *Aaron*, Ex. 6:20.
b *Moses, face of, transfigured*, Ex. 2:10.
c *Countenance, transfigured*, Prov. 15:13.
d *Transfiguration, of Moses*, Matt. 17:2.
**31**
e *Rulers*, Ex. 18:21.
f *Government, Mosaic*, Isa. 22:21.
**32**
g *Prophets, inspiration of*, Isa. 3:2.
h *Sinai*, Ex. 16:1.
**33**
i 2 Cor. 3:13, 16.
j *Veil, worn by Moses*, Gen. 24:65.

h *Commandment, enjoining liberality to the house of God*, Deut. 8:2. i *First Fruits, presented at tabernacle*, Deut. 18:4. j *Church, called house of the Lord*, 1 Kin. 9:3. k *Goat, kid*, Deut. 14:4. l *Milk*, Job 10:10.

* **HARVEST.** *Sabbath to be observed in*, Ex. 34:21. *Sabbath desecrated in*, Neh. 13:15–22.
*Of wheat in Palestine, at Pentecost*, Ex. 34:22; Lev. 23:15, 17; *and before vintage*, Lev. 26:5. *Of barley, before wheat*, **Ex. 9:31, 32.**
*Celebrated with joy*, Judg. 9:27; Isa. 9:3; 16:10; Jer. 48:33. *Promises of*, Gen. 8:22; Jer. 5:24; Joel 2:23, 24.
**Figurative**, Jer. 8:20; Joel 3:13; Matt. 9:37; 13:39; Mark 4:29; Luke 10:2; John 4:35; Rev. 14:15.

† **FACE.** *Character revealed in*, Isa. 3:9. TRANSFIGURED

v.1-1533 BC
See footnote, *Time*, Rev. 10:6.

## CHAPTER 35

*The Sabbath. 4 The free gifts for the tabernacle. 20 The readiness of the people to offer. 30 Bezaleel and Aholiab are called to the work.*

AND [a]Mō′ṣeṣ gathered all
the congregation of the
children of [b]Ĭṣ′ra-el together,
and said unto them, These *are*
the [c]words which the LORD hath
commanded, that *ye* should do
them.
2 [d]Six days shall [e,f]work be
done, but on the seventh day
there shall be to you an holy
day, a [g]sabbath of [h]rest to the
LORD: whosoever doeth work
therein shall be [i]put to [j]death.
3 Ye shall kindle no [k]fire
throughout your habitations upon the [g]sabbath day.
4 ¶ And Mō′ṣeṣ spake unto all
the congregation of the children
of Ĭṣ′ra-el, saying, This *is* the
thing which the LORD [l]com-
manded, saying,
5 [l]Take ye from among you an
[m]offering unto the LORD: whosoever *is* of a willing heart, let
him bring it, an offering of the
LORD; [n]gold, and [o]silver, and
[p]brass,[GS]
6 And [q]blue, and [q]purple, and
[q]scarlet, and fine linen, and goats'
*hair*,
7 And rams' skins dyed [q]red,
and [1,r]badgers' skins, and
[s]shittim wood.
8 And [t]oil for the light, and
[u]spices for anointing oil, and for
the sweet [v]incense,
9 And [w]onyx stones, and stones
to be set for the [x]ephod,[C] and for
the [y]breastplate.
10 And every wise hearted
among you shall come, and
make all that the LORD hath
commanded:
11 The [z]tabernacle, his tent,
and his covering, [2]his taches,[C]
and his boards, his bars, his pillars, and his sockets,
12 The [a]ark, and the staves
thereof, *with* the [b]mercy seat,
and the *vail of the covering,
13 The table, and his staves,
and all his vessels, and the
†shewbread,
14 The candlestick[C] also for the
light, and [3]his furniture,[C] and his
[c]lamps, with the [d]oil for the
light,
15 And the incense [e]altar, and
his staves, and the anointing [d]oil,
and the sweet incense, and the
hanging for the door at the entering in of the tabernacle,
16 The [f]altar of burnt offering,
with his brasen[C] grate, his staves,
and all his vessels, the laver and
his foot,
17 The hangings of the [g]court,
his pillars, and their sockets, and
the hanging for the door of the
court,
18 The pins of the tabernacle,
and the pins of the [g]court, and
their cords,
19 The cloths of service, to do
service in the holy *place*, the holy
[h]garments for Aâr′on the priest,
and the [i]garments of his sons, to
minister in the priest's office.
20 ¶ And all the congregation
of the children of Ĭṣ′ra-el departed from the presence of
Mō′ṣeṣ.
21 And [j]they came, every one
whose heart stirred him up, and
every one whom his spirit made
willing, *and* they [k]brought the
LORD's offering to the work of
the [4]tabernacle of the congregation, and for all his service, and
for the holy [h,i]garments.[T]

1
a *Moses*, Ex. 2:10.
b *Israel*, Ex. 4:22.
c *Word of God, inspired*, Psa. 119:9.

2
d *Commandment, enjoining labor*, Deut. 8:2.
e *Labor, enjoined*, Luke 10:7.
f *Industry, enjoined*, 1 Kin. 11:28.
g *Sabbath*, Ex. 16:23.
h *Rest, on the Sabbath, enjoined*, Ex. 23:12.
i *Punishment, for Sabbath desecration*, Lev. 26:41.
j *Death, penalty*, Num. 23:10.

3
k *Fire, not to be kindled on the Sabbath*, Ex. 12:8.

4
l *Commandment, enjoining liberality to the house of God*, vs. 4-9; Deut. 8:2.

5
m *Offerings, free will*, Lev. 6:17.
n *Gold*, Ezek. 7:19.
o *Silver*, 1 Chr. 28:14.
p *Brass*, Job 28:2.

6
q *Colors, symbolical*, Ezek. 16:16.

7
r *Badger*, Ex. 25:5.
s *Acacia*, Ex. 26:15.
1 R. V. sealskins,

8
t *Oil*, Deut. 12:17.
u *Spices*, 1 Kin. 10:2.
v *Incense*, Ex. 37:29.

9
w *Onyx, for the priests' vestments*, Ezek. 28:13.
x *Ephod*, Ex. 28:6.
y *Breastplate, free will offering of materials for*, Ex. 28:4.

v.11-1533 BC
See footnote, *Time*, Rev. 10:6.

11
z *Tabernacle, materials for, voluntarily offered*, vs. 20-29; Ex. 27:9.
2 R. V. its clasps,

12
a *Ark, of tabernacle*, Ex. 25:10.
b *Mercy Seat*, Ex. 25.17.

14
c *Lamp*, Ex. 27:20.
d *Oil*, Deut. 12:17.
3 R. V. its vessels,

15
e *Altar, of incense*, Ex. 30:1.

16
f *Altar, of burnt offerings*, Gen. 8:20.

17
g *Court, of tabernacle*, Ex. 38:9.

19
h *High Priest, vestments of*, Lev. 21:10.
i *Priest, vestments, of*, Lev. 1:5.

21
j *Israel, gifts consecrated by, for the tabernacle*, Ex. 4:22.
k *Liberality, instances of*, vs. 21-29; 1 Tim. 6:18.
4 R. V. tent of meeting,

*Of Moses*, Ex. 34:29-35; *of Jesus*, Matt. 17:2; Luke 9:29. *Covering of*, Isa. 6:2. *Disfigured, in fasting*, Matt. 6:16.

* **VAIL.** *A covering for the ark*, Ex. 35:12; 39:34; 40:21, Num. 4:5.

† **SHEWBREAD,** Heb. 9:2. *Called* HALLOWED BREAD, 1 Sam. 21:6. *Ordinance concerning*, Lev. 24:5-9. *Required to be kept before the Lord continually*, Ex. 25:30; 2 Chr. 2:4. *Provided by a yearly per capita tax*, Neh. 10:32, 33. *Prepared by the Levites*, 1 Chr. 9:32; 23:29. *Unlawfully eaten by David*, 1 Sam. 21:6; Matt. 12:3, 4, Mark 2:25, 26; Luke 6:3, 4. *Placed on the table of shewbread*, Ex. 40:22, 23.

**Table of,** Heb. 9:2. *Ordinances concerning*, Ex. 25:23-30; 37:10-15. *Its situation in the tabernacle*, Ex. 26:35; 40:22. *Furniture of*, Ex. 25:29, 30; 37:16; Num. 4:7. *Consecration of*, Ex. 30:26, 27, 29. *How removed*, Num. 4:7, 15. *For the temple*, 1 Kin. 7:48; 2 Chr. 4:19.

v.22–1533 BC
See footnote, *Time,* Rev. 10:6.

**22**
l *Women, consecrated jewels to the tabernacle,* Prov. 31:10.
m *Bracelet,* Gen. 24:22.
n *Earring,* Prov. 25:12.
o *Ring,* Gen. 41:42.
p *Jewels,* Gen. 24:53.
q *Gold,* Ezek. 7:19.
5 R. V. brooches,
6 R. V. signet-rings,
7 R. V. armlets,
**23**
r *Colors, symbolical,* Ezek. 16:16.
s *Linen,* Ezek. 27:16.
t *Goat, hair of, used for curtains of tabernacle,* Deut. 14:4.
u *Badger,* Ex. 25:5.
**24**
v *Silver,* 1 Chr. 28:14.
w *Brass,* Job 28:2.
x *Acacia, gifts of, for tabernacle,* Ex. 26:15.
8 R. V. acacia
**25**
y *Women, domestic duties of,* v. 26; Prov. 31:10.
z *Spinning,* Prov. 31:19.

a *Art,* 2 Chr. 16:14.
b *Liberality, instances of,* 1 Tim. 6:18.
c *Colors, symbolical,* Ezek. 16:16.
d *Linen,* Ezek. 27:16.
**26**
e *Wisdom,* Prov. 2:2.
**27**
f *Rulers,* Ex. 18:21.
g *Onyx,* Ezek. 28:13.
h *Precious Stones,* Ex. 39:10.
i *Ephod,* Ex. 28:6.
j *Breastplate,* Ex. 28:4.
**28**
k *Spices,* 1 Kin. 10:2.
l *Oil,* Deut. 12:17.
m *Incense,* Ex. 37:29.
n *Perfume,* Prov. 27:9.
**29**
o *Israel, gifts consecrated by, for tabernacle,* Ex. 4:22.
p *Offerings, free will,* Lev. 6:17.
q *Moses,* Ex. 2:10.

22 And [j]they came, both men and [l]women, as many as were willing hearted, *and* [k]brought [5,m]bracelets, and [n]earrings, and [6,o]rings, and [7]tablets,[G] all [p]jewels of [q]gold: and every man that offered *offered* an offering of gold unto the LORD.

23 And [j]every man, with whom was found [r]blue, and [r]purple, and [r]scarlet, and fine [s]linen, and [t]goats' *hair,* and red skins of rams, and [1,u]badgers' skins, [k]brought *them.*

24 [j]Every one that did offer an offering of [v]silver and [w]brass[G] brought the LORD's offering: and every man, with whom was found [8,x]shittim wood for any work of the service, brought *it.*

25 And all the [y]women that were wise hearted did [z,a]spin with their hands, and [b]brought that which they had spun, *both* of [c]blue, and of [c]purple, *and* of [c]scarlet, and of fine [d]linen.

26 And all the women whose heart stirred them up in [e]wisdom [a]spun goats' *hair.*

27 And the [f]rulers brought [g]onyx stones, and [h]stones to be set, for the [i]ephod, and for the [j]breastplate;

28 And [k]spice, and [l]oil for the light, and for the anointing oil, and for the sweet [m,n]incense.

29 The children of [o]Īṣ'ra-el [b]brought a [p]willing offering unto the LORD, every man and woman, whose heart made them willing to bring for all manner of work, which the LORD had commanded to be made by the hand of [q]Mō'ṣeṣ.

30 ¶ And [q]Mō'ṣeṣ said unto the children of Īṣ'ra-el, See, the LORD hath called by name [r,s,t]Bĕ-zăl'e-el the son of ‡Ū'rī, the son of [u]Hûr, of the tribe of [v]Jū'dah;

31 And he hath [w,x]filled him with the [y]spirit[G] of God, in [e]wisdom, in understanding, and in knowledge, and in all manner of workmanship;[T]

32 And to devise curious[G] works, to work in [z]gold, and in [a]silver, and in [b]brass,

33 And in the [c]cutting of [d]stones, to set *them,* and in ‖carving of wood, to make any manner of cunning[G] work.

34 And he hath [e]put in [f,g]his heart that he may teach, *both* he, and [h]Ā-hō'li-ăb, the son of [i]Ā-hĭs'a-măch, of the tribe of [j]Dăn.

35 Them hath he [e]filled with [k,l]wisdom of heart, to work all manner of [m]work, of the [n]engraver, and of the cunning[G] workman, and of the [o]embroiderer, in [p]blue, and in [p]purple, in [p]scarlet, and in fine [q]linen, and of the [r]weaver, *even* of them that do any work, and of those that devise cunning[G] work.

## CHAPTER 36

*The offerings are delivered to the workmen. 5 The liberality of the people is restrained. 8 The curtain with cherubim. 14 The curtains of goats' hair. 19 The covering of skins. 20 The boards with their sockets. 31 The bars. 35 The vail. 37 The hanging for the door.*

THEN wrought [a]Bē-zăl'e-el and *Ā-hō'li-ăb, and every wise hearted man, in whom the LORD [b,c]put [d]wisdom and understanding to know how to [e]work all manner of work for the service of the [f]sanctuary, according to all that the LORD had commanded.

2 And [g]Mō'ṣeṣ called [a]Bē-zăl'e-el and *Ā-hō'li-ăb, and

v.30–1533 BC
See footnote, *Time,* Rev. 10:6.

**30**
r *Bezaleel,* vs. 30–35; Ex. 31:2.
s *Artisan,* vs. 30–35; 1 Chr. 29:5.
t *Master Workman, instances of,* 1 Cor. 3:10.
u *Hur,* Ex. 31:2.
v *Judah, tribe of,* Num. 10:14.
**31**
w *Inspiration, of tabernacle workmen,* Job 32:8.
x *Genius, mechanical, divinely inspired,* Ex. 28:3.
y *Holy Spirit, inspiration of,* Acts 1:2.
**32**
z *Gold,* Ezek. 7:19.

a *Silver,* 1 Chr. 28:14.
b *Brass,* Job 28:2.
**33**
c *Lapidary,* Ex. 31:5.
d *Precious Stones,* Ex. 39:10.
**34**
e *Inspiration, of tabernacle workmen,* Job 32:8.
f *Bezaleel,* Ex. 31:2.
g *Master Workman, instances of,* 1 Cor. 3:10.
h *Aholiab,* Ex. 36:1.
i *Ahisamach,* Ex. 31:6.
j *Dan, tribe of,* Gen. 30:6.
**35**
k *Wisdom,* Prov. 2:2.
l *Genius, mechanical, divinely inspired,* Ex. 28:3.
m *Art,* 2 Chr. 16:14.
n *Engraving,* Ex. 32:4.
o *Embroidery,* Ezek. 26:16.
p *Colors, symbolical,* Ex. 16:16.
q *Linen,* Ezek. 27:16.
r *Weaving,* Isa. 38:12.

**1**
a *Bezaleel,* Ex. 31:2.
b *Inspiration,* Job 32:8.
c *Genius, mechanical, divinely inspired,* Ex. 28:3.
d *Wisdom, of skilled artisans,* Prov. 2.2.
e *Art.* 2 Chr. 16:14.
f *Sanctuary,* Lev. 4:6.
**2**
g *Moses,* Ex. 2:10.

‡ **URI** (fiery). *Father of Bezaleel,* Ex. 31:2; 35:30; 38:22, 1 Chr. 2:20; 2 Chr. 1:5.

‖ **CARVING.** *Woodwork of the temple was decorated with carvings of flowers, cherubim, and palm trees,* 1 Kin. 6:18, 29, 32, 35; Psa. 74:6. *Beds decorated with,* Prov. 7:16. *Idols manufactured by,* Deut. 7:5; Isa. 44:9–17; 45:20; Hab. 2:18, 19. Persons skilled in: *Bezaleel,* Ex. 31:5; *Hiram* 1 Kin. 7:13–51; 2 Chr. 2:13, 14.

* **AHOLIAB.** *An artificer of the tabernacle,* Ex. 31:6; 35:34; 36:1, 2; 38:23.

v.2–1533 BC
See footnote, *Time*, Rev. 10:6.

every wise hearted man, in whose heart the LORD had [b,c]put [d]wisdom, *even* every one whose heart stirred him up to come unto the work to do it:

3 And they received of [g]Mō'ṣeṣ all the offering, which the children of [h]Ĭṣ'ra-el had brought for the work of the service of the [l]sanctuary, to make it *withal*. And they [i]brought yet unto him free offerings every morning.

4 ¶ And all the wise men, that wrought all the work of the [l]sanctuary, came every man from his work which they made;

5 And they spake unto [g]Mō'ṣeṣ, saying, [h]The people [i]bring much more than enough for the service of the work, which the LORD commanded to make.

6 And [g]Mō'ṣeṣ gave commandment, and they caused it to be proclaimed throughout the camp, saying, Let neither man nor woman make any more work for the offering of the [l]sanctuary. So [h]the people were restrained from bringing.

7 [i]For the stuff they had was sufficient for all the work to make it, and too much.

8 ¶ And every wise hearted man among them that wrought the work of the [j]tabernacle made ten [k,l]curtains *of* fine twined [m]linen, and [n]blue, and [n]purple, and [n]scarlet: *with* [o]cherubims of cunning[G] work made he them.

9 The length of one [k]curtain *was* twenty and eight †cubits,[G] and the breadth of one curtain four cubits:[G] the curtains *were* all of one size.

10 And he coupled the five [k]curtains one unto another: and *the other* five curtains he coupled one unto another.

11 And he made loops of [n]blue on the edge of one [k]curtain from the selvedge[G] in the coupling: likewise he made in the uttermost[G] side of *another* curtain, in the coupling of the second.

12 Fifty loops made he in one [k]curtain, and fifty loops made he in the edge of the curtain which *was* in the coupling of the second: the loops held one *curtain* to another.

13 And he made fifty [1]taches[G] of [p]gold, and coupled the [k]curtains one unto another with the [1]taches: so it became one [j]tabernacle.

14 ¶ And he made [k]curtains *of* [q]goats' *hair* for the tent over the tabernacle: eleven curtains he made them.

15 The length of one [k]curtain *was* thirty †cubits,[G] and four cubits[G] *was* the breadth of one curtain: the eleven curtains *were* of one size.

16 And he coupled five [k]curtains by themselves, and six curtains by themselves.

17 And he made fifty loops upon the uttermost[G] edge of the [k]curtain in the coupling,[G] and fifty loops made he upon the edge of the curtain which coupleth the second.

18 And he made fifty [1]taches[G] *of* [r]brass to couple the tent together, that it might be one.

19 ¶ And he made a covering for the tent *of* rams' skins dyed [n]red, and a covering *of* [2,s]badgers' skins above *that*.

20 ¶ And he made boards for the [j]tabernacle *of* [t]shittim wood, standing up.

21 The length of a board *was* ten †cubits,[G] and the breadth of a board one cubit[G] and a half.

22 One board had two tenons,[G] [3]equally distant one from another: thus did he make for all the boards of the [j]tabernacle.

**3**
*h* *Israel, consecrate gifts for tabernacle*, Ex. 4:22.
*i* *Liberality, instances of*, vs.3–7; 1 Tim. 6:18.

**8**
*j* *Tabernacle*, Ex. 27:9.
*k* *Curtains, for the tabernacle*, Ex. 26:1.
*l* *Tapestry, of the tabernacle*, vs. 8–18; Prov. 7:16.
*m* *Linen*, Ezek. 27:16.
*n* *Colors, symbolical*, Ezek. 16:16.
*o* *Cherubim*, Ex. 37:7.

v.11–1533 BC
See footnote, *Time*, Rev. 10:6.

**13**
*p* *Gold*, Ezek. 7:19
1 R. V. clasps

**14**
*q* *Goat*, Deut. 14:4.

**18**
*r* *Brass*, Job 28:2.

**19**
*s* *Badger, skins of*, Ex. 25:5.
2 R. V. sealskins

**20**
*t* *Acacia*, Ex. 26:15.

**22**
3 R. V. joined one to

† **CUBIT.** About 17.5 inches. Cubit of Ezekiel, about 20.5 inches. *A measure of distance, equal to*, Gen. 6:16; Deut. 3:11; Ezek. 40:5; 43:13; Rev. 21:17. *Who can add to his height one*, Matt. 6:27; Luke 12:25.

v.23–1533 BC
See footnote, *Time*, Rev. 10:6.

24
*u Silver*, 1 Chr. 28:14.

29
4 R. V. double

31
5 R. V. acacia

35
*v Vail*, Ex. 26:31.

23 And he made boards for the [j]tabernacle; twenty boards for the south side southward:

24 And forty sockets of [u]silver he made under the twenty boards; two sockets under one board for his two tenons, and two sockets under another board for his two tenons.

25 And for the other side of the [j]tabernacle, *which is* toward the north corner, he made twenty boards,

26 And their forty sockets of [u]silver; two sockets under one board, and two sockets under another board.

27 And for the sides of the [j]tabernacle westward he made six boards.

28 And two boards made he for the corners of the [j]tabernacle in the two sides.

29 And they were [4]coupled beneath, and coupled together at the head[G] thereof, to one ring: thus he did to both of them in both the corners.

30 And there were eight boards; and their sockets *were* sixteen sockets of [u]silver, under every board two sockets.

31 ¶ And he made bars of [5,t]shittim wood; five for the boards of the one side of the [j]tabernacle,

32 And five bars for the boards of the other side of the [j]tabernacle, and five bars for the boards of the tabernacle for the sides westward.

33 And he made the middle bar to shoot[G] through the boards from the one end to the other.

34 And he overlaid the boards with [p]gold, and made their rings *of* gold *to be* places for the bars, and overlaid the bars with gold.

35 ¶ And he made a [v]vail *of* [n]blue, and [n]purple, and [n]scarlet, and fine twined [m]linen: *with* [o]cherubims made he it of cunning[G] work.[Q]

36 And he made thereunto four [w]pillars *of* [5,t]shittim *wood*, and overlaid them with [p]gold: their [‡]hooks *were of* gold; and he cast for them four sockets of [u]silver.

37 ¶ And he made an [k,l]hanging for the [6,j]tabernacle door *of* [n]blue, and [n]purple, and [n]scarlet, and fine twined [m]linen, of [x]needlework;

38 And the five [w]pillars of it with their [‡]hooks: and he overlaid their [y]chapiters[C] and their fillets[C] with [p]gold: but their five sockets *were of* [r]brass.[C]

## CHAPTER 37

*The ark. 6 The mercy seat with cherubim. 10 The table with its vessels. 17 The candlestick with its lamps and instruments. 25 The altar of incense. 29 The anointing oil and sweet incense.*

[a] AND [b]Bĕ-zăl′e-el made the [c]ark *of* [d]shittim wood: two [e]cubits[C] and a half *was* the length of it, and a cubit[G] and a half the breadth of it, and a cubit[G] and a half the height of it:

2 And he overlaid [c]it with pure [f]gold within and without, and made a crown[C] of gold to it round about.

3 And he [g]cast for [c]it four rings of [f]gold, *to be set* by the four corners of it; even two rings upon the one side of it, and two rings upon the other side of it.

4 And he made s t a v e s[C] *of* [d]shittim wood, and overlaid them with [f]gold.

5 And he put the staves into the rings by the sides of the [c]ark, to bear the ark.

6 ¶ [a]And he made the [h]mercy seat *of* pure [f]gold: two [e]cubits and a half *was* the length thereof, and one cubit and a half the breadth thereof.

v.35–1533 BC
See footnote, *Time*, Rev. 10:6.

36
*w Pillars, of the tabernacle*, Gen. 28:18.

37
*x Embroidery*, Ezek. 26:16.
6 R. V. tent

38
*y Chapiter*, 1 Kin. 7:16.

1
*a Tabernacle, furniture of*, vs. 1–29: Ex. 27:9.
*b Bezaleel*, Ex. 31:2.
*c Ark, of tabernacle*, Ex. 25:10.
*d Acacia*, Ex. 26.15.
*e Cubit*, Ex. 36:9.

2
*f Gold*, Ezek. 7:19.

3
*g Molding*, 1 Kin. 7:16.

6
*h Mercy Seat*, Ex. 25:17.

‡ **HOOKS.** *For tabernacle, made of gold*, Ex. 26:32, 37; 36:36; *made of silver*, Ex. 27:10; 38:10–12, 17, 19. *In the temple, seen in Ezekiel's vision*, Ezek. 40:43. *Used, for catching fish*, Ezek. 29:4; Matt. 17:27; *for pruning*, Isa. 2:4; 18:5; Joel 3:10. **Figurative**, Ezek. 38:4.

v.7-1533 BC
See footnote, *Time*, Rev. 10:6.

7 [a]And he made two *cherubims *of* [f]gold, beaten out of one piece made he them, on the two ends of the [h]mercy seat;

8 One cherub on the end on this side, and another cherub on the *other* end on that side: out of the [h]mercy seat made he the *cherubims on the two ends thereof.

9 And the *cherubims spread out *their* wings on high, *and* covered with their wings over the [h]mercy seat, with their faces one to another; *even* to the mercy seatward[G] were the faces of the cherubims.

10 ¶ And he made the [i]table *of* [1,d]shittim wood: two [e]cubits *was* the length thereof, and a cubit the breadth thereof, and a cubit and a half the height thereof:

11 And he overlaid [i]it with pure [f]gold, and made thereunto a crown[G] of gold round about.

12 Also he made thereunto a border of an [j]handbreadth[G] round about; and made a crown[G] of [f]gold for the border thereof round about.

13 And he cast for [i]it four rings of [f]gold, and put the rings upon the four corners that *were* in the four feet thereof.

14 Over against the border were the rings, the places for the staves to bear the [i]table.

15 And he made the staves *of* [1,d]shittim wood, and overlaid them with [f]gold, to bear the [i]table.

16 [a]And he made the vessels which *were* upon the [i]table, his dishes, and his spoons, and his [k]bowls, and [2]his covers to cover[G] withal,[G] *of* pure [f]gold.

17 ¶ [a]And he made the [l]candlestick *of* pure gold: *of* [m]beaten work made he the candlestick;[G] his shaft, and his branch, his bowls, his knops,[G] and his flowers, were of the same:

18 And six branches going out of the sides thereof; three branches of the [l]candlestick[G] out of the one side thereof, and three branches of the [l]candlestick out of the other side thereof:

19 Three bowls made [3]after the fashion of [n]almonds in one branch, a knop[G] and a flower; and three bowls made [3]like almonds in another branch, a knop and a flower: so throughout the six branches going out of the candlestick,[G]

20 And in the [l]candlestick[G] *were* four bowls made [3]like [n]almonds, his knops,[G] and his flowers:

21 And a knop[G] under two branches of the same, and a knop under two branches of the same, and a knop under two branches of the same, according to the six branches going out of it.

22 Their knops[G] and their branches were of the same: all of it *was* one [m]beaten work *of* pure [f]gold.

23 And he made his seven [o]lamps, and his snuffers, and his snuffdishes, *of* pure gold.

24 *Of* a talent[G] of pure [f]gold made he it, and all the vessels thereof.

25 ¶ [a]And he made the incense [p]altar *of* [1,d]shittim wood: the length of it *was* a [e]cubit, and the breadth of it a cubit; *it was* foursquare; and two cubits *was* the height of it; the horns thereof were of the same.

26 And he overlaid [p]it with pure [f]gold, *both* the top of it, and

**10**
*i Shewbread, table of*, vs. 10-15; Ex. 35:13.
1 R. V. acacia

**12**
*j Measure, linear*, Deut. 25:15.

**16**
*k Bowl, made of gold*, Ex. 25:29.
2 Am. R. V. the flagons thereof, to pour out therewith,

**17**
*l Candlestick*, vs. 17-24; Ex. 25:31.
*m* Ex. 25:18; Num. 8:4.

v.17-1533 BC
See footnote, *Time*, Rev. 10:6.

**19**
*n Almond*, Gen. 43:11.
3 R.V. like almond blossoms

**23**
*o Lamp*, Ex. 27:20.

**25**
*p Altar, of incense*, vs. 25-28; Ex. 30:1.

* **CHERUBIM.** *Eastward of the garden of Eden*, Gen. 3:24.
**In the Tabernacle,** Ex. 25:18-20; 37:7-9. *Figures of, embroidered on walls of tabernacle*, Ex. 26:1; 36:8; *and on the vail*, Ex. 26:31; 36:35.
**In the Temple,** 1 Kin. 6:23-29; 2 Chr. 3:10-13. *Ark rested beneath the wings of*, 1 Kin. 8:6, 7; 2 Chr. 5:7, 8; Heb. 9:5. *Figures of, on the vail*, 2 Chr. 3:14; *on the walls*, 1 Kin. 6:29-35 2 Chr. 3:7; *on the lavers*, 1 Kin. 7:29, 36. *In Ezekiel's vision of the temple*, Ezek. 41:18-20, 25.
**Figurative,** Ezek. 28:14, 16.
**Symbolical,** Ezek. 1; 10.

v.26–1533 BC
See footnote, *Time*, Rev. 10:6.

29
*q* *Oil, sacred*, Deut. 12:17.
*r* *Ointment, sacred*, Eccl. 7:1.
*s* *Spices*, 1 Kin. 10:2.
*t* *Apothecary*, Neh. 3:8.

1
*a* *Tabernacle, furniture of*, vs. 1–8; Ex. 27:9.
*b* *Bezaleel*, Ex. 31:2.
*c* *Altar, of burnt offerings*, Gen. 8:20.
*d* *Offerings, burnt*, Lev. 6:17.
*e* *Acacia*, Ex. 26:15.
*f* *Cubit*, Ex. 36:9.

2
*g* *Brass*, Job 28:2.

3
*h* *Shovel*, Num. 4:14.
*i* *Basin*, 1 Kin. 7:50.
*j* *Fleshhook*. Ex. 27:3.
*k* *Firepan*, 2 Kin. 25:15.

4
1 R. V. ledge round it

the sides thereof round about,
and the horns of it: also he made
unto it a crown[G] of gold round
about.
27 And he made two rings of
[f]gold for [p]it under the crown[G]
thereof, by the two corners of it,
upon the two sides thereof, to be
places for the staves to bear
it withal.
28 And he made the staves *of*
[1,d]shittim wood, and overlaid
them with [f]gold.
29 ¶ [a]And he made the holy
anointing [q,r]oil, and the pure
[†]incense of sweet [s]spices, according to the work of the
[t]apothecary.[G]

## CHAPTER 38

*The altar of burnt offering. 8 The laver of brass. 9 The court. 21 The sum of what the people offered.*

[a] AND [b]he made the [c]altar of
[d]burnt offering *of* [e]shittim
wood: five [f]cubits[G] *was* the length
thereof, and five cubits the
breadth thereof; *it was* foursquare; and three cubits[G] the
height thereof.
2 And he made the horns
[c]thereof on the four corners of it;
the horns thereof were of the
same: and he overlaid it with
[g]brass.
3 And he made all the vessels
of the [c]altar, the pots, and the
[h]shovels, and the [i]basons, *and*
the [j]fleshhooks, and the [k]fire-
pans: all the vessels thereof
made he *of* [g]brass.
4 And he made for the [c]altar a
brasen[G] grate[G] of network under
the [1]compass thereof beneath
unto the midst of it.
5 And he cast four rings for the
four ends of the grate of [g]brass,
*to be* places for the staves.
6 And he made the staves *of*
[2,e]shittim wood, and overlaid
them with [g]brass.
7 And he put the staves into the
rings on the sides of the [c]altar,
to bear it withal; he made the
altar hollow with boards.
8 ¶ [a]And he made the [l]laver[G] *of*
[g]brass,[G] and the foot of it *of* brass,
[m]of the [3,n]looking-glasses of *the*
[4,o]*women* assembling, which assembled *at* the door of the [5]tab-
ernacle of the congregation.
9 ¶ And he made the [*,p]court:
on the south side southward the
[q]hangings of the court *were of* fine
twined [r]linen, an hundred [f]cubits:[G]
10 Their [s]pillars *were* twenty,
and their brasen[G] sockets twenty;
the [t]hooks of the pillars and
their fillets[G] *were of* [u]silver.
11 And for the north side *the*
[q]*hangings were* an hundred [f]cu-
bits, their [s]pillars *were* twenty,
and their sockets of [g]brass[G] twenty; the [t]hooks of the pillars and
their fillets[G] *of* [u]silver.
12 And for the west side *were*
[q]hangings of fifty cubits, their
[s]pillars ten, and their sockets
ten; the [t]hooks of the pillars and
their fillets[G] *of* [u]silver.
13 And for the east side eastward fifty cubits.[G]
14 The [q]hangings of the one
side *of the gate were* fifteen [f]cu-
bits[G]; their [s]pillars three, and
their sockets three.
15 And for the other side of the
[*,p]court gate, on this hand and
that hand, *were* hangings of fifteen cubits[G]; their [s]pillars three,
and their sockets three.

v.5–1533 BC
See footnote, *Time*, Rev. 10:6.

6
2 R. V. acacia

8
*l* *Laver*, Ex. 30:18.
*m* *Liberality, instances of*, 1 Tim. 6:18.
*n* *Mirror*, Job 37:18.
*o* *Women, consecrated mirrors to the tabernacle*, Prov. 31:10.
3 R. V. mirrors
4 R. V. serving women which served at
5 R. V. tent of meeting.

9
*p* *Tabernacle, court of*, Ex. 27:9.
*q* *Curtains*, Ex. 26:1.
*r* *Linen*, Ezek. 27:16.

10
*s* *Pillars, of court of tabernacle*, Gen. 28:18.
*t* *Hooks, of silver*, Ex. 36:36.
*u* *Silver*, 1 Chr. 28:14.

† **INCENSE.** *Formula for compounding*, Ex. 30:34, 35. *Uses of*, Ex. 30:36–38, Lev. 16:12, 13; Num. 16:17, 18, 35, 40, 46; Deut. 33:10. *Compounded, by Bezaleel*, Ex. 37:29; *by priests*, 1 Chr. 9:30. *Offered morning and evening*, Ex. 30:7, 8; 2 Chr. 13:11. *Offered on the golden altar*, Ex. 30:1–7; 40:5, 27; 2 Chr. 2:4; 32:12. *Offered in making atonement*, Lev. 16:12, 13; Num. 16:46, 47; Luke 1:10. *Unlawfully offered, by Nadab and Abihu*, Lev. 10:1, 2; *by Korah, Dathan, and Abiram*, Num. 16:16–35; *by Uzziah*, 2 Chr. 26:16–21. *Offered in idolatrous worship*, 1 Kin. 11:8; 12:33; 2 Kin. 17:11; 2 Chr. 25:14; 28:3; Jer. 19:13; Ezek. 8:11.
*Presented by the wise men to Jesus*, Matt. 2:11.
See footnote, ALTAR OF INCENSE, Ex. 30:1.
**Figurative:** *Of prayer*, Psa. 141:2. *Of praise*, Mal. 1:11. *Of an acceptable sacrifice*, Eph. 5:2.
**Symbolical:** *Of the prayers of saints*, Rev. 5:8; 8:3, 4.

* **COURT. Of the tabernacle,** Ex. 27:9, 12, 16–19; 35:17, 18; 38:9, 15–20, 31; 39:40; 40:8, 33; Lev. 6:16, 26; Num. 3:26, 37; 4:26.
**Of the temple,** 1 Chr. 28:12; 2 Chr. 4:9; 6:13; 23:5; 33:5.
*The inner court*, 1 Kin. 6:36; 7:12.
*The middle court*, 1 Kin. 8:64; 2 Chr. 7:7.

v.16–1533 BC
See footnote, *Time*, Rev. 10:6.

16 All the hangings of the *,[p]court round about *were* of fine twined [r]linen.

17 And the sockets for the [s]pillars *were of* brass[G]; the [t]hooks of the pillars and their fillets[G] *of* [u]silver; and the overlaying of their chapiters[G] *of* silver; and all the pillars of the court *were* filleted[G] with silver.

18 And the [q]hanging for the gate of the *,[p]court *was* needlework, *of* [v]blue, and [v]purple, and [v]scarlet, and fine twined linen: and twenty cubits *was* the length, and the height in the breadth *was* five cubits, answerable to the hangings of the court.

19 And their [s]pillars *were* four, and their sockets *of* brass[G] four; their [t]hooks *of* [u]silver, and the overlaying of their chapiters[G] and their fillets[G] *of* silver.

20 And all the pins of the tabernacle, and of the court round about, *were of* brass.

21 ¶ This is the sum of the tabernacle, *even* of the tabernacle of testimony, as it was counted, according to the commandment of [w]Mō′ṣeṣ, *for* the service of the [x]Lē′vītes, by the hand of †Ĭth′a-mär, son to [y]Aâr′on the priest. [Q]

22 And [z]Bĕ-zăl′e-el the son of Ū′rī, the son of [a]Hûr, of the tribe of [b]Jū′dah, made all that the LORD commanded Mō′ṣeṣ.

23 And with him *was* [c]Ă-hō′-li-ăb, son of [d]Ă-hĭs′a-măch, of the tribe of [e]Dăn, an [f]engraver, and a cunning[G] workman, and an [g]embroiderer in [h]blue, and in [h]purple, and in [h]scarlet, and in fine linen.

24 All the [i]gold that was occupied[G] for the work in all the work of the [6,j]holy *place*, even the gold of the offering, was twenty and nine ‡talents[G], and seven hundred and thirty [k]shekels[G], after the shekel of the [l]sanctuary.

25 And the [m]silver of them that were [n]numbered of the congregation *was* an hundred ‡talents[G], and a thousand seven hundred and threescore and fifteen [k]shekels[G], after the shekel of the [l]sanctuary:

26 A [o]bekah for every man, *that is*, half a [k]shekel[G], after the shekel of the [l]sanctuary, for every one that went to be [n]numbered, from twenty years old and upward, for six hundred thousand and three thousand and five hundred and fifty *men*. [Q]

27 And of the hundred ‡talents[G] of [m]silver were [p]cast the sockets of the [l]sanctuary, and the sockets of the [q]vail; an hundred sockets of the hundred talents, a talent for a socket.

28 And of the thousand seven hundred seventy and five [k]*shekels*[G] he made [r]hooks for the [s]pillars, and overlaid their chapiters[G], and filleted[G] them.

29 And the [t]brass of the offering *was* seventy ‡talents[G], and two thousand and four hundred [k]shekels[G].

30 And therewith he made the sockets to the door of the [7,u]tabernacle of the congregation, and the brasen [v]altar, and the brasen[G] grate for it, and all the vessels of the altar,

31 And the sockets of the *court round about, and the sockets of the court gate, and all the pins of the [u]tabernacle, and all the pins of the court round about.

**18**
*Colors, symbolical*, Ezek. 16:16.

**21**
*w Moses*, Ex. 2:10.
*x Levites*, Deut. 10:8.
*y Aaron*, Ex. 6:20.

**22**
*z Bezaleel*, Ex. 31:2.

*a Hur*, Ex. 31:2.
*b Judah, tribe of*, Num. 10:14.

**23**
*c Aholiab*, Ex. 36:1.
*d Ahisamach*, Ex. 31:6.
*e Dan, tribe of*, Gen. 30:6.
*f Engraving*, Ex. 32:4.
*g Embroidery*, Ezek. 26:16.
*h Colors, symbolical*, Ezek. 16:16.

**24**
*i Gold, for the tabernacle*, Ezek. 7:19.

v.24–1533 BC
See footnote, *Time* Rev. 10:6.

*j Holy Place*, Ex. 26:33.
*k Shekel*, Ex. 30:13.
*l Sanctuary*, Lev. 4:6.
6 R. V. sanctuary

**25**
*m Silver, for the tabernacle*, 1 Chr. 28:14.
*n Census*, 2 Sam. 24:1.

**26**
*o Tax*, Neh. 10:32.

**27**
*p Molding*, 1 Kin. 7:16.
*q Vail*, Ex. 26:31.

**28**
*r Hooks*, Ex. 36:36.
*s Pillar*, Gen. 28:18.

**29**
*t Brass*, Job 28:2.

**30**
*u Tabernacle*, Ex. 27:9.
*v Altar, of burnt offerings*, Gen. 8:20.
7 R. V. tent of meeting.

† **ITHAMAR.** *Son of Aaron*, Ex. 6:23; 28:1; 1 Chr. 6:3. *Intrusted with moneys of the tabernacle*, Ex. 38:21. *Charged with duties of the tabernacle*, Num. 4:28; 7:8. *Forbidden to lament the death of his brothers, Nadab and Abihu*, Lev. 10:6, 7. *Descendants of*, 1 Chr. 24:1–19.

‡ **TALENT.** Value of, of gold, about six thousand pounds, or, twenty-nine thousand, one hundred and fifty dollars; of silver, four hundred and ten pounds, or, nearly two thousand dollars, 1 Kin. 9:14, 28; 10:10, 14. *A weight equal to three thousand shekels—about one hundred and twenty-five pounds*, Ex. 38:25, 26.
*Parables of the*, Matt. 18:23–35; 25:15, 28.

v.1–1533 BC
See footnote, *Time,*
Rev. 10:6.

1
a *Colors, symbolical,* Ezek. 16:16.
b *Holy Place, priest ministered in,* Ex. 26:33.
c *High Priest, vestments of,* vs. 1–31; Lev. 21:10.
d *Aaron,* Ex. 6:20.
e *Moses,* Ex. 2:10.
1 R. V. finely wrought garments.

2
f *Ephod,* vs. 2–26; Ex. 28:6.
g *Gold,* Ezek. 7:19.
h *Linen,* Ezek. 27:16.

3
i *Embroidery, gold thread used in,* Ezek. 26:16.

5
j *Girdle,* Prov. 31:24.

6
k *Onyx,* Ezek. 28:13.
l *Engraving,* Ex. 32:4.
m *Seal,* 1 Kin. 21:8.

7
n *Memorial,* Num. 16:40.

8
o *Breastplate,* Ex. 28:4.

## CHAPTER 39

*The clothes of service and holy garments. 2 The ephod. 8 The breastplate. 22 The robe of the ephod. 27 The coats, mitre, and girdle of fine linen. 30 The plate of the holy crown. 32 All is viewed and approved by Moses.*

AND of the [a]blue, and [a]purple, and [a]scarlet, they
made [1]cloths of service, to do
service in the [b]holy *place,* and
made the holy [c]garments for
[d]Aâr′on; as the LORD commanded
[e]Mō′ṣeṣ.
2 And he made the [f]ephod[G] *of*
[g]gold, [a]blue, and [a]purple, and
[a]scarlet, and fine twined [h]linen.
3 And they did beat the [g]gold
into thin plates, and cut *it into*
wires, to [i]work *it* in the [a]blue,
and in the [a]purple, and in the
[a]scarlet, and in the fine [h]linen,
*with* cunning[G] work.
4 They made shoulderpieces
for [f]it, to couple *it* together: by
the two edges was it coupled
together.
5 And the curious[G] [j]girdle of his
[f]ephod,[G] that *was* upon it, *was* of
the same, according to the work
thereof; *of* [g]gold, [a]blue, and [a]purple,
and [a]scarlet, and fine twined
[h]linen; as the LORD commanded
[e]Mō′ṣeṣ.
6 ¶ And they wrought [k]onyx
stones inclosed in ouches[G] of
[g]gold, [l]graven, as [m]signets[G] are
graven,[G] with the names of the
children of Ĭṣ′ra-el.
7 And he put them on the
shoulders of the [f]ephod, *that*
*they should be* stones for a [n]memorial
to the children of Ĭṣ′ra-el;
as the LORD commanded [e]Mō′ṣeṣ.
8 ¶ And he made the [o]breastplate
*of* cunning[G] [i]work, like the
work of the [f]ephod; *of* [g]gold,
[a]blue, and purple, and scarlet,
and fine twined [h]linen.
9 It was foursquare; they made
the [o]breastplate double: a [p]span[G]
*was* the length thereof, and a
span the breadth thereof, *being*
doubled.
10 And they set in it four rows
of *stones: *the first* row *was* a
[q]sardius, a [r]topaz, and a [s]carbuncle:
this *was* the first row.
11 And the second row, an
[t]emerald, a [u]sapphire, and a
†diamond.
12 And the third row, a
[2,v]ligure, an [w]agate, and an
[x]amethyst.
13 And the fourth row, a
[y]beryl, an [k]onyx, and a [z]jasper:
*they were* inclosed in ouches[G] of
[a]gold in their inclosings.
14 And the *stones *were* according
to the names of the
children of Ĭṣ′ra-el, twelve, according
to their names, *like* the
[b]engravings of a [c]signet, every
one with his name, according to
the twelve tribes.
15 And they made upon the
[d]breastplate [e]chains [3]at the ends,
*of* wreathen[G] work *of* pure [a]gold.
16 And they made two ouches[G]
*of* [a]gold, and two gold rings; and
put the two rings in the two ends
of the [d]breastplate.
17 And they put the two
wreathen[G] [e]chains of [a]gold in the
two rings on the ends of the
[d]breastplate.
18 And the two ends of the two
wreathen[G] [e]chains they fastened
in the two ouches,[G] and put them
on the shoulderpieces of the
[f]ephod, before it.

v.8–1533 BC
See footnote, *Time,*
Rev. 10:6.

9
p *Span,* Ex. 28:16.

10
q *Sardius,* Ex. 28:17.
r *Topaz,* Ezek. 28:13.
s *Carbuncle,* Isa. 54:12.

11
t *Emerald,* Rev. 4:3.
u *Sapphire,* Job 28:6.

12
v Ex. 28:19.
w *Agate,* Ex. 28:19.
x *Amethyst,* Rev. 21:20.
2 R. V. jacinth.

13
y *Beryl,* Ezek. 1:16.
z *Jasper,* Rev. 21:19.

a *Gold,* Ezek. 7:19.

14
b *Engraving,* Ex. 32:4.
c *Seal,* 1 Kin. 21:8.

15
d *Breastplate,* Ex. 28:4.
e *Chains,* Dan. 5:7.
3 R. V. like cords.

18
f *Ephod,* Ex. 28:6.

*** PRECIOUS STONES.** In the breastplate of the high priest the stones were set, probably, in the order of the tribes of the children of Israel, reading from the right upper corner to the left. The first stone, sardius was probably the tribal stone for Reuben; topaz, for Simeon; carbuncle, for Levi; emerald, for Judah; sapphire, for Issachar; diamond, for Zebulun; ligure, or jacinth, for Dan; agate, for Naphtali; amethyst, for Asher; beryl, for Gad; onyx, for Joseph; jasper, for Benjamin, Ex. 28:9–21; 39:6–14. *Voluntary offerings of, by the Israelites for the breastplate and ephod,* Ex. 35:27. *Exported, from Sheba,* 1 Kin. 10:2, 10; 2 Chr. 9:1, 9; Ezek. 27:22; *from Ophir,* 1 Kin. 10:11; 2 Chr. 9:10. *Partial catalogue of,* Ezek. 28:13. *Seen in the foundation of the New Jerusalem in John's apocalyptic vision,* Rev. 21:19–21. *In kings' crowns,* 2 Sam. 12:30; 1 Chr. 20:2.

**Figurative,** Isa. 54:11, 12.

See footnotes: AGATE, Ex. 28:19; AMETHYST, Rev. 21:20; BERYL, Ezek. 1:16; CARBUNCLE, Isa. 54:12; CRYSTAL, Rev. 4:6; DIAMOND, Ex. 39:11; EMERALD, Rev. 4:3; JASPER, Rev. 21:19; RUBY, Job 28:18; SAPPHIRE, Job 28:6; SARDIUS, Ex. 28:17; TOPAZ, Ezek. 28:13.

**† DIAMOND,** possibly Sardonyx. *One of, the jewels in the breastplate,* Ex. 28:18; 39:11; Jer. 17:1; Ezek. 28:13.

v.19–1533 BC
See footnote, *Time*, Rev. 10:6.

19 And they made two rings of
gold, and put *them* on the two
ends of the [d]breastplate, upon
the border of it, which *was* on
the side of the [f]ephod inward.
20 And they made two *other*
golden rings, and put them on
the two sides of the [f]ephod underneath,
toward the forepart of
it, over against the *other* coupling
thereof, above the curious[G]
[g]girdle of the ephod.
21 And they did bind the
[d]breastplate by his rings unto
the rings of the [f]ephod with a
lace of [h]blue, that it might be
above the curious[G] [g]girdle of the
ephod, and that the breastplate
might not be loosed from the
ephod; as the LORD commanded
[i]Mō′ṣeṣ.
22 ¶ And he made the robe of
the [f]ephod *of* [j]woven work, all
*of* [h]blue.
23 And *there was* an hole in the
midst of the robe, as the hole
of an [k]habergeon,[G] *with* a band
round about the hole, that it
should not rend.
24 And they made upon the
hems of the robe [l]pomegranates
*of* [h]blue, and [h]purple, and [h]scarlet,
*and* twined [m]*linen.*
25 And they made [n]bells *of*
pure gold, and put the bells between
the [l]pomegranates upon
the hem of the robe, round about
between the pomegranates;
26 A [n]bell and a [l]pomegranate,
a bell and a pomegranate, round
about the hem of the robe to
minister[G] *in*; as the LORD commanded
[i]Mō′ṣeṣ.
27 ¶ And they made [o,p]coats *of*
fine [m]linen *of* [j]woven work for
[q]Aâr′on, and for his sons,
28 And a [r]mitre *of* fine [m]linen,
and goodly [4,s,t]bonnets[G] *of* fine
linen, and linen [u]breeches *of* fine
twined linen,
29 And a [g]girdle *of* fine twined
[m]linen, and [h]blue, and [h]purple,
and [h]scarlet, *of* [5,v]needlework;
as the LORD commanded
[i]Mō′ṣeṣ.
30 ¶ And they made the plate
of the holy [w]crown *of* pure [a]gold,
and wrote upon it a [x]writing,
*like to* the [b]engravings of a [c]signet,
[‡,y]HOLINESS TO THE
LORD.
31 And they tied unto it a lace
of [h]blue, to fasten *it* on high up-

**20**
*g Girdle*, Prov. 31:24.

**21**
*h Colors, symbolical*, Ezek. 16:16.
*i Moses*, Ex. 2:10.

**22**
*j Weaving*, Isa. 38:12.

**23**
*k Coat of Mail*, 1 Sam. 17:5.

**24**
*l Pomegranate*, Num. 13:23.

v.24–1533 BC
See footnote, *Time*, Rev. 10:6.

*m Linen*, Ezek. 27:16.

**25**
*n Bell*, Ex. 28:33.

**27**
*o High Priest, vestments of*, Lev. 21:10.
*p Priest, vestments of*, Lev. 1:5.
*q Aaron*, Ex. 6:20.

**28**
*r Miter*, Ex. 28:4.
*s Turban*, Ex. 28:40.
*t Dress, of the head*, Zech. 3:4.
*u Breeches*, Ex. 28:42.
4 R. V. headtires

**29**
*v Embroidery*, Ezek. 26:16.
5 R. V. the work of the embroiderer;

**30**
*w Crown*, Ex. 29:6.
*x Legends*, Zech. 14:20.
*y Instruction, by legends*, Prov. 23:23.

‡ **HOLINESS.** [Sin and Holiness, sinful man and the Holy Jehovah, were the dominant ideas in the Mosaic law. To impress the nation of Israel, which was to become a separated and holy people, and through them, as the medium of the divine revelation, to impress all people for all time with the great and central truth of the true religion, namely, that a holy God can be pleased by none but holy people, was the supreme purpose of the system of Mosaic ordinances. The student must, therefore, seek for this spiritual purpose through all the ordinances of the law. Defilement and uncleanness, exclusion of the unclean from the congregation, atonements and atoning sacrifices, washings and purifications, *whole* burnt offerings, *unblemished* priests and *unblemished* offerings typical of *unblemished* and *uncorrupted* motives in worship and service, were ordained as object lessons to teach that there is a difference between unholiness and holiness, and between the unholy and the holy, and thus to exalt holiness as the supreme lesson of life.

As in the books of the Mosaic law, so throughout the Holy Scriptures, the attainment of holiness is the dominant theme.]

**Attribute of God,** Josh. 24:19; 1 Sam. 6:20; Job 6:10; Psa. 22:3; 47:8; 60:6; 89:35; 111:9; 145:17; Isa. 5:16; 6:3; 29:19, 23; 41:14; 43:14, 15; 47:4; 49:7; 57:15; Ezek. 36:21, 22; 39:7, 25; Hos. 11:9; Hab. 1:12, 13; Luke 1:49; John 17:11; Rom. 1:23; Rev. 4:8; 6:10; 15:4.

**Described,** Rom. 14:17. *As walking in uprightness*, Isa. 57:2. *As a highway*, Isa. 35:8. *As departing from evil*, Psa. 34:14; 37:27. *As satisfying*, John 6:35. *As crucifying the flesh*, Gal. 5:24. *As a new creature*, Gal. 6:15. *As a new man*, Eph. 4:24; Col. 3:10. *As a rest*, Heb. 4:3, 9. *As pure, peaceable, gentle*, Jas. 3:17.

**Enjoined,** Gen. 17:1; Ex. 22:31; Lev. 10:8–10; 11:44, 45; 19:2; 20:7, 26; Num. 15:40; Deut. 13:17; 18:13; Josh. 7:13; 2 Chr. 20:21; Job 5:24; Psa. 4:4; 97:10; Isa. 52:1, 11; Mic. 6:8; Zeph. 2:3; Matt. 5:29, 30, 48; 12:33; John 5:14 Rom. 6:1–23; 1 Cor. 3:16; 5:7; 15:34; 2 Cor. 6:14–17; 7:1 Eph. 1:4; 5:1, 3, 8–11; 1 Thess. 4:3, 4, 7; 5:22, 23; 2 Thess 2:13; 1 Tim. 4:12; 5:22; 6:11, 12; 2 Tim. 2:19, 21, 22 1 Pet. 1:5; 2 Pet. 1:5–8; 1 John 2:1, 5, 29; 2 John 4; Rev. 18:4

*Upon the church*, Ex. 19:6; 22:31; Deut. 7:6; 26:19; 28:9 Isa. 4:3; 52:1, 11; 60:1, 21; Zech. 8:3; 14:20, 21; 2 Cor. 11 2; 1 Pet. 2:5, 9; Rev. 19:8.

**Exhortations to,** Matt. 5:30; John 5:14; Rom. 6:13, 19 12:1, 2; 13:12–14; 1 Cor. 6:13, 19, 20; 10:31; 2 Cor. 13:7, 8 Eph. 4:22–24; Col. 3:5, 12–15; 1 Thess. 2:12; 3:13; 1 Tim 4:12; Tit. 2:9, 10, 12; 1 Pet. 4:1; 2 Pet. 3:11, 12, 14; 3 John 11

**Motives to:** *God's holiness*, Gen. 17:1; Lev. 11:44, 45 19:2; 20:26; Isa. 6:1–8; Matt. 5:48; 1 Pet. 1:15, 16; *God's mercies*, Rom. 12:1.

**A condition of eternal salvation,** Heb. 12:14.

**Taught:** *By figures*, Isa. 61:9–11; Matt. 12:33; 1 Cor 3:17; Eph. 2:21. *By mottoes*, Ex. 28:36; Zech. 14:20.

BY DISFELLOWSHIP: *Of the uncircumcised*, Gen. 17:14 *Of those who violated the law, of unleavened bread*, Ex. 12:15 *of sacrifices*, Lev. 17:9; 19:5–7; *of purification*, Num. 19:20 *Of those who were defiled*, Lev. 7:25, 27; 13:5, 21, 26; 17:10; 18 29; 19:8; 20:3–6; Num. 5:2, 3; 19:13. *Of those who were guilty of blasphemy*, Num. 15:31.

**Typified:** *In unblemished offerings*, Ex. 12:5; Lev. 1:3 10; 3:1, 6; 4:3, 23; 5:15; 6:6; 9:2, 3; 22:19, 21; Num. 28:3 9, 11, 19, 31; 29:2, 8, 13, 17, 20, 23, 26, 29, 32, 36. *In washing of offerings*, Lev. 1:9, 13. *In washing of priests*, Ex. 29:4 Lev. 8:6; 1 Chr. 15:14. *In washing of garments*, Lev. 11:28 40; 13:6, 34; 14:8, 9, 47; 15:5–13; Num. 19:7, 8, 10, 19, 21 *In purifications*, Lev. 12:4, 6–8; 15:16–18, 21, 22, 27; 16:4 24, 26, 28; 17:15, 16. *By making a difference between clean and unclean animals*, Lev. 11:1–47; 20:25; Deut. 14:3–20.

See footnotes: GOD, *Holiness of*, Gen. 2:2; SANCTIFICATION, 1 Pet. 1:2.

v.31–1533 BC
See footnote, *Time,* Rev. 10:6.

**32**
z *Tabernacle, completed,* Ex. 27:9.

a *Obedience, instances of,* Heb. 5:8.
b *Moses,* Ex. 2:10.
7 R. V. meeting.

**33**
c *Tabernacle, completed,* Ex. 27:9.

8 R. V. its clasps,

**34**
d *Colors, symbolical,* Ezek. 16:16.
e *Badger,* Ex. 25:5.
f *Vail,* Ex. 35:12.
9 R. V. sealskins,
10 R. V. screen;

**35**
g *Ark,* Ex. 25:10.
h *Mercy Seat,* Ex. 25:17.

**36**
i *Shewbread,* Ex. 35:13.

**37**
j *Candlestick,* Ex. 25:31.
k *Lamp,* Ex. 27:20.
l *Oil, illuminating,* Deut. 12:17.

**38**
m *Altar, of incense,* Ex. 30:1.
n *Oil, sacred,* Deut. 12:17.
o *Incense,* Ex. 37:29.
11 R. V. tent

**39**
p *Altar, of burnt offerings,* Gen. 8:20.
q *Brass,* Job 28:2.
r *Laver,* Ex. 30:18.

**40**
s *Court, of the tabernacle,* Ex. 38:9.
12 R. V. instruments

**41**
t *Holy Place,* Ex. 26:33.
u *High Priest, vestments of,* Lev. 21:10.
v *Priest, vestments of,* Lev. 1:5.

on the [7]mitre; as the LORD commanded [t]Mō′ṣeṣ.
32 Thus was all the work of the
[z]tabernacle of the tent of [7]the
congregation finished: and the
children of Ĭṣ′ra-el [a]did according
to all that the LORD commanded
[b]Mō′ṣeṣ, so did they.
33 ¶ And they brought the [c]tabernacle
unto [b]Mō′ṣeṣ, the tent,
and all his furniture, [8]his taches,[G]
his boards, his bars, and his pillars,
and his sockets,
34 And the covering of ‖rams'
skins dyed [d]red, and the covering
of [9,e]badgers' skins, and the
[f]vail of the [10]covering,
35 The [g]ark of the testimony,
and the staves thereof, and the
[h]mercy seat,
36 The table, *and* all the vessels
thereof, and the [i]shewbread,[G]
37 The pure [j]candlestick,[G] *with*
the [k]lamps thereof, *even with* the
lamps to be set in order, and all
the vessels thereof, and the [l]oil
for light,
38 And the golden [m]altar, and
the anointing [n]oil, and the sweet
[o]incense, and the hanging for the
[11]tabernacle door,
39 The brasen[G] [p]altar, and his
grate of [q]brass, his staves, and
all his vessels, the [r]laver and his
foot,[G]
40 The hangings of the [s]court,
his pillars, and his sockets, and
the hanging for the court gate,
his cords, and his pins, and all
the [12]vessels of the service of the
[c]tabernacle, for the tent of [6]the
congregation,
41 The cloths of service to do
service in the [t]holy *place,* and
the holy [u]garments for Aâr′on
the priest, and his sons' [v]garments,
to minister[G] in the priest's
office.
42 According to all that the
LORD commanded [b]Mō′ṣeṣ, [a]so
the children of Ĭṣ′ra-el made all
the work.
43 And Mō′ṣeṣ did look upon
all the work, and, behold, they
[a]had done it as the LORD had
commanded, even so had they
done it: and Mō′ṣeṣ [w]blessed
them.

## CHAPTER 40

*Moses is commanded to set up the tabernacle, 9 and to anoint it; 13 and to consecrate Aaron and his sons. 16 Moses performs all things accordingly. 34 A cloud covers the tabernacle.*

AND the LORD spake unto
[a]Mō′ṣeṣ, saying,
2 [b]On the first day of the first
[c]month shalt thou set up the
[d,e]tabernacle of the tent of [1]the
congregation.
3 And thou shalt put [f]therein
the [g]ark of the [h]testimony,[G] and
cover the ark with the [i]vail.
4 And thou shalt bring in the
[j]table, and set in order the things
that are to be set in order upon
it; and thou shalt bring in
the [k]candlestick,[G] and light the
[l]lamps thereof.
5 And thou shalt set the [m]altar
of gold for the [n]incense before
the [g]ark of the [h]testimony, and
put the hanging of the door to
the [d]tabernacle.
6 And thou shalt set the [o]altar
of the burnt offering before the
door of the [d]tabernacle of the
tent of [1]the congregation.
7 And thou shalt set the [p]laver
between the tent of [1]the congregation
and the altar, and shalt
put water therein.
8 And thou shalt set up the
[q,r]court round about, and hang
up the hanging at the court gate.
9 And thou shalt take the
anointing [s]oil, and [t]anoint the
[u]tabernacle, and all that *is* therein,
and shalt [v,w]hallow it, and all
the [2]vessels thereof: and it shall
be holy.
10 And thou shalt [t]anoint the

v.42–1533 BC
See footnote, *Time,* Rev. 10:6.

**43**
w *Benedictions,* Deut. 21:5.

**1**
a *Moses,* Ex. 2:10.

**2**
b *Statute, enjoining erection and furnishing of a house for public worship,* Deut. 8:2.
c *Month, Abib, tabernacle set up in,* Ex. 12:2.
d *Tabernacle,* Ex. 27:9.
e *Types, the sanctuary a type of the heavenly sanctuary,* Heb. 10:1.
1 R. V. meeting.

**3**
f *Holy Place, contents of,* Ex. 26:33.
g *Ark, of testimony,* Ex. 25:10.
h *Testimony,* Ex. 25:16.
i *Vail,* Ex. 35:12.

**4**
j *Shewbread, table of,* Ex. 35:13.
k *Candlestick,* Ex. 25:31.
l *Lamp,* Ex. 27:20.

**5**
m *Altar, of incense,* Ex. 30:1.
n *Incense, on the golden altar,* Ex. 37:29.

**6**
o *Altar, of burnt offerings,* Gen. 8:20.

**7**
p *Laver,* Ex. 30:18.

**8**
q *Court, of the tabernacle,* Ex. 38:9.
r *Tabernacle, court of,* Ex. 27:9.

**9**
s *Oil, sacred,* Deut. 12:17.
t *Anointing, in consecration,* Lev. 8:12.
u *Tabernacle, sanctified,* Ex. 27:9.
v *Sanctification, material things sanctified,* 1 Pet. 1:2.
w *Holiness, typified,* Ex. 39:30.
2 R. V. furniture

‖**RAM.** *Skins of, used for the roof of the tabernacle,* Ex. 26:14; 39:34. *Seen in Daniel's vision,* Dan. 8:2–25. *Used in sacrifice,* Gen. 22:13; Ex. 29:1, 3, 15; 29:15–32; Lev. 5:15; 8:2, 18–29. *Trumpets made of the horns of,* Josh. 6:4–6, 8, 13.

v.10–1533 BC
See footnote, *Time,* Rev. 10:6.

11
x *Laver, sanctified,* Ex. 30:18.
12
y *Statute, establishing and providing for the ordination of a holy ministry,* Deut. 8:2.
z *Ordination, of priests,* Ex. 29:1.

a *Priest, consecration of,* Lev. 1:5.
b *Ceremonial Washing,* Ex. 19:10.
c *Purification,* Num. 19:19.
3 R. V. tent of meeting,
13
d *Jesus, priesthood of, typified,* Matt. 1:21.
e *High Priest, vestments of,* Lev. 21:10.
f *Anointing, in consecration,* Lev. 8:12.
g *Ordination, of priests,* Ex. 29:1.
h *Sanctification,* 1 Pet. 1:2.
i *Holiness, typified,* Ex. 39:30.
16
j *Obedience, instances of,* Heb. 5:8.
k *Moses, character of,* Ex. 2:10.

v.17–1532 BC
See footnote, *Time,* Rev. 10:6.

17
l *Month,* Ex. 12:2.
m *Tabernacle,* Ex. 27:9.

20
n *Decalogue,* Ex. 20:3.
o *Ark, contents of, the law,* Ex. 25:10.
p *Mercy Seat, placed on ark of testimony,* Ex. 25:17.
21
q *Ark, place of,* Ex. 25:10.

[o]altar of the burnt offering, and
all his vessels, and [v,w]sanctify[C]
the altar: and it shall be an altar
most holy.
11 And thou shalt [t]anoint the
[x]laver and his foot,[C] and [v,w]sanc-
tify it.
12 And [y]thou shalt [z]bring
[a]Aâr′on and his sons unto the
door of the [3]tabernacle of the
congregation, and [b,c]wash them
with water.
13 And thou shalt put upon
[a,d]Aâr′on the holy [e]garments,
and [f,g]anoint him, and [h,i]sancti-
fy him; that he may minister unto me in the priest's office.
14 And thou shalt bring his
sons, and clothe them with coats:
15 And thou shalt [f,g]anoint
[a]them, as thou didst anoint their
father, that they may minister
unto me in the priest's office: for
their anointing shall surely be an
everlasting priesthood throughout their generations.
16 Thus [j]did [k]Mō′ṣeṣ: according to all that the LORD commanded him, so did he.
17 ¶ And it came to pass in the
first [l]month in the second year,
on the first *day* of the month,
*that* the [m]tabernacle was reared
up.
18 And Mō′ṣeṣ reared up the
[m]tabernacle, and fastened his
sockets, and set up the boards
thereof, and put in the bars
thereof, and reared up his
pillars.
19 And he spread abroad the
tent over the [m]tabernacle, and
put the covering of the tent
above upon it; as the LORD commanded Mō′ṣeṣ.
20 ¶ And he took and put the
[n]testimony into the [o]ark, and set
the staves on the ark, and put
the [p]mercy seat above upon the
ark:
21 And he brought the [q]ark into
the [m]tabernacle, and set up the
[r,s,t]vail of the covering, and covered the ark of the testimony; as
the LORD commanded Mō′ṣeṣ.
22 ¶ And he put the [u]table in
the tent of [4]the congregation, upon the side of the tabernacle
northward, [v]without[C] the vail.
23 And he set the [u]bread in
order upon it before the LORD;
as the LORD had commanded
Mō′ṣeṣ.
24 ¶ And he put the [w]candle-
stick[C] in the tent of [4]the congregation, over against the [u]table,
on the side of the [m]tabernacle
southward.
25 And he lighted the [w]lamps
before the LORD; as the LORD
commanded Mō′ṣeṣ.
26 ¶ And he put the golden
[x]altar in the tent of [4]the congregation before the vail:
27 And he burnt sweet [y]incense
thereon; as the LORD commanded Mō′ṣeṣ.
28 ¶ And he set up the hanging
*at* the door of the [m]tabernacle.
29 And he put the [z]altar of
burnt offering *by* the door of the
tabernacle of the tent of [4]the
congregation, and offered upon
it the [a]burnt offering and the
[b]meat[C] offering: as the LORD
commanded [c]Mō′ṣeṣ.
30 ¶ And he set the [d]laver between the tent of [4]the congregation and the [e]altar, and put water there, to [f]wash *withal.*[C]
31 And [c]Mō′ṣeṣ and [g]Aâr′on
and his sons [f,h,i]washed their
hands and their feet thereat:
32 When [c,g]they went into the
tent of [4]the congregation, and
when they came near unto the
[e]altar, they [f,h,i]washed; as the
LORD commanded [c]Mō′ṣeṣ.
33 And he reared up the [j]court
round about the [k]tabernacle and
the [e]altar, and set up the hanging of the court gate. So [c]Mō′ṣeṣ
finished the work.
34 ¶ Then[Q] a [l]cloud covered the

v.21–1532 BC
See footnote, *Time,* Rev. 10:6.
r *Vail,* Ex. 35:12.
s *Jesus, the vail a type of humanity of,* (with Heb. 10:20); Matt. 1:21.
t *Types, of the Savior,* Heb. 10:1.
22
u *Shewbread, table of,* Ex. 35:13.
v *Holy Place,* Ex. 26:33.
4 R. V. meeting,

24
w *Lamp,* Ex. 27:20.

26
x *Altar, of incense,* Ex. 30:1.

27
y *Incense,* Ex. 37:29.

29
z *Altar, of burnt offerings,* Gen. 8:20.

a *Offerings, burnt,* Lev. 6:17.
b *Offerings, meat,* Lev. 6:17.
c *Moses,* Ex. 2:10.
30
d *Laver,* Ex. 30:18.
e *Altar, of burnt offerings,* Gen. 8:20.
f *Ablution,* Judg. 19:21.
31
g *Aaron,* Ex. 6:20.
h *Priest, ablutions of,* Lev. 1:5.
i *Ceremonial Washing,* Ex. 19:10.

33
j *Court, of the tabernacle,* Ex. 38:9.
k *Tabernacle, court of,* Ex. 27:9.
34
l *Pillar, of cloud and fire,* Ex. 13:21.

v.34–1532 BC
See footnote, *Time*, Rev. 10:6.

*m God, glory of*, Gen. 2:2.
*n Tabernacle, filled with cloud of glory*, Ex. 27:9.

36
*o God, guide*, Gen. 2:2.
*p Israel*, Ex. 4:22.

tent of [4]the congregation, and the [m]glory of the LORD filled the [n]tabernacle.

35 And [c]Mō′ṣeṣ was not able to enter into the tent of [4]the congregation, because the [l]cloud abode thereon, and the [m]glory of the LORD filled the [n]tabernacle.[Q]

36 And [o]when the [l]cloud was taken up from over the [n]tabernacle, the children of [p]Ĭṣ′ra-el went onward in all their journeys:

37 But if the [l]cloud were not taken up, then [p]they journeyed not till the day that it was taken up.

38 For the [l]cloud of the LORD *was* upon the [n]tabernacle by day, and fire was on it by night, in the sight of all the house of [p]Ĭṣ′ra-el, throughout all their journeys.

v.36–1532 BC
See footnote, *Time*, Rev. 10:6.

---

THE THIRD BOOK OF MOSES,

CALLED

# LEVITICUS

1
*a Moses*, Ex. 2:10.
*b Inspiration*, Job 32:8.
*c Revelation, concerning offerings*, vs. 1–17; 2 Cor. 12:1.
*d Tabernacle, the Lord revealed himself at*, Ex. 27:9.
1 R. V. tent of meeting.

2
*e Israel*, Ex. 4:22.
*f Offerings, burnt*, Lev. 6:17.
*g Jesus, typified in offerings*, Matt. 1:21.
2 R. V. oblation

3
*h Holiness, typified*, Ex. 39:30.
*i Blemish*, Lev. 14:10.
*j Sin, typified*, Rom. 5:12.
*k Offerings, offered at the door of the tabernacle*, Lev. 6:17.
3 R. V. offering

4
*l Hand, imposition of*, Ezra 10:19.
*m Atonement, made by animal sacrifices*, Lev. 17:11.
*n Jesus, atonement by, typified*, Matt. 1:21.

5
*o Jesus, vicarious death of, typified*, Matt. 1:21.
*p Blood, sacrificial*, Heb. 9:19.
*q Jesus, atoning blood of, typified*, Matt. 1:21.

## CHAPTER 1

*The burnt offerings of the herd; 10 of the flocks; 14 and of the fowls.*

AND the LORD called unto [a]Mō′ṣeṣ, and [b,c]spake unto him out of the [1,d]tabernacle of the congregation, saying,

2 Speak unto the children of [e]Ĭṣ′ra-el, and say unto them, If any man of you bring an [2,f,g]offering unto the LORD, ye shall bring your [2]offering of the cattle, *even* of the herd, and of the flock.

3 If his [2]offering *be* a [f]burnt [3,g]sacrifice[c] of the herd, let him offer a male [h]without [i,j]blemish: he shall offer [k]it of his own voluntary will at the door of the [1]tabernacle of the congregation before the LORD.

4 And he shall put his [l]hand upon the head of the [f]burnt [g]offering; and it shall be accepted *for him to make [m,n]atonement for him.

5 And he shall [o]kill the bullock before the LORD: and the †priests, Aâr′on's sons, shall bring the [p,q]blood, and sprinkle the blood round about upon the [r]altar that *is by* the door of the [1]tabernacle of the congregation.

6 And †he shall flay[c] the [f]burnt offering, and cut it into his pieces.

7 And the sons of Aâr′on the †priest shall put fire upon the [r]altar, and lay the wood in order upon the fire:

8 And the †priests, Aâr′on's sons, shall lay the parts, the head, and the [s]fat, in order upon the wood that *is* on the fire which *is* upon the [r]altar:

9 But his inwards and his legs shall he [h,t,u]wash in water: and the †priest shall burn all on the [r]altar, *to be* a [f]burnt [3]sacrifice, an offering made by fire, of a sweet[c] savour unto the LORD.

10 ¶ And if his [2]offering *be* of the flocks, *namely*, of the [v]sheep, or of the [w]goats, for a [f]burnt [g]sacrifice; he shall bring it a male [h]without [i,j]blemish.

11 And he shall [o]kill it on the side of the [r]altar northward before the LORD: and the †priests, Aâr′on's sons, shall sprinkle his

v.5–1532 BC
*r Altar*, Gen. 8:20.

8
*s Fat, offered in sacrifice*, Lev. 7:24.

9
*t Ceremonial Washing*, Ex. 19:10.
*u Purification*, Num. 19:19.

10
*v Sheep*, Deut. 32:14.
*w Goat*, Deut. 14:4.

---

* **SUBSTITUTION**, Gen. 22:13. *The offering for the offerer*, Lev. 1:4; 16:21, 22. *The Levites for the firstborn of the Israelites*, Num. 3:12, 41, 45; 8:18. *The life of Ahab for that of Ben-hadad*, 1 Kin. 20:42. *Of Christ for us*, Isa. 53:4–6; 1 Cor. 5:7; 2 Cor. 5:21; Gal. 3:13; 1 Pet. 2:24.

† **PRIEST. Antemosaic:** *Melchizedek*, Gen. 14:18; Heb. 5:6, 10; 6:20; 7:1–21. *Jethro*, Ex. 2:16. *Priests in Israel before the giving of the law*, Ex. 19:22, 24. **Mosaic**, Ex. 28:1–4; 29:9, 44; Num. 3:10; 18:7; 1 Chr. 23:13. *Hereditary descent of office*, Ex. 27:21; 28:43; 29:9.

v.11–1532 BC
See footnote, *Time*, Rev. 10:6.

[p,q]blood round about upon the altar.

12 And he shall cut it into his pieces, with his head and his [s]fat: and the [†]priest shall lay them in order on the wood that *is* on the fire which *is* upon the [r]altar:

13 But he shall [h,t,u]wash the inwards and the legs with water: and the [†]priest shall bring *it* all, and burn *it* upon the [r]altar: it *is* a [l]burnt [3]sacrifice, an offering made by fire, of a sweet savour unto the LORD.

14 And if the [l]burnt [3]sacrifice for his [2]offering to the LORD *be* of fowls, then he shall bring his [2]offering of [x]turtledoves, or of young [y]pigeons.

15 And the [†]priest shall bring it unto the [r]altar, and wring off his head, and burn *it* on the altar; and the [p,q]blood thereof shall be wrung out at the side of the altar:

16 And he shall pluck away his crop with [4]his feathers, and cast it beside the altar on the east part, by the place of the ashes:

17 And he shall cleave it with the wings thereof, *but* shall not divide *it* asunder: and the [†]priest shall burn it upon the [r]altar, upon the wood that *is* upon the fire: it *is* a [l]burnt sacrifice, an offering made by fire, of a sweet savour unto the LORD.

**14**
*x Dove*, Gen. 8:8.
*y Pigeon*, Gen. 15:9.

**16**
4 R. V. the filth thereof.

## CHAPTER 2

*The meat offering of flour with oil and incense, 4 baken in the oven, 5 or on a plate, 7 or in a fryingpan. 12 The oblation of the first fruits. 13 The salt of the meat offering.*

AND when any will offer a [1,a]meat[G] offering unto the LORD, his [2]offering shall be *of* fine flour; and he shall pour [b]oil upon it, and put [c]frankincense thereon:

2 And he shall bring it to Aâr′on's sons the priests: and he shall take thereout his handful of the flour thereof, and of the [b]oil thereof, with all the [c]frankincense thereof; and the [d]priest shall burn the memorial of it upon the [e]altar, *to be* an offering made by fire, of a sweet savour unto the LORD:

3 And the [f,g]remnant of the [1,a]meat offering *shall be* Aâr′on's and his sons': *it is* a thing most holy[G] of the offerings of the LORD made by fire.

4 ¶ And if thou bring an oblation of a [1,a]meat[G] offering baken[G] in the [h]oven, *it shall be* unleavened [i]cakes of fine flour mingled[G] with [b]oil, or unleavened wafers anointed[G] with oil.

5 ¶ And if thy oblation *be* a [1,a]meat[G] offering *baken* in a pan, it shall be *of* fine flour unleavened, mingled[G] with [b]oil.

6 Thou shalt part it in pieces, and pour oil thereon: it *is* a [1,a]meat[G] offering.

v.1–1532 BC
See footnote, *Time*, Rev. 10:6.

**1**
*a Offerings, meat*, Lev. 6:17.
*b Oil*, Deut. 12:17.
*c Frankincense*, 1 Chr. 9:29.
1 R. V. meal
2 R. V. oblation

**2**
*d Priest, duties of*, Lev. 1:5.
*e Altar*, Gen. 8:20.

**3**
*f High Priest, emoluments of*, Lev. 21:10.
*g Priest, emoluments of*, Lev. 1:5.

**4**
*h Oven*, Ex. 8:3.
*i Bread*, vs. 5, 7; Ezek. 4:13.

*Consecration of*, Ex. 29:1–9, 19–35; 40:12–16; Lev. 6:20–23; 8:6–35; 21:8; Heb. 7:21. *Is holy*, Lev. 21:6, 7; 22:9, 16. *Ablutions of*, Ex. 30:19–21; 40:30–32; Lev. 16:24. *Must be without blemish*, Lev. 21:17–23. *Vestments of*, Ex. 28: 2–43; 29:29, 30; 31:10; 39:1–29; Lev. 6:10, 11; 8:13; Ezek. 44:17–19. *Don vestments in temple*, Ezek. 42:14; 44:18. *Atonement for*, Lev. 4:3–12; 16:6, 24; Ezek. 44:27. *Defilement and purification of*, Lev. 21:1–5; Ezek. 44:25, 26. *Marriage of*, Lev. 21:7–15; Ezek. 44:22. *Chambers for, in temple*, Ezek. 40:45, 46. *Exempt from tax*, Ezra 7:24. *Armed and organized for war at the time of the disaffection toward Saul*, 1 Chr. 12:27, 28. *Beard and hair of*, Ezek. 44:20.

*Twenty-four courses of*, 1 Chr. 24:1–19; 28:13, 21; 2 Chr. 8:14; 31:2; 35:4, 5; Ezra 2:36–39; Neh. 13:30. *Chosen for service by lot*, Luke 1:8, 9, 23.

*Usurpations of office of*, Num. 3:10; 16; 18:7; 2 Chr. 26: 18. *Priests were appointed by Jeroboam, who were not of the sons of Levi*, 1 Kin. 12:31; 13:33.

See footnotes: LEVITES, Deut. 10:8; MINISTERS, Rom. 15:16.

**Duties of:**. *To offer sacrifices*, Lev. 1:4–17; 2:2, 16; 3:5, 11, 13, 16; 4:5–12, 17, 25, 26, 30–35; 1 Chr. 16:39, 40; 2 Chr. 13:11; 29:34; 35:11–14; Ezra 6:20; Heb. 10:11; see footnote, OFFERINGS, Lev. 6:17. *To offer the first fruits*, Lev. 23:10, 11; Deut. 26:3, 4. *To pronounce benedictions*, Num. 6:22–27; Deut. 21:5; 2 Chr. 30:27. *To teach the law*, Lev. 10:11; Deut. 24:8; 27:14–26; 31:9–13; 33:10; Ezra 7:10; Neh. 8: 1–18; Jer. 2:8; Mal. 2:7. *To light the lamps in the tabernacle*, Ex. 27:20, 21; Lev. 24:3, 4; 2 Chr. 13:11. *To keep the sacred fire burning*, Lev. 6:12, 13. *To furnish a quota of wood for the house of God*, Neh. 10:34. *To have charge of the sanctuary*, Num. 3:38; 18:1, 5. *To prepare the tabernacle and its contents for removal*, Num. 4:5–15. *To act as scribes*, Ezra 7:1–6; Neh. 8:9. *To be present at and supervise the tithing*, Neh. 10:38. *To act as treasurers*, Neh. 13:13. *To sound the trumpet in calling assemblies, and in battle*, Num. 10:2–10; 31:6; Josh. 6:1–20; 2 Chr. 13:12. *To examine lepers*, Lev. 13:1–56; 14:1–32; Matt. 8:4; Luke 5:14. *To purify the unclean*, Lev. 12:7; 15:15, 30, 31. *To value things devoted*, Lev. 27:8, 12. *To officiate in the holy place*, Heb. 9:6. *To be chiefs of Levites*, Num. 3:9, 32; 4:19, 28, 33; 1 Chr. 9:20. *To act as magistrates*, Num. 5:14–31; Deut. 17:8–13; 19:17; 21:5; 2 Chr. 19:8; Ezek. 44:23, 24. *To encourage the army on the eve of battle*, Deut. 20:2–4. *To bear the ark, through the Jordan*, Josh. 3; 4:15–18; *in battle*, Josh. 6:6, 12; 1 Sam. 4:3–5.

**Emoluments of:** *No part of Canaan allotted to*, Num.

v.7-1532 BC
See footnote, *Time*, Rev. 10:6.

7 ¶ And if any oblation *be* a [1,a]meat[G] offering *baken* in the fryingpan, it shall be made *of* fine flour with [b]oil.

8 And thou shalt bring the [1,a]meat[G] offering that is made of these things unto the LORD: and when it is presented unto the [d]priest, he shall bring it unto the [e]altar.

9 And the [d]priest shall take from the [1,a]meat[G] offering a memorial thereof, and shall burn *it* upon the [e]altar: *it is* an offering made by fire, of a sweet savour unto the LORD.

10 And [f,g]that which is left of the [1,a]meat[G] offering *shall be* Aâr′on's and his sons': *it is* a thing most holy of the offerings of the LORD made by fire.

11 No [1,a]meat[G] offering, which ye shall bring unto the LORD, shall be made with [j]leaven: for ye shall burn no leaven, nor any [k]honey, in any offering of the LORD made by fire.

12 ¶ As for the oblation[G] of the [l]firstfruits, ye shall offer them unto the LORD: but they shall not be burnt on the [e]altar for a sweet savour.

13 And every [m]oblation of thy [1]meat[G] [a]offering shalt thou season with [n]salt; neither shalt thou suffer[G] the salt of the [o]covenant of thy God to be lacking from thy [1,a]meat[G] offering: with all thine [2]offerings thou shalt offer salt.

14 And if thou offer a [1,a]meat[G] offering of thy [l]firstfruits unto the LORD, thou shalt offer for the [1]meat offering of thy firstfruits green ears of corn dried by the fire, *even* corn[G] beaten out of full ears.

15 And thou shalt put oil upon it, and lay frankincense thereon: it *is* a [1]meat offering.

16 And the priest shall burn the memorial[G] of it, *part* of the beaten corn[G] thereof, and *part* of the oil thereof, with all the frankincense thereof: *it is* an offering made by fire unto the LORD.

11
*j Leaven, forbidden*, Lev. 23:17.
*k Honey, not to be offered*, Prov. 25:27.

12
*l First Fruits, required as an offering*, Deut. 18:4.

13
*m Offerings, must be salted*, Lev. 6:17.
*n Salt*, 2 Kin. 2:20.
*o Covenant, of God with men*, Deut. 29:1.

## CHAPTER 3

*The peace offering of the herd; 6 of the flock; 7 either a lamb, 12 or a goat.*

AND if his oblation *be* a sacrifice of [a]peace [b]offering, if he offer *it* of the herd; whether *it be* a male or female, he shall offer it [c]without [d,e]blemish before the LORD.

2 And he shall [f]lay his [g]hand upon the head of his [1,h]offering, and [i]kill it *at* the door of the [2]tabernacle of the congregation: and Aâr′on's sons the [j]priests shall sprinkle the [k,l]blood upon the [m]altar round about.

3 And he shall offer of the sacrifice of the [a]peace [b]offering an

v.13-1532 BC
See footnote, *Time* Rev. 10:6.

1
*a Offerings, peace*, Lev. 6:17.
*b Jesus, typified in offerings*, Matt. 1:21.
*c Holiness, typified*, Ex. 39:30.
*d Blemish*, Lev. 14 10.
*e Sin, typified*, Rom. 5:12.

2
*f Sin, confession of*, Rom. 5:12.
*g Hand, imposition of*, Ezra 10:19.
*h Offerings, offered at the door of tabernacle*, Lev. 6:17.
*i Jesus, vicarious death of, typified*, Matt. 1:21.
*j Priest, duties of*, Lev. 1:5.
*k Blood, sacrificial*, Heb. 9:19.
*l Jesus, atoning blood of, typified*, Matt. 1:21.
*m Altar*, Gen. 8:20.
1 R. V. oblation.
2 R. V. tent of meeting:

18:20; Deut. 10:9; 14:27; 18:1, 2; Josh. 13:14, 33; 14:3; 18:7; Ezek. 44:28. *Provided with cities and suburbs*, Josh. 21:13–19; 1 Chr. 6:57–60; Neh. 11:3 20; Ezek. 48:8–13. *Own lands sanctified to the Lord*, Lev. 27:21. *Part of the spoils of war, including captives*, Num. 31:25–29. *First fruits*, Lev. 23:20; 24:9; Num. 18:12, 13, 17, 18; Deut. 18:3–5; Neh. 10:36. *Redemption money*, Lev. 27:23; *of firstborn*, Num. 3:46–51; 18:15, 16. *Things devoted*, Lev. 27:21; Num. 5:9, 10: 18:14. *Fines*, Lev. 5:16; 22:14; Num. 5:8. *Trespass money and other trespass offerings*, Lev. 5:15, 18; Num. 5:5–10; 18:9; 2 Kin. 12:16. *The shewbread*, Ex. 25:30; Lev. 24:5–9; 2 Chr. 2:4; Neh. 10:33; Matt. 12:4; Heb. 9:2. *Portions of sacrifices and offerings*, Ex. 29:27–34; Lev. 2:2, 3, 9, 10; 5:12, 13, 16; 6:15–18, 26; 7:6–10, 31–34; 10:12–14; 14:12, 13; Num. 6:19, 20; 18:8–19; Deut. 18:3–5; 1 Sam. 2:13, 14; Ezek. 44:28–31; 45:1–4; 1 Cor. 9:13; 10:18.

*Regulations by Hezekiah concerning*, 2 Chr. 31:4–19. *Portion of land allotted to, in redistribution in Ezekiel's vision*, Ezek. 48:8–14.

*For sustenance of their families*, Lev. 22:11–13; Num. 18:11, 19.

**Miscellaneous facts concerning:** *Loyal to Rehoboam, at the time of the revolt of the ten tribes*, 2 Chr. 11:13. *Zeal of, in purging the temple*, 2 Chr. 29:4–17. *Wickedness of*, 2 Chr. 36:14. *Taken captive to Babylon*, Jer. 29:1. *Return from the captivity*, Ezra 1:5; 2:36–39, 61, 70; 3:8; 7:7; 8:24–30; Neh. 7:39–42, 63–73; 10:1–8; 12:1–7. *Polluted by marrying idolatrous wives*, Ezra 9:1, 2; 10:5, 18, 19. *Restore the altar, and offer sacrifices*, Ezra 3:1–7. *Supervise the building of the temple*, Ezra 3:8–13. *Drunken*, Isa. 28:7. *Inquire of John the Baptist whether he were the Christ*, John 1:19. *Conspire to destroy Jesus*, Matt. 26:3–5, 14, 15, 47, 51; Mark 14:10, 11, 43, 47, 53–66; 15:1; Luke 22:1–6, 50, 54, 66–71; 23:1, 2; John 11:47; 19:15, 16, 18. *Try, and condemn Jesus*, Matt. 26:57–68; 27:1, 2; Mark 14:53–65; Luke 22:54–71; 23:13–24; John 18:15–32. *Incite the people to ask that Barabbas be released and Jesus destroyed*, Matt. 27:20; Mark 15:11; Luke 23:18. *Persecute the disciples*, Acts 22:5. *Reprove and threaten Peter and John*, Acts 4:6–21; 5:17–41. *Try, condemn, and stone Stephen*, Acts 6:12–15; 7. *Paul brought before*, Acts 22:30; 23:1–5. *Many converts among*, Acts 6:7.

*Zealous*, 1 Chr. 9:10–13. *Priestly office performed by prophets*, 1 Sam. 16:5.

**Corrupt**, Jer. 23:11, 12; Ezek. 22:26; Luke 10:31. INSTANCES OF: *Eli's sons*, 1 Sam. 2:12–17, 22. *Of the captivity*, Ezra 9:1, 2; 10:18–22; Neh. 13:4–9, 28, 29.

**Figurative**, Ex. 19:6; Isa. 61:6; 1 Pet. 2:5, 9; Rev. 1:6; 5:10; 20:6.

**Idolatrous**, 1 Kin. 12:32; 2 Kin. 10:19; 11:18; 23:5; 2 Chr. 23:17; 34:4, 5; Jer. 48:35; Hos. 10:5; Zeph. 1:4.

v.3–1532 BC
See footnote, *Time*, Rev. 10:6.

3
*n* *Fat, offered in sacrifice*, Lev. 7:24.

4
*o* *Caul, burnt with sacrifice*, Ex. 29:13.
3 R. V. loins,

7
*p* *Lamb, offering of*, Num. 7:15.

offering made by fire unto the LORD; the [n]fat that covereth the inwards[C], and all the fat that *is* upon the inwards,

4 And the two *kidneys, and the [n]fat that *is* on them, which *is* by the [3]flanks[C], and the [o]caul[C] above the †liver, with the kidneys, it shall he take away.

5 And Aâr′on's [j]sons shall burn it on the [m]altar upon the burnt sacrifice, which *is* upon the wood that *is* on the fire: *it is* an offering made by fire, of a sweet savour unto the LORD.

6 ¶ And if his [1]offering for a sacrifice of [a]peace [b]offering unto the LORD *be* of the flock; male or female, he shall offer it [c]without [d,e]blemish.

7 If he offer a [b,p]lamb for his [1]offering, then shall he offer it before the LORD.

8 And he shall [f]lay his hand upon the head of his [1]offering, and [i]kill it before the [2]tabernacle of the congregation: and Aâr′on's [j]sons shall sprinkle the [k,l]blood thereof round about upon the [m]altar.

9 And he shall offer of the sacrifice of the [a]peace [b]offering an offering made by fire unto the LORD; the [n]fat thereof, *and* the whole rump, it shall he take off hard[C] by the backbone; and the fat that covereth the inwards, and all the fat that *is* upon the inwards[C],

10 And the two *kidneys, and the [n]fat that *is* upon them, which *is* by the [3]flanks, and the [o]caul[C] above the †liver, with the kidneys, it shall he take away.

11 And the [j]priest shall burn it upon the [m]altar: *it is* the food of the offering made by fire unto the LORD.

12 ¶ And if his [1,a]offering *be* a goat, then he shall offer it before the LORD.

13 And he shall [f]lay his [g]hand upon the head of it, and [i]kill it before the [2]tabernacle of the congregation: and the [j]sons of Aâr′on shall sprinkle the [k,l]blood thereof upon the altar round about.

14 And he shall offer thereof his [1]offering, *even* an [a]offering made by fire unto the LORD; the [n]fat that covereth the inwards, and all the fat that *is* upon the inwards,

15 And the two *kidneys, and the [n]fat that *is* upon them, which *is* by the [3]flanks, and the [o]caul[C] above the †liver, with the kidneys, it shall he take away.

16 And the [j]priest shall burn them upon the [m]altar: *it is* the food of the offering made by fire for a sweet savour: all the [n]fat *is* the LORD's.

17 *It shall be* a perpetual statute for your generations throughout all your dwellings, that ye eat neither [q]fat nor [r]blood.[Q]

## CHAPTER 4

*The sin offering of ignorance; 3 for the priest; 13 for the congregation; 22 for the ruler; 27 and for any of the people.*

AND the LORD [a]spake unto [b]Mō′ṣeṣ, saying,

2 Speak unto the children of Iṣ′ra-el, saying, If a soul shall sin through [c]ignorance against any of the commandments of the LORD *concerning things* which ought not to be done, and shall do against any of them:

3 If the [d]priest that is [e]anointed[C] do sin [1]according to the sin of the people; then let him bring for his sin, which he hath sinned, a young [f,g]bullock [h]without [i]blemish unto the LORD for a [j]sin offering.

4 And he shall bring the [f,g]bul-

v.12–1532 BC
See footnote, *Time*, Rev. 10:6.

17
*q* *Fat, forbidden as food*, Lev. 7:24.
*r* *Blood, forbidden as food*, Gen. 9:4.

1
*a* *Revelation, concerning sins of ignorance*, vs. 1–35; 2 Cor. 12:1.
*b* *Moses*, Ex. 2:10.

2
*c* *Ignorance, sins of*, Acts 3:17.

3
*d* *Priest, atonement for*, Lev. 1:5.
*e* *Anointing*, Lev. 8:12.
*f* *Bullock*, Ex. 29:3.
*g* *Jesus, typified in offerings*, Matt. 1:21.
*h* *Holiness, typified*, Ex. 39:30.
*i* *Sin, typified*, Rom. 5:12.
*j* *Offerings, sin*, Lev. 6:17.
1 R. V. so as to bring guilt on the people;

***KIDNEY.** *Burnt offering of*, Ex. 29:13, 22; Lev. 3; 4:9, 10; 7:4, 5; 8:16; 9:10; Deut. 32:14.
**† LIVER.** *Of offerings, the caul upon, burned*, Ex. 29:13, 22; Lev. 3:4, 5, 10, 15; 4:9; 7:4; 8:16, 25; 9:10, 19. *Wound in, mortal*, Prov. 7:23. *Superstitious rites with*, Ezek. 21:21. **Figurative:** *Of the emotions*, Lam. 2:11.

v.4–1532 BC
See footnote, *Time,* Rev. 10:6.

4
*k* *Sin, confession of,* Rom. 5:12.
*l* *Hand, imposition of,* Ezra 10:19.
*m* *Jesus, vicarious death of, typified,* Matt. 1:21.
2 R. V. tent of meeting

5
*n* *Priest, duties of,* Lev. 1:5.
*o* *Blood, sacrificial,* Heb. 9:19.
*p* *Jesus, atoning blood of, typified,* Matt. 1:21.

6
*q* *Vail,* Ex. 26:31.

7
*r* *Altar, of incense,* Ex. 30:1.
*s* *Altar, of burnt offerings,* Gen. 8:20.

8
*t* *Fat, offered in sacrifice,* Lev. 7:24.

9
*u* *Kidney,* Lev. 3:4.
*v* *Caul,* Ex. 29:13.
*w* *Liver,* Lev. 3:4.
3 R. V. loins,

10
*x* *Offerings, peace,* Lev. 6:17.

12
*y* Heb. 13:11.

lock unto the door of the [2]taber-
nacle of the congregation before[C]
the LORD[C]; and shall [k]lay his
[l]hand upon the bullock's head,
and [m]kill the bullock before the
LORD.
5 And the [d,n]priest that is
[e]anointed[C] shall take of the bullock's [o,p]blood, and bring it to
the [2]tabernacle of the congregation:
6 And the [n]priest shall dip his
finger in the [o,p]blood, and sprinkle of the blood seven times before the LORD, before the [q]vail
of the *sanctuary.
7 And the [n]priest shall put *some*
of the [o,p]blood upon the horns of
the [r]altar of sweet incense before
the LORD, which *is* in the [2]tab-
ernacle of the congregation; and
shall pour all the blood of the
bullock at the bottom of the [s]al-
tar of the burnt offering, which
*is at* the door of the [2]tabernacle
of the congregation.
8 And he shall take off from it
all the [t]fat of the [j]bullock for
the [j]sin [g]offering; the fat that
covereth the inwards, and all the
fat that *is* upon the inwards.
9 And the two [u]kidneys, and
the [t]fat that *is* upon them, which
*is* by the [3]flanks[C] and the [v]caul[C]
above the [w]liver, with the kidneys, it shall he take away,
10 As it was taken off from the
[j]bullock of the sacrifice of [x]peace
offerings: and the [n]priest shall
burn them upon the [s]altar of the
burnt offering.
11 And the skin of the [j]bullock,
and all his flesh, with his head,
and with his legs, and his inwards, and his dung,
12 Even the whole bullock shall
he carry forth [y]without[C] the camp
unto a clean place, where the
ashes are poured out, and burn
him on the wood with fire: where
the ashes are poured out shall he
be burnt.
13 ¶ And if the whole [z]congre-
gation of Is'ra-el [4]sin through
[a]ignorance, and the thing be hid[C]
from the eyes of the assembly,
and they have done [5]*somewhat*
*against* any of the commandments of the LORD *concerning*
*things* which should not be done,
and are guilty;
14 When the [a]sin, which they
have sinned against it, is known,
then the congregation shall offer
a young [b,c,d]bullock for [6]the sin,
and bring him before the tabernacle of the congregation.
15 And the [e]elders of the [f]con-
gregation shall [g]lay their [h]hands
upon the head of the [b,c]bullock
before the LORD: and the bullock shall be [i]killed before the
LORD.
16 And the [j]priest that is
anointed shall bring of the bullock's [k,l]blood to the tabernacle
of the congregation:
17 And the [j]priest shall dip his
finger *in some* of the [k,l]blood,
and sprinkle *it* seven times before the LORD, *even* before the
[m]vail.
18 And he shall put *some* of the
[k,l]blood upon the horns of the
[n]altar which *is* before the LORD,
that *is* in the [2]tabernacle of the
congregation, and shall pour out
all the blood at the bottom of
the [o]altar of the burnt offering, which *is at* the door of the
[2]tabernacle of the congregation.
19 And he shall take all his [p]fat
from him, and burn *it* upon the
altar.
20 And he shall do with the

v.12–1532 BC
See footnote, *Time,* Rev. 10:6.

13
*z* *Church,* Matt.16:18.
*a* *Ignorance, sins of,* Acts 3:17.
4 R. V. shall err, and the thing be
5 R. V. any of the things which the Lord hath commanded not to be done,

14
*b* *Bullock,* Ex.29:3.
*c* *Offerings, sin,* Lev. 6:17.
*d* *Jesus, typified in offerings,* Matt. 1:21.
6 R. V. a sin offering,

15
*e* *Senate,* Num. 11:16.
*f* *Church,* Matt.16:18.
*g* *Sin, confession of,* Rom. 5:12.
*h* *Hand, imposition of,* Ezra 10:19.
*i* *Jesus, vicarious death of, typified,* Matt. 1:21.

16
*j* *Priest, duties of,* Lev. 1:5.
*k* *Blood, sacrificial,* Heb. 9:19.
*l* *Jesus, atoning blood of, typified,* Matt. 1:21.

17
*m* *Vail,* Ex. 26:31.

18
*n* *Altar, of incense,* Ex. 30:1.
*o* *Altar, of burnt offerings,* Gen. 8:20.

19
*p* *Fat, offered in sacrifice,* Lev. 7:24.

* **SANCTUARY,** Lev. 26:31; Num. 7:13; 1 Chr. 28:10.
**Signifying:** *Canaan,* Psa. 78:54 (with Ex. 15:17). *God's dwelling place,* Psa. 102:19. *The tabernacle,* Ex. 25:8; 36:1–4, 6; 38:24–27; Lev. 19:30; 26:2; 27:3, 25; Num. 3:31, 32, 47, 50; 8:19; 18:1, 3, 5; 1 Chr. 9:29; Heb. 9:1. *The contents of the tabernacle,* Num. 4:15; 7:9; 10:21. *The temple,* 1 Chr. 22:19; 2 Chr. 20:8; 29:21; 30:8; 36:17; Psa. 73:17; 74:7 *The holy place,* 2 Chr. 26:18. *The holy of holies,* Lev. 4:6, 10:4; 16:33.
**Figurative:** *Of God's goodness to his people,* Isa. 8:14; Ezek. 11:16.
See footnotes: HOLY OF HOLIES, Ex. 26:33; HOLY PLACE, Ex. 26:33; TABERNACLE, Ex. 27:9; TEMPLE, 1 Kin. 6:17.

v.20–1532 BC
See footnote, *Time*, Rev. 10:6.

**20**

q *Atonement, made by animal sacrifices*, Lev. 17:11.
r *Jesus, atonement by, typified*, Matt. 1:21.
s *Sin, forgiveness of*, Rom. 5:12.

**22**

t *Rulers, atonement for sins of*, Ex. 18:21.

**23**

u *Holiness, typified*, Ex. 39:30.
v *Blemish*, Lev. 14:10.
w *Sin, typified*, Rom. 5:12.
7 R. V. for his oblation a goat,

**24**

x *Offerings, burnt*, Lev. 6:17.

**26**

y *Offerings, peace*, Lev. 6:17.

[b]bullock as he did with the bullock for a [c]sin [d]offering, so shall he do with this: and the [j]priest shall make an [q,r]atonement[C] for them, and it shall be [s]forgiven them.

21 And he shall carry forth the [b]bullock without[C] the camp, and burn him as he burned the first bullock: it *is* a [c]sin [d]offering for the congregation.

22 ¶ When a [t]ruler hath sinned, and done *somewhat* through [a]ignorance *against* any of the commandments of the LORD his God *concerning things* which should not be done, and is guilty;

23 Or if [t]his [a]sin, wherein he hath sinned, come to his knowledge; he shall bring [7]his [c,d]offering, a kid of the goats, a male [u]without [v,w]blemish:

24 And he shall [g]lay his [h]hand upon the head of the goat, and [i]kill it in the place where they kill the [x]burnt offering before the LORD: it *is* a [c]sin [d]offering.

25 And the [j]priest shall take of the [k,l]blood of the [c]sin [d]offering with his finger, and put *it* upon the horns of the [o]altar of burnt offering, and shall pour out his blood at the bottom of the altar of burnt offering.

26 And he shall burn all his [p]fat upon the [o]altar, as the fat of the sacrifice of [y]peace offerings: and the priest shall make an [q,r]atonement for him as concerning his sin, and it shall be [s]forgiven him.

27 ¶ And if any one of the common people sin through [a]ignorance, while he doeth *somewhat against* any of the commandments of the LORD *concerning things* which ought not to be done, and be guilty;

28 Or if his [a]sin, which he hath sinned, come to his knowledge: then he shall bring [7]his [c]offering, a kid of the goats, a female [u]without [v,w]blemish, for his sin which he hath sinned.

29 And he shall [g]lay his [h]hand upon the head of the [c]sin [d]offering, and [i]slay the sin offering in the place of the [x]burnt offering.

30 And the priest shall take of the [k,l]blood thereof with his finger, and put *it* upon the horns of the [o]altar of burnt offering, and shall pour out all the blood thereof at the bottom of the altar.

31 And he shall take away all the [p]fat thereof, as the fat is taken away from off the sacrifice of [y]peace offerings; and the [j]priest shall burn *it* upon the altar for a sweet savour unto the LORD; and the priest shall make an [q,r]atonement for him, and it shall be [s]forgiven him.

32 And if he bring a [z]lamb for a [c]sin [d]offering, he shall bring it a female [u]without [v,w]blemish.

33 And he shall [a]lay his [b]hand upon the head of the [c]sin [d]offering, and [e]slay it for a sin offering in the place where they kill the [f]burnt offering.

34 And the [g]priest shall take of the [h,i]blood of the [c]sin [d]offering with his finger, and put *it* upon the horns of the [j]altar of burnt offering, and shall pour out all the blood thereof at the bottom of the altar:

35 And he shall take away all the [k]fat thereof, as the fat of the lamb is taken away from the sacrifice of the [l]peace offerings; and the [g]priest shall burn them upon the [j]altar according to the offerings made by fire unto the LORD: and the priest shall make an [m,n]atonement for his sin that he hath committed, and it shall be [o]forgiven him.

v.28–1532 BC
See footnote, *Time*, Rev. 10:6.

**32**

z *Lamb, offerings of*, Num. 7:15.

**33**

a *Sin, confession of*, Rom. 5:12.
b *Hand, imposition of*, Ezra 10:19.
c *Offerings, sin*, Lev. 6:17.
d *Jesus, typified in offerings*, Matt. 1:21.
e *Jesus, vicarious death of, typified*, Matt. 1:21.
f *Offerings, burnt*, Lev. 6:17.

**34**

g *Priest, duties of*, Lev. 1:5.
h *Blood, sacrificial*, Heb. 9:19.
i *Jesus, atoning blood of, typified*, Matt. 1:21.
j *Altar, of burnt offerings*, Gen. 8:20.

**35**

k *Fat, offered in sacrifice*, Lev. 7:24.
l *Offerings, peace*, Lev. 6:17.
m *Atonement, made by animal sacrifices*, Lev. 17:11.
n *Jesus, atonement by, typified*, Matt. 1:21.
o *Sin, forgiveness of*, Rom. 5:12.

v.1–1532 BC
See footnote, *Time*, Rev. 10:6.

1
*a* *Witness*, Num. 35:30.
*b* *Sin, punishment of*, Rom. 5:12.

2
*c* *Sanitation and Hygiene, carcasses*, Num. 31:23.
*d* *Creeping Things, unclean*, Rom. 1:23.
*e* *Sin, typified*, Rom. 5:12.

3
*f* *Ignorance, sins of*, Acts 3:17.

4
*g* *Vows*. Num. 30:2.
*h* *Oath*, Num. 5:19.

5
*i* *Sin, confession of*, Rom. 5:12.

6
*j* *Jesus, typified in offerings*. Matt. 1:21.
*k* *Offerings, sin*, Lev. 6:17.
*l* *Priest, duties of*, Lev. 1:5.
*m* *Atonement, made by animal sacrifices*, Lev. 17:11.
*n* *Jesus, atonement by, typified*, Matt. 1:21.
1 R. V. guilt

# CHAPTER 5

*For him that sins in concealing his knowledge, 2 in touching an unclean thing, 4 or in making an oath, there shall be a trespass offering of the flock, 7 of fowls, 11 or of flour. 14 The trespass offering for sacrilege, 17 and for sins of ignorance.*

AND if a soul sin, and hear the voice of swearing,[C] and *is* a [a]witness, whether he hath seen or known *of it*; if he do not utter[C] *it*, then he shall bear his [b]iniquity.

2 [c]Or if a soul touch any unclean[C] thing, whether *it be* a carcase of an unclean beast, or a carcase of unclean cattle, or the carcase of unclean [d]creeping things, and *if* it be hidden from him; he also shall be *,[e]unclean, and guilty.

3 Or if he touch the uncleanness of man, whatsoever uncleanness *it be* that a man shall be[C] *,[e]defiled withal, and it be [f]hid from him; when he knoweth *of it*, then he shall be guilty.

4 Or if a soul [g]swear,[C] pronouncing with *his* lips to do evil, or to do good, whatsoever *it be* that a man shall pronounce with an [h]oath, and it be [f]hid from him; when he knoweth *of it*, then he shall be guilty[C] in one of these.

5 And it shall be, when he shall be guilty in one of these *things*, that he shall [i]confess that he hath sinned in that *thing*:

6 And he shall bring his [1]trespass[C] [j]offering unto the LORD for his sin which he hath sinned, a female from the flock, a lamb or a kid of the goats, for a [k]sin [j]offering; and the [l]priest shall make an [m,n]atonement for him concerning his sin.

7 And if [o]he be not able to bring a [p]lamb, then he shall bring for his [1]trespass which he hath committed, two [q]turtledoves, or two young [r]pigeons, unto the LORD; one for a [k]sin [j]offering, and the other for a [s]burnt offering.

8 And he shall bring them unto the [l]priest, who shall offer *that* which *is* for the [k]sin [j]offering first, and wring off his head from his neck, but shall not divide *it* asunder:

9 And he shall sprinkle of the [t,u]blood of the [k]sin [j]offering upon the side of the altar; and the rest of the blood shall be wrung out at the bottom of the altar: it *is* a sin offering.

10 And he shall offer the second *for* a [s]burnt offering, according to the [2]manner:[C] and the [l]priest shall make an [m,n]atonement for him for his sin which he hath sinned, and it shall be [v]forgiven him.

11 But if [o]he be not able to bring two [k,q]turtledoves, or two young [k,r]pigeons, then he that sinned shall bring for his [3]offering the tenth part of an [w]ephah[C] of fine flour for a sin offering; he shall put no [x]oil upon it, neither shall he put *any* [y]frankincense thereon: for it *is* a sin offering.[Q]

12 Then shall he bring it to the priest, and the [l]priest shall take his handful of it, *even* a memorial thereof, and burn *it* on the altar, according to the offerings made by fire unto the LORD: it *is* a sin offering.

13 And the [l]priest shall make an atonement for him as touch-

v.7–1532 BC
See footnote, *Time*. Rev. 10:6.

7
*o* *Poor, inexpensive offerings of*. Prov. 21:13.
*p* *Lamb*, Num. 7:15.
*q* *Dove*, Gen. 8:8.
*r* *Pigeon*, Gen. 15:9.
*s* *Offerings, burnt*, Lev. 6:17.

9
*t* *Blood, sacrificial*, Heb. 9:19.
*u* *Jesus, atoning blood of, typified*, Matt. 1:21

10
*v* *Sin, forgiveness of*, Rom. 5:12.
2 R. V. ordinance

11
*w* *Measure, dry, ephah*, Deut. 25:15.
*x* *Oil, on sin offerings, forbidden*, Deut. 12:17.
*y* *Frankincense, prohibited in sin offerings*, 1 Chr. 9:29.
3 R. V. oblation

* **DEFILEMENT.** In studying the Mosaic law relating to defilement, it must be kept in mind that sin defiles. To keep this great truth constantly before the mind of the Israelites specific ordinances concerning defilement were given to Moses. The obvious purpose of this object lesson was to teach that sin pollutes the soul and separates from God, and that only the *clean*, that is, the *pure in heart*, can have fellowship with Him.

*Laws relating to*, Lev. 7:18–21; 11:43; 22:2–7. *Caused, by leprosy*, Lev. 13:3, 44–46; 14; 22:4; *by gonorrhea*, Lev. 15:1–15; 22:4; Deut. 23:10, 11; *by copulation*, Lev. 15:17; *by spermatorrhea*, Lev. 15:16, 17; *by childbirth*, Lev. 12:2–8; Luke 2:22; *by menses*, Lev. 15:19–33; 2 Sam. 11:4; *by touching the dead*, Lev. 21:1–4, 11; Num. 5:2, 3; 9:6–11; 19:11–22; 31:19, 20; *by eating carcass of any unclean animal*, Lev. 11:39, 40; 17:15, 16; 22:8; *by touching carcass of an unclean thing*, Lev. 5:2–13; 11:8, 24–28, 31–38; *by slaying in battle*, Num. 31:19, 20.

*Of priests*, Lev. 21:1–5; Num. 19:7–10; Ezek. 44:25, 26.
*Contact with sinners falsely supposed to cause*, John 18:28.

*Egyptian usage, concerning*, Gen. 43:32.

See footnotes: CEREMONIAL WASHING, Ex. 19:10; PURIFICATION, Num. 19:19.

v.13–1532 BC
See footnote, *Time*, Rev. 10:6.

13
z *Priest, emoluments of*, Lev. 1:5.

a *Offerings, meat*, Lev. 6:17.
4 R. V. the meal
14
b *Revelation, concerning offerings*, vs. 14–19; 2 Cor. 12:1.
c *Moses*, Ex. 2:10.
15
d *Ignorance, sins of*, Acts 3:17.
e *Jesus, typified in offerings*, vs. 16–19; Matt. 1:21.
f *Holiness, typified*, Ex. 39:30.
g *Sin, typified*, Rom. 5:12.
h *Shekel*, Ex. 30: 13.
5 R. V. guilt
16
i *Restitution, required*, Ex. 22:3.
j *Fine, a penalty*, Ex. 22:1.
k *Priest, emoluments of*, Lev. 1:5.
l *Priest, duties of*, Lev. 1:5.
m *Atonement, made by animal sacrifices*, Lev. 17:11.
n *Jesus, atonement by, typified*, Matt. 1:21.
o *Sin, forgiveness of*, Rom. 5:12.
17
p *Sin, punishment of*, Rom. 5:12.
18
*Offerings, trespass*, Lev. 3:17.

1
a *Revelation, concerning offerings*, vs. 1–30; 2 Cor. 12:1.
b *Inspiration*, vs. 1–30; Job 32:8.
c *Moses*, Ex. 2:10.

ing his sin that he hath sinned
in one of these, and it shall be
[v]forgiven him: and *the* [z]remnant
shall be the priest's, as [4]a [a]meat[G]
offering.
14 ¶ And the LORD [b]spake unto [c]Mō′ṣeṣ, saying,
15 If a soul commit a trespass,
and sin through [d]ignorance, in
the holy things of the LORD;
then he shall bring for his [1]tres-
pass unto the LORD a [e]ram [f]with-
out [g]blemish out of the flocks,
with thy estimation[G] by [h]shekels
of silver, after the shekel of the
sanctuary, for a [5]trespass offering:
16 And he shall make
[i]amends for the harm that he
hath done in the holy thing, and
shall add the [j]fifth part thereto,
and give [k]it unto the priest:
and the [l]priest shall make an
[m,n]atonement for him with the
ram of the [5]trespass offering,
and it shall be [o]forgiven him.
17 ¶ And if a soul sin, and commit any of these things which are
forbidden to be done by the commandments of the LORD; though
he [d]wist[G] *it* not, yet he is guilty,
and shall bear[G] his [p]iniquity[G].
18 And he shall bring a [e]ram
[f]without [g]blemish out of the
flock, with thy estimation[G], for a
[5,q]trespass offering, unto the
priest: and the [l]priest shall make
an [m,n]atonement for him concerning his [d]ignorance wherein
he erred and wist[G] *it* not, and it
shall be [o]forgiven him.
19 It *is* a [5,q]trespass offering: he
hath certainly trespassed against
the LORD.

## CHAPTER 6

*The trespass offering for sins done wittingly. 8 The law of the burnt offering, 14 and of the meat offering. 19 The offering at the consecration of a priest. 24 The law of the sin offering.*

AND the LORD [a,b]spake unto [c]Mō′ṣeṣ, saying,
2 If a soul[G] sin, and commit a
trespass against the LORD, and
[1,d]lie unto his [e]neighbour in that
which was delivered him *to
keep, or in fellowship[G], or in a
thing [f]taken away by violence,
or hath [2]deceived his neighbour;
3 Or have found [g]that which
was lost, and [3,h]lieth concerning it, and [4,i,j]sweareth[G] falsely;
in any of all these that a man
doeth, sinning therein:
4 Then it shall be, because he
hath sinned, and is guilty[G], that
he shall [k]restore that which he
[l]took [5]violently away, or the
thing which he hath [6]deceitfully
gotten, or that which was delivered him to *keep, or the lost
thing which he found,
5 Or all that about which he
hath [i,j]sworn[G] falsely; [l]he shall
even [k]restore [g]it in the principal,
and shall add the [m]fifth part
more thereto, *and* give it unto
him to whom it appertaineth[G], in
the day of his [7]trespass offering.
6 And he shall bring his [8]tres-
pass [n]offering unto the LORD,
a ram [o]without [p,q]blemish out of
the flock, with thy estimation[G],
for a [8]trespass offering, unto the
priest:
7 And the [r]priest shall make an
[s,t]atonement for him before the
LORD: and [u]it shall be [v]forgiven
him for any thing of all that he
hath done in trespassing therein.
8 ¶ And the LORD spake unto
Mō′ṣeṣ, saying,
9 Command [w]Aâr′on and his
sons, saying, This *is* the law of
the burnt offering: It *is* the
burnt offering, because[G] of the
burning upon the [x]altar all night
unto the morning, and the fire of
the altar shall be burning in it.
10 And the priest shall put on
his [y]linen [z]garment, and his lin-
en [a]breeches shall he put upon
his flesh, and take up the ashes

v.2–1532 BC
See footnote, *Time*, Rev. 10:6.
2
d *Dishonesty*, Ezek. 22:13.
e *Neighbor*, Luke 10:29.
f *Robbery*, Ezek. 22:29.
1 R. V. deal falsely with
2 R. V. have oppressed
3
g *Property, personal*, Lev. 27:15.
h *False Witness*, Matt. 19:18.
i *Oath*, Num. 5:19.
j *Perjury*, 1 Tim. 1:10.
3 R. V. deal falsely therein,
4 R. V. swear to a lie;
4
k *Restitution*, Ex. 22:3.
5 R. V. by robbery,
6 R. V. gotten by oppression,
5
l *Statute, fixing penalty for false dealing*, Deut. 8:2.
m *Fine, a penalty*, Ex. 22:1.
7 R. V. being found guilty.
6
n *Jesus, typified in offerings*, Matt. 1:21.
o *Holiness, typified*, Ex. 39:30.
p *Blemish*, Lev. 14: 10.
q *Sin, typified*, Rom. 5:12.
8 R. V. guilt
7
r *Priest, duties of*, Lev. 1:5.
s *Atonement, made by animal sacrifices*, Lev. 17:11.
t *Jesus, atonement by, typified*, Matt. 1:21.
u *Promises, to the penitent, of forgiveness*, 2 Cor. 1:20.
v *Sin, forgiveness of*, Rom. 5:12.
9
w *Aaron*, Ex. 6:20.
x *Altar, of burnt offerings*, Gen. 8:20.
10
y *Linen*, Ezek. 27:16.
z *Priest, vestments of*, Lev. 1:5.
a *Breeches*, Ex. 28:42.

* **TRUST**, involving Property. *Mosaic law concerning*, Ex. 22:7–13; Lev. 6:2–7. *The parable of the pounds*, Matt. 25:14–28; Luke 19:12–27. See footnote, STEWARD Gen. 43:19.

v.10–1532 BC
See footnote, *Time*, Rev. 10:6.

*b Altar, of burnt offerings*, Gen. 8: 20.

11
*c Priest, vestments of*, Lev. 1:5.

12
*d Fire*, Ex. 12:8.
*e Priest, duties of*, Lev. 1:5.

14
9 R. V. meal

which the fire hath consumed
with the burnt †offering on the
[b]altar, and he shall put them beside the altar.
11 And he shall put off his [c]gar-
ments, and put on other garments, and carry forth the ashes
without[G] the camp unto a clean
place.
12 And the [d]fire upon the [b]altar
shall be burning in it; it shall not
be put out: and the [e]priest shall
burn wood on it every morning,
and lay the burnt †offering in
order upon it; and he shall burn
thereon the fat of the peace
offerings.
13 The [d]fire shall ever be burning upon the [b]altar; it shall never
go out.
14 ¶ And this *is* the law of the
[9]meat[G] †offering: the [e]sons of
Aâr′on shall offer it before the
LORD, before the [b]altar.
15 And he shall take of it his
handful, of the flour of the [9]meat[G]
†offering, and of the [f]oil thereof,
and all the [g]frankincense which
*is* upon the [9]meat offering, and
shall burn *it* upon the [b]altar *for*
a sweet savour, *even* the memorial[G] of it, unto the LORD.
16 And the [h,i]remainder thereof
shall Aâr′on and his sons eat:
[10,j]with unleavened bread shall it
be eaten in the holy place;
in the [k]court of the [11,l]tabernacle
of the congregation they shall
eat it.[Q]
17 It shall not be baken with
[j]leaven. I have given [h,i]it *unto*
*them for* their portion of my †of-
ferings made by fire; it *is* most
holy[G], as *is* the sin offering, and
as the [8]trespass offering.
18 All the males among the
children of Aâr′on shall eat of
[h,i]it. *It shall be* a statute for ever
in your generations concerning
the †offerings of the LORD made
by fire: every one that toucheth
them shall be holy.

v.15–1532 BC
See footnote, *Time*, Rev. 10:6.

15
*f Oil*, Deut. 12:17.
*g Frankincense*, 1 Chr. 9:29.

16
*h High Priest, emoluments of*, Lev. 21:10.
*i Priest, emoluments of*, Lev. 1:5.
*j Leaven, forbidden with meat offerings*, Lev. 23:17.
*k Court, inner*, Ex. 38:9.
*l Tabernacle, court of*, Ex. 27:9.
10 R. V. without leaven
11 R. V. tent of meeting

† **OFFERINGS.** *Holy*, Lev. 2:3; 6:17, 25, 27, 29; 7:1, 6; 10:12; Num. 18:9, 10. *Offered, at the tabernacle*, Lev. 1:3; 3:2; 17:4, 8, 9; *at the temple*, 1 Kin. 8:62; 12:27; 2 Chr. 7:12. *All animal sacrifices, must be eight days old or over*, Lev. 22: 27; *must be without blemish*, Ex. 12:5; 29:1; Lev. 1:3, 10; 22:18–22; Deut. 15:21; 17:1; Ezek. 43:23; Mal. 1:8, 14; Heb. 9:14; 1 Pet. 1:19; *must be salted*, Lev. 2:13; Ezek. 43:24. *Must be, with leaven*, Lev. 7:13; Amos 4:5; *without leaven*, Ex. 23:18; 34:25. *Eaten*, 1 Sam. 9:13. *Ordinance relating to scapegoat*, Lev. 16:7–26.

*Insufficiency of*, Heb. 8:7–13; 9:1–15; 10:1–12, 18–20. *Unavailing, when not accompanied by piety*, 1 Sam. 15:22; Psa. 40:6; 50:8–14; 51:16, 17; Prov. 21:3, 27; Isa. 1:11–14; 66:3; Jer. 6:20; 7:21–23; 14:12; Hos. 6:6; 8:13; Amos 5:21–24; Mic. 6:6–8; Matt. 9:13; 12:7; Mark 12:33.

**Animal Sacrifices:** *A type of Christ*, Psa. 40:6–8 (with Heb. 10:1–14); Isa. 53:11, 12 (with Lev. 16:21); John 1:29; 1 Cor. 5:7; 2 Cor. 5:21; Heb. 9:19–28; 10:1, 10, 12; 13:10–13.

**Atonement for sin made by,** see footnote, ATONEMENT, Lev. 17:11.

**Burnt,** Lev. 9:2, 3. *Offered by Noah*, Gen. 8:20. *Its purpose was to make an atonement for sin*, Lev. 1:4. *Ordinances concerning*, Ex. 29:15–18; Lev. 1; 5:7–10; 6:9–13; 17:8, 9; 23:18, 26–37; Num. 15:24, 25; 19:9; 28:26–31; 29. *For cleansing leprosy*, Lev. 14.

*Accompanied by other offerings*, Num. 15:3–16. *Skins of, belonged to priests*, Lev. 7:8. *Accompanied with music*, Num. 10:10.

*Offered in idolatrous worship*, Ex. 32:6; 1 Kin. 18:26; 2 Kin. 10:25; Acts 14:13.

**Daily:** *Sacrificial*, Ex. 29:38–42; Lev. 6:20; Num. 28:3–8; 29:6; 1 Kin. 18:29; 1 Chr. 16:40; 2 Chr. 2:4; 13:11; Ezra 3:3–6; 9:4, 5; Psa. 141:2; Ezek. 46:13–15; Dan. 9:21, 27; 11:31.

**Drink:** *Libations of wine offered with the sacrifices*, Gen. 35:14; Ex. 29:40, 41; 30:9; Lev. 23:13, 18; Num. 6:17; 15:24; 28:5–15, 24–31; 29:6–11, 18–40; 2 Kin. 16:13; 1 Chr. 29:21; 2 Chr. 29:35; Ezra 7:17; Ezek. 45:17.

**Free Will,** Lev. 23:38; Num. 29:39; Deut. 12:6; 2 Chr. 31:14; Ezra 3:5. *Must be perfect*, Lev. 22:17–25. *To be eaten at the tabernacle*, Deut. 12:17, 18. *To be eaten by priests*, Lev. 7:16, 17. *With meat and drink offerings*, Num. 15:1–16. *Obligatory*, Deut. 16:10; *when signified in a vow*, Deut. 23:23.

**Heave:** *Given to the priests' families as part of their emoluments*, Lev. 10:14; Num. 5:9; 18:10–19, 24. *Consecrated by being elevated by the priest*, Ex. 29:27. *Consisted, of the right thigh or hind quarter* [Am. R. V.], Ex. 29:27, 28; Lev. 7:32, 34; 10:15; *of spoils, including captives and other spoils of war*, Num. 31:29, 41. *When offered*, Lev. 7:12–14; Num. 6:20; 15:19–21. *In certain instances this offering was brought to the tabernacle, or temple*, Deut. 12:6, 11, 17, 18. *To be offered on taking possession of the land of Canaan*, Num. 15:18–21.

**Meat** (R. V. Meal, but better stated *food offering*, as it provided food for the priests): *Ordinances concerning*, Ex. 29:40, 41; 30:9; 40:29; Lev. 2; 5:11, 12; 6:14–23; 7:9–13, 37; 9:17; 23:13, 16, 17; Num. 4:16; 5:15, 18, 25, 26; 8:8; 15:3–16, 24; 18:9; 28:5, 9, 12, 13, 20, 21, 26–31; 29:3, 4, 14. *To be eaten in the holy place*, Lev. 10:13; Num. 18:9, 10. *Offered with animal sacrifices*, Num. 15:3–16. *Not mixed with leaven*, Lev. 2:4, 11; 6:14–18; 10:12, 13; Num. 6:15, 17. *Storerooms for, in the temple*, Neh. 12:44; 13:5, 6.

**Peace:** *Laws concerning*, Ex. 20:24; 24:5; Lev. 3:6; 7: 11–18; 9:3, 4, 18–22; 19:5; 23:19; Num. 6:14; 10:10. *Offered, by the princes*, Num. 7:17; 23:29, 35, 41, 47, 53, 59, 65, 71, 77, 83, 88; *by Joshua*, Josh. 8:31; *by David*, 2 Sam. 6:17; 24:25.

*Offered in idolatrous worship*, Ex. 32:6. *Offered by harlots*, Prov. 7:14.

**Sin:** *Ordinances concerning*, Ex. 29:10–14 (with Heb. 13: 11–13); Lev. 4:5; 6:1–7, 26–30; 9:1–21; 12:6–8; 14:19, 22, 31; 15:15, 30; 23:19; Num. 6:10, 11, 14, 16; 8:8, 12; 15:27; 28:15, 22–24, 30; 29:5, 6, 11, 16–38; Ezek. 45:19–25. *Temporary*, Dan. 11:31; Heb. 9; 10.

**Thank,** Lev. 7:11–15; 22:29; Deut. 12:11, 12.

**Trespass** (R. V. guilt): *Ordinances concerning*, Lev. 5; 6:1–7; 7:1–7; 14:10–22; 19:21, 22; Num. 6:12; Ezra 10:19. *To be eaten by the priests*, Lev. 7:6, 7; 14:13; Num. 18:9, 10. *Offered by idolaters*, 1 Sam. 6:3, 8, 17, 18. See SIN OFFERING, above.

**Vow,** Lev. 7:16, 17; 22:17–25; Deut. 23:21–23.

**Wave:** *Ordinances concerning*, Ex. 29:22, 26–28; Lev. 7:29–34; 8:25–29; 9:19–21; 10:14, 15; 23:10, 11, 17–20; Num. 5:25; 6:19, 20. *Belonged to the priests*, Ex. 29:26–28; Lev. 7:31, 34; 8:29; 23:20; Num. 18:11, 18. *To be eaten*, Lev. 10:14, 15; Num. 18:11, 18, 19, 31.

**Wood:** *Fuel for the temple*, Neh. 10:34; 13:31.

**Figurative,** Psa. 51:17; Jer. 33:11; Rom. 12:1; Phil. 4:18; Heb. 13:15.

v.19–1532 BC
See footnote, *Time*, Rev. 10:6.

**19**
*m Revelation*, 2 Cor. 12:1.
*n Inspiration*, Job 32:8.
*o Moses*, Ex. 2:10.

**20**
*p Aaron*, Ex. 6:20.
*q Priest, consecration of*, Lev. 1:5.
*r Anointing*, Lev. 8:12.
*s Measure, dry, ephah*, Deut. 25:15.
12 R. V. oblation
13 R. V. meal

**21**
14 R. V. when it is soaked,

**22**
*t High Priest, duties of*, Lev. 21:10.

**25**
*u Jesus, typified in offerings*, Matt. 1:21.
*v Jesus, vicarious death of, typified*, Matt. 1:21.

**26**
15 R. V. tent of meeting.

**27**
*w Holiness*, Ex. 39:30.
*x Sanctification*, 1 Pet. 1:2.

19 ¶ And the LORD [m,n]spake unto [o]Mō′ṣeṣ, saying,

20 This *is* the [12]offering of [p]Aâr′on and of his sons, which they shall offer unto the LORD in the day when he is [q,r]anointed; the tenth part of an [s]ephah[G] of fine flour for a [13]meat[G]†offering perpetual, half of it in the morning, and half thereof at night.

21 In a pan it shall be made with [j]oil; [14]*and when it is* baken, thou shalt bring it in: *and* the baken pieces of the [13]meat[G]†offering shalt thou offer *for* a sweet[G] savour unto the LORD.

22 And the [t]priest of [p]his sons that is [r]anointed in his stead shall offer it: *it is* a statute for ever unto the LORD; it shall be wholly burnt.

23 For every [13]meat[G]†offering for the priest shall be wholly burnt: it shall not be eaten.

24 ¶ And the LORD [m,n]spake unto [o]Mō′ṣeṣ, saying,

25 Speak unto [p]Aâr′on and to his sons, saying, This *is* the law of the sin [†,u]offering: In the place where the burnt offering is [v]killed shall the sin offering be [v]killed before the LORD: it *is* most holy.[G]

26 The [t]priest that offereth it for sin shall eat it: in the holy place shall it be eaten, in the [k]court of the [15,l]tabernacle of the congregation.[Q]

27 Whatsoever shall touch the flesh thereof shall be [w,x]holy: and when there is sprinkled of the blood thereof upon any garment, thou shalt wash that whereon it was sprinkled in the holy place.

28 But the earthen vessel wherein it is sodden[G] shall be broken: and if it be sodden in a brasen[G] pot, it shall be both scoured, and rinsed in water.

29 All the males among the [t]priests shall eat thereof: it *is* most holy.

30 And no sin †offering, whereof *any* of the [y,z]blood is brought into the [15]tabernacle of the congregation to reconcile[G] *withal* in the holy *place*, shall be eaten: it shall be burnt in the fire.

## CHAPTER 7

*The law of the trespass offering, 11 and of the peace offerings, 12 whether it be for a thanksgiving, 16 or a vow, or a freewill offering. 22 The fat, 26 and the blood, are forbidden. 28 The priest's portion in the peace offerings.*

LIKEWISE this *is* the law of the [1,a]trespass[G] [b]offering: it *is* most holy.

2 In the place where they [c]kill the [d]burnt offering shall they [c]kill the [1,a]trespass [b]offering: and the [e,f]blood thereof shall he sprinkle round about upon the [g]altar.

3 And he shall offer of it all the fat thereof; the [2]rump, and the fat that covereth the inwards,

4 And the two [h]kidneys, and the fat that *is* on them, which *is* by the [3]flanks, and the [i]caul[G] *that is* above the [j]liver, with the kidneys, it shall he take away:

5 And the [k]priest shall burn them upon the [g]altar *for an* offering made by fire unto the LORD: it *is* a [1,a]trespass offering.

6 Every male among the priests shall eat [l]thereof: it shall be eaten in the holy place: it *is* most holy.[Q]

7 As the [m]sin offering *is*, so *is* the [1,a]trespass offering: *there is* one law for them: the priest that maketh [n]atonement therewith shall have [l]*it*.

8 And the priest that offereth any man's [d]burnt offering, *even* the priest shall have to himself the [l]skin of the burnt offering which he hath offered.

9 And all the [4,l,o]meat[G] offering that is baken in the [p]oven, and all that is dressed[G] in the frying-

v.29–1532 BC
See footnote, *Time*, Rev. 10:6.

**30**
*y Blood, sacrificial*, Heb. 9:19.
*z Jesus, atoning blood of, typified*, Matt. 1:21.

**1**
*a Offerings, trespass*, vs. 1–6; Lev. 6:17.
*b Jesus, typified in offerings*, Matt. 1:21.
1 R. V. guilt

**2**
*c Jesus, vicarious death of, typified*, Matt. 1:21.
*d Offerings, burnt*, Lev. 6:17.
*e Blood, sacrificial*, Heb. 9:19.
*f Jesus, atoning blood of, typified*, Matt. 1:21.
*g Altar, of burnt offerings*, Gen. 8:20.

**3**
2 R. V. fat tail,

**4**
*h Kidney*, Lev. 3:4.
*i Caul*, Ex. 29:13.
*j Liver*, Lev. 3:4.
3 R. V. loins,

**5**
*k Priest, duties of*, Lev. 1:5.

**6**
*l Priests, emoluments of*, Lev. 1:5.

**7**
*m Offerings, sin*, Lev. 6:17.
*n Atonement, made by animal sacrifices*, Lev. 17:11.

**9**
*o Offerings, meat*, Lev. 6:17.
*p Oven*, Ex. 8:3.
4 R. V. meal

pan, and in the pan, shall be the priest's that offereth it.

10 And every[4,l,o] meat[G] offering, mingled with [q]oil, and dry, shall all the sons of Aâr'on have, one *as much* as another.

11 ¶ And this *is* the law of the sacrifice of [r]peace offerings, which he shall offer unto the LORD.

12 If he offer it for a [s]thanksgiving, then he shall offer with the sacrifice of thanksgiving unleavened [t]cakes mingled[G] with [q]oil, and unleavened wafers anointed with oil, and cakes mingled with oil, of fine flour [5]fried.[Q]

13 Besides the [t]cakes, he shall offer *for* his [6]offering [u]leavened bread with the sacrifice of [s]thanksgiving of his peace [r]offerings.

14 And of it he shall offer one out of the whole oblation *for* an [v]heave offering unto the LORD, *and* [l]it shall be the priest's that sprinkleth the blood of the [r]peace offerings.

15 And the flesh of the sacrifice of his [r]peace offerings for thanksgiving shall be eaten the same day [7]that it is offered; [w]he shall not leave any of it until the morning.[Q]

16 But if the sacrifice of his [6,x]offering *be* a [y]vow[G], or a voluntary offering, it shall be eaten the same day that he offereth his sacrifice: and on the morrow[G] also the remainder of it shall be eaten:

17 But [w]the remainder of the flesh of the sacrifice on the third day shall be burnt with fire.

18 And if *any* of the flesh of the sacrifice of his [r]peace offerings be eaten at all on the third day, it shall not be accepted, neither shall it be imputed unto him that offereth it: it shall be an abomination, and the soul that eateth of it shall bear his [z]iniquity.

19 And [a]the flesh that toucheth any unclean *thing* shall not be eaten; it shall be burnt with fire: and as for the flesh, all that be [b]clean shall eat thereof.

20 But the soul that eateth *of* the flesh of the sacrifice of [c]peace offerings, that *pertain* unto the LORD, having his [d,e]uncleanness upon him, even that soul shall be [f]cut off from his [g]people.

21 Moreover [a]the soul that shall touch any unclean *thing, as* the [d,e]uncleanness of man, or *any* unclean [h]beast, or any abominable unclean *thing*, and eat of the flesh of the sacrifice of [c]peace offerings, which *pertain* unto the LORD, even that soul shall be [f]cut off from his [g]people.

22 ¶ And the LORD [i]spake unto [j]Mō'ṣeṣ, saying,

23 Speak unto the children of Iṣ'ra-el, saying, Ye shall eat no manner of *fat, of ox, or of sheep, or of goat.

24 And the *fat of the beast that dieth of itself, and the fat of that which is torn with beasts, may be used in any other use: but ye shall in no wise[G] eat of it.

25 For whosoever eateth the *fat of the beast, of which men offer an offering made by fire unto the LORD, even the soul that eateth *it* shall be [f]cut off from his [g]people.

26 Moreover ye shall eat no manner of [k]blood, *whether it be* of fowl or of beast, in any of your dwellings.

27 Whatsoever soul[G] *it be* that eateth any manner of [k]blood, even that soul shall be [f]cut off from his [g]people.

28 ¶ And the LORD [i]spake unto [j]Mō'ṣeṣ, saying,

v.9–1532 BC
See footnote, *Time,* Rev. 10:6.

10
q *Oil, for food,* Deut. 12:17.

11
r *Offerings, peace,* vs. 11–15; Lev. 6:17.

12
s *Offerings, thank,* Lev. 6:17.
t *Bread,* Ezek. 4:13.
5 R. V. soaked.

13
u *Leaven,* Lev. 23:17.
6 R. V. oblation

14
v *Offerings, heave,* Lev. 6:17.

15
w *Sanitation and Hygiene,* Num. 31:23.
7 R. V. of his oblation;

16
x *Offerings, vow,* Lev. 6:17.
y *Vows, edible things offered in,* Num. 30:2.

v.18–1532 BC
See footnote, *Time,* Rev. 10:6.

18
z *Sin, punishment of,* Rom. 5:12.

19
a *Sanitation and Hygiene, contagion,* Num. 31:23.
b *Holiness, typified,* Ex. 39:30.

20
c *Offerings, peace,* Lev. 6:17.
d *Defilement, laws relating to,* Lev. 5:2.
e *Sin, pollution of, typified,* Rom. 5:12.
f *Disfellowship,* Num. 15:31.
g *Church, rules of discipline in Mosaic,* Matt. 16:18.

21
h *Animals, clean and unclean,* Jer. 27:5.

22
i *Inspiration,* Job 32:8.
j *Moses,* Ex. 2:10.

26
k *Blood, forbidden as food,* Gen. 9:4.

* **FAT.** *Offered in sacrifice,* Ex. 23:18; 29:13, 22; Lev. 1:8; 3:3–5, 9–11, 14–16; 4:8–10; 7:3–5; 8:16, 25, 26; 10:15; 17:6; 1 Sam. 2:15, 16; Isa. 43:24. *Belonged to the Lord,* Lev. 3:16. *Forbidden as food,* Lev. 3:16, 17; 7:23. *Idolatrous sacrifices of,* Deut. 32:38. **Figurative,** Gen. 45:18; Isa. 25:6.

v.29–1532 BC
See footnote, *Time*, Rev. 10:6.

30
*l Offerings, wave,* Lev. 6:17.

31
*m Priest, duties of,* Lev. 1:5.
*n Priest, emoluments of,* Lev. 1:5.

32
*o Offerings, heave,* Lev. 6:17.
8 R. V. thigh

34
9 R. V. as a due

35
*p Anointing,* Lev. 8:12.
*q Ordination, of priests,* Ex. 29:1.
*r Priest, consecration of,* Lev. 1:5.

36
10 R. V. It is a due

29 Speak unto the children of Ĭṣ′ra-el, saying, He that offereth the sacrifice of his [c]peace offerings unto the LORD shall bring his oblation[G] unto the LORD of the sacrifice of his peace offerings.

30 His own hands shall bring the offerings of the LORD made by fire, the *fat with the breast, it shall he bring, that the breast may be waved *for* a [l]wave offering before the LORD.

31 And the [m]priest shall burn the *fat upon the altar: but the [n]breast shall be Aâr′on's and his sons'.

32 And the [n]right [8]shoulder shall ye give unto the priest *for* an [o]heave offering of the sacrifices of your [c]peace offerings.

33 He among the sons of Aâr′on, that offereth the blood of the [c]peace offerings, and the *fat, shall have the [n]right [8]shoulder for *his* part.

34 For the wave breast and the heave [8]shoulder have I taken of the children of Ĭṣ′ra-el from off the sacrifices of their [c]peace offerings, and have given [n]them unto Aâr′on the priest and unto his sons [9]by a statute for ever from among the children of Ĭṣ′ra-el.

35 ¶ This *is the portion* of the [p,q]anointing of [r]Aâr′on, and of the [p,q]anointing of his [r]sons, out of the offerings of the LORD made by fire, in the day *when* he presented [m]them to minister unto the LORD in the priest's office;

36 Which the LORD commanded to be given them of the children of Ĭṣ′ra-el, in the day that he [p,q]anointed them, [10]*by* a statute for ever throughout their generations.

37 This *is* the [s]law of the burnt [t]offering, of the [11]meat[G] [t]offering, and of the sin [t]offering, and of the [12]trespass [t]offering, and of the †consecrations, and of the sacrifice of the peace [t]offerings;

38 Which the LORD commanded Mō′ṣeṣ in mount [u]Sī′nāi, in the day that he commanded the children of Ĭṣ′ra-el to offer their oblations[G] unto the LORD, in the wilderness of Sī′nāi.

## CHAPTER 8

*Moses consecrates Aaron and his sons.* 14 *Their sin offering.* 18 *Their burnt offering.* 22 *The ram of consecration.* 31 *The place and time of their consecration.*

AND the LORD [a,b]spake unto Mō′ṣeṣ, saying,

2 Take [c,d]Aâr′on and his [d]sons with him, and the [e]garments, and the anointing [f]oil, and a bullock for the [g]sin offering, and two rams, and a [h]basket of unleavened bread;

3 And gather thou all the congregation together unto the door of the [1]tabernacle of the congregation.

4 And Mō′ṣeṣ did as the LORD commanded him; and the assembly was gathered together unto the door of the [1]tabernacle of the congregation.

5 And Mō′ṣeṣ said unto the congregation, This *is* the thing which the LORD [a,b]commanded to be done.

6 And Mō′ṣeṣ [i]brought [c,d]Aâr′on and his [d]sons, and [j,k]washed them with water.

7 [i]And he put upon [c,d]him the [e]coat, and girded him with the [l]girdle, and clothed him with the robe, and put the [m]ephod[G] upon him, and he girded him with the curious[G] girdle of the ephod[G], and bound *it* unto him therewith.

v.37–1532 BC
See footnote, *Time*, Rev. 10:6.

37
*s Law, of Moses,* Deut. 33:2.
*t Offerings,* Lev. 6:17.
11 R. V. meal
12 R. V. guilt

38
*u Sinai, the law delivered on,* Ex. 16:1.

1
*a Revelation, concerning offerings,* 2 Cor. 12:1.
*b Inspiration,* Job 32:8.

2
*c Aaron, consecration of,* Ex. 6:20.
*d Priest, consecration of,* Lev. 1:5.
*e Priest, vestments of,* Lev. 1:5.
*f Oil, sacred,* Deut. 12:17.
*g Offerings, sin,* Lev. 6:17.
*h Basket,* Ex. 29:3.

3
1 R. V. tent of meeting.

6
*i Ordination, of priests,* Ex. 29:1.
*j Ceremonial Washing,* Ex. 19:10.
*k Holiness, typified,* Ex. 39:30.

7
*l Girdle,* Prov. 31:24.
*m Ephod,* Ex. 28:6.

† **CONSECRATION,** Psa. 51:17; Matt. 13:44, 45, 46; Rom. 6:13, 16, 19; 12:1; 2 Cor. 8:5.
*Enjoined,* Ex. 32:29.
*Conditional,* Gen. 28:20–22; 2 Sam. 15:7, 8.
**Instances of:** *Abraham, of Isaac,* Gen. 22:9–12. *Of Aaron,* Ex. 28; 29; Lev. 8. *Of priests,* Ex. 29:1–9, 19–35; 40: 12–16; Lev. 6:20–23; 8:6–35; Heb. 7:21. *Of the altar,* Ex. 29: 36, 37, 44; 30:26–28; 40:10; Lev. 8:10, 11; Num. 7. *Jephthah, of his daughter,* Judg. 11:30, 31, 34–40. *Hannah, of Samuel,* 1 Sam. 1:11, 24–28. *David consecrates the water obtained by his valiant warriors,* 2 Sam. 23:16; 1 Chr. 11:18. *Amasiah, of himself,* 2 Chr. 17:16.
See footnote, DEDICATION, Ezra 6:17.

v.8–1532 BC
See footnote, *Time*, Rev. 10:6.

**8**
*n Breastplate*, Ex. 28:4.
**9**
*o Miter*, Ex. 28:4.
*p Crown, for priest*, Ex. 29:6.
**10**
*q Tabernacle, anointed with holy oil*, Ex. 27:9.
*r Church, holy*, 1 Kin. 9:3.
*s Sanctification*, 1 Pet. 1:2.
**11**
*t Altar, of burnt offerings, how sanctified*, Gen. 8:20.
*u Laver, sanctified*, Ex. 30:18.
**12**
*v Jesus, priesthood of, typified in Aaron*, Matt. 1:21.
**13**
*w Priest, vestments of*, Lev. 1:5.
*x Turban*, Ex. 28:40.
2 R. V. headtires
**14**
*y Jesus, typified in offerings*, Matt. 1:21.
*z Sin, confession of*, Rom. 5:12.

*a Hand, imposition of*, Ezra 10:19.
**15**
*b Jesus, vicarious death of, typified*, Matt. 1:21.
*c Moses*, Ex. 2:10.
*d Blood, sacrificial*, Heb. 9:19.
*e Jesus, atoning blood of, typified*, Matt. 1:21.
*f Altar, of burnt offerings*, Gen. 8:20.
*g Sanctification*, 1 Pet. 1:2.
*h Holiness, typified*, Ex. 39:30.
*i Atonement, by animal sacrifice*, Lev. 17:11.
*j Jesus, atonement by, typified*, Matt. 1:21.
3 R. V. atonement for

8 [i]And he put the [n]breastplate
upon him: also he put in the
breastplate the *Ū'rim[G] and the
Thŭm'mim.[G]
9 [i]And he put the [o]mitre upon
his head; also upon the mitre,
*even* upon his forefront,[G] did he
put the golden plate, the holy
[p]crown; as the LORD [a,b]com-
manded Mō'ṣeṣ.
10 And Mō'ṣeṣ took the anointing [l]oil, and †anointed the
[q,r]tabernacle and all that *was*
therein, and [k,s]sanctified them.
11 And he sprinkled thereof upon the [t]altar seven times, and
†anointed the altar and all his
vessels, both the [u]laver and his
foot, to [k,s]sanctify them.
12 [i]And he poured of the
anointing [l]oil upon [c,v]Aâr'on's
head, and †anointed him, to
[s,k]sanctify him.
13 [i]And Mō'ṣeṣ brought Aâr'-
on's [d]sons, and put [w]coats upon
them, and girded them with
[l]girdles, and put [2,x]bonnets[G] upon them; as the LORD com-
manded Mō'ṣeṣ.
14 ¶ And he brought the bullock for the [g]sin [y]offering: and
Aâr'on and his sons [z]laid their
[a]hands upon the head of the bullock for the sin offering.
15 And he [b]slew *it*; and [c]Mō'ṣeṣ
took the [d,e]blood, and put *it* upon the horns of the [f]altar round
about with his finger, and purified the altar, and poured the
blood at the bottom of the altar,
and [g,h]sanctified it, to make
[3,i,j]reconciliation[G] upon it.[Q]

16 And he took all the [k]fat that
*was* upon the inwards, and the
[l]caul[G] *above* the [m]liver, and the
two [n]kidneys, and their fat, and
[c]Mō'ṣeṣ burned *it* upon the
[f]altar.
17 But [o]the bullock, and his
hide, his flesh, and his dung,
he burnt with fire without[G] the
camp; as the LORD commanded
Mō'ṣeṣ.
18 ¶ And he brought the ram
for the [p]burnt offering: and
[q,r]Aâr'on and his sons laid their
[a]hands upon the head of the
ram.
19 And he [b]killed *it*; and [c]Mō'-
ṣeṣ sprinkled the [d,e]blood upon
the [f]altar round about.[Q]
20 And he cut the ram into
pieces; and [c]Mō'ṣeṣ burnt the
head, and the pieces, and the
[k]fat.
21 And he [h]washed the inwards
and the legs in water; and Mō'-
ṣeṣ burnt the whole ram upon
the [f]altar: it *was* a [p]burnt [4]sac-
rifice for a sweet[G] savour, *and* an
offering made by fire unto the
LORD; as the LORD commanded
Mō'ṣeṣ.
22 ¶ And he brought the other
ram, the ram of [s]consecration:[G]
and [q,r]Aâr'on and his sons laid
their [a]hands upon the head of
the ram.
23 And he [b]slew *it*; and [c]Mō'ṣeṣ
took of the [d,e]blood of it, and put
*it* upon the tip of [s]Aâr'on's right
‡ear, and upon the ‖thumb of
his right hand, and upon the
great [t]toe of his right foot.

v.16–1532 BC
See footnote, *Time*, Rev. 10:6.

**16**
*k Fat*, Lev. 7:24.
*l Caul*, Ex. 29:13.
*m Liver*, Lev. 3:4.
*n Kidney*, Lev. 3:4.
**17**
*o Sanitation and Hygiene, filth, disposition of*, Num. 31:23.
**18**
*p Offerings, burnt*, Lev. 6:17.
*q Aaron*, Ex. 6:20.
*r Jesus, priesthood of, typified in Aaron*, vs. 19–30; Matt. 1:21.
**21**
4 R. V. offering
**22**
*s Priest, consecration of*, Lev. 1:5.
**23**
*t Toe*, Lev. 14:14.

***URIM AND THUMMIM,** signifying light and perfection. *In the breastplate*, Ex. 28:30; Lev. 8:8. *Eleazar to ask counsel for Joshua, according to the judgment of*, Num. 27:21. *Priests only might interpret*, Deut. 33:8; Ezra 2:63; Neh. 7:65. *Israelites consult*, Judg. 1:1; 20:18, 23. *Withheld answer from King Saul*, 1 Sam. 28:6.

† **ANOINTING. Of High Priests,** Ex. 29:7, 29; 40:13; Lev. 6:20; 8:12; 16:32; Num. 35:25; Psa. 133:2.

**Of Priests,** Ex. 28:41; 30:30; 40:15; Lev. 4:3; 8:30; Num. 3:3.

**Of Kings,** Judg. 9:8, 15. *Saul*, 1 Sam. 9:16; 10:1; 15:1. *David*, 1 Sam. 16:3, 12, 13; 2 Sam. 2:4; 5:3; 12:7; 19:21; 1 Chr. 11:3. *Solomon*, 1 Kin. 1:39; 1 Chr. 29:22. *Jehu*, 1 Kin. 19:16; 2 Kin. 9:1–3, 6, 12. *Hazael*, 1 Kin. 19:15. *Joash*, 2 Kin. 11:12; 2 Chr. 23:11. *Jehoahaz*, 2 Kin. 23:30. *Cyrus*, Isa. 45:1.

**Of Prophets,** 1 Kin. 19:16.

**Of the Tabernacle,** Ex. 30:26; 40:9; Lev. 8:10; Num. 7:1. *Altars in*, Ex. 30:26–28; 40:10; Lev. 8:11; Num. 7:1. *Vessels of*, Ex. 30:27, 28; 40:9, 10; Lev. 8:10, 11; Num. 7:1.

See footnote, ANOINTING, Deut. 28:40.

‡ **EAR.** *Blood put upon, in consecration of priests*, Ex. 29:20; Lev. 8:23; *in cleansing lepers*, Lev. 14:14, 25. *Anointed with oil in purifications*, Lev. 14:17, 28. *Bored as a sign of servitude*, Ex. 21:5, 6.

**Figurative:** *Of desire for false teaching*, 2 Tim. 4:3. *Of the understanding*, Matt. 13:15; Mark 8:18. *Of attention*, Job 29:21.

*Anthropomorphic uses of*, Psa. 17:6; 39:12; 77:1; 80:1; 84:8.

‖ **THUMB.** *Blood put on, in consecration*, Ex. 29:20; Lev. 8:23; *in purification*, Lev. 14:14, 25. *Oil put on*, Lev. 14:17, 28. *Of prisoners cut off*, Judg. 1:6, 7.

See footnote, HAND, Ezra 10:19.

v.24–1532 BC
See footnote, *Time*, Rev. 10:6.

25
5 R. V. fat tail,
6 R. V. thigh:

27
*u Offerings, wave*, Lev. 6:17.

30
*v Oil, sacred*, Deut. 12:17.

24 And he brought Aâr′on's [s]sons, and Mō′şeş put of the [d,e]blood upon the tip of their right [‡]ear, and upon the [‖]thumbs of their right hands, and upon the great [t]toes of their right feet: and Mō′şeş sprinkled the blood upon the [f]altar round about.

25 And he took the [k]fat, and the [5]rump, and all the fat that *was* upon the inwards, and the [l]caul[G] *above* the [m]liver, and the two [n]kidneys, and their fat, and the right [6]shoulder:

26 And out of the basket of unleavened bread, that *was* before the LORD, he took one unleavened cake, and a cake of oiled bread, and one wafer, and put *them* on the [k]fat, and upon the right [6]shoulder:

27 And he put all upon [s]Aâr′on's hands, and upon his [s]sons' hands, and waved them *for* a wave [u]offering before the LORD.

28 And [c]Mō′şeş took them from off their hands, and burnt *them* on the [f]altar upon the [p]burnt offering: they *were* consecrations for a sweet savour: it *is* an offering made by fire unto the LORD.

29 And Mō′şeş took the breast, and waved it *for* a [u]wave offering before the LORD: *for* of the ram of [s]consecration it was Mō′şeş' part; as the LORD commanded Mō′şeş.

30 And [c]Mō′şeş took of the [†]anointing [v]oil, and of the [d,e]blood which *was* upon the [f]altar, and sprinkled *it* upon [q]Aâr′on, *and* upon his garments, and upon his sons, and upon his sons' garments with him; and [g,h,s]sanctified Aâr′on, *and* his garments, and his sons, and his sons' garments with him.

31 ¶ And [c]Mō′şeş said unto [q]Aâr′on and to his sons, Boil the flesh *at* the door of the [7,w]tabernacle of the congregation: and there eat it with the bread that *is* in the basket of consecrations, as I commanded, saying, Aâr′on and his sons shall eat it.

32 And [o]that which remaineth of the flesh and of the bread shall ye burn with fire.

33 And ye shall not go out of the door of the [7,w]tabernacle of the congregation *in* [x]seven days, until the days of your [s]consecration[G] be at an end: for seven days shall he consecrate you.

34 As he hath done this day, *so* the LORD hath commanded to do, to make an [i,j]atonement[G] for you.

35 Therefore shall ye abide *at* the door of the [7,w]tabernacle of the congregation day and night [x]seven days, and [y]keep[G] the charge[G] of the LORD, that ye die not: for so I am commanded.

36 So Aâr′on and his sons did all things which the LORD commanded by the hand of Mō′şeş.

## CHAPTER 9

*The first offerings of Aaron, for himself and the people.* 8 *The sin offering,* 12 *and the burnt offering for himself.* 15 *The offerings for the people.* 23 *Moses and Aaron bless the people.* 24 *Fire comes from the Lord upon the altar.*

AND it came to pass on the eighth day, *that* [a]Mō′şeş called [b]Aâr′on and his sons, and the [c]elders of Īş′ra-el;

2 And he said unto [b]Aâr′on, Take thee a [1]young calf for a [d]sin [e]offering, and a ram for a [f]burnt offering, [g]without [h,i]blemish, and offer *them* before the LORD.

3 And unto the children of Īş′ra-el thou shalt speak, saying, Take ye a [2]kid of the goats for a [d]sin [e]offering; and a calf and a lamb, *both* of the first year, [g]without [h,i]blemish, for a [f]burnt offering;

4 Also a bullock and a ram for [f]peace offerings, to sacrifice be-

v.31–1532 BC
See footnote, *Time*, Rev. 10:6.

31
*w Tabernacle*, Ex. 27:9.
7 R. V. tent of meeting:

33
*x Seven, days*, Gen. 7:2.

35
*y Priest, duties of*, Lev. 1:5.

1
*a Moses*, Ex. 2:10.
*b Aaron, enters upon the priestly office*, vs. 1–24; Ex. 6:20.
*c Senate*, Num. 11:16.

2
*d Offerings, sin*, vs. 1–21; Lev. 6:17.
*e Jesus, typified in the offerings*, Matt. 1:21.
*f Offerings, burnt*, Lev. 6:17.
*g Holiness, typified*, Ex. 39:30.
*h Blemish*, Lev. 14 10.
*i Sin, typified*, Rom. 5:12.
1 R. V. bull

3
2 R. V. he-goat

4
*f Offerings, peace*, Lev. 6:17.

v.4–1532 BC
See footnote, *Time*, Rev. 10:6.

*k Offerings, meat*, Lev. 6:17.
3 R. V. meal

**5**
4 R. V. tent of meeting:

**7**
*l High priest, duties of*, Lev. 21:10.
*m Altar, of burnt offerings*, Gen. 8:20.
*n Atonement, made by animal sacrifices*, Lev. 17:11.
*o Jesus, atonement by, typified*, Matt. 1:21.
5 R. V. oblation

**8**
*p Jesus, vicarious death of, typified*, Matt. 1:21.

**9**
*q Blood, sacrificial*, Heb. 9:19.
*r Jesus, atoning blood of, typified*, Matt. 1:21.

**10**
*s Fat, offered in sacrifice*, Lev. 7:24.
*t Kidney*, Lev. 3:4.
*u Caul*, Ex. 29:13.
*v Liver*, Lev. 3:4.

**11**
*w Sanitation and Hygiene, filth, disposition of*, Num. 31:23.

**14**
*x Ceremonial Washing*, Ex. 19:10.
*y Purification, by Washing*, Num. 19:19.

fore the LORD; and a [3,k]meat[G] offering mingled[G] with oil: for to day
the LORD will appear unto you.
5 ¶ And they brought *that*
which Mō'ṣeṣ commanded before the [4]tabernacle of the congregation: and all the congregation drew near and stood before
the LORD.
6 And [a]Mō'ṣeṣ said, This *is* the
thing which the LORD com-
manded that ye should do: and
the glory of the LORD shall appear unto you.
7 And [a]Mō'ṣeṣ said unto
[b,l]Aâr'on, Go unto the [m]altar,
and offer thy [d]sin [e]offering, and
thy [f]burnt offering, and make an
[n,o]atonement for thyself, and for
the people: and offer the [5]offer-
ing of the people, and make an
atonement for them; as the
LORD commanded.[G]
8 ¶ [b,l]Aâr'on therefore went
unto the altar, and [p]slew the calf
of the [d]sin [e]offering, which *was*
for himself.
9 And the sons of [b]Aâr'on
brought the [q,r]blood unto him:
and [l]he dipped his finger in the
blood, and put *it* upon the horns
of the [m]altar, and poured out the
blood at the bottom of the altar:
10 But the [s]fat, and the [t]kid-
neys, and the [u]caul[G] above the
[v]liver of the [d]sin offering, he
burnt upon the altar; as the
LORD commanded Mō'ṣeṣ.
11 And [w]the flesh and the hide
he burnt with fire without[G] the
camp.
12 And [l]he [p]slew the [f]burnt
[e]offering; and Aâr'on's sons
presented unto him the [q,r]blood,
which he sprinkled round about
upon the [m]altar.
13 And they presented the
[f]burnt offering unto him, with the
pieces thereof, and the head: and
he burnt *them* upon the [m]altar.
14 And he did [q,x,y]wash the
inwards and the legs, and burnt
*them* upon the [f]burnt offering on
the altar.
15 ¶ And he brought the people's [5]offering, and took the
goat, which *was* the [d]sin [e]offer-
ing for the people, and [p]slew it,
and offered it for sin, as the first.
16 And he brought the [f]burnt
[e]offering, and offered it according to the [6]manner.[G]
17 And he brought the [3,k]meat[G]
offering, and took an handful
thereof, and burnt *it* upon the
[m]altar, beside the burnt [7]sacri-
fice[G] of the morning.
18 He [p]slew also the bullock
and the ram *for* a sacrifice of
[j]peace [e]offerings, which *was* for
the people: and Aâr'on's sons
presented unto him the [q,r]blood,
which [l]he sprinkled upon the
altar round about,
19 And the [s]fat of the bullock
and of the ram, the [8]rump, and
that which covereth *the inwards*,[G]
and the [t]kidneys, and the [u]caul
*above* the [v]liver:
20 And they put the [s]fat upon
the breasts, and he burnt the fat
upon the [m]altar:
21 And the breasts and the
right [9]shoulder Aâr'on waved
*for* a [z]wave offering before the
LORD; as Mō'ṣeṣ commanded.
22 And [a]Aâr'on lifted up his
[b]hand toward the people, and
[c]blessed them, and came down
from offering of the [d]sin [e]offer-
ing, and the [f]burnt offering, and
[g]peace offerings.
23 And [h]Mō'ṣeṣ and [a]Aâr'on
went into the [4]tabernacle of the
congregation, and came out, and
[c]blessed the people: and the
[i]glory of the LORD appeared unto all the people.
24 And there came a [j,k]fire out
from before the LORD, and consumed upon the altar the [f]burnt
offering and the fat: *which*
when all the people saw, they[S]
shouted, and fell on their faces.

v.14–1532 BC
See footnote, *Time*, Rev. 10:6.

**16**
6 R. V. ordinance.

**17**
7 R. V. offering

**19**
8 R. V. fat tail,

**21**
*z Offerings, wave*, Lev. 6:17.
9 R. V. thigh

**22**
*a Aaron*, Ex. 6:20.
*b Hand, lifted up in benediction*, Ezra 10:19.
*c Benediction, instances of*, Deut. 21:5.
*d Offerings, sin*, Lev. 6:17.
*e Jesus, typified in offerings*, Matt. 1:21.
*f Offerings, burnt*, Lev. 6:17.
*g Offerings, peace*, Lev. 6:17.

**23**
*h Moses*, Ex. 2:10.
*i God, glory of*, Gen. 2:2.

**24**
*j Fire, miraculous*, Ex. 12:8.
*k Miracles*, Luke 23:8.

v.1–1532 BC
See footnote, *Time*, Rev. 10:6.

1
*a* *Minister, false and corrupt*, Rom. 15:16.
*b* *Nadab*, Ex. 24:1.
*c* *Abihu*, Ex. 6:23.
*d* *Aaron*, Ex. 6:20.
*e* *Censer*, Lev. 16:12.
*f* *Incense, unlawfully offered*, Ex. 37:29.
*g* *Sacrilege, instances of*, Lev. 19:8.
*h* *Presumption, instances of*, Psa. 19:13.

2
*i* *Fire, miraculous*, Ex. 12:8.
*j* *Miracles, destruction of Nadab and Abihu*, Luke 23:8.
*k* *Judgments, on Nadab and Abihu*, Ex. 6:6.

3
*l* *Moses*, Ex. 2:10.
*m* *Minister, character and qualifications of*, Rom. 15:16.
*n* *Resignation, exemplified*, Job 5:17.

4
*o* Ex. 6:22.
*p* Or, *Elzaphan*, Ex. 6:22; Num. 3:30; 1 Chr. 15:8.
*q* *Uzziel*, Num. 3:19.

5
*r* *Ephod*, Ex. 28:6.

6
*s* *Eleazar*, Num. 3:2.
*t* *Ithamar*, Ex. 38:21.
*u* *Bereavement*, Hos. 9:12.
*v* *Mourning*, Lam. 2:5.
*w* *Rending of Garments*, 2 Chr. 34:27.
1 R. V. let not the hair of your heads go loose,

7
*x* *Anointing*, Lev. 8:12.
*y* *Oil, sacred*, Deut. 12:17.
2 R. V. tent of meeting,

## CHAPTER 10

*Nadab and Abihu, for offering strange fire, are consumed. 6 Aaron and his sons are forbidden to mourn for them. 8 The priests are forbidden wine when they go into the tabernacle. 12 The law of eating the holy things. 16 Aaron's excuse for transgressing thereof.*

AND [a,b]Nā′dăb and [a,c]Ā-bī′-hū, the sons of [d]Aâr′on, took either of them his [e]censer, and put fire therein, and put [f]incense thereon, and [g,h]offered strange fire before the LORD, which he commanded them not.

2 And there went out [i,j]fire from the LORD, and [k]devoured them, and they died before the LORD.

3 Then [l]Mō′ṣeṣ said unto [d]Aâr′on, This *is it* that the LORD spake, saying, I will be sanctified in [m]them that come nigh me, and before all the people I will be glorified. And Aâr′on [n]held his peace.

4 And [l]Mō′ṣeṣ called [o]Mĭsh′a-el and [p]Ĕl′za-phăn, the sons of [q]Ŭz′zĭ-el the uncle of Aâr′on, and said unto them, Come near, carry your brethren from before the sanctuary out of the camp.

5 So they went near, and carried them in their [r]coats out of the camp; as [l]Mō′ṣeṣ had said.

6 And [l]Mō′ṣeṣ said unto [d]Aâr′-on, and unto [s]Ē-le-ā′zar and unto [t]Ĭth′a-mär, his sons, [1,u,v]Uncover not your heads, neither [w]rend your clothes; lest ye die, and lest wrath come upon all the people: but let your brethren, the whole house of Īṣ′ra-el, bewail the burning which the LORD hath kindled.

7 And ye shall not go out from the door of the [2]tabernacle of the congregation, lest ye die: for the [x]anointing [y]oil of the LORD *is* upon you. And they did according to the word of [l]Mō′ṣeṣ.

8 ¶ And the LORD [z]spake unto [a]Aâr′on, saying,

9 [*,b]Do not drink [c]wine nor strong drink, thou, nor thy sons with thee, when ye go into the [2]tabernacle of the congregation, lest ye die: *it shall be* a statute for ever throughout your generations:

10 And [d]that ye may put difference between [e]holy and unholy, and between [f]unclean and clean;

11 And that [g]ye may [h]teach the children of Īṣ′ra-el all the [i]statutes which the LORD hath spoken unto them by the hand of Mō′ṣeṣ.

12 ¶ And [j]Mō′ṣeṣ spake unto [a]Aâr′on, and unto [k]Ē-le-ā′zar and unto [l]Ĭth′a-mär, his sons that were left, Take the [3,m]meat [m,n]offering that remaineth of the offerings of the LORD made by fire, and eat it without leaven beside the altar: for [o]it *is* most holy:

13 And ye shall eat it in the holy place, because [n]it *is* thy due, and thy sons' due, of the [4]sacrifices of the LORD made by fire: for so I am commanded.

14 And the wave breast and heave [5]shoulder shall ye eat in a clean place; thou, and thy sons, and thy daughters with thee: for [n]*they be* thy due, and thy sons' due, *which* are given out of the sacrifices of [p]peace offerings of the children of Īṣ′ra-el.

15 The heave [5]shoulder and the wave breast shall they bring with the offerings made by fire of the [q]fat, to wave *it for* a [r]wave offering before the LORD; and [n]it shall be thine, and thy sons' with thee, [6]by a statute for ever; as the LORD hath commanded.

16 ¶ And [j]Mō′ṣeṣ diligently sought the goat of the [s]sin offer-

v.8–1532 BC
See footnote, *Time*, Rev. 10:6.
*z* *Inspiration*, Job 32:8.

*a* *Aaron*, Ex. 6:20.

9
*b* *Commandment, forbidding use of, strong drink*, Deut. 8:2.
*c* *Wine, forbidden to priests on duty*, Prov. 23:31.

10
*d* *Commandment, enjoining holiness*, Deut. 8:2.
*e* *Holiness*, Ex. 39:30.
*f* *Defilement*, Lev. 5:2.

11
*g* *Priest, duties of*, Lev. 1:5.
*h* *Instruction, in religion*, Prov. 23:23.
*i* *Law, of Moses*, Deut. 33:2.

12
*j* *Moses*, Ex. 2:10.
*k* *Eleazar*, Num. 3:2.
*l* *Ithamar*, Ex. 38:21.
*m* *Offerings, meat*, Lev. 6:17.
*n* *High Priest, emoluments of*, Lev. 21:10.
*o* *Offerings, holy*, Lev. 6:17.
3 R. V. meal

13
4 R. V. offerings

14
*p* *Offerings, peace*, Lev. 6:17.
5 R. V. thigh

15
*q* *Fat*, Lev. 7:24.
*r* *Offerings, wave*, Lev. 6:17.
6 R. V. as a due

16
*s* *Offerings, sin*, Lev. 6:17.

*** TOTAL ABSTINENCE FROM INTOXICATING BEVERAGES. Enjoined**, Prov. 23:20, 31, 32. *Upon priests when officiating*, Lev. 10:8–10. *Upon Nazirites*, Num. 6:3, 4. *Upon Samson's mother*, Judg. 13:4, 13, 14. *Upon kings*, Prov. 31:4.
**Exemplified by:** *Israelites in the wilderness*, Deut. 29:6. *Daniel and his companions while pupils in the civil service school of Nebuchadnezzar*, Dan. 1:8, 12. *Rechabites*, Jer. 35:6–14. *John the Baptist*, Matt. 11:18; Luke 7:33, with 1:15.

v.16–1532 BC
See footnote, *Time*, Rev. 10:6.

t *Anger, instances of*, Psa. 37:8.
17
u *Reproof, faithfulness in*, Prov. 17:10.
v *Intercession, of man with God*, Jer. 27:18.
w *Church, called the congregation*, Matt. 16:18.
x *Atonement, made by animal sacrifices*, Lev. 17:11.
y *Jesus, atonement by, typified*, Matt. 1:21.
18
z *Sanctuary*, Lev. 4:6.
7 R. V. sanctuary

19
a *Aaron*, Ex. 6:20.
b *Moses*, Ex. 2:10.
c *Offerings, sin*, Lev. 6:17.
d *Offerings, burnt*, Lev. 6:17.

1
a *Revelation, concerning clean and unclean animals*, vs. 2–47; 2 Cor. 12:1.
b *Inspiration*, Job 32:8.
c *Moses*, Ex. 2:10.
d *Aaron*, Ex. 6:20.
2
e *Israel, taught to be holy by eating none but clean animals*, Ex. 4:22.
f Deut. 14:3–20.
g *Animals, clean and unclean*, Jer. 27:5.
1 R. V. living things
3
h *Hoof*, Deut. 14:3–8.
i *Cud*, Deut. 14:3–8.
4
j *Food, things prohibited as*, Psa. 136:25.

ing, and, behold, it was burnt:
and he was [t]angry with [k]Ē-le-ā′-
zar and [l]Ĭth′a-mär, the sons of
Aâr′on *which were* left *alive*,
saying,
17 [u]Wherefore have ye not eat-
en the sin offering in the holy
place, seeing [o]it *is* most holy,
and *God* hath given it you to
[v]bear the iniquity of the [w]con-
gregation, to make [x,y]atone-
ment for them before the LORD?
18 Behold, the blood of it was
not brought in within the [7,z]holy
*place*: ye should indeed have
eaten it in the [7]holy *place*, as I
commanded.
19 And [a]Aâr′on said unto
[b]Mō′şeş, Behold, this day have
they offered their [c]sin offering
and their [d]burnt offering before
the LORD; and such things have
befallen[G] me: and *if* I had eaten
the sin offering to day, should it
have been accepted in the sight
of the LORD?
20 And when Mō′şeş heard
*that*, he was content.

## CHAPTER 11

*What may, and what may not be eaten, of beasts, 9 of fishes, 13 and fowls. 29 The creeping things which are unclean. 44 Sanctification.*

AND[Q] the LORD [a,b]spake unto [c]Mō′şeş and to [d]Aâr′-
on, saying unto them,
2 Speak unto the children of
[e]Ĭş′ra-el, saying, [f,g]These *are* the
[1]beasts which ye shall eat among
all the beasts that *are* on the
earth.[Q]
3 [g]Whatsoever parteth[G] the
[h]hoof, and is clovenfooted, *and*
cheweth the [i]cud, among the
beasts, that shall ye eat.
4 Nevertheless [j]these shall ye
not eat of them that chew the
[i]cud, or of them that divide the
[h]hoof: *as* the [k]camel, because he
cheweth the cud, but divideth
not the hoof; he *is* [l,m]unclean[G]
unto you.
5 And the *coney, because he
cheweth the [i]cud, but divideth
not the [h]hoof; he *is* [l,m]unclean[G]
unto you.
6 And the [n]hare, because he
cheweth the [i]cud, but divideth
not the [h]hoof; he *is* [l,m]unclean
unto you.
7 And the †swine, though he
divide the [h]hoof, and be cloven-
footed, yet he cheweth not the
[i]cud; he *is* [l,m]unclean to you.
8 [j]Of their flesh shall ye not
eat, and their carcase shall ye
not touch; they *are* [l,m]unclean
to you.
9 ¶ These shall ye eat of [o]all
that *are* in the waters: whatsoever hath fins and scales in the
waters, in the seas, and in the
rivers, them shall ye eat.
10 And [j]all that have not fins
and scales in the seas, and in the
rivers, of all that move in the
waters, and of any living thing
which *is* in the waters, they *shall
be* an abomination[G] unto you:
11 [j]They shall be even an
abomination unto you; ye shall
not eat of their flesh, but ye
shall have their carcases in
abomination.
12 [j]Whatsoever hath no fins nor
scales in the waters, that *shall be*
an abomination unto you.
13 ¶ And [j]these *are they which*
ye shall have in abomination
among the [p]fowls; they shall not
be eaten, they *are* an abomination: the ‡eagle, and the [2,q]ossi-
frage, and the [r]ospray;
14 And the [s]vulture, and the
[t]kite after his kind;
15 Every [u]raven after his kind;

v.4–1532 BC
See footnote, *Time*, Rev. 10:6.

k *Camel, forbidden as food*, 1 Sam. 30:17.
l *Unclean Creatures*, Deut. 14.
m *Sin, typified, in unclean animals*, Rom. 5:12.
6
n Deut. 14:7.
9
o *Fish, clean and unclean*, Matt. 17:27.
13
p *Birds, unclean*, Eccl. 12:4.
q Deut. 14:12.
r Deut. 14:12.
2 R. V. gier eagle.
14
s Deut. 14:13.
t Deut. 14:13.
15
u *Raven*, Job 38:41.

***CONEY**, Lev. 11:5; Deut. 14:7; Psa. 104:18; Prov. 30:26.

†**SWINE.** *Forbidden as food*, Lev. 11:7; Deut. 14:8. *Used, for food*, Isa. 65:4; 66:17; *for sacrifice*, Isa. 66:3. *Wild boar*, Psa. 80:13. *Jewels in the nose of*, Prov. 11:22. *Viciousness of*, Matt. 7:6. *Jesus sends devils into*, Matt. 8:28–32; Mark 5:11–14; Luke 8:32, 33. *Feeding of*, Luke 15:15, 16. *Sow returns to her wallow*, 2 Pet. 2:22.
**Figurative:** *Of the wicked*, Matt. 7:6.

‡**EAGLE**, Ex. 19:4; Deut. 32:11; Psa. 103:5; Jer. 48:40; Hos. 8:1. *Forbidden as food*, Lev. 11:13; Deut. 14:12. *Swift flight of*, Deut. 28:49; Job 9:26; Prov. 30:19; Jer. 4:13.

v.16–1532 BC
See footnote, *Time*, Rev. 10:6.

**16**
*v* Deut. 14:15.
*w* Deut. 14:15.
*x* *Hawk,* Deut. 14: 15.
3 R. V. seamew,
**18**
*y* Deut. 14:16.
*z* Deut. 14:17; Psa. 102:6.

*a* Deut. 14:17.
4 R. V. horned owl,
5 R. V. vulture,
**19**
*b* Deut. 14:18.
*c* Deut. 14:18.
*d* Deut. 14:18; Isa. 2:20.
6 R. V. hoopoe,
**20**
*e* Deut. 14:19.
*f* *Creeping Things,* Rom. 1:23.
7 R. V. winged creeping things
**22**
*g* *Locust,* Nah. 3:17.
*h* *Grasshopper,* Num. 13:33.
8 R. V. cricket

**24**
*i* *Defilement,* Lev. 5:2.
*j* *Sin, typified,* Rom. 5:12.
**25**
*k* *Ceremonial Washing,* Ex. 19:10.
*l* *Holiness, typified,* Ex. 39:30.
**26**
*m* *Animals, clean and unclean,* Jer. 27:5.
9 R. V. *omits* The carcases *of*

16 And the ‖owl, and the [v]night hawk, and the [3,w]cuckow, and the [x]hawk after[C] his kind,

17 And the little ‖owl, and the §cormorant, and the great owl,

18 And the [4,y]swan, and the [z]pelican, and the [5,a]gier eagle,

19 And the +stork, the [b]heron after her kind, and the [6,c]lapwing, and the [d]bat.

20 All [7,e]fowls that [f]creep, going upon *all* four, *shall be* an abomination unto you.

21 Yet these may ye eat of every [7,e]flying [f]creeping thing that goeth upon *all* four, which have legs above their feet, to leap withal[C] upon the earth;

22 *Even* these of them ye may eat; the [g]locust after his kind, the bald locust after his kind, and the [8]beetle after his kind, and the [h]grasshopper after his kind.

23 But all [7]*other* [e]flying [f]creeping things, which have four feet, *shall be* an abomination unto you.

24 And for these ye shall be [i,j]unclean: whosoever toucheth the carcase of them shall be unclean until the even.

25 And whosoever beareth *ought* of the carcase of them shall [k,l]wash his clothes, and be [i,j]unclean until the even.[Q]

26 [9]*The carcases* of every [m]beast which divideth the hoof, and *is* not clovenfooted, nor cheweth the cud, *are* unclean unto you: every one that toucheth them shall be [i,j]unclean.

27 And [m]whatsoever goeth upon his paws, among all manner of beasts that go on *all* four, those *are* unclean unto you: whoso toucheth their carcase shall be [i,j]unclean until the even.

28 And he that beareth the carcase of them shall [k,l]wash his clothes, and be unclean until the even: they *are* unclean unto you.

29 ¶ These also *shall be* [i,j]unclean unto you among the [f]creeping things that creep upon the earth; the weasel, and the ⊙mouse, and the [10]tortoise after his kind.

30 And the [11]ferret, and the [12]chameleon, and the lizard, and the [13]snail, and the [14]mole.

31 [e]These *are* unclean to you among all that [f]creep: whosoever doth touch them, when they be dead, shall be [i,j]unclean until the even.

32 And upon whatsoever *any* of them, when they are dead, doth fall, it shall be [i,j]unclean; whether *it be* any vessel of wood, or [n]raiment, or skin, or sack, whatsoever vessel *it be,* wherein *any* work is done, it must be [k]put into water, and it shall be unclean until the even; so it shall be [l]cleansed.

33 And every earthen vessel, whereinto *any* of them falleth, whatsoever *is* in it shall be [i,j]unclean; and ye shall break it.

34 Of all meat[C] which may be eaten, *that* on which *such* water cometh shall be [i,j]unclean: and all drink that may be drunk in every *such* vessel shall be unclean.

35 And every *thing* whereupon *any part* of their carcase falleth shall be [i,j]unclean; *whether it be* [o]oven, or ranges[G] for pots, they shall be broken down: *for* they *are* unclean, and shall be unclean unto you.

v.27–1532 BC
See footnote, *Time.* Rev. 10:6.

**29**
10 R. V. great lizard
**30**
11 R. V. gecko,
12 R. V. land crocodile,
13 R. V. sand-lizard,
14 R. V. chameleon.
**32**
*n* *Dress, ceremonial purification of,* Zech. 3:4.
**35**
*o* *Oven,* Ex. 8:3.

49:22; Lam. 4:19. *Nest of,* Deut. 32:11; Job 39:27–30; Jer. 49: 16. *Bald,* Mic. 1:16. *Gier* [R.V.], Lev. 11:13; Deut. 14:12.

*Parable of,* Ezek. 17:3–7; *Similitudes of,* Ezek. 1:10; 10:14; 17:3; Dan. 7:4; Rev. 4:7; 12:14.

‖ **OWL,** or more probably, ostrich. *Unclean,* Lev. 11: 16, 17; Deut. 14:15, 16; Job 30:29; Isa. 13:21; 34:11, 13; 43:20; Jer. 50:39, Mic. 1:8.

§ **CORMORANT.** *A bird forbidden as food,* Lev. 11:17; Deut. 14:17; Isa. 34:11; Zeph. 2:14.

+ **STORK,** Zech. 5:9. *Forbidden as food,* Lev. 11:19; Deut. 14:18. *Nest of, in fir trees,* Psa. 104:17. *Migratory,* Jer. 8:7.

⊙ **MOUSE.** *Forbidden as food,* Lev. 11:29. *Used as food,* Isa. 66:17. *Images of,* 1 Sam. 6:4, 5, 11, 18.

v.36–1532 BC
See footnote, *Time,* Rev. 10:6.

36 Nevertheless a fountain or pit,[G] *wherein there is* plenty of water, shall be clean: but that which toucheth their carcase shall be [i,j]unclean.

37 And if *any part* of their carcase fall upon any sowing seed which is to be sown, it *shall be* clean.

38 But if *any* water be put upon the seed, and *any part* of their carcase fall thereon, it *shall be* [i,j]unclean[G] unto you.

39 And if any beast, of which ye may eat, die; he that toucheth the carcase thereof shall be [i,j]unclean until the even.

40 And he that eateth of the carcase of it shall [k,l]wash his clothes, and be unclean until the even: he also that beareth the carcase of it shall wash his clothes, and be unclean until the even.

41 And every [j]creeping thing that creepeth upon the earth *shall be* an abomination[G]; [p]it shall not be eaten.

42 Whatsoever goeth upon the belly, and whatsoever goeth upon *all* four, or whatsoever hath more[G] feet among all [j]creeping things that creep upon the earth, [p]them ye shall not eat; for they *are* an abomination.

43 Ye shall not make your selves abominable[G] with any creeping thing that creepeth, neither shall ye make yourselves unclean with them, that ye should be [i,j]defiled thereby.

44 For I *am* the LORD your God: ye shall therefore [q]sanctify yourselves, and [r,s]ye shall be [t]holy; [u]for [v]I *am* holy: neither shall ye [i]defile yourselves with any manner of [j]creeping thing that creepeth upon the earth.[Q S]

45 For [w]I *am* the LORD that bringeth you up out of the land of E′gypt, to be your God: [s]ye shall therefore be [t]holy,[G] [u]for [v]I *am* holy.

46 This *is* the law of the beasts, and of the fowl, and of every living creature that moveth in the waters, and of every creature that creepeth upon the earth:

47 To make a difference between the [j]unclean and the [l]clean, and between the [15]beast that may be eaten and the [14,p]beast that may not be eaten.[Q]

## CHAPTER 12

*The purification of a woman after childbirth. 6 Her offerings for her purifying.*

AND the LORD [a]spake unto [b]Mō′ṣeṣ, saying,

2 Speak unto the children of [c]Iṣ′ra-el, saying, If a [d]woman have conceived seed, and born a man child: then she shall be [e]unclean[G] [f]seven days; according to the days of the [1]separation for her infirmity shall she be unclean.

3 And in the eighth day the flesh of his foreskin shall be [g]circumcised.[Q]

4 And [d]she then shall continue in the blood of her [h]purifying three and thirty days; she shall touch no hallowed thing, nor come into the sanctuary, until the days of her [i]purifying be fulfilled.

5 But if [d]she bear a maid[G] child, then she shall be [e]unclean two weeks, as in her [2]separation: and she shall continue in the blood of her purifying threescore and six days.

6 And when the days of [d]her [h,i]purifying are fulfilled, for a son, or for a *daughter, she shall

41
p *Food, things prohibited as,* Psa. 136:25.

44
q *Sanctification,* 1 Pet. 1:2.
r Lev. 19:2; 1 Pet. 1:16.
s *Commandment, enjoining holiness,* Deut. 8:2.
t *Holiness, enjoined,* Ex. 39:30.
u *Example, God, our,* John 13:15.
v *God, holiness of,* Gen. 2:2.

v.45–1532 BC
See footnote, *Time,* Rev. 10:6.

45
w *God, love of, exemplified,* Gen. 2:2.

47
15 R. V. living thing

1
a *Revelation, concerning purification,* vs. 1–8; 2 Cor. 12:1.
b *Moses,* Ex. 2:10.

2
c *Israel, the law delivered to,* Ex. 4:22.
d *Women, purification of,* vs. 1–8; Prov. 31:10.
e *Defilement,* Lev. 5:2.
f *Seven, days,* Gen. 7:2.
1 R. V. impurity of her sickness

3
g *Circumcision, institution of,* Gen. 17:10.

4
h *Purification,* Num. 19:19.
i *Holiness, typified,* Ex. 39:30.

5
2 R. V. impurity:

* **DAUGHTER.** *Affectionate,* Josh. 2:12, 13. *Dutiful,* Judg. 11:36–39. *Sold in concubinage,* Ex. 21:7–10. *Offered in sacrifice by idolaters,* Deut. 12:31; 2 Kin. 17:17; Jer. 7:31; 32:35. *Given in marriage by parents,* Judg. 1:12, 13; 1 Sam. 17:25; 18:20, 21. *Spared, by Pharaoh,* Ex. 1:16, 22; *by Herod,* Matt. 2:16. *Property rights of,* Num. 27:1–11; 36; Josh. 17:3–6; Ruth 4:5. *Wicked, instances of,* Gen. 19:30–38; 34:7. **Ordinance concerning:** *Offerings at birth of,* Lev. 12:6. *Prescribing damages for injury of,* Ex. 21:31. *Relating to priest's,* Lev. 21:9; 22:12, 13. *Forbidden to be the wife of her mother's husband,* Lev. 20:14.

v.6–1532 BC
See footnote, *Time*, Rev. 10:6.

6
*j Lamb, offering of*, Num. 7:15.
*k Offerings, burnt*, Lev. 6:17.
*l Jesus, typified in offerings*, Matt. 1:21.
*m Pigeon*, Gen. 15:9.
*n Dove*, Gen. 8:8.
*o Offerings, sin*, Lev. 6:17.
*p Priest, duties of*, Lev. 1:5.
3 R. V. tent of meeting,

7
*q Atonement, made by animal sacrifices*, Lev. 17:11.
*r Jesus, atonement by, typified*, Matt. 1:21.
4 R. V. fountain

8
*s Poor*, Prov. 21:13.
*t* Luke 2:24.
5 R. V. her means suffice not for

bring a [j]lamb of the first year
for a [k]burnt [l]offering, and a
young [m]pigeon, or a turtle [n]dove,
for a [o]sin offering, unto the door
of the [3]tabernacle of the congregation, unto the [p]priest:[Q]
7 [p]Who shall offer it before the
LORD, and make an [q,r]atone-
ment[C] for [d]her; and she shall be
[h,i]cleansed from the [4]issue of her
blood. This *is* the law for her
that hath born a male or a
*female.
8 And if [5,d]she be [s]not able to
bring a [j]lamb, then she shall
bring [t]two [n]turtles,[C] or two
young [m]pigeons; the one for the
[k]burnt [l]offering, and the other
for a [o]sin offering: and the
[p]priest shall make an [q,r]atone-
ment for her, and she shall be
[h,i]clean.[C Q]

## CHAPTER 13

*Laws and tokens whereby the priest is to be guided in discerning the plague of leprosy.*

1
*a Revelation, concerning treatment of diseases*, vs. 1–59; 2 Cor. 12:1.
*b Moses*, Ex. 2:10.
*c Aaron*, Ex. 6:20.

2
*d Scab*, Lev. 14:56.

3
*e Priest, duties of*, Lev. 1:5.
*f Disease, diagnosis of*, vs. 3–46; Ex. 15:26.
*g Defilement*, Lev. 5:2.
*h Sin, typified*, Rom. 5:12.

AND the LORD [a]spake unto
[b]Mō'ṣeṣ and [c]Aâr'on, saying,
2 When a man shall have in the
skin of his flesh a rising,[C] a [d]scab,
or bright spot, and it be in the
skin of his flesh *like* the plague
of *leprosy; then he shall be
brought unto [c]Aâr'on the priest,
or unto one of his sons the
priests:
3 And the [e]priest shall [f]look on
the plague in the skin of the
flesh: and *when* the hair in the
plague is turned white, and the
plague in sight *be* deeper than
the skin of his flesh, it *is* a plague
of leprosy: and the priest shall
look on him, and pronounce him
[g,h]unclean.[C]
4 If the bright spot *be* white in
the skin of his flesh, and in sight
*be* not deeper than the skin, and
the hair thereof be not turned
white; then the [e]priest shall
[i]shut up *him that hath* the
plague [j]seven days:
5 And the [e]priest shall [f]look on
him the seventh day: and, behold, *if* the plague in his sight be
at a stay,[C] *and* the plague spread
not in the skin; then the priest
shall [i]shut him up [j]seven days
more:
6 And the [e]priest shall [f]look on
him again the seventh day: and,
behold, *if* the plague [1]*be* somewhat dark, *and* the plague
spread not in the skin, the priest
shall pronounce him clean: it *is*
*but* a scab: and he shall [k]wash
his clothes, and be [l]clean.
7 But if the scab spread much
abroad in the skin, after that he
hath been seen of the priest for
his cleansing, he shall be seen of
the priest again:
8 And *if* the priest [f]see that,
behold, the scab spreadeth in the
skin, then the priest shall pronounce him [g,h]unclean[C]: it *is* a
*leprosy.
9 ¶ When the plague of *leprosy is in a man, then he shall be
brought unto the priest;
10 And the [e]priest shall [f]see
*him*: and, behold, *if* the rising *be*
white in the skin, and it have
turned the hair white, and *there*
*be* quick[C] raw flesh in the rising;
11 It *is* an old[C] *leprosy in the
skin of his flesh, and the [e]priest
shall pronounce him [g,h]unclean,[C]
and shall not [i]shut him up: for
he *is* unclean.
12 And if a *leprosy break out
abroad in the skin, and the leprosy cover all the skin of *him*
*that hath* the plague from his
head even to his foot, wheresoever the [e]priest [f]looketh;
13 Then the [e]priest shall [f]con-
sider: and, behold, *if* the *lep-

v.4–1532 BC
See footnote, *Time*, Rev. 10:6.

4
*i Sanitation and Hygiene, isolation*, Num. 31:23.
*j Seven, days*, Gen. 7:2.

6
*k Ceremonial Washing*, Ex. 19:10.
*l Holiness, typified*, Ex. 39:30.
1 R. V. be dim,

*** LEPROSY.** *Law concerning*, Lev. 13:14; 22:4; Num. 5:1–3; 12:14; Deut. 24:8; Matt. 8:4; Mark 1:44; Luke 5:14; 17:14. *Of Moses' hand*, Ex. 4:6, 7. Sent as a judgment: *On Miriam*, Num. 12:1–10; Deut. 24:9; *on Gehazi*, 2 Kin. 5:27; *on Uzziah*, 2 Chr. 26:19–41. *Entailed*, 2 Kin. 5:27. *Isolation of lepers*, Lev. 13:46; Num. 5:2; 12:14; 2 Kin. 15:5; 2 Chr. 26:21. *Separate burial of*, 2 Chr. 26:23. Instances of, not mentioned above: *Four lepers outside Samaria*, 2 Kin. 7:3; *Azariah*, 2 Kin. 15:5; *Simon*, Mark 14:3.

v.13–1532 BC
See footnote, *Time*, Rev. 10:6.

rosy have covered all his flesh, he shall pronounce *him* clean *that hath* the plague: it is all turned white: he *is* clean.

14 But when raw flesh appeareth in him, he shall be [g,h]unclean.

15 And the [e]priest shall [f]see the raw flesh, and pronounce him to be [g,h]unclean: *for* the raw flesh *is* unclean: it *is* a *leprosy.

16 Or if the raw flesh turn again, and be changed unto white, he shall come unto the priest;

17 And the [e]priest shall [f]see him: and, behold, *if* the plague be turned into white; then the priest shall pronounce *him* clean *that hath* the plague: he *is* clean.

18 ¶ The flesh also, in which, *even* in the skin thereof, was a [m]boil, and is healed,

19 And in the place of the [m]boil there be a white rising,[C] or a bright spot, white, and somewhat reddish, and it be shewed to the priest;

20 And if, when the [e]priest [f]seeth it, behold, it *be* in sight lower than the skin, and the hair thereof be turned white; the priest shall pronounce him [g,h]unclean: it *is* a plague of *leprosy broken out of the [m]boil.

21 But if the priest [f]look on it, and, behold, *there be* no white hairs therein, and *if* it *be* not lower than the skin, but [2]*be* somewhat dark; then the [e]priest shall [n]shut him up [j]seven days:

22 And if it spread much abroad in the skin, then the priest shall pronounce him [g,h]unclean: it *is* a plague.[C]

23 But if the bright spot stay[C] in his place, *and* spread not, it [3]*is* a burning [m]boil; and the priest shall pronounce him clean.

24 ¶ Or if there be *any* flesh, in the skin whereof *there is* a hot burning, and the quick[C] *flesh* that burneth have a white bright spot, somewhat reddish, or white;

25 Then the [e]priest shall [f]look upon it: and, behold, *if* the hair in the bright spot be turned white, and it *be in* sight deeper than the skin; it *is* a *leprosy broken out of the burning: wherefore the priest shall pronounce him [g,h]unclean: it *is* the plague[C] of leprosy.

26 But if the priest [f]look on it, and, behold, *there be* no white hair in the bright spot, and it *be* no lower[C] than the *other* skin, but [2]*be* somewhat dark; then the [e]priest shall [n]shut him up [j]seven days:

27 And the [e]priest shall [f]look upon him the seventh day: *and* if it be spread much abroad in the skin, then the priest shall pronounce him [g,h]unclean: it *is* the plague of *leprosy.

28 And if the bright spot stay in his place, *and* spread not in the skin, but it [2]*be* somewhat dark; it *is* a rising[C] of the burning, and the priest shall pronounce him clean: for it [4]*is* an inflammation of the burning.

29 ¶ If a man or woman have a plague upon the head or the [o]beard;

30 Then the [e]priest shall [f]see the plague: and, behold, if it *be* in sight deeper than the skin; *and there be* in it a yellow thin hair; then the priest shall pronounce him [g,h]unclean: it *is* a dry scall,[C] *even* a *leprosy upon the head or beard.

31 And if the priest [f]look on the plague[C] of the scall,[C] and, behold, it *be* not in sight deeper than the skin, and *that there is* no black hair in it; then the priest shall

v.24–1532 BC
See footnote, *Time*, Rev. 10:6.

**18** *m* ***Boil***, Ex. 9:9.

**21** *n Sanitation and Hygiene, isolation*, Num. 31:23.
**2** R. V. be dim,

**23** **3** R. V. is the scar of the boil;

**28** 4 R. V. is the scar

**29** *o Beard*, 1 Sam. 21:13.

**Healed:** *Naaman*, 2 Kin. 5:8–14. *By Jesus*, Matt. 8:3; Mark 1:40–42; Luke 5:13; 17:12–14. *Apostles empowered to heal*, Matt. 10:8.

v.31–1532 BC
See footnote, *Time*,
Rev. 10:6.

[n]shut up *him that hath* the
plague of the scall [j]seven days:
32 And in the seventh day the
[e]priest shall [f]look on the plague:
and, behold, *if* the scall[G] spread
not, and there be in it no yellow
hair, and the scall[G] *be* not in sight
deeper than the skin;
33 He shall be shaven, but the
scall[G] shall he not shave; and the
priest shall [n]shut up *him that*
*hath* the scall[G] [j]seven days more:
34 And in the seventh day the
priest shall [f]look on the scall[G]:
and, behold, *if* the scall be not
spread in the skin, nor *be* in
sight deeper than the skin; then
the priest shall pronounce him
clean: and he shall [k]wash his
clothes, and be [l]clean.
35 But if the scall[G] spread much
in the skin after his cleansing;
36 Then the priest shall [f]look
on him: and, behold, if the scall[G]
be spread in the skin, the priest
shall not seek for yellow hair;
he *is* [g,h]unclean.
37 But if the scall[G] be in his
sight at a stay, and *that* there is
black hair grown up therein; the
scall[G] is healed, he *is* [l]clean: and
the priest shall pronounce him
[l]clean.
38 ¶ If a man also or a woman
have in the skin of their flesh
bright spots, *even* white bright
spots;
39 Then the [e]priest shall [f]look:
and, behold, *if* the bright spots
in the skin of their flesh *be* dark-
ish white; it [5]*is* a freckled spot
*that* groweth in the skin; he *is*
clean.
40 And the man whose hair is
fallen off his head, he *is* [p]bald;
*yet is* he clean.
41 And he that hath his hair
fallen off from the part of his
head toward his face, he *is* forehead [p]bald: *yet is* he clean.
42 And if there be in the [p]bald
head, or bald forehead, a white

39
5 R. V. is a tetter, it hath broken out in the skin;

40
p *Baldness*, Lev. 21:5.

reddish sore; it *is* a *leprosy
sprung up in his bald head, or
his bald forehead.
43 Then the priest shall [f]look[G]
upon it: and, behold, *if* the rising
of the sore *be* white reddish in
his [p]bald head, or in his bald
forehead, as the *leprosy appeareth in the skin of the flesh;
44 He is a *leprous man, he *is*
unclean[G]: the priest shall pronounce him utterly [g,h]unclean;
his plague *is* in his head.
45 And the *leper in whom the
plague *is*, his clothes shall be
[q]rent,[G] and his head bare, and he
shall put a covering upon his upper lip, and shall cry, Unclean,
Unclean.
46 All the days wherein the
plague *shall be* in him he shall
be [6,g]defiled; he *is* [h]unclean: he
shall dwell [n]alone; without[G] the
camp *shall* his habitation *be*.[Q]
47 ¶ The [r]garment also that the
plague of *leprosy is in, *whether*
*it be* a [s]woollen garment, or a
[t]linen garment;
48 Whether [r]*it be* in the warp,
or woof; of [t]linen, or of [s]woollen;
whether in a skin, or in any
thing made of skin;
49 And if the plague be greenish or reddish in the [r]garment, or
in the skin, either in the warp,[G] or
in the woof,[G] or in any thing of
skin; it *is* a plague of *leprosy,
and shall be shewed unto the
priest:[Q]
50 And the [e]priest shall [f]look
upon the plague, and [n]shut up *it*
*that hath* the plague [j]seven days:
51 And [e]he shall [f]look on the
plague on the seventh day: if the
plague be spread in the [r]gar-
ment, either in the warp, or in
the woof, or in a skin, *or* in any
work that is made of skin; the
plague *is* a fretting[G] *leprosy; it
*is* unclean.
52 [e]He shall therefore [u]burn
that garment, whether warp or

v.42–1532 BC
See footnote, *Time*,
Rev. 10:6.

45
q *Rending of Garments*, 2 Chr. 34:27.

46
6 R. V. unclean;

47
r *Dress, ceremonial purification of*, Zech. 3:4.
s *Wool*, Judg. 6:37.
t *Linen*, Ezek. 27:16.

52
u *Sanitation and Hygiene, disinfection*, Num. 31:23.

v.52–1532 BC
See footnote, *Time,* Rev. 10:6.

woof, in [s]woollen or in [t]linen, or
any thing of skin, wherein the
plague is: for it *is* a fretting[G] leprosy; it shall be [u]burnt in the
fire.
53 And if the [e]priest shall [f]look,
and, behold, the plague be not
spread in the [r]garment, either in
the warp, or in the woof, or in
any thing of skin;
54 Then the priest shall command that they [k]wash *the* [r]*thing*
wherein the plague *is,* and he
shall [n]shut it up [i]seven days
more:
55 And the priest shall [f]look on
the plague, after that [r]it is
washed: and, behold, *if* the
plague have not changed his
colour, and the plague be not
spread; it *is* unclean; thou shalt
[u]burn it in the fire; it *is* fret[G] inward, *whether* it *be* bare within
or without.
56 And if the priest look, and,
behold, the plague [7]*be* somewhat
dark after the washing of it; then
he shall rend[G] it out of the [r]gar-
ment, or out of the skin, or out
of the warp, or out of the
woof:
57 And if it appear still in
the [r]garment, either in the warp,[G]
or in the woof, or in any thing
of skin; it *is* a spreading *plague:*
thou shalt [u]burn that wherein
the plague *is* with fire.
58 And the [r]garment, either
warp, or woof, or whatsoever
thing of skin *it be,* which thou
shalt wash, if the plague be departed from them, then it shall
be [k]washed the second time, and
shall be clean.
59 This *is* the law of the
plague of leprosy in a [r]garment
of [s]woollen or [t]linen, either in
the warp, or woof, or any thing
of skins, to pronounce it clean,
or to pronounce it unclean.

56
7 R. V. be dim

## CHAPTER 14

*The rites and sacrifices in cleansing the leper. 33 The signs of leprosy in a house. 48 The cleansing of that house.*

AND the LORD [a]spake unto
[b]Mō′ṣeṣ, saying,[Q]
2 This shall be the law of the
[c]leper in the day of his [d]cleans-
ing: He shall be brought unto
the priest:
3 And the [e]priest shall go forth
out of the camp; and the priest
shall [f]look, and, behold, *if* the
plague of [c]leprosy be healed in
the leper;[Q]
4[Q] Then shall the [e]priest command to take for him that is to
be [d]cleansed two birds alive *and*
clean, and [g]cedar wood, and
[h]scarlet and [i]hyssop:
5 And the [e]priest shall command that one of the birds be
[j]killed in an earthen vessel over
running water:
6 As for the living bird, he shall
take it, and the [g]cedar wood,
and the [h]scarlet, and the [i]hyssop,
and shall dip them and the living
bird in the [k,l]blood of the bird
*that was* [j]killed over the running
water:
7 And [e]he shall *sprinkle upon
him that is to be [d]cleansed from
the [c]leprosy seven times, and
shall pronounce him [m,n]clean,
and shall let the living bird loose
into the open field.
8 And he that is to be cleansed
shall [o,p]wash his clothes, and
shave off all his hair, and wash
himself in water, that he may be
[n]clean: and after that he shall
come into the camp, and shall
tarry[G] abroad[G] out of his tent
seven days.
9 But it shall be on the seventh
day, that he shall shave all his
hair off his head and his [q]beard
and his eyebrows, even all his
hair he shall shave off: and he
shall [o]wash his clothes, also he

v.1–1532 BC
See footnote, *Time,* Rev. 10:6.

1
a *Revelation, concerning purification,* vs. 1–57; 2 Cor. 12:1.
b *Moses,* Ex. 2:10.

2
c *Leprosy, law concerning,* vs. 1–57; Lev. 13:2.
d *Purification,* vs. 2–29; Num. 19:19.

3
e *Priests, duties of.* Lev. 1:5.
f *Disease, diagnosis of,* Ex. 15:26.

4
g *Cedar,* Isa. 9:10.
h *Colors, symbolical,* Ezek. 16:16.
i *Hyssop,* Ex. 12:22.

5
j *Jesus, vicarious death of, typified,* Matt. 1:21.

6
k *Blood, sacrificial,* Heb. 9:19.
l *Jesus, atoning blood of, typified,* Matt. 1:21.

7
m *Purification, by blood,* Num. 19:19.
n *Holiness, typified,* Ex. 39:30.

8
o *Ceremonial Washing, for defilement,* Ex. 19:10.
p *Sanitation and Hygiene, disinfection,* Num. 31:23.

9
q *Beard,* 1 Sam. 21:13.

* **SPRINKLING.** *Of blood,* Lev. 14:7, 51; 16:14; 17:6; Num. 19:4; Heb. 9:13, 19, 21; 11:28; 12:24; 1 Pet. 1:2. *Of water,* Num. 8:7; 19:18–21; Ezek. 36:25; Heb. 9:19. *Of oil,* Lev. 14:16, 27. See footnote, PURIFICATION, Num. 19:19.

v.8–1532 BC
See footnote, *Time*, Rev. 10:6.

**10**
r *Lamb, offering of*, Num. 7:15.
s *Sin, typified*, Rom. 5:12.
t *Measure*, Deut. 25:15.
u *Offerings, meat*, Lev. 6:17.
v *Oil*, Deut. 12:17.
1 R. V. meal

**11**
w *Tabernacle*, Ex. 27:9.
2 R. V. tent of meeting:

**12**
x *Offerings, trespass*, Lev. 6:17.
y *Jesus, typified in offerings*, Matt. 1:21.
z *Offerings, wave*, Lev. 6:17.
3 R. V. guilt

**13**
a *Priest, duties of*, Lev. 1:5.
b *Jesus, vicarious death of, typified*, Matt. 1:21.
c *Offerings, sin*, Lev. 6:17.
d *Offerings, burnt*, Lev. 6:17.
e *Court, of tabernacle*, Ex. 38:9.
f *Priest, emoluments of*, Lev. 1:5.
4 R. V. place of the sanctuary:

**14**
g *Blood, sacrificial*, Heb. 9:19.
h *Jesus, atoning blood of, typified*, Matt. 1:21.
i *Offerings, trespass*, Lev. 6:17.
j *Ear*, Lev. 8:23.
k *Purification*, Num. 19:19.
l *Thumb*, Lev. 8:23.

**15**
m *Oil*, Deut. 12:17.

**16**
n *Seven*, Gen. 7:2.

shall wash his flesh in water, and
he shall be [n]clean.
10 And on the eighth day he
shall take two he [r]lambs [n]without
[†,s]blemish, and one ewe[G]
lamb of the first year without
blemish, and three [t]tenth deals[G]
of fine flour *for* a [1,u]meat[G] offering,
mingled[G] with [v]oil, and one
[t]log[G] of oil.
11 And the [e]priest that maketh
*him* [d]clean shall present the man
that is to be made clean, and
those things, before the LORD,
*at* the door of the [2,w]tabernacle
of the congregation:
12 And the [e]priest shall take
one he [r]lamb, and offer him for
a [3,x]trespass [y]offering, and the
[t]log of [v]oil, and wave them *for* a
[z]wave offering before the LORD:
13 And [a]he shall [b]slay the lamb
in the place where he shall kill
the [c]sin offering and the [d]burnt
offering, in the [4,e]holy place:
for as the sin offering *is* the
[f]priest's, *so is* the [3]trespass offering:
it *is* most holy:
14 And the [a]priest shall take
*some* of the [g,h]blood of the [3,i]trespass
offering, and the priest
shall put *it* upon the tip of the
right [j]ear of him that is to be
[k]cleansed, and upon the [l]thumb
of his right hand, and upon the
great [‡]toe of his right foot:
15 And the priest shall take
*some* of the log[G] of [m]oil, and pour
*it* into the palm of his own left
hand:
16 And the priest shall dip his
right finger in the oil that *is* in
his left hand, and shall *sprinkle
of the oil with his finger [n]seven
times before the LORD:
17 And of the rest of the [m]oil
that *is* in his hand shall the
[a]priest put upon the tip of the
right [j]ear of him that is to be
[k]cleansed, and upon the [l]thumb
of his right hand, and upon the
great [‡]toe of his right foot, upon
the [g,h]blood of the [3,i]trespass
offering:
18 And the remnant of the [m]oil
that is in the priest's hand he
shall pour upon the [o]head of him
that is to be [k]cleansed: and the
[a]priest shall make an [p,q]atonement[G]
for him before the LORD.
19 And the [a]priest shall offer
the [c]sin offering, and make an
[p,q]atonement for him that is to
be [k]cleansed from his uncleanness;
and afterward he shall
[b]kill the [d]burnt offering:
20 And the [a]priest shall offer
the [d]burnt offering and the
[5,r]meat offering upon the altar:
and the priest shall make an
[p,q]atonement for him, and he
shall be [k,s]clean.
21 And if he *be* [t]poor, and cannot
get so much; then he shall
take one [6,u]lamb *for* a [i]trespass[G]
offering to be waved, to make
an [p,q]atonement for him, and
one [v]tenth deal[G] of fine flour mingled[G]
with [m]oil for a [5,r]meat[G] offering,
and a log[G] of oil;
22 And two [w]turtledoves, or
two young [x]pigeons, such as he
is able to get; and the one shall
be a [c]sin offering, and the other
a [d]burnt offering.
23 And he shall bring them on
the eighth day for his [k]cleansing
unto the priest, unto the door of
the [2]tabernacle of the congregation,
before the LORD.
24 And the [a]priest shall take
the [u]lamb of the [3,i]trespass offer-

v.17–1532 BC
See footnote, *Time*, Rev. 10:6.

**18**
o *Head, anointed*, Psa. 133:2.
p *Atonement, made by animal sacrifices*, Lev. 17:11.
q *Jesus, atonement by, typified*, Matt. 1:21.

**20**
r *Offerings, meat*, Lev. 6:17.
s *Holiness, typified*, Ex. 39:30.
5 R. V. meal

**21**
t *Poor*, Prov. 21:13.
u *Lamb*, Num. 7:15.
v *Measure*, Deut. 25:15.
6 R. V. he-lamb for a guilt

**22**
w *Dove*, Gen. 8:8.
x *Pigeon*, Gen. 15:9.

† **BLEMISH,** a physical deformity. The Mosaic law prohibited blemished persons from exercising the functions of the priest's office and prohibited the offering of blemished animals for sacrifices. The blemish was an imperfection, and this imperfection disqualified persons and things for sacred uses. It was intended to teach by this object lesson that no one whose *heart* was *imperfect* could enjoy the privileges of divine worship. The *blemish* thus became *a type of sin* and the offering *without blemish* became *a type of holiness*. *Debarred sons of Aaron from exercise of priestly offices*, Lev. 21:17–23. *Animals with, forbidden to be used for sacrifice*, Ex. 12:5; Lev. 1:3, 10; 3:16; 4:23, 28, 32; 6:6; 9:3; 22:19–25; Num. 28:19; 29:8, 26; Deut. 15:21; 17:1; Mal. 1:8, 14.
**Figurative,** Eph. 5:27; Heb. 9:14; 1 Pet. 1:19.

‡ **TOE.** *Anointed, in consecration*, Ex. 29:20; Lev. 8:23, 24; *in purification*, Lev. 14:14, 17, 25, 28. *Of prisoners of war cut off*, Judg. 1:6, 7. *Six, on each foot*, 2 Sam. 21:20; 1 Chr. 20:6.

v.24–1532 BC
See footnote, *Time*, Rev. 10:6.

24
*y* *Offerings, wave*, Lev. 6:17.

ing, and the [v]log of oil, and the
priest shall wave them *for* a [y]wave
offering before the LORD:
25 And he shall [b]kill the lamb
of the [3,i]trespass offering, and the
priest shall take *some* of the
[g,h]blood of the [3]trespass offering, and put *it* upon the tip of
the right [j]ear of him that is to be
[k]cleansed, and upon the [l]thumb
of his right hand, and upon the
great [‡]toe of his right foot:
26 And the priest shall pour of
the [m]oil into the palm of his own
left hand:
27 And the priest shall [*]sprin-
kle with his right finger *some* of
the [m]oil that *is* in his left hand
[n]seven times before the LORD:
28 And the priest shall put of
the [m]oil that *is* in his hand upon
the tip of the right [j]ear of him
that is to be [k]cleansed, and upon
the [l]thumb of his right hand,
and upon the great [‡]toe of his
right foot, upon the place of the
[g,h]blood of the [3]trespass offering:
29 And the rest of the [m]oil that
*is* in the priest's hand he shall
put upon the [o]head of him that
is to be [k]cleansed, to make an
[p,q]atonement for him before the
LORD.
30 And he shall offer the one
of the [w]turtledoves, or of the
young [x]pigeons, such as he can
get;
31 *Even* such as [t]he is able to
get, the one *for* a [c]sin offering,
and the other *for* a [d]burnt offering, with the [5,r]meat offering:
and the [a]priest shall make an
[p,q]atonement for him that is to
be [k]cleansed before the LORD.
32 This *is* the law *of him* in
whom *is* the plague of [z]leprosy,
[t]whose hand is not able to get
*that which pertaineth* to his
[k]cleansing.[Q]
33 ¶ And the LORD [a]spake unto [b]Mō′ṣeṣ and unto [c]Aâr′on,
saying,
34 When ye be come into the
land of [d]Cā′năan, which I give to
you for a possession, and I put
the plague of [e]leprosy in a [f]house
of the land of your possession;
35 And he that owneth the
[f]house shall come and tell the
[g]priest, saying, It seemeth[C] to me
*there is* as it were a plague[C] in the
house:
36 Then the [g]priest shall command that they [h]empty the
[f]house, before the priest go *into*
*it* to see the plague, that all that
*is* in the house be not made unclean: and afterward the priest
shall go in to see the house:
37 And [g]he shall look on the
plague, and, behold, *if* the
plague *be* in the walls of the
[f]house with hollow strakes,[C]
greenish or reddish, which in
sight *are* lower[C] than the wall;
38 Then the [g]priest shall go out
of the [f]house to the door of the
house, and [h]shut up the house
[i]seven days:
39 And the [g]priest shall come
again the seventh day, and shall
look: and, behold, *if* the plague
be spread in the walls of the
[f]house;
40 Then the [g]priest shall command that they [h]take away the
stones in which the plague *is*,
and they shall cast them into an
unclean place without[C] the city:
41 And [g]he [h]shall cause the
[f]house to be scraped within
round about, and they shall pour
out the [7]dust that they scrape off
without[C] the city into an unclean
place:
42 And they shall take other
stones, and put *them* in the place
of those stones; and he shall take
other [‖]morter, and shall plaister
the [f]house.

32
*z* *Leprosy*, Lev. 13:2.

33
*a* *Revelation, concerning leprosy in houses*, 2 Cor. 12:1.

v.33–1532 BC
See footnote, *Time*, Rev. 10:6.

*b* *Moses*, Ex. 2:10.
*c* *Aaron*, Ex. 6:20.

34
*d* *Canaan*, Gen. 37:1.
*e* *Leprosy*, Lev. 13:2.
*f* *House*, Esth. 8:1.

35
*g* *Priest, duties of*, Lev. 1:5.

36
*h* *Sanitation and Hygiene*, vs. 37–47; Num. 31:23.

38
*i* *Seven*, Gen. 7:2.

41
7 R. V. mortar

‖ **MORTAR.** *A cement*, Ex. 1:14. *Slime used as, in building tower of Babel*, Gen. 11:3. *Used, to plaster houses*, Lev. 14:42, 43, 45, 48; Dan. 5:5; *in building altars*, Deut. 27:2–5. *Untempered, not enduring*, Ezek. 13:10–15; 22:28. *To be trodden to make firm*, Nah. 3:14. **Figurative**, Isa. 41:25.

v.43–1532 BC
See footnote, *Time*, Rev. 10:6.

**46**
*j* *Defilement*, Lev. 5:2.
*k* *Sin, typified*, Rom. 5:12.

**47**
*l* *Ceremonial Washing*, Ex. 19:10.

**49**
*m* *Purification*, Num. 19:19
*n* *Cedar*, Isa. 9:10.
*o* *Colors, symbolical*, Ezek. 16:16.
*p* *Hyssop*, Ex. 12:22.

**50**
*q* *Jesus, vicarious death of, typified*, Matt. 1:21.

**51**
*r* *Jesus, atoning blood of, typified*, Matt. 1:21.

43 And if the plague come again, and break out in the [f]house, after that he hath taken away the stones, and after he hath scraped the house, and after it is plaistered;

44 Then the [g]priest shall come and look, and, behold, *if* the plague be spread in the house, it *is* a fretting[C] [e]leprosy in the house: it *is* unclean.

45 And he shall [h]break down the [f]house, the stones of it, and the timber thereof, and all the ‖morter of the house; and he shall carry *them* forth out of the city into an unclean place.

46 Moreover he that goeth into the house all the while that it is shut up shall be [j,k]unclean until the even.

47 And he that lieth in the house shall [l]wash his clothes; and he that eateth in the house shall wash his clothes.

48 And if the priest shall come in, and look *upon it*, and, behold, the plague hath not spread in the [f]house, after the house was plaistered: then the priest shall pronounce the house clean, because the plague is healed.

49 And he shall take to [m]cleanse the house two birds, and [n]cedar wood, and [o]scarlet, and [p]hyssop:

50 And he shall [q]kill the one of the birds in an earthen vessel over running water:

51 And he shall take the [n]cedar wood, and the [p]hyssop, and the [o]scarlet, and the living bird, and dip them in the [r]blood of the slain bird, and in the running water, and *sprinkle the house [i]seven times:

52 And he shall [m]cleanse[C] the [f]house with the [r]blood of the bird, and with the running water, and with the living bird, and with the [n]cedar wood and with the [p]hyssop, and with the [o]scarlet:

53 But he shall let go the living bird out of the city into the open fields, and make an [s]atonement for the house: and it shall be [t]clean.

54 This *is* the [u]law for all manner of plague of [e]leprosy, and scall,[C]

55 And for the [e]leprosy of a [v]garment, and of a [f]house,

56 And for a rising,[C] and for a §scab, and for a bright spot:

57 To teach when *it is* unclean, and when *it is* clean: this *is* the law of [e]leprosy.

## CHAPTER 15

*The uncleanness of men in their issues. 13 The cleansing of them. 19 The uncleanness of women in their issues. 28 Their cleansing.*

AND the LORD [a]spake unto [b]Mō'ṣeṣ and to [c]Aâr'on, saying,

2 Speak unto the children of [d]Iṣ'ra-el, and say unto them, When any man hath [1]a running issue[C] out of his flesh, *because of* his issue he *is* [e,f]unclean.

3 And this shall be his [e,f]uncleanness in his issue: whether his flesh run with his issue, or his flesh be stopped from his issue, it *is* his uncleanness.

4 Every bed, whereon he lieth that hath the issue, is [e,f]unclean: and every thing, whereon he sitteth, shall be unclean.

5 And [g]whosoever toucheth his bed shall [h,i]wash his clothes, and bathe *himself* in water, and be [e,f]unclean until the even.

6 And [g]he that sitteth on *any* thing whereon he sat that hath the issue shall [h,i]wash his clothes, and bathe *himself* in water, and be [e,f]unclean until the even.

v.52–1532 BC
See footnote, *Time* Rev. 10:6.

**53**
*s* *Atonement, made for houses*, Lev. 17:11.
*t* *Holiness, typified*, Ex. 39:30.

**54**
*u* *Law, of Moses*, Deut. 33:2.

**55**
*v* *Dress, purification of*, Zech. 3:4

**1**
*a* *Revelation, concerning defilement*, 2 Cor. 12:1.
*b* *Moses*, Ex. 2:10.
*c* *Aaron*, Ex. 6:20.

**2**
*d* *Israel*, Ex. 4:22.
*e* *Defilement*, Lev. 5:2.
*f* *Sin, typified*, Rom. 5:12.
1 R. V. an issue

**5**
*g* *Sanitation and Hygiene*, vs. 6–13 Num. 31:23.
*h* *Ceremonial Washing*, Ex. 19:10.
*i* *Purification*, vs. 4–13, 16–33; Num. 19:19.

§ **SCAB.** *A disease of the skin*, Lev. 13:2, 6–8; 14:56; 21:20; 22:22; Deut. 28:27; Isa. 3:17. See footnote, DISEASE, Ex. 15:26.

v.7–1532 BC
See footnote, *Time*, Rev. 10:6.

7 And [g]he that toucheth the flesh of him that hath the issue shall [h,i]wash his clothes, and bathe *himself* in water, and be [e,f]unclean until the even.

8 And [g]if he that hath the issue [j]spit upon him that is clean; then he shall [h,i]wash his clothes, and bathe *himself* in water, and be [e,f]unclean until the even.

9 And what saddle soever he rideth upon that hath the issue shall be unclean.

10 And whosoever toucheth any thing that was under him shall be [e,f]unclean until the even: and [g]he that beareth *any of* those things shall [h,i]wash his clothes, and bathe *himself* in water, and be unclean until the even.

11 And [g]whomsoever he toucheth that hath the issue[C], and hath not rinsed his hands in water, he shall [h,i]wash his clothes, and bathe *himself* in water, and be [e,f]unclean until the even.

12 And [g]the vessel of earth, that he toucheth which hath the issue, shall be broken: and every vessel of wood shall be rinsed in water.

13 And when he that hath an issue is [i]cleansed of his issue; then he shall number to himself [k]seven days for his cleansing, and [h]wash his clothes, and bathe his flesh in running water, and shall be [l]clean.

14 And on the eighth day he shall take to him two [m]turtledoves, or two young [n]pigeons, and come before the LORD unto the door of the [2]tabernacle of the congregation, and give them unto the priest:

15 And the [o]priest shall offer them, the one *for* a sin [p,q]offering, and the other *for* a burnt [q]offering; and the priest shall make an [r,s]atonement[C] for him before the LORD for his issue.

16 And [g]if any man's seed[C] of *copulation go out from him, then he shall [h,i]wash all his flesh in water, and be [e,f]unclean until the even.

17 And [g]every [t]garment, and every skin, whereon is the seed of copulation, shall be [h,i]washed with water, and be [e,f]unclean until the even.

18 The woman also with whom man shall lie *with* seed of *copulation, they shall *both* [h,i]bathe *themselves* in water, and be [e,f]unclean until the even.[Q]

19 ¶ And if a [u]woman have an [v,w]issue[C], *and* her issue in her flesh be blood, she shall be [3]put apart [k]seven days: and whosoever toucheth her shall be [e,f]unclean until the even.

20 And every thing that [u]she lieth upon in her [3,v]separation shall be [e,f]unclean: every thing also that she sitteth upon shall be unclean.

21 And [g]whosoever toucheth her bed shall [h,i]wash his clothes, and bathe *himself* in water, and be [e,f]unclean until the even.

22 And [g]whosoever toucheth any thing that she sat upon shall [h,i]wash his clothes, and bathe *himself* in water, and be [e,f]unclean until the even.

23 And if it *be* on *her* bed, or on any thing whereon she sitteth, when he toucheth it, he shall be [e,f]unclean until the even.

24 And if any man lie with her at all, and her [4,v]flowers[C] be upon him, he shall be [e,f]unclean [k]seven days; and all the bed whereon he lieth shall be unclean.

25 And if a [u]woman have an [w]issue of her blood many days out of the time of her [4,v]separation, or if [5]it run beyond the

8
j *Spitting*, Num. 12:14.

13
k *Seven, days*, Gen. 7:2.
l *Holiness, typified*, Ex. 39:30.

14
m *Dove*, Gen. 8:8.
n *Pigeon*, Gen. 15:9.
2 R. V. tent of meeting,

15
o *Priest, duties of*, Lev. 1:5.
p *Offerings*, Lev. 6:17.
q *Jesus, typified in offerings*, Matt. 1:21.

v.15–1532 BC
See footnote, *Time*, Rev. 10:6.

r *Atonement, made by animal sacrifices*, Lev. 17:11.
s *Jesus, atonement by, typified*, Matt. 1:21.

17
t *Dress, purification of*, Zech. 3:4.

19
u *Women, purifications of*, vs. 19–33; Prov. 31:10.
v *Menstruation*, Ezek. 18:6
w *Hemorrhage*, Matt. 9:20.
3 R. V. in her impurity

24
4 R. V. impurity

25
5 R. V. she have an issue

* **COPULATION.** *Between persons near of kin, forbidden*, Lev. 18:6–16. *During menses, forbidden*, Lev. 18:19 *With animals, forbidden*, Ex. 22:19; Lev. 18:23; 20:15, 16.

v.25–1532 BC
See footnote, *Time*, Rev. 10:6.

time of her [4]separation; all the days of the issue of her [e,f]uncleanness shall be as the days of her separation: she *shall be* unclean.[Q]

26 Every bed whereon she lieth all the days of her [w]issue shall be unto her as the bed of her [4,v]separation: and whatsoever she sitteth upon shall be [e,f]unclean, as the uncleanness of her [4]separation.

27 And whosoever toucheth those things shall be unclean, and shall [h,i]wash his clothes, and bathe *himself* in water, and be [e,f]unclean until the even.

28 But if [u]she be [i]cleansed of her issue, then she shall number to herself [k]seven days, and after that she shall be [l]clean.

29 And on the eighth day she shall take unto her two [m]turtles,[C] or two young [n]pigeons, and bring them unto the priest, to the door of the [2]tabernacle of the congregation.

30 And the [o]priest shall offer the one *for* a sin [p,q]offering, and the other *for* a burnt [q]offering; and the priest shall make an [r,s]atonement for her before the LORD for the issue of her [e,f]uncleanness.

31 Thus shall ye [i]separate the children of [d]Is′ra-el from their [e,f]uncleanness; that they die not in their [e,f]uncleanness, when they defile my [x]tabernacle that *is* among them.

32 This *is* the [y]law of him that hath an issue, and *of him* whose seed goeth from him, and is [e,f]defiled therewith;

33 And of her that is sick of her [4,v]flowers,[C] and of him that hath an issue, of the man, and of the [u]woman, and of him that lieth with her that is [e,f]unclean.

31
x *Tabernacle, defilement of*, Ex. 27:9.

32
y *Law, of Moses*, Deut. 33:2.

## CHAPTER 16

*How the high priest must enter into the holy place. 11 The sin offering for himself. 15 The sin offering for the people. 20 The scapegoat. 29 The yearly atonement.*

AND the LORD [a]spake unto [b]Mō′ṣeṣ after the death of the two sons of Aâr′on, when they offered before the LORD, and died;

2 And the LORD said unto [b]Mō′ṣeṣ, Speak unto [c]Aâr′on thy brother, that he come not at all times into the [d]holy *place* within the [e]vail before the [f]mercy seat, which *is* upon the [g]ark; that he die not: for I will appear in the [*,h]cloud upon the mercy seat.[Q]

3 [T]Thus shall [c]Aâr′on come into the [d]holy *place*: with a young [i]bullock for a [j]sin [k]offering, and a ram for a [l]burnt offering.[Q]

4 He shall put on the [m]holy linen coat, and he shall have the linen [n]breeches upon his flesh, and shall be girded with a linen [o]girdle, and with the linen [p]mitre[C] shall he be attired:[C] these *are* [m]holy garments; therefore shall he [q,r]wash his flesh in water, and *so* put them on.

5 And he shall take of the congregation of the children of Is′ra-el two [1]kids of the goats for a [j]sin [k]offering, and one ram for a [l]burnt offering.

6 And [c]Aâr′on shall offer his [i]bullock of the [j]sin offering, which *is* for himself, and make an [s,t]atonement[C] for [u]himself, and for his house.[Q]

7 And [c]he shall take the two goats, and present them before the LORD *at* the door of the [2]tabernacle of the congregation.[T]

8 And [c]Aâr′on shall cast [v]lots upon the two goats; one lot for the LORD, and the other lot [3]for the scapegoat.[C]

9 And [c]Aâr′on shall bring the goat upon which the LORD's [v]lot

v.1–1532 BC
See footnote, *Time*, Rev. 10:6.

1
a *Revelation, concerning the ceremonies on the day of atonement*, 2 Cor. 12:1.
b *Moses*, Ex. 2:10

2
c *High Priest, duties of*, vs. 1–34; Lev. 21:10.
d *Holy of Holies*, Ex. 26:33.
e *Vail*, Ex. 26:31.
f *Mercy Seat*, Ex 25:17.
g *Ark*, Ex. 25:10.
h *God, incomprehensible, symbolized*, Gen. 2:2.

3
i *Bullock*, Ex. 29:3
j *Offerings, sin*, Lev. 6:17.
k *Jesus, typified in offerings*, Matt 1:21.
l *Offerings, burnt*, Lev. 6:17.

4
m *Holiness, typified*, Ex. 39:30.
n *Breeches*, Ex. 28:42.
o *Girdle*, Prov. 31:24.
p *Miter*, Ex. 28:4
q *Ceremonial Washing, of priests*, Ex. 19:10.
r *Purification*, Num. 19:19.

5
1 R. V. he-goats

6
s *Atonement, made by animal sacrifices*, Lev. 17:11.
t *Jesus, atonement by, typified*, Matt. 1:21.
u *High Priest, atonement for*, Lev. 21:10.

7
2 R. V. tent of meeting.

8
v *Lot*, Esth. 3:7.
3 R. V. for Azazel.

* **SHEKINAH.** *The visible sign of God's presence on the ark of testimony in the Holy of holies*, Ex. 25:22; 29:42, 43; 30:6, 36; Lev. 16:2; Num. 7:89; 17:4; 1 Sam. 4:4; 2 Sam. 6:2; 2 Kin. 19:14, 15; Psa. 80:1; Isa. 37:16; Ezek. 9:3; 10:18.

v.9–1532 BC
See footnote, *Time,* Rev. 10:6.

10
4 R. V. send him away for Azazel

11
w *Jesus, vicarious death of, typified,* Matt. 1:21.

12
x *Altar, of incense,* Ex. 30:1.
y *Incense,* Ex. 37:29.

14
z *Blood, sacrificial,* Heb. 9:19.
a *Jesus, atoning blood of, typified,* Matt. 1:21.
b *Bullock,* Ex. 29:3.
c *Sprinkling, of blood,* Lev. 14:7.
d *Mercy Seat,* Ex. 25:17.

15
e *High Priest, duties of,* Lev. 21:10.
f *Jesus, vicarious death of, typified,* Matt. 1:21.
g *Offerings,* Lev. 6:17.
h *Jesus, typified in offerings,* Matt. 1:21.
i *Blood, sacrificial,* Heb. 9:19.
j *Vail,* Ex. 26:31.

16
k *Atonement,* Lev. 17:11.
l *Jesus, atonement by, typified,* Matt. 1:21.
m *Holy of Holies,* Ex. 26:33.
n *Defilement,* Lev. 5:2.
o *Sin, typified,* Rom. 5:12.

fell, and offer him *for* a sin
[j,k]offering.
10 But the goat, on which the
[v]lot fell [3]to be the scapegoat,
shall be presented alive before
the LORD, to make an [s,t]atone-
ment with him, *and* to [4]let him
go for a scapegoat into the wilderness.
11 And [e]Aâr′on shall bring the
[i]bullock of the [j]sin [k]offering,
which *is* for himself, and shall
make an atonement for [u]him-
self, and for his house, and shall
[w]kill the bullock of the sin offering which *is* for himself:
12 And [e]he shall take a †censer
full of burning coals of fire from
off the [x]altar before the LORD,
and his hands full of sweet [y]in-
cense beaten small, and bring *it*
within the [e]vail:[T Q]
13 And [e]he shall put the [y]in-
cense upon the fire before the
LORD, that the cloud of the incense may cover the [f]mercy seat
that *is* upon the testimony, that
he die not:[Q]
14 And he shall take of the
[z,a]blood of the [b]bullock, and
[c]sprinkle *it* with his finger upon
the [d]mercy seat eastward; and
before the mercy seat shall he
sprinkle of the blood with his
finger seven times.[Q]
15 Then shall [e]he [f]kill the goat
of the sin [g,h]offering, that *is* for
the people, and bring his [i,a]blood
within the [j]vail, and do with that
blood as he did with the blood of
the [b]bullock, and [c]sprinkle it upon the [d]mercy seat, and before
the mercy seat:[T Q]
16 And [e]he shall make an
[k,l]atonement for the [m]holy *place,*
because of the [n,o]uncleanness of
the children of Ĭs̱′ra-el, and because of their transgressions in
all their sins: and so shall he do
for the [p]tabernacle of the congregation, that remaineth among
them in the midst of their uncleanness.
17 And there shall be no man
in the [2,p]tabernacle of the congregation when he goeth in to
make an [k,l]atonement in the
[m]holy *place,* until he come out,
and have made an atonement for
[q]himself, and for his household,
and for all the congregation of
Ĭs̱′ra-el.
18 And [e]he shall go out unto the
[r]altar that *is* before the LORD,
and make an [k,l]atonement for it;
and shall take of the [i,a]blood of
the [b]bullock, and of the blood of
the goat, and put *it* upon the
horns of the altar round about.
19 And he shall [c]sprinkle of the
[i,a]blood upon it with his finger
seven times, and [s]cleanse it, and
[t]hallow[G] it from the [n,o]unclean-
ness of the children of Ĭs̱′ra-el.
20 ¶ And when he hath made
an end of [5]reconciling[G] the [m]holy
*place,* and the [2,p]tabernacle of
the congregation, and the [r]altar,
he shall bring the live goat:
21 And [e]Aâr′on shall lay both
his [u]hands upon the head of the
live goat, and [v]confess over him
all the iniquities[G] of the children
of Ĭs̱′ra-el, and all their transgressions in all their sins, putting
them upon the head of the goat,
and shall send *him* away by the
hand of a fit man into the wilderness:[Q]
22 And the goat shall [w]bear[G] upon him all their iniquities unto a
land not inhabited: and he shall
let go the goat in the ‡wilder-
ness.
23 And Aâr′on shall come into
the [2,p]tabernacle of the congregation, and shall put off the linen
garments, which he put on when

v.16—1532 BC
See footnote, *Time.* Rev. 10:6.

p *Tabernacle,* Ex. 27:9.

17
q *High Priest, atonement for,* Lev. 21:10.

18
r *Altar, of incense,* Ex. 30:1.

19
s *Purification,* Num. 19:19.
t *Holiness, typified,* Ex. 39:30.

20
5 R. V. atoning for

21
u *Hand, imposition of,* Ezra 10:19.
v *Sin, confession of,* Rom. 5:12.

22
w *Substitution,* Lev. 1:4.

† **CENSER,** or fire pan. *Used for offering incense,* Lev. 16:12; Num. 4:14; 16:6, 7, 16–18, 46. *For the temple, made of gold,* 1 Kin. 7:50; 2 Kin. 25:15; 2 Chr. 4:22. *Those which Korah used were converted into plates,* Num. 16:37–39. *Used in idolatrous rites,* Ezek. 8:11.
**Symbolical,** Rev. 8:3, 5.

‡ **DESERT.** *An arid region bearing only a sparse vegetation,* Lev. 16:22; Deut. 8:15; Jer. 2:2, 6; 17:6.
**Figurative,** Isa. 35:1.

v.23–1532 BC
See footnote, *Time*, Rev. 10:6.

**24**
x *Ceremonial Washing*, Ex. 19:10.

**25**
y *Fat*, Lev. 7:24.
z *Altar, of burnt offerings*, Gen. 8:20.

**26**
a *Defilement, of priests*, Lev. 5:2.
b *Substitution*, Lev. 1:4.
c *Ceremonial Washing*, Ex. 19:10.
d *Purification*, Num. 19:19.

**27**
e *Offerings, sin*, Lev. 6:17.
f *Blood, sacrificial*, Heb. 9:19.
g *Jesus, atoning blood of, typified*, Matt. 1:21.
h *Atonement*, Lev. 17:11.
i *Jesus, atonement by, typified*, Matt. 1:21.
j *Holy of Holies*, Ex. 26:33.
k *Sanitation and Hygiene, filth, disposition of*, Num. 31:23.

**29**
l *Month*, Ex. 12:2.
m *Humility*, Prov. 22:4.
n *Rest, on day of atonement*, Ex. 23:12.
o *Foreigner*, Deut. 23:20.

**30**
p *Day of Atonement*, Lev. 23:27.
q *Holiness, typified*, Ex. 39:30.

**32**
r *High Priest, consecration of*, Lev. 21:10.
s *Anointing*, Lev. 8:12.

he went into the [m]holy *place*, and shall leave them there:

24 And [e]he shall [s, x]wash his flesh with water in the [m]holy place, and put on his garments, and come forth, and offer his burnt [g]offering, and the burnt offering of the people, and make an [k, l]atonement[C] for [q]himself, and for the people.

25 And the [y]fat of the sin [g]offering shall he burn upon the [z]altar.

26 And [a]he that let go the goat for the [b]scapegoat shall [c, d]wash his clothes, and bathe his flesh in water, and afterward come into the camp.

27 And the bullock *for* the [e]sin offering, and the goat *for* the [e]sin offering, whose [f, g]blood was brought in to make [h, i]atonement in the [j]holy *place*, shall *one* carry forth without[C] the camp; and [k]they shall burn in the fire their skins, and their flesh, and their dung.[Q]

28 And [a]he that burneth them shall [c, d]wash his clothes, and bathe his flesh in water, and afterward he shall come into the camp.

29 ¶ And *this* shall be a statute for ever unto you: *that* in the seventh [l]month, on the tenth *day* of the month, ye shall [m]afflict[G] your souls,[C] and [n]do no work at all, *whether it be* one of your own country, or a [o]stranger that sojourneth among you:[Q]

30 For on that day shall *the priest* make an [p, i]atonement[G] for you, to [d]cleanse you, *that* ye may be [q]clean from all your sins before the LORD.[Q]

31 It *shall be* a sabbath[G] of [n]rest unto you, and ye shall [m]afflict[G] your souls, by a statute for ever.

32 And the [r]priest, whom he shall [s]anoint, and whom he shall consecrate to minister in the priest's office in his father's stead, shall make the [h, i]atonement, and shall put on the linen [t]clothes, *even* the holy garments:

33 And he shall make an [h, i]atonement for the [j]holy sanctuary, and he shall make an atonement for the [2, u]tabernacle of the congregation, and for the [v]altar, and he shall make an atonement for the priests, and for all the people of the congregation.

34 And this shall be an everlasting statute unto you, to make an [p]atonement for the children of Iș'ra-el for all their sins [w]once a year. And he did as the LORD commanded Mō'şeş.

## CHAPTER 17

*All sacrifices must be offered to the Lord at the door of the tabernacle. 7 Sacrifices must not be offered to devils. 10 The eating of blood is forbidden, 15 and of that which dies of itself, or is torn.*

AND the LORD [a]spake unto [b]Mō'şeş, saying,

2 Speak unto [c]Aâr'on, and unto his sons, and unto all the children of [d]Iș'ra-el, and say unto them; This *is* the thing which the [e]LORD hath commanded, saying,

3 What man soever *there be* of the house of [d]Iș'ra-el, that killeth an ox, or lamb, or goat, in the camp, or that killeth *it* out of the camp,

4 And bringeth it not unto the door of the [1, f]tabernacle of the congregation, to offer [2]an [g]offering unto the LORD before the tabernacle of the LORD; blood shall be imputed unto that man; he hath shed blood; and that man shall be [h, i]cut[G] off from among his people:

5 To the end that the children of [d]Iș'ra-el may bring their [g]sacrifices, which they [3]offer in the open field, even that they may bring them unto the LORD, unto the door of the [1, f]tabernacle of the congregation, unto the priest,

v.32–1532 BC
See footnote, *Time*, Rev. 10:6.

t *High Priest, vestments of*, Lev. 21:10.

**33**
u *Tabernacle, atonement for*, Ex. 27:9.
v *Altar, of incense, atonement for*, Ex. 30:1.

**34**
w Heb. 9:7, **27**.

**1**
a *Revelation, concerning offerings and blood*, 2 Cor. 12:1.
b *Moses*, Ex. 2:10.

**2**
c *Aaron*, Ex. 6:20.
d *Israel*, Ex. 4:22.
e *God, sovereign*, Gen. 2:2.

**4**
f *Tabernacle*, Ex. 27:9.
g *Offerings, must be offered by the priests*, Lev. 6:17.
h *Church, discipline in*, Matt. 16:18.
i *Disfellowship*, Num. 15:31.
1 R. V. tent of meeting,
2 R. V. it as an oblation

**5**
3 R. V. sacrifice

v.5–1532 BC
See footnote, *Time*, Rev. 10:6.

**6**

*j Offerings, peace,* Lev. 6:17.
*k Sprinkling, of blood,* Lev. 14:7.
*l Blood, sacrificial, Heb.* 9:19.
*m Jesus, atoning blood of, typified,* Matt. 1:21.
*n Fat,* Lev. 7:24.

**7**

*o Satyr,* Isa. 13:21.
4 R. V. the he-goats,

**8**

*p Foreigners,* Deut. 23:20.
*q Offerings, burnt,* Lev. 6:17.

**10**

*r Sanitation and Hygiene, food,* Num. 31:23.
*s Blood, forbidden as food,* Gen. 9:4.

**11**

*t Blood, is the life,* Gen. 9:4.
*u Jesus, atonement by, typified,* Matt. 1:21.
5 R. V. by reason of the life.

and [3]offer them *for* [j]peace offerings unto the LORD.
6 And the priest shall [k]sprinkle
the [l,m]blood upon the altar of the
LORD *at* the door of the [1,l]taber-
nacle of the congregation, and
burn the [n]fat for a sweet savour
unto the LORD.
7 And they shall no more [3]offer
their [q]sacrifices unto [4,o]devils,[G]
after whom they have gone a[G]
whoring. This shall be a statute
for ever unto them throughout
their generations.
8 And thou shalt say unto them,
Whatsoever man *there be* of the
house of [d]Ĭṣ′ra-el, or of the
[p]strangers which sojourn among
you, that offereth a [q]burnt offering or sacrifice,
9 And bringeth [q]it not unto the
door of the [1,l]tabernacle of the
congregation, to offer it unto the
LORD; even that man shall be
[h,i]cut[G] off from among his people.
10 ¶ [Q]And whatsoever man
*there be* of the house of [d]Ĭṣ′ra-el,
or of the [p]strangers that sojourn
among you, that [r]eateth any
manner of [s]blood; I will even set
my face against that soul that
eateth blood, and will [h,i]cut[G] him
off from among his people.
11 For the life of the flesh *is* in
the [t]blood: and I have given it to
you upon the altar to make an
[*,u]atonement for your souls: for
it *is* the [l,m]blood *that* maketh an
atonement [5]for the soul.[T] [Q]
12 Therefore I said unto the
children of [d]Ĭṣ′ra-el, No soul[G] of
you shall eat [s]blood, neither
shall any [p]stranger that sojourneth among you eat blood.

13 And whatsoever man *there*
*be* of the children of Ĭṣ′ra-el, or
of the [p]strangers that sojourn
among you, which [v]hunteth and
catcheth any [w]beast or fowl that
may be eaten; [r]he shall even
pour out the [s]blood thereof, and
cover it with dust.
14 For *it is* the life of all flesh;
the [t]blood [6]of it *is* for the life
thereof: therefore I said unto the
children of [d]Ĭṣ′ra-el, Ye shall
[r,w]eat the [s]blood of no manner of
flesh: for the life of all flesh *is* the
blood thereof: whosoever eateth
it shall be [h,i]cut off.[Q]
15 And every soul that [r,w]eateth
that which died *of itself*, or that
which was torn *with beasts*,
*whether it be* one of your own
country, or a [p]stranger,[G] he shall
both [x,y]wash his clothes, and
bathe *himself* in water, and be
[z,a]unclean until the even: then
shall he be [b]clean.
16 But if he [c,d]wash *them* not,
nor bathe his flesh; then he shall
bear his [e]iniquity.

## CHAPTER 18

*Imitating the corrupt doings of the heathen forbidden. 6 Unlawful marriages. 19 Abominable lusts.*

AND the LORD [a]spake unto
[b]Mō′ṣeṣ, saying,
2 Speak unto the children of
Ĭṣ′ra-el, and say unto them, [c]I
*am* the LORD your God.
3 [d]After the [e]doings of the land
of [f]Ē′ġy̆pt, wherein ye dwelt,
shall ye not do: and after the doings of the land of [g]Cā′năan,
whither I bring you, shall ye not
do: neither shall ye walk in their
ordinances.

v.13–1532 BC
See footnote, *Time*, Rev. 10:6.

**13**

*v Hunting,* Gen. 27:5.
*w Food,* Psa. 136:25.

**14**

6 R. V. thereof is all one with the life

**15**

*x Ceremonial Washing, for defilement,* Ex. 19:10.
*y Purification,* Num. 19:19.
*z Defilement,* Lev. 5:2.

*a Sin, typified,* Rom. 5:12.
*b Holiness, typified,* Ex. 39:30.

**16**

*c Ceremonial Washing, for defilement,* Ex. 19:10.
*d Purification,* Num. 19:19.
*e Sin, punishment of,* Rom. 5:12.

**1**

*a Revelation, concerning marriage and evil desires,* 2 Cor. 12:1.
*b Moses,* Ex. 2:10.

**2**

*c God, sovereign,* Gen. 2:2.

**3**

*d Evil Company, forbidden,* Prov. 13:20.
*e Example, bad,* John 13:15.
*f Egypt,* Gen. 41:8.
*g Canaan,* Gen. 37:1.

* **ATONEMENT.** *For tabernacle and furniture,* Lev. 16:15–20, 33. *In consecration of the Levites,* Num. 8:21. *For those defiled by the dead,* Num. 6:11. *Made for houses,* Lev. 14:53.

*By meat offerings,* Lev. 5:11–13 *By jewels,* Num. 31:50. *By money,* Ex. 30:12–16; 2 Kin. 12:16. *By incense,* Num. 16:46–50.

**By animal sacrifices:** *In burnt offerings,* Lev. 1:4; 4:13–21; 12:6–8; Num. 15:22–28; 28:27–31; 29. *In trespass offerings,* Lev. 5:6–9; 6:7; 14:12–32. *In sin offerings,* Ex. 29:36; Lev. 4:22–35; 9:7; 10:17; 16:6–34; Num. 28:22; 29. *Forgiveness of sins through,* Lev. 5:10; 19:22.

**By Jesus,** Rom. 3:24–26; 5:11–15; 1 Thess. 1:10; Heb. 13:12; 1 John 2:2; 3:5; 4:10; Rev. 5:6, 9; 13:8. TYPIFIED: *In passover lamb,* Ex. 12:5, 11, 14; 1 Cor. 5:7; *in sacrifices,* Ex. 24:8; Lev. 16:30, 34; 17:11; 19:22; Heb. 9:11–28.

*Once for all,* Heb. 7:27; 9:24–28; 10:10, 12, 14; 1 Pet. 3:18. *Vicarious,* Isa. 53:4–12; Matt. 20:28; John 6:51; 11:49–51; Gal. 3:13; Eph. 5:2; 1 Thess. 5:9, 10; Heb. 2:9; 1 Pet. 2:24. *Through his blood,* Luke 22:20; 1 Cor. 1:23; Eph. 2:13–15, Heb. 9:12–15, 25, 26; 12:24; 13:12, 20, 21; 1 John 5:6; Rev. 1:5; 5:9; 7:14; 12:11. *For reconciliation,* Rom. 5:1–21; 2 Cor. 5:18, 19, 21; Eph. 2:16, 17; Col. 1:20–22; Heb. 2:17. *For remission of sins,* Zech. 13:1; Matt. 26:28; Luke 24:46, 47; John 1:29; Rom. 4:25; 1 Cor. 15:3; Gal. 1:3, 4; Eph. 1:7; Col. 1:14; Heb. 1:3; 10:1–20; John 1:7; 3:5.

v.4–1532 BC
See footnote, *Time,* Rev. 10:6.

4
[h] *Commandment, enjoining obedience,* Deut. 8:2.

5
[i] *Contingencies, in divine government,* 1 Kin. 3:14.

6
[j] *Commandment, forbidding incest,* vs. 7–17; Deut. 8:2.

7
[k] *Father, to be revered,* Psa. 27:10.
[l] *Mother, reverence for, enjoined,* 1 Kin. 2:20.

4 [h]Ye shall do my judgments,[G] and keep mine ordinances,[G] to walk therein: [c]I *am* the LORD your God.

5 [h]Ye shall therefore keep my statutes, and my judgments:[G] which [i]if a man *do he shall live in them: [c]I *am* the LORD.[T Q]

6 ¶ [j]None of you shall approach to any that is near of kin to him, to †uncover *their* nakedness: [c]I *am* the LORD.

7 The[Q] nakedness of thy [k]father, or the nakedness of thy [l]mother, shalt thou not †uncover: she *is* thy mother; thou shalt not uncover her nakedness.

8 [j]The nakedness of thy father's wife shalt thou not †uncover: it *is* thy father's nakedness.[Q]

9 [j]The nakedness of thy sister, the daughter of thy father, or daughter of thy mother, *whether she be* born at home, or born abroad, *even* their nakedness thou shalt not †uncover.

10 [j]The nakedness of thy son's daughter, or of thy daughter's daughter, *even* their nakedness thou shalt not †uncover: for their's *is* thine own nakedness.

11 [j]The nakedness of thy father's wife's daughter, begotten of thy father, she *is* thy sister, thou shalt not †uncover her nakedness.

12 [j]Thou shalt not †uncover the nakedness of thy father's sister: she *is* thy father's near kinswoman.

13 [j]Thou shalt not †uncover the nakedness of thy mother's sister: for she *is* thy mother's near kinswoman.

14 [j]Thou shalt not †uncover the nakedness of thy father's brother, thou shalt not approach to his wife: she *is* thine aunt.

15 [j]Thou shalt not †uncover the nakedness of thy daughter in law: she *is* thy son's wife; thou shalt not uncover her nakedness.

16 [j]Thou shalt not †uncover the nakedness of thy brother's wife: it *is* thy brother's nakedness.[Q]

17 [j]Thou shalt not †uncover the nakedness of a woman and her daughter, neither shalt thou take her son's daughter, or her daughter's daughter, to uncover her nakedness; *for* they *are* her near kinswoman: it *is* wickedness.

18 Neither shalt thou take a wife to her sister, to [1]vex[G] *her,* to †uncover her nakedness, beside the other in her life *time.*

19 Also thou shalt not approach unto a woman to uncover her nakedness, as long as she is put apart for her [m]uncleanness.

20 Moreover [n]thou shalt not [o]lie[G] carnally[G] with thy neighbour's wife, to defile thyself with her.

21 And [p]thou shalt not let any of thy [q]seed pass through *the fire* to [r]Mō'lech, neither shalt thou [s]profane[G] the name of thy [t]God: [c]I *am* the LORD.

22 [u]Thou shalt not ‡lie with mankind, as with womankind: it *is* abomination.[G Q]

23 [v]Neither shalt thou ‖lie with any beast to defile thyself therewith: neither shall any woman stand before a beast to lie down thereto: it *is* confusion.[G]

24 Defile not ye yourselves in any of these [w]things: for in all these the [x, y]nations are defiled which I cast out before you:

25 And the land is defiled:

v.14–1532 BC
See footnote, *Time,* Rev. 10:6.

18
1 R. V. be a rival to her,

19
[m] *Menstruation,* Ezek. 18:6.

20
[n] *Commandment, forbidding adultery,* Deut. 8:2.
[o] *Adultery, forbidden,* Lev. 20:10.

21
[p] *Commandment, forbidding idolatry and forbidding profanation of God's name,* Deut. 8:2.
[q] *Human Sacrifices, forbidden,* Deut. 12:31.
[r] *Molech,* 1 Kin. 11:7.
[s] *Profanation, forbidden,* Lev. 22:32.
[t] *God, name of, not to be profaned,* Gen. 2:2.

22
[u] *Commandment, forbidding sodomy,* Deut. 8:2.

23
[v] *Commandment, forbidding bestiality,* Deut. 8:2.

24
[w] *Sin, repugnant to God,* vs. 24–30; Rom. 5:12.
[x] *Nation, punishment of,* vs. 24–30; Isa. 2:4.
[y] *Canaanites, to be destroyed,* Ex. 23:28.

* **WORKS UNDER THE LAW,** Lev. 18:5; Ezek. 20:11, 13, 20; Luke 10:28; Rom. 10:5; Gal. 3:12.

† **INCEST.** *Defined and forbidden,* Lev. 18:6–18; 20:11, 12, 17, 19–21; Deut. 22:30; 27:20, 22, 23; Ezek. 22:11; 1 Cor. 5:1.
**Instances of:** *Lot with his daughters,* Gen. 19:31–36. *Abraham,* Gen. 20:12, 13. *Nahor,* Gen. 11:29. *Reuben,* Gen. 35:22; 49:4. *Amram,* Ex. 6:20. *Judah,* Gen. 38:16–18; 1 Chr. 2:4. *Amnon,* 2 Sam. 13:14. *Absalom,* 2 Sam. 16:21, 22.

‡ **SODOMY,** Gen. 19:5–8; Ex. 22:19; Lev. 18:22; 20:13; Deut. 23:17; Judg. 19:22; 1 Kin. 14:24; 15:12; 22:46; 2 Kin. 23:7; Rom. 1:24, 26, 27; 1 Cor. 6:9; 1 Tim. 1:10.
See footnote, SODOMITES, Gen. 19:25.

‖ **BESTIALITY.** *Forbidden,* Ex. 22:19; Lev. 18:23; 20:15, 16; Deut. 27:21.

v.25–1532 BC
See footnote, *Time*, Rev. 10:6.

**25**
*z Judgments*, Ex. 6:6.

*a Canaanites, wickedness of*, Ex. 23:28.

**26**
*b Commandment, enjoining obedience*, Deut. 8:2.
*c Foreigner*, Deut. 23:20.

**28**
*d Judgments*, Ex. 6:6.
*e Nations, punishments of*, Isa. 2:4.

**29**
*f Disfellowship*, Num. 15:31.

**30**
*g Sin, typified*, Rom. 5:12.
*h God, sovereign*, Gen. 2:2.

**1**
*a Revelation, of various ordinances*, 2 Cor. 12:1.
*b Moses*, Ex. 2:10.

**2**
*c Commandment, enjoining holiness*, Deut. 8:2.
*d* Lev. 11:44; 1 Pet. 1:16.
*e Holiness, enjoined*, Ex. 39:30.
*f Example, God our, in holiness*, John 13:15.
*g God, holiness of*, Gen. 2:2.
*h Holiness, attribute of God*, Ex. 39:30.

therefore I do [z]visit the iniquity
thereof upon it, and the land itself
vomiteth out her [a]inhabitants.
26 Ye shall therefore [b]keep[G] my
statutes and my judgments,[C] and
shall not commit *any* of these
[§]abominations[G]; *neither* any of
your own nation, nor any [c]stranger
that sojourneth among you:
27 (For all these [§]abominations
have the [a]men of the land
done, which *were* before you,
and the land is defiled;)
28 That the land [d]spue not you
out also, when ye defile it, as it
spued out the [e]nations that *were*
before you.
29 For whosoever shall commit
any of these [§]abominations,
even the souls[G] that commit *them*
shall be [f]cut[C] off from among
their people.
30 [b]Therefore shall ye keep
mine ordinance, that *ye* commit
not *any one* of these [§]abominable
customs, which were committed
before you, and that ye
[g]defile not yourselves therein:
[h]I *am* the LORD your God.

## CHAPTER 19

*Holiness. 3 Reverence for parents. 4 Idolatry forbidden. 5 Peace offerings. 9 The law of gleanings. 11 Theft, forbidden. 16 Talebearing, forbidden. 19 Sundry laws.*

AND the LORD [a]spake unto
[b]Mō′ṣeṣ, saying,
2 Speak unto all the congregation
of the children of Ĭṣ′ra-el,
and say unto them, [c,d,e]Ye shall
be holy: for [f,g]I the LORD your
God *am* [h]holy.[G S Q]
3 ¶ [i,j]Ye shall fear[C] every man
his [k]mother, and his [l]father, and
keep my [m]sabbaths: [n]I *am* the
LORD your God.
4 ¶ Turn ye not unto [o]idols,[G]
nor [p]make to yourselves molten[G]
gods: [n]I *am* the LORD your God.
5 ¶ And if ye offer a sacrifice of
[q]peace offerings unto the LORD,
ye shall offer it [1]at your own will.
6 It shall be eaten the same day
ye offer it, and on the morrow:[G]
and if ought[C] remain until the
third day, [r]it shall be burnt in
the fire.
7 And if it be eaten at all on the
third day, it *is* abominable; it
shall not be accepted.
8 Therefore *every one* that eateth
it shall bear his [s]iniquity, because
he hath [*]profaned the hallowed
thing of the LORD: and
that soul shall be [t]cut off from
among his people.
9 ¶ And [u]when ye [v]reap the
[w]harvest of your land, thou shalt
not wholly reap the corners of
thy field, neither shalt thou gather
the [x]gleanings of thy harvest.
10 And [u]thou shalt not [x]glean
thy vineyard, neither shalt thou
gather [2]*every* grape of thy vineyard;
thou shalt leave them for
the [y]poor and stranger:[G] [n]I *am*
the LORD your God.
11 ¶ [z]Ye shall not [a]steal,
neither deal falsely, neither [b]lie
one to another.
12 ¶ And [c]ye shall not [d]swear
by my name [e]falsely, neither
shalt thou [f,g]profane the name
of thy [h]God: I *am* the LORD.[Q]
13 ¶ [i,j]Thou shalt not defraud
thy [k]neighbour, neither [l]rob *him*:
the [m]wages of [n,o]him that is

v.3–1532 BC
See footnote, *Time*, Rev. 10:6.
*m Sabbath*, Ex. 16:23.
*n God, sovereign*, Gen. 2:2.

**4**
*o Idolatry, forbidden*, 1 Sam. 15:23.
*p Molding, of images*, 1 Kin. 7:16.

**5**
*q Offerings, peace*, Lev. 6:17.
1 R. V. that ye may be accepted.

**6**
*r Sanitation and Hygiene*, Num. 31:23.

**8**
*s Sin, punishment for*, Rom. 5:12.
*t Disfellowship*, Num. 15:31.

**9**
*u Commandment, enjoining liberality to the poor*, v. 10; Deut. 8:2.
*v Agriculture*, Gen. 3:23.
*w Harvest*, Ex. 34:21.
*x Gleaning*, Lev. 23:22.

**10**
*y Poor, duty to*, Prov. 21:13.
2 R. V. the fallen fruit

**11**
*z Commandment, forbidding theft, fraud and falsehood*, Deut. 8:2.
*a Theft*, Mark 7:22.
*b Falsehood, forbidden*, Job 21:34.

**12**
*c Commandment, forbidding perjury, and profaning God's name*, Deut. 8:2.
*d False Witness, forbidden*, Matt. 19:18.
*e Perjury, forbidden*, 1 Tim. 1:10
*f Profanation, forbidden*, Lev. 22:32.
*g Blasphemy, forbidden*, 2 Sam. 12:14.
*h God, name of, not to be profaned*, Gen. 2:2.

**13**

**3** *i Commandment, enjoining reverence for parents, and keeping the Sabbath*, Deut. 8:2. *j Children, commandments to*, Mark 10:14. *k Mother, reverence for, enjoined*, 1 Kin. 2:20. *l Father, to be revered*, Psa. 27:10.

*i Honesty, enjoined*, Rom. 13:13. *j Commandment, forbidding fraud, robbery and oppression*, Deut. 8:2. *k Neighbor, honesty toward, enjoined*, Luke 10:29. *l Robbers*, Hos. 6:9. *m Wages*, Gen. 31:7. *n Employee, rights of*, Deut. 24:14. *o Hired Servant, rights of*, Lev. 25:40.

§ **ABOMINATION,** Prov. 6:16–19. *Idolatry*, Deut. 7:25; 27:15; 32:16. *Unjust weights and measures*, Deut. 25:13–16; Prov. 11:1; 20:10, 23. *Incest*, Lev. 18:6–18. *Lying with a woman in her menses*, Lev. 18:19. *Adultery*, Lev. 18:20; Deut. 24:4. *Sodomy*, Lev. 18:22, 23; 20:13. *Offering seed to Molech*, Lev. 18:21; *or children in sacrifice*, Deut. 18:10. *Sorcery and necromancy*, Deut. 18:10, 11. *The hire of a whore and price of a dog, as a consecrated gift*, Deut. 23:18. *For a woman to wear man's apparel*, Deut. 22:5. *Frowardness*, Prov. 3:32; 11:20. *Unrighteousness*, Prov. 17:15. *Wickedness*, Prov. 8:7. *Falsehood*, Prov. 12:22. *Pride*, Prov. 16:5. *Scorners*, Prov. 24:9. *Prayer, ways and thoughts of the wicked*, Prov. 15:8, 9, 26; 21:27; 28:9; 29:27.

* **SACRILEGE,** profaning holy things. **Forbidden**, **Lev.** 19:8.

**Instances of:** *Nadab and Abihu offer strange fire*, Lev. 10:1–7; Num. 3:4. *Korah and his company*, Num. 16:1–35, 40. *The people of Beth-shemesh*, 1 Sam. 6:19. *Uzzah*, 2 Sam. 6:6, 7; 1 Chr. 13:9, 10. *Uzziah*, 2 Chr. 26:16–21. *Ahaz*, 2 Chr. 28:24. *Money changers in the temple*, Matt. **21:12**, 13; Mark 11:15–17; Luke 19:45; John 2:14–16. *Those who profaned the holy eucharist*, 1 Cor. 11:20–22, **27**, **29**.

v.13–1532 BC
See footnote, *Time*, Rev. 10:6.

*p Master*, Col. 4:1.
*q Employer, to be prompt in payment*, Deut. 24:14.
**14**
*r Malice, forbidden*, Eph. 4:31.
*s Commandment, forbidding malicious mischief, and enjoining the fear of God*, Deut. 8:2.
*t Deafness, law concerning*, Matt. 11:5.
*u Blind, cruelty to, forbidden*, Deut. 27:18.
*v Fear of God, enjoined*, Acts 9:31.
**15**
*w Commandment, enjoining justice*, Deut. 8:2.
*x Injustice, forbidden*, Isa. 26:10.
*y Poor*, Prov. 21:13.
*z Judge, character of*, Judg. 2:18.
*a Rulers, duties of*, Ex. 18:21.
**16**
*b Commandment, forbidding talebearing and false witness*, Deut. 8:2.
*c Talebearing*, Prov. 11:13.
*d False Witness, forbidden*, Matt. 19:18.
*e False Accusation, forbidden*, 2 Tim. 3:3.
*f Neighbor, false witness against, forbidden*, Luke 10:29.
*g God, sovereign*, Gen 2:2.
**17**
*h Commandment, forbidding hatred, and enjoining rebuke of sin*, Deut. 8:2.
*i Hatred, forbidden*, Prov. 15:17.
*j Reproof, enjoined*, Prov. 17:10.
*k Neighbor, hatred of, forbidden*, Luke 10:29.
3 R. V. bear sin because of him.

hired shall not abide with [p,q]thee
all night until the morning.
14 ¶ [r,s]Thou shalt not curse the
[t]deaf, nor put a stumblingblock
before the [u]blind, but shalt [v]fear
thy God: I *am* the LORD.
15 ¶ [w]Ye shall do no [x]unright-
eousness in judgment: thou shalt
not respect the person of the
[y]poor, nor honour the person of
the mighty: *but* in righteousness
shalt [z,a]thou judge thy neighbour.
16 ¶ [b]Thou shalt not go up and
down *as* a †,[c]talebearer among
thy people: neither shalt thou
[d,e]stand against the blood of thy
[f]neighbour: [g]I *am* the LORD.
17 ¶ [h]Thou shalt not [i]hate thy
brother in thine heart: thou shalt
in any wise [j]rebuke thy [k]neigh-
bour, and not [3]suffer sin upon him.
18 ¶ [l]Thou shalt not [m,n]avenge,
nor bear any grudge against the
children of thy people, but [o]thou
shalt [p,q]love thy [r]neighbour as
thyself: [g]I *am* the LORD.
19 ¶ [s,t]Ye shall keep my [u]stat-
utes. Thou shalt not let thy
[v]cattle gender with a diverse
kind: [w]thou shalt not sow thy
field with mingled ‡seed: [x]neither
shall a garment mingled of linen
and woollen come upon thee.
20 ¶ And whosoever [y]lieth carnally with a woman, that *is* a
[z]bondmaid, betrothed to an husband, and not at all redeemed,
nor freedom given her; she shall
be [4,a,b]scourged; they shall not
be put to death, because she was
not free.

**18** *l Commandment, forbidding revenge and grudge, and enjoining love*, Deut. 8:2. *m Retaliation, malicious, forbidden*, Deut. 19:19. *n Revenge, forbidden*, Ezek. 25:15. *o Royal Law*, Jas. 2:8. *p Duty, of man to man*, Eccl. 12:13. *q Love, of man for man*, 1 John 4:7. *r Neighbor, love for, enjoined*, Luke 10:29. **19** *s Obedience, enjoined*, Heb. 5:8. *t Commandment, enjoining obedience*, Deut. 8:2. *u Law, of Moses, obedience to, enjoined*, Deut. 33:2. *v Animals, laws concerning*, Jer. 27:5. *w* Deut. 22:9. *x* Deut. 22:11. **20** *y Adultery, penalties for*, Lev. 20:10. *z Servant*, Jer. 2:14.—*a Punishment*, Lev. 26:41. *b Sin, punishment of*, Rom. 5:12. 4 R. V. punished;

21 And he shall bring his [5,c]tres-
pass [d]offering unto the LORD,
unto the door of the [6]tabernacle
of the congregation, *even* a ram
for a [5]trespass offering.
22 And the priest shall make
an [e,f]atonement for him with the
ram of the [5,c]trespass [d]offering
before the LORD for his sin
which he hath done: and the
[g,h]sin which he hath done shall
be forgiven him.
23 ¶ And when ye shall come
into the land, and shall have
[i]planted all manner of trees for
food, then ye shall count the
fruit thereof as uncircumcised:
three years shall it be as uncircumcised unto you: it shall not
be eaten of.
24 But in the fourth year all the
fruit thereof shall be holy to
[j]praise the LORD *withal*.
25 And in the fifth year shall
ye eat of the fruit thereof, that it
may yield unto you the increase
thereof: [k]I *am* the LORD your
God.
26 ¶ Ye shall not eat *any thing*
with the [l]blood: neither shall ye
use [m]enchantment, nor [7]observe
times.
27 Ye shall not round the corners of your heads, neither shalt
thou mar the corners of thy
[n]beard.
28 Ye shall not make any ‖cut-
tings in your flesh for the dead,
nor print any marks upon you:
[k]I *am* the LORD.
29 ¶ [o,p]Do not prostitute thy
daughter, to cause her to be a
whore; lest the land fall to
whoredom, and the land become
full of wickedness.
30 ¶ [q]Ye shall keep my [r]sab-
baths, and §reverence my [s,t]sanc-
tuary: [k]I *am* the LORD.

v.21–1532 BC
See footnote, *Time*, Rev. 10:6.

**21**
*c Offerings, trespass*, Lev. 6:17.
*d Jesus, typified in offerings*, Matt. 1:21.
5 R. V. guilt
6 R. V. tent of meeting,
**22**
*e Atonement, made by animal sacrifices*, Lev. 17:11.
*f Jesus, atonement by, typified*, Matt. 1:21.
*g Sin, forgiveness of*, Rom. 5:12.
*h Promises, to penitent*, 2 Cor. 1:20.
**23**
*i Horticulture, encouraged*, vs. 23–25; Deut. 20:19.
**24**
*j Thankfulness, enjoined*, Acts 24:3.
**25**
*k God, sovereign*, Gen. 2:2.
**26**
*l Blood, forbidden as food*, Gen. 9:4.
*m Sorcery, forbidden*, Isa. 47:9.
7 R. V. practise augury.
**27**
*n Beard*, 1 Sam. 21:13.
**29**
*o Adultery, forbidden*, Lev. 20:10.
*p Commandment, to parents, forbidding harlotry*, Deut. 8:2.
**30**
*q Commandment, enjoining Sabbath keeping and reverence for God's house*, Deut. 8:2.
*r Sabbath, rest on, enjoined*, Ex. 16:23.
*s Sanctuary, reverence for*, Lev. 4:6.
*t Church, holy*, 1 Kin. 9:3.

† **GOSSIP,** Prov. 16:28; 26:20.
**Forbidden,** Lev. 19:16; Psa. 50:20; Prov. 11:13; 20:19. See footnotes: SLANDER, Prov. 10:18; SPEECH, *Evil*, Col. 4:6.

‡ **SEED.** *Law fixing production of*, Gen. 1:11, 12, 29. *Each produces its own kind*, Gal. 6:7, 8. *Each has a body of its own*, 1 Cor. 15:38. *Different kinds must not be mixed in sowing*, Lev. 19:19; Deut. 22:9. *Parable of the sower of*, Matt. 13:3–8, 18–23; Mark 4:3–8, 13–20; Luke 8:5–8, 11–15. *Lessons from the sowing of*, Eccl. 11:6; Hos. 10:12; 2 Cor. 9:6. *Sowing of, a type of burial*, 1 Cor. 15:36–38.

‖ **CUTTING.** *Of the flesh for the dead, forbidden*, Lev. 21:5; Deut. 14:1; Jer. 16:6.

§ **REVERENCE.** *For God*, Gen. 17:3; Ex. 3:5; 19:16–

v.31–1532 BC
See footnote, *Time*, Rev. 10:6.

**31**
*u Commandment, forbidding witchcraft*, Deut. 8:2.
*v Familiar Spirits*, Deut. 18:11.
*w Witchcraft*, Ex. 22:18.

**32**
*x Commandment, enjoining reverence for the aged, and fear of God*, Deut. 8:2.
*y Manners*, Gen. 18:2.
*z Respect, to the aged, enjoined*, Isa. 22:11.

*a Fear of God, enjoined*, Acts 9:31.
*b God, sovereign*, Gen. 2:2.

**33**
*c Commandment, enjoining justice to and love for foreigners*, Deut. 8:2.
*d Foreigners, justice toward, enjoined*, Deut. 23:20.
8 R. V. do him wrong.

**34**
*e Love, of man for man, enjoined*, 1 John 4:7.

**35**
*f Honesty, enjoined*, Rom. 13:13.
*g Commandment, enjoining honesty in business*, v.36; Deut. 8:2.
*h Injustice, forbidden*, Isa. 26:10.
*i Dishonesty, forbidden*, Ezek. 22:13.
*j Measure*, Deut. 25:15.

**36**
*k Balances*, Prov. 11:1.
*l Hin*, Ex. 29:40.

**37**
*m Commandment, enjoining obedience*, Deut. 8:2.
*n Obedience, enjoined*, Heb. 5:8.
*o Law, of Moses, obedience to, enjoined*, Deut. 33:2.

31 ¶ [u]Regard not them that
have [v]familiar spirits, neither
seek after [w]wizards, to be defiled
by them: [k]I *am* the LORD your
God.
32 ¶ [x]Thou shalt [§, y]rise up before the hoary head, and [z]hon-
our the face of the old man, and
[a]fear thy God: [b]I *am* the LORD.
33 ¶ And [c]if a [d]stranger sojourn
with thee in your land, ye shall
not [8]vex him.
34 *But* the [d]stranger that dwelleth with you shall be unto you as
one born among you, and thou
shalt [e]love him as thyself; for ye
were strangers in the land of
Ē′gȳpt: [b]I *am* the LORD your
God.
35 ¶ [f, g]Ye shall do no [h, i]un-
righteousness in judgment, in
meteyard, in [+]weight, or in
[j]measure.
36 Just [k]balances, just [+]weights,
a just [j]ephah, and a just [l]hin,
shall ye have: [b]I *am* the LORD
your God, which brought you
out of the land of Ē′gȳpt.
37 [m]Therefore shall ye [n]ob-
serve all my [o]statutes, and all my
judgments, and do them: [b]I *am*
the LORD.

## CHAPTER 20

*The punishment denounced against him that offers his children to Molech; 6 that consults wizards; 9 that curses his parents; 10 and that commits adultery, incest, sodomy, and other abominations. 22 Obedience is required. 27 Wizards must be put to death.*

AND the LORD [a]spake unto
[b]Mō′ṣeṣ, saying,
2 Again, thou shalt say to the
children of Ĭṣ′ra-el, Whosoever
*he be* of the children of Ĭṣ′ra-el,
or of the strangers that sojourn
in Ĭṣ′ra-el, that [c]giveth *any* of his
[d]seed unto [e]Mō′lech; he shall
surely be [f]put to [g]death: the people of the land shall stone him
with stones.
3 And I will set my face against
that man, and will [h]cut him off
from among his people; because
he hath [c]given of his [d]seed unto
[e]Mō′lech, to defile my [i]sanc-
tuary, and to [j]profane my holy
[k]name.
4 And if the people of the land
do any ways [*]hide their eyes
from the man, when he [c]giveth
of his [d]seed unto [e]Mō′lech, and
[f, g]kill him not:
5 Then I will set my face
against that [l]man, and against
his [m]family, and will [h]cut him
off, and all that go a whoring
after him, to commit [c]whoredom
with [e]Mō′lech, from among their
people.
6 ¶ And [n]the soul that turneth
after such as have [o]familiar spirits, and after [p, q]wizards, to go a
whoring after them, I will even
set my face against that soul, and
will [h]cut him off from among his
people.
7 [r]Sanctify yourselves therefore,
and [s]be ye holy: for [t]I *am* the
LORD your God.
8 And [u]ye shall [v]keep my statutes, and do them: I *am* the
LORD which [w]sanctify you.
9 ¶ For [x, y]every one that curseth his [z]father or his [a]mother
shall be surely [b]put to [c]death: he
hath cursed his father or his
mother; his [d]blood *shall be* upon
him.
10 ¶ And [e]the man that committeth [†]adultery with *another*
man's wife, *even he* that committeth adultery with his neighbour's wife, the adulterer and

v.2–1532 BC
See footnote. *Time*, Rev. 10:6.

*d Human Sacrifices, forbidden*, Deut. 12:31.
*e Molech*, 1 Kin. 11:7.
*f Punishment, death penalty*, Lev. 26:41.
*g Death, penalty*, Num. 23:10.

**3**
*h Disfellowship*, Num. 15:31.
*i Church, holy*, 1 Kin. 9:3.
*j Profanation, of God's name*, Lev. 22:32.
*k God, name of, not to be profaned*, Gen. 2:2.

**5**
*l Parents, curses upon, entailed*, 2 Cor. 12:14.
*m Children, involved in sin of parents*, Mark 10:14.

**6**
*n Statute, forbidding witchcraft*, Deut. 8:2.
*o Familiar Spirits*, Deut. 18:11.
*p Witchcraft*, Ex. 22:18.
*q Sorcery, forbidden*, Isa. 47:9.

**7**
*r Commandment, enjoining holiness*, Deut. 8:2.
*s Holiness, enjoined*, Ex. 39:30.
*t God, sovereign*, Gen. 2:2.

**8**
*u Commandment, enjoining obedience*, Deut. 8:2.
*v Obedience, enjoined*, Heb. 5:8.
*w Sanctification*, 1 Pet. 1:2.

**9**
*x Commandment, enjoining reverence for parents*, Deut. 8:2.
*y Children, punishment of*, Mark 10:14.
*z Father*, Psa. 27:10.

*a Mother*, 1 Kin. 2:20.
*b Punishment, death penalty*, Lev. 26:41.
*c Death, penalty*, Num. 23:10.
*d Blood, figurative*, Gen. 9:4.

**10**
*e Statute, defining incest and forbidding evil lusts*, vs. 10–25; Deut. 8:2.

**1** *a Revelation, of various commandments*, 2 Cor. 12:1. *b Prophet, inspiration of*, Isa. 3:2. **2** *c Idolatry, wicked practices of*, 1 Sam. 15:23.

24. *For God's house*, Lev. 19:30; 26:2. *For sacred places*, Ex. 3:5; Josh. 5:15; Acts 7:33. *For kings*, 1 Sam. 24:6; 26:9, 11; 2 Sam. 1:14; Eccl. 10:20; 1 Pet. 2:17. *For rulers*, Ex. 33:8. *For magistrates*, Ex. 22:28; 2 Pet. 2:10; Jude 8. *For parents*, Ex. 20:12; Lev. 19:3. *For the aged*, Lev. 19:32; Job 32:4–7.

+ **WEIGHTS.** *Must be just*, Deut. 25:13–15; Prov. 11:1; 16:11; 20:10, 23; Mic. 6:10, 11.

**Maneh,** a weight. *Rendered pound*, 1 Kin. 10:17; Ezra 2:49; Neh. 7:71, 74. *Equal to 2 lb Troy*, 1 Kin. 10:17; 2 Chr. 9:16. See footnote, MEASURE, Deut. 25:15.

* **CONNIVANCE,** Lev. 20:4; 1 Sam. 3:11–13; Prov. 10:10.

† **ADULTERY,** Prov. 29:3; Jer. 23:10; Matt. 15:19; Mark 7:21.
*Defined*, Matt. 5:28, 32; 19:9; Mark 10:11, 12; Luke 16:

v 10–1532 BC
See footnote, *Time*, Rev. 10:6.

11
*f* *Incest*, Lev. 18:6.

13
*g* *Sodomy*, Lev. 18:22.
*h* *Abomination*, Lev. 18:27.

14
*i* *Marriage, incestuous, forbidden*, Gen. 34:9.
*j* *Mother-in-law*, Matt. 10:35.

15
*k* *Bestiality*, Lev. 18:23.

17
*l* *Disfellowship*, Num. 15:31.

the adulteress shall surely be [b]put to [c]death.

11 And [e]the man that †,[f]lieth with his father's wife hath uncovered his father's nakedness: both of them shall surely be [b]put to [c]death; their [d]blood *shall be* upon them.

12 And [e]if a man [f]lie with his ‡daughter in law, both of them shall surely be [b]put to [c]death: they have wrought confusion; their [d]blood *shall be* upon them.

13 ¶ [e]If a man also [g]lie with mankind, as he lieth with a woman, both of them have committed an [h]abomination: they shall surely be [b]put to [c]death; their [d]blood *shall be* upon them.

14 And [e]if a man [f,i]take a wife and [j]her mother, it *is* wickedness: they shall be [b,c]burnt with fire, both he and they; that there be no wickedness among you.

15 And [e]if a man [k]lie with a beast, he shall surely be [b]put to [c]death: and ye shall slay the beast.

16 And [e]if a woman approach unto any beast, and [k]lie down thereto, thou shalt [b,c]kill the woman, and the beast: they shall surely be put to death; their [d]blood *shall be* upon them.

17 And [e]if a man shall [i]take his sister, his father's daughter, or his mother's daughter, and [f]see her nakedness, and she see his nakedness; it *is* a wicked thing; and they shall be [l]cut off in the sight of their people: he hath uncovered his sister's nakedness; he shall bear his iniquity.

18 And [e]if a man shall lie with a woman having her [m]sickness, and shall uncover her nakedness; he hath discovered her fountain, and she hath uncovered the fountain of her blood: and both of them shall be [l]cut off from among their people.

19 And [e]thou shalt not [f,i]uncover the nakedness of thy mother's sister, nor of thy father's sister: for he uncovereth his near kin: they shall bear their iniquity.

20 And [e]if a man shall [f]lie with his uncle's wife, he hath uncovered his uncle's nakedness: they shall bear their sin; they shall die childless.

21 And [e]if a man shall [f,i]take his brother's wife, it [1]*is* an unclean thing: he hath uncovered his brother's nakedness; they shall be childless.

22 ¶ Ye shall therefore [n]keep all my statutes, and all my judgments, and do them: that the land, whither I bring you to dwell therein, spue you not out.

23 And ye shall not walk in the [o]manners of the [p,q]nation, which I cast out before you: for they committed all these things, and therefore I abhorred them.

24 But I have said unto you, Ye shall inherit their [r]land, and I will give it unto you to possess it, a land that floweth with [s]milk and [t]honey: I *am* the LORD your

v.17–1532 BC
See footnote, *Time*, Rev. 10:6.

18
*m* *Menstruation*, Ezek. 18:6.

21
1 R.V. is impurity

22
*n* *Obedience, enjoined*, Heb. 5:8

23
*o* *Example, bad*, John 13:15.
*p* *Canaanites*, Ex. 23:28.
*q* *Evil Company*, Prov. 13:20.

24
*r* *Canaan*, Gen. 37:1.
*s* *Milk, figurative*, Job 10:10.
*t* *Honey, figurative* Prov. 25:27.

---

18; Rom. 7:3. *Repugnant to righteous*, Job 31:1, 9–12; Ezek. 18:5, 6, 9. *Law concerning wife accused of*, Num. 5:11–30; Deut. 22:13–19. *Fatal consequences of*, Prov. 2:16–19; 5:3–22; 6:24–33; 7:5–23; 9:13–18; 22:14; 23:27. *Secrecy in*, Job 24:15–18; 2 Tim. 3:6. *Moral corruption by*, Jer. 3:1; 5:7, 8; Hos. 4:1, 2, 11.

*Impenitence in*, Prov. 30:18–20; Jer. 7:9, 10; 2 Cor. 12:21; 1 Pet. 4:3, 4; Rev. 9:2.

**Forbidden**, Ex. 25:14; Lev. 18:20; 19:29; Deut. 5:18; 23:17; Matt. 5:27; 19:18; Mark 10:19; Luke 18:20 (*with* Eph. 4:17–19); Acts 15:20, 29; Rom. 13:9, 13; 1 Cor. 6:13, 15, 16, 18; 10:8; Col. 3:5; Eph. 5:3; 1 Thess. 4:3–5, 7; 1 Tim. 1:10; Jas. 2:11.

**Penalties for:** *Fines*, Ex. 22:16,17; Deut. 18:19,28, 29. *Curses*, Deut. 27:20, 22, 23. *Divine judgments*, 2 Sam. 12:10–12; Jer. 29:22, 23; Ezek. 16:38, 40, 41; Mal. 3:5; 1 Cor. 10:8; Heb. 13:4; Rev. 2:20–22. *Death*, Gen. 20:3, 7; 26:11; 38:24; Lev. 20:10–12; 21:9; Deut. 22:20–27; 2 Sam. 12:14; Ezek. 23:45, 47, 48; John 8:4, 5. *Excommunication*, 1 Cor. 5:1–13; Eph. 5:11, 12. *Exclusion from kingdom of God*, 1 Cor. 6:9, 10; Gal. 5:19, 21; Eph. 5:5, 6; Jude 7; Rev. 21:8; 22:15

**Forgiveness of,** Judg. 19:1–4; John 8:10, 11.

**Instances of:** *Sodomites*, Gen. 19:5–8. *Lot*, Gen. 19:31–38. *Shechem*, Gen. 34:2. *Reuben*, Gen. 35:22. *Judah* Gen. 38:1–24. *The Levite's concubine*, Judg. 19:2. *The Gibeanites*, Judg. 19:22–25. *Gilead*, Judg. 11:1. *Samson* Judg. 16:1. *Sons of Eli*, 1 Sam. 2:22. *David*, 2 Sam. 11:1–5. *Amnon*, 2 Sam. 13:1–20. *Absalom*, 2 Sam. 16:22. *Israelites*, Jer. 29:23; Ezek. 29:9–11; 33:26; Hos. 7:4. *Herod* Mark 6:17, 18; Luke 3:19. *Samaritan woman*, John 4:17, 18. *The woman brought to Jesus in the temple*, John 8:4–11 *Corinthians*, 1 Cor. 5:1–5. *Heathen*, Eph. 4:17–19; 1 Pet. 4:3

**Figurative**, Jer. 3:2; Ezek. 16:15, 16; Hos. 4:1.

‡ **DAUGHTER-IN-LAW. Filial:** INSTANCE OF, *Ruth* Ruth 1:11–18; 4:15.

**Unfilial:** *Prophecy of*, Mic. 7:6; Matt. 10:35.

v.24–1532 BC
See footnote, *Time*, Rev. 10:6.

*u* *God, love of, exemplified*, Gen. 2:2.
*v* *Israel, taught to be holy*, Ex. 4:22.
**25**
*w* *Holiness, typified*, Ex. 39:30.
*x* *Animals, clean and unclean*, Jer. 27:5.
*y* *Sin, typified*, Rom. 5:12.
2 R. V. thing wherewith the ground teemeth,
**26**
*z* *Holiness, enjoined*, Ex. 39:30.

*a* *Commandment, enjoining holiness*, Deut. 8:2.
*b* *God, holiness of*, Gen. 2:2.
**27**
*c* *Familiar Spirits*, Deut. 18:11.
*d* *Sorcery*, Isa. 47:9.
*e* *Punishment, death penalty*, Lev. 26:41.
*f* *Death, penalty*, Num. 23:10.
*g* *Blood, figurative*, Gen. 9:4.

**1**
*a* *Revelation, concerning priests*, 2 Cor. 12:1.
*b* *Prophets, inspiration of*, Isa. 3:2.
*c* *Priest, defilement of*, Lev. 1:5.
*d* *Mourning*, vs. 1–5; Lam. 2:5.
*e* *Defilement, of priests*, vs. 1–15; Lev. 5:2.
1 R. V. defile himself

God, which [u]have separated[G] [v]you from *other* people.

25 Ye shall therefore put difference between [w]clean [x]beasts and [y]unclean, and between unclean fowls and clean: and ye shall not make your souls abominable by beast, or by fowl, or by any [2]manner of living thing that creepeth on the ground, which I have separated from you as unclean.

26 And [z,a]ye shall be holy unto me: for I the LORD *am* [b]holy, and have severed you from *other*[S] people, that ye should be mine.

27 ¶ A man also or woman that hath a [c]familiar spirit, or that is a [d]wizard[G], shall surely be [e]put to [f]death: they shall stone them with stones: their [g]blood *shall be* upon them.

## CHAPTER 21

*Of the priests' mourning. 6 Of their holiness. 13 Of their marriages. 16 Any priest having a blemish must not minister in the sanctuary.*

AND the LORD [a]said unto [b]Mō'ṣeṣ, Speak unto the [c]priests the sons of Aâr'on, and say unto them, [d]There shall none [1]be [e]defiled for the dead among his people:

2 But for [c]his kin, that is near unto him, *that is*, for his mother, and for his father, and for his son, and for his daughter, and for his brother,

3 And for [c]his sister a virgin, that is nigh[G] unto him, which hath had no husband; for her may he [1]be [e]defiled.

4 *But* he shall not [e]defile himself, *being* a chief man among his people, to profane himself.

5 [c]They shall not make *,[f]baldness upon their head, neither shall they shave off the corner of their beard, nor make any cuttings in their flesh.

6 [g,h]They shall be [i]holy unto their God, and not [j]profane the [k]name of their God: for the [l]offerings of the LORD made by fire, *and* the [m]bread of their God, [n]they do offer: therefore [i]they shall be holy.

7 [o,p]They shall not take a wife *that is* a whore, or profane; neither shall they take a woman put away from her husband: for [q]he *is* holy unto his God.

8 Thou shalt sanctify[G] him therefore; for [n]he offereth the [m]bread of thy God: [q]he shall be holy unto thee: for I the [r]LORD, which [s,t]sanctify you, *am* holy.[S]

9 And the [u]daughter of any priest, if she profane[G] herself by playing the [v,w]whore, she profaneth her father: she shall be burnt with [x]fire.[Q]

10 ¶ And *he that is* the †high priest among his brethren, upon whose head the [y]anointing [z]oil was poured, and that is consecrated to put on the garments, shall not uncover his head, nor rend[G] his clothes;

11 Neither shall †he go in to any dead body, nor [a]defile himself for his father, or for his mother;

12 Neither shall he go out of the [b]sanctuary, nor profane the sanctuary of his God; for the crown of the [c]anointing [d]oil of his God *is* upon him: I *am* the LORD.

v.5–1532 BC
See footnote, *Time*, Rev. 10:6.

**5**
*f* *Idolatry, wicked practices of, forbidden*, 1 Sam. 15:23.
**6**
*g* *Commandment, enjoining holiness upon ministers*, Deut. 8:2.
*h* *Minister, character and qualifications of*, vs. 6–23; Rom. 15:16.
*i* *Holiness, enjoined*, Ex. 39:30.
*j* *Profanation, forbidden*, Lev. 22:32.
*k* *God, name of, not to be profaned*, Gen. 2:2.
*l* *Offerings, burnt*, Lev. 6:17.
*m* *Bread, figurative*, Ezek. 4:13.
*n* *Priest, duties of*, Lev. 1:5.
**7**
*o* *Minister, marriage of*, Rom. 15:16.
*p* *Priest, marriage of*, Lev. 1:5.
*q* *Priest, holy*, Lev. 1:5.
**8**
*r* *God, holiness of*, Gen. 2:2.
*s* *Sanctification*, 1 Pet. 1:2.
*t* *Spiritual Blessings, sanctification*, Eph. 1:3.
**9**
*u* *Daughter, of priest*, Lev. 12:6.
*v* *Harlot, punishment of*, Prov. 7:10.
*w* *Adultery, penalties for*, Lev. 20:10.
*x* *Fire, torture by*, Ex. 12:8.
**10**
*y* *Anointing*, Lev. 8:12.
*z* *Oil, sacred*, Deut. 12:17.

**11**
*a* *Defilement, of priests*, Lev. 5:2.
**12**
*b* *Sanctuary*, Lev. 4:6.
*c* *Anointing*, Lev. 8:12.
*d* *Oil, sacred*, Deut. 12:17.

* **BALDNESS**, Lev. 13:40, 41. *A judgment*, Isa. 3:24; Jer. 47:5; 48:37; Ezek. 7:18. *Artificial, a sign of mourning*, Isa. 22:12; Jer. 16:6; Ezek. 27:31; 29:18; Amos 8:10; Mic. 1:16. *Artificial, as an idolatrous practice, forbidden*, Lev. 21:5; Deut. 14:1.

**Instances of:** *Elisha*, 2 Kin. 2:23.

† **HIGH PRIEST.** Moses did not denominate Aaron chief or high priest. The function he served was superior to that of other priests. The office appears after the institution of the priesthood, Lev. 21:10–15; Num. 3:32.

*Two apparently co-ordinate high priests, Zadok and Abiathar*, 2 Sam. 15:24, 29; *and Annas and Caiaphas*, Luke 3:2.

*Must be without blemish*, Lev. 21:17–23. *Consecration of*, Ex. 29:1–9, 19–35; 40:12–16; Lev. 6:20–23; 8:6–35; 21:10; Heb. 7:21.

*Vestments of*, Ex. 28:2–43; 29:29; 31:10; 39:1–31; Lev. 8:7–9. *Respect due to*, Acts 23:5.

**Duties of:** *Had charge of the sanctuary and altar*, Num. 18:2, 5, 7. *To offer sacrifices*, Heb. 5:1; 8:3. *To designate subordinate priests for duty*, Num. 4:19; 1 Sam. 2:36. *To officiate in consecrations, of Levites*, Num. 8:11–21; *of kings*, 1 Kin. 1:34. *To have charge of the treasury*, 2 Kin. 12:10; 22:4; 2 Chr. 24:6–14; 34:9. *To light the lamps of tabernacle*, Ex. 27:20, 21; 30:8; Lev. 24:3, 4; Num. 8:3. *To burn in-*

v.13–1532 BC
See footnote, *Time*, Rev. 10:6.

**13**
e *Priest, marriage of*, Lev. 1:5.
f *Marriage*, Gen. 34:9.
**14**
g *Widow*, 2 Sam. 14:5.
h *Virgin*, Isa. 62:5.
**15**
i *Sanctification, the Lord the sanctifier*, 1 Pet. 1:2.
**16**
j *Prophets, inspiration of*, Isa. 3:2.
**17**
k *Priest*, Lev. 1:5.
l *Minister, character and qualifications of*, Rom. 15:16.
m *Jesus, perfection of, typified*, vs. 17–23; Matt. 1:21.
n *Blemish*, Lev. 14:10.
o *Sin, typified*, Rom. 5:12.
p *Bread, figurative*, Ezek. 4:13.
**18**
q *Blindness*, 2 Kin. 6:18.
**20**
r *Scab*, Lev. 14:56.
**21**
s *Offerings, burnt*, Lev. 6:17.
**23**
t *Vail*, Ex. 26:31.
u *Altar*, Gen. 8.20.

13 And [e]he shall [f]take a wife in her virginity.

14 A [g]widow, or a divorced woman, or profane, *or* an harlot, these shall he not take: but he shall [f]take a [h]virgin of his own people to wife.

15 Neither shall he profane his seed among his people: for I the LORD do [i]sanctify him.

16 ¶ And the LORD spake unto [j]Mō'ṣeṣ, saying,

17 Speak unto [k]Aâr'on, saying, [l,m]Whosoever *he be* of thy seed in their generations that hath *any* [n,o]blemish, let him not approach to offer the [p]bread of his God.

18 For whatsoever man *he be* that hath a [n,o]blemish, he shall not approach: a [q]blind man, or a ‡lame, or he that hath a flat nose, or any thing superfluous,

19 Or a man that is ‡brokenfooted, or brokenhanded,

20 Or crookbackt, or a dwarf, or that hath a [n,o]blemish in his eye, or be scurvy, or [r]scabbed, or hath his stones broken;

21 No [l]man that hath a [n,o]blemish of the seed of Aâr'on the [k]priest shall come nigh to offer the [s]offerings of the LORD made by fire: he hath a blemish; he shall not come nigh[G] to offer the [p]bread of his God.

22 He shall eat the [p]bread of his God, *both* of the most holy, and of the holy.

23 Only he shall not go in unto the [t]vail, nor come nigh[G] unto the [u]altar, because he hath a [n,o]blemish; that he profane[G] not my sanctuaries: for I the LORD do [i]sanctify them.

24 And Mō'ṣeṣ told *it* unto Aâr'on, and to his sons, and unto all the children of Ĭṣ'ra-el.

## CHAPTER 22

*The priests in their uncleanness must abstain from the holy things. 6 How they shall be cleansed. 10 Who of the priest's house may eat of the holy things. 17 The sacrifices must be without blemish. 26 The age of the sacrifice. 29 The law of eating the sacrifice of thanksgiving.*

AND the LORD [a]spake unto [b]Mō'ṣeṣ, saying,

2 Speak unto [c]Aâr'on and to his sons, that they separate themselves from the holy things of the children of Ĭṣ'ra-el, and that they profane not my holy [d]name *in those things* which they hallow unto me: I *am* the LORD.

3 Say unto them, Whosoever *he be* of all your seed among your generations, that goeth unto the holy things, which the children of Ĭṣ'ra-el hallow unto the LORD, having his [e]uncleanness upon him, that soul shall be [f,g]cut off from my presence: I *am* the LORD.

4 What man soever of the seed of [c]Aâr'on *is* a [e,h,i]leper, or hath [1]a running issue; he shall not eat of the holy things, until he be clean. And whoso toucheth any thing *that is* unclean *by* the dead, or a man whose seed goeth from him;

5 Or whosoever toucheth any [j]creeping thing, whereby he may be made [e,k]unclean, or a man of whom he may take unclean-

v.23–1532 BC
See footnote, *Time*, Rev. 10:6.

**1**
a *Revelation, relating to priests*, vs. 1–16; 2 Cor. 12:1
b *Prophets, inspiration of*, Isa. 3:2.
**2**
c *Priest*, Lev. 1:5.
d *God, name of, not to be profaned*, Gen. 2:2.
**3**
e *Defilement*, Lev. 5:2.
f *Church, rules of discipline in*, Matt. 16:18.
g *Disfellowship*, Num. 15:31.
**4**
h *Leprosy, law concerning*, Lev. 13:2.
i *Disease*, Ex. 15:26.
1 R. V. an issue;
**5**
j *Creeping Things*, Rom. 1:23.
k *Sin, typified*, Rom. 5:12.

---

*cense*, Ex. 30:7, 8; 1 Sam. 2:28; 1 Chr. 23:13. *To place shewbread on the table every Sabbath*, Lev. 24:8. *To make atonement for his own sins*, Lev. 4:3–12; 9:7; 16:6, 11, 17, 24, 33.

*On the day of atonement*, Ex. 30:10; Lev. 16; Heb. 5:3; 9:7.

*Judicial*, Num. 5:15–18; 1 Sam. 4:18; Matt. 26:3, 57, 62; Acts 5:21–28; 23:1–5. *To officiate at choice of ruler*, Num. 27:18, 19, 21. *To distribute spoils of war*, Num. 31:26–29.

**Emoluments of:** *Provided with cities and suburbs*, Josh. 21:13–19; 1 Chr. 6:57–60; Neh. 11:3, 20; Ezek. 45:1–6; 48:8–13. *Possessed land sanctified to the Lord*, Lev. 27:21. *Portion, of tithe of the tithes*, Num. 18:8–18, 26–32; Neh. 10:38; *of the spoils of war, including captives*, Num. 31:25–29; *of first fruits*, Lev. 23:20; 24:9; Num. 18:12, 13, 17, 18; Deut. 18:3–5; Neh. 10:36; *of redemption money*, Lev. 27:23; *of redemption money of firstborn*, Num. 3:46–51; 18:15, 16; *of things devoted*, Num. 5:9, 10; 18:14; *of fines*, Num. 5:8; *of trespass money and other trespass offerings*, Num. 5:5–10; 18:9; *of the shewbread*, Lev. 24:5–9; Matt. 12:4; *of sacrifices and offerings*, Ex. 29:27–34; Lev. 2:2, 3, 9, 10; 5:12, 13, 16; 6:15–18; 10:12–14; 14:12, 13; Num. 6:19, 20; 18:8–19; Deut. 18:3–5; 1 Sam. 2:13, 14; Ezek. 45:1–4; 1 Cor. 9:13.

*Regulations by Hezekiah concerning*, 2 Chr. 31:4–19. *Portion of land allotted to, in redistribution in Ezekiel's vision*, Ezek. 48:8–14. *Sustenance of their families*, Lev. 22:11–13; Num. 18:11, 19.

See footnote, PRIEST, Lev. 1:5.

‡ **LAMENESS.** *Disqualified priests from exercising the priestly office*, Lev. 21:18. *Disqualified animals for sacrificial uses*, Deut. 15:21. *Hated by David*, 2 Sam. 5:8. *Healed, by Jesus*, Matt. 11:5; 15:31; 21:14; Luke 7:22; *by Peter*, Acts 3:2–11.

**Figurative**, Heb. 12:13.

v.5–1532 BC
See footnote, *Time*, Rev. 10:6.

6
*l* *Ablution*, Judg. 19:21.

7
*m* *Purification*, Num. 19:19.
*n* *Holiness, typified*, Ex. 39:30.

8
*o* *Sanitation and Hygiene, food*, Num. 31:23.

9
*p* *Obedience, enjoined*, Heb. 5:8.
*q* *Sin, punishment for*, Rom. 5:12.
*r* *Sanctification*, 1 Pet. 1:2.

10
*s* *Foreigners*, Deut. 23:20.
*t* *Hired Servant*, Lev. 25:40.

11
*u* *Servant, bought and sold*, Jer. 2:14.
*v* *Money*, Jer. 32:9.

12
*w* *Daughter, of priest*, Lev. 12:6.
*x* *Marriage*, Gen. 34:9.
2 R. V. the heave offering

13
*y* *Widow*, 2 Sam. 14:5.

14
*z* *Ignorance, sins of*, Acts 3:17.

*a* *Fine*, Ex. 22:1.
*b* *Restitution*, Ex. 22:3.
*c* *Priest, emoluments of*, Lev. 1:5.

16
3 R. V. that bringeth guilt,

ness, whatsoever uncleanness he hath;

6 The soul which hath touched any such shall be [e,k]unclean until even, and shall not eat of the holy things, unless he [l]wash his flesh with water.

7 And when the sun is down, he shall be [m,n]clean, and shall afterward eat of the holy things; because it *is* his food.

8 [o]That which dieth of itself, or is torn *with beasts*, he shall not eat to defile himself therewith: I *am* the LORD.

9 [c]They shall therefore [p]keep[G] mine ordinance,[G] lest they bear [q]sin for it, and die therefore, if they profane it: I the LORD do [r]sanctify them.

10 There shall no [s]stranger eat *of* the holy thing: a sojourner of the priest, or an [t]hired servant, shall not eat *of* the holy thing.

11 But if the [c]priest buy *any* [u]soul[G] with his [v]money, he shall eat of it, and he that is born in his house: they shall eat of his meat.[G]

12 If the priest's [w]daughter also be [x]*married* unto a [s]stranger,[G] she may not eat of [2]an offering of the holy things.

13 But if the priest's [w]daughter be a [y]widow, or divorced, and have no child, and is returned unto her father's house, as in her youth, she shall eat of her father's meat:[G] but there shall no [s]stranger[G] eat thereof.

14 And if a man eat *of* the holy thing [z]unwittingly,[G] then he shall put the [a]fifth *part* thereof unto it, and shall [b]give [c]*it* unto the priest with the holy thing.

15 And they shall not profane the holy things of the children of Is'ra-el, which they offer unto the LORD;

16 Or suffer[G] them to bear the iniquity [3]of trespass, when they eat their holy things: for I the LORD do [d]sanctify them.

17 ¶ And the LORD [e]spake unto [f]Mō'ṣeṣ, saying,

18 Speak unto [g]Aâr'on, and to his sons, and unto all the children of [h]Is'ra-el, and say unto them, Whatsoever *he be* of the house of Is'ra-el, or the [i]strangers[G] in Is'ra-el, that will offer his [j]oblation for all his [k]vows, and for all his [l]freewill offerings, which they will offer unto the LORD for a [m]burnt offering;

19 *Ye shall* [n,o]*offer* at your own will a male [p]without [q,r]blemish, of the beeves,[G] of the [s]sheep, or of the [t]goats.

20 *But* whatsoever hath a [q,r]blemish, [n]*that* shall ye not offer: for it shall not be acceptable for you.

21 And whosoever offereth a sacrifice of [u]peace offerings unto the LORD to accomplish *his* [k]vow, or a [l]freewill offering [4]in beeves[G] or [s]sheep, [n]it shall be [p]perfect to be accepted; there shall be no [q,r]blemish therein.

22 [v]Blind, or broken,[G] or maimed, or having a wen,[G] or scurvy, or [w]scabbed, ye shall not offer these unto the LORD, nor make an offering by fire of them upon the [x]altar unto the LORD.

23 Either a [y]bullock or a [z]lamb that hath any thing superfluous or lacking in his parts, that mayest thou offer *for* a [l]freewill offering; but for a [k]vow[G] it shall not be accepted.

24 Ye shall not offer unto the LORD [a]that which is [b,c]bruised, or crushed, or broken, or cut; neither shall ye make *any offering thereof* in your land.

25 Neither from a [d]stranger's[G] hand shall ye offer the [e]bread of your God of any of these; because their [f]corruption *is* in them, *and* [b,c]blemishes *be* in

v.16–1532 BC
See footnote, *Time*, Rev. 10:1.

*d* *Sanctification, the Lord the sanctifier*, 1 Pet. 1:2.

17
*e* *Revelation, concerning offerings*, vs. 17–33; 2 Cor. 12:1.
*f* *Prophets, inspiration of*, Isa. 3:2.

18
*g* *Priest*, Lev. 1:5
*h* *Israel*, Ex. 4:22.
*i* *Foreigners*, Deut. 23:20.
*j* *Jesus, typified in the offerings*, vs. 18–22, 24; Matt. 1:21.
*k* *Vows*, Num. 30:2.
*l* *Offerings, free will*, Lev. 6:17.
*m* *Offerings, burnt*, Lev. 6:17.

19
*n* *Offerings, must be without blemish*, Lev. 6:17.
*o* *Dedication*, Ezra 6:17.
*p* *Holiness, typified*, Ex. 39:30.
*q* *Blemish*, Lev. 14:10.
*r* *Sin, typified*, Rom. 5:12.
*s* *Sheep*, Deut. 32:14.
*t* *Goat*, Deut. 14:4.

21
*u* *Offerings, peace*, Lev. 6:17.
4 R. V. of the herd or of the flock,

22
*v* *Blindness, of animals*, 2 Kin. 6:18.
*w* *Scab*, Lev. 14:56.
*x* *Altar, of burnt offerings*, Gen. 8:20.

23
*y* *Bullock*, Ex. 29:3.
*z* *Lamb, offering of*, Num. 7:15.

24
*a* *Offerings, must be without blemish*, Lev. 6:17.
*b* *Blemish*, Lev. 14:10.
*c* *Sin, typified*, Rom. 5:12.

25
*d* *Foreigners*, Deut. 23:20.
*e* *Bread, figurative* Ezek. 4:13.
*f* *Corruption*, Job 17:14.

v.25–1532 BC
See footnote, *Time*, Rev. 10:6.

**26**
g *Inspiration*, Job 32:8.
h *Moses*, Ex. 2:10.
**27**
i *Bullock*, Ex. 29:3.
j *Sheep*, Deut. 32:14.
k *Goat*, Deut. 14:4.
l *Offerings*, Lev. 6:17.
**29**
m *Offerings, thank*, Lev. 6:17.
5 R. V. sacrifice
6 R. V. ye shall sacrifice it that ye may be accepted.
**30**
n *Sanitation and Hygiene, food*, Num. 31:23.
o *God, sovereign*, Gen. 2:2.
**31**
p *Obedience, enjoined*, Heb. 5:8.
**32**
q *Blasphemy, forbidden*, 2 Sam. 12:14.
r *God, name of, not to be profaned*, Gen. 2:2.
s *Sanctification, the Lord the sanctifier*, 1 Pet. 1:2.
**33**
t *God, love of, exemplified*, Gen. 2:2.
u *Egypt*, Gen. 41:8.

**1**
a *Revelation, concerning the Sabbath*, vs. 1–8; 2 Cor. 12:1.
b *Prophets, inspiration of*, Isa. 3:2.
**2**
c *Annual Feasts*, Num. 15:3.
**3**
d *Commandment, enjoining labor and rest*, Deut. 8:2.
e *Labor*, Luke 10:7.
f *Sabbath*, Ex. 16:23.

them: they shall not be accepted for you.

26 ¶ And the LORD [g]spake unto [h]Mō'ṣeṣ, saying,

27 When a [i]bullock, or a [j]sheep, or a [k]goat, is brought forth, then it shall be seven days under the dam; and from the eighth day and thenceforth it shall be accepted for an [l]offering made by fire unto the LORD.

28 And *whether it be* cow or ewe, ye shall not kill it and her young both in one day.

29 ¶ And when ye [5]will offer a [m]sacrifice of thanksgiving unto the LORD, [6]offer *it* at your own will.

30 On the same day it shall be eaten up; [n]ye shall leave none of it until the morrow: [o]I *am* the LORD.

31 Therefore shall ye [p]keep my commandments, and do them: [o]I *am* the LORD.

32 Neither shall ye [*,q]profane my holy [r]name; but I will be hallowed among the children of Ĭṣ'ra-el: I *am* the LORD which [s]hallow you,

33 That [t]brought you out of the land of [u]Ē'ġy̆pt, to be your God: [o]I *am* the LORD.

## CHAPTER 23

*The feasts of the Lord. 3 The sabbath. 2 The passover. 9 The sheaf of first fruits. 15 The feast of pentecost. 22 Gleanings to be left for the poor. 23 The feast of trumpets. 26 The day of atonement. 33 The feast of tabernacles.*

AND the LORD [a]spake unto [b]Mō'ṣeṣ, saying,

2 Speak unto the children of Ĭṣ'ra-el, and say unto them, *Concerning* the [c]feasts of the LORD, which ye shall proclaim *to be* holy convocations, *even* these *are* my feasts.

3 [d]Six days shall [e]work be done: but the seventh day *is* the [f]sabbath of rest, an holy convocation; [g]ye shall do no work *therein*: it *is* the sabbath of the LORD in all your dwellings.

4 ¶ These *are* the [c]feasts of the LORD, *even* holy convocations, which ye shall proclaim in their seasons.

5 In the fourteenth *day* of the [h]first [i]month at even *is* the LORD's [j]passover.

6 And on the fifteenth day of the same [h,i]month *is* the feast of unleavened bread unto the LORD: [k]seven days ye must eat [l]unleavened bread.

7 In the first day ye shall have an holy convocation: [d]ye shall [l]do no servile work therein.

8 But ye shall offer an [m]offering made by fire unto the LORD [k]seven days: in the seventh day *is* an holy convocation: [d,l]ye shall do no servile work *therein*.

9 ¶ And the LORD [n]spake unto [b]Mō'ṣeṣ, saying,

10 [n]Speak unto the children of Ĭṣ'ra-el, and say unto them, When ye be come into the land which I give unto you, and shall reap the [o]harvest thereof, then ye shall bring a sheaf of the [p]firstfruits of your harvest unto the priest:

11 And [q]he shall [r]wave the sheaf before the LORD, to be accepted for you: on the morrow after the [f]sabbath the priest shall wave it.

12 And ye shall offer that day when ye wave the sheaf an he [s,t]lamb [u]without [v,w]blemish of the first year for a [x]burnt offering unto the LORD.

13 And the [1,y]meat offering thereof *shall be* two [z]tenth deals of fine flour mingled with [a]oil, an offering made by fire unto the LORD *for* a sweet savour: and

v.3–1532 BC
See footnote, *Time*, Rev. 10:6.
g *Sanitation and Hygiene, rest enjoined*, vs. 3–8, 24–42; Num. 31:23.
**5**
h *Abib*, Ex. 13:4.
i *Month*, Ex. 12:2.
j *Passover*, Num. 9:5.
**6**
k *Seven, days*, Gen. 7:2.
**7**
l *Rest, enjoined*, Ex. 23:12.
**8**
m *Offerings*, Lev. 6:17.
**9**
n *Revelation, concerning first fruits*, 2 Cor. 12:1.
**10**
o *Harvest*, Ex. 34:21.
p *First Fruits*, Deut. 18:4.
**11**
q *Priest, duties of*, Lev. 1:5.
r *Offerings, wave*, Lev. 6:17.
**12**
s *Lamb, offerings of*, Num. 7:15.
t *Jesus, typified in the offerings*, Matt. 1:21.
u *Holiness, typified*, Ex. 39:30.
v *Blemish*, Lev. 14:10.
w *Sin, typified*, Rom. 5:12.
x *Offerings, burnt*, Lev. 6:17.
**13**
y *Offerings, meat*, Lev. 6:17.
z *Measure, dry*, Deut. 25:15.
a *Oil, used for food*, Deut. 12:17.
1 R. V. meal

* **PROFANATION. Of God's Name,** Lev. 20:3; Prov. 30:9.
FORBIDDEN, Ex. 20:7 (with Deut. 5:11); Lev. 18:21; 19:12; 21:6; 22:2, 32.
INSTANCES OF, Psa. 139:20; Isa. 52:5; Rom. 2:24.
**Of the Sabbath,** Neh. 13:15–22; Ezek. 20:12, 13, 16; 22:8; 23:38.
**Of the house of God,** 2 Chr. 33:7; Neh. 13:7; Jer. 7:11; Matt. 21:13; Mark 11:17; Luke 19:46.
**Of holy things:** *Forbidden*, Lev. 22:15.

v.13–1532 BC
See footnote, *Time*, Rev. 10:6.

b *Offerings, drink*, Lev. 6:17.
c *Wine*, Prov. 23:31.
d *Measure, liquid*, Deut. 25:15.

14
e *Thankfulness, cultivated by offerings*, Acts 24:3.
2 R. V. the oblation of

15
f *Sabbath*, Ex. 16:23.
g *Offerings, wave*, Lev. 6:17.
h *Seven, weeks*, Gen. 7:2.
i *Pentecost, institution of*, Acts 2:1.

16
j *Offerings, meat*, Lev. 6:17.

17
k *Measure, dry*, Deut. 25:15.
l *First Fruits*, Deut. 18:4.

18
m *Bread*, Ezek. 4:13.
n *Jesus, typified in offerings*, Matt. 1:21.
o *Holiness, typified*, Ex. 39:30.
p *Blemish*, Lev. 14:10.
q *Sin, typified*, Rom. 5:12.
r *Offerings, burnt*, Lev. 6:17.

19
s *Offerings, sin*, Lev. 6:17.
t *Offerings, peace*, Lev. 6:17.
3 R. V. offer
4 R. V. he-goat

20
u *Priests, duties of*, Lev. 1:5.

the [b]drink offering thereof *shall*
*be* of [c]wine, the fourth *part* of
an [d]hin.[G]
14 And ye shall eat neither
bread, nor parched corn,[G] nor
green ears, until the selfsame[G]
day that ye have [e]brought [2]an
offering unto your God: *it shall*
*be* a statute for ever throughout
your generations in all your
dwellings.
15 ¶ [T]And[Q] ye shall count unto
you from the morrow[G] after the
[f]sabbath, from the day that ye
brought the sheaf of the [g]wave
offering; [h,i]seven sabbaths shall
be complete:
16 Even unto the morrow[G] after
the seventh [f]sabbath shall ye
number fifty days; and ye shall
offer a new [1,j]meat[G] offering unto
the LORD.[T]
17 Ye shall bring out of your
habitations two [g]wave[G] loaves of
two [k]tenth deals[G]: they shall be
of fine flour; they shall be baken
with *leaven; *they are* the [l]first-
fruits unto the LORD.
18 And ye shall offer with the
[m]bread seven [n]lambs [o]without
[p,q]blemish of the first year, and
one young bullock, and two
rams: they shall be *for* a [r]burnt
offering unto the LORD, with
their [1,j]meat[G] offering, and their
[b]drink offerings, *even* an offering made by fire, of sweet savour
unto the LORD.
19 Then ye shall [3]sacrifice one
[4]kid of the goats for a [s]sin [n]of-
fering, and two lambs of the
first year for a sacrifice of [t]peace
offerings.
20 And the [u]priest shall wave[G]
them with the [m]bread of the
[l]firstfruits *for* a [g]wave offering
before the LORD, with the two
lambs: [v]they shall be holy[G] to
the LORD for the priest.
21 And ye shall proclaim on the
selfsame[G] day, *that* it may be an
holy convocation unto you: ye
shall [w]do no servile[G] work *therein*:
*it shall be* a statute for ever in all
your dwellings throughout your
generations.[Q]
22 ¶ And [x]when ye reap the
[y]harvest of your land, thou shalt
not make clean riddance of the
corners of thy field when thou
reapest, neither shalt thou gather any †gleaning of thy harvest:
[z]thou shalt leave them unto the
[a]poor, and to the [b]stranger[G]: I *am*
the LORD your God.
23 ¶ And the LORD [c]spake unto [d]Mō′ṣeṣ, saying,
24 Speak unto the children of
Ĭṣ′ra-el, saying, In the [e]seventh
[f]month, in the first *day* of the
month, shall [5]ye have a [g]sab-
bath, a memorial of blowing of
‡trumpets, an holy convocation.[G]
25 Ye shall do [g]no servile [h]work
*therein*: but ye shall offer an[i] offering made by fire unto the
LORD.
26 ¶ And the LORD [j]spake unto
[d]Mō′ṣeṣ, saying,
27 Also on the tenth *day* of this
[e]seventh [f]month *there shall be* a
day of ‖,[k]atonement: it shall be
an holy convocation unto you;
and ye shall [l,m]afflict your souls,
and offer an [i]offering made by
fire unto the LORD.
28 And [g]ye shall do no work in
that same day: for it *is* a day of
‖atonement, to make an atone-

v.20–1532 BC
See footnote, *Time*, Rev. 10:6.

v *Priest, emoluments of*, Lev. 1:5.

21
w *Rest, enjoined*, Ex. 23:12.

22
x *Agriculture*, Gen. 3:23.
y *Harvest*, Ex. 34:21.
z *Liberality, enjoined*, 1 Tim. 6:18.

a *Poor, duty to*, Prov. 21:13.
b *Foreigner*, Deut. 23:20.

23
c *Revelation, concerning the feast of trumpets*, 2 Cor. 12:1.
d *Prophets, inspiration of*, Isa. 3:2.

24
e *Ethanim, October*, 1 Kin. 8:2.
f *Month*, Ex. 12:2.
g *Rest, enjoined*, Ex. 23:12.
5 R. V. be a solemn rest unto you,

25
h *Labor*, Luke 10:7.
i *Offerings, burnt*, Lev. 6:17.

26
j *Revelation, concerning the day of atonement*, 2 Cor. 12:1.

27
k *Jesus, atonement by, typified*, Matt. 1:21.
l *Humility*, vs. 26–32; Prov. 22:4.
m *Repentance, enjoined*, vs. 26–32; Mark 1:4.

* **LEAVEN** (*yeast*). *For bread*, Ex. 12:34, 39; Hos. 7:4; Matt. 13:33. *Leavened bread used, with peace offering*, Lev. 7:13; Amos 4:5; *with wave offering*, Lev. 23:15–17.
*A type of sin*, 1 Cor. 5:6–8. *Forbidden to be used in the passover*, Ex. 12:19, 20; 13:3, 4, 7; 23:18; Num. 9:11. *Forbidden also with meat offerings*, Lev. 2:11; 6:17; 10:12; *and with blood*, Ex. 23:18; 34:25.
**Figurative:** *Of the hypocrisy of the Pharisees*, Matt. 16:6–12; Mark 8:15; Luke 12:1. *Of other evils*, 1 Cor. 5:6–8; Gal. 5:9.
**Parable of**, Matt. 13:33; Luke 13:21.

† **GLEANING.** *Laws concerning*, Lev. 19:9, 10; 23:22; Deut. 24:19, 20.
**Instances of:** *Ruth in the field of Boaz*, Ruth 2:2, 3.
**Figurative**, Judg. 8:2; Isa. 17:6; Jer. 49:9; Mic. 7:1.

‡ **TRUMPETS. Feast of:** *When and how observed*, Lev. 23:24, 25; Num. 29:1–6. *Celebrated after the captivity with joy*, Neh. 8:2, 9–12.
See footnote, ANNUAL FEASTS, Num. 15:3.

‖ **DAY OF ATONEMENT.** *Time of*, Ex. 30:10; Lev. 23:27; 25:9; Num. 29:7. *How observed*, Ex. 30:10; Lev 16:2–34; 23:27–32; Num. 29:7–11; Heb. 9:7.

v.26–1532 BC
See footnote, *Time*, Rev. 10:6.

29
*n* *Impenitence, judgments denounced against*, Rom. 2:5.
*o* *Disfellowship*, Num. 15:31.

31
*p* *Sanitation and Hygiene, rest enjoined*, Num. 31:23.

33
*q* *Revelation, concerning the feast of tabernacles*, 2 Cor. 12:1.

34
*r* *Tabernacles, feast of*, vs. 34–43; Deut. 16:13.
*s* *Seven, days*, Gen. 7:2.

37
*t* *Annual Feasts*, Num. 15:3.
*u* *Offerings, meat*, Lev. 6:17.
*v* *Offerings, drink*, Lev. 6:17.
6 R. V. meal

38
*w* *Sabbath*, Ex. 16:23.
*x* *Vows*, Num. 30:2.

ment for you before the LORD
your God.
29 For whatsoever soul[C] *it be*
that shall [n]not be [l,m]afflicted in
that same ‖day, he shall be [o]cut
off from among his people.[Q]
30 And whatsoever soul *it be*
that doeth any [h]work in that
same ‖day, the same soul will I
destroy from among his people.
31 [g,p]Ye shall do no manner of
[h]work: *it shall be* a statute for
ever throughout your generations in all your dwellings.
32 It *shall be* unto you a sabbath of [g]rest, and ye shall [l,m]afflict your souls: in the ninth *day*
of the [l]month at even, from even
unto even, shall ye celebrate
your sabbath.
33 ¶ And the LORD [q]spake unto [d]Mō'ṣeṣ, saying,
34 Speak unto the children of
Ĭṣ'ra-el, saying, The fifteenth
day of this [e]seventh month *shall*
*be* the feast of [r]tabernacles *for*[Q]
[s]seven days unto the LORD.
35 On the first day *shall be* an
holy convocation: [g]ye shall do no
servile [h]work *therein*.
36 [s]Seven days ye shall offer an
offering made by fire unto the
LORD: on the eighth day shall be
an holy convocation unto you;
and ye shall offer an offering
made by fire unto the LORD: it
*is* a solemn assembly; *and* [g]ye
shall do no servile [h]work *therein*.[Q]
37 These *are* the [t]feasts of the
LORD, which ye shall proclaim
*to be* holy convocations, to offer
an offering made by fire unto the
LORD, a [i]burnt offering, and a
[6,u]meat[C] offering, a sacrifice, and
[v]drink offerings, every thing upon his day:
38 Beside the [w]sabbaths of the
LORD, and beside your gifts,
and beside all your [x]vows, and
beside[C] all your [y]freewill offerings, which ye give unto the
LORD.
39 Also in the fifteenth day of
the [e]seventh [l]month, when ye
have gathered in the fruit of the
land, ye shall keep a [r,t]feast unto
the LORD [s]seven days: on the
first day *shall be* a [7]sabbath,[C] and
on the eighth day *shall be* a
[7]sabbath.
40 And ye shall take you on the
first day the boughs of goodly
trees, branches of [z]palm trees,
and the boughs of thick trees,
and §willows of the brook; and
ye shall rejoice before the LORD
your God seven days.
41 And ye shall keep it a [a]feast
unto the LORD [b]seven days in
the year. *It shall be* a statute for
ever in your generations: ye shall
celebrate it in the [c]seventh
[d]month.
42 Ye shall dwell in †booths[C]
[b]seven days; all that are Ĭṣ'ra-el-
ītes born shall dwell in booths:
43 That your generations may
know that I made the children
of Ĭṣ'ra-el to dwell in †booths,
when I [e]brought them out of the
land of Ē'ġy̆pt: I *am* the LORD
your God.
44 And Mō'ṣeṣ declared unto
the children of Ĭṣ'ra-el the
[f]feasts of the LORD.

## CHAPTER 24

*The oil for the lamps of the tabernacle. 5 The shewbread. 10 Shelomith's son blasphemes. 13 The law of blasphemy, 17 of murder, 18 and of damage. 23 The blasphemer is stoned.*

AND the LORD [a]spake unto
[b]Mō'ṣeṣ, saying,
2 Command the children of
[c]Ĭṣ'ra-el, that they bring unto
thee pure [d]oil [e]olive beaten for
the light, to cause the [f]lamps to
burn continually.
3 Without[C] the vail of the testi-

v.38–1532 BC
See footnote, *Time*, Rev. 10:6.
*y* *Offerings, free will*, Lev. 6:17.

39
7 R. V. solemn rest.

40
*z* *Palm Tree*, Song 7:7.

41
*a* *Tabernacles, feast of*, Deut. 16:13.
*b* *Seven, days*, Gen. 7:2.
*c* *Ethanim, October*, 1 Kin. 8:2.
*d* *Month*, Ex. 12:2.

43
*e* *God, preserver*, Gen. 2:2.

44
*f* *Annual Feasts*, Num. 15:3.

1
*a* *Revelation, of sundry laws*, 2 Cor. 12:1.
*b* *Prophets, inspiration of*, Isa. 3:2.

2
*c* *Israel*, Ex. 4.22.
*d* *Oil, illuminating*, Deut. 12:17.
*e* *Olive*, Deut. 6:11.
*f* *Lamp*, Ex. 27:20.

§ **WILLOW.** Job 40:4. *In Canaan*, Lev 23:40; Isa. 15:7, 44:4; Ezek. 17:5. *By the rivers of Babylon*, Psa. 137:2.

† **BOOTH.** *Made of boughs*, Jonah 4:5. *Made, for cattle*, Gen. 33:17; *for watchmen*, Job 27:18; Isa. 1:8. *Prescribed for the Israelites to dwell in, during the feast of tabernacles, to celebrate their wanderings in the wilderness*, Lev. 23:40–43; Neh. 8:15–17.

v.3–1532 BC
See footnote, *Time*, Rev. 10:6.

3
g *High Priest, duties of*, Lev. 21: 10.
1 R. V. tent of meeting.

4
h *Candlestick*, Ex. 25:31.

5
i *Shewbread*, Ex. 35:13.
j *Measure, dry*, Deut. 25:15.

7
k *Frankincense*, 1 Chr. 9:29.
l *Memorial*, Num. 16:40.
m *Offerings*, Lev. 6: 17.

8
n *Sabbath*, Ex. 16:23.

9
o *High Priest, emoluments of*, Lev. 21:10.

11
p *Blasphemy*, 2 Sam. 12:14.

12
q *Prison*, Gen. 39: 20.

mony, in the [1]tabernacle of the
congregation, shall [g]Aâr′on order it from the evening unto the
morning before the LORD continually: *it shall be* a statute for
ever in your generations.
4 [g]He shall order[G] the [j]lamps upon the pure [h]candlestick[G] before
the LORD continually.
5 ¶ [Q]And thou shalt take fine
flour, and bake twelve [i]cakes
thereof: two [j]tenth deals[G] shall
be in one cake.
6 And thou shalt set [i]them in
two rows, six on a row, upon the
pure table before the LORD.
7 And thou shalt put pure
[k]frankincense upon *each* row,
that it may be on the [i]bread
for a [l]memorial, *even* an [m]of-
fering made by fire unto the
LORD.
8 Every [n]sabbath [g]he shall set
it in order before the LORD continually, *being taken* from the
children of Ĭṣ′ra-el by an everlasting covenant.[C]
9 And [i, o]it shall be Aâr′on's and
his sons'; and they shall eat it in
the holy place: for it *is* most holy
unto him of the [m]offerings of the
LORD made by fire by a perpetual statute.[Q]
10 ¶ And the son of an Ĭṣ′ra-el-
ĭt-ĭsh woman, whose father *was*
an Ē-ġȳp′tian, went out among
the children of [c]Ĭṣ′ra-el: and
this son of the Ĭṣ′ra-el-ĭt-ĭsh
*woman* and a man of Ĭṣ′ra-el
strove[G] together in the camp;
11 And the Ĭṣ′ra-el-ĭt-ĭsh woman's son [p]blasphemed the name
*of the* LORD and *cursed. And
they brought him unto Mō′ṣeṣ:
(and his mother's name *was*
Shĕl′o-mĭth, the daughter of
Dĭb′rī, of the tribe of Dăn:)
12 And they put him in [q]ward,[G]
that the mind of the LORD might
be shewed them.

13 And the LORD [r]spake unto
Mō′ṣeṣ, saying,
14 Bring forth him that hath
*cursed without the camp; and
[s]let [t]all that heard *him* lay their
[u]hands upon his head, and let all
the [v]congregation [w]stone him.
15 And [r]thou shalt speak unto
the children of [c]Ĭṣ′ra-el, saying,
Whosoever *,[p]curseth his God
shall bear[G] his sin.
16 And he that [p]blasphemeth
the name of the LORD, he shall
surely be [x]put to [y]death, *and* all
the congregation shall certainly
[w]stone him: as well the [z]stranger,[G]
as he that is born in the land,
when he blasphemeth the name
*of the* LORD, shall be put to
death.[Q]
17 And he that [a]killeth any
man shall surely be [b]put to
[c]death.[Q]
18 And he that killeth a [d]beast
shall [e]make it good; [2]beast for
beast.
19 And if a man cause a blemish in his neighbour; as he hath
done, [f]so shall it be done to
him;
20 [f]Breach for breach, eye for
eye, tooth for tooth: as he
hath caused a blemish in a
man, [f]so shall it be done to him
*again*.[Q]
21 And he that killeth a [d]beast,
he shall [e]restore it: and he that
[a]killeth a man, he shall be [b]put
to [c]death.
22 Ye shall have [g]one manner
of law, as well for the [h]stranger,[G]
as for one of your own country:
for I *am* the LORD your God.
23 ¶ And Mō′ṣeṣ spake to the
children of Ĭṣ′ra-el, that they
should bring forth him that had
*cursed out of the camp, and
[b, c, i]stone him with stones. And
the children of Ĭṣ′ra-el did as the
LORD commanded Mō′ṣeṣ.

v.13–1532 BC
See footnote, *Time*, Rev. 10:6.

13
r *Revelation, concerning the punishment of crimes*, vs. 14–22; 2 Cor. 12:1.

14
s *Evidence*, Deut. 17:6.
t *Witness*, Num. 35:30.
u *Hand, imposition of*, Ezra 10:19.
v *Church, called the congregation*, Matt. 16:18.
w *Stoning*, 1 Sam. 30:6.

16
x *Punishment, death penalty*, Lev. 26:41.
y *Death, penalty*, Num. 23:10.
z *Foreigners, forbidden to blaspheme*, Deut. 23:20.

17
a *Homicide, punishment of*, Deut. 5:17.
b *Punishment, death penalty*, Lev. 26:41.
c *Death, penalty*, Num. 23:10.

18
d *Property, personal*, Lev. 27:15.
e *Restitution*, Ex. 22:3.
2 R. V. life for life.

19
f *Retaliation, judicial*, Deut. 19:19.

22
g *Legislation, class, forbidden*, Ex.12: 49.
h *Foreigners*, Deut. 23:20.

23
i *Stoning*, 1 Sam. 30:6.

* **CURSING.** *God, death penalty for*, Lev. 24:11, 15. *Parents, death penalty for*, Ex. 21:17, Matt. 15:4, Mark 7.10. *David, by Goliath*, 1 Sam. 17:43; *by Shimei*, 2 Sam. 16:5–8. *The precepts of Jesus concerning*, Luke 6:28. *Apostolic precepts concerning*, Rom. 12:14.
See footnote, GOD, *Name of, not to be profaned*, Gen. 2:2.

v.1–1532 BC
See footnote, *Time*, Rev. 10:6.

1

a *Revelation, concerning the sabbatic year and jubilee*, vs. 1–17; 2 Cor. 12:1.
b *Prophets, inspiration of*, Isa.3:2.
c *Sinai*, Ex. 16:1.

2

d *Israel, the law delivered to*, vs. 2–55; Ex. 4:22.
e *Canaan*, Gen. 37:1.

3

f *Agriculture, laws concerning*, Gen. 3:23.
g *Pruning*, Isa. 18:5.

4

h *Rest, enjoined*, Ex. 23:12.

5

i *Harvest*, Ex. 34:21.

6

j *Servant, rights of*, Jer. 2:14.
k *Employee, rights of*, Deut. 24:14.
l *Foreigner*, Deut. 23:20.

7

m *Animals, kindness to*, Jer. 27:5.
1 R. V. food.

## CHAPTER 25

*The sabbath of the seventh year. 8 The jubilee in the fiftieth year. 14 Of oppression. 18 The blessing upon obedience. 23 The redemption of land. 29 and of houses. 35 Compassion for the poor. 39 The law respecting bondmen. 47 The redemption of Israelitish servants.*

AND the LORD [a]spake unto
[b]Mō′ṣeṣ in mount [c]Sī′nāi,
saying,
2 Speak unto the children of
[d]Ĭṣ′ra-el, and say unto them,
When ye come into the [e]land
which I give you, then shall the
land keep a *sabbath unto the
LORD.
3 [f]Six years thou shalt sow thy
field, and six years thou shalt
[g]prune thy vineyard, and gather
in the †fruit thereof;
4 But in the seventh year shall
be a *sabbath[G] of [h]rest unto the
land, a sabbath[G] for the LORD:
thou shalt neither [f]sow thy field,
nor [g]prune thy vineyard.
5 That which groweth of its
own accord of thy [i]harvest thou
shalt not reap, neither gather the
†grapes of thy vine undressed:[G]
*for* it is a year of [h]rest unto the
land.
6 And the sabbath of the land
shall be meat[G] for you; for thee
and for thy [j]servant, and for thy
maid, and for thy [k]hired servant,
and for thy [l]stranger that
sojourneth with thee,
7 And for thy [m]cattle, and for
the beast that *are* in thy land,
shall all the increase thereof be
[1]meat.[G]
8 ¶ And thou shalt number seven
*sabbaths of years unto thee,
seven times [n]seven years; and
the space of the seven sabbaths
of years shall be unto thee forty
and nine years.
9 Then shalt thou [2]cause the
[o]trumpet of the ‖jubile to
sound on the tenth *day* of the
[p]seventh [q]month, in the day of
[r]atonement shall ye make the
trumpet sound throughout all
your land.
10 And ye shall hallow the fiftieth
year, and proclaim ‡,[s]liberty
throughout *all* the land unto
all the inhabitants thereof: it
shall be a ‖jubile unto you; and
ye shall return every man unto
his possession, and ye shall return
every man unto his family.
11 A ‖jubile shall that fiftieth
year be unto you: [t]ye shall not
sow, neither reap that which
groweth of itself in it, nor gather
*the* †*grapes* in it of thy vine undressed.[G]
12 For it *is* the ‖jubile; it shall
be holy[G] unto you: ye shall eat the
increase thereof out of the field.
13 In the year of this ‖jubile ye
shall return every man unto his
possession.
14 And if thou [u]sell [v]ought[G] unto
thy neighbour, or buyest *ought*
of thy neighbour's hand, [w]ye
shall not oppress one another:
15 According to the number of
years after the ‖jubile thou shalt
[u,v]buy of thy neighbour, *and* according
unto the number of

v.8–1532 BC
See footnote, *Time*, Rev. 10:6.

8

n *Seven, years*, Gen. 7:2.

9

o *Trumpet*, Josh. 6:4.
p *Ethanim, October*, 1 Kin. 8:2.
q *Month*, Ex. 12:2.
r *Day of Atonement*, Lev. 23:27.
2 R.V. send abroad the loud trumpet on the tenth day

10

s *Emancipation*, Deut. 15:12.

11

t *Rest, enjoined*, Ex. 23:12.

14

u *Commerce*, 1 Kin. 10:15.
v *Land, sale and redemption of*, Ruth 4:3.
w *Kindness, enjoined*, Acts 28:2.

* **SABBATIC YEAR**, a rest recurring every seventh year. *Called* YEAR OF RELEASE, Deut. 15:9; 31:10. *Ordinances concerning*, Ex. 23:9–11; Lev. 25. *Israelitish bondservants set free in*, Ex. 21:2; Deut. 15:12; Jer. 34:14. *Creditors required to release debtors in*, Deut. 15:1–6, 12–18; Neh. 10:31. *Ordinances concerning instruction in the law during*, Deut. 31:10–13. *Enforced observance of*, Lev. 26:34, 35; Jer. 34:12–22.

† **GRAPE.** *Cultivated in vineyards, by Noah*, Gen. 9:20; *by the Canaanites*, Num. 13:24; Deut. 6:11; Josh. 24:13; *by the Edomites*, Num. 20:17; *by the Amorites*, Num. 21:22; Isa. 16:8, 9. *Grown, at Shechem*, Judg. 9:27; *at Abel*, Judg. 11:33 [marg.]; *at Timnath*, Judg. 14:5; *at Shiloh*, Judg. 21:20, 21; *at Jezreel*, 1 Kin. 21: 1–18; *at Carmel*, 2 Chr. 26:10; *at En-gedi*, Song 1:14; *at Baal-hamon*, Song 8:11; *at Lebanon*, Hos. 14:7; *at Samaria*, Jer. 31:5.

*Gleanings of, for the poor*, Lev. 19:9, 10; Deut. 24:21.

*Culture of*, Lev. 25:3, 11; Deut. 28:39; 2 Chr. 26:10, Isa. 5:1, 2; Jer. 31:5.

*Wine made of*, Jer. 25:30. *Wine of, forbidden to Nazarites*, Num. 6:4. See footnote, WINE, Prov. 23:31.

**Figurative**, Deut. 32:32, 33; Psa. 128:3; Isa. 5:1–10; Jer. 2:21, 31:29; Ezek. 15; 18:2; Hos. 10:1; Rev. 14:18–20.

FABLE OF, Judg. 9:12, 13.

PARABLES OF THE VINE, Psa. 80:8–14; Ezek. 17:6–10; 19:10–14; John 15:1–5.

PROVERB OF, Jer. 31:29; Ezek. 18:2.

‡ **LIBERTY.** *Of Hebrew bondservants, in Sabbatic year*, Ex. 21:2; Deut. 15:12; Jer. 34:14; *in year of Jubilee*, Lev. 25:10, 9, 40.

**Political**, Acts 22:28.

**Religious:** *In Rome*, Acts 28:31.

**Spiritual**, Psa. 119:45; Isa. 61:1; Luke 4:18; John 8:32, 33, 36, Rom. 6:6, 22; 8:1, 2; 1 Cor. 7:22, 2 Cor. 3:17; Gal. 2:4; 1 Pet. 2:16.

**Figurative:** *Of the gospel*, Jas. 1:25; 2:12.

‖ **JUBILEE.** *Called* ACCEPTABLE YEAR OF THE LORD, Isa. 61:2; THE YEAR OF LIBERTY, Ezek. 46:17.

**Laws Concerning**, Lev. 25:8–55; 27:17–24; **Num. 36:4.** See footnote, SABBATIC YEAR, Lev. 25:2.

v.15–1532 BC See footnote, *Time,* Rev. 10:6.

years of the fruits he shall sell unto thee:

16 According to the multitude of years thou shalt increase the price [v]thereof, and according to the fewness of years thou shalt diminish the price of it: for *according* to the number *of the years* of the fruits doth he [u]sell unto thee.

17 [x]Ye shall not therefore oppress one another; but thou shalt [y]fear thy God: for I *am* the LORD your God.

18 ¶ [§]Wherefore ye shall [z,a]do my statutes, and keep my judgments,[C] and do them; and [b,c,d]ye shall dwell in the land in safety.

19 And the land shall yield her fruit, and [b,c,d]ye shall eat your fill, and [d]dwell therein in safety.

20 And if ye shall say, What shall we eat the [*]seventh year? behold, we shall not sow, nor gather in our increase:

21 Then [e]I will command my [f]blessing upon you in the sixth year, and it shall bring forth fruit for three years.

22 And ye shall sow the eighth year, and eat *yet* of old fruit until the ninth year; until her fruits come in ye shall eat *of* the old *store.*[S]

23 ¶ The [g]land shall not be sold for ever: for the land *is* mine; for ye *are* strangers and sojourners[C] with me.

24 And in all the [g]land of your possession ye shall grant a [§]redemption for the land.

25 ¶ If thy brother be waxen[C] [h]poor, and hath sold away *some* of his [g]possession, and if any of his kin come to [§]redeem it, then shall he redeem that which his brother sold.

26 And if the man have none to [§]redeem [g]it, and himself be able to redeem it;

27 Then let him count the years of the [g]sale thereof, and restore the overplus[C] unto the man to whom he sold it; that he may return unto his possession.

28 But if he be not able to restore [g]*it* to him, then that which is sold shall remain in the hand of him that hath bought it until the year of jubile: and in the jubile it shall go out, and he shall return unto his possession.

29 And if a man sell a dwelling [i]house in a walled city, then he may [§]redeem it within a whole [+]year after it is sold; *within* a full year may he redeem it.

30 And if it be not [§]redeemed within the space of a full [+]year, then the [i,j]house that *is* in the walled city shall be established for ever to him that bought it throughout his generations: it shall not go out in the [‖]jubile.

31 But [k]the houses of the villages which have no wall round about them shall be counted as the fields of the country: they may be [§]redeemed, and they shall go out in the [‖]jubile.

32 Notwithstanding the cities of the [l]Lē′vītes, *and* the [k]houses of the cities of their possession, may the Lē′vītes [§]redeem at any time.

33 And if [3]a man purchase of the [l]Lē′vītes, then the [k]house that was sold, and the city of his possession, shall go out in *the year of* [‖]jubile: for the houses of the cities of the Lē′vītes *are* their possession among the children of Iṣ′ra-el.

34 But the [k]field of the suburbs[C] of their cities may not be sold; for it *is* their perpetual possession.

v.26–1532 BC See footnote, *Time,* Rev. 10:6.

17
x *Commandment, forbidding oppression, and enjoining the fear of God,* Deut. 8:2.
y *Fear of God,* Acts 9:31.

18
z *Commandment, enjoining obedience,* Deut. 8:2.
a *Obedience, enjoined,* Heb. 5:8.
b *Promises, to the obedient,* 2 Cor. 1:20.
c *Righteous, promises to,* Psa. 64:10.
d *Reward, a motive to obedience,* Matt. 5:12.

21
e *God, providence of,* Gen. 2:2.
f *Temporal Blessings, from God,* Psa. 103:2.

23
g *Land, sale and redemption of,* vs. 23–33; Ruth 4:3.

25
h *Poor, duty to,* vs. 25–28, 39–43; Prov. 21:13.

29
i *House, laws regarding sale of,* vs. 29–33; Esth. 8:1.

30
j *Property, alienated,* vs. 29–33; Lev. 27:15.

31
k *Property, inalienable,* Lev. 27:15.

32
l *Levites,* Deut. 10:8.

33
3 R. V. one of the Levites redeem

§ **REDEMPTION.** *Of persons or property,* Ex. 13:13; Lev. 25:25–34; 27:2–33; Ruth 4:3–10. *Redemption money paid to priests,* Num. 3:46–51. *Of firstborn,* Ex. 13:13; 34:20; Lev. 27:27; Num. 3:40–51; 18:15–17. *Of land,* Lev. 25:23–33; 27:19, 20; Jer. 32:7.

**Of our souls,** see footnote, REDEMPTION OF OUR SOULS, Eph. 1:7.

+ **YEAR,** Gen. 1:14. *Divided into months,* Ex. 12:2; Num. 10:10; 28:11.

*Redemption of houses sold, limited to one,* Lev. 25:29, 30. *Land to rest one, in seven,* Lev. 25:5. *Of release,* Deut. 15:9.

Age by: *Of Abraham,* Gen. 25:7; *of Jacob,* Gen. 47:9.

*A thousand, with the Lord as one day,* Psa. 90:4; 2 Pet. 3:8. *Satan to be bound a thousand,* Rev. 20:2–4, 7.

v.35–1532 BC
See footnote, *Time*, Rev. 10:6.

**35**
*m Alms, enjoined*, Matt. 6:2.
*n Lending, to the poor, enjoined*, vs. 35–37; Deut. 15:2.
*o Foreigners, kindness to the poor of, required*, Deut. 23:20.

**36**
*p Creditor*, Deut. 15:2.
*q Interest*, Ex. 22: 25.
*r Fear of God, enjoined*, Acts 9:31.

**37**
*s Money*, Jer. 32:9.

**38**
*t God, love of, exemplified*, Gen. 2:2.
*u Egypt*, Gen. 41:8.
*v Canaan*, Gen. 37:1.

**39**
*w Servant*, Jer. 2:14.

**41**
*x Emancipation*, Deut. 15:12.

**42**
*y Servant, figurative*, Jer. 2:14.
*z God, providence of*, Gen. 2:2.

**43**
*a Employer*, Deut. 24:14.
*b Master*, Col. 4:1.
*c Fear of God, enjoined*, Acts 9:31.

**44**
*d Servant*, Jer. 2:14.

35 ¶ [Q]And if thy brother be
waxen[G] [h]poor, and fallen in decay[G]
with thee; then thou shalt [m,n]re-
lieve him: *yea, though he be* a
[o]stranger, or a sojourner; that he
may live with thee.
36 Take [p]thou no [q]usury[G] of
[h,o]him, or increase[G]: but [r]fear thy
God; that thy brother may live
with thee.[Q]
37 Thou shalt not give [h,o]him
[s]money upon [q]usury,[G] nor [n]lend
him thy victuals[G] for increase.[G]
38 I *am* the LORD your God,
which [t]brought you forth out of
the land of [u]Ē′ġȳpt, to give you
the land of [v]Cā′năan, *and* to be
your God.
39 ¶ And if thy brother *that*
*dwelleth* by thee be waxen[G] [h]poor,
and be sold unto thee; thou shalt
not compel him to serve as a
[w]bondservant:[G]
40 *But* as an ⊙hired servant,
*and* as a sojourner, he shall be
with thee, *and* shall serve thee
unto the year of ‖jubile:
41 And [x]*then* shall he depart
from thee, *both* he and his children with him, and shall return
unto his own family, and unto
the possession of his fathers shall
he return.
42 For they *are* my [y]servants,
which I [z]brought forth out of the
land of Ē′ġȳpt: they shall not be
sold as bondmen.[G]
43 [a,b]Thou shalt not rule over
him with rigour;[G] but shalt [c]fear
thy God.[Q]
44 Both thy [d]bondmen, and thy
[d]bondmaids,[G] which thou shalt
have, *shall be* of the heathen[G] that
are round about you; of them
shall ye buy bondmen and
bondmaids.
45 Moreover of the children of
the [e]strangers that do sojourn
among you, of them shall ye buy,
and of their families that *are*
with you, which they begat in
your land: and they shall be your
possession.
46 And ye shall take them as an
inheritance for your children after you, to inherit *them for* a
possession; they shall be your
[d]bondmen for ever: but over
your brethren the children of Ĭş′-
ra-el, [a,b]ye shall not rule one
over another with rigour.
47 ¶ And if a sojourner or
[e]stranger wax[G] rich by thee, and
thy brother *that dwelleth* by him
wax poor, and [f]sell [g]himself unto
the stranger *or* sojourner by thee,
or to the stock of the stranger's[G]
family:
48 [T]After that [f,g]he is sold he
may be §redeemed again; one of
his brethren may redeem him:
49 Either his uncle, or his
uncle's son, may §redeem [f,g]him,
or *any* that is nigh[G] of kin unto
him of his family may redeem
him; or if he be able, he may
redeem himself.[T]
50 And [f,g]he shall reckon with
him that bought him from the
year that he was sold to him unto
the year of ‖jubile: and the price
of his sale shall be according unto the number of years, according to the time of an ⊙hired servant shall it be with him.
51 If *there be* yet many years *be-*
*hind*, according unto them he
shall give again the price of his
§redemption out of the [h]money
that he was bought for.
52 And if there remain but few
years unto the year of ‖jubile,
then [i]he shall count with him,
*and* according unto his years

v.45–1532 BC
See footnote, *Time*, Rev. 10:6.

**45**
*e Foreigners*, Deut. 23:20.

**47**
*f Servant, voluntary servitude of*, Jer. 2:14.
*g Debtor*, Luke 7:41.

**51**
*h Money*, Jer. 32:9.

**52**
*i Master*, Col. 4:1.

⊙ **HIRED SERVANT.** *Jacob*, Gen. 29:15; 30:26; *re-employed*, Gen. 30:27–34; 31:6, 7, 41. *Laborers for a vineyard*, Matt. 20:1–15. *The prodigal*, Luke 15:15–19.

*Kindness to*, Ruth 2:4. *Treatment of, more considerate than that accorded slaves*, Lev. 25:53.

**Rights of:** *To receive wages*, Matt. 10:10; Luke 10:7; Rom. 4:4; 1 Tim. 5:18; Jas. 5:4. *To daily payment of wages*, Lev. 19:13; Deut. 24:15. *To share in spontaneous products of land in Sabbatic year*, Lev. 25:6. *Wages of, paid in portion of flocks or products*, Gen. 30:31, 32; 2 Chr. 2:10; *or in money*, Matt. 20:2, 9, 10. *Oppression of, forbidden*, Deut. 24:14; Col. 4:1. *Oppressors of, punished*, Mal. 3:5.

*Mercenary*, Job 7:2. *Unfaithful*, John **10:12, 13.**

See footnotes: MASTER, Col. 4:1; SERVANT, Jer. 2:14; WAGES, Gen. 31:7.

shall he give him again the price of his [§]redemption.

53 *And* as a yearly [⊙]hired servant shall [g]he be with him: *and the [i]other* shall not rule with rigour over him in thy sight.[Q]

54 And if [g]he be not [§]redeemed in these *years*, then he shall go out in the year of [‖]jubile, *both* he, and his children with him.

55 For unto me the children of Is'ra-el *are*[j] servants; they *are* my servants whom I [k]brought forth out of the land of E'gypt: [l]I *am* the LORD your God.

## CHAPTER 26

*Idolatry forbidden. 2 Sabbath keeping. 3 Blessings to them that keep the commandments. 14 A curse to those that break them. 40 God promises to remember them that repent.*

[a]YE shall make you no [b]idols nor graven[C] image[C], neither rear you up a [1]standing image,[C] neither shall ye set up *any* [2]image[C] of stone in your land, to [c]bow down unto it: for I *am* the LORD your God.[C]

2 [d]Ye shall keep[C] my [e]sabbaths, and [f]reverence my [g,h]sanctuary: I *am* the LORD.

3 ¶ [i,j]If ye [k]walk in my statutes, and [l]keep my commandments, and [l]do them;

4 [m]Then [n,o]I will give [p]you [q,r]rain in due season, and the land shall yield her increase,[C] and the trees of the field shall yield their fruit.

5 [S]And [r]your [s]threshing shall reach unto the vintage, and the vintage shall reach unto the sowing time: and [o,p]ye shall eat your bread to the full, and dwell in your land safely.

6 And [n,o]I will give [r,t]peace in the [u]land, and [p]ye shall lie down, and none shall make *you* afraid: and I will rid[C] evil beasts out of the land, neither shall the sword go through your land.[S]

7 And [p,v]ye shall chase your enemies, and they shall fall before you by the sword.

8 And [v]five of you shall chase an hundred, and an hundred of you shall put ten thousand to flight: and your enemies shall fall before you by the sword.

9 [T]For [n,o]I will have respect unto you, and make you fruitful, and multiply you, and establish my [w]covenant with you.

10 And [o]ye shall eat old store,[C] and bring forth the old because of the new.

11 [S]And[Q] I will set my tabernacle among you: and my soul shall not abhor you.

12 And [x,y]I will [z]walk among you, and will be your God, and ye shall be my people.[S] [Q]

13 I *am* the LORD your God, which [a]brought you forth out of the land of E'gypt, that ye should not be their bondmen[C]; and I have broken the bands of your [b]yoke, and made you go upright.[T] [C]

14 ¶ But [c]if [d]ye will not hearken unto me, and will [e]not do all these commandments;

15 And [c]if [d]ye shall despise my statutes, or if your soul abhor my judgments,[C] so that ye will [e]not do all my commandments, *but* that ye break my [f]covenant:

16 I also will [g]do this unto [h]you; I will even appoint over you terror, [i,j]consumption,[C] and the [k]burning ague,[C] that shall consume the eyes, and cause sorrow of heart: and ye shall sow your seed in vain, for your enemies shall eat it.

17 And I will set my face against you, and [d,h]ye shall be [g,l]slain before your enemies: they that hate you shall reign over you; and ye shall flee when none pursueth you.

18 And if [d,h]ye will not yet for all this hearken[C] unto me, then I

v.52–1532 BC
ee footnote, *Time*, Rev. 10:6.

55
*Servant, figurative*, Jer. 2:14.
*God, providence of*, Gen. 2:2.
*God, sovereign*, Gen. 2:2.

1
*Commandment, forbidding idolatry*, Deut. 8:2.
*Idol*, 1 Kin. 15:12.
*Idolatry, forbidden*, 1 Sam. 15:23.
R. V. pillar,
R. V. figured stone
2
*Commandment, enjoining keeping the Sabbath holy*, Deut. 8:2.
*Sabbath*, Ex. 16:23.
*Reverence, for God's house*, Lev. 19:30.
*Sanctuary*, Lev. 4:6.
*Church, should be reverenced*, 1 Kin. 9:3.
3
*Blessings, contingent upon obedience*, vs. 3–43; Deut. 11:26.
*Contingencies, in divine government of man*, vs. 3–28; 1 Kin. 3:14.
*Faithfulness, rewards of*, Luke 16:10.
*Obedience*, vs. 3–13; Heb. 5:8.
4
m *Reward, a motive to obedience*, Matt. 5:12.
n *God, providence of*, Gen. 2:2.
o *Promises, to the obedient*, 2 Cor. 1:20.
p *Righteous, promises to*, Psa. 64:10.
q *Rain*, 2 Sam. 1:21.
r *Temporal Blessings, from God*, vs. 4–10; Psa. 103:2.
5
s *Harvest*, Ex. 34:21. 6 t *Social Peace, promised*, Jer. 29:7. u *Nation*, Isa. 2:4.

v.7–1532 BC
See footnote, *Time*, Rev. 10:6.

7
v *Victories, from God*, vs. 6–9; Deut. 28:7.

9
w *Covenant, of God with men*, Deut. 29:1.

12
x *God, presence of*, Gen. 2:2.
y 2 Cor. 6:16.
z *Fellowship, with God*, 1 Cor. 1.9.

13
a *God, providence of*, Gen. 2:2.
b *Yoke, figurative*, 1 Sam. 6:7.

14
c *Backsliding, admonitions against*, Hos. 11:7.
d *Nation, punishment of*, Isa. 2:4
e *Disobedience, to God*, vs. 14–46; Eph. 5:6.
15
f *Covenant*, Deut. 29:1.
16
g *Judgments, denounced against disobedience*, Ex 6:6.
h *Wicked, punishment of*, Psa. 73:3.
i *Consumption*, Deut. 28:22.
j *Disease, threatened as judgments*, Ex. 15:26.
k *Fever*, Deut. 28:22.
17
l *War, God uses as a judgment*, vs. 31–39; Judg. 3:2.

v.18–1532 BC
See footnote, *Time*, Rev. 10:6.

**18**

m *Chastisement, divine*, Job 33:19.
n *Seven*, Gen. 7:2.
o *Sin, repugnant to God*, Rom. 5:12.
3 R. V. chastise

**19**

p *Pride*, Prov. 16: 18.
q *Brass, figurative*, Job 28:2.

**20**

r *Famine, sent as a judgment*, 2 Kin. 8:1.

**21**

s *Obduracy*, Prov. 29:1.
t *Impenitence, judgments denounced against*, Rom. 2:5.
u *Plague, denounced as judgment*, Ex. 11:1.

**22**

v *Animals, sent as judgment*, Jer. 27:5.

**23**

w *Afflictions, impenitence in*, Psa. 34:19.

**25**

4 R. V. execute the vengeance of the

**26**

x *Oven*, Ex. 8:3.

will [3,m]punish[G] you [n]seven times
more for your [o]sins.
19 And I will [q]break the [p]pride
of [h]your power; and I will make
your heaven as iron, and your
earth as [q]brass:
20 And your strength shall be
spent in vain: for [h]your land
shall [g,r]not yield her increase,
neither shall the trees of the land
yield their fruits.
21 And if ye [e]walk contrary
unto me, and will [s,t]not hearken
unto me; I will bring [n]seven
times more [g,u]plagues upon you
according to your [o]sins.[Q]
22 I will also [g]send wild beasts
among [h]you, which shall rob you
of your children, and destroy
your cattle, and make you few in
number; and your *high* ways
shall be desolate.[S]
23 And if [d,h]ye will [s,t]not be reformed by me by [w]these things,
but will [e]walk contrary unto me;
24 Then will I also walk contrary unto you, and will [m]punish[G]
you yet [n]seven times for your
[o]sins.
25 And I will [g]bring a sword
upon you, that shall [4]avenge the
quarrel[G] of *my* [l]covenant: and
when ye are gathered together
within your cities, I will send the
[u]pestilence among you; and ye
shall be delivered unto the hand
of the enemy.
26 *And* when I have broken the
staff of your bread, ten women
shall bake your bread in one
[x]oven, and they shall deliver *you*
your bread again by weight: and
ye shall eat, and not be satisfied.

27 And if ye [s]will not for all
this hearken unto me, but walk
contrary unto me;
28 Then I will walk contrary
unto [h]you also in fury; and I,
even I, will [m]chastise you [n]seven
times for your [o]sins.
29 And ye shall [y]eat the flesh of
your sons, and the flesh of your
daughters shall ye eat.
30 And I will destroy your [z]high
places, and cut down your [5]images, and [a]cast your carcases upon the carcases of your [b]idols,
and my soul shall abhor you.
31 And I will [a]make your cities
waste,[G] and bring your sanctuaries unto desolation, and I will
not smell the savour[G] of your
sweet odours.
32 And I will bring the land into desolation: and your enemies
which dwell therein shall be
astonished at it.
33 And I will [c,d]scatter [e,f]you
among the heathen,[G] and will
draw out a [g]sword after you: and
your land shall be desolate, and
your cities waste.
34 Then shall the land enjoy
her [h,i]sabbaths, as long as it lieth
desolate, and [d,e]ye *be* in your
enemies' land; *even* then shall
the land rest, and enjoy her
sabbaths.
35 As long as it lieth desolate it
shall rest; because it did not rest
in your sabbaths, when ye dwelt
upon it.
36 And upon [j,k]them that are
left *alive* of you I will [a]send a
*faintness[G] into their hearts in the
lands of their enemies; and the

v.27–1532 BC
See footnote, *Time*, Rev. 10:6.

**29**

y *Cannibalism*, Lam. 2:20.

**30**

z *High Places*, 1 Kin. 3:2.
5 R.V. sun-images,
a *Judgments, denounced against disobedience*, Ex. 6:6.
b *Idol*, 1 Kin. 15: 12.

**33**

c *Dispersion*, Gen. 11:8.
d *Captivity, of Israelites, foretold*, Isa. 5:13.
e *Israel, dispersion of*, Ex. 4:22.
f *Nation, punishment of*, Isa. 2:4.
g *War, God uses as a judgment*, Judg. 3:2.

**34**

h *Sabbath, signifying a rest period*, Ex. 16:23.
i *Sabbatic Year, enforced observance of*, Lev. 25:2.

**36**

j *Children, involved in sin of parents*, vs. 39–45; Mark 10:14.
k *Sin, consequences of, entailed upon children*, Rom. 5: 12.

***COWARDICE.** *Described*, Josh. 7:5. *From God*, Josh. 23:10. *Inflicted as a judgment*, Lev. 26:36, 37; Deut. 32:30. *Disqualifies for military service*, Deut. 20:8; Judg. 7:3.

*Caused, by adversity*, Job 15:24; 18:11; *by wickedness*, Prov. 28:1.

*Cause of adversity*, Prov. 29:25.

*Rebuke for*, Isa. 51:12, 13.

**Instances of:** *Adam, in attempting to shift upon Eve the responsibility for his sin*, Gen. 3:12. *Abraham, in calling his wife his sister*, Gen. 12:11–19; 20:2–12. *Isaac, in calling his wife his sister*, Gen. 26:7–9. *Jacob, in fleeing from Laban*, Gen. 31:31. *Aaron, in yielding to the Israelites, when they demanded an idol*, Ex. 32:22–24. *The ten spies*, Num. 13: 28, 31–33. *Israelites, in fearing to attempt the conquest of Canaan*, Num. 14:1–5; Deut. 1:26–28; *in the battle with the people of Ai*, Josh. 7:5; *in fearing to meet Goliath*, 1 Sam. 17: 24; *in fearing to fight the Philistines*, 1 Sam. 13:6, 7. *Twenty thousand of Gideon's army*, Judg. 7:3. *Ephraimites*, Psa. 78:9. *Ephraimites and Manassehites*, Josh. 17:14–18. *Amoritish kings*, Josh. 10:16. *Canaanites*, Josh. 2:11; 5:1. *Samuel, fearing to obey God's command to anoint a king in Saul's stead*, 1 Sam. 16:2. *David, in fleeing from Absalom*, 2 Sam. 15:13–17. *Nicodemus, in coming to Jesus by night*, John 3: 1, 2. *Joseph of Arimathea secretly a disciple*, John 19:38. *Parents of the blind man, who was restored to sight*, John 9: 22. *Early converts among the rulers*, John 12:42, 43. *Disciples, in the storm at sea*, Matt. 8:26; Mark 4:38; Luke 8:25; *when Jesus was apprehended*, Matt. 26:56. *Peter, in denying the Lord*, Matt. 26:69–74, Mark 14:66–72; Luke 22:54–60; John 18:16, 17, 25, 27. *Pilate, in condemning Jesus*,

v.36–1532 BC
See footnote, *Time*, Rev. 10:6.

sound of a shaken leaf shall
chase them; and they shall flee,
as fleeing from a sword; and
they shall fall when none pursueth.
37 And [a]they shall fall one upon another, as it were before a
sword, when none pursueth: and
ye shall have *no power to stand
before your enemies.
38 And [a,j]ye shall perish among
the heathen,[C] and the land of your
enemies shall eat you up.
39 And [j,k]they that are left of
you shall pine away in their iniquity in your enemies' lands;
and also in the iniquities of their
fathers shall they pine away
with them.
40 If [l,m,n]they shall [o]confess
their [p]iniquity, and the iniquity
of their fathers, with their
trespass which they trespassed
against me, and that also they
have walked contrary unto
me;
41 And *that* I also have walked
contrary unto them, and have
[c]brought them into the land of
their enemies; if then their [q]un-
circumcised hearts be [r]humbled,
and they then accept of the †pun-
ishment of their iniquity:[Q]
42 Then [l,s]will I [t]remember my
[u]covenant with Jā'cob, and also
my covenant with Ī'ṣaac, and also my covenant with Ā'brā-hăm
will I remember; and I will remember the land.[Q]
43 The land also shall be left
of them, and shall enjoy her sabbaths, while she lieth desolate
without them: and they shall accept of the [j]punishment of their
iniquity: because, even because
they despised my [a]judgments,[C]
and because their soul abhorred
my statutes.
44 And yet for all that, when
they be in the land of their enemies, [v]I [s]will not cast them
away, neither will I abhor them:
to destroy them utterly, and to
break my [u]covenant with them:
for I *am* the LORD their God.[S]
45 But I will for their sakes [t]re-
member the [u]covenant of their
ancestors, whom I brought forth
out of the land of Ē'ġy̆pt in the
sight of the heathen,[C] that I might
be their God: I *am* the LORD.[S]
46 These *are* the [w]statutes and
judgments[G] and [x]laws, which the
LORD made between him and
the children of Ĭṣ'ra-el in mount
[y]Sī'nai by the hand of Mō'ṣeṣ.

**40**
*l* *Backsliders, promises to*, vs. 40–42; Jer. 3:22.
*m* *Nation, penitent, promises to*, vs. 40–42, Isa. 2:4.
*n* *Penitent, promises to*, vs. 40–42; Psa. 51:17.
*o* *Prayer, confession in*, Acts 6:4.
*p* *Sin, confession of*, Rom. 5:12.

**41**
*q* *Circumcision, figurative*, Gen. 17:10.
*r* *Repentance, condition of forgiveness*, Mark 1:4.

**42**
*s* *Promises, to penitents*, 2 Cor. 1:20.
*t* *God, faithfulness of*, Gen. 2:2.
*u* *Covenant, of God with men*, Deut. 29:1.

v.42–1532 BC
See footnote, *Time*, Rev. 10:6.

**44**
*v* *God, mercy of*, Gen. 2:2.

**46**
*w* *Word of God, inspiration of*, Psa. 119:9.
*x* *Law, of Moses, divine authority for*, Deut. 33:2.
*y* *Sinai*, Ex. 16:1.

## CHAPTER 27

*Of special vows. 3 The estimation of a person consecrated, 9 of a beast, 14 of a house, 16 and of a field. 19 Precepts respecting the redemption of consecrated things. 28 No devoted thing may be redeemed. 32 The tithe may not be changed.*

AND the LORD [a]spake unto
[b]Mō'ṣeṣ, saying,
2 Speak unto the children of

**1**
*a* *Revelation, relating to vows*, 2 Cor. 12:1.
*b* *Prophets, inspiration of*, Isa. 3:2.

*through fear of the people*, John 19:12–16. *Peter and other Christians, at Antioch*, Gal. 2:11–14. *Companions of Paul*, 2 Tim. 4:16. *False teachers*, Gal. 6:12.
See footnote, COURAGE, Deut. 31:7.

† **PUNISHMENT.** *Assumed for others*, Gen. 27:13; 1 Sam. 25:24; 2 Sam. 14:9; Matt. 27:25.
*By scourging*, Deut. 22:18; 25:2, 3; Prov. 17:10; 19:29; 20:30; Matt. 27:26; Mark 15:15; Luke 23:16; John 19:1; Acts 22:24; 2 Cor. 6:5; 11:23. *By imprisonment*, Gen. 39:20; 40; see footnote, PRISONERS, Psa. 79:11. *By confinement within limits*, 1 Kin. 2:26, 36–38.

**Death Penalty:** *For murder*, Gen. 9:5, 6; Lev. 24:17; Num. 35:16–21, 30–33; Deut. 17:6. *For adultery*, Lev. 20:10; Deut. 22:24. *For incest*, Lev. 20:11, 12, 14. *For bestiality*, Ex. 22:19; Lev. 20:15, 16. *For sodomy*, Lev. 18:22; 20:13. *For incontinence*, Deut. 22:21–24. *For rape of a betrothed virgin*, Deut. 22:25. *For kidnapping*, Ex. 21:16; Deut. 24:7. *Upon a priest's daughter who committed fornication*, Lev. 21:9. *For witchcraft*. Ex. 22:18. *For offering human sacrifice*, Lev. 20:2–5. *For striking or cursing father or mother*, Ex. 21:15, 17; Lev. 20:9; Matt. 15:4; Mark 7:10. *For disobedience to parents*, Deut. 21:18–21. *For blasphemy*, Lev. 24:11–14, 16, 23. *For Sabbath desecration*, Ex. 35:2; Num. 15:32–36. *For prophesying falsely, or propagating false doctrines*, Deut. 13:1–10. *For sacrificing to false gods*, Ex. 22:20. *For refusing to abide by the decision of court*, Deut. 17:12. *For treason*, 1 Kin. 2:25; Esth. 2:23. *For sedition*, Acts 5:36, 37.
*Shall not be remitted*, Num. 35:31.
*Not inflicted on testimony of less than two witnesses*, Num. 35:30; Deut. 17:6; 19:15.
MODES OF EXECUTION OF: *Burning*, Gen. 38:24; Lev. 20:14; 21:9; Jer. 29:22; 3:19–23. *Stoning*, Ex. 19:13; Lev. 20:2, 27; 24:14; Num. 15:33–36; Deut. 13:10; 17:5; 22:21, 24; Josh. 7:25; 1 Kin. 21:10, 13; Ezek. 16:40; Acts 7:57, 58. *Hanging*, Gen. 40:22; Deut. 21:22, 23; Josh. 8:29. *Beheading*, Matt. 14:10; Mark 6:16, 27, 28. *Crucifixion*, Matt. 27:35, 38; Mark 15:24, 27; Luke 23:33. *The sword*, Ex. 32:27, 28.
*Executed, by the witnesses*, Deut. 13:9; 17:7; Acts 7:58; *by the congregation*, Num. 15:35, 36; Deut. 13:9.
**In Divine Government:** *According to deeds*, Job 34:11; Prov. 12:14; 24:12; Isa. 59:18; Jer. 17:10; Ezek. 7:3, 27; 16:59; 39:24; Zech. 1:6; Matt. 5:22; 16:27; 25:14–30; Luke 12:47, 48; 2 Pet. 3:7.
*Entailed, on children*, Ex. 34:7; Jer. 31:29; Lam. 5:7
*Not entailed, on children*, Deut. 24:16; 2 Chr. 25:4.
*Delayed*, Psa. 50:21; Prov. 1:24–31; Eccl. 8:11–13; Hab. 1:2–4.
*Design of, to secure obedience*, Gen. 2:17; Ex. 20:3–5; Lev. 26:14–39; Deut. 13:10, 11; 17:13; 19:19, 20; 21:21, 22; Prov. 19:25; 21:11; 26:3.
*No escape from*, Gen. 3:7–19; 4:9–11; Job 11:20; 34:21.

v.2–1532 BC
See footnote, *Time*, Rev. 10:6.

2
c *Vows*, vs. 1–13; Num. 30:2.
d *Dedication*, Ezra 6:17.
1 R. V. accomplish a vow

3
e *Shekels*, Ex. 30: 13.

8
f *Priest, duties of*, Lev. 1:5.

9
g *Offerings*, Lev. 6:17.
2 R. V. oblation

Iṣ′ra-el, and say unto them, When a man shall [1]make a singular [c,d]vow, the persons *shall be* for the LORD by thy estimation.

3 And thy estimation shall be of the male from twenty years old even unto sixty years old, even thy estimation shall be fifty [e]shekels of silver, after the shekel of the sanctuary.

4 And if [c,d]it *be* a female, then thy estimation shall be thirty [e]shekels.

5 And if [c,d]*it be* from five years old even unto twenty years old, then thy estimation shall be of the male twenty [e]shekels, and for the female ten shekels.

6 And if [c,d]*it be* from a month old even unto five years old, then thy estimation shall be of the male five [e]shekels of silver, and for the female thy estimation *shall be* three shekels of silver.

7 And if [c,d]*it be* from sixty years old and above; if *it be* a male, then thy estimation shall be fifteen [e]shekels, and for the female ten shekels.

8 But if he be poorer than thy estimation, then he shall present himself before the priest, and the priest [f]shall value him; according to his ability that [c,d]vowed shall the priest value him.

9 And if *it be* a *beast, whereof men [c,d]bring an [2,g]offering unto the LORD, all that *any man* giveth of such unto the LORD shall be holy.

10 He shall not alter [c,d]it, nor change it, a good for a bad, or a bad for a good: and if he shall at all change beast for beast, then it and the exchange thereof shall be holy.

11 And if [c,d]*it be* any unclean *beast, of which they do not offer [3]a [g]sacrifice unto the LORD, then he shall present the beast before the priest:

12 And the priest [f]shall value it, whether it be good or bad: as thou valuest it, *who art* the priest, so shall it be.

13 But if he will at all [h]redeem it, then he shall add a fifth *part* thereof unto thy estimation.

14 ¶ And when a man shall [c,d]sanctify his *house *to be* holy unto the LORD, then the priest [f]shall estimate it, whether it be good or bad: as the priest shall estimate it, so shall it stand.

15 And if he that [c,d]sanctified it will [h]redeem his *house, then he shall add the fifth *part* of the [i]money of thy estimation unto it, and it shall be his.

16 And if a man shall [c,d]sanctify unto the LORD *some part* of a *,[j]field of his possession, then thy estimation shall be according to the seed thereof: [4]an [k]homer of [l]barley seed *shall be valued* at fifty [e]shekels of silver.

17 If he [c,d]sanctify his *,[j]field from the year of [m]jubile, according to thy estimation it shall stand.

18 But if he [c,d]sanctify his *,[j]field after the [m]jubile, then the priest [f]shall reckon unto him the [i]money according to the years that remain, even unto the year of the jubile, and it shall be abated from thy estimation.

19 And if he that [c,d]sanctified the *,[j]field will in any wise [h]redeem it, then he shall add the fifth *part* of the [i]money of thy estimation unto it, and it shall be assured to him.

v.11–1532 BC

11
3 R. V. an oblation

13
h *Redemption, of property*, Lev. 25:24.

15
i *Money*, Jer. 32:9.

16
j *Land, dedication and redemption of*, vs. 17–24; Ruth 4:3.
k *Measure, dry*, Deut. 25:15.
l *Barley*, Ex. 9:31.
4 R. V. the sowing of a homer

17
m *Jubilee, laws concerning*, Lev. 25: 10.

22; Prov. 1:24–31; 11:21; 16:5; 29:1; Isa. 10:3; Jer. 11:11; 15:1; 25:28, 29; Ezek. 7:19; Amos 2:14–16; 9:1–4; Zeph. 1: 18; Matt. 10:28; 23:33; Rom. 2:3; 1 Thess. 5:2, 3; Col. 3: 25, Heb. 2:3; 12:25, 26; Rev. 6:15–17.
*Eternal*, Isa. 34:8–10; Dan. 12:2, Matt. 3:12; 10:28; 18: 8; 25:41, 46; Mark 3:29; Luke 3:17, John 5:29, Heb. 6:2; 10:28–31; Rev. 14:10, 11; 19:3; 20:10.
See footnote, WICKED, *Punishment of*, Psa. 73:3.

* **PROPERTY. Personal:** *Rights in, sacred*, Ex. 20: 17; Deut. 5:21. *Laws concerning trespass of, and violence to*, Ex. 21:28–36; 22:9; Lev. 24:18, 21; Deut. 23:25. *Strayed, to be returned to owner*, Ex. 23:4; Deut. 22:1–3. *Hired*, Ex. 22:14, 15. *Loaned*, Ex. 22:10–15. *Sold for debt*, Prov. 22: 26, 27. *Rights of redemption of*, Jer. 32:7. *Dedicated to God, redemption of*, Lev. 27:9–13, 26–33. *In slaves*, Ex. 21:2, 4.
**In real estate,** Gen. 23:17, 18; 26:20. *Rights in*

v.20–1532 BC
See footnote, *Time*, Rev. 10:6.

20
n *Land, alienated by dedication*, Ruth 4.3.

21
o *Priest, emoluments of*, Lev. 1:5.

22
p *Land, transfer of, temporary*, vs. 22–24; Ruth 4:3.

26
q *Firstborn, of man and beast, reserved to himself by God*, Zech. 12:10.

20 And if he will not [h]redeem the [*, n]field, or if he have sold the field to another man, it shall not be redeemed any more.

21 But the [*, i]field, when it goeth out in the [m]jubile, shall be holy unto the LORD, as a field devoted; the [o]possession thereof shall be the priest's.

22 And if *a man* [c, d]sanctify unto the LORD a [*, p]field which he hath bought, which *is* not of the fields of his possession;

23 Then the priest [f]shall reckon unto him the worth of thy estimation[c], *even* unto the year of the [m]jubile: and he shall give thine estimation in that day, *as* a holy thing unto the LORD.

24 In the year of the [m]jubile the [*, p]field shall return unto him of whom it was bought, *even* to him to whom the possession of the land *did belong*.

25 And all thy estimations[c] shall be according to the [e]shekel[c] of the sanctuary: twenty [†]gerahs shall be the shekel.

26 ¶ Only the [q]firstling[c] of the beasts, which should be the LORD's firstling, no man shall [c, d]sanctify it; whether *it be* ox, or sheep: it *is* the LORD's.

27 And if [q]*it be* of an unclean [*]beast, then he shall [h]redeem *it*[c] according to thine estimation, and shall add a fifth *part* of it thereto: or if it be not redeemed, then it shall be sold according to thy estimation.

28 Notwithstanding no [d]devoted thing, that a man shall devote unto the LORD of all that he hath, *both* of man and beast, and of the field of his possession, shall be sold or [h]redeemed: every devoted thing *is* most holy unto the LORD.

29 None [d]devoted, which shall be devoted of men, shall be [h]redeemed; *but* shall surely be put to death.

30 And all the [r]tithe of the land, *whether* of the seed of the land, *or* of the fruit of the tree, *is* the LORD's: *it is* holy[c] unto the LORD.[Q]

31 And if a man will at all [h]redeem *ought*[c] of his [r]tithes, he shall add thereto the fifth *part* thereof.

32 And concerning the [r]tithe of the herd, or of the flock, *even* of whatsoever passeth under the rod, the tenth shall be holy unto the LORD.

33 He shall not search whether it be good or bad, neither shall he change it: and if he change it at all, then both it and the change thereof shall be holy; it shall not be [h]redeemed.

34 These *are* the commandments, which the LORD commanded [b]Mō'ṣeṣ for the children of Īṣ'ra-el in mount [s]Sī'nāi.

v.27–1532 BC
See footnote, *Time*, Rev. 10:6.

30
r *Tithes, Mosaic law concerning*, vs. 30–33; Num. 18:24.

34
s *Sinai*, Ex. 16:1.

*violated*, Gen. 21:25–32; 26:18–22. *Dedicated*, Lev. 27:16–25.
See footnote, LAND, Ruth 4:3.
*Dwellings, alienated*, Lev 25:29, 30; *alienated by absence*, 2 Kin. 8:1–6. *In villages, inalienable*, Lev. 25:31–33. *dedicated*, Lev. 27:14, 15.
*Confiscation of* (*Naboth's vineyard*), 1 Kin. 21:15, 16. *Entail of*. Num. 27:1–11; 36:1–9. *Landmarks of, not to be removed*, Deut. 19:14; 27:17.

† **GERAH.** A weight equal to thirteen and seventenths grains. *Also a coin, equivalent to about three cents American money, and one and a half pence in English money*. Ex. 30:13; Lev 27:25; Num. 3:47; 18:16, Ezek. 45:12.
See footnote, WEIGHTS, Lev. 19:35.

THE FOURTH BOOK OF MOSES,

CALLED

# NUMBERS

## CHAPTER 1

*God commands Moses to number the people. 5 The princes of the tribes. 17 The number of every tribe. 47 The Levites are not to be numbered, but are appointed for the service of the tabernacle.*

AND the LORD [a]spake unto [b]Mō′ṣeṣ in the wilderness of [c]Sī′nāi, in the [d]tabernacle of the congregation, on the first *day* of the second [e]month, in the second year after they were come out of the land of [f]Ē′ġȳpt, saying,

2 Take ye the [g]sum[G] of all the congregation of the children of [h]Ĭṣ′ra-el, after their families, by the house of their fathers, with the number of *their* names, every male by their polls[G];

3 From twenty years old and upward, all that are able to go forth to war in Ĭṣ′ra-el: thou and [i,j]Aâr′on shall number them by their [k]armies[G].

4 [l]And with you there shall be a man of every tribe; every one [m]head of the house of his fathers.

5 ¶ And these *are* the names of the men that shall stand with you: of *the* [n]*tribe of* Reu̇′ben; [o]Ė-lī′zur the son of [p]Shĕd′e-ur.

6 Of [q]Sĭm′e-on; [r]Shė-lū′mĭ-el the son of [s]Zū-rĭ-shăd′da-ī.

7 Of [t]Jū′dah; [u]Näh′shŏn the son of [v]Ăm-mĭn′a-dăb.

8 Of Ĭs′sa-char; [w]Nė-thăn′e-el the son of [x]Zū′ar.

9 Of [y]Zĕb′u-lŭn; [z]Ė-lī′ab the son of [a]Hē′lon.

10 Of the children of [b]Jō′ṣeph: of [c]Ē′phră-ĭm; [d]Ė-lĭsh′a-mȧ the son of [e]Ăm-mī′hŭd: of [f]Mȧ-năs′seh; [g]Gȧ-mā′lĭ-el the son of [h]Pė-däh′zur.

11 Of Bĕn′ja-mĭn; [i]Ăb′i-dăn the son of [j]Ġĭd-e-ō′nī.

12 Of [k]Dăn; [l]Ā-hĭ-ē′zĕr the son of [l]Ăm-mī-shăd′da-ī.

13 Of Ăsh′ĕr; [m]Pā′ġi-el the son of [n]Ŏc′ran.

14 Of [o]Găd; [p]Ė-lī′a-săph the son of [q]Deū′el.

15 Of Năph′ta-lī; [r]Ȧ-hī′rȧ the son of [s]Ē′nan.

16 [t]These *were* the renowned of the congregation, [u]princes of the tribes of their fathers, heads of thousands[G] in Ĭṣ′ra-el.

17 ¶ And [v]Mō′ṣeṣ and [w]Aâr′on took these men which are expressed by *their* names:

18 And they assembled all the congregation together on the first *day* of the second [x]month, and they declared their [y]pedigrees[G] after their families, by the house of their fathers, according to the number of the names, from twenty years old and upward, by their polls[G].

19 As the LORD commanded Mō′ṣeṣ, so he [z,a]numbered them in the wilderness of [b]Sī′nāi.

20 ¶ And the [c]children of Reu̇′ben, Ĭṣ′ra-el's eldest son, by their generations, after their families, by the house of their fathers, according to the number of the names, by their polls[G], every male from twenty years old and upward, [d]all that were able to go forth to [e]war;

21 [a]Those that were numbered of them, *even* of the [c]tribe of Reu̇′ben, *were* forty and six thousand and five hundred.

22 ¶ Of the children of [f]Sĭm′-e-on, by their generations, after their families, by the house of

---

v.1–1532 BC
See footnote, *Time*, Rev. 10:6.

1
a *Revelation, concerning the organization of Israel*, vs. 1–54; 2 Cor. 12:1.
b *Prophets, inspiration of*, Isa.3:2.
c *Sinai, wilderness of*, Ex. 16:1.
d *Tabernacle, the Lord reveals himself at*, Ex. 27:9.
e *Month, Zif (May)*, Ex. 12:2.
f *Egypt*, Gen. 41:8.

2
g *Census*, vs. 2–46; 2 Sam. 24:1.
h *Israel, numbered*, Ex. 4:22.

3
i *Aaron*, Ex. 6:20.
j *High Priest, duties of*, Lev. 21:10.
k *Armies, enumeration of*, Deut. 11:4.

4
l *Government, Mosaic*, Isa. 22:21.
m *Senate*, Num. 11:16.

5
n *Reubenites*, Josh. 22:1.
o *Elizur*, Num. 10:18.
p Num. 2:10; 7:30, 35; 10:18.

6
q *Simeon, tribe of*, Num. 2:12.
r Num. 2:12; 7:36, 41; 10:19.
s *Zurishaddai*, Num. 7:36.

7
t *Judah, tribe of*, Num. 10:14.
u *Nahshon*, Num. 7:12.
v *Amminadab*, Num. 2:3.

8
w *Nethaneel*, Num. 2:5.
x Num. 2:5; 7:18, 23; 10:15.

9
y *Zebulun, tribe of*, Gen. 49:13.
z Num. 2:7; 7:24, 29; 10:16.

---

a *Helon*, Num. 2:7.

10
b *Joseph*, Gen. 33:2.

c *Ephraim, tribe of*, Gen. 41:52. d Num. 2:18; 7:48, 53; 10:22; 1 Chr. 7:26. e *Ammihud*, Num. 2:18. f *Manasseh, tribe of*, Gen. 46:20. g *Gamaliel*, Num. 2:20. h *Pedahzur*, Num. 2:20.

v.1 –1532 BC
See footnote, *Time*, Rev. 10:6.

11
i Num. 2:22.
j *Gideoni*, Num. 10:24.

12
k *Dan, tribe of*, Gen. 30:6.
l Num. 2:25.

13
m *Pagiel*, Num. 2:27.
n Num. 2:27; 7:72, 77; 10:26.

14
o *Gad, tribe of*, Deut. 33:20.
p Num. 2:14; 7:42, 47; 10:20.
q Or, *Reuel*, Num. 2:14; 7:42, 47; 10:20.

15
r *Ahira*, Num. 2:29.
s Num. 2:29; 7:78, 83; 10:27.

16
t *Government, Mosaic*, Isa. 22:21.
u *Senate*, Num. 11:16.

17
v *Moses*, Ex. 2:10.
w *Aaron*, Ex. 6:20.

18
x *Month, Zif (May)*, Ex. 12:2.
y *Genealogy*, 1 Chr. 5.1.

19
z *Census*, 2 Sam. 24:1.

---

a *Israel, numbered at Sinai*, Ex. 4:22.
b *Sinai*, Ex. 16:1.

20
c *Reubenites, military enrollment of, at Sinai*, Josh. 22:1.
d *Armies, enumeration of*, Deut. 11:4.
e *War*, Judg. 3:2.

22
f *Simeon, tribe of*, Num. 2:12.

v.22–1532 BC
See footnote, *Time*, Rev. 10:6.

24
g *Gad, tribe of,* Deut. 33:20.

26
h *Judah, tribe of, numbered at Sinai,* Num. 10:14.

30
i *Zebulun, tribe of, enrollment of,* Gen. 49:13.

their fathers, those that were numbered of them, according to the number of the names, by their polls[c], every male from twenty years old and upward, [d]all that were able to go forth to [e]war;

23 [a]Those that were numbered of them, *even* of the tribe of [f]Sĭm′e-on, *were* fifty and nine thousand and three hundred.

24 ¶ Of the children of [g]Găd, by their generations, after their families, by the house of their fathers, according to the number of the names, from twenty years old and upward, [d]all that were able to go forth to [e]war;

25 [a]Those that were numbered of them, *even* of the tribe of [g]Găd, *were* forty and five thousand six hundred and fifty.

26 ¶ Of the children of [h]Jū′-dah, by their generations, after their families, by the house of their fathers, according to the number of the names, from twenty years old and upward, [d]all that were able to go forth to [e]war;

27 [a]Those that were numbered of them, *even* of the tribe of [h]Jū′-dah, *were* threescore and fourteen thousand and six hundred.

28 ¶ Of the children of *Ĭs′sa-char, by their generations, after their families, by the house of their fathers, according to the number of the names, from twenty years old and upward, [d]all that were able to go forth to [e]war;

29 [a]Those that were numbered of them, *even* of the tribe of Ĭs′-sa-char, *were* fifty and four thousand and four hundred.

30 ¶ Of the children of [i]Zĕb′u-lŭn, by their generations, after their families, by the house of their fathers, according to the number of the names, from twenty years old and upward, [d]all that were able to go forth to [e]war;

31 [a]Those that were numbered of them, *even* of the tribe of [i]Zĕb′u-lŭn, *were* fifty and seven thousand and four hundred.

32 ¶ Of the children of [j]Jō′-ṣeph, *namely,* of the children of [k]Ē′phră-ĭm, by their generations, after their families, by the house of their fathers, according to the number of the names, from twenty years old and upward, [d]all that were able to go forth to [e]war;

33 [a]Those that were numbered of them, *even* of the tribe of [k]Ē′phră-ĭm, *were* forty thousand and five hundred.

34 ¶ Of the children of [l]Mă-năs′seh, by their generations, after their families, by the house of their fathers, according to the number of the names, from twenty years old and upward, [d]all that were able to go forth to [e]war;

35 [a]Those that were numbered of them, *even* of the tribe of [l]Mă-năs′seh, *were* thirty and two thousand and two hundred.

36 ¶ Of the children of †Bĕn′ja-mĭn, by their generations, after their families, by the house of their fathers, according to the number of the names, from twenty years old and upward, [d]all that were able to go forth to war;

37 [a]Those that were numbered of them, *even* of the tribe of †Bĕn′ja-mĭn, *were* thirty and

v.30–1532 BC
See footnote, *Time* Rev. 10:6.

32
j *Joseph,* Gen. 33:2.
k *Ephraim, tribe of, numbered at Sinai,* Gen. 41:52.

34
l *Manasseh, tribe of, numbered at Sinai,* Gen. 46:20.

* **ISSACHAR. Tribe of:** *Military census of, taken, at Sinai,* Num. 1:28, 29; 2:6; *on the plains of Moab,* Num. 26; 25; *in the time of David,* 1 Chr. 7:1-5. *Moses' blessing upon,* Deut. 33:18, 19. *Place in march and camp,* Num. 2:3, 5; 10:14, 15. *Parts of Canaan allotted to,* Josh. 19:17-23 (with 17:10, 11). *Cities of, allotted to the sons of Gershom,* 1 Chr. 6:71-73.
*Joins Deborah and Barak in war against Sisera,* Judg. 5:15. *Insurgents from, join David,* 1 Chr. 12:32, 40. *Joins with the kingdom of Judah after the conquest of Samaria by the king of Assyria,* 2 Chr. 30:18 (with 2 Kin. 18:9-12).
*Facts relating to, that were common to all the tribes,* see footnote, ISRAEL, Ex. 4:22.

† **BENJAMIN. Tribe of:** *Census of, at Sinai,* Num. 1:37; *in the plain of Moab,* Num. 26:41. *Clans of,* Num. 26:38-40; 1 Chr. 7:6-12; 8. *Position of, in camp and march,*

B.C. 1490 ?
See footnote, *Time*,
Rev. 10:6.

five thousand and four hundred.
38 ¶ Of the children of [m]Dăn,
by their generations, after their
families, by the house of their
fathers, according to the number
of the names, from twenty years
old and upward, [d]all that were
able to go forth to [e]war;
39 [a]Those that were numbered
of them, *even* of the tribe of
[m]Dăn, *were* threescore and two
thousand and seven hundred.
40 ¶ Of the children of ‡Ăsh′ẽr,
by their generations, after their
families, by the house of their
fathers, according to the number
of the names, from twenty years
old and upward, [d]all that were
able to go forth to [e]war;
41 [a]Those that were numbered
of them, *even* of the tribe of
‡Ăsh′ẽr, *were* forty and one
thousand and five hundred.
42 ¶ Of the children of ‖Năph′-
ta-lī, throughout their generations, after their families, by the
house of their fathers, according
to the number of the names,
from twenty years old and upward, [d]all that were able to go
forth to [e]war;
43 [a]Those that were numbered
of them, *even* of the tribe of
‖Năph′ta-lī, *were* fifty and three
thousand and four hundred.
44 ¶ [a]These *are* those that were
numbered, which [n]Mō′ṣeṣ and
[o]Aâr′on numbered, and the princes of Ĭṣ′ra-el, *being* twelve men:

**39**
*m Dan, tribe of, census of, at Sinai*, Gen. 30:6.

**44**
*n Moses*, Ex. 2:10.
*o Aaron*, Ex. 6:20.

each one was for the house of
his fathers.
45 So were all those that were
numbered of the children of
[a]Ĭṣ′ra-el, by the house of their
fathers, from twenty years old
and upward, [d]all that were able
to go forth to [e]war in Ĭṣ′ra-el;
46 Even all they that were numbered were six hundred thousand
and three thousand and five hundred and fifty.
47 ¶ But the [p]Lē′vītes after the
tribe of their fathers were [q]not
numbered among them.
48 For the LORD had spoken
unto [r]Mō′ṣeṣ, saying,
49 Only thou shalt [q]not number
the tribe of [p]Lē′vī, neither take
the sum of them among the children of Ĭṣ′ra-el:
50 But thou shalt appoint the
[p]Lē′vītes over the [s]tabernacle of
[t]testimony, and over all the vessels thereof, and over all things
that *belong* to it: they shall bear
the tabernacle, and all the vessels thereof; and they shall minister unto it, and shall encamp
round about the tabernacle.
51 And when the [s]tabernacle
setteth forward, the Lē′vītes
shall take it down: and when the
tabernacle is to be pitched, the
Lē′vītes shall set it up: and the
[u]stranger that cometh nigh shall
be [v]put to [w]death.
52 And the children of Ĭṣ′ra-el
shall pitch their tents, every man
by his own camp, and every man

v.44–1532 BC
See footnote, *Time*,
Rev. 10:6

**47**
*p Levites, exempt from military duty*, Deut. 10:8.
*q Armies, those exempt from service in*, Deut. 11:4.

**48**
*r Prophets, inspiration of*, Isa. 3:2.

**50**
*s Tabernacle, of testimony*, Ex. 27:9.
*t Testimony, the commandments revealed to Moses*, Ex. 25:10.

**51**
*u Foreigners*, Deut 23:20.
*v Punishment, death penalty*, Lev. 26:41.
*w Death, penalty*, Num. 23:10.

Num. 2:18, 22. *Moses' benediction upon*, Deut. 33:12. *Allotment to, in the land of Canaan*, Josh. 18:11–28. *Prophecy of reallotment to*, Ezek. 48:23. *Did not exterminate the Jebusites*, Judg. 1:21. *Joins Deborah in the war against Sisera*, Judg. 5:14. *Territory of, invaded by the Ammonites*, Judg. 10:9. *Did not avenge the crime of the Gibeanites against the Levite's concubine; the war that followed*, Judg. 19: 20. *Saul, the first king of Israel, from*, 1 Sam. 9:1, 17; 10:20, 21. *Its rank in the time of Samuel*, 1 Sam. 9:21. *Jerusalem within the territory of*, Josh. 15:7; 18:28; Jer. 6:1. *A company of, joins David at Ziklag*, 1 Chr. 12:1, 2, 16. *Not enrolled by Joab when he took a census of the military forces of Israel*, 1 Chr. 6:21. *Loyal to Ish-bosheth, the son of Saul*, 2 Sam. 2:9, 15, 31; 1 Chr. 12:29. *Subsequently joins David*, 2 Sam. 3:19; 19:16, 17; 1 Chr. 12:29. *Loyal to Rehoboam*, 1 Kin. 12:21; 2 Chr. 11:1. *Military forces of, in the reign, of Asa*, 2 Chr. 14:8; *of Jehoshaphat*, 2 Chr. 17:17. *Skilled in archery and as slingers of stones*, Judg. 3:15; 20:16; 1 Chr. 8:40; 12:2. *Returns to Palestine from the exile in Babylon*, 1 Chr. 9:7–9; Ezra 1:5. *Paul, of the tribe of*, Rom. 11:1; Phil. 3:5. ***Saints of, seen in John's vision*, Rev. 7:8.**

‡ **ASHER. Tribe of:** *Census of*, Num. 1:40, 41; 26. 44–47; 1 Chr. 7:40; 12:36. *Position of, in camp and march*, Num. 2:25,27. *Prophecies concerning, by Moses*, Deut. 33:24, 25; *by John*, Rev. 7:6. *Allotment to, of land in Canaan*, Josh. 91:24–31. *Prophecy of allotment to, of land in Canaan*, Ezek. 48:2. *Cities of, allotted to the Gershomites*, 1 Chr. 6:71, 74, 75. *Upbraided by Deborah*, Judg. 5:17. *Summoned by Gideon*, Judg. 6:35; 7:23. *Joins Hezekiah*, 2 Chr. 30:11.

‖ **NAPHTALI. Tribe of:** *Census of*, Num. 1:42, 43; 26:48–50; 1 Chr. 7:13; 12:34. *Position assigned to, in camp and march*, Num. 2:25–31; 10:25–27. *Moses' benediction on*, Deut. 33:23. *Inheritance of*, Josh. 19:32–39; Judg. 1: 33. *Prophecy of inheritance of*, Ezek. 48:3. *Cities of, allotted to the Gershomites*, 1 Chr. 6:71, 76.

*Defeats Sisera*, Judg. 4:6, 10; 5:18. *Follows Gideon*, Judg. 6:35; 7:23. *Joins in triumphal celebration*, Psa. 68:27. *Military operations of*, 1 Chr. 12:34, 40. *Military operations against*, 1 Kin. 15:20; 2 Kin. 15:29; 2 Chr. 16:4.

***Prophecies concerning*, Isa. 9:1, 2; Rev. 7:6.**

v.52–1532 BC
See footnote. *Time*, Rev. 10:6.

53
x *Levites, place of, in camp and march*, Deut. 10:8.

54
y *Obedience, instances of*, Heb. 5:8.

1
a *Revelation, concerning the camp and order of march of the Israelites*, vs. 1–34; 2 Cor. 12:1.
b *Moses*, Ex. 2:10.
c *Prophets, inspiration of*, Isa. 3:2.
d *Aaron*, Ex. 6:20.

2
e *Israel, order of camp and march*, Ex. 4:22.
f *Standard*, Num. 1:52.
g *Armies, standards of*, Deut. 11:4.
h *Tabernacle*, Ex. 27:9.
1 R.V. over against the tent of meeting

3
i *Judah, tribe of*, Num. 10:14.
j *Armies, how officered*, vs. 3–31; Deut. 11:4.
k *Nahshon*, Num. 7:12.
l *Captain*, Num. 31:48.

5
m *Issachar, tribe of*, Num. 1:28.
n Num. 1:8; 7:18–23; 10:15.
o *Zuar*, Num. 1:8.

7
p *Zebulun, tribe of*, Gen. 49:13.
q *Eliab*, Num. 1:9.
r Num. 1:9; 7:24–29; 10:16.

by his own [§]standard, throughout their hosts.
53 But the [x]Lē′vītes shall pitch[C]
round about the [s]tabernacle of
[t]testimony, that there be no
wrath upon the congregation of
the children of Is̱′ra-el: and the
Lē′vītes shall keep the charge[C] of
the tabernacle of testimony.
54 And the children of Ĭs̱′ra-el
[y]did according to all that the
LORD commanded Mō′s̱es̱, so
did they.

## CHAPTER 2

*The order of the tribes in their tents.*

AND the LORD [a]spake unto
[b,c]Mō′s̱es̱ and unto [d]Aâr′-
on, saying,
2 Every man of the children of
[e]Is̱′ra-el shall pitch[C] by his own
[f,g]standard, with the ensign[C] of
their father's house: [1]far off
about[C] the [h]tabernacle of the congregation shall they pitch[C].
3 ¶ And [e]on the east side toward the rising of the sun shall
they of the [f,g]standard of the
camp of [i]Jū′dah pitch[C] throughout their [j]armies[C]: and [k]Näh′-
shŏn the son of *Ăm-mĭn′a-dăb
*shall be* [l]captain of the children
of Jū′dah.
4 And [j]his host, and those that
were numbered of them, *were*
threescore and fourteen thousand and six hundred.
5 And [e]those that do pitch[C] next
unto him *shall be* the tribe of
[m]Ĭs′sa-char: and [n]Nē-thăn′e-el
the son of [o]Zū′ar *shall be* [j,l]cap-
tain of the children of Ĭs′sa-char.
6 And [j]his host, and those that
were numbered thereof, *were*
fifty and four thousand and four
hundred.
7 [e]*Then* the tribe of [p]Zĕb′u-lŭn:
and [q]Ē-lī′ab the son of [r]Hē′lon
*shall be* [j,l]captain of the children
of Zĕb′u-lŭn.
8 And his [j]host, and those that
were numbered thereof, *were*
fifty and seven thousand and
four hundred.
9 All that were numbered in the
camp of [i]Jū′dah *were* an hundred
thousand and fourscore thousand and six thousand and four
hundred, throughout their [j]ar-
mies. [e]These shall first set forth.
10 ¶ [e]On the south side *shall be*
the [f,g]standard of the camp of
[s]Reu̱′ben according to their [j]ar-
mies: and the [l]captain of the
children of Reu̱′ben *shall be*
[t]Ē-lī′zur the son of [u]Shĕd′e-ur.
11 And his [j]host, and those that
were numbered thereof, *were*
forty and six thousand and five
hundred.
12 And [e]those which pitch by
him *shall be* the tribe of †Sĭm′e-on:
and the [j,l]captain of the children
of Sĭm′e-on *shall be* [v]Shē-lū′mĭ-el
the son of [w]Zū-rĭ-shăd′da-ī.
13 And [j]his host, and those that
were numbered of them, *were*
fifty and nine thousand and three
hundred.
14 [e]Then the tribe of [x]Găd:
and the [j,l]captain of the sons of
Găd *shall be* [y]Ē-lī′a-săph the son
of [z]Reu̱′el.
15 And [a]his host, and those that
were numbered of them, *were*
forty and five thousand and six
hundred and fifty.
16 All that were numbered in
the camp of [b]Reu̱′ben *were* an
hundred thousand and fifty and
one thousand and four hundred
and fifty, throughout their [a]ar-
mies. And [c]they shall set forth
in the second rank.
17 ¶ [c]Then the [d]tabernacle of
the congregation shall set[C] for-

v.7–1532 BC
See footnote, *Time*, Rev. 10:6.

10
s *Reubenites*, Josh. 22:1.
t *Elizur*, Num. 10:18.
u *Shedeur*, Num. 1:5.

12
v *Shelumiel*, Num. 1:6.
w *Zurishaddai*, Num. 7:36.

14
x *Gad, tribe of*, Deut. 33:20.
y *Eliasaph*, Num. 1:14.
z Or, *Deuel*, Num. 1:14.

15
a *Armies, how officered*, Deut. 11:4.

16
b *Reubenites*, Josh 22:1.
c *Israel, order of camp and march* Ex. 4:22.

17
d *Tabernacle*, Ex. 27:9.

§ **STANDARD**, Song 6:4. *Used, to designate the different tribes of Israel*, Num. 1:52; 2:2; *in war*, Jer. 4:19, 21; *to mark the way to defensed cities*, Jer. 4:6; *to call attention to news*, Jer. 50:2.
**Figurative**, Psa. 20:5; 60:4; 74:4; Song 2:4; Isa. 5:26; 11:10, 12; 13:2; 18:3; 30:17; 31:9; Jer. 4:21; 51:12.

* **AMMINADAB** (*kindred of the prince*). *Father-in-law of Aaron*, Ex. 6:23. *Father of Nahshon*, Num. 1:7; 2:3; 7:12, 17; 10:14. *Lineage of*, Ruth 4:18–20; 1 Chr. 2:10; Matt. 1:4; Luke 3:33.
† **SIMEON**. **Tribe of**: *Military enrollment of, at Sinai*, Num. 1:22, 23; 2:12; *in the plains of Moab*, Num. 26:

ward with the camp of the [e]Lē′-
vītes in the midst of the camp: as
they encamp, so shall they set
forward, every man in his place
by their [f,g]standards.
18 ¶ [c]On the west side *shall be*
the [f,g]standard of the camp of
[h]Ē′phră-ĭm according to their
[2]armies: and the [i,j]captain of
the sons of Ē′phră-ĭm *shall be*
[k]Ĕ-lĭsh′-a-mȧ the son of [l]Ăm-
mī′hŭd.
19 And [i]his host, and those that
were numbered of them, *were*
forty thousand and five hundred.
20 And [c]by him *shall be* the
tribe of [m]Mȧ-năs′seh: and the
[i,j]captain of the children of Mȧ-
năs′seh *shall be* [n]Gȧ-mā′lĭ-el the
son of [o]Pĕ-dăh′zur.
21 And [i]his host, and those that
were numbered of them, *were*
thirty and two thousand and two
hundred.
22 [c]Then the tribe of [p]Bĕn′ja-
mĭn: and the [i,j]captain of the
sons of Bĕn′ja-mĭn *shall be* [q]Ăb′-
i-dăn the son of [r]Gĭd-e-ō′nī.
23 And [i]his host, and those that
were numbered of them, *were*
thirty and five thousand and
four hundred.
24 All that were numbered of
the camp of [h]Ē′phră-ĭm *were* an
hundred thousand and eight thousand and an hundred, throughout their armies. And [c]they shall
go forward in the third rank.
25 ¶ [c]The [f,g]standard of the
camp of [s]Dăn *shall be* on the
north side by their armies: and
the captain of the children of
Dăn *shall be* [t]Ā-hĭ-ē′zēr the son
of [u]Ăm-mĭ-shăd′da-ī.
26 And [i]his host, and those that
were numbered of them, *were*
threescore and two thousand
and seven hundred.
27 And [c]those that encamp by
him *shall be* the tribe of [v]Ăsh′ēr:
and the captain of the children
of Ăsh′ēr *shall be* [w]Pā′gĭ-el the
son of [x]Ŏc′ran.
28 And [i]his host, and those that
were numbered of them, *were*
forty and one thousand and five
hundred.
29 ¶ [c]Then the tribe of [y]Năph′-
ta-lī: and the [i,j]captain of the
children of Năph′ta-lī *shall be*
[z]Ā-hī′rȧ the son of [a]Ē′nan.
30 And [i]his host, and those that
were numbered of them, *were*
fifty and three thousand and
four hundred.
31 All they that were [b]num-
bered in the camp of [c]Dăn *were*
an hundred thousand and fifty
and seven thousand and six hundred. [d]They shall go hindmost
with their standards.
32 ¶ These *are* those which
were numbered of the children
of Ĭș′ra-el by the house of their
fathers: all those that were numbered of the camps throughout
their hosts *were* six hundred
thousand and three thousand
and five hundred and fifty.
33 But the [e]Lē′vītes were [f]not
numbered among the children of
Ĭș′ra-el; as the LORD commanded [g]Mō′șeș.
34 And the children of Ĭș′ra-el
[h]did according to all that the
LORD commanded [g]Mō′șeș: so
[d]they pitched by their [i,j]stand-
ards, and so they set forward,
every one after their families, according to the house of their
fathers.

## CHAPTER 3

*The sons of Aaron. 5 The Levites are given to the priests for the service of the tabernacle, 11 instead of the firstborn. 14 The Levites are numbered by their families. 21 The families, number, and charge of the Gershonites, 27 of the Kohathites, 33 and of the Merarites. 38 The place and charge of Moses and Aaron. 40 The Levites are taken instead of the firstborn. 46 The overplus of the firstborn are redeemed.*

THESE also *are* the generations of [a]Aâr′on and [b]Mōșeș

v.17–1532 BC See footnote, *Time*, Rev. 10:6.

e *Levites*, Deut. 10:8.
f *Standard*, Num. 1:52.
g *Armies, standard of*, Deut. 11:4.

18

h *Ephraim, tribe of*, Gen. 41:52.
i *Armies, how officered*, Deut. 11:4.
j *Captain*, Num. 31:48.
k *Elishama*, Num. 1:10.
l Num. 1:10; 7:48, 53; 10:22.
2 R. V. hosts:

20

m *Manasseh, tribe of*, Gen. 46:20.
n Num. 1:10; 7:54, 59; 10:23.
o Num. 1:10; 7:54, 59; 10:23.

22

p *Benjamin, tribe of*, Num. 1:37.
q Num. 1:11; 7: 60–65; 10:24.
r *Gideoni*, Num. 10:24.

25

s *Dan, tribe of*, Gen. 30:6.
t Num. 1:12; 7:66–71; 10:25.
u Num. 1:12; 7: 66–71; 10:25.

27

v *Asher, tribe of*, Num. 1:40.

v.27–1532 BC See footnote, *Time*, Rev. 10:6.

w Num. 1:13; 7: 72–77; 10:26.
x *Ocran*, Num. 1:13.

29

y *Naphtali, tribe of*, Num. 1:42.
z Num. 1:15; 7: 78–83; 10:27.
a Num. 1:15.

31

b *Israel, numbered*, Ex. 4:22.
c *Dan, tribe of*, Gen. 30:6.
d *Israel, line of camp and march*, Ex. 4:22.

33

e *Levites, not enrolled*, Deut. 10:8.
f *Armies, those exempt from service in*, Deut. 11:4.
g *Moses*, Ex. 2:10.

34

h *Obedience, instances of*, Heb. 5:8.
i *Standards*, Num. 1:52.
j *Armies, standards of*, Deut. 11:4.

B.C. 1491? See footnote, *Time*, Rev. 10:6.

1

a *Aaron, descendants of*, Ex. 6:20.
b *Moses*, Ex. 2:10.

14. *Place of, in camp and march*, Num. 2:10–12. *Inheritance allotted to*, Josh. 19:1–9; 1 Chr. 4:24–43. *Stood on Mount Gerizim to bless at the time of the rehearsal of the law*, Deut. 27:12. *Joined with the people of Judah and Benjamin in the renewal of the passover*, 2 Chr. 15:9 (with vs. 1–15). *Idolatry of*, 2 Chr. 34:6 (with vs. 1–7).

v.1–1532 BC
ee footnote, *Time*, Rev. 10:6.

*Sinai*, Ex. 16:1.

2
*Nadab*, Ex. 24:1.
*Abihu*, Ex. 6:23.
*Ithamar*, Ex. 38:21.

3
*Priest, consecration of*, Lev. 1:5.
*Anointing*, Lev. 8:12.

B.C. 1490?
ee footnote, *Time*, Rev. 10:6.

4
*Sacrilege, instances of*, Lev. 19:8.

5
*Revelation, concerning the Levites*, vs. 5–50; 2 Cor. 12:1.
*Prophets, inspiration of*, Isa. 3:2.

6
*Levites, duties of*, Deut. 10:8.
*Minister, call of*, Rom. 15:16.

7
*Tabernacle*, Ex. 27:9.

8
*Israel*, Ex. 4:22.
R. V. furniture

10
*Foreigner*, Deut. 23:20.
*Priest, usurpations of office of*, Lev. 1:5.

in the day *that* the LORD spake
with Mō′ṣeṣ in mount [c]Sī′nāi.
2 And these *are* the names of
the sons of Aâr′on; [d]Nā′dăb the
firstborn, and [e]Ă-bī′hū, *Ē-le-ā′-
zar, and [f]Ĭth′a-mär.
3 These *are* the names of the
sons of [a]Aâr′on, the [g]priests
which were [h]anointed, whom he
consecrated to minister in the
priest's office.
4 And [d]Nā′dăb and [e]Ă-bī′hū
died before the LORD, when
they [i]offered strange fire before
the LORD, in the wilderness of
[c]Sī′nāi, and they had no children: and *Ē-le-ā′zar and [f]Ĭth′-
a-mär ministered in the priest's
office in the sight of Aâr′on
their father.
5 ¶ And the LORD[j,k]spake unto
[b]Mō′ṣeṣ, saying,
6 Bring the [l,m]tribe of Lē′vī
near, and present them before
Aâr′on the priest, that they may
minister unto him.
7 And [l]they shall keep his
charge, and the charge of the
whole congregation before the
[n]tabernacle of the congregation, to do the service of the
tabernacle.
8 And [l]they shall keep all the
[1]instruments of the tabernacle of
the congregation, and the charge
of the children of [o]Ĭṣ′ra-el, to do
the service of the tabernacle.
9 And thou shalt give the
[l]Lē′vītes unto [a]Aâr′on and to
his sons: they *are* wholly given
unto him out of the children of
[o]Ĭṣ′ra-el.
10 And thou shalt appoint
[a]Aâr′on and his sons, and they
shall wait on their priest's office:
and the [p,q]stranger that cometh
nigh shall be put to death.

11 ¶ And the LORD [j]spake unto [k]Mō′ṣeṣ, saying,
12 And I, behold, I have taken
the [m,r]Lē′vītes from among the
children of [o]Ĭṣ′ra-el [s]instead of
all the [t]firstborn that openeth the
[2]matrix among the children of
Ĭṣ′ra-el: therefore the Lē′vītes
shall be mine:
13 Because all the [u]firstborn
*are* mine; *for* on the day that I
smote all the firstborn in the
land of [v]Ē′ġypt I hallowed unto
me all the firstborn in [o]Ĭṣ′ra-el,
both man and beast: mine shall
they be: I *am* the LORD.
14 ¶ And the LORD [j]spake unto
[k]Mō′ṣeṣ in the wilderness of
[c]Sī′nāi, saying,
15 [w]Number the [x]children of
Lē′vī after the house of their
fathers, by their families: every
male from a month old and upward shalt thou number them.
16 And Mō′ṣeṣ [w]numbered
them according to the word of
the LORD, as he was com-
manded.
17 And these were the [x]sons of
Lē′vī by their names; [y]Ġēr′-
shŏn, and [z]Kō′hăth, and [a]Mē-
rā′rī.
18 And these *are* the names of
the [b]sons of Ġēr′shŏn by their
families; [c]Lĭb′nī, and [d]Shĭm′e-ī.
19 And the sons of Kō′hăth by
their families; [e]Ăm′răm, and
[f]Ĭz′e-här, †Hē′bron, and ‡Ŭz′-
zĭ-el.
20 And the [g]sons of Mē-rā′rī by
their families; [h]Mäh′lī, and
[i]Mū′shī. These *are* the families
of the [j]Lē′vītes according to the
house of their fathers.
21 ¶ Of Ġēr′shŏn *was* the family of the [c]Lĭb′nītes, and the
family of the Shĭm′ītes: these *are*

v.11–1532 BC
See footnote, *Time*, Rev. 10:6.

12
r *Levites, substituted for the firstborn*, Deut. 10:8.
s *Substitution, the Levites for the firstborn*, Lev. 1:4.
t *Firstborn, Levites taken instead of*, Zech. 12:10.
2 R. V. womb.

13
u *Firstborn, reserved to himself, by God*, Zech. 12:10.
v *Egypt*, Gen. 41:8.

15
w *Census*, vs. 14–43; 2 Sam. 24:1
x *Levites, enrollment of*, vs. 14–39; Deut. 10:8.

17
y *Gershon*, vs. 17–26; Gen. 46:11.
z *Kohath*, Num. 26:58.

a *Merari*, Gen. 46:11.

18
b *Gershonites*, Num. 4:27.
c *Libni*, Ex. 6:17.
d *Shimei*, Ex. 6:17.

19
e *Amram, head of one of the branches of Levites*, v. 27; Ex. 6:18.
f *Izhar*, 1 Chr. 6:2.

20
g *Merarites*, Num. 26:57.
h *Mahli*, Ex. 6:19.
i *Mushi*, Ex. 6:19.
j *Levites, enrollment of*, Deut. 10:8.

* **ELEAZAR** (*whom God hath helped*). *Son of Aaron*, x. 6:23; 28:1. *Married a daughter of Putiel, who bore him* *hinehas*, Ex. 6:25. *After the death of Nadab and Abihu* *made chief of the tribe of Levi*, Num. 3:32. *Duties of*, um. 4:16. *Succeeds Aaron as high priest*, Num. 20:26, 28; Deut. 10:6. *ssists Moses in the census*, Num. 26:63. *With Joshua*, *ivides Palestine*, Num. 34:17; Josh. 14:1; 19:51. *Death nd burial of*, Josh. 24:33. *Descendants of*, 1 Chr. 24:1–19.

† **HEBRON.** *Son of Kohath*, Ex. 6:18; Num. 3:19; 1 Chr. 6:2, 18; 23:12, 19; 24:23.

‡ **UZZIEL**, a Levite. *One of the sons of Kohath*, Ex. 6:18; Num. 3:19. *Names of his sons*, Ex. 6:22; 1 Chr. 6:2; 23:12. *Elizaphan, chief of his house*, Num. 3:30. *His sons carried out Nadab and Abihu*, Lev. 10:4. *His descendants, appointed by David to carry the ark, and minister before the Lord*, 1 Chr. 15:10, *apportioned for the temple service*, 1 Chr. 23:20; 24:24.

v.21–1532 BC
See footnote, *Time*, Rev. 10:6.

22
*k* *Census*, 2 Sam. 24:1.

23
*l* *Gershonites, duties of*, vs. 23–26; Num. 4:27.
*m* *Tabernacle*, Ex. 27:9.

24
*n* *Eliasaph*, Num. 1:14.

26
*o* *Court, of tabernacle*, Ex. 38:9.

30
*p* Or, *Elzaphan*, Lev. 10:4.

the families of the [b]Gĕr′shon-
ītes.

22 Those that were [j,k]num-
bered of them, according to the
number of all males, from a
month old and upward, *even*
those that were numbered of
them *were* seven thousand and
five hundred.

23 The families of the [l]Gĕr′-
shon-ītes shall pitch[G] behind the
[m]tabernacle westward.

24 And the chief of the house of
the father of the [l]Gĕr′shon-ītes
*shall be* [n]Ē-lī′a-săph the son of
Lā′el.

25 And the charge of the [l]sons
of Gĕr′shŏn in the [m]tabernacle
of the congregation *shall be* the
tabernacle, and the tent, the covering thereof, and the hanging
for the door of the tabernacle of
the congregation,

26 And the hangings of the
[o]court, and the curtain for the
door of the court, which *is* by the
[m]tabernacle, and by the altar
round about, and the cords of it
for all the service thereof.

27 ¶ And of Kō′hăth *was* the
family of the [e]Ăm′răm-ītes, and
the family of the [f]Ĭz′e-har-ītes,
and the family of the ‖Hē′bron-
ītes, and the family of the Ŭz′-
zĭ-el-ītes: these *are* the families
of the §Kō′hath-ītes.

28 In the [j,k]number of all the
males, from a month old and upward *were* eight thousand and
six hundred, keeping the charge[G]
of the sanctuary.

29 The families of the §sons of
Kō′hăth shall pitch[G] on the side
of the [m]tabernacle southward.

30 And the chief of the house
of the father of the families of
the Kō′hath-ītes *shall be* [p]Ē-lĭz′-
a-phăn the son of ‡Ŭz′zĭ-el.

31 And §their charge[G] *shall be*
the [q]ark, and the [r]table, and the
[s]candlestick,[G] and the [t]altars, and
the vessels of the [u]sanctuary
wherewith they minister, and the
hanging, and all the service
thereof.

32 And *,[v]Ē-le-ā′zar the son of
[w]Aâr′on the priest *shall be* chief[G]
over the chief of the Lē′vītes,
*and have* the oversight of them
that keep the charge of the
[u]sanctuary.

33 ¶ Of [a]Mė-rā′rī *was* the family of the [h]Măh′lītes, and the
family of the [i]Mū′shītes: these
*are* the [g]families of Mė-rā′rī.

34 And those that were [j,k]num-
bered of them, according to the
number of all the males, from a
month old and upward, *were* six
thousand and two hundred.

35 And the chief[G] of the house of
the father of the [g]families of Mė-
rā′rī *was* Zū′rĭ-el the son of Ăb-i-
hā′il: *these* shall pitch[G] on the
side of the [m]tabernacle northward.

36 And *under* the custody and
charge[G] of the [x]sons of Mė-rā′rī
*shall be* the boards of the [m]taber-
nacle, and the bars thereof, and
the [y]pillars thereof, and the
sockets thereof, and all the
[3]vessels thereof, and all that
serveth thereto,

37 And the pillars of the [o]court
round about, and their sockets,
and their pins, and their cords.

38 ¶ But those that encamp before the [m]tabernacle toward the
east, *even* before the tabernacle
of the congregation eastward,
*shall be* [z]Mō′ṣeṣ, and [v,w]Aâr′on
and his sons, keeping the charge
of the [u]sanctuary for the charge
of the children of Ĭṣ′ra-el; and
the [a]stranger that cometh nigh[G]
shall be put to [b]death.

39 All that were [c]numbered

v.31–1532 BC
See footnote, *Time*, Rev. 10:6.

31
*q* *Ark, carried by Kohathites*, Ex. 25:10.
*r* *Shewbread, table of*, Ex. 35:13.
*s* *Candlestick*, Ex. 25:31.
*t* *Altar, carried by Kohathites*, Ex. 30:1.
*u* *Sanctuary*, Lev. 4:6.

32
*v* *High Priest, duties of*, Lev. 21:10.
*w* *Aaron*, Ex. 6:20.

36
*x* *Merarites, duties of*, v. 37; Num. 26:57.
*y* *Pillar, of tabernacle*, Gen. 28:18.
3 R. V. instruments

38
*z* *Moses*, Ex. 2:10.

*a* *Foreigner*, Deut. 23:20.
*b* *Death, penalty*, Num. 23:10.

39
*c* *Census*, 2 Sam. 24:1.

‖ **HEBRONITES.** *A division of the Levites*, Num. 3:27; 26:58. *Duties of*, 1 Chr. 26:30–32.

§ **KOHATHITES.** *A division of the Levites*, Num. 3:19, 27; 4:34; 26:57. *In four families, or subdivisions*, Num. 3:27. *Duties of*, Num. 3:29–31; 4:18–20, 37; 10:21; 1 Chr. 6:33; 9:32; 2 Chr. 20:19; 29:11, 12–15; 34:12. *Cities of*, Josh. 21:4, 10, 11; 1 Chr. 6:54, 55, 66. See footnote, LEVITES, Deut. 10:8.

v.39–1532 BC See footnote, *Time*, Rev. 10:6.

d *Levites, enrollment of*, Deut. 10:8.
e *Moses*, Ex. 2:10.
f *Aaron*, Ex. 6:20.

of the [d]Lē′vītes, which [e]Mō′ṣeṣ
and [f]Aâr′on numbered at the
commandment of the LORD,
throughout their families, all the
males from a month old and
upward, *were* twenty and two
thousand.
40 ¶ And the LORD [g]said unto
[e]Mō′ṣeṣ, [c]Number all the [h]first-
born of the males of the children
of Ĭṣ′ra-el from a month old and
upward, and take the number of
their names.
41 And thou shalt take the [i]Lē′-
vītes for me ([j]I *am* the LORD)
[k]instead of all the [h]firstborn
among the children of Ĭṣ′ra-el;
and the cattle of the Lē′vītes instead of all the firstlings among
the cattle of the children of
Ĭṣ′ra-el.
42 And [e]Mō′ṣeṣ [c]numbered, as
the LORD commanded him, all
the [h]firstborn among the children
of Ĭṣ′ra-el.
43 And all the [h]firstborn males
by the number of names, from a
month old and upward, of those
that were numbered of them,
were twenty and two thousand
two hundred and threescore and
thirteen.
44 ¶ And the LORD [g]spake unto [e]Mō′ṣeṣ, saying,
45 Take the [i]Lē′vītes [k]instead
of all the [h]firstborn among the
children of Ĭṣ′ra-el, and the cattle of the Lē′vītes instead of
their cattle; and the Lē′vītes
shall be mine: [j]I *am* the LORD.
46 And for those that are to be
[l]redeemed of the two hundred
and threescore and thirteen of
the [h]firstborn of the children of
Ĭṣ′ra-el, which are more than the
Lē′vītes;
47 Thou shalt even take five
[m]shekels[c] apiece by the poll, after
the shekel of the sanctuary shalt
thou take *them*: (the shekel *is*
twenty [n]gerahs:)
48 And thou shalt give the

40
g *Prophets, inspiration of*, Isa. 3:2.
h *Firstborn, redemption of*, vs. 40–51; Zech. 12:10.

41
i *Levites, substituted for firstborn*, Deut. 10:8.
j *God, sovereign*, Gen. 2:2.
k *Substitution, the Levites for the firstborn*, Lev. 1:4.

46
l *Redemption*, Lev. 25:24.

47
m *Shekel*, Ex. 30:13.
n *Gerah, a weight*, Lev. 27:25.

[o,p,q]money, wherewith the odd
number of them is to be [l]re-
deemed, unto [p]Aâr′on and to
his [q]sons.
49 And [e]Mō′ṣeṣ took the redemption [o]money of them that
were over and above them that
were [l]redeemed by the Lē′vītes:
50 Of the [h]firstborn of the children of Ĭṣ′ra-el took he the
[o]money; a thousand three hundred and threescore and five
[m]*shekels*[c], after the shekel of the
sanctuary:
51 And [e]Mō′ṣeṣ gave the
[o,p,q]money of them that were [l]re-
deemed unto [p]Aâr′on and to his
[q]sons, according to the word of
the LORD, as the LORD commanded Mō′ṣeṣ.

v.48–1532 BC See footnote, *Time*, Rev. 10:6.

48
o *Money*, Jer. 32:9.
p *High Priest, emoluments of*, Lev. 21:10.
q *Priest, emoluments of*, Lev. 1:5.

## CHAPTER 4

*The age and time of the Levites' service. 4 The service of the Kohathites, when the priests have taken down the tabernacle. 16 The charge of Eleazar. 17 The office of the priests. 21 The service of the Gershonites, 29 and of the Merarites. 34 The number of the Kohathites, 38 of the Gershonites, 42 and of the Merarites.*

AND the LORD [a,b]spake unto [c]Mō′ṣeṣ and unto Aâr′-
on, saying,
2 Take the [d]sum of the [e]sons of
Kō′hăth from among the [f,g]sons
of Lē′vī, after their families, by
the house of their fathers,
3 From [f]thirty years old and
upward even until [g]fifty years
old, all that enter [1]into the host,
to do the work in the [h]tabernacle
of the congregation.
4 ¶ This *shall be* the service of
the [e]sons of Kō′hăth in the
[h]tabernacle of the congregation,
*about* the most holy things:
5 And when the camp setteth
forward, [i]Aâr′on shall come, and
his sons, and they shall take
down the covering [j]vail, and
cover the [k]ark of testimony with
it:
6 And shall put thereon the
covering of [2,l]badgers' skins, and
shall spread over *it* a cloth

1
a *Revelation, concerning the Levites*, vs. 1–49; 2 Cor. 12:1.
b *Inspiration*, Job 32:8.
c *Prophets, inspiration of*, Isa. 3:2.

2
d *Census*, 2 Sam. 24:1.
e *Kohathites*, Num. 3:27.
f *Levites, age of, when inducted into office*, Deut. 10:8.
g *Levites, age of, when retired from office*, Deut. 10:8.

3
h *Tabernacle*, vs. 3–33; Ex. 27:9.
1 R. V. upon the service.

5
i *High Priest, duties of*, vs. 5–15; Lev. 21:10.
j *Vail*, Ex. 35:12.
k *Ark, carried by the Kohathites*, Ex. 25:10.

6
l *Badger*, Ex. 25:5.
2 R. V. sealskin.

v.6–1532 BC
See footnote, *Time*, Rev. 10:6.

*m Colors, symbolical*, Ezek. 16:16.

**7**
*n Shewbread, table of*, Ex. 35:13.
*o Bowl*, Ex. 25:29.
3 R. V. the cups to pour out withal:

**9**
*p Candlestick*, Ex. 25:31.
*q Tongs*, Ex. 25:38.

**10**
4 R. V. the frame.

**11**
*r Altar, of incense*, Ex. 30:1.

**12**
*s Sanctuary*, Lev. 4:6.
5 R. V. vessels

**13**
*t Altar, of burnt offerings*, Gen. 8:20.

**14**
*u Censer*, Lev. 16:12.
*v Flesh Hook*, Ex. 27:3.
6 R.V. the firepans,

wholly of [m]blue, and shall put in the staves thereof.

7 And upon the table of [n]shewbread they shall spread a cloth of [m]blue, and put thereon the dishes, and the *spoons, and the [o]bowls, and [3]covers to cover withal: and the continual bread shall be thereon:

8 And they shall spread upon them a cloth of [m]scarlet, and cover the same with a covering of [2,l]badgers' skins, and shall put in the staves thereof.

9 And they shall take a cloth of [m]blue, and cover the [p]candlestick[G] of the light, and his lamps, and his [q]tongs, and his snuffdishes, and all the oil vessels thereof, wherewith they minister unto it:

10 And they shall put it and all the vessels thereof within a covering of [2,l]badgers' skins, and shall put *it* upon [4]a bar[G].

11 And upon the golden [r]altar they shall spread a cloth of [m]blue, and cover it with a covering of [2,l]badgers' skins, and shall put to the staves thereof:

12 And they shall take all the [5]instruments[G] of ministry, wherewith they minister in the [s]sanctuary, and put *them* in a cloth of [m]blue, and cover them with a covering of [2]badgers' skins, and shall put *them* on [4]a bar:

13 And they shall take away the ashes from the [t]altar, and spread a [m]purple cloth thereon:

14 And they shall put upon it all the vessels thereof, wherewith they minister about it, [6]*even* the [u]censers, the [v]fleshhooks, and the †shovels, and the basons, all the vessels of the [t]altar; and they shall spread upon it a covering of [2,l]badgers' skins, and put to the staves of it.

15 And when Aâr′on and his sons have made an end of[G] covering the [s]sanctuary, and all the [7]vessels of the sanctuary, as the camp is to set[G] forward; after that, the [e]sons of Kō′hath shall come to bear *it*: but they shall not touch [8]*any* holy thing, lest they die. These *things are* the burden of the sons of Kō′hath in the tabernacle of the congregation.

16 ¶ And to the office of [i,w]Ē-le-ā′zar the son of Aâr′on the priest *pertaineth* the [x]oil for the light, and the sweet [y]incense, and the [9]daily [z]meat[G] offering, and the anointing oil, *and* the oversight of all the [h]tabernacle, and of all that therein *is*, in the [s]sanctuary, and in the [7]vessels thereof.

17 ¶ And the LORD [a]spake unto Mō′ṣeṣ and unto Aâr′on, saying,

18 Cut ye not off the tribe of the families of the [b]Kō′hath-ītes from among the [c]Lē′vītes:

19 But thus do unto [b]them, that they may live, and not die, when they approach unto the most holy things: [d]Aâr′on and his [e]sons shall go in, and appoint them every one to his service and to his burden:

20 But [b]they shall not go in to see [10]when the holy things are covered, lest they die.

21 ¶ And the LORD [a]spake unto Mō′ṣeṣ, saying,

22 Take also the sum of the ‡sons of Gēr′shŏn, throughout the houses of their fathers, by their families;

23 From [f]thirty years old and upward until [g]fifty years old shalt thou number them; all that enter in to perform the service, to do the work in the [h]tabernacle of the congregation.

24 This *is* the service of the

v.15–1532 BC
See footnote, *Time*, Rev. 10:6.

**15**
7 R. V. furniture
8 R. V. the sanctuary,

**16**
*w Eleazer, duties of*, Num. 3:2.
*x Oil*, Deut. 12:17
*y Incense*, Ex. 37:29.
*z Offerings, meat*, Lev. 6:17.
9 R. V. continual meal

**17**
*a Prophets, inspiration of*, Isa. 3:2

**18**
*b Kohathites*, Num. 3:27.
*c Levites*, Deut. 10:8.

**19**
*d High Priest, duties of*, Lev. 21:10.
*e Priest, duties of*, vs. 28, 33; Lev. 1:5.

**20**
10 R. V. the sanctuary even for a moment,

**23**
*f Levites, age of, when inducted into office*, Deut. 10:8.
*g Levites, age of, when retired from office*, Deut. 10:8
*h Tabernacle*, Ex. 27:9.

***SPOONS.** *Of the tabernacle*, Ex. 25:29; Num. 4:7; 7:14–86. *Of the temple*, 1 Kin. 7:50; 2 Kin. 25:14; 2 Chr. 4:22.

† **SHOVEL.** *A utensil, in the tabernacle*, Ex. 27:3; 38:3 Num. 4:14; *in the temple*, 1 Kin. 7:40; 2 Kin. 25:14; 2 Chr 4:11; Jer. 52:18.

v 24–1532 BC
See footnote, *Time*, Rev. 10:6.

25
11 R. V. sealskin.

26
*i Court, of tabernacle*, Ex. 38:9.

28
*j Ithamar*, Ex. 38:21.

29
*k Merarites*, vs. 29–33; Num. 26:57.

families of the ‡Gē̄r′shon-ītes, to
serve, and for burdens:
25 And they shall bear the curtains of the [h]tabernacle, and the
tabernacle of the congregation,
his covering, and the covering of
the [11]badgers' skins that *is* above
upon it, and the hanging for the
door of the tabernacle of the
congregation,
26 And the hangings of the
[i]court, and the hanging for the
door of the gate of the court,
which *is* by the [h]tabernacle and
by the altar round about, and
their cords, and all the instruments of their service, and all
that is made for them: so shall
they serve.
27 At the appointment of [d]Aâr′-
on and his [e]sons shall be all the
service of the sons of the ‡Gē̄r′-
shon-ītes, in all their burdens,
and in all their service: and ye
shall appoint unto them in
charge all their burdens.
28 This *is* the service of the
families of the ‡sons of Gē̄r′shŏn
in the [h]tabernacle of the congregation: and their charge [G] *shall be*
under the hand of [j]Ĭth′a-mär the
son of Aâr′on the priest.
29 ¶ As for the [k]sons of Mē̇-
rā′rī, thou shalt number them
after their families, by the house
of their fathers;
30 From [f]thirty years old and
upward even unto [g]fifty years
old shalt thou number them,
every one that entereth into the
service, to do the work of the
[h]tabernacle of the congregation.
31 And this *is* the charge of
[k]their burden, according to all
their service in the [h]tabernacle
of the congregation; the boards
of the tabernacle, and the bars
thereof, and the pillars thereof,
and sockets thereof,
32 And the pillars of the [i]court
round about, and their sockets,
and their pins, and their cords,
with all their instruments, and
with all their service [G]: and by
name ye shall reckon the instruments of the charge of their
burden.
33 This *is* the service of the
families of the [k]sons of Mē̇-rā′rī,
according to all their service, in
the [h]tabernacle of the congregation, under the hand of [j]Ĭth′a-
mär the son of Aâr′on the priest.
34 ¶ And [l]Mō′ṣeṣ and [m]Aâr′on
and the chief of the congregation [n, o]numbered the sons of the
[b]Kō′hath-ītes after their families, and after the house of their
fathers,
35 From [f]thirty years old and
upward even unto [g]fifty years
old, every one that entereth into
the service, for the work in the
[h]tabernacle of the congregation:
36 And those that were [n, o]num-
bered of them by their families
were two thousand seven hundred and fifty.
37 These *were* they that were
[n, o]numbered of the families of
the [b]Kō′hath-ītes, all that might
do service in the [h]tabernacle of
the congregation, which [l]Mō′ṣeṣ
and [m]Aâr′on did [n, o]number according to the commandment of
the Lord by the hand of Mō′ṣeṣ.
38 ¶ And those that were
[n, o]numbered of the ‡sons of
Gē̄r′shŏn, throughout their families, and by the house of their
fathers,
39 From [f]thirty years old and
upward even unto [g]fifty years
old, every one that entereth into
the service, for the work in the
[h]tabernacle of the congregation,
40 Even those that were
[n, o]numbered of them, throughout their families, by the house
of their fathers, were two thou-

v.32–1532 BC
See footnote, *Time*, Rev. 10:6.

34
*l Moses*, Ex. 2:10.
*m Aaron*, Ex. 6:20.

36
*n Levites, enrollment of*, Deut. 10:8.
*o Census*, 2 Sam. 24:1.

‡ **GERSHONITES**. *Sons of Gershon*, Num. 3:18; 4:22, 23, 38; 26:57; 1 Chr. 6:17, 20, 43; 15:7; 23:7. *Duties of*, Num. 3:23–26; 4:24–28; 7:7 (with vs. 3–5); 10:17; 2 Chr. 29:12–15. *Cities assigned to*, Josh. **21:6**; **1 Chr. 6:62, 71**.
See footnote, Levites, Deut. **10:8**.

v 40–1532 BC
See footnote, *Time*, Rev. 10:6.

sand and six hundred and thirty.

41 These *are* they that were
[n,o]numbered of the families of
the [‡]sons of Gēr′shŏn, of all that
might do service in the tabernacle of the congregation, whom
[l]Mō′ṣeṣ and [m]Aâr′on did number according to the commandment of the LORD.

42 ¶ And those that were
[n,o]numbered of the families of
the [k]sons of Mē-rā′rī, throughout their families, by the house
of their fathers,

43 From [j]thirty years old and
upward even unto [g]fifty years
old, every one that entereth into
the service, for the work in the
tabernacle of the congregation,

44 Even those that were
[n,o]numbered of them after their
families, were three thousand
and two hundred.

45 These *be* those that were
[n,o]numbered of the families of
the [k]sons of Mē-rā′rī, whom
[l]Mō′ṣeṣ and [m]Aâr′on numbered
according to the word of the
LORD by the hand of Mō′ṣeṣ.

46 All those that were [o]numbered of the [n]Lē′vītes, whom
[l]Mō′ṣeṣ and [m]Aâr′on and the
chief of Ĭṣ′ra-el numbered, after
their families, and after the
house of their fathers,

47 From [j]thirty years old and
upward even unto [g]fifty years
old, every one that came to do
the service of the ministry, and
the service of the burden in the
tabernacle of the congregation,

48 Even those that were [n,o]numbered of them, were eight thousand and five hundred and fourscore.

49 According to the commandment of the LORD they were
[n,o]numbered by the hand of
[l]Mō′ṣeṣ, every one according to
his service, and according to his
burden: thus were they numbered of him, as the LORD commanded Mō′ṣeṣ.

## CHAPTER 5

*The unclean are to be removed out of the camp. 5 Restitution is to be made in case of trespass. 11 The trial in a case of jealousy.*

AND the LORD [a]spake unto
[b]Mō′ṣeṣ, saying,

2 Command the children of
Ĭṣ′ra-el, that they [c]put out of the
camp every [d,e]leper, and every
one that hath an issue, and whosoever is [f,g]defiled by the dead:

3 Both male and female shall ye
[c]put out, without the camp shall
ye put them; that they [f,g]defile
not their camps, in the midst
whereof I dwell.

4 And the children of Ĭṣ′ra-el
did so, and [c]put them out without the camp: as the LORD
spake unto Mō′ṣeṣ, so did the
children of Ĭṣ′ra-el.

5 ¶ And the LORD [a]spake unto
[b]Mō′ṣeṣ, saying,

6 Speak unto the children of
Ĭṣ′ra-el, When a man or woman
shall commit any sin that men
commit, to do a trespass against
the LORD, and that person be
guilty;

7 Then [h]they shall [i]confess their
sin which they have done: and
he shall [1,j]recompense his trespass with the principal thereof,
and add unto it the [k]fifth *part*
thereof, and give *it* unto *him*
against whom he hath trespassed.

8 But if the man have no kinsman to [2,j]recompense the trespass unto, let the [l]trespass be
recompensed unto the LORD,
*even* to the priest; beside the
ram of the [m,n]atonement, whereby an atonement shall be made
for him.

9 And every [l,o]offering of all the
holy things of the children of
Ĭṣ′ra-el, which they bring unto
the [l]priest, shall be his.

v.49–1532 BC
See footnote, *Time*, Rev. 10:6.

1
a *Revelation, of various ordinances,* vs. 1–31; 2 Cor. 12:1.
b *Prophets, inspiration of,* Isa. 3:2

2
c *Sanitation and Hygiene, isolation,* Num. 31:23
d *Disease,* Ex. 15:26.
e *Leprosy, isolation of lepers,* Lev. 13:2.
f *Defilement, by dead,* Lev. 5:2.
g *Sin, typified,* Rom. 5:12.

7
h *Commandment, requiring confession and restitution,* Deut. 8:2.
i *Sin, confession of,* Rom. 5:12.
j *Restitution,* Ex. 22:3.
k *Fine,* Ex. 22:1.
1 R. V. make restitution for his guilt in full,

8
l *Priest, emoluments of,* Lev. 1:5.
m *Atonement, made by animal sacrifice,* Lev. 17:11.
n *Jesus, atonement by, typified,* Matt. 1:21.
2 R. V. whom restitution may be made for guilt, the restitution for guilt which is made unto the Lord shall be the priest's;

9
o *Offerings, heave,* Lev. 6:17.

v.10–1532 BC
See footnote, *Time,* Rev. 10:6.

10 And every man's hallowed things shall be his: [l]whatsoever any man giveth the priest, it shall be his.

11 ¶ And the LORD [a]spake unto [b]Mō'ṣeṣ, saying,

12 Speak unto the children of Iṣ'ra-el, and say unto them, If any [p]man's [q]wife go aside, and commit a [r]trespass against him,

13 And a man [r]lie with [q]her carnally, and it be hid from the eyes of her [p]husband, and be kept close, and she be [g,s]defiled, and *there be* no witness against her, neither she be taken [3]*with the manner;*

14 And the spirit of [t]jealousy come upon him, and he be jealous of his [q]wife, and she be [s]defiled: or if the spirit of jealousy come upon him, and he be jealous of his wife, and she be not defiled:

15 Then shall the [p]man bring his [q]wife unto the [u]priest, and he shall bring her [v]offering for her, the tenth *part* of an [w]ephah of [x]barley meal; he shall pour no oil upon it, nor put [y]frankincense thereon; for it *is* [4]an offering of [t]jealousy, an offering of memorial, bringing iniquity to remembrance.

16 And the [u]priest shall bring [q]her near, and set her before the LORD;

17 And the [u]priest shall take holy water in an earthen vessel; and of the dust that is in the floor of the [z]tabernacle the priest shall take, and put *it* into the water:

18 And the [u]priest shall set the [q]woman before the LORD, and uncover the woman's head, and put the [v]offering of memorial in her hands, which *is* the [5,t]jealousy offering: and the priest shall have in his hand the bitter water that causeth the curse:

19 And the [a]priest shall charge [b,c]her by an *oath, and say unto the woman, If no man have [d]lain with thee, and if thou hast not gone aside to uncleanness [6]*with another* instead of thy [e]husband, be thou free from this bitter water that causeth the curse:

20 But if thou hast [d]gone aside *to another* instead of thy [e]husband, and if thou be [f]defiled, and some man have lain with thee beside thine husband:

21 Then the [a]priest shall charge the [b]woman with an oath of cursing, and the priest shall say unto the woman, [g]The LORD make thee a curse and an oath among thy people, when the LORD doth make thy thigh to [7]rot, and thy belly to swell;

22 [g]And this water that causeth the curse shall go into thy bowels, to make *thy* belly to swell, and *thy* thigh to [7]rot: And the woman shall say, Ā-mĕn, ā-mĕn.

**12**
p *Husband,* Num. 30:6.
q *Wife, unfaithful,* vs. 12–31; Prov. 5:18.
r *Adultery, penalties for,* vs. 12–31; Lev. 20:10.

**13**
s *Defilement,* Lev. 5:2.
3 R. V. in the act;

**14**
t *Jealousy,* vs. 14–31; Psa. 78:58.

**15**
u *High Priest, duties of, judicial,* Lev. 21:10.
v *Offerings, meat,* Lev. 6:17.
w *Measure, dry,* Deut. 25.15.
x *Barley, used in offerings,* Ex. 9:31.
y *Frankincense,* 1 Chr. 9:29.
4 R. V. a meal offering of

v.17–1532 BC
See footnote, *Time,* Rev. 10:6.

**17**
z *Tabernacle,* Ex. 27:9.

**18**
5 R. V. meal offering of jealousy:

**19**
a *High Priest, duties of, judicial,* Lev. 21:10.
b *Wife,* Prov. 5:18.
c *Witness, qualified by oath,* Num. 35.30.
d *Adultery,* Lev. 20:10.
e *Husband,* Num. 30:6.
6 R.V. being under thy husband,

**20**
f *Defilement,* Lev. 5:2.

**21**
g *Judgments,* Ex. 6:6.
7 R. V. fall away.

*** OATH,** a solemn qualification. *Attributed to God,* Gen. 22:16; 26:3; Num. 14:30; Psa. 89:35; 95:11; 105:9; 132:11; Isa. 14:24; 45:23; Jer. 11:5; 22:5; 49:13; 51:14; Luke 1:73; Heb. 3:11, 18; 4:3; 6:13, 17; 7:21, 28.

Used in solemnizing covenants: *Between Abraham, and the King of Sodom,* Gen. 14:22, 23; *and Abimelech,* Gen. 21:22, 23. *Between Isaac and Abimelech,* Gen. 26:26–29, 31. *Between Abraham and his servant,* Gen. 24:2, 3, 9, 37, 41. *Between, Jacob and Esau,* Gen. 25:33; *Jacob and Laban,* Gen. 31:53; *Jacob and Joseph,* Gen. 47:28 31. *Between Joseph and Israel,* Gen. 50:25. *Between Rahab and the spies,* Josh. 2:12–14; 6:22. *Between Israelites and Hivites,* Josh. 9:3–20. *Between Moses and Caleb,* Josh. 14:9. *Between elders of Gilead and Jephthah,* Judg. 11:10. *By Israelites,* Judg. 21:5. *Between Ruth, and Naomi,* Ruth 1:17; *and Boaz,* Ruth 3:13. *Between Jonathan and David,* 1 Sam. 20:3, 13–17. *Between David and Saul,* 1 Sam. 24:21, 22; 2 Sam. 21:7. *Israelites confirm covenants by,* Jer. 42:4–6.

*Used, in solemnizing testimony,* Ex. 22:10, 11; Num. 5:19–24; Deut. 6:13; 10:20; 1 Kin. 8:31, 32; Psa. 15:1, 2, 4; Heb. 6:16; *in confirming allegiance to sovereigns,* Eccl. 8:2.

Other uses of: *Samuel affirms his honesty of administration by,* 1 Sam. 12:5. *Saul swears by, to Jonathan,* 1 Sam. 19:6; *to witch of Endor,* 1 Sam. 28:10. *David swears by,* 2 Sam. 3:35; *to Bath-sheba,* 1 Kin. 1:28, 29. *Zedekiah swears to Jeremiah by,* Jer. 38:16. *Joab confirms his word by,* 2 Sam. 19:7. *Word confirmed by, by Solomon,* 1 Kin. 2:23; *by Shimei,* 1 Kin. 2–42; *by the king of Samaria,* 2 Kin. 6:31; *by Gedaliah,* Jer. 40:9. *Elisha seals his vow to follow Elijah by,* 2 Kin. 2:2. *Gehazi confirms his lie by,* 2 Kin. 5:20. *Zedekiah violates,* 2 Chr. 36:13.

*Required, of rulers by Jehoiada,* 2 Kin. 11:4; *of the priests and Levites by Ezra,* Ezra 10:5, 19; *of the priests by Nehemiah,* Neh. 5:12, 13. *Heard in Daniel's vision,* Dan. 12:7. *Heard in John's vision,* Rev. 10:5, 6. *Peter confirms his denial of Jesus by,* Mark 14:71. *Required of Christ,* Matt. 26:63. *Paul confirms certain statements by,* 2 Cor. 1:23; Gal. 1:20. *Christ's teaching concerning,* Matt. 23:18–22.

**Profane:** *Forbidden,* Ex. 20:7; Lev. 19:12; Deut. 5:11; Matt. 5:33–37; Jas. 5:12. *Unrighteous, forbidden,* Lev. 19: 12; Hos. 4:15. *Unrighteous, punishment for,* Lev. 6:2–5. *Wicked, made by Israelites,* Isa. 48:1; Jer. 5:2, 7; 7:8, 9; *made by Herod,* Matt. 14:7, 9; Mark 6:23, 26; *made by enemies of Paul,* Acts 23:12–14.

**Idolatrous,** Jer. 12:16.

See footnote, PERJURY, 1 Tim. 1:10.

v.23–1532 BC
See footnote, *Time*, Rev. 10:6.

23 And the [a]priest shall write
these curses in a †book, and he
shall blot *them* out with the bitter water:
24 And [a]he shall cause the
[b]woman to drink the bitter water
that causeth the curse: and the
water that causeth the curse
shall enter into her, *and become*
bitter.
25 Then the [a]priest shall take
the [8,h]jealousy [i]offering out of
the woman's hand, and shall
[j]wave the offering before the
LORD, and offer it upon the
[k]altar:
26 And the [a]priest shall take an
handful of the [i]offering, *even* the
memorial thereof, and burn *it*
upon the [k]altar, and afterward
shall cause the [b]woman to drink
the water.
27 And when he hath made her
to drink the water, then it shall
come to pass, *that,* if she be [f]de-
filed, and have [d]done trespass
against her [e]husband, [g]that the
water that causeth the curse
shall enter into her, *and become*
bitter, and her belly shall swell,
and her thigh shall rot: and the
woman shall be a curse among
her people.
28 And if the [b]woman be not
[f]defiled, but be clean; then she
shall be free, and shall conceive
seed.
29 This *is* the law of [h]jealous-
ies, when a [b]wife [9]goeth aside *to*
*another* instead of her [e]husband,
and is [f]defiled;
30 Or when the spirit of [h]jeal-
ousy cometh upon [e]him, and he
be jealous over his [b]wife, and
shall set the woman before the
LORD, and the [a]priest shall execute upon her all this law.
31 Then shall the man be
guiltless from iniquity, and this
woman shall bear her iniquity.

25
*h Jealousy,* Psa. 78:58.
*i Offerings, meat,* Lev. 6:17.
*j Offerings, wave,* Lev. 6:17.
*k Altar, of burnt offerings,* Gen. 8:20.
8 R. V. meal offering of jealousy

29
9 R. V. being under her husband, goeth

v.30–1532 BC
See footnote, *Time*, Rev. 10:6.

## CHAPTER 6

*The law of the Nazarites. 22 The form of blessing the people.*

AND the LORD [a]spake unto
[b,c]Mō'ṣeṣ, saying,
2 Speak unto the children of
[d]Iṣ'ra-el, and say unto them,
When either man or woman
shall [e]separate *themselves* to
[f]vow a vow of a *Năz'a-rīte, to
separate *themselves* unto the
LORD:
3 *He shall [g]separate *himself*
from [h]wine and strong drink,
and shall drink no †vinegar of
wine, or vinegar of strong drink,
neither shall he drink any liquor
of [i]grapes, nor eat moist grapes,
or dried.
4 All the days of *his separation shall he eat nothing that is
made of the [i]vine tree, from the
kernels even to the husk.
5 All the days of the [f]vow of
*his separation there shall [j]no
[k,l]razor come upon his head: until the days be fulfilled, in the
which he separateth *himself* unto
the LORD, [m]he shall be holy, *and*
shall let the locks of the hair of
his head grow.
6 All the days that *he separateth *himself* unto the LORD

1
*a Revelation, concerning the Nazarite,* 2 Cor. 12:1.
*b Moses,* Ex. 2:10.
*c Prophets, inspiration of,* Isa.3:2.

2
*d Israel,* Ex. 4:22.
*e Consecration,* Lev. 7:37.
*f Vows,* Num. 30:2.

3
*g Total Abstinence, from intoxicating beverages,* Lev. 10:9.
*h Wine, forbidden to Nazarites,* Prov. 23:31.
*i Grape, wine of,* Lev. 25:5.

5
*j* Judg. 13:5; 16:17.
*k* 1 Sam. 1:11.
*l Shaving,* Ezek. 44:20.
*m Holiness, enjoined,* Ex. 39:30.

---

† **BOOK.** *Genealogies kept in,* Gen. 5:1. *Law of Moses written in,* Num. 5:23; Deut. 17:18; 31:9, 24, 26; 2 Kin. 22:8. *Topography of Palestine recorded in,* Josh. 18:9.

Chronicles of the times kept in: *By Jasher,* Josh. 10:13; 2 Sam. 1:18; *by Samuel, Nathan, and Gad,* 1 Sam. 10:25; 1 Chr. 29:29; *by Shemaiah and Iddo,* 2 Chr. 12:15; 13:22; *by Isaiah,* 2 Chr. 26:22; 32:32; Isa. 8:1.

Of the kings of Judah and Israel: *Of David,* 1 Chr. 27:24; *of Solomon,* 1 Kin. 11:41; *of Jehu,* 2 Chr. 20:34; *of other kings,* 2 Chr. 16:11; 24:27; 25:26; 27:7; 28:26; 35:27; 36:8; *of the kings of Israel,* 1 Kin. 14:19; 2 Chr. 20:34; 33:18.

*Other records kept in,* Ezra 4:15; 6:1, 2; Esth. 6:1; 9:32; Jer. 32:12.

*Prophecies written in, by Jeremiah,* Jer. 25:13; 30:2; 45:1; 51:60, 63; Dan. 9:2. *Other prophecies written in,* 2 Chr. 33:18, 19. *Lamentations written in,* 2 Chr. 35:25. *Numerous,* Eccl. 12:12. *Eating of, figurative,* Jer. 15:16; Ezek. 2:8-10; 3:1-3; Rev. 10:2-10. *Of magic,* Acts 19:19.

*Paul's, left at Troas,* 2 Tim. 4:13.

*Made in a roll,* Jer. 36:4; Zech. 5:1. *Sealed,* Isa. 29:11; Dan. 12:4; Rev. 5:1-5.

*Debir was called* KIRJATH-SEPHER, *which signifies a city of books,* Josh. 15:15, 16; Judg. 1:11, 12.

See footnote, BOOK, figurative, p. 906.

* **NAZIRITE.** *Vows of,* Num. 6:1-21. *Character of,* Amos 2:11, 12.

**Instances of ;** *Samson,* Judg. 13:5, 7; 16:17. *Samuel,* 1 Sam. 1:11. *Rechabites,* Jer. 35. *John the Baptist,* Matt. 11:18; Luke 1:15; 7:33.

† **VINEGAR,** a sour wine. *Forbidden to Nazirites,* Num. 6:3. *Used with food,* Ruth 2:14; Psa. 67:21; Prov. 10:26. *Offered to Christ on the cross,* Matt. 27:34, 48; John 19:29 (with Mark 15:23).

v.6–1532 BC
See footnote, *Time*, Rev. 10:6.

6
n *Defilement*, Lev. 5:2.
7
1 R. V. separation unto God
10
o *Dove*, Gen. 8:8.
p *Pigeon*, Gen. 15:9.
q *Tabernacle*, Ex. 27:9.
2 R. V. turtle-doves,
11
r *Priest, duties of*, Lev. 1:5.
s *Offerings, sin*, Lev. 6:17.
t *Jesus, typified in offerings*, Matt. 1:21.
u *Offerings, burnt*, Lev. 6:17.
v *Atonement*, Lev. 17:11.
w *Jesus, atonement by, typified*, Matt. 1:21.
12
x *Lamb, offering of*, Num. 7:15.
y *Offerings, trespass*, Lev. 6:17.
3 R. V. separate
4 R. V. guilt
14
z *Holiness, typified*, Ex. 39:30.

a *Blemish*, Lev.14:10.
b *Sin, typified*, Rom. 5:12.
c *Offerings, burnt*, Lev. 6:17.
d *Holiness, typified*, Ex. 39:30.
e *Offerings, sin*, Lev. 6:17.
f *Offerings, peace*, Lev. 6:17.
15
g *Oil*, Deut. 12:17.

he [n]shall come at no dead
body.
7 *,[m]He shall not make himself
[n]unclean for his father, or for his
mother, for his brother, or for
his sister, when they die: because
the [1,e]consecration of his God *is*
upon his head.
8 All the days of his separation
[m]he *is* holy unto the LORD.
9 And if any man die very suddenly by *him, and he hath [n]de-
filed the head of his consecration; then he shall [l]shave his
head in the day of his cleansing, on the seventh day shall he
shave it.
10 And on the eighth day he
shall bring two [2,o]turtles, or
two young [p]pigeons, to the
priest, to the door of the [q]taber-
nacle of the congregation:
11 And the [r]priest shall offer
the one for a [s]sin [t]offering, and
the other for a [u]burnt offering,
and make an [v,w]atonement for
him, for that he sinned by the
dead, and shall hallow his head
that same day.
12 And he shall [3]consecrate unto the LORD the days of his separation, and shall bring a [x]lamb
of the first year for a [4,y]trespass
[t]offering: but the days that were
before shall be lost, because his
separation was [n]defiled.
13 ¶ And this *is* the law of the
*Năz′a-rīte, when the days of his
separation are fulfilled: he shall
be brought unto the door of the
[q]tabernacle of the congregation:
14 And he shall offer his offering unto the LORD, one he
*lamb of the first year [z]without
[a,b]blemish for a [c]burnt offering,
and one ewe lamb of the first
year [d]without [a,b]blemish for a
[e]sin offering, and one ram without blemish for [f]peace offerings,
15 And a basket of unleavened
bread, cakes of fine flour mingled with [g]oil, and wafers of unleavened bread anointed with
oil, and their [5,h]meat offering,
and their [i]drink offerings.
16 And the [j]priest shall bring
*them* before the LORD, and shall
offer his [e]sin [k]offering, and his
[c]burnt offering:
17 And he shall offer the ram
*for* a sacrifice of [f]peace offerings
unto the LORD, with the basket
of unleavened bread: the [j]priest
shall offer also [6]his [h]meat offering, and his [i]drink offering.
18 And the *Năz′a-rīte shall
[l]shave the head of his separation
*at* the door of the [m]tabernacle of
the congregation, and shall take
the hair of the head of his separation, and put *it* in the fire
which *is* under the sacrifice of
the [f]peace offerings.
19 And the [j]priest shall take the
sodden shoulder of the ram, and
one unleavened cake out of
the basket, and one unleavened
[n]wafer, and shall put *them* upon
the hands of the *Năz′a-rīte, after *the hair of* his separation is
[l]shaven:
20 And the [j]priest shall wave
them *for* a [o]wave offering before
the LORD: [p]this *is* holy for the
priest, with the wave breast and
[q]heave shoulder: and after that
the *Năz′a-rīte may drink [r]wine.
21 This *is* the law of the *Năz′-
a-rīte who hath [s]vowed, *and of*
his offering unto the LORD for
his separation, beside *that* that
his hand shall get: according to
the vow which he vowed, so he
must do after the law of his
separation.
22 ¶ And the LORD [t]spake unto
[u,v]Mō′ṣeṣ, saying,
23 Speak unto [w]Aâr′on and unto his sons, saying, [x]On this
wise ye shall [y]bless the children
of [z]Ĭṣ′ra-el, saying unto them,
24 [a,b,c]The LORD [d]bless thee,
and keep thee:
25 [a,b,c]The LORD make his

v.15–1532 BC
See footnote, *Time*, Rev. 10:6.

h *Offerings, meat*, Lev. 6:17.
i *Offerings, drink*, Lev. 6:17.
5 R. V. meal
16
j *Priest, duties of*, Lev. 1:5.
k *Jesus, typified in offerings*, Matt. 1:21.
17
6 R. V. the meal
18
l *Shaving*, Ezek. 44:20.
m *Tabernacle*, Ex. 27:9.
19
n *Wafer*, Ex. 29:23.
20
o *Offerings, wave*, Lev. 6:17.
p *Priest, emoluments of*, Lev. 1:5.
q *Offerings, heave*, Lev. 6:17.
r *Wine*, Prov. 23:31.
21
s *Vows*, Num. 30:2.
22
t *Revelation, of priestly benediction*, 2 Cor. 12:1.
u *Moses*, Ex. 2:10.
v *Prophets, inspiration of*, Isa.3:2.
23
w *Aaron*, Ex. 6:20.
x *Statute, prescribing priestly benediction*, Deut.8:2.
y *Benedictions*, Deut. 21:5.
z *Israel*, Ex. 4:22.

24
a *Intercession, of man with God*, Jer. 27:18.
b *Prayer, intercessory*, Acts 6:4.
c *Benedictions*, Deut. 21:5.
d *Spiritual Blessings*, Eph. 1:3.

v.25–1532 BC
See footnote, *Time,* Rev. 10:6.

25
e *Grace of God,* Rom. 4:16.
26
f *Spiritual Peace,* Gal. 1:3.
27
g *Spiritual Adoption,* Rom. 8:15.
h *Israel,* Ex. 4:22.
i *Promise, of blessing upon the church,* 2 Cor. 1:20.

1
a *Moses,* Ex. 2:10.
b *Tabernacle, sanctified,* Ex. 27:9.
c *Anointing,* Lev. 8:12.
d *Dedication, of the tabernacle,* vs. 1–89; Ezra 6:17.
e *Church, holy,* 1 Kin. 9:3.
f *Altar, of burnt offerings,* vs. 1–89; Gen. 8:20.
1 R. V. furniture

2
g *Senate,* Num. 11:16.

3
h *Wagon,* Gen. 45:19, 27.
i *Bullock,* Ex.29:3.

4
j *Prophets, inspiration of,* Isa.3:2.

face shine upon thee, and be
[e]gracious unto thee:
26 The LORD lift up his
countenance upon thee, and give
thee [f]peace. T Q
27 And they shall [g]put my
name upon the children of [h]Ĭṣ'-
ra-el; and [i]I will [d]bless them.

## CHAPTER 7

*The offering of the princes at the dedication of the tabernacle. 10 Their several offerings at the dedication of the altar. 89 God speaks to Moses from the mercy seat.*

AND it came to pass on the
day that [a]Mō'ṣeṣ had
fully set up the [b]tabernacle, and
had [c,d]anointed it, and sanctified
[e]it, and all the [1]instruments
thereof, both the [f]altar and all
the vessels thereof, and had
anointed them, and sanctified
them;
2 That the [g]princes of Ĭṣ'ra-el,
heads of the house of their fathers,
who *were* the princes of
the tribes, and were over them
that were numbered, offered:
3 And they brought their offering
before the LORD, six covered
[h]wagons, and twelve [i]oxen;
a wagon for two of the princes,
and for each one an ox: and they
brought them before the tabernacle.
4 And the LORD spake unto
[a,j]Mō'ṣeṣ, saying,
5 Take *it* of them, that they
may be to do the service of the
tabernacle of the congregation;
and thou shalt give them unto
the Lē'vītes, to every man according
to his service.
6 And [a]Mō'ṣeṣ took the [h]wagons
and the [i]oxen, and gave
them unto the Lē'vītes.
7 Two wagons and four oxen
he gave unto the [k]sons of Gĕr'-
shŏn, according to their service:
8 And four wagons and eight
oxen he gave unto the [l]sons of
Mē-rā'rī, according unto their
service, under the hand of [m]Ĭth'-
a-mär the son of Aâr'on the
priest.
9 But unto the [n]sons of Kō'hath
he gave none: because the service
of the [o]sanctuary belonging
unto them *was that* they should
bear upon their shoulders.
10 ¶ And the [q]princes offered
for [p]dedicating of the [f]altar in
the day that it was [c]anointed,
even the princes offered their
offering before the altar.
11 And the LORD said unto
[j]Mō'ṣeṣ, They shall offer their
offering, each [g]prince on his day,
for the [p]dedicating of the [f]altar.
12 ¶ And he that offered his
offering the first day was *Näh'-
shŏn the son of [q]Ăm-mĭn'a-dăb,
of the tribe of [r]Jū'dah:
13 And *his offering *was* one
[s]silver [t]charger, the weight
whereof *was* an hundred and
thirty [u]*shekels,* one silver [v]bowl
of seventy shekels, after the
shekel of the sanctuary; both of
them *were* full of fine flour
mingled with oil for a [2,w]meat
offering;
14 One [x]spoon of ten [u]*shekels*
of [y]gold, full of [z]incense;
15 One young [a]bullock, one
ram, one †lamb of the first year,
for a [b]burnt [c]offering:
16 One kid of the goats for a
[d]sin offering:
17 And for a sacrifice of [e]peace
offerings, two oxen, five rams,
five he goats, five †lambs of the
first year: this *was* the offering

v.7–1532 BC
See footnote, *Time,* Rev. 10:6.

7
k *Gershonites, duties of,* Num. 4:27.
8
l *Merarites, duties of,* Num. 26:57.
m *Ithamar,* Ex. 38:21.
9
n *Kohathites, duties of,* Num. 3:27.
o *Tabernacle, how and by whom carried,* vs. 6–9; Ex. 27:9.

10
p *Dedication, of the altar,* Ezra 6:17.

12
q *Amminadab,* Num. 2:3.
r *Judah,* Num. 10:14.
13
s *Silver,* 1 Chr. 28:14.
t *Charger,*Ezra 1:9.
u *Shekel,*Ex.30:13.
v *Bowl, made of silver,* Ex. 25:29.
w *Offerings, meat,* Lev. 6:17.
2 R. V. meal
14
x *Spoons,* Num. 4:7.
y *Gold,* Ezek. 7:19.
z *Incense,* Ex. 37:29.

15
a *Bullock,*Ex.29:3.
b *Offerings, burnt,* Lev. 6:17.
c *Jesus, typified in offerings,* Matt. 1:21.
16
d *Offerings, sin,* Lev. 6:17.
17
e *Offerings, peace,* Lev. 6:17.

***NAHSHON** (*enchanter*). *Son of Amminadab,* Ex. 6:23; Num. 1:7; Ruth 4:20; 1 Chr. 2:10. *Captain of the host of Judah,* Num. 2:3; 10:14; 1 Chr. 2:10. *Liberality of,* Num. 7:12, 17. *In the lineage of Jesus,* Matt. 1:4; Luke 3:32.

**†LAMB.** *Offering of,* Lev. 3:7; 5:6; 22:23, 23:12; Num. 7:15, 21, 28:3–8; *at the daily morning and evening sacrifices,* Ex. 29:38–42. *Offering of, at the feast, of the passover,* Ex. 12:15; *of pentecost,* Lev. 23:18–20; *of tabernacles,* Num. 29:13–40; *of the new moon,* Num. 28:11; *of trumpets,* Num. 29:2. *Offering of, on the Sabbath day,* Num. 28:9, *at purifications,* Lev. 12:6; 14:10–25; *by the Nazarite,* Num. 6:12; *for sin of ignorance,* Lev. 4:32.

**Figurative:** *The wolf dwelling with, a figure of Messiah's reign,* Isa. 11:6; 65:25. *A type of young believers,* John 21:15. *A name given to Christ,* John 1:29, 36; Rev. 5:6, 8, 12, 13; 6:1, 16; 7:9, 10, 14; 12:11; 13:8; 14:4, 10; 17:14; 19:7, 9; 21:9, 14, 22, 23, 27; 22:1, 3. *Jesus compared to,* Isa. 53:7; Acts 8:32; 1 Pet. 1:19.

v 17–1532 BC
See footnote, *Time*,
Rev. 10:6.

*f* *Amminadab*, Num. 2:3.
18
*g* *Nethaneel*, Num. 2:5.
*h* *Zuar*, Num. 1:8.
*i* *Issachar*, Num. 1:28.
19
*j* *Silver*, 1 Chr. 28: 14.
*k* *Charger*, Ezra 1:9.
*l* *Shekel*, Ex. 30: 13.
*m* *Bowl, made of silver*, Ex. 25:29.
*n* *Offerings, meat*, Lev. 6:17.
20
*o* *Spoons*, Num. 4:7.
*p* *Gold*, Ezek. 7:19.
*q* *Incense*, Ex. 37: 29.
24
*r* *Eliab*, Num. 1:9.
*s* *Helon*, Num. 2:7.
*t* *Zebulun*, Gen. 49:13.
30
*u* *Elizur*, Num. 10: 18.
*v* *Shedeur*, Num. 1:5.

of *Näh′shŏn the son of [f]Ăm-
mĭn′a-dăb.
18 ¶ On the second day [g]Nĕ-
thăn′e-el the son of [h]Zū′ar,
prince of [i]Is′sa-char, did offer:
19 [g]He offered *for* his offering
one [j]silver [k]charger, the weight
whereof *was* an hundred and
thirty [l]*shekels*, one silver [m]bowl
of seventy shekels, after the
shekel of the sanctuary; both of
them full of fine flour mingled
with oil for a [3,n]meat offering:
20 One [o]spoon of [p]gold of ten
[l]*shekels*, full of [q]incense:
21 One young [a]bullock, one
ram, one †lamb of the first year,
for a [b]burnt [c]offering:
22 One kid of the goats for a
[d]sin [c]offering:
23 And for a sacrifice of [e]peace
offerings, two [a]oxen, five rams,
five he goats, five †lambs of the
first year: this *was* the offering
of [g]Nĕ-thăn′e-el the son of Zū′ar.
24 ¶ On the third day [r]Ē-lī′ab
the son of [s]Hē′lon, prince of
the children of [t]Zĕb′u-lŭn, *did
offer*:
25 [r]His offering *was* one [j]silver
[k]charger, the weight whereof
*was* an hundred and thirty [l]*shekels*, one silver [m]bowl of seventy
shekels, after the shekel of the
sanctuary; both of them full of
fine flour mingled with oil for
a [2,n]meat offering:
26 One golden [o]spoon of ten
[l]*shekels*, full of [q]incense:
27 One young [a]bullock, one
ram, one †lamb of the first year,
for a [b]burnt [c]offering:
28 One kid of the goats for a
[d]sin [c]offering:
29 And for a sacrifice of [e]peace
offerings, two oxen, five rams,
five he goats, five lambs of the
first year: this *was* the offering
of [r]Ē-lī′ab the son of [s]Hē′lon.
30 ¶ On the fourth day [u]Ē-lī′-
zur the son of [v]Shĕd′e-ur, prince
of the [w]children of Reu′ben, *did
offer*:
31 [u]His offering *was* one [j]silver
[k]charger of the weight of an hundred and thirty [l]*shekels*, one silver [m]bowl of seventy shekels,
after the shekel of the sanctuary;
both of them full of fine flour
mingled with oil for a [3,n]meat
offering:
32 One golden [o]spoon of ten
[l]*shekels*, full of [q]incense:
33 One young [a]bullock, one
ram, one †lamb of the first year,
for a [b]burnt [c]offering:
34 One kid of the goats for a
[d]sin [c]offering:
35 And for a sacrifice of [e]peace
offerings, two oxen, five rams,
five he goats, five lambs of the
first year: this *was* the offering
of [u]Ē-lī′zur the son of [v]Shĕd′e-ur.
36 ¶ On the fifth day [x]Shĕ-lū′-
mĭ-el the son of ‡Zū-rĭ-shăd′-
da-ī, prince of the children of
[y]Sĭm′e-on, *did offer*:
37 [x]His offering *was* one [j]silver
[k]charger, the weight whereof
*was* an hundred and thirty [l]*shekels*, one silver [m]bowl of seventy
shekels, after the shekel of the
sanctuary; both of them full of
fine flour mingled with oil for
a [3,n]meat offering:
38 One golden [o]spoon of ten
[l]*shekels*, full of [q]incense:
39 One young [a]bullock, one
ram, one †lamb of the first year,
for a [b]burnt [c]offering:
40 One kid of the goats for a
[d]sin offering:
41 And for a sacrifice of [e]peace
offerings, two oxen, five rams,
five he goats, five lambs of the
first year: this *was* the offering
of [x]Shĕ-lū′mĭ-el the son of ‡Zū-
rĭ-shăd′da-ī.
42 ¶ On the sixth day [z]Ē-lī′a-
săph the son of [a]Deū′el, prince
of the children of [b]Găd, *offered*:
43 His offering *was* one [c]silver

v.30–1532 BC
See footnote, *Time*,
Rev. 10:6.

*w* *Reubenites*, Josh. 22:1.
36
*x* *Shelumiel*, Num. 1:6.
*y* *Simeon*, Num. 2:12.
42
*z* *Eliasaph*, Num. 1:14.

*a* *Deuel*, Num. 1:14.
*b* *Gad*, Deut. 33:20
43
*c* *Silver*, 1 Chr. 28: 14.

‡ **ZURISHADDAI** (*my rock is the Almighty*). *Father of Shelumiel*, Num. 1:6; 2:12; 7:36, 41; 10:19.

v.43–1532 BC
See footnote, *Time*, Rev. 10:6.

*d* *Charger*, Ezra 1:9.
*e* *Shekels*, Ex. 30: 13.
*f* *Bowl*, Ex. 25:29.
*g* *Offerings, meat*, Lev. 6:17.
3 R. V. meal

**44**
*h* *Spoons*, Num. 4:7.
*i* *Incense*, Ex. 37: 29.

**45**
*j* *Bullock*, Ex. 29:3.
*k* *Offerings, burnt*, Lev. 6:17.
*l* *Jesus, typified in offerings*, Matt. 1:21.

**46**
*m* *Offerings, sin*, Lev. 6:17.

**47**
*n* *Offerings, peace*, Lev. 6:17.
*o* *Eliasaph*, Num. 1:14.

**48**
*p* *Elishama*, Num. 1:10.
*q* *Ammihud*, Num. 2:18.
*r* *Ephraim, tribe of*, Gen. 41:52.

**54**
*s* *Gamaliel*, Num. 2:20.
*t* *Pedahzur*, Num. 2:20.
*u* *Manasseh, tribe of*, Gen. 46:20.

[d]charger of the weight of an hundred and thirty [e]*shekels*, a silver [f]bowl of seventy shekels, after the shekel of the sanctuary; both of them full of fine flour mingled with oil for a [3,g]meat offering:

44 One golden [h]spoon of ten [e]*shekels*, full of [i]incense:

45 One young [j]bullock, one ram, one †lamb of the first year, for a [k]burnt [l]offering:

46 One kid of the goats for a [m]sin offering:

47 And for a sacrifice of [n]peace offerings, two oxen, five rams, five he goats, five lambs of the first year: this *was* the offering of [o]Ê-lī'a-săph the son of [a]Deū'el.

48 ¶ On the seventh day [p]Ê-lĭsh'a-mȧ the son of [q]Ăm-mī'hŭd, prince of the children of [r]Ē'phră-ĭm, *offered*:

49 His offering *was* one [c]silver [d]charger, the weight whereof *was* an hundred and thirty [e]*shekels*, one silver [f]bowl of seventy shekels, after the shekel of the sanctuary; both of them full of fine flour mingled with oil for a [3,g]meat offering:

50 One golden [h]spoon of ten [e]*shekels*, full of [i]incense:

51 One young [j]bullock, one ram, one †lamb of the first year, for a [k]burnt [l]offering:

52 One kid of the goats for a [m]sin offering:

53 And for a sacrifice of [n]peace offerings, two oxen, five rams, five he goats, five lambs of the first year: this *was* the offering of [p]Ê-lĭsh'a-mȧ the son of [q]Ăm-mī'hŭd.

54 ¶ On the eighth day *offered* [s]Gă-mā'lĭ-el the son of [t]Pē-däh'-zur, prince of the children of [u]Mȧ-năs'seh:

55 His offering *was* one [c]silver [d]charger of the weight of an hundred and thirty [e]*shekels*, one silver [f]bowl of seventy shekels, after the shekel of the sanctuary; both of them full of fine flour mingled with oil for a [3,g]meat offering:

56 One golden [h]spoon of ten [e]*shekels*, full of [i]incense:

57 One young [j]bullock, one ram, one †lamb of the first year, for a [k]burnt [l]offering:

58 One kid of the goats for a [m]sin offering:

59 And for a sacrifice of [n]peace offerings, two oxen, five rams, five he goats, five lambs of the first year: this *was* the offering of [s]Gă-mā'lĭ-el the son of [t]Pē-däh'zur.

60 ¶ On the ninth day [v]Ăb'ĭ-dăn the son of [w]Ḡĭd-e-ō'nī, prince of the children of [x]Bĕn'-ja-mĭn, *offered*:

61 His offering *was* one [c]silver [d]charger, the weight whereof *was* an hundred and thirty [e]*shekels*, one silver [f]bowl of seventy shekels, after the shekel of the sanctuary; both of them full of fine flour mingled with oil for a [3,g]meat offering:

62 One golden [h]spoon of ten *shekels* full of [i]incense:

63 One young [j]bullock, one ram, one †lamb of the first year, for a [k]burnt [l]offering:

64 One kid of the goats for a [m]sin offering:

65 And for a sacrifice of [n]peace offerings, two oxen, five rams, five he goats, five lambs of the first year: this *was* the offering of [v]Ăb'ĭ-dăn the son of [w]Ḡĭd-e-ō'nī.

66 ¶ On the tenth day [y]Ā-hĭ-ē'zēr the son of [z]Ăm-mĭ-shăd'-da-ī, prince of the children of [a]Dăn, *offered*:

67 His offering *was* one [b]silver [c]charger, the weight whereof *was* an hundred and thirty [d]*shekels*, one silver [e]bowl of seventy shekels, after the shekel of the sanctuary; both of them full of fine flour mingled with oil for a [3,f]meat offering:

v.55–1532 BC
See footnote, *Time*, Rev. 10:6.

**60**
*v* *Abidan*, Num. 2:22.
*w* *Gideoni*, Num. 10:24.
*x* *Benjamin*, Num. 1:37.

**66**
*y* *Ahiezer*, Num. 2:25.
*z* *Ammishaddai*, Num. 2:25.

*a* *Dan, tribe of*, Gen. 30:6.

**67**
*b* *Silver*, 1 Chr. 28: 14.
*c* *Charger*, Ezra 1:9.
*d* *Shekel*, Ex. 30:13
*e* *Bowl*, Ex. 25:29.
*f* *Offerings, meat*, Lev. 6:17.

v.68–1532 BC
See footnote, *Time*, Rev. 10:6.

**68**
g *Spoons*, Num. 4:7.
h *Incense*, Ex. 37:29.

**69**
i *Bullock*, Ex. 29:3.
j *Offerings, burnt*, Lev. 6:17.
k *Jesus, typified in offerings*, Matt. 1:21.

**70**
l *Offerings, sin*, Lev. 6:17.

**71**
m *Offerings, peace*, Lev. 6:17.
n Num. 2:25.

**72**
o *Pagiel*, Num. 2:27.
p *Ocran*, Num. 1:13.
q *Asher*, Num. 1:40.

**78**
r *Ahira*, Num. 2:29.
s *Enan*, Num. 1:15.
t *Naphtali*, Num. 1:42.

68 One golden [g]spoon of ten [d]*shekels*, full of [h]incense:

69 One young [i]bullock, one ram, one †lamb of the first year, for a [j]burnt [k]offering:

70 One kid of the goats for a [l]sin offering:

71 And for a sacrifice of [m]peace offerings, two oxen, five rams, five he goats, five lambs of the first year: this *was* the offering of [n]Ā-hī-ē'zēr the son of [n]Ăm-mĭ-shăd'da-ī.

72 ¶ On the eleventh day [o]Pā'-ḡi-el the son of [p]Ŏc'ran, prince of the children of [q]Ăsh'ēr, *offered*:

73 [o]His offering *was* one [b]silver [c]charger, the weight whereof *was* an hundred and thirty [d]*shekels*, one silver [e]bowl of seventy shekels, after the shekel of the sanctuary; both of them full of fine flour mingled with oil for a [3,f]meat offering:

74 One golden [g]spoon of ten *shekels*, full of [h]incense:

75 One young [i]bullock, one ram, one †lamb of the first year, for a [j]burnt [k]offering:

76 One kid of the goats for a [l]sin offering:

77 And for a sacrifice of [m]peace offerings, two oxen, five rams, five he goats, five lambs of the first year: this *was* the offering of [o]Pā'ḡi-el the son of [p]Ŏc'ran.

78 ¶ On the twelfth day [r]Ā-hī'-rȧ the son of [s]Ē'nan, prince of the children of [t]Năph'ta-lī, *offered*:

79 His offering *was* one [b]silver [c]charger, the weight whereof *was* an hundred and thirty [d]*shekels*, one silver [e]bowl of seventy shekels, after the shekel of the sanctuary; both of them full of fine flour mingled with oil for a [3,f]meat offering:

80 One golden [g]spoon of ten [d]*shekels*, full of [h]incense:

81 One young [i]bullock, one ram, one lamb of the first year, for a [j]burnt [k]offering:

82 One kid of the goats for a [l]sin offering:

83 And for a sacrifice of [m]peace offerings, two oxen, five rams, five he goats, five lambs of the first year: this *was* the offering of [r]Ā-hī'rȧ the son of [s]Ē'nan.

84 This *was* the [u]dedication of the [v]altar, in the day when it was [w]anointed, by the [x]princes of Ĭṣ'ra-el: twelve [c]chargers of [b]silver, twelve silver [e]bowls, twelve [g]spoons of [y]gold:

85 Each [c]charger of [b]silver *weighing* an hundred and thirty [d]*shekels*, each [e]bowl seventy: all the silver vessels *weighed* two thousand and four hundred *shekels*, after the shekel of the sanctuary:

86 The golden [g]spoons *were* twelve, full of [h]incense, *weighing* ten [d]*shekels* apiece, after the shekel of the sanctuary: all the [y]gold of the spoons *was* an hundred and twenty *shekels*.

87 All the oxen for the [j]burnt [k]offering *were* twelve [i]bullocks, the rams twelve, the †lambs of the first year twelve, with their [3,f]meat offering: and the kids of the goats for [l]sin offering twelve.

88 And all the oxen for the sacrifice of the [m]peace offerings *were* twenty and four [i]bullocks, the rams sixty, the he goats sixty, the †lambs of the first year sixty. This *was* the [u]dedication of the [v]altar, after that it was [w]anointed.

89 And when Mō'ṣeṣ was gone into the [z]tabernacle of the congregation to speak with him, then he heard the voice of one speaking unto him from off the [a,b]mercy seat that *was* upon the [c]ark of testimony, from between the two [d]cherubims: and he spake unto him.

v.81–1532 BC
See footnote, *Time*, Rev. 10:6.

**84**
u *Dedication, by anointing*, Ezra 6:17.
v *Altar, of burnt offerings*, Gen. 8:20.
w *Anointing*, Lev. 8:12.
x *Senate*, Num. 11:16.
y *Gold*, Ezek. 7:19.

**89**
z *Tabernacle, the Lord reveals himself at*, Ex. 27.9.

a *Mercy Seat*, Ex. 25:17.
b *Shekinah*, Lev. 16:2.
c *Ark*, Ex. 25:10.
d *Cherubim*, Ex. 37:7.

## CHAPTER 8

*The lighting of the lamps. 5 The consecration of the Levites. 23 The age and time of their service.*

AND the LORD [a]spake unto [b, c]Mō′ṣeṣ, saying,

2 Speak unto [d, e]Aâr′on, and say unto him, When thou lightest the [f]lamps, the seven lamps shall give light over against the [g]candlestick[G].

3 And [d, e]Aâr′on did so; he lighted the [f]lamps thereof over against the [g]candlestick[G], as the LORD commanded [c]Mō′ṣeṣ.

4 And this work of the [g]candlestick[G] *was of* [h]beaten [i]gold, unto the shaft thereof, unto the flowers thereof, *was* beaten work: according unto the pattern which the LORD had [a]shewed Mō′ṣeṣ, so he made the candlestick.

5 ¶ And the LORD [a]spake unto [c]Mō′ṣeṣ, saying,

6 [j]Take the [k]Lē′vītes from among the children of [l]Ĭṣ′ra-el, and [m, n]cleanse them.

7 And thus shalt thou do unto them, to [m]cleanse them: [o]Sprinkle water of [1]purifying upon them, and let them shave all their flesh, and let them [p]wash their clothes, and *so* make themselves [n]clean.

8 Then let them take a young [q]bullock with his [2, r]meat[G] offering, *even* fine flour mingled[G] with oil, and another young bullock shalt thou take for a [s]sin [t]offering.

9 And thou shalt bring the [k]Lē′vītes before the [u]tabernacle of the congregation: and thou shalt gather the whole assembly of the children of [l]Ĭṣ′ra-el together:

10 And thou shalt bring the [k]Lē′vītes before the LORD: and the children of [l]Ĭṣ′ra-el shall put their [v]hands upon the Lē′vītes:

11 And [d, w]Aâr′on shall offer the [k]Lē′vītes before the LORD *for* an offering[G] of the children of [l]Ĭṣ′ra-el, that they may execute[G] the service of the LORD.

12 And the [k]Lē′vītes shall [x, y]lay their [v]hands upon the heads of the [q]bullocks: and thou shalt offer the one *for* a [z]sin [a]offering, and the other *for* a [b]burnt offering, unto the LORD, to make an [c, d]atonement for the Lē′vītes.

13 And thou shalt set the [e]Lē′vītes before [f, g]Aâr′on, and before his sons, and offer them [3]*for* an offering[G] unto the LORD.

14 [h]Thus shalt thou separate the [e]Lē′vītes from among the children of Ĭṣ′ra-el: and the Lē′vītes shall be mine.

15 And after that shall the [e]Lē′vītes go in to do the service of the [i]tabernacle of the congregation: and thou shalt [j, k]cleanse them, and offer them [3]*for* an offering.

16 For [e]they *are* wholly given unto me from among the children of [l]Ĭṣ′ra-el; [m]instead of such as open every womb, *even instead of* the [n]firstborn of all the children of Ĭṣ′ra-el, have I taken them unto me.

17 For all the [n]firstborn of the children of [l]Ĭṣ′ra-el *are* mine, *both* man and beast: on the day that I smote every firstborn in the land of [o]Ē′ġўpt I sanctified[G] them for myself.

18 And I have taken the [e]Lē′vītes [m]for all the [n]firstborn of the children of [l]Ĭṣ′ra-el.

19 And I have given the Lē′vītes *as* a gift to Aâr′on and to his sons from among the children of [l]Ĭṣ′ra-el, to [p]do the service of the children of Ĭṣ′ra-el in the [i]tabernacle of the congregation, and to make an [q, r]atonement for the children of Ĭṣ′ra-el: that there be no plague[G] among the children of Ĭṣ′ra-el, when the children of Ĭṣ′ra-el come nigh[G] unto the [s]sanctuary.

20 And [t]Mō′ṣeṣ, and [f, g]Aâr′on,

---

v.1–1532 BC
See footnote, *Time,* Rev. 10:6.

**1**

a *Revelation, of various ordinances,* 2 Cor. 12:1.
b *Moses,* Ex. 2:10.
c *Prophets, inspiration of,* Isa. 3:2.

**2**

d *Aaron,* Ex. 6:20.
e *High Priest, duties of,* Lev. 21:10.
f *Lamp,* Ex. 27:20.
g *Candlestick, of the tabernacle,* Ex. 25:31.

**4**

h Ex. 25:18; 37:17.
i *Gold,* Ezek. 7:19.

**6**

j *Commandment, enjoining holiness in ministers,* v. 7; Deut. 8:2.
k *Levites,* Deut. 10:8.
l *Israel,* Ex. 4:22.
m *Purification,* Num. 19:19.
n *Holiness, typified,* Ex. 39:30.

**7**

o *Sprinkling,* Lev. 14:7.
p *Ceremonial Washing,* Ex. 19:10.
1 R. V. expiation

**8**

q *Bullock,* Ex. 29:3.
r *Offerings, meat,* Lev. 6:17.
s *Offerings, sin,* Lev. 6:17.
t *Jesus, typified in offerings,* Matt. 1:21.
2 R. V. meal

**9**

u *Tabernacle,* Ex. 27:9.

**10**

v *Hand, imposition of,* Ezra 10:19.

**11**

w *High Priest, duties of,* Lev. 21:10.

---

v.11–1532 BC
See footnote, *Time,* Rev. 10:6.

**12**

x *Sin, confession of,* Rom. 5:12.
y *Commandment, enjoining confession of sin,* Deut. 8:2.
z *Offerings, sin,* Lev. 6:17.

a *Jesus, typified in offerings,* Matt. 1:21.
b *Offerings, burnt,* Lev. 6:17.
c *Atonement,* Lev. 17:11.
d *Jesus, atonement by, typified,* Matt. 1:21.

**13**

e *Levites, taken instead of firstborn,* Deut. 10:8.
f *Aaron,* Ex. 6:20.
g *High Priest,* Lev. 21:10.
3 R. V. for a wave

**14**

h *Commandment, enjoining holiness in ministers,* Deut. 8:2.

**15**

i *Tabernacle,* Ex. 27:9.
j *Purification,* Num. 19:19.
k *Holiness, typified,* Ex. 39:30.

**16**

l *Israel,* Ex. 4:22.
m *Substitution,* Lev. 1:4.
n *Firstborn, reserved to God,* Zech. 12:10.

**17**

o *Egypt,* Gen. 41:[illegible]

**19**

p *Levites, duties of,* Deut. 10:8.
q *Atonement,* Lev. 17:11.
r *Jesus, atonement by, typified,* Matt. 1:21.
s *Church, holy,* 1 Kin. 9:3.

**20**

t *Moses,* Ex. 2:10

v.20–1532 BC
See footnote, *Time*, Rev. 10:6.

and all the congregation of the children of [l]Ĭṣ′ra-el, did to the [e]Lē′vītes according unto all that the LORD commanded Mō′ṣeṣ concerning the Lē′vītes, so did the children of Ĭṣ′ra-el unto them.

21 And the [e]Lē′vītes were [j,k]purified, and they [u]washed their clothes; and [g]Aâr′on offered them [3]*as* an offering before the LORD; and Aâr′on made an [q,r]atonement for them to cleanse them.

22 And after that went the [p]Lē′vītes in to do their service in the [i]tabernacle of the congregation before Aâr′on, and before his sons: as the LORD had commanded [t]Mō′ṣeṣ concerning the Lē′vītes, so did they unto them.

23 ¶ And the LORD [v]spake unto Mō′ṣeṣ, saying,

24 This *is it* that *belongeth* unto the [p]Lē′vītes: [w]from twenty and five years old and upward they shall go in to wait upon the service of the [i]tabernacle of the congregation:

25 And [x]from the age of fifty years they shall cease waiting upon the service *thereof*, and shall serve no more:

26 But shall minister with their brethren in the tabernacle of the congregation, to keep the charge, and shall do no service. Thus shalt thou do unto the Lē′vītes touching their charge.

## CHAPTER 9

*The passover is commanded again. 6 A second passover allowed for them that were unclean or absent. 15 The cloud guides the removings and encampings of the Israelites.*

AND the LORD [a]spake unto [b,c]Mō′ṣeṣ in the wilderness of [d]Sī′nāi, in the first [e]month of the second year after they were come out of the land of [f]Ē′ġȳpt, saying,

2 Let the children of [g]Ĭṣ′ra-el also keep the [*,h]passover at his appointed season.

3 In the fourteenth day of this [e]month, at even, ye shall keep it in his appointed season: according to all the rites of it, and according to all the ceremonies thereof, shall ye keep it.

4 And [b]Mō′ṣeṣ spake unto the children of [g]Ĭṣ′ra-el, that they should keep the [*,h]passover.

5 And they kept the [*]passover on the fourteenth day of the first [e]month at even in the wilderness of [d]Sī′nāi: according to all that the LORD [a]commanded [b]Mō′ṣeṣ, so did the children of [g]Ĭṣ′ra-el.

6 ¶ And there were certain men, who were [i,j]defiled by the dead body of a man, that they could not keep the [*]passover on that day: and they came before [b]Mō′ṣeṣ and before [k]Aâr′on on that day:

7 And those men said unto him, We *are* [i,j]defiled by the dead body of a man: wherefore are we kept back, that we may not offer an [l]offering of the LORD in his appointed season among the children of Ĭṣ′ra-el?

8 And [b]Mō′ṣeṣ said unto them, Stand still, and [c]I will hear what the LORD will command concerning you.

9 ¶ And the LORD [a]spake unto [b,c]Mō′ṣeṣ, saying,

10 Speak unto the children of [g]Ĭṣ′ra-el, saying, If any man of you or of your posterity shall be [i,j]unclean by reason of a dead body, or *be* in a journey afar off,

---

21
*u Ceremonial Washing*, Ex. 19:10.

23
*v Prophets, inspiration of*, Isa. 3:2.

24
*w Levites, age of, when inducted into office*, Deut. 10:8.

25
*x Levites, age of, when retired from office*, Deut. 10:8.

1
*a Revelation, concerning the passover*, vs. 1–14; 2 Cor. 12:1.
*b Moses*, Ex. 2:10.
*c Prophets, inspiration of*, Isa. 3:2.
*d Sinai*, Ex. 16:1.
*e Month*, Ex. 12:2.

v.1–1532 BC
See footnote, *Time*, Rev. 10:6.

*f Egypt*, Gen. 41:8.

2
*g Israel*, Ex. 4:22.
*h Jesus, our passover, typified*, Matt. 1:21.

6
*i Defilement, by touching the dead*, Lev. 5:2.
*j Sin, typified*, Rom. 5:12.
*k Aaron*, Ex. 6:20.

7
*l Offerings*, Lev. 6:17.

---

* **PASSOVER.** *Institution of*, Ex. 12:3–49; 23:15–18; 34:18; Lev. 23:4–8; Num. 9:2–5; 28:16–25; Deut. 16:1–8, 16; Psa. 81:3, 5. *Design of*, Ex. 12:21–28.
*Special passover, for those who were unclean, or on journey, to be held in second month*, Num. 9:6–12; 2 Chr. 30:2–4. *Lamb of, killed by Levites, for those who were ceremonially unclean*, 2 Chr. 30:17; 35:3–11; Ezra 6:20. *Strangers authorized to celebrate*, Ex. 12:48, 49; Num. 9:14.
*Observed, at place designated by God*, Deut. 16:5–7; *with unleavened bread*, Ex. 12:8, 15–20; 13:3, 6; 23:15; Lev. 23:6; Num. 9:11; 28:17; Deut. 16:3, 4; Mark 14:12; Luke 22:7; Acts 12:3; 1 Cor. 5:8. *Penalty for neglecting to observe*, Num. 9:13.
*Reinstituted by Ezekiel*, Ezek. 45:21–24.
Observation of: *Renewed, by the Israelites on entering Canaan*, Josh. 5:10, 11; *by Hezekiah*, 2 Chr. 30:1; *by Josiah*,

v.10–1532 BC
See footnote, *Time*, Rev. 10:6.

11
*m* Ex. 12:8.

12
*n* Ex. 12:46; John 19:36.

13
*o Disfellowship*, Num. 15:31.

14
*p Foreigners*, Deut. 23:20.
*q Legislation, class, forbidden*, Ex. 12:49.

15
*r Tabernacle, called tent of the testimony*, Ex. 27:9.
*s Pillar, of cloud and fire*, Ex. 13:21.

17
*t God, guide*, Gen. 2:2.
*u Tent, used for dwelling*, Gen. 13:5.

yet he shall keep the *passover unto the LORD.

11 The fourteenth day of the second [e]month at even they shall keep it, *and* eat it with unleavened bread and [m]bitter *herbs*.

12 They shall leave none of it unto the morning, [n]nor break any bone of it: according to all the ordinances of the *passover they shall keep it.

13 But the man that *is* clean, and is not in a journey, and forbeareth to keep the *passover, even the same soul shall be [o]cut off from among his people: because he brought not the offering of the LORD in his appointed season, that man shall bear his sin.

14 And if a [p]stranger shall sojourn among you, and will keep the *passover unto the LORD; according to the †ordinance of the passover, and according to the manner thereof, so shall he do: ye shall have [q]one ordinance, both for the stranger, and for him that was born in the land.

15 ¶ And on the day that the [r]tabernacle was reared up the [s]cloud covered the tabernacle, *namely*, the tent of the testimony: and at even there was upon the tabernacle as it were the appearance of fire, until the morning.

16 So it was alway: the [s]cloud covered it *by day*, and the appearance of fire by night.

17 And when the [s,t]cloud was taken up from the tabernacle, then after that the children of [g]Ĭs′ra-el journeyed: and in the place where the cloud abode, there the children of Ĭs′ra-el pitched their [u]tents.

18 [t]At the commandment of the LORD the children of Ĭs′ra-el [v]journeyed, and at the commandment of the LORD they pitched: as long as the [s]cloud abode upon the [r]tabernacle they rested in their [u]tents.

19 And when the [s,t]cloud tarried long upon the [r]tabernacle many days, then the children of [g]Ĭs′ra-el [v]kept the charge of the LORD, and journeyed not.

20 And *so* it was, when the [s]cloud was a few days upon the [r]tabernacle; [v]according to the commandment of the LORD they abode in their [u]tents, and according to the commandment of the LORD they journeyed.

21 And *so* it was, when the [s]cloud abode from even unto the morning, and *that* the cloud was taken up in the morning, then they journeyed: whether *it was* by day or by night that the cloud was taken up, they journeyed.

22 Or *whether it were* two days, or a month, or a year, that the [s,t]cloud tarried upon the [r]tabernacle, remaining thereon, the children of [g]Ĭs′ra-el abode in their [u]tents, and journeyed not: but when it was taken up, they journeyed.

23 At the commandment of the LORD they rested in the tents, and at the commandment of the LORD they journeyed: they [v]kept the charge of the LORD, at the commandment of the LORD by the hand of Mō′ṣeṣ.

## CHAPTER 10

*The use of the silver trumpets.* 11 *The Israelites remove from Sinai to Paran.* 14 *The order of their march.* 29 *Hobab is entreated by Moses not to leave them.* 35 *The prayer of Moses at the removing and resting of the ark.*

AND the LORD [a]spake unto [b]Mō′ṣeṣ, saying,

2 Make thee two [c]trumpets of

v.18–1532 BC
See footnote, *Time*, Rev. 10:6.

18
*v Obedience*, Heb. 5:8.

1
*a Revelation, concerning trumpets*, 2 Cor. 12:1.
*b Prophets, inspiration of*, Isa. 3:2.

2
*c Trumpet*, Josh. 6:4.

2 Kin. 23:22, 23; 2 Chr. 35:1, 18; *after return from captivity*, Ezra 6:19, 20. *Observed by Jesus*, Matt. 26:17–20; Luke 22:15; John 2:13, 23; 13. *Jesus, at the age of twelve, in the temple at time of*, Luke 2:41–50. *Jesus crucified at time of*, Matt. 26:2; Mark 14:1, 2; John 18:28. *The lamb of, a type of Christ*, 1 Cor. 5:7. *Lord's supper ordained at*, Matt 26:26–28; Mark 14:12–25; Luke 22:7–20.

*Prisoners released at, by the Romans*, Matt. 27:15; Mark 15:6; Luke 23:17, 25; John 18:39. *Peter imprisoned at time of*, Acts 12:3. *Christ called* OUR PASSOVER, 1 Cor. 5:7. See footnote, ANNUAL FEASTS, Num. 15:3

† **ORDINANCE.** *A decree*, Ex. 15:25; **Num. 10:8; 15:15;** 18:8; 1 Sam. 30:25; Isa. 24:5; Mal. 4:4.

v.2–1532 BC
See footnote, *Time*, Rev. 10:6.

*d Silver, trumpets of*, 1 Chr. 28:14.
1 R. V. beaten work

3
*e Tabernacle*, Ex. 27:9.

4
*f Senate*, Num. 11:16.
*g Israel*, Ex. 4:22.

8
*h Aaron*, Ex. 6:20.
*i Priest, duties of*, Lev. 1:5.
*j Ordinance, a decree*, Num. 9:14.

9
*k Armies, rendezvous of*, Deut. 11:4.
*l Promise, to the obedient, of deliverance from enemies*, 2 Cor. 1:20.

10
*m Annual Feasts*, Num. 15:3.
*n Offerings, burnt*, Lev. 6:17.
*o Offerings, peace*, Lev. 6:17.
2 R. V. set feasts,

[d]silver; of [1]a whole piece shalt
thou make them: that thou mayest use them for the calling of the
assembly, and for the journeying
of the camps.
3 And when they shall blow
with [c]them, all the assembly shall
assemble themselves to thee at
the door of the [e]tabernacle of the
congregation.
4 And if they blow *but* with one
[c]*trumpet*, then the [f]princes,
*which are* heads of the thousands
of [g]Īṣ′ra-el, shall gather themselves unto thee.
5 [c]When ye blow an alarm,
then the camps that lie on the
east parts shall go forward.
6 [c]When ye blow an alarm the
second time, then the camps that
lie on the south side shall take
their journey: they shall blow an
alarm for their journeys.
7 But [c]when the congregation
is to be gathered together, ye
shall blow, but ye shall not
sound an alarm.
8 And the sons of [h]Aâr′on, the
[i]priests, shall blow with the
[c]trumpets; and they shall be to
you for an [j]ordinance for ever
throughout your generations.
9 And [k]if ye go to war in your
land against the enemy that oppresseth you, then ye shall blow
an alarm with the [c]trumpets;
and [l]ye shall be remembered before the LORD your God, and ye
shall be saved from your enemies.
10 Also in the day of your gladness, and in your [2,m]solemn
days, and in the beginnings of
your months, ye shall blow with
the trumpets over your [n]burnt
offerings, and over the sacrifices
of your [o]peace offerings; that
they may be to you for a memorial before your God: [p]I *am*
the LORD your God.
11 ¶ And it came to pass on the
twentieth *day* of the second
[q]month, in the second [r]year,
that the [s]cloud was taken up
from off the [e]tabernacle of the
testimony.
12 And the children of [g]Īṣ′ra-el
took their journeys out of the
wilderness of [t]Sī′nāi; and the
[s]cloud rested in the wilderness
of [u]Pā′ran.
13 And [g]they first took their
journey according to the commandment of the LORD by the
hand of Mō′ṣeṣ.
14 ¶ In the first *place* went the
[v,w]standard of the camp of the
children of *Jū′dah according to
their armies: and over his host
*was* [x]Näh′shŏn the son of [y]Ăm-mĭn′a-dăb.
15 And over the host of the
tribe of the children of [z]Ĭs′sa-char *was* [a]Nē-thăn′e-el the son
of [b]Zū′ar.
16 And over the host of the
tribe of the children of [c]Zĕb′u-lŭn *was* [d]Ē-lī′ab the son of
[e]Hē′lon.
17 And the [f]tabernacle was
taken down; and the [g]sons of
Gēr′shŏn and the [h]sons of Mē-rā′rī set forward, bearing the
tabernacle.
18 And the [i]standard of the
camp of [j]Reu̇′ben set forward
according to their armies: and
over his host *was* [k]Ē-lī′zur the
son of [l]Shĕd′e-ur.
19 And over the host of the
tribe of the children of [m]Sĭm′e-on
*was* [n]Shē-lū′mĭ-el the son of
[o]Zū-rĭ-shăd′da-ī.
20 And over the host of the

v.10–1532 BC
See footnote, *Time*, Rev. 10:6.

*p God, sovereign*, Gen. 2:2.

11
*q Month, Zif*, Ex. 12:2.
*r Year, divided into months*, Lev. 25:29.
*s Pillar, of cloud and fire*, Ex. 13:21.

12
*t Sinai*, Ex. 16:1.
*u Paran*, Gen. 21:21.

14
*v Standard*, Num. 1:52.
*w Armies, standards of*, Deut. 11:4.
*x Nahshon*, Num. 7:12.
*y Amminadab*, Num. 2:3.

15
*z Issachar, tribe of*, Num. 1:28.

*a Nethaneel*, Num. 2:5.
*b Zuar*, Num. 1:8.

16
*c Zebulun, tribe of*, Gen. 49:13.
*d Eliab*, Num. 1:9.
*e Helon*, Num. 2:7.

17
*f Tabernacle, by whom carried*, Ex. 27:9.
*g Gershonites, duties of*, Num. 4:27.
*h Merarites, duties of*, Num. 26:57.

18
*i Standard*, Num. 1:52.
*j Reubenites*, Josh. 22:1.
*k* Num. 1:5; 2:10; 7:30, 35.
*l Shedeur*, Num. 1:5.

19
*m Simeon, tribe of*, Num. 2:12.
*n Shelumiel*, Num. 1:6.
*o Zurishaddai*, Num. 7:36.

***JUDAH. Tribe of:** *Prophecies concerning*, Gen. 49:10. *Enrollment of the military forces of, at Sinai*, Num. 1:26, 27; 2:4; *in the plain of Moab*, Num. 26:22; *at Bezek*, 1 Sam. 11:8; 2 Sam. 24:9. *Place of, in camp and march*, Num. 2:3, 9. *By whom commanded*, Num. 2:3; 10:14. *Moses' benediction upon*, Deut. 33:7. *Commissioned of God to lead in the conquest of the promised land*, Judg. 1:1–19. *Inheritance of*, Josh. 15; 18:5; 19:1, 9. *Makes David king*, 2 Sam. 2:1–11; 5:4, 5. *Upbraided by David for lukewarmness toward him after Absalom's defeat*, 2 Sam. 19:11–15. *Accused by the other tribes of stealing the heart of David*, 2 Sam. 19:41–43. *Loyal to David at the time of the insurrection led by Sheba*, 2 Sam. 20:1, 2. *Men of, join David against Saul*, 1 Chr. 12:16. *Loyal to the house of David at the time of the revolt of the ten tribes*, 1 Kin. 12:20. *The kingdom of Judah and Benjamin after the revolt takes the name of*, see footnote, JUDAH, *Kingdom of*, 2 Chr. 11:17.

v.20—1532 BC
See footnote, *Time*, Rev. 10:6.

20
p *Gad, tribe of*, Deut. 33:20.
q *Eliasaph*, Num. 1:14.
r *Deuel*, Num. 1:14.

21
s *Kohathites, duties of*, Num. 3:27.
t *Sanctuary*, Lev. 4:6.

22
u *Ephraim, tribe of*, Gen. 41:52.
v *Elishama*, Num. 1:10.
w *Ammihud*, Num. 2:18.

23
x *Manasseh, tribe of*, Gen. 46:20.
y *Gamaliel*, Num. 2:20.
z *Pedahzur*, Num. 2:20.

24
a *Benjamin, tribe of*, Num. 1:37.
b *Abidan*, Num. 2:22.
c Num. 1:11; 2:22; 7:60, 65.

25
d *Standard*, Num. 1:52.
e *Dan, tribe of*, Gen. 30:6.
f *Ahiezer*, Num. 2:25.
g *Ammishaddai*, Num. 2:25.

26
h *Asher, tribe of*, Num. 1:40.
i *Pagiel*, Num. 2:27.
j *Ocran*, Num. 1:13.

27
k *Naphtali, tribe of*, Num. 1:42.
l *Ahira*, Num. 2:29.
m *Enan*, Num. 1:15.

28
n *Israel*, Ex. 4:22.

29
o *Moses*, Ex. 2:10.
p Judg. 4:11.
q Or, *Jethro*, Ex. 3:1.
r *Faith, instances of*, Mark 11:22.
s *God, providence of*, Gen. 2:2.
t *Temporal Blessings, from God*, Psa. 103:2.

tribe of the children of [p]Găd *was* [q]Ĕ-lī′a-săph the son of [r]Deū′el.

21 And the [s]Kō′hath-ītes set forward, bearing the [t]sanctuary: and *the other* did [g]set up the tabernacle against they came.

22 And the [t]standard of the camp of the children of [u]Ē′phră-ĭm set forward according to their armies: and over his host *was* [v]Ĕ-lĭsh′a-mȧ the son of [w]Ăm-mī′hŭd.

23 And over the host of the tribe of the children of [x]Mȧ-năs′seh *was* [y]Gȧ-mā′lĭ-el the son of [z]Pĕ-däh′zur.

24 And over the host of the tribe of the children of [a]Bĕn′ja-mĭn *was* [b]Ăb′i-dăn the son of [c]Gĭd-e-ō′nī.

25 And the [d]standard of the camp of the children of [e]Dăn set forward, *which was* the rereward of all the camps throughout their hosts: and over his host *was* [f]Ā-hī-ē′zēr the son of [g]Ăm-mĭ-shăd′da-ī.

26 And over the host of the tribe of the children of [h]Ăsh′ēr *was* [i]Pā′ğī-el the son of [j]Ŏc′ran.

27 And over the host of the tribe of the children of [k]Năph′ta-lī *was* [l]Ā-hī′rȧ the son of [m]Ē′nan.

28 Thus *were* the journeyings of the children of [n]Ĭṣ′ra-el according to their armies, when they set forward.

29 ¶ And [o]Mō′ṣeṣ said unto [p]Hō′băb, the son of [q]Rȧ-gū′el the Mĭd′ĭ-an-īte, Mō′ṣeṣ′ father in law, [r]We are journeying unto the place of which the LORD said, I will [s]give [t]it you: come thou with us, and we will do thee good: for the LORD hath spoken good concerning Ĭṣ′ra-el.

30 And he said unto him, I will not go; but I will depart to mine own land, and to my kindred.

31 And he said, Leave us not, I pray thee; forasmuch as thou knowest how we are to encamp in the wilderness, and thou mayest be to us instead of eyes.

32 And it shall be, if thou go with us, yea, it shall be, that what [t]goodness the LORD shall do unto us, the same will we do unto thee.

33 ¶ And [n]they departed from the mount of the LORD three days' journey: and the [u,v]ark of the covenant of the LORD went before them in the three days' journey, to search out a resting place for them.

34 And the [w]cloud of the LORD *was* upon them by day, when they went out of the camp.

35 And it came to pass, when the [u]ark set forward, that [o]Mō′ṣeṣ [x]said, Rise up, LORD, and let thine enemies be scattered; and let them that hate thee flee before thee.

36 And when it rested, he [x]said, Return, O LORD, unto the many thousands of Ĭṣ′ra-el.

## CHAPTER 11

*The burning at Taberah quenched at the prayer of Moses. 4 The people lust for flesh, and loathe the manna. 10 Moses complains of the burden of his charge. 16 Seventy elders are appointed to bear it with him. 24 Their inspiration. 31 Quails are given at Kibroth-hattaavah.*

AND *when* the people [a]complained, it displeased the LORD: and the LORD heard *it*; and his [b]anger was kindled; and [c]the [d]fire of the LORD burnt among them, and consumed *them that were* in the uttermost parts of the camp.

2 And the people cried unto [e]Mō′ṣeṣ; and when Mō′ṣeṣ [f]prayed unto the LORD, the fire was quenched.

3 And he called the name of the place [g]Tăb′e-rah: because the [d]fire of the LORD burnt among them.

4 ¶ And the mixt multitude that *was* among [h]them fell a [i]lusting: and the children of Ĭṣ′-

B.C. 1490?
See footnote, *Time*, Rev. 10:6.

33
u *Ark, called ark of covenant*, Ex. 25:10.
v *God, guide*, Gen. 2:2.

34
w *Pillar, of cloud and fire*, Ex. 13:21.

35
x *Prayer*, Acts 6:4.

1
a *Murmuring, instances of*, Num. 14:2.
b *Anger of God*, 2 Kin. 13:3.
c *Judgments, upon Israelites*, Ex. 6:6.
d *Miracles*, Luke 23:8.

2
e *Moses*, Ex. 2:10.
f *Intercession, answered*, Jer. 27:18.

3
g Deut. 9:22.

4
h *Israel, accompanied by mixed multitude*, Ex. 4:22.
i *Appetite, a source of temptation*, Prov. 23:2.

v.4–1532 BC
See footnote, *Time*, Rev. 10:6.

*j* *Borrowing Trouble, instances of*, vs. 4–30; Matt. 6:25.

5
*k* *Egypt*, Gen. 41:8.
*l* *Cucumber*, Isa. 1:8.
1 R. V. for naught;

6
*m* *Manna*, Ex. 16:31.

7
*n* Ex. 16:31.
*o* Gen. 2:12.

8
*p* *Mill*, Ex. 11:5.
*q* Prov. 27:22.
*r* *Bread, made of manna*, Ezek. 4:13.
2 R. V. mortars, and seethed it in pots, and made cakes of it:

10
*s* *Moses, impatience of*, vs. 10–15; Ex. 2:10.

11
*t* *Presumption, instances of*, Psa. 19:13.

ra-el also wept again, and said, [j]Who shall give us flesh to eat?[Q]

5 We remember the fish, which we did eat in [k]Ē′ġy̆pt [1]freely;[G] the [l]cucumbers, and the melons, and the leeks, and the onions, and the garlick:

6 But now our soul *is* dried[G] away: *there is* nothing at all, beside this [m]manna, *before* our eyes.

7[Q] And the manna *was* as [n]coriander seed, and the colour thereof as the colour of [o]bdellium.

8 *And* the people went about, and gathered [m]*it*, and ground *it* in [p]mills, or beat *it* in [2]a [q]mortar, and baked *it* in pans, and made [r]cakes of it: and the taste of it was as the taste of fresh oil.

9 And when the dew fell upon the camp in the night, the [m]manna fell upon it.[Q]

10 ¶ Then Mō′ṣeṣ heard the people weep throughout their families, every man in the door of his tent: and the [b]anger of the Lord was kindled[G] greatly; [s]Mō′ṣeṣ also was displeased.

11 And [s]Mō′ṣeṣ [a]said unto the Lord, [t]Wherefore hast thou afflicted thy servant? and wherefore have I not found favour in thy sight, that thou layest the burden of all this people upon me?[S]

12 [a,t]Have I conceived all this people? have I begotten them, that thou shouldest say unto me, Carry them in thy bosom, as a nursing father beareth the sucking child, unto[G] the [u]land which thou [v]swarest unto their fathers?

13 [a,t]Whence should I have flesh to give unto all this people? for they weep unto me, saying, Give us flesh, that we may eat.

14 [w]I am not able to bear[G] all this people alone, because *it is* too heavy for me.

15 And [w]if thou deal thus with me, [x]kill me, I pray thee, out[G] of hand, if I have found favour in thy sight; and let me not see my wretchedness.

16 ¶ And the Lord said unto [e]Mō′ṣeṣ, Gather unto me *seventy men of the †elders of Ĭṣ′-ra-el, whom thou knowest to be the elders of the people, and officers over them; and bring them unto the [y]tabernacle of the congregation, that they may stand there with thee.

17 And I will come down and [z]talk with [a]thee there: and I will take of the spirit which *is* upon thee, and will [b]put *it* upon them; and they shall bear the burden of the people with thee, that thou bear *it* not thyself alone.[T]

18 And say thou unto the people,[G] [c]Sanctify yourselves against to morrow, and ye shall eat flesh: for ye have wept in the ears of the Lord, [d]saying, Who shall give us flesh to eat? for *it was* well with us in Ē′ġy̆pt: therefore the Lord will give you flesh,[G] and ye shall eat.

19 Ye shall not eat one day, nor

v.12–1532 BC
See footnote, *Time*, Rev. 10:6.

12
*u* *Canaan, promised to Abraham and his seed*, Gen. 37:1.
*v* *Covenant, of God with men*, Deut. 29:1.

14
*w* *Despondency, instances of*, Eccl. 2:20.

15
*x* *Death, desired, by Moses*, Num. 23:10.

16
*y* *Tabernacle*, Ex. 27:9.

17
*z* *Communion with God*, 2 Cor. 13:14.

*a* *Prophets, inspiration of*, Isa. 3:2.
*b* *Inspiration*, Job 32:8.

18
*c* *Purification*, Num. 19:19.
*d* *Murmuring, instances of*, Num. 14:2.

*** SEVENTY.** *The senate of the Israelites composed of seventy elders*, Ex. 24:1, 9; Num. 11:16, 24, 25. *Seventy disciples sent forth by Jesus*, Luke 10:1–17. *The Jews in captivity in Babylon seventy years*, Jer. 25:11, 12; 29:10; Dan. 9:2; Zech. 1:12; 7:5.

*Seventy weeks in the vision of Daniel*, Dan. 9:24.

**† SENATE.** *Chosen elders of the nation, vested with representative, judicial, and executive authority*, Ex. 4:29; 5:15, 19; 6:14–25; 12:21; Num. 11:16–30.

*Closely associated with Moses and subsequent leaders*, Ex. 3:16–18; 4:29; 12:21; 17:5, 6; 18:12; 19:7; 24:1, 14; Num. 16:25; Deut. 5:23; 27:1; 29:10; 31:9, 28; Josh. 7:6; 8:10, 33; 23:2; 24:1; Judg. 11:5–11; Acts 5:17, 18, 21. *Made confession of sin in behalf of the nation*, Lev. 4:15; 9:1.

Miscellany of Facts Relating to the Senate and Senators or Elders. *Demands a king*, 1 Sam. 8:4–10, 19–22. *Saul pleads to be honored before*, 1 Sam. 15:30. *Chooses David as king*, 2 Sam. 3:17–21; 5:3; 1 Chr. 11:3. *Closely associated with David*, 2 Sam. 12:17; 1 Chr. 15:25; 21:16. *Joins Absalom in his usurpation*, 2 Sam. 17:4. *David upbraids*, 2 Sam. 19:11. *Assists Solomon at the dedication of the temple*, 1 Kin. 8:1–3; 2 Chr. 5:2–4. *Counsels king Rehoboam*, 1 Kin. 12:6–8, 13. *Counsels king Ahab*, 1 Kin. 20:7, 8. *Josiah assembles, to hear the law of the Lord*, 2 Kin. 23:1; 2 Chr. 34:29, 31.

*Legislates with Ezra in reforming certain marriages with the heathen*, Ezra 10:8–14. *Legislates in later times*, Matt. 15:2, 7–9; Mark 7:1–13. *Sits as a court*, Jer. 26:10–24. *Constitutes, with priests and scribes, a court for the trial of both civil and ecclesiastical causes*, Matt. 21:23; 26:3–5, 57–68; 27:1, 2; Mark 8:31; 14:53–65; 15:1; Luke 22:52–71; Acts 4:1–21; 6:12–15. *Seeks counsel from prophets*, Ezek. 8:1; 14:1; 20:1, 3. *Corrupt*, 1 Kin. 21:8–14; Ezek. 8:11, 12; Matt. 26:14, 15; 27:3, 4.

*A similar senate existed among, the Egyptians*, Gen. 50:7; *the Midianites and Moabites*, Num. 22:4, 7, 8; *the Gibeonites*, Josh. 9:11.

v.19–1532 BC
See footnote, *Time*, Rev. 10:6.

**20**
*e Gluttony*, Prov. 30:22.
*f Sarcasm, instances of*, Judg. 10:14.

**21**
*g Moses*, Ex. 2:10.
*h Doubting, of Moses*, Rom. 14:23.
*i Israel, number of*, Ex. 4:22.

**23**
*j God, power of*, Gen. 2:2.
*k Hand, figurative*, Ezra 10:19.

**24**
*l Tabernacle*, Ex. 27:9.

**25**
*m Pillar, of cloud and fire, symbol of the Lord's presence*, Ex. 13:21.
*n Prophets, inspiration of*, Isa. 3:2.

two days, nor five days, neither
ten days, nor twenty days;
20 [e,f]*But* even a whole month,
until it come out at your nostrils,
and it be loathsome unto you:
because that ye have despised
the LORD which *is* among you,
and have wept before him, [d]saying,
Why came we forth out of
Ē′gy̆pt?
21 And [g]Mō′şeş [h]said, The
[i]people, among whom I *am*, *are*
six hundred thousand footmen;
and thou hast said, I will give
them flesh, that they may eat a
whole month.
22 [f]Shall the flocks and the
herds be slain for them, to suffice
them? or shall all the fish of the
sea be gathered together for
them to suffice them?
23 And the LORD said unto
[g]Mō′şeş, Is the LORD's [j,k]hand
waxed short? thou shalt see now
whether my word shall come to
pass unto thee or not.
24 ¶ And [g]Mō′şeş went out,
and told the people the words of
the LORD, and gathered the
*seventy men of the †elders of
the people, and set them round
about the [l]tabernacle.
25 And the LORD came down
in a [m]cloud, and spake unto
[n]him, and took of the spirit that
*was* upon him, and [b]gave *it* unto
the seventy elders: and it came
to pass, *that*, when the spirit
rested upon them, they prophesied,
and did not cease.
26 But there remained two *of*
*the* men in the camp, the name of
the one *was* Ĕl′dăd, and the
name of the other Mē′dăd: and
the [b]spirit rested upon them, and
they *were* of them that were written,
but went not out unto the
[l]tabernacle: and they prophesied
in the camp.
27 And there ran a young man,
and told Mō′şeş, and said, Ĕl′dăd
and Mē′dăd do prophesy in
the camp.
28 And [o]Jŏsh′u-ȧ the son of
Nŭn, the servant of Mō′şeş, *one*
of his young men, answered and
said, My lord Mō′şeş, [‡,p]forbid
them.
29 And [q]Mō′şeş said unto him,
[r]Enviest thou for my sake?
[s,t]would God that all the LORD's
people were [n]prophets, *and* that
the LORD would [b]put his spirit
upon them!
30 And Mō′şeş gat him into the
camp, he and the †elders of Iş′ra-el.
31 ¶ And there went forth a
[u]wind from the LORD, and
[v]brought [w,x]quails from the sea,
and let *them* fall by the camp,
as it were a day's journey on this
side, and as it were a day's journey
on the other side, round
about the camp, and as it were
two cubits *high* upon the face of
the earth.
32 And the people stood up all
that day, and all *that* night, and
all the next day, and they gathered
the [w]quails: he that gathered
least gathered ten [y]homers:
and they spread *them* all abroad
for themselves round about the
‖camp.
33 And while the flesh *was* yet
between their teeth, ere it was
chewed, the [z]wrath of the LORD
was kindled against the people,
and the LORD [a]smote the people
with a very great [b]plague.
34 And he called the name of
that place ‖Kĭb′roth–hat-tā′a-vah:
because there they buried
the people that lusted.

v.26–1532 BC
See footnote, *Time*, Rev. 10:6.

**28**
*o Joshua*, Josh. 1:1.
*p Bigotry, instances of*, Isa. 65:5.

**29**
*q Moses, character of*, Ex. 2.10.
*r Envy, instances of*, Prov. 14:30.
*s Zeal, instances of*, 2 Cor. 7:11.
*t Unselfishness, instances of, Moses*, 1 Cor. 10:24.

**31**
*u Meteorology*, Matt. 16:2.
*v God, providence of*, Gen. 2:2.
*w Quail*, Ex. 16:13.
*x Temporal Blessings, from God*, Psa. 103:2.

**32**
*y Measure, dry*, Deut. 25:15.

**33**
*z Anger of God*, 2 Kin. 13:3.

*a Judgments, upon the Israelites*, Ex. 6:6.
*b Plague, on the Israelites*, Ex. 11:1.

‡ **INTOLERANCE**, religious. Exemplified: *By Joshua*, Num. 11:24–28; *by James and John*, Mark 9:38, 39; Luke 9:49. *By the Jews, in persecuting the disciples*, Acts 4:1–3, 15–21; 17:13; *in persecuting Stephen*, Acts 6:9–15; 7:57–59; 8:1–3; *in persecuting Paul*, Acts 13:50; 17:5; 18:13; 21:28–31; 22:22, 23; 23:2.

See footnote, PERSECUTION, John 15:20.

*Of idolatrous religions, taught by Moses*, Ex. 22:20; Deut. 13; 17:1–7. Exemplified: *By Elijah*, 1 Kin. 18:40; *by Jehu*, 2 Kin. 10:18–31; *by the Jews, at the time of the religious revival under the leadership of Azariah*, 2 Chr. 15:12, 13.

‖ **KIBROTH-HATTAAVAH** (*the graves of lust*). *A station where the Israelites were miraculously fed with quails*, Num. 11:31–35; 33:16, 17; Deut. 9:22.

v.35–1532 BC
See footnote, *Time*, Rev. 10:6.

35 *And* the people journeyed from Kĭb′roth–hat-tā′a-vah unto [§]Hă-zē′roth; and abode at Hă-zē′roth.

## CHAPTER 12

*God rebukes the sedition of Miriam and Aaron. 10 Miriam's leprosy. 13 Moses' prayer for the healing of Miriam. 14 God commands that she be shut out from the camp seven days.*

AND [a,b,c]Mĭr′ĭ-am and [d,e]Aâr′on [f,g]spake against [h]Mō′ṣeṣ because of the [1]Ē-thĭ-ō′pĭ-an woman whom he had [i]married: for he had married an Ē-thĭ-ō′pĭ-an woman.

2 And they said, [j]Hath the LORD indeed spoken only by [h]Mō′ṣeṣ? [k]hath he not spoken also by us? And the LORD heard *it*.

3 (Now the man [m]Mō′ṣeṣ *was* very [n]meek, above all the men which *were* upon the face of the earth.)

4 And the LORD spake suddenly unto [h]Mō′ṣeṣ, and unto [d]Aâr′on, and unto [a]Mĭr′ĭ-am, Come out ye three into the [o]tabernacle of the congregation. And they three came out.

5 And the LORD came down in the [p]pillar of the cloud, and stood *in* the door of the [o]tabernacle, and called [d]Aâr′on and [a]Mĭr′ĭ-am: and they both came forth.

6 And he said, Hear now my words: If there be a [q]prophet among you, I the LORD will make myself known unto him in a [r]vision, *and* will speak unto him in a [s]dream.

7 My servant [t]Mō′ṣeṣ *is* not so, who *is* [u]faithful in all mine house.[Q]

8 With [t]him will I [v]speak mouth to mouth, even apparently,[G] and not in dark[G] speeches; and the similitude of the LORD shall he behold: wherefore then were ye not afraid to speak against my servant Mō′ṣeṣ?[Q]

9 And the [w]anger of the LORD was kindled against them; and he departed.[S]

10 [S]And the [p]cloud departed from off the [o]tabernacle; and, behold, [a]Mĭr′ĭ-am [x]*became* [y]leprous, *white* as snow: and [d]Aâr′on looked upon Mĭr′ĭ-am, and, behold, *she was* leprous.

11 And [d]Aâr′on said unto [h]Mō′ṣeṣ, Alas, my lord, I beseech thee, lay not the sin upon us, wherein [z]we have done foolishly, and wherein we have sinned.

12 [a]Let her not be as one dead, of whom the flesh is half consumed when he cometh out of his mother's womb.

13 And Mō′ṣeṣ [b,c]cried unto the LORD, saying, [d]Heal her now, O God, I beseech thee.

14 ¶ And the LORD said unto Mō′ṣeṣ, If her father had but [*]spit in her face, should she not be ashamed [e]seven days? let her be [f,g]shut out from the camp seven days, and after that let her be received in *again*.

15 And [h]Mĭr′ĭ-am was [f,g]shut out from the camp [e]seven days: and the people journeyed not till Mĭr′ĭ-am was brought in *again*.[S]

16 And afterward the [i]people removed[G] from [j]Hă-zē′roth, and pitched in the wilderness of [k]Pā′ran.

## CHAPTER 13

*The names of the men who were sent to search the land. 17 Their instructions. 21 Their acts. 26 Their report.*

AND the LORD [a]spake unto Mō′ṣeṣ, saying,

2 Send thou men, that they may search the land of [b]Cā′năan, which I give unto the children of Ĭṣ′ra-el: of every tribe of their fa-

**1**
a *Miriam*, Ex. 15:20.
b *Women, wicked, instances of*, Prov. 31:10.
c *Citizens, wicked and treasonable, instances of*, Luke 15:15.
d *Aaron*, Ex. 6:20.
e *Minister, false and corrupt, instances of*, Rom. 15:16.
f *Treason, instances of*, 2 Kin. 11:14.
g *Conspiracy, instances of*, vs. 1–16; 1 Kin. 16:9.
h *Moses*, Ex. 2:10.
i *Miscegenation, instances of*, Josh. 23:12.
1 R. V. Cushite

**2**
j *Envy, instances of*, Prov. 14:30.
k *Ambition, instances of*, vs. 2–10; Hab. 2:5.
l *Sin, known to God*, Rom. 5:12.

**3**
m *Moses, character of*, Ex. 2:10.
n *Meekness, instances of*, Psa. 45:4.

**4**
o *Tabernacle*, Ex. 27:9.

**5**
p *Pillar, of cloud and fire, symbol of the Lord's presence*, Ex. 13:21.

**6**
q *Prophets, inspiration of*, vs. 6–8; Isa. 3:2.
r *Vision*, Acts 9:10.
s *Dream, instances of*, Dan. 1:17.

**7**
t *Moses, prophecies of*, Ex. 2:10.
u *Faithfulness, instances of*, Luke 16:10.

**8**
v *Communion, with God*, 2 Cor. 13:14.

v.8–1532 BC
See footnote, *Time*, Rev. 10:6.

**9**
w *Anger of God*, 2 Kin. 13:3.

**10**
x *Miracles*, Luke 23:8.
y *Leprosy, as a judgment*, Lev. 13:2.

**11**
z *Sin, confession of*, Rom. 5:2.

**12**
a *Intercession, of man with man*, Jer. 27:18.

**13**
b *Intercession, of man with God*, Jer. 27:18.
c *Affliction, prayer in*, Psa. 34:19.
d *Healing, the Lord the healer*, Acts 4:22.

**14**
e *Seven, days*, Gen. 7:2.
f *Leprosy, isolation of lepers*, Lev. 13:2.

**15**
g *Sanitation and Hygiene, isolation*, Num. 31:23.
h *Miriam*, Ex. 15:20.

**16**
i *Israel*, Ex. 4:22.
j *Hazeroth*, Num. 11:35.
k *Paran, desert of*, Gen. 21:21.

**1**
a *Prophets, inspiration of*, Isa. 3:2.

**2**
b *Canaan, land of*, Gen. 37:1.

§ **HAZEROTH** (*village*). *A station in the journeyings of the children of Israel*, Num. 11:35; 12:16; 33:17, 18; Deut. 1:1.

* **SPITTING**. *In the face, as an indignity*, Num. 12:14; Deut. 25:9; Job 30:10; Isa. 50:6; Matt. 26:67; 27:30; Mark 14:65. *Jesus used spittle in healing*, Mark 7:33; 8:23.

v.2–1532 BC
See footnote, *Time*, Rev. 10:6.

**3**
*c* *Israel, sends twelve spies to view the land,* Ex. 4:22.
*d* *Paran, wilderness of,* Gen. 21:21.

**4**
*e* *Reubenites,* Josh. 22:1.

**5**
*f* *Simeon, tribe of,* Num. 2:12.

**6**
*g* *Judah, tribe of,* Num. 10:14.
*h* *Caleb,* Num. 14:6.

**7**
*i* *Issachar, tribe of,* Num. 1:28.

**8**
*j* *Ephraim, tribe of,* Gen. 41:52.
*k* Or, *Joshua,* Josh. 1:1.

**9**
*l* *Benjamin, tribe of,* Num. 1:37.

**10**
*m* *Zebulun, tribe of,* Gen. 49:13.

**11**
*n* *Manasseh, tribe of,* Gen. 46:20.

**12**
*o* *Dan, tribe of,* Gen. 30:6.

**13**
*p* *Asher, tribe of,* Num. 1:40.

**14**
*q* *Naphtali, tribe of,* Num. 1:42.

**15**
*r* *Gad, tribe of,* Deut. 33:20.

**16**
*s* *Spies,* Josh. 6:23.

thers shall ye send a man, every
one a ruler among them.
3 And [a]Mō′ṣeṣ by the commandment of the LORD [c]sent
them from the wilderness of
[d]Pā′ran: all those men *were*
heads of the children of Ĭṣ′ra-el.
4 And these *were* their names:
of the [e]tribe of Reu̦′ben, Shăm-
mū′ȧ the son of Zăc′cur.
5 Of the tribe of [f]Sĭm′e-on,
Shā′phat the son of Hō′rī.
6 Of the tribe of [g]Jū′dah, [h]Cā′-
leb the son of Jĕ-phŭn′neh.
7 Of the tribe of [i]Ĭs′sa-char,
Ī′găl the son of Jō′ṣeph.
8 Of the tribe of [j]Ē′phrā-ĭm,
[k]Ō-shē′ȧ the son of Nŭn.
9 Of the tribe of [l]Bĕn′ja-mĭn,
Păl′tī the son of Rā′phu.
10 Of the tribe of [m]Zĕb′u-lŭn,
Găd′dĭ-el the son of Sō′dī.
11 Of the tribe of Jō′ṣeph,
*namely,* of the tribe of [n]Mȧ-năs′-
seh, Găd′dī the son of Sū′sī.
12 Of the tribe of [o]Dăn, Ăm′-
mĭ-el the son of Ġĕ-măl′lī.
13 Of the tribe of [p]Ăsh′ĕr, Sē′-
thu̦r the son of Mī′chaĕl.
14 Of the tribe of [q]Năph′ta-lī,
Näh′bī the son of Vŏph′sī.
15 Of the tribe of [r]Găd, Ġĕ-ū′el
the son of Mā′chī.
16 These *are* the names of the
[s]men which [a]Mō′ṣeṣ sent to spy
out the land. And Mō′ṣeṣ called
[k]Ō-shē′ȧ the son of Nŭn Jĕ-
hŏsh′u-ȧ.
17 ¶ And [a]Mō′ṣeṣ sent [s]them to
spy out the land of [b]Cā′năan,
and said unto them, Get you up
this *way* southward, and go up
into the mountain:
18 And see the [b]land, what it *is*;
and the people that dwelleth
therein, whether they *be* strong
or weak, few or many;
19 And what the land *is* that
they dwell in, whether it *be* good
or bad; and what cities *they be*
that they dwell in, whether in
[1]tents, or in strong holds:
20 And what the land *is*, whether it *be* fat or lean, whether there
be wood therein, or not. And be ye
of good courage, and bring of the
fruit of the land. Now the time *was*
the time of the first ripe [i]grapes.
21 So [s]they went up; and
searched the [b]land from the wilderness of *Zĭn unto [u]Rē′hŏb, as
men come to [v]Hā′math.
22 And [s]they ascended by the
south, and came unto [w]Hē′bron;
where [x]Ȧ-hī′man, [y]Shē′shāi, and
[z]Tăl′māi, the children of Ā′năk,
*were*. (Now Hē′bron was built
seven years before [a]Zō′an in
Ē′ġy̆pt.)
23 And [b]they came unto the
[2]brook of [c]Ĕsh′cŏl, and cut down
from thence a branch with one
cluster of [d]grapes, and they bare
it between two upon a staff; and
*they brought* of the †pomegran-
ates and of the [e]figs.
24 The place was called the
[2]brook [c]Ĕsh′cŏl, because of the
cluster of [d]grapes which the
[b]children of Ĭṣ′ra-el cut down
from thence.
25 And [b]they returned from
searching of the land after [f]forty
days.
26 ¶ And [b]they went and came
to Mō′ṣeṣ, and to Aăr′on, and to
all the congregation of the children of Ĭṣ′ra-el, unto the wilderness of [g]Pā′ran, to [h]Kā′desh;
and [i]brought back word unto
them, and unto all the congregation, and shewed them the fruit
of the land.
27 And [b]they told him, and
said, We came unto the land
whither thou sentest us, and surely it [j]floweth with [k]milk and [l]hon-
ey; and this *is* the fruit of it.

v.19–1532 BC
See footnote, *Time*, Rev. 10:6.
1 R. V. camps.

**20**
*i* *Grape,* Lev. 25:5.

**21**
*u* Or, *Beth-rehob,* Judg. 18:28.
*v* *Hamath,* 1 Chr. 18:3.

**22**
*w* *Hebron,* Gen. 23:2.
*x* Josh. 15:14.
*y* Josh. 15:14; Judg. 1:10.
*z* Josh. 15:14; Judg. 1:10.

*a* *Zoan,* Isa. 30:4.

**23**
*b* *Spies,* Josh. 6:23.
*c* Num. 32:9; Deut. 1:24.
*d* *Grape,* Lev. 25:5.
*e* *Fig Tree,* Luke 13:6.
2 R. V. valley of

**25**
*f* *Forty, days,* Jonah 3:4.

**26**
*g* *Paran, wilderness of,* Gen. 21:21.
*h* *Kadesh, Israel encamps at,* Gen. 14:7.
*i* *Israel, spies bring reports to,* vs. 26–33; Ex. 4:22.

**27**
*j* *Canaan, fruitfulness of,* Gen. 37:1.
*k* *Milk, figurative,* Job 10:10.
*l* *Honey, figurative,* Prov. 25:27.

* **ZIN** (*a low palm tree*). *A desert W. of Mt. Seir,* Num. 13:21; 20:1; 27:14; 33:36; 34:3, 4; Deut. 32:51; Josh. 15:1, 3.
† **POMEGRANATE,** a fruit. *Abounded in the land of Canaan,* 1 Sam. 14:2. *Brought by the spies to show the fruitfulness of the land of Canaan,* Num. 13:23. *Figures of the fruits of, were embroidered on the ephod,* Ex. 28:33, 34; 39: 24–26; *carved on the pillars of the temple,* 1 Kin. 7:18, 20, 42; 2 Kin. 25:17; Jer. 52:22, 23. *Wine made of,* Song 8:2.

v.28–1532 BC
See footnote, *Time*, Rev. 10:6.

28
*m Anakim*, Deut. 1:28.
*n Hittites*, Judg. 1:26.
*o Jebusites*, Deut. 7:1.
*p Amorites, territory of*, Gen. 14:13.
*q Canaanites*, Ex. 23:28.
*r Jordan, river of*, Gen. 32:10.

30
*s Caleb*, Num. 14:6.
*t Courage, instances of*, Deut. 31:7.
*u Faith, instances of*, Mark 11:22.

31
*v Cowardice, instances of*, Lev. 26:36.

32
*w Borrowing Trouble, instances of*, Matt. 6:25.

33
*x* Eccl. 12:5; Isa. 40:22; Nah. 3:17.

1
*a Cowardice, instances of*, Lev. 26:36.
*b Disobedience to God, instances of*, Eph. 5:6.

28 Nevertheless the people *be* strong that dwell in the land, and the cities *are* walled, *and* very great: and moreover we saw the [m]children of Ā′năk there.

29 The ‡Ăm′a-lĕk-ītes dwell in the land of the south: and the [n]Hĭt′tītes, and the [o]Jĕb′u-sītes, and the [p]Ăm′ôr-ītes, dwell in the mountains: and the [q]Cā′năan-ītes dwell by the sea, and by the coast of [r]Jôr′dan.

30 And [s]Cā′leb stilled the people before Mō′ṣeṣ, and said, [t]Let us go up at once, and possess it; for [u]we are well able to overcome it.

31 But the men that went up with him [v]said, We be not able to go up against the people; for they *are* stronger than we.

32 And they brought up an evil report of the land which they had searched unto the children of Ĭṣ′ra-el, [w]saying, The land, through which we have gone to search it, *is* a land that eateth up the inhabitants thereof; and all the people that we saw in it *are* men of a great stature.

33 And there we saw the giants, the [m]sons of Ā′năk, *which come* of the giants: and [v]we were in our own sight as [x]grasshoppers, and so we were in their sight.

## CHAPTER 14

*The people murmur. 6 Joshua and Caleb labor to still them. 11 God threatens them. 13 Moses intercedes with God for them, and obtains pardon. 26 The murmurers are not to enter the promised land. 36 The men who brought up the evil report die by a plague. 40 The people attempting to go up against the will of God are smitten.*

[a,b]AND all the congregation lifted up their voice, and cried; and the people wept that night.

2 And all the children of [c]Ĭṣ′ra-el *murmured against [d]Mō′ṣeṣ and against [e]Aâr′on: and the whole congregation said unto them, Would God that we had died in the land of Ē′ġȳpt! or would God we had died in this wilderness!

3 And *·[e]wherefore hath the LORD brought us unto this land, to fall by the sword, that our wives and our children should be a prey? were it not better for us to return into Ē′ġȳpt?

4 And they [f]said one to another, Let us make a captain, and let us return into Ē′ġȳpt.

5 Then Mō′ṣeṣ and Aâr′on fell on their faces before all the assembly of the congregation of the children of Ĭṣ′ra-el.

6 And [g]Jŏsh′u-ȧ the son of Nŭn, and †Cā′leb the son of Jė-phŭn′neh, *which were* of them that searched the land, [h]rent their clothes:

7 And [i,j]they spake unto all the company of the children of Ĭṣ′ra-el, saying, The [k]land, which we passed through to search it, *is* an exceeding good land.

8 If the LORD delight in us, then [l]he will bring us into this [k]land, and give it us; a land which floweth with [m]milk and [n]honey.

9 Only rebel not ye against the LORD, neither fear ye the people of the land; for they *are* bread for us: their defence is departed from them, and [l]the [o]LORD *is* with us: fear them not.

10 But all the congregation bade stone [q]them with stones. And the [p]glory of the LORD ap-

v.2–1532 BC
See footnote, *Time*, Rev. 10:6.

2
*c Israel, murmuring of*, Ex. 4:22.
*d Moses, murmured against*, Ex. 2:10.
*e Aaron, murmured against*, Ex. 6:20.

4
*f Conspiracy, instances of*, 1 Kin. 16:9.

6
*g Joshua*, Josh. 1:1.
*h Rending of Garments*, 2 Chr. 34:27.

7
*i Courage, instances of*, vs. 7–9; Deut. 31:7.
*j Decision, instances of*, vs. 7–9; Isa. 50:7.
*k Canaan, fruitfulness of*, Gen. 37:1.

8
*l Faith, instances of*, Mark 11:22.
*m Milk, figurative*, Job 10:10.
*n Honey, figurative*, Prov. 25:27.

9
*o God, preserver*, Gen. 2:2.

10
*p Pillar, of cloud and fire*, Ex. 13:21.

‡ **AMALEKITES.** *A people inhabiting the country S. of Idumea and E. of the Red Sea*, Num. 13:29; 14:25; 1 Sam. 15:7; 27:8. *Defeated, by Chedorlaomer*, Gen. 14:7; *by Joshua*, Ex. 17:8, 13; *by Gideon*, Judg. 7; *by Saul*, 1 Sam. 14:47, 48; 15:1–33; *by David*, 1 Sam. 27:8, 9; 30:1–20; *by the Simeonites*, 1 Chr. 4:42, 43. *Defeat the Israelites*, Num. 14:45; Judg. 3:13. *Israel commanded to destroy*, Deut. 25:17–19; 1 Sam. 28:18. *Prophecies against*, Ex. 17:14, 16; Num. 24:20.

* **MURMURING.** *Forbidden*, 1 Cor. 10:10; Phil. 2:14; Jas. 5:9. *Rebuked*, Job 15:11–13; Eccl. 7:10; Lam. 3:39; Rom. 9:19, 20. *Punishment for*, Num. 14:26–37; 17:10, 11. **Instances of:** *Hezekiah*, Isa. 38:10–18. *Jeremiah*, Jer. 15:10; 20:14–18; Lam. 3. *Martha*, Luke 10:40. *Prodigal's brother*, Luke 15:29, 30.
**Against God:** *By Cain*, Gen. 4:13, 14. *By Moses*, Ex. 5:22, 23; Num. 11:11–15. *By the Israelites*, Ex. 16:8, 12; Num. 11:1–10; 21:5; Deut. 1:26–28; Psa. 44:9–26; 106:24, 25. *By Job*, Job 3; 6; 7:2–6; 9:18; 16:6–14; 19:7–20; 30; 34:37. *By the Psalmist*, Psa. 73:13–22. *By Jonah*, Jonah 4.
**Against Moses:** *By the Israelites*, Ex. 5:21; 14:11, 12; 15:24; 16:2, 3; 17:2, 3; Num. 14; 16:2, 3, 13, 14, 41; 20:2–5.

† **CALEB** *(a dog)*. *Son of Jephunneh*, Num. 13:6; 14:6; 1 Chr. 4:15. *One of the two survivors of the Israelites per*

v.10–1532 BC
See footnote, *Time*, Rev. 10:6.

*q Tabernacle*, Ex. 27:9.

11

*r Disobedience to God*, Eph. 5:6.
*s Unbelief, instances of*, Heb. 3:12.
*t Miracles, design of*, Luke 23:8.
1 R. V. despise

12

*u Judgments*, Ex. 6:6.
*v Moses, character of, magnified of God*, Ex. 2:10.

13

*w Unselfishness, instances of*, 1 Cor. 10:24.
*x Intercession, of man with God*, vs. 13–18; Jer. 27:18.
*y Prayer, pleas offered in*, vs. 13–18; Acts 6:4.
*z Egyptians*, Gen. 50:3.

14

*a Pillar, of cloud and fire*, Ex. 13:21.

16

*b Canaan, promised to Abraham and his seed*, Gen. 37:1.
*c Covenant, of God with men*, Deut. 29:1.

17

*d Intercession, of man with God*, Jer. 27:18.

18

*e God, longsuffering of*, Gen. 2:2.
*f God, mercy of*, Gen. 2:2.
*g Sin, forgiveness of*, Rom. 5:12.
*h Children, involved in sin of parents*, Mark 10:14.
2 R. V. slow to anger, and plenteous in

peared in the [q]tabernacle of the
congregation before all the children of Iș'ra-el.
11 ¶ And the LORD said unto
Mō'şeş, How long will this people [1, r]provoke me? and how
long will it be ere they [‡, s]believe
me, for all the [t]signs which I
have shewed among them?
12 I will [u]smite [‡]them with the
pestilence, and disinherit them,
and will make of [v]thee a greater
nation and mightier than they.
13 [w]And Mō'şeş [x, y]said unto
the LORD, Then the [z]Ē-ġўp'-tianș shall hear *it*, (for thou
broughtest up this people in thy
might from among them;)
14 [x, y]And they will tell *it* to the
inhabitants of this land: *for* they
have heard that thou LORD *art*
among this people, that thou
LORD art seen face to face, and
*that* thy cloud standeth over
them, and *that* thou goest before
them, by day time in a [a]pillar of
a cloud, and in a pillar of fire by
night.
15 Now *if* thou shalt [‡]kill *all*
this people as one man, then the
nations which have heard the
fame of thee will speak, saying,
16 Because the LORD was not
able to bring this people into the
[b]land which he [c]sware unto
them, therefore he hath slain
them in the wilderness.
17 And now, I [d]beseech thee,
let the power of my LORD be
great, according as thou hast
spoken, saying,
18 The LORD *is* [2, e]longsuffering, and of great [f]mercy, [g]forgiving iniquity and transgression,
and by no means clearing *the
guilty*, visiting the iniquity of the
fathers upon the [h]children unto
the third and fourth *generation*.
19 [d]Pardon, I beseech thee, the
iniquity of this people according
unto the greatness of thy [f]mercy,
and as thou hast [g]forgiven this
people, from [i]Ē'ġўpt even until
now.
20 And the LORD said, I have
[g]pardoned according to thy
word:
21 But *as* truly *as* I live, all the
earth shall be filled with the
[j]glory of the LORD.
22 Because all those [k]men
which have seen my [j]glory, and
my [l]miracles, which I did in
[i]Ē'ġўpt and in the wilderness,
and have tempted me now these
ten times, and have [m, n, o]not
hearkened to my voice;
23 Surely [k]they [p]shall not see
the [b]land which I [c]sware unto
their fathers, neither shall any of
them that [3]provoked me see it:
24 But my servant [q]Cā'leb, because he had another spirit with
him, and [r, s]hath followed me
fully, [t]him will I bring into the
[b]land whereinto he went; and
his seed shall possess it.
25 (Now the [u]Ăm'a-lĕk-ītes
and the [v]Cā'năan-ītes dwelt in
the valley.) To morrow [w]turn
you, and get you into the wilderness by the way of the [x]Red
sea.
26 ¶ And the LORD [y]spake unto
Mō'şeş and unto Aâr'on, saying,
27 How long *shall I bear with*
this evil congregation, which
murmur against me? [z]I have
[a]heard the *murmurings of the
children of Ĭș'ra-el, which they
murmur against me.
28 Say unto them, *As truly as* I
live, saith the LORD, as ye have
spoken in mine ears, so will I do
to you:
29 [‡, b]Your carcases shall fall in
this wilderness; and all that were

v.19–1532 BC
See footnote, *Time*, Rev. 10:6.

19

*i Egypt*, Gen. 41:8.

21

*j God, glory of*, Gen. 2:2.

22

*k Reprobates*, 1 Cor. 9:27.
*l Miracles*, Luke 23:8.
*m Disobedience to God*, Eph. 5:6.
*n Impenitence, instances of*, Rom. 2:5.
*o Obduracy, instances of*, Prov. 29:1.

23

*p Judgments, upon the Israelites for murmuring*, Ex. 6:6.
3 R. V. despised

24

*q Caleb*, Num. 14:6.
*r Obedience, exemplified*, Heb. 5:8.
*s Perseverance, instances of*, Eph. 6:18.
*t Promise, to the obedient*, 2 Cor. 1:20.

25

*u Amalekites*, Num. 13:29.
*v Canaanites*, Ex. 23:28.
*w Israel, return to the wilderness*, Ex. 4:22.
*x Red Sea*, Ex. 10:19.

26

*y Prophets, inspiration of*, Isa. 3:2.

27

*z God, knowledge of*, Gen. 2:2.

*a Sin, known to God*, Rom. 5:12.

29

*b Judgments, upon the Israelites for murmuring*, Ex. 6:6.

*mitted to enter the land of promise*, Num. 14:30, 38; 26:63–65; 32:11–13; Deut. 1:34–36; Josh. 14:6–15. *Sent to Canaan as a spy*, Num. 13:6. *Brings favorable report*, Num. 13:26–30; 14:6–9. *Assists in dividing Canaan*, Num. 34:19. *Life of, miraculously saved*, Num. 14:10–12. *Age of*, Josh. 14:7–10. *Inheritance of*, Josh. 14:6–15; 15:13–16. *Descendants of*, 1 Chr. 4:15.

‡ **UNBELIEVING ISRAELITES DESTROYED**, Num. 14:11, 13–39; 32:11; Deut. 1:34, 35; Psa. 95:11; 106:26; 1 Cor. 10:5, 10; Heb. 3:17; Jude 5.

v.29–1532 BC
See footnote, *Time*, Rev. 10:6.

**30**
c *Canaan*, Gen. 37:1.
d *Oath, attributed to God*, Num. 5:19.
e *Joshua, rewarded for his courage*, Josh. 1:1.

**31**
4 R. V. rejected.

**33**
f *Children, involved in sin of parents*, Mark 10:14.
g *Sin, consequence of, entailed on children*, Rom. 5:12.
h *Adversity*, Psa. 10:6.
i *Forty, years*, Jonah 3:4.

**34**
5 R. V. alienation.

**36**
j *Spies*, Josh. 6:23.

**37**
k *Plague*, Ex. 11:1.

numbered of you, according to your whole number, from twenty years old and upward, which have *murmured against me,

30 Doubtless ye shall not come into the [c]land, *concerning* which I [d]sware to make you dwell therein, save †Cā'leb the son of Jĕ-phŭn'neh, and [e]Jŏsh'u-ȧ the son of Nŭn.

31 But your little ones, which ye said should be a prey, them will I bring in, and they shall know the [c]land which ye have [4]despised.

32 But *as for* ‡you, your carcases, they shall fall in this wilderness.

33 And your [f,g]children shall [h]wander in the wilderness [i]forty years, and bear your whoredoms, until your carcases be wasted in the wilderness.

34 After the number of the days in which ye searched the [c]land, *even* forty days, each day for a year, shall ye bear your iniquities, *even* [i]forty years, and ye shall know my [5]breach of promise.

35 I the LORD have said, I will surely do it unto all this evil congregation, that are gathered together against me: in this wilderness they shall be [b]consumed, and there they shall ‡die.

36 And the [j]men, which Mō'ṣeṣ sent to search the [c]land, who returned, and made all the congregation to *murmur against him, by bringing up a slander upon the land,

37 Even those [j]men that did bring up the evil report upon the land, died by the [k]plague before the LORD.

38 But [e]Jŏsh'u-ȧ the son of Nŭn, and †Cā'leb the son of Jĕ-phŭn'neh, *which were* of the [j]men that went to search the [c]land, lived *still*.

39 And Mō'ṣeṣ told these sayings unto all the children of Iṣ'ra-el: and the people [l]mourned greatly.

40 And they rose up early in the morning, and gat them up into the top of the mountain, saying, [m]Lo, we *be here*, and will go up into the place which the LORD hath promised: for we have [n]sinned.

41 And Mō'ṣeṣ said, [o]Wherefore now do ye transgress the commandment of the LORD? but [p]it shall not prosper.

42 [o]Go not up, for the [q]LORD *is* not among you; that ye be not smitten before your enemies.

43 For the [r]Ăm'a-lĕk-ītes and the [s]Cā'năan-ītes *are* there before you, and ye [b]shall fall by the sword: because [t]ye are [u]turned away from the LORD, therefore the LORD will not be with you.

44 But they [v]presumed to go up unto the hill top: nevertheless the [w]ark of the covenant of the LORD, and Mō'ṣeṣ, departed not out of the camp.

45 Then the [r]Ăm'a-lĕk-ītes came down, and the [s]Cā'năan-ītes which dwelt in that hill, and [x]smote them, and discomfited them, *even* unto [y]Hôr'mah.

## CHAPTER 15

*The law of the meat offering and the drink offering. 17 The law of the first of the dough for a heave offering. 22 The sacrifice for sins of ignorance. 30 The punishment of presumption. 32 The sabbath-breaker is stoned. 37 Fringes on their garments.*

AND the LORD [a]spake unto [b]Mō'ses, saying,

2 Speak unto the children of [c]Iṣ'ra-el, and say unto them, When ye be come into the [d]land of your habitations, which I give unto you,

3 And will make an offering by fire unto the LORD, a [e]burnt offering, or a sacrifice in performing a [f]vow, or in a [g]freewill offer-

v.39–1532 BC
See footnote, *Time*, Rev. 10:6.

**39**
l *Conviction of Sin, instances of*, John 16:8.

**40**
m *Repentance, unavailing*, vs. 39–45; Mark 1:4.
n *Sin, confession of*, Rom. 5:12.

**41**
o *Reproof, faithfulness in, instances of*, Prov. 17:10.
p *Opportunity, lost*, vs. 40–43; Gal. 6:10.

**42**
q *Holy Spirit, withdrawn, instances of*, Acts 1:2.

**43**
r *Amalekites*, Num. 13:29.
s *Canaanites*, Ex. 23:28.
t *Reprobates*, 1 Cor. 9:27.
u *Backsliding, instances of Israel's*, Hos. 11:7.

**44**
v *Presumption, instances of*, Psa. 19:13.
w *Ark, in the tabernacle*, Ex. 25:10.

**45**
x *Israel, defeated by the Amalekites*, Ex. 4.22.
y *Hormah*, Deut. 1:44.

**1**
a *Revelation, concerning offerings*, 2 Cor. 12:1.
b *Prophets, inspiration of*, Isa. 3:2.

**2**
c *Israel*, Ex. 4:22.
d *Canaan*, Gen. 37:1.

**3**
e *Offerings, burnt*, Lev. 6:17.
f *Vows* Num. 30:2
g *Offerings, free will*, Lev. 6:17.

1 R. V. set

**4**
*h Offerings, meat,* Lev. 6:17.
*i Measure, dry,* Deut. 25:15.
*j Hin,* Ex. 29:40.
*k Oil, sacred,* Deut. 12:17.
2 R. V. meal

**5**
*l Wine,* Prov. 23: 31.
*m Offerings, drink, libations of wine offered with the sacrifice,* Lev. 6: 17.
*n Lamb,* Num. 7:15.

**8**
*o Bullock,* Ex. 29:3.
*p Offerings, peace,* Lev. 6:17.

ing, or in your [1]solemn *feasts,
to make a sweet savour unto the
LORD, of the herd, or of the
flock:
4 Then shall he that offereth
his offering unto the LORD bring
a [2,h]meat offering of a [i]tenth deal
of flour mingled with the fourth
*part* of an [j]hin of [k]oil.
5 And the fourth *part* of an [j]hin
of [l]wine for a [m]drink offering
shalt thou prepare with the
burnt offering or sacrifice, for
one [n]lamb.
6 Or for a ram, thou shalt prepare *for* a [2,h]meat offering two
[i]tenth deals of flour mingled
with the third *part* of an [j]hin
of [k]oil.
7 And for a [m]drink offering
thou shalt offer the third *part* of
an [j]hin of [l]wine, *for* a sweet
savour unto the LORD.
8 And when thou preparest a
[o]bullock *for* a [e]burnt offering, or
*for* a sacrifice in performing a
[f]vow, or [p]peace offerings unto
the LORD:
9 Then shall he bring with a
[o]bullock a [2,h]meat offering of
three [i]tenth deals of flour mingled with half an [j]hin of [k]oil.
10 And thou shalt bring for a
[m]drink offering half an [j]hin of
[l]wine, *for* an offering made by
fire, of a sweet savour unto the
LORD.
11 Thus shall it be done for one
[o]bullock, or for one ram, or for a
[n]lamb, or a kid.
12 According to the number
that ye shall prepare, so shall ye
do to every one according to
their number.
13 All that are born of the country shall do these things after
this manner, in offering an [e]of-
fering made by fire, of a sweet
savour unto the LORD.
14 And if a [q]stranger sojourn
with you, or whosoever *be* among
you in your generations, and will
offer an [e]offering made by fire, of
a sweet savour unto the LORD;
as ye do, so he shall do.
15 [r]One [s]ordinance *shall be*
*both* for you of the congregation,
and also for the [q]stranger that
sojourneth *with you,* an ordinance for ever in your generations: as ye *are,* so shall the
stranger be before the LORD.
16 [r]One law and one manner
shall be for you, and for the
[q]stranger that sojourneth with
you.

**14**
*q Foreigners, religious privileges of,* Deut. 23:20.

**15**
*r Legislation, class, forbidden,* Ex. 12: 49.
*s Ordinance, a decree,* Num. 9:14.

---

* **ANNUAL FEASTS,** Instituted by Moses. *Designated as,* SOLEMN FEASTS, Num. 15:3; 2 Chr. 8:13; Lam. 2:6; Ezek. 46:9; SET FEASTS, Num. 29:39; Ezra 3:5; APPOINTED FEASTS, Isa. 1:14; HOLY CONVOCATIONS, Lev. 23:4. *First and last days were Sabbatic,* Lev. 23:39, 40; Num. 28:18–25; 29:12, 35; Neh. 8:1–18. *Kept with rejoicing,* Lev. 23: 40; Deut. 16:11–14; 2 Chr. 30:21–26; Ezra 6:22; Neh. 8:9–12, 17; Psa. 122:4; Isa. 30:29; Zech. 8:19. *Divine protection given during,* Ex. 34:24.

*All males were required to attend,* Ex. 23:17; 34:23; Deut. 16:16; Ezek. 36:38; Luke 2:41, 42; John 4:45; 7. *Aliens permitted to attend,* John 12:20; Acts 2:1–11. *Attended by women,* 1 Sam. 1:3, 9; Luke 2:41. Observed: *By Jesus,* Matt. 26:17–20; Luke 2:41, 42; 22:15; John 2:13, 23; 5:1; 7:10; 10:22; *by Paul,* Acts 20:6, 16; 24:11, 17.

**Of New Moon,** Num. 10:10; 28:11–15; 1 Chr. 23:31; 2 Chr. 31:3; Ezra 3:5. *Traffic at time of, suspended,* Amos 8:5.

**The Passover:** *Institution of,* Ex. 12:3–49; 23:15–18; 34:18; Lev. 23:4–8; Num. 9:2–5, 13, 14; 28:16–25; Deut. 16:1–8, 16; Psa. 81:3, 5. *Design of,* Ex. 12:21–28.

*Special passover, for those who were unclean, or on journey, to be held in second month,* Num. 9:6–12; 2 Chr. 30:2–4. *Lamb killed by Levites, for those who were ceremonially unclean,* 2 Chr. 30:17; 35:3–11; Ezra 6:20. *Strangers authorized to celebrate,* Ex. 12:48, 49; Num. 9:14.

*Observed at place designated by God,* Deut. 16:5–7; *with unleavened bread,* Ex. 12:8, 15–20; 13:3, 6; 23:15; Lev. 23:6; Num. 9:11; 28:17; Deut. 16:3, 4; Mark 14:12; Luke 22:7; Acts 12:3; 1 Cor. 5:8. *Penalty for neglecting to observe,* Num. 9:13.

*Reinstituted by Ezekiel,* Ezek. 45:21–24.

Observation of: *Renewed, by the Israelites on entering Canaan,* Josh. 5:10, 11; *by Hezekiah,* 2 Chr. 30:1; *by Josiah,* 2 Kin. 23:22, 23; 2 Chr. 35:1, 18; *after return from captivity,* Ezra 6:19, 20. *Observed by Jesus,* Matt. 26:17–20; Luke 22:15; John 2:13, 23; 13. *Jesus, when twelve years old, in the temple at time of,* Luke 2:41–50. *Jesus crucified at time of,* Matt. 26:2; Mark 14:1, 2; John 18:28. *Lord's supper ordained at,* Matt. 26:26–28; Mark 14:12–25; Luke 22:7–20. *The lamb of, a type of Christ,* 1 Cor. 5:7

*Prisoners released at, by the Romans,* Matt. 27:15; Mark 15:6; Luke 23:16, 17; John 18:39. *Peter imprisoned at time of,* Acts 12:3.

*Christ called* OUR PASSOVER, 1 Cor. 5:7.

**Pentecost:** *Called,* FEAST OF WEEKS, Ex. 34:22; Deut. 16:10; FEAST OF HARVEST, Ex. 23:16; DAY OF FIRST FRUITS, Num. 28:26; DAY OF PENTECOST, Acts 2:1; 20:16; 1 Cor. 16:8.

*Institution of,* Ex. 23:16; 34:22; Lev. 23:15–21; Num. 28:26–31; Deut. 16:9–12, 16.

*Holy Ghost given to the apostles on the day of,* Acts 2.

**Of Purim:** *Instituted to commemorate the deliverance of the Jews from the plot of Haman,* Esth. 9:20–32.

**Of Tabernacles,** called also FEAST OF INGATHERING: *Instituted,* Ex. 23:16; 34:22; Lev. 23:34–43; Num. 29:12–40; Deut. 16:13–16. *Design of,* Lev. 23:42, 43. *The law read in connection with, every seventh year,* Deut. 31:10–12; Neh. 8:18.

Observance of: *After the captivity,* Ezra 3:4; Neh. 8:14–18; *by Jesus,* John 7:2, 14. *Observance of, omitted,* Neh. 8:17. *Penalty for not observing,* Zech. 14:16–19.

*Jeroboam institutes an idolatrous feast to correspond to, in the eighth month,* Kin. 12:32, 33; 1 Chr. 27:11.

**Of Trumpets:** *When and how observed,* Lev. 23:24, 25; Num. 29:1–6. *Celebrated after the captivity with joy,* Neh. 8:2, 9–12.

17 ¶ And the LORD [a]spake unto [b]Mō'ṣeṣ, saying,
18 Speak unto the children of
[c]Ĭṣ'ra-el, and say unto them,
When ye come into the [d]land
whither I bring you,
19 Then it shall be, that, when
ye eat of the bread of the [d]land,
ye shall offer up an [t]heave offering unto the LORD.
20 Ye shall offer up a cake of
the [u]first of your dough *for* an
[t]heave offering: as *ye do* the
heave offering of the threshingfloor, so shall ye heave it.
21 Of the [u]first of your dough
ye shall give unto the LORD an
[t]heave offering in your generations.
22 ¶ And if ye have erred, and
[v]not observed all these commandments, which the LORD
hath [a]spoken unto [b]Mō'ṣeṣ,
23 *Even* all that the LORD hath
commanded you by the hand of
Mō'ṣeṣ, from the day that the
LORD commanded Mō'ṣeṣ, and
henceforward among your generations;
24 Then it shall be, if *ought* be
committed by [w]ignorance without the knowledge of the congregation, that all the congregation shall offer one young [o]bul-
lock for a [e]burnt [x]offering, for
a sweet savour unto the LORD,
with his [2,h]meat offering, and his
[m]drink offering, according to the
[3]manner, and one kid of the
goats for a [y]sin offering.
25 And the priest shall make an
[z,a]atonement for all the congregation of the children of Ĭṣ'ra-el,
and [b]it shall be [c]forgiven them;
for it [4]*is* [d]ignorance: and they
shall bring their offering, a sacrifice made by fire unto the
LORD, and their [e]sin offering
before the LORD, for their [5]igno-
rance:
26 And [b]it shall be [c]forgiven all
the congregation of the children
of Ĭṣ'ra-el, and the [f]stranger
that sojourneth among them;
seeing all the people *were* in
[d]ignorance.
27 ¶ And if any soul sin
through [d]ignorance, then he
shall bring a she goat of the first
year for a [e]sin [g]offering.
28 And the priest shall make an
[a,h]atonement for the soul that
[6]sinneth ignorantly, when he sinneth by [d]ignorance before the
LORD, to make an atonement
for him; and [b]it shall be [c]for-
given him.
29 [i]Ye shall have [j]one law for
him that sinneth through [d]igno-
rance, *both for* him that is born
among the children of Ĭṣ'ra-el,
and for the [f]stranger that sojourneth among them.
30 ¶ But the soul that doeth
*ought* [7,l]presumptuously, *whether he be* born in the land, or a
stranger, the same [8]reproacheth
the LORD; and [m]that soul shall
be †,[k,n]cut off from among his
people.
31 Because he hath despised
the word of the LORD, and hath
broken his commandment, that
soul [o]shall utterly be †,[n]cut off;
his iniquity *shall be* upon him.
32 ¶ And while the children of

19
t *Offerings, heave,* Lev. 6:17.

20
u *First Fruits,* Deut. 18:4.

22
v *Disobedience to God,* Eph. 5:6.

24
w *Ignorance, sins of,* Acts 3:17.
x *Jesus, typified in offerings,* Matt. 1:21.
y *Offerings, sin,* Lev. 6:17.
3 R. V. ordinance,

25
a *Atonement,* Lev. 17:11.

z *Jesus, atonement by, typified,* Matt. 1:21.

b *Promise, to penitents, of forgiveness,* 2 Cor. 1:20.
c *Sin, forgiveness of,* Rom. 5:12.
d *Ignorance, sins of,* Acts 3:17.
e *Offerings, sin,* Lev. 6:17.
4 R. V. was an error,
5 R. V. error:

26
f *Foreigner,* Deut. 23:20.

27
g *Jesus, typified in offerings,* Matt. 1:21.

28
h *Atonement,* Lev. 17:11.
6 R. V. erreth,

29
i *Statute, forbidding class legislation,* Deut. 8:2.
j *Legislation, class, forbidden,* Ex. 12:49.

30
k *Sin, punishment of,* Rom. 5:12.
l *Presumption,* Psa. 19:13.
m *Statute, fixing penalty for disobedience,* Deut. 8:2.
n *Church, rules of discipline in,* Matt. 16:18.
7 R. V. with an high hand,
8 R. V. blasphemeth

31
o *Wicked, punishment of,* Psa. 73:3.

† **DISFELLOWSHIP.** In order to impress the children of Israel with the necessity of holiness as the only ground of fellowship with God and with the righteous, we find many lessons on holiness in the Mosaic ordinances. The design of these lessons was to teach the Israelites, and through them all people for all time, that holiness is the supreme attribute of those who please God; and that without it man must be forever separated from Him. The following Scriptures describe one of the object-lessons by which this great central truth of the system of Mosaic instruction was kept prominently before the public mind. They teach that defilement must separate the defiled from the undefiled and hence sin must separate the unholy from the holy. Therefore the soul that violated the ordinances was "cut off from Israel," or "cut off from the congregation," etc., that is, was deprived of the privileges enjoyed by those who were obedient to the law.

Jesus ordained this mode of discipline, Matt. 15:18. It was enjoined as a corrective measure in apostolic times, see under sub-head ENJOINED, below.

*Of the uncircumcised,* Gen. 17:14. *Of those who violated the law, of unleavened bread,* Ex. 12:15; *of sacrifices,* Lev. 17:9; 19:5–7; *of purification,* Num. 19:20. *Of those who were defiled, by eating prohibited food,* Lev. 7:25, 27; 17:10; 19:8; *by touching the dead,* Num. 19:13; *by committing abominations,* Lev. 18:29; 20:3–6.

**Enjoined:** *For blasphemy,* Num. 15:31. *For schism,* Rom. 16:17. *For heresy,* 1 Tim. 6:3–5; Tit. 3:10, 11; 2 John 10, 11. *For immorality,* Matt. 18:17, 18; 1 Cor. 5:1–7, 11, 13; 2 Thess. 3:6.

[p]Ĭṣ′ra-el were in the wilderness,
they found a man that gathered sticks upon the [q]sabbath
day.
33 And they that found him
gathering sticks brought him unto Mō′ṣeṣ and Aâr′on, and unto
all the congregation.
34 And they put him in [r]ward,
because it was not declared what
should be done to him.
35 And the LORD said unto
Mō′ṣeṣ, [s]The man shall be
surely [t]put to [u]death: all
the congregation shall [v]stone
him with stones without the
camp.
36 And all the congregation
brought him without the camp,
and [i,v]stoned him with stones,
and he died; as the LORD commanded Mō′ṣeṣ.
37 ¶ And the LORD [w]spake unto
Mō′ṣeṣ, saying,
38 [x]Speak unto the children of
Ĭṣ′ra-el, and bid them that
they make them [y,z]fringes in
the borders of their garments
throughout their generations,
and that they put upon the
fringe of the borders a ribband
of [a]blue:
39 [b,c,d]And [e]it shall be unto you
for a fringe, that ye may look upon it, and remember all the commandments of the LORD, and
[f]do them; and that ye seek not
after your own heart and your
own eyes, after which ye use to
go a whoring:
40 [g]That ye may remember,
and [f]do all my command-
ments, and be [h]holy unto your
God.
41 [i]I *am* the LORD your
God, which brought you out
of the land of Ē′gy̆pt, to be
your God: I *am* the LORD your
God.

## CHAPTER 16

*The rebellion of Korah, Dathan, and Abiram. 23 Moses separates the people from the rebels' tents. 31 The earth swallows up Korah and his company: and a fire consumes the others. 36 Their censers used to cover the altar. 41 Fourteen thousand and seven hundred are slain by a plague for murmuring against Moses and Aaron. 46 The plague is stayed by Aaron.*

NOW *,[a]Kō′rah, the son of
Ĭz′här, the son of Kō′-
hath, the son of Lē′vī, and †Dā′-
than and ‡Ā-bī′ram, the sons of
[b]Ē-lī′ab, and Ŏn, the son of Pē′-
leth, [c]sons of Reu′ben, took *men*:
2 And [d,e,f]they [g,h]rose up before [i]Mō′ṣeṣ, with certain of the
children of Ĭṣ′ra-el, two hundred
and fifty princes of the assembly,
famous in the congregation, men
of renown:
3 And they [j]gathered themselves together [k]against [i]Mō′ṣeṣ
and against [l]Aâr′on, and [m]said
unto them, [n]*Ye take* too much
upon you, seeing all the congregation *are* holy, every one of
them, and the LORD *is* among
them: wherefore then [o]lift ye up
yourselves above the congregation of the LORD?
4 And when [p]Mō′ṣeṣ heard *it*,
he [q]fell upon his face:
5 And he spake unto [a,]*Kō′rah
and unto all his company, saying, Even to morrow the LORD
will shew who *are* his, and [r]*who*
*is* holy; and will cause *him* to
come near unto him: even *him*
whom he hath [t]chosen will he
cause to come near unto him.
6 This do; Take you [u]censers,
*Kō′rah, and all his company;
7 And put fire therein, and put
[v]incense in them before the
LORD to morrow: and it shall be
*that* the man whom the LORD
doth [t]choose, he *shall be* [r,s]holy:
*ye take* too much upon you, ye
[d]sons of Lē′vī.
8 And Mō′ṣeṣ said unto *Kō′-

32
p *Israel,* Ex. 4:22.
q *Sabbath, profanation of,* vs. 32–36; Ex. 16:23.

34
r *Prison,* Gen. 39:20.

35
s *Legislation,* Ex. 12:49.
t *Punishment, death penalty,* Lev. 26:41.
u *Death, penalty,* Num. 23:10.
v *Stoning,* 1 Sam. 30:6.

37
w *Prophets, inspiration of,* Isa. 3:2.

38
x *Statute, prescribing methods of religious instruction,* Deut. 8:2.
y *Fringes,* Deut. 22:12.
z Deut. 22:12.

a *Colors, symbolical,* Ezek. 16:16.

39
b *Statute, prescribing methods of religious instruction,* Deut. 8:2.
c *Instruction, by object lessons,* Prov. 23:23.
d *Instruction, in religion,* Prov. 23:23.
e *Token,* Psa. 86:17.
f *Obedience, enjoined,* Heb. 5:8.

40
g *Commandment, enjoining obedience and holiness,* Deut. 8:2.
h *Holiness, enjoined,* Ex. 39:30.

41
i *God, love of, exemplified,* Gen. 2:2.

1
a *Minister, false and corrupt, instances of,* Rom. 15:16.
b *Eliab,* Num. 26:8.
c *Reubenites,* Josh. 22:1.

2
d *Levites, sedition among,* vs. 1–50; Deut. 10:8.
e *Citizens, treasonable, instances of,* Luke 15:15.
f *Treason, instances of,* vs. 1–33; 2 Kin. 11:14.
g *Ambition, instances of,* Hab. 2:5.
h *Envy, instances of,* Prov. 14:30.
i *Moses,* Ex. 2:10.

3
j *Conspiracy, instances of,* 1 Kin. 16:9.
k *Presumption, instances of,* Psa. 19:13.
l *Aaron,* Ex. 6:20.
m *Murmuring, of the Israelites,* Num. 14:2.
n *False Accusation,* 2 Tim. 3:3.
o *Usurpation, of executive power,* 2 Sam. 15:1.

4
p *Moses, character of,* vs. 4–11; Ex. 2:10.
q *Meekness, instances of,* vs. 4–11; Psa. 45:4.

5
r *Minister, character and qualifications of,* Rom. 15:16.
s *Holiness,* Ex. 39:30.
t *Minister, call of,* v. 9; Rom. 15:16.

6
u *Censer,* Lev. 16:12.

7
v *Incense,* Ex. 37:29.

*** KORAH.** *A Kohathite,* Ex. 6:18, 21, 24. *Jealous of Moses, leads two hundred and fifty princes in an insurrection, and is swallowed up in the earth,* Num. 16; 26:9, 10; Deut. 11:6; Psa. 106:17; Jude 11. *Descendants of, porters after the return from captivity,* 1 Chr. 9:19.

† **DATHAN.** *A conspirator against Moses,* Num. 16:1–35; 26:9; Deut. 11:6; Psa. 106:17.

‡ **ABIRAM** (*lofty, proud*). *An Israelite who conspired with Dathan against Moses and Aaron,* Num. 16; 26:9, 10; Deut. 11:6; Psa. 106:17.

9
w *Reproof, instances of*, Prov. 17:10.
x *Levites, set apart as ministers of religion*, Deut. 10:8.

10
y *Ambition*, Hab. 2:5.
z *Priest*, Lev. 1:5.

11
a *Aaron*, Ex. 6:20.
b *Murmuring, instances of*, Num. 14:2.

12
c *Moses*, Ex. 2:10.
d *Ingratitude, of man to man*, Rom. 1:21.

13
e *Ambition*, Hab. 2:5.

15
f *Anger*, Psa. 37:8.
g *Prayer, imprecatory*, Acts 6:4.
h *Rulers, righteous*, Ex. 18:21.
i *Integrity, instances of*, Job 2:3.

17
j *Censer*, Lev. 16. 12.
k *Incense*, Ex. 37: 29.

rah, Hear, I pray you, ye [d]sons
of Lē'vī.
9 [w]*Seemeth it but* a small thing
unto you, that the God of Ĭṣ'-
ra-el hath separated [x]you from
the congregation of Ĭṣ'ra-el, to
bring you near to himself to do
the service of the tabernacle of
the LORD, and to stand before
the congregation to minister unto them?
10 And he hath brought thee
near *to him*, and all thy brethren
the [x]sons of Lē'vī with thee: and
[y]seek ye the [z]priesthood also?
11 For which cause *both* thou
and all thy company *are* gathered together against the LORD:
and what *is* [a]Aâr'on, that ye
[b]murmur against him?
12 ¶ And [c]Mō'ṣeṣ sent to call
†Dā'than and ‡Ā-bī'ram, the
sons of Ē-lī'ab: which said,
[b,d]We will not come up:
13 [b,d]*Is it* a small thing that
thou hast brought us up out of a
land that floweth with milk and
honey, to kill us in the wilderness, except thou [e]make thyself
altogether a prince over us?
14 [b,d]Moreover thou hast not
brought us into a land that floweth with milk and honey, or giv-
en us inheritance of fields and
vineyards: wilt thou put out the
eyes of these men? we will not
come up.
15 And [c]Mō'ṣeṣ was very
[f]wroth,[c] and [g]said unto the
LORD, Respect not thou their
offering: [h,i]I have not taken
one ass from them, neither have
I hurt one of them.
16 And [c]Mō'ṣeṣ said unto *Kō'-
rah, Be thou and all thy company before the LORD, thou,
and they, and [a]Aâr'on, to
morrow:
17 And take every man his
[j]censer, and put [k]incense in
them, and bring ye before the
LORD every man his censer, two
hundred and fifty censers; thou
also, and Aâr'on, each *of you* his
censer.
18 And they took every man his
[j]censer, and put fire in them, and
laid [k]incense thereon, and stood
in the door of the [l]tabernacle of
the congregation with Mō'ṣeṣ
and Aâr'on.
19 [Q]And *Kō'rah gathered all
the congregation against them
unto the door of the [l]tabernacle
of the congregation: and the
[m]glory of the LORD appeared
unto all the congregation.
20 And the LORD [n]spake unto
[c]Mō'ṣeṣ and unto [a]Aâr'on, saying,
21 Separate yourselves from
among this [o]congregation, that
I may [p]consume[c] them in a
moment.
22 And [a,c]they fell upon their
faces, and [q,r]said, O [s]God, the
[t]God of the spirits of all flesh,
shall one man sin, and wilt thou
be wroth[c] with all the congregation?[Q]
23 ¶ And the LORD spake unto
Mō'ṣeṣ, saying,
24 Speak unto the congregation, saying, Get you up from
about the tabernacle of *Kō'-
rah, †Dā'than, and ‡Ā-bī'ram.
25 And [c]Mō'ṣeṣ rose up and
went unto †Dā'than and ‡Ā-bī'-
ram; and the [u]elders of Ĭṣ'ra-el
followed him.
26 And he spake unto the congregation, saying, [v]Depart, I
pray you, from the tents of these
[o]wicked men, and touch nothing
of their's, lest ye be consumed in
all their sins.[Q]
27 So they gat up from the tabernacle of *Kō'rah, †Dā'than,
and ‡Ā-bī'ram, on every side:
and Dā'than and Ā-bī'ram came
out, and stood in the door of
their tents, and their wives, and
their sons, and their little children.

18
l *Tabernacle*, Ex. 27:9.

19
m *Pillar, of cloud and fire*, Ex. 13. 21.

20
n *Inspiration*, Job 32:8.

21
o *Evil Company*, Prov. 13:20.
p *Anger of God*, 2 Kin. 13:3.

22
q *Prayer, intercessory*, Acts 6:4.
r *Intercession, instances of*, Jer. 27:18.
s *God, justice of*, Gen. 2:2.
t *God, a spirit*, Gen. 2:2.

25
u *Senate*, Num. 11 16.

26
v *Fellowship, with the wicked forbidden*, 1 Cor. 1:9.

28
w *Miracles, design of*, vs. 28–30; Luke 23:8.
x *Prophets, inspiration of*, Isa. 3:2.

30
y *Death, of the wicked, a judgment*, Num. 23:10.
1 R. V. alive
2 R. V. despised

31
z *Earthquakes*, Isa. 29:6.

a *Miracles, destruction of Korah*, Luke 23:8.

32
b *Death, of the wicked, sudden*, Num. 23:10.

34
c *Israel*, Ex. 4:22.

35
d *Fire*, Ex. 12:8.

36
e *Moses*, Ex. 2:10.
f *Prophets, inspiration of*, Isa. 3:2.

37
g *Eleazar*, Num. 3:2.
h *Priest*, Lev. 1:5.
i *Censer*, Lev. 16:12.
3 R. V. holy;

28 And Mō'ṣeṣ said, [w]Hereby ye shall know that the LORD hath [x]sent me to do all these works; for *I have* not *done them* of mine own mind.

29 If these men die the common death of all men, or if they be visited after the visitation of all men; *then* the LORD hath not sent me.

30 But if the LORD make a new thing, and the earth open her mouth, and [y]swallow them up, with all that *appertain* unto them, and they go down [1]quick into the pit; then ye shall understand that these men have [2]provoked the LORD.

31 ¶ And it came to pass, as he had made an end of speaking all these words, that the ground [z,a]clave asunder that *was* under them:

32 And the earth [a]opened her mouth, and [b]swallowed them up, and their houses, and all the men that *appertained* unto *Kō'rah, and all *their* goods.

33 They, and all that *appertained* to them, went down alive into the pit, and the earth closed upon them: and they [b]perished from among the congregation.

34 And all [c]Ĭṣ'ra-el that *were* round about them fled at the cry of them: for they said, Lest the earth swallow us up *also*.

35 And there came out a [d]fire from the LORD, and consumed the two hundred and fifty men that offered incense.

36 ¶ And the LORD spake unto [e,f]Mō'ṣeṣ, saying,

37 Speak unto [g]Ē-le-ā'zar the son of Aâr'on the [h]priest, that he take up the [i]censers out of the burning, and scatter thou the [d]fire yonder; for they are hallowed.[3]

38 The [i]censers of these sinners against their own souls, let them make them broad plates *for* a covering of the [j]altar: for they offered them before the LORD, therefore they are hallowed: and they shall be a [k]sign unto the children of Ĭṣ'ra-el.

39 And [g]Ē-le-ā'zar the [h]priest took the brasen [i]censers, wherewith they that were burnt had offered; and they were made broad *plates for* a covering of the altar:

40 *To be* a ‖memorial unto the children of Ĭṣ'ra-el, that no stranger, which *is* not of the seed of Aâr'on, [l]come near to offer [m]incense before the LORD; that he be not as *Kō'rah, and as his company: as the LORD said to him by the hand of Mō'ṣeṣ.

41 ¶ But on the morrow all the congregation of the children of [n]Ĭṣ'ra-el [o]murmured against [e]Mō'ṣeṣ and against [p]Aâr'on, saying, Ye have killed the people of the LORD.

42 And it came to pass, when the congregation was gathered against [e]Mō'ṣeṣ and against [p]Aâr'on, that they looked toward the [q]tabernacle of the congregation: and, behold, the [r]cloud covered it, and the [s]glory of the LORD appeared.

43 And [e]Mō'ṣeṣ and [p]Aâr'on came before the [q]tabernacle of the congregation.

44 And the LORD spake unto [e]Mō'ṣeṣ, saying,

45 Get you up from among this congregation, that [t]I may consume them as in a moment. And they fell upon their faces.

46 And [e]Mō'ṣeṣ said unto [p]Aâr'on, Take a [i]censer, and put fire therein from off the altar, and put on [m]incense, and go quickly unto the congregation, and [u]make an [v]atonement for

38
j *Altar, of incense*, Ex. 30:1.
k *Token*, Psa. 86:17.

40
l *Sacrilege, instances of*, Lev. 19:8.
m *Incense*, Ex. 37:29.

41
n *Israel, murmuring of*, Ex. 4:22.
o *Murmuring, of Israelites*, Num. 14:2.
p *Aaron*, Ex. 6:20.

42
q *Tabernacle*, Ex. 27:9.
r *Pillar, of cloud and fire*, Ex. 13:21.
s *God, glory of*, Gen. 2:2.

45
t *Anger of God*, 2 Kin. 13:3.

46
u *Intercession, of man with God*, Jer. 27:18.
v *Atonement*, Lev. 17:11.

‖ **MEMORIAL.** *Passover*, Ex. 12:14. *Firstborn set apart as a*, Ex. 13:12–16. *Pot of manna*, Ex. 16:32–34. *Feast of tabernacles*, Lev. 23:43. *Stones upon shoulder of the ephod*, Ex. 28:12; 39:7. *Atonement money*, Ex. 30:16. *The twelve stones of Jordan*, Josh. 4:1–9. *Lord's Supper*, Luke 22:19; 1 Cor. 11:24–26. See footnote, PILLAR, Gen. 28:18.

them: for there is [t]wrath gone out from the LORD; the [w, x]plague is begun.

47 And [p]Aâr'on took as [e]Mō'ṣeṣ commanded, and ran into the midst of the congregation; and, behold, the [w, x]plague was begun among the people: and he put on [m]incense, and made an [v]atonement for the people.

48 And he [u]stood between the dead and the living; and the [w]plague was stayed.[C]

49 Now they that died in the [w]plague were fourteen thousand and seven hundred, beside them that died about the matter of *Kō'rah.[S Q]

50 And Aâr'on returned unto Mō'ṣeṣ unto the door of the [q]tabernacle of the congregation: and the [w]plague was stayed.

## CHAPTER 17

*God commands the tribes to bring their rods. 8 Only Aaron's rod flourishes. 10 It is kept for a token against the rebels.*

AND the[S] LORD spake unto [a]Mō'ṣeṣ, saying,

2 Speak unto the children of [b]Ĭṣ'ra-el, and take of every one of them a rod according to the house of *their* fathers, of all their [c]princes according to the house of their fathers twelve rods: write thou every man's name upon his rod.

3 And thou shalt write [d]Aâr'on's name upon the rod of [e]Lē'vī: for one rod *shall be* for the head of the house of their fathers.

4 And thou shalt lay them up in the [f]tabernacle of the congregation before the testimony, [g]where I will meet with you.

5 And it shall come to pass, *that* the man's rod, whom I shall choose, [h]shall blossom: and I will make to cease from me the [i]murmurings of the children of [b]Ĭṣ'ra-el, whereby they murmur against you.

6 ¶ And [a]Mō'ṣeṣ spake unto the children of [b]Ĭṣ'ra-el, and every one of their [c]princes gave him a rod apiece, for each prince one, according to their father's houses, *even* twelve rods: and the [j]rod of Aâr'on *was* among their rods.

7 And [a]Mō'ṣeṣ laid up the rods before the LORD in the [f]tabernacle of witness.

8[Q] And it came to pass, that on the morrow[G] [a]Mō'ṣeṣ went into the [f]tabernacle of witness; and, behold, the [j]rod of Aâr'on for the house of [e]Lē'vī was budded, and brought forth buds, and bloomed blossoms, and [1]yielded [k]almonds.

9 And [a]Mō'ṣeṣ brought out all the rods from before the LORD unto all the children of [b]Ĭṣ'ra-el: and they looked, and took every man his rod.

10 ¶ And the LORD said unto Mō'ṣeṣ, Bring Aâr'on's [j]rod again before the [l]testimony, to be kept for a [m]token[C] against the rebels; and thou shalt quite take away their [n]murmurings from me, that they die not.[Q]

11 And [a]Mō'ṣeṣ did *so*: as the LORD commanded him, so did he.[S]

12 And the children of [b]Ĭṣ'ra-el spake unto [a]Mō'ṣeṣ, saying, Behold, [o]we die, we perish, we all perish.

13 Whosoever cometh any thing[G] near unto the [f]tabernacle of the LORD shall die: shall we be consumed[G] with dying?

## CHAPTER 18

*The charge of the priests and Levites. 8 The priests' portion. 21 The Levites' portion. 25 The heave offering to the priests out of the Levites' portion.*

AND the LORD said unto [a, b]Aâr'on, [c]Thou and thy sons and thy father's house with thee shall bear the iniquity of the sanctuary: and thou and thy

v Plague, on the Israelites, Ex. 11:1.
x Miracles, plague, Luke 23:8.

1
a Moses, Ex. 2:10.

2
b Israel, Ex. 4:22.
c Government, Mosaic, Isa. 22:21.

3
d Aaron, Ex. 6:20.
e Levites, Deut. 10:8.

4
f Tabernacle, Ex. 27:9.
g Shekinah, Lev. 16:2.

5
h Miracles, design of, Luke 23:8.
i Murmuring, Num. 14:2.

6
j Rod of Aaron, Ex. 7:9.

8
k Almond, Gen. 43 11.
1 R. V. bare ripe

10
l Ark, contents of, Ex. 25:10.
m Token, Psa. 86 17.
n Murmuring, against God, Num. 14:2.

12
o Despondency, Eccl. 2:20.

1
a Aaron, Ex. 6:20.
b Minister, charge delivered to, vs. 1-7; Rom. 15:16.
c Priest, duties of, Lev. 1:5.

sons with thee shall bear the iniquity of your priesthood.

2 And thy brethren also of the tribe of [d]Lē′vī, the tribe of thy father, bring thou with thee, that they may be joined unto thee, and minister unto thee: but [c]thou and thy sons with thee *shall minister* before the tabernacle of witness.

3 And [d]they shall keep thy charge, and the charge of all the [e]tabernacle: only they shall not come nigh the vessels of the sanctuary and the altar, that neither they, nor ye also, die.

4 And [d]they shall be joined unto thee, and keep the charge of the [e]tabernacle of the congregation, for all the service of the tabernacle: and a [f]stranger shall not come nigh unto you.

5 And [c]ye shall keep the charge of the [g]sanctuary, and the charge of the altar: that there be no wrath any more upon the children of Ĭş′ra-el.

6 And I, behold, I have taken your brethren the [d]Lē′vītes from among the children of Ĭş′ra-el: to you *they are* given *as* a gift for the LORD, to do the service of the [e]tabernacle of the congregation.

7 Therefore [c]thou and thy sons with thee shall keep your priest's office for every thing of the altar, and within the vail: and ye shall serve: I have given your priest's office *unto you as* a service of gift: and the [f]stranger that cometh nigh shall be [h]put to [i]death.

8 ¶ And the LORD spake unto [a]Aâ′ron, Behold, I also have given thee the charge of mine [j]heave offerings of all the hallowed things of the children of Ĭş′ra-el; unto thee have I given [k]them by reason of the anointing, and to thy sons, by an ordinance for ever.

9 [k]This shall be thine of the most holy things, *reserved* from the fire: every oblation of their's, every [1,l]meat offering of their's, and every [m]sin offering of their's, and every [2,n]trespass offering of their's, which they shall render unto me, *shall be* most [o]holy for thee and for thy sons.

10 [3]In the most holy *place* shalt thou eat [k]it; every male shall eat it: it shall be [o]holy unto thee.

11 And [k]this is thine; the [j]heave offering of their gift, with all the [p]wave offerings of the children of Ĭş′ra-el: I have given them unto thee, and to thy sons and to thy daughters with thee, [4]by a statute for ever: every one that is [q]clean in thy house shall eat of it.

12 All the best of the [r]oil, and all the best of the [s]wine, and of the [t]wheat, the [u]firstfruits of them which they shall offer unto the LORD, [k]them have I given thee.

13 *And* [k]whatsoever is [u]first ripe in the land, which they shall bring unto the LORD, shall be thine; every one that is [q]clean in thine house shall eat *of* it.

14 [k]Every thing [v,w]devoted in Ĭş′ra-el shall be thine.

15 [k,x]Every thing that openeth the [5]matrix in all flesh, which they bring unto the LORD, *whether it be* of men or beasts, shall be thine: nevertheless the [y]firstborn of man shalt thou surely [z]redeem, and the firstling of unclean beasts shalt thou redeem.

16 And those that are to be [x,z]redeemed from a month old shalt thou redeem, according to thine estimation, for the [a]money of five [b]shekels, after the shekel of the sanctuary, which *is* twenty [c]gerahs.

17 But the [d]firstling of a cow, or the firstling of a sheep, or the firstling of a goat, thou shalt not [e]redeem; they *are* holy: thou

---

2
d *Levites, duties of,* Deut. 10:8.

3
e *Tabernacle,* Ex. 27:9.

4
f *Foreigners, Mosaic law relating to,* Deut. 23:20.

5
g *Sanctuary, in charge of priests,* Lev. 4:6.

7
h *Punishment, death penalty,* Lev. 26:41.
i *Death, penalty,* Num. 23:10.

8
j *Offerings, heave,* Lev. 6:17.
k *Priest, emoluments of,* Lev. 1:5.

9
l *Offerings, meat,* Lev. 6:17.
m *Offerings, sin,* Lev. 6:17.
n *Offerings, trespass,* Lev. 6:17.
o *Offerings, holy,* Lev. 6:17.
1 R. V. meal
2 R. V. guilt

10
3 R. V. As the most holy thing shalt thou eat thereof:

11
p *Offerings, wave,* Lev. 6:17.
q *Holiness, typified,* Ex. 39:30.
4 R. V. as a due for ever:

12
r *Oil, offerings of,* Deut. 12:17.
s *Wine, offerings of,* Prov. 23:31.
t *Wheat,* Ezra 6:9.
u *First Fruits,* Deut. 18:4.

14
v *Dedication, law concerning dedicated things,* Ezra 6:17.
w *Vows, things offered in, belonged to the priest,* Num. 30:2.

15
x *Priest, emoluments of,* v. 16; Lev. 1:5.
y *Firstborn, redemption of,* vs. 15–17; Zech. 12: 10.
z *Redemption,* Lev. 25:24.
5 R. V. womb,

16
a *Money,* Jer. 32:9.
b *Shekel,* Ex. 30:13.
c *Gerah,* Lev. 27: 25.

17
d *Firstborn, redemption of,* Zech. 12:10.
e *Redemption,* Lev. 25:24.

shalt sprinkle their [f,g]blood upon
the altar, and shalt burn their
fat *for* an offering made by fire,
for a sweet savour unto the
LORD.
18 And the [h]flesh of them shall
be thine, as the wave breast and
as the right [6]shoulder are thine.
19 [h]All the [i]heave offerings of
the holy things, which the children of Iş'ra-el offer unto the
LORD, have I given thee, and
thy sons and thy daughters with
thee, [4]by a statute for ever: it *is*
a [j,k]covenant of [l,m]salt for ever
before the LORD unto thee and
to thy seed with thee.
20 ¶ And the LORD spake unto
Aâr'on, Thou shalt have no inheritance in their land, neither
shalt thou have any part among
them: [h,n,o]I *am* thy part and
thine inheritance among the
children of Iş'ra-el.
21 And, behold, I have given
the children of Lē'vī all the
[*,p]tenth in Iş'ra-el for an inheritance, for their service which
they serve, *even* the service of the
[q]tabernacle of the congregation.
22 Neither must the children of
Iş'ra-el henceforth come nigh
the [q]tabernacle of the congregation, lest they bear sin, and die.
23 But the [r]Lē'vītes shall do the
service of the [q]tabernacle of the
congregation, and they shall
bear their iniquity: *it shall be* a
statute for ever throughout your
generations, that among the children of Iş'ra-el they have no
inheritance.
24 But the [*,p]tithes of the children of Iş'ra-el, which they offer
*as* an heave [i]offering unto the
LORD, I have given to the Lē'-
vītes to inherit: therefore I have
said unto them, Among the children of Iş'ra-el they shall have
no inheritance.
25 ¶ And the LORD [s]spake unto [t]Mō'şeş, saying,
26 Thus speak unto the Lē'-
vītes, and say unto them, When
ye take of the children of Iş'ra-el
the [*,p]tithes which I have given
you from them for your inheritance, then ye shall offer up an
[i]heave offering of it for the
LORD, *even* a tenth *part* of the
tithe.
27 And *this* your [i]heave offering shall be reckoned unto you,
as though *it were* the corn of the
threshingfloor, and as the fulness
of the [u]winepress.
28 Thus ye also shall offer an
[i]heave offering unto the LORD of
all your [*]tithes, which ye receive
of the children of Iş'ra-el; and ye
shall give thereof the LORD's
[h]heave offering to Aâr'on the
priest.
29 Out of all your gifts ye shall
offer every [i]heave offering of the
LORD, of all the best thereof,
*even* the hallowed part thereof
out of it.
30 Therefore thou shalt say unto them, When ye have heaved
the best thereof, then it shall be
counted unto the Lē'vītes as the
increase of the threshingfloor,
and as the increase of the [u]wine-
press.
31 And ye shall eat it in every
place, ye and your households:
for it *is* your [h]reward for your
service in the [q]tabernacle of the
congregation.
32 And ye shall bear no sin
by reason of it, when ye have
heaved from it the best of it: neither shall ye pollute the holy
things of the children of Iş'ra-el,
lest ye die.

f *Blood sacrificial,* Heb. 9:19.
g *Jesus, atoning blood of, typified,* Matt. 1:21.

18
h *Priest, emoluments of,* Lev. 1:5.
6 R. V. thigh,

19
i *Offerings, heave,* Lev. 6:17.
j *Covenant, of God with men,* Deut. 29:1.
k *Covenant, ratified with salt,* Deut. 29:1.
l *Salt,* 2 Kin. 2:20.
m *Symbols and Similitudes,* Heb. 9:9.

20
n *Minister, emoluments of,* Rom. 15:16.
o *Promise, to ministers,* 2 Cor. 1:20.

21
p *Levites, emoluments of,* Deut. 10:8.
q *Tabernacle,* Ex. 27:9.

23
r *Levites, duties of,* Deut. 10:8.

25
s *Revelation, concerning emoluments of priests and Levites,* vs. 25–31: 2 Cor. 12:1.
t *Prophets, inspiration of,* Isa. 3:2.

27
u *Wine Press,* Isa. 5:2.

*** TITHES.** *Paid by Abraham to Melchizedek,* Gen. 14:20; Heb. 7:2–6. *Jacob vows a tenth of all his property to God,* Gen. 28:22.
*Mosaic laws concerning,* Lev. 27:30–33; Num. 18:21, 24; Deut. 12:6, 7, 17–19; 14:22–29; 26:12–15. *Poor entitled to share in,* Deut. 14:28, 29; 26:12, 13.
*Customs relating to,* Neh. 10:37, 38; Amos 4:4; Heb. 7:5–9. *Tithe of tithes for priests,* Num. 18:26; Neh. 10:38. *Stored in the temple,* Neh. 10:38, 39; 12:44; 13:5, 12; 2 Chr. 31:11, 12; Mal. 3:10.
Payment of: *Resumed, in Hezekiah's reign,* 2 Chr. 31:5–10; *under Nehemiah,* Neh. 13:12. *Withheld,* Neh. 13:10; Mal. 3:8.
*Customary in later times,* Matt. 23:23; Luke 11:42; 18:12. *Observed by idolaters,* Amos 4:4, 5.

## CHAPTER 19

*The water of separation. 11 The law for the use of it in purification of the unclean.*

AND the LORD [a]spake unto Mō'ṣeṣ and unto Aâr'on, saying,

2 This *is* the ordinance of the law which the LORD hath commanded, saying, Speak unto the children of Ĭṣ'ra-el, that they bring thee a [b]red [*,c,d]heifer [e]without [f,g]spot,[C] wherein *is* [e]no [f,g]blemish, *and* upon which never came yoke:

3 And ye shall give her unto [h]Ē-le-ā'zar the [i]priest, that he may bring her forth without[C] the camp, and *one* shall slay her before his face:

4 And [h]Ē-le-ā'zar the [i]priest shall take of her [j,k]blood with his finger, and [l]sprinkle of her blood [1]directly before the [m]tabernacle of the congregation seven times:

5 And *one* shall burn the [*]heifer in his sight; her skin, and her flesh, and her blood, with her dung, shall he burn:

6 And the [i]priest shall take [n]cedar wood, and [o]hyssop, and [b]scarlet, and cast *it* into the midst of the burning of the heifer.[Q]

7 Then the priest shall [p]wash his clothes, and he shall [‡,p]bathe his flesh in water, and afterward he shall come into the camp, and the priest shall be [g,q]unclean until the even.

8 And he that burneth her shall wash his clothes in water, and [p]bathe his flesh in water, and shall be [g,q]unclean until the even.

9 And a man *that is* [e]clean shall gather up the [†]ashes of the [*,r]heifer, and lay *them* up without[C] the camp in a clean place, and it shall be kept for the congregation of the children of Ĭṣ'ra-el for a [s]water of separation: it *is* a [2]purification for sin.[Q]

10 And he that gathereth the [†]ashes of the heifer shall wash his clothes, and be [g,q]unclean until the even: and it shall be unto the children of Ĭṣ'ra-el, and unto the [t]stranger that sojourneth among them, for a statute for ever.

11 ¶ He that [u]toucheth the dead body of any man shall be [g,v]unclean seven days.

12 He shall [‡]purify himself with it on the third day, and on the seventh day he shall be [e]clean: but if he purify not himself the third day, then the seventh day he shall not be clean.

13 Whosoever [u]toucheth the dead body of any man that is dead, and [‡]purifieth not himself, defileth the [w]tabernacle of the LORD; and that soul shall be [x]cut off from Ĭṣ'ra-el: because the [s]water of separation was not [l]sprinkled upon him, he shall be [g,v]unclean; his uncleanness *is* yet upon him.[Q]

14 This *is* the law, when a man dieth in a tent: all that come into the tent, and all that *is* in the tent, shall be [v]unclean seven days.

15 And [u]every open vessel, which hath no covering bound upon it, *is* unclean.

16 And [u]whosoever toucheth one that is slain with a sword in the open fields, or a dead body, or a bone of a man, or a [y]grave, shall be [g,v]unclean seven days.

17[Q] And for an unclean *person* they shall take of the [†]ashes of the [3]burnt [*]heifer of [‡]purification for sin, and running water shall be put thereto in a vessel:

18 And a [e]clean person shall take [o]hyssop, and dip *it* in the water, and [l]sprinkle *it* upon the tent, and upon all the vessels,

**1**
a *Inspiration*, Job 32:8.

**2**
b *Colors, symbolical*, Ezek. 16:16.
c *Types, of the Savior*, Heb. 10:1.
d *Jesus, typified in offerings*, Matt. 1:21.
e *Holiness, typified*, Ex. 39:30.
f *Blemish*, Lev. 14:10.
g *Sin, typified*, Rom. 5:12.

**3**
h *Eleazar*, Num. 3:2.
i *Priest, duties of*, Lev. 1:5.

**4**
j *Blood, sacrificial*, Heb. 9:19.
k *Jesus, atoning blood of, typified*, Matt. 1:21.
l *Sprinkling*, Lev. 14:7.
m *Tabernacle*, Ex. 27:9.
1 R. V. toward the front of the tent of meeting

**6**
n *Cedar*, Isa. 9:10.
o *Hyssop*, Ex. 12:22.

**7**
p *Ceremonial Washing*, Ex. 19:10.
q *Defilement, of priests*, Lev. 5:2.

**9**
r *Offerings, burnt*, Lev. 6:17.
s *Water*, 1 Kin. 17:10.
2 R. V. sin offering.

**10**
t *Foreigners*, Deut. 23:20.

**11**
u *Sanitation and Hygiene, contagion*, Num. 31:23.
v *Defilement, caused by touching the dead*, Lev. 5:2.

**13**
w *Tabernacle, defilement of, punished*, Ex. 27:9.
x *Disfellowship*, Num. 15:31.

**16**
y *Burying Places*, Gen. 23:4.

**17**
3 R. V. burning of the sin offering

---

*** HEIFER.** *When used as sacrifice, must be without blemish and must not have come under the yoke*, Num. 19:2; Deut. 21:3. *An atonement for murder*, Deut. 21:1-9.
**Red Heifer:** *A type of atonement by Jesus*, Heb. 9:13, 14. *Ashes from burning of, used for water of separation*, Num. 19. **Figurative:** *Of backsliders*, Hos. 4:16. *Of the obedient*, Hos. 10:11.

**† ASHES.** *Uses of, in purification*, Num. 19:9, 10, 17; Heb. 9:13. *A symbol of mourning*, 2 Sam. 13:19; Esth. 4:1, 3. *Sitting in*, Job 2:8; Isa. 58:5; Jer. 6:26; Ezek. 27:30;

and upon the persons that were there, and upon him that touched a bone, or one slain, or one dead, or a [u]grave:

19 And the [e]clean *person* shall [l]sprinkle upon the unclean on the third day, and on the seventh day: and on the seventh day he shall ‡purify himself, and [p]wash his clothes, and [p]bathe himself in water, and shall be [e]clean at even.

20 But the man that shall be unclean, and shall not ‡purify himself, that soul shall be [x]cut off from among the congregation, because he hath defiled the [w]sanctuary of the LORD: the [s]water of separation hath not been [l]sprinkled upon him; he *is* [g,v]unclean.

21 And it shall be a perpetual statute unto them, that he that [l]sprinkleth the [s]water of separation shall wash his clothes; and he that toucheth the water of separation shall be [g,v]unclean until even.

22 And [u]whatsoever the unclean *person* toucheth shall be unclean; and the soul that toucheth *it* shall be [g,v]unclean until even.

## CHAPTER 20

*The children of Israel come to Zin, where Miriam dies. 2 They murmur for want of water. 7 Moses smites the rock at Meribah, and water comes forth. 14 Moses at Kadesh desires a passage through Edom, which is denied. 22 Aaron dies at mount Hor, and the high-priesthood passes to Eleazar.*

THEN came the children of Is′ra-el, *even* the whole congregation, into the desert of [a]Zin in the first [b,c]month: and the people abode in [d]Kā′desh; and [e]Mĭr′ĭ-am died there, and was buried there.

2 And there was no water for the congregation: and they gathered themselves together against [f]Mō′ṣeṣ and against [g]Aâr′on.

3 And the [h]people [1]chode with Mō′ṣeṣ, and spake, [i]saying, Would God that we had died when our brethren died before the LORD!

4 And [i]why have ye brought up the congregation of the LORD into this wilderness, [j]that we and our cattle should die there?

5 And [i]wherefore have ye made us to come up out of Ē′gy̆pt, to bring us in unto this evil place? it *is* no place of seed, or of figs, or of vines, or of pomegranates; neither *is* there any water to drink.

6 And [f]Mō′ṣeṣ and [g]Aâr′on went from the presence of the assembly unto the door of the [k]tabernacle of the congregation, and they fell upon their faces: and the [l]glory of the LORD appeared unto them.

7 ¶ And the LORD spake unto Mō′ṣeṣ, saying,

8 [m]Take the rod, and gather thou the assembly together, thou, and Aâr′on thy brother, and speak ye unto the rock before their eyes; and it shall give forth his water, and thou shalt bring forth to them water out of the rock: so thou shalt give the congregation and their beasts drink.

v.1–1494 BC
See footnote, *Time,* Rev. 10:6.

1
a *Zin,* Num. 13:21.
b *Abib,* Ex. 13:4.
c *Month, Abib,* Ex. 12:2.

v.1–1494 BC
See footnote, *Time,* Rev. 10:6.

d *Kadesh.* Gen. 14:7.
e *Miriam,* Ex. 15:20.

2
f *Moses, murmured against,* Ex. 2:10.
g *Aaron, murmured against,* Ex. 6:20.

3
h *Israel, murmur against Moses,* Ex. 4:22.
i *Murmuring, of the Israelites,* Num. 14:2.
1 R. V. strove

4
j *Borrowing Trouble,* vs. 1–13; Matt. 6:25.

6
k *Tabernacle,* Ex. 27:9.
l *God, glory of,* Gen. 2:2.

8
m *God, providence of,* Gen. 2:2.

Jonah 3:6. *Repenting in,* Job 42:6; Dan. 9:3; Matt. 11:21; Luke 10:13.

‡ **PURIFICATION.** In studying the Mosaic law relating to purifications, it must be kept in mind that sin defiles. To keep this great truth constantly before the mind of the Israelites specific ordinances concerning purifications were given to Moses; the purpose being, by this object lesson, to teach that sin defiles and only the pure in heart can see God. Therefore certain incidents, such as eating that which had died of itself, touching the dead, etc., were signified as defiling, and definite ceremonies were prescribed for persons who were defiled. During the period of defilement, and when performing the ceremonies required of them, the defiled were expected to contemplate the defilement of sin and the need of purification of the heart.

*Sanitary and symbolical,* Ex. 19:10, 14; Heb. 9:10. *For women, after childbirth,* Lev. 12:6–8; Luke 2:22; *after menstruation,* Lev. 15:19–33; 2 Sam. 11:4. *After copulation,* Lev. 15:16–18. *For spermatorrhea,* Lev. 15:4–18. *For eating that which died of itself,* Lev. 17:15. *For those who had slain in battle,* Num. 31:19–24. *Of priests,* Ex. 29:4; 30:18–21; 40:12, 30–32; Lev. 8:6; 16:4, 24, 26, 28; 22:3; Num. 19:7, 8; 2 Chr. 4:6. *Of Levites,* Num. 8:6, 7, 21. *Of lepers,* see footnote, LEPROSY, Lev. 13:2. *Of the Jews before the passover,* John 11:55. *By fire, for things that resist fire,* Num. 31:23. *By blood,* Ex. 24:5–8; Lev. 14:6, 7; Heb. 9:12–14, 19–22. *By abstaining from sexual intercourse,* Ex. 19:15. *By washing in water parts of animal sacrifices,* Lev. 1:9, 13; 9:14; 2 Chr. 4:6. *Penalty to be imposed upon those who do not observe the ordinances concerning,* Lev. 7:20, 21; 22:3; Num. 19:13, 20.

*Water of,* Num. 19:17–21; 31:23. *Washing hands in water, symbolical of innocency,* Deut. 21:6; Psa. 26:6. *Tradi-*

9 And Mō′ṣeṣ took the rod from before the LORD, as he commanded him.

10 And [n]Mō′ṣeṣ and [o]Aâr′on gathered the congregation together before the rock, and he said unto them, [p]Hear now, ye rebels; must we fetch you water out of this rock?

11 And [n]Mō′ṣeṣ lifted up his hand, and with his rod he [q]smote the rock twice: and the [r,s,t]water came out abundantly, and the congregation drank, and their beasts *also*.

12 ¶ And the LORD spake unto [n]Mō′ṣeṣ and [o]Aâr′on, Because [u]ye [v]believed me not, to sanctify me in the eyes of the children of Ĭṣ′ra-el, therefore [w,x]ye shall not bring this congregation into the land which I have given them.

13 This *is* the water of [y]Měr′i-bah; because the children of [h]Ĭṣ′ra-el [i]strove with the LORD, and he was sanctified in them.

14 ¶ And Mō′ṣeṣ sent [z]messengers from [a]Kā′desh unto the king of [b]Ē′dom, Thus saith thy brother [c]Ĭṣ′ra-el, Thou knowest all the travel that hath befallen us:

15 How our fathers went down into [d]Ē′ġy̆pt, and we have dwelt in Ē′ġy̆pt a long time; and the [e]Ē-ġy̆p′tianṣ vexed us, and our fathers:

16 And when we [f]cried unto the LORD, he heard our voice, and sent an [g]angel, and hath brought us forth out of [d]Ē′ġy̆pt: and, behold, we *are* in [a]Kā′desh, a city in the uttermost of thy border:

17 Let us pass, I pray thee, through thy country: we will not pass through the fields, or through the [h]vineyards, neither will we drink *of* the water of the wells: we will go by the king's [i]*high* way, we will not turn to the right hand nor to the left, until we have passed thy borders.

18 And [b]Ē′dom said unto him, [j]Thou shalt not pass by me, lest I come out against thee with the sword.

19 And the children of [c]Ĭṣ′ra-el said unto him, We will go by the [i]high way: and if I and my cattle drink of thy water, then I will pay for it: I will only, without *doing* anything *else*, go through on my feet.

20 And he said, [c,j]Thou shalt not go through. And [b]Ē′dom came out against him with much people, and with a strong hand.

21 Thus [b]Ē′dom [c,j]refused to give Ĭṣ′ra-el passage through his border: wherefore Ĭṣ′ra-el turned away from him.

22 ¶ And the children of Ĭṣ′ra-el, *even* the whole congregation, journeyed from [a]Kā′desh, and came unto mount *Hôr.

23 And the LORD spake unto Mō′ṣeṣ and Aâr′on in mount *Hôr, by the coast of the land of [k]Ē′dom, saying,

24 [l]Aâr′on shall be gathered unto his people: for he shall not enter into the land which I have given unto the children of Ĭṣ′ra-el, because ye [m]rebelled against my word at the water of [n]Měr′i-bah.

25 Take [l]Aâr′on and [o]Ē-le-ā′zar his son, and bring them up into mount *Hôr:

26 And strip Aâr′on of his garments, and put them upon [o]Ē-leā′zar his son: and [l]Aâr′on shall be gathered *unto his people*, and shall die there.

27 And Mō′ṣeṣ did as the LORD commanded: and they went up into mount *Hôr in the sight of all the congregation.

v.9–1494 BC
See footnote, *Time*, Rev. 10:6.

10
n *Moses, character of*, Ex. 2:10.
o *Aaron, presumption of*, vs. 10–12; Ex. 6:20.
p *Anger, instances of*, Psa. 37:8.

11
q *Disobedience to God*, Eph. 5:6.
r *Water, miraculously supplied*, 1 Kin. 17:10.
s *Temporal Blessings, from God*, Psa. 103:2.
t *Miracles, water from the rock of Kadesh*, Luke 23:8.

12
u *Unbelievers*, 1 Cor. 6:6.
v *Unbelief*, Heb. 3:12.
w *Moses, not permitted to enter Canaan*, Ex. 2:10.
x *Aaron, not permitted to enter Canaan*, Ex. 6:20.

13
y *Meribah*, Ex. 17:7.

14
z *Ambassadors*, Josh. 9:4.

a *Kadesh*, Gen. 14:7.
b *Edomites*, 2 Kin. 8:21.
c *Israel, refused passage through the country of Edom*, vs. 14–21; Ex. 4:22.

15
d *Egypt*, Gen. 41:8.
e *Egyptians*, Gen. 50:3.

16
f *Adversity, prayer in*, Psa. 10:6.
g *Angel, functions of*, Heb. 1:13.

17
h *Grape*, Lev. 25:5.

v.17–1494 BC
See footnote, *Tim* Rev. 10:6.

i *Highway*, Deut. 2:27.

18
j *Inhospitablenes* Luke 9:53.

23
k *Edom*, Obad. 1.

24
l *Aaron, death of*, vs. 24–29; Ex. 6:20.
m *Disobedience to God*, Eph. 5:6.
n *Meribah*, Ex. 17:7.

25
o *Eleazar, succeed Aaron as high priest*, Num. 3:

*tions of the elders concerning*, Matt. 15:2; Mark 7:2–5, 8, 9; Luke 11:38. *Of Paul, to show his fidelity to the law*, Acts 21:24, 26.
**Figurative**, Psa. 26:6; 51:7; Ezek. 36:25.

See footnotes: DEFILEMENT, Lev. 5:2; SPIRITUAL PURIF CATION, Psa. 51:2.
* **HOR** (*the mountain of mountains*). *Aaron died on*, Nu 20:22–29; 21:4; 33:38, 39; 34:7, 8; Deut. 32:50.

v.28–1494 BC
See footnote, *Time*, Rev. 10:6.

28
p *Death, of Aaron*, Num. 23:10.

29
q *Mourning*, Lam. 2:5.

1
a Num. 33:40; Josh. 12:14.

2
b *Vows*, Num. 30:2.

3
c *Canaanites*, Ex. 23:28.
d *Israel, defeats the Canaanites*, Ex. 4:22.
e *Hormah*, Deut. 1:44.

4
f *Hor*, Num. 20:22.
g *Red Sea*, Ex. 10:19.
h *Edom*, Obad. 1.

5
i *Blasphemy, instances of*, 2 Sam. 12:14.
j *Moses, people murmur against*, Ex. 2:10.
k *Murmuring, instances of*, Num. 14:2.

28 And Mō′ṣeṣ stripped Aâr′on of his garments, and put them upon [o]Ē-le-ā′zar his son; and [l]Aâr′on [p]died there in the top of the mount: and Mō′ṣeṣ and [o]Ē-le-ā′zar came down from the mount.

29 And when all the congregation saw that Aâr′on was dead, they [q]mourned for Aâr′on thirty days, *even* all the house of Ĭṣ′ra-el.

## CHAPTER 21

*The Israelites destroy the Canaanites at Hormah. 4 They murmur, and are plagued with fiery serpents. 7 They repent, and are healed in looking upon the brazen serpent. 10 Sundry journeys of the Israelites. 21 Sihon is overcome, 33 and also Og.*

AND *when* king [a]Ā′răd the Cā′năan-īte, which dwelt in the south, heard tell that Ĭṣ′ra-el came by the way of the spies; then he fought against Ĭṣ′ra-el, and took *some* of them prisoners.

2 And Ĭṣ′ra-el vowed a [b]vow[C] unto the LORD, and said, If thou wilt indeed deliver this people into my hand, then I will utterly destroy their cities.

3 And the LORD hearkened to the voice of Ĭṣ′ra-el, and delivered up the [c]Cā′năan-ītes; and [d]they utterly destroyed them and their cities: and he called the name of the place [e]Hôr′mah.

4 ¶ And they journeyed from mount [f]Hôr by the way of the [g]Red sea, to compass the land of [h]Ē′dom: and the soul of the people was much discouraged because of the way.

5 [T Q]And the people [i]spake against God, and against [j]Mō′ṣeṣ, [k]Wherefore have ye brought us up out of Ē′ġypt to die in the wilderness? for *there is* no bread, neither *is there any* water; and our soul loatheth this light[C] bread.

6 And the LORD [l,m]sent fiery *,[n]serpents among the [o]people, and they bit the people; and much[C] people of Ĭṣ′ra-el died.[T Q]

7 [p]Therefore the people came to Mō′ṣeṣ, and said, [q,r]We have sinned, for we have spoken against the LORD, and against thee; pray unto the LORD, that he take away the serpents from us. And Mō′ṣeṣ [s]prayed for the people.

8 And the [t]LORD said unto Mō′ṣeṣ, Make thee a fiery *serpent, and set it upon a pole: and it shall come to pass, that every one that is bitten, when he looketh upon it, shall live.

9 [u]And Mō′ṣeṣ made a *,[v,w]serpent of brass, and put it upon a pole, and it came to pass, that if a serpent had bitten any man, when he beheld the serpent of brass, he lived.[Q]

10 ¶ And the children of Ĭṣ′ra-el set forward, and pitched[C] in [x]Ō′both.

11 And they journeyed from [x]Ō′both, and pitched at [y]Ĭj′e-ăb′a-rĭm, in the wilderness which *is* before [z]Mō′ab, toward the sunrising.

12 ¶ From thence they removed, and pitched[C] in the valley of [a]Zā′red.

13 From thence they removed, and pitched[C] on the other side of [b]Är′nŏn, which *is* in the wilderness that cometh out of the coasts[C] of the [c]Ăm′ôr-ītes: for Är′nŏn *is* the border of [d]Mō′ab, between Mō′ab and the Ăm′ôr-ītes.

14 Wherefore it is said in the

v.5–1494 BC
See footnote, *Time*, Rev. 10:6.

6
l *Judgments, upon the Israelites*, Ex. 6:6.
m *Miracles, scourge of serpents*, Luke 23:8.
n *Plague*, Ex. 11:1.
o *Israel, scourged with serpents*, Ex. 4:22.

7
p *Afflictions, benefits of*, Psa. 34:19.
q *Repentance, instances of*, Mark 1:4.
r *Conviction of Sin, instances of*, John 16:8.
s *Intercession, instances of*, Jer. 27:18.

8
t *God, mercy of*, Gen. 2:2.

9
u John 3:14, 15.
v *Brazen Serpent*, 2 Kin. 18:4.
w *Jesus, atonement by, typified*, Matt. 1:21.

10
x Num. 33:43, 44.

11
y Num. 33:44.
z *Moab*, Num. 26:3.

12
a Deut. 2:13, 14.

13
b *Arnon*, Num. 22:36.
c *Amorites*, Gen. 14:13.
d *Moab*, Num. 26:3.

* **SERPENT.** *Satan appears in the form of, to Eve*, Gen. 3:1–15; 2 Cor. 11:3; Rev. 12:9. *Subtlety of*, Gen. 3:1; Eccl. 10:8; Matt. 10:16. *Curse upon*, Gen. 3:14, 15; 49:17. *Feeds upon the dust*, Gen. 3:14; Isa. 65:25; Mic. 7:17. *Unfit for food*, Matt. 7:10. *Venom of*, Deut. 32:24, 33; Job 20:16; Psa. 58:4; 140:3; Acts 28:5, 6. *Intoxicating wine compared to the venomous*, Prov. 23:31, 32. *The staff of Moses transformed into*, Ex. 4:3; 7:15. *Fiery, sent as a plague upon the Israelites*, Num. 21:6, 7; Deut. 8:15; 1 Cor. 10:9. *The wound of, miraculously healed by looking upon the brazen, set up by Moses*, Num. 21:8, 9. *Charming of*, Psa. 58:4, 5; Eccl. 10:11; Jer. 8:17. *Mentioned in Solomon's riddle*, Prov. 30:19. *Sea serpent*, Amos 9:3. *The seventy endued with power over*, Luke 10:19. *The apostles given power over*, Mark 16:18; Acts 28:5.
**Figurative**, Isa. 14:29; 30:6; 65:25.

v.14–1494 BC
See footnote, *Time*, Rev. 10:6.

14
e *War*, Judg. 3:2.
1 R. V. valleys

15
f Deut. 2:9, 18, 29; Isa. 15:1.
2 R. V. the slope of valleys that inclineth toward the

16
g *Moses*, Ex. 2:10.

17
h *Israel*, Ex. 4:22.
i *Thankfulness, exemplified*, Acts 24:3.
j *Music*, 2 Chr. 5:13.

19
k Or, *Bamoth-baal*, Josh. 13:17.

20
l *Pisgah*, Deut. 3:27.
3 R. V. down upon the desert.

21
m *Ambassadors*, Josh. 9:4.

22
n *Grape*, Lev. 25:5.
o *Highways*, Deut. 2:27.

23
p *Inhospitableness, instances of*, Luke 9:53.
q *Jahaz*, Judg. 11:20.

book of the [e]wars of the LORD, What he did in the Red sea, and in the [1]brooks of [b]Är′nŏn,

15 And [2]at the stream of the brooks that goeth down to the dwelling of [f]Är and lieth upon the border of [d]Mō′ab.

16 ¶ And from thence *they went* to Bē′er: that *is* the well whereof the LORD spake unto [g]Mō′ṣeṣ, Gather the people together, and I will give them water.

17 Then [h]Ĭṣ′ra-el [i]sang this [j]song, Spring up, O well; sing ye unto it:

18 The princes digged the well, the nobles of the people digged it, by *the direction of* the lawgiver, with their staves. And from the wilderness *they went* to Măt′ta-nah:

19 And from Măt′ta-nah to Nȧ-hā′lĭ-el: and from Nȧ-hā′lĭ-el to [k]Bā′mŏth:

20 And from [k]Bā′mŏth *in* the valley, that *is* in the country of [d]Mō′ab, to the top of [l]Pĭṣ′gah, which looketh [3]toward Jĕsh′ĭ-mŏn.

21 ¶ And [h]Ĭṣ′ra-el sent [m]messengers unto †Sī′hŏn king of the [c]Ăm′ôr-ītes, saying,

22 Let me pass through thy land: we will not turn into the fields, or into the [n]vineyards; we will not drink *of* the waters of the well: *but* we will go along by the king's [o]*high* way, until we be past thy borders.

23 And †Sī′hŏn [p]would not suffer[c] Ĭṣ′ra-el to pass through his border: but Sī′hŏn gathered all his people together, and went out against Ĭṣ′ra-el into the wilderness: and he came to [q]Jā′hăz, and fought against Ĭṣ′ra-el.

24 And [r]Ĭṣ′ra-el smote him with the edge of the sword, and possessed his land from Är′nŏn unto ‡Jăb′bŏk, even unto the [s]children of Ăm′mŏn: for the border of the children of Ăm-mŏn *was* strong.

25 And [r]Ĭṣ′ra-el took all these cities: and Ĭṣ′ra-el dwelt in all the cities of the [c]Ăm′ôr-ītes, in [t]Hĕsh′bŏn, and in all the villages thereof.

26 For Hĕsh′bŏn *was* the city of †Sī′hŏn the king of the Ăm′ôr-ītes, who had fought against the former king of [u]Mŏ′ab, and taken all his land out of his hand, even unto Är′nŏn.

27 Wherefore they that speak in proverbs[c] say, [v]Come into Hĕsh′bŏn, let the city of †Sī′hŏn be built and prepared:

28 [v]For there is a fire gone out of [t]Hĕsh′bŏn, a flame from the city of †Sī′hŏn: it hath consumed [f]Är of Mō′ab, *and* the lords of the high places of [b]Är′nŏn.

29 [v]Woe to thee, [u]Mō′ab! thou art undone, O people of Chē′mŏsh: he hath given his sons [4]that escaped, and his daughters, into captivity unto †Sī′hŏn king of the [c]Ăm′ôr-ītes.

30 [v]We have shot at them; [t]Hĕsh′bŏn is perished even unto ‖Dī′bŏn, and we have laid them waste even unto Nō′phah, which *reacheth* unto §Mĕd′e-bȧ.

31 ¶ Thus [r]Ĭṣ′ra-el dwelt in the land of the [c]Ăm′ôr-ītes.

32 And Mō′ṣeṣ sent to [w]spy out [x]Jȧ-ā′zer, and they took the villages thereof, and drove out the Ăm′ôr-ītes that *were* there.

33 ¶ And they turned and went up by the way of Bā′shăn: and ✝Ŏg

v.24–1494 BC
See footnote, *Tim*[e], Rev. 10:6.

24
r *Israel, defeats th*[e] *Amorites*, Ex. 4:22.
s *Ammonites*, Deut. 2:20.

25
t *Heshbon*, Isa. 16:8.

26
u *Moabites*, Gen. 19:37.

27
v *War Song*, vs. 27–30; Judg. 5:[1]

29
4 R. V. as fugitives.

32
w *Spies*, Josh. 6:2[3]
x *Jazer*, Josh. 13:25.

† **SIHON**, king of the Amorites. *His seat of government at Heshbon*, Num. 21:26. *The proverbial chant celebrating the victory of, over the Moabites*, Num. 21:26–30. *Conquest of his kingdom by the Israelites*, Num. 21:21–25; Deut. 2:24–37; 3:2, 6, 8; Josh. 13:10, 21, 27; Judg. 11:19–21.

‡ **JABBOK** (*a pouring out*). *A stream on the E. of the Jordan*, Gen. 32:22. *The northern boundary of the possessions, of the Ammonites*, Num. 21:24; Judg. 11:13; *of the Amorites*, Judg. 11:22; *of the Reubenites and the Gadites*, Deut. 3:16; Josh. 12:2.

‖ **DIBON**, called also DIBON-GAD and DIMON. *A cit*[y] *on the northern banks of the Arnon*, Num. 21:30. *Israelite*[s] *encamp at*, Num. 33:45. *Allotted to Gad and Reuben*, Num 32:3, 34; Josh. 13:9, 17. *Taken by Moab*, Isa. 15:2, 9; Jer 48:18, 22.

§ **MEDEBA** (*waters of quiet or rest*). *A city of Moab* Num. 21:30. *An idolatrous high place*, Isa. 15:2. *Allotte*[d] *to Reuben*, Josh. 13:9, 16. *David defeats the Syrians and th*[e] *Ammonites at*, 1 Chr. 19:7–15.

✝ **OG**, king of Bashan. *A man gigantic of stature*, Num

v.33–1494 BC
See footnote, *Time*, Rev. 10:6.

33
*y* *Edrei*, Josh. 13:12.

35
*z* *Israel, defeats king of Bashan*, Ex. 4:22.

1
*a* *Israel, arrives in the plains of Moab*, Ex. 4:22.
*b* *Moab, plains of*, Num. 26:3.
*c* *Jordan, plain of*, Gen. 32:10.

2
*d* Num. 23:18; Josh. 24:9.
*e* *Amorites*, Gen. 14:13.

3
*f* *Moabites*, Gen. 19:37.

4
*g* *Senate*, Num. 11:16.
*h* *Midianites*, Gen. 37:28.

5
*i* *Balaam*, Deut. 23:4.
*j* Or, *Bosor*, 2 Pet. 2:15.

the king of Bā'shăn went out against them, he, and all his people, to the battle at [y]Ĕd're-ī.

34 And the LORD said unto Mō'ṣeṣ, Fear him not: for I have delivered him into thy hand, and all his people, and his land; and thou shalt do to him as thou didst unto †Sī'hŏn king of the [c]Ăm'ôr-ītes, which dwelt at [t]Hĕsh'bŏn.

35 So [z]they smote[C] him, and his sons, and all his people, until there was none left him alive: and they possessed his land.

## CHAPTER 22

*Balak sends for Balaam, who at first refuses to come. 15 He sends again and obtains him. 22 The angel of the Lord would have slain Balaam, if his ass had not turned aside. 34 Balaam's penitence. 36 Balak entertains Balaam.*

AND the children of [a]Īṣ'ra-el set forward, and pitched[C] in the plains of [b]Mō'ab on this side [c]Jôr'dan *by* *Jĕr'ĭ-chō.

2 ¶ And †Bā'lăk the son of [d]Zĭp'por saw all that Īṣ'ra-el had done to the [e]Ăm'ôr-ītes.[S]

3 And [f]Mō'ab was sore[C] afraid of the people, because they *were* many: and Mō'ab was distressed because of the children of [a]Īṣ'ra-el.

4 And [f]Mō'ab said unto the [g]elders of [h]Mĭd'ĭ-an, Now shall this company lick up all *that are* round about us, as the ox licketh up the grass of the field. And †Bā'lăk the son of [d]Zĭp'por *was* king of the Mō'ab-ītes at that time.

5 He sent messengers therefore unto [i]Bā'laam the son of [j]Bē'or to [k]Pē'thôr, which *is* by the river of the land of the children of his people, to call him, saying, Behold, there is a people come out from Ē'ġy̆pt: behold, they cover the face of the earth, and they abide over[C] against me:

6 Come now therefore, I pray thee, curse[C] me this people; for they *are* too mighty for me: peradventure[C] I shall prevail, *that* we may smite them, and *that* I may drive them out of the land: for I wot[C] that he whom thou blessest *is* blessed, and he whom thou cursest is cursed.

7 And the [g]elders of [f]Mō'ab and the [g]elders of [h]Mĭd'ĭ-an departed with the rewards of divination[C] in their hand; and they came unto [i]Bā'laam, and spake unto him the words of †Bā'lăk.[Q]

8 And he said unto them, Lodge here this night, and I will bring you word again, as the LORD shall speak unto me: and the [g]princes of Mō'ab abode with [i]Bā'laam.

9 And God came unto [i]Bā'laam, and said, What men *are* these with thee?

10 And [i]Bā'laam said unto God, †Bā'lăk the son of [d]Zĭp'por, king of [f]Mō'ab, hath sent unto me, *saying*,

11 Behold, *there is* a people come out of Ē'ġy̆pt, which covereth the face of the earth: come now, curse me them; peradventure[C] I shall be able to overcome them, and drive them out.

12 And [l,m]God said unto [i]Bā'laam, Thou shalt not go with

v.5–1494 BC
See footnote, *Time*, Rev. 10:6.

*k* Deut. 23:4.

12
*l* *God, preserver*, Gen. 2:2.
*m* *God, providence of, overruling interpositions of*, Gen. 2:2.

21:33; Deut. 3:11; Josh. 12:4; 13:12. *Defeated and slain by Moses*, Num. 21:33–35; Deut. 1:4; 3:1–7; 29:7; 31:4; Josh. 2:10; 9:10; Psa. 135:10, 11; 136:18–20. *Land of, given to Gad, Reuben, and Manasseh*, Num. 32:33; Deut. 3:8–17; 4:47–49; 29:7, 8; Josh. 12: 4–6; 13:12, 30, 31.

* **JERICHO** (*city of the moon, or place of fragrance*). *A city E. of Jerusalem and near the Jordan*, Num. 22:1; 26:3; Deut. 34:1. *Called the* CITY OF PALM TREES, Deut. 34:3. *Situation of, pleasant*, 2 Kin. 2:19. *Rahab the harlot lived in*, Josh. 2; Heb. 11:31. *Joshua sees the captain of the host of the Lord near*, Josh. 5:13–15. *Besieged by Joshua seven days; fall and destruction of*, Josh. 6; 24:11. *Situated within the territory allotted to Benjamin*, Josh. 18:12, 21. *The Kenites dwelt at*, Judg. 1:16. *King of Moab makes conquest of, and establishes his capital at*, Judg. 3:13. *Rebuilt by Hiel*, 1 Kin. 16:34. *Company of the sons of the prophets dwelt at*, 2 Kin. 2:4, 5, 15, 18. *Captives of Judah, taken by the king of Israel, released at, on account of the denunciation of the prophet Oded*, 2 Chr. 28:7–15. *Inhabitants of, taken captive to Babylon, return to, with Ezra and Nehemiah*, Ezra 2:34; Neh. 7:36; *assist in repairing the walls of Jerusalem*, Neh. 3:2. *Blind men healed at, by Jesus*, Matt. 20:29–34; Mark 10:46–52; Luke 18:35–43. *Zacchæus dwelt at*, Luke 19:1–10.

**Plain of**, 2 Kin. 25:5; Jer. 52:8.

**Waters of**, Josh. 16:1. *Purified by Elisha*, 2 Kin. 2:18–22.

† **BALAK.** *King of Moab*, Num. 22:4; Josh. 24:9; Judg. 11:25; Mic. 6:5. *Tries to bribe Balaam to curse Israel*, Num. 22:5–7, 15–17.

v.12–1494 BC
See footnote, *Time*, Rev. 10:6.

them; thou shalt not curse[s] the people: for they *are* blessed.[s]

13 And Bā′laam rose up in the morning, and said unto the princes of [†]Bā′lăk, Get you into your land: for the LORD refuseth to give me leave[G] to go with you.

14 And the princes of Mō′ab rose up, and they went unto Bā′lăk, and said, Bā′laam [n]refuseth to come with us.

14
*n* *Temptation, resisted, instances of,* Luke 11:4.

15 ¶ And Bā′lăk sent yet again princes, more, and more honourable than they.

16 And they came to [i]Bā′laam, and said to him, Thus saith [†]Bā′lăk the son of [d]Zĭp′por, Let nothing, I pray thee, hinder thee from coming unto me:

17 For I will [o]promote thee unto very great honour, and I will do whatsoever thou sayest unto me: come therefore, I pray thee, curse me this people.

17
*o* *Bribery, instances of,* 1 Sam. 8:3.

18 And [p]Bā′laam answered and said unto the servants of Bā′lăk, If Bā′lăk would give me his house full of [q]silver and [r]gold, [s]I [n,t]cannot go beyond the word of the LORD my God, to do less or more.

18
*p* *Minister, incorruptible,* vs. 37, 38; Rom. 15:16.
*q* *Silver,* 1 Chr. 28:14.
*r* *Gold,* Ezek. 7:19.
*s* *Prophets, inspiration of,* Isa. 3:2.
*t* *Decision, instances of,* Isa 50:7.

19 Now therefore, I pray you, tarry ye also here this night, that [s]I may know what the LORD will say unto me more.

20 And God came unto [s]Bā′laam at night, and said unto him, If the men come to call thee, rise up, *and* go with them; but yet the word which I shall say unto thee, that shalt thou do.

21 And Bā′laam rose up in the morning, and saddled his ass, and went with the [g]princes of [f]Mō′ab.

22 ¶ [T]And God's [u]anger was kindled because [v]he went: and the [w]angel of the LORD stood in the way for an adversary against him. Now he was riding upon his ass, and his two servants *were* with him.[s]

22
*u* *Anger of God,* 2 Kin. 13:3.
*v* *Disobedience to God, instances of,* Eph. 5:6.
*w* *Angel, functions of,* Heb. 1:13.

v.23–1494 BC
See footnote, *Time,* Rev. 10:6.

23[s] And the ass saw the [w]angel of the LORD standing in the way, and his sword drawn in his hand: and the ass turned aside out of the way, and went into the field: and [i]Bā′laam [x]smote the ass, to turn her into the way.

23
*x* *Animals, cruelty to,* Jer. 27:5.

24 But the [w]angel of the LORD stood in a path of the vineyards, a wall *being* on this side, and a wall on that side.

25 And when the ass saw the [w]angel of the LORD, she thrust herself unto the wall, and crushed Bā′laam's foot against the wall: and he [x]smote her again.

26 And the [w]angel of the LORD went further, and stood in a narrow place, where *was* no way to turn either to the right hand or to the left.

27 And when the ass saw the angel of the LORD, she fell down under Bā′laam: and Bā′laam's [y]anger was kindled, and he [x]smote the ass with a staff.[G]

27
*y* *Anger, instances of,* Psa. 37:8.

28[s] And the LORD [z]opened the mouth of the ass, and she said unto Bā′laam, What have I done unto thee, that thou hast [x]smitten me these three times?[Q]

28
*z* *Miracles, Balaam's ass speaks,* Luke 23:8.

29 And Bā′laam said unto the ass, Because thou hast mocked me: [y]I would there were a sword in mine hand, for now would I kill thee.

30 And the ass said unto Bā′laam, *Am* not I thine ass, upon which thou hast ridden [1]ever since *I was* thine unto this day? was I ever wont[G] to do so unto thee? And he said, Nay.[s]

30
1 R. V. all thy life long unto this day?

31 Then the LORD opened the eyes of [a]Bā′laam, and he saw the [b]angel of the LORD standing in the way, and his sword drawn in his hand: and he bowed down his head, and fell flat on his face.

31
*a* *Balaam,* Deut. 23:4.
*b* *Angel, functions of,* Heb. 1:13.

32 And the [b]angel[G] of the LORD said unto him, Wherefore hast

v.32–1494 BC
See footnote, *Time*, Rev. 10:6.

32
*c* *Animals, cruelty to*, Jer. 27:5.
*d* *Sin, repugnant to God*, Rom. 5:12.

33
*e* *Wicked, punishment of*, Psa. 73:3.

34
*f* *Repentance, instances of*, Mark 1:4.

35
*g* *Prophets, inspiration of*, Isa. 3:2.

36
*h* *Moab*, Num. 26:3.

37
*i* *Temptation*, Luke 11:4.
*j* *Bribery*, 1 Sam. 8:3.

41
*k* *High Places*, 1 Kin. 3:2.
*l* *Baal*, 2 Kin. 17:16.

thou [c]smitten thine ass these three times? behold, I went out to withstand thee, because *thy* [d]way is perverse before me:

33 And the ass saw me, and turned from me these three times: unless she had turned from me, surely now also I had [e]slain thee, and saved her alive.

34 And [a]Bā'laam said unto the angel of the LORD, [f]I have sinned; for I knew not that thou stoodest in the way against me: now therefore, if it displease thee, I will get me back again.

35 And the [b]angel of the LORD said unto Bā'laam, Go with the men: but only [g]the word that I shall speak unto thee, that thou shalt speak. So Bā'laam went with the princes of †Bā'lăk.

36 ¶ And when †Bā'lăk heard that [a]Bā'laam was come, he went out to meet him unto a city of [h]Mō'ab, which *is* in the border of ‡Ăr'nŏn, which *is* in the utmost coast.

37 And †Bā'lăk said unto [a]Bā'laam, Did I not earnestly send unto thee to call thee? wherefore camest thou not unto me? am I not able indeed to [i,j]promote thee to honour?

38 And Bā'laam said unto Bā'lăk, Lo, I am come unto thee: have I now any power at all to say any thing? [g]the word that God putteth in my mouth, that shall I speak.

39 And [a]Bā'laam went with †Bā'lăk, and they came unto Kĭr'jath–hū'zoth.

40 And Bā'lăk offered oxen and sheep, and sent to Bā'laam, and to the princes that *were* with him.

41 And it came to pass on the morrow, that †Bā'lăk took [a]Bā'laam, and brought him up into the [k]high places of [l]Bā'al, that thence he might see the utmost *part* of the people.

## CHAPTER 23

*Balak's sacrifices and Balaam's parables.*

AND [a]Bā'laam said unto [b]Bā'lăk, Build me here [c]seven [d]altars, and prepare me here seven oxen and seven rams.

2 And [b]Bā'lăk did as [a]Bā'laam had spoken; and Bā'lăk and Bā'laam offered on *every* [d]altar a [e]bullock and a ram.

3 And [a]Bā'laam said unto [b]Bā'lăk, Stand by thy [f]burnt offering, and I will go: peradventure the LORD will come to meet me: and whatsoever he [g]sheweth me I will tell thee. And he went to an high place.

4 And God met [a]Bā'laam: and he said unto him, I have prepared [c]seven [d]altars, and I have offered upon *every* altar a [e]bullock and a ram.

5 And the LORD [g]put a word in [a]Bā'laam's mouth, and said, Return unto [b]Bā'lăk, and thus thou shalt speak.

6 And he returned unto him, and, lo, he stood by his [f]burnt sacrifice, he, and all the princes of [h]Mō'ab.

7 And he took up his parable, and said, [b]Bā'lăk the king of [i]Mō'ab hath brought me from Ā'ram, out of the mountains of the east, *saying*, Come, curse me Jā'cob, and come, defy [j]Iş'ra-el.

8 How shall [k,l]I curse, whom God hath not cursed? or how shall I defy, *whom* the LORD hath not defied?

9 For from the top of the rocks I see him, and from the hills I behold him: lo, the people shall dwell alone, and shall not be reckoned among the nations.

10 Who can count the dust of

v.41–1494 BC
See footnote, *Time*, Rev. 10:6.

1
*a* *Balaam*, Deut. 23:4.
*b* *Balak*, Num. 22:4.
*c* *Seven*, Gen. 7:2.
*d* *Altar*, Gen. 8:20.

2
*e* *Bullock*, Ex. 29:3.

3
*f* *Offerings, burnt*, Lev. 6:17.
*g* *Prophets, inspiration of*, Isa. 3:2.

6
*h* *Moab*, Num. 26:3.

7
*i* *Moabites*, Gen 19:37.
*j* *Israel*, Ex. 4:22.

8
*k* *Minister, incorruptible*, Rom. 15:16.
*l* *Minister, faithful*, Rom. 15:16.

‡ **ARNON** (*noisy, a murmurer*). A river emptying into the Dead Sea from the east. *Boundary between Moabites and Amorites*, Num. 21:13, 14, 26; 22:36; Deut. 2:24, 36; 3:8, 16; Josh. 12:1. *Fords of*, Isa. 16:2. *Miracles at*, Num. 21:14.

v.10–1494 BC
See footnote, *Time*,
Rev. 10:6.

Jā′cob, and the number of the
fourth *part* of [i]Ĭs′ra-el? Let me
die the *death of the righteous,
and let my last end be like his!
11 And [b]Bā′lăk said unto [a]Bā′-
laam, What hast thou done unto
me? I took thee to curse mine
enemies, and, behold, thou hast
blessed *them* altogether.
12 And [a]he answered and said,
Must [g]I not take heed to speak
that which the LORD hath put in
my mouth?
13 And [b]Bā′lăk said unto [a]him,
Come, I pray thee, with me unto
another place, from whence thou
mayest see them: thou shalt see
but the utmost part of them, and
shalt not see them all: and curse
me them from thence.
14 ¶ And he brought him into
the field of Zō′phim, to the top
of [m]Pĭs′gah, and built [c]seven
[d]altars, and offered a [e]bullock
and a ram on *every* altar.
15 And he said unto [b]Bā′lăk,
Stand here by thy [f]burnt offering, while I meet *the* LORD
yonder.
16 And the LORD met [a]Bā′-
laam, and [g]put a word in his
mouth, and said, Go again unto
[b]Bā′lăk, and say thus.
17 And when he came to him,
behold, he stood by his [f]burnt
offering, and the princes of
[i]Mō′ab with him. And [b]Bā′lăk
said unto him, What hath the
LORD spoken?
18 And he took up his parable,
and said, Rise up, [b]Bā′lăk, and
hear; hearken unto me, thou son
of [n]Zĭp′por:
19 [o,p]God *is* not a man, [q]that

v.13–1494 BC
See footnote, *Time*
Rev. 10:6.

14
*m Pisgah*, Deut. 3:27.

18
*n Zippor*, Num. 22:2.

19
*o God, truth*, Gen. 2:2.
*p God, perfection of*, Gen. 2:2.
*q God, immutable*, Gen. 2:2.

* **DEATH.** *Universal to mankind*, Eccl. 3:2, 19–21; Rom. 5:12, 14; 1 Pet. 1:24.
*Time of, unknown*, Gen. 27:2; Psa. 39:4, 13.
*Nearness to*, Josh. 23:14; 1 Sam. 20:3.
*Separates spirit and body*, Eccl. 12:5, 7.
*Does not end conscious existence*, Luke 20:34–38; 23:39–43; Rev. 20:12, 13; *exemplified in the appearance of Moses and Elijah at the transfiguration of Jesus*, Matt. 17:2, 3; Mark 9:4, 5; Luke 9:30–33.
*Not to be feared by the righteous*, Matt. 10:28.
*Brings rest to the righteous*, Job 3:13, 17–19.
*Dispossesses of earthly goods*, Job 1:21; Psa. 49:17; Luke 12:16–20; 1 Tim. 6:7.
*A judgment*, Gen. 2:17; 3:19; 6:7, 11–13; 19:12, 13, 24, 25; Josh. 5:4–6; 1 Chr. 10:13, 14.
*God's power over*, Deut. 32:39; 1 Sam. 2:6; Psa. 68:20; 2 Tim. 1:10.
*Christ's power over*, Heb. 2:14, 15; Rev. 1:18.
*To be destroyed*, Isa. 25:8; Hos. 13:14; 1 Cor. 15:21, 22, 26, 55–57; Rev. 20:14; 21:4.
*Preparation for*, 2 Kin. 20:1; Luke 12:35–37; *by Moses*, Num. 27:12–23; *by David*, 1 Kin. 2:1–10; *by Ahithophel*, 2 Sam. 17:23.
*Apostrophe to*, Hos. 13:14; 1 Cor. 15:55.
**Described as:** *Giving up the ghost*, Gen. 25:8; 35:29; Lam. 1:19; Acts 5:10. *King of terrors*, Job 18:14. *A change*, Job 14:14. *Going to thy fathers*, Gen. 15:15; 25:8; 35:29. *Putting off this tabernacle*, 2 Pet. 1:14. *Requiring the soul*, Luke 12:20. *Going the way whence there is no return*, Job 16:22. *Being gathered to our people*, Gen. 49:33. *In silence*, Psa. 94:17; 115:17. *Returning to dust*, Gen. 3:19. *Being cut down*, Job 14:2. *Fleeing as a shadow*, Job 14:2. *Departing*, Phil. 1:23.
**Called Sleep,** Deut. 31:16; 1 Kin. 14:31; 15:8, 24; 16:6, 28; Job 7:21; 14:12; Psa. 76:5, 6; Jer. 51:39; Dan. 12:2; John 11:11; Acts 7:60; 13:36; 1 Cor. 15:6, 18, 51; 1 Thess. 4:13–15.
**Exemption from:** *Enoch*, Gen. 5:24; Heb. 11:5. *Elijah*, 2 Kin. 2. *Promised to saints at the second coming of Christ*, 1 Cor. 15:51; 1 Thess. 4:15, 17. *No death in heaven*, Luke 20:36; Rev. 21:4.
**Desired,** Jer. 8:3; Rev. 9:6. *By Moses*, Num. 11:15. *By Elijah*, 1 Kin. 19:4. *By Job*, Job 3; 6:8–11; 7: 1–3, 15, 16; 10:1. *By Jonah*, Jonah 4:8. *By Simeon*, Luke 2:29. *By Paul*, 2 Cor. 5:2, 8; Phil. 1:20–23.
**Inevitable,** 2 Sam. 14:14; Job 7:1, 8–10, 21; 10:21, 22; 14: 2, 5, 7–12, 14, 19–21; 16:22; 21:23, 25, 26, 32, 33; 30:23; 34: 15, 19; Psa. 49:7–10; 82:7; 89:48; 144:4; Eccl. 2:14–18; 5: 15; 8:8; 9:5, 10; Isa. 51:12; Jer. 9:21; Zech. 1:5; John 9:4; Heb. 9:27; 13:14; Jas. 1:10, 11.
**Of the Righteous:** *A transition*, Luke 16:22; 23:43. *Balaam extols*, Num. 23:10. *Peaceful*, Psa. 37:37. *Precious in the sight of the Lord*, Psa. 116:15. *A merciful providence in*, Isa. 57:1, 2. *Anticipated with confidence*, Prov. 14:32; Luke 2:29; Acts 7:59; Rom. 14:7, 8; 1 Cor. 3:21–2 2 Cor. 5:1, 4, 8; 1 Thess. 5:9, 10; 2 Tim. 4:6–8; Heb. 11:1 *Hope in*, Dan. 12:13; 1 Cor. 15:51–57; 2 Cor. 1:9, 1 1 Thess. 4:13, 14; 2 Pet. 1:11, 14; Rev. 14:13.
**Of the Wicked,** Job 18:14, 18; 20:4, 5, 8, 11; 21:13, 1 18, 23–26; 24:20, 24, 27:8, 19–23; Psa. 37:1, 2, 9, 10, 35, 3 49:7, 9, 10, 14, 17, 19, 20; Prov. 5:22, 23; 11:7, 10; 21:1 Eccl. 8:10; Isa. 14:11, 15.
*Sudden*, Num. 16:32; Prov. 10:25, 27; Isa. 17:14; Acts 5:3–1
*A judgment*, Num. 16:29, 30; 1 Sam. 25:38; Job 36:1 14, 18, 20; Psa. 55:23; 58:9; 78:50; 92:7; Prov. 2:22; 14:3 Isa. 26:14; Jer. 16:3, 4; Ezek. 28:8, 10; Amos 9:10; Luk 12:20.
**Scenes of:** *Of Jacob*, Gen. 49:1–33; Heb. 11:21. *O Moses*, Deut. 34:1–7. *Of Samson*, Judg. 16:25–30. *Of El* 1 Sam. 4:12–18. *Of the wife of Phinehas*, 1 Sam. 4:19–2 *Of Zechariah*, 2 Chr. 24:22. *Of Jesus*, Matt. 27:34–53; Mar 15:23–38; Luke 23:27–49; John 19:16–30. *Of Stephen*, Act 7:59, 60.
**Penalty:** *Shall not be remitted*, Num. 35:31. *In th Mosaic law the death penalty was inflicted, for murder*, Ge 9:5, 6; Num. 35:16–21, 30–33; Deut. 17:6; *for adultery*, Le 20:10; Deut. 22:24; *for incest*, Lev. 20:11, 12, 14; *for bes tiality*, Ex. 22:19; Lev. 20:15, 16; *for sodomy*, Lev. 18:2 20:13; *for rape of a betrothed virgin*, Deut. 22:25; *for perjur* Zech. 5:4; *for kidnapping*, Ex. 21:16; Deut. 24:7; *upon priest's daughter, who committed fornication*, Lev. 21:9; *f witchcraft*, Ex. 22:18; *for offering human sacrifice*, Lev. 2 2–5; *for striking or cursing father or mother*, Ex. 21:15, 1 Lev. 20:9; *for disobedience to parents*, Deut. 21:18–21; *f theft*, Zech. 5:3, 4; *for blasphemy*, Lev. 24:23; *for Sabbat desecration*, Ex. 35:2; Num. 15:32–36; *for prophesying falsel or propagating false doctrines*, Deut. 13:1–10; *for sacrificin to false gods*, Ex. 22:20; *for refusing to abide by the decisio of court*, Deut. 17:12; *for treason*, 1 Kin. 2:25; Esth. 2:2 *for sedition*, Acts 5:36, 37.
*Not inflicted on testimony of less than two witnesses*, Num 35:30; Deut. 17:6; 19:15.
MODES OF EXECUTION OF DEATH PENALTY: *Burnin* Gen. 38:24; Lev. 20:14; 21:9; Jer. 29:22; Ezek. 23:25; Da 3:19–23. *Stoning*, Lev. 20:2, 27; Num. 14:10; 15:33–3 Deut. 13:10; 17:5; 22:21, 24; Josh. 7:25; 1 Kin. 21:10; Eze 16:40. *Hanging*, Gen. 40:22; Deut. 21:22, 23; Josh. 8:2 Esth. 7:10. *Beheading*, Matt. 14:10; Mark 6:16, 27, 28. *Cr cifixion*, Matt. 27:35, 38; Mark 15:24, 27; Luke 23:33. *Th sword*, Ex. 32:27, 28; 1 Kin. 2:25, 34, 46; Acts 12:2.
*Executed, by the witnesses*, Deut. 13:9; 17:7; Acts 7:58; *b the congregation*, Num. 15:35, 36; Deut. 13:9.
**Figurative,** Rom. 6:2–11; 7:1–11; 8:10, 11; Col. 2:2 2 Tim. 2:11.
**Symbolized:** *By the pale horse*, Rev. 6:8.
See footnotes: SPIRITUAL DEATH, **1 John 3:14; THE SEC OND DEATH,** Rev. 20:14.

v.19–1494 BC
See footnote, *Time*, Rev. 10:6.

r *God, faithfulness of*, Gen. 2:2.

20
s *Grace of God*, Rom. 4:16.

22
t *God, providence of*, Gen. 2:2.
u *God, power of*, Gen. 2:2.
v *Unicorn*, Job 39:9.
1 R. V. the wild-ox.

23
w *Sorcery, practiced by Balaam*, Isa. 47:9.
x *God, preserver*, Gen. 2:2.

28
R. V. down upon the desert.

he should lie; neither the son of
man, that he should repent: hath
he said, and [r]shall he not do *it*?
or hath he spoken, and shall he
not make it good? [Q]
20 Behold, [g]I have received
*commandment* to bless: and he
hath [s]blessed; and I cannot reverse it.
21 He hath not beheld iniquity
in Jā′cob, neither hath he seen
perverseness in [i]Ĭṣ′ra-el: the
LORD his God *is* with him, and
the shout of a king *is* among
them.
22 [t,u]God brought them out of
Ē′ġy̆pt; he hath as it were the
strength of [1]an [v]unicorn.
23 Surely *there is* no [w]enchant-
ment[C] against Jā′cob, neither *is*
*there* any divination against
Ĭṣ′ra-el: according to this time
it shall be said of Jā′cob and
of Ĭṣ′ra-el[S], What hath [x]God
wrought!
24 Behold, the people shall rise
up as a great lion, and lift up
himself as a young lion: he shall
not lie down until he eat *of* the
prey, and drink the blood of the
slain.
25 ¶ And [b]Bā′lăk said unto
[a]Bā′laam, Neither curse them at
all, nor bless them at all.
26 But [a]Bā′laam answered and
said unto [b]Bā′lăk, Told not I
thee, saying, [g]All that the LORD
speaketh, that I must do?
27 ¶ And [b]Bā′lăk said unto
[a]Bā′laam, Come, I pray thee, I
will bring thee unto another
place; peradventure[C] it will please
God that thou mayest curse me
them from thence.
28 And [b]Bā′lăk brought [a]Bā′-
laam unto the top of Pē′or, that
looketh toward [2]Jĕsh′ĭ-mŏn.
29 And [a]Bā′laam said unto
[b]Bā′lăk, Build me here [c]seven
[d]altars, and prepare me here sev-
en [e]bullocks and seven rams.
30 And [b]Bā′lăk did as [a]Bā′-
laam had said, and offered a
[e]bullock and a ram on *every*
[d]altar.

## CHAPTER 24

*Balaam foretells the happiness of Israel. 10 Balak in anger dismisses him. 15 He prophesies of the Star of Jacob, and of the destruction of sundry nations.*

AND when [a]Bā′laam saw
that it pleased the LORD
to bless [b]Ĭṣ′ra-el, he went not,
as at other times, to seek for
[c]enchantments[C], but he set his
face toward the wilderness.
2 And [a]Bā′laam lifted up his
eyes, and he saw Ĭṣ′ra-el abiding
*in his tents* according to their
tribes; and the [d]spirit of God
[e]came upon [f]him.[T]
3 And he took up his parable[C],
and said, [a]Bā′laam the son of
Bē′or hath said, and the man
whose [1]eyes are open hath said:
4 He hath said, which heard the
words of God, which saw the
[g]vision of the Almighty, falling
[2]*into a trance*, but having his eyes
open:
5 How goodly are thy [h]tents, O
Jā′cob, *and* thy tabernacles, O
Ĭṣ′ra-el!
6 As the valleys are they spread
forth, as gardens by the river's
side, as the trees of lign[C] [i]aloes
which the LORD hath planted,
*and* as [j]cedar trees beside the
waters.[Q]
7 He shall pour the water out
of his [k]buckets, and his seed
*shall be* in many waters, and his
king shall be higher than Ā′găg,
and his kingdom shall be exalted.
8 God brought him forth out of
Ē′ġy̆pt; he hath as it were the
strength of [3]an [l]unicorn: he shall
eat up the nations his enemies,
and shall break their bones, and
pierce *them* through with his
[m]arrows.
9 He couched[C], he lay down as a
[n]lion, and as a great lion: who
shall stir him up? Blessed *is* he

v.30–1494 BC
See footnote, *Time*, Rev. 10:6.

1
a *Balaam*, Deut. 23:4.
b *Israel*, Ex. 4:22.
c *Sorcery*, Isa. 47:9.

2
d *Holy Spirit, inspiration of*, Acts 1:2.
e *Inspiration*, Job 32:8.
f *Prophets, inspiration of*, Isa. 3:2.

3
1 R. V. eye was closed saith:

4
g *Vision, a mode of revelation*, Acts 9:10.
2 R. V. *omits* into a trance,

5
h *Tent*, Gen. 13:5.

6
i *Aloes*, Psa. 45:8.
j *Cedar*, Isa. 9:10.

7
k Isa. 40:15.

8
l *Unicorn*, Job 39:9.
m *Arrow, figurative*, 1 Sam. 20:20.
3 R. V. the wild-ox:

9
n *Lion*, Mic. 5:8.

v.9–1494 BC
See footnote, *Time*, Rev. 10:6.

that blesseth thee, and cursed *is*
he that curseth thee.
10 ¶ And [o]Bā′lăk's [p]anger was
kindled against [a]Bā′laam, and
he smote his hands together: and
Bā′lăk said unto Bā′laam, I
called thee to curse mine enemies, and, behold, thou hast altogether blessed *them* these three
times.
11 Therefore now flee thou to
thy place: [q]I thought to promote
thee unto great honour; [r]but, lo,
the [s]LORD hath kept thee back
from honour.
12 And [t]Bā′laam said unto Bā′-
lăk, Spake I not also to thy messengers which thou sentest unto
me, saying,
13 If Bā′lăk would give me his
house full of [u]silver and [v]gold, [t]I
[r,w]cannot go beyond the commandment of the LORD, to do
*either* good or bad of mine own
mind; *but* what the LORD saith,
that will I speak?
14 And now, behold, I go unto
my people: come *therefore, and*
I will advertise[G] thee what this
people shall do to thy people in
the latter days.
15 And he took up his parable,[G]
and said, [a]Bā′laam the son of
Bē′or hath said, and the man
whose [1]eyes are open hath
said:
16 [f]He hath said, which heard
the words of God, and knew the
knowledge of the most High,
*which* saw the [g]vision of the
Almighty, falling [2]*into a trance,*
but having his eyes open:
17 I shall see him, but not now:
I shall behold him, but not
nigh[G]: there shall come a [x,y,z]Star
out of Jā′cob, and a [a]Sceptre
shall rise out of Ĭṣ′ra-el, and
shall smite the corners of Mō′-
ab, and destroy all the [4]children
of Shēth.[Q]

18 And [b]Ē′dom shall be a possession, [c]Sē′ïr also shall be a
possession for his enemies; and
Ĭṣ′ra-el shall do valiantly.[G]
19 Out of Jā′cob shall come he
that shall have dominion, and
shall destroy him that remaineth
of the city.
20 And when he looked on
[d]Ăm′a-lĕk, he took up his parable,[G] and said, Ăm′a-lĕk *was* the
first of the nations: but his latter
end *shall be* that he perish for
ever.
21 And he looked on the [e]Kĕn′-
ītes, and took up his parable,
and said, Strong is thy dwelling-
place, and thou puttest thy [f]nest
in a rock.
22 Nevertheless the [e]Kĕn′īte
shall be wasted, until [g]Ăs′shur
shall carry thee away captive.
23 And he took up his parable,
and said, Alas, who shall live
when God doeth this!
24 And [h]ships *shall come* from
the coast of [i]Chĭt′tim, and shall
afflict [g]Ăs′shur, and shall afflict
[j]Ē′bēr, and he also shall perish
for ever.
25 And [k]Bā′laam rose up, and
went and returned to his place:
and [l]Bā′lăk also went his way.

## CHAPTER 25

*Israel at Shittim commits whoredom and idolatry.* 6 *Phinehas kills Zimri and Cozbi.* 10 *God therefore gives him the covenant of an everlasting priesthood.* 16 *The Midianites are to be smitten.*

AND [Q] [a]Ĭṣ′ra-el abode in
*Shĭt′tim, and the people
began to commit [b]whoredom[G]
with the daughters of [c]Mō′ab.
2 And they called the people
unto the sacrifices of their gods:
and the people did eat, and
[b]bowed down to their [d]gods.[Q]
3[S] And [a]Ĭṣ′ra-el [e]joined himself
unto †Bā′al–pē′or: and the [f]an-
ger of the LORD was kindled[G]
against Ĭṣ′ra-el.[Q]

**10**
o *Balak*, Num. 22:4.
p *Anger, instances of*, Psa. 37:8.

**11**
q *Bribery, instances of*, 1 Sam. 8:3.
r *Temptation, resisted, instances of*, Luke 11:4.
s *Grace of God*, Rom. 4:16.

**12**
t *Minister, incorruptible*, Rom. 15:16.

**13**
u *Silver*, 1 Chr. 28:14.
v *Gold*, Ezek. 7:19.
w *Decision, instances of*, Isa. 50:7.

**17**
x *Jesus, prophecies concerning (according to many commentators)*, Matt. 1:21.
y *Stars, figurative*, Judg. 5:20.
z *Messianic Hope*, Gen. 49:10.

a *Scepter, figurative*, Esth. 4:11.
4 R V. sons of tumult.

v.18–1494 BC
See footnote, *Time*, Rev. 10:6.

**18**
b *Edomites, prophecies concerning*, 2 Kin. 8:21.
c *Seir*, Deut. 1:2.

**20**
d *Amalekites, prophecies against*, Num. 13:29.

**21**
e *Kenites*, 1 Sam. 15:6.
f Deut. 32:11.

**22**
g *Assyria*, Gen. 25:18.

**24**
h *Ship*, 2 Chr. 8:18
i *Chittim*, Dan. 11 30.
j *Eber*, Gen. 10:21

**25**
k *Balaam*, Deut. 23:4.
l *Balak*, Num. 22:4.

**1**
a *Israel*, Ex. 4:22.
b *Idolatry, wicked practices of*, 1 Sam. 15:23.
c *Moabites*, Gen. 19:37.

**2**
d *Idol*, 1 Kin. 15:12.

**3**
e *Fellowship, with the wicked*, 1 Cor 1:9.
f *Anger of God, provoked*, 2 Kin 13:3.

* **SHITTIM** (*acacia*). *Called also* ABEL-SHITTIM, Num. 33:49. *A camping place of Israel*, Num. 25:1; 33:49. *Joshua sends spies from*, Josh. 2:1. *Valley of*, Joel 3:18.

† **BAAL-PEOR**, an idol of Moab. *Licentious practices in the worship of, a snare to the Israelites*, Num. 25:3, 5, 31:16 Deut. 4:3; Josh. 22:17; Psa. 106:28; Hos. 9:10.

v.4–1494 BC
See footnote, *Time*, Rev. 10:6.

4
*g Moses*, Ex. 2:10.
*h Judgments, on the Israelites for murmuring*, Ex. 6:6.

6
*i Midianites*, Gen. 37:28.
*j Women, wicked, instances of*, Prov. 31:10.
1 R. V. tent of meeting.

7
*k Decision, instances of*, Isa. 50:7.
*l Zeal, instances of*, 2 Cor. 7:11.

8
*m Plague*, Ex. 11:1.
*n Israel, visited by a plague*, Ex. 4:22.
2 R. V. pavilion.

10
*o Prophets, inspiration of*, Isa. 3:2.

11
*p Anger of God, appeased*, 2 Kin. 13:3.
*q Jealousy, attributed to God*, Psa. 78:58.
3 R. V. in that he was jealous with my jealousy among them.

12
*r Covenant, of God with men, instances of*, Deut. 29:1.

4 And the LORD said unto [g]Mō′ṣeṣ, Take all the heads of the people, and [h]hang[c] them up before the LORD against the sun, that the fierce [j]anger[c] of the LORD may be turned away from Ĭṣ′ra-el.[s]

5 And Mō′ṣeṣ said unto the judges of Ĭṣ′ra-el, [h]Slay ye every one his men that were joined unto †Bā′al–pē′or.

6 ¶ And, behold, one of the children of Ĭṣ′ra-el came and brought unto his brethren a [i]Mĭd′ĭ-an-īt-ish [j]woman in the sight of [g]Mō′ṣeṣ, and in the sight of all the congregation of the children of Ĭṣ′ra-el, who *were* weeping *before* the door of the [1]tabernacle of the congregation.

7 And when ‡Phĭn′e-has, the son of Ē-le-ā′zar, the son of Aâr′on the priest, saw *it*, he [k]rose up from among the congregation, and [l]took a javelin in his hand;

8 And he [l]went after the man of Ĭṣ′ra-el into the [2]tent, and thrust both of them through, the man of Ĭṣ′ra-el, and the woman through her belly. So the [m,n]plague was stayed from the children of Ĭṣ′ra-el.

9 And those that died in the [m]plague were twenty and four thousand.[Q]

10 ¶ And the LORD spake unto [o]Mō′ṣeṣ, saying,

11 ‡Phĭn′e-has, the son of Ē-le-ā′zar, the son of Aâr′on the priest, hath turned my [p]wrath away from the children of Ĭṣ′ra-el, [3]while he was zealous for my sake among them, that I consumed[c] not the children of Ĭṣ′ra-el in my [q]jealousy.

12 [T]Wherefore say, Behold, I give unto him my [r]covenant of peace:

13 And he shall have it, and his seed after him, *even* the [r]covenant of an everlasting priesthood; because he was [4]zealous for his God, and made an [s]atonement[c] for the children of Ĭṣ′ra-el.[T]

14 Now the name of the Ĭṣ′ra-el-īte that was slain, *even* that was slain with the [i]Mĭd′ĭ-an-īt-ish [j]woman, *was* Zĭm′rī, the son of Sā′lu, a prince of a chief house among the [t]Sĭm′e-on-ītes.

15 And the name of the [i]Mĭd′ĭ-an-īt-ish [j]woman that was slain *was* Cŏz′bī, the daughter of [u]Zûr; he *was* head over a people, *and* of a chief house in Mĭd′ĭ-an.

16 ¶ And the LORD spake unto [o]Mō′ṣeṣ, saying,

17 Vex[c] the [i]Mĭd′ĭ-an-ītes, and smite them:

18 For [i]they vex you with their wiles,[c] wherewith they have beguiled[c] you in the matter of Pē′or, and in the matter of Cŏz′bī, the daughter of a prince of Mĭd′ĭ-an, their sister, which was slain in the day of the [m]plague for Pē′or's sake.

## CHAPTER 26

*The number of all Israel is taken in the plains of Moab. 52 The land is to be divided by lot. 57 The families and number of Levites. 63 Of all the men numbered at Sinai, only Caleb and Joshua are left.*

AND it came to pass after the [a]plague, that the LORD spake unto [b]Mō′ṣeṣ and unto Ē-le-ā′zar the son of Aâr′on the priest, saying,

2 Take the [c,d]sum[c] of all the congregation of the children of Ĭṣ′ra-el, from twenty years old and upward, throughout their fathers' house, [e]all that are able to go to war in Ĭṣ′ra-el.

3 And [f]Mō′ṣeṣ and [g]Ē-le-ā′zar the priest spake with them in the plains of *Mō′ab by [h]Jôr′dan *near* [i]Jĕr′ĭ-chō, saying,

v.13–1494 BC
See footnote, *Time*, Rev. 10:6.

13
*s Atonement*, Lev. 17:11.
4 R. V. jealous

14
*t Simeon, tribe of*, Num. 2:12.

15
*u* Num. 31:8; Josh. 13:21.

1
*a Plague*, Ex. 11:1.
*b Prophets, inspiration of*, Isa. 3:2.

2
*c Census*, 2 Sam. 24:1.
*d Armies, enumeration of Israel's military forces*, Deut. 11:4.
*e Soldiers, enrollment of*, vs. 1–65; Ezra 8:22.

3
*f Moses*, Ex. 2:10.
*g Eleazar*, Num. 3:2.
*h Jordan*, Gen. 32:10.
*i Jericho*, Num. 22:1.

‡ **PHINEHAS.** *High priest*, Ex. 6:25; Josh. 22:30; 1 Chr. 6:4, 50. *Religious zeal of*, Num. 25:7–15; Psa. 106:30. *Chief of the Korahite Levites*, 1 Chr. 9:19, 20. *Sent to sound the trumpets in the battle with the Midianites*, Num. 31:6. *A commissioner to the Israelites east of the Jordan*, Josh. 22:13–32. *Inheritance allotted to*, Josh. 24:33. *Mediator in behalf of the people*, Judg. 20:28.

* **MOAB.** *The territory E. of the Jordan, bounded on the*

v.4–1494 BC
See footnote, *Time*, Rev. 10:6.

4
*i* *Egypt*, Gen. 41:8.

5
*k* *Hanoch*, Ex. 6:14.
*l* *Pallu*, Gen. 46:9.

6
*m* *Hezron*, 1 Chr. 5:3.
*n* *Carmi*, Gen. 46:9.

7
*o* *Reubenites, enrollment of, in Moab*, Josh. 22:1.

8
*p* Num. 16:1, 12: Deut. 11:6.

9
*q* *Dathan*, Num. 16:1.
*r* *Abiram*, Num. 16:1.
*s* *Citizens, wicked and treasonable, instances of*, Luke 15:15.
*t* *Korah*, Num. 16:1.

10
*u* *Earthquake*, Isa. 29:6.
*v* *Fire*, Ex. 12:8.

12
*w* 1 Chr. 4:24.
*x* *Jamin*, Gen. 46:10.

13
*y* 1 Chr. 4:24.
*z* *Shaul*, Ex. 6:15.

4 *Take the* [c,d]*sum of the people*, from twenty years old and upward; as the LORD commanded Mō′ṣeṣ and the children of Ĭṣ′ra-el, which went forth out of the land of [i]Ē′ġȳpt.

5 ¶ Reu′ben, the eldest son of Ĭṣ′ra-el: the children of Reu′ben; [k]Hā′nŏch, *of whom cometh* the family of the Hā′noch-ītes: of [l]Păl′lu, the family of the Păl′lu-ītes:

6 Of [m]Hĕz′rŏn, the family of the Hĕz′ron-ītes: of [n]Cär′mī, the family of the Cär′mītes.

7 These *are* the families of the [o]Reu′ben-ītes: and they that were numbered of them were forty and three thousand and seven hundred and thirty.

8 And the sons of [l]Păl′lu; [p]Ē-lī′ab.

9 And the sons of Ē-lī′ab; Nē-mū′el, and [q]Dā′than, and [r]Ă-bī′ram. This is that Dā′than and Ă-bī′ram, *which were* famous in the congregation, [s]who strove [c] against Mō′ṣeṣ and against Aăr′on in the company of [t]Kō′rah, when they strove against the LORD:

10 And the earth [u]opened her mouth, and swallowed them up together with [t]Kō′rah, when that company died, what time the [v]fire devoured two hundred and fifty men: and they became a sign.

11 Notwithstanding the children of [t]Kō′rah died not.

12 ¶ The sons of Sĭm′e-on after their families: of [w]Nē-mū′el, the family of the Nē-mū′el-ītes: of [x]Jā′min, the family of the Jā′min-ītes: of †Jā′chin, the family of the Jā′chin-ītes:

13 Of [y]Zē′rah, the family of the Zär′hītes: of [z]Shā′ul, the family of the Shā′ul-ītes.

14 These *are* the families of the [a]Sĭm′e-on-ītes, twenty and two thousand and two hundred.

15 ¶ The children of [b]Găd after their families: of Zē′phon, the family of the Zē′phon-ītes: of [c]Hăg′gī, the family of the Hăg′gītes: of [d]Shu′nī, the family of the Shu′nītes:

16 Of [e]Ŏz′nī, the family of the Ŏz′nītes: of Ē′rī, the family of the Ē′rītes:

17 Of [f]Ā′rŏd, the family of the Ā′rod-ītes: of Ă-rē′lī, the family of the Ă-rē′lītes.

18 These *are* the families of the children of [b]Găd according to those that were numbered of them, forty thousand and five hundred.

19 ¶ The sons of Jū′dah *were* [g]Ēr and [h]Ō′nan: and Ēr and Ō′nan died in the land of Cā′năan.

20 And the sons of Jū′dah after their families were; of [i]Shē′lah, the family of the [j]Shē′lan-ītes: of [k]Phā′rĕz, the family of the Phär′zītes: of [l]Zē′rah, the family of the Zär′hītes.

21 And the sons of [k]Phā′rĕz were; of [m]Hĕz′rŏn, the family of the Hĕz′ron-ītes: of [n]Hā′mŭl, the family of the Hā′mul-ītes.

22 These *are* the families of [o]Jū′dah according to those that were numbered of them, threescore and sixteen thousand and five hundred.

23 ¶ *Of* the sons of Ĭs′sa-char after their families: *of* [p]Tō′lă, the family of the Tō′la-ītes: of [q]Pū′ă, the family of the Pū′nītes:

24 Of [r]Jăsh′ŭb, the family of the Jăsh′ub-ītes: of [s]Shĭm′rŏn, the family of the Shĭm′ron-ītes.

25 These *are* the families of [t]Ĭs′sa-char according to those

v.14–1494 BC
See footnote, *Time*, Rev. 10:6.

14
*a* *Simeon, tribe of, military enrollment of*, Num. 2:12.

15
*b* *Gad, tribe of, enumeration of*, Deut. 33:20.
*c* Gen. 46:16.
*d* Gen. 46:16.

16
*e* Or, *Ezbon*, Gen. 46:16.

17
*f* Or, *Arodi*, Gen. 46:16.

19
*g* *Er*, Gen. 38:3.
*h* *Onan*, Gen. 38:8.

20
*i* *Shelah*, Gen. 38:5
*j* Or, *Shilonites*, 1 Chr. 9:5.
*k* *Pharez*, Gen. 38 29.
*l* Or, *Zarah*, Gen. 38:30.

21
*m* *Hezron*, 1 Chr. 2:5.
*n* *Hamul*, 1 Chr. 2:5.

22
*o* *Judah, tribe of, enrollment of*, Num. 10:14.

23
*p* Gen. 46:13; 1 Chr. 7:1, 2.
*q* Or, *Phuvah*, Gen. 46:13.

24
*r* *Jashub*, 1 Chr. 7:1.
*s* *Shimron*, Gen. 46:13.

25
*t* *Issachar, tribe of*, Num. 1:28.

---

*N. by the river Arnon*, Num. 21:13; Judg. 11:18. *Israelites come into*, Deut. 2:17, 18. *Military forces numbered in*, Num. 26:3, 63. *The law rehearsed in, by Moses*, Num. 35, 36; Deut. chapters 29, 31, 33. *The Israelites renew their covenant in*, Deut. 29:1. *Belonged to the land of promise*, Josh. 13:32.

† **JACHIN** (*firm*). *Son of Simeon*, Gen. 46:10; Ex. 6:15. *Called* JARIB, 1 Chr. 4:24.

v.25–1494 BC
See footnote, *Time*, Rev. 10:6.

that were numbered of them, threescore and four thousand and three hundred.

26 ¶ *Of* the sons of Zĕb′u-lŭn after their families: of [u]Sē′red, the family of the Sär′dītes: of [v]Ē′lŏn, the family of the Ē′lon-ītes: of [w]Jăh′lĕ-el, the family of the Jăh′lĕ-el-ītes.

27 These *are* the families of the [x]Zĕb′u-lun-ītes according to those that were numbered of them, threescore thousand and five hundred.

28 ¶ The sons of [y]Jō′şeph after their families *were* Mă-năs′seh and Ē′phră-ĭm.

29 Of the sons of [z]Mă-năs′seh: of [a]Mā′chĭr, the family of the Mā′chir-ītes: and Mā′chĭr begat ‡Ḡĭl′e-ăd: of Ḡĭl′e-ăd *come* the family of the Ḡĭl′e-ăd-ītes.

30 These *are* the sons of ‡Ḡĭl′e-ăd: *of* [b]Jē-ē′zēr, the family of the Jē-ē′zer-ītes: of [c]Hē′lĕk, the family of the Hē′lek-ītes:

31 And *of* Ăs′rĭ-el, the family of the Ăs′rĭ-el-ītes: and *of* [d]Shē′chem, the family of the Shē′chem-ītes:

32 And *of* [e]Shē-mī′dȧ, the family of the Shē-mī′da-ītes: and *of* [f]Hē′phēr, the family of the Hē′pher-ītes.

33 And [g]Zē-lō′phe-hăd the son of [f]Hē′phēr had no şons, but daughters: and the names of the daughters of Zē-lō′phe-hăd *were* ‖Măh′lah, and §Nō′ah, [h]Hŏg′lah, +Mĭl′cah, and [i]Tĭr′zah.

34 These *are* the families of [j]Mă-năs′seh, and those that were numbered of them, fifty and two thousand and seven hundred.

35 ¶ These *are* the sons of [k]Ē′phră-ĭm after their families: of [l]Shụ′the-lah, the family of the Shụ′thal-hītes: of [m]Bē′chēr, the family of the Băch′rītes: of Tā′hăn, the family of the Tā′han-ītes.

36 And these *are* the sons of [l]Shụ′the-lah: of Ē′răn, the family of the Ē′ran-ītes.

37 These *are* the families of the sons of [k]Ē′phră-ĭm according to those that were numbered of them, thirty and two thousand and five hundred. These *are* the sons of Jō′şeph after their families.

38 ¶ The sons of [n]Bĕn′ja-mĭn after their families: of ⊙Bē′lȧ, the family of the Bē′la-ītes: of [o]Ăsh′bĕl, the family of the Ăsh′bel-ītes: of [p]Ȧ-hī′ram, the family of the Ȧ-hī′ram-ītes:

39 Of Shụ′pham, the family of the Shụ′pham-ītes: of Hū′pham, the family of the Hū′pham-ītes.

40 And the sons of ⊙Bē′lȧ were Ärd and Nā′a-man: *of Ard*, the family of the Ärd′ītes: *and* of [q]Nā′a-man, the family of the Nā′a-mītes.

41 These *are* the sons of [n]Bĕn′ja-mĭn after their families: and they that were numbered of them *were* forty and five thousand and six hundred.

42 ¶ These *are* the sons of [r]Dăn after their families: of [s]Shụ′ham, the family of the Shụ′ham-ītes. These *are* the families of Dăn after their families.

43 All the families of the Shụ′ham-ītes, according to those that were numbered of them, *were* threescore and four thousand and four hundred.

44 ¶ *Of* the children of [t]Ăsh′ēr after their families: of [u]Jĭm′nȧ, the family of the Jĭm′nītes: of [v]Jĕs′u-ī, the family of the Jĕs′u-

26
*u* Gen 46:14.
*v* Gen. 46:14.
*w* Gen. 46:14.

27
*x* *Zebulun, tribe of*, Gen. 49:13.

28
*y* *Joseph*, Gen. 33:2.

29
*z* *Manasseh, tribe of, enumeration of*, Gen. 46:20.

*a* *Machir*, Gen. 50:23.

30
*b* Or, *Abiezer*, Josh. 17:2.
*c* Josh. 17:2.

31
*d* Josh. 17:2.

32
*e* Josh. 17:2; or, *Shemidah*, 1 Chr. 7:19.
*f* Num. 27:1; Josh. 17:2, 3.

33
*g* *Zelophehad*, Num. 27:1.
*h* *Hoglah*, Num. 27:1.
*i* *Tirzah*, Josh. 17:3.

34
*j* *Manasseh, tribe of, enumeration of*, Gen. 46:20.

35
*k* *Ephraim, tribe of*, Gen. 41:52.
*l* 1 Chr. 7:20.

v.35–1494 BC
See footnote, *Time*, Rev. 10:6.

*m* Or, *Bered*, 1 Chr. 7:20.

38
*n* *Benjamin, tribe of*, vs. 38–40; Num. 1:37.
*o* *Ashbel*, Gen. 46:21.
*p* Or, *Ehud*, 1 Chr. 8:6.

40
*q* 1 Chr. 8:4.

42
*r* *Dan, tribe of, census of*, Gen. 30:6.
*s* Or, *Hushim*, Gen. 46:23.

44
*t* *Asher tribe of, census of*, Num. 1:40.
*u* Or, *Jimnah*, Gen. 46:17; and *Imnah*, 1 Chr. 7:30.
*v* Or, *Isuah*, 1 Chr. 7:30.

‡ **GILEAD**, from whom the land of Gilead took its name. *Grandson of Manasseh*, Num. 26:29, 30; 27:1; 36:1; Josh. 17:1, 3; 1 Chr. 2:21, 23; 7:14, 17.

‖ **MAHLAH.** One of the daughters of Zelophehad. *Special legislation in regard to the inheritance of*, Num. 27:1–7; 36:1–12; Josh. 17:3, 4.

§ **NOAH** (*rest, quiet*). A daughter of Zelophehad. *Special legislation in regard to the inheritance of*, Num. 26:33; 27:1–7; 36:1–12; Josh. 17:3–7.

+ **MILCAH** (*advice*). A daughter of Zelophehad. *Special legislation in regard to the inheritance of*, Num. 27:1–7; 36:1–12; Josh. 17:3, 4.

⊙ **BELA.** *Son of Benjamin*, Num. 26:38, 40; 1 Chr. 7:6, 7; 8:1, 3. *Called* Belah, Gen. 46:21.

v.44–1494 BC
See footnote, *Time*, Rev. 10:6.

*w* *Beriah*, 1 Chr. 7:30.

45
*x* *Heber*, Gen. 46:17.
*y* *Malchiel*, Gen. 46:17.

46
*z* Gen. 46:17; 1 Chr. 7:30.

47
*a* *Asher, tribe of, census of*, Num. 1:40.

48
*b* *Naphtali, tribe of, census of*, vs. 48–50; Num. 1:42.
*c* Or, *Jahziel*, 1 Chr. 7:13.
*d* *Guni*, Gen. 46:24.

49
*e* *Jezer*, Gen. 46:24.
*f* Gen. 46:24; or, *Shallum*, 1 Chr. 7:13.

51
*g* *Israel, census of*, Ex. 4:22.

52
*h* *Prophets, inspiration of*, Isa. 3:2.

53
*i* *Canaan, land of, divided by lot*, Gen. 37:1.

55
*j* *Lot, decisions made by*, Esth. 3:7.

ītes: of [w]Bė-rī′ah, the family of the Bė-rī′ītes.

45 Of the sons of Bė-rī′ah: of [x]Hē′bēr, the family of the Hē′ber-ītes: of [y]Măl′chĭ-el, the family of the Măl′chĭ-el-ītes.

46 And the name of the daughter of Ăsh′ēr *was* [z]Sā′rah.

47 These *are* the families of the sons of [a]Ăsh′ēr according to those that were numbered of them; *who were* fifty and three thousand and four hundred.

48 ¶ *Of* the sons of [b]Năph′ta-lī after their families: of [c]Jăh′zē-el, the family of the Jăh′zē-el-ītes: of [d]Gū′nī, the family of the Gū′nītes:

49 Of [e]Jē′zēr, the family of the Jē′zer-ītes: of [f]Shĭl′lem, the family of the Shĭl′lem-ītes.

50 These *are* the families of [b]Năph′ta-lī according to their families: and they that were numbered of them *were* forty and five thousand and four hundred.

51 These *were* the numbered of the children of [g]Īṣ′ra-el, six hundred thousand and a thousand seven hundred and thirty.

52 ¶ And the LORD spake unto [h]Mō′ṣeṣ, saying,

53 Unto these the [i]land shall be divided for an inheritance according to the number of names.

54 To many thou shalt give the more inheritance, and to few thou shalt give the less inheritance: to every one shall his inheritance be given according to those that were numbered of him.

55 Notwithstanding the [i]land shall be divided by [j]lot: according to the names of the tribes of their fathers they shall inherit.

56 According to the [j]lot shall the possession thereof be divided between many and few.

57 ¶ And these *are* they that were numbered of the [k]Lē′vītes after their families: of [l]Gēr′shŏn, the family of the [m]Gēr′shon-ītes: of Kō′hăth, the family of the [n]Kō′hath-ītes: of [o]Mėrā′rī, the family of the ▲Mėrā′rītes.

58 These *are* the families of the [k]Lē′vītes: the family of the [p]Lĭb′nītes, the family of the [q]Hē′bron-ītes, the family of the Mäh′lītes, the family of the Mū′shītes, the family of the Kō′rath-ītes. And ●Kō′hăth begat [r]Ăm′răm.

59 And the name of [r]Ăm′răm's wife *was* [s]Jŏch′e-bĕd, the daughter of Lē′vī, whom *her mother* bare to Lē′vī in Ē′ġўpt: and she bare unto Ăm′răm [t]Aâr′on and [u]Mō′ṣeṣ, and [v]Mĭr′ĭ-am their sister.

60 And unto [t]Aâr′on was born [w]Nā′dăb, and [x]Ă-bī′hū, [y]Ē-le-ā′zar, and [z]Ĭth′a-mär.

61 And [w]Nā′dăb and [x]Ă-bī′hū died, when they offered strange fire before the LORD.

62 And those that were numbered of [a]them were twenty and three thousand, all males from a month old and upward: for they were not numbered among the children of Īṣ′ra-el, because there was [b]no inheritance given them among the children of Īṣ′ra-el.

63 ¶ These *are* they that were numbered by [c]Mō′ṣeṣ and [d]Ē-le-ā′zar the priest, who numbered the children of [e]Īṣ′ra-el in the plains of *Mō′ab by [f]Jôr′dan *near* [g]Jĕr′ĭ-chō.

64 But among these there was not a man of them whom [c]Mō′ṣeṣ and [h]Aâr′on the priest numbered, when they numbered the

v.56–1494 BC
See footnote, *Time*, Rev. 10:6.

57
*k* *Levites, enrollment of*, Deut. 10:8.
*l* *Gershon*, Gen. 46:11.
*m* *Gershonites*, Num. 4:27.
*n* *Kohathites*, Num. 3:27.
*o* *Merari*, Gen. 46:11.

58
*p* *Libni*, Ex. 6:17.
*q* *Hebronites*, Num. 3:27
*r* *Amram*, Ex. 6:18.

59
*s* *Jochebed*, Ex. 6:20.
*t* *Aaron*, Ex. 6:20.
*u* *Moses*, Ex. 2:10.
*v* *Miriam*, Ex. 15:20.

60
*w* *Nadab*, Ex. 24:1.
*x* *Abihu*, Ex. 6:23.
*y* *Eleazar*, Num. 3:2.
*z* *Ithamar*, Ex. 38:21.

62
*a* *Levites, enrollment of*, Deut. 10:8.
*b* *Levites, emoluments of*, Deut. 10:8.

63
*c* *Moses*, Ex. 2:10.
*d* *Eleazar*, Num. 3:2.
*e* *Israel*, Ex. 4:22.
*f* *Jordan*, Gen. 32:10.
*g* *Jericho*, Num. 22:1.

64
*h* *Aaron*, Ex. 6:20.

▲ **MERARITES.** *Sons of Merari, the Levite*, Num. 26:57; 1 Chr. 6:29, 44–46; 15:6; 23:21; 26:10; Ezra 8:19. *Cities assigned to*, 1 Chr. 6:63, 77–81. *Duties of*, Num. 3:36, 37; 1 Chr. 15:17, 18; 26:19; 2 Chr. 29:12–15; 34:12.
See footnote, LEVITES, Deut. 10:8.

● **KOHATH** (*assembly*). *Son of Levi*, Gen. 46:11; Ex. 6:16. *Grandfather of Moses, Aaron, and Miriam*, Num. 26:58, 59. *Father of the Kohathites, one of the divisions of the Levites*, Ex. 6:18; Num. 3:19, 27.
See footnote, KOHATHITES, Num. 3:27.

v.64–1494 BC See footnote, *Time,* Rev. 10:6.

*i Sinai, wilderness of,* Ex. 16:1.

65

*j Judgments,* Ex. 6:6.

*k Caleb,* Num. 14:6.

*l Joshua,* Josh.1:1.

children of Iş′ra-el in the wilderness of [i]Sī′nāi.

65 For the LORD had said of them, They [j]shall surely die in the wilderness. And there was not left a man of them, save [k]Cā′leb the son of Jė-phŭn′neh, and [l]Jŏsh′u-ȧ the son of Nŭn.

## CHAPTER 27

*The daughters of Zelophehad plead for an inheritance. 6 The law of inheritances. 12 Moses, being told of his death, prays for a successor. 18 Joshua is appointed to succeed him.*

1

*a Hepher,* Num. 26:32.

*b Gilead,* Num. 26:29.

*c Manasseh,* Gen. 46:20.

*d Joseph,* Gen. 33:2.

*e Women, property rights of,* vs. 1–11; Prov. 31:10.

*f Mahlah,* Num. 26:33.

*g Noah,* Num. 26:33.

*h Milcah,* Num. 26:33.

*i Tirzah,* Josh. 17:3.

2

*j Moses,* Ex. 2:10.

*k Court, civil,* Ex. 18:26.

*l Government, popular, by a national assembly or its representatives,* Isa. 22:1.

*m Eleazar,* Num. 3:2.

3

*n Orphan, instances of,* Lam. 5:3.

*o Korah,* Num. 16:1.

4

*p Petition, right of,* Esth. 5:6.

*q Land, unmarried woman's rights in,* Ruth 4:5.

*r Property, in real estate, entailed,* Lev. 27:15.

5

*s Mediation,* Gal. 3:19.

*t Revelation, concerning property rights of women,* 2 Cor. 12:1.

THEN came the daughters of *Zė-lō′phe-hăd, the son of [a]Hē′phĕr, the son of [b]Gĭl′e-ăd, the son of Mā′chĭr, the son of [c]Mȧ-năs′seh, of the families of Mȧ-năs′seh the son of [d]Jō′şeph: and these *are* the names of his [e]daughters; [f]Mäh′lah, [g]Nō′ah, and †Hŏg′lah, and [h]Mĭl′cah, and [i]Tĭr′zah.

2 And [e]they stood before [j,k,l]Mō′şeş, and before [m]Ē-le-ā′zar the priest, and before the princes and all the congregation, *by* the door of the tabernacle of the congregation, saying,

3 [n]Our father died in the wilderness, and he was not in the company of them that gathered themselves together against the LORD in the company of [o]Kō′rah; but died in his own sin, and had no sons.

4 Why should the name of our father be done away from among his family, because he hath no son? [p]Give unto us *therefore* a [q,r]possession among the brethren of our father.

5 And Mō′şeş [s]brought their cause before the LORD.

6 ¶ And the LORD [t]spake unto Mō′şeş, saying,

v.7–1494 BC See footnote, *Time,* Rev. 10:6.

7

*u Daughter, property rights of,* Lev. 12:6.

*v Legislation, concerning inheritance,* Ex. 12:49.

8

*w Israel,* Ex. 4:22.

*x Heir, Mosaic law relating to inheritance of,* vs. 8–11; Gen. 15:3.

12

*y Moses, not permitted to enter Canaan,* vs. 12–14; Ex. 2:10.

*z* Num. 33:47, 48; Deut. 32:49.

*a Canaan,* Gen. 37:1.

13

*b Aaron, death of,* Ex. 6:20.

14

*c Disobedience to God, instances of,* Eph. 5:6.

*d Zin, a desert,* Num. 13:21.

*e Meribah,* Ex. 17:7.

*f Kadesh,* Gen. 14:7.

7 The [e,u]daughters of *Zė-lō′phe-hăd speak right: [v]thou shalt surely give them a possession of an ‡inheritance among their father's brethren; and thou shalt cause the inheritance of their father to pass unto them.

8 And thou shalt speak unto the children of [w]Iş′ra-el, saying, [v]If a man die, and have no son, then ye shall cause his ‡,[q,r]inheritance to pass unto his [u,x]daughter.

9 And [v]if he have no daughter, then ye shall give his ‡,[r]inheritance unto his brethren.

10 And [v]if he have no brethren, then ye shall give his ‡,[r]inheritance unto his father's brethren.

11 And [v]if his father have no brethren, then ye shall give his ‡,[r]inheritance unto his kinsman that is next to him of his family, and he shall possess it: and it shall be unto the children of [w]Iş′ra-el a statute of judgment, as the LORD commanded Mō′şeş.

12 ¶ And the LORD said unto [y]Mō′şeş, Get thee up into this mount [z]Ăb′a-rĭm, and see the [a]land which I have given unto the children of Iş′ra-el.

13 And when thou hast seen it, thou also shalt be gathered unto thy people, as [b]Aâr′on thy brother was gathered.

14 For ye [c]rebelled against my commandment in the desert of [d]Zĭn, in the strife of the congregation, to sanctify me at the water before their eyes: that *is* the water of [e]Mĕr′i-bah in [f]Kā′desh in the wilderness of Zĭn.

15 ¶ And Mō′şeş spake unto the LORD, saying,

* **ZELOPHEHAD,** grandson of Gilead. *His daughters petition for his inheritance,* Num. 27:1–11; 36; Josh. 17:3–6; 1 Chr. 7:15.

† **HOGLAH,** a daughter of Zelophehad. *Special legislation in regard to the inheritance of,* Num. 27:1–11; 36:1–12; Josh. 17:3, 4.

‡ **INHERITANCE,** Num. 27:6–11; Job 42:15; Eccl. 2:18, 19; Luke 15:12, 25–31. *Of children,* Gen. 24:36; 25:5; 2 Chr. 21:3. *Of children of concubines,* Gen. 15:3; 21:9–11; 25:6. *Of children of polygamous marriages,* Deut. 21:15. *Of servants,* Prov. 17:2. *Of real estate inalienable,* 1 Kin. 21:3; Jer. 32:6–8; Ezek. 46:16–18. *Provisions for inheritance under Levirate marriages,* Gen. 38:7–11; Num. 36:6–9; Deut. 25:5–10; Ruth 4:1–17.

See footnote, HEIR, Gen. 15:3.

**Figurative,** Matt. 25:34; Acts 20:32; 26:18; Rom. 8:16, 17; Gal. 4:7; Eph. 1:11–14; Col. 3:24; Tit. 3:7; Heb. 1:14; 9:15–17.

v.16–1494 BC See footnote, *Time*, Rev. 10:6.

16 *g* *Intercession, of man with God*, Jer. 27:18. *h* *God, a spirit*, Gen. 2:2.
17 *i* *Rulers, duties of*, Ex. 18:21.
18 *j* *Moses*, Ex. 2:10. *k* *Call, to special religious duty*, Phil. 3:14. *l* *Joshua, commissioned*, Josh. 1:1. *m* *Hand, imposition of*, Ezra 10:19.
19 *n* *Government, Mosaic, popular, by a national assembly or its representatives*, Isa. 22:1. *o* *Eleazar*, Num. 3:2. *p* *High Priest*, Lev. 21:10.
20 *q* *Citizens, duties of*, Luke 15:15. *r* *Loyalty, enjoined*, Eccl. 8:2.
21 *s* *Wisdom, prayer for*, Prov. 2:2. *t* *Urim and Thummim*, Lev. 8:8.
22 *u* *Moses, appoints Joshua as his successor*, Ex. 2:10.

16 [g]Let the LORD, the [h]God of
the spirits of all flesh, set a man
over the congregation.[Q]
17 [h,i]Which may go out before
them, and which may go in before them, and which may lead
them out, and which may bring
them in; that the congregation of
the LORD be not as sheep which
have no shepherd.[Q]
18 ¶ And the LORD said unto
[j]Mō'ṣeṣ, [k]Take thee [l]Jŏsh'u-ȧ
the son of Nŭn, a man in whom
*is* the spirit,[C] and lay thine [m]hand
upon him;[T]
19 [n]And set [l]him before [o]Ē-le-ā'zar the [p]priest, and before all
the congregation; and give him a
charge[C] in their sight.
20 And thou shalt put *some* of
thine honour upon [l]him, that all
the [q]congregation of the children
of Ĭṣ'ra-el may be [r]obedient.
21 And [l]he shall stand before
[o]Ē-le-ā'zar the [p]priest, who shall
[s]ask *counsel* for him after the
judgment of [t]Ū'rim before the
LORD: at his word shall [q]they go
out, and at his word they shall
come in, *both* he, and all the children of Ĭṣ'ra-el with him, even
all the congregation.
22 And [u]Mō'ṣeṣ did as the
LORD commanded him: and he
took [l]Jŏsh'u-ȧ, and set him before [o]Ē-le-ā'zar the [p]priest, and
before all the congregation:
23 And he laid his [m]hands upon
him, and gave [l]him a charge, as
the LORD commanded by the
hand of Mō'ṣeṣ.

## CHAPTER 28

*Offerings are to be observed. 3 The continual burnt offering. 9 The offering on the sabbath, 11 on the first day of the months, 16 at the passover, 26 and in the day of first fruits.*

1 *a* *Revelation, concerning offerings*, 2 Cor. 12:1.
2 *b* *Offerings, burnt, offered daily*, Lev. 6:17. 1 R. V. offerings

AND the LORD [a]spake unto
Mō'ṣeṣ, saying,
2 Command the children of
Ĭṣ'ra-el, and say unto them, My
[b]offering, *and* my bread for my
[1]sacrifices made by fire, *for* a
sweet savour unto me, shall ye
observe to offer unto me in their
due season.
3 And thou shalt say unto them,
This *is* the [b,c]offering made by
fire which ye shall offer unto the
LORD; two [d]lambs of the first
year [e]without [2,f]spot[C] day by
day, *for* a [b]continual burnt offering.
4 The one [c,d]lamb shalt thou
offer in the morning, and the
other lamb shalt thou offer at
even;
5 And a tenth *part* of an [g]ephah
of flour for a [3,h]meat[C] offering,
mingled[C] with the fourth *part* of
an hin of beaten [i]oil.
6 *It is* a continual [b]burnt offering, which was ordained[C] in
mount [j]Sī'nāi for a sweet savour,
[4]a sacrifice made by fire unto
the LORD.
7 And the [k]drink offering thereof *shall be* the fourth *part* of an
hin[C] for the one [c,d]lamb: in the
holy *place* shalt thou cause the
strong [l]wine to be poured unto
the LORD *for* a drink offering.
8 And the other [c,d]lamb shalt
thou offer at even: as the [3,h]meat[C]
offering of the morning, and as
the [k]drink offering thereof, thou
shalt offer *it*, [4]a sacrifice made
by fire, of a sweet[C] savour unto
the LORD.
9 ¶[Q]And on the [m]sabbath day
two [c,d]lambs of the first year
[e]without spot, and two [g]tenth
deals[C] of flour *for* a [h]meat[C] offering, mingled[C] with [i]oil, and the
[k]drink offering thereof:
10 *This is* the burnt offering of
every [m]sabbath, beside the [b]continual burnt offering, and his
drink [k]offering.[Q]
11 ¶ And in the [n]beginnings of
your months ye shall offer a
burnt [c]offering unto the LORD;
two young [o]bullocks, and one
ram, seven [d]lambs of the first
year [e]without [f]spot;

v.2–1494 BC See footnote, *Time*, Rev. 10:6.

3 *c* *Jesus, typified in offerings*, Matt. 1:21. *d* *Lamb, offering of*, Num. 7:15. *e* *Holiness, typified*, Ex. 39:30. *f* *Sin, typified*, Rom. 5:12. 2 R. V. blemish,
5 *g* *Measure, dry*, Deut. 25:15. *h* *Offerings, meat*, Lev. 6:17. *i* *Oil*, Deut. 12:17. 3 R. V. meal
6 *j* *Sinai*, Ex. 16:1. 4 R. V. an offering
7 *k* *Offerings, drink*, Lev. 6:17. *l* *Wine, offered with sacrifices*, Prov. 23:31.
9 *m* *Sabbath, sacrifices on*, Ex. 16:23.
11 *n* *Moon, feast of the new*, vs. 11–15; Song 6:10. *o* *Bullock, used for sacrifices*, vs. 11–31; Ex. 29:3.

v.12–1494 BC
See footnote, *Time*, Rev. 10:6.

12 And three [g]tenth deals of flour *for* a [3,h]meat offering, mingled with [i]oil, for one [o]bullock; and two tenth deals of flour *for* a meat offering, mingled with oil, for one ram;

13 And a several tenth deal of flour mingled with oil *for* a [h]meat offering unto one lamb; *for* a burnt [b]offering of a sweet savour, a sacrifice made by fire unto the LORD.

14 And their [k]drink offerings shall be half an hin of [l]wine unto a [o]bullock, and the third *part* of an hin unto a ram, and a fourth *part* of an hin unto a lamb: this *is* the burnt offering of every month throughout the months of the year.

15 And one kid of the goats for a [p]sin [c]offering unto the LORD shall be offered, beside the [b]continual burnt offering, and his [k]drink offering.

16 ¶ And in the fourteenth day of the first month *is* the [q,r]passover of the LORD.

17 And in the fifteenth day of this month *is* the [s]feast: seven days shall unleavened bread be eaten.

18 In the first day *shall be* an holy convocation; ye shall do [t]no manner of servile work therein:

19 But ye shall offer [4]a sacrifice made by fire *for* a burnt [c]offering unto the LORD; two young [o]bullocks, and one ram, and seven [d]lambs of the first year: they shall be unto you [e]without [f,u]blemish:

20 And their [3,h]meat offering *shall be of* flour mingled with [i]oil: three [g]tenth deals shall ye offer for a [o]bullock, and two tenth deals for a ram;

21 A several [g]tenth deal shalt thou offer for every lamb, throughout the seven [d]lambs:

22 And one goat *for* a [p]sin offering, to make an [v,w]atonement for you.

23 Ye shall offer these beside the [b]burnt offering in the morning, which *is* for a continual burnt offering.

24 After this manner ye shall offer daily, throughout the seven days, the meat of the [5]sacrifice made by fire, of a sweet savour unto the LORD: it shall be offered beside the continual [b]burnt offering, and his [k]drink offering.

25 And on the seventh day ye shall have an holy convocation; ye shall do [t]no servile work.

26 ¶ Also in the [x]day of the firstfruits, when ye bring a new [3,h]meat offering unto the LORD, [6]after your weeks *be out*, ye shall have an holy convocation; ye shall do [t]no servile work:

27 But ye shall offer the burnt [c]offering for a sweet savour unto the LORD; two young [o]bullocks, one ram, seven [d]lambs of the first year;

28 And their [3,h]meat offering of flour mingled with [i]oil, three [g]tenth deals unto one [o]bullock, two tenth deals unto one ram,

29 A several [g]tenth deal unto one [d]lamb, throughout the seven lambs;

30 *And* one kid of the goats, to make an [v,w]atonement for you.

31 Ye shall offer *them* beside the continual [b]burnt offering, and his [3,h]meat offering, (they shall be unto you [e]without [f,u]blemish) and their [k]drink offerings.

## CHAPTER 29

*The offering at the feast of trumpets, 7 on the day of afflicting their souls, 13 and on the eight days of the feast of tabernacles.*

AND in the seventh month on the first *day* of the month, ye shall have an holy convocation; ye shall do [a]no servile work: it is a day of blowing the [b]trumpets unto you.

---

15
*p Offerings, sin*, Lev. 6:17.

16
*q Passover*, Num. 9:5.
*r Jesus, our passover, typified*, Matt. 1:21.

17
*s Annual Feasts*, Num. 15:3.

18
*t Rest, enjoined*, Ex. 23:12.

19
*Blemish*, Lev. 14:10.

v.22–1494 BC
See footnote, *Time*, Rev. 10:6.

22
*v Atonement, made by animal sacrifices*, Lev. 17:11.
*w Jesus, atonement by, typified*, Matt. 1:21.

24
5 R. V. offering

26
*x Pentecost*, Acts 2:1.
6 R. V. in your feast of weeks.

1
*a Rest, enjoined*, Ex. 23:12.
*b Trumpets, feast of*, vs. 1–6; Lev. 23:24.

v.2–1494 BC
See footnote, *Time*, Rev. 10:6.

**2**

*c* *Offerings, burnt*, Lev. 6:17.
*d* *Jesus, typified in offerings*, vs. 2–39; Matt. 1:21.
*e* *Bullock*, Ex. 29:3.
*f* *Lamb, offering of*, Num. 7:15.
*g* *Holiness, typified*, Ex. 39:30.
*h* *Blemish*, Lev. 14:10.
*i* *Sin, typified*, Rom. 5:12.

**3**

*j* *Offerings, meat*, Lev. 6:17.
*k* *Oil*, Deut. 12:17.
*l* *Measure, dry*, Deut. 25:15.
1 R. V. meal.

**5**

*m* *Offerings, sin*, Lev. 6:17.
*n* *Atonement, made by animal sacrifices*, Lev. 17:11.
*o* *Jesus, atonement by, typified*, Matt. 1:21.

**6**

*p* *Offerings, drink*, Lev. 6:17.
2 R. V. new moon.
3 R. V. an offering

**7**

*q* *Day of Atonement*, Lev. 23:27.

2 And ye shall offer a [c]burnt [d]offering for a sweet savour unto the LORD; one young [e]bullock, one ram, *and* seven [f]lambs of the first year [g]without [h,i]blemish:

3 And their [1,j]meat offering *shall be of* flour mingled with [k]oil, three [l]tenth deals for a [e]bullock, *and* two tenth deals for a ram,

4 And one [l]tenth deal for one [f]lamb, throughout the seven lambs:

5 And one kid of the goats *for* a [m]sin offering, to make an [n,o]atonement for you:

6 Beside the [c]burnt offering of the [2]month, and his [1,j]meat offering, and the daily burnt offering, and his [1]meat offering, and their [p]drink offerings, according unto their manner, for a sweet savour, [3]a sacrifice made by fire unto the LORD.

7 ¶ And ye shall have on the tenth [q]*day* of this seventh month an holy convocation; and ye shall afflict your souls: ye shall [a]not do any work *therein*:

8 But ye shall offer a [c]burnt [d]offering unto the LORD *for* a sweet savour; one young [e]bullock, one ram, *and* seven lambs of the first year; they shall be unto you [g]without [h,i]blemish:

9 And their [1,j]meat offering *shall be of* flour mingled with [k]oil, three [l]tenth deals to a [e]bullock, *and* two tenth deals to one ram,

10 A several [l]tenth deal for one [f]lamb, throughout the seven lambs:

11 One kid of the goats *for* a [m]sin offering; beside the sin offering of [n,o]atonement, and the continual [c]burnt offering, and the [1,j]meat offering of it, and their [p]drink offerings.

12 ¶ And on the fifteenth day of the seventh month ye shall have an [r]holy convocation; ye shall do [a]no servile work, and ye shall keep a [s]feast unto the LORD seven days:

13 And ye shall offer a [c]burnt [d]offering, [3]a sacrifice made by fire, of a sweet savour unto the LORD; thirteen young [e]bullocks, two rams, *and* fourteen [f]lambs of the first year; they shall be [g]without [h,i]blemish:

14 And their [1,j]meat offering *shall be of* flour mingled with oil, three [l]tenth deals unto every [e]bullock of the thirteen bullocks, two tenth deals to each ram of the two rams,

15 And a several [l]tenth deal to each [f]lamb of the fourteen lambs:

16 And one kid of the goats *for* a [m]sin [d]offering; beside the continual [c]burnt offering, his [1,j]meat offering, and his [p]drink offering.

17 ¶ And on the second day *ye shall offer* twelve young [e]bullocks, two rams, fourteen [f]lambs of the first year [g]without [t]spot:

18 And their [1,j]meat offering and their [p]drink offerings for the bullocks, for the rams, and for the lambs, *shall be* according to their number, after the manner:

19 And one kid of the goats *for* a [m]sin [d]offering; beside the continual [c]burnt offering, and the meat offering thereof, and their [p]drink offerings.

20 ¶ And on the third day eleven [e]bullocks, two rams, fourteen [f]lambs of the first year [g]without [h,i]blemish;

21 And their [1,j]meat offering and their [p]drink offerings for the [e]bullocks, for the rams, and for the [f]lambs, *shall be* according to their number, after the manner:

22 And one goat *for* a [m]sin [d]offering; beside the continual [c]burnt offering, and his [1,j]meat offering, and his [p]drink offering.

23 ¶ And on the fourth day ten

v.12–1494 BC
See footnote, *Time*, Rev. 10:6.

**12**

*r* *Tabernacles, feast of*, vs. 12–40; Deut. 16:13.
*s* *Annual Feasts*, Num. 15:3.

v.23–1494 BC
See footnote, *Time*, Rev. 10:6.

[e]bullocks, two rams, *and* fourteen [f]lambs of the first year
[g]without [h,i]blemish:
24 Their [4,j]meat offering and
their [p]drink offerings for the
[e]bullocks, for the rams, and for
the [f]lambs, *shall be* according to
their number, after the manner:
25 And one kid of the goats *for*
a [m]sin [d]offering; beside the continual [c]burnt offering, his [4,j]meat
offering, and his [p]drink offering.
26 ¶ And on the fifth day nine
bullocks, two rams, *and* fourteen lambs of the first year
[g]without [h,i]spot:
27 And their [4,j]meat offering
and their [p]drink offerings for the
[e]bullocks, for the rams, and for
the [f]lambs, *shall be* according to
their number, after the manner:
28 And one goat *for* a [m]sin [d]of-
fering; beside the continual
[c]burnt offering, and his [4,j]meat
offering, and his [p]drink offering.
29 ¶ And on the sixth day eight
[e]bullocks, two rams, *and* fourteen [f]lambs of the first year
[g]without [h,i]blemish:
30 And their [4,j]meat offering
and their [p]drink offerings for the
[e]bullocks, for the rams, and for
the [f]lambs, *shall be* according to
their number, after the manner:
31 And one goat *for* a [m]sin [d]of-
fering; beside the continual
[c]burnt offering, his [4,j]meat offering, and his [p]drink offering.
32 ¶ And on the [t]seventh day
[t]seven [e]bullocks, two rams, *and*
fourteen lambs of the first year
[g]without [h,i]blemish:
33 And their [4,j]meat offering
and their [p]drink offerings for the
[e]bullocks, for the rams, and for
the [f]lambs, *shall be* according to
their number, after the manner:
34 And one goat *for* a [m]sin [d]of-
fering; beside the continual
[c]burnt offering, his [4,j]meat offering, and his [p]drink offering.
35 ¶ On the eighth day ye shall
have a solemn assembly: ye shall
do [a]no servile work *therein*:
36 But ye shall offer a [c]burnt
[d]offering, [5]a sacrifice made by
fire, of a sweet savour unto the
LORD: one [e]bullock, one ram,
seven [f]lambs of the first year
[g]without [h,i]blemish:
37 Their [4,j]meat offering and
their [p]drink offerings for the
[e]bullock, for the ram, and for the
[f]lambs, *shall be* according to
their number, after the manner:
38 And one goat *for* a [m]sin [d]of-
fering; beside the continual
[c]burnt offering, and [4,j]his meat
offering, and his [p]drink offering.
39 These *things* ye shall do
unto the LORD in your set
[s]feasts, beside your [u]vows, and
your [v]freewill offerings, for your
[c]burnt offerings, and for your
[4,j]meat offerings, and for your
[p]drink offerings, and for your
[w]peace offerings.
40 And Mō′ṣeṣ told the children of Ĭṣ′ra-el according to all
that the LORD commanded
Mō′ṣeṣ.

## CHAPTER 30

*Vows not to be broken. 3 Of a maid's vow; 6 of a wife's; 9 of a widow's, and of her that is divorced.*

AND Mō′ṣeṣ spake unto the
[a]heads of the tribes concerning the children of Ĭṣ′ra-el,
saying, This *is* the thing which
the LORD hath commanded.
2 If a man vow a *vow unto the
LORD, or swear an [b]oath to bind
his soul with a bond; he shall not
break his word, he shall [c]do according to all that proceedeth
out of his mouth.
3 If a [d]woman also vow a *vow

**24**
4 R. V. meat

**32**
t *Seven*, Gen. 7:2.

v.34–1494 BC
See footnote, *Time*, Rev. 10:6.

**36**
5 R. V. an offering

**39**
u *Vows*, Num.30:2.
v *Offerings, free will*, Lev. 6:17.
w *Offerings, peace*, Lev. 6:17.

**1**
a *Government, Mosaic*, Isa. 22:1.

**2**
b *Oath*, Num. 5:19.
c *Obedience, enjoined*, Heb. 5:8.

**3**
d *Women, vows of*, Prov. 31:10.

* **VOWS**, Psa. 22:25; 61:8; 65:1. *Heard of God*, Psa. 61:5. *Obligatory*, Num. 30:2; Deut. 23:21-23; Job 22:27; Psa. 50:14; 56:12; 66:13, 14; 76:11; Eccl. 5:4, 5; Nah. 1:15. *In affliction*, Psa. 116:14-19. *Rash*, Prov. 20:25; Eccl. 5:6; *by Jephthah*, Judg. 11:29-40; *by Israelites*, Judg. 20:7-11.
**Mosaic laws concerning:** *Of women*, Num. 30:3-16. *Of Nazirites*, Num. 6:1-21. *Offerings devoted under*, Lev. 7:16-18; 27:1-25; Num. 15:2-16. *Things offered in, must be perfect*, Lev. 22:18-25. *Things forbidden to be offered in*, Deut. 23:18.
See footnote, COVENANT, Deut. 29:1.
**Instances of:** *Jacob*, Gen. 28:20-22. *The mother of*

v.3–1494 BC
See footnote, *Time*, Rev. 10:6.

unto the LORD, and bind *herself* by a bond, *being* in her father's house in her youth;

4 And [d]her [e]father hear her *vow, and her bond wherewith she hath bound her soul, and her father shall hold[C] his peace at her: then all her vows shall stand, and every bond wherewith she hath bound her soul shall stand.

4
*e Father*, Psa. 27:10.

5 But if [d]her [e]father disallow[C] her in the day that he heareth; not any of her *vows, or of her bonds wherewith she hath bound her soul, shall stand: and the LORD shall forgive her, because her father disallowed[C] her.

6 And if [d,f]she had at all an †husband, [1]when she vowed, or uttered ought[C] out of her lips, wherewith she bound her soul;

6
*f Wife, vows of*, vs. 6–16; Prov. 5:18.
1 R. V. while her vows are upon her, or the rash utterance of her lips,

7 And [d,f]her †husband heard *it*, and held[C] his peace at her in the day that he heard *it*: then her *vows shall stand, and her bonds wherewith she bound her soul shall stand.

8 But if [d,f]her †husband disallowed[C] her on the day that he heard *it*; then he shall make her *vow which she vowed, and that which she uttered with her lips, wherewith she bound her soul, of none effect: and the LORD shall forgive her.

9 But every *vow of a [g]widow, and of her that is divorced, wherewith they have bound their souls, shall stand against her.

9
*g Widow, vows of*, 2 Sam. 14:5.

10 And if [d,f]she vowed in her †husband's house, or bound her soul by a bond with an [b]oath;

11 And [d,f]her †husband heard *it*, and held[C] his peace at her, *and* disallowed her not: then all her *vows shall stand, and every bond wherewith she bound her soul shall stand.

v.11–1494 BC
See footnote, *Time*, Rev. 10:6

12 But if [d,f]her †husband hath utterly made them void[C] on the day he heard *them*; *then* whatsoever proceedeth out of her lips concerning her *vows, or concerning the bond of her soul, shall not stand: her husband hath made them void[C]; and the LORD shall forgive her.

13 Every *vow, and every binding [b]oath to afflict the soul, [d,f]her †husband may establish it, or her husband may make it void.

14 But if [d,f]her †husband altogether hold[C] his peace at her from day to day; then he establisheth all her *vows, or all her bonds, which *are* upon her: he confirmeth them, because he held his peace at her in the day that he heard *them*.

15 But if †he shall any ways make them void[C] after that he hath heard *them*; then he shall bear [d,f]her iniquity.

16 These *are* the statutes, which the LORD commanded Mō´ṣeṣ, between a †man and his [d,f]wife, between the [e]father and his [h]daughter, *being yet* in her youth in her father's house.

16
*h Daughter*, Lev. 12:6.

## CHAPTER 31

*The Midianites are spoiled, and Balaam slain.* 13 *Moses is wroth with the officers for saving the women alive.* 19 *How the soldiers, with their captives and spoil, are to be purified.* 25 *The proportion in which the prey is to be divided.* 48 *The voluntary oblation unto the treasury of the Lord.*

AND the LORD spake unto [a]Mō´ṣeṣ, saying,

1
*a Moses*, Ex. 2:10.

2 Avenge[C] the children of [b]Ĭṣ´-ra-el of the [c]Mĭd´ĭ-an-ītes: after-

2
*b Israel*, Ex. 4:22.
*c Midianites*, Gen. 37:28.

---

*Micah, dedication of silver for making an idol*, Judg. 17:2, 3. *Hannah, consecrating Samuel*, 1 Sam. 1:11, 27, 28. *Elkanah*, 1 Sam. 1:21. *Absalom*, 2 Sam. 15:7, 8. *Job, not to entertain thoughts of fornication*, Job 31:1. *David*, Psa. 132:2–5. *Jonah*, Jonah 2:9. *Jews, to slay Paul*, Acts 23:12–15.

† **HUSBAND.** *Relation of, to wife*, Gen. 2:23, 24; Matt. 19:5, 6; Mark 10:7; 1 Cor. 7:3–5; Eph. 5:22–33. *May give wife bill of divorcement*, Deut. 24:1–4. *Law relating to, in cases where wife's virtue is questioned*, Num. 5:11–31; Deut. 22:13–21. *Exemptions for*, Deut. 24:5. *Chastity of*, Prov. 5:15–20; Mal. 2:14–16. *Duties of*, Eccl. 9:9; Col. 3:19; 1 Pet. 3:7; *to provide for family*, Gen. 30:30; 1 Tim. 5:8. *Rights of*, 1 Cor. 7:3, 5. *Sanctified in the wife*, 1 Cor. 7:14, 16. *Headship of*, 1 Cor. 11:3. Faithful: *Isaac*, Gen. 24:67; *Joseph*, Matt. 1:19, 20. *Unreasonable and oppressive* Esth. 1:10–22.
**Figurative**, Isa. 54:5, 6; Jer. 3:14; 31:32; Hos. 2:19, 20.

v.2–1494 BC
See footnote, *Time*, Rev. 10:6.

3
*d War*, Judg. 3:2.

4
*e Armies, levies for*, Deut. 11:4.

6
*f Phinehas*, Num. 25:7.
*g Eleazar*, Num. 3:2.
*h Priest, duties of*, Lev. 1:5.
*i Trumpet*, Josh. 6:4.
1 R. V. vessels of the sanctuary

7
*j Massacre, instances of*, Esth. 3:13.

8
*k* Josh. 13:21.
*l* Josh. 13:21.
*m Zur*, Num. 25:15.
*n* Josh. 13:21.
*o* Josh. 13:21.
*p Balaam*, Deut. 23:4.

9
*q Women, taken captive*, Prov. 31:10.
*r Captive*, 1 Sam. 30:3.
*s Spoils*, 1 Chr. 26:27.

ward shalt [a]thou be gathered unto thy people.

3 And Mō′ṣeṣ spake unto the people, saying, Arm some of yourselves unto the [d]war, and let them go against the [c]Mĭd′ĭ-an-ītes, and avenge the LORD of Mĭd′ĭ-an.

4 Of every tribe a [e]thousand, throughout all the tribes of [b]Ĭṣ′ra-el, shall ye send to the [d]war.

5 So there were delivered out of the thousands of Ĭṣ′ra-el, a thousand of *every* tribe, [e]twelve thousand armed for [d]war.

6 And Mō′ṣeṣ sent them to the [d]war, a [e]thousand of *every* tribe, them and [f]Phĭn′e-has the son of [g]Ē-le-ā′zar the [h]priest, to the war, with the [1]holy instruments, and the [i]trumpets to blow in his hand.

7 And [b]they [d]warred against the [c]Mĭd′ĭ-an-ītes, as the LORD commanded Mō′ṣeṣ; and they [j]slew all the males.

8 And they [j]slew the kings of Mĭd′ĭ-an, beside the rest of them that were slain; *namely*, [k]Ē′vī, and [l]Rē′kem, and [m]Zûr, and [n]Hûr, and [o]Rē′bȧ, five kings of Mĭd′ĭ-an: [p]Bā′laam also the son of Bē′or they slew with the sword.

9 And the children of [b]Ĭṣ′ra-el took *all* the [q]women of Mĭd′ĭ-an [r]captives, and their little ones, and took the [s]spoil of all their cattle, and all their flocks, and all their goods.

10 And they burnt all their cities wherein they dwelt, and all their goodly castles, with fire.

11 And they took all the [s]spoil, and all the prey, *both* of men and of beasts.

12 And they brought the [r]captives, and the prey, and the [s]spoil, unto Mō′ṣeṣ, and Ē-le-ā′zar the priest, and unto the congregation of the children of Ĭṣ′ra-el, unto the camp at the plains of [t]Mō′ab, which *are* by [u]Jôr′dan *near* [v]Jĕr′ĭ-chō.

13 ¶ [w]And Mō′ṣeṣ, and Ē-le-ā′zar the priest, and all the princes of the congregation, went forth to meet them without the camp.

14 And [x]Mō′ṣeṣ was [y]wroth with the officers of the host, *with* the [z]captains over thousands, and captains over hundreds, which came from the [2]battle.

15 And [x]Mō′ṣeṣ said unto them, Have ye saved all the women alive?

16 Behold, [a]these caused the children of Ĭṣ′ra-el, through the counsel of [b]Bā′laam, to commit trespass against the LORD in the matter of [c]Pē′or, and there was a [d]plague among the congregation of the LORD.

17 Now therefore [e]kill every male among the [f]little ones, and kill every woman that hath known man by lying with him.

18 But all the women children, that have not known a man by lying with him, keep alive for yourselves.

19 And do [g]ye abide without the camp seven days: whosoever hath killed any person, and whosoever hath [h]touched any slain, [i]purify *both* yourselves and your captives on the third day, and on the seventh day.

20 [g]And purify all *your* [j]raiment, and all that is made of skins, and all work of goats' *hair*, and all things made of wood.

21 ¶ And [k]Ē-le-ā′zar the priest said unto the men of war which went to the battle, This *is* the ordinance of the law which the LORD commanded Mō′ṣeṣ;

22 Only the [l]gold, and the [m]silver, the [n]brass, the [o]iron, the [p]tin, and the [q]lead,

v.12–1494 BC
See footnote, *Time*, Rev. 10:6.

12
*t Moab*, Num. 26:3.
*u Jordan*, Gen. 32:10.
*v Jericho*, Num. 22:1.

13
*w Government, Mosaic*, Isa. 22:1.

14
*x Moses, character of*, Ex. 2:10.
*y Anger*, Psa. 37:8.
*z Armies, how officered*, Deut. 11:4.
2 R. V. service of the war.

16
*a Women, active in instigating iniquity*, Prov. 31:10.
*b Balaam, counsel of*, Deut. 23:4.
*c Baal-Peor*, Num. 25:3.
*d Plague*, Ex. 11:1.

17
*e Captive, prisoners of war put to death*, 1 Sam. 30:3.
*f Infanticide*, Ex. 1:16.

19
*g Armies, religious ceremonies attending*, Deut. 11:4.
*h Defilement*, Lev. 5:2.
*i Purification*, Num. 19:19.

20
*j Dress, ceremonial purification of*, Zech. 3:4.

21
*k Eleazar*, Num. 3:2.

22
*l Gold*, Ezek. 7:19.
*m Silver*, 1 Chr. 28:14.
*n Brass*, Job 28:2.
*o Iron*, Prov. 27:17.
*p* Isa. 1:25; Ezek. 22:18, 20; 27:12.
*q Lead*, Ezek. 22:18.

v.23–1494 BC
See footnote, *Time*,
Rev. 10:6.

23 *Every thing that may abide
the fire, ye shall make *it* go
through the fire, and it shall be
clean; nevertheless it shall be
[i]purified[G] with the water of separation: and all that abideth not
the fire ye shall make go through
the water.
24 [q]And ye shall [r]wash your
clothes on the seventh day, and
ye shall be clean, and afterward
ye shall come into the camp.
25 ¶ And the LORD spake unto
Mō′ṣeṣ, saying,
26 Take the sum of the [s]prey[G]
that was taken, *both* of man
and of beast, thou, and [k]Ē-le-ā′-
zar the [t]priest, and the chief fathers of the congregation:
27 And divide the [s]prey[G] into
two parts; between [u]them that
took the war upon them, who
went out to battle, and between
all the congregation:
28 And levy a [v]tribute unto the
LORD of the men of war which
went out to battle: one soul of
five hundred, *both* of the [w]per-
sons, and of the beeves[G], and of
the asses, and of the sheep:
29 Take *it* of their half, and
give [v]*it* unto [k]Ē-le-ā′zar the
priest, *for* an [x]heave[G] offering of
the LORD.
30 And of the children of Ĭṣ′-
ra-el's half, thou shalt take one
portion of fifty, of the persons,
of the beeves[G], of the asses, and of
the flocks, of all manner of
beasts, and give [y]them unto the

**24**
*r Ceremonial Washing*, Ex. 19:10.

**26**
*s Spoils*, 1 Chr. 26:27.
*t High Priest, duties of*, Lev. 21:10.

**27**
*u Armies, rewards for meritorious conduct in*, Deut. 11:4.

**28**
*v Priest, emoluments of*, Lev. 1:5.
*w Servant, captives of war made*, Jer. 2:14.

**29**
*x Offerings, heave*, Lev. 6:17.

**30**
*y Levites, emoluments of*, Deut. 10:8.

Lē′vītes, which keep the charge
of the tabernacle of the LORD.
31 And Mō′ṣeṣ and Ē-le-ā′zar
the priest did as the LORD commanded Mō′ṣeṣ.
32 And the booty, *being* the
rest of the [s]prey which the men
of war had caught, was six hundred thousand and seventy thousand and five thousand sheep,
33 And threescore[G] and twelve
thousand beeves[G],
34 And threescore[G] and one
thousand [z]asses,
35 And thirty and two thousand [a]persons in all, of [b]women
that had not known man by lying with him.
36 And the [c]half, *which was* the
portion of [d]them that went out to
war, was in number three hundred thousand and seven and
thirty thousand and five hundred sheep:
37 And the LORD's [e]tribute of
the sheep was six hundred and
threescore and fifteen.
38 And the beeves[G] *were* thirty
and six thousand; of which the
LORD's [e]tribute *was* threescore
and twelve.
39 And the [f]asses *were* thirty
thousand and five hundred; of
which the LORD's [e]tribute[G] *was*
threescore and one.
40 And the [a]persons *were* sixteen thousand; of which the
LORD's [e]tribute *was* thirty and
two persons.
41 And Mō′ṣeṣ gave the [e]trib-

v.30–1494 BC
See footnote, *Time*,
Rev. 10:6.

**34**
*z Ass, domesticated*, 2 Chr. 28:15.

**35**
*a Servant, captives of war made*, Jer. 2:14.
*b Women, taken captive*, Prov. 31:10.

**36**
*c Spoils, of war*, 1 Chr. 26:27.
*d Armies, rewards for meritorious conduct in*, Deut. 11:4.

**37**
*e Priest, emoluments of*, Lev. 1:5.

**39**
*f Ass, domesticated*, 2 Chr. 28:15.

***SANITATION AND HYGIENE.** *Relating, to carcases*, Lev. 5:2; 10:4, 5; 11:24–40; 22:4, 6; Num. 9:6, 10; 19:11–16; 31:19; *to contagion*, Lev. 5:2, 3; 7:19, 21; 11:24–40; Num. 9:6, 10; 19:11–16, 22; 31:19, 20; *to leprosy*, Lev. 13:2–59; 14:2, 3, 8, 9, 34–57; Num. 5:2–4; Deut. 24:8; *to venereal diseases*, Lev. 15:2–33; 22:4–8.

**For prevention of the spread of disease:** *By washing*, Lev. 13:6, 34, 53, 54, 58, 59; 14:8, 9, 46–48, 54–57; 15:2–28; Num. 31:19, 20, 22–24; Deut. 23:10, 11. *By burning*, Lev. 7:19; 13:51, 52, 55–57; Num. 31:19, 20, 22, 23. *By isolation*, Lev. 13:2–5, 31–33, 45, 46–50; 14:34–38; Num. 5:2, 3; 12:10, 14, 15; 2 Kin. 7:3; 15:5; 2 Chr. 26:21; Luke 17:12. *By demolishing infected houses*, Lev. 14:39–45.

**Food.** ARTICLES PRESCRIBED AS: *Cloven-footed, cud-chewing beasts*, Lev. 11:2, 3; Deut. 14:6. *Aquatic animals having fins and scales*, Lev. 11:9; Deut. 14:9. *Certain insects*, Lev. 11:22.

ARTICLES FORBIDDEN AS: *Fat*, Lev. 3:17; 7:23–25. *Blood*, Lev. 3:17; 7:26, 27; 17:10–14; 19:26; Deut. 12: 16, 20–25; 15:22, 23. *Flesh having touched any unclean thing*, Lev. 7:19. *Flesh of peace and thank offerings remaining till the second day*, Lev. 7:15; 22:30. *Flesh of vow or voluntary offerings remaining till the third day*, Lev. 7:16–18; 19:5–8. *All beasts that are not both cloven-footed and cud-chewing*, Lev. 11:4–8, 26; Deut. 14:7, 8. *Aquatic animals not having fins and scales*, Lev. 11:10–12; Deut. 14:10. *Animals dying of themselves or torn by beasts*, Ex. 22:31; Lev. 17:15; 22:8; Deut. 14:21. *Certain insects*, Lev. 11:23. *Certain creeping things*, Lev. 11:20, 21, 28–31, 41. *Certain birds*, Lev. 11:13–18.

**Gluttony:** *Disease resulting from*, Num. 11:18–20, 31–33.

**Filth:** *Disposition of*, Ex. 29:14, 34; Lev. 4:11, 12, 21; 6:30; 7:17, 19; 8:17, 32; 9:11; 16:27, 28; 19:6; Deut. 23:12, 13; Heb. 13:11.

**Rest:** *Enjoined, on the Sabbath*, Ex. 20:9–11; 31:13–17; 34:21; 35:2; Deut. 5:12–14; *on the first and last days of annual feasts*, Ex. 34:22; Lev. 23:3–8, 24, 25, 33–42; Num. 9:2, 3; 28:16–18, 25, 26; 29:1, 7; *on the day of atonement*, Lev. 23:26–32; *in the sabbatic year*, Lev. 25:2–7; *in the jubilee*, Lev. 25:8–12.

**Women in childbirth,** Lev. 12:2, 4, 5.

v.41–1494 BC
See footnote, *Time*, Rev. 10:6.

41
g *Offerings, heave*, Lev. 6:17.

47
h *Levites, emoluments of*, Deut. 10:8.

48
i *Armies, check roll-call*, Deut. 11:4.

50
j *Thankfulness, to God, instances of*, vs. 50–54; Acts 24:3.
k *Liberality, instances of*, 1 Tim. 6:18.
l *Jewels*, Gen. 24:53.
m *Gold*, Ezek. 7:19.
n *Chains*, Dan. 5:7.
o *Bracelet*, Gen. 24:22.
p *Ring*, Gen. 41:42.
q *Atonement*, Lev. 17:11.

ute, *which was* the LORD's
[g]heave offering, unto Ē-le-ā'zar
the priest, as the LORD commanded Mō'ṣeṣ.
42 And of the children of Iṣ'-
ra-el's [c]half, which Mō'ṣeṣ divided from the men that warred,
43 (Now the [c]half *that pertained unto* the congregation was
three hundred thousand and
thirty thousand *and* seven thousand and five hundred sheep,
44 And thirty and six thousand
beeves,
45 And thirty thousand [l]asses
and five hundred,
46 And sixteen thousand [a]per-
sons;)
47 Even of the children of Iṣ'-
ra-el's [c]half, Mō'ṣeṣ took one
portion of fifty, *both* of [a]man and
of beast, and gave [h]them unto
the Lē'vītes, which kept the
charge of the tabernacle of the
LORD; as the LORD commanded
Mō'ṣeṣ.
48 ¶ And the officers which
*were* over thousands of the [i]host,
the †captains of thousands, and
captains of hundreds, came near
unto Mō'ṣeṣ:
49 And they said unto Mō'ṣeṣ,
Thy servants have taken the
[i]sum of the men of war which
*are* under our charge, and there
lacketh not one man of us.
50 [j]We have therefore [k]brought
an oblation for the LORD, what
every man hath gotten, of [l]jew-
els of [m]gold, [n]chains, and [o]brace-
lets, [p]rings, earrings, and tablets, to make an [q]atonement for
our souls before the LORD.
51 And Mō'ṣeṣ and Ē-le-ā'zar
the priest took the [m]gold of them,
*even* all wrought [l]jewels.
52 And all the [m]gold of the offering that they offered up to the
LORD, of the †captains of thousands, and of the captains of
hundreds, was sixteen thousand
seven hundred and fifty [r]shekels.
53 (*For* the men of war had taken [c]spoil, every man for himself.)
54 And Mō'ṣeṣ and Ē-le-ā'zar
the priest took the [m]gold of the
captains of thousands and of
hundreds, and brought it into
the [s]tabernacle of the congregation, *for* a memorial for the children of Iṣ'ra-el before the LORD.

## CHAPTER 32

*The Reubenites and the Gadites ask for their inheritance on the east of Jordan. 6 Moses reproves them. 16 They offer satisfactory conditions, 33 and he assigns them the land. 39 They take possession of it.*

NOW the [a]children of Reu'-
ben and the children of
[b]Găd had a very great multitude
of cattle: and when they saw the
land of [c]Jā'zēr, and the land of
[d]Gĭl'e-ăd, that, behold, the place
*was* a place for cattle;
2 The children of [b]Găd and
the [a]children of Reu'ben came
and spake unto [e]Mō'ṣeṣ, and to
[e]Ē-le-ā'zar the priest, and unto
the [e]princes of the congregation,
saying,
3 Ăt'a-rōth, and [f]Dī'bŏn, and
[c]Jā'zēr, and [g]Nĭm'rah, and
[h]Hĕsh'bŏn, and [i]Ē-le-ā'leh, and
Shē'bam, and *Nē'bō, and
Bē'ŏn,
4 *Even* the country which the
LORD smote before the congregation of Iṣ'ra-el, *is* a land for
cattle, and thy servants have
cattle:
5 Wherefore, said they, [i]if we
have found grace in thy sight,
let this [d]land be given unto thy

v.52–1494 BC
See footnote, *Time*, Rev. 10:6.

52
r *Shekel*, Ex. 30:13.

54
s *Tabernacle, offerings brought to*, Ex. 27:9.

1
a *Reubenites*, Josh. 22:1.
b *Gad, tribe of*, Deut. 33:20.
c *Jazer*, Josh. 13:25.
d *Gilead*, Deut. 3:13.

2
e *Government, Mosaic*. Isa. 22:1.

3
f *Dibon*, Num. 21:30.
g Or, *Beth-Nimrah*, Josh. 13:27.
h *Heshbon*, Isa. 16:8.
i Isa. 15:4; 16:9.

5
i *Petition, right of, recognized by Israel*, Esth. 5:6.

† **CAPTAIN.** *Commander-in-chief of an army*, Deut. 20:9; Judg. 4:2; 1 Sam. 14:50; 1 Kin. 2:35; 16:16; 1 Chr. 27:34. *Of the tribes*, Num. 2. *Of thousands*, Num. 31:48; 1 Sam. 17:18; 1 Chr. 28:1. *Of hundreds*, 2 Kin. 11:15. *Of fifties*, 2 Kin. 1:9; Isa. 3:3. *Of the guard*, Gen. 37:36; 2 Kin. 25:8. *Of the ward*, Jer. 37:13.
*Signifying any commander*, 1 Sam. 9:16; 22:2; 2 Kin. 20:5; *or leader*, 1 Chr. 11:21; 12:34; 2 Chr. 17:14–19; John 18:12.
*David's captains, or chief heroes*, 2 Sam. 23:8–39; 1 Chr. 11; 12. *King appoints*, 1 Sam. 18:13; 2 Sam. 17:25; 18:1.
*Angel of the Lord called*, Josh. 5:14. *Christ called* (R. V. AUTHOR), Heb. 2:10.
See footnote, ARMIES, Deut. 11:4.

* **NEBO.** *A city allotted to Reuben*, Num. 32:3, 38; 1 Chr. 5:8. *Prophecies concerning*, Isa. 15:2; Jer. 48:1, 22.

**v.5–1494 BC**
See footnote, *Time,* Rev. 10:6.

*k Jordan,* Gen. 32: 10.

**6**
*l Motive, misunderstood,* Psa. 106:8.
*m Uncharitableness, instances of,* Matt. 7:1.

**7**
*n Canaan, promised to Abraham and his seed,* Gen. 37:1.

**8**
*o Israel, sends twelve spies to view the land,* Ex. 4:22.
*p Kadesh,* Gen. 14:7.

**9**
*q Eshcol,* Num. 13: 23.

**10**
*r Anger of God,* 2 Kin. 13:3.

**11**
*s Unbelieving Israelites destroyed,* Num. 14:11.
*t Egypt,* Gen. 41:8.
*u Covenant, of God with men,* Deut. 29:1.
*v Abraham,* Gen. 17:5.
*w Isaac,* Gen. 21:3.
*x Jacob,* Gen. 27: 11.

**12**
*y Caleb,* Num.14:6.
*z Joshua,* Josh.1:1.

**13**
*a Anger of God,* 2 Kin. 13:3.
*b Forty, years,* Jonah 3:4.
*c Unbelieving Israelites destroyed,* Num. 14:11.

**14**
*d Reproof, faithfulness in,* Prov. 17: 10.
*e Children, wicked,* Mark 10:14.

**15**
*f Fear of God, a motive of obedience,* Acts 9:31.

servants for a possession, *and*
bring us not over [k]Jôr′dan.
6 ¶ And Mō′ṣeṣ said unto the
children of [b]Găd and to the
[a]children of Reu̥′ben, [†,l]Shall
your brethren go to war, and
[m]shall ye sit here?
7 And wherefore discourage ye
the heart of the children of Ĭṣ′-
ra-el from going over into the
[n]land which the LORD hath
given them?
8 [†,l]Thus did your fathers,
when I sent [o]them from [p]Kā′-
desh–bär′ne-ȧ to see the [n]land.
9 For when [o]they went up unto
the valley of [q]Ĕsh′cŏl, and saw
the [n]land, they discouraged the
heart of the children of Ĭṣ′ra-el,
that they should not go into the
land which the LORD had given
them.
10 And the LORD's [r]anger was
kindled the same time, and he
sware, saying,
11 Surely none of the [s]men that
came up out of [t]Ē′ġy̆pt, from
twenty years old and upward,
shall see the [n]land which I
[u]sware unto [v]Ā′brā-hăm, unto
[w]Ī′ṣaac, and unto [x]Jā′cob; because they have not wholly followed me:
12 Save [y]Cā′leb the son of Jē-
phŭn′neh the Kĕn′ez-īte, and
[z]Jŏsh′u-ȧ the son of Nŭn: for
they have wholly followed the
LORD.
13 And the LORD's [a]anger was
kindled against Ĭṣ′ra-el, and he
made them wander in the wilderness [b]forty years, until all the
[c]generation, that had done evil
in the sight of the LORD, was
consumed.
14 And, [d]behold, [e]ye are risen
up in your father's stead, an increase of sinful men, to augment
yet the fierce [a]anger of the LORD
toward Ĭṣ′ra-el.
15 For [d,f]if ye turn away from
after him, he will yet again leave
them in the wilderness; and ye
shall destroy all this people.
16 ¶ And [g,h]they came near unto him, and said, [i]We will build
sheepfolds here for our cattle,
and cities for our little ones:
17 But [g,h]we ourselves will go
ready armed before the children
of Ĭṣ′ra-el, until we have brought
them unto their place: and our
little ones shall dwell in the
fenced cities because of the inhabitants of the land.
18 [g,h]We will not return unto
our houses, until the children of
Ĭṣ′ra-el have inherited every
man his inheritance.
19 For [g,h]we will not inherit
with them on yonder side [j]Jôr′-
dan, or forward; because our inheritance is fallen to us on this
side Jôr′dan eastward.
20 ¶ And [k]Mō′ṣeṣ said unto
them, If ye will do this thing, if
ye will go armed before the
LORD to [l]war,
21 And will go all of you armed
over [j]Jôr′dan before the LORD,
until he hath driven out his enemies from before him,
22 And the [m]land be subdued
before the LORD: then afterward ye shall return, and be
guiltless before the LORD, and
before Ĭṣ′ra-el; and this [n]land
shall be your possession before
the LORD.
23 But if ye will not do so, behold, ye have sinned against the
LORD: and be sure your [o]sin
will find [p]you out.
24 Build you cities for your
little ones, and folds for [i]your
sheep; and do that which hath
proceeded out of your mouth.
25 And the children of [g]Găd
and the [h]children of Reu̥′ben
spake unto Mō′ṣeṣ, saying, Thy
servants will do as my lord
commandeth.

**v.15–1494 BC**
See footnote, *Time,* Rev. 10:6.

**16**
*g Gad, tribe of,* Deut. 33:20.
*h Reubenites,* Josh. 22:1.
*i Shepherd,* Jer.31: 10.

**19**
*j Jordan,* Gen. 32: 10.

**20**
*k Moses,* Ex. 2:10.
*l War,* Judg. 3:2.

**22**
*m Canaan,* Gen. 37:1.
*n Gilead,* Deut. 3:13.

**23**
*o Sin, known to God,* Rom. 5:12
*p Wicked, punishment of,* Psa. 73:3.

† **MISJUDGMENT. Instances of:** *Of the Reubenites and Gadites,* Num. 32:1–33; Josh. 22:11–31. *Of Hannah,* 1 Sam. 1:14–17. See footnote, UNCHARITABLENESS, Matt. 7:1.

v.26–1494 BC
See footnote, *Time*, Rev. 10:6.

26 Our little ones, our wives,
our flocks, and all our cattle,
shall be there in the cities of
[n]Gĭl'e-ăd:
27 But thy servants will pass
over, every man armed for [l]war,
before the LORD to battle, as my
lord saith.
28 So concerning them [k]Mō'ṣeṣ
commanded [q]Ē-le-ā'zar the
priest, and [r]Jŏsh'u-ȧ the son of
Nŭn, and the chief fathers of the
tribes of the children of Ĭṣ'ra-el:
29 And Mō'ṣeṣ said unto them,
If the children of [g]Găd and the
[h]children of Reu̯'ben will pass
with you over [j]Jôr'dan, every
man armed to [l]battle, before the
LORD, and the [m]land shall be
subdued before you; then ye
shall give them the land of [n]Gĭl'-
e-ăd for a possession:
30 But if they will not pass over
with you armed, they shall have
possessions among you in the
land of [m]Cā'năan.
31 And the children of [g]Găd
and the [h]children of Reu̯'ben
answered, saying, As the LORD
hath said unto thy servants, so
will we do.
32 We will pass over armed before the LORD into the land of
[m]Cā'năan, that the possession of
our inheritance on this side Jôr'-
dan *may be* our's.
33 And Mō'ṣeṣ gave unto them,
*even* to the children of [g]Găd, and
to the [h]children of Reu̯'ben, and
unto half the tribe of [s]Mȧ-năs'-
seh the son of Jō'ṣeph, the kingdom of [t]Sī'hŏn king of the [u]Ăm'-
ôr-ītes, and the kingdom of [v]Ŏg
king of ‡Bā'shăn, the land, with
the cities thereof in the coasts,
*even* the cities of the country
round about.

34 ¶ And the children of Găd
built [w]Dī'bŏn, and Ăt'a-rŏth,
and [x]Ăr'ŏ-ĕr,
35 And Ăt'rŏth, Shō'phan, and
[y]Jȧ-ā'zĕr, and [z]Jŏg'be-hah,
36 And Bĕth–nĭm'rah, and
[a]Bĕth–hā'ran, [b]fenced cities: and
folds for sheep.
37 And the [c]children of Reu̯'-
ben built [d]Hĕsh'bŏn, and [e]Ē-le-
ā'leh, and ‖Kĭr-jath-ā'im,
38 And *Nē'bō, and §Bā'al-
mē'on, (their names being
changed,) and Shĭb'mah: and
gave other names unto the [b]cities
which they builded.
39 And the children of [f]Mā'-
chĭr the son of Mȧ-năs'seh went
to [g]Gĭl'e-ăd, and took it, and dispossessed the [h]Ăm'ôr-īte which
*was* in it.
40 And Mō'ṣeṣ gave [g]Gĭl'e-ăd
unto [f]Mā'chĭr the son of Mȧ-
năs'seh; and he dwelt therein.
41 And [i]Jā'īr the son of Mȧ-
năs'seh went and took the small
towns thereof, and called them
[j]Hā'voth–jā'īr.
42 And Nō'bah went and took
[k]Kē'năth, and the villages thereof, and called it Nō'bah, after
his own name.

## CHAPTER 33

*Forty-two journeys of the Israelites. 50 The Canaanites are to be destroyed. 54 Law for allotment of inheritances in Canaan.*

THESE *are* the [a]journeys of
the children of [b]Ĭṣ'ra-el,
which went forth out of the land
of [c]Ē'ġy̆pt with their armies under the hand of [d]Mō'ṣeṣ and
[e]Aâr'on.
2 And [d]Mō'ṣeṣ wrote their goings out according to their [a]jour-
neys by the commandment of
the LORD: and these *are* their

28
q *Eleazar*, Num. 3:2.
r *Joshua*, Josh. 1:1.

33
s *Manasseh, tribe of*, Gen. 46:20.
t *Sihon*, Num. 21:21.
u *Amorites, territory of*, Gen. 14:13.
v *Og*, Num. 31:33.

v.34–1494 BC
See footnote, *Time*, Rev. 10:6.

34
w *Dibon*, Num. 21:30.
x Josh. 13:25; Judg. 11:33.

35
y Or, *Jazer*, Josh. 13:25.
z Judg. 8:11.

36
a Or, *Beth-aram*, Josh. 13:27.
b *Cities, fortified*, Num. 35:8.

37
c *Reubenites*, Josh. 22:1.
d *Heshbon*, Isa. 16:8.
e Isa. 15:4; 16:9.

39
f *Machir*, Gen. 50:23.
g *Gilead*, Deut. 3:13.
h *Amorites*, Gen. 14:13.

41
i *Jair*, Josh. 13:30.
j *Havoth-jair*, Judg. 10:4.

42
k 1 Chr. 2:23.

1
a *Itinerary, of the Israelites*, vs. 1–56; Deut. 10:6,7.
b *Israel, itinerary of*, vs. 1–56; Ex. 4:22.
c *Egypt*, Gen. 41:8.
d *Moses*, Ex. 2:10.
e *Aaron*, Ex. 6:20.

‡ **BASHAN** (*light or sandy soil*), a region E. of the Jordan and N. of Arnon. *Og, king of*, Josh. 13:12. *Allotted to the two and one-half tribes, which had their possession E. of the Jordan*, Num. 32:33; Deut. 3:10–14; Josh. 12:4–6; 13:29–31; 17:1. *Invaded and taken by Hazael, king of Syria*, 2 Kin. 10:32, 33. *Retaken by Jehoash*, 2 Kin. 13:25. *Fertility and productiveness of*, Isa. 33:9; Jer. 50:19; Nah. 1:4. *Forests of, famous*, Isa. 2:13; Ezek. 27:6, Zech. 11:2. *Distinguished for its fine cattle*, Deut. 32:14; Psa. 22:12; Ezek. 39:18; Amos 4:1; Mic. 7:14.

‖ **KIRJATHAIM** (*double city*), called also KIRIATHAIM. *A city of Reuben*, Num. 32:37; Josh. 13:19. *Prophecies concerning*, Jer. 48:1, 23; Ezek. 25:9.

§ **BAAL-MEON** (*lord of dwelling*). *A city of the Reubenites*, Num. 32:38; 1 Chr. 5:8; Ezek. 25:9. *Called* BETH-MEON, Jer. 48:23; BETH-BAAL-MEON, Josh. 13:17; BEON, Num. 32:3.

v.2–1494 BC
See footnote, *Time*, Rev. 10:6.

3
[f] *Rameses*, Gen. 47:11.
[g] *Abib*, Ex. 13:4.
[h] *Month*, Ex. 12:2.
[i] *Passover*, Num. 9:5.

4
[j] *Egyptians, firstborn of, destroyed*, Gen. 50:3.
[k] *Firstborn, of Egyptians, slain*, Zech. 12:10.
[l] *Judgments*, Ex. 6:6.
[m] *Idolatry*, 1 Sam. 15:23.

5
[n] *Succoth*, Ex. 12:37.

6
[o] Ex. 13:20.

7
[p] Ex. 14:2, 9.
[q] Ex. 14:2, 9.
[r] Ex. 14:2.

8
[s] *Red Sea, Israelites cross*, Ex. 10:19.
[t] Ex. 15:22–25.

9
[u] Ex. 15:27.

11
[v] *Sin, wilderness of*, Ex. 17:1.

journeys according to their goings out.
3 And they departed from [f]Ră-
mē′sēṣ in the [g]first [h]month, on
the fifteenth day of the first
month; on the morrow after the
[i]passover the children of Ĭṣ′ra-el
went out with an high hand in
the sight of all the Ė-ġy̆p′tianṣ.
4 For the [j]Ė-ġy̆p′tianṣ buried
all *their* [k]firstborn, which the
LORD had [l]smitten among them:
upon [m]their gods also the LORD
executed judgments.
5 And the children of [b]Ĭṣ′ra-el
removed from [f]Ră-mē′sēṣ, and
pitched in [n]Sŭc′coth.
6 And [b]they departed from
[n]Sŭc′coth, and pitched in
[o]Ē′tham, which *is* in the edge
of the wilderness.
7 And [b]they removed from
[o]Ē′tham, and turned again
unto [p]Pī′–ha-hī′roth, which *is*
before [q]Bā′al–zē′phon: and they
pitched before [r]Mĭg′dol.
8 And [b]they departed from before [p]Pī′–ha-hī′roth, and passed
through the midst of the [s]sea into the wilderness, and went three
days' journey in the wilderness
of Ē′tham, and pitched in [t]Mā′-
rah.
9 And [b]they removed from
[t]Mā′rah, and came unto [u]Ē′lim:
and in Ē′lim *were* twelve fountains of water, and threescore
and ten palm trees; and they
pitched there.
10 And they removed from
Ē′lim, and encamped by the
[s]Red sea.
11 And they removed from the
[s]Red sea, and encamped in the
wilderness of [v]Sĭn.
12 And they took their journey
out of the wilderness of [v]Sĭn, and
encamped in Dŏph′kah.
13 And they departed from
Dŏph′kah, and encamped in
Ā′lụsh.
14 And [b]they removed from
Ā′lụsh, and encamped at
[w]Rĕph′i-dĭm, where was no water for the people to drink.
15 And [b]they departed from
[w]Rĕph′i-dĭm, and pitched in the
wilderness of [x]Sī′nāi.
16 And they removed from the
desert of [x]Sī′nāi, and pitched at
[y]Kĭb′roth–hat-tā′a-vah.
17 And they departed from
[y]Kĭb′roth–hat-tā′a-vah, and encamped at [z]Hȧ-zē′roth.
18 And [a]they departed from
Hȧ-zē′roth, and pitched in Rĭth′-
mah.
19 And [a]they departed from
Rĭth′mah, and pitched at Rĭm′-
mon–pā′rez.
20 And [a]they departed from
Rĭm′mon–pā′rez, and pitched in
Lĭb′nah.
21 And they removed from
Lĭb′nah, and pitched at Rĭs′sah.
22 And [a]they journeyed from
Rĭs′sah, and pitched in Kĕ-hĕl′-
a-thah.
23 And [a]they went from Kĕ-
hĕl′a-thah, and pitched in mount
Shā′pher.
24 And [a]they removed from
mount Shā′pher, and encamped
in Hăr′a-dah.
25 And [a]they removed from
Hăr′a-dah, and pitched in Măk-
hē′loth.
26 And [a]they removed from
Măk-hē′loth, and encamped at
Tā′hăth.
27 And [a]they departed from
Tā′hăth, and pitched at Tā′rah.
28 And [a]they removed from
Tā′rah, and pitched in Mĭth′-
cah.
29 And [a]they went from Mĭth′-
cah, and pitched in Hăsh-mō′-
nah.
30 And [a]they departed from
Hăsh-mō′nah, and encamped at
Mō-sē′roth.
31 And [a]they departed from
Mō-sē′roth, and pitched in [b]Bĕn-
e–jā′a-kăn.

14
[w] *Rephidim*, Ex. 17:1.

15
[x] *Sinai, wilderness of*, Ex. 16:1.
16
[y] *Kibroth-hattaavah*, Num. 11:34.
17
[z] *Hazeroth*, Num. 11:35.

18
[a] *Israel, itinerary of*, Ex. 4:22.

31
[b] Deut. 10:6.

32 And [a]they removed from Běn-e-jā'a-kăn, and encamped at [c]Hôr'-hā-ġĭd'găd.

33 And [a]they went from [c]Hôr'-hā-ġĭd'găd, and pitched in Jŏt'ba-thah.

34 And [a]they removed from Jŏt'ba-thah, and encamped at Ē-brō'nah.

35 And [a]they departed from Ē-brō'nah, and encamped at *Ē'zĭ-on-gā'bĕr.

36 And [a]they removed from *Ē'zĭ-on-gā'bĕr, and pitched in the wilderness of [d]Zĭn, which *is* [e]Kā'desh.

37 And [a]they removed from [e]Kā'desh, and pitched in mount [f]Hôr, in the edge of the land of [g]Ē'dom.

38 And [h]Aâr'on the priest went up into mount [f]Hôr at the commandment of the LORD, and died there, in the fortieth year after the children of [a]Iṣ'ra-el were come out of the land of [i]Ē'ġўpt, in the first *day* of the fifth [j]month.

39 And [h]Aâr'on *was* an [k]hundred and twenty and three years old when he died in mount [f]Hôr.

40 And [1]king [l]Ā'răd the [m]Cā'năan-īte, which dwelt in the south in the land of Cā'năan, heard of the coming of the children of Iṣ'ra-el.

41 And [a]they departed from mount [f]Hôr, and pitched in Zăl-mō'nah.

42 And [a]they departed from Zăl-mō'nah, and pitched in Pū'non.

43 And [a]they departed from Pū'non, and pitched in [n]Ō'both.

44 And they departed from [n]Ō'both, and pitched in [o]Ĭj'e-ăb'a-rĭm, in the border of [p]Mō'ab.

45 And [a]they departed from Ī'ĭm, and pitched in [q]Dī'bŏn-găd.

46 And [a]they removed from Dī'bŏn-găd, and encamped in [r]Ăl'mŏn-dĭb-la-thā'ĭm.

47 And [a]they removed from [r]Ăl'mŏn-dĭb-la-thā'ĭm, and pitched in the mountains of [s]Ăb'a-rĭm, before Nē'bō.

48 And [a]they departed from the mountains of [s]Ăb'a-rĭm, and pitched in the plains of [p]Mō'ab by [t]Jôr'dan *near* [u]Jĕr'ĭ-chō.

49 And [a]they pitched by Jôr'dan, from [v]Bĕth-jĕs'i-mŏth *even* unto [w]Ā'bel-shĭt'tim in the plains of Mō'ab.

50 ¶ And the LORD spake unto [x]Mō'ṣeṣ in the plains of [s]Mō'ab by [t]Jôr'dan *near* [u]Jĕr'ĭ-chō, saying,

51 Speak unto the children of Iṣ'ra-el, and say unto them, When ye are passed over [t]Jôr'dan into the land of [y]Cān'ăan;

52 Then ye shall drive out all the inhabitants of the [y]land from before you, and destroy all their [2]pictures, and †destroy all their molten [z]images, and quite [a]pluck down all their high places:

53 And ye shall dispossess *the inhabitants of* the [b]land, and dwell therein: for I have given you the land to possess it.

54 And ye shall divide the [b]land by [c]lot for an inheritance among your families: *and* to the more ye shall give the more inheritance, and to the fewer ye shall give the less inheritance: every man's *inheritance* shall be in the place where his lot falleth; according to the tribes of your fathers ye shall inherit.

55 But if ye will not drive out the [d]inhabitants of the land from

32
c *Probably identical with Gudgodah*, Deut. 10:7.

36
d *Zin*, Num. 13:21.
e *Kadesh*, Gen. 14:7.

37
f *Hor*, Num. 20:22.
g *Edom*, Obad. 1.

38
h *Aaron, death of*, Ex. 6:20.
i *Egypt*, Gen. 41:8.
j *Month, Ab (August)*, Ex. 12:2.

v.39–1494 BC
See footnote, *Time*, Rev. 10:6.

39
k *Longevity, instances of*, Psa. 91:16.

40
l *Arad*, Num. 21:1.
m *Canaanites*, Ex. 23:28.
1 R. V. king of Arad,

43
n Num. 21:10, 11.

44
o Num. 21:11.
p *Moab*, Num. 26:3.

v.45–1494 BC
See footnote, *Time*, Rev. 10:6.

45
q *Dibon*, Num. 21:30.

46
r Or, *Beth-diblathaim*, Jer. 48:22 or, *Diblath*, Ezek 6:14.

47
s *Abarim*, Num. 27:12.

48
t *Jordan*, Gen. 32:10.
u *Jericho*, Num. 22:1.

49
v *Beth-jesimoth*, Josh. 12:3.
w Or, *Shittim*, Num. 25:1.

50
x *Moses*, Ex. 2:15.

51
y *Canaan*, Gen. 37:1.

52
z *Idolatry, objects of*, 1 Sam. 15:23.

a *High Places, idolatrous, to be destroyed*, 1 Kin. 3:2.
2 R. V. figured stones,

53
b *Canaan*, Gen. 37:1.

54
c *Lot, the land of Canaan divided among the tribes by*, Esth. 3:7.

55
d *Evil Company, perils of*, Prov. 13:20.

* **EZION-GABER** (*the giant backbone*). *Last encampment of Israel before coming to the wilderness of Zin*, Num. 33:35, 36; Deut. 2:8. *Solomon built a navy at*, 1 Kin. 9:26. *Solomon visits*, 2 Chr. 8:17. *Jehoshaphat built a navy at*, 2 Chr. 20:36. *Ships of Jehoshaphat wrecked at*, 1 Kin. 22:48.

† **ICONOCLASM.** *Idols to be destroyed*, Ex. 23:24; 34:13; Num. 33:52; Deut. 7:5, 25, 26; 12:1–4; Judg. 2:2; Jer. 50:2. *Idols destroyed, by Moses*, Ex. 32:20; *by Gideon*, Judg. 6:28–32; *by David*, 2 Sam. 5:21; 1 Chr. 14:12; *by Jehu*, 2 Kin. 10:26–28; *by Jehoiada*, 2 Kin. 11:18; *by Hezekiah*, 2 Kin. 18:3–6; *by Josiah*, 2 Kin. 23:4–20; *by Asa*, 2 Chr. 14:3–5; 15:8–16; *by Jehoshaphat*, 2 Chr. 17:6; 19:3; *by the Jews*, 2 Chr. 30:14; *by Manasseh*, 2 Chr. 33:15.
See footnotes: IDOL, 1 Kin. 15:12; IDOLATRY, 1 Sam. 15:23.

before you; then it shall come to pass, that [e]those which ye let remain of them *shall be* pricks in your eyes, and [f]thorns in your sides, and shall vex you in the land wherein ye dwell.

56 Moreover it shall come to pass, *that* I shall do unto you, as I thought to do unto them.

## CHAPTER 34

*The borders of the promised land. 16 The names of the men appointed to divide it.*

AND the LORD [a]spake unto [b]Mō′ṣeṣ, saying,

2 Command the children of Ĭṣ′ra-el, and say unto them, When ye come into the [c]land of Cā′năan; (this *is* the land that shall fall unto you for an inheritance, *even* the land of Cā′năan with the [d]coasts thereof:)

3 Then [d]your south quarter shall be from the wilderness of [e]Zĭn along by the coast of [f]Ē′dom, and your south border shall be the outmost coast of the salt sea eastward:

4 And your border shall turn from the south to the ascent of [g]Ȧ-krăb′bim, and pass on to [e]Zĭn: and the going forth thereof shall be from the south to [h]Kā′desh-bär′ne-ȧ, and shall go on to [i]Hā′zar-ăd′dar, and pass on to [j]Ăz′mŏn:

5 And the [d]border shall fetch a compass from [j]Ăz′mŏn unto the [1]river of [k]Ē′ġȳpt, and the goings out of it shall be at the sea.

6 And *as for* the [d]western border, ye shall even have the [l]great sea for a border: this shall be your west border.

7 And this shall be your [d]north border: from the [l]great sea ye shall point out for you mount [m]Hôr:

8 From mount [m]Hôr ye shall point out *your border* unto the entrance of [n]Hā′math; and the goings forth of the [d]border shall be to [o]Zē′dăd:

9 And the border shall go on to Zĭph′rŏn, and the goings out of it shall be at [p]Hā′zar-ē′nan: this shall be your north border.

10 And ye shall point out your [d]east border from [p]Hā′zar-ē′nan to Shē′pham:

11 And the [d]coast shall go down from Shē′pham to *Rĭb′lah, on the east side of Ā′in; and the border shall descend, and shall reach unto the side of the [q]sea of Chĭn′ne-rĕth eastward:

12 And the border shall go down to [r]Jôr′dan, and the goings of it shall be at the [s]salt sea: this shall be your land with the coasts thereof round about.

13 And Mō′ṣeṣ commanded the children of Ĭṣ′ra-el, saying, This *is* the [t]land which ye shall inherit by [u]lot, which the LORD commanded to give unto the nine tribes, and to the half tribe:

14 For the tribe of the [v]children of Reu′ben according to the house of their fathers, and the tribe of the children of [w]Găd according to the house of their fathers, have received *their inheritance*; and half the tribe of [x]Mȧ-năs′seh have received their inheritance:

15 The two tribes and the half tribe have received their inheritance on this side [r]Jôr′dan *near* [y]Jĕr′ĭ-chō eastward, toward the sunrising.

16 ¶ And the LORD spake unto Mō′ṣeṣ, saying,

17 These *are* the names of the [z]men which shall divide the [a]land unto you: [b]Ē-le-ā′zar the priest, and [c]Jŏsh′u-ȧ the son of Nŭn.

18 And ye shall take one prince of every tribe, to divide the land by inheritance.

v.55–1494 BC
See footnote, *Time*, Rev. 10:6.

e *Fellowship, with the wicked,* 1 Cor. 1:9.
f *Thorn, figurative,* Hos. 2:6.

1
a *Revelation, defining the boundaries of Canaan,* 2 Cor. 12:1.
b *Prophets, inspiration of,* Isa. 3:2.

2
c *Canaanites, territory of,* vs. 2–12; Ex. 23:28.
d *Topography,* Josh. 13:16.

3
e *Zin,* Num. 13:21.
f *Edom,* Obad. 1.

4
g Josh. 15:3; Judg. 1:36.
h *Kadesh,* Gen. 14:7.
i Or, *Addar,* Josh. 15:3.
j Josh. 15:4.

5
k *Egypt, river of,* Gen. 15:18.
1 R. V. brook

6
l *Mediterranean Sea,* Ex. 23:31.

7
m *Hor,* Num. 20:22.

8
n *Hamath,* 1 Chr. 18:3.

v.8–1494 BC
See footnote, *Time*, Rev. 10:6.

o Ezek. 47:15.

9
p Ezek. 47:17; 48:1.

11
q *Sea of Galilee,* Matt. 4:18.

12
r *Jordan,* Gen. 32:10.
s *Dead Sea,* Gen. 14:3.

13
t *Canaan, divided by lot,* Gen. 37:1.
u *Lot, Canaan divided by,* Esth. 3:7.

14
v *Reubenites,* Josh. 22:1.
w *Gad,* Deut. 33:20.
x *Manasseh, tribe of,* Gen. 46:20.

15
y *Jericho,* Num. 22:1.

17
z *Israel, men chosen to allot the land of Canaan,* vs. 17–29; Ex. 4:22.

a *Canaan, divided by lot,* Gen. 37:1.
b *Eleazar,* Num. 3:2.
c *Joshua,* Josh. 1:1.

* **RIBLAH** (*fertility*). *A border town of the promised land,* Num. 34:10, 11. *King Jehoahaz overthrown in, by Pharaoh,* 2 Kin. 23:33. *Headquarters of Nebuchadnezzar in siege of Jerusalem,* 2 Kin. 25:6, 20, 21; Jer. 39:5, 6; 52:9, 26.

v.19–1494 BC
See footnote, *Time*, Rev. 10:6.

19
*d* *Judah, tribe of,* Num. 10:14.
*e* *Caleb,* Num. 14:6.
20
*f* *Simeon, tribe of,* Num. 2:12.
21
*g* *Benjamin, tribe of,* Num. 1:37.
22
*h* *Dan, tribe of,* Gen. 30:6.
23
*i* *Manasseh, tribe of,* Gen. 46:20.
24
*j* *Ephraim, tribe of,* Gen. 41:52.
25
*k* *Zebulun, tribe of,* Gen. 49:13.
26
*l* *Issachar, tribe of,* Num. 1:28.
27
*m* *Asher, tribe of,* Num. 1:40.
28
*n* *Naphtali, tribe of,* Num. 1:42.

19 And the names of the men *are* these: Of the tribe of [d]Jū'dah, [e]Cā'leb the son of Jĕ-phŭn'neh.

20 And of the tribe of the children of [f]Sĭm'e-on, Shĕ-mū'el the son of Ăm-mī'hŭd.

21 Of the tribe of [g]Bĕn'ja-mĭn, Ĕ-lī'dăd the son of Chĭs'lon.

22 And the prince of the tribe of the children of [h]Dăn, Bŭk'kī the son of Jŏg'lī.

23 The prince of the children of Jō'ṣeph, for the tribe of the children of [i]Mă-năs'seh, Hăn'nĭ-el the son of Ē'phŏd.

24 And the prince of the tribe of the children of [j]Ē'phră-ĭm, Kĕ-mū'el of the son of Shĭph'tan.

25 And the prince of the tribe of the children of [k]Zĕb'u-lŭn, Ĕ-lĭz'a-phăn the son of Pär'-năch.

26 And the prince of the tribe of the children of [l]Ĭs'sa-char, Păl'tĭ-el the son of Ăz'zan.

27 And the prince of the tribe of the children of [m]Ăsh'ēr, Ă-hī'-hụd the son of Shĕl'o-mī.

28 And the prince of the tribe of the children of [n]Năph'ta-lī, Pĕd'a-hĕl the son of Ăm-mī'-hŭd.

29 These *are they* whom the LORD commanded to divide the inheritance unto the children of Ĭṣ'ra-el in the land of [a]Cā'năan.

## CHAPTER 35

*Forty-eight cities with their suburbs are to be given to the Levites. 6 Six of them to be cities of refuge. 9 The laws concerning manslaying and murder. 31 No satisfaction to be taken for the life of the murderer.*

1
*a* *Moab,* Num. 26:3.
*b* *Jordan,* Gen. 32:10.
*c* *Jericho,* Num. 22:1.

1 AND the LORD spake unto Mō'ṣeṣ in the plains of [a]Mō'ab by [b]Jôr'dan *near* [c]Jĕr'ĭ-chō, saying,

v.2–1494 BC
See footnote, *Time*, Rev. 10:6.

2
*d* *Levites, emoluments of,* Deut. 10:8.
*e* Josh. 14:4.

2 Command the children of Ĭṣ'ra-el, that they give unto the Lē'vītes of the inheritance of their possession *,[d]cities to dwell in; and ye shall give *also* unto the Lē'vītes [e]suburbs for the cities round about them.

3 And the *,[d]cities shall they have to dwell in; and the [e]suburbs of them shall be for their cattle, and for their goods, and for all their beasts.

4 And the [e]suburbs of the *,[d]cities, which ye shall give unto the Lē'vītes, *shall reach* from the wall of the city and outward a thousand cubits round about.

5 And ye shall measure from without the city on the east side two thousand cubits, and on the south side two thousand cubits, and on the west side two thousand cubits, and on the north side two thousand cubits; and the city *shall be* in the midst: this shall be to them the [e]suburbs of the cities.

6 And among the [d]cities which ye shall give unto the Lē'vītes *there shall be* six *cities for refuge, which ye shall appoint for the manslayer, that he may flee thither: and to them ye shall add forty and two cities.

7 *So* all the [d]cities which ye shall give to the Lē'vītes *shall be* forty and eight cities: them *shall ye give* with their suburbs.

8
*f* *Liberality, according to ability,* 1 Tim. 6:18.

8 And the *cities which ye shall give *shall be* of the possession of the children of Ĭṣ'ra-el: from *them that have* many ye shall [f]give many; but from *them that have* few ye shall give few: every one shall give of his [d]cities unto the Lē'vītes according to his inheritance which he inheriteth.

* **CITIES.** *Ancient,* Gen. 4:17; 10:10-12. *Fortified,* Num. 32:36; Deut. 9:1; Josh. 10:20; 14:12; 2 Chr. 8:5; 11:10-12; 17:2, 19; 21:3; Isa. 23:11. *Gates of,* Deut. 3:5; Josh. 6:26; 1 Sam. 23:7; 2 Sam. 18:24; 2 Chr. 8:5.
Designated as: *Royal,* Josh. 10:2; 1 Sam. 27:5; 2 Sam. 12:26; 1 Chr. 11:7; *treasure,* Gen. 41:48; Ex. 1:11; 1 Kin. 9:19; 2 Chr. 8:4; 16:4; 17:12; *chariot,* 2 Chr. 1:14; 8:6; 9:25; *merchant,* Isa. 23:11; Ezek. 17:4; 27:3.
*Town clerk of,* Acts 19:35. *Government of, by rulers,* Neh. 3:9, 12, 17, 18; 7:2.
*Suburbs of,* Num. 35:3-5; Josh. 14:4.
**Figurative,** Heb. 11:10, 16; 12:22; 13:14.
**Priestly,** Josh. 21:1-4, 13-19; 1 Chr. 6:57-60; Neh. 11:3, 20.
**Levitical,** Lev. 25:32; Num. 35:2-8; Josh. 14:4; 1 Chr. 6:54-81; 13:2.
**Refuge:** *From the avenger of blood,* Ex. 21:13, 14; Num

v.9–1494 BC See footnote, *Time*, Rev. 10:6.

9 *g Prophets, inspiration of*, Isa. 3:2.
10 *h Canaan*, Gen. 37:1.
11 *i Homicide, accidental*, Deut. 5:17.
12 *j Court*, Ex. 18:26.
15 *k Foreigners, privilege of, under Mosaic law*, Deut. 23:20.
1 R. V. unwittingly
16 *l Homicide, felonious*, Deut. 5:17.
*m Iron*, Prov. 27:17.
*n Punishment, death penalty*, Lev. 26:41.
*o Death, penalty*, Num. 23:10.
2 R. V. manslayer:
19 *p Avenger of Blood*, Deut. 19:6.
3 R. V. avenger

9 ¶ And the LORD spake unto
[g]Mō′şeş, saying,
10 Speak unto the children of
Ĭş′ra-el, and say unto them,
When ye be come over [b]Jôr′dan
into the land of [h]Cā′năan;
11 Then ye shall appoint you
cities to be *cities of refuge for
you; that the slayer may flee
thither, which [i]killeth any person
at unawares.
12 And they shall be unto you
*cities for refuge from the avenger;
that the manslayer die not,
until he stand before the [j]congregation
in judgment.
13 And of these *cities which
ye shall give six cities shall ye
have for refuge.
14 Ye shall give three *cities
on this side [b]Jôr′dan, and three
cities shall ye give in the land of
[h]Cā′năan, *which* shall be cities
of refuge.
15 These six *cities shall be a
refuge, *both* for the children of
Ĭş′ra-el, and for the [k]stranger,
and for the sojourner among
them: that every one that [i]killeth
any person [1]unawares may flee
thither.
16 And if he [l]smite him with an
instrument of [m]iron, so that he
die, he *is* a [2]murderer: the [2]murderer
shall surely be [n]put to
[o]death.
17 And if he [l]smite him with
throwing a stone, wherewith he
may die, and he die, he *is* a
[2]murderer: the [2]murderer shall
surely be [n]put to [o]death.
18 Or *if* he [l]smite him with an
hand weapon of wood, wherewith
he may die, and he die, he
*is* a [2]murderer: the [2]murderer
shall surely be [n]put to [o]death.
19 The [3,p]revenger of blood
himself shall [n]slay the [2]murderer:
when he meeteth him, he
shall slay him.

20 But if he [l]thrust him of hatred,
or hurl at him by laying of
wait, that he die;
21 Or in enmity [l]smite with his
hand, that he die: he that smote
*him* shall surely be [n]put to
[o]death; *for* he *is* a [2]murderer:
the [3,p]revenger of blood shall
[n]slay the [2]murderer, when he
meeteth him.
22 But if he [i]thrust him suddenly
without enmity, or have
cast upon him any thing without
laying of wait,
23 Or with any stone, wherewith
a man may die, seeing
*him* not, and cast *it* upon
him, [i]that he die, and *was* not
his enemy, neither sought his
harm:
24 Then the [j]congregation shall
judge between the [4]slayer and
the [3,p]revenger of blood according
to these judgments:
25 And the [j]congregation shall
deliver the slayer out of the hand
of the [3,p]revenger of blood, and
the congregation shall restore
him to the *city of his refuge,
whither he was fled: and he shall
abide in it unto the death of the
[q]high priest, which was [r]anointed
with the holy [s]oil.
26 But if the slayer shall at any
time come without the border of
the *city of his refuge, whither
he was fled;
27 And the [3,p]revenger of blood
find him without the borders of
the *city of his refuge, and the
[3,p]revenger of blood kill the
slayer; he shall not be guilty of
blood:
28 Because he should have remained
in the *city of his refuge
until the death of the [q]high
priest: but after the death of the
high priest the slayer shall return
into the land of his possession.

v.20–1494 BC See footnote, *Time*, Rev. 10:6.

24 4 R V. smiter
25 *q High Priest*, Lev. 21:10.
*r Anointing*, Lev. 8:12.
*s Oil, sacred*, Deut. 12:17.

35:6, 11–32; Deut. 4:41–43; 19:2–13; Josh. 20:1–6. *List of*, Josh. 20:7–9. *Roads made to*, Deut. 19:3. FIGURATIVE: *Of Christ*, Heb. 6:18.

v.29–1494 BC
See footnote, *Time,* Rev. 10:6.

30
*Evidence,* Deut. 17:6.
*Punishment, death penalty, not inflicted on testimony of less than two witnesses,* Lev. 26:41.

31
*Ransom,* Ex. 21: 30.
*Punishment, death penalty, not to be remitted,* Lev. 26:41.
R.V. ransom

34
*Defilement,* Lev. 5:2.

1
*Gilead, grandson of Manasseh,* Num. 26:29.
*Machir,* Gen. 50:23.
*Manasseh, tribe of,* Gen. 46:20.
*Petition, right of, recognized by Israel,* vs. 1–5; Esth. 5:6.
*Government, Mosaic,* Isa. 22:21.
*Israel,* Ex. 4:22.

2
*Property, in real estate,* Lev. 27: 15.

29 So these *things* shall be for a
statute of judgment unto you
throughout your generations in
all your dwellings.
30 Whoso [l]killeth any person,
the [2]murderer shall be [n]put to
[o]death by the [t]mouth of †wit-
nesses: but [u]one witness shall
not testify against any person *to*
*cause him* to die.
31 Moreover ye shall take no
[5,v]satisfaction for the life of a
[2]murderer, which *is* guilty of
death: but [w]he shall be surely
put to death.
32 And ye shall take no [5,v]sat-
isfaction for him that is fled to
the *city of his refuge, that he
should come again to dwell in
the land, until the death of the
[q]priest.
33 So ye shall not pollute the
land wherein ye *are*: for blood it
defileth the land: and the land
cannot be cleansed of the blood
that is shed therein, but by the
blood of him that shed it.
34 [x]Defile not therefore the
land which ye shall inherit,
wherein I dwell: for I the LORD
dwell among the children of
Iṣ′ra-el.

## CHAPTER 36

*The inheritance of daughters secured to their own tribe by their marrying only in that tribe. 10 The daughters of Zelophehad marry their father's brothers' sons.*

AND the chief fathers of the
families of the children of
[a]Gĭl′e-ăd, the son of [b]Mā′chir,
the son of [c]Mā-năs′seh, of the
families of the sons of Jō′ṣeph,
came near, and [d]spake before
[e]Mō′ṣeṣ, and before the princes,
the chief fathers of the children
of [f]Iṣ′ra-el:
2 And they [d]said, The LORD
commanded my lord to give the
[g]land for an inheritance by lot to
the children of [f]Iṣ′ra-el: and my
lord was commanded by the
LORD to give the [h]inheritance of
[i]Zĕ-lō′phe-hăd our brother unto
his [j,k,l]daughters.
3 And if [j,l]they be married to
any of the sons of the *other* tribes
of the children of [f]Iṣ′ra-el, then
shall their [g]inheritance be taken
from the inheritance of our fathers, and shall be put to the inheritance of the tribe whereunto
they [1]are received: so shall it be
taken from the lot of our inheritance.
4 And when the [m]jubile of the
children of [f]Iṣ′ra-el shall be,
then shall their [g]inheritance be
put unto the inheritance of the
tribe whereunto they are received: so shall their inheritance
be taken away from the inheritance of the tribe of our
fathers.
5 And Mō′ṣeṣ commanded the
children of Iṣ′ra-el according to
the word of the LORD, saying,
The [c]tribe of the sons of Jō′ṣeph
hath [d]said well.
6 This *is* the thing which the
LORD doth command concerning the daughters of [i]Zĕ-lō′phe-
hăd, saying, Let them [n]marry to
whom they think best; only to
the family of the tribe of their
father shall they marry.
7 So shall not the [g,o]inheritance
of the children of [f]Iṣ′ra-el remove from tribe to tribe: for
every one of the children of Iṣ′-
ra-el shall keep himself to the inheritance of the tribe of his
fathers.
8 And every [j,l]daughter, that
possesseth an [g,o]inheritance in
any tribe of the children of Iṣ′-
ra-el, shall be [n]wife unto one of
the family of the tribe of her fa-

v.2 1494 BC
See footnote, *Time,* Rev. 10:6.

h *Land, unmarried woman's rights in,* Ruth 4:3.
i *Zelophehad,* Num. 27:1.
j *Daughters, property rights of,* Lev. 12:6.
k *Heir, Mosaic law relating to inheritance of,* Gen. 15:3.
l *Women, property rights of,* Prov. 31:10.

3
1 R V. shall belong:

4
m *Jubilee, laws concerning,* Lev. 25: 10.

6
n *Marriage, Mosaic laws concerning,* Gen. 34:9.

7
o *Inheritance, provision for, under Levirate marriages,* vs. 6–9; Num. 27:7.

† **WITNESS,** Lev. 5:1; Prov. 18:17. *Qualified, by oath,* Ex. 22:11; Num. 5:19; 1 Kin. 8:31, 32; *by laying hands on the accused,* Lev. 24:14. *Two, necessary to establish a fact,* Num. 35:30; Deut. 17:6; 19:15; Matt. 18:16; John 8:17; 2 Cor. 13:1; 1 Tim. 5:19; Heb. 10:28. *Required to cast the first stone in executing sentence,* Deut. 13:9; 17:5–7; Acts 7:58. *To the transfer of land,* Gen. 23:11, 16–18; Ruth 4:1–9; Jer. 32:9–12, 25, 44. *To marriage,* Ruth 4:10, 11. *Incorruptible,* Psa. 15:4. *Corrupted by money,* Matt. 28:11–15; Acts 6:11, 13.
See footnote, FALSE WITNESS, Matt. 19:18.

v.8–1494 BC
See footnote, *Time*,
Rev. 10:6.

ther, that the children of [f]Is̱′ra-el
may enjoy every man the inheritance of his fathers.
9 Neither shall the [g,o]inherit-
ance remove[c] from *one* tribe to
another tribe; but every one of
the tribes of the children of Is̱′-
ra-el shall keep himself to his
own inheritance.
10 Even as the LORD com-
manded Mō′ṣeṣ, so did the
daughters of [i]Zē-lō′phe-hăd:
11 For [p]Mäh′lah, [q]Tĭr′zah, and
[r]Hŏg′lah, and [s]Mĭl′cah, and
[t]Nō′ah, the daughters of [i]Zē-
lō′phe-hăd, were married unto
their father's brothers' sons:
12 *And* they were [n]married into
the families of the sons of [c]Mă-
năs′seh the son of Jō′ṣeph, and
their [g,o]inheritance remained in
the tribe of the family of their
father.
13 These *are* the commandments and the judgments[c], which
the LORD commanded by the
hand of [u]Mō′ṣeṣ unto the children of Is̱′ra-el in the plains of
[v]Mō′ab by [w]Jôr′dan *near* [x]Jĕr′-
ĭ-chō.

11
*p Mahlah*, Num. 26:33.
*q Tirzah*, Josh. 17:3.
*r Hoglah*, Num. 27:1.
*s Milcah*, Num. 26:33.
*t Noah*, Num. 26:33.

v.11–1494 BC
See footnote, *Time*,
Rev. 10:6.

13
*u Prophets, inspiration of*, Isa. 3:2.
*v Moab, the law rehearsed in, by Moses*, Num. 26:3.
*w Jordan, a river of Palestine*, Gen 32:10.
*x Jericho*, Num. 22:1.

THE FIFTH BOOK OF MOSES,

CALLED

# DEUTERONOMY

## CHAPTER 1

*Moses' speech in the end of the fortieth year: in which he briefly rehearses the promise of God; 13 the appointment of officers for them; 19 the sending of the spies to search the land; 34 and God's anger for their incredulity and disobedience.*

v.1–1494 BC
See footnote, *Time*,
Rev. 10:6.

THESE *be* the [a]words which
Mō′ṣeṣ spake unto all
[b]Is̱′ra-el on this side [c]Jôr′dan in
the wilderness, in the plain over[c]
against the [d]Red *sea*, between
[e]Pā′ran, and Tō′phel, and Lā′-
ban, and [f]Hă-zē′roth, and Dĭz′-
a-hăb[s].
2 (*There are* eleven days' *journey* from [g]Hō′reb by the way of
mount *Sē′ĭr unto [h]Kā′desh-
bär′ne-ȧ.)
3 And it came to pass in the
fortieth year, in the eleventh
[i]month, on the first *day* of the
month, *that* [j]Mō′ṣeṣ spake unto
the children of Is̱′ra-el, according unto all that the LORD had
given him in commandment unto them;
4 After he had slain [k]Sī′hŏn the
king of the [l]Ăm′ôr-ītes, which
dwelt in [m]Hĕsh′bŏn, and [n]Ŏg
the king of Bā′shăn, which dwelt
at †Ăs′ta-rŏth in [o]Ĕd′re-ī:
5 On this side [c]Jôr′dan, in the
land of [p]Mō′ab, began [j]Mō′ṣeṣ
to declare[c] this [a]law, saying,
6 The LORD our God spake un-
to [j]us in [g]Hō′reb, saying, Ye have
dwelt long enough in this mount:
7 Turn you, and take your
journey, and go to the mount of
the [l]Ăm′ôr-ītes, and unto all *the
places* nigh[c] thereunto, in the
plain, in the hills, and in the
vale, and in the south, and by
the sea side, to the land of the
[q]Cā′năan-ītes, and unto ‡Lĕb′a-
non, unto the great river, the
river [r]Eū-phrā′tēṣ.[c]

1
*a Law, of Moses*, Deut. 33:2.
*b Israel*, Ex. 4:22.
*c Jordan*, Gen. 32:10.
*d Red Sea*, Ex. 10:19.
*e Paran*, Gen. 21:21.
*f Hazeroth*, Num. 11:35.

2
*g Horeb*, Ex. 3:1.
*h Kadesh*, Gen. 14:7.

3
*i Month, Sebat (February)*, Ex. 12:2.
*j Prophets, inspiration of*, Isa. 3:2.

v.3–1494 BC
See footnote, *Time*,
Rev. 10:6.

4
*k Sihon*, Num. 21:21.
*l Amorites, territory of*, Gen. 14:13.
*m Heshbon*, Isa. 16:8.
*n Og*, Num. 21:33.
*o Edrei*, Josh. 13:12.

5
*p Moab*, Num. 26:3.

7
*q Canaanites*, Ex. 23:28.
*r Euphrates*, Gen. 15:18.

* **SEIR**, a range of hills trending southwest from the Dead Sea. *The route from Horeb to Kadesh-barnea on the west of*, Deut. 1:1, 2. *Children of Israel journey by*, Deut. 1:2; 2:1; 33:2. *Originally inhabited by Horites*, Gen. 14:6; 36:6; 36:20–30; Deut. 2:12; *and later by the children of Esau after they destroyed the Horim*, Deut. 2:4, 5, 12, 22 (with Gen. 32:3; 33:14, 16; 36:8, 9; Num. 24:18); Josh. 24:4. *The southern boundary of the conquests of Joshua*, Josh. 11:15–18.

† **ASHTAROTH.** *The capital city of Bashan*, Josh. 9:10. *Giants dwell at*, Josh. 12:4. *Allotted to Manasseh*, Josh. 13:31; 1 Chr. 6:71. *Possibly identical with* ASHTEROTH KARNAIM, *mentioned in* Gen. 14:5. *Called* BEESH-TERAH, Josh. 21:27.

‡ **LEBANON,** a mountain range. *Northern boundary of the land of Canaan*, Deut. 3:25; 11:24; Josh. 1:4; 9:1. *Early inhabitants of*, Judg. 3:3. *Snow of*, Jer. 18:14. *Streams of*, Song 4:15. *Cedars of*, Judg. 9:15; 2 Kin. 19:23; 2 Chr. 2:8; Psa. 29:5; 104:16; Isa. 2:13; 14:8; Ezek. 27:5. *Other trees of*, 2 Kin. 19:23; 2 Chr. 2:8. *Beasts of*, Isa. 40:16. *Fertility and productiveness of*, Hos. 14:5–7. *Solomon's house built of the forest of*, 1 Kin. 7:2–5.

*Valley of*, Josh. 11:17; 12:7. *Tower of*, Song 7:4. *Solomon had cities of store in*, 1 Kin. 9:19.

**Figurative**, Isa. 29:17; Jer. 22:6.

v.8–1494 BC
See footnote, *Time*, Rev. 10:6.

**8**
s *Canaan, promised to Abraham*, Gen. 37:1.
t *Covenant, of God with men*, Deut. 29:1.
u *Abraham*, Gen. 17:5.
v *Isaac*, Gen. 21:3.
w *Jacob*, Gen. 27:11.

**10**
x *God, providence of*, Gen. 2:2.
y *Temporal Blessings, from God*, Psa. 103:2.

**11**
z *Children, the gift of God*, Mark 10:14.

**12**
a *Moses*, Ex. 2:10.
b *Strife*, Prov. 20:3.

**13**
c *Commandment, enjoining the choice of wise men for rulers*, Deut. 8:2.
d *Court, civil, composition of, and mode of procedure by*, vs. 15–17; Ex. 18:26.
e *Government, representative*, vs. 13–15; Isa. 22:21.
f *Judge, character of, and precepts relating to*, vs. 13–17; Judg. 2:18.
g *Rulers, character and qualifications of*, Ex. 18:21.
h Ex. 18:24-26.

**16**
i *Commandment, enjoining justice*, Deut. 8:2.
j *Judge, must judge righteously*, Judg. 2:18.
k *Court, justice required of*, Ex. 18:26.
l *Foreigners, justice toward, enjoined*, Deut. 23:20.

8 Behold, I have set the [s]land before you: go in and possess the land which the LORD [t]sware[c] unto your fathers, [u]Ā'brä-hăm, [v]Ī'ṣaac, and [w]Jā'cob, to give unto them and to their seed after them.

9 ¶ And I spake unto you at that time, saying, I am not able to bear[c] you myself alone:

10 The LORD your [x]God hath [y]multiplied you, and, behold, ye *are* this day as the stars of heaven for multitude.[Q]

11 (The LORD God of your fathers make you a thousand times so many [z]more as ye *are*, and [y]bless you, as he hath promised you!)

12 How can [a]I myself alone bear your cumbrance[c], and your burden, and your [b]strife?

13 [c,d,e]Take you [f,g]wise men, and understanding[c], and known among your tribes, and I will make them [h]rulers over you.

14 And ye answered me, and said, The thing which thou hast spoken *is* good *for us* to do.

15 So I took the [h]chief of your tribes, [f,g]wise men, and known, and [d,e]made them heads over you, captains over thousands, and captains over hundreds, and captains over fifties, and captains over tens, and officers among your tribes.

16 And I [i]charged your [j,k]judges at that time, saying, Hear *the causes*[c] between your brethren, and judge righteously between *every* man and his brother, and the [l]stranger[G] *that is* with him.[Q]

17 [i,j,k]Ye shall not respect persons in judgment; *but* ye shall hear the small as well as the great; ye shall not be afraid of the face of man; for the judgment *is* God's: and the cause[c] that is too hard for you, bring *it* unto me, and I will hear it.[Q]

18 And [a]I commanded you at that time all the things which ye should do.

19 ¶ And when we departed from [m]Hō'reb, we went through all that great and terrible wilderness, which ye saw by the way of the mountain of the [n]Ăm'ôr-ītes, as the LORD our God commanded us; and we came to [o]Kā'desh–bär'ne-ȧ.

20 And I said unto you, Ye are come unto the mountain of the [n]Ăm'ôr-ītes, which the LORD our God doth give unto us.

21 Behold, the LORD thy God hath set the land before thee: go up *and* possess *it*, as the LORD God of thy fathers hath said unto thee; [p]fear not, neither be discouraged.

22 ¶ And ye came near unto me every one of you, and said, [q]We will send [r]men before us, and they shall search us out the land, and bring us word again by what way we must go up, and into what cities we shall come.

23 And the saying pleased me well: and I took [r]twelve men of you, one of a tribe:

24 And [r]they turned and went up into the mountain, and came unto the valley of [s]Ĕsh'cŏl, and searched it out.

25 And [r]they took of the fruit of the land in their hands, and brought *it* down unto us, and brought us word again, and said *It is* a good land which the LORD our God doth give us.

26 Notwithstanding [t]ye would not go up, but [u]rebelled against the commandment of the LORD your God:

27 And ye [v]murmured in your tents, and said, Because the LORD hated us, he hath brought us forth out of the land of [w]Ē'ġўpt, to deliver us into the hand of the [n]Ăm'ôr-ītes, to destroy us.

28 Whither shall we go up? our

v.18–1494 BC
See footnote, *Time*, Rev. 10:6.

**19**
m *Horeb*, Ex. 3:1.
n *Amorites*, Gen. 14:13.
o *Kadesh*, Gen. 14:7.

**21**
p *Faith, enjoined, in time of public danger*, vs. 21–31; Mark 11:22.

**22**
q *Israel, sends twelve spies to view the land*, Ex. 4:22.
r *Spies*, Josh. 6:23.

**24**
s *Eshcol*, Num. 13:23.

**26**
t *Cowardice, instances of*, Lev. 26:36.
u *Disobedience, to God, instances of*, Eph. 5:6.

**27**
v *Murmuring, instances of*, Num. 14:2.
w *Egypt*, Gen. 41:8.

v.28–1494 BC
See footnote, *Time*,
Rev. 10:6.

30
*x God, preserver*, Gen. 2:2.
*y Assurance, of divine help*, Heb. 10:22.
*z War, God in*, Judg. 3:2.

32
*a Unbelief*, Heb. 3:12.
33
*b God, providence of*, Gen. 2:2.
*c Pillar, of cloud and fire, a guide to Israel*, Ex. 13:21.
34
*d Sin, known to God*, Rom. 5:12.
*e Anger of God*, 2 Kin. 13:3.

v.34–1494 BC
See footnote, *Time*,
Rev. 10:6.

35
*f Reprobates*, 1 Cor. 9:27.
*g Unbelieving Israelites destroyed*, Num. 14:11.
*h Canaan, promised to Abraham*, Gen. 37:1.
*i Covenant, of God with men*, Deut. 29:1.
36
*j Caleb*, Num.14:6.
*k Obedience, instances of*, Heb. 5:8.
*l Decision, instances of*, Isa. 50:7.
37
*m Moses, not permitted to enter Canaan*, Ex. 2:10.
38
*n Joshua, commissioned*, Josh. 1:1.

[r]brethren have [t]discouraged our
heart, saying, The people *is*
greater and taller than we; the
cities *are* great and walled up to
heaven; and moreover we have
seen the sons of the ‖Ăn′a-kĭms
there.
29 Then I said unto you, Dread
not, neither be afraid of them.
30 The[s] LORD your God [x]which
goeth before you, [y]he shall [z]fight
for you, according to all that he
did for you in [w]Ē′gy̆pt before
your eyes;
31 And in the wilderness, where
thou hast seen how that the
LORD thy God [x]bare thee, as a
man doth bear his son, in all the
way that ye went, until ye came
into this place.[s Q]
32 Yet in this thing ye did [a]not
believe the LORD your God,
33 [b]Who went in the way before you, to search you out a
place to pitch your tents *in*, in
[c]fire by night, to shew you by
what way ye should go, and in a
cloud by day.
34 And the LORD [d]heard the
voice of your words, and was
[e]wroth[C], and sware, saying,
35 Surely there shall not one of
[f, g]these men of this evil generation see that good [h]land, which I
[i]sware[C] to give unto your fathers,
36 Save[C] [j]Cā′leb the son of Jē-
phŭn′neh; he shall see it, and to
him will I give the [h]land that he
hath trodden[C] upon, and to his
children, because he hath wholly
[k, l]followed the LORD.
37 Also the LORD was [e]angry
with [m]me for your sakes, saying,
Thou also shalt not go in thither.
38 *But* [n]Jŏsh′u-ȧ the son of
Nŭn, which standeth before
thee, he shall go in thither: encourage him: for he shall cause
Ĭṣ′ra-el to inherit it.

39 Moreover your little ones,
which ye said should be a prey[C],
and your children, which in that
day had no knowledge between
good and evil, they shall go in
thither, and unto them will I
give [h]it, and they shall possess it.
40 But *as for* [f, g]you, turn you,
and take your journey into the
wilderness by the way of the
[o]Red sea.
41 Then ye answered and said
unto me, [p]We have sinned
against the LORD, we will go up
and fight, according to all that
the LORD our God commanded
us. And when ye had girded on
every man his weapons of war, ye
were ready to go up into the hill.
42 And the LORD said unto me,
Say unto them, Go not up, neither fight; for [q]I *am* not among
you; lest ye be smitten[C] before
your enemies.
43 So I [r]spake unto you; and
[f]ye [s]would not hear, but rebelled
against the commandment of the
LORD, and went [t]presumptu-
ously[C] up into the hill.
44 And the [u]Ăm′ôr-ītes, which
dwelt in that mountain, came
out against you, and chased you,
as §bees do, and destroyed [v]you
in *Sē′ïr, *even* unto +Hôr′mah.
45 And ye returned and wept
before the LORD; but the LORD
would not hearken to [w]your
voice, nor give ear unto you.
46 So [x]ye abode in [y]Kā′desh
many days, according unto the
days that ye abode *there*.

## CHAPTER 2

*Israel's history continued: they were not to meddle with the Edomites; 9 nor with the Moabites; 17 nor with the Ammonites; 24 but Sihon the Amorite was subdued by them.*

THEN we turned, and took
our journey into the wil-
derness by the way of the [a]Red

v.39–1494 BC
See footnote, *Time*,
Rev. 10:6.

40
*o Red Sea*, Ex. 10:19.

41
*p Sin, confession of*, Rom. 5:12.

42
*q Holy Spirit, withdrawn from incorrigible sinner*, Acts 1:2.

43
*r Reproof, faithfulness in*, Prov. 1:10.
*s Disobedience to God*, Eph. 5:6.
*t Presumption, instances of*, Psa. 19:13.

44
*u Amorites*, Gen. 14:13.
*v Israel, defeated battle*, Ex. 4 22.

45
*w Wicked, prayer of, not answered*, Psa. 73:3.

B.C. 1451?
See footnote, *Time*,
Rev. 10:6.

46
*x Israel, abides at Kadesh*, Ex. 4:22.
*y Kadesh*, Gen. 14:7.

1
*a Red Sea*, Ex. 10:19.

‖ **ANAKIM.** *A race of giants*, Num. 13:28–33; Deut. 2:10; 9:2.
**Defeated:** *By Joshua*, Josh. 11:21, 22. *By Caleb*, Josh. 14:12, 15, 15:13, 14; Judg. 1:20.
§ **BEE.** *In Palestine*, Judg. 14:8; Psa. 118:12; Isa. 7:18.

**Figurative**, Isa. 7:18.
+**HORMAH** (*utter destruction*). *A city S. W. of the Dead Sea*, Num. 14:45; 21:1–3. *Taken by Judah and Simeon*, Judg. 1.17. *Allotted to Simeon*, Josh. 19:4; 1 Chr. 4:30. *With the territory allotted to Judah*, Josh. 15:30; 1 Sam. 30:30.

v.1–1494 BC
See footnote, *Time*, Rev. 10:6.

sea, as the LORD spake unto me: and we compassed mount [b]Sē′ĭr many days.

2 And the LORD [c]spake unto me, saying,

3 Ye have compassed this [b]mountain long enough: turn you northward.

4 And command thou the [d]people, saying, Ye *are* to pass through the coast of your brethren the [e]children of [f]Ē′sa̤u, which dwell in [b]Sē′ĭr; and they shall be afraid of you: take ye good heed unto yourselves therefore:

5 Meddle not with [e]them; for I will not give you of their land, no, not so much as a foot breadth; because I have given mount [b]Sē′ĭr unto [f]Ē′sa̤u *for* a possession.

6 Ye shall buy meat of [e]them for [g]money, that ye may eat; and ye shall also buy water of them for money, that ye may drink.

7 For the LORD thy God hath [h]blessed thee in all the works of thy hand: [i]he knoweth thy walking through this great wilderness: these forty years the LORD thy God *hath been* with thee; [j]thou hast lacked nothing.

8 And when we passed by from our brethren the [e]children of [f]Ē′sa̤u, which dwelt in [b]Sē′ĭr, through the way of the plain from *Ē′lăth, and from [k]Ē′zĭ-on–gā′bĕr, we turned and passed by the way of the wilderness of [l]Mō′ab.

9 And the LORD said unto me, Distress not the [m]Mō′ab-ītes, neither contend with them in battle: for I will not give thee of their land *for* a possession; because I have given [n]Är unto the children of Lŏt *for* a possession.

10 The [o]Ē′mimṣ dwelt therein in times past, a people great, and many, and tall, as the [p]Ăn′a-kĭmṣ;

11 Which also were accounted [q]giants, as the [p]Ăn′a-kĭmṣ; but the [m]Mō′ab-ītes call them [o]Ē′mimṣ.

12 The Hō′rĭmṣ also dwelt in [b]Sē′ĭr beforetime; but the [e]children of Ē′sa̤u succeeded them, when they had destroyed them from before them, and dwelt in their stead; as Ĭṣ′ra-el did unto the land of his possession, which the LORD gave unto them.

13 Now rise up, *said I*, and get you over the [r]brook [s]Zē′red. And we went over the brook Zē′red.

14 And the space in which we came from [t]Kā′desh–bär′ne-ȧ, until we were come over the [r]brook [s]Zē′red, *was* thirty and eight years; until all the generation of the men of war [u]were wasted out from among the host, as the LORD sware unto them.

15 For indeed the hand of the LORD was against [v]them, to destroy them from among the host, until they were consumed.

16 ¶ So it came to pass, when all the [v]men of war [u]were consumed and dead from among the people,

17 That the LORD spake unto [c]me, saying,

18 Thou art to pass over through [n]Är, the coast of [l]Mō′ab, this day:

19 And *when* thou comest nigh over against the children of Ăm′mŏn, distress them not, nor meddle with them: for I will not give thee of the land of the children of Ăm′mŏn *any* possession; because I have given it unto the children of Lŏt *for* a possession.

20 (That also was accounted a land of giants: giants dwelt therein in old time; and the

b *Seir*, Deut. 1:2.

2
c *Prophets, inspiration of*, Isa. 3:2.

4
d *Israel*, Ex. 4:22.
e *Edomites*, 2 Kin. 8:21.
f *Esau*, Gen. 25:25.

6
g *Money*, Jer. 32:9.

7
h *Temporal Blessings, from God*, Psa. 103:2.
i *God, knowledge of*, Gen. 2:2.
j *God, providence of*, Gen. 2:2.

8
k *Ezion-gaber*, Num. 33:35.
l *Moab*, Num. 26:3.

9
m *Moabites*, Gen. 19:37.
n *Ar*, Num. 21:15.

10
o Gen. 14:5.

v.10–1494 BC
See footnote, *Time*, Rev. 10:8.

p *Anakim*, Deut. 1:28.

11
q Or, *Rephaim*, Gen. 14:5.

13
r *Brook*, Deut. 8:7.
s Or, *Zared*, Num. 21:12.

14
t *Kadesh*, Gen. 14:7.
u *Judgments, upon the Israelites*, Ex. 6:6.

15
v *Wicked, punishment of*, Psa. 73:3.

* **ELATH**, called also ELOTH. *A city of Idumea*, 1 Kin. 9:26; 2 Chr. 8:17. **Conquest of**: *By Uzziah*, 2 Kin. 14:22; 2 Chr. 26:2. *By the Syrians*, 2 Kin. 16:6.

v.20–1494 BC
See footnote, *Time*, Rev. 10:6.

20
w Or, *Zuzims*, Gen. 14:5.

23
x Or, *Avites*, Josh. 13:3.
y Or, *Gaza*, Gen. 10:19.
1 R. V. villages as far as Gaza,

24
z *Arnon*, Num. 22: 36.
a *Sihon*, Num. 21: 21.
b *Heshbon*, Isa. 16:8.
2 R. V. valley of Arnon:

26
c *Kedemoth*, Josh. 13:18.

28
d *Food*, Psa. 136: 25.

[†]Ăm′mon-ītes call them [w]Zăm-
zŭm′mims̩;
21 A people great, and many,
and tall, as the [p]Ăn′a-kĭms̩; but
the LORD destroyed them before
them; and they succeeded them,
and dwelt in their stead:
22 As he did to the [e]children of
Ē′sa̩u, which dwelt in [b]Sē′ïr,
when he destroyed the Hō′rĭms̩
from before them; and they succeeded them, and dwelt in their
stead even unto this day:
23 And the [x]Ā′vĭms̩ which
dwelt in [1]Hă-zē′rĭm, *even* unto
[y]Ăz′zah, the [‡]Căph′tŏ-rĭms̩,
which came forth out of Căph′-
tôr, destroyed them, and dwelt
in their stead. )
24 ¶ Rise ye up, take your journey, and pass over the [2]river
[z]Är′nŏn: behold, I have given into thine hand [a]Sī′hŏn the Ăm′-
ôr-īte, king of [b]Hĕsh′bŏn, and
his land: begin to possess *it*, and
contend with him in battle,
25 This day will I begin to put
the dread of thee and the fear of
thee upon the nations *that are*
under the whole heaven, who
shall hear report of thee, and
shall tremble, and be in anguish
because of thee.
26 ¶ And I sent messengers out
of the wilderness of [c]Kĕd′e-
mŏth unto [a]Sī′hŏn king of
[b]Hĕsh′bŏn with words of peace,
saying,
27 Let me pass through thy
land: I will go along by the [‖]high
way, I will neither turn unto the
right hand nor to the left.
28 Thou shalt sell me [d]meat[C] for
[e]money, that I may eat; and give
me water for money, that I may
drink: only I will pass through
on my feet;
29 (As the [f]children of Ē′sa̩u
which dwell in [g]Sē′ïr, and the
[h]Mō′ab-ītes which dwell in [i]Är,
did unto me;) until I shall pass
over [j]Jôr′dan into the land
which the LORD our God giveth
us.
30 But [a]Sī′hŏn king of [b]Hĕsh′-
bŏn would not let us pass by
him: for the LORD thy [k]God
hardened his spirit, and made
his [l]heart obstinate, that he
might deliver him into thy hand,
as *appeareth* this day.
31 And the LORD said unto me,
Behold, I have begun to give
[a]Sī′hŏn and his land before thee:
begin to possess, that thou mayest inherit his land.
32 Then [a]Sī′hŏn came out
against us, he and all his people,
to fight at [m]Jā′hăz.
33 And the LORD our God [k]de-
livered [a]him before us; and [n]we
smote him, and his sons, and all
his people.
34 And [n]we took all his cities
at that time, and [o,p]utterly destroyed the men, and the women,
and the little ones, of every city,
we left none to remain:
35 Only the cattle we took for a
prey[C] unto ourselves, and the
[q]spoil of the cities which we
took.
36 From [r]Ăr′ŏ-ēr, which *is* [3]by
the brink of the river of [s]Är′nŏn,
and *from* the city that *is* [4]by the
river, even unto [t]Gĭl′e-ăd, there

v.28–1494 BC
See footnote, *Time*, Rev. 10:6.

e *Money*, Jer. 32:9.

29
f *Edomites*, 2 Kin. 8:21.
g *Seir*, Deut. 1:2.
h *Moabites*, Gen. 19:37.
i *Ar*, Num. 21:15.
j *Jordan*, Gen. 32: 10.

30
k *God, providence of, overruling interpositions of*, Gen. 2:2.
l *Heart, hardened*, Psa. 44:21.

32
m *Jahaz*, Judg. 11 20.

33
n *Israel, defeats the Amorites*, Ex. 4: 22.

34
o *War, of extermination*, Judg. 3:2.
p *Massacre, instances of*, Esth. 3:13.

35
q *Spoils*, 1 Chr. 26 27.

36
r *Aroer*, Deut. 4:48.
s *Arnon*, Num. 22 36.
t *Gilead*, Deut. 3:13.
3 R. V. on the edge of the valley of Arnon,
4 R. V. in the valley,

† **AMMONITES.** *Descendants of Ben-ammi, one of the sons of Lot*, Gen. 19:38. *Character of*, Judg. 10:6; 2 Kin. 23:13; 2 Chr. 20:25; Jer. 27:3, 9; Ezek. 25:3, 6; Amos 1:13; Zeph. 2:10. *Territory of*, Num. 21:24; Deut. 2:19; Josh. 12:2; 13:10, 25; Judg. 11:13.

*Israelites forbidden to disturb*, Deut. 2:19, 37. *Excluded from the congregation of Israel*, Deut. 23:3–6. *Confederate with Moabites and Amalekites against Israel*, Judg. 3:12, 13. *Defeated by the Israelites*, Judg. 10:7–18; 11:32, 33; 12:1–3; 1 Sam. 11:1–11; 2 Sam. 8:11, 12; 10:1–14; 11:1; 12:26–31; 1 Chr. 18:11; 19:15, 19; 20:1–3; 2 Chr. 20:1–25; 26:7, 8; 27:5. *Conspire against the Jews*, Neh. 4:7, 8.

*Solomon takes wives from*, 1 Kin. 11:1; 2 Chr. 12:13; Neh. 13:26. *Jews intermarry with*, Ezra 9:1, 2; 10:10–44; Neh. 13:23, 24.

**Kings of:** *Baalis*, Jer. 40:14. *Hanun*, 2 Sam. 10:1–15; 1 Chr. 19:1–15. *Nahash*, 1 Sam. 11:1–11; 2 Sam. 10:1, 2 1 Chr. 19:1, 2.

**Idols of:** *Milcom*, 2 Kin. 23:13. *Molech*, 1 Kin. 11:7.

**Prophecies concerning**, Isa. 11:14; Jer. 9:25, 26; 25 15–21; 27:1–11; 49:1–6; Ezek. 21:20, 28–32; 25:1–11; Dan 11:41; Amos 1:13–15; Zeph. 2:8–11.

‡ **CAPHTORIM.** *People of Caphtor*, Gen. 10:14; 1 Chr 1:12; Jer. 47:4; Amos 9:7.

‖ **HIGHWAYS.** *From Gibeon to Beth-horon*, Josh. 10:10 *From Beth-el to Shechem*, Judg. 21:19. *From Judæa to Galilee, by way of Samaria*, John 4:3–5, 43. *To Bethel*, Judg. 20:31 *To Gibeah*, Judg. 20:31. *To cities of refuge*, Deut. 19:3 *Built by rulers*, Num. 20:17; 21:22.

**Figurative**, Prov. 16:17; Isa. 11:16; 35:8–10; 40:3, 4; Matt 3:3; 7:13, 14.

v.36–1494 BC
See footnote, *Time,* Rev. 10:6.

37
u *Jabbok,* Num. 21: 24.

1
a *Bashan,* Num. 32:33.
b *Og,* Num. 21:33.
c *Edrei,* Josh. 13: 12.

2
d *Faith, enjoined, in time of public danger,* Mark 11: 22.
e *Sihon,* Num. 21: 21.
f *Amorites,* Gen. 14:13.

3
g *Israel, defeats the king of Bashan,* Ex. 4:22.
h *War, of extermination,* Judg. 3:2.

4
i 1 Kin. 4:13.

5
j *Walls, of cities,* 1 Sam. 20:25.

was not one city too strong for
us: the LORD our God [k]delivered
all unto [n]us:
37 Only unto the land of the
children of Ăm′mŏn thou camest not, *nor* unto any place of the
river [u]Jăb′bŏk, nor unto the cities in the mountains, nor unto
whatsoever the LORD our God
forbad us.

## CHAPTER 3

*The history of the conquest of Og king of Bashan, the last of the giants. 12 The distribution of the lands east of Jordan to the two tribes and a half. 23 Moses' prayer to enter into the land. 26 He is permitted only to see it.*

THEN we turned, and went
up the way to [a]Bā′shăn:
and [b]Ŏg the king of Bā′shăn
came out against us, he and all
his people, to battle at [c]Ĕd′re-ī.
2 And the LORD said unto me,
[d]Fear [b]him not: for I will deliver him, and all his people, and
his land, into thy hand; and thou
shalt do unto him as thou didst
unto [e]Sī′hŏn king of the [f]Ăm′-
ôr-ītes, which dwelt at Hĕsh′bŏn.
3 So the LORD our God de-
livered into our hands [b]Ŏg also,
the king of [a]Bā′shăn, and all his
people: and [g]we smote[G] him until
[h]none was left to him remaining.
4 And [g]we took all [b]his cities at
that time, there was not a city
which we took not from them,
threescore cities, all the region of
[i]Är′gŏb, the kingdom of Ŏg in
[a]Bā′shăn.
5 All these cities *were* fenced[G]
with high [j]walls, *gates, and
bars; beside unwalled[G] towns a
great many.

6 And [g]we [h, k]utterly destroyed
them, as we did unto [e]Sī′hŏn
king of Hĕsh′bŏn, utterly destroying the men, women, and
children, of every city.
7 But all the cattle, and the
[l]spoil of the cities, we took for a
prey to ourselves.
8 And we took at that time out
of the hand of the two kings of
the [f]Ăm′ôr-ītes the land that *was*
on this side [m]Jôr′dan, from the
[1]river of [n]Är′nŏn unto mount
[o]Hĕr′mon;
9 (*Which* [o]Hĕr′mon the Sī-dō′-
nĭ-anș call Sĭr′ĭ-ŏn; and the [f]Ăm′-
ôr-ītes call it Shē′nir;)
10 All the cities of the plain,
and all Ḡĭl′e-ăd, and all [a]Bā′-
shăn, unto †Săl′chah and [c]Ĕd′-
re-ī, cities of the kingdom of [b]Ŏg
in Bā′shăn.
11 For only [b]Ŏg king of [a]Bā′-
shăn remained of the remnant of
[p]giants; behold, his [q]bedstead
*was* a bedstead of [r]iron; *is* it not
in ‡Răb′bath of the children of
Ăm′mŏn? nine [s]cubits *was* the
length thereof, and four cubits
the breadth of it, after the cubit
of a man.
12 And this land, *which* we
possessed at that time, from
[t]Ăr′ō-ēr, which *is* by the [1]river
[n]Är′nŏn, and half mount ‖Ḡĭl′-
e-ăd, and the cities thereof, gave
I unto the [u]Reu̥′ben-ītes and to
the [v]Găd′ītes.
13 And the rest of ‖Ḡĭl′e-ăd,
and all [a]Bā′shăn, *being* the kingdom of [b]Ŏg, gave I unto the half
tribe of [w]Mă-năs′seh; all the re-

v.6–1494 BC
See footnote, *Time,* Rev. 10:6.

6
k *Massacre instances of,* Esth. 3:13.

7
l *Spoils,* 1 Chr. 26: 27.

8
m *Jordan,* Gen. 32: 10.
n *Arnon, boundary between Moabites and Amorites,* Num. 22:36.
o *Hermon,* Deut. 4:48.
1 R. V. valley of

11
p Or, *Rephaim,* Gen. 14:5.
q *Bed,* Amos 6:4.
r *Iron,* Prov. 27: 17.
s *Cubit,* Ex. 36:9.

12
t *Aroer,* Deut. 4:48.
u *Reubenites,* Josh 22:1.
v *Gad, tribe of,* Deut. 33:20.

13
w *Manasseh, tribe of,* Gen. 46:20.

***GATES.** *Of cities,* Josh. 6:26; 1 Sam. 23:7; 2 Sam. 18:24; 2 Chr. 8:5. *Made, of iron,* Acts 12:10; *of wood,* Neh. 1:3; *of brass,* Psa. 107:16.

*Closed, at night,* Josh. 2:5, 7; *on the Sabbath,* Neh. 13:19. *Guards at,* 2 Kin. 7:17; Neh. 13:19, 22. *Jails made in the towers of,* Jer. 20:2. *Bodies of slain exposed to view at,* 2 Kin. 10:8. *Punishment of criminals required outside of,* Deut. 17:5; Acts 7:58; Heb. 13:12.

**The open square of:** *A place, for idlers,* Gen. 19:1; 23: 10; 1 Sam. 4:18; Psa. 69:12; Prov. 1:21; 8:3; Jer. 17:19, 20; 22:2; *for religious services,* Acts 14:13; *for reading of the law,* Neh. 8; *for the transaction of public business, announcement of legal transactions,* Gen. 23:10, 16; *for conferences on public affairs,* Gen. 34:20; *for holding courts of justice,* Deut. 16:18; 21:19; 22:15; Josh. 20:4; Ruth 4:1; 2 Sam. 15:2; Prov. 22:22; Zech. 8:16; *for thrones of kings* 1 Kin. 22:10; 2 Chr. 18:9; Jer. 38:7.

**Figurative:** *Of the people of a city,* Isa. 3:26; Jer. 14:2. *Of the powers of hell,* Matt. 16:18. *Of death,* Job 38:17; Psa. 9:13; Isa. 38:10. *Of righteousness,* Psa. 118:19. *Of salvation,* 118:19, 20; Isa. 26:2; Matt. 7:13; Luke 13:24.

**Symbolical,** Rev. 21:12, 13, 21, 25.

† **SALCAH,** called also SALCHAH. *A city of Gad,* Josh. 12:5; 13:11; 1 Chr. 5:11.

‡ **RABBAH,** called also RABBATH. *A city E. of the Jordan, originally belonging to the Ammonites,* Josh. 13:25. *Bedstead of the giant Og kept at,* Deut. 3:11. *Taken by David,* 2 Sam. 11:1; 12:26–31; 1 Chr. 20:1–3. *Possessed again by the Ammonites; prophesied against,* Jer. 49:2, 3; Ezek. 21:20; 25:5; Amos 1:14.

‖ **GILEAD** (*stony, heap of testimony*), a region E. of the Jordan. *A grazing country,* Num. 32:1; 1 Chr. 5:9. *Allotted to the tribes of Reuben and Gad and half tribe of Manasseh.*

v.13–1494 BC
See footnote, *Time*, Rev. 10:6.

14
x *Jair*, Josh. 13:30.
y Or, *Geshur*, 2 Sam. 3:3.
z Or, *Maachah*, 2 Sam. 10:6, 8; 1 Chr. 19:7.

a Or, *Havoth-jair*, Judg. 10:4.

15
b *Machir*, Gen. 50:23.

16
c *Reubenites*, Josh. 22:1.
d *Gad, tribe of*, Deut. 33:20.
e *Arnon*, Num. 22:36.
f *Jabbok*, Num. 21:24.
g *Ammonites*, Deut. 2:20.
1 R. V. valley of

17
h *Jordan*, Gen. 32:10.
i *Sea of Galilee*, Matt. 4:18.
j *Dead Sea*, Gen. 14:3.
2 R. V. the slopes of Pisgah eastward.

18
k *Canaan, land of*, Gen. 37:1.

gion of [i]Ăr′gŏb, with all Bā′-
shăn, which was called the land
of [p]giants.
14 [x]Jā′ïr the son of Mȧ-năs′seh
took all the country of [i]Ăr′gŏb
unto the coasts of [y]Gēsh′u-rī
and [z]Mȧ-ăch′a-thī; and called
them after his own name, [a]Bā′-
shăn–hā′voth–jā′ïr, unto this
day.
15 And I gave ‖Gĭl′e-ăd unto
[b]Mā′chïr.
16 And unto the [c]Reu′ben-ītes
and unto the [d]Găd′ītes I gave
from ‖Gĭl′e-ăd even unto the
[1]river [e]Är′nŏn half the valley,
and the border even unto the
river [f]Jăb′bŏk, *which is* the
border of the [g]children of Ăm′-
mŏn;
17 The plain also, and [h]Jôr′-
dan, and the coast *thereof*, from
[i]Chĭn′ne-rĕth even unto the sea
of the plain, *even* the salt sea,
under [2,§]Ăsh′dŏth–pĭṣ′gah eastward.
18 ¶ And I commanded you at
that time, saying, The LORD
your God hath given you this
[k]land to possess it: ye shall pass
over armed before your brethren
the children of Ĭṣ′ra-el, all *that
are* meet for the war.
19 But your wives, and your
little ones, and your cattle, (*for* I
know that ye have much cattle,)
shall abide in your cities which I
have given you;
20 Until the LORD have given
rest unto your brethren, as well
as unto you, and *until* they also
possess the [k]land which the
LORD your God hath given
them beyond [h]Jôr′dan: and *then*
shall ye return every man unto
his possession, which I have giv-
en you.
21 ¶ And I commanded [l]Jŏsh′-
u-ȧ at that time, saying, Thine
eyes have seen all that the LORD
your God hath done unto these
two kings: so shall the LORD do
unto all the kingdoms whither
thou passest.
22 [m]Ye shall not fear them: for
the LORD your God he shall
[n]fight for you.
23 ¶ And [o]I besought the LORD
at that time, saying,
24 O LORD God, thou hast begun to shew thy servant thy
greatness, and thy [p]mighty
hand: for what [3]God *is there* in
heaven or in earth, that can do
according to thy works, and according to thy might?
25 [o,q]I pray thee, let me go
over, and see the good [k]land that
*is* beyond [h]Jôr′dan, that goodly
mountain, and [r]Lĕb′a-non.
26 But the LORD was [s]wroth
with me for your sakes, and
would not hear me: and the
LORD [t]said unto me, Let it suffice thee; speak no more unto me
of this matter.
27 [q]Get thee up into the top of
[§]Pĭṣ′gah, and lift up thine eyes
westward, and northward, and
southward, and eastward, and behold *it* with thine eyes: for thou
shalt not go over this [h]Jôr′dan.
28 But charge [u]Jŏsh′u-ȧ, and
encourage him, and strengthen
him: for he shall go over before
this people, and he shall cause
them to inherit the land which
thou shalt see.
29 So we abode in the valley
over against [+]Bĕth–pē′ôr.

v.20–1494 BC
See footnote, *Time*, Rev. 10:6.

21
l *Joshua*, Josh. 1:1

22
m *Faith, enjoined, in time of publi[c] danger*, Mark 11:22.
n *War, God in*, Judg. 3:2.

23
o *Moses, not permitted to enter Canaan*, vs. 23–29; Ex. 2:10.

24
p *God, power of*, Gen. 2:2.
3 R. V. god

25
q *Prayer, answer to, different fro[m] the request*, vs. 26, 27; Acts 6:4
r *Lebanon*, Deut. 1:7.

26
s *Anger of God*, 2 Kin. 13:3.
t *Prayer, rebuked*, Acts 6:4.

28
u *Joshua, commissioned*, Josh. 1:

Num. 32; Deut. 34:1; 2 Kin. 10:33. *Reubenites expel the Hagarites from*, 1 Chr. 5:9, 10, 18–22. *Ammonites make war against; defeated by Jephthah*, Judg. 11; Amos 1:13. *The prophet Elijah dwelt in*, 1 Kin. 17:1. *David retreats to, at the time of Absalom's rebellion*, 2 Sam. 17:16, 22, 24; *pursued into, by Absalom*, 2 Sam. 17:26. *Absalom defeated and slain in the forests of*, 2 Sam. 18:6–15.

*Hazael, king of Syria, smites the land of*, 2 Kin. 10:32, 33; Amos 1:3. *Invaded by Tiglath-pileser, king of Syria*, 2 Kin. 15:29. *Exported spices, balm, and myrrh*, Gen. 37:25; Jer. 8:22; 46:11.

**Figurative:** *Of prosperity*, Jer. 22:6; 50:19.

§ **PISGAH** (*piece, section, or the height*), a ridge or mounta[in] E. of the Jordan, opposite to Jericho. *The Israelites com[e] to*, Num. 21:20. *A boundary of the country assigned to t[he] Reubenites and Gadites*, Deut. 3:17 [R. V.]; 4:49; Josh. 12 [R. V.]. *Balaam prophesies on*, Num. 23:14–24. *Moses vie[ws] Palestine from*, Deut. 34:1–4.

+ **BETH-PEOR.** *A place in territory allotted to the tribe* [of] *Reuben*, Deut. 4:46; 34:6. *Near the burial place of Mose[s]*, Josh. 13:20.

v.1–1494 BC
See footnote, *Time*, Rev. 10:6.

1
*a Commandment, enjoining obedience*, Deut. 8:2.
*b Instruction, in religion*, Prov. 23:23.
*c Obedience, enjoined*, vs. 1–40; Heb. 5:8.
*d Blessings, contingent upon obedience*, Deut. 11:26.

2
*e Commandment, forbidding adding to, or taking from, God's law*, Deut. 8:2.
*f Word of God, not to be added to, or taken from*, Psa. 119:9.

3
*g Baal-peor*, Num. 25:3.

4
*h Decision, instances of*, Isa. 50:7.
*i God, providence of*, Gen. 2:2.
*j Temporal Blessings, from God*, Psa. 103:2.

5
*k Law, of Moses, divine authority for*, Deut. 33:2.
*l Word of God, inspiration of*, Psa. 119:9.
*m Canaan, land of*, Gen. 37:1.

6
*n Wisdom, spiritual*, Prov. 2:2.

7
*o Access to God*, Eph. 3:12.
*p Prayer*, Acts 6:4.
1 R. V. a god

9
*q Commandment, enjoining watchfulness, and instruction of children in the law of God*, Deut. 8:2.
*r Watchfulness, against backsliding, enjoined*, Matt. 24:42.
*s Diligence, required*, Rom. 12:8.
*t Backsliding, admonitions against*, Hos. 11:7.

## CHAPTER 4

*An exhortation to obedience. 41 Moses appoints the three cities of refuge on the east of the Jordan.*

NOW therefore [a]hearken, O
Is'ra-el, unto the statutes
and unto the judgments, which I
[b]teach you, for to [c]do *them*, [d]that
ye may live, and go in and possess the land which the LORD
God of your fathers giveth you.
2 [e]Ye shall not add unto the
[f]word which I command you,
neither shall ye diminish *ought*
from it, that ye may [c]keep the
commandments of the LORD
your God which I command
you.
3 Your eyes have seen what the
LORD did because of [g]Bā'al-
pē'or: for all the men that followed Bā'al-pē'or, the LORD
thy God hath destroyed them
from among you.
4 But ye that did [h]cleave unto
the [i]LORD your God *are* [j]alive
every one of you this day.
5 Behold, I have [b]taught you
[k,l]statutes and judgments, even
as the LORD my God commanded me, that ye should [c]do
so in the [m]land whither ye go to
possess it.
6 [a,c]Keep therefore and do
*them*; for this *is* your [n]wisdom
and your understanding in the
sight of the nations, which shall
hear all these statutes, and say,
Surely this great nation *is* a wise
and understanding people.
7 For what nation *is there so*
great, who *hath* [1]God *so* nigh
unto them, as the LORD our
[o]God *is* in all *things that* we [p]call
upon him *for*?
8 And what nation *is there so*
great, that hath statutes and
judgments *so* righteous as all
this [k,l]law, which I set before
you this day?
9 Only [q,r]take heed to thyself,
and keep thy soul [s]diligently,
[t]lest thou forget the things which
thine eyes have seen, and lest
they depart from thy heart all
the days of thy life: but [u,v]teach
them [w]thy [x,y]sons, and thy sons'
sons:
10 *Specially* the day that thou
stoodest before the LORD thy
God in [z]Hō'reb, when the LORD
said unto me, Gather me the
people together, and I will make
them hear my [a]words, that they
may learn to [b]fear me all the
days that they shall live upon
the earth, and *that* [c]they may
[d,e]teach their children.
11 And ye came near and stood
under the [f]mountain; and [g]the
mountain burned with fire unto
the midst of heaven, with [h]darkness, clouds, and thick darkness.
12 And the [i]LORD spake unto
you out of the midst of the fire:
ye heard the voice of the words,
but saw no [2]similitude; only *ye
heard* a voice.
13 And he declared unto you
his [j]covenant, which he commanded you to [k]perform, *even*
ten [l]commandments; and he
wrote them upon two [m]tables of
[n]stone.
14 ¶ And [o]the LORD commanded me at that time to
[p]teach you statutes and judgments, that ye might [k]do them
in the land whither ye go over to
possess it.
15 [q,r]Take ye therefore good
heed unto yourselves; for ye saw
no manner of [2]similitude on the
day *that* the LORD spake unto
you in [s]Hō'reb out of the midst
of the fire:
16 [t]Lest ye corrupt *yourselves*,
and [u]make you a graven image,
[3]the similitude of any figure, the
likeness of male or female,
17 The likeness of any beast
that *is* on the earth, the likeness
of any winged fowl that flieth in
the air,
18 The likeness of any thing

v.9–1494 BC
See footnote, *Time*, Rev. 10:6.
*u Instruction, of children*, Prov. 23:23.
*v School, in the home*, Acts 19:9.
*w Parents, duty of, to instruct children in righteousness*, 2 Cor. 12:14.
*x Children, instruction of*, Mark 10:14.
*y Family, religion of the*, 1 Chr. 13:14.

10
*z Horeb*, Ex. 3:1.

*a Law, of Moses, divine authority for*, Deut. 33:2.
*b Fear of God, enjoined*, Acts 9:31
*c Parents, duty of, to instruct children in righteousness*, 2 Cor. 12:14.
*d Instruction, of children*, Prov. 23:23.
*e School, in the home*, Acts 19:9.

11
*f Mountain*, Mic. 7:12.
*g* Heb. 12:18.
*h God, incomprehensible, symbolized by darkness*, Gen. 2:2.

12
*i God, invisible*, Gen. 2:2.
2 R. V. form;

13
*j Decalogue*, Ex. 20:3.
*k Obedience, enjoined*, Heb. 5:8.
*l Law, of Moses, engraved on stone*, Deut. 33:2.
*m Table, of testimony*, Ex. 31:18.
*n Stones, commandments engraved upon*, Ex. 24:12.

14
*o Word of God, inspiration of*, Psa. 119:9.
*p Instruction, in religion*, Prov. 23:23.

15
*q Commandment, enjoining watchfulness*, Deut. 8:2.
*r Watchfulness, enjoined*, Matt. 24:42.
*s Sinai*, Ex. 16:1.

16
*t Commandment, forbidding idolatry*, Deut. 8:2.
*u Idolatry*, 1 Sam. 15:23.
3 R. V. in the form

v.18–1494 BC
See footnote, *Time*, Rev. 10:6.

18
*v Creeping Things*, Rom. 1:23.
19
*w Sun, worship of, forbidden*, Josh. 10:12.
*x Moon, worship of, forbidden*, Song 6:10.
*y Stars, worship of, forbidden*, Judg. 5:20.
4 R. V. thou be drawn away and
20
*z God, love of, exemplified*, Gen. 2:2.

*a Iron*, Prov. 27:17.
*b Furnace, figurative of afflictions*, Prov. 17:3.
*c Egypt*, Gen. 41:8.
21
*d Anger of God*, 2 Kin. 13:3.
*e Moses, not permitted to enter Canaan*, Ex. 2:10.
*f Oath, attributed to God*, Num. 5:19.
*g Jordan*, Gen. 32:10.
*h Canaan, land of*, Gen. 37:1.
22
*i Death*, Num. 23:10.
23
*j Commandment, enjoining watchfulness*, Deut. 8:2.
*k Watchfulness, enjoined against backsliding*, Matt. 24:42.
*l Covenant, of God with men*, Deut. 29:1.
*m Idol*, 1 Kin. 15:12.
24
*n* Heb. 12:29.
*o Fire, figurative of judgments*, Ex. 12:8.
*p God, jealous*, Gen. 2:2.
25
*q Idolatry, denounced*, 1 Sam. 15:23.
26
*r Minister, faithful, instances of*, Rom. 15:16.
*s Judgments*, Ex. 6:6.

that [v]creepeth on the ground, the
likeness of any fish that *is* in the
waters beneath the earth:
19 And lest thou lift up thine
eyes unto heaven, and when thou
seest the [w]sun, and the [x]moon,
and the [y]stars, *even* all the host[G]
of heaven, [4]shouldest be driven
to [u]worship them, and serve
them, which the LORD thy God
hath divided unto all the nations
under the whole heaven.[Q]
20 But the [z]LORD hath taken
you, and brought you forth out
of the [a]iron [b]furnace, *even* out of
[c]Ē′gӯpt, to be unto him a people
of inheritance, as *ye are* this day.[Q]
21 Furthermore the LORD was
[d]angry with [e]me for your sakes,
and [f]sware that I should not go
over [g]Jôr′dan, and that I should
not go in unto that good [h]land,
which the LORD thy God giveth
thee *for* an inheritance:
22 But [e]I must [i]die in this land,
I must not go over [g]Jôr′dan: but
ye shall go over, and possess that
good [h]land.
23 [j,k]Take heed unto yourselves,
lest ye forget the [l]covenant[G]
of the LORD your God,
which he made with you, and
make you a graven[G] [m]image, [3]*or*
the likeness of any *thing*, which
the LORD thy God hath forbidden
thee.
24 For the LORD thy [n]God *is* a
consuming[G] [o]fire, *even* a [p]jealous
God.[S Q]
25 ¶ When thou shalt beget
children, and children's children,
and ye shall have remained
long in the land, and shall [q]corrupt
*yourselves*, and make a
graven[G] [m]image, [3]*or* the likeness
of any *thing*, and shall do evil in
the sight of the LORD thy God,
to provoke him to [d]anger:[S]
26 [r]I call heaven and earth to
witness against you this day,
that ye shall soon utterly [s]perish
from off the [h]land whereunto ye
go over Jôr′dan to possess it; ye
shall not prolong *your* days upon
it, but shall utterly be destroyed.
27 And the LORD shall [s]scatter
[t]you among the nations, and ye
shall be left few in number
among the heathen,[G] whither the
LORD shall lead you.
28 And there ye shall [u]serve
[m]gods, the work of men's hands,
wood and [v]stone, which neither
see, nor hear, nor eat, nor smell.
29 But if from thence [w,x,y]thou
shalt [z,a]seek the LORD thy God,
[b,c]thou shalt find *him*, if thou
seek him with all thy heart and
with all thy soul.
30 When thou art in [d]tribulation,[G]
and all these things are
come upon thee, *even* in the latter
days, if [c,e]thou turn to the
LORD thy God, and shalt be
obedient unto his voice;
31 (For the LORD thy God *is*
a [f]merciful God;) [g,h]he will not
forsake [c,e]thee, neither destroy
thee, nor forget the [i]covenant of
thy fathers which he sware unto
them.[S T]
32 For ask now of the days that
are past, which were before thee,
since the day that [j]God created
[k]man upon the earth, and *ask*
from the one side of heaven unto
the other, whether there hath
been *any such thing* as this great
thing *is*, or hath been heard
like it?
33 Did *ever* people hear the
voice of God [l]speaking out of the
midst of the fire, as thou hast
heard, and live?
34 Or hath [m]God assayed[G] to go
*and* take him a nation from the
midst of *another* nation, by
temptations,[G] by [l]signs, and by
wonders, and by war, and by a
mighty hand, and by a stretched
out [n]arm, and by great terrors,
according to all that the LORD
your God did for you in [o]Ē′gӯpt
before your eyes?

v.26–1494 BC
See footnote, *Time*, Rev. 10:6.

27
*t Backsliders, punishment of*, Jer. 3:22.
28
*u Idolatry, folly of*, 1 Sam. 15:23.
*v Stones, idols made of*, Ex. 24:12.
29
*w Backsliders, promises to penitent*, Jer. 3:22.
*x Seekers*, Isa. 55:6.
*y Nation, penitent, promises to*, Isa. 2:4.
*z Repentance, condition of divine favor*, Mark 1:4.

*a Spiritual Desire, reward for*, Psa. 42:1.
*b Promises, to the penitent, of forgiveness and favor*, 2 Cor. 1:20.
*c Penitent, promises to*, Psa. 51:17.
30
*d Afflictions, benefits of*, Psa. 34:19.
*e Backsliders, promises to penitent*, Jer. 3:22.
31
*f God, mercy of*, Gen. 2:2.
*g God, faithfulness of*, Gen. 2:2.
*h Promise, to the righteous, not to be forsaken*, 2 Cor. 1:20.
*i Covenant, of God with men*, Deut. 29:1.
32
*j God, creator of man*, Gen. 2:2.
*k Man, created*, Job 4:17.
33
*l Miracles*, Luke 23:8.
34
*m God, power of*, Gen. 2:2.
*n Arm, figurative*, Psa. 89:13.
*o Egypt*, Gen. 41:8.

v.35–1494 BC
See footnote, *Time,* Rev. 10:6.

**35**
p *Miracles, design of,* Luke 23:8.
q *Wisdom, spiritual,* Prov. 2:2.
r Mark 12:32.

**37**
s *God, love of,* Gen. 2:2.
t *Foreordination,* Rom. 8:30.
u *Children, of the righteous, blessed of God,* Mark 10:14.
5 R. V. with his presence, with

**38**
v *Canaan, land of, promised to Abraham and his seed,* Gen. 37:1.

**39**
w *God, sovereign,* Gen. 2:2.

**40**
x *Commandment, enjoining obedience,* Deut. 8:2.
y *Blessings, contingent upon obedience,* Deut. 11:26.
z *Reward, a motive to faithfulness,* Matt. 5:12.

a *Faithfulness, rewards of,* Luke 16:10.
b *Promises, to the obedient, of prosperity and long life,* 2 Cor. 1:20.
c *Temporal Blessings,* Psa. 103:2.
d *Children, of the righteous, blessed of God,* Mark 10:14.
e *Life, long, promised to the obedient,* Eccl. 8:15.

**41**
f *Cities, of refuge,* Num. 35:8.
g *Jordan,* Gen. 32:10.

**42**
h *Homicide, accidental,* Deut. 5:17.

**43**
i *Reubenites,* Josh. 22:1.
j *Ramoth-gilead,* Josh. 20:8.
k *Gad, tribe of,* Deut. 33:20.

35 Unto thee it was shewed,
[p]that thou mightest [q]know that
the LORD he *is* God; [r]*there is*
none else beside him.
36 Out of heaven he made thee
to hear his voice, that he might
instruct thee: and upon earth he
shewed thee his great [l]fire; and
thou heardest his words out of
the midst of the fire.
37 And because he [s]loved thy
fathers, therefore he [t]chose their
[u]seed after them, and brought
thee out [5]in his sight with his
mighty [m]power out of Ē′ġ̆ypt;
38 To drive out nations from
before thee greater and mightier
than thou *art,* to bring thee in, to
give thee their [v]land *for* an inheritance,
as *it is* this day.
39 Know therefore this day,
and consider *it* in thine heart,
that the LORD he *is* [w]God in
heaven above, and upon the
earth beneath: [r]*there is* none
else.
40 [x]Thou shalt keep therefore
his statutes, and his commandments,
which I command thee
this day, [y,z,a]that [b]it may [c]go
well with thee, and with thy
[d]children after thee, and that
thou mayest [e]prolong *thy* days
upon the earth, which the LORD
thy God giveth thee, for ever.
41 ¶ Then Mō′ṣeṣ severed three
[f]cities on this side [g]Jôr′dan toward
the sunrising;
42 That the slayer might flee
[f]thither, which should [h]kill his
neighbour unawares, and hated
him not in times past; and that
fleeing unto one of these cities
he might live:
43 *Namely,* [*,f]Bē′zēr in the
wilderness, in the plain country,
of the [i]Reu′ben-ītes; and [f,j]Rā′moth
in Ġĭl′e-ăd, of the [k]Găd′ītes;
and [†,f]Gō′lan in Bā′shăn,
of the [l]Mă-năs′sītes.
44 ¶ And this *is* the [m]law which
Mō′ṣeṣ set before the children of
Ĭṣ′ra-el:
45 These *are* the [n]testimonies,
and the [m]statutes, and the judgments,
which Mō′ṣeṣ spake unto
the children of [o]Ĭṣ′ra-el, after
they came forth out of [p]Ē′ġ̆ypt.
46 On this side [g]Jôr′dan, in the
valley over against [q]Bĕth–pē′ôr,
in the land of [r]Sī′hŏn king of the
[s]Ăm′ôr-ītes, who dwelt at Hĕsh′bŏn,
whom Mō′ṣeṣ and the children
of Ĭṣ′ra-el smote, after they
were come forth out of Ē′ġ̆ypt:
47 And they possessed his land,
and the land of [t]Ŏg king of Bā′shăn,
two kings of the [s]Ăm′ôr-ītes,
which *were* on this side
[g]Jôr′dan toward the sunrising;
48 From [‡]Ăr′ŏ-ēr, which *is* [6]by
the bank of the river [u]Ăr′nŏn,
even unto mount Sī′ŏn, which *is*
[‖]Hēr′mon,
49 And all the plain on this side
[g]Jôr′dan eastward, even unto
the [v]sea of the plain, under the
[7]springs of [w]Pĭṣ′gah.

## CHAPTER 5

*The history of the covenant in Horeb; 6 of the giving of the ten commandments; 22 and of Moses receiving the law from God.*

AND [a]Mō′ṣeṣ called all [b]Ĭṣ′ra-el, and said unto them,
Hear, O Ĭṣ′ra-el, the [c]statutes
and judgments which I speak
in your ears this day, that ye
may learn them, and [d]keep, and
do them.
2 The LORD our God made a
[e]covenant with us in [f]Hō′reb.
3 The LORD made not this
[e]covenant with our fathers, but
with us, *even* us, who *are* all of
us here alive this day.
4 The LORD talked with you

v.43–1494 BC
See footnote, *Time,* Rev. 10:6.
l *Manasseh, tribe of,* Gen. 46:20.

**44**
m *Law, of Moses,* Deut. 33:2.

**45**
n *Testimony,* Ex. 25:16.
o *Israel,* Ex. 4:22.
p *Egypt,* Gen. 41:8.

**46**
q *Beth-peor,* Deut. 3:29.
r *Sihon,* Num. 21:21.
s *Amorites,* Gen. 14:13.

**47**
t *Og,* Num. 21:33.

**48**
u *Arnon,* Num. 22:36.
6 R. V. on the edge of the valley of Arnon.

**49**
v *Dead Sea,* Gen. 14:3.
w *Pisgah,* Deut. 3:27.
7 R. V. slopes of

**1**
a *Moses,* Ex. 2:10.
b *Israel, the law delivered to,* vs. 1–33; Ex. 4:22.
c *Law, of Moses, divine authority for,* vs. 1–22; Deut. 33:2.
d *Obedience, enjoined,* Heb. 5:8.

**2**
e *Covenant, of God with men,* Deut. 29:1.
f *Horeb,* Ex. 3:1.

* **BEZER.** *A city of refuge, E. of the Jordan,* Josh. 20:8; 21:36; 1 Chr. 6:78.

† **GOLAN,** a town in Bashan. *Given to Manasseh as a city of refuge,* Josh. 20:8. *A Levitical city,* Josh. 21:27; 1 Chr. 6:71.

‡ **AROER.** *A city of the Amorites in the valley of the river Arnon,* Deut. 4:48. *Conquered by Israelites,* Deut. 2:36; 3:12; Judg. 11:26, 33. *Taken by Hazael,* 2 Kin. 10:33.

‖ **HERMON** (*lofty*). *A mountain in the N. of Palestine,* 1 Chr. 5:23; Psa. 133:3. *Called,* SIRION, Deut. 3:8, 9; Psa. 29:6; SHENIR, Deut. 3:9; Song 4:8; SENIR, Ezek. 27:5.

v.4–1494 BC
See footnote, *Time*, Rev. 10:6.

4
*g* *Sinai, the law delivered to Moses upon*, Ex. 16:1.

5
*h* *Mediation*, Gal. 3:19.

6
*i* *God, providence of*, Gen. 2:2.
*j* *Egypt*, Gen. 41:8.

7
*k* *Commandment, forbidding idolatry*, Deut. 8:2.
*l* *Decalogue*, vs. 7–21; Ex. 20:3.
*m* *Idolatry, forbidden*, 1 Sam. 15:23.

8
*n* *Commandment, forbidding the making of idolatrous images*, Deut. 8:2.

9
*o* *Commandment, forbidding the worship of images*, Deut. 8:2.
*p* *God, jealous*, Gen. 2:2.
*q* *Sin, consequences of, entailed upon children*, Rom. 5:12.
*r* *Wicked, punishment of*, Psa. 73:3.

10
*s* *God, mercy of*, Gen. 2:2.
*t* *Blessings, contingent upon obedience*, Deut. 11:26.
*u* *Love, of man for God*, 1 John 4:19.
*v* *Obedience, rewarded*, Heb. 5:8.

11
*w* *Commandment, forbidding the profaning of God's name*, Deut. 8:2.
*x* *Blasphemy*, 2 Sam. 12:14.
*y* *Oath, profane, forbidden*, Num. 5:19.
*z* *Profanation, of God's name, forbidden*, Gen. 2:2.—*a God, name of, not to be profaned*, Gen. 2:2.

**12** *b Decalogue*, Ex. 20:3. *c Fourth Commandment*, vs. 12–14; Ex. 20:8. *d Commandment, enjoining the keeping of the Sabbath holy*, Deut. 8:2. *e Sabbath*, Ex. 16:23.

**13** *f Commandment, enjoining labor*, Deut. 8:2. *g Industry, enjoined*, 1 Kin. 11:28. *h Labor*, Luke 10:7.

face to face in the [g]mount out of
the midst of the fire,
5 ([a]I [h]stood between the LORD
and you at that time, to shew
you the word of the LORD: for
ye were afraid by reason of the
fire, and went not up into the
[g]mount;) saying,
6 ¶ I *am* the LORD thy God,
which [i]brought thee out of the
land of [j]E'gypt, from the house
of bondage.[T]
7 [k,l,m]Thou shalt have none
other gods before[G] me.
8 [l,n]Thou shalt not make thee
*any* graven[G] image, *or* any likeness
*of any thing* that *is* in heaven
above, or that *is* in the earth
beneath, or that *is* in the waters
beneath the earth:
9 [o]Thou shalt not [m]bow down
thyself unto them, nor serve
them: for I the LORD thy God
*am* a [p]jealous God, visiting the
[q]iniquity of the [r]fathers upon the
children unto the third and
fourth *generation* of them that
hate me,[S]
10 And [s]shewing *,[t]mercy unto
thousands of them that [u]love me
and [v]keep[G] my commandments.
11 [w]Thou shalt not [x,y,z]take
the [a]name of the LORD thy God
in vain: for the LORD will not
hold *him* guiltless that taketh
his name in vain.[Q]
12 [b,c,d]Keep[Q] the [e]sabbath[G] day
to sanctify[G] it, as the LORD thy
God hath commanded thee.
13[Q] [f,g]Six days thou shalt [h]labour,
and do all thy work:
14 But the seventh day *is* the
[e]sabbath[G] of the LORD thy God:
*in it* [i,j]thou shalt [k,l]not do any
work, thou, nor thy son, nor thy
daughter, nor thy [m]manservant,
nor thy maidservant, nor thine
[n]ox, nor thine ass, nor any of thy
cattle, nor thy stranger that *is*
within thy gates[G]; that thy manservant
and thy maidservant
may rest as well as thou.[Q]
15 And [o]remember that thou
wast a servant in the land of
[p]E'gypt, and *that* the LORD thy
[q]God brought thee out thence
through a mighty hand and by a
stretched out [r,s]arm: therefore
the LORD thy God commanded
thee to keep[G] the [e]sabbath[G] day.
16 ¶ [t,u]Honour[Q] [v]thy [w,x]father
and thy [y]mother, as the LORD
thy God hath commanded thee;
that [z,a]thy [b]days may be prolonged,
and [c]that it may go well
with thee, in the land which the
LORD thy God giveth thee.
17 [d,e]Thou[Q] shalt [1]not [†]kill.
18 [f,g]Neither[Q] shalt thou commit
[h]adultery.
19 [i,j]Neither shalt thou [k]steal.
20 [l,m]Neither shalt thou bear
[n,o]false witness[G] against thy
neighbour.[Q]
21 [p,q]Neither shalt thou [2,r]desire
thy neighbour's wife, neither
shalt thou [3]covet[G] thy neighbour's
[s]house, his field, or his

v.14–1494 BC
See footnote, *Time*, Rev. 10:6.

14
*i* *Employer*, Deut. 24:14.
*j* *Master, duties of*, Col. 4:1.
*k* *Rest, on the Sabbath day, enjoined*, Ex. 23:12.
*l* *Sanitation and Hygiene, rest enjoined*, Num. 31:23.
*m* *Servant, to have rest on the Sabbath*, Jer. 2:14.
*n* *Animals, laws concerning*, Jer. 27:5.

15
*o* *Commandment, enjoining a remembrance of God's mercies*, Deut. 8:2.
*p* *Egypt*, Gen. 41:8.
*q* *God, preserver*, Gen. 2:2.
*r* *Arm, figurative*, Psa. 89:13.
*s* *Anthropomorphisms*, Gen. 11:5.

16
*t* *Commandment, enjoining reverence for parents*, Deut. 8:2.
*u* *Fifth Commandment*, Ex. 20:12.
*v* *Children, commandments to*, Mark 10:14.
*w* *Father, to be revered*, Psa. 27:10.
*x* *Parents, to be reverenced*, 2 Cor. 12:14.
*y* *Mother, reverence for, enjoined*, 1 Kin. 2:20.
*z* *Children, promises and assurances to*, Mark 10:14.

*a* *Promise, to obedient children, of long life and prosperity*, 2 Cor. 1:20.
*b* *Life, long, promised to those who honor parents*, Eccl. 8:15. *c Blessings, contingent upon obedience*, Deut. 11:26.

**17** *d Commandment, forbidding murder*, Deut. 8:2. *e Sixth Commandment*, Ex. 20:13. 1 R. V. do no murder.

**18** *f Commandment, forbidding adultery*, Deut. 8:2. *g Seventh Commandment*, Ex. 20:14. *h Adultery, forbidden*, Lev. 20:10.

**19** *i Commandment, forbidding theft*, Deut. 8:2. *j Eighth Commandment*, Ex. 20:15. *k Theft*, Mark 7:22.

**20** *l Commandment, forbidding false witness*, Deut. 8:2. *m Ninth Commandment*, Ex. 20:16. *n False Witness*, Matt. 19:18. *o Falsehood*, Job 21:34.

**21** *p Commandment, forbidding covetousness*, Deut. 8:2. *q Tenth Commandment*, Ex. 20:17. *r Covetousness, commandments against*, Isa. 57:17. *s Property, personal rights in, sacred*, Lev. 27:15. 2 R. V. covet 3 R. V. desire

---

* **MERCY**, Psa. 85:10; Prov. 20:28; Hos. 4:1; Jas. 2:13. *A grace of the godly*, Psa. 37:25, 26; Prov. 11:17; 12:10; 14:22, 31; Rom. 12:8. *Of the wicked, cruel*, Prov. 12:10. *Iniquity atoned by*, Prov. 16:6.

*Enjoined*, Prov. 3:3; Hos. 12:6; Mic. 6:8; Matt. 9:13; 12:7; 23:23; Luke 6:36; Col. 3:12, 13. *To be shown with cheerfulness*, Rom. 12:8. *Rewards of*, 2 Sam. 22:26; Psa. 18:25; 37:25, 26; Prov. 14:21; 21:21; Matt. 5:7.

See footnote, KINDNESS, Acts 28:2.

**Instances of:** *The prison keeper to Joseph*, Gen. 39:21–23. *Joshua to Rahab*, Josh. 6:25. *The Israelites to the man of Bethel*, Judg. 1:23–26. *David to Saul*, 1 Sam. 24:10–13, 17.

**Of God,** see footnote, GOD, *Mercy of*, Gen. 2:2.

† **HOMICIDE. Accidental,** Ex. 21:13; Num. 35:11–15, 22–28, 32; Deut. 4:41–43; 19:1–10; Josh. 20:1–9.

**Felonious, or murder,** Job 24:14; Psa. 10:8; 38:12; 94:3, 6; Prov. 12:6; 28:17; Isa. 59:3; Jer. 2:34; 7:9, 10; 19:4; Ezek. 22:9; Hos. 4:1–3; Hab. 2:10, 12. *God's abhorrence of*, Psa. 5:6; 9:12; Prov. 6:16, 17.

v.21–1494 BC
See footnote, *Time,* Rev. 10:6.

**22**
*t* *Decalogue,* Ex. 20:3.
*u* *God, incomprehensible, symbolized by darkness,* Gen. 2:2.
*v* *God, invisible,* Gen. 2:2.
*w* *Sinai,* Ex. 16:1.
*x* *Stones, commandments engraved upon,* Ex. 24:12.

**23**
*y* *Senate,* Num. 11:16.

**24**
*z* *God, glory of,* Gen. 2:2.

**27**
*a* *Mediation,* Gal. 3:19.
*b* *Moses,* Ex. 2:10.
*c* *Israel,* Ex. 4:22.
*d* *Decision, instances of,* Isa. 50:7.

manservant, or his maidservant, his ox, or his ass, or [s]any *thing* that *is* thy neighbour's.[S Q]

22 ¶ These [t]words the [u,v]LORD spake unto all your assembly in the [w]mount out of the midst of the fire, of the cloud, and of the thick darkness, with a great voice: and he added no more. And he wrote them in two tables of [x]stone, and delivered them unto me.[Q]

23 And it came to pass, when ye heard the voice out of the midst of the [u]darkness, (for the [w]mountain did burn with fire,) that ye came near unto me, *even* all the heads of your tribes, and your [y]elders;[T Q]

24 And ye said, Behold, the LORD our God hath shewed us [z]his glory and his greatness, and we have heard his voice out of the midst of the fire: we have seen this day that God doth talk with man, and he liveth.

25 Now therefore why should we die? for this great fire will consume[G] us: if we hear the voice of the LORD our God any more, then we shall die.[Q]

26 For who *is there of* all flesh, that hath heard the voice of the living God speaking out of the midst of the fire, as we *have,* and lived?[T]

27 [a]Go [b]thou near, and hear all that the LORD our God shall say: and speak thou unto [c]us all that the LORD our God shall speak unto thee; and [d]we will hear *it,* and do *it.*

28 And the LORD heard the voice of your words, when [c]ye spake unto [b]me; and the LORD said unto me, I have heard the voice of the words of this people, which they have spoken unto thee: they have well said all that they have spoken.[T]

29 O that there were such an [e]heart in [f]them, that they would [g]fear me, and keep[G] all my commandments always, [h]that [i]it might be well with them, and with their [j]children for ever![S]

30 Go say to them, Get you into your tents again.[S]

31 But as for [b]thee, stand thou here by me, and I will [k]speak unto thee all the [l]commandments, and the statutes, and the judgments,[G] which thou shalt teach [c]them, that they may do *them* in the land which I give them to possess it.

32 [m]Ye shall observe to [n]do therefore as the LORD your God hath commanded you: ye shall not turn aside to the right hand or to the left.

33 [m,n]Ye shall walk in all the ways which the LORD your God hath commanded you, that ye may [o]live, and *that it may be* well with you, and *that* ye may prolong *your* days in the land which ye shall possess.[S]

## CHAPTER 6

*An exhortation to obey the law, and to teach it diligently to their children.*

NOW these *are* the [a,b]commandments, the statutes, and the judgments,[G] which the

v.28–1494 BC
See footnote, *Time,* Rev. 10:6.

**29**
*e* *Heart,* Psa. 44:21.
*f* *Wicked, God's love for,* Psa. 73:3.
*g* *Fear of God,* Acts 9:31.
*h* *Blessings, contingent upon obedience,* Deut. 11:26.
*i* *Promises, to the righteous,* 2 Cor. 1:20.
*j* *Children, of the righteous, blessed of God,* Mark 10:14.

**31**
*k* *Inspiration, of Moses,* Job 32:8.
*l* *Law, of Moses,* Deut. 33:2.

**32**
*m* *Commandment, enjoining obedience,* Deut. 8:2.
*n* *Obedience, enjoined,* Heb. 5:8.

**33**
*o* *Temporal Blessings, from God,* Psa. 103:2.

**1**
*a* *Word of God, inspired,* Psa. 119:9.
*b* *Law,* vs. 4–9; Deut. 33:2.

*Forbidden,* Ex. 20:13; Deut. 5:17; Prov. 1:15, 16; Jer. 22:3; Matt. 5:21; 19:18; Mark 10:19; Luke 18:20; Rom. 13:9; 1 Tim. 1:9; Jas. 2:11; 1 Pet. 4:15; 1 John 3:12, 15.

*Through conspiracy,* Psa. 37:32; Prov. 1:11, 12. *In hearts of wicked,* Matt. 15:19; Mark 7:21. *Impenitence for,* Rev. 9:21. *Penitence for,* Psa. 51:1–17. *Inquest over suspected,* Deut. 21:1–9.

**Instances of:** *By Cain,* Gen. 4:8. *By Lamech,* Gen. 4:23, 24. *By Simeon and Levi,* Gen. 34:25–31. *By Pharaoh,* Ex. 1:16, 22. *By Moses,* Ex. 2:12. *By Ehud,* Judg. 3:16–23. *By Abimelech,* Judg. 9:5, 18, 56. *By Joab,* 2 Sam. 3:24–27; 2 Sam. 20:9, 10; 1 Kin. 2:5. *By Solomon,* 1 Kin. 2:23–46. *By Rechab and Baanah,* 2 Sam. 4:5–8. *By David,* 2 Sam. 11:14–17; 2 Sam. 12:9. *By Absalom,* 2 Sam. 13:22–29. *By Baasha,* 1 Kin. 15:27–29. *By Zimri,* 1 Kin. 16:9–11. *By Ahab and Jezebel,* 1 Kin. 21:10–24. *By Hazael,* 2 Kin. 8:15. *By Jehu,* 2 Kin. 9:24–37. *By Athaliah,* 2 Kin. 11:1. *Of Joash, by his servants,* 2 Kin. 12:20, 21. *By Menahem,* 2 Kin. 15:16. *Of Sennacherib, by his sons,* 2 Kin. 19:37; Isa. 37:38. *By Manasseh,* 2 Kin. 21:16; 24:4. *Of Amon, by his servants,* 2 Kin. 21:23. *By Jehoram,* 2 Chr. 21:4. *By Joash,* 2 Chr. 24:21. *By Amaziah's soldiers,* 2 Chr. 25:12. *By Nebuchadnezzar,* Jer. 39:6. *By Ishmael,* Jer. 41:1–7. *By Herod I,* Matt. 2:16. *By Herod,* Matt. 14:10; Mark 6:27. *By Barabbas,* Mark 15:7; Acts 3:14.

**Punishment for,** Lev. 24:17; Deut. 19:11–13; Psa. 55:23. *By a curse,* Gen. 4:9–12; 49:7; Deut. 27:24, 25. *By death,* Gen. 9:5, 6; Ex. 21:12, 14; Num. 35:16–21, 30–33; Deut. 17:6; 1 Kin. 21:19; Ezek. 35:6; Hos. 1:4. *By everlasting punishment,* Rev. 21:8; 22:15.

INSTANCES OF PUNISHMENT FOR: *Cain,* Gen. 4:11–15. *The murderer of Saul,* 2 Sam. 1:15, 16. *David,* 2 Sam. 12:9–18. *Joab,* 1 Kin. 2:31–34. *Haman,* Esth. 7:10. *The murderers of Ish-bosheth,* 2 Sam. 4:11, 12; *of Joash,* 2 Kin. 14:5.

v.1–1494 BC
See footnote, *Time*, Rev. 10:6.

c *Instruction, in religion*, Prov. 23:23.
d *Obedience, enjoined*, vs. 1–25; Heb. 5:8.
e *Canaan*, Gen. 37:1.

2
f *Fear of God*, Acts 9:31.
g *Reward, a motive to faithfulness*, Matt. 5:12.
h *Promise, to the obedient*, 2 Cor. 1:20.
i *Temporal Blessings, from God*, Psa. 103:2.

3
j *Faithfulness, rewards of*, Luke 16:10.

4
k Mark 12:29.
l *God, unity of*, Gen. 2:2.

5
m *Commandment, enjoining supreme love to God*, Deut. 8:2.
n Matt. 22:37–39; Mark 12:30; Luke 10:27.
o *Love, of man for God, enjoined*, 1 John 4:19.
p *Duty, of man to God*, Eccl. 12:13.

6
q *Commandment, enjoining remembrance of God's law*, Deut. 8:2.

7
r *Commandment, enjoining religious instruction of children*, Deut. 8:2.
s *Parents, duty of, to instruct children in righteousness*, vs. 20–24; 2 Cor. 12:14.
t *Instruction, of children*, Prov. 23:23.
u *Children, instruction of*, Mark 10:14.
v *School, in the home*, Acts 19:9.

8
w *Phylactery*, Matt. 23:5.
x *Frontlets*, Ex. 13:16.

9
y *Legends*, Zech. 14:20.
z *House*, Esth. 8:1.

10
a *Canaan, land of, promised to Abraham and his seed*, Gen. 37:1.
b *Covenant, of God with men*, Deut. 29:1.

LORD your God commanded to
[c]teach you, that ye might [d]do
*them* in the [e]land whither ye go
to possess it:
2 That thou mightest [f]fear the
LORD thy God, to [d]keep all his
statutes and his commandments,
which I command thee, thou,
and thy son, and thy son's son,
all the days of thy life; and
[g,h]that thy [i]days may be prolonged.
3 ¶ Hear therefore, O Iṣ'ra-el,
and observe to [d,j]do *it*; [g,h]that
it may be well with thee, and
that ye may [i]increase mightily,
as the LORD God of thy fathers
hath promised thee, in the [e]land
that floweth with milk and
honey.
4 Hear, O Iṣ'ra-el: [k]The LORD
our [l]God *is* one LORD:
5 And [m,n]thou shalt [o,p]love the
LORD thy God with all thine
heart, and with all thy soul, and
with all thy might.
6 And [q]these words, which I
command thee this day, shall be
in thine heart:
7 And [r,s]thou shalt [t]teach
them diligently unto thy [u]children,
and shalt [v]talk of them
when thou sittest in thine house,
and when thou walkest by the
way, and when thou liest down,
and when thou risest up.
8 And thou shalt bind them
for a [w]sign upon thine hand, and
they shall be as [x]frontlets between
thine eyes.
9 And thou shalt write [y]them
upon the posts of thy [z]house, and
on thy gates.
10 And it shall be, when the
LORD thy God shall have
brought thee into the [a]land
which he [b]sware unto thy fathers,
to Ā'brā-hăm, to Ī'ṣaac,
and to Jā'cob, to give thee [c]great
and goodly cities, which thou
buildedst not,
11 And [c]houses full of all good
*things*, which thou filledst not,
and wells digged, which thou
diggedst not, [d]vineyards and
*olive trees, which thou plantedst
not; when thou shalt have
eaten and be full;
12 *Then* [e]beware lest thou [f]forget
the LORD, which brought
thee forth out of the land of
[g]Ē'gȳpt, from the house of bondage.
13 [h,i]Thou shalt [j]fear the
LORD thy God, and serve him,
and shalt [k]swear by his name.
14 [l,m]Ye shall not go after other
gods, of the gods of the people
which *are* round about you;
15 (For the LORD thy God *is* a
[n]jealous God among you) lest
the [o]anger of the LORD thy God
be kindled against thee, and [p]destroy
thee from off the face of the
earth.
16 ¶ [q,r]Ye shall not tempt the
LORD your God, as ye tempted
*him* in [s]Măs'sah.
17 [t]Ye shall [u,v]diligently [w]keep
the commandments of the LORD
your God, and his testimonies,
and his statutes, which he hath
commanded thee.
18 And [x]thou shalt do *that*
*which is* right and good in the
sight of the LORD: [y,z]that it may
be well with thee, and that thou
mayest go in and possess the
good [a]land which the LORD
sware unto thy fathers.
19 To cast out all thine enemies
from before thee, as the LORD
hath spoken.
20 ¶ *And* when thy [a]son asketh

y *Reward, a motive to faithfulness*, Matt. 5:12. z *Blessings, contingent upon obedience*, Deut. 11:26.—**20** a *Children, instruction of*, Mark 10:14.

v.10–1494 BC
See footnote, *Time*, Rev. 10:6.

c *Riches, a snare*, vs. 10–12; Eccl. 4:8.

11
d *Grape*, Lev. 25:5.

12
e *Commandment, enjoining watchfulness*, Deut. 8:2.
f *Ingratitude, of man to God*, Rom. 1:21.
g *Egypt*, Gen. 41:8.

13
h *Commandment, enjoining the fear and service of God, and to solemnize oaths in the name of God rather than of idolatrous gods*, Deut. 8:2.
i Matt. 4:10; Luke 4:8.
j *Fear of God*, Acts 9:31.
k *Oath, a solemn qualification*, Num. 5:19.

14
l *Commandment, forbidding idolatry*, Deut. 8:2.
m *Idolatry, forbidden*, 1 Sam. 15:23.

15
n *God, jealous*, Gen. 2:2.
o *Anger of God*, 2 Kin. 13:3.
p *Judgments*, Ex. 6:6.

16
q Matt. 4:7; Luke 4:12.
r *Commandment, forbidding tempting God*, Deut. 8:2.
s Or, *Meribah*, Ex 17:7.

17
t *Commandment, enjoining obedience*, Deut. 8:2.
u *Diligence, required*, Rom. 12:8.
v *Watchfulness*, Matt. 24:42.
w *Obedience, enjoined*, Heb. 5:8.

18
x *Commandment, enjoining right conduct*, Deut. 8:2.

***OLIVE**, a fruit tree. *Leaf of, brought by the dove to Noah's ark*, Gen. 8:11. *Common to the land of Canaan*, Ex. 23:11; Deut. 8:8. *Israelites commanded to cultivate, in the land of promise*, Deut. 28:40. *Branches of, used for booths*, Neh. 8:15. *Precepts concerning gleaning the fruit of*, Deut. 24:20. *Cherubim made of the wood of*, 1 Kin. 6:23. *Fable of*, Judg. 9:8. **Fruit of:** *Oil extracted from, used, in compounding the sacred ointment*, Ex. 30:24; *as illuminating oil in the tabernacle* Ex. 25:6; 27:20; 35:14, 28; 39:37; Lev. 24:2. **Figurative:** *The wild, a figure of the Gentiles; the cultivated, of the Jews*, Rom. 11:17–21, 24. **Symbolical**, Zech. 4:2–12; Rev. 11:4.

v.20–1494 BC
See footnote, *Time,* Rev. 10:6.

b *Word of God,* Psa. 119:9.

21
c *Pharaoh, at the time of the exodus,* Ex. 3:10.
d *Servant,* Jer. 2:14.
e *God, providence of,* Gen. 2:2.

22
f *Miracles,* Luke 23:8.
g *Egyptians, visited by plagues,* Gen. 50:3.

23
h *Canaan,* Gen. 37:1.
i *Covenant, of God with men,* Deut. 29:1.

24
j *Obedience, enjoined,* Heb. 5:8.
k *Fear of God, enjoined,* Acts 9:31.
l *Blessings, contingent upon obedience,* Deut. 11:26.

25
m *Righteousness, imputed on account of obedience,* Psa. 15:2.

thee in time to come, saying,
What *mean* the [b]testimonies, and
the statutes, and the judgments,
which the LORD our God hath
commanded you?
21 Then thou shalt say unto
thy [a]son, We were [c]Phā'raōh's
[d]bondmen in Ē'ġy̆pt; and the
LORD [e]brought us out of Ē'ġy̆pt
with a mighty hand:
22 And the LORD shewed
[f]signs and wonders, great and
sore, upon [g]Ē'ġy̆pt, upon [c]Phā'-
raōh, and upon all his household, before our eyes:
23 And he brought us out from
thence, that he might bring us
in, to give us the [h]land which he
[i]sware unto our fathers.
24 And the LORD commanded
us to [j]do all these statutes, to
[k]fear the LORD our God, for our
good always, [l]that he might preserve us alive, as *it is* at this day.
25 And it shall be our [m]right-
eousness, if we observe to [l]do all
these commandments before the
LORD our God, as he hath commanded us.

## CHAPTER 7

*All intercourse with the nations of Canaan is forbidden, 4 for fear of idolatry, 6 to promote the holiness of the people, 9 and to secure the favor of God. 17 A promise of victory over those nations. 25 Their idols to be destroyed.*

1
a *Canaan,* Gen. 37:1.
b *Judgments, upon the Canaanites,* vs. 1–26; Ex. 6:6.
c Acts 13:19.
d *Hittites,* Judg. 1:26.
e *Girgashites,* Neh. 9:8.
f *Amorites,* Gen. 14:13.
g *Canaanites,* Ex. 23:28.
h *Perizzites,* Gen. 15:20.
i *Hivites,* Gen. 10:17.

2
j *Fellowship, with the wicked, forbidden,* 1 Cor. 1:9.

WHEN the LORD thy God
shall bring thee into the
[a]land whither thou goest to possess it, and hath [b,c]cast out many
nations before thee, the [d]Hĭt'-
tītes, and the [e]Gĭr'ga-shītes, and
the [f]Ăm'ôr-ītes, and the [g]Cā'-
năan-ītes, and the [h]Pĕr'ĭz-zītes,
and the [i]Hī'vītes, and the *Jĕb'-
u-sītes, seven nations greater
and mightier than thou;
2 And when the LORD thy God
shall deliver them before thee;
thou shalt smite them, *and* utterly destroy them; [j]thou shalt
make no [k]covenant with [l]them,
nor shew mercy unto them:
3 Neither shalt thou make
[m,n]marriages with them; thy
daughter thou shalt not give unto his son, nor his daughter shalt
thou take unto thy son.
4 For they will turn away thy
son from following me, that they
may [o]serve other gods: so will
the [p,q]anger of the LORD be
kindled against you, and destroy thee suddenly.
5 But thus shall ye deal with
them; ye shall destroy their altars, and [r]break down their [1]im-
ages, and cut down their groves,
and burn their [s]graven images
with fire.
6 For thou *art* an [t,u,v]holy people unto the LORD thy God: the
LORD thy [w]God hath [x]chosen
[y]thee to be a special people unto
himself, above all people that
*are* upon the face of the earth.
7 The LORD did not set his
[w]love upon you, nor [x]choose you,
because ye were more in number
than any people; for ye *were* the
fewest of all people:
8 But because the LORD [w]loved
you, and because he would keep
the [z]oath which he had [a]sworn
unto your fathers, hath the
LORD [b]brought you out with a
mighty hand, and redeemed you
out of the house of bondmen,
from the hand of [c]Phā'raōh king
of Ē'ġy̆pt.
9 Know therefore that the
LORD thy God, he *is* God, the
faithful [b]God, [d]which [e]keepeth
[f]covenant and [g]mercy with them
that [h]love him and [i]keep his
commandments to a thousand
generations;
10 And repayeth [j,k]them that
hate him to their face, to destroy
them: he will not be slack to him

v.2–1494 BC
See footnote, *Time,* Rev. 10:6.

k *Alliances, with idolaters, forbidden,* Josh. 9:15.
l *Evil Company, forbidden,* Prov. 13:20.

3
m *Marriage, wives among the Israelites must be Israelites,* Gen. 34:9.
n *Miscegenation, forbidden,* Josh. 23:12.

4
o *Idolatry,* 1 Sam. 15:23.
p *Anger of God,* 2 Kin. 13:3.
q *Anthropomorphisms,* Gen. 11:5.

5
r *Iconoclasm,* Num. 33:52.
s *Carving,* Ex. 35:33.
1 R. V. pillars,

6
t *The Holy, described,* Col. 3:12.
u *Holiness,* Ex. 39:30.
v *Righteous, described,* Psa. 64:10.
w *God, love of, exemplified,* Gen. 2:2.
x *Election of Grace,* Rom. 11:5.
y *Israel, taught to be holy by being separate,* Ex. 4:22.

8
z *Covenant, of God with men,* Deut. 29:1.

a *Anthropomorphisms, oath attributed to God,* Gen. 11:5.
b *God, faithfulness of,* Gen. 2:2.
c *Pharaoh, of the exodus,* Ex. 3:10.

9
d *Promise, to the obedient,* 2 Cor. 1:20.
e *Blessings, contingent upon obedience,* Deut. 11:26.
f *Covenant, of God with men,* Deut. 29:1.
g *God, mercy of,* Gen. 2:2.
h *Love, of man for God,* 1 John 4:19.
i *Obedience, rewarded,* Heb. 5:8.

10
j *Wicked, punishment of,* Psa. 73:3.
k *The Godless, to be punished,* Job 8:13.

* **JEBUSITES.** *One of the tribes of Canaan,* Deut. 7:1. *Land of, given to Abraham and his descendants,* Gen. 15:21; Ex. 3:8, 17; 23:23, 24; 33:2; 34:10, 11; Deut. 20:17. *Conquered, by Joshua,* Josh. chapters 10–12; 24:11; *by David,* 2 Sam. 5:6–9. *Jerusalem within the territory of,* Josh. 18:28. *Not exterminated, but intermarry with the Israelites,* Judg. 3:5, 6; Ezra 9:1, 2; 10:18–44. *Paid tribute to Solomon,* 1 Kin. 9:20, 21.

v.10–1494 BC
See footnote, *Time*, Rev. 10:6.

11
*l* *Commandment, enjoining obedience to God's law*, Deut. 8:2.
*m* *Obedience, enjoined*, Heb. 5:8.
*n* *Word of God*, Psa. 119:9.

12
*o* *Contingencies, in divine government*, 1 Kin. 3:14.

13
*p* *God, love of*, Gen. 2:2.
*q* *Temporal Blessings, from God*, Psa. 103:2.
*r* *God, providence of*, vs. 13–24; Gen. 2:2.

15
*s* *Disease, healing of, from God*, Ex. 15:26.

16
*t* *Pity*, Job 19:21.
*u* *Idolatry, forbidden*, 1 Sam. 15:23.

17
*v* *Doubting*, Rom. 14:23.
*w* *Canaanites*, Ex. 23:28.

18
*x* *Faith, enjoined*, Mark 11:22.
*y* *Egypt*, Gen. 41:8.

that hateth him, he will repay him to his face.

11 [l,m]Thou shalt therefore keep the [n]commandments, and the statutes, and the judgments[G], which I command thee this day, to do them.

12 Wherefore it shall come to pass, [o]if ye hearken to these judgments, and [m]keep, and do them, that [d,e]the LORD thy God shall keep unto thee the [f]covenant and the [g]mercy which he sware unto thy fathers:[T]

13 [S]And [p]he will love thee, and [q]bless thee, and multiply thee: [r]he will also bless the fruit[G] of thy womb, and the fruit of thy land, thy corn[G], and thy wine, and thine oil, the in crease of thy kine[G], and the flocks of thy sheep, in the land which he [a,f]sware[G] unto thy fathers to give thee.

14 [d]Thou shalt be [q]blessed above all people: there shall not be male or female †barren among you, or among your cattle.

15 And the [r]LORD will take away from thee all [s]sickness, and will put none of the evil diseases of Ē′ġȳpt, which thou knowest, upon thee; but will lay them upon all *them* that hate thee.

16 And thou shalt consume[G] all the people which the LORD thy God shall deliver thee; thine eye shall have no [t]pity upon them: neither shalt thou [u]serve their gods; for that *will be* a snare unto thee.

17 If thou shalt [v]say in thine heart, These [w]nations *are* more than I; how can I dispossess them?

18 Thou shalt [x]not be afraid of them: *but* shalt well remember what the LORD thy God did unto [c]Phā′raōh, and unto all [y]Ē′ġȳpt;

19 The great temptations[G] which thine eyes saw, and the [z]signs, and the wonders, and the mighty hand, and the stretched out [a]arm, whereby the LORD thy [b]God brought thee out: so shall the LORD thy God do unto all the people of whom thou art afraid.

20 Moreover the LORD thy God will [c]send the [d]hornet among them, until they that are left, and hide themselves from thee, be destroyed.

21 [e]Thou shalt not be affrighted[G] at them: for the LORD thy [f]God *is* among you, a [g]mighty God and terrible.[G S]

22 And the LORD thy God will put out those [h]nations before thee by little and little: thou mayest not consume[G] them at once, lest the beasts of the field increase upon thee.[S]

23 [S]But the LORD thy God shall deliver them unto thee, and shall [2]destroy [h]them with a [3]mighty destruction, until they be destroyed.

24 And he shall deliver their kings into thine hand, and thou shalt destroy their name from under heaven: there shall no man be able to stand before thee, until thou have destroyed them.[S]

25 [i]The [j]graven[G] [k]images of their gods shall ye [l]burn with fire: thou shalt not [4,m]desire the silver or gold *that is* on them, nor take *it* unto thee, lest thou be [n]snared[G] therein: for it *is* an [o]abomination[G] to the LORD thy God.

26 Neither shalt thou bring an [o]abomination into thine house, lest thou be a cursed thing like it: *but* thou shalt utterly detest it, and thou shalt utterly abhor it; for it *is* a cursed thing.

v.19–1494 BC
See footnote, *Time*, Rev. 10:6.

19
*z* *Miracles*, Luke 23:8.
*a* *Arm, figurative*, Psa. 89:13.
*b* *God, providence of*, Gen. 2:2.

20
*c* *Judgments*, Ex. 6:6.
*d* Ex. 23:28; Josh. 24:12.

21
*e* *Faith, enjoined*, Mark 11:22.
*f* *God, presence of*, Gen. 2:2.
*g* *God, power of*, Gen. 2:2.

22
*h* *Canaanites, to be destroyed*, Ex. 23:28.

23
2 R. V. discomfit
3 R. V. great discomfiture,

25
*i* *Statute, enjoining destruction of idols, and forbidding covetousness*, Deut. 8:2.
*j* *Carving*, Ex. 35:33.
*k* *Idols*, 1 Kin. 15:12.
*l* *Iconoclasm*, Num. 33:52.
*m* *Covetousness*, Isa. 57:17.
*n* *Temptation, admonitions against yielding to*, Luke 11:4.
*o* *Abomination*, Lev. 18:27.
4 R. V. covet

† **BARRENNESS**, Ex. 23:26. *Sterility of women*, Prov. 30:15, 16. *Of women, a reproach*, Gen. 16:2; 29:32; 30:1–3, 13, 22, 23; 1 Sam. 1:6, 7; 2:1–11; Isa. 4:1; Luke 1:25. *Sent as a judgment*, Gen. 20:17, 18; 2 Sam. 6:23. Of women, providentially removed: *Of Sarah*, Gen. 11:30; 16:1; 17:15–21; *of Rebecca*, Gen. 25:21; *of Leah*, Gen. 29:31; *of Manoah's wife*, Judg. 13; *of Hannah*, 1 Sam. 1:6–20; 2:1–10; *of Elisabeth*, Luke 1:5–25, 36.

v.1–1494 BC
See footnote, *Time*, Rev. 10:6.

## CHAPTER 8

*An exhortation to obedience in view of God's mercy and goodness to them. 19 The penalty of disobedience.*

1 ALL the *commandments which I command [a]thee this day shall ye observe[C] to [b]do, that ye may [c]live, and multiply, and go in and possess the [d]land which the LORD [e]sware[C] unto your fathers.

2 And *thou shalt remember all the way which the LORD thy

a *Israel*, Ex. 4:22.
b *Obedience, enjoined*, Heb. 5:8.

v.1–1494 BC
c *Temporal Blessings, from God*, v. 18; Psa. 103:2.
d *Canaan*, Gen. 37:1.
e *Covenant, of God with men*, Deut. 29:1.

* **COMMANDMENTS AND STATUTES.**
**Admonishing Against:**
*Backsliding*, Deut. 8:11–17; 29:18; Ezek. 33:12, 13, 18; Luke 9:62; 1 Cor. 10:12; Heb. 3:12, 13; 12:15; 2 Pet. 2:20, 21.
*Conspiracy*, Ex. 23:1, 2.
*Hypocrisy*, Matt. 6:1–5, 16; Luke 20:46, 47; 1 Pet. 2:1.
*Lusts*, Prov. 31:3; Rom. 13:13, 14; Gal. 5:16; 1 Pet. 2:11.
*Oppression of foreigners*, Ex. 22:21; 23:9; Deut. 24:14; Zech. 7:10.
*Popular corruption*, Ex. 23:2.
*Reviling rulers*, Ex. 22:28; Acts 23:5.
**Concerning:** *Indissolubility of marriage*, Gen. 2:24; Matt. 19:6; Mark 10:9; 1 Cor. 7:1–16.
*Lost property*, Ex. 23:4; Deut. 22:1–3.
*Ministers*, 3:10; Acts 20:31; 1 Tim. 1:4; 3:2–13; 4:12–16; 5:20–22; 2 Tim. 2:2, 3, 14–16, 22–24; Tit. 1:5–9; 2:1–10, 15; 1 Pet. 5:2, 3.
*Restitution*, Ex. 21:30–36; 22:1–15; Lev. 6:4, 5; 24:18; Num. 5:7.
*Vicious animals*, Ex. 21:28–32, 35, 36.
*Women*, Eph. 5:22, 24; Tit. 2:3–5; 1 Pet. 3:1–3.
**Enjoining:** *Abhorrence, of the abominations of the wicked*, Deut. 7:25, 26; *of evil*, Rom. 12:9–21.
*Abiding in Christ*, John 15:4, 9; 1 John 2:28.
*Abstinence from evil*, 1 Thess. 5:22.
*Accord with Christ, and concord with one another*, Phil. 2:2–5.
*Admonition and encouragement*, 1 Thess. 5:14.
*Altruistic service*, Matt. 20:26; Mark 9:35; 10:42–45; Luke 22:26; John 13:14; Rom. 15:1, 2; 1 Cor. 10:24; Gal. 6:10; Phil. 2:3, 4.
*Assistance to the distressed*, Psa. 82:4; Prov. 24:11.
*Building a sanctuary*, Ex. 25:8.
*Casting anxiety upon the Lord*, 1 Pet. 5:7.
*Charitableness*, Matt. 18:10; Luke 6:37, 38; Rom. 14:1–3, 13, 19.
*Chastity*, Prov. 5:15–19; Matt. 5:27, 28.
*Cheerfulness*, Eccl. 9:7–9.
*Choice of wise men for rulers*, Ex. 18:21; Deut. 1:13.
*Christian graces*, 2 Cor. 13:11; Col. 3:12–17; 2 Tim. 2:22.
*Christian tolerance toward the weak*, Rom. 15:1.
*Confession of sin*, Num. 8:12; Jas. 5:16.
*Contentment*, Luke 3:14; Heb. 13:5.
*Courage*, Deut. 31:6, 7; Josh. 1:6, 7, 9; 1 Kin. 2:2, 3; 1 Chr. 28:20; Neh. 4:14; Jer. 1:8; Ezek. 2:6.
*Cross-bearing*, Matt. 16:24; Mark 8:34.
*Destruction of idols*, Ex. 23:24; 34:13; Num. 33:52; Deut. 7:25; 12:13.
*Diligence*, Eccl. 9:10; 11:6.
*Diligence in business*, Prov. 27:23.
*Discipleship*, Matt. 19:21; Mark 10:21; Luke 18:22.
*Discipline of disorderly church members*, 2 Thess. 3:6.
*Discipling of children*, Matt. 19:14; Mark 10:14; Luke 18:16, 17.
*Discreet conduct*, Rom. 12:17; Eph. 4:1–3; 5:15, 16; Phil. 1:27; 4:5; 1 Pet. 2:11, 12.
*Doing all to the glory of God*, 1 Cor. 10:31; Col. 3:17, 23.
*Establishing, and providing for the ordination of, a holy ministry*, Ex. 28:1–3; 40:12–15; Lev. 8:1–13.
*Esteem for pastors*, 1 Thess. 5:12, 13; 1 Tim. 5:17; Heb. 13:7.
*Evangelism*, Matt. 28:19.
*Faith*, Ex. 14:13; 2 Chr. 20:20; Psa. 37:3, 5; 62:8; 115:9, 11; Prov. 3:5; Isa. 26:4; 50:10; Jer. 49:11; Mark 1:15; 5:36; 11:22; John 6:29; 12:36; 14:1, 11; 20:27; *in Christ*, 1 John 3:23.
*Faithfulness to friends*, Prov. 27:10.
*Family support*, 1 Tim. 5:8.
*Fear of God*, Lev. 19:14, 32; 25:17; Deut. 6:13; 10:12, 20; 13:4; Josh. 24:14; 1 Sam. 12:24; 2 Kin. 17:39; Prov. 3:7; 23:17; 24:21; Eccl. 12:13; Isa. 8:13; 1 Pet. 2:17.
*Fidelity in wedlock*, Gen. 2:24; Matt. 19:6; Mark 10:8; 1 Cor. 7:10, 11.
*Fidelity to God*, 1 Sam. 12:20; Matt. 22:21.
*Fidelity to God and government*, Matt. 22:21; Mark 12:17; Luke 20:25.
*Fidelity to vows*, Num. 30:2; Deut. 23:21–23; Psa. 50:14; Eccl. 5:4.
*Forbearance*, Eph. 4:2; Col. 3:13.
*Forgiveness*, Matt. 18:22; Mark 11:25; Luke 17:3, 4; Rom. 12:14; Eph. 4:32; Col. 3:13.
*Fortitude under persecution*, Matt. 10:26–28; Mark 13:9, 11–13; Rev. 2:10.
*Fraternal reproof*, Matt. 18:15–17; Luke 17:3, 4.
*Fruits of righteousness*, Luke 3:11, 14.
*Gentleness*, Tit. 3:2.
*Godliness*, Eph. 5:1
*Golden Rule, in conduct*, Matt. 7:12; Luke 6:31.
*Good works*, 1 Pet. 3:10.
*Growth in grace*, Heb. 6:1; 2 Pet. 1:5–8; 3:18; Jude 20, 21.
*Heed to instruction*, Prov. 4:10; 19:20; 22:17.
*Heed to parental instruction*, Prov. 1:8; 23:22.
*Heed to the truth*, Matt. 11:15; Mark 4:9; Rev. 2:7.
*Helpfulness*, 1 Cor. 10:24; Gal. 6:1, 2; Phil. 2:4; 1 Thess. 5:11.
*Holiness*, Ex. 22:31; 30:29; Lev. 11:44; 20:7, 25, 26; 21:7; Num. 15:40; Deut. 18:13; Josh. 7:13; Isa. 1:16, 17; Jer. 6:16; Amos 5:14, 15; 1 Cor. 5:7; 2 Cor. 7:1; Eph. 4:22–32; Col. 3:5, 8, 9; 1 Thess. 4:3–7; 2 Tim. 2:19, 22; Heb. 12:14; Jas. 1:21; 4:8; 1 Pet. 1:13–16; 2:11, 12; 3:15; 3 John 11.
*Holiness in ministers*, Lev. 21:6; Num. 8:14, 15.
*Honesty*, Lev. 19:35, 36; Deut. 25:13–16; 1 Thess. 4:12.
*Honesty in service*, 1 Cor. 4:2; Eph. 6:5–7; Col. 3:22, 23; Tit. 2:9, 10.
*Honesty in office*, Luke 3:13.
*Honor to civil rulers*, 1 Pet. 2:17.
*Hospitality*, Rom. 12:13; Heb. 13:2; 1 Pet. 4:9.
*Humility*, Rom. 12:16; Phil. 2:3; Jas. 4:10; 1 Pet. 3:8; 5:6, 7.
*Imitation of Christ*, Rom. 13:14; Col. 2:6, 7.
*Industry*, Prov. 6:6; Eph. 4:28; 1 Thess. 4:11; 2 Thess. 3:12.
*Influence for righteousness*, Matt. 5:16; Phil. 2:15.
*Joyfulness*, Rom. 12:12; Phil. 3:1; 4:4; 1 Thess. 5:16.
*Justice*, Lev. 19:15; Isa. 56:1; Zech. 7:9, 10; John 7:24.
*Justice in courts*, Deut. 1:17; 25:1, 2.
*Justice to, and love for, foreigners*, Lev. 19:33, 34; 24:22.
*Keeping the Sabbath holy*, Ex. 16:29; 20:8; 31:12–16; 35:2, 3; Lev. 19:3, 30; 26:2; Deut. 5:12.
*Kindness*, Prov. 3:27, 28; Eph. 4:32; Col. 3:12; 1 Thess. 5:15.
*Kindness to animals*, Deut. 25:4.
*Kindness to enemies*, Ex. 23:4, 5; Prov. 25:21; Rom. 12:20.
*Labor*, Ex. 20:9; 35:2; Deut. 5:13.
*Laying up treasure in heaven*, Matt. 6:20.
*Liberality*, Prov. 3:9; Eccl. 11:1; Matt. 5:42; Luke 6:30; 12:33, 34; 2 Cor. 8:7; Heb. 13:16.
*Liberality in God's service*, Mal. 3:10.
*Liberality in support of religion*, Deut. 15:19; 16:17.
*Liberality toward house of God*, Ex. 22:29; 30:12–16; 34:26; 35:4-9.
*Liberality to the poor*, Lev. 19:9, 10; 23:22; Deut. 15:7–15; 24:19–21, Rom. 12:13; Heb. 13:16; 1 John 3:17.
*Love for enemies*, Matt. 5:44; Luke 6:27–29; Rom. 12:14, 15.
*Love for foreigners*, Lev. 19:34; Deut. 10:19.
*Love for God*, Deut. 6:5; 10:12; 11:1, 8, 13; 30:16; Josh. 22:5; 23:11; Matt. 22:37; Mark 12:30; Luke 10:27.
*Love for man*, Lev. 19:18, 33, 34; Matt. 19:19; 22:39; Mark 12:31; Luke 10:27; John 13:34; 15:12, 17; Rom. 12:9, 10; 13:8–10; 1 Cor. 16:14; Gal. 5:14; Eph. 5:2; Col. 3:14; 1 Thess. 3:12; 4:9; Heb. 13:1; Jas. 2:8; 1 Pet. 2:17; 3:8; 4:8; 1 John 3:11, 18, 23; 4:7, 21; 2 John 5.
*Loving truth and peace*, Zech. 8:19.
*Manliness*, 1 Cor. 16:13, 14.
*Manly gravity*, 1 Cor. 14:20; Tit. 2:2.
*Meekness*, Matt. 5:39, 40; Luke 6:29; Eph. 4:2; Col. 3:12; Tit. 3:12.
*Mercy*, Prov. 3:3; Zech. 7:9, 10; Luke 6:36.
*Mercy to debtors*, Deut. 24:6.
*Oaths in God's name*, Deut. 6:13; 10:20.
*Obedience*, Lev. 18:4, 5, 26, 30; 19:19, 37; 20:8, 22; 22:31; 25:18; Num. 15:40; Deut. 4:1, 6, 23, 40; 5:32, 33; 6:17, 18; 7:11; 8:1, 6; 10:12, 13; 11:1, 8, 13, 32; 12:28, 32; 13:4; 27:1, 10; 29:9; 30:2, 8, 16; 1 Sam. 15:1; 1 Kin. 2:2, 3; 2 Kin. 17:37, 38; 1 Chr. 28:20; Prov. 3:6; 4:20, 21; 5:7; 7:1–14; Eccl. 12:13; John 13:15.
*Obedience to Christ as Lord*, 1 Pet. 3:15.
*Obedience to civil government*, Eccl. 8:2; Mark 12:17; Luke 20:25; Rom. 13:1, 7; Tit. 3:1; 1 Pet. 2:13.
*Obedience to God's law*, Deut. 11:8, 13, 32; 30:16; Josh. 22:5; 2 Kin. 17:37, 38; 1 Chr. 28:8.
*Orderly conduct of divine worship*, 1 Cor. 14:26–33.
*Patience*, Jas. 1:4; 5:7–9.
*Patience under afflictions*, Prov. 3:11.
*Patience under tribulations*, Rom. 12:12; Jas. 1:2–4; 1 Pet. 4:1.
*Peaceableness*, Rom. 12:18; Col. 3:15; 1 Thess. 4:11; Heb. 12:14.
*Perfection*, Gen. 17:1; Matt. 5:48.
*Praise*, Psa. 146 to 150. See footnote, PRAISE, Psa. 150:1.
*Prayer*, Jer. 33:3; Matt. 7:7–11; Luke 11:9–13; Phil. 4:6; Col. 4:2; 1 Thess. 5:17, 18; 1 Tim. 2:8.
*Prayer for more laborers in the Lord's vineyard*, Matt. 9:38.
*Prayer for rulers*, 1 Tim. 2:1, 2.
*Prayerfulness*, Luke 22:40; Rom. 12:12; 1 Thess. 5:17.

v.2–1494 BC
**2**
*f* *God, providence of*, Gen. 2:2.
*g* *Forty, years*, Jonah 3:4.
*h* *Adversity, design of*, Psa. 10:6.
*i* *Temptation, a test of obedience*, Luke 11:4.

God *f*led *a*thee these *g*forty years
in the wilderness, to *h*humble
thee, *and* to *i*prove[c] thee, to know
what *was* in thine heart, whether
thou wouldest keep his commandments, or no.

3 [s]And *f*he *h*humbled thee, and
suffered thee to *j*hunger, and *f*fed
*k*thee with *l*manna, which thou
knewest not, neither did thy fathers know; that he might make
thee know that *m*man doth not

v.3–1494 BC
**3**
*j* *Hunger, a source, of temptation*, Neh. 9:15.
*k* *Israel, providentially cared for*, Ex. 4:22.
*l* *Manna*, Ex. 16:31.
*m* Matt. 4:4; Luke 4:4.

**COMMANDMENTS, Enjoining**—(CONTINUED):
*Preparation for the Sabbath*, Ex. 16:23.
*Preparedness*, Matt. 24:44; 25:13 (with vs. 1–12); 1 Thess. 5:8.
*Propagation of children*, Gen. 9:1, 7.
*Propriety in worship*, 1 Cor. 14:26–33, 40.
*Prudence*, Col. 4:5.
*Prudence in guests*, Prov. 23:1, 2.
*Prudence in speech*, Eccl. 5:2, 6; 7:21; 10:20.
*Public instruction in the word of God*, Deut. 31:10–13.
*Public worship*, Ex. 34:23; Deut. 12:5–7, 11–14, 17, 18, 26, 27; 16:16.
*Pure conversation*, Eph. 4:29; 1 Pet. 3:10.
*Purity*, 2 Cor. 7:1; Eph. 5:1–4; 1 Tim. 5:22; Heb. 13:4.
*Purity in family of a minister*, Lev. 21:9.
*Purity of thought*, Phil. 4:8.
*Quietness*, 1 Thess. 4:11.
*Rebuke of sin*, Lev. 19:17; Eph. 5:11.
*Reconciliation between brethren*, Matt. 5:23–25.
*Regard for consciences of others*, 1 Cor. 10:28.
*Regulated enjoyments*, Eccl. 11:9, 10.
*Religious instruction of children*, Deut. 4:9; 6:7–9; 11:19, 20; 32:46; Eph. 6:14.
*Remembrance of God in youth*, Eccl. 12:1.
*Remembrance of God's mercies*, Deut. 5:15; 8:2.
*Remembrance of the law*, Deut. 6:6–9; 11:18; 32:46; 1 Chr. 16:15.
*Renunciation of sources of temptation*, Matt. 5:29, 30; 18:8, 9; Mark 9:43–48.
*Repentance*, Prov. 1:23; Ezek. 33:11; Mal. 3:7; Matt. 3:2; 7:13, 14; Mark 1:15; Acts 2:38; 17:30; Rev. 3:19.
*Reproof of the erring*, 1 Tim. 5:20.
*Resistance of evil*, Jas. 4:7.
*Respect for religious instruction*, 1 Thess. 5:20.
*Rest on the Sabbath*, Ex. 20:10; 23:12; 34:21; 35:2, 3; Lev. 23:3, 24; Deut. 5:14.
*Restraint of temper*, Eccl. 7:9; Eph. 4:26, 31; Jas. 1:19.
*Returning good for evil*, Matt. 5:4; 1 Cor. 6:7; 1 Pet. 3:9.
*Reverence for God's house*, Lev. 19:30; 26:2; Eccl. 5:1.
*Reverence for holy places*, Ex. 3:5; Josh. 5:15; Acts 7:33.
*Reverence, for parents*, Ex. 20:12; Lev. 19:3, 30; 20:9; Deut. 5:16; Prov. 23:22; Matt. 15:4; 19:19; Luke 18:20; Eph. 6:1, 2; *for the aged*, Lev. 19:32.
*Right conduct*, Deut. 6:18; Prov. 4:26, 27; Phil. 1:27; Jas. 1:19.
*Righteousness*, Ex. 23:7; Ezek. 45:9; Hos. 12:6; Luke 13:24; Rom. 13:7, 8.
*Rulers to study God's law*, Deut. 17:18–20.
*Secrecy in giving alms*, Matt. 6:3.
*Seeking the Lord*, 1 Chr. 16:11; Isa. 55:6; Amos 5:4, 6.
*Seeking the kingdom of God*, Matt. 6:33; Luke 12:31.
*Self-denial*, Matt. 16:24; Mark 8:34; 10:21; Luke 9:23; 18:22; Rom. 15:2.
*Self-discipline*, Matt. 5:29, 30; Mark 9:45–48.
*Self-examination*, 2 Cor. 13:5.
*Service for God*, Ex. 23:25; Deut. 6:13; 10:12, 20.
*Simplicity in worship*, Matt. 6:7.
*Six days of labor, and one day of rest*, Ex. 20:9–11; 35:2.
*Sobermindedness*, Tit. 2:6.
*Sobriety*, 1 Thess. 5:8; 1 Pet. 1:13; 4:7; 5:8, 9.
*Social peace*, 1 Thess. 5:13.
*Spiritual diligence*, Rom. 12:11; 13:12; Heb. 4:11; 2 Pet. 1:10; 3:14.
*Spirituality*, Gal. 5:16.
*Steadfastness*, Deut. 13:8, 10; Rom. 12:21; 1 Cor. 15:58; 16:13; Gal. 5:1; Eph. 6:11, 13, 14, 18; Phil. 1:27; 4:1; 1 Thess. 5:21; 2 Thess. 2:15; 2 Tim. 1:13; 1 Pet. 1:13; Jude 21; Rev. 3:11.
*Steadfastness in prayer*, Rom. 12:12; Eph. 6:18; 1 Thess. 5:17.
*Submission to God*, 2 Chr. 30:8; Prov. 3:11; Jas. 4:7.
*Submission to fraternal counsel*, Eph. 5:21.
*Suffering, one for another*, 1 John 3:16–17.
*Sympathy*, Rom. 12:15; Heb. 13:3; 1 Pet. 3:8.
*Support of ministers*, Deut. 12:19; Gal. 6:6; 1 Tim. 5:17, 18.
*Thankfulness*, Deut. 8:10; Col. 3:15.
*Thanksgiving*, Eph. 5:4, 20; Phil. 4:6; Col. 3:17; 1 Thess. 5:17, 18; 1 Tim. 2:1; Heb. 13:15.
*Tithing*, Deut. 12:6; 14:22.
*Truthfulness*, Prov. 3:3; Zech. 8:16, 17, 19; Eph. 4:25.
*Various Christian duties*, Rom. 12:6–8; Eph. 6:10–20; Jas. 4:8–11; 5:7–9, 12, 14; 1 Pet. 1:13–17; 2:11–25; 3:8, 9, 15; 4:7–15; 5:5–8; 2 Pet. 1:5–7.
*Watchfulness*, Prov. 4:23; Matt. 24:42, 44; 25:13; Mark 13:35–37; Luke 12:35–40; 21:36; 1 Cor. 16:13, 14; Eph. 5:15; Phil. 3:2; Col. 4:2; 1 Thess. 5:6; 1 Pet. 5:8, 9; Rev. 3:2.
*Watchfulness against backsliding*, Deut. 4:9; 8:11; 11:16, 28; 2 Pet. 3:17.
*Watchfulness against covetousness*, Deut. 15:9; Luke 12:15.
*Watchfulness against false christs*, Matt. 24:23–26; Mark 13:21–23; Luke 17:23.
*Whole-hearted service*, Josh. 22:5; 24:14; 1 Sam. 12:24; 1 Chr 28:9; Eccl. 9:10.
*Wisdom*, Prov. 3:21; 4:5, 13; 5:1; 8:5, 6, 32, 33; 23:12, 23; *in speech*, Prov. 23:9; 26:4, 5; Col. 4:6.
*Wise self-restraint*, Eccl. 7:16, 18, 21.
*Witnessing for Christ*, Mark 5:19; 1 Pet. 3:15.
*Worship*, Gen. 35:1; Ex. 20:24; Rev. 19:10; 22:9.
*Worship, social*, Eph. 5:19; Col. 3:16.
*Zeal for righteousness*, John 6:27; 1 Cor. 15:58.
*Zeal for the faith*, Jude 3.
*Zeal in one's calling*, Rom. 12:6–8.

**Fixing Penalty for:**
*Adultery*, Lev. 20:10; 21:9; 1 Cor. 6:9, 10; Gal. 5:19, 21.
*Arson*, Ex. 22:6.
*Bestiality*, Ex. 22:19; Lev. 20:13, 15, 16.
*Blasphemy*, Lev. 24:16.
*Carnality*, Lev. 19:20.
*Contempt of authority*, Deut. 17:12.
*Criminal neglect to safeguard life*, Ex. 21:28–36.
*Cursing parents*, Ex. 21:17; Lev. 20:9.
*Destruction of neighbor's property*, Lev. 24:18.
*Disobedience*, Num. 15:30, 31.
*False witness*, Deut. 19:18, 19.
*Fornication*, Acts 15:20; 1 Cor. 6:18; 10:8.
*Idolatry*, Lev. 20:2–5; Deut. 17:5; *propagandism of idolatry*, Deut. 13:5, 9, 10, 15.
*Impenitence*, Lev. 23:29.
*Incest*, Lev. 20:11, 12, 14, 17, 19–21.
*Laziness*, 2 Thess. 3:10.
*Loss of borrowed property*, Ex. 22:14, 15.
*Loss of property held in trust*, Ex. 22:7–13.
*Manstealing*, Ex. 21:16; Deut. 24:7.
*Murder*, Ex. 21:12; Lev. 24:17; Num. 35:31; Deut. 19:11–13.
*Personal injury*, Ex. 21:18–27; Lev. 24:19, 20.
*Sabbath breaking*, Ex. 31:14; 35:2.
*Seduction*, Ex. 22:16.
*Theft*, Ex. 22:1–4.
*Trespass*, Ex. 22:5.
*Untimely cohabitation*, Lev. 20:18.
*Witchcraft*, Ex. 22:18; Lev. 20:27.

**Forbidding:**
*Adultery*, Ex. 20:14; Lev. 18:20; Deut. 5:18; Matt. 5:27; 19:18; Luke 18:20; Rom. 13:9; 1 Cor. 10:8.
*Anxiety*, Matt. 6:25–34; 10:19–23; Luke 12:11, 22–32; John 14:27; Phil. 4:6.
*Association with bad men*, Prov. 1:10–19.
*Association with harlots*, Prov. 2:16; 5:3–21; 6:20, 24–26; 7:1–27; 23:26–28.
*Bestiality*, Lev. 18:23; 20:13, 15, 16.
*Boasting*, Deut. 9:4.
*Bribe taking*, Ex. 23:8; Deut. 16:19; 27:25.
*Causeless strife*, Prov. 3:30.
*Change in God's law*, Deut. 4:2; 12:32.
*Class, distinction*, Ex. 23:3; Lev. 19:15; Num. 15:29; Deut. 16:19; *legislation*, Lev. 24:22.
*Company with winebibbers*, Prov. 23:20.
*Conformity to the world*, Lev. 20:23.
*Contention*, Rom. 13:13; Phil. 2:14; 2 Tim. 2:14; Tit. 3:2.
*Corrupt conversation*, Eph. 4:29; 5:4; Col. 3:8.
*Covetousness*, Ex. 20:17; Deut. 5:21; 7:25, 26; Luke 12:15; Rom. 13:9; Eph. 5:3; Col. 3:5; 1 Tim. 6:10, 11; Heb. 13:5.
*Dishonesty in business*, Lev. 19:13, 35; 25:14; Deut. 25:13–15; Mark 10:19.
*Divorce*, 1 Cor. 7:10, 11 (with Matt. 5:32; 19:9; Mark 10:11, 12; Luke 16:18).
*Drunkenness*, Rom. 13:13; Eph. 5:18.
*Envy*, Prov. 3:31; 23:17; 24:1, 19; Rom. 13:13; 1 Pet. 2:1.
*Evil speech*, Psa. 34:13; Prov. 4:24; 30:10; Tit. 3:2; 1 Pet. 3:10.
*Evil to a neighbor*, Ex. 20:16; Lev. 19:13, 16; Prov. 3:29.
*False dealing*, Lev. 6:1–5; 19:11.
*False swearing*, Lev. 19:12.
*False witness*, Ex. 20:16; 23:1; Lev. 19:16; Deut. 5:20; Prov. 24:28; Matt. 19:18; Luke 18:20.
*Falsehood*, Lev. 19:11; Eph. 4:25; Col. 3:9.
*Fellowship with the wicked*, Prov. 1:10–15; 4:14, 15; Rom. 16:17; 1 Cor. 5:9–11; 2 Cor. 6:14, 17; Eph. 5:11; 2 Thess. 3:6; 2 Tim. 3:5.

**v.3–1494 BC**
See footnote, *Time,* Rev. 10:6.

*n Word of God,* Psa. 119:9.

**4**
*o* Deut. 29:5; Neh. 9:21.

**5**
*p Divine Chastisement, administered in love,* Job 33:19.
*q Adversity,* Psa. 10:6.

**6**
*r Fear of God, a motive to obedience,* Acts 9:31.

live by bread only, but by every
[n]*word* that proceedeth out of the
mouth of the LORD doth man
live.[T] [Q]
4 Thy [o]raiment waxed[G] not old
upon thee, neither did thy foot
swell, these [g]forty years.[S]
5 Thou shalt also consider in
thine heart, that, as a man chasteneth
his son, *so* the LORD thy
God [p,q]chasteneth thee.[Q]
6 Therefore *thou shalt [b]keep
the commandments of the LORD
thy God, to walk in his ways,
and to [r]fear him.
7 For the LORD thy God
[c]bringeth thee into a good land,
a [s]land of †brooks of water, of
fountains and depths that spring
out of valleys and hills;
8 A [s]land of [t]wheat, and [u]barley,
and vines, and [v]fig trees,
and pomegranates; a land of
oil [w]olive, and [x]honey;[S]
9 A [s]land wherein thou shalt eat
bread without scarceness,[G] thou
shalt not lack any *thing* in it; a
land whose stones *are* [y]iron, and
out of whose hills thou mayest
dig [z]brass.
10 When thou hast eaten and
art full, then *thou shalt [a]bless
the LORD thy God for the good
land which he hath given thee.

**v.7–1494 BC**
See footnote, *Time,* Rev. 10:6.

**7**
*s Canaan, fertility of,* Gen. 37:1.

**8**
*t Wheat,* Ezra 6:9.
*u Barley,* Ex. 9:31.
*v Fig Tree, common to Palestine,* Luke 13:6.
*w Olive,* Deut. 6:11.
*x Honey,* Prov. 25:27.

**9**
*y Iron,* Prov. 27:17.
*z Brass,* Job 28:2.

**10**
*a Praise,* Psa. 150:1.

---

*Fraud,* Lev. 19:11, 13, 35; 1 Thess. 4:6.
*Giving cause for stumbling,* 1 Cor. 8:9; 10:32.
*Grudge,* Lev. 19:18.
*Haste for riches,* Prov. 23:4.
*Haste in litigation,* Prov. 25:8, 9.
*Hatred,* Lev. 19:17; Eph. 4:31; Col. 3:8.
*Heed to false teachers,* Deut. 13:1–18.
*Idolatry,* Ex. 20:3–5, 23; Lev. 18:21; 20:2–5; 26:1; Deut. 4:16–19, 23; 5:7–9; 6:14; 13:2, 3; 16:21, 22; Josh. 24:14; 2 Kin. 17:35; Ezek. 20:18; 1 Cor. 10:7; 1 John 5:21.
*Impure marriages,* Lev. 21:7.
*Incest,* Lev. 18:6; 20:11, 12, 14, 17, 19–21; Deut. 22:30.
*Indulgence in wine,* Prov. 23:31; Eph. 5:18; Tit. 2:3.
*Injustice,* Ex. 23:2, 3; Lev. 19:15; 25:17; Deut. 16:19.
*Injustice to foreigners,* Ex. 12:49; 22:21; Lev. 19:33, 34; Deut. 1:16; 24:14, 17.
*Injustice to the poor,* Ex. 23:6.
*Intolerance,* Mark 9:39; Luke 9:49, 50.
*Invidious respect of persons,* Jas. 2:1–9.
*Labor on Sabbath,* Ex. 20:10; 23:12; 34:21; 35:2, 3; Lev. 23:3; Deut. 5:14.
*Lasciviousness,* Prov. 31:3; Rom. 13:13; Eph. 4:17–39; 5:3; 1 Thess. 4:2–6; 2 Tim. 2:22.
*Lawlessness,* Deut. 12:8.
*Laziness,* 2 Thess. 3:10.
*Love of the world,* 1 John 2:15.
*Malice,* Lev. 19:17, 18; Eph. 4:31; Col. 3:8; 1 Pet. 2:1.
*Malicious mischief,* Lev. 19:14.
*Meddling,* 1 Pet. 4:15.
*Murder,* Ex. 20:13; Deut. 5:17; Matt. 5:21; 19:18; Rom. 13:9; Jas. 2:11; 1 Pet. 4:15.
*Murmuring,* 1 Cor. 10:10; Phil. 2:14; Jas. 5:9.
*Offerings with blemish, which implied, in its teaching purpose, the forbidding of insincere or imperfect service of God,* Lev. 1:3, 10; 3:1, 6; 4:3, 23, 28, 32; 5:15, 18; 6:6; 9:2, 3; 22:18–22; Deut. 15:21; 17:1.
*Oppression,* Lev. 19:13; Prov. 22:22.
*Oppression of the poor,* Deut. 24:14.
*Oppression of widows and orphans,* Ex. 22:22–24; Jer. 22:3; Zech. 7:10.
*Ostentation in giving, in fasting, and in prayer,* Matt. 6:1, 5, 6, 17, 18.
*Perjury,* Lev. 19:12.
*Perversion of justice,* Deut. 16:19, 20; 24:17.
*Prejudice,* Ex. 23:3.
*Profane swearing,* Matt. 5:34–36; Jas. 5:12.
*Profaning God's name,* Ex. 20:7; Lev. 18:21; 19:12; 21:6; 22:32; Deut. 5:11.
*Prostitution of a daughter,* Lev. 19:29.
*Putting a neighbor's life in peril by false witness,* Lev. 19:16.
*Removal of landmarks,* Deut. 19:14; Prov. 22:28; 23:10.
*Resistance,* Matt. 5:39.
*Retaliation,* Lev. 19:18; Prov. 24:29; Matt. 5:38–42; Rom. 12:17; 1 Thess. 5:15; 1 Pet. 3:9.
*Robbery,* Lev. 19:13; Prov. 22:22.
*Sabbath breaking,* Ex. 31:14; Jer. 17:21, 22.
*Self-confidence,* Prov. 3:5, 7.
*Self-esteem,* Rom. 12:3.
*Self-praise,* Prov. 27:2.
*Selfishness,* 1 Cor. 10:24; Phil. 2:4.
*Sodomy,* Lev. 18:22; 20:13.
*Taking of interest,* Ex. 22:25; Lev. 25:35, 37.
*Talebearing,* Lev. 19:16.
*Theft,* Ex. 20:15; Lev. 19:11; Deut. 5:19; Matt. 19:18; Luke 18:20; Rom. 13:9; Eph. 4:28; 1 Pet. 4:15.
*Uncharitable judgments,* Matt. 7:1–5; Luke 6:37, 42; Rom. 14:1–3, 13.
*Uncharitableness,* Prov. 24:17; Matt. 18:10.
*Unholy ambition,* Phil. 2:3.
*Unrighteous anger,* Matt. 5:22.
*Unrighteous judgments,* Lev. 19:15.
*Use of strong drink by priests,* Lev. 10:9.
*Vain repetitions in prayer,* Matt. 6:7, 8.
*Various vices,* Rom. 13:12, 13; Gal. 5:19–21; Eph. 4:28–31; 5:3–6, 11, 18; Col. 3:5, 8, 9; 1 Thess. 4:3–6; 5:15, 22; 1 Tim. 3:3, 8; 6:17; 2 Tim. 3:2–5; Tit. 2:3, 10; Heb. 13:5; Jas. 1:21; 2:11; 4:11; 5:9, 12; 1 Pet. 2:11; 3:9; 4:3.
*Witchcraft,* Lev. 19:26, 31; 20:6.
*Withholding a servant's wages,* Lev. 19:13.
*Worldliness,* Matt. 6:19; Rom. 12:2; 1 John 2:15.
**Implied:** *Enjoining an exact conscience,* Matt. 6:22–24. *Against self-righteousness,* Matt. 7:3.
**Miscellaneous:**
*Against quenching the spirit,* 1 Thess. 5:19.
*Limiting the number of stripes in punishment,* Deut. 25:3.
*Ordaining man's supremacy over the animal kingdom,* Gen. 9:2.
*Ordaining places of public worship,* Deut. 12:11.
*Protecting debtors,* Deut. 24:10, 12, 13.
*To children, enjoining obedience to parents,* Prov. 6:20; Eph. 6:1–3; Col. 3:20. See COMMANDMENT, *Enjoining reverence for parents,* above.
*To fathers, concerning children,* Eph. 6:4; Col. 3:21.
*To husbands, enjoining, love of wife,* Eph. 5:25; Col. 3:19; *honor to wife,* 1 Pet. 3:7.
*To judges of courts, enjoining justice,* Deut. 1:16.
*To masters, enjoining equity,* Col. 4:1.
*To masters, enjoining humane treatment of servants,* Eph. 6:9.
*To ministers,* 2 Tim. 2:1, 2.
*To ministers, enjoining faithfulness,* Col. 4:17; 1 Tim. 6:11, 12, 14; 2 Tim. 1:8, 13.
*To ministers, enjoining fortitude,* 2 Tim. 2:3.
*To ministers, forbidding, worldly entanglements,* 2 Tim. 2:4, 5; *foolish and unlearned questions,* 2 Tim. 2:23; *strife,* 2 Tim. 2:24.
*To servants, enjoining obedience,* Eph. 6:5–8; Col. 3:22–25; Tit. 2:9, 10; 1 Pet. 2:18, 19.
*To soldiers, enjoining obedience,* Deut. 20:3; Luke 3:14.
*To wives, enjoining obedience,* Eph. 5:22; Col. 3:18; 1 Pet. 3:1–4.
*To young men, enjoining obedience to parents,* Prov. 6:20; 23:22.
**Prescribing:** *Law of evidence,* Deut. 17:6; 19:15.
*Priestly benedictions,* Num. 6:23–26.
*Stimulants for the perishing,* Prov. 31:6.
**Warning:** *The rich,* 1 Tim. 6:17–19.
**Warning against:** *Covetousness,* Luke 12:15.
*False teachers,* Matt. 7:15; Eph. 5:6, 7; Col. 2:8.
*Love of money,* Heb. 13:5.
*Sensuality,* Prov. 6:24, 25.
*Sinful indulgence,* Luke 21:34.
*Sinning against the Holy Spirit,* Eph. 4:30; 1 Thess. 5:19.
*Temptations,* Prov. 1:10–15; 19:27.
† **BROOK,** Psa. 42:1. *Zered,* Deut. 2:13, 14. *Besor,* 1 Sam. 30:9, 10. *Kidron,* 2 Sam. 15:23; 1 Kin. 15:13; 2 Kin. 23:6, 12; 2 Chr. 15:16; 29:16; 30:14; Jer. 31:40; John 18:1. *Gaash,* 2 Sam. 23:30; 1 Chr. 11:32. *Cherith,* 1 Kin. 17:3–7. *Kison,* Psa. 83:9.

v.11–1494 BC
See footnote, *Time,* Rev. 10:6.

**11**
b *Watchfulness, enjoined,* Matt. 24:42.
c *Temptation, admonitions against,* vs. 11–20; Luke 11:4.
d *Backsliding, warnings against,* Hos. 11:7.
e *Ingratitude, to God, prosperity tempts to,* Rom. 1:21.
f *Word of God,* Psa. 119:9.

**12**
g *Riches, a snare,* Eccl. 4:8.
h *Prosperity, dangers of,* Eccl. 7:14.

**14**
i *Pride,* Prov. 16:18.
j *God, providence of,* Gen. 2:2.

**15**
k *Desert,* Lev. 16:22.
l *Serpent, fiery,* Num. 21:6.
m *Scorpion,* Luke 10:19.
n *Meribah,* Ex. 17:7.

**16**
o *Manna,* Ex. 16:31.
p *Afflictions, design of,* Psa. 34:19.

**17**
q *Presumption,* Psa. 19:13.

**18**
r *Thankfulness, enjoined,* Acts 24:3.
s *Temporal Blessings, from God,* Psa. 103:2.
t *Covenant, of God with men,* Deut. 29:1.

**19**
u *Idolatry, punishment of,* 1 Sam. 15:23.

**20**
v *Judgments,* Ex. 6:6.

11 *[b,c]Beware that thou [d,e]forget not the LORD thy God, in not keeping his [f]commandments, and his judgments[G], and his statutes, which I command thee this day:

12 Lest [c,g,h]*when* thou hast eaten and art full, and hast built goodly houses, and dwelt *therein*;

13 And [c,g,h]*when* thy herds and thy flocks multiply, and thy silver and thy gold is multiplied, and all that thou hast is multiplied;

14 Then thine heart be [i]lifted up, and thou [d,e]forget the LORD thy God, which [j]brought thee forth out of the land of Ē'gȳpt, from the house of bondage;

15 [j]Who led thee through that great and terrible [k]wilderness, *wherein were* fiery [l]serpents, and [m]scorpions, and drought, where *there was* no water; who brought thee forth water out of the [n]rock of ‡flint;

16 [j]Who fed thee in the [k]wilderness with [o]manna, which thy fathers knew not, [p]that he might humble thee, and that he might prove[G] thee, to do thee good at thy latter end;

17 And thou [e,i,q]say in thine heart, My power and the might of *mine* hand hath gotten me this wealth.

18 But *thou shalt [r]remember the LORD thy God: for *it is* [j]he that giveth thee [s]power to get wealth, that he may establish his [t]covenant[G] which he sware unto thy fathers, as *it is* this day.[S]

19 And it shall be, if thou do at all [d,e]forget the LORD thy God, and walk after other gods, and [u]serve them, and worship them, I testify against you this day that ye shall surely perish.

20 As the nations which the LORD [v]destroyeth before your face, so shall ye perish; because ye would not be obedient unto the voice of the LORD your God.

## CHAPTER 9

*Moses dissuades Israel from self-righteousness, by rehearsing their rebellions. 26 His prayer for them.*

[a]HEAR, O [b]Is̱'ra-el: Thou *art* to pass over [c]Jôr'dan this day, to go in to possess nations greater and mightier than thyself, cities great and [d]fenced[G] up to heaven,

2 A people great and tall, the children of the [e]Ăn'a-kĭms̱, whom thou knowest, and *of whom* thou hast heard *say,* Who can stand before the children of Ā'năk!

3 [a]Understand therefore this day, that the LORD thy God *is* [f]he which goeth ever before thee; *as* a consuming fire he shall destroy [g]them, and he shall bring them down before thy face: so shalt thou drive them out, and destroy them quickly, as the LORD hath said unto thee.[Q]

4 [h,i,j]Speak not thou in thine heart, after that the LORD thy [f]God hath cast them out from before thee, saying, For my [k]righteousness the LORD hath brought me in to possess this land: but for the wickedness of these [l]nations the LORD doth drive them out from before thee.[Q]

5 Not for thy righteousness, or for the uprightness of thine heart, dost thou go to possess their land: but for the wickedness of these [l]nations the LORD thy God doth drive them out from before thee, and that [m]he may perform the [n]word which the LORD sware unto thy fathers, Ā'brā-hăm, Ī's̱aac, and Jā'cob.[S]

6 Understand therefore, that the LORD thy [f]God giveth thee not this good land to possess it

v.20–1494 BC
See footnote, *Time,* Rev. 10:6.

**1**
a *Preaching,* Matt. 9:35.
b *Israel,* Ex. 4:22.
c *Jordan,* Gen. 32:10.
d *Cities, fortified,* Num. 35:8.

**2**
e *Anakim,* Deut. 1:28.

**3**
f *God, providence of,* Gen. 2:2.
g *Canaanites, to be destroyed,* Ex. 23:28.

**4**
h *Commandment, forbidding boasting,* Deut. 8:2.
i *Presumption, admonitions against,* vs. 4–29; Psa. 19:13.
j *Humility, enjoined,* Prov. 22:4.
k *Self-righteousness,* Luke 18:11.
l *Nation, punishment of,* Isa. 2:4.

**5**
m *God, faithfulness of,* Gen. 2:2.
n *Covenant, of God with men,* Deut. 29:1.

‡ **FLINT,** Deut. 32:13; Psa. 114:8; Isa. 50:7; Ezek. 3:9.

v.6–1494 BC
See footnote, *Time,* Rev. 10:6.

6
o *Self-will,* Gen. 49:6.

7
p *Anger of God,* 2 Kin. 13:3.
q *Disobedience to God,* Eph. 5:6.

8
r *Horeb,* Ex. 3:1.

9
s *Sinai,* Ex. 16:1.
t *Table, of testimony,* Ex. 31:18.
u *Forty, days,* Jonah 3:4.
v *Fasting, forty days,* Zech. 8:19.

10
w *Decalogue,* Ex. 20:3.
x *Law, of Moses, divine authority for,* Deut. 33:2.

12
y *Backsliding, of Israel,* Hos. 11:7.
z *Molding, of images,* 1 Kin. 7:16.

13
a *Israel, obduracy of,* Ex. 4:22.
b *Wicked, described,* Psa. 73:3.

14
c *Judgments,* Ex. 6:6.
d *Moses,* Ex. 2:10.

for thy [k]righteousness; for thou
*art* a [o]stiffnecked people.
7 ¶ Remember, *and* forget not,
how thou provokedst[G] the LORD
thy God to [p]wrath[G] in the wilderness: from the day that thou
didst depart out of the land of
Ē′g̃ȳpt, until ye came unto this
place, ye have been [q]rebellious
against the LORD.
8 Also in [r]Hō′reb ye provoked
the LORD to [p]wrath[G], so that the
LORD was angry with you to
have destroyed you.
9 When I was gone up into the
[s]mount to receive the tables of
stone, *even* the [t]tables of the
covenant[G] which the LORD made
with you, then I abode[G] in the
mount forty days and [u]forty
nights, I [v]neither did eat bread
nor drink water:
10[Q] And the LORD delivered unto me two [t]tables of stone written with the finger of God; and
on them *was written* according
to all the [w, x]words, which the
LORD spake with you in the
[s]mount out of the midst of the
fire in the day of the assembly.[T]
11 And it came to pass at the
end of [u]forty days and forty
nights, *that* the LORD gave me
the two tables of stone, *even* the
[t]tables of the covenant.[Q]
12 And the LORD said unto me,
Arise, get thee down quickly
from hence; for thy people which
thou hast brought forth out of
Ē′g̃ȳpt have corrupted *themselves*; they are quickly [y]turned
aside out of the way which I
commanded them; they have
made them a [z]molten[G] image.
13 Furthermore the LORD
spake unto me, saying, I have
seen this [a]people, and, behold,
it *is* a [b]stiffnecked people:
14 Let me alone, that I may
[c]destroy [a]them, and blot out
their name from under heaven:
and I will make of [d]thee a nation mightier and greater than
they.[S]
15 So I turned and came down
from the [e]mount, and the mount
burned with fire: and the two
[f]tables of the covenant *were* in
my two hands.
16 And I looked, and, behold,
[g]ye had sinned against the LORD
your God, *and* had made you a
[h]molten[G] [i]calf: ye had [j]turned
aside quickly out of the way
which the LORD had commanded you.
17 And [d]I took the two [f]tables,
and cast them out of my two
hands, and brake them before
your eyes.
18 And [d]I [k, l]fell down before
the LORD, as at the first, [m]forty
days and forty nights: I did
[n]neither eat bread, nor drink
water, because of all your sins
which ye sinned, in doing wickedly in the sight of the LORD, to
provoke him to [o]anger.[S]
19 For I was afraid of the [o]an-
ger and hot displeasure, wherewith the LORD was wroth[G]
against you to destroy you. But
[p]the [q]LORD hearkened unto me
at that time also.[S] [Q]
20 And the LORD was very
[o]angry with [r]Aăr′on to have destroyed him: and I [l]prayed for
Aăr′on also the same time.[S]
21 And [d]I took your sin, the
[s, t]calf which ye had made, and
[t]burnt it with fire, and stamped
it, *and* ground *it* very small, *even*
until it was as small as dust: and
I cast the dust thereof into the
brook that descended out of the
mount.
22 And at [u]Tăb′e-rah, and at
Măs′sah, and at [v]Kĭb′roth-hat-
tā′a-vah, ye provoked[G] the LORD
to [o]wrath.
23 Likewise when the LORD
sent you from [w]Kā′desh–bär′-
ne-ȧ, saying, Go up and possess
the [x]land which I have given

v.14–1494 BC
See footnote, *Time,* Rev. 10:6.

15
e *Sinai,* Ex. 16:1.
f *Table, of testimony,* Ex. 31:18.

16
g *Israel, idolatry of,* Ex. 4:22.
h *Molding, of images,* 1 Kin. 7:16.
i *Calf, golden,* Mic. 6:6.
j *Backsliding, of Israel,* Hos. 11:7.

18
k *Zeal, exemplified,* 2 Cor. 7:11.
l *Prayer, intercessory,* Acts 6:4.
m *Forty, days,* Jonah 3:4.
n *Fasting,* Zech. 8:19.
o *Anger of God,* 2 Kin. 13:3.

19
p *Intercession, answered, instances of,* Jer. 27:18.
q *God, mercy of,* Gen. 2:2.

20
r *Aaron,* Ex. 6:20.

21
s *Idolatry, objects of,* 1 Sam. 15:23.
t *Iconoclasm,* Num. 33:52.

22
u Num. 11:3.
v *Kibroth-hattaavah,* Num. 11:34.

23
w *Kadesh,* Gen. 14:7.
x *Canaan,* Gen. 37:1.

v.23–1494 BC
See footnote, *Time*, Rev. 10:6.

*y* *Disobedience to God*, Eph. 5:6.
*z* *Unbelief, instances of*, Heb. 3:12.

24
*a* *Wicked, described*, Psa. 73:3.
*b* *Disobedience to God*, Eph. 5:6.

25
*c* *Prayer, importunity in*, Acts 6:4.
*d* *Forty, days*, Jonah 3:4.

26
*e* *Prayer, intercessory*, Acts 6:4.
*f* *God, providence of*, Gen. 2:2.
*g* *God, power of*, Gen. 2:2.
*h* *Egypt*, Gen. 41:8.

27
*i* *Intercession, influence of righteous*, Jer. 27:18.
*j* *Self-will*, Gen. 49:6.
*k* *Israel, obduracy of*, Ex. 4:22.

29
*l* *Arm, figurative*, Psa. 89:13.

1
*a* *Moses*, Ex. 2:10.
*b* *Table, of testimony*, Ex. 31:18.

you; then ye [y]rebelled against the commandment of the LORD your God, and ye [z]believed him not, nor hearkened[C] to his voice.

24 [a]Ye have been [b]rebellious against the LORD from the day that I knew you.

25 Thus I [c]fell down before the LORD [d]forty days and forty nights, as I fell down *at the first:* because the LORD had said he would destroy you.

26 I [e]prayed therefore unto the LORD, and said, O Lord GOD, destroy not thy people and thine inheritance, which thou hast redeemed through thy greatness, which [f,g]thou hast brought forth out of [h]Ē′ġypt with a mighty hand.

27 [e,i]Remember thy servants, Ā′brā-hăm, Ī′ṣaac, and Jā′cob; look not unto the [j]stubbornness of this [k]people, nor to their wickedness, nor to their sin:

28 [e]Lest the land whence thou broughtest us out say, Because the LORD was not able to bring them into the land which he promised them, and because he hated them, he hath brought them out to slay them in the wilderness.

29 [e]Yet they *are* thy people and thine inheritance, which [f]thou broughtest out by [g]thy mighty power and by thy stretched out [l]arm.[S]

## CHAPTER 10

*God's mercy in restoring the two tables; 6 in continuing the priesthood; 8 in separating the tribe of Levi; 10 and in hearkening unto the prayer of Moses for the people. 12 An exhortation to obedience. 22 God's blessing on Israel.*

AT that time the LORD said unto [a]me, Hew thee two [b]tables of stone like unto the first, and come up unto me into the [c]mount, and make thee an [d]ark of wood.

2 And I will write on the [b]tables the [e]words that were in the first tables which thou brakest, and thou shalt put them in the [d]ark.

3 [Q]And I made an [d]ark *of* [1]shittim wood, and hewed two tables of stone like unto the first, and went up into the [c]mount, having the two tables in mine hand.

4 And he wrote on the [b]tables, according to the first writing, the ten [e,f]commandments, which the LORD spake unto you in the [c]mount out of the midst of the fire in the day of the assembly: and the LORD gave them unto me.

5 And [a]I turned myself and came down from the [c]mount, and put the [b]tables in the [d]ark which I had made; and there they be, as the LORD commanded me.[Q]

6 ¶ And the children of Iṣ′ra-el took their [g]journey from [h]Bē-ē′roth of the children of [i]Jā′a-kăn to Mō-sē′rā: there [j]Aâr′on died, and there he was buried; and [k]Ē-le-ā′zar his son ministered in the priest's office in his stead.[C]

7 From thence they [g]journeyed unto [l]Gŭd′go-dah; and from Gŭd′go-dah to [m]Jŏt′băth, a land of [2]rivers of waters.

8 ¶ [C]At that time the LORD separated the *tribe of Lē′vī, to bear the [d]ark of the covenant of the LORD, to stand before the LORD to minister unto him, and to [n]bless in his name, unto this day.

9 Wherefore *Lē′vī hath no

v.1–1494 BC
See footnote, *Time*, Rev. 10:6.

*c* *Sinai*, Ex. 16:1.
*d* *Ark*, Ex. 25:10.

2
*e* *Law, of Moses, divine authority for*, Deut. 33:2.

3
1 R. V. acacia

4
*f* *Decalogue*, Ex. 20:3.

6
*g* *Itinerary*, Num. 33.
*h* Or, *Bene-jaakan*, Num. 33:31, 32.
*i* Or, *Akan*, Gen. 36:27.
*j* *Aaron*, Ex. 6:20.
*k* *Eleazar*, Num. 3:2.

7
*l* Or, *Hor-hagidgad*, Num. 33:32, 33.
*m* 2 Kin. 21:19.
2 R. V. brooks

8
*n* *Benedictions*, Deut. 21:5.

* **LEVITES**, the descendants of Levi. *Exempt from military service and set apart as ministers of religion*, Num. 1:47–54; 3:6–16; 16:9, 10; 18:6; 26:57–62; Deut. 10:8; 1 Chr. 15:2. *Taken instead of the firstborn*, Num. 3:12, 41–45; 8:14, 16–18. *Not enrolled at Sinai*, Num. 1:47–49; 2:33. *Enrolled, in wilderness of Sinai*, Num. 3:14–39; 4:2, 3; *in plains of Moab*, Num. 26:57–62; *by David*, 1 Chr. 23:3–5.

*Age of, when inducted into office*, Num. 4:3, 30, 47; 8:23–26; 1 Chr. 23:3, 24, 27; Ezra 3:8; *when retired from office*, Num. 4:3, 30, 47; 8:25, 26.

*Consecration of*, Num. 8:6–21. *Subordinate to the sons of Aaron*, Num. 3:9; 8:19; 18:6.

*Place of, in camp and march*, Num. 1:50–53; 2:17; 3:23–35. *Cities assigned to, in the land of Canaan*, Josh. 21. *Porters and singers of, lodged in the chambers of the temple*, 1 Chr. 9:27, 33; Ezek. 40:44. *Singers of, resided also in villages outside of Jerusalem*, Neh. 12:29.

*Three divisions of, each having the name of one of its progenitors, Gershon, Kohath, and Merari*, Num. 3:17.

GERSHONITES, Num. 3:18, 21–26; 4:23–26; 10:17. *Ruling chief over the Gershonites was Ithamar*, Num. 4:28. See footnote, GERSHONITES, Num. 4:27.

KOHATHITES, *consisting of the families of the Amramites, Izeharites, Hebronites, Uzzielites*, Num. 3:27. *Of the Amram-*

part nor inheritance with his brethren; [o]the LORD *is* [p]his inheritance, according as the LORD thy God promised him.

10 ¶ And I stayed in the [c]mount, according to the first time, [q]forty days and forty nights; and [r]the LORD hearkened unto me at that time also, *and* the LORD would not destroy thee.

11 And the LORD said unto me, Arise, take *thy* journey before the people, that they may go in and possess the [s]land, which I [t]sware unto their fathers to give unto them.

12 ¶ And now, Iṣ'ra-el, what doth the LORD thy God [u,v]require of thee, but to [w]fear the LORD thy God, to walk in all his ways, and to [x]love him, and to serve the LORD thy God with all thy [y]heart and with all thy soul,[Q]

13 To [z]keep the [a]commandments of the LORD, and his statutes, which I command thee this day for thy good?

14 Behold, the heaven and the heaven of heavens *is* the LORD's thy [b]God, the [c]earth *also*, with all that therein *is*.[S]

15 Only the [d]LORD had a delight in thy fathers to love them, and he [e]chose their [f]seed[G] after them, *even* you above all people, as *it is* this day.[S Q]

16 [g,h,i]Circumcise therefore the foreskin of your heart, and be no more stiffnecked.[T]

17 For the LORD your God *is* [b]God of gods, and Lord of lords, a great God, a mighty, and a terrible,[G] [j]which [k]regardeth not persons, nor taketh reward:[S Q]

18 [l,m]He doth execute the judgment[G] of the [n,o]fatherless and [p]widow, and loveth the [q]stranger,[G] in giving him [r]food and raiment.[S]

19 [s]Love ye therefore the [q]stranger[G]: for ye were strangers[G] in the land of [t]Ē'ġy̆pt.

20 [u,v]Thou shalt [w]fear the LORD thy God; him shalt thou serve, and to him shalt thou cleave, and [x]swear by his name.

21 He *is* thy [y]praise, and he *is* thy God, that hath done for thee these great and terrible[G] things, which thine eyes have seen.

22 Thy [z]fathers went down into [t]Ē'ġy̆pt with threescore and ten persons; and now the LORD thy God hath made thee as the stars of heaven for multitude.[Q]

## CHAPTER 11

*The people are exhorted to obedience, 2 by their own experience of God's great works; 8 by the promise of God's special blessings; 16 and in view of his judgments. 18 These words to be laid up in their hearts, and taught to their children. 22 Rewards of obedience. 26 A blessing and a curse set before them.*

THEREFORE [a]thou shalt [b,c]love the LORD thy God, and [d]keep his charge,[G] and his statutes, and his judgments,[G] and his commandments, alway.[S]

2 And know ye this day: for *I speak* not with your children which have not known, and which have not seen the [e]chastisement of the LORD your God, his greatness, [f]his mighty hand, and his stretched out [g]arm,

v.9–1494 BC See footnote, *Time,* Rev. 10:6.

**9**

o *Promise, to ministers,* 2 Cor. 1:20.

p *Minister, emoluments of,* Rom. 15:16.

**10**

q *Forty, days,* Jonah 3:4.

r *Intercession, answered,* Jer. 27:18.

**11**

s *Canaan,* Gen. 37:1.

t *Covenant, of God with men,* Deut. 29:1.

**12**

u *Duty, of man to God, to obey,* Eccl. 12:13.

v *Commandment, enjoining fear of God, obedience and love,* Deut. 8:2.

w *Fear of God, a motive to obedience,* Acts 9:31.

x *Love, of man for God,* 1 John 4:19.

y *Heart,* Psa. 44:21.

**13**

z *Obedience, enjoined,* Heb. 5:8.

a *Law, of Moses,* Deut. 33:2.

**14**

b *God, sovereign,* Gen. 2:2.

c *Earth, the Lord's,* Prov. 8:23.

**15**

d *God, love of, exemplified,* Gen. 2:2.

e *Foreordination,* Rom. 8:30.

f *Children, of the righteous blessed of God,* Mark 10:14.

**16**

g *Circumcision, figurative,* Gen. 17:10.

h *Commandment, enjoining consecration of heart,* Deut. 8:2.

i *Repentance, enjoined,* Mark 1:4.

v.17–1494 BC See footnote, *Time,* Rev. 10:6.

**17**

j *God, judge,* Gen. 2:2.

k *Respect of persons,* Prov. 24:23.

**18**

l *God, providence of,* Gen. 2:2.

m *Promise, implied, to the fatherless, widows and strangers,* 2 Cor. 1:20.

n *Children, God's care of,* Mark 10:14.

o *Orphan,* Lam. 5:3.

p *Widow,* 2 Sam. 14:5.

q *Foreigners,* Deut. 23:20.

r *Temporal Blessings, from God,* Psa. 103:2.

**19**

s *Commandment, enjoining love of foreigners,* Deut. 8:2.

t *Egypt,* Gen. 41:8.

**20**

u *Commandment, enjoining the fear and service of God, and solemnization of testimony in the name of God, rather than of idolatrous gods,* Deut. 8:2.

v Matt. 4:10; Luke 4:8.

w *Fear of God,* Acts 9:31.

x *Oath,* Num. 5:19

**21**

y *Praise,* Psa. 150:1.

**22**

z *Israel, number of, who went into Egypt,* Ex. 4:22.

**1**

a *Commandment, enjoining love and obedience to God,* Deut. 8:2.

b *Duty, of man to God,* Eccl. 12:13.

c *Love, of man for God,* 1 John 4:19.

d *Obedience, enjoined,* Heb. 5:8.

2 e *Divine Chastisement, corrective,* Job 33:19. f *God, power of,* Gen. 2:2. g *Arm, figurative,* Psa. 89:13.

*ites, Aaron and his family were set apart as priests,* Ex. 28:1; 29:9; Num. 3:38; 8:1–14; 17; 18:1; *the remaining families appointed to take charge of the ark, table, candlestick, altars, and vessels of the sanctuary, the hangings, and all the service,* Num. 3:27–32; 4:2–15, 18–20. *Chief over the Kohathites was Elizaphan,* Num. 3:30. See footnote, KOHATHITES, Num. 3:27.

MERARITES, Num. 3:20, 33–37; 4:31–33; 7:8; 10:17; 1 Chr. 6:19, 29, 30; 23:21–23. *Ruling chief over the Merarites was Ithamar,* Num. 4:33; 7:8. See footnote, MERARITES, Num. 26:57.

**Duties of:** *Had charge of the tabernacle,* Num. 1:50–53; 3:6–9, 21–37; 4:1–15, 17–49; 8:19, 22; 18:3–6; 1 Chr. 9:27–29; 23:2–32; *and of the temple,* Ezra 8:24–34.

*Bore the ark of the covenant,* Deut. 10:8; 1 Chr. 15:2, 26, 27. *Ministered before the ark,* 1 Chr. 16:4. *Custodians and administrators of the tithes and other offerings,* 1 Chr. 9:26–29; 26:20–26, 28; 29:8; 2 Chr. 24:5, 11; 31:11–19; 34:9; Ezra 8:29, 30, 33; Neh. 12:44. *Prepared the shewbread,* 1 Chr. 23:28, 29. *Assisted the priests in preparing the sacrifices,* 2 Chr. 29:12–36; 35:1–18. *Killed the passover for the children of the captivity,* Ezra 6:20, 21. *Teachers of the law,* Deut. 33:10; 2 Chr. 17:8, 9; 35:3; Neh. 8:7–13; Mal. 2:6, 7. *Were judges,* Deut. 17:9; 1 Chr. 23:4; 26:29; 2 Chr. 19:8–11.

*Joined with the other tribes in pronouncing the blessings of the law in the responsive service at Mount Gerizim,* Deut. 27:12; Josh. 8:13. *Were porters,* 1 Chr. 9:26, 27; 26:13–19; 2 Chr. 23:4, 5; 34:13; 35:15. *Were overseers in building, and of the repairs of, the temple,* 1 Chr. 23:2–4; Ezra 3:8, 9. *Supervised weights and measures,* 1 Chr. 23:29.

**Emoluments of:** *In lieu of landed inheritance, forty-eight cities with suburbs were assigned to them,* Num. 35:2–8; Josh. 14:3, 4; 1 Chr. 6:54–81; 13:2; *assigned to, by families,* Josh. 21:4–40. *Suburbs of their cities were inalienable for*

v.3–1494 BC
See footnote, *Time*, Rev. 10:6.

3
h *Miracles*, Luke 23:8.
i *Egypt*, Gen. 41:8.
j *Pharaoh, at the time of the exodus*, Ex. 3:10.
1 R. V. signs,

4
k *Red Sea*, Ex. 10:19.
l *Israel, pass through the Red Sea*, Ex. 4:22.

6
m *Dathan*, Num. 16:1.
n *Abiram*, Num. 16:1.
o *Eliab*, Num. 26:8.

3 And his [1,h]miracles, and his
acts, which he did in the midst
of [i]Ē'ġȳpt unto [j]Phā'raōh the
king of Ē'ġȳpt, and unto all his
land;
4 And what he did unto the
*army of [i]Ē'ġȳpt, unto their
horses, and to their chariots;
how he made the water of the
[k]Red sea to [h]overflow[G] them as
they pursued after [l]you, and *how*
the LORD hath destroyed them
unto this day;
5 And what he did unto you in
the wilderness, until ye came into this place;[Q]
6 And what he did unto [m]Dā'-
than and [n]Ă-bī'ram, the sons of
[o]Ē-lī'ab, the son of Reu'ben:
how the [p]earth opened her
mouth, and swallowed them up,
and their households, and their
tents, and all the substance[G] that
*was* in their possession, in the
midst of all Is'ra-el:
7 [S]But your eyes have seen all
the great acts of the [q]LORD
which he did.
8 Therefore [r]shall ye [d]keep all
the commandments which I
command you this day, [s]that ye
may be strong, and go in and
possess the [t]land, whither ye go
to possess it;[S]
9 And [s]that ye may prolong
*your* days in the [t]land, which the
LORD [u]sware unto your fathers
to give unto them and to their

v.6–1494 BC
See footnote, *Time*, Rev. 10:6.

p *Miracles, destruction of Korah*, Luke 23:8.

7
q *God, providence of*, Gen. 2:2.

8
r *Commandment, enjoining obedience*, Deut. 8:2.
s *Promise, implied, to the obedient, of prosperity*, 2 Cor. 1:20.
t *Canaan*, Gen. 37:1.

9
u *Covenant, of God with men*, Deut. 29:1.

*debt*, Lev. 25:34. *Tithes and other offerings*, Num. 18:24, 26–32; Deut. 18:1–8; 26:11–13; Josh. 13:14; Neh. 10:38, 39; 12:44, 47. *First fruits*, Neh. 12:44, 47. *Spoils of war, including captives*, Num. 31:30, 42–47. *Pensioned*, 2 Chr. 31:16–18. *Owned lands*, Deut. 18:8; 1 Kin. 2:26. *Land allotted to, by Ezekiel*, Ezek. 48:13, 14.

**Historical facts relating to:** *Religious zeal of*, Ex. 32:26–28; Deut. 33:9, 10; Mal. 2:4, 5. *Sedition among, led by Korah, Dathan, Abiram, and On, on account of jealousy toward Moses and Aaron*, Num. 16 (with 4:19, 20). *Degraded from the Levitical office by Jeroboam*, 2 Chr. 11:13–17; 13:9–11. *Tithes withheld from*, Neh. 13:10–13; Mal. 3:10.

*Rebel against Saul, and join David armed for war*, 1 Chr. 12:26. *Intermarry with Canaanites*, Ezra 9:1, 2; 10:2–24.

*List of those who returned from captivity*, Ezra 2:40–63; **7**:7; 8:16–20; Neh. 7:43–73; 12. *Sealed the covenant with Nehemiah*, Neh. 10:9–28.

**Prophecies concerning,** Jer. 33:18–22; Ezek. 44:10–14; Mal. 3:3. *Of their repentance for the crucifixion of the Messiah*, Zech. 12:10–13. *John's vision concerning*, Rev. 7:7.

See footnote, PRIEST, Lev. 1:5.

*** ARMIES.** *Who of the Israelites were subject to service in*, Num. 1:2, 3; 26:2; 2 Chr. 25:5. *Who were exempt from service in*, Num. 1:47–50; 2:33; Deut. 20:5–9; Judg. 7:3. *Age when subject to military service*, Num. 1:18. *Enumeration of Israel's military forces*, Num. 1:2–46; 26:1–51; 1 Sam. 11:8; 2 Sam. 18:1, 2; 24:1–9; 1 Kin. 20:15; 2 Chr. 25:5. *Levies for*, Num. 31:4; Judg. 20:10. *Compulsory service in*, 1 Sam. 14:52.

*Composed, of insurgents*, 1 Sam. 22:1, 2; *of mercenaries*, 2 Sam. 10:6; 1 Chr. 19:6, 7; 2 Chr. 25:6. *Confederated*, Josh. 10:1–5; 11:1–5; Judg. 1:3; 2 Sam. 10:6, 15, 16, 19; 1 Kin. 15:20; 22:1–4; 2 Kin. 18:19–21; 1 Chr. 19:6, 7; 2 Chr. 16:2–9; 18:1, 3; 20:1; 22:5; 28:16, 20; Psa. 83:1–12; Isa. 7:1–9.

*Standards of*, Num. 2:2, 3, 10, 17, 18, 25, 31, 34; 10:14, 18, 22, 25. *Uniforms of*, Ezek. 23:6, 12; Nah. 2:3. *Standing armies*, 1 Sam. 13:2; 1 Chr. 27; 2 Chr. 1:14; 17:12–19; 26:11–15.

*Determine royal succession*, 2 Sam. 2:8–10; 1 Kin. 16:16; 2 Kin. 11:4–12.

*Exhorted before battle*, Deut. 20:1–9. *Battle shouts*, Josh. 6:20; Judg. 7:18, 20; 1 Sam. 17:20, 52; 2 Chr. 13:15.

Triumphs of, celebrated: *With songs*, Judg. 5; 1 Sam. 18:6, 7; *with music*, 2 Chr. 20:28; *with dancing*, 1 Sam. 18:6, 7. *Taught martial songs*, 2 Sam. 1:18.

*Insubordination in, punished, Achan*, Josh. **7**. *Check roll-call*, Num. 31:48, 49; 1 Sam. 14:17.

*Champions fight instead of*, 1 Sam. 17:4–53; 2 Sam. 2:14–17; 21:15–22. *Confidence in, vain*, Psa. 33:16; 44:6. *Escort duty performed by*, 2 Kin. 1:9; Ezra 8:22; Neh. 2:9; Acts 23:23, 24, 31–33. *Non-combatants share equally in spoils*, 1 Sam. 30:21–25.

*Engines used*, 2 Chr. 26:15; Ezek. 26:9. *Fortifications*, 2 Sam. 5:9; 2 Kin. 25:1; 2 Chr. 11:11; 26:9; Neh. 3:8; 4:2; Isa. 22:10; 25:12; 29:3; 32:14; Jer. 6:6; 32:24; 33:4; 51:53; Ezek. 4:2; 17:17; 21:22; 26:8; 33:27; Dan. 11:15, 19; Nah. 2:1; 3:14.

**Religious ceremonies in:** *Seeking counsel from God before battle*, Num. 27:21; Judg. 1:1; 1 Sam. 14:19, 37–41; 23:2–12; 30:8; 2 Sam. 2:1; 5:19, 23; 1 Kin. 22:7–28; 2 Kin. 3:11–19; 1 Chr. 14:10, 14; Jer. 37:3–10. *Sacrifices*, 1 Sam. 13:8, 12. *Purifications*, Num. 31:19–24. *Prophets prophesy before*, 2 Chr. 20:14–17. *Priests exhort*, Deut. 20:2–4. *Holiness enjoined*, Deut. 23:9. *Officers consecrate themselves to God*, 2 Chr. 17:16. *Army choir and songs*, 2 Chr. 20:21, 22. *Ark taken to battle*, Josh. 6:6, 7, 13.

**Divine assistance to:** *When Aaron and Hur held up Moses' hands*, Ex. 17:11, 12. *In siege of Jericho*, Josh. **6**. *Sun stands still*, Josh. 10:11–14. *Gideon's victory*, Judg. **7**. *Samaria's deliverances*, 1 Kin. 20; 2 Kin. **7**. *Jehoshaphat's victories*, 2 Kin. 3:18; 2 Chr. 20:17. *Angel of the Lord smites the Assyrians*, 2 Kin. 19:35.

**Rewards for meritorious conduct in:** *The general offers his daughter in marriage*, Josh. 15:16, 17. *King offers his daughter*, 1 Sam. 17:25; 18:17–28. *Promotion*, 2 Sam. 23:8–39; 1 Chr. 11:6, 10–47. *Share of spoils*, Num. 31:25–47. *Roll of honor for distinguished heroes*, 2 Sam. 23:8–39.

**How officered:** *Commander-in-chief*, 1 Sam. 14:50; 2 Sam. 2:8; 8:16; 17:25; 19:13; 20:23. *Generals of corps and divisions*, Num. 2:3–31; 1 Chr. 27:1–22; 2 Chr. 17:12–19. *Captains, of thousands*, Num. 31:14, 48; 1 Sam. 17:18; 1 Chr. 28:1; 2 Chr. 17:14; 25:5; *of hundreds*, Num. 31:14, 48; 2 Kin. 11:15; 1 Chr. 28:1; 2 Chr. 25:5; *of fifties*, 2 Kin. 1:9; Isa. 3:3.

**Rendezvous of.** Methods employed in effecting: *Sounding a trumpet*, Num. 10:9; Judg. 3:27; 6:34; 1 Sam. 13:3, 4; *cutting oxen in pieces, and sending the pieces throughout Israel*, 1 Sam. 11:7. *Refusal to obey the summons, instance of*, Judg. 21:5–11 (with chapter 20).

**Tactics of:** *Camp and march*, Num. **2**. *March in ranks*, Joel 2:7. *Move, in attack, in three divisions*, Judg. 7:16; 9:43; 1 Sam. 11:11; 13:17, 18; 2 Sam. 18:2; Job 1:17. *Flanks called wings*, Isa. 8:8. *Night attacks*, Gen. 14:15; Judg. 7:16–22; Isa. 15:1. *Decoy*, Josh. 8:4–22; Judg. 20:29–43; Neh. 6. *Delay*, 2 Sam. 17:7–14. *Spies used in*, 2 Sam. 15:32, 34.

*Orders delivered with trumpets*, 2 Sam. 2:28; 18:16; 20:1, 22; Neh. 4:18, 20.

STRATAGEMS: Ambushes, Jer. 51:12. *At Ai*, Josh. 8:2–22. *At Shechem*, Judg. 9:25, 34. *At Gibeah*, Judg. 20:29–43. *At Zemaraim*, 2 Chr. 13:13. *By Jehoshaphat*, 2 Chr. 20:22.

Reconnoissances: *Of Jericho*, Josh. 2:1–24. *Of Ai*, Josh. 7:2, 3. *Of Beth-el*, Judg. 1:23, 24. *Of Laish*, Judg. 18:2–10.

Celerity of action: *Abraham, in pursuit of Chedorlaomer*, Gen. 14:14, 15. *Joshua, against the Amorites*, Josh. 10:6, 9. *The confederated kings*, Josh. 11:7. *David's attack upon the Philistines*, 2 Sam. 5:23–25.

FORCED MARCHES, Isa. 5:26, 27.

SIEGES, Jer. 39:1. *Of Jericho*, Josh. **6**. *Of Samaria*, 2 Kin. 6:24–33; **7**. *Of Jerusalem*, 2 Kin. 25:1–3.

**Panics:** *Among Canaanites*, Ex. 15:14–16. *Among army of Israel*, Lev. 26:17; Deut. 32:30. *Among the Midianites*, Judg. 7:21, 22. *Among the Philistines*, 1 Sam. 14:15–19. *Among the Syrians*, 2 Kin. 7:6–15. *Among Ammonites, Moabites and Edomites*, 2 Chr. 20:22, 23. *From God*, Gen. 35:5; Josh. 23:10. *Soldiers destroy each other to escape captivity*, 1 Sam. 14:20; 31:4–6.

**Roman army:** *Captains* [R. V. marg., military tribunes] *of*, Acts 22:24–29. *Centurions of*, Matt. 8:5, 8, 9; 27:54; Luke 7:2, 8; 23:47; Acts 10:1, 22; 21:32; 22:26; 23:17, 23; 24:23; 27:1, 11, 43; 28:16. *Divided into bands* [R. V. marg., cohorts], Acts 10:1; 27:1.

**Figurative.** Deut. 33:2; 2 Kin. 6:17; Psa. 68:17; Rev. 9:16.

v.9–1494 BC
See footnote, *Time*, Rev. 10:6.

*v Milk, figurative*, Job 10:10.
*w Honey, figurative*, Prov. 25:27.
**10**
*x Irrigation*, Eccl. 2:6.
**11**
*y Canaan, fertility of*, Gen. 37:1.
**12**
*z Eye, figurative*, Matt. 6:22.

**13**
*a Diligence, required*, Rom. 12:8.
*b Law, of Moses*, Deut. 33:2.
*c Word of God*, Psa. 119:9.
*d Commandment, enjoining obedience, love to God and faithful service*, Deut. 8:2.
*e Love, of man for God*, 1 John 4:19.
*f Duty, of man to God*, Eccl. 12:13.
*g Faithfulness, enjoined*, Luke 16:10.
*h Heart*, Psa. 44:21.
**14**
*i Promise, to the obedient, of prosperity*, 2 Cor. 1:20.
*j God, providence of*, Gen. 2:2.
*k Reward*, Matt. 5:12.
*l Rain*, 2 Sam. 1:21.
*m Temporal Blessings, from God*, Psa. 103:2.
*n Wine*, Prov. 23:31.
*o Oil*, Deut. 12:17.
**16**
*p Commandment, enjoining watchfulness*, Deut. 8:2.
*q Watchfulness, enjoined*, Matt. 24:42.
*r Idolatry, forbidden*, 1 Sam. 15:23.
**17**
*s Anger of God*, 2 Kin. 13:3.
*t Judgments*, Ex. 6:6.
*u Rain, withheld as a judgment*, 2 Sam. 1:21.
2 R. V. And the anger of the Lord
*v Commandment, enjoining remembrance of the law*, Deut. 8:2.

seed, a land that floweth with
[v]milk and [w]honey.
10 ¶ For the [i]land, whither
thou goest in to possess it, *is* not
as the land of [i]Ē′ġȳpt, from
whence ye came out, where thou
sowedst thy seed, and [x]water-
edst[G] *it* with thy foot, as a garden
of herbs:
11 But the [y]land, whither ye go
to possess it, *is* a land of hills and
valleys, *and* drinketh water of
the rain of heaven:
12[S] A [y]land which the LORD
thy [q]God careth for: the [z]eyes
of the LORD thy God *are* always
upon it, from the beginning of
the year even unto the end of the
year.
13 ¶ And it shall come to pass,
if ye shall hearken [a]diligently
unto my [b,c]commandments
which I [d]command you this day,
to [e,f]love the LORD your God,
and to [g]serve him with all your
[h]heart and with all your soul,
14 [i]That [j]I will [k]give *you* the
[l,m]rain of your land in his due
season, the first rain and the latter rain, that thou mayest gather
in thy corn[G], and thy [n]wine, and
thine [o]oil.[Q]
15 And I will send [m]grass in thy
fields for thy cattle, that thou
mayest eat and be full.[S]
16 [p,q]Take heed to yourselves,
that your heart be not deceived,
and ye turn aside, and [r]serve
other gods, and worship them;
17 [2]And *then* the LORD's
[s]wrath[G] be kindled[G] against you,
and he [t]shut up the heaven, that
there be no [u]rain, and that the
land yield not her fruit; and *lest*
ye perish quickly from off the
good land which the LORD giveth you.[T]
18 ¶ [v]Therefore shall ye lay up
these my [b,c]words in your heart
and in your soul, and bind [w]them
for a [x]sign upon your hand, that
they may be as [y]frontlets[G] between your eyes.[T]
19 And [z,a]ye shall [b]teach
[c,d]them your [e]children, [f]speak-
ing of them when thou sittest in
thine house, and when thou
walkest by the way, when thou
liest down, and when thou risest
up.
20 And thou shalt write [c,d]them
upon the †door posts of thine
house, and upon thy gates:
21 [g]That your days may be
multiplied, and the days of your
children, in the [h]land which the
LORD sware unto your fathers to
give them, as the days[G] of heaven
upon the earth.
22 ¶ For if ye shall [i]diligently
[j]keep all these commandments
which I command you, to do
them, to [k]love the LORD your
God, to walk in all his ways, and
to cleave[G] unto him;
23 [g]Then will the [l]LORD drive
out all these [m]nations from before you, and ye shall possess
greater nations and mightier
than yourselves.
24 [g]Every place whereon the
soles of your feet shall tread shall
be your's: from the wilderness
and [n]Lĕb′a-non, from the river,
the river [o]Eū-phrā′tēş, even unto
the uttermost [p]sea shall your
coast[G] be.
25 [g]There shall no man be able
to stand[G] before you: *for* the
[l]LORD your God shall lay the
fear of you and the dread of you
upon all the land that ye shall
tread upon, as he hath said unto
you.[S]
26 ¶ Behold, I set before you
this day a ‡blessing[G] and a [q]curse[G];
27 A ‡blessing[G], [r]if ye [s]obey the
commandments of the LORD

v.18–1494 BC
See footnote, *Time*, Rev. 10:6.

**18**
*w Legends*, Zech. 14:20.
*x Phylactery*, Matt. 23:5.
*y Frontlets*, Ex. 13:16.
**19**
*z Parents, duty of, to instruct children in righteousness*, 2 Cor. 12:14.

*a Commandment, enjoining religious instruction of children*, Deut. 8:2.
*b Instruction, of children*, Prov. 23:23.
*c Word of God*, Psa. 119:9.
*d Law, of Moses*, Deut. 33:2.
*e Children, instruction of*, Mark 10:14.
*f School, in the home*, Acts 19:9.
**21**
*g Promise, to the obedient*, 2 Cor. 1:20.
*h Canaan*, Gen. 37:1.
**22**
*i Diligence*, Rom. 12:8.
*j Obedience, enjoined*, Heb. 5:8.
*k Love, of man for God*, 1 John 4:19.
**23**
*l God, providence of*, Gen. 2:2.
*m Canaanites*, Ex. 23:28.

**24**
*n Lebanon*, Deut. 1:7.
*o Euphrates*, Gen. 15:18.
*p Mediterranean Sea*, Ex. 23:31.

**26**
*q Curse*, Judg. 5:23.
**27**
*r Contingencies, in divine government of man*, 1 Kin. 3:14.
*s Obedience, rewarded*, Heb. 5:8.

† **DOOR.** *Posts of, sprinkled with the blood of the paschal lamb*, Ex. 12:22. *The law to be written on*, Deut. 11:20. *Hinges for*, Prov. 26:14; *of Solomon's temple made of gold*, 1 Kin. 7:50. *Of the temple made of two leaves; cherubim and flowers carved upon, covered with gold*, 1 Kin. 6:31–35. **Figurative:** *Of hope*, Hos. 2:15. *Of opportunity*, 1 Cor. 16:9; Rev. 3:8. *Of lost opportunity*, Matt. 25:10, Luke 13:25; Rev. 3:7. *Christ, the door of salvation*, John 10:7, 9.

‡ **BLESSINGS, CONTINGENT UPON OBEDIENCE.**
**Temporal:** *Longevity*, Ex. 20:12; Deut. 4:40; 5:16; 1 Kin.

your God, which I command
you this day:
28 And a [q]curse, if [t]ye will [u]not
obey the commandments of the
LORD your God, but turn aside
out of the way which I command
you this day, to [v]go after other
gods, which ye have not known.
29 And it shall come to pass,
when the LORD thy [l]God hath
brought thee in unto the [h]land
whither thou goest to possess it,
that thou shalt put the blessing
upon mount ‖Gĕr′ĭ-zĭm, and the
curse upon mount §Ē′bal.
30 *Are* they not on the other
side [w]Jôr′dan, by the way where
the sun goeth down, in the land
of the [m]Cā′năan-ītes, which
dwell in the champaign over
against Gĭl′găl, beside the
[3]plains of [x]Mō′reh?
31 For ye shall pass over [w]Jôr′-
dan to go in to possess the [h]land
which the LORD your [l]God giveth you, and ye shall possess it,
and dwell therein.
32 And [y]ye shall observe to [i]do
all the statutes and judgments
which I set before you this day.

## CHAPTER 12

*The monuments of idolatry are to be destroyed. 5 All offerings are to be brought to the place chosen of God. 17 Holy things must be eaten in the holy place. 20 Exceptions. 29 The rites of idolatry not to be inquired into.*

THESE *are* the [a]statutes and
judgments, which ye shall
observe to do in the [b]land, which
the LORD [c]God of thy fathers
giveth thee to possess it, all the
days that ye live upon the earth.
2 [d]Ye shall utterly [e]destroy all
the places, wherein the [f]nations
which ye shall possess [g]served
their gods, upon the high [h]moun-
tains, and upon the hills, and
under every green tree:
3 And [d]ye shall [e]overthrow
their altars, and break their [i]pil-
lars, and burn their [j]groves with
fire; and ye shall hew down the
graven [k]images of their gods,
and destroy the names of them
out of that place.
4 Ye shall not do so unto the
LORD your God.
5 But [l]unto the [m,n]place which
the LORD your God shall choose
out of all your tribes to put his
name there, *even* unto his habitation shall ye [o]seek, and thither
thou shalt come:
6 And [m]thither ye shall bring
your [p]burnt offerings, and your
sacrifices, and your [q]tithes, and
[r]heave offerings of your hand,
and your [s]vows, and your [t]free-
will offerings, and the firstlings
of your herds and of your
flocks:
7 And there ye shall eat before
the LORD your God and ye shall
[u]rejoice in all that ye put your
hand unto, ye and your [v]house-
holds, wherein the LORD thy
[c]God hath [w]blessed thee.
8 [x]Ye shall not do after all *the
things* that we do here this day,
every man whatsoever *is* right in
his own [y]eyes.
9 For ye are not as yet come to
the rest and to the inheritance,
which the LORD your God giveth you.
10 But *when* ye go over [z]Jôr′-
dan, and dwell in the [a]land
which the LORD your God giveth you to inherit, and *when* he
giveth you rest from all your ene-

**v.27–1494 BC** See footnote, *Time*, Rev. 10:6.

**28**
*t Wicked, punishment of*, Psa. 73:3.
*u Disobedience to God*, Eph. 5:6.
*v Idolatry, forbidden*, 1 Sam. 15:23.

**30**
*w Jordan*, Gen. 32:10.
*x* Gen. 12:6.
3 R. V. oaks

**32**
*y Commandment, enjoining obedience*, Deut. 8:2.

**1**
*a Law, of Moses*, Deut. 33:2.
*b Canaan*, Gen. 37:1.
*c God, providence of*, Gen. 2:2.

**2**
*d Statute, against idolatry*, Deut. 8:2.
*e Iconoclasm*, Num. 33:52.
*f Canaanites*, Ex. 23:28.
*g Idolatry*, 1 Sam. 15:23.

**v.2–1494 BC** See footnote, *Time*, Rev. 10:6.

*h Mountain*, Mic. 7:12.

**3**
*i Pillar*, Gen. 28:18.
*j Groves*, Judg. 6:28.
*k Idols, to be destroyed*, 1 Kin. 15:12.

**5**
*l Statute, enjoining public worship*, Deut. 8:2.
*m Tabernacle, offerings brought to*, Ex. 27:9.
*n Church*, 1 Kin. 9:3.
*o Worship, enjoined*, Gen. 22:5.

**6**
*p Offerings, burnt*, Lev. 6:17.
*q Tithes*, Num. 18:24.
*r Offerings, heave*, Lev. 6:17.
*s Vows*, Num. 30:2.
*t Offerings, free will*, Lev. 6:17.

**7**
*u Thankfulness, enjoined*, Acts 24:3.
*v Family, religion in the*, 1 Chr. 13:14.
*w Temporal Blessings, from God*, Psa. 103:2.

**8**
*x Commandment, forbidding lawlessness*, Deut. 8:2.
*y Reasoning, not a sufficient guide in human affairs*, Job 13:6.

**10**
*z Jordan*, Gen. 32:10.

*a Canaan*, Gen. 37:1.

3:14; Prov. 3:1, 2. *Deliverence from enemies*, Ex. 23:22; Lev. 26:6–8; Deut. 28:7; 30:1–4; Prov. 16:7; Jer. 15:19–21. *Prosperity*, Lev. 26:3–5; Deut. 7:12–14; 15:4, 5; 28:2–6, 8, 10–12; 29:9; 30:1–5, 9–20; Josh. 1:8; 1 Kin. 2:3, 4; 9:3–9; 1 Chr. 22:13; 28:7, 8; 2 Chr. 7:17–22; 26:5; 27:6; 31:10; Job 36:11; Isa. 1:19; Jer. 7:3–7; 11:1–5; 12:16; 17:24–27; 22:4, 5, 15, 16; Mal. 3:10–12. *Favors to children*, Deut. 4:1, 40; 5:29; 7:9; 12:25, 28. *Pre-eminent honors*, Deut. 28:1, 13; Zech. 3:7. *Averted judgments*, Ex. 15:26; Deut. 7:15.
**Spiritual:** *Divine favor*, Ex. 19:5; Jer. 7:23. *Mercy*, Ex. 20:6; Deut. 5:10, 16; 7:9; 1 Kin. 8:23; 2 Chr. 30:9. *Holiness*, Deut. 28:9; 30:1–3, 6; Col. 1:22, 23. *Eternal salvation*, Matt. 10:22; 24:13; Mark 13:13; Heb. 3:6, 14; 10:36; Rev. 2:10.
See footnotes: SPIRITUAL BLESSINGS, *From God*, Eph. 1:3; TEMPORAL BLESSINGS, *From God*, Psa. 103:2.

‖ **GERIZIM.** *Mount of blessing*, Deut. 27:12; Josh. 8:33. *Jotham addresses the Shechemites from*, Judg. 9:7. *Samaritans worship at*, John 4:20.

§ **EBAL**, a mountain of Ephraim. *Half of the tribes of Israel stand on, to respond Amen to the curses of the law*, Deut. 11:29; 27:12, 13; Josh. 8:33. *Altar built on*, Josh. 8:30.

**v.10–1494 BC**
See footnote, *Time*, Rev. 10:6.

**11**
b *Statute, ordaining places of public worship*, Deut. 8:2.
c *Tabernacle, offerings brought to*, Ex. 27:9.
d *Church, divinely instituted*, 1 Kin. 9:3.
e *Offerings, burnt*, Lev. 6:17.
f *Tithes*, Num. 18:24.
g *Offerings, heave*, Lev. 6:17.
h *Vows*, Num. 30:2.

**12**
i *Thankfulness, enjoined*, Acts 24:3.
j *Children, to enjoy religious privileges*, Mark 10:14.
k *Servant, to enjoy religious privileges*, Jer. 2:14.

**13**
l *Commandment, enjoining watchfulness*, Deut. 8:2.
m *Watchfulness, enjoined*, Matt. 24:42.

**14**
n *Obedience, enjoined*, Heb. 5:8.

**15**
o *Deer*, Deut. 14:5.
1 R. V. gazelle,

**16**
p *Statute, forbidding eating of blood*, Deut. 8:2.
q *Sanitation and Hygiene, food*, Num. 31:23.
r *Blood, forbidden as food*, Gen. 9:4.

mies round about, so that ye
dwell in safety;
11 Then [b]there shall be a
[c,d]place which the LORD your
God shall choose to cause his
name to dwell there; thither
shall ye bring all that I command
you; your [e]burnt offerings,
and your sacrifices, your
[f]tithes, and the [g]heave offering
of your hand, and all your choice
[h]vows which ye vow unto the
LORD:
12 And ye shall [i]rejoice before
the LORD your God, ye, and
your [j]sons, and your [j]daughters,
and your [k]menservants, and
your [k]maidservants, and the Lē′vīte
that *is* within your gates;
forasmuch as he hath no part
nor inheritance with you.
13 [l,m]Take heed to thyself that
thou offer not thy [e]burnt offerings
in every place that thou
seest;
14 But in the [c,d]place which the
LORD shall choose in one of thy
tribes, there thou shalt offer thy
[e]burnt offerings, and there thou
shalt [n]do all that I command
thee.
15 Notwithstanding thou mayest
kill and eat flesh in all thy
gates, whatsoever thy soul lusteth
after, according to the blessing
of the LORD thy God which
he hath given thee: the unclean
and the clean may eat thereof, as
of the [1,o]roebuck, and as of the
hart.
16 Only [p,q]ye shall not eat the
[r]blood; ye shall pour it upon the
earth as water.
17 ¶ Thou mayest not eat within
thy gates the [f]tithe of thy
corn, or of thy wine, or of thy
*oil, or the firstlings of thy herds
or of thy flock, nor any of thy
[h]vows which thou vowest, nor
thy [s]freewill offerings, or [g]heave
offering of thine hand:
18 But thou must eat them before
the LORD thy God in the
[c]place which the LORD thy God
shall choose, thou, and thy [j]son,
and thy [j]daughter, and thy [k]manservant,
and thy [k]maidservant,
and the Lē′vīte that *is* within
thy gates: and thou shalt [i]rejoice
before the LORD thy God
in all that thou puttest thine
hands unto.
19 [m,t]Take heed to thyself that
thou [u]forsake not the Lē′vīte as
long as thou livest upon the earth.
20 ¶ When the LORD thy God
shall [v]enlarge thy border, as [w]he
hath promised thee, and thou
shalt say, I will eat flesh, because
thy soul longeth to eat
flesh: thou mayest eat flesh,
whatsoever thy soul lusteth after.
21 If the [c]place which the
LORD thy God hath chosen to
put his name there be too far
from thee, then thou shalt kill of
thy herd and of thy flock, which
the LORD hath given thee, as I
have commanded thee, and thou
shalt eat in thy gates whatsoever
thy soul lusteth after.
22 Even as the [1,o]roebuck and
the hart is eaten, so thou shalt
eat them: the unclean and the
clean shall eat *of* them alike.
23 Only [p,q]be sure that thou eat
not the [r]blood: for the blood *is*
the life; and thou mayest not eat
the life with the flesh.
24 [p,q]Thou shalt not eat [r]it;
thou shalt pour it upon the earth
as water.

**v.17–1494 BC**
See footnote, *Time*, Rev. 10:6.

**17**
s *Offerings, free will*, Lev. 6:17.

**19**
t *Commandment, enjoining the care of ministers*, Deut. 8:2.
u *Liberality, enjoined*, 1 Tim. 6:18.

**20**
v *Temporal Blessings, from God*, Psa. 103:2.
w *God, faithfulness of*, Gen. 2:2.

---

*** OIL.** *Extracted from olives*, Ex. 30:24; Lev. 24:2. *Offerings of*, Num. 18:12.
*Used, for food*, Lev. 2:4, 5; 14:10, 21; 1 Kin. 17:12–16; Prov. 21:17; Ezek. 16:13; Hos. 2:5; *for the head*, Psa. 23:5; Luke 7:46; *for anointing pillars*, Gen. 28:18; *for anointing kings*, 1 Sam. 10:1; 16:1, 13; 1 Kin. 1:39.
*On sin offering, forbidden*, Lev. 5:11.
*Tribute paid in*, Hos. 12:1. *Commerce in*, 2 Kin. 4:1–7; 2 Chr. 2:10, 15.
*Illuminating*, Matt. 25:3, 8; *for tabernacle*, Ex. 25:6; 27:20; 35:8, 14, 28; Lev. 24:2–4; Num. 4:16.
**Sacred,** Ex. 30:23–25; 31:11; 35:8, 15, 28; 37:29; 39:38; Num. 4:16; 1 Chr. 9:30. *Used, for anointing the tabernacle*, Lev. 8:10; *for anointing priests*, Ex. 29:7; 30:30; Lev. 8:12. *Punishment for profaning*, Ex. 30:31–33. *Used in idolatrous worship*, Ezek. 23:41.
**Figurative,** Matt. 25:3, 4, 8.

25 [p,q]Thou shalt not eat [r]it; [x,y]that it may go well with thee, and with thy children after thee, when thou shalt [z]do *that which is* right in the sight of the LORD.

26 Only thy holy things which thou hast, and thy [a]vows,[G] thou shalt take and go unto the [b]place which the LORD shall choose:

27 And thou shalt offer thy [c]burnt [d]offerings, the flesh and the [e,f]blood, upon the altar of the LORD thy God: and the blood of thy sacrifices shall be poured out upon the altars of the LORD thy God, and thou shalt eat the flesh.

28 [g]Observe and hear all these words which I command thee, [h,i,j]that it may go well with thee, and with thy [k]children after thee for ever, when thou doest *that which is* good and right in the sight of the LORD thy God.

29 ¶ When the LORD thy God shall [l]cut[G] off the [m]nations from before thee, whither thou goest to possess them, and thou [2]succeedest them, and dwellest in their [n]land;

30 [o]Take heed to thyself that thou be not [3]snared by [p]following [m,q]them, after that they be destroyed from before thee; and that thou enquire[G] not after their gods, saying, How did these nations [r]serve their gods? even so will I do likewise.

31 Thou shalt not do so unto the LORD thy God: for every abomination[G] to the LORD, which he hateth, have they done unto their gods; for even their †sons and their daughters they have [r]burnt in the fire to their gods.

32 [s]What thing soever I command you, observe[G] to do it: thou shalt not add [t]thereto, nor diminish from it.[Q]

v.25–1494 BC
See footnote, *Time*, Rev. 10:6.

**25**
x *Blessings, contingent upon obedience*, Deut. 11:26.
y *Promise, to the obedient*, 2 Cor. 1:20.
z *Obedience, rewarded*, Heb. 5:8.

**26**
a *Vows*, Num. 30:2.
b *Tabernacle, offerings brought to*, Ex. 27:9.

**27**
c *Offerings, burnt*, Lev. 6:17.
d *Jesus, typified in offerings*, Matt. 1:21.
e *Blood, sacrificial*, Heb. 9:19.
f *Jesus, atoning blood of, typified*, Matt. 1:21.

**28**
g *Commandment, enjoining obedience*, Deut. 8:2.
h *Blessings, contingent upon obedience*, Deut. 11:26.
i *Promise, to the obedient*, 2 Cor. 1:20.
j *Obedience, rewarded*, Heb. 5:8.
k *Children, of the righteous, blessed of God*, Mark 10:14.

**29**
l *Judgments, upon the Canaanites*, vs. 29–32; Ex. 6:6.
m *Canaanites, to be destroyed*, Ex. 23:28.
n *Canaan*, Gen. 37:1.
2 R. V. possessest

**30**
o *Commandment, enjoining watchfulness*, Deut. 8:2.
p *Fellowship, with the wicked, forbidden*, 1 Cor. 1:9.
q *Evil Company, forbidden*, Prov. 13:20.
r *Idolatry, wicked practices of*, 1 Sam. 15:23.
3 R. V. ensnared to follow

**32**
s *Commandment, enjoining obedience, and forbidding any change of God's word*, Deut. 8:2.
t *Word of God*, Psa. 119:9.

## CHAPTER 13

*Enticers to idolatry, 6 even one's nearest kindred, 9 are to be stoned to death. 12 Idolatrous cities are not to be spared.*

IF[Q] there arise among you a [a,b,c]prophet, or a dreamer of [d]dreams, and giveth thee a [e]sign or a wonder,

2 And[Q] the [e]sign or the wonder come to pass, whereof [a,b,c]he spake unto thee, saying, [f]Let us [g]go after other gods, which thou hast not known, and let us serve them;

3 [h,i]Thou shalt not hearken unto the words of that [a,b,c]prophet, or that dreamer of [d]dreams: for the LORD your God [j]proveth[G] you, to know whether ye [k]love the LORD your God with all your [l]heart and with all your soul.[Q]

4 [m]Ye shall walk after the LORD your God, and [n]fear him, and [o]keep his commandments, and obey his voice, and ye shall serve him, and cleave unto him.[Q]

5 And that [a,b,c]prophet, or that dreamer of [d]dreams, shall be [p]put to death; because he hath spoken [1]to turn *you* away from the LORD your God, which brought you out of the land of E'gypt, and redeemed you out of the house of bondage, to thrust thee out of the way which the LORD thy God commanded thee to walk in. So shalt thou put the evil away from the midst of thee.

6 ¶ If thy brother, the son of thy mother, or thy son, or thy daughter, or the [q]wife of thy bosom, or thy [r,s]friend, which *is* as thine own soul, entice thee secretly, saying, [f]Let us go and [g]serve other gods, which thou hast not known, thou, nor thy fathers;

7 *Namely*, of the gods of the

v.1–1494 BC
See footnote, *Time*, Rev. 10:6.

**1**
a *Prophets, false*, Isa. 3:2.
b *Minister, false and corrupt*, Rom. 15:16.
c *False Teachers*, 2 Pet. 2:1.
d *Dream*, Dan. 1:17.
e *Miracles, wrought in support of false religion*, Luke 23:8.

**2**
f *Heresy, propagandism of, forbidden*, vs. 2–5; Tit. 3:10.
g *Idolatry*, 1 Sam. 15:23.

**3**
h *Statute, forbidding heed to false teachers*, Deut. 8:2.
i *Intolerance, of idolatrous religions, taught by Moses*, Num. 11:28.
j *Temptation, a test*, Luke 11:4.
k *Love, of man for God*, 1 John 4:19.
l *Heart*, Psa. 44:21.

**4**
m *Commandment, enjoining the fear of God and obedience*, Deut. 8:2.
n *Fear of God*, Acts 9:31.
o *Obedience, enjoined*, Heb. 5:8.

**5**
p *Punishment, death penalty*, Lev. 26:41.
1 R. V. rebellion against the Lord

**6**
q *Marriage, obligations under, inferior to duty to God*, vs. 6–10; Gen. 34:9.
r *Friendship, temptations in*, vs. 6–9; Prov. 22:24.
s *Friends*, Ex. 33:11.

† **HUMAN SACRIFICES.** *Forbidden*, Lev. 18:21; 20:2–5; Deut. 12:31. *Offered, by Abraham, who was deterred by the angel of the Lord*, Gen. 22:1–19; Heb. 11:17–19; *by Canaanites*, Deut. 12:31; *by Moabites*, 2 Kin. 3:27; *by Israelites*, 2 Kin. 16:3; 23:10; 2 Chr. 28:3; Isa. 57:5; Jer. 7:31; 19:5; 32:35; Ezek. 16:20, 21; 20:26, 31; 23:37, 39; *by the Sepharvites to idols*, 2 Kin. 17:31. *Offered, to demons*, Psa. 106:37, 38; *to Baal*, Jer. 19:5, 6.

v.7–1494 BC
See footnote, *Time*, Rev. 10:6.

7
t *Canaanites*, Ex. 23:28.
8
u *Commandment, enjoining steadfastness*, Deut. 8:2.
v *Fellowship, with the wicked forbidden*, 1 Cor. 1:9.
w *Pity, forbidden to idolatrous proselytizers*, Job 19:21.
9
x *Witness*, Num. 35:30.
10
y *Stoning*, 1 Sam. 30:6.
z *Punishment, stoning*, Lev. 26:41.
12
2 R. V. tell concerning one
13
a *Apostasy*, Acts 1:25.
b *Heresy, propagandism of, forbidden*, vs. 13–18; Tit. 3:10.
c *Idolatry*, 1 Sam. 15:23.
3 R. V. Certain base fellows are
14
d *Abomination*, Lev. 18:27.
15
e *Punishment, death penalty*, Lev. 26:41.

[t]people which *are* round about you, nigh[G] unto thee, or far off from thee, from the *one* end of the earth even unto the *other* end of the earth;

8 [u,v]Thou shalt not consent unto him, nor hearken unto him; neither shall thine eye [w]pity him, neither shalt thou spare, neither shalt thou conceal him:

9 But thou shalt surely [p]kill him; [x]thine hand shall be first upon him to put him to death, and afterwards the hand of all the people.

10 And thou shalt [y,z]stone him with stones, that he die; because he hath sought to thrust thee away from the LORD thy God, which brought thee out of the land of Ē'gy̆pt, from the house of bondage.

11 And all Ĭş'ra-el shall hear, and fear, and shall do no more any such wickedness as this is among you.

12 ¶ If thou shalt hear [2]say[G] in one of thy cities, which the LORD thy God hath given thee to dwell there, saying,

13 [3]*Certain* men, the children of Bē'lĭ[G]-ăl, are [a]gone out from among you, and have withdrawn the inhabitants of their city, saying, [b]Let us go and [c]serve other gods, which ye have not known;

14 Then shalt thou enquire, and make search, and ask diligently; and, behold, *if it be* truth, *and* the thing certain, *that* such [d]abomination is wrought among you;

15 Thou shalt surely smite[G] the inhabitants of that city with the edge of the sword, [e]destroying it utterly, and all that *is* therein and the cattle thereof, with the edge of the sword.

16 And thou shalt gather all the [f]spoil of it into the midst of the street thereof, and shalt burn with fire the city and all the spoil thereof every whit, for the LORD thy God: and it shall be an heap for ever; it shall not be built again.

17 And there shall cleave[C] nought[G] of the [4]cursed [d]thing to thine hand: that the [g]LORD may turn from the fierceness of his [h]anger, and shew thee [i]mercy, and have compassion upon thee, and multiply thee, as he hath [j]sworn unto thy fathers;[S]

18 When thou shalt hearken to the voice of the LORD thy God, to [k]keep all his [l]commandments which I command thee this day, to do *that which is* right in the eyes of the LORD thy God.[S]

## CHAPTER 14

*God's children are not to disfigure themselves in their mourning. 3 What may and what may not be eaten, 4 of beasts, 9 of fishes, 11 and of fowls. 21 That which dies of itself may not be eaten. 23 Tithes and firstlings to be eaten before the Lord. 28 The third year's tithe of alms and charity.*

YE[Q] *are* the [a]children of the LORD your [b]God: ye shall not [c,d,e]cut yourselves, nor make any [f]baldness between your eyes for the dead.

2 For thou *art* an [g,h]holy people unto the LORD thy God, and the [i]LORD hath chosen thee to be a peculiar[C] people unto himself, above all the nations that *are* upon the earth.[T Q]

3 ¶ [j,k]Thou shalt not eat any [l]abominable[G] thing.

4 [m]These *are* the [n]beasts which ye shall eat: the ox, the sheep, and the *goat,

5 The hart, and the [1]roebuck, and the [2]fallow †deer, and the wild goat, and the pygarg, and the [3]wild ox, and the chamois.

v.16–1494 BC
See footnote, *Time*, Rev. 10:6.

16
f *Spoils*, 1 Chr. 26:27.
17
g *God, providence of*, Gen. 2:2.
h *Anger of God*, 2 Kin. 13:3.
i *God, mercy of*, Gen. 2:2.
j *Covenant, of God with men*, Deut. 29:1.
4 R. V. devoted
18
k *Obedience*, Heb. 5:8.
l *Law, of Moses*, Deut. 33:2.
1
a *Spiritual Adoption*, Rom. 8:15.
b *God, fatherhood of*, Gen. 2:2.
c *Idolatry, wicked practices of*, 1 Sam. 15:23.
d *Mourning, cutting the flesh*, Lam. 2:5.
e *Cutting, the flesh*, Lev. 19:28.
f *Baldness*, Lev. 21:5.
2
g *The Holy, described*, Col. 3:12.
h *Israel, a separate people*, Ex. 4:22.
i *God, love of, exemplified*, Gen. 2:2.
3
j *Israel, taught to be holy by eating none but clean animals*, vs. 3–21; Ex. 4:22.
k *Sanitation and Hygiene, food*, vs. 3–21; Num. 31:23.
l *Sin, typified, in unclean animals*, Rom. 5:12.
4
m Lev. 11:2–47.
n *Animals, ordained as food for man*, vs. 3–21; Jer. 27:5.
5
1 R. V. gazelle,
2 R. V. roebuck,
3 R. V. antelope,

* **GOAT.** *Designated as one of the clean animals to be eaten*, Deut. 14:4 (with Lev. 11:1–8). *Used, for food*, Gen. 27:9; 1 Sam. 16:20; 2 Chr. 17:11; *for the paschal feast*, Ex. 12:5; 2 Chr. 35:7. *Used as a sacrifice, by Abraham*, Gen. 15:9; *by Gideon*, Judg. 6:19; *by Manoah*, Judg. 13:19. *Milk of, used for food*, Prov. 27:27. *Hair of, used, for clothing*, Num. 31:20; *for pillows*, 1 Sam. 19:13; *for curtains of the tabernacle*, Ex. 26:7; 35:23; 36:14. *Regulations of Mosaic law required that a kid should not be killed for food before it is eight days old*, Lev. 22:27; *nor seethed in its mother's milk*, Ex. 23:19; 34:26. *Numerous*, 1 Sam. 25:2; 2 Chr. 17:11. *In Palestine*, 1 Sam. 24:2; Psa. 104:18; Song 4:1; 6:5.

† **DEER**, called also FALLOW DEER, HART, HIND. *Designated among the clean animals, to be eaten*, Deut. 12:15;

v.6–1494 BC
See footnote, *Time*, Rev. 10:6.

**6**
o *Hoof*, Lev. 11: 3–8.
p *Cud*, Lev. 11: 3–8.

**7**
q Lev. 11:6.
r *Coney*, Lev. 11:5.
s *Unclean creatures*, Lev. 11.

**8**
t *Swine*, Lev. 11:7.

**9**
u *Fish*, Matt. 17: 27.

**11**
v *Holiness, typified, in clean animals*, Ex. 39:30.
w *Birds*, Eccl. 12:4.

**12**
x *Eagle*, Lev. 11: 13.
y Lev. 11:13.
z Lev. 11:13.
4 R. V. gier eagle,

**13**
a Lev. 11:14.
b Lev. 11:14.
5 R. V. falcon,
6 R. V. kite

**14**
c *Raven*, Job 38: 41.

**15**
d *Owl*, Lev. 11:17.
e Lev. 11:16.
f Lev. 11:16.
g Lev. 11:16; Job 39:26.
7 R. V. ostrich,
8 R. V. seamew,

**16**
h Lev. 11:18.
9 R. V. horned owl,

**17**
i Lev. 11:18.
j Lev. 11:18.
k *Cormorant*, Lev. 11:17.
10 R. V. vulture,

**18**
l *Stork*, Lev. 11: 19.
m Lev. 11:19.
n Lev. 11:19.
o Lev. 11:19.
11 R. V. hoopoe,

**19**
p *Creeping Things*, Rom. 1:23.
q Lev. 11:23–25.
r *Sin, typified*, Rom. 5:12.

**20**
s *Holiness, typified*, Ex. 39:30.
t *Birds*, Eccl. 12:4.

6 And every beast that parteth the [o]hoof, and cleaveth the cleft into two claws, *and* cheweth the [p]cud among the beasts, that ye shall eat.

7 Nevertheless these ye shall not eat of them that chew the [p]cud, or of them that divide the cloven [o]hoof; *as* the camel, and the [q]hare, and the [r]coney: for they chew the cud, but divide not the hoof; *therefore* they *are* [l,s]unclean unto you.

8 And the [t]swine, because it divideth the [o]hoof, yet cheweth not the [p]cud, it *is* [l,s]unclean unto you: [j,k]ye shall not eat of their flesh, nor touch their dead carcase.

9 ¶ These ye shall eat of [u]all that *are* in the waters: all that have fins and scales shall ye eat:

10 And [u]whatsoever hath not fins and scales ye may not eat; it *is* [l,s]unclean unto you.

11 ¶ *Of* all [v]clean [w]birds ye shall eat.

12 But these *are they* of which ye shall not eat: the [x]eagle, and the [4,y]ossifrage, and the [z]ospray,

13 And the glede, and the [5,a]kite, and the [6,b]vulture after his kind,

14 And every [c]raven after his kind,

15 And the [7,d]owl, and the [e]night hawk, and the [8,f]cuckow, and the [g]hawk after his kind,

16 The little [d]owl, and the great owl, and the [9,h]swan,

17 And the [i]pelican, and the [10,j]gier eagle, and the [k]cormorant,

18 And the [l]stork, and the [m]heron after her kind, and the [11,n]lapwing, and the [o]bat.

19 And every [p,q]creeping thing that flieth *is* [r]unclean unto you: they shall not be eaten.

20 *But of* all [s]clean [t]fowls ye may eat.

21 ¶ Ye shall not eat *of* any thing that dieth of itself: thou shalt give it unto the [u]stranger that *is* in thy gates, that he may eat it; or thou mayest sell it unto [12]an alien: for [v]thou *art* an holy people unto the LORD thy God. Thou shalt not seethe a kid in his mother's milk.

22 [w]Thou shalt truly [x]tithe all the increase of thy seed, that the field bringeth forth year by year.

23 And thou shalt eat before the LORD thy God, in the [y]place which he shall choose to place his name there, the [x]tithe of thy corn, of thy wine, and of thine oil, and the firstlings of thy herds and of thy flocks; that thou mayest learn to [z]fear the LORD thy God always.

24 And if the way be too long for thee, so that thou art not able to carry it; *or* if the [y]place be too far from thee, which the LORD thy God shall choose to set his name there, when the LORD thy God hath blessed thee:

25 Then shalt thou turn *it* into [a]money, and bind up the money in thine hand, and shalt go unto the place which the LORD thy God shall choose:

26 And thou shalt bestow that [a]money for whatsoever thy soul lusteth after, for oxen, or for sheep, or for [b]wine, or for strong drink, or for whatsoever thy soul desireth: and thou shalt eat there before the LORD thy God, and thou shalt [c]rejoice, thou, and thine household,

27 And the [d,e]Lē′vīte that *is* within thy gates; [f,g]thou shalt not forsake him; for he hath no part nor inheritance with thee.

28 ¶ At the end of three years thou shalt bring forth all the [h]tithe of thine increase the same

v.21–1494 BC
See footnote, *Time*, Rev. 10:6.

**21**
u *Foreigners*, Deut. 23:20.
v *Israel, a separate people*, Ex. 4:22.
12 R.V. a foreigner:

**22**
w *Commandment, enjoining tithes*, Deut. 8:2.
x *Tithes*, Num. 18: 24.

**23**
y *Tabernacle*, Ex. 27:9.
z *Fear of God, enjoined*, Acts 9:31.

**25**
a *Money*, Jer. 32:9.

**26**
b *Wine*, Prov. 23: 31.
c *Thankfulness*, Acts 24:3.

**27**
d *Levites, emoluments of*, vs. 27–29; Deut. 10:8.
e *Priest, emoluments of*, Lev. 1:5.
f *Liberality, enjoined*, vs. 27–29; 1 Tim. 6:18.
g *Church, duty of, to ministers*, Matt. 16:18.

**28**
h *Tithes*, Num. 18: 24.

14:5. *Provided for Solomon's household*, 1 Kin. 4:23. *Fleetness of*, 2 Sam. 2:18; 1 Chr. 12:8; Prov. 6:5; Song 8:14; Isa. 35:6. *Surefootedness of*, 2 Sam. 22:34. *Gentleness of* Prov. 5:19.

v.28–1494 BC
See footnote, *Time*, Rev. 10:6.

**29**

*i Foreigners*, Deut. 23:20.
*j Poor, duty to*, Prov. 21:13.
*k Orphan, beneficent provision for*, Lam. 5:3.
*l Widow*, 2 Sam. 14:5.
*m Blessings, contingent upon obedience*, Deut. 11: 26.

year, and shalt lay *it* up within
thy gates.[C]
29 And the [d,e]Lē′vīte, (because
he hath no part nor inheritance
with thee,) and the [i,j]stranger,[C]
and the [k]fatherless, and the
[l]widow, which *are* within thy
gates, shall come, and shall eat
and be satisfied; [m]that the LORD
thy God may bless thee in all the
work of thine hand which thou
doest.

## CHAPTER 15

*The seventh year of release for the poor. 7 This must not deter from lending or giving. 12 A Hebrew servant is to go forth free and well furnished in the seventh year, unless he choose not to depart. 19 All firstling males of the cattle are to be consecrated unto the Lord.*

**1**

*a Sabbatic Year, creditors required to release debtors in*, Lev. 25:2.

**2**

*b Poor, duty to*, Prov. 21:13.

**3**

*c Foreigners, not accorded the privileges of the seventh year release*, Deut. 23: 20.

**4**

*d Promise, to the obedient, of prosperity*, 2 Cor. 1:20.
*e Canaan*, Gen. 37:1.
*f Temporal Blessings, from God*, Psa. 103:2.
*g God, providence of*, Gen. 2:2.
1 R. V. Howbeit there

**5**

*h Obedience, rewarded*, Heb. 5:8.

[a]AT the end of *every* seven
years thou shalt make a
release.[C]
2 And this *is* the manner of
the release: Every *creditor that
†lendeth *ought*[C] unto his [b]neighbour shall release[C] *it;* he shall not
exact *it* of his neighbour, or of
his brother; because it is called
the LORD's release.
3 Of a [c]foreigner thou mayest
exact *it again:* but *that* which
is thine with thy brother thine
hand shall release;
4[S] [1]Save[C] when there shall be no
[b]poor among you; for [d]the LORD
shall greatly [f]bless thee in the
[e]land which the LORD thy [g]God
giveth thee *for* an inheritance to
possess it:
5 Only if thou carefully hearken[C] unto the voice of the LORD
thy God, to observe to [h]do all
these commandments which I
command thee this day.
6 For the LORD thy [g]God
[f]blesseth thee, as he promised
thee: and [d]thou shalt †lend unto
many nations, but thou shalt not
borrow; and thou shalt reign
over many nations, but they
shall not reign over thee.[S]
7 ¶ If[Q] there be among you a
[b]poor man of one of thy brethren
within any of thy gates[C] in thy
land which the LORD thy [g]God
giveth thee, [i]thou shalt not harden thine heart, nor shut thine
hand from thy poor brother:
8 But [i]thou shalt [j]open thine
hand wide unto [b]him, and shalt
surely †lend him sufficient for
his need, *in that* which he
wanteth.[C] [Q]
9 [k]Beware that there be not a
[2]thought in thy wicked heart,
saying, The [a]seventh year, the
[l]year of release, is at hand; and
thine [m]eye[C] be evil against thy
[b]poor brother, and thou [n]givest
him nought;[C] and he cry unto the
LORD against thee, and it be sin
unto thee.[T]
10 [i]Thou shalt surely [j]give
[b]him, and thine heart shall not
be grieved when thou givest unto
him: because that [d]for this thing
the LORD thy God shall [f,o]bless
thee in all thy works, and in all
that thou puttest thine hand
unto.
11 For the poor shall never
cease out of the land: therefore I
[i]command thee, saying, Thou
shalt [j]open thine hand wide unto
thy brother, to thy [b]poor, and to
thy needy, in thy land.[Q]
12 ¶ *And* if thy brother, an
[p]Hē′brew man, or an Hē′brew
woman, be sold unto thee, and

v.6–1494 BC
See footnote, *Time*, Rev. 10:6.

**7**

*i Commandment, enjoining liberality to the poor*, vs. 7–15; Deut. 8:2.

**8**

*j Liberality, enjoined*, 1 Tim. 6:18.

**9**

*k Commandment, enjoining watchfulness against covetousness*, Deut. 8:2.
*l Year, of release*, Lev. 25:29.
*m Covetousness, warnings against*, Isa. 57:17.
*n Selfishness*, 2 Tim. 3:2.
2 R. V. base thought in thine heart,

**10**

*o Reward, a motive to faithfulness*, Matt. 5:12.

**12**

*p Hebrew*, Gen. 40: 15.

---

*** CREDITOR. Mosaic laws concerning:** *Manumission of debtor-servants*, Ex. 21:2-6. *Must return pawned raiment*, Ex. 22:25-27; Deut. 24:10-13. *Must not take widow's raiment for pledge*, Deut. 24:17; *nor millstones*, Deut. 24:6. *Must not exact interest of the poor*, Lev. 25:35-37; Deut. 15:2, 3; 23:19, 20.
**Christ's injunctions to,** Matt. 5:42; Luke 6:34.
**Oppressions by:** *In seizing debtor's personal property*, Job 22:6; 24:3, 10; Prov. 22:26, 27. *In seizing debtor's houses*, Job 20:18-20. *In imprisoning debtor*, Matt. 5:25, 26; 18: 28-35; Luke 12:58, 59. *In enslaving debtor's children*, 2 Kin. 4:1; Neh. 5:1-13; Job 24:9.
**Merciful,** Psa. 112:5; Matt. 18:23-27; Luke 7:41-43.

**† LENDING,** Psa. 37:25, 26; 112:5; Prov. 19:17. *To the poor, enjoined*, Lev. 25:35; Deut. 15:7-11; *enjoined by Christ*, Matt. 5:42; Luke 6:34, 35. *Borrower to be released in the year of release*, Deut. 15:1-6.
**Things forbidden as security of loans:** *Millstones*, Deut. 24:6. *Widow's raiment*, Deut. 24:17.
**Lender:** *Forbidden, to take interest from poor Hebrews*, Ex. 22:25-27; Lev. 25:36, 37; Deut. 23:19, 20; *to enter debtor's house for security*, Deut. 24:10, 11; *to keep pawned raiment over night*, Deut. 24:12, 13. *Oppression of*, Neh. 5:1-13. *Is master of borrower*, Prov. 22:7. *Wicked, punished*, Prov. 28:8; Ezek. 18:13.
See footnote, BORROWING, Ex. 22:14.

serve thee six years; then in the [a]seventh year thou shalt let [q,r,s]him go ‡free from thee.[Q]

13 And when thou sendest [b,q]him out ‡free from thee, [i]thou shalt not let him go away empty:

14 [i]Thou shalt furnish him [j]liberally out of thy flock, and out of thy floor,[C] and out of thy [t]winepress: [3]*of that* wherewith the LORD thy God hath blessed thee thou shalt give unto him.

15 And [u]thou shalt remember that thou wast a bondman[C] in the land of Ē′ġўpt, and the LORD thy God redeemed thee: therefore I command thee this thing to day.[S]

16 And it shall be, if [v]he say unto thee, I will not go away from thee; because he loveth thee and thine house, because he is well with thee;[Q]

17 Then thou shalt take an [w]aul, and thrust *it* through his ear unto the door, and he shall be thy [v]servant for ever. And also unto thy maidservant thou shalt do likewise.

18 It shall not seem hard unto [x]thee, when thou sendest [s]him away ‡free from thee; for [4]he hath been worth a double [y]hired servant *to thee,* in serving thee six years: and [z]the LORD thy God shall bless thee in all that thou doest.

19 ¶ [a]All the [b]firstling males that come of thy herd and of thy flock thou shalt sanctify[C] unto the LORD thy God: thou shalt do no work with the firstling of thy bullock, nor shear the firstling of thy sheep.

20 Thou shalt eat *it* before the LORD thy God year by year in the [c]place which the LORD shall choose, thou and thy household.

21 And [d]if there be *any* [e,f]blemish therein, *as if it be* [g]lame, or [h]blind, *or have* any ill blemish, thou shalt not sacrifice[C] [i]it unto the LORD thy God.

22 Thou shalt eat it within thy gates: the unclean and the clean *person shall eat it* alike, as the [5]roebuck, and as the hart.

23 Only [j]thou shalt not eat the [k]blood thereof; thou shalt pour it upon the ground as water.

## CHAPTER 16

*The feast of the passover, 9 of weeks, 13 of tabernacles. 16 Every male must offer, as he is able, at these three feasts. 18 Of judges and justice. 21 Groves and images are forbidden.*

OBSERVE[Q] the[S] [a]month of [b]Ā′bĭb, and keep the [c]passover unto the LORD thy God: for in the month of Ā′bĭb the LORD thy God brought thee forth out of [d]Ē′ġўpt by night.

2 Thou shalt therefore sacrifice[C] the [e]passover unto the LORD thy God, of the flock and the herd, in the [e]place which the LORD shall choose to place his name there.

3 Thou shalt eat no leavened bread with it; seven days shalt thou eat unleavened bread therewith, *even* the bread of affliction[C]; for thou camest forth out of the land of [d]Ē′ġўpt in haste: that thou mayest remember the day when thou camest forth out of the land of Ē′ġўpt all the days of thy life.[Q]

4 And there shall be no leavened bread seen with thee in all thy coast[C] seven days; neither shall there *any thing* of the flesh, which thou sacrificedst the first day at even, remain all night until the morning.

5 Thou mayest not sacrifice[C] the [e]passover within any of thy gates,[C] which the LORD thy God giveth thee:

6 But at the [e]place which the LORD thy God shall choose to

---

v.12–1494 BC See footnote, *Time,* Rev. 10:6.

*q* *Poor, to be released in sabbatic year,* Prov. 21:13.
*r* *Debtor,* Luke 7:41.
*s* *Servant, law of Moses concerning,* Jer. 2:14.

**14**
*t* *Wine-press,* Isa. 5:2.
3 R. V. as the Lord

**15**
*u* *Humility, enjoined,* Prov. 22:4.

**16**
*v* *Servant, voluntary servitude of,* Jer. 2:14.

**17**
*w* Ex. 21:6.

**18**
*x* *Employer,* Deut. 24:14.
*y* *Hired Servant,* Lev. 25:40.
*z* *Promise, to those who are liberal to the poor,* 2 Cor. 1:20.
4 R. V. to the double of the hire of an hireling hath he served thee

**19**
*a* *Commandment, enjoining liberality in support of religion,* Deut. 8:2.
*b* *Firstborn,* Zech. 12:10.

**20**
*c* *Tabernacle, offerings brought to,* Ex. 27:9.

**21**
*d* *Statute, forbidding faulty service of God,* Deut. 8:2.
*e* *Blemish,* Lev. 14:10.
*f* *Sin, typified,* Rom. 5:12.

v.21–1494 BC See footnote, *Time,* Rev. 10:6.

*g* *Lameness,* Lev. 21:18.
*h* *Blindness, of animals,* 2 Kin. 6:18.
*i* *Offerings, must be without blemish,* Lev. 6:17.

**22**
5 R. V. gazelle,

**23**
*j* *Statute, forbidding eating blood* Deut. 8:2.
*k* *Blood, forbidden as food,* Gen. 9:4

**1**
*a* *Month,* Ex. 12:2.
*b* *Abib,* Ex. 13:4.
*c* *Passover,* Num. 9:5.
*d* *Egypt,* Gen. 41:8.

**2**
*e* *Tabernacle, offerings brought to,* Ex. 27:9.

---

‡ **EMANCIPATION.** *Of all Jewish servants, in seventh year of servitude,* Ex. 21:2; *at the Jubilee,* Lev. 25:8–17, 39–41 Proclamation of: *By Zedekiah,* Jer. 34:8–11; *by Cyrus,* 2 Chr. 36:23; Ezra 1:1–4. See footnotes: JUBILEE, Lev 25:10; SABBATIC YEAR, Lev. 25:2.

v.6–1494 BC
See footnote, *Time*, Rev. 10:6.

6

f *Worship, enjoined*, Gen. 22:5.

place his name in, there [f]thou
shalt sacrifice[G] the [c]passover at
even, at the going down of the
sun, at the season[G] that thou
camest forth out of Ē'ġȳpt.
7 And thou shalt roast and eat
*it* in the [e]place which the LORD
thy God shall choose: and thou
shalt turn in the morning, and
go unto thy tents.
8 Six days thou shalt eat unleavened bread: and on the seventh day *shall be* a solemn assembly to the LORD thy God:
thou shalt do no work *therein*.[Q]
9 ¶[Q] [g]Seven weeks shalt thou
number unto thee: begin to number the seven weeks from *such
time as* thou beginnest *to put* the
sickle to the corn.[G]
10 And thou shalt keep the
[g,h]feast of weeks unto the LORD
thy God with a tribute[G] of a [i]free-
will offering of thine hand,
which thou shalt [j]give *unto the
LORD thy God*, according as the
LORD thy God hath blessed
thee:
11 And thou shalt [h,k]rejoice before the LORD thy God, [l]thou,
and thy son, and thy daughter,
and thy [m]manservant, and thy
maidservant, and the [n]Lē'vīte
that *is* within thy gates, and the
[o]stranger,[G] and the [p]fatherless,
and the [q]widow, that *are* among
you, in the [e]place which the
LORD thy God hath chosen to
place his name there.[Q]
12 And thou shalt remember
that thou wast a bondman[G] in
[d]Ē'ġȳpt and [r]thou shalt observe[G]
and [s]do these statutes.
13 ¶ Thou shalt observe the
feast of *tabernacles seven days,
after that thou hast gathered in
thy corn[G] and thy wine:
14 And thou shalt rejoice in thy
*,[h]feast, [l]thou, and thy son, and

9

g *Pentecost*, vs 9–12; Acts 2:1.

10

h *Annual Feasts, kept with rejoicing*, vs. 11–14; Num. 15:3.

i *Offerings, free will*, Lev. 6:17.

j *Liberality, according to ability*, 1 Tim. 6:18.

11

k *Thankfulness, enjoined*, Acts 24:3.

l *Family Worship*, 1 Sam. 1:19.

m *Servant, must enjoy religious privileges*, Jer. 2:14.

n *Levites*, Deut. 10:8.

o *Foreigners*, Deut. 23:20.

p *Orphan*, Lam. 5:3.

q *Widow*, 2 Sam. 14:5.

12

r *Commandment, enjoining obedience*, Deut. 8:2.

s *Obedience, enjoined*, Heb. 5:8.

thy daughter, and thy [m]man-
servant, and thy maidservant,
and the [n]Lē'vīte, the [o]stranger,[G]
and the [p]fatherless, and the
[q]widow, that *are* within thy
gates.
15 Seven days shalt thou keep
a solemn *feast unto the LORD
thy God in the place which the
LORD shall choose: because the
LORD thy God shall [t]bless thee
in all thine increase, and in all
the works of thine hands, therefore thou shalt surely rejoice.
16 ¶ [u,v]Three times in a year
shall all thy males appear before
the LORD thy God in the place
which he shall choose; in the
[c]feast of unleavened bread, and
in the [g]feast of weeks, and in the
feast of *tabernacles: [w]and they
shall not appear before the
LORD empty:
17 [w]Every man *shall* [1]*give* as he
is able, according to the blessing
of the LORD thy God which he
hath given thee.
18 ¶ [x]Judges and officers shalt
thou make thee in all thy gates,[G]
which the LORD thy God giveth
thee, throughout thy tribes: and
they shall judge the people with
[y]just judgment.
19 [z,a]Thou shalt not [b]wrest[G]
judgment[G]; thou shalt not respect
persons, neither take a [c]gift[G]: for
a gift doth blind the eyes of the
wise, and pervert the words of
the righteous.
20 [a]That which is altogether
just shalt thou follow, [d]that thou
mayest live, and inherit the
[e]land which the LORD thy God
giveth thee.
21 [f,g]Thou shalt not plant thee
a [1,h]grove of any trees near unto
the altar of the LORD thy God,
which thou shalt make thee.
22 [f,g]Neither shalt thou set thee

v.14–1494 BC
See footnote, *Time*, Rev. 10:6.

15

t *Temporal Blessings, from God*, Psa. 103:2.

16

u *Commandment, enjoining public worship*, Deut. 8:2.

v *Annual Feasts, all males were required to attend*, Num. 15:3.

w *Commandment, enjoining liberality in support of religion*, Deut. 8:2.

18

x *Judge, precepts relating to*, vs. 18–20: Judg. 2:18.

y *Justice*, vs. 18–20; Deut. 33:21.

19

z *Commandment, forbidding perversion of justice, and taking of bribes*, v. 20; Deut. 8:2.

a *Integrity, enjoined*, v. 20; Job 2:3.

b *Injustice, forbidden*, Isa. 26:10.

c *Bribery, corrupts conscience*, 1 Sam. 8:3.

20

d *Blessings, contingent upon obedience*, Deut. 11:26.

e *Canaan*, Gen. 37:1.

21

f *Commandment, forbidding idolatry*, v. 22; Deut. 8:2.

g *Idolatry, forbidden*, 1 Sam. 15:23.

h *Groves, forbidden to be established*, Judg. 6:28.

1 R. V. Asherah

*** TABERNACLES, FEAST OF,** called also FEAST OF INGATHERING. *Instituted*, Ex. 23:16; 34:22; Lev. 23:34–43; Num. 29:12–40; Deut. 16:13–16. *Design of*, Lev. 23:42, 43. *The law read in connection with, every seventh year*, Deut. 31:10–12; Neh. 8:18. *Observance of, after the captivity*, Ezra 3:4; Neh. 8:14–18; *by Jesus*, John 7:2, 14. *Observance of, omitted*, Neh. 8:17. *Penalty for not observing*, Zech. 14:16–19.
*Jeroboam institutes an idolatrous feast to correspond to, in the eighth month*, 1 Kin. 12:32, 33.

v.22–1494 BC
See footnote, *Time*, Rev. 10:6.

22
2 R. V. a pillar;

1
a *Offerings, must be without blemish*, Lev. 6:17.
b *Blemish*, Lev. 14:10.
c *Sin, typified*, Rom. 5:12.
d *Abomination*, Lev. 18:27.

2
e *Intolerance, of idolatrous religion, taught by Moses*, Num. 11:28.
f *Idolatry*, 1 Sam. 15:23.
g *Sun*, Josh. 10:12.
h *Moon*. Song 6:10.

5
i *Statute, fixing penalty for idolatry*, Deut. 8:2.
j *Gates*, Deut. 3:5.
k *Punishment, stoning*, Lev. 26:41.
l *Stoning*, 1 Sam. 30:6.

6
m *Statute, prescribing law of evidence*, Deut. 8:2.
n *Witness, two necessary to establish a fact*, Num. 35:30.
o *Punishment, death penalty*, Lev. 26:41.
1 R. V. to die

7
p *Witness, required to cast first stone in executing sentence*, Num. 35:30.
q *Punishment, executed by witnesses*, Lev. 26:41.

up [2]*any* image; which the LORD
thy God hateth.[S]

## CHAPTER 17

*Things sacrificed to be without blemish. 2 Idolaters are to be slain. 8 Hard matters of controversy are to be determined by the priests and judges. 12 Death penalty for contempt of court. 14 The election, 16 and duty of a king.*

THOU [S]shalt not sacrifice unto the LORD thy God *any*
[a]bullock, or sheep, wherein is
[b,c]blemish, *or* any evilfavouredness[C]: for that *is* an [d]abomination
unto the LORD thy God.
2 ¶ [e]If there be found among
you, within any of thy gates[C]
which the LORD thy God giveth
thee, man or woman, that hath
wrought wickedness in the sight
of the LORD thy God, in transgressing his covenant,[C]
3 [e]And hath gone and [f]served
other gods, and worshipped
them, either the [g]sun, or [h]moon,
or any of the host of heaven,
which I have not commanded;
4 [e]And it be told thee, and thou
hast heard *of it*, and enquired
diligently, and, behold, *it be* true,
*and* the thing certain, *that* such
[d]abomination[C] is wrought[C] in Is'-
ra-el:
5 [e,i]Then shalt thou bring forth
that man or that woman, which
have committed that wicked
[d]thing, unto thy [j]gates,[C] *even* that
man or that woman, and shalt
[k,l]stone them with stones, till
they die.
6 [m]At the *mouth of two [n]wit-
nesses, or three witnesses, shall
he that is [1]worthy of death be
[o]put to death; *but* at the mouth
of one witness he shall not be
put to death.[Q]
7 The hands of the [p]witnesses
shall be first upon him to [o,q]put
him to death, and afterward the
hands of all the people. So thou
shalt put the evil away from
among you.[Q]
8 ¶ [T][r]If there arise a matter too
hard for thee in judgment, between blood and blood, between
†plea and plea, and between
[s]stroke and stroke, *being* matters of controversy within thy
gates: then shalt thou arise, and
get thee up into the place which
the LORD thy God shall choose;
9 And thou shalt come unto the
[t]priests the [u]Le'vites, and unto
the [v]judge that shall be in those
days, and enquire; and [w]they
shall shew thee the sentence of
judgment:
10 And thou shalt do according
to the sentence, which [w]they of
that place which the LORD shall
choose shall shew thee; and thou
shalt observe to do according to
all that they inform thee:
11 According to the [2]sentence
of the law which [x]they shall
teach thee, and according to the
judgment which they shall tell
thee, thou shalt do: thou shalt
not decline[C] from the sentence
which they shall shew thee, *to*
the right hand, nor *to* the left.[T]
12 [y]And the man that will do
presumptuously, and will [z]not
hearken[C] unto the priest that
standeth to minister there before
the LORD thy God, or unto the
judge, even that man shall [a]die:
and thou shalt put away the evil
from Is'ra-el.
13 [b]And all the people shall
hear, and [c]fear, and do no more
presumptuously.[C]
14 ¶ When thou art come unto
the [d]land which the LORD thy
God giveth thee, and shalt possess it, and shalt dwell therein,
and shalt say, I will set a [e]king

v.7–1494 BC
See footnote, *Time*, Rev. 10:6.

8
r *Court, superior and inferior*, vs. 8–13; Ex. 18:26.
s *Assault and Battery*, Ex. 21:15.

9
t *Priest, duties of*, vs. 8–13; Lev. 1:5.
u *Levites, were judges*, Deut. 10:8.
v *Judge*, Judg. 2:18.
w *Court, civil*, Ex. 18:26.

11
x *Court, sentence of, final and obligatory*, Ex. 18:26.
2 R. V. tenor

12
y *Statute, fixing penalty for contempt of authority*, Deut. 8:2.
z *Court, contempt of*, Ex. 18:26.

a *Punishment, death penalty*, Lev. 26:41.

13
b *Punishment, design of*, Lev. 26:41.
c *Fear of God, a motive to obedience*, Acts 9:31.

14
d *Canaan*, Gen. 37:1.
e *King*, vs. 14–19; 2 Kin. 3:10.

***EVIDENCE.** *Concealment of, punished*, Lev. 5:1. *Two or more witnesses required in, to sustain an allegation*, Num. 35:30; Deut. 17:6, 7; 19:15; Matt. 18:16; Heb. 10:28. *False, forbidden*, Ex. 20:16; 23:1, 7; Prov. 24:28; Matt. 19:18. *Punishment for falsehood in*, Deut. 19:16–21. *Self-criminating, extorted*, Josh. 7:19–21.

†**PLEADING.** *Of the guilty*, Josh. 7:19–21. *Of Jesus, to the charge that he professed to be the Son of God*, Matt. 26:62–64; Mark 14:61, 62; Luke 22:70; *to the charge that he was a king*, Matt. 27:11; Mark 15:2; Luke 23:2, 3; John 33:34.
See footnote, DEFENSE, Acts 19:23.

v.14–1494 BC
ee footnote, *Time,*
Rev. 10:6.

**15**
*Foreigners, Israel not permitted to make kings of,* Deut. 23:20.
3 R. V. put a foreigner

**16**
*Horse,* Job 39:19.

**18**
*Commandment, enjoining upon rulers to study God's law,* vs. 19–20; Deut. 8:2.
*King, constitutional restrictions of,* vs. 18–20; 2 Kin. 3:10.
*Constitution,* Dan. 6:12.
*Law, of Moses,* Deut. 33:2.
*Word of God,* Psa. 119:9.
*Book, law of Moses written in,* Num. 5:23.

**20**
*Pride,* Prov. 16:18.
*Blessings, contingent upon obedience,* Deut. 11:26.

over me, like as all the nations
that *are* about me;
15 Thou shalt in any wise[c] set
*him* [e]king over thee, whom the
LORD thy God shall choose: *one*
from among thy brethren shalt
thou set king over thee: thou
mayest not [3]set a [f]stranger[c] over
thee, which *is* not thy brother.
16 But [e]he shall not multiply
[g]horses to himself, nor cause the
people to return to Ē′ġȳpt, to the
end that he should multiply
horses: forasmuch as the LORD
hath said unto you, Ye shall
henceforth return no more that
way.
17 Neither shall [e]he ‡multiply
wives to himself, that his heart
turn not away: neither shall he
greatly multiply to himself silver
and gold.
18 [h]And it shall be, when he
sitteth upon the throne of his
kingdom, that he shall write
[i]him a [j]copy of this [k,l]law in a
[m]book out of *that which is* before
the priests the Lē′vītes:
19 [h]And it shall be with him,
and he shall read therein all the
days of his life: that he may
learn to [c]fear[c] the LORD his God,
to keep all the [l]words of this
[k]law and these statutes, to do
them:
20 [h]That his heart be not [n]lifted
up above his brethren, and that
he turn not aside from the
[k,l]commandment, *to* the right
hand, or *to* the left: to the end
[o]that he may prolong *his* days in
his kingdom, he, and his children, in the midst of Ĭş′ra-el.[s]

## CHAPTER 18

*The Lord is the inheritance of the priests and Levites. 3 The portion of the priest, 6 and of the Levite. 9 The abominations of the nations are to be avoided. 15 A Prophet is promised to Israel. 20 The false prophet is to die.*

[a]THE[Q] priests the Lē′vītes, *and*
all the tribe of Lē′vī, shall
have no part nor inheritance
with Ĭş′ra-el: [b,c]they shall eat
the offerings of the LORD made
by fire, and his inheritance.
2 Therefore shall [c]they have no
inheritance among their brethren: the LORD *is* their inheritance, as he hath said unto them.
3 ¶ And this shall be the
[b]priest's due from the [a]people,
from them that offer a [d]sacrifice,
whether *it be* ox or sheep; and
they shall give unto the priest the
shoulder, and the two cheeks,
and the maw.[c Q]
4 The *firstfruit *also* of thy
corn,[c] of thy wine, and of thine
oil, and the first of the [b,e]fleece of
thy sheep, shalt [a]thou [f]give him.
5 For the LORD thy God hath
chosen [g]him out of all thy tribes,
to stand to minister in the name
of the LORD, him and his sons
for ever.
6 ¶ And if a [h]Lē′vīte come from
any of thy gates[c] out of all Ĭş′ra-el, where he sojourned,[c] and
come with all the desire of his
mind unto the place which the
LORD shall choose;
7 Then [h]he shall minister in the
name of the LORD his God, as
all his brethren the Lē′vītes *do,*
which stand there before the
LORD.
8 [c]They shall have like portions

v.1–1494 BC
See footnote, *Time,*
Rev. 10:6.

**1**
a *Church, duty of, to ministers,* vs. 1–8; Matt. 16:18.
b *Priest, emoluments of,* Lev. 1:5.
c *Levites, emoluments of,* Deut. 10:8.

**3**
d *Offerings,* Lev. 6:17.

**4**
e *Wool,* Judg. 6:37.
f *Liberality, enjoined,* 1 Tim. 6:18.

**5**
g *Priest, duties of,* Lev. 1:5.

**6**
h *Levites, duties of,* Deut. 10:8.

‡ **POLYGAMY.** *Forbidden,* Lev. 18:18; 1 Tim. 3:2, 12; 'it. 1:6. *Authorized,* 2 Sam. 12:8.
*Tolerated,* Ex. 21:10; 1 Sam. 1:2; 2 Chr. 24:3. *Practiced, y Lamech,* Gen. 4:19; *by Abraham,* Gen. 16; *by Esau,* Gen. 6:34; 28:9; *by Jacob,* Gen. 29:30; *by Ashur,* 1 Chr. 4:5; *by Gideon,* Judg. 8:30; *by Elkanah,* 1 Sam. 1:2; *by David,* 1 Sam. 5:39–44; 2 Sam. 3:2–5; 5:13; 1 Chr. 14:3; *by Solomon,* Kin. 11:1–8; *by Rehoboam,* 2 Chr. 11:18–23; *by Abijah,* Chr. 13:21; *by Jehoram,* 2 Chr. 21:14; *by Joash,* 2 Chr. 24:3; *y Jehoiachin,* 2 Kin. 24:15; *by Belshazzar,* Dan. 5:2. *Mosaic law respecting the firstborn in,* Deut. 21:15–17.
*Sought by women,* Isa. 4:1.
**The evil effects of:** *Husband's favoritism in,* Deut. 1:15–17; *Jacob's,* Gen. 29:30; 30:15; *Elkanah's,* 1 Sam. 1: ; *Rehoboam's,* 2 Chr. 11:21. *Domestic infelicity, in Abraham's family,* Gen. 16; 21:9–16; *in Jacob's,* Gen. 29:30–34; 30:1–23; *in Elkanah's,* 1 Sam. 1:4–7. *Solomon's idolatry on account of,* 1 Kin. 11:4–8. See footnotes: CONCUBINAGE, 2 Sam. 21:11; MARRIAGE, Gen. 34:9.

* **FIRST FRUITS.** *First ripe of fruits, grain, oil, wine, and first of fleece, required as an offering,* Lev. 2:12–16; Num. 18:12, 13; 2 Chr. 31:5; Neh. 10:35, 37, 39; Prov. 3:9; Jer. 2:3. *Offerings of, must be free from blemish,* Num. 18:12; *must be presented at the tabernacle,* Ex. 22:29; 23:19; 34:26; Deut. 26:3–10; *belonged to the priests,* Lev. 23:20; Num. 18:12, 13; Deut. 18:3–5. *Free will offerings of, given to the prophets,* 2 Kin. 4:42.
*Wave offering of,* Lev. 23:10–14, 17. *Heave offering of,* Num. 15:20; Neh. 10:37; Ezek. 44:30. *To be offered as a thank offering upon entrance into the land of promise,* Deut. 26:1–10.
**Figurative,** Rom. 8:23; 11:16; 16:5; 1 Cor. 15:20, 23; Jas. 1:18.

v.8–1494 BC
See footnote, *Time*, Rev. 10:6.

9
*i* *Canaan*, Gen. 37:1.
*j* *Example, bad, admonitions against*, John 13:15.

10
*k* *Idolatry, wicked practices of*, 1 Sam. 15:23.
*l* *Sorcery, forbidden*, vs. 9–14; Isa. 47:9.
1 R. V. one that practiseth augury,
2 R. V. sorcerer,

11
*m* *Charmers*, Isa. 19:3.

13
*n* *Commandment, enjoining holiness*, Deut. 8:2.
*o* *Holiness, enjoined*, Ex. 39:30.
*p* *Perfection*, Heb. 6:1.

14
*q* *Canaanites*, Ex. 23:28.

15
*r* *Prophecies, concerning the Messiah and their fulfillment*, Gen. 12:3.
*s* Vs. 18, 19; Acts 3:22; 7:37.
*t* *Jesus, prophecies concerning*, Matt. 1:21.
*u* *Moses, a type of Christ*, Ex. 2:10.
*v* *Types, of the Savior*, Heb. 10:1.

16
*w* *Horeb*, Ex. 3:1.

to eat, beside that which cometh
of the sale of his patrimony.[C]
9 ¶ When thou art come into
the [i]land which the LORD thy
God giveth thee, [j]thou shalt not
learn to do after the abominations[C] of those nations.
10 There shall not be found
among you *any one* that [k]maketh
his son or his daughter to pass[C]
through the fire, *or* that useth
[l]divination, [1]*or* an observer of
times, or an enchanter, or a
[2]witch,[C]
11 Or a [m]charmer, or a con-
sulter with †familiar[C] spirits, or a
wizard,[C] or a ‡ necromancer.[C]
12 For all that do [k,l,m]these
things *are* an abomination unto
the LORD: and because of these
abominations the LORD thy God
doth drive them out from before
thee.
13 [n,o]Thou shalt be [p]perfect[C]
with the LORD thy God.[Q]
14 For these [q]nations, which
thou shalt possess, hearkened
unto observers of times, and unto [l,m]diviners:[C] but as for thee,
the LORD thy God hath not suffered[C] thee so *to do*.[Q]
15 ¶ [r,s]The LORD thy God will
raise up unto thee a [t]Prophet
from the midst of thee, of thy
brethren, like unto [u,v]me; unto
him ye shall hearken;[T Q]
16 According to all that thou
desiredst of the LORD thy God
in [w]Hō'reb in the day of the assembly, saying, Let me not hear
again the voice of the LORD my
God, neither let me see this
great fire any more, that I die
not.
17 And the LORD said unto me,
They have well *spoken that*
which they have spoken.
18 [r,s]I will raise them up a
[t]Prophet from among their
brethren, like unto [u,v]thee, and
will put my words in his mouth;
and [x]he shall speak unto them
all that I shall command him.[Q]
19 And it shall come to pass,
*that* whosoever will [y]not hearken
unto my words which [x]he shall
speak in my name, I will require
*it* of him.[Q]
20 But the [z]prophet, which shall
presume to speak a word in my
name, which I have not commanded him to speak, or that
shall speak in the name of other
gods, even that prophet shall die.
21 And if thou say in thine
heart, How shall we know the
word which the LORD hath not
spoken?
22 When a [z]prophet speaketh
in the name of the LORD, if the
thing follow not, nor come to
pass, that *is* the thing which the
LORD hath not spoken, *but* the
prophet hath spoken it presumptuously: thou shalt not be afraid
of him.

## CHAPTER 19

*The cities of refuge. 4 The privilege thereof for the manslayer. 14 Landmarks not to be removed. 15 Two witnesses required to establish a matter. 16 The punishment of a false witness.*

WHEN the LORD thy God
hath cut[C] off the [a]nations,
whose land the LORD thy God
giveth thee, and thou succeedest
them, and dwellest in their cities,
and in their houses;
2 Thou shalt separate[C] three
[b]cities for thee in the midst of thy
land, which the LORD thy God
giveth thee to possess it.
3 Thou shalt prepare thee a
[c]way, and divide the coasts[C] of
thy land, which the LORD thy
God giveth thee to inherit, into
three parts, that every slayer
may flee thither.
4 ¶ And this *is* the case of the

v.18–1494 BC
See footnote, *Time*, Rev. 10:6.

18
*x* *Jesus, mediation of*, Matt. 1:21.

19
*y* *Disobedience to God, denunciations against*, Eph. 5:6.

20
*z* *Prophets, false, denunciations against*, Isa. 3:2

1
*a* *Canaanites*, Ex. 23:28.

2
*b* *Cities, of refuge*, vs. 2–13; Num. 35:8.

3
*c* *Highways*, Deut 2:27.

† **FAMILIAR SPIRITS.** *Consulting of, forbidden*, Lev. 19:31; 20:6, 27; Deut. 18:10, 11; *vain*, Isa. 8:19; 19:3. *Those who consulted, to be cut off*, Lev. 20:6, 27.
*Consulted by Saul*, 1 Sam. 28:3–25; 1 Chr. 10:13.
See footnote, WITCHCRAFT, Ex. 22:18.

‡ **NECROMANCY,** Deut. 18:11; 1 Sam. 28:7–19; Isa 8:19; 29:4.
See footnotes: SORCERY, Isa. 47:9; WITCHCRAFT, Ex. 22:18

v.4–1494 BC
See footnote, *Time*, Rev. 10:6.

4
*d Homicide, accidental*, Deut. 5:17.
1 R. V. unawares,

6
*e Hatred*, Prov. 15:17.

9
*f Love, of man for God, enjoined*, 1 John 4:19.

11
*g Statute, fixing penalty for murder*, vs. 12, 13; Deut. 8:2.
*h Homicide, felonious*, Deut. 5:17.

slayer, which shall flee [b]thither,
that he may live: Whoso [d]killeth
his neighbour [1]ignorantly,[c] whom
he hated not in time past;
5 As when a man goeth into the
wood[c] with his neighbour to hew
wood, and his hand fetcheth[c] a
stroke with the *ax to cut down
the tree, and the head[c] slippeth
from the helve,[c] and lighteth[c] upon his neighbour, [d]that he die;
he shall flee unto one of those
[b]cities, and live:
6 Lest the †avenger of the
blood pursue the slayer, while
his heart is hot and overtake
him, because the way is long,
and slay him; whereas he *was*
not worthy of death, inasmuch
as he [e]hated him not in time
past.
7 Wherefore I command thee,
saying, Thou shalt separate[c]
three [b]cities for thee.
8 And if the LORD thy God enlarge thy coast,[c] as he hath sworn
unto thy fathers, and give thee
all the land which he promised
to give unto thy fathers;
9 If thou shalt keep all these
commandments to do them,
which I command thee this day,
to [f]love the LORD thy God, and
to walk ever in his ways; then
shalt thou add three [b]cities more
for thee, beside these three:
10 That innocent blood be not
shed in thy land, which the
LORD thy God giveth thee *for*
an inheritance, and *so* blood be
upon thee.
11 ¶ [g]But if any man [e]hate his
neighbour, and lie in wait [h]for
him, and rise up against him,
and smite him mortally that he
die, and fleeth into one of these
[b]cities:
12 Then the [i]elders of his city
shall send and fetch him thence,
and deliver him into the hand of
the †avenger of blood, that he
may die.
13 Thine eye shall not [j]pity
him, but thou shalt put away *the*
*guilt of* innocent blood from Ĭs′-
ra-el, that it may go well with
thee.
14 ¶ [k]Thou shalt not remove
thy neighbour's ‡landmark,
which they of old time have set
in thine [l]inheritance, which thou
shalt inherit in the land that the
LORD thy God giveth thee to
possess it.
15 ¶ [m]One witness shall not rise
up against a man for any iniquity, or for any sin, in any sin
that he sinneth: [n]at the [o]mouth
of two [p]witnesses, or at the
mouth of three witnesses, shall
the matter be established. Q
16 [q]If a [r]false witness[c] rise up
against any man to [s]testify
against him [2]*that which is*
wrong;
17 Then both the men, between
whom the controversy *is*, shall
stand before the LORD, before
the [t]priests and the [q]judges,
which shall be in those days;
18 And the [q]judges shall make
[u]diligent inquisition[c]: and, behold, [v]*if* the witness *be* a [r]false
witness,[c] *and* hath testified [w]false-
ly against his brother;
19 [v]Then shall ye ‖do unto
him, as he had thought to have
[w]done unto his brother: [x]so shall
thou put the evil away from
among you. Q

v.11–1494 BC
See footnote, *Time*, Rev. 10:6.

12
*i Government, municipal*, Isa. 22:21.

13
*j Pity, forbidden to murderers*, Job 19:21.

14
*k Commandment, forbidding fraud in metes and bounds*, Deut. 8:2.
*l Property, in real estate*, Lev. 27:15.

15
*m Statute, fixing laws of evidence*, Deut. 8:2.
n Matt. 18:16; 2 Cor. 13:1.
*o Evidence, two or more witnesses required in*, vs. 15–21; Deut. 17:6.
*p Witness, two necessary to establish a fact*, Num. 35:30.

16
*q Judge, precepts relating to*, vs 16–19; Judg. 2:18.
*r False Witness, punishment for*, vs. 16–20; Matt. 19:18.
*s Evidence, punishment for falsehood in*, Deut. 17:6.
2 R. V. of wrong doing;

17
*t Priest, duties of, to act as magistrate*, Lev. 1:5.

18
*u Diligence, required in discharging official duties*, Rom. 12:8.
*v Statute, fixing penalty for false witness*, v. 19; Deut. 8:2.
*w Slander, punishment for*, Prov. 10:18.

19
*x Punishment, design of*, Lev. 26:41.

* **AX,** 1 Sam. 13:20 21: 2 Sam. 12:31; 1 Chr. 20:3; Psa. 74:5, 6. *Elisha causes, to swim*, 2 Kin. 6:5, 6. *Battle-ax*, Ezek. 26:9.
**Figurative,** Jer. 46:22; 51:20; Matt. 3:10.

† **AVENGER OF BLOOD.** *Premosaic*, Gen. 9:5, 6. *Cain feared*, Gen. 4:14.
*Mosaic law concerning*, Num. 35:19–29; *set aside by David*, 2 Sam. 14:4–11.
**Figurative,** Psa. 8:2; 44:16; Rom. 13:14.

‡ **LANDMARKS.** *Protected from fraudulent removal*, Deut. 27:17; Job 24:2; Prov. 22:28; 23:10; Hos. 5:10.

‖ **RETALIATION,** Psa. 10:2. *Judicial, ordained in Mosaic law*, Ex. 21:23–25; Lev. 24:17–22; Deut. 19:19–21. *Malicious, forbidden*, Lev. 19:18; Prov. 20:22; 24:29; Matt. 5:38–44; Luke 9:54; Rom. 12:17, 19; 1 Cor. 6:7, 8; 1 Thess. 5:15; 1 Pet. 3:9.
**Instances of:** *Israelites, on the Amalekites*, Deut. 25:17–19; 1 Sam. 15:1–9. *Gideon, on the princes of Succoth*, Judg. 8:7, 13–16; *on kings of Midian*, Judg. 8:18–21; *on the men of Penuel*, Judg. 8:8, 17. *Joab, on Abner*, 2 Sam. 3:27, 30. *David, on Michal*, 2 Sam. 6:21–23; *on Joab*, 1 Kin. 2:5, 6; *on Shimei*, 1 Kin. 2:8, 9. *Jews, on the Chaldeans*, Esth. 9.
See footnote, REVENGE, Ezek. 25:15.

v.20–1494 BC
See footnote, *Time*, Rev. 10:6.

20
*y* *Fear of God, a motive to truthfulness*, Acts 9:31.

21
*z* *Pity, forbidden, to false witnesses*, Job 19:21.

1
*a* *War, God in*, Judg. 3:2.
*b* *Commandment, to soldiers, enjoining courage*, Deut. 8:2.
*c* *Faith, enjoined, in time of public danger*, Mark 11:22.

2
*d* *Priest, duties of*, Lev. 1:5.
*e* *Armies, priests exhort, before battle*, vs. 2–4; Deut. 11:4.

4
*f* *God, providence of, in delivering from enemies*, Gen. 2:2.

5
*g* *Armies, who were exempt from service in*, Deut. 11:4.
*h* *Dedication*, Ezra 6:17.

6
*i* *Agriculture*, Gen. 3:23.

20 And those which remain shall hear, and [y]fear, and shall henceforth commit no more any such evil among you.

21 And thine eye shall not [z]pity; *but* ‖life *shall go* for life, eye for eye, tooth for tooth, hand for hand, foot for foot.[Q]

## CHAPTER 20

*The priest's exhortation to the people before battle. 5 The officers' declaration to those exempt from the war. 10 How to deal with the cities that accept or refuse the proclamation of peace. 16 What cities must be destroyed. 19 Fruit trees not to be destroyed in the siege.*

WHEN thou goest out to [a]battle against thine enemies, and seest horses, and chariots, *and* a people more than thou, [b,c]be not afraid of them: for the LORD thy God *is* with thee, which brought thee up out of the land of E′gy̆pt.

2 And it shall be, when ye are come nigh[C] unto the battle, that the [d]priest shall approach and speak unto the [e]people,

3 [d]And shall [e]say unto them, Hear, O Is̱′ra-el, ye approach this day unto battle against your enemies: [c]let not your hearts faint, fear not, and do not tremble, neither be ye terrified because of them;

4 For the LORD your [f]God *is* he that goeth with you, to [b]fight for you against your enemies, to save you.

5 ¶ And the officers shall speak unto the [g]people, saying, What man *is there* that hath built a new house, and hath not [h]dedicated it? let him go and return to his house, lest he die in the battle, and another man dedicate it.

6 And what man *is he* that hath [i]planted a vineyard, and hath not *yet* eaten of it? let him *also* go and return unto his house, lest he die in the battle, and another man eat of it.

7 And what man *is there* that hath *betrothed a wife, and hath not taken her? let him go and return unto his house, lest he die in the battle, and another man take her.

8 And the officers shall speak further unto the [g]people, and they shall say, What [j]man *is there that is* [k]fearful and fainthearted? let him go and return unto his house, lest his brethren's heart faint as well as his heart.

9 And it shall be, when the officers have made an end of speaking unto the [g]people, that they shall make [l]captains of the armies to lead the people.

10 ¶ When thou comest nigh[C] unto a city to [m]fight against it, then proclaim[C] [n]peace unto it.

11 And it shall be, if it make thee answer of [n]peace, and open unto thee, then it shall be, *that* all the people *that is* found therein shall be tributaries[C] unto thee, and they shall serve thee.

12 And if it will make no [n]peace with thee, but will make [o]war against thee, then thou shalt [m]besiege it:

13 And when the LORD thy God hath delivered it into thine hands, thou shalt [p,q]smite every male thereof with the edge of the sword:

14 But the [r,s]women, and the little ones, and the cattle, and all that is in the city, *even* all the [t]spoil thereof, shalt thou take unto thyself; and thou shalt eat the spoil of thine enemies, which the LORD thy God hath given thee.

15 Thus shalt thou do unto all the cities *which are* very far off from thee, which *are* not of the cities of these nations.

16 But of the cities of these [u]people, which the LORD thy

v.7–1494 BC
See footnote, *Tim*
Rev. 10:6.

8
*j* *Soldiers, cowar excused from dut as*, Ezra 8:22.
*k* *Cowardice, disqualifies for mili tary service*, Lev 26:36.

9
*l* *Captain*, Num. 31:48.

10
*m* *Siege*, Deut. 28:53.
*n* *Peace*, Jer. 29:7.

12
*o* *War*, Judg. 3:2.

13
*p* *Massacre, authorized by Moses*, Esth. 3:13.
*q* *War, of extermination*, vs. 13–18 Judg. 3:2.

14
*r* *Captive, enslaved* 1 Sam. 30:3.
*s* *Servant, captives of war made*, Jer. 2:14.
*t* *Spoils*, 1 Chr. 26 27.

16
*u* *Canaanites, to be destroyed*, Ex. 23:28.

***BETROTHAL.** *Of Jacob*, Gen. 29:18–30. *Exempts from military duty*, Deut. 20:7. *A quasi marriage*, Matt. 1:18; Luke 1:27. **Figurative** Isa. 62:4; Hos. 2:19, 20; 2 Cor. 11:2. **See footnote, MARRIAGE, Gen. 34:9.**

v.16–1494 BC
See footnote, *Time*, Rev. 10:6.

17
*v Hittites*, Judg. 1:26.
*w Amorites*, Gen. 14:13.
*x Perizzites*, Gen. 15:20.
*y Hivites*, Gen. 10:17.
*z Jebusites*, Deut. 7:1.

18
*a Idolatry*, 1 Sam. 15:23.

19
*b Siege*, Deut. 28:53.
*c War*, Judg. 3:2.
*d Horticulture, encouraged*, v. 20; Lev. 19:23–25.

1
*a Homicide, felonious*, vs. 1–9; Deut. 5:17.
*b Canaan*, Gen. 37:1.

2
*c Government, municipal*, Isa. 22:21.

God doth give thee *for* an inheritance, thou shalt save alive
nothing that breatheth:
17 But thou shalt [p]utterly destroy them; *namely*, the [v]Hĭt′-
tītes, and the [w]Ăm′ôr-ītes, the
[u]Cā′năan-ītes, and the [x]Pĕr′ĭz-
zītes, the [y]Hī′vītes, and the
[z]Jĕb′u-sītes; as the LORD thy
God hath commanded thee:
18 That they teach you not to
do after all their abominations,[c]
which they have done unto their
[a]gods; so should ye sin against
the LORD your God.
19 ¶ When thou shalt [b]besiege
a city a long time, in making
[c]war against it to take it, thou
shalt [d]not destroy the trees thereof by forcing an ax against them:
for thou mayest eat of them, and
thou shalt not cut them down
(for the tree of the field *is* man's
*life*) to employ *them* in the siege:
20 Only the trees which thou
knowest that they *be* not trees
for meat,[c] thou shalt destroy and
cut them down; and thou shalt
build [†]bulwarks[c] against the city
that maketh [c]war with thee, until it be subdued.

## CHAPTER 21

*The expiation for murder where the murderer is unknown. 10 The treatment of a captive taken to wife. 15 The firstborn not to be disinherited for the sake of another wife's offspring. 18 A stubborn son is to be stoned to death. 22 The body of a malefactor must not hang all night on a tree.*

IF *one* be found [a]slain in the
[b]land which the LORD thy
God giveth thee to possess it, lying in the field, *and* it be not
known who hath slain him:
2 Then thy [c]elders and thy
judges shall come forth, and
they shall measure unto the cities which *are* round about him
that is [a]slain:
3 And it shall be, *that* the city
*which is* next unto the [a]slain
man, even the [c]elders of that city
shall take an [d]heifer, which hath
not been wrought[c] with, *and*
which hath not drawn[c] in the
yoke;
4 And the [c]elders of that city
shall bring down the [d]heifer unto
a rough valley, which is neither
eared[c] nor sown, and shall strike
off the heifer's neck there in the
valley:
5 And the priests the sons of
Lē′vī shall come near; for them
the LORD thy God hath chosen
to minister unto him, and to
*bless in the name of the LORD;
and by [e]their word shall every
controversy and every stroke[c] be
*tried*:
6 [Q]And all the [c]elders of that
city, *that are* next unto the [a]slain
*man*, shall [f]wash their hands
over the [d]heifer that is beheaded
in the valley:
7 And they shall answer and
say, Our hands have not shed
this blood, neither have our eyes
seen *it*.
8 [g,h]Be merciful, O LORD, unto
thy people Ĭş′ra-el, whom thou
hast redeemed, and lay not innocent blood unto thy people of
Ĭş′ra-el's charge. And the blood
shall be forgiven them.
9 So shalt thou put away the
*guilt of* innocent blood from
among you, when thou shalt do

v.2–1494 BC
See footnote, *Time*, Rev. 10:6.

3
*d Heifer*, Num. 19:2.

5
*e Priest, duties of, to act as magistrate*, Lev. 1:5.

6
*f Ablution, of hands, a token of innocency*, Judg. 19:21.

8
*g Prayer, intercessory*, Acts 6:4.
*h Intercession, of man with God*, Jer. 27:18.

† **BULWARK**, 2 Chr. 26:15; Eccl. 9:14.
**Figurative**, Psa. 48:13; Isa. 26:1.

* **BENEDICTIONS.** *By God, upon creatures he had made*, Gen. 1:22; *upon man*, Gen. 1:28; *upon Noah*, Gen. 9:1, **2.** *Divinely appointed*, Deut. 10:8; 21:5. *Form of, to be used by priests*, Num. 6:23–26.
**Instances of:** *By Melchizedek, upon Abraham*, Gen. 14:19, 20; Heb. 7:7. *By Bethuel's household, upon Rebekah*, Gen. 24:60. *By Isaac, upon Jacob*, Gen. 27:23–29, 37; 28: 1–4; *upon Esau*, Gen. 27:39, 40. *By Jacob, upon Pharaoh*, Gen. 47:7–10; *upon Joseph's sons*, Gen. 48; *upon his own sons*, Gen. 49. *By Moses, upon the tribes of Israel*, Deut. 33. *By Aaron*, Lev. 9:22, 23. *By half the tribes, who stood on mount Gerizim*, Deut. 11:29, 30; 27:11–13; Josh. 8:33. *By Joshua, upon Caleb*, Josh. 14:13; *upon the Reubenites, Gadites, and half tribe of Manasseh*, Josh. 22:6, 7. *By Naomi, upon Ruth and Orpah*, Ruth 1:8, 9. *By the people, upon Ruth*, Ruth 4:11, 12. *By Eli, upon Elkanah*, 1 Sam. 2:20. *By Saul, upon David*, 1 Sam. 17:37. *By David, upon the people*, 2 Sam. 6:18; *upon Barzillai*, 2 Sam. 19:39. *By Araunah, upon David*, 2 Sam. 24:23. *By Solomon, upon the people*, 1 Kin. 8:14, 55–58; 2 Chr. 6:3. *By Simeon, upon Jesus*, Luke 2:34. *By Jesus*, Luke 24:50.
**Apostolic**, Rom. 1:7; 15:5, 13, 33; 16:20; 1 Cor. 1:3; 16:23; 2 Cor. 1:2; 13:14; Gal. 1:3; 6:16, 18; Eph. 1:2; 6:23, 24; Phil. 1:2; 4:23; Col. 1:2; 1 Thess. 1:1; 5:28; 2 Thess. 1:2; 3:16, 18; 1 Tim. 1:2; 6:21; 2 Tim. 1:2; 4:22; Tit. 3:15; Philemon 3, 25; Heb. 13:20, 21, 25; 1 Pet. 1:2; 5:10, 11, 14; 2 Pet. 1:2–4; 2 John 3; Jude 2; Rev. 22:21.

v.9–1494 BC
See footnote, *Time,* Rev. 10:6.

10
*i* *Israel,* Ex. 4:22.
*j* *War,* Judg. 3:2.
*k* *Servant, captives of war made,* vs. 11–14; Jer. 2:14.

13
*Marriage,* Gen. 34:9.

14
*m* *Divorce,* Matt. 19:7.
*n* *Money,* Jer. 32:9.
1 R. V. deal with her as a slave,

15
*o* *Concubinage,* 2 Sam. 21:11.
*p* *Polygamy,* Deut. 17:17.
*q* *Children,* Mark 10:14.
*r* *Firstborn, birthright of,* Zech. 12:10.

16
*s* *Heir,* Gen. 15:3.
*t* *Inheritance,* Num. 27:7.

17
*u* *Birthright, entitles firstborn to double portion of inheritance,* 2 Chr. 21:3.

*that which is* right in the sight of
the LORD.[Q]
10 ¶ When [i]thou goest forth to
[j]war against thine enemies, and
the LORD thy God hath delivered them into thine hands, and
thou hast taken them [k]captive,
11 And seest among the [k]cap-
tives a beautiful woman, and
hast a desire unto her, that thou
wouldest have her to thy wife;
12 Then thou shalt bring her
home to thine house; and she
shall shave her head, and pare[c]
her nails;
13 And she shall put the raiment of her [k]captivity from off
her, and shall remain in thine
house, and bewail her father and
her mother a full month: and after that thou shalt go in unto her,
and [l]be her husband, and she
shall be thy wife.
14 And it shall be, if thou have
no delight in her, then thou shalt
[m]let her go whither she will; but
thou shalt not sell her at all for
[n]money, thou shalt not [1]make
merchandise of her, because
thou hast humbled her.
15 ¶ If a man have [o,p]two
wives, one beloved, and another
hated, and they have born him
[q]children, *both* the beloved and
the hated; and *if* the [r]firstborn
son be her's that was hated:[s]
16 Then it shall be, when he
maketh his sons to [s,t]inherit *that*
which he hath, *that* he may not
make the son of the beloved
[r]firstborn before the son of the
hated, *which is indeed* the firstborn:
17 But he shall acknowledge
the son of the hated *for* the
[r]firstborn, by giving him a [u]dou-
ble portion of all that he hath:
for he *is* the beginning of his
strength; the right of the firstborn *is* his.

18 ¶ If a man have a stubborn
and rebellious son, which will
not obey the voice of his [v]father,
or the voice of his [w]mother, and
*that,* when they have [x]chastened
him, will not hearken unto
them:
19 Then shall [x]his [v]father and
his [w]mother lay hold on him, and
bring him out unto the [c, y]elders
of his city, and unto the [z]gate of
his place;
20 And they shall say unto the
[a]elders of his city, This our son
*is* [b]stubborn and rebellious, he
will not obey our voice; *he is* a
[2, c]glutton, and a [d]drunkard.
21 And all the men of his city
shall [e,f]stone [g]him with stones,
that he die: so shalt thou put evil
away from among you; and all
Is'ra-el shall hear, and [h]fear.
22 ¶[Q]And if a man have committed a sin worthy of death,
and he be to be put to [i]death,
and thou [j]hang him on a tree:
23 [k]His body shall not remain
all night upon the tree, but thou
shalt in any wise[c] [l]bury him that
day; (for [m]he that is hanged *is*
[†]accursed of God;) that thy
land be not defiled, which the
LORD thy God giveth thee *for* an
inheritance.[Q]

## CHAPTER 22

*Of humanity toward brethren. 5 The sexes to be distinguished by apparel. 6 The dam not to be taken with her young ones. 8 The house must have battlements. 9 Divers things to be avoided. 12 Fringes upon the vesture. 13 The punishment of him that slanders his wife. 22 Of adultery; 25 of rape; 28 and of fornication. 30 Incest.*

[a]THOU shalt not see thy
[b]brother's [c]ox or his sheep
go [d]astray, and hide thyself[c] from
them: [e]thou shalt in any case
bring them again unto thy
brother.
2 [a]And if thy [b]brother *be* not
nigh[c] unto thee, or if thou know
him not, then [e]thou shalt bring

v.18–1494 BC
See footnote, *Time* Rev. 10:6.

18
*v* *Father, to be obeyed,* Psa. 27:10.
*w* *Mother, to be obeyed,* 1 Kin. 2:20.
*x* *Children, punishment of,* vs. 18–21; Mark 10:14.

19
*y* *Court, civil,* Ex. 18:26.
*z* *Gates, place for holding courts of justice,* Deut. 3:5

20
*a* *Court, civil,* Ex. 18:26.
*b* *Self-will,* Gen. 49:6.
*c* *Gluttony,* Prov. 30:22.
*d* *Drunkard, punishment of,* Psa. 69:12.
2 R. V. riotous liver,

21
*e* *Punishment, design of,* Lev. 26:41.
*f* *Stoning,* 1 Sam. 30:6.
*g* *Children, punishment of,* Mark 10 14.
*h* *Fear of God, a motive to filial obedience,* Acts 9:31.

22
*i* *Death, penalty,* Num. 23:10.
*j* *Hanging,* Josh. 8:29.

23
*k* John 19:31.
*l* *Burial,* Acts 8:2
*m* Gal. 3:13.

1
*a* *Commandment, respecting lost property,* Deut. 8:2.
*b* *Neighbor, kindness to, enjoined* Luke 10:29.
*c* *Property, personal, strayed,* vs. 1–3; Lev. 27:15.
*d* Ex. 23:4.
*e* *Kindness, enjoined,* vs. 2–4; Acts 28:2.

† **ACCURSED.** *Things devoted irredeemably to God, as a field or firstling consecrated to God,* Lev. 27:21, 29. *Silver gold, and vessels of brass and iron in the siege of Jericho,* Josh. 6:19; 7:1–26. *Persons under the divine curse,* Deut. 21:23 Gal. 1:8; 3:13.

v.2–1494 BC
See footnote, *Time*, Rev. 10:6.

3
f *Ass, domesticated*, 2 Chr. 28: 15.

4
g *Commandment, defining duty to neighbor*, Deut. 8:2.
h *Animals*, Jer. 27:5.

5
i *Women*, Prov. 31:10.
j *Dress*, Zech. 3:3.

6
k *Birds*, Eccl. 12:4.

7
l *Promise, to the obedient, of long life*, 2 Cor. 1:20.
m *Reward, a motive to show kindness*, Matt. 5:12.
n *Life, long, promised to the obedient*, Eccl. 8:15.

8
o *Statute, safeguarding human life*, Deut. 8:2.
p *House, architecture of*, Esth. 8:1.
q Jer. 5:10.
r *Homicide, felonious*, Deut. 5:17.

9
s *Agriculture, Mosaic laws concerning*, Gen. 3:23.
t *Seed*, Lev. 19:19.
1 R. V. two kinds of seed, lest the whole fruit be forfeited, the seed which thou hast sown, and the increase of the vineyard.

10
u *Bullock*, Ex. 29:3.
v *Ass*, 2 Chr. 28: 15.

11
w *Wool*, Judg. 6:37.
x *Linen*, Ezek. 27: 16.

[c]it unto thine own house, and it
shall be with thee until thy
brother seek after it, and thou
shalt restore it to him again.
3 In like manner shalt thou do
with his [f]ass; and so shalt thou
do with his raiment; and with all
lost thing of thy brother's, which
he hath lost, and thou hast
found, shalt thou do likewise:
thou mayest not hide[c] thyself.
4 ¶ [g]Thou shalt not see thy
brother's ass or his ox fall down
by the way,[c] and hide[c] thyself
from [h]them: thou shalt surely
help him to lift *them* up again.
5 ¶ The [i]woman shall not wear
that which pertaineth unto a
man, neither shall a man put on
a woman's [j]garment: for all that
do so *are* abomination unto the
LORD thy God.
6 ¶ If a [k]bird's nest chance to
be before thee in the way in any
tree, or on the ground, *whether
they be* young ones, or eggs, and
the dam[c] sitting upon the young,
or upon the eggs, thou shalt not
take the dam with the young:
7 *But* thou shalt in any wise[c] let
the dam go, and take the young
to thee; [l,m]that it may be well
with thee, and *that* thou mayest
prolong *thy* [n]days.
8 ¶ [o]When thou buildest a new
[p]house, then thou shalt make a
[q]battlement[c] for thy roof, that
thou [r]bring not blood upon thine
house, if any man fall from
thence.
9 ¶ Thou shalt not [s]sow thy
vineyard with [1]divers[c] [t]seeds: lest
the fruit of thy seed which thou
hast sown, and the fruit of thy
vineyard, be defiled.
10 ¶ Thou shalt not *plow with
an [u]ox and an [v]ass together.
11 ¶ Thou shalt not wear a
[j]garment of divers[c] sorts, *as* of
[w]woollen and [x]linen together.

12 ¶ Thou shalt make thee
[y]fringes upon the four quarters[c]
of thy vesture,[c] wherewith thou
coverest *thyself*.
13 ¶ If any [z]man [a]take a wife,
and go in unto her, and [b]hate
her,
14 [2]And [c,d]give occasions of
speech against her, and bring up
an evil name upon her, and say,
I took this woman, and when I
came to her, I found [3]her not a
maid:
15 Then shall the father of the
damsel, and her mother, take
and bring forth *the tokens of*
the damsel's [e]virginity unto the
[f,g]elders of the city in the [h]gate:
16 And the damsel's father
shall say unto the [f,g]elders, I
[a]gave my daughter unto this
man to[c] wife, and he [b]hateth her;
17 And, lo, he hath [4,c,d]given
occasions of speech *against her*,
saying, I found not [5]thy daughter a maid[c]; and yet these *are the
tokens of* my daughter's [e]virgin-
ity. And they shall spread the
cloth before the [f,g]elders of the
city.
18 And the [f,g]elders of that city
shall take that man and [i,j]chas-
tise him;
19 And they shall [k]amerce[c] him
in an hundred [l]*shekels*[c] of silver,
and give *them* unto the father
of the damsel, because he hath
brought up an [c,d]evil name upon
a [e]virgin of Is'ra-el: and she shall
be his wife; he may not put her
away all his days.
20 But if this thing be true, *and
the tokens of* [e]virginity be not
found for the damsel:
21 Then they shall bring out
the damsel to the door of her
father's house, and the men of
her city shall [m,n]stone her with
stones that she die: because she
hath wrought folly in Is'ra-el, to

v.12–1494 BC
See footnote, *Time*, Rev. 10:6.

12
y Num. 15:38–41.

13
z *Husband*, Num. 30:6.

a *Marriage*, Gen. 34:9.
b *Hatred*, Prov. 15: 17.

14
c *Character, defamation of*, vs. 13–19; Phil. 2:15.
d *Slander*, Prov. 10:18.
2 R. V. and lay shameful things to her charge,
3 R. V. not in her the tokens of virginity:

15
e *Virgin*, Isa. 62:5.
f *Court, civil*, Ex. 18:26.
g *Government, municipal*, Isa. 22: 21.
h *Gates, place for holding courts of justice*, Deut. 3:5.

17
4 R. V. laid shameful things to her charge,
5 R. V. in thy daughter the tokens of virginity;

18
i *Punishment, by scourging*, Lev. 26:41.
j *Scourging*, Acts 22:24.

19
k *Damages and Compensation*, Ex. 21:19.
l *Shekel*, Ex. 30:13.

21
m *Stoning*, 1 Sam. 30:6.
n *Punishment, death penalty*, Lev. 26:41.

***PLOW.** *Shares of, sharpened by smiths of the Philistines*, 1 Sam. 13:20. *Used, by Elisha with twelve yoke of oxen*, 1 Kin. 19:19; *by Job's servants*, Job 1:14.
**Figurative:** *Of afflictions*, Psa. 129:3.

v.21–1491 BC
See footnote, *Time,* Rev. 10:6.

o *Adultery, penalties for,* Lev. 20:10.

23
p *Betrothal, a quasi marriage,* v. 24; Deut. 20:7.

play the [o]whore[C] in her father's house: so shalt thou put evil away from among you.[Q]

22 ¶ If a man be found [o]lying with a woman married to an husband, then they shall both of them [n]die, *both* the man that lay with the woman, and the woman: so shalt thou put away evil from Īș'ra-el.[Q]

23 If a damsel *that is* a [e]virgin be [p]betrothed unto an husband, and a man find her in the city and †lie with her;

24 Then ye shall bring them both out unto the gate of that city, and ye shall [m,n]stone them with stones that they die; the damsel, because she cried not, *being* in the city; and the man, because he hath †humbled his neighbour's wife: so thou shalt put away evil from among you.[Q]

25 ¶ But if a man find a [p]betrothed damsel in the field, and the man ‡force[C] her, and lie with her: then the man only that lay with her [n]shall die:

26 But unto the damsel thou shalt do nothing; *there is* in the damsel no sin *worthy* of death: for as when a man riseth against his neighbour, and slayeth him, even so *is* this matter:

27 ‡For he found her in the field, *and* the betrothed damsel cried, and *there was* none to save her.

28 ¶ If a man find a damsel *that is* a [e]virgin, which is not [p]betrothed, and lay hold on her, and †lie with her, and they be found;

29 Then the man that †lay with her shall [k]give unto the damsel's father fifty [l]*shekels*[C] of silver, and she shall be his wife; because he hath humbled her, he may not put her away all his days.

30 ¶ A man shall not [q]take his father's wife, nor discover[C] his father's skirt.[Q]

## CHAPTER 23

*Who may and who may not enter into the congregation. 9 Uncleanness to be avoided in the camp. 15 Of the fugitive servant. 17 Of lewdness. 18 Of abominable sacrifices. 19 Of usury. 21 Of vows. 24 Of trespasses.*

HE that is wounded in the stones, or [a]hath his privy[C] member cut off, shall not enter into the congregation of the LORD.

2 A *bastard shall not enter into the congregation of the LORD; even to his tenth generation shall he not enter into the congregation of the LORD.

3 An [b]Ăm'mon-īte or [c]Mō'ab-īte shall not enter into the congregation of the LORD; even to their tenth generation shall they not enter into the congregation of the LORD for ever:

4 Because they [d]met [e]you not with bread and with water in the way, when ye came forth out of [f]Ē'ġy̆pt; and because they [g]hired against thee †Bā'laam the son of Bē'or of [h]Pē'thôr of [i]Mĕs-o-pō-tā'mĭ-ȧ, to curse thee.

5 Nevertheless the LORD thy God [j]would not hearken[C] unto Bā'laam; but the LORD thy [k]God turned the curse into a blessing unto thee, because the LORD thy [l]God loved thee.[S]

6 Thou shalt not seek their

v.29–1494 BC
See footnote, *Time,* Rev. 10:6.

30
q *Incest,* Lev. 18:6.

1
a *Eunuch,* Matt. 19:12.

3
b *Ammonites,* Deut. 2:20.
c *Moabites,* Gen. 19:37.

4
d *Inhospitableness, instances of,* Luke 9:53.
e *Israel,* Ex. 4:22.
f *Egypt,* Gen. 41:8.
g *Malice, instances of,* Eph. 4:31.
h Num. 22:5.
i *Mesopotamia,* Gen. 24:10.

5
j *Prayer, answer to, withheld,* Acts 6:4.
k *God, providence of,* Gen. 2:2.
l *God, love of, exemplified,* Gen. 2:2.

† **SEDUCTION.** *Laws concerning,* Ex. 22:16, 17; Deut. 22:23–29.
See footnote, RAPE, Deut. 22:25.
**Instances of:** *Of Dinah,* Gen. 34:2. *Of Tamar,* 2 Sam. 13:1–14.

‡ **RAPE.** *Law imposes death penalty for,* Deut. 22:25–27. *Captives subjected to,* Isa. 13:16; Lam. 5.11; Zech. 14:2.
**Instances of:** *Of the concubine of a Levite, by Benjamites; tribe of Benjamin nearly exterminated by the army of the other tribes, as punishment for,* Judg. 19:22–30; 20:35. *Of Tamar, by Amnon; avenged in the death of Amnon at the hand of Absalom, Tamar's brother,* 2 Sam. 13:6–29, 32, 33.

* **BASTARD.** *Excluded from the congregation,* Deut. 23:2.
**Instances of:** *Ishmael,* Gen. 16:3, 15; Gal. 4:22. *Moab and Ammon,* Gen. 19:36, 37. *Sons of Tamar by Judah,* Gen 38:12–30. *Jephthah,* Judg. 11:1.
**Figurative,** Zech. 9:6; Heb. 12:8.

† **BALAAM** (*foreigner*), son of Beor. *From Mesopotamia,* Deut. 23:4. *A soothsayer,* Josh. 13:22. *A prophet,* Num. 24:2–9; 2 Pet. 2:15, 16. *Balak sends for, to curse Israel,* Num. 22:5–7; Josh. 24:9; Neh. 13:2; Mic. 6:5. *Anger of, rebuked by his ass,* Num. 22:22–35; 2 Pet. 2:16. *Counsel of, an occasion of Israel's corruption with the Midianites,* Num. 31:16; Rev. 2:14. *Covetousness of,* 2 Pet. 2:15; Jude 11. *Death of,* Num. 31:8; Josh. 13:22.

v.6–1494 BC
See footnote, *Time*, Rev. 10:6.

7
*m* *Edomites*, 2 Kin. 8:21.
*n* *Egyptians*, Gen. 50:3.

9
*o* *Armies*, Deut. 11:4.

10
*p* *Defilement*, Lev. 5:2.
*q* *Sin, typified*, Rom. 5:12.
*r* *Disfellowship, of the righteous and wicked, typified*, Num. 15:31.

11
*s* *Ablution*, Judg. 19:21.
*t* *Holiness, typified*, Ex. 39:30.

12
*u* *Sanitation and Hygiene, filth, disposition of*, Num. 31:23.

14
*v* *God, preserver*, Gen. 2:2.
*w* *Anthropomorphisms*, Gen. 11:5.

peace nor their prosperity all thy days for ever.

7 Thou shalt not abhor an [m]Ē′dom-īte; for he *is* thy brother: thou shalt not abhor an [n]Ē-ġȳp′tian; because thou wast a ‡stranger[C] in his land.

8 The children that are begotten of them shall enter into the congregation of the LORD in their third generation.

9 ¶ When the [o]host goeth forth against thine enemies, then keep thee from every wicked thing.

10 If there be among you any man, that is not clean by reason of [p,q]uncleanness that chanceth him by night, then shall he [r]go abroad out of the camp, he shall not come within the camp:

11 But it shall be, when evening cometh on, he shall [s,t]wash *himself* with water: and when the sun is down, he shall come into the camp *again*.

12 [u]Thou shalt have a place also without[C] the camp, whither thou shalt go forth abroad:

13 [u]And thou shalt have a paddle[C] upon thy weapon; and it shall be, when thou wilt ease thyself abroad, thou shalt dig therewith, and shalt turn back and cover that which cometh from thee:

14 For the LORD thy [v]God [w]walketh in the midst of thy camp, to deliver thee, and to give up thine enemies before thee; therefore shall thy camp be [t]holy: that he see no [p,q]unclean thing in thee, and turn away from thee.[S]

15 ¶ Thou shalt not deliver unto his master the [x,y]servant which is escaped from his master unto thee:

16 [x,y]He shall dwell with thee, *even* among you, in that place which he shall choose in one of thy gates, where it liketh[C] him best: thou shalt not [z]oppress him.

17 ¶ There shall be no [a,b,c]whore[C] of the daughters of Ĭṣ′ra-el, nor a [d]sodomite of the sons of Ĭṣ′ra-el.

18 Thou shalt not bring the hire of a [b]whore[C], or the [1]price of a [e]dog[C], into the [f]house of the LORD thy God for any [g]vow: for even both these *are* [h]abomination[C] unto the LORD thy God.

19 ¶ [i]Thou shalt not [j]lend upon[C] [k]usury[C] to thy brother; usury of [l]money, usury of victuals, usury of any thing that is lent upon usury:

20 Unto a [2,‡]stranger[C] thou mayest [j]lend upon [k]usury[C]; but unto thy brother thou shalt not lend upon usury: that the LORD thy God may [m]bless thee in all that thou settest thine hand to in the [n]land whither thou goest to possess it.

21 ¶ [o]When thou shalt [g]vow a [p]vow unto the LORD thy God, thou shalt not slack[C] to pay it: for the LORD thy God will surely require it of thee; and it would be sin in thee.[Q]

22 But if thou shalt forbear[C] to [g]vow[C], it shall be no sin in thee.

23 That which is gone out of thy lips thou shalt keep and perform; *even* a [q]freewill offering, according as thou hast [g,p]vowed

v.15–1494 BC
See footnote, *Time*, Rev. 10:6.

15
*x* *Fugitives*, Judg. 12:4.
*y* *Servant*, Jer. 2:14.

16
*z* *Oppression, forbidden*, Eccl. 5:8.

17
*a* *Adultery, forbidden*, Lev. 20:10.
*b* *Harlot*, Prov. 7:10.
*c* *Prostitution, forbidden*, Lev. 19:29.
*d* *Sodomy*, Lev. 18 22.

18
*e* *Dog*, 1 Kin. 21:19.
*f* *Church*, 1 Kin. 9:3.
*g* *Vows*, Num. 30:2.
*h* *Abomination*, Lev. 18:27.
1 R. V. wages

19
*i* *Creditor*, Deut. 15:2.
*j* *Lending*, Deut. 15:2.
*k* *Interest*, Ex. 22:25.
*l* *Money*, Jer. 32:9.

20
*m* *Temporal Blessings, from God*, Psa. 103:2.
*n* *Canaan*, Gen. 37:1.
2 R. V. foreigner

21
*o* *Commandment, enjoining fidelity to vows*, Deut. 8:2.
*p* *Offerings, vow* Lev. 6:17.

23
*q* *Offerings, free will*, Lev. 6:17.

‡ **FOREIGNERS.** *Numerous in days of Solomon*, 2 Chr. 2:17. *Love of, enjoined*, Lev. 19:33, 34; Deut. 10:18, 19. *Justice toward, enjoined*, Lev. 24:22; Deut. 1:16; 24:17; 27:19; Jer. 7:6. *Kindness to poor of, required*, Lev. 25:35. *Hospitality to, required by Jesus*, Matt. 25:35, 38, 43. *David's kindness to*, 2 Sam. 15:19, 20.

*Israelites forbidden, to abhor*, Deut. 23:7; *to oppress*, Ex. 22:21; 23:9; Deut. 24:14; Jer. 22:3; Zech. 7:10; *to marry*, Deut. 25:5; *to make kings of*, Deut. 17:15.

*Israelites authorized, to purchase as slaves*, Lev. 25:44–46; *to take interest from*, Deut. 23:20.

*Not accorded the privileges of the seventh year release of debts*, Deut. 15:3. *Oppressed*, Ezek. 22:29. *Oppressors of, judged*, Mal. 3:5. *Separate burial place provided for*, Matt. 27:7. *Inheritance of, in Ezekiel's vision*, Ezek. 47:22, 23.

**Privileges of, under Mosaic law:** *To offer sacrifices*, Lev. 17:8. *To eat the passover*, Ex. 12:43–49; Num. 9:14. *To eat food forbidden to Israel*, Deut. 14:21. *To asylum in cities of refuge*, Num. 35:15; Josh. 20:9.

**Requirements of:** *To assemble for religious instruction*, Deut. 31:12. *To conform to Mosaic ordinances in offering sacrifices*, Num. 15:14, 15; 19:10. *To observe the Sabbath*, Ex. 20:10; 23:12.

**Forbidden:** *To eat things offered in sacrifice*, Ex. 29:33; Lev. 22:10, 12. *To eat blood*, Lev. 17:10. *To blaspheme*, Lev. 24:16.

v.23–1494 BC
See footnote, *Time*, Rev. 10:6.

unto the LORD thy God, which thou hast promised with thy mouth.

24 ¶ [r,s]When[Q] thou comest into thy neighbour's vineyard, then[C] thou mayest eat grapes thy fill at thine own pleasure; but thou shalt not [t]put *any* in thy vessel.

25 When thou comest into the standing [u,v]corn[C] of thy neighbour, then thou mayest pluck the ears with thine hand; but thou shalt not move a ‖sickle unto thy neighbour's standing corn.[Q]

## CHAPTER 24

*Of divorce. 5 The newly married man exempt from going to war. 7 Of manstealers. 8 Of leprosy. 10 Of pledges. 14 Of the hire of a servant. 16 Of justice. 19 Of charity.*

WHEN a [a]man hath taken a wife, and [b]married her, and it come to pass that she find no favour in his eyes, because he hath found some [1]uncleanness in her: then let him write her a bill of [c]divorcement[C], and give *it* in her hand, and send her out of his house.[Q]

2 And when she is departed out of his house, she may go and be another man's *wife*.

3 And *if* the latter [a]husband hate her, and write her a bill of [c]divorcement, and giveth *it* in her hand, and sendeth her out of his house; or if the latter husband die, which took her *to be* his wife;[Q]

4 Her former [a]husband, which sent her away, may not take her again to be his wife, after that she is defiled; for that *is* [d]abomination[C] before the LORD: and thou shalt not cause the [e]land to sin, which the LORD thy God giveth thee *for* an inheritance.

5 ¶ When a [a,f]man hath [b]taken a new wife, [g]he shall not go out to [h]war, neither shall he be charged with any business: *but* he shall be free at home one year, and shall cheer up his wife which he hath taken.

6 ¶ [i,j,k]No [l]man shall take the nether[C] or the upper [m]millstone to [n]pledge: for he taketh *a man's* life to pledge.

7 ¶ If a man be found [o,p]stealing any of his brethren of the children of Ĭṣ′ra-el, and [2,q]maketh merchandise of him, or selleth him; then that *thief shall [r]die; and thou shalt put[Q] evil away from among you.

8 ¶ Take heed in the plague of [s]leprosy, that thou observe[C] diligently, and do according to all that the [t]priests the Lē′vītes shall [u]teach you: as I commanded them, *so* ye shall observe to do.

9 Remember what the LORD thy God did unto [v]Mĭr′ĭ-am by the way, after that ye were come forth out of [w]Ē′ġўpt.

10 ¶ [j,x]When [l]thou dost [k]lend thy [3]brother any thing, thou shalt not go into his [y]house to fetch[C] his [n]pledge.[C]

11 [l]Thou shalt stand abroad, and the man to whom thou dost [k]lend shall bring out the [n]pledge abroad unto thee.

12 [x]And if the man *be* [z]poor, [a]thou shalt not sleep with his [b]pledge:[C]

13 In any case [a]thou shalt deliver [c]him the [b]pledge again when the sun goeth down, that he may sleep in his own raiment, and bless thee: and [d]it shall be righteousness unto thee before the LORD thy God.

14 ¶ [†,e,f]Thou shalt not op-

**24**
r *Commandment, forbidding theft*, Deut. 8:2.
s *Agriculture, laws concerning trespass*, Gen. 3:23.
t *Theft*, Mark 7:22.

**25**
u *Corn*, Psa. 65:13.
v *Property, personal*, Lev. 27.15.

**1**
a *Husband*, Num. 30:6.
b *Marriage*, Gen. 34:9.
c *Divorce*, Matt. 19:7.
1 R. V. unseemly thing

**4**
d *Abomination*, Lev. 18:27.
e *Canaan*, Gen. 37:1.

v.5–1494 BC
See footnote, *Time*, Rev. 10:6.

**5**
f *Bridegroom*, Isa. 61:10.
g *Armies, who are exempt from service in*, Deut. 11:4.
h *War*, Judg. 3:2.

**6**
i *Commandment, enjoining mercy to debtors*, Deut. 8:2.
j *Debt*, 1 Sam. 22:2.
k *Lending*, Deut. 15:2.
l *Creditor*, Deut. 15:2.
m *Millstone*, Judg. 9:53.
n *Pawn*, Job 24:3.

**7**
o *Kidnapping*, Ex. 21:16.
p *Servant, man-stealing forbidden*, Jer. 2:14.
q *Commerce, slaves*, 1 Kin. 10:15.
r *Punishment, death penalty*, Lev. 26:41.
2 R. V. he deal with him as a slave,

**8**
s *Leprosy*, Lev. 13:2.
t *Priest, duties of, to teach the law*, Lev. 1:5.
u *Instruction, in sanitation and hygiene*, Prov. 23:23.

**9**
v *Miriam*, Ex. 15:20.
w *Egypt*, Gen. 41:8.

**10**
x *Commandment, protecting debtors*, Deut. 8:2.
y *House, a man's castle*, Esth. 8:1.
3 R. V. neighbor

**12**
z *Poor, duty to*, Prov. 21:13.

a *Creditor*, Deut. 15:2.
b *Pawn*, Job 24:3.

**13**
c *Debtor*, Luke 7:41.
d *Works, good*, 2 Tim. 1:9.

**14**
e *Commandment, forbidding oppression of the poor*, Deut. 8:2.
f *Master, duties of, to servants*, Col. 4:1.

‖ **SICKLE.** *Used for cutting grain*, Deut. 23:25; Jer. 50:16; Mark 4:29.
**Figurative:** *Of the judgments of God*, Joel 3:13; Rev. 14:14–19.

* **THIEVES**, Matt. 6:19, 20; John 10:1; Rom. 2:21; 1 Pet. 4:15; Rev. 3:3. *Ignominious*, Jer. 2:26. *Desecrated the temple*, Matt. 21:13; Mark 11:17; Luke 19:45, 46. *Excluded from the kingdom of God*, 1 Cor. 6:10. *Collusion with*, Psa. 50:18. ***Worship of, offensive to God***, Jer. 7:9, 10. *Penalty for*, Deut. 24:7; Prov. 6:30, 31; Ezek. 18:10, 13; Zech. 5:3; Matt. 27:38, 44; Mark 15:27.
See footnote, THEFT, Mark 7:22.

† **EMPLOYER. Required:** *To be kind*, Lev. 25:40–43; Job 31:13–15; Eph. 6:9; Phil. 15, 16. *To grant Sabbath rest*, Ex. 20:10; Deut. 5:14. *To accord just compensation*, Jer. 22:13; Matt. 10:10; 20:1–15; Luke 10:7; Rom. 4:4; Col. 4:1; 1 Tim. 5:18. *To make prompt payment*, Lev. 19:13; Deut. 24:15; Jas. 5:4, 5. ***Not to oppress***, Deut. 24:14; Mal. 3:5.

v.14–1494 BC
See footnote, *Time*, Rev. 10:6.

*g Hired Servant,* Lev. 25:40.
*h Poor, oppression of,* Prov. 21:13.
*i Foreigners, Israelites forbidden to oppress,* Deut. 23:20.
15
*j Wages,* Gen. 31:7.
16
*k* 2 Kin. 14:6; 2 Chr. 25:4.
*l Punishment, not entailed on children,* Lev. 26:41.
*m Sin, punishment for, not to be inflicted on children,* Rom. 5:12.
17
*n Commandment, forbidding perversion of justice,* Deut. 8:2.
*o Injustice, forbidden,* Isa. 26:10.
*p Foreigners, justice toward, enjoined,* Deut. 23:20.
*q Orphan, justice to, required,* Lam. 5:3.
*r Widow,* 2 Sam. 14:5.
18
*s Servant,* Jer. 2:14.
*t Egypt,* Gen. 41:8.
*u God, providence of,* Gen. 2:2.
19
*v Commandment, enjoining liberality to the poor,* Deut. 8:2.
*w Gleaning, laws concerning,* Lev. 23:22.
*x Liberality, enjoined,* vs. 19–21; 1 Tim. 6:18.
*y Poor, gleanings reserved for,* Prov. 21:13.
*z Orphan,* Lam. 5:3.

*a Widow,* 2 Sam. 14:5.
*b Reward, a motive to bestow charity,* Matt. 5:12.
20
*c Olive,* Deut. 6:11.
*d Poor, gleanings reserved for,* Prov. 21:13.
*e Orphan, beneficent provision for,* Lam. 5:3.
21
*f Grape,* Lev. 25:5.
*g Gleaning, laws concerning,* Lev. 23:22.

press an [‡,g]hired servant *that is*
[h]poor and needy, *whether he be*
of thy brethren, or of thy [i]stran-
gers[G] that *are* in thy land within
thy gates:[Q]
15 At[G] his day [†,j]thou shalt give
[‡]*him* his [j]hire[G], neither shall the
sun go down upon it; for he *is*
poor, and setteth his heart upon
it: lest he cry against thee unto
the LORD, and it be sin unto
thee.[Q]
16 ¶ [‖,k]The fathers shall not be
put to death for the children,
[l]neither shall the children be put
to death for the fathers: every
man shall be put to death for his
own [m]sin.
17 ¶ [a,n,o]Thou shalt not pervert the judgment[G] of the [p]stran-
ger[G], *nor* of the [q]fatherless; nor
take a [r]widow's raiment to
[b]pledge:
18 But thou shalt remember
that thou wast a [s]bondman[G] in
[t]E'gypt, and the LORD thy [u]God
redeemed thee thence: therefore
I command thee to do this thing.
19 ¶ [v,w]When thou cuttest
down thine harvest in thy field,
and hast forgot a sheaf in the
field, [x]thou shalt not go again
to fetch it: it shall be for the
[p,y]stranger[G], for the [y,z]fatherless,
and for the [a,d]widow: [b]that the
LORD thy God may bless thee
in all the work of thine hands.
20 When thou beatest thine
[c]olive tree, thou shalt not go over
the boughs again: it shall be for
the [d]stranger[G], for the [d,e]father-
less, and for the [a,d]widow.
21 When thou gatherest the
[f]grapes of thy vineyard, thou
shalt not [g]glean *it* afterward: it
shall be for the [d]stranger[G], for
the [d,e]fatherless, and for the
[a,d]widow.

22 And thou shalt remember
that thou wast a [h]bondman[G] in
the land of [i]E'gypt: therefore I
command thee to do this thing.

## CHAPTER 25

*Stripes not to exceed forty. 4 The ox not to be muzzled. 5 Of raising seed unto a brother. 11 Of the immodest woman. 13 Of unjust weights. 17 The memory of Amalek is to be blotted out.*

[a]IF there be a controversy between men, and they come
unto [b]judgment, that *the* [c,d]*judg-*
*es* may judge them; then they
shall [e]justify[G] the righteous, and
condemn the wicked.[T]
2 And it shall be, if the wicked
man *be* worthy[G] to be beaten, that
the [c,d]judge shall cause him to
lie down, and to be [f,g]beaten before his face, according to his
fault, by a certain number.
3 [h]Forty stripes he may give
him, *and* not exceed: lest, *if* he
should exceed, and [f,g]beat him
above these with many stripes,
then thy brother should seem
vile unto thee.
4 ¶ [i,j]Thou shalt not muzzle
the [k]ox when he [l,m]treadeth[G] out
*the corn*.[G][Q]
5 ¶ If brethren dwell together,
and one of them die, and have
no child, the [n]wife of the dead
shall not [o]marry without[G] unto a
[p]stranger[G]: her husband's [q]broth-
er shall go in unto her, and take
her to him to wife, and perform
the duty of an husband's brother
unto her.[Q]
6 And it shall be, *that* the
[r]firstborn which she beareth
shall [s]succeed in the name of his
brother *which is* dead, that his
name be not put out of Is'ra-el.
7 And if the man like[G] not to
[o]take his brother's [n]wife, then
let his brother's wife go up to the
gate unto the [t,u]elders, and say,

v.22–1494 BC
See footnote, *Time*, Rev. 10:6.

22
*h Servant,* Jer. 2:14.
*i Egypt,* Gen. 41:8.

1
*a Commandment, enjoining justice in courts,* Deut. 8:2.
*b Court, justice required of,* Ex. 18:26.
*c Judge, precepts relating to,* Judg. 2:18.
*d Rulers, duties of,* Ex. 18:21.
*e Justice,* Deut. 33:21.
2
*f Scourging,* Acts 22:24.
*g Punishment, by scourging,* Lev. 26:41.

3
*h Forty, stripes,* Jonah 3:4.
4
*i Commandment, enjoining kindness to animals,* Deut. 8:2.
*j* 1 Cor. 9:9; 1 Tim. 5:18.
*k Animals, kindness to,* Jer. 27:5
*l Labor, compensation for,* Luke 10:7.
*m Threshing,* 1 Chr. 21:20.
5
*n Widow,* 2 Sam. 14:5.
*o Marriage, levirate,* Gen. 34:9.
*p Foreigners,* Deut. 23:20.
*q Brother, levirate marriage of,* vs. 5–10; Prov. 18:24.

6
*r Firstborn,* Zech. 12:10.
*s Inheritance,* Num. 27:7.

7
*t Court, civil,* Ex. 18:26.
*u Government, municipal,* Isa. 22:21.

‡ **EMPLOYEE.** *Character of unrighteous,* Job 7:1–3; 14:1, 6; Matt. 20:1–15.
**Rights of:** *Just compensation,* Matt. 10:10; Luke 10:7; Rom. 4:4; Col. 4:1; 1 Tim. 5:18. *Prompt payment,* Lev. 19:13. *Hebrew, to participation in products of the land during Sabbatic year,* Lev. 25:6.

**Kindness to:** *Exemplified,* Ruth 2:4; Luke 15:17, 19.
**Oppressions of,** Prov. 22:16; Mal. 3:5; Luke 15:15–17; Jas. 5:4.

‖ **INNOCENT.** *Shall not suffer for the guilty,* Deut. 24:16; 2 Kin. 14:6; 2 Chr. 25:4; Jer. 31:29, 30; Ezek. 18:20.

v.7–1494 BC
See footnote, *Time*, Rev. 10:6.

My husband's brother refuseth
to raise up unto his brother a
name in Is'ra-el, he will not perform the duty of my husband's
brother.
8 Then the [t,u]elders of his city
shall call him, and speak unto
him: and *if* he stand[c] *to it*, and
say, I like[c] not to take her;
9 Then shall his [q]brother's
[n]wife come unto him in the presence of the elders, and loose his
[v]shoe[c] from off his foot, and [w]spit
in his face, and shall answer and
say, So shall it be done unto that
man that will not build up his
brother's house.
10 And his name shall be called
in Is'ra-el, The house of him
that hath his [v]shoe loosed.
11 ¶ When men [x]strive together one with another, and the
wife of the one draweth near for
to deliver her husband out of the
hand of him that smiteth him,
and putteth forth her hand, and
taketh him by the secrets[c]:
12 Then thou shalt cut off her
hand, thine eye shall not [y]pity
*her*.
13 ¶ [z,a]Thou shalt not have in
thy bag divers[c] [b]weights, a great
and a small.
14 [c]Thou shalt not have in
thine house divers[c] *measures, a
great and a small.
15 *But* thou shalt [d]have a perfect and just [b]weight, a perfect
and just *measure shalt thou
have: [e,f,g]that thy days may be
lengthened in the land which
the LORD thy God giveth thee.
16 For all that do such things,
*and* all that do [h]unrighteously,
*are* an [i]abomination[c] unto the
LORD thy God.
17 ¶ Remember what [j]Ăm'a-
lĕk did unto [k]thee by the way,
when ye were come forth out of
[l]Ē'ġўpt;
18 How [j]he met [k]thee by the
way, and smote the hindmost[c] of
thee, *even* all *that were* feeble behind thee, when thou *wast* faint
and weary; and he feared not
God.
19 Therefore it shall be, when
the LORD thy [m]God hath given
thee rest from all thine enemies
round about, in the [n]land which
the LORD thy God giveth thee
*for* an inheritance to possess it,
*that* [k]thou shalt [o]blot out the
remembrance of [j]Ăm'a-lĕk from
under heaven; thou shalt not
forget *it*.

## CHAPTER 26

*The profession of him that offers the basket of first fruits. 12 The prayer of him that gives his third year's tithes. 16 The covenant between God and the people.*

AND it shall be, when thou
*art* come in unto the
[a]land which the LORD thy [b]God
giveth thee *for* an inheritance,
and possessest it, and dwellest
therein;

**9**
v *Shoe*, Josh. 5:15.
w *Spitting*, Num. 12:14.

**11**
x *Strife*, Prov. 20:3.

**12**
y *Pity, not to be shown offenders*, Job 19:21.

**13**
z *Commandment, forbidding dishonesty in business*, Deut. 8:2.

a *Dishonesty, forbidden*, Ezek. 22:13.
b *Weights, must be just*, Lev. 19:35.

**14**
c *Commandment, forbidding dishonesty in business*, Deut. 8:2.

**15**
d *Honesty*, Rom. 13:13.

v.15–1494 BC
See footnote, *Time*, Rev. 10:6.

e *Reward, a motive to honesty*, Matt. 5:12.
f *Promise, to the honest, of long life*, 2 Cor. 1:20.
g *Faithfulness, rewards of*, Luke 16:10.

**16**
h *Sin, repugnant to God*, Rom. 5:12.
i *Abomination*, Lev. 18:27.

**17**
j *Amalekites*, Num. 13:29.
k *Israel*, Ex. 4:22.
l *Egypt*, Gen. 41:8.

**19**
m *God, providence of*, Gen. 2:2.
n *Canaan*, Gen. 37:1.
o *Retaliation*, Deut. 19:19.

**1**
a *Canaan*, Gen. 37:1.
b *God, providence of*, Gen. 2:2.

* **MEASURE.** *False*, Hos. 12:7–9. *False, an abomination*, Prov. 11:1; 20:10, 23; Mic. 6:10–12. *Just, required*, Lev. 19:35, 36; Deut. 25:13–16; Prov. 16:11.

The following modern equivalents of ancient measurements are based upon the latest researches, and are probably as nearly correct as it is possible at this time to make them:

**Dry:** BUSHEL, *about a peck*, Matt. 5:15; Mark 4:21; Luke 11:33.

CAB, or kab, *about two quarts*, 2 Kin. 6:25.

COR, *equal to one homer or ten ephahs, equal to about eleven bushels*, 1 Kin. 4:22; 5:11; 2 Chr. 2:10; 27:5; Ezra 7:22; Ezek. 45:14.

EPHAH, *equal to three seah (and in liquid, to a bath), containing about a bushel*, Ex. 16:36; Lev. 5:11; 6:20; 19:36; Num. 5:15; 28:5; Judg. 6:19; Ruth 2:17; 1 Sam. 1:24; 17:17; Isa. 5:10; Ezek. 45:10, 11, 13, 24; 46:5, 7, 11, 14; Amos 8:5; Zech. 5:6–10.

HALF-HOMER, *about five and a half bushels*, Hos. 3:2.

HOMER, *about eleven bushels, equal to a cor or ten ephahs*, Lev. 27:16; Num. 11:32; Isa. 5:10; Ezek. 45:11–14; Hos. 3:2.

OMER, *about seven pints*, Ex. 16:16, 18, 22, 32, 33, 36.

SEAH, *about a peck and a half*, Gen. 18:6; 1 Sam. 25:18; 1 Kin. 18:32; 2 Kin. 7:1, 16, 18.

TENTH DEAL, *about a gallon, equal to one-tenth of an ephah*, Ex. 29:40; Lev. 14:10, 21; 23:13, 17; 24:5; Num. 15:4, 6, 9; 28:9, 12, 13, 20, 21, 28, 29; 29:3, 4, 9, 10, 14, 15.

**Liquid:** BATH, *about eight gallons and a half*, 1 Kin. 7:26, 38; 2 Chr. 2:10; 4:5; Ezra 7:22; Isa. 5:10; Ezek. 45:10, 11, 14; Luke 16:6.

FIRKIN, *nearly nine gallons*, John 2:6.

HIN, *about a gallon and a half*, Ex. 29:40; 30:24; Lev. 19:36; 23:13; Num. 15:4–10; 28:5, 7, 14; Ezek. 4:11; 45:24; 46:5, 7, 11, 14.

LOG, *about a pint, one-twelfth of a hin*, Lev. 14:10, 12, 15, 21, 24.

**Linear:** CUBIT, *about seventeen and a half inches, the length of the forearm*. See footnote, CUBIT, Ex. 36:9.

FATHOM, *about six feet*, Acts 27:28.

FINGER, *about three-fourths of an inch*, Jer. 52:21.

FURLONG, Luke 24:13.

HANDBREADTH, *about three inches*, Ex. 25:25; 37:12; 1 Kin. 7:26; 2 Chr. 4:5; Psa. 39:5; Ezek. 40:5, 43; 43:13.

MILE, probably nine-tenths of an English mile, Matt. 5:41.

PACE, 2 Sam. 6:13.

REED, *probably six cubits*, Ezek. 40:5.

SABBATH DAY'S JOURNEY (the distance is uncertain, probably 1,000 yards), Acts 1:12.

SPAN, *about nine inches*, Ex. 28:16; 1 Sam. 17:4; Isa. 40:12; Ezek. 43:13.

v.2–1494 BC
See footnote, *Time*, Rev. 10:6.

**2**
c *First Fruits, offerings of, presented at the tabernacle*, Deut. 18:4.
d *Basket*, Ex. 29:3.
e *Tabernacle*, Ex. 27:9.

**3**
f *Priest, duties of*, Lev. 1:5.
g *Patriotism*, vs. 1–11; Psa. 137:1.

**5**
h *Egypt*, Gen. 41:8.
i *Israel, number of, who went into Egypt*, Ex. 4:22.

**6**
j *Egyptians*, Gen. 50:3.
k *Servant, cruelty to*, Jer. 2:14.

**7**
l *Prayer, answered*, Acts 6:4.
m *Afflictions*, Psa. 34:19.

**8**
n *Miracles*, Luke 23:8.

**9**
o *Milk, figurative*, Job 10:10.
p *Honey, figurative*, Prov. 25:27.

2 That thou shalt take of the
[c]first of all the fruit of the earth,
which thou shalt bring of thy
[a]land that the LORD thy God
giveth thee, and shalt put *it* in a
[d]basket, and shalt go unto the
[e]place which the LORD thy God
shall choose to place[C] his name
there.
3 And thou shalt go unto the
[f]priest that shall be in those
days, and say unto him, [g]I profess[C]
this day unto the LORD thy
God, that I am come unto the
country which the LORD sware
unto our fathers for to give
us.
4 And the [f]priest shall take the
[d]basket out of thine hand, and
set it down before the altar of the
LORD thy God.
5 And thou shalt speak and say
before the LORD thy God, A
Sўr′ĭ-an ready to perish *was* my
father, and he went down into
[h]Ē′ġȳpt, and sojourned there
with a [i]few, and became there a
nation, great, mighty, and populous:
6 And the [j]Ē-ġȳp′tians evil[C] entreated[C]
us, and afflicted us, and
laid upon [k]us hard bondage[C]:
7 And when we cried unto the
LORD God of our fathers, the
LORD heard our [l]voice, and
looked on our [m]affliction, and
our labour, and our oppression:
8 And the [b]LORD brought us
forth out of [h]Ē′ġȳpt with a
mighty hand, and with an outstretched
arm, and with great
terribleness[C], and with [n]signs,
and with wonders:
9 And he hath brought us into
this place, and hath given us
this [a]land, *even* a land that floweth
with [o]milk and [p]honey.
10 And now, behold, I have
brought the [c]firstfruits of the
[a]land, which [b]thou, O LORD,
hast given me. And thou shalt
set it before the LORD thy God,
and worship before the LORD
thy God:
11 And thou shalt [q]rejoice in
every good *thing* which the
LORD thy God hath given unto
thee, and unto thine house, thou,
and the Lē′vīte, and the stranger[C]
that *is* among you.
12 ¶ When thou hast made an
end of tithing all the [r]tithes of
thine increase the third year,
*which is* the year of tithing, and
hast given [s]*it* unto the Lē′vīte,
the [t]stranger[C], the [u]fatherless,
and the [v]widow, that they may
eat within thy gates, and be
filled;
13 Then thou shalt say before
the LORD thy God, I have
brought away the hallowed[C]
things out of *mine* house, and
also have given [s]them unto the
Lē′vīte, and unto the [t]stranger[C],
to the [u]fatherless, and to the
[v]widow, [w]according to all thy
commandments which thou hast
commanded me: I have not
transgressed thy commandments,
neither have I forgotten
*them*:
14 I have not eaten thereof in
my [x]mourning, neither have I
taken away *ought*[C] thereof for *any*
unclean[C] *use*, nor given *ought*
thereof for the dead: *but* I have
hearkened to the voice of the
LORD my God, *and* have [w]done
according to all that thou hast
commanded me.
15 Look down from thy holy
habitation, from [y]heaven, and
[z]bless thy people Ĭṣ′ra-el, and
the land which thou hast given
us, as [a]thou swarest unto our fathers,
a land that floweth with
milk and honey.
16 ¶ [b]This day the LORD thy
God hath commanded thee to
[c]do these statutes and judgments[C]:
thou shalt therefore keep
and do them with all thine
[d]heart, and with all thy soul.[S]

v.10–1494 BC
See footnote, *Time*, Rev. 10:6.

**11**
q *Thankfulness, enjoined*, Acts 24:3.

**12**
r *Tithes*, Num. 18:24.
s *Levites, emoluments of*, Deut. 10:8.
t *Poor, duty to*, Prov. 21:13.
u *Orphan, beneficent provision for*, Lam. 5:3.
v *Widow*, 2 Sam. 14:5.

**13**
w *Obedience*, Heb. 5:8.

**14**
x *Mourning*, Lam. 2:5.

**15**
y *Heaven, God's dwelling place*, Luke 18:22.
z *Temporal Blessings, prayer for*, Psa. 103:2.

a *God, faithfulness of*, Gen. 2:2.

**16**
b *Commandment, enjoining obedience*, Deut. 8:2.
c *Obedience, enjoined*, Heb. 5:8.
d *Heart*, Psa. 44:21.

v.17–1494 BC
See footnote, *Time,* Rev. 10:6.

**17**

e *Decision, instances of, Israelites,* Isa. 50:7.

**18**

f *God, love of, exemplified,* Gen. 2:2.
g *Spiritual Adoption, of Israel,* Rom. 8:15.
h *Israel, a holy people,* Ex. 4:22.
i *The Holy, described,* Col. 3:12.

**19**

j *God, providence of,* Gen. 2:2.
k *Temporal Blessings, from God, national greatness,* Psa. 103:2.
l *Holiness,* Ex. 39:30.

**1**

a *Senate,* Num. 11:16.
b *Israel,* Ex. 4:22.
c *Commandment, enjoining obedience,* Deut. 8:2.
d *Obedience, enjoined,* Heb. 5:8.

**2**

e *Jordan,* Gen. 32:10.
f *Canaan,* Gen. 37:1.
g *God, providence of,* Gen. 2:2.
h *Pillar,* Gen. 28:18.

**3**

i *Law, of Moses, engraved upon monuments,* Deut. 33:2.
j *Milk, figurative,* Job 10:10.
k *Honey, figurative,* Prov. 25:27.

**4**

l *Ebal,* Deut. 11:29.

**5**

m *Altar,* Gen. 8:20.

17 Thou hast [e]avouched[C] the LORD this day to be thy God, and to walk in his ways, and to keep his statutes, and his commandments, and his judgments,[C] and to hearken unto his voice:

18 And the [f]LORD hath [g]avouched[C] [h]thee this day to be his [i]peculiar[C] people, as [a]he hath promised thee, and that *thou* shouldest [c]keep all his commandments;

19 And [j]to [k]make thee high above all nations which he hath made, in praise, and in name, and in honour; and that thou mayest be an [h,l]holy[C] people unto the LORD thy God, as he hath spoken.[S]

## CHAPTER 27

*The people are commanded to write the law upon stones; 5 and to build an altar of whole stones. 11 The tribes divided on Gerizim and Ebal. 14 The curses pronounced from mount Ebal.*

AND Mō'ṣeṣ with the [a]elders of [b]Ĭṣ'ra-el commanded the people, saying, [c,d]Keep[C] all the commandments which I command you this day.

2 And it shall be on the day when ye shall pass over [e]Jôr'dan unto the [f]land which the LORD thy [g]God giveth thee, that thou shalt [h]set thee up great stones, and plaister them with plaister:

3 And thou shalt write upon them all the words of this [i]law, when thou art passed over, that thou mayest go in unto the [f]land which the LORD thy [g]God giveth thee, a land that floweth with [j]milk and [k]honey; as the LORD God of thy fathers hath promised thee.

4 Therefore it shall be when ye be gone over [e]Jôr'dan, *that* ye shall set up these stones, which I command you this day, in mount [l]Ē'bal, and thou shalt plaister them with plaister.

5 And there shalt thou build an [m]altar unto the LORD thy God, an altar of stones: thou shalt not lift up *any* iron *tool* upon them.

6 Thou shalt build the [m]altar of the LORD thy God of whole[C] stones: and thou shalt offer [n]burnt offerings thereon unto the LORD thy God:

7 And thou shalt offer [o]peace offerings, and shalt eat there, and rejoice before the LORD thy God.

8 And thou shalt write upon the stones all the words of this [i]law very plainly.

9 ¶ And Mō'ṣeṣ and the priests the Lē'vītes spake unto all [b]Ĭṣ'ra-el, saying, [1,p]Take heed, and hearken, O Ĭṣ'ra-el; this day thou art [q]become the people of the LORD thy [r]God.

10 [s,t]Thou shalt therefore obey the voice of the LORD thy God, and do his commandments and his statutes, which I command thee this day.

11 ¶ And Mō'ṣeṣ charged the [b]people the same day, saying,

12 [u]These shall stand upon mount [v]Gĕr'ĭ-zĭm to [w]bless the people, when ye are come over Jôr'dan; [x]Sĭm'e-on, and [y]Lē'vī, and [z]Jū'dah, and [a]Ĭs'sa-char, and [b,c]Jō'ṣeph, and [d]Bĕn'ja-mĭn:

13 And these shall stand upon mount [e]Ē'bal to [f]curse; [g]Reu'ben, [h]Găd, and [i]Āsh'ĕr, and [j]Zĕb'u-lŭn, [k]Dăn, and [l]Năph'ta-lī.

14 ¶ And the [m]Lē'vītes shall speak, and [n]say unto all the men of Ĭṣ'ra-el with a loud voice,

15 [f,o]Cursed *be* the man that maketh *any* graven[C] or molten[C] [p]image, an [q]abomination[C] unto the LORD, the work of the hands of the craftsman,[C] and putteth *it* in *a* secret[C] *place.* And all the people shall answer and say, Amen.

16 [f]Cursed *be* [r]he that setteth[C] light by his father or his mother. And all the people shall say, Amen.

v.5–1494 BC
See footnote, *Time,* Rev. 10:6.

**6**

n *Offerings, burnt,* Lev. 6:17.

**7**

o *Offerings, peace,* Lev. 6:17.

**9**

p *Watchfulness, enjoined,* Matt. 24:42.
q *Spiritual Adoption,* Rom. 8:15
r *God, love of, exemplified,* Gen. 2:2.
1 R. V. Keep silence,

**10**

s *Commandment, enjoining obedience,* Deut. 8:2.
t *Obedience, enjoined,* Heb. 5:8.

**12**

u *Law, of Moses, blessings and curses of,* Deut. 33:2.
v *Gerizim,* Deut. 11:29.
w *Benedictions,* Deut. 21:5.
x *Simeon, tribe of,* Num. 2:12.
y *Levites,* Deut. 10:8.
z *Judah, tribe of,* Num. 10:14.

a *Issachar, tribe of,* Num. 1:28.
b *Ephraim, tribe of,* Gen. 41:52.
c *Manasseh, tribe of,* Gen. 46:20.
d *Benjamin, tribe of,* Num. 1:37.

**13**

e *Ebal,* Deut. 11:29.
f *Curse,* Judg. 5:23.
g *Reubenites,* Josh. 22:1.
h *Gad, tribe of,* Deut. 33:20.
i *Asher, tribe of,* Num. 1:40.
j *Zebulun, tribe of,* Gen. 49:13.
k *Dan, tribe of,* Gen. 30:6.
l *Naphtali, tribe of,* Num. 1:42.

**14**

m *Levites,* Deut. 10:8.
n *Instruction, in religion,* Prov. 23:23.

**15**

o *Idolatry, denounced,* 1 Sam. 15:23.
p *Idol, manufacture of, forbidden,* 1 Kin. 15:12.
q *Abomination,* Lev. 18:27.

**16**

r *Children, wicked,* Mark 10:14.

v.17–1494 BC
See footnote, *Time*, Rev. 10:6.

**17**
*s Landmarks, protected from fraudulent removal,* Deut. 19:14.

**19**
*t Injustice, forbidden,* Isa. 26:10.
*u Court, justice required of,* Ex. 18:26.
*v Foreigners, justice toward, enjoined,* Deut. 23:20.
*w Orphan, justice to, required,* Lam. 5:3.
*x Widow,* 2 Sam. 14:5.

**20**
*y Adultery, penalties for,* Lev. 20:10.
*z Incest, forbidden,* Lev. 18:6.

**21**
*a Curse,* Judg. 5:23.
*b Bestiality,* Lev. 18:23.

**22**
*c Incest, forbidden,* Lev. 18:6.

**23**
*d Mother-in-law, not to be defiled,* Matt. 10:35.

**24**
*e Homicide, felonious,* Deut. 5:17.

**25**
*f Bribery,* 1 Sam. 8:3.

**26**
*g* Gal. 3:10.
*h Law, of Moses,* Deut. 33:2.

**1**
*a Blessings, contingent upon obedience,* Deut. 11:26.

17 [f]Cursed *be* he that removeth
his neighbour's [s]landmark. And
all the people shall say, Amen.
18 [f]Cursed *be* he that maketh
the *blind to wander out of the
way. And all the people shall
say, Amen.
19 [f,t,u]Cursed *be* he that perverteth[c] the judgment[c] of the
[v]stranger,[c] [w]fatherless, and [x]wid-
ow. And all the people shall say,
Amen.
20 [f]Cursed *be* he that [y,z]lieth
with his father's wife; because
he uncovereth his father's skirt.
And all the people shall say,
Amen.[Q]
21 [a]Cursed *be* he that [b]lieth
with any manner of beast. And
all the people shall say, Amen.
22 [a]Cursed *be* he that [c]lieth
with his sister, the daughter of
his father, or the daughter of his
mother. And all the people shall
say, Amen.
23 [a]Cursed *be* he that [c]lieth
with his [d]mother in law. And all
the people shall say, Amen.
24 [a]Cursed *be* he that †,[e]smit-
eth[c] his neighbour secretly. And
all the people shall say, Amen.
25 [a]Cursed *be* he that taketh
[f]reward to slay an innocent person. And all the people shall
say, Amen.
26 [a,g]Cursed *be* he that confirmeth[c] not *all* the words of this
[h]law to do them. And all the
people shall say, Amen.[Q]

## CHAPTER 28

*The blessings for obedience.* 15 *The curses for disobedience.*

AND it shall come to pass,
[a]if thou shalt hearken diligently unto the voice of the
LORD thy God, to observe *and*
to [b]do all his commandments
which I command thee this day,
[c]that the LORD thy God [d,e]will
set thee on high above all nations of the earth:[s]
2[s]And [c]all these [a]blessings shall
come on [d]thee, and overtake
thee, [a]if thou shalt hearken[c] unto
the voice of the LORD thy God.
3 [c,f]Blessed *shalt* [d]thou *be* in the
city, and blessed *shalt* thou *be* in
the field.
4 [c,f]Blessed *shall be* the fruit[c] of
thy body, and the fruit of thy
ground, and the fruit of thy cattle, the increase of thy kine,[c] and
the flocks of thy sheep.[Q]
5 [c,f]Blessed *shall be* thy [g]basket
and thy [1,h]store.[c s]
6 [c,f]Blessed *shalt* [d]thou *be* when
thou comest in, and blessed *shalt*
thou *be* when thou goest out.[s]
7 *,[c]The [e]LORD shall [f]cause
thine enemies that rise up
against thee to be smitten[c] before
thy face: they shall come out
against thee one way, and flee
before thee seven ways.[s]
8 [c]The [e]LORD shall command
the [f]blessing upon thee in thy
storehouses, and in all that thou
settest thine hand unto; and he
shall bless thee in the land
which the LORD thy God giveth
thee.[s]
[s]
9 [i]The [j]LORD shall [a]establish
thee an [k]holy people unto himself, as he hath sworn unto thee,
[a]if thou shalt keep the commandments of the LORD thy God, and
[l]walk in his ways.
10 And all people of the earth
shall see that thou art [m]called
by the name of the LORD; and
they shall be afraid of thee.
11 And the [e]LORD shall make
thee plenteous[c] [2]in [f]goods, and

v.1–1494 BC
See footnote, *Time*, Rev. 10:6.

*b Obedience, rewarded,* Heb. 5:8.
*c Promise, to obedient, of prosperity,* 2 Cor. 1:20.
*d Righteous, promises to,* Psa. 64:10.
*e God, providence of,* Gen. 2:2.

**3**
*f Temporal Blessings, from God,* Psa. 103:2.

**5**
*g Basket,* Ex. 29:3.
*h Kneading-trough,* Ex. 8:3.
1 R. V. kneading-trough.

**9**
*i Spiritual Blessings, from God,* Eph. 1:3.
*j God, love of, exemplified,* Gen. 2:2.
*k Holiness,* Ex. 39:30.
*l Walking, figurative,* Gen. 5:22.

**10**
*m Spiritual Adoption, of Israel,* Rom. 8:15.

**11**
2 R.V. for good.

* **BLIND.** *Cruelty to, forbidden,* Lev. 19:14; Deut. 27:18. *Hated by David,* 2 Sam. 5:8.
See footnote, BLINDNESS, 2 Kin. 6:18.

† **ASSASSINATION.** *Denounced,* Deut. 27:24. *David's abhorrence of,* 2 Sam. 4:9, 12.

**Instances of:** *Of Eglon, by Ehud,* Judg. 3:15–22. *Of Abner, by Joab,* 2 Sam. 3:27. *Of Ish-bosheth, by the sons of Rimmon,* 2 Sam. 4:5–7. *Of Amnon, by Absalom,* 2 Sam. 13:28, 29. *Of Amasa, by Joab,* 2 Sam. 20:9, 10. *Of Joash, by his servants,* 2 Kin. 12:20. *Of Sennacherib, by his sons,* 2 Kin. 19:37; Isa. 37:38.

* **VICTORIES.** *In battle, from God,* Lev. 26:6–9; Deut. 28:7; 32:30; Josh. 23:10; Psa. 55:18; 76:5, 6. *Celebrated in song,* Judg. 5; 2 Sam. 22; *by women,* Judg. 5; 1 Sam. 18:6, 7; 2 Sam. 1:20.

v.11–1494 BC
See footnote, *Time*, Rev. 10:6.

*n* *Canaan*, Gen. 37:1.
*o* *Covenant, of God with men*, Deut. 29:1.

**14**
*p* *Idolatry*, 1 Sam. 15:23.

**15**
*q* *Disobedience to God, denunciations against*, vs. 16–62; Eph. 5:6.
*r* *Curse*, Judg. 5:23.
*s* *Afflictions, from God*, vs. 15–68; Psa. 34:19.
*t* *Judgments, denounced against disobedience*, vs. 15–68; Ex. 6:6.
*u* *Wicked, punishment of*, vs. 15–68; Psa. 73:3.

**18**
3 R. V. young of thy flock.

**20**
*v* *Adversity, dispensation from God*, Psa. 10:6.

the fruit of thy body, and in the
fruit of thy cattle, and in the
fruit of thy ground, in the [n]land
which the LORD [o]sware unto thy
fathers to give thee.
12 The [e]LORD shall open unto
thee his good treasure, the heav-
en to give the rain unto thy land
in his season, and to bless all the
work of thine hand: and thou
shalt lend unto many nations,
and thou shalt not borrow.
13 And the [e]LORD shall [f]make
thee the head, and not the tail;
and thou shalt be above only,
and thou shalt not be beneath;
[a]if that thou hearken[C] unto the
commandments of the LORD thy
God, which I command thee
this day, to observe[C] and to do
*them*:[s]
14 And thou shalt not go aside
from any of the words which I
command thee this day, *to* the
right hand, or *to* the left, to go
after other gods to [p]serve them.
15 ¶ But it shall come to pass,
if thou wilt [q]not hearken[C] unto
the voice of the LORD thy God,
to observe to do all his commandments and his statutes
which I command thee this day;
that all these [r,s,t]curses shall
come upon [u]thee, and overtake
thee:
16 [r]Cursed *shalt* thou *be* in the
city, and cursed *shalt* thou *be* in
the field.
17 [r]Cursed *shall be* thy [g]basket
and thy [1,h]store.[C]
18 [r]Cursed *shall be* the fruit[C] of
thy body, and the fruit of thy
land, the increase of thy kine,[C]
and the [3]flocks of thy sheep.
19 [r]Cursed *shalt* thou *be* when
thou comest in, and cursed *shalt*
thou *be* when thou goest out.
20 The LORD shall send upon
thee [r]cursing, [s,v]vexation, and
rebuke, in all that thou settest
thine hand unto for to do, until
[u]thou be destroyed, and until
thou perish quickly; because of
the [w]wickedness of thy doings,
whereby thou hast forsaken me.[s]
21 The LORD shall make the
[x]pestilence[C] cleave[C] unto thee, until he have consumed[C] thee from
off the [n]land, whither thou goest
to possess it.
22 The LORD shall smite thee
with a [y]consumption, and with a
†fever, and with an inflammation, and with an extreme burning, and with the sword, and
with blasting,[C] and with [z]mil-
dew; and they shall pursue thee
until thou perish.
23 [a,b,c]And thy heaven that *is*
over thy head shall be brass, and
the earth that *is* under thee *shall*
*be* iron.
24 [a,b,c]The LORD shall make
the [d]rain of thy land powder and
dust: from heaven shall it come
down upon thee, until thou be
destroyed.
25 [a,e]The LORD shall cause
thee to be smitten before thine
enemies: thou shalt go out one
way against them, and flee seven
ways before them: and shalt be
[4]removed into all the kingdoms
of the earth.
26 [a]And thy carcase shall be
meat[C] unto all fowls of the air,
and unto the beasts of the earth,
and no man shall fray[C] *them*
away.
27 The LORD will smite thee
with the [5,a,f]botch[C] of Ē′gy̆pt,
and with the [g]emerods,[C] and
with the [6,h]scab, and with the
itch, whereof thou canst not
be healed.
28 The LORD shall smite thee
with [a,i]madness,[C] and [j]blindness,
and astonishment[C] of heart:
29 [a]And thou shalt grope at
noonday, as the [j]blind gropeth
in darkness, and thou shalt not
prosper in thy ways: and thou

v.20–1494 BC
See footnote, *Time*, Rev. 10:6.

*w* *Sin, punishment of*, Rom. 5:12.

**21**
*x* *Plague*, Ex. 11:1.

**22**
*y* *Consumption*, Lev. 26:16.
*z* Amos 4:9; Hag. 2:17.

**23**
*a* *Curse*, Judg. 5:23.
*b* *Drought, as a judgment*, Gen. 31:40.
*c* *Famine, as a judgment*, 2 Kin. 8:1.

**24**
*d* *Rain, withheld as a judgment*, 2 Sam. 1:21.

**25**
*e* *War, as a judgment*, Judg. 3:2.
4 R. V. tossed to and fro among

**27**
*f* *Boil*, Ex. 9:9.
*g* *Tumor*, 1 Sam. 5:6.
*h* *Scab*, Lev. 14:56.
5 R. V. boil
6 R. V. scurvy

**28**
*i* *Insanity, as a judgment from God*, Prov. 26:18.
*j* *Blindness*, 2 Kin. 6:18.

† **FEVER**, Lev. 26:16; Job 30:30; Psa. 22:15; Matt. 8:14; Acts 28:8. See footnote, DISEASE, Ex. 15:26.

v.29–1494 BC
See footnote, *Time*, Rev. 10:6.

shalt be only oppressed and
spoiled[c] evermore, and no man
shall save *thee*.
30 [a]Thou shalt betroth a wife,
and another man shall lie with
her: thou shalt build an house,
and thou shalt not dwell therein:
thou shalt plant a vineyard, and
shalt not gather the [k]grapes
thereof.
31 [a]Thine ox *shall be* slain before thine eyes, and thou shalt
not eat thereof: thine ass *shall*
*be* violently taken away from
before thy face, and shall not
be restored to thee: thy sheep
*shall be* given unto thine enemies, and thou shalt have none
to rescue *them*.
32 [a]Thy sons and thy daughters *shall be* given unto another
people, and thine eyes shall look,
and fail[c] *with longing* for them all
the day long: and *there shall be*
no might in thine hand.
33 [a]The fruit of thy land, and
all thy labours, shall a nation
which thou knowest not eat up[c];
and thou shalt be only oppressed
and crushed alway:
34 [a]So that thou shalt be [i]mad
for the sight of thine eyes which
thou shalt see.
35 [a]The LORD shall smite thee
in the knees, and in the legs,
with a sore [5,i]botch[c] that cannot
be healed, from the sole of thy
foot unto the top of thy head.[Q]
36 [a,l]The LORD shall bring
thee, and thy king which thou
shalt set over thee, unto a nation
which neither thou nor thy fathers have known; and there
shalt thou [m]serve other gods,
wood and [n]stone.
37 [a]And thou shalt become
an astonishment, a proverb, and
a byword, among all nations
whither the LORD shall lead
thee.
38 [a,c]Thou shalt carry much
seed out into the field, and shalt
gather *but* little in; for the [o]lo-
cust shall consume[c] it.
39 [a]Thou shalt plant vineyards, and dress *them*, but shalt
neither drink *of* the wine, nor
gather *the* [k]*grapes*; for the
[p]worms shall eat them.
40 [a]Thou shalt have [q]olive
trees throughout all thy coasts[c],
but thou shalt not [†]anoint *thy-*
*self* with the oil; for thine olive[c]
shall cast *his fruit*.
41 [a]Thou shalt beget sons and
daughters, but thou shalt not enjoy them; for they shall go into
[l]captivity[c].
42 [a]All thy trees and fruit of thy
land shall the [o]locust consume[c].
43 [a]The stranger[c] that *is* within
thee shall get up above thee very
high; and thou shalt come down
very low.
44 [a]He shall lend to thee, and
thou shalt not lend to him: he
shall be the head, and thou shalt
be the tail.
45 Moreover all these [a,r]curses
shall come upon thee, and shall
pursue thee, and overtake thee,
till thou be destroyed; because
thou [s]hearkenedst not unto the
voice of the LORD thy God, to
keep his commandments and his
statutes which he commanded
thee:
46 And they shall be upon thee
for a sign and for a wonder[c], and
upon thy seed for ever.
47 Because thou [t]servedst not
the LORD thy God with joyfulness, and with gladness of heart,
for the abundance of all *things*;
48 [a]Therefore shalt thou serve
thine enemies which the LORD

**30**
*k* *Grapes*, Lev. 25:5.

**36**
*l* *Captivity, of the Israelites, foretold*, Isa. 5:13.
*m* *Idolatry*, 1 Sam. 15:23.
*n* *Stones, idols made of*, Ex. 24:12.

v.37–1494 BC
See footnote, *Time*, Rev. 10:6.

**38**
*o* *Locust*, Nah. 3:17.

**39**
*p* *Worm*, Jonah 4:7.

**40**
*q* *Olive*, Deut. 6:11.

**45**
*r* *Judgments*, Ex. 6:6.
*s* *Disobedience to God*, Eph. 5:6.

**47**
*t* *Ingratitude, of man to God*, Rom. 1:21.

‡ **ANOINTING.** *Of the body*, Deut. 28:40; Ruth 3:3; Esth. 2:12; Psa. 92:10; 104:15; 141:5; Prov. 27:9, 16; Eccl. 9:8; Song 4:10; Isa. 57:9; Amos 6:6; Mic. 6:15. *Of guests*, Luke 7:46. *Of captives*, 2 Chr. 28:15. *Of the sick*, Isa. 1:6; Mark 6:13; Luke 10:34; Jas. 5:14; Rev. 3:18. *Of the dead*, Matt. 26:12; Mark 14:8; 16:1; Luke 23:56. *Of Jesus, as a token of love*, Luke 7:37, 38, 46; John 11:2; 12:3. See footnote, ANOINTING, *of High Priests, etc.*, page 173.
**Figurative:** *Of Christ's kingly and priestly office*, Psa. 45:7; Isa. 61:1; Dan. 9:24; Luke 4:18; Acts 4:27; 10:38; Heb. 1:9. *Of spiritual gifts*, 2 Cor. 1:21; 1 John 2:20, 27.
**Symbolical:** *Of Jesus*, Matt. 26:7–12; John 12:3–7.

v.48–1494 BC
See footnote, *Time*, Rev. 10:6.

**48**
*u* ***Iron, articles made of,*** Prov. 27:17.

**49**
*v* ***Israel, prophecies concerning,*** vs. 49–57; Ex. 4:22.
*w* ***Eagle,*** Lev. 11: 13.
*x* ***Language,*** Dan. 3:29.

**50**
*y* ***Countenance, fierce,*** Prov. 15: 13.

**51**
7 R. V. the young of thy flock,

**53**
*z* ***Cannibalism,*** Lam. 2:20.

**54**
*a* ***Curse,*** vs. 54–68; Judg. 5:23.

**55**
*b* ***Cannibalism,*** Lam. 2:20.

shall send against thee, in [c]hun-
ger, and in thirst, and in nakedness, and in want[c] of all *things*:
and he shall put a yoke[c] of [u]iron
upon thy neck, until he have destroyed thee.
49 [a]The LORD shall bring a nation against [v]thee from far, from
the end of the earth, *as swift* as
the [w]eagle flieth; a nation whose
[x]tongue[c] thou shalt not understand;
50 A nation of fierce [y]counte-
nance, which shall not regard[c]
the person of the old, nor shew
favour to the young:
51 And he shall eat the fruit of
thy cattle, and the fruit of thy
land, until thou be destroyed:
which *also* shall not leave thee
*either* corn[c], wine, or oil, *or* the
increase of thy kine[c], or [7]flocks of
thy sheep, until he have de-
troyed thee.
52 And he shall besiege thee in
all thy gates, until thy high and
fenced[c] walls come down, wherein thou trustedst, throughout all
thy land: and he shall besiege
thee in all thy gates throughout
all thy land, which the LORD thy
God hath given thee.
53 And thou shalt [z]eat the fruit[c]
of thine own body, the flesh of
thy sons and of thy daughters,
which the LORD thy God hath
given thee, in the ‖siege, and in
the straitness[c], wherewith thine
enemies shall distress[c] thee:
54 [a]*So that* the man *that is* tender among you, and very delicate, his eye[c] shall be evil toward
his brother, and toward the wife
of his bosom, and toward the
remnant of his children which he
shall leave:
55 So that he will not give to
any of them of the flesh of his
children whom he shall [b]eat: because he hath nothing left him
in the ‖siege, and in the straitness[c], wherewith thine enemies
shall distress thee in all thy
gates.
56 The tender[c] and delicate[c]
woman among you, which would
not adventure[c] to set the sole of
her foot upon the ground for
delicateness[c] and tenderness, her
eye[c] shall be evil toward the husband of her bosom, and toward
her son, and toward her daughter,
57 And toward her young one
that cometh out from between
her feet, and toward her children
which she shall bear: for she
shall [b]eat them for want[c] of all
*things* secretly in the ‖siege and
straitness[c], wherewith thine enemy shall distress thee in thy
gates.
58 If [c]thou wilt not observe to
do all the words of this [d]law that
are written in this book, that
thou mayest [e,f]fear this glorious
and fearful name, THE LORD
THY GOD;[s]
59 [a]Then the LORD will make
thy [g]plagues[c] wonderful[c], and the
plagues of thy seed, *even* great
plagues, and of long continuance, and sore[c] sicknesses, and of
long continuance.
60 [a]Moreover he will bring
upon thee all the [h]diseases of
E'gypt, which thou wast afraid
of; and they shall cleave[c] unto
thee.
61 Also every [h]sickness, and
every [g]plague, which *is* not written in the book of this [d]law, them
will the LORD bring upon thee,
until thou be destroyed.
62 And ye shall be left few in
number, whereas ye were as the
stars of heaven for multitude;
because thou wouldest [i]not obey

v.55–1494 BC
See footnote, *Time*, Rev. 10:6.

**58**
*c* ***Backsliders, warnings to,*** Jer. 3:22.
*d* ***Law, of Moses,*** Deut. 33:2.
*e* ***Fear of God,*** Acts 9:31.
*f* ***God, name of, to be reverenced,*** Gen. 2:2.

**59**
*g* ***Plague, as a judgment,*** Ex. 11:1.

**60**
*h* ***Disease, threatened as judgment,*** Ex. 15:26.

**62**
*i* ***Disobedience to God,*** Eph. 5:6.

‖ **SIEGE.** *Offer of peace must be made to the city before beginning,* Deut. 20:10–12. *Conducted by erecting embankments parallel to the walls of the besieged city,* Deut. 20:19, 20; Isa. 29:3; 37:33. *Distress of the inhabitants during,* 2 Kin. 6:24–29; 25:2, 3; Isa. 36:12; Jer. 19:9. *Cannibalism in,* 2 Kin. 6:28, 29.
**Instances of:** *Of Jericho,* Josh. 6. *Of Rabbah,* 2 Sam. 11:1; 1 Chr. 20:1. *Of Abel,* 2 Sam. 20:15. *Of Gibbethon,* 1 Kin.

v.62–1494 BC
See footnote, *Time*, Rev. 10:6.

the voice of the LORD thy
God.
63 And it shall come to pass,
*that* as the LORD [j,k]rejoiced over
you to do you good, and to multiply you; so the LORD will rejoice over [l]you to destroy you,
and to bring you to nought; and
ye shall be plucked from off the
land whither thou goest to possess it.
64 [a]And the LORD shall [m]scat-
ter thee among all people, from
the one end of the earth even unto
the other; and there thou shalt
[n]serve other gods, which neither
thou nor thy fathers have
known, *even* wood and stone.
65 [a]And among these nations
shalt thou find no ease, neither
shall the sole of thy foot have
rest: but the LORD shall give
thee there a [o]trembling heart,
and failing of eyes, and [8]sorrow
of mind:
66 [a,o]And thy life shall hang in
doubt before thee; and thou
shalt fear day and night, and
shalt have none assurance of thy
life:
67 [a,o]In the morning thou shalt
say, Would God it were even!
and at even thou shalt say,
Would God it were morning!
for the fear of thine heart wherewith thou shalt fear, and for the
sight of thine eyes which thou
shalt see.
68 And the LORD shall bring
thee into Ē′ġy̆pt again with
ships, by the way whereof I
spake unto thee, Thou shalt see
it no more again: and there ye
shall be sold unto your enemies
for [p]bondmen and bondwomen,
and no man shall buy *you*.

63
*j* *Joy, attributed to God*, Psa. 5:11.
*k* *Anthropomorphisms*, Gen. 11:5.
*l* *Backsliders, punishment of*, Jer. 3:22.

64
*m* *Israel, dispersion of*, Ex. 4:22.
*n* *Idolatry*, 1 Sam. 15:23.

65
*o* *Despondency, caused by corrective judgments*, Eccl. 2:20.
8 R. V. pining of soul:

## CHAPTER 29

*Moses exhorts the people to obedience, in view of the works they have seen. 10 All are presented before the Lord to enter into covenant with him. 18 The great wrath which shall come on him that flatters himself in his wickedness. 29 Secret things belong unto God.*

THESE *are* the words of the
*covenant, which the
LORD commanded Mō′ṣeṣ to
make with the children of [a]Is′-
ra-el in the land of [b]Mō′ab, beside the covenant which he
made with them in [c]Hō′reb.
2 ¶ And Mō′ṣeṣ called unto all
Iṣ′ra-el, and said unto them, Ye
have seen all that the [d]LORD did
before your eyes in the land of
Ē′ġy̆pt unto [e]Phā′raōh, and unto
all his servants, and unto all his
land;
3 The great temptations which
thine eyes have seen, the signs,
and those great [f]miracles:
4 Yet [g]the LORD hath not given

v.67–1494 BC
See footnote, *Time*, Rev. 10:6.

68
*p* *Servant, bought and sold*, Jer. 2:14.

1
*a* *Israel, renew the covenant*, vs. 1–29; Ex. 4:22.
*b* *Moab*, Num. 26:3.
*c* *Horeb*, Ex. 3:1.

2
*d* *God, providence of*, Gen. 2:2.
*e* *Pharaoh*, Ex. 3:10.

3
*f* *Miracles*, Luke 23:8.

4
*g* *Spiritual Blindness*, 2 Cor. 4:4.

---

15:27. *Of Tirzah*, 1 Kin. 16:17. *Of Jerusalem, by Rezin, king of Syria, and Pekah, son of Remaliah, king of Israel*, 2 Kin. 16:5; *by Nebuchadnezzar*, 2 Kin. 24:10, 11; 25:1–3; Jer. 52:4–34; Dan. 1:1; *by Sennacherib*, 2 Chr. 32:1–23. *Of Samaria*, 1 Kin. 20:1; 2 Kin. 6:24; 17:5; 18:9–11.

*** COVENANT. Of God with men:** *Salt an emblem of*, Lev. 2:13; Num. 18:19; 2 Chr. 13:5. *Confirmed with an oath*, Gen. 22:16; 26:3; 50:24; Ex. 34:27, 28; Num. 32:11; Psa. 89:35; 105:9; Luke 1:73; Heb. 6:13, 17, 18.

*Binding*, Jer. 11:2, 3; Gal. 3:15. *Everlasting*, Gen. 8:20–22; 9:1–17; Psa. 105:8, 10; Isa. 54:10; 61:8.

*God faithful to*, Lev. 26:44, 45; Deut. 4:31; 7:8, 9; Judg. 2:1; 1 Kin. 8:23; Psa. 105:8–11; 106:45; 111:5; Mic. 7:20. *Repudiated by God on account of Jews' idolatry*, Jer. 44:26, 27; Heb. 8:9. *Broken by the Jews*, Jer. 22:9; Ezek. 16:59; Heb. 8:9.

*Punishments for breaking of*, Lev. 26:25–46.

INSTANCES OF: *The sabbath*, Ex. 31:16. *The Ten Commandments*, Ex. 34:28; Deut. 5:2, 3; 9:9. *With Noah*, Gen. 6:18; 8:16; 9:8–17. *With Abraham*, Gen. 12:1–3; 15; 17:1–22; Ex. 6:4–8; Psa. 105:8–11; Rom. 9:7–13; Gal. 3. *With Isaac*, Gen. 17:19. *With Jacob*, Gen. 28:13–15. *With the Israelites to deliver them from Egypt*, Ex. 6:4–8. *With Phinehas*, Num. 25:12, 13. *With Israel, to destroy Amalek*, Ex. 17:14–16. *With Israel, at Horeb*, Ex. 34:27; Deut. 5:2, 3; *in Moab*, Deut. 29:1–15. *With the Levites*, Mal. 2:4, 5. *With David*, 2 Sam. 7:12–16; 1 Chr. 17:11–14; 2 Chr. 6:16. *With David and his house*, 2 Sam. 23:5; Psa. 89:20–37; Jer. 33:21. *With God's people*, Isa. 55:3; 59:21.

See footnote, BLOOD OF COVENANT, Ex. 24:8.

**Of man with God:** *By Jacob*, Gen. 28:20–22. *By Joshua*, Josh. 24:25 (with vs. 19–28). *By Absalom*, 2 Sam. 15:7, 8. *By Jehoiada and Joash*, 2 Kin. 11:17. *By Josiah*, 2 Kin. 23:3. *By Asa*, 2 Chr. 15:12–15. *By Nehemiah*, Neh. 9:38; 10. *By Israelites*, Ex. 24:3, 7; 19:8; Deut. 5:27; 26:17; Jer. 50:5. See footnote, Vows, Num. 30:2.

**Of men with men:** *Sacred*, Josh. 9:18–21; Gal. 3:15. *Binding*, Josh. 9:18–20; Jer. 34:8–21; Ezek. 17:14–18; Gal. 3:15. *Binding not only on those who make them, but on those who are represented*, Deut. 29:14, 15.

*Breach of, punished*, 2 Sam. 21:1–6; Jer. 34:8–22; Ezek. 17:13–19.

RATIFIED: *By giving the hand*, Ezra 10:19; Lam. 5:6; Ezek. 17:18. *By loosing the shoe*, Ruth 4:7–11. *By writing and sealing*, Neh. 9:38; Jer. 32:10–12. *By giving presents*, Gen. 21:27–30; 1 Sam. 18:3, 4. *By making a feast*, Gen. 26:30 *By erecting a monument*, Gen. 31:45, 46, 49–53. *By offering a sacrifice*, Gen. 15:9–17; Jer. 34:18, 19. *By taking an oath*, Gen. 21:23, 24; 25:33; 26:28–31; 31:53; Josh. 2:12–14; 14:9.

See footnote, CONTRACTS, Matt. 20:2.

INSTANCES OF: *Abraham and Abimelech*, Gen. 21:22–32. *Abimelech and Isaac*, Gen. 26:26–31. *Jacob and Laban*, Gen. 31:44–54. *Jonathan and David*, 1 Sam. 18:3, 4; 20:16, 42; 2 Sam. 21:7. *Jews with each other, to serve God*, 2 Chr. 15:12–15; Neh. 10:28–32. *King Zedekiah and his subjects*, Jer. 34:8. *Ahab with Benhadad*, 1 Kin. 20:34. *Subjects with sovereign*, 2 Chr. 23:1–3, 16.

v.4–1494 BC
See footnote, *Time*, Rev. 10:6.

*h* *Wisdom, spiritual.* Prov. 2:2.

**5**
*i* *Temporal Blessings, from God,* Psa. 103:2.
*j* *Israel, providentially cared for,* Ex. 4:22.
*k* *Miracles, design of,* Luke 23:8.
*l* *Dress,* Zech. 3:3.
*m* *Shoe,* Josh. 5:15.

**6**
*n* *Total Abstinence, from intoxicating beverages, instances of,* Lev. 10:9.
*o* *Wine,* Prov. 23: 31.

**7**
*p* *Sihon,* Num. 21: 21.
*q* *Heshbon,* Isa. 16:8.
*r* *Og,* Num. 21:33.
*s* *Bashan,* Num. 32:33.

**8**
*t* *Reubenites,* Josh. 22:1.
*u* *Gad, tribe of,* Deut. 33:20.
*v* *Manasseh, tribe of,* Gen. 46:20.

**9**
*w* *Commandment, enjoining obedience,* Deut. 8:2.
*x* *Obedience, enjoined,* Heb. 5:8.
*y* *Blessings, contingent upon obedience,* Deut. 11: 26.

**10**
*z* *Senate,* Num. 11: 16.

**11**
*a* *Foreigners,* Deut. 23:20.

**13**
*b* *God, love of, exemplified,* Gen. 2:2.
*c* *God, faithfulness of,* Gen. 2:2.

you an [h]heart to perceive, and
eyes to see, and ears to hear,
unto this day. [Q]
5 And [d,i]I have led [j]you forty
years in the wilderness: [k]your
[l]clothes are not waxen[c] old upon
you, and thy [m]shoe is not waxen[c]
old upon thy foot.[s]
6 [j]Ye have not eaten bread,
[n]neither have ye drunk [o]wine
or strong drink: [k]that ye might
know that I *am* the LORD your
God.
7 And when ye came unto this
place, [p]Sī′hŏn the king of
[q]Hĕsh′bŏn, and [r]Ŏg the king of
[s]Bā′shăn, came out against us
unto battle, and we smote them:
8 And we took their land, and
gave it for an inheritance unto
the [t]Reṳ′ben-ītes, and to the
[u]Găd′ītes, and to the half tribe
of [v]Mă-năs′seh.
9 [w,x]Keep therefore the words
of this *covenant[c], and do them,
[y]that ye may prosper in all that
ye do.
10 ¶ Ye stand this day all of
you before the LORD your God;
your captains of your tribes,
your [z]elders, and your officers,
*with* all the men of Ĭṣ′ra-el,
11 Your little ones, your wives,
and thy [a]stranger[c] that *is* in thy
camp, from the hewer of thy
wood unto the drawer of thy
water:
12 That thou shouldest enter
into *covenant[c] with the LORD
thy God, and into his oath,
which the LORD thy God maketh with thee this day:
13 That he may establish thee
to day for a people unto himself,
and *that* he may be unto thee a
[b]God, as he hath said unto thee,
and as [c]he hath *sworn unto thy
fathers, to Ā′brā-hăm, to Ī′ṣaac,
and to Jā′cob.
14 Neither with you only do I
make this *covenant and this
oath;
15 But with *him* that standeth
here with us this day before the
LORD our God, and also with *him*
that *is* not here with us this day:
16 (For ye know how we have
dwelt in the land of [d]Ē′ġȳpt; and
how we came through the nations which ye passed by;
17 And ye have seen their
abominations[c], and their [e]idols,
wood and stone, silver and gold,
which *were* among them:)
18 Lest there should be among
you man, or woman, or family,
or tribe, [f]whose heart [g]turneth
away this day from the LORD
our God, to go *and* [e]serve the
gods of these nations; lest there
should be among you a root that
beareth [h]gall and †wormwood;[Q]
19 And it come to pass, when
he heareth the words of this
curse, that he [i,j,k]bless himself in
his heart, saying, I shall have
peace, though I walk in the
[1]imagination of mine heart, to
[2]add drunkenness to thirst:[s]
20 The LORD will not [3]spare
him, but then the [l,m]anger of the
LORD and [n]his [o,m]jealousy shall
smoke[c] against that man, and all
the [p]curses that are written in
this book shall lie upon him, and
the LORD shall blot out his
name from under heaven.[s Q]
21 And the LORD shall separate
him unto evil out of all the tribes
of [q]Ĭṣ′ra-el, according to all the
curses of the *covenant that are
written in this book of the [r]law:
22 So that the generation to
come of your children that shall
rise up after you, and the
[4,a]stranger that shall come from
a far land, shall say, when they
see the [s]plagues of that land and
the [t]sicknesses which the LORD
hath laid upon it;

v.14–1494 BC
See footnote, *Time*, Rev. 10:6.

**16**
*d* *Egypt,* Gen. 41:8

**17**
*e* *Idolatry,* 1 Sam. 15:23.

**18**
*f* *Backsliders,* vs. 18–28; Jer. 3:22.
*g* *Backsliding,* Hos. 11:7.
*h* *Gall,* Job 16:13.

**19**
*i* *False Confidence,* Psa. 30:6.
*j* *Impenitence, judgments denounced against,* Rom. 2:5.
*k* *Delusion,* 2 Thess. 2:11.
1 R. V. stubbornness
2 R. V. destroy the moist with the dry:

**20**
*l* *Anger of God,* 2 Kin. 13:3.
*m* *Anthropomorphisms,* Gen. 11:5.
*n* *God, jealous,* Gen. 2:2.
*o* *Jealousy, attributed to God,* Psa 78:58.
*p* *Judgments, denounced against disobedience,* Ex 6:6.
3 R. V. pardon

**21**
*q* *Israel, tribes of,* Ex. 4:22.
*r* *Law, of Moses,* Deut. 33:2.

**22**
*s* *Plague,* Ex. 11:1.
*t* *Disease, threatened, as judgments,* Ex. 15:26
4 R. V. foreigner

† **WORMWOOD.** *A bitter plant,* Deut. 29:18.
**Figurative,** Deut. 29:18; Prov. 5:4; Jer. 9:15; 23:15; Lam. 3:19.
**Symbolical,** Rev. 8:11.

v.23–1494 BC
ee footnote, *Time*, Rev. 10:6.

**23**
*Sodom*, Gen. 13:10.
*Gomorrah*, Gen. 13:10.
Gen. 10:19; 14:2; Hos. 11:8.
*Zeboim*, Hos. 11:8.

**29**
*Mysteries*, Mark 4:11.
*God, unsearchable*, Gen. 2:2.

*Revelation*, 2 Cor. 12:1.
*Word of God, inspired*, Psa. 119:9.
*Law, of Moses*, Deut. 33:2.

**1**
*Adversity, design of*, vs. 1–3; Psa. 10:6.
*Backsliders, promises to penitent*, vs. 1–10; Jer. 3:22.
*Nation, penitent, promises to*, vs. 1–10; Isa. 2:4.

23 *And that* the whole land thereof *is* ‡brimstone, and salt, *and* burning, *that* it is not sown, nor beareth, nor any grass groweth therein, like the overthrow of [u]Sŏd′om, and [v]Gō-mŏr′rah, [w]Ăd′mah, and [x]Ze-bō′im, which the LORD overthrew in his [l]anger, and in his wrath:[S][T]

24 Even all nations shall say, Wherefore hath the LORD done thus unto this land? what *meaneth*[S] the heat of this great [l]anger?

25 Then men shall say, Because [f]they have [g]forsaken[C] the *covenant[C] of the LORD God of their fathers, which he made with them when he brought them forth out of the land of [c]Ē′ġўpt:

26 For they went and [e]served other gods, and worshipped them, gods whom they knew not, and *whom* he had not given unto them:

27 And the [l]anger of the LORD was kindled against this land, to bring upon it all the [p]curses that are written in this book:[S]

28 And the LORD rooted them out of their land in [l]anger, and in wrath, and in great indignation, and cast them into another land, as *it is* this day.[S]

29 The [y]secret[C] *things belong* unto the LORD our [z]God: but those *things which are* [a]revealed *belong* unto us and to our children for ever, that *we* may do all the [b]words of this [c]law.[S]

## CHAPTER 30

*Great mercies promised unto the repentant. 11 The commandment is manifest. 15 Life and death are set before them.*

AND it shall come to pass, when all these things are come upon thee, the blessing and the [a]curse, which I have set before thee, and [b,c]thou shalt call[G] *them* to mind among all the nations, whither the LORD thy God hath driven thee,

2 [b,c,d]And shalt [e]return unto the LORD thy God, and shalt obey his voice according to all that I [f]command thee this day, thou and thy children, with all thine heart, and with all thy soul;

3 [b,c,d,g]That then [h]the LORD thy [i]God will turn thy captivity,[C] and have compassion upon thee, and will return and gather thee from all the nations, whither the LORD thy God hath scattered thee.

4 [b,c]If *any* of thine be driven out unto the outmost *parts* of heaven, from thence will the LORD thy [j]God gather thee, and from thence will he fetch thee:[S][Q]

5 [d,g,h]And the LORD thy [j]God will bring [b,c]thee into the [k]land which thy fathers possessed, and thou shalt possess it; and he will do thee good and multiply thee above thy fathers.

6 And the LORD thy God will [l,m]circumcise [d]thine [n]heart, and the heart of thy seed, to [o,p]love the LORD thy God with all thine heart, and with all thy soul, that thou mayest live.[S][T][Q]

7 And the LORD thy God will put all these [q]curses upon [c]thine enemies, and on them that hate thee, which persecuted thee.

8 And [d,f]thou shalt [e]return and obey the voice of the LORD, and do all his commandments which I command thee this day.

9 [b,c,d,g]And the LORD thy [r]God will make thee plenteous[C] in every work of thine hand, in the fruit[C] of thy body, and in the fruit of thy cattle, and in the fruit of thy land, for good: for the LORD will again [s]rejoice over thee for good, as he rejoiced over thy fathers:[S]

v.1–1494 BC
See footnote, *Time*, Rev. 10:6.

**2**
d *Penitent, promises to*, Psa. 51:17.
e *Repentance*, Mark 1:4.
f *Commandment, enjoining obedience*, Deut. 8:2.

**3**
g *Blessings, contingent upon obedience*, Deut. 11:26.
h *Promise, to the obedient, of prosperity*, vs. 4–10; 2 Cor. 1:20.
i *God, mercy of*, Gen. 2:2.

**4**
j *God, providence of, delivers from enemies*, Gen. 2:2.

**5**
k *Canaan*, Gen. 37:1.

**6**
l *Circumcision, figurative*, Gen. 17:10.
m *Regeneration, circumcision of the heart*, Tit. 3:5.
n *Heart, renewed*, Psa. 44:21.
o *Love, of man for God*, 1 John 4:19.
p *Duty, of man to God*, Eccl. 12:13.

**7**
q *Afflictions*, Psa. 34:19.

**9**
r *God, goodness of*, Gen. 2:2.
s *Joy, attributed to God*, Psa. 5:11.

‡ **BRIMSTONE.** *Rained upon Sodom*, Gen. 19:24; Luke 17:29. *In Palestine*, Deut. 29:23. **Figurative:** *Of judgments on wicked*, Job 18:15; Psa. 11:6; Isa. 30:33; Ezek. 38:22. *Of destruction*, Rev. 9:17, 18. *Of future punishment*, Rev. 14:10; 19:20; 21:8.

v.10–1494 BC
See footnote, *Time*, Rev. 10:6.

10
t *Law, of Moses*, Deut. 33:2.

11
1 R. V. too hard for

12
u *Excuses, for disobedience*, vs. 11–14; Luke 14:18.

14
v *Word of God*, Psa. 119:9.

15
w *Minister, faithful, instances of*, Rom. 15:16.

17
x *Backsliding*, Hos. 11:7.
y *Idolatry, denounced*, 1 Sam. 15:23.

18
z *Judgments, denounced against disobedience*, Ex. 6:6.

19
a *Minister, faithful, instances of*, Rom. 15:16.
b *Blessings, contingent upon obedience*, Deut. 11:26.

10 [s] [g]If thou shalt hearken unto the voice of the LORD thy God, to keep his commandments and his statutes which are written in this book of the [t]law, *and* if thou [e]turn unto the LORD thy God with all thine heart, and with all thy soul.

11 ¶ For this [f]commandment which I command thee this day, it *is* not [1]hidden from thee, neither *is* it far off. [T] [Q]

12 It [Q] *is* not in heaven, that thou shouldest [u]say, Who shall go up for us to heaven, and bring it unto us, that we may hear it, and do it?

13 Neither *is* it beyond the sea, that thou shouldest [u]say, Who shall go over the sea for us, and bring it unto us, that we may hear it, and do it?

14 But the [v]word *is* very nigh[C] unto thee, in thy mouth, and in thy heart, that thou mayest [Q] do [T] it. [S]

15 ¶ [S] See, [w]I have set before thee this day life and good, and death and evil;

16 In that [f]I command thee this day to [o,p]love the LORD thy God, to walk in his ways, and to keep his commandments and his statutes and his judgments,[C] that thou mayest live and multiply: and the LORD thy God shall bless thee in the [k]land whither thou goest to possess it.

17 But if thine heart [x]turn away, so that thou wilt not hear, but shalt be drawn away, and [y]worship other gods, and serve them;

18 I [y,z]denounce[C] unto you this day, that ye shall surely perish, *and that* ye shall not prolong *your* days upon the land, whither thou passest over Jôr′dan to go to possess it. [S]

19 [a]I call heaven and earth to record[C] this day against you, *that* I have set before you life and death, [b]blessing and cursing: therefore [c,d]choose life, that both thou and thy seed may live: [S]

20 That thou mayest [e,f]love the LORD thy God, *and* [g]that thou mayest obey his voice, and that thou mayest cleave unto him: for he *is* thy life, and the length of thy days: [b,h]that thou mayest dwell in the land which the LORD sware unto thy fathers, to Ā′brā-hăm, to Ī′ṣaac, and to Jā′cob, to give them. [S] [T]

## CHAPTER 31

*Moses encourages the people*, 7 *and Joshua*. 9 *He delivers the law unto the priests to be read every seventh year to the people*. 14 *God calls Moses and Joshua into the tabernacle*. 19 *He gives them a song to testify against the people*. 23 *Joshua receives a charge*. 24 *Moses delivers the book of the law to the Levites to keep*. 28 *He makes a protestation to the elders*.

AND [a]Mō′ṣeṣ went and spake these words unto all Ĭṣ′ra-el.

2 And [a]he said unto them, I *am* [b]an hundred and twenty years old this day; I can no more go out and come in: also the LORD hath said unto me, Thou shalt not go over this [c]Jôr′dan.

3 The LORD thy [d]God, he will go over before thee, *and* he will destroy these [e]nations from before thee, and thou shalt possess them: *and* [f]Jŏsh′u-ȧ, he shall go over before thee, as the LORD hath said. [S]

4 And the LORD shall do unto them as he did to [g]Sī′hŏn and to [h]Ŏg, kings of the [i]Ăm′ôr-ītes, and unto the land of them, whom he destroyed.

5 And the [d]LORD shall give [e]them up before your face, that ye may do unto them according unto all the commandments which I have commanded you.

6 [j,k]Be strong and of a good *courage, fear not, nor be afraid of them: for [l]the LORD thy God, [d]he *it is* that doth go with [m]thee; [n]he will not fail thee, nor forsake thee. [S] [Q]

7 ¶ And [o]Mō′ṣeṣ called unto

v.19–1494 BC
See footnote, *Time*, Rev. 10:6.
c *Choice*, 2 Sam. 24:12.
d *Decision, injunction concerning*, Isa. 50:7.

20
e *Love, of man to God*, 1 John 4:19
f *Duty, of man to God*, Eccl. 12:13
g *Obedience, enjoined*, Heb. 5:8
h *Reward, a motive to obedience*, Matt. 5:12.

1
a *Moses, his virility*, Ex. 2:10.

2
b *Longevity*, Psa. 91:16.
c *Jordan*, Gen. 32:10.

3
d *God, providence of, delivers from enemies*, Gen. 2:2.
e *Canaanites, to be destroyed*, vs. 3–5; Ex. 23:28.
f *Joshua, commissioned*, Josh. 1:1

4
g *Sihon*, Num. 21:21.
h *Og*, Num. 21:33
i *Amorites*, Gen. 14:13.

6
j *Commandment, enjoining courage*, Deut. 8:2.
k *Faith, enjoined*, Mark 11:22.
l *Promise, to the righteous, of divine help*, 2 Cor. 1:20.
m *Righteous, promises to*, Psa. 64:10.
n *God, faithfulness of*, Gen. 2:2.

7
o *Moses, appoints Joshua his successor* Ex. 2:10.

[l]Jŏsh′u-ȧ, and said unto him in
the sight of all Ĭş′ra-el, [j,k]Be
strong and of a good *courage:
for thou must go with this people
unto the [p]land which the LORD
hath sworn unto their fathers to
give them; and thou shalt cause
them to inherit it.[Q]
8 And [q]the LORD, he *it is* that
doth go before thee; he will be
with thee, he will not fail thee,
neither forsake thee: fear not,
neither be dismayed.[Q]
9 ¶[S]And Mō′şeş wrote this [r]law,
and delivered it unto the [s]priests
the sons of Lē′vī, which bare the
ark of the covenant of the LORD,
and unto all the [t]elders of Ĭş′-
ra-el.
10 And Mō′şeş commanded
them, saying, At the end of *every*
[u]seven [v]years, in the [1]solemnity
of the year of release, in the
feast of [w]tabernacles,
11 When all Ĭş′ra-el is come to
[x]appear before the LORD thy
God in the place which he shall
choose, [s]thou shalt [y]read this
[r,z]law before all Ĭş′ra-el in their
hearing.
12 [a]Gather the people together,
men, and [b]women, and [c]chil-
dren, and thy [d]stranger[C] that *is*
within thy gates, [e]that they may
hear, and that they may learn,
and [f]fear the LORD your God,
and observe to do all the words
of this law:
13 And *that* their [c]children,
which have not known *any*
*thing*, may hear, and learn to
[f]fear the LORD your God, as
long as ye live in the [g]land
whither ye go over [h]Jôr′dan to
possess it.
14 ¶ And the LORD said unto
Mō′şeş, Behold, thy days approach that thou must [i]die: [j]call
[k]Jŏsh′u-ȧ, and present yourselves in the [l]tabernacle of the
congregation, that I may give
him a charge.[C] And Mō′şeş and
Jŏsh′u-ȧ went, and presented
themselves in the tabernacle of
the congregation.[S]
15 And the [m]LORD appeared in
the [l]tabernacle in a [n]pillar of a
cloud: and the pillar of the cloud
stood over the door of the tabernacle.
16 ¶ And the LORD said unto
Mō′şeş, Behold, thou shalt [i]sleep
with thy fathers; and this [o]peo-
ple will rise up, and go a
[†,p]whoring[C] after the gods[C] of the
strangers[C] of the land, whither
they go *to be* among them, and
will forsake me, and [q]break my
covenant which I have made
with them.
17 Then my [r]anger shall be
kindled against [o,s]them in that
day, and I will [t]forsake them,
and I will [u]hide my face from
them, and they shall be devoured,[C] and many [v]evils and
troubles shall befall them; so
that they will say in that day,

v.7–1494 BC
See footnote, *Time*, Rev. 10:6.

p *Canaan*, Gen. 37:1.

**8**

q *Faith, instances of*, Mark 11:22.

**9**

r *Law, of Moses, preserved in the ark of the covenant*, Deut. 33:2.

s *Priest, duties of, to teach the law*, Lev. 1:5.

t *Senate*, Num. 11:16.

**10**

u *Sabbatic Year, called year of release*, Lev. 25:2.

v *Year*, Lev. 25:29.

w *Tabernacles, feast of*, Deut. 16:13.

1 R. V. set time

**11**

x *Worship, the whole nation required to assemble for*, vs. 11–13; Gen. 22:5.

y *Instruction, in religion*, Prov. 23:23.

z *Word of God, to be read in public assemblies*, vs. 11–13; Psa. 119:9.

**12**

a *Commandment, enjoining public instruction in the word of God*, Deut. 8:2.

b *Women, required to attend reading of the law*, Prov. 31:10.

c *Children, instruction of, in the law*, Mark 10:14.

d *Foreigners, required to assemble for religious instruction*, Deut. 23:20.

e *Instruction, in religion*, Prov. 23:23.

f *Fear of God, a motive to obedience*, Acts 9:31.

v.13–1494 BC
See footnote, *Time*, Rev. 10:6.

**13**

g *Canaan*, Gen. 37:1.

h *Jordan*, Gen. 32:10.

**14**

i *Death*, Num. 23:10.

j *Call, personal*, Phil. 3:14.

k *Joshua*, Josh. 1:1.

l *Tabernacle*, Ex. 27:9.

**15**

m *God, appearances of*, Gen. 2:2.

n *Pillar, of cloud and fire*, Ex. 13:21.

**16**

o *Backsliders, warnings to*, Jer. 3:22.

p *Idolatry, denounced*, 1 Sam. 15:23.

q *Disobedience to God*, Eph. 5:6.

**17**

r *Anger of God*, 2 Kin. 13:3.

s *Reprobates*, 1 Cor. 9:27.

t *Holy Spirit, withdrawn from incorrigible sinners*, Acts 1:2.

u *Sin, separates from God*, Rom. 5:12.

v *Adversity, design of*, Psa. 10:6.

* **COURAGE**, Prov. 28:1.

**Exhortations to**, Psa. 31:24; Isa. 51:7, 12–16; Ezek. 2:6; 3:9; Matt. 10:28; Luke 12:4; Phil. 1:27, 28.

**Enjoined:** *Upon Joshua*, Deut. 31:7, 8, 22, 23; Josh. 1:1–9. *Upon the Israelites*, Josh. 23:6; 1 Chr. 19:13; 2 Chr. 32:7, 8; Isa. 41:10; 51:7, 12–16. *Upon Solomon*, 1 Chr. 22:13; 28:20. *Upon Asa*, 2 Chr. 15:1–7. *Upon the disciples*, Matt. 10:26, 28; Luke 12:4. *Upon Paul*, Acts 18:9, 10. *Upon other Christians*, 1 Cor. 16:13; Phil. 1:27, 28.

*By Jehoshaphat upon judicial and executive officers*, 2 Chr. 19:11.

**Instances of:** *Abraham, in leaving his fatherland*, Gen. 12:1–9; *in offering Isaac*, Gen. 22:1–14. *Gideon, in destroying the altar of Baal*, Judg. 6:25–31. *Joshua and Caleb, in advising that Israel go at once and possess the land*, Num. 13:30; 14:6–12. *Othniel, in smiting Kirjathsepher*, Josh. 15:16, 17. *Gideon, in attacking the confederate armies of the Midianites and Amalekites with three hundred men*, Judg. 7:7–23. *Deborah, in leading Israel's armies*, Judg. 4. *Jael, in slaying Sisera*, Judg. 4:18–22. *Agag, in the indifference with which he faced death*, 1 Sam. 15:32, 33. *Jonathan and his armor bearer*, 1 Sam. 14:6–16, 45. *David, in slaying Goliath*, 1 Sam. 17:32–50; 19:5; *in entering into the tent of Saul, and carrying away Saul's spear*, 1 Sam. 26:7–12. *David's captains*, 2 Sam. 23. *Joab, in reproving king David*, 2 Sam. 19:5–7. *Esther, in going to the king to save her people*, Esth. 4:8, 16; chapters 5–7. *The three Hebrews, who refused to bow down to the image of Nebuchadnezzar*, Dan. 3:16–18. *Daniel, in persisting in prayer, regardless of the edict against praying*, Dan. 6:10. *Nehemiah, in refusing to take refuge in the temple*, Neh. 6:10–13. *Ezra, in undertaking the perilous journey from Babylon to Palestine without a guard*, Ezra 8:22, 23. *The Jews, in returning answer to Tatnai*, Ezra 5:11. *Joseph of Arimathea, in caring for the body of Jesus*, Mark 15:43. *Thomas, in being willing to die with Jesus*, John 11:16. *Peter and other disciples*, Acts 3:12–26; 4:9–13, 19, 20, 31; 5:29. *The apostles, under persecution*, Acts 5:21, 29–32. *Paul, in going to Jerusalem, despite his impressions that bonds and imprisonments awaited him*, Acts 20:22–24; 24:14, 25.

† **WHOREDOM.** *Licentious rites of, in idolatrous worship*, Lev. 19:29; Deut. 31:16; Judg. 2:17; 2 Kin. 9:22.

See footnote, IDOLATRY, *Wicked practices of*, 1 Sam. 15:23.

**Figurative**, Ezek. 16; 23; Rev. 17:1–6.

Are not these [w]evils come upon us, because our God *is* not among us?[S]

18 And I will surely [u]hide my face in that day for all the evils which [s]they shall have wrought, in that [o]they are turned unto other gods.[S]

19 Now therefore write ye this [x]song for you, and [e]teach it the children of Ĭs̱′ra-el: put it in their mouths, that this song may be a witness for me against the children of Ĭs̱′ra-el.

20 For when I shall have brought them into the [g]land which I sware unto their fathers, that floweth with milk and honey; and they shall have eaten and filled themselves, and waxen[G] [y, z]fat; then will they [a]turn unto other gods, and [b]serve them, and [2]provoke me, and break my covenant.

21 And it shall come to pass, when many evils and troubles are befallen them, that this [c]song shall testify against them as a witness; for it shall not be forgotten out of the mouths of their seed: for [d]I know their [e]imagination which they go[C] about[C], even now, before I have brought them into the [f]land which I sware.

22 Mō′s̱es̱ therefore wrote this [c]song the same day, and [g]taught it the children of Ĭs̱′ra-el.

23 And he gave [h]Jŏsh′u-ȧ the son of Nŭn a charge, and said, [i]Be strong and of a good *courage: for thou shalt bring the children of [j]Ĭs̱′ra-el into the land which I sware unto them: and I will be with thee.

24 ¶ And it came to pass, when Mō′s̱es̱ had made an end of writing the words of this [k]law in a [l]book, until they were finished,

25 That Mō′s̱es̱ commanded the [m]Lē′vītes, which bare the [n]ark of the covenant of the LORD, saying,

26 [Q]Take this [l]book of the [k]law, and put it in the side of the [n]ark of the covenant of the LORD your God, that it may be there for a witness against thee.

27 [o]For I know thy rebellion[C], and thy [p]stiff neck: behold, while I am yet alive with you this day, ye have been [q]rebellious against the LORD; and how much more after my death?[Q]

28 Gather unto me all the [r]elders of your tribes, and your officers, that I may speak these words in their ears, and call heaven and earth to record against them.

29 For I know that after my death ye will utterly corrupt *yourselves*, and turn aside from the way which I have commanded you; and evil will befall [s]you in the latter days; because ye will do evil in the sight of the LORD, to provoke him to [t, u]anger through the work of your hands.[S]

30 And Mō′s̱es̱ spake in the ears of all the congregation of Ĭs̱′ra-el the words of this [c]song, until they were ended.

## CHAPTER 32

*Moses' song in which he sets forth God's mercy and vengeance. 46 He exhorts them to lay it up in their hearts. 48 God sends him up to mount Nebo, to see the land, and die.*

GIVE ear, O ye heavens, and I will speak; and hear, O earth, the words of my mouth.

2 My doctrine[C] shall drop as the rain, my speech shall distil as the dew, as the small rain upon the tender herb, and as the showers upon the grass:

3 Because I will publish[C] the name of the LORD: ascribe ye greatness unto our God.[S]

4 *He is* the [a]Rock, his [b]work *is* perfect: for all [c]his ways *are* judgment[C]: a [d]God of [1]truth and [e]without iniquity, just and right *is* he.[S T Q]

---

v.17–1494 BC See footnote, *Time*, Rev. 10:6.

*w Judgments*, Ex. 6:6.

19
*x Song, didactic*, Psa. 77:6.

20
*y Riches, a snare*, Eccl. 4:8.
*z Prosperity, dangers of*, Eccl. 7:14.

*a Backsliding, temptations to*, Hos. 11:7.
*b Idolatry*. 1 Sam. 15:23.
2 R. V. despise

21
*c Song, didactic*, Psa. 77:6.
*d God, knowledge of*, Gen. 2:2.
*e Sin, known to God*, Rom. 5:12.
*f Canaan*, Gen. 37:1.

22
*g Instruction, in religion*, Prov. 23:23.

23
*h Joshua*, Josh. 1:1.
*i Faith, enjoined, in time of public danger*, Mark 11:22.
*j Israel, Joshua appointed leader of*, Ex. 4:22.

24
*k Law, of Moses*, Deut. 33:2.
*l Book, law of Moses written in*, Num. 5:23.

25
*m Levites, duties of*, Deut. 10:8.
*n Ark, in the tabernacle*, Ex. 25:10.

v.26–1494 BC See footnote, *Time*, Rev. 10:6.

27
*o Reproof, faithfulness in*, Prov. 17:10.
*p Self-will*, Gen. 49:6.
*q Disobedience to God*, Eph. 5:6.

28
*r Senate*, Num. 11:16.

29
*s Wicked, punishment of*, Psa. 73:3.
*t Anger of God*, 2 Kin. 13:3.
*u Anthropomorphisms*, Gen. 11:5.

4
*a Rock*, Psa. 78:15
*b Works of God*, Psa. 40:5.
*c God, judge*, Gen. 2:2.
*d God, faithfulness of*, Gen. 2:2.
*e God, holiness of*, Gen. 2:2.
1 R. V. faithfulness

v.5–1494 BC
ee footnote, *Time,*
Rev. 10:6.

5
*Backsliders,* Jer. 3:22.
R. V. dealt corruptly with him, they are not his children, it is their blemish;

6
*Ingratitude, of man to God,* Rom. 1:21.
*God, fatherhood of,* Gen. 2:2.
*God, creator of man,* Gen. 2:2.

8
*God, sovereign,* Gen. 2:2.
*Earth, early divisions of,* Prov. 8:23.
*Dispersion,* Gen. 11:8.
ı *Adam,* Gen. 2:19.
. *Forordination,* Rom. 8:30.

9
*God, love of, exemplified,* vs. 9–12; Gen. 2:2.

10
• *God, guide,* Gen. 2:2.
*God, preserver,* Gen. 2:2.

11
*Eagle,* Lev. 11:13.

13
• *Temporal Blessings, from God,* Psa. 103:2.
*Honey,* Prov. 25:27.
ı *Flint,* Deut. 8:15.
› *Rock, oil from,* Psa. 78:15.

14
ʋ *Butter,* Gen. 18:8.
ɛ *Milk,* Job 10:10.
ʮ *Bashan,* Num. 32:33.

5 [f]They have [2]corrupted themselves, their spot *is* not *the spot*
of his children: *they are* a perverse and crooked generation.[T Q]
6 [g]Do ye thus requite[C] the
LORD, O foolish people and
unwise? *is* not [h]he thy father
*that* hath bought thee? hath [i]he
not made thee, and established
thee?[T Q]
7 Remember the days of old,
consider the years of many generations: ask thy father, and he
will shew thee; thy elders, and
they will tell thee.[S]
8 When the [j]Most High divided
to the nations their [k]inheritance,
when he [l]separated the sons of
[m]Ăd′ăm, he [n]set the bounds of
the people according to the number of the children of Is̩′ra-el.[S Q]
9 For the [o]LORD's portion *is*
his people; Jā′cob *is* the lot of
his inheritance.[S]
10 [o]He found him in a desert
land, and in the waste howling
wilderness; [p]he led him about,
he instructed him, [q]he kept him
as the apple[C] of his eye.[S]
11 As an [r]eagle stirreth up her
nest, fluttereth over her young,
spreadeth abroad her wings, taketh them, beareth them on her
wings:
12 *So* the [p]LORD alone did lead
him, and *there was* no strange
god with him.[S]
13 [s]He made him ride on the
high places of the earth, that he
might eat the increase of the
fields; and he made him to suck
[t]honey out of the rock, and oil
out of the [u]flinty [v]rock;
14 [w]Butter of kine,[C] and [x]milk
of *sheep, with fat of lambs, and
rams of the breed of [y]Bā′shăn,
and [z]goats, with the fat of kidneys of wheat; and thou didst
drink the pure blood of the
grape.[S]
15 But †Jĕsh′u-rŭn waxed[G]
[a, b]fat, and kicked: thou art wax-
en[C] fat, thou art grown thick,
thou art covered *with fatness*;
then he [c, d, e]forsook [f]God *which*
made him, and lightly esteemed
the [g, h]Rock of his [i]salvation.[C]
16 [j]They provoked [k]him to
[l]jealousy with strange [m]*gods*,
with [n]abominations[C] provoked
they him to [o]anger.[S]
17 [j]They [m]sacrificed unto
[3, p]devils,[C] not to God; to gods
whom they knew not, to new
*gods that* came newly up, whom
your fathers feared not.[S Q T]
18 Of the [g]Rock *that* begat thee
thou art [q]unmindful, and hast
forgotten [f]God that formed thee.[Q]
19 And when the LORD saw [r]*it*,
he abhorred[C] *them*, because of the
provoking of his sons, and of his
daughters.
20 And he said, I will hide my
face[C] from them, I will see what
their end *shall be*: for they *are* a
very froward[C] generation, children in whom *is* no faith.[Q]
21 They have moved [k]me to
[l]jealousy with *that which is* not
God; they have provoked me to
[o]anger with their vanities:[C] and
[s]I will move[C] them to jealousy
with *those which are* not a people; I will provoke them to anger
with a foolish nation.[S Q]
22 For a [t]fire is kindled in mine
[o]anger, and shall burn unto the
lowest [u]hell,[C] and shall consume
the earth with her increase, and
set on fire the foundations of the
mountains.[S]

v.14–1494 BC
See footnote, *Time,* Rev. 10:6.

z *Goat,* Deut. 14:4.

15
a *Prosperity, dangers of,* Eccl. 7:14.
b *Riches, a snare,* Eccl. 4:8.
c *Backsliding, temptations to,* Hos. 11:7.
d *Apostasy,* Acts 1:25.
e *Infidelity, danger of, in prosperity,* 2 Cor. 6:15.
f *God, creator,* Gen 2:2.
g *Rock,* Psa. 78:15.
h *God, savior,* Gen. 2:2.
i *Salvation,* Acts 16:17.

16
j *Backsliders, corrective judgments upon,* vs. 16–25; Jer. 3:22.
k *God, jealous,* Gen. 2:2.
l *Jealousy, attributed to God,* Psa. 78:58.
m *Idolatry,* 1 Sam. 15:23.
n *Abomination,* Lev. 18:27.
o *Anger of God, provoked,* 2 Kin. 13:3.

17
p *Demons, worship of,* Matt. 4:24.
3 R. V. demons,

18
q *Ingratitude,* Rom. 1:21.

19
r *Sin, repugnant to God,* Rom. 5:12.

21
s Rom. 10:19.

22
t *Fire, figurative,* Ex. 12:8.
u *Hell,* Mark 9:43.

*** SHEEP.** *Used for food,* Deut. 14:4; 1 Kin. 4:23; 2 Chr. 17:11; Neh. 5:18. *Offered in sacrifice, by Abraham,* Gen. 22:13; *by Solomon,* 1 Kin. 8:63. *Required in the Mosaic offerings,* Ex. 20:24; Lev. 1:10; 22:19; Deut. 18:3. *The land of Bashan adapted to the raising of,* Deut. 32:14; *so also of Bozrah,* Mic. 2:12; *and Kedar,* Ezek. 27:21; *and Nebaioth,* Isa. 60:7; *and Sharon,* Isa. 65:10.
*Jacob's management of,* Gen. 30:32–43. *Milk of, used for food,* Deut. 32:14. *Shearing of,* Gen. 31:19; 38:12, 13; Isa. 53:7. *Feasting at the time of shearing,* 1 Sam. 25:11, 36; 2 Sam. 13:23. *First fleece of, belonged to priests and Levites,* Deut. 18:4. *Tribute paid in,* 2 Kin. 3:4; 1 Chr. 5:21; 2 Chr. 17:11.
**Figurative,** 1 Chr. 21:17; Psa. 74:1; 95:7; 100:3; Jer. 13:20. *Of backsliders,* Jer. 50:6. *Of lost sinners,* Matt. 9:36; 10:6. *Of the righteous,* Jer. 50:17; Ezek. 34; Matt. 26:31; Mark 14:27; Luke 12:32; John 10:1–16; 21:15, 16; Acts 20:28; Heb. 13:20; 1 Pet. 5:2. *Of the defenselessness of ministers,* Matt. 10:16. *Parable of the lost,* Matt. 18:11–13; Luke 15:4–7.

**† JESHURUN.** *A name used poetically for Israel,* Deut. 32:15; 33:5, 26; Isa. 44:2.

v.23–1494 BC
See footnote, *Time*, Rev. 10:6.

**23**
v *Judgments, denounced against disobedience*, Ex. 6:6.
w *Arrow, figurative*, 1 Sam. 20:20.

**24**
x *Serpent, venom of*, Num. 21:6.

**25**
y *War*, Judg. 3:2.
z *Women*, Prov. 31:10.

**26**
a *Backsliders*, Jer. 3:22.

**27**
4 R. V. judge amiss, lest they should say, Our hand is exalted,

**28**
b *Spiritual Blindness*, 2 Cor. 4:4.

**29**
· *Wicked, God's love for*, Psa. 73:3.
d *Wisdom, spiritual*, Prov. 2:2.
e *Death, preparation for*, Num. 23:10.

**30**
f *Armies, panic in*, Deut. 11:4.
g *Cowardice, inflicted as a judgment*, Lev. 26:36.
h *Panic*, Judg. 7:22.
i *Holy Spirit, withdrawn from incorrigible sinners*, Acts 1:2.
j *Nation, punishment of*, Isa. 2:4.
5 R. V. delivered

**32**
k *Wicked, described*, Psa. 73:3.
l *Sodom*, Gen. 13:10.
m *Gomorrah*, Gen. 13:10.
n *Grape, figurative*, Lev. 25:5.
o *Gall*, Job 16:13.

**33**
p *Asp*, Job 20:14.

23 I will heap [v]mischiefs upon them; I will spend mine [w]arrows upon them.

24 [i,v]*They shall be* burnt with hunger, and devoured with burning heat, and with bitter destruction: I will also send the teeth of beasts upon them, with the poison of [x]serpents of the dust.

25 The [v,y]sword without, and terror within, shall destroy both the young man and the [z]virgin, the suckling[G] *also* with the man of gray hairs.

26 I said, I would scatter [a]them into corners, I would make the remembrance of them to cease from among men:

27 Were it not that I feared the wrath of the enemy, lest their adversaries should [4]behave themselves strangely, *and* lest they should say, Our hand *is* high, and the LORD hath not done all this.

28 For they *are* a nation void of counsel, [b]neither *is there any* understanding in them.

29 O that [a,c]they were [d]wise, *that* they understood this, *that* they would consider their latter [e]end![S Q]

30 [f,g]How should one chase a thousand, and two put ten thousand to [h]flight, except [i]their Rock had sold [j]them, and the LORD had [5]shut them up?

31 For their rock *is* not as our Rock, even our enemies themselves *being* judges.

32 For [k]their vine *is* of the vine of [l]Sŏd′om, and of the fields of [m]Gō-mŏr′rah: their [n]grapes *are* grapes of [o]gall, their clusters *are* bitter:

33 Their wine *is* the poison of ‡dragons, and the cruel ‖venom of [p]asps.

34 [q]*Is* not this laid up in store with me, *and* sealed up among my treasures?[Q]

35 [r]To me *belongeth* vengeance, and recompence; their foot shall slide in *due* time: for the day of their calamity *is* at hand, and the things that shall come upon them make haste.

36 For the [s]LORD shall judge his people, and [t]repent [u]himself for his servants, when he seeth that *their* power is gone, and *there is* none shut up, or left.[Q T S]

37 And he shall say, Where *are* their [v]gods, *their* rock in whom they trusted,

38 [v]Which did eat the fat of their sacrifices, *and* drank the wine of their drink offerings? let them rise up and help you, *and* be your protection.

39 See now that [w]I, *even* I, *am* he, and *there is* no god with me: [x]I [y]kill, and I make [z]alive; I [a]wound, and I [b]heal: neither *is there any* that can deliver out of my hand.[S T]

40 For I lift up my hand to heaven, and say, [c]I live for ever.[Q S]

41 If I whet my glittering [d]sword, and mine hand take hold on judgment; I will render [e]vengeance to mine enemies, and will reward them that hate me.

42 I will make mine arrows drunk with blood, and my sword shall devour flesh; *and that* with the blood of the slain and of the captives, [6]from the beginning of revenges upon the enemy.

43 [f]Rejoice, O ye nations, *with* his people: for he will avenge the blood of his servants, and will render vengeance to his adversaries, and will [7]be merciful unto his land, *and* to his people.[Q]

44 ¶ And [g]Mō′ṣeṣ came and

v.34–1494 BC
See footnote, *Time*, Rev. 10:6.

**34**
q *Sin, known to God*, Rom. 5:1

**35**
r *Vengeance, belongs to God*, Psa. 94:1.

**36**
s *God, judge*, Gen. 2:2.
t *Repentance, attributed to God*, Mark 1:4.
u *God, mercy of, manifested in withholding punishment*, Gen. 2:2.

**37**
v *Idolatry, folly of*, 1 Sam. 15:23.

**39**
w *God, sovereign*, Gen. 2:2.
x *God, power of*, Gen. 2:2.
y *Death, God's power over*, Num. 23:10.
z *Life, from God*, Eccl. 8:15.
a *Adversity, dispensation from God*, Psa. 10:6.
b *Healing, the Lord the healer*, Acts 4:22.

**40**
c *God, eternity of*, Gen. 2:2.

**41**
d *Sword, figurative of judgments*, 1 Chr. 21:5.
e *Judgments*, Ex. 6:6.

**42**
6 R. V. From the head of the leaders of the enemy

**43**
f Rom. 15:10.
7 R. V. make expiation for

**44**
g *Moses*, Ex. 2:10

‡ **DRAGON.** *The Hebrew word translated* DRAGON *signified any terrible creature as, a venomous serpent*, Deut. 32:33; Psa. 91:13; *a sea serpent*, Psa. 74:13; 148:7; Isa. 27:1; *a jackal*, Isa. 13:22; 34:13; 35:7; 43:20; Jer. 9:11; 10:22; 14:6; 49:33; 51:37; Mic. 1:8; Mal. 1:3. *A term applied, to Pharaoh*, Isa. 51:9; *to Satan*, Rev. 20:2. **Symbolical,** Ezek. 29:3; 32:2; Rev. 12; 13; 16:13.

‖ **VENOM. Figurative:** *Of evil in the heart*, Job 20:14, 16. *Of the wicked tongue*, Psa. 140:3; Rom. 3:13. *Of the infurious effects of wine*, Deut. 32:33; Prov. 23:32.

v.44–1494 BC
See footnote, *Time*, Rev. 10:6.

h *Song, didactic*, Psa. 77:6.
i *Joshua*, Josh.1:1.

46
j *Commandment, enjoining obedience*, Deut. 8:2.
k *Parents, duties of, to instruct children*, 2 Cor. 12:14.
l *Obedience, enjoined*, Heb. 5:8.

47
m *Obedience, rewarded*, Heb. 5:8.
n *Jordan*, Gen. 32:10.

49
o Deut. 34:1.
p *Moab*, Num. 26:3.
q *Jericho*, Num. 22:1.
r *Canaan*, Gen. 37:1.

50
s *Death*, Num. 23:10.
t *Aaron*, Ex. 6:20.
u *Hor*, Num. 20:22.

spake all the words of this [h]song
in the ears of the people, he, and
[i]Hō-shē′ȧ the son of Nŭn.
45 And [g]Mō′ṣeṣ made an end
of speaking all these words to
all Īṣ′ra-el:
46 And he said unto them, [j]Set
your hearts unto all the words
which I testify[c] among you this
day, which [k]ye shall command
your children to observe to [l]do,
all the words of this law.
47 For it *is* not a vain thing for
you; because it *is* your life: and
[m]through this thing ye shall prolong
*your* days in the land,
whither ye go over [n]Jôr′dan to
possess it.[s]
48 ¶ And the LORD spake
unto [g]Mō′ṣeṣ that selfsame[c] day,
saying,
49 Get thee up into this[s] mountain
Ăb′a-rĭm, *unto* mount [o]Nē′bō,
which *is* in the land of
[p]Mō′ab, that *is* over against
[q]Jĕr′ĭ-chō; and behold the land
of [r]Cā′năan, which I give unto
the children of Īṣ′ra-el for a
possession:[Q]
50 And [s]die in the [o]mount
whither thou goest up, and be
gathered unto thy people; as
[t]Aâr′on thy brother died in
mount [u]Hôr, and was gathered
unto his people:
51 Because ye trespassed
against me among the children
of Īṣ′ra-el at the waters of [v]Mĕr′-
i-bah–Kā′desh, in the wilderness
of [w]Zĭn; because ye sanctified
me not in the midst of the children
of Īṣ′ra-el.
52 Yet thou shalt see the [r]land
before *thee*; but thou shalt not go
thither unto the land which I
give the children of Īṣ′ra-el.

## CHAPTER 33

*Moses' blessing. 2 The majesty of God. 6 The blessings on the several tribes. 26 The excellency of Israel's God.*

AND this *is* the [a]blessing,
wherewith [b]Mō′ṣeṣ the
[c]man of God blessed the children
of [d]Īṣ′ra-el before his
[e]death.
2 And he said, The LORD came
from [f]Sī′nāi, and rose up from
[g]Sē′ĭr unto them; [h]he shined
forth from mount [i]Pā′ran, and
he came [1]with ten thousands of
saints: from [j]his right hand
*went* a fiery *law for them.[Q]
3 Yea,[Q] [k]he loved the people; all
his saints *are* in thy hand: and
they sat down at thy [l]feet; *every
one* shall receive of thy words.
4 Mō′ṣeṣ commanded us a
*law, *even* the inheritance of
the congregation of Jā′cob.[Q]
5 And he was king in [m]Jĕsh′u-
rŭn, when the heads of the people
*and* the tribes of Īṣ′ra-el were
gathered together.
6 ¶ [n]Let [o]Reu′ben live, and not

v.51–1494 BC
See footnote, *Time*, Rev. 10:6.

51
v *Meribah*, Ex. 17:7.
w *Zin*, Num. 13:21.

B.C. 1491?
See footnote, *Time*, Rev. 10:6.

1
a *Benedictions, by Moses*, vs. 1:29; Deut. 21:5.
b *Moses, benedictions of*, Ex. 2:10.
c *Minister, called man of God*, Rom. 15:16.
d *Israel, prophecies concerning*, vs. 1–29; Ex. 4:22.
e *Death*, Num. 23:10.

2
f *Sinai*, Ex. 16:1.
g *Seir*, Deut. 1:2.
h *God, glory of*, Gen. 2:2.
i *Paran*, Gen. 21:21.
j *Theocracy, established*, vs. 2–5; Judg. 8:23.
1 R. V. from the ten thousands of holy ones: At his right hand was a fiery law unto them.

3
k *God, love of*, Gen. 2:2.
l *Feet, figurative*, 2 Sam. 4:4.

B.C. 1451?

5
m *Jeshurun*, Deut. 32:15.

6
n *Intercession, Moses for Israel*, vs. 6–25; Jer. 27:18.
o *Reubenites*, Josh. 22:1.

---

*** LAW.** *Made for the lawless*, 1 Tim. 1:8–10. *To be obeyed*, Matt. 22:21; Luke 20:22–25.

**Of God**, Psa. 119:1–8. *Holy*, Rom. 7:12. *Perfect*, Psa. 19:7–9; Jas. 1:25. *Spiritual*, Rom. 7:14. *To be obeyed*, 1 John 5:3. *Love, the fulfilling of*, Rom. 13:10; 1 Tim. 1:5.

OF MOSES: *Divine authority for*, Ex. 19:16–24; 20:1, 2; 24:12–18; 31:18; 32:15, 16; 34:1–4, 27, 28; Lev. 26:46; Deut. 4:10–13, 36; 5:1–22; 9:10; 10:1–5; 33:2–4; 1 Kin. 8:9; Ezra 7:6; Neh. 1:7; 8:1; 9:14; Psa. 78:5; 103:7; Isa. 33:22; Mal. 4:4; Acts 7:38, 53; Gal. 3:19; Heb. 9:18–21. *Given at Sinai*, Ex. 19; Deut. 1:1; 4:10–36, 44–46; 33:2. *Received by the disposition of angels*, Deut. 33:2; Acts 7:53; Gal. 3:19; Heb. 2:2. *Engraved, on stone*, Ex. 20:3–17; 24:12; 31:18; 32:16; 34:29; 40:20; Deut. 4:13; 5:4–22; 9:10; *on monuments*, Deut. 27:2–8; Josh. 8:30–35.

*Preserved in the ark of the covenant*, Ex. 25:16; Deut. 31:9, 26. *To be written, on door posts*, Deut. 6:9; 11:20; *on frontlet for the forehead, and on parchment for the hand*, Ex. 13:9, 16; Deut. 6:4–9; 11:18–21. *Children instructed in*, see footnote, CHILDREN, Mark 10:14.

*Expounded, by priests and Levites*, Lev. 10:11; Deut. 33:10; 2 Chr. 35:3; *by princes, priests, and Levites*, Ezra 7:10; Neh. 8:1–18; *from city to city*, 2 Chr. 17:7–10; *in synagogues*, Acts 13:14–52; 15:21 (with 9:20; 14:1); 17:1–3; 18:4, 26. *Expounded to the assembled nation at the feast of tabernacles in the sabbatic year*, Deut. 31:10–13. *Rehearsed by Moses, with many admonitions*, Deut. 4:44–46; chapters 5–34.

*Obedience to, enjoined*, Deut. 4:40; 5:32; 6:17; 7:11; 8:1, 6; 10:12, 13; 11:1, 8, 32; 13:4; 16:12; 27:1; 30:16; 32:46; Josh. 1:7; 22:5; 1 Kin. 2:3; 8:61; 2 Kin. 17:37. *Found by Hilkiah in the house of the Lord*, 2 Kin. 22:8.

*Blessings and curses of, responsively read by Levites and people at Ebal and Gerizim*, Deut. 27:12–26; Josh. 8:33–35.

*Formed a constitution on which the civil government of the Israelites was founded, and according to which rulers were required to rule*, Deut. 17:18–20; 2 Kin. 11:12; 2 Chr. 23:11.

*Was given because of transgressions until the coming of the Messiah*, Gal. 3:19. *Was committed to the Jews*, Rom. 3:1, 2. *Brings the knowledge of sin*, Rom. 3:20; 7:7.

*Prophecies in, of the Messiah*, Luke 24:44; John 1:45; 5:46; 12:34; Acts 26:22, 23; 28:23; Rom. 3:21, 22.

*Epitomized by Jesus*, Matt. 22:40; Mark 12:29–33; Luke 10:27.

*Temporary*, Jer. 3:16; Dan. 9:27; Heb. 10:1–18. *Weakness of*, Rom. 8:3, 6.

*Fulfilled by Christ*, Matt. 5:17–45; Acts 6:14; 13:39; Rom. 10:3, 4; Eph. 2:15; Heb. 8:4–13; 9:8–24; 10:3–9.

*Superseded by the gospel*, Luke 16:16, 17; John 1:17; 4:20–24; 8:35 (with Gal. 4:30, 31); Acts 10:28; 15:1–29; 21:20–25; Rom. 7:1–6; 2 Cor. 3:7–14; Gal. 2:3–9, 19; 4:4–31; 5:1–18; Col. 2:14–23; Heb. 7:5–9.

v.6–1494 BC
See footnote, *Time*, Rev. 10:6.

7
*p Judah, tribe of*, Num. 10:14.

8
*q Levites*, Deut. 10:8.
*r Urim and Thummim*, Lev. 8:8.
*s Meribah*, Ex. 17:7.

9
*t Obedience, exemplified*, Heb. 5:8.

10
*u Levites, teachers of the law*, Deut. 10:8.
*v Instruction, in religion*, Prov. 23:23.
*w Incense*, Ex. 37:29.
*x Offerings, burnt*, Lev. 6:17.

11
*y Temporal Blessings, prayer for*, Psa. 103:2.

12
*z Benjamin, tribe of*, Num. 1:37.

*a Intercession, of Moses for Israel*, Jer. 27:18.
*b God, preserver of the righteous*, Gen. 2:2.

13
*c Ephraim, tribe of*, Gen. 41:52.
*d Manasseh, tribe of*, Gen. 46:20.
*e Dew, figurative*, Dan. 4:15.

14
*f Sun*, Josh. 10:12.

die; and let *not* his men be
few.
7 ¶ And this *is the blessing* of
[p]Jū′dah: and he [n]said, Hear,
LORD, the voice of Jū′dah, and
bring him unto his people: let his
hands be sufficient for him; and
be thou an help *to him* from his
enemies.
8 ¶ And of [q]Lē′vī he [n]said, *Let*
thy [r]Thŭm′mim and thy Ū′rim[C]
*be* with thy holy one, whom thou
didst prove[C] at Măs′sah, *and with*
whom thou didst strive at the
waters of [s]Mĕr′i-bah;
9 Who said unto his father and
to his mother, I have not seen
him; neither did he acknowledge
his brethren, nor knew his own
children: for they have [t]observed[C]
thy word, and kept thy covenant.[Q]
10 [u]They shall [v]teach Jā′cob
thy judgments[C], and Ĭṣ′ra-el thy
*law: they shall put [w]incense be-
fore thee, and whole [x]burnt sacrifice upon thine altar.
11 [n, y]Bless, LORD, his substance, and accept the work of
his hands: smite through the
loins of them that rise against
him, and of them that hate him,
that they rise not again.
12 ¶ *And* of [z]Bĕn′ja-mīn he
[a]said, The beloved of the LORD
shall dwell in safety by him; *and*
*the* [b]LORD shall cover him all the
day long, and he shall dwell between his shoulders.[Q]
13 ¶ And of [c, d]Jō′ṣeph he [a]said,
Blessed of the LORD *be* his land,
for the precious things of heaven,
for the [e]dew, and for the deep
that coucheth[C] beneath,
14 And for the precious fruits
*brought forth* by the [f]sun, and for
the precious things put forth by
the [g]moon,
15 And for the chief things of
the ancient mountains, and for
the precious things of the [2]last-
ing [h]hills,
16 And for the precious things
of the earth and fulness thereof,
and *for* the good will of him that
dwelt in the [i]bush: [a]let *the bless-*
*ing* come upon the head of
[c, d]Jō′ṣeph, and upon the top of
the head of him *that was* separated from his brethren.
17 His glory *is like* the firstling
of his bullock, and his horns *are*
*like* the horns of [3, j]unicorns:
with them he shall push the people together to the ends of the
earth: and they *are* the ten thousands of [c]Ē′phră-ĭm, and they
*are* the [4]thousands of [d]Mă-năs′-
seh.
18 ¶ And of [k]Zĕb′u-lŭn he said,
Rejoice, Zĕb′u-lŭn, in thy going
out; and, [l]Ĭs′sa-char, in thy
tents.
19 They shall call the people
unto the mountain; there they
shall [m]offer sacrifices of righteousness: for they shall suck *of*
the abundance of the seas, and
*of* treasures hid in the sand.
20 ¶ And of †Găd he said,
Blessed *be* he that enlargeth
Găd: he dwelleth as a [4]lion, and
teareth the arm with the crown
of the head.
21 And he provided the first
part for himself, because there,
*in* a portion of the lawgiver, *was*
*he* seated; and he came with the
heads of the people, he executed
the ‡justice[C] of the LORD, and
his judgments[C] with Ĭṣ′ra-el.

v.14–1494 BC
See footnote, *Time*, Rev. 10:6.

*g Moon*, Song 6:10.

15
*h Earth, perpetuity of*, Prov. 8:23.
2 R. V. everlasting

16
*i Burning Bush*, Ex. 3:2.

17
*j Unicorn*, Job 39:9.
3 R. V. the wild-ox:

18
*k Zebulun, tribe of*, Gen. 49:13.
*l Issachar, tribe of*, Num. 1:28.

19
*m Worship, enjoined*, Gen. 22:5.

20
4 R. V. lioness,

† **GAD** (*fortune*), a tribe of Israel. *Military enrollment of, at Sinai*, Num. 1:14, 24, 25; *in the plains of Moab*, Num. 26:15–18; *in the reign of Jotham*, 1 Chr. 5:11–17. *Place of, in camp and march*, Num. 2:10, 14, 16. *Wealth of, in cattle and spoils*, Josh. 22:8.

*Petitions for their portion of land E. of the Jordan*, Num. 32:1–5; Deut. 3:12, 16, 17; 29:8. *Boundaries of territory of*, Josh. 13:24–28. *Cities of, given to the sons of Merari*, 1 Chr. 6:80. *Aids in the conquest of the region W. of the Jordan*, Num. 32:16–32; Josh. 4:12, 13; 22:1–8. *Erects a monument to signify the unity of the tribes E. of the Jordan with the tribes W. of that river*, Josh. 22:10, 24–28.

*Blessed by Moses*, Deut. 33:20.

*Disaffected toward Saul as king, and joins the faction under David in the wilderness of Hebron*, 1 Chr. 12:8–15, 37, 38. *Joins the Reubenites in the war against the Hagarites*, 1 Chr. 5:10, 18–22. *Smitten by the king of Syria*, 2 Kin. 10:32, 33. *Carried into captivity to Assyria*, 1 Chr. 5:26. *Land of, occupied by the Ammonites, after the tribe is carried into captivity*, Jer. 49:1. *Reallotment of territory to, by Ezekiel*, Ezek. 48:27, 29.

‡ **JUSTICE.** *From God*, Psa. 72:1, 2; Prov. 29:26. *Enjoined*, Ex. 23:1–3, 6–8; Lev. 19:13–15; Deut. 16:18–20; 25:1–4; Psa. 82:3, 4; 106:3; Prov. 18:5; Isa. 1:17; Jer. 7:5, 7;

v.22–1494 BC
See footnote, *Time*, Rev. 10:6.

**22**
n *Dan, tribe of*, Gen. 30:6.
o *Bashan*, Num. 32:33.
**23**
p *Naphtali, tribe of*, Num. 1:42.
**24**
q *Asher, tribe of*, Num. 1:40.
r *Children*, Mark 10:14.
**25**
s *Brass, figurative*, Job 28:2.
t *Spiritual Blessings*, Eph. 1:3.
**26**
u *God, power of*, Gen. 2:2.
v *Jeshurun*, Deut. 32:15.
**27**
w *Adversity, consolation in*, Psa. 10:6.
x *Promise, to the righteous*, 2 Cor. 1:20.
y *God, eternity of*, Gen. 2:2.
z *Righteous, promises to*, Psa. 64:10.
a *Arm, figurative*, Psa. 89:13.
**28**
b *Israel, prophecies concerning*, Ex. 4:22.
c *Corn*, Psa. 65:13.
d *Wine*, Prov. 23:31.
e *Dew, figurative*, Dan. 4:15.
**29**
f *Righteous, happiness of*, Psa. 64:10.
g *God, preserver*, Gen. 2:2.
h *Shield, figurative*, 1 Kin. 14:27.
5 R. V. submit themselves unto thee

22 ¶ And of [n]Dăn he said, Dăn *is* a lion's whelp: he shall leap from [o]Bā'shăn.

23 ¶ And of [p]Năph'ta-lī he said, O Năph'ta-lī, satisfied with favour, and full with the blessing of the LORD: possess thou the west and the south.

24 ¶ And of [q]Ăsh'ēr he said, *Let* Ăsh'ēr *be* blessed with [r]children; let him be acceptable to his brethren, and let him dip his foot in oil.

25 Thy shoes *shall be* iron and [s]brass; and as thy days, [t]*so shall* thy strength *be*.

26 ¶ *There is* none like unto the [u]God of [v]Jĕsh'u-rŭn, *who* rideth upon the heaven in thy help, and in his excellency on the sky.

27 [w, x]The eternal [y]God *is* [z]*thy* refuge, and underneath *are* the everlasting [a]arms: and he shall thrust out the enemy from before thee; and shall say, Destroy *them*.

28 [b]Ĭs'ra-el then shall dwell in safety alone: the fountain of Jā'cob *shall be* upon a land of [c]corn and [d]wine; also his heavens shall drop down [e]dew.

29 Happy *art* [f]thou, O [b]Ĭs'ra-el: who *is* like unto thee, O people saved by the [g]LORD, the [h]shield of thy help, and who *is* the sword of thy excellency! and thine enemies shall [5]be found liars unto thee; and thou shalt tread upon their high places.

## CHAPTER 34

*Moses from mount Nebo views the land. 5 His death and burial. 7 His age. 8 The people mourn for him thirty days. 9 Joshua succeeds him. 10 The praise of Moses.*

**1**
a *Moses, views the land*, Ex. 2:10.
b *Moab*, Num. 26:3.
c Deut. 32:49, 50.
d *Pisgah*, Deut. 3:27.
e *Jericho*, Num. 22:1.

AND [a]Mō'ṣeṣ went up from the plains of [b]Mō'ab unto the mountain of [c]Nē'bō, to the top of [d]Pĭṣ'gah, that *is* over against [e]Jĕr'ĭ-chō. And the LORD shewed him all the land of [f]Gĭl'e-ăd, unto [g]Dăn,

2 And all [h]Năph'ta-lī, and the land of [i]Ē'phră-ĭm, and [j]Mă-năs'seh, and all the land of [k]Jū'dah, unto the utmost sea,

3 And the south, and the plain of the valley of [e]Jĕr'ĭ-chō, the city of [l]palm trees, unto *Zō'ar.

4 And the LORD said unto [a]him, This *is* the [m]land which I [n]sware unto Ā'bră-hăm, unto Ī'ṣaac, and unto Jā'cob, saying, I will give it unto thy seed: I have caused thee to see *it* with thine eyes, but thou shalt not go over thither.

5 ¶ So [a]Mō'ṣeṣ the servant of the LORD [o]died there in the land of [b]Mō'ab, according to the word of the LORD.

6 And he buried him in a valley in the land of [b]Mō'ab, over against [p]Bĕth–pē'ôr: but no man knoweth of his sepulchre unto this day.

7 ¶ And [a]Mō'ṣeṣ *was* [q, r]an hundred and twenty years old when he [o]died: his eye was not dim, nor his natural force abated.

8 ¶ And the children of [s]Ĭṣ'ra-el [t]wept for [a]Mō'ṣeṣ in the plains of [b]Mō'ab thirty days: so the days of weeping *and* mourning for Mō'ṣeṣ were ended.

9 ¶ And [u]Jŏsh'u-ȧ the son of Nŭn was [v]full of the spirit of wisdom; for [a]Mō'ṣeṣ had laid his [w]hands upon him: and the children of Ĭṣ'ra-el hearkened unto him, and did as the LORD commanded Mō'ṣeṣ.

10 ¶ And there arose not a prophet since in Ĭṣ'ra-el like unto [a]Mō'ṣeṣ, whom the LORD knew face to face,

11 In all the [x]signs and the

v.1–1494 BC
See footnote, *Time*, Rev. 10:6.
f *Gilead*, Deut. 3:13.
g *Dan*, Judg. 18:29.
**2**
h *Naphtali, tribe of*, Num. 1:42.
i *Ephraim, tribe of*, Gen. 41:52.
j *Manasseh, tribe of*, Gen. 46:20.
k *Judah, tribe of*, Num. 10:14.
**3**
l *Palm Tree*, Song 7:7.
**4**
m *Canaan*, Gen. 37:1.
n *Covenant, of God with men*, Deut. 29:1.
**5**
o *Death*, Num. 23:10.
**6**
p *Beth-peor*, Deut. 3:29.
**7**
q *Longevity, of Moses*, Psa. 91:16.
r *Old Age*, Isa. 46:4.
**8**
s *Israel, mourns for Moses*, Ex. 4:22.
t *Mourning*, Lam. 2:5.
v.8–1493 BC
**9**
u *Joshua, divinely inspired*, Josh. 1:1.
v *Inspiration, of Joshua*, Job 32:8.
w *Hand, imposition of*, Ezra 10:19.
**11**
x *Miracles*, Luke 23:8.

Lam. 3:35, 36; Mic. 6:8; Zech. 7:9; 8:16; John 7:24, 51. *Without respect of persons*, Prov. 24:23; 28:21. *Perverted*, Eccl. 3:16; 5:8; Isa. 59:14, 15; Jer. 22:3; Amos 5:7, 11, 12; Mic. 7:3; Hab. 1:4; Matt. 12:7. *Rewarded*, Jer. 22:4, 15, 16; Ezek. 18:5–9.
**Of God**, see footnote, GOD, *Justice of*, Gen. 2:2.

See footnotes: COURT, Ex. 18:26; INJUSTICE, Isa. 26:10; JUDGE, Judg. 2:18.
***ZOAR.** *A city of the Moabites, near the Jordan*, Gen. 13:10; Deut. 34:3; Isa. 15:5; Jer. 48:34. *King of, fought against Chedorlaomer*, Gen. 14:2, 8. *Not destroyed with Sodom and Gomorrah*, Gen. 19:20–23, 30.

*y Egypt*, Gen. 41:8.
*z Pharaoh*, Ex. 3:10.

wonders, which the LORD sent him to do in the land of [y]Ē'ġȳpt to [z]Phā'raōh, and to all his servants, and to all his land,

12 And in all that mighty hand, and in all the great terror[C] which Mō'şeş [1]shewed in the sight of all Ĭş'ra-el.

12
1 R.V. wrought

THE

# BOOK OF JOSHUA

## CHAPTER 1

*The Lord appoints Joshua to succeed Moses. 3 The extent of the promised land. 5 God encourages and instructs Joshua. 10 Joshua prepares the people to pass over Jordan. 12 He puts the two tribes and a half in mind of their promise to Moses. 16 They promise him obedience.*

v.1–1493 BC

1
*a Death*, Num. 23:10.
*b Moses*, Ex. 2:10.
*c Call, personal*, Phil. 3:14.
*d Rulers, ordained of God*, Ex. 18:21.

2
*e Jordan*, Gen. 32:10.
*f Canaan*, Gen. 37:1.
*g Israel*, Ex. 4:22.

3
*h God, faithfulness of*, Gen. 2:2.

4
*i Canaanites, territory of*, Ex. 23:28.
*j Lebanon*, Deut. 1:7.
*k Euphrates*, Gen. 15:18.
*l Hittites*, Judg. 1:26.
*m Mediterranean Sea*, Ex. 23:31.

5
*n Promise, to the righteous, of divine help*, 2 Cor. 1:20.
*o Righteous; promises to*, Psa. 64:10.
*p God, preserver*, Gen. 2:2.
*q God, presence of*, Gen. 2:2.
*r* Heb. 13:5.
*s Grace of God*, Rom. 4:16.

6
*t Commandment, enjoining courage*, Deut. 8:2.
*u Faith, enjoined*, Mark 11:22.

NOW after the [a]death of [b]Mō'şeş the servant of the LORD it came to pass, that the LORD [c,d]spake unto *Jŏsh'u-ȧ the son of Nŭn, Mō'şeş' minister, saying,

2 Mō'şeş my servant is dead; now therefore [c]arise, go over this [e]Jôr'dan, thou, and all this people, unto the [f]land which I do give to them, *even* to the children of [g]Ĭş'ra-el.

3 Every place that the sole of your foot shall tread[C] upon, that have [h]I given unto you, as I said unto Mō'şeş.

4 [i]From the wilderness and this [j]Lĕb'a-non even unto the great river, the river [k]Eū-phrā'tēş, all the land of the [l]Hĭt'tītes, and unto the [m]great sea toward the going down of the sun, shall be your coast.[C]

5 [n]There shall not any man be able to stand before [o]thee all the days of thy life: as I was with [b]Mō'şeş, *so* [p,q]I will be with thee: [h,r]I [s]will not fail thee, nor forsake thee.[S] [Q]

6 [t,u]Be strong and of a good [v]courage: for [1]unto this people shalt thou divide for an inheritance the [f]land, which I [w]sware unto their fathers to give them.

7 Only [t,u]be *, [x]thou strong and very [v]courageous, that thou mayest observe to [y]do according to all the [z]law, which Mō'şeş my servant commanded thee: turn not from it *to* the right hand or *to* the left, [a]that thou mayest [b]prosper whithersoever thou goest.

8 [c]This [d]book of the [e]law shall not depart[C] out of thy mouth; but [f,g]thou shalt [h]meditate therein day and night, that thou mayest observe to do according to all that is written therein: [a,i]for then [j]thou shalt make thy way [b,k]prosperous, and then thou shalt have good success.[S]

9 Have not [l]I commanded thee? [m]Be strong and of a good courage; [n]be not afraid, neither be thou dismayed: for [o]the [p]LORD thy God *is* with thee whithersoever thou goest.[S]

10 ¶ Then *Jŏsh'u-ȧ commanded the [q]officers of the [r]people, saying,

11 Pass through the [r]host, and command the [s]people, saying,

*o Promise, to the righteous, of divine help*, 2 Cor. 1:20. *p God, presence of*, Gen. 2:2. **10** *q Rulers*, Ex. 18:21. *r Armies, officers of*, Deut. 11:4. **11** *s Israel*, Ex. 4:22.

*v Courage*, vs. 1–9 Deut. 31:7.
*w Covenant, of God with men*, Deut. 29:1.
1 R. V. thou shalt cause this people to inherit the land which

7
*x Rulers, duties of* Ex. 18:21.
*y Obedience, enjoined*, Heb. 5:8.
*z Law, of Moses*, Deut. 33:2.

*a Blessings, contingent upon obedience*, Deut. 11:26.
*b Prosperity*, Eccl. 7:14.

8
*c Commandment, enjoining knowledge of God's word*, Deut. 8:2.
*d Book*, Num. 5:23.
*e Word of God*, Psa. 119:9.
*f Minister, duties of*, Rom. 15:16.
*g Rulers, righteous* Ex. 18:21.
*h Meditation, on the law, enjoined* Psa. 49:3.
*i Obedience, rewarded*, Heb. 5:8
*j Promise, to the righteous, of prosperity*, 2 Cor. 1:20.
*k Temporal Blessings, from God*, Psa. 103:2.

9
*l God, sovereign*, Gen. 2:2.
*m Commandment, enjoining courage*, Deut. 8:2.
*n Faith, enjoined upon public leaders*, vs. 5–9; Mark 11:22.

* **JOSHUA** (*Jehovah his help*), called also JEHOSHUA, JEHOSHUAH, and OSHEA. *Son of Nun*, Num. 13:8; 1 Chr. 7:27. *Intimately associated with Moses*, Ex. 24:13; 32:17; 33:11. *A religious zealot*, Num. 11:28. *Sent to view Canaan*, Num. 13:3–8. *Makes favorable report*, Num. 14:6–10. *Miraculously preserved when he made a favorable report of the land*, Num. 14:10. *Rewarded for his courage and fidelity*, Num. 14:30, 38; 32:12.

*Charged with responsibilities of Moses' office*, Num. 27:18–23; Deut. 1:38; 3:28; 31:3, 7, 23; 34:9. *Divinely inspired*, Num. 27:18; Deut. 34:9; Josh. 1:5, 9; 3:7; 8:8. *Promises to*, Josh. 1:5–9.

*Leads the people into Canaan*, Josh. chapters 1–4; Acts 7:45; Heb. 4:8. *Renews circumcision; re-establishes the passover, has a vision of the angel of God*, Josh. 5. *Besieges and takes Jericho*, Josh. 6. *Takes Ai*, Josh. 7; 8. *The kings of six nations of Canaanites combine against him*, Josh. 9:1, 2; *are defeated and slain*, Josh. 10:1–27. *Makes league with Gibeonites*, Josh. 9:3–27. *Defeats, successively, seven kings*, Josh. 10:23–43. *Takes Hazor*, Josh. 11:1–17. *Completes conquest of whole land*, Josh. 11:18–23. *List of kings whom Joshua smote*, Josh. 12.

*Allots land*, Josh. chapters 13–19. *Sets the tabernacle in Shiloh*, Josh. 18:1. *Designates, cities of refuge*, Josh. 20; *forty-eight cities for the Levites*, Josh. 21.

*Exhorts the people before his death*, Josh. 23; 24. *Survives*

v.11–1493 BC
See footnote, *Time*, Rev. 10:6.

*t Food*, Psa. 136:25.
*u Jordan*, Gen. 32:10.
*v Canaan*, Gen. 37:1.
*w God, providence of*, Gen. 2:2.

12
*x Reubenites, assist in conquest of the region west of the Jordan*, vs. 12–18; Josh. 22:1.
*y Gad, tribe of*, Deut. 33:20.
*z Manasseh, tribe of, the eastern half assist in the conquest of the country west of the Jordan*, vs. 12–15; Gen. 46:20.

13
*a Moses*, Ex. 2:10.
*b God, providence of*, Gen. 2:2.
*c Canaan*, Gen. 37:1.

14
*d Wife*, Prov. 5:18.
*e Children*, Mark 10:14.
*f Cattle*, Ex. 12:29.
*g Moab*, Num. 26:3.
*h Jordan*, Gen. 32:10.
*i Courage*, Deut. 31:7.

16
*j Loyalty, instances of*, vs. 16–18; Eccl. 8:2.

17
*k Decision*, Isa. 50:7.
*l Prayer, intercessory*, Acts 6:4.

18
*m Death, penalty*, Num. 23:10.

Prepare you [t]victuals[c]; for within
three days ye shall pass over this
[u]Jôr′dan, to go in to possess the
[v,k]land, which the [w]LORD your
God giveth you to possess it.
12 ¶ And to the [x]Reu̦′ben-ītes,
and to the [y]Găd′ītes, and to half
the tribe of [z]Må-năs′seh, spake
*Jŏsh′u-å, saying,
13 Remember the word which
[a]Mō′se̦s the servant of the LORD
commanded you, saying, The
[b]LORD your God hath given you
rest, and hath given you this
[c]land.
14 Your [d]wives, your [e]little
ones, and your [f]cattle, shall remain in the [g]land which Mō′se̦s
gave you on this side [h]Jôr′dan;
but ye shall pass before your
brethren armed, all the mighty
men of [i]valour[c], and help
them;
15 Until the [b]LORD have given
your brethren rest[c], as *he hath
given* you, and they also have
possessed the [c]land which the
LORD our God giveth them:
then ye shall return unto the
[g]land of your possession, and enjoy it, which Mō′se̦s the LORD's
servant gave you on this side
[h]Jôr′dan toward the sunrising[c].
16 ¶ And they answered
*Jŏsh′u-å, saying, [j]All that thou
commandest us we will do, and
whithersoever thou sendest us,
we will go.
17 According as we hearkened
unto Mō′se̦s in all things, so
[k]will we hearken unto thee: only
[l]the LORD thy God be with thee,
as he was with Mō′se̦s.
18 Whosoever *he be* that doth
rebel against thy commandment,
and will not hearken unto thy
words in all that thou commandest him, he [m]shall be put to
death: only be strong and of a
good courage.

## CHAPTER 2

*Rahab receives and conceals the two spies sent from Shittim. 8 The covenant between her and them. 18 The token of the scarlet thread. 23 Their return and report.*

AND [a]Jŏsh′u-å the son of
Nŭn sent out of [b]Shĭt′tim
two [c]men to spy secretly, saying,
Go view the land, even [d]Jĕr′ĭ-
chō. And they went, and came
into an [e,f]harlot's house, named
*Rā′hăb, and [g]lodged there.
2 And it was told the [h]king of
[d]Jĕr′ĭ-chō, saying, Behold, there
came [c]men in hither[c] to night of
the children of Ĭs̱′ra-el to search
out the country.
3 And the [h]king of [d]Jĕr′ĭ-chō
sent unto *Rā′hăb, saying,
Bring forth the [c]men that are
come to thee, which are entered
into thine house: for they be
come to search out all the
country.
4 And the *,[e]woman took the
two men, and [i]hid them, and
said thus, There came men unto
me, but [j]I wist not[c] whence they
*were*:[Q]
5 [j]And it came to pass *about the
time* of shutting of the [k]gate,
when it was dark, that the men
went out: whither[c] the men went
I wot[c] not: pursue after them
quickly; for ye shall overtake
them.
6 But *she had brought them
up to the [l]roof of the house, and
[i]hid them with the stalks of
[m]flax, which she had laid in
order upon the roof.
7 And the men pursued after
[c]them the way to [n]Jôr′dan unto
the fords: and as soon as they
which pursued after them were
gone out, they shut the [k]gate.

v.18–1493 BC
See footnote, *Time*, Rev. 10:6.

1
*a Joshua*, Josh. 1:1.
*b Shittim*, Num. 25:1.
*c Spies*, Josh. 6:23
*d Jericho*, Num. 22:1.
*e Harlot*, Prov. 7:10.
*f Women, wicked*, Prov. 31:10.
*g Hospitality*, Rom. 12:13.

2
*h Rulers*, Ex. 18:21.

4
*i Kindness, instances of*, Acts 28:2.
*j Falsehood, instances of*, Job 21:34.

5
*k Gates, closed at night*, Deut. 3:5.

6
*l House, architecture of*, Esth. 8:1.
*m Flax*, Ex. 9:31.

7
*n Jordan*, Gen. 32:10.

*Israelites who refused to enter Canaan*, Num. 26:63–65. *Allotment of land to*, Josh. 19:49, 50.
*Death and burial of*, Josh. 24:29, 30; Judg. 2:8, 9. *Esteem in which he was held*, Josh. 1:16–18. *Faith of, at the taking of Jericho*, Josh. 6:16. *Military genius of, as exhibited, at the defeat of the Amalekites*, Ex. 17:13; *at the taking of Ai*, Josh. 8:1–29; *at Gibeon, and other cities*, Josh. chapters 10, 11.

* **RAHAB**, a woman of Jericho. *Assists the spies of Israel*, Josh. 2. *Is spared at the taking of Jericho*, Josh. 6:17–25. *Ancestor of Joseph*, see R. V. Matt. 1:5. *Faith of, commended*, Heb. 11:31; Jas. 2:25.

v.8–1493 BC
See footnote, *Time*, Rev. 10:6.

**9**

o *Faith, instances of*, vs. 9–11; Mark 11:22.

p *Canaan*, Gen. 37:1.

**10**

q *Miracles, design of*, Luke 23:8.

r *Red Sea*, Ex. 10:19.

s *Egypt*, Gen. 41:8.

t *Amorites*, Gen. 14:13.

u *Sihon*, Num. 21:21.

v *Og*, Num. 21:33.

**11**

w *Cowardice, instances of*, Lev. 26:36.

x *God, sovereign*, Gen. 2:2.

**12**

y *Daughter, affectionate*, Lev. 12:6.

z *Intercession, of man with man*, Jer. 27:18.

---

a *Oath*, Num. 5:19.

b *Token*, Psa. 86:17.

**13**

c *Father*, Psa. 27:10.

d *Mother*, 1 Kin. 2:20.

e *Death*, Num. 23:10.

**14**

f *Spies*, Josh. 6:23.

g *Covenant, of men with men*, Deut. 29:1.

**15**

h *Walls, houses built upon*, 1 Sam. 20:25.

8 ¶ And before [c]they were laid down, *she came up unto them upon the roof;

9 And she said unto the men, I [o]know that the LORD hath given you the [p]land, and that your terror is fallen upon us, and that all the inhabitants of the land faint because of you.

10 For we have heard how the LORD [q]dried up the water of the [r]Red sea for you, when ye came out of [s]Ē′ġ̆ypt; and what ye did unto the two kings of the [t]Ăm′ôr-ītes, that *were* on the other side Jôr′dan, [u]Sī′hŏn and [v]Ŏg, whom ye utterly destroyed.

11[Q]And as soon as we had heard *these things*, [w]our hearts did melt, neither did there remain any more courage in any man, because of you: for the LORD your God, he *is* [x]God in heaven above, and in earth beneath.

12 Now therefore, [y]I [z]pray you, [a]swear[C] unto me by the LORD, since I have shewed you kindness, that ye will also shew kindness unto my father's house, and give me a true [b]token:[Q]

13 And *that* ye will save alive my [c]father, and my [d]mother, and my brethren, and my sisters, and all that they have, and deliver our lives from [e]death.

14 And the [f]men answered *her, [g]Our life for your's, if ye utter not this our business. And it shall be, when the LORD hath given us the land, that we will deal kindly and truly with thee.

15 Then *she let [f]them down by a cord through the †window: for her house *was* upon the town [h]wall, and she dwelt upon the wall.[Q]

16 And she said unto them, Get you to the mountain, lest the pursuers meet you; and hide yourselves there three days, until the pursuers be returned: and afterward may ye go your way.

17 And the men said unto her, We *will be* [1]blameless[C] of this thine [a]oath which thou hast made us swear.

18 Behold, *when* we come into the land, thou shalt bind this line of [b]scarlet thread in the †window which thou didst let us down by: and thou shalt bring thy [c]father, and thy [d]mother, and thy brethren, and all thy [c]father's household, home unto thee.

19 [g]And it shall be, *that* whosoever shall go out of the doors of thy house into the street, his blood *shall be* upon his head, and we *will be* guiltless: and whosoever shall be with thee in the house, his blood[C] *shall be* on our head, if *any* hand be upon him.

20 And if thou utter this our business, then we will be [1]quit[C] of thine [a]oath which thou hast made us to swear.

21 And she said, [g]According unto your words, so *be* it. And she sent them away, and they departed: and she bound the [b]scarlet line in the window.

22 And [f]they went, and came unto the mountain, and abode there three days, until the pursuers were returned: and the pursuers sought *them* throughout all the way, but found *them* not.

23 So the two [f]men returned, and descended from the mountain, and passed over, and came to [i]Jŏsh′u-ȧ the son of Nŭn, and told him all *things* that befell them:

24 And they said unto [i]Jŏsh′u-ȧ, Truly the [j]LORD hath delivered into our hands all the [k]land; for even all the inhabitants of the country do faint because of us.

v.16–1493 BC
See footnote, *Time*, Rev. 10:6.

**17**

1 R. V. guiltless

**23**

i *Joshua*, Josh. 1:1.

**24**

j *God, providence of*, Gen. 2:2.

k *Canaan*, Gen. 37:1.

---

† **WINDOW**, Gen. 6:16; 26:8; Josh. 2:15, 21; 1 Sam. 19:12; 1 Kin. 6:4; Ezek. 40:16–36; Acts 20:9.

v.1–1493 BC
See footnote, *Time*, Rev. 10:6.

## CHAPTER 3

*The Israelites come to Jordan. 2 The officers instruct them how they are to pass over it. 7 The Lord encourages Joshua. 9 Joshua encourages the people. 14 The waters of Jordan are divided.*

AND [a]Jŏsh'u-ȧ rose early in the morning; and they removed from [b]Shĭt'tim, and came to [c]Jôr'dan, he and all the children of [d]Ĭṣ'ra-el, and lodged there before they passed over.

2 And it came to pass after three days, that the officers went through the [1]host;

3 And they commanded the people, saying, When ye see the [e]ark of the covenant of the LORD your God, and the [f]priests the Lē'vītes bearing it, then ye shall remove from your place, and go after it.

4 Yet there shall be a space between you and it, about two thousand [g]cubits by measure: come not near unto it, that ye may know the way by which ye must go: for ye have not passed *this* way heretofore.

5 And [a]Jŏsh'u-ȧ said unto the people, [h]Sanctify yourselves: for to morrow the LORD will do wonders among you.

6 And [a]Jŏsh'u-ȧ spake unto the [f]priests, saying, Take up the [e]ark of the covenant, and pass over before the people. And they took up the ark of the covenant, and went before the people.

7 ¶ And the LORD said unto [a]Jŏsh'u-ȧ, This day will I begin to magnify thee in the sight of all [d]Ĭṣ'ra-el, that they may know that, as [i]I was with Mō'ṣeṣ, *so* [i]I will be with thee.

8 And thou shalt command the [f]priests that bear the [e]ark of the covenant, saying, When ye are come to the brink of the water of [c]Jôr'dan, ye shall stand still in Jôr'dan.

9 ¶ And [a]Jŏsh'u-ȧ said unto the children of Ĭṣ'ra-el, Come hither, and hear the [j]words of the LORD your God.

10 And [a]Jŏsh'u-ȧ said, Hereby ye shall know that the living God [i]*is* among you, and *that* he will without fail drive out from before you the [k]Cā'năan-ītes, and the [l]Hĭt'tītes, and the [m]Hī'vītes, and the [n]Pĕr'ĭz-zītes, and the [o]Ğīr'ga-shītes, and the [p]Ăm'ôr-ītes, and the [q]Jĕb'u-sītes.

11 Behold, the [e]ark of the covenant of the [r]LORD of all the earth passeth over before you into [c]Jôr'dan.

12 Now therefore take you twelve men out of the tribes of [s]Ĭṣ'ra-el, out of every tribe a man.

13 And it shall come to pass, as soon as the soles of the feet of the [f]priests that bear the [e]ark of the LORD, the [r]LORD of all the earth, shall rest in the waters of [c]Jôr'dan, *that* the waters of Jôr'dan shall be cut off [2]*from* the waters that come down from above; and they shall stand upon an heap.

14 ¶ And it came to pass, when the [d]people removed from their tents, to pass over [c]Jôr'dan, and the [f]priests bearing the [e]ark of the covenant before the people;

15 And as they that bare the [e]ark were come unto [c]Jôr'dan, and the feet of the [f]priests that bare the ark were dipped in the brim of the water, (for Jôr'dan overfloweth all his banks all the time of harvest,)

16 That the waters which came down from above [t]stood *and* rose up upon an heap very far from the city Ăd'ăm, that *is* beside [u]Zăr'e-tăn: and those that came down toward the [v]sea of the [3]plain, *even* the salt sea, failed, *and* were cut off: and the people passed over right against [w]Jĕr'ĭ-chō.

17 And the [f]priests that bare the [e]ark of the covenant of the

---

1
a *Joshua*, Josh. 1:1.
b *Shittim*, Num. 25:1.
c *Jordan*, Gen. 32:10.
d *Israel*, Ex. 4:22.

2
1 R. V. midst of the camp;

3
e *Ark, of the covenant*, Ex. 25:10.
f *Priest, duties of*, Lev. 1:5.

4
g *Cubit*, Ex. 36:9.

5
h *Sanctification*, 1 Pet. 1:2.

7
i *God, presence of*, Gen. 2:2.

v.9–1493 BC
See footnote, *Time*, Rev. 10:6.

9
j *Word of God*, Psa. 119:9.

10
k *Canaanites*, Ex. 23:28.
l *Hittites*, Judg. 1:26.
m *Hivites*, Gen. 10:17.
n *Perizzites*, Gen. 15:20.
o *Girgashites*, Neh. 9:8.
p *Amorites*, Gen. 14:13.
q *Jebusites*, Deut. 7:1.

11
r *God, sovereign*, Gen. 2:2.

12
s *Israel, tribes of*, Ex. 4:22.

13
2 R. V. even the waters

16
t *Miracles, Jordan divided*, Luke 23:8.
u Or, *Zartanah*, 1 Kin. 4:12; or, *Zarthan*, 1 Kin. 7:46.
v *Dead Sea*, Gen. 14:3.
w *Jericho*, Num. 22:1.
3 R. V. Arabah.

v.17–1493 BC
See footnote, *Time*, Rev. 10:6.

1
*a Israel*, Ex. 4:22.
*b Jordan*, Gen. 32: 10.
*c Prophets, inspiration of*, Isa. 3:2.
*d Joshua*, Josh. 1:1.

3
*e Stones, memorial pillars of*, Ex. 24: 12.

5
*f Ark, in the tabernacle*, Ex. 25:10.

6
*g Token, memorial stones*, Psa. 86: 17.

7
*h Instruction, by object lessons*, Prov. 23:23.
*i Memorial*, Num. 16:40.

LORD [l]stood firm on dry ground
in the midst of Jôr′dan, and all
the [d]Ĭṣ′ra-el-ītes passed over on
dry ground, until all the people
were passed clean[c] over Jôr′dan.[Q S]

## CHAPTER 4

*Twelve men are appointed to take twelve stones for a memorial out of Jordan. 9 Twelve other stones are set up in the midst of Jordan. 10 The people pass over. 14 God magnifies Joshua. 20 The twelve stones are pitched in Gilgal.*

AND it came to pass, when
all the [a]people were clean[c]
passed over [b]Jôr′dan, that the
LORD [c]spake unto [d]Jŏsh′u-ȧ,
saying,
2 Take you twelve men out of
the people, out of every tribe a
man,
3 And command ye them, saying, Take you hence out of the
midst of [b]Jôr′dan, out of the
place where the priests′ feet
stood firm, twelve [e]stones, and
ye shall carry them over with
you, and leave them in the lodging place, where ye shall lodge
this night.
4 Then [d]Jŏsh′u-ȧ called the
twelve men, whom he had prepared of the children of [a]Ĭṣ′ra-el,
out of every tribe a man:
5 And [d]Jŏsh′u-ȧ said unto
them, Pass over before the [f]ark
of the LORD your God into the
midst of [b]Jôr′dan, and take you
up every man of you a [e]stone
upon his shoulder, according
unto the number of the tribes
of the children of Ĭṣ′ra-el:
6 That this may be a [g]sign[c]
among you, *that* when your children ask *their fathers* in time to
come, saying, What *mean* ye by
these [e]stones?
7 Then ye shall [h]answer them,
That the waters of [b]Jôr′dan were
cut off[c] before[c] the [f]ark of the
covenant of the LORD; when it
passed over Jôr′dan, the waters
of Jôr′dan were cut off: and
these stones shall be for a [i]me-
morial unto the children of [a]Ĭṣ′-
ra-el for ever.
8 And the children of Ĭṣ′ra-el
did so as [d]Jŏsh′u-ȧ commanded,
and took up twelve [e]stones out of
the midst of [b]Jôr′dan, as the
LORD [c]spake unto Jŏsh′u-ȧ,
according to the number of the
tribes of the children of Ĭṣ′ra-el,
and carried them over with
them unto the place where
they lodged, and laid them down
there.
9 And Jŏsh′u-ȧ set up twelve
[j]stones in the midst of [b]Jôr′dan,
in the place where the feet of the
[k]priests which bare the [f]ark of
the covenant stood: and they are
there unto this day.
10 ¶ For the [k]priests which
bare the [f]ark stood in the midst
of [b]Jôr′dan, until everything was
finished that the LORD [c]com-
manded [d]Jŏsh′u-ȧ to speak unto
the people, according to all that
[l]Mō′ṣeṣ commanded Jŏsh′u-ȧ:
and the people hasted[c] and
passed over.
11 And it came to pass, when
all the people were clean[c] passed
over, that the [f]ark of the LORD
passed over, and the [k]priests, in
the presence of the people.
12 And the [m]children of Reu̇′-
ben, and the children of [n]Găd,
and half the tribe of [o]Mā-năs′-
seh, passed over armed before
the children of [a]Ĭṣ′ra-el, as Mō′-
ṣeṣ spake unto them:
13 About [p]forty thousand prepared for war passed over before
the LORD unto battle, to the
plains of [q]Jĕr′ī-chō.
14 ¶ On that day the LORD
magnified[c] [d]Jŏsh′u-ȧ in the sight
of all Ĭṣ′ra-el; and they feared[c]
him, as they feared Mō′ṣeṣ, all
the days of his life.
15 ¶ And the LORD [c]spake
unto [d]Jŏsh′u-ȧ, saying,
16 Command the [k]priests that
bear the [f]ark of the testimony,

v.7–1493 BC
See footnote, *Time*, Rev. 10:6.

9
*j Pillar*, Gen. 28: 18.
*k Priest, duties of*, Lev. 1:5.

10
*l Moses*, Ex. 2:10

12
*m Reubenites*, Josh. 22:1.
*n Gad, tribe of*, Deut. 33:20.
*o Manasseh, tribe of*, Gen. 46:20.

13
*p Armies*, Deut. 11:4.
*q Jericho*, Num. 22:1.

v.16–1493 BC
See footnote, *Time*, Rev. 10:6.

18 *Miracles*, Luke 23:8.

19 *Abib*, Ex. 13:4.
*Month*, Ex. 12:2.

23 *God, providence of*, Gen. 2:2.
*Miracles, design of*, Luke 23:8.
*Red Sea*, Ex. 10:19.

24 *Hand, figurative*, Ezra 10:19.
*Fear of God*, Acts 9:31.

that they come up out of [b]Jôr'dan.

17 [d]Jŏsh'u-ȧ therefore commanded the [k]priests, saying, Come ye up out of [b]Jôr'dan.

18 And it came to pass, when the priests that bare the [l]ark of the covenant of the LORD were come up out of the midst of Jôr'dan, *and* the soles of the priests' feet were lifted up unto the dry land, that the waters of Jôr'dan [r]returned unto their place, and flowed over all his banks, as *they did* before.[s]

19 ¶ And the [a]people came up out of [b]Jôr'dan on the tenth *day* of the [s]first [t]month, and encamped in *Gĭl'găl, in the east border of [q]Jĕr'ĭ-chō.

20 And those twelve [e]stones, which they took out of [b]Jôr'dan, did [d]Jŏsh'u-ȧ pitch[c] in *Gĭl'găl.

21 And he spake unto the children of Ĭs'ra-el, saying, When your children shall ask their fathers in time to come, saying, What *mean* these [e]stones?

22 Then ye shall [h]let your children know, saying, [a]Ĭs'ra-el came over this [b]Jôr'dan on dry land.

23 [s]For the [u]LORD your God [v]dried up the waters of [b]Jôr'dan from before you, until ye were passed over, as the LORD your God did to the [w]Red sea, which he [v]dried up from before us, until we were gone over:

24 [v]That all the people of the earth might know the [x]hand of the LORD, that it *is* mighty: that ye might [y]fear[c] the LORD your God for ever.[s]

## CHAPTER 5

*The Canaanites are afraid. 2 Joshua renews circumcision. 10 The passover is kept at Gilgal. 12 The manna ceases. 13 An angel appears to Joshua.*

AND it came to pass, when all the kings of the [a]Ăm'ôr-ītes, which *were* on the side of [b]Jôr'dan westward, and all the kings of the [c]Cā'năan-ītes, which *were* by the sea, heard that the [d]LORD had dried up the waters of Jôr'dan from before the children of [e]Ĭs'ra-el, until we were passed over, [f]that [g]their heart melted[c], neither was there spirit in them any more, because of the children of Ĭs'ra-el.

2 ¶ At that time the LORD said unto [h]Jŏsh'u-ȧ, Make thee [1]sharp knives, and circumcise again the children of Ĭs'ra-el the second time.

3 And [h]Jŏsh'u-ȧ made him [1]sharp knives, and [i]circumcised the children of Ĭs'ra-el at the hill of the foreskins.

4 And this *is* the cause[c] why Jŏsh'u-ȧ did [i]circumcise: All the people that came out of [j]Ē'ġy̆pt, *that were* males, *even* all the men of war, [k]died in the wilderness by the way, after they came out of Ē'ġy̆pt.

5 Now all the people that came out were [i]circumcised: but all the people *that were* born in the wilderness by the way as they came forth out of Ē'ġy̆pt, *them* they had not circumcised.

6 For the children of [e]Ĭs'ra-el walked [l]forty years in the wilderness, till all the people *that were* men of war, which came out of [j]Ē'ġy̆pt, were consumed, because they [m]obeyed not the voice of the LORD: unto whom the

v.1–1493 BC
See footnote, *Time*, Rev. 10:6.

1
a *Amorites*, Gen. 14:13.
b *Jordan*, Gen. 32:10.
c *Canaanites*, Ex. 23:28.
d *God, providence of*, Gen. 2:2.
e *Israel*, Ex. 4:22.
f *Miracles, convincing effect of*, Luke 23:8.
g *Cowardice, instances of*, Lev. 26:36.

2
h *Joshua*, Josh. 1:1.
1 R. V. knives of flint.

3
i *Circumcision, instances of*, Gen. 17:10.

4
j *Egypt*, Gen. 41:8.
k *Death, a judgment*, Num. 23:10.

6
l *Forty, years*, Jonah 3:4.
m *Disobedience to God, instances of*, Eph. 5:6.

*** GILGAL** (*a rolling away*). *Place of the first encampment of the Israelites W. of the Jordan*, Josh. 4:19; 9:6; 10:6, 43; 14:6. *Monument erected in, to commemorate the passage of the Jordan by the children of Israel*, Josh. 4:19–24. *Circumcision renewed at*, Josh. 5:2–9. *Passover kept at*, Josh. 5:10, 11. *Manna ceased at, after the passover*, Josh. 5:12. *Quarries at*, Judg. 3:19. *Eglon, king of Moab, resides and is slain at*, Judg. 3:14–26. *A judgment seat, where Israel, in that district, came to be judged by Samuel*, 1 Sam. 7:16. *Saul proclaimed king over all Israel at*, 1 Sam. 11:15. *An altar built at, and sacrifice offered*, 1 Sam. 11:15; 13:4–15; 15:6–23. *Agag, king of the Amalekites, slain at, by Samuel*, 1 Sam. 15:33. *Tribe of Judah assembles at, to proceed to the E. side of the Jordan to conduct king David back after the defeat of Absalom*, 2 Sam. 19:14, 15, 40–43. *A school of the prophets at*, 2 Kin. 4:38–40. *Prophecies concerning*, Hos. 4:15; 9:15; 12:11; Amos 4:4; 5:5.

v.6–1493 BC
See footnote, *Time*, Rev. 10:6.

*n Canaan*, Gen. 37:1.
*o Covenant, of God with men*, Deut. 29:1.

9
*p Gilgal*, vs. 2–9; Josh. 4:19.

10
*q Passover*, Num. 9:5.
*r Jericho*, Num. 22:1.

11
*s Corn*, Psa. 65:13.

12
*t Manna*, Ex. 16: 31.

LORD sware that he would not
shew them the [n]land, which the
LORD [o]sware unto their fathers
that he would give us, a land
that floweth with milk and
honey.
7 And their children, *whom* he
raised up in their stead, them
[h]Jŏsh'u-ȧ [i]circumcised: for they
were uncircumcised, because
they had not circumcised them
by the way.
8 And it came to pass, when
they had done [i]circumcising all
the people, that they abode in
their places in the camp, till they
were whole.[C]
9 And the LORD said unto
[h]Jŏsh'u-ȧ, This day have I rolled
away the reproach of [j]Ē'ġy̆pt
from off you. Wherefore the
name of the place is called
[p]Ḡĭl'găl unto this day.
10 ¶ And the children of [e]Ĭṣ'-
ra-el encamped in [p]Ḡĭl'găl, and
kept the [q]passover on the fourteenth day of the month at even
in the plains of [r]Jĕr'ĭ-chō.
11 And they did eat of the old
[s]corn[C] of the land on the morrow[C]
after the [q]passover, unleavened
cakes, and parched[C] *corn* in the
selfsame[C] day.
12 ¶ And the [t]manna ceased on
the morrow[C] after they had eaten
of the old [s]corn[C] of the land; neither had the children of [e]Ĭṣ'ra-el
manna any more; but they did
eat of the fruit of the land of
[n]Cā'năan that year.
13 ¶[T] And it came to pass, when
[h]Jŏsh'u-ȧ was by [r]Jĕr'ĭ-chō, that
he lifted up his eyes and looked,
and, behold, [u]there stood a [v]man
over[C] against him with his [w]sword
drawn in his hand: and Jŏsh'u-ȧ
went unto him, and said unto
him, *Art* thou for us, or for our
adversaries?[Q]
14 And [v]he said, Nay; but *as*
captain of the host of the LORD
am I now come. And [h]Jŏsh'u-ȧ
fell on his face to the earth, and
did worship, and said unto him,
What saith my lord unto his
servant?
15 And the [v]captain of the
LORD's host said unto Jŏsh'u-ȧ,
[x]Loose thy *shoe from off thy
foot; for the place whereon thou
standest *is* holy. And Jŏsh'u-ȧ
did so.[Q]

## CHAPTER 6

*Jericho is shut up. 2 God instructs Joshua how to besiege it. 12 The city is compassed seven days. 20 The walls fall down. 21 All that are in the city destroyed. 22 Only Rahab and her family are saved. 26 The rebuilder of Jericho is cursed.*

NOW [a]Jĕr'ĭ-chō was straitly[C]
shut up because of the
children of [b]Ĭṣ'ra-el: none went
out, and none came in.
2 And the LORD said unto
[c]Jŏsh'u-ȧ, See, I have given into
thine hand [a]Jĕr'ĭ-chō, and the
king thereof, *and* the mighty
men of valour.[G T]
3 And ye shall [d]compass[C] the
city, all *ye* [e]men of war, *and* go
round about the city once. Thus
shalt thou do six days.
4 And [f]seven [g]priests shall bear
before the ark seven *trumpets
of rams' horns: and the [h]seventh
day ye shall compass the city
seven times, and the priests shall
blow with the trumpets.

v.13–1493 BC
See footnote, *Tim*
Rev. 10:6.

13
*u Vision*, Acts 9: 10.
*v Angel, appearances of*, Heb. 1:13.
*w Sword, symbolic al*, 1 Chr. 21:5.

15
*x Reverence, for sacred places*, Lev. 19:30.

1
*a Jericho*, Num. 22:1.
*b Israel, Jericho taken by*, vs. 2–21; Ex. 4:22.

2
*c Joshua*, Josh. 1:1.

3
*d Siege, instances of*, Deut. 28:53
*e Armies, sieges*, Deut. 11:4.

4
*f Seven*, Gen. 7:
*g Priest, duties* Lev. 1:5.
*h Seven, days*, Ge 7:2.

* **SHOE.** *Taken off on holy ground*, Ex. 3:5; Josh. 5:15; Acts 7:33. *Put off in mourning*, Ezek. 24:17. *Of the children of Israel did not wax old*, Deut. 29:5. *Loosed in token of refusal to observe the levirate marriage*, Deut. 25:9; Ruth 4:7, 8. *Poor sold for a pair of*, Amos 2:6; 8:6. *Made of badgers'* (R. V. seal) *skins*, Ezek. 16:10. *Latchet of*, Gen. 14:23; Isa. 5:27. *Loosing of the latchet of, a humble service*, Mark 1:7; Luke 3:16.

* **TRUMPET.** *Made, of ram's horn*, Josh. 6:4–6, 8, 13; *of silver*, Num. 10:2.

*Used, at Sinai*, Ex. 19:13–19; 20:18; Heb. 12:19; *to assemble the Israelites*, Num. 10:1–10; *on day of atonement*, Lev. 25:9; Isa. 27:13; *at jubilee*, Lev. 25:9; *at the bringing up of the ark*, 2 Sam. 6:5, 15; 1 Chr. 13:8; 15:28; *at anointing of kings*, 1 Kin. 1:34, 39; 2 Kin. 9:13; 11:14; *at dedication of Solomon's temple*, 2 Chr. 5:12, 13; 7:6; *in worship*, 1 Chr. 15:24; 16:42; 25:5; Psa. 81:3, 4; *at Jehoshaphat's triumph*, 2 Ch 20:28; *at founding of second temple*, Ezra 3:10, 11; *at dedic tion of the wall*, Neh. 12:35, 41; *in war*, Job 39:24, 25; Jer. 19; 6:1, 17; 42:14; 51:27; Ezek. 7:14; Amos 2:2; 3:6; Zep 1:16; 1 Cor. 14:8; *in the siege of Jericho*, Josh. 6:4–20. *Us to summon soldiers, by Phinehas*, Num. 31:6; *by Ehu* Judg. 3:27; *by Gideon*, Judg. 6:34; *by Saul*, 1 Sam. 13: *by Joab*, 2 Sam. 2:28; 18:16; 20:22; *by Absalom*, 2 Sa 15:10; *by Sheba*, 2 Sam. 20:1; *by Nehemiah*, Neh. 4:1 20. *Used by Gideon's soldiers*, Judg. 7:8–22. *Used in wa by Abijah*, 2 Chr. 13:12, 14.

*Sounded as a signal of danger*, Ezek. 33:3–6; Joel 2:1.

**Figurative,** Ezek. 33:3; Joel 2:1; Zech. 9:14; Matt. 6:2.

**Symbolical,** Matt. 24:31; 1 Cor. 15:52; 1 Thess. 4:16. *John's vision*, Rev. 1:10; 4:1; 8; 9:1–14; 10:7; 11:15.

v.5–1493 BC
See footnote, *Time*, Rev. 10:6.

5 And it shall come to pass, that when they make a long *blast* with the ram's horn, *and* when ye hear the sound of the *trumpet, all the people shall shout with a great shout; and the [i]wall of the city shall fall down flat, and the people shall ascend up every man straight before him.

6 ¶ And [c]Jŏsh'u-ȧ the son of Nŭn called the [g]priests, and said unto them, Take up the [j,k]ark of the covenant, and let [f]seven priests bear seven *trumpets of rams' horns before the ark of the LORD.

7 And [1]he said unto the people, Pass on, and compass the city, and let him that is armed pass on before the ark of the LORD.

8 ¶ And it came to pass, when [c]Jŏsh'u-ȧ had spoken unto the [b]people, that the [f]seven [g]priests bearing the seven *trumpets of rams' horns passed on before the LORD, and blew with the trumpets: and the [k]ark of the covenant of the LORD followed them.

9 And the [e]armed men went before the [g]priests that blew with the *trumpets, and the rereward[C] came after the ark, *the priests* going on, and blowing with the trumpets.

10 And [c]Jŏsh'u-ȧ had commanded the people, saying, Ye shall not shout, nor make any noise with your voice, neither shall *any* word proceed out of your mouth, until the day I bid you shout; then shall ye shout.

11 So the [j]ark of the LORD compassed the city, going about *it* once: and they came into the camp,[Q] and lodged in the camp.

12 ¶ And [c]Jŏsh'u-ȧ [l]rose early in the morning, and the [g]priests took up the [k]ark of the LORD.

13 And [f]seven [g]priests bearing seven *trumpets of rams' horns before the [j,k]ark of the LORD went on continually, and blew with the *trumpets: and the [e]armed men went before them; but the rereward[C] came after the ark of the LORD, *the priests* going on, and blowing with the trumpets.

14 And the second day they compassed[C] the city once, and returned into the camp: so they did six days.

15 And it came to pass on the seventh day, that [b]they [l]rose early about the dawning of the day, and compassed the [a]city after the same manner [f]seven times: only on that day they compassed the city seven times.

16 And it came to pass at the seventh time, when the [g]priests blew with the *trumpets, Jŏsh'u-ȧ said unto the people, [m]Shout; for the LORD hath given you the city.

17 And the city shall be [2]accursed, *even* it, and all that *are* therein, to the LORD: only [n]Rā'hăb the [o]harlot shall live, she and all that *are* with her in the house, because she [p]hid the messengers that we sent.[Q]

18 And ye, in any wise[C] keep *yourselves* from the [3]accursed thing, lest [4]ye make *yourselves* accursed, [5]when ye take of the accursed thing, and make the camp of Ĭṣ'ra-el [6]a curse[C], and trouble it.

19 But [q]all the silver, and gold, and vessels of brass and iron, [7]*are* consecrated[C] unto the LORD: they shall come into the [r]treasury of the LORD.

20 So the people [m]shouted when *the* [g]*priests* blew with the *trumpets: and it came to pass, when the people heard the sound of the trumpet, and the people shouted with a great shout, [t]hat the [s]wall [t]fell down flat, so that the people went up into the city, every man straight before him, and they took the city.[s]

5
i *Walls*, 1 Sam. 20:25.

6
j *Ark, taken to battle*, Ex. 25:10.
k *Ark, carried by priests*, Ex. 25:10.

7
1 R. V. they

12
l *Rising, early, instances of*, Gen. 19:2.

v.13–1493 BC
See footnote, *Time*, Rev. 10:6.

16
m *Shouting, in battle*, 2 Chr. 15:14.

17
n *Rahab*, Josh. 2:1.
o *Harlot*, Prov. 7:10.
p *Hospitality, rewarded*, Rom. 12 13.
2 R. V. devoted,

18
3 R. V. devoted
4 R. V. when ye have devoted it
5 R. V. *omits* when.
6 R. V. accursed,

19
q *Spoils*, 1 Chr. 26:27.
r *Treasuries*, Ezra 5:17.
7 R. V. are holy

20
s Heb. 11:30.
t *Miracles*, Luke 23:8.

v.21–1493 BC
See footnote, *Time,* Rev. 10:6.

**21**

*u War, of extermination,* Judg. 3:2.

**22**

*v Thankfulness, of man to man,* Acts 24:3.

*w Oath,* Num. 5:19.

**24**

*x Iron,* Prov. 27: 17.

*y Church, called house of the Lord,* 1 Kin. 9:3.

*z Tabernacle, called house of the Lord,* Ex. 27:9.

**25**

*a Joshua,* Josh. 1:1.

*b Mercy, instances of,* Deut. 5:10.

*c Rahab,* Josh. 2:1.

*d Israel,* Ex. 4:22.

*e Jericho,* Num. 22:1.

**26**

*f* 1 Kin. 16:34.

*g Prophecies, miscellaneous,* Dan. 9:24.

*h Gates, of cities,* Deut. 3:5.

8 R. V. charged them with an oath

9 R. V. with the loss of his firstborn shall he lay the foundation thereof, and with the loss of his

21 [Q] [u]And they utterly destroyed all that *was* in the city, both man and woman, young and old, and ox, and sheep, and ass, with the edge of the sword.

22 But [v]Jŏsh′u-ȧ had said unto the two †men that had spied out the country, Go into the [n, o]harlot's house, and bring out thence the woman, and all that she hath, as ye [w]sware unto her.

23 And the young men that were †spies went in, and brought out [n]Rā′hăb, and her father, and her mother, and her brethren, and all that she had; and they brought out all her kindred[c] and left them without[c] the camp of Īs̹′ra-el.

24 And they burnt the city with fire, and all that *was* therein: only [q]the silver, and the gold, and the vessels of brass and of [x]iron, they put into the [r]treasury of the [y, z]house of the LORD.

25 And [a]Jŏsh′u-ȧ [b]saved [c]Rā′hăb the harlot alive, and her father's household, and all that she had; and she dwelleth in [d]Īs̹′ra-el *even* unto this day; because she hid the †messengers, which Jŏsh′u-ȧ sent to spy out [e]Jĕr′ĭ-chō. [Q]

26 ¶ And [a]Jŏsh′u-ȧ [8]adjured[c] *them* at that time, saying, Cursed *be* the [f]man before the LORD, that riseth up and buildeth this city [e]Jĕr′ĭ-chō: [9, g]he shall lay the foundation thereof in his firstborn, and in his youngest *son* shall he set up the [h]gates of it.

27 So the LORD was with [a]Jŏsh′u-ȧ; and his fame was *noised*[c] throughout all the country.

## CHAPTER 7

*Achan's trespass. 2 The Israelites are smitten at Ai. 6 Joshua's complaint. 10 God instructs him what to do. 16 Achan is taken by lot. 19 His confession. 22 He and all he had are destroyed in the valley of Achor.*

BUT the children of [a]Īs̹′ra-el committed a trespass in the [1, b]accursed thing: for [c]Ā′chăn, the son of [d]Cär′mī, the son of Zăb′dī, the son of Zē′rah, of the tribe of Jū′dah, took of the [1]accursed thing: and the [e]anger of the LORD was kindled[c] against the children of Īs̹′ra-el. [s]

2 And [f]Jŏsh′u-ȧ sent men from [g]Jĕr′ĭ-chō to *Ā′ī, which *is* beside [h]Bĕth–ā′ven, on the east side of [i]Bĕth′–el, and spake unto them, saying, Go up and view the country. And the men went up and [j]viewed Ā′ī.

3 And they returned to [f]Jŏsh′u-ȧ, and said unto him, Let not all the people go up; but let about two or three thousand men go up and smite *Ā′ī; *and* make not all the people to labour thither; for they *are but* few.

4 So there went up thither of the people about three thousand men: and they [k]fled before the men of *Ā′ī.

5 And the men of *Ā′ī smote of them about thirty and six men: for they chased them *from* before the gate *even* unto Shĕb′a-rĭm, and smote them in the going[c] down: wherefore [k]the hearts of the people melted, and became as water.

6 ¶ And [f, l]Jŏsh′u-ȧ rent[c] his clothes, and fell to the earth upon his face before the [m]ark of the LORD until the eventide[c], he and the [n]elders of Īs̹′ra-el, and [o]put dust[c] upon their heads.

7 And [f]Jŏsh′u-ȧ [p, q]said, Alas, O Lord GOD, wherefore hast

v.1–1493 BC
See footnote, *Time,* Rev. 10:6.

**1**

*a Israel,* Ex. 4:22.

*b Accursed,* Deut. 21:23.

*c* Josh. 22:20; 1 Chr. 2:7.

*d* 1 Chr. 2:7.

*e Anger of God,* 2 Kin. 13:3.

1 R. V. devoted

**2**

*f Joshua,* Josh. 1:1.

*g Jericho,* Num. 22:1.

*h Beth-aven,* Josh. 18:12.

*i Bethel,* Josh. 18: 13.

*j Armies, reconnoissances of,* Deut. 11:4.

**4**

*k Cowardice,* Lev. 26:36.

**6**

*l Zeal, instances of,* 2 Cor. 7:11.

*m Ark,* Ex. 25:10.

*n Senate,* Num. 11: 16.

*o Mourning, dust on the head,* Lam. 2:5.

**7**

*p Intercession, instances of,* vs. 7–26; Jer. 27:18.

*q Prayer, intercessory,* Acts 6:4.

† **SPIES,** Gen. 42:9. *Sent to investigate, Canaan,* Num. 13; 32:8, 9; Deut. 1:22–25; Josh. 14:7; *Jaazer,* Num. 21:32; *Jericho,* Josh. 2:1. *Used, by David,* 1 Sam. 26:4; *at the court of Absalom,* 2 Sam. 15:10; 17:1–17. *Pharisees acted as, in order to entrap Jesus,* Luke 20:20. *In the church of Galatia,* Gal. 2:4.

* **AI** (*mass or heap of ruins*), called also AIJA, AIATH, and HAI. *Abraham pitched tent at,* Gen. 12:8; 13:3. *A royal city of the Canaanites,* Josh. 10:1. *Conquest and destruction of,* Josh. 7:2–5; 8:1–29. *Population of,* 12,000, Josh. 8:25. *Rebuilt* Ezra 2:28. *Inhabited by the Benjamites after the captivity,* Ezra 2:28; Neh. 7:32; 11:31.

v.7–1493 BC
ee footnote, *Time*, Rev. 10:6.

*Jordan*, Gen. 32: 10.
*Amorites*, Gen. 14:13.
R. V. that we

9
*Prayer, pleas offered in*, Acts 6:4.
*Canaanites*, Ex. 23:28.
R. V. for

10
*Prayer, rebuked*, Acts 6:4.
*Indecision, instances of*, 1 Kin. 18:21.

11
*Sin, known to God*, Rom. 5:12.
*Sacrilege*, Lev. 19:8.
*Theft, instances of*, Mark 7:22.

12
*Sin, separates from God*, Rom. 5:12.
*Accursed*, Deut. 21:23.
R. V. devoted thing

13
*Commandment, enjoining holiness*, Deut. 8:2.
*Holiness, enjoined*, Ex. 39: 30.
R. V. There is a devoted
R. V. devoted

14
R. V. near by

thou at all brought this [a]people
over [r]Jôr′dan, to deliver us into
the hand of the [s]Ăm′ôr-ītes, to
destroy us? would [2]to God we
had been content, and dwelt on
the other side Jôr′dan!
8 [p,q]O Lord, what shall I say,
when Ĭş′ra-el turneth their backs
before their enemies!
9 [t]For the [u]Cā′năan-ītes and all
the inhabitants of the land shall
hear *of it*, and shall environ[C] us
round, and cut off our name
from the earth: and what wilt
thou do [3]unto thy great name?
10 ¶ And the LORD said unto
[l]Jŏsh′u-ȧ, [v]Get thee up; [w]where-
fore[C] liest thou thus upon thy
face?
11 Ĭş′ra-el hath [x]sinned, and
they have also transgressed my
covenant which I commanded
them: for they have even [y]taken
of the [1,b]accursed thing, and
have also [z]stolen, and [†]dissem-
bled[C] also, and they have put *it*
even among their own stuff.[C]
12 Therefore the children of
Ĭş′ra-el could not stand before
their enemies, *but* turned *their*
backs before their enemies, because they were accursed[C]: [a]nei-
ther will I be with you any more,
except ye destroy the [4,b]accursed[C]
from among you.
13 Up, sanctify the people, and
say, [c,d]Sanctify[C] yourselves
against to morrow: for thus saith
the LORD God of Ĭş′ra-el,
[5]*There is* an [b]accursed thing in
the midst of thee, O Ĭş′ra-el:
thou canst not stand before thine
enemies, until ye take away the
[6]accursed thing from among
you.
14 In the morning therefore ye
shall be brought [7]according to
your tribes: and it shall be, *that*
the tribe which the LORD taketh
shall come [7]according to the
families *thereof*; and the family
which the LORD shall take shall
come by households; and the
household which the LORD shall
take shall come man by man.
15 And it shall be, *that* he that
is taken with the [6,b]accursed
thing shall be [e]burnt with fire, he
and all that he hath: because he
hath [f]trangressed[C] the covenant[C]
of the LORD, and because he
hath wrought folly in Ĭş′ra-el.
16 ¶ So [g]Jŏsh′u-ȧ [h]rose up
early in the morning, and
brought Ĭş′ra-el by their tribes;
and the tribe of [i]Jū′dah was
taken[C]:
17 And he brought the family
of [i]Jū′dah; and he took the family of the Zär′hītes: and he
brought the family of the Zär′-
hītes man by man; and Zăb′dī
was taken:
18 And he brought his household man by man; and [j]Ā′chăn,
the son of [k]Cär′mī, the son of
Zăb′dī, the son of Zē′rah, of the
tribe of [i]Jū′dah, was taken.
19 And [g]Jŏsh′u-ȧ said unto
[j]Ā′chăn, My son, give, I pray
thee, glory to the LORD God of
Ĭş′ra-el, and make confession
unto him; and tell me now what
thou hast done; hide *it* not from
me.[Q]
20 And [j]Ā′chăn answered
[g]Jŏsh′u-ȧ, and said, [‡,l,m,n]In-
deed [o,p]I have sinned against the
LORD God of Ĭş′ra-el, and thus[C]
and thus have I done:
21 [‡,l,n]When I saw among the
[q]spoils a goodly[C] Băb-y̆-lō′nish
[8]garment, and two hundred
[r]shekels[C] of silver, and a wedge
of [s]gold of fifty shekels[C] weight,
then I [t]coveted[C]them, and [u]took

v.14–1493 BC
See footnote, *Time*, Rev. 10:6.

15
e *Punishment, death penalty*, Lev. 26:41.
f *Disobedience to God*, Eph. 5:6.

16
g *Joshua*, Josh. 1:1.
h *Rising, early*, Gen. 19:2.
i *Judah, tribe of*, Num. 10:14.

18
j Josh. 22:20; 1 Chr. 2:7.
k 1 Chr. 2:7.

20
l *Evidence, self-criminating*, Deut. 17:6.
m *Pleading, of the guilty*, vs. 19–21 Deut. 17:8.
n *Self-condemnation, instances of*, vs. 19–25; Job 9:20.
o *Repentance, instances of*, Mark 1:4.
p *Sin, confession of*, Rom. 5:12.

21
q *Spoils*, 1 Chr. 26: 27.
r *Shekel*, Ex. 30: 13.
s *Gold, wedge of*, Ezek. 7:19.
t *Covetousness, instances of*, Isa. 57:17.
u *Temptation, yielding to*, Luke 11:4.
8 R. V. mantle.

† **DISSEMBLING.** *Practiced by the wicked*, Prov. 26:24. *Abhorred by the righteous*, Psa. 26:4.
**Instances of:** *Joseph*, Gen. 42:7–20; 43:26–34. *The Israelites*, Josh. 7:11. *David*, 1 Sam. 21:13–15. *The Jews*, Gal. 2:13.
See footnotes: DECEPTION, Josh. 9:4; HYPOCRISY, Jas. 3:17.

‡ **SELF-CRIMINATION.** Under ancient customs accused persons were required to give self-criminating testimony if guilty of the offence charged, and were, on occasions, scourged for the purpose of forcing self-criminating testimony whether guilty or innocent. Num. 5:11–27; 2 Sam. 1:10, 16; 1 Kin. 8:31, 32; 2 Chr. 6:22; Acts 22:24.
See footnote, SELF-CONDEMNATION, Job 9:20.
**Instances of:** *Achan*, Josh. 7:19–25.

v.21–1493 BC
See footnote, *Time*, Rev. 10:6.

24
v Josh. 15:7; Isa. 65:10, Hos. 2:15.

25
w *Death, penalty*, Num. 23:10.
x *Stoning*, 1 Sam. 30:6.
9 R. V. and stoned

26
y *Anger of God*, 2 Kin. 13:3.

1
a *Joshua, military genius of*, Josh. 1:1.
b *Courage, enjoined*, Deut. 31:7.
c *Ai*, Josh. 7:2.
d *God, providence of*, Gen. 2:2.
e *Canaan*, Gen. 37:1.

them; and, behold, they *are* hid
in the earth in the midst of my
tent, and the silver under it.
22 So [g]Jŏsh'u-ȧ sent messengers, and they ran unto the tent;
and, behold, *it was* hid in his
tent, and the silver under it.
23 And they took them out of
the midst of the tent, and
brought them unto [g]Jŏsh'u-ȧ,
and unto all the children of Ĭṣ'-
ra-el, and laid them out before
the LORD.
24 And [g]Jŏsh'u-ȧ, and all Ĭṣ'-
ra-el with him, took [j]Ā'chăn the
son of Zē'rah, and the silver, and
the [s]garment, and the wedge of
[s]gold, and his sons, and his
daughters, and his oxen, and his
asses, and his sheep, and his
tent, and all that he had: and
they brought them unto the valley of [v]Ā'chôr.
25 And [g]Jŏsh'u-ȧ said, Why
hast thou troubled us? the
LORD shall trouble thee this
day. And all Ĭṣ'ra-el [e,w,x]stoned
him with stones, and [||]burned
them with fire, [9]after they had
stoned them with stones.
26 And they raised over him a
great heap of stones unto this
day. So the LORD turned from
the fierceness of his [y]anger.
Wherefore the name of that
place was called, The valley of
[v]Ā'chôr, unto this day. [s]

## CHAPTER 8

*God encourages Joshua. 3 The stratagem whereby Ai is taken. 29 The king thereof is hanged. 30 Joshua builds an altar, 32 writes the law on stones, 34 and pronounces blessings and cursings.*

AND the LORD said unto
[a]Jŏsh'u-ȧ, [b]Fear not, neither be thou dismayed: take all
the people of war with thee, and
arise, go up to [c]Ā'ī: see, [d]I have
given into thy hand the king of
Ā'ī, and his people, and his city,
and his [e]land:
2 And thou shalt do to [c]Ā'ī and
her king as thou didst unto [f]Jĕr'-
ĭ-chō and her king: only the
[g]spoil thereof, and the cattle
thereof, shall ye take for a prey
unto yourselves: [h]lay thee an
[*,i]ambush for the city behind it.
3 ¶ So [a]Jŏsh'u-ȧ arose, and all
the [h]people of war, to go up
against [c]Ā'ī: and Jŏsh'u-ȧ chose
out thirty thousand mighty men
of valour, and [i]sent them away
by night.
4 And he commanded them,
saying, Behold, [h]ye shall [i]lie in
[*]wait against the [c]city, *even* behind the city: go not very far
from the city, but be ye all
ready:
5 And I, and all the people that
*are* with me, will approach unto the [c]city: and it shall come
to pass, when they come out
against us, as at the first, that
[i]we will flee before them,
6 (For they will come out after
us) till we have drawn them
from the city; for they will say,
They flee before us, as at the
first: therefore [i]we will flee before them.
7 Then ye shall rise up from the
[*]ambush, and seize upon the
city: for the LORD your God
will [d]deliver it into your hand.
8 And it shall be, when ye have
taken the city, *that* ye shall set
the city on fire: [j]according to the
commandment of the LORD
shall ye do. See, I have commanded you.
9 [a]Jŏsh'u-ȧ therefore sent them
forth: and they went to [i]lie in
[*]ambush, and abode between
[k]Bĕth'–el and [c]Ā'ī, on the west
side of Ā'ī: but Jŏsh'u-ȧ lodged
that night among the people.
10 And [a]Jŏsh'u-ȧ rose up early
in the morning, and [1,l]numbered
the people, and went up, he and

v.2–1493 BC
See footnote, *Time*, Rev. 10:6.

2
f *Jericho*, Num. 22:1.
g *Spoils*, 1 Chr. 26: 27.
h *Armies, stratagems at Ai*, vs. 2–22; Deut. 11:4.
i *Strategy*, vs. 2–25; Judg. 7:16.

8
j *Joshua, divinely inspired*, Josh. 1:1.

9
k *Bethel*, Josh. 18: 13.

10
l *Armies, mustered*, Deut. 11:4
1 R. V. mustered

|| **CREMATION**, Josh. 7:25; 1 Sam. 31:12; 2 Kin. 23:20; 2 Chr. 34:5; Amos 2:1; 6:10.
***AMBUSH.** *At Ai*, Josh. 8:2–22. *At Shechem*, Judg. 9:25, 34. *At Gibeah*, Judg. 20:29–41. *Near Zemaraim*, 2 Chr. 13:13. *By Jehoshaphat*, 2 Chr. 20:22. **Figurative**, Jer. 51:12.

v.10–1493 BC
See footnote, *Time*, Rev. 10:6.

*m Senate*, Num. 11:16.

the [m]elders of Ĭş′ra-el, before the people to [c]Ā′ī.

11 And all the people, *even the* [h]*people* of war that *were* with him, went up, and drew nigh[c], and came before the city, and pitched[c] on the north side of [c]Ā′ī: now *there was* a valley between them and Ā′ī.

12 And he took about five thousand men, and set them to [i]lie in *ambush between [k]Bĕth′–el and Ā′ī, on the west side of the city.

13 And when they had set the people, *even* all the [h]host that *was* on the north of the city, and their liers[c] in wait on the west of the city, [a]Jŏsh′u-ȧ went that night into the midst of the valley.

14 And it came to pass, when the king of [c]Ā′ī saw *it*, that they hasted and rose up early, and the men of the city went out against [n]Ĭş′ra-el to battle, he and all his people, at a time appointed, before the [2]plain; but he wist[c] not that *there were* liers[c] in *ambush against him behind the city.

14
*n Israel*, Ex. 4:22.
2 R. V. Arabah;

15 And [a]Jŏsh′u-ȧ and all [n]Ĭş′ra-el [i]made[c] as if they were beaten before them, and fled by the way of the wilderness.

16 And all the people that *were* in [c]Ā′ī were called together to pursue after them: and they pursued after [a]Jŏsh′u-ȧ, and were drawn away from the city.

17 And there was not a man left in [c]Ā′ī or [k]Bĕth′–el, that went not out after Ĭş′ra-el: and they left the city open, and pursued after [n]Ĭş′ra-el.

18 And the LORD [f]said unto Jŏsh′u-ȧ, Stretch out the [3]spear that *is* in thy hand toward [c]Ā′ī; for I will give it into thine hand. And Jŏsh′u-ȧ [o]stretched out the [3]spear that *he had* in his hand toward the city.

18
*o Faith, instances of*, Mark 11:22.
3 R. V. javelin

19 And the *ambush arose quickly out of their place, and they ran as soon as he had stretched out his hand: and they entered into the city, and took it, and hasted[c] and set the city on fire.

v.19–1493 BC
See footnote, *Time*, Rev. 10:6.

20 And when the men of [c]Ā′ī looked behind them, they saw, and, behold, the smoke of the city ascended up to heaven, and they had no power to flee this way or that way: and the people that fled to the wilderness turned back upon the pursuers.

21 And when [a]Jŏsh′u-ȧ and all [n]Ĭş′ra-el saw that the *ambush had taken the city, and that the smoke of the city ascended, then they turned again, and slew the men of [c]Ā′ī.

22 And the other issued out of the city against them; so they were in the midst of [n]Ĭş′ra-el, some on this side, and some on that side: and they smote[c] them, so that they let none of them remain or escape.

23 And the king of [c]Ā′ī they took alive, and brought him to [a]Jŏsh′u-ȧ.

24 And it came to pass, when [n]Ĭş′ra-el had made an end of [p,q]slaying all the inhabitants of [c]Ā′ī in the field, in the wilderness wherein they chased them, and when they were all fallen on the edge of the sword, until they were consumed, that all the Ĭş′ra-el-ītes returned unto Ā′ī, and smote it with the edge of the sword.

24
*p War, of extermination*, Judg. 3:2.
*q Massacre*, Esth. 3:13.

25 And *so* it was, *that* all that fell that day, both of men and women, *were* twelve thousand, *even* all the men of [c]Ā′ī.

26 For [a]Jŏsh′u-ȧ drew not his hand back, wherewith he stretched out the spear, until he had [p,q]utterly destroyed all the inhabitants of [c]Ā′ī.

27 Only the cattle and the [g]spoil of that city Ĭş′ra-el took for a prey unto themselves, according unto the word of the

v.27–1493 BC
See footnote, *Time*, Rev. 10:6.

LORD which he [j]commanded
Jŏsh'u-ȧ.
28 And [a]Jŏsh'u-ȧ burnt [c]Ā'ī,
and made it an heap[c] for ever,
*even* a desolation unto this
day.
29 And the king of [c]Ā'ī he
[†, r, s]hanged on a tree until eventide: and as soon as the sun
was down, [a]Jŏsh'u-ȧ commanded
that they should take his carcase[c]
down from the tree, and [t]cast it
at the entering of the gate of the
city, and raise thereon a great
heap of stones, *that remaineth*
unto this day.
30 ¶ Then Jŏsh'u-ȧ built an
[u]altar unto the LORD God of
Ĭs̱'ra-el in mount [v]Ē'bal,
31 As Mō'ṣeṣ the servant of the
LORD commanded the children
of [w]Ĭs̱'ra-el, as it is written in the
book of the [x, y]law of Mō'ṣeṣ, an
[u]altar of whole stones, over
which no man hath lift up *any*
iron: and they offered thereon
[z]burnt offerings unto the LORD,
and sacrificed [a]peace offerings.
32 And he wrote there upon the
stones a copy of the [b, c]law of
Mō'ṣeṣ, which he wrote in the
presence of the children of
Ĭs̱'ra-el.
33 And all Ĭs̱'ra-el, and their
[d]elders, and officers, and their
judges, stood on this side the
[e]ark and on that side before the
priests the [f]Lē'vītes, which bare
the ark of the covenant of the
LORD, as well the [g]stranger,[c] as
he that was born among them;
half of them over against mount
[h]Gĕr'ĭ-zĭm, and half of them
over against mount [i]Ē'bal; as
Mō'ṣeṣ the servant of the LORD
had commanded before, that
they should [j]bless the people of
Ĭs̱'ra-el.[Q]
34 And afterward he [k]read all
the words of the [b, c]law, the blessings and [l]cursings, according to
all that is written in the book of
the law.
35 There was not a word of all
that Mō'ṣeṣ commanded, which
Jŏsh'u-ȧ read not before all the
[4]congregation of Ĭs̱'ra-el, with
the [m]women, and the [n, o]little
ones, and the [g]strangers[c] that
were conversant[c] among them.

## CHAPTER 9

*The kings combine against Israel. 3 The Gibeonites by craft obtain a league; 16 for which they are condemned to perpetual bondage.*

AND it came to pass, when
all the kings which *were*
on this side [a]Jôr'dan, in the hills,
and in the valleys, and in all the
coasts[c] of the [b]great sea over
against [c]Lĕb'a-non, the [d]Hĭt'-
tīte, and the [e]Ăm'ôr-īte, the
[f]Cā'-năan-īte, the [g]Pĕr'ĭz-zīte,
the [h]Hī'vīte, and the [i]Jĕb'u-sīte,
heard *thereof*;
2 That they [j]gathered themselves together, to fight with
[k]Jŏsh'u-ȧ and with Ĭs̱'ra-el, with[c]
one accord.
3 ¶ And when the inhabitants
of [l]Gĭb'e-on heard what [k]Jŏsh'-
u-ȧ had done unto [m]Jĕr'ĭ-chō
and to [n]Ā'ī,
4 They did *work wilily, and
went and [o, p]made as if they had
been †ambassadors, and took
old sacks upon their asses, and

**29**
*r* *Death, penalty*, Num. 23:10.
*s* *Punishment, hanging*, Lev. 26:41.
*t* *Burial*, Acts 8:2.

**30**
*u* *Altar*, Gen. 8:20.
*v* *Ebal*, Deut. 11:29.

**31**
*w* *Israel, required to assemble for reading of the law*, vs. 30–34; Ex. 4:22.
*x* *Word of God*, Psa. 119:9.
*y* *Law, of Moses*, Deut. 33:2.
*z* *Offerings, burnt*, Lev. 6:17.

*a* *Offerings, peace*, Lev. 6:17.

**32**
*b* *Word of God*, Psa. 119:9.
*c* *Law, of Moses*, Deut. 33:2.

**33**
*d* *Senate*, Num. 11:16.
*e* *Ark, of the covenant*, Ex. 25:10.
*f* *Levites*, Deut. 10:8.
*g* *Foreigners, required to assemble for religious instruction*, Deut. 23:20.
*h* *Gerizim*, Deut. 11:29.

v.33–1493 BC
See footnote, *Time*, Rev. 10:6.

*i* *Ebal*, Deut. 11:29.
*j* *Benedictions*, Deut. 21:5.

**34**
*k* *Instruction, in religion*, Prov. 23:23.
*l* *Curse*, Judg. 5:23.

**35**
*m* *Women, required to attend reading of the law*, Prov. 31:10.
*n* *Children, instruction of*, Mark 10:14.
*o* *Children, attend divine worship*, Mark 10:14.
4 R. V. assembly

**1**
*a* *Jordan*, Gen. 32:10.
*b* *Mediterranean Sea*, Ex. 23:31.
*c* *Lebanon*, Deut. 1:7.
*d* *Hittites*, Judg. 1:26.
*e* *Amorites*, Gen. 14:13.
*f* *Canaanites*, Ex. 23:28.
*g* *Perizzites*, Gen. 15:20.
*h* *Hivites*, Gen. 10:17.
*i* *Jebusites*, Deut. 7:1.

**2**
*j* *Armies, confederated*, Deut. 11:4.
*k* *Joshua*, Josh. 1:1.

**3**
*l* *Gibeon*, Jer. 41:16.
*m* *Jericho*, Num. 22:1.
*n* *Ai*, Josh. 7:2.

**4**
*o* *Craftiness, instances of*, Psa. 83:3.
*p* *Diplomacy, instances of*, 2 Kin. 16:7.

† **HANGING.** *Capital punishment by*, Gen. 40:19–22; Josh. 8:29; Esth. 7:10. *A disgrace*, Deut. 21:22, 23; Gal. 3:13. See footnote, PUNISHMENT, Lev. 26:41.

* **DECEPTION. Instances of:** *By the serpent*, Gen. 3:4. *Abraham, in stating that Sarah was his sister*, Gen. 12:13; 20:2. *Isaac, in stating that his wife was his sister*, Gen. 26:7. *Jacob and Rebekah, in imposing Jacob on his father; and Jacob's impersonating of Esau*, Gen. 27:6–23. *Laban, in substituting Leah for Rachel*, Gen. 29:23. *Jacob's sons, in entrapping the Shechemites*, Gen. 34:13–31; *in representing to their father that Joseph had been destroyed by wild beasts*, Gen. 37:31–35. *Joseph, in his ruse with his brethren*, Gen. 42; 43; 44. *The Gibeonites, in misrepresenting their place of residence*, Josh. 9:3–15. *Ehud deceives Eglon, and slays him*, Judg. 3:15–22. *Jael deceives Sisera*, Judg. 4:18–21. *Delilah deceives Samson*, Judg. 16:4–20. *Michal deceives messengers of Saul*, 1 Sam. 19:13, 14. *David feigns madness*, 1 Sam. 21:10–15. *Amnon deceives Tamar by feigning sickness*, 2 Sam. 13:6–14. *Hushai deceives Absalom*, 2 Sam. 16:15–19. *By Absalom, when he avenged his sister*, 2 Sam. 13:23–28; *when he began his conspiracy*, 2 Sam. 15:7. *By Rabshakeh*, 2 Kin. 18:17–31. *By the old prophet*, 1 Kin. 13:18. *By Gehazi*, 2 Kin. 5:20–24. *Sanballat tries to deceive Nehemiah*, Neh. 6. *By Job's friends*, Job 6:15. *By Ananias and Sapphira*, Acts 5:1–8.
See footnotes: DECEIT, Psa. 36:3; FALSEHOOD, Job 21:34; HYPOCRISY, Jas. 3:17.

† **AMBASSADORS.** *Sent, by Moses to Edom*, Num. 20:14; *to the Amorites*, Num. 21:21; *by Israelites to various nations*, Judg. 11:12–28; *by Hiram to David*, 2 Sam. 5:11; *and to Solomon*, 1 Kin. 5:1; *by Benhadad to Ahab*, 1 Kin. 20:2–

v.4–1493 BC
See footnote, *Time*, Rev. 10:6.

*q* *Bottle*, Gen. 21:14.
*r* *Bread*, Ezek. 4:13.
1 R. V. wine-skins,

6
*s* *Gilgal*, Josh. 4:19.
*t* *Falsehood*, Job 21:34.

9
*u* *Egypt*, Gen. 41:8.

10
*v* *Sihon*, Num. 21:21.
*w* *Og*, Num. 21:33.
*x* *Ashtaroth*, Deut. 1:4.

11
*y* *Senate*, Num. 11:16.

[1]wine [q]bottles[c], old, and rent[c],
and bound up;
5 And old shoes and clouted[c]
upon their feet, and old garments upon them; and all the
[r]bread of their provision was
dry *and* mouldy.
6 And they went to [k]Jŏsh′u-ȧ
unto the camp at [s]Gĭl′găl, and
[t]said unto him, and to the men
of Ĭs̤′ra-el, We be come from a
far country: now therefore make
ye a ‡league[c] with us.
7 And the men of Ĭs̤′ra-el said
unto the [h]Hī′vītes, Peradventure[c]
ye dwell among us; and how
shall we make a league with you?
8 And they said unto [k]Jŏsh′u-ȧ,
We *are* thy servants. And Jŏsh′-
u-ȧ said unto them, Who *are* ye?
and from whence come ye?
9 And they [t]said unto him,
From a very far country thy
servants are come because of the
name[c] of the LORD thy God: for
we have heard the fame of him,
and all that he did in [u]Ē′gy̆pt,
10 And all that he did to the
two kings of the [e]Ăm′ôr-ītes,
that *were* beyond Jôr′dan, to
[v]Sī′hŏn king of Hĕsh′bŏn, and
to [w]Ŏg king of Bā′shăn, which
*was* at [x]Ăsh′ta-rŏth.
11 Wherefore our [y]elders and
all the inhabitants of our country spake to us, saying, Take
victuals[c] with you for the journey, and go to meet them, and
say unto them, We *are* your
servants: therefore now make
ye a ‡league[c] with us.
12 This our [r]bread we took hot
*for* our provision out of our
houses on the day we came forth
to go unto you; but now, behold,
it is dry, and it is mouldy:
13 And these [1,q]bottles[c] of wine
which we filled, *were* new; and,
behold, they be rent[c]: and these
our garments and our shoes are
become old by reason of the very
long journey.
14 And the men took of their
victuals[c], and [z]asked not *counsel*[c] at the mouth of the LORD.
15 And [a]Jŏsh′u-ȧ made peace
with them, and made a ‡,[b]league
with them, to let them live: and
the [c]princes of the [d]congrega-
tion sware unto them.
16 ¶ And it came to pass at the
end of three days after they had
made a ‡,[b]league with them,
that they heard that they *were*
their neighbours, and *that* they
dwelt among them.
17 And the children of Ĭs̤′ra-el
journeyed, and came unto their
cities on the third day. Now
their cities *were* [e]Gĭb′e-on, and
[f]Chē-phī′rah, and ‖Bē-ē′rŏth,
and [g]Kĭr′jath-jē′a-rĭm.
18 And the children of Ĭs̤′ra-el
smote them not, because the
[c]princes of the congregation had
[h,i]sworn unto them by the LORD
God of Ĭs̤′ra-el. And all the congregation murmured against the
princes.
19 But all the [c]princes said unto
all the congregation, We have
[h,i]sworn[c] unto them by the LORD
God of Ĭs̤′ra-el: now therefore
we may not touch them.
20 This we will do to them; we
will even let them live, lest
[j]wrath[c] be upon us, because of the
[i]oath which we sware unto them.

v.12–1493 BC
See footnote, *Time*, Rev. 10:6.

14
*z* *Prayerlessness*, Job 21:15.

15
*a* *Joshua*, Josh. 1:1.
*b* *Treaty*, 1 Kin. 5:12.
*c* *Government*, vs. 15–21; Isa. 22:21.
*d* *Israel, makes a league with the Gibeonites*, Ex. 4:22.

17
*e* *Gibeon*, Jer. 41:16.
*f* Josh. 18:26; Ezra 2:25; Neh. 7:29.
*g* *Kirjath-jearim*, Josh. 15:9.

18
*h* *Covenant, sacred*, Deut. 29:1.
*i* *Oath, used to solemnize covenants*, Num. 5:19.

20
*j* *Anger of God*, 2 Kin. 13:3.

5; *by Amaziah to Jehoash*, 2 Kin. 14:8; *by Ahaz to Tiglath*, 2 Kin. 16:7; *by Hoshea to So*, 2 Kin. 17:4; *by Sennacherib through Rabshakeh to Hezekiah*, 2 Kin. 19:9; *by Berodach to Hezekiah*, 2 Kin. 20:12; 2 Chr. 32:31; *by Zedekiah to Egypt*, Jer. 37:5–7; Ezek. 17:15.

*Other references to*, Prov. 13:17; Isa. 18:2; 30:4; 33:7; 36:11; 39:1, 2; Luke 14:32.

**Figurative,** Obad. 1; 2 Cor. 5:20; Eph. 6:20.

‡ **ALLIANCES.** *With idolaters forbidden*, Ex. 23:32, 33; 34:12–15; Deut. 7:2; Judg. 2:2; 2 Chr. 19:2; 20:37; Isa. 30:2; 31:1; Hos. 4:17; 5:13; 12:1; Ezek. 17:15.

**Ratification of:** *By oaths*, Gen. 21:23; 26:28–31; Josh. 9:15–20. *By giving the hand*, Lam. 5:6.

See footnote, TREATY, 1 Kin. 5:12.

**Instances of:** *Between, Abraham and Mamre, Eshcol, and Aner*, Gen. 14:13; *Abraham and Abimelech*, Gen. 21:22–32; *Isaac and Abimelech*, Gen. 26:26–31; *Canaanitish nations against Israel*, Josh. 9:1, 2; *Joshua and the Gibeonites*, Josh. 9; *Moabites, Amalekites, and Ammonites*, Judg. 3:12, 13; *Solomon and Hiram*, 1 Kin. 5:12; Amos 1:9; *Asa and Benhadad*, 1 Kin. 15:18, 19; 2 Chr. 16:3; *Jehoshaphat and Ahab*, 1 Kin. 22; 2 Chr. 18:1; *Jehoshaphat and Ahaziah*, 2 Chr. 20:35; *Ahaz and Tiglath*, 2 Kin. 16:7, 8; 2 Chr. 28:16, 21; *Rezin and Pekah*, 2 Kin. 16:5; *Zedekiah and Pharaoh*, Jer. 37:1–8; Ezek. 17:15–17.

‖ **BEEROTH.** *A city of the Hivites*, Josh. 9:17 *Allotted to Benjamin*, Josh. 18:25; 2 Sam. 4:2. *Captivity from, return to, from Babylon*, Ezra 2:25; Neh. 7:29.

21 And the [c]princes said unto them, Let them live; but let them be hewers of wood and drawers of water unto all the congregation; as the princes had promised them.

22 ¶ And [a]Jŏsh′u-ȧ called for them, and he spake unto them, saying, Wherefore[C] have ye beguiled us, saying, We *are* very far from you; when ye dwell among us?

23 Now therefore ye *are* cursed, and there shall [2]none of you be freed from being bondmen[C], and hewers of wood and drawers of water for the [k]house of my God.

24 And they answered [a]Jŏsh′u-ȧ, and said, Because it was certainly told thy servants, how that the LORD thy God commanded his servant Mō′ṣeṣ to give you all the land, and to destroy all the inhabitants of the land from before you, therefore we were sore[C] afraid of our lives because of you, and have done this thing.

25 And now, behold, we *are* in thine hand; as it seemeth good and right unto thee to do unto us, do.

26 And so did he unto them, and delivered them out of the hand of the children of Ĭṣ′ra-el, that they slew them not.

27 And [a]Jŏsh′u-ȧ made them that day hewers of wood and drawers of water for the congregation, and for the altar of the LORD, even unto this day, in the place which he should choose.

## CHAPTER 10

*Five kings war against Gibeon. 6 Joshua rescues it. 10 God fights against them with hailstones. 12 The sun and moon stand still at the word of Joshua. 16 The five kings are shut up in a cave. 23 They are brought forth, 24 scornfully used, 26 and hanged. 28 Seven other kings are conquered. 43 Joshua returns to Gilgal.*

NOW it came to pass, when Ȧ-dō′nī-zē′dĕc king of [a]Jĕ-ru̥′sȧ-lĕm had heard how [b]Jŏsh′u-ȧ had taken [c]Ā′ī, and had [d]utterly destroyed it; as he had done to [e]Jĕr′ī-chō and her king, so he had done to Ā′ī and her king; and how the inhabitants of [f]Gĭb′e-on had made peace with Ĭṣ′ra-el, and were among them;

2 That they feared greatly, because [f]Gĭb′e-on *was* a great [g]city, as one of the royal cities, and because it *was* greater than [c]Ā′ī, and all the men thereof *were* mighty.

3 Wherefore Ȧ-dō′nī-zē′dĕc king of [a]Jĕ-ru̥′sȧ-lĕm sent unto Hō′ham king of [h]Hē′bron, and unto Pī′ram king of [i]Jär′mŭth, and unto Jȧ-phī′ȧ king of *Lā′chish, and unto Dē′bīr king of [j]Ĕg′lŏn, saying,

4 Come up unto me, and help me, that we may smite[C] [f]Gĭb′e-on: for it hath made peace with [b]Jŏsh′u-ȧ and with the children of Ĭṣ′ra-el.

5 Therefore the five kings of the [k]Ăm′ôr-ītes, the king of [a]Jĕ-ru̥′sȧ-lĕm, the king of [h]Hē′bron, the king of [i]Jär′mŭth, the king of *Lā′chish, the king of [j]Ĕg′lŏn, gathered themselves together, and went up, they and all their [l]hosts, and encamped before [f]Gĭb′e-on, and made war against it.

6 ¶ And the men of [f]Gĭb′e-on sent unto [b]Jŏsh′u-ȧ to the camp to [m]Gĭl′găl, saying, Slack[C] not thy hand from thy servants; come up to us quickly, and save us, and help us: for all the kings of the [k]Ăm′ôr-ītes that dwell in the mountains are [l]gathered together against us.

7 So [b]Jŏsh′u-ȧ ascended from [m]Gĭl′găl, he, and all the people of war with him, and all the mighty men of valour[C].

8 ¶ And the LORD [n]said unto

23
k *Church, called house of God,* 1 Kin. 9:3.
2 R. V. never fail to be of you bondmen.

1
a *Jerusalem,* Judg. 19:10.

b *Joshua,* Josh. 1:1
c *Ai,* Josh. 7:2.
d *War, of extermination,* Judg. 3.2
e *Jericho,* Num. 22:1.
f *Gibeon,* Jer. 41:16.

2
g *Cities, royal,* Num. 35:8.

3
h *Hebron,* Gen. 23:2.
i Josh. 12:11; 15:35; Neh. 11:29.
j Josh. 15:39.

5
k *Amorites,* Gen. 14:13.
l *Armies, confederated,* Deut. 11:4

6
m *Gilgal,* Josh. 4:19.

8
n *Prophets, inspiration of,* Isa. 3:2.

* **LACHISH,** a city. *King of, besieges Gibeon,* Josh. 10:5. *Captured by Joshua,* Josh. 10:31, 32. *Allotted to Judah,* Josh. 15:39; Neh. 11:30. *Fortified by Rehoboam,* 2 Chr. 11:9. *Assassination of Amaziah at,* 2 Kin. 14:19. *War against By Sennacherib,* 2 Kin. 18:13–17; 19:8; 2 Chr. 32:9; *by Nebuchadnezzar,* Jer. 34:7. *Prophecy concerning,* Mic. 1:13.

[b]Jŏsh′u-ȧ, Fear them not: for
[o]I have delivered them into thine
hand; there shall not a man of
them stand[C] before thee.
9 Jŏsh′u-ȧ therefore [p]came unto them suddenly, *and* went up
from [m]Gĭl′găl all night.
10 And the [o]LORD discomfited[C]
them before Ĭṣ′ra-el, and slew
them with a great slaughter at
[l]Gĭb′e-on, and chased them
along the [q]way that goeth up to
†Bĕth–hō′rŏn, and smote them
to ‡Ȧ-zē′kah, and unto [r]Măk-
kē′dah.
11 [S]And it came to pass, as [k]they
fled from before Ĭṣ′ra-el, *and*
were in the going down to
†Bĕth–hō′rŏn, that the LORD
[s,t]cast down great stones from
heaven upon them unto ‡Ȧ-zē′-
kah, and they died: *they were*
more which died with [u]hail-
stones than *they* whom the children of Ĭṣ′ra-el slew with the
sword.
12 ¶ Then spake [b]Jŏsh′u-ȧ to
the LORD in the day when the
LORD delivered up the [k]Ăm′ôr-
ītes before the children of Ĭṣ′-
ra-el, and he said in the sight
of Ĭṣ′ra-el, ‖,[v]Sun, [w]stand thou
still upon [l]Gĭb′e-on; and thou,
[x]Moon, in the valley of [y]Ăj′a-
lŏn.
13 And the ‖,[v]sun [w]stood still,
and the [x]moon stayed, until the
people had avenged themselves
upon their enemies. *Is* not this
written in the [z]book of [1]Jā′shēr?
So the sun stood still in the
midst of heaven, and hasted[C] not
to go down about a whole day.[S]
14 And there was no day like
that before it or after it, that the
[a]LORD hearkened[G] unto the voice
of a man: for the LORD [b]fought
for Ĭṣ′ra-el.
15 ¶ And [c]Jŏsh′u-ȧ returned,
and all [d]Ĭṣ′ra-el with him, unto
the camp to [e]Gĭl′găl.
16 But these five kings [f]fled,
and hid themselves in a [g]cave at
[h]Măk-kē′dah.
17 And it was told [c]Jŏsh′u-ȧ,
saying, The five kings are found
hid in a [g]cave at [h]Măk-kē′dah.
18 And [c]Jŏsh′u-ȧ said, Roll
great stones upon the mouth of
the [g]cave, and set men by it for
to keep[C] them:
19 And stay[C] ye not, *but* pursue
after your enemies, and smite
the hindmost[C] of them; suffer[C]
them not to enter into their
cities: for the [a]LORD your God
hath delivered them into your
hand.
20 And it came to pass, when
[c]Jŏsh′u-ȧ and the children of
[d]Ĭṣ′ra-el had made an end of
slaying them with a very great
slaughter, till they were consumed,[C] that the rest *which* remained of them entered into
[i]fenced[C] cities.
21 And all the people returned
to the camp to [c]Jŏsh′u-ȧ at
[h]Măk-kē′dah in peace: none
moved his tongue against any
of the children of Ĭṣ′ra-el.
22 Then said [c]Jŏsh′u-ȧ, Open
the mouth of the [g]cave, and
bring out those five kings unto
me out of the cave.
23 And they did so, and
brought forth those five kings
unto him out of the cave, the
king of [j]Jē-rụ′sȧ-lĕm, the king of
[k]Hē′bron, the king of [l]Jär′mŭth,
the king of *Lā′chish, *and* the
king of [m]Ĕg′lŏn.

*o* *God, providence of,* Gen. 2:2.

**9**
*p* *Armies, stratagems,* Deut. 11:4.

**10**
*q* *Highways,* Deut. 2:27.
*r* Josh. 12:16.

**11**
*s* *Meteorology,* Matt. 16:2.
*t* *Miracles, hail on the confederated kings,* Luke 23:8.
*u* *Hail,* Job 38:22.

**12**
*v* *Celestial Phenomena,* Luke 23:44.
*w* *Miracles, sun and moon stand still,* Luke 23:8.
*x* *Moon,* Song 6:10.
*y* Or, *Aijalon,* Josh. 21:24.

**13**
*z* *Book,* Num. 5:23.
1 R. V. (marg.) *Or,* The Upright?

**14**
*a* *God, overruling providence of,* Gen. 2:2.

*b* *War, God in,* Judg. 3:2.

**15**
*c* *Joshua,* Josh. 1:1.
*d* *Israel,* Ex. 4:22.
*e* *Gilgal,* Josh. 4:19.

**16**
*f* *Cowardice, instances of,* Lev. 26:36.
*g* *Cave,* Judg. 6:2.
*h* Josh. 12:16.

**20**
*i* *Cities, fortified,* Num. 35:8.

**23**
*j* *Jerusalem,* Judg. 19:10.
*k* *Hebron,* Gen. 23:2.
*l* Josh. 12:11; 15:35; Neh. 11:29.
*m* Josh. 15:39.

† **BETH-HORON.** *Two ancient cities of Canaan, near which Joshua defeated the Amorites,* Josh. 10:10, 11; 16:3, 5; 18:13; 1 Sam. 13:18; 1 Chr. 7:24. *Assigned to the Levites,* Josh. 21:22; 1 Chr. 6:68. *Solomon builds,* 1 Kin. 9:17; 2 Chr. 8:5. *Taken from Judah by the ten tribes,* 2 Chr. 25:13.

‡ **AZEKAH.** *A town of Judah,* Josh. 10:10, 11; 15:35; 1 Sam. 17:1; 2 Chr. 11:9; Neh. 11:30; Jer. 34:7.

‖ **SUN.** *Created,* Gen. 1:14–18; Psa. 74:16; 136:7, 8; Jer. 31:35. *Worship of, forbidden,* Deut. 4:19; 17:3. *Worshiped,* Job 31:26–28; Jer. 8:2; Ezek. 6:4, 6 [R. V.]; 8:16. *Kings of Judah dedicate horses to,* 2 Kin. 23:11.
*Darkening of,* Ex. 10:21–23; Amos 8:9; Matt. 24:29; 27:45; Mark 13:24; 15:33; Luke 23:44, 45; Acts 2:20. *Stands still,* Josh. 10:12, 13; Hab. 3:11. *Light from, causes shadow to go back on dial of Ahaz,* 2 Kin. 20:11; Isa. 38:8.
**Figurative,** Judg. 5:31; Psa. 84:11; Isa. 30:26; 60:19, 20; Ezek. 32:7; Jer. 15:9; Joel 2:10, 31; 3:15; Mic. 3:6; Mal. 4:2; Luke 21:25. *In John's vision,* Rev. 6:12; 8:12; 9:2; 12:1; 16:8; 19:17.

24 And it came to pass, when they brought out those kings unto [c]Jŏsh′u-ȧ, that Jŏsh′u-ȧ called for all the men of Ĭș′ra-el, and said unto the [2]captains of the men of war which went with him, Come near, put[c] your feet upon the necks of these kings. And they came near, and put their feet upon the necks of them.

25 And [c]Jŏsh′u-ȧ said unto them, [n]Fear not, nor be dismayed, be strong and of good [o]courage: for thus shall the LORD do to all your enemies against whom ye fight.

26 And afterward [c]Jŏsh′u-ȧ smote [p]them, and slew them, and hanged them on five trees: and they were hanging upon the trees until the evening.

27 And it came to pass at the time of the going down of the ‖sun, *that* Jŏsh′u-ȧ commanded, and they took them down off the trees, and cast them into the [g,q]cave wherein they had been hid, and laid great stones in the cave's mouth, *which remain* until this very day.

28 ¶ And that day [c]Jŏsh′u-ȧ took [h]Măk-kē′dah, and [r]smote it[c] with the edge of the sword, and the king thereof he [s]utterly destroyed, them, and all the souls that *were* therein; he let none remain: and he did to the king of Măk-kē′dah as he did unto the king of [t]Jĕr′ĭ-chō.

29 Then [c]Jŏsh′u-ȧ passed from [h]Măk-kē′dah, and all [d]Ĭș′ra-el with him, unto §Lĭb′nah, and fought against Lĭb′nah:

30 And the LORD [a]delivered it also, and the king thereof, into the hand of Ĭș′ra-el; and he smote it with the edge of the sword, and [s]all the souls[c] that *were* therein; he let none remain in it; but did unto the king thereof as he did unto the king of [t]Jĕr′ĭ-chō.

31 ¶ And [c]Jŏsh′u-ȧ passed from §Lĭb′nah, and all Ĭș′ra-el with him, unto *Lā′chish, and encamped against it, and fought against it:

32 And the LORD [a]delivered *Lā′chish into the hand of [d]Ĭș′ra-el, which took it on the second day, and [r,s]smote it with the edge of the sword, and all the souls that *were* therein, according to all that he had done to Lĭb′nah.

33 ¶ Then Hō′ram king of +Gē′zēr came up to help *Lā′chish; and [c]Jŏsh′u-ȧ smote him and his people, until he had left him none remaining.

34 ¶ And from *Lā′chish [c]Jŏsh′u-ȧ passed unto [m]Ĕg′lŏn, and all Ĭș′ra-el with him; and they encamped against it, and fought against it:

35 And they took it on that day, and [r]smote it with the edge of the sword, and all the souls that *were* therein he [s]utterly destroyed that day, according to all that he had done to *Lā′chish.

36 And [c]Jŏsh′u-ȧ went up from [m]Ĕg′lŏn, and all Ĭș′ra-el with him, unto [k]Hē′bron; and they fought against it:

37 And they took it, and [r,s]smote it with the edge of the sword, and the king thereof, and all the cities thereof, and all the souls that *were* therein; he left none remaining, according to all that he had done to [m]Ĕg′lŏn; but [r,s]destroyed it utterly, and all the souls that *were* therein.

38 ¶ And [c]Jŏsh′u-ȧ returned,

24
2 R. V. chiefs

25
n *Faith, enjoined,* Mark 11:22.
o *Courage, enjoined,* Deut. 31:7.

26
p *Captive, cruelty to,* 1 Sam. 30:3.

27
q *Burying Places,* Gen. 23:4.

28
r *War, of extermination,* Judg. 3:2.
s *Massacre, instances of,* Esth. 3:13.
t *Jericho,* Num. 22:1.

§ **LIBNAH** (*whiteness*). *A city of the Canaan′ites, captured by Joshua,* Josh. 10:29–32, 39; 12:15. *Allotted to the priests,* Josh. 13; 1 Chr. 6:57. *Sennacherib besieges; his army defeated near,* 2 Kin. 19:8, 35; Isa. 37:8–36.

+ **GEZER**, a Canaanitish royal city; called also GAZER, GAZARA, GAZERA, and GOB. *King of, defeated by Joshua,* Josh. 10:33; 12:12. *Canaanites not expelled from, but made to pay tribute,* Josh. 16:10; Judg. 1:29. *Allotted to Ephraim,* Josh. 16:3, 10; 1 Chr. 7:28. *Assigned to Levites,* Josh. 21:21; 1 Chr 6:67. *Battle with Philistines at,* 2 Sam. 21:18; 1 Chr. 20:4. *Smitten by David,* 1 Sam. 27:8. *Fortified by Solomon,* 1 Kin. 9:15–17.

38
[u] *Debir*, Josh. 15: 15.

40
[v] *Obedience, exemplified*, Heb. 5:8.
3 R. V. slopes,

41
[w] *Kadesh*, Gen. 14:7.
[x] Josh. 11:16; 15: 51.

B.C. 1450?
See footnote, *Time*, Rev. 10:6.

1
[a] Josh. 12:19.
[b] Josh. 19:15.
[c] Josh. 12:20.

and all Ĭş'ra-el with him, to
[u]Dē'bĭr; and fought against it:
39 And [r]he took it, and the king
thereof, and all the cities thereof;
and they smote them with the
edge of the sword, and [s]utterly
destroyed all the souls that *were*
therein; he left none remaining:
as he had done to [k]Hē'bron, so
he did to [u]Dē'bĭr, and to the king
thereof; as he had done also to
[§]Lĭb'nah, and to her king.
40 ¶ [v]So [c]Jŏsh'u-ȧ smote[c] all the
country of the hills, and of the
south, and of the vale, and of the
[3]springs, and all their kings: he
left none remaining, but utterly
destroyed all that breathed, as
the LORD God of Ĭş'ra-el commanded.
41 And Jŏsh'u-ȧ smote them
from [w]Kā'desh–bär'ne-ȧ even
unto Gā'zȧ, and all the country
of [x]Gō'shen, even unto Gĭb'-
e-on.
42 And all these kings and their
land did [c]Jŏsh'u-ȧ take at one
time, because the LORD God of
Ĭş'ra-el [b]fought for Ĭş'ra-el.
43 And Jŏsh'u-ȧ returned, and
all Ĭş'ra-el with him, unto the
camp to [e]Gĭl'găl.

## CHAPTER 11

*Divers kings overcome at the waters of Merom. 10 Hazor taken and burnt. 16 All the country taken by Joshua. 21 The Anakim cut off.*

AND it came to pass, when
Jā'bin king of *Hā'zôr
had heard *those things*, that he
sent to Jō'băb king of [a]Mā'dŏn
and to the king of [b]Shĭm'rŏn,
and to the king of [c]Ăch'shăph,
2 And to the kings that *were* on
the north of the mountains, and
of the [1]plains south of [d]Chĭn'ne-
rŏth, and in the valley, and in
the [2]borders of †Dôr on the
west,
3 *And to* the [e]Cā'năan-īte on
the east and on the west, and *to*
the [f]Ăm'ôr-īte, and the [g]Hĭt'tīte,
and the [h]Pĕr'ĭz-zīte, and the
[i]Jĕb'u-sīte in the mountains, and
*to* the [j]Hī'vīte under Hēr'mon in
the land of Mĭz'peh.
4 And they went out, they and
all their hosts with them, much[c]
people, even as the sand that *is*
upon the sea shore in multitude,
with horses and ‡chariots very
many.
5 And when all these kings
were [k]met together, they came
and pitched[c] together at the waters of Mē'rom, to fight against
Ĭş'ra-el.
6 ¶ And the LORD said unto
[l]Jŏsh'u-ȧ, Be not afraid because
of them: for to morrow about
this time will I deliver them up
all slain before Ĭş'ra-el: thou
shalt hough[c] their [m]horses, and
burn their ‡chariots with fire.
7 So [l]Jŏsh'u-ȧ came, and all the
people of war with him, against
them by the waters of Mē'rom
suddenly; and they fell upon
them.
8 And the [n]LORD delivered
them into the hand of Ĭş'ra-el,
[o]who smote them, and chased
them unto great Zī'dŏn, and
unto [p]Mĭs're-phŏth–mā'im, and
unto the valley of Mĭz'peh eastward; and they smote them, until they [o]left them none remaining.
9 And Jŏsh'u-ȧ did unto them
as the LORD bade him: he

2
[d] 1 Kin. 15:20.
1 R. V. Arabah
2 R. V. heights

3
[e] *Canaanites*, Ex. 23:28.
[f] *Amorites*, Gen. 14:13.
[g] *Hittites*, Judg. 1:26.
[h] *Perizzites*, Gen. 15:20.
[i] *Jebusites*, Deut. 7:1.
[j] *Hivites*, Gen. 10: 17.

5
[k] *Armies, confederated*, Deut. 11:4.

6
[l] *Joshua*, Josh. 1:1.
[m] *Horse, houghing of*, Job 39:19.

8
[n] *God, providence of*, Gen. 2:2.
[o] *War, of extermination*, Judg. 3:2.
[p] Josh. 13:6.

* **HAZOR.** *A fortified city of Naphtali*, Josh. 11:1, 10, 11, 13; 12:19; 19:36; Judg. 4:2, 17; 1 Sam. 12:9; 2 Kin. 15:29; Neh. 11:33.

† **DOR.** *A town and district of Palestine*, Josh. 11:2. *Conquered by Joshua*, Josh. 12:23; 1 Kin. 4:11. *Allotted to Manasseh, although situated in the territory of Asher*, Josh. 17:11; Judg. 1:27; 1 Chr. 7:29.

‡ **CHARIOT.** *For war*, Ex. 14:7, 9, 25; Josh. 11:4; 1 Sam. 13:5; 1 Kin. 20:1, 25; 2 Kin. 6:14; 2 Chr. 12:2, 3; Psa. 20:7; 46:9; Jer. 46:9; 47:3; 51:21, 22; Joel 2:5; Nah. 2:3, 4; 3:2. *Wheels of Pharaoh's, providentially taken off*, Ex. 14:25.

*Made of iron*, Josh. 17:18; Judg. 1:19. *Commanded by captains*, Ex. 14:7; 1 Kin. 9:22; 22:31–33; 2 Kin. 8:21. *Introduced among Israelites by David*, 2 Sam. 8:4. *Imported from Egypt by Solomon*, 1 Kin. 10:26–29. *Cities for*, 1 Kin. 9:19; 2 Chr. 1:14; 8:6; 9:25. *Traffic in*, Rev. 18:13.

*Royal*, Gen. 41:43; 46:29; 2 Kin. 5:9; 2 Chr. 35:24; Jer. 17: 25; 22:4; Acts 8:28, 29.

**Figurative,** 2 Kin. 6:17; Psa. 68:17; 104:3; Isa. 66:15; Hab. 3:8.

**Symbolical,** Zech. 6:1–8; 2 Kin. 2:11, 12.

10
[q] *Government, imperial,* Isa. 22:21.

11
[r] *Captive, cruelty to,* 1 Sam. 30:3.
[s] *Massacre,* Esth. 3:13.

12
[t] *Moses,* Ex. 2:10.

13
3 R. V. on their mounds,

14
[u] *Spoils,* 1 Chr. 26:27.

15
[v] *Obedience, exemplified,* Heb. 5:8.

16
[w] Josh. 10:41.
4 R. V. Arabah,

17
[x] Josh. 12:7.

houghed[c] their [m]horses, and
burnt their ‖chariots with fire.
10 ¶ And [l]Jŏsh'u-ȧ at that time
turned back, and took *Hā'zôr,
and smote the king thereof with
the sword: for Hā'zôr beforetime
was the [q]head of all those kingdoms.
11 And [o]they smote[c] all the
[r]souls[c] that *were* therein with the
edge of the sword, [s]utterly destroying *them*: there was not any
left to breathe: and he burnt
*Hā'zôr with fire.
12 And all the cities of those
kings, and all the kings of them,
did Jŏsh'u-ȧ take, and smote
them with the edge of the sword,
*and* he utterly destroyed them,
as [t]Mō'ṣeṣ the servant of the
LORD commanded.
13 But *as for* the cities that
stood still [3]in their strength, Ĭṣ'-
ra-el burned none of them, save[c]
*Hā'zôr only; *that* did Jŏsh'u-ȧ
burn.
14 And all the [u]spoil of these
cities, and the cattle, the children of Ĭṣ'ra-el took for a prey
unto themselves; but every man
they smote with the edge of
the sword, [o]until they had [s]de-
stroyed them, neither left they
any to breathe.
15 As the LORD commanded
[t]Mō'ṣeṣ his servant, so did Mō'-
ṣeṣ command Jŏsh'u-ȧ, and so
[v]did Jŏsh'u-ȧ; he left nothing
undone of all that the LORD
commanded Mō'ṣeṣ.
16 So Jŏsh'u-ȧ took all that
land, the hills, and all the south
country, and all the land of
[w]Gō'shen, and the valley, and
the [4]plain, and the mountain of
Ĭṣ'ra-el, and the valley of the
same;
17 *Even* from the mount [x]Hā'-
lăk, that goeth up to [y]Sē'ïr, even
unto [z]Bā'al-găd in the valley of
[a]Lĕb'a-non under mount [b]Hĕr'-
mon: and all their kings he took,
and [c]smote them, and slew them.
18 [d]Jŏsh'u-ȧ made war a long
time with all those kings.
19 There was not a city that
made peace with the children of
Ĭṣ'ra-el, save the [e]Hī'vītes the inhabitants of Gĭb'e-on: all *other*
they took in battle.
20 For [f]it was of the [g]LORD to
harden their [h]hearts, that they
should come against Ĭṣ'ra-el in
battle, that he might destroy
them utterly, *and* that they
might have no favour[c], but that
he might destroy them, as the
LORD commanded Mō'ṣeṣ.[s]
21 ¶ And at that time came
[d]Jŏsh'u-ȧ, and cut off the [i]Ăn'a-
kĭmṣ from the mountains, from
[j]Hē'bron, from [k]Dē'bïr, from
[l]Ā'năb, and from all the mountains of Jū'dah, and from all the
mountains of Ĭṣ'ra-el: Jŏsh'u-ȧ
[c]destroyed them utterly with
their cities.
22 There was none of the [i]Ăn'a-
kĭmṣ left in the land of the children of Ĭṣ'ra-el: only in [m]Gā'zȧ,
in ‖Găth, and in [n]Ăsh'dŏd, there
remained.
23 So [d]Jŏsh'u-ȧ took the whole
[o]land, according to all that the
LORD said unto [p]Mō'ṣeṣ; and
Jŏsh'u-ȧ gave it for an inheritance unto Ĭṣ'ra-el according to
their divisions by their tribes.
And the land rested from [c]war.

## CHAPTER 12

*The two kings on the east of Jordan, whose countries Moses took and disposed of. 7 The thirty-one kings on the west of Jordan, whom Joshua smote.*

NOW these *are* the kings of
the [a]land, which the children of Ĭṣ'ra-el smote[c], and pos-

[y] *Seir,* Deut. 1:2.
[z] Josh. 12:7; 13:5.
[a] *Lebanon,* Deut. 1:7.
[b] *Hermon,* Deut. 4:48.
[c] *War, of extermination,* Judg. 3:2.

18
[d] *Joshua,* Josh. 1:1.

19
[e] *Hivites,* Gen. 10:17.

20
[f] *Foreordination,* Rom. 8:30.
[g] *God, providence of,* Gen. 2:2.
[h] *Heart, hardened, instances of,* Psa. 44:21.

21
[i] *Anakim,* Deut. 1:28.
[j] *Hebron,* Gen. 23:2.
[k] *Debir,* Josh. 15:15.
[l] Josh. 15:50.

22
[m] *Gaza,* Gen. 10:19.
[n] *Ashdod,* 1 Sam. 6:17.

v.23—1489 BC

23
[o] *Canaan,* Gen. 37:1.
[p] *Moses,* Ex. 2:10.

1
[a] *Canaan, conquest of, by the Israelites,* vs. 1–24; Gen. 37:1.

‖ **GATH** (*wine-press*). *One of the five chief cities of the Philistines,* Josh. 13:3; 1 Sam. 6:17; 2 Sam. 21:20; 1 Chr. 8:13; Amos 6:2; Mic. 1:10. *Anakim, a race of giants, inhabitants of,* Josh. 11:22. *Goliath dwelt in,* 1 Sam. 17:4; 1 Chr. 20:5–8. *Obed-edom belonged to,* 2 Sam. 6:10. *The ark taken to,* 1 Sam. 5:8. *Inhabitants of, called* GITTITES, Josh. 13:3; *slew sons of Ephraim,* 1 Chr. 7:20, 21. *David takes refuge at,* 1 Sam. 21:10–15; 27:2–7. *Band of Gittites attached to David,* 2 Sam. 15:18–22. *Taken by David,* 1 Chr. 18:1. *Shimei's servants escape to,* 1 Kin. 2:39–41. *Fortified by Rehoboam,* 2 Chr. 11:8. *Taken by Hazael,* 2 Kin. 12:17. *Recovered by Jehoash,* 2 Kin. 13:25. *Besieged by Uzziah,* 2 Chr. 26:6.

sessed their land on the other
side [b]Jôr′dan toward the rising
of the sun, from the [1]river [c]Är′-
nŏn unto mount [d]Hẽr′mon, and
all the [2]plain on the east:
2 [e]Sī′hŏn king of the [f]Ăm′ôr-
ītes, who dwelt in [g]Hĕsh′bŏn,
*and* ruled from [h]Ăr′ō-ẽr, which
[3]*is* upon the bank of the river
[c]Är′nŏn, and from the middle of
the river, and from half [i]Gĭl′e-
ăd, even unto the river [j]Jăb′bŏk,
*which is* the border of the [k]chil-
dren of Ăm′mŏn;
3 And from [4]the plain to the
[l]sea of Chĭn′ne-rŏth on the east,
and unto the [m]sea of the [5]plain,
*even* the salt sea on the east, the
way to *Bĕth–jĕsh′i-mŏth; and
from the south, under [6,n]Ăsh′-
dŏth–pĭs̤′gah:
4 And the [7]coast of [o]Ŏg king of
[p]Bā′shăn, *which was* of the remnant of the [q]giants, that dwelt at
[r]Ăsh′ta-rŏth and at [s]Ĕd′re-ī,
5 And reigned in mount
[d]Hẽr′mon, and in [t]Săl′cah, and
in all [p]Bā′shăn, unto the border
of the [u]Gĕsh′u-rītes, and the
[v]Mȧ-ăch′a-thītes, and half [i]Gĭl′e-
ăd, the border of [e]Sī′hŏn king of
[g]Hĕsh′bŏn.
6 Them did [w]Mō′s̤es̤ the servant of the LORD and the children of Ĭs̤′ra-el smite: and Mō′-
s̤es̤ the servant of the LORD
gave it *for* a possession unto the
[x]Reu̥′ben-ītes, and the [y]Găd′-
ītes, and the half tribe of [z]Mȧ-
năs′seh.
7 ¶ And these *are* the kings of
the [a]country which [b]Jŏsh′u-ȧ
and the children of Ĭs̤′ra-el
smote on this side [c]Jôr′dan on
the west, from [d]Bā′al–găd in the
valley of [e]Lĕb′a-non even unto
the mount [f]Hā′lăk, that goeth up
to [g]Sē′ïr; which Jŏsh′u-ȧ gave
unto the tribes of Ĭs̤′ra-el *for*
a possession according to their
divisions;
8 In the mountains, and in the
valleys, and in the [5]plains, and
in the [8]springs, and in the wilderness, and in the south country; the [h]Hĭt′tītes, the [i]Ăm′ôr-
ītes, and the [j]Cā′năan-ītes, the
[k]Pĕr′ĭz-zītes, the [l]Hī′vītes, and
the [m]Jĕb′u-sītes:
9 The king of [n]Jĕr′ĭ-chō, one;
the king of [o]Ā′ī, which *is* beside
[p]Bĕth′-el, one;
10 The king of [q]Jē-ru̥′sȧ-lĕm,
one; the king of [r]Hē′bron, one;
11 The king of [s]Jär′mu̇th, one;
the king of [t]Lā′chish, one;
12 The king of [u]Ĕg′lŏn, one;
the king of [v]Gē′zẽr, one;
13 The king of [w]Dē′bĭr, one;
the king of †Gē′dẽr, one;
14 The king of [x]Hôr′mah, one;
the king of [y]Ā′răd, one;
15 The king of [z]Lĭb′nah, one;
the king of [a]Ȧ-dŭl′lăm, one;
16 The king of [b]Măk-kē′dah,
one; the king of [c]Bĕth′–el, one;
17 The king of [d]Tăp′pu̥-ah,
one; the king of [e]Hē′phẽr, one;
18 The king of [f]Ā′phek, one;
the king of Lȧ-shâr′on, one;
19 The king of [g]Mā′dŏn, one;
the king of [h]Hā′zôr, one;
20 The king of Shĭm′ron–mē′-
ron, one; the king of [i]Ăch′shăph,
one;
21 The king of ‡Tā′a-năch,
one; the king of [j]Mė-gĭd′dō,
one;
22 The king of [k]Kē′desh, one;
the king of [l]Jŏk′ne-ăm of Cär′-
mel, one;
23 The king of [m]Dôr in the
[9]coast of Dôr, one; the king of
the nations of Gĭl′găl, one;

b *Jordan*, Gen. 32:10.
c *Arnon*, Num. 22:36.
d *Hermon*, Deut. 4:48.
1 R. V. valley of
2 R. V. Arabah eastward:

**2**
e *Sihon*, Num. 21:21.
f *Amorites*, Gen. 14:13.
g *Heshbon*, Isa. 16:8.
h *Aroer*, Deut. 4:48.
i *Gilead*, Deut. 3:13.
j *Jabbok*, Num. 21:24.
k *Ammonites*, Deut. 2:20.
3 R. V. is on the edge of the valley of Arnon, and the city that is in the middle of the valley,

**3**
l *Sea of Galilee*, Matt. 4:18.
m *Dead Sea*, Gen. 14:3.
n *Pisgah*, Deut. 3:27.
4 R. V. the Arabah unto
5 R. V. Arabah,
6 R. V. the slopes of Pisgah:

**4**
o *Og*, Num. 21:33.
p *Bashan*, Num. 32:33.
q *Rephaim*, Gen. 14:5.
r *Ashtaroth*, Deut. 1:4.
s *Edrei*, Josh. 13:12.
7 R. V. border

**5**
t *Salcah*, Deut. 3:10.
u *Geshur*, 2 Sam. 3:3.
v Deut. 3:14; or, *Maachah*, 1 Chr. 19:7.

**6**
w *Moses*, Ex. 2:10.
x *Reubenites*, Josh. 22:1.
y *Gad, tribe of*, Deut. 33:20.
z *Manasseh, tribe of*, Gen. 46:20.

7—a *Canaan, conquest of, by the Israelites*, Gen. 37:1. b *Joshua*, Josh. 1:1. c *Jordan*, Gen. 32:10. d *Baal-gad*, Josh. 11:17. e *Lebanon*, Deut. 1:7.

f Josh. 11:17.
g *Seir*, Deut. 1:2.

**8**
h *Hittites*, Judg. 1:26.
i *Amorites*, Gen. 14:13.
j *Canaanites*, Ex. 23:28.
k *Perizzites*, Gen. 15:20.
l *Hivites*, Gen. 10:17.
m *Jebusites*, Deut. 7:1.
8 R. V. slopes,

**9**
n *Jericho*, Num. 22:1.
o *Ai*, Josh. 7:2.
p *Bethel*, Josh. 18:13.

**10**
q *Jerusalem*, Judg. 19:10.
r *Hebron*, Gen. 23:2.

**11**
s Josh. 15:35; Neh. 11:29.
t *Lachish*, Josh. 10:5.

**12**
u Josh. 10:34, 36, 37.
v *Gezer*, Josh. 10:33.

**13**
w *Debir*, Josh. 15:15.

**14**
x *Hormah*, Deut. 1:44.
y *Arad*, Num. 21:1.

**15**
z *Libnah*, Josh. 10:29.

a *Adullam*, 2 Chr. 11:7.

**16**
b Josh. 10:16-28.
c *Bethel*, Josh. 18:13.

**17**
d Josh. 15:34.
e 1 Kin. 4:10.

**18**
f *Aphek*, 1 Sam. 4:1.

**19**
g Josh. 11:1.
h *Hazor*, Josh. 11:1.

**20**
i Josh. 11:1.

**21**
j *Megiddo*, Josh. 17:11.

**22**
k Josh. 19:37; 1 Chr. 6:72; or, *Kishon*, Josh. 21:28.
l Josh. 19:11; 21:34.

**23**
m *Dor*, Josh. 11:2.
9 R. V. height

* **BETH-JESHIMOTH** (*house of desolations*, or, *waste*). *A place in Moab*, Num. 33:49; Josh. 12:3; 13:20; Ezek. 25:9. *Called* BETH-JESIMOTH, Num. 33:49.

† **BETH-GADER.** *A place in Judah*, 1 Chr. 2:51. *Probably identical with* GEDER, Josh. 12:13; *and with* GEDOR, Josh. 15:58.

‡ **TAANACH** (*sandy soil*), called also TANACH. *A city conquered by Joshua*, Josh. 12:21. *Allotted to Manasseh*, Josh. 17:11; 1 Chr. 7:29. *Canaanites not driven from*, Josh. 17:12; Judg. 1:27. *Assigned to the Levites*, Josh. 21:25. *The scene of Barak's victory*, Judg. 5:19. *One of Solomon's commissaries at*, 1 Kin. 4:12.

24 The king of [n]Tĭr′zah, one:
all the kings thirty and one.

## CHAPTER 13

*Much land yet to be possessed. 8 The inheritance of the two tribes and a half. 14 The inheritance of Levi is the sacrifices of the Lord. 15 The inheritance of Reuben. 22 Balaam slain. 24 The inheritance of Gad, 29 and of the half tribe of Manasseh.*

NOW [a]Jŏsh′u-ȧ was [b]old *and*
stricken in years; and the
LORD said unto him, Thou art
old *and* stricken[c] in years, and
there remaineth yet very much
land to be possessed.
2 This *is* the land that yet remaineth: all the [1]borders of the
[c]Phĭ-lĭs′tĭneṣ, and all [d]Gĕsh′u-rī,
3 From *Sī′hôr, which *is* before [e]Ē′ġy̆pt, even unto the borders of [f]Ĕk′rŏn northward,
*which* is counted to the [g]Cā′-
năan-īte: five lords of the [c]Phĭ-
lĭs′tĭneṣ; the [h]Gā′zath-ītes, and
the [i]Ăsh′dŏth-ītes, the [j]Ĕsh′ka-
lŏn-ītes, the [k]Gĭt′tītes, and the
Ĕk′ron-ītes; also the [l]Ā′vītes:
4 From the south, all the land
of the [g]Cā′năan-ītes, and Mē-
ā′rah that [2]*is* beside the [m]Sĭ-
dō′nĭ-anṣ, unto [n]Ā′phek, to the
borders of the [o]Ăm′ôr-ītes:
5 And the [p]land of the Ġĭb′-
lītes, and all [q]Lĕb′a-non, toward
the sunrising, from [r]Bā′al–găd
under mount [s]Hĕr′mon unto the
entering into [t]Hā′math.
6 All the inhabitants of the hill
country from [q]Lĕb′ȧ-non unto
[u]Mĭs′re-phŏth–mā′im, *and* all
the [m]Sĭ-dō′nĭ-anṣ, them will I
drive out from before the children of [v]Ĭṣ′ra-el: only divide
thou it by lot unto the Ĭṣ′ra-el-
ītes for an inheritance, as I have
commanded thee.
7 Now therefore divide this
land for an inheritance unto the
nine tribes, and the half tribe of
[w]Mȧ-năs′seh,
8 With whom the [x]Reu̇′ben-
ītes and the [y]Găd′ītes have received their inheritance, which
[z]Mō′ṣeṣ gave them, beyond [a]Jôr′-
dan eastward, *even* as Mō′ṣeṣ the
servant of the LORD gave them;
9 From [b]Ăr′ŏ-ēr, that [3]*is* upon
the bank of the river [c]Ăr′nŏn,
and the city that [4]*is* in the midst
of the river, and all the plain of
[d]Mĕd′e-bȧ unto [e]Dī′bŏn;
10 And all the cities of [f]Sī′hŏn
king of the [g]Ăm′ôr-ītes, which
reigned in [h]Hĕsh′bŏn, unto the
border of the [i]children of Ăm′-
mŏn;
11 And [j]Ġĭl′e-ăd, and the border of the [k]Ġĕsh′u-rītes and
[l]Mȧ-ăch′a-thītes, and all mount
[m]Hĕr′mon, and all [n]Bā′shăn unto [o]Săl′cah;
12 All the kingdom of [p]Ŏg
in [n]Bā′shăn, which reigned in
[q]Ăsh′ta-rŏth and in †Ĕd′re-ī,
who remained of the remnant of
the [r]giants: for these did [s]Mō′-
ṣeṣ smite[c], and cast them out.
13 Nevertheless the children of
Ĭṣ′ra-el expelled not the [k]Ġĕsh′-
u-rītes, nor the [l]Mȧ-ăch′a-thītes:
but the Ġĕsh′u-rītes and the Mȧ-
ăch′a-thītes dwell among the
Ĭṣ′ra-el-ītes until this day.
14 Only unto the tribe of Lē′vī
he gave none inheritance; [t]the
sacrifices[c] of the LORD God of
Ĭṣ′ra-el made by fire *are* their
inheritance, as he said unto
them.
15 ¶ And [s]Mō′ṣeṣ gave unto the
tribe of the [u]children of Reu̇′-
ben *inheritance* according to
their families.
16 And their [5,] ‡coast[c] was from
[b]Ăr′ŏ-ēr, that *is* on the [6]bank
of the river [c]Ăr′nŏn, and the
city that *is* in the [7]midst of
the river, and all the plain by
[d]Mĕd′e-bȧ;

24
n *Tirzah,* 1 Kin. 14:17.

B.C. 1445?
See footnote, *Time,* Rev. 10:6.

1
a *Joshua, allots the land,* vs. 1–33; Josh. 1:1.
b *Old age,* Isa. 46:4.

2
c *Philistines,* Gen. 26:14.
d Or, *Geshur,* 2 Sam. 3:3.
1 R. V. regions

3
e *Egypt,* Gen. 41:8.
f *Ekron,* Amos 1:8.
g *Canaanites,* Ex. 23:28.
h Or, *Gazites,* Judg. 16:2.
i *Ashdod,* 1 Sam. 6:17.
j *Ashkelon,* Judg. 1:18.
k *Gath,* Josh. 11:22.
l Or, *Avims,* Deut. 2:23.

4
m *Zidon,* Ezek. 28:21.
n Josh. 19:30; or, *Aphik,* Judg. 1:31.
o *Amorites,* Gen. 14:13.
2 R. V. belongeth to the Zidonians,

5
p *Gebal,* Ezek. 27:9.
q *Lebanon,* Deut. 1:7.
r *Baal-gad,* Josh. 11:17.
s *Hermon,* Deut. 4:48.
t *Hamath,* 1 Chr. 18:3.

6
u Josh. 11:8.
v *Israel,* Ex. 4:22.

7
w *Manasseh, tribe of,* Gen. 46:20.

8
x *Reubenites,* Josh. 22:1.
y *Gad, tribe of,* Deut. 33:20.
z *Moses,* Ex. 2:10.
a *Jordan,* Gen. 32:10.

9
b *Aroer,* Deut. 4:48.
c *Arnon,* Num. 22:36.
d *Medeba,* Num. 21:30.
e *Dibon,* Num. 21:30.
3 R. V. is on the edge of the valley of Arnon,
4 R. V. is in the middle of the valley,

10
f *Sihon,* Num. 21:21.
g *Amorites,* Gen. 14:13.
h *Heshbon,* Isa. 16:8.
i *Ammonites,* Deut. 2:20.

11
j *Gilead,* Deut. 3:13.
k Or, *Geshur,* 2 Sam. 3:3.
l Deut. 3:14; or, *Maachah,* 1 Chr. 19:7.
m *Hermon,* Deut. 4:48.
n *Bashan,* Num. 32:33.
o *Salcah,* Deut. 3:10.

12
p *Og,* Num. 21:33.
q *Ashtaroth,* Deut. 1:4.
r *Rephaim,* Gen. 14:5.
s *Moses,* Ex. 2:10.

14
t *Levites, emoluments of,* Deut. 10:8.

15
u *Reubenites,* Josh. 22:1.

16
5 R. V. border
6 R. V. edge of the valley of Arnon,
7 R. V. middle of the valley,

* **SIHOR** (*black, or turbid*), called also SHIHOR. *A river of Egypt, supposed by some authorities to be the Nile,* 1 Chr. 13:5; Isa. 23:3; Jer. 2:18.

† **EDREI** (*strength, or stronghold*). *A town in Bashan,* Josh. 12:4. *Allotted to Manasseh,* Josh. 13:12, 31. *Joshua defeats Og at,* Num. 21:33–35; Deut. 1:4; 3:1–3.

‡ **TOPOGRAPHY.** *Of Canaan,* Num. 34:2–15; Josh. 13:15–33; 15; 16; 18:9–20.

17
v Or, *Bamoth,* Num. 21:19, 20.
w *Baal-meon,* Num. 32:38.
18
x *Jahaz,* Judg. 11:20.
19
y *Kirjathaim,* Num. 32:37.
20
z *Beth-peor,* Deut. 3:29.

a *Pisgah,* Deut. 3:27.
b *Beth-jesimoth,* Josh. 12:3.
8 R. V. the slopes of Pisgah,
21
c *Sihon,* Num. 21:21.
d *Amorites,* Gen. 14:13.
e *Heshbon,* Isa. 16:8.
f *Moses,* Ex. 2:10.
g Num. 31:8.
h Num. 31:8.
i Num. 31:8.
j Num. 31:8.
k *Duke,* Gen. 36:15.
22
l *Balaam,* Deut. 23:4.
m *Sorcery,* Isa. 47:9.
23
n *Reubenites,* Josh. 22:1.
o *Jordan,* Gen. 32:10.
24
p *Gad, tribe of,* Deut. 33:20.
25
q *Gilead,* Deut. 3:13.
r *Ammonites,* Deut. 2:20.
s Num. 32:34; Judg. 11:33.
t *Rabbah,* Deut. 3:11.
26
u *Mahanaim,* Gen. 32:2.
v *Debir,* Josh. 15:15.
27
w Or, *Beth-haran,* Num. 32:36.
x Or, *Nimrah,* Num. 32:3.

17 [h]Hĕsh′bŏn, and all her cities that *are* in the plain; [e]Dī′bŏn, and [v]Bā′moth–bā′al, and [w]Bĕth–bā′al–mē′on,

18 And [x]Jȧ-hā′zȧ, and ‖Kĕd′e-mŏth, and §Mĕph′a-ăth,

19 And [y]Kĭr-jath-ā′im, and +Sĭb′mah, and Zā′reth–shā′har in the mount of the valley,

20 And [z]Bĕth–pē′ôr, and [8,a]Ăsh′dŏth–pĭs′gah, and [b]Bĕth–jĕsh′i-mŏth,

21 And all the cities of the plain, and all the kingdom of [c]Sī′hŏn king of the [d]Ăm′ôr-ītes, which reigned in [e]Hĕsh′bŏn, whom [f]Mō′ṣeṣ smote with the princes of Mĭd′ĭ-an, [g]Ē′vī, and [h]Rē′kem, and Zûr, and [i]Hûr, and [j]Rē′bȧ, *which were* [k]dukes[C] of Sī′hŏn, dwelling in the country.

22 ¶ [l]Bā′laam also the son of Bē′or, the [m]soothsayer[C], did the children of Ĭṣ′ra-el slay with the sword among them that were slain by them.

23 And the border of the [n]children of Reu̧′ben was [o]Jôr′dan, and the border *thereof.* This *was* the inheritance of the children of Reu̧′ben after their families, the cities and the villages thereof.

24 ¶ And [f]Mō′ṣeṣ gave *inheritance* unto the tribe of [p]Găd, *even* unto the children of Găd according to their families.

25 And their [5]coast[C] was ⊙Jā′zēr, and all the cities of [q]Gĭl′e-ăd, and half the land of the [r]children of Ăm′mŏn, unto [s]Ăr′ŏ-ēr that *is* before [t]Răb′bah;

26 And from [e]Hĕsh′bŏn unto Rā′math–mĭz′peh, and Bĕt′o-nĭm; and from [u]Mā-hȧ-nā′im unto the border of [v]Dē′bĭr;

27 And in the valley, [w]Bĕth–ā′ram, and [x]Bĕth–nĭm′rah, and [y]Sŭc′coth, and Zā′phŏn, the rest of the kingdom of [c]Sī′hŏn king of [e]Hĕsh′bŏn, [o]Jôr′dan and *his* border, *even* unto the [9]edge of the [z]sea of Chĭn′ne-rĕth on the other side Jôr′dan eastward.

28 This *is* the inheritance of the children of [a]Găd after their families, the cities, and their villages.

29 ¶ And [b]Mō′ṣeṣ gave *inheritance* unto the half tribe of [c]Mȧ-năs′seh: and *this* was *the possession* of the half tribe of the children of Mȧ-năs′seh by their families.

30 And their coast[C] was from [d]Mā-hȧ-nā′im, all [e]Bā′shăn, all the kingdom of [f]Ŏg king of Bā′shăn, and all the towns of ▲Jā′ïr, which *are* in Bā′shăn, threescore cities:

31 And half [g]Gĭl′e-ăd, and [h]Ăsh′ta-rŏth, and †Ĕd′re-ī, cities of the kingdom of [f]Ŏg in [e]Bā′shăn, *were*[C] *pertaining* unto the children of [i]Mā′chĭr the son of Mȧ-năs′seh, *even* to the one half of the children of Mā′chĭr by their families.

32 These *are the countries* which [b]Mō′ṣeṣ did distribute for inheritance in the plains of [j]Mō′ab, on the other side [k]Jôr′dan, by [l]Jĕr′ĭ-chō, eastward.

33 But unto the tribe of Lē′vī [b]Mō′ṣeṣ gave not *any* inheritance: [m]the LORD God of Ĭṣ′ra-el *was* their inheritance, as he said unto them.

## CHAPTER 14

*The nine tribes and a half are to have their inheritance by lot. 6 Caleb by favor obtains Hebron.*

AND these *are the countries* which the children of [a]Ĭṣ′ra-el inherited in the land of [b]Că′năan, which [c]Ē-le-ā′zar the

y *Succoth,* Judg. 8:5.
z *Sea of Galilee,* Matt. 4:18.
9 R. V. uttermost part
28
a *Gad, tribe of,* Deut. 33:20.
29
b *Moses,* Ex. 2:10.
c *Manasseh, tribe of,* Gen. 46:20.
30
d *Mahanaim,* Gen. 32:2.
e *Bashan,* Num. 32:33.
f *Og,* Num. 21:33.
31
g *Gilead,* Deut. 3:13.
h *Ashtaroth,* Deut. 1:4.
i *Machir,* Gen. 50:23.
32
j *Moab,* Num. 26:3.
k *Jordan,* Gen. 32:10.
l *Jericho,* Num. 22:1.
33
m *Levites, emoluments of,* Deut. 10:8.

v.1–1489 BC
See footnote, *Time,* Rev. 10:6.
1
a *Israel,* Ex. 4:22.
b *Canaan, divided by Joshua,* Gen. 37:1.
c *Eleazar,* Num. 3:2.

‖ **KEDEMOTH,** a city of Moab. *Allotted to tribe of Reuben and the Merarite Levites,* Josh. 13:18; 21:37; 1 Chr. 6:79. *Encircled by a wilderness of same name,* Deut. 2:26.

§ **MEPHAATH.** *A Levitical city in Reuben,* Josh. 13:18; 21:37; 1 Chr. 6:79; Jer. 48:21.

+ **SIBMAH** (*coolness or fragrance*). *A city of Reuben,* Josh. 13:19; Isa. 16:8, 9; Jer. 48:32. *Apparently identical with* SHEBAM, Num. 32:3; *and* SHIBMAH, Num. 33:28.

⊙ **JAZER,** called also JAAZER. *A Levitical city in Gilead, allotted to Gad, and given to the Levites,* Num. 21:32; 32:1, 3, 35; Josh. 13:25; 21:39; 2 Sam. 24:5; 1 Chr. 6:81; Jer. 48:32.

▲ **JAIR** (*whom Jehovah enlightens*). *Son of Manasseh,* Num. 32:41; Deut. 3:14; Josh. 13:30; 1 Kin. 4:13.

v.1–1489 BC
See footnote, *Time*, Rev. 10:6.

*d Joshua*, Josh. 1:1.

2
*e Lot*, Esth. 3:7.
*f Moses*, Ex. 2:10.

3
*g Levites, emoluments of*, Deut. 10:8.

4
*h Joseph*, Gen. 33:2.
*i Manasseh, tribe of*, Gen. 46:20.
*j Ephraim, tribe of*, Gen. 41:52.
*k Cities, suburbs of*, Num. 35:8.
*l* Num. 35:3–5.

6
*m Judah, tribe of*, Num. 10:14.
*n Gilgal*, Josh. 4:19.
*o Caleb*, Num. 14:6.
*p* Or, *Kadesh*, Gen. 14:7.

8
*q Cowardice*, Lev. 26:36.
*r Obedience, exemplified*, Heb. 5:8.

9
*s Oath*, Num. 5:19.

priest, and [d]Jŏsh'u-ȧ the son of Nŭn, and the heads of the fathers of the tribes of the children of Ĭṣ'ra-el, distributed for inheritance to them.[Q]

2 By [e]lot *was* their inheritance, as the LORD commanded by the hand of [f]Mō'ṣeṣ, for the nine tribes, and *for* the half tribe.

3 For [f]Mō'ṣeṣ had given the inheritance of two tribes and an half tribe on the other side Jôr'dan: but unto the Lē'vītes he gave [g]none inheritance among them.

4 For the children of [h]Jō'ṣeph were two tribes, [i]Mȧ-năs'seh and [j]Ē'phrā-ĭm: therefore they gave no part unto the Lē'vītes in the land, save[C] [g, k]cities to dwell *in*, with their [l]suburbs[C] for their cattle and for their substance.

5 As the LORD commanded [f]Mō'ṣeṣ, so the children of Ĭṣ'ra-el did, and they divided the land.

6 ¶ Then the children of [m]Jū'dah came unto [d]Jŏsh'u-ȧ in [n]Gĭl'găl: and [o]Ca'leb the son of Jē-phŭn'neh the Kĕn'ez-īte said unto him, Thou knowest the thing that the LORD said unto [f]Mō'ṣeṣ the man of God concerning me and thee in [p]Kā'desh–bär'ne-ȧ.

7 Forty years old *was* [o]I when [f]Mō'ṣeṣ the servant of the LORD sent me from [p]Kā'desh–bär'ne-ȧ to espy[C] out the land; and I brought him word again as *it was* in mine heart.

8 Nevertheless my brethren that went up with me made the [q]heart of the people melt: but I wholly [r]followed the LORD my God.

9 And [f]Mō'ṣeṣ [s]sware[C] on that day, saying, Surely the land whereon thy feet have trodden shall be thine inheritance, and thy children's for ever, because thou hast wholly followed the LORD my God.

10 And now, behold, the [t]LORD hath kept me alive, as he said, these forty and five years, even since the LORD spake this word unto Mō'ṣeṣ, while *the children of* Ĭṣ'ra-el wandered in the wilderness: and now, lo, I *am* this day fourscore and five years old.

11 [u]As yet [o]I *am as* strong this day as *I was* in the day that Mō'ṣeṣ sent me: as my strength *was* then, even so *is* my strength now, for war, both to go out, and to come in.

12 Now therefore give me this mountain, whereof the LORD spake in that day; for thou heardest in that day how the [v]Ăn'a-kĭmṣ *were* there, and *that* the [w]cities *were* great *and* fenced:[C] if so be the LORD *will be* with me, then I shall be able to drive them out, as the LORD said.

13 And [d]Jŏsh'u-ȧ [x]blessed him, and gave unto [o]Cā'leb the son of Jē-phŭn'neh [y]Hē'bron for an inheritance.

14 [y]Hē'bron therefore became the inheritance of [o]Cā'leb the son of Jē-phŭn'neh the Kĕn'ez-īte unto this day, because that he wholly [r]followed the LORD God of Ĭṣ'ra-el.

15 And the name of [y]Hē'bron before *was* Kĭr'jath–är'bȧ; *which Ar'ba was* [1]a great man among the [v]Ăn'a-kĭmṣ. And the [z]land had rest[C] from war.

## CHAPTER 15

*The borders of the lot of Judah. 13 Caleb takes possession of his portion. 16 Othniel, for his valor, has Achsah, Caleb's daughter, to wife. 18 She obtains a blessing of her father. 21 The cities of Judah. 63 The Jebusites not conquered.*

THIS then was the [a]lot[C] of the tribe of the children of [b]Jū'dah by their families; [c]*even* to the border of [d]Ē'dom the wilderness of [e]Zĭn southward *was* the uttermost[C] part of the south coast.[C]

2 And [c]their south border was

v.10–1489 BC
See footnote, *Time*, Rev. 10:6.

10
*t God, preserver*, Gen. 2:2.

11
*u Infirmity, physical, Caleb exempt from*, John 5:5.

12
*v Anakim*, Deut. 1:28.
*w Cities, fortified*, Num. 35:8.

13
*x Benedictions*, Deut. 21:5.
*y Hebron*, Gen. 23:2.

15
*z Nation, peace of*, Isa. 2:4.
1 R. V. the greatest

1
*a Lot*, Esth. 3:7.
*b Judah, tribe of*, Num. 10:14.
*c Topography*, Josh. 13:16.
*d Edom*, Obad. 1
*e Zin*, Num. 13 21.

v.2–1489 BC
See footnote, *Time*, Rev. 10:6.

**2**
*f* *Dead Sea*, Gen. 14:3.

**3**
*g* Or, *Akrabim*, Num. 34:4.
*h* Or, *Kadesh*, Gen. 14:7.
*i* Or, *Hazar-addar*, Num. 34:4.

**4**
*j* Num. 34:4, 5.
*k* *Egypt*, Gen. 15:18.
1 R. V. brook
2 R. V. the border

**5**
*l* *Jordan*, Gen. 32:10.

**6**
*m* Josh. 18:19, 21.
*n* *Pillar*, Gen. 28:18.
*o* Josh. 18:17.
*p* *Reuben*, Gen. 35:22.

**7**
*q* Josh. 7:24, 26; Isa. 65:10; Hos. 2:15.
*r* Or, *Geliloth*, Josh. 18:17.
*s* Josh. 18:17.

**8**
*t* *Hinnom*, Jer. 7:31.
*u* *Jerusalem*, Judg. 19:10.

from the shore of the [f]salt sea, from the bay that looketh southward:

3 And [c]it went out to the south side to [g]Mā-ăl′eh-ā-crăb′bim, and passed along to [e]Zĭn, and ascended up on the south side unto [h]Kā′desh–bär′ne-ȧ, and passed along to Hĕz′rŏn, and went up to [i]Ā′där, and fetched[C] a compass to Kär′ka-ȧ:

4 [c]*From thence* it passed toward [j]Ăz′mŏn, and went out unto the [1]river of [k]Ē′ġy̆pt; and the goings[C] out of [2]that coast[C] were at the sea: this shall be your south coast.

5 And [c]the east border *was* the [f]salt sea, *even* unto the end of [l]Jôr′dan. And *their* border in the north quarter *was* from the bay of the sea at the uttermost[C] part of Jôr′dan:

6 And [c]the border went up to [m]Bĕth–hŏg′lȧ, and passed along by the north of *Bĕth–är′a-bah; and the border went up to the [n]stone[C] of [o]Bō′hăn the son of [p]Reu′ben:

7 And [c]the border went up toward ‖Dē′bĭr from the valley of [q]Ā′chôr, and so northward, looking toward [r]Ġĭl′găl, that *is* before the going[C] up to [s]Ā-dŭm′-mĭm, which *is* on the south side of the river: and the border passed toward the waters of [s]Ĕn-shē′mesh, and the goings[C] out thereof were at †Ĕn–rō′ġel:

8 And [c]the border went up by the valley of the son of [t]Hĭn′nom unto the south side of the Jĕb′u-sīte; the same *is* [u]Jĕ-ru′să-lĕm: and the border went up to the top of the mountain that *lieth* before the valley of Hĭn′nom westward, which *is* at the end of the [v]valley of the giants northward:

9 And [c]the border was drawn[C] from the top of the hill unto the fountain of the water of [w]Nĕph′to-ah, and went out to the cities of mount Ē′phron; and the border was drawn to Bā′al-ah, which *is* ‡Kĭr′jath–jē′a-rĭm:

10 And the border [3]compassed[C] from ‡Bā′al-ah westward unto mount [x]Sē′ĭr, and passed along unto the side of mount Jē′a-rĭm, which *is* Chĕs′a-lŏn, on the north side, and went down to [y]Bĕth–shē′mesh, and passed on to [z]Tĭm′nah:

11 And the border went out unto the side of [a]Ĕk′rŏn northward: and the border was drawn[C] to Shĭ′crŏn, and passed along to mount Bā′al-ah, and went out unto Jăb′ne-el; and the goings[C] out of the border were at the sea.

12 And the west border *was* to the [b]great sea, and the [2]coast[C] *thereof*. This *is* the [2]coast[C] of the children of [c]Jū′dah round about according to their families.

13 ¶ And unto [d]Cā′leb the son of Jĕ-phŭn′neh he gave a part among the children of [c]Jū′dah, according to the commandment of the LORD to Jŏsh′u-ȧ, *even* the city of Är′bȧ the father of [e]Ā′năk, which *city is* [f]Hē′bron.

14 And [d]Cā′leb drove thence the three sons of Ā′năk, [g]Shē′-shāi, and [h]Ā-hī′man, and [i]Tăl′-māi, the [j]children of Ā′năk.

15 And he went up thence[C] [4]to the inhabitants of ‖Dē′bĭr: and

v.8–1489 BC
See footnote, *Time*, Rev. 10:6.

*v* *Rephaim*, 1 Chr. 11:15.

**9**
*w* Josh. 18:15.

**10**
*x* *Seir*, Deut. 1:2.
*y* *Beth-shemesh*, Josh. 21:16.
*z* 2 Chr. 28:18.
3 R. V. turned about

**11**
*a* *Ekron*, Amos 1:8.

**12**
*b* *Mediterranean Sea*, Ex. 23:31.
*c* *Judah, tribe of*, Num. 10:14.

**13**
*d* *Caleb*, Num. 14:6.
*e* Josh. 21:11.
*f* *Hebron*, Gen. 23:2.

**14**
*g* Num. 13:22.
*h* Num. 13:22.
*i* Num. 13:22; Judg. 1:10.
*j* *Anakim*, Deut. 1:28.

**15**
4 R. V. against

* **BETH-ARABAH** (*house of the desert*). *A place in the wilderness of Judea*, Josh. 15:6, 61. *Assigned to Benjamin*, Josh. 18:22. *John the Baptist preaches in*, Matt. 3:1; Mark 1:4; Luke 3:3. *Called* ARABAH, Josh. 18:18.

† **EN-ROGEL** (*spring of the fuller*). *A spring near Jerusalem*, Josh. 15:7; 18:16; 2 Sam. 17:17. *Adonijah holds seditious feast at*, 1 Kin. 1:9.

‡ **KIRJATH-JEARIM** (*city of woods*), called also BAALAH. *One of the four cities of the Gibeonites*, Josh. 15:9. *Inhabitants of, not smitten, on account of the covenant made by the Israelites with the Gibeonites, but put under servitude*, Josh. 9:17 (with verses 3–27). *In the territory allotted to Judah*, Josh. 15:9, 60; 18:14. *The Philistines bring the ark to*, 1 Sam. 6:21 (with vs. 1–21). *Ark remains twenty years at*, 1 Sam. 7:1, 2; 1 Chr. 13:5, 6. *David brings the ark from*, 2 Sam. 6:1–11; 1 Chr. 13:5–8; 2 Chr. 1:4. *Inhabitants of, who were taken into captivity to Babylon, return*, Ezra 2:25; Neh. 7:29. *Urijah, the prophet, an inhabitant of*, Jer. 26:20.

‖ **DEBIR** (*a sanctuary*), a town in the mountains of Judah. *Called also* KIRJATH-SANNAH, Josh. 15:49; *and* KIRJATH-SEPHER, *which signifies a city of books*, Josh. 15:15, 16. *Anakim expelled from, by Joshua*, Josh. 11:21. *Taken by Othniel*, Josh. 15:15–17, 49; Judg. 1:12, 13. *Allotted to the priests*, Josh. 21:15.

v.15–1489 BC See footnote, *Time,* Rev. 10:6.

**15** k *Book,* Num. 5:23.
**16** l *Armies, reward for meritorious conduct in,* Deut. 11:4.
m *Daughter, given in marriage by parents,* Lev. 12:6.
**17** n Judg. 1:13.
**21** o *Edom,* Obad. 1.
p *Kabzeel,* 2 Sam. 23:20.
5 R. V. border
**23** q 1 Kin. 9:15.
**27** r Or, *Beth-phelet,* Neh. 11:26.
**28** s Josh. 19:3; 1 Chr. 4:28; Neh. 11:27.
t *Beer-sheba,* Judg. 20:1.
**29** u Or, *Balah,* Josh. 19:3; or, *Bilhah,* 1 Chr. 4:29.
v Josh. 19:3; or, *Ezem,* 1 Chr. 4:29.

the name of ‖Dē′bĭr before *was*
[k]Kĭr′jath–sē′phẽr.
16 And [d]Cā′leb said, [l]He that
smiteth Kĭr′jath–sē′phẽr, and
taketh it, to him will I give
§Ăch′sah my daughter to[c] wife.
17 And +Ŏth′nĭ-el the son of
[n]Kē′năz, the brother of [d]Cā′leb,
took it: and he gave him §Ăch′-
sah his daughter to wife.
18 And it came to pass, as she
came *unto him,* that she moved
him to ask of her father a field:
and she lighted[c] off *her* ass; and
[d]Cā′leb said unto her, What
wouldest thou?
19 Who answered, Give me a
blessing; for thou hast given me
a south land; give me also
springs of water. And he gave
her the upper springs, and the
nether[c] springs.
20 This *is* the inheritance of the
tribe of the children of [c]Jū′dah
according to their families.
21 ¶ And the uttermost cities of
the tribe of the children of [c]Jū′-
dah toward the [5]coast[c] of [o]Ē′dom
southward were [p]Kăb′ze-el, and
Ē′dẽr, and Jā′gŭr,
22 And Kī′nah, and Dĭ-mō′-
nah, and Ăd′a-dah,
23 And Kē′desh, and [q]Hā′zôr,
and Ĭth′nan,
24 Zĭph, and Tē′lem, and Bē′a-
lŏth,
25 And Hā′zôr, Hȧ-dăt′tah,
and Kē′rĭ-ŏth, *and* Hĕz′rŏn,
which *is* Hā′zôr,
26 Ā′măm, and Shē′mȧ, and
Mŏl′a-dah,
27 And Hā′zar–găd′dah, and
Hĕsh′mŏn, and [r]Bĕth–pā′let,
28 And [s]Hā′zar–shụ′al, and
[t]Bē′er–shē′bȧ, and Bĭz-jŏth′jah,
29 [u]Bā′al-ah, and Ī′ĭm, and
[v]Ā′zem,
30 And [w]Ĕl′to-lăd, and [x]Chē′-
sĭl, and [y]Hôr′mah,
31 And ⊙Zĭk′lăg, and [z]Măd-
măn′nah, and Săn-săn′nah,
32 And [a]Lĕb′a-ŏth, and [b]Shĭl′-
him, and [c]Ā′in, and [d]Rĭm′mon.
all the cities *are* twenty and nine,
with their villages:
33 *And* in the valley, [e]Ĕsh′ta-ŏl,
and Zō′re-ah, and Ăsh′nah,
34 And [f]Zȧ-nō′ah, and Ĕn-găn′-
nim, [g]Tăp′pụ-ah, and Ē′nam,
35 [h]Jär′mŭth, and [i]Ȧ-dŭl′lăm,
[j]Sō′coh, and [k]Ȧ-zē′kah,
36 And [l]Shȧ-rā′im, and Ăd-i-
thā′im, and Ḡē-dē′rah, and Ḡĕd-
e-rŏth-ā′im; fourteen cities with
their villages:
37 [m]Zē′nan, and Hăd′a-shah,
and Mĭg′dal–găd,
38 And Dĭl′e-ăn, and Mĭz′peh,
and Jŏk′the-el,
39 [n]Lā′chish, and [o]Bŏz′kăth,
and [p]Ĕg′lŏn,
40 And Căb′bon, and Läh′-
mam, and Kĭth′lish,
41 And [q]Ḡē-dē′roth, Bĕth–dā′-
gon, and Nā′a-mah, and Măk-
kē′dah; sixteen cities with their
villages:
42 Lĭb′nah, and [r]Ē′thẽr, and
[s]Ā′shan,
43 And Jĭph′tah, and Ăsh′nah,
and Nē′zib,
44 And [t]Kēi′lah, and [u]Ăch′zĭb,
and ▲Mȧ-rē′shah; nine cities
with their villages:
45 [v,w]Ĕk′rŏn, with her towns
and her villages:
46 [w]From [v]Ĕk′rŏn even unto
the sea, all that *lay* near [x]Ăsh′-
dŏd, with their villages:
47 [w,x]Ăsh′dŏd with her towns
and her villages, [y]Gā′zȧ with her
towns and her villages, unto the
[6]river of [z]Ē′ġy̆pt, and the [a]great
sea, and the border *thereof*:

v.30–1489 BC See footnote, *Time,* Rev. 10:6.

**30** w Josh. 19:4; or, *Tolad,* 1 Chr. 4:29.
x Or, *Bethul,* Josh. 19:4; or, *Bethuel,* 1 Chr. 4:30.
y *Hormah,* Deut. 1:44.
**31** z Or, *Beth-marcaboth,* Josh. 19:5.
**32** a Or, *Beth-lebaoth,* Josh. 19:6.
b Or, *Sharuhen,* Josh. 19:6.
c *Ain,* Josh. 19:7.
d *Rimmon,* Zech. 14:10.
**33** e *Eshtaol,* Judg. 18:2.
**34** f Neh. 3:13; 11:30.
g Josh. 12:17.
**35** h Neh. 11:29.
i *Adullam,* 2 Chr. 11:7.
j *Socoh,* 1 Sam. 17:1.
k *Azekah,* Josh. 10:10.
**36** l Or, *Shaaraim,* 1 Sam. 17:52.
**37** m Or, *Zaanan,* Mic. 1:11.
**39** n *Lachish,* Josh. 10:5.
o 2 Kin. 22:1.
p Josh. 10:3, 5, 23, 34.
**41** q 2 Chr. 28:18.
**42** r *Ether,* Josh. 19:7.
s Josh. 19:7; 1 Chr. 4:32.
**44** t *Keilah,* 1 Sam. 23:1.
u Mic. 1:14.
**45** v *Ekron,* Amos 1:8.
w *Philistines, territory of,* Gen. 26:14.
**46** x *Ashdod,* 1 Sam. 6:17.
**47** y *Gaza,* Gen. 10:19.
z *Egypt, brook of,* Gen. 15:18.
a *Mediterranean Sea,* Ex. 23:31.
6 R. V. brook

§ **ACHSAH,** Caleb's daughter. *Given to Othniel as a reward of valor,* Josh. 15:16–19; Judg. 1:9–13. *Called* ACHSA, 1 Chr. 2:49.

+ **OTHNIEL** (*lion of God*), son of Kenaz and nephew of Caleb. *Conquers Kirjath-sepher, and as reward secures Caleb's daughter to wife,* Josh. 15:16–20; Judg. 1:12, 13. *Becomes deliverer and judge of Israel,* Judg. 3:8–11. *Death of,* Judg. 3:11. *Descendants of,* 1 Chr. 4:13, 14.

⊙ **ZIKLAG.** *A city within the territory allotted to the tribe of Judah,* Josh. 15:31. *Reallotted to the tribe of Simeon,* Josh. 19:5. *David dwells at,* 1 Sam. 27:5, 6; 2 Sam. 1:1; 1 Chr. 12:1. *Amalekites destroy,* 1 Sam. 30. *Inhabited by the returned exiles of Judah,* Neh. 11:28.

▲ **MARESHAH.** *A city of Judah,* Josh. 15:44; 2 Chr. 11:8; 14:9, 10. *Birthplace of Eliezer the prophet,* 2 Chr. 20:37. *Prophecy concerning,* Mic. 1:15.

v.48–1489 BC
See footnote, *Time*, Rev. 10:6.

48 And in the mountains, Shā′-
mĭr, and [b]Jăt′tir, and Sō′coh,
49 And Dăn′nah, and Kĭr′jath-
săn′nah, which *is* ‖Dē′bĭr,
50 And [c]Ā′năb, and [d]Ĕsh′te-
mōh, and Ā′nĭm,
51 And [e]Gō′shen, and [f]Hō′lŏn,
and [g]Gī′loh; eleven cities with
their villages:
52 Ā′rab, and Du′mah, and
Ē′she-ăn,
53 And Jā′num, and Bĕth-
tăp′pu-ah, and Ă-phē′kah,
54 And Hŭm′tah, and Kĭr′-
jath-är′bȧ, which *is* [h]Hē′bron,
and Zī′or; nine cities with their
villages:
55 •Mā′on, [i]Cär′mel, and
[j]Zĭph, and [k]Jŭt′tah,
56 And [l]Jĕz′re-el, and Jŏk′de-
ăm, and Zȧ-nō′ah,
57 Cāin, Gĭb′e-ah, and Tĭm′-
nah; ten cities with their villages:
58 Hăl′hŭl, [m]Bĕth′–zûr, and
Gē′dôr,
59 And Mā′a-răth, and Bĕth-
ā′noth, and Ĕl′te-kŏn; six cities
with their villages:
60 Kĭr′jath–bā′al, which *is*
‡Kĭr′jath–jē′a-rĭm, and Răb′-
bah; two cities with their villages:
61 In the wilderness, *Bĕth-
är′a-bah, Mĭd′din, and Sĕc′a-cah,
62 And Nĭb′shăn, and the city
of [n]Salt, and [o]Ĕn–gē′dī; six cities
with their villages.
63 ¶ As for the [p]Jĕb′u-sītes the
inhabitants of [q]Jē-ru′sȧ-lĕm, the
children of [r]Jū′dah could not
drive them out: but the Jĕb′u-
sītes dwell with the children of
Jū′dah at Jē-ru′sȧ-lĕm unto this
day.

## CHAPTER 16

*The general borders of the sons of Joseph. 5 The border of the inheritance of Ephraim. 10 The Canaanites not conquered.*

AND the lot of the children
of [a,b]Jō′seph fell [c]from
[d]Jôr′dan by [e]Jĕr′ī-chō, unto the
water of Jĕr′ī-chō on the east,
to the wilderness that goeth
up from Jĕr′ī-chō [1]throughout
mount [f]Bĕth′–el,
2 [c]And goeth out from [f]Bĕth′–
el to Lŭz, and passeth along unto
the borders of Är′chī to [g]Ăt′a-
rŏth,
3 [c]And goeth down westward
to the [2]coast[c] of Jăph-lē′tī, unto
the [2]coast of [h]Bĕth–hō′rŏn the
nether[c], and to [i]Gē′zēr: and the
goings[c] out thereof are at the sea.
4 So the children of Jō′seph,
[b]Mȧ-năs′seh and [a]Ē′phră-ĭm,
took their inheritance.
5 ¶ And [c]the border of the children of [a]Ē′phră-ĭm according to
their families was *thus*: even the
border of their inheritance on the
east side was [g]Ăt′a-rŏth–ăd′dar,
unto [h]Bĕth–hō′rŏn the upper;
6 And [c]the border went out [3]to-
ward the sea to [j]Mĭch′me-thah
on the north side; and the border
went about eastward unto Tā′a-
năth–shī′lōh, and passed by it
on the east to Jȧ-nō′hah;
7 And [c]it went down from Jȧ-
nō′hah to [g]Ăt′a-rŏth, and to Nā′-
a-răth, and came to [e]Jĕr′ī-chō,
and went out at [d]Jôr′dan.
8 [c]The border went out from
[k]Tăp′pu-ah westward unto the
[4]river [l]Kā′nah; and the goings[c]
out thereof were at the sea. This
*is* the inheritance of the tribe of
the children of [a]Ē′phră-ĭm by
their families.
9 And the separate cities for
the children of [a]Ē′phră-ĭm *were*
among the inheritance of the
children of [b]Mȧ-năs′seh, all the
cities with their villages.
10 And they drave[c] not out
the [m]Cā′năan-ītes that dwelt in
[i]Gē′zēr: but the Cā′năan-ītes
dwell among the [a]Ē′phră-ĭm-ītes
unto this day, and [5]serve under
tribute.

48
b Josh. 21:14; 1 Chr. 6:57.
50
c Josh. 11:21.
d Or, *Eshtemoa*, 1 Sam. 30:28.
51
e Josh. 10:41; 11:16.
f Josh. 21:15; or, *Hilen*, 1 Chr. 6:58.
g 2 Sam. 15:12.
54
h *Hebron*, Gen. 23:2.
55
i *Carmel*, 2 Chr. 26:10.
j 2 Chr. 11:8.
k Josh. 21:16.
56
l 1 Sam. 25:43; 27:3; 29:1, 11.
58
m *Beth-zur*, Neh. 3:16.
62
n *Salt*, 2 Kin. 2:20.
o *En-gedi*, 2 Chr. 20:2.
63
p *Jebusites*, Deut. 7:1.
q *Jerusalem*, Judg. 19:10.
r *Judah, tribe of*, Num. 10:14.
1
a *Ephraim, tribe of*, Gen. 41:52.
b *Manasseh, tribe of*, Gen. 46:20.
c *Topography*, Josh. 13:16.
d *Jordan*, Gen. 32:10.
e *Jericho*, Num. 22:1.

v.1–1489 BC
See footnote, *Time*, Rev. 10:6.
f *Bethel*, Josh. 18:13.
1 R. V. through the hill country to Bethel;
2
g Or, *Atarothadar*, Josh. 18:13.
3
h *Beth-horon*, Josh. 10:10.
i *Gezer*, Josh. 10:33.
2 R. V. border
6
j Josh. 17:7.
3 R. V. westward at Michmethath
8
k Josh. 17:8.
l Josh. 17:9.
4 R. V. brook of
10
m *Canaanites*, Ex. 23:28.
5 R. V. became servants to do taskwork.

•**MAON.** *A city allotted to Judah*, Josh. 15:55. *Dwelling place of Nabal*, 1 Sam. 25:2. *David, with his insurgents, encamps near*, 1 Sam. 23:24, 25. *Uzziah engages in war against the people of, called* MEHUNIMS, 2 Chr. 26:7.

v.1–1489 BC
See footnote, *Time*, Rev. 10:6.

**1**
*a Manasseh, tribe of*, Gen. 46:20.
*b Joseph*, Gen. 33:2.
*c Machir*, Gen. 50:23.
*d Gilead*, Num. 26:29.
*e Gilead*, Deut. 3:13.
*f Bashan*, Num. 32:33.

**2**
*g* Num. 26:30.
*h* 1 Chr. 7:14.
*i* Num. 26:31.
*j* Num. 26:32; 27:1.
*k* Num. 26:32; or, *Shemidah*, 1 Chr. 7:19.

**3**
*l Zelophehad*, Num. 27:1.
*m Daughter, property rights of*, vs. 3–6; Lev. 12:6.
*n Heir*, Gen. 15:3.
*o Women, property rights of*, vs. 3–6; Prov. 31:10.
*p Mahlah*, Num. 26:33.
*q Noah*, Num. 26:33.
*r Hoglah*, Num. 27:1.
*s Milcah*, Num. 26:33.

**4**
*t Eleazar*, Num. 3:2.
*u Government, executive officers of*, Isa. 22:21.
*v Joshua*, Josh. 1:1.
*w Petition, rights of, recognized by Israel*, Esth. 5:6.

## CHAPTER 17

*The lot of Manasseh. 7 His coast. 12 The Canaanites not driven out. 14 The children of Joseph obtain an additional lot.*

THERE was also a lot for the tribe of [a]Mȧ-năs′seh; for he *was* the firstborn of [b]Jō′ṣeph; *to wit*, for [c]Mā′chĭr the firstborn of Mȧ-năs′seh, the father of [d]Ḡĭl′e-ăd: because he was a man of war, therefore he had [e]Ḡĭl′eăd and [f]Bā′shăn.

2 There was also *a lot* for the rest of the children of [a]Mȧ-năs′seh by their families; for the children of *Ā-bĭ-ē′zēr, and for the children of [g]Hē′lĕk, and [f]or the children of [h]Ăs′rĭ-el, and for the children of [i]Shē′chem, and for the children of [j]Hē′phēr, and for the children of [k]Shē-mī′dȧ: these *were* the male children of Mȧ-năs′seh the son of [b]Jō′ṣeph by their families.

3 ¶ But [l]Zē-lō′phe-hăd, the son of [j]Hē′phēr, the son of [d]Ḡĭl′e-ăd, the son of [c]Mā′chĭr, the son of Mȧ-năs′seh, had no sons, but [m,n,o]daughters: and these *are* the names of his daughters, [p]Mäh′lah, and [q]Nō′ah, [r]Hŏg′lah, [s]Mĭl′cah, and †Tĭr′zah.

4 And they came near before [t,u]Ē-le-ā′zar the priest, and before [u,v]Jŏsh′u-ȧ the son of Nŭn, and before the [u]princes, [w]saying, The LORD commanded Mō′ṣeṣ to give us an inheritance among our brethren. Therefore according to the commandment of the LORD he gave them an inheritance among the brethren of their father.

5 And there fell ten portions to [a]Mȧ-năs′seh, beside the land of [e]Ḡĭl′e-ăd and [f]Bā′shăn, which *were* on the other side Jôr′dan;

6 Because the [m,n,o]daughters of Mȧ-năs′seh had an inheritance among his sons: and the rest of Mȧ-năs′seh's sons had the land of [e]Ḡĭl′e-ăd.

7 ¶ And the [1]coast[c] of [a]Mȧ-năs′seh was from Ăsh′ēr to [x]Mĭch′me-thah, that *lieth*[c] before [y]Shē′chem; and the border went along on the right hand unto the inhabitants of Ĕn–tăp′pu̥-ah.

8 *Now* [a]Mȧ-năs′seh had the land of [z]Tăp′pu̥-ah: but Tăp′pu̥-ah on the border of [a]Mȧ-năs′seh *belonged* to the children of [b]Ē′phrā-ĭm;

9 And the [1]coast[c] descended unto the [2]river [c]Kā′nah, southward of the [3]river: these cities of [b]Ē′phrā-ĭm *are* among the cities of [a]Mȧ-năs′seh: the [1]coast of Mȧ-năs′seh also *was* on the north side of the [2]river, and the outgoings[c] of it were at the sea:

10 Southward *it was* [b]Ē′phră-ĭm's, and northward *it was* [a]Mȧ-năs′seh's, and the sea is his border; and they met together in [d]Ăsh′ēr on the north, and in [e]Ĭs′sa-char on the east.

11 And [a]Mȧ-năs′seh had in [e]Ĭs′sa-char and in [d]Ăsh′ēr ‡Bĕth–shē′an and her towns, and [f]Ĭb′le-ăm and her towns, and the inhabitants of [g]Dôr and her towns, and the inhabitants of Ĕn′–dôr and her towns, and the inhabitants of [h]Tā′a-năch and her towns, and the inhabitants of ‖Mĕ-ḡĭd′dō and her towns, [4]*even* three countries.

12 Yet the children of [a]Mȧ-năs′seh could not drive out *the inhabitants of* those cities; but the [i]Cā′năan-ītes would dwell in that land.

v.6–1489 BC
See footnote, *Time*, Rev. 10:6.

**7**
*x* Josh. 16:6.
*y Shechem*, Josh. 20:7.
1 R. V. border

**8**
*z* Josh. 16:8.

*a Manasseh, tribe of*, Gen. 46:20.
*b Ephraim, tribe of*, Gen. 41:52.

**9**
*c* Josh. 16:8.
2 R. V. brook of
3 R. V. brook:

**10**
*d Asher, tribe of*, Num. 1:40.
*e Issachar, tribe of*, Num. 1:28.

**11**
*f* Or, *Gath-rimmon*, Josh. 21:25.
*g Dor*, Josh. 11:2.
*h Taanach*, Josh. 12:21.
4 R. V. even the three heights.

**12**
*i Canaanites*, Ex. 23:28.

* **ABIEZER** (*helpful*), called also JEEZER. *Descendants of*, Num. 26:30; Josh. 17:2; Judg. 6:34; 8:2; 1 Chr. 7:18.

† **TIRZAH** (*delight*). *A daughter of Zelophehad*, Num. 26:33; 36:11; Josh. 17:3. *Special legislation in regard to the inheritance of*, Num. 27:1–11; 36; Josh. 17:3, 4.

‡ **BETH-SHEAN** (*security*). *A city of Manasseh*, Josh. 17:11; 1 Chr. 7:29. *Not subdued*, Judg. 1:27. *Bodies of Saul and his sons exposed in*, 1 Sam. 31:10, 12. *Called* BETH-SHAN, 1 Sam. 31:10, 12; 2 Sam. 21:12. *District of, under tribute to Solomon's commissariat*, 1 Kin. 4:12.

‖ **MEGIDDO** (*place of troops*), called also MEGIDDON, and probably ARMAGEDDON. *A city in Issachar, situated on the southern edge of the plain of Esdraelon*, Josh. 17:11; 1 Chr. 7:29. *Conquest of, by Joshua*, Josh. 12:21. *Walled by Solomon*, 1 Kin. 9:15. *Included in one of Solomon's*

v.13–1489 BC. See footnote, *Time*, Rev. 10:6.

13 Yet it came to pass, when
the children of Ĭş'ra-el were
waxen[c] strong, that they put the
[i]Cā'năan-ītes to [5]tribute[c]; but did
not utterly drive them out.
14 ¶ And the children of [a,b]Jō'-
şeph spake unto [j]Jŏsh'u-à, [k]say-
ing, [l]Why hast thou given me
*but* one lot[c] and one portion to
inherit, seeing I *am* a great people, forasmuch as the LORD
hath blessed me hitherto?
15 And [j]Jŏsh'u-à answered
them, [m]If thou *be* a great people,
*then* get thee up to the wood[c] *coun-*
*try,* and cut down for thyself there
in the land of the [n]Pĕr'ĭz-zītes
and of the [o]giants, if mount [§]Ē'-
phră-ĭm be too narrow for thee.
16 And the children of [a,b]Jō'-
şeph said, The hill is not enough
for us: and all the [i]Cā'năan-ītes
that dwell in the land of the valley have [p]chariots of [q]iron, *both*
*they* who *are* of [‡]Bĕth-shē'an
and her towns, and *they* who *are*
of the valley of [+]Jĕz're-el.
17 And [j]Jŏsh'u-à spake unto
the house of Jō'şeph, *even* to
[b]Ē'phră-ĭm and to [a]Mă-năs'seh,
saying, Thou *art* a great people,
and hast great power: thou shalt
not have one lot[c] *only*:
18 But the mountain shall be
thine; for it *is* a wood[c], and thou
shalt cut it down: and the outgoings[c] of it shall be thine: for
thou shalt drive out the [i]Cā'-
năan-ītes, though they have
[q]iron [p]chariots, *and* though they
*be* strong.

13 — 5 R. V. taskwork.

14 — *j Joshua,* Josh. 1:1. *k Murmuring, instances of,* Num. 14:2. *l Avarice,* Eccl. 5:10.

15 — *m Sarcasm, instances of,* Judg. 10:14. *n Perizzites,* Gen. 15:20. *o Rephaim,* Gen. 14:5.

16 — *p Chariots,* Josh. 11:4. *q Iron,* Prov. 27:17.

## CHAPTER 18

*The tabernacle is set up at Shiloh. 2 The remainder of the land is divided into seven parts, which are distributed by lot. 11 The lot and border of Benjamin. 21 Their cities.*

AND the whole congregation
of the children of [a]Ĭş'ra-el
assembled together at [b]Shī'lōh,
and set up the [1,c]tabernacle of
the congregation there. And the
land was subdued before them.[Q]
2 And there remained among
the children of [a]Ĭş'ra-el seven
tribes, which had not yet received their inheritance.
3 And [d]Jŏsh'u-à said unto the
children of Ĭş'ra-el, How long
*are* ye slack[c] to go to possess the
[e]land, which the LORD God of
your fathers hath given you?
4 Give[c] out from among you
three men for *each* tribe: and I
will send them, and they shall
rise, and go through the [e]land,
and describe it according to the
inheritance of them; and they
shall come *again* to me.
5 And they shall divide it into
seven parts[c]: [f]Jū'dah shall abide
in [2]their coast[c] on the south,
and the house of [g,h]Jōş'eph shall
abide in their [3]coasts[c] on the
north.
6 Ye shall therefore describe[c]
the [e]land *into* seven parts, and
bring *the description* hither to
me, that I may cast [i]lots for you
here before the LORD our God.
7 But the Lē'vītes have no part
among you; for the priesthood
of the LORD *is* [j,k,l]their inheritance: and [m]Găd, and [n]Reu'-
ben, and half the tribe of [g]Mă-
năs'seh, have received their inheritance beyond [o]Jôr'dan on
the east, which Mō'şeş the servant of the LORD gave them.
8 ¶ And the men arose, and
went away: and [d]Jŏsh'u-à
charged them that went to describe the land, saying, Go and
walk through the land, and describe it, and come again to me,
that I may here cast lots for you
before the LORD in [b]Shī'lōh.
9 And the men went and passed

1 — *a Israel,* Ex. 4:22. *b Shiloh,* Judg. 21:12.

v.1–1489 BC. See footnote, *Time*, Rev. 10:6.

*c Tabernacle, pitched at Shiloh,* Ex. 27:9. 1 R. V. tent of meeting

3 — *d Joshua,* Josh. 1:1. *e Canaan,* Gen. 37:1.

5 — *f Judah, tribe of,* Num. 10:14. *g Manasseh, tribe of,* Gen. 46:20. *h Ephraim, tribe of,* Gen. 41:52. 2 R. V. his border 3 R. V. border

6 — *i Lot,* Esth. 3:7.

7 — *j Levites, emoluments of,* Deut. 10:8. *k Minister, emoluments of,* Rom. 15:16. *l Priest, emoluments of,* Lev. 1:5. *m Gad, tribe of,* Deut. 33:20. *n Reubenites,* Josh. 22:1. *o Jordan,* Gen. 32:10.

*commissary districts,* 1 Kin. 4:12. *Ahaziah dies at,* 2 Kin. 9:27. *Josiah slain at, by Pharaoh-nechoh,* 2 Kin. 23:29, 30; 2 Chr. 35:22–24. *Prophecy concerning,* Zech. 12:11.

§ **EPHRAIM** (*fruitful*). *A range of low mountains,* Josh. 17:15–18. *Joshua has his inheritance in,* Judg. 2:9. *Residence of Micah,* Judg. 17:8. *A place of hiding for Israelites,* 1 Sam. 14:22. *Sheba resides in,* 2 Sam. 20:21. *Noted for rich pastures,* Jer. 50:19.

+ **JEZREEL.** *A valley,* Josh. 17:16. *Place of Gideon's battle with the Midianites,* Judg. 6:33. *Place of the defeat of the Israelites under Saul and Jonathan,* 1 Sam. 29:1, 11; 31:1–6; 2 Sam. 4:4.

v.10–1489 BC
See footnote, *Time*, Rev. 10:6.

through the [e]land, and [p]described it by cities into seven parts in a [q]book,[C] and came *again* to [d]Jŏsh′u-ȧ [4]to the host at [b]Shī′lōh.

10 And [d]Jŏsh′u-ȧ cast[C] [i]lots for them in Shī′lōh before the LORD: and there Jŏsh′u-ȧ divided the [e]land unto the children of [a]Iṣ′ra-el according to their divisions.[C]

11 ¶ And the [i]lot[C] of the tribe of the children of [r]Bĕn′ja-mĭn came up according to their families: and the [5]coast[C] of their lot came forth between the children of [f]Jū′dah and the children of [g,h]Jō′ṣeph.

12 And [p]their border on the north side was from [o]Jôr-dăn; and the border went up to the side of [s]Jĕr′ĭ-chō on the north side, and went up through the mountains westward; and the goings[C] out thereof were at the wilderness of *Bĕth–ā′vĕn.

13 And [p]the border went over from thence toward Lŭz, to the side of Lŭz, which *is* †Bĕth′–el, southward; and the border descended to [t]Ăt′ă-rōth–ā′där, near the hill that *lieth* on the south side of the nether[C] [u]Bĕth–hō′rŏn.

14 And [p]the border was drawn[C] *thence*, and compassed the corner of the sea southward, from the hill that *lieth* before [u]Bĕth–hō′rŏn southward; and the goings[C] out thereof were at Kĭr′jath–bā′al, which *is* [v]Kĭr′jath–jē′a-rĭm, a city of the children of [f]Jū′-dah: this *was* the west quarter.[C]

15 And [p]the south quarter *was* from the end of [v]Kĭr′jath–jē′a-rĭm, and the border went out on the west, and went out to the well of waters of [w]Nĕph′to-ah:

16 And [p]the border came down to the end of the mountain that *lieth* before the valley of the son of [x]Hĭn′nom, *and* which *is* in the [6, y]valley of the giants on the north, and descended to the valley of Hĭn′nom, to the side of [z]Jĕ-bū′sī on the south, and descended to [a]Ĕn–rō′gel,

17 [b]And was drawn[C] from the north, and went forth to [c]Ĕn–shē′mesh, and went forth toward [d]Gĕl′ĭ-lŏth, which *is* over[C] against the going[C] up of [e]Ă-dŭm′-mĭm, and descended to the [f]stone[C] of [g]Bō′-hăn the son of Reu̇′ben,

18 [b]And passed along toward the side over against [h]Ăr′a-bah northward, and went down unto Ăr′a-bah:

19 And [b]the border passed along to the side of [i]Bĕth–hŏg′-lah northward: and the outgoings[C] of the border were at the north bay of the [j]salt sea at the south end of [k]Jôr′dan: this *was* the south [5]coast.[C]

20 And [k]Jôr′dan was the [b]border of it on the east side. This *was* the inheritance of the children of [l]Bĕn′ja-mĭn, by the [5]coasts[C] thereof round about, according to their families.

21 Now the cities of the tribe of the children of [l]Bĕn′ja-mĭn according to their families were [m]Jĕr′ĭ-chō, and [i]Bĕth–hŏg′lah, and [7]the valley of Kē′ziz,

22 And [h]Bĕth–ăr′a-bah, and Zĕm-a-rā′im, and †Bĕth′–el,

23 And Ā′vĭm, and Pā′rah, and [n]Ŏph′rah,

9
p *Topography*, Josh. 13:16.
q *Book, topography of Palestine recorded in*, Num. 5:23.
4 R. V. unto the camp at Shiloh.

11
r *Benjamin, tribe of*, Num. 1:37.
5 R. V. border

12
s *Jericho*, Num. 22:1.

13
t Josh. 16:2, 5, 7.
u *Beth-horon*, Josh. 10:10.

14
v *Kirjath-jearim*, Josh. 15:9.

v.15–1489 BC
See footnote, *Time*, Rev. 10:6.

15
w Josh. 15:9.

16
x *Hinnom*, Jer. 7:31.
y *Rephaim*, 1 Chr. 11:15.
z *Jerusalem*, Judg. 19:10.
a *Enrogel*, Josh. 15:7.
6 R. V. vale of Rephaim

17
b *Topography*, Josh. 13:16.
c Josh. 15:7.
d Or, *Gilgal*, Josh. 15:7.
e Josh. 15:7.
f *Pillar*, Gen. 28:18.
g Josh. 15:6.

18
h Or, *Beth-arabah*, Josh. 15:6.

19
i Josh. 15:6.
j *Dead Sea*, Gen. 14:3.
k *Jordan*, Gen. 32:10.

20
l *Benjamin, tribe of*, Num. 1:37.

21
m *Jericho*, Num. 22:1.
7 R. V. Emek-keziz.

23
n 1 Sam. 13:17.

* **BETH-AVEN.** *A place on the mountains of Benjamin*, Josh. 7:2; 18:12; 1 Sam. 13:5; 14:23; Hos. 4:15; 5:8; 10:5.

† **BETH-EL** (*house of God*), a city N. of Jerusalem. *The ancient city adjacent to, and finally embraced in, was called* LUZ, Josh. 18:13; Judg. 1:23–26. *Abraham establishes an altar at*, Gen. 12:8; 13:3, 4. *The place where Jacob sees the vision of the ladder*, Gen. 28:10–22; 31:13; Hos. 12:4; *and builds an altar*, Gen. 35:1–15. *Deborah dies at*, Gen. 35:8. *Conquered, by Joshua*, Josh. 8:17; 12:16; *by the house of Joseph*, Judg 1:22–26. *Allotted to Benjamin*, Josh. 18:13, 22. *Court of justice held at, by Deborah*, Judg. 4:5; *by Samuel*, 1 Sam. 7:16. *Tabernacle at*, Judg. 20:18, 26, 27; 21:2. *Jeroboam institutes idolatrous worship at*, 1 Kin. 12:25–33; 2 Kin. 10:29. *Idolatry at*, Jer. 48:13; Amos 4:4. *Shalmanezer sends a priest to*, 2 Kin. 17:27, 28. *Prophecies against the idolatrous altars at*, 1 Kin. 13:1–6, 32; 2 Kin. 23:4, 15–20; Amos 3:14. *The school of prophets at*, 2 Kin. 2:3. *Children of, mock Elisha*, 2 Kin. 2:23, 24. *People of, return from Babylon*, Ezra 2:28; Neh. 7:32. *Prophecies against*, Amos 5:5.

v.24–1489 BC
See footnote, *Time*, Rev. 10:6.

24
o Ezra 2:26; Neh. 7:30.

25
p *Gibeon*, Jer. 41:16.
q *Beeroth*, Josh. 9:17.

26
r Josh. 9:17; Ezra 2:25; Neh. 7:29.

28
s 2 Sam. 21:14.
t *Jerusalem*, Judg. 19:10.

1
a *Simeon, tribe of*, Num. 2:12.
b *Judah, tribe of*, Num. 10:14.

2
c *Beer-sheba*, Judg. 20:1.

3
d Josh. 15:28; 1 Chr. 4:28.
e Or, *Baal*, 1 Chr. 4:33.
f Josh. 15:29.

4
g Josh. 15:30.
h Or, *Chesil*, Josh. 15:30; or, *Bethuel*, 1 Chr. 4:30.
i *Hormah*, Deut. 1:44.

5
j *Ziklag*, Josh. 15:31.
k 1 Chr. 4:31.
l Or, *Hazar-susim*, 1 Chr. 4:31.

6
m Or, *Lebaoth*, Josh. 15:32; or, *Bethbirei*, 1 Chr. 4:31.

7
n Zech. 14:10.
o 1 Chr. 4:32; 6:59.

24 And Chē′phar–hȧ–ăm′mo-
nāi, and Ŏph′nī, and [o]Gā′bȧ;
twelve cities with their villages:
25 [p]Gĭb′e-on, and Rā′mah, and
[q]Bē-ē′roth,
26 And [‡]Mĭz′peh, and [r]Chē-
phī′rah, and Mō′zah,
27 And Rē′kem, and Ĭr′pe-el,
and Tăr′a-lah,
28 And [s]Zē′lah, Ē′leph, and
Jē-bū′sī, which *is* [t]Jē-ru′să-lĕm,
Gĭb′e-ath, *and* Kĭr′jath; fourteen cities with their villages.
This *is* the inheritance of the
children of [l]Bĕn′ja-mĭn according to their families.

## CHAPTER 19

*The lot of Simeon, 10 of Zebulun, 17 of Issachar, 24 of Asher, 32 of Naphtali, 40 and of Dan. 49 The children of Israel give an inheritance to Joshua.*

AND the second lot came
forth to [a]Sĭm′e-on, *even*
for the tribe of the children of
Sĭm′e-on according to their families: and their inheritance was
within the inheritance of the
children of [b]Jū′dah.
2 And they had in their inheritance [c]Bē′er–shē′bȧ, and Shē′bȧ,
and Mŏl′a-dah,
3 And [d]Hā′zar–shu′al, and
[e]Bā′lah, and [f]Ā′zem,
4 And [g]Ĕl′to-lăd, and [h]Bē′thŭl,
and [i]Hôr′mah,
5 And [j]Zĭk′lăg, and [k]Bĕth–
mär′ca-bŏth, and [l]Hā′zar-sū′-
sah,
6 And [m]Bĕth–lĕb′a-ŏth, and
Shȧ-ru′hen; thirteen cities and
their villages:
7 [*]Ā′in, [n]Rĕm′mon, and
[†]Ē′thēr, and [o]Ā′shan; four cities
and their villages:
8 And all the villages that *were*
round about these cities to [e]Bā′-
al-ăth–bē′ēr, [p]Rā′math of the
south. This *is* the inheritance of
the tribe of the children of [a]Sĭm′-
e-on according to their families.
9 Out of the portion of the children of [b]Jū′dah *was* the inheritance of the children of [a]Sĭm′e-
on: for the part of the children of
Jū′dah was too much for them:
therefore the children of Sĭm′e-
on had their inheritance within
the inheritance of them.
10 ¶ And the third lot came up
for the children of [q]Zĕb′u-lŭn
according to their families: and
the border of their inheritance[G]
was unto Sā′rid:
11 And their border went up
[1]toward the sea, and Măr′a-lah,
and reached to Dăb′ba-shĕth,
and reached to the [2]river that *is*
before [r]Jŏk′ne-ăm;
12 And turned from Sā′rid
eastward toward the sunrising
unto the border of [s]Chĭs′loth–
tā′bôr, and then goeth out to
[t]Dăb′e-răth, and goeth up to
Jȧ-phī′ȧ,
13 And from thence passeth on
along on the east to Gĭt′tah–hē′-
phēr, to Ĭt′tah–kā′zin, and goeth
out to [3]Rĕm′mon–mĕth′o-är to
Nē′ah;
14 And the border [4]compasseth
it on the north side to Hăn′na-
thŏn: and the outgoings[G] thereof
are in the valley of Jĭph′thah–el:
15 And Kăt′tath, and [u]Nȧ-
hăl′lal, and [v]Shĭm′rŏn, and Ĭd′a-
lah, and [w]Bĕth′–lĕ-hĕm: twelve
cities with their villages.
16 This *is* the inheritance of the
children of [q]Zĕb′u-lŭn according
to their families, these cities with
their villages.
17 ¶ *And* the fourth lot[G] came

v.8–1489 BC
See footnote, *Time*, Rev. 10:6.

8
p Or, *Ramoth*, 1 Sam. 30:27.

10
q *Zebulun, tribe of*, Gen. 49:13.

11
r Josh. 12:22; 21:34.
1 R. V. westward, even to
2 R. V. brook

12
s Or, *Tabor*, 1 Chr. 6:77.
t Josh. 21:28; 1 Chr. 6:72.

13
3 R. V. Rimmon which stretcheth unto

14
4 R. V. turned about it

15
u Josh. 21:35; Judg. 1:30.
v Josh. 11:1.
w Judg. 12:10.

16
x *Issachar, tribe of*, Num. 1:28.

‡ **MIZPAH** (*watch tower*), a city north of Jerusalem. *Allotted to Benjamin*, Josh. 18:26. *The Israelites assemble at*, Judg. 20:1–3; *and decree the penalty to be visited upon the Benjamites for their maltreatment of the Levite's concubine*, Judg. 20:10. *Israel assembled at, by Samuel, that he might reprove them for their idolatry*, 1 Sam. 7:5. *A judgment seat of Samuel*, 1 Sam. 7:16. *Saul crowned king of Israel at*, 1 Sam. 10:17–25. *Built, or perhaps fortified, by Asa*, 1 Kin. 15:22; 2 Chr. 16:6. *Temporarily the capital of the country after the children of Israel had been carried away captive*, 2 Kin. 25:23, 25; Jer. 40:6–15; 41:1–14. *Captivity returned to*, Neh. 3:7, 15, 19.

* **AIN** (*an eye, or spring*). *A city in Judah, allotted to Simeon*, Josh. 15:32; 19:7; 21:16; 1 Chr. 4:32. *Called, by error*, ASHAN, 1 Chr. 6:59. *Possibly identical with En-Rimmon*, Neh. 11:29.

† **ETHER**, a city of Canaan. *Assigned to Judah*, Josh. 15:42. *Subsequently allotted to Simeon*, Josh. 19:7. *Called* TOCHEN, 1 Chr. 4:32.

v.17–1489 BC
See footnote, *Time*, Rev. 10:6.

18
*y Jezreel*, 1 Kin. 18:45.

20
*z* Or, *Kedesh*, Josh. 12:22.

21
*a* Josh. 21:29.

22
*b Tabor*, Judg. 8:18.
*c Jordan*, Gen. 32: 10.
5 R. V. border

23
*d Issachar, tribe of*, Num. 1:28.

24
*e Lot*, Esth. 3:7.
*f Asher, tribe of*, Num. 1:40.

25
*g* Josh. 21:31; or, *Hukok*, 1 Chr. 6:75.

26
*h* Or, *Mishal*, Josh. 21:30;
*i Carmel*, Jer. 46: 18.

27
*j Zebulun, tribe of*, Gen. 49:13.

28
*k Zidon*, Ezek. 28: 21.

out to [x]Ĭs′sa-char, for the children of Ĭs′sa-char according to
their families.
18 And their border was toward
[y]Jĕz′re-el, and Chĕ-sŭl′loth, and
‡Shụ′nem,
19 And Hăph-rā′im, and Shī′-
hŏn, and Ăn-a-hā′rath,
20 And Răb′bĭth, and [z]Kĭsh′-
ĭ-ŏn, and Ā′bĕz,
21 And Rē′meth, and [a]Ĕn-
găn′nim, and Ĕn–hăd′dah, and
Bĕth–păz′zez;
22 And the [5]coast[c] reacheth to
[b]Tā′bôr, and Shâ-hăz′i-mah,
and Bĕth–shē′mesh; and the outgoings[c] of their border were at
[c]Jôr′dan: sixteen cities with their
villages.
23 This *is* the inheritance of the
tribe of the children of [d]Ĭs′sa-
char according to their families,
the cities and their villages.
24 ¶ And the fifth [e]lot came
out for the tribe of the children
of [f]Ăsh′ēr according to their
families.
25 And their border was [g]Hĕl′-
kăth, and Hā′lī, and Bē′ten, and
Ăch′shăph,
26 And Â-lăm′mē-lĕch, and
Ā′măd, and [h]Mī′she-al; and
reacheth to [i]Cär′mel westward,
and to Shī′hôr–lĭb′nath;
27 And turneth toward the sunrising to Bĕth–dā′gon, and
reacheth to [j]Zĕb′u-lŭn, and to
the valley of Jĭph′thah–el toward
the north side of Bĕth–ē′mek,
and Nĕ-ī′el, and goeth out to
Cā′bŭl on the left hand,
28 And Hē′bron, and Rē′hŏb,
and Hăm′mŏn, and Kā′nah,
*even* unto great [k]Zī′dŏn;
29 And *then* the [5]coast[c] turneth
to Rā′mah, and to the [6]strong
city ‖Tȳre; and the [5]coast[c] turneth to Hō′sah; and the outgoings[c] thereof are at the sea [7]from
the coast to [l]Ăch′zĭb:
30 Ŭm′mah also, and [m]Ā′phek,
and §Rē′hŏb: twenty and two
cities with their villages.
31 This *is* the inheritance of the
tribe of the children of [f]Ăsh′ēr
according to their families, these
cities with their villages.
32 ¶ The sixth lot came out to
the children of [n]Năph′ta-lī, *even*
for the children of Năph′ta-lī
according to their families.
33 And their [5]coast[c] was from
Hē′leph, from [8]Ăl′lŏn to [o]Zā-a-
năn′nim, and Ăd′a-mī, Nē′keb,
and Jăb′ne-el, unto Lā′kŭm;
and the outgoings[c] thereof were
at [c]Jôr′dan:
34 And *then* the [5]coast[c] turneth
westward to Ăz′noth–tā′bôr, and
goeth out from thence to Hŭk′-
kok, and reacheth to [j]Zĕb′u-lŭn
on the south side, and reacheth
to [f]Ăsh′ēr on the west side, and
to [p]Jū′dah upon [c]Jôr′dan toward the sunrising[c].
35 And the fenced[c] [q]cities *are*
Zĭd′dim, Zēr, and Hăm′math,
Răk′kath, and Chĭn′ne-rĕth,
36 And Ăd′a-mah, and Rā′-
mah, and [r]Hā′zôr,
37 And Kē′desh, and Ĕd′re-ī,
and Ĕn–hā′zôr,
38 And Ī′ron, and Mĭg′dal–el,
Hō′rem, and [s]Bĕth–ā′nath, and
[t]Bĕth–shē′mesh; nineteen cities
with their villages.
39 This *is* the inheritance of the
tribe of the children of [n]Năph′-
ta-lī according to their families,
the cities and their villages.

v.29–1489 BC
See footnote, *Time*, Rev. 10:6.

29
*l* Judg. 1:31.
6 R. V. fenced
7 R. V. by the region of

30
*m* Josh. 13:4.

32
*n Naphtali, tribe of*, Num. 1:42.

33
*o* Judg. 4:11.
8 R. V. the oak in

34
*p Judah, tribe of*, Num. 10:14.

35
*q Cities, fortified*, Num. 35:8.

36
*r Hazor*, Josh. 11:1.

38
*s* Judg. 1:33.
*t* Judg. 1:33.

‡ **SHUNEM.** *A city allotted to the tribe of Issachar*, Josh. 19:18. *Elisha dwells at, with the Shunammite*, 2 Kin. 4. *A maid found in, to nourish David*, 1 Kin. 1:3.

‖ **TYRE** (*rock*), a city situated on the shore of the Mediterranean. *On the northern boundary of Asher*, Josh. 19: 29. *Pleasant site of*, Hos. 9:13. *Fortified*, Josh. 19:29; 2 Sam. 24:7. *Commerce of*, 1 Kin. 9:26–28; 10:11; Ezra 3:7; Isa. 23; Ezek. 27; 28:1–19; Zech. 9:2; Acts 21:3. *Merchants of*, Isa. 23:8. *Antiquity of*, Isa. 23:7. *Riches of*, Isa. 23:8; Zech. 9:3. *Besieged by Nebuchadnezzar*, Ezek. 26:7; 29:18. *Jesus, goes to the coasts of*, Matt. 15:21; *heals the daughter of the Syrophenician woman near*, Matt. 15:21–28; Mark 7: 24–31. *People from, come to hear Jesus, and to be healed of their diseases*, Mark 3:8; Luke 6:17. *Herod's hostility toward*, Acts 12:20–23. *Paul visits*, Acts 21:3–7. *To be judged according to its opportunity and privileges*, Matt. 11:21, 22; Luke 10:13, 14. *Prophecies relating to*, Psa. 45:12; 87:4; Isa. 23; Jer. 25: 22; 27:1–11; 47:4; Ezek. chapters 26–28; Joel 3:4–8; Amos 1:9, 10; Zech. 9:2–4.

§ **REHOB** (*broad place*) *A Levitical city of Asher*, Josh. 19: 30; 21:31; 1 Chr. 6:75. *Canaanites not driven from*, Judg. 1:31.

40 ¶ *And* the seventh lot came out for the tribe of the children of [u]Dăn according to their families.

41 And the [5]coast[C] of their inheritance was +Zō′rah, and [v]Ĕsh′ta-ŏl, and [w]Ĭr–shē′mesh,

42 And [x]Shă-al-ăb′bin, and [y]Ăj′a-lŏn, and Jĕth′lah,

43 And Ē′lŏn, and Thĭm′na-thah, and [z]Ĕk′rŏn,

44 And [a]Ĕl′te-keh, and [b]Gĭb′be-thŏn, and [c]Bā′al-ăth,

45 And Jē′hŭd, and Bĕn′e-bē′răk, and Găth–rĭm′mon,

46 And Mē–jăr′kon, and Răk′kon, with the border before [d]Jā′phō.

47 And the [5]coast[C] of the children of [e]Dăn went out [9]*too little* for them: therefore the children of Dăn went up to fight against Lē′shem, and took it, and smote it with the edge of the sword, and possessed it, and dwelt therein, and called Lē′shem, [f]Dăn, after the name of Dăn their father.

48 This *is* the inheritance of the tribe of the children of [e]Dăn according to their families, these cities with their villages.

49 ¶ When they had made an end of dividing the land for inheritance by [10]their coasts[C], the children of Ĭș′ra-el gave an inheritance to [g]Jŏsh′u-ȧ the son of Nŭn among them:

50 According to the word of the LORD they gave him the city which he asked, *even* [h]Tĭm′nath–sē′rah in mount [i]Ē′phră-ĭm: and he built the city, and dwelt therein.

51 These *are* the inheritances, which [j]Ē-le-ā′zar the priest, and [g]Jŏsh′u-ȧ the son of Nŭn, and the heads of the fathers of the tribes of the children of Ĭș′ra-el, divided for an inheritance by [k]lot in [l]Shī′lōh before the LORD, at the door of the [11,m]tabernacle of the congregation. So they made an end of dividing the [n]country.

## CHAPTER 20

*Six cities of refuge are appointed. 9 Their uses.*

THE LORD also [a]spake unto Jŏsh′u-ȧ, saying,

2 Speak to the children of Ĭș′ra-el, saying, Appoint[C] out for you [b]cities of refuge, whereof I spake unto you by the hand of Mō′șeș:

3 That the slayer that [c]killeth *any* person unawares[C] *and* unwittingly[C] may flee thither: and they shall be your refuge from the [d]avenger of blood.

4 And when he that doth flee unto one of those [h]cities shall stand at the entering of the [e]gate of the city, and shall declare his cause[C] in the ears of the [f,g]elders of that city, they shall take him into the city unto them, and give him a place, that he may dwell among them.

5 And if the [d]avenger of blood pursue after him, then they shall not deliver the slayer up into his hand; because he [c]smote his neighbour unwittingly[C], and [h]hated him not beforetime[C].

6 And he shall dwell in that [b]city, until he stand before the congregation[C] for judgment, *and* until the death of the [i]high priest that shall be in those days: then shall the slayer return, and come unto his own city, and unto his own house, unto the city from whence he fled.

7 ¶ And they appointed[C b,j]Kē′desh in [b,k]Găl′ĭ-lee in mount Năph′ta-lī, and *Shē′chem in mount [l]Ē′phră-ĭm, and Kĭr′-

v.40–1489 BC
See footnote, *Time*, Rev. 10:6.

**40**
*u Dan, tribe of*, Gen. 30:6.

**41**
*v Eshtaol*, Judg. 18:2.
*w* Or, *Beth-shemesh*, Josh. 21:16.

**42**
*x Possibly identical with Shaalabim*, Judg. 1:35; 1 Kin. 4:9.
*y Aijalon*, Josh. 21:24.

**43**
*z Ekron*, Amos 1:8.

**44**
*a* Josh. 21:23.
*b Gibbethon*, 1 Kin. 15:27.
*c* 1 Kin. 9:18.

**46**
*d* Or, *Joppa*, 2 Chr. 2:16.

**47**
*e Dan, tribe of*, Gen. 30:6.
*f Dan*, Judg. 18:29.
9 R. V. beyond them:

**49**
*g Joshua*, Josh. 1:1.
10 R. V. the borders thereof; and

**50**
*h* Josh. 24:30; or, *Timnath-heres*, Judg. 2:9.
*i Ephraim*, Josh. 17:15.

**51**
*j Eleazar*, Num. 3:2.

v.51–1489 BC
See footnote, *Time*, Rev. 10:6.
*k Lot*, Esth. 3:7.
*l Shiloh*, Judg. 21:12.
*m Tabernacle, pitched at Shiloh*, Ex. 27:9.
*n Canaan, land of, divided*, Gen. 37:1.
11 R. V. tent of meeting.

**1**
*a Prophets, inspiration of*, Isa. 3:2.

**2**
*b Cities, of refuge*, Num. 35:8.

**3**
*c Homicide, accidental*, Deut. 5:17.
*d Avenger of Blood*, Deut. 19:6.

**4**
*e Gates, place for holding courts of justice*, Deut. 3:5.
*f Court, civil, held at the gates of cities*, Ex. 18:26.
*g Government, municipal*, Isa. 22:21.

**5**
*h Hatred*, Prov. 15:17.

**6**
*i High Priest*, Lev. 21:10.

**7**
*j Kedesh*, Josh. 21:32.
*k Galilee*, Mark 6:21.
*l Ephraim, mount of*, Josh. 17:15.

+ **ZORAH** (*hornet's nest*), called also ZAREAH and ZOREAH *A city of Dan or Judah*, Josh. 15:33; 19:41. *The city of Samson*, Judg. 13:2, 24, 25; 16:31. *Representatives of the tribe of Dan sent from, to spy out the land with a view to its conquest*, Judg. 18. *Fortified by Rehoboam*, 2 Chr. 11:10. *Repeopled after the captivity*, Neh. 11:29.

* **SHECHEM**, called also SICHEM; a city on the side of Mount Gerizim. *Abraham built an altar at, and dwelt at,*

jath–är′bȧ, which *is* [b,m]Hē′bron,
in the mountain of Jū′dah.
8 And on the other side [n]Jôr′-
dan by [o]Jĕr′ĭ-chō eastward, they
assigned [b,p]Bē′zēr in the wilderness upon the plain out of the
[q]tribe of Reụ′ben, and [†,b]Rā′-
moth in Gĭl′e-ăd out of the tribe
of [r]Găd, and [b,s]Gō′lan in [t]Bā′-
shăn out of the tribe of [u]Mȧ-
năs′seh.
9 These were the [b]cities appointed[G] for all the children of
Iṣ′ra-el, and for the [v]stranger
that sojourneth[G] among them,
that whosoever [c]killeth *any* person at unawares[G] might flee
thither, and not die by the hand
of the [d]avenger of blood, until he
stood before the congregation.

## CHAPTER 21

*Forty-eight cities given by lot, out of the other tribes, unto the Levites. 43 God gave the land unto the Israelites, and rest, according to his promise.*

THEN came near the heads[G]
of the fathers of the [a]Lē′-
vītes unto [b]Ē-le-ā′zar the priest,
and unto [c]Jŏsh′u-ȧ the son of
Nŭn, and unto the [d]heads[G] of the
fathers of the tribes of the children of Iṣ′ra-el;
2 And they spake unto them at
[e]Shī′lōh in the land of Cā′năan,
[f]saying, The LORD commanded
by the hand of Mō′ṣeṣ to give us
cities to dwell in, with the suburbs[G] thereof for our cattle.
3 And the children of Iṣ′ra-el
gave unto the [a]Lē′vītes out of
their inheritance, at the commandment of the LORD, these
cities and their suburbs[G].
4 And the [g]lot[G] came out for
the families of the [h]Kō′hath-ītes:
and the children of [i]Aâr′on the
[j]priest, *which were* of the Lē′-
vītes, had by lot out of the
tribe of [k]Jū′dah, and out of the
tribe of [l]Sĭm′e-on, and out of
the tribe of [m]Bĕn′ja-mĭn, thirteen cities.
5 And the rest of the children of
Kō′hăth *had* by [g]lot out of the
families of the tribe of [n]Ē′phră-
ĭm, and out of the tribe of [o]Dăn,
and out of the half tribe of [p]Mȧ-
năs′seh, ten cities.
6 And the [q]children of Ḡēr′-
shŏn *had* by [g]lot out of the families of the tribe of [r]Ĭs′sa-char,
and out of the tribe of [s]Ăsh′ēr,
and out of the tribe of [t]Năph′-
ta-lī, and out of the half tribe of
[p]Mȧ-năs′seh in Bā′shăn, thirteen cities.
7 The [u]children of Mē-rā′rī by
their families *had* out of the
[v]tribe of Reụ′ben, and out of the
tribe of [w]Găd, and out of the
tribe of [x]Zĕb′u-lŭn, twelve cities.
8 And the children of Iṣ′ra-el
gave by [g]lot unto the [a]Lē′vītes
these cities with their suburbs[G],
as the LORD commanded by the
hand of Mō′ṣeṣ.
9 ¶ And they gave out of the
tribe of the children of [k]Jū′dah,
and out of the tribe of the children of [l]Sĭm′e-on, these cities
which are *here* mentioned by
name,
10 Which the children of [i]Aâr′-
on, *being* of the families of the
[h]Kō′hath-ītes, *who were* of the
children of Lē′vī, had: for their's
was the first [g]lot.
11 And they gave them the city
of Är′bȧ the father of [y]Ā′năk,
which *city is* [z]Hē′bron, in the
hill *country* of Jū′dah, with the
suburbs[G] thereof round about it.

v.7–1489 BC
See footnote, *Time*, Rev. 10:6.

*m Hebron*, Gen. 23:2.

8
*n Jordan*, Gen. 32:10.
*o Jericho*, Num. 22:1.
*p Bezer*, Deut. 4:43.
*q Reubenites*, Josh. 22:1.
*r Gad, tribe of*, Deut. 33:20.
*s Golan*, Deut. 4:43.
*t Bashan*, Num. 32:33.
*u Manasseh, tribe of*, Gen. 46:20.

9
*v Foreigners, privileges of, under Mosaic laws*, Deut. 23:20.

1
*a Levites, cities assigned to, in the land of Canaan*, vs. 1–45; Deut. 10:8.
*b Eleazar*, Num. 3:2.
*c Joshua, sets apart forty-eight cities for the Levites*, vs. 1–45; Josh. 1:1.
*d Senate*, Num. 11:16.

2
*e Shiloh*, Judg. 21:12.
*f Petition, rights of recognized by Israel*, Esth. 5:6.

4
*g Lot*, Esth. 3:7.
*h Kohathites, cities of*, Num. 3:27.
*i Aaron*, Ex. 6:20.

v.4–1489 BC
See footnote, *Time*, Rev. 10:6.

*j Priest, emoluments of*, Lev. 1:5.
*k Judah, tribe of*, Num. 10:14.
*l Simeon, tribe of*, Num. 2:12.
*m Benjamin, tribe of*, Num. 1:37.

5
*n Ephraim, tribe of*, Gen. 41:52.
*o Dan, tribe of*, Gen. 30:6.
*p Manasseh, tribe of*, Gen. 46:20.

6
*q Gershonites*, Num. 4:27.
*r Issachar, tribe of*, Num. 1:28.
*s Asher, tribe of*, Num. 1:40.
*t Naphtali, tribe of*, Num. 1:42.

7
*u Merarites*, Num. 26:57.
*v Reubenites*, Josn. 22:1.
*w Gad, tribe of*, Deut. 33:20.
*x Zebulun, tribe of*, Gen. 49:13.

11
*y Anakim*, Deut. 1:28.
*z Hebron*, Gen. 23:2.

Gen. 12:6, 7. *Jacob bought a parcel of ground in, and erected an altar at*, Gen. 33:18–20. *Simeon and Levi slew the men of*, Gen. 34:24–26. *Jacob purged his house of idols at*, Gen. 35:2–4. *The flocks of Jacob kept at*, Gen. 37:12–14. *Joseph buried in*, Josh. 24:32. *Jacob buried in*, Acts 7:16 (with Gen. 50:13).

*Allotted to Ephraim*, Josh. 20:7; 1 Chr. 6:66, 67; 7:28. *Designated as a city of refuge*, Josh. 20:7; 21:21. *Joshua assembled tribes of Israel, and renewed covenant at*, Josh. 24:1–27. *Abimelech made king at*, Judg. 9:1–6. *Destroyed by Abimelech*, Judg. 9:45. *Rehoboam made king at*, 1 Kin. 12:1; 2 Chr. 10:1. *Rebuilt by Jeroboam*, 1 Kin. 12:25. *Men of, slain by Ishmael*, Jer. 41:5–7.

*Called* SYCHAR, John 4:5. *Jesus made disciples in*, John 4:1–42.

† **RAMOTH-GILEAD.** *Called also* RAMAH, 2 Kin. 8:29; 2 Chr. 22:6. *A city of Gad, and a city of refuge*. Deut. 4:43; Josh. 20:8; 1 Chr. 6:80. *One of Solomon's commis*

v.12–1489 BC
See footnote, *Time*, Rev. 10:6.

12
a *Caleb*, Num. 14:6.
13
b *Hebron*, Gen. 23:2.
c *Cities, of refuge*, Num. 35:8.
d *Libnah*, Josh. 10:29.
14
e Josh. 15:48; 1 Chr. 6:57.
f *Eshtemoa*, 1 Sam. 30:28.
15
g Josh. 15:51; or, *Hilen*, 1 Chr. 6:58.
h *Debir*, Josh. 15:15.
16
i *Ain*, Josh. 19:7.
j Josh. 15:55.
17
k *Benjamin, tribe of*, Num. 1:37.
l *Gibeon*, Jer. 41:16.
18
m *Anathoth*, Jer. 1:1.
n Or, *Alemeth*, 1 Chr. 6:60.
20
o *Kohathites*, Num. 3:27.
p *Ephraim, tribe of*, Gen. 41:52.
21
q *Shechem*, Josh. 20.7.
r *Gezer*, Josh. 10:33.

12 But the fields of the city, and
the villages thereof, gave they to
[a]Cā′leb the son of Jĕ-phŭn′neh
for his possession.
13 Thus they gave to the children of Aâr′on the priest [b]Hē′-
bron with her suburbs[c], *to be* a
[c]city of refuge for the slayer; and
[d]Lĭb′nah with her suburbs[c],
14 And [e]Jăt′tĭr with her suburbs[c], and [f]Ĕsh-te-mō′ȧ with her
suburbs[c],
15 And [g]Hō′lŏn with her suburbs[c], and [h]Dē′bĭr with her suburbs[c],
16 And [i]Ā′in with her suburbs[c],
and [j]Jŭt′tah with her suburbs[c],
*and* *Bĕth–shē′mesh with her
suburbs[c]; nine cities out of those
two tribes.
17 And out of the tribe of
[k]Bĕn′ja-mĭn, [l]Gĭb′e-on with her
suburbs[c], †Gē′bȧ with her suburbs[c],
18 [m]Ăn′a-thŏth with her suburbs[c], and [n]Ăl′mŏn with her suburbs[c]; four cities.
19 All the cities of the children
of Aâr′on, the priests, *were* thirteen cities with their suburbs[c].
20 ¶ And the families of the
[o]children of Kō′hăth, the Lē′-
vītes which remained of the children of Kō′hăth, even they had
the cities of their lot out of the
tribe of [p]Ē′phrā-ĭm.
21 For they gave them [q]Shē′-
chem with her suburbs[c] in mount
Ē′phrā-ĭm, *to be* a [c]city of refuge
for the slayer; and [r]Gē′zēr with
her suburbs[c],

22 And Kĭb′za-im with her suburbs[c], and [s]Bĕth–hō′rŏn with her
suburbs[c]; four cities.
23 And out of the tribe of [t]Dăn,
[u]Ĕl′te-keh with her suburbs[c],
[v]Gĭb′be-thŏn with her suburbs[c],
24 ‡Ăij′a-lŏn with her suburbs[c],
‖Găth–rĭm′mon with her suburbs[c]; four cities.
25 And out of the half tribe of
[w]Mă-năs′seh, [x]Tā′năch with her
suburbs[c], and ‖Găth–rĭm′mon
with her suburbs[c]; two cities.
26 All the cities *were* ten with
their suburbs[c] for the families of
the [o]children of Kō′hăth that remained.
27 ¶ And unto the [y]children of
Gēr′shŏn, of the families of the
Lē′vītes, out of the *other* half
tribe of [w]Mă-năs′seh *they gave*
[z]Gō′lan in Bā′shăn with her suburbs[c], *to be* a [a]city of refuge for
the slayer; and Bē-ĕsh′–te-răh
with her suburbs[c]; two cities.
28 And out of the tribe of
[b]Ĭs′sa-char, [c]Kĭ′shŏn with her
suburbs[c], [d]Dăb′a-reh with her
suburbs[c],
29 Jär′mŭth with her suburbs[c],
[e]Ĕn–găn′nim with her suburbs[c];
four cities.
30 And out of the tribe of [f]Ăsh′-
ēr, [g]Mĭ′shal with her suburbs[c],
[h]Ăb′dŏn with her suburbs[c],
31 [i]Hĕl′kăth with her suburbs[c],
and [j]Rē′hŏb with her suburbs[c];
four cities.
32 And out of the tribe of
[k]Năph′ta-lī, §Kē′desh in [l]Găl′ĭ-
lee with her suburbs[c], *to be*

v.22–1489 BC
See footnote, *Time*, Rev. 10:6.

22
s *Beth-horon*, Josh. 10:10.
23
t *Dan, tribe of*, Gen. 30:6.
u Josh. 19:44.
v *Gibbethon*, 1 Kin. 15:27.
25
w *Manasseh, tribe of*, Gen. 46:20.
x Or, *Taanach*, Josh. 12:21.
27
y *Gershonites*, Num. 4:27.
z *Golan*, Deut. 4:43.

a *Cities, of refuge*, Num. 35:8.
28
b *Issachar, tribe of*, Num. 1:28.
c Or, *Kedesh*, 1 Chr. 6:72.
d Or, *Daberath*, Josh. 19:12; 1 Chr. 6:72.
29
e Josh. 19:21.
30
f *Asher, tribe of*, Num. 1:40.
g Or, *Misheal*, Josh. 19:26.
h 1 Chr. 6:74.
31
i Josh. 19:25; or, *Hukok*, 1 Chr. 6:75.
j *Rehob*, Josh. 19:30.
32
k *Naphtali, tribe of*, Num. 1:42.
l *Galilee*, Mark 6:21.

*aries at*, 1 Kin. 4:13. *In the possession of the Syrians*, 1 Kin. 22:3. *Besieged by Israel and Judah; Ahab slain at*, 1 Kin. 22:29–36; 2 Chr. 18. *Recovered by Joram; Joram wounded at*, 2 Kin. 8:28, 29; 9:14, 15; 2 Chr. 22:5, 6. *Elisha anoints Jehu king at*, 2 Kin. 9:1–6.

* **BETH-SHEMESH** (*house of the sun*). *A priestly city of Dan*, Josh. 21:16; 1 Sam. 6:15; 1 Chr. 6:59. *On the northern border of Judah*, Josh. 15:10; 1 Sam. 6:9, 12. *In later times transferred to Judah*, 2 Kin. 14:11. *Mentioned in Solomon's commissary districts*, 1 Kin. 4:9. *Amaziah taken prisoner at*, 2 Kin. 14:11–13; 2 Chr. 25:21–23. *Retaken by the Philistines*, 2 Chr. 28:18. *Called* IR-SHEMESH, Josh. 19:41.

† **GEBA** (*hill*), called also GABA. *A city of Benjamin, assigned to the sons of Aaron*, Josh. 21:17; 1 Sam. 13:3; 2 Sam. 5:25; 1 Kin. 15:22; 2 Kin. 23:8; 1 Chr. 6:60; 8:6; 2 Chr. 16:6; Neh. 11:31; 12:29; Isa. 10:29; Zech. 14:10.

‡ **AIJALON.** *A valley and Levitical city in the tribe of Dan*, Josh. 10:12; 19:42; 21:24. *Taken from Dan by the Amorites*, Judg. 1:35.

(In 1 Chr. 6:69 this city, or possibly another, as there is confusion in the records, is mentioned as a city belonging to Ephraim; while again this or possibly another city of the same name is mentioned in 2 Chr. 11:10 as a city of Judah.)

‖ **GATH-RIMMON.** *A city of Manasseh*, Josh. 21:25. *Called* IBLEAM, Josh. 17:11; Judg. 1:27; 2 Kin. 9:27; *and* BILEANO, 1 Chr. 6:70.

(A Gath-rimmon is mentioned in Josh. 21:24 as being in the tribe of Dan. This may be another city, but it is probably identical with the Gath-rimmon of v. 25. Another Gath-rimmon is mentioned as belonging to the tribe of Ephraim, see 1 Chr. 6:69.)

§ **KEDESH,** called also KEDESH-NAPHTALI. *A city of refuge*, Josh. 20:7; 21:32. *Given to the Gershonites*, 1 Chr. 6:76. *Home of Barak and Heber*, Judg. 4:6, 9, 11. *Captured by Tiglath-pileser*, 2 Kin. 15:29.

v.32–1489 BC
See footnote, *Time*, Rev. 10:6.

**33**
*m Gershonites*, Num. 4:27.

**34**
*n Merarites*, Num. 26:57.
*o Zebulun, tribe of*, Gen. 49:13.
*p* Josh. 12:22; 19:11.

**35**
*q* Josh. 19:15; Judg. 1:30.

**36**
*r Reubenites*, Josh. 22:1.
*s Bezer*, Deut. 4:43.
*t Jahaz*, Judg. 11:20.

**37**
*u Kedemoth*, Josh. 13:18.
*v Mephaath*, Josh. 13:18.

**38**
*w Gad, tribe of*, Deut. 33:20.
*x Ramoth-gilead*, Josh. 20:8.
*y Mahanaim*, Gen. 32:2.

**39**
*z Heshbon*, Isa. 16:8.

---

*a Jazer*, Josh. 13:25.

**40**
*b Merarites*, Num. 26:57.

**41**
*c Levites, cities assigned to*, Deut. 10:8.

**43**
*d Israel, conquest of the land*, Ex. 4:22.
*e Canaan, promised to Abraham and his seed*, Gen. 37:1.

a [a]city of refuge[c] for the slayer; and +Hăm'moth-dôr with her suburbs, and Kär'tan with her suburbs[c]; three cities.

33 All the cities of the [m]Gēr'-shon-ītes according to their families *were* thirteen cities with their suburbs.[c]

34 ¶ And unto the families of the [n]children of Mė-rā'rī, the rest of the Lē'vītes, out of the tribe of [o]Zĕb'u-lŭn, [p]Jŏk'ne-ăm with her suburbs[c], and Kär'tah with her suburbs[c],

35 Dĭm'nah with her suburbs[c], [q]Nā'ha-lăl with her suburbs[c]; four cities.

36 And out of the [r]tribe of Reu̇'ben, [s]Bē'zēr with her suburbs[c], and [t]Jȧ-hā'zah with her suburbs[c],

37 [u]Kĕd'e-mŏth with her suburbs[c], and [v]Mĕph'a-ăth with her suburbs[c]; four cities.

38 And out of the tribe of [w]Găd, [x]Rā'moth in Ḡĭl'e-ăd with her suburbs[c], *to be* a city of refuge for the slayer; and [y]Mā-hȧ-nā'ĭm with her suburbs[c],

39 [z]Hĕsh'bŏn with her suburbs[c], [a]Jā'zēr with her suburbs[c]; four cities in all.

40 So all the cities for the [b]children of Mė-rā'rī by their families, which were remaining of the families of the Lē'vītes, were *by* their lot twelve cities.

41 All the [c]cities of the Lē'vītes within the possession of the children of Īṣ'ra-el *were* forty and eight cities with their suburbs.[c]

42 These cities were every one with their suburbs[c] round about them: thus *were* all these cities.

43 ¶ And the LORD gave unto [d]Īṣ'ra-el all the [e]land which he [f]sware to give unto their fathers; and they possessed it, and dwelt therein.[s]

44[s] And the [g]LORD gave [h]them rest round about, according to all that he [f]sware unto their fathers: and there stood not a man of all their enemies before them; the [g]LORD delivered all their enemies into their hand.

45 [i]There failed not ought[c] of any good thing which the [i]LORD had spoken unto the house of Īṣ'ra-el; all came to pass.[s]

## CHAPTER 22

*Joshua dismisses the two tribes and a half with a blessing. 10 They build an altar of testimony by Jordan. 11 The other tribes are offended thereat. 21 A satisfactory explanation is given.*

THEN [a]Jŏsh'u-ȧ called the *Reu̇'ben-ītes, and the [b]Găd'ītes, and the half tribe of [c]Mȧ-năs'seh,

2 And said unto them, Ye have kept[c] all that [d]Mō'ṣeṣ the servant of the LORD commanded you, and have [e]obeyed my voice in all that I commanded you:

3 Ye have not left your brethren these many days unto this day, but [e]have kept[c] the charge[c] of the commandment of the LORD your God.

4 And now the [f]LORD your God hath given rest unto your brethren, as he promised them: therefore now return ye, and get you unto your tents, *and* unto the [g]land of your possession, which Mō'ṣeṣ the servant of the LORD gave you on the other side [h]Jôr'dan.[Q]

5 But [i,j]take [k]diligent heed to [l,m]do the commandment and the law, which Mō'ṣeṣ the servant of the LORD charged you, to [n]love

v.43–1489 BC
See footnote, *Time*, Rev. 10:6.

*f Covenant, of God with men*, Deut. 29:1.

**44**
*g God, providence of*, Gen. 2:2.
*h Nation, peace given to, by God*, Isa. 2:4.

**45**
*i God, faithfulness of, exemplified*, Gen. 2:2.

**1**
*a Joshua*, Josh. 1:1.
*b Gad, tribe of*, Deut. 33:20.
*c Manasseh, tribe of*, Gen. 46:20.

**2**
*d Moses*, Ex. 2:10
*e Obedience, exemplified*, Heb. 5:8

**4**
*f God, faithfulness of*, Gen. 2:2.
*g Gilead*, Deut. 3:13.
*h Jordan*, Gen. 32:10.

**5**
*i Commandment, enjoining obedience, love to God and whole-hearted service*, Deut. 8:2.
*j Watchfulness, enjoined*, Matt. 24:42.
*k Diligence, required, in keeping commandments*, Rom. 12:8.
*l Obedience, enjoined*, Heb. 5:8
*m Duty, of man to God, to obey*, Eccl 12:13.
*n Love, of man for God*, 1 John 4:19

---

**+HAMMOTH-DOR.** *A city of Naphtali assigned to Levites*, Josh. 21:32. *Possibly identical with* HAMMATH, Josh. 19:35. *Called* HAMMON, 1 Chr. 6:76.

***REUBENITES**, the descendants of Reuben. *Military enrollment of, at Sinai*, Num. 1:20, 21, *in Moab*, Num. 26:7. *Place of, in camp and march*, Num. 2:10. *Standard of*, Num. 10:18. *Certain of, conspire against Moses and Aaron*, Num. 16:1–3; Deut. 11:6. *Have their inheritance east of the Jordan*, Num. 32; Deut. 3:16, 17; Josh. 12:6; 13:15–23, 18:7. *Cities of, given to the sons of Merari*, 1 Chr 6:78. *Assist the other tribes in conquest of the region west of the Jordan*, Josh. 1:12–18; 22:1–6. *Unite with the other tribes in building a monument to signify the unity of the tribes on the east of the Jordan with the tribes on the west of the river; monument misunderstood; the explanation and reconciliation*, Josh. 22:10–34. *Reproached by Deborah*, Judg 5:15, 16. *Taken captive into Assyria*, 2 Kin. 15.29; 1 Chr. 5.26.

v.5–1489 BC
See footnote, *Time*, Rev. 10:6.

6
o *Benedictions, instances of*, Deut. 21:5.

7
p *Bashan*, Num. 32:33.
1 R. V. inheritance

8
q *Silver*, 1 Chr. 28: 14.
r *Gold*, Ezek. 7:19.
s *Brass*, Job 28:2.
t *Iron*, Prov. 27: 17.
u *Spoils*, 1 Chr. 26: 27.

9
v *Shiloh*, Judg. 21: 12.
w *Canaan*, Gen. 37:1.

10
x *Altar*, Gen. 8:20.

11
y *Israel*, Ex. 4:22.

the LORD your God, and to walk in all his ways, and to keep his commandments, and to cleave unto him, and to serve him with all your heart and with all your soul.

6 So [a]Jŏsh'u-ȧ [o]blessed them, and sent them away: and they went unto their tents.

7 ¶ Now to the *one* half of the tribe of [c]Mȧ-năs'seh [d]Mō'ṣeṣ had given [1]*possession* in [p]Bā'-shăn: but unto the *other* half thereof gave [a]Jŏsh'u-ȧ among their brethren on this side [h]Jôr'dan westward. And when Jŏsh'u-ȧ sent them away also unto their tents, then he [o]blessed them,

8 And he spake unto them, saying, Return with much riches unto your tents, and with very much cattle, with [q]silver, and with [r]gold, and with [s]brass, and with [t]iron, and with very much raiment: divide the [u]spoil of your enemies with your brethren.

9 And the *children of Reu̥'ben and the children of [b]Găd and the half tribe of [c]Mȧ-năs'seh returned, and departed from the children of Ĭṣ'ra-el out of [v]Shī'-lōh, which *is* in the land of [w]Cā'-năan, to go unto the country of [g]Gĭl'e-ăd, to the land of their possession, whereof they were possessed, according to the word of the LORD by the hand of Mō'ṣeṣ.

10 ¶ And when they came unto the borders of [h]Jôr'dan, that *are* in the land of [w]Cā'năan, the *children of Reu̥'ben and the children of [b]Găd and the half tribe of [c]Mȧ-năs'seh built there an [x]altar by Jôr'dan, a great altar to see to.

11 ¶ And the children of [y]Ĭṣ'-ra-el heard say, Behold, the *children of Reu̥'ben and the children of [b]Găd and the half tribe of [c]Mȧ-năs'seh have built an [x]altar [2]over against the land of [w]Cā'năan, in the borders of [h]Jôr'dan, [3]at the passage of the children of Ĭṣ'ra-el.

12 And when the children of Ĭṣ'ra-el heard *of it*, [z]the whole congregation of the children of Ĭṣ'ra-el gathered themselves together at Shī'lōh, to go up to war against them.

13 And the children of [a]Ĭṣ'ra-el sent unto the *children of Reu̥'-ben, and to the children of [b]Găd, and to the half tribe of [c]Mȧ-năs'-seh, into the land of [d]Gĭl'e-ăd, [e]Phĭn'e-has the son of [f]Ē-le-ā'-zar the priest,

14 And with [e]him ten princes, of each chief house a prince throughout all the tribes of [a]Ĭṣ'-ra-el; and each one *was* an head of the house of their fathers among the thousands of Ĭṣ'ra-el.

15 And they came unto the *children of Reu̥'ben, and to the children of [b]Găd, and to the half tribe of [c]Mȧ-năs'seh, unto the land of [d]Gĭl'e-ăd, and they spake with them, saying,

16 Thus [g,h]saith the whole congregation of the LORD, [i,j]What trespass *is* this that ye have committed against the God of Ĭṣ'-ra-el, to turn away this day from following the LORD, in that ye have builded you an [k]altar, that ye might rebel this day against the LORD?

17 [i,j]*Is* the iniquity of Pē'or too little for us, from which we are not cleansed until this day, although there was a [l]plague in the congregation of the LORD,

18 [h,i,j]But that ye must turn away this day from following the LORD? and it will be, *seeing* ye rebel to day against the LORD, that to morrow he will be [m]wroth with the whole congregation of Ĭṣ'ra-el.

19 Notwithstanding, if the land

v.11–1489 BC
See footnote, *Time*, Rev. 10:6.

2 R. V. in the forefront of
3 R. V. on the side that pertaineth to the

12
z *Rashness*, 2 Sam. 6:7.

13
a *Israel*, Ex. 4:22.
b *Gad, tribe of*, Deut. 33:20.
c *Manasseh, tribe of*, Gen. 46:20.
d *Gilead*, Deut. 3:13.
e *Phinehas*, Num. 25:7.
f *Eleazar*, Num. 3:2.

16
g *Reproof, faithfulness in*, Prov. 17: 10.
h *False Accusation*, 2 Tim. 3:3.
i *Misjudgment, instances of*, Num. 32:6.
j *Motive, misunderstood*, vs. 16–29; Psa. 106:8.
k *Altar*, Gen. 8:20.

17
l *Plague, on the Israelites*, Ex. 11:1.

18
m *Anger of God*, 2 Kin. 13:3.

v.19–1489 BC
See footnote, *Time*, Rev. 10:6.

19
*n* *Tabernacle*, Ex. 27:9.

20
*o* Josh. 7; or, *Achar*, 1 Chr. 2:7.
*p* *Judgments*, Ex. 6:6.
4 R. V. devoted

22
*q* *God, knowledge of*, Gen. 2:2.

23
*r* *Offerings, burnt*, Lev. 6:17.
*s* *Offerings, meat*, Lev. 6:17.
*t* *Offerings, peace*, Lev. 6:17.
5 R. V. meal

24
*u* *Prudence, instances of*, 2 Chr. 2:12.
6 R. V. out of carefulness done this, and of purpose,

25
*v* *Jordan*, Gen. 32: 10.
*w* *Fear of God*, Acts 9:31.

of your possession *be* unclean[G], *then* pass ye over unto the land of the possession of the LORD, wherein the LORD's [n]tabernacle dwelleth, and take possession among us: [i,j]but rebel not against the LORD, nor rebel against us, in building you an [k]altar beside[G] the altar of the LORD our God.

20 Did not [o]Ā'chăn the son of Zē'rah commit a trespass in the [4]accursed[G] thing, and [p]wrath fell on all the congregation of [a]Ĭș'ra-el? and that man perished not alone in his iniquity.

21 ¶ Then the *children of Reu̥'ben and the children of [b]Găd and the half tribe of [c]Mă-năs'seh answered, and said unto the heads of the thousands of Ĭș'ra-el,

22 The LORD God of gods, the LORD God of gods, [q]he knoweth, and [a]Ĭș'ra-el he shall know; if *it be* in rebellion, or if in transgression against the LORD, (save[G] us not this day,)

23 That we have built us an [k]altar to turn from following the LORD, or if to offer thereon [r]burnt offering or [5,s]meat[G] offering, or if to offer [t]peace offerings thereon, let the LORD himself require[G] *it*;

24 And [j,u]if we have not *rather* [6]done it for fear of *this* thing, saying, In time to come your children might speak unto our children, saying, What have ye to do with the LORD God of Ĭș'ra-el?

25 For the LORD hath made [v]Jôr'dan a border between us and you, ye *children of Reu̥'ben and children of [b]Găd; ye have no part in the LORD: so shall your children make our children cease from [w]fearing the LORD.

26 Therefore we said, [j]Let us now prepare to build us an [k]altar, not for [r]burnt offering, nor for sacrifice[G]:

27 But *that* it *may be* a [x]witness between us and you, and our generations after us, that we might do the service of the LORD before him with our [r]burnt offerings, and with our sacrifices, and with our peace offerings; [j]that your children may not say to our children in time to come, Ye have[G] no part in the LORD.

28 Therefore said we, that it shall be, when they should *so* say to us or to our generations in time to come, that we may say *again*, Behold the pattern of the [k]altar of the LORD, which our fathers made, not for [r]burnt offerings, nor for sacrifices; but it *is* a witness between us and you.

29 [j]God forbid that we should rebel against the LORD, and turn this day from following the LORD, to build an [k]altar for [r]burnt offerings, for [5,s]meat[G] offerings, or for sacrifices, beside the altar of the LORD our God that *is* before his [n]tabernacle.

30 ¶ And when [e]Phĭn'e-has the priest, and the princes of the congregation and heads of the thousands of Ĭș'ra-el which *were* with him, heard the words that the *children of Reu̥'ben and the children of [b]Găd and the children of [c]Mă-năs'seh spake, it pleased them.

31 And [e]Phĭn'e-has the son of [f]Ē-le-ā'zar the priest said unto the *children of Reu̥'ben, and to the children of Găd, and to the children of Mă-năs'seh, This day we perceive that the LORD *is* among us, because [y]ye have not committed this trespass against the LORD: now ye have delivered the children of Ĭș'ra-el out of the hand of the LORD.

32 And [e]Phĭn'e-has the son of [f]Ē-le-ā'zar the priest, and the princes, returned from the *chil-

v.26–1489 BC
See footnote, *Time*, Rev. 10:6.

27
*x* *Memorial*, Num 16:40.

31
*y* *Righteousness, fruits of*, Psa. 15:2.

v.32–1489 BC
See footnote, *Time*, Rev. 10:6.

**32**
z *Canaan*, Gen. 37:1.

**33**
a *Thankfulness, to God*, Acts 24:3.
7 R. V. spake no more of going

**34**
b *Memorial*, Num. 16:40.

**1**
a *Israel, Joshua's exhortation to*, vs. 1–16; Ex. 4:22.
b *Joshua, exhortation of*, vs. 1–16; Josh. 1:1.
c *Longevity, instances of*, Psa. 91:16.

**2**
d *Senate*, Num. 11:16.

**3**
e *Canaanites*, Ex. 23:28.
f *War, God in*, Judg. 3:2.

**4**
g *Lot*, Esth. 3:7.
h *Jordan*, Gen. 32:10.
i *Mediterranean Sea*, Ex. 23:31.

dren of Reṳ′ben, and from the
children of Găd, out of the land
of [d]Ḡil′e-ăd, unto the land of
[z]Cā′năan, to the children of Ĭṣ′-
ra-el, and brought them word
again.
33 And the thing pleased the
children of Ĭṣ′ra-el; and the children of Ĭṣ′ra-el [a]blessed God,
and [7]did not intend to go up
against them in battle, to destroy the land wherein the children of Reṳ′ben and Găd dwelt.
34 And the children of Reṳ′ben
and the children of Găd called
the altar *Ed*: for it *shall be* a
[b]witness between us that the
LORD *is* God.

## CHAPTER 23

*Joshua's exhortation to the children of Israel in his old age. 3 God's benefits, 5 promises, 11 threatenings. 16 Judgments on idolatry.*

AND it came to pass a long
time after that the LORD
had given rest unto [a]Ĭṣ′ra-el
from all their enemies round
about, that [b]Jŏsh′u-ȧ waxed[C] [c]old
*and* stricken in age.
2 And Jŏsh′u-ȧ called for all
Ĭṣ′ra-el, *and* for their [d]elders,
and for their heads, and for their
judges, and for their officers, and
said unto them, I am old *and*
stricken in age:
3 And ye have seen all that the
LORD your God hath done unto
all these [e]nations because of you;
for the LORD your God *is* he
that hath [f]fought for you.
4 Behold, I have divided unto
you by [g]lot these nations that
remain, to be an inheritance for
your tribes, from [h]Jôr′dan, with
all the nations that I have cut[C]
off, even unto the [i]great sea
westward.
5 And the LORD your God, he
shall expel them from before
you, and drive them from out of
your sight; and ye shall possess
their land, [j]as the LORD your
God hath promised unto you.
6 [k,l]Be ye therefore very courageous to keep and to [m]do all
that is written in the book of the
[n]law of Mō′ṣeṣ, that ye turn not
aside therefrom *to* the right hand
or *to* the left;
7 That ye [o]come not among
these [p]nations, these that remain
among you; neither make mention of the name of their gods,
nor cause to swear *by them*, [q]nei-
ther serve them, nor bow yourselves unto them:
8 But [r]cleave[C] unto the LORD
your God, as ye have done unto
this day.
9 For the LORD hath [s]driven
out from before you great nations and strong: but *as for* you,
no man hath been able to stand[C]
before you unto this day.[Q]
10 One man of you shall chase
a thousand: for the [s,t]LORD your
God, he *it is* that fighteth for
you, as he hath promised you.[S]
11 [u,v]Take good heed therefore
unto yourselves, that ye [w,x]love
the LORD your God.
12 Else if ye do in any wise[C] go
back, and [y]cleave[C] unto the remnant of these nations, *even* these
that remain among you, and
shall make *marriages with them,
and go[C] in unto them, and they
to you:
13 [y]Know for a certainty that
the LORD your God will no more
drive out *any of* these nations
from before you; but [z]they shall
be snares and [a]traps unto you,
and scourges in your sides, and
thorns in your eyes, until ye
perish from off this good land
which the LORD your God hath
given you.

**5**
j *God, faithfulness of*, Gen. 2:2.

**6**
k *Commandment, enjoining courage and fidelity*, Deut. 8:2.
l *Courage, enjoined*, Deut. 31:7.
m *Obedience, enjoined*, Heb. 5:8.
n *Law, of Moses*, Deut. 33:2.

**7**
o *Fellowship, with the wicked, forbidden*, 1 Cor. 1:9.
p *Evil Company, forbidden*, Prov. 13:20.
q *Idolatry, forbidden*, 1 Sam. 15:23.

**8**
r *Faithfulness, exhortations to*, Luke 16:10.

**9**
s *God, providence of*, Gen. 2:2.

**10**
t *Victories, in battle, from God*, Deut. 28:7.

**11**
u *Commandment, enjoining love of God*, Deut. 8:2.
v *Watchfulness, enjoined*, Matt. 24:42.
w *Love, of man for God*, 1 John 4:19.
x *Duty, of man to God, to love*, Eccl. 12:13.

**12**
y *Fellowship, with the wicked, punishment on account of*, 1 Cor. 1:9.

**13**
z *Judgments*, Ex. 6:6.

a Job 18:10; Jer. 5:26.

*** MISCEGENATION,** mixture of blood of different peoples. *Forbidden, by Abraham*, Gen. 24:37; *by Isaac*, Gen. 28:1; *by Moses*, Ex. 34:12–16; Deut. 7:3, 4; *by Joshua*, Josh. 23:12; *by Ezra*, Ezra 9:2, 11–15; *by Nehemiah*, Neh. 13:25. *Reasons for prohibition of*, Ex. 34:16; Deut. 7:4; Josh. 23:12, 13. *Prohibition of, observed by the Jews*, Neh. 10:30.
*Results of*, Judg. 3:6, 7.
**Instances of:** *Esau*, Gen. 26:34, 35. *Moses*, Num. 12:1. *Israel*, Num. 25:1, 6–8; Judg. 3:5–8. *Solomon*, 1 Kin. 11:1, 2.

14 And, behold, this day I *am* going[c] the way of all the earth: and ye know in all your hearts and in all your souls, that not one thing hath failed of all the good things which the [b]LORD your God spake concerning you; all are come to pass unto you, *and* not one thing hath failed thereof.

15 Therefore it shall come to pass, *that* as all good things are come upon you, which the LORD your God promised you; so shall the LORD [c]bring upon you all [d]evil things, until he have destroyed you from off this good [e]land which the LORD your God hath given you.

16 When ye have [f]transgressed the [g]covenant of the LORD your God, which he commanded you, and have gone and [h]served other gods, and bowed yourselves to them; then shall the [i]anger of the LORD be kindled against you, and ye shall [d]perish quickly from off the good land which he hath given unto you.[s]

## CHAPTER 24

*Joshua assembles the tribes at Shechem. 2 A brief history of God's benefits from Terah onward. 14 He renews the covenant between them and God, 26 and sets up a stone as a witness thereof. 29 Joshua's age, death, and burial. 32 Joseph's bones are buried. 33 Eleazar dies.*

AND [a]Jŏsh'u-ȧ gathered all the tribes of [b,c]Ĭṣ'ra-el to [d]Shē'chem, and called for the [e]elders of Ĭṣ'ra-el, and for their heads, and for their judges, and for their officers; and they presented themselves before God.

2 And [a]Jŏsh'u-ȧ said unto all the people, Thus saith the LORD God of Ĭṣ'ra-el, Your fathers dwelt [1]on the other side of the flood[G] in old time, *even* [f]Tē'rah, the father of [g]Ā'bră-hăm, and the father of Nā'chôr: and they [h]served other gods.

3 And [i]I took your father [g]Ā'bră-hăm from the other side of the flood, and led him throughout all the land of [j]Cā'-năan, and multiplied his seed, and gave him [k]Ī'ṣaac.

4 And [i]I gave unto [k]Ī'ṣaac [l]Jā'-cob and [m]Ē'sa̤u: and I gave unto Ē'sa̤u mount [n]Sē'īr, to possess it; but Jā'cob and his children went down into [o]Ē'ġy̆pt.

5 [t]I sent [p]Mō'ṣeṣ also and [q]Aâr'-on, and I [r,s]plagued [o]Ē'ġy̆pt, according to that which I did among them: and afterward I [t]brought you out.

6 And [t]I brought your fathers out of [o]Ē'ġy̆pt: and ye came unto the sea; and the [u]Ē-ġy̆p'tianṣ pursued after your fathers with chariots and [v]horsemen unto the [w]Red sea.

7 And when they [x]cried unto the LORD, he [y]put darkness between you and the [u]Ē-ġy̆p'tianṣ, and brought the [w]sea upon them, and covered[C] them; and your eyes have seen what I have done in [o]Ē'ġy̆pt: and ye dwelt in the wilderness a long season.

8 And [i]I [t]brought you into the [j]land of the [z]Ăm'ôr-ītes, which dwelt on the other side [a]Jôr'dan; and they fought with you: and I gave them into your hand, that ye might possess their land; and I destroyed them from before you.

9 Then [b]Bā'lăk the son of [c]Zĭp'-por, king of [d]Mō'ab, arose and warred against Ĭṣ'ra-el, and sent and called [e]Bā'laam the son of Bē'or to curse you:

10 [f]But I would not hearken unto [e]Bā'laam; therefore he blessed you still: so [g]I delivered you out of his hand.

11 And ye went over [a]Jôr'dan, and came unto [h]Jĕr'ĭ-chō: and the men of Jĕr'ĭ-chō fought against you, the [i]Ăm'ôr-ītes, and the [j]Pĕr'ĭz-zītes, and the [k]Cā'-năan-ītes, and the [l]Hĭt'tītes, and the [m]Ġĭr'ga-shītes, the [n]Hī'vītes,

**14**
*b God, faithfulness of, exemplified,* Gen. 2:2.

**15**
*c God, providence of,* Gen. 2:2.
*d Judgments,* Ex. 6:6.
*e Canaan,* Gen. 37:1.

**16**
*f Disobedience to God,* Eph. 5:6.
*g Covenant, of God with men,* Deut. 29:1.
*h Idolatry,* 1 Sam. 15:23.
*i Anger of God,* 2 Kin. 13:3.

**1**
*a Joshua, exhortation of,* vs. 1–23; Josh. 1:1.
*b Israel, covenant renewed to,* vs. 1–33; Ex. 4:22.
*c Nation,* Isa. 2:4.
*d Shechem,* Josh. 20:7.
*e Senate,* Num. 11:16.

**2**
*f Terah,* Gen. 11:24.
*g Abraham,* Gen. 17:5.
*h Idolatry,* 1 Sam. 15:23.
1 R. V. of old time beyond the River, even

**3**
*i God, providence of,* Gen. 2:2.
*j Canaan,* Gen. 37:1.
*k Isaac,* Gen. 21:3.

**4**
*l Jacob,* Gen. 27:11.
*m Esau,* Gen. 25:25.
*n Seir,* Deut. 1:2.
*o Egypt,* Gen. 41:8.

**5**
*p Moses,* Ex. 2:10.
*q Aaron,* Ex. 6:20.
*r Plague,* Ex. 11:1.
*s Judgments,* Ex. 6:6.
*t Israel, led of God,* Ex. 4:22.

**6**
*u Egyptians,* Gen. 50:3.
*v Armies,* Deut. 11:4.
*w Red Sea,* Ex. 10:19.

**7**
*x Prayer, answered,* Acts 6:4.
*y Miracles,* Luke 23:8.

**8**
*z Amorites,* Gen. 14:13.
*a Jordan,* Gen. 32 10.

**9**
*b Balak,* Num. 22:4.
*c Zippor,* Num. 22:2.
*d Moabites,* Gen. 19:37.
*e Balaam,* Deut. 23:4.

**10**
*f Prayer, answer to, withheld,* Act 6:4.
*g God, preserver,* Gen. 2:2.

**11**
*h Jericho,* Num. 22:1.
*i Amorites,* Gen. 14:13.
*j Perizzites,* Gen. 15:20.
*k Canaanites,* Ex. 23:28.
*l Hittites,* Judg. 1:26.
*m Girgashites,* Neh 9:8.
*n Hivites,* Gen. 10 17.

and the [o]Jĕb′u-sītes; and I delivered them into your hand.
12 And [p]I sent the [q, r]hornet before you, which drave them out
from before you, *even* the two
kings of the [i]Ăm′ôr-ītes; *but* not
with thy sword, nor with thy
bow.
13 And [p]I have given you a
[s]land for which ye did not labour, and cities which ye built
not, and ye dwell in them; of the
[t]vineyards and oliveyards which
ye planted not do ye eat.
14 ¶ [u, v]Now therefore [w]fear the
LORD, and [x]serve him in [y]sin-
cerity and in [z]truth: and put
away the gods which your fathers served [2]on the other side
of the flood,[c] and in [a]Ē′ġy̆pt; and
serve ye the LORD.
15 And if it seem evil unto you
to serve the LORD, [b]choose you
this day whom ye will serve;
[c]whether the gods which your
fathers [d]served that [3]*were* on the
other side of the flood,[c] or the
gods of the [e]Ăm′ôr-ītes, in whose
land ye dwell: but as for [f]me and
[g]my house, [h, i]we will serve the
LORD.[S]
16 And the people answered
and said, [h]God forbid that we
should forsake the LORD, to
[d]serve other gods;
17 For the [j]LORD our God, he
*it is* that brought us up and
our fathers out of the land of
[a]Ē′ġy̆pt, from the house of bondage, and which did those great
[k]signs in our sight, and preserved us in all the way wherein
we went, and among all the people through whom we passed:
18 And the [l]LORD drave out
from before us all the people,
even the [e]Ăm′ôr-ītes which dwelt
in the [m]land: *therefore* [h]will we
also serve the LORD; for he *is*
our God.[Q]
19 And [f]Jŏsh′u-à said unto
the people, Ye cannot serve the
LORD: for he *is* an [n]holy [o]God;
he *is* a [p]jealous God; he will not
forgive your transgressions nor
your sins.[S T]
20 If ye [q]forsake the LORD, and
[d]serve strange[c] gods, then he will
turn and do you hurt,[c] and consume[c] you, after that he hath
done you good.
21 And the people said unto
[f]Jŏsh′u-à, Nay; but [h]we will
serve the LORD.
22 And [f]Jŏsh′u-à said unto the
people, Ye *are* witnesses against
yourselves that ye have chosen
you the LORD, to serve him.
And they said, [h]*We are* witnesses.
23 Now therefore put away,
*said he*, the strange[c] [d]gods which
*are* among you, and incline[c] your
heart unto the LORD God of
Iṣ′ra-el.
24 And the people said unto
[f]Jŏsh′u-à, [h]The LORD our God
will we serve, and his voice will
we [r]obey.
25 So [f]Jŏsh′u-à made a [s]cove-
nant with the people that day,
and set them a statute and an
ordinance in [t]Shē′chem.
26 And [f]Jŏsh′u-à wrote these
words in the book of the [u]law of
God, and took a great [v]stone,
and set it up there under an oak,
that *was* by the [w]sanctuary of
the LORD.
27 And [f]Jŏsh′u-à said unto all
the people, Behold, this [v]stone
shall be a witness unto us; for it
hath heard all the words of the
LORD which he spake unto us:
it shall be therefore a witness unto you, lest ye [q]deny your God.
28 So [f]Jŏsh′u-à let the people
depart, every man unto his inheritance.
29 ¶ And it came to pass after
these things, that [f]Jŏsh′u-à the
son of Nŭn, the servant of the
LORD, [x]died, *being* [y]an hundred
and ten years old.

o *Jebusites*, Deut. 7:1.

**12**

p *God, providence of*, Gen. 2:2.

q Ex. 23:28; Deut. 7:20.

r *Animals, instruments of God's will*, Jer. 27.5.

**13**

s *Canaan*, Gen. 37:1.

t *Grape*, Lev. 25.5.

**14**

u *Commandment, enjoining fear of God, whole-hearted service and to abstain from idolatry*, Deut. 8:2.

v *Zeal, enjoined*, 2 Cor. 7:11.

w *Fear of God, enjoined*, Acts 9:31.

x *Obedience, enjoined*, Heb. 5:8.

y *Sincerity*, 1 Cor. 5:8.

z *Truth*, John 18: 37.

a *Egypt*, Gen. 41:8.

2 R. V. beyond the River,

**15**

b *Choice*, 2 Sam. 24:12.

c *Good and Evil*, Gen. 3:5.

d *Idolatry*, 1 Sam. 15:23.

e *Amorites*, Gen. 14:13.

f *Joshua*, Josh. 1:1.

g *Family, religion in*, 1 Chr. 13:14.

h *Faithfulness, instances of*, Luke 16:10.

i *Character, stability of*, Phil. 2:15.

3 R. V. were beyond the River,

**17**

j *God, preserver*, Gen. 2:2.

k *Miracles*, Luke 23:8.

**18**

l *God, providence of*, Gen. 2:2.

m *Canaan*, Gen. 37:1.

**19**

n *Holiness, attribute of God*, **Ex.** 39:30.

o *God, holiness of*, Gen. 2:2.

p *Jealousy, attributed to God*, **Psa.** 78:58.

**20**

q ***Backsliding, admonitions against***, **Hos. 11:7.**

**24**

r ***Obedience***, **Heb.** 5:8.

**25**

s *Covenant, of man with God*, Deut. 29:1.

t *Shechem*, Josh. 20:7.

**26**

u *Word of God*, Psa. 119:9.

v *Pillar*, Gen. 28: 18.

w *Tabernacle*, Ex. 27:9.

**29**

x *Death*, Num. 23 10.

y *Longevity*, Psa 91:16.

**B.C. 1426?**

30 And they [z]buried him in the border of his inheritance in [a]Tĭm'nath–sē'rah, which *is* in mount [b]Ē'phră-ĭm, on the north [4]side of the hill of [c]Gā'ăsh.

31 And [d]Ĭs̱'ra-el served the LORD all the days of [e]Jŏsh'u-ȧ, and all the days of the elders that overlived[C] Jŏsh'u-ȧ, and which had known all the works of the LORD, that he had done for Ĭs̱'ra-el.

32 ¶ And the bones of [f]Jō's̱eph, which the children of Ĭs̱'ra-el brought up out of [g]Ē'ġy̆pt, buried they in [h]Shē'chem, in a parcel[C] of ground which [i]Jā'cob bought of the sons of [j]Hā'mor the father of [k]Shē'chem for an hundred pieces of [5,l]silver: and it became the inheritance of the children of Jō's̱eph.[Q]

33 ¶ And [m]Ē-le-ā'zar the son of [n]Aâr'on died; and they buried him in a [o]hill *that pertained to* [p]Phĭn'e-has his son, which was given him in mount [b]Ē'phră-ĭm.

30
z *Burial*, Acts 8:2.

a Josh. 19:50.
b *Ephraim, mount of*, Josh. 17:15.
c Judg. 2:9; 2 Sam. 23:30.
4 R. V. of the mountain

31
d *Israel, religious fidelity of, during the life of Joshua*, Ex. 4:22.
e *Joshua*, Josh. 1:1.

32
f *Joseph*, Gen. 33:2.

g *Egypt*, Gen. 41:
h *Shechem, Joseph buried at*, Josh. 20:7.
i *Jacob*, Gen. 27: 11.
j *Hamor*, Gen. 34 18.
k *Shechem*, Gen. 34:2.
l *Silver*, 1 Chr. 28 14.
5 R. V. money:

33
m *Eleazar*, Num. 3:2.
n *Aaron*, Ex. 6:20
o *Burying Places*, Gen. 23:4.
p *Phinehas*, Num. 25:7.

THE

# BOOK OF JUDGES

## CHAPTER 1

*The acts of Judah and Simeon. 6 Adoni-bezek justly requited. 8 Jerusalem taken. 10 Hebron taken. 11 Othniel has Achsah to wife for taking of Debir. 16 The Kenites dwell in Judah. 17 Hormah, Gaza, Askelon, and Ekron taken. 21 The acts of Benjamin; 22 of the house of Joseph; 30 of Zebulun; 31 of Asher; 33 of Naphtali; 34 and of Dan.*

NOW after the death of [a]Jŏsh'u-ȧ it came to pass, that the [b]children of [c]Ĭs̱'ra-el [d]asked the LORD, saying, Who shall go up for us against the [e]Cā'năan-ītes first, to fight against them?

2 And the LORD said, [f]Jū'dah shall go up: behold, [g]I have delivered the land into his hand.

3 And [f]Jū'dah said unto [h]Sĭm'e-on his brother, Come up with me into my lot[C], that we may fight against the [e]Cā'năan-ītes; and I likewise will go with thee into thy lot[C]. So Sĭm'e-on went with him.

4 And Jū'dah went up; and the [i]LORD [j]delivered the [e]Cā'năan-ītes and the [k]Pĕr'ĭz-zītes into their hand: and they slew of them in Bē'zĕk ten thousand men.

5 And they found Ȧ-dō'nī–bē'zek in Bē'zĕk: and they fought against him, and they slew the [e]Cā'năan-ītes and the [k]Pĕr'ĭz-zītes.

6 But Ȧ-dō'nī–bē'zek fled; and they pursued after him, and caught [l]him, and [m]cut off his [n]thumbs and his great [o]toes.

7 And [p]Ȧ-dō'nī–bē'zek said, Threescore and ten kings, having their thumbs and their great toes cut off, gathered *their* meat[C] under my *table: as I have done, so God hath requited me. And they brought him to [q]Jē-ru̇'sȧ-lĕm, and there he died.

8 ¶ Now the children of [f]Jū'dah had fought against [q]Jē-ru̇'sȧ-lĕm, and had [j]taken it, and smitten it with the edge of the sword, and set the city on fire.

9 And afterward the children of [f]Jū'dah went down to fight against the [e]Cā'năan-ītes, that dwelt in the mountain, and in the south, and in the valley.

10 And [f]Jū'dah went[C] against the [e]Cā'năan-ītes that dwelt in [r]Hē'bron: (now the name of Hē'bron before *was* Kĭr'jath–är'bȧ:) and they slew [s]Shē'shāi, and Ȧ-hī'man, and [t]Tăl'māi.

1
a *Joshua, death of*, Josh. 1:1.
b *Armies, religious ceremonies in*, Deut. 11:4.
c *Israel, conquest of the land*, vs. 1–36; Ex. 4:22.
d *Guidance, prayer for*, Psa. 48:14.
e *Canaanites*, Ex. 23:28.

2
f *Judah, tribe of*, Num. 10:14.
g *War, God in*, Judg. 3:2.

3
h *Simeon, tribe of*, Num. 2:12.

4
i *God, Providence of*, Gen. 2:2.
j *Victories, in battle*, Deut. 28:7.
k *Perizzites*, Gen. 15:20.

6
l *Captive, cruelty to*, 1 Sam. 30:3.
m *Cruelty, instances of*, Psa. 27:12
n *Thumb, of prisoners cut off*, Lev. 8:23.
o *Toe, of prisoners cut off*, Lev. 14: 14.

7
p *Rulers, wicked*, Ex. 18:21.
q *Jerusalem*, Judg 19:10.

10
r *Hebron*, Gen. 23:2.
s Num. 13:22; Josh. 15:14.
t Num. 13:22; Josh. 15:14.

* **TABLE.** *An article of furniture*, Judg. 1:7; 1 Sam. 20:29, 34; 2 Kin. 4:10; John 2:15. *Made of silver*, 1 Chr. 28:16. **Figurative:** *Of the altar*, Mal. 1:7, 12. *Of the Lord's supper*, 1 Cor. 10:21. *Of idolatrous feasts*, 1 Cor. 10:21. *Of charities*, Acts 6:2.

11
[t] Debir, Josh. 15: 15.
[v] Kirjath-sepher, a city of books; see Debir, Josh. 15: 15.
12
[w] Caleb, Num. 14:6.
[x] Armies, rewards for meritorious conduct in, v. 13; Deut. 11:4.
[y] Reward, a motive for valor, Matt. 5:12.
[z] Achsah, vs. 12–15; Josh. 15:16.
13
[a] Othniel, Josh. 15: 17.
[b] Caleb, Num. 14:6.
16
[c] Kenites, 1 Sam. 15:6.
[d] Jericho, Num. 22:1.
[e] Judah, tribe of, Num. 10:14.
1 R. V. brother in law,
17
[f] Simeon, tribe of, Num. 2:12.
[g] Canaanites, Ex. 23:28.
[h] Hormah, Deut. 1:44.
18
[i] Gaza, Gen. 10: 19.
[j] Ekron, Amos 1:8.
2 R. V. border
19
[k] God, providence of, Gen. 2:2.

11 And from thence [t]he went
against the inhabitants of [u]Dē′-
bĭr: and the name of Dē′bĭr before *was* [v]Kĭr′jath–sē′phẽr:
12 And [w]Cā′leb said, [x]He that
smiteth [v]Kĭr′jath–sē′phẽr, and
taketh it, [y]to him will I give
[z]Ăch′sah my daughter to wife[C].
13 And [a]Ŏth′nĭ-el the son
of †Kē′năz, [b]Cā′leb's younger
brother, took it: and he gave him
Ăch′sah his daughter to wife[C].
14 And it came to pass, when
she came *to him*, that she moved
him to ask of her father a field:
and she lighted[C] from off *her* ass;
and [b]Cā′leb said unto her, What
wilt thou?
15 And she said unto him, Give
me a blessing: for thou hast giv-
en me a south land; give me also
springs of water. And [b]Cā′leb
gave her the upper springs and
the nether[C] springs.
16 ¶ And the children of the
[c]Kĕn′īte, Mō′ṣeṣ′ [1]father in law,
went up out of the [d]city of palm
trees with the children of [e]Jū′-
dah into the wilderness of Jū′-
dah, which *lieth* in the south of
Ā′răd; and they went and dwelt
among the people.
17 And [e]Jū′dah went with
[f]Sĭm′e-on his brother, and they
slew the [g]Cā′năan-ītes that inhabited Zē′phath, and utterly
destroyed it. And the name of
the city was called [h]Hôr′mah.
18 Also [e]Jū′dah took [i]Gā′zȧ
with the [2]coast[C] thereof, and
‡Ăs′ke-lŏn with the [2]coast thereof, and [j]Ĕk′rŏn with the [2]coast
thereof.
19 And the [k]LORD was with
[e]Jū′dah; and he drave out *the*
*inhabitants of* the mountain; but
could not drive out the [l]inhabi-
tants of the valley, because they
had [m]chariots of [n]iron.
20 And they gave [o]Hē′bron unto [b]Cā′leb, as Mō′ṣeṣ said: and
he expelled thence[C] the three
[p]sons of Ā′năk.
21 ¶ And the children of [q]Bĕn′-
ja-mĭn did not drive out the
[r]Jĕb′u-sītes that inhabited [s]Jē-
rṳ′sȧ-lĕm; but the Jĕb′u-sītes
dwell with the children of Bĕn′-
ja-mĭn in Jē-rṳ′sȧ-lĕm unto this
day.
22 ¶ And the [t,u]house[C] of Jō′-
ṣeph, they also went up against
[v]Bĕth′–el: and the [k]LORD *was*
with them.
23 And the house[C] of [t,u]Jō′ṣeph
sent to [3,w]descry[C] [v]Bĕth′–el. (Now
the name of the city before *was*
Lŭz.)
24 And the spies saw a man
come forth out of the [v]city, and
they said unto him, Shew us,
we pray thee, the entrance into
the city, and we will shew thee
[x]mercy.
25 And when [y,z]he shewed
them the entrance into the [v]city,
they smote the city with the edge
of the sword; but they let go the
man and all his family.
26 And the man went into the
land of the ‖Hĭt′tītes, and built
a city, and called the name
thereof Lŭz: which *is* the name
thereof unto this day.
27 ¶ Neither did [a]Mȧ-năs′seh
drive out *the inhabitants of*
[b]Bĕth–shē′an and her towns, nor
[c]Tā′a-năch and her towns, nor
the inhabitants of [d]Dôr and her
towns, nor the inhabitants of
[e]Ĭb′le-ăm and her towns, nor the
inhabitants of [f]Mē-gĭd′dō and

[l] Canaanites, not expelled from the land, Ex. 23:28.
[m] Chariot, Josh. 11:4.
[n] Iron, Prov. 27: 17.
20
[o] Hebron, Gen. 23:2.
[p] Anakim, Deut. 1:28.
21
[q] Benjamin, tribe of, Num. 1:37.
[r] Jebusites, Deut. 7:1.
[s] Jerusalem, Judg. 19:10.
22
[t] Manasseh, tribe of, Gen. 46:20.
[u] Ephraim, tribe of, Gen. 41:52.
[v] Beth-el, Josh. 18: 13.
23
[w] Armies, reconnoissances by, Deut. 11:4.
3 R. V. spy out
24
[x] Mercy, Deut. 5:10.
25
[y] Betrayal, Matt. 26:46.
[z] Treason, instances of, 2 Kin. 11: 14.
27
[a] Manasseh, tribe of, Gen. 46:20.
[b] Beth-shean, Josh. 17:11.
[c] Taanach, Josh. 12:21.
[d] Dor, Josh. 11:2.
[e] Josh. 17:11; 2 Kin. 9:27.
[f] Megiddo, Josh. 17:11.

† **KENAZ** (*hunting*). *Brother of Caleb*, Josh. 15:17; Judg. :13; 3:9, 11; 1 Chr. 4:13.

‡ **ASKELON** (*migration*), called also ASHKELON. *One of e five chief cities of the Philistines*, Josh. 13:3. *Captured by e people of Judah*, Judg. 1:18. *Samson slays thirty men of*, udg. 14:19. *People of, suffer from plague of emerods* R. V. tumors), 1 Sam. 6:17. *Prophecies concerning*, Jer. 5:20; 47:5, 7; Amos 1:8; Zeph. 2:4, 7; Zech. 9:5.

‖ **HITTITES** (*fear*), a tribe of Canaanites. *Children of Heth*, Gen. 10:15; 23:10. *Sell a burying-ground to Abraham*, Gen. 23. *Esau marries a woman of*, Gen. 26:34; 36:2. *Dwelling-place of*, Gen. 23:17–20; Num. 13:29; Josh. 1:4; Judg. 1:26. *Their land given to the Israelites*, Ex. 3:8; Deut 7:1; Josh. 1:4. *Conquered by Joshua*, Josh. 9:1, 2; chapters 10–12; 24:11. *Intermarry with Israelites*, Judg. 3:5–7; Ezra 9:1. *Solomon marries woman of*, 1 Kin. 11:1; Neh. 13:26. *Pay tribute to Solomon*, 1 Kin. 9:20, 21. *Retain their own kings*, 1 Kin. 10:29; 2 Kin. 7:6; 2 Chr. 1:17. *Officers from, in David's army*, 1 Sam. 26:6; 2 Sam. 11:3; 23:39.

her towns: but the [g]Cā′năan-ītes would[C] dwell in that land.

28 And it came to pass, when Ĭş′ra-el was strong, that they put the [g]Cā′năan-ītes to [4,h]tribute,[C] and did not utterly drive them out.

29 Neither did [i]Ē′phră-ĭm drive out the [g]Cā′năan-ītes that dwelt in [j]Ḡē′zēr; but the Cā′năan-ītes dwelt in Ḡē′zēr among them.

30 Neither did [k]Zĕb′u-lŭn drive out the inhabitants of Kĭt′ron, nor the inhabitants of [l]Nā′ha-lŏl; but the [g]Cā′năan-ītes dwelt among them, and became [h]tributaries.[C]

31 Neither did [m]Ăsh′ēr drive out the inhabitants of [n]Ăc′chō, nor the inhabitants of [o]Zī′dŏn, nor of Äh′lăb, nor of [p]Ăch′zĭb, nor of Hĕl′bah, nor of [q]Ā′phĭk, nor of [r]Rē′hŏb:

32 But the Ăsh′ēr-ītes dwelt among the [g]Cā′năan-ītes, the inhabitants of the land: for they did not drive them out.

33 Neither did [s]Năph′ta-lī drive out the inhabitants of [t]Bĕth–shē′mesh, nor the inhabitants of [u]Bĕth–ā′nath; but he dwelt among the [g]Cā′năan-ītes, the inhabitants of the land: nevertheless the inhabitants of Bĕth–shē′mesh and of Bĕth–ā′nath became [h]tributaries[C] unto them.

34 And the [v]Ăm′ôr-ītes forced the children of [w]Dăn into the mountain: for they would not suffer[C] them to come down to the valley:

35 But the [v]Ăm′ôr-ītes would dwell in mount Hē′rēş in [x]Ăij′a-lŏn, and in Shā-ăl′bim: yet the hand of the [a,i]house of Jō′şeph prevailed, so that they became [h]tributaries.[C]

36 And the [5]coast[C] of the [v]Ăm′ôr-ītes *was* from the going[C] up to [y]Ā-krăb′bim, from the rock, and upward.

g *Canaanites, not expelled from the land,* Ex. 23:28.
**28**
h *Tribute,* Ezra 4:13.
4 R. V. taskwork,
**29**
i *Ephraim, tribe of,* Gen. 41:52.
j *Gezer,* Josh. 10:33.
**30**
k *Zebulun, tribe of,* Gen. 49:13.
l Or, *Nahallal,* Josh. 19:15; 21:35.
**31**
m *Asher, tribe of,* Num. 1:40.
n Or, *Ptolemais,* Acts 21:7.
o *Zidon,* Ezek. 28:21.
p Josh. 19:29.
q Or, *Aphek,* Josh. 13:4; 19:30.
r *Rehob,* Josh. 19:30.
**33**
s *Naphtali, tribe of,* Num. 1:42.
t Josh. 19:38.
u Josh. 19:38.
**34**
v *Amorites,* Gen. 14:13.
w *Dan, tribe of,* Gen. 30:6.
**35**
x *Aijalon,* Josh. 21:24.
**36**
y *Akrabbim,* Num 34:4.
5 R. V. border

## CHAPTER 2

*An angel rebukes the people at Bochim. 6 The wickedness of the next generation after Joshua. 14 God's dealings with them in judgment and mercy. 20 The nations left to prove Israel.*

AND[T] an [a]angel of the LORD came up from Ḡĭl′găl to Bō′chim, and said, I made [b]you to go up out of Ē′ġўpt, and have brought you unto the [c]land which I sware unto your fathers; and I said, [d]I will never break my [e]covenant[C] with you.[s]

2 And ye shall make no [f]league with the [g]inhabitants of this land; ye shall throw[C] down their altars: but ye have [h]not obeyed my voice: why have ye done this?

3 Wherefore I also said, I will not drive [i]them out from before you; but they shall be *as thorns* in your sides, and their [j]gods shall be a snare[C] unto you.

4 And it came to pass, when the [a]angel of the LORD spake these words unto all the children of [b]Ĭş′ra-el, that the people [k]lifted up their voice, and [l]wept.[s]

5 And they called the name of that place Bō′chim: and they sacrificed there unto the LORD.

6 ¶ And when [m]Jŏsh′u-ȧ had let the people go, the children of Ĭş′ra-el went every man unto his inheritance to possess the [c]land.

7 And the [n]people [o]served the LORD all the days of Jŏsh′u-ȧ, and all the days of the elders that outlived Jŏsh′u-ȧ, who had seen all the great [p]works of the LORD, that he did for Ĭş′ra-el.

8 And [m]Jŏsh′u-ȧ the son of Nŭn, the servant of the LORD, [q]died, *being* an [r]hundred and ten years old.

9 And they buried him in the border of his inheritance in [s]Tĭm′nath–hē′rēş, in the mount[C] of [t]Ē′phră-ĭm, on the north [1]side of the hill [u]Gā′ăsh.

10 And also all that generation were gathered[C] unto their fathers:

**1**
a *Angel,* Ex. 14:19
b *Israel, under the judges,* Ex. 4:22
c *Canaan, promised to Abraham and his seed,* Gen. 37:1.
d *God, faithfulness of,* Gen. 2:2.
e *Covenant, of God with men,* Deut. 29:1.
**2**
f *Alliances,* Josh. 9:15.
g *Evil Company, forbidden,* Prov. 13:20.
h *Disobedience to God,* Eph. 5:6.
**3**
i *Canaanites, not expelled,* Ex. 23:28.
j *Idolatry,* 1 Sam. 15:23.
**4**
k *Repentance,* Mark 1:4.
l *Weeping,* Ezra 3:13.
**6**
m *Joshua,* Josh. 1:1.
**7**
n *Israel, religious fidelity of, during the life of Joshua,* Ex. 4:22.
o *Obedience,* Heb. 5:8.
p *Miracles,* Luke 23:8.
**B.C. 1444?**
**8**
q *Death,* Num. 23:10.
r *Old Age,* Isa. 46:4.
**B.C. 1426?**
**9**
s Or, *Timnath-serah,* Josh. 19:50.
t *Ephraim,* Josh. 17:15.
u *Gaash,* Josh. 24:30.
1 R. V. of the mountain of

**B.C. 1426?**
See footnote, *Time*, Rev. 10:6.

**10**
v *Ingratitude, to God*, Rom. 1:21.

**11**
w *Backsliding, of Israel*, Hos. 11:7.
x *Idolatry*, 1 Sam. 15:23.
y *Baal*, 2 Kin. 17:16.

**12**
z *Backsliders*, Jer. 3:22.

a *God, providence of*, Gen. 2:2.
b *Idolatry*, 1 Sam. 15:23.
c *Anger of God*, 2 Kin. 13:3.

**13**
d *Backsliding*, Hos. 11:7.
e *Baal*, 2 Kin. 17:16.
f *Ashtoreth*, 1 Kin. 11:5.

**14**
g *Nation, chastisement of*, Isa. 2:4.

**16**
h Acts 13:20.
i *Oppression, national, relieved*, Eccl. 5:8.
j *Israel, under the Judges*, Ex. 4:22.

**17**
k *Whoredom*, Deut. 31:16.
l *Instability, instances of*, Jas. 1:8.

and there arose another [b]generation after them, which [v]knew not the LORD, nor yet the [p]works which he had done for Ĭş'ra-el.[Q]

11 ¶ And the children of Ĭş'ra-el did evil in the sight of the LORD, and [w, x]served [y]Bā'al-ĭm:

12 [S]And [z]they [w]forsook the LORD God of their fathers, which [a]brought them out of the land of Ē'ġȳpt, and [b]followed other gods, of the gods of the people that *were* round about them, and bowed[C] themselves unto them, and provoked the LORD to [c]anger.

13 And they [d]forsook the LORD, and served [e]Bā'al and [f]Ăsh'ta-rŏth.

14 And the [c]anger of the LORD was hot against Ĭş'ra-el, and he delivered [g]them into the hands of spoilers that spoiled them, and he sold them into the hands of their enemies round about, so that they could not any longer stand before their enemies.[S] [T]

15 Whithersoever [g]they went out, the hand[C] of the LORD was against them for evil, as the LORD had said, and as the LORD had sworn unto them: and they were greatly distressed.

16 ¶ [h]Nevertheless the LORD raised up *judges, which [i]delivered [j]them out of the hand of those that spoiled[C] them.[Q]

17 And yet [j]they would not hearken unto their *judges, but they [d]went a[C] [k]whoring after other gods, and [b]bowed themselves unto them: they [d, l]turned quickly out of the way which their fathers walked in, obeying the commandments of the LORD; *but* they did not so.

18 And when the [m]LORD raised them up judges, then the LORD was with the *judge, and [i]delivered them out of the hand of their enemies all the days of the judge: for it [n, o]repented the LORD because of their groanings by reason of them that oppressed them and vexed[C] them.

19 And it came to pass, when the *judge was dead, *that* they [l]returned, and corrupted[C] *themselves* more than their fathers, in following other gods to [b]serve them, and to bow down unto them; they ceased not from their own doings, nor from their [p]stubborn way.

20 ¶ And the [c]anger of the LORD was hot against [j]Ĭş'ra-el; and he said, Because that this people hath [q]transgressed my covenant which I commanded their fathers, and have not hearkened unto my voice;[S]

21 I also will not henceforth drive out any from before them of the nations which Jŏsh'u-ȧ left when he died:

22 [r]That through them I may prove[C] Ĭş'ra-el, whether they will keep the way of the LORD to walk therein, as their fathers did [s]keep *it*, or not.

23 Therefore the [t]LORD left those nations, without driving them out hastily; neither delivered he them into the hand of Jŏsh'u-ȧ.

**18**
m *God, mercy of*, Gen. 2:2.
n *Repentance, attributed to God*, Mark 1:4.
o *Anthropomorphisms*, Gen. 11:5.

**19**
p *Self-will*, Gen. 49:6.

**20**
q *Disobedience to God*, Eph. 5:6.

**22**
r *Adversity, design of*, Psa. 10:6.
s *Obedience*, Heb. 5:8.

**23**
t *God, providence of*, Gen. 2:2.

*** JUDGE.** *Must be, righteous*, Ex. 18:21, 22; Lev. 19:15; Deut. 16:18–20; 1 Kin. 3:9; Psa. 58:1, 2; 72:1, 2, 4; *intelligent*, Deut. 1:12, 13; Isa. 28:6. *Must judge righteously*, Deut. 1:16, 17. *Jurisdiction of*, 1 Sam. 2:25. *Inferior and superior*, Deut. 17:8–11. *Held circuit courts*, 1 Sam. 7:16. *Rules for guidance of*, Ex. 18:22; Deut. 19:16–19; 25:1–3; 2 Chr. 19:5–10; Prov. 24:23; Ezek. 44:24; John 7:24.

*Kings and other rulers as*, 2 Sam. 8:15; 15:2; 1 Kin. 3:16–28; 10:9; 2 Kin. 8:1–6· Psa. 72:1–4; Matt. 27:11–26; Acts 23:34, 35; 24; 25:11, 12. *Priests and Levites as*, Deut. 17:9; 1 Chr. 23:4; 2 Chr. 19:8; Ezek. 44:23, 24; Matt. 26:57–62. *Women as, Deborah*, Judg. 4:4.

*Persian government provided*, Ezra 7:25.

**Corrupt,** 1 Sam. 8:3; Psa. 82:2–4; Isa. 5:22, 23; Dan. 9:12; Mic. 7:3; Zeph. 3:3.

INSTANCES OF CORRUPT: *Eli's sons*, 1 Sam. 2:12–17, 22–25. *Samuel's sons*, 1 Sam. 8:1–5. *The judges of Jezreel*, 1 Kin. 21:8–13. *Pilate*, Matt. 27:24, 26; Mark 15:15, 19–24. *Felix*, Acts 24:26, 27.

See footnotes: GOD, *Judge*, Gen. 2:2; COURT, Ex. 18:26.

**Of Israel,** executives and leaders of the nation. *During the time when the land was ruled by judges*, Judg. 2:16–19; Acts13:20.

*Othniel*, Judg. 3:9–11. *Ehud*, Judg. 3:15–30. *Shamgar*, Judg. 3:31. *Deborah*, Judg. 4:4, 5. *Gideon*, Judg. 6:11–40; 7:8. *Abimelech*, Judg. 9:1–54. *Tola*, Judg. 10:1–2. *Jair*, Judg. 10:3–5. *Jephthah*, Judg. 12:7. *Ibzan*. Judg. 12:8–10. *Elon*, Judg. 12:11, 12. *Abdon*, Judg. 12:13, 14. *Samson*, Judg. 15:20; 16:31.

*Eli*, 1 Sam. 4:18. *Samuel*, 1 Sam. 7:6, 15–17. *The sons of Samuel*, 1 Sam. 8:1–5.

## CHAPTER 3

*The nations which were left to prove Israel. 5 The Israelites dwelling among them are led into idolatry. 8 Othniel delivers them from Chushan-rishathaim; 12 Ehud from Egion; 31 and Shamgar from the Philistines.*

NOW these *are* the nations
which the [a]LORD left, to
prove[c] [b]Ĭṣ′ra-el by them, *even*
as many *of Is′ra-el* as had not
known[c] all the *wars of Cā′-
năan;
2 Only that the generations of
the children of Ĭṣ′ra-el might
know,[c] to teach them *war,[c] at
the least such as before knew
nothing thereof;
3 *Namely,* five lords of the [c]Phĭ-
lĭs′tīneṣ, and all the [d]Cā′năan-
ītes, and the [e]Sĭ-dō′nĭ-anṣ, and
the [f]Hī′vītes that dwelt in mount
[g]Lĕb′a-non, from mount Bā′al–
hĕr′mon unto the entering in of
Hā′math.
4 And they were to prove[c] Ĭṣ′-
ra-el by them, to know whether
they would hearken unto the
commandments of the LORD,
which he commanded their
fathers by the hand of Mō′ṣeṣ.
5 ¶ And the children of Ĭṣ′ra-el
[h]dwelt among the [d]Cā′năan-ītes,
[i]Hĭt′tītes, and [j]Ăm′ôr-ītes, and
[k]Pĕr′ĭz-zītes, and [f]Hī′vītes, and
[l]Jĕb′u-sītes:
6 And [b,h]they [m]took their
daughters to be their wives, and
gave their daughters to their
sons, and [n]served their gods.
7 And the children of Ĭṣ′ra-el
did evil in the sight of the LORD,
and forgat the LORD their God,
and [n]served Bā′al-ĭm and the
[1]groves.[c]
8 Therefore the [o]anger of the
LORD was hot against [b]Ĭṣ′ra-el,
and he sold them into the hand
of Chū′shan–rĭsh-a-thā′im king
of [p]Mĕs-o-pŏ-tā′mĭ-ȧ: and the
children of Ĭṣ′ra-el served
Chū′shan–rĭsh-a-thā′im eight
years.[s]
9 And when the children of
[q]Ĭṣ′ra-el [r,s]cried unto the LORD,
the [a,t]LORD raised up a deliverer
to the children of Ĭṣ′ra-el, who
delivered them, *even* [u]Ŏth′nĭ-el
the son of [v]Kē′năz, Cā′leb's
younger brother.
10 And the [w]Spirit of the LORD
came upon [u]him, and he [x]judged
Ĭṣ′ra-el, and went out to war:
and the [a]LORD delivered Chū′-
shan–rĭsh-a-thā′im king of Mĕs-
o-pŏ-tā′mĭ-ȧ into his hand; and
his hand prevailed against Chū′-
shan–rĭsh-a-thā′im.[T]
11 And the [y]land had rest forty
years. And [u,x]Ŏth′nĭ-el the son
of Kē′năz died.
12 ¶ And the children of Ĭṣ′-
ra-el did evil again in the sight
of the LORD: and the LORD
strengthened Ĕg′lŏn the king
of [z]Mō′ab against [a]Ĭṣ′ra-el, because they had done evil in the
sight of the LORD.
13 And he [b]gathered unto him
the children of [c]Ăm′mŏn and
[d]Ăm′a-lek, and went and smote[c]
[a]Ĭṣ′ra-el, and possessed[c] the [e]city
of palm trees.
14 So the children of [a]Ĭṣ′ra-el

**1**
a *God, providence of,* Gen. 2:2.
b *Israel, under the judges,* vs. 1-7; Ex. 4:22.

**3**
c *Philistines,* Gen. 26:14.
d *Canaanites,* Ex. 23:28.
e Or, *Zidon,* Ezek. 28:21.
f *Hivites,* Gen. 10:17.
g *Lebanon,* Deut. 1:7.

**5**
h *Fellowship, with the wicked,* 1 Cor. 1:9.
i *Hittites,* Judg. 1:26.
j *Amorites,* Gen. 14:13.
k *Perizzites,* Gen. 15:20.
l *Jebusites,* Deut. 7:1.

**6**
m *Miscegenation, instances of,* Josh. 23:12.
n *Idolatry,* 1 Sam. 15:23.

v.8–1473 BC
See footnote, *Time,* Rev. 10:6.

**7**
1 R. V. Asheroth.

**8**
o *Anger of God,* 2 Kin. 13:3.
p *Mesopotamia,* Gen. 24:10.

**9**
q *Nation, in adversity, prayer of,* Isa. 2:4.
r *Adversity, prayer in,* Psa. 10:6.
s *Prayer, instances of, answered,* Acts 6:4.
t *God, preserver,* Gen. 2:2.
u *Othniel,* Josh. 15:17.
v *Kenaz,* Judg. 1:13.

**10**
w *Holy Spirit, inspiration of,* Acts 1:2.
x *Judges,* Judg. 2:16.

v.10–1465 BC

**11**
y *Nation, peace of,* Isa. 2:4.

**12**
z *Moabites,* Gen. 19:37.

a *Nation, punishment of,* Isa. 2:4.

v.12–1425 BC

**13**
b *Alliances,* Josh. 9:15.
c *Ammonites,* Deut. 2:20.
d *Amalekites,* Num. 13:29.
e *Jericho,* Num. 22:1.

---

* **WAR.** *Civil,* Josh. 22:12, 33; Judg. 12:1–6; 20; 2 Sam. 2:12–31; 3:1; 17:24–26; 18:1–8; 20; 1 Kin. 14:30; 15:6; 16:21; Isa. 19:2. *Averted,* Josh. 22:11–34.

*Enemy harangued by general of opposing side,* 2 Kin. 18:19–36; 2 Chr. 13:4–12.

*Of extermination,* Num. 31.7–17; Deut. 2:33, 34; 3:6; 20:13–18; Josh. 6:21, 24; 8:24, 25; 10:2–40; 11:11–23; 1 Sam. 15:3–9; 27:8–11.

*God in,* Deut. 7:17–24; 20:1, 4; 31:6–8, 23; Josh. 10:14, 42; Judg. 1:2; 6:16; 7:9; 1 Sam. 17:45–47; 19:5; 30:7, 8; 2 Sam. 5:22–24; 22:18; Psa. 18:34; 76:3; Jer. 46:15; Amos 5:8, 9; Zech. 10:5. *God uses, as a judgment,* Lev. 26:17, 31–39; Deut. 28:25–68; 32:30; Judg. 2:14; 2 Kin. 15:37; 1 Chr. 5:22, 26; 14:10–15; 21:12; 2 Chr. 12:1–12; 15:6; 24:23, 24; 33:11; 36; Job 19:29; Psa. 44:9–16; Isa. 5:25–30; 9:8–12; 13:3, 4; 19:2; 34:2–6; Jer. 12:7, 12; 46:15–17, 21; 47:6, 7; 50:25; Ezek. 23:22–25; Amos 4:11; Zeph. 1:7–18; Zech. 8:10; 14:2. *God, sends panic in,* Ex. 15:14–16; 2 Kin. 7:6, 7; *threatens defeat in,* 2 Chr. 18:12–16; Isa. 30:15–17; Ezek. 21:9–17; *inflicts defeat in,* Josh. 7:4, 5, 12, 13; 2 Chr. 12:5–8; 24:23, 24; Psa. 78:66; Isa. 5:25; Jer. 46:15, 16.

*Repugnant to the righteous,* Psa. 120:7.

*Repugnant to God,* 1 Chr. 22:8, 9; 28:3; Psa. 68:30.

*Councils of,* 2 Sam. 17:1–15; 1 Chr. 13:1. *Wisdom required in,* Prov. 24:6; Eccl. 9:14–18; Luke 14:31, 32. *Chronicles of,* Num. 21:14.

*Evils of,* Psa. 79:1–3; Isa. 3:25, 26; 5:29, 30; 6:11, 12; 9:5, 19–21; 13:15, 16; 15; 16:9, 10; 18:6; 19:2–16; Jer. 4:19–31; 5:16, 17; 6:24–26; 7:33, 34; 8:16, 17; 9:10–21; 13:14; 14:18; 15:8, 9; 19:7–9; 25:33; 46:3–12; 47:3; 48:28, 33; 51:30–58; Hos. 10:14; 13:16; Joel 2:2–10; Amos 1:13; 6:9, 10; 8:3; Nah. 2:10; 3:3, 10; Zech. 14:2; Luke 21:20–26. *Slain in, neglected,* Isa 14:19.

*To cease,* Psa. 46:9; Isa. 2:4; Mic. 4:3.

*Prophecies of,* Matt. 24:6; Mark 13:7; Luke 21:9.

See footnote, ARMIES, Deut. 11:4.

**In heaven:** SYMBOLICAL, Rev. 12:7.

v.14–1425 BC
See footnote, *Time*, Rev. 10:6.

14
*f* *Moabites*, Gen. 19:37.

15
*g* *Prayer, in adversity*, Acts 6:4.
*h* *Adversity, prayer in*, Psa. 10:6.
*i* *God, providence of*, Gen. 2:2.
*j* *Benjamin, tribe of*, Num. 1:37.
*k* Judg. 20:16.

v.15–1407 BC

19
*l* *Gilgal*, Josh. 4:19.
*m* *Deception, instances of*, Josh. 9:4.
*n* *Falsehood, instances of*, Job 21:34.

20
*o* *Summer*, Isa. 28:4.
*p* *House, architecture of*, Esth. 8:1.
*q* *Hypocrisy, instances of*, Jas. 3:17.
2 Heb. cool upper chamber.

21
*r* *Confidence, betrayed*, Mic. 7:5.
*s* *Homicide, felonious*, Deut. 5:17.
*t* *Assassination*, Deut. 27:24.
*u* *Regicide*, 2 Sam. 1:10.

22
3 R. V. it came out behind.

23
*v* Neh. 3:3, 13, 14.

served Ĕg′lŏn the king of [f]Mō′ab
eighteen years.
15 But when the children of
[a]Ĭṣ′ra-el [g,h]cried unto the LORD,
the [i]LORD raised them up a
deliverer, Ē′hŭd the son of †Gē′-
rȧ, a [j]Bĕn′ja-mīte, a man [k]left-
handed: and by him the children
of Ĭṣ′ra-el sent a present unto
Ĕg′lŏn the king of Mō′ab.
16 But Ē′hŭd made him a dagger which had two edges, of a
cubit[c] length; and he did gird[c] it
under his raiment upon his right
thigh.
17 And he brought the present
unto Ĕg′lŏn king of Mō′ab: and
Ĕg′lŏn *was* a very fat man.
18 And when he had made an
end to offer the present, he sent
away the people that bare the
present.
19 But he himself turned[c] again
from the quarries that *were* by
[l]Gĭl′găl, and [m]said, [n]I have a
secret errand unto thee, O king:
who said, Keep silence. And all
that stood by him went out from
him.
20 And Ē′hŭd came unto him;
and he was sitting in a [2,o]sum-
mer [p]parlour, which he had for
himself alone. And Ē′hŭd [q]said,
[n]I have a message from God unto
thee. And he arose out of *his* seat.
21 [r]And Ē′hŭd put forth his
left hand, and took the dagger from his right thigh, and
[s,t,u]thrust it into his belly:
22 And the haft[c] also went in
after the blade; and the fat
closed upon the blade, so that he
could not draw the dagger out of
his belly; and [3]the dirt came out.
23 Then Ē′hŭd went forth
through the [p]porch, and shut the
doors of the parlour upon him,
and [v]locked them.
24 When he was gone out, his
servants came; and when they
saw that, behold, the doors of
the [p]parlour *were* locked, they
said, Surely he covereth[c] his feet
in his [o]summer chamber.
25 And they tarried till they
were ashamed[c]: and, behold, he
opened not the doors of the [p]par-
lour; therefore they took a ‡key,
and opened *them*: and, behold,
their lord *was* fallen down dead
on the earth.
26 And Ē′hŭd escaped while
they tarried, and passed beyond
the quarries, and escaped unto
Sē′i-răth.
27 And it came to pass, when
he was come, that he blew a
[w]trumpet in the mountain[c] of
[x]Ē′phră-ĭm, and the [y]children
of Ĭṣ′ra-el went down with him
from the mount, and he before
them.
28 And he said unto them,
Follow after me: for the LORD
hath delivered your enemies the
[f]Mō′ab-ītes into your hand.
And they went down after him
and took the fords of [z]Jŏr′dan
[4]toward Mō′ab, and suffered[c] not
a man to pass over.
29 And they slew of [a]Mō′ab at
that time about ten thousand
men, all lusty,[c] and all men of
valour[c]; and there escaped not a
man.
30 So [a]Mō′ab was subdued that
day under the hand of Ĭṣ′ra-el.
And the [b]land had rest fourscore
years.
31 ¶ And after him was [c]Shăm′-
găr the son of Ā′năth, which
slew of the [d]Phĭ-lĭs′tĭneṣ six hundred men with an ox goad: and
he also delivered [e]Ĭṣ′-ra-el.

## CHAPTER 4

*Deborah and Barak deliver Israel from Jabin and Sisera. 18 Jael kills Sisera.*

AND the children of Ĭṣ′ra-el
again [a]did evil in the sight of
the LORD, when Ē′hŭd was dead.

See footnote, *Time*, Rev. 10:6.

27
*w* *Trumpet*, Josh. 6:4.
*x* *Ephraim*, Josh. 17:15.
*y* *Armies, rendezvous of*, Deut. 11:4.

28
*z* *Jordan, fords of*, Gen. 32:10.
4 R. V. against the Moabites,

29
*a* *Moabites*, Gen. 19:37.

30
*b* *Nation, instances of national peace*, Isa. 2:4.

31
*c* Judg. 5:6.
*d* *Philistines*, Gen. 26:14.
*e* *Israel, under the judges*, Ex. 4:22.

v.1–1327 BC
See footnote, *Time*, Rev. 10:6.

1
*a* *Disobedience to God*, Eph. 5:6.

† **GERA.** Possibly the name of three men; more probably of one. *The son of Bela*, Gen. 46:21; Judg. 3:15; 2 Sam. 16:5; 19:16, 18; 1 Kin. 2:8; 1 Chr. 8:3, 5, 7.

‡ **KEY**, Judg. 3:25. *A symbol of authority*, Isa. 22:22; Matt. 16:19; Rev. 1:18; 3:7; 9:1; 20:1. **Figurative**, Luke 11:52.

v.2–1327 BC
See footnote, *Time*, Rev. 10:6.

**2**
b *Divine Chastisement*, Job 33:19.
c See Josh. 11:1.
d *Canaanites*, Ex. 23:28.
e *Hazor*, Josh. 11:1.
f *Captain*, Num. 31:48.

**3**
g *Israel, under the judges*, Ex. 4:22.
h *Adversity, prayer in*, Psa. 10:6.
i *Prayer, instances of*, Acts 6:4.

**4**
j Judg. 5.
k *Women, as prophetesses*, v. 14; Prov. 31:10.
l *Women, as rulers*, Prov. 31:10.
m *Judges of Israel*, Judg. 2:16.

**5**
n *Palm Tree*, Song 7:7.
o *Ramah*, 1 Sam. 1:19.
p *Bethel*, Josh. 18:13.
q *Ephraim*, Josh. 17:15.
r *Court, civil*, Ex. 18:26.

**6**
s *Courage*, vs. 6–16; Deut. 31:7.
t Judg. 5; Heb. 11:32.
u *Kedesh*, Josh. 21:32.
v *Tabor*, Judg. 8:18.
w *Naphtali, tribe of*, Num. 1:42.
x *Zebulun, tribe of*, Gen. 49:13.

v.4–1307 BC

**7**
y *God, providence of*, Gen. 2:2.

2 And the LORD [b]sold[C] them into the hand of [c]Jā'bin king of [d]Cā'năan, that reigned in [e]Hā'zôr; the [f]captain of whose host *was* *Sĭs'e-rȧ, which dwelt in Hȧ-rō'sheth of the Ġĕn'tīleṣ.[C]

3 And the children of [g]Ĭṣ'ra-el [h,i]cried unto the LORD: for he had nine hundred chariots of iron; and twenty years he mightily oppressed the children of Ĭṣ'ra-el.

4 ¶ And [j,k]Dĕb'o-rah, a †prophetess, the wife of Lăp'i-dŏth, [l]she [m]judged Ĭṣ'ra-el at that time.

5 And she dwelt under the [n]palm tree of Dĕb'o-rah between [o]Rā'mah and [p]Bĕth'–el in mount [q]Ē'phră-ĭm: and the children of Ĭṣ'ra-el came up to [r]her for judgment.

6 And [j,s]she sent and called [t]Bā'răk the son of Ȧ-bĭn'o-ăm out of [u]Kē'desh–năph'ta-lī, and said unto him, Hath not the LORD God of Ĭṣ'ra-el commanded, *saying*, Go and draw toward mount [v]Tā'bôr, and take with thee ten thousand men of the children of [w]Năph'ta-lī and of the children of [x]Zĕb'u-lŭn?

7 And I will draw unto thee to the river ‡Kī'shŏn *Sĭs'e-rȧ, the [f]captain of [c]Jā'bin's army, with his chariots and his multitude; and I will [y]deliver[C] him into thine hand.

8 And [t]Bā'răk said unto her, If thou wilt go with me, then I will go: but if thou wilt not go with me, *then* I will not go.

9 And [j]she said, [s]I will surely go with thee: notwithstanding the journey that thou takest shall not be for thine honour; for [†,k]the LORD shall sell Sĭs'e-rȧ into the hand of a woman. And Dĕb'o-rah arose, and went with [t]Bā'răk to Kē'desh.

10[Q] And [t]Bā'răk called [x]Zĕb'u-lŭn and [w]Năph'ta-lī to [u]Kē'desh; and he went up[C] with ten thousand men at his feet: and Dĕb'o-rah went up with him.

11 Now [z]Hē'bēr the Kĕn'īte, *which was* of the children of Hō'băb the [1]father in law of Mō'ṣeṣ, had severed[C] himself from the [a]Kĕn'ītes, and pitched his tent [2]unto the plain of [b]Zā-a-nā'im, which *is* by Kē'desh.

12 And they shewed *Sĭs'e-rȧ that [c]Bā'răk the son of Ȧ-bĭn'o-ăm was gone up[C] to mount [d]Tā'bôr.

13 And *Sĭs'e-rȧ gathered together all his chariots, *even* nine hundred chariots of iron, and all the people that *were* with him, from Hȧ-rō'sheth of the Ġĕn'tīleṣ[C] unto the river of ‡Kī'shŏn.

14 And [e]Dĕb'o-rah said unto [c]Bā'răk, Up; for [f]this *is* the day in which the LORD hath delivered Sĭs'e-rȧ into thine hand: is not the LORD gone out before thee? So Bā'răk went down from mount [d]Tā'bôr, and ten thousand men after him.

15 And [g]the LORD discomfited[C] *Sĭs'e-rȧ, and all *his* chariots, and all *his* host, with the edge of the sword before [c]Bā'răk; so that Sĭs'e-rȧ lighted[C] down off *his* chariot, and fled away on his feet.

16 But [c]Bā'răk pursued after the chariots, and after the host,[C] unto Hȧ-rō'sheth of the Ġĕn'tīleṣ:[C] and all the host of *Sĭs'e-rȧ fell upon the edge of the sword; *and* there was not a man left.

17 Howbeit[C] *Sĭs'e-rȧ fled away on his feet to the tent of [h]Jā'el the wife of Hē'bēr the [a]Kĕn'īte: for *there was* peace between [i]Jā'-

v.9–1307 BC
See footnote, *Time*, Rev. 10:6.

**11**
z Judg. 5:24.
a *Kenites*, 1 Sam. 15:6.
b Or, *Zaanannim*, Josh. 19:33.
1 R. V. brother in law
2 R. V. as far as the oak in Zaanannim,

**12**
c Judg. 5; Heb. 11:32.
d *Tabor*, Judg. 8:18.

**14**
e Judg. 5.
f *Faith, instances of*, Mark 11:22.

**15**
g *War, God in*, Judg. 3:2.

**17**
h Judg. 5:6, 24.
i See Josh. 11:1.

* **SISERA.** *Captain of a Canaanitish army, defeated by Barak, slain by Jael*, Judg. 4: 5:20–31; 1 Sam. 12:9; Psa. 83:9.

† **PROPHETESS,** Ezek. 13:17; Joel 2:28, 29; Acts 2:16–18. *Miriam*, Ex. 15:20. *Deborah*, Judg. 4:4, 5. *Huldah*, 2 Kin. 22:14. *Noadiah, a false prophetess*, Neh. 6:14. *Elisabeth*, Luke 1:41–45. *Mary*, Luke 1:46–55. *Anna*, Luke 2:36–38. *Daughters of Philip*, Acts 21:9. See footnote, WOMEN, Prov. 31:10.

‡ **KISHON** (*tortuous, winding stream*), called also KISON, a river of Palestine emptying into the Mediterranean near the northern base of Mount Carmel. *Sisera defeated at, and his army destroyed in*, Judg. 4:7, 13; 5:21; Psa. 83:9. *Prophets of Baal destroyed by Elijah at*, 1 Kin. 18:40.

v.17–1307 BC
See footnote, *Time*, Rev. 10:6.

*j* *Hazor*, Josh. 11:1.

18
*k* *Hypocrisy, instances of*, Jas. 3:17.
3 R. V. rug.

19
*l* *Milk*, Job 10:10.

20
*m* *Falsehood*, Job 21:34.

21
*n* *Nail*, Isa. 41:7.

23
*o* *God, providence of*, Gen. 2:2.
*p* *Canaanites, defeated by Israelites*, Ex. 23:28.

1
*a* *Armies, triumphs of, celebrated*, vs. 1–31; Deut. 11:4.
*b* *Patriotism*, vs. 1–31; *instances of*, Psa. 137:1.
*c* *Music*, 2 Chr. 5:13.
*d* *Victories, celebrated in song*, vs. 1–31; Deut. 28:7.
*e* Judg. 4:4–16.
*f* *Judges, of Israel*, Judg. 2:16.
*g* *Women, as poets*, Prov. 31:10.
*h* *Women, patriotic*, Prov. 31:10.
*i* Judg. 4:6–16.

bin the king of [j]Hā'zôr and the house of Hē'bēr the Kĕn'īte.[Q]

18 And [h]Jā'el went out to meet *Sĭs'e-rȧ, and [k]said unto him, Turn in[C], my lord, turn in to me; fear not. And when he had turned in unto her into the tent, she covered[C] him with a [3]mantle.

19 And *he said unto her, Give me, I pray thee, a little water to drink; for I am thirsty. And she opened a bottle[C] of [l]milk, and gave him drink, and covered him.

20 Again he said unto her, Stand in the door of the tent, and it shall be, when any man doth come and enquire of thee, and say, Is there any man here? that [m]thou shalt say, No.

21 Then [h]Jā'el Hē'bēr's wife took a nail of the tent, and took an hammer in her hand, and went softly unto him, and smote the [n]nail into his temples, and fastened it into the ground: for he was fast asleep and weary. So he died.

22 And, behold, as [c]Bā'răk pursued *Sĭs'e-rȧ, [h]Jā'el came out to meet him, and said unto him, Come, and I will shew thee the man whom thou seekest. And when he came into her *tent*, behold, Sĭs'e-rȧ lay dead, and the nail *was* in his temples.

23 So [o]God subdued on that day [i]Jā'bin the king of [p]Cā'năan before the children of Ĭş'ra-el.

24 And the hand of the children of Ĭş'ra-el prospered, and prevailed against [i]Jā'bin the king of [p]Cā'năan, until they had destroyed Jā'bin king of Cā'năan.

## CHAPTER 5

*The song of Deborah and Barak.*

THEN *[,a,b,c,d]sang [e,f,g,h]Dĕb'-o-rāh and [i]Ba'rak the son of Ā-bĭn'o-ăm on that day, saying,

2 [1,*,j,k,l]Praise ye the LORD for the avenging of Ĭş'ra-el, when the people willingly offered[C] themselves.

3 Hear, O ye kings; give ear, O ye princes; I, *even* I, will sing unto the LORD; I will sing *praise* to the LORD God of Ĭş'ra-el.

4 LORD, when thou wentest out of Sē'ïr, when thou marchedst out of the field of Ē'dom, the earth trembled, and the heavens dropped, the clouds also dropped water.[Q]

5 The mountains melted from before the LORD, *even* that Sī'-nāi from before the LORD God of Ĭş'ra-el.

6 In the days of [m]Shăm'gär the son of Ā'năth, in the days of [n]Jā'el, the highways were unoccupied, and the travellers walked through byways.

7 [2]*The inhabitants of* the villages ceased, they ceased in Ĭş'ra-el, until that I [e,h]Dĕb'o-rah arose, that I arose a mother in Ĭş'ra-el.

8 They chose new [o]gods; then *was* war in the gates: was there a shield or spear seen among forty thousand in Ĭş'ra-el?

9 My heart *is* toward[C] the governors of Ĭş'ra-el, that offered[C] themselves willingly among the people. [p]Bless ye the LORD.

10 [3]Speak, ye that ride[C] on white [q]asses, ye that sit [4]in judgment, and walk by the way.

11 [5]*They that are delivered* from the noise of [r]archers in the places of drawing water, there shall they rehearse[C] the [s]righteous acts of the LORD, *even* the righteous acts [6]*toward the inhabitants* of his villages in Ĭş'ra-el: then shall the people of the LORD go down to the gates.

12 Awake, awake, [e,h]Dĕb'o-rah: awake, awake, utter a song:

v.2–1307 BC
See footnote, *Time*, Rev. 10:6.

2
*j* *Poetry, epic*, Acts 17:28.
*k* *Praise, song of Deborah*, vs. 1–31; Psa. 150:1.
*l* *Thankfulness, to God*, Acts 24:3.
1 R. V. For that the leaders took the lead in Israel, For that the people offered themselves willingly, Bless ye the Lord.

6
*m* Judg. 3:31.
*n* Judg. 4:17–22.

7
2 R. V. The rulers ceased in Israel, they ceased, Until

8
*o* *Idolatry*, 1 Sam. 15:23.

9
*p* *Thankfulness, enjoined*, Acts 24:3.

10
*q* *Ass, domesticated*, 2 Chr. 28:15.
3 R. V. tell of it,
4 R. V. on rich carpets,

11
*r* *Archery*, Gen. 21:20.
*s* *God, righteousness of*, Gen. 2:2
5 R. V. Far from
6 R. V. of his rule in Israel.

* **WAR SONGS.** *Celebrating, the destruction of Pharaoh's army*, Ex. 15:1–21; *victory over Sihon, king of the Amorites*, Num. 21:24–30; *victory over Sisera*, Judg. 5. *David's lament over the defeat of Saul*, 2 Sam. 1:19–27. *Celebrating David's victories over his enemies and his deliverances from Saul*, 2 Sam. 22.

v.12–1307 BC
See footnote, *Time*, Rev. 10:6.

**12**
*t Captivity, figurative*, Isa. 5:13.

**13**
7 R. V. came down a remnant of the nobles and the people;
8 R. V. came down for me against the mighty.

**14**
*u Ephraim, tribe of*, Gen. 41:52.
*v Amalekites*, Num. 13:29.
*w Benjamin, tribe of*, Num. 1:37.
*x Zebulun, tribe of*, Gen. 49:13.
9 R. V. came down they whose root is in Amalek;
10 R. V. marshal's staff.

**15**
*y Issachar, tribe of*, Num. 1:28.
*z Reubenites*, Josh. 22:1.
11 R. V. Into the valley they rushed forth at his feet. By the watercourses of Reuben There were great resolves of heart.

**16**
*a Patriotism, lack of*, Psa. 137:1.
*b Lukewarmness, instances of*, Rev. 3:16.
12 R. V. At the watercourses of

**17**
*c Gilead*, Num. 26:29.
*d Dan, tribe of*, Gen. 30:6.
*e Asher, tribe of*, Num. 1:40.
13 R. V. sat still at the haven of the sea,
14 R. V. by his creeks.

**18**
*f Zebulun, tribe of*, Gen. 49:13.
*g Patriotism, instances of*, Psa. 137:1.
*h Naphtali, tribe of*, Num. 1:42.

**19**
*i Taanach*, Josh. 12:21.
*j Megiddo*, Josh. 17:11.

**20** *k Celestial Phenomena*, Luke 23:44. *l Sisera*, Judg. 4:2.

arise, [i]Bā′răk, and lead thy [t]cap-
tivity captive, thou son of Ă-bĭn′-
o-ăm.
13 Then [7]he made him that
remaineth have dominion over
the nobles among the people: the
LORD [8]made me have dominion
over the mighty.
14 Out of [u]Ē′phră-ĭm [9]*was*
*there* a root of them against
[v]Ăm′a-lĕk; after thee, [w]Bĕn′ja-
mĭn, among thy people; out of
Mā′chĭr came down governors,
and out of [x]Zĕb′u-lŭn they that
handle the [10]pen of the writer.
15 And the princes[G] of [y]Ĭs′sa-
char *were* with [e]Dĕb′o-rah; even
Ĭs′sa-char, and also [i]Bā′răk: [11]he
was sent on foot into the valley.
For the divisions of [z]Reu′ben
*there were* great thoughts of
heart.
16 [a, b]Why abodest thou among
the sheepfolds, to hear the bleat-
ings of the flocks? [12]For the
divisions of Reu′ben *there were*
great searchings of heart.
17 [a, b, c]Gĭl′e-ăd abode beyond
Jôr′dan: and why did [d]Dăn remain in ships? [e]Ăsh′ēr [13]con-
tinued on the sea shore, and
abode [14]in his breaches.[G]
18 [f, g]Zĕb′u-lŭn and [h]Năph′-
ta-lī *were* a people *that* jeoparded[G]
their lives unto the death in the
high places of the field.
19 The kings came *and* fought,
then fought the kings of Cā′năan
in [i]Tā′a-năch by the waters of
[j]Mĕ-gĭd′dō; they took no gain of
money.[Q]
20 They fought from heaven;
[k]the [†]stars in their courses
fought against [l]Sĭs′e-ră.
21 The river of [m]Kī′shŏn swept
them away, that ancient river,
the river Kī′shŏn. O my
soul, [15]thou hast trodden down
strength.
22 Then were the horsehoofs
broken by the means of the
pransings, the pransings of their
mighty ones.
23 [‡]Curse ye Mē′rŏz, said the
angel of the LORD, curse ye
bitterly the inhabitants thereof;
[a, b]because they came not to the
help of the LORD, to the help of
the LORD against the mighty.[T]
24 Blessed above women shall
[n]Jā′el the wife of [o]Hē′bēr the
Kĕn′īte be, blessed shall she be
above women in the tent.[Q]
25 He asked water, *and* she
gave *him* milk; she brought forth
[p]butter in a lordly dish.
26 [n]She put her hand to the
nail, and her right hand to the
workmen's hammer; and with
the hammer she smote [l]Sĭs′e-ră,
she smote off his head, when
she had pierced and stricken
through his temples.
27 At her feet he bowed, he fell,
he lay down: at her feet he
bowed, he fell: where he bowed,
there he fell down dead.
28 The mother of [l]Sĭs′e-ră
looked out at a [q]window, and
cried through the lattice, Why is
his chariot *so* long in coming?
why tarry the wheels of his
chariots?
29 Her wise ladies answered
her, yea, she returned answer to
herself,
30 Have they not sped[G]? have
they *not* divided the prey[G]; to
every man a damsel *or* two; to

v.21–1307 BC
See footnote, *Time*, Rev. 10:6.

**21**
*m Kishon*, Judg. 4:7.
15 R. V. march on with strength.

**24**
*n* Judg. 4:17–22.
*o* Judg. 4:11, 17, 21.

**25**
*p Butter*, Gen. 18:8.

**28**
*q House, architecture of*, Esth. 8:1

† **STARS.** *Created by God*, Gen. 1:16; Job 26:13; Psa. 8:3; 136:7, 9; Amos 5:8. *Differ in splendor*, 1 Cor. 15:41.
*Worship of, forbidden*, Deut. 4:19. *Worshiped*, 2 Kin. 17:16; 21:3; 23:5; Jer. 19:13; Amos 5:26; Zeph. 1:5; Acts 7:42, 43.
*Constellations of*, Isa. 13:10; *Arcturus* [R. V. Bear], *Orion*, *Pleiades*, Job 9:9; 38:31; Amos 5:8; *serpent*, Job 26:13.
*Planets*, 2 Kin. 23:5; *the morning star*, Job 38:7; Rev. 2:28; 22:16.
*Darkening of*, Job 9:7; Eccl. 12:2; Isa. 13:10; 34:4; Joel 2:10; 3:15; Rev. 8:12. *Comets*, Jude 13. *Falling of*, Dan. 8:10; Matt. 24:29; Mark 13:25; Rev. 6:13. *Courses of*, Judg. 5:20. *Guides the wise men*, Matt. 2:2, 7, 9, 10.

**Figurative:** *Of the deliverer*, Num. 24:17. *Seven stars, of the seven churches*, Rev. 1:16, 20. *Of Jesus*, Rev. 22:16. *Crown of twelve stars*, Rev. 12:1.

‡ **CURSE.** *Denounced, against the serpent*, Gen. 3:14, 15; *against Adam and Eve*, Gen. 3:15–19; *against the ground*, Gen. 3:17, 18; *against Cain*, Gen. 4:11–16; *against Canaan*, Gen. 9:24–27; *against the disobedient*, Deut. 28:15–68; Jer. 11:3; *against Meroz*, Judg. 5:23; *against Gehazi*, 2 Kin. 5:27.
*Assumed for others*, Matt. 27:25. *Paul wishes he could assume, for Israel*, Rom. 9:3.
*Paternal*, Gen. 27:12, 13; 49:5–7.
*Of the Mosaic law*, Deut. 27:15–26; Josh. 8:30–34.

v.30–1307 BC
See footnote, *Time*, Rev. 10:6.

30
r *Embroidery*, Ezek. 26:16.

31
s *Prayer, intercessory*, Acts 6:4.
t *Righteous*, Psa. 64:10.
u *Sun*, Josh. 10:12.
v *Forty*, Jonah 3:4.

v.1–1267 BC
See footnote, *Time*, Rev. 10:6.

1
a *Israel, under the judges*, Ex. 4:22.
b *Disobedience to God*, Eph. 5:6.
c *Divine Chastisement*, Job 33:19.
d *Judgments*, Ex. 6:6.
e *Midianites*, Gen. 37:28.

2
f *Fortification*, Ezek. 17:17.

3
g *Amalekites*, Num. 13:29.

4
h 1 Chr. 7:28.

5
i *Tent*, Gen. 13:5.
1 R. V. locusts

[t]Sĭs′e-rȧ a prey of divers[c]colours,
a prey[G] of divers colours of [r]nee-
dlework, of divers colours of
needlework on both sides, *meet*[G]
for the necks of *them that take*
the spoil?
31 So let all thine enemies perish, O LORD: but [s]*let* [t]them that
love him *be* as the [u]sun when he
goeth forth in his might. And
the land had rest [v]forty years.[Q]

## CHAPTER 6

*The Israelites for their sin are oppressed by Midian. 8 A prophet rebukes them. 11 An angel sends Gideon for their deliverance. 17 Gideon asks for a sign. 21 His present is consumed with fire. 25 Gideon destroys Baal's altar, and offers a sacrifice unto the Lord. 28 The men of the city demand his death. 31 Joash defends his son, and calls him Jerubbaal. 33 Gideon's army. 36 The sign of the fleece.*

AND the children of [a]Ĭṣ′ra-el
[b]did evil in the sight of
the LORD: and the LORD [c,d]de-
livered them into the hand[c] of
[e]Mĭd′ĭ-an seven years.
2 And the hand of [e]Mĭd′ĭ-an
prevailed against [a]Ĭṣ′ra-el: *and*
because of the Mĭd′ĭ-an-ītes the
children of Ĭṣ′ra-el made them
the dens which *are* in the mountains, and *caves, and [f]strong
holds.
3 And *so* it was, when [a]Ĭṣ′ra-el
had sown, that the [e]Mĭd′ĭ-an-
ītes came up, and the [g]Ăm′a-lĕk-
ītes, and the children of the east,
even they came[c]up against them;
4 And they encamped against
them, and destroyed the increase[c]
of the earth, till thou come unto
[h]Gā′zȧ, and left no sustenance[c]
for Ĭṣ′ra-el, neither sheep, nor
ox, nor ass.
5 For they came up with their
cattle and their [i]tents, and they
came as [1]grasshoppers for multitude; *for* both they and their
camels were without number:
and they entered into the land
to destroy it.
6 And Ĭṣ′ra-el was greatly im-
poverished because of the Mĭd′-
ĭ-an-ītes; and the children of
Ĭṣ′ra-el [j]cried unto the LORD.
7 ¶ And it came to pass, when
the children of [k]Ĭṣ′ra-el cried
unto the LORD because of the
[e]Mĭd′ĭ-an-ītes,
8 That the LORD [l]sent a prophet unto the children of Ĭṣ′ra-el,
which said unto them, Thus
saith the LORD God of Ĭṣ′ra-el,
[m]I brought you up from Ē′gy̆pt,
and brought you forth out of the
house of bondage;
9 And [m]I delivered you out of
the hand of the [n]Ē-gy̆p′tianṣ,
and out of the hand of all that
oppressed you, and drave them
out from before you, and gave
you their land;
10 And I said unto you, [o]I *am*
the LORD your God; fear[c]not the
gods of the [p]Ăm′ôr-ītes, in whose
land ye dwell: but ye [b]have not
obeyed my voice.
11 ¶[T]And there came an [q]angel
of the LORD, and sat under an
oak which *was* in [r]Ŏph′rah, that
*pertained* unto [s]Jō′ăsh the Ā′bĭ-
ĕz′rīte: and his son †Gĭd′e-on
threshed[c] wheat by the [t]wine-
press, to hide *it* from the [e]Mĭd′-
ĭ-an-ītes.
12 And the [q]angel of the LORD
appeared unto †him, and said
unto him, [o]The LORD *is* with
thee, thou mighty man of [u]val-
our.[c]
13 And †Gĭd′e-on said unto
him, Oh my Lord, [v]if the LORD

v.5–1267 BC
See footnote, *Time*, Rev. 10:6.

6
j *Adversity, prayer in*, Psa. 10:6.

7
k *Nation, in adversity, prayer of*, Isa. 2:4.

v.7–1260 BC

8
l *Prophets, inspiration of*, Isa. 3:2.
m *God, providence of*, Gen. 2:2.

9
n *Egyptians*, Gen. 50:3.

10
o *God, love of*, Gen. 2:2.
p *Amorites*, Gen. 14:13.

11
q *Angel, appearances of*, Heb. 1:13.
r Judg. 8:27, 32; 9:5.
s Judg. 7:14; 8:13, 29–32.
t *Wine-press*, Isa. 5:2.

12
u *Courage*, Deut. 31:7.

13
v *Doubting*, Rom. 14:23.

---

*** CAVE.** *Used as a dwelling, by Lot*, Gen. 19:30; *by Elijah*, 1 Kin. 19:9; *by the Israelites*, Ezek. 33:27; *by saints*, Heb. 11:38. *Place of refuge*, Josh. 10:16–27; Judg. 6:2; 1 Sam. 13:6; 1 Kin. 18:4, 13; 19:9, 13. *Burial place*, Gen. 23:9–20; 25:9; 49:29–32; 50:13; John 11:38.

*Of Adullam*, 1 Sam. 22:1; 2 Sam. 23:13; 1 Chr. 11:15. *Of En-gedi*, 1 Sam. 24:1, 3–8.

**† GIDEON** (*warrior*), called also JERUBBAAL. *Son of Joash*, Judg. 6:11, 29; 7:14; 8:13. *Call of, by an angel*, Judg. 6:11, 14. *His excuses*, Judg. 6:15. *Promises of the Lord to*, Judg. 6:16. *Angel attests the call of, by miracles*, Judg. 6:21–24. *He destroys the altar of Baal, and builds one to the Lord*, Judg. 6:25–27. *His prayer tests*, Judg. 6:36–40. *Leads an army against, and defeats the Midianites*, Judg. 6:33–35; 7; 8:4–12. *Ephraimites chide, for not inviting them to join in the campaign against the Midianites*, Judg. 8:1–3. *Avenges himself upon the people of Succoth*, Judg. 8:14–17. *Israel desires to make him king; he refuses*, Judg. 8:22, 23. *Makes an ephod which becomes a snare to the Israelites*, Judg. 8:24–27. *Had seventy sons*, Judg. 8:30. *Death of*, Judg. 8:32. *Faith of*, Heb. 11:32.

v.13–1260 BC
See footnote, *Time*, Rev. 10:6.

*w Despondency*, Eccl. 2:20.
2 R. V. wondrous works

**14**
*x Call, personal*, Phil. 3:14.
*y Faith, enjoined*, Mark 11:22.

**15**
*z Excuses*, Luke 14:18.

*a Manasseh, tribe of*, Gen. 46:20.

**16**
*b War, God in*, Judg. 3:2.

**17**
*c Faith, strengthened by miracles*, vs. 36–40; Mark 11.22.
*d Miracles, convincing effects of*, Luke 23:8.

**19**
*e Goat*, Deut. 14:4.
*f Measure, dry*, Deut. 25:15.
3 R. V. meal:

**20**
*g Angel, appearances of*, Heb. 1:13.

be with us, why then is all this befallen[c] us? and where *be* all his [2]miracles[c] which our fathers told us of, saying, Did not the LORD bring us up from Ē'ġy̆pt? but [w]now the LORD hath forsaken us, and delivered us into the hands of the [e]Mĭd'ĭ-an-ītes.

14 And the LORD looked upon him, and said, [x]Go in this thy might, and thou shalt save Ĭş'ra-el from the hand of the [e]Mĭd'ĭ-an-ītes: [y]have not I sent thee?

15 And he said unto him, Oh my Lord, [v]wherewith shall I save Ĭş'ra-el? behold, [z]my family *is* poor in [a]Mȧ-năs'seh, and I *am* the least in my father's house.

16 And the LORD said unto [†]him, Surely [b]I will be with thee, and thou shalt smite[c] the Mĭd'ĭ-an-ītes as one man.

17 And he said unto him, If now I have found grace in thy sight, then [c]shew me a [d]sign that thou talkest with me.

18 Depart not hence, I pray thee, until I come unto thee, and bring forth my present, and set *it* before thee. And he said, I will tarry until thou come again.

19 And [†]Ḡĭd'e-on went in, and made ready a [e]kid, and unleavened cakes of an [f]ephah[c] of [3]flour: the flesh he put in a basket, and he put the broth in a pot, and brought *it* out unto him under the oak, and presented *it*.

20 And the [g]angel of God said unto him, Take the flesh and the unleavened cakes, and lay *them* upon this rock, and pour out the broth. And he did so.

21 Then the [g]angel of the LORD put forth the end of the staff that *was* in his hand, and touched the flesh and the unleavened cakes; and [h]there rose up fire out of the rock, and consumed the flesh and the unleavened cakes. Then the angel of the LORD departed out of his sight.[s]

22 And when [†]Ḡĭd'e-on perceived that he *was* an [g]angel of the LORD, Ḡĭd'e-on said, [i]Alas, O Lord GOD! for because I have seen an angel of the LORD face to face.

23 And the LORD said unto him, Peace *be* unto thee; fear not: thou shalt not die.

24 Then [†]Ḡĭd'e-on built an [j]altar there unto the LORD, and called it Jē̇-hō'vah–shā'lom: unto this day it *is* yet in Ŏph'rah of the Ā'bĭ–ĕz'rītes.[T]

25 ¶ And it came to pass the same night, that the LORD said unto him, Take thy father's young bullock, even the second bullock of seven years old, and throw down the altar of [k,l]Bā'al that thy father hath, and cut down the [‡]grove[c] that *is* by it:

26 And build an [j]altar unto the LORD thy God upon the top of this rock, in the [4]ordered place, and take the second bullock, and offer a burnt [m]sacrifice[c] with the wood of the [‡]grove[c] which thou shalt cut down.

27 Then [†]Ḡĭd'e-on [n,o]took ten men of his servants, and [p]did as the LORD had said unto him: and *so* it was, because he feared his father's household, and the men of the city, that he could not do *it* by day, that he did *it* by night.

28 ¶ And when the men of the city arose early in the morning, behold, the altar of [k]Bā'al was [q]cast down; and the [‡]grove[c] was cut down that *was* by it, and the

v.21–1260 BC
See footnote, *Time*, Rev. 10:6.

**21**
*h Miracles*, Luke 23:8.

**22**
*i Prayer, exemplified*, Acts 6:4.

**24**
*j Altar*, Gen. 8:20

**25**
*k Baal*, 2 Kin. 17 16.
*l Idolatry*, 1 Sam. 15:23.

**26**
*m Jesus, typified in offerings*, Matt. 1:21.
4 R. V. orderly manner,

**27**
*n Courage, instances of*, Deut. 31:7.
*o Decision, instances of*, Isa. 50:7.
*p Obedience, exemplified*, Heb. 5:8.

**28**
*q Iconoclasm*, Num. 33:52.

‡ **GROVES** [R. V. Asheroth, Asherah, Asherim, and in Gen. 21:33 tamarisk tree], probably an image or images of the Canaanitish goddess Asherah. See footnote, ASHTORETH, 1 Kin. 11:15.

*Forbidden to be established*, Deut. 16:21; Isa. 17:8; 27:9; Mic. 5:14. *To be destroyed*, Deut. 12:3. *Worshiped by Israelites*, Judg. 3:7; 1 Kin. 14:15, 23; 15:13; 18:19; 2 Kin. 13:6; 17:10, 16; 21:3–7; 2 Chr. 24:18; Isa. 1:29; 57:5; Jer. 17:2.

*Destroyed, by Gideon*, Judg. 6:28; *by Hezekiah*, 2 Kin. 18:4; 2 Chr. 31:1; *by Josiah*, 2 Kin. 23:6, 14, 15; 2 Chr. 34:3, 4; *by Asa*, 2 Chr. 14:3; *by Jehoshaphat*, 2 Chr. 17:6; 19:3.

See footnote, IDOLATRY, 1 Sam. 15:23.

second bullock was offered upon
the [i]altar *that was* built.
29 And they said one to another,
Who hath done this
thing? And when they enquired
and asked, they said, †Gĭd′e-on
the son of [r]Jō′ăsh hath done this
thing.
30 Then the men of the city
said unto [r]Jō′ăsh, [s]Bring out thy
son, that he may die: because he
hath cast down the altar of
Bā′al, and because he hath cut
down the grove[c] that *was* by it.
31 And Jō′ăsh said unto all that
stood against him, Will ye plead
for [k]Bā′al? will ye save him? he
that will plead for him, let him
be put to death whilst *it is yet*
morning: [t]if he *be* a god, let him
plead for himself, because *one*
hath cast down his altar.
32 Therefore on that day he
called him Jĕ-rŭb′ba-ăl, saying,
Let Bā′al plead[c] against him, because
he hath thrown down his
altar.
33 ¶ Then all the [u]Mĭd′ĭ-an-ītes
and the [v]Ăm′a-lĕk-ītes and
the children of the east were
gathered together, and went
over, and pitched[c] in the valley of
[w]Jĕz′re-el.
34 But the [x]Spirit of the LORD
came upon †Gĭd′e-on, and he
blew a [y]trumpet; and [z]Ā′bĭ-ē′zĕr
was [a]gathered after him.[T]
35 And †he sent messengers
throughout all [b]Mă-năs′seh; who
also was gathered after him: and
he sent messengers unto [c]Ăsh′ĕr,
and unto [d]Zĕb′u-lŭn, and unto
[e]Năph′ta-lī; and they came up
to meet them.
36 ¶ And †Gĭd′e-on said unto
God, [f,g]If thou wilt save Ĭş′ra-el
by mine hand[c], as thou hast said,
37 Behold, I will put a fleece of
‖wool in the floor; *and* [i]if the
[h,i,j,k]dew be on the fleece only,
and *it be* dry upon all the earth
*beside*, then shall I know that
thou wilt save Ĭş′ra-el by mine
hand, as thou hast said.
38 And it was so: for he [l]rose
up early on the morrow[c], and
thrust the fleece together, and
wringed the [h]dew out of the
fleece, a bowl full of water.
39 And Gĭd′e-on said unto
God, [m]Let not thine anger be hot
against me, and I will speak but
this once: [j]let me prove[c], I pray
thee, but this once with the
fleece; let it now be dry only upon
the fleece, and upon all the
ground let there be dew.
40 And God did so that night:
for it was [j]dry upon the fleece
only, and there was dew on all
the ground.

## CHAPTER 7

*Gideon's army of thirty-two thousand is reduced to three hundred. 9 He is encouraged by the dream and interpretation of the barley cake. 15 His stratagem of trumpets and lamps in pitchers. 24 The Ephraimites take Oreb and Zeeb.*

THEN Jĕ-rŭb′ba-ăl, who *is*
[a]Gĭd′e-on, and all the [b]people
that *were* with him, [c]rose
up early, and pitched[c] beside the
[1]well of Hā′rod: so that the host
of the [d]Mĭd′ĭ-an-ītes were on the
north side of them, by the hill of
Mō′reh, in the valley.
2 And [e]the LORD said unto
[a]Gĭd′e-on, The [f]people that *are*
with thee *are* too many for me to
give the [d]Mĭd′ĭ-an-ītes into their
hands, lest Ĭş′ra-el vaunt[c] themselves
against me, [g]saying, Mine
own hand hath saved me.
3 Now therefore go to, proclaim
in the ears of the people,
saying, [h]Whosoever *is* [i]fearful
and afraid, let him return and
depart early from mount [j]Gĭl′e-ăd.
And there returned of the
people twenty and two thousand;
and there remained ten
thousand.

v.28–1260 BC
See footnote, *Time*, Rev. 10:6.

29
r Judg. 7:14; 8:13, 29–32.

30
s *Persecution, of the righteous*, John 15:20.

31
t *Idolatry, folly of*, 1 Sam. 15:23.

33
u *Midianites*, Gen. 37:28.
v *Amalekites*, Num. 13:29.
w *Jezreel*, Josh. 17:16.

34
x *Holy Spirit, inspiration of*, Acts 1:2.
y *Trumpet*, Josh. 6:4.
z *Abiezer*, Josh. 17:2.

a *Armies, rendezvous of*, Deut. 11:4.

35
b *Manasseh, tribe of*, Gen. 46:20.
c *Asher, tribe of*, Num. 1:40.
d *Zebulun, tribe of*, Gen. 49:13.
e *Naphtali, tribe of*, Num. 1:42.

36
f *Faith, strengthened by miracles*, vs. 36–40; Mark 11:22.
g *Prayer, tokens asked for*, Acts 6:4.

37
h *Dew*, Dan. 4:15.
i *Token*, Psa. 86:17.
j *Miracles, dew on Gideon's fleece*, Luke 23:8.
k *Meteorology, phenomena of*, Matt. 16:2.

v.37–1260 BC
See footnote, *Time*, Rev. 10:6.

38
l *Rising, early*, Gen. 19:2.

39
m *Prayer, boldness in*, Acts 6:4.

1
a *Gideon*, Judg. 6:11.
b *Israel, under the judges*, vs. 1–25; Ex. 4:22.
c *Decision, instances of*, Isa. 50:7.
d *Midianites, defeated by Gideon*, vs. 1–25; Gen. 37:28.
1 R. V. spring

2
e *Faith, trial of*, vs. 1–25; Mark 11:22.
f *Armies, divine assistance to*, vs. 2–25; Deut. 11:4.
g *Presumption*, Psa. 19:13.

3
h *Soldiers, cowards excused from duty as*, Ezra 8:22.
i *Cowardice, disqualifies for military service*, Lev. 26:36.
j *Gilead*, Deut. 3:13.

‖ **WOOL.** *Used for clothing*, Lev. 13:47–52, 59; Prov. 31:13; Ezek. 34:3; 44:17. *Prohibited in the priest's temple dress*, Ezek. 44:17. *Mixing of, with other fibers forbidden*, Lev. 19:19; Deut. 22:11. *Tribute paid in*, 2 Kin. 3:4. *Fleece of*, Judg. 6:37. *First fleece of, belonged to the priests*, Deut. 18:4.

v.4–1260 BC
See footnote, *Time,* Rev. 10:6.

4 And [e]the LORD said unto [a]Gĭd′e-on, The people *are* yet *too* many; bring them down unto the water, and I will try[c]them for thee there: and it shall be, *that* of whom I say unto thee, This shall go with thee, the same shall go with thee; and of whomsoever I say unto thee, This shall not go with thee, the same shall not go.

5 So he brought down the people unto the water: and the LORD said unto [a]Gĭd′e-on, Every one that lappeth of the water with his tongue, as a dog lappeth, him shalt thou set by himself; likewise every one that boweth down upon his knees to drink.

6 And the number of them that lapped, *putting* their hand to their mouth, were three hundred men: but all the rest of the people bowed down upon their knees to drink water.

7 And [e]the LORD said unto Gĭd′e-on, By the three hundred men that lapped will [k]I save you, and deliver the [d]Mĭd′ĭ-an-ītes into thine hand: and let all the *other* people go every man unto his place[c].

8 So the people took victuals[c] in their hand, and their [l]trumpets: and he sent all *the rest of* Ĭṣ′ra-el every man unto his tent, and retained those three hundred men: and the host[c]of Mĭd′ĭ-an was beneath him in the valley.

9 ¶ And it came to pass the same night, that the LORD said unto him, Arise, get thee down unto the host; for [k,m]I have delivered it into thine hand.

10 But if thou fear to go down, go thou with Phū′rah thy servant down to the host:

11 And thou shalt hear what they say; and afterward shall thine hands be strengthened to go down unto the host[c]. Then went he down with Phū′rah his servant unto the outside[c] of the armed men that *were* in the host.

12 And the [d]Mĭd′ĭ-an-ītes and the [n]Ăm′a-lĕk-ītes and all the children of the east lay along in the valley like [2]grasshoppers for multitude; and their camels *were* without number[c], as the sand by the sea side for multitude.

13 And when [a]Gĭd′e-on was come, behold, *there was* a man that told a [o]dream unto his fellow, and said, Behold, I dreamed a dream, and, lo, a cake of barley [p]bread tumbled into the host of Mĭd′ĭ-an, and came unto a tent, and smote it that it fell, and overturned it, that the tent lay along[c].

14 And his fellow answered and said, This *is* nothing else save[c] the sword of Gĭd′e-on the son of [q]Jō′ăsh, a man of Ĭṣ′ra-el: *for* into his hand hath God delivered Mĭd′ĭ-an, and all the host.

15 ¶ And it was so, when [a]Gĭd′e-on heard the telling of the [o]dream, and the interpretation thereof, that he worshipped, and returned into the host[c]of Ĭṣ′ra-el, and said, Arise; for the LORD hath delivered into your hand the host of Mĭd′ĭ-an.

16 And he *divided the three hundred men *into* three companies, and he put a [l]trumpet in every man's hand, with empty [r]pitchers, [3]and lamps[c]within the pitchers.

17 And he said unto them, Look on me, and do likewise: and, behold, when I come to the outside of the camp, it shall be *that,* as I do, so shall ye do.

18 When I blow with a [l]trumpet, I and all that *are* with me, then blow ye the trumpets also on every side of all the camp,

7
k *God, providence of,* Gen. 2:2.

8
l *Trumpet, used by Gideon's soldiers,* Josh. 6:4.

9
m *War, God in,* Judg. 3:2.

v.11–1260 BC
See footnote, *Time,* Rev. 10:6.

12
n *Amalekites,* Num. 13:29.
2 R. V. locusts

13
o *Dream,* Dan. 1:17.
p *Bread,* Ezek. 4:13.

14
q Judg. 6:11, 29, 31; 8:13, 29–32

16
r Eccl. 12:6; Lam. 4:2.
3 R. V. with torches

***STRATEGY.** *In war,* Gen. 14:14, 15; 32:7, 8; Josh. 8:3–25; Judg. 7:16–23; 20:29–43; Neh. 6; Isa. 15:1; Jer. 6:5; 2 Chr. 32:3, 4. See footnote, ARMIES, *Tactics,* Deut. 11:4.

v.18–1260 BC
See footnote, *Time*, Rev. 10:6.

**18**
4 R. V. For the Lord and for Gideon.

**19**
*s Night, divided into watches*, Gen. 1:5.

**20**
*Battle, shouting in*, 1 Sam. 17:20.
*u Sword*, 1 Chr. 21:5.
5 R. V. torches

**21**
6 R. V. and they shouted, and put them to flight.

**22**
*v God, providence of*, Gen. 2:2.
*w* 1 Kin. 4:12; 19:16.

**23**
*x Naphtali, tribe of*, Num. 1:42.
*y Asher, tribe of*, Num. 1:40.
*z Manasseh, tribe of*, Gen. 46:20.

**24**
*a Gideon*, Judg. 6:11.
*b Ephraim, mount of*, Josh. 17:15.
*c Midianites*, Gen. 37:28.
*d Jordan*, Gen. 32:10.
*e Ephraim, tribe of*, Gen. 41:52.

**25**
*f Captive, cruelty to*, 1 Sam. 30:3.
*g* Judg. 8:3; Psa. 83:11.

and say, [4]*The sword* of the
LORD, and of Gĭd′e-on.
19 ¶ So [a]Gĭd′e-on, and the hundred men that *were* with him,
came unto the outside of the
camp in the beginning of the
middle [s]watch; and they had but
newly set the watch[G]: and they
blew the [l]trumpets, and brake
the [r]pitchers that *were* in their
hands.
20 And the three companies
blew the [l]trumpets, and brake
the [r]pitchers, and held the
[5]lamps[c] in their left hands, and
the [l]trumpets in their right hands
to blow *withal*: and they [t]cried,
The [u]sword of the LORD[c], and of
Gĭd′e-on.
21 And they stood every man in
his place round about the camp:
and all the host[c] ran and [6]cried,
and fled.
22 And the three hundred blew
the trumpets, and the [v]LORD set
every man's sword against his
fellow, even throughout all the
host: and the host [†]fled to
Bĕth-shĭt′tah in Zĕr′e-răth, *and*
to the border of [w]Ā′bel-mē-hō′lah, unto Tăb′bath.[s]
23 And the men of Ĭṣ′ra-el
gathered themselves together out
of [x]Năph′ta-lī, and out of [y]Ăsh′-ēr, and out of all [z]Mă-năs′seh
and pursued after the Mĭd′ĭ-an-ītes.
24 And [a]Gĭd′e-on sent messengers throughout all mount
[b]Ē′phră-ĭm, saying, Come down
against the [c]Mĭd′ĭ-an-ītes, and
take before them the waters
unto Bĕth-bā′rah and [d]Jôr′dan.
Then all the men of [e]Ē′phră-ĭm
gathered themselves together,
and took the waters unto Bĕth-bā′rah and Jôr′dan.
25 And they took two [f]princes
of the [c]Mĭd′ĭ-an-ītes, [g]Ō′reb and
[g]Zē′eb; and they slew Ō′reb upon the rock [h]Ō′reb, and Zē′eb
they slew at the winepress of
Zē′eb, and pursued Mĭd′ĭ-an,
and brought the heads of Ō′reb
and Zē′eb to Gĭd′e-on on the
other side Jôr′dan.

## CHAPTER 8

*Gideon pacifies the Ephraimites. 4 Succoth and Penuel refuse to relieve Gideon's army. 10 Zebah and Zalmunna are taken. 13 Succoth and Penuel are destroyed. 18 Gideon avenges his brethren's death on Zebah and Zalmunna. 22 He refuses the office of ruler. 24 He makes an ephod which becomes the cause of idolatry. 29 Gideon's children, and death. 33 The Israelites' idolatry and ingratitude.*

AND the men of [a]Ē′phră-ĭm
said unto [b]him, [c,d]Why
hast thou served us thus, that
thou calledst us not, when thou
wentest to fight with the [e]Mĭd′-ĭ-an-ītes? And they did chide[c]
with him sharply.
2 And [b]he [f,g]said unto them,
What have I done now in
comparison of you? [h]*Is* not
the [i]gleaning of the grapes of
Ē′phră-ĭm better than the vintage of [j]Ā′bĭ-ē′zēr?
3 God hath delivered into your
hands the princes of Mĭd′ĭ-an,
[k]Ō′reb and [k]Zē′eb: and what
was I able to do in comparison
of you? Then their [c]anger was
abated[G] toward him, when he had
said that.
4 ¶ And [b]Gĭd′e-on came to
[l]Jôr′dan, *and* passed over, he,
and the three hundred men that
*were* with him, faint, yet pursuing *them*.
5 And he said unto the men
of *Sŭc′coth, Give, I pray you,
loaves of bread unto the people
that follow me; for they *be* faint,
and I am pursuing after [m]Zē′-bah and [m]Zăl-mŭn′nȧ, kings of
Mĭd′-ĭ-an.
6 And the princes of *Sŭc′coth
said, *Are*[c] the hands of [m]Zē′bah

v.25–1260 BC
See footnote, *Time*, Rev. 10:6.
*h* Isa. 10:26.

**1**
*a Ephraim, tribe of*, Gen. 41:52.
*b Gideon*, Judg. 6:11.
*c Anger, instances of*, Psa. 37:8.
*d Jealousy, instances of*, Psa. 78:58.
*e Midianites*, Gen. 37:28.

**2**
*f Tact*, Prov. 15:1.
*g Meekness, instances of*, Psa. 45:4.
*h Flattery*, Prov. 6:24.
*i Gleaning, figurative*, Lev. 23:22.
*j Abiezer*, Josh. 17:2.

**3**
*k* Judg. 7:25; Psa. 83:11.

**4**
*l Jordan, fords of*, Gen. 32:10.

**5**
*m* Psa. 83:11.

† **PANIC.** *In armies*, Lev. 26:17; Deut. 32:30; Josh. 23:10; 1 Sam. 4:10; 1 Chr. 19:14, 15, 18. *From God*, Gen. 35:5; Ex. 15:14–16; 1 Sam. 14:15–20; 2 Kin. 7:6, 7; 2 Chr. 20:22, 23. See footnote, ARMIES, Deut. 11:4.

* **SUCCOTH** (*booths*), a city probably east of the Jordan. *Jacob builds a house in*, Gen. 33:17. *Allotted to Gad*, Josh. 13:27. *People of, punished by Gideon*, Judg. 8:5–8, 14–16. *Located near the Jordan*, 1 Kin. 7:46; 2 Chr. 4:17.

v.6–1260 BC
See footnote, *Time*, Rev. 10:6.

7
*n* *Retaliation*, Deut. 19:19.

8
*o* *Penuel*, Gen. 32: 31.

9
*p* *Tower*, 2 Chr. 26:9.

11
*q* Num. 32:35.

13
*r* Judg. 6:11, 29, 31: 7:14.
1 R. V. from the ascent of Heres.

14
*s* *Government, municipal*, Isa. 22:21.

and [m]Zăl-mŭn′nȧ now in thine
hand, that we should give bread
unto thine army?
7 And [b]Gĭd′e-on said, Therefore when the LORD hath delivered [m]Zē′bah and [m]Zăl-mŭn′nȧ
into mine hand, then I will [n]tear
your flesh with the thorns of the
wilderness and with briers.
8 And [b]he went up thence to
[o]Pē-nū′el, and spake unto them
likewise: and the men of Pē-nū′-
el answered him as the men of
*Sŭc′coth had answered *him*.
9 And [b]he spake also unto the
men of Pē-nū′el, saying, When
I come again in peace, I will
[n]break down this [p]tower.
10 ¶ Now [m]Zē′bah and [m]Zăl-
mŭn′nȧ *were* in Kär′kôr, and
their hosts with them, about fifteen thousand *men*, all that were
left of all the hosts of the children of the east: for there fell an
hundred and twenty thousand
men that drew[c] sword.
11 ¶ And [b]Gĭd′e-on went up by
the way of them that dwelt in
tents on the east of Nō′bah and
[q]Jŏg′be-hah, and smote[c] the host:
for the host was secure[c].
12 And when [m]Zē′bah and
[m]Zăl-mŭn′nȧ fled, he pursued
after them, and took the two
kings of Mĭd′ĭ-an, Zē′bah and
Zăl-mŭn′nȧ, and discomfited[c] all
the host.
13 ¶ And [b]Gĭd′e-on the son of
[r]Jō′ăsh returned from battle [1]be-
fore the sun *was up*,
14 And caught a young man of
the men of *Sŭc′coth, and enquired of him: and he described[c]
unto him the [s]princes of Sŭc′-
coth, and the [s]elders thereof, *even*
threescore and seventeen men.
15 And he came unto the men
of *Sŭc′coth, and said, Behold
[m]Zē′bah and [m]Zăl-mŭn′nȧ, with
whom ye did upbraid me, saying, *Are* the hands of Zē′bah and
Zăl-mŭn′nȧ now in thine hand,
that we should give bread unto
thy men *that are* weary?
16 And he took the elders of the
city, and thorns of the wilderness and briers, and with them
he taught the men of Sŭc′coth.
17 And he beat down the [p]tower
of [o]Pē-nū′el, and [n]slew the men
of the city.
18 ¶ Then said he unto [m]Zē′-
bah and [m]Zăl-mŭn′nȧ, What
manner of men *were they* whom
ye slew at †Tā′bôr? And they
answered, As thou *art*, so *were*
they; each one resembled the
children of a king.
19 And he said, They *were* my
brethren, *even* the sons of my
mother: *as* the LORD liveth, if
ye had saved them alive, I would
not slay you.
20 And he said unto Jē′thĕr
his firstborn, Up, *and* slay them.
But the youth drew not his
sword: for he feared, because
he *was* yet a youth.
21 Then [m]Zē′bah and [m]Zăl-
mŭn′nȧ said, Rise thou, and fall
upon us: for as the man *is*, *so*
*is* his strength. And [b]Gĭd′e-on
arose, and [t,u]slew Zē′bah and
Zăl-mŭn′nȧ, and took [2]away the
ornaments that *were* on their
camels' necks.
22 ¶ Then the men of Ĭṣ′ra-el
[v]said unto [b]Gĭd′e-on, Rule thou
over us, both thou, and thy son,
and thy son's son also: [v]for thou
hast delivered us from the hand
of Mĭd′ĭ-an.
23 And [b,w]Gĭd′e-on said unto
them, I will not rule over you,
neither shall my son rule over
you: ‡,[x]the LORD shall rule over
you.
24 And [b]Gĭd′e-on said unto
them, I would desire a request of
you, that ye would give me every

v.15–1260 BC
See footnote, *Time*, Rev. 10:6.

21
*t* *Retaliation, instances of*, Deut. 19:19.
*u* *Captive, cruelty to*, 1 Sam. 30:3.
2 R. V. the crescents that were

22
*v* *Thankfulness, of man to man*, Acts 24:3.

23
*w* *Unselfishness, instances of*, 1 Cor. 10:24.
*x* *Government, theocratic*, Isa. 22:21.

† **TABOR.** *A mountain on the border of Issachar*, Josh. 19:22; Judg. 8:18; Psa. 89:12; Jer. 46:18; Hos. 5:1. *Assembling place of Barak's army*, Judg. 4:6, 12, 14.

‡ **THEOCRACY.** *Established*, Ex. 19:8; 24:3, 7; Deut. 33:2–5; Josh. 24:24; Judg. 8:23; 1 Sam. 12:12. *Rejected by Israel*, 1 Sam. 8:7, 19; 10:19; 2 Chr. 13:8.

v.24–1260 BC
See footnote, *Time*, Rev. 10:6.

**24**
y *Spoils*, 1 Chr. 26: 27.
z *Ishmaelites*, Gen. 39:1.

**26**
a *Shekel*, Ex. 30: 13.
b *Gold*, Ezek. 7:19.
c *Colors*, Ezek. 16: 16.
d *Chains*, Dan. 5:7.
3 R. V. the crescents,
4 R. V. the pendants,

**27**
e *Gideon*, Judg. 6: 11.
f *Ephod*, Ex. 28:6.
g Judg. 6:11; 9:5.
h *Temptation, leading into*, Luke 11:4.

**28**
i *Midianites*, Gen. 37:28.
j *Forty*, Jonah 3:4.

**30**
k *Polygamy*, Deut. 17:17.

**31**
l *Concubinage*, 2 Sam. 21:11.
m *Shechem*, Josh. 20:7.
n Judg. 9; 2 Sam. 11:21.

**32**
o *Old Age*, Isa. 46:4.

v.33 1220 BC

**33**
p *Backsliding, of Israel*, Hos. 11:7.
q Judg. 9:4; called *Berith*, Judg. 9:46.

man the [y]earrings of his prey[C]. (For they had golden earrings, because they *were* [z]Ĭsh′ma-el-ītes.)

25 And [v]they answered, We will willingly give *them*. And they spread a garment, and did cast therein every man the [y]earrings of his prey[C].

26 And the weight of the golden [y]earrings that he requested was a thousand and seven hundred [a]*shekels*[C] of [b]gold; beside [3]ornaments, and [4]collars, and [c]purple raiment that *was* on the kings of Mĭd′ĭ-an, and beside the [d]chains that *were* about their camels' necks.

27 And [e]Gĭd′e-on made an [f]ephod[C] thereof, and put it in his city, *even* in [g]Ŏph′rah: and all Ĭş′ra-el went thither[C] a[C] whoring after it: which thing became a [h]snare unto Gĭd′e-on, and to his house.

28 ¶ Thus was [i]Mĭd′ĭ-an subdued before the children of Ĭş′ra-el, so that they lifted[C] up their heads no more. And the country was in quietness [j]forty years in the days of Gĭd′e-on.

29 And [e]Jĕ-rŭb′ba-ăl the son of Jō′ăsh went and dwelt in his own house.

30 And [e]Gĭd′e-on had threescore and ten sons of his body begotten: for he had [k]many wives.

31 And his [l]concubine[C] that *was* in [m]Shē′chem, she also bare him a son, whose name he called [n]Ă-bĭm′e-lĕch.

32 And [e]Gĭd′e-on the son of Jō′ăsh died in a good [o]old age, and was buried in the sepulchre of Jō′ăsh his father, in Ŏph′rah of the Ā′bĭ–ĕz′rītes.

33 And it came to pass, as soon as [e]Gĭd′e-on was dead, that the children of Ĭş′ra-el [p]turned again, and went a[C] whoring after Bā′al-ĭm, and made [q]Bā′al–bē′rith their god.

34 And the children of Ĭş′ra-el [r]remembered not the LORD their God, [s]who had delivered them out of the hands of all their enemies on every side:

35 [t]Neither shewed they kindness to the house of Jĕ-rŭb′ba-ăl, *namely*, [e]Gĭd′e-on, according to all the goodness which he had shewed unto Ĭş′ra-el.

## CHAPTER 9

*Abimelech by conspiracy with the Shechemites, and murder of his brethren, is made king. 7 Jotham by a parable rebukes them, and foretells their ruin. 22 Gaal conspires with the Shechemites against Abimelech. 30 Zebul reveals it. 34 Abimelech overcomes them, and sows the city with salt. 46 He burns the hold of the god Berith. 50 At Thebez he is slain by a piece of a millstone. 56 Jotham's curse is fulfilled.*

AND [a]Ă-bĭm′e-lĕch the son of [b]Jĕ-rŭb′ba-ăl went to [c]Shē′chem unto his mother's brethren, and communed[C] with them, and with all the family of the house of his mother's father, saying,

2 [d]Speak, I pray you, in the ears of all the men of Shē′chem, Whether[C] *is* better for you, either that all the sons of Jĕ-rŭb′ba-ăl, *which are* threescore and ten persons, reign over you, or that one reign over you? remember also that I *am* your bone[C] and your flesh.

3 And his mother's brethren spake of him in the ears of all the men of Shē′chem all these words: and their hearts inclined to follow Ă-bĭm′e-lĕch; for they said, He *is* our brother.

4 And they gave him threescore and ten *pieces* of silver out of the house of [e]Bā′al–bē′rith, wherewith Ă-bĭm′e-lĕch hired vain[C] and light[C] persons, which followed him.

5 And he went unto his father's house at [f]Ŏph′rah, and [g,h,i]slew his brethren the sons of Jĕ-rŭb′ba-ăl, *being* threescore and ten persons, upon one stone: notwithstanding yet Jō′tham the

v.34–1220 BC
See footnote, *Time*, Rev. 10:6.

**34**
r *Ingratitude, to God*, Rom. 1:21.
s *God, providence of*, Gen. 2:2.

**35**
t *Ingratitude, of man to man*, Rom. 1:21.

**1**
a Judg. 8:31; 2 Sam. 11:21.
b Or *Gideon*, Judg. 6:11.
c *Shechem*, Josh. 20:7.

**2**
d *Ambition, instances of*, Hab. 2:5.

**4**
e Judg. 8:33.

**5**
f *Ophrah*, Judg. 6:11.
g *Homicide, felonious*, Deut. 5:17.
h *Fratricide, instances of*, Gen. 4:8.
i *Treachery*, 2 Kin. 9:23.

v.5–1220 BC
See footnote, *Time*, Rev. 10:6.

6
*j* *Pillar*, Gen. 28:18.
1 R. V. oak

7
*k* *Gerizim*, Deut. 11:29.

8
*l* *Allegory*, Gal. 4:24.
*m* *Sarcasm, instances of*, vs. 7–19; Judg. 10:14.
*n* *Parables*, Ezek. 20:49.
*o* *Anointing*, Lev. 8:12.
*p* *Olive, fable of*, Deut. 6:11.

9
2 R. V. wave to and fro over the trees?

10
*q* *Fig Tree*, Luke 13:6.

12
*r* *Vine, fable of*, Judg. 13:14.

14
*s* Luke 6:44.

15
*t* *Lebanon, cedars of*, Deut. 1:7.

16
3 R. V. uprightly

youngest son of Jĕ-rŭb′ba-ăl was
left; for he hid himself.
6 And all the men of [c]Shē′chem
gathered together, and all the
house of Mĭl′lō, and went, and
made [a]Ā-bĭm′e-lĕch king, by the
[1]plain of the [j]pillar that *was* in
Shē′chem.
7 And when they told *it* to
Jō′tham, he went and stood in
the top of mount [k]Gĕr′ĭ-zĭm, and
lifted up his voice, and cried,
and said unto them, Hearken[c]
unto me, ye men of [c]Shē′chem,
that God may hearken unto you.
8 [l,m,n]The trees went forth *on*
*a time*[c] to [o]anoint a king over
them; and they said unto the
[p]olive tree, Reign thou over us.
9 But the [p]olive tree said unto
them, Should I leave my fatness,
wherewith by me they honour
God and man, and go to [2]be
promoted over the trees?
10 And the trees said to the [q]fig
tree, Come thou, *and* reign over
us.
11 But the [q]fig tree said unto
them, Should I forsake my
sweetness, and my good fruit,
and go to [2]be promoted over the
trees?
12 Then said the trees unto
the [r]vine, Come thou, *and* reign
over us.
13 And the [r]vine said unto
them, Should I leave my wine,
which cheereth God and man,
and go to [2]be promoted over the
trees?
14 Then said all the trees unto
the [s]bramble, Come thou, *and*
reign over us.
15 And the bramble said unto
the trees, If in truth ye anoint
me king over you, *then* come *and*
put your trust in my shadow:
and if not, let fire come out of
the bramble, and devour the
cedars of [t]Lĕb′a-non.
16 Now therefore, if ye have
done truly and [3]sincerely, in
that ye have made [a]Ā-bĭm′e-lĕch
king, and if ye have dealt well
with [u]Jĕ-rŭb′ba-ăl and his
house, and have done unto him
according to the deserving of his
hands;
17 (For my father fought for
you, and adventured[c] his life far,
and delivered you out of the
hand of [v]Mĭd′ĭ-an:
18 And [w]ye are risen up against
my father's house this day, and
have [g,h]slain his sons, threescore
and ten persons, upon one stone,
and have made Ā-bĭm′e-lĕch,
the son of his maidservant, king
over the men of Shē′chem, because he *is* your brother;)
19 If ye then have dealt truly
and [3]sincerely with [u]Jĕ-rŭb′ba-ăl
and with his house this day, *then*
rejoice ye in Ā-bĭm′e-lĕch, and
let him also rejoice in you:
20 But if not, let fire come out
from Ā-bĭm′e-lĕch, and devour
the men of Shē′chem, and the
house of Mĭl′lō; and let fire come
out from the men of Shē′chem,
and from the house of Mĭl′lō,
and devour Ā′bĭm′e-lĕch.
21 And Jō′tham ran away, and
fled, and went to Bē′er, and
dwelt there, for fear of Ā-bĭm′e-
lĕch his brother.
22 ¶ When [a]Ā-bĭm′e-lĕch had
reigned three years over Iṣ′ra-el,
23 Then [x]God sent an [y,z]evil
spirit between Ā-bĭm′e-lĕch and
the [a]men of [b]Shē′chem; and
the men of Shē′chem [c,d,e]dealt
treacherously with [f]Ā-bĭm′e-
lĕch:[s]
24 That the cruelty *done* to the
threescore and ten sons of [g]Jĕ-
rŭb′ba-ăl might come, and their
[h]blood be laid upon [f]Ā-bĭm′e-
lĕch their brother, which [i]slew
them; and upon the men of
Shē′chem, which aided him in
the killing of his brethren.
25 And the men of Shē′chem
set [j]liers[c] in wait for him in the

v.16–1220 BC
See footnote, *Time*, Rev. 10:6.

*u* Judg. 6:32: or, *Gideon*, Judg. 6:11.

17
*v* *Midianites*, Gen 37:28.

18
*w* *Ingratitude, of man to man*, Rom. 1:21.

v.22–1218 BC

23
*x* *God, providence of*, Gen. 2:2.
*y* *Demons*, Matt. 4:24.
*z* *Evil Spirit*, 1 Sam. 18:10.

*a* *Citizens, wicked and treasonable*, Luke 15:15.
*b* *Shechem*, Josh. 20:7.
*c* *Conspiracy, instances of*, vs. 23–41; 1 Kin. 16:9.
*d* *Treachery*, 2 Kin. 9:23.
*e* *Treason*, 2 Kin. 11:14.
*f* Judg. 8:31; 2 Sam. 11:21.

24
*g* Judg. 6:32; or, *Gideon*, Judg. 6:11.
*h* *Sin, punishment of*, Rom. 5:12.
*i* *Homicide, felonious*, Deut. 5:17.

25
*j* *Ambush*, Josh. 8:2.

v.25–1218 BC
See footnote, *Time*, Rev. 10:6.

*k Robbery*, Ezek. 22:29.

27
*l Harvest, celebrated with joy*, Ex. 34:21.
*m Grape, grown at Shechem*, Lev. 25:5.
*n Idolatry*, 1 Sam. 15:23.

28
*o Shechem*, Gen. 34:2.
*p Hamor*, Gen. 34: 18.

30
*q Anger*, Psa. 37:8.

31
4 R. V. craftily.
5 R. V. constrain the city to take part against thee.

32
*r Armies, tactics of*, Deut. 11:4.

top of the mountains, and they [k]robbed all that came along that way by them: and it was told Ȧ-bĭm′e-lĕch.

26 And Gā′al the son of Ē′bed came with his brethren, and went over to Shē′chem: and the men of Shē′chem put their confidence in him.

27 And they went out into the fields, and [l]gathered their vineyards, and trode *the* [m]*grapes*, and made[c] merry, and went into the house of their [n]god, and did eat and drink, and cursed [f]Ȧ-bĭm′e-lĕch.

28 And Gā′al the son of Ē′bed said, Who *is* Ȧ-bĭm′e-lĕch, and who *is* [o]Shē′chem, that we should serve him? *is* not *he* the son of [g]Jė-rŭb′ba-ăl? and Zē′bul his officer? serve the men of [p]Hā′mor the father of Shē′chem: for why should we serve him?

29 And would to God this people were under my hand! then would I remove Ȧ-bĭm′e-lĕch. And he said to Ȧ-bĭm′e-lĕch, Increase thine army, and come out.

30 ¶ And when Zē′bul the ruler of the city heard the words of Gā′al the son of Ē′bed his [q]anger was kindled[c].

31 And he sent messengers unto [f]Ȧ-bĭm′e-lĕch [4]privily,[c] saying, Behold, Gā′al the son of Ē′bed and his brethren be come to [b]Shē′chem; and, behold, they [5]fortify the city against thee.

32 Now therefore [r]up[c] by night, thou and the people that *is* with thee, and [j]lie[c] in wait in the field:

33 And it shall be, *that* in the morning, as soon as the sun is up, thou shalt rise early, and set upon[c] the city: and, behold, *when* he and the people that *is* with him come out against thee, then mayest thou do to them as thou shalt find occasion.

34 ¶ And [f]Ȧ-bĭm′e-lĕch rose up, and all the people that *were* with him, by night, and they [j]laid wait against [b]Shē′chem in four companies.

35 And Gā′al the son of Ē′bed went out, and stood in the entering of the gate of the city: and Ȧ-bĭm′e-lĕch rose up, and the people that *were* with him, from [j]lying[c] in wait.

36 And when Gā′al saw the people, he said to Zē′bul, Behold, there come people down from the top of the mountains. And Zē′bul said unto him, Thou seest the shadow of the mountains as *if they were* men.

37 And Gā′al spake again and said, See there come people down by the middle of the land, and another company [6]come along by the plain of Mė-ŏn′e-nĭm.

38 Then said Zē′bul unto him, Where *is* now thy mouth[c], wherewith thou saidst, Who *is* Ȧ-bĭm′-e-lĕch, that we should serve him? *is* not this the people that thou hast despised? go out, I pray now, and fight with them.

39 And Gā′al went out before the men of Shē′chem, and fought with [f]Ȧ-bĭm′e-lĕch.

40 And [f]Ȧ-bĭm′e-lĕch chased him, and he fled before him, and many were overthrown *and* wounded, *even* unto the entering of the gate.

41 And [f]Ȧ-bĭm′e-lĕch dwelt at Ȧ-ru′mah: and Zē′bul thrust[c] out Gā′al and his brethren, that they should not dwell in [b]Shē′chem.

42 And it came to pass on the morrow,[c] that the people went out into the field; and they told [f]Ȧ-bĭm′e-lĕch.

43 And he took the people, and [r]divided them into three companies, and [j,r]laid wait in the field, and looked, and, behold, the people *were* come forth out of the city; and he rose up against them, and smote them.

v.34–1218 BC
See footnote *Time*, Rev. 10:6.

37
6 R. V. cometh by the way of the oak of

v.44–1218 BC
See footnote, *Time,* Rev. 10:6.

44 And [f]Ā-bĭm'e-lĕch, and [r]the company that *was* with him, rushed forward, and stood in the entering of the gate of the city: and [r]the two *other* companies ran upon all *the people* that *were* in the fields, and slew them.

45 And Ā-bĭm'e-lĕch fought against [b]the city all that day; and he took the city, and slew the people that *was* therein, and beat down the city, and sowed it with salt.

46 ¶ And when all the men of the [s]tower of [b]Shē'chem heard *that,* they entered into an hold[c] of the house of the [t]god [u]Bē'rith.

47 And it was told [f]Ā-bĭm'e-lĕch, that all the men of the tower of Shē'chem were gathered together.

48 And [f]Ā-bĭm'e-lĕch gat[c] him up to mount [v]Zăl'mŏn, he and all the people that *were* with him; and Ā-bĭm'e-lĕch took an ax in his hand, and cut down a bough from the trees, and took it, and laid *it* on his shoulder, and said unto the people that *were* with him, What ye have seen me do, make haste, *and* do as I *have done.*

49 And all the people likewise cut down every man his bough, and followed Ā-bĭm'e-lĕch, and put *them* to the hold,[c] and set the hold on fire upon them; so that all the men of the tower of Shē'chem died also, about a thousand men and women.

50 ¶ Then went [f]Ā-bĭm'e-lĕch to [w]Thē'bĕz, and encamped[c] against Thē'bĕz, and took it.

51 But there was a strong tower within the city, and thither fled all the men and women, and all they of the city, and shut [7]*it* to them, and gat[c] them up to the top of the tower.

52 And [f]Ā-bĭm'e-lĕch came unto the tower, and fought against it, and went hard[c] unto the door of the tower to burn it with fire.

53 And a certain [x]woman [y]cast [8]a piece of a *millstone upon Ā-bĭm'e-lĕch's head, and all[c] to brake his scull.

54 Then he called hastily unto the young man his †armourbearer, and said unto him, Draw thy sword, and slay me, that men say not of me, A woman slew him. And his young man thrust him through, and he died.

55 And when the men of Ĭṣ'ra-el saw that Ā-bĭm'e-lĕch was dead, they departed every man unto his place.[c]

56 ¶ Thus God [9, y, z]rendered the wickedness of Ā-bĭm'e-lĕch, which he did unto his father, in slaying his seventy brethren:[s]

57 And all the evil of the men of Shē'chem did God [10, z]render upon their heads: and upon them came the curse of Jō'tham the son of Jė-rŭb'ba-ăl.[s]

## CHAPTER 10

*Tola judges Israel. 3 Jair also, whose thirty sons had thirty cities. 6 The Philistines and Ammonites oppress Israel. 10 In their misery God sends them to their false gods. 15 Upon their repentance he pities them.*

AND after [a]Ā-bĭm'e-lĕch there arose to defend[c] [b]Ĭṣ'ra-el [c]Tō'lȧ the son of Pū'ah, the son of Dō'dō, a man of [d]Ĭs'sa-char; and he dwelt in Shā'mĭr in [e]mount Ē'phră-ĭm.

2 And [c]he judged [b]Ĭṣ'ra-el twenty and three years, and died, and was buried in Shā'mĭr.

3 ¶ And after him arose [c]Jā'ĭr, a Gĭl'e-ăd-īte, and judged [b]Ĭṣ'ra-el twenty and two years.

4 And he had thirty sons that rode on thirty ass colts, and they had thirty cities, which are

**46**
s *Tower, of Shechem,* 2 Chr 26:9.
t *Idolatry,* 1 Sam. 15:23.
u Or, *Baal-berith,* Judg. 8:33.

**48**
v Or, *Salmon,* Psa. 68:14.

**50**
w 2 Sam. 11:21.

**51**
7 R. V. themselves in,

v.52–1218 BC
See footnote, *Time,* Rev. 10:6.

**53**
x *Women,* Prov. 31:10.
y *Judgments, upon Abimelech,* with v. 56; Ex. 6:6.
8 R. V. an upper millstone

**56**
z *Sin, punishment of,* Rom. 5:12.
9 R. V. requited

**57**
10 R. V. requite

**1**
a *Abimelech,* Judg. 8:31.
b *Israel, under the judges,* Ex. 4:22.
c *Judges of Israel,* Judg. 2:16.
d *Issachar, tribe of,* Num. 1:28.
e *Ephraim, mount of,* Josh. 17:15.

v.1–1217 BC

v 3–1 94 BC

* **MILLSTONE,** Isa. 47:2; Jer. 25:10. *Not to be taken in pledge,* Deut. 24:6. *Probably used in executions by drowning,* Matt. 18:6; Mark 9:42; Luke 17:2. *Abimelech killed by one being hurled upon him,* Judg. 9:53.
**Figurative:** *Of the hard heart,* Job 41:24.

† **ARMOR-BEARER,** an attendant who carried a soldier's equipment. *Of Abimelech,* Judg. 9:54. *Of Jonathan,* 1 Sam. 14:6, 7, 12, 14, 17. *Of Saul,* 1 Sam. 16:21; 31:4–6; 1 Chr. 10:4, 5. *Of Goliath,* 1 Sam. 17:7. *Of Joab,* 2 Sam. 18:15.

called *Hā′voth–jā′ĭr unto this day, which *are* in the land of [f]Gĭl′e-ăd.

5 And Jā′ĭr died, and was buried in Cā′mŏn.

6 ¶ And the children of Ĭs̹′ra-el did evil again in the sight of the LORD, and [g]served [h]Bā′al-ĭm, and [i]Ăsh′ta-rŏth, and the gods of Sy̆r′ĭ-ȧ, and the gods of [j]Zī′dŏn, and the gods of [k]Mō′ab, and the gods of the [l]children of Ăm′mŏn, and the gods of the [m]Phĭ-lĭs′tĭnes̹, and [n]forsook the LORD, and served not him.

7 And the [o]anger of the LORD was hot against Ĭs̹′ra-el, and [p]he sold them into the hands of the [m]Phĭ-lĭs′tĭnes̹, and unto the hands of the [l]children of Ăm′mŏn.[S]

8 And that year they vexed[C] and [q]oppressed the children of Ĭs̹′ra-el: eighteen years, all the children of Ĭs̹′ra-el that *were* on the other side [r]Jôr′dan in the land of the [s]Ăm′ôr-ītes, which *is* in [f]Gĭl′e-ăd.

9 Moreover the [l]children of Ăm′mŏn passed over [r]Jôr′dan to fight also against [t]Jū′dah, and against [u]Bĕn′ja-mĭn, and against the house of [v]Ē′phră-ĭm; so that Ĭs̹′ra-el was sore[C] distressed.

10 ¶ And the children of [w]Ĭs̹′ra-el [x]cried unto the LORD, saying, [y]We have sinned against thee, both because we have forsaken our God, and also [g]served [h]Bā′al-ĭm.

11 And the LORD said unto the children of Ĭs̹′ra-el, *Did* not [p]I *deliver you* from the [z]Ē-ġy̆p′tians̹, and from the [a]Ăm′ôr-ītes, from the [b]children of Ăm′mŏn, and from the [c]Phĭ-lĭs′tĭnes̹?

12 The Zī-dō′nĭ-ans̹ also, and the [d]Ăm′a-lĕk-ītes, and the Mā′on-ītes, did oppress you; and [e]ye cried to me, and I [f]delivered you out of their hand.

13 Yet [g]ye [h]have forsaken me, and served other gods: wherefore I will deliver you no more.

14 †Go and cry[C] unto the [i]gods which ye have chosen; let them deliver you in the time of your [j]tribulation.[C]

15 And the children of Ĭs̹′ra-el said unto the LORD, [k,l]We have sinned: [m]do thou unto us whatsoever seemeth good unto thee; [m]deliver us only, we pray thee, this day.

16 And they [n]put away the strange[C] gods from among them, and served the LORD: and [o]his soul was [p]grieved[C] for the misery of Ĭs̹′ra-el.

17 Then the [b]children of Ăm′mŏn were gathered together, and encamped in [q]Gĭl′e-ăd. And the children of Ĭs̹′ra-el assembled themselves together, and encamped in Mĭz′peh.

18 And the people *and* princes of [q]Gĭl′e-ăd said one to another, What man *is he* that will begin to fight against the children of Ăm′mŏn? he shall be head[C] over all the inhabitants of Gĭl′e-ăd.

## CHAPTER 11

*The covenant between Jephthah and the Gileadites, that he should be their head. 12 Jephthah's messages to the Ammonites. 30 His vow. 32 His conquest of the Ammonites. 34 His daughter first meets him. 39 He performs his vow.*

NOW *Jĕph′thah the Gĭl′e-ăd-īte was a mighty man of valour,[C] and he *was* the [a]son of

v.4–1194 BC
see footnote, *Time*, Rev. 10:6.

**4**
[f] *Gilead*, Deut. 3:13.

**6**
[g] *Idolatry*, 1 Sam. 15:23.
[h] *Baal*, 2 Kin. 17:16.
[i] *Ashtoreth*, 1 Kin. 11:5.
[j] *Zidon*, Ezek. 28:21.
[k] *Moabites*, Gen. 19:37.
[l] *Ammonites*, Deut. 2:20.
[m] *Philistines*, Gen. 26:14.
[n] *Backsliding, of Israel*. Hos. 11:7.

v.6–1172 BC

**7**
[o] *Anger of God, provoked*, 2 Kin. 13:3.
[p] *God, providence of*, Gen. 2:2.

**8**
[q] *Oppression, national, relieved*, vs. 1–18; Eccl. 5:8.
[r] *Jordan*, Gen. 32:10.
[s] *Amorites*, Gen. 14:13.

**9**
[t] *Judah, tribe of*, Num. 10:14.
[u] *Benjamin, tribe of*, Num. 1:37.
[v] *Ephraim, tribe of*, Gen. 41:52.

**10**
[w] *Nation, in adversity, prayer of*, Isa. 2:4.
[x] *Prayer, confession in*, Acts 6:4.
[y] *Sin, confession of*, Rom. 5:12.

**11**
[z] *Egyptians*, Gen. 50:3.
[a] *Amorites*, Gen. 14:13.

[b] *Ammonites*, Deut. 2:20.
[c] *Philistines*, Gen. 26:14.

**12**
[d] *Amalekites*, Num. 13:29.
[e] *Adversity, benefits of*, Psa. 10:6.
[f] *God, providence of*, Gen. 2:2.

**13**
[g] *Backsliders, punishment of*, Jer. 3:22.
[h] *Ingratitude, of man to God*, Rom. 1:21.

**14**
[i] *Idolatry, folly of*, 1 Sam. 15:23.
[j] *Adversity*, Psa. 10:6.

**15**
[k] *Sin, confession of*, Rom. 5:12.
[l] *Nation in adversity, prayer of*, Isa. 2:4.
[m] *Resignation, exemplified*, Job 5:17.

**16**
[n] *Repentance, instances of*, Mark 1:4.
[o] *God, love of*, Gen. 2:2.
[p] *Anthropomorphisms*, Gen. 11:5.

**17**
[q] *Gilead*, Deut. 3:13.

**1**
[a] *Bastard*, Deut. 23:2.

* **HAVOTH-JAIR.** *Certain villages E. of the Jordan* Num. 32:41; Judg. 10:4. *Called also* BASHAN-HAVOTH-JAIR, Deut. 3:14.

† **SARCASM.** **Instances of:** *Cain's self-justifying argument*, Gen. 4:9. *Israelites reproaching Moses*, Ex. 14:11. *God reproaching Israel*, Num. 11:20; Judg. 10:14. *Balak reproaching Balaam*, Num. 24:11. *Joshua to descendants of Joseph*, Josh. 17:15–18. *By Jotham*, Judg. 9:7–19. *By Samson*, Judg. 14:18. *The men of Jabesh to Nahash*, 1 Sam. 11:10. *Eliab to David*, 1 Sam. 17:28. *David reproaching Abner*, 1 Sam. 26:15. *Elijah to the priests of Baal*, 1 Kin. 18:27. *David's reply to Michal's irony*, 2 Sam. 6:21. *Ahab's reply to Ben-hadad*, 1 Kin. 20:11. *Jehoash to Amaziah*, 2 Kin. 14:9, 10; 2 Chr. 25:18, 19. *Rabshakeh to Hezekiah*, 2 Kin. 18:23, 24. *Sanballat's address to the army of Samaria*, Neh. 4:2, 3. *Zophar to Job*, Job 11:12. *Job to Zophar*, Job 12:2, 3. *The persecutors of Jesus to Jesus*, Matt. 27:28, 29; John 19:3, 15. *Paul, to the Corinthians*, 2 Cor. 11:19; *to Timothy*, 1 Tim. 4:7. *Agrippa to Paul*, Acts 26:28.
See footnote, IRONY, Mark 12:14.

* **JEPHTHAH** (*opener*), a judge of Israel. *Illegitimate, and therefore not entitled to inherit his father's property*, Judg. 11:1, 2. *Escapes the violence of his half-brothers; dwells in the land of Tob*, Judg. 11:3. *Recalled from the land of Tob by the elders of Gilead*, Judg. 11:5. *Made captain of the host*, Judg. 11:5–11. *Made head of the land of Gilead*, Judg. **11:7–11.**

2
*b Strife, instances of,* Prov. 20:3.
1 R. V. another

3
*c Or, Ish-tob,* 2 Sam. 10:6, 8.

4
*d Ammonites,* Deut. 2:20.

5
*e Government, municipal,* Isa. 22:21.
*f Senate,* Num. 11:16.
*g Gilead,* Deut. 3:13.

10
*h Oath,* Num. 5:19.

an harlot: and Gĭl′e-ăd begat
Jĕph′thah.
2 And Gĭl′e-ăd's wife bare him
sons; and his wife's sons grew
up, and they [b]thrust out Jĕph′-
thah, and said unto him, Thou
shalt not inherit in our father's
house; for thou *art* the son of [1]a
strange woman.
3 Then *Jĕph′thah fled from
his brethren, and dwelt in the
land of [c]Tŏb: and there were
gathered vain[c] men to Jĕph′-
thah, and went out with him.
4 ¶ And it came to pass in[c] process of time, that the [d]children
of Ăm′mŏn made war against
Ĭs′ra-el.
5 And it was so, that when the
children of Ăm′mŏn made war
against Ĭs′ra-el, the [e,f]elders of
[g]Gĭl′e-ăd went to fetch[c] Jĕph′-
thah out of the land of Tŏb:
6 And they said unto *Jĕph′-
thah, Come, and be our captain,
that we may fight with the
[d]children of Ăm′mŏn.
7 And *Jĕph′thah said unto the
elders of Gĭl′e-ăd, Did not ye
hate me, and expel me out of my
father's house? and why are ye
come unto me now when ye are
in distress[c]?
8 And the elders of Gĭl′e-ăd
said unto *Jĕph′thah, Therefore
we turn again to thee now, that
thou mayest go with us, and
fight against the [d]children of
Ăm′mŏn, and be our head[c] over
all the inhabitants of Gĭl′e-ăd.
9 And *Jĕph′thah said unto the
elders of Gĭl′e-ăd, If ye bring me
home again to fight against the
[d]children of Ăm′mŏn, and the
LORD deliver them before me,
shall I be your head?
10 And the [f]elders of Gĭl′e-ăd
said unto *Jĕph′thah, [h]The
LORD be witness between us, if
we do not so according to thy
words.
11 Then *Jĕph′thah went with
the elders of Gĭl′e-ăd, and the
people made him head and captain over them: and Jĕph′thah
uttered all his words before the
LORD in Mĭz′peh.
12 ¶ And *Jĕph′thah [i]sent
[j]messengers unto the king of
the [d]children of Ăm′mŏn, saying,
What hast thou to do with me,
that thou art come against me
to fight in my land?
13 And the king of the [d]chil-
dren of Ăm′mŏn answered unto
the messengers of *Jĕph′thah,
Because [k]Ĭs′ra-el took away my
land, when they came up out of
[l]Ē′ġўpt, from [m]Är′nŏn even unto [n]Jăb′bŏk, and unto [o]Jôr′dan:
now therefore restore those *lands*
again peaceably.
14 And *Jĕph′thah sent [j]mes-
sengers again unto the king of
the [d]children of Ăm′mŏn:
15 And said unto him, Thus
saith *Jĕph′thah, [k]Ĭs′ra-el took
not away the land of [p]Mō′ab,
nor the land of the [d]children of
Ăm′mŏn:
16 But when [k]Ĭs′ra-el came up
from Ē′ġўpt, and walked through
the wilderness unto the [q]Red sea,
and came to [r]Kā′desh:
17 Then [k]Ĭs′ra-el sent [j]messen-
gers unto the king of [s]Ē′dom,
saying, Let me, I pray thee, pass
through thy land: but the king of
Ē′dom would not hearken[c] *thereto*. And in like manner they sent
unto the king of [t]Mō′ab: but he
would not *consent*: and Ĭs′ra-el
abode in [r]Kā′desh.
18 Then they went along
through the wilderness, and
compassed[c] the land of [s]Ē′dom,
and the land of [p]Mō′ab, and
came by the east side of the land

12
*i Diplomacy, instances of,* vs. 12-28; 2 Kin. 16:7.
*j Ambassadors,* Josh. 9:4.
v.12-1154 BC

13
*k Israel,* Ex. 4:22.
*l Egypt,* Gen. 41:8.
*m Arnon,* Num. 22:36.
*n Jabbok,* Num. 21:24.
*o Jordan,* Gen. 32:10.

15
*p Moab,* Num. 26:3.

16
*q Red Sea,* Ex. 10:19.
*r Kadesh,* Gen. 14:7.

17
*s Edomites,* 2 Kin. 8:21.
*t Moabites,* Gen. 19:37.

*His message to the king of the Ammonites,* Judg. 11:12–28. *Leads the host of Israel against the Ammonites,* Judg. 11:29–33. *His rash vow,* Judg. 11:31. *His daughter comes to meet him; his grief; her resignation to her fate,* Judg. 11:34–40. *Falsely accused by the Ephraimites,* Judg. 12:1. *Leads the army of the Gileadites against the Ephraimites,* Judg. 12:4. *Judges Israel six years; dies, and is buried in Gilead,* Judg. 12:7. *Faith of,* Heb. 11:32.

v.18–1154 BC
See footnote, *Time*, Rev. 10:6.

19
*u Sihon*, Num. 21:21.

20
2 R. V. border:

21
*v God, providence of*, Gen. 2:2.
*w Amorites*, Gen. 14:13.

24
*x Amorites, idolatry of*, Gen. 14:13.

25
*y Balak*, Num. 22:4.

26
*z Aroer*, Deut. 4:48.
3 R. V. side

of Mō'ab, and pitched[G] on the
other side of [m]Är'nŏn, but came
not within the border of Mō'ab:
for Är'nŏn *was* the border of
Mō'ab.
19 And [k]Ĭṣ'ra-el sent messengers unto [u]Sī'hŏn king of the
Am'ôr-ītes, the king of Hĕsh'-
bŏn; and Ĭṣ'ra-el said unto him,
Let us pass, we pray thee,
through thy land into my place.
20 But [u]Sī'hŏn trusted not Ĭṣ'-
ra-el to pass through his [2]coast[G]:
but Sī'hŏn gathered all his people together, and pitched[G] in [†]Jā'-
hăz, and fought against Ĭṣ'ra-el.
21 And the [v]LORD God of Ĭṣ'-
ra-el delivered [u]Sī'hŏn and all
his people into the hand of Ĭṣ'-
ra-el, and they smote them: so
Ĭṣ'ra-el possessed all the land of
the [w]Ăm'ôr-ītes, the inhabitants
of that country.
22 And they possessed all the
[2]coasts[G] of the Ăm'ôr-ītes, from
[m]Är'nŏn even unto [n]Jăb'bŏk,
and from the wilderness even
unto [o]Jôr'dan.
23 So now the LORD God of
Ĭṣ'ra-el hath dispossessed the
[w]Ăm'ôr-ītes from before his people Ĭṣ'ra-el, and shouldest thou
possess it?
24 Wilt not [x]thou possess that
which [‡]Chē'mŏsh thy god giveth
thee to possess? So whomsoever
the LORD our God [v]shall drive
out from before us, them will
we possess.
25 And now *art* thou any thing
better than [y]Bā'lăk the son of
Zĭp'por, king of [t]Mō'ab? did he
ever strive against [k]Ĭṣ'ra-el, or
did he ever fight against them,
26 While [k]Ĭṣ'ra-el dwelt in
Hĕsh'bŏn and her towns, and in
[z]Ăr'ŏ-ēr and her towns, and in
all the cities that *be* along by the
[3]coasts[G] of Är'nŏn, three hundred
years? why therefore did ye not
recover *them* within that time?
27 Wherefore I have not sinned
against thee, but thou doest me
wrong to war against me: the
LORD the [a]Judge be judge this
day between the children of Ĭṣ'-[T][T][S]
ra-el and the children of Ăm'mŏn.
28 Howbeit the king of the
children of Ăm'mŏn hearkened
not unto the words of [*]Jĕph'-
thah which he sent him.
29 ¶ Then the [b]Spirit of the
LORD came upon [*]Jĕph'thah,
and he passed over [c]Gĭl'e-ăd,
and [d]Mȧ-năs'seh, and passed
over Mĭz'peh of Gĭl'e-ăd, and
from Mĭz'peh of Gĭl'e-ăd he
passed over *unto* the [e]children
of Ăm'mŏn.[T]
30 And [*]Jĕph'thah [f,g]vowed[G] a
[h]vow[G] unto the LORD, and said,
If thou shalt without fail deliver
the [e]children of Ăm'mŏn into
mine hands,
31 Then it shall be, that whatsoever cometh forth of the doors
of my house to meet me, when I
return in peace[G] from the children
of Ăm'mŏn, [i]shall surely be the
LORD's, and I will offer it up
for a [j]burnt offering.
32 ¶ So[Q] [*]Jĕph'thah passed over
unto the [e]children of Ăm'mŏn to
fight against them; and the [k]LORD
delivered[G] them into his hands.
33 And he smote[G] them from
[l]Ăr'ŏ-ēr, even till thou come to
Mĭn'nith, *even* twenty cities, and
unto the plain of the vineyards,
with a very great slaughter.
Thus the [e]children of Ăm'mŏn
were subdued before the children of Ĭṣ'ra-el.[Q]
34 ¶ And [*]Jĕph'thah came to
Mĭz'peh unto his house, and, behold, his [m]daughter came out to
meet him with [n,o]timbrels[G] and
with [p]dances: and she *was his*

v.26–1154 BC
See footnote, *Time*, Rev. 10:6.

27
*a God, judge*, Gen. 2:2.

29
*b Holy Spirit, inspiration of*, Acts 1:2.
*c Gilead*, Deut. 3:13.
*d Manasseh, tribe of*, Gen. 46:20
*e Ammonites*, Deut. 2:20.

30
*f Zeal, exemplified*, 2 Cor. 7:11.
*g Rashness, instances of*, 2 Sam. 6:7.
*h Vows, rash*, Num. 30:2.

31
*i Consecration*, Lev. 7:37.
*j Offerings, burnt*, Lev. 6:17.

32
*k God, providence of*, Gen. 2:2.

33
*l Aroer*, Num. 32:34.

34
*m Women, mirthful*, Prov. 31:10.
*n Timbrel*, Ex. 15:20.
*o Music*, 2 Chr. 5:13.
*p Dancing*, Eccl. 3:4.

† **JAHAZ** (*a place trodden down*), called also JAHAZA, JAHAZAH, and JAHZAH. *A Levitical city in Reuben, taken from the Moabites*, Josh. 13:18; 21:36; Isa. 15:4; Jer. 48:21. *Given to the sons of Merari*, 1 Chr. 6:78. *Sihon, king of the Amorites, defeated at*, Num. 21:23; Deut. 2:32; Judg. 11:20.

‡ **CHEMOSH.** *An idol of the Moabites*, 1 Kin. 11:7, 33; 2 Kin. 23:13, 21; Jer. 48:7, 13, 46; Judg. 11:24.

v.34–1154 BC
See footnote, *Time*, Rev. 10:6.

35
q *Mourning*, Lam. 2:5.

36
r *Children, good*, Mark 10:14.

37
s *Virgin*, Isa. 62:5.
t *Women*, Prov. 31:10.
u *Celibacy, deplored*, 1 Tim. 4:3.

40
4 **R. V** celebrate

1
a *Jealousy*, Psa. 78:58.
b *Citizens, wicked and treasonable*, Luke 15:15.
c *Ephraim, tribe of*, Gen. 41:52.

only child; beside her he had neither son nor daughter.

35 And it came to pass, when he saw her, that he [q]rent[C] his clothes, and said, Alas, my daughter! thou hast brought me very low, and thou art one of them that trouble me: for I have [h]opened my mouth unto the LORD, and I cannot go back.

36 And [r]she said unto him, My father, *if* thou hast opened thy mouth unto the LORD, do to me according to that which hath proceeded out of thy mouth; forasmuch as the [k]LORD hath taken vengeance for thee of thine enemies, *even* of the [e]children of Ăm′mŏn.

37 And [s,t]she said unto her father, Let this thing be done for me: let me alone two months, that I may go up and down upon the mountains, and bewail[C] my [u]virginity, I and my fellows[C].

38 And he said, Go. And he sent her away *for* two months: and [s,t]she went with her companions, and bewailed her [u]virginity upon the mountains.

39 And it came to pass at the end of two months, that she returned unto her father, who did with her *according* to his [h]vow which he had vowed: and she knew no man. And it was a custom in Ĭş′ra-el,

40 *That* the daughters of Ĭş′ra-el went yearly to [4]lament the daughter of Jĕph′thah the Ḡĭl′e-ăd-īte four days in a year.

## CHAPTER 12

*The Ephraimites, quarreling with Jephthah, are detected by the word Shibboleth, and slain by the Gileadites. 7 Jephthah dies. 8 Ibzan, 11 Elon, 13 and Abdon, successively judge Israel.*

AND [a]the [b]men of [c]Ē′phră-ĭm gathered themselves together, and went northward, and said unto [d]Jĕph′thah, Wherefore[C] passedst thou over to fight against the [e]children of Ăm′mŏn, and didst not call us to go with thee? we will burn thine house upon thee with fire.

2 And Jĕph′thah said unto them, I and my [f]people were at great [g]strife with the [e]children of Ăm′mŏn; and when I called you, ye delivered me not out of their hands.

3 And when I saw that ye delivered *me* not, I put my life in my hands, and passed over[C] against the [e]children of Ăm′mŏn, and the [h]LORD delivered them into my hand: wherefore[C] then are ye come up unto me this day, to fight against me?

4 [i]Then Jĕph′thah gathered together all the men of [j]Ḡĭl′e-ăd, and fought with [k]Ē′phră-ĭm: and the men of Ḡĭl′e-ăd smote Ē′phră-ĭm, because they said, Ye Ḡĭl′e-ăd-ītes *are* *fugitives of Ē′phră-ĭm among the Ē′phră-ĭm-ītes, *and* among the Mă-năs′sītes.

5 And the Ḡĭl′e-ăd′ītes took the passages[C] of [l]Jôr′dan before the [k]Ē′phră-ĭm′ītes: and it was *so*, that when those Ē′phră-ĭm-ītes which were escaped said, Let me go over; that the men of Ḡĭl′e-ăd said unto him, *Art* thou an Ē′phră-ĭm-īte? If he said, Nay;

6 [m]Then said they unto him, Say now Shĭb′bo-lĕth: and he said Sĭb′bo-lĕth: for he could not frame[C] to pronounce *it* right. Then they took him, and slew him at the passages[C] of [l]Jôr′dan: and there fell at that time of the Ē′phră-ĭm-ītes forty and two thousand.

7 And [n,o]Jĕph′thah judged [p]Ĭş′ra-el six years. Then died Jĕph′thah the Ḡĭl′e-ăd-īte, and

v.1–1154 BC
See footnote, *Time*, Rev. 10:6.

d *Jephthah*, Judg. 11:1.
e *Ammonites*, Deut. 2:20.

2
f *Israel, under the judges*, Ex. 4:22.
g *Strife, instances of*, vs. 1–6; Prov. 20:3.

3
h *God, providence of*, Gen. 2:2.

4
i *War, civil*, Judg. 3:2.
j *Gilead*, Deut. 3:13.
k *Ephraim, tribe of* Gen. 41:52.

5
l *Jordan, fords of*, Gen. 32:10.

6
m *Language, dialects of the Jews* Dan. 3:29.

7
n *Jephthah, judge*, Judg. 11:1.
o *Judges of Israel*, Judg. 2:16.
p *Israel, under the judges*, Ex. 4:22.

* **FUGITIVES.** *From servitude, not to be returned*, Deut. 23:15, 16.
From slavery: *Shimei's servants*, 1 Kin. 2:39; *Onesimus*, Philemon 10.
From justice: *Moses*, Ex. 2:15; *Absalom*, 2 Sam. 13: 34–38.
From the wrath of the king: *David*, 1 Sam. 21:10; 27:2; *Jeroboam*, 1 Kin. 11:40; *Joseph, to Egypt*, Matt. 2:13–15.

v.8–1148 BC
See footnote, *Time*, Rev. 10:6.

8
q *Possibly identical with Bethlehem in Zebulun*, Josh. 19:15.

v.11–1141 BC

12
r *Zebulun, tribe of*, Gen. 49:13.

v.13–1131 BC

14
1 R. V. sons' sons,

15
s 2 Sam. 23:30; 1 Chr. 11:31; 27:14.

v.1–1123 BC
See footnote, *Time*, Rev. 10:6.

1
a *Israel, under the judges, backsliding of*, Ex. 4:22.
b *God, providence of*, Gen. 2:2.
c *Judgments*, Ex. 6:6.
d *Philistines*, Gen. 26:14.

2
e *Zorah*, Josh. 19:41.
f *Dan, tribe of*, Gen. 30:6.
g *Barrenness*, Deut. 7:14.

3
h *Angel, appearances of*, Heb. 1:13.
i *Conception*, Gen. 21:2.

was buried in *one of* the cities of Gĭl'e-ăd.

8 ¶ And after him [o]Ĭb'zăn of [q]Bĕth'–le-hĕm judged [p]Ĭs̱'ra-el.

9 And he had thirty sons, and thirty daughters, *whom* he sent abroad,[C] and took in thirty daughters from abroad[C] for his sons. And he judged Ĭs̱'ra-el seven years.

10 Then died Ĭb'zăn, and was buried at [q]Bĕth'–lĕ-hĕm.

11 ¶ And after him [o]Ē'lŏn, a Zĕb'u-lon-īte, judged [p]Ĭs̱'ra-el; and he judged Ĭs̱'ra-el ten years.

12 And Ē'lŏn the Zĕb'u-lon-īte died, and was buried in Ăij'a-lŏn in the country of [r]Zĕb'u-lŭn.

13 ¶ And after him [o]Ăb'dŏn the son of Hĭl'lel, a Pĭr'a-thon-īte, judged [p]Ĭs̱'ra-el.

14 And he had forty sons and thirty [1]nephews,[C] that rode on threescore and ten ass colts: and he judged Ĭs̱'ra-el eight years.

15 And Ăb'dŏn the son of Hĭl'lel the [s]Pĭr'a-thon-īte died, and was buried in Pĭr'a-thŏn in the land of [c]Ē'phră-ĭm, in the mount of the Ăm'a-lĕk-ītes.

## CHAPTER 13

*Israel delivered into the hand of the Philistines. 2 An angel appears to Manoah's wife, 8 and again to her and to Manoah. 15 Manoah's sacrifice, during which the angel is discovered. 24 Samson is born.*

AND the children of [a]Ĭs̱'ra-el did evil again in the sight of the LORD; and the [b]LORD [c]delivered them into the hand of the [d]Phĭ-lĭs'tĭnes forty years.

2 ¶ And there was a certain man of [e]Zō'rah, of the family of the [f]Dăn'ītes, whose name *was* Mā-nō'ah; and his wife *was* [g]barren, and bare not.

3 [T]And the [h]angel of the LORD appeared unto the woman, and said unto her, Behold now, thou *art* [g]barren, and bearest not: but thou shalt [i]conceive, and bear a son.[Q]

4 Now therefore beware,[C] I pray thee, and [j]drink not [k]wine nor strong drink, and eat not any unclean *thing*:[Q]

5 For, lo, thou shalt [i]conceive, and bear a son; and no [l]razor shall come on his head: for the [m]child shall be a [n]Năz'a-rīte unto God from the womb: and he shall begin to deliver Ĭs̱'ra-el out of the hand of the [d]Phĭ-lĭs'tĭnes̱.[Q]

6 ¶ Then the woman came and told her husband, saying, A man of God came unto me, and his countenance *was* like the countenance of an [h]angel of God, very terrible[C]: but I asked him not whence he *was*, neither told he me his name:

7 But he said unto me, Behold, thou shalt [i]conceive, and bear a son; and now [j]drink no [k]wine nor strong drink, neither eat any unclean *thing*: for the child shall be a [n]Năz'a-rīte to God from the womb to the day of his death.[Q]

8 ¶ Then Mā-nō'ah [o]intreated the LORD, and said, O my Lord, let the man of God which thou didst send come again unto us, and teach us what we shall do unto the child that shall be born.

9 And God [o]hearkened[C] to the voice of Mā-nō'ah; and the [h]angel[C] of God came again unto the woman as she sat in the field: but Mā-nō'ah her husband *was* not with her.

10 And the woman made haste, and ran, and shewed[C] her husband, and said unto him, Behold, the man hath appeared unto me, that came unto me the *other* day.

11 And Mā-nō'ah arose, and went after his wife, and came to the man, and said unto him, *Art* thou the man that spakest unto the woman? And he said, I *am*.

12 And Mā-nō'ah said, Now let thy words come to pass. [1]How

4
j *Total Abstinence*, Lev. 10:9.
k *Wine, admonitions against the use of*, Prov. 23:31.

5
l *Shaving*, Ezek. 44:20.
m *Children, dedicated to God*, Mark 10:14.
n *Nazarite*, Num. 6:2.

8
o *Prayer, answered*, Acts 6:4.

12
1 R. V. what shall be the manner of the child, and what shall be his work?

shall we order the child, and *how* shall we do unto him?

13 And the [h]angel of the LORD said unto Mā-nō'ah, Of all that I said unto the woman let her beware.

14 She [i]may not eat of any *thing* that cometh of the *vine, [j]neither let her drink [k]wine or strong drink, nor eat any unclean *thing*: all that I commanded her let her observe.

15 ¶ And Mā-nō'ah said unto the [h]angel of the LORD, I pray thee, let us detain thee, until we shall have made ready a kid for thee.

16 And the [h]angel of the LORD said unto Mā-nō'ah, Though thou detain me, I will not eat of thy bread[C]: and if thou wilt offer a [p]burnt offering, thou must offer it unto the LORD. For Mā-nō'ah knew not that he *was* an angel[C] of the LORD.

17 And Mā-nō'ah said unto the [h]angel of the LORD, What *is* thy name, that when thy sayings come to pass we may do[C] thee honour?

18 And the [h]angel[C] of the LORD said unto him, Why askest thou thus after my name, seeing it *is* [2]secret?

19[S] So Mā-nō'ah took a [q]kid with a [3,r]meat[C] offering, and offered *it* upon a rock unto the LORD: and *the* [h]*angel* did wonderously; and Mā-nō'ah and his wife looked on.

20 For it came to pass, when the flame went up toward heaven from off the altar, that the [h]angel[C] of the LORD ascended[C] in the flame of the altar. And Mā-nō'ah and his wife looked on *it*, and fell on their faces to the ground.[S]

21 But the [h]angel of the LORD did no more appear to Mā-nō'ah and to his wife. Then Mā-nō'ah knew that he *was* an angel of the LORD.

22 And Mā-nō'ah said unto his wife, We shall surely die, because we have seen God.

23 But his [s]wife said unto him, [t]If the LORD were pleased to kill us, he would not have received a [p]burnt offering and a [3,r]meat[C] offering at our hands, neither would he have shewed us all these *things*, nor would as at this time have told us *such things* as these.[T]

24 ¶ And the woman bare a son, and called his name †Săm'son: and the child grew, and the LORD blessed him.

25 And the [u]Spirit of the LORD began to move[C] him at times in the camp of [v]Dăn between [w]Zō'rah and [x]Ĕsh'ta-ŏl.[T]

## CHAPTER 14

*Samson desires a wife of the Philistines. 5 In his journey he kills a lion. 8 In a second journey he finds honey in the carcass. 10 Samson's marriage feast. 12 His riddle is made known by his wife. 19 He slays and spoils thirty Philistines. 20 His wife is given to another.*

AND [a]Săm'son went down to Tĭm'nath and saw a woman in Tĭm'nath of the daughters of the [b]Phĭ-lĭs'tīneș.

2 And he came up, and told his father and his mother, and said, I have seen a woman in Tĭm'nath of the daughters of the Phĭ-lĭs'tīneș: now therefore get her for me [c]to[C] wife.[S]

3 Then his father and his mother

16
p *Offerings, burnt,* Lev. 6.17.

18
2 R.V. wonderful?

19
q *Goat,* Deut. 14 4.
r *Offerings, meal,* Lev. 6:17.
3 R. V. meal

23
s *Women, good, instances of,* Prov. 31:10.
t *Faith, instances of,* Mark 11:22.

25
u *Holy Spirit, inspiration of,* Acts 1:2.
v *Dan, tribe of,* Gen. 30:6.
w *Zorah,* Josh. 19:41.
x *Eshtaol,* Judg. 18:2.

1
a *Samson,* Judg. 13:24.
b *Philistines,* Gen. 26:14.

2
c *Marriage,* Gen. 34:9.

* **VINE.** *Degeneracy of,* Isa. 5:2–6; Jer. 2:21. *Fable of,* Judg. 9:12, 13. *Pruned,* Isa. 5:6; John 15:1–5. *Parables of,* Psa. 80:8–16; Ezek. 17:6–10; 19:10–14.
SYMBOLICAL, John 15:1–5.
See footnote, VINEYARD, Isa. 1:8.

† **SAMSON** (*sunlike*). *A judge of Israel,* Judg. 16:31. *A Danite, son of Manoah; miraculous birth of; a Nazarite from his mother's womb; the mother forbidden to drink wine or strong drink, or to eat any unclean thing during gestation,* Judg. 13:2–7, 24, 25. *Desires a Philistine woman for his wife; slays a lion,* Judg. 14:1–7. *His marriage feast and the riddle propounded,* Judg. 14:8–19. *Slays thirty Philistines,* Judg. 14:19. *Wife of, estranged,* Judg. 14:20; 15:1, 2. *Is avenged for the estrangement of his wife,* Judg. 15:3–8. *His great strength,* Judg. 15:7–14. *Slays a thousand Philistines with the jawbone of an ass,* Judg. 15:13–17. *Miraculously supplied with water,* Judg. 15:18, 19. *Carries off the gate of Gaza,* Judg. 16:1–3. *Cohabits with Delilah, an harlot; her machinations with the Philistines to overcome him,* Judg. 16:4–20. *Is blinded by the Philistines and confined to hard labor in prison; pulls down the pillars of the temple; meets his death, and slays a multitude of his enemies,* Judg. 16:21–31; Heb. 11:32.

said unto him, *Is there* never a
woman among the daughters of
thy brethren, or among all my
people, that thou goest to take a
wife of the uncircumcised [b]Phĭ-
lĭs′tĭneṣ? And Săm′son said unto his father, Get her for me; for
she pleaseth me well.
4 But his father and his mother
knew not that [d]it *was* of the
LORD, that he sought an occasion[C] against the [b]Phĭ-lĭs′tĭneṣ:
for at that time the Phĭ-lĭs′tĭneṣ
had dominion over Iṣ′ra-el.[S]
5 Then went [a]Săm′son down,
and his father and his mother, to
Tĭm′nath, and came to the vineyards of Tĭm′nath: and, behold,
a young [e]lion roared against him.
6[Q] And the Spirit of the LORD
came mightily upon him, and he
rent[C] him as he would have rent[C] a
kid, and *he had* nothing in his
hand: but he told not his father
or his mother what he had done.[T S]
7 And he went down, and
talked with the woman; and
she pleased Săm′son well.[Q]
8 ¶ And after a time he returned to take her, and he
turned aside to see the carcase
of the lion: and, behold, *there
was* a swarm of [f]bees and [g]honey
in the carcase of the lion.
9 And he took thereof in his
hands, and went on eating, and
came to his father and mother,
and he gave them, and they did
eat: but he told not them that he
had taken the honey out of the
carcase of the lion.
10 ¶ So his father went down
unto the woman: and [a]Săm′son
made there a [h,i]feast; for so used
the young men to do.
11 And it came to pass, when
they saw [j]him, that they brought
thirty companions to be with
him.
12 And [a]Săm′son said unto
them, I will now put forth a [k]rid-
dle unto you: if ye can certainly

4
c *Foreordination,* Rom. 8:30.

5
e *Lion,* Mic. 5.8.

8
f *Bee,* Deut. 1:44.
g *Honey,* Prov. 25: 27.

10
h *Feasts,* Mark 12: 39.
i *Marriage, nuptial feasts,* Gen. 34:9.

11
j *Bridegroom,* Isa. 61:10.

12
k Ezek. 17:2–10.

declare it me within the seven
days of the [h,i]feast, and find *it*
out, then I will give you thirty
[1]sheets and thirty change of
garments:
13 But if ye cannot declare *it*
me, then shall ye give me thirty
[1]sheets and thirty change of garments. And they said unto him,
Put forth thy riddle[C], that we may
hear it.
14 And he said unto them, Out
of the [e]eater came forth meat[C],
and out of the strong came forth
[g]sweetness. And they could
not in three days expound the
[k]riddle[C].
15 And it came to pass on the
seventh day, that they said unto
[a]Săm′son's wife, Entice thy husband, that he may declare unto
us the [k]riddle[C], lest we burn thee
and thy father's house with fire:
have ye called us to [2]take that
we have? *is it* not *so*?
16 And [a]Săm′son's wife wept
before him, and said, Thou dost
but hate me, and lovest me not:
thou hast put forth a [k]riddle[C] unto the children of my people, and
hast not told *it* me. And he said
unto her, Behold, I have not told
*it* my father nor my mother, and
shall I tell *it* thee?
17 And she wept before him the
seven days, while their [h,i]feast
lasted: and it came to pass on
the seventh day, that he told her,
because she lay[C] sore upon him:
and she told the riddle[C] to the
children of her people.
18 And the men of the city said
unto him on the seventh day before the sun went down, What *is*
sweeter than [g]honey? and what
*is* stronger than a [e]lion? And he
[l]said unto them, If ye had not
plowed with my [m]heifer, ye had
not found out my [k]riddle[C].
19 And the Spirit of the LORD
came upon [a]him, and he went
down to [n]Ăsh′ke-lŏn, and slew

1 R. V. linen garments

15
2 R. V. impoverish us?

18
l *Sarcasm, instances of,* Judg. 10: 14.
m *Heifer,* Num. 19:2.

19
n Or, *Askelon,* Judg. 1:18.

thirty men of them, and took their spoil, and gave change of garments unto them which expounded[c] the riddle[c]. And his [o]anger was kindled, and he went up to his father's house.[T]

20 But Săm'son's wife was *given* to his companion, whom he had used as his friend[c].

## CHAPTER 15

*Samson is denied his wife. 3 He burns the Philistines' corn by means of foxes. 6 His wife and her father are burnt by the Philistines; 7 for which Samson smites them hip and thigh. 9 He is bound by the men of Judah, and delivered to the Philistines; 14 of whom he kills a thousand with the jawbone of an ass. 18 God makes a fountain for him in Lehi.*

BUT it came to pass within a while after, in the time of wheat harvest, that [a]Săm'son visited his wife with a kid; and he said, I will go in to my wife into the chamber. But her father would not suffer[c] him to go in.

2 And her father said, I verily thought that thou hadst utterly hated her; therefore I gave her to thy companion: *is* not her younger sister fairer than she? take her, I pray thee, instead of her.

3 ¶ And Săm'son said concerning them, Now shall I be more blameless than the [b]Phĭ-lĭs'tīneş, though I do them a [1]displeasure[c].

4 And Săm'son went and caught three hundred [c]foxes, and took firebrands[c], and turned tail to tail, and put a firebrand in the midst between two tails.

5 And when he had set the brands[c] on fire, he let *them* go into the standing [d]corn[c] of the [b]Phĭ-lĭs'tīneş, and [e]burnt up both the shocks[c], and also the standing corn[c], [2]with the vineyards *and* olives.

6 Then the [b]Phĭ-lĭs'tīneş said, Who hath done this? And they answered, [a]Săm'son, the son in law of the Tĭm'nīte, because he had taken his wife, and given her to his companion. And the Phĭ-lĭs'tīneş came up, and [f]burnt her and her father with fire.

7 ¶ And [a]Săm'son said unto them, Though ye have done this, yet will I be [g]avenged of you, and after that I will cease.

8 And [g]he smote them hip and thigh with a great slaughter: and he went down and dwelt in the [3]top of the rock Ē'tam.

9 ¶ Then the [b]Phĭ-lĭs'tīneş went up, and pitched[c] in [h]Jū'dah, and spread themselves in Lē'hī.

10 And the men of Jū'dah said, Why are ye come up against us? And they answered, To bind[c] [a]Săm'son are we come up, to do to him as he hath done to us.

11 Then three thousand men of [h]Jū'dah went to the [3]top of the rock Ē'tam, and said to [a]Săm'son, Knowest thou not that the Phĭ-lĭs'tīneş *are* rulers over us? what *is* this *that* thou hast done unto us? And he said unto them, [i]As they did unto me, so have I done unto them.

12 And they said unto him, We are come down to bind thee, that we may deliver thee into the hand of the Phĭ-lĭs'tīneş. And Săm'son said unto them, Swear unto me, that ye will not fall upon me yourselves.

13 And they spake unto him, saying, No; but we will bind thee fast[c], and deliver thee into their hand: but surely we will not kill thee. And they bound him with two new cords, and brought him up from the rock.

14 ¶ *And* when [a]he came unto Lē'hī, the [b]Phĭ-lĭs'tīneş shouted against him: and the Spirit of the LORD came mightily upon him, and the cords that *were* upon his arms became as flax that was burnt with fire, and his bands loosed from off his hands.[T]

15 And he found a new[c] jawbone of an [j]ass, and put forth his

---

*o* *Anger*, Psa. 37:8.

**B.C. 1140?** See footnote, *Time*, Rev. 10:6.

1 *a* *Samson*, Judg. 13:24.

3 *b* *Philistines*, Gen. 26:14.
1 R. V. mischief.

4 *c* *Fox*, Psa. 63:10.

5 *d* *Corn*, Psa. 65:13.
*e* *Arson, instances of*, 2 Sam. 14.30.
2 R. V. and also the olive yards.

6 *f* *Homicide, felonious*, Deut. 5:7.

7 *g* *Revenge*, Ezek. 25:15.

8 3 R. V. cleft

9 *h* *Judah, tribe of*, Num. 10:14.

11 *i* *Retaliation*, Deut. 19:19.

15 *j* *Ass*, 2 Chr. 28:15.

hand, and took it, and slew a
thousand men therewith.
16 And [a]Săm′son said, With
the jawbone of an [i]ass, heaps
upon heaps, with the jaw of an
ass have I slain a thousand men.
17 And it came to pass, when
he had made an end of speaking,
that he cast away the jawbone
out of his hand, and called that
place Rā′math–lē′hī.
18 ¶ And he was sore athirst,
and called on the LORD, and
said, [k]Thou hast given this great
deliverance into the hand of thy
servant: and now shall I die for
thirst, and fall into the hand of
the uncircumcised?
19 But God clave[C] an hollow
place that [4]*was* in the jaw, and
there came [l]water thereout; and
when he had drunk, his spirit
came again, and he revived:
wherefore he called the name
thereof Ĕn–hăk′kō-rē, which *is*
in Lē′hī unto this day.[s]
20 And [a,m]he judged [n]Ĭs′ra-el
in the days of the Phĭ-lĭs′tĭneş
twenty years.

## CHAPTER 16

*Samson carries away the gates of the city of Gaza. 4 Delilah, bribed by the Philistines, entices Samson. 6 Thrice he deceives her. 15 At last he reveals to her the secret of his strength. 21 The Philistines take him, and put out his eyes. 22 His strength returning, he pulls down the house of Dagon upon the Philistines, and dies.*

THEN went [a]Săm′son to
[b]Gā′zȧ, and saw there an
harlot, and [c]went in unto her.
2 *And it was told* the [d]Gā′zītes,
saying, [a]Săm′son is come thither.[C]
And they compassed *him* in, and
laid wait for him all night in the
gate of the city, and were quiet
all the night, saying, In the
morning, when it is day, we
shall kill him.
3 And [a]Săm′son lay till midnight, and arose at midnight,
and took the doors of the gate of
the city, and the two posts, and
went away with them, bar and
all, and put *them* upon his shoulders, and carried them up to the
top of an hill that *is* before
Hē′bron.
4 ¶ And it came to pass afterward, that [a]he loved a [e]woman
in the valley of Sō′rek, whose
name *was* [f]Dē-lī′lah.
5 And the lords of the [g]Phĭ-lĭs′-
tĭneş came up unto her, and said
unto her, Entice him, and see
wherein his great strength *lieth*,
and by what *means* we may prevail against him, that we may
bind[C] him to afflict[C] him: and we
will [h]give thee every one of us
eleven hundred *pieces* of silver.
6 And [f]Dē-lī′lah said to [a]Săm′-
son, Tell me, I pray thee, wherein thy great strength *lieth*, and
wherewith thou mightest be
bound to afflict thee.
7 And [a]Săm′son said unto her,
If they bind me with seven green
withs[C] that were never dried, then
shall I be weak, and be as another man.
8 Then the lords of the [g]Phĭ-
lĭs′tĭneş brought up to her seven
green withs[C] which had not been
dried, and she bound him with
them.
9 Now *there were* men lying in
wait, abiding with her in the
chamber. And [e,f]she said unto
him, The Phĭ-lĭs′tĭneş *be* upon
thee, [a]Săm′son. And he brake
the withs,[C] as a thread of [i]tow[C] is
broken when it toucheth the fire.
So his strength was not known.
10 And [e,f]Dē-lī′lah said unto
[a]Săm′son, Behold, thou hast
mocked me, and told me lies:
now tell me, I pray thee, wherewith thou mightest be bound.
11 And he said unto her, If they
bind me fast[C] with new ropes
[1]that never were occupied,[C] then
shall I be weak, and be as another man.
12 [e,f]Dē-lī′lah therefore took
new ropes, and bound him there-

18
k *God, providence of,* Gen. 2:2.

19
l *Water,* 1 Kin. 17: 10.
4 R. V. is in Lehi.

20
m *Judges of Israel,* Judg. 2:16.
n *Israel, under the judges,* Ex. 4:22.

B.C. 1120?
See footnote, *Time,* Rev. 10:6.

1
a *Samson,* Judg. 13:24.
b *Gaza,* Gen. 10: 19.
c *Adultery, instances of,* Lev. 20: 10.

2
d Or, *Gazathites,* Josh. 13:3.

4
e *Woman, wicked,* Prov. 31:10.
f *Friends, false,* vs. 4–20; Ex. 33: 11.

5
g *Philistines, lords of,* Gen. 26:14.
h *Bribery, instances of,* 1 Sam. 8:3.

9
i Isa. 1:31.

11
1 R. V. wherewith no work hath been done.

with, and said unto him, The [g]Phĭ-lĭs′tĭneş *be* upon thee, Săm′-son. And *there were* liers[c] in wait abiding in the chamber. And he brake them from off his arms like a thread.

13 And [e,f]Dē-lī′lah said unto [a]Săm′son, Hitherto thou hast mocked me, and told me lies: tell me wherewith thou mightest be bound. And he said unto her, If thou [j]weavest the seven locks of my head with the web.

14 And she fastened *it* with the pin, and said unto him, The [g]Phĭ-lĭs′tĭneş *be* upon thee, [a]Săm′son. And he awaked out of his sleep, and went away with the pin of the beam, and with the web.

15 ¶ And [e,f]she said unto [a]him, How canst thou say, I love thee, when thine heart *is* not with me? thou hast mocked me these three times, and hast not told me wherein thy great strength *lieth*.

16 And it came to pass, when she pressed him daily with her words, and urged him, *so* that his soul was vexed unto death;

17 That he told her all his heart, and said unto her, There hath not come a razor upon mine head; for I *have been* a [k]Năz′a-rīte unto God from my mother's womb: if I be shaven, then my strength will go from me, and I shall become weak, and be like any *other* man.[s]

18 And when [e,f]Dē-lī′lah saw that he had told her all his heart, she sent and called for the lords of the [g]Phĭ-lĭs′tĭneş, saying, Come up this once, for he hath shewed me all his heart. Then the lords of the Phĭ-lĭs′tĭneş came up unto her, and [h]brought [l]money in their hand.

19 And [e,f]she made him sleep upon her knees; and she called for a man, and she caused him to shave off the seven locks of his head; and she began to afflict him, and his strength went from him.

20 And [e,f]she said, The [g]Phĭ-lĭs′tĭneş *be* upon thee, [a]Săm′son. And he awoke out of his sleep, and said, I will go out as at other times before, and shake myself. And he [m]wist[c] not that the [n]LORD was departed from him.

21 But the [g]Phĭ-lĭs′tĭneş took [o]him, and [p]put out his eyes, and brought him down to [b]Gā′zȧ, and bound him with [q]fetters of [r]brass; and [s]he did [t]grind in the prison house.

22 Howbeit the hair of his head began to grow again after he was shaven.

23 Then the lords of the [g]Phĭ-lĭs′tĭneş gathered them together for to offer a great sacrifice unto [*]Dā′gon their god, and to rejoice: for they said, Our god hath delivered [a]Săm′son our enemy into our hand.

24 And when the people saw him, they [u]praised their god: for they said, Our god hath delivered into our hands our enemy, and the destroyer of our country, which slew many of us.

25 And it came to pass, when their hearts were merry, that they said, Call for [a,s]Săm′son, that he may make us sport.[c] And they called for Săm′son out of the prison house; and he made them sport[c]: and they set him between the pillars.

26 And [a,s]Săm′son said unto the lad that held him by the hand, Suffer[c] me that I may feel the pillars whereupon the [v]house standeth, that I may lean upon them.

27 Now the [v]house was full of men and women; and all the lords of the [g]Phĭ-lĭs′tĭneş *were* there; and *there were* upon the

13
j *Weaving*, Isa. 38:12.

17
k *Nazarite*, Num. 6:2.

18
l *Money*, Jer. 32:9.

20
m *Spiritual Blindness*, 2 Cor. 4:4.
n *Holy Spirit, withdrawn*, Acts 1:2.

21
o *Captive, cruelty to*, 1 Sam. 30:3.
p *Cruelty, instance of*, Psa. 27:12.
q *Fetters*, Mark 5:4.
r *Brass*, Job 28:2.
s *Prisoners*, Psa. 79:11.
t *Mill*, Ex. 11:5.

24
u *Idolatry*, 1 Sam. 15:23.

26
v *House, architecture of*, Esth. 8:1

* **DAGON.** *An idol of the Philistines*, Judg. 16:23, 24; 1 Sam. 5:1–5. *Temple of*, 1 Chr. 10:10.

roof about three thousand men
and women, that beheld while
[a,s]Săm′son made sport.
28[Q]And [a]Săm′son [w]called unto
the LORD, and said, O Lord
GOD, remember me, I pray
thee, and strengthen me, I pray
thee, only this once, O God, that
I may be at[c] once [x]avenged[c] of
the [g]Phĭ-lĭs′tĭnes for my two
eyes.
29 And Săm′son took hold of
the two middle pillars upon
which the house stood, and on
which it was borne up,[c] of the
one with his right hand, and of
the other with his left.
30 And Săm′son [y]said, Let me
die with the [g]Phĭ-lĭs′tĭnes. And
he bowed himself with *all his*
might; and the house fell upon
the lords, and upon all the people that *were* therein. [x]So the
dead which he slew at his death
were more than *they* which he
slew in his life. [S Q]
31 Then his brethren and all the
house of his father came down,
and took him, and brought
*him* up, and buried him between [z]Zŏ′rah and [a]Ĕsh′ta-ŏl in
the [b]buryingplace of Mă-nō′ah
his father. And [c,d]he judged
[e]Ĭs′ra-el twenty years.

## CHAPTER 17

*The idolatry of Micah and his mother. 7 He hires a Levite to be his priest.*

AND there was a man of
mount [a]Ē′phră-ĭm, whose
name *was* Mī′cah.
2 And [b]he said unto his mother,
The eleven hundred [1,*,c]*shekels*
of silver that were taken from
thee, about which thou cursedst,
and spakest of also in mine ears,
behold, the silver *is* with me;
I [d,e]took it. And his mother said,
Blessed *be thou* of the LORD, my
son.
3 And when he had [f]restored
the [*]eleven hundred [1,c]*shekels*[C]
of silver to his mother, his mother said, I had wholly [g]dedicated
the silver unto the LORD from
my hand for my son, to make a
graven[C] image and a molten[C] image: now therefore I will restore
it unto thee.
4 Yet he restored the [*,h]money
unto his mother; and his mother
took two hundred [1]*shekels*[c] of silver, and gave them to the founder,[C] who made thereof a graven[C]
image and a molten[C] image: and
they were in the house of Mī′cah.
5 And the man Mī′cah had an
house of gods, and made an
[i]ephod,[C] and [†]teraphim, and consecrated[C] one of his sons, who became his priest.
6 In those days *there was* no
king in Ĭs′ra-el, *but* [j]every man
did *that which was* right in his
own eyes.
7 ¶ And there was a young
[k]man out of [l]Bĕth′-lĕ-hĕm–jū′-
dah of the family of Jū′dah,
who *was* a [m]Lē′vīte, and he sojourned there.
8 And the man departed out of
the city from [l]Bĕth′-lĕ-hĕm–jū′-
dah to sojourn where he could
find *a place*: and he came to
mount [a]Ē′phră-ĭm to the house
of Mī′cah, as he journeyed.
9 And Mī′cah said unto him,
Whence comest thou? And he
said unto him, I *am* a Lē′vīte of
Bĕth′-lĕ-hĕm–jū′dah, and I go
to sojourn where I may find *a
place*.
10 And Mī′cah said unto him,
Dwell with me, and be unto me
a [n]father and a [o]priest, and I
will give thee ten [1]*shekels*[C] of
silver by the year, and a suit
of apparel, and thy victuals.[C]
So the [m]Lē′vīte went in.
11 And the Lē′vīte was content

28
w *Prayer, imprecatory,* Acts 6:4.
x *Revenge,* Ezek. 25:15.

30
y *Suicide, instances of,* 1 Kin. 16:18.

31
z *Zorah,* Josh. 19:41.
a *Eshtaol,* Judg. 18:2.
b *Burying Places,* Gen. 23:4.
c *Samson, judge of Israel,* Judg. 13:24.
d *Judges of Israel,* Judg. 2:16.
e *Israel, under the judges,* Ex. 4:22.

**B.C. 1406?**
See footnote, *Time,* Rev. 10:6.

1
a *Ephraim, mount of,* Josh. 17:15.

2
b *Conscience, guilty, instances of,* Acts 23:1.
c *Shekel,* Ex. 30:13.
d *Dishonesty, instances of,* Ezek. 22:13.
e *Theft, instances of,* Mark 7:22.
1 R. V. pieces

3
f *Restitution,* Ex. 22:3.
g *Vows, instances of,* Num. 30:2.

4
h *Money, silver used as,* Jer. 32:9.

5
i *Ephod,* Ex. 28:6.

6
j *Liberty, political,* Lev. 25:10.

7
k Judg. 18:3–30.
l *Bethlehem,* Gen. 48:7.
m *Minister, false and corrupt, instances of,* vs. 7–13; Rom. 15:16.

10
n *Father,* Psa. 27:10.
o *Minister, hired,* Rom. 15:16.

* **CONSCIENCE MONEY,** money returned for conscience sake. *By Micah,* Judg. 17:2–4. *By Judas,* Matt. 27:3–5.
† **TERAPHIM,** household idols. *Used by Laban; stolen by Rachel,* Gen. 31:19, 30–35. *Used by Micah; stolen by the Danites,* Judg. 17:5; 18:14, 17–20. *Used by Michal,* 1 Sam. 19:13. *Condemned and disposed of by Jacob,* Gen. 35:2–4.

to dwell with the man; and the young man was unto him as one of his sons.

12 And Mī′cah consecrated the Lē′vīte; and the young man became his [o]priest, and was in the house of Mī′cah.

13 Then said Mī′cah, Now know I that the LORD will do me good, seeing I have a Lē′vīte to *my* [o]priest.

## CHAPTER 18

*The Danites send five men to seek out an inheritance. 3 At the house of Micah they consult with his priest, and are encouraged in their way. 7 They visit Laish, and bring back a good report. 11 Six hundred men are sent to surprise it. 14 In the way they rob Micah of his priest and his consecrated things. 27 They win Laish, and call it Dan. 30 They set up Micah's graven image, and Jonathan becomes their priest.*

IN those days *there was* no king in Ĭṣ′ra-el: and in those days the tribe of the [a]Dăn′ītes sought them an inheritance to dwell in; for unto that day *all their* inheritance had not fallen[C] unto them among the tribes of Ĭṣ′ra-el.

2 And the children of [a]Dăn sent of their family five men from their [1]coasts, men of valour, from [b]Zō′rah, and from *Ĕsh′ta-ŏl, to [c]spy out the land, and to search it; and they said unto them, Go, search the land: who when they came to mount [d]Ē′phră-ĭm, to the house of Mī′cah, they lodged there.

3 When they *were* by the house of Mī′cah, they knew the voice of the young [e]man the [f]Lē′vīte: and they turned in thither[C], and said unto him, Who brought thee hither[C]? and what makest[C] thou in this *place*? and what hast thou here?

4 And he said unto them, Thus and thus dealeth Mī′cah with me, and hath [g]hired me, and I am his priest.

5 And they said unto him, [h]Ask counsel, we pray thee, of God, that we may know whether our way which we go shall be prosperous.

6 And the priest said unto them, Go in peace: before the LORD *is* your way wherein ye go.

7 ¶ Then the five men departed, and came to Lā′ish, and saw the people that *were* therein, how they dwelt [2]careless[C], after the manner of the [i]Zī-dō′nĭ-anṣ, quiet and secure[C]; and *there was* no [j]magistrate in the land, that might put *them* to shame in *any* thing; and they *were* far from the Zī-dō′nĭ-anṣ, and had no business with *any* man.

8 And they came unto their brethren to [b]Zō′rah and *Ĕsh′ta-ŏl: and their brethren said unto them, What *say* ye?

9 And they said, Arise, that we may go up against them: for we have seen the land, and, behold, it *is* very good: and *are* ye still? be not slothful to go, *and* to enter to possess the land.

10 When ye go, ye shall come unto a people secure, and to a large land: for God hath given it into your hands; a place where *there is* no want of any thing that *is* in the earth.

11 ¶ And there went from thence of the family of the [a]Dăn′ītes, out of [b]Zō′rah and out of *Ĕsh′ta-ŏl, six hundred men appointed[C] with weapons of war.

12 And they went up, and pitched[C] in [k]Kĭr′jath–jē′a-rĭm, in Jū′dah: wherefore they called that place Mā′hă-neh–dăn unto this day: behold, *it is* behind Kĭr′jath–jē′a-rĭm.

13 And they passed thence unto mount [d]Ē′phră-ĭm, and came unto the house of Mī′cah.

14 Then answered the five men that went to [c]spy out the country

1 *a Dan, tribe of,* Gen. 30:6.

2 *b Zorah,* Josh. 19:41.
*c Armies, reconnoissance by,* Deut. 11:4.
*d Ephraim, mount of,* Josh. 17:15.
1 R. V. whole number.

3 *e* Judg. 17:7-13.
*f Minister, false and corrupt, instances of,* Rom. 15:16.

4 *g Minister, hired,* Rom. 15:16.

5 *h Guidance, prayer for,* Psa. 48:14.

7 *i Zidon,* Ezek. 28:21.
*j Magistrate,* Ezra 7:25.
2 R. V. in security.

12 *k Kirjath-jearim,* Josh. 15:9.

* **ESHTAOL.** *A town of Judah,* Josh. 15:33. *Allotted to Dan,* Josh. 19:41; Judg. 18:2, 8, 11. *Samson moved by the spirit of the Lord near,* Judg. 13:25. *Samson buried near,* Judg. 16:31.

of Lā'ish, and said unto their brethren, Do ye know that [l]there is in these houses an [m]ephod,[C] and [n]teraphim, and a graven[C] [o]image, and a molten[C] image? now therefore consider what ye have to do.

14 *Idolatry*, 1 Sam. 15:23.
*Ephod*, Ex. 28:6.
*Teraphim*, Judg. 17:5.
*Idol*, 1 Kin. 15: 12.

15 And they turned thitherward,[C] and came to the house of the young [e]man the [l]Lē'vīte, *even* unto the house of Mī'cah, and saluted[C] him.

16 And the six hundred men appointed with their weapons of war which *were* of the [a]children of Dăn, stood by the entering of the gate.

17 And the five men that went to [c]spy out the land went up, *and* came in thither,[C] *and* [p]took the graven[C] [o]image, and the [m]ephod, and the [n]teraphim, and the molten[C] [o]image: and the [l]priest stood in the entering of the gate with the six hundred men *that were* appointed with weapons of war.

17 p *Theft, instances of*, Mark 7:22.

18 And these went into Mī'cah's house, and fetched the carved [o]image, the [m]ephod, and the [n]teraphim, and the molten[C] [o]image. Then said the priest unto them, What do ye?

19 And they said unto him, Hold thy peace, lay thine hand upon thy mouth, and go with us, and be to us a father and a priest: *is it* better for thee to be a priest unto the house of one man, or that thou be a priest unto a tribe and a family in Iș'ra-el?

20 And the [l]priest's heart was glad, and he [p, q]took the [m]ephod, and the [n]teraphim, and the graven[C] [o]image, and went in the midst of the people.

20 q *Dishonesty, instances of*, Ezek. 22:13.

21 So they turned and departed, and put the little ones and the cattle and the [3]carriage[C] before them.

21 3 R. V. goods

22 ¶ *And* when they were a good way from the house of Mī'cah, the men that *were* in the houses near to Mī'cah's house were gathered together, and overtook the children of [a]Dăn.

23 And they cried unto the children of [a]Dăn. And they turned their faces, and said unto Mī'cah, What aileth thee, that thou comest with such a company?

24 And he said, Ye have taken away my [o]gods[C] which I made, and the priest, and ye are gone away: and what have I more[C]? and what *is* this *that* ye say unto me, What aileth thee?

25 And the children of [a]Dăn said unto him, Let not thy voice be heard among us, lest angry fellows run upon thee, and thou lose thy life, with the lives of thy household.

26 And the children of [a]Dăn went their way: and when Mī'cah saw that they *were* too strong for him, he turned and went back unto his house.

27 And they [p]took *the things* which Mī'cah had made, and the [l]priest which he had, and came unto Lā'ish, unto a people *that were* at[C] quiet and secure: and they [r]smote[C] them with the edge of the sword, and burnt the city with fire.

27 r *War, evils of*, Judg. 3:2.

28 And *there was* no deliverer, because it *was* far from [s]Zī'dŏn, and they had no business with *any* man; and it was in the valley that *lieth* by †Bĕth-rē'hŏb. And they built a city, and dwelt therein.

28 s *Zidon*, Ezek. 28: 21.

29 And they called the name of the city ‡Dăn, after the name of Dăn their father, who was born unto Iș'ra-el: howbeit the name of the city *was* Lā'ish at the first.

30 And the children of [a]Dăn

† **BETH-REHOB.** *A place in Dan*, 2 Sam. 10:6. *Called* REHOB, Num. 13:21; 2 Sam. 10:8.
‡ **DAN** (*a judge*), a city of the tribe of Dan. *Called also* LAISH *and* LESHEM. Gen. 14:14; Deut. 34:1; Judg. 20:1; Jer. 8:16. *Captured by the people of Dan*, Josh. 19:47; Judg. 18: 27-29. *Idolatry established at*, Judg. 18; 1 Kin. 12:28, 29; Amos 8: 14. *Captured by Ben-hadad*, 1 Kin. 15:20; 2 Chr. 16:4.

**30**
*t Manasseh*, Gen. 46:20.
4 R. V. Moses,

**31**
*u Tabernacle*, Ex. 27:9.
*v Church, house of God*, 1 Kin. 9:3.
*w Shiloh*, Judg. 21:12.

[l]set up the graven[c] [o]image: and
[e]Jŏn′a-than, the son of Gēr′-
shŏm, the son of [4,t]Mă-năs′seh,
he and his sons were priests to
the tribe of Dăn until the day of
the captivity of the land.
31 And they [l]set them up Mī′-
cah's graven[c] [o]image, which he
made, all the time that the
[u,v]house of God was in [w]Shī′lōh.

## CHAPTER 19

*A Levite goes to Bethlehem to fetch home his concubine. 16 An old man entertains him at Gibeah. 22 The men of the city abuse his concubine to death. 29 He divides her into twelve pieces, and sends them to the twelve tribes.*

**1**
*a Israel, under the judges*, Ex. 4:22.
*b Ephraim, mount of*, Josh. 17:15.
*c Concubinage*, 2 Sam. 21:11.
*d* Or, *Bethlehem*, Gen. 48:7.

AND it came to pass in those
days, when *there was* no
king in [a]Is̹′ra-el, that there was a
certain Lē′vīte sojourning on the
side of mount [b]Ē′phră-ĭm, who
took to him a [c]concubine out of
[d]Bĕth′–lĕ-hĕm–jū′dah.
2 And his [c]concubine played
the whore[c] against him, and went
away from him unto her father's
house to [d]Bĕth′–lĕ-hĕm–jū′dah,
and was there four whole months.

**3**
*e Ass, domesticated*, 2 Chr. 28:15.

3 And her husband arose, and
went after her, to speak friendly
unto her, *and* to bring her again,
having his servant with him, and
a couple of [e]asses: and she
brought him into her father's
house: and when the *father of
the damsel[c] saw him, he rejoiced
to meet him.

**4**
*f Hospitality*, Rom. 12:13.

4 And his *father in law, the
damsel's[c] father, [f]retained[c] him;
and he abode with him three
days: so they did eat and drink,
and lodged there.
5 And it came to pass on the
fourth day, when they arose
early in the morning, that he
rose up to depart: and the damsel's father said unto his son in
law, [f]Comfort[c] thine heart with a
morsel of bread, and afterward
go your way.
6 And they sat down, and did
eat and drink both of them together: for the damsel's[c] father
had said unto the man, Be content, I pray thee, and [f]tarry all
night, and let thine heart be
merry.[c]
7 And when the man rose up to
depart, his *father in law urged
him: therefore he lodged there
again.
8 And he arose early in the
morning on the fifth day to depart: and the damsel's[c] father
said, Comfort[c] thine heart, I pray
thee. [1,f]And they tarried until
afternoon, and they did eat both
of them.
9 And when the man rose up to
depart, he, and his concubine,
and his servant, his father in
law, the damsel's[c] father, said
unto him, Behold, now the day
draweth toward evening. I pray
you [f]tarry all night: behold, the
day groweth to an end, lodge
here, that thine heart may be
merry; and to morrow get you
early on your way, that thou
mayest go home.
10 But the man would not tarry
that night, but he rose up and
departed, and came over against
Jē′bus, which *is* †Jē-ru̇′să-lĕm;

**8**
1 R. V. and tarry ye until the da declineth;

* **FATHER-IN-LAW.** *Hospitable to son-in-law, a man of Bethlehem-judah*, Judg. 19:3–9. *Unjust, Laban to Jacob*, Gen. 29:21–23; 31:7, 39–42. *Judah to Tamar*, Gen. 38:12–26.

† **JERUSALEM** (*habitation of peace*). *Called*, Jebus, Josh. 18:28; Judg. 19:10; Zion, 1 Kin. 8:1; Zech. 9:13; City of David, 2 Sam. 5:7; 1 Kin. 8:1; Isa. 22:9; Salem, Gen. 14:18; Psa. 76:2; Ariel, Isa. 29:1; City of Judah, 2 Chr. 25:28. *To be called*, The Lord our Righteousness, Jer. 33:16; The Lord is There, Ezek. 48:35.

Described as: *The Perfection of Beauty, the Joy of the whole Earth*; Lam. 2:15; *the Throne of the Lord*, Jer. 3:17; *Holy Mountain*, Dan. 9:16, 20; *Holy City*, Neh. 11:1, 18; Isa. 52:1; Matt. 4:5; *City of Solemnities*, Isa. 33:20; *City of Truth*, Zech. 8:3.

*Situation and appearance of*, Psa. 122:3; 125:2; Song 6:4; Mic. 4:8.

*Melchizedek, ancient king and priest of*, Gen. 14:18. *King of, confederated with the four other kings of the Amorite against Joshua and the hosts of Israel*, Josh. 10:1–5; *slai by Joshua*, Josh. 10:15–26. *Allotted to tribe of Benjamir* Josh. 18:28.

*Conquest of, made by David*, 2 Sam. 5:7. *The inhabitan of, not expelled*, Josh. 15:63; Judg. 1:21. *Conquest of Mour Zion in, made by David*, 1 Chr. 11:4–6.

*The capital of David's kingdom by divine appointmen* 1 Kin. 15:4; 2 Kin. 19:34; 2 Chr. 6:6; 12:13. *The citadel o Mount Zion, occupied by David, and called the* City of Davi 2 Sam. 5:5–9; 1 Chr. 11:7.

*Ark brought to, by David*, 2 Sam. 6:12–19. *The threshing floor of Araunah within the citadel of*, 2 Sam. 24:16; *Davi purchases and erects an altar upon it*, 2 Sam. 24:16–25. *Th city built around the citadel*, 1 Chr. 11:8. *Dwellers in*, 1 Chr 9:3–44.

*The chief Levites dwelt in*, 1 Chr. 9:34. *The high pries*

and *there were* with him two
[e]asses saddled, his [c]concubine
also *was* with him.
11 *And* when they *were* by [†]Jē′-
bus, the day was far spent; and
the servant said unto his master,
Come, I pray thee, and let us
turn in into this city of the
Jĕb′u-sītes, and lodge in it.
12 And his master said unto
him, We will not turn aside hith-
12 *Gibeah*, Hos. 9:9. er[C] into the city of a stranger[C], that
*is* not of the children of Iṣ′ra-el;
we will pass over to [g]Gĭb′e-ah.
13 And he said unto his servant, Come, and let us draw near
to one of these places to lodge[C]
all night, in [g]Gĭb′e-ah, or in
[‡]Rā′mah.
14 And they passed on and
14 *Benjamin, tribe of*, Num. 1:37. went their way; and the sun
went down upon them *when
they were* by [g]Gĭb′e-ah, which
*belongeth* to [h]Bĕn′ja-mĭn.
15 And they turned aside thith-
er[C], to go in *and* to lodge[C] in [g]Gĭb′-
15 *Inhospitableness, instances of*, Luke 9:53. e-ah: and when he went in, he
sat him down in a street of the
city: for [i]*there was* no man that
took them into his house to
lodging.
16 ¶ And, behold, there came
an old man from his work out of
the field at even, which *was* also
of mount [b]Ē′phră-ĭm; and he sojourned in [g]Gĭb′e-ah: but the
men of the place *were* [h]Bĕn′ja-
mītes.
17 And when he had lifted up
his eyes, he saw a wayfaring[C] man
in the street of the city: and the
old man said, Whither[C] goest
thou? and whence comest thou?
18 And he said unto him, We
*are* passing from [d]Bĕth′-lĕ-hĕm-
jū′dah [2]toward the side of mount 18
[b]Ē′phră-ĭm; from whence *am* I: [j] *Church, house of the Lord*, 1 Kin. 9:3.
and I went to Bĕth′-lĕ-hĕm-jū′- [2] R. V. unto the farther side of the hill country of
dah, but I *am now* going to the
[j]house of the LORD; and [i]there
*is* no man that receiveth me to
house.
19 Yet there is both straw and
provender[C] for our [e]asses; and
there is bread and wine also for
me, and for thy handmaid, and
for the young man *which is* with
thy servants: *there is* no want of
any thing.
20 And the old man said, Peace
*be* with thee; howsoever [k]*let* all 20 [k] *Hospitality, instances of*, Rom. 12:13.
thy wants *lie* upon me; only
lodge not in the street.
21 So he [k]brought him into his

*welt at*, John 18:15. *Annual feasts kept at*, Ezek. 36:38 (with Deut. 16:16 and Psa. 122:3–5); Luke 2:41; John 4:20; 5:1; :1–14; 12:20. *Prayers of the Israelites made toward*, 1 Kin. :38; Dan. 6:10. *Beloved*, Psa. 122:6; 137:1–7; Isa. 62:1–7. *aths taken in the name of*, Matt. 5:35.

*Fortified by Solomon*, 1 Kin. 3:1; 9:15. *Walls of*, Jer. 39:4. *Walls of, restored, by Uzziah*, 2 Chr. 26:9, 10; *by Jotham*, Chr. 27:3; *by Manasseh*, 2 Chr. 33:14; *by Nehemiah*, Neh. 2: 1–20; 3; 4; 5; 6:1–15. *Dedicated by Nehemiah*, Neh. 12: 7–43.

*Water supply for, brought into, from the Gihon by Hezekiah*, Kin. 18:17; 20:20; 2 Chr. 32:3, 4, 30; Neh. 2:13–15; Isa. 7:3; 2:9–11; 36:2.

Roman rulers resided at: *Herod I*, Matt. 2:3; *Pontius Pilate*, Matt. 27:2; Mark 15:1; Luke 23:1–7; John 18:28, 29; *Herod III*, Acts 12:1–23.

*Gospel first preached at*, Mic. 4:2; Luke 24:47; Acts 1:4; :14. *Pentecostal revival occurred at*, Acts 2. *Stephen martyred at*, Acts 6:8–15; 7. *Disciples persecuted and dispersed from*, Acts 8:1–4; 11:19–21.

**Besieged:** *By Pekah*, 2 Kin. 16:5. *By the Philistines*, Chr. 21:16, 17. *By Sennacherib*, 2 Kin. 18:13–37; 19:20–37; Chr. 32.

**Captured and pillaged by:** *Shishak, king of Egypt*, Kin. 14:25, 26; 2 Chr. 12:9. *By Jehoash, king of Israel*, Kin. 14:13, 14; 2 Chr. 25:23, 24. *By Nebuchadnezzar, king of Babylon*, 2 Kin. 24:8–16; 25:1–17; 2 Chr. 36:10, 17–21; Jer. :3; 32:2; 39; 52:4–7, 12–24; Lam. 1:5–8.

**Rebuilding of:** *Ordered by proclamation of Cyrus*, 2 Chr. 6:23; Ezra 1:1–4. *Rebuilt by Nehemiah under the direction of Artaxerxes*, Neh. chapters 2–6.

**Gates of:** *Old gate, fish gate, sheep gate, prison gate*, Neh. :1, 3, 6, 32; 12:39. *Gate of Ephraim*, 2 Chr. 25:23; Neh. 12: 9. *Gate of Benjamin*, Jer. 37:13; Zech. 14:10. *Gate of Joshua*, 2 Kin. 23:8. *Corner gate*, Zech. 14:10. *Valley gate*, Neh. 2:13; 3:13. *Dung gate*, Neh. 2:13; 3:13; 12:31. *Gate of the fountain*, Neh. 2:14; 3:15; 12:37. *Water gate*, Neh. 3: 26; 8:1; 12:37. *Horse gate*, Neh. 3:28. *King's gate*, 1 Chr. 9:18. *Shallecheth*, 1 Chr. 26:16. *High gate*, 2 Chr. 23:20. *East gate*, Neh. 3:29. *Miphkad*, Neh. 3:31. *Middle gate*, Jer. 39:3. *First gate*, Zech. 14:10.

**Buildings of:** *High priest's palace*, John 18:15. *Castle*, Acts 21:34. *Stairs*, Neh. 3:15.

**Streets of:** *Street or plaza of*, Ezra 10:9. *Street or open square of the water gate, and of Ephraim gate*, Neh. 8:16. *Baker's street*, Jer. 37:21.

**Towers of:** *Hananeel*, Neh. 3:1; 12:39; Jer. 31:38; Zech. 14:10. *Meah*, Neh. 3:1; 12:39. *Millo*, 2 Sam. 5:9; 1 Kin. 9:15, 24; 11:27; 1 Chr. 11:8; 2 Chr. 32:5. *Ophel*, 2 Chr. 27:3; 33:14; Neh. 3:26, 27.

**Wickedness of,** Luke 13:33, 34. *Catalogue of abominations in*, Ezek. 22:3–12, 25–30; 23; 33:25, 26. *Led Judah to sin*, Mic. 1:5.

**Prophecies against,** Isa. 3:1–8; Jer. 9:11; 19:6, 15; 21: 10; 26:9, 11; Dan. 9:2, 26, 27; Mic. 1:1; 3:12. *Of pestilence, famine, and war in*, Jer. 34:2; Ezek. 5:12; Amos 2:5. *Of the destruction of*, Jer. 7:32–34; 26:18; 32:29, 31, 32; Dan. 9:24–27. *Destruction of, foretold by Jesus*, Matt. 23:37, 38; 24:15; Mark 13:14–23; Luke 13:34, 35; 17:26–37; 19:41–44; 21: 20–24.

Concerning: *The rebuilding of*, Isa. 44:28; Jer. 31:38–40; Ezek. 48:15–22; Dan. 9:25; Zech. 14:8–11; *final restoration of*, Joel 3:20, 21; Zech. 2:2–5; 8; *measurement of, in Ezekiel's vision*, Ezek. 45:6; *names of the gates of, in Ezekiel's vision*, Ezek. 48:31–34.

‡ **RAMAH.** *Called* RAMA, Matt. 2:18. *A city allotted to Benjamin*, Josh. 18:25; Judg. 19:13. *Attempted fortification of, by King Baasha; destruction of, by Asa*, 1 Kin. 15:17–22;

house, and gave provender[C] unto the [l]asses: and they ‖washed their [m]feet, and did eat and drink.

22 ¶ *Now* as they were making their hearts merry, behold, the men of the city, certain sons of Bē′lĭ-al,[C] beset the house round about, *and* beat at the door, and spake to the master of the house, the old man, saying, Bring forth the man that came into thine house, that we may [n]know him.

23 And the man, the master of the house, went out unto them, and said unto them, Nay, my brethren, *nay,* I pray you, do not *so* wickedly; seeing that this man is [k]come into mine house, do not this folly.

24 Behold, *here is* my daughter a maiden, and his [c]concubine; them I will bring out now, and humble ye them, and do with them what seemeth good unto you: but unto this man do not so vile a [n]thing.

25 But the men would not hearken to him: so the man took his [c]concubine, and brought her forth unto them; and they [o, p]knew her, and [q]abused[C] her all the night until the morning: and when the day began to spring,[C] they let her go.

26 Then came the woman in the dawning of the day, and fell down at the door of the man's house where her lord *was,* till it was light.

27 And her lord rose up in the morning, and opened the doors of the house, and went out to go his way: and, behold, the woman his [c]concubine[C] was fallen down *at* the door of the house, and her hands *were* upon the threshold.

28 And he said unto her, Up, and let us be going. But none answered. Then the man took her *up* upon an ass, and the man rose up, and gat him unto his place.

29 ¶ And when he was come into his house, he took a knife, and laid hold on his [c]concubine, and divided[C] her, [3]*together* with her bones, into twelve pieces, and sent her into all the [4]coasts[C] of Ĭs̹′ra-el.

30 And it was so, that all that saw it said, There was no such deed done nor seen from the day that the children of [a]Ĭs̹′ra-el came up out of the land of [r]Ē′gy̆pt unto this day: consider of it, take [5]advice, and speak *your minds.*

## CHAPTER 20

*The Levite in an assembly of the people declares his wrong. 8 The decree of the assembly. 12 The Benjamites, being required to deliver up the guilty persons, refuse and prepare for war. 18 The Israelites in two battles lose forty thousand. 26 By stratagem they destroy all the Benjamites, except six hundred.*

THEN all the children of [a]Ĭs̹′ra-el went out, and the congregation was [b]gathered together as one man, from [c]Dăn to *Bē′er–shē′bȧ, with the land of Gĭl′e-ăd, unto the LORD in [d]Mĭz′peh.

2 And the chief of all the people, *even* of all the tribes of [a]Ĭs̹′ra-el, presented themselves in the assembly of the people of God, four hundred thousand footmen that drew sword.

3 (Now the children of [e]Bĕn′ja-mĭn heard that the children of Ĭs̹′ra-el were gone up to [d]Mĭz′peh.) Then said the children of Ĭs̹′ra-el, Tell *us,* how was this wickedness?

4 And the Lē′vīte, the husband

---

21
l *Animals,* Jer. 27:5.
m *Feet,* 2 Sam. 4:4.

22
n *Sodomy,* Lev. 18: 22.

25
o *Adultery, instances of,* Lev. 20: 10.
p *Lasciviousness, instances of,* 1 Pet. 4:3.
q *Rape, instances of,* Deut. 22:25.

29
3 R. V. limb by limb,
4 R. V. borders

30
r *Egypt,* Gen. 41:8
5 R. V. counsel, and speak.

1
a *Israel, under the Judges,* Ex. 4:22
b *Armies, rendezvous of,* Deut. 11:4.
c *Dan,* Judg. 18: 29.
d *Mizpah,* Josh. 18:26.

3
e *Benjamin, tribe of,* Num. 1:37.

---

2 Chr. 16:1–6. *People of, return from the Babylonish captivity,* Ezra 2:26; Neh. 7:30; 11:33. *Jeremiah imprisoned in,* Jer. 40:1. *Prophecies concerning,* Isa. 10:29; Jer. 31:15; Hos. 5:8; Matt. 2:18.

‖ **ABLUTION.** *Of the feet,* Gen. 18:4; 19:2; 24:32; 43; 24; Judg. 19:21; 2 Sam. 11:8; Song 5:3. *Of the hands, as a token of innocency,* Deut. 21:6, 7; Psa. 26:6; 73:13; Matt. 27: 24. *Of the face,* Matt. 6:17. *Of the dead,* Acts 9:37. *Of infants,* Ezek. 16:4.
See footnote, CEREMONIAL WASHINGS, Ex. 19:10.
**Figurative:** See footnote, SPIRITUAL PURIFICATION Psa. 51:2.

* **BEER-SHEBA** *(the well of the oath). The most southern city of Palestine,* Judg. 20:1. *Named by Abraham, who dwel*

4
[f] *Gibeah,* Hos. 9:9.
[g] *Concubinage,* 2 Sam. 21:11.

8
[h] *Vows,* Num. 30:2.

10
[i] *Armies, levies for,* Deut. 11:4.

12
[j] *Reproof, faithfulness in,* Prov. 17:10.

13
1 R. V. sons

of the woman that was slain, answered and said, I came into
[f]Ḡĭb′e-ah that *belongeth* to Bĕn′-
ja-mĭn, I and my [g]concubine, to
lodge.
5 And the men of [f]Ḡĭb′e-ah
rose against me, and beset the
house round about upon me by
night, *and* thought to have slain
me: and my [g]concubine have
they forced,[c] that she is dead.
6 And I took my [g]concubine,
and cut her in pieces, and sent
her throughout all the country of
the inheritance of [a]Ĭs̱′ra-el: for
they have committed lewdness[c]
and folly[c] in Ĭs̱′ra-el.
7 Behold, ye *are* all children of
[a]Ĭs̱′ra-el: give here your advice
and counsel.
8 ¶ And all the [a]people arose as
one man, [h]saying, We will not
any *of us* go to his tent, neither
will we any *of us* turn into his
house.
9 But now this *shall be* the
thing which we will do to
[f]Ḡĭb′-e-ah; *we will go up* by[c]
lot against it;
10 And we will take [i]ten men
of an hundred throughout all the
tribes of [a]Ĭs̱′ra-el, and an hundred of a thousand, and a thousand out of ten thousand, to
fetch[c] victual[c] for the people, that
they may do, when they come
to [f]Ḡĭb′e-ah of [e]Bĕn′ja-mĭn, according to all the folly[c] that they
have wrought in Ĭs̱′ra-el.
11 So all the men of Ĭs̱′ra-el
were gathered against the city,
knit together as one man.
12 ¶ And the tribes of [a]Ĭs̱′ra-el
sent men through all the tribe
of [e]Bĕn′ja-mĭn, [j]saying, What
wickedness *is* this that is done
among you?
13 Now therefore deliver *us* the
men, the [1]children of Bē′lĭ-al,[c]
which *are* in [f]Ḡĭb′e-ah, that we
may put them to death, and put
away evil from Ĭs̱′ra-el. But the
children of [e]Bĕn′ja-mĭn would
not hearken to the voice of
their brethren the children of
[a]Ĭs̱′-ra-el:
14 But the children of [e]Bĕn′ja-
mĭn gathered themselves together out of the cities unto [f]Ḡĭb′e-
ah, to go out to [k]battle against
the children of [a]Ĭs̱′ra-el.
15 And the children of [e]Bĕn′ja-
mĭn were numbered at that time
out of the cities twenty and six
thousand men that drew sword,
beside the inhabitants of [f]Ḡĭb′e-
ah, which were numbered seven
hundred chosen men.
16 Among all this people *there*
*were* seven hundred chosen men
[l]lefthanded; every one could
[m]sling stones at an hair *breadth,*
and not miss.
17 And the men of [a]Ĭs̱′ra-el,
beside [e]Bĕn′ja-mĭn, were numbered four hundred thousand
men that drew sword: all these
*were* men of war.
18 ¶ And [n]the children of Ĭs̱′-
ra-el arose, and went up to [2]the
[o, p]house of God, and [q]asked
counsel[c] of God, and said, Which
of us shall go up first to the
[k]battle against the children of
[e]Bĕn′ja-mĭn? And [r]the LORD
said, [s]Jū′dah *shall go up* first.
19 And the children of [a]Ĭs̱′ra-el
rose up in the morning, and encamped against [f]Ḡĭb′e-ah.
20 And the men of Ĭs̱′ra-el went
out to [k]battle against [e]Bĕn′ja-
mĭn; and the men of [a]Ĭs̱′ra-el
put themselves in array[c] to fight
against them at [f]Ḡĭb′e-ah.
21 And the children of [e]Bĕn′ja-
mĭn came forth out of [f]Ḡĭb′e-ah,
and destroyed down to the
ground of the Ĭs̱′ra-el-ītes that

14
[k] *War,* Judg. 3:2.

16
[l] Judg. 3:15.
[m] *Sling,* 1 Sam. 17:40.

18
[n] *Armies, religious ceremonies in,* Deut. 11:4.
[o] *Bethel, tabernacle at,* Josh. 18:13.
[p] *Tabernacle,* Ex. 27:9.
[q] *Guidance, prayer for,* Psa. 48:14.
[r] *Prayer, answered,* Acts 6:4.
[s] *Judah, tribe of,* Num. 10:14.
2 R. V. Beth-el,

*there,* Gen. 21:31–33; 22:19. *The dwelling place of Isaac,* Gen. 26:23. *Jacob went out from, toward Haran,* Gen. 28:10. *Sacrifices offered at, by Jacob when journeying to Egypt,* Gen. 46:1. *In the inheritance of Judah,* Josh. 15:20, 28; 2 Sam. 24:7; Neh. 11:30. *Afterward assigned to Simeon,* Josh. 19: 2, 9; 1 Chr. 4:28. *Two sons of Samuel were judges at,* 1 Sam. 8:2. *Became a seat of idolatrous worship,* Amos 5:5; 8:14. *Wilderness of,* Gen. 21:14–19.

day twenty and two thousand
men.
22 And the people the men of
[a]Ĭş′ra-el encouraged themselves,
and set their [k]battle again in array in the place where they put
themselves in array the first day.
23 (And the children of Ĭş′ra-el
went up and wept before the
LORD until even, and [q]asked
counsel of the LORD, saying,
Shall I go up again to [k]battle
against the children of Bĕn′ja-
mĭn my brother? And [r]the
LORD said, Go up against him.)
24 And the children of [a]Ĭş′ra-el
came near against the children
of [e]Bĕn′ja-mĭn the second day.
25 And [e]Bĕn′ja-mĭn went forth
against them out of [f]Ğĭb′e-ah
the second day, and destroyed
down to the ground of the children of Ĭş′ra-el again eighteen
thousand men; all these drew
the sword.
26 ¶ Then all the children of
Ĭş′ra-el, and all the people, went
up, and came unto [2]the [o,p]house
of God, and wept, and sat there
before the LORD, and [t]fasted
that day until even, and offered
[u]burnt [v]offerings and [w]peace
offerings before the LORD.
27 And the children of Ĭş′ra-el
[q]enquired[c] of the LORD, (for the
[x]ark of the covenant of God *was*
[o]there in those days,
28 And [y,z]Phĭn′e-has, the son
of Ē′le-ā′zar, the son of Aâr′on,
stood before it in those days,)
[q]saying, Shall I yet again go out
to [k]battle against the children of
Bĕn′ja-mĭn my brother, or shall
I cease? And [r]the LORD said,
Go up; for to morrow I will
deliver them into thine hand.
29 ¶ And [a]Ĭş′ra-el [b]set [c]liers[c] in
wait round about [d]Ğĭb′e-ah.
30 And the children of [a]Ĭş′ra-el
went up against the children of
[e]Bĕn′ja-mĭn on the third day,
and put themselves in array
against [d]Ğĭb′e-ah, as at other
times.
31 And the children of [e]Bĕn′ja-
mĭn went out against the people,
*and* were [b]drawn away from the
city; and they began to smite of
the people, *and* kill, as at other
times, in the [f]highways, of which
one goeth up to [2]the [g]house of
God, and the other to [d]Ğĭb′e-ah
in the field, about thirty men of
Ĭş′ra-el.
32 And the children of [e]Bĕn′ja-
mĭn said, They *are* smitten down
before us, as at the first. But the
children of Ĭş′ra-el said, [b]Let us
flee, and draw them from the
city unto the highways.
33 And all the men of [a]Ĭş′ra-el
rose up out of their place, and
put themselves in array at Bā′-
al–tā′mar: and the [b,c]liers[c] in
wait of Ĭş′ra-el came forth out of
their places, *even* out of the
meadows of [d]Ğĭb′e-ah.
34 And there came against
Ğĭb′e-ah ten thousand chosen
men out of all Ĭş′ra-el, and the
battle was sore[c]: but they knew
not that evil *was* near them.
35 And the LORD smote [e]Bĕn′-
ja-mĭn before Ĭş′ra-el: and the
children of Ĭş′ra-el destroyed of
the Bĕn′ja-mītes that day twenty
and five thousand and an hundred men: all these drew[c] the
sword.
36 So the children of [e]Bĕn′ja-
mĭn saw that they were smitten:
for the men of [a]Ĭş′ra-el gave
place to the Bĕn′ja-mītes, because they trusted unto the [c]liers[c]
in wait which they had set beside [d]Ğĭb′e-ah.
37 And the [c]liers[c] in wait hasted[c],
and rushed upon Ğĭb′e-ah; and
the [c]liers[c] in wait drew *themselves*
along, and smote all the city with
the edge of the sword.
38 Now there was an appointed
sign between the men of Ĭş′ra-el
and the [c]liers[c] in wait, that they

26

t *Fasting*, Zech. 8.19.
u *Offerings, burnt*, Lev. 6:17.
v *Jesus, typified in offerings*, Matt. 1:21.
w *Offerings, peace*, Lev. 6:17.

27

x *Ark, of the covenant*, Ex. 25:10.

28

y *Phinehas, mediator*, Num. 25:7.
z *Jesus, priesthood of, typified*, Matt. 1:21.

29

a *Israel, under the judges*, Ex. 4:22.
b *Strategy, in war*, Judg. 7:16.
c *Ambush, instances of*, Josh. 8:2.
d *Gibeah, of Saul*, Hos. 9.9.

30

e *Benjamin, tribe of*, Num. 1:37.

31

f *Highways*, Deut. 2:27.
g *Bethel*, Josh. 18:13.

should make a great [3,h]flame
with smoke rise up out of the
city.

39 And when the men of Ĭṣ′ra-el [b]retired in the [i]battle, [e]Bĕn′ja-mĭn began to smite *and* kill of the men of Ĭṣ′ra-el about thirty persons: for they said, Surely they are smitten down before us, as *in* the first battle.

40 But when the [4,h]flame began to arise up out of the city with a pillar of smoke, the [e]Bĕn′ja-mītes looked behind them, and, behold, the [5]flame of the city [6]ascended up to heaven.

41 And when the men of Ĭṣ′ra-el turned again, the men of [e]Bĕn′ja-mĭn were amazed[C]: for they saw that evil was come upon them.

42 Therefore they turned *their backs* before the men of Ĭṣ′ra-el unto the way of the wilderness; but the [i]battle overtook them; and them which *came* out of the cities they destroyed in the midst of them.

43 *Thus* they [b]inclosed the [e]Bĕn′ja-mītes round about, *and* chased them, *and* trode[C] them down with ease over against [d]Gĭb′e-ah toward the sunrising[C].

44 And there fell of [e]Bĕn′ja-mĭn eighteen thousand men; all these *were* men of valour[C].

45 And they turned and fled toward the wilderness unto the rock of [j]Rĭm′mon: and they gleaned[C] of them in the [j]highways five thousand men; and pursued hard after them unto Gī′dom, and slew two thousand men of them.

46 So that all which fell[C] that day of [e]Bĕn′ja-mĭn were twenty and five thousand men that drew the sword; all these *were* men of valour[C].

47 But six hundred men turned and fled to the wilderness unto the rock [j]Rĭm′mon, and abode in the rock Rĭm′mon four months.

48 And the men of [a]Ĭṣ′ra-el turned again upon the children of [e]Bĕn′ja-mĭn, and smote them with the edge of the sword, [7]as well the men of *every* city, as the beast, and all that came to hand: also they set on fire all the cities that they came to.

**38**
*h Fire, used as signal in war,* Ex. 12:8.
3 R. V. cloud of smoke

**39**
*i War,* Judg. 3:2.

**40**
4 R. V. cloud
5 R. V. whole
6 R. V. went up in smoke to heaven.

**45**
*j* **Judg. 21:13.**

**48**
7 R. V. both the entire city, and the cattle,

## CHAPTER 21

*The people bewail the desolation of Benjamin. 8 By the destruction of Jabesh-gilead four hundred Benjamites are provided with wives. 16 The rest of the Benjamites obtain wives at Shiloh.*

NOW the men of [a]Ĭṣ′ra-el had [b,c]sworn in [d]Mĭz′peh, saying, There shall not any of us give his daughter unto [e]Bĕn′ja-mĭn to[C f]wife.

2 And the [g]people came to [1]the [h,i]house of God, and abode there till even before God, and lifted up their voices, and wept sore[C];

3 And [j]said, O LORD God of [a]Ĭṣ′ra-el, why is this come to pass in Ĭṣ′ra-el, that there should be to day one tribe lacking in Ĭṣ′ra-el?

4 And it came to pass on the morrow[C], that the people rose early, and built there an [k]altar, and offered [l]burnt [m]offerings and [n]peace offerings.

5 And the children of [a]Ĭṣ′ra-el said, Who *is there* among all the tribes of Ĭṣ′ra-el that came not up[C] with the congregation unto the LORD? For they had made a great [o]oath concerning him that came not up to the LORD to [d]Mĭz′peh, saying, He shall surely be put to [p]death.

6 And the children of [a]Ĭṣ′ra-el repented[C] them for [e]Bĕn′ja-mĭn their brother, and said, There is one tribe cut off from Ĭṣ′ra-el this day.

7 How shall we do for [f]wives for them that remain, seeing we have [b]sworn by the LORD that

**1**
*a Israel, under the judges,* Ex. 4:22.
*b Vows, rash,* Num. 30:2.
*c Rashness, instances of,* 2 Sam. 6:7.
*d Mizpah,* Josh. 18:26.
*e Benjamin, tribe of,* Num. 1:37.
*f Wife,* Prov. 5:18.

**2**
*g Nation, in adversity, prayer of,* Isa. 2:4.
*h Bethel,* Josh. 18:13.
*i Church,* 1 Kin. 9:3.
1 R. V. Beth-el,

**3**
*j Prayer,* Acts 6:4.

**4**
*k Altar,* Gen. 8:20.
*l Offerings, burnt,* Lev. 6:17.
*m Jesus, typified in offerings,* Matt. 1:21.
*n Offerings, peace,* Lev. 6:17.

**5**
*o Oath,* Num. 5:19.
*p Death, penalty,* Num. 23:10.

we will not give them of our daughters to[c] wives?

8 ¶ And they said, What one *is there* of the tribes of [a]Ĭş′ra-el that came not up to [d]Mĭz′peh to the LORD? And, behold, there came none to the camp from *Jā′besh–gĭl′e-ăd to the assembly.

9 For the people were numbered,[c] and, behold, *there were* none of the inhabitants of *Jā′besh–gĭl′e-ăd there.

10 And the congregation sent thither[c] [q]twelve thousand men of the valiantest,[c] and commanded them, saying, Go and smite the inhabitants of *Jā′besh–gĭl′e-ăd with the edge of the sword, with the women and the children.

11 And this *is* the thing that ye shall do, Ye shall utterly destroy every [r]male, and every [r]woman that hath lain by man.

12 And they found among the inhabitants of *Jā′besh–gĭl′e-ăd four hundred young [s]virgins, that had known no man by lying with any male: and they brought them unto the camp to †Shī′lōh, which *is* in the land of Cā′năan.

13 And the whole [a]congregation sent *some* to speak to the children of [e]Bĕn′ja-mĭn that *were* in the rock [t]Rĭm′mon, and [2]to call peaceably unto them.

14 And [e]Bĕn′ja-mĭn came again at that time; and they gave them [l]wives which they had saved alive of the women of *Jā′besh–gĭl′e-ăd: and yet so they sufficed them not.

15 And the people repented[c] them for [e]Bĕn′ja-mĭn, because that the LORD had made a breach in the tribes of Ĭş′ra-el.

16 ¶ Then the [u]elders of the congregation said, How shall we do for [l]wives for them that remain, seeing the women are destroyed out of [e]Bĕn′ja-mĭn?

17 And they said, *There must be* an inheritance for them that be escaped of [e]Bĕn′ja-mĭn, that a tribe be not destroyed out of Ĭş′ra-el.

18 Howbeit we may not give them wives of our daughters: for the children of Ĭş′ra-el have [b,c]sworn, saying, Cursed *be* he that giveth a wife to [e]Bĕn′ja-mĭn.

19 Then they said, Behold, *there is* a [v]feast of the LORD in †Shī′lōh yearly *in a place* which *is* on the north side of [h]Bĕth′–el, on the east side of the [w]highway that goeth up from Bĕth′–el to [x]Shē′chem, and on the south of Lē-bō′nah.

20 Therefore they commanded the children of [c]Bĕn′ja-mĭn, saying, Go and lie[c] in wait in the vineyards:

21 And see, and, behold, if the [y]daughters of †Shī′lōh come out to [z]dance in dances, then come ye out of the vineyards, and [a]catch you every man his [b]wife of the daughters of Shī′lōh, and go to the land of Bĕn′ja-mĭn.

22 And it shall be, when their fathers or their brethren come unto us to complain, that we will say unto them, [3]Be favourable[c] unto them for our sakes: because we reserved not to each man his wife in the war: for ye did not give unto them at this time, *that* ye should be guilty.

23 And the children of [c]Bĕn′ja-mĭn did so, and took *them* [b]wives, according to their number, of them that danced, whom they [a]caught: and they went and returned unto their inheri-

10
q *Armies*, Deut. 11:4.

11
r *Captive, cruelty to*, 1 Sam. 30:3.

12
s *Virgin*, Isa. 62:5.

13
t Judg. 20:45, 47.
2 R. V. proclaimed peace unto them.

16
u *Senate*, Num. 11: 16.

19
v *Annual Feasts*, Num. 15:3.
w *Highways*, Deut. 2:27.
x *Shechem*, Josh. 20:7.

21
y *Women*, Prov. 31:10.
z *Dancing*, Eccl. 3:4.

a *Wife, obtained by kidnapping*, Prov. 5:18.
b *Marriage*, Gen. 34:9.

22
3 R. V. Grant them graciously unto us:

23
c *Benjamin, tribe of*, Num. 1:37.

* **JABESH-GILEAD** (*dry land in Gilead*). *A city E. of the Jordan*, Judg. 21:8–15. *Besieged by the Ammonites*, 1 Sam. 11:1–11. *Saul and his sons buried at*, 1 Sam. 31:11–13; 1 Chr. 10:11, 12; 2 Sam. 2:4. *Bones of Saul and his son removed from, by David, and buried at Zelah*, 2 Sam. 21:12–14.

† **SHILOH.** *A city of Ephraim, north of Beth-el, and on the highway from Beth-el to Shechem*, Judg. 21:19. *Tabernacle at*, Josh. 18:1, 8–10; 19:51; Judg. 18:31; 21:19; 1 Sam. 1:3, 9, 21, 24; 2:14; 14:3; Psa. 78:60; Jer. 7:12, 14; 26:6. 7. *Seat of government during the time of Joshua*, Josh. 21:.1, 2. *The place of rendezvous for the tribes*, Josh. 22:9, 12; Judg 21: 12. *Eli, dwelt at*, 1 Sam. 1:9; 4:12, 13; *dies at*, 1 Sam. 4:18. *Ahijah the prophet dwells at*, 1 Kin. 14:2. *Devoted men from, slain by Ishmael*, Jer. 41:5–9.

tance, and repaired[c] the cities, and dwelt in them.

24 And the children of Ĭṣ′ra-el departed thence at that time, every man to his tribe and to his family, and they went out from thence every man to his inheritance.

25 In those days *there was* no king in Ĭṣ′ra-el: [d]every man did *that which was* right in his own eyes.

25
*d Liberty*, Lev. 25:10.

THE

# BOOK OF RUTH

## CHAPTER 1

*Elimelech, driven by famine into Moab, dies there. 4 His two sons, having married wives of Moab, die also. 6 Naomi returning homeward, 8 dissuades her two daughters-in-law from going with her. 14 Orpah leaves her, but Ruth cleaves unto her. 19 They two come to Beth-lehem.*

NOW it came to pass in the days when the [a]judges ruled, that there was a famine in the [b]land. And a certain man of [c]Bĕth′-lĕ-hĕm–jū′dah went to sojourn[c] in the country of [d]Mō′ab, he, and his wife, and his two sons.

2 And the name of the man *was* [e]Ĕ-lĭm′e-lĕch, and the name of his wife *Nā-ō′mī, and the name of his two sons [f]Mäh′lon and [g]Chĭl′ĭ-on, Ĕph′rath-ītes of Bĕth′-lĕ-hĕm–jū′dah. And they came into the country of Mō′ab, and continued[c] there.

3 And [e]Ĕ-lĭm′e-lĕch *Nā-ō′mī's husband [h]died; and [i]she was left, and her two sons.

4 And they took them [j]wives of the women of [d]Mō′ab; the name of the one *was* Ôr′pah, and the name of the other †Ruth: and they dwelled there about ten years.

5 And [f]Mäh′lon and [g]Chĭl′ĭ-on died also both of them; and the woman was left[c] of her two sons and her husband.

6 ¶ Then *she arose with her [k]daughters in law, that she might return from the country of [d]Mō′ab: for she had heard in the country of Mō′ab how that the LORD had visited his people in [l]giving them [m]bread.[C] [s]

7 Wherefore she went forth out of the place where she was, and her two [k]daughters in law with her; and they went on the way to return unto the land of [n]Jū′dah.

8 And *Nā-ō′mī said unto her two [k]daughters in law, Go, return each to her mother's house: [o, p, q]the LORD deal kindly with you, as ye have dealt with the dead, and with me.

9 [o, p, q]The LORD grant you that ye may find rest, each *of you* in the house of her husband. Then she ‡kissed them; and they lifted up their voice, and wept.

10 And [k, q]they said unto her, Surely we will return with thee unto thy people.

11 And *Nā-ō′mī said, Turn again, my daughters: why [q]will ye go with me? *are* there yet *any more* sons in my womb, that they may be your husbands?

12 Turn again, my daughters, go *your way*; for I am too old to have an husband. If I should say, I have hope, *if* I should

1
*a Judges of Israel*, Judg. 2:16.
*b Canaan*, Gen. 37:1.
*c Bethlehem*, Gen. 48:7.
*d Moabites*, Gen. 19:37.

2
*e* Ruth 2:1, 3; 4:3, 9.
*f* Ruth 4:9, 10.
*g* Ruth 4:9.

3
*h Death*, Num. 23:10.
*i Widow*, 2 Sam. 14:5.

4
*j Wife*, Prov. 5:18.

6
*k Daughter-in-law*, Lev. 20:12.
*l God, providence of*, Gen. 2:2.
*m Temporal Blessings, from God*, Psa. 103:2.

7
*n Judah, tribe of*, Num. 10:14.

8
*o Prayer, intercessory*, Acts 6:4.
*p Benedictions*, Deut. 21:5.
*q Love, instances of*, 1 John 4:7.

* **NAOMI** (*pleasant*). *Lived in Bethlehem*, Ruth 1:1, 2. *Wife of Elimelech*, Ruth 1:2. *Removed to Moab*, Ruth 1:1, 2. *Bereaved of her husband and sons*, Ruth 1:3, 5. *Returns after ten years to Bethlehem*, Ruth 1:4, 6, 7, 19, 22. *Beloved by Ruth*, Ruth 1:16, 17.

† **RUTH** (*a female friend*). *The daughter-in-law of Naomi*, Ruth 1:4. *Her devotion to Naomi*, Ruth 1:16, 17 (with vs. 6–18). *Goes to Bethlehem*, Ruth 1:19, 22. *Gleaned in the field of Boaz*, Ruth 2:3. *Receives kindness from Boaz*, Ruth 2:4–17; 3:15. *Under Naomi's instructions claims from Boaz the duty of a kinsman*, Ruth. 3:1–9. *Marries Boaz*, Ruth 4:9–13. *An ancestor of Jesus*, Ruth 4:13, 21, 22; Matt. 1:5.

‡ **KISS.** *Of affection*, Gen. 27:26, 27; 31:55; 33:4; 48:10; 50:1; Ex. 18:7, Ruth 1:14; 2 Sam. 14:33; 19:39; Luke 15:20; Acts 20:37. *The feet of Jesus kissed by the penitent woman*, Luke 7:38.
*Holy*, Rom. 16:16; 2 Cor. 13:12; 1 Thess. 5:26; 1 Pet. 5:14.
*Deceitful*, Prov. 27:6; *of Joab, when he slew Amasa*, 2 Sam. 20:9, 10; *of Judas, when he betrayed Jesus*, Matt. 26:48; Mark 14:45; Luke 22:48.

13
r *Marriage, levirate,* Gen. 34:9.

14
s *Mother-in-law,* Matt. 10:35.

15
t *Idolatry,* 1 Sam. 15:23.

16
u *Faithfulness, instances of,* Luke 16:10.

17
v *Oath,* Num. 5:19.

19
1 R. V. the women

20
w *Adversity, dispensation from God,* Psa. 10:6.

have an husband also to night,
and should also bear sons;
13 [r]Would ye tarry for them till
they were grown? would ye stay[c]
for them from having husbands?
nay my daughters; for it grieveth me much [q]for your sakes
that the hand[c] of the LORD is
gone out against me.
14 And [k,q]they lifted up their
voice, and wept again: and Ôr′-
pah ‡kissed her [s]mother in law;
but †Rṳth clave[c] unto her.
15 And she said, Behold, thy
sister in law is gone back unto
her people, and unto her [t]gods:
return thou after thy sister in
law.
16 And †Rṳth [q]said, Intreat
me not to leave thee, *or* to return[c]
from following after thee: for
whither[c] thou goest, I [u]will go;
and where thou lodgest,[c] I will
lodge:[c] [u]thy people *shall be*
my people, and thy God my
God:
17 [q]Where thou diest, [u]will I
die, and there will I be buried:
[v]the LORD do so to me, and
more also, *if ought*[c] but death
part thee and me.
18 When she saw that †she
was stedfastly minded[c] to go with
her, then she left[c] speaking unto
her.
19 ¶ So they two went until
they came to [c]Bĕth′-lĕ-hĕm.
And it came to pass, when they
were come to Bĕth′-lĕ-hĕm, that
all the city was moved about
them, and [1]they said, *Is* this
Nā̇-ō′mī?
20 And she said unto them,
Call me not Nā̇-ō′mī, call me
Mā′rā̇: for the Almighty hath
[w]dealt very bitterly with me.
21 I went out full, and the
LORD hath brought me home
again empty: why *then* call ye
me Nā̇-ō′mī, seeing the LORD
hath testified against me, and
the Almighty hath afflicted me?
22 So Nā̇-ō′mī returned, and
†Rṳth the Mō′ab-īt-ess, her
daughter in law, with her, which
returned out of the country of
Mō′ab: and they came to
Bĕth′-lĕ-hĕm in the beginning
of barley harvest.

## CHAPTER 2

*Ruth gleans in the fields of Boaz. 4 Boaz inquires concerning her, 8 and shews her great favor. 18 That which she gleans she carries to Naomi.*

AND [a]Nā̇-ō′mī had a kinsman of her husband's, a
mighty man of wealth, of the
family of [b]Ē-lĭm′e-lĕch; and his
name *was* *Bō′ăz.
2 And [c]Rṳth the [d]Mō′ab-īt-ess
said unto [a]Nā̇-ō′mī, Let me now
go to the field, and [e]glean[c] ears of
corn[c] after *him* in whose sight I
shall find grace. And she said
unto her, Go, my daughter.
3 And she went, and came, and
[e]gleaned in the field after the
reapers: and her hap[c] was to light[c]
on a part of the field *belonging*
unto *Bō′ăz, who *was* of the kindred of [b]Ē-lĭm′e-lĕch.
4 ¶ And, behold, *Bō′ăz came
from [f]Bĕth′-lĕ-hĕm, and said
unto the [g]reapers, [h]The LORD *be*
with you. And they answered
him, [h]The LORD bless thee.
5 Then said *Bō′ăz unto his
servant that was set over the
reapers, Whose damsel *is* this?
6 And the servant that was
set over the reapers answered
and said, It *is* the Mō′ab-īt-ish
[c]damsel that came back with
[a]Nā̇-ō′-mī out of the country
of [d]Mō′ab:
7 And [c]she said, I pray you, let
me [e,i]glean and gather after the
reapers among the sheaves: so
she came, and hath continued
even from the morning until

1
a *Naomi,* Ruth 1:2.
b Ruth 1:1–3; 4:3, 9.

2
c *Ruth,* Ruth 1:4.
d *Moabites,* Gen. 19:37.
e *Gleaning,* Lev. 23:22.

4
f *Bethlehem,* Gen. 48:7.
g *Servant, kindness to,* Jer. 2:14.
h *Salutations,* Luke 1:44.

7
i *Women, gleaned,* Prov. 31:10.

* **BOAZ** (*alacrity*), called also Booz. *In the lineage of,* David, 1 Chr. 2:11–15. *A man of wealth,* Ruth 2:1. *Kindness of, to his servants,* Ruth 2:4; *to Ruth,* Ruth 2:8–13; 3:15–17. *Obtains right to redeem Naomi's inheritance,* Ruth 4:1–12. *Marries Ruth,* Ruth 4:13. *Ancestor of Jesus,* Matt. 1:5; Luke 3:32.

now, that she tarried a little in
the house.
8 Then [j]said *Bō′ăz unto
[c]Ruth, Hearest thou not, my
daughter? Go not to [e,i]glean in
another field, neither go from
hence,[c] but abide here fast[c] by my
maidens:
9 [j]*Let* thine eyes *be* on the field
that they do reap, and [i]go thou
after them: have I not charged
the young men that they shall
not touch[G] thee? and when thou
art athirst, go unto the vessels,
and drink of *that* which the
young men have drawn.
10 Then [c]she fell on her face,
and bowed herself to the ground,
and said unto him, Why have I
found grace in thine eyes, that
thou shouldest [j]take knowledge[G]
of me, seeing I *am* a [k]stranger[G]?
11 And *Bō′ăz answered and
said unto her, It hath fully been
shewed me, all that [l]thou hast
done unto thy mother in law
since the death of thine husband: and *how* [l]thou hast left
thy father and thy mother, and
the land of thy nativity, and art
come unto a people which thou
knewest not heretofore.
12 [m]The LORD recompense[G] thy
work, and a full reward be given
thee of the [n]LORD God of Is′-
ra-el, under whose wings thou
art come to [1]trust.
13 Then [c]she said, Let me find
favour in thy sight, my lord; for
that thou [j]hast comforted me
and for that thou [j]hast spoken
friendly unto thine handmaid,
though I be not like unto one
of thine handmaidens.
14 And *Bō′ăz said unto [c,o]her,
At mealtime come thou hither,[c]
and eat of the bread, and dip thy
morsel in the [p]vinegar. And she
sat beside the reapers: and [o]he
reached her parched [q]*corn*,[c] and
she did eat, and was sufficed,[c]
and left.

8
j *Kindness, instances of*, Acts 28:2.

10
k *Foreigners*, Deut. 23:20.

11
l *Daughter-in-law, filial*, Lev. 20:12.

12
m *Prayer, intercessory*, Acts 6:4.
n *God, preserver*, Gen. 2:2.
1 R. V. take refuge.

14
o *Poor, kindness to*, vs. 14–16; Prov. 21:13.
p *Vinegar*, Num. 6:3.
q *Corn, parched*, Psa. 65:13.

15 And when she was risen
up to [e]glean,[c] *Bō′ăz commanded
his young men, [j]saying, Let her
glean even among the sheaves,
and reproach[c] her not:
16 [j]And let fall also *some* of the
handfuls of purpose for her, and
leave *them*, that she may glean
*them*, and rebuke her not.
17 So [c]she [e]gleaned in the field
until even, and [r]beat out that she
had gleaned: and it was about an
[s]ephah[G] of barley.
18 ¶ And [i]she took *it* up, and
went into the city: and her
[a,t]mother in law saw what she
had [e]gleaned: and [l]she brought
forth,[c] and gave to her that she had
reserved after she was sufficed.[c]
19 And her [a]mother in law
said unto her, Where hast thou
gleaned to day? and where
wroughtest thou? [u]blessed be he
that did take knowledge of thee.
And she shewed her [t]mother in
law with whom she had wrought,
and said, The man's name
with whom I wrought to day *is*
*Bō′ăz.
20 And [a]Nā-ō′mī said unto her
daughter in law, [u]Blessed *be* he
of the LORD, who hath not left[c]
off his kindness to the living and
to the dead. And Nā-ō′mī said
unto her, The man *is* near of kin
unto us, one of our next kinsmen.[c T]
21 And [c]Ruth the [d]Mō′ab-īt-ess
said, He said unto me also, Thou
shalt keep fast[c] by my young
men, until they have ended all
my harvest.
22 And [a]Nā-ō′mī said unto
[c]Ruth her daughter in law, *It is*
good, my daughter, that thou go
out with his maidens, that they
meet thee not in any other field.
23 So she kept fast[c] by the maidens of *Bō′ăz to [e,i]glean unto the
end of barley harvest and of
wheat harvest; and dwelt with
her mother in law.

17
r *Threshing*, 1 Chr. 21:20.
s *Measure, dry, ephah*, Deut. 25:15.

18
t *Mother-in-law*, Matt. 10:35.

19
u *Thankfulness, of man to man*, Acts 24:3.

1
a *Naomi,* Ruth 1:2.
b *Ruth,* Ruth 1:4.
c *Mother-in-law,* Matt. 10:35.
d *Love, instances of,* 1 John 4:7.

2
e *Boaz,* Ruth 2:1.
f *Threshing,* 1 Chr. 21:20.

3
g *Anointing,* Deut. 28:40.

10
h *Kindness, instances of,* Acts 28:2.

## CHAPTER 3

*By Naomi's instruction, 5 Ruth lies down at the feet of Boaz. 8 He acknowledges the duty of a kinsman; 14 and sends her away with six measures of barley.*

THEN [a]Nā-ō'mī [b]her [c]mother
in law [d]said unto her, My
daughter, shall I not seek rest[G]
for thee, that it may be well with
thee?
2 And now *is* not [e]Bō'ăz of
our kindred, with whose maidens thou wast? Behold, he*winnoweth barley to night in the
[f]threshingfloor.
3 Wash thyself therefore, and
[g]anoint thee, and put thy raiment upon thee, and get thee
down to the floor: *but* make not
thyself known unto the man, until he shall have done eating and
drinking.
4 And it shall be, when he lieth
down, that thou shalt mark[G] the
place where he shall lie, and thou
shalt go in, and uncover his feet,
and lay thee down; and he will
tell thee what thou shalt do.
5 And she said unto her, All
that thou sayest unto me I
will do.
6 ¶ And [b]she went down unto the
floor[C], and did according to all that
her [a,c]mother in law bade her.
7 And when [e]Bō'ăz had eaten
and drunk, and his heart was
merry[G], he went to lie down at the
end of the heap of corn[C]: and she
came softly, and uncovered his
feet, and laid her down.
8 ¶ And it came to pass at midnight, that the man was afraid,
and turned himself: and, behold,
a woman lay at his feet.
9[T] And [e]he said, Who *art* thou?
And she answered, I *am* [b]Ruth
thine handmaid: spread therefore thy skirt over thine handmaid; for thou *art* a near kinsman[C].
10 And [e]he [h]said, Blessed *be*
thou of the LORD, my daughter:
*for* thou hast shewed more kindness[G] in the latter end than at the
beginning, inasmuch as thou fol-
lowedst not young men, whether
poor or rich.
11 And [h]now, my daughter,
fear not; I will do to thee all that
thou requirest: for all the city of
my people doth know that thou
*art* a virtuous woman.
12 And now it is true that I *am*
*thy* near kinsman[C]: howbeit there
is a kinsman[G] nearer than I.
13 [h]Tarry this night, and it
shall be in the morning, *that* if he
will perform unto [b]thee the part
of a kinsman[C], well; let him do
the kinsman's[G] part: but if he will
not do the part of a kinsman[G] to
thee, then will I do the part
of a kinsman[C] to thee, [i]*as* the
LORD liveth: lie down until the
morning.[T]
14 ¶ And she lay at his feet until the morning: and [b]she rose up
before one could know[C] another.
And [e]he said, Let it not be
known that a woman came into
the floor.
15 Also he said, Bring the [1]vail[C]
that *thou hast* upon thee, and
hold it. And when she held it,
[h,j]he measured six *measures* of
[k]barley, and laid *it* on her: and
[2]she went into the city.
16 And when she came to her
mother in law, she said, Who *art*
thou, my daughter? And she
told her all that the man had
done to her.
17 And she said, These six
*measures* of barley gave he me;
for he said to me, Go not empty
unto thy mother in law.
18 Then said she, Sit still, my
daughter, until thou know how
the matter will fall[C]: for the man
will not be in rest, until he have
finished the thing this day.

13
i *Oath,* Num. 5:19.

15
j *Poor, kindness to, instances of,* Prov. 21:13.
k *Barley,* Ex. 9:31.
1 R. V. mantle
2 R. V. he

* **WINNOWING.** *Of grain,* Ruth 3:2; Isa. 30:24.
**Figurative:** *Of the separation of the wicked from the righteous,* Matt. 3:12; Luke 3:17.

## CHAPTER 4

*Boaz calls the next kinsman before the elders; 6 but he refuses to redeem the inheritance of Elimelech according to the manner in Israel. 9 Boaz buys it. 10 He marries Ruth. 13 She bears Obed, the grandfather of David. 18 The generations of Pharez.*

THEN[T] went [a]Bō'ăz up to the gate, and sat him down there: and, behold, the [b]kinsman[G] of whom Bō'ăz spake came by; unto whom he said, Ho, such a one! turn aside, sit down here. And he turned aside, and sat down.

2 And he took [c]ten men of the [d]elders of the city, and said, Sit ye down here. And they sat down.

3 And [a]he said unto the [b]kinsman,[G] [e]Nā-ō'mī, that is come again out of the country of [f]Mō'ab, selleth a parcel[G] of *land, which *was* our brother [g]Ĕ-lĭm'e-lĕch's:

4 And I thought to [1]advertise[G] thee, saying, Buy [h]*it* before[G] [2]the [i]inhabitants, and before the [c,d]elders of my people. If thou wilt [j]redeem *it*, redeem *it*: but if thou wilt not redeem *it*, *then* tell me, that I may know: for *there is* none to redeem *it* beside thee; and I *am* after thee. And [b]he said, I will redeem *it*.

5 Then said [a]Bō'ăz, What day thou buyest the field of the hand [G]of [e]Nā-ō'mī, thou must buy *it* also of [k]Ruth the Mō'ab-ī-tess, the wife of the dead, to [l]raise up the name of the dead upon his [h]inheritance.

6 And the [b]kinsman[G] said, I cannot redeem *it* for myself, lest I mar[G] mine own [h]inheritance: redeem[G] thou my right[G] to thyself; for I cannot redeem *it*.

7 Now this *was the manner* in former time in Ĭs'ra-el concerning [j]redeeming[G] and concerning changing,[G] for to [m]confirm all things; a man plucked[G] off his [n]shoe,[G] and gave *it* to his neighbour: and this [3]*was* a testimony in Ĭs'ra-el.

8 Therefore the [b]kinsman[G] said unto [a]Bō'ăz, Buy [h]*it* for thee. So he drew off his [n]shoe.[G]

9 ¶ And [a]Bō'ăz said unto the [c,d]elders, and *unto* all the people, Ye *are* [i]witnesses this day, that I have [o]bought *all that *was* [g]Ĕ-lĭm'e-lĕch's, and all that *was* [p]Chĭl'ĭ-on's and [q]Mäh'lon's, of the hand of [e]Nā-ō'mī.

10 Moreover [k]Ruth the [f]Mō'ab-īt-ess, the wife of Mäh'lon, have I [r]purchased to be my [l]wife, to raise up the name of the dead upon his inheritance, that the name of the dead be not cut off from among his brethren, and from the gate of his place: ye *are* witnesses this day.

11 And all the people that *were* in the gate, and the [c,d]elders, said, *We are* [i]witnesses. [s]The LORD make the woman that is come into thine house like [t]Rā'chel and like [u]Lē'ah, which two did build the house of Ĭs'ra-el: and do thou worthily in Ĕph'ratah, and be famous in [v]Bĕth'-lĕ-hĕm:[T]

12 [s]And let thy house be like the house of [w]Phā'rĕz, whom [x]Tā'mar bare[G] unto [y]Jū'dah, of the seed which the LORD shall give thee of this young woman.[Q]

13 ¶ So [z]Bō'ăz took [a]Ruth, and she was his [b]wife: and when he went in unto her, the LORD gave her conception, and she bare[G] a [c]son.[Q]

---

1
a *Boaz*, Ruth 2:1.
b *Heir*, vs. 1–12; Gen. 15:3.

2
c *Court, civil*, Ex. 18:26.
d *Government, municipal*, Isa. 22:21.

3
e *Naomi*, Ruth 1:2.
f *Moabites*, Gen. 19:37.
g Ruth 1:1–3; 2:1, 3.

4
h *Inheritance*, Num. 27:7.
i *Witness*, Num. 35:30.
j *Redemption, of property*, vs. 3–9; Lev. 25:24.
1 R. V. disclose it unto thee,
2 R. V. them that sit here,

5
k *Ruth*, Ruth 1:4.
l *Marriage, levirate*, Gen. 34:9.

7
m *Covenant, of men with men*, Deut. 29:1.
n *Shoe*, Josh. 5:15.
3 R. V. was the manner of attestation,

9
o *Contracts*, Matt. 20.2.
p Ruth 1:2, 4, 5.
q Ruth 1:2, 5.

10
r *Wife, bought*, Prov. 5:18.

11
s *Benedictions*, Deut. 21:5.
t *Rachel*, Gen. 29:6.
u *Leah*, Gen. 29:16.
v *Bethlehem*, Gen. 48:7.

12
w *Pharez*, Gen. 38:29.
x *Tamar*, Gen. 38:6.
y *Judah*, Gen. 37:26.

13
z *Boaz*, Ruth 2:1.

a *Ruth*, Ruth 1.4.
b *Wife*, Prov. 5:18.
c *Children, the gift of God*, Mark 10:14.

---

***LAND.** *Appeared on third creative day*, Gen. 1:9. *Original title to, from God*, Gen. 13:14–17; 15:7; Ex. 23:31; Lev. 25:23. *Bought and sold*, Gen. 23:3–18; 33:19; Acts 4:34; 5:1–8. *Entailment of title to*, Num. 27:8–11.

*Sale and redemption of, laws concerning*, Lev. 25:15, 16, 23–33; Num. 36:4, Jer. 32:7–16, 25, 44; Ezek. 46:18. *Dedication and redemption of*, Lev. 27:14–25. *Alienated, by dedication*, Lev. 27:20, 21; *by absence of owner*, 2 Kin. 8:1–6.

*Inalienable*, Lev. 27:22–24; Num. 36:7.

*Conveyance of, by written deeds and other forms*, Gen. 23:3–20; Ruth 4:3–8, 11; Jer. 32:9–14. *Conveyance of, witnessed*, Gen. 23:10, 11; Ruth 4:9–11; Jer. 32:9–14. *Transfer of temporary*, Lev. 27:22–25.

*Mortgaged for debt*, Neh. 5:3–5. *Leased*, Matt. 21:33–41; Mark 12:1–9; Luke 20:9–16.

*Priest's part in*, Gen. 47:22; Ezek. 48:10. *King's part in* Ezek. 48:21. *Widow's dower in*, Ruth 4:3–9. *Unmarried woman's rights in*, Num. 27:1–11, 36:1–11.

*To rest every seventh year*, Ex. 23:11.

14 d Naomi, Ruth 1:2.
e Temporal Blessings, from God, Psa. 103:2.
f Thankfulness, exemplified, Acts 24:3.
15 g Daughter-in-law, filial, Lev. 20:12.
16 h Nurse, 2 Chr. 22:11.

14 And the women said unto [d]Nā-ō'mī, [e,f]Blessed *be* the LORD, which hath not left thee this day without a kinsman,[G] that his name may be famous in Iş'ra-el.
15 And he shall be unto thee a restorer of *thy* life, and a nourisher[G] of thine old age: for thy [a]daughter in law, which [g]loveth thee, which is better to thee than seven sons, hath born him.[C]
16 And [d]Nā-ō'mī took the child, and laid it in her bosom, and became [h]nurse unto it.
17 [Q]And the women her neighbours gave it a name, saying, There is a son born to [d]Nā-ō'mī; and they called his name †Ō'bed: he *is* the father of ‡Jĕs'se, the father of [i]Dā'vid.
18 ¶ Now [j]these *are* the generations of [k]Phā'rĕz: Phā'rĕz begat [l]Hĕz'rŏn,
19 And [l]Hĕz'rŏn begat ‖Răm, and Răm begat [m]Ăm-mĭn'a-dăb,
20 And [m]Ăm-mĭn'a-dăb begat [n]Näh'shŏn, and Näh'shŏn begat §Săl'mŏn,
21 And §Săl'mŏn begat [o]Bō'ăz, and Bō'ăz begat †Ō'bed,
22 And †Ō'bed begat ‡Jĕs'se, and Jĕs'se begat [i]Dā'vid.[Q]

17 i David, 1 Sam. 16:13.
18 j Genealogy, vs. 18–22; 1 Chr. 5:1.
k Pharez, Gen. 38:29.
l Hezron, 1 Chr. 2:5.
19 m Amminadab, Num. 2:3.
20 n Nahshon, Num. 7:12.
21 o Boaz, Ruth 2:1.

THE

# FIRST BOOK OF SAMUEL

## CHAPTER 1

*Elkanah and his two wives worship yearly at Shiloh. 9 Hannah prays for a child and makes a vow. 12 Eli first rebukes her, afterward blesses her. 19 Having borne Samuel, 24 she presents him unto the* LORD, *according to her vow.*

1 a Ephraim, mount of, Josh. 17:15.
b 1 Sam. 2:11, 20; 1 Chr. 6:27, 34.
c 1 Chr. 6:27, 34.
d Or, *Eliab*, 1 Chr. 6:27; or, *Eliel*, 1 Chr. 6:34.
2 e Polygamy, evil effects of, vs. 4–7; Deut. 17:17.

NOW there was a certain man of Rā-math-ā'im-zō'phim, of mount [a]Ē'phră-ĭm, and his name *was* [b]Ĕl'kă-nah, the son of [c]Jĕr'o-hăm, the son of [d]Ē-lī'hū, the son of Tō'hu, the son of Zŭph, an Ĕph'rath-īte:
2 And he had [e]two wives; the name of the one *was* *Hăn'nah, and the name of the other Pĕ-nĭn'nah: and Pĕ-nĭn'nah had children, but Hăn'nah had no children.
3 And this [b]man went up out of his city[C] yearly to [f]worship and to sacrifice unto the LORD of hosts in [g]Shī'lōh. And the two sons of +Ē'lī, ⊙Hŏph'nī and [h]Phĭn'e-has, the priests of the LORD, *were* there.
4 And when the time was that [b]Ĕl'kă-nah offered,[C] he gave to Pĕ-nĭn'nah his wife, and to all her sons and her daughters, portions:
5 But unto *Hăn'nah he gave a [1,i]worthy portion; for he loved Hăn'nah: but the LORD had shut up her womb.
6 And [e,j]her [2,k]adversary also [l]provoked her sore, for to make her fret, because the LORD had [m]shut up her womb.

3 f Annual Feasts, Num. 15:3.
g Shiloh, tabernacle at, Judg. 21:12.
h Phinehas, 1 Sam. 2:34.
5 i Partiality, Elkanah for Hannah, 1 Tim. 5:21.
1 R. V. double
6 j Family, infelicity in, 1 Chr. 13:14.
k Women, wicked, Prov. 31:10.
l Cruelty, Psa. 27:12.
m Barrenness, Deut. 7:14.
2 R. V. rival

*Products of, for all*, Eccl. 5:9. *Monopoly of*, Gen. 47:20–26; Isa. 5:8.
*Of Canaan divided into portions for tribes and families by Joshua, Eleazar and a prince from each tribe, and assigned by lot*, Num. 34:16–29; 35:1–8; Josh. chapters 14–19.

† **OBED** (*serving Jehovah*). *Son of Boaz and grandfather of David*, Ruth 4:17–22; 1 Chr. 2:12; Matt. 1:5; Luke 3:32.

‡ **JESSE** (*strong* or *living*). *Father of David*, Ruth 4:17; 1 Sam. 17:12. *Samuel visits, under divine command, to select from his sons a successor to Saul*, 1 Sam. 16:1–13. *Saul asks, to send David to become a member of his court*, 1 Sam. 16:19–23. *Sons in Saul's army*, 1 Sam. 17:13–28. *Dwells with David in Moab*, 1 Sam. 22:3, 4. *Descendants of*, 1 Chr. 2:13–17. *Ancestor of Jesus*, Matt. 1:5, 6; Luke 3:32.

‖ **RAM.** *Son of Hezron, and an ancestor of Jesus*, Ruth 4:19; 1 Chr. 2:9, 10. *Called* ARAM, Matt. 1:3, 4; Luke 3:33.

§ **SALMON,** called also SALMA. *Father of Boaz*, Ruth 4:20, 21; 1 Chr. 2:11. *In the lineage of Joseph*, Matt. 1:4, 5; Luke 3:32.

* **HANNAH** (*grace, favor*), mother of Samuel. *Trials and prayer of; and promise to*, 1 Sam. 1:1–18. *Samuel born to; dedicates him to God; leaves him at the temple*, 1 Sam. 1:19–28. *Her hymn of praise*, 1 Sam. 2:1–10. *Visits Samuel at the temple from year to year*, 1 Sam. 2:18, 19. *Children of*, 1 Sam. 2:20, 21.

+ **ELI.** *High priest*, 1 Sam. 1:25; 2:11; 1 Kin. 2:27. *Judge of Israel*, 1 Sam. 4:18. *Mis-judges and rebukes Hannah*, 1 Sam. 1:14. *His benediction upon Hannah*, 1 Sam. 1:17, 18; 2:20. *Officiates when Samuel is presented at the tabernacle*, 1 Sam. 1:24–28. *Indulgent to his corrupt sons*, 1 Sam. 2:22–25, 29; 3:11–14. *His solicitude for the ark*, 1 Sam. 4:11–18. *Death of*, 1 Sam. 4:18.
*Prophecies of judgments upon his house*, 1 Sam. 2:27–36; 3; 1 Kin. 2:27.

⊙ **HOPHNI** (*a fighter*). *Son of Eli*, 1 Sam. 1:3. *Wickedness of*, 1 Sam. 2:12–17, 22–36; 3:11–14. *Death of*, 1 Sam. 4:4, 11, 17.

7 And *as* he [i]did so year by year, when she went up to the [n]house of the LORD, so she provoked her; therefore she [o]wept, and did not eat.

8 Then said [b]Ĕl'kă-nah her husband to her, *Hăn'nah, why weepest thou? and why eatest thou not? and why is thy heart grieved? *am* not I better to thee than ten sons?

9 ¶ So *,[p]Hăn'nah rose up after they had eaten in [q]Shī'lōh, and after they had drunk. Now +Ē'lī the priest sat upon a seat by a post of the [n,r]temple of the LORD.

10 And she *was* in [s]bitterness of soul, and [t]prayed unto the LORD, and [o]wept sore.

11 And *she vowed a [u]vow, and [s,t]said, O LORD of hosts, if thou wilt indeed look on the [m]affliction of thine handmaid, and remember me, and not forget thine handmaid, but wilt give unto thine handmaid a [v]man child, [w]then I will give him unto the LORD all the days of his life, and [x]there shall no razor come upon his head.

12 ¶ And it came to pass, as *she continued [t]praying before the LORD, that +Ē'lī marked her mouth.

13 Now *Hăn'nah, she spake in her [y]heart; only her lips moved, but her voice was not heard: therefore Ē'lī [z]thought she had been [a]drunken.

14 And +Ē'lī said unto her, [b,c]How long wilt thou be [a]drunken? put away thy wine from thee.

15 And *Hăn'nah answered and said, [d]No, my lord, I *am* a woman of a sorrowful spirit: I have drunk neither wine nor strong drink, but have [e]poured out my soul before the LORD.

16 Count not thine handmaid for a daughter of Bē'lĭ-ăl: for out of the abundance of my complaint and [3]grief have I spoken hitherto.

17 Then +Ē'lī answered and said, Go in peace: and [f]the God of Ĭş'ra-el grant *thee* thy petition that thou hast asked of him.

18 And she said, Let thine handmaid find grace in thy sight. So the woman went her way, and did eat, and [g]her [h]countenance was no more *sad*.

19 ¶ And they [i]rose up in the morning early, and ‖worshipped before the LORD, and returned, and came to their house to §Rā'mah: and [j]Ĕl'kă-nah knew *Hăn'nah his wife; and the LORD [k,l]remembered her.

20 Wherefore it came to pass, when the time was come about after *Hăn'nah had [l]conceived, that she bare a son, and called his name [m]S ă m'u-e l, *saying*, Because I have asked [n]him of the LORD.

21 And the man [j]Ĕl'kă-nah, and all his house, went up to offer unto the LORD the [o]yearly sacrifice, and his [p]vow.

22 But *Hăn'nah went not up; for she said unto her husband, *I will not go up* until the child be [q]weaned, and *then* I will [r,s]bring him, that he may appear before the LORD, and there abide for ever.

23 And [j]Ĕl'kă-nah her husband said unto her, Do what seemeth thee good; tarry until thou have [q]weaned him; only the LORD establish his word. So the woman abode, and gave her son suck until she weaned him.

24 ¶ And when she had [q]weaned him, *she took him up with her, with three [t]bullocks,

---

**7**
- *n Church,* 1 Kin. 9:3.
- *o Weeping, instances of,* Ezra 3:13.

**9**
- *p Women, good, instances of,* vs. 9–18; Prov. 31:10.
- *q Shiloh,* Judg. 21:12.
- *r Tabernacle,* Ex. 27:9.

**10**
- *s Affliction, prayer in,* Psa. 34:19.
- *t Prayer, importunity in,* Acts 6:4.

**11**
- *u Vows, instances of,* Num. 30:2.
- *v Temporal Blessings, prayer for,* Psa. 103:2.
- *w Consecration, conditional,* Lev. 7:37.
- *x Nazirite,* Num. 6:2.

**13**
- *y Heart,* Psa. 44:21.
- *z Mis-judgment, instances of,* Num. 32:6.

- *a Drunkenness,* Luke 21:34.

**14**
- *b False Accusation,* 2 Tim. 3:3.
- *c Uncharitableness, instances of,* Matt. 7:1.

**15**
- *d Meekness, instances of,* Psa. 45:4.
- *e Prayer, instances of,* Acts 6:4.

**16**
- 3 R. V. my provocation

**17**
- *f Prayer, intercessory,* Acts 6:4.

**18**
- *g Faith, instances of,* Mark 11:22.
- *h Countenance,* Prov. 15:13.

**19**
- *i Rising, early,* Gen. 19:2.
- *j* 1 Sam. 2:11, 20; 1 Chr. 6:27, 34.
- *k Prayer, answered,* Acts 6:4.
- *l God, providence of,* Gen. 2:2.

**20**
- *m Samuel,* 1 Sam. 3:1.
- *n Children, in answer to prayer,* Mark 10:14.

**21**
- *o Annual Feasts,* Num. 15:3.
- *p Vows, instances of,* Num. 30:2.

**22**
- *q Children, weaning of,* Mark 10:14.
- *r Dedication,* Ezra 6:17.
- *s Children, dedicated to God in infancy,* Mark 10:14.

**B.C. 1165?**

**24**
- *t Bullock,* Ex. 29:3.

---

‖ **FAMILY WORSHIP,** Deut. 16:11, 14; *of Abraham,* Gen. 12:7, 8; 13:4, 18; *of Jacob,* Gen. 35:2, 3; *of Job,* Job 1:5; *of the Philippian jailer,* Acts 16:34.

§ **RAMAH** (*a high place*), called also RAMATHAIM-ZOPHIM. *A city in Mount Ephraim,* Judg. 4:5; 1 Sam. 1:1. *Home, of Elkanah,* 1 Sam. 1:1, 19; 2:11; *of Samuel,* 1 Sam. 1:19, 20; 7:17; 8:4; 15:34; 16:13. *David flees to,* 1 Sam. 19:18. *Samuel dies and is buried in,* 1 Sam. 25:1; 28:3.

and one [u]ephah[G] of [4]flour, and a bottle[G] of [v]wine, and [r,s]brought him unto the [w]house of the LORD in [x]Shī′lōh: and the child *was* young.

25 And they [y]slew a [t]bullock, and [r,s]brought the child to +Ē′lī.

26 And she said, Oh my lord, *as* thy soul liveth, my lord, I *am* the woman that stood by thee here, praying unto the LORD.

27 For this [m,n]child I prayed; and the LORD hath [k]given me my petition which I asked of him:

28 [z]Therefore also I have [5,a,b]lent [c]him to the LORD; as long as he liveth he shall be [4]lent to the LORD. And he worshipped the LORD there.

## CHAPTER 2

*Hannah's song of thanksgiving. 12 The sin of Eli's sons. 18 Samuel's ministry. 20 Hannah's other children. 22 Eli reproves his sons. 27 A prophecy against Eli's house.*

AND [a]Hăn′nah [b]prayed, and [c]said, [d,e]My heart [f]rejoiceth in the LORD, mine horn[G] is exalted in the LORD: my mouth is enlarged over mine enemies; because I rejoice in thy salvation.[G] [Q]

2 [d,e]*There is* none holy as the [g]LORD: for *there is* none beside thee: neither *is there* any rock like our God.[S]

3 *Talk no more so exceeding [h]proudly; let *not* [i]arrogancy come out of your mouth: for the LORD *is* a God of [j]knowledge, and by him actions are [k]weighed.[G] [S]

4 [d,e]The bows of the mighty men *are* broken, and they that stumbled are girded with [l]strength.

5 *They that were* full have hired out themselves for bread; and *they that were* hungry ceased: so that the [m]barren hath born [n]seven; and she that hath many children is waxed[G] feeble.[Q]

6 The LORD [o]killeth, and [p,q,r]maketh alive: he [o]bringeth down to the grave,[G] and [p,q,r]bringeth up.[S]

7 The LORD maketh [s]poor, and [l]maketh [t]rich: he bringeth low, and lifteth up.[S] [Q]

8 [l]He raiseth up the [u]poor out of the dust, *and* lifteth up the [1,v]beggar from the dunghill,[G] to set *them* among princes, and to make them inherit the throne of glory: [w]for the pillars of the [x]earth *are* the LORD's, and [y]he hath set the world upon them.[S]

9 [z]He will keep the feet of his saints, and the wicked shall be silent in [a]darkness; for by strength shall no man prevail.[T] [S]

10 The adversaries of the [b]LORD shall be broken to pieces; out of heaven shall he thunder upon them: the LORD shall [c]judge the ends of the earth; and he shall give strength unto his king, and exalt the horn[G] of his anointed.[S] [T] [Q]

11 ¶ And [d]Ĕl′kă-nah went to [e]Rā′mah to his house. And the [f]child did minister[G] unto the LORD before [g]Ē′lī the [h]priest.

12 Now the [i,j]sons of Ē′lī *were* [k]sons of Bē′lī-al;[G] they [l]knew not the LORD.

13 And the priest's custom with the people *was, that,* when any man offered sacrifice, the priest's servant came, while the flesh was in seething,[G] with a [m]fleshhook of three teeth in his hand;

14 And he struck *it* into the pan, or kettle, or †caldron, or pot; [n]all that the [m]fleshhook brought up the priest took for himself. So they did in [o]Shī′lōh unto all the Iṣ′ra-el-ītes that came thither.[G]

u *Measure, dry,* Deut. 25:15.
v *Wine,* Prov. 23:31.
w *Tabernacle,* Ex. 27:9.
x *Shiloh,* Judg. 21:12.
4 R. V. meal,

25
y *Offerings,* Lev. 6.17.

28
z *Thankfulness, to God,* Acts 24:3.

a *Dedication, of Samuel by his mother,* Ezra 6:17.
b *Consecration,* Lev. 7:37.
c *Children, dedicated to God in infancy,* Mark 10:14.
5 R. V. granted

1
a *Hannah,* 1 Sam. 1:2.
b *Prayer,* Acts 6:4.
c *Women, as poets,* vs. 1–10; Prov. 31:10.
d *Poetry, lyrics, sacred,* vs. 1–10; Acts 17:28.
e *Praise,* vs. 1–10; Psa. 150:1.
f *Joy, instances of,* Psa. 5:11.

2
g *God, holiness of,* Gen. 2:2.

3
h *Pride,* Prov. 16:18.
i Prov. 8.13; Isa. 13:11.
j *God, knowledge of,* Gen. 2.2.
k *God, judge,* Gen. 2:2.

4
l *Temporal Blessings, from God,* Psa. 103:2.

5
m *Barrenness,* Deut. 7:14.
n *Seven,* Gen. 7:2.

6
o *God, power of,* Gen. 2:2.
p *God, preserver,* Gen. 2:2.
q *Death, God's power over,* Num. 23:10.
r *Life, from God,* Eccl. 8:15.

7
s *Poverty,* Prov. 30:8.
t *Riches,* Eccl. 4:8.

8
u *Poor, God's care of,* Prov. 21:13.
v *Beggars,* Luke 16:20.
w *Geology,* Psa. 104:5.
x *Earth,* Prov. 8:23.
y *God, creator,* Gen. 2:2.
1 R. V. needy

9
z *Righteous, promises to,* Psa. 64:10.

a *Death,* Num. 23:10.

10
b *God, power of,* Gen. 2:2.
c *God, judge,* Gen. 2:2.

11
d 1 Sam. 1:1–8, 19–23.
e *Ramah,* 1 Sam. 1:19.
f *Samuel,* 1 Sam. 3:1.
g *Eli,* 1 Sam. 1:3.
h *High Priest,* Lev. 21:10.

12
i *Minister, false and corrupt,* Rom. 15:16.
j *Priest, corrupt,* Lev. 1:5.
k *Children, wicked,* Mark 10:14.
l *Spiritual Blindness, instances of.* 2 Cor. 4:4.

13
m *Fleshhook,* Ex. 27:3.

14
n *Priest, emoluments of,* Lev. 1:5.
o *Shiloh,* Judg. 21:12.

*** SATIRE.** *In Hannah's song of exultation over Peninnah,* 1 Sam. 2:1-10 (with 1:5-10). *Of Jesus against hypocrites,* Matt. 23:1-33; Mark 12:13-40; Luke 11:39-54. See footnotes: IRONY, Mark 12:14; SARCASM, Judg. 10:14.

**† CALDRON,** used for cooking the flesh of sacrifices for food of priests and Levites. *In the tabernacle,* 1 Sam. 2:14. *In the temple,* 2 Chr. 35:13; Jer. 52:18, 19. **Figurative,** Ezek. 11:3-11.

15 Also before they burnt the [p]fat, the priest's servant came, and said to the man that sacrificed, Give [n]flesh to roast for the priest; for he will not have sodden flesh of thee, but raw.

16 And *if* any man said unto him, [2]Let them not fail to burn the [p]fat presently, and *then* take *as much* as thy soul desireth; then he would answer him, *Nay*; but thou shalt give *it me* now: and if not, I will take *it* by force.

17 Wherefore the sin of the [i,j,k]young men was very great before the LORD: for men abhorred the offering of the LORD.

18 ¶ But [l,q]Săm′u-el ministered before the LORD, *being* a child, girded with a linen [r]ephod.

19 Moreover his [s,t,u]mother made him a little [v]coat, and brought *it* to him from year to year, when she came up with her husband to offer the yearly sacrifice.

20 And [g]Ē′lī blessed [d]Ĕl′kă-nah and his [s]wife, and said, [w]The LORD give thee seed of this [s]woman for the [3]loan which is lent to the LORD. And they went unto their own home.

21 And the LORD visited [s]Hăn′nah, so that she conceived, and bare three [x]sons and two daughters. And the child [l]Săm′u-el grew before the LORD.

22 ¶ Now [y]Ē′lī was very [z]old, and heard all that his sons did unto all Ĭş′ra-el; and how [a,b]they [c,d]lay with the [e]women that [4]assembled *at* the door of the [5]tabernacle of the congregation.

23 And he [f]said unto [a,b]them, Why do ye such things? for I hear of your evil dealings by all this people.

24 Nay, my sons; for *it is* no good report that I hear: ye [g]make the LORD's people to transgress.

25 If one man sin against another, [6]the judge shall judge him: but if a man sin against the LORD, who shall intreat for him? Notwithstanding they [h,i]hearkened not unto the voice of their father, because the LORD [j]would slay them.

26 And the [k]child [l]Săm′u-el grew on, and was in favour both with the LORD, and also with men.

27 ¶ And there came a man of God unto [m]Ē′lī, and said unto him, Thus saith the LORD, Did I [7]plainly appear unto the house of thy father, when they were in [n]Ē′ġўpt [8]in [o]Phā′raōh's house?

28 And did I choose him out of all the tribes of Ĭş′ra-el *to be* my priest, to offer upon mine [p]altar, to burn [q]incense, to wear an [r]ephod before me? and did I give unto the house of thy father [s]all the offerings made by fire of the children of Ĭş′ra-el?

29 Wherefore kick ye at my sacrifice and at mine offering, which I have commanded *in my* habitation; and honourest thy sons above me, to make yourselves fat with the chiefest of all the offerings of Ĭş′ra-el my people?

30 Wherefore the LORD God of Ĭş′ra-el saith, I said indeed *that* thy house, and the house of thy father, should walk before me for ever: but now the LORD saith, Be it far from me; for them that honour me I will honour, and [t]they that despise me shall be lightly esteemed.

31 Behold, the days come, that I will [u]cut off thine arm, and the arm of thy father's house, that there shall not be an old man in thine house.

32 And [u]thou shalt [9]see an enemy *in my* habitation, in all *the wealth* which *God* shall give Ĭş′ra-el: and there shall not be an old man in thine house for ever.

**15**
*p* *Fat*, Lev. 7:24.

**16**
2 R. V. They will surely burn

**18**
*q* *Children, early piety of*, Mark 10:14.
*r* *Ephod*, Ex. 28:6.

**19**
*s* *Hannah*, 1 Sam. 1:2.
*t* *Parents, affection of, exemplified*, 2 Cor. 12:14.
*u* *Women, domestic duties of*, Prov. 31:10.
*v* *Dress*, Zech. 3:3.

**20**
*w* *Benedictions*, Deut. 21:5.
3 Am. R. V. petition which was asked of Jehovah.

**21**
*x* *Children, the gift of God*, Mark 10: 14.

**22**
*y* *Eli*, 1 Sam. 1:3.
*z* *Longevity*, Psa. 91:16.
*a* *Priest, corrupt*, Lev. 1:5.
*b* *Minister, false and corrupt*, Rom. 15:16.
*c* *Lasciviousness, instances of*, 1 Pet. 4:3.
*d* *Adultery*, Lev. 20:10.
*e* *Women, wicked*, Prov. 31:10.
4 R. V. did service
5 R. V. tent of meeting.

**23**
*f* *Reproof*, Prov. 17:10.

**24**
*g* *Temptation, leading into*, Luke 11:4.

**25**
*h* *Impenitence, instances of*, Rom. 2:5.
*i* *Obduracy*, Prov. 29:1.
*j* *Foreordination*, Rom. 8:30.
6 R. V. God shall

**26**
*k* *Children, good*, Mark 10:14.
*l* *Samuel*, 1 Sam. 3:1.

**27**
*m* *Eli*, 1 Sam. 1:3
*n* *Egypt*, Gen. 41:8.
*o* *Pharaoh, at the time of the Exodus*, Ex. 3:10.
7 R. V. reveal myself unto
8 R. V. in bondage to

**28**
*p* *Altar*, Gen. 8:20.
*q* *Incense*, Ex. 37: 29.
*r* *Ephod*, Ex. 28:6.
*s* *Priest, emoluments of*, Lev. 1:5.

**30**
*t* *The Godless, described as despising God*, Job 8:13.

**31**
*u* *Judgments*, vs. 31–36; Ex. 6:6.

**32**
9 R. V. behold the affliction of my

34
[v] *Hophni*, 1 Sam. 1:3.

35
[w] *Minister, character and qualifications of*, Rom. 15:16.

36
[x] *High Priest, duties of*, Lev. 21:10.
10 R. V. loaf
11 R. V. morsel

1
[a] *Children, early piety of*, Mark 10:14.
[b] *Eli*, 1 Sam. 1:3.
[c] *Word of God*, Psa. 119:9.
[d] *Vision*, Acts 9:10.

2
[e] *Infirmity, physical*, John 5:5.

3
[f] *Candlestick*, Ex. 25:31.
[g] *Tabernacle*, Ex. 27:9.
[h] *Church, place of worship*, 1 Kin. 9:3.

33 And the man of thine, *whom* I shall not cut off from mine altar, *shall be* [u]to consume thine eyes, and to grieve thine heart: and all the increase of thine house [u]shall die in the flower of their age.

34 And this *shall be* a sign unto thee, that shall come upon thy two sons, on [v]Hŏph′nī and ‡Phĭn′e-has; [u]in one day they shall die both of them.

35 And I will raise me up a [w]faithful priest, *that* shall do according to *that* which *is* in mine heart and in my mind: and I will build him a sure house; and he shall walk before mine anointed for ever.

36 And it shall come to pass, *that* every one that is left in thine house shall come *and* [u]crouch to [x]him for a piece of silver and a [10]morsel of bread, and shall say, Put me, I pray thee, into one of the priest's offices, that I may eat a [11]piece of bread.

## CHAPTER 3

*How the word of the Lord was first revealed to Samuel. 11 God foretells to Samuel the destruction of Eli's house. 15 Samuel, though unwilling, tells Eli the vision. 20 Samuel established to be a prophet.*

AND the [a]child *Săm′u-el ministered unto the LORD before [b]Ē′lī. And the [c]word of the LORD was precious in those days; *there was* no open [d]vision.

2 And it came to pass at that time, when [b]Ē′lī *was* laid down in his place, and [e]his eyes began to wax dim, *that* he could not see;

3 And ere the [f]lamp of God went out in the [g,h]temple of the LORD, where the [i]ark of God *was*, and *Săm′u-el was laid down *to sleep*;

4 That the LORD [j]called *Săm′u-el: and he answered, Here *am* I.

5 And he ran unto [b]Ē′lī, and said, Here *am* I; for thou calledst me. And he said, I called not; lie down again. And he went and lay down.

6 And the LORD called yet again, *Săm′u-el. And Săm′u-el arose and went to [b]Ē′lī, and said, Here *am* I; for thou didst call me. And he answered, I called not, my son; lie down again.

7 Now *Săm′u-el did not yet know the LORD, neither was the word of the LORD yet revealed unto him.

8 And the LORD called *Săm′u-el again the third time. And [k]he arose and went to [b]Ē′lī, and said, Here *am* I; for thou didst call me. And Ē′lī perceived that the LORD had called the child.

9 Therefore [b]Ē′lī said unto *Săm′u-el, Go, lie down: and it shall be, if he call thee, that thou shalt say, Speak, LORD; for thy servant heareth. So Săm′u-el went and lay down in his place.

10 And the LORD came, and stood, and called as at other times, *·[k]Săm′u-el, Săm′u-el. Then Săm′u-el answered, Speak; for thy servant heareth.

11 ¶ And the LORD [l]said to *Săm′u-el, Behold, I will do a thing in Iṣ′ra-el, at which both the ears of every one that heareth it shall tingle.

12 In that day I will perform

[i] *Ark*, Ex. 25:10.

4
[j] *Call, personal*, Phil. 3:14.

8
[k] *Children, good*, Mark 10:14.

11
[l] *Revelation*, 2 Cor. 12:1.

‡ **PHINEHAS.** *Son of Eli*, 1 Sam. 1:3; 14:3. *Sin of*, 1 Sam. 2:12-17, 22-36; 3:11-14. *Death of*, 1 Sam. 4:4, 11, 17, 19.

* **SAMUEL** (*asked of God*). *Providential birth of*, 1 Sam. 1:7-20. *Consecrated to God before his birth*, 1 Sam. 1:11, 22, 24-28. *His mother's song of thanksgiving*, 1 Sam. 2:1-10. *Ministered in the house of God*, 1 Sam. 2:11, 18, 19. *Blessed of God*, 1 Sam. 2:21; 3:19. *His vision concerning the house of Eli*, 1 Sam. 3:1-18. *A prophet of the Israelites*, 1 Sam. 3:20, 21; 4:1. *A judge of Israel; his judgment seats at Bethel, Gilgal, Mizpeh, and Ramah*, 1 Sam. 7:15-17. *Organizes the tabernacle service*, 1 Chr. 9:22; 26:28; 2 Chr. 35:18. *Israelites repent under his reproofs and admonitions*, 1 Sam. 7:3-6. *The Philistines defeated through his intercession and sacrifices*, 1 Sam. 7:7-14. *Makes his corrupt sons judges in Israel*, 1 Sam. 8:1-3. *People desire a king; he protests*, 1 Sam. 8:4-22. *Anoints Saul king of Israel*, 1 Sam. 9:10. *Renews the kingdom of Saul*, 1 Sam. 11:12-15. *Reproves Saul; foretells that his kingdom shall not be established*, 1 Sam. 13:11-15; 15. *Anoints David to be king*, 1 Sam. 16:1-13. *Shelters David when escaping from Saul*, 1 Sam. 19:18. *Death of; the lament for him*, 1 Sam. 25:1.

*Called up by the witch of Endor*, 1 Sam. 28:3-20. *His integrity as judge and ruler*, 1 Sam. 12:1-5; Psa. 99:6; Jer. 15:1; Heb. 11:32. *Chronicles of*, 1 Chr. 29:29. *Sons of*, 1 Chr. 6:28, 33. *Called* SHEMUEL, 1 Chr. 6:33.

against [b]Ē'lī all *things* which I have spoken concerning his [m]house: [1]when I begin, I will also make an end.

13 For I have told him that I will [n]judge his house for ever for the iniquity which he knoweth; because his [o]sons [2]made themselves vile, and [p,q]he restrained them not.

14 And therefore I have sworn unto the house of [b]Ē'lī, that the [r]iniquity of Ē'lī's [m,s]house shall not be purged with sacrifice nor offering for ever.

15 ¶ And *Săm'u-el lay until the morning, and opened the doors of the house of the LORD. And Săm'u-el feared to shew [b]Ē'lī the [d]vision.

16 Then [b]Ē'lī called *Săm'u-el, and said, Săm'u-el, my son. And he answered, Here *am* I.

17 And he said, What *is* the thing that *the* LORD hath said unto thee? I pray thee hide *it* not from me: God do so to thee, and more also, if thou hide *any* thing from me of all the things that he said unto thee.

18 And *Săm'u-el told him every whit, and hid nothing from him. And he said, [t]It *is* the LORD: let him do what seemeth him good.

19 And *,[k]Săm'u-el grew, and the LORD was with him, and did let none of his words fall to the ground.

20 And all Ĭṣ'ra-el from [u]Dăn even to [v]Bē'er–shē'bȧ knew that *Săm'u-el *was* established *to be* a [w]prophet of the LORD.[Q]

21 And the LORD appeared again in [x]Shī'lōh: for the LORD [w]revealed himself to *Săm'u-el in Shī'lōh by the word of the LORD.

## CHAPTER 4

*The Israelites are overcome by the Philistines at Eben-ezer. 3 They fetch the ark to the terror of the Philistines. 10 They are smitten again, the ark is taken, and Hophni and Phinehas slain. 12 Eli, at the news, falling backward, breaks his neck. 19 Phinehas' wife, in her travail with Ichabod, dies.*

AND the word of [a]Săm'u-el came to all [b]Ĭṣ'ra-el. Now Ĭṣ'ra-el went out against the [c]Phĭ-lĭs'tĭneṣ to battle, and pitched[C] beside †Ēb'en-ē'zẽr: and the Phĭ-lĭs'tĭneṣ pitched in ‡Ā'phek.

2 And the [c]Phĭ-lĭs-tĭneṣ put themselves in array against [b]Ĭṣ'ra-el: and when they joined battle, Ĭṣ'ra-el was smitten before the Phĭ-lĭs'tĭneṣ: and they slew of the [d]army in the field about four thousand men.

3 ¶ And when the people were come into the camp, the elders of [b]Ĭṣ'ra-el said, Wherefore hath the LORD smitten us to day before the [c]Phĭ-lĭs'tĭneṣ? Let us fetch the [e]ark of the covenant of the LORD out of [f]Shī'lōh unto us, that, when it cometh among us, it may save us out of the hand[C] of our enemies.

4 So the people sent to [f]Shī'lōh, that they might bring from thence the [e]ark of the covenant of the LORD of hosts, [1]which dwelleth [g]*between* the cherubims: and the two sons of Ē'lī, [h]Hŏph'nī and [i]Phĭn'e-has, *were* there with the ark of the covenant of God.

5 And when the [e]ark of the covenant of the LORD came into the camp, all Ĭṣ'ra-el [j]shouted with a great shout, so that the earth rang again.

6 And when the [c]Phĭ-lĭs'tĭneṣ heard the noise of the [j]shout, they said, What *meaneth* the noise of this great shout in the camp of the [k]Hē'brewṣ? And they

12
m *Wicked, punishment of,* Psa. 73:3.
1 R. V. from the beginning even unto the end.

13
n *Judgments,* Ex. 6:6.
o *Children, death of, as a judgment upon parents,* Mark 10:14.
p *Parents, indulgent,* 2 Cor. 12:14.
q *Connivance,* Lev. 20:4.
2 R. V. did bring a curse upon themselves.

14
r *Sin, unpardonable,* Rom. 5:12.
s *Reprobates,* 1 Cor. 9:27.

18
t *Resignation, exemplified,* Job 5:17.

20
u *Dan, a city,* Judg. 18:29.
v *Beersheba,* Judg. 20:1.
w *Prophets, inspiration of,* Isa. 3:2.

21
x *Shiloh,* Judg. 21:12.

v.1–1044 BC See footnote, *Time,* Rev. 10:6.

1
a *Samuel,* 1 Sam. 3:1.
b *Israel, under the judges,* Ex. 4:22.
c *Philistines,* Gen. 26:14.

2
d *Armies,* Deut. 11:4.

3
e *Ark,* Ex. 25:10.
f *Shiloh,* Judg. 21:12.

4
g *Shekinah,* Lev. 16:2.
h *Hophni,* 1 Sam. 1:3.
i *Phinehas,* 1 Sam. 2:34.
1 Am. R. V. who sitteth above the cherubim:

5
j *Shouting,* 2 Chr. 15:14.

6
k *Hebrew,* Gen. 40:15.

† **EBENEZER** *(stone of help). A memorial stone, erected by Samuel to commemorate Israel's victory over the Philistines,* 1 Sam. 7:12. *Philistines defeat the Israelites at,* 1 Sam. 4. *Philistines remove the ark from,* 1 Sam. 5:1.

‡ **APHEK** *(strength),* a city of the tribe of Issachar. *Philistines defeat Israelites at,* 1 Sam. 4:1–11. *Saul slain at,* 1 Sam. 29:1; 31. Probably the same mentioned in Josh. 12:18 as a royal city of the Canaanites.

v.6–1044 BC
See footnote, *Time*, Rev. 10:6.

7
*l Cowardice*, Lev. 26:36.

8
*m Egyptians*, Gen. 50:3.

9
*n Courage, exhortation to*, Deut. 31:7.

10
*o Battle*, 1 Sam. 17:20.
*p Judgments*, Ex. 6:6.
*q Panic*, Judg. 7:22.

11
*r Eli*, 1 Sam. 1:3.

12
*s Benjamin, tribe of*, Num. 1:37.

15
*t Longevity*, Psa. 91:16.
*u Blindness, instances of*, 2 Kin. 6:18.

understood that the [e]ark of the
LORD was come into the camp.
7 And the [c]Phĭ-lĭs′tĭneș were
[l]afraid, for they said, God is
come into the camp. And they
said, Woe unto us! for there hath
not been șuch a thing heretofore.
8 Woe unto us! [l]who shall deliver us out of the hand of these
mighty Gods? these *are* the
Gods that smote the [m]Ē-ġўp′-
tianș with all the plagues in the
wilderness.
9 [n]Be strong, and quit yourselves like men, O ye [c]Phĭ-lĭs′-
tĭneș, that ye be not servants
unto the [k]Hē′brewș, as they
have been to you: [n]quit yourselves like men, and fight.
10 ¶ And the [c]Phĭ-lĭs′tĭneș
[o]fought, and Ĭș′ra-el [p]was smitten, and they [q]fled every man
into his tent: and there was a
very great slaughter; for there
fell of Ĭș′ra-el thirty thousand
footmen.
11 And the [e]ark of God was
taken; and the two sons of
[r]Ē′lī, [h]Hŏph′nī and [i]Phĭn′e-has,
were [p]slain.
12 ¶ And there ran a man of
[s]Bĕn′ja-mĭn out of the [d]army,
and came to [f]Shī′lōh the same
day with his clothes rent, and
with earth upon his head.
13 And when he came, lo, [r]Ē′lī
sat upon a seat by the wayside
watching: for his heart trembled
for the [e]ark of God. And when
the man came into the city, and
told *it*, all the city cried out.
14 And when [r]Ē′lī heard the
noise of the crying, he said,
What *meaneth* the noise of this
tumult? And the man came in
hastily, and told Ē′lī.
15 Now [r]Ē′lī was [t]ninety and
eight years old; and his eyes were
dim, that he [u]could not see.
16 And the man said unto [r]Ē′lī,
I *am* he that came out of the
[d]army, and I fled to day out of
the army. And he said, What
is there done, my son?
17 And the messenger answered
and said, [v]Ĭș′ra-el is fled before
the [c]Phĭ-lĭs′tĭneș, and there hath
been also a great slaughter
among the people, and thy two
sons also, [h]Hŏph′nī and [i]Phĭn′e-
has, are dead, and the [e]ark of
God is taken.
18 And it came to pass, when he
made mention of the [e]ark of
God, that [r]he fell from off the
seat backward by the side of the
[w]gate, and his neck brake, and
he [x]died: for he was an old
man, and heavy. And [r, y]he had
[z]judged [a]Ĭș′ra-el forty years.
19 ¶ And his daughter in
law, [b]Phĭn′e-has′ wife, was with
child, *near* to be delivered: and
when she heard the tidings that
the [c]ark of God was taken, and
that her father in law and her
husband were dead, she bowed
herself and [2]travailed; for her
pains came upon her.
20 And about the time of her
death the women that stood by
her said unto her, Fear not; for
thou hast born a son. But she
answered not, neither did she
regard *it*.
21 And she named the child
[d]Ī′-cha-bŏd, saying, The glory
is departed from Ĭș′ra-el: because the [c]ark of God was taken,
and because of her father in law
and her husband.
22 And she said, The glory is
departed from Ĭș′ra-el: for the
[c]ark of God is taken.

## CHAPTER 5

*The Philistines bring the ark into the house of Dagon at Ashdod. 3 Dagon falls down before the ark; and the men of Ashdod are smitten with emerods. 8 The ark being brought to Gath and to Ekron, the same judgments follow.*

AND the [a]Phĭ-lĭs′tĭneș took
the [b]ark of God, and
brought it from [c]Ĕb′en–ē′zēr
unto [d]Ăsh′dŏd.
2 When the Phĭ-lĭs′tĭneș took

v.16–1044 BC
See footnote, *Time*, Rev. 10:6.

17
*v Israel, under the judges*, Ex. **4:22.**

18
*w Gates*, Deut. **3:5.**
*x Death*, Num. 23: 10.
*y High Priest, duties of, judicial*, Lev. 21:10.
*z Judges of Israel*, Judg. 2:16.
*a Israel, under the judges*, Ex. **4:22.**

19
*b Phinehas*, 1 Sam. 2.34.
*c Ark*, Ex. **25:10.**
2 R. V. brought forth;

21
*d* 1 Sam. **14:3.**

1
*a Philistines*, Gen. 26:14.
*b Ark*, Ex. 25:10.
*c Ebenezer*, 1 Sam. 4:1.
*d Ashdod*, **1** Sam. 6:17.

v.2–1044 BC
See footnote, *Time,* Rev. 10:6.

2
*e* *Temple, idolatrous,* 1 Kin. 6:17.
*f* *Dagon,* Judg. 16:23.

5
*g* *Priest, idolatrous,* Lev. 1:5.

6
*h* *Judgments,* Ex. 6:6.
*i* 1 Sam. 6:4, 5, 11, 17.
1 R. V. tumours,
2 R. V. borders

8
*j* *Gath,* Josh. 11:22.

9
3 R. V. discomfiture:

the [b]ark of God, they brought it into the [e]house of [f]Dā′gon, and set it by Dā′gon.

3 ¶ And when they of [d]Ăsh′dŏd arose early on the morrow, behold, [f]Dā′gon *was* fallen upon his face to the earth before [b]the ark of the LORD. And they took Dā′gon, and set him in his place again.

4 And when they arose early on the morrow morning, behold, [f]Dā′gon *was* fallen upon his face to the ground before the [b]ark of the LORD; and the head of Dā′gon and both the palms of his hands *were* cut off upon the threshold; only *the stump of* Dā′gon was left to him.

5 Therefore neither the [g]priests of [f]Dā′gon, nor any that come into Dā′gon's house, tread on the threshold of Dā′gon in [d]Ăsh′dŏd unto this day.

6 ¶ But the hand of the LORD was heavy upon them of [d]Ăsh′dŏd, and he destroyed them, and [h]smote them with [1,i]emerods, *even* Ăsh′dŏd and the [2]coasts thereof.

7 And when the men of [d]Ăsh′dŏd saw that *it was* so, they said, The [b]ark of the God of Ĭṣ′ra-el shall not abide with us: for his hand is sore upon us, and upon [f]Dā′gon our god.

8 They sent therefore and gathered all the lords of the [a]Phĭ-lĭs′tīneṣ unto them, and said, What shall we do with the [b]ark of the God of Ĭṣ′ra-el? And they answered, Let the ark of the God of Ĭṣ′ra-el be carried about unto [j]Găth. And they carried the ark of the God of Ĭṣ′ra-el about *thither.*

9 And it was *so,* that, after they had carried it about, the hand of the LORD was against the city with a very great [3]destruction: and he [h]smote the men of the city, both small and great, and [i]they had [i]emerods in their secret parts.

10 ¶ Therefore they sent the [b]ark of God to [k]Ĕk′rŏn. And it came to pass, as the ark of God came to Ĕk′rŏn, that the Ĕk′ron-ītes cried out, saying, They have brought about the [b]ark of the God of Ĭṣ′ra-el to us, to slay us and our people.

11 So they sent and gathered together all the lords of the [a]Phĭ-lĭs′tīneṣ, and said, Send away the [b]ark of the God of Ĭṣ′ra-el, and let it go again to his own place, that it slay us not, and our people: for there was a deadly [3,h]destruction throughout all the city; the [l]hand of God was very heavy there.

12 And the men that died not were smitten with the [1,i]emerods: and the cry of the city went up to heaven.

## CHAPTER 6

*After seven months the Philistines take counsel how to send back the ark.* 10 *They bring it on a new cart unto Beth-shemesh.* 13 *The people of that place are smitten for looking into the ark.* 21 *They send to the men of Kirjath-jearim to fetch it.*

AND the [a]ark of the LORD was in the country of the [b]Phĭ-lĭs′tīneṣ seven months.

2 And the [b]Phĭ-lĭs′tīneṣ called for the priests and the [c]diviners, saying, What shall we do to the [a]ark of the LORD? tell us wherewith we shall send it to his place.

3 And they said, If ye send away the [a]ark of the God of Ĭṣ′ra-el, send it not empty; but in any wise return him a [1,d]trespass offering: then ye shall be healed, and it shall be known to you why his hand is not removed from you.

4 Then said they, What *shall be* the [1]trespass [d]offering which we shall return to him? They answered, Five golden [2,e]emerods, and five golden [f]mice, *according to* the number of the lords of the

v.9–1044 BC
See footnote, *Time,* Rev. 10:6.

4 R. V. tumours brake out upon them.

10
*k* *Ekron,* Amos 1:8.

11
*l* *Divine Chastisement,* Job 33:19.

v.1–1043 BC
See footnote, *Time,* Rev. 10:6.

1
*a* *Ark,* Ex. 25:10.
*b* *Philistines,* Gen. 26:14.

2
*c* *Sorcery,* Isa. 47:9.

3
*d* *Offerings, trespass,* Lev. 6:17.
1 R. V. guilt

4
*e* 1 Sam. 5:6, 9, 12
*f* *Mouse,* Lev. 11:29.
2 R. V. tumours.

v.4–1043 BC
See footnote, *Time*, Rev. 10:6.

*g Plague*, Ex. 11:1.

**6**
*h Heart*, Psa. 44:21.
*i Egyptians*, Gen. 50:3.
*j Pharaoh, at the time of the exodus*, Ex. 3:10.
*k Miracles, design of*, Luke 23:8.
*l Adversity, design of*, Psa. 10:6.
*m Israel, in Egypt*, Ex. 4:22.

**7**
*n* 2 Sam. 6:3; 1 Chr. 13:7.
*o Cattle*, Ex. 12:29.

**8**
*p Jewels*, Gen. 24:53.

**9**
*q Bethshemesh*, Josh. 21.16.
3 R. V. its own border

[b]Phĭ-lĭs′tĭneș: for one [g]plague *was* on you all, and on your lords.

5 Wherefore ye shall make images of your [2,e]emerods, and images of your [f]mice that [g]mar the land; and ye shall give glory unto the God of Ĭș′ra-el: peradventure he will lighten his hand from off you, and from off your gods, and from off your land.

6 Wherefore then do ye [h]harden your hearts, as the [i]Ė-ġȳp′tianș and [j]Phā′raōh [h]hardened their hearts? when he had wrought [k]wonderfully among them, [l]did they not let the [m]people go, and they departed?

7 Now therefore make a new [n]cart, and take two milch [o]kine, on which there hath come no *yoke, and tie the kine to the cart, and bring their calves home from them:

8 And take the [a]ark of the LORD, and lay it upon the [n]cart; and put the [p]jewels of gold, which ye return him *for* a [1,d]trespass offering, in a coffer by the side thereof; and send it away, that it may go.

9 And see, if it goeth up by the way of [3]his own coast to [q]Běth–shē′mesh, *then* he hath done us this great evil: but if not, then we shall know that *it is* not his hand *that* smote us; it *was* a chance *that* happened to us.

10 ¶ And the men did so; and took two milch [o]kine, and tied them to the [n]cart, and shut up their calves at home:

11 And they laid the [a]ark of the LORD upon the [n]cart, and the coffer with the [f]mice of gold and the images of their [2,e]emerods.

12 And the [o]kine took the straight way to the way of [q]Běth–shē′mesh, *and* went along the highway, lowing as they went, and turned not aside *to* the right hand or *to* the left; and the lords of the [b]Phĭ-lĭs′tĭneș went after them unto the border of Běth–shē′mesh.

13 And *they of* [q]Běth–shē′mesh *were* †reaping their wheat [r]harvest in the valley: and they lifted up their eyes, and saw the [a]ark, and rejoiced to see *it*.

14 And the [n]cart came into the field of Jŏsh′u-ȧ, a Běth–shē′mīte, and stood there, where *there was* a great stone: and they clave the wood of the cart, and offered the kine a [s]burnt offering unto the LORD.

15 And the Lē′vītes took down the [a]ark of the LORD, and the coffer that *was* with it, wherein the [p]jewels of gold *were*, and put *them* on the great stone: and the men of Běth–shē′mesh offered [s]burnt offerings and sacrificed sacrifices the same day unto the LORD.

16 And when the five lords of the [b]Phĭ-lĭs′tĭneș had seen *it*, they returned to [t]Ĕk′rŏn the same day.

17 And these *are* the golden [2,e]emerods which the [b]Phĭ-lĭs′tĭneș returned *for* a [1,d]trespass offering unto the LORD; for ‡Ăsh′dŏd one, for [u]Gā′zȧ one, for [v]Ăs′ke-lŏn one, for [w]Găth one, for [t]Ĕk′rŏn one;

18 And the golden [f]mice, *according to* the number of all the cities of the [b]Phĭ-lĭs′tĭneș *belonging to* the five lords, *both* of fenced cities, and of country

v.12–1043 BC
See footnote, *Time*, Rev. 10:6.

**13**
*r Harvest*, Ex. 34:21.

**14**
*s Offerings, burnt*, Lev. 6:17.

**16**
*t Ekron*, Amos 1:8.

**17**
*u Gaza*, Gen. 10:19.
*v Askelon*, Judg. 1:18.
*w Gath*, Josh. 11:22.

* **YOKE**, Num. 19:2; Deut. 21:3; 1 Sam. 6:7; 11:7.

**Figurative:** *Of oppression*, Lev. 26:13; 1 Kin. 12:4; 2 Chr. 10:4, 9–11; Isa. 9:4; 10:27; Jer. 28:2, 4, 10; 30:8. *Of the bondage of sin*, Lam. 1:14. *Of burdensome ordinances*, Acts 15:10; Gal. 5:1. *Of discipleship to Christ*, Matt. 11:29, 30. *Of discipline*, Lam. 3:27.

† **REAPING**, Psa. 129:7. *Laws concerning gleaning at the time of*, Lev. 19:9, 10; 23:22; Deut. 24:19, 20.

**Figurative**, Psa. 126:6; Hos. 10:12, 13; John 4:35–38.

‡ **ASHDOD** (*a stronghold*). *A city of the Philistines*, Josh. 13:3; 1 Sam. 6:17; Amos 3:9. *Anakim inhabit*, Josh. 11:22. *Assigned to Judah*, Josh. 15:47. *Dagon's temple in, in which was deposited the ark*, 1 Sam. 5:1–8. *Conquest of, by Uzziah*, 2 Chr. 26:6; *by Tartan*, Isa. 20:1. *People of, conspire against the Jews*, Neh. 4:7, 8. *Jews intermarry with*, Neh. 13:23, 24. *Prophecies concerning*, Jer. 25:20; Amos 1:8; 3:9–15; Zeph. 2:4; Zech. 9:6. *Called* AZOTUS, Acts 8:40.

v.18–1043 BC
See footnote, *Time,* Rev. 10:6.

18
x *Stones, landmarks,* Ex. 24: 12.
4 R. V. stone, whereon

19
y *Divine Chastisement,* Job 33:19.
z *Curiosity, instances of,* Prov. 27: 20.

a *Ark,* Ex. 25:10.

20
b *Bethshemesh,* Josh. 21:16.
c *God, holiness of,* Gen. 2:2.

21
d *Kirjath-jearim,* Josh. 15:9.
e *Philistines,* Gen. 26:14.

1
a *Kirjath-jearim,* Josh. 15:9.
b *Ark,* Ex. 25:10.

3
c *Samuel,* 1 Sam. 3:1.
d *Promise, to penitents, of deliverance from adversity,* 2 Cor. 1:20.
e *God,* Gen. 2:2.

villages, even unto the great
[4,x]*stone of* Ā′bĕl, whereon they
set down the ark of the LORD:
*which stone remaineth* unto this
day in the field of Jŏsh′u-ȧ, the
Bĕth–shē′mīte.
19 ¶ And he [y]smote the men of
[q]Bĕth–shē′mesh; because they
had [z]looked into the [a]ark of the
LORD, even he smote[G] of the people
fifty thousand and threescore
and ten men: and the people
lamented, because the LORD
had smitten *many* of the people
with a great slaughter.[s]
20 And the men of [b]Bĕth–shē′-
mesh said, Who is able to stand
before this [c]holy LORD God?
and to whom shall he go up
from us?[s]
21 And they sent messengers to
the inhabitants of [d]Kĭr′jath–jē′-
a-rĭm, saying, The [e]Phĭ-lĭs′tĭnes
have brought again the [a]ark of
the LORD; come ye down, *and*
fetch[G] it up to you.

## CHAPTER 7

*They of Kirjath-jearim bring the ark into the house of Abinadab, where it remains twenty years. 3 The Israelites, at Samuel's exhortation, repent at Mizpeh. 9 While Samuel prays and sacrifices, the Lord discomfits the Philistines. 13 They are subdued. 15 Samuel judges Israel.*

AND the men of [a]Kĭr′jath–jē′-
a-rĭm came, and fetched
up the [b]ark of the LORD, and
brought it into the house of
*Ā-bĭn′a-dăb in the hill, and
sanctified[G] Ē-le-ā′zar his son to
keep the ark of the LORD.
2 And it came to pass, while the
[b]ark abode in [a]Kĭr′jath–jē′a-
rĭm, that the time was long; for
it was twenty years: and all the
house of Ĭs′ra-el lamented after
the LORD.
3 ¶ And [c]Săm′u-el spake unto
all the house of Ĭs′ra-el, saying,
[d]If ye do return unto the [e]LORD
with all your hearts, *then* put
away the strange[G] gods and [f]Ăsh′-
ta-rŏth from among you, and
prepare your hearts unto the
LORD, and serve him only: and
he will deliver[G] you out of the
hand[C] of the Phĭ-lĭs′tĭnes.
4 Then [g]the children of Ĭs′ra-el
[h]did put away [i]Bā′al-ĭm and
[f]Ăsh′ta-rŏth, and served the
LORD only.
5 And [c]Săm′u-el said, [g]Gather
all Ĭs′ra-el to [j]Mĭz′peh, and I
will [k,l]pray for you unto the
LORD.
6 And [g]they gathered together
to [j]Mĭz′peh, and drew [m]water,
and poured *it* out before the
LORD, and [n]fasted on that day,
and said there, [h,o]We have
sinned against the LORD. And
[c,p]Săm′u-el judged the children
of Ĭs′ra-el in Mĭz′peh.
7 And when the [q]Phĭ-lĭs′tĭnes
heard that the children of Ĭs′-
ra-el were gathered together to
[j]Mĭz′peh, the lords of the Phĭ-
lĭs′tĭnes went up against Ĭs′ra-el.
And when the children of Ĭs′-
ra-el heard *it,* they were afraid
of the Phĭ-lĭs′tĭnes.
8 And the children of Ĭs′ra-el
said to [c,p]Săm′u-el, Cease not to
[k,l]cry[G] unto the LORD our God
for us, that he will [r]save us out
of the hand of the [q]Phĭ-lĭs′tĭnes.
9[Q] And [c,p]Săm′u-el took a sucking
lamb, and offered *it for* a
[1,s]burnt [t]offering wholly unto
the LORD: and Săm′u-el [k,l]cried
unto the LORD for Ĭs′ra-el; and
the LORD [2]heard him.
10 And as [c,p]Săm′u-el was offering
up the [s]burnt [t]offering,
the [q]Phĭ-lĭs′tĭnes drew near to
battle against Ĭs′ra-el: but the
LORD [u]thundered with a great
[†,v]thunder on that day upon

f Or, *Ashtoreth,* 1 Kin. 11:5.

4
g *Religious revivals,* Hab. 3:2.
h *Repentance, instances of,* Mark 1:4.
i *Baal,* 2 Kin. 17: 16.

5
j *Mizpah,* Josh. 18:26.
k *Prayer, intercessory,* Acts 6:4.
l *Intercession, of man with God,* Jer. 27:18.

6
m *Water, libation of,* 1 Kin. 17:10
n *Fasting,* Zech. 8:19.
o *Sin, confession of,* Rom. 5:12.
p *Judges of Israel,* Judg. 2:16.

7
q *Philistines,* Gen. 26:14.

8
r *God, preserver,* Gen. 2:2.

9
s *Offerings, burnt,* Lev. 6:17.
t *Jesus, typified in offerings,* Matt. 1:21.
1 R. V. whole burnt offering unto
2 R. V. answered

10
u *God, providence of,* Gen. 2:2.
v *Meteorology, phenomena of,* Matt. 16:2.

* **ABINADAB** *(noble). A Levite, in whose house the ark of God rested twenty years,* 1 Sam. 7:1, 2; 2 Sam. 6:3, 4; 1 Chr. 13:7.

† **THUNDER.** *On Sinai,* Ex. 19:16; Psa. 77:18. *A manifestation of divine power,* Job 26:14; Psa. 77:18. *A token of divine anger,* 1 Sam. 12:17, 18. *Sent, as a plague upon the Egyptians,* Ex. 9:23–34; Psa. 78:48; *upon the Philistines, in battle with the children of Israel,* 1 Sam. 7:10. *Sent as a judgment,* Isa. 29:6. *Sons of Zebedee called sons of,* Mark 3:17.

the Phĭ-lĭs′tĭneṣ, and discomfited
them; and they were smitten
before Ĭṣ′ra-el.
11 And the men of Ĭṣ′ra-el went
out of [i]Mĭz′peh, and pursued the
[q]Phĭ-lĭs′tĭneṣ, and smote them,
until *they came* under Bĕth′–cär.
12 Then [c,p]Săm′u-el took a
[w,x]stone, and set *it* between
[i]Mĭz′peh and Shĕn, and called
the name of it [y]Ĕb′en–ē′zĕr,
saying, Hitherto hath the LORD
helped us.
13 So the [q]Phĭ-lĭs′tĭneṣ were
subdued, and they came no
more [3]into the coast of [z]Ĭṣ′ra-el:
and the [a]hand of the LORD was
against the Phĭ-lĭs′tĭneṣ all the
days of [b]Săm′u-el.
14 And the cities which the
[c]Phĭ-lĭs′tĭneṣ had taken from Ĭṣ′-
ra-el were restored to Ĭṣ′ra-el,
from [d]Ĕk′rŏn even unto [e]Găth;
and the [4]coasts thereof did Ĭṣ′-
ra-el deliver out of the hands of
the Phĭ-lĭs′tĭneṣ. And there was
peace between Ĭṣ′ra-el and the
[f]Ăm′ôr-ītes.
15 ¶ And [b]Săm′u-el [g]judged
Ĭṣ′ra-el all the days of his life.
16 And [b,g]he went from year
to year in [h]circuit to [i]Bĕth′–el,
and [j]Gĭl′găl, and [k]Mĭz′peh, and
[g]judged Ĭṣ′ra-el in all those places.
17 And [b]his return *was* to [l]Rā′-
mah; for there *was* his house;
and there [g]he judged Ĭṣ′ra-el;
and there he built an [m]altar
unto the LORD.

## CHAPTER 8

*Because of the ill government of Samuel's sons, the Israelites ask a king. 6 Samuel, displeased thereat, is comforted of God. 10 He describes to them the manner of a king. 19 Because of their importunity, God directs Samuel to make them a king.*

AND it came to pass, when
[a]Săm′u-el was [b]old, that
he made his sons [c,d]judges over
[e]Ĭṣ′ra-el.
2 Now the name of his firstborn
was [f]Jō′el; and the name of
his second, [g]Ā-bī′ah: *they were*
judges in [h]Bē′er–shē′bȧ.
3 And his [i]sons walked not in
his ways, but [c,d,j]turned aside
after lucre, and took *bribes,
and perverted judgment.
4 Then all the [k,l]elders of
[e]Ĭṣ′ra-el gathered themselves together, and came to [a]Săm′u-el
unto [m]Rā′mah,
5 And said unto him, Behold,
thou art [n]old, and thy [i]sons walk
not in thy ways: now make [e]us
a [o]king to judge us like all the
nations.
6 ¶ But the thing displeased
[a]Săm′u-el, when they said, Give
us a [n]king to judge us. And
Săm′u-el [p]prayed unto the
LORD.
7 And the LORD said unto
[a]Săm′u-el, Hearken unto the
voice of the people in all that
they say unto thee: for they have
not rejected thee, but [q]they have
rejected [r]me, that [s]I should not
[1]reign over them.
8 According to all the works
which they have done since the
day that I [t]brought them up out
of [u]Ē′ġȳpt even unto this day,
[2]wherewith they have forsaken
me, and [v]served other gods, so
do they also unto thee.
9 Now therefore hearken unto
their voice: howbeit [3]yet protest
solemnly unto them, and shew
them the manner of the king
that shall reign over them.
10 ¶ And [a]Săm′u-el told all the
words of the LORD unto the people that asked of him a [o]king.
11 And he said, [w]This will be
the manner of the [x]king that
shall reign over you: He will take
your sons, and appoint *them* for

---

12
w *Stones, memorial pillars*, Ex. 24:12.
x *Pillar*, Gen. 28:18.
y *Ebenezer*, 1 Sam. 4:1.

13
z *Israel*, Ex. 4:22.

a *Hand, figurative*, Ezra 10:19.
b *Samuel*, 1 Sam. 3:1.
3 R. V. within the border

14
c *Philistines*, Gen. 26:14.
d *Ekron*, Amos 1:8.
e *Gath*, Josh. 11:22.
f *Amorites*, Gen. 14:13.
4 R. V. border

15
g *Judge*, Judg. 2:16.

16
h *Court, circuit*, Ex. 18:26.
i *Bethel*, Josh. 18:13.
j *Gilgal*, Josh. 4:19.
k *Mizpah*, Josh. 18:26.

17
l *Ramah*, 1 Sam. 1:19.
m *Altar*, Gen. 8:20.

1
a *Samuel*, 1 Sam. 3:1.
b *Old Age*, Isa. 46:4.
c *Judge, corrupt*, vs. 1–5; Judg. 2:16.
d *Minister, false and corrupt*, vs. 1–5; Rom. 15:16.
e *Israel, under the judges*, Ex. 4:22.

2
f Or, *Vashni*, 1 Chr. 6:28.
g 1 Chr. 6:28.
h *Beersheba*, Judg. 20:1.

3
i *Children, wicked*, Mark 10:14.
j *Covetousness, instances of*, Isa. 57:17.

4
k *Government*, Isa. 22:21.
l *Senate*, Num. 11:16.
m *Ramah*, 1 Sam. 1:19.

5
n *Longevity*, Psa. 91:16.
o *King*, 2 Kin. 3:10.

v.4–1023 BC

6
p *Prayer, exemplified*, Acts 6:4.

7
q *Ingratitude, of man to God*, Rom. 1:21.
r *Rejection, of God*, Sam. 5.22.
s *Theocracy*, Judg. 8:23.
1 R. V. be king

8
t *God, providence of*, Gen. 2:2.
u *Egypt*, Gen. 41:8.
v *Idolatry*, 1 Sam. 15:23.
2 R. V. in that they

9
3 R. V. thou shalt protest

11
w *Government, monarchical, tyranny in*, Isa. 22.21.
x *Rulers, wicked*, vs. 11–18; Ex. 18:21.

---

***BRIBERY**, Psa. 26:9, 10; Prov. 15:27; Isa. 33:15, 16.
*Corrupts conscience*, Ex. 23:8; Deut. 16:18, 19; Eccl. 7:7. *Perverts justice*, 1 Sam. 8:1, 3; 12:3; Prov. 17:23; 28:21; Isa. 1:23; 5:22, 23; Ezek. 22:12; Amos 5:12; Mic. 7:3. *Destroys national welfare*, Prov. 29:4. *Profanes God*, Ezek. 13:19.
*Denunciation against*, Job 15:34; Ezek. 22:12, 13.
*Punishment for*, Deut. 27:25; Amos 2:6.
**Instances of:** *Balak attempts to bribe Balaam*, Num 22:17, 37. *Of Delilah*, Judg. 16:5. *Of Samuel's sons*, 1 Sam. 8:3. *Of the false prophet, Shemaiah*, Neh. 6:10–13. *Of Benhadad*, 1 Kin. 15:19. *Haman bribes Ahasuerus to destroy the Jews*, Esth. 3:9. *Chief priests bribe Judas*, Matt. 26:15; 27:3–9; Mark 14:11; Luke 22:5. *Soldiers bribed to declare that the*

v.11–1023 BC
See footnote, *Time,* Rev. 10:6.

4 R. V. they shall

12
*y Art,* 2 Chr. 16:14.
5 R. V. them unto him for
6 R. V. he will set some to plow

14
*z Vineyard,* Isa. 1:8.
*a Olive,* Deut. 6:11.

15
*b Rulers, wicked,* Ex. 18:21.
*c Government, monarchical, tyranny in,* Isa. 22:21.
*d Tithes,* Num. 18: 24.

17
7 R. V. flocks:

18
*e Adversity, prayer in,* Psa. 10:6.
8 R. V. answer

19
*f Samuel,* 1 Sam. 3:1.
*g Self-will,* Gen. 49:6.
*h Worldliness, instances of,* 1 John 2:15.

himself, for his chariots, and *to be* his horsemen; and [4]*some* shall run before his chariots.

12 And [x]he will appoint [5]him captains over thousands, and captains over fifties; and [6,w]*will set them* to ear his ground, and to reap his harvest, and to [y]make his instruments of war, and instruments of his chariots.

13 And [w,x]he will take your daughters *to be* confectionaries, and *to be* cooks, and *to be* †bakers.

14 And [w,x]he will take your fields, and your [z]vineyards, and your [a]oliveyards, *even* the best *of them,* and give *them* to his servants.

15 And [b,c]he will take the [d]tenth of your seed, and of your vineyards, and give to his officers, and to his servants.

16 And [b,c]he will take your menservants, and your maidservants, and your goodliest young men, and your asses, and put *them* to his work.

17 He will take the [d]tenth of your [7]sheep: and [c]ye shall be his servants.

18 And ye shall [e]cry out in that day because of your [b]king which ye shall have chosen you; and the LORD will not [8]hear you in that day.

19 ¶ Nevertheless the people refused to obey the voice of [f]Săm′u-el; and they said, Nay; but [g,h]we will have a king over us;

20 That we also may be [h]like all the nations; and [h]that our king may judge us, and go out before us, and fight our battles.

21 And [f]Săm′u-el heard all the words of the people, and he [i]rehearsed them in the ears of the LORD.

22 And the LORD said to [f]Săm′u-el, Hearken unto their voice, and make them a king. And Săm′u-el said unto the men of Ĭṣ′ra-el, Go ye every man unto his city.

## CHAPTER 9

*Saul, not finding his father's asses, 18 comes to Samuel. 19 Samuel entertains him at the feast; 25 and the next morning brings him on his way.*

NOW there was a man of [a]Bĕn′ja-mĭn, whose name *was* *Kĭsh, the son of Ȧ-bī′el, the son of Zē′rôr, the son of Bė-chō′rath, the son of Ȧ-phī′ah, a Bĕn′ja-mīte, a mighty man of [1]power.

2 And he had a son, whose name *was* †Sạul, a choice young man, and a goodly: and *there was* not among the children of Ĭṣ′ra-el a goodlier person than he: from his shoulders and upward *he was* higher than any of the people.

3 And the asses of *Kĭsh †Sạul's father were lost. And Kĭsh said to Sạul his son, Take now one of the servants with thee, and arise, go seek the asses.

4 And he passed through mount [b]Ē′phră-ĭm, and passed through

v.20–1023 BC
See footnote, *Time,* Rev. 10:6.

21
*i Mediation, instances of,* Gal. 3:19.

1
*a Benjamin, tribe of,* Num. 1:37.
1 R. V. valour.

4
*b Ephraim, mount of,* Josh. 17:15.

---

*disciples stole the body of Jesus,* Matt. 28:12–15. *Felix seeks a bribe from Paul,* Acts 24:26.

† **BAKER,** 1 Sam. 8:13; Jer. 37:21; Hos. 7:4, 6. *Pharaoh's chief,* Gen. 40.

* **KISH.** *Father of Saul,* 1 Sam. 9:1–3; 10:21; 2 Sam. 21: 14; 1 Chr. 8:33; 9:39. *Called* CIS, Acts 13:21.

† **SAUL** *(asked for),* king of Israel. *A Benjamite, son of Kish,* 1 Sam. 9:1, 2. *His personal appearance,* 1 Sam. 9:2; 10:23. *Made king of Israel,* 1 Sam. 9; 10; 11:12–15; Hos. 13: 11. *Dwells at Gibeah of Saul,* 1 Sam. 14:2; 15:34; Isa. 10:29. *Sons of,* 1 Chr. 8:33; 9:39. *Defeats the Philistines,* 1 Sam. 13; 14:46, 52. *Smites the Amalekites,* 1 Sam. 15. *Is reproved by Samuel, for usurping priestly functions,* 1 Sam. 13:11–14; *for disobedience in not slaying the Amalekites,* 1 Sam. 15:16–26. *Dedicates the spoils of war,* 1 Sam. 15:21–25; 1 Chr. 26: 28. *Loss of his kingdom foretold,* 1 Sam. 15:27–29. *Sends messengers to Jesse, asking that David be sent to him as musician and armor-bearer,* 1 Sam. 16:17–23. *Defeats the Philistines after Goliath is slain by David,* 1 Sam. 17. *His jealousy of David; gives his daughter, Michal, to David to be his wife; becomes David's enemy,* 1 Sam. 18. *Tries to slay David; Jonathan intercedes and incurs his father's displeasure; David's loyalty to him; Saul's repentance; prophesies,* 1 Sam. 19. *Hears Doeg against Ahimelech, and slays the priest and his family,* 1 Sam. 22:9–19. *Pursues David to the wilderness of Ziph; the Ziphites betray David to,* 1 Sam. 23:14–29. *Pursues David to Engedi,* 1 Sam. 24:1–6. *His life spared by David,* 1 Sam. 24:5–8. *Saul's contrition for his bad faith,* 1 Sam. 24: 16–22. *David is again betrayed to, by the Ziphites; Saul pursues him to the hill of Hachilah; his life spared again by David; his confession, and his blessing upon David,* 1 Sam. 26. *Slays the Gibeonites; crime avenged by the death of seven of his sons,* 2 Sam. 21:1–9. *His kingdom invaded by Philistines; seeks counsel of the witch of Endor, who foretells his death,* 1 Sam. 28:3–25; 29:1. *Is defeated and commits suicide,* 1 Sam. 31: 1–6; 1 Chr. 10:1–6. *His three sons slain; and their bodies, and Saul's, exposed in Bethshan, rescued by the people of Jabesh, and burned; bones of, buried under a tree at Jabesh,* 1 Sam. 31: 8–13; 1 Chr. 10:8–14. *His death, a judgment on account of his sins,* 1 Chr. 10:13. *David's lamentation over Saul and Jonathan,* 2 Sam. 1:17–27.

v.4–1023 BC
See footnote, *Time,*
Rev. 10:6.

c Or, *Baal-shalisha,* 2 Kin. 4:42.

5
d *Children, good, instances of,* Mark 10:14.

6
e *Prophets,* Isa. 3:2.

7
f *Prophets, emoluments of,* Isa. 3:2.

8
g *Shekel,* Ex. 30:13.

11
h *Women, duties of,* Prov. 31:10.

the land of [c]Shăl'i-shȧ, but they
found *them* not: then they passed
through the land of Shā'lim, and
*there they were* not: and he
passed through the land of the
[a]Bĕn'ja-mītes, but they found
*them* not.
5 *And* when they were come
to the land of Zŭph, [d]Sa̤ul said
to his servant that *was* with
him, Come, and let us return;
lest my father leave *caring*
for the asses, and take thought
for us.
6 And he said unto him, Behold now, *there is* in this city a
[e]man of God, and *he is* an honourable man; all that he saith
cometh surely to pass: now let
us go thither; peradventure he
can shew us our way that we
should go.
7 Then said [†]Sa̤ul to his servant, But, behold, *if* we go, [f]what
shall we bring the man? for
the bread is spent in our vessels,
and *there is* not a present to
bring to the man of God: what
have we?
8 And the servant answered
[†]Sa̤ul again, and said, Behold,
I have here at hand the fourth
part of a [g]shekel of silver: [f]*that*
will I give to the man of God, to
tell us our way.
9 (Beforetime in Ĭṣ'ra-el, when
a man went to enquire of God,
thus he spake, Come, and let us
go to the seer: for *he that is* now
*called* a Prophet was beforetime
called a Seer.)
10 Then said [†]Sa̤ul to his servant, Well said; come, let us go.
So they went unto the city where
the man of God *was.*
11 ¶ *And* as they went up the
hill to the city, they found young
[h]maidens going out to draw
water, and said unto them, Is
the seer here?
12 And they answered them,
and said, He is; behold, *he is* before you: make haste now, for he
came to day to the city; for *there*
*is* a sacrifice of the people to day
in the [i]high place:
13 As soon as ye be come into
the city, ye shall straightway
find him, before he go up to the
[i]high place to eat: for the people
will not eat until he come, because he doth [j]bless the [k]sacrifice; *and* afterwards they eat
that be bidden. Now therefore
get you up; for about this time
ye shall find him.
14 And they went up into the
city: *and* when they were come
into the city, behold, [l]Săm'u-el
came out against them, for to go
up to the [i]high place.
15 ¶ Now the LORD had told
[e,l,m]Săm'u-el in his ear a day
before [†]Sa̤ul came, saying,
16 To morrow about this time I
will send thee a man out of the
land of [a]Bĕn'ja-mĭn, and thou
shalt [n]anoint him *to be* [o]captain
over my people Ĭṣ'ra-el, that he
may save my people out of the
hand of the [p]Phĭ-lĭs'tĭneṣ: for
[q]I have looked upon my people,
because their cry is come
unto me.
17 And when [l]Săm'u-el saw
[†]Sa̤ul, the [r]LORD said unto him,
Behold the man whom I spake
to thee of! [s]this same shall reign
over my people.
18 Then [†]Sa̤ul drew near to
[l]Săm'u-el in the gate, and said,
Tell me, I pray thee, where the
seer's house *is.*
19 And [l]Săm'u-el answered
[†]Sa̤ul, and said, I *am* the [t]seer:
go up before me unto the [i]high
place; for ye shall eat with me to
day, and to morrow I will let
thee go, and will tell thee all
that *is* in thine heart.
20 And as for thine asses that
were lost three days ago, set not
thy mind on them; for they are
found. And [2]on whom *is* all the

v.12–1023 BC
See footnote, *Time,*
Rev. 10:6.

12
i *High Places,* 1 Kin. 3:2.

13
j *Thanksgiving, for food,* Luke 24:30.
k *Offerings, eaten,* Lev. 6:17.

14
l *Samuel,* 1 Sam. 3:1.

15
m *Minister, influential in public affairs,* vs. 15–27; Rom. 15:16.

16
n *Anointing,* Lev. 8:12.
o *King, divinely authorized,* 2 Kin. 3:10.
p *Philistines,* Gen. 26:14.
q *God, preserver,* Gen. 2:2.

17
r *Government, God in,* Isa. 22:21.
s *Rulers, appointed by God,* Ex. 18:21.

19
t *Prophets,* Isa. 3:2.

20
2 R. V. for whom is all that is desirable in Israel?

v.20–1023 BC
See footnote, *Time*, Rev. 10:6.

3 R. V. for

desire of Ĭş'ra-el? *Is it* not [3]on thee, and [3]on all thy father's house?

21 And †Sạul answered and said, [u]*Am* not I a Bĕn'ja-mīte, of the smallest of the tribes of Ĭş'ra-el? and [u]my family the least of all the families of the tribe of [a]Bĕn'ja-mĭn? wherefore then speakest thou so to me?

22 And [l]Săm'u-el took †Sạul and his servant, and brought them into the [4]parlour, and made them sit in the [v]chiefest place among them that were bidden, which *were* about thirty persons.

23 And Săm'u-el said unto the cook, Bring the portion which I gave thee, of which I said unto thee, Set it by thee.

24 And the cook took up the [5]shoulder, and *that* which *was* upon it, and set *it* before †Sạul. And [l]*Sam'u-el* said, Behold that which [6]is left! set *it* before thee, *and* eat: for unto this time hath it been kept for thee since I said, I have invited the people. So Sạul did eat with Săm'u-el that day.

25 ¶ And when they were come down from the [i]high place into the city, [l]*Sam'u-el* communed with †Sạul upon the top of the [w]house.

26 And they [x]arose early: and it came to pass about the spring of the day, that [l]Săm'u-el called [7] †Sạul to the top of the [w]house, saying, Up, that I may send thee away. And Sạul arose, and they went out both of them, he and Săm'u-el, abroad.

27 *And* as they were going down to the end of the city, [l]Săm'u-el said to †Sạul, Bid the servant pass on before us, (and he passed on,) but stand thou still awhile, that I may shew thee the word of God.

21
u *Modesty, instances of,* 1 Tim. 2:9.

22
v *Feasts, guests arranged at, according to rank,* Mark 12:39.
4 R. V. guest-chamber,

24
5 R. V. thigh.
6 R. V. hath been reserved!

25
w *House,* Esth. 8:1.

26
x *Rising, early,* Gen. 19:2.
7 R. V. to Saul on the housetop,

## CHAPTER 10

*Samuel anoints Saul. 2 He confirms him by prediction of three signs. 9 Saul's heart is changed, and he prophesies. 17 Saul is chosen at Mizpeh by lot. 26 The people variously affected toward him.*

THEN [a, b, c]Săm'u-el took a vial of [d]oil, and poured *it* upon [e]his head, and kissed him, and said, *Is it* not because [f]the [g]LORD hath [h]anointed thee *to be* captain over his [i]inheritance?

2 When [e]thou art departed from me to day, then thou shalt find two men by [j]Rā'chel's sepulchre in the border of [k]Bĕn'ja-mĭn at Zĕl'zah; and they will say unto thee, The asses which thou wentest to seek are found: and, lo, thy father hath left the care of the asses, and [1, l]sorroweth for you, saying, What shall I do for my son?

3 Then shalt [e]thou go on forward from thence, and thou shalt come to the [2]plain of Tā'bôr, and there shall meet thee three men going up to God to [m]Bĕth'-el, one carrying three kids, and another carrying three loaves of [n]bread, and another carrying a bottle of [o]wine:

4 And they will [p]salute thee, and give thee two *loaves* of bread; which thou shalt receive of their hands.

5 After that [e]thou shalt come to the hill of God, where *is* the garrison of the [q]Phĭ-lĭs'tĭneş: and it shall come to pass, when thou art come thither to the city, that thou shalt meet a company of prophets coming down from the [r]high place with a [s]psaltery, and a [t]tabret, and a [u]pipe, and a [v]harp, before them; and they shall prophesy:

6 And the [w]Spirit of the LORD will come upon thee, and thou shalt prophesy with them, and shalt be turned into another man.

7 And let it be, when these signs are come unto thee, *that*

v.1–1023 BC
See footnote, *Time*, Rev. 10:6.

1
a *Samuel,* 1 Sam. 3:1.
b *Minister, influential in public affairs,* vs. 1–27; Rom. 15:16.
c *Church and State, ecclesiastical power superior to civil, appoints kings,* 1 Sam. 16:1.
d *Oil,* Deut. 12:17.
e *Saul, made king,* vs. 1–27; 1 Sam. 9:2.
f *King, how chosen,* 2 Kin. 3:10.
g *Government, God in,* Isa. 22:21.
h *Anointing,* Lev. 8:12.
i *Israel, under the kings,* Ex. 4:22.

2
j *Rachel,* Gen. 29:6.
k *Benjamin, tribe of,* Num. 1:37.
l *Parents, love of,* 2 Cor. 12:14.
1 R. V. taketh thought

3
m *Bethel,* Josh. 18:13.
n *Bread,* Ezek. 4:13.
o *Wine,* Prov. 23:31.
2 R. V. oak

4
p *Salutations,* Luke 1:44.

5
q *Philistines,* Gen. 26:14.
r *High Places,* 1 Kin. 3:2.
s *Music,* 2 Chr. 5:13.
t *Timbrel,* Ex. 15:20.
u 1 Kin. 1:40; Isa. 30:29.
v *Harp,* Dan. 3:10.

6
w *Prophets, inspiration of,* Isa. 3:2.

v.7–1023 BC
See footnote, *Time*, Rev. 10:6.

8
[x] *Gilgal*, Josh. 4:19.
[y] *Offerings, burnt*, Lev. 6:17.
[z] *Offerings, peace*, Lev. 6:17.
[a] *Seven, days*, Gen. 7:2.

9
[b] *Saul*, 1 Sam. 9:2.
[c] *Samuel*, 1 Sam. 3:1.

12
[f] *Proverbs*, 1 Sam. 24:13.

13
[g] *High Places*, 1 Kin. 3:2.

thou do as occasion serve thee; for God *is* with thee.

8 And thou shalt go down before me to [x]Gĭl′găl; and, behold, I will come down unto thee, to offer [y]burnt offerings, *and* to sacrifice sacrifices of [z]peace offerings: [a]seven days shalt thou tarry, till I come to thee, and shew thee what thou shalt do.

9 ¶ And it was *so*, that when [b]he had turned his back to go from [c]Săm′u-el, God gave him [d]another[G] [e]heart: and all those signs came to pass that day.

10 And when they came thither[G] to the hill, behold, a company of prophets met [b]him; and the Spirit of God came upon him, and he prophesied among them.[T]

11 And it came to pass, when all that knew him beforetime[G] saw that, behold, he prophesied among the prophets, then the people said one to another, What *is* this *that* is come unto the son of Kĭsh? *Is* [b]Saul also among the prophets?

12 And one of the same place answered and said, But who *is* their father? Therefore it became a proverb, [f]*Is* Saul also among the prophets?

13 And when [b]he had made an end of prophesying, he came to the [g]high place.

14 ¶ And [b]Saul's uncle said unto him and to his servant, Whither[G] went ye? And he said, To seek the asses: and when we saw that *they were* no where, we came to [c]Săm′u-el.

15 And [b]Saul's uncle said, Tell me, I pray thee, what [c]Săm′u-el said unto you.

16 And [b]Saul said unto his uncle, He told us plainly that the asses were found. But of the matter of the kingdom, whereof [c]Săm′u-el spake, he told him not.

17 ¶ And [c]Săm′u-el called the people together unto the LORD to [h]Mĭz′peh;

18 And said unto the children of [i]Ĭs′ra-el, Thus saith the LORD God of Ĭs′ra-el, I [j]brought up Ĭs′ra-el out of Ē′ġypt, and [j]delivered you out of the hand[G] of the [k]Ē-ġy̆p′tians, and out of the hand[G] of all kingdoms, *and* of them that oppressed you:

19 And ye have this day [l,m]rejected your God, who himself [n]saved you out of all your [3,o]adversities and your [4]tribulations; and ye have said unto him, *Nay*, but set a [p]king over us. Now therefore present yourselves before the LORD by your tribes, and by your thousands.

20[Q] And when [c]Săm′u-el had caused all the tribes of [i]Ĭs′ra-el to come near, the tribe of [q]Bĕn′ja-mĭn [r]was taken.

21 When he had caused the tribe of [q]Bĕn′ja-mĭn to come near by their families, the family of Mā′trī was taken, and [b,s]Saul the son of [t]Kĭsh [r]was taken: and when they sought him, he could not be found.[Q]

22 Therefore they enquired[G] of the LORD further, if the man should yet come thither.[G] And the LORD answered, Behold, he hath[G] hid himself among the stuff.

23 And they ran and fetched[G] [b]him thence[G]: and when he stood among the people, he was higher than any of the people from his shoulders and upward.

24 And [c]Săm′u-el said to all the people, See ye [b]him whom the [u]LORD hath [v]chosen, that *there is* none like him among all the people? And all the people [w]shouted, and [x]said, God save the [p]king.[Q]

25 [y]Then [z,a]Săm′u-el told the people the manner of the kingdom, and wrote [b]*it* in a [c]book, and laid *it* up before the LORD.

v.17–1023 BC
See footnote, *Tim* Rev. 10:6.

17
[h] *Mizpah*, Josh. 18:26.

18
[i] *Israel*, Ex. 4:22.
[j] *God, providence of*, Gen. 2:2.
[k] *Egyptians*, Gen. 50:3.

19
[l] *Ingratitude, of man to God*, Rom 1:21.
[m] *Theocracy, rejec ed by Israel*, Judg 8:23.
[n] *God, preserver*, Gen. 2:2.
[o] *Adversity*, Psa. 10:6.
[p] *King*, 2 Kin. 3:10.
3 R. V. calamities
4 R. V. distresses;

20
[q] *Benjamin, tribe of*, Num. 1:37.
[r] *Lot, Saul chose by*, Esth. 3:7.

21
[s] *King, chosen by lot*, 2 Kin. 3:10.
[t] *Kish*, 1 Sam. 9:1

24
[u] *Government, Go in*, Isa. 22:21.
[v] *Rulers, appointe by God*, Ex. 18 21.
[w] *Shouting*, 2 Chr 15:14.
[x] *Salutations*, Luke 1:44.

25
[y] *King, constitutional restriction of*, 2 Kin. 3:10.
[z] *Samuel*, 1 Sam. 3:1.
[a] *Minister, influential in public affairs*, Rom. 15 16.
[b] *Constitution*, Dan. 6:12.
[c] *Book*, Num. 5:23

v.25–1023 BC
See footnote, *Time*, Rev. 10:6.

26
*d Gibeah*, Hos. 9:9.

27
*e Citizens, wicked and treasonable*, Luke 15:15.
*f Treason, instances of*, 2 Kin. 11:14.
*g Meekness, instances of*, Psa. 45:4.
*h Tact, of Saul*, Prov. 15:1.

1
*a Ammonites*, Deut. 2:20.
*b Jabesh-gilead*, Judg. 21:8.

3
*c Government, municipal*, Isa. 22:21.
*d Seven, days*, Gen. 7:2.
R. V. borders

4
*e Gibeah*, Hos. 9:9.
*f Saul*, 1 Sam. 9:2.

6
*g Anger, instances of*, Psa. 37:8.

And Săm'u-el sent all the people
away, every man to his house.
26 And Saul also went home to
[d]Gĭb'e-ah; and there went with
him a band of men, whose hearts
God had touched.
27 But the [e]children of Bē'lĭ-al
said, How shall this man save
us? And [f]they despised him,
and brought him no presents.
But [g,h]he held his peace.

## CHAPTER 11

*The cruel condition offered to the men of Jabesh-gilead. 4 They send messengers to Saul, and are delivered by him. 12 Saul spares his enemies. 14 His kingdom renewed at Gilgal.*

THEN *Nā'hăsh the [a]Ăm'-
mon-īte came up, and en-
camped against [b]Jā'besh–gĭl'e-ăd:
and all the men of Jā'besh said
unto Nā'hăsh, Make a covenant
with us, and we will serve thee.
2 And *Nā'hăsh the Ăm'mon-
īte answered them, On this *condition* will I make *a covenant*
with you, that I may thrust out
all your right eyes, and lay it *for*
a reproach upon all Ĭs'ra-el.
3 And the [c]elders of Jā'besh
said unto him, Give us [d]seven
days' respite, that we may send
messengers unto all the [1]coasts
of Ĭs'ra-el: and then, if *there be*
no man to save us, we will come
out to thee.
4 ¶ Then came the messengers
to [e]Gĭb'e-ah of [f]Saul, and told
the tidings in the ears of the people: and all the people lifted up
their voices, and wept.
5 And, behold, [f]Saul came after
the herd out of the field; and
Saul said, What *aileth* the people
that they weep? And they told
him the tidings of the men of
Jā'besh.
6 And the Spirit of God came
upon [f]Saul when he heard those
tidings, and his [g]anger was kindled greatly.[T]

7 And he took a yoke of oxen,
and hewed them in pieces, and
sent *them* throughout all the
[1]coasts of Ĭs'ra-el by the hands
of messengers, saying, [h]Whoso-
ever cometh not forth after [f]Saul
and after [i]Săm'u-el, so shall it
be done unto his oxen. And the
fear of the LORD fell on the
people, and they came out with
one consent.
8 And when he [j]numbered
[k]them in Bē'zĕk, the children
of [l]Ĭs'ra-el were three hundred
thousand, and the men of [m]Jū'-
dah thirty thousand.
9 And they said unto the messengers that came, Thus shall ye
say unto the men of [b]Jā'besh–
gĭl'e-ăd, To morrow, by *that
time* the sun be hot, ye shall have
help. And the messengers came
and shewed *it* to the men of
Jā'besh; and they were glad.
10 Therefore the men of Jā'-
besh said, [n]To morrow we will
come out unto you, and ye shall
do with us all that seemeth good
unto you.
11 And it was *so* on the morrow, that Saul put the people in
[o]three companies; and they
came into the midst of the host
in the morning [p]watch, and slew
the [a]Ăm'mon-ītes until the heat
of the day: and it came to pass,
that they which remained were
scattered, so that two of them
were not left together.
12 ¶ And the people said unto
[i]Săm'u-el, Who *is* he that said,
Shall [f,q]Saul reign over us?
bring the men, that we may put
them to death.
13 And [f,q]Saul said, [r,s]There
shall not a man be put to death
this day: for to day the LORD
hath wrought salvation in Ĭs'-
ra-el.
14 ¶ Then said [i]Săm'u-el to the

v.7–1023 BC
See footnote, *Time*, Rev. 10:6.

7
*h Armies, rendezvous of*, Deut. 11:4.
*i Samuel*, 1 Sam. 3:1.

8
*j Muster*, 2 Kin. 25:19.
*k Armies, Israel's military forces*, Deut. 11:4.
*l Israel, under the kings*, Ex. 4:22.
*m Judah, tribe of*, Num. 10:14.

10
*n Sarcasm, instances of*, Judg. 10:14.

11
*o Armies, tactics of*, Deut. 11:4.
*p Night, divided into watches*, Gen. 1:5.

12
*q Rulers, righteous, instances of*, Ex. 18:21.

13
*r Statecraft, wisdom in*, Prov. 28:2.
*s Prudence, instances of*, 2 Chr. 2:12.

***NAHASH** (*serpent*), an Ammonite king. *Attacked abesh-gilead*, 1 Sam. 11:1–3; 12:12. *Defeated by Saul*, 1 Sam. 1:11–11. *Kindness of, to David; and death of*, 2 Sam. 10:1, 2; 1 Chr. 19:1, 2. *David's purpose to show kindness to son of, misunderstood and his messengers treated with indignities; the war that followed*, 1 Chr. 19:1–19; 20:1–3.

v.14–1023 BC
See footnote, *Time*, Rev. 10:6.

14
t *Government, Mosaic*, Isa. 22:21.

15
u *Gilgal*, Josh. 4:19.
v *Saul, made king over Israel*, 1 Sam. 9:2.
w *Offerings, peace*, Lev 6:17.

1
a *Samuel*, 1 Sam. 3:1.
b *Minister, influential in public affairs*, vs. 1–14; Rom. 15:16.
c *King*, 2 Kin. 3:10.

2
d *Longevity*, Psa. 91:16.

3
e *Rulers, righteous, instances of*, Ex. 18:21.
f *Honesty, instances of*, Rom. 13. 13.
g *Bribery*, 1 Sam. 8:3.
1 R. V. taken a ransom

4
h *Integrity, instances of*, Job 2:3.

5
i *Oath*, Num. 5:19.

6
j *God, providence of*, Gen. 2:2.
k *Moses*, Ex. 2:10.
l *Aaron*, Ex. 6:20.
m *Egypt*, Gen. 41:8.

people, Come, and let [t]us go to
[u]Gĭl′găl, and renew the kingdom
there.
15 And all the people went to
[u]Gĭl′găl; and there they made
[v]Saul king before the LORD in
Gĭl′găl; and there they sacrificed
sacrifices of [w]peace offerings before
the LORD; and there Saul
and all the men of Iṣ′ra-el rejoiced
greatly.

## CHAPTER 12

*Samuel testifies to Israel his integrity. 6 He recounts God's dealings with their fathers; 16 and, by means of thunder in harvest, convinces them of their sin in asking a king: 20 but comforts them in the hope of God's mercy, if obedient.*

AND [a, b]Săm′u-el said unto
all Iṣ′ra-el, Behold, I have
hearkened unto your voice in
all that ye said unto me, and
have made a [c]king over you.
2 And now, behold, the king
walketh before you: and I am
[d]old and grayheaded; and, behold,
my sons *are* with you: and
I have walked before you from
my childhood unto this day.
3 Behold, here [e]I *am*: witness
against me before the LORD,
and before his anointed: [f]whose
ox have I taken? or whose ass
have I taken? or whom have I
defrauded? whom have I oppressed?
or of whose hand have
I [1]received *any* [g]bribe to blind
mine eyes therewith? and I will
restore it you.
4 And they said, Thou [h]hast
not defrauded us, nor oppressed
us, neither hast thou taken ought
of any man's hand.
5 And he said unto them, The
LORD *is* witness against you,
and his anointed *is* witness this
day, that ye have not found
ought in my hand. And they
answered, [i]*He is* witness.
6 ¶ And [a]Săm′u-el said unto
the people, *It is* the [j]LORD that
advanced [k]Mō′ṣeṣ and [l]Aâr′on,
and that [j]brought your fathers
up out of the land of [m]Ē′ġy̆pt.

7 Now therefore stand still, that
[n]I may reason with you before
the LORD of all the righteous
acts of the LORD, which he did
to you and to your fathers.
8 When [o]Jā′cob was come into
[m]Ē′ġy̆pt, and your fathers [p]cried
unto the LORD, then the LORD
sent [k]Mō′ṣeṣ and [l]Aâr′on, which
brought forth your fathers out of
Ē′ġy̆pt, and made them dwell in
[q]this place.
9 And when they forgat the
LORD their God, he [r, s]sold them
into the hand of [t]Sĭs′e-râ, captain
of the host of [u]Hā′zôr, and
into the hand of the [v]Phĭ-lĭs′-tĭneṣ,
and into the hand of the
king of [w]Mō′ab, and they fought
against them.
10 And [r]they [x]cried unto the
LORD, and said, [y]We have
sinned, because we have forsaken
the LORD, and have
served [z]Bā′al-ĭm and [a]Ăsh′ta-rŏth:
but now deliver us out
of the hand of our enemies, and
we will serve thee.
11 And the LORD [b]sent [c]Jĕ-rŭb′-ba-ăl,
and Bē′dăn, and [d]Jĕph′-thah,
and [e]Săm′u-el, and [b]delivered
you out of the hand of
your enemies on every side, and
ye dwelled safe.
12 And when ye saw that
Nā′hăsh the king of the [f]children
of Ăm′mŏn came against
you, ye said unto me, Nay; but
a [g]king shall reign over us: when
[h]the LORD your God *was* your
king.
13 Now therefore, behold the
king whom ye have chosen, *and*
whom ye have desired! and, behold,
[i]the LORD hath set a king
over you.
14 If ye will [j]fear the LORD,
and serve him, and [k]obey his
voice, and not rebel against the
commandment of the LORD,
then shall both ye and also the
king that reigneth over you con-

v.7–1023 BC
See footnote, *Time*, Rev. 10:6.

7
n *Minister, influential in public affairs*, Rom. 15:16.

8
o *Jacob*, Gen. 27:11.
p *Prayer*, Acts 6:4
q *Canaan*, Gen. 37:1.

9
r *Adversity, benefits of, illustrated* v. 10; Psa. 10:6
s *Divine Chastisement*, Job. 33:19
t *Sisera*, Judg. 4:2
u *Hazor*, Josh. 11:1.
v *Philistines*, Gen. 26:14.
w *Moabites*, Gen. 19:37.

10
x *Prayer, confession in*, Acts 6:4
y *Sin, confession of*, Rom. 5:12.
z *Baal*, 2 Kin. 17 16.

a Or, *Ashtoreth*, 1 Kin. 11:5.

11
b *God, providence of*, Gen. 2:2.
c Or, *Gideon*, Judg 6:11.
d *Jephthah*, Judg. 11:1.
e *Samuel*, 1 Sam. 3:1.

12
f *Ammonites*, Deut. 2:20.
g *King*, 2 King. 3:10.
h *Theocracy*, Judg 8:23.

13
i *Rulers, appointed by God*, Ex. 18 21.

14
j *Fear of God*, Acts 9:31.
k *Obedience*, Heb. 5:8.

v.14–1023 BC
See footnote, *Time*, Rev. 10:6.

tinue following the LORD your God:

15 But if ye will not obey the voice of the LORD, but rebel against the commandment of the LORD, then shall the hand of the LORD be against you, as *it was* against your fathers.

16 Now therefore stand and see this great thing, which the LORD will do before your eyes.

17 *Is it* not wheat harvest to day? I will call unto the LORD, and he shall send [l,m]thunder and [m,n]rain; [o]that ye may perceive and see that your wickedness *is* great, which ye have done in the sight of the LORD, in asking you a [g]king.

18 So [e]Săm′u-el [p]called unto the LORD; and the LORD sent [l,m]thunder and [n]rain that day: and [o]all the people greatly [j]feared the LORD and Săm′u-el.

19 And all the people said unto [e]Săm′u-el, [q]Pray for thy servants unto the LORD thy God, that we die not: for [r]we have added unto all our sins *this* evil, to ask us a [g]king.

20 And [e]Săm′u-el said unto the people, Fear not: ye have done all this wickedness: yet [s]turn not aside from following the LORD, but [k]serve the LORD with all your [t]heart;

21 And turn ye not aside: for *then should ye go* after [u]vain *things*, which cannot profit nor deliver; for they *are* vain.

22 For [v]the LORD [w]will not forsake his people for his great name's sake: because it hath pleased the LORD to [x]make you his people.

23 Moreover [y]as for me, God forbid that I should sin against the LORD in ceasing to [z,a]pray for you: but I will [b]teach you the good and the right [c]way:

24 Only [d,e]fear the LORD, and [e,f]serve him in [g]truth with [h]all your heart: for consider how great *things* he hath done for you.

25 But if ye shall still do wickedly, [i]ye shall be consumed, both ye and your king.

## CHAPTER 13

*Saul's select band. 3 He calls the Israelites to Gilgal against the Philistines. 5 The great host of the Philistines. 6 The distress of the Israelites. 8 Saul, weary of staying for Samuel, sacrifices. 11 Samuel reproves him. 17 The three bands of the Philistines. 19 The Philistines suffer no smith in Israel.*

[a]SAUL [1]reigned one year; and when he had reigned two years over [b]Ĭṣ′ra-el,

2 [a]Saul chose him three thousand [c]*men* of [b]Ĭṣ′ra-el; *whereof* two thousand were with Saul in [d]Mĭch′mash and in mount Bĕth′-el, and a thousand were with [e]Jŏn′a-than in [f]Ḡĭb′e-ah of Bĕn′ja-mĭn: and the rest of the people he sent every man to his tent.

3 And [e]Jŏn′a-than smote the *garrison of the [g]Phĭ-lĭs′tĭneṣ that *was* in [h]Ḡē′bȧ, and the Phĭ-lĭs′tĭneṣ heard *of it*. And [a]Saul blew the [i]trumpet throughout all the land, saying, Let the [j]Hē′brewṣ hear.

4 And all [b]Ĭṣ′ra-el heard say *that* [a]Saul had smitten a *garrison of the [g]Phĭ′lĭs′tĭneṣ, and *that* Ĭṣ′ra-el also was had in abomination with the Phĭ-lĭs′tĭneṣ. And the people were called together after Saul to [k]Ḡĭl′ḡăl.

5 And the [g]Phĭ-lĭs′tĭneṣ gathered themselves together to fight with [b]Ĭṣ′ra-el, [c]thirty thousand [l]chariots, and [c]six thousand †horsemen, and [c]people as the sand which *is* on the sea shore in multitude: and they came up,

17
l *Thunder*, 1 Sam. 7:10.
m *Meteorology*, Matt. 16:2.
n *Rain*, 2 Sam. 1:21.
o *Miracles, design of*, Luke 23:8.

18
p *Prayer, answered*, Acts 6:4.

19
q *Intercession, solicited*, Jer. 27:18.
r *Repentance, instances of*, Mark 1:4.

20
s *Commandment, enjoining obedience*, Deut. 8:2.
t *Heart*, Psa. 44:21.

21
u *Idolatry, folly of*, 1 Sam. 15:23.

22
v *Promise, to God's people, that he will not forsake them*. 2 Cor. 1:20.
w *God, faithfulness of*, Gen. 2:2.
x *Foreordination*, Rom. 8:30.

23
y *Zeal, instances of*, 2 Cor. 7:11.
z *Intercession, of man with God, instances of*, Jer. 27:18.
a *Prayer, intercessory*, Acts 6:4.

v.23–1023 BC
See footnote, *Time*, Rev. 10:6.

b *Instruction, in religion*, Prov. 23:23.
c *Way*, Isa. 35:8.

24
d *Fear of God, enjoined*, Acts 9:31.
e *Commandment, enjoining the fear of the Lord, and wholehearted service*, Deut. 8:2.
f *Obedience, enjoined*, Heb. 5:8.
g *Truth*, John 18:37.
h *Diligence*, Rom. 12:8.

25
i *Wicked, punishment of*, Psa. 73:3.

1
a *Saul*, 1 Sam. 9:2.
b *Israel, under the kings*, Ex. 4:22.
1 R. V. was [thirty] years old when he began to reign;

2
c *Armies*, Deut. 11:4.
d *Michmash*, 1 Sam. 14:5.
e *Jonathan, son of Saul*, 1 Sam. 14:1.
f *Gibeah, of Saul*, Hos. 9:9.

3
g *Philistines*, Gen. 26:14.
h *Geba*, Josh. 21:17.
i *Trumpet*, Josh. 6:4.
j *Hebrew*, Gen. 40:15.

4
k *Gilgal*, Josh. 4:19.

5
l *Chariot*, Josh. 11:4.

* **GARRISON.** *A military camp*, 1 Sam. 13:3; 14:1; 2 Sam. 8:6, 14; 23:14; 1 Chr. 11:16. *Roman, in Jerusalem*, Acts 21:31–33.

† **CAVALRY.** *Mounted, on horses*, Ex. 14:23; 15:19; 1 Sam. 13:5; 2 Sam. 8:4; 1 Kin. 4:26; 2 Chr. 8:6; 9:25; 12:3; Isa. 30:16; 31:1; Jer. 4:29; Zech. 10:5; Rev. 9:16–18; *on camels*, 1 Sam. 30:17. See footnote, ARMIES, Deut. 11:4.

m *Bethaven*, Josh. 18:12.

**6**

n *Cave*, Judg. 6:2.
2 R. V. holds,

**7**

o *Jordan*, Gen. 32: 10.

**8**

p *Church and State, ecclesiastical power superior to civil*, 1 Sam. 16:1.
q *Seven, days*, Gen. 7:2.
r *Samuel*, 1 Sam. 3:1.

**9**

s *Offerings, burnt*, Lev. 6:17.
t *Offerings, peace*, Lev. 6:17.
u *Usurpation*, vs. 8–14; 2 Sam. 15:1.
v *Presumption, instances of*, Psa. 19:13.

**11**

w *Minister, expostulates with rulers*, vs. 11–14; Rom. 15:16.
x *Reproof, faithfulness in*, Prov. 17: 10.

**12**

y *Armies, religious ceremonies attending*, Deut. 11:4.

**13**

z *Disobedience to God, instances of*, v. 14; Eph. 5:6.

and pitched in [d]Mĭch′mash,
eastward from [m]Bĕth–ā′ven.
6 When the men of [b]Īṣ′ra-el
saw that they were in a strait,
(for the people were distressed,)
then the people did hide themselves in [n]caves, and in thickets, and in rocks, and in [2]high
places, and in pits.
7 And *some of* the [f]Hē′brewṣ
went over [o]Jôr′dan to the land
of Găd and Gĭl′e-ăd. As for
[a]Sa̤ul, he *was* yet in [k]Ḡĭl′găl,
and all the people followed
him trembling.
8 [p]And he tarried seven days,
[q]according to the set time that
[r]Săm′u-el *had appointed*: but
Săm′u-el came not to [k]Ḡĭl′găl;
and the people were scattered
from him.
9 And [a]Sa̤ul said, Bring hither
a [s]burnt offering to me, and
[t]peace offerings. And [u,v]he offered the burnt offering.
10 And it came to pass, that as
soon as he had made an end of
offering the [s]burnt offering, behold, [r]Săm′u-el came; and [a]Sa̤ul
went out to meet him, that he
might salute him.
11 And [r,w]Săm′u-el [x]said, What
hast thou done? And Sa̤ul said,
Because I saw that the people
were scattered from me, and *that*
thou camest not within the days
appointed, and *that* the [g]Phĭ-
lĭs′tĭneṣ gathered themselves together at [d]Mĭch′mash;
12 Therefore said I, The [g]Phĭ-
lĭs′tĭneṣ will come down now
upon me to [k]Ḡĭl′găl, and I have
not [y]made supplication unto the
LORD: I forced myself therefore, and offered a [s]burnt offering.
13 And [r]Săm′u-el [x]said to
[a]Sa̤ul, Thou hast done foolishly:
thou [z]hast not kept the commandment of the LORD thy
God, which he commanded thee:
for now would the LORD have
established thy kingdom upon
Īṣ′ra-el for ever.
14 But now thy kingdom shall
not continue: the LORD hath
sought him [a]a [b,c]man after his
own heart, and the LORD hath
commanded him *to be* captain
over his people, because thou
hast not kept *that* which the
LORD commanded thee.
15 And [d]Săm′u-el arose, and
gat him up from [e]Ḡĭl′găl unto
[f]Gĭb′e-ah of Bĕn′ja-mĭn. And
[g]Sa̤ul numbered the people *that*
*were* present with him, about six
hundred men.
16 And [g]Sa̤ul, and [h]Jŏn′a-than
his son, and the people *that were*
present with them, abode in
[f]Gĭb′e-ah of Bĕn′ja-mĭn: but
the [i]Phĭ-lĭs′tĭneṣ encamped in
[j]Mĭch′mash.
17 ¶ And the spoilers came out
of the camp of the Phĭ-lĭs′tĭneṣ
[k]in three companies: [k]one company turned unto the way *that*
*leadeth to* [l]Ŏph′rah, unto the
land of Shṳ′al:
18 And [k]another company
turned the way *to* [m]Bĕth–hō′rŏn:
and [k]another company turned *to*
the way of the border that looketh to the valley of [n]Ze-bō′im toward the wilderness.
19 ¶ Now there was no [o]smith
found throughout all the [p]land
of Īṣ′ra-el: for the [i]Phĭ-lĭs′tĭneṣ
said, Lest the [q]Hē′brewṣ make
*them* swords or spears:
20 But all the Īṣ′ra-el-ītes went
down to the [i]Phĭ-lĭs′tĭneṣ, to
sharpen every man his [r,s]share,
and his [r]coulter, and his [r,t]ax,
and his [r,u]mattock.
21 Yet they had a file for the
[u]mattocks, and for the coulters,
and for the forks, and for the
[t]axes, and to sharpen the [v]goads.
22 So it came to pass in the day
of battle, that there was neither
[w]sword nor [w]spear found in the
hand of any of the people that

**14**

a Acts 13:22.
b *David*, 1 Sam. 16:13.
c *Righteous, described*, Psa. 64: 10.

**15**

d *Samuel*, 1 Sam. 3:1.
e *Gilgal*, Josh. 4:19.
f *Gibeah*, Hos. 9:9.
g *Saul*, 1 Sam. 9:2.

**16**

h *Jonathan*, 1 Sam. 14:1.
i *Philistines*, Gen. 26:14.
j *Michmash*, 1 Sam. 14:5.

**17**

k *Armies, tactics of*, Deut. 11:4.
l Josh. 18:23.

**18**

m *Bethhoron*, Josh. 10:10.
n Neh. 11:34.

**19**

o *Smith*, Isa. 54: 16.
p *Canaan*, Gen. 37:1.
q *Hebrew*, Gen. 40 15.

**20**

r *Agriculture, implements of*, Gen 3:23.
s *Plow*, Deut. 22: 10.
t *Ax*, Deut. 19:5.
u Isa. 7:25.

**21**

v Judg. 3:31.

**22**

w *Armor*, 1 Sam. 17:54.

*were* with [g]Sa̤ul and [h]Jŏn′a-
than: but with Sa̤ul and with
Jŏn′a-than his son was there
found.
23 And the garrison of the [i]Phĭ-
lĭs′tĭnes̤ went out to the passage[G]
of [j]Mĭch′mash.

## CHAPTER 14

*Jonathan, unknown to his father, surprises a garrison of the Philistines. 17 Saul and his men come to the battle. 24 His unadvised adjuration distresses the people. 26 Jonathan, through ignorance, transgresses. 32 Saul restrains the people from eating blood. 36 For his transgression, Jonathan is condemned to die by his father; 45 but is rescued by the people. 47 Saul's wars. 49 His family.*

NOW it came to pass upon a
day, that *Jŏn′a-than the
son of [a]Sa̤ul said unto the [b]young
man that bare[G] his armour,
Come, and let us go over to the
[c]Phĭ-lĭs′tĭnes̤' [d]garrison, that *is*
on the other side. But he told
not his father.
2 And [a]Sa̤ul tarried in the uttermost[G] part of [e]Gĭb′e-ah under a
[f]pomegranate tree which *is* in
[g]Mĭg′rŏn: and the people that
*were* with him *were* about six
hundred men;
3 And [h]Ā-hī′ah, the son of
[i]Ā-hī′tub, [j]Ī′-cha-bŏd's brother,
the son of [k]Phĭn′e-has, the son of
Ē′lī, the LORD's [l]priest in [m]Shī′-
lōh, wearing an ephod.[G] And the
people knew not that Jŏn′a-than
was gone.
4 ¶ And between the passages,[G]
by which *Jŏn′a-than sought to
go over unto the [c]Phĭ-lĭs′tĭnes̤'
[d]garrison, *there was* a sharp rock
on the one side, and a sharp rock
on the other side: and the name
of the one *was* Bō′zĕz, and the
name of the other Sē′neh.
5 The forefront of the one *was*
situate northward over against[G]
†Mĭch′mash, and the other
southward over against [e]Gĭb′-
e-ah.
6 And *Jŏn′a-than said to the
[b]young man that bare his armour, [n]Come, and let us go over
unto the [d]garrison of these [c]un-
circumcised: it may be that the
LORD will work for us: for [o]*there
is* no restraint to the [p,q]LORD to
save by many or by few.[S]
7 And his [b]armourbearer said
unto him, Do all that *is* in thine
heart: turn thee; behold, I *am*
with thee according to thy heart.
8 Then said *Jŏn′a-than, Behold, we will pass over unto *these*
men, and we will discover[G] ourselves unto them.
9 If they say thus unto us, Tarry
until we come to you; then we
will stand still in our place, and
will not go up unto them.
10 But if they say thus, Come
up unto us; then we will go up:
for the LORD hath delivered
them into our hand:[G] and this
*shall be* a sign unto us.
11 And both of them discovered[G]
themselves unto the [d]garrison of
the [c]Phĭ-lĭs′tĭnes̤: and the Phĭ-
lĭs′tĭnes̤ said, Behold, the [r]Hē′-
brews̤ come forth out of the holes
where they had hid themselves.
12 And the men of the [d]garrison
answered *Jŏn′a-than and his
[b]armourbearer, and said, Come
up to us, and we will shew you a
thing. And Jŏn′a-than said unto
his armourbearer, [n,o]Come up
after me: for the LORD hath delivered them into the hand of
Ĭs̤′ra-el.
13 And *Jŏn′a-than climbed up
upon his hands and upon his
feet, and his [b]armourbearer after
him: and they fell before Jŏn′a-

**1**
[a] *Saul*, 1 Sam. 9:2.
[b] *Armor-bearer*, Judg. 9:54.
[c] *Philistines*, Gen. 26:14.
[d] *Garrison*, 1 Sam. 13:3.

**2**
[e] *Gibeah, of Saul*, Hos. 9:9.
[f] *Pomegranate*, Num. 13:23.
[g] Isa. 10:28.

**3**
[h] Or, *Ahimelech*, 1 Sam. 21:1.
[i] 1 Sam. 22:9, 11, 12, 20.
[j] 1 Sam. 4:21.
[k] *Phinehas*, 1 Sam. 2:34.
[l] *High Priest*, Lev. 21:10.
[m] *Shiloh*, Judg. 21:12.

**6**
[n] *Courage, instances of*, vs. 6–16, 45: Deut. 31:7.
[o] *Faith, instances of*, Mark 11:22.
[p] *God, power of*, Gen. 2:2.
[q] *God, providence of*, Gen. 2:2.

**11**
[r] *Hebrew*, Gen. 40:15.

* **JONATHAN** (*God given*). *Son of Saul*, 1 Sam. 14:49. *Victory of, over the Philistine garrison of Geba*, 1 Sam. 13:3, 4, 16; *over Philistines at Michmash*, 1 Sam. 14:1–16. *Under Saul's curse pronounced against any who might take food before he was avenged of his enemies*, 1 Sam. 14:24–30, 43; *rescued by the people*, 1 Sam. 14:43–45. *Love of, for David*, 1 Sam. 18:1–4; 19:1–7; 20; 23:16–18.
*Killed in battle with Philistines, and his body with those of his father and brothers exposed on the wall of Bethshan*, 1 Sam. 31:2, 6; 1 Chr. 10:2. *Buried by inhabitants of Jabesh-gilead*, 1 Sam. 31:11–13. *Mourned by David*, 2 Sam. 1:11, 12, 17–27. *Bones of, removed from Jabesh-gilead by David to Zelah, and buried in the sepulchre of Kish*, 2 Sam. 21:12–14. *Ishbosheth, the lame son of, cared for by David*, 2 Sam. 4:4; 9.

† **MICHMASH** (*something hidden*). *A city of Benjamin*, 1 Sam. 13:5, 11. *Is garrisoned by Saul*, 1 Sam. 13:2. *Philistines smitten at, by Jonathan*, 1 Sam. 14:31. *People of the captivity return to, and dwell in*, Ezra 2:27; Neh. 7:31; 11:31. *Prophecy concerning the king of Assyria storing his baggage at*, Isa. 10:28.

than; and his armourbearer slew after him.

14 And that first slaughter, which *Jŏn′a-than and his [b]armourbearer made, was about twenty men, within as it were [1]an half [s]acre of land, *which* a yoke *of oxen might plow.*

15 ¶ And there was [t, u]trembling in the [2]host, in the field, and among all the people: the [d]garrison, and the spoilers, they also trembled, and the earth [v]quaked: so it was a very great trembling.

16 And the watchmen of [a]Sa̤ul in [e]Gĭb′e-ah of Bĕn′ja-mĭn looked; and, behold, the multitude [u]melted away, and they went [3]on beating down *one another.*

17 ¶ Then said [a]Sa̤ul unto the people that *were* with him, [w, x]Number now, and see who is gone from us. And when they had numbered, behold, *Jŏn′a-than and his [b]armourbearer *were* not *there.*

18 And [a]Sa̤ul said unto [h, l]Ā-hī′-ah, Bring hither the [y]ark of God. For the ark of God was at that time with the children of Ĭs̤′ra-el.

19 ¶ And it came to pass, while [a]Sa̤ul talked unto the [l]priest, that the noise that *was* in the [2]host of the [c]Phĭ-lĭs′tĭnes̤ went on and increased: and Sa̤ul said unto the priest, Withdraw thine hand.

20 And [a]Sa̤ul and all the people that *were* with him assembled themselves, and they came to the battle: and, behold, [u]every man's sword was against his fellow, *and there was* a very great discomfiture.

21 Moreover the [r]Hē′brews̤ *that* were with the [c]Phĭ-lĭs′tĭnes̤ before that time, which went up with them into the camp *from the country* round about, even they also *turned* to be with the [z]Ĭs̤′ra-el-ītes that *were* with [a]Sa̤ul and *Jŏn′a-than.

22 Likewise all the men of Ĭs̤′ra-el which had hid themselves in mount [b]Ē′phră-ĭm, *when* they heard that the [c]Phĭ-lĭs′tĭnes̤ fled, even they also followed hard after them in the battle.

23 So the LORD [d]saved [e]Ĭs̤′ra-el that day: and the battle passed over unto [f]Bĕth–ā′ven.

24 ¶ And the men of Ĭs̤′ra-el were distressed that day: [4, g]for [a]Sa̤ul had adjured the people, saying, Cursed *be* the man that eateth *any* food until evening, that I may be avenged on mine enemies. So [h]none of the people tasted *any* food.

25 And all *they of* the land came to a wood; and there was [i]honey upon the ground.

26 And when the people were come into the wood, behold, the [i]honey dropped; but no man put his hand to his mouth: for the people feared the [j]oath.

27 But *Jŏn′a-than heard not when his father charged the people with the [j]oath: wherefore he put forth the end of the rod that *was* in his hand, and dipped it in an honeycomb, and put his hand to his mouth; and his eyes were enlightened.

28 Then answered one of the people, and said, Thy father straitly charged the people with an [j]oath, [g]saying, Cursed *be* the man that eateth *any* food this day. And the people were faint.

29 Then said *Jŏn′a-than, My father hath troubled the land: see, I pray you, how mine eyes have been enlightened, because I tasted a little of this [i]honey.

30 How much more, if haply the people had eaten freely to day of the [k]spoil of their enemies which they found? for

**14**
*s* Isa. 5:10.
1 R. V. half a furrow's length in an acre of land.

**15**
*t Panic,* Judg. 7:22.
*u Armies, panic in,* Deut. 11:4.
*v Earthquakes, instances of,* Isa. 29:6.
2 R. V. camp,

**16**
3 R. V. hither and thither.

**17**
*w Muster,* 2 Kin. 25:19.
*x Armies, check roll-call in,* Deut. 11:4.

**18**
*y Ark.* Ex. 25:10.

**21**
*z Israel,* Ex. 4:22.
*a Saul,* 1 Sam. 9:2.

**22**
*b Ephraim,* Josh. 17:15.
*c Philistines,* Gen. 26:14.

**23**
*d God, preserver,* Gen. 2:2.
*e Israel,* Ex. 4:22.
*f Bethaven,* Josh. 18:12.

**24**
*g Rashness, of Saul.* 2 Sam. 6:7.
*h Fasting, instances of,* Zech. 8:19.
4 R. V. but

**25**
*i Honey,* Prov. 25:27.

**26**
*j Oath,* Num. 5:19.

**30**
*k Spoils,* 1 Chr. 26:27.

5 R. V. now hath there been no great slaughter

31
*l Aijalon,* Josh. 21:24.

32
*m Sheep,* Deut. 32: 14.

33
*n Sin,* Rom. 5:12.
*o Blood, eaten with food,* Gen. 9:4.
6 R. V. dealt treacherously:

34
*p Blood, forbidden as food,* Gen. 9:4.

35
*q Altar,* Gen. 8:20.

36
*r Priest,* Lev. 1:5.

37
*s Prayer, answer to, delayed,* Acts 6:4.

[5]had there not been now a much
greater slaughter among the
[c]Phĭ-lĭs′tĭneş?
31 And they smote the [c]Phĭ-
lĭs′tĭneş that day from †Mĭch′-
mash to [l]Ăij′a-lŏn: and the people were very faint.
32 And the people flew upon
the [k]spoil, and took [m]sheep, and
oxen, and calves, and slew *them*
on the ground: and the people
did eat *them* with the blood.
33 Then they told Sa̤ul, saying,
Behold, the people [n]sin against
the LORD, in that they eat with
the [o]blood. And he said, Ye
have [6]transgressed: roll a great
stone unto me this day.
34 And [a]Sa̤ul said, Disperse
yourselves among the people,
and say unto them, Bring me
hither every man his ox, and
every man his [m]sheep, and slay
*them* here, and eat; and sin not
against the LORD in eating with
the [p]blood. And all the people
brought every man his ox with
him that night, and slew *them*
there.
35 And [a]Sa̤ul built an [q]altar
unto the LORD: the same was
the first altar that he built unto
the LORD.
36 ¶ And [a]Sa̤ul said, Let us go
down after the [c]Phĭ-lĭs′tĭneş by
night, and spoil them until the
morning light, and let us not
leave a man of them. And they
said, Do whatsoever seemeth
good unto thee. Then said the
[r]priest, Let us draw near hither
unto God.
37 And [a]Sa̤ul asked counsel of
God, Shall I go down after the
[c]Phĭ-lĭs′tĭneş? wilt thou deliver
them into the hand of [e]Ĭş′ra-el?
But he [s]answered him not that
day.
38 And [a]Sa̤ul said, Draw ye
near hither, all the chief of the
people: and know and see wherein this [n]sin hath been this day.

39 For, *as* the LORD liveth,
which saveth [e]Ĭş′ra-el, though
it be in *Jŏn′a-than my son,
[g]he shall surely die. But
*there was* not a man among
all the people *that* answered
him.
40 Then said he unto all [e]Ĭş′-
ra-el, Be ye on one side, and [a]I
and *Jŏn′a-than my son will be
on the other side. And the people said unto [a]Sa̤ul, Do what
seemeth good unto thee.
41 Therefore [a]Sa̤ul said unto the LORD God of Ĭş′ra-el,
[7]Give a perfect [t]*lot*. And Sa̤ul
and *Jŏn′a-than were [8]taken:
but the people escaped.
42 And [a]Sa̤ul said, Cast [t]*lots*
between me and *Jŏn′a-than
my son. And Jŏn′a-than was
taken.
43 Then [a]Sa̤ul said to *Jŏn′a-
than, Tell me what thou hast
done. And Jŏn′a-than told him,
and said, I did but taste a little
[i]honey with the end of the rod
that *was* in mine hand, *and*, lo,
I must die.
44 [u]And [a]Sa̤ul answered, God
do so and more also: for thou
shalt surely die, *Jŏn′a-than.
45 And the [v]people [w]said unto
[a]Sa̤ul, Shall *Jŏn′a-than die,
who hath wrought this great salvation in Ĭş′ra-el? God forbid:
*as* the LORD liveth, there shall
not one hair of his head fall to
the ground; for he hath wrought
with God this day. [x]So the people rescued Jŏn′a-than, that he
died not.
46 Then [a]Sa̤ul went up from
following the [c]Phĭ-lĭs′tĭneş: and
the Phĭ-lĭs′tĭneş went to their
own place.
47 ¶ So [a]Sa̤ul took the kingdom over [e]Ĭş′ra-el, and fought
against all his enemies on every
side, against [y]Mō′ab, and against
the [z]children of Ăm′mŏn, and
against [a]Ē′dom, and against the

41
*t Lot,* Esth. 3:7.
7 R. V. Shew the right.
8 R. V. taken by lot:

44
*u Government, monarchical, tyranny in,* Isa. 22: 21.

45
*v Public Opinion,* John 12:42.
*w Intercession, of man with man,* Jer. 27:18.
*x King, influenced by popular opinion,* 2 Kin. 3:10.

47
*y Moabites,* Gen. 19:37.
*z Ammonites,* Deut. 2:20.
*a Edomites,* 2 Ki. 8:21.

*b Philistines*, Gen. 26:14.

48
*c Amalekites*, Num. 13:29.
*d Israel*, Ex. 4:22.
9 R. V. did valiantly,

49
*e Saul*, 1 Sam. 9:2.
*f* Or, *Abinadab*, 1 Sam. 31:2.
*g* 1 Sam. 18:17–19.
*h Michal*, 1 Sam. 18:20.

50
*i Armies, how officered*, Deut. 11:4.
*j* 1 Chr. 8:33; 9:39.
*k Nepotism, of Saul*, Gen. 47:11.

51
*l Kish*, 1 Sam. 9:1.

52
*m War*, Judg. 3:2.
*n Armies, compulsory service in*, Deut. 11:4.

kings of [‡]Zō′bah, and against
the [b]Phĭ-lĭs′tĭneş: and whithersoever he turned himself, he
vexed *them.*
48 And he [9]gathered an host,
and smote the [c]Ăm′a-lĕk-ītes,
and delivered [d]Ĭş′ra-el out of the
hands of them that spoiled them.
49 ¶ Now the sons of [e]Saụl
were *Jŏn′a-than, and [f]Ĭsh′u-ī,
and ‖Mĕl′chī–shụ′ă: and the
names of his two daughters *were*
*these*; the name of the firstborn
[g]Mē′răb, and the name of the
younger [h]Mī′chal:
50 And the name of Saụl's wife
*was* Ă-hĭn′o-ăm, the daughter of
Ă-hĭm′a-ăz; and the name of the
[i]captain of his host *was* §Ăb′nēr,
the son of [j]Nēr, Saụl's [k]uncle.
51 And [l]Kĭsh *was* the father of
Saụl; and [j]Nēr the father of
§Ăb′nēr *was* the son of Ă-bī′el.
52 And there was sore [m]war
against the [b]Phĭ-lĭs′tĭneş all the
days of [e]Saụl: and when Saụl
saw any strong man, or any
valiant man, he [n]took him unto
him.

## CHAPTER 15

*Samuel sends Saul to destroy Amalek. 6 Saul favors the Kenites. 8 He spares Agag and the best of the spoil. 10 Samuel announces unto Saul God's rejection of him for his disobedience. 24 Saul's humiliation. 32 Samuel kills Agag. 34 Samuel and Saul part.*

1
*a Samuel*, 1 Sam. 3:1.
*b Church and State, ecclesiastical power superior to civil*, 1 Sam. 16:1.
*c Saul*, 1 Sam. 9:2.
*d Anointing*, Lev. 8:12.
*e Israel, under the kings*, vs. 1–35; Ex. 4:22.
*f Commandment, enjoining obedience*, Deut. 8:2.
2
*g Amalekites*, Num. 13:29.

[a, b]SĂM′U-EL also said unto
[c]Saụl, The LORD sent me
to [d]anoint thee *to be* king over
his people, over [e]Ĭş′ra-el: now
therefore [f]hearken thou unto the
voice of the words of the LORD.
2 Thus saith the LORD of
hosts, I remember *that* which
[g]Ăm′a-lĕk did to Ĭş′ra-el, how
he laid *wait* for him in the way,
when he came up from [h]Ē′ġўpt.
3 Now [i]go and [j]smite Ăm′a-lĕk,
and utterly destroy all that they
have, and spare them not; but
[k]slay both man and woman, infant and suckling, ox and sheep,
camel and ass.
4 And [c]Saụl gathered the [e]peo-
ple together, and numbered
them in Tĕl′a-ĭm, two hundred
thousand footmen, and ten thousand men of [l]Jū′dah.
5 And [c]Saụl came to a city of
[g]Ăm′a-lĕk, and laid wait in the
valley.
6 ¶ And [c]Saụl said unto the
*Kĕn′ītes, Go, depart, get you
down from among the [g]Ăm′a-
lĕk-ītes, lest I destroy you with
them: [m]for ye shewed kindness
to all the children of Ĭş′ra-el,
when they came up out of
[h]Ē′ġўpt. So the Kĕn′ītes departed from among the Ăm′a-
lĕk-ītes.
7 And [c]Saụl smote the [g]Ăm′a-
lĕk-ītes from [n]Hăv′i-lah *until*
thou comest to †Shûr, that *is*
over against [h]Ē′ġўpt.
8 And he took Ā′găg the king
of the [g]Ăm′a-lĕk-ītes alive, and
[k]utterly destroyed all the people
with the edge of the sword.
9 But [c]Saụl and the people
[o]spared Ā′gag, and the best of
the sheep, and of the oxen, and
of the fatlings, and the lambs,
and all *that was* good, and
[o]would not utterly destroy them:
but every thing *that was* vile
and refuse, that they destroyed
utterly.
10 ¶ Then [p]came the word

*h Egypt*, Gen. 41:8.
3
*i Agency, in executing judgments*, vs. 1–19; Mark 1:17.
*j Retaliation*, Deut. 19:19.
*k War, of extermination*, Judg. 3:2.

4
*l Judah, tribe of*, Num. 10:14.

6
*m Thankfulness, of man to man*, Acts 24:3.

7
*n* Gen. 25:18.

9
*o Disobedience to God, instances of*, Eph. 5:6.

10
*p Prophets, inspiration of*, Isa. 3:2.

‡ **ZOBAH,** called also ZOBA, ARAM-ZOBAH, and HAMATH-ZOBAH. *A kingdom in the N. of Palestine*, 1 Sam. 14:47. *Conquest of, by David*, 2 Sam. 8:3–8, 12; 1 Kin. 11:23, 24; 1 Chr. 18:2–9. *Its inhabitants mercenaries of the Ammonites against David*, 2 Sam. 10:6–19; 1 Chr. 19:6–19. *David writes a psalm after the conquest of*, see title of Psa. 60. *Invaded by Solomon*, 2 Chr. 8:3.

‖ **MELCHISHUA** (*king of help*), called also MALCHISHUA. *Son of king Saul*, 1 Sam. 14:49; 31:2; 1 Chr. 8:33; 9:39; 10:2.

§ **ABNER** (*enlightening*), son of Ner. *Uncle of Saul*, 1 Sam. 14:50, 51 (with 9:1). *Captain of the host*, 1 Sam. 14:50; 17:55; 26:5, 14. *Dedicated spoils of war to the tabernacle*, 1 Chr. 26:27, 28. *Loyalty of, to the house of Saul*, 2 Sam. 2:8–32. *Alienation of, from the house of Saul*, 2 Sam. 3:6–21. *Murdered by Joab; David's sorrow for*, 2 Sam. 3:27–39.

* **KENITES** (*smiths, or dwellers in a nest*). *A Canaanitish tribe whose country was given to Abraham*, Gen. 15:19. *Moses married a woman of*, Ex. 2:21; Judg. 1:16. *Showed kindness to Israel in the wilderness*, Ex. 18:1–23; 1 Sam. 15:6. *Balaam's prophecy concerning*, Num. 24:21–23; 1 Sam. 27:10. *Dwelt with Israel in Jericho and in wilderness of Judah*, Judg. 1:16. *Heber, whose wife slew Sisera, was one of*, Judg. 4:17–21. *Rechabites descended from*, 1 Chr. 2:55.

† **SHUR.** *A wilderness southwest of Palestine*, Gen. 16:7; 20:1; 25:18; Ex. 15:22; 1 Sam. 15:7; 27:8.

11
[q] *Repentance, attributed to God,* Mark 1:4.
[r] *Backsliders, instances of,* Jer. 3:22.

12
[s] *Carmel,* 2 Chr. 26:10.
[t] *Gilgal,* Josh. 4:19.
1 R. V. monument,

13
[u] *Salutions,* Luke 1:44.
[v] *Self-righteousness, instances of,* Luke 18:11.
[w] *Falsehood, instances of,* Job 21:34.

14
[x] *Minister, expostulates with rulers,* Rom. 15:16.
[y] *Reproof, faithfulness in,* vs. 14–35; Prov. 17:10.

15
[z] *Spoils, dedicated to the Lord,* 1 Chr. 26:27.

16
[a] *Samuel,* 1 Sam. 3:1.
[b] *Saul,* 1 Sam. 9:2.
[c] *Prophets, inspiration of,* Isa. 3:2.

of the LORD unto [a]Săm′u-el,
saying,
11 [q]It repenteth me that I have
set up [c]Sa̤ul *to be* king: for [r]he
is turned back from following
me, and [o]hath not performed my
commandments. And it grieved
[a]Săm′u-el; and he cried unto the
LORD all night.
12 And when [a]Săm′u-el rose
early to meet [c]Sa̤ul in the morning,
it was told Săm′u-el, saying,
Sa̤ul came to [s]Cär′mel, and, behold,
he set him up a [1]place, and
is gone about, and passed on,
and gone down to [t]Gĭl′găl.
13 And [a]Săm′u-el came to
[c]Sa̤ul: and Sa̤ul said unto him,
[u]Blessed *be* thou of the LORD:
[v,w]I have performed the commandment
of the LORD.
14 And [a]Săm′u-el [x,y]said, What
*meaneth* then this bleating of
the sheep in mine ears, and
the lowing of the oxen which I
hear?
15 And Sa̤ul said, They have
brought them from the [g]Ăm′a-lĕk-ītes:
for the people spared
the best of the [z]sheep and of the
[z]oxen, to sacrifice unto the LORD
thy God; and the rest we have
utterly destroyed.
16 Then [a]Săm′u-el said unto
[b]Sa̤ul, Stay, and I will tell thee
what the LORD hath [c]said to me
this night. And he said unto
him, Say on.
17 And Săm′u-el said, When
thou *wast* little in thine own
sight, *wast* thou not *made* the
head of the tribes of Ĭs̤′ra-el, and
[d,e]the LORD anointed thee king
over Ĭs̤′ra-el?
18 And the LORD [f]sent thee
on a journey, and said, Go and
utterly [g]destroy the sinners the
[h]Ăm′a-lĕk-ītes, and fight against
them until they be consumed.
19 [i]Wherefore then [j]didst thou
not obey the voice of the LORD,
but didst [k]fly upon the spoil, and
didst evil in the sight of the
LORD?
20 And [b]Sa̤ul said unto [a]Săm′u-el,
Yea, [l]I have obeyed the
voice of the LORD, and have
gone the way which the LORD
sent me, and have brought Ā′găg
the king of Ăm′a-lĕk, and have
utterly destroyed the Ăm′a-lĕk-ītes.
21 But [m]the people took of the
[n]spoil, sheep and oxen, the chief
of the [2]things [3]which should
have been utterly destroyed, to
sacrifice unto the LORD thy God
in [o]Gĭl′găl.
22 And [a]Săm′u-el said, Hath
the LORD *as great* delight in
burnt [p]offerings and sacrifices,
as in obeying the voice of the
LORD? Behold, to [‡,q]obey *is*
better than sacrifice, *and* to
hearken than the fat of rams.
23 [i]For [r]rebellion *is as* the sin
of [s]witchcraft, and [t]stubbornness
*is as* [4]iniquity and [‖]idol-

17
[d] *Government, God in,* Isa. 22:21.
[e] *Rulers, appointed by God,* Ex. 18:21.

18
[f] *Agency, in executing judgments,* Mark 1:17.
[g] *War, of extermination,* Judg. 3:2.
[h] *Amalekites,* Num. 13:29.

19
[i] *Reproof, faithfulness in,* Prov. 17:10.
[j] *Self-will, exemplified,* Gen. 49:6.
[k] *Disobedience to God, instances of,* Eph. 5:6.

20
[l] *Falsehood,* Job 21:34.

21
[m] *Responsibility, attempts to shift,* Ezek. 18:20.
[n] *Spoils,* 1 Chr. 26:27.
[o] *Gilgal,* Josh. 4:19.
2 R. V. devoted things,
3 R. V. *omits:* which should have been utterly destroyed,

22
[p] *Offerings,* Lev. 6:17.
[q] *Obedience, enjoined,* Heb. 5:8.

23
[r] *Disobedience to God,* Eph. 5:6.
[s] *Sorcery,* Isa. 47:9.
[t] *Impenitence, judgments denounced against,* Rom. 2:5.
4 R. V. idolatry and teraphim.

‡ **OBEDIENCE BETTER THAN SACRIFICE,** 1 Sam. 15:22; Psa. 40:6–9; Prov. 21:3; Jer. 7:22, 23; Hos. 6:6; Mic. 6:6–8; Matt. 9:13; 12:7; Mark 12:33; Heb. 10:8, 9.

‖ **IDOLATRY. Objects of:** *Sun, moon, and stars,* Deut. 4:19; 2 Kin. 17:16; 21:3, 5; 2 Chr. 33:3, 5; Job 31:26–28; Jer. 7:17–20; 8:2; Ezek. 8:15, 16; Zeph. 1:4, 5; Acts 7:42. *Images, of Asherah,* 2 Kin. 21:7; *of angels,* Col. 2:18; *of animals,* Rom. 1:23. *Golden calf,* Ex. 32:4. *Brazen serpent,* 2 Kin. 18:4. *Net and drag,* Hab. 1:16. *Idolatrous pictures on monuments,* Num. 33:52. *Pictures on walls,* Ezek. 8:10.

**Wicked practices of:** *Human sacrifices,* Lev. 18:21; 20:2–5; Deut. 12:31; 18:10; 2 Kin. 3:26, 27; 16:3; 17:17, 18; 21:6; 23:10; 2 Chr. 28:3; 33:6; Psa. 106:37, 38; Isa. 57:5; Jer. 7:31; 19:4–7; 32:35; Ezek. 16:20, 21; 20:26, 31; 23:37, 39; Mic. 6:7. *Licentiousness,* Ex. 32:6, 25; Num. 25:1–3; 1 Kin. 14:24; 15:12; 2 Kin. 17:30; 23:7; Ezek. 16:17; 23:1–44; Hos. 4:12–14; Amos 2:8; Mic. 1:7; Rom. 1:24, 26, 27; 1 Cor. 10:7, 8; 1 Pet. 4:3, 4; Rev. 2:14, 20–22; 9:20, 21; 14:8; 17:1–6.

**Other Customs of:** *Offered, burnt offerings,* Ex. 32:6; 1 Kin. 13:26; 2 Kin. 10:25; Acts 14:13; *libations,* Isa. 57:6; 65:11; Jer. 7:18; 19:13; 32:29; 44:17, 19, 25; Ezek. 20:28; *libations of wine,* Deut. 32:38; *libations of blood,* Psa. 16:4; Zech. 9:7. *Meat* (R. V. meal) *offerings,* Isa. 57:6; Jer. 7:18; 44:17; Ezek. 16:19. *Peace offerings,* Ex. 32:6.

*Incense burned on altars,* 1 Kin. 12:33; 2 Chr. 30:14; 34:25; Isa. 65:3; Jer. 1:16; 11:12, 17; 44:3; 48:35; Ezek. 16:18; 23:41; Hos. 11:2. *Prayers to idols,* Judg. 10:14; 1 Kin. 18:25–29; Isa. 16:12; 44:17; 45:20; 46:7; Jonah 1:5. *Praise,* Judg. 16:24; Dan. 5:4.

*Singing and dancing,* Ex. 32:18, 19. *Music,* Dan. 3:5–7 *Cutting the flesh,* 1 Kin. 18:28; Jer. 41:5. *Kissing,* 1 Kin. 19:18; Hos. 13:2; Job 31:27. *Bowing,* 1 Kin. 19:18; 2 Kin. 5:18. *Tithes and gifts,* 2 Kin. 23:11; Dan. 11:38; Amos 4:4, 5.

*Annual feasts,* 1 Kin. 12:32; Ezek. 18:6, 11, 12, 15; 22:9; Dan. 3:2, 3.

**Folly of,** Deut. 4:28; 32:37, 38; Judg. 6:31; 10:14; 1 Sam. 5:3, 4; 12:21; 1 Kin. 18:25–29; 2 Kin. 19:18; 2 Chr. 25:15; Psa. 106:19, 20; 115:4, 5, 8; 135:15–18; Isa. 37:19; 44:9–20; 45:20; 46:1, 2, 6, 7; Jer. 2:28; 11:12; 16:19, 20; 48:13; 51:17; Hos. 8:5, 6; Zech. 10:2; Acts 14:13, 15; 17:22, 23, 29; Rom. 1:22, 23; 1 Cor. 8:4; 10:5; 12:2; Gal. 4:8; Rev. 9:20.

*Folly of, illustrated by contrast of idols with the true God,* Psa. 96:5; Isa. 40:12–26; 41:23–29; Jer. 10:5; 14:22; Dan. 5:23; Hab. 2:18, 19, 20.

*Folly of, exemplified in the ruin of Israel,* 2 Chr. 28:22. 23.

u *Reprobates*, 1 Cor. 9:27.

24

v *Conviction of Sin, instances of*, John 16:8.
w *Sin, confession of*, Rom. 5:12.
x *King, influenced by popular opinion*, 2 Kin. 3:10.
y *Cowardice*, Lev. 26:36.
z *Public Opinion*, John 12:42.

26

a *Samuel*, 1 Sam. 3:1.
b *Saul*, 1 Sam. 9:2.
c *Reprobates*, 1 Cor. 9:27.
d *God, rejected*, Gen. 2:2.
e *Government, God in*, vs. 26–28; Isa. 22:21.

27

5 R. V. robe,

28

f *Judgments*, Ex. 6:6.

29

g *God, truth*, Gen. 2:2.
h *God, immutable*, Gen. 2:2.

30

i *Sin, confession of*, Rom. 5:12.
j *Senate*, Num. 11:16.
k *Government, Mosaic*, Isa. 22:21.

atry. Because [b,u]thou hast rejected the word of the LORD, he
hath also rejected thee from *being* king.
24 And [b]Saul said unto [a]Săm'-
u'el, [v,w]I have sinned: for I have
transgressed the commandment
of the LORD, and thy words:
because [x]I [y]feared [z]the people,
and obeyed their voice.
25 Now therefore, I pray thee,
pardon my sin, and turn again
with me, that I may worship the
LORD.
26 And [a]Săm'u-el said unto
[b]Saul, I will not return with
thee: for [c]thou hast [d]rejected the
word of the LORD, and [e]the
LORD hath rejected thee from
being king over Is'ra-el.
27 And as [a]Săm'u-el turned
about to go away, [b]he laid hold
upon the skirt of his [5]mantle,
and it rent.
28 And [a]Săm'u-el said unto
him, The LORD hath [f]rent the
kingdom of Is'ra-el from thee
this day, and hath given it to a
neighbour of thine, *that is* better
than thou.
29 And also the Strength of
Is'ra-el will [g]not lie nor [h]repent:
for he *is* not a man, that he
should repent.
30 Then he said, [i]I have sinned: *yet* honour me now, I
pray thee, before the [j,k]elders of
my people, and before [l]Is'ra-el,
and turn again with me, that I
may worship the LORD thy God.
31 So [a]Săm'u-el turned again
after [b]Saul; and Saul worshipped
the LORD.
32 ¶ Then said [a]Săm'u-el,
Bring ye hither to me Ā'găg the
king of the [m]Ăm'a-lĕk-ītes. And
Ā'găg came unto him delicately.
And Ā'găg said, Surely the bitterness of death is past.
33 And [a]Săm'u-el said, [n]As
thy sword hath made women
childless, [n]so shall thy mother
be childless among women. And
Săm'u-el hewed [o]Ā'găg in pieces
before the LORD in [p]Gĭl'găl.
34 ¶ Then [a]Săm'u-el went to
[q]Rā'mah; and [b]Saul went up to
his house to [r]Gĭb'e-ah of Saul.
35 And [a]Săm'u-el came no
more to see [b]Saul until the day
of his [s]death: nevertheless Săm'-
u-el [t]mourned for Saul: and the
LORD [u,v]repented that he had
made Saul king over Is'ra-el.

## CHAPTER 16

*Samuel sent to Bethlehem to anoint one of the sons of Jesse. 6 Seven of his sons pass before Samuel. 12 David is chosen, and anointed. 14 Saul, troubled by an evil spirit, sends for David.*

1 *AND the LORD said unto
[a,b]Săm'u-el, How long
wilt thou [c]mourn for [d]Saul, seeing I have rejected him from
reigning over [e]Is'ra-el? fill thine

l *Israel, under the kings*, Ex. 4:22.

32

m *Amalekites*, Num. 13:29.

33

n *Retaliation*, Deut. 19:19.
o *Captive, cruelty to*, 1 Sam. 30:3.
p *Gilgal*, Josh. 4:19.

34

q *Ramah*, 1 Sam. 1:19.
r *Gibeah*, Hos. 9:9.

35

s *Death*, Num. 23:10.
t *Friendship, instances of*, Prov. 22:24.
u *God, repentance attributed to*, Gen. 2:2.
v *Anthropomorphisms*, Gen. 11:5.

1

a *Samuel*, 1 Sam. 3:1.
b *Minister, influential in public affairs*, vs. 1–35; Rom. 15:16.
c *Friendship*, Prov. 22:24.
d *Saul*, 1 Sam. 9:2.
e *Israel, under the kings*, Ex. 4:22.

**Denounced,** Deut. 12:31; 27:15; Job 31:26–28; Psa. 44:20, 21; 97:7; Isa. 42:17; 45:16; Jer. 3:1–11; 32:34, 35; Ezek. 16:15–63; 43:7–9; Hos. 1:2; 2:2–5; 4:12–19; 5:1–3; 9:10; 13:2, 3; Jonah 2:8; Amos 4:4, 5; Hab. 1:16; Acts 17:16–29; Rom. 1:25; 1 Cor. 6:9, 10.

**Forbidden,** Gen. 35:2; Ex. 20:3–6, 23; 23:13, 24, 32, 33; 34:14, 17; Lev. 19:4; 26:1, 30; Deut. 4:15–28; 5:7–9; 7:2–5, 16; 11:16, 17; 16:21, 22; Psa. 81:9; Ezek. 8:8–18; 14:1–8; 16:15–63; 20:7, 8, 16, 18, 24, 27–32, 39; 23:7–49; Acts 15:20–29; 1 Cor. 10:14, 20–22; 1 John 5:21.

**Prophecies relating to,** Isa. 46:1, 2. *Its punishments*, Num. 33:4; Deut. 31:16–21, 29; Isa. 21:9; Jer. 51:44, 47, 52. *Its end*, Isa. 2:8, 18, 20; 17:7, 8; 27:9; 31:7; Jer. 10:11, 15; Hos. 10:2; 14:8; Mic. 5:13, 14; Zeph. 2:11; Zech. 13:2.

**Punishment of,** Deut. 8:19; 11:28; 13:6–9; 17:2–5; 28:14–18; 30:17, 18; 32:15–26; Judg. 2:3; 1 Kin. 9:6–9; Neh. 9:27–37; Psa. 16:4; 59:8; 78:58–64; 106:34–42; Isa. 1:29–31; 2:6–22; 30:22; 65:3–7; Jer. 1:15, 16; 5:1–17; 7; 8:1, 2, 19; 13:9–27; 16; 17:1–6; 18:13–17; 19; 22:5–9; 44; Ezek. 6; 8:8–18; 9; 14:1–8; 16:15–63; 20:7, 8, 24–39; 22:4; 23:9, 10, 22–49; 44:10–12; Hos. 8:5–14; 10; 13:1–4; Amos 3:14; 5:5; Mic. 1:1–9; 5:12–14; 6:16; Zeph. 1; Mal. 2:11–13; Rev. 21:8; 22:15.

See footnote, IDOL, 1 Kin. 15:12.

*** CHURCH AND STATE. Ecclesiastical power superior to civil:** *Appoints kings*, 1 Sam. 10:1. *Directs administration*, 1 Sam. 15:1–4. *Reproves rulers*, 1 Sam. 15:14–33. *Withdraws support, and anoints a successor*, 1 Sam. 15:34, 35; 16:1–13; 2 Kin. 9:1–26; 11:4–12. *Attempted usurpation of ecclesiastical functions by civil authorities, reproved*, 1 Sam. 13:8–14; 2 Chr. 26:16–21.

**Civil power superior to the ecclesiastical:** *David, in organizing the priests and Levites in courses, and appointing musicians, instruments, and other details of religious services*, 1 Chr. 23; 24; 25; 2 Chr. 35:4. *Solomon, in thrusting Abiathar out of the high priest's office*, 1 Kin. 2:26, 27, 35; *in overshadowing the ecclesiastical in building the temple, and officiating primarily in the dedication, intercessory or priestly prayer, pronouncing the benediction, etc.*, 1 Kin. chapters 5–8. *Hezekiah, in reorganizing temple service*, 2 Chr. 31:2–21. *Jeroboam, in subverting the Jewish religion*, 1 Kin. 12:26–33. *Manasseh, in subverting, and afterward restoring, the true religion*, 2 Chr. 33:2–9, 15–17. *Jehoash, in supervising the repairs of the temple*, 2 Kin. 12:4–18. *Ahaz, in transforming the altars*, 2 Kin. 16:10–16. *Josiah, in exercising the function of the priests in the temple*, 2 Chr 34:29–33.

**State favorable to religion:** *In exempting priests from taxation*, Gen. 47:26; *and other functionaries of religious worship*, Ezra 7:24. *Cyrus, in his proclamation to restore the temple at Jerusalem*, 2 Chr. 36:22, 23; Ezra 1:1–11. *Darius, in his edict furthering the restoration of the temple*, Ezra 6:1–14. *Artaxerxes, in exempting priests, Levites, and other temple functionaries from taxes*, Ezra 7:24.

[f]horn with [g]oil, and go, I will
send thee to [h]Jĕs′se the Bĕth′–
lĕ-hĕm-īte: for [i]I have provided
me a [j]king among his sons.
2 And Săm′u-el [k,l]said, How
can I go? if Saul hear *it*, he
will kill me. And the LORD
said, Take an heifer with thee,
and say, I am come to sacrifice
to the LORD.
3 And call [h]Jĕs′se to the sacrifice, and [i]I [m]will shew thee what
thou shalt do: and thou shalt
[n]anoint unto me [j]*him* whom [i]I
name unto thee.
4 And [a]Săm′u-el did that which
the LORD spake, and came to
[o]Bĕth′–lĕ-hĕm. And the [p]elders
of the town [q]trembled at his
coming, and said, Comest thou
peaceably?
5 And he said, Peaceably: I
am come [r]to sacrifice unto the
LORD: [s]sanctify yourselves, and
come with me to the sacrifice.
And he sanctified [h]Jĕs′se and his
sons, and called them to the
sacrifice.
6 And it came to pass, when
they were come, that he looked
on †Ē-lī′ab, and said, Surely
the LORD's anointed *is* before
him.
7 But the LORD said unto
[a]Săm′u-el, Look not on his countenance, or on the height of his
stature; because I have refused
him: for *the* LORD *seeth* not as
man seeth; for man looketh on
the outward appearance, but the
LORD [t]looketh on the [u]heart.
8 Then [h]Jĕs′se called [v]Ā-bĭn′a-
dăb, and made him pass before
[a]Săm′u-el. And he said, Neither
hath the LORD chosen this.
9 Then [h]Jĕs′se made ‡Shăm′-
mah to pass by. And he said,
Neither hath the LORD chosen
this.
10 Again, [h]Jĕs′se made seven
of his sons to pass before [a]Săm′-
u-el. And Săm′u-el said unto
Jĕs′se, The LORD hath not
chosen these.
11 And [a]Săm′u-el said unto
[h]Jĕs′se, Are here all *thy* children? And he said, There remaineth yet the youngest, and,
behold, he [w]keepeth the sheep.
And Săm′u-el said unto Jĕs′se,
Send and fetch him: for we
will not sit down till he come
hither.
12 And he sent, and brought
him in. Now he *was* ruddy, *and*
withal of a [x]beautiful countenance, and goodly to look to.
And the [i]LORD said, Arise,
anoint him: for this *is* [j]he.
13 Then [a]Săm′u-el took the
horn of [g]oil, and [n]anointed him
in the midst of his brethren: and
the [y]Spirit of the LORD [z]came
upon ‖Dā′vid from that day for-

*f Horn*, 1 Kin. 1:39.
*g Oil*, Deut. 12:17.
*h Jesse*, Ruth 4:17.
*i Government, God in*, Isa. 22:21.
*j King, divinely authorized*, 2 Kin. 3:10.

2
*k Cowardice, instances of*, Lev. 26:36.
*l Doubting*, Rom. 14:23.

3
*m Prophets, inspiration of*, Isa. 3:2.
*n Anointing*, Lev. 8:12.

4
*o Bethlehem*, Gen. 48:7.
*p Government, municipal*, Isa. 22: 21.
*q Minister, fear of*, Rom. 15:16.

5
*r Priest, priestly office performed by prophets*, Lev. 1:5.
*s Purification*, Num. 19:19.

7
*t God, knowledge of*, Gen. 2:2.
*u Heart, known to God*, Psa. 44:21.

8
*v* 1 Sam. 17:13; 1 Chr. 2:13.

11
*w Shepherd*, Jer. 31:10.

12
*x Beauty, instances of*, Prov. 6:25.

13
*y Holy Spirit, inspiration of*, Acts 1:2.
*z Inspiration*, Job 32:8.

† **ELIAB** (*to whom God is father*). *Son of Jesse, and eldest brother of David*, 1 Sam. 16:6; 17:13, 28; 1 Chr. 2:13. *A prince in the tribe of Judah*, 1 Chr. 27:18.

‡ **SHAMMAH** (*astonishment or desolation*). *David's brother*, 1 Sam. 16:9; 17:13. *Called*, SHIMEAH, 2 Sam. 13:3, 32; 21:21; SHIMMA, 1 Chr. 2:13; SHIMEA, 1 Chr. 20:7.

‖ **DAVID** (*affectionate or beloved*), king of Israel. *Genealogy of*, Ruth 4:18–22; 1 Sam. 16:11; 17:12; 1 Chr. 2:3–15; Matt. 1:1–6; Luke 3:31–38. *A shepherd*, 1 Sam. 16:11. *Kills a lion and a bear*, 1 Sam. 17:34–36. *Anointed king, while a youth, by the prophet Samuel, and inspired*, 1 Sam. 16: 1, 13; Psa. 89:19–37. *Chosen of God*, 1 Sam. 16:1; Psa. 78:70.

*Described to Saul*, 1 Sam. 16:18. *Detailed as armor-bearer and musician at Saul's court*, 1 Sam. 16:21–23. *Slays Goliath*, 1 Sam. 17. *Love of Jonathan for*, 1 Sam. 18:1–4. *Popularity and discreetness of*, 1 Sam. 18.

*Saul's jealousy of*, 1 Sam. 18:8–30. *Is defrauded of Merab, and given Michal to wife*, 1 Sam. 18:17–27. *Jonathan intercedes for*, 1 Sam. 19:1–7.

*Conducts a campaign against, and defeats, the Philistines*, 1 Sam. 19:8. *Saul attempts to slay him; he escapes to Ramah, and dwells at Naioth, whither Saul pursues him*, 1 Sam. 19:9–24. *Returns, and Jonathan makes covenant with him*, 1 Sam. 20. *Escapes by way of Nob, where he obtains shewbread and Goliath's sword from Abimelech*, 1 Sam. 21:1–6; Matt. 12:3, 4. *Escapes to Gath*, 1 Sam. 21:10–15. *Recruits an army of insurgents; goes to Moab; returns to Hareth*, 1 Sam. 22. *Saves Keilah*, 1 Sam. 23:1–13. *Makes second covenant with Jonathan*, 1 Sam. 23:16–18. *Goes to the wilderness of Ziph; is betrayed to Saul*, 1 Sam. 23:13–26. *Writes a psalm on the betrayal*, Psa. 54. *Saul is diverted from pursuit of*, 1 Sam. 23: 27, 28. *Goes to Engedi*, 1 Sam. 23:29. *Refrains from slaying Saul*, 1 Sam. 24. *Covenants with Saul*, 1 Sam. 26. *Marries Nabal's widow, Abigail, and Ahinoam*, 1 Sam. 25.

*Dwells in the wilderness of Ziph; has opportunity to slay Saul, but takes his spear only; Saul is contrite*, 1 Sam. 26. *Flees to Achish and dwells in Ziklag*, 1 Sam. 27. *List of men who join him*, 1 Chr. 12:1–22. *Conducts an expedition against Amalekites; misstates the facts to Achish*, 1 Sam. 27:8–12. *Is refused permission to accompany the Philistines to battle against the Israelites*, 1 Sam. 28:1, 2; 29; 1 Chr. 12:19. *Rescues the people of Ziklag, who had been captured by the Amalekites*, 1 Sam. 30.

*Slays the pretended murderer of Saul*, 2 Sam. 1:1–16. *Laments Saul's death*, 2 Sam. 1:17–27.

*After dwelling one year and four months at Ziklag*, 1 Sam. 27:7; *goes to Hebron, and is anointed king by Judah*, 2 Sam. 2: 1–4, 11; 5:5; 1 Kin. 2:11; 1 Chr. 3:4; 11:1–3. *List of those who join him at Hebron* 1 Chr. 12:23–40. *Ishbosheth, son of Saul, crowned*, 2 Sam. chapters 2–4. *David wages war against, and defeats, Ishbosheth*, 2 Sam. 2:13–32; 3:1. *Demands the restoration of Michal, his wife*, 2 Sam. 3:14–16. *Abner revolts from Ishbosheth, and joins David, but is slain by*

**14**
*a Holy Spirit, withdrawn from incorrigible sinners,* Acts 1:2.
*b Saul,* 1 Sam. 9:2.
*c Evil Spirit,* 1 Sam. 18:10.
*d Demons,* Matt. 4:24.
*e Insanity, demoniacal,* Prov. 26: 18.
*f Reprobates,* 1 Cor. 9:27.

**16**
*g Harp,* Dan. 3:10.
*h Music, physical effect of, on man,* 2 Chr. 5:13.

ward. So Săm′u-el rose up, and
went to Rā′mah.[T Q]
14 ¶[S] But the [a]Spirit of the
LORD departed from [b]Saul, and
an [c,d,e]evil spirit from the LORD
troubled [f]him.[T]
15 And [b]Saul's servants said
unto him, Behold now, an [c]evil
spirit from God troubleth thee.
16 Let our lord now command
thy servants, *which are* before
thee, to seek out a man, *who is* a
cunning[G] player on an [g]harp: and
it shall come to pass, when the
[c]evil spirit from God is upon
thee, that he shall play with his
hand, and [h]thou shalt be well.[S]
17 And [b]Saul said unto his
servants, Provide me now a man
that can play well, and bring
*him* to me.
18 Then answered one of the
[1]servants, and said, Behold, I
have seen a son of [i]Jĕs′se the
[j]Bĕth′-lĕ-hĕm-īte, *that is* cunning[G] in playing, and a mighty
valiant man, and a man of war,
and prudent in [2]matters, and a
[k]comely[G] person, and the LORD
*is* with [l]him.
19 ¶ Wherefore [b]Saul sent
messengers unto [i]Jĕs′se, and
said, Send me ‖Dā′vid thy son,
which *is* [m]with the sheep.
20 And [i]Jĕs′se took an ass
*laden* with bread, and a bottle[G]
of wine, and a [n]kid, and sent
[o,p]*them* by ‖Dā′vid his son unto
[b]Saul.
21 And ‖Dā′vid came to [b]Saul,
and stood[G] before him: and he
[q]loved him greatly; and he became his [r]armourbearer.
22 And [b]Saul sent to [i]Jĕs′se,

**18**
*i Jesse,* Ruth 4:17.
*j Bethlehem,* Gen. 48:7.
*k Beauty, instances of,* Prov. 6:25.
*l God, dwells with the righteous,* Gen. 2:2.
1 R. V. young men,
2 R. V. speech.

**19**
*m Shepherd,* Jer. 31:10.

**20**
*n Goat,* Deut. 14:4.
*o Presents,* Gen. 32:13.
*p King, emoluments of,* 2 Kin. 3:10.

**21**
*q Love, of man for man, instances of* 1 John 4:7.
*r Armor-bearer,* Judg. 9:54.

*Joab,* 2 Sam. 3:6–38. *Punishes Ishbosheth's murderers,* 2 Sam. 4.

*Anointed king over all Israel, after reigning over Judah at Hebron seven years and six months; and reigns thirty-three years,* 2 Sam. 2:11; 5:5; 1 Chr. 3:4; 11:1–3; 29:27. *Makes conquest of Jerusalem,* 2 Sam. 5:6; 1 Chr. 11:4–8; Isa. 29:1. *Builds a palace,* 2 Sam. 5:11; 2 Chr. 2:3. *Friendship of, with Hiram, king of Tyre,* 2 Sam. 5:11; 1 Kin. 5:1. *Prospered of God,* 2 Sam. 5:10, 12; 1 Chr. 11:9. *Fame of,* 1 Chr. 14:17. *Philistines make war against, and are defeated by him,* 2 Sam. 5:17, 25.

*Assembles thirty thousand men to escort the ark to Jerusalem with music and thanksgiving,* 2 Sam. 6:1–5; 1 Chr. 13:1–8. *Uzzah is stricken when he attempts to steady the ark,* 2 Sam. 6:6–8; 1 Chr. 13:9–11. *David is terrified, and leaves the ark at the house of Obed-edom,* 2 Sam. 6:9–11; 1 Chr. 13:12–14. *After three months brings the ark to Jerusalem with dancing and great joy,* 2 Sam. 6:12–16; 1 Chr. 15; 16:1. *Organizes the tabernacle service,* 1 Chr. 9:22; 15:16–24; 16:4–6, 37–43. *Offers sacrifice, distributes gifts, and blesses the people,* 2 Sam. 6:17–19; 1 Chr. 16:2, 3 *Michal upbraids him for his religious enthusiasm,* 2 Sam. 6:20–23; 1 Chr. 15:29.

*Desires to build a temple; is forbidden, but receives promise that his seed should reign forever,* 2 Sam. 7:4–16; 23:5; 1 Chr. 17:1–14; 2 Chr. 6:16; Psa. 89:3, 4; 132:11, 12; Jer. 33:17–21; Acts 15:16; Rom. 15:12. *Interpretation and fulfillment of this prophecy,* Acts 13:22, 23. *Conquers the Philistines, Moabites, and Syrians,* 2 Sam. 8:1–14.

*Treats Mephibosheth, the lame son of Jonathan, with great kindness,* 2 Sam. 9:4–13; 19:24–30. *Sends commissioners with a message of sympathy to Hanun, son of the king of Ammon; the message misinterpreted, and commissioners treated with indignity; David retaliates by invading his kingdom, and defeating the combined armies of the Ammonites and Syrians,* 2 Sam. 10; 1 Chr. 19.

*Commits adultery with Bathsheba,* 2 Sam. 11:2–5. *Wickedly causes the death of Uriah,* 2 Sam. 11:6–25. *Takes Bathsheba to be his wife,* 2 Sam. 11:26, 27. *Is rebuked by the prophet Nathan,* 2 Sam. 12:1–14. *Repents of his crime and confesses his guilt,* Psa. 6; 32; 38; 39; 40; 51. *Is chastised with grievous affliction on account of his crime,* Psa. 38; 41; 69. *Death of his infant son by Bathsheba,* 2 Sam. 12:15–23. *Solomon is born to,* 2 Sam. 12:24, 25.

*Ammonites defeated and tortured by,* 2 Sam. 12:26–31. *Amnon's crime; his murder by Absalom, and Absalom's flight,* 2 Sam. 13. *Absalom's return,* 2 Sam. 14:1–24.

*Absalom's usurpation,* 2 Sam. 15. *David's flight from Jerusalem,* 2 Sam. 15:13–37. *Shimei curses him,* 2 Sam. 16:5–14. *Crosses the Jordan,* 2 Sam. 17:21–29. *Absalom's defeat and death,* 2 Sam. 18. *Laments the death of Absalom,* 2 Sam. 18:33; 19:1–4 *Upbraided by Joab,* 2 Sam. 19:5–7. *David upbraids the priests for not showing loyalty amid the murmurings of the people against him,* 2 Sam. 19:9–15. *Shimei sues for clemency,* 2 Sam. 19:16–23. *Mephibosheth sues for the king's favor,* 2 Sam. 19:24–30. *Barzillai rewarded,* 2 Sam. 19:31–40.

*Judah accused by the ten tribes of stealing him away,* 2 Sam. 19:41–43. *Returns to Jerusalem,* 2 Sam 20:1–3.

*Sheba's conspiracy against, and his death,* 2 Sam. 20. *Makes Amasa general,* 2 Sam. 19:13. *Amasa is slain,* 2 Sam. 20:4–10. *Consigns seven sons of Saul to the Gibeonites to be slain to atone for Saul's persecution of the Gibeonites,* 2 Sam. 21:1–14. *Buries Saul's and his son's bones,* 2 Sam. 21:12–14.

*Defeats the Philistines,* 2 Sam. 21:15–22; 1 Chr. 20:4–8. *Takes the military strength of Israel without divine authority, and is reproved,* 2 Sam. 24; 1 Chr. 21; 27:24. *Marries Abishag,* 1 Kin. 1:1–4

*Reorganizes the tabernacle service,* 1 Chr. chapters 23–26; 2 Chr. 7:6; 8:14; 23:18; 29:27–30; 35:15; Ezra 3:10; 8:20

*Adonijah usurps the scepter; Solomon appointed to the throne,* 1 Kin. 1; 1 Chr. 23:1. *Delivers his charge to Solomon,* 1 Kin. 2:1–11; 1 Chr. 22:6–19; 28; 29.

*Last words of,* 2 Sam. 23:1–7. *Death of,* 1 Kin. 2:10; 1 Chr. 29:28; Acts 2:29, 30. *Sepulchre of,* Acts 2:29. *Age of, at death,* 2 Sam. 5:4, 5; 1 Chr. 29:28. *Length of reign, forty years,* 1 Kin. 2:11; 1 Chr. 29:27, 28.

*Wives of,* 2 Sam. 3:2–5; 11:3, 27; 1 Chr. 3:5. *Children born to, at Hebron,* 2 Sam. 3:2–5; 1 Chr. 3:4; *at Jerusalem,* 2 Sam. 5:14–16; 1 Chr. 3:5–8; 14:4–7. *Descendants of,* 1 Chr. 3.

*Civil and military officers of,* 2 Sam. 8:16–18. See footnote, CABINET, Ezra 7:14.

*Lists of his heroes, and of their exploits,* 2 Sam. 23:8–39; 1 Chr. 11; 12:23–40.

*Devoutness of,* 1 Sam. 13:14; 2 Sam. 6:5, 14–18; 7:18–29; 8:11; 24:25· 1 Kin. 3:14; 1 Chr. 17:16–27; 29:10–20; 2 Chr. 7:17; Zech. 12:8; Psa. 6; 7; 11; 13; 17; 22; 26; 27:7–14; 28; 31; 35; 37; 38; 39; 40:11–17; 51; 54; 55; 56; 57; 59; 60; 61; 62; 64:1–6; 69; 70; 71; 86; 101; 108; 120:1–2; 140; 141; 142; 143; 144; Acts 13:22.

*Justice of, in administration,* 1 Sam. 30:23, 24; 2 Sam. 8:15; 1 Chr. 18:14. *Meekness of,* 1 Sam. 24:7; 26:11; 2 Sam. 16:11; 19:22, 23. *Merciful,* 2 Sam. 19:23. *His intercessional influence with God,* 1 Kin. 11:12, 13, 32, 34; 15:4; 2 Kin. 8:19; 19:34; 20:6; Psa. 132:10; Isa. 37:35.

*As musician,* 1 Sam. 16:21–23; 23:5; 2 Chr. 7:6; 29:26; Neh. 12:36; Amos 6:5. *As poet,* 2 Sam. 22. *As prophet,* 2 Sam. 23:2–7; 1 Chr. 28:19; Matt. 22:41–46; Acts 2:25–35; 4:25.

*Type of Christ,* Psa. 2; 16; 18:43; 69:7–9, 20, 21, 26, 29; 89:19–37.

*Jesus called son of,* Matt. 9:27; 12:23; 15:22; 20:30, 31; 21:9; 22:42; Mark 10:47, 48; Luke 18:37, 39.

*Prophecies concerning him and his kingdom,* 2 Sam. 7:11–16; 1 Chr. 17:9–14; 22; 2 Chr. 6:5–17; 13:5; 21:7; Psa. 89:19–37; Isa. 9:7; 16:5; 22:20–25; Jer. 23:5; 33:15–26; Luke 1; 32, 33.

*Chronicles of, written by Samuel, Nathan, and Gad,* 1 Chr. 29:29,30.

saying, Let ‖Dā′vid, I pray thee, stand before me; for he hath found favour in my sight.

23 And it came to pass, when the [c]*evil* spirit from God was upon Sa̤ul, that Dā′vid took an harp, and played with his hand: [h]so Sa̤ul was refreshed, and was well, and the evil spirit departed from him.

## CHAPTER 17

*The armies of the Israelites and Philistines arrayed for battle. 4 Goliath's challenge. 12 David is sent by his father to visit his brethren. 28 Eliab chides him. 32 David accepts the challenge, and shows the ground of his confidence. 38 He slays Goliath. 55 Saul asks about David.*

NOW the [a]Phĭ-lĭs′tĭne̤s gathered together their [b]armies to battle, and were gathered together at *Shō′choh, which *belongeth* to [c]Jū′dah, and pitched between Shō′choh and [d]Ā-zē′kah, in Ē′phĕs–dăm′mim.

2 And [e]Sa̤ul and the men of [f]Ĭs̤′ra-el were gathered together, and pitched by the valley of [g]Ē′lah, and set the battle in array against the [a]Phĭ-lĭs′tĭne̤s.

3 And the [a]Phĭ-lĭs′tĭne̤s stood on a mountain on the one side, and [f]Ĭs̤′ra-el stood on a mountain on the other side: and *there was* a valley between them.

4 And there went out a champion out of the camp of the [a]Phĭ-lĭs′tĭne̤s, named †Gō-lī′ath, of [h]Găth, whose height *was* six [i]cubits and a [j]span.

5 And †*he had* an [k]helmet of [l]brass upon his head, and he *was* armed with a ‡coat of mail; and the weight of the coat *was* five thousand shekels of brass.

6 And †*he had* greaves of [l]brass upon his legs, and a [1]target of brass between his shoulders.

7 And the staff of his spear *was* like a [m]weaver's beam; and his [n]spear's head *weighed* six hundred [o]shekels of [p]iron: and [q]one bearing a shield went before him.

8 And he stood and [r]cried unto the [s]armies of [f]Ĭs̤′ra-el, and said unto them, Why are ye come out to set *your* battle in array? *am* not I a [a]Phĭ-lĭs′tĭne, and ye servants to [e]Sa̤ul? choose you a man for you, and let him come down to me.

9 If he be able to fight with me, and to kill me, then will we be your [t]servants: but if I prevail against him, and kill him, then shall ye be our servants, and serve us.

10 And the †Phĭ-lĭs′tĭne said, I defy the [s]armies of [f]Ĭs̤′ra-el this day; give me a man, that we may fight together.

11 When [e]Sa̤ul and all [f]Ĭs̤′ra-el heard those words of the Phĭ-lĭs′tĭne, they were dismayed, and greatly [u]afraid.

12 ¶ Now [v]Dā′vid *was* the son of that Ĕph′rath-īte of [w]Bĕth′–lĕ-hĕm–jū′dah, whose name *was* [x]Jĕs′se; and he had eight sons: and the man went among men *for* an old man in the days of [e]Sa̤ul.

13 And the three eldest sons of [x]Jĕs′se went *and* followed [e]Sa̤ul to the battle: and the names of his three sons that went to the battle *were* [y]Ē-lī′ab the firstborn, and next unto him [z]Ā-bĭn′-a-dăb, and the third [a]Shăm′mah.

14 And [b]Dā′vid *was* the youngest: and the three eldest followed [c]Sa̤ul.

15 But [b]Dā′vid went and returned from [c]Sa̤ul to [d]feed his father's sheep at [e]Bĕth′–lĕ-hĕm.

16 And the †Phĭ-lĭs′tĭne drew

1
*a* *Philistines*, Gen. 26:14.
*b* *Armies*, Deut. 11:4.
*c* *Judah, tribe of*, Num. 10:14.
*d* *Azekah*, Josh. 10:10.

2
*e* *Saul*, 1 Sam. 9:2.
*f* *Israel, under the kings*, Ex. 4:22.
*g* 1 Sam. 21:9.

4
*h* *Gath*, Josh. 11:22.
*i* *Cubit*, Ex. 36:9.
*j* *Measure, linear*, Deut. 25:15.

5
*k* *Helmet*, Jer. 46:4.
*l* *Brass*, Job 28:2.

6
1 R. V. javelin

7
*m* 2 Sam. 21:19.
*n* *Spear*, 2 Kin. 11:10.
*o* *Shekel*, Ex. 30:13.
*p* *Iron*, Prov. 27.17.
*q* *Armor-bearer*, Judg. 9:54.

8
*r* *Boasting, instances of*, Prov. 25:14.
*s* *Armies, champions fight instead of*, Deut. 11:4.

9
*t* *Servant*, Jer. 2:14.

11
*u* *Cowardice*, Lev. 26:36.

12
*v* *David*, 1 Sam. 16:13.
*w* *Beth-lehem*, Gen. 48:7.
*x* *Jesse*, Ruth 4:17.

13
*y* *Eliab*, 1 Sam. 16:6.
*z* 1 Sam. 16:8; 1 Chr. 2:13.

*a* *Shammah*, 1 Sam. 16:9.

14
*b* *David*, 1 Sam. 16:13.
*c* *Saul*, 1 Sam. 9:2.

15
*d* *Shepherd*, Jer. 31:10.
*e* *Beth-lehem*, Gen. 48:7.

* **SHOCHOH** (*branches, hedge*), called also SHOCHO, SHOCOH, SHOCO, SOCHOH, SOCOH. *A city of Judah*, Josh. 15:35; 1 Sam. 17:1. *One of Solomon's commissaries in*, 1 Kin. 4:10. *Rebuilt and fortified by Rehoboam*, 2 Chr. 11:7. *Taken by Philistines*, 2 Chr. 28:18.

† **GOLIATH** (*an exile*), a giant champion of Gath. *Defies armies of Israel, and is slain by David*, 1 Sam 17; 21:9; 22:10. *His sons*, 2 Sam. 21:15–22; 1 Chr. 20:4–8.

‡ **COAT OF MAIL**, 1 Sam. 17:5, 38; 1 Kin. 22:34; 2 Chr. 18:33. *Called habergeon*, Ex. 28:32; 39:23; 2 Chr. 26:14; Neh. 4:16. *Called breastplate*, Isa. 59:17.
**Figurative:** *Of the Christian armor*, Eph. 6:14; 1 Thess. 5:8.

near morning and evening, and
presented himself [f]forty days.
17 And [g,h]Jĕs′se said unto
[b]Dā′vid his son, Take now for
thy brethren an [i]ephah of this
parched [j]corn, and these ten
[k]loaves, and run to the camp
to thy brethren;
18 And carry these ten [l,m]chees-
es unto the [n,o]captain of *their*
thousand, and look how thy
brethren fare, and take their
pledge.
19 Now [c]Sa̤ul, and they, and all
the men of [p]Ĭṣ′ra-el, *were* in the
valley of [q]Ē′lah, fighting with
the [r]Phĭ-lĭs′tĭneṣ.
20 And [b]Dā′vid [s]rose up early
in the morning, and [d]left the
sheep with a keeper, and took,
and went, as [g]Jĕs′se had commanded him; and he came to the
[2]trench, as the host was going
forth to the fight, and [t]shouted
for the ‖battle.
21 For [p]Ĭṣ′ra-el and the [r]Phĭ-
lĭs′tĭneṣ had put the ‖battle in
array, army against army.
22 And [b]Dā′vid left his [3]car-
riage in the hand of the keeper
of the [3]carriage, and ran into the
army, and came and [u]saluted
his brethren.
23 And as he talked with them,
behold, there came up the
§champion, the Phĭ-lĭs′tĭne of
Găth, †Gŏ-lī′ath by name, out
of the armies of the [r]Phĭ-lĭs′-
tĭneṣ, and spake according to the
same words: and [b]Dā′vid heard
*them*.
24 And all the men of Ĭṣ′ra-el,
when they saw the man, [v]fled
from him, and were sore afraid.
25 And the men of Ĭṣ′ra-el
said, Have ye seen this man that
is come up? surely to defy Ĭṣ′-
ra-el is he come up: and it shall
be, *that* the man who killeth him,
the king will [w]enrich him with
great [x]riches, and will [w,y]give
him his [z]daughter, and [w]make
his father's house free in Ĭṣ′ra-el.
26 And [a]Dā′vid spake to the
men that stood by him, saying,
What shall be done to the man
that killeth this Phĭ-lĭs′tĭne, and
taketh away the reproach from
Ĭṣ′ra-el? for [b]who *is* this uncircumcised Phĭ-lĭs′tĭne, that he
should defy the armies of the
living God?
27 And the people answered
him after this manner, saying,
So shall it be done to the man
that killeth him.
28 And [c]Ē-lī′ab his eldest brother heard when he spake unto
the men; and Ē-lī′ab's [d]anger
was kindled against [a]Dā′vid,
and he said, Why camest thou
down hither? and [e]with whom
hast thou left those few sheep
in the wilderness? [f]I know thy
pride, and the naughtiness of
thine [g]heart; for thou art come
down that thou mightest see the
‖battle.
29 And [a]Dā′vid [h]said, What
have I now done? *Is there* not
a cause?
30 And he turned from him toward another, and spake after
the same manner: and the people answered him again after the
former manner.
31 And when the words were
heard which [a]Dā′vid spake, they
rehearsed *them* before [i]Sa̤ul: and
he sent for him.
32 ¶ And [a]Dā′vid said to [i]Sa̤ul,
Let no man's heart fail because
of him; [j]thy servant [k]will go and
fight with this †Phĭ-lĭs′tĭne.
33 And [i]Sa̤ul said to [a]Dā′vid,
Thou art not able to go against
this †Phĭ-lĭs′tĭne to fight with
him: for thou *art but* a youth,

16
*f* *Forty, days*, Jonah 3:4.
17
*g* *Jesse*, Ruth 4:17.
*h* *Parents, affection of, exemplified*, 2 Cor. 12:14.
*i* *Measure, dry*, Deut. 25:15.
*j* *Corn*, Psa. 65:13.
*k* *Bread*, Ezek. 4:13.
18
*l* 2 Sam. 17:29; Job 10:10.
*m* *Presents*, Gen. 32:13.
*n* *Captain, of thousands*, Num. 31:48.
*o* *Armies, how officered*, Deut. 11:4.
19
*p* *Israel, under the kings*, Ex. 4:22.
*q* 1 Sam. 21:9.
*r* *Philistines*, Gen. 26:14.
20
*s* *Rising, early*, Gen. 19:2.
*t* *Armies, battle shouts*, Deut. 11:4.
2 R. V. place of the wagons, as the host that was going forth to the fight shouted for the battle.
22
*u* *Salutations*, Luke 1:44.
3 R. V. baggage
24
*v* *Cowardice, instances of*, Lev. 26:36.

25
*w* *Armies, rewards for meritorious conduct in*, Deut. 11:4.
*x* *Riches*, Eccl. 4:8.
*y* *Marriage*, Gen. 34:9.
*z* *Daughter, given in marriage by parents*, Lev. 12:6.
26
*a* *David*, 1 Sam. 16:13.
*b* *Zeal*, 2 Cor. 7:11.
28
*c* *Eliab*, 1 Sam. 16:6.
*d* *Anger*, Psa. 37:8.
*e* *Sarcasm, instances of*, Judg. 10:14.
*f* *Uncharitableness, instances of*, Matt. 7:1.
*g* *Heart*, Psa. 44:21.
29
*h* *Meekness, instances of*, Psa. 45:4.
31
*i* *Saul*, 1 Sam. 9:2.
32
*j* *Courage, instances of*, Deut. 31:7.
*k* *Decision, instances of*, Isa. 50:7.

‖ **BATTLE.** *Shouting in*, Judg. 7:20; 1 Sam. 17:20. *Priests in*, 2 Chr. 13:12.
Prayer before: *By Asa*, 2 Chr. 14:11; *by Jehoshaphat*, 2 Chr. 20:3–12. See footnotes: ARMIES, Deut. 11:4; WAR, Judg. 3:2.

§ **CHAMPIONSHIP.** Battles were decided by: *By Goliath and David*, 1 Sam. 17:8–53; *by young men of David's and Abner's armies*, 2 Sam. 2:14–17; *by representatives of the Philistines' and David's armies*, 2 Sam. 21:20–22.

and he a [l]man of war from his
youth.
34 And [a]Dā′vid said unto Sa̤ul,
Thy servant [m]kept his father's
sheep, and there came a [n]lion,
and a [o]bear, and took a lamb out
of the flock:
35 And [j]I went out after him,
and smote him, and delivered *it*
out of his mouth: and when he
arose against me, I caught *him*
by his beard, and smote him,
and slew him.
36 [j]Thy servant slew both the
[n]lion and the [o]bear: and [p]this
uncircumcised Phĭ-lĭs′tĭne shall
be as one of them, seeing he
hath defied the armies of the
living God.
37 [a]Dā′vid said moreover, The
LORD that [q]delivered me out of
the paw of the [n]lion, and out of
the paw of the [o]bear, [p]he will deliver me out of the hand of †this
Phĭ-lĭs′tĭne. And [i]Sa̤ul said unto
Dā′vid, Go, and [r]the LORD be
with thee.
38 ¶ And [i]Sa̤ul [4]armed Dā′vid
with his [5]armour, and he put an
[s]helmet of brass upon his head;
also he [4]armed him with a ‡coat
of mail.
39 And [a]Dā′vid girded his
[t]sword upon his [5]armour, and he
assayed to go; for he had not
proved *it*. And Dā′vid said unto [i]Sa̤ul, I cannot go with these;
for I have not proved *them*.
And Dā′vid put them off him.
40 And he took his staff in his
hand, and chose him five smooth
stones out of the brook, and put
them in a shepherd's bag which
he had, even in a scrip; and his
+sling *was* in his hand: and [j]he
drew near to †the Phĭ-lĭs′tĭne.
41 And †the Phĭ-lĭs′tĭne came
on and drew near unto [a]Dā′vid;
and the man that bare the shield
*went* before him.

33
l *Soldiers*, Ezra 8:22.
34
m *Shepherd*, Jer. 31:10.
n *Lion*, Mic. 5:8.
o *Bear*, 2 Sam. 17:8.
36
p *Faith, instances of*, Mark 11:22.
37
q *God, his preserving care, exemplified*, Gen. 2:2.
r *Benedictions*, Deut. 21:5.
38
s *Helmet*, Jer. 46:4.
4 R. V. clad
5 R. V. apparel,
39
t *Sword*, 1 Chr. 21:5.

42 And when †the Phĭ-lĭs′tĭne
looked about, and saw Dā′vid,
he disdained him: for he was *but*
a youth, and ruddy, and of a
fair countenance.
43 And the †Phĭ-lĭs′tĭne said
unto [a]Dā′vid, *Am* I a [u]dog, that
thou comest to me with staves?
And the Phĭ-lĭs′tĭne cursed Dā′-
vid by his [v]gods.
44 And the Phĭ-lĭs′tĭne [w]said to
Dā′vid, Come to me, and I will
give thy flesh unto the fowls of the
air, and to the beasts of the field.
45 [i]Then said [a]Dā′vid to the
†Phĭ-lĭs′tĭne, Thou comest to me
with a sword, and with a spear,
and with a [6]shield: but [p]I come
to thee in the name of the
[x]LORD of hosts, the God of the
armies of Ĭs̤′ra-el, whom thou
hast defied.
46 [p]This day will the LORD deliver thee into mine hand; and I
will smite thee, and take thine
head from thee; and I will give
the carcases of the host of the
[y]Phĭ-lĭs′tĭnes̤ this day unto the
fowls of the air, and to the wild
beasts of the earth; that all the
earth may know that there is a
God in Ĭs̤′ra-el.
47 And all this assembly shall
know that the LORD [x]saveth not
with sword and spear: for the
[z]battle *is* the LORD's, and he
will [a]give you into our hands.
48 And it came to pass, when
the Phĭ-lĭs′tĭne arose, and came
and drew nigh to meet Dā′vid,
that Dā′vid hasted, and ran
toward the army to meet the
Phĭ-lĭs′tĭne.
49 And [b]Dā′vid put his hand in
his bag, and took thence a stone,
and slang *it*, and smote †the Phĭ-
lĭs′tĭne in his forehead, that the
stone sunk into his forehead;
and he fell upon his face to the
earth.

43
u *Dog*, 1 Kin. 21:19.
v *Idolatry*, 1 Sam. 15:23.
44
w *Boasting, instances of*, Prov. 25:14.
45
x *God, preserver* Gen. 2:2.
6 R. V. javelin:
46
y *Philistines*, Gen. 26:14.
47
z *War, God in*, Judg. 3:2.
a *God, providence of*, Gen. 2:2.
49
b *David*, 1 Sam. 16:13.

---

**+SLING.** *David slays Goliath with*, 1 Sam. 17:40–50. *Dexterous use of*, Judg. 20:16; 1 Chr. 12:2. *Used in war*. Judg. 20:16; 2 Kin. 3:25; 2 Chr. 26:14.

50 So [b]Dā′vid prevailed over †the Phĭ-lĭs′tĭne with a +sling and with a stone, and smote the Phĭ-lĭs′tĭne, and slew him; but *there was* no sword in the hand of Dā′vid.

51 Therefore [b]Dā′vid ran, and stood upon †the Phĭ-lĭs′tĭne, and took his sword, and drew it out of the sheath thereof, and slew him, and cut off his head therewith. And when the [c]Phĭ-lĭs′tĭneș saw their §champion was dead, they fled.

52 And the men of [d]Ĭș′ra-el and of Jū′dah arose, and shouted, and pursued the [e]Phĭ-lĭs′tĭneș, until thou come to the valley, and to the gates of [e]Ĕk′rŏn. And the wounded of the Phĭ-lĭs′tĭneș fell down by the way to [f]Shā-a-rā′im, even unto [g]Găth, and unto Ĕk′rŏn.

53 And the children of Ĭș′ra-el returned from chasing after the Phĭ-lĭs′tĭneș, and they [h]spoiled their [7]tents.

54 And [b]Dā′vid took the [i]head of †the Phĭ-lĭs′tĭne, and brought it to [j]Jĕ-ru̥′să-lĕm; but he put his ⊙armour in his tent.

55 ¶ And when [k]Sa̤ul saw [b]Dā′vid go forth against †the Phĭ-lĭs′tĭne, he said unto [l]Ăb′nēr, the captain of the host, Ăb′nēr, whose son *is* this youth? And Ăb′nēr said, *As* thy soul liveth, O king, I cannot tell.

56 And the king said, Enquire thou whose son the stripling *is*.

57 And as [b]Dā′vid returned from the slaughter of †the Phĭ-lĭs′tĭne, [l]Ăb′nēr took him, and brought him before [k]Sa̤ul with the head of the Phĭ-lĭs′tĭne in his hand.

58 And [k]Sa̤ul said to him, Whose son *art* thou, *thou* young man? And [b]Dā′vid answered, *I am* the son of thy servant [m]Jĕs′se the Bĕth′-lĕ-hĕm-īte.

## CHAPTER 18

*Jonathan's affection for David. 5 Saul promotes him; 8 but afterward envies his praise, 10 and in fury seeks to kill him. 20 Offers his daughter as a snare; 25 but David escapes the danger. 28 Saul's hatred and David's glory increase.*

AND it came to pass, when he had made an end of speaking unto [a]Sa̤ul, that the soul of [b]Jŏn′a-than was [c,d]knit with the soul of [e]Dā′vid, and Jŏn′a-than [f]loved him as his own soul.

2 And [a]Sa̤ul took [e]him that day, and would let him go no more home to his father's house.

3 Then [b]Jŏn′a-than and [e]Dā′vid made a [g]covenant, because he loved him as his own soul.

4 And [b]Jŏn′a-than stripped himself of the [h]robe that *was* upon him, and [i]gave it to [e]Dā′vid, and his garments, even to his sword, and to his bow, and to his [i]girdle.

5 ¶ And [e]Dā′vid went out whithersoever [a]Sa̤ul sent him, *and* behaved himself [j]wisely: and Sa̤ul set him over the men of war, and he was accepted in the sight of all the people, and also in the sight of Sa̤ul's servants.

6 ¶ And it came to pass as [k]they came, when [e]Dā′vid was returned from the slaughter of the [l]Phĭ-lĭs′tĭne, that the [m,n]women came out of all cities of Ĭș′ra-el, singing and [o]danc-

**51**
c *Philistines*, Gen. 26:14.

**52**
d *Israel, under the kings*, Ex. 4:22.
e *Ekron*, Amos 1:8.
f Or, *Sharaim*, Josh. 15:36.
g *Gath*, Josh. 11:22.

**53**
h *Spoils*, 1 Chr. 26:27.
7 R. V. camp.

**54**
i *Trophies*, 1 Sam. 21:9.
j *Jerusalem*, Judg. 19:10.

**55**
k *Saul*, 1 Sam. 9:2.
l *Abner*, 1 Sam. 14:50.

**58**
m *Jesse*, Ruth 4:17.

**1**
a *Saul*, 1 Sam. 9:2.
b *Jonathan, love of, for David*, 1 Sam. 14:1.
c *Friendship, instances of*, Prov. 22:24.
d *Fraternity*, Zech. 11:14.
e *David*, 1 Sam. 16:13.
f *Love, of man for man, instances of*, 1 John 4:7.

**3**
g *Covenant, of men with men*, Deut. 29:1.

**4**
h *Dress*, Zech. 3:3.
i *Girdle*, Prov. 31:24.

**5**
j *Prudence, instances of*, 2 Chr. 2:12.

**6**
k *Armies, triumphs of, celebrated*, Deut. 11:4.
l *Goliath*, 1 Sam. 17:4.
m *Women, patriotic*, Prov. 31:10.
n *Victories, celebrated by women*, Deut. 28:7.
o *Dancing, of women*, Eccl. 3:4.

---

⊙ **ARMOR.** *The equipment of a soldier*, 1 Sam. 13:22; Jer. 46:3, 4; Eph. 6:14–17.

**Defensive:** *Helmet*, 1 Sam. 17:5, 38; 2 Chr. 17:17; 26:14; Jer. 46:4; Ezek. 23:24. *Breastplate*, Rev. 9:9–17. *Coat of mail*, 1 Sam. 17:5, 38; 1 Kin. 22:34; 2 Chr. 18:33. *Greave, protection for the leg*, 1 Sam. 17:6.

*Shield*, 2 Sam. 1:21; 8:7; 1 Kin. 10:16, 17; 14:27; 2 Chr. 9:16; 26:14; Neh. 2:3.

**Offensive:** *Bows*, Gen. 21:16, 20; *made, of steel* [R. V. brass], 2 Sam. 22:35; Job 20:24; Psa. 18:34; *of wood*, Ezek. 39:9. *David instructed the Israelites in the use of, by writing war song to*, 2 Sam. 1:18. *Arrows*, 1 Sam. 31:3; 2 Sam. 22:15; 1 Kin. 22:34; 2 Kin. 19:32; 2 Chr. 17:17; Psa. 7:13; Isa. 22:3; Jer. 51:3.

*Battle ax*, Jer. 51: 20. *Dart, a light javelin*, Num. 25:7; 1 Sam. 18:10; 2 Sam. 18:14; Job 41:29. *Javelin, a heavy lance*, Ezek. 39:9; *used, by Goliath*, 1 Sam. 16:6; *by Saul*, 1 Sam. 18:11; 19:9, 10.

*Sling, used for throwing stones*, Prov. 26:8. *David slays Goliath with*, 1 Sam. 17:40–50. *Dexterous use of*, Judg. 20:16. *Used in war*, Judg. 20:16; 2 Kin. 3:25; 2 Chr. 26:14.

*Sword, used, by Gideon*, Judg. 7:20; *by Peter*, Matt. 26:51; John 18:10. *David's army equipped with*, 1 Chr. 21:5.

**Figurative,** Rom. 13:12; 2 Cor. 6:7; 10:4; Eph. 6:11–17; 1 Thess. 5:8.

ing, to meet king Sa̤ul, with
[1, p]tabrets, with joy, and with
instruments of [q]musick.
7 And the [m]women [2]answered
*one another* as they played, and
said, [a]Sa̤ul hath slain his thousands, and [e]Dā'vid his ten
thousands.
8 And [a, r]Sa̤ul was very [s, t]wroth,
and the saying displeased him;
and he [u]said, They have ascribed unto [e]Dā'vid ten thousands, and to me they have ascribed *but* thousands: and *what*
can he have more but the kingdom?
9 And [a]Sa̤ul [u]eyed [e]Dā'vid from
that day and forward.
10 ¶ And it came to pass on the
morrow, that the [*, v, w]evil spirit
from God came upon [a]Sa̤ul, and
he prophesied in the midst of the
house: and Dā'vid played with
his hand, as [3]at other times: and
*there was* a [4, x]javelin in Sa̤ul's
hand.
11 And [r]Sa̤ul [u]cast the [4, x]jave-
lin; for he [u]said, I will smite
Dā'vid even to the wall *with it.*
And [e]Dā'vid avoided out of his
presence twice.
12 ¶ And Sa̤ul was afraid of
Dā'vid, because the LORD was
with him, and was [y]departed
from [z]Sa̤ul.
13 Therefore [a]Sa̤ul removed
[b]him from him, and made him
his [c, d]captain over a thousand;
and he went out and came in
before the people.
14 And [b]Dā'vid behaved himself [e]wisely in all his ways; and
the LORD *was* [f]with him.
15 Wherefore when [a]Sa̤ul saw
that he behaved himself very
[e]wisely, he [5]was afraid of him.
16 But all Ĭs̜'ra-el and Jū'dah
[g]loved [b]Dā'vid, because he went
out and came in before them.
17 ¶ And [a]Sa̤ul said to [b]Dā'vid,
Behold my elder daughter [h]Mē'-
răb, her will I [i]give thee to [j]wife:
only be thou valiant for me, and
fight the LORD's battles. For
Sa̤ul said, Let not mine hand be
upon him, but let the hand of
the [k]Phĭ-lĭs'tĭneṣ be upon him.
18 And [b]Dā'vid said unto Sa̤ul,
[l]Who *am* I? and what *is* my life,
*or* my father's family in Ĭs̜'ra-el,
that I should be [m]son in law to
the king?
19 But it came to pass at
the time when [h]Mē'răb Sa̤ul's
daughter should have been given
to [b]Dā'vid, that she was given
unto [n]Ā'drĭ-el the [o]Mĕ-hŏl'ath-
īte to wife.
20 And [†]Mī'chal Sa̤ul's
[p]daughter loved [b]Dā'vid: and
they told [a]Sa̤ul, and the thing
pleased him.
21 And [a]Sa̤ul said, I will give
him [†, p]her, that she may be
a snare to him, and that the
hand of the [k]Phĭ-lĭs'tĭneṣ may
be against him. Wherefore Sa̤ul
said to [b]Dā'vid, Thou shalt this
day be my [m]son in law [6]in *the
one of* the twain.
22 And [a]Sa̤ul commanded his
servants, *saying,* Commune with
[b]Dā'vid secretly, and say, Behold, the king hath delight in
thee, and all his servants love
thee: now therefore be the king's
[m]son in law.
23 And [a]Sa̤ul's servants spake
those words in the ears of [b]Dā'-
vid. And Dā'vid said, Seemeth
it to you *a* light *thing* to be a
king's son in law, [l]seeing that I
*am* a poor man, and lightly
esteemed?
24 And the servants of [a]Sa̤ul
told him, saying, On this manner spake [b]Dā'vid.
25 And [a]Sa̤ul said, Thus shall

p *Timbrel,* Ex. 15:20.
q *Music,* 2 Chr. 5:13.
1 R. V. timbrels,

**7**
2 R. V. sang one to another in their play,

**8**
r *Rulers, wicked, instances of,* Ex. 18:21.
s *Jealousy, instances of,* Psa. 78:58.
t *Envy, instances of,* Prov. 14:30.
u *Malice, instances of,* vs. 8–29; Eph. 4:31.

**10**
v *Demons,* Matt. 4:24.
w *Insanity, demoniacal,* Prov. 26:18.
x *Spear,* 2 Kin. 11:10.
3 R. V. he did day by day:
4 R. V. spear

**12**
y *Holy Spirit, withdrawn from incorrigible sinners,* Acts 1:2.
z *Reprobates,* 1 Cor. 9:27.

**13**
a *Saul,* 1 Sam. 9:2.
b *David,* 1 Sam. 16:13.
c *Captain,* Num. 31:48.
d *Armies, how officered,* Deut. 11:4.

**14**
e *Prudence, instances of,* 2 Chr. 2:12.
f *God, dwells with the righteous,* Gen. 2:2.

**15**
5 R. V. stood in awe

**16**
g *Love, of man for man, instances of,* 1 John 4:7.

**17**
h 1 Sam. 14:49.
i *Armies, rewards for meritorious conduct in,* Deut. 11:4.
j *Marriage,* Gen. 34:9.
k *Philistines,* Gen. 26:14.

**18**
l *Humility, instances of,* Prov. 22:4.
m *Son-in-law,* Gen. 19:12.

**19**
n 2 Sam. 21:8, 9.
o 2 Sam. 21:8.

**20**
p *Daughter,* Lev. 12:6.

**21**
6 R. V. a second time.

* **EVIL SPIRIT.** *Sent, upon Saul,* 1 Sam. 16:14; 18:10; 19:9: *between Abimelech and the men of Shechem,* Judg. 9:23. *Volunteers to incite Ahab to evil,* 1 Kin. 22:21–23; 2 Chr. 18:19–22.

† **MICHAL,** daughter of Saul. *Given to David as a reward for slaying Goliath,* 1 Sam. 18:20–28. *Rescues David from death,* 1 Sam. 19:9–17. *Saul forcibly separates them, and she is given in marriage to Phalti,* 1 Sam. 25:44. *David recovers, to himself,* 2 Sam. 3:13–16. *Ridicules David on account of his religious zeal,* 2 Sam. 6:16, 20–23.

ye say to [b]Dā'vid, The king desireth not any [q]dowry, but an hundred foreskins of the [k]Phĭ-lĭs'tĭneș, to be [r]avenged of the king's enemies. But Saul thought to make Dā'vid fall by the hand of the Phĭ-lĭs'tĭneș.

26 And when his servants told [b]Dā'vid these words, it pleased Dā'vid well to be the king's [m]son in law: and the days were not expired.

27 Wherefore [b]Dā'vid arose and went, he and his men, and slew of the [k]Phĭ-lĭs'tĭneș two hundred men; and Dā'vid brought their foreskins, and they gave them in full tale to the king, that he might be the king's [m]son in law. And [a]Saul gave him †Mī'chal his daughter to wife.

28 And [a]Saul saw and knew that the [f]LORD *was* with Dā'vid, and *that* †Mī'chal Saul's daughter loved him.

29 And Saul was yet the more afraid of Dā'vid; and Saul became Dā'vid's [s]enemy continually.

30 Then the princes of the [k]Phĭ-lĭs'tĭneș went forth: and it came to pass, after they went forth, *that* Dā'vid behaved himself more wisely than all the servants of Saul; so that his name was much set by.

## CHAPTER 19

*Jonathan discloses his father's purpose to kill David. 4 He persuades his father to reconciliation. 8 By reason of David's success, Saul's rage breaks out against him; 12 but he is rescued by Michal. 18 David comes to Samuel in Naioth. 20 Saul sends to take David. His messengers, 22 and Saul himself, prophesy.*

AND [a,b]Saul spake to [c]Jŏn'a-than his son, and to all his servants, [d,e]that they should kill [f]Dā'vid.

2 But [c]Jŏn'a-than [a]Saul's son [g]delighted much in [f]Dā'vid: and Jŏn'a-than told Dā'vid, saying, Saul my father seeketh to kill thee: now therefore, I pray thee, take heed to thyself until the morning, and abide in a secret *place*, and hide thyself:

3 And I will go out and stand beside my father in the field where thou *art* and I will commune with my father of thee; and what I see, that I will tell thee.

4 And [c]Jŏn'a-than spake good of [f]Dā'vid unto [a]Saul his father, and [h,i]said unto him, Let not the king sin against his servant, against Dā'vid; because he hath not sinned against thee, and because his works *have been* to theeward very good:

5 For he [j]did put his life in his hand, and slew [k]the Phĭ-lĭs'tĭne, and the [l]LORD wrought a great [1]salvation for all Ĭș'ra-el: thou sawest *it*, and didst rejoice: [h,i]wherefore then wilt thou sin against innocent blood, to slay Dā'vid without a cause?

6 And [a]Saul hearkened unto the [m]voice of [c]Jŏn'a-than: and Saul [n]sware, *As* the LORD liveth, he shall not be slain.

7 And [c]Jŏn'a-than called [f]Dā'vid, and Jŏn'a-than shewed him all those things. And Jŏn'a-than brought Dā'vid to Saul, and he [o]was in his presence, as in times past.

8 ¶ And there was [p]war again: and [f]Dā'vid went out, and fought with the [q]Phĭ-lĭs'tĭneș, and slew them with a great slaughter; and they fled from him.

9 And the [r,s]evil spirit from the LORD was upon [a]Saul, as he sat in his house with his [2]javelin in his hand: and [f]Dā'vid played with *his* hand.

10 And [a]Saul [d,e]sought to smite [f]Dā'vid even to the wall with the [2]javelin; but he slipped away out of Saul's presence, and he smote the [2]javelin into the wall: and Dā'vid fled, and escaped that night.

25
*q* *Dowry*, Gen. 34:12.
*r* *Revenge*, Ezek. 25:15.

29
*s* *Enemy*, Prov. 24:17.

1
*a* *Saul*, 1 Sam. 9:2.
*b* *Rulers, wicked, instances of*, Ex. 18:21.
*c* *Jonathan*, 1 Sam. 14:1.
*d* *Evil for good, instances of*, Psa. 35:12.
*e* *Malice, instances of*, Eph. 4:31.
*f* *David*, 1 Sam. 16:13.

2
*g* *Friendship, instances of*, Prov. 22:24.

4
*h* *Intercession, of man with man*, Jer. 27:18.
*i* *Reproof, faithfulness in*, Prov. 17:10.

5
*j* *Courage, instances of*, Deut. 31:7.
*k* *Goliath*, 1 Sam. 17:4.
*l* *War, God in*, Judg. 3:2.
1 R. V. victory

6
*m* *Influence, good*, 1 Cor. 7:14.
*n* *Oath*, Num. 5:19.

7
*o* *Reconciliation, between man and man*, 2 Cor. 5:18.

8
*p* *War*, Judg. 3:2.
*q* *Philistines*, Gen. 26:14.

9
*r* *Evil Spirit*, 1 Sam. 18:10.
*s* *Demons, possession by*, Matt. 4:24.
2 R. V. spear

11 [a]Sa̤ul also sent messengers unto [l]Dā'vid's house, to watch him, and to [d,e]slay him in the morning: and [t]Mī'chal Dā'vid's wife told him, saying, If thou save not thy life to night, to morrow thou shalt be slain.

12 So [t]Mī'chal let [l]Dā'vid down through a [u]window: and he went, and fled, and escaped.

13 [v]And [t]Mī'chal took an [w]image, and laid *it* in the bed, and put a pillow of [x]goat's *hair* for his bolster[c], and covered *it* with a cloth.

14 And when [a]Sa̤ul sent messengers to take [l]Dā'vid, she [y]said, He *is* sick.

15 And [a]Sa̤ul sent the messengers *again* to see [l]Dā'vid, saying, Bring him up to me in the bed, that I may [d,e]slay him.

16 And when the messengers were come in, behold, [3]*there was* an [w]image in the bed, with a pillow of [x]goats' *hair* for his bolster[c].

17 And [a]Sa̤ul said unto [t]Mī'chal, Why hast thou deceived me so and sent away mine enemy, that he is escaped? And Mī'chal answered Sa̤ul, He said unto me, Let me go; why should I kill thee?

18 ¶[T]So [l]Dā'vid fled, and escaped, and came to [z]Săm'u-el to [a]Rā'mah, and told him all that [b]Sa̤ul had done to him. And he and Săm'u-el went and dwelt in [c]Nā'ioth.

19 And it was told [b]Sa̤ul, saying, Behold, [d]Dā'vid *is* at [c]Nā'ioth in [a]Rā'mah.

20 And [b]Sa̤ul sent messengers to take [d]Dā'vid: and when they saw the [e]company of the [f]prophets prophesying, and [g,h,i]Săm'u-el standing *as* appointed over them, [j]the Spirit of God was upon the messengers of Sa̤ul, and they also prophesied.

21 And when it was told [b]Sa̤ul, he sent other messengers, and they prophesied likewise. And Sa̤ul sent messengers again the third time, and they prophesied also.

22 Then went he also to [a]Rā'mah, and came to a great well that *is* in Sē'chu: and he asked and said, Where *are* [g]Săm'u-el and [d]Dā'vid? And *one* said, Behold, *they be* at Nā'ioth in Rā'mah.

23 And he went thither[c] to [c]Nā'ioth in [a]Rā'mah: and the Spirit of God was upon him also, and he went on, and prophesied, until he came to Nā'ioth in Rā'mah.

24 And he stripped off his clothes also, and prophesied before [g]Săm'u-el in like manner, and lay down naked all that day and all that night. Wherefore they say, [k]*Is* Sa̤ul also among the prophets?[T]

## CHAPTER 20

*David consults with Jonathan for his safety. 11 They renew their covenant by oath. 18 Jonathan's token to David. 24 Saul, missing David, seeks to kill Jonathan. 36 Jonathan makes known to David his danger. 41 They lovingly separate.*

AND [a]Dā'vid fled from [b]Nā'ioth in [c]Rā'mah, and came and said before [d]Jŏn'a-than, What have I done? what *is* mine iniquity? and what *is* my sin before thy [e]father, that he seeketh my life?

2 And [d]he said unto him, [f]God forbid; thou shalt not die: behold, my [e]father will do nothing either great or small, but that he will shew it me: and why should my father hide this thing from me? it *is* not *so*.

3 And Dā'vid [g]sware moreover, and said, Thy father certainly knoweth that I have found grace in thine eyes; and he saith, Let not Jŏn'a-than know this, [l]lest he be grieved: but truly *as* the LORD liveth, and *as* thy soul

11
*Michal*, 1 Sam. 18:20.

12
u *Window*, Josh. 2:15.

13
v *Deception, instances of*, Josh. 9:4.
w *Teraphim*, Judg. 17:5.
x *Goat*, Deut. 14:4.

14
y *Falsehood, instances of*, Job 21:34.

16
3 R. V. the teraphim was in

18
z *Samuel*, 1 Sam. 3:1.

a *Ramah*, 1 Sam. 1:19.
b *Saul*, 1 Sam. 9:2.
c 1 Sam. 20:1.

19
d *David*, 1 Sam. 16:13.

20
e *School*, Acts 19:9.
f *Students*, 2 Kin. 2:3.
g *Samuel*, 1 Sam. 3:1.
h *Teachers*, 1 Chr. 25:8.
i *Minister, teachers of schools*, Rom. 15:16.
j *Prophets, inspiration of*, Isa. 3:2.

24
k *Proverbs*, 1 Sam. 24:13.

1
a *David*, 1 Sam. 16:13.
b 1 Sam. 19:18, 19, 22.
c *Ramah*, 1 Sam. 1:19.
d *Jonathan*, 1 Sam. 14:1.
e *Saul*, 1 Sam. 9:2.

2
f *Love, of man for man*, 1 John 4:7.

3
g *Oath*, Num. 5:19.

*h Life, brevity and uncertainty of,* Eccl. 8:15.
*i Death,* Num. 23: 10.

4
*j Friendship, instances of,* Prov. 22:24.

5
*k Feasts, given by kings,* Mark 12: 39.

6
*l Bethlehem,* Gen. 48:7.

7
*m Anger,* Psa. 37:8.

8
*n Covenant, of men with men,* Deut. 29:1.

12
1 R. V. The Lord, the God of Israel, be witness;

liveth, *there is* [h]but a step between me and [i]death.
4 Then said [d]Jŏn′a-than unto
[a]Dā′vid, [f,j]Whatsoever thy soul
desireth, I will even do *it* for
thee.
5 And [a]Dā′vid said unto [d]Jŏn′-
a-than, Behold, to morrow *is* the
new moon, and I should not[G] fail
to sit with the king at [k]meat: but
let me go, that I may hide myself in the field unto the third
*day* at even.
6 If thy father at all miss me,
then say, Dā′vid earnestly asked
*leave* of me that he might run to
[l]Bĕth′-lĕ-hĕm his city: for *there*
*is* a yearly sacrifice there for all
the family.
7 If he say thus, *It is* well; thy
servant shall have peace: but if
he be very [m]wroth[G], *then* be sure
that evil is determined by him.
8 Therefore thou shalt deal
kindly with thy servant; for thou
hast brought thy servant into a
[n]covenant[G] of the LORD with
thee: notwithstanding, if there
be in me iniquity, slay me thyself; for why shouldest thou
bring me to thy father?
9 And [d]Jŏn′a-than said, Far be
it from thee: for if I knew certainly that evil were determined
by my father to come upon thee,
then [f,j]would not I tell it thee?
10 Then said [a]Dā′vid to [d]Jŏn′-
a-than, Who shall tell me? or
what *if* thy father answer thee
roughly?
11 And [d]Jŏn′a-than said unto
[a]Dā′vid, Come, and let us go out
into the field. And they went
out both of them into the field.
12 And [d]Jŏn′a-than said unto
[a]Dā′vid, [1]O LORD God of Ĭṣ′-
ra-el, when I have sounded my
[e]father about to morrow any
time, *or* the third *day*, and, behold, *if there be* good toward
Dā′vid, and I then send not unto
thee, and shew it thee;
13 [o]The LORD do so and much
more to Jŏn′a-than: but if it
please my [e]father *to do* thee evil,
then I will shew it thee, and send
thee away, that thou mayest go
in peace: and [o]the LORD be with
thee, as he hath been with my
father.
14 And thou shalt not only
while yet I live shew me the
kindness of the LORD, that I
die not:
15[T] But *also* thou shalt not cut
off thy kindness from my house
for ever: no, not when the LORD
[p]hath cut off the enemies of Dā′-
vid every one from the face of
the earth.
16 So[G] [d]Jŏn′a-than made *a*
[n]*covenant* with the house[G] of
Dā′vid, *saying*, Let the LORD
even require *it* at the hand[G] of
Dā′vid's enemies.[T]
17 And [d]Jŏn′a-than caused
[a]Dā′vid to [g]swear[G] again, because
he [f]loved him: for he [f]loved him
as he loved his own soul.
18 Then [d]Jŏn′a-than said to
[a]Dā′vid, To morrow *is* the new
[q]moon: and thou shalt be
missed, because thy seat will be
empty.
19 And *when* thou hast stayed
three days, *then* thou shalt go
down quickly, and come to the
place where thou didst hide thyself when the business was *in*
*hand*, and shalt remain by the
[r,s]stone Ē′zĕl.
20 And I will [t]shoot three *arrows on the side *thereof*, as
though I shot at a mark.
21 And, behold, I will send a
lad, *saying*, Go, find out the *arrows. If I expressly say unto the
lad, Behold, the arrows *are* on

13
*o Prayer, intercessory,* Acts 6:4.

15
*p God, providence of,* Gen. 2:2.

18
*q New Moon, feast of,* Amos 8:5.

19
*r Stones,* Ex. 24: 12.
*s Pillar,* Gen. 28: 18.

20
*t Archery,* Gen. 21: 20.

* **ARROW,** a weapon. *Used, in hunting,* Gen. 21:20; 27:3; *in war,* 1 Sam. 31:3; 2 Kin. 19:32; Psa. 7:13; Isa. 22:3; Jer. 51:3. *Divination by,* Ezek. 21:21. *Shot by Jonathan as a sign to David,* 1 Sam. 20:20–42. *Shot by Joash as a sign against the Syrians,* 2 Kin. 13:14–19.

**Figurative:** *Of divine judgments,* Num. 24:8; Deut. 32:23, 42; 2 Sam. 22:15; Job 6:4; Psa. 11:2; 38:2; 144:6; Lam. 3:12, 13; Ezek. 5:16.
*Of the malice of wicked men,* Psa. 57:4; 58:7; 120:4. *Of daily perils,* Psa. 91:5.

this side of thee, take them; then come thou: for *there is* peace to thee, and no hurt; *as* the LORD liveth.

22 But if I say thus unto the young man, Behold, the arrows *are* beyond thee; go thy way: for the LORD [p]hath sent thee away.

23 And *as touching* the matter which thou and I have spoken of, behold, [o]the LORD *be* between thee and me for ever.

24 ¶ So [a]Dā′vid hid himself in the field: and when the new [q]moon was come, the [e]king sat him down to eat meat.

25 And the [e]king sat upon his seat, as at other times, *even* upon a seat by the [†]wall: and [d]Jŏn′a-than then arose, and [u]Ăb′nēr sat by [e]Saul's side, and Dā′vid's place was empty.

26 Nevertheless [e]Saul spake not any thing that day: for he thought, Something hath befallen him, he *is* [v]not clean; surely he *is* not clean.

27 And it came to pass on the morrow, *which was* the second *day* of the month, that [a]Dā′vid's place was empty: and [e]Saul said unto [d]Jŏn′a-than his son, Wherefore cometh not the son of [w]Jĕs′se to meat, neither yesterday, nor to day?

28 And [d]Jŏn′a-than answered [e]Saul, Dā′vid earnestly asked *leave* of me *to go* to [x]Bĕth′-lĕ-hĕm:

29 And he said, Let me go, I pray thee; for our family hath a sacrifice in the city; and my brother, he hath commanded me *to be there*: and now, if I have found favour in thine eyes, let me get away, I pray thee, and see my brethren. Therefore he cometh not unto the king's [y]table.

24
u *Abner*, 1 Sam. 14:50.

26
v *Defilement*, Lev. 5:2.

27
w *Jesse*, Ruth 4:17.

28
x *Bethlehem*, Gen. 48:7.

29
y *Table*, Judg. 1:7.

30 Then Saul's [z]anger was kindled against [a]Jŏn′a-than, and he [b]said unto him, Thou son of the perverse rebellious *woman*, do not I know that thou hast chosen the [c]son of [d]Jĕs′se to thine own confusion, and unto the confusion of thy mother's nakedness?

31 [e,f]For as long as the son of Jĕs′se liveth upon the ground, thou shalt not be established, nor thy kingdom. Wherefore now send and fetch him unto me, for [b]he shall surely die.

32 And [a]Jŏn′a-than answered Saul his father, and [g]said unto him, Wherefore shall he be slain? what hath he done?

33 And Saul cast [2]a javelin at him to smite him: whereby Jŏn′a-than knew that it was determined of his father to slay [c]Dā′vid.

34 So [a]Jŏn′a-than arose from the [h]table in fierce [i]anger, and did eat no meat the second day of the [j]month: for he was grieved for Dā′vid, because his father had done him shame.

35 ¶ And it came to pass in the morning, that [a]Jŏn′a-than went out into the field at the time appointed with [c]Dā′vid, and a little lad with him.

36 And he said unto his lad, Run, find out now the [*]arrows which I [k]shoot. *And* as the lad ran, he shot an arrow beyond him.

37 And when the lad was come to the place of the arrow which [a]Jŏn′a-than had shot, Jŏn′a-than cried after the lad, and said, *Is* not the arrow beyond thee?

38 And [a]Jŏn′a-than cried after the lad, Make speed, haste, stay not. And Jŏn′a-than's lad gath-

30
z *Anger, instances of*, Psa. 37:8.

a *Jonathan*, 1 Sam. 14:1.
b *Malice, instances of*, Eph. 4:31.
c *David*, 1 Sam. 16:13.
d *Jesse*, Ruth 4:17.

31
e *Envy, instances of*, Prov. 14:30.
f *Jealousy*, Psa. 78:58.

32
g *Friendship, instances of*, Prov. 22:24.

33
2 R. V. his spear

34
h *Table*, Judg. 1:7.
i *Anger*, Psa. 37:8.
j *Month*, Ex. 12:2.

36
k *Archery*, Gen. 21:20.

† **WALLS**, of cities. *Of Bashan, destroyed by the Israelites*, Deut. 3:5, 6. *Of Jericho*, Josh. 2:15; 6. *Of Babylon*, Jer. 51:44; *broad*, Jer. 51:58. *Of Beth-shan*, 1 Sam. 31:10. *Of Rabbah*, 2 Sam. 11:20. *Of Abel*, 2 Sam. 20:15, 21. *Houses built upon*, Josh. 2:15. *Double*, 2 Kin. 25:4; Isa. 22:11. *Sentinels on*, see footnote, WATCHMAN, 2 Sam. 18:24. *Of Jerusalem*, see footnote, JERUSALEM, Judg. 19:10. **Figurative:** *Of the new Jerusalem*, Rev. 21:12, 14, 17–21.

ered up the arrows, and came to his master.

39 But the lad knew not any thing: only [a]Jŏn′a-than and [c]Dā′vid knew the matter.

40 And [a]Jŏn′a-than gave his [3]artillery unto his lad, and said unto him, Go, carry *them* to the city.

41 ¶ *And* as soon as the lad was gone, [c]Dā′vid arose out of *a place* toward the south, and [l]fell on his face to the ground, and bowed himself three times: and [g,m]they kissed one another, and wept one with another, until Dā′vid exceeded.

42 And [a]Jŏn′a-than said to [c]Dā′vid, Go in peace, forasmuch as we have [n,o]sworn both of us in the name of the LORD, saying, The LORD be between me and thee and between my seed and thy seed for ever. And he arose and departed: and Jŏn′a-than went into the city.

40
3 R. V. weapons

41
*l Salutations,* Luke 1:44.
*m Love, of man for man, instances of,* 1 John 4:7.

42
*n Covenant, of men with men,* Deut. 29:1.
*o Oath,* Num. 5:19.

## CHAPTER 21

*David at Nob obtains of Ahimelech hallowed bread. 7 Doeg was present. 8 David takes Goliath's sword. 10 David flees to Gath. 13 He feigns himself mad.*

THEN came [a]Dā′vid to [b]Nŏb to *Ă-hĭm′e-lĕch the [c]priest: and Ă-hĭm′e-lĕch [1]was afraid at the meeting of Dā′vid, and said unto him, Why *art* thou alone, and no man with thee?

2 And [a]Dā′vid [d]said unto *Ă-hĭm′e-lĕch the priest, The [e]king hath commanded me a business, and hath said unto me, Let no man know any thing of the business whereabout I send thee, and what I have commanded thee: and I have appointed [2]*my* servants to such and such a place.

3 Now therefore what is under thine hand? give *me* five *loaves of* bread in mine hand, or what there is present.

1
*a David,* 1 Sam. 16:13.
*b Nob,* Neh. 11:32.
*c High Priest,* Lev. 21:10.
1 R. V. came to meet David trembling.

2
*d Falsehood, instances of,* Job 21:34.
*e King,* 2 Kin. 3:10.
2 R. V. the young men

4 And the [c]priest answered [a]Dā′vid, and said, *There is* no common bread under mine hand, but there is [f]hallowed bread; if the young men have kept themselves at least from women.

5 And [a]Dā′vid answered the [c]priest, and said unto him, Of a truth women *have been* kept from us about these three days, since I came out, and the vessels of the young men are holy, [3]and *the bread is* in a manner common, yea, though it were sanctified this day in the vessel.

6 So the priest gave him [f]hallowed *bread*: for there was no bread there but the shewbread, that was taken from before the LORD, to put hot bread in the day when it was taken away.

7 Now a certain man of the servants of [g]Saul *was* there that day, detained before the LORD; and his name *was* †Dō′eg, an [h]Ē′dom-īte, the chiefest of the herdmen that *belonged* to Saul.

8 And [a]Dā′vid said unto *Ă-hĭm′e-lĕch, And is there not here under thine hand [i]spear or [j]sword? for I have neither brought my sword nor my weapons with me, because the king's business required haste.

9 And the priest said, The ‡,[j]sword of [k]Gō-lī′ath the Phĭ-lĭs′tĭne, whom thou slewest in the valley of [l]Ē′lah, behold, it *is here* wrapped in a cloth behind the [m]ephod: if thou wilt take that, take *it*: for *there is* no other save that here. And Dā′vid said, *There is* none like that; give it me.

10 ¶ And [a]Dā′vid arose, and [n]fled that day for fear of [g]Saul,

4
*f Shewbread,* Ex. 35:13.

5
3 R. V. though it was but a common journey; how much more then to-day shall their vessels be holy?

7
*g Saul,* 1 Sam. 9:2.
*h Edomites,* 2 Kin. 8:21.

8
*i Spear,* 2 Kin. 11:10.
*j Sword,* 1 Chr. 21:5.

9
*k Goliath,* 1 Sam. 17:4.
*l* 1 Sam. 17:2, 19.
*m Ephod,* Ex. 28:6.

10
*n Fugitives,* Judg. 12:4.

* **AHIMELECH,** called also AHIAH. *Mentioned as son, while, in fact, he was father, of Abiathar,* 2 Sam. 8:17; 1 Chr. 18:16. *A high priest, during the reign of Saul,* 1 Sam. 14:3, 18. *Gives shewbread and the sword of Goliath to David,* 1 Sam. 21:1–9; Mark 2:26. *Betrayed by Doeg, an Edomite, and slain by command of Saul,* 1 Sam. 22:9–22.

† **DOEG** (*fearful*). *An Edomite, present when Ahimelech helped David,* 1 Sam. 21:7; 22:9, 22; title to Psa. 52. *Slew eighty-five priests,* 1 Sam. 22:18, 19.

‡ **TROPHIES.** *Goliath's head and armor,* 1 Sam. 17:54; 21:9; *Saul's,* 1 Sam. 31:8–10. *Placed in temples,* 1 Sam. 31:10; 1 Chr. 10:9, 10; Dan. 1:2.

and went to ‖Ā′chish the king of [o]Găth.

11 And the servants of ‖Ā′chish said unto him, *Is* not this [a]Dā′vid the king of the land? did they not sing one to another of him in [p]dances, saying, [q]Saul hath slain his thousands, and Dā′vid his ten thousands?

12 And [a]Dā′vid laid up these words in his heart, and was sore afraid of ‖Ā′chish the king of [o]Găth.

13 And he changed his behaviour before them, and [q]feigned himself [r]mad in their hands, and scrabbled on the doors of the gate, and let his spittle fall down upon his §beard.

14 Then said Ā′chish unto his servants, Lo, ye see the man is [r]mad: wherefore *then* have ye brought him to me?

15 Have I need of mad men, that ye have brought this *fellow* to play the mad man in my presence? shall this *fellow* come into my house?

## CHAPTER 22

*Many persons resort unto David at Adullam. 3 He commends his parents unto the king of Moab. 5 Admonished by Gad, he comes to Hareth. 6 Saul pursuing him complains of his servants' unfaithfulness. 9 Doeg accuses Ahimelech. 11 Saul commands to kill the priests. 17 His servants refusing, Doeg slays them. 20 Abiathar escaping brings David the news.*

[a]DĀ′VID therefore departed thence, and escaped to the [b]cave *Ă-dŭl′lăm: and when his brethren and all his father's house heard *it,* they went down thither to him.

2 And every one *that was* in distress, and every one that *was* in †debt, and every one *that was* discontented, gathered themselves unto him; and he became a [c]captain over [d]them: and there were with him about four hundred men.

3 ¶ And [a]Dā′vid went thence to Mĭz′peh of [e]Mō′ab: and [f]he said unto the king of Mō′ab, Let my [g]father and my mother, I pray thee, come forth, *and be* with you, [h]till I know what God will do for me.

4 And he brought them before the king of [e]Mō′ab: and they dwelt with him all the while that Dā′vid was in the hold.

5 ¶ And the [i]prophet [j]Găd said unto [a]Dā′vid, Abide not in the hold; depart, and get thee into the land of [k]Jū′dah. Then Dā′vid departed, and came into the forest of Hā′reth.

6 ¶ When [l]Saul heard that [a]Dā′vid was discovered, and the men that *were* with him, (now Saul abode in [m]Gĭb′e-ah under [1]a tree in [n]Rā′mah, having his spear in his hand, and all his servants *were* standing about him;)

7 Then [l,o]Saul [p]said unto his servants that stood about him, Hear now, ye [q]Bĕn′ja-mītes; will the [a]son of [g]Jĕs′se give every one of you fields and vineyards, *and* make you all captains of thousands, and captains of hundreds;

8 That all of you have [r]conspired against me, and *there is* none that sheweth me that my son hath made a league with the son of Jĕs′se, and *there is* none of you that is sorry for me, or sheweth unto me that my son hath stirred up my servant against me, to lie in wait, as at this day?

9 ¶ Then answered [s]Dō′eg the [t]Ē′dom-īte, which was set over

o *Gath,* Josh. 11:22.

11

p *Dancing,* Eccl. 3:4.

13

q *Dissembling, instances of,* Josh. 7:11.

r *Insanity, feigned by David,* Prov. 26:18.

1

a *David,* 1 Sam. 16:13.

b *Cave,* Judg. 6:2.

2

c *Captain,* Num. 31:48.

d *Armies, composed of insurgents,* Deut. 11:4.

3

e *Moabites,* Gen. 19:37.

f *Children, good, instances of,* Mark 10:14.

g *Jesse,* Ruth 4:17.

h *Doubting,* Rom. 14:23.

5

i *Prophets,* Isa. 3:2.

j *Gad,* 2 Sam. 24:11.

k *Judah, tribe of,* Num. 10:14.

6

l *Saul,* 1 Sam. 9:2.

m *Gibeah,* Hos. 9:9.

n *Ramah,* 1 Sam. 1:19.

1 R. V. the tamarisk tree

7

o *Rulers, wicked, instances of,* Ex. 18:21.

p *Malice, instances of,* Eph. 4:31.

q *Benjamin, tribe of,* Num. 1:37.

8

r *Conspiracy,* 1 Kin. 16:9.

9

s *Doeg,* 1 Sam. 21:7.

t *Edomites,* 2 Kin. 8:21.

‖ **ACHISH.** *King of the Philistines, called also* ABIMELECH, title to Psa. 34. *David escapes to,* 1 Sam. 21:10–15; 27; 28:1, 2; 29. *Shimei's servants escape to,* 1 Kin. 2:39, 40.

§ **BEARD,** Ezek. 5:1. *Worn long, by Aaron,* Psa. 133:2; *by Samson,* Judg. 16:17; *by David,* 1 Sam. 21:13. *Shaven by Egyptians,* Gen. 41:14. *Untrimmed in mourning,* 2 Sam. 19:24. *Plucked, as a sign of mourning,* Ezra 9:3 *Cut, as a sign of mourning,* Jer. 41:5; 48:37. *Lepers required to shave,* Lev. 13:29–33; 14:9. *Beards of David's ambassadors half shaven by the king of the Amorites,* 2 Sam. 10:4; 1 Chr. 19:4. *Idolatrous practice of marring, forbidden,* Lev. 19:27; 21:5.

* **ADULLAM,** a cave near the Dead Sea. *David takes refuge in.* 1 Sam. 22:1; 2 Sam. 23:13; 1 Chr. 11:15; titles to Psa. 57; 142 Late researches, contrary to former opinions, locate it in the vicinity of the city of Adullam, see footnote ADULLAM, 2 Chr. 11:7.

† **DEBT.** *Apostolic precept to Christians against contracting,* Rom. 13:8.

**Security for:** *Warnings against becoming surety for others,* Prov. 11:15; 22:26. *Raiment taken as, must be returned to the debtor before sundown,* Ex. 22:25–27; Deut. 24:10–13; Job 22:6; Amos 2:8. *Houses and lands,* Neh. 5:3, 4. *Children,* Job 24:9. *Millstones, forbidden as security for,* Deut. 24:6.

the servants of Sa̤ul, and [u]said, I saw the son of Jĕs′se coming to [v]Nŏb, to [w]Ȧ-hĭm′e-lĕch the son of [x]Ȧ-hī′tub.

10 And [w]he [y]enquired of the LORD for him, and gave him [z]victuals, and gave him the [a]sword of [b]Gō-lī′ath the Phĭ-lĭs′tīne.

11 ¶ Then the [c,d]king sent to call [e]Ȧ-hĭm′e-lĕch the [f]priest, the son of Ȧ-hī′tub, and all his father's house, the priests that *were* in [g]Nŏb: and they came all of them to the king.

12 And [c,d]Sa̤ul said, Hear now, thou son of Ȧ-hī′tub. And he answered, Here I *am*, my lord.

13 And [c,d]Sa̤ul [h]said unto him, Why have ye [i]conspired against me, [e]thou and the [j]son of Jĕs′se, in that thou hast given him bread, and a [a]sword, and hast enquired of God for him, that he should rise against me, to lie in wait, as at this day?

14 Then [e]Ȧ-hĭm′e-lĕch answered the [c]king, and said, And who *is so* faithful among all thy servants as [j]Dā′vid, which is the king's son in law, and [2]goeth at thy bidding, and is honourable in thine house?

15 Did I then begin to enquire of God for him? be it far from me: let not the king impute *any* thing unto his servant, *nor* to all the house of my father: for thy servant knew nothing of all this, less or more.

16 And the king [k,l]said, Thou shalt surely die, [e]Ȧ-hĭm′e-lĕch, thou, and all thy father's house.

17 And the king [k,l]said unto the [3]footmen that stood about him, Turn, and slay the [f]priests of the LORD; because their hand also *is* with [j]Dā′vid, and because they knew when he fled, and did not shew it to me. But the servants of the king would not put forth their hand to fall upon the priests of the LORD.

18 And the king [k,l]said to [m]Dō′eg, Turn thou, and fall upon the [f]priests. And Dō′eg the Ē′dom-īte turned, and he fell upon the priests, and slew on that day fourscore and five persons that did wear a linen [n]ephod.

19 And [g]Nŏb, the city of the [f]priests, [o]smote he with the edge of the sword, both men and women, children and sucklings, and oxen, and asses, and sheep, with the edge of the sword.

20 ¶ And one of the sons of [e]Ȧ-hĭm′e-lĕch the son of [p]Ȧ-hī′tub, named ‡Ȧ-bī′a-thär, escaped, and fled after [j]Dā′vid.

21 And ‡Ȧ-bī′a-thär shewed [j]Dā′vid that [c]Sa̤ul [k,l]had slain the LORD's [f]priests.

22 And [j]Dā′vid said unto ‡Ȧ-bī′a-thär, I knew *it* that day, when [m]Dō′eg the Ē′dom-īte *was* there, that he would surely tell [c]Sa̤ul: I have occasioned *the death* of all the persons of thy father's house.

23 [q]Abide thou with me, fear not: for he that seeketh my life seeketh thy life: but with me thou *shalt be* in safeguard.

## CHAPTER 23

*David rescues Keilah. 7 God shewing him the coming of Saul, and the treachery of the Keilites, he escapes from Keilah. 14 In Ziph Jonathan comforts him. 19 The Ziphites discover him to Saul. 25 At Maon he is rescued from Saul by the invasion of the Philistines. 29 He dwells at En-gedi.*

THEN they told [a]Dā′vid, saying, Behold, the [b]Phĭ-lĭs′tīne̤s [c]fight against *Kēi′lah,

---

*u Betrayal, of David*, Matt. 26:46.
*v Nob*, Neh. 11:32.
*w Ahimelech*, 1 Sam. 21:1.
*x* 1 Sam. 14:3.

**10**
*y Guidance, prayer for*, Psa. 48:14.
*z Food*, Psa. 136:25.

*a Sword*, 1 Chr. 21:5.
*b Goliath*, 1 Sam. 17:4.

**11**
*c Saul*, 1 Sam. 9:2.
*d King*, 2 Kin. 3:10.
*e Ahimelech*, 1 Sam. 21:1.
*f Priest*, Lev 1:5.
*g Nob*, Neh. 11:32.

**13**
*h False Accusation*, 2 Tim. 3:3.
*i Conspiracy*, 1 Kin. 16:9.
*j David*, 1 Sam. 16:13.

**14**
2 R. V. is taken into thy council,

**16**
*k Rulers, wicked, instances of*, Ex. 18:21.
*l Government, monarchical, tyranny in*, Isa. 22:21.

**17**
3 R. V. guard

**18**
*m Doeg*, 1 Sam. 21:7.
*n Ephod*, Ex. 28:6.

**19**
*o Cruelty, instances of*, Psa. 27:12.

**20**
*p* 1 Sam. 14:3.

**23**
*q Friendship, instances of*, Prov. 22:24.

**1**
*a David*, 1 Sam. 16:13.
*b Philistines*, Gen. 26:14.
*c War*, Judg. 3:2.

---

‡ **ABIATHAR,** high priest. *Called, apparently by error,* AHIMELECH 1 Chr. 24:3, 6, 31; *and* ABIMELECH, 1 Chr. 18:16. *Apparently, by error, the father of, while, in fact, he was the son of, Ahimelech*, 2 Sam. 8:17; *or Abimelech*, 1 Chr. 18:16. *Son of Ahimelech*, 1 Sam. 22:20. *Escapes to David from the vengeance of Saul, who slew the priests in the city of Nob*, 1 Sam. 22:20–23 (with vs. 6–19). *Consults the ephod for David*, 1 Sam, 23:9–12; 30:7, 8. *Associate high priest with Zadok in the reign of David*, 2 Sam 15:35; 20:25; 1 Kin. 4:4; 1 Chr. 15:11. *Loyal to David when Absalom rebelled; leaves Jerusalem with the ark of the covenant, but is directed by David to return with the ark*, 2 Sam. 15:24–29. *Aids David by sending his son from Jerusalem to David with secret information concerning the counsel of Ahithophel*, 2 Sam. 15:35, 36; 17:15–22; 1 Kin. 2:26. *Supports Adonijah's pretensions to the throne*, 1 Kin. 1:7. *Thrust out of office by Solomon*, 1 Kin. 2:26, 27, with 1 Sam. 2:31–35

* **KEILAH** (*fortress*). *One of a group of nine cities in the*

and they [d]rob the [e]threshing-
floors.
2 Therefore [a]Dā'vid [f,g]enquir-
ed of the LORD, saying,
Shall I go and smite these [b]Phĭ-
lĭs'tīneṣ? And the LORD said
unto Dā'vid, Go, and smite the
Phĭ-lĭs'tīneṣ, and save *Kē'i'lah.
3 And Dā'vid's men said unto
him, Behold, we be afraid here
in [h]Jū'dah: how much more then
if we come to *Kē'i'lah against
the armies of the Phĭ-lĭs'tīneṣ?
4 Then Dā'vid [f,g]enquired of
the LORD yet again. And the
LORD answered him and said,
Arise, go down to *Kē'i'lah; for
I will [i]deliver the [b]Phĭ-lĭs'tīneṣ
into thine hand.
5 So [a]Dā'vid and his men went
to *Kē'i'lah, and fought with the
[b]Phĭ-lĭs'tīneṣ, and brought away
their [j]cattle, and smote them
with a great slaughter. So Dā'-
vid saved the inhabitants of
Kē'i'lah.
6 And it came to pass, when
[k]Ā-bī'a-thär the son of [l]Ā-hĭm'-
e-lĕch fled to Dā'vid to Kē'i'lah,
*that* he came down *with* an
[m]ephod in his hand.
7 ¶ And it was told [n]Saul that
[a]Dā'vid was come to *Kē'i'lah.
And Saul [o]said, God hath delivered him into mine hand; for he
is shut in, by entering into a
town that hath [p]gates and bars.
8 And [n]Saul called all the people together to [c]war, to go down
to *Kē'i'lah, to besiege Dā'vid
and his men.
9 And [a]Dā'vid knew that [n]Saul
[1]secretly practised mischief
against him; and he said to
[k]Ā-bī'a-thär the priest, Bring
hither the [m]ephod.
10 Then [g]said [a]Dā'vid, O
LORD God of Ĭṣ'ra-el, thy servant hath certainly heard that
Saul seeketh to come to Kē'i'lah,
to destroy the city for my sake.
11 Will the men of *Kē'i'lah deliver me up into his hand? will
Saul come down, as thy servant
hath heard? O LORD God of
Ĭṣ'ra-el, I beseech thee, tell thy
servant. And the [q]LORD [r]said,
He will come down.
12 Then said Dā'vid, Will the
men of *Kē'i'lah deliver me and
my men into the hand of Saul?
And the [q]LORD [r]said, [s]They
will deliver *thee* up.
13 Then [a]Dā'vid and his men,
*which were* about six hundred,
arose and departed out of *Kē'i'-
lah, and went whithersoever they
could go. And it was told [n]Saul
that Dā'vid was escaped from
Kē'i'lah; and he forbare to go
forth.
14 And [a]Dā'vid abode in the
wilderness in strong holds, and
remained in a mountain in the
wilderness of [t]Zĭph. And [n]Saul
[o]sought him every day, but God
[u]delivered him not into his hand.
15 And [a]Dā'vid saw that [n]Saul
was come out to seek his life:
and Dā'vid *was* in the wilderness of [t]Zĭph in a wood.
16 ¶ And [v]Jŏn'a-than Saul's
son arose, and [w]went to [a]Dā'vid
into the wood, and strengthened
his hand in God.
17 And [v]he said unto him, Fear
not: for the hand of Saul my
father shall not find thee; and
[x]thou shalt be king over Ĭṣ'ra-el,
and I shall be next unto thee;
and that also Saul my father
knoweth.
18 And they two made a [y]cove-
nant before the LORD: and Dā-
vid abode in the wood, and
[v]Jŏn'a-than went to his house.
19 ¶ Then came up the Zĭph'-
ītes to Saul to [z]Gĭb'e-ah, saying,
Doth not [a]Dā'vid hide himself
with us in strong holds in the

d *Theft*, Mark 7:22.
e *Threshing*, 1 Chr. 21:20.
2
f *Armies, religious ceremonies in*, Deut. 11:4.
g *Guidance, prayer for*, Psa. 48:14.
3
h *Judah, tribe of*, Num. 10:14.
4
i *God, providence of*, Gen. 2:2.
5
j *Spoils*, 1 Chr. 26:27.
6
k *Abiathar*, 1 Sam. 22:20.
l *Ahimelech*, 1 Sam. 21:1.
m *Ephod*, Ex. 28:6.
7
n *Saul*, 1 Sam. 9.2.
o *Malice, instances of*, Eph. 4:31.
p *Gates*, Deut. 3:5.
9
1 R. V. devised
11
q *God, foreknowledge of*, Gen. 2:2.
r *Prayer, answered*, vs. 10–12; Acts 6:4.
12
s *Ingratitude, of man to man*, Rom. 1:21.
14
t 1 Sam. 26:2.
u *God, preserver*, Gen. 2:2.
16
v *Jonathan*, 1 Sam 14:1.
w *Friendship, instances of*, Prov. 22:24.
17
x *Unselfishness, instances of*, 1 Cor. 10:24.
18
y *Covenant, of men with men*, Deut. 29:1.
19
z *Gibeah*, Hos. 9:9.
a *David*, 1 Sam. 16:13.

*southern part of Palestine allotted to Judah*, Josh. 15:44. *Philistines make a predatory excursion against. after harvest*, 1 Sam. 23:1. *David rescues*, 1 Sam. 23:2–13. *Rulers of, aid in restoring the wall of Jerusalem after the captivity*, Neh. 3:17, 18.

wood, in the hill of [b]Hăch′i-lah, which *is* on the south of [2,c]Jĕsh′-i-mŏn?

20 Now therefore, O king, come down according to all the desire of thy soul to come down; and our part *shall be* to deliver him into the king's hand.

21 And [d]Saul said, Blessed *be* ye of the LORD; for ye have compassion on me.

22 [e]Go, I pray you, [3]prepare yet, and know and see his place where his haunt is, *and* who hath seen him there: for it is told me *that* he dealeth very subtilly.

23 [e]See therefore, and take knowledge of all the lurking places where he hideth himself, and come ye again to me with the certainty, and I will go with you: and it shall come to pass, if he be in the land, that I will search him out throughout all the thousands of [f]Jū′dah.

24 And they arose, and went to [g]Zĭph before [d]Saul: but [a]Dā′vid and his men *were* in the wilderness of Mā′on, in the [4]plain on the south of [2,c]Jĕsh′i-mŏn.

25 [d]Saul also and his men went to seek *him*. And they told [a]Dā′vid: wherefore he came down into a rock, and abode in the wilderness of Mā′on. And when Saul heard *that*, he pursued after Dā′vid in the wilderness of Mā′on.

26 And [d]Saul went on this side of the mountain, and [a]Dā′vid and his men on that side of the mountain: and Dā′vid made haste to get away for fear of Saul; for Saul and his men compassed Dā′vid and his men round about to take them.

27 ¶ But there came a messenger unto Saul, saying, Haste thee, and come; for the [h]Phĭ-lĭs′tĭnes have invaded the land.

28 Wherefore [d]Saul returned from pursuing after [a]Dā′vid, and went against the [h]Phĭ-lĭs′tĭnes: therefore they called that place Sē′lȧ–hăm-mah-lē′koth.

29 ¶ And [a]Dā′vid went up from thence, and dwelt in strong holds at [i]Ĕn–gē′dī.

## CHAPTER 24

*David in a cave at En-gedi cuts off Saul's skirt but spares his life. 8 He shews thereby his innocency. 16 Saul, acknowledging his fault, takes an oath of David, and departs.*

AND it came to pass, when [a]Saul was returned from following the [b]Phĭ-lĭs′tĭnes, that it was told him, saying, Behold, [c]Dā′vid *is* in the wilderness of [d]Ĕn–gē′dī.

2 Then [a]Saul took three thousand chosen men out of all [e]Iṣ′ra-el, and went to seek [c]Dā′vid and his men upon the rocks of the wild [f]goats.

3 And he came to the sheepcotes by the way, where *was* a [g]cave; and [a]Saul went in to cover his feet: and [c]Dā′vid and his men [1]remained in the sides of the cave.

4 And the men of [c]Dā′vid said unto him, Behold the day of which the LORD said unto thee, Behold, I will deliver thine enemy into thine hand, that thou mayest do to him as it shall seem good unto thee. Then Dā′vid arose, and cut off the skirt of [a]Saul's robe privily.

5 And it came to pass afterward, that [c]Dā′vid's [h,i]heart smote him, because he had cut off Saul's skirt.

6 And [j]he said unto his men, [k]The LORD forbid that I should do this thing unto my master, the LORD's anointed, to stretch forth mine hand against him, seeing he *is* the anointed of the LORD.

7 So [l]Dā′vid stayed his servants with these words, and suffered them not to rise against [a]Saul. But Saul rose up out

b 1 Sam. 26:1, 3.
c 1 Sam. 26:1.
2 R. V. the desert?

21
d *Saul*, 1 Sam. 9:2.

22
e *Malice, instances of*, Eph. 4:31.
3 R. V. make yet more sure,

23
f *Judah, tribe of*, Num. 10:14.

24
g 1 Sam. 26:2.
4 R. V. Arabah

27
h *Philistines*, Gen. 26:14.

29
i *En-gedi*, 2 Chr. 20:2.

1
a *Saul*, 1 Sam. 9:2
b *Philistines*, Gen. 26:14.
c *David*, 1 Sam. 16:13.
d *En-gedi*, 2 Chr. 20:2.

2
e *Israel, under the kings*, Ex. 4:22.
f *Goat*, Deut. 14:4.

3
g *Cave, of En-gedi*, Judg. 6:2.
1 R. V. were abiding in the innermost parts

5
h *Heart*, Psa. 44:21.
i *Conscience, guilty*, Acts 23:1.

6
j *Citizens, loyal*, Luke 15:15.
k *Loyalty, instances of*, Eccl. 8:2.

7
l *David, meekness of*, 1 Sam. 16:13.

of the [g]cave, and went on *his* way.

8 ¶ [c]Dā′vid also arose afterward, and went out of the [g]cave, and cried after [a]Sa̤ul, saying, [m]My lord the king. And when Sa̤ul looked behind him, Dā′vid stooped with his face to the earth, and bowed himself.

9 And [c]Dā′vid said to [a]Sa̤ul, Wherefore hearest thou men's [n]words, saying, Behold, Dā′vid seeketh thy hurt?

10 Behold, this day thine eyes have seen how that the LORD had delivered thee to day into mine hand in the [g]cave: and *some* bade *me* kill thee: but *mine eye* [o]spared [p]thee; and [l]I said, I will not put forth mine hand against my lord; for he *is* the LORD's anointed.

11 Moreover, my father, see, yea, see the skirt of thy robe in my hand: for in that I cut off the skirt of thy robe, and [s]killed thee not, know thou and see that *there is* neither evil nor transgression in mine hand, and I have not sinned against thee; yet thou huntest my soul to take it.

12 The LORD [q]judge between me and thee, and the LORD avenge me of thee: but mine hand shall not be upon thee.

13 As saith the *proverb of the ancients, Wickedness proceedeth from the [r]wicked: but mine hand shall not be upon thee.

14 [s]After whom is the king of Is̤′ra-el come out? after whom dost thou pursue? after a dead [t]dog, after a [u]flea.

15 The LORD therefore be [q]judge, and judge between me and thee, and see, and plead my cause, and [v]deliver me out of thine hand.

16 ¶ And it came to pass, when

8
*m Salutations*, Luke 1:44.

9
*n Slander*, Prov. 10:18.

10
*o Good, for evil*, Luke 6:27.
*p Enemy, forgiveness of*, Prov. 24: 17.

12
*q God, judge*, Gen. 2:2.

13
*r Wicked*, Psa. 73:3.

14
*s Humility, instances of*, Prov. 22:4.
*t Dog*, 1 Kin. 21: 19.
*u* 1 Sam. 26:20.

15
*v God, providence of*, Gen. 2:2.

[l]Dā′vid had made an end of speaking these words unto [a]Sa̤ul, that Sa̤ul said, *Is* this thy voice, my son Dā′vid? And Sa̤ul lifted up his voice, and wept.

17 And he said to Dā′vid, Thou *art* more righteous than I: for thou hast rewarded me [o]good, [w]whereas I have rewarded thee evil.

18 And thou hast shewed this day how that thou hast [o]dealt well with me: forasmuch as when the LORD had delivered me into thine hand, thou [o]killedst me not.

19 For if a man find his enemy, [p]will he let him go well away? wherefore the LORD reward thee good for that thou hast done unto me this day.

20 And now, behold, I know well that thou shalt surely be king, and that the kingdom of Is̤′ra-el shall be established in thine hand.

21 [x]Swear now therefore unto me by the LORD, that thou wilt not cut off my seed after me, and that thou wilt not destroy my name out of my father's house.

22 And Dā′vid [x]sware unto Sa̤ul. And Sa̤ul went home; but Dā′vid and his men gat them up unto the hold.

## CHAPTER 25

*Samuel dies. 2 David's message to Nabal; 10 Nabal's churlish answer provokes him. 14 Abigail by her wisdom pacifies David. 36 Nabal's death. 39 David takes Abigail and Ahinoam to be his wives. 44 Michal is given to Phalti.*

AND [a]Săm′u-el died; and all the Is̤′ra-el-ītes were gathered together, and [b]lamented him, and [c]buried him in his house at [d]Rā′mah. And [e]Dā′vid arose, and went down to the wilderness of [f]Pā′ran.

2 And *there was* a man in [g]Mā′on, whose possessions *were* in [h]Cär′mel; and the man *was* very

17
*w Ingratitude*, Rom. 1:21.

21
*x Oath*, Num. 5:19

1
*a Samuel*, 1 Sam. 3:1.
*b Mourning*, Lam. 2:5.
*c Burying Places*, Gen. 23:4.
*d Ramah*, 1 Sam. 1:19.
*e David*, 1 Sam. 16:13.
*f Paran*, Gen. 21: 21.

2
*g Maon*, Josh. 15: 55.
*h Carmel*, 2 Chr. 26:10.

* **PROVERBS**, 1 Sam. 10:12; 24:13, 14; 2 Sam. 3:8; 20: 18; 1 Kin. 20:11; Prov. 1:17; Ezek. 12:22, 23; 16:44; 18:2, 3 (with Jer. 31:29), 4; Hos. 4:9, Matt. 12:33 (with Luke 6:44); Luke 4:23; 14:34; John 1:46; 1 Cor. 15:33; Gal. 6:7. *Design of*, Prov. 1:1–4. *Written by Solomon*, Prov. 1:1; 25:1. See the BOOK OF PROVERBS.

great, and he had three thousand
[i]sheep, and a thousand [j]goats:
and he was shearing his sheep in
Cär′mel.
3 Now the name of the man *was*
Nā′bal; and the name of his wife
*Ăb′ĭ-gail: and *she was* a woman
of [k]good understanding, and of a
[l]beautiful countenance: but the
man *was* churlish and evil in his
doings; and he *was* of the house
of [m]Cā′leb.
4 And [e]Dā′vid heard in the
wilderness that Nā′bal did shear
his sheep.
5 And Dā′vid sent out ten
young men, and Dā′vid said unto the young men, Get you up to
[h]Cär′mel, and go to Nā′bal, and
greet him in my name:
6 And thus shall ye say to him
that liveth *in prosperity*, [n]Peace
*be* both to thee, and peace *be* to
thine house, and peace *be* unto
all that thou hast.
7 And now I have heard that
thou hast shearers: now thy
shepherds which were with us,
we hurt them not, neither was
there ought missing unto them,
all the while they were in [h]Cär′-
mel.
8 Ask thy young men, and they
will shew thee. Wherefore let the
young men find favour in thine
eyes: for we come in a good day:
give, I pray thee, whatsoever
cometh to thine hand unto thy
servants, and to thy son [e]Dā′vid.
9 And when [e]Dā′vid's young
men came, they spake to Nā′bal
according to all those words in
the name of Dā′vid, and ceased.
10 And Nā′bal answered [e]Dā′-
vid's servants, and said, Who *is*
Dā′vid? and who *is* the son of
[o]Jĕs′se? there be many servants
now a days that break away
every man from his master.

*i* *Sheep*, Deut. 32:14.
*j* *Goat*, Deut. 14:4.

3
*k* *Tact*, Prov. 15:1.
*l* *Beauty, instances of*, Prov. 6:25.
*m* *Caleb*, Num. 14:6.

6
*n* *Salutations*, Luke 1:44.

10
*o* ***Jesse***, Ruth 4:17.

11 Shall I then take my bread,
and my water, and my flesh that
I have killed for my shearers,
and give *it* unto men, whom I
know not whence they *be*?
12 So [e]Dā′vid's young men
turned their way, and went
again, and came and told him
all those sayings.
13 And [e]Dā′vid said unto his
men, Gird ye on every man his
sword. And they girded on every
man his sword; and Dā′vid also
girded on his sword: and there
went up after Dā′vid about four
hundred men; and two hundred
abode by the stuff.
14 ¶ But one of the young
[p]men told *Ăb′ĭ-gail, Nā′bal's
wife, saying, Behold, [e]Dā′vid
sent messengers out of the wilderness to salute our master;
and he railed on them.
15 But the men *were* very good
unto us, and we were not hurt,
[r]neither missed we any thing, as
long as we were conversant with
them, when we were in the fields:
16 They were a wall unto us
both by night and day, all the
while we were with them keeping the sheep.
17 Now therefore know and
consider what thou wilt do; for
evil is determined against our
master, and against all his
household: for he *is such* a son
of Bē′lĭ-ăl, that *a man* cannot
speak to him.
18 [s,t]Then *Ăb′ĭ-gail made
haste, and took two hundred
[u]loaves, and two bottles of [v]wine,
and five [w]sheep ready dressed,
and five [x]measures of parched
[y]*corn*, and an hundred clusters
of †raisins, and two hundred
cakes of [z]figs, and laid *them* on
asses.
19 And she said unto her [1]serv-

14
*p* *Young Men*, Prov. 1:4.
*q* *Servant, good, instances of*, Jer. 2:14.

15
*r* *Integrity, instances of*, Job 2:3.

18
*s* *Tact, of Nabal's wife*, Prov. 15:1.
*t* *Diplomacy, instances of*, 2 Kin. 16:7.
*u* *Bread*, Ezek. 4:13.
*v* *Wine*, Prov. 23:31.
*w* *Sheep*, Deut. 32:14.
*x* *Measure, dry*, Deut. 25:15.
*y* *Corn, parched*, Psa. 65:13.
*z* *Fig*, Mark 11:13.

19
1 R. V. young men,

* **ABIGAIL** (*exaltation*), Nabal's wife. *Her wisdom and tact, and marriage to David*, 1 Sam. 25; 27:3; 2 Sam. 2:2. *Mother of Chileab by David*, 2 Sam. 3:3; 1 Chr. 3:1. *Taken captive and rescued by David*, 1 Sam. 30:5–18.

† **RAISINS.** *Given by Abigail to David*, 1 Sam. 25:18. *Given to the famishing Egyptian to revive him*, 1 Sam. 30:12. *Given by Ziba to David*, 2 Sam. 16:1. ***Given to David at Ziklag***, 1 Chr. 12:40.

**20**
a *David,* 1 Sam. 16:13.

**21**
b *Ingratitude, of man to man,* Rom. 1:21.
c *Evil for Good, instances of,* Psa. 35:12.

**22**
d *Oath,* Num. 5:19.
e *Revenge,* Ezek. 25:15.
2 R. V. so much as one man child.

**23**
f *Diplomacy, instances of,* vs. 23–31; 2 Kin. 16:7.
g *Salutations,* Luke 1:44.

**24**
h *Intercession, of man with man, instances of,* Jer. 27:18.
i *Punishment, assumed for others,* Lev. 26:41.

**26**
3 R. V. bloodguiltiness,

ants, Go on before me; behold,
I come after you. But she told
not her husband Nā'bal.
20 And it was *so, as* she rode on
the ass, that she came down by
the covert of the hill, and, behold, [a]Dā'vid and his men came
down against her; and she met
them.
21 Now [a]Dā'vid had said, Surely in vain have I kept all that
this *fellow* hath in the wilderness, so that nothing was
missed of all that *pertained* unto him: and he [b]hath requited
me [c]evil for good.
22 [d]So and more also do God
unto the enemies of Dā'vid, [e]if
I leave of all that *pertain* to him
by the morning light [2]any that
pisseth against the wall.
23 And when *Ăb'ĭ-gail saw
[a]Dā'vid, [f]she hasted, and lighted
off the ass, and [g]fell before Dā'-
vid on her face, and bowed herself to the ground.
24 And fell at his feet, and
[h]said, ‡Upon me, my lord, [i]*upon*
me *let this* iniquity *be*: and let
thine handmaid, I pray thee,
speak in thine audience, and hear
the words of thine handmaid.
25 [h]Let not my lord, I pray
thee, regard this man of Bē'lĭ-al,
*even* Nā'bal: for as his name *is*,
so *is* he; Nā'bal *is* his name, and
folly *is* with him: but I thine
handmaid saw not the young
men of my lord, whom thou
didst send.
26 [j]Now therefore, my lord, *as*
the LORD liveth, and *as* thy soul
liveth, seeing the LORD hath
withholden thee from [3]coming to
*shed* blood, and from avenging
thyself with thine own hand,
now let thine enemies, and they
that seek evil to my lord, be as
Nā'bal.
27 [j]And now this [4,j]blessing
which thine handmaid hath
brought unto my lord, let it even
be given unto the young men
that follow my lord.
28 I pray thee, forgive the trespass of thine handmaid: [j,k]for
the LORD will certainly make
my lord a sure house; because
my lord fighteth the battles of
the LORD, and evil hath not
been found in thee *all* thy days.
29 [k]Yet a man is risen to pursue
thee, and to seek thy soul: but
the soul of my lord shall be
bound in the bundle of life with
the LORD thy God; and the
souls of thine enemies, them
shall he sling out, *as out* of the
middle of a sling.
30 [k]And it shall come to pass,
when the LORD shall have done
to my lord according to all the
good that he hath spoken concerning thee, and shall have [l]ap-
pointed thee ruler over Ĭş'ra-el;
31 That this shall be no grief
unto thee, nor offence of heart
unto my lord, either that thou
hast shed blood causeless, or
that my lord hath avenged himself: but when the LORD shall
have dealt well with my lord,
then remember thine handmaid.
32 ¶ And [a]Dā'vid said to *Ăb'ĭ-
gail, Blessed be the LORD God
of Ĭş'ra-el, which sent thee this
day to meet me:
33 And blessed *be* thy advice,
and blessed *be* thou, which hast
kept me this day from [5]coming
to *shed* blood, and from avenging myself with mine own hand.
34 For in very deed, *as* the
LORD God of Ĭş'ra-el liveth,
which hath kept me back from
hurting thee, except thou hadst
hasted and come to meet me,
surely there had not been left un-

**27**
j *Presents, propitiatory,* Gen. 32:13.
4 R. V. present

**28**
k *Tact, of Nabal's wife,* Prov. 15:1.

**30**
l *Government, God in,* Isa. 22:21.

**33**
5 R. V. bloodguiltiness.

‡ **PENALTY. Vicariously assumed:** *By Rebekah,* Gen. 27:13. *By Abigail,* 1 Sam. 25:24. *By the woman of Tekoa,* 2 Sam. 14:9. *By the persecutors of Jesus,* Matt. 27:25. *By Jesus for the human race,* Gal. 3:13. *Paul desires to assume, for Israel,* Rom. 9:3.

See footnote, VICARIOUS SUFFERING, Rom. 9:3.
For a study of Penalties see the scriptures under each crime, as, for the penalties for Arson, see the footnote, ARSON, etc.
See footnote, PUNISHMENT, Lev. 26:41.

to Nā′bal by the morning light [6]any that pisseth against the wall.

35 So Dā′vid received of her hand [j]*that* which she had brought him, and said unto her, Go up in peace to thine house; see, I have hearkened to thy voice, and have accepted thy person.

36 ¶ And *Ăb′ĭ-gail came to Nā′bal; and, behold, he held a [m]feast in his house, like the feast of a king; and Nā′bal's heart *was* merry within him, for he *was* very [n]drunken: wherefore she told him nothing, less or more, until the morning light.

37 But it came to pass in the morning, when the [n]wine was gone out of Nā′bal, and his wife had told him these things, that his heart died within him, and he became *as* a stone.

38 And it came to pass about ten days *after*, that the LORD [o]smote Nā′bal, that he [p]died.

39 And when [a]Dā′vid heard that Nā′bal was dead, he said, Blessed *be* the LORD, that hath pleaded the cause of my reproach from the hand of Nā′bal, and hath kept his servant from evil: for the LORD hath returned the wickedness of Nā′bal upon his own head. And Dā′vid sent and [7]communed with *Ăb′ĭ-gail, to take her to him to wife.

40 And when the servants of Dā′vid were come to *Ăb′ĭ-gail to [q]Cär′mel, they spake unto her, saying, [a]Dā′vid sent us unto thee, to take thee to him to wife.

41 And she arose, and [g]bowed herself on *her* face to the earth, and said, Behold, *let* thine handmaid *be* a servant to [r]wash the feet of the servants of my lord.

42 And *Ăb′ĭ-gail hasted, and arose, and rode upon an ass, with five damsels of her's that went after her; and she went after the messengers of Dā′vid, and became his wife.

43 [a]Dā′vid also took ‖Ā-hĭn′-o-ăm of [s]Jĕz′re-el; and [t]they were also both of them his wives.

44 But [u]Saul had given [v]Mī′-chal his daughter, Dā′vid's wife, to [w]Phăl′tī the son of [x]Lā′ish, which *was* of [y]Găl′lim.

## CHAPTER 26

*Saul, upon the information of the Ziphites, pursues David. 5 David stays Abishai from killing Saul, but takes his spear and cruse. 13 David reproves Abner, 18 and exhorts Saul. 21 Saul acknowledges his sin.*

AND the Zĭph′ītes came unto [a]Saul to [b]Gĭb′e-ah, saying, Doth not [c]Dā′vid hide himself in the hill of [d]Hăch′i-lah, *which is* before [1,e]Jĕsh′i-mŏn?

2 [f]Then [a]Saul arose, and went down to the wilderness of [g]Zĭph, having three thousand chosen [h]men of Ĭs′ra-el with him, to seek [c]Dā′vid in the wilderness of Zĭph.

3 And [a]Saul pitched in the hill of [d]Hăch′i-lah, which *is* before [e]Jĕsh′i-mŏn, by the way. But [c]Dā′vid abode in the wilderness, and he saw that Saul came after him into the wilderness.

4 [c]Dā′vid therefore sent out [i]spies, and understood that [a]Saul was come in very deed.

5 ¶ And [c]Dā′vid arose, and came to the place where [a]Saul had pitched: and Dā′vid beheld the place where Saul lay, and [j]Ăb′nēr the son of [k]Nēr, the captain of his host: and Saul lay [2]in the trench, and the people pitched round about him.

6 Then answered [c]Dā′vid and said to Ā-hĭm′e-lĕch the [l]Hĭt′-tīte, and to [m]Ā-bĭsh′a-ī the son of Zĕr-u-ī′ah, brother to [n]Jō′ăb, saying, Who will go down with me to [a]Saul to the camp? And

**34**
6 R. V. so much as one man child.

**36**
*m* *Feasts,* Mark 12: 39.
*n* *Drunkenness, instances of,* Luke 21:34.

**38**
*o* *Disease, sent from God,* Ex. 15:26.
*p* *Death, of the wicked, a judgment,* Num. 23: 10.

**39**
7 R. V. spake concerning

**40**
*q* *Carmel,* 2 Chr. 26:10.

**41**
*r* *Ablution, of the feet,* Judg. 19:21.

**43**
*s* Josh. 15:56.
*t* *Polygamy,* Deut. 17:17.

**44**
*u* *Saul,* 1 Sam. 9:2.
*v* *Michal,* 1 Sam. 18:20.
*w* Or, *Phaltiel,* 2 Sam. 3:15, 16.
*x* 2 Sam. 3:15.
*y* Isa. 10:30.

**1**
*a* *Saul,* 1 Sam. 9:2
*b* *Gibeah,* Hos. 9:9.
*c* *David,* 1 Sam. 16:13.
*d* 1 Sam. 23:19.
*e* 1 Sam. 23:19, 24
1 R. V. the desert?

**2**
*f* *Malice,* Eph. 4:31.
*g* 1 Sam. 23:14, 15 24.
*h* *Armies,* Deut. 11:4.

**4**
*i* *Spies,* Josh. 6:23.

**5**
*j* *Abner,* 1 Sam. 14:50.
*k* 1 Sam. 14:50; 1 Chr. 8:33; 9:39
2 R. V. within the place of the wagons,

**6**
*l* *Hittites,* Judg. 1:26.
*m* *Abishai,* 2 Sam. 3:30.
*n* *Joab,* 2 Sam. 20: 23.

‖ **AHINOAM** (*pleasant*). *One of the wives of David,* 1 Sam. 25:43; 27:3; 2 Sam. 3:2. *Taken captive by the Amalekites,* 1 Sam. 30:5, 18.

Ȧ-bĭsh'a-ī said, I will go down with thee.

7 [o]So [c]Dā'vid and [m]Ȧ-bĭsh'a-ī came to the people by night: and, behold, [a]Saul lay sleeping [2]within the trench, and his [p]spear stuck in the ground at his [q]bolster: but [j]Ab'nēr and the people lay round about him.

8 Then said [m]Ȧ-bĭsh'a-ī to Dā'vid, God hath delivered thine [r]enemy into thine hand this day: now therefore let me smite him, I pray thee, with the [p]spear even to the earth at once, and I will not *smite* him the second time.

9 And [c,s]Dā'vid said to [m]Ȧ-bĭsh-a-ī, [t,u,v]Destroy him not: for who can stretch forth his hand against the LORD's anointed, and be guiltless?

10 [c]Dā'vid said furthermore, *As* the LORD liveth, the LORD shall smite him; or his day shall come to [w]die; or he shall descend into battle, and perish.

11 [x]The LORD forbid that [y]I should stretch forth mine hand against the LORD's anointed: but, I pray thee, take thou now the spear that *is* at his bolster, and the *cruse of water, and let us go.

12 So [c]Dā'vid took the [p]spear and the *cruse of water from Saul's [q]bolster; and they gat them away, and no man saw *it*, nor knew *it*, neither awaked: for they *were* all [z]asleep; because a deep sleep from the LORD was fallen upon them.

13 ¶ Then [a]Dā'vid went over to the other side, and stood on the top of an hill afar off; a great space *being* between them:

14 And Dā'vid cried to the people, and to [b]Ăb'nēr the son of [c]Nēr, saying, Answerest thou not, Ăb'nēr? Then Ăb'nēr answered and said, Who *art* thou *that* criest to the [d]king?

15 And [a]Dā'vid said to [b]Ăb'nēr, *Art* not thou a *valiant* man? and who *is* like to thee in Ĭṣ'ra-el? wherefore then hast thou not kept thy lord the [d]king? for there came one of the people in to destroy the king thy lord.

16 This thing *is* not good that thou hast done. *As* the LORD liveth, ye *are* worthy to die, because ye have not kept your master, the LORD's anointed. And now see where the king's [e]spear *is*, and the *cruse of water that *was* at his [f]bolster.

17 And [g]Saul knew [a]Dā'vid's voice, and said, *Is* this thy voice, my son Dā'vid? And Dā'vid said, *It is* my voice, my lord, O king.

18 And he said, Wherefore doth my lord [h]thus pursue after his servant? for what have I done? or what evil *is* in mine hand?

19 Now therefore, I pray thee, let my lord the king hear the words of his servant. If the LORD have stirred thee up against me, let him accept an offering: but if *they be* the children of men, cursed *be* they before the LORD: for they have driven me out this day from abiding in the inheritance of the LORD, saying, Go, serve other gods.

20 Now therefore, let not my blood fall to the earth [3]before the face of the LORD: for the king of Ĭṣ'ra-el is come out to seek a [i]flea, as when one doth [j]hunt a [k]partridge in the mountains.

21 ¶ Then said [g]Saul, [l]I have sinned: return, my son [a]Dā'vid: for I will no more do thee harm, because my [4]soul was precious in thine eyes this day: behold, I have played the fool, and have erred exceedingly.

7
o *Courage, instances of*, Deut. 31:7.
p *Spear*, 2 Kin. 11:10.
q 1 Sam. 19:13.

8
r *Enemy*, Prov. 24:17.

9
s *Citizens, loyal, instance of*, Luke 15:15.
t *Forgiveness, instances of*, Matt. 18:21.
u *Good for Evil, instances of*, Luke 6:27.
v *Temptation, resistance to*, Luke 11:4.

10
w *Death*, Num. 23:10.

11
x *Loyalty, instances of*, Eccl. 8:2.
y *David, meekness of*, 1 Sam. 16:13.

12
z *Sleep*, Psa. 127:2.

13
a *David*, 1 Sam. 16:13.

14
b *Abner*, 1 Sam. 14:50.
c 1 Sam. 14:50; 1 Chr. 8:33; 9:39.

d *King*, 2 Kin. 3:10.

16
e *Spear*, 2 Kin. 11:10.
f 1 Sam. 19:13.

17
g *Saul*, 1 Sam. 9:2.

18
h *Malice, instances of*, Eph. 4:31.

20
i 1 Sam. 24:14.
j *Hunting, fowling*, Gen. 27:5.
k Jer. 17:11.
3 R. V. away from the presence of the Lord:

21
l *Sin, confession of*, Rom. 5:12.
4 R. V. life

***CRUSE.** *A vessel for liquids*, 1 Sam. 26:11; 1 Kin. 14:3; 2 Kin. 2:20; Matt. 26:7; Mark 14:3; Luke 7:37.

22 And [a]Dā′vid answered and said, Behold the king's [e]spear! and let one of the young men come over and fetch it.

23 The LORD [5,m]render to every man his righteousness and his faithfulness: for the LORD delivered [n]thee into *my* hand to day, but I would not stretch forth mine hand against the LORD's anointed.

24 And, behold, as thy life was much set[G] by this day in mine eyes, so let my life be much set by in the eyes of the LORD, and let him [o]deliver me out of all [p]tribulation.

25 Then [g]Saul said to Dā′vid, [q]Blessed *be* thou, my son Dā′vid: thou shalt both do great *things*, and also shalt still prevail. So Dā′vid went on his way, and Saul returned to his place.

## CHAPTER 27

*David flees to Gath, and Saul seeks no more for him. 5 Achish gives Ziklag to David. 8 He deceives Achish.*

AND [a]Dā′vid said in his heart, I shall now perish one day by the hand[G] of [b]Saul: [c]*there is* nothing better for me than that I should speedily escape into the land of the [d]Phĭ-lĭs′tĭneș; and Saul shall despair of me, to seek me any more in [1]any coast[G] of Ĭș′ra-el: so shall I escape out of his hand.[G]

2 And [a]Dā′vid arose, and he passed over with the six hundred men that *were* with him unto [e]Ā′chish, the son of Mā′ŏch, king of [f]Găth.

3 And [a]Dā′vid dwelt with [e]Ā′chish at [f]Găth, he and his men, every man with his household, *even* Dā′vid with his [g]two wives, [h]Ă-hĭn′o-ăm the Jĕz′re-el-ĭt-ess, and [i]Ăb′ĭ-gail the Cär′mel-ĭt-ess, Nā′bal's wife.

4 And it was told [b]Saul that [a]Dā′vid was fled to [f]Găth: and he sought no more again for him.

5 ¶ And [a]Dā′vid said unto [e]Ā′chish, If I have now found grace in thine eyes, let them give me a place in some town in the country, that I may dwell there: for why should thy servant dwell in the royal [j]city with thee?

6 Then [e]Ā′chish gave him [k]Zĭk′lăg that day: wherefore Zĭk′lăg pertaineth unto the kings of Jū′dah unto this day.

7 And the time that [a]Dā′vid dwelt in the country of the [d]Phĭ-lĭs′tĭneș was a full year and four months.

8 ¶ And [a]Dā′vid and his men went up, and invaded the [l]Gĕsh′u-rītes, and the [m]Gĕz′rītes, and the [n]Ăm′a-lĕk-ītes: for those *nations were* of old the inhabitants of the land, as thou goest to [o]Shûr, even unto the land of [p]Ē′ġўpt.

9 And [a]Dā′vid smote[G] the land, and left [q]neither man nor woman alive, and took away the [r]sheep, and the oxen, and the asses, and the camels, and the apparel, and returned, and came to Ā′chish.

10 And [e]Ā′chish said, Whither[G] have ye made[G] a road[G] to day? And Dā′vid [s,t]said, Against the south of [u]Jū′dah, and against the south of the Jĕ-răh′me-el-ītes, and against the south of the Kĕn′ītes.

11 And [a]Dā′vid saved neither [v]man nor woman alive, to bring *tidings* to [f]Găth, saying, Lest they should tell on[G] us, saying, So did Dā′vid, and so *will be* his manner all the while he dwelleth in the country of the [d]Phĭ-lĭs′-tĭneș.

12 And [e]Ā′chish believed [a]Dā′vid, saying, He hath made his people Ĭș′ra-el utterly to abhor him; therefore he shall be my servant for ever.

**23**
m *God, justice of*, Gen. 2:2.
n *Enemy*, Prov. 24:17.
5 R. V. shall render

**24**
o *God, preserver*, Gen. 2:2.
p *Adversity*, Psa. 10:6.

**25**
q *Benedictions, instances of*, Deut. 21:5.

**1**
a *David*, 1 Sam. 16:13.
b *Saul*, 1 Sam. 9:2.
c *Prudence*, 2 Chr. 2:12.
d *Philistines*, Gen. 26:14.
1 R. V. all the borders

**2**
e *Achish*, 1 Sam. 21:10.
f *Gath*, Josh. 11:22.

**3**
g *Polygamy*, Deut. 17:17.
h *Ahinoam*, 1 Sam. 25:43.
i *Abigail*, 1 Sam. 25:3.

**5**
j *Cities, royal*, Num. 35:8.

**6**
k *Ziklag*, Josh. 15:31.

**8**
l *Geshur*, 2 Sam. 3:3.
m *Gezer*, Josh. 10:33.
n *Amalekites*, Num. 13:29.
o *Shur*, 1 Sam. 15:7.
p *Egypt*, Gen. 41:8

**9**
q *War, of extermination*, Judg. 3:2
r *Spoils*, 1 Chr. 26:27.

**10**
s *Falsehood, instances of*, Job 21:34.
t *Deception, instances of*, Josh. 9:4.
u *Judah, tribe of*, Num. 10:14.

**11**
v *Captive, put to death*, 1 Sam. 30:3.

1
*a Philistines*, Gen. 26:14.
*b Armies*, Deut. 11:4.
*c War*, Judg. 3:2.
*d Israel*, Ex. 4:22.
*e Achish*, 1 Sam. 21:10.
*f David*, 1 Sam. 16:13.

3
*g Samuel*, 1 Sam. 3:1.
*h Mourning*, Lam. 2:5.
*i Burying Places*, Gen. 23:4.
*j Ramah*, 1 Sam. 1:19.
*k Saul*, 1 Sam. 9:2.
*l Familiar Spirits*, Deut. 18:11.
*m Witchcraft*, Ex. 22:18.

4
*n* 1 Sam. 31:1–8: 1 Chr. 10:1–8.

5
*o Cowardice*, Lev. 26:36.

6
*p Wicked, prayer of, not answered*, Psa. 73:3.
*q Guidance, prayer for, not heard*, Psa. 48:14.
*r Dream, revelations by*, Dan. 1:17.
*s Urim and Thummim*, Lev. 8:8.
*t Prophets*, Isa. 3:2.

7
*u Sorcery*, Isa. 47:9.

## CHAPTER 28

*Achish puts confidence in David 3 Saul, forsaken of God, resorts unto a witch at En-dor. 12 Samuel appears, and makes known to Saul his approaching ruin.*

AND it came to pass in those
days, that the [a]Phĭ-lĭs′-
tĭneṣ gathered their [b]armies together for [c]warfare, to fight with
[d]Ĭṣ′ra-el. And [e]Ā′chish said unto [f]Dā′vid, Know thou assuredly, that thou shalt go out with
me to battle, thou and thy men.
2 And [f]Dā′vid said to [e]Ā′chish,
Surely thou shalt know what thy
servant can do. And Ā′chish
said to Dā′vid, Therefore will I
make thee keeper of mine head
for ever.
3 ¶ Now [g]Săm′u-el was dead,
and all Ĭṣ′ra-el had [h]lamented
him, and [i]buried him in [j]Rā′-
mah, even in his own city. And
[k]Sạul had put away those that
had [l]familiar spirits, and the
[m]wizards, out of the land.
4 And the [a, b]Phĭ-lĭs′tĭneṣ gathered themselves together, and
came and pitched in Shụ′nem:
and [k]Sạul gathered all Ĭṣ′ra-el
together, and they pitched in
[n]Gĭl-bō′ȧ.
5 And when [k]Sạul saw the
[b]host of the Phĭ-lĭs′tĭneṣ, he was
[o]afraid, and his heart greatly
trembled.
6 And when [k]Sạul enquired
of the LORD, the LORD [p, q]an-
swered him not, neither by
[r]dreams, nor by [s]Ū′rim, nor by
[t]prophets.
7 Then said [k]Sạul unto his
servants, Seek me a woman that
[u]hath a [l]familiar spirit, that I
may go to her, and enquire of
her. And his servants said to
him, Behold, *there is* a woman
that hath a familiar spirit at
*Ĕn′-dôr.
8 And [k]Sạul disguised himself,
and put on other raiment, and he
went, and two men with him,
and they came to the woman by
night: and he said, I pray thee,
[v]divine unto me by the [l]familiar
spirit, and bring me *him* up,
whom I shall name unto thee.
9 And the woman said unto
him, Behold, thou knowest what
[k]Sạul hath done, how he hath
cut off those that have [l]familiar
spirits, and the [m]wizards, out of
the land: wherefore then layest
thou a snare for my life, to cause
me to die?
10 And Sạul [w]sware to her by
the LORD, saying, *As* the LORD
liveth, there shall no punishment happen to thee for this
thing.
11 Then said the woman,
Whom shall I bring up unto
thee? And he said, Bring me
up [g]Săm′u-el.
12 And when the woman saw
[g]Săm′u-el, she cried with a loud
voice: and the woman spake to
[k]Sạul, saying, Why hast thou deceived me? for thou *art* [k]Sạul.
13 And the king said unto her,
Be not afraid: for what sawest
thou? And the woman said unto
Sạul, I [1]saw gods ascending out
of the earth.
14 And he said unto her, What
form *is* he of? And she said, An
old man cometh up; and he *is*
covered with a [2]mantle. And
[k]Sạul perceived that it *was*
[g]Săm′u-el, and he stooped with
*his* face to the ground, and
bowed himself.
15 And [g]Săm′u-el said to [k]Sạul,
Why hast thou disquieted me, to
bring me up? And Sạul an-
swered, I am sore distressed;
for the Phĭ-lĭs′tĭneṣ make war
against me, and God is [x]depart-
ed from [y]me, and answereth me
no more, neither by [z]prophets,
nor by [a]dreams: therefore I have

8
*v Necromancy*, Deut. 18:11.

10
*w Oath*, Num. 5:19.

13
1 R. V. see a god coming up

14
2 R. V. robe.

15
*x Holy Spirit, withdrawn from incorrigible sinners*, Acts 1:2.
*y Reprobates*, 1 Cor. 9:27.
*z Prophets*, Isa. 3:2.

*a Dream*, Dan. 1:17.

* **EN-DOR** (*fountain of Dor*). *A city of Manasseh*, Josh. 17:11. *The witch of, consulted by Saul*, 1 Sam. 28:7–25. *Deborah triumphs at, over Sisera*, Judg. 4; Psa. 83:10.

called thee, that thou mayest make known unto me what I shall do.

16 Then said [b]Săm'u-el, Wherefore then dost thou ask of me, seeing the LORD is departed from thee, and is become thine enemy?

17 And the LORD hath [3]done to him, as he spake by me: for [c]the LORD hath [d]rent the kingdom out of thine hand, and given it to thy neighbour, *even* to [e]Dā'vid:

18 Because thou [f]obeyedst not the voice of the LORD, nor executedst his fierce [g]wrath upon [h]Ăm'a-lĕk, therefore hath the LORD done [d]this thing unto thee this day.

19 Moreover the LORD will also [d]deliver Ĭṣ'ra-el with thee into the hand of the [i]Phĭ-lĭs'tĭneṣ: and to morrow *shalt* thou and thy [j]sons *be* with me: the LORD also shall [d]deliver the host of Ĭṣ'ra-el into the hand of the Phĭ-lĭs'tĭneṣ.

20 Then [k]Sa̤ul fell straightway all along on the earth, and was sore [l]afraid, because of the words of [b]Săm'u-el: and there was no strength in him; for he had [m]eaten no bread all the day nor all the night.

21 ¶ And the woman came unto [k]Sa̤ul, and saw that he was sore troubled, and said unto him, Behold, thine handmaid hath obeyed thy voice, and I have put my life in my hand, and have hearkened unto thy words which thou spakest unto me.

22 Now therefore, I pray thee, hearken thou also unto the voice of thine handmaid, and [n]let me set a morsel of [o]bread before thee; and eat, that thou mayest have strength, when thou goest on thy way.

23 But he refused, and said, I will not eat. But his servants, together with the woman, compelled him; and he hearkened unto their voice. So he arose from the earth, and sat upon the bed.

24 [n]And the woman had a fat calf in the house; and she hasted, and killed it, and took flour, and kneaded *it*, and did bake unleavened bread thereof:

25 [n]And she brought *it* before Sa̤ul, and before his servants; and they did eat. Then they rose up, and went away that night.

## CHAPTER 29

*The lords of the Philistines mistrust David. 6 Achish dismisses him, with commendations of his fidelity.*

NOW the [a]Phĭ-lĭs'tĭneṣ gathered together all their [b]armies to [c]Ā'phek: and the [d]Ĭṣ'ra-el-ītes pitched by a fountain which *is* in [e]Jĕz're-el.

2 And the lords of the [a]Phĭ-lĭs'tĭneṣ passed on by hundreds, and by thousands: but [f]Dā'vid and his men passed on in the rearward with [g]Ā'chish.

3 Then said the princes of the Phĭ-lĭs'tĭneṣ, What *do* these [h]Hē'brewṣ *here*? And [g]Ā'chish said unto the princes of the Phĭ-lĭs'tĭneṣ, *Is* not this [f]Dā'vid, the servant of Sa̤ul the king of Ĭṣ'ra-el, which hath been with me these days, or these years, and I have found no fault in him since he fell *unto me* unto this day?

4 And the princes of the [a]Phĭ-lĭs'tĭneṣ were wroth with him; and the princes of the Phĭ-lĭs'tĭneṣ said unto him, [i]Make this fellow return, that he may go again to his place which thou hast appointed him, and let him not go down with us to battle, lest in the battle he be an adversary to us: for wherewith should he reconcile himself unto his master? *should it* not *be* with the heads of these men?

5 *Is* not this [f]Dā'vid, of whom they sang one to another in dances, saying, [j]Sa̤ul slew his

16
b *Samuel,* 1 Sam. 3:1.

17
c *Government, God in,* Isa. 22:21.
d *Judgments,* Ex. 6:6.
e *David,* 1 Sam. 16:13.
3 R. V. wrought for himself,

18
f *Disobedience to God,* Eph. 5:6.
g *Anger of God, provoked,* 2 Kin. 13:3.
h *Amalekites,* Num. 13:29.

19
i *Philistines,* Gen. 26:14.
j *Children, death of, as a judgment upon parents,* Mark 10:14.

20
k *Saul,* 1 Sam. 9:2.
l *Cowardice,* Lev. 26:36.
m *Fasting,* Zech. 8:19.

22
n *Hospitality,* Rom. 12:13.
o *Bread,* Ezek. 4:13.

1
a *Philistines,* Gen. 26:14.
b *Armies,* Deut. 11:4.
c *Aphek,* 1 Sam. 4:1.
d *Israel,* Ex. 4:22.
e Josh. 15:56.

2
f *David,* 1 Sam. 16:13.
g *Achish,* 1 Sam. 21:10.

3
h *Hebrew,* Gen. 40 15.

4
i *Prudence, instances of,* 2 Chr. 2:12.

5
j *Saul,* 1 Sam. 9:2

thousands, and Dā′vid his ten thousands?

6 ¶ Then [g]Ā′chish called [f]Dā′vid, and said unto him, Surely, *as* the LORD liveth, thou hast been upright, and thy going out and thy coming in with me in the host *is* good in my sight: for I have not found evil in thee since the day of thy coming unto me unto this day: [i]nevertheless the lords favour thee not.

7 [i]Wherefore now return, and go in peace, that thou displease not the lords of the Phĭ-lĭs′tĭneș.

8 And [f]Dā′vid said unto [g]Ā′chish, But what have I done? and what hast thou found in thy servant so long as I have been with thee unto this day, that I may not go fight against the enemies of my lord the king?

9 And [g]Ā′chish answered and said to [f]Dā′vid, I know that thou *art* good in my sight, as an angel of God: notwithstanding the princes of the [a]Phĭ-lĭs′tĭneș have [i]said, He shall not go up with us to the battle.

10 Wherefore now rise up early in the morning with thy master's servants that are come with thee: and as soon as ye be up early in the morning, and have light, depart.

11 So [f]Dā′vid and his men rose up early to depart in the morning, to return into the land of the Phĭ-lĭs′tĭneș. And the Phĭ-lĭs′tĭneș went up to [e]Jĕz′re-el.

## CHAPTER 30

*The Amalekites spoil Ziklag. 4 David by God's direction pursues them, 11 and recovers the spoil. 22 David's law for dividing spoil. 26 He sends presents to his friends.*

1 AND it came to pass, when [a]Dā′vid and his men were come to [b]Zĭk′lăg on the third day, that the [c]Ăm′a-lĕk-ītes had invaded the south, and Zĭk′lăg, and smitten Zĭk′lăg, and burned it with fire;

2 And had taken the women *captives, that *were* therein: they slew not any, either great or small, but carried *them* away, and went on their way.

3 So [a]Dā′vid and his men came to the city, and, behold, *it was* burned with fire; and their wives, and their sons, and their daughters, were taken *captives.

4 Then Dā′vid and the people that *were* with him lifted up their voice and [d]wept, until they had no more power to weep.

5 And Dā′vid's [e]two wives were taken captives, [f]Ă-hĭn′o-ăm the Jĕz′re-el-ĭt-ess, and [g]Ăb′ĭ-gail the wife of Nā′bal the Cär′mel-īte.

6 And Dā′vid was greatly distressed; for the people spake of †stoning him, because the soul of all the people was [d]grieved, every man for his sons and for his daughters: but Dā′vid encouraged himself in the LORD his God.

7 And [a]Dā′vid said to [h]Ă-bī′a-thär the [i]priest, [j]Ă-hĭm′e-lĕch's son, I pray thee, bring me hither the [k]ephod. And Ă-bī′a-thär brought thither the ephod to Dā′vid.

8 And [a]Dā′vid [l]enquired at the LORD, saying, Shall I pursue after this troop? shall I overtake them? And he [m]answered him, Pursue: for thou shalt surely overtake *them*, and without fail recover *all*.

9 So [a]Dā′vid went, he and the six hundred men that *were* with

1
a *David*, 1 Sam. 16:13.
b *Ziklag*, Josh. 15:31.
c *Amalekites*, Num. 13:29.

4
d *Mourning*, Lam. 2:5.

5
e *Polygamy*, Deut. 17:17.
f *Ahinoam*, 1 Sam. 25:43.
g *Abigail*, 1 Sam. 25:3.

7
h *Abiathar*, 1 Sam. 22:20.
i *High Priest*, Lev. 21:10.
j *Ahimelech*, 1 Sam. 21:1.
k *Ephod*, Ex. 28:6.

8
l *Armies, religious ceremonies in*, Deut. 11:4.
m *Guidance, prayer for, answered*, Psa. 48:14.

* **CAPTIVE.** *Prisoner of war*, Gen. 14:12; Deut. 21:10–14; 1 Sam. 30:1, 2.
**Cruelty to:** *Put to death*, Num. 31:9–20; Deut. 20:13; Josh. 8:29; 10:15–40; 11:11; Judg. 7:25; 8:21; 21:11; 1 Sam. 15:32, 33; 27:11; 2 Sam. 8:2; 12:31; 2 Kin. 8:12; Jer. 39:6; Lam. 3:34. *Ripping women with child*, 2 Kin. 8:12; 15:16; Hos. 13:16; Amos 1:13. *Tortured under saws and harrows*, 2 Sam. 12:31; 1 Chr. 20:3. *Blinded*, Judg. 16:21; 2 Kin. 25:7; Jer. 39:7. *Maimed*, Judg. 1:6, 7. *Ravished*, Lam. 5:11–13; Zech. 14:2. *Enslaved*, Deut. 20:14; 2 Kin. 5:2; Psa. 44:12; Joel 3:6. *Robbed*, Ezek. 23:25, 26. *Other indignities to*, Isa. 20:4.
**Kindness to**, 2 Kin. 25:27–30; 2 Chr. 28:11–15; Psa. 106:46. *Advanced to positions in state*, *Esther*, Esth. 2:8–17; *Mordecai*, Esth. 8:1, 2; *Daniel and his three companions*, Dan. 1. See footnote, PRISONERS, Psa. 79:11.

† **STONING.** *Punishment by*, Ex. 19:13; **Lev.** 20:2, 27; 24:14, 16; Num. 14:10; Deut. 13:10; 17:5; 22:21, 24; Ezek. 16:40; Heb. 11:37.
**Instances of:** *The blasphemer*, Lev. 24:13–23. *Sabbath*

9
*n Brook*, Deut. 8:7.

12
*o Food*, Psa. 136: 25.
*p Fig*, Mark 11:13.
*q Raisins*, 1 Sam. 25:18.
*r Fasting*, Zech. 8:19.

13
*s Servant, cruelty to*, Jer. 2:14.

14
*Judah, tribe of*, Num. 10:14.

15
*u Oath*, Num. 5:19.
*v Treason, instances of*, 2 Kin. 11: 14.

16
*w Dancing*, Eccl. 3:4.
*x Spoils*, 1 Chr. 26: 27.

him, and came to the [n]brook
Bē′sôr, where those that were
left behind stayed.
10 But [a]Dā′vid pursued, he and
four hundred men: for two hundred abode behind, which were
so faint that they could not go
over the [n]brook Bē′sôr.
11 ¶ And they found an Ē-ġўp′-
tian in the field, and brought
him to [a]Dā′vid, and gave him
bread, and he did eat; and they
made him drink water;
12 And they gave him a piece of
a [o]cake of [p]figs, and two clusters
of [q]raisins: and when he had
eaten, his spirit came again to
him: for he had [r]eaten no bread,
nor drunk *any* water, three days
and three nights.
13 And [a]Dā′vid said unto him,
To whom *belongest* thou? and
whence *art* thou? And he said,
I *am* a young man of Ē′ġўpt,
servant to an Ăm′a-lĕk-īte; and
my master [s]left me, because
three days agone I fell sick.
14 [c]We made an invasion *upon*
the south of the ‡Chĕr′e-thītes,
and upon *the coast* which *be-*
*longeth* to [t]Jū′dah, and upon the
south of Cā′leb; and we burned
[b]Zĭk′lăg with fire.
15 And Dā′vid said to him,
Canst thou bring me down to
this company? And he said,
[u]Swear unto me by God, that
thou wilt neither kill me, nor
deliver me into the hands of my
master, and [v]I will bring thee
down to this [c]company.
16 And when he had brought
him down, behold, *they were*
spread abroad upon all the
earth, eating and drinking, and
[w]dancing, because of all the
great [x]spoil that they had taken
out of the land of the [y]Phĭ-lĭs′-
tīneș, and out of the land of
[t]Jū′dah.
17 And [a]Dā′vid smote them
from the twilight even unto the
evening of the next day: and
there escaped not a man of them,
save four hundred young men,
[z]which rode upon ‖camels, and
fled.
18 And [a]Dā′vid recovered all
that the Ăm′a-lĕk-ītes had carried away: and Dā′vid rescued
his [b]two wives.
19 And there was nothing lacking to them, neither small nor
great, neither sons nor daughters, neither [c]spoil, nor any *thing*
that they had taken to them:
Dā′vid recovered all.
20 And [a]Dā′vid took all the
flocks and the herds, *which* they
drave before those *other* cattle,
and said, This *is* Dā′vid's [c]spoil.
21 ¶ And [a]Dā′vid came to the
two hundred men, which were so
faint that they could not follow
Dā′vid, whom they had made also to abide at the [d]brook Bē′sôr:
and they went forth to meet Dā′-
vid, and to meet the people that
*were* with him: and when Dā′-
vid came near to the people, he
[e]saluted them.
22 Then answered all the wicked men and *men* of Bē′lĭ-ăl, of
those that went with Dā′vid, and
said, Because they went not with
us, we will not give them *ought*
of the [c]spoil that we have recovered, save to every man his wife
and his children, that they may
lead *them* away, and depart.
23 Then said [a]Dā′vid, Ye shall
not do so, my brethren, with that
which the LORD hath given us,
who hath [f]preserved us, and de-

*y Philistines*, Gen. 26:14.

17
*z Cavalry*, 1 Sam. 13:5.

18
*a David*, 1 Sam. 16:13.
*b Polygamy*, Deut. 17:17.

19
*c Spoils*, 1 Chr. 26: 27.

21
*d Brook*, Deut. 8:7.
*e Salutations*, Luke 1:44.

23
*f God, preserver*, Gen. 2:2.

*breaker*, Num. 15:36. *Achan*, Josh. 7:25. *Naboth*, 1 Kin. 21:10–13. *Stephen*, Acts 7:59. *Paul*, Acts 14:19; 2 Cor. 11:25. See footnote, PUNISHMENT, Lev. 26:41.

‡ **CHERETHITES,** a Philistine tribe. *David's bodyguard*, 1 Sam. 30:14, 16; 2 Sam. 8:18; 15:18; 20:7, 23; 1 Kin. 1:38, 44; 1 Chr. 18:17; Ezek. 25:16; Zeph. 2:5. *Solomon's escort at his coronation*, 1 Kin. 1:38.

‖ **CAMEL.** *Herds of*, Gen. 12:16; 24:35; Gen. 30:43; 1 Sam. 30:17; 1 Chr. 27:30; Job 1:3, 17; Isa. 60:6. *Ornaments of*, Judg. 8:21, 26. *Stables for*, Ezek. 25:5. *Docility of*, Gen. 24:11.

**Uses of:** *For riding*, Gen. 24:10, 61, 64; 31:17. *For drawing chariots*, Isa. 21:7. *For carrying burdens*, Gen. 24 10; 37:25; 1 Kin. 10:2; 2 Kin. 8:9; 1 Chr. 12:40; Isa. 30:6. *For milk*, Gen. 32:15. *Forbidden as food*, Lev. 11:4. *Hair of made into cloth*, Matt. 3:4; Mark 1:6.

livered the company that came against us into our hand.

24 For who will hearken unto you in this matter? but as his [c]part *is* that goeth down to the battle, so *shall* his [c]part *be* that tarrieth by the stuff: they shall part alike.

25 And it was *so* from that day forward, that he made it a statute and an [g]ordinance for Ĭṣ′ra-el unto this day.

26 ¶ And when [a]Dā′vid came to [h]Zĭk′lăg, he sent of the [c]spoil unto the [i]elders of [j]Jū′dah, *even* to his friends, saying, Behold a [k]present for you of the spoil of the enemies of the LORD;

27 To *them* which *were* in Bĕth′-el, and to *them* which *were* in south [l]Rā′moth, and to *them* which *were* in [m]Jăt′tĭr,

28 And to *them* which *were* in Ăr′ō-ēr, and to *them* which *were* in Sĭph′moth, and to *them* which *were* in §Ĕsh-te-mō′ȧ,

29 And to *them* which *were* in Rā′chăl, and to *them* which *were* in the cities of the Jĕ-räh′me-el-ītes, and to *them* which *were* in the cities of the Kĕn′ītes,

30 And to *them* which *were* in [n]Hôr′mah, and to *them* which *were* in Chôr-ā′shan, and to *them* which *were* in Ā′thăch,

31 And to *them* which *were* in [o]Hē′bron, and to all the places where Dā′vid himself and his men were wont to haunt.

## CHAPTER 31

*Saul's army defeated. 2 His sons slain. 4 He and his armor-bearer kill themselves. 7 The Philistines possess the forsaken towns of the Israelites. 8 They triumph over the dead bodies of Saul and his sons. 11 The men of Jabesh-gilead recover the bodies by night, burn them, and bury their bones at Jabesh.*

NOW the [a]Phĭ-lĭs′tĭneṣ fought against [b]Ĭṣ′ra-el: and the men of Ĭṣ′ra-el fled from before the Phĭ-lĭs′tĭneṣ, and fell down slain in mount [c]Gĭl-bō′ȧ.

2 And the [a]Phĭ-lĭs′tĭneṣ followed hard upon [d]Saul and upon his sons; and the Phĭ-lĭs′tĭneṣ slew [e]Jŏn′a-than, and *Ȧ-bĭn′a-dăb, and [f]Mĕl′chĭ-shu′ȧ, Saul's sons.

3 And the battle went sore against Saul, and the [g]archers [1]hit him; and he was [2]sore wounded of the archers.

4 Then said Saul unto his [h]armourbearer, Draw thy sword, and thrust me through therewith; lest these [a]uncircumcised come and [i]thrust me through, and abuse me. But his armourbearer would not; for he was sore afraid. Therefore Saul took a sword, and [j]fell upon it.

5 And when his [h]armourbearer saw that Saul was dead, he [j]fell likewise upon his sword, and died with him.

6 So [d]Saul died, and his three *,[e],[f]sons, and his [h]armourbearer, and all his men, that same day together.

7 ¶ And when the men of [b]Ĭṣ′ra-el that *were* on the other side of the valley, and *they* that *were* on the other side [k]Jôr′dan, saw that the men of Ĭṣ′ra-el fled, and that [d]Saul and his sons were dead, they forsook the cities, and fled; and the [a]Phĭ-lĭs′tĭneṣ came and dwelt in them.

8 ¶ And it came to pass on the morrow, when the Phĭ-lĭs′tĭneṣ came to [l]strip the slain, that they found Saul and his three sons fallen in mount [m]Gĭl-bō′ȧ.

9 And they cut off his [n]head, and stripped off his armour, and sent into the land of the Phĭ-lĭs′tĭneṣ round about, to publish *it in* the house of their [o]idols, and among the people.

10 And they put his [n]armour in the [p]house of [q]Ăsh′ta-rŏth: and they fastened his body to the [r]wall of [s]Bĕth′-shăn.

11 And when the inhabitants of

---

25
g *Ordinance*, Num. 9:14.

26
h *Ziklag*, Josh. 15:31.
i *Government*, Isa. 22:21.
j *Judah, tribe of*, Num. 10:14.
k *Presents*, Gen. 32:13.

27
l Josh. 19:8.
m Josh. 15:48; 21:14; 1 Chr. 6:57.

30
n *Hormah*, Deut. 1:44.

31
o *Hebron*, Gen. 23:2.

1
a *Philistines*, Gen. 26:14.
b *Israel, under the kings*, Ex. 4:22.
c 1 Sam. 28:4; 1 Chr. 10:1–8.

2
d *Saul*, 1 Sam. 9:2.
e *Jonathan*, 1 Sam. 14:1.
f *Melchi-shua*, 1 Sam. 14:49.

3
g *Archery*, Gen. 21:20.
1 R. V. overtook
2 R. V. greatly distressed by reason

4
h *Armor-bearer*, Judg. 9:54.
i *Captive, cruelty to*, 1 Sam. 30:3.
j *Suicide, instances of*, 1 Kin. 16:18.

7
k *Jordan*, Gen. 32:10.

8
l *Spoils*. 1 Chr. 26:27.
m 1 Sam. 28:4; 1 Chr. 10:1–8.

9
n *Trophies*, 1 Sam. 21:9.
o *Idolatry*, 1 Sam. 15:23.

10
p *Temple, idolatrous*, 1 Kin. 6:17.
q Or, *Ashtoreth, temple of*, 1 Kin. 11:5.
r *Walls*, 1 Sam. 20:25.
s Or, *Beth-shean*, Josh. 17:11.

---

§ **ESHTEMOA**, called also ESHTEMOH. *A town of Canaan assigned to Judah*, Josh. 15:50. *Allotted to the Aaronites*, Josh. 21:14; 1 Chr. 6:57. *David shared spoil with*, 1 Sam. 30:28.

* **ABINADAB**. *Second son of Saul by Ahinoam*, 1 Sam. 31:2; 1 Chr. 8:33; 9:39; 10:2. *Called* ISHUI, 1 Sam 14:49.

11 [t] Jabesh-gilead, Judg. 21:8.

[t]Jā′besh–gĭl′e-ăd heard of that
which the [a]Phĭ-lĭs′tĭneș had done
to [d]Sa̤ul;
12 All the valiant men arose,
and went all night, and took the
body of Sa̤ul and the bodies of
his *,[e,f]sons from the wall of
[s]Bĕth′–shăn, and came to [t]Jā′-
besh, and [u]burnt them there.
13 And they took their bones,
and buried *them* [v]under [3]a tree
at Jā′besh, and [w,x]fasted [y]seven
days.

12 *u* *Cremation*, Josh. 7:25.

13 *v* *Burying Places*, Gen. 23:4. *w* *Fasting*, Zech. 8:19. *x* *Mourning, fasting*, Lam. 2:5. *y* *Seven, days, fasts of*, Gen. 7:2. 3 R. V. the tamarisk tree in

THE

# SECOND BOOK OF SAMUEL

## CHAPTER 1

*An Amalekite, bringing tidings of the overthrow of the Israelites, and claiming to have slain Saul, is put to death. 17 David's lamentation over Saul and Jonathan.*

v.1–984 BC

1 *a* *Saul*, 1 Sam. 9:2. *b* *David*, 1 Sam. 16:13. *c* *Amalekites*, Num. 13:29. *d* *Ziklag*, Josh. 15: 31.

2 *e* *Rending of Garments, a token of affliction*, 2 Chr. 34:27. *f* *Dust, put on the head in mourning*, Eccl. 3:20.

3 *g* *Israel, under the kings*, Ex. 4:22.

4 *h* *Death*, Num. 23: 10. *i* *Jonathan*, 1 Sam. 14:1.

6 *j* 1 Sam. 28:4, 1 Chr. 10.1–8.

NOW it came to pass after
the death of [a]Sa̤ul, when
[b]Dā′vid was returned from the
slaughter of the [c]Ăm′a-lĕk-ītes,
and Dā′vid had abode two days
in [d]Zĭk′lăg;
2 It came even to pass on the
third day, that, behold, a man
came out of the camp from Sa̤ul
with his clothes [e]rent, and [f]earth
upon his head: and *so* it was,
when he came to [b]Dā′vid, that
he fell to the earth, and did
obeisance.
3 And [b]Dā′vid said unto him,
From whence comest thou?
And he said unto him, Out of the
camp of [g]Ĭș′ra-el am I escaped.
4 And [b]Dā′vid said unto him,
How went the matter? I pray
thee, tell me. And he answered,
That the people are fled from the
battle, and many of the people
also are fallen and [h]dead; and
[a]Sa̤ul and [i]Jŏn′a-than his son
are dead also.
5 And [b]Dā′vid said unto the
young man that told him, How
knowest thou that [a]Sa̤ul and
[i]Jŏn′a-than his son be dead?
6 And the young man that
told him said, As I happened by
chance upon mount [j]Gĭl-bō′ȧ,
behold, Sa̤ul leaned upon his
[k]spear; and, lo, the chariots and
horsemen followed hard after
him.
7 And when he looked behind
him, he saw me, and called unto
me. And I answered, Here *am* I.
8 And he said unto me, Who
*art* thou? And I answered him,
I *am* an Ăm′a-lĕk-īte.
9 He said unto me again, Stand,
I pray thee, upon me, and slay
me: for anguish is come upon
me, because my life *is* yet whole
in me.
10 So I stood upon him, and
*slew him, because I was sure
that he could not live after that
he was fallen: and I took the
[l]crown that *was* upon his head,
and the [m]bracelet that *was* on
his arm, and have brought them
hither unto my lord.
11 Then [b]Dā′vid took hold on
his clothes, and [e]rent them; and
likewise all the men that *were*
with him:
12 And they [n]mourned, and
wept, and [o]fasted until even, for
[a]Sa̤ul, and for [i]Jŏn′a-than his
son, and for the people of the
LORD, and for the house of Ĭș′-
ra-el; because they were fallen
by the sword.
13 ¶ And [b]Dā′vid said unto
the young man that told him,
Whence *art* thou? And he

v.6–984 BC See footnote, *Time*, Rev. 10:6. *k* *Spear*, 2 Kin. 11: 10.

10 *l* *Crown, worn by kings*, Ex. 29:6. *m* *Bracelet*, Gen. 24:22.

12 *n* *Mourning*, Lam. 2:5. *o* *Fasting, instances of*, Zech. 8:19.

* **REGICIDE.** *Of Eglon*, Judg. 3:16–23 *Of Saul*, 2 Sam. 1:10. *Of Ish-bosheth*, 2 Sam. 4:5–8 *Of Nadab*, 1 Kin. 15: 27–29. *Of Elah* 1 Kin. 16:9–11. *Of Jehoram*, 2 Kin. 9:24. *Of Ahaziah*, 2 Kin. 9:27. *Of Joash*, 2 Kin. 12:20, 21. *Of Amaziah*, 2 Kin. 14:19, 20. *Of Zachariah*, 2 Kin. 15:10. *Of Shallum*, 2 Kin. 15:14. *Of Pekahiah*, 2 Kin. 15:25. *Of Pekah*, 2 Kin. 15:30. *Of Sennacherib*, 2 Kin. 19:36, 37; Isa. 37:37, 38. See footnote, HOMICIDE, Deut. 5:17.

v.13–984 BC
See footnote, *Time*, Rev. 10:6.

13
p *Foreigners*, Deut. 23:20.
14
q *Citizens, loyal, insuances of, David*, Luke 15:15.
r *Loyalty, instances of, David*, Eccl. 8:2.
s *Reverence, for kings*, Lev. 19:30.
15
t *Homicide, punishment for*, Deut. 5:17.
u *Death, penalty*, Num. 23:10.
16
v *Blood, figurative*, Gen. 9:4.
w *Self-crimination*, Josh. 7:20.
17
x *Friendship, instances of*, Prov. 22:24.
y *Forgiveness*, Matt. 18:21.
z *Mourning*, vs. 17–27; Lam. 2:5.

a *Elegy*, vs. 17–27; 2 Sam. 3:33, 34.
b *Saul*, 1 Sam. 9:2.
c *Jonathan*, 1 Sam. 14:1.
18
d *Book*, Num. 5:23.
1 R. V. song
19
e *Poetry*, vs. 19–27; Acts 17:28.
f *War Songs*, vs. 19–27; Judg. 5:1.
20
g *Gath*, Josh. 11:22.
h *Askelon*, Judg. 1:18.
i *Philistines*, Gen. 26:14.
21
j 1 Sam. 28:4; 1 Chr. 10:1–8.
k *Shield*, 1 Kin. 14:27.
l *Anointing*, Lev. 8:12.
2 R. V. not anointed with oil.

answered, I *am* the son of a
[p]stranger, an [c]Ăm′a-lĕk-īte.
14 And [q,r]Dā′vid said unto
him, [s]How wast thou not afraid
to stretch forth thine hand to
destroy the LORD's anointed?
15 And [b]Dā′vid called one of
the young men, and said, Go
near, *and* fall upon him. And
he [t]smote him that he [u]died.
16 And Dā′vid said unto him,
Thy [v]blood *be* upon thy head;
for [w]thy mouth hath testified
against thee, saying, I have
*slain the LORD's anointed.
17 ¶ And Dā′vid [x,y,z]lamented
with this [a]lamentation over [b]Sa̤ul
and over [c]Jŏn′a-than his son:
18 (Also he bade them teach
the children of Jū′dah *the* [1]*use of*
the †bow: behold, *it is* written
in the [d]book of Jā′shēr.)
19 [a,e,f]The beauty of Ĭs̤′ra-el is
slain upon thy high places: how
are the mighty fallen!
20 Tell *it* not in [g]Găth, publish *it* not in the streets of [h]Ăs′-
ke-lŏn; lest the daughters of the
[i]Phĭ-lĭs′tĭnes̤ rejoice, lest the
daughters of the uncircumcised
triumph.
21 Ye mountains of [j]Gĭl-bō′ȧ,
*let there be* no dew, neither *let*
*there be* ‡rain, upon you, nor
fields of offerings: for there the
[k]shield of the mighty is vilely
cast away, the shield of [b]Sa̤ul,
[2]*as though he had* not *been*
[l]anointed with oil.
22 From the blood of the slain,
from the fat of the mighty, the
†bow of [c]Jŏn′a-than turned not
back, and the sword of [b]Sa̤ul
returned not empty.
23 [b]Sa̤ul and [c]Jŏn′a-than *were*
lovely and pleasant in their lives,
and in their [m]death they were
not divided: they were swifter
than eagles, they were stronger
than lions.
24 Ye daughters of Ĭs̤′ra-el,
[n]weep over [b]Sa̤ul, who clothed
you in [o]scarlet, [3]with *other* delights, who put on ornaments of
gold upon your apparel.
25 [n]How are the mighty fallen
in the midst of the battle! O
Jŏn′a-than, *thou wast* slain in
thine high places.
26 [n]I am distressed for thee, my
brother Jŏn′a-than: very pleasant hast thou been unto me:
thy [p]love to me was wonderful,
passing the love of women.
27 How are the mighty fallen,
and the weapons of war perished!

## CHAPTER 2

*David, by God's direction, goes up to Hebron, where he is made king of Judah. 5 He commends the men of Jabesh-gilead for their kindness to Saul. 8 Abner makes Ish-bosheth king of Israel. 12 A skirmish between the men of Abner and of Joab. 18 Asahel is slain. 25 At Abner's request Joab sounds a retreat. 32 Asahel's burial.*

AND it came to pass after
this, that [a]Dā′vid [b]en-
quired of the LORD, saying,
Shall I go up into any of the
cities of [c]Jū′dah? And the LORD
[d]said unto him, Go up. And
Dā′vid said, Whither shall I
go up? And he said, Unto
[e]Hē′bron.
2 So [a]Dā′vid went up thither,
and his [f]two wives also, [g]Ă-
hĭn′o-ăm the Jĕz′re-el-īt-ess,
and [h]Ăb′ĭ-gail Nā′bal's wife the
Cär′mel-īte.

v.23–984 BC
See footnote, *Time*, Rev. 10:6.

23
m *Death*, Num. 23:10.
24
n *Mourning*, Lam. 2:5.
o *Colors, symbolical*, Ezek. 16:16.
3 R. V. delicately.
26
p *Love, of man for man*, 1 John 4:7.

1
a *David*, 1 Sam. 16:13.
b *Armies, religious ceremonies in*, Deut. 11:4.
c *Judah, tribe of*, Num. 10:14.
d *Guidance, prayer for, answered*, Psa. 48:14.
e *Hebron*, Gen. 23:2.
2
f *Polygamy*, Deut. 17:17.
g *Ahinoam*, 1 Sam. 25:43.
h *Abigail*, 1 Sam. 25:3.

† **BOW.** *A weapon*, Gen. 21:16, 20. *Made, of steel* [R. V. brass], 2 Sam. 22:35; Job 20:24; Psa. 18:34; *of wood*, Ezek. 39:9. *Used in war*, Isa. 13:18; Lam. 2:4; Ezek. 39:3. *Used by the Elamites*, Jer. 49:35. *David instructed the Israelites in the use of, writing war song to*, 2 Sam. 1:18. *Used in hunting*, Gen. 27:3.
See footnotes: ARCHERY, Gen. 21:20; ARROW, 1 Sam. 20:20.
**Figurative**, Gen. 49:24; Job 16:13; 29:20; Psa. 78:57; Lam. 3:12; Hos. 1:5; Hab. 3:9; Rev. 6:2.

‡ **RAIN.** *Forty days of, at the time of the flood*, Gen. 7:4, 10–12, 17–24. *The earth shall no more be destroyed by*, Gen. 9:8–17. *The plague of, upon Egypt*, Ex. 9:22–26, 33, 34. *Sent by God*, Deut. 11:13, 14; Job 37:6; Isa. 30:23; Jer. 5:24; 14:22. *Withheld, as judgment*, Deut. 11:17; 28:24; 1 Kin. 8:35; 2 Chr. 7:13; Jer. 3:3; Amos 4:7; Zech. 14:17. *Miraculously caused, by Samuel*, 1 Sam. 12:16–19; *by Elijah*, 1 Kin. 18:41–45.
*Contingent upon obedience*, Lev. 26:3, 4; Deut. 11:13, 14. *Prayer for*, 1 Kin. 8:35, 36; 2 Chr. 6:26, 27. *Withheld, in answer to prayer*, Jas. 5:17, 18.
*Rainy season in Palestine in the ninth month, corresponding to December*, Ezra 10:9, 13.
*North wind brings, in Palestine* [R. V.], Prov. 25:23.
See footnote, METEOROLOGY, Matt. 16:2.
**Figurative**, Psa. 72:6; Matt. 7:25, 27.

3 And his men that *were* with
him did [a]Dā′vid bring up, every
man with his household: and
they dwelt in the cities of [e]Hē′-
bron.
4 And the men of [c]Jū′dah
came, and there they [i]anointed
[a]Dā′vid [j]king over the house of
Jū′dah. And they told Dā′vid,
saying, *That* the men of [k]Jā′-
besh–ğĭl′e-ăd *were they* that
buried [l]Sa̤ul.
5 ¶ And [a]Dā′vid sent messengers unto the men of [k]Jā′besh–
ğĭl′e-ăd, and said unto them,
[m,n]Blessed *be* ye of the LORD,
that ye have shewed this kindness unto your lord, *even* unto
Sa̤ul, and have buried him.
6 [o]And now the LORD shew
kindness and [p]truth unto you:
and [m]I also will requite you this
kindness, because ye have done
this thing.
7 Therefore now let your hands
be strengthened, and be ye valiant: for your master [l]Sa̤ul is
dead, and also the house of
[c]Jū′dah have [i]anointed me [j]king
over them.
8 ¶ But [q]Ăb′nēr the son of Nēr,
[r,s]captain of Sa̤ul's host, took
*Ĭsh–bō′sheth the son of Sa̤ul,
and brought him over to [t]Mā-
hă-nā′im;
9 And made him king over
[u]Ğĭl′e-ăd, and over the [v]Ăsh′ŭr-
ītes, and over [w]Jĕz′re-el, and
over [x]Ē′phră-ĭm, and over
[y]Bĕn′ja-mĭn, and over all [z]Ĭs̤′-
ra-el.
10 *Ĭsh–bō′sheth Sa̤ul's son
*was* forty years old when he
began to reign over Ĭs̤′ra-el,
and reigned two years. But
the house of [a]Jū′dah followed
[b]Dā′vid.
11 And the time that Dā′vid
was king in [c]Hē′bron over the
house of Jū′dah was seven years
and six months.
12 ¶ And [d]Ăb′nēr the son of
Nēr, and the servants of *Ĭsh–
bō′sheth the son of [e]Sa̤ul, went
out from [f]Mā′hă-nā′im to [g]Ğĭb′-
e-on.
13 And [h]Jō′ăb the son of [i]Zĕr-
u̯-ī′ah, and the servants of [b]Dā′-
vid, went out, and met together
by the †pool of Ğĭb′e-on: and
they sat down, the one on the
one side of the pool, and the
other on the other side of the
pool.
14 And [d]Ăb′nēr said to [h]Jō′ăb,
[j]Let the young men now arise,
and play before us. And Jō′ăb
said, Let them arise.
15 Then there arose and went
over by number twelve [1]of
[k]Bĕn′ja-mĭn, [2]which *pertained* to
*Ĭsh–bō′sheth the son of [e]Sa̤ul,
and twelve of the servants of
[b]Dā′vid.
16 And they caught every one
his fellow by the head, and
*thrust* his sword in his fellow's
side; so they fell down together:
wherefore that place was called
Hĕl′kăth–hăz′zu-rĭm, which *is*
in Ğĭb′e-on.
17 And there was a very sore
[l]battle that day; and [d]Ăb′nēr
was beaten, and the men of
Ĭs̤′ra-el, before the servants of
Dā′vid.
18 ¶ And there were three sons
of [i]Zĕr-u̯-ī′ah there, [h]Jō′ăb, and
[m]Ā-bĭsh′a-ī, and ‡Ā′sa-hĕl: and
Ā′sa-hĕl *was as* light of foot as
a wild [n]roe.
19 And ‡Ā′sa-hĕl pursued after
[d]Ăb′nēr; and in going he turned
not to the right hand nor to the
left from following Ăb′nēr.
20 Then [d]Ăb′nēr looked behind

4
*i* *Anointing*, Lev. 8:12.
*j* *King*, 2 Kin. 3:10.
*k* *Jabesh-gilead*, Judg. 21:8.
*l* *Saul*, 1 Sam. 9:2.
v.4–983 BC

5
*m* *Thankfulness, of man to man*, Acts 24:3.
*n* *Benedictions*, Deut. 21:5.

6
*o* *Prayer, intercessory*, Acts 6:4.
*p* *Truth*, John 18:37.

8
*q* *Abner*, 1 Sam. 14:50.
*r* *Captain*, Num. 31:48.
*s* *Armies, how officered*, Deut. 11:4.
*t* *Mahanaim*, Gen. 32:2.

9
*u* *Gilead*, Deut. 3:13.
*v* Ezek. 27:6.
*w* *Jezreel*, 1 Kin. 18:45.
*x* *Ephraim, tribe of*, Gen. 41:52.
*y* *Benjamin, tribe of*, Num. 1:37.
*z* *Israel, under the kings*, Ex. 4:22.

10
*a* *Judah, tribe of*, Num. 10:14.
*b* *David*, 1 Sam. 16:13.

v.11–983 BC

11
*c* *Hebron*, Gen. 23:2.

12
*d* *Abner*, 1 Sam. 14:50.
*e* *Saul*, 1 Sam. 9:2.
*f* *Mahanaim*, Gen. 32:2.
*g* *Gibeon*, Jer. 41:16.

13
*h* *Joab*, 2 Sam. 20:23.
*i* *Zeruiah, sister of David*, 1 Chr. 2:16.

14
*j* *Championship*, 1 Sam. 17:23.

15
*k* *Benjamin, tribe of*, Num. 1:37.
1 R. V. for
2 R. V. and for Ish-bosheth

17
*l* *War, civil*, Judg. 3:2.

18
*m* *Abishai*, 2 Sam. 3:30.
*n* *Deer*, Deut. 14:5.

* **ISH-BOSHETH,** son of Saul. *Called* ESH-BAAL, 1 Chr. 8:33; 9:39. *Made king by Abner*, 2 Sam. 2:8–10. *Deserted by Abner*, 2 Sam. 3:6–12. *Restores Michal, David's wife, to David*, 2 Sam. 3:14–16. *Assassinated*, 2 Sam. 4:5–8. *Assassination of, avenged by David*, 2 Sam. 4:9–12.

† **POOL.** *Of Gibeon*, 2 Sam. 2:13; Jer. 41:12. *Of Hebron*, 2 Sam. 4:12. *Of Samaria*, 1 Kin. 22:38. *Of Heshbon*, Song. 7:4. Of Jerusalem: *Upper pool*, 2 Kin. 18:17; Isa. 36:2; *lower pool*, Isa. 22:9. *Siloam*, John 9:7, 11; *called* SILOAH, Neh. 3:15; *and probably identical with king's pool*, Neh. 2:14.

‡ **ASAHEL.** *Nephew of David and one of his captains*, 2 Sam. 2:18–24, 32; 3:27; 23:24; 1 Chr. 2:16; 11:26; 27:7. *Slain by Abner*, 2 Sam. 2:20–28. *Death of, avenged by Joab*, 2 Sam. 3:27.

him, and said, *Art* thou ‡Ā′sa-hĕl? And he answered, I *am*.

21 And [d]Ăb′nēr said to him, Turn thee aside to thy right hand or to thy left, and lay thee hold on one of the young men, and take thee his armour. But ‡Ā′sa-hĕl would not turn aside from following him.

22 And [d]Ăb′nēr said again to ‡Ā′sa-hĕl, Turn thee aside from following me: wherefore should I smite thee to the ground? how then should I hold up my face to Jō′ăb thy brother?

23 Howbeit he refused to turn aside: wherefore [d]Ăb′nēr with the hinder end of the spear smote him [3]under the fifth *rib*, that the spear came out behind him; and he fell down there, and died in the same place: and it came to pass, *that* as many as came to the place where Ā′sa-hĕl fell down and died stood still.

24 [h]Jō′ăb also and [m]Ā-bĭsh′a-ī pursued after [d]Ăb′nēr: and the sun went down when they were come to the hill of Ăm′mah, that *lieth* before Ḡī′ah by the way of the wilderness of [g]Ḡĭb′e-on.

25 ¶ And the children of [k]Bĕn′ja-mĭn gathered themselves together after [d]Ăb′nēr, and became one troop, and stood on the top of an hill.

26 Then [d]Ăb′nēr called to [h]Jō′ăb, and said, [o]Shall the sword devour for ever? knowest thou not that it will be bitterness in the latter end? how long shall it be then, ere thou bid the people return from following their brethren?

27 And [h]Jō′ăb said, *As* God liveth, unless thou hadst spoken, surely then in the morning the people had gone up every one from following his brother.

28 So [h]Jō′ăb blew a [p]trumpet, and all the [q]people stood still, and pursued after Ĭs′ra-el no more, neither fought they any more.

29 And Ăb′nēr and his men walked all that night through the plain, and passed over [r]Jôr′dan, and went through all Bĭth′rŏn, and they came to [l]Mā-hă-nā′im.

30 And [h]Jō′ăb returned from following [d]Ăb′nēr: and when he had gathered all the people together, there lacked of [b]Dā′vid's servants nineteen men and †Ā′sa-hĕl.

31 But the servants of Dā′vid had smitten of [k]Bĕn′ja-mĭn, and of [d]Ăb′nēr's men, *so that* three hundred and threescore men died.

32 ¶ And they took up ‡Ā′sa-hĕl, and [s]buried him in the sepulchre of his father, which *was in* [t]Bĕth′-lĕ-hĕm. And Jō′ăb and his men went all night, and they came to [u]Hē′bron at break of day.

## CHAPTER 3

*During the war David waxes stronger. 2 Six sons born to him in Hebron. 6 Abner, displeased with Ish-bosheth, 12 seeks terms of David. 13 David requires him first to bring to him Michal, his wife. 14 This being done, Abner is entertained by David, and dismissed. 22 Joab, returning from battle, kills Abner. 23 David curses Joab, 31 and mourns for Abner.*

NOW there was long [a]war between the house of [b]Saul and the house of [c]Dā′vid: but Dā′vid waxed stronger and stronger, and the house of Saul waxed weaker and weaker.

2 ¶ And unto [c]Dā′vid were sons born in [d]Hē′bron: and his firstborn was [e]Ăm′nŏn, of [f]Ă-hĭn′o-ăm the Jĕz′re-el-īt-ess;

3 And his second, [g]Chĭl′e-ăb, of [h]Ăb′ĭ-gail the wife of Nā′bal the Cär′mel-īte; and the third, *Ăb′sa-lŏm the son of [i]Mā′a-cah the

23
3 R. V. in the belly.

26
o *Intercession, of man with man,* Jer. 27:18.

28
p *Trumpet,* Josh. 6:4.
q *Armies,* Deut. 11:4.

29
r *Jordan, fords of,* Gen. 32:10.

32
s *Burying Places,* Gen. 23:4.
t *Beth-lehem,* Gen. 48:7.
u *Hebron,* Gen. 23:2.

1
a *War, civil,* Judg. 3:2.
b *Saul,* 1 Sam. 9:2.
c *David,* 1 Sam. 16:13.

2
d *Hebron,* Gen. 23:2.
e 2 Sam. 13:1–33; 1 Chr. 3:1.
f *Ahinoam,* 1 Sam. 25:43.

3
g Or, *Daniel,* 1 Chr. 3:1.
h *Abigail,* 1 Sam. 25:3.
i 1 Chr. 3:2.

* **ABSALOM** (*father of peace*), called also ABISHALOM. *Son of David by Maacah,* 2 Sam. 3:3; 1 Chr. 3:2. *Beauty of,* 2 Sam. 14:25. *Slays Amnon,* 2 Sam. 13:22–29. *Flees to Geshur,* 2 Sam. 13:37, 38. *Is permitted by David to return to Jerusalem,* 2 Sam. 14:1–24. *His demagogism,* 2 Sam. 15:1–6,13; *conspiracy,* 2 Sam. chapters 15–17; *death and burial,* 2 Sam. 18:9–17. *David's mourning for,* 2 Sam. 18:33; 19:1–8. *Children of,* 2 Sam. 14:27; 18:18; 1 Kin. 15:2; 2 Chr. 11:20. *Pillar of,* 2 Sam. 18:18.

daughter of [i]Tăl'māi king of
†Gē'shŭr;
4 And the fourth, [k]Ăd-o-nī'jah
the son of [l]Hăg'gĭth; and the
fifth, [m]Shĕph-a-tī'ah the son of
[m]Ăb'i-tăl;
5 And the sixth, [m]Ĭth're-ăm, by
[m]Ĕg'lah [c]Dā'vid's wife. These
were born to Dā'vid in [d]Hē'-
bron.
6 ¶ And it came to pass, while
there was [a]war between the
house of [b]Saul and the house of
[c]Dā'vid, that [n]Ăb'nēr made himself strong for the house of Saul.
7 And Saul had a [o]concubine,
whose name *was* [p]Rĭz'pah, the
daughter of [p]Ā-ī'ah: and [q]*Ish-
bo'sheth* said to [n]Ăb'nēr, Wherefore hast thou gone in unto my
father's concubine?
8 Then was [n]Ăb'nēr very
[r]wroth for the words of [q]Ĭsh-
bō'sheth, and said, [s]*Am* I a
[t]dog's head, [1]which against Jū'-
dah do shew kindness this day
unto the house of [b]Saul thy
father, to his brethren, and to his
friends, and have not delivered
thee into the hand of [c]Dā'vid,
that thou chargest me to day
with a fault concerning this
woman?
9 [u]So do God to Ăb'nēr, and
more also, except, as the LORD
hath [v]sworn to Dā'vid, even so I
do to him;
10 To translate the kingdom
from the house of [b]Saul, and to
set up the throne of Dā'vid over
[w]Ĭs'ra-el and over Jū'dah, from
[x]Dăn even to [y]Bē'er-shē'bȧ.
11 And he could not answer
[n]Ăb'nēr a word again, because
he feared him.
12 ¶ And [n]Ăb'nēr sent messengers to Dā'vid on his behalf, saying, Whose *is* the land? saying
*also*, Make thy [z]league with me,
and, behold, my hand *shall be*
with thee, to bring about all
Ĭs'ra-el unto thee.
13 And he said, Well; I will
make a [z]league with thee: but
one thing I require of thee, that
is, Thou shalt not see my face,
except thou first bring [a]Mī'chal
Saul's daughter, when thou comest to see my face.
14 And [b]Dā'vid sent messengers to [c]Ĭsh-bō'sheth [d]Saul's
son, saying, Deliver *me* my [e]wife
[a]Mī'chal, which I espoused to
me for an hundred foreskins of
the [f]Phĭ-lĭs'tĭnes.
15 And [c]Ĭsh-bō'sheth sent, and
took her from *her* husband,
*even* from [g]Phăl'tī-el the son of
[g]Lā'ish.
16 And her husband went with
her along weeping behind her to
‡Bȧ-hū'rim. Then said [h]Ăb'nēr
unto him, Go, return. And he
returned.
17 ¶ And [h]Ăb'nēr [i]had communication with the [j]elders of
Ĭs'ra-el, saying, Ye sought for
[b]Dā'vid in times past *to be* [k]king
over you:
18 Now then do *it*: for the
LORD hath spoken of Dā'vid,
saying, By the hand of my servant Dā'vid I will [l]save my people Ĭs'ra-el out of the hand of
the [f]Phĭ-lĭs'tĭnes, and out of
the hand of all their enemies.
19 And [h]Ăb'nēr also [i]spake in
the ears of [m]Bĕn'ja-mĭn: and
Ăb'nēr went also to speak in the
ears of [b]Dā'vid in [n]Hē'bron all
that seemed good to Ĭs'ra-el, and
that seemed good to the whole
house of Bĕn'ja-mĭn.
20 So [h]Ăb'nēr came to Dā'vid
to [n]Hē'bron, and twenty men
with him. And [b]Dā'vid made
Ăb'ner and the men that *were*
with him a [o]feast.

i 2 Sam. 13:37; 1 Chr. 3:2.

4

k *Adonijah,* 1 Kin. 1:5.

l 1 Kin. 1:5, 11; 1 Chr. 3:2.

m 1 Chr. 3:3.

6

n *Abner,* 1 Sam. 14:50.

7

o *Concubinage,* 2 Sam. 21:11.

p 2 Sam. 21:8–11.

q *Ish-bosheth,* 2 Sam. 2:8.

8

r *Anger,* Psa. 37:8.

s *Proverbs,* 1 Sam. 24:13.

t *Dog,* 1 Kin. 21:19.

1 R. V. that belongeth to Judah? This day do I shew kindness unto

9

u *Oath,* Num. 5:19.

v *Covenant, of God with men,* Deut. 29:1.

10

w *Israel, under the kings,* Ex. 4:22.

x *Dan,* Judg. 18:29.

y *Beer-sheba,* Judg. 20:1.

12

z *Covenant, of men with men,* Deut. 29:1.

v.12–976 BC
See footnote, *Time,* Rev. 10:6.

13

a *Michal,* 1 Sam. 18:20.

14

b *David,* 1 Sam. 16:13.

c *Ish-bosheth,* 2 Sam. 2:8.

d *Saul,* 1 Sam. 9:2.

e *Wife,* Prov. 5:18.

f *Philistines,* Gen. 26:14.

15

g Or, *Phalti,* 1 Sam. 25:44.

16

h *Abner,* 1 Sam. 14:50.

17

i *Diplomacy,* vs. 18–21; 2 Kin. 16:7.

j *Senate,* Num. 11:16.

k *King,* 2 Kin. 3:10.

18

l *God, preserver,* Gen. 2:2.

19

m *Benjamin, tribe of,* Num. 1:37.

n *Hebron,* Gen. 23:2.

20

o *Feasts,* Mark 12:39.

† **GESHUR,** also called GESHURI, a district E. of the sources of the Jordan. *The inhabitants of, not subdued by the Israelites,* Deut. 3:14; Josh. 13:2–13; 1 Chr. 2:23. *Inhabitants of one of the villages of, exterminated, and the spoils taken by David,* 1 Sam. 27:8. *David marries a princess of,* 2 Sam. 3:3; 1 Chr. 3:2. *Absalom takes refuge in, after the murder of Amnon, and remains there three years,* 2 Sam. 13:37, 38. *Absalom returns from,* 2 Sam. 15:8.

‡ **BAHURIM.** *A village between the fords of the Jordan and Jerusalem,* 2 Sam. 3:16; 16:5; 17:18, 19:16; 1 Kin. 2:8.

v.21–976 BC
See footnote, *Time*, Rev. 10:6.

21
p *Covenant, of men with men*, Deut. 29:1.

22
q *Joab*, 2 Sam. 20:23.
r *Spoils*, 1 Chr. 26:27.
2 R. V. a foray.

23
s *Talebearer*, Prov. 11:13.

24
t *Jealousy, instances of*, vs. 24–27; Psa. 78:58.

25
u *False Accusation*, 2 Tim. 3:3.

27
v *Confidence, betrayed, instances of*, Mic. 7:5.
w *Treachery, of Joab*, 2 Kin. 9:23.
x *Homicide, felonious, instances of*, Deut. 5:17.
y *Assassination, instances of*, Deut. 27:24.
z *Revenge, instances of*, Ezek. 25:15.

a *Asahel*, 2 Sam. 2:18.
3 R. V. in the belly.

21 And Ăb′nēr [t]said unto Dā′vid, I will arise and go, and will gather all Īṣ′ra-el unto my lord the king, that they may make a [p]league with thee, and that thou mayest reign over all that thine heart desireth. And Dā′vid sent Ăb′nēr away; and he went in peace.

22 ¶ And, behold, the servants of [b]Dā′vid and [q]Jō′ăb came from [2]*pursuing* a troop, and brought in a great [r]spoil with them: but [h]Ăb′nēr *was* not with Dā′vid in [n]Hē′bron; for he had sent him away, and he was gone in peace.

23 When [q]Jō′ăb and all the host that *was* with him were come, [s]they told Jō′ăb, saying, Ăb′nēr the son of Nēr came to the king, and he hath sent him away, and he is gone in peace.

24 [t]Then Jō′ăb came to the king, and said, What hast thou done? behold, Ăb′nēr came unto thee; why *is* it *that* thou hast sent him away, and he is quite gone?

25 [u]Thou knowest Ăb′nēr the son of Nēr, that he came to deceive thee, and to know thy going out and thy coming in, and to know all that thou doest.

26 And when [q]Jō′ăb was come out from [b]Dā′vid, he sent messengers after [h]Ăb′nēr, which brought him again from the well of Sī′rah: but Dā′vid knew *it* not.

27 And when Ăb′nēr was returned to [n]Hē′bron, [q]Jō′ăb took him aside in the gate to [v]speak with him quietly, and [w, x, y]smote him there [3]under the fifth *rib*, that he died, [z]for the blood of [a]Ā′sa-hĕl his brother.

28 ¶ And afterward when [b]Dā′vid heard *it*, he [c]said, I and my kingdom *are* guiltless before the LORD for ever from the blood of [d]Ăb′nēr the son of Nēr:

29 [e]Let it rest on the head of [e]Jō′ăb, and on all his father's house; and let there not fail from the house of Jō′ăb one that hath an issue, or that is a leper, or that leaneth on a staff, or that falleth on the sword, or that lacketh bread.

30 So [c]Jō′ăb and ‖Ă-bĭsh′a-ī his brother slew [d]Ăb′nēr, [f]because he had slain their brother [a]Ā′sa-hĕl at [g]Gĭb′e-on in the battle.

31 ¶ [c]And [b]Dā′vid said to [e]Jō′ăb, and to all the people that *were* with him, [h]Rend your clothes, and gird you with sackcloth, and [i]mourn before [d]Ăb′nēr. And king Dā′vid *himself* followed the [j]bier.

32 And they [k]buried [d]Ăb′nēr in [l]Hē′bron: and the king lifted up his voice, and [m]wept at the §grave of Ăb′nēr; and all the people wept.

33 And the king [q]lamented over Ăb′nēr, and said, [n, o]Died Ăb′nēr as a fool dieth?

34 [n, o]Thy hands *were* not bound, nor thy [p]feet put into [q]fetters: as a man falleth before wicked men, *so* fellest thou. And all the people [m]wept again over him.

35 And when all the people came to cause Dā′vid to eat meat while it was yet day, Dā′vid [r]sware, saying, So do God to me, and more also, [s]if I taste bread, or ought else, till the sun be down.

36 And all the people took no-

v.28–976 BC
See footnote, *Time*, Rev. 10:6.

28
b *David*, 1 Sam. 16:13.
c *Diplomacy*, vs. 28–38; 2 Kin. 16:7.
d *Abner*, 1 Sam. 14:50.

29
e *Joab*, 2 Sam. 20:23.

30
f *Revenge, instances of*, Ezek. 25:15.
g *Gibeon*, Jer. 41:16.

31
h *Rending of Garments*, 2 Chr. 34:27.
i *Mourning*, Lam. 2:5.
j Luke 7:14.

32
k *Burial*, Acts 8:2
l *Hebron*, Gen. 23:2.
m *Weeping, instances of*, Ezra 3:13.

33
n *Elegy*, 2 Sam. 1:17–27.
o *Poetry, elegy on the death of Abner*, Acts 17:28.

34
p *Feet*, 2 Sam. 4:4.
q *Fetters*, Mark 5:4.

35
r *Oath*, Num. 5:19.
s *Fasting*, Zech. 8:19.

‖ **ABISHAI.** *Son of Zeruiah, David's sister, and brother of Joab and Asahel, two of David's most gallant leaders*, 2 Sam. 2:18; 1 Chr. 2:16. *One of David's chief men*, 2 Sam. 23:18. *Seeks Saul's life*, 1 Sam. 26:6–8. *Pursues and slays Abner*, 2 Sam. 2:24. *Defeats, the Edomites*, 1 Chr. 18:12, *the Ammonites*, 2 Sam. 10:10, 14; 1 Chr. 19:10–15. *Seeks the life of Shimei*, 2 Sam. 16:9; 19:21. *Leads a division of David's army against Absalom*, 2 Sam. 18:2, 5. *Commanded army which overthrew Sheba*, 2 Sam. 20:1–22. *Saves David from being slain by a Philistine*, 2 Sam. 21:17. *Obtains water from the well of Beth-lehem for David*, 1 Chr. 11:15–20.

§ **GRAVE.** *Prepared by Jacob*, Gen. 50:5. *Defilement from touching*, Num. 19:16, 18. *Weeping at*, 2 Sam. **3:32**; John 11:31; 20:11. *Of parents, honored*, 2 Sam. 19:**38**. *Welcomed*, Job 3:20–22. *Apostrophe to*, Hos. **13:14**.

See footnote, BURYING PLACES, Gen. **23:4**.

v.36–976 BC
See footnote, *Time*, Rev. 10:6.

37
t *Israel, under the kings.* Ex. 4:22.

39
u *Zeruiah, sister of David,* 1 Chr. 2:16.
v *Wicked, punishment of,* Psa. 73:3.

1
a *Saul,* 1 Sam. 9:2.
b *Ish-bosheth,* 2 Sam. 2:8.
c *Abner,* 1 Sam. 14:50.
d *Hebron,* Gen. 23:2.

2
e *Benjamin, tribe of,* Num. 1:37.
f *Beeroth,* Josh. 9:17.

3
g Neh. 11:33.

4
h *Jonathan,* 1 Sam. 14:1.
i *Jezreel, Israelites defeated at,* Josh. 17:16.
j *Nurse,* 2 Chr. 22: 11.
k *Mephibosheth,* 2 Sam. 9:6.

tice *of it,* and it pleased them: as
whatsoever the king did pleased
all the people.
37 For all the people and all
[t]Ĭṣ′ra-el understood that day
that it was not of the king to slay
[d]Ăb′nēr the son of Nēr.
38 And the king said unto his
servants, Know ye not that there
is a prince and a great man
fallen this day in Ĭṣ′ra-el?
39 And I *am* this day weak,
though anointed king; and these
men the sons of [u]Zĕr-ụ-ī′ah *be*
too hard for me: the LORD shall
[v]reward the doer of evil according to his wickedness.

## CHAPTER 4

*The Israelites being troubled at the death of Abner, 2 Baanah and Rechab slay Ish-bosheth, and bring his head to Hebron. 9 David causes them to be slain, and Ish-bosheth's head to be buried.*

AND when [a]Sạul's [b]son heard
that [c]Ăb′nēr was dead in
[d]Hē′bron, his hands were feeble,
and all the Ĭṣ′ra-el-ītes were
troubled.
2 And Sạul's son had two men
*that were* captains of bands: the
name of the one *was* Bā′a-nah,
and the name of the other Rē′-
chăb, the sons of Rĭm′mon a
Bė-ē′roth-īte, of the children of
[e]Bĕn′ja-mĭn: (for [f]Bė-ē′roth also
was reckoned to Bĕn′ja-mĭn.
3 And the Bė-ē′roth-ītes fled to
[g]Ğĭt′ta-ĭm, and were sojourners
there until this day.)
4 And [h]Jŏn′a-than, [a]Sạul's son,
had a son *that was* lame of *his*
*feet. He was five years old
when the tidings came of Sạul
and Jŏn′a-than out of [i]Jĕz′re-el,
and his [j]nurse took him up, and
fled: and it came to pass, as she
made haste to flee, that he fell,
and became lame. And his name
*was* [k]Mė-phĭb′o-shĕth.
5 ¶ And the sons of Rĭm′mon
the Bė-ē′roth-īte, Rē′chăb and
Bā′a-nah, went, and came about
the heat of the day to the house
of [b]Ĭsh–bō′sheth, who lay on a
bed at noon.
6 And they came thither into
the midst of the house, *as though*
they would have fetched wheat;
and they [l,m,n]smote him [1]under
the fifth *rib*: and Rē′chăb and
Bā′a-nah his brother escaped.
7 For when they came into the
house, he lay on his bed in his
bedchamber, and they smote
him, and slew him, and beheaded him, and took his head,
and gat them away through
the [2]plain all night.
8 And they brought the head of
[b]Ĭsh–bō′sheth unto [o]Dā′vid to
[d]Hē′bron, and said to the king,
Behold the head of Ĭsh–bō′sheth
the son of [a]Sạul thine enemy,
which sought thy life; and the
LORD hath avenged my lord the
king this day of Sạul, and of his
seed.
9 ¶ [p]And Dā′vid answered Rē′-
chăb and Bā′a-nah his brother,
the sons of Rĭm′mon the Bė-ē′-
roth-īte, and said unto them, *As*
the LORD liveth, who hath redeemed my soul out of all adversity,
10 When one told me, saying,
Behold, Sạul is dead, thinking
to have brought good tidings, I
took hold of him, and slew him
in Zĭk′lăg, [3]who *thought* that I
would have given him a reward
for his tidings:
11 How much more, when
wicked men have slain a righteous person in his own house upon his bed? shall I not therefore
now require his blood of your
hand, and take you away from
the earth?
12 And Dā′vid commanded his

v.5–976 BC
See footnote, *Time*, Rev. 10:6.

6
l *Treachery,* 2 Kin. 9:23.
m *Assassination, instances of,* Deut. 27:24.
n *Homicide, felonious, instances of,* Deut. 5:17.
1 R. V. in the belly:

7
2 R. V. Arabah

8
o *David,* 1 Sam. 16:13.

9
p *Government, monarchical, tyranny in,* vs. 9–12; Isa. 22:21.

10
3 R. V. which was the reward I gave him for his tidings.

* **FEET.** *Washing of,* Gen. 18:4; 19:2; 24:32; 43:24; Judg. 19:21; *by priests,* Ex. 30:19, 21; 40:31; *by disciples,* 1 Tim. 5:10; *by Jesus, as an example,* John 13:4–14.
*Of Jesus, anointed by Mary,* John 11:2; 12:3; *kissed by a sinful but penitent woman,* Luke 7:38. *Lame,* 2 Sam. 4:4; Acts 14:8. *In fetters or stocks,* 2 Sam. 3:34; Job 13:27; *of Paul and Silas in the prison in Philippi,* Acts 16:24.
**Figurative,** Psa. 58:10; Isa. 52:7; Matt. 18:8; Rom. 10:15. *Sitting at, figurative of being instructed,* Luke 10:39; Acts 22:3.

v.12–976 BC
See footnote, *Time*, Rev. 10:6.

12
q *Punishment, death penalty*, Lev. 26:41.
r *Hanging*, Josh. 8:29.
s *Pool*, 2 Sam. 2:13.

young men, and they [q]slew
them, and cut off their hands
and their feet, and [r]hanged *them*
up over the [s]pool in Hē′bron.
But they took the head of Ĭsh-
bō′sheth, and buried *it* in the
sepulchre of Ăb′nēr in Hē′bron.

## CHAPTER 5

*The tribes come to Hebron to anoint David king over Israel. 4 His age. 6 He takes Zion from the Jebusites and dwells in it. 11 Hiram sends to David. 14 Eleven sons are born to David in Jerusalem. 17 He smites the Philistines at Baal-perazim, 22 and again at the mulberry trees.*

1
a *Israel, under the kings*, Ex. 4:22.
b *David*, 1 Sam. 16:13.
c *Hebron*, Gen. 23:2.

THEN came all the tribes
of [a]Ĭṣ′ra-el to [b]Dā′vid unto
[c]Hē′bron, and spake, saying,
Behold, we *are* thy bone and
thy flesh.
2 Also in time past, when [d]Saul
was king over us, thou wast he
that leddest out and broughtest
in Ĭṣ′ra-el: and the LORD said to
thee, Thou shalt feed my people
Ĭṣ′ra-el, and thou shalt be a captain over Ĭṣ′ra-el.
3 So all the [e]elders of Ĭṣ′ra-el
came to the king to [c]Hē′bron;
and king [b]Dā′vid [f]made a league
with them in Hē′bron before the
LORD: and they [g]anointed Dā′-
vid [h,i]king over Ĭṣ′ra-el.
4 [b]Dā′vid *was* thirty years old
when he began to reign, *and* he
reigned forty years.
5 In [c]Hē′bron he reigned over
[j]Jū′dah seven years and six
months: and in [k]Jĕ-ru′sā-lĕm he
reigned thirty and three years
over all [a]Ĭṣ′ra-el and Jū′dah.
6 ¶ And the [b,h]king and his
men went to [k]Jĕ-ru′sā-lĕm [1]unto
the [l]Jĕb′u-sītes, the inhabitants
of the land: which spake unto
Dā′vid, saying, Except thou take
away the [m]blind and the [n]lame,
thou shalt not come in hither:
thinking, Dā′vid cannot come in
hither.
7 Nevertheless Dā′vid took the
strong hold of *Zī′ŏn: the same
*is* the [k]city of Dā′vid.
8 And [b]Dā′vid said on that day,
Whosoever [2]getteth up to the
gutter, and smiteth the [l]Jĕb′u-
sītes, and the [n]lame and the
[m]blind, *that are* hated of Dā′vid's
soul, *he shall be chief and captain*. [3]Wherefore they said, The
blind and the lame shall not
come into the house.
9 So Dā′vid dwelt in the [o]fort,
and called it the [k]city of Dā′vid.
And Dā′vid built round about
from †Mĭl′lō and inward.
10 And [b]Dā′vid went on, and
grew great, and the LORD God
of hosts *was* with him.
11 ¶ And ‡Hī′ram king of
[p]Tȳre sent [q]messengers to [b]Dā′-
vid, and [r]cedar trees, and [s]car-
penters, and ‖masons: and they
[t]built Dā′vid an [u]house.
12 And Dā′vid perceived that
the [v]LORD had established him
king over [a]Ĭṣ′ra-el, and that he
had exalted his kingdom for his
people Ĭṣ′ra-el's sake.
13 ¶ And [b]Dā′vid [w]took *him*
more [x]concubines and wives out
of [k]Jĕ-ru′sā-lĕm, after he was
come from [c]Hē′bron: and there
were yet sons and daughters
born to Dā′vid.
14 And these *be* the names of
those that were born unto him in

2
d *Saul*, 1 Sam. 9:2.

3
e *Senate*, Num. 11:16.
f *Constitution*, Dan. 6:12.
g *Anointing*, Lev. 8:12.
h *King*, 2 Kin. 3:10.
i *Government, monarchical*, Isa. 22:21.

5
j *Judah, tribe of*, Num. 10:14.
k *Jerusalem*, Judg 19:10.

6
l *Jebusites*, Deut. 7:1.
1 R. V. against

v.6–976 BC
See footnote, *Time*, Rev. 10:6.

m *Blind*, Deut. 27:18.
n *Lameness*, Lev. 21:18.

8
2 R. V. smiteth the Jebusites, let him get up to the watercourse, and smite the lame
3 R. V. Wherefore they say, There are the blind and the lame; he cannot come into the house.

9
o *Fortification*, Ezek. 17:17.

11
p *Tyre*, 1 Kin. 5:1.
q *Ambassadors*, Josh. 9:4.
r *Cedar*, Isa. 9:10.
B.C. 1043?
s *Carpentry*, 2 Kin. 12:11.
t *Art*, 2 Chr. 16:14.
u *House*, Esth. 8:1.

12
v *Government, God in*, Isa. 22:21.

13
w *Polygamy*, Deut. 17:17.
x *Concubinage*, 2 Sam. 21:11.

* **ZION,** called also SION, a stronghold of Jerusalem. *Taken from the Jebusites by David*, 2 Sam. 5:6–9; 1 Chr. 11:5–7. *Called thereafter the* CITY OF DAVID, 2 Sam. 5:7, 9; 1 Kin. 8:1; 1 Chr. 11:5, 7; 15:1, 29; 2 Chr. 5:2. *Ark placed in*, 2 Sam. 6:12, 16; 1 Kin 8:1; 1 Chr. 15:1, 29; 2 Chr. 5:2.
*Collectively, the place, the forms, and the assemblies of Israelitish worship*, 2 Kin. 19:21, 31; Psa. 9:11; 48:2, 11, 12; 74:2; 132:13; 137:1; Isa. 35:10; 40:9; 49:14; 51:16; 52:1, 2, 7, 8; 60:14; 62:1, 11; Jer. 31:6; 50:5; Lam. 1:4; Joel 2:1, 15; Matt 21:5; John 12:15; Rom. 9:33; 11:26; 1 Pet. 2:6.
*Applied to Jerusalem*, Psa. 87:2, 3, 5; 149:2; Song 3:11; Isa. 33:14, 20; 60:14; Jer. 9:19; 30:17; Zech. 9:13.
*Restoration of, promised*, Isa. 51:3, 11, 16; 52:1, 2, 7, 8; 59:20; 60:14; Obad. 17, 21; Zeph. 3:14, 16; Zech. 1:14, 17; 2:7, 10; 8:2, 3; 9:9, 13.
*City of the redeemed*, Heb. 12:22; Rev. 14:1.

† **MILLO.** *Part of the citadel of Jerusalem*, 1 Chr. 11:8. *King Solomon raises a levy to repair*, 1 Kin. 9:15, 24; 11:27. *Repaired by King Hezekiah*, 2 Chr. 32:5. *King Joash murdered at*, 2 Kin. 12:20.

‡ **HIRAM,** king of Tyre, called also HURAM. *Builds a house for David*, 1 Chr. 14:1; 2 Chr. 2:3. *Love of, for David*, 1 Kin. 5:1. *Aids Solomon in building the temple*, 1 Kin. 5; 2 Chr. 2:3–16. *Dissatisfied with cities given by Solomon*, 1 Kin. 9:11–13. *Makes presents of gold and seamen to Solomon*, 1 Kin. 9:14, 26–28; 10:11.

‖ **MASON.** *A trade, in the time of David*, 2 Sam. 5:11; *in later times*, 2 Kin. 12:12; 22:6; 1 Chr. 14:1; Ezra 3:7.

[k]Jē-ru̧'sȧ-lĕm; [y]Shăm-mū'ah, and [z]Shō'băb, and [z]Nā'than, and [a]Sŏl'o-mon,

15 [b]Ĭb'här also, and Ĕl-ĭ-shu̧'ȧ, and [c]Nē'pheg, and [d]Jȧ-phī'ȧ,

16 And [e]Ē-lĭsh'a-mȧ, and [f]Ē-lī'a-dȧ, and [g]Ē-lĭph'a-lĕt.

17 ¶ But when the [h]Phĭ-lĭs'tĭneș heard that they had [i]anointed [j]Dā'vid [k]king over Ĭș'ra-el, all the Phĭ-lĭs'tĭneș came up to seek Dā'vid; and Dā'vid heard *of it*, and went down to the [l]hold.

18 The Phĭ-lĭs'tĭneș also came and spread themselves in the valley of [m]Rĕph'a-ĭm.

19 And Dā'vid [n]enquired of the LORD, saying, Shall I go up to the Phĭ-lĭs'tĭneș? wilt thou deliver them into mine hand? And the LORD [o]said unto Dā'vid, Go up: for I will doubtless deliver the Phĭ-lĭs'tĭneș into thine hand.

20 And [j]Dā'vid came to [p]Bā'al-pĕr'a-zĭm, and Dā'vid smote them there, and said, The LORD hath broken forth upon mine enemies before me, as the breach of waters. Therefore he called the name of that place Bā'al-pĕr'a-zĭm.

21 And there they left their [q]images, and [j]Dā'vid and his men [4]burned them.

22 ¶ And the [h]Phĭ-lĭs'tĭneș came up yet again, and spread themselves in the valley of [m]Rĕph'a-ĭm.

23 And when [j]Dā'vid [n]enquired of the LORD, he [o]said, [r]Thou shalt not go up; [5]*but* [s]fetch a compass behind them, and come upon them over against the [t]mulberry trees.

24 And let it be, when thou hearest the sound of [6]a going in the tops of the [t]mulberry trees, that then thou shalt bestir thyself: for then shall the [u]LORD go out before thee, to smite the host of the [h]Phĭ-lĭs'tĭneș.

25 And [j]Dā'vid did so, as the LORD had commanded him; and smote the [h]Phĭ-lĭs'tĭneș from [v]Gē'bȧ until thou come to [w]Gā'zĕr.

## CHAPTER 6

*David fetches the ark from Kirjath-jearim on a new cart. 6 Uzzah is smitten. 11 God blesses Obed-edom. 12 David bringing the ark into Zion dances before it. 17 He places it in the tabernacle. 20 Michal, reproving David for his religious joy, is childless to her death.*

AGAIN, [a]Dā'vid gathered together all *the* chosen *men* of [b]Ĭș'ra-el, thirty thousand.

2 And [a]Dā'vid arose, and went with all the people that *were* with him from Bā'al-ē of Jū'dah, to bring up from thence the [c]ark of God, whose name is called by the name of the LORD of hosts that [1,d,e]dwelleth *between* the cherubims.

3 And they set the [c]ark of God upon a new [f]cart, and brought it out of the house of [g]Ȧ-bĭn'a-dăb that *was* in [2,h]Gĭb'e-ah: and [i]Ŭz'zah and [j]Ȧ-hī'ō, the sons of Ȧ-bĭn'a-dăb, drave the new cart.

4 And they brought it out of the house of [g]Ȧ-bĭn'a-dăb which *was* at [2,h]Gĭb'e-ah, accompanying the ark of God: and Ȧ-hī'ō went before the ark.

5 And [a]Dā'vid and all the house of Ĭș'ra-el [k]played before the LORD on all manner of *instruments made of* *fir wood, even on [l]harps, and on [m]psalteries, and on [n]timbrels, and [3]on cornets, and on [o]cymbals.

6 And [p]when they came to Nā'chŏn's [q]threshingfloor, [i]Ŭz'zah [r]put forth *his hand* to the [c]ark of God, and took hold of it; for the oxen [4]shook *it*.

7 And the [s]anger of the LORD was kindled against [i]Ŭz'zah; and God [t]smote him there for

**14**
y Or, *Shimea*, 1 Chr. 3:5; or, *Shammua*, 1 Chr. 14:4.
z 1 Chr. 3:5; 14:4.
a *Solomon*, 2 Sam. 12:24.
**15**
b 1 Chr. 3:6; 14:5.
c 1 Chr. 3:7; 14:6.
d 1 Chr. 3:7.
**16**
e 1 Chr. 3:8; 14:7.
f 1 Chr. 3:8; or, *Beeliada*, 1 Chr. 14:7.
g *Eliphelet*, 1 Chr. 3:8.
**17**
h *Philistines*, Gen. 26:14.
i *Anointing, of kings*, Lev. 8:12.
j *David*, 1 Sam. 16:13.
k *King*, 2 Kin. 3:10.
l *Fortification*, Ezek. 17:17.
**18**
m *Rephaim*, 1 Chr. 11:15.
**19**
n *Armies, religious ceremonies in*, Deut. 11:4.
o *Prayer, answered*, Acts 6:4.
**20**
p 1 Chr. 14:11; or, *Perazim* Isa. 28:21.
**21**
q *Idol*, 1 Kin. 15:12.
4 R. V. took them away.
**23**
r *God, providence of*, Gen. 2:2.
s *Strategy*, Judg. 7:16.
t 1 Chr. 14:14, 15.
5 R. V. make a circuit behind them,
**24**
u *War, God in*, Judg. 3:2.
6 R. V. marching in

**25**
v *Geba*, Josh. 21:17.
w 1 Chr. 14:16.
**1**
a *David*, 1 Sam. 16:13.
b *Israel, under the kings*, Ex. 4:22.
**2**
c *Ark, in the tabernacle*, Ex. 25:10.
d *Mercy Seat*, Ex. 25:17.
e *Shekinah*, Lev. 16:2.
1 R. V. sitteth upon the cherubim.
**3**
f 1 Sam. 6:7–14; 1 Chr. 13:7.
g *Abinadab*, 1 Sam. 7:1.
h *Gibeah*, Hos. 9:9.
i 1 Chr. 13:7, 9–11.
j 1 Chr. 13:7.
2 R. V. the hill:
**5**
k *Music*, 2 Chr. 5:13.
l *Harp*, Dan. 3.10.
m *Psaltery*, 1 Chr. 16:5.
n *Timbrel*, Ex. 15:20.
o *Cymbal*, 1 Chr. 13:8.
3 R. V. with castanets,
**6**
p 1 Chr. 13:9, 10.
q *Threshing, floors for*, 1 Chr. 21:20.
r *Sacrilege, instances of*, Lev. 19:8.
4 R. V. stumbled.
**7**
s *Anger of God*, 2 Kin. 13:3.
t *Judgments*, Ex. 6:6.

* **FIR TREE.** *Wood of, used for building*, 1 Kin. 6:15, 34; 2 Chr. 2:8; Song 1:17. *Ships made of*, Ezek. 27:5. *Instruments of music made of*, 2 Sam. 6:5. **Figurative**, Isa. 55:13.

his †error; and there he died by
the ark of God.
8 And Dā'vid was displeased,
because the LORD had made a
breach upon Ŭz'zah: and he
called the name of the place
[u]Pē'rez–ŭz'zah to this day.
9 And Dā'vid was afraid of the
LORD that day, and said, How
shall the [c]ark of the LORD come
to me?
10 So Dā'vid would not remove
the [c]ark of the LORD unto him
into the [v]city of Dā'vid: but Dā'-
vid carried it aside into the
house of ‡Ō'bed–ē'dom the Ḡĭt'-
tīte.
11 And the ark of the LORD
continued in the house of
‡Ō'bed–ē'dom the Ḡĭt'tīte three
months: and the LORD [w]blessed
Ō'bed–ē'dom, and all his household.
12 ¶ And it was told king [a]Dā'-
vid, saying, The LORD hath
blessed the house of ‡Ō'bed–ē'-
dom, and all that *pertaineth* unto
him, because of the [c]ark of God.
So Dā'vid went and brought up
the ark of God from the house of
Ō'bed–ē'dom into the [v]city of
Dā'vid with gladness.
13 And it was *so,* that when
they that bare the [c]ark of the
LORD had gone six [x]paces, he
sacrificed [5]oxen and fatlings.
14 And Dā'vid [y]danced before
the LORD with all *his* might; and
[z]Dā'vid *was* girded with a linen
[a]ephod.
15 So [b]Dā'vid and all the house
of Ĭṣ'ra-el brought up the [c]ark of
the LORD with [d]shouting, and
with the sound of the trumpet.
16 And as the [c]ark of the LORD
came into the [e]city of Dā'vid,
[f]Mī'chal Saul's daughter looked
through a window, and saw king
Dā'vid leaping and [g]dancing before the LORD; and [h]she despised him in her heart.
17 ¶ And they brought in the
[c]ark of the LORD, and set it in
his place, in the midst of the
[6]tabernacle that [b]Dā'vid had
pitched for it: and Dā'vid offered [i]burnt offerings and [j]peace
offerings before the LORD.
18 And as soon as [b]Dā'vid had
made an end of offering [i]burnt
offerings and [j]peace offerings, he
[k]blessed the people in the name
of the LORD of hosts.
19 And he dealt among all the
people, *even* among the whole
multitude of Ĭṣ'ra-el, as well to
the women as men, to every one
a cake of bread, and a good
piece *of flesh,* and a [7]flagon *of
wine.* So all the people departed
every one to his house.
20 ¶ Then [b]Dā'vid returned to
bless his household. And [l]Mī'-
chal the daughter of Saul came
out to meet Dā'vid, and [l,m]said,
How glorious was the king of
Ĭṣ'ra-el to day, who uncovered
himself to day in the eyes of the
handmaids of his servants, as
one of the vain fellows shame-
lessly uncovereth himself!
21 And Dā'vid said unto Mī'-
chal, *It was* before the LORD,
which [n]chose me before thy father, and before all his house, to
appoint me ruler over the people of the LORD, over Ĭṣ'ra-el:
therefore will I play before the
LORD.
22 And I will yet be more vile

**8**
u 1 Chr. 13:11.

**10**
v *Jerusalem,* Judg. 19:10.

**11**
w *Temporal Blessings, from God,* Psa. 103:2.

**13**
x *Measure, linear,* Deut. 25:15.
5 R. V. an ox and a fatling.

**14**
y *Dancing,* Eccl. 3:4.
z 1 Chr. 15:27–29.
a *Ephod,* Ex. 28:6.

**15**
b *David,* 1 Sam. 16:13.
c *Ark,* Ex. 25:10.
d *Shouting,* 2 Chr. 15:14.

**16**
e *Jerusalem,* Judg. 19:10.
f *Michal,* 1 Sam. 18:20.
g *Dancing,* Eccl. 3:4.
h *Women, wicked, instances of,* Prov. 31:10.

**17**
i *Offerings, burnt,* Lev. 6:17.
j *Offerings, peace,* Lev. 6:17.
6 R. V. tent

**18**
k *Benedictions,* Deut. 21:5.

**19**
7 R. V. cake of raisins.

**20**
l *Family, infelicity in,* 1 Chr. 13:14.
m *Irony, instances of,* Mark 12:14.

**21**
n *Sarcasm, instances of,* Judg. 10:14.

† **RASHNESS,** Psa. 116:11. *Admonitions against,* Prov. 25:8; Eccl. 5:2; 7:9. *Folly of,* Prov. 14:29; 29:20. *Tends to want,* Prov. 21:5.

**Instances of:** *Moses, in slaying the Egyptian,* Ex. 2:11, 12; Acts 7:24, 25; *when he smote the rock,* Num. 20:10–12. *Jephthah's vow,* Judg. 11:30–39. *Israel's vow to destroy the Benjamites,* Judg. 21:1–6. *Uzzah, in steadying the ark,* 2 Sam. 6:6, 7. *David, in his generosity to Ziba,* 2 Sam. 16:4; 19:26–29. *Rehoboam, in forsaking the counsel of the old men,* 1 Kin. 12:8–15. *Josiah, in fighting against Necho,* 2 Chr. 35:20–24. *Naaman, in refusing to wash in Jordan for his cleansing from leprosy,* 2 Kin. 5:11, 12. *Peter, in cutting off the ear of Malchus,* Matt. 26:51; Mark 14:47; Luke 22:50. *James and John, in desiring to call down fire on the Samaritans for refusing hospitality to Jesus,* Luke 9:54. *Paul, in persisting in going to Jerusalem, against the admonitions of the Holy Spirit,* Acts 21:4, 10–15. *The centurion, in rejecting Paul's counsel to winter in Crete,* Acts 27:11.

‡ **OBED-EDOM** (*servant of Edom*), a Korhite Levite. *Doorkeeper of the ark,* 1 Chr. 15:18, 24; 26:4–8. *David leaves ark with,* 2 Sam. 6:10; 1 Chr. 13:13, 14. *Ark removed from house of,* 2 Sam. 6:12; 1 Chr. 15:25. *Appointed, to minister before the ark,* 1 Chr. 16:4, 5, 37, 38; *to sound with harps,* 1 Chr. 15:21.

than thus, and will be base in
mine own sight: and of the maidservants which thou hast spoken
of, of them shall I be had in
honour.
23 [o]Therefore [l]Mī′chal the
daughter of Saul had no child
unto the day of her death.

## CHAPTER 7

*Nathan approves the purpose of David to build God a house. 4 Afterward by the command of God he forbids him; 12 but promises blessings to his seed. 18 David's prayer and thanksgiving.*

AND it came to pass, when
the [a, b]king sat in his
house, and the LORD had given
him rest round about from all
his enemies;
2 That the [a, b]king said unto
*Nā′than the prophet, [c]See now,
I dwell in an [d]house of cedar,
but the [e]ark of God dwelleth
within curtains[G].
3 And *Nā′than said to the
king, Go, do all that *is* in thine
heart; for the LORD *is* with thee.
4 ¶ And it came to pass that
night, that [f]the word of the LORD
came unto *Nā′than, saying,
5 Go and tell my servant [b]Dā′-
vid, Thus saith the LORD, Shalt
thou build me an [g]house for me
to dwell in?
6 Whereas I have not dwelt in
*any* house since the time that I
[h]brought up the children of [i]Ĭs′-
ra-el out of [j]Ē′gy̆pt, even to this
day, but have walked[G] in a tent
and in a [k]tabernacle.
7 In all *the places* wherein I
have walked with all the children of [i]Ĭs′ra-el spake I a word
with any of the tribes of Ĭs′-
ra-el, whom I commanded to
feed my people Ĭs′ra-el, saying,
Why build ye not me an house
of cedar?
8[S] Now therefore so shalt thou
say unto my servant Dā′vid,

23
o *Retaliation,* Deut. 19:19.

1
a *King,* 2 Kin. 3:10.
b *David,* 1 Sam. 16:13.

2
c *Zeal, instances of,* 2 Cor. 7:11.
d *Palace,* 1 Kin. 21:1.
e *Ark,* Ex. 25:10.

4
f *Prophets, inspiration of,* Isa. 3:2.

5
g *Church,* 1 Kin. 9:3.

6
h *God, providence of,* Gen. 2:2.
i *Israel,* Ex. 4:22.
j *Egypt,* Gen. 41:8.
k *Tabernacle,* Ex. 27:9.

Thus saith the LORD of hosts, [l]I
[m]took thee from the sheepcote[G],
from [n]following the sheep, to be
ruler over my people, over Ĭs′ra-el:
9 And I was with thee whithersoever[G] thou wentest, and [h]have
cut[G] off all thine enemies out of
thy sight, and have [o]made thee a
great name, like unto the name
of the great *men* that *are* in the
earth.[S]
10 Moreover I will [h]appoint a
place for my people [i]Ĭs′ra-el, and
will plant them, that they may
dwell in a place of their own, and
move no more; neither shall
the children of wickedness afflict
them any more, as beforetime[G],
11 And as since the time that
[l]I commanded judges *to be* over
my people [p]Ĭs′ra-el, and have
caused thee to rest from all thine
enemies. Also the LORD telleth
thee that he will make thee an
house[G].
12 And [q]when thy days be fulfilled, and thou shalt sleep with
thy fathers, [l, m]I will [r]set up thy
[s]seed after thee, which shall proceed out of thy bowels[G], and I
will establish his kingdom.
13 [q]He shall build an [t]house for
my name, and [l]I will stablish[G]
[u]the throne of [s]his kingdom [r]for
ever.
14 [q, v]I[T] will be his [w]father, and
[x]he shall be my son. If he commit iniquity, I will [y, z, a]chasten
him with the [b]rod of men, and
with the stripes of the children
of men:[S]
15 But my [c]mercy shall not depart away from him, as I took
*it* from [d]Saul, whom I put away
before thee.
16 And thine house and thy
kingdom shall be established for
ever before thee: [e]thy throne
shall be established for ever.[T]

8
l *Government, God in,* Isa. 22:21.
m *Rulers, appointed by God,* Ex. 18:21.
n *Shepherd,* Jer. 31:10.

9
o *Temporal Blessings, from God,* Psa. 103:2.

11
p *Israel, under the judges,* Ex. 4:22.

12
q 1 Chr. 17:11–14.
r *King, hereditary succession of,* 2 Kin. 3:10.
s *Solomon, prophecies concerning,* 2 Sam. 12:24.

13
t *Temple, Solomon's,* 1 Kin. 6:17.
u *Messianic Hope,* Gen. 49:10.

14
v Heb. 1:5.
w *God, fatherhood of,* Gen. 2:2.
x *Spiritual Adoption,* Rom. 8:15.
y *Divine Chastisement,* Job 33:19.
z *Adversity, design of, for correction,* Psa. 10:6.

a *Wicked, punishment of,* Psa. 73:3.
b *Agency, in executing judgment,* Mark 1:17.

15
c *God, mercy of,* Gen. 2:2.
d *Saul,* 1 Sam. 9:2.

16
e *Messianic Hope,* Gen. 49:10.

* **NATHAN,** a prophet in the time of David. *His message to David concerning the building of a temple,* 2 Sam. 7:1–17; 1 Chr. 17:1–15. *Reproves David for his adultery with Bath-sheba and his murder of Uriah,* 2 Sam. 12:1–15. *Gives Solomon the name Jedidiah,* 2 Sam. 12:25. *Assists Bath-sheba in securing to Solomon, her son, the succession to the throne,* 1 Kin. 1:10–14, 22–27. *Assists in anointing Solomon,* 1 Kin. 1:32–45.

*Kept the chronicles,* 1 Chr. 29:29; 2 Chr. 9:29. *Assists David in the organization of the tabernacle services,* 2 Chr. 29:25.

**17**
[f] *Vision*, Acts 9:10.
[g] *David*, 1 Sam. 16:13.

**18**
[h] *Prayer, exemplified*, Acts 6:4.
[i] *Humility, exemplified*, Prov. 22:4.

**20**
[j] *God, knowledge of*, Gen. 2:2.
[k] *Heart, known to God*, Psa. 44:21.

**21**
[l] *God, goodness of*, Gen. 2:2.

**22**
[m] *God, sovereign*, Gen. 2:2.

**23**
[n] *Israel*, Ex. 4:22.
[o] *God, love of, exemplified*, Gen. 2:2.
[p] *Miracles*, Luke 23:8.
[q] *Egypt*, Gen. 41:8.

17 According to all these words, and according to all this [l]vision, so did Nā′than speak unto [g]Dā′vid.

18 ¶ Then went king [g]Dā′vid in, and sat before the LORD, and he [h]said, [i]Who *am* I, O Lord GOD? and what *is* my house[G], that thou hast brought me hitherto[C]?

19 And this was yet a small thing in thy sight, O Lord GOD; but thou hast spoken also of thy servant's house for a great while to come. And *is* this the manner of man, O Lord GOD?

20 And what can [g]Dā′vid say more unto thee? for thou, Lord GOD, [j,k]knowest thy servant.[S]

21 For thy word's sake, and according to [l]thine own heart, hast thou done all these great things, to make thy servant know *them*.

22 Wherefore thou art great, O LORD God: for *there is* none like thee, neither *is there any* [m]God beside thee, according to all that we have heard with our ears.

23 And what one nation in the earth *is* like thy people, *even* like [n]Ĭs′ra-el, whom God went to [o]redeem for a people to himself, and to make him a name, and to do for you [p]great things and terrible[C], for thy land, before thy people, which thou redeemedst to thee from [q]Ē′ġy̆pt, *from* the nations and their gods?[T]

24 For thou hast confirmed[C] to thyself thy people [n]Ĭs′ra-el *to be* a people unto thee for ever: and thou, LORD, art become their God.

25 [h]And now, O LORD God, the word that thou hast spoken concerning thy servant, and concerning his house, establish *it* for ever, and do as thou hast said.

26 [h]And let thy name be magnified for ever, saying, The LORD of hosts *is* the God over Ĭs′ra-el: and let the house of thy servant Dā′vid be established before thee.

27 For thou, O LORD of hosts, God of Ĭs′ra-el, hast revealed to thy servant, saying, I will build thee an house: therefore hath thy servant found in his heart to [h]pray this prayer unto thee.

28 And now, O Lord GOD, [r]thou *art* that God, and thy words [s]be true, and thou hast promised this goodness unto thy servant:[S]

29 [h]Therefore now let it please thee to bless the house of thy servant, that it may continue for ever before thee: for thou, O Lord GOD, hast spoken *it*: and with thy blessing let the house of thy servant be blessed for ever.

## CHAPTER 8

*David subdues the Philistines and the Moabites. 3 He smites Hadadezer and the Syrians. 7 Toi sends Joram to him with presents. 11 The presents and the spoil David dedicates to God. 14 He puts garrisons in Edom. 16 David's officers.*

AND after this it came to pass, that [a]Dā′vid smote[G] the [b]Phĭ-lĭs′tĭnes, and subdued them: and Dā′vid took [1,c]Mē′theg-ăm′mah out of the hand of the Phĭ-lĭs′tĭnes.

2 And [a]he smote [d]Mō′ab, and measured [e]them with a line, casting them down to the ground; even with two lines measured he to put to death, and with one full line to keep alive. And *so* the [d]Mō′ab-ītes became Dā′vid's servants, *and* brought [f,g]gifts.

3 ¶ [a]Dā′vid smote[G] also *Hăd-ăd-ē′zēr, the son of Rē′hŏb, king of [h]Zō′bah, as he went to recover his [2]border at the river [i]Eū-phrā′tēs.

4 And [a]Dā′vid took from him a thousand [3]*chariots*, and seven hundred [j]horsemen, and twenty

**28**
[r] *Faith, instances of*, Mark 11:22.
[s] *God, faithfulness of*, Gen. 2:2.

**1**
[a] *David*, 1 Sam. 16:13.
[b] *Philistines*, Gen. 26:14.
[c] Or, *Gath*, Josh. 11:22.
1 R. V. the bridle of the mother city out of

**2**
[d] *Moabites, David conquers*, Gen. 19:37.
[e] *Captive, cruelty to*, 1 Sam. 30:3.
[f] *King, emoluments of*, 2 Kin. 3:10.
[g] *Tribute*, Ezra 4:13.

**3**
[h] *Zobah*, 1 Sam. 14:47.
[i] *Euphrates*, Gen. 15:18.
2 R. V. dominion at the River.

**4**
[j] *Cavalry*, 1 Sam. 13:5.
3 R. V. *omits* chariots.

* **HADADEZER**, called also HADAREZER. *King of Zobah, vanquished by David*, 2 Sam. 8:3–13; 10:15–19; 1 Kin. 11:23; 1 Chr. 18:3–10; 19:6–19.

k *Animals, cruelty to,* Jer. 27:5.
l *Horses, houghing of,* Job 39:19.
m *Chariot,* Josh. 11:4.
5
n *Damascus,* Isa. 8:4.
6
o *Garrison,* 1 Sam. 13:3.
p *Syria,* 2 Kin. 6:23.
q *Servant, captives of war made,* Jer. 2:14.
r *God, providence of,* Gen. 2:2.
4 R. V. gave victory to
7
s *Shield,* 1 Kin. 14:27.
t *Gold,* Ezek. 7:19.
u *Jerusalem,* Judg. 19:10.
8
v *Brass,* Job 28:2.
9
w Or, *Tou,* 1 Chr. 18:9, 10.
x *Hamath,* 1 Chr. 18:3.
10
y *Diplomacy, instances of,* 2 Kin. 16:7.
z Or, *Hadoram,* 1 Chr. 18:10.

a *Silver,* 1 Chr. 28:14.
b *Gold,* Ezek. 7:19.
c *Brass,* Job 28:2.
11
d *David,* 1 Sam. 16:13.
e *Liberality, instances of,* 1 Tim. 6:18.
f *Zeal, instances of,* 2 Cor. 7:11.
12
g *Syria,* 2 Kin. 6:23.
h *Moabites,* Gen. 19:37.
i *Ammonites,* Deut. 2:20.
j *Philistines,* Gen. 26:14.
k *Amalekites,* Num. 13:29.
l *Zobah,* 1 Sam. 14:47.

thousand footmen: and Dā'vid
[k]houghed all the chariot [l]*horses,*
but reserved of them *for* an hundred [m]chariots.
5 And when the Sy̆r'ĭ-ans̤ of
[n]Dȧ-măs'cus came to succour
Hăd-ăd-ē'zẽr king of [h]Zō'bah,
[a]Dā'vid slew of the Sy̆r'ĭ-ans̤ two
and twenty thousand men.
6 Then Dā'vid put [o]garrisons
in [p]Sy̆r'ĭ-ȧ of Dȧ-măs'cus: and
the Sy̆r'ĭ-ans̤ became [q]servants
to Dā'vid, *and* brought gifts.
And the LORD [4,r]preserved Dā'-
vid whithersoever he went.
7 And Dā'vid took the [s]shields
of [t]gold that were on the servants of Hăd-ăd-ē'zẽr, and
brought them to [u]Jē-ru̇'sȧ-lĕm.
8 And from Bē'tah, and from
Bĕr'o-thāi, cities of Hăd-ăd-ē'-
zẽr, king Dā'vid took exceeding
much [v]brass.
9 ¶ When [w]Tō'ī king of [x]Hā'-
math heard that [a]Dā'vid had
smitten all the host of Hăd-ăd-
ē'zẽr,
10 [y]Then [w]Tō'ī sent [z]Jō'ram
his son unto king Dā'vid, to
salute him, and to bless him,
because he had fought against
Hăd-ăd-ē'zẽr, and smitten him:
for Hăd-ăd-ē'zẽr had wars with
Tō'ī. And *Jo'ram* brought with
him vessels of [a]silver, and vessels of [b]gold, and vessels of
[c]brass:
11 Which also king [d]Dā'vid did
[e,f]dedicate unto the LORD, with
the [a]silver and [b]gold that he had
dedicated of all nations which he
subdued;
12 Of [g]Sy̆r'ĭ-ȧ, and of [h]Mō'ab,
and of the [i]children of Ăm'mŏn,
and of the [j]Phĭ-lĭs'tīnes̤, and of
[k]Ăm'a-lĕk, and of the spoil of
Hăd-ăd-ē'zẽr, son of Rē'hŏb,
king of [l]Zō'bah.
13 And [d]Dā'vid gat *him* a name
when he returned from smiting
of the [g]Sy̆r'ĭ-ans̤ in the valley
of salt, *being* eighteen thousand
*men.*
14 ¶ And he put [m]garrisons in
Ē'dom; throughout all Ē'dom
put he garrisons, and all [n]they of
Ē'dom became Dā'vid's [o]serv-
ants. And the LORD [4]preserved
Dā'vid whithersoever he went.
15 And [d]Dā'vid reigned over all
[p]Is̤'ra-el; and Dā'vid executed
judgment and [q]justice unto all
his people.
16 [r]And [s]Jō'ăb the son of
[t]Zĕr-u-ī'ah *was* over the [u]host;
and [v]Jė-hŏsh'a-phăt the son of
[v]Ȧ-hī'lu̇d *was* [w]recorder;
17 And [x]Zā'dŏk the son of
[y]Ȧ-hī'tub, and [z]Ȧ-hĭm'e-lĕch the
son of Ȧ-bī'a-thär, *were* the
[a]priests; and [b]Sĕr-a-ī'ah *was*
the [c]scribe;
18 And [d]Bė-nā'iah the son of
[e]Jė-hoi'a-dȧ *was over* both the
[f]Chĕr'e-thītes and the [g]Pĕl'e-
thītes; and Dā'vid's [h]sons were
[5]chief rulers.

## CHAPTER 9

*David inquires for the descendants of Saul.*
*6 His kind reception of Mephibosheth.*
*9 The provision made for him by David.*

AND [a]Dā'vid said, Is there
yet any that is left of the
house of [b]Saul, that I may [c]shew
him [d]kindness for [e]Jŏn'a-than's
sake?
2 And *there was* of the house
of [b]Saul a [f]servant whose name
*was* *Zī'bȧ. And when they had
called him unto [a]Dā'vid, the
[g]king said unto him, *Art* thou
Zī'bȧ? And he said, Thy servant *is he.*
3 And the king said, *Is* there
not yet any of the house of Saul,
that I may [c]shew the kindness
of God unto him? And *Zī'bȧ
said unto the king, Jŏn'a-than
hath yet a [h]son, *which is* [i]lame
on *his* feet.

14
m *Garrison,* 1 Sam. 13:3.
n *Edomites,* 2 Kin. 8:21.
o *Servant, captives of war made,* Jer. 2:14.
15
p *Israel, under the kings,* Ex. 4:22.
q *Justice,* Deut. 33:21.
16
r *Nepotism,* Gen. 47:11.
s *Joab,* 2 Sam. 20:23.
t *Zeruiah, sister of David,* 1 Chr. 2:16.
u *Armies,* Deut. 11:4.
v 2 Sam. 20:24; 1 Kin. 4:3; 1 Chr. 18:15.
w 2 Sam. 20:23-26.
17
x *Zadok,* 2 Sam. 19:11.
y 1 Chr. 18:16.
z 1 Chr. 24:6.

a *High Priest,* Lev. 21:10.
b Or, *Sheva,* 2 Sam. 20:25; or, *Shisha,* 1 Kin. 4:3; or, *Shavsha,* 1 Chr. 18:16.
c *Scribe,* 1 Kin. 4:3.
18
d *Benaiah,* 1 Kin. 4:4.
e 1 Kin. 1:26, 32, 36; 1 Chr. 11:22.
f *Cherethites,* 1 Sam. 30:14.
g *Pelethites,* 2 Sam. 20:7.
h *Nepotism,* Gen. 47:11.
5 R. V. priests.
1
a *David,* 1 Sam. 16:13.
b *Saul,* 1 Sam. 9:2.
c *Friendship, instances of,* Prov. 22:24.
d *Kindness,* Acts 28:2.
e *Jonathan,* 1 Sam. 14:1.
2
f *Servants, good, instances of,* vs. 1–13; Jer. 2:14.
g *King,* 2 Kin. 3:10.
3
h *Orphan, instances of,* Lam. 5:3.
i *Lameness,* Lev. 21:18.

* **ZIBA,** Saul's servant. *His fidelity to Mephibosheth,* 2 Sam. 9. *Deserts and villainously slanders Mephibosheth; joins David, and is given title to Mephibosheth's estate,* 2 Sam. 16:1–4; 19:17; *Mephibosheth obtains a hearing with David and regains half the estate,* 2 Sam. 19:26–29.

4 And the king said unto him,
Where *is* he? And *Zī′bȧ said
unto the king, Behold, he *is* in
the house of [j]Mā′chĭr, the son of
[j]Ăm′mĭ-el, in [j]Lō–dē′bär.
5 Then king Dā′vid sent, and
fetched him out of the house of
[j]Mā′chĭr, the son of [j]Ăm′mĭ-el,
from [j]Lō–dē′bär.
6 Now when †Mē-phĭb′o-shĕth,
the son of [e]Jŏn′a-than, the son
of [b]Sa̤ul, was come unto [a]Dā′-
vid, he [k]fell on his face, and did
[1,l]reverence. And [b]Dā′vid said,
Mē-phĭb′o-shĕth. And he answered, Behold thy servant!
7 ¶ And [a]Dā′vid said unto him,
Fear not: for I will surely shew
thee kindness for [e]Jŏn′a-than
thy father's sake, and will restore thee all the land of Sa̤ul thy
father: and [m,n]thou shalt eat
bread at my table continually.
8 And †he [2,l]bowed himself,
and said, [o]What *is* thy servant,
[p]that thou shouldest look upon
such a dead [q]dog as I *am*?
9 ¶ Then the [a,g]king called to
*Zī′bȧ, [b]Sa̤ul's servant, and said
unto him, I have [m]given unto thy
master's son all that pertained to
Sa̤ul and to all his house.
10 Thou therefore, and thy
sons, and thy [r]servants, shall
[s]till the land for him, and thou
shalt bring in *the fruits*, that thy
master's son may have food to
eat: but †Mē-phĭb′o-shĕth thy
master's son shall eat bread
alway at my table. Now *Zī′bȧ
had fifteen sons and twenty
servants.
11 Then said Zī′bȧ unto the
king, According to all that my
lord the king hath commanded
his servant, so shall thy servant
do. As for †Mē-phĭb′o-shĕth,
*said the king*, he shall eat at
my table, as one of the king's
sons.
12 And †Mē-phĭb′o-shĕth had
a young son, whose name *was*
[t]Mī′chȧ. And all that dwelt in
the house of Zī′bȧ *were* servants
unto Mē-phĭb′o-shĕth.
13 So †Mē-phĭb′o-shĕth dwelt
in [u]Jē-ru̧′sȧ-lĕm: for he did eat
continually at the king's table;
and was lame on both his feet.

4
*j* 2 Sam. 17:27.

6
*k* *Salutations*, Luke 1:44.
*l* *Reverence, for kings*, Lev. 19:30.
1 R. V. obeisance.

7
*m* *Generosity, instances of*, Gen. 20:14.
*n* *Hospitality, instances of*, Rom. 12:13.

8
*o* *Humility, instances of*, Prov. 22:4.
*p* *Flattery, instances of*, Prov. 6:24.
*q* *Dog, epithet of contempt*, 1 Kin. 21:19.
2 R. V. did obeisance.

10
*r* *Servant*, Jer. 2:14.
*s* *Agriculture*, Gen. 3:23.

12
*t* Or, *Micah*, 1 Chr. 8:34, 35; 9:40, 41.

13
*u* *Jerusalem*, Judg. 19:10.

## CHAPTER 10

*David's messengers, sent to comfort Hanun, are shamefully treated. 6 The Ammonites, strengthened by the Syrians, are overcome by Joab and Abishai. 15 The Syrians are again defeated.*

AND [a]it came to pass after
this, that the king of the
[b]children of Ăm′mŏn died, and
[c]Hā′nŭn his son reigned in his
stead.
2 Then [d]said [e]Dā′vid, I will
shew [f]kindness unto [c]Hā′nŭn the
son of [g]Nā′hăsh, as his father
shewed kindness unto me. And
Dā′vid sent to *,[h]comfort him
by the hand of his servants
for his father. And Dā′vid's
servants came into the land of
the [b]children of Ăm′mŏn.
3 And the princes of the [b]chil-
dren of Ăm′mŏn [i]said unto [c]Hā′-
nŭn their lord, [j,k]Thinkest thou
that [e]Dā′vid doth honour thy father, that he hath sent comforters unto thee? hath not Dā′vid
*rather* sent his servants unto
thee, to search the city, and to
spy it out, and to overthrow it?
4 Wherefore [c,l]Hā′nŭn took
[e]Dā′vid's servants, and shaved
off the one half of their [m]beards,
and cut off their garments in the
middle, *even* to their buttocks,
and sent them away.
5 When they told *it* unto [e]Dā′-
vid, he sent to meet them, because the men were greatly

1
*a* 1 Chr. 19:1–19.
*b* *Ammonites*, Deut. 2:20.
*c* 1 Chr. 19:1–6.

2
*d* *Friendship, instances of*, Prov. 22:24.
*e* *David*, 1 Sam. 16:13.
*f* *Thankfulness, of man to man*, Acts 24:3.
*g* *Nahash, kindness of*, 1 Sam. 11:1.
*h* *Sympathy*, 1 Pet. 3:8.

3
*i* *Uncharitableness, instances of*, Matt. 7:1.
*j* *False Accusation*, 2 Tim. 3:3.
*k* *Motive, misunderstood*, Psa. 106:8.

4
*l* *Rulers, wicked, instances of*, Ex. 18:21.
*m* *Beard, half shaven*, 1 Sam. 21:13.

† **MEPHIBOSHETH.** *Son of Jonathan*, 2 Sam. 4:4. *Called* MERIB-BAAL, 1 Chr. 8:34; 9:40. *Was lame*, 2 Sam. 4:4. *A guest of David*, 2 Sam. 9:1–13; 21:7. *Property of his father given to*, 2 Sam. 9:9, 10. *Is slandered to David by his servant Ziba; acting hastily, David gives his property to Ziba; later David restores part of his property*, 2 Sam. 16:1–4; 19:24–30.

* **CONDOLENCE.** **Instances of:** *David, with Hanun, which is resented by Hanun; the war that followed*, 2 Sam. 10:2. *The three friends, with Job*, Job 2:11. *Jews with Mary and Martha*, John 11:31, 33.
See footnotes: AFFLICTIONS, *Consolation in*, Psa. 34:19; SYMPATHY, Jas. 1:27.

ashamed: and the king said, Tarry at [n]Jĕr′ĭ-chō until your beards be grown, and *then* return.

6 ¶ And when the [b]children of Ăm′mŏn saw that they [1]stank before [e]Dā′vid, the children of Ăm′mŏn sent and hired the [o,p]Sy̆r′ĭ-anṣ of [q]Bĕth–rē′hŏb, and the Sy̆r′ĭ-anṣ of [r]Zō′bȧ, twenty thousand footmen, and of king [s]Mā′a-cah a thousand men, and of [2,t]Ĭsh′–tŏb twelve thousand men.

7 And when [e]Dā′vid heard of *it,* he sent [u]Jō′ăb, and all the host of the mighty men.

8 And the [b]children of Ăm′mŏn came out, and put the battle in array at the entering in of the gate: and the [o]Sy̆r′ĭ-anṣ of [r]Zō′bȧ, and of [q]Rē′hŏb, and [2,t]Ĭsh′–tŏb, and [s]Mā′a-cah, *were* by themselves in the field.

9 When [u]Jō′ăb saw that the front of the battle was against him before and behind, he chose of all the choice *men* of [v]Ĭṣ′ra-el, and put *them* in array against the [o]Sy̆r′ĭ-anṣ:

10 And the rest of the people he delivered into the hand of [w]Ȧ-bĭsh′a-ī his brother, that he might put *them* in array against the [b]children of Ăm′mŏn.

11 And he said, If the [o]Sy̆r′ĭ-anṣ be too strong for me, then thou shalt help me: but if the [b]children of Ăm′mŏn be too strong for thee, then I will come and help thee.

12 Be of good courage, and [x]let us play the men for our people, and for the cities of our God: and the LORD do that which seemeth him good.

13 And [u]Jō′ăb drew nigh, and the people that *were* with him, unto the battle against the [o]Sy̆r′ĭ-anṣ: and they fled before him.

14 And when the [b]children of Ăm′mŏn saw that the Sy̆r′ĭ-anṣ were fled, then fled they also before [w]Ȧ-bĭsh′a-ī, and entered into the city. So [u]Jō′ăb returned from the children of Ăm′mŏn, and came to [y]Jĕ-ru̥′sȧ-lĕm.

15 ¶ And when the [o]Sy̆r′ĭ-anṣ saw that they were [3]smitten before [v]Ĭṣ′ra-el, they gathered themselves together.

16 And [z]Hăd-är-ē′zēr sent, and brought out the [o]Sy̆r′ĭ-anṣ that *were* beyond the river: and they came to Hē′lam; and [a]Shō′băch the [b]captain of the host of Hăd-är-ē′zēr *went* before them.

17 And when it was told [c]Dā′vid, he gathered all [d]Ĭṣ′ra-el together, and passed over [e]Jôr′dan, and came to Hē′lam. And the Sy̆r′ĭ-anṣ set themselves in array against Dā′vid, and fought with him.

18 And the Sy̆r′ĭ-anṣ fled before Ĭṣ′ra-el; and [c]Dā′vid slew *the men of* seven hundred [f]chariots of the Sy̆r′ĭ-anṣ, and forty thousand [g]horsemen, and smote Shō′băch the captain of their host, who died there.

19 And when all the kings *that were* servants to [h]Hăd-är-ē′zēr saw that they were [3]smitten before Ĭṣ′ra-el, they made peace with Ĭṣ′ra-el, and served them. So the Sy̆r′ĭ-anṣ feared to help the children of Ăm′mŏn any more.

## CHAPTER 11

*Joab besieges Rabbah. 2 David commits adultery with Bath-sheba. 3 His attempt to conceal his adultery. 14 He plots the death of Uriah. 17 Uriah is slain; and Joab sends word to David. 26 David takes Bath-sheba to wife.*

AND it came to pass, after the year was expired, at the time when kings go forth *to battle,* that [a]Dā′vid sent [b]Jō′ăb, and his servants with him, and all [c]Ĭṣ′ra-el; and they destroyed the [d]children of Ăm′mŏn, and [e]besieged [f]Răb′bah. But Dā′vid tarried still at [g]Jĕ-ru̥′sȧ-lĕm.

2 ¶ And it came to pass in an

5
n *Jericho,* Num. 22:1.

6
o *Syria, armies of,* 2 Kin. 6:23.
p *Armies, composed of mercenaries,* Deut. 11:4.
q Judg. 18:28.
r *Zobah,* 1 Sam. 14:47.
s 1 Chr. 19:7.
t Or, *Tob,* Judg. 11:3, 5.
1 R. V. were become odious to
2 R. V. the men of Tob

7
u *Joab,* 2 Sam. 20:23.

9
v *Israel, under the kings,* Ex. 4:22.

10
w *Abishai,* 2 Sam. 3:30.

12
x *Patriotism, instances of,* Psa. 137:1.

14
y *Jerusalem,* Judg. 19:10.

15
3 R. V. put to the worse

16
z Or, *Hadadezer,* 2 Sam. 8:3.
a Or, *Shophach,* 1 Chr. 19:16, 18.
b *Captain,* Num. 31:48.

17
c *David,* 1 Sam. 16:13.
d *Israel, under the kings,* Ex. 4:22.
e *Jordan,* Gen. 32:10.

18
f *Chariot,* Josh. 11:4.
g *Cavalry,* 1 Sam. 13:5.

19
h Or, *Hadadezer,* 2 Sam. 8:3.

1
a *David,* 1 Sam. 16:13.
b *Joab,* 2 Sam. 20:23.
c *Israel, under the kings,* Ex. 4:22.
d *Ammonites,* Deut. 2:20.
e *Siege, instances of,* Deut. 28:53.
f *Rabbah,* Deut. 3:11.
g *Jerusalem,* Judg. 19:10.

eveningtide, that [a]Dā′vid arose
from off his bed, and walked upon the roof of the king's [h]house:
and from the roof he saw a
woman washing herself; and the
woman *was* very [i]beautiful [j]to
look upon.
3 And [a]Dā′vid sent and [k]en-
quired after the woman. And
*one* said, *Is* not this [l]Băth′-shĕ-
bȧ, the daughter of [m]Ė-lī′am, the
[n]wife of *U-rī′ah the Hĭt′tīte?
4 And [a]Dā′vid sent messengers,
and [o]took her; and [p]she came in
unto him, and he [q]lay with her;
for she was [r]purified from her
[s]uncleanness: and she returned
unto her house.
5 And the woman conceived,
and sent and told [a]Dā′vid, and
said, I *am* with child.
6 And [a]Dā′vid sent to [b]Jō′ăb,
*saying*, Send me *U-rī′ah the
Hĭt′tīte. And Jō′ăb sent U-rī′ah
to Dā′vid.
7 And when *U-rī′ah was come
unto him, [a]Dā′vid demanded *of
him* how Jō′ăb did, and how the
people did, and how the [t]war
prospered.
8 And [a]Dā′vid said to *U-rī′-
ah, Go down to thy house, and
[u]wash thy [v]feet. And U-rī′ah
departed out of the king's house,
and there followed him a mess *of*
*meat* from the king.
9 [w]But *U-rī′ah slept at the
door of the king's house with all
the servants of his lord, and went
not down to his house.
10 And when they had told
[a]Dā′vid, saying, *U-rī′ah went
not down unto his house, Dā′vid
said unto U-rī′ah, Camest thou
not from *thy* journey? why *then*
didst thou not go down unto
thine house?
11 And U-rī′ah said unto [a]Dā′-
vid, The [x]ark, and Ĭṣ′ra-el, and
Jū′dah, abide in [1]tents; and my
lord [b]Jō′ăb, and the servants of
my lord, are encamped in the
open fields; [y]shall I then go into
mine house, to eat and to drink,
and to lie with my wife? *as* thou
livest, and *as* thy soul liveth, [z]I
will not do this thing.
12 And Dā′vid said to U-rī′ah,
Tarry here to day also, and to
morrow I will let thee depart. So
U-rī′ah abode in [a]Jė-ru̦′sȧ-lĕm
that day, and the morrow.
13 And when Dā′vid had called
him, he did eat and drink before
him; and he made him [b]drunk:
and at even he went out to lie on
his bed with the servants of his
lord, but went not down to his
house.
14 ¶ And it came to pass in the
morning, that [c,d]Dā′vid wrote a
[e]letter to [f]Jō′ăb, and sent *it* by
the hand of *U-rī′ah.
15 And [g]he wrote in the [e]let-
ter, saying, [h,i,j]Set ye U-rī′ah in
the forefront of the hottest battle,
and retire ye from him, that he
may be smitten, and die.
16 And it came to pass, when
[f]Jō′ăb observed the city, that he
assigned *U-rī′ah unto a place
where he knew that valiant men
*were*.
17 And the men of the city went
out, and fought with [f]Jō′ăb: and
there fell *some* of the people of
the servants of Dā′vid; and
*U-rī′ah the Hĭt′tīte died also.
18 ¶ Then [f]Jō′ăb sent and told
Dā′vid all the things concerning
the [k]war;
19 And charged the messenger,
saying, When thou hast made an
end of telling the matters of the
[k]war unto the king,
20 And if so be that the king's
[l]wrath arise, and he say unto
thee, Wherefore approached ye
so nigh unto the city when ye
did fight? knew ye not that

2
*h* *House, architecture of*, Esth. 8:1.
*i* *Beauty, instances of*, Prov. 6:25.
*j* *Temptation*, Luke 11:4.

3
*k* *Covetousness*, Isa. 57:17.
*l* *Bath-sheba*, 1 Kin. 1:11.
*m* Or, *Ammiel*, 1 Chr. 3:5.
*n* *Wife*, Prov. 5:18.

4
*o* *Lasciviousness, instances of*, 1 Pet. 4:3.
*p* *Women, wicked*, vs. 5–27; Prov. 31:10.
*q* *Adultery, instances of*, Lev. 20:10.
*r* *Purification*, Num. 19:19.
*s* *Defilement*, Lev. 5:2.

7
*t* *War*, Judg. 3:2.

8
*u* *Ablution, of the feet*, Judg. 19:21.
*v* *Feet*, 2 Sam. 4:4.

9
*w* *Loyalty, instances of*, Eccl. 8:2.

11
*x* *Ark, of the covenant*, Ex. 25:10.
1 R. V. booths;
*y* *Patriotism, instances of*, Psa. 137:1.
*z* *Continence, instances of*, Matt. 19:12.

12
*a* *Jerusalem*, Judg. 19:10.

13
*b* *Drunkenness, instances of*, Luke 21:34.

14
*c* *David*, 1 Sam. 16:13.
*d* *Government, monarchical, tyranny in*, vs. 14–17; Isa. 22: 21.
*e* *Letters*, Isa. 37: 14.
*f* *Joab*, 2 Sam 20: 23.

15
*g* *Friends, false*, Ex. 33:11.
*h* *Evil for Good*, Psa. 35:12.
*i* *Ingratitude, of man to man*, Rom. 1:21.
*j* *Treachery*, 2 Kin. 9:23.

18
*k* *War*, Judg. 3:2.

20
*l* *Anger*, Psa. 37:8.

* **URIAH.** *One of David's mighty men*, 2 Sam. 23:39; 1 Chr. 11:41. *David's adultery with the wife of*, 2 Sam. 11:2–5; 1 Kin. 15:5. *Summoned from seat of war by David*, 2 Sam. 11:6–13. *Noble spirit of*, 2 Sam. 11:11. *David compasses the death of*, 2 Sam. 11:14–25. *David marries the widow of*, 2 Sam. 11:26, 27. *Called* URIAS, Matt. 1:6.

they would shoot from the
[m]wall?
21 Who smote [n]Ă-bĭm′e-lĕch
the son of Jĕ-rŭb′be-shĕth? did
not a woman cast [2]a piece of a
millstone upon him from the
[m]wall, that he died in [o]Thē′bĕz?
why went ye nigh the wall? then
say thou, Thy servant *U-rī′ah
the Hĭt′tīte is dead also.
22 ¶ So the messenger went,
and came and shewed [c]Dā′vid
all that [f]Jō′ăb had sent him for.
23 And the messenger said unto
[c]Dā′vid, Surely the men prevailed against us, and came out
unto us into the field, and we
were upon them even unto the
entering of the gate.
24 And the shooters shot from
off the [m]wall upon thy servants;
and *some* of the king's servants
be dead, and thy servant *U-rī′-
ah the Hĭt′tīte is dead also.
25 Then Dā′vid said unto the
messenger, Thus shalt thou say
unto [f]Jō′ăb, Let not this thing
displease thee, for the sword
devoureth one as well as another: make thy battle more strong
against the city, and overthrow
it: and encourage thou him.
26 ¶ And when the [p]wife of
U-rī′ah heard that *U-rī′ah her
husband was dead, she [q]mourned
for her husband.
27 And when the mourning was
past, [c]Dā′vid sent and fetched
her to his house, and she became
his wife, and bare him a son.
But the [r]thing that Dā′vid had
done displeased the LORD.

## CHAPTER 12

*Nathan's parable of the ewe lamb.* 7 *He applies it to David, who confesses his sin and is pardoned.* 15 *David's conduct upon the sickness and death of the child.* 24 *Solomon is born.* 26 *Rabbah is taken.*

AND the LORD [a]sent [b,c]Nā′-
than unto [d]Dā′vid. And
he came unto him, and [e]said unto him, [f]There were two men in
one city; the one rich, and the
other poor.
2 The rich *man* had exceeding
many flocks and herds:
3 But the poor *man* had nothing, save one little ewe lamb,
which he had bought and nourished up: and it grew up together
with him, and with his children;
it did eat of his own meat, and
drank of his own cup, and lay in
his bosom, and was unto him as
a daughter.
4 And there came a traveller
unto the rich man, and he spared
to take of his own flock and of
his own herd, to dress for the
wayfaring man that was come
unto him; but he took the poor
man's lamb, and dressed it for
the man that was come to him.
5 And Dā′vid's [g]anger was
greatly kindled against the man;
and he said to [b]Nā′than, [h]*As* the
LORD liveth, [i]the man that hath
done this [1]*thing* shall surely die:
6 And he shall [j]restore the lamb
fourfold, because he did this
thing, and because he had no
pity.
7 ¶ And [b]Nā′than [e]said to
[d]Dā′vid, Thou *art* the man.
Thus saith the LORD God of
Ĭş′ra-el, [k]I [l]anointed thee king
over [m]Ĭş′ra-el, and I [n]delivered
thee out of the hand of [o]Saul;
8 And [p]I gave thee thy master's
house, and thy master's [q]wives
into thy bosom, and gave thee
the house of Ĭş′ra-el and of Jū′-
dah; and if *that had been* too little, I would moreover have given
unto thee such and such things.
9 Wherefore hast thou despised
the commandment of the LORD,
to [r]do evil in his sight? thou hast
[s]killed [t]U-rī′ah the Hĭt′tīte with
the sword, and hast taken his
[u]wife *to be* thy wife, and hast
slain him with the sword of the
[v]children of Ăm′mŏn.
10 Now therefore [w,x]the sword

m *Walls,* 1 Sam. 20:25.

21

n Judg. 8:31; 9.
o Judg. 9:50–56.
2 R. V. an upper millstone

26

p *Bath-sheba,* 1 Kin. 1:11.
q *Mourning,* Lam. 2:5.

27

r *Sin, repugnant to God,* Rom. 5:12.

1

a *Prophets, inspiration of,* Isa. 3:2.
b *Nathan,* 2 Sam. 7:2.
c *Minister, influential in public affairs,* Rom. 15:16.
d *David,* 1 Sam. 16:13. e *Reproof, faithfulness in,* Prov. 17:10.
f *Parables, of the lamb,* vs. 1–6; Ezek. 20.49.

5

g *Anger,* Psa. 37:8.
h *Oath,* Num. 5:19.
i *Self-condemnation, instances of,* Job 9:20.
1 R. V. is worthy to die:

6

j *Restitution,* Ex. 22:3.

7

k *King, by divine appointment,* 2 Kin. 3:10.
l *Anointing,* Lev. 8:12.
m *Israel, under the kings,* Ex. 4:22.
n *God, providence of,* Gen. 2.2.
o *Saul,* 1 Sam. 9:2.

8

p *Government, God in,* Isa. 22:21.
q *Polygamy, authorized,* Deut. 17:17.

9

r *Disobedience to God,* Eph. 5:6.
s *Homicide, felonious, instances of,* Deut. 5:17.
t *Uriah,* 2 Sam. 11:3.
u *Women, wicked, instances of,* Prov. 31:10.
v *Ammonites,* Deut. 2:20.

10

w *Adultery, penalties for,* Lev. 20:10.
x *Judgments,* Ex. 6:6.

shall never depart from thine
house; because thou hast despised me, and hast taken the
wife of [t]U-rī'ah the Hĭt'tīte to be
thy wife.
11 Thus saith the LORD, Be-
hold,[w,x]I will raise up evil against
thee out of thine own house, and
I will take thy wives before thine
eyes, and give *them* unto thy
neighbour, and he shall lie with
thy wives in the sight of this sun.
12 For thou didst *it* secretly:
but I will do this thing before all
Is'ra-el, and before the sun.
13 And Dā'vid said unto Nā'-
than, [y,z]I have sinned against
the LORD. And [a]Nā'than said
unto [b]Dā'vid, The LORD also
hath [c,d]put away thy sin; thou
shalt not die.
14 Howbeit, because by this
[e]deed thou hast given great occasion to the enemies of the
LORD to *blaspheme, the child
also *that is* born unto thee [f]shall
surely die.
15 ¶ And [a]Nā'than departed
unto his house. And the LORD
[g]struck the child that U-rī'ah's
[h]wife bare unto [b]Dā'vid, and it
was very sick.
16 Dā'vid therefore [i,j,k]be-
sought God for the child; and
Dā'vid [l]fasted, and went in, and
lay all night upon the earth.
17 And the elders of his house
arose, *and went* to him, to raise
him up from the earth: but he
would not, [l]neither did he eat
bread with them.
18 And it came to pass on the
[m]seventh day, that [n]the child
[o]died. And the servants of [b]Dā'-
vid feared to tell him that the
child was dead: for they said,
Behold, while the child was yet
alive, we spake unto him, and
he would not hearken unto our
voice: how will he then vex himself, if we tell him that the child
is dead?
19 But when [b]Dā'vid saw that
his servants whispered, Dā'vid
perceived that the child was
[o]dead: therefore Dā'vid said unto his servants, Is the child
dead? And they said, He is
dead.
20 Then [b]Dā'vid arose from the
earth, and washed, and [p]anoint-
ed *himself*, and changed his apparel, and came into the [q]house
of the LORD, and worshipped:
then he came to his own house;
and when he required, they set
bread before him, and he did
eat.
21 Then said his servants unto
him, What thing *is* this that thou
hast done? thou didst fast and
weep for the child, *while it was*
alive; but when the child was
dead, thou didst rise and eat
bread.
22 And he said, While the child
was yet alive, I fasted and wept:
for I said, Who can tell *whether*
GOD will be gracious to me, that
the child may live?
23 [r,s,t]But now he is dead,
wherefore should I fast? can I
bring him back again? [u]I shall
go to him, but he shall not return to me.
24 ¶ And [b]Dā'vid comforted

13
y *Repentance, instances of*, Mark 1:4.
z *Sin, confession of*, Rom. 5:12.
a *Nathan*, 2 Sam. 7:2.
b *David*, 1 Sam. 16:13.
c *God, mercy of, manifested in granting forgiveness*, Gen. 2:2.
d *Sin, forgiveness of*, Rom. 5.12.
14
e *Adultery*, Lev. 20:10.
f *Children, death of, as a judgment upon parents*, Mark 10:14.
15
g *Divine Chastisement*, Job 33:19.
h *Bath-sheba*, 1 Kin. 1:11.
16
i *Afflictions, prayer in*, Psa. 34:19.
j *Parents, affection of, exemplified*, 2 Cor. 12:14.
k *Children, prayer in behalf of*, Mark 10:14.
l *Fasting, instances of*, Zech. 8:19.
18
m *Seven*, Gen. 7:2.
n *Bereavement, instances of*, Hos. 9:12.

o *Death*, Num. 23:10.
20
p *Anointing*, Deut. 28:40.
q *Church, called house of the Lord*, 1 Kin. 9:3.
23
r *Bereavement, resignation in*, Hos. 9:12.
s *Afflictions, resignation in, exemplified*, Psa. 34:19.
t *Resignation, exemplified*, Job 5:17.
u *Immortality*, 1 Cor. 15:54.

* **BLASPHEMY.** *Reproaching God*, 2 Kin. 19:22; 2 Chr. 32:19; Psa. 73:9, 11; 74:18; 139:20; Prov. 30:9; Isa. 5:19; 8:21, 22; 37:23; 45:9; 52:5; Ezek. 35:12, 13; Dan. 7:25; Matt. 10:25. *Defying God*, Isa. 29:15, 16; 36:15, 18, 20, 21; 37:10; Ezek. 8:12; 9:9; Mal. 3:13, 14. *Denying the word of God*, Jer. 17:15. *Speaking lies against God*, Hos. 7:13. *Imputing ignorance to God*, Psa. 10:11, 13; Isa. 40:27; *unrighteousness to God*, Jer. 20:7; Ezek. 18:25; 33:17–20. *Exalting oneself above God*, Dan. 11:36, 37; 2 Thess. 2:4. *Calling Jesus accursed*, 1 Cor. 12:3; Jas. 2:7.
*Occasioned by sins of believers*, 2 Sam. 12:14; Rom. 2:24.
**Foretold,** 2 Pet. 3:3, 4. *John's vision of*, Rev. 13:1, 5, 6; 16:9, 11, 21; 17:3.
**Forbidden,** Ex. 20:7; 22:28; Lev. 19:12; 22:32; Jas. 3:10; 5:12.
**Against the Holy Spirit,** Matt. 12:31, 32; Mark 3:29, 30; Luke 12:10.
**Punishment for,** Lev. 24:10–16; Isa. 65:7; Heb. 10:29.
**Instances of:** *The depraved son of Shelomith, who, in an altercation with an Israelite, cursed God*, Lev. 24:10–16. *Those who used the adultery of David as an occasion to blaspheme*, 2 Sam. 12:14. *Rabshakeh, in the siege of Jerusalem*, 2 Kin. 18:22–26, 32–35; 19; Isa. 36:15–20; 37:10–36. *Israel*, Ezek. 20:27, 28. *Saul of Tarsus*, 1 Tim. 1:13. *The early Christians, persecuted by Saul of Tarsus, compelled to blaspheme the name of Jesus*, Acts 26:11. *Two disciples, Hymenæus and Alexander, who were delivered unto Satan that they might learn not to blaspheme*, 1 Tim. 1:20. *Backslidden Ephesians*, Rev. 2:9.
**False accusations of:** *Against Naboth*, 1 Kin. 21:13. *Against Jesus*, Matt. 9:3; 26:65; Mark 2:7; 14:58; Luke 5:21; 22:70, 71; John 5:18; 10:33; 19:7. *Against Stephen*, Acts 6:11, 13.

[h]Băth′–shĕ-bȧ his wife, and went unto her, and lay with her: and she bare a son, and he called his name †Sŏl′o-mon: and the LORD [v]loved him.[s]

25 And he sent by the hand of [a]Nā′than the prophet; and he called his name Jĕd-ĭ-dī′ah, because of the LORD.

26 ¶ And [w]Jō′ăb fought against [x]Răb′bah of the [y]children of Ăm′mŏn, and took the royal [z]city.

27 And [w]Jō′ăb sent messengers to Dā′vid, and said, I have fought against [x]Răb′bah, and have taken the city of waters.

28 [a]Now therefore gather the rest of the people together, and encamp against[c] the city, and take it: lest I take the city, and it be called after my name.

29 And [b]Dā′vid gathered all the people together, and went to [c]Răb′bah, and fought against it, and took it.

30 And he took their king's [d]crown from off his head,[G] the weight whereof *was* a [e]talent of gold with the [f]precious stones: and it was *set* on Dā′vid's head. And he brought forth the [g]spoil of the city in great abundance.

31 And he brought forth the people that *were* therein, and [h]put *them* under ‡saws, and under [i]harrows of iron, and under [j]axes of iron, and made them pass[G] through the [k]brick kiln: and thus did he unto all the cities of the [l]children of Ăm′mŏn. So Dā′vid and all the people returned unto Jĕ-ru̇′sȧ-lĕm.

**24**
*v* *God, love of*, Gen. 2:2.

**26**
*w* *Joab*, 2 Sam. 20: 23.
*x* *Rabbah*, Deut. 3:11.
*y* *Ammonites, defeated by the Israelites*, Deut. 2:20.
*z* *Cities, royal*, Num. 35:8.

**28**
*a* *Unselfishness, instances of*, 1 Cor. 10:24.

**29**
*b* *David*, 1 Sam. 16:13.
*c* *Rabbah*, Deut. 3:11.

**30**
*d* *Crown*, Ex. 29:6.
*e* *Talent*, Ex. 38: 25.
*f* *Precious Stones*, Ex. 39:10.
*g* *Spoils*, 1 Chr. 26: 27.

**31**
*h* *Captive, cruelty to*, 1 Sam. 30:3.
*i* 1 Chr. 20:3.
*j* *Ax*, Deut. 19:5.
*k* *Brick*, Gen. 11:3.
*l* *Ammonites, defeated by the Israelites*, Deut. 2:20.

## CHAPTER 13

*Amnon defiles Tamar, his sister. 15 He thereupon hates her, and turns her away. 19 Absalom receives her, 23 and purposes the death of his brother. 28 Amnon is slain. 30 David's grief at the news of it. 37 Absalom flees to Talmai at Geshur.*

AND it came to pass after this, that [a]Ăb′sa-lŏm the son of [b]Dā′vid had a [c]fair sister, whose name *was* [d]Tā′mar; and[G] [e]Ăm′nŏn the son of Dā′vid loved her.

2 And [e]Ăm′nŏn was so vexed,[G] that he fell sick for his sister [d]Tā′mar; for she *was* a virgin; and Ăm′nŏn thought it hard[G] for him to do any thing to her.

3 But [e]Ăm′nŏn had a friend, whose name *was* Jŏn′a-dăb, the son of [f]Shĭm′e-ah Dā′vid's brother: and Jŏn′a-dăb *was* a very subtil[G] man.

4 And he said unto him, Why *art* thou, *being* the king's son, lean[G] from day to day? wilt thou not tell me? And [e]Ăm′nŏn said unto him, I love [d]Tā′mar, my brother Ăb′sa-lŏm's sister.

5 And Jŏn′a-dăb said unto him, Lay thee down on thy bed, and

**1**
*a* *Absalom*, 2 Sam. 3:3.
*b* *David*, 1 Sam. 16:13.
*c* *Beauty, instances of*, Prov. 6:25.
*d* 1 Chr. 3:9.
*e* 2 Sam. 3:2.

**3**
*f* Or, *Shammah*, 1 Sam. 16:9.

---

† **SOLOMON** (*peace*). *Son of David by Bath-sheba*, 2 Sam. 12:24; 1 Kin. 1:13, 17, 21. *Named Jedidiah, by Nathan the prophet*, 2 Sam. 12:24, 25. *Ancestor of Joseph*, Matt. 1:6. *Succeeds David to the throne of Israel*, 1 Kin. 1:11–48; 2:12; 1 Chr. 23:1; 28. *Anointed king a second time*, 1 Chr. 29:22. *His vision and prayer for wisdom*, 1 Kin. 3:5–14; 2 Chr. 1:7–12. *Covenant of God with, renewed in a vision after the dedication of the temple*, 1 Kin. 9:1–9; 2 Chr. 7:12–22. *His rigorous reign*, 1 Kin. 2.

*Builds the temple*, 1 Kin. 5; 6; 1 Chr. 6:10; 2 Chr. 2; 3; 4; 5:1; 7:11; Jer. 52:20; Acts 7:45–47. *Dedicates the temple*, 1 Kin. 8; 2 Chr. 6. *Renews the courses of the priests and Levites, and the forms of service according to the commandment of Moses and the regulations of David*, 2 Chr. 8:12–16; 35:4; Neh. 12:45.

*Builds, his palace*, 1 Kin. 3:1; 7:1, 8; 9:10; 2 Chr. 7:11; 8:1; *his house of the forest of Lebanon*, 1 Kin. 7:2–7; *palace for Pharaoh's daughter*, 1 Kin. 7:8–12; 9:24; 2 Chr. 8:11. *Thrones of*, 1 Kin. 7:7; 10:18–20. *Builds Millo; the wall of Jerusalem; the cities of Hazor, Megiddo, Gezer, Beth-horon, Baalath, Tadmor; store cities, and cities for chariots and for cavalry*, 1 Kin. 9:15–19; 2 Chr. 9:25. *Provides an armory*, 1 Kin. 10:16, 17. *Imports apes and peacocks*, 1 Kin. 10:22. *Drinking vessels of his houses*, 1 Kin. 10:21; 2 Chr. 9:20. *Musicians and musical instruments of his court*, 1 Kin. 10:12; 2 Chr. 9:11. *The splendor of his court*, 1 Kin. 10:5–9, 12; 2 Chr. 9:3–8; Matt. 6:29; Luke 12:27.

*Commerce of* 1 Kin. 9:28; 10:11, 12, 22, 28, 29; 2 Chr. 1:16, 17; 8:17, 18; 9:13–22, 28. *Presents received by*, 1 Kin. 10:10; 2 Chr. 9:9, 23, 24. *Is visited by the queen of Sheba*, 1 Kin. 10:1–13; 2 Chr. 9:1–12. *Wealth of*, 1 Kin. 9; 10:10, 14, 15, 23, 27; 2 Chr. 1:15; 9:1, 9, 13, 24, 27. *Has seven hundred wives and three hundred concubines* 1 Kin. 11:3; *their influence over him*, 1 Kin. 11:4. *Marries one of Pharaoh's daughters*, 1 Kin. 3:1. *Builds idolatrous temples*, 1 Kin. 11:1–8; 2 Kin. 23:13. *His idolatry*, 1 Kin. 3:3, 4; 2 Kin. 23:13; Neh. 13:26.

*Extent of his dominions*, 1 Kin. 4:21, 24; 8:65; 2 Chr. 7:8; 9:26. *Receives tribute*, 1 Kin. 4:21; 9:21; 2 Chr. 8:8. *Officers of*, 1 Kin. 2:35; 4:1–19; 2 Chr. 8:9, 10. *His purveyors*, 1 Kin. 4:7–19. *Divides his kingdom into subsistence departments, the daily subsistence rate for his court*, 1 Kin. 4:7–23, 27, 28.

*Military equipment of*, 1 Kin. 4:26, 28; 10:16, 17, 26, 28; 2 Chr. 1:14; 9:25. *Cedes certain cities to Hiram*, 1 Kin. 9:10–13; 2 Chr. 8:2. *Wisdom and fame of*, 1 Kin. 4:29–34; 10:3, 4, 8, 23, 24; 1 Chr. 29:24, 25; 2 Chr. 9:2–7, 22, 23; Matt. 12:42. *Piety of*, 1 Kin. 3:5–15; 4:29; 8. *Beloved of God*, 2 Sam. 12: 24. *Justice of, illustrated in his judgment of the two harlots*, 1 Kin. 3:16–28. *Oppressions of*, 1 Kin. 12:4; 2 Chr. 10:4.

*Reigns forty years*, 2 Chr. 9:30. *Death of*, 2 Chr. 9:29–31. *Prophecies concerning*, 2 Sam. 7:12–16; 1 Kin. 11:9–13 1 Chr. 17:11–14; 28:6, 7; Psa. 132:11.

*A type of Christ*, Psa. 45:2–17; 72.

‡ **SAW.** *Used, as an instrument of torture*, 2 Sam 12:31 1 Chr. 20:3; Heb. 11:37; *for cutting stone*, 1 Kin. 7:9; *for cutting wood*, Isa. 10:15.

5
1 R. V. feign

6
2 R. V. feigned

8
3 R. V. dough.

11
g *Seduction, instances of,* Deut. 22:23.
h *Lasciviousness, instances of,* 1 Pet. 4:3.

[1]make thyself sick: and when thy father cometh to see thee, say unto him, I pray thee, let my sister [d]Tā′mar come, and give me meat, and dress the meat in my sight, that I may see *it*, and eat *it*, at her hand.

6 So [e]Ăm′nŏn lay down, and [2]made himself sick: and when the king was come to see him, Ăm′nŏn said unto the king, I pray thee, let [d]Tā′mar my sister come, and make me a couple of cakes in my sight, that I may eat at her hand.

7 Then [b]Dā′vid sent home to [d]Tā′mar, saying, Go now to thy brother [e]Ăm′nŏn's house, and dress him meat.

8 So [d]Tā′mar went to her brother [e]Ăm′nŏn's house; and he was laid down. And she took [3]flour, and kneaded *it*, and made cakes in his sight, and did bake the cakes.

9 And she took a pan, and poured *them* out before him; but he refused to eat. And [e]Ăm′nŏn said, Have out all men from me. And they went out every man from him.

10 And Ăm′nŏn said unto [d]Tā′mar, Bring the meat into the chamber, that I may eat of thine hand. And Tā′mar took the cakes which she had made, and brought *them* into the chamber to Ăm′nŏn her brother.

11 And when she had brought *them* unto him to eat, he [g]took hold of her, and [h]said unto her, Come lie with me, my sister.

12 And she answered him, Nay, my brother, do not force me; for no such thing ought to be done in Ĭș′ra-el: do not thou this folly.

13 And I, whither shall I cause my shame to go? and as for thee, thou shalt be as one of the fools in Ĭș′ra-el. Now therefore, I pray thee, speak unto the king; for he will not withhold me from thee.

14 Howbeit he would not hearken unto her voice: but, being stronger than she, [i]forced her, and [j]lay with her.

15 ¶ Then [e]Ăm′nŏn [k]hated her exceedingly; so that the hatred wherewith he hated her *was* greater than the love wherewith he had loved her. And Ăm′nŏn said unto her, Arise, be gone.

16 And [d]she said unto him, *There is* no cause: this evil in sending me away *is* greater than the other that thou didst unto me. But he would not hearken unto her.

17 Then he called his servant that ministered unto him, and said, Put now this *woman* out from me, and bolt the door after her.

18 And *she had* a [l]garment of divers colours upon her: for with such robes were the king's daughters *that were* [m]virgins apparelled. Then his servant brought her out, and bolted the door after her.

19 ¶ And [d]Tā′mar put [n]ashes on her head, and [o]rent her garment of divers colours that *was* on her, and laid her hand on her head, and went on [p]crying.

20 And [a]Ăb′sa-lŏm her brother said unto her, Hath [e]Ăm′nŏn thy brother been with thee? but hold now thy peace, my sister: he *is* thy brother; regard not this thing. So [d]Tā′mar remained desolate in her brother Ăb′sa-lŏm's house.

21 ¶ But when king [b]Dā′vid heard of all these things, he was very [q]wroth.

22 And [a]Ăb′sa-lŏm spake unto his brother [e]Ăm′nŏn neither good nor bad: for Ăb′sa-lŏm [k]hated Ăm′nŏn, because he had [i]forced his sister [d]Tā′mar.

23 ¶ And it came to pass after

14
i *Rape, instances of,* Deut. 22:25.
j *Incest, instances of,* Lev. 18:6.

15
k *Hatred,* Prov. 15 17.

18
l *Dress,* Zech. 3:3.
m *Virgin,* Isa. 62:5.

19
n *Ashes,* Num. 19:9.
o *Rending of Garments,* 2 Chr. 34: 27.
p *Weeping,* Ezra 3:13.

21
q *Anger,* Psa. 37:8.

23
*r* *Sheep*, Deut. 32: 14.
*s* *Hospitality*, Rom. 12:13.

25
*t* *Benedictions*, Deut. 21:5.
4 R. V. burdensome unto thee.

26
*u* *Amnon*, 2 Sam. 3:2.

28
*v* *Malice, instances of*, Eph. 4:31.
*w* *Drunkenness, instances of*, Luke 21:34.
*x* *Wine, instances of intoxication from*, Prov. 23: 31.

29
*y* *Fratricide, instances of*, Gen. 4:8.
*z* *Assassination, instances of*, Deut. 27:24.

*a* *Amnon*, 2 Sam. 3:2.
*b* *Mule*, 2 Sam. 18:9.

30
*c* *David*, 1 Sam. 16:13.
*d* *Absalom*, 2 Sam. 3:3.

31
*e* *Rending of Garments*, 2 Chr. 34:27.
*f* *Mourning*, Lam. 2:5.

32
*g* Or, *Shammah*, 1 Sam. 16.9.

two full years, that [a]Ăb′sa-lŏm
had [r]sheepshearers in Bā′al–hā′-
zôr, which *is* beside Ē′phră-ĭm:
and Ăb′sa-lŏm [s]invited all the
king's sons.
24 And [a]Ăb′sa-lŏm came to the
king, and said, Behold now, thy
servant hath sheepshearers; let
the king, I beseech thee, and his
servants go with thy servant.
25 And the king said to Ăb′sa-
lŏm, Nay, my son, let us not all
now go, lest we be [4]chargeable
unto thee. And he pressed him:
howbeit he would not go, but
[t]blessed him.
26 Then said Ăb′sa-lŏm, If not,
I pray thee, let my brother [u]Ăm′-
nŏn go with us. And the king
said unto him, Why should he go
with thee?
27 But [a]Ăb′sa-lŏm pressed him,
that he let Ăm′nŏn and all the
king's sons go with him.
28 ¶ Now [a]Ăb′sa-lŏm had commanded his servants, saying,
[v]Mark ye now when [u]Ăm′nŏn's
heart is [w]merry with [x]wine, and
when I say unto you, Smite Ăm′-
nŏn; then kill him, fear not: have
not I commanded you? be courageous, and be valiant.
29 And the servants of Ăb′sa-
lŏm [y,z]did unto [a]Ăm′nŏn as Ăb′-
sa-lŏm had commanded. Then
all the king's sons arose, and
every man gat him up upon his
[b]mule, and fled.
30 ¶ And it came to pass, while
they were in the way, that tidings came to [c]Dā′vid, saying,
[d]Ăb′sa-lŏm hath slain all the
king's sons, and there is not one
of them left.
31 Then the king arose, and
[e,f]tare his garments, and lay on
the earth; and all his servants
stood by with their clothes rent.
32 And Jŏn′a-dăb, the son of
[g]Shĭm′e-ah Dā′vid's brother, answered and said, Let not my
lord suppose *that* they have slain
all the young men the king's
sons; for [a]Ăm′nŏn only is dead:
for by the appointment of [d]Ăb′-
sa-lŏm this hath been determined from the day that he
[h]forced his sister [i]Tā′mar.
33 Now therefore let not my
lord the king take the thing to
his heart, to think that all the
king's sons are dead: for Ăm′-
nŏn only is dead.
34 But [d]Ăb′sa-lŏm [j]fled. And
the [k]young man that kept the
watch lifted up his eyes, and
looked, and, behold, there came
much people by the way of the
hill side behind him.
35 And Jŏn′a-dăb said unto
the king, Behold, the king's sons
come: as thy servant said, so
it is.
36 And it came to pass, as soon
as he had made an end of speaking, that, behold, the king's sons
came, and lifted up their voice
and [l]wept: and the king also and
all his servants wept very sore.
37 ¶ But [d]Ăb′sa-lŏm fled, and
went to [m]Tăl′māi, the son of
Ăm-mī′hŭd, king of [n]Gē′shŭr.
And *Da′vid* [f]mourned for his
son every day.
38 So [d]Ăb′sa-lŏm [j]fled, and
went to [n]Gē′shŭr, and was there
three years.
39 And *the soul of* king [c]Dā′vid
[o]longed to go forth unto Ăb′sa-
lŏm: for he was comforted concerning [a]Ăm′nŏn, seeing he was
dead.

## CHAPTER 14

*Joab, seeking the return of Absalom, fetches a widow of Tekoah to the king. 4 Her parable. 21 Joab is sent to bring Absalom to Jerusalem. 25 Absalom's beauty and family. 28 After two years he is admitted to the presence of the king.*

NOW [a]Jō′ăb the son of [b]Zĕr-
u-ī′ah [c]perceived that the
[d]king's [e]heart *was* toward [f]Ăb′-
sa-lŏm.
2 And [a] [g]Jō′ăb sent to [h]Tē-kō′-
ah, and fetched thence a wise
woman, and said unto her, I

*h* *Rape*, Deut. 22: 25.
*i* 1 Chr. 3:9.

34
*j* *Fugitives, from justice*, Judg. 12.4.
*k* *Watchman*, 2 Sam. 18:24.

36
*l* *Weeping, instances of*, Ezra 3:13.

37
*m* 2 Sam. 3:3; 1 Chr. 3:2.
*n* *Geshur*, 2 Sam. 3.3.

39
*o* *Parents, affection of, exemplified*, 2 Cor. 12:14.

1
*a* *Joab*, 2 Sam. 20: 23.
*b* *Zeruiah, sister of David*, 1 Chr. 2:16.
*c* *Kindness, instances of*, vs. 1–24; Acts 28:2.
*d* *David*, 1 Sam. 16:13.
*e* *Parents, affection of, exemplified*, 2 Cor. 12:14.
*f* *Absalom*, 2 Sam. 3:3.

2
*g* *Tact*, Prov. 15:1.
*h* *Tekoah*, Jer. 6:1.

pray thee, feign thyself to be a [i]mourner, and put on now mourning apparel, and [j]anoint not thyself with oil, but be as a woman that had a long time mourned for the dead:

3 And come to the king, and speak on this manner unto him. So [a,g]Jō'ăb put the words in her mouth.

4 ¶ And when the woman of [h]Tē-kō'ah spake to the king, she fell on her face to the ground, and did obeisance, and said, [k]Help, O king.

5 And the king said unto her, What aileth thee? And she answered, [l]I *am* indeed a *widow woman, and mine husband is dead.

6 And thy handmaid had two sons, and they two strove together in the field, and *there was* none to part them, but the one [m]smote the other, and slew him.

7 And, behold, the whole family is risen against thine handmaid, and they said, Deliver him that smote his brother, that we may kill him, for the life of his brother whom he slew; and we will destroy the heir also: and so they shall quench my [n]coal which is left, and shall not leave to my husband *neither* name nor remainder upon the earth.

8 And the [d]king said unto the woman, Go to thine house, and I will give charge concerning thee.

9 And the woman of [h]Tē-kō'ah said unto the king, My lord, O king, [o]the iniquity *be* on me, and on my father's house: and the king and his throne *be* guiltless.

10 And the king said, Whosoever saith *ought* unto thee, bring him to me, and he shall not touch thee any more.

11 Then said she, I pray thee, let the king remember the LORD thy God, that thou wouldest not suffer the [p]revengers of blood to destroy any more, lest they destroy my son. And he said, [q]*As* the LORD liveth, there shall not one hair of thy son fall to the earth.

12 Then the woman said, [k]Let thine handmaid, I pray thee, speak *one* word unto my lord the [d]king. And he said, Say on.

13 And the woman [r]said, Wherefore then hast thou thought such a thing against the people of God? for the king doth speak this thing as one which is [1]faulty, in that the king doth not fetch home again his banished.

14 [s]For we [t]must needs die, and *are* as water spilt on the ground, which can not be gathered up again; neither doth God [2]respect *any* person: yet doth [u]he devise means, that his banished be not expelled from him.

15 Now therefore that I am come to [k]speak of this thing unto my lord the king, *it is* because the people have made me afraid: and thy handmaid said, I will now speak unto the king; it may be that the king will perform the request of his handmaid.

16 For the king will hear, to deliver his handmaid out of the hand of the man *that would* destroy me and my son together out of the inheritance of God.

17 Then thine handmaid said, The word of my lord the king shall now be comfortable: [v]for as

i *Mourning*, Lam. 2:5.
j *Anointing*, Deut. 28:40.

4
k *Intercession, of man with man, instances of. Joab*, vs. 1–22; Jer. 27:18.

5
l *Parables, of the woman of Tekoa*, Ezek. 20:49.

6
m *Fratricide*, Gen. 4:8.

7
n Prov. 25:22; Isa. 6:6, 7.

9
o *Penalty, vicariously assumed*, 1 Sam. 25:24.

11
p *Avenger of Blood*, Deut. 19:6.
q *Oath*, Num. 5:19.

13
r *Reproof, faithfulness in*, Prov. 17:10.
1 R. V. guilty.

14
s *Life, brevity and uncertainty of*, Eccl. 8:15.
t *Death, inevitable*, Num. 23:10.
u *God, mercy of*, Gen. 2:2.
2 R. V. take away life.

17
v *Flattery, instances of*, Prov. 6:24.

* **WIDOW**, 1 Tim. 5:3–6, 9–12, 16. *High priest forbidden to marry*, Lev. 21:14. *Supported by father, when daughter of priest*, Lev. 22:13. *Vows of, binding*, Num. 30:9. *Entitled to glean in orchards and harvest fields*, Deut. 24:19–21.

*Levirate marriage of*, Deut. 25:5–10. *Marriage of, authorized*, Rom. 7:3; 1 Cor. 7:39; 1 Tim. 5:14 [R. V.]. *Marriage of, discouraged*, 1 Cor. 7:8, 9.

*Kindness to, exemplified by Job*, Job 29:13; 31:16, 22. *God, the friend of*, Deut. 10:18; Psa. 68:5; 146:9; Prov. 15:25; Jer. 49:11.

*Care of, in the Christian churches*, Acts 6:1–7; 1 Tim. 5:9, 16. *Care of, enjoined*, Deut. 14:28, 29; 16:11, 14; Isa. 1:17, Jer. 7:6, 7, 1 Tim. 5:3; Jas. 1:27.

*Neglected*, Acts 6:1. *Oppressed*, Job 24:3, 21; Psa 94:6; Isa. 1:23; Ezek. 22.7, Mark 12:40; Luke 20:47. *Oppression of, forbidden*, Ex. 22:22–24; Deut. 24:17; 27:19; Isa. 10:2; Jer. 22:3; Zech. 7:10; Mal. 3:5.

an angel of God, so *is* my lord
the king to discern good and
bad: therefore the LORD thy
God will be with thee.

18 Then the [d]king answered
and said unto the woman, Hide
not from me, I pray thee, the
thing that I shall ask thee. And
the woman said, Let my lord the
king now speak.

19 And the king said, *Is not* the
hand of [a]Jō'ăb with thee in all
this? And the woman answered
and said, *As* thy soul liveth, my
lord the king, none can turn to
the right hand or to the left from
ought that my lord the king hath
spoken: for thy servant Jō'ăb, he
bade me, and he put all these
words in the mouth of thine
handmaid:

20 [3]To fetch about this form of
speech hath thy servant Jō'ăb
done this thing: and [v]my lord *is*
wise, according to the wisdom of
an angel of God, to know all
*things* that *are* in the earth.

21 ¶ And the king said unto
[a]Jō'ăb, Behold now, I have done
this thing: go therefore, bring
the young man Ăb'sa-lŏm again.

22 And Jō'ăb fell to the ground
on his face, and [4]bowed himself,
and [w]thanked the king: and
Jō'ăb said, To day thy servant
knoweth that I have found grace
in thy sight, my lord, O king, in
that the king hath fulfilled the
request of his servant.

23 So Jō'ăb arose and went to
[x]Gē'shŭr, and brought Ăb'sa-
lŏm to [y]Jē-ru'să-lĕm.

24 And the king said, Let him
turn to his own house, and let
him not see my face. So [l]Ăb'sa-
lŏm returned to his own house,
and saw not the king's face.

25 ¶ But in all Is'ra-el there
was none to be so much praised
as [l]Ăb'sa-lŏm for his [z]beauty:
from the sole of his foot even to
the crown of his head there was
no blemish in him.

26 And when he polled his
head, (for it was at every year's
end that he polled *it*: because *the
hair* was heavy on him, therefore he polled it:) he weighed the
hair of his head at two hundred
shekels after the king's weight.

27 And unto [a]Ăb'sa-lŏm there
were born three sons, and one
daughter, whose name *was* Tā'-
mar: she was a woman of a fair
countenance.

28 ¶ So [a]Ăb'sa-lŏm dwelt two
full years in [b]Jē-ru'să-lĕm, and
saw not the king's face.

29 Therefore Ăb'sa-lŏm sent
for [c]Jō'ăb, to have sent him to
the king; but he would not come
to him: and when he sent again
the second time, he would not
come.

30 Therefore he said unto his
servants, See, Jō'ăb's field is
near mine, and he hath [d]barley
there; go and †set it on fire. And
Ăb'sa-lŏm's servants set the field
on fire.

31 Then [c]Jō'ăb arose, and
came to [a]Ăb'sa-lŏm unto *his*
house, and said unto him,
Wherefore have thy servants
set my field on fire?

32 And [a]Ăb'sa-lŏm answered
[c]Jō'ăb, Behold, I sent unto thee,
saying, Come hither, that I may
send thee to the king, to say,
Wherefore am I come from [e]Gē'-
shŭr? *it had been* good for me *to
have been* there still: now therefore let me see the king's face;
and if there be *any* iniquity in
me, let him kill me.

33 So [c]Jō'ăb came to the king,
and [f]told him: and when he had
called for [a]Ăb'sa-lŏm, he came
to the king, and bowed himself
on his face to the ground before

20
3 R. V. to change the face of the matter hath

22
w *Thankfulness, of man to man,* Acts 24:3.
4 R. V. did obeisance,

23
x *Geshur,* 2 Sam. 3:3.
y *Jerusalem,* Judg. 19:10.

25
z *Beauty,* Prov. 6:25.

27
a *Absalom,* 2 Sam. 3:3.

28
b *Jerusalem,* Judg. 19:10.

29
c *Joab,* 2 Sam. 20:23.

30
d *Barley,* Ex. 9:31.

32
e *Geshur,* 2 Sam. 3:3.

33
f *Intercession, of man with man,* Jer. 27:18.

† **ARSON,** Psa. 74:7, 8. *Law concerning,* Ex. 22:6.
**Instances of** *By Samson,* Judg. 15:4, 5. *By Danites,* Judg. 18:27. *By Absalom,* 2 Sam. 14:30.

the king: and the [g]king [h,i]kissed
Ăb′sa-lŏm.

## CHAPTER 15

*Absalom steals the hearts of Israel. 7 Under cover of a vow he obtains leave to go to Hebron. 10 He makes a great conspiracy there. 13 David upon the news flees from Jerusalem. 19 Ittai refuses to leave him. 24 Zadok and Abiathar are sent back with the ark. 30 David and his people pass over mount Olivet, weeping. 32 Hushai is sent back with instructions.*

AND it came to pass after
this, that [a,b]Ăb′sa-lŏm *pre
pared him chariots and horses,
and fifty men to run before
him.
2 And [a,c,d]Ăb′sa-lŏm rose up
early, and stood beside the way
of the [e]gate: and it was *so*, that
when any man that had a
controversy came to the [f]king
for [g]judgment, †then Ăb′sa-lŏm
[h]called unto him, and said, Of
what city *art* thou? And he said,
Thy servant *is* of one of the
tribes of [i]Iṣ′ra-el.
3 And [a]Ăb′sa-lŏm †,[d]said unto
him, See, [j]thy matters *are* good
and right; but *there is* no man
*deputed* of the king to hear thee.
4 [a,c,d]Ăb′sa-lŏm said moreover,
†Oh that I were made judge in
the land, that every man which
hath any suit or cause might
come unto me, and I would do
him justice!
5 And it was *so*, that [h]when any
man came nigh *to him* to do him
obeisance, he put forth his hand,
and took him, and kissed him.
6 And †on this manner did
[a,c,d]Ăb′sa-lŏm to all Iṣ′ra-el that
came to the king for judgment:
so Ăb′sa-lŏm [k]stole the hearts of
the men of Iṣ′ra-el.
7 ¶ And it came to pass after
[l]forty years, that [a]Ăb′sa-lŏm
said unto the [f,m]king, [n,o]I pray
thee, let me go and pay my [p]vow,
which I have [q]vowed unto the
LORD, in [r]Hē′bron.
8 For thy servant vowed a
[p]vow while I abode at [s]Gē′shŭr
in [t]Sy̆r′ĭ-ȧ, saying, [u]If the LORD
shall bring me again indeed to
[v]Jė-ru̥′sȧ-lĕm, then I will serve
the LORD.
9 And the [f,m]king said unto
him, Go in peace. So he arose,
and went to H[r]ē′bron.
10 ¶ But [a,c]Ăb′sa-lŏm [d]sent
[w]spies throughout all the tribes
of Iṣ′ra-el, saying, As soon as ye
hear the sound of the [x]trumpet,
then ye shall say, Ăb′sa-lŏm
reigneth in [r]Hē′bron.
11 And with [a]Ăb′sa-lŏm went
two hundred men out of [v]Jė-
ru̥′sȧ-lĕm, *that were* called; and
they went in their simplicity, and
they knew not any thing.
12 And [c]Ăb′sa-lŏm sent for
‡Ȧ-hĭth′o-phĕl the Gī′lo-nīte,
[y]Dā′vid's [z]counsellor, from his
city, *even* from [a]Gī′loh, while he
offered sacrifices. And the [b]con-
spiracy was strong; for the people increased continually with
[c]Ăb′sa-lŏm.
13 ¶ And there came a messenger to [d]Dā′vid, saying, The
hearts of the men of Iṣ′ra-el are
after [c]Ăb′sa-lŏm.
14 And [d]Dā′vid said unto all
his servants that *were* with him
at [e]Jė-ru̥′sȧ-lĕm, Arise, and [f]let
us flee; for we shall not *else*
escape from [c]Ăb′sa-lŏm: make
speed to depart, lest he overtake
us suddenly, and bring evil upon
us, and smite the city with the
edge of the sword.

g *David,* 1 Sam. 16:13.
h *Kiss,* Ruth 1:14.
i *Parents, affection of, exemplified,* 2 Cor. 12:14.

1
a *Absalom,* 2 Sam. 3:3.
b *Ambition, instances of,* Hab. 2:5.

2
c *Children, wicked, instances of,* vs. 2–12: Mark 10:14.
d *Treason, instances of,* 2 Kin. 11:14.
e *Gates,* Deut. 3:5.
f *King,* 2 Kin. 3:10.
g *Judge,* Judg. 2:16.
h *Diplomacy, instances of,* vs. 2–6; 2 Kin. 16:7.
i *Israel, under the kings,* Ex. 4:22.

3
j *Flattery, instances of,* Prov. 6:24.

6
k *Treachery,* 2 Kin. 9:23.

7
l *Forty, years,* Jonah 3:4.

m *David,* 1 Sam. 16:13.
n *Hypocrisy,* Jas. 3:17.
o *Deception, instances of,* Josh. 9:4.
p *Vows,* Num. 30:2.
q *Covenant, of man with God,* Deut. 29:1.
r *Hebron,* Gen. 23:2.

8
s *Geshur,* 2 Sam. 3:3.
t *Syria,* 2 Kin. 6:23.
u *Consecration, conditional,* Lev. 7:37.
v *Jerusalem,* Judg. 19:10.

10
w *Spies,* Josh. 6:23
x *Trumpet,* Josh. 6:4.

12
y *Friends, false,* Ex. 33:11.
z *Cabinet,* Ezra 7:14.

a Josh. 15:51.
b *Conspiracy, instances of,* 1 Kin 16:9.
c *Absalom,* 2 Sam. 3:3.

13
d *David,* 1 Sam. 16:13.

14
e *Jerusalem,* Judg. 19:10.
f *Cowardice, instances of,* Lev. 26:36.

* **USURPATION. Of political functions:** *By Absalom,* 2 Sam. 15:1–12. *By Adonijah,* 1 Kin. 1:5–9. *By Baasha,* 1 Kin. 15:27, 28 *By Zimri,* 1 Kin. 16:9, 10 *By Athaliah,* 2 Kin. 11:1–16 *By Shallum,* 2 Kin. 15:10

**Of executive power:** *In the scheme of Joseph to dispossess the Egyptians of their real and personal property,* Gen. 47:13–26. *By Pharaoh, making bondservants of the Israelites,* Ex. 1:9–22 *By Ahab, in ordering Naboth's death and confiscation of his vineyard,* 1 Kin. 21:7–19.
*Moses accused of,* Num. 16:3.

**In Ecclesiastical affairs:** *By Saul, in assuming priestly functions,* 1 Sam. 13:8–14. *By Solomon, in thrusting Abiathar out of the priesthood,* 1 Kin. 2:26, 27. *By Uzziah, in assuming priestly offices,* 2 Chr. 26:16–21. *By Ahaz,* 2 Kin. 16:12, 13. See footnote, CHURCH AND STATE, 1 Sam. 16:1.

† **DEMAGOGISM. Instances of:** *Absalom,* 2 Sam. 15:1–6. *Pilate,* Matt. 27:17–26; Mark 15:6–15; Luke 23:13–25; John 18:38–40; 19:4–16. *Herod,* Acts 12:3. *Felix,* Acts 24:27

‡ **AHITHOPHEL** *(foolish brother).* *One of David's counselors,* 2 Sam. 15:12; 1 Chr. 27:33. *Joins Absalom,* 2 Sam. 15:31, 34; 16:15, 20–23; 17:1–23. *Suicide of,* 2 Sam. 17:1–5, 23.

**15**
*g King*, 2 Kin. 3:10.

**16**
*h Concubinage*, 2 Sam. 21:11.

**17**
1 R. V. Beth-merhak.

**18**
*i Cherethites*, 1 Sam. 30:14.
*j Pelethites*, 2 Sam. 20:7.
*k Gath*, vs. 18-22. Josh. 11:22.

**19**
*l* 2 Sam. 18:2, 5, 12.
*m Foreigners*, Deut. 23:20.

**20**
*n Unselfishness, instances of*, 1 Cor. 10:24.

**21**
*o Oath*, Num. 5:19.
*p Friendship, instances of*, Prov. 22:24.
*q Loyalty, instances of*, Eccl. 8:2.
2 R. V. for death or for life,

**23**
*r Citizens, loyal, instances of*, Luke 15:15.
*s Weeping, instances of*, Ezra 3:13.
*t Brook*, Deut. 8:7.

15 And the [g]king's servants said unto the king, Behold, thy servants *are ready to do* whatsoever my lord the king shall appoint.

16 And the [g]king went forth, and all his household after him. And the king left ten women, *which were* [h]concubines, to keep the house.

17 And the [g]king went forth, and all the people after him, and tarried in [1]a place that was far off.

18 And all his servants passed on beside him; and all the [i]Chĕr′e-thītes, and all the [j]Pĕl′e-thītes, and all the Gĭt′tītes, six hundred men which came after him from [k]Găth, passed on before the [g]king.

19 ¶ Then said the [g]king to [l]Ĭt′ta-ī the Gĭt′tīte, Wherefore goest thou also with us? return to thy place, and abide with the king: for thou *art* a [m]stranger, and also an exile.

20 [n]Whereas thou camest *but* yesterday, should I this day make thee go up and down with us? seeing I go whither I may, return thou, and take back thy brethren: mercy and truth *be* with thee.

21 And [l]Ĭt′ta-ī answered the king, and said, [o]*As* the LORD liveth, and *as* my lord the king liveth, [p,q]surely in what place my lord the king shall be, whether [2]in death or life, even there also will thy servant be.

22 And [d,g]Dā′vid said to [l]Ĭt′ta-ī, Go and pass over. And Ĭt′ta-ī the Gĭt′tīte passed over, and all his men, and all the little ones that *were* with him.

23 And all the [r]country [s]wept with a loud voice, and all the people passed over: the king also himself passed over the [t]brook [u]Kĭd′ron, and all the people passed over, toward the way of the wilderness.

24 ¶ And lo [v,w]Zā′dŏk also, and all the [x]Lē′vītes *were* with him, bearing the [y]ark of the covenant of God: and they set down the ark of God; and [z]Ā-bī′a-thär went up, until all the people had done passing out of the city.

25 And the [a]king said unto [b]Zā′dŏk, Carry back the [c]ark of God into the city: if I shall find [d]favour in the eyes of the LORD, he will bring me again, and shew me *both* it, and his habitation:

26 But if he thus say, I have no delight in thee, behold, *here am* I, [e,f]let him do to me as seemeth good unto him.

27 The [a]king said also unto [b]Zā′dŏk the priest, *Art not* thou a [g]seer? return into the city in peace, and your two sons with you, ‖Ā-hĭm′a-ăz thy son, and §Jŏn′a-than the son of [h]Ā-bī′a-thär.

28 See, I will tarry [3]in the plain of the wilderness, until there come word from you to certify me.

29 [b]Zā′dŏk therefore and [h]Ā-bī′a-thär carried the [c]ark of God again to [i]Jē-ru′sā-lĕm: and they tarried there.

30 ¶ And [a]Dā′vid went up by the ascent of [4,j]*mount* Ŏl′ĭ-vĕt, and [k,l]wept as he went up, and had his head covered, and he went barefoot: [m]and all the people that *was* with him covered every man his head, and they went up, weeping as they went up.

31 And *one* told [a]Dā′vid, saying, ‡Ā-hĭth′o-phĕl [n]*is* among the [o]conspirators with Ăb′sa-lŏm. And Dā′vid [p]said, O

*u Kidron*, 1 Kin. 2:37.

**24**
*v Zadok*, 2 Sam. 19:11.
*w High Priest*, Lev. 21:10.
*x Levites*, Deut. 10:8.
*y Ark*, Ex. 25:10.
*z Abiathar*, 1 Sam. 22:20.

**25**
*a David*, 1 Sam. 16.13.
*b Zadok*, vs. 24-36; 2 Sam. 19:11.
*c Ark*, Ex. 25:10.
*d Grace of God*, Rom. 4.16.

**26**
*e Resignation, exemplified*, Job 5:17.
*f Adversity, resignation in, exemplified*, Psa. 10:6.

**27**
*g Prophets, called seers*, Isa. 3:2.
*h Abiathar*, 1 Sam. 22:20.

**28**
3 R. V. at the fords of

**29**
*i Jerusalem*, Judg. 19:10.

**30**
*j Mount of Olives*, Mark, 11:1.
*k Weeping*, Ezra 3:13.
*l Mourning*, Lam. 2:5.
*m Love, of man for man*, 1 John 4:7.
4 R. V. the mount of Olives,

**31**
*n Treachery, of Ahithophel*, 2 Kin. 9.23.
*o Conspiracy, instances of*, 1 Kin. 16:9.
*p Adversity, prayer in*, Psa. 10:6.

‖ **AHIMAAZ**, son of Zadok, the high priest. *Loyal to David*, 2 Sam. 15:27, 36; 17:17-21; 18:19-33, 1 Chr. 6:8, 9, 53.
§ **JONATHAN** (*God-given*). *Son of Abiathar*, 2 Sam. 15:27. *Acts as spy for David*, 2 Sam. 15.27, 28, 17:17-21. *Informs Adonijah of Solomon's succession to the throne of David*, 1 Kin. 1:42-48.

LORD, I pray thee, turn the
counsel of Ā-hīth'o-phĕl into
foolishness.

32 ¶ And it came to pass, that
*when* [a]Dā'vid was come to the
top *of the mount*, where he
[q]worshipped God, behold, [r]Hū'-
shāi the Är'chīte came to meet
him with his coat [l,s]rent, and
[t]earth upon his head:

33 Unto whom Dā'vid [u,v]said,
If thou passest on with me, then
thou shalt be a burden unto
me:

34 But [v,w]if [r]thou return to the
city, and say unto [x]Ăb'sa-lŏm,
[y]I will be thy servant, O king; *as*
I *have been* thy father's servant
hitherto, so *will* I now also *be*
thy servant: then mayest thou
for me defeat the counsel of
‡Ā-hīth'o-phĕl.

35 And *hast thou* not there with
thee [b]Zā'dŏk and [h]Ā-bī'a-thär
the priests? therefore it shall be,
*that* what thing soever thou shalt
hear out of the king's house,
thou shalt tell *it* to Zā'dŏk and
Ā-bī'a-thär the priests.

36 Behold, *they have* there with
them their two sons, ‖Ā-hĭm'a-
ăz Zā'dŏk's *son*, and §Jŏn'a-
than Ā-bī'a-thär's *son*; and by
them ye shall send unto me
every thing that ye can hear.

37 So [r]Hū'shāi [a]Dā'vid's [z]friend
came into the city, and
[x]Ăb'sa-lŏm came into [i]Jē-ru'-
să-lĕm.

## CHAPTER 16

*Ziba, by false suggestions, obtains his master's inheritance. 6 Shimei curses David. 9 David abstains from revenge. 15 Hushai is received into Absalom's confidence. 20 Ahithophel's counsel.*

AND when [a]Dā'vid was a
little past the top *of the*
*hill*, behold, [b]Zī'bȧ the [c]servant
of [d]Mē-phĭb'o-shĕth met him,
with a couple of [e]asses saddled,
and upon them [f]two hundred
*loaves* of [g]bread, and an hundred
bunches of [h]raisins, and an hundred of [i]summer fruits, and a
bottle of [j]wine.

2 And the king said unto [b]Zī'bȧ,
What meanest thou by [f]these?
And Zī'bȧ said, The [e]asses *be* for
the king's household to ride on;
and the [g]bread and [i]summer
fruit for the [k]young men to
eat; and the [j]wine, that such as
be faint in the wilderness may
drink.

3 And the [a]king said, And
where *is* thy master's son? And
[b]Zī'bȧ said unto the king, Behold, he abideth at [l]Jē-ru'să-
lĕm: for he said, To day shall
the house of [m]Ĭs'ra-el restore me
the kingdom of my father.

4 Then said the king to [b]Zī'-
bȧ, Behold, [n,o,p]thine *are* all
that *pertained* unto [d]Mē-phĭb'o-
shĕth. And Zī'bȧ said, [1]I humbly beseech thee *that* I may find
grace in thy sight, my lord, O
king.

5 ¶ And when king [a]Dā'vid
came to [q]Bā-hū'rim, behold,
thence came out a man of the
family of the house of [r]Saul,
whose name *was* [s]Shĭm'e-ī, the
son of [t]Gē'rȧ: he came forth, and
[u,v]cursed still as he came.

6 And he cast stones at [a]Dā'-
vid, and at all the servants of
king Dā'vid: and all the people
and all the mighty men *were*
on his right hand and on his
left.

7 And thus said [s]Shĭm'e-ī when
he [u]cursed, [2,w]Come out, come
out, thou bloody man, and thou
man of Bē'lĭ-al:

8 The LORD hath returned upon thee all the blood of the house
of [r]Saul, in whose stead thou
hast reigned; and the LORD hath
delivered the kingdom into the
hand of [x]Ăb'sa-lŏm thy son:
and, behold, thou *art taken* in
thy mischief, because thou *art*
a [3]bloody man.

9 ¶ Then said [y]Ā-bĭsh'a-ī the

---

32
q *Worship*, Gen. 22:5.
r 2 Sam. 16:16–19:17:5–16.
s *Rending of Garments, a token of affliction*, 2 Chr. 34:27.
t *Dust*, Eccl. 3:20.

33
u *Prudence, instances of*, 2 Chr. 2:12.
v *Diplomacy, instances of*, vs. 34–36; 2 Kin. 16:7.

34
w *Craftiness, instances of*, vs. 34–36; Psa. 83:3.
x *Absalom*, 2 Sam. 3:3.
y *Falsehood*, Job 21:34.

37
z *Friendship, instances of*, Prov. 22:24.

1
a *David*, 1 Sam. 16:13.
b *Ziba*, 2 Sam. 9:2.
c *Servant, wicked and unfaithful*, Jer. 2:14.
d *Mephibosheth*, 2 Sam. 9:6.
e *Ass, domesticated*, 2 Chr. 28:15.
f *Presents*, Gen. 32:13.
g *Bread*, Ezek. 4:13.
h *Raisins*, 1 Sam. 25:18.
i *Summer, fruits of*, Isa. 28:4.
j *Wine*, Prov. 23:31.

2
k *Young Men*, Prov. 1:4.

3
l *Jerusalem*, Judg. 19:10.
m *Israel, under the kings*, Ex. 4:22.

4
n *Confiscation, of property*, Ezra 10:8.
o *Government, monarchical, tyranny in*, Isa. 22:21.
p *Rashness, instances of*, 2 Sam. 6:7.
1 R. V. I do obeisance; let me find favour in

5
q *Bahurim*, 2 Sam. 3:16.
r *Saul*, 1 Sam. 9:2.
s *Shimei*, 1 Kin. 2:36.
t *Gera*, Judg. 3:15.
u *Cursing*, Lev. 24:11.
v *Malice, instances of*, Eph. 4:31.

7
w *Railing, instances of*, Jude 9.
2 R. V. Begone, begone, thou man of blood, and man of Belial:

8
x *Absalom*, 2 Sam. 3:3.
3 R. V. man of blood.

9
y *Abishai*, 2 Sam. 3:30.

z *Zeruiah, sister of David*, 1 Chr. 2:16.

a *Dog*, 1 Kin. 21: 19.

b *Rulers*, Ex. 18: 21.

**10**

c *David, meekness of*, 1 Sam. 16:13.

d *Resignation, exemplified*, Job 5:17.

e *Enemy, forgiveness of*, Prov. 24: 17.

f *Cursing*, Lev. 24: 11.

**11**

g *Meekness, instances of*, Psa. 45 4.

h *Forgiveness, instances of*, Matt. 18:21.

**12**

i *Adversity*, Psa. 10:6.

4 R. V. the wrong done unto me,

5 R. V. of me this day.

**13**

j *Shimei*, 1 Kin. 2:36.

k *Dust, casting of, in anger*, Eccl. 3:20.

**15**

l *Absalom*, 2 Sam. 3:3.

m *Jerusalem*, Judg. 19:10.

n *Ahithophel*, 2 Sam. 15:12.

**16**

o 2 Sam. 15:32-37; 17:5-16; 1 Chr. 27:33.

p *Friendship, instances of*, Prov. 22:24.

q *Falsehood, instances of*, Job 21:34.

r *Diplomacy, instances of*, 2 Kin. 16:7.

s *Salutations*, Luke 1:44.

**18**

t *Deception, instances of*, Josh. 9:4.

son of [z]Zĕr-ụ-ī'ah unto the king,
Why should this dead [a]dog curse
my lord the [b]king? let me go
over, I pray thee, and take off
his head.

10 And the [c]king said, What
have I to do with you, ye sons of
Zĕr-ụ-ī'ah? [d]so let [e]him curse,
because the LORD hath said unto him, [f]Curse Dā'vid. Who
shall then say, Wherefore hast
thou done so?

11 [g,h]And [c]Dā'vid said to
Ā-bĭsh'a-ī, and to all his servants, Behold, my son, which
came forth of my bowels, seeketh my life: how much more now
*may this* Bĕn'ja'mīte *do it*? *let
him alone, and let him curse; for
the LORD hath bidden him.

12 It may be that the LORD
will look on [4]mine [i]affliction,
and that the LORD will requite
me good for his [f]cursing [5]this
day.

13 And as [c]Dā'vid and his men
went by the way, [j]Shĭm'e-ī went
along on the hill's side over
against him, and cursed as he
went, and threw stones at him,
and cast [k]dust.

14 And the king, and all the
people that *were* with him, came
weary, and refreshed themselves
there.

15 ¶ And [l]Ăb'sa-lŏm, and all
the people the men of Ĭṣ'ra-el,
came to [m]Jē-rụ'sā-lĕm, and [n]Ā-
hĭth'o-phĕl with him.

16 And it came to pass, when
[o]Hū'shāi the Är'chīte, Dā'vid's
[p]friend, was come unto Ăb'sa-
lŏm, that Hū'shāi [q,r]said unto
Ăb'sa-lŏm, [s]God save the king,
God save the king.

17 And [l]Ăb'sa-lŏm said to
[o]Hū'shāi, *Is* this thy kindness to
thy [p]friend? why wentest thou
not with thy friend?

18 And [o]Hū'shāi [q,r,t]said unto
Ăb'sa-lŏm, Nay; but whom the
LORD, and this people, and all
the men of Ĭṣ'ra-el, choose, his
will I be, and with him will I
abide.

19 And again, whom should I
serve? *should I* not *serve* in the
presence of his son? [t]as I have
served in thy father's presence,
so will I be in thy presence.

20 ¶ Then said [l]Ăb'sa-lŏm
to [n]Ā-hĭth'o-phĕl, Give counsel
among you what we shall do.

21 And [n]Ā-hĭth'o-phĕl said unto [l]Ăb'sa-lŏm, Go in unto thy
father's [u]concubines, which he
hath left to keep the house; and
all Ĭṣ'ra-el shall hear that thou
art abhorred of thy father: then
shall the hands of all that *are*
with thee be strong.

22 So they spread [l]Ăb'sa-lŏm a
tent upon the top of the [v]house;
and Ăb'sa-lŏm [w]went in unto his
father's [u]concubines in the sight
of all Ĭṣ'ra-el.

23 And the [x]counsel of [n]Ā-
hĭth'o-phĕl, which he counselled in those days, *was* as if a
man had enquired at the oracle
of God: so *was* all the counsel of
Ā-hĭth'o-phĕl both with Dā'vid
and with Ăb'sa-lŏm.

## CHAPTER 17

*Ahithophel's counsel is defeated by Hushai. 15 Secret intelligence is sent unto David. 23 Ahithophel hangs himself. 24 Absalom passes over Jordan, and makes Amasa captain. 27 David at Mahanaim is furnished with supplies.*

MOREOVER [a]Ā-hĭth'o-phĕl
[b,c]said unto [d]Ăb'sa-lŏm,
Let me now choose out twelve
thousand men, and I will arise
and pursue after [e]Dā'vid this
night:

2 [b,c]And I will come upon him
while he *is* weary and weak
handed, and will make him
afraid: and all the people that
*are* with him shall flee; and I
will smite the king only:

**21**

u *Concubinage*, 2 Sam. 21:11.

**22**

v *House*, Esth. 8:1.

w *Incest, instances of*, Lev. 18:6.

**23**

x *Counselor*, Prov. 11:14.

**1**

a *Ahithophel*, 2 Sam. 15:12.

b *War, councils of*, Judg. 3:2.

c *Treason, instances of*, 2 Kin. 11: 14.

d *Absalom*, 2 Sam 3:3.

e *David*, 1 Sam. 16:13.

* **CLEMENCY.** *Of David toward disloyal subjects, to Shimei*, 2 Sam. 16:5-13; 19:16-23; *to Amasa*, 2 Sam. 19:13, with 17:25. *Of Solomon to Abiathar*, 1 Kin. 2:26.

3 [b,c]And I will bring back all the people unto thee: the man whom thou seekest *is* as if all returned: *so* all the people shall be in peace.

4 And the saying pleased [d]Ăb′-sa-lŏm well, and all the [f]elders of [g]Ĭṣ′ra-el.

5 Then said [d]Ăb′sa-lŏm, Call now [h]Hū′shāi the Är′chīte also, and let us hear likewise what he saith.

6 And when [h]Hū′shāi was come to [d]Ăb′sa-lŏm, Ăb′sa-lŏm spake unto him, saying, [a]Ȧ-hĭth′o-phĕl [b]hath spoken after this manner: shall we do *after* his saying? if not; speak thou.

7 And [h]Hū′shāi [i]said unto Ăb′-sa′lŏm, The [b]counsel that [a]Ȧ-hĭth′o-phĕl hath given *is* not good at this time.

8 [j]For, said Hū′shāi, thou knowest thy father and his men, that they *be* mighty men, and they *be* chafed in their minds, as a *bear robbed of her whelps in the field: and thy father *is* a man of war, and will not lodge with the people.

9 Behold, he is hid now in some pit, or in some *other* place: and it will come to pass, when some of them be overthrown at the first, that whosoever heareth it will say, There is a slaughter among the people that follow Ăb′sa-lŏm.

10 And he also *that is* valiant, whose heart *is* as the heart of a lion, shall utterly melt: for all Ĭṣ′ra-el knoweth that thy father *is* a mighty man, and *they* which *be* with him *are* valiant men.

11 Therefore I [b]counsel that all Ĭṣ′ra-el be generally gathered unto thee, from [k]Dăn even to [l]Bē′er–shē′bȧ, as the sand that *is* by the sea for multitude; and that thou go to battle in thine own person.

12 So shall we come upon him in some place where he shall be found, and we will light upon him as the dew falleth on the ground: and of him and of all the men that *are* with him there shall not be left so much as one.

13 Moreover, if he be gotten into a city, then shall all Ĭṣ′ra-el bring ropes to that city, and we will draw it into the river, until there be not one small stone found there.

14 And [d]Ăb′sa-lŏm and all the men of Ĭṣ′ra-el said, The [b]counsel of [h]Hū′shāi the Är′chīte *is* better than the counsel of [a]Ȧ-hĭth′o-phĕl. For the LORD [m]had appointed to defeat the good counsel of Ȧ-hĭth′o-phĕl, to the intent that the LORD might bring evil upon Ăb′sa-lŏm.

15 ¶ [n,o]Then said [h]Hū′shāi unto [p]Zā′dŏk and to [q]Ȧ-bī′a-thär the [r]priests, Thus and thus did [a]Ȧ-hĭth′o-phĕl [b]counsel [d]Ăb′sa-lŏm and the [f]elders of [g]Ĭṣ′ra-el; and thus and thus have I counselled.

16 [n,o]Now therefore send quickly, and tell [e]Dā′vid, saying, Lodge not this night [1]in the plains of the wilderness, but speedily pass over; lest the king be swallowed up, and all the people that *are* with him.

17 Now [s]Jŏn′a-than and [t]Ȧ-hĭm′a-ăz stayed by [u]Ĕn–rō′-gel; for they might not be seen to come into the city: and a wench went and told them; and they went and told king [e]Dā′vid.

18 Nevertheless a lad saw them, and told [d]Ăb′sa-lŏm: but they went both of them away quickly, and came to a man's house in [v]Bȧ-hū′rim, which had a well in his court; whither they went down.

19 And [w]the woman took and

4
f *Senate*, Num. 11:16.
g *Israel, under the kings*, Ex. 4:22.

5
h 2 Sam. 15:32–37; 16:16; 1 Chr. 27:33.

7
i *Friendship, instances of, of David and Hushai*, Prov. 22:24.

8
j *Diplomacy*, vs. 8–14; 2 Kin. 16:7.

11
k *Dan*, Judg. 18:29.
l *Beer-sheba*, Judg. 20:1.

14
m *God, providence of*, Gen. 2:2.

15
n *Citizens, loyal, instances of*, Luke 15:15.
o *Loyalty, instances of, to David*, Eccl. 8:2.
p *Zadok*, 2 Sam. 19:11.
q *Abiathar*, 1 Sam 22:20.
r *High Priest*, Lev. 21:10.

16
1 R. V. at the fords of

17
s *Jonathan*, 2 Sam. 15:27.
t *Ahimaaz*, 2 Sam. 15:27.
u *En-rogel*, Josh. 15:7.

18
v *Bahurim*, 2 Sam. 3:16.

19
w *Kindness, instances of*, Acts 28:2.

***BEAR.** *Ferocity of*, 2 Sam. 17:8; Prov. 17:12; 28:15; Isa. 11:7; 59:11; Lam. 3:10; Hos. 13:8; Amos 5:19. *Killed by David*, 1 Sam. 17:34–37. *Two destroy the children of Beth-el, who mocked Elisha*, 2 Kin. 2:24.
**Similitudes of:** *The beast in Daniel's vision*, Dan. 7:5. *Ceasing to be ravenous, illustrative of millennial peace*, **Isa. 11:7.**

spread a covering over the well's
mouth, and spread ground corn
thereon; and the thing was not
known.
20 And when [d]Ăb′sa-lŏm's
servants came to the woman
to the house, they said, Where
*is* [t]Ă-hĭm′a-ăz and [s]Jŏn′a-than?
And the woman [x]said unto
them, They be gone over the
brook of water. And when they
had sought and could not find
*them,* they returned to [y]Jĕ-ru′-
sȧ-lĕm.
21 And it came to pass, after
they were departed, that [s,t]they
came up out of the well, and
[n,o]went and told king [e]Dā′vid,
and said unto Dā′vid, Arise, and
pass quickly over the water: for
thus hath Ă-hĭth′o-phĕl counselled against you.
22 Then Dā′vid arose, and all
the people that *were* with him,
and they passed over [z]Jôr′dan:
by the morning light there lacked not one of them that was not
gone over Jôr′dan.
23 ¶ And [a,b]when [c]Ă-hĭth′o-
phĕl saw that his counsel was
not followed, he saddled *his* ass,
and arose, and gat him home to
his house, to his city, and [d]put
his household in order, and
[e]hanged himself, and died, and
was buried in the sepulchre of
his father.
24 [f]Then [g]Dā′vid came to [h]Mā-
hȧ-nā′im. And [i]Ăb′sa-lŏm passed over [j]Jôr′dan, he and all the
men of Ĭṣ′ra-el with him.
25 And [i]Ăb′sa-lŏm made
†Ăm′a-sȧ [k]captain of the host
instead of [l]Jō′ăb: which Ăm′a-
sȧ *was* a man's son, whose name
*was* [m]Ĭth′rȧ an Ĭṣ′ra-el-īte, that
went in to [n]Ăb′ĭ-gail the daughter of Nā′hăsh, sister to [o]Zĕr-u-
ĭ′ah Jō′ăb's mother.

**20**
*x Falsehood, instances of,* Job 21:34.
*y Jerusalem,* Judg. 19:10.

**22**
*z Jordan,* Gen. 32:10.

**23**
*a Ambition, disappointed,* Hab. 2:5.
*b Pride, instances of,* Prov. 16:18.
*c Ahithophel,* 2 Sam. 15:12.
*d Death, preparation for,* Num. 23:10.
*e Suicide, instances of,* 1 Kin. 16:18.

**24**
*f War, civil,* Judg. 3:2.
*g David,* 1 Sam. 16:13.
*h Mahanaim,* Gen. 32:2.
*i Absalom,* 2 Sam. 3:3.
*j Jordan,* Gen. 32:10.

**25**
*k Captain,* Num. 31:48.
*l Joab,* 2 Sam. 20:23.
*m* Or, *Jether,* 1 Chr. 2:17.
*n* 1 Chr. 2:16, 17.
*o Zeruiah,* 1 Chr. 2:16.

26 [l]So Ĭṣ′ra-el and Ăb′sa-lŏm
pitched in the land of [p]Gĭl′e-ăd.
27 ¶ And it came to pass, when
[g]Dā′vid was come to [h]Mā-hȧ-
nā′im, that Shō′bī the son of
Nā′hăsh of [q]Răb′bah of the
[r]children of Ăm′mŏn, and [s]Mā′-
chĭr the son of [s]Ăm′mĭ-el of
[s]Lō-dē′bär, and ‡Bär-zĭl′la-ī the
Gĭl′e-ăd-īte of [t]Rō-gē′lim,
28 [u,v,w]Brought [x]beds, and [y]ba-
sons, and earthen vessels, and
[z]wheat, and [a]barley, and flour,
and parched [b]*corn,* and [c]beans,
and [d]lentiles, and parched
[e]*pulse,*
29 [f]And [g]honey, and [h]butter,
and [i]sheep, and [j]cheese of kine,
for [k]Dā′vid, and for the people
that *were* with him, to eat: for
they said, The people *is* [l]hungry,
and weary, and thirsty, in the
wilderness.

## CHAPTER 18

*David musters his army for battle, and gives charge concerning Absalom. 6 The defeat of the Israelites in the wood of Ephraim. 9 Absalom, caught by his head in an oak, is slain by Joab. 19 The tidings are brought to David. 33 His mourning for Absalom.*

AND [a]Dā′vid [b]numbered the
people that *were* with
him, and set [c,d]captains of thousands and captains of hundreds
over them.
2 And [a]Dā′vid [e]sent forth a
[f]third part of the people under
the hand of [g]Jō′ăb, and a third
part under the hand of [h]Ă-bĭsh′-
a-ī the son of [i]Zĕr-u-ī′ah, Jō′-
ăb's brother, and a third part
under the hand of [j]Ĭt′ta-ī the
Gĭt′tīte. And the king said unto
the people, I will surely go forth
with you myself also.
3 But the [k]people answered,
[l,m]Thou shalt not go forth: for if
we flee away, they will not care
for us; neither if half of us die,
will they care for us: but now

**26**
*p Gilead,* Deut. 3:13.

**27**
*q Rabbah,* Deut. 3:11.
*r Ammonites,* Deut. 2:20.
*s* 2 Sam. 9:4, 5.
*t* 2 Sam. 19:31.

**28**
*u Love, of man for man, instances of,* 1 John 4:7.
*v Liberality,* 1 Tim. 6:18.
*w Patriotism,* Psa. 137:1.
*x Bed,* Amos 6:4.
*y Basin,* 1 Kin. 7:50.
*z Wheat,* Ezra 6:9.
*a Barley,* Ex. 9:31.
*b Corn,* Psa. 65:13.
*c* Ezek. 4:9.
*d Lentiles,* Gen. 25:34.
*e* Dan. 1:12, 16.

**29**
*f Love, of man for man,* 1 John 4:7.
*g Honey,* Prov. 25:27.
*h Butter,* Gen. 18:8.
*i Sheep,* Deut. 32:14.
*j* 1 Sam. 17:18; Job 10:10.
*k David,* 1 Sam. 16:13.
*l Hunger,* Neh. 9:15.

**1**
*a David,* 1 Sam. 16:13.
*b Muster,* 2 Kin. 25:19.
*c Armies, how officered,* Deut. 11:4.
*d Captain,* Num. 31:48.

**2**
*e War, civil,* Judg. 3:2.
*f Armies, tactics of,* Deut. 11:4.
*g Joab,* 2 Sam. 20:23.
*h Abishai,* 2 Sam. 3:30.
*i Zeruiah* 1 Chr. 2:16.
*j* 2 Sam. 15:19–22.

**3**
*k Citizens, loyal, instances of,* Luke 15:15.
*l Love, of man for man,* 1 John 4:7.
*m Loyalty, instances of,* Eccl. 8:2.

† **AMASA** *(burden-bearer). Nephew of David,* 2 Sam. 17:25; 1 Chr. 2:17. *Joins Absalom,* 2 Sam. 17:25. *Returns to David, and is made captain of the host,* 2 Sam. 19:13, 14. *Slain by Joab,* 2 Sam. 20:8–12; 1 Kin. 2:5, 32.

‡ **BARZILLAI.** *A generous friend of David,* 2 Sam 17:27–29. *Is invited by David to become a royal guest in Jerusalem,* 2 Sam. 19:31–39; 1 Kin. 2:7. *Descendants of, return from Babylon,* Ezra 2:61; Neh. 7:63.

*thou art* worth ten thousand of us: therefore now *it is* better that thou succour us out of the city.

4 And the king said unto them, What seemeth you best I will do. And the king stood by the gate-side, and all the people came out by hundreds and by thousands.

5 And the king [n]commanded [g]Jō'ăb and [h]Ă-bĭsh'a-ī and [j]Ĭt'-ta-ī, saying, *Deal* gently for my sake with the young man, *even* with [o]Ăb'sa-lŏm. And all the people heard when the king gave all the captains charge concerning Ăb'sa-lŏm.

6 ¶ [e]So the people went out into the field against Ĭs'ra-el: and the battle was in the wood of Ē'phră-ĭm;

7 [e]Where the people of [p]Ĭs'ra-el were slain before the servants of [a]Dā'vid, and there was there a great slaughter that day of twenty thousand *men*.

8 [e]For the battle was there scattered over the face of all the country: and the wood devoured more people that day than the sword devoured.

9 ¶ And [o]Ăb'sa-lŏm met the servants of [a]Dā'vid. And Ăb'-sa-lŏm rode upon a mule, and the *mule went under the thick boughs of a great [q]oak, and his head caught hold of the oak, and he was taken up between the heaven and the earth; and the mule that *was* under him went away.

10 And a certain man saw *it*, and told [g]Jō'ăb, and said, Behold, I saw [o]Ăb'sa-lŏm hanged in an [q]oak.

11 And [g]Jō'ăb said unto the man that told him, And, behold, thou sawest *him*, and why didst thou not smite him there to the ground? and I would have given thee ten [1]*shekels* of silver, and a girdle.

12 And the [k]man [l]said unto [g]Jō'ăb, Though I should receive a thousand [1]*shekels* of silver in mine hand, *yet* would I not put forth mine hand against the king's son: for in our hearing the [n]king charged thee and [h]Ă-bĭsh'-a-ī and [j]Ĭt'ta-ī, saying, Beware that none *touch* the young man [o]Ăb'sa-lŏm.

13 Otherwise [2]I should have wrought falsehood against mine own life: for there is no matter hid from the king, [3]and thou thyself wouldest have set thyself against *me*.

14 Then said [g]Jō'ăb, I may not tarry thus with thee. And he took three †darts in his hand, and thrust them through the heart of [o]Ăb'sa-lŏm, while he *was* yet alive in the midst of the [q]oak.

15 And ten [r]young men that bare [g]Jō'ăb's armour compassed about and [s]smote Ăb'sa-lŏm, and slew him.

16 And [g]Jō'ăb blew the [t]trumpet, and the people returned from pursuing after [p]Ĭs'ra-el: for Jō'-ăb held back the people.

17 And they took [o]Ăb'sa-lŏm, and cast him into a great [u]pit in the wood, and laid a very great heap of stones upon him: and all [p]Ĭs'ra-el fled every one to his tent.

18 ¶ Now [o]Ăb'sa-lŏm in his lifetime had taken and reared up for himself a [v]pillar which *is* in the [w]king's dale: for he said, I have no son to keep my name in remembrance: and he called the pillar after his own name: and it is called unto this day, Ăb'sa-lŏm's [4]place.

19 ¶ Then said [x]Ă-hĭm'a-ăz the

5
n *Parents, affection of, exemplified*, 2 Cor. 12:14.
o *Absalom*, 2 Sam. 3:3.

7
p *Israel, under the kings*, Ex. 4:22.

9
q *Oak*, Gen. 35:4.

11
1 R. V. pieces

13
2 R. V. if I had dealt falsely against his life.
3 R. V. then thou thyself wouldest have stood aloof.

15
r *Armor-bearer*, Judg. 9:54.
s *Homicide, felonious, instances of*, Deut. 5:17.

16
t *Trumpet*, Josh. 6:4.

17
u *Burying Places*, Gen. 23:4.

18
v *Pillar*, Gen. 28:18.
w Gen. 14:17.
4 R. V. monument.

19
x *Ahimaaz*, 2 Sam. 15:27.

* **MULE.** **Uses of:** *As pack animals*, 2 Kin. 5:17; 1 Chr. 12:40. *In barter*, Ezek. 27:14. *By the captivity in returning from Babylon*, Ezra 2:66; Neh. 7:68. *In war*, Zech. 14:15. *For royal riders*, 2 Sam. 13:29; 18:9; 1 Kin. 1:33, 38. *Ridden, by posts*, Esth. 8:10, 14; *by saints in Isaiah's prophetic vision of the kingdom of Christ*, Isa. 66:20. *Tribute paid in*, 1 Kin. 10:25.

† **DART.** *A light javelin*, Num. 35:7; 1 Sam. 18:10; 2 Sam. 18:14; Job 41:29. **Figurative**, Eph. 6:16.

[y] *Zadok*, 2 Sam. 19:11.

22

5 R. V. wilt have no reward for the tidings?

24

z *Gates*, Deut. 3:5.

25

a *David*, 1 Sam. 16:13.

son of [y]Zā′dŏk, Let me now run,
and bear the king tidings, how
that the LORD hath avenged
him of his enemies.
20 And [g]Jō′ăb said unto him,
Thou shalt not bear tidings this
day, but thou shalt bear tidings
another day: but this day thou
shalt bear no tidings, because
the king's son is dead.
21 Then said [g]Jō′ăb to Cṳ′shī,
Go tell the king what thou hast
seen. And Cṳ′shī bowed himself unto Jō′ăb, and ran.
22 Then said [x]Ā-hĭm′a-ăz the
son of [y]Zā′dŏk yet again to
[g]Jō′ăb, But howsoever, let me, I
pray thee, also run after Cṳ′shī.
And Jō′ăb said, Wherefore wilt
thou run, my son, seeing that
thou [5]hast no tidings ready?
23 But howsoever, *said he*, let
me run. And he said unto him,
Run. Then [x]Ā-hĭm′a-ăz ran by
the way of the plain, and overran
Cṳ′shī.
24 And [a]Dā′vid sat between the
two [z]gates: and the ‡watchman
went up to the roof over the gate
unto the wall, and lifted up his
eyes, and looked, and behold a
man running alone.
25 And the ‡watchman cried,
and told the [a]king. And the king
said, If he *be* alone, *there is* tidings in his mouth. And he came
apace, and drew near.
26 And the watchman saw another man running: and the
watchman called unto the ‖por-
ter, and said, Behold *another*
man running alone. And the
[a]king said, He also bringeth
tidings.
27 And the ‡watchman said,
Me thinketh the running of the
foremost is like the running of
[b]Ā-hĭm′a-ăz the son of [c]Zā′dŏk.
And the king said, He *is* a good
man, and cometh with good
tidings.
28 And [b]Ā-hĭm′a-ăz called, and
said unto the [a]king, All is well.
And he [d]fell down to the earth
upon his face before the king,
and said, Blessed *be* the LORD
thy God, which hath [e]delivered
up the men that lifted up their
hand against my lord the king.
29 And the king said, Is the
young man [f]Ăb′sa-lŏm safe?
And [b]Ā-hĭm′a-ăz answered,
When [g]Jō′ăb sent the king's
servant, and *me* thy servant, I
saw a great tumult, but I knew
not what *it was*.
30 And the king said *unto him*,
Turn aside, *and* stand here. And
he turned aside, and stood still.
31 And, behold, Cṳ′shī came;
and Cṳ′shī said, Tidings, my
lord the [a]king: for the LORD
hath avenged thee this day of
all them that rose up against
thee.
32 And the king said unto Cṳ′-
shī, *Is* the young man [f]Ăb′sa-
lŏm safe? And Cṳ′shī an-
swered, The enemies of my lord
the king, and all that rise against
thee to do *thee* hurt, be as *that*
young man *is*.
33 ¶ [h]And the [a]king was much
moved, and went up to the
[i]chamber over the gate, and
[j, k]wept: and as he went, [l]thus he
said, O my son Ăb′sa-lŏm, my
son, my son Ăb′sa-lŏm! would
God I had died for thee, O Ăb′-
sa-lŏm, my son, my son!

27

b *Ahimaaz*, 2 Sam. 15:27.

c *Zadok*, 2 Sam. 19:11.

28

d *Salutations*, Luke 1:44.

e *God, providence of*, Gen. 2:2.

29

f *Absalom*, 2 Sam. 3:3.

g *Joab*, 2 Sam. 20:23.

33

h *Bereavement, instances of*, Hos. 9:12.

i *House*, Esth. 8:1.

j *Weeping, instances of*, Ezra 3:13.

k *Mourning*, Lam. 2:5.

l *Parents, affection of, exemplified*, 2 Cor. 12:14.

‡ **WATCHMAN.** *A sentinel*, Song 3:3; 5:7. *On the walls, of Jerusalem*, 2 Sam. 13:34; Neh. 4:9; 7:3; Isa. 52:8; 62:6; *of Mahanaim*, 2 Sam. 18:24, 25; *of Babylon*, Jer. 51:12. *On towers*, 2 Kin. 9:17; 2 Chr. 20:24; Isa. 21:5–12. *On hills*, Jer. 31:6. *At the gates of the temple*, 2 Kin. 11:6, 7. *Alarm of, given by trumpets*, Ezek. 33:3–6. *Unfaithfulness in the discharge of duty of, punished by death*, Ezek. 33:6; Matt. 28:14; Acts 12:19.

**Figurative:** *Of spiritual teachers*, Isa. 52:8; 56:10; 62:6; Jer. 6:17; Ezek. 3:17; 33:7–9, with vs. 2–6.

‖ **PORTERS.** *Guards at, the city gates; the doors of the king's palace; the doors of the temple*, 2 Kin. 23:4; 25:18; 1 Chr. 9:17–32; 2 Chr. 34:13; 35:15; Esth. 2:21; 6:2; Psa. 84:10; Jer. 35:4; 52:24; *the door of the ark*, 1 Chr. 15:23, 24; 16:38. *Lodged about the temple in order to be present for opening the doors*, 1 Chr. 9:27. *Collected money for the temple*, 2 Kin. 22:4; 2 Chr. 34:9.

*One-third were porters of the temple*, 2 Chr. 23:4. *One-third were porters of the king's house*, 2 Chr. 23:5. *One-third were porters at the gate of the foundation*, 2 Chr. 23:5. *They served, also, as porters at the gates of the walls*, Neh. 12:25.

*They served in twenty-four courses*, 1 Chr. 26:13–19. *Their posts were determined by lot*, 1 Chr. 24:31; 26:13–19.

## CHAPTER 19

*Joab causes the king to cease his mourning. 9 The Israelites bring the king back. 11 David sends to incite the men of Judah. 18 Shimei is pardoned. 24 Mephibosheth is restored to his possessions in part. 32 Barzillai's kindness is remembered. 41 The Israelites expostulate with Judah for bringing home the king without them.*

AND it was told [a]Jō'ăb, Behold, the [b]king weepeth
and [c,d]mourneth for [e]Ăb'sa-lŏm.
2 And the victory that day was
*turned* into [d]mourning unto all
the people: [f]for the people heard
say that day how the king was
grieved for his son.
3 [f]And the people gat them by
stealth that day into the city, as
people being ashamed steal away
when they flee in battle.
4 But the [b]king covered his
face, and the king [c,d]cried with a
loud voice, O my son Ăb'sa-lŏm,
O Ăb'sa-lŏm, my son, my son!
5 And [a,g]Jō'ăb came into the
house to the king, and [h,i,j]said,
Thou hast shamed this day the
faces of all thy servants, which
this day have saved thy life, and
the lives of thy sons and of thy
daughters, and the lives of thy
[k]wives, and the lives of thy [l]con-
cubines;
6 [h,j]In that thou lovest thine
[m]enemies, and hatest thy friends.
For thou hast declared this day,
that thou regardest neither princes nor servants: for this day I
perceive, that if Ăb'sa-lŏm had
lived, and all we had died this
day, then it had pleased thee
well.
7 [h,j]Now therefore arise, go
forth, and speak comfortably
unto thy servants: for I [n]swear
by the LORD, if thou go not
forth, there will not tarry one
with thee this night: and that
will be worse unto thee than all
the evil that befell thee from thy
youth until now.
8 Then the king arose, and sat
in the [o]gate. And they told unto
all the people, saying, Behold,
the king doth sit in the gate.
And all the people came before
the king: for Ĭs̹'ra-el had fled
every man to his tent.
9 ¶ And all the people were at
strife throughout all the tribes of
Ĭs̹'ra-el, saying, The [b]king saved
us out of the hand of our enemies, and he delivered us out of
the hand of the [p]Phĭ-lĭs'tĭnes̹;
and now he is fled out of the land
for Ăb'sa-lŏm.
10 And [e]Ăb'sa-lŏm, whom we
anointed over us, is dead in battle. Now therefore why speak
ye not a word of bringing the
king back?
11 ¶ And king [b]Dā'vid sent to
*Zā'dŏk and to [q]Ā-bī'a-thär the
[r]priests, [s]saying, Speak unto the
[t]elders of Jū'dah, saying, Why
are ye the last to bring the king
back to his house? seeing the
speech of all Ĭs̹'ra-el is come to
the king [1]*even* to his house.
12 Ye *are* my brethren, ye *are*
my bones and my flesh: wherefore then are ye the last to bring
back the king?
13 [s]And say ye to [u]Ăm'a-să,
[v]*Art* thou not of my bone, and of
my flesh? God do so to me, and
more also, if [w]thou be not [x]cap-
tain of the host before me continually in the room of [a]Jō'ăb.
14 And he bowed the heart of
all the men of [y]Jū'dah, even as
*the heart of* one man; so that they
sent *this word* unto the king, Return thou, and all thy servants.
15 So the king returned, and
came to [z]Jôr'dan. And [a]Jū'dah
came to [b]Gĭl'găl, to go to meet
the king, to conduct the king
over Jôr'dan.
16 ¶ And [c]Shĭm'e-ī the son of

1
*a* *Joab*, 2 Sam. 20:23.
*b* *David*, 1 Sam. 16:13.
*c* *Parents, parental affection, exemplified*, vs. 1–6; 2 Cor. 12:14.
*d* *Mourning*, Lam. 2:5.
*e* *Absalom*, 2 Sam. 3:3.
2
*f* *Sympathy*, Jas. 1:27.
5
*g* *Citizens, loyal, instances of*, Luke 15:15.
*h* *Courage, instances of*, Deut. 31:7.
*i* *Loyalty*, Eccl. 8:2.
*j* *Reproof, faithfulness in*, Prov. 17:10.
*k* *Polygamy*, Deut. 17:17.
*l* *Concubinage*, 2 Sam. 21:11.
6
*m* *Enemy, instances of forgiveness of*, Prov. 24:17.
7
*n* *Oath*, Num. 5:19.

8
*o* *Gates*, Deut. 3:5.
9
*p* *Philistines*, Gen. 26:14.
11
*q* *Abiathar*, 1 Sam. 22:20.
*r* *High Priest*, Lev. 21:10.
*s* *Diplomacy*, 2 Kin. 16:7.
*t* *Senate*, Num. 11:16.
1 R. V. to bring him to his house.
13
*u* *Amasa*, 2 Sam. 17:25.
*v* *Clemency, of David*, 2 Sam. 16:11.
*w* *Nepotism, of David*, Gen. 47:11.
*x* *Armies, how officered*, Deut. 11:4.
14
*y* *Judah, tribe of*, Num. 10:14.
15
*z* *Jordan*, Gen. 32:10.
*a* *Judah, tribe of*, Num. 10:14.
*b* *Gilgal*, Josh. 4:19.
16
*c* *Shimei*, 1 Kin. 2:36.

* **ZADOK** (*righteous*). *High priest in time of David's reign*, 2 Sam. 19:11; 20:25; 1 Chr. 15:11; 16:39; 27:17. *Removes the ark from Jerusalem at the time of Absalom's usurpation; returns with it at David's command*, 2 Sam. 15:24–36; 17:15. *Stands aloof from Adonijah at the time of his attempted usurpation*, 1 Kin. 1:8, 26. *Summoned by David to anoint Solomon*, 1 Kin. 1:32–40, 44, 45. *Performs the function of high priest after Abiathar was deposed by Solomon*, 1 Kin. 2:35; 1 Chr. 29:22. *Sons of, faithful when the people went astray*, Ezek. 43:19; 44:15, 16; 48:11.

d *Gera*, Judg. 3:15.
e *Benjamin, tribe of*, Num. 1:37.
f *Bahurim*, 2 Sam. 3:16.
g *David*, 1 Sam. 16:13.

17
h *Ziba*, 2 Sam. 9:2.
i *Saul*, 1 Sam. 9:2.
j *Jordan*, Gen. 32:10.

18
k *Ship*, 2 Chr. 8:18.

19
l *Jerusalem*, Judg. 19:10.

21
m *Abishai*, 2 Sam. 3:30.
n *Zeruiah*, 1 Chr. 2:16.
o *Death, penalty*, Num. 23:10.
p *Rulers, must not be reviled*, Ex. 18:21.

22
q *David, meekness of*, 1 Sam. 16:13.
r *Israel, under the kings*, Ex. 4:22.

23
s *Forgiveness, of enemies, instances of*, Matt. 18:21.
t *Clemency, of David*, 2 Sam. 16:11.

24
u *Mephibosheth*, 2 Sam. 9:6.

[d]Gē′rȧ, a [e]Bĕn′ja-mīte, which *was* of [f]Bȧ-hū′rim, hasted and came down with the men of Jū′dah to meet king [g]Dā′vid.

17 And *there were* a thousand men of [e]Bĕn′ja-mĭn with him, and [h]Zī′bȧ the servant of the house of [i]Sa̤ul, and his fifteen sons and his twenty servants with him; and they went over [j]Jôr′dan before the king.

18 And there went over a ferry [k]boat to carry over the king's household, and to do what he thought good. And [c]Shĭm′e-ī the son of [d]Gē′rȧ fell down before the king, as he was come over Jôr′dan;

19 And said unto the king, Let not my lord impute iniquity unto me, neither do thou remember that which thy servant did perversely the day that my lord the king went out of [l]Jē-rṳ′sȧ-lĕm, that the king should take it to his heart.

20 For thy servant doth know that I have sinned: therefore, behold, I am come the first this day of all the house of Jō′s̤eph to go down to meet my lord the king.

21 But [m]Ȧ-bĭsh′a-ī the son of [n]Zĕr-ṳ-ī′ah answered and said, Shall not [c]Shĭm′e-ī be put to [o]death for this, because he cursed the LORD's [p]anointed?

22 And [q]Dā′vid said, What have I to do with you, ye sons of Zĕr-ṳ-ī′ah, that ye should this day be adversaries unto me? shall there any man be put to death this day in [r]Ĭs̤′ra-el? for do not I know that I *am* this day king over Ĭs̤′ra-el?

23 Therefore the [g]king said unto [c]Shĭm′e-ī, [†, s, t]Thou shalt not die. And the king sware unto him.

24 ¶ And [u]Mē-phĭb′o-shĕth the son of [i]Sa̤ul came down to meet the [g]king, and had neither dressed his feet, nor trimmed his beard, nor washed his clothes, from the day the king departed until the day he came *again* in peace.

25 And it came to pass, when he was come to [l]Jē-rṳ′sȧ-lĕm to meet the king, that the king said unto him, Wherefore wentest not thou with me, [u]Mē-phĭb′o-shĕth?

26 And he answered, My lord, O king, my [v]servant deceived me: for thy servant said, I will saddle me an ass, that I may ride thereon, and go [2]to the king; because thy servant *is* lame.

27 And he hath [w]slandered thy servant unto my lord the king; but my lord the king *is* as an angel of God: do therefore *what is* good in thine eyes.

28 For all *of* my father's house were but dead men before my lord the king: yet didst thou set thy servant among them that did eat at thine own table. What right therefore have I yet to cry any more unto the king?

29 And the king said unto him, Why speakest thou any more of thy matters? I have said, Thou and [h]Zī′bȧ divide the land.

30 And [u]Mē-phĭb′o-shĕth said unto the king, Yea, let him take all, forasmuch as my lord the king is come again in peace unto his own house.

31 ¶ And [x]Bär-zĭl′la-ī the Gĭl′e-ăd-īte came down from [y]Rō-gē′lim, and went over [j]Jôr′dan with the king, to conduct him over Jôr′dan.

32 Now [x]Bär-zĭl′la-ī was a [z]very aged man, *even* fourscore years old: and [a, b]he [c]had provided the king of sustenance while he lay at [d]Mā-hȧ-nā′im; for he *was* a very great man.

33 And the [e]king [f]said unto

26
v *Servant, wicked and unfaithful*, Jer. 2:14.
2 R.V. with

27
w *Slander, instances of*, Prov. 10:18.

31
x *Barzillai*, 2 Sam. 17:27.
y 2 Sam. 17:27.

32
z *Longevity, instances of*, Psa. 91:16.

a *Citizens, loyal, instances of*, Luke 15:15.
b *Loyalty, instances of*, Eccl. 8:2.
c *Liberality, instances of*, 1 Tim. 6:18.
d *Mahanaim*, Gen. 32:2.

33
e *David*, 1 Sam. 16:13.
f *Friendship, instances of*, Prov. 22:24.

† **AMNESTY**, for political offenses. *To Shimei*, 2 Sam. 19:16–23. *To Amasa*, 2 Sam. 19:13, with 17:25.

g *Barzillai*, 2 Sam. 17:27.
h *Jerusalem*, Judg. 19:10.

35
i *Old Age*, Isa. 46:4.
j *Music*, 2 Chr. 5:13.

36
k *Jordan*, Gen. 32: 10.

37
l *Contentment, instances of*, 1 Tim. 6:6.
m *Grave*, 2 Sam. 3:32.
n Jer. 41:17.

39
o *Kiss, of affection*, Ruth 1:14.
p *Benedictions, instances of*, Deut. 21:5.

40
q *Gilgal*, Josh. 4:19

41
r *Jealousy, instances of*, Psa. 78:58.
s *Israel, under the kings*, Ex. 4:22.
t *Flattery, instances of*, vs. 41–43; Prov. 6:24.

[g]Bär-zĭl′la-ī, Come thou over
with me, and I will feed thee
with me in [h]Jĕ-ru̧′să-lĕm.
34 And [g]Bär-zĭl′la-ī said unto
the [e]king, How long have I to
live, that I should go up with the
king unto Jĕ-ru̧′să-lĕm?
35 I *am* this day fourscore years
[i]old: *and* can I discern between
good and evil? can thy servant
taste what I eat or what I drink?
can I hear any more the [j]voice of
singing men and singing women?
wherefore then should thy
servant be yet a burden unto my
lord the king?
36 Thy servant will go a little
way over [k]Jôr′dan with the king:
and why should the king recompense
it me with such a reward?
37 [l]Let thy servant, I pray thee,
turn back again, that I may die
in mine own city, *and be buried*
by the [m]grave of my father and
of my mother. But behold thy
servant [n]Chĭm′hăm; [l]let him go
over with my lord the king; and
do to him what shall seem good
unto thee.
38 And the [e]king answered,
[n]Chĭm′hăm shall go over with
me, and I will do to him that
which shall seem good unto thee:
and [l]whatsoever thou shalt require
of me, *that* will I do for
thee.
39 And all the people went over
[k]Jôr′dan. And when the [e]king
was come over, the king [o]kissed
[g]Bär-zĭl′la-ī, and [p]blessed him;
and he returned unto his own
place.
40 Then the [e]king went on to
[q]Gĭl′găl, and [n]Chĭm′hăm went
on with him: and all the people
of Jū′dah conducted the king,
and also half the people of Ĭş′ra-el.
41 ¶ And, behold, [r]all the men
of [s]Ĭş′ra-el came to the [e]king,
and said unto the king, [t]Why
have our brethren the men of
[u]Jū′dah stolen thee away, and
have brought the king, and
his household, and all [e]Dā′vid's
men with him, over [k]Jôr′dan?
42 And all the men of [u]Jū′dah
answered the men of [s]Ĭş′ra-el,
Because the king *is* near of kin
to us: wherefore then be ye [v]angry
for this matter? have we
eaten at all of the king's *cost*?
or hath he given us any gift?
43 [r]And the men of [s]Ĭş′ra-el answered
the men of [u]Jū′dah, and
said, We have ten parts in the
king, and we have also more
*right* in Dā′vid than ye: why
then did ye despise us, that our
advice should not be first had in
bringing back our king? And
the words of the men of Jū′dah
were fiercer than the words of
the men of Ĭş′ra-el.

## CHAPTER 20

*Sheba makes a party in Israel. 3 David's ten concubines are put in ward unto the day of their death. 4 Amasa, made captain over Judah, is slain by Joab. 14 Joab pursues Sheba unto Abel. 16 A wise woman saves the city. 23 David's officers.*

AND there happened to be
there a man of Bē′lĭ-al,
whose name *was* [a]Shē′bȧ, the
son of Bĭch′rī, a Bĕn′ja-mīte:
and he blew a [b]trumpet, and
[c]said, We have no part in [d]Dā′vid,
neither have we inheritance
in the son of Jĕs′se: every man to
his tents, O [e]Ĭş′ra-el.
2 So every man of [e]Ĭş′ra-el went
up from after [d]Dā′vid, *and* followed
[a]Shē′bȧ the son of Bĭch′rī:
but the men of [f]Jū′dah clave unto
their king, from [g]Jôr′dan even
to [h]Jĕ-ru̧′să-lĕm.
3 ¶ And [d]Dā′vid came to his
house at [h]Jĕ-ru̧′să-lĕm; and the
king took the ten women *his*
[i]concubines, whom he had left to
keep the house, and put them in
ward, and fed them, but went
not in unto them. So they were
shut up unto the day of their
death, living in widowhood.

u *Judah, tribe of*, Num. 10:14.

42
v *Anger*, Prov. 37:8.

1
a *Citizens, wicked and treasonable*, Luke 15:15.
b *Trumpet*, Josh. 6:4.
c *Treason*, 2 Kin. 11:14.
d *David*, 1 Sam. 16:13.
e *Israel, under the kings*, Ex. 4:22.

2
f *Judah, tribe of*, Num. 10:14.
g *Jordan*, Gen. 32: 10.
h *Jerusalem*, Judg. 19:10.

3
i *Concubinage*, 2 Sam. 21:11.

4 ¶ Then said the [d]king to [j]Ăm′a-sȧ, [k]Assemble me the men of [l]Jū′dah within three days, and be thou here present.

5 So [j]Ăm′a-sȧ went to [k]assemble *the men of* Jū′dah: but he tarried longer than the set time which he had appointed him.

6 And [d]Dā′vid said to [l]Ā-bĭsh′-a-ī, Now shall [a]Shē′bȧ the son of Bĭch′rī do us more harm than *did* [m]Ăb′sa-lŏm: take thou thy lord's servants, and pursue after him, lest he get him fenced cities, and escape us.

7 And there went out after him Jō′ăb's men, and the [n]Chĕr′e-thītes, and the *Pĕl′e-thītes, and all the mighty men: and they went out of [h]Jē-ru̦′sȧ-lĕm, to pursue after [a]Shē′bȧ the son of Bĭch′rī.

8 When they *were* at the great [o]stone which *is* in Gĭb′e-on, [j]Ăm′a-sȧ [1]went before them. And Jō′ăb's garment that he had put on was girded unto him, and upon it a [p]girdle *with* a [q]sword fastened upon his loins in the sheath thereof; and as he went forth it fell out.

9 And Jō′ăb said to [j]Ăm′a-sȧ, [2]*Art* thou in health, my brother? And Jō′ăb took Ăm′a-sȧ by the beard with the right hand to [r,s]kiss him.

10 But [j]Ăm′a-sȧ took no heed to the sword that *was* in Jō′ăb's hand: [t,u]so he [v,w]smote him therewith in the [3]fifth *rib*, and shed out his bowels to the ground, and struck him not again; and he died. So Jō′ăb and [l]Ā-bĭsh′a-ī his brother pursued after Shē′bȧ the son of Bĭch′rī.

11 And one of Jō′ăb's men stood by him, and said, He that favoureth Jō′ăb, and he that *is* for [d]Dā′vid, *let him go* after Jō′ăb.

4
j *Amasa*, 2 Sam. 17:25.
k *Muster*, 2 Kin. 25:19.

6
l *Abishai*, 2 Sam. 3:30.
m *Absalom*, 2 Sam. 3:3.

7
n *Cherethites*, 1 Sam. 30:14.

8
o *Pillar*, Gen. 28:18.
p *Girdle*, Prov. 31:24.
q *Sword*, 1 Chr. 21:5.
1 R. V. came to meet

9
r *Kiss*, Ruth 1:14.
s *Salutations, by kissing*, Luke 1:44.
2 R. V. Is it well with thee,

10
t *Confidence, betrayed*, Mic. 7:5.
u *Treachery*, 2 Kin. 9:23.
v *Assassination, instances of*, Deut. 27:24.
w *Homicide, felonious, instances of*, Deut. 5:17.
3 R. V. belly,

12 And [j]Ăm′a-sȧ wallowed in blood in the midst of the highway. And when the man saw that all the people stood still, he removed Ăm′a-sȧ out of the highway into the field, and cast a cloth upon him, when he saw that every one that came by him stood still.

13 When he was removed out of the highway, all the people went on after Jō′ăb, to pursue after Shē′bȧ the son of Bĭch′rī.

14 ¶ And he went through all the tribes of Ĭṣ′ra-el unto [x]Ā′bĕl, and to Bĕth–mā′a-chah, and all the Bē′rītes: and they were gathered together, and went also after him.

15 And they came and [y]besieged him in [x]Ā′bĕl of Bĕth–mā′a-chah, and they cast up a bank against the city, and it stood [4]in the trench: and all the people that *were* with Jō′ăb [z]battered the [a]wall, to throw it down.

16 ¶ [b,c]Then cried a wise [d]woman out of the city, Hear, hear; say, I pray you, unto [e]Jō′ăb, Come near hither, that I may speak with thee.

17 And when he was come near unto her, the [d]woman said, *Art* thou [e]Jō′ăb? And he answered, I *am he*. Then [c]she said unto him, Hear the words of thy handmaid. And he answered, I do hear.

18 Then she [b,c]spake, saying, They were wont to speak in old time, saying, [f]They shall surely ask *counsel* at Ā′bĕl: and so they ended *the matter*.

19 [g]I *am one of them that are* peaceable *and* faithful in Ĭṣ′ra-el: thou seekest to destroy a city and a mother in Ĭṣ′ra-el: why wilt thou swallow up the inheritance of the LORD?

20 And [e]Jō′ăb answered and

14
x *Abel-beth-maachah*, 2 Kin. 15:29.

15
y *Siege, instances of*, Deut. 28:53.
z Ezek. 4:2; 21:22.
a *Walls*, 1 Sam. 20:25.
4 R. V. against the rampart:

16
b *Diplomacy, instances of*, 2 Kin. 16:7.
c *Statecraft, women in*, Prov. 28:2.
d *Women*, Prov. 31:10.
e *Joab*, 2 Sam. 20:23.

18
f *Proverbs*, 1 Sam. 24:13.

19
g *Tact*, Prov. 15:1.

***PELETHITES.** *A part of David's bodyguard*, 1 Kin. 1:38; 2 Sam. 8:18; 20:7, 23; 1 Chr. 18:17; *of Absalom's escort*, 2 Sam. 15:18.

said, Far be it, far be it from me, that I should swallow up or destroy.

21 The matter *is* not so: but a man of mount [h]Ē′phră-ĭm, [i]Shē′bȧ the son of Bĭch′rī by name, hath lifted up his hand against the king, *even* against [j]Dā′vid: deliver him only, and I will depart from the city. And the [c,d]woman said unto [e]Jō′ăb, Behold, his head shall be thrown to thee over the wall.

22 Then the [b,d]woman went unto all the people in her wisdom. And they cut off the head of Shē′bȧ the son of Bĭch′rī, and cast *it* out to Jō′ăb. And he blew a trumpet, and they retired from the city, every man to his tent. And [e]Jō′ăb returned to [k]Jē-ru̥′sȧ-lĕm unto the king.

23 ¶ [l]Now †Jō′ăb *was* over all the [m]host of Ĭṣ′ra-el: and [n]Bē-nā′iah the son of Jē-hoi′a-dȧ *was* over the [o]Chĕr′e-thītes and over the [p]Pĕl′e-thītes:

24 And [q]Ā-dō′ram *was* over the [r]tribute: and [s]Jē-hŏsh′a-phăt the son of [t]Ā-hī′lu̥d *was* recorder:

25 And Shē′vȧ *was* [u]scribe: and [v]Zā′dŏk and [w]Ā-bī′a-thär *were* the [x]priests:

26 And Ī′rȧ also the Jā′ïr-īte was [5]a [y]chief ruler about Dā′vid.

## CHAPTER 21

*The Gibeonites are avenged by famine, and by the death of seven of Saul's sons.* 10 *Rizpah's kindness unto the dead.* 12 *David buries the bones of Saul and Jonathan in the sepulchre of Kish.* 15 *Four battles against the Philistines, wherein four giants are slain.*

THEN there was a [a,b,c]famine in the days of [d]Dā′vid three years, year after year; and Dā′vid [e]enquired of the LORD. And the LORD answered, [f]*It is* for [g]Sa̤ul, and for *his* bloody house, because he slew the Ḡĭb′e-on-ītes.

2 And the [d]king called the Ḡĭb′e-on-ītes, and said unto them; (now the Ḡĭb′e-on-ītes *were* not of the children of Ĭṣ′ra-el, but of the remnant of the [h]Ăm′ôr-ītes; and the children of [i]Ĭṣ′ra-el had [j]sworn unto them: and [g]Sa̤ul sought to slay them in his zeal to the children of Ĭṣ′ra-el and Jū′dah.)

3 Wherefore Dā′vid said unto the Ḡĭb′e-on-ītes, What shall I do for you? and wherewith shall I make the [k]atonement, that ye may bless the inheritance of the LORD?

4 And the Ḡĭb′e-on-ītes said unto him, We will have no silver nor gold of Sa̤ul, nor of his house; neither [1]for us shalt thou kill any man in Ĭṣ′ra-el. And he said, What ye shall say, *that* will I do for you.

5 And they answered the king, The man that consumed us, and that devised against us *that* we should be destroyed from remaining in any of the [2]coasts of Ĭṣ′ra-el,

6 Let seven men of his sons be delivered unto us, and we will hang them up unto the LORD in Ḡĭb′e-ah of Sa̤ul, *whom* the LORD did choose. And the king said, I will give *them*.

7 But the [d]king spared [l]Mē-phĭb′o-shĕth, the son of [m]Jŏn′a-than the son of [g]Sa̤ul, because of the LORD's [j,n]oath that *was* between them, between Dā′vid and Jŏn′a-than the son of Sa̤ul.

8 But the king took the two sons of [o]Rĭz′pah the daughter of

**21**
*h Ephraim, mount of*, Josh. 17:15.
*i Citizens, wicked and treasonable*, Luke 15:15.
*j David*, 1 Sam. 16:13.

**22**
*k Jerusalem*, Judg. 19:10.

**23**
*l Cabinet, David's*, vs. 23–26; Ezra 7:14.
*m Armies*, Deut. 11:4.
*n Benaiah*, 1 Kin. 4:4.
*o Cherethites*, 1 Sam. 30:14.
*p Pelethites*, 2 Sam. 20:7.

**24**
*q* Or, *Adoniram*, 1 Kin. 5:14.
*r Tax, collectors of*, Neh. 10:32.
*s* 2 Sam. 8:16.
*t* 2 Sam. 8:16.

**25**
*u Scribe*, 1 Kin. 4:3.
*v Zadok*, 2 Sam. 19:11.
*w Abiathar*, 1 Sam. 22:20.
*x High Priest*, Lev. 21:10.

**26**
*y Minister*, 2 Chr. 9:4.
5 R. V. priest unto

**1**
*a Famine, instances of*, 2 Kin. 8:1.
*b Canaan, famine in*, Gen. 37:1.
*c Judgments*, Ex. 6:6.
*d David*, 1 Sam. 16:13.
*e Prayer*, Acts 6:4.
*f Sin, punishment of, instances of*, Rom. 5:12.
*g Saul*, 1 Sam. 9:2.

**2**
*h Amorites*, Gen. 14:13.
*i Israel, under the kings*, Ex. 4:22.
*j Covenant, of men with men*, Deut. 29:1.

**3**
*k Atonement*, Lev. 17:11.

**4**
1 R. V. is it for us to put any man to death in Israel.

**5**
2 R. V. borders

**7**
*l Mephibosheth*, 2 Sam. 9:6.
*m Jonathan*, 1 Sam. 14:1.
*n Oath*, Num. 5:19.

**8**
*o* 2 Sam. 3:7.

† **JOAB.** *Son of David's sister*, 1 Chr. 2:16. *Commander of David's army*, 2 Sam. 8:16; 20:23; 1 Chr. 11:6; 18:15; 27:34. *Dedicates spoils of his battles*, 1 Chr. 26:28. *Defeats the Jebusites*, 1 Chr. 11:6. *Defeats and slays Abner*, 2 Sam. 2:13–32; 3:27; 1 Kin. 2:5. *Destroys all the males in Edom*, 1 Kin. 11:16; title to Psa. 60. *Defeats the Ammonites*, 2 Sam. 10:7–14; 1 Chr. 19:6–15. *Captures Rabbah*, 2 Sam. 11:1, 15–25; 12:26–29; 1 Chr. 20:1. *Procures the return of Absalom to Jerusalem*, 2 Sam. 14:1–24. *Barley field of, burned by Absalom*, 2 Sam. 14:29–33. *Pursues and kills Absalom*, 2 Sam. 18:1–16. *Censures David for lamenting the death of Absalom*, 2 Sam. 19:1–8. *Replaced by Amasa as commander of David's army*, 2 Sam. 17:25; 19:13. *Kills Amasa* 2 Sam. 20:8–13; 1 Kin. 2:5. *Causes Sheba to be put to death*, 2 Sam. 20:16–22. *Opposes the numbering of the people*, 2 Sam. 24:3; 1 Chr. 21:3. *Numbers the people*, 2 Sam. 24:4–9; 1 Chr. 21:4, 5; 27:23, 24. *Supports Adonijah as successor to David*, 1 Kin. 1:7; 2:28. *Condemned to death by David*, 1 Kin. 2:5, 6. *Slain by Benaiah, under Solomon's order*, 1 Kin. 2:29–34

[o]Ȧ-ī′ah, whom she bare unto [q]Saul, Är-mō′nī and [l]Mė-phĭb′-o-shĕth; and the five sons of [p]Mī′chal the daughter of Saul, whom she [3]brought up for [q]Ā′drĭ-el the son of Bär-zĭl′la-ī the [q]Mė-hŏl′ath-īte:

9 And he delivered them into the hands of the Ḡĭb′e-on-ītes, and they hanged them in the hill before the LORD: and they fell *all* seven together, and were put to death in the days of harvest, in the first *days,* in the beginning of barley harvest.

10 ¶ And [o, r]Rĭz′pah the daughter of [o]Ȧ-ī′ah took sackcloth, and spread it for her upon the rock, from the beginning of harvest until water dropped upon them out of heaven, and suffered neither the birds of the air to rest on them by day, nor the beasts of the field by night.

11 And it was told [d]Dā′vid what Rĭz′pah the daughter of Ȧ-ī′ah, the *concubine of Saul, had done.

12 And [d]Dā′vid went and took the bones of [q]Saul and the bones of [m]Jŏn′a-than his son from the men of [s]Jā′besh–ḡĭl′e-ăd, which had stolen them from the street of [t]Bĕth′–shăn, where the [u]Phĭ-lĭs′tĭneș had hanged them, when the Phĭ-lĭs′tĭneș had slain Saul in [v]Ḡĭl-bō′ȧ:

13 And he brought up from thence the bones of [q]Saul and the bones of [m]Jŏn′a-than his son; and they gathered the bones of them that were hanged.

14 And the bones of Saul and Jŏn′a-than his son [w]buried they in the country of [x]Bĕn′ja-mĭn in [y]Zē′lah, in the sepulchre of [z]Kĭsh his father: and they performed all that the king commanded. And after that God was intreated for the land.

15 ¶ Moreover the [a]Phĭ-lĭs′tĭneș had yet [b]war again with Ĭș′ra-el; and [c]Dā′vid went down, and his servants with him, and fought against the Phĭ-lĭs′tĭneș: and Dā′vid waxed faint.

16 And Ĭsh′bĭ–bē′nŏb, which *was* of the sons of the giant, the weight of whose spear *weighed* three hundred *shekels* of brass in weight, he being girded with a new *sword,* thought to have slain Dā′vid.

17 But [d]Ȧ-bĭsh′a-ī the son of Zĕr-u-ī′ah succoured him, and smote the [a]Phĭ-lĭs′tĭne, and killed him. [e]Then the [f]men of Dā′vid sware unto him, saying, Thou shalt go no more out with us to battle, that thou quench not the light of Ĭș′ra-el.

18 And it came to pass after this, that there was again a battle with the [a]Phĭ-lĭs′tĭneș at [g]Gŏb: then [h]Sĭb′be-chāi the Hū′shath-īte slew [i]Săph, which *was* of the sons of the giant.

19 And there was again a battle in [g]Gŏb with the [a]Phĭ-lĭs′tĭneș, where [j]Ĕl-hā′nan the son of Jȧ-är′e–ŏr′e-ḡĭm, a Bĕth′-lĕ-hĕm-īte, slew [4]*the brother of* [k]Gō-lī′ath the Ḡĭt′tīte, the staff of whose [l]spear *was* like a [m]weaver's [n]beam.

20 And there was yet a battle in [o]Găth, where was a man of *great* stature, that had on every hand six fingers, and on every foot six [p]toes, four and twenty in number; and he also was born to the giant.

21 And when [q]he defied Ĭș′ra-el, [r]Jŏn′a-than the son of [s]Shĭm′e-ah the brother of Dā′vid slew him.

*p* *Michal,* 1 Sam. 18:27.
*q* 1 Sam. 18:19.
3 R. V. bare to

10
*r* *Parents, affection of, exemplified,* 2 Cor. 12:14.

12
*s* *Jabesh-gilead,* Judg. 21:8.
*t* Or, *Beth-shean,* Josh. 17:11.
*u* *Philistines,* Gen. 26:14.
*v* 1 Sam. 28:4; 31:1–8.

14
*w* *Burial,* Acts 8:2.
*x* *Benjamin, tribe of,* Num. 1:37.
*y* Josh. 18:28.
*z* *Kish,* 1 Sam. 9:1.

15
*a* *Philistines,* Gen. 26:14.
*b* *War,* Judg. 3:2.
*c* *David,* 1 Sam. 16:13.

17
*d* *Abishai,* 2 Sam. 3:30.
*e* *Loyalty, instances of,* Eccl. 8:2.
*f* *Citizens, loyal, instances of,* Luke 15:15.

18
*g* Or, *Gezer,* Josh. 10:33.
*h* 1 Chr. 11:29; 2[illegible] 4; 27:11.
*i* Or, *Sippai,* 1 Chr. 20:4.

19
*j* 1 Chr. 20:5.
*k* *Goliath,* 1 Sam. 17:4.
*l* *Spear,* 2 Kin. 11:10.
*m* *Weaving,* Isa. 38:12.
*n* 1 Sam. 17:7.
4 R. V. *omits* the brother of

20
*o* *Gath,* Josh. 11:22.
*p* *Toe,* Lev. 14:14.

21
*q* *Championship,* 1 Sam. 17:23.
*r* 1 Chr. 20:7.
*s* Or, *Shammah,* 1 Sam. 16:9.

* **CONCUBINAGE.** *Laws concerning,* Ex. 21:7–11; Lev. 19:20–22; Deut. 21:10–14. *Concubines might be dismissed,* Gen. 21:9–14. *Concubines called wives,* Gen. 37:2; Judg. 19:3–5. *Children of, not heirs,* Gen. 21:10. *Children of concubines of Jacob had equal status in his benedictions with those of his wives,* Gen. 49.

*Practiced, by Abraham,* Gen. 16:3; 25:6; 1 Chr. 1:32; *b[y] Nahor,* Gen. 22:23, 24; *by Jacob,* Gen. 30:4; *by Eliphaz,* Ge[n]. 36:12; *by Gideon,* Judg. 8:31; *by Caleb,* 1 Chr. 2:46–48; *b[y] Manasseh,* 1 Chr. 7:14; *by Saul,* 2 Sam. 3:7; *by David,* 2 Sam. 5:13; 15:16; *by Solomon,* 1 Kin. 11:3; *by Rehoboam,* 2 Chr. 1[1]:21; *by Abijah,* 2 Chr. 13:21; *by Belshazzar,* Dan. 5:2.

22 These four were born to the
giant in [o]Găth, and fell by the
hand of Dā′vid, and by the hand
of his servants.

## CHAPTER 22

*David's psalm of thanksgiving to God for his deliverance, and manifold blessings.*

AND[T] [a]Dā′vid [b]spake unto
the LORD the words of
this [c,d]song in the day *that* the
LORD had [e,f]delivered him out
of the hand of all his enemies,
and out of the hand of Saul:
2 And he said, [c,g]The [e]LORD *is*
my [h]rock, and my [i]fortress, and
my deliverer;
3 The God of my [h]rock; [g]in him
will I trust: *he is* my [j]shield, and
the [k]horn of my [l]salvation,[G] my
high [m]tower, and my refuge, my
[e]saviour; thou savest me from
violence.[T]
4 I will call on the LORD, *who
is* worthy to be [b]praised: so shall
I be saved from mine enemies.
5 When the waves of death
compassed me, the floods of [1]un-
godly men made me afraid;
6 The [2]sorrows of [n]hell compassed me about; the snares of
death [3]prevented[G] me;
7 In my [o]distress I [p]called upon
the LORD, and cried to my God:
and he did hear my voice out of
his temple, and my cry *did enter*
into his ears.
8[S] Then the earth shook and
trembled; the foundations of
heaven moved and shook, because he was [q]wroth.[G]
9 There went up a smoke out of
his nostrils, and fire out of his
mouth devoured: coals were kindled by it.[S T]
10 He bowed the heavens also,
and came down; and darkness
*was* under his feet.
11 And he rode upon a cherub,
and did fly: and he was seen upon the wings of the wind.
12 And he made darkness pavilions round about him, [4]dark
waters, *and* thick clouds of the
skies.
13 Through the brightness before him were coals of fire kindled.
14 The LORD thundered from
heaven, and the most High
uttered his voice.
15 And he sent out arrows, and
scattered them; lightning, and
discomfited[G] them.
16 And the channels of the [r]sea
appeared, the foundations of
the world were discovered,[G] at
the rebuking of the [s]LORD, at
the blast of the [t]breath of his
nostrils.
17 He sent from above, he took
me; he drew me out of many
[u]waters;
18 [v]He [w]delivered me from my
strong enemy, *and* from them
that hated me: for they were too
strong for me.
19 They [5]prevented[G] me in the
day of my calamity: but the
LORD was my stay.[G]
20 He brought me forth also
into a large place: he [w]delivered
me, because [x]he delighted in me.[S]
21 The LORD rewarded me
according to my righteousness:
according to the cleanness[G] of my
hands hath he recompensed me.
22 For I [y]have kept the ways
of the LORD, and have not wickedly departed from my God.
23 For all his judgments[G] *were*
before me: and *as for* his statutes, I [y]did not depart from
them.
24 [y]I was also upright before
him, and have kept myself from
mine iniquity.
25 Therefore the LORD hath
recompensed me according to
my righteousness; according to
my cleanness[G] in his eye sight.[S]
26[S] With the merciful thou wilt
shew thyself [z]merciful, *and* with
the upright man thou wilt shew
thyself upright.

**1**
a *David,* 1 Sam. 16:13.
b *Praise,* vs. 1–31; Psa. 150:1.
c *Poetry, epic,* vs. 1–51; Acts 17:28.
d *War Songs,* vs. 1–51; Judg. 5:1.
e *God, preserver,* Gen. 2:2.
f *Victories,* Deut. 28:7.

**2**
g *Faith, instances of,* Mark 11:22.
h *Rock, figurative,* Psa. 78:15.
i *Fortification, figurative,* Ezek. 17:17.

**3**
j *Shield, figurative,* 1 Kin. 14:27.
k *Horn, figurative,* 1 Kin. 1:39.
l *Salvation,* Acts 16:17.
m *Tower, figurative,* 2 Chr. 26:9.

**5**
1 R. V. ungodliness made

**6**
n *Hell,* Mark 9:43.
2 R. V. cords of Sheol were round about me:
3 R .V. came upon me.

**7**
o *Adversity, prayer in,* Psa. 10:6.
p *Prayer, in adversity,* Acts 6:4.

**8**
q *Anger of God,* 2 Kin. 13:3.

**12**
4 R. V. Gathering of waters,

**16**
r *Red Sea,* Ex. 10 19.
s *God, power of,* Gen. 2:2.
t *Breath, of God,* Gen. 7:15.

**17**
u *Water, figurative,* 1 Kin. 17: 10.

**18**
v *War, God in,* Judg. 3:2.
w *God, providence of,* Gen. 2:2.

**19**
5 R. V. came upon me

**20**
x *Grace of God,* Rom. 4:16.

**22**
y *Faithfulness, instances of,* Luke 16:10.

**26**
z *God, mercy of,* Gen. 2:2.

27 With the pure thou wilt shew thyself pure; and with the [6,a]froward thou wilt shew thyself [7]unsavoury.

28 And the [b]afflicted people thou wilt [c]save: but thine eyes *are* upon the haughty, *that* thou mayest bring *them* down.

29 For [d]thou *art* my lamp, O LORD: and the LORD will lighten my darkness.

30 For by thee I [8]have run through a troop: by my God [9]have I leaped over a wall.

31 [e]*As for* God, his way *is* perfect; the word of the LORD *is* tried: he *is* a [10,c]buckler to all them that trust in him.

32 For who *is* God, save the LORD? and who *is* a [f]rock, save our God?

33 God *is* my [11]strength *and* power: and he maketh my way perfect.

34 He maketh my feet like hinds' *feet*: and setteth me upon my high places.

35 He teacheth my hands to war; so that [12]a bow of steel is broken by mine arms.

36 Thou hast also given me the [g]shield of thy [h]salvation: and thy [i]gentleness hath made me great.

37 Thou hast enlarged my steps under me; so that my feet did not slip.

38 I have pursued mine enemies, and destroyed them; and turned not again until I had consumed them.

39 And I have consumed them, and wounded them, that they could not arise: yea, they are fallen under my feet.

40 For thou hast girded me with strength to battle: them that rose up against me hast thou subdued under me.

41 Thou hast also [13]given me the necks of mine enemies, that I might destroy them that hate me.

42 They [j]looked, but *there was* none to save; *even* unto the LORD, but he answered them not.

43 Then did I beat them as small as the dust of the earth, I did stamp them as the mire of the street, *and* did spread them abroad.

44 Thou also hast delivered me from the strivings of my people, thou hast kept me *to be* head of the [14]heathen: a people *which* I knew not shall serve me.

45 [k]Strangers shall submit themselves unto me: as soon as they hear, they shall be obedient unto me.

46 [k]Strangers shall fade away, and [15]they shall be afraid out of their close places.

47 [l]The LORD liveth; and blessed *be* my rock; and exalted be the God of the [f]rock of my [h]salvation.

48 It *is* God that [m]avengeth me, and that bringeth down the people under me,

49 And that [m]bringeth me forth from mine enemies: thou also hast lifted me up on high above them that rose up against me: thou hast delivered me from the violent man.

50 Therefore I will give [n]thanks unto thee, O LORD, among the [14]heathen, and I will sing [l]praises unto thy name.

51 [16]*He is* the tower of [h]salvation for his king: and sheweth [17]mercy to his anointed, unto Dā'vid, and to his seed for evermore.

## CHAPTER 23

*David, in his last words, professes his faith in God's promises; 6 and describes the condition of the wicked. 8 A catalogue of David's mighty men.*

1 NOW these *be* the last words of [a]Dā'vid. Dā'vid the son of Jĕs'se said, and the man *who was* raised up on high, the anointed of the God of Jā'cob,

---

27
a *Wicked, punishment of,* Psa. 73:3.
6 R. V. perverse
7 R. V. froward.

28
b *Afflictions, consolation in,* Psa. 34:19.
c *God, preserver,* Gen. 2:2.

29
d *God, guide,* Gen. 2:2.

30
8 R. V. run upon
9 R. V. do I leap

31
e *Faith, exemplified,* Mark 11:22.
10 R. V. shield unto

32
f *Rock, figurative,* Psa. 78:15.

33
11 R. V. strong fortress: And he guideth the perfect in his way.

35
12 R. V. mine arms do bend a bow of brass.

36
g *Shield, figurative,* 1 Kin. 14:27.
h *Salvation,* Acts 16:17.
i *Gentleness, of God,* 2 Cor. 10:1.

41
13 R. V. made mine enemies turn their backs unto me,

42
j *Wicked, prayer of,* Psa. 73:3.

44
14 R. V. nations:

45
k *Foreigners,* Deut. 23:20.

46
15 R. V. shall come trembling out

47
l *Praise,* Psa. 150:1.

48
m *God, providence of,* Gen. 2:2.

50
n *Thankfulness, to God,* Acts 24:3.

51
16 R. V. Great deliverance giveth he to his king:
17 R. V. lovingkindness

1
a *David,* 1 Sam. 16:13.

and the sweet psalmist of Ĭş′ra-el, said,

2 [T]The Spirit of the LORD [b]spake by me, and his word *was* in my tongue.[T]

3 The God of Ĭş′ra-el said, the [c]Rock of Ĭş′ra-el spake to me, [1,d]He that ruleth over men *must be* just, ruling in the [e]fear of God.

4 And *he shall be* as the light of the morning, *when* the sun riseth, *even* a morning without clouds; *as* the tender grass *springing* out of the earth by clear shining after rain.

5 Although my house *be* not so with God; yet [f]he hath made with me an everlasting [g]covenant, ordered in all *things*, and [h]sure: for *this is* all my salvation, and all *my* desire, although he make *it* not to grow.[S T]

6 [S]But [2,i]*the sons* of Bē′lĭ-al *shall be* all of them as thorns thrust away, because they cannot be taken with hands:

7 But the man *that* shall touch them must be [3]fenced with [j]iron and the staff of a spear; and [k]they shall be utterly burned with fire in the *same* place.[S]

8 ¶ [l]These *be* the names of the mighty men whom Dā′vid had: The [m]Tăch′mo-nīte that sat in the seat, chief among the captains; the same *was* Ăd′ĭ-nō the Ĕz′nīte: [4]*he lift up his spear* against eight hundred, whom he slew at one time.

9 And after him *was* [n]Ē-le-ā′-zar the son of [5]Dō′dō the Ā-hō′-hīte, *one* of the three mighty men with [u]Dā′vid, when they defied the [o]Phĭ-lĭs′tīneş *that* were there gathered together to battle, and the men of Ĭş′ra-el were gone away:

10 [p]He arose, and smote the Phĭ-lĭs′tīneş until his hand was weary, and his hand clave unto the sword: and the [q]LORD [r]wrought a great victory that day; and the people returned after him only to spoil.

11 And after him *was* Shăm′-mah the son of Ăg′e-ē the Hā′ra-rīte. And the [o]Phĭ-lĭs′tīneş were gathered together into a troop, where was a piece of ground full of lentiles: and the people fled from the Phĭ-lĭs′tīneş.

12 But he stood in the midst of the [6]ground, and defended it, and slew the [o]Phĭ-lĭs′tīneş: and the [q]LORD [r]wrought a great victory.

13 And three of the thirty chief went down, and came to [a]Dā′vid in the harvest time unto the [s]cave of [t]Ā-dŭl′lăm: and the troop of the [o]Phĭ-lĭs′tīneş pitched in the valley of [u]Rĕph′a-ĭm.

14 And Dā′vid *was* then in an hold, and the [v]garrison of the [o]Phĭ-lĭs′tīneş *was* then *in* [w]Bĕth′–lĕ-hĕm.

15 And Dā′vid longed, and said, Oh that one would give me drink of the water of the well of [w]Bĕth′–lĕ-hĕm, which *is* by the gate!

16 [x]And the three mighty men [p]brake through the host of the Phĭ-lĭs′tīneş, and drew water out of the well of [w]Bĕth′–lĕ-hĕm, that *was* by the gate, and took *it*, and brought *it* to [y]Dā′vid: nevertheless he would not drink thereof, but [z]poured it out unto the LORD.[S]

17 And he said, Be it far from me, O LORD, that I should do this: [7]*is not this* the blood of the men that went in jeopardy of their lives? therefore he would not drink it. These things did these three mighty men.

18 And [a]Ā-bĭsh′a-ī, the brother of [b]Jō′ăb, the son of Zĕr-u-ī′ah, was chief among three. And [c]he lifted up his spear against three hundred, *and* slew *them*, and had the name among three.

2
*b* *Inspiration*, Job 32:8.

3
*c* *Rock, figurative*, Psa. 78:15.
*d* *Rulers, character and qualifications of*, Ex. 18:21.
*e* *Fear of God*, Acts 9:31.
1 R. V. One that ruleth over men righteously, That ruleth

5
*f* *Faith, exemplified*, Mark 11:22.
*g* *Covenant, of God with men*, Deut. 29:1.
*h* *God, faithfulness of*, Gen. 2:2.

6
*i* *Evil Company, perils of*, Prov. 13:20.
2 R. V. the ungodly

7
*j* *Iron, figurative*, Prov. 27:17.
*k* *Wicked, punishment of*, Psa. 73:3.
3 R. V. armed

8
*l* *Armies, rewards for meritorious conduct in, roll of honor*, vs. 8–39; Deut. 11:4.
*m* Or, *Jashobeam*, 1 Chr. 27:2.
4 R. V. *omits* he lift up his spear

9
*n* 1 Chr. 11:12.
*o* *Philistines*, Gen. 26:14.
5 R. V. Dodai the son of an Ahohite,

10
*p* *Courage, instances of*, Deut. 31:7.
*q* *War, God in*, Judg. 3:2.
*r* *God, providence of*, Gen. 2:2.

12
6 R. V. plot,

13
*s* *Cave*, Judg. 6:2.
*t* *Adullam*, 1 Sam 22:1.
*u* *Rephaim*, 1 Chr. 11:15.

14
*v* *Garrison*, 1 Sam 13:3.
*w* *Beth-lehem*, Gen. 48:7.

16
*x* 1 Chr. 11:18.
*y* *David*, 1 Sam. 16:13.
*z* *Consecration, instances of*, Lev. 7:37.

17
7 R. V. shall I drink the

18
*a* *Abishai*, 2 Sam 3:30.
*b* *Joab*, 2 Sam. 20 23.
*c* *Courage, instances of*, Deut. 31:7.

19 Was he not most honourable
of three? therefore he was their
captain: howbeit he attained not
unto the *first* three.
20 And [d]Bĕ-nā′iah the son of
Jĕ-hoi′a-dȧ, the son of a valiant
man, of [e]Kăb′ze-el, who had
done many acts, he slew [8]two
lionlike men of Mō′ab: he went
down also and slew a [f]lion in the
midst of a pit in time of [g]snow:
21 And he slew an [h]Ē-ġy̆p′tian,
a goodly man: and the Ē-ġy̆p′-
tian had a [i]spear in his hand;
but he went down to him with a
staff, and plucked the spear out
of the Ē-ġy̆p′tian's hand, and
slew him with his own spear.
22 These *things* did [d]Bĕ-nā′iah
the son of Jĕ-hoi′a-dȧ, and had
the name among three mighty
men.
23 He was more honourable
than the thirty, but he attained
not to the *first* three. And [j]Dā′-
vid set him over his guard.
24 [k]Ā′sa-hĕl, the brother of
[b]Jō′ăb, *was* one of the thirty;
[l]Ĕl-hā′nan the son of [l]Dō′dō of
Bĕth′-lĕ-hĕm,
25 [m]Shăm′mah the Hā′rod-īte,
Ĕl′i-kȧ the Hā′rod-īte,
26 [n]Hĕ′lez the Păl′tīte, [o]Ī′rȧ the
son of [p]Ĭk′kĕsh the Tĕ-kō′īte,
27 [q]Ā-bĭ-ē′zĕr the Ăn′e-thŏth-
īte, Mĕ-bŭn′nāi the Hū′shath-īte,
28 Zăl′mŏn the Ā-hō′hīte, [r]Mȧ-
hăr′a-ī the Nĕ-tŏph′a-thīte,
29 [s]Hĕ′lĕb the son of [t]Bā′a-nah,
a Nĕ-tŏph′a-thīte, [u]Ĭt′ta-ī the
son of [v]Rī′bāi out of Ḡĭb′e-ah of
the children of [w]Bĕn′ja-mĭn,
30 [x]Bĕ-nā′iah the Pĭr′a-thon-
īte, [y]Hĭd′da-ī of the [z]brooks of
[a]Gā′ăsh,
31 [b]Ā′bĭ-ăl′bŏn the Är′bath-īte,
[c]Ăz′ma-vĕth the Bär-hū′mīte,
32 [c]Ē-lī′ah-bȧ the Shȧ-ăl′bo-
nīte, of the sons of Jā′shen, Jŏn′-
a-than,
33 Shăm′mah the Hā′ra-rīte,
[d]Ā-hī′am the son of [e]Shā′rär the
Hā′ra-rīte,
34 Ē-lĭph′e-lĕt the son of
[f]Ā-hăs′ba-ī, the son of the Mȧ-
ăch′a-thīte, [g]Ē-lī′am the son of
Ā-hĭth′o-phĕl the Ḡī′lo-nīte,
35 [h]Hĕz′ra-ī the Cär′mel-īte,
[i]Pā′a-rāi the Är′bīte,
36 [j]Ī′găl the son of Nā′than of
Zō′bah, Bā′nī the Găd′īte,
37 [k]Zē′lek the Ăm′mon-īte,
[k]Nā′ha-rī the Bĕ-ē′roth-īte, armourbearer to Jō′ăb the son of
Zĕr-u-ī′ah,
38 [l]Ī′rȧ an Ĭth′rīte, [l]Gā′rĕb an
Ĭth′rīte,
39 [m]U-rī′ah the Hĭt′tīte: thirty
and seven in all.

## CHAPTER 24

*David's sin in numbering the people. 10 His confession thereof. 11 Of three judgments offered, he chooses the three days' pestilence. 16 The destroying angel is stayed and Jerusalem spared. 18 David erects an altar and offers a sacrifice unto the Lord.*

AND again the [a]anger of
the LORD was kindled
against [b]Ĭṣ′ra-el, and he moved
[c]Dā′vid against them [1]to say,
[d]Go, *,[e,f]number Ĭṣ′ra-el and
Jū′dah.
2 For the king said to [g]Jō′ăb
the captain of the [f]host, which
*was* with him, Go now through
all the tribes of Ĭṣ′ra-el, from
[h]Dăn even to [i]Bē′er-shē′bȧ, and
*,[f]number ye the people, that I
may know the number of the
people.
3 And [g]Jō′ăb [j]said unto the
king, Now the LORD thy God
add unto the people, how many
soever they be, an hundredfold,
and that the eyes of my lord the
king may see *it*: but why doth
my lord the king delight in this
thing?
4 Notwithstanding the king's
[k]word prevailed against [g]Jō′ăb,
and against the captains of the

**20**
d *Benaiah,* 1 Kin. 4:4.
e Josh. 15:21; 1 Chr. 11:22.
f *Lion,* Mic. 5:8.
g *Snow, in Palestine,* Jer. 18:14.
8 R. V. the two sons of Ariel of Moab:

**21**
h *Egyptians,* Gen. 50:3.
i *Spear,* 2 Kin. 11:10.

**23**
j *David,* 1 Sam. 16:13.

**24**
k *Asahel,* 2 Sam. 2:18.
l 1 Chr. 11:26.

**25**
m Or, *Shammoth,* 1 Chr. 11:27.

**26**
n 1 Chr. 11:27; 27:10.
o 1 Chr. 11:28.
p 1 Chr. 27:9.

**27**
q 1 Chr. 11:28; 27:12.

**28**
r 1 Chr. 11:30; 27:13.

**29**
s Or, *Heled,* 1 Chr. 11:30; or, *Heldai,* 1 Chr. 27:15.
t 1 Chr. 11:30.
u Or, *Ithai,* 1 Chr. 11:31.
v 1 Chr. 11:31.
w *Benjamin, tribe of,* Num. 1:37.

**30**
x *Benaiah,* 1 Chr. 27:14.
y Or, *Hurai,* 1 Chr. 11:32.
z *Brook,* Deut. 8:7.
a *Gaash,* Josh. 24:30.

**31**
b Or, *Abiel,* 1 Chr. 11:32.
c 1 Chr. 11:33.

**33**
d 1 Chr. 11:35.
e Or, *Sacar,* 1 Chr. 11:35.

**34**
f Or, *Ur,* 1 Chr. 11:35.
g Or, *Ahijah,* 1 Chr. 11:36.

**35**
h Or, *Hezro,* 1 Chr. 11:37.
i Or, *Naarai,* 1 Chr. 11:37.

**36**
j Or, *Joel,* 1 Chr. 11:38.

**37**
k 1 Chr. 11:39.

**38**
l 1 Chr. 11:40.

**39**
m *Uriah,* 2 Sam. 11:3.

**1**
a *Anger of God,* 2 Kin. 13:3.
b *Israel, under the kings,* Ex. 4:22.
c *David,* 1 Sam. 16:13.
d 1 Chr. 21.
e *Muster,* 2 Kin. 25:19.
f *Armies, enumeration of,* Deut. 11:4.
1 R. V. saying,

**2**
g *Joab,* 2 Sam. 20:23.
h *Dan,* Judg. 18:29.
i *Beer-sheba,* Judg. 20:1.

**3**
j *Reproof, faithfulness in,* Prov. 17:10.

**4**
k *Self-will,* Gen. 49:6.

*** CENSUS.** *Numbering of Israel, by Moses,* Ex. 38:26; Num. 1; 3:14–43; 26; *by David,* 2 Sam. 24:1–9; 1 Chr. 21:1–8; 27:24. *A poll tax to be levied at each,* Ex. 30:12–16; 38:26. *Of the Roman Empire, by Cæsar, when Quirinius was governor of Syria,* Luke 2:1–3 [R. V.].

5
[l] *Jordan,* Gen. 32:10.
[2] R. V. is in the middle of the valley of

6
[m] *Zidon,* Ezek. 28:21.

7
[n] *Tyre, fortified,* Josh. 19:29.
[o] *Hivites,* Gen. 10:17.

8
[p] *Jerusalem,* Judg. 19:10.

9
[q] *Judah, tribe of,* Num. 10:14.

10
[r] *Conscience, guilty, instances of,* Acts 23:1.
[s] *Repentance,* Mark 1:4.
[t] *Sin, confession of,* Rom. 5:12.

11
[u] *Prophets, called seers,* Isa. 3:2.

12
[v] *Contingencies, in divine government of man,* 1 Kin. 3:14.
[w] *Judgments,* Ex. 6:6.

host. And Jō′ăb and the captains of the host went out from
the presence of the king, to
*number the people of Ĭṣ′ra-el.
5 And they passed over [l]Jôr′-
dan, and pitched in Ăr′ŏ-ēr, on
the right side of the city that
[2]*lieth* in the midst of the river of
Găd, and toward Jā′zēr:
6 Then they came to Ḡĭl′e-ăd,
and to the land of Täh′tim–hŏd′-
shī; and they came to Dăn–jā′-
an, and about to [m]Zī′dŏn,
7 And came to the strong hold
of [n]Tȳre, and to all the cities of
the [o]Hī′vītes, and of the Cā′-
năan-ītes: and they went out to
the south of Jū′dah, *even* to
[i]Bē′er–shē′bȧ.
8 So when they had gone
through all the land, they came
to [p]Jĕ-rṳ′să-lĕm at the end of
nine months and twenty days.
9 And [g]Jō′ăb gave up the *sum
of the number of the people unto
the king: and there were in Ĭṣ′-
ra-el [f]eight hundred thousand
valiant men that drew the sword;
and the men of [q]Jū′dah *were*
[f]five hundred thousand men.
10 ¶ And [c]Dā′vid's [r]heart
smote him after that he had
numbered the people. And Dā′-
vid said unto the LORD, [s,t]I have
sinned greatly in that I have
done: and now, I beseech thee,
O LORD, take away the iniquity
of thy servant; for I have done
very foolishly.
11 For when [c]Dā′vid was up in
the morning, the word of the
LORD came unto the prophet
†Găd, Dā′vid's [u]seer, saying,
12 Go and say unto Dā′vid,
Thus saith the LORD, [v]I offer
thee [w]three *things*; ‡choose thee
one of them, that I may *do it*
unto thee.

13 So †Găd came to [c]Dā′vid,
and told him, and said unto him,
[w]Shall seven years of famine
come unto thee in thy [x]land? or
wilt thou flee three months before thine enemies, while they
pursue thee? or that there be
three days' [y]pestilence in thy
land? now advise, and see what
answer I shall return to him that
sent me.
14 And Dā′vid said unto †Găd.
I am in a great strait: [z,a]let us
fall now into the hand of the
LORD; [b]for his [c]mercies *are*
great: and let me not fall into the
hand of man.
15 ¶ So the LORD [d,e]sent a
[f]pestilence upon [g]Ĭṣ′ra-el from
the morning even to the time
appointed: and there died of
the people from [h]Dăn even to
[i]Bē′er–shē′bȧ seventy thousand
men.
16 And when the [j]angel stretched out his hand upon [k]Jĕ-rṳ′să-
lĕm to destroy it, the [l]LORD
[m,n]repented him of the evil, and
said to the angel that destroyed
the people, It is enough: stay
now thine hand. And the angel
of the LORD was by the [o]thresh-
ingplace of [p]Ȃ-rạu′nah the Jĕb′-
u-sīte.
17 And [q]Dā′vid [r]spake unto the
LORD when he saw the [j]angel
that smote the people, and said,
Lo, [s]I have sinned, and I have
done [3]wickedly: [t]but these sheep
what have they done? let thine
hand, I pray thee, be against me,
and against my father's house.
18 ¶ And †Găd came that day
to [q]Dā′vid, and said unto him,
Go up, rear an [u]altar unto the
LORD in the [o]threshingfloor of
[p]Ȃ-rạu′nah the Jĕb′u-sīte.
19 And [q]Dā′vid, according to

13
[x] *Canaan,* Gen. 37:1.
[y] *Plague,* Ex. 11:1.

14
[z] *Adversity, resignation in, exemplified,* Psa. 10:6.
[a] *Resignation, exemplified,* Job 5:17.
[b] *Faith, instances of,* Mark 11:22.
[c] *God, mercy of,* Gen. 2:2.

15
[d] *God, providence of,* Gen. 2:2.
[e] *Sin, punishment of,* Rom. 5:12.
[f] *Plague,* Ex. 11:1.
[g] *Nation, involved in sins of rulers,* Isa. 2:4.
[h] *Dan,* Judg. 18:29.
[i] *Beer-sheba,* Judg. 20:1.

16
[j] *Angel, functions of,* Heb. 1:13.
[k] *Jerusalem,* Judg. 19:10.
[l] *God, mercy of,* 2:2.
[m] *Repentance, attributed to God,* Mark 1:4.
[n] *Anthropomorphisms,* Gen. 11:5.
[o] *Threshing,* 1 Chr. 21:20.
[p] Or, *Ornan,* 1 Chr. 21:15–25.

17
[q] *David,* 1 Sam. 16:13.
[r] *Prayer, intercessory,* Acts 6:4.
[s] *Self-condemnation,* Job 9:20.
[t] *Intercession, exemplified,* Jer. 27:18.
[3] R. V. perversely:

18
[u] *Altar,* Gen. 8:20.

† **GAD** *(fortune). A prophet,* 2 Sam. 24:11. *Bids David leave Adullam,* 1 Sam. 22:5. *Bears the divine message to David offering choice between three evils, for his presumption in numbering Israel,* 2 Sam. 24:11–14; 1 Chr. 21:9–13. *Bids David build an altar on threshing floor of Ornan,* 2 Sam. 24:18, 19; 1 Chr. 21:18, 19. *Assists David in arranging tabernacle service,* 2 Chr. 29:25. *Is one of the court historians during the reign of David,* 1 Chr. 29:29.

‡ **CHOICE.** *Between life and death,* Deut. 30:19, 20. *Between God and false gods,* Josh. 24:15–18. *Between judgments, by David,* 2 Sam. 24:12–14; 1 Chr. 21:11–13. *Between God and Baal,* 1 Kin. 18:21, 39, 40. *Of Moses,* Heb. 11:24, 25.

the saying of Găd, went up as the LORD commanded.

20 And [p]Ā-ra̤u′nah looked, and saw the [q]king and his servants coming on toward him: and Ā-ra̤u′nah went out, and [v]bowed himself before the king on his face upon the ground.

21 And [p]Ā-ra̤u′nah said, Wherefore is my lord the king come to his servant? And [q]Dā′vid said, To buy the [o]threshingfloor of thee, to build an [u]altar unto the LORD, [t]that the [f]plague may be stayed from the people.

22 And [p]Ā-ra̤u′nah said unto Dā′vid, [w, x]Let my lord the king take and offer up what *seemeth* good unto him: behold, *here be* oxen for [y]burnt [4]sacrifice, and [o]threshing instruments and [5]*other* instruments of the oxen for wood.

23 All these *things* did [p]Ā-ra̤u′nah, *as* a king, give unto the king. And Ā-ra̤u′nah said unto the king, [z]The LORD thy God accept thee.

24 And the king said unto Ā-ra̤u′nah, Nay; but I will surely buy *it* of thee at a price: [a, b]neither will I offer [c]burnt offerings unto the LORD my God of that which doth cost me nothing. So Dā′vid bought the threshingfloor and the oxen for fifty [d]shekels of silver.

25 And Dā′vid built there an [e]altar unto the LORD, and offered [b]burnt offerings and [f]peace offerings. So the LORD was intreated for the land, and the [g]plague was stayed from Ĭṣ′ra-el.

20
v *Salutations*, Luke 1:44.

22
w *Liberality, instances of*, 1 Tim. 6:18.
x *Unselfishness, instances of*, 1 Cor 10:24.
y *Offerings, burnt*, Lev. 6:17.
4 R. V. offering,

5 R. V. the furniture

23
z *Benedictions, instances of*, Deut. 21:5.

24
a *Self-denial*, Mark 8:34.
b *Zeal*, 2 Cor. 7:11.
c *Offerings, burnt*, Lev. 6:17.
d *Shekel*, Ex. 30:13.

25
e *Altar*, Gen. 8:20.
f *Offerings, peace*, Lev. 6:17.
g *Plague*, Ex. 11:1.

THE

# FIRST BOOK OF THE KINGS

## CHAPTER 1

*Abishag cherishes David in his extreme age. 5 Adonijah aspires to the kingdom. 11 Nathan and Bath-sheba induce the king to secure the succession to Solomon. 32 Solomon anointed king. 41 At the tidings thereof, Adonijah flees to the horns of the altar. 51 He is spared by Solomon.*

NOW king [a]Dā′vid was [b]old *and* stricken in years; and they covered him with clothes, but he gat no heat.

2 Wherefore his servants said unto him, Let there be sought for my lord the king a young [c]virgin: and let her stand before the [d]king, and let her cherish him, and let her lie in thy bosom, that my lord the king may get heat.

3 So they sought for a fair damsel throughout all the coasts of Ĭṣ′ra-el, and found [e]Ăb′ĭ-shăg a *Shṳ′nam-mīte, and brought her to the king.

4 And the [e]damsel *was* very [f]fair, and cherished the [d]king, and ministered to him: but the king [g]knew her not.

5 ¶ Then †,[h]Ăd-o-nī′jah the son of [i]Hăg′gĭth [j]exalted himself, saying, [k]I will be [d]king: and he prepared him [l]chariots and [m]horsemen, and fifty men to run before him.

6 And his father [n]had not displeased him at any time in saying, Why hast thou done so? and he also *was a* very goodly *man*; and *his mother* bare him after [o]Ăb′sa-lŏm.

7 And he [p]conferred with [q]Jō′ăb the son of [r]Zĕr-ṳ-ī′ah, and with [s]Ā-bī′a-thär the priest: and they following †Ăd-o-nī′jah helped *him*.

8 But [t]Zā′dŏk the priest, and

1
a *David*, 1 Sam. 16:13.
b *Old Age*, Isa. 46:4.

2
c *Virgin*, Isa. 62:5.
d *King*, 2 Kin. 3:10.

3
e 1 Kin. 2:13-25.

4
f *Beauty, instances of*, Prov. 6:25.
g *Continence*, Matt. 19:12.

5
h *Children, wicked, instances of*, Mark 10:14.
i 1 Chr. 3:2.
j *Ambition, instances of*, Hab. 2:5.
k *Usurpation*, v. 11; 2 Sam. 15:1.
l *Chariots*, Josh. 11:4.
m *Cavalry*, 1 Sam. 13:5.

6
n *Parents, indulgent*, 2 Cor. 12:14.
o *Absalom*, 2 Sam. 3:2.

7
p *Counsel*, Prov. 12:15.
q *Joab*, 2 Sam. 20:23.
r *Zeruiah*, 1 Chr. 2.16.
s *Abiathar*, 1 Sam. 22:20. 8 t *Zadok*, 2 Sam. 19:11.

* **SHUNAMMITE**, a person from Shunem. *Abishag, the damsel who nourished David*, 1 Kin. 1:3; *desired by Adonijah as wife*, 1 Kin. 2:13–25. *A woman who gave hospitality to Elisha, and whose son he raised to life*, 2 Kin. 4:8–37.

† **ADONIJAH.** *Son of David and Haggith*, 2 Sam. 3:4, 1 Kin. 1:5, 6, 1 Chr. 3:2. *Plots to succeed his father as king; is crowned by Abiathar the priest, and proclaimed king; his downfall*, 1 Kin. 1. *Executed by Solomon*, 1 Kin. 2:13–25.

*u Benaiah*, 1 Kin. 4:4.
*v Jehoiada*, 2 Kin. 12:2.
*w Nathan*, 2 Sam. 7:2.
*x Shimei*, 1 Kin. 2:36.

**9**
*y Pillar*, Gen. 28: 18.
*z En-rogel*, Josh. 15:7.
*a Feasts*, Mark 12: 39.
*b Judah, tribe of*, Num. 10:14.
1 R. V. fatlings

**10**
*c Nathan*, 2 Sam. 7:2.
*d Benaiah*, 1 Kin. 4:4.
*e Solomon*, 2 Sam. 12:24.

**11**
*f Statecraft ministers in*, Prov. 28:2.
*g Friendship, instances of*, Prov. 22:24.
*h* 1 Chr. 3:2.

**12**
*i Counsel*, Prov. 12:15.
*j Wisdom, worldly*, Prov. 2:2.

**13**
*k Oath*, Num. 5:19.
*l Covenant*, Deut. 29:1.

**14**
*m Diplomacy*, 2 Kin. 16:7.

**15**
*n Statecraft, women in*, Prov. 28:2.
*o Old Age*, Isa. 46:4.
*p* 1 Kin. 2:13–25.

**16**
*q Homage*, Acts 10:25.
*r Petition, right of, recognized by David*, vs. 15–21: Esth. 5:6.

[u]Bē-nā'iah the son of [v]Jē-hoi'-
a-dȧ, and [w]Nā'than the prophet,
and [x]Shĭm'e-ī, and Rē'ī, and
the mighty men which *belonged*
to Dā'vid, were not with †Ăd-o-
nī'jah.
9 And †Ăd-o-nī'jah slew sheep
and oxen and [1]fat cattle by the
[y]stone of Zō'he-lĕth, which *is* by
[z]Ĕn-rō'gel, and [a]called all his
brethren the king's sons, and all
the men of [b]Jū'dah the king's
servants:
10 But [c]Nā'than the prophet,
and [d]Bē-nā'iah, and the mighty
men, and [e]Sŏl'o-mon his brother,
he called not.
11 ¶ Wherefore [e]Nā'than
[f,g]spake unto ‡Băth'-shĕ-bȧ the
mother of [e]Sŏl'o-mon, saying,
Hast thou not heard that †Ăd-
o-nī'jah the son of [h]Hăg'gĭth
doth reign, and Dā'vid our
lord knoweth *it* not?
12 Now therefore come, [g]let me,
I pray thee, give thee [i,j]counsel,[G]
that thou mayest save thine own
life, and the life of thy son
[e]Sŏl'o-mon.
13 Go and get thee in unto king
Dā'vid, and say unto him, Didst
not thou, my lord, O king,
[k,l]swear unto thine handmaid,
saying, Assuredly [e]Sŏl'o-mon thy
son shall reign after me, and he
shall sit upon my throne? why
then doth †Ăd-o-nī'jah reign?
14 Behold, [m]while thou yet
talkest there with the king, [f]I
also will come in after thee, and
confirm thy words.
15 ¶ And ‡,[n]Băth'-shĕ-bȧ went
in unto the king into the chamber: and the king was very [o]old;
and [p]Ăb'ĭ-shăg the Shu̧'nam-
mīte ministered unto the king.
16 And ‡Băth'-shĕ-bȧ bowed,
and did [q]obeisance unto the
king. And the king said, [r]What
wouldest[G] thou?

17 And she said unto him, My
lord, thou [k,l]swarest by the
LORD thy God unto thine
‡handmaid, *saying*, Assuredly
[e]Sŏl'o-mon thy son shall reign
after me, and he shall sit upon
my throne.
18 And, now behold, †Ăd-o-nī'-
jah [s]reigneth; and now, my lord
the king, thou knowest *it* not:
19 And †he hath slain oxen and
[1]fat cattle and sheep in abundance, and hath [a]called all the
sons of the king, and [t]Ā-bī'a-
thär the [u]priest, and [v]Jō'ăb the
[w]captain of the host: but [e]Sŏl'o-
mon thy servant hath he not
called.
20 And thou, my lord, O king,
the eyes of all Ĭṣ'ra-el *are* upon
thee, that thou shouldest tell
them [x]who shall sit on the
throne of my lord the king
after him.
21 Otherwise it shall come to
pass, when my lord the king
shall [y]sleep with his fathers, that
I and my son Sŏl'o-mon shall be
counted offenders.[G]
22 ¶ And, lo, while she yet
talked with the king, [z,a,b]Nā'-
than the prophet also came in.
23 And they told the king, saying, Behold [a]Nā'than the prophet. And when he was come in
before the king, he [c]bowed himself before the king with his face
to the ground.
24 And [a]Nā'than [d,e]said, My
lord, O king, hast thou said,
†Ăd-o-nī'jah shall reign after
me, and he shall sit upon my
throne?
25 For he is gone down this
day, and hath slain oxen and
[1]fat cattle and sheep in abundance, and [f]hath called all the
king's sons, and the [g]captains
of the host, and [h]Ā-bī'a-thär the
[i]priest; and, behold, they eat and

**18**
*s Usurpation, of political functions*, 2 Sam. 15:1.

**19**
*t Abiathar*, 1 Sam. 22:20.
*u High Priest*, Lev. 21:10.
*v Joab*, 2 Sam. 20. 23.
*w Captain*, Num. 31:48.

**20**
*x King, hereditary succession of*, 2 Kin. 3:10.

**21**
*y Death, called sleep*, Num. 23:10.

**22**
*z Ministers, influential in public affairs*, Rom. 15:16.
*a Nathan*, 2 Sam. 7:2.
*b Statecraft, ministers in*, Prov. 28:2.

**23**
*c Homage*, Acts 10:25.

**24**
*d Tact*, Prov. 15:1.
*e Prudence*, 2 Chr. 2:12.

**25**
*f Feasts*, Mark 12: 39.
*g Armies, how officered*, Deut. 11:4.
*h Abiathar*, 1 Sam. 22:20.
*i High Priest*, Lev. 21:10.

‡ **BATH-SHEBA**, wife of Uriah and later wife of David. *Called* BATH-SHUA, 1 Chr. 3:5. *Adultery of*, 2 Sam. 11:2–5. *Mother of Solomon*, 1 Kin. 1:11–31; 2:13–21; 1 Chr. 3:5

*j Salutations*, Luke 1:44.

**26**

*k Jealousy, instances of*, Psa. 78:58.
*l Zadok*, 2 Sam. 19:11.
*m Benaiah*, 1 Kin. 4:4.
*n Jehoiada*, 2 Sam. 8:18.
*o Solomon*, 2 Sam. 12:24.

**27**

*p King, hereditary succession of*, 2 Kin. 3:10.

**28**

*q David*, 1 Sam. 16:13.

**29**

*r Oath*, Num. 5:19.
*s God, preserver*, Gen. 2:2.

**30**

*t Covenant, of men with men*, Deut. 29:1

**31**

2 R. V. obeisance

**33**

*u Mule*, 2 Sam. 18:9.

**34**

*v Prophets, officiate at installation of kings*, Isa. 3.2.
*w Anointing, of kings*, Lev. 8:12.
*x King, modes of induction into office*, 2 Kin. 3:10.
*y Israel, under the kings*, Ex. 4:22.

drink before him, and say, [j]God
save[c] king †Ăd-o-nī′jah.
26 [k]But [a]me, *even* me thy servant, and [l]Zā′dŏk the [i]priest, and
[m]Bē-nā′iah the son of [n]Jē-hoi′a-
dȧ, and thy servant [o]Sŏl′o-mon,
hath he not called.
27 Is this thing done by my
lord the king, and thou hast not
shewed *it* unto thy servant, [p]who
should sit on the throne of my
lord the king after him?
28 ¶ Then king [q]Dā′vid answered and said, Call me
‡Băth′-shĕ-bȧ. And she came
into the king's presence, and
stood before the king.
29 And the king [r]sware, and
said, *As* the LORD liveth, that
[s]hath redeemed my soul out of
all distress,
30 Even as I [t]sware unto thee
by the LORD God of Ĭṣ′ra-el,
saying, Assuredly [o,p]Sŏl′o-mon
thy son shall reign after me, and
he shall sit upon my throne in
my stead; even so will I certainly
do this day.
31 Then ‡Băth′-shĕ-bȧ bowed
with *her* face to the ground, and
did [2,c]reverence to the king, and
said, [j]Let my lord king Dā′vid
live for ever.
32 ¶ And king [q]Dā′vid said,
Call me [l]Zā′dŏk the [i]priest, and
[a]Nā′than the prophet, and [m]Bē-
nā′iah the son of [n]Jē-hoi′a-dȧ.
And they came before the king.
33 The king also said unto
them, Take with you the servants of your lord, and cause
[o]Sŏl′o-mon my son to ride upon
mine own [u]mule, and bring him
down to ‖Gī′hon:
34 And let [l]Zā′dŏk the [i]priest
and Nā′than the [v]prophet [w]an-
oint him there [x]king over [y]Ĭṣ′-
ra-el: and blow ye with the
[z]trumpet, and say, [a]God save
king [b]Sŏl′o-mon.
35 Then ye shall come up after
him, that he may come and sit
upon my throne; for he shall be
king in my stead: and I have appointed him to be ruler over
[c]Ĭṣ′ra-el and over Jū′dah.
36 And [d]Bē-nā′iah the son of
[e]Jē-hoi′a-dȧ answered the king,
and said, Amen: [f]the LORD
God of my lord the king say so
*too*.
37 [f]As the LORD hath been
with my lord the king, even so be
he with [b]Sŏl′o-mon, and make
his [g]throne greater than the
throne of my lord king [h]Dā′vid.
38 So [i]Zā′dŏk the priest, and
[j]Nā′than the prophet, and [d]Bē-
nā′iah the son of [e]Jē-hoi′a-dȧ,
and the [k]Chĕr′e-thītes, and the
[l]Pĕl′e-thītes, went down, and
caused Sŏl′o-mon to ride upon king [h]Dā′vid's mule, and
brought him to ‖Gī′hon.
39 And [i]Zā′dŏk the priest took
an §horn of [m]oil out of the [3,n]tab-
ernacle, and [o]anointed [b]Sŏl′o-
mon. And they blew the [p]trump-
et; and all the people said, [a]God
save king Sŏl′o-mon.
40 And all the people came up
after him, and the people piped
with [q]pipes[G], and rejoiced with
great [r]joy, so that the earth rent[G]
with the sound of them.
41 ¶ And †Ăd-o-nī′jah and all
the [s]guests that *were* with him
heard *it* as they had made an
end of [t]eating. And when [u]Jō′ăb
heard the sound of the [p]trumpet,
he said, Wherefore[G] *is this* noise
of the city being in an uproar?
42 And while he yet spake, behold, [v]Jŏn′a-than the son of
[w]Ă-bī′a-thär the priest came:
and †Ăd-o-nī′jah said unto him,

*z Trumpet*, Josh. 6:4.

*a Salutations*, Luke 1:44.
*b Solomon*, 2 Sam. 12:24.

**35**

*c Israel, under the kings*, Ex. 4:22.

**36**

*d Benaiah*, 1 Kin. 4:4.
*e Jehoiada*, 2 Sam. 8:18.
*f Prayer, intercessory*, Acts 6:4.

**37**

*g Throne, figurative*, 1 Kin. 2:19.
*h David*, 1 Sam. 16.13.

**38**

*i Zadok*, 2 Sam. 19:11.
*j Nathan*, 2 Sam. 7:2.
*k Cherethites*, 1 Sam. 30:14.
*l Pelethites*, 2 Sam 20:7.

**39**

*m Oil*, Deut. 12:17.
*n Tabernacle*, Ex. 27:9.
*o Anointing, of kings*, Lev. 8:12.
*p Trumpet*, Josh. 6:4.
3 R. V. Tent,

**40**

*q* 1 Sam. 10:5; Isa. 30:29.
*r Joy*, Psa. 5:11.

**41**

*s Guests*, Zeph. 1:7.
*t Feasts*, Mark 12: 39.
*u Joab*, 2 Sam. 20: 23.

**42**

*v Jonathan*, 2 Sam. 15:27.
*w Abiathar*, 1 Sam. 22:20.

‖ **GIHON.** *A fountain or spring north of Jerusalem, the waters of which were conducted by Hezekiah into Jerusalem and stored in pools*, 2 Chr. 32:4, 30; 33:14; Neh. 2:14, 15; 3:15, 16; Isa. 7:3; 22:9–11; 36:2. *Solomon crowned at*, 1 Kin. 1:33, 38, 45.

§ **HORN.** *Used to hold the anointing oil*, 1 Sam. 16:1; 1 Kin. 1:39. *Used for a trumpet*, Josh. 6:4–6, 8, 13. *Horns of the altar*, Ex. 27:2; 1 Kin. 1:50; 2:28.
**Figurative:** *Of divine protection*, 2 Sam. 22:3. *Of power*, Psa. 89; 92:10; 132:17; Mic. 4.
SYMBOLICAL, Dan. 7:7–24; 8:3–9, 20; Zech. 1:18–21; Rev. 5:6; 12:3; 13:1, 11; 17:3–16.

*x* *Flattery, instances of*, Prov. 6:24.
4 R. V. worthy

Come in; for [x]thou *art* a [4]valiant[c]
man, and bringest good tidings.
43 And Jŏn′a-than answered
and said to †Ăd-o-nī′jah, Verily
our lord king [h]Dā′vid hath made
[b]Sŏl′o-mon king.
44 And the king hath sent with
him [i]Zā′dŏk the priest, and
[j]Nā′than the prophet, and [d]Bĕ-
nā′iah the son of [e]Jė-hoi′a-dȧ,
and the [k]Chĕr′e-thītes, and the
[l]Pĕl′e-thītes, and they have
caused him to ride upon the
king's mule:
45 And [i]Zā′dŏk the priest and
[j]Nā′than the prophet have [o]an-
ointed him king in ‖Gī′hon:
and they are come up from
thence[c] rejoicing, so that the city
rang again. This *is* the noise
that ye have heard.
46 And also Sŏl′o-mon sitteth
on the throne of the kingdom.
47 And moreover the king's
servants came to bless our lord
king [h]Dā′vid, saying, [f]God make
the name of Sŏl′o-mon better
than thy name, and make his
[g]throne greater than[c] thy throne.
And the king bowed[c] himself upon the bed.
48 And also thus said the king,
[y]Blessed be the LORD God of
Ịṣ′ra-el, which hath given *one* to
sit on my throne this day, mine
eyes even seeing it.
49 And all the [s]guests that *were*
with †Ăd-o-nī′jah [z]were afraid,
and rose up, and went every man
his way.
50 And †Ăd-o-nī′jah [z]feared because of [a]Sŏl′o-mon, and arose,
and went, [b]and caught hold on
the horns of the [c]altar.
51 And it was told [a]Sŏl′o-mon,
saying, Behold, †Ăd-o-nī′jah
feareth king Sŏl′o-mon: for, lo,
he hath caught hold on the horns
of the [c]altar, saying, Let king
Sŏl′o-mon [d]swear unto me to day
that he will not [e]slay his servant
with the sword.

48
*y* *Praise*, Psa. 150:1.

49
*z* *Cowardice*, Lev. 26:36.

50
*a* *Solomon*, 2 Sam. 12:24.
*b* 1 Kin. 2 28.
*c* *Altar*, Gen. 8:20.

51
*d* *Oath*, Num. 5:19.
*e* *Punishment, death penalty*, Lev. 26:41.

52 And [a]Sŏl′o-mon said, If he
will shew himself a worthy man,
there shall not an hair of him
fall to the earth: but if wickedness shall be found in him, he
shall die.
53 So king [a]Sŏl′o-mon sent, and
they brought him down from
the [c]altar. And he came and
[2,f]bowed[c] himself to king Sŏl′o-
mon: and Sŏl′o-mon said unto
him, [g]Go to thine house.

## CHAPTER 2

*David's charge to Solomon.* 5 *His directions concerning Joab,* 7 *Barzillai,* 8 *and Shimei.* 10 *His death.* 12 *Solomon succeeds him.* 13 *Adonijah, suing for Abishag, is put to death.* 26 *Abiathar is deprived of the priesthood.* 28 *Joab, fleeing to the horns of the altar, is there slain.* 35 *Benaiah is put in Joab's place, and Zadok in Abiathar's* 36 *Shimei is ordered to remain in Jerusalem;* 39 *but disobeying, he is put to death.*

NOW the days of [a]Dā′vid
drew nigh[c] that he should
[b]die; and he charged[c] [c]Sŏl′o-mon
his son, saying,
2 I go the way of all the earth:
be thou strong therefore, and
shew thyself a man;
3 [s]And [d]keep the charge of the
LORD thy God, to walk in his
ways, to [e]keep his statutes, and
his commandments, and his
judgments[c], and his [f]testimonies,
as it is written in the [g]law of Mō′-
ṣeṣ, [h,i]that thou mayest prosper
in all that thou doest, and whithersoever[c] thou turnest thyself:
4 That the LORD may [1]con-
tinue his [j]word which he spake
concerning me, saying, If thy
children take heed to thy way, to
walk before me in truth with all
their [k]heart and with all their
soul, [l]there shall not fail thee
(said he) a man on the throne of
Ịṣ′ra-el.[s]
5 Moreover thou knowest also
what [m]Jō′ăb the son of Zĕr-ụ-
ī′ah [n,o]did to me, *and* what he
did to the two [p]captains of the
hosts of Ịṣ′ra-el, unto [q]Ăb′nĕr
the son of Nĕr, and unto [r]Ăm′a-
sȧ the son of [s]Jē′thĕr, whom he

53
*f* *Salutations*, Luke 1:44.
*g* *Forgiveness, instances of*, Matt. 18:21.

1
*a* *David*, 1 Sam. 16:13.
*b* *Death, preparation for*, Num. 23:10.
*c* *Solomon*, 2 Sam. 12:24.

3
*d* *Watchfulness*, Matt. 24:42.
*e* *Obedience, enjoined*, Heb. 5:8.
*f* *Testimony, the commandments revealed to Moses* Ex. 25:16.
*g* *Law, of Moses*, Deut. 33:2.
*h* *Obedience, rewarded*, Heb. 5:8.
*i* *Blessings, contingent upon obedience*, Deut. 11:26

4
*j* *Covenant, of God with men*, Deut. 29:1.
*k* *Heart*, Psa. 44:21.
*l* *Promise, of reward, to the obedient*, 2 Cor. 1:20.
1 R. V. establish his

5
*m* *Joab*, 2 Sam. 20 23.
*n* *Ingratitude, of man to man, instances of*, Rom. 1:21.
*o* *Evil for Good*, Psa. 35:12.
*p* *Armies, how officered*, Deut. 11:4.
*q* *Abner*, 1 Sam. 14:50.
*r* *Amasa*, 2 Sam. 17:25.
*s* *Jether*, 1 Chr. 2:17.

[t]slew, and shed the blood of war in [u]peace, and put the blood of war upon his [v]girdle[G] that *was* about his loins, and in his shoes that *were* on his feet.

6 Do therefore according to thy wisdom, and [w]let not his hoar[G] head go down to the grave[G] in peace.

7 But [x]shew [y]kindness unto the sons of [z]Bär-zĭl′la-ī the Ḡĭl′e-ăd-īte, and [a]let them be of those that eat at thy table: for so they came to me when I fled [2]because of [b]Ăb′sa-lŏm thy brother.

8 And, behold, *thou hast* with thee Shĭm′e-ī the son of [c]Ḡē′rȧ, a Bĕn′ja-mīte of [d]Bȧ-hū′rim, which [e,f]cursed me with a grievous curse in the day when I went to [g]Mā-hȧ-nā′im: but he came down to meet me at [h]Jôr′dan, and I [i]sware[G] to him by the LORD, saying, I will not put thee to death with the sword.

9 Now therefore hold him not guiltless: for thou *art* a wise man, and knowest what thou oughtest to do unto him; but [j]his hoar[G] head bring thou down to the grave[G] with blood.

10 ¶ So [k]Dā′vid [l]slept with his fathers, and was [m]buried in the [n]city of Dā′vid.[Q]

11 And the days that Dā′vid reigned over Ĭṣ′ra-el *were* forty years: seven years reigned he in [o]Hē′bron, and thirty and three years reigned he in [n]Jē-ru̥′sȧ-lĕm.

12 ¶ Then sat [p]Sŏl′o-mon upon the *throne of Dā′vid his father; and his kingdom was established greatly.

*t Homicide, felonious*, Deut. 5:17.
*u Peace*, Jer. 29:7.
*v Girdle*, Prov. 31:24.

**6**
*w Retaliation, instances of*, Deut. 19:19.

**7**
*x Thankfulness, of man to man*, Acts 24:3.
*y Kindness*, Acts 28:2.
*z Barzillai*, 2 Sam. 17:27.

*a Hospitality*, Rom. 12:13.
*b Absalom*, 2 Sam. 3:3.
2 R. V. from

**8**
*c Gera*, Judg. 3:15.
*d Bahurim*, 2 Sam. 3:16.
*e Cursing*, Lev. 24:11.
*f Malice, instances of*, Eph. 4:31.
*g Mahanaim*, Gen. 32:2.
*h Jordan*, Gen. 32:10.
*i Covenant, of men with men*, Deut. 29:1.

**9**
*j Retaliation, instances of*, Deut. 19:19.

**10**
*k David, death of*, 1 Sam. 16:13.
*l Death, called sleep*, Num. 23:10.
*m Burying Places*, Gen. 23:4.
*n Jerusalem*, Judg. 19:10.

**11**
*o Hebron*, Gen. 23:2.

v.12–943 BC
**12**
*p Solomon*, 2 Sam. 12:24.

13 ¶ And [q]Ăd-o-nī′jah the son of [r]Hăg′ḡĭth came to [s]Băth′-shĕ-bȧ the mother of [p]Sŏl′o-mon. And she said, Comest thou peaceably? And he said, Peaceably.

14 He said moreover, I have somewhat to say unto thee. And she said, Say on.

15 And he said, Thou knowest that the [t]kingdom was mine, and *that* all Ĭṣ′ra-el set their faces on [u,v]me, that I should reign: howbeit the kingdom is turned about, and is become my brother's: for [w]it was his [x,y]from the LORD.

16 And now I ask one petition of thee, deny me not. And she said unto him, Say on.

17 And he said, [z]Speak, I pray thee, unto [a]Sŏl′o-mon the king, (for he will not say[G] thee nay,) that he give me [b]Ăb′ī-shăg the Shu̥′nam-mīte to[G] wife.

18 And [c]Băth′-shĕ-bȧ said, Well; I will speak for thee unto the king.

19 ¶ [c]Băth′-shĕ-bȧ therefore went unto king [a]Sŏl′o-mon, to [d]speak unto him for [e]Ăd-o-nī′jah. And the king rose up to meet her, and [f]bowed[G] himself unto her, and sat down on his *throne, and caused a [3]seat to be set for the king's †mother; and she sat on his right hand.

20 Then she said, I desire one small [g]petition of thee; *I pray thee*, say[G] me not nay. And the king said unto her, Ask on, my †mother: for I will not say[G] thee nay.

**13**
*q Adonijah*, 1 Kin. 1:5.
*r* 1 Kin. 1:5, 11; 1 Chr. 3:2.
*s Bath-sheba*, 1 Kin. 1:11.

**15**
*t Birthright*, 2 Chr. 21:3.
*u Firstborn, birthright of, set aside*, Zech. 12:10.
*v King, hereditary succession of*, 2 Kin. 3:10.
*w Government, God in*, Isa. 22:21.
*x God, providence of*, Gen. 2:2.
*y Rulers, appointed by God*, Ex. 18:21.

**17**
*z Influence, solicited*, 1 Cor. 7:14.

*a Solomon*, 2 Sam. 12:24.
*b* 1 Kin. 1:1–4.

**18**
*c Bath-sheba*, 1 Kin. 1:11.

**19**
*d Intercession, of man with man*, Jer. 27:18.
*e Adonijah*, 1 Kin. 1:5.
*f Salutations*, Luke 1:44.
3 R. V. throne to

**20**
*g Petition, right of*, Esth. 5:6.

* **THRONE**, 1 Kin. 1:30; 2:19; Acts 12:21. *Made of ivory*, 1 Kin. 10:18–20; 2 Chr. 9:17–19. *Of Solomon, called* THE THRONE OF THE LORD, 1 Chr. 29:23. *Abdicated by David*, 1 Kin. 1:32–40.

**Figurative:** *Of sovereign power*, Gen. 41:40; Ex. 11:5; 1 Kin. 2:12, 24; 8:20; 10:9; 2 Chr. 6:10; 9:8; Psa. 132:11, 12; Isa. 9:7. *Of the sovereign power of God*, 2 Chr. 18:18; Psa. 9:4, 7; 11:4; 47:8; 89:14; 97:2; 103:19; Isa. 6:1; 66:1; Matt. 5:34; 23:22; Acts 7:49; Heb. 8:1; 12:2; Rev. 1:4; 3:21; 4:2–11; 7:9–17; 14:3; 19:4; 21:5. *Of the sovereign power of Christ*, Isa. 9:7; Matt. 19:28; 25:31; Luke 1:32; Acts 2:30; Rev. 3:21; 22:1, 3. *Seen in John's vision*, Rev. 4:3–6; 5:1, 7, 11, 13; 6:16; 7:9–11, 15, 17; 20:11; 21:5.

† **MOTHER.** *Reverence for, enjoined*, Ex. 20:12; Lev. 19:3; Deut. 5:16; Prov. 23:22; Matt. 15:4; 19:19; Mark 7:10; 10:19; Luke 18:20; Eph. 6:2. *To be obeyed*, Deut. 21:18; Prov. 1:8; 6:20. *Love for*, 1 Kin. 19:20. *Love for, must be subordinate to love for Christ*, Matt. 10:37.

*Sanctifying influence of*, 2 Tim. 1:5. *Dishonoring of, to be punished*, Ex. 21:15, 17; Lev. 20:9; Prov. 20:20; 28:24; 30:11, 17; Matt. 15:4–6; Mark 7:10–12.

*Love of*, Isa. 49:15; 66:13.

Love of, exemplified: *By Hagar*, Gen. 21:14–16; *by the mother of Moses*, Ex. 2:1–3; *by Hannah*, 1 Sam. 1:20–28; *by Rizpah*, 2 Sam. 21:8–11; *by Bath-sheba*, 1 Kin. 1:16–21; *by the mother whose child was brought to Solomon for him to arbitrate upon*, 1 Kin. 3:16–26; *by the woman whose sons were to be taken for debt*, 2 Kin. 4:1–7; *by the Shunammitess*, 2 Kin

21 And she said, Let [b]Ăb′ĭ-shăg
the Shṳ′nam-mīte be given to
[e]Ăd-o-nī′jah thy brother to[c]
wife.
22 And king [a]Sŏl′o-mon answered and said unto his †moth-
er, And why dost thou ask [b]Ăb′-
ĭ-shăg the Shṳ′nam-mīte for
[e,h]Ăd-o-nī′jah? ask for him the
kingdom also; for he *is* mine
elder brother; even for him,
and for [i]Ā-bī′a-thär the priest,
and for [j]Jō′ăb the son of Zĕr-
u̧-ī′ah.
23 Then [k]king [a]Sŏl′o-mon
[l]sware by the LORD, saying,
God do so to me, and more also,
if Ăd-o-nī′jah have not spoken
this word against his own life.
24 Now therefore, [l]*as* the LORD
liveth, which hath established
me, and set me on the *throne of
Dā′vid my father, and who hath
made me an house, as he [m]prom-
ised, [e,k]Ăd-o-nī′jah shall be put
to death this day.
25 And king [a]Sŏl′o-mon [n]sent
by the hand of [o]Bē-nā′iah the
son of Jē-hoi′a-dȧ; and he [p]fell
upon him that he died.
26 ¶ [q,r]And unto [i]Ā-bī′a-thär
the [s]priest [k]said the king, Get
thee to [t]Ăn′a-thŏth, unto thine
own [u]fields; for thou *art* worthy
of death: but I will not at this
time put thee to death, because
thou barest the [v]ark of the Lord
GOD before [w]Dā′vid my father,
and because thou hast been afflicted in all wherein my father
was afflicted.
27 So [a]Sŏl′o-mon thrust out
[i]Ā-bī′a-thär from being [s]priest
unto the LORD; that he might
fulfil the word of the LORD,
which he spake concerning the
house of [x]Ē′lī in Shī′lōh.
28 ¶ Then tidings came to
[j]Jō′ăb: for Jō′ăb had turned after Ăd-o-nī′jah, though he turned
not after [y]Ăb′sa-lŏm. And
Jō′ăb fled unto the [4]tabernacle
of the LORD, [z]and caught hold
on the horns of the [a]altar.
29 And it was told king [b]Sŏl′o-
mon that [c]Jō′ăb was fled unto
the [4]tabernacle of the LORD;
and, behold, *he is* by the [a]altar.
Then Sŏl′o-mon sent [d]Bē-nā′iah
the son of Jē-hoi′a-dȧ, saying,
Go, fall upon him.
30 And [d]Bē-nā′iah came to the
[4]tabernacle of the LORD, and
said unto him, Thus saith the
king, Come forth. And he said,
Nay[c]; but I will die here. And
Bē-nā′iah brought the king word
again, saying, Thus said [c]Jō′ăb,
and thus he answered me.
31 And the king said unto him,
Do as he hath said, and [e]fall upon him, and bury him; that thou
mayest take away the innocent
blood, which Jō′ăb shed, from
me, and from the house of my
father.
32 And the LORD shall return
his blood upon his own head,
who fell upon two men more
righteous and better than he,
and [f]slew them with the sword,
my father Dā′vid not knowing
*thereof, to wit,* [g]Ăb′nēr the son of
Nēr, captain of the host of Ĭs̞′-
ra-el, and [h]Ăm′a-sȧ the son of
Jē′thēr, captain of the host of
Jū′dah.
33 Their blood[c] shall therefore
return upon the head of Jō′ăb,
and upon the head of his seed for
ever: but upon Dā′vid, and upon
his seed, and upon his house,
and upon his *throne, shall
there be peace for ever from the
LORD.
34 So [d]Bē-nā′iah the son of Jē-
hoi′a-dȧ went up, and fell upon
him, and [e,i]slew him: and he was
buried in his own [j]house in the
wilderness.

**22**
h *Firstborn,* Zech. 12:10.
i *Abiathar,* 1 Sam. 22:20.
j *Joab,* 2 Sam. 20:23.

**23**
k *Government, monarchical, tyranny in,* Isa. 22:21.
l *Oath,* Num. 5:19.

**24**
m *Covenant, of God with men,* Deut. 29:1.

**25**
n *Fratricide,* Gen. 4:8.
o *Benaiah,* 1 Kin. 4:4.
p *Punishment, death penalty,* Lev. 26:41.

**26**
q *Church and State, civil power superior to ecclesiastical,* v. 27; 1 Sam. 16:1.
r *Usurpation, in ecclesiastical affairs,* v. 27; 2 Sam. 15:1.
s *High Priest,* Lev. 21:10.
t *Anathoth,* Jer. 1:1.
u *Levites, emoluments of,* Deut. 10:8.
v *Ark,* Ex. 25:10.
w *David,* 1 Sam. 16:13.

**27**
x *Eli,* 1 Sam. 1:3.

**28**
y *Absalom,* 2 Sam. 3:3.
z 1 Kin. 1:50.
a *Altar, of burnt offerings,* Gen. 8:20.
4 R. V. Tent

**29**
b *Solomon,* 2 Sam. 12:24.
c *Joab,* 2 Sam. 20:23.
d *Benaiah,* 1 Kin. 4:4.

**31**
e *Homicide, punishment of,* Deut. 5:17.

**32**
f *Homicide, felonious,* Deut. 5:17.
g *Abner,* 1 Sam. 14:50.
h *Amasa,* 2 Sam. 17:25.

**34**
i *Punishment, death penalty,* Lev. 26:41.
j *Burying Places,* Gen. 23:4.

4:18–37; *by Mary the mother of Jesus,* Luke 2:41–50; *by the bereaved mothers of Beth-lehem,* Matt. 2:16–18; *by the Syrophenician woman,* Matt. 15:21–28; Mark 7:24–30.

*Grieves over wayward children,* Prov. 10:1; 19:26; 29:15. *Rejoices over good children,* Prov. 23:23–25. *Incest with, forbidden,* Lev. 18:7. *Wicked,* Gen. 27:6–17.

35 ¶ And the [b]king put [d]Bĕ-nā'iah the son of Jĕ-hoi'a-dȧ in his [k]room[G] over the host: and [l]Zā'dŏk the priest did the [m]king put in the room[G] of [n]Ā-bī'a-thär.

36 ¶ And the [b]king sent and called for ‡Shĭm'e-ī, and said unto him, Build thee an house in [o]Jĕ-ru̥'sȧ-lĕm, and dwell there, and go not forth thence[G] any whither.[G]

37 For it shall be, *that* on the day thou goest out, and passest over the brook ‖Kĭd'ron, thou shalt know for certain that thou shalt [i]surely die: thy blood[G] shall be upon thine own head.

38 And ‡Shĭm'e-ī said unto the king, The saying *is* good: as my lord the king hath said, so will thy servant do. And Shĭm'e-ī dwelt in [o]Jĕ-ru̥'sȧ-lĕm many days.

39 And it came to pass at the end of three years, that two of the [p]servants of ‡Shĭm'e-ī [q]ran away unto [r]Ā'chish son of Mā'a-chah king of [s]Găth. And they told Shĭm'e-ī, saying, Behold, thy servants *be* in Găth.

40 And Shĭm'e-ī arose, and saddled his ass, and went to [s]Găth to [r]Ā'chish to seek his [p]servants: and Shĭm'e-ī went, and brought his servants from Găth.

41 And it was told [b]Sŏl'o-mon that ‡Shĭm'e-ī had gone from [o]Jĕ-ru̥'sȧ-lĕm to [s]Găth, and was come again.

42 And the king sent and called for Shĭm'e-ī, and said unto him, Did I not make thee to [t]swear by the LORD, and protested unto thee, saying, Know for a certain, on the day thou goest out, and walkest abroad[G] any whither,[G] that thou shalt surely die? and thou saidst unto me, The word *that* I have heard *is* good.

43 Why then hast thou not kept the [t]oath of the LORD, and the commandment that I have charged thee with?

44 The king said moreover to ‡Shĭm'e-ī, Thou knowest all the wickedness which thine heart is privy[G] to, that thou didst to [u]Dā'vid my father: therefore the LORD shall return thy wickedness upon thine own head;

45 And king [b]Sŏl'o-mon *shall be* blessed, and the throne of Dā'vid shall be established before the LORD for ever.

46 So the king commanded [d]Bĕ-nā'iah the son of Jĕ-hoi'a-dȧ; which went out, and [i]fell upon him, that he died. And the kingdom was established in the hand of Sŏl'o-mon.

## CHAPTER 3

*Solomon marries Pharaoh's daughter. 2 High places being in use, Solomon sacrifices at Gibeon the great high place. 5 His prayer for wisdom. 10 God's answer. 16 Solomon's decision between the two mothers.*

AND [a]Sŏl'o-mon made affinity[G] with *Phā'raōh king of Ē'gȳpt, and took Phā'raōh's daughter, and brought her into the [b]city of Dā'vid, until he had made an end of building his own house, and the [c]house of the LORD, and the wall of Jĕ-ru̥'sȧ-lĕm round about.

2 Only the people sacrificed[G] in †high places, because there was no house built unto the name of the LORD, until those days.

3 And [a,d]Sŏl'o-mon loved the

35
k *Captain*, Num. 31:48.
l *Zadok*, 2 Sam. 19:11.
m *Church and State, civil power superior to ecclesiastical*, 1 Sam. 16:1.
n *Abiathar*, 1 Sam. 22:20.

36
o *Jerusalem*, Judg. 19:10.

39
p *Servant*, Jer. 2:14.
q *Fugitives, instances of*, Judg. 12:4.
r *Achish*, 1 Sam. 21:10.
s *Gath*, Josh. 11:22.

42
t *Oath*, Num. 5:19.

44
u *David*, 1 Sam 16:13.

1
a *Solomon*, 2 Sam. 12:24.
b *Jerusalem*, Judg. 19:10.
c *Temple, Solomon's*, 1 Kin. 6:17.

3
d *Children, good, instances of*, Mark 10:14.

‡ **SHIMEI.** *A Benjamite*, 1 Kin. 2:8. *Curses David*, 2 Sam. 16:5–8. *David's magnanimity toward*, 2 Sam. 16:9–13; 19:16–23. *Dwelt in Jerusalem*, 1 Kin. 2:36–40. *Slain by order of Solomon*, 1 Kin. 2:41–46.

‖ **KIDRON** (*turbid*), called also CEDRON. *A valley and stream between Jerusalem and the Mount of Olives*, 1 Kin. 2:37; Neh. 2:15; Jer. 31:40. *David flees across, from Absalom*, 2 Sam. 15:23. *Destruction of idols at, by Asa, Josiah, and the Levites*, 1 Kin. 15:13; 2 Kin. 23:4, 6, 12; 2 Chr. 29:16. *The garden of Gethsemane, where Jesus endured the night of agony and where he was arrested, situated in*, John 18:1.

* **PHARAOH.** *At the time of Solomon*, 1 Kin. 3:1; 7:8; 9:16, 24; 11:1, 18–22; 2 Chr. 8:11; Song 1:9.

† **HIGH PLACES.** *Places, of worship*, Gen. 12:8; 22:2, 14; 31:54; 1 Sam. 9:12, 13; 2 Sam. 24:25; 1 Kin. 18:30, 38; 2 Chr. 1:3; 33:17; *of idolatrous worship*, Num. 22:41; 1 Kin. 11:7; 12:31; 14:23; 15:14; 22:43; 2 Kin. 17:9–11, 29; Jer. 7:31. *Licentious practices at*, Ezek. 16:24–43. *The idolatrous, to be destroyed*, Lev. 26:30; Num. 33:52. *Destroyed, by Asa*, 2 Chr. 14:3; *by Jehoshaphat*, 2 Chr. 17:6; *by Hezekiah*, 2 Kin. 18:4; 2 Chr. 31:1; *by Josiah*, 2 Kin. 23:8.

See footnotes: GROVES, Judg. 6:28; IDOLATRY, 1 Sam. 15:23.

LORD, walking in the statutes of Dā'vid his father: only he sacrificed[c] and burnt incense in †high places.

4 And the king went to [e]Gĭb'e-on to sacrifice there; for that *was* the great †high place: a thousand [f]burnt offerings did Sŏl'o-mon offer upon that altar.

5 ¶ In [e]Gĭb'e-on the LORD [g]appeared to [a]Sŏl'o-mon in a [h]dream by night: and God said, Ask what I shall give thee.

6 And [a]Sŏl'o-mon said, Thou hast shewed unto thy servant [i]Dā'vid my father great [1]mercy, according as he walked before thee in truth, and in righteousness, and in uprightness of heart with thee; and thou hast kept for him this great kindness, that thou hast given him a son to sit on his throne, as *it is* this day.

7 And now, O LORD my God, [j]thou hast made thy servant king instead of Dā'vid my father: and I *am* [k]*but* a little child: I know not *how* to go out or come in.

8 And thy servant *is* in the midst of thy people which thou hast chosen, a great people, that cannot be numbered nor counted for multitude.

9 Give therefore thy servant an [l]understanding[c] [m]heart to [n]judge thy people, [o]that I may discern between good and bad: for who is able to judge this thy so great a people?

10 And the speech pleased the Lord, that [a]Sŏl'o-mon had asked this thing.

11 And God said unto him, Because thou hast asked this thing, and [p]hast not asked for thyself [q]long life; neither hast asked riches for thyself, nor hast asked the life of thine enemies; but hast asked for thyself [l]understanding to discern judgment[c];

12 Behold, [r]I have done according to thy words: lo, I have given thee a [s]wise and an understanding heart; so that there was none like thee before thee, neither after thee shall any arise like unto thee.

13 And [t]I have also given thee that which thou hast not asked, both [u]riches, and honour: so that there shall not be any among the kings like unto thee all thy days.

14 And [‡,v]if thou wilt walk in my ways, to keep[c] my statutes and my commandments, as thy father [w]Dā'vid did walk, [x]then I will lengthen thy days.

15 And Sŏl'o-mon awoke; and, behold, *it was* a [h]dream. And he came to Jē-ru'sā-lĕm, and stood before the [y]ark of the covenant of the LORD, and offered up burnt [z]offerings, and offered peace offerings, and made a feast to all his servants.

16 ¶ ‖Then came there two women, *that were* [a]harlots, unto the [b,c,d]king, and stood before him.

17 And the one woman said, O my lord, I and this woman dwell in one house; and I was delivered of a child with her in the house.

18 And it came to pass the third day after that I was delivered, that this woman was delivered also: and we *were* together; *there was* no stranger with us in the house, save[c] we two in the house.

19 And this woman's child died in the night; because she overlaid[c] it.

20 And she arose at midnight, and took my son from beside me,

**4**
e *Gibeon,* Jer. 41:16.
f *Offerings, burnt,* Lev. 6:17.

**5**
g *God, appearances of,* Gen. 2:2.
h *Dream, instances of,* Dan. 1:17.

**6**
i *David,* 1 Sam. 16:13.
1 R. V. kindness,

**7**
j *Government, God in,* Isa. 22:21.
k *Humility, exemplified,* Prov. 22:4.

**9**
l *Wisdom, spiritual, prayer for,* Prov. 2:2.
m *Heart,* Psa. 44:21.
n *Judge, character of,* Judg. 2:18.
o *Knowledge, desire for,* Luke 11:52.

**11**
p *Unselfishness,* 1 Cor. 10:24.
q *Longevity,* Psa. 91:16.

**12**
r *Prayer, answered,* Acts 6:4.
s *Wisdom, of Solomon,* Prov. 2:2.

**13**
t *Prayer, answer to, exceeds petition,* Acts 6:4.
u *Temporal Blessings, from God,* Psa. 103:2.

**14**
v *Probation,* Rom. 5:4.
w *David, devoutness of,* 1 Sam. 16:13.
x *Blessings, contingent upon obedience,* Deut. 11:26.

**15**
y *Ark, in the tabernacle,* Ex. 25:10.
z *Jesus, typified in offerings,* Matt. 1:21.

**16**
a *Harlot,* Prov. 7:10.
b *King, acts as judge,* 2 Kin. 3:10.
c *Solomon,* 2 Sam. 12:24.
d *Rulers, righteous,* Ex. 18:21.

‡ **CONTINGENCIES IN DIVINE GOVERNMENT OF MAN.** *Conditional rewards,* Gen. 4:7; 18:19; Ex. 19:5; Lev. 26:3; Deut. 7:12; 11:26, 27; 1 Chr. 28:7; 2 Chr. 26:5; Job 36:11; Jer. 11:4; 18:9, 10; 22:4, 5; Matt. 23:37; John 14:23; Col. 1:22, 23; Heb. 3:14; Rev. 22:17.
*Conditional punishments,* Gen. 2:16, 17; 3:3; Lev. 26:14–16; Deut. 11:28; 1 Kin. 20:42; Job 36:12; Jer. 12:17; 18:8; Ezek. 33:14–16; Jonah 3:10; Rev. 2:22; 3:3.

‖ **ARBITRATION. Instances of:** *Between Laban and Jacob,* Gen. 31:37. *The two harlots before Solomon,* 1 Kin. 3:16–28. *Urged by Paul, as a mode of action for Christians,* 1 Cor. 6:1–8. See footnote, COURT, Ex. 18:26.

while thine handmaid slept, and laid it in her bosom, and laid her dead child in my bosom.

21 And when I rose in the morning to give my child suck, behold, it was dead: but when I had considered it in the morning, behold, it was not my son, which I did bear.

22 And the other woman said, Nay; but the living *is* my son, and the dead *is* thy son. And this said, No; but the dead *is* thy son, and the living *is* my son. Thus they spake before the king.

23 Then said the [b,c,d]king, The one saith, This *is* my son that liveth, and thy son *is* the dead: and the other saith, Nay; but thy son *is* the dead, and my son *is* the living.

24 And the [b,c,d]king said, Bring me a sword. And they brought a sword before the king.

25 [e]And the [b,c,d]king said, Divide the living child in two, and give half to the one, and half to the other.

26 Then spake the [f]woman whose the living child *was* unto the king, for her [§]bowels[G] yearned[G] upon her son, and she said, O my lord, give her the living child, and in no wise[G] slay it. But the other said, Let it be neither mine nor thine, *but* divide *it*.

27 Then the [b,c,d]king answered and said, Give her the living child, and in no wise[G] slay it: she *is* the mother thereof.

28 And all Ĭṣ′ra-el heard of the judgment[G] which the king had judged; and they [g]feared the king: for they saw that the [h]wisdom of God *was* in him, to do judgment.

25 *e Tact,* Prov. 15:1.

26 *f Parents, affection of, exemplified,* 2 Cor. 12:14.

28 *g Reverence, for kings,* Lev. 19:30.
*h Wisdom, of Solomon,* Prov. 2:2.

## CHAPTER 4

*Solomon's princes. 7 His twelve officers over twelve commissary districts. 20 The prosperity and extent of his kingdom. 22 His daily provision. 26 His stables. 29 His wisdom.*

SO king [a]Sŏl′o-mon was [b]king over all [c]Ĭṣ′ra-el.

2 And these *were* the [d]princes which he had; Ăz-a-rī′ah the son of [e]Zā′dŏk the [f]priest,

3 Ĕl-ĭ-hō′reph and Ă-hī′ah, the sons of [g]Shī′shȧ, [*]scribes; [h]Jė-hŏsh′a-phăt the son of [i]Ă-hī′lụd, the recorder.

4 And [†]Bė-nā′iah the son of Jė-hoi′a-dȧ *was* over the host: and [e]Zā′dŏk and [j]Ă-bī′a-thär *were* the [f]priests:

5 And Ăz-a-rī′ah the son of Nā′than *was* over the officers: and Zā′bud the son of Nā′than *was* [1]principal officer, *and* the king's friend:

6 And Ă-hī′shär *was* over the household: and [k]Ăd-o-nī′ram the son of Ăb′dȧ *was* over the [2,l,m]tribute[G].

7 ¶ And [a]Sŏl′o-mon had twelve officers over all [n]Ĭṣ′ra-el, which provided [l,m]victuals[G] for the king and his household: each man his month in a year made provision.

8 And these *are* their names: [3]The son of Hûr, in mount Ē′phră-ĭm:

9 [4]The son of Dē′kär, in Mā′kăz, and in [o]Shā-ăl′bim, and [p]Bĕth–shē′mesh, and [q]Ē′lon-bĕth–hā′năn:

10 [5]The son of Hē′sed, in Ăr′ụ-bŏth; to him *pertained* [r]Sō′choh, and all the land of [s]Hē′phẽr:

1 *a Solomon,* 2 Sam. 12:24.
*b King,* 2 Kin. 3:10.
*c Israel, under the kings,* Ex. 4:22.

2 *d Cabinet, Solomon's,* Ezra 7:14.
*e Zadok,* 2 Sam. 19:11.
*f High Priest,* Lev. 12:10.

3 *g* Or, *Seraiah,* 2 Sam. 8:17.
*h* 2 Sam. 8:16.
*i* 2 Sam. 8:16; 1 Chr. 18:15.

4 *j Abiathar,* 1 Sam. 22:20.

5 1 R. V. priest,

6 *k Adoniram,* 1 Kin. 5:14.
*l Tax,* Neh. 10:32.
*m King, emoluments of,* 2 Kin. 3:10.
2 R. V. levy.

7 *n Canaan, land of, divided into twelve provinces,* vs. 7–19; Gen. 37:1.

8 3 R. V. Ben-hur,

9 *o* Judg. 1:35.
*p Beth-shemesh,* Josh. 21:16.
*q* Or, *Elon,* Josh. 19:43.
4 R. V. Ben-deker,

10 *r* Or, *Shocoh,* 1 Sam. 17:1.
*s* Josh. 12:17.
5 R. V. Ben-hesed,

§ **BOWELS.** *Disease of,* 2 Chr. 21:15–19. *Of Judas burst out,* Acts 1:18.

**Figurative:** *Of the sensibilities,* Gen. 43:30; 1 Kin. 3:26; Job 30:27; Psa. 22:14; Song 5:4; Jer. 4:19; 31:20; Lam. 1:20.

* **SCRIBE.** *A writer and transcriber of the law,* 2 Sam. 8:17; 20:25; 1 Kin. 4:3; 2 Kin. 12:10; 18:18, 37; 19:2; 1 Chr. 24:6; 27:32; Neh. 13:13; Jer. 36:12. *King's secretary,* 2 Kin. 12:10–12; 22:3–14; Esth. 3:12; 8:9. *Mustering officer of the army,* 2 Kin. 25:19; 2 Chr. 26:11. *Instructor in the law,* Matt. 7:29; 13:52; 17:10; 23:2, 3. *Test Jesus with questions, bringing to Jesus a woman taken in adultery,* John 8:3. *Members of the council,* Matt. 2:4; 20:18; Luke 22:66. *Impute blasphemy to Jesus,* Matt. 9:3; Mark 2:6, 7; Luke 5:21. *Conspire against Jesus,* Matt. 26:3, 57; 27:41; Mark 14:1; Luke 22:66. *Hypocrisy of, reproved by Jesus,* Matt. 5:20; 15:1–9.

† **BENAIAH.** *Son of Jehoiada,* 1 Kin. 1:8, 10, 26. *Commander of the Cherethites and Pelethites,* 2 Sam. 8:18; 1 Kin. 1:38; 1 Chr. 18:17. *A distinguished warrior,* 2 Sam. 23:20–23; 1 Chr. 11:22–25; 27:5, 6. *Loyal to Solomon,* 1 Kin. 1:32–36; 4:4. *By Solomon's command slays, Adonijah,* 1 Kin. 2:25; *Joab,* 1 Kin. 2:29–34; *Shimei,* 1 Kin. 2:44–46. *Succeeds Joab,* 1 Kin. 2:35. *By error written Jehoiada, son of Benaiah, instead of Benaiah, son of Jehoiada,* 1 Chr. 27:34.

11 The son of Ȧ-bĭn′a-dăb, in all the [6]region of [t]Dôr; which had Tā′phath the daughter of Sŏl′o-mon to wife:

12 Bā′a-nȧ the son of Ȧ-hī′lụd; *to him pertained* [u]Tā′a-năch and [v]Mė-gĭd′dō, and all [w]Bĕth–shē′-an, which *is* by [x]Zär′ta-nah beneath Jĕz′re-el, from Bĕth–shē′-an to [y]Ā′bel–mė-hō′lah, *even* unto *the place that is* beyond Jŏk′ne-ăm:

13 [7]The son of Gē′bĕr, in [z]Rā′-moth–gĭl′e-ăd; to him *pertained* the towns of [a]Jā′īr the son of [b]Mȧ-năs′seh, which *are* in [c]Gĭl′-e-ăd; to him *also pertained* the region of [d]Är′gŏb, which *is* in [e]Bā′shăn, threescore great cities with [f]walls and brasen bars:

14 Ȧ-hĭn′a-dăb the son of Ĭd′-dō *had* [g]Mā-hȧ-nā′im:

15 Ȧ-hĭm′a-ăz *was* in [h]Năph′-ta-lī; he also took Băs′măth the daughter of Sŏl′o-mon to wife:

16 Bā′a-nah the son of Hū′shāi *was* in [i]Ăsh′ēr and [8]in Ā′lŏth:

17 Jė-hŏsh′a-phăt the son of Păr′ụ-ah, in [j]Ĭs′sa-char:

18 Shĭm′e-ī the son of Ē′lah, in [k]Bĕn′ja-mīn:

19 Gē′bĕr the son of Ū′rī *was* in the country of [c]Gĭl′e-ăd, *in* the country of [l]Sī′hŏn king of the [m]Ăm′ŏr-ītes, and of [n]Ŏg king of [e]Bā′shăn; and *he was* the only officer which *was* in the land.

20 ¶ Jū′dah and [o]Ĭṣ′ra-el *were* many, as the sand which *is* by the sea in multitude, [p]eating and drinking, and making merry.

21 And [q]Sŏl′o-mon reigned over [r]all kingdoms [s]from the [t]river unto the land of the [u]Phĭ-lĭs′tīneṣ, and unto the border of [v]Ē′ġy̆pt: they brought [w]presents, and served Sŏl′o-mon all the days of his life.

22 ¶ And Sŏl′o-mon's provision for one day was thirty [x]measures of fine flour, and threescore measures of meal.

23 Ten fat oxen, and twenty oxen out of the pastures, and an hundred sheep, beside harts, and [9]roebucks, and [10]fallowdeer, and fatted fowl.

24 For he had dominion over all *the* [s]*region* on this side the river, from Tĭph′sah even to [11, y]Ăz′zah, over all the kings on this side the river: and he had [z, a]peace on all sides round about him.

25 And Jū′dah and Ĭṣ′ra-el dwelt safely, every man under his vine and under his fig tree, from [b]Dăn even to [c]Bē′er–shē′-bȧ, all the days of [d]Sŏl′o-mon.

26 ¶ And [d]Sŏl′o-mon had forty thousand stalls of horses for his [e]chariots, and twelve thousand [f]horsemen.

27 And those officers provided victual for king [d]Sŏl′o-mon, and for all that came unto king Sŏl′o-mon's table, every man in his month: they [12]lacked nothing.

28 [g]Barley also and straw for the horses and [13]dromedaries brought they unto the place where *the officers* were, every man according to his charge.

29 ¶ And God gave [d]Sŏl′o-mon [h]wisdom and understanding exceeding much, and largeness of heart, even as the sand that *is* on the sea shore.

30 And [d]Sŏl′o-mon's [h]wisdom excelled the wisdom of all the children of the east country, and all the wisdom of [i]Ē′ġy̆pt.

31 For he was [h]wiser than all men; than Ē′than the Ĕz′ra-hīte, and [j]Hē′man, and [j]Chăl′-cŏl, and [j]Där′dȧ, the sons of Mā′hŏl: and his fame was in all nations round about.

32 And he spake three thousand [k]proverbs: and his [l]songs were a thousand and five.

33 And he spake of trees, from the [m]cedar tree that *is* in [n]Lĕb′a-

**11**
*t Dor*, Josh. 11:2.
6 R. V. height of Dor:

**12**
*u Taanach*, Josh. 12:21.
*v Megiddo*, Josh. 17:11.
*w Beth-shean*, Josh. 17:11.
*x* Or, *Zaretan*, Josh. 3:16.
*y* Judg. 7:22.

**13**
*z Ramoth-gilead*, Josh. 20:8.

*a Jair*, Josh. 13:30.
*b Manasseh*, Gen. 46:20.
*c Gilead*, Deut. 3:13.
*d* Deut. 3:4–13, 14.
*e Bashan*, Num. 32:33.
*f Cities, walled*, Num. 35:8.
7 R. V. Ben-geber,

**14**
*g Mahanaim*, Gen. 32:2.

**15**
*h Naphtali, tribe of*, Num. 1:42.

**16**
*i Asher, tribe of*, Num. 1:40.
8 R. V. Bealoth:

**17**
*j Issachar, tribe of*, Num. 1:28.

**18**
*k Benjamin, tribe of*, Num. 1:37.

**19**
*l Sihon*, Num. 21:21.
*m Amorites*, Gen. 14:13.
*n Og*, Num. 21:33.

**20**
*o Israel, under the kings*, Ex. 4:22.
*p Feasts*, Mark 12:39.

**21**
*q Solomon*, 2 Sam. 12:24.
*r Government, imperial*, Isa. 22:21.
*s Canaan, extent of*, Gen. 37:1.
*t Euphrates*, Gen. 15:18.
*u Philistines*, Gen. 26:14.
*v Egypt*, Gen. 41:8.
*w Tribute*, Ezra 4:13.

**22**
*x Measure, dry*, Deut. 25:15.

**23**
9 R. V. gazelles,
10 R. V. roebucks,

**24**
*y* Or, *Gaza*, Gen. 10:19.
*z Nation, peace of*, Isa. 2:4.

*a Peace*, Jer. 29:7.
11 R. V. Gaza,

**25**
*b Dan*, Judg. 18:29.
*c Beer-sheba*, Judg. 20:1.
*d Solomon*, 2 Sam. 12:24.

**26**
*e Chariots*, Josh. 11:4.
*f Cavalry*, 1 Sam. 13:5.

**27**
12 R. V. let nothing be lacking.

**28**
*g Barley*, Ex. 9:31.
13 R. V. swift steeds

**29**
*h Wisdom, of Solomon*, Prov. 2:2.

**30**
*i Egyptians, wisdom of*, Gen. 50:3.

**31**
*j* 1 Chr. 2:6.

**32**
*k Proverbs*, 1 Sam. 24:13.
*l Song*, Psa. 77:6.

**33**
*m Cedar*, Isa. 9:10.
*n Lebanon*, Deut. 1:7.

o *Hyssop*, Ex. 12: 22.
p *Animals*, Jer. 27:5.
q *Birds*, Eccl. 12:4.
r *Creeping Things*, Rom. 1:23.
s *Fish*, Matt. 17: 27.

1
a *Hiram*, 2 Sam. 5:11.
b *Diplomacy, instances of*, 2 Kin. 16:7.
c *Ambassadors*, Josh. 9:4.
d *Solomon*, 2 Sam. 12:24.
e *Friendship, instances of*, Prov. 22:24.
f *Love, of man for man*, 1 John 4:7.
g *David*, 1 Sam. 16:13.

4
h *Peace*, Jer. 29:7.

5
i *Temple, Solomon's*, 1 Kin. 6:17.

6
j *Cedar*, Isa. 9:10.
k *Lebanon*, Deut. 1:7.

non even unto the [o]hyssop that
springeth out of the wall: he
spake also of [p]beasts, and of
[q]fowl, and of [r]creeping things,
and of [s]fishes.
34 And there came of all people
to hear the [h]wisdom of Sŏl′o-
mon, from all kings of the earth,
which had heard of his wisdom.

## CHAPTER 5

*Hiram congratulates Solomon. 2 He is informed of his purpose to build the temple; and desired to furnish him with timber. 7 Their agreement concerning this matter. 13 The number of Solomon's workmen.*

AND [a]Hī′ram king of *Tȳre
[b]sent his [c]servants unto
[d]Sŏl′o-mon; for he had heard
that they had anointed him king
in the room of his father: [e]for
Hī′ram was ever a [f]lover of
[g]Dā′vid.
2 And [d]Sŏl′o-mon sent to [a]Hī′-
ram, saying,
3 Thou knowest how that [g]Dā′-
vid my father could not build an
house unto the name of the
LORD his God for the wars
which were about him on every
side, until the LORD put them
under the soles of his feet.
4 But now the LORD my God
hath given me [h]rest on every
side, *so that there is* neither adversary nor evil occurrent.
5 And, behold, I purpose to
build an [i]house unto the name of
the LORD my God, as the LORD
spake unto Dā′vid my father,
saying, Thy son, whom I will set
upon thy throne in thy room, he
shall build an house unto my
name.
6 Now therefore command thou
that they hew me [j]cedar trees
out of [k]Lĕb′a-non; and my servants shall be with thy servants:
and unto thee will I give hire for
thy servants according to all that
thou shalt appoint: for thou
knowest that *there is* not among
us any that can skill to hew timber like unto the [l,m]Sī-dō′nī-ans.
7 ¶ And it came to pass, when
[a]Hī′ram heard the words of
[d]Sŏl′o-mon, that he rejoiced
greatly, and said, Blessed *be* the
LORD this day, which hath given
unto Dā′vid a [n]wise son over
this great people.
8 And [a]Hī′ram sent to [d]Sŏl′o-
mon, saying, I have [1]considered
the things which thou sentest to
me for: *and* [o]I will do all thy desire concerning timber of [j]cedar,
and concerning timber of [p]fir.
9 [q]My servants shall bring *them*
down from [k]Lĕb′a-non unto the
sea: and I will convey them by
sea in floats unto the place that
thou shalt appoint me, and will
cause them to be discharged
there, and thou shalt receive
*them*: and [q]thou shalt accomplish my desire, in giving food
for my household.
10 So [a]Hī′ram [q]gave [d]Sŏl′o-
mon [j]cedar trees and [p]fir trees
*according to* all his desire.
11 And Sŏl′o-mon [q]gave Hī′-
ram twenty thousand [r]measures
of [s]wheat *for* food to his household, and twenty measures of
pure [t]oil: thus gave Sŏl′o-mon to
Hī′ram year by year.
12 And the LORD gave [d]Sŏl′o-
mon [n]wisdom, as he promised
him: and there was [h]peace between Hī′ram and Sŏl′o-mon;
and they two made a [†,u]league
together.
13 ¶ And king [d]Sŏl′o-mon
raised a [v]levy out of all Ĭṣ′ra-el;
and the levy was thirty thousand
men.
14 And he sent them to [k]Lĕb′a-
non, ten thousand a month by
courses: a month they were in
Lĕb′a-non, *and* two months at

l *Zidon*, Ezek. 28: 21.
m *Artisans*, 1 Chr. 29:5.

7
n *Wisdom, of Solomon*, Prov. 2:2.

8
o *Contracts*, Matt. 20:2.
p *Fir Tree*, 2 Sam. 6:5.
1 R. V. heard the message which thou hast sent unto me:

9
q *Reciprocity*, 1 Cor. 9:11.

11
r *Measure, dry*, Deut. 25:15.
s *Wheat*, Ezra 6:9.
t *Oil*, Deut. 12:17.

12
u *Alliances, instances of*, Josh. 9:15.

13
v *Tax, levies of men*, Neh. 10:32.

* **TYRE,** kingdom of. *Hiram, king of*, 1 Kin. 5:1; 2 Chr. 2:3. *Men and materials sent from, to Solomon, for the erection of the temple and his castles*, 1 Kin. 5:1-11; 9:10, 11; 2 Chr. 2:3-16. Josh. 9:3-15; *Judah and Syria*, 1 Kin. 15:19; 2 Chr. 16:3. *Cession of territory by*, 1 Kin. 9:10-14; 20:34. *Sacredness of*. Josh. 9:16-21, with 2:8-21.

† **TREATY.** Between nations: *Israelites and Gibeonites*, *Of reciprocity*, 1 Kin. 5:1-12. *With idolatrous nations forbidden*, Ex. 34:12, 15.

home: and [‡]Ăd-o-nī′ram *was*
over the [v]levy.[G]
15 And [d]Sŏl′o-mon had threescore and ten thousand that bare
burdens, and fourscore thousand hewers in the mountains;
16 Beside the chief of Sŏl′o-
mon's officers which *were* over
the work, three thousand and
three hundred, which ruled over
the people that wrought in the
work.
17 And the king commanded,
and they [2]brought great [w]stones,
costly stones, [3]*and* hewed stones,
to lay the foundation of the
[x]house.
18 And Sŏl′o-mon's builders
and Hī′ram's builders [4]did hew[G]
[w]*them*, and the stonesquarers:[G] so
they prepared timber and stones
to build the house.

## CHAPTER 6

*The building of Solomon's temple. 5 The chambers thereof 11 God's promise concerning it. 15 The ceiling and adorning of the house. 23 The cherubim. 31 The doors. 36 The court. 37 The time spent in building it.*

AND[Q] it came to pass in [a]the
four hundred and eighti-
eth year after the children of
[b]Ĭş′ra-el were come out of the
land of Ē′ġy̆pt, in the fourth
year of [c]Sŏl′o-mon's reign over
Ĭş′ra-el, in the [d]month Zĭf, which
*is* the second month, that [e]he began to build the house of the
LORD.
2 And the house which king
Sŏl′o-mon built for the LORD,
the length thereof *was* threescore[G] [f]cubits,[G] and the breadth
thereof twenty *cubits*,[G] and the
height thereof thirty cubits.[GQ]
3 And the porch before the temple of the house, twenty cubits[G]
*was* the length thereof, according to the breadth of the house;
*and* ten cubits[G] *was* the breadth
thereof before the house.
4 And for the house he made
[g]windows of [1]narrow lights.[G]
5 And against the wall of the
house he built [2]chambers[G] round
about, *against* the walls of
the house round about, *both* of
the temple and of the [*]oracle:[G]
and he made chambers round
about:
6 The nethermost[G] [3]chamber
*was* five cubits broad, and the
middle *was* six cubits broad, and
the third *was* seven cubits
broad: for [4]without[G] *in the wall*
of the house he made narrowed[G]
rests round about, that *the beams*
should not be fastened in the
walls of the house.
7 And the house, when it was
in building, was built of [h]stone
made ready before it was
brought thither:[G] so that there
*was* neither [i]hammer nor [j]ax
*nor* any tool of [k]iron heard in the
house, while it was in building.
8 The door for the middle
[5]chamber *was* in the right side of
the house: and they went up
with winding stairs into the
middle *chamber*, and out of the
middle into the third.
9 So he built the house, and
finished it; and covered the
house with beams and boards of
[l]cedar.
10 And *then* he built [6]cham-
bers[G] against all the house, five
[f]cubits high: and they rested on
the house with timber of [l]cedar.
11 ¶ And the word of the LORD
[m]came to [d]Sŏl′o-mon, saying,
12 *Concerning* this house which
thou art in building, [n]if thou wilt
walk in my statutes, and execute
my judgments,[G] and [o]keep all my
commandments to walk in them;
then [p]will I [7]perform my [q]word
with thee, which I spake unto
Dā′vid thy father:

**17**
*w Stones*, Ex. 24:12.
*x Temple, Solomon's*, 1 Kin. 6:17.
2 R. V. hewed out
3 R. V. to lay the foundation of the house with wrought stone.

**18**
4 R. V. and the Gebalites did fashion them,

**v.1–940 BC**
See footnote, *Time*, Rev. 10:6.

**1**
*a Time, from the exodus*, Rev. 10:6.
*b Israel, under the kings*, Ex. 4:22.
*c Solomon*, 2 Sam. 12:24.
*d Month, Zif (May)*, Ex. 12:2.
*e* 2 Chr. chapters 3,4.

**2**
*f Cubit*, Ex. 36:9.

**v.4–940 BC**
See footnote, *Time*, Rev. 10:6.

**4**
*g Window*, Josh. 2:15.
1 R. V. fixed lattice-work.

**5**
2 R. V. stories

**6**
3 R. V. story
4 R. V. on the outside he made rebatements in the wall of the house round about,

**7**
*h Stones*, Ex. 24:12.
*i* Isa. 41:7.
*j Ax*, Deut. 19:5.
*k Iron*, Prov. 27:17.

**8**
5 R. V. side-chambers

**9**
*l Cedar*, Isa. 9:10.

**v.9–933 BC**

**10**
6 R. V. the stories

**11**
*m Inspiration*, Job 32:8.

**12**
*n Blessings contingent upon obedience*, Deut. 11:26.
*o Obedience, enjoined*, Heb. 5:8.
*p Promise, to the obedient, of divine favor*, 2 Cor. 1:20.
*q Covenant, of God with men*, Deut. 29:1.
7 R. V. establish

‡ **ADONIRAM**, called also ADORAM and HADORAM. *A tax-gatherer*, 2 Sam. 20:24; 1 Kin. 4:6; 5:14; 12:18; 2 Chr. 10:18.

* **ORACLE**. *The most holy place*, 1 Kin. 6:5; 2 Chr. 5:7, 9; Psa. 28:2. *The scriptures called oracles*, Acts 7:38; Rom. 3:2; Heb. 5:12; 1 Pet. 4:11.

v.13–933 BC
See footnote, *Time*, Rev. 10:6.

13
r *Righteous, promises to*, Psa. 64:10.
s *Fellowship, with God*, 1 Cor. 1:9.

15
8 R. V. from
9 R. V. unto
t *Fir Tree*, 2 Sam. 6:5.

13 And [†,r]I will [s]dwell among
the children of Is'ra-el and will
not forsake my people Is'ra-el.[S]
14 So [d]Sŏl'o-mon built the
house, and finished it.[Q]
15 And he built the walls of the
house within with boards of [l]ce-
dar, [8]both the floor of the house,
[9]and the walls of the ceiling[G]: *and*
he covered *them* on the inside
with wood, and covered the floor
of the house with planks of [t]fir.
16 And he built twenty [l]cubits[G]
on the [10]sides of the house, both
the floor [9]and the walls with
boards of cedar: he even built
*them* for it within, *even* for the
[*]oracle[G], *even* for the [u]most holy
*place*.
17 And the house, that *is*, the
[‡]temple[G] before [11]it, was forty
cubits[G] *long*.
18 And the [l]cedar of the house
within *was* [v]carved with knops[G]

v.16–933 BC
See footnote, *Time*, Rev. 10:6.

16
u *Holy of Holies, in the temple*, Ex. 26:33.
10 R.V. hinder part of the house with boards of cedar from the floor unto the walls:

17
11 R. V. the oracle,

18
v *Carving*, Ex. 35:33.

---

† **GOD, dwells with the righteous,** Ex. 25: 8; 29:45; Lev. 26:11, 12; 1 Kin. 6:13; Ezek. 37:26, 27; 2 Cor. 6:16; Rev. 21:3.

‡ **TEMPLE, Solomon's.** *Called*, TEMPLE OF THE LORD, 2 Kin. 11:10; HOLY TEMPLE, Psa. 79:1; HOLY HOUSE, 1 Chr 29:3; HOUSE OF GOD, 1 Chr. 29:2; 2 Chr. 23:9; HOUSE OF THE LORD, 2 Chr. 23:5, 12; Jer. 28:5. ZION, Psa. 20:2; 74:2; Isa. 2:3.

Described as: *House of the God of Jacob*, Isa. 2:3; *House of my Glory*, Isa. 60:7; *House of Prayer*, Isa. 56:7; *House of Sacrifice*, 2 Chr. 7:12; *House of their Sanctuary*, 2 Chr. 36:17; *Holy and Beautiful House*, Isa. 64:11; *Mountain of the Lord's House*, Isa. 2:2; *Palace*, 1 Chr. 29:1, 19; *Sanctuary*, 2 Chr. 20:8; *Tabernacle of Witness*, 2 Chr. 24:6.

*Greatness of*, 2 Chr. 2:5, 6. *Beauty of*, Isa. 64:11; Hag. 2: 3, 9. *Holiness of*, 1 Kin. 8:10; 9:3.

*David undertakes the building of*, 2 Sam. 7:2, 3; 1 Chr. 22:7; 28:2; Psa. 132:2–5; Acts 7:46; *but is forbidden of God because he was a man of war*, 2 Sam. 7:4–12; 1 Kin. 5:3; 1 Chr. 22:8; 28:3. *Not asked for by God*, 2 Sam. 7:7. *The building of, committed to Solomon*, 2 Sam. 7:13. *David makes preparation for*, 1 Chr. 22; 28:14-18; 29:1–5; 2 Chr. 3:1; 5:1. *Built by Solomon*, 1 Kin. 6:14; 8:20; 9:1, 10; Acts 7:47. *Solomon makes levies of men for the building of*, 1 Kin. 5:13–16; 2 Chr. 2:1, 2, 17, 18.

*Materials for, furnished by Hiram*, 1 Kin. 5:8–18. *Pattern and building of*, 1 Kin. 6; 7:13 51; 1 Chr. 28:11–19; 2 Chr. 3; 4. *Time when begun*, 1 Kin. 6:1, 37; 2 Chr. 3:2. *Time when finished*, 1 Kin. 6:38. *Site of*, 1 Chr. 21:28–30; 22:1; 2 Chr. 3:1. *Site of, supposed to be where Abraham offered Isaac*, Gen. 22:2, 4.

*Materials prepared for*, 1 Kin. 5:17, 18. *No tools used in the erection of*, 1 Kin. 6:7. *Foundations of*, 1 Kin. 5:17, 18; 2 Chr. 3:3.

*Prayer made toward*, 1 Kin. 8:38; Dan. 6:10; Jonah 2:4. *Jews swore by*, Matt. 23:16–22; *Ezekiel's vision concerning*, Ezek. 8:16.

ORACLE, OR HOLY OF HOLIES, IN, 1 Kin. 6:19, 20; 8:6. *Called*, MOST HOLY HOUSE, 2 Chr. 3:8; INNER HOUSE, 1 Kin. 6:27; HOLIEST OF ALL, Heb. 9:3.

*Description of*, 1 Kin. 6:16, 19–35; 2 Chr. 3:8–14; 4:22. *Gold used in*, 2 Chr. 3:8–10. Contents of: *Ark*, 1 Kin. 6:19; 8:6; 2 Chr. 5:2–10; *cherubims*, 1 Kin. 6:23–28; 2 Chr. 3:10–13; 5:7, 8.

HOLY PLACE IN, 1 Kin. 8:8, 10. *Called*, THE GREATER HOUSE, 2 Chr. 3:5; TEMPLE, 1 Kin. 6:17. *Description of*, 1 Kin. 6:16–18; 2 Chr. 3:5–7.

CONTENTS OF THE HOLY PLACE: *The table of shewbread*, 1 Kin. 7:48; 2 Chr. 29:18. *Other tables of gold and silver*, 1 Chr. 28:16; 2 Chr. 4:18, 19. *Candlesticks and their utensils*, 1 Kin. 7:49, 50; 1 Chr. 28:15; 2 Chr. 4:7, 20–22. *Altar of incense and its furniture*, 1 Kin. 6:20; 7:48, 50; 1 Chr. 28: 17, 18; 2 Chr. 4:19, 22.

CHAMBERS OF, 1 Kin. 6:5–10; 2 Kin. 11:2, 3. *Offerings brought to*, Neh. 10:37–39.

COURTS OF: *Of the priests*, 2 Chr. 4:9. *Inner*, 1 Kin. 6:36. *Surrounded by rows of stones and cedar beams*, 1 Kin. 6:36; 7: 12.

CONTENTS OF THE COURTS: *Altar of burnt offerings*, 2 Chr. 15:8. *The brazen sea*, 1 Kin. 7:23–37, 44, 46; 2 Chr. 4:2–5, 10. *Ten lavers*, 1 Kin. 7:38–46; 2 Chr. 4:6.

GREAT COURT OF, 2 Cor. 4:9; Jer. 19:14; 26:2. *Covered place for the Sabbath, and king's entry*, 2 Kin. 16:18.

GATES OF: *Higher gate*, 2 Kin. 15:35. *New gate*, Jer. 26:10; 36:10. *Beautiful gate*, Acts 3:2. *Eastern gate, closed on working days, open on the Sabbath*, Ezek. 46:1, 12. *Gifts received at*, 2 Chr. 24:8–11.

PORCH OF: *Called* PORCH OF THE LORD, 2 Chr. 15:8. *Dimensions of*, 1 Kin. 6:3; 2 Chr. 3:4. *Overlaid with gold*, 2 Chr. 3:4. *Doors of*, 2 Chr. 29:7. *Pillars of*, 1 Kin. 7:15–22; 2 Kin. 11: 14; 23:3; 25:17; 2 Chr. 3:15–17; 4:12, 13.

DESIGN OF: *For a dwelling place of the Lord*, 1 Kin. 8:10, 11, 13; 9:3; 2 Kin. 21:7; 1 Chr. 29:1; 2 Chr. 5:13, 14; 7:1–3, 16; Ezek. 10:3, 4. *To contain the ark of the covenant*, 1 Kin. 8:21. *For the offering of sweet incense*, 2 Chr. 2:4. *For the continual shewbread and the burnt offerings*, 2 Chr. 2:4. *For prayer and worship*, 1 Kin. 8; 2 Kin. 19:14, 15; 2 Chr. 30:27; Isa. 27:13; 56:7; Jer. 7:2; 26:2; Ezek. 46:2, 3, 9; Zech. 7:2, 3; 8:21, 22; Matt. 21:13; Mark 11:17; Luke 1:10; 2:37; 18:10; 19:46; Acts 3:1; 22:17. *For an armory*, 2 Kin. 11:10; 2 Chr. 23:9, 10. *For refuge*, 1 Kin. 1:50; 2:28; Neh. 6:10, 11.

MISCELLANEOUS FACTS ABOUT: *Dedication of*, 1 Kin. 8; 2 Chr. 5; 6; 7. *Pillaged, by Shishak*, 1 Kin. 14:25, 26; *by Jehoash, king of Israel*, 2 Kin. 14:14. *Repaired, by Jehoash, king of Judah*, 2 Kin. 12:4–14; 2 Chr. 24:7–14; *by Josiah*, 2 Kin. 22:3–7; 2 Chr. 34:8–13. *Ahaz constructs an altar in, after the pattern of one in Damascus*, 2 Kin. 16:10–17. *Purified by Hezekiah*, 2 Chr. 29:15–19. *Converted into an idolatrous shrine by Manasseh*, 2 Kin. 21:4–7; 2 Chr. 33:4–7.

Treasures of: *Used in the purchase of peace, by Jehoash, from Hazael*, 2 Kin. 12:18; *by Hezekiah, from the king of Assyria*, 2 Kin. 18:15, 16. *Used in securing help in war, by Asa, from Benhadad*, 1 Kin. 15:18.

*Destroyed by Nebuchadnezzar, and the valuable contents of, carried to Babylon*, 2 Kin. 24:13; 25:9–17; 2 Chr. 36:7, 19; Ezra 1:7; Psa. 79:1; Isa. 64:11; Jer. 27:16, 19–22; 28:3; 52; 13, 17–23; Lam. 2:7; 4:1. *Vessels of, used by Belshazzar*, Dan. 5:2, 3; *returned to Jerusalem*, Ezra, 1:7–11; 5:14, 15.

*Destruction of, foretold*, Jer. 27:18–22; Ezek. 7:22, 25; Matt. 24:2; Luke 21:5, 6.

*Restoration of, ordered by Cyrus*, Ezra 1:2–4; 6:3–5.

**The Second:** *Restored by Zerubbabel*, Ezra 3:2–13; 4; 5:2–17; Hag. 2:4. *Building of, suspended*, Ezra 4; *resumed*, Ezra 4:24; 5; 6; Hag. 1:1, 12–15; Zech. 8:9; *finished*, Ezra 6:14, 15. *Dedicated*, Ezra 6:15–18. *Artaxerxes' favorable action toward*, Ezra 7:11–28. *Profaned*, Neh. 13:7.

*Prophecies of the building of*, Isa. 44:28; Dan. 8:13, 14; Hag. 1; 2; Zech. 1:16; 4:8–10; 6:12–15; 8:9–15.

*Ezekiel's vision of*, Ezek. 37:26, 28; chapters 40–48.

**Herod's:** *Forty-six years in building*, John 2:20. *Goodly stones of*, Mark 13:1; Luke 21:5. *Beautiful gate of*, Acts 3:10. *Solomon's porch*, John 10:23; Acts 3:11; 5:12. *Treasury of*, Mark 12:41–44; John 8:20. *Zacharias, officiating priest, has a vision of an angel in; receives promise of a son*, Luke 1:5–23, with vs. 57–64. *Jesus brought to, according to the law and custom*, Luke 2:21–39. *Simeon blesses Jesus in*, Luke 2:25–35. *Anna, the prophetess, dwells in*, Luke 2:36, 37. *Jesus, when a youth, in*, Luke 2:46; *is taken to the pinnacle of, in his temptation*, Matt. 4:5–7; Luke 4:9–12; *teaches in*, Matt. 26:55; Mark 11:27–33; 12:35–44; 14:49; John 5:14–47; 7:14–28; 8; 10:23–38; 18:20; *performs miracles in*, Matt. 21:14, 15; *drives money changers from*, Matt. 21: 12, 13; Mark 11:15–17; Luke 19:45, 46; John 2:15, 16.

*Captains of*, Luke 22:52; Acts 4:1; 5:24, 26. *Judas casts down the pieces of silver in*, Matt. 27:5.

*Vail of, rent at the time of the crucifixion*, Matt. 27:51. *The disciples worship in, after the resurrection*, Luke 24:53; Acts 2:46; 3:1. *Peter heals the lame man at the gate of*, Acts 3:1–16. *Disciples preach in*, Acts 5:20, 21, 42. *Paul's vision in*, Acts 22:17–21. *Paul, observes ceremonial forms in*, Acts 21:26–30; *is apprehended in*, Acts 21:33.

*Prophecies by Daniel concerning its destruction*, Dan. 8:11–15; 9:26, 27; 11:30, 31. *Jesus foretells the destruction of*, Matt. 24:1, 2; Mark 13:2; Luke 21:6.

**Figurative:** *Of the body of Jesus*, Matt. 26:61; 27:40; John 2:19, 21. *Of the indwelling of God*, 1 Cor. 3:16, 17; 6: 19; 2 Cor. 6:16. *Of the Church*, Eph. 2:21; 2 Thess. 2:4; Rev. 3:12. *Seen in John's vision*, Rev. 15:5–8; 16:1–17.

**Idolatrous:** *Of Dagon, at Ashdod*, 1 Sam. 5:2. *Of the calves, at Beth-el*, 1 Kin. 12:31–33. *Of Rimmon, at Damascus*, 2 Kin. 5:18. *Of Baal, at Samaria*, 2 Kin. 10:21–27. *At*

and open flowers: all *was* cedar;
there was no stone seen.
19 And the *,[u]oracle he prepared in the house within, to set
there the [w]ark of the covenant of
the LORD.
20 And [12]the *oracle in the forepart *was* twenty cubits in length,
and twenty cubits in breadth,
and twenty cubits in the height
thereof: and he overlaid it with
pure [x]gold; and [13]*so* covered the
[y]altar [14]*which was of* cedar.
21 So Sŏl′o-mon overlaid the
‡house within with pure [x]gold:
and he [15]made a partition by the
[z]chains of gold before the *oracle; and he overlaid it with gold.
22 And the whole ‡house he
overlaid with [a]gold, until he had
finished all the house: also the
whole [b]altar that [16]*was* by the
*oracle he overlaid with gold.
23 ¶ And within the *,[c]oracle
he made two [d]cherubims *of*
[e]olive tree, *each* ten [f]cubits high.
24 And five [f]cubits *was* the one
wing of the cherub, and five cubits the other wing of the cherub: from the uttermost part of
the one wing unto the uttermost
part of the other *were* ten cubits.
25 And the other cherub *was*
ten [f]cubits: both the cherubims
*were* of one measure and one size.
26 The height of the one cherub
*was* ten cubits, and so *was it* of
the other cherub.
27 And he set the [d]cherubims
within the inner house: and they
stretched forth the wings of the
cherubims, so that the wing of
the one touched the *one* wall,
and the wing of the other cherub
touched the other wall; and their
wings touched one another in the
midst of the house.
28 And he overlaid the cherubims with [a]gold.
29 And he carved all the walls
of the house round about with
[g]carved figures of [d]cherubims
and [h]palm trees and open flowers, within and without.
30 And the floor of the ‡house
he overlaid with [a]gold, within
and without.
31 ¶ And for the entering of the
*,[c]oracle he made doors *of* [e]olive
tree: the lintel *and* side posts
*were* a fifth part *of the wall.*
32 The two doors also *were of*
[e]olive tree; and he [g]carved upon
them carvings of [d]cherubims and
[h]palm trees and open flowers,
and overlaid *them* with [a]gold,
and spread gold upon the cherubims, and upon the palm trees.
33 So also made he for the door
of the temple posts *of* olive tree,
a fourth part *of the wall.*
34 And the two doors *were of* [i]fir
tree: the two leaves of the one door
*were* folding, and the two leaves
of the other door *were* folding.
35 And he carved *thereon* cherubims and palm trees and open
flowers: and covered *them* with
gold fitted upon the carved work.
36 And he built the inner [j]court
with three rows of hewed [k]stone,
and a row of [l]cedar beams.
37 ¶ In the fourth year was the
foundation of the ‡,[m]house of
the LORD laid, in the [n]month Zĭf:
38 And in the eleventh year, in
the [n]month Bŭl, which *is* the
eighth month, was the ‡house
finished throughout all the parts
thereof, and according to all the
fashion of it. So was he seven
years in building it.

## CHAPTER 7

*The building of Solomon's three houses.* 13 *For the temple Hiram, the workman, makes the two pillars,* 23 *the molten sea,* 27 *the ten bases,* 38 *the ten lavers,* 40 *and all the utensils.*

BUT [a]Sŏl′o-mon was building
his own [b]house thirteen years,
and he finished all his house.

---

**v.18–933 BC**
See footnote, *Time,* Rev. 10:6.

**19**
*w* *Ark,* Ex. 25:10.

**20**
*x* *Gold,* Ezek. 7:19.
*y* *Altar, of incense,* Ex. 30:1.
12 R. V. within the oracle was a space of
13 R. V. he covered
14 R. V. with cedar.

**21**
*z* *Chains,* Dan. 5:7.
15 R. V. drew chains of gold across before

**22**
*a* *Gold,* Ezek. 7:19.
*b* *Altar, of incense,* Ex. 30:1.
16 R. V. belonged to the

**23**
*c* *Holy of Holies,* Ex. 26:33.
*d* *Cherubim,* Ex. 37:7.
*e* *Olive,* Deut. 6:11.
*f* *Cubit,* Ex. 36:9.

**v.29–933 BC**
See footnote, *Time,* Rev. 10:6.

**29**
*g* *Carving,* Ex. 35:33.
*h* *Palm Tree,* Song 7:7.

**34**
*i* *Fir Tree,* 2 Sam. 6:5.

**36**
*j* *Court, of the temple,* Ex. 38:9.
*k* *Stones,* Ex. 24:12.
*l* *Cedar,* Isa. 9:10.

**37**
*m* *Church,* 1 Kin. 9:3.
*n* *Month,* Ex. 12:2

**1**
*a* *Solomon,* 2 Sam. 12:24.
*b* *Palace, of Solomon,* 1 Kin. 21:1.

---

*Babylon,* 2 Chr. 36:7; Dan. 1:2. *Of Diana, at Ephesus,* Acts 19:27. *Destroyed,* 2 Kin. 10:27; 11:18. *Trophies stored in,* 1 Sam. 31:8–10; 1 Chr. 10:9, 10; Dan. 1:2.

v.2–933 BC
See footnote, *Time*, Rev. 10:6.

**2**
c *Lebanon*, Deut. 1:7.
d *House, architecture of*, Esth. 8:1.
e *Cubit*, Ex. 36:9.
f *Cedar*, Isa. 9:10.
g *Pillar*, Gen. 28:18.

**3**
1 R. V. over the forty and five beams, that were upon the pillars;

**4**
2 R. V. prospects in

**5**
3 R. V. in prospect:

**7**
h *Throne*, 1 Kin. 2:19.
4 R. V. floor to floor.

**8**
i *Pharaoh, at the time of Solomon*, 1 Kin. 3:1.
5 R. V. He made
6 R. V. Solomon had

**9**
j *Stones*, Ex. 24:12.
k *Saw*, 2 Sam. 12:31.
7 R. V. unto the

2 ¶ He built also the house of
the forest of [c]Lĕb′a-non; the
[d]length thereof *was* an hundred
[e]cubits[G], and the breadth thereof
fifty cubits[G], and the height thereof thirty cubits[G], upon four rows
of [f]cedar [g]pillars, with cedar
beams upon the pillars.
3 And *it was* covered with [f]ce-
dar above [1]upon the beams, that
*lay* on forty five pillars, fifteen
*in* a row.
4 And *there were* [2]windows *in*
three rows, and light *was* against
light *in* three ranks[G].
5 And [d]all the doors and posts
*were* square [3]with the windows:
and light *was* against light *in*
three ranks[G].
6 ¶ And he made a porch of
[g]pillars; the length thereof *was*
fifty cubits[G], and the breadth
thereof thirty cubits[G]: and the
porch *was* before them: and the
*other* pillars and the thick beam
*were* before them.
7 Then he made a porch for the
[h]throne where he might judge,
*even* the porch of judgment: and
*it was* covered with [f]cedar from
[4]one side of the floor to the other.
8 And his [d]house where he
dwelt *had* another court within
the porch, *which* was of the like
work. [5]Sŏl′o-mon made also an
house for [i]Phā′raōh's daughter,
whom [6]he had taken *to*[G] *wife*, like[G]
unto this porch.
9 [d]All these *were of* costly
[j]stones, according to the measures of hewed stones, sawed
with [k]saws, within and without,
even from the foundation unto
the coping[G], and *so* on the outside
[7]toward the great court.
10 And the foundation *was of*
costly [j]stones, even great stones,
stones of ten [e]cubits[G], and stones
of eight cubits[G].
11 And above *were* costly
stones, after the measures of
hewed stones, and [f]cedars.
12 And the great court round
about *was* with three rows of
hewed stones, and a row of cedar
beams, [8]both for the [l]inner court
of the [m]house of the LORD, and
for the porch of the house.
13 ¶ And king [a]Sŏl′o-mon sent
and fetched *Hī′ram out of
[n]Tȳre.
14 *He *was* a widow's son of
the tribe of [o]Năph′ta-lī, and his
father *was* a man of [n]Tȳre, a
[p, q]worker in brass: and he was
filled with [r]wisdom, and understanding, and cunning[G] to work
all works in brass. And he came
to king [a]Sŏl′o-mon, and wrought
all his work.
15 [s]For he cast two [g]pillars of
brass[G], of eighteen [e]cubits[G] high
apiece: and a line of twelve cubits[G] did compass[G] either of them
about.
16 And he †made two ‡chapi-
ters[G] *of* molten[G] brass, to set upon the tops of the [g]pillars: the
height of the one chapiter[G] *was*
five [e]cubits, and the height of the
other chapiter[G] *was* five cubits:
17 *And* [t]nets of checker work,
and wreaths of [u]chain work,
for the ‡chapiters[G] which *were*
upon the top of the pillars;
seven for the one chapiter[G], and
seven for the other chapiter[G].
18 And he made the [g]pillars,
and two rows round about upon
the one network, to cover the
‡chapiters[G] that *were* upon the
top, [9]with [v]pomegranates: and
so did he for the other chapiter[G].
19 And the ‡chapiters[G] that *were*
upon the top of the pillars, *were*
of [w]lily work in the porch, four
[e]cubits[G].
20 And [10]the chapiters[G] upon the

v.11–933 BC
See footnote, *Time*, Rev. 10:6.

**12**
l *Court, of the temple, the inner court*, Ex. 38:9.
m *Temple, Solomon's*, 1 Kin. 6:17.
8 R. V. like as the

**13**
n *Tyre*, 1 Kin. 5:1.

**14**
o *Naphtali, tribe of*, Num. 1:42.
p *Master Workman*, 1 Cor. 3:10.
q *Artisan*, 1 Chr. 29:5.
r *Wisdom*, Prov. 2:2.

**15**
s 2 Chr. 4:12.

**17**
t *Net*, Isa. 51:20.
u *Chains*, Dan. 5:7.

**18**
v *Pomegranate*, Num. 13:23.
9 R. V. of the pillars:

**19**
w *Lily*, Matt. 6:28.

**20**
10 R. V. there were chapiters above also upon the two pillars, close by the belly

*** HIRAM,** called also HURAM. *An artificer sent by King Hiram to execute the artistic work of the interior of the temple*, 1 Kin. 7:13–45; 2 Chr. 2:13, 14; 4:11–16.

**† MOLDING,** Ezek. 24:11. *Of images*, Ex. 32:4, 8; 34:17; Lev. 19:4; Deut. 9:12. *Of the laver*, 1 Kin. 7:23. *Of mirrors*, Job 37:18. *Done in the plain of Jordan*, 1 Kin. 7:46; 2 Chr. 4:17.

**‡ CHAPITER,** head of a pillar. *In the tabernacle*, Ex. 36:38. *In the temple*, 1 Kin. 7:16–42; 2 Kin. 25:17; 2 Chr. 4:12, 13; Jer. 52:22.

v.20–933 BC
ee footnote, *Time*, Rev. 10:6.

21
2 Chr. 3:17.

23
*Laver, brazen*, Ex. 30:18.

24
1 R. V. for ten cubits,

25
*Bullock*, Ex. 29:3.

26
*Measure, linear*, Deut. 25:15.
*Lily*, Matt. 6:28.
*Measure, liquid*, Deut. 25:15.

27
*Brass*, Job 28:2.
*Cubit*, Ex. 36:9.

two [g]pillars *had pomegranates*
also above, over against the
belly[C] which *was* by the network:
and the [v]pomegranates *were* two
hundred in rows round about
upon the other chapiter.[C]
21 And he set up the [g]pillars in
the porch of the temple: and
he set up the right pillar, and
called the name thereof [x]Jā′chin:
and he set up the left pillar,
and called the name thereof
[x]Bō′ăz.
22 And upon the top of the
[g]pillars *was* [w]lily work: so was
the work of the pillars finished.
23 ¶ And he [†]made a molten[C]
[y]sea, ten [e]cubits[C] from the one
brim to the other: *it was* round
all about, and his height *was*
five cubits[C]: and a line of thirty
cubits[C] did compass it round
about.
24 And under the brim of [y]it
round about *there were* knops[C]
compassing it, [11]ten in a cubit,[C]
compassing the sea round about:
the knops[C] *were* cast in two rows,
when it was cast.
25 [y]It stood upon twelve [z]oxen,
three looking toward the north,
and three looking toward the
west, and three looking toward
the south, and three looking toward the east: and the sea *was*
*set* above upon them, and all
their hinder parts *were* inward.
26 And it *was* an [‖,a]hand
breadth[C] thick, and the brim
thereof was wrought like the
brim of a cup, with flowers of
[b]lilies: it contained two thous-
and [§,c]baths.[C]
27 ¶ And he made ten bases[C] of
[d]brass[C]; four [e]cubits[C] *was* the
length of one base, and four cubits[C] the breadth thereof, and
three cubits[C] the height of it.
28 And the work of the bases
*was* on this *manner*: they had
borders, and the borders *were*
between the ledges:
29 And on the borders that *were*
between the ledges *were* [f]lions,
[g]oxen, and [h]cherubims: and upon the ledges *there was* a [12]base[C]
above: and beneath the lions
and oxen *were* [13]certain additions made of thin work.
30 And every base had four
brasen wheels, and [14]plates of
[d]brass: and the four [15]corners
thereof had undersetters[C]: under
the [i]laver *were* undersetters[C] molten,[C] [16]at the side of every addition.
31 And the mouth of it within
the [‡]chapiter[C] and above *was* a
[e]cubit: but the mouth thereof
*was* round *after* the work of
[17]the base,[C] a cubit and an half:
and also upon the mouth of it
*were* gravings[C] with their borders, foursquare, not round.
32 And under the borders *were*
four wheels; and the axletrees of
the wheels *were joined* to the
base: and the height of a wheel
*was* a [e]cubit and half a cubit.
33 And the work of the wheels
*was* like the work of a chariot
wheel: their axletrees, and their
naves,[C] and their felloes,[C] and
their spokes, *were* all [†]molten.[C]
34 And *there were* four undersetters[C] to the four corners of one
base: *and* the undersetters[C] *were*
of the very base itself.
35 And in the top of the base
*was there* a round compass of
half a [e]cubit high: and on the top
of the base the [18]ledges thereof
and the borders thereof *were* of
the same.
36 For on the plates of the
[18]ledges thereof, and on the borders thereof, he [j]graved[C] [h]cheru-
bims, [f]lions, and [k]palm trees,
according to the [19]proportion of
every one, and additions round
about.

v.28–933 BC
See footnote, *Time*, Rev. 10:6.

29
*f Lion*, Mic. 5:8.
*g Bullock*, Ex. 29:3.
*h Cherubim, figures of*, Ex. 37:7
12 R. V. pedestal above:
13 R. V. wreaths of hanging work.

30
*i Laver, brazen*, Ex. 30:18.
14 R. V. axles of
15 R. V. feet there of
16 R. V. with wreaths at the side of each.

31
17 R. V. a pedestal.

35
18 R. V. stays thereof

36
*j Carving*, Ex. 35:33.
*k Palm Tree*, Song 7:7.
19 R. V. space of each, with wreaths round about.

‖ **HANDBREADTH.** *A measure, about four inches*, Ex. 25:25; 1 Kin. 7:26; 2 Chr. 4:5; Psa. 39:5; Jer. 52:21; Ezek. 40:5, 43.

§ **BATH.** *A Hebrew measure for liquids, containing about eight gallons and three quarts*, 1 Kin. 7:26, 38; Ezra 7:22; Isa. 5:10; Ezek. 45:10, 11, 14.

v.37–933 BC
See footnote, *Time*, Rev. 10:6.

39
*l* *Temple, Solomon's*, 1 Kin. 6:17.

40
*m* *Shovel*, Num. 4:14.
*n* *Solomon*, 2 Sam. 12:24.
*o* *Church, called house of the Lord*, 1 Kin. 9:3.

41
*p* *Pillar*, Gen. 28:18.

42
*q* *Pomegranate*, Num. 13:23.

46
*r* *Jordan*, Gen. 32:10.
*s* *Succoth*, Judg. 8:5.
*t* *Zaretan*, Josh. 3:16.

37 After this *manner* he made the ten bases: all of them had one casting, one measure, *and* one size.

38 Then made he ten [i]lavers[G] of [d]brass[G]: one laver[G] contained forty [§,c]baths: *and* every laver[G] was four [e]cubits: *and* upon every one of the ten bases one laver[G].

39 And he put five bases on the right side of the [l]house, and five on the left side of the house: and he set the sea on the right side of the house eastward over against the south.

40 ¶ And *Hī′ram made the [i]lavers, and the [m]shovels, and the ⊙basons. So Hī′ram made an end of doing all the work that he made king [n]Sŏl′o-mon for the [l,o]house of the LORD:

41 The two [p]pillars, and the *two* bowls of the ‡chapiters[G] that *were* on the top of the two pillars; and the two networks, to cover the two bowls of the chapiters[G] which *were* upon the top of the pillars;

42 And four hundred [q]pomegranates for the two networks, *even* two rows of pomegranates for one network, to cover the two bowls of the ‡chapiters[G] that *were* upon the pillars;

43 And the ten bases, and ten [i]lavers on the bases;

44 And one [i]sea, and twelve [g]oxen under the sea;

45 And the pots, and the [m]shovels, and the basons: and all these vessels, which *Hī′ram made to king [n]Sŏl′o-mon for the [l,o]house of the LORD, *were of* bright [d]brass[G].

46 In the plain of [r]Jôr′dan did the king †cast them, in the clay ground between [s]Sŭc′coth and [t]Zär′than.

47 And [n]Sŏl′o-mon left all the vessels *unweighed*, because they were exceeding many: neither was the weight of the [d]brass[G] found out.

48 And [n]Sŏl′o-mon made all the vessels that *pertained* unto the [l]house of the LORD: the [u]altar of [v]gold, and the table of gold, whereupon[G] the [w]shewbread *was*,

49 And the [x]candlesticks of pure [v]gold, five on the right *side*, and five on the left, before the [y]oracle[G], with the flowers, and the [z]lamps, and the [a]tongs *of* gold,

50 And the [b]bowls, and the +snuffers, and the ⊙basons, and the [c]spoons, and the [20,d]censers[G] *of* pure [e]gold; and the hinges *of* gold, *both* for the doors of the inner house, the most holy *place*, *and* for the doors of the house, *to*[G] *wit*, of the temple.

51 So was ended all the work that king [f]Sŏl′o-mon made for the [g]house of the LORD. And Sŏl′o-mon brought in the things which [h,i]Dā′vid his father had dedicated; *even* the silver, and the gold, and the vessels, did he put [21]among the treasures of the [j]house of the LORD.

## CHAPTER 8

*The elders and chief men of Israel assemble for the dedication of the temple. 3 The ark is brought into the most holy place. 12 Solomon's blessing. 22 His prayer. 62 His sacrifice.*

[a,b]THEN [c]Sŏl′o-mon assembled the [d]elders of Ĭs′ra-el, and all the heads of the tribes, the chief[G] of the fathers of the children of Ĭs′ra-el, unto king Sŏl′o-mon in [e]Jĕ-ru′sā-lĕm, that they might bring up the [f]ark of the covenant of the LORD out of the city of Dā′vid, which *is* [g]Zī′ŏn.[Q]

2 And all the men of Ĭs′ra-el assembled themselves unto king Sŏl′o-mon at the [h]feast in the [i]month Ĕth′a-nĭm, which *is* the seventh month.

v.47–933 BC
See footnote, *Time* Rev. 10:6.

48
*u* *Altar, of incense*, Ex. 30:1.
*v* *Gold*, Ezek. 7:19.
*w* *Shewbread, table of*, Ex. 35:13.

49
*x* *Candlestick, of the temple*, Ex. 25:31.
*y* *Oracle*, 1 Kin. 6:5.
*z* *Lamp*, Ex. 27:20.
*a* *Tongs*, Ex. 25:38.

50
*b* *Bowl*, Ex. 25:29.
*c* *Spoons*, Num. 4:7.
*d* *Censer*, Lev. 16:12.
*e* *Gold*, Ezek. 7:19.
20 R. V. firepans.

51
*f* *Solomon*, 2 Sam. 12:24.
*g* *Temple*, 1 Kin. 6:17.
*h* *Liberality, instances of*, 1 Tim. 6:18.
*i* *David*, 1 Sam. 16:13.
*j* *Treasure Houses*, Ezra 5:17.
21 R. V. in the treasuries

1
*a* *Dedication, of Solomon's temple*, vs. 1–66; Ezra 6:17.
*b* *Temple, Solomon's, dedication of*, vs. 1–66; 1 Kin. 6:17.
*c* *Solomon*, 2 Sam. 12:24.
*d* *Senate*, Num. 11:16.
*e* *Jerusalem*, Judg. 19:10.
*f* *Ark, transferred to Solomon's temple*, Ex. 25:10.
*g* *Zion*, 2 Sam. 5:7.

2
*h* *Annual Feasts*, Num. 15:3.
*i* *Month, Ethanim*, Ex. 12:2.

**+ SNUFFERS.** *For the lamps, in the tabernacle,* Ex. 25:38; Num. 4:9; *in the temple,* 1 Kin. 7:50; 2 Kin. 12:13; 25:14; Jer. 52:18.

**⊙ BASIN.** *For the temple, made of gold,* 1 Kin. 7:50; 1 Chr. 28:17; 2 Chr. 4:8, 22. *For the tabernacle, made of brass,* Ex. 27:3; 38:3; 1 Kin. 7:45.

3 And all the [d]elders of Is͎'ra-el came, and the [j]priests took up the [k]ark.

4 And they brought up the [k]ark of the LORD, and the [l]tabernacle of the congregation, and all the holy vessels that *were* in the tabernacle, even those did the [j]priests and the [m]Lē'vītes bring up.

5 And king [c]Sŏl'o-mon, and all the congregation of Ĭs͎'ra-el, that were assembled unto him, *were* with him before the [k]ark, sacrificing sheep and oxen, that could not be told[C] nor numbered for multitude.

6 And the priests brought in the [k]ark of the covenant of the LORD unto his place, into the [n]oracle[C] of the house, to the [o]most holy *place*, *even* under the wings of the [p]cherubims.[Q]

7 For the [p]cherubims spread forth *their* two wings over the place of the [k]ark, and the cherubims covered the ark and the staves thereof above.

8 And [1]they drew out the staves, that the ends[C] of the staves were seen out in the holy *place* before the oracle[C], and they were not seen without[C]: and there they are unto this day.

9 *There was* nothing in the [k]ark save[C] the two [q]tables of stone, which [r]Mō'ṣeṣ put there at [s]Hō'reb, when the LORD made *a* [t]*covenant* with the children of Ĭs͎'ra-el, when they came out of the land of Ē'ġȳpt.

10[Q] And it came to pass, when the [j]priests were come out of the [u]holy *place*, that the [v]cloud filled the [w]house of the LORD,

11 So that the [j]priests could not stand to minister because of the [v]cloud: for the [x]glory of the LORD had filled the house of the LORD.[Q]

12 ¶ [y]Then spake Sŏl'o-mon, The [z,a,b]LORD said that he would dwell in the thick [c]darkness.[S]

13 I have surely built thee an house to dwell in, a settled[C] place for thee to abide in for ever.[Q]

14 And the [d]king turned his face about, and [e]blessed all the congregation of Ĭs͎'ra-el: (and all the congregation of Ĭs͎'ra-el stood;)

15 And he said, Blessed *be* the LORD God of Ĭs͎'ra-el, which [e]spake with his mouth unto [f]Dā'vid my father, and hath with his hand [g]fulfilled *it*, saying,[S]

16 Since the day that I brought forth my people Ĭs͎'ra-el out of [h]Ē'ġȳpt, I chose no city out of all the tribes of Ĭs͎'ra-el to build an [i]house, that my name might be therein; but [j]I chose [k]Dā'vid to be over my people Ĭs͎'ra-el.

17[Q] And it was in the heart of [f]Dā'vid my father to build an [i]house for the name of the LORD God of Ĭs͎'ra-el.

18 And the LORD said unto [f]Dā'vid my father, Whereas it was in thine heart to build an [i]house unto my name, thou didst well that it was in thine heart.[Q]

19[Q] Nevertheless thou shalt not build the [i]house; but thy son that shall come forth out of thy loins, he shall build the house unto my name.

20 And the LORD [g]hath performed his word that he spake, and [d]I am risen up in the room[C] of Dā'vid my father, and sit on the [l]throne of Ĭs͎'ra-el, as the LORD promised, and have built an house for the name of the LORD God of Ĭs͎'ra-el.[S Q]

21 And I have set there a place for the [m]ark, wherein *is* the [n]covenant of the LORD, which he made with our fathers, when he brought them out of the land of [h]Ē'ġȳpt.

22 ¶ And [d]Sŏl'o-mon [o]stood be-

---

3
j *Priests*, Lev. 1:5.
k *Ark*, Ex. 25:10.
4
l *Tabernacle, brought to the temple*, Ex. 27:9.
m *Levites*, Deut. 10:8.
6
n *Oracle*, 1 Kin. 6:5.
o *Holy of Holies*, Ex. 26:33.
7
p *Cherubim*, Ex. 37:7.
8
1 R. V. the staves were so long that
9
q *Table, of testimony*, Ex. 31:18.
r *Moses*, Ex. 2:10.
s *Horeb*, Ex. 3:1.
t *Covenant, of God with men*, Deut. 29:1.
10
u *Holy Place*, Ex. 26:33.
v *Pillar of Cloud and Fire*, Ex. 13:21.
w *Church, called house of the Lord*, 1 Kin. 9:3.
11
x *God, glory of*, Gen. 2:2.
12
y 2 Chr. 6:1–39.
z *God, incomprehensible*, Gen. 2:2.
a *God, unsearchable*, Gen. 2:2.
b *God, invisible*, Gen. 2:2.

c *Darkness*, Gen. 1:2.
14
d *Solomon*, 2 Sam. 12:24.
e *Covenant, of God with men*, Deut. 29:1.
15
f *David*, 1 Sam. 16:13.
g *God, faithfulness of*, Gen. 2:2.
16
h *Egypt*, Gen. 41:8.
i *Church, place of worship*, 1 Kin. 9:3.
j *Government, God in*, Isa. 22:21.
k *Rulers, appointed by God*, Ex. 18:21.
20
l *Throne, figurative*, 1 Kin. 2:19.
21
m *Ark*, Ex. 25:10.
n *Covenant, of God with men*, Deut. 29:1.
22
o *Prayer, postures in*, Acts 6:4.

fore the altar of the LORD in the
presence of all the congregation
of Is'ra-el, and spread forth his
hands toward heaven:
23 [s]And he [p]said, LORD God
of Is'ra-el, *there is* no God like
thee, in heaven above, or on
earth beneath, [q]who keepest
[n]covenant[G] and [q]mercy with thy
servants that [r, s]walk before thee
with all their heart:
24 [q]Who hast kept with thy
servant [t]Dā'vid my father that
thou promisedst him: thou spakest also with thy mouth, and
[q]hast fulfilled *it* with thine hand,
as *it is* this day.[S]
25 [t]Therefore now, LORD God
of Is'ra-el, keep with thy servant Dā'vid my father that thou
[n]promisedst him, saying, There
shall not fail thee a man in my
sight to sit on the throne of Is'-
ra-el; [r]so that thy children [u]take
heed to their way, that they walk
before me as thou hast walked
before me.
26 [t]And now, O God of Is'ra-el,
let thy [n]word, I pray thee, be
verified, which thou spakest unto
thy servant Dā'vid my father.
27 But will God indeed dwell
on the earth? behold, the heav-
en and heaven of heavens cannot
contain [v, w]thee; how much less
this[i, x]house that I have builded[Q][S]?
28 [p]Yet have thou respect[G] unto
the prayer of thy servant, and to
his supplication, O LORD my
God, to hearken unto the cry
and to the prayer, which thy servant prayeth before thee to day:
29 That thine eyes may be
opened toward[G] this house night
and day, *even* toward the place
of which thou hast said, My
name shall be there: that thou
mayest hearken unto the prayer
which thy servant shall make toward this place.

23

p *Prayer, exemplified*, vs. 23–30; Acts 6:4.

q *God, mercy of*, Gen. 2:2.

r *Blessings, contingent upon obedience*, Deut. 11:26.

s *Obedience, rewarded*, Heb. 5:8.

25

t *Prayer, pleas offered in*, Acts 6:4.

u *Watchfulness, enjoined*, Matt. 24:42.

27

v *God, infinite*, Gen. 2:2.

w *God, omnipresent*, Gen. 2:2.

x *Temple, Solomon's*, 1 Kin. 6:17.

30 And hearken thou to the
supplication of thy servant, and
[y]of thy people Is'ra-el, when
they shall pray toward[G] this
place: and hear thou in [z]heaven
thy dwelling place: and when
thou hearest, [a]forgive.
31 ¶ If any man trespass[G]
against his neighbour, and an
[b]oath[G] be laid upon [c]him to
[d, e]cause him to swear, and [2]the
oath[G] come before thine altar in
this house:
32 Then hear thou in heaven,
and do, and [f]judge thy servants,
condemning the wicked, to bring
his way upon his head; and justifying the righteous, to give him
according to his righteousness.[S]
33 ¶ When thy people Is'ra-el
be smitten down before the enemy, [g, h]because they have sinned
against thee, and [i]shall turn
again to thee, and confess thy
name, and [j]pray, and make supplication unto thee in this house:
34 Then hear thou in heaven,
and [a]forgive the sin of thy people Is'ra-el, and bring them
again unto the land which thou
gavest unto their fathers.
35 ¶ When heaven is [k]shut up,
and there is [l]no [m, n]rain, because
they have sinned[G] against thee; if
they [j]pray toward this place, and
confess thy name, and [h, i]turn
from their sin, when thou afflict-
est them:
36 [j, k]Then hear thou in [o]heaven,
and [a]forgive the sin of thy servants, and of thy people Is'ra-el,
that [p]thou [q, r]teach them the
[s]good way wherein they should
walk, and give [m, n]rain upon thy
land, which thou hast given to
thy people for an inheritance.
37 ¶ If there be in the land
[t]famine, if there be [u]pestilence,
*blasting,[G] mildew, [v]locust, *or* if
there be †caterpiller; if their en-

30

y *Prayer, intercessory*, Acts 6:4.

z *Heaven, God's dwelling place*, Luke 18:22.

a *Sin, forgiveness of*, Rom. 5:12.

31

b *Oath*, Num. 5:19

c *Witness*, Num. 35:30.

d *Self-condemnation*, Job 9:20.

e *Self-crimination* Josh. 7:20.

2 R. V. he come and swear befor

32

f *God, judge*, Gen. 2:2.

33

g *Backsliders, corrective judgment upon*, Jer. 3:22.

h *Adversity, desig of*, Psa. 10:6.

i *Repentance, condition of forgiveness*, vs. 33–50; Mark 1:4.

j *Prayer, in adversity*, Acts 6:4.

35

k *Adversity, prayer in*, Psa. 10:6.

l *Drought*, Gen. 31:40.

m *Rain*, 2 Sam. 1:21.

n *Temporal Blessings, prayer for* Psa. 103:2.

36

o *Heaven, God's dwelling place*, Luke 18:22.

p *God, guide*, Gen 2:2.

q *Instruction*, Prov. 23:23.

r *Wisdom, spiritual, prayer for*, Prov. 2:2.

s *Way, of holines* Isa. 35:8.

37

t *Famine*, 2 Kin 8:1.

u *Plague*, Ex. 11:

v *Locust*, Nah. 3:17.

* **BLASTING**, 1 Kin. 8:37. *Sent as a judgment*, Deut. 28:22; Amos 4:9; Hag. 2:17.
**Figurative**, Job 4:9; Psa. 18:16.

† **CATERPILLAR**. *Sent as a judgment upon Israe* 1 Kin. 8:37; Psa. 78:46; Joel 1:4; 2:25; (R. V. cankerworn Jer. 51:27.

**38**
*w Prayer,* Acts 6:4.
*x Temple, Solomon's,* 1 Kin. 6:17.

**39**
*y Sin, forgiveness of,* Rom. 5:12.
*z Heart, known to God,* Psa. 44:21.
*a God, knowledge of,* Gen. 2:2.

**40**
*b Fear of God,* Acts 9:31.

**41**
*c Foreigners,* Deut. 23:20.

**43**
*d Prayer, intercessory,* Acts 6:4.
*e Catholicity, instances of,* Eph. 2:14.
*f Heaven, God's dwelling place,* Luke 18:22.
*g Temple, Solomon's,* 1 Kin. 6:17.

**44**
*h God, providence of,* Gen. 2:2.
*i Prayer, in adversity,* Acts 6:4.
*j Jerusalem,* Judg. 19:10.

**46**
*k Depravity,* Job 15:14.
*l Sin,* Rom. 5:12.

emy besiege them in the land of their cities; whatsoever plague, whatsoever sickness *there be*;

38 What [w]prayer and supplication soever be *made* by any man, *or* by all thy people Ĭṣ'ra-el, which shall know every man the plague of his own heart, and spread forth his hands toward this [x]house:

39[S] Then hear thou in [o]heaven thy dwelling place, and [y]forgive, and do, and give to every man according to his ways, whose [z]heart [a]thou knowest; (for thou, *even* thou only, knowest the hearts of all the children of men;)

40 That they may [b]fear[G] thee all the days that they live in the land which thou gavest unto our fathers.

41 ¶ Moreover concerning a [c]stranger,[G] that *is* not of thy people Ĭṣ'ra-el; but cometh out of a far country for thy name's sake;

42 (For they shall hear of thy great name, and of thy strong hand, and of thy stretched out[G] arm:) when he shall come and pray toward this house;

43 [d,e]Hear thou in [f]heaven thy dwelling place, and do according to all that the [c]stranger[G] calleth to thee for: that all people of the earth may know thy name, to [b]fear thee, as *do* thy people Ĭṣ'ra-el; and that they may know that this [g]house, which I have builded, is called by thy name.

44 ¶ If thy people go out to battle against their enemy, whithersoever[G] thou shalt [h]send them, and shall [i]pray unto the LORD toward the [j]city which thou hast chosen, and *toward* the [g]house that I have built for thy name:

45 [d]Then hear thou in heaven their prayer and their supplication, and maintain their cause.[G]

46 If they sin against thee, ([k,l]for *there is* no man that sinneth not,) and thou be [m]angry with them, and deliver them to the enemy, so that they carry them away [n]captives unto the land of the enemy, far or near;[S]

47 [d]*Yet* if they shall bethink[G] themselves in the land whither they were carried captives, and [o]repent, and make [p]supplication[G] unto thee in the land of them that carried them [n]captives, [q]saying, We have sinned, and have done perversely,[G] we have committed wickedness;

48 And *so* [o]return unto thee with all their heart, and with all their soul, in the land of their enemies, which led them away [n]captive, and [p]pray unto thee toward their land, which thou gavest unto their fathers, the [j]city which thou hast chosen, and the [g]house which I have built for thy name:

49 Then [d]hear thou their [p]prayer and their supplication in [f]heaven thy dwelling place, and maintain their cause,[G]

50 And [d;r]forgive thy people that have sinned against thee, and all their transgressions wherein they have transgressed against thee, and give them compassion before them who carried them [n]captive, that they may have compassion on them:

51[S] [s]For they *be* thy people, and thine inheritance, which thou [h]broughtest forth out of Ē'gy̆pt, from the midst of the [t]furnace of iron:

52 That thine [u]eyes may be open unto the supplication of thy servant, and unto the supplication of thy people Ĭṣ'ra-el, to hearken unto them in all that they call for unto thee.

53 For thou didst separate [v]them from among all the people of the earth, *to be* thine inheritance, as thou spakest by the hand of [w]Mō'ṣeṣ thy servant,

*m Anger of God,* 2 Kin. 13:3.
*n Captivity, as a judgment,* Isa. 5:13.

**47**
*o Repentance,* Mark 1:4.
*p Prayer, confession in,* Acts 6:4.
*q Sin, confession of,* Rom. 5:12.

**50**
*r Sin, forgiveness of,* Rom. 5:12.

**51**
*s Prayer, pleas offered in,* Acts 6:4.
*t Furnace, figurative,* Prov. 17:3.

**52**
*u Anthropomorphisms,* Gen. 11:5.

**53**
*v Israel, a holy people,* Ex. 4:22.
*w Moses,* Ex. 2:10.

when thou [h]broughtest our fathers out of [x]Ē'ġy̆pt, O Lord GOD.[s]

54 ¶ And it was *so*, that when [y]Sŏl'o-mon had made an end of praying all this prayer and supplication unto the LORD, he arose from before the altar of the LORD, from [z]kneeling on his knees with his hands spread up to heaven.

55 And he stood, and [a]blessed all the congregation of Ĭş'ra-el with a loud voice, saying,

56 [b]Blessed *be* the LORD, that hath given rest unto his people Ĭş'ra-el, [c]according to all that he promised: there [c]hath not failed one word of all his good promise, which he promised by the hand of Mō'şeş his servant.[s]

57 The [d]LORD our God be with us, as he was with our fathers: let him not leave us, nor forsake us:

58 That he may incline our hearts unto him, to walk in all his ways, and to keep his commandments, and his statutes, and his judgments,[C] which he commanded our fathers.

59 And let these my words, wherewith I have made [e]supplication before the LORD, be nigh[C] unto the LORD our God day and night, that he maintain the cause of his servant, and the cause of his people Ĭş'ra-el [3]at all times, as the matter shall require:

60 That all the people of the earth may know that the [f]LORD *is* God, *and that there is* none else.

61 Let your [g]heart therefore be [h]perfect[C] with the LORD our God, to walk in his statutes, and to [i]keep his commandments, as at this day.

62 ¶ [j]And the [k]king, and all Ĭş'ra-el with him, [l]offered sacrifice[C] before the LORD.

63 And [k]Sŏl'o-mon offered a sacrifice of [m]peace offerings, which he offered unto the LORD, two and twenty thousand [n]oxen, and an hundred and twenty thousand [o]sheep. So the king and all the children of Ĭş'ra-el [p]dedicated the [q]house of the LORD.

64 The same day did the king hallow[C] the middle of the [r]court that *was* before the house of the LORD: for there he offered [s]burnt offerings, and [4,t]meat[C] offerings, and the fat of the [m]peace offerings: because the brasen [u]altar that *was* before the LORD *was* too little to receive the burnt offerings, and [4]meat[C] offerings, and the fat of the peace offerings.

65 ¶ And at that time [k]Sŏl'o-mon held a [v,w]feast, and all Ĭş'ra-el with him, a great congregation, from the entering in of [x]Hā'math unto the river of [y]Ē'ġy̆pt, before the LORD our God, seven days and seven days, *even* fourteen days.

66 On the eighth day he sent the people away: and they blessed[C] the king, and went unto their tents [z]joyful and glad of heart for all the goodness that the LORD [a]had done for [b]Dā'vid his servant, and for Ĭş'ra-el his people.

## CHAPTER 9

*God's covenant with Solomon. 10 The mutual presents of Solomon and Hiram. 15 The houses and cities built by Solomon. 20 Bondservice levied by him upon the Canaanites, but not on the Israelites. 25 His solemn sacrifices thrice a year. 26 His navy fetches gold from Ophir.*

AND it came to pass, when [a]Sŏl'o-mon had finished the building of the [*,b]house of the LORD, and the king's [c]house, and all Sŏl'o-mon's desire which he was pleased to do,

2 That the LORD [d]appeared to [a]Sŏl'o-mon the second time, as he had appeared unto him at [e]Ḡĭb'e-on.

3 And the LORD said unto him,

x *Egypt*, Gen. 41:8.

54
y *Solomon*, 2 Sam. 12:24.
z *Prayer, postures in*, Acts 6:4.

55
a *Benedictions*, Deut. 21:5.

56
b *Thankfulness, to God*, Acts 24:3.
c *God, faithfulness of*, Gen. 2:2.

57
d *God, dwells with the righteous*, 1 Kin. 6:13.

59
e *Prayer*, Acts 6:4.
3 R. V. as every day shall require:

60
f *God, sovereign*, Gen. 2:2.

61
g *Heart, perfect*, Psa. 44:21.
h *Perfection*, Heb. 6:1.
i *Obedience, enjoined*, Heb. 5:8.

62
j 2 Chr. 7:4–10.
k *Solomon*, 2 Sam. 12:24.
l *Worship*, Gen. 22:5.

63
m *Offerings, peace*, Lev. 6:17.
n *Cattle, used for sacrifice*, Ex. 12:29.
o *Sheep, offered in sacrifice*, Deut. 32:14.
p *Dedication, of Solomon's temple*, Ezra 6:17.
q *Temple, Solomon's*, 1 Kin. 6.17.

64
r *Court, of the temple*, Ex. 38:9.
s *Offerings, burnt*, Lev. 6:17.
t *Offerings, meat*, Lev. 6:17.
u *Altar, of burnt offerings*, Gen. 8:20.
4 R. V. meal

65
v *Dedication, feast of*, Ezra 6:17.
w *Feasts*, Mark 12 39.
x *Hamath*, 1 Chr. 18:3.
y *Egypt, brook of*, Gen. 15:18.

66
z *Thankfulness, to God*, Acts 24:3.
a *God, providence of*, Gen. 2:2.
b *David*, 1 Sam 16:13.

v.1–920 BC
See footnote, *Time*, Rev. 10:6.

1
a *Solomon*, 2 Sam. 12:24.
b *Temple, Solomon's*, 1 Kin. 6:17.
c *Palace*, 1 Kin. 21:1.

2
d *God, appearances of*, Gen. 2:2.
e *Gibeon*, Jer. 41:16.

v.3–920 BC
See footnote, *Time*, Rev. 10:6.

**3**
*f* *Prayer, answered*, Acts 6:4.
*g* *Temple, Solomon's, holiness of*, 1 Kin. 6:17.

**4**
*h* *Probation*, Rom. 5:4.
*i* *Obedience, rewarded*, Heb. 5:8.
*j* *Example, good*, John 13:15.
*k* *Integrity*, Job 2:3.

**5**
*l* *God, providence of*, Gen. 2:2.
*m* *Blessings, contingent upon obedience*, Deut. 11:26.
*n* *Covenant, of God with men*, Deut. 29:1.

**6**
*o* *Backsliders, warnings to*, Jer. 3:22.
*p* *Disobedience to God*, Eph. 5:6.
*q* *Idolatry*, 1 Sam. 15:23.

**7**
*r* *Judgments, denounced against disobedience*, Ex. 6:6.
*s* *Canaan*, Gen. 37:1.

I have heard thy [f]prayer and
thy supplication, that thou hast
made before me: I have [g]hal-
lowed this *house, which thou
hast built, to put my name there
for ever; and mine eyes and mine
heart shall be there perpetually.
4 And [h]if thou [i]wilt walk before me, [j]as Dā'vid thy father
walked, in [k]integrity of heart,
and in uprightness, to do according to all that I have commanded thee, *and* will keep my
statutes and my judgments:
5 Then [l]I will [m]establish the
throne of thy kingdom upon
Ĭs'ra-el for ever, as I [n]promised
to Dā'vid thy father, saying,
There shall not fail thee a man
upon the throne of Ĭs'ra-el.
6 *But* if ye shall at all [o]turn
from following me, ye or your
children, and [p]will not keep my
commandments *and* my statutes
which I have set before you, but
go and [q]serve other gods, and
worship them:
7 Then will I [r]cut off Ĭs'ra-el
out of the [s]land which I have
given them; and this house,
which I have hallowed for my
name, will I cast out of my sight;
and Ĭs'ra-el shall be a proverb
and a byword among all people:
8 And at this *,[b]house, *which* is
high, every one that passeth by
it shall be astonished, and shall
hiss; and they shall say, Why
hath the LORD done thus unto
this land, and to this house?
9 And they shall answer Because [o]they forsook the LORD
their God, [l]who brought forth
their fathers out of the land of
[t]Ē'ġy̆pt, and have taken hold
upon other gods, and have
[q]worshipped them, and served
them: [r]therefore hath the LORD
brought upon them all this evil.
10 ¶ And it came to pass at the
end of twenty years, when [a]Sŏl'-
o-mon had built the two houses,
the *,[b]house of the LORD, and
the king's [c]house,
11 ([u]*Now* Hī'ram the king of
[v]Tȳre had furnished [a]Sŏl'o-mon
with [w]cedar trees and [x]fir trees,
and with gold, according to all
his desire,) that [u]then king Sŏl'o-
mon [y]gave Hī'ram twenty cities
in the land of [z]Găl'ĭ-lee.
12 And [a]Hī'ram came out from
[b]Tȳre to see the cities which
[c]Sŏl'o-mon had given him; and
they pleased him not.
13 And he [d]said, What cities
*are* these which thou hast given
me, my brother? And he called
them the land of Cā'bŭl unto
this day.
14 And [a]Hī'ram sent to the
king sixscore [e]talents of gold.
15 ¶ And this *is* the reason of
the [f]levy which king [c]Sŏl'o-mon
raised; for to build the [g]house of
the LORD, and his own [h]house,
and [i]Mĭl'lō, and the wall of
[j]Jē̇ru'sā-lĕm, and [k]Hā'zôr, and
[l]Mē̇-ḡĭd'dō, and [m]Ḡē'zēr.
16 *For* [n]Phā'raōh king of
[o]Ē'ġy̆pt had gone up, and taken
[m]Ḡē'zēr, and burnt it with fire,
and slain the [p]Cā'năan-ītes that
dwelt in the city, and given it *for*

v 9–920 BC
See footnote, *Time*, Rev. 10:6.

**9**
*t* *Egypt*, Gen. 41:8.

**11**
*u* *Reciprocity*, 1 Cor. 9:11.
*v* *Tyre*, 1 Kin. 5:1.
*w* *Cedar*, Isa. 9:10.
*x* *Fir Tree*, 2 Sam. 6:5.
*y* *Treaty, cession of territory by*, 1 Kin. 5:12.
*z* *Galilee*, Mark 6:21.

**12**
*a* *Hiram*, 2 Sam. 5:11.
*b* *Tyre*, 1 Kin. 5:1.
*c* *Solomon*, 2 Sam. 12:24.

**13**
*d* *Sarcasm*, Judg. 10:14.

**14**
*e* *Talent*, Ex. 38:25.

**15**
*f* *Tax, levies of men*, Neh. 10:32.
*g* *Temple, Solomon's*, 1 Kin. 6:17.
*h* *Palace*, 1 Kin. 21:1.
*i* *Millo*, 2 Sam. 5:9.
*j* *Jerusalem, fortified by Solomon*, Judg. 19:10.
*k* Josh. 15:23.
*l* *Megiddo*, Josh. 17:11.
*m* *Gezer*, Josh. 10:33.

**16**
*n* *Pharaoh, at the time of Solomon*, v. 24; 1 Kin. 3:1.
*o* *Egypt*, Gen. 41:8.
*p* *Canaanites*, Ex. 23:28.

* **CHURCH**, place of worship. *Called*, COURTS, Psa. 65:4; 84:2, 10; 92:13; 96:8; 100:4; Isa. 1:12; 62:9; HOLY ORACLE, Psa. 28:2; HOLY PLACE, Psa. 24:3; 68:17; Acts 6:13; 21:28; HOLY TEMPLE, Psa. 5:7; 11:4; 65:4; 79:1; 138:2; Jonah 2:4, 7; HOUSE OF GOD, Josh. 9:23; Judg. 18:31; 1 Chr. 9:11; 2 Chr. 5:14; 22:12; 24:13; 33:7; 36:19; Ezra 5:8, 15; 7:20, 23; Neh. 6:10; 11:11; 13:11; Psa. 42:4; 52:8; 55:14; 84:10; Eccl. 5:1; Isa. 2:3; Hos. 9:8; Joel 1:16; Mic. 4:2; Matt. 12:4; 1 Tim. 3:15; Heb. 10:21; 1 Pet. 4:17; HOUSE OF THE LORD, Ex. 23:19; 34:26; Deut. 23:18; Josh. 6:24; Judg. 19:18; 1 Sam. 1:7, 24; 2 Sam. 12:20; 1 Kin. 3:1; 6:37; 7:40; 8:10, 63; 10:5; 2 Kin. 11:3, 4, 15, 18, 19; 12:4, 9, 10, 13, 16; 16:18; 20:8; 23:2, 7, 11; 25:9; 1 Chr. 6:31; 22:1, 11, 14; 23:4; 26:12; 2 Chr. 8:16; 26:21; 29:5, 15; 33:15; 34:15; 36:14; Ezra 7:27; Psa. 27:4; 92:13; 116:19; 118:26; 122:1, 9; 134:1; Isa. 37:14; Jer. 17:26; 20:1, 2; 26:2, 7; 28:1, 5; 29:26; 35:2; Zech. 8:9; HOUSE OF PRAYER, Isa. 56:7; Matt. 21:13; Mark 11:17; Luke 19:46; MY FATHER'S HOUSE, John 2:16; SANCTUARY, Ex. 25:8; Lev. 19:30; 21:12; Num. 8:19; 19:20; 1 Chr. 22:19; 24:5; 2 Chr. 20:8; 26:18; 29:21; 30:8, 19; Psa. 20:2; 28:2 (marg.); 63:2; 68:24; 73:17; 74:3, 7; 77:13; 78:69; 96:6; 150:1; Isa. 16:12; 63:18; Lam. 2:7, 20; 4:1; Ezek. 5:11; Dan. 8:11, 13, 14; 9:17, 26; 11:31; TABERNACLE, Ex. 26:1; Lev. 26:11; Josh. 22:19; Psa. 15:1; 61:4; 76:2; TEMPLE, 1 Sam. 1:9; 3:3; 2 Kin. 11:10, 13; Ezra 4:1; Psa. 5:7; 11:4; 27:4; 29:9; 48:9; 68:29; Mal. 3:1; Matt. 4:5; 23:16; Luke 18:10; 24:53; ZION, Psa. 132:13; 137:1; Isa. 35:10; Jer. 31:6; 50:5; Joel 2:1, 15.

*Instituted by divine authority*, Ex. 25:8, 9; Deut. 12:11–14. *Holy*, Ex. 30:26–29; 40:9; Lev. 8:10, 11; 26:2; Num. 7:1; 8:19; 1 Chr. 29:3; 2 Chr. 3:8; Isa. 64:11; Ezek. 23:39; 43:12. *Should be reverenced*, Lev. 19:30; 26:2.

See footnotes: CHURCH, *The body of believers*, Matt. 16:18; TABERNACLE, Ex. 27:9; TEMPLE, 1 Kin. 6:17.

a [q]present unto his daughter, Sŏl′o-mon's wife.

17 And [c]Sŏl′o-mon built [m]Gē′-zēr, and [r]Bĕth–hō′rŏn the nether,[G]

18 And [s]Bā′al-ăth, and [t]Tăd′-môr in the wilderness, in the land,

19 And all the [u]cities of store[G] that [c]Sŏl′o-mon had, and cities for his [v]chariots, and cities for his [w]horsemen, and that which Sŏl′o-mon desired to build [1]in Jĕ′ru-sā-lĕm, and in [x]Lĕb′a-non, and in all the land of his dominion.

20 *And* all the people *that were* left of the [y]Ăm′ôr-ītes, [z]Hĭt′-tītes, [a]Pĕr′ĭz-zītes, [b]Hī′vītes, and [c]Jĕb′u-sītes, which *were* not of the children of Ĭş′ra-el,

21 Their children that were left after them in the land, whom the children of Ĭş′ra-el also were not able utterly to destroy, [2]upon those did [d]Sŏl′o-mon levy[G] a [e]tribute[G] of bondservice[G] unto this day.

22 But of the children of Ĭş′-ra-el did [d]Sŏl′o-mon make no bondmen[G]: but they *were* men of war, and his servants, and his princes, and his [f]captains, and rulers of his [g]chariots, and his horsemen.

23 These *were* the chief[G] of the officers that *were* over [d]Sŏl′o-mon's work, five hundred and fifty, which bare rule over the people that wrought in the work.

24 ¶ But [h]Phā′raōh's daughter came up out of the [i]city of Dā′-vid unto her house which [d]*Sol′o-mon* had built for her: then did he build [j]Mĭl′lō.

25 ¶ And three times in a year did [d]Sŏl′o-mon offer [k]burnt offerings and [l]peace offerings upon the [m]altar which he built unto the LORD, and he burnt incense upon the [n]altar that *was* before the LORD. So he finished the house.

26 ¶ And king [d]Sŏl′o-mon [o]made a [p]navy of [q]ships in [r]Ē′zī-on–gē′bēr, which *is* beside [s]Ē′lōth, on the shore of the [t]Red sea, in the land of [u]Ē′dom.

27 And [v]Hī′ram sent in the [q]navy his servants, [w]shipmen[G] that had knowledge of the sea, with the servants of [d]Sŏl′o-mon.

28 And [x]they came to †Ō′phīr, and fetched from thence[G] [y]gold, four hundred and twenty [z]talents,[G] and brought *it* to king [d]Sŏl′o-mon.

## CHAPTER 10

*The Queen of Sheba admires the wisdom of Solomon. 14 Solomon's gold and the use made of it. 24 The presents received by him. 26 His chariots and horsemen.*

AND[Q] [a]when the [b,c]queen of *Shē′bȧ heard of the fame of [d]Sŏl′o-mon concerning the name of the LORD, she came to prove[G] him with hard questions.

2 And she came to [e]Jĕ-ru′sā-lĕm with a very great train,[G] with [f]camels that bare †,[g]spices, and very much [g,h]gold, and [g,i]precious stones: and when she was come to [d]Sŏl′o-mon, she communed[G] with him of all that was in her heart.

3 And [d]Sŏl′o-mon told her all her questions: there was not *any* thing hid from the king, which he told[G] her not.

4[Q] And when the [b]queen of *Shē′bȧ had seen all Sŏl′o-mon's

q *Presents*, Gen. 32:13.

17

r *Beth-horon*, Josh. 10:10.

18

s Josh. 19:44; 2 Chr. 8:6.
t 2 Chr. 8:4.

19

u *Treasure Cities*, Ex. 1:11.
v *Chariot*, Josh. 11:4.
w *Cavalry*, 1 Sam. 13:5.
x *Lebanon*, Deut. 1:7.
1 R. V. for his pleasure in Jerusalem,

20

y *Amorites*, Gen. 14:13.
z *Hittites*, Judg. 1:26.
a *Perizzites*, Gen. 15:20.
b *Hivites*, Gen. 10:17.
c *Jebusites*, Deut. 7:1.

21

d *Solomon*, 2 Sam. 12:24.
e *Tax, levies of men*, Neh. 10:32.
2 R. V. of them did Solomon raise a levy of bondservants unto this day.

22

f *Captain*, Num. 31:48.
g *Chariot*, Josh. 11:4.

24

h *Pharaoh, at the time of Solomon*, 1 Kin. 3:1.
i *Jerusalem*, Judg. 19:10.
j *Millo*, 2 Sam. 5:9.

25

k *Offerings, burnt*, Lev. 6:17.
l *Offerings, peace*, Lev. 6:17.
m *Altar, of burnt offerings*, Gen. 8:20.
n *Altar, of incense*, Ex. 30:1.

26

o *Art*, 2 Chr. 16:14.
p 1 Kin. 10:11.
q *Ship*, 2 Chr. 8:18.
r *Ezion-geber*, Num. 33:35.
s Or, *Elath*, Deut. 2:8.
t *Red Sea*, Ex. 10:19.
u *Edom*, Obad. 1.

27

v *Hiram*, 2 Sam. 5:11.
w *Mariner*, Ezek. 27:27.

28

x *Commerce, of the Israelites*, 1 Kin. 10:15.
y *Gold*, Ezek. 7:19.
z *Talent*, Ex. 38:25.

1

a 2 Chr. 9:1-24.
b *Queen, of Sheba*, 1 Kin. 11:19.
c *Women, as rulers*, Prov. 31:10.
d *Solomon*, 2 Sam. 12:24.

2

e *Jerusalem*, Judg. 19:10.
f *Camel, uses of*, 1 Sam. 30:17.
g *Presents*, Gen. 32:13.
h *Gold*, Ezek. 7:19.
i *Precious Stones*, Ex. 39:10.

† **OPHIR,** a country celebrated for its gold and other valuable merchandise. *Products of, used by Solomon and Hiram*, 1 Kin. 9:28; 10:11; 2 Chr. 8:18; 9:10, 11. *Jehoshaphat sends ships to, which are wrecked*, 1 Kin. 22:48. *Gold of*, 1 Chr. 29:4; Job 22:24; 28:16; Psa. 45:9; Isa. 13:12.

* **SHEBA.** *Queen of, visits Solomon*, 1 Kin. 10:1-13; 2 Chr. 9:1-12. *Rich, in gold*, Psa. 72:15; *in spices*, Jer. 6:20; Ezek. 27:22. *Merchandise of*, Ezek. 27:22, 23; 38:13. *Prophecies concerning the people of, coming into the kingdom of Messiah*, Isa. 60:6.

† **SPICES.** *Stores of*, 2 Kin. 20:13. *In the formula for the sacred oil*, Ex. 25:6; 35:8. *Used in the temple*, 1 Chr. 9:29. *Exported from Gilead*, Gen. 37:25. *Sent as a present by Jacob to Joseph*, Gen. 43:11. *Presented by the queen of Sheba to Solomon*, 1 Kin. 10:2, 10; 2 Chr. 9:1, 9. *Sold in the markets of Tyre*, Ezek. 27:22. *Used in the embalming of Asa*, 2 Chr. 16:14. *Prepared by Mary Magdalene, Mary the mother of James, and Salome, and by Joseph of Arimathea, for embalming the body of Jesus*, Mark 16:1; Luke 23:56; 24:1; John 19:39, 40.

4
*j* *Wisdom, of Solomon,* Prov. 2:2.

5
*k* *Temple, Solomon's,* 1 Kin. 6:17.
1 R. V. (marg.) burnt offering which he offered in the house of the Lord;

9
*l* *Throne, figurative,* 1 Kin. 2:19.
*m* *Judge, kings and other rulers as,* Judg. 2:18.
*n* *King, acts as judge,* 2 Kin. 3:10.

10
*o* *Liberality, instances of,* 1 Tim. 6:18.
*p* *Talent,* Ex. 38: 25.

[j]wisdom, and the house that he
had built,
5 And the meat[G] of his table, and
the sitting of his servants, and
the attendance of his ministers,
and their apparel, and his
‡cupbearers, and his [1]ascent by
which he went up unto the
[k]house of the LORD; there was
no more spirit in her.
6 And she said to the [d]king, It
was a true report that I heard in
mine own land of thy acts[G] and of
thy [j]wisdom.
7 Howbeit I believed not the
words, until I came, and mine
eyes had seen *it*: and, behold, the
half was not told me: thy [j]wisdom
and prosperity exceedeth
the fame[G] which I heard.[Q]
8 Happy *are* thy men, happy
*are* these thy servants, which
stand continually before thee,
*and* that hear thy [j]wisdom.
9 Blessed be the LORD thy
God, which delighted in thee, to
set thee on the [l]throne of Ĭş'ra-el:
because the LORD loved
Ĭş'ra-el for ever, therefore made
he thee king, to do [m,n]judgment
and justice.
10 And she [o]gave the [d]king
an [g]hundred and twenty [p]talents[G]
of [h]gold, and of †,[g]spices very
great store, and [g,i]precious
stones: there came no more such
abundance of spices as these
which the [b]queen of *Shē'bȧ
gave to king [d]Sŏl'o-mon.[Q]

11 And the [q,r]navy also of [s]Hī'ram,
that ‖brought [h]gold from
[t]Ō'phīr, brought in from Ō'phīr
great plenty of [u]almug trees,
and [i]precious stones.
12 And the king made of the
[u]almug trees [v]pillars for the
[k]house of the LORD, and for the
king's [w]house, [x,y]harps also and
psalteries for singers: there came
no such almug trees, nor were
seen unto this day.
13 And king [d]Sŏl'o-mon gave
unto the queen of *Shē'bȧ all
her desire, whatsoever she asked,
beside *that* which Sŏl'o-mon
[z]gave her of his royal bounty.
So she turned and went to her
own country, she and her servants.
14 ¶ Now the weight of [a,b]gold
that came to [c]Sŏl'o-mon in one
year was six hundred threescore[G]
and six [d]talents[G] of gold,
15 Beside [a]*that* [2]*he had* of the
[e]merchantmen, and of the §traffick
of the spice merchants, and
of all the kings of [3,f]Ȧ-rā'bĭ-ȧ,
and of the governors of the
country.
16 ¶ And king [c]Sŏl'o-mon
made two hundred targets[G] *of*
beaten [b]gold: six hundred
[g]*shekels*[G] of gold went to one
target.[G]
17 And *he made* three hundred
[h]shields *of* beaten [b]gold; three
pound[G] of gold went to one shield:
and the king put them in the

11
*q* 1 Kin. 9:26, 27.
*r* *Ship,* 2 Chr. 8:18.
*s* *Hiram,* 2 Sam. 5:11.
*t* *Ophir,* 1 Kin. 9:28.
*u* Or, *algum,* 2 Chr. 2:8; 9:10, 11.

12
*v* *Pillar,* Gen. 28: 18.
*w* *Palace,* 1 Kin. 21:1.
*x* *Harp,* Dan. 3:10.
*y* *Music, instruments of,* 2 Chr. 5:13.

13
*z* *Presents,* Gen. 32:13.

14
*a* *King, emoluments of,* 2 Kin. 3:10.
*b* *Gold,* Ezek. 7:19.
*c* *Solomon,* 2 Sam. 12:24.
*d* *Talent,* Ex. 38: 25.

15
*e* *Merchant,* Neh. 3:32.
*f* *Arabia,* 2 Chr. 9:14.
2 R. V. which the chapmen brought, and the traffic of the merchants,
3 R. V. the mingled people,

16
*g* *Shekel,* Ex. 30: 13.

17
*h* *Shield, made of gold,* 1 Kin. 14:27.

‡ **CUPBEARER,** or butler, an officer of very considerable importance in Oriental courts. Gen. 40:1, 11; 1 Kin. 10:5; 2 Chr. 9:4; Neh. 1:11; 2:1.

‖ **IMPORTS.** From Egypt: *Of horses and chariots, and linen yarn,* 1 Kin. 10:28, 29; 2 Chr. 1:16, 17. From Gilead: *Of spices,* Gen. 37:25. From Ophir: *Of Gold,* 1 Kin. 10:11; 22:48; 1 Chr. 29:4. From Tarshish: *Of gold, ivory, apes, and peacocks,* 1 Kin. 10:22; 2 Chr. 9:21; *silver, iron, tin, lead, brass, slaves,* Ezek. 27:12, 13. From Arabia: *Of sheep and goats,* Ezek. 27:21.

*Of Tyre,* Ezek. 27:12–25.

§ **COMMERCE.** *Laws concerning,* Lev. 19:36, 37; 25:14, 17. *Carried on, by caravans,* Gen. 37:25, 27; Isa. 60:6; *by ships,* 1 Kin. 9:27, 28; 10:11; Psa. 107:23; Prov. 31:14; Rev. 18:19.

*Of the Arabians,* Isa. 60:6; Jer. 6:20; Ezek. 27:21–24. *Of the Ethiopians,* Isa. 45:14. *Of the Ishmaelites,* Gen. 37:27, 28. *Of the Israelites,* 1 Kin. 9:26–28; Neh. 3:31–32; Ezek. 27:17. *Of the Ninevites,* Nah. 3:16. *Of the Syrians.* Ezek. 27:16, 18. *Of the Tyrians,* Isa. 23:8; Ezek. 27; 28:5. *Of the Zidonians,* Isa. 23:2. *Of the Jews,* Ezek. 27:17. *From Tarshish,* Jer. 10:9; Ezek. 27:25.

*Evil practices connected with,* Ezek. 22:13; Hos. 12:7.

Articles of: *Apes,* 1 Kin. 10:22; *balm,* Gen. 37:25; *blue cloth,* Ezek. 27:24; *brass,* Ezek. 27:13; Rev. 18:12; *cinnamon,* Rev. 18:13; *chests of rich apparel,* Ezek. 27:24; *chariots,* 1 Kin. 10:29; Rev. 18:13; *cloths for chariots,* Ezek. 27:20; *corn,* 1 Kin. 5:11; Ezek. 27:17; *embroidery,* Ezek. 27:16, 24; *frankincense,* Jer. 6:20; Rev. 18:13; *gold,* 1 Kin. 9:28; 10:22; 2 Chr. 8:18; Isa. 60:6; Rev. 18:12; *honey,* Ezek. 27:17; *horses,* 1 Kin. 10:29; Ezek. 27:14; Rev. 18:13; *ivory,* 1 Kin. 10:22; 2 Chr. 9:21; Ezek. 27:15; Rev. 18:12; *iron,* Ezek. 27:12, 19; *land,* Gen. 23:13–16; *lead,* Ezek. 27:12; *oil,* 1 Kin. 5:11; Ezek. 27: 17; *pearls,* Rev. 18:12; *peacocks,* 1 Kin. 10:22; *perfumes,* Song 3:6; *precious stones,* Ezek. 27:16, 22; 28:13; Rev. 18:12; *purple,* Ezek. 27:16; Rev. 18:12; *sheep,* Ezek. 27:21; Rev. 18: 13; *slaves,* Gen. 37:28, 36; Deut. 24:7; *silk,* Rev. 18:12; *silver,* 1 Kin. 10:22; 2 Chr. 9:21; Rev. 18:12; *sweet cane,* Jer. 6:20; *thyine wood,* Rev. 18:12; *timber,* 1 Kin. 5:6, 8; *tin,* Ezek. 27:12; *wheat,* Rev. 18:13; *white wool,* Ezek. 27:18; *wine,* 2 Chr. 2:15; Ezek. 27:18; Rev. 18:13; *bodies and souls of men,* Rev. 18:13.

*Transportation of passengers,* Jonah 1:3; Acts 21:2; 27:2, 6, 37.

See footnote, IMPORTS, 1 Kin. 10:11.

[i]house of the forest of [j]Lĕb′a-
non.
18 ¶ Moreover the king made
a great [k]throne of [l]ivory, and
overlaid it with the best [b]gold.
19 The [k]throne had six steps,
and the top of the throne *was*
round behind: and *there were*
stays[c] on either side on the place
of the seat, and two [m]lions stood
beside the stays.[c]
20 And twelve [m]lions stood
there on the one side and on the
other upon the six steps: there
was not the like made in any
kingdom.
21 And all king [c]Sŏl′o-mon's
drinking vessels *were of* [b]gold,
and all the vessels of the [i]house
of the forest of [j]Lĕb′a-non *were*
*of* pure gold; none *were of* [n]sil-
ver: it was nothing[c] accounted of
in the days of Sŏl′o-mon.
22 For the king had at sea a
[o]navy of [p]Thär′shish with the
navy of [q]Hī′ram: once in three
years came the navy of Thär′-
shish, §bringing [b]gold, and [n]silver,
[l]ivory, and [r]apes, and [r]peacocks.
23 So king [c]Sŏl′o-mon exceeded all the kings of the earth for
[s]riches and for [t]wisdom.
24 ¶ And all the earth sought[c] to
[c]Sŏl′o-mon, to hear his [t]wisdom,
which God had put in his heart.
25 And they brought every
man his [u,v]present, vessels of [n]sil-
ver, and vessels of gold, and garments, and armour, and †spices,
[w]horses, and [x]mules, a rate[c] year
by year.
26 ¶ [y]And Sŏl′o-mon gathered
together chariots and [z]horse-
men: and he had a thou-
sand and four hundred chariots,
and twelve thousand horsemen,
whom he bestowed[c] in the [a]cities
for chariots, and with the king at
[b]Jĕ-ru̧′să-lĕm.
27 And the king made [c]silver *to*
*be* in [b]Jĕ-ru̧′să-lĕm as stones, and
cedars made he *to be* as the
[d]sycomore trees that *are* in the
vale, for abundance.
28 ¶ And [e]Sŏl′o-mon had
‖,[f]horses brought out of [g]Ē′ġy̆pt,
[4]and linen yarn: the king's [h]mer-
chants received the linen yarn
at a price.
29 And a ‖,[i]chariot came up
and went out of [g]Ē′ġy̆pt for six
hundred [j]*shekels*[c] of [c]silver, and
an [f]horse for an hundred and
fifty[c]: and so for all the kings of
the [k]Hĭt′tītes, and for the kings
of [l]Sy̆r′ĭ-ȧ, did they bring *them*
out by their means.[c]

## CHAPTER 11

*Solomon's wives and concubines. 4 In his old age they turn him unto idolatry. 9 God threatens him. 14 Solomon's adversaries, namely, Hadad, 23 Rezon, 26 and Jeroboam. 41 Solomon's reign, and death.*

BUT king [a,b]Sŏl′o-mon [c,d]loved
[e]many strange[c] [f]women, together with the daughter of
[g]Phā′raōh, women of the [h]Mō′-
ab-ītes, [i]Ăm′mon-ītes, [j]Ē′dom-
ītes, [k]Zī-dō′nĭ-anș, *and* [l]Hĭt′tītes;
2 Of the nations *concerning*
which the LORD said unto the
children of Ĭș′ra-el, Ye shall not
[m]go in to them, neither shall they
come in unto you: *for* surely they
will turn away your heart [n]after
their gods: Sŏl′o-mon [c]clave[c] unto these in love.
3 And [d]he [o]had seven hundred
wives, princesses, and three hundred [p]concubines: and his [q]wives
[r,s]turned away his heart.
4 For it came to pass, when
[a]Sŏl′o-mon was old, *that* his
[q]wives [r,s]turned away his heart
[t]after[c] other gods: and [u]his heart
was not perfect[c] with the LORD
his God, as *was* the heart of
[v]Dā′vid his father.
5 For [a]Sŏl′o-mon [t]went after
*Ăsh′to-rĕth the goddess of the

i *Armory,* Neh. 3:19.
j *Lebanon,* Deut. 1:7.
18
k *Throne, of ivory,* 1 Kin. 2:19.
l *Ivory,* 2 Chr. 9:17.
19
m *Lion,* Mic. 5:8.
21
n *Silver,* 1 Chr. 28:14.
22
o 1 Kin. 9:26, 27.
p *Tarshish,* 2 Chr. 20:36.
q *Hiram,* 2 Sam. 5:11.
r 2 Chr. 9:21.
23
s *Rich, instances of,* Jas. 5:1.
t *Wisdom, of Solomon,* Prov. 2:2.
25
u *King, emoluments of,* 2 Kin. 3:10.
v *Tribute,* Ezra 4:13.
w *Horse,* Job 39:19.
x *Mule,* 2 Sam. 18:9.
26
y 2 Chr. 1:14-17.
z *Cavalry,* 1 Sam. 13:5.

a *Cities, chariot,* Num. 35:8.
b *Jerusalem,* Judg. 19:10.
27
c *Silver,* 1 Chr. 28:14.

d *Sycamore,* 2 Chr. 1:15.
28
e *Solomon,* 2 Sam. 12:24.
f *Horse,* Job 39:19.
g *Egypt,* Gen. 41:8.
h *Merchant,* Neh. 3:32.
4 R. V. and the king's merchants received them in droves, each drove at a price.
29
i *Chariot,* Josh. 11:4.
j *Shekel,* Ex. 30:13.
k *Hittites,* Judg. 1:26.
l *Syria,* 2 Kin. 6:23.
1
a *Solomon,* 2 Sam. 12:24.
b *Rulers, wicked, instances of,* vs. 1-13; Ex. 18:21.
c *Fellowship, with the wicked,* 1 Cor. 1:9.
d *Lasciviousness, instances of,* 1 Pet. 4:3.
e *Instability, instances of,* Jas. 1:8.
f *Women, wicked,* Prov. 31:10.
g *Pharaoh, father-in-law of Solomon,* 1 Kin. 3:1.
h *Moabites,* Gen. 19:37.
i *Ammonites,* Deut. 2:20.
j *Edomites,* 2 Kin. 8:21.
k *Zidon,* Ezek. 28:21.
l *Hittites,* Judg. 1:26.
2
m *Miscegenation,* Josh. 23:12.
n *Idolatry,* 1 Sam. 15:23.
3
o *Polygamy,* Deut. 17:17.
p *Concubinage,* 2 Sam. 21:11.
q *Wife, idolatrous,* Prov. 5:18.
r *Influence, evil,* 1 Cor. 7:14.
s *Temptation, yielding to, instances of,* Luke 11:4.
4
t *Backsliders, instances of,* Jer. 3:22.
u *Character, instability of,* Phil. 2:15.
v *David,* 1 Sam. 16:13.

* **ASHTORETH,** an idol of the Philistines, Zidonians, and Phenicians. *Probably identical with queen of heaven,* Jer. 7:18. *Worshiped by Israelites,* Judg. 2:13; 10:6; 1 Sam. 7:3, 4; 12:10; 1 Kin. 11:5, 33; 2 Kin. 23:13. *Temple of,* 1 Sam. 31:10. *High places of, at Jerusalem, destroyed,* 2 Kin. 23:13.

6
w *Disobedience to God, instances of,* Eph. 5:6.
x *Obedience, exemplified,* Heb. 5:8.
7
y *High Places,* 1 Kin. 3:2.
z *Chemosh,* Judg. 11:24.

a *Jerusalem,* Judg. 19:10.
b *Ammonites,* Deut. 2:20.
8
c *Incense, offered in idolatrous worship,* Ex. 37:29.
d *Idolatry,* 1 Sam. 15:23.
9
e *Anger of God,* 2 Kin. 13:3.
f *Solomon,* 2 Sam. 12:24.
g *Backsliding,* Hos. 11:7.
h *God, appearances of,* Gen. 2:2.
10
i *Disobedience to God,* Eph. 5:6.
11
j *Government, God in,* Isa. 22:21.
k *Judgments, denounced against Solomon,* Ex. 6:6.
12
l *Children, of the righteous, blessed of God,* Mark 10:14.
m *Intercession, influence of the righteous,* Jer. 27:18.
n *David, intercessional influence of,* 1 Sam. 16:13.
14
o *God, providence of,* Gen. 2:2.

[k]Zī-dō'nĭ-anş, and after Mĭl'com the abomination of the [i]Ăm'mon-ītes.

6 And Sŏl'o-mon [w]did evil in the sight of the LORD, and [u]went not fully after the LORD, [x]as *did* [v]Dā'vid his father.

7 Then did Sŏl'o-mon build an [y]high[G] place for [z]Chē'mŏsh, the abomination of Mō'ab, in the hill that *is* before [a]Jē-ru'să-lĕm, and for †Mō'lech, the abomination of the [b]children of Ăm'mŏn.

8 And likewise did he for all his strange[G] wives, which burnt [c]incense and [d]sacrificed unto their gods.

9 ¶ And the LORD was [e]angry with [f]Sŏl'o-mon, because his heart [g]was turned from the LORD God of Ĭş'ra-el, which had [h]appeared unto him twice,[s]

10 And had commanded him concerning this thing, that he should not [d]go after other gods: but he [i]kept[G] not that which the LORD commanded.

11 Wherefore the LORD said unto [f]Sŏl'o-mon, Forasmuch as this is done of thee, and thou hast not kept my covenant and my statutes, which I have commanded thee, [j,k]I will surely rend[G] the kingdom from thee, and will give it to thy servant.

12 Notwithstanding in [l]thy days I will not do it [m]for [n]Dā'vid thy father's sake: *but* I [k]will rend[G] it out of the hand of thy son.

13 Howbeit I will not rend[G] away all the kingdom; *but* will give one tribe to thy [l]son [m]for [n]Dā'vid my servant's sake, and for [a]Jē-ru'să-lĕm's sake which I have chosen.

14 ¶ And the LORD [o]stirred up an adversary unto [f]Sŏl'o-mon, Hā'dăd the Ē'dom-īte: he *was* of the king's seed in Ē'dom.

15 For it came to pass, when Dā'vid was in Ē'dom, and [p]Jō'ăb the captain of the host was gone up to bury the slain, after he had smitten every male in Ē'dom;

16 (For six months did [p]Jō'ăb remain there with all Ĭş'ra-el, until he had cut off every male in Ē'dom:)

17 That Hā'dăd [q]fled, he and certain Ē'dom-ītes of his father's servants with him, to go into [r]Ē'ġўpt; Hā'dăd *being* yet a little child.

18 And they arose out of Mĭd'ĭ-an, and came to [s]Pā'ran: and they took men with them out of Pā'ran, and they came to [r]Ē'ġўpt, unto Phā'raōh king of Ē'ġўpt; which gave him an house, and appointed[G] him victuals,[G] and gave him land.

19 And Hā'dăd found great favour in the sight of Phā'raōh, so that he gave him to[G] wife the sister of his own wife, the sister of Täh'pen-ēş the ‡queen.

20 And the sister of Täh'pen-ēş bare him Ġē-nū'băth his son, whom Täh'pen-ēş weaned in Phā'raōh's house: and Ġē-nū'băth was in Phā'raōh's household among the sons of Phā'raōh.

21 And when Hā'dăd heard in Ē'ġўpt that Dā'vid [t]slept with his fathers, and that Jō'ăb the captain of the host was dead, Hā'dăd said to Phā'raōh, Let me depart, that I may go to [u]mine own country.

22 Then Phā'raōh said unto him, But what hast thou lacked with me, that, behold, thou seek-

15
p *Joab,* 2 Sam. 20:23.
17
q *Fugitives, instances of,* Judg. 12:4.
r *Egypt,* Gen. 41:8.
18
s *Paran,* Gen. 21:21.
21
t *Death, called sleep,* Num. 23:10.
u *Patriotism,* Psa. 137:1.

† **MOLECH,** called also MOLOCH and MILCOM. *An idol of the Ammonites,* 1 Kin. 11:5, 33; 2 Kin. 23:13; Acts 7:43. *Worshiped by the wives of Solomon, and by Solomon,* 1 Kin. 11: 1–8. *Altar of, situated in the valley of Hinnom,* 2 Kin. 23:10; 2 Chr. 28:3; Jer. 7:31; 32:35. *Children sacrificed to,* Ezek. 23:37, 39; see Lev. 18:21; 20:2–5.

‡ **QUEEN.** *The wife of a king,* 1 Kin. 11:19. *Crowned,* Esth. 1:11; 2:17. *Divorced,* Esth. 1:10–22. *Sits on the throne with the king,* Neh. 2:6. *Makes feasts for the women of the royal household,* Esth. 1:9. *Exerts an evil influence in public affairs,* 1 Kin. 21:5–16. *Counsels the king,* Dan. 5:10–12. *Of Sheba visits Solomon,* 1 Kin. 10:1–13; 2 Chr. 9:1–12. *Candace, of Ethiopia,* Acts 8:27.

*The reigning sovereign, Athaliah,* 2 Kin. 11:1–3; 2 Chr. 22: 12.

*The moon called* QUEEN OF HEAVEN, Jer. 7:18; 44:17–19, 25.

**23**
*v Hadadezer,* 2 Sam. 8:3.
*w Zobah,* 1 Sam. 14:47.

**24**
*x Damascus,* Isa. 8:4.

**25**
*y Syria,* 2 Kin. 6:23.

**26**
*z Jeroboam,* 1 Kin. 14:5.

---

*a* 1 Kin. 12:2.
*b Solomon,* 2 Sam. 12:24.
*c Treason,* 2 Kin. 11:14.
1 R. V. Ephraimite

**27**
*d Millo,* 2 Sam. 5:9.
*e Jerusalem,* Judg. 19:10.

**28**
*f Jeroboam,* 1 Kin. 14:5.
*g Promotion, instances of,* Psa. 75:6.
*h Civil Service,* Dan. 1:5.

**29**
2 R. V. now Ahijah had
**B.C. 980?**

est to go to thine own country?
And he answered, Nothing:
howbeit[G] let me go in any wise.[G]
23 ¶ And God [o]stirred him up
*another* adversary, Rē′zŏn the
son of Ē-lī′a-dah, which [q]fled
from his lord [v]Hăd-ăd-ē′zēr king
of [w]Zō′bah:
24 And he gathered men unto
him, and became captain over a
band, when Dā′vid slew them
*of* [w]*Zo′bah*: and they went to
[x]Dă-măs′cus, and dwelt therein, and reigned in Dă-măs′cus.
25 And he was an adversary to
Ĭṣ′ra-el all the days of Sŏl′o-
mon, beside the mischief[G] that
Hā′dăd *did*: and he abhorred[G]
Ĭṣ′ra-el, and reigned over
[y]Sўr′ĭ-ă.
26 ¶ And [z]Jĕr-o-bō′am the son
of [a]Nē′băt, an [1]Ĕph′rath-īte of
Zĕr′e-dă, [b]Sŏl′o-mon's servant,
whose mother's name *was* Zĕ-
ru′ah, a widow woman, even [c]he
lifted[G] up *his* hand against the
king.
27 And this *was* the cause[G] that
[c]he lifted up *his* hand against the
king: Sŏl′o-mon built [d]Mĭl′lō,
*and* repaired the breaches of the
[e]city of Dā′vid his father.
28 And the man [f]Jĕr-o-bō′am
*was* a mighty man of valour[G]: and
Sŏl′o-mon seeing the young man
that he was ‖industrious, he
[g,h]made him ruler over all the
charge[G] of the house of Jō′ṣeph.
29 And it came to pass at that
time when [f]Jĕr-o-bō′am went
out of [e]Jĕ-ru′să-lĕm, that the
prophet §Ă-hī′jah the Shī′lo-
nīte found him in the way; [2]and
he had clad himself with a new
garment; and they two *were*
alone in the field:
30 And §Ă-hī′jah caught the

new garment that *was* on him,
and rent[G] it *in* twelve pieces:
31 And he said to [f]Jĕr-o-bō′am,
Take thee ten pieces: for thus
saith the LORD, the God of
Ĭṣ′ra-el, Behold, [i]I will [j]rend[G]
the kingdom out of the hand
of [b]Sŏl′o-mon, and will give
ten tribes to thee:
32 (But he shall have one tribe
[k]for my servant Dā′vid's sake,
and for [e]Jĕ-ru′să-lĕm's sake, the
city which I have chosen out of
all the tribes of Ĭṣ′ra-el:)
33 Because that they have forsaken me, and have [l]worshipped
*Ash′to-rĕth the goddess of the
[m]Zĭ-dō′nĭ-anṣ, [n]Chē′mŏsh the
god of the [o]Mō′ab-ītes, and Mĭl′-
com the god of the [p]children of
Ăm′mŏn, and [q]have not walked
in my ways, to do *that which is*
right in mine eyes, and *to keep*
my statutes and my judgments[G],
as *did* Dā′vid his father.
34 Howbeit I will not take the
whole kingdom out of his hand:
but I will make him prince all
the days of his life for Dā′vid my
servant's sake, whom I chose,
because he [r]kept my commandments and my statutes:
35 But I will take the kingdom
out of his son's hand, and will
give it unto thee, *even* ten tribes.
36 And unto his son will I give
one tribe, that Dā′vid my servant may have a [s]light alway before me in [e]Jĕ-ru′să-lĕm, the city
which I have chosen me to put
my name there.
37 And [i]I will take [t]thee, and
thou shalt reign according to all
that thy soul desireth, and shalt
be king over Ĭṣ′ra-el.
38 And it shall be, [u]if thou wilt
hearken unto all that I command

**31**
*i Government, God in,* Isa. 22:21.
*j Judgments, denounced against Solomon,* Ex. 6:6.

**32**
*k Intercession, intercessional influence of the righteous,* Jer. 27:18.

**33**
*l Idolatry,* 1 Sam. 15:23.
*m Zidon,* Ezek. 28:21.
*n Chemosh,* Judg. 11:24.
*o Moabites,* Gen. 19:37.
*p Ammonites,* Deut. 2:20.
*q Disobedience to God,* Eph. 5:6.

**34**
*r Obedience, rewarded,* Heb. 5:8.

**36**
*s Light, figurative,* Matt. 5:14.

**37**
*t Rulers, appointed by God,* Ex. 18:21.

**38**
*u Blessings, contingent upon obedience,* Deut. 11:26.

---

‖ **INDUSTRY,** Prov. 16:26.
**Exemplified:** *By ants,* Prov. 30:25. *By prudent wife,* Prov. 31:27, with vs. 13–26.
**Enjoined,** Gen. 2:15; Ex. 23:12; 35:2; Deut. 5:13; Prov. 27:23–27; Eccl. 9:10; 11:4, 6; Rom. 12:11; Eph. 4:28; 1 Thess. 4:11, 12; 2 Thess. 3:10–12; 1 Tim. 5:8.
*Brings prosperity,* Prov. 10:4, 5; 12:11, 24, 27; 13:4, 11; 21:5; 22:29; 28:19. *Reflections concerning,* Eccl. 1:3; 2:10, 11, 17–22.
**Instances of:** *Jeroboam,* 1 Kin. 11:28. *Paul,* Acts 18:3; 20:33, 34; 1 Cor. 4:12; 1 Thess. 2:9; 2 Thess. 3:8.

§ **AHIJAH,** a prophet of Shiloh. *Foretells the revolt of the ten tribes,* 1 Kin. 11:29, 30; 12:15; *divine judgments on Jeroboam and his house,* 1 Kin. 14:2–18; 15:29; 2 Chr. 10:15.

thee, and wilt walk in my ways,
and do *that is* right in my sight,
to [r]keep my statutes and my
commandments, as Dā′vid my
servant did; that I will be with
thee, and build thee a sure
house,[c] as I built for Dā′vid, and
will give Ĭṣ′ra-el unto thee.
39 And I will for this [v]afflict[c] the
seed of Dā′vid, [w]but not for ever.
40 [b]Sŏl′o-mon sought therefore
to kill [f]Jĕr-o-bō′am. And Jĕr-
o-bō′am arose, and [x]fled into
[y]Ē′ġy̆pt, unto +Shī′shăk king of
Ē′ġy̆pt, and was in Ē′ġy̆pt until
the death of Sŏl′o-mon.
41 ¶ And the rest of the acts[c] of
Sŏl′o-mon, and all that he did,
and his [z]wisdom, *are* they not
written in the [a]book of the acts
of Sŏl′o-mon?
42 And the time that [b]Sŏl′o-
mon reigned in [c]Jē-ru̩′să-lĕm
over all [d]Ĭṣ′ra-el *was* forty years.
43 And Sŏl′o-mon [e]slept[c] with
his fathers, and was [f]buried in
the city of Dā′vid his father: and
⊙Rē-ho-bō′am his son reigned in
his stead.

39
v *Divine Chastisement*, Job 33:19.
w *God, mercy of*, Gen. 2:2.

40
x *Fugitives, instances of*, Judg. 12:4.
y *Egypt*, Gen. 41:8.

41
z *Wisdom, of Solomon*, Prov. 2:2.

a *Book, chronicles of*, Num. 5:23.

42
b *Solomon*, 2 Sam. 12:24.
c *Jerusalem*, Judg. 19:10.
d *Israel, under the kings*, Ex. 4:22.

43
e *Death, called sleep*, Num. 23:10.

v.43–904 BC

f *Burial*, Acts 8:2.

## CHAPTER 12

*The people ask Rehoboam for a redress of grievances. 6 He refuses their request, and answers them roughly. 16 Ten tribes revolt, and make Jeroboam king. 21 God forbids Rehoboam to war against them. 25 Jeroboam strengthens himself by the idolatry of the two calves.*

[a]AND [b]Rē-ho-bō′am went to
[c]Shē′chem: for all *Ĭṣ′-
ra-el were come to Shē′chem to
make him [d]king.

1
a 2 Chr. 10:1-19.
b *Rohoboam*, 1 Kin. 11:43.
c *Shechem*, Josh. 20:7.
d *Government, monarchical*, Isa. 22:21.

2 And it came to pass, when
[e]Jĕr-o-bō′am the son of [f]Nē′băt,
who was yet in [g]Ē′ġy̆pt, heard
*of it* (for he was [h]fled from
the presence of king Sŏl′o-
mon, and Jĕr-o-bō′am dwelt in
Ē′ġy̆pt;)
3 That they sent and called
him. And [e]Jĕr-o-bō′am and all
the congregation of Ĭṣ′ra-el
came, and spake unto [b]Rē-ho-
bō′am, [i]saying,
4 [j]Thy [j]father [k]made our [l]yoke
grievous[c]: now therefore make
thou the grievous service of thy
father, and his heavy yoke
which he put upon us, lighter,
and we will serve thee.
5 And he said unto them, Depart yet *for* three days, then
come again to me. And the people departed.
6 ¶ And king [b]Rē-ho-bō′am
[m]consulted with the [n]old men,
that stood before [o]Sŏl′o-mon his
father while he yet lived, and
said, How do ye advise that I
may answer this people?
7 And they spake unto him,
saying, If [p]thou wilt be a servant
unto this people this day, and
wilt serve them, and answer
them, and speak good words to
them, then they will be thy servants for ever.
8 But [b]he [q]forsook the [m]coun-
sel of the old men, which they
had given him, and consulted
with the [r]young men that were

v.2–903 BC
See footnote, *Time*, Rev. 10:6.

2
e *Jeroboam*, 1 Kin. 14:5.
f 1 Kin. 11:26.
g *Egypt*, Gen. 41:8.
h *Fugitives*, Judg. 12:4.

3
i *Petition*, Esth. 5:6.

4
j *Solomon, oppression of*, 2 Sam. 12:24.
k *Oppression*, Eccl. 5:8.
l *Yoke, figurative*, 1 Sam. 6:7.

6
m *Counsel*, Prov. 12:15.
n *Old Age, wise*, Isa. 46:4.
o *Solomon*, 2 Sam. 12:24.

7
p *Rulers, character and qualifications of*, Ex. 18:21.

8
q *Rashness, instances of*, 2 Sam. 6:7.
r *Young Men*, Prov. 1:4.

---

+**SHISHAK**, king of Egypt. *Gives asylum to Jeroboam*, 1 Kin. 11:40. *Pillages Jerusalem*, 1 Kin. 14:25, 26; 2 Chr. 12:2–9.

⊙**REHOBOAM.** *Son and successor to Solomon as king*, 1 Kin. 11:43; 2 Chr. 9:31. *Refuses to reform abuses*, 1 Kin. 12:1–15; 2 Chr. 10:1–15. *Ten tribes, under leadership of Jeroboam, successfully revolt from*, 1 Kin. 12:16–24; 2 Chr. 10:16–19; 11:1–4. *Builds fortified cities; is temporarily prosperous*, 2 Chr. 11:5–23. *Kingdom of, invaded by king of Egypt and despoiled*, 1 Kin. 14:25–28; 2 Chr. 12:1–12. *Reigned over Judah seventeen years*, 1 Kin. 14:21; 2 Chr. 12:13. *Death of*, 1 Kin. 14:31; 2 Chr. 12:16. *Genealogy and descendants of*, 1 Chr. 3; Matt. 1. *Called* ROBOAM, Matt. 1:7.

***ISRAEL AFTER THE REVOLT**, consisting of the Ten Tribes who seceded from the house of David. *Called also* JACOB, Hos. 12:2. Foreshadowing circumstances indicating the separation: *Disagreement and war after Saul's death*, 2 Sam. chapters 2–4; 1 Chr. 12:23–40; *lukewarmness of the ten tribes, and zeal of Judah for David in Absalom's rebellion*, 2 Sam. 19:41–43; *the rebellion of Sheba*, 2 Sam. 20. *The two factions are distinguished as Israel and Judah during David's reign*, 2 Sam. 21:2. *Revolt consummated under Rehoboam, son and successor of Solomon*, 1 Kin. 12; 2 Chr. 10.

Kings of, and the period of time during which each reigned.
1. *Jeroboam, twenty-two years*, 1 Kin. 14:5.
2. *Nadab, about two years*, 1 Kin. 14:20.
3. *Baasha, twenty-four years*, 1 Kin. 15:16.
4. *Elah, two years*, 1 Kin. 16:6.
5. *Zimri, seven days*, 1 Kin. 16:9.
6. *Omri, twelve years*, 1 Kin. 16:16.
7. *Ahab, twenty-two years*, 1 Kin. 16:29.
8. *Ahaziah, two years*, 1 Kin. 22:40.
9. *Jehoram, twelve years*, 2 Kin. 1:17.
10. *Jehu, twenty-eight years*, 2 Chr. 22:8.
11. *Jehoahaz, seventeen years*, 2 Kin. 10:35.
12. *Jehoash, sixteen years*, 2 Kin. 13:10.
13. *Jeroboam II, forty-one years*, 1 Chr. 5:17.
14. *Zachariah, six months*, 2 Kin. 14:29.
15. *Shallum, one month*, 2 Kin. 15:10.
16. *Menahem, ten years*, 2 Kin. 15:13.
17. *Pekahiah, two years*, 2 Kin. 15:25.
18. *Pekah, twenty years*, Isa. 7:1.
19. *Hoshea, nine years*, 2 Kin. 15:30.

grown up with him, *and* which stood[C] before him:

9 And he said unto them, What counsel[C] give ye that we may answer this people, who have spoken to me, saying, Make the [l]yoke which thy father did put upon us lighter?

10 And the [r]young men that were grown up with him spake unto him, saying, Thus shalt thou speak unto this people that spake unto thee, saying, Thy father made our [l]yoke heavy, but make thou *it* lighter unto us; thus shalt thou say unto them, My little *finger* shall be thicker than my father's loins.

11 And now whereas my father did lade[C] you with a heavy [l]yoke, I [k]will add to your yoke: my father hath [s]chastised[C] you with whips, but I will chastise you with [t]scorpions.[C]

12 ¶ So [e]Jĕr-o-bō'am and all the people came to [b]Rē-ho-bō'am the third day, as the king had appointed, saying, Come to me again the third day.

13 And the king answered the people roughly[C], and [q]forsook[C] the [n]old men's [m]counsel[C] that they gave him;

14 And spake to them after[C] the counsel of the [r]young men, saying, My father made your [l]yoke heavy, and I [u]will add to your yoke: my father *also* [s]chastised you with whips, but I will chastise you with [t]scorpions.

15 Wherefore the king hearkened not unto the people; [v]for [1]the cause[C] was from the [w]LORD[C], that he might perform his [x]saying, which the LORD spake by [y]Ă-hī'jah the Shī'lo-nīte unto Jĕr-o-bō'am the son of Nē'băt.[S]

16 ¶ So when all *Ĭş'ra-el saw that the king hearkened not unto them, the [z]people answered the king, saying, What portion have we in Dā'vid? neither *have we* inheritance in the son of Jĕs'se: [a]to your tents, O Ĭş'ra-el: now see to thine own house, Dā'vid. So Ĭş'ra-el departed unto their tents.

17 But *as for* the children of Ĭş'ra-el which dwelt in the cities of Jū'dah, [b]Rē-ho-bō'am reigned over them.

18 Then king [b]Rē-ho-bō'am sent [c]Ă-dō'ram, who *was* over the [2,d,e]tribute[C]; and all Ĭş'ra-el [f]stoned him with stones, that he died. Therefore king Rē-ho-bō'am made speed to get him up to his chariot, to [g]flee to [h]Jē-ru'să-lĕm.

19 So *Ĭş'ra-el rebelled against the house[C] of Dā'vid unto this day.

20 ¶ And it came to pass, when all Ĭş'ra-el heard that [i]Jĕr-o-bō'am was come again, that they sent and called him unto the congregation, and made him king over all Ĭş'ra-el: there was none that followed the house of Dā'vid, but the tribe of Jū'dah only.

21 ¶ [j]And when [b]Rē-ho-bō'am was come to [h]Jē-ru'să-lĕm, he assembled all the house of Jū'dah, with the tribe of [k]Bĕn'ja-mĭn, an hundred and fourscore thousand chosen men, which were warriors, to fight against the house of *Ĭş'ra-el, to bring the kingdom again to Rē-ho-bō'am the son of [l]Sŏl'o-mon.

v.8–903 BC See footnote, *Time*, Rev. 10:6.

11
- s *Scourging, figurative*, Acts 22:24.
- t *Scorpion, figurative*, Luke 10:19.

14
- u *Oppression, instances of*, Eccl. 5:8.

15
- v *Government, God in*, Isa. 22:21.
- w *God, providence of, overruling interpositions of*, Gen. 2:2.
- x *Foreordination*, Rom. 8:30.
- 1 R. V. it was a thing brought about of the Lord,

v.15–903 BC See footnote, *Time*, Rev. 10:6.

- y *Ahijah*, 1 Kin. 11:29.

16
- z *Citizens, wicked and treasonable, instances of*, Luke 15.15.
- a *Treason, instances of*, 2 Kin. 11:14.

17
- b *Rehoboam*, 1 Kin 11:43.

18
- c Or, *Adoniram*, 1 Kin. 5:14.
- d *Tax, resisted*, Neh. 10:32.
- e *King, emoluments of*, 2 Kin. 3:10.
- f *Homicide, felonious*, Deut. 5:17.
- g *Cowardice*, Lev. 26.36.
- h *Jerusalem*, Judg 19 10.
- 2 R. V. levy;

20
- i *Jeroboam*, 1 Kin 14:5.

21
- j 2 Chr. 11:1–4.
- k *Benjamin, tribe of*, Num. 1:37.
- l *Solomon*, 2 Sam. 12:24.

**History of:** *War continued, between the two kingdoms all the days of Rehoboam and Jeroboam*, 1 Kin. 14:30; *between Jeroboam and Abijam*, 1 Kin. 15:7; *between Baasha and Asa*, 1 Kin. 15:16, 32. *Famine prevails in the reign of Ahab*, 1 Kin. 18:1–6. *Invaded by, but defeats, Ben-hadad, king of Syria*, 1 Kin. 20. *Moab rebels against*, 2 Kin. 1:1; 3. *Army of Syria invades, but peacefully withdraws through the tact of the prophet Elisha*, 2 Kin. 6:8–23. *Samaria besieged*, 2 Kin. 6:24–33; 7; *city of, taken, and the people carried to Assyria*, 2 Kin. 17. *The land repeopled by colonization from various cities of Assyria*, 2 Kin. 17:24, *The remnant that remained after the able-bodied were carried into captivity affiliated with the kingdom of Judah*, 2 Chr. 30 18–26; 34:6; 35:18.

**Prophecies Concerning:** *Of captivity, famine, and judgments*, 1 Kin. 14:15, 16; 17:1; 2 Kin. 8:1; Isa. 9:8–21; 17:3–11; 28:1–8; Hos. 2:1–13; chapters 4; 8; 9; 10; 11:5, 6; 12:7–14; 13; Amos 2:6, 13–16; chapters 3–9.

*Of restoration*, Jer. 30:3–24; Hos. 2:14–23; 11:9–11; 13:13, 14; 14:8.

*Of the reunion of the ten tribes and Judah*, Jer. 3:18; Ezek. 37: 16–22. See footnote, JUDAH, *Kingdom of*, 2 Chr. 11:17.

v.22–903 BC
See footnote, *Time*, Rev. 10:6.

**23**
m *Judah, kingdom of*, 2 Chr. 11:17.

**24**
n *Government, God in*, Isa. 22:21.
o *God, providence of*, Gen. 2.2.

**25**
p *Shechem*, Josh. 20·7.
q *Ephraim*, Josh. 17.15.
r *Penuel*, Gen. 32:31.

**26**
s *Rulers, wicked, instances of*, vs. 26–33; Ex. 18:21.

**27**
t *Offerings*, Lev. 6:17.
u *Temple, Solomon's*, 1 Kin. 6:17.

**28**
v *Church and State, civil power superior to ecclesiastical*, 1 Sam. 16:1.
w *Statecraft*, Prov. 28:2.
x *Idolatry*, 1 Sam. 15:23.
y *Calf, images of*, Mic. 6:6.
z *Idol, made of gold*, 1 Kin. 15:12.

**29**
a *Beth-el*, Josh. 18:13.
b *Dan*, Judg. 18:29.

22 But the word of God came
unto †Shĕm-a-ī′ah the man of
God, saying,
23 Speak unto [b]Rē-ho-bō′am,
the son of [l]Sŏl′o-mon, king of
[m]Jū′dah, and unto all the house
of Jū′dah and Bĕn′ja-mĭn, and
to the remnant of the people,
saying,
24 Thus saith the LORD, Ye
shall not go up, nor fight against
your brethren the children of
Ĭs′ra-el: return every man to
his house; for [n]this thing is from
[o]me. They hearkened therefore
to the word of the LORD, and
returned to depart, according to
the word of the LORD.
25 ¶ Then [i]Jĕr-o-bō′am built
[p]Shē′chem in mount [q]Ē′phră-
ĭm, and dwelt therein; and went
out from thence, and built [r]Pē-
nū′el.
26 ¶ And [s]Jĕr-o-bō′am said in
his heart, Now shall the kingdom
return to the house of Dā′vid:
27 If this people go up to do
[t]sacrifice in the [u]house of the
LORD at [h]Jē-ru′sā-lĕm, then
shall the heart of this people turn
again unto their lord, *even* unto
[b]Rē-ho-bō′am king of Jū′dah,
and they shall kill me, and go
again to Rē-ho-bō′am king of
Jū′dah.
28 [v,w]Whereupon the [s]king
took counsel, and [x]made two
[y,z]calves *of* gold, and said unto them, It is too much for
you to go up to Jē-ru′sā-lĕm:
behold thy gods, O Ĭs′ra-el,
which brought thee up out of
the land of Ē′gȳpt.
29 And he set the one in [a]Bĕth′–
el, and the other put he in [b]Dăn.
30 And this thing became a sin:
for the people went *to* [c]*worship*
before the one, *even* unto Dăn.
31 And [d,e]he made an [f]house of
[g]high places, and made [h,i]priests
[3]of the lowest of the people,
which were not of the sons of
Lē′vī.
32 And [d,e]Jĕr-o-bō′am ordained a [j]feast in the eighth
[k]month, on the fifteenth day of
the month, like unto the feast
that *is* in Jū′dah, and he [4]of-
fered upon the [l]altar. So did
he in [a]Bĕth′–el, [c]sacrificing unto
the calves that he had made:
and he placed in Bĕth′–el the
[h]priests of the [g]high places which
he had made.
33 So he [5]offered upon the altar
which he had made in [a]Bĕth′–el
the fifteenth day of the eighth
[k]month, *even* in the month which
he had devised of his own heart;
and ordained a [j]feast unto the
children of Ĭs′ra-el: and he [5]of-
fered upon the [m]altar, and burnt
[o]incense.

## CHAPTER 13

*A prophet cries against the altar at Beth-el. 4 Jeroboam's hand withers; 6 but is restored at the prayer of the prophet; 7 who refuses the king's entertainment, and departs. 11 An old prophet deceives him, and brings him back. 20 He is reproved of God, 24 slain by a lion, 26 and buried by the old prophet. 33 Jeroboam's obstinacy.*

AND, behold, there came a
[a]man of God out of Jū′-
dah by the word of the LORD
unto [b]Bĕth′–el: and [c,d]Jĕr-o-bō′-
am stood by the [e]altar to burn
[f]incense.
2 And he [g,h]cried against the
altar in the word of the LORD,
and said, O altar, altar, thus
saith the LORD; Behold, a child
shall be born unto the house of
Dā′vid, *Jō-sī′ah by name; and

**30**
c *Idolatry*, 1 Sam. 15:23.

**31**
d *Jeroboam*, 1 Kin. 14:5.
e *Rulers, wicked, instances of*, Ex. 18:21.
f *Temple, idolatrous*, 1 Kin. 6:17.
g *High Places*, 1 Kin. 3:2.
h *Priest, appointed by Jeroboam*, Lev. 1:5.
i *Minister, false and corrupt*, Rom. 15:16.
3 R. V. from among all the people,

**32**
j *Tabernacles, feast of*, Deut. 16:13.
k *Month, Bul*, Ex. 12:2.
l *Altar, used in idolatrous worship*, Gen. 8:20.
4 R. V. went up unto the altar;

**33**
m *Altar, of incense*, Ex. 30:1.
n *Incense, offered in idolatrous worship*, Ex. 37:29.
5 R. V. went up unto the altar,

**1**
a *Prophets, inspiration of*, Isa. 3:2.
b *Beth-el*, Josh. 18:13.
c *Jeroboam*, 1 Kin. 14:5.
d *Rulers, wicked, instances of*, Ex. 18:21.
e *Altar, of incense*, Ex. 30:1.
f *Incense, offered in idolatrous worship*, Ex. 37:29.

**2**
g *Prophecies*, Dan. 9:24.
h *Reproof, faithfulness in*, Prov. 17:10.

† **SHEMAIAH** (*heard of Jehovah*), a prophet in the time of Rehoboam. *Prevents Rehoboam from war with Jeroboam*, 1 Kin. 12:22–24; 2 Chr. 11:2–4. *Foretells the punishment of Rehoboam by Shishak, king of Egypt*, 2 Chr. 12:5, 7. *Writes chronicles*, 2 Chr. 12:15.

* **JOSIAH** (*whom Jehovah heals*). *King of Judah*, 2 Kin. 21:24–26; 1 Chr. 3:14; 2 Chr. 33:25. *Called* JOSIAS, Matt. 1:10, 11. *Ancestor of Jesus*, Matt. 1:10, 11. *Destroys the altars and high places of idolatry*, 2 Kin. 23:3–20, 24, 25; 2 Chr. 34:1–4. *Slain in battle with Pharaoh-nechoh*, 2 Kin. 23:29, 30; 2 Chr. 35:20–24. *Reigned thirty-one years*, 2 Kin. 22:1; 2 Chr. 34:1. *Lamentations for*, 2 Chr. 35:25.

Piety of: *Exemplified, in his repairing of the temple*, 2 Kin. 22:3–6; *in his solicitude when the copy of the law was discovered and read to him*, 2 Kin. 22:8–20; 2 Chr. 34:14–33; *in keeping a solemn passover*, 2 Kin. 23:21–23; 2 Chr. 35:1–19.

*Prophecies concerning his zeal against idolatry*, 1 Kin. 13:1–3; 2 Kin. 23:15–20.

3
*i* ***Sign***, Mark 8:11.

4
*j* *Presumption, instances of*, Psa. 19:13.
*k* *Miracles*, Luke 23:8.

5
*l* *Prophecies, fulfilled*, Dan. 9:24.

6
*m* *Good for Evil*, Luke 6:27.
*n* *Intercession, answered*, Jer. 27:18.
1 R. V. favor of

7
*o* ***Hospitality***, Rom. 12:13.
*p* *Prophets, emoluments of*, Isa. 3:2.

8
*q* *Temptation, resistance to, instances of*, Luke 11:4.
*r* *Fellowship, with the wicked, instances of those who avoided*, 1 Cor. 1:9.

upon thee shall he offer the priests of the high places that burn incense upon thee, and men's bones shall be burnt upon thee.

3 And he gave a [i]sign the same day, saying, This *is* the sign which the LORD hath spoken; Behold, the altar shall be rent,[c] and the ashes that *are* upon it shall be poured out.

4 ¶ And it came to pass, when king [c,d]Jĕr-o-bō'am heard the saying of the [a]man of God, which had cried against the altar in [b]Bĕth'–el, that [j]he put forth his hand from the altar, saying, Lay hold on him. And his hand, which he put forth against him, [k]dried up, so that he could not pull it in again to him.

5 [l]The altar also [k]was rent,[c] and the ashes poured out from the altar, according to the [i]sign which the man of God had given by the word of the LORD.

6 And the [c]king answered and said unto the [a]man of God, Intreat[c] now the [1]face of the LORD thy God, and pray for me, that my hand may be restored me again. [m]And the man of God [n]besought the LORD, and the king's hand was restored him again, and became as *it was* before.

7 ¶ And the [c]king said unto the [a]man of God, [o]Come home with me, and refresh thyself, and I will give thee a [p]reward.[c]

8 And the [a]man of God said unto the king, If thou wilt give me half thine house, [q,r]I will not go in with thee, neither will I eat bread nor drink water in this place:

9 For so was it charged me by the word of the LORD, saying, Eat no bread, nor drink water, nor turn again by the same way that thou camest.

10 So he went another way, and returned not by the way that he came to [b]Bĕth'–el.

11 ¶ Now there dwelt an old [s]prophet in [b]Bĕth'–el; and his sons came and told him all the works that the man of God had done that day in Bĕth'–el: the words which he had spoken unto the [c]king, them they told also to their father.

12 And their father said unto them, What way went he? For his sons had seen what way the man of God went, which came from [t]Jū'dah.

13 And he said unto his sons, Saddle me the ass. So they saddled him the ass: and he rode thereon,

14 And went after the man of God, and found him sitting under an oak: and he said unto him, *Art* thou the man of God that camest from [t]Jū'dah? And he said, I *am*.

15 Then he said unto him, [u]Come home with me, and eat bread.[c]

16 And he [q]said, I may not return with thee, nor go in with thee: neither will I eat bread nor drink water with thee in this place:

17 For it was said to me by the word of the LORD, Thou shalt eat no bread nor drink water there, nor turn again to go by the way that thou camest.

18 He said unto him, I *am* a [s]prophet also as thou *art*; [v]and an angel spake unto me by the word of the LORD, saying, Bring him back with thee into thine house, that he may eat bread and drink water. *But* he [w]lied unto him.

19 So he [x,y]went back with him, and did eat bread in his house, and drank water.

20 ¶ And it came to pass, as they sat at the table, that the word of the LORD came unto

11
*s* *Prophets, false*, Isa. 3:2.

12
*t* *Judah, kingdom of*, 2 Chr. 11:17.

15
*u* *Temptation, leading into*, Luke 11:4.

18
*v* *Deception, instances of*, Josh. 9:4.
*w* *Falsehood, instances of*, Job 21:34.

19
*x* *Disobedience to God, instances of*, Eph. 5:6.
*y* *Temptation, yielding to, instances of*, Luke 11:4.

the prophet that brought him
back:
21 And he cried unto the man
of God that came from Jū′dah,
saying, Thus saith the LORD,
Forasmuch as thou hast [x]dis-
obeyed the mouth of the LORD,
and hast not kept the commandment which the LORD thy God
commanded thee,
22 But [y]camest back, and hast
eaten bread and drunk water
in the place, of the which [2]*the*
*LORD* did say to thee, Eat no
bread, and drink no water; [z]thy
carcase shall not come unto the
sepulchre of thy fathers.
23 ¶ And it came to pass, after
he had eaten bread, and after he
had drunk, that he saddled for
him the [a]ass, *to wit,* for the
prophet whom he had brought
back.
24 And when he was gone, a
[b]lion met him by the way, and
slew him: and [c]his carcase was
cast in the way, and the ass
stood by it, the lion also stood by
the carcase.
25 And, behold, men passed by,
and saw the carcase cast in the
way, and the [b]lion standing by
the carcase: and they came and
told *it* in the city where the old
prophet dwelt.
26 ¶ And when the prophet
that brought him back from the
way heard *thereof,* he said, It *is*
the man of God, who was [d]dis-
obedient unto the [3]word of the
LORD: therefore the LORD [e]hath
delivered him unto the [b]lion,
which hath torn him, and slain
him, [c]according to the word of
the LORD, which he spake unto
him.
27 And he spake to his sons,
saying, Saddle me the [a]ass. And
they saddled *him.*
28 And he went and found his
carcase cast in the way, and the
[a]ass and the [b]lion standing by

**22**
z *Judgments, upon the prophet of Judah,* Ex. 6:6.
2 R. V. he said to thee,

**23**
a *Ass, domesticated,* 2 Chr. 28:15.

**24**
b *Lion,* Mic. 5:8.
c *Prophecies, fulfilled,* Dan. 9:24.

**26**
d *Disobedience to God, instances of,* Eph. 5:6.
e *Judgments, upon the prophet of Judah,* Ex. 6:6.
3 R. V. mouth of

the carcase: the lion had not eat-
en the carcase, nor torn the ass.
29 [f]And the prophet took up
the carcase of the man of God,
and laid it upon the [a]ass, and
brought it back: and [4]the old
prophet came to the city, to
mourn and to bury him.
30 And he [g]laid his carcase in
his own grave; and they [h]mourn-
ed over him, *saying,* Alas, my
brother!
31 And it came to pass, after he
had buried him, that he spake to
his sons, saying, When I am
dead, then [g]bury me in the sepulchre wherein the man of God
*is* buried; lay my bones beside
his bones:
32 For the saying which he
cried by the word of the LORD
against the [i]altar in [j]Bĕth′-el,
and against all the [k]houses of
the [l]high places which *are* in the
cities of [m]Sā-mā′rĭ-ȧ, shall surely
come to pass.
33 ¶ After this thing [n,o]Jĕr-
o-bō′am returned not from his
evil way, but made again [5]of
the lowest of the people [p]priests
of the [l]high places: whosoever
would, he consecrated him, [6]and
he became *one* of the priests of
the high places.
34 And this thing became [q]sin
unto the house of [n]Jĕr-o-bō′am,
even to [r]cut *it* off, and to destroy
*it* from off the face of the earth.

## CHAPTER 14

*Abijah being sick, Jeroboam sends his wife disguised to the prophet Ahijah at Shiloh. 5 Ahijah, forewarned of God, announces God's judgment upon his house. 17 Abijah dies, and is buried. 19 Nadab succeeds Jeroboam. 21 Rehoboam's wicked reign. 25 Shishak spoils Jerusalem. 29 Abijam succeeds Rehoboam.*

AT that time Ȧ-bī′jah the son
of Jĕr-o-bō′am fell sick.
2 And [a]Jĕr-o-bō′am said to his
wife, Arise, I pray thee, and disguise thyself, that thou be not
known to be the wife of Jĕr-o-
bō′am; and get thee to [b]Shī′lōh:

**29**
f *Conscience, guilty,* vs. 29–32; Acts 23:1.
4 R. V. he came to the city of the old prophet,

**30**
g *Burial,* Acts 8:2.
h *Mourning,* Lam. 2:5.

**32**
i *Altar, used in idolatrous worship,* Gen. 8:20.
j *Beth-el,* Josh. 18.13.
k *Temple, idolatrous,* 1 Kin. 6:17.
l *High Places,* 1 Kin. 3:2.
m *Samaria,* Isa. 7:9.

**33**
n *Jeroboam,* 1 Kin. 14:5.
o *Rulers, wicked, instances of,* Ex. 18:21.
p *Priest,* Lev. 1:5.
5 R. V. from among all the people
6 R. V. that there might be priests of

**34**
q *Sin, fruits of,* Rom. 5:12.
r *Judgments,* Ex. 6:6.

**2**
a *Parents, affection of, exemplified,* 2 Cor. 12:14.
b *Shiloh,* Judg. 21:12.

c *Ahijah*, 1 Kin. 11:29.
d *Israel, after the revolt*, 1 Kin. 12:1.

3
e *Bread*, Ezek. 4:13.
f *Prophets, emoluments of*, Isa. 3:2.
g *Honey*, Prov. 25:27.

4
h *Blindness, instances of*, 2 Kin. 6:18.

5
i *Prophecies, fulfilled*, vs. 5–18; Dan. 9:24.
j *Prophets, inspiration of*, Isa. 3:2.
k *Deception, instances of*, Josh. 9:4.

7
l *Government, God in*, Isa. 22:21.
m *Rulers, appointed by God*, Ex. 18:21.

8
n *Obedience, exemplified*, Heb. 5:8.

9
o *Idolatry*, 1 Sam. 15:23.

behold, there *is* [c]Ā-hī′jah the
prophet, which told me that I
*should be* king over this [d]people.
3 And take with thee ten
[e,f]loaves, and cracknels[G], and a
cruse[G] of [g]honey, and go to him:
he shall tell thee what shall become of the child.
4 And Jĕr-o-bō′am's wife did
so, and arose, and went to [b]Shī′-
lōh, and came to the house of
[c]Ā-hī′jah. But Ā-hī′jah could
[h]not see; for his eyes were set[G] by
reason of his age.
5 ¶ And the LORD [i,j]said unto
[c]Ā-hī′jah, Behold, the wife of
*Jĕr-o-bō′am cometh to ask a
thing of thee for her son; for he
*is* sick: thus and thus shalt thou
say unto her: for it shall be,
when she cometh in, that she
shall [k]feign[G] herself *to be* another
*woman*.
6 And it was *so*, when Ā-hī′jah
heard the sound of her feet, as
she came in at the door, that he
said, Come in, thou wife of Jĕr-
o-bō′am; why [k]feignest[G] thou thyself *to be* another? for I *am* sent
to thee *with* heavy[G] *tidings*[G].
7 Go, tell *Jĕr-o-bō′am, Thus
[j]saith the LORD God of Ĭṣ′-
ra-el, Forasmuch as [l]I exalted
thee from among the people,
and [m]made thee prince over my
people Ĭṣ′ra-el,
8 And [l]rent[G] the kingdom away
from the house of Dā′vid, and
gave it thee: and *yet* thou hast
not been as my servant Dā′vid,
who [n]kept my commandments,
and who followed me with all
his heart, to do *that* only *which*
*was* right in mine eyes;
9 But hast done evil above all
that were before thee: for thou
hast gone and [o]made thee other
gods, and molten[G] images, to provoke me to [p]anger, and hast cast
me behind thy back:[S]
10 Therefore, behold, I will
bring [q]evil upon the house of
*Jĕr-o-bō′am, and will cut off
from Jĕr-o-bō′am [1]him that
pisseth[G] against the wall, *and* him
that is shut up and left in Ĭṣ′-
ra-el, and will take away the
remnant of the house of Jĕr-o-
bō′am, as a man taketh away
dung[G], till it be all gone.[S]
11 [q]Him that dieth of *Jĕr-o-
bō′am in the city shall the dogs
eat; and him that dieth in the
field shall the fowls of the air
eat: for the LORD hath spoken *it*.
12 Arise thou therefore, get
thee to thine own house: *and*
when thy feet enter into the city,
the child shall die.
13 And all Ĭṣ′ra-el shall [r]mourn
for him, and bury him: for [s]he
only of *Jĕr-o-bō′am shall come
to the [t]grave, because in him
there is found *some* good thing
toward the LORD God of Ĭṣ′ra-el
in the house of Jĕr-o-bō′am.
14 Moreover the LORD shall
raise him up a king′ over [d]Ĭṣ′-
ra-el, who shall cut off the house
of *Jĕr-o-bō′am that day: but
what? even now.
15 For the LORD shall smite[G]
[u]Ĭṣ′ra-el, as a [v]reed is shaken in
the water, and he shall root up
Ĭṣ′ra-el out of this good land,
which he gave to their fathers,
and shall scatter them beyond
the [2]river, because they have
made their [3,w]groves[G], provoking
the LORD to [p]anger.[S]
16 And he shall give [x]Ĭṣ′ra-el
up because of the sins of *,[y]Jĕr-
o-bō′am, who did sin, and who
made Ĭṣ′ra-el to sin.[Q]

p *Anger of God*, 2 Kin. 13:3.

10
q *Judgments, denounced against Jeroboam*, Ex. 6:6.
1 R. V. every man child,

13
r *Mourning*, Lam. 2:5.
s *Children, good, instances of*, Mark 10:14.
t *Burying Places*, Gen. 23:4.

15
u *Israel, prophecies concerning*, 1 Kin. 12:1.
v *Reed, figurative*, Ezek. 40:3.
w *Groves*, Judg. 6:28.
2 R. V. River;
3 R. V. Asherim,

16
x *Nation, involved in sins of rulers*, Isa. 2:4.
y *Rulers, wicked, instances of*, Ex. 18:21.

***JEROBOAM,** first king of Israel after the revolt. *Promoted by Solomon*, 1 Kin. 11:28. *Ahijah's prophecies concerning*, 1 Kin. 11:29–39; 14:5–16. *Flees to Egypt to escape from Solomon*, 1 Kin. 11:26–40. *Recalled from Egypt by the ten tribes on account of disaffection toward Rehoboam, and made king*, 1 Kin. 12:1–20; 2 Chr. 10:12–19. *Subverts the religion of Moses*, 1 Kin. 12:25–33; 13:33, 34; 14:9, 16; 16:2, 26, 31; 2 Chr. 11:14; 13:8, 9. *Hand of, paralyzed*, 1 Kin. 13:1–10. *His wife sent to consult the prophet Ahijah concerning her child; the prophet foretells the death of the child and divine judgments on, and on his house*, 1 Kin. 14:1–18. *His wars with Rehoboam*, 1 Kin. 14:19, 30; 15:6; 2 Chr. 11:1–4. *His war with Abijam*, 1 Kin. 15:7, 2 Chr. 13:1–20. *Reigned twenty-two years*, 1 Kin. 14:20. *Death of*, 1 Kin. 14:20; 2 Chr. 13:20

17 ¶ And *Jĕr-o-bō′am's wife
arose, and departed, and came
to †Tĭr′zah: *and* when she came
to the threshold of the door, the
child died;
18 And they buried him; and
all Ĭş′ra-el [r]mourned for him, according to the word of the LORD,
which he [j]spake by the hand of
his servant Ă-hī′jah the prophet.
19 And the rest of the acts of
*Jĕr-o-bō′am, how he warred,
and how he reigned, behold, they
*are* written in the [z]book of the
chronicles[G] of the kings of Ĭş′ra-el.
20 And the days which *Jĕr-
o-bō′am reigned *were* two and
twenty years: and he slept with
his fathers, and [a]Nā′dăb his son
reigned in his stead.
21 ¶ And [b]Rē-ho-bō′am the son
of [c]Sŏl′o-mon reigned in [d]Jū′-
dah. Rē-ho-bō′am *was* forty and
one years old when he began to
reign, and he reigned seventeen
years in [e]Jĕ-ru̧′să-lĕm, the city
which the LORD did choose out
of all the tribes of Ĭş′ra-el, to put
his name there. And his mother's name *was* [f]Nā′a-mah an
Ăm′mon-ĭt-ess.
22 And [d]Jū′dah did evil in the
sight of the LORD, and they provoked him to [g]jealousy with
their [h]sins which they had committed, above all that their
fathers had done.
23 For they also built them
[i]high places, and [4]images, and
[3]groves, on every high hill, and
under every green tree.
24 And there were also [j]sodom-
ites in the land: *and* they did according to all the [k]abominations of
the nations which the LORD cast
out before the children of Ĭş′ra-el.

**19**
*z Book*, Num. 5:23.

**20**
*a* 1 Kin. 15:25–31.
v.20–882 BC

**21**
*b Rehoboam*, 1 Kin. 11:43.
*c Solomon*, 2 Sam. 12:24.
v.21–903 BC
*d Judah, kingdom of*, 2 Chr. 11:17.
*e Jerusalem*, Judg. 19:10.
*f* 2 Chr. 12:13.

**22**
*g Jealousy, attributed to God*, Psa. 78:58.
v.22–900 BC
*h Sin, repugnant to God*, Rom. 5:12.

**23**
*i High Places*, 1 Kin. 3:2.
4 R. V. pillars,

**24**
*j Sodomy*, Lev. 18:22.
*k Idolatry, wicked practices of*, 1 Sam. 15:23.

25 ¶ And it came to pass in the
fifth year of king [b]Rē-ho-bō′am,
*that* [l]Shī′shăk king of [m]Ē′ġy̆pt
came up against [e]Jĕ-ru̧′să-lĕm:
26 And he took away the treasures of the house of the LORD,
and the treasures of the king's
house; he even took away all: and
he took away all the ‡shields of
gold which [c]Sŏl′o-mon had made.
27 And king [b]Rē-ho-bō′am
made in their stead brasen
‡shields, and committed *them*
unto the hands of the chief[G] of the
guard, which [n]kept the door of
the king's house.
28 And it was *so*, when the king
went into the house of the LORD,
that the guard bare[G] them, and
brought them back into the
guard chamber[G].
29 ¶ Now the rest of the acts of
[b]Rē-ho-bō′am, and all that he
did, *are* they not written in the
[o]book of the chronicles[G] of the
kings of [d]Jū′dah?
30 And there was [p]war between
Rē-ho-bō′am and Jĕr-o-bō′am
all *their* days.
31 And [b]Rē-ho-bō′am [q]slept[G]
with his fathers, and was buried
with his fathers in the [e]city of
Dā′vid. And his mother's name
*was* [f]Nā′a-mah an Ăm′mon-ĭt-
ess. And [r]Ă-bī′jam his son
reigned in his stead.

## CHAPTER 15

*Abijam's wicked reign. 8 Asa succeeds him. 9 Asa's good reign. 16 His war with Baasha causes him to make a league with Ben-hadad. 23 Jehoshaphat succeeds Asa. 25 Nadab's wicked reign. 27 Baasha, conspiring against him, executes Ahijah's prophecy. 31 Nadab's acts and death. 33 Baasha's wicked reign.*

NOW in the eighteenth year
of king [a]Jĕr-o-bō′am the
son of Nē′băt reigned *Ă-bī′jam
over [b]Jū′dah.

v.25–899 BC
See footnote, *Time*, Rev. 10:6.

**25**
*l Shishak*, 1 Kin. 11:40.
*m Egyptians*, Gen. 50:3.

**27**
*n Porters*, 2 Sam. 18:26.

**29**
*o Book*, Num. 5:23

**30**
*p War*, Judg. 3:2.

**31**
*q Death, called sleep*, Num. 23:10.
v.31–886 BC
*r Abijam*, 1 Kin. 15:1.

**1**
*a Jeroboam*, 1 Kin. 14:5.
*b Judah, kingdom of*, 2 Chr. 11:17.

† **TIRZAH,** a city of Canaan. *Captured by Joshua*, Josh. 12:24. *Becomes the residence of the kings of Israel*, 1 Kin. 14:17; 15:21, 33; 16:6, 8, 9, 15, 17, 23. *Royal residence moved from*, 1 Kin. 16:23, 24. *Base of military operations of Menahem*, 2 Kin. 15:14, 16. *Beauty of*, Song 6:4.

‡ **SHIELD,** defensive armor. *Different kinds of, designated as buckler, shield, target*, Psa. 35:2; Ezek. 38:4. *Used, by Saul*, 2 Sam. 1:21; *by the Benjamites*, 2 Chr. 14:8; 17:17. *Uzziah equipped the children of Israel with*, 2 Chr. 26:14. *Made, of brass*, 1 Kin. 14:27; *of gold*, 2 Sam. 8:7; 1 Kin. 10:16, 17; 1 Chr. 18:7; 2 Chr. 9:15, 16; *of wood*, Ezek. 39:9, 10; *with bosses*, Job 15:26. *Stored, in armories*, 1 Kin. 10:17; 2 Chr. 11:12; 32:5, 27; *in the tabernacle*, 2 Kin. 11:10; 2 Chr. 23:9. *Covered when not in use*, Isa. 22:6. *Painted red*, Nah. 2:3.
**Figurative**: Eph. 6:16. *Of God's protection*, Gen. 15:1; Deut. 33:29; 2 Sam. 22:3, 36; Psa. 3:3; 5:12; 18:2, 35; 33:20; 84:9, 11; Prov. 30:5. *Of God's truth*, Psa. 91:4. *Of an army*, Jer. 46:3.

* **ABIJAM,** called also ABIJAH and ABIA. *Son of Reho-*

v.2–886 BC
See footnote, *Time*, Rev. 10:6.

2
c *Jerusalem*, Judg. 19:10.
d 2 Chr. 11:20–22; 15:16; or, *Michaiah*, 2 Chr. 13:2.

3
e *Rulers, wicked, instances of*, Ex. 18:21.

4
f *David, intercessional influence of*, 1 Sam. 16:13.
g *Intercession, intercessional influence of the righteous*, Jer. 27:18.

5
h *Obedience, exemplified*, Heb. 5:3.
i *Uriah*, 2 Sam. 11:3.

6
j *War*, Judg. 3:2.
k *Rehoboam*, 1 Kin. 11:43.

7
l *Book*, Num. 5:23.

8
m *Death, called sleep*, Num. 23:10.

v.8–884 BC
n *Burial*, Acts 8:2.

2 Three years reigned he in
[c]Jē-ru̧′sȧ-lĕm. And his mother's name *was* [d]Mā′a-chah, the
daughter of Ȧ-bĭsh′a-lom.
3 And [e]he walked in all the sins
of his father, which he had done
before him: and his heart was
not perfect with the LORD his
God, as the heart of Dā′vid his
father.
4 Nevertheless for [f]Dā′vid's
[g]sake did the LORD his God give
him a lamp in [c]Jē-ru̧′sȧ-lĕm, to
set up his son after him, and to
establish Jē-ru̧′sȧ-lĕm:
5 Because [f]Dā′vid [h]did *that*
*which was* right in the eyes of the
LORD, and turned not aside
from any *thing* that he commanded him all the days of his
life, save[G] only in the matter of
[i]U-rī′ah the Hĭt′tīte.
6 And there was [j]war between
[k]Rē-ho-bō′am and [a]Jĕr-o-bō′am
all the days of his life.
7 Now the rest of the acts of
*Ȧ-bī′jam, and all that he did,
*are* they not written in the [l]book
of the chronicles[G] of the kings of
[b]Jū′dah? And there was [j]war
between Ȧ-bī′jam and [a]Jĕr-o-
bō′am.
8 And *Ȧ-bī′jam [m]slept[G] with his
fathers; and they [n]buried him in
the [c]city of Dā′vid: and †Ā′sȧ his
son reigned in his stead.
9 ¶ And in the twentieth year of
[a]Jĕr-o-bō′am king of Ĭs̹′ra-el
reigned †Ā′sȧ over [b]Jū′dah.
10 And forty and one years
reigned he in [c]Jē-ru̧′sȧ-lĕm. And
his mother's name *was* [d]Mā′a-
chah, the daughter of Ȧ-bĭsh′a-
lom.

11 And †,[o]Ā′sȧ did *that which*
*was* right in the eyes of the
LORD, as *did* Dā′vid his father.
12 And he [p]took away the
[q,r,s]sodomites out of the land,
and removed all the ‡idols that
his fathers had made.
13 And also [d]Mā′a-chah his
mother, even her he removed
from *being* queen, because she
had made an [1]idol in a [t]grove[G];
and †Ā′sȧ [2]destroyed her idol,
and burnt *it* by the [u]brook
[v]Kĭd′ron.
14 But the [w]high places were
not removed: nevertheless †Ā′-
sȧ's heart was [x]perfect with the
LORD all his days.
15 And he [y]brought in the
things which his father had dedicated, and the things which
himself had dedicated, into the
[z]house of the LORD, [a]silver, and
[b]gold, and vessels.
16 ¶ And there was war between †Ā′sȧ and ‖Bā′a-shȧ king
of [c]Ĭs̹′ra-el all their days.
17 [d]And ‖Bā′a-shȧ king of Ĭs̹′-
ra-el went up against [e]Jū′dah,
and built [f]Rā′mah, that he
might not suffer[G] any to go out
or come in to Ā′sȧ king of Jū′-
dah.
18 Then †Ā′sȧ took all the [a]sil-
ver and the [b]gold *that were* left in
the treasures[G] of the [g]house of the
LORD, and the treasures of the
king's [h]house, and delivered
them into the hand of his servants: and king Ā′sȧ sent them to
[i]Bĕn–hā′dăd, the son of Tăb′rĭ-
mon, the son of Hē′zī-on, king of
[j]Sȳr′ĭ-ȧ, that dwelt at [k]Dȧ-măs′-
cus, saying,

v.11–884 BC

11
o *Rulers, righteous, instances of*, Ex. 18:21.

12
p *Zeal, instances of*, 2 Cor. 7:11.
q *Idolatry, wicked practices of*, 1 Sam. 15:23.
r *Sodomites*, Gen. 19:25.
s *Sodomy*, Lev. 18:22.

13
t *Groves*, Judg. 6:28.
u *Brook*, Deut. 8:7.
v *Kidron*, 1 Kin. 2:37.
1 R. V. abominable image for an Asherah;
2 R. V. cut down her image,

14
w *High Places*, 1 Kin. 3:2.
x *Perfection*, Heb. 6:1.

15
y *Liberality, instances of*, 1 Tim. 6:18.
z *Temple, Solomon's*, 1 Kin. 6:17.

a *Silver*, 1 Chr. 28:14.
b *Gold*, Ezek. 7:19.

16
c *Israel, after the revolt*, 1 Kin. 12:1.

17
d 2 Chr. 16:1–6.
e *Judah, kingdom of*, 2 Chr. 11:17.
f *Ramah*, Judg. 19:13.

18
g *Temple, Solomon's*, 1 Kin. 6:17.
h *Palace*, 1 Kin. 21:1.
i 2 Chr. 16:2–4.
j *Syria*, 2 Kin. 6:23.
k *Damascus*, Isa. 8:4.

*boam*, 1 Chr. 3:10; Matt. 1:7. *King of Judah*, 1 Kin. 14:31; 15:1; 2 Chr. 12:16. *Reigned three years*, 1 Kin. 15:1, 2; 2 Chr. 13:1, 2. *History of*, 1 Kin. 15:1–8; 2 Chr. 11:20, 22; 13. *Succeeded by Asa*, 1 Kin. 15:8; 2 Chr. 14:1.

† **ASA** (*physician*). *King of Judah*, 1 Kin. 15:8–24; 1 Chr. 3:10. *Destroyed idolatry*, 2 Chr. 14; 15. *Death and burial of*, 2 Chr. 16. *Reigned forty-one years*, 1 Kin. 15:9, 10. *Genealogy of*, Matt. 1:7.

‡ **IDOL.** *Manufacture of*, Ex. 20:4; 32:4, 20; Deut. 4:23; Isa. 40:19, 20; 44:9–17; Hab. 2:18; Acts 19:24, 25. *Manufacture of, forbidden*, Ex. 20:4; 34:17; Deut. 5:8; 27:15. *Made, of gold*, Ex. 32:3, 4; Dan. 3:1, 5, 10, 12; *of silver and gold*, Psa. 115:4–7; 135:15–17; Isa. 2:20; 30:22; 31:7; Hos. 8:4; *of wood and stone*, Lev. 26:1; Deut. 4:28; 2 Kin. 19:18; Isa. 37:19; 44:13–19; Ezek. 20:32. *Stolen*, Gen. 31:19, 30; Judg. 18:17–27, 30, 31. *Covering of*, Isa. 30:22.
*Prayer to, unanswered*, 1 Kin. 18:25–29. *Falls down before the ark of Jehovah*, 1 Sam. 5:1–5. *Used by Michal to save the life of David*, 1 Sam. 19:13–17. *Derided*, Psa. 115:4–8; 135:15–18; Isa. 44:9–17. *To be abandoned*, Isa. 2:20. *To be destroyed*, Deut. 12:3. *Things offered to, not to be eaten*, Ex. 34:15. *Paul's instructions concerning eating things offered to*, 1 Cor. 8; 10:25–33.
See footnote, IDOLATRY, 1 Sam. 15:23.

‖ **BAASHA.** *King of Israel*, 1 Kin. 15:16–22, 27–34; 16:1–7; 21:22; 2 Kin. 9:9; 2 Chr. 16:1–6; Jer. 41:9. *Reigned twenty-four years*, 1 Kin. 15:33.

19
*l* *Treaty, between Judah and Syria,* 1 Kin. 5:12.
*m* *Alliances, instances of,* Josh. 9:15.
*n* *Bribery, instances of,* 1 Sam. 8:3.
20
*o* *Captain,* Num. 31:48.
*p* *Armies, confederated,* Deut. 11:4.
*q* 2 Kin. 15:29; 2 Chr. 16:4.
*r* *Dan,* Judg. 18:29.
*s* *Abel-beth-maachah,* 2 Kin. 15:29.
*t* Josh. 11:2.
*u* *Naphtali, tribe of,* Num. 1:42.
21
*v* *Tirzah,* 1 Kin. 14:17.
22
*w* *Geba,* Josh. 21:17.
*x* *Benjamin, tribe of,* Num. 1:37.
*y* *Mizpah,* Josh. 18:26.
23
*z* *Book,* Num. 5:23.

*a* *Judah, kingdom of,* 2 Chr. 11:17.
*b* *Old Age,* Isa. 46:4.
24
*c* *Death, called sleep,* Num. 23:10.
v.24–843 BC
*d* *Jehoshaphat,* 2 Kin. 12:18.
25
*e* 1 Kin. 14:20.
*f* *Jeroboam,* 1 Kin. 14:5.
v.25–882 BC
*g* *Israel, after the revolt,* 1 Kin. 12:1.

19 *There is* a [l,m]league[G] between me and thee, *and* between my father and thy father: behold, I [n]have sent unto thee a present of silver and gold; come and break thy [l,m]league with ‖Bā′a-shȧ king of Ĭṣ′ra-el, that he may depart from me.

20 So [i]Bĕn–hā′dăd hearkened unto king †Ā′sȧ, and sent the [o]captains of the [p]hosts which he had against the cities of Ĭṣ′ra-el, and smote [q]Ī′jon, and [r]Dăn, and [s]Ā′bel–bĕth–mā′a-chah, and all [t]Çĭn′ne-rŏth, with all the land of [u]Năph′ta-lī.

21 And it came to pass, when ‖Bā′a-shȧ heard *thereof*, that he left off building of [l]Rā′mah, and dwelt in [v]Tĭr′zah.

22 Then king †Ā′sȧ made a §proclamation throughout all [e]Jū′dah; none *was* exempted: and they took away the stones of [l]Rā′mah, and the timber thereof, wherewith ‖Bā′a-shȧ had builded; and king Ā′sȧ built with them [w]Ḡē′bȧ of [x]Bĕn′ja-mĭn, and [y]Mĭz′pah.

23 The rest of all the acts of †Ā′sȧ, and all his might, and all that he did, and the cities which he built, *are* they not written in the [z]book of the chronicles[G] of the kings of [a]Jū′dah? Nevertheless in the time of his [b]old age he was diseased in his feet.

24 And †Ā′sȧ [c]slept[G] with his fathers, and was buried with his fathers in the city of Dā′vid his father: and [d]Jĕ-hŏsh′a-phăt his son reigned in his stead.

25 ¶ And [e]Nā′dăb the son of [f]Jĕr-o-bō′am began to reign over [g]Ĭṣ′ra-el in the second year of †Ā′sȧ king of [a]Jū′dah, and reigned over Ĭṣ′ra-el two years.

26 And [h]he did evil in the sight of the LORD, and [i]walked [j]in the way of his [k]father, and in his sin wherewith [l]he [i]made Ĭṣ′ra-el to sin.[S]

27 ¶ And ‖[m]Bā′a-shȧ the son of [n]Ā-hī′jah, of the house of [o]Ĭs′sa-char, [p]conspired against him; and Bā′a-shȧ smote[G] him at +Ḡĭb′be-thŏn, which *belonged* to the [q]Phĭ-lĭs′tĭneş; for [e]Nā′dăb and all Ĭṣ′ra-el laid [r]siege to Ḡĭb′be-thŏn.

28 Even in the third year of †Ā′sȧ king of [a]Jū′dah did ‖Bā′a-shȧ [s,t]slay him, and [u]reigned in his stead.

29 And it came to pass, when he reigned, *that* he smote all the house of [f]Jĕr-o-bō′am; he left not to Jĕr-o-bō′am any that breathed, until he had destroyed him, according unto the [v]saying of the LORD, which he spake by his servant [w]Ā-hī′jah the Shī′lo-nīte:

30 Because of the sins of [f]Jĕr-o-bō′am which he sinned, and which [x]he [i]made [l]Ĭṣ′ra-el sin, by his provocation wherewith he provoked the LORD God of Ĭṣ′ra-el to [y]anger.[S]

31 ¶ Now the rest of the acts of Nā′dăb, and all that he did, *are* they not written in the [z]book of the chronicles of the kings of [a]Ĭṣ′ra-el?

32 And there was [b]war between †Ā′sȧ and ‖Bā′a-shȧ king of Ĭṣ′ra-el all their days.

33 ¶ In the third year of †Ā′sȧ king of [c]Jū′dah began ‖Bā′a-shȧ the son of Ā-hī′jah to reign over all [a]Ĭṣ′ra-el in [d]Tĭr′zah, twenty and four years.[S]

34 And ‖he did evil in the sight of the LORD, and [e]walked [f]in the way of [g]Jĕr-o-bō′am, and in his sin wherewith he [e]made [h]Ĭṣ′ra-el to sin.

v.26–882 BC
See footnote, *Time,* Rev. 10:6.
26
*h* *Rulers, wicked, instances of,* Ex. 18:21.
*i* *Sin, fruits of,* Rom. 5:12.
*j* *Influence, evil,* 1 Cor. 7:14.
*k* *Parents, evil influence of,* 2 Cor. 12:14.
*l* *Nation, involved in sins of rulers,* Isa. 2:4.
27
*m* *Citizens, wicked and treasonable,* Luke 15:15.
*n* 2 Kin. 9:9.
*o* *Issachar, tribe of,* Num. 1:28.
*p* *Conspiracy, instances of,* 1 Kin 16:9.
*q* *Philistines,* Gen. 26:14.
*r* *Siege, instances of,* Deut. 28.53.
28
*s* *Homicide, felonious, instances of,* Deut. 5:17.
*t* *Regicide,* 2 Sam. 1:10.
*u* *Usurpation, of political functions,* 2 Sam. 15:1.
29
*v* *Prophecies, fulfilled,* Dan. 9:24.
*w* *Ahijah,* 1 Kin. 11:29.
30
*x* *Temptation, leading into,* Luke 11:4.
*y* *Anger of God,* 2 Kin. 13:3.
31
*z* *Book,* Num. 5:23.

*a* *Israel, after the revolt,* 1 Kin. 12:1.
32
*b* *War,* Judg. 3:2.
33
*c* *Judah, kingdom of,* 2 Chr. 11:17.
v.33–881 BC
*d* *Tirzah,* 1 Kin. 14:17.
34
*e* *Sin, fruits of,* Rom. 5:12.
*f* *Influence, evil,* 1 Cor. 7:14.
*g* *Jeroboam,* 1 Kin 14:5.
*h* *Nation, involved in sins of rulers,* Isa. 2:4.

§ **PROCLAMATION.** *Imperial,* 2 Chr. 30:1-10; Ezra 7:13-26; Esth. 1:22; 8:10-14; Isa. 40:3, 9; Dan. 3:4-7; 4:1; 5:29. *Of emancipation.* 2 Chr. 36:22, 23; Ezra 1:1-4; 7:13.

+ **GIBBETHON.** *A city of Dan,* Josh. 19:44. *Allotted to the Levites,* Josh. 21:23. *Besieged by Israel, while in possession of Philistines,* 1 Kin. 15:27; 16:15, 17.

v.1–858 BC
See footnote, *Time*, Rev. 10:6.

1
a *Jehu*, 2 Chr. 19:2.
b 2 Chr. 19:2; 20:34.
c *Baasha*, 1 Kin. 15:16.

2
d *Government, God in*, Isa. 22:21.
e *Promotion, instances of*, Psa. 75:6.
f *Rulers, appointed by God*, Ex. 18:21.
g *Ingratitude, of man to God*, Rom. 1:21.
h *Jeroboam*, 1 Kin. 14:5.
i *Temptation, leading into*, Luke 11:4.

3
j *Judgments*, Ex. 6:6.

5
k *Book*, Num. 5:23.
l *Israel, after the revolt*, 1 Kin. 12:1.

6
m *Death, called sleep*, Num. 23:10.
n *Burial*, Acts 8:2.
o *Tirzah*, 1 Kin. 14:17.

7
p *Prophets, inspiration of*, Isa. 3:2.
q *Sin, repugnant to God*, Rom. 5:12.

## CHAPTER 16

*Jehu's prophecy against Baasha. 6 Elah succeeds him. 8 Zimri, conspiring against Elah, succeeds him; 11 and executes Jehu's prophecy. 15 Omri is made king. 18 Zimri destroys himself. 21 The kingdom being divided, Omri prevails against Tibni; 23 and builds Samaria. 25 His wicked reign. 27 Ahab succeeds him. 29 Ahab's wicked reign. 34 The rebuilding of Jericho.*

THEN the word of the LORD
came to [a]Jē'hū the son
of [b]Hă-nā'nī against [c]Bā'a-shȧ,
saying,
2 Forasmuch as [d]I [e]exalted[G]
[f]thee out of the dust, and made
thee prince over my people Ĭṣ'-
ra-el; and [g]thou hast walked in
the way of [h]Jĕr-o-bō'am, and
hast [i]made my people Ĭṣ'ra-el to
sin, to provoke me to anger with
their sins;[S]
3 Behold, I [j]will take away the
posterity of [c]Bā'a-shȧ, and the
posterity of his house; and will
make thy house like the house of
[h]Jĕr-o-bō'am the son of Nē'băt.
4 Him that dieth of [c]Bā'a-shȧ
in the city [j]shall the dogs eat:
and him that dieth of his in the
fields shall the fowls of the air
eat.
5 Now the rest of the acts of
[c]Bā'a-shȧ, and what he did, and
his might, *are* they not written in
the [k]book of the chronicles of the
kings of [l]Ĭṣ'ra-el?
6 So [c]Bā'a-shȧ [m]slept[G] with his
fathers, and was [n]buried in [o]Tĭr'-
zah: and Ē'lah his son reigned
in his stead.
7 And also by the hand of the
prophet [a]Jē'hū the son of *Hă-
nā'nī [p]came the word of the LORD
against [c]Bā'a-shȧ, and against
his house, even for all the evil
that he did in the sight of the
LORD, [q]in provoking him to
anger with the work of his
hands, in being like the house of
[h]Jĕr-o-bō'am; and because he
[r]killed him.[S]
8 ¶ In the twenty and sixth
year of [s]Ā'sȧ king of [t]Jū'dah began Ē'lah the son of [c]Bā'a-shȧ to
reign over Ĭṣ'ra-el in [o]Tĭr'zah,
two years.
9 And his [u,v]servant [w]Zĭm'rī,
captain of half *his* chariots,
*,[x]conspired against him, as he
was in [o]Tĭr'zah, drinking himself [y,z]drunk in the house of
Är'zȧ steward of *his* house in
Tĭr'zah.
10 And [a]Zĭm'rī went in and
smote him, and [b,c]killed him,
in the twenty and seventh year
of [d]Ā'sȧ king of [e]Jū'dah, and
[f]reigned in his stead.
11 ¶ And it came to pass, when
[a]he began to reign, as soon as he
sat on his throne, *that* he [c]slew
all the house of [g]Bā'a-shȧ: he
left him not [1]one that pisseth[G]
against a wall, neither of his
kinsfolks, nor of his friends.
12 Thus did [a]Zĭm'rī destroy all
the [h]house of Bā'a-shȧ, according to the [i]word of the LORD,
which he spake against Bā'a-shȧ
by Jē'hū the prophet,
13 For all the sins of Bā'a-shȧ,
and the sins of Ē'lah his son,
by which they sinned, and by
which they [j,k]made Ĭṣ'ra-el to
sin, [l]in provoking the LORD God
of Ĭṣ'ra-el to anger with their
vanities.[GS]
14 Now the rest of the acts of
Ē'lah, and all that he did, *are*
they not written in the [m]book of
the chronicles of the kings of
[n]Ĭṣ'ra-el?

v.7–858 BC
See footnote, *Time*, Rev. 10:6.

r *Homicide, felonious, instances of*, Deut. 5:17.

8
s *Asa*, 1 Kin. 15:8.
t *Judah, kingdom of*, 2 Chr. 11:17.

9
u *Citizens, wicked and treasonable, instances of*, Luke 15:15.
v *Servant, wicked and unfaithful*, Jer. 2:14.
w 2 Kin. 9:31.
x *Treason, instances of*, 2 Kin. 11:14.
y *King, drunken, instances of*, 2 Kin. 3:10.
z *Drunkenness, instances of*, Luke 21:34.

v.10–857 BC

10
a 2 Kin. 9:31.
b *Regicide, of Elah*, 2 Sam. 1:10.
c *Homicide, felonious, instances of*, Deut. 5:17.
d *Asa*, 1 Kin. 15:8.
e *Judah kingdom of*, 2 Chr. 11:17.
f *Usurpation, of political functions*, 2 Sam. 15:1.

11
g *Baasha*, 1 Kin. 15:16.
1 R. V. a single man child,

12
h *Children, involved in sins of parents*, Mark 10:14.
i *Prophecies, fulfilled*, Dan. 9:24.

13
j *Temptation, leading into*, Luke 11:4.
k *Influence, evil*, 1 Cor. 7:14.
l *Sin, repugnant to God*, Rom. 5:12.

14
m *Book*, Num. 5:23.
n *Israel, after the revolt*, 1 Kin. 12:1.

---

* **CONSPIRACY. Law against,** Ex. 23:1, 2.
**Instances of:** *Joseph's brethren, against Joseph*, Gen. 37:18–20. *Miriam and Aaron, against Moses*, Num. 12. *Israelites, against Moses and Aaron*, Num. 14:4; 16:1–35. *Abimelech, against Gideon's sons*, Judg. 9:1–6. *Gaal, against Abimelech*, Judg. 9:23–41. *Delilah, against Samson*, Judg. 16:4–21. *Abner, against Ish-bosheth*, 2 Sam. 3:7–21. *Absalom*, 2 Sam. 15:10–13. *Baasha*, 1 Kin. 15:27. *Zimri*, 1 Kin. 16:9. *Jezebel, against Naboth*, 1 Kin. 21:8–13. *Jehu*, 2 Kin. 9:14–24. *Servants of Joash, against Joash*, 2 Kin. 12:20. *People in Jerusalem, against Amaziah*, 2 Kin. 14:19; 2 Chr. 25:27. *Shallum, against Zachariah*, 2 Kin. 15:10. *Pekah, against Pekahiah*, 2 Kin. 15:23–25. *Hoshea, against Pekah*, 2 Kin. 15:30. *Servants of Amon, against Amon*, 2 Kin. 21:23. *Bigthan and Teresh, against Ahasuerus*, Esth. 2:21–23. *Chaldeans, against Shadrach, Meshach, and Abed-nego*, Dan. 3:8–18; *against Daniel*, Dan. 6:4–17.
*Against Jesus*, Jer. 11:9, 19; Matt. 12:14; 21:38–41; 26:3, 4; 27:1, 2; Mark 3:6. *Against Paul*, Acts 18:12; 23:12–15.
Falsely accused of: *Jonathan*, 1 Sam. 22:8.
See footnotes: COMPLICITY, Prov. 29:24; CONNIVANCE, Lev. 20:4.

v.15–857 BC
See footnote, *Time*, Rev. 10:6.

15
o *Tirzah*, 1 Kin. 14:17.
p *Gibbethon*, 1 Kin. 15:27.
q *Philistines*, Gen. 26:14.

16
r *Captain*, Num. 31:48.
s *Armies, how officered*, Deut. 11:4.

17
t *Siege, instances of*, Deut. 28:53.

18
u *Palace*, 1 Kin. 21:1.

19
v *Rulers, wicked, instances of*, Ex. 18:21.
w *Jeroboam*, 1 Kin. 14:5.

20
x *Treason, instances of*, 2 Kin. 11:14.

15 ¶ In the twenty and seventh
year of [d]Ā′sȧ king of [e]Jū′dah did
[a]Zĭm′rī reign seven days in [o]Tĭr′-
zah. And the people *were* encamped against [p]Gĭb′be-thŏn,
which *belonged* to the [q]Phĭ-lĭs′-
tīneș.
16 And the people *that were* encamped heard[C] say, [a]Zĭm′rī hath
*conspired, and hath also slain
the king: wherefore all Ĭș′ra-el
made †Ŏm′rī, the [r,s]captain of
the host, king over Ĭș′ra-el that
day in the camp.
17 And †Ŏm′rī went up from
[p]Gĭb′be-thŏn, and all Ĭș′ra-el
with him, and they [t]besieged
[o]Tĭr′zah.
18 And it came to pass, when
[a]Zĭm′rī saw that the city was
taken[C], that he went into the
[u]palace of the king's house, and
burnt the king's house over him
with fire, and ‡died,
19 For his sins which [v]he sinned
in doing evil in the sight of the
LORD, in walking in the way of
[w]Jĕr-o-bō′am, and in his sin
which he did, to [j,k]make Ĭș′ra-el
to sin.
20 Now the rest of the acts of
Zĭm′rī, and his [x]treason that he
wrought, *are* they not written in
the [m]book of the chronicles of
the kings of [n]Ĭș′ra-el?
21 ¶ Then were the people of
[n]Ĭș′ra-el divided into two parts:
half of the people followed Tĭb′-
nī the son of Gī′năth, to make
him king; and half followed
†Ŏm′rī.

22 But the people that followed
†Ŏm′rī prevailed[C] against the
people that followed Tĭb′nī the
son of Gī′năth: so Tĭb′nī died,
and Ŏm′rī reigned.
23 ¶ In the thirty and first year
of Ā′sȧ king of Jū′dah began
†Ŏm′rī to reign over [n]Ĭș′ra-el,
twelve years: six years reigned
he in [o]Tĭr′zah.
24 And he bought the hill ‖Sȧ-
mā′rĭ-ȧ of Shē′mēr for two [y]tal-
ents[C] of [z]silver, and built on the
hill, and called the name of
the city which he built, after the
name of Shē′mēr, owner of the
hill, Sȧ-mā′rĭ-ȧ.
25 ¶ But †Ŏm′rī [a]wrought[C] evil
in the eyes of the LORD, and did
worse than all that *were* before
him.
26 For he walked in all the way
of [b]Jĕr-o-bō′am the son of Nē′-
băt, and in his sin wherewith he
[c,d]made Ĭș′ra-el to sin, to provoke the LORD God of Ĭș′ra-el
to anger with their vanities.[C]
27 Now the rest of the acts of
†Ŏm′rī which he did, and his
might that he shewed, *are* they
not written in the [e]book of the
chronicles of the kings of [f]Ĭș′-
ra-el?
28 So †Ŏm′rī [g]slept with his
fathers, and was [h]buried in
‖Sȧ-mā′rĭ-ȧ: and §Ā′hăb his son
reigned in his stead.
29 ¶ And in the thirty and
eighth year of [i]Ā′sȧ king of
[j]Jū′dah began §Ā′hăb the son
of †Ŏm′rī to reign over [f]Ĭș′ra-

v.22–856 BC
See footnote, *Time*, Rev. 10:6.

v.23–853 BC

24
y *Talent*, Ex. 38:25.
z *Money, silver used as*, Jer. 32:9.

25
a *Rulers, wicked, instances of*, Ex. 18:21.

26
b *Jeroboam*, 1 Kin. 14:5.
c *Temptation, leading into*, Luke 11:4.
d *Influence, evil*, 1 Cor. 7:14.

27
e *Book*, Num. 5:23.
f *Israel, after the revolt*, 1 Kin. 12:1.

28
g *Death, called sleep*, Num. 23:10.
h *Burial*, Acts 8:2.

29
i *Asa*, 1 Kin. 15:8.
v.29–846 BC
j *Judah, kingdom of*, 2 Chr. 11:17.

† **OMRI,** king of Israel. *Was commander of the army of Israel, and was proclaimed king by the army upon news of assassination of king Elah*, 1 Kin. 16:16. *Slays king Zimri; defeats his rival, Tibni, and establishes himself*, 1 Kin. 16:17–22. *Built city of Samaria*, 1 Kin. 16:24. *Surrendered cities to king of Syria*, 1 Kin. 20:34. *Reigned twelve years*, 1 Kin. 16:23. *Wicked reign and death of*, 1 Kin. 16:23–28. *Denounced by Micah*, Mic. 6:16.

‡ **SUICIDE.** *Temptation to, of the Philippian jailer*, Acts 16:27.
See footnote, DEATH, *Desired*, Num. 23:10.
**Instances of:** *Samson*, Judg. 16:29, 30. *Saul and his armor-bearer*, 1 Sam. 21:4, 5; 1 Chr. 10:4, 5. *Ahithophel*, 2 Sam. 17:23. *Zimri*, 1 Kin. 16:18. *Judas*, Matt. 27:5; Acts 1:18.

‖ **SAMARIA** (*watch mountain*). *City of, built by Omri*, 1 Kin. 16:24. *Capital of the kingdom of the ten tribes*, 1 Kin. 16:29; 22:51; 2 Kin. 13:1, 10; 15:8. *Besieged by Ben-hadad*, 1 Kin. 20:1–22; 2 Kin. 6:24–33; 7. *The king of Syria is led into, by Elisha, who miraculously blinds him and his army*, 2 Kin. 6:8–23. *Ahab ruled in*, 1 Kin. 16:29. *Besieged by Shalmaneser, king of Assyria, three years; taken; the people carried away to Halah and Habor, cities of the Medes*, 2 Kin. 17:5, 6; 18:9–11.
*Idolatry of*, 1 Kin. 16:32; 2 Kin. 13:6. *Temple of, destroyed and worshipers of Baal slain*, 2 Kin. 10:17–28; 23:19.
*Visited by Philip, Peter, and John*, Acts 8:5–25.

§ **AHAB.** *King of Israel*, 1 Kin. 16:29. *Marries Jezebel*, 1 Kin. 16:31. *Idolatry of*, 1 Kin. 16:30–33; 18:18, 19; 21:25, 26. *Other wickedness of*, 2 Kin. 3:2; 2 Chr. 21:6; 22:3, 4; Mic. 6:16. *Reproved by Elijah*, 1 Kin. 17:1; 18:17, 18. *Assembles the prophets of Baal*, 1 Kin. 18:17–46. *Fraudulently confiscates Naboth's vineyard*, 1 Kin. 21:1–26. *His repentance*, 1 Kin. 21:27–29. *Defeats Ben-hadad*, 1 Kin. 20. *Reigned twenty-two years*, 1 Kin. 16:29. *Closing history and death of*, 1 Kin. 22; 2 Chr. 18. *Succeeded by his son, Ahaziah*, 1 Kin. 22:40. *Prophecies against*, 1 Kin. 20:42; 21:19–24; 22:19–28; 2 Kin. 9:8, 25, 26. *Sons of, murdered*, 2 Kin. 10:1–8.

el: and Ā'hăb the son of Ŏm'rī
reigned over Ĭs'ra-el in ‖Să-mā'-
rĭ-ȧ twenty and two years.
30 And §Ā'hăb the son of
†Ŏm'rī [a]did evil in the sight of
the LORD above[G] all that *were*
before him.
31 And it came to pass, as if it
had been a light thing for him to
walk in the sins of [b]Jĕr-o-bō'am
the son of Nē'băt, that he took
to wife +Jĕz'e-bĕl the daughter
of Ĕth-bā'al king of the [k]Zī-dō'-
nĭ-ans, and went and [l]served
[m]Bā'al, and worshipped him.[Q]
32 And he reared up an [n]altar
for [m]Bā'al in the house of Bā'al,
which he had built in ‖Să-mā'rĭ-ȧ.
33 And §Ā'hăb made [2]a [o]grove[G];
and Ā'hăb [a]did more to provoke
the LORD God of Ĭs'ra-el to anger than all the kings of Ĭs'ra-el
that were before him.
34 ¶ In his days did [p]Hī'el
the Bĕth'-el-īte build [q]Jĕr'ĭ-chō:
he laid the foundation thereof
[3]in Ā-bī'ram his firstborn, and
set up the gates thereof [4]in his
youngest *son* Sē'gub, according
to the [r]word of the LORD, which
he [s]spake by [t]Jŏsh'u-ȧ the son
of Nŭn.

## CHAPTER 17

*Elijah, having prophesied against Ahab, is sent to the brook Cherith, where the ravens feed him. 8 He is sent to the widow of Zarephath. 17 He restores the widow's son to life.*

AND *Ē-lī'jah the Tĭsh'bīte,
*who was* of the inhabitants
of [a]Gĭl'e-ăd, said unto [b]Ā'hăb,
*As* the LORD God of Ĭs'ra-el
liveth, before whom I stand,
[c]there shall not be [d]dew nor
rain these years, but according
to my word.[Q]
2 And the word of the LORD
[e]came unto *him, saying,
3 Get thee hence[G], and turn thee
eastward, and hide thyself by the
[f]brook Chē'rĭth, that *is* before
[g]Jôr'dan.
4 And it shall be, *that* thou shalt
drink of the [f]brook; and [h]I have
commanded the [i]ravens to [j]feed
[k]thee there.
5 So *he went and [l]did according unto the word of the LORD:
for he went and dwelt[G] by the
[f]brook Chē'rĭth, that *is* before
[g]Jôr'dan.
6 And the [i]ravens [m]brought
him bread and flesh in the morning, and bread and flesh in the
evening; and he drank of the
[f]brook.[S]
7 And it came to pass after a
while, that the [f]brook dried up,
because there had been [n]no rain
in the [o]land.
8 ¶ And the word of the LORD
[e]came unto *him, saying,
9 [Q]Arise, get thee to [p,q]Zăr'e-
phăth, which *belongeth* to [r]Zī'-
dŏn, and dwell there: behold,
[h]I have commanded a [s]widow
[t]woman there to sustain[G] thee.
10 So *he arose and went to
[p]Zăr'e-phăth. And when he
came to the gate of the city,
behold, the [s]widow woman *was*

v 29–846 BC

31
k *Zidon*, Ezek. 28:21.
l *Idolatry*, 1 Sam. 15:23.
m *Baal*, 2 Kin. 17:16.

32
n *Altar, used in, idolatrous worship*, Gen. 8:20.

33
o *Groves*, Judg. 6:28.
2 R. V. the Asherah;

34
p Josh. 6:26.
q *Jericho*, Num. 22:1.
r *Prophecies, fulfilled*, Dan. 9:24.
s *Prophets, inspiration of*, Isa. 3:2.
t *Joshua*, Josh. 1:1.
3 R. V. with the loss of Abiram
4 R. V. with the loss of his youngest

1
a *Gilead*, Deut. 3:13.
b *Ahab*, 1 Kin. 16:29.
c Luke 4:25.
d *Dew, absence of*, Dan. 4:15.

2
e *Prophets, inspiration of*, Isa. 3:2.

3
f *Brook, Cherith*, Deut. 8:7.
g *Jordan*, Gen. 32:10.

4
h *God, providence of*, Gen. 2:2.
i *Raven*, Job 38:41.
j *Temporal Blessings, from God*, v. 6; Psa. 103:2.
k *Minister, God's care of*, v. 6; Rom. 15:16.

5
l *Obedience, exemplified*, Heb. 5:8.

6
m *Miracles*, Luke 23:8.

7
n *Drought*, Gen. 31:40.
o *Canaan, famines in*, Gen. 37:1.

9
p Or, *Sarepta*, Luke 4:26.
q Luke 4:26.
r *Zidon*, Ezek. 28:21.
s *Widow*, 2 Sam. 14:5.
t *Women, good, instances of*, Prov. 31:10.

**+ JEZEBEL.** *Daughter of Ethbaal, a king of Zidon, and wife of Ahab*, 1 Kin. 16:31. *Was an idolatress and persecuted the prophets of God*, 1 Kin. 18:4, 13, 19; 2 Kin. 3:2, 13; 9:7, 22. *Vowed to kill Elijah*, 1 Kin. 19:1–3. *Wickedly accomplishes the death of Naooth*, 1 Kin. 21:5–16. *Death of, foretold*, 1 Kin. 21:23; 2 Kin. 9:10. *Death of, at the hand of Jehu*, 2 Kin. 9:30–37.

*** ELIJAH,** the Tishbite, a Gileadite and prophet, called ELIAS in the authorized version of the N. T. *Persecuted by Ahab*, 1 Kin. 17:1–7; 18:7–10. *Escapes to the wilderness, where he is miraculously fed by ravens*, 1 Kin. 17:1–7. *By divine direction goes to Zarephath, where he is sustained in the household of a widow, whose meal and oil are miraculously increased*, 1 Kin. 17:8–16. *Returns, and sends a message to Ahab*, 1 Kin. 18:1–16. *Meets Ahab and directs him to assemble the prophets of Baal*, 1 Kin. 18:17–20. *Derisively challenges the priests of Baal to offer sacrifices*, 1 Kin. 18:25–29. *Slays the prophets of Baal*, 1 Kin. 18:40. *Escapes from the fierce wrath of Jezebel to the wilderness, thence to Mt. Horeb*, 1 Kin. 19:1–18. *Fasts forty days*, 1 Kin. 19:8. *Despondency and murmuring of*, 1 Kin. 19:10, 14. *Consolation given to*, 1 Kin. 19:11–18. *Flees to the wilderness of Damascus; directed to anoint Hazael king over Syria, Jehu king over Israel, and Elisha to be a prophet in his own stead*, 1 Kin. 19:9–21.

*Personal aspect of*, 2 Kin. 1:8. *Piety of*, 1 Kin. 19:10, 14; Luke 1:17; Rom. 11:2; Jas. 5:17, 18. *Is translated*, 2 Kin. 2:11. *Appears to Jesus at his transfiguration*, Matt. 17:3, 4; Mark 9:4; Luke 9:30. *Ante-type of John the Baptist*, Mal. 4:5; Matt. 11:14; 16:14; 17:10–12; Mark 9:12, 13; Luke 1:17; John 1:21–25.

**Miracles of:** *Increases the oil of the widow of Zarephath*, 1 Kin. 17:14–16. *Raises from the dead the son of the woman of Zarephath*, 1 Kin. 17:17–24. *Causes rain after a drought of three and a half years*, 1 Kin. 18:41–45; Luke 4:25; Jas. 5:17, 18. *Causes fire to consume the sacrifice*, 1 Kin. 18:24, 36–38. *Calls fire down upon the soldiers of Ahaziah*, 2 Kin. 1:10–12; Luke 9:54.

**Prophecies of:** *Foretells, a drought*, 1 Kin. 17:1; *the destruction of Ahab and his house*, 1 Kin. 21:17–29; 2 Kin. 9:25–37; *the death of Ahaziah*, 2 Kin. 1:2–17; *the plague sent as a judgment upon the people in the time of Jehoram, king of Israel*, 2 Chr. 21:12–15.

there gathering of sticks: and he
called to her, and said, Fetch
me, I pray thee, a little †water in
a vessel, that I may drink.
11 And as she was going to
fetch *it,* he called to her, and
said, Bring me, I pray thee, a
morsel of [u]bread in thine
hand.
12 And she said, *As* the LORD
thy God liveth, I have not a
cake, but an handful of meal in
a [v]barrel, and a little [w]oil in a
cruse: and, behold, I *am* gathering two sticks, that I may go in
and dress[C] it for me and my son,
that we may eat it, and die.
13 And *Ē-lī'jah said unto her,
Fear not; go *and* do as thou hast
said: but make me thereof a little cake first, and bring *it* unto
me, and after make for thee and
for thy son.
14 For thus saith the LORD
God of Iș'ra-el, The [v]barrel of
meal shall not waste[C], neither
shall the cruse of [w]oil fail, until
the day *that* the LORD sendeth
rain upon the earth.[S]
15 And she went and [x]did according to the saying of Ē-lī'jah:
and she, and he, and her house,
did eat *many* days.
16 *And* [y,z]the barrel of meal
wasted[C] not, neither did the cruse
of [a]oil fail, according to the word
of the LORD, which he spake by
Ē-lī'jah.[S]
17 ¶[Q]And it came to pass after
these things, *that* the son of
the woman, the mistress of the
house, fell sick; and his sickness
was so sore[C], that there was no
breath left in him.
18 And she said unto *Ē-lī'jah,
What have I to do with thee, O

11
*u Bread,* Ezek. 4:13.

12
*v* 1 Kin. 18:33.
*w Oil,* Deut. 12:17.

15
*x Faith, instances of,* Mark 11:22.

16
*y Prophecies, fulfilled,* Dan. 9:24.
*z Hospitality, rewarded, instances of,* vs. 10–24; Rom. 12:13.

*a Oil,* Deut. 12:17.

thou man of God? art thou
come unto me to call my [b]sin to
remembrance, and to slay my
son?[Q]
19 And he said unto her, Give
me thy son. And he took him
out of her bosom, and carried
him up into a [c]loft[C], where he
abode, and laid him upon his
own bed.
20 And he [d]cried unto the
LORD, and said, O LORD my
God, hast thou also brought evil
upon the widow with whom I sojourn, by slaying her son?
21 And he stretched himself
upon the child three times, and
cried unto the LORD, and said,
O LORD my God, I pray thee,
[d]let this child's soul come into
him again.[Q]
22 And the LORD [e,f]heard the
voice of *Ē-lī'jah; and the soul
of the child came into him again,
and [g,h]he revived.[S]
23 And *Ē-lī'jah took the child,
and brought him down out of
the chamber[C] into the house, and
delivered him unto his mother:
and Ē-lī'jah said, See, thy son
liveth.[Q]
24 And the woman said to
*Ē-lī'jah, Now [i]by this I know
that thou *art* a man[C] of God, *and*
that the word of the LORD in thy
mouth *is* truth.[Q]

## CHAPTER 18

*In the extremity of famine Elijah is sent to Ahab, and meets Obadiah, 9 who brings Ahab to him. 17 Elijah reproves Ahab. 20 At Mount Carmel Baal's prophets are convinced by fire from heaven, and are slain. 41 Elijah by prayer obtains rain.*

AND it came to pass *after*
many days, that the word
of the LORD came to [a]Ē-lī'jah in
the third year, saying, Go, shew

18
*b Conviction of Sin,* John 16:8.

19
*c House, chambers in,* Esth. 8:1.

20
*d Temporal Blessings, prayer for,* Psa. 103:2.

22
*e Intercession, answered,* Jer. 27:18.
*f Prayer, answered,* Acts 6:4.
*g Dead, raised to life,* 2 Kin. 4:32.
*h Children, miracles in behalf of,* vs. 17–23; Mark 10:14.

24
*i Miracles, convincing effect of,* Luke 23:8.

1
*a Elijah,* 1 Kin. 17:1.

† **WATER.** *Creation of,* Psa. 95:5; 148:4, 5. *Covered the whole earth,* Gen. 1:9. *Daily allowance of,* Ezek. 4:11. *City supply of,* 2 Kin. 20:20. *Vision of, by Ezekiel,* Ezek. 47:1–5. *Of separation,* Num. 19:2–22. *Libation of,* 1 Sam. 7:6. *Irrigation with,* Deut. 11:10; Eccl. 2:6; Isa. 58:11. *Miraculously supplied, to the Israelites,* Ex. 17:1, 6; Num. 20:11; *to Samson,* Judg. 15:19; *to Jehoshaphat's army,* 2 Kin. 3:16–20. *Purified by Elisha,* 2 Kin. 2:19–22. *Red Sea divided,* Ex. 14:21, 22. *The river Jordan divided,* Josh. 3:14–17; 2 Kin. 2:6–8, 14. *Jesus walks on,* Matt. 14:25. *Changed, to blood,* Ex. 7:17–25; Rev. 16:3–6; *to wine,* John 2:1–11. *Of affliction,* 1 Kin. 22:27; 2 Chr. 18:26; Isa. 30:20.

**Figurative:** *Water of life,* John 4:10–14; 7:37–39; Rev. 21:6; 22:17. *Of adversity,* 2 Sam. 22:17; Psa. 69:1; Isa. 43:2. *Of spiritual cleansing,* Ezek. 36:25. *Of salvation,* Isa. 12:3; 44:3, 4; 49:10; 55:1; Jer. 2:13; John 7:38. *Of domestic love,* Prov. 5:15.

**Symbolical,** Isa. 8:7, 8; Rev. 8:11; 12:15; 16:4; 17:1, 15.

b *Ahab*, 1 Kin. 16:29.

2

c *Famine, instances of*, 2 Kin. 8:1.

d *Samaria*, Isa. 7:9.

3

e *Fear of God*, Acts 9:31.

4

f *Jezebel*, 1 Kin. 16:31.

g *Women, wicked, instances of*, Prov. 31:10.

h *Martyrdom, instances of*, Rev. 17:6.

i *Persecution, instances of*, John 15:20.

j *Zeal, instances of*, 2 Cor. 7:11.

k *Kindness, instances of*, Acts 28:2.

l *Love, of man for man, instances of*, 1 John 4:7.

m *Cave*, Judg. 6:2.

thyself unto [b]Ā'hăb; and I will
send rain upon the earth.[Q]
2 And [a]Ē-lī'jah went to shew
himself unto [b]Ā'hăb. And *there*
*was* a sore[C] [c]famine in [d]Să-mā'rĭ-ȧ.
3 And [b]Ā'hăb called Ō-ba-
dī'ah, which *was* the governor
of *his* house. (Now Ō-ba-dī'ah
[e]feared the LORD greatly:
4 For it was *so*, when [f,g]Jĕz'e-
bĕl [h,i]cut[C] off the prophets of the
LORD, that Ō-ba-dī'ah [j]took an
hundred prophets, and [k,l]hid
them by fifty in a [m]cave, and fed
them with bread and water.)[Q]
5 And [b]Ā'hăb said unto Ō-ba-
dī'ah, Go into the land, unto all
fountains of water, and unto all
brooks: peradventure[C] we may
find grass to save the horses and
mules alive, that we lose not all
the beasts.
6 So they divided the land between them to pass throughout
it: [b]Ā'hăb went one way by himself, and Ō-ba-dī'ah went another way by himself.
7 ¶ And as Ō-ba-dī'ah was in
the way, behold, [a]Ē-lī'jah met
him: and he knew him, and fell[C]
on his face, and said, *Art*[C] thou
that my lord Ē-lī'jah?
8 And he answered him, I *am*:
go, tell thy lord, Behold, [a]Ē-lī'-
jah *is here*.
9 And he said, What have I
sinned, that thou wouldest deliver thy servant into the hand[G] of
Ā'hăb, to slay me?
10 *As* the LORD thy God liveth,
*there is no nation or kingdom,
whither[G] my lord hath not sent to
seek thee: and when they said,
*He is* not *there*; he took[G] an oath
of the kingdom and nation, that
they found thee not.
11 And now thou sayest, Go, tell
thy lord, Behold, [a]Ē-lī'jah *is here*.
12 And it shall come to pass, *as*
*soon as* I am gone from [a]thee,
that the [1]Spirit of the LORD
shall carry thee whither[G] I know
not; and *so* when I come and
tell [b]Ā'hăb, and he cannot find
thee, he shall slay me: but I thy
servant fear the LORD from my
[n]youth.[T Q]
13 Was it not told my lord what
I [j]did when [f,g]Jĕz'e-bĕl [h,i]slew[G]
the prophets of the LORD, how I
[k,l]hid an hundred men of the
LORD's prophets by fifty in a
[m]cave, and fed them with bread
and water?[Q]
14 And now thou sayest, Go,
tell thy lord, Behold, [a]Ē-lī'jah *is*
*here*: and he shall slay me.
15 And [a]Ē-lī'jah said, *As* the
LORD of hosts liveth, before
whom I stand, I will surely shew
myself unto him to day.
16 So Ō-ba-dī'ah went to meet
[b]Ā'hăb, and told him: and Ā'hăb
went to meet Ē-lī'jah.
17 ¶ And it came to pass, when
[b]Ā'hăb saw Ē-lī'jah, that Ā'hăb
[o]said unto him, *Art*[G] thou he that
troubleth Ĭs'ra-el?[Q]
18 And he [p]answered, I have
not troubled Ĭs'ra-el; [q]but [b]thou,
and thy father's house, in that ye
have forsaken the commandments of the LORD, and thou
hast followed [r]Bā'al-ĭm.
19 Now therefore send, *and*
gather to me all Ĭs'ra-el unto
mount [s]Cär'mel, and the [t]proph-
ets of [r]Bā'al four hundred and
fifty, and the prophets of the
[2,u]groves[G] four hundred, which
eat at Jĕz'e-bĕl's table.
20 So [b]Ā'hăb sent unto all the
children of Ĭs'ra-el, and gathered the prophets together unto
mount [s]Cär'mel.
21 ¶ And [a]Ē-lī'jah came unto
all the people, and said, How
long †halt ye between two opin-

12

n *Children, good, instances of*, Mark 10:14.

1 R. V. spirit

17

o *False Accusation, instances of*, 2 Tim. 3:3.

18

p *Minister, expostulates with rulers*, Rom. 15:16.

q *Reproof*, Prov. 17:10.

r *Baal*, 2 Kin. 17:16.

19

s *Carmel*, Jer. 46:18.

t *National Religion, ministers supported by the state*, Gal. 1:13.

u *Groves*, Judg. 6:28.

2 R. V. Asherah

* **EXTRADITION**, 1 Kin. 18:7, 10; Jer. 26:21–23; Acts 9:2, 14; 22:5.

† **INDECISION**, 1 Kin. 18:21; Jas. 1:6–8; 4:17; Rev. 3:15.

See footnotes: DECISION, Isa. 50:7; INSTABILITY, Jas. 1:8; LUKEWARMNESS, Rev. 3:16.

**Instances of:** *Moses at the Red Sea*, Ex. 14:15. *Joshua after the defeat at Ai*, Josh. 7:6–10. *Felix*, Acts 24:25.

ions ? if the LORD *be* God, [v,w]fol-
low him: but if Bā′al, *then* follow
him. And the people answered
him not a word.[s]
22 Then said [a]Ē-lī′jah unto the
people, I, *even* I only, remain a
prophet of the LORD; but Bā′-
al's prophets *are* four hundred
and fifty men.
23 Let them therefore give us
two bullocks; and let them
choose one bullock for themselves, and cut it in pieces, and
lay *it* on wood, and put no fire
*under*: and I will dress[G] the other
bullock, and lay *it* on wood, and
put no fire *under*:
24[Q] And [x]call[G] ye on the name of
your gods, and [a]I will call on the
name of the LORD: and the God
that [y]answereth by fire, let him
be God. And all the people
answered and said, It is well
spoken.
25 And Ē-lī′jah said unto the
prophets of [r]Bā′al, Choose you
one bullock for yourselves, and
dress[G] *it* first; for ye *are* many;
and call on the name of your
gods, but put no fire *under*.
26 And they took the bullock
which was given them, and they
dressed[G] *it*, and [z]called on the
name of [a]Bā′al from morning
even until noon, saying, O Bā′al,
hear[G] us. But *there was* no voice,
nor any that answered. And
they leaped [3]upon the [b]altar
which was made.
27 And it came to pass at noon,
that [c]Ē-lī′jah ‡mocked them,
and said, [d]Cry aloud: for he *is* a
god; either he is talking, or he is
pursuing, or he is in a journey,
*or* peradventure[G] he sleepeth, and
must be awaked.
28 And they cried aloud, and
[e]cut themselves after their manner with knives and lancets[G], till
the blood gushed out upon them.
29 And it came to pass, when
midday was past, and they
prophesied until the *time* of the
offering of the *evening* [f]sacrifice,
that *there was* neither voice, nor
any to answer, nor any that regarded.[G]
30 [g]And [c]Ē-lī′jah said unto all
the people, Come near unto me.
And all the people came near
unto him. And he repaired the
[h]altar of the LORD *that was*
broken down.
31 And [c]Ē-lī′jah took twelve
stones, according to the number
of the [i]tribes of the sons of [j]Jā′-
cob, unto whom the word of the
LORD came, saying, Ĭṣ′ra-el
shall be thy name:
32 And with the stones he built
an [h]altar in the name of the
LORD: and he made a trench
about the altar, as great as would
contain two [k]measures[G] of seed.
33 And he put the wood in
order, and cut the bullock in
pieces, and laid *him* on the
wood, and said, Fill four [l]bar-
rels with water, and pour *it* on
the [m]burnt [4]sacrifice, and on the
wood.
34 And he said, Do *it* the second time. And they did *it* the
second time. And he said, Do *it*
the third time. And they did *it*
the third time.
35 And the water ran round
about the [h]altar; and he filled
the trench also with water.
36 And it came to pass at *the*
*time of* the offering of the *even-*
*ing* sacrifice, that [c]Ē-lī′jah the
prophet came near, and [n]said,
LORD God of Ā′brā-hăm, Ī′ṣaac
and of Ĭṣ′ra-el, let it be known
this day that thou *art* God in

**21**
v *Choice*, 2 Sam. 24:12.
w *Decision*, Isa. 50:7.

**24**
x *Prayer, test of*, Acts 6:4.
y *Miracles, convincing effect of*, Luke 23:8.

**26**
z *Idolatry, customs of*, 1 Sam. 15:23.

a *Idol, prayer to, unanswered*, 1 Kin. 15:12.
b *Altar, used in idolatrous worship*, Gen. 8:20.
3 R. V. about

**27**
c *Elijah*, 1 Kin. 17:1.
d *Sarcasm, instances of*, Judg. 10:14.

**28**
e *Idolatry, customs of*, 1 Kin. 15:23.

**29**
f *Offerings, burnt, offered in idolatrous worship*, Lev. 6:17.

**30**
g *Faith, instances of*, Mark 11:22.
h *Altar*, Gen. 8:20.

**31**
i *Israel, tribes of*, Ex. 4:22.
j *Jacob*, Gen. 27:11.

**32**
k *Measure, dry*, Deut. 25:15.

**33**
l 1 Kin. 17:12, 14, 16.
m *Offerings, burnt*, Lev. 6:17.
4 R. V. offering.

**36**
n *Prayer, pleas offered in*, Acts 6:4.

‡ **MOCKING. Instances of:** *At affliction*, Job 12:5; Prov. 17:5. *Ishmael, at Sarah*, Gen. 21:9. *Elijah, at the priests of Baal*, 1 Kin. 18:27. *Zedekiah, at Micaiah*, 1 Kin. 22:24. *Children, at Elisha*, 2 Kin. 2:23. *The false friends, at Job*, Job 15:12; 30:1. *Rabshakeh mocks God*, Isa. 36:18–20; 37:22–38. *The Ammonites mocked God*, Ezek. 25:3. *Tyre, at Jerusalem*, Ezek. 26:2. *The obdurately wicked mock*, Isa. 28:15, 22; 2 Pet. 3:3. *The persecutors, at Jesus*, Matt. 26:67, 68; 27:28–31, 39–44; Mark 10:34; 14:65; 15:17–20, 29–32; Luke 23:11; John 19:2, 3, 5; 1 Pet. 2:23.
See footnote, SCOFFING, Hab. 1:10.
**Figurative,** Prov. 1:26.

Iș′ra-el, and *that* I *am* thy servant, and *that* I have done all
these things at thy word.[s]
37 [n]Hear me, O LORD, hear
me, that this people may know
that thou *art* the LORD God, and
*that* thou hast turned their heart
back again.[s]
38 [o]Then [p]the [q]fire of the
LORD fell, and consumed the
[m]burnt [4]sacrifice, and the wood,
and the stones, and the dust, and
licked up the water that *was* in
the trench.[s]
39 And when all the people saw
*it*, [r]they fell on their faces: and
they said, The LORD, he *is* the
God; the LORD, he *is* the God.[Q]
40 And [c]Ē-lī′jah said unto
them, [s]Take the prophets of
[t]Bā′al; let not one of them escape. And they took them: and
Ē-lī′jah brought them down to
the brook [u]Kī′shŏn, and [v]slew
them there.
41 ¶ And [c]Ē-lī′jah said unto
[w]Ā′hăb, Get thee up, eat and
drink; for *there is* a sound of
abundance of [x]rain.
42[Q] So [w]Ā′hăb went up to eat
and to drink. And Ē-lī′jah went
up to the top of [y]Cär′mel; and
he [z]cast himself down upon the
earth, and put his face between
his knees,
43 And said to his servant, Go
up now, look toward the sea.
And he went up, and looked,
and said, *There is* nothing. And
he said, Go again [a]seven times.
44 And it came to pass at the
[a]seventh time, that he said, Behold, there ariseth a little [b]cloud
out of the sea, like a man's hand.
And he said, Go up, say unto
[c]Ā′hăb, Prepare *thy chariot*, and
get thee down, that the [d]rain
stop thee not.
45 And it came to pass in the
meanwhile, that the heaven was
black with clouds and wind, and
there was [e]a great rain. And
[c]Ā′hăb rode and went to ‖Jĕz′-
re-el.[Q]
46 And the [f]hand of the LORD
was on [g]Ē-lī′jah; and he girded
up his loins, and ran before
[c]Ā′hăb to the entrance of ‖Jĕz′-
re-el.[Q]

## CHAPTER 19

*Elijah, threatened by Jezebel, flees to Beer-sheba. 4 In the wilderness he is comforted by an angel. 9 God's appearance unto him at Horeb. 15 He is sent to anoint Hazael, Jehu, and Elisha. 19 Elisha follows Elijah.*

AND [a]Ā′hăb told [b]Jĕz′e-bĕl all
that [c]Ē-lī′jah had done,
and withal[c] how he had slain
all the prophets with the sword.
2 Then [b,d]Jĕz′e-bĕl sent a messenger unto [c]Ē-lī′jah, saying,
[e,f,g]So let the gods do *to me*, and
more also, if I make not thy life
as the life of one of them by to
morrow about this time.
3 And when he saw *that*, [h]he
arose, and went for his life, and
came to [i]Bē′er-shē′bȧ, which *be-*
*longeth* to Jū′dah, and left his
servant there.
4 ¶ But [c]he himself went a
*day's journey into the wilder-
ness, and came and sat down
under a [j]juniper tree: and [k]he
requested for himself that he
might [l]die; and said, It is
enough; now, O LORD, take
away my life; for I *am* not better
than my fathers.
5 And as [c]he lay and slept under a [j]juniper tree, behold, then
an [m]angel touched him, and said
unto him, Arise *and* eat.
6 And [c]he looked, and, behold,
*there was* a [n,o]cake baken[c] on the
coals, and a cruse[c] of [p]water at
his head. And he did eat and
drink, and laid him down again.
7 And the [m]angel of the LORD

**38**
o *Prayer, answered,* Acts 6:4.
p *Miracles,* Luke 23:8.
q *Fire, miraculous,* Ex. 12:8.

**39**
r *Religious Revivals, instances of,* Hab. 3:2.

**40**
s *Intolerance,* Num. 11:28.
t *Baal,* 2 Kin. 17:16.
u *Kishon,* Judg. 4:7.
v *Massacre,* Esth. 3:13.

**41**
w *Ahab,* 1 Kin. 16:29.
x *Rain,* 2 Sam. 1:21.

**42**
y *Carmel,* Jer. 46:18.
z *Prayer, postures in,* Acts 6:4.

**43**
a *Seven,* Gen. 7:2.

**44**
b *Meteorology, weather affected by good men's prayers,* Matt. 16:2.
c *Ahab,* 1 Kin. 16:29.
d *Rain,* 2 Sam. 1:21.

**45**
e *Miracles,* Luke 23:8.

**46**
f *Hand, figurative,* Ezra 10:19.
g *Elijah,* 1 Kin. 17:1.

**1**
a *Ahab,* 1 Kin. 16:29.
b *Jezebel,* 1 Kin. 16:31.
c *Elijah,* 1 Kin. 17:1.

**2**
d *Women, wicked, instances of,* Prov. 31:10.
e *Persecution, instances of,* John 15:20.
f *Malice, instances of,* Eph. 4:31.
g *Revenge, exemplified,* Ezek. 25:15.

**3**
h *Prudence, instances of,* 2 Chr. 2:12.
i *Beer-sheba,* Judg. 20:1.

**4**
j Psa. 120:4.
k *Despondency, instances of,* Eccl. 2:20.
l *Death, desired,* Num. 23:10.

**5**
m *Angel, appearances of,* Heb. 1:13.

**6**
n *Temporal Blessings, from God,* Psa. 103:2.
o *Bread,* Ezek. 4:13.
p *Water,* 1 Kin. 17:10.

‖ **JEZREEL.** *A city of Issachar,* Josh. 19:18; 2 Sam. 2:9. *Ahab's residence in,* 1 Kin. 18:45, 46; 21:1. *Naboth's vineyard in, which Ahab took from Naboth by conspiracy and violence through Jezebel's evil counsel,* 1 Kin. 21:1. *Joram's residence in,* 2 Kin. 8:29. *Jehu kills king Ahab, his wife, and friends, and king Ahaziah at,* 2 Kin. 9:15–37; 10:11. *Prophecies concerning,* Hos. 1:4, 5, 11.

* **DAY'S JOURNEY.** *Eighteen or twenty miles,* Ex. 3:18; 1 Kin. 19:4; Jonah 3:4. *Sabbath day's journey, about two thousand paces,* Acts 1:12.

came again the second time, and touched him, and said, Arise *and* eat; because the journey *is* too great for thee.

8 And [c]he arose, and did eat and drink, and went [q]in the strength of that meat[G] [r]forty days and forty nights unto [s]Hō′reb the mount of God.

9 ¶ And [c]he came thither[G] unto a [t]cave, and lodged there; and, behold, the word of the LORD [u]*came* to him, and he said unto him, What doest thou here, [c]Ē-lī′jah?

10 And [c]he said, I have been [v,w]very jealous for the LORD God of hosts: for the children of Ĭs′ra-el have forsaken thy covenant, [x]thrown down thine altars, and slain thy prophets with the sword; and I, *even* I only, am left; and they[Q] seek my life, to take it away.

11 [S]And he said, Go forth, and stand upon the [s]mount before the LORD. And, behold, the LORD passed by, and a great and strong [y]wind rent[G] the mountains, and brake in pieces the rocks before the LORD; *but* the LORD *was* not in the wind: and after the wind an [z]earthquake; *but* the LORD *was* not in the earthquake:

12 And after the [z]earthquake a fire; *but* the LORD *was* not in the fire: and after the fire a still small voice.[S]

13 And it was *so,* when [a]Ē-lī′jah heard *it,* that he wrapped his face in his [b]mantle, and went out, and stood in the entering in of the cave. And, behold, *there came* a voice unto him, and said, What doest thou here, Ē-lī′jah[S]?

14 And he said, I have been [c,d]very jealous[G] for the LORD God of hosts: because the children of Ĭs′ra-el have forsaken thy covenant, thrown down thine altars, and slain thy [e]prophets with the sword; and I, *even* I only, am left; and [f]they seek my life, to take it away.[Q]

15 And the LORD said unto him, Go, return on thy way to the wilderness of [g]Dȧ-măs′-cus: and when thou comest, [h]anoint[G] [i]Hăz′a-el *to be* [j]king over [k]Sўr′ĭ-ȧ:

16 And [l]Jē′hū the son of Nĭm′-shī shalt thou [h]anoint[G] *to be* king over Ĭs′ra-el: and [†,m]Ē-lī′shȧ the son of [n]Shā′phat of [o]Ā′bel–mē-hō′lah shalt thou [p]anoint *to be* prophet in thy room.[G]

17 And it shall come to pass, *that* him that escapeth the sword of [i]Hăz′a-el shall [l]Jē′hū slay: and him that escapeth from the sword of Jē′hū shall [†]Ē-lī′shȧ slay.[S]

18 [q]Yet I have left *me* seven thousand in Ĭs′ra-el, all the knees which have not [r]bowed unto [s]Bā′al, and every mouth which hath not kissed him.[S T Q]

19 ¶ So he departed thence[G], and found [†]Ē-lī′shȧ the son of [n]Shā′phat, who *was* [t]plowing *with* twelve yoke *of* [u]oxen before him, and he with the twelfth: and [a]Ē-lī′jah passed by him, and cast his [v]mantle upon him.

20 And [†]he left the oxen, and

**8**
q *Fasting, prolonged,* Zech. 8:19.
r *Forty, days,* Jonah 3:4.
s *Horeb,* Ex. 3:1.

**9**
t *Cave,* Judg. 6:2.
u *Prophets, inspiration of,* Isa. 3:2.

**10**
v *Faithfulness, instances of,* Luke 16:10.
w *Zeal, instances of,* 2 Cor. 7:11.
x Rom. 11:3.

**11**
y *Meteorology,* Matt. 16:2.
z *Earthquakes,* Isa. 29:6.

**13**
a *Elijah,* 1 Kin. 17:1.
b *Dress,* Zech. 3:3.

**14**
c *Zeal,* 2 Cor. 7:11.
d *Faithfulness, instances of,* Luke 16:10.
e *Minister, trials and persecutions of,* Rom. 15:16.
f *Despondency,* Eccl. 2:20.

**15**
g *Damascus,* Isa. 8:4.
h *Anointing, of kings,* Lev. 8:12.
i *Hazael,* 2 Kin. 9:14.
j *King, appointed by God,* 2 Kin. 3:10.
k *Syria,* 2 Kin. 6:23.

**16**
l *Jehu,* 2 Chr. 22:8.
m *Minister, call of,* Rom. 15:16.
n 2 Kin. 3:11; 6:31.
o 1 Kin. 4:12; Judg. 7:22.
p *Anointing, of prophets,* Lev. 8:12.

**18**
q Rom. 11:4.
r *Idolatry, customs of,* 1 Sam. 15:23.
s *Baal,* 2 Kin. 17:16.

**19**
t *Plow,* Deut. 22:10.
u *Bullock, uses of,* Ex. 29:3.
v *Mantle,* Ezra 9:3.

† **ELISHA** (*God his salvation*), successor to the prophet Elijah. *Elijah instructed to anoint,* 1 Kin. 19:16. *Called by Elijah,* 1 Kin. 19:19. *Ministers to Elijah,* 1 Kin. 19:21. *Witnesses Elijah's translation; receives a double portion of his spirit,* 2 Kin. 2:1–15; 3:11. *Mocked by the children of Beth-el,* 2 Kin. 2:23, 24. *Directs that Jehu be anointed king of Israel,* 2 Kin. 9:1–3. *Life of, sought by Jehoram,* 2 Kin. 6:31–33. *Death of,* 2 Kin. 13:14–20. *Bones of, restore a dead man to life,* 2 Kin. 13:21.

**Miracles of:** *Divides the Jordan,* 2 Kin. 2:14. *Purifies the waters of Jericho by casting salt into the fountain,* 2 Kin. 2:19–22. *Increases the oil of the woman whose sons were to be sold for debt,* 2 Kin. 4:1–7. *Raises from the dead the son of the Shunammite,* 2 Kin. 4:18–37. *Neutralizes the poison of the pottage,* 2 Kin. 4:38–41. *Increases the bread to feed one hundred men,* 2 Kin. 4:42–44. *Heals Naaman the leper,* 2 Kin. 5:1–19; Luke 4:27. *Sends leprosy as a judgment upon Gehazi,* 2 Kin. 5:26, 27. *Recovers the ax that had fallen into a stream by causing it to float,* 2 Kin. 6:6. *Reveals the counsel of the king of Syria,* 2 Kin. 6:8–12. *Opens the eyes of his servant to see the hosts of the Lord,* 2 Kin. 6:17. *Brings blindness upon the army of Syria, and by his consummate tact prevents a battle and establishes a lasting peace,* 2 Kin. 6:18–23.

**Prophecies of:** *Foretells, the birth of a son to the Shunammite woman,* 2 Kin. 4:16; *plenty to the starving in Samaria,* 2 Kin. 7:1; *death of the unbelieving prince,* 2 Kin. 7:2; *seven years' famine in the land of Canaan,* 2 Kin. 8:1–3; *death of Ben-hadad, king of Syria,* 2 Kin. 8:7–10; *elevation of Hazael to the throne,* 2 Kin. 8:11–15; *the victory of Jehoash over Syria,* 2 Kin. 13:14–19.

ran after Ê-lī′jah, and said, [w, x]Let me, I pray thee, kiss my [y]father and my [y]mother, and *then* I will follow thee. And he said unto him, Go back again: for what have I done to thee?[Q]

21 And he returned back from him, and took a yoke of oxen, and slew them, and boiled their flesh with the instruments[G] of the oxen, and [z]gave unto the people, and [a]they did eat. Then he arose, and [b]went after Ê-lī′jah, and ministered unto him.

## CHAPTER 20

*Ben-hadad besieges Samaria. 13 Under direction of a prophet, the Syrians are slain. 22 The next year the Syrians come up against Ahab to Aphek; 28 but are again smitten. 31 The Syrians humbling themselves, Ahab sends Ben-hadad away with a covenant. 35 The prophet by a parable denounces God's judgment against Ahab.*

AND *Bĕn–hā′dăd the king of [a]Sȳr′ĭ-à gathered all his host together: and *there were* thirty and two kings with him, and [b]horses, and [c]chariots: and he went up and [d]besieged [e]Să-mā′rĭ-à, and warred against it.

2 And *he sent [f]messengers to [g]Ā′hăb king of [h]Ĭṣ′ra-el into the city, and said unto him, Thus saith Bĕn–hā′dăd,

3 Thy [i]silver and thy [j]gold *is* mine; thy wives also and thy children, *even* the goodliest[G], *are* mine.

4 And the king of Ĭṣ′ra-el answered and said, My lord, O king, according to thy saying, I *am* thine, and all that I have.

5 And the [f]messengers came again, and said, Thus speaketh *Bĕn–hā′dăd, saying, Although I have sent unto thee, saying, [k, l]Thou shalt deliver me thy [i]silver, and thy [j]gold, and thy wives, and thy children;

6 Yet I will send my servants unto thee to morrow about this time, and they shall search thine house, and the houses of thy servants; and it shall be, *that* whatsoever is pleasant in thine eyes, they shall put *it* in their hand, and take *it* away.

7 Then the king of [h]Ĭṣ′ra-el [m]called all the [n]elders of the land, and said, Mark, I pray you, and see how this *man* seeketh mischief[G]: for he sent unto me for my wives, and for my children, and for my silver, and for my gold; and I denied him not.

8 And all the [n]elders and all the people said unto him, Hearken not *unto him*, nor consent.

9 Wherefore he said unto the messengers of *Bĕn–hā′dăd, Tell my lord the king, All that thou didst send for to thy servant at the first I will do: but this thing I may not do. And the [f]messengers departed, and brought him word again.

10 And Bĕn–hā′dăd sent unto him, and [o]said, The gods do so unto me, and more also, if the dust of Să-mā′rĭ-à shall suffice for handfuls for all the people that follow me.

11 And the king of Ĭṣ′ra-el answered and said, Tell *him*, [p, q, r]Let not him that girdeth on *his* [1]*harness*[G] boast himself as he that putteth it off.

12 And it came to pass, when **Ben–ha′dad* heard this message, as he *was* drinking, he and the kings in the pavilions, that he said unto his servants, Set *yourselves in array*[G]. And they set *themselves in array*[G] against the city.

13 ¶ And, behold, there came a [s]prophet unto [g]Ā′hăb king of [t]Ĭṣ′ra-el, saying, [u]Thus saith the LORD, Hast thou seen all this great multitude? behold, I will deliver it into thine hand this

20
w *Procrastination, instances of,* Acts 24:25.
x *Excuses,* Luke 14:18.
y *Parents, love for,* 2 Cor. 12:14.

21
z *Liberality, instances of,* 1 Tim. 6:18.

a *Feasts,* Mark 12:39.
b *Obedience, instances of,* Heb. 5:8.

1
a *Syria,* 2 Kin. 6:23.
b *Horse,* Job 39:19.
c *Chariot,* Josh. 11:4.
d *Siege,* Deut. 28:53.
e *Samaria,* 1 Kin. 16:24.

2
f *Ambassadors,* Josh. 9:4.
g *Ahab,* 1 Kin. 16:29.
h *Israel, after the revolt,* 1 Kin. 12:1.

3
i *Silver,* 1 Chr. 28:14.
j *Gold,* Ezek. 7:19.

5
k *Government, monarchical, tyranny in,* Isa. 22:21.
l *Oppression,* Eccl. 5:8.

7
m *War, councils of,* Judg. 3:2.
n *Senate,* Num. 11:16.

10
o *Boasting, instances of,* Prov. 25:14.

11
p *False Confidence, warnings against,* Psa. 30:6.
q *Proverbs,* 1 Sam. 24:13.
r *Sarcasm, instances of,* Judg. 10:14.
1 R. V. armour

13
s *Prophets, inspiration of,* Isa. 3:7
t *Israel, prophecies concerning,* vs. 13–28; 1 Kin. 12:1.
u *Prophecies, fulfilled,* vs. 13–30 Dan. 9:24.

* **BEN-HADAD**, a king of Syria. *Besieges Samaria; his drunkenness and his defeat; renews invasion and is again defeated; Ahab denounced for not destroying him,* 1 Kin. 20. *Sends captain of his host to Elisha to be healed of leprosy,* 2 Kin. 5:1–7, 18. *Besieges Samaria again, and flees in panic,* 2 Kin. 6:24–33; 7:1–16. *Death of,* 2 Kin. 8:7–15.

day; and thou shalt know that I
*am* the LORD.
14 And [g]Ā'hăb said, By whom?
And he said, [s]Thus saith the
LORD, *Even* by the young men
of the princes of the provinces.
Then he said, Who shall order
the battle? And he answered,
Thou.
15 Then he numbered the
young men of the princes of the
provinces, and they were two
hundred and thirty two: and
after them he numbered all the
[v]people, *even* all the children of
Is̩'ra-el, *being* seven thousand.
16 And they went out at noon.
But *Bĕn-hā'dăd *was* drinking
himself [w,x]drunk in the pavilions,
he and the kings, the thirty and
two kings that helped him.
17 And the young men of the
princes of the provinces went out
first; and *Bĕn-hā'dăd sent out,
and they told him, saying, There
are men come out of [e]Să-mā'rĭ-ȧ.
18 And he said, Whether they
be come out for peace, take them
alive; or whether they be come
out for [y]war, take them alive.
19 So these young men of the
princes of the provinces came
out of the city, and the [v]army
which followed them.
20 And they slew every one
his man: and the Sy̆r'ĭ-ans̩ fled;
and Ĭs̩'ra-el pursued them: and
*Bĕn-hā'dăd the king of [a]Sy̆r'-
ĭ-ȧ escaped on an horse with the
horsemen.
21 And the king of Ĭs̩'ra-el went
out, and smote[c] the [b]horses and
[c]chariots, and slew the Sy̆r'ĭ-ans̩
with a great slaughter.
22 ¶ And the [s]prophet came to
the king of Ĭs̩'ra-el, and said unto him, Go, strengthen thyself,
and mark, and see what thou
doest: for at the return of the
year the king of [a]Sy̆r'ĭ-ȧ will
come up against thee.
23 And the servants of the king

15
v *Armies*, Deut. 11:4.

16
w *King, drunken, instances of*, 2 Kin. 3:10.
x *Drunkenness, instances of*, Luke 21:34.

18
y *War*, Judg. 3:2.

of Sy̆r'ĭ-ȧ said unto him, [z]Their
gods *are* gods of the hills; therefore they were stronger than we;
but let us fight against them in
the plain, and surely we shall be
stronger than they.
24 And do this thing, Take the
kings away, every man out of
his place, and put [a,b]captains in
their rooms[c]:
25 And number[c] thee an army,
like the army that thou hast lost,
horse for horse, and chariot for
chariot: and we will fight against
them in the plain, *and* surely we
shall be stronger than they. And
he hearkened unto their voice,
and did so.
26 And it came to pass at the
return of the year, that *Bĕn-
hā'dăd [c]numbered the Sy̆r'ĭ-ans̩,
and went up to Ā'phek, to fight
against Ĭs̩'ra-el.
27 And the children of [d]Ĭs̩'ra-
el were [c]numbered, and were
[2]all present, and went against
them: and the children of Ĭs̩'-
ra-el pitched[c] before them like
two little flocks of kids; but
the Sy̆r'ĭ-ans̩ filled the country.
28 ¶ And there came a man of
God, and spake unto the [e]king of
Ĭs̩'ra-el, and said, Thus saith the
[f]LORD, Because the Sy̆r'ĭ-ans̩
have said, [g]The LORD *is* God of
the hills, but he *is* not God of the
valleys, therefore will [h]I deliver
all this great multitude into thine
hand, and ye shall know that I
*am* the LORD.
29 And they pitched[c] one over[c]
against the other [i]seven days.
And *so* it was, that in the seventh
day the battle was joined: and
the children of [d]Ĭs̩'ra-el slew of
the Sy̆r'ĭ-ans̩ an hundred thousand footmen in one day.
30 But the rest fled to Ā'phek,
into the city; and *there* a wall fell
upon twenty and seven thousand
of the men *that were* left. And
*Bĕn-hā'dăd fled, and came in-

23
z *Delusion, exemplified*, 2 Thess. 2:11.

24
a *Captain*, Num. 31:48.
b *Armies, how officered*, Deut. 11:4.

26
c *Muster, of troops*, 2 Kin. 25:19.

27
d *Israel, after the revolt*, 1 Kin. 12:1.
2 R. V. victualled,

28
e *Ahab*, 1 Kin. 16:29.
f *God, unity of*, Gen. 2:2.
g *Delusion, exemplified*, 2 Thess. 2:11.
h *War, God in*, Judg. 3:2.

29
i *Seven, days*, Gen. 7:2.

to the city, into an inner chamber.
31 ¶ And his servants said unto
him, Behold now, we have heard
that the kings of the house of
Ĭş'ra-el *are* merciful kings: [i]let
us, I pray thee, put [k]sackcloth
on our loins, and †ropes upon
our heads, and go out to the king
of Ĭş'ra-el: peradventure[c] he will
save thy life.
32 So they girded [k]sackcloth on
their loins, and *put* †ropes on
their heads, and came to the
king of Ĭş'ra-el, and said, Thy
servant *Běn–hā'dăd saith, I
pray thee, let me live. And [l]he
said, *Is* he yet alive? he *is* my
[m]brother.
33 Now the men [3]did diligently
observe whether *any thing would
come* from him, and did hastily
catch *it*: and they said, Thy
[m]brother *Běn–hā'dăd. Then he
said, Go ye, bring him. Then
Běn–hā'dăd came forth to him;
and he caused him to come up
into the chariot.
34 And **Ben–ha'dad* said unto
him, The cities, which my father took from thy father, I will
restore; and thou shalt make
streets for thee in [n]Dă-măs'cus,
as my father made in [o]Sā-mā'-
rĭ-ȧ. Then *said* [e]*A'hab,* I will
send thee away with this [p,q]cove-
nant. So he made a covenant[c]
with him, and sent him away.
35 ¶ And a certain man of the
[r,s]sons of the prophets said unto
his neighbour in the word of the
LORD, Smite me, I pray thee.
And the man refused to smite
him.
36 Then said he unto him, Because thou [t]hast not obeyed the
voice of the LORD, behold, as
soon as thou art departed from
me, a [u]lion shall slay thee. And
[v]as soon as he was departed from
him, a lion found him, and slew
him.
37 Then he found another man,
and said, Smite me, I pray thee.
And the man smote him, so that
in smiting he wounded *him*.
38 So the [w]prophet departed,
and waited for the king by the
way, and disguised himself with
[4, x]ashes upon his face.
39 And as the king passed by,
he cried unto the king: and he
[y]said, Thy servant went out into
the midst of the battle; and, behold, a man turned aside, and
brought a man unto me, and
said, Keep[c] this man: if by any
means he be missing, then shall
thy life be for his life, or else thou
shalt pay a talent[c] of silver.
40 And as thy servant was busy
here and there, he was gone.
And the king of Ĭş'ra-el said unto him, [z]So *shall* thy judgment
*be*; thyself hast decided *it*.
41 And he hasted, and took the
[5, x]ashes away from his face; and
the king of Ĭş'ra-el discerned
him that he *was* of the [w]proph-
ets.
42 And he said unto him, Thus
saith the LORD, Because [a]thou
[b]hast let go out of *thy* hand a
man whom I [c]appointed to utter
destruction, therefore [d]thy life
shall go for his life, and thy people for his people.[s]
43 And the king of Ĭş'ra-el
went to his house [e]heavy[c] and
displeased, and came to Sā-mā'-
rĭ-ȧ.

## CHAPTER 21

*Naboth refuses Ahab his vineyard. 5 Jezebel causes Naboth to be stoned for blasphemy. 15 Ahab takes possession of the vineyard. 17 Thereupon Elijah denounces judgments against Ahab and Jezebel. 25 Ahab humbling himself, God defers the judgment against him.*

AND it came to pass after
these things, *that* [a]Nā'bŏth
the Jĕz're-el-īte had a [b]vine-

31
*i* *Diplomacy, instances of*, 2 Kin. 16:7.
*k* *Sackcloth, a symbol of mourning*, Isa. 15:3.

32
*l* *Kindness, instances of*, Acts 28:2.
*m* *Brother*, Prov. 18:24.

33
3 R. V. observed diligently, and hasted to catch whether it were his mind;

34
*n* *Damascus*, Isa. 8:4.
*o* *Samaria*, 1 Kin. 16:24.
*p* *Covenant, of men with men*, Deut. 29:1.
*q* *Treaty, cession of territory by*, 1 Kin. 5:12.

35
*r* *Prophets, schools of*, Isa. 3:2.
*s* *Students*, 2 Kin. 2:3.

36
*t* *Disobedience to God, instances of*, Eph. 5:6.
*u* *Lion*, Mic. 5:8.
*v* *Prophecies, fulfilled*, Dan. 9:24.

38
*w* *Prophets*, Isa. 3:2.
*x* *Ashes, disguises in*, Num. 19:9.
4 R. V. his headband over his eyes.

39
*y* *Parables*, Ezek. 20:49.

40
*z* *Self-condemnation, instances of*, Job 9:20.

41
5 R. V. headband away from his eyes;

42
*a* *Ahab, prophecies against*, 1 Kin. 16:29.
*b* *Disobedience to God, instances of*, Eph. 5:6.
*c* *Foreordination*, Rom. 8:30.
*d* *Substitution*, Lev. 1:4.

43
*e* *Despondency*, Eccl. 2:20.

1
*a* 2 Kin. 9:21-36.
*b* *Vineyard*, Isa. 1:8.

† **ROPE.** *Threefold*, Eccl. 4:12. *Put on the head as an emblem of servitude*, 1 Kin. 20:31, 32. *Used in casting lots*, Mic. 2:5. **Figurative:** *Of temptations*, Psa. 140:5; Prov. 5:22.

yard, which *was* in [c]Jĕz′re-el,
hard[G] by the *palace of [d]Ā′hăb
[e]king of [f]Sȧ-mā′rĭ-ȧ.
2 And [d]Ā′hăb spake unto [a]Nā′-
bŏth, [g]saying, Give me thy
[b]vineyard, that I may have it for
a garden of herbs, because it *is*
near unto my house: and I will
give thee for it a better vineyard
than it; *or*, if it seem good to
thee, I will give thee the worth of
it in [h]money.
3 And [a]Nā′bŏth said to [d]Ā′hăb,
The LORD forbid it me, that I
should give the [i]inheritance of
my fathers unto thee.
4 And [d]Ā′hăb came into his
house heavy[G] and [j]displeased
because of the word which
[a]Nā′bŏth the Jĕz′re-el-īte had
spoken to him: for he had said,
I will not give thee the [i]inherit-
ance of my fathers. And he laid
him down upon his bed, and
turned away his face, and would
eat no bread.
5 ¶ But [k]Jĕz′e-bĕl his wife
came to him, and said unto him,
Why is thy spirit so sad, that
thou eatest no bread[G]?
6 And he said unto her, Because I spake unto [a]Nā′bŏth the
Jĕz′re-el-īte, and said unto him,
Give me thy [b]vineyard for [h]mon-
ey; or else, if it please thee, I will
give thee *another* vineyard for it:
and he answered, I will not give
thee my vineyard.
7 And [k]Jĕz′e-bĕl his wife said
unto him, Dost thou now [l]govern
the kingdom of Ĭṣ′ra-el? arise,
*and* eat bread[G], and let thine
heart be merry: [m]I will give thee
the vineyard of [a]Nā′bŏth the
Jĕz′re-el-īte.
8 [m]So [k,n]she wrote letters [o]in
[d]Ā′hăb's name, and sealed *them*
with his †seal, and sent the letters unto the [p]elders and to the
nobles that *were* in his city,
dwelling with [a]Nā′bŏth.
9 And she wrote in the letters,
saying, Proclaim a fast, and set
[a]Nā′bŏth on high among the
people:
10 And set two men, sons of
Bē′lĭ-al[G], before him, to [q]bear
witness against him, [r]saying,
Thou didst [1]blaspheme God and
the king. And *then* carry him
out, and stone him, that he may
die.
11 And the men of his city, *even*
the [s,t]elders and the nobles who
were the inhabitants in his city,
did as [k,n]Jĕz′e-bĕl had sent unto
them, *and* as it *was* written in
the letters which she had sent
unto them.
12 They proclaimed a fast, and
set [a]Nā′bŏth on high among the
people.
13 And there came in two men,
children of Bē′lĭ-al[G], and sat before him: and the men of Bē′-
lĭ-al[G] [u,v]witnessed against him,
*even* against Nā′bŏth, in the
presence of the people, saying,
[w]Nā′bŏth did [1,x]blaspheme God
and the king. Then they carried
him forth out of the city, and
[y]stoned him with stones, that he
died.
14 Then they sent to [k]Jĕz′e-
bĕl, saying, [z]Nā′bŏth is stoned,
and is dead.
15 ¶ And it came to pass, when
[a]Jĕz′e-bĕl heard that [b]Nā′bŏth
was stoned, and was dead, that
Jĕz′e-bĕl said to [c]Ā′hăb, Arise,

*Jezreel*, 1 Kin. 18:45.
*Ahab*, 1 Kin. 16:29.
*King*, 2 Kin. 3:10.
*Samaria*, 1 Kin. 16:24.

2
*Covetousness, instances of*, Isa. 57:17.

**B.C. 899?**
*Money*, Jer. 32:9.

3
*Inheritance*, Num. 27:7.

4
*Anger, instances of*, Psa. 37:8.

5
*Jezebel*, 1 Kin. 16:31.

7
*Government, monarchical, tyranny in*, Isa. 22:21.
*Conspiracy, instances of*, 1 Kin. 16:9.

8
n *Women, wicked, instances of*, Prov. 31:10.
o *Usurpation, of executive power*, 2 Sam. 15:1.
p *Government, municipal*, Isa. 22:21.

10
q *False Witness*, Matt. 19:18.
r *Slander*, Prov. 10:18.
1 R. V. curse.

11
s *Court, corrupt*, Ex. 18:26.
t *Rulers, wicked, instances of*, Ex. 18:21.

13
u *False Accusation*, 2 Tim. 3:3.
v *Falsehood*, Job 21:34.
w *Indictments*, Matt. 27:37.
x *Blasphemy, false indictments for*, 2 Sam. 12:14.
y *Stoning*, 1 Sam. 30:6.

14
z 2 Kin. 9:21–36.

15
a *Jezebel*, 1 Kin. 16:31.
b 2 Kin. 9:21–36.
c *Ahab*, 1 Kin. 16:29.

* **PALACE.** *For kings*, 1 Kin. 21:1; 2 Kin. 15:25; Jer. 39:27; Amos 1:12; Nah. 2:6. *Of David*, 2 Sam. 7:2. *Of Solomon*, 1 Kin. 7:1–12; 10:17; 2 Chr. 9:11, 16, 20. *At Babylon*, Dan. 4:29; 5:5; 6:18. *At Shushan*, Neh. 1:1; Esth. 1:2; 7:7; Dan. 8:2. *Archives kept in*, Ezra 6:2. *Proclamations issued in*, Amos 3:9.

**Figurative:** *Of governments*, Amos 1:12; 2:2; Nah. 2:6.

† **SEAL,** a stamp used for attesting documents. *Engraved*, Ex. 28:11, 21, 36; 39:6, 14, 30; 2 Tim. 2:19. *Decrees attested by*, 1 Kin. 21:8; Esth. 8:8.

Documents sealed with: *Ahab's letter*, 1 Kin. 21:8; *covenants*, Neh. 9:38; 10:1; Isa. 8:16; *decrees*, Esth. 8:8; Dan. 6:9; *deeds*, Jer. 32:10.

*Treasures secured by*, Deut. 32:34. *Lion's den made sure by*, Dan. 6:17; *also sepulchre of Jesus*, Matt. 27:66.

*In John's vision*, Rev. 6; 8:1; 10:4. *Of God*, Rev. 7:2; *put on* 144,000 *of the twelve tribes*, Rev. 7:3–8.

**Figurative:** *Of secrecy*, Dan. 12:9; Rev. 5:1. *Of certainty of divine approval*, John 6:27; Rom. 15:28; 2 Cor. 1:22; Eph. 1:13; 4:30; Rev. 7:2–4. *Circumcision a seal of righteousness*, Rom. 4:11.

take possession of the vineyard
of Nā'bŏth the Jĕz're-el-īte,
which he refused to give thee for
money: for Nā'bŏth is not alive,
but dead.
16 And it came to pass, when
[c]Ā'hăb heard that [b]Nā'bŏth was
dead, that Ā'hăb rose up to go
down to the [d]vineyard of Nā'-
bŏth the Jĕz're-el-īte, to [e,f]take
possession of it.
17 ¶And the [g]word of the LORD
came to [h]Ē-lī'jah the Tĭsh'bīte,
saying,
18 Arise, go down to meet
[c]Ā'hăb king of Ĭṣ'ra-el, which *is*
in [i]Să-mā'rĭ-ȧ: behold, *he is* in
the [d]vineyard of Nā'bŏth, whither he is gone down to possess it.
19 And [g,h]thou shalt speak unto [c]him, saying, Thus saith the
LORD, Hast thou [j]killed, and
also [e,f]taken possession? And
thou shalt speak unto him, saying, Thus saith the LORD, [k]In
the place where ‡dogs licked the
blood of [b]Nā'bŏth shall dogs
lick thy blood, even thine.
20 And [c]Ā'hăb said to [h]Ē-lī'-
jah, Hast thou found me, O
mine enemy? And he answered,
I have found *thee*: because [l]thou
hast [m]sold thyself to work evil in
the sight of the LORD.
21 Behold, I will [n]bring [k]evil
upon [o]thee, and will take away
thy posterity, and will cut off
from Ā'hăb [2]him that pisseth
against the wall, and him that is
shut up and left in Ĭṣ'ra-el,
22 And will make thine house
like the house of [p]Jĕr-o-bō'am
the son of Nē'băt, and like the
house of [q]Bā'a-shȧ the son of
Ȧ-hī'jah, for the provocation
wherewith thou hast provoked
*me* to [r]anger, and [s]made Ĭṣ'ra-el
to sin.
23 And of [a]Jĕz'e-bĕl also [t]spake
the LORD, saying, The ‡dogs
shall eat Jĕz'e-bĕl by the wall of
[u]Jĕz're-el.
24 Him that dieth of [c]Ā'hăb in
the city the ‡dogs shall eat; and
him that dieth in the field shall
the fowls of the air eat.
25 But there was none like unto
[c]Ā'hăb, which did sell himself to
work wickedness in the sight of
the LORD, whom [v]Jĕz'e-bĕl his
wife [w]stirred up.
26 And he did very abominably
in [x]following idols, according to
all *things* as did the [y]Ăm'ôr-ītes,
whom the LORD cast out before
the children of Ĭṣ'ra-el.
27 And it came to pass, when
Ā'hăb heard those words, that
he [z,a]rent his clothes, and put
[b]sackcloth upon his flesh, and
fasted, and lay in sackcloth, and
went softly.
28 And the word of the LORD
[c]came to Ē-lī'jah the Tĭsh'bīte,
saying,
29 Seest thou how Ā'hăb [d]hum-
bleth himself before me? because he humbleth himself before me, [e]I will not bring the evil
in his days: *but* in his [f]son's days
will I bring the evil upon his
house.

## CHAPTER 22

*Ahab, misled by false prophets, is slain at Ramoth-gilead. 37 The dogs lick his blood. 40 Ahaziah succeeds him. 41 Jehoshaphat's good reign. 50 Jehoram succeeds him. 51 Ahaziah's evil reign.*

AND they continued three
years without [a]wars be-
tween [b]Sўr'ĭ-ȧ and [c]Ĭṣ'ra-el.
2 [d]And it came to pass in the
third year, that [e]Jĕ-hŏsh'a-phăt
the [f]king of [g]Jū'dah came down
to the [h]king of [c]Ĭṣ'ra-el.
3 And the king of Ĭṣ'ra-el said
unto his servants, Know ye that
[i]Rā'moth in Ḡĭl'e-ăd *is* our's,
and we *be* still, *and* take it not
out of the hand of the king of
[b]Sўr'ĭ-ȧ?

**16**
d *Vineyard,* Isa. 1:8.
e *Confiscation,* Ezra 10:8.
f *Property, confiscation of,* Lev. 27:15.
**17**
g *Prophets, inspiration of,* Isa. 3:2.
h *Elijah,* 1 Kin. 17:1.
**18**
i *Samaria,* 1 Kin. 16:24.
**19**
j *Homicide, felonious,* Deut. 5:17.
k *Judgments, denounced against Ahab and Jezebel,* Ex. 6:6.
**20**
l *Reproof, faithfulness in,* Prov. 17:10.
m *Wicked, described,* Psa. 73:3.
**21**
n *Wicked, punishment of,* Psa. 73:3.
o *Rulers, wicked,* Ex. 18:21.
2 R. V. every man child, and him that is shut up and him that is left at large in Israel,
**22**
p *Jeroboam,* 1 Kin. 14:5.
q *Baasha,* 1 Kin. 15:16.
r *Anger of God,* 2 Kin. 13:3.
s *Temptation, leading into,* Luke 11:4.
**23**
t *Prophecies,* Dan. 9:24.

u *Jezreel,* 1 Kin. 18:45.
**25**
v *Women, wicked,* Prov. 31:10.
w *Influence, evil,* 1 Cor. 7:14.
**26**
x *Idolatry,* 1 Sam. 15:23.
y *Amorites,* Gen. 14:13.
**27**
z *Repentance,* Mark 1:4.

a *Rending of Garments,* 2 Chr. 34:27.
b *Sackcloth,* Isa. 15:3.
**28**
c *Prophets, inspiration of,* Isa. 3:2.
**29**
d *Humility, instances of,* Prov. 22:4.
e *God, mercy of,* Gen. 2:2.
f *Children, involved in sins of parents,* Mark 10:14.

**v.1–825 BC**
See footnote, *Time,* Rev. 10:6.
**1**
a *War,* Judg. 3:2.
b *Syria,* 2 Kin. 6:23.
c *Israel, after the revolt,* 1 Kin. 12:1.
**2**
d 2 Chr. 18:2–34.
e *Jehoshaphat,* 2 Kin. 12:18.
f *King,* 2 Kin. 3:10.
g *Judah, kingdom of,* 2 Chr. 11:17.
h *Ahab,* 1 Kin. 16:29.
**3**
i *Ramoth-gilead,* Josh. 20:8.

‡ **DOG.** *Shepherd,* Job 30:1. *Greyhound,* Prov. 30:31. *Price of, not to be brought into the sanctuary,* Deut. 23:18. *Licked the blood, of Naboth,* 1 Kin. 21:19; *of Ahab,* 1 Kin. 22:38. *Epithet of contempt,* 1 Sam. 17:43; 24:14; 2 Sam. 3:8; 9:8; 16:9; 2 Kin. 8:13; Isa. 56:10, 11; Matt. 15:26, 27. **Figurative,** Matt. 7:6; Phil. 3:2; Rev. 22:15.

v.4–825 BC
See footnote, *Time*, Rev. 10:6.

4
*j* *Alliances*, Josh. 9:15.
*k* *Armies, confederated*, Deut. 11:4.
*l* *Horse*, Job 39:19.

5
*m* *Armies, religious ceremonies in*, vs. 7–28; Deut. 11:4.
*n* *Guidance, prayer for*, Psa. 48:14.

6
*o* *Prophets, false*, Isa. 3:2.

7
*p* *Prophets*, Isa. 3:2.

8
*q* 2 Chr. 18:4–27.
*r* *Reproof, despised*, Prov. 17:10.

10
*s* *Throne*, 1 Kin. 2:19.
*t* *Gates, thrones of kings at*, Deut. 3:5.
*u* *Samaria*, 1 Kin. 16:24.

11
*v* 2 Chr. 18:10, 23.
*w* *Horn, symbolical*, 1 Kin. 1:39.

4 And he said unto [e]Jė-hŏsh′a-phăt, Wilt thou go with me to battle to [i]Rā′moth–gĭl′e-ăd? And Jė-hŏsh′a-phăt said to the king of Ĭṣ′ra-el, [j]I *am* as thou *art*, my [k]people as thy people, my [l]horses as thy horses.

5 ¶ And [e]Jė-hŏsh′a-phăt said unto the [h]king of Ĭṣ′ra-el, [m,n]Enquire, I pray thee, at the word[C] of the LORD to day.

6 Then the king of Ĭṣ′ra-el gathered the [o]prophets together, about four hundred men, and said unto them, Shall I go against [i]Rā-moth–gĭl′e-ăd to battle, or shall I forbear? And they said, Go up; for the LORD shall deliver *it* into the hand of the king.

7 And [e]Jė-hŏsh′a-phăt said, *Is there* not here a [p]prophet of the LORD besides, that we might enquire of him?

8 And the [h]king of Ĭṣ′ra-el said unto [e]Jė-hŏsh′a-phăt, [q]*There is* yet one man, Mī-cā′iah the son of Ĭm′lah, by whom we may enquire of the LORD: but I [r]hate him; for he doth not prophesy[C] good concerning me, but evil. And Jė-hŏsh′a-phăt said, Let not the king say so.

9 Then the [h]king of Ĭṣ′ra-el called an officer[C], and said, Hasten *hither* Mī-cā′iah the son of Ĭm′lah.

10 And the [h]king of Ĭṣ′ra-el and [e]Jė-hŏsh′a-phăt the king of [f]Jū′dah sat each on his [s]throne, having put on their robes, in a void[C] place in the entrance of the [t]gate of [u]Sȧ-mā′rĭ-ȧ; and all the [o]prophets prophesied before them.

11 And *Zĕd-e-kī′ah the son of [v]Chĕ-nā′a-nah made him [w]horns of iron: and he said, Thus saith the LORD, With these shalt thou push the [b]Sȳr′ĭ-anṣ, until thou have consumed them.

12 And all the [o]prophets prophesied so, saying, Go up to [i]Rā′moth–gĭl′e-ăd, and prosper: for the LORD shall deliver *it* into the king's hand.

13 And the messenger that was gone to call Mī-cā′iah spake unto him, saying, Behold now, the words of the prophets *declare* good unto the king with one mouth: let thy word, I pray thee, be like the word of one of them, and speak *that which is* good.

14 And [x]Mī-cā′iah said, [y,z,a]*As* the LORD liveth, what the LORD [b]saith unto me, that will I speak.

15 So [c]he came to the king. And the king said unto him, Mī-cā′iah, shall we go against [d]Rā′moth–gĭl′e-ăd to battle, or shall we forbear? And he answered him, Go, and prosper: for the LORD shall deliver *it* into the hand of the king.

16 And the king said unto him, How many times shall I adjure[C] thee that thou tell me nothing but *that which is* true in the name of the LORD?

17 And he said, I [e]saw all Ĭṣ′ra-el scattered upon the hills, as sheep that have not a [f]shepherd: and the LORD said, These have no master: let them return every man to his house in peace.[Q]

18 And the [g]king of Ĭṣ′ra-el said unto [h]Jė-hŏsh′a-phăt, Did I not tell thee that he would prophesy no good concerning me, but evil?

19 And he said, Hear thou therefore the word of the LORD: I saw the [i]LORD sitting on his throne, and all the host of heaven standing by him on his right hand and on his left.[Q]

20 And the LORD said, Who shall persuade [g]Ā′hăb, that he may go up and fall at [d]Rā′moth–gĭl′e-ăd? And one said on this

v.12–825 BC
See footnote, *Time*, Rev. 10:6.

14
*x* *Minister, faithful*, Rom. 15:16.
*y* *Temptation, resistance to*, vs. 13–28; Luke 11:4.
*z* *Decision, instances of*, Isa. 50:7.
*a* *Zeal, exemplified*, 2 Cor. 7:11.
*b* *Prophets, inspiration of*, Isa. 3:2.

15
*c* 2 Chr. 18:4–27.
*d* *Ramoth-gilead*, Josh. 20:8.

17
*e* *Vision, of Micaiah*, Acts 9:10.
*f* *Shepherd*, Jer. 31:10.

18
*g* *Ahab*, 1 Kin. 16:29.
*h* *Jehoshaphat*, 2 Kin. 12:18.

19
*i* *God, glory of*, Gen. 2:2.

* **ZEDEKIAH**, a false prophet. *Prophesies to Ahab of victory over the Syrians, instead of defeat*, 1 Kin. 22:11; 2 Chr. 18:10. *Smites Micaiah, the true prophet*, 1 Kin. 22:24, 25; 2 Chr. 18:23, 24.

v.20–825 BC See footnote, *Time,* Rev. 10:6.

21
*Evil Spirit,* 1 Sam. 18:10.

24
*k* *Presumption,* Psa. 19:13.
*l* *Minister, persecutions of,* Rom. 15:16.
*m* *Mocking,* 1 Kin. 18:27.
1 R. V. spirit

25
*n* *House, architecture of,* Esth. 8:1.

26
*o* 2 Chr. 18:25.
*p* 2 Chr. 18:25.

27
*q* *Persecution, instances of,* John 15:20.
*r* *Revenge, exemplified,* Ezek. 25:15.
*s* *Prisoners,* Psa. 79:11.
*t* *Bread, of affliction,* Ezek. 4:13.
*u* *Water, of affliction,* 1 Kin. 17:10.

manner, and another said on that manner.

21 And there came forth a [j]spirit, and stood before the LORD, and said, I will persuade him.

22 And the LORD said unto him, Wherewith[G]? And he said, I will go forth, and I will be a lying [j]spirit in the mouth of all his prophets. And he said, Thou shalt persuade *him,* and prevail also: go forth, and do so.

23 Now therefore, behold, the LORD hath put a lying [j]spirit in the mouth of all these thy prophets, and the LORD hath spoken evil concerning thee.[S]

24 ¶ But *Zĕd-e-kī′ah the son of Chĕ-nā′a-nah went near, and [k]smote[G] [l]Mī-cā′iah on the cheek, and [m]said, Which way went the [1]Spirit of the LORD from me to speak unto thee?

25 And Mī-cā′iah said, Behold, thou shalt see in that day, when thou shalt go into an [n]inner chamber to hide thyself.

26[Q] And the [g]king of Ĭş′ra-el said, Take [l]Mī-cā′iah, and carry him back unto [o]Ā′mon the governor of the city, and to [p]Jō′ăsh the king's son;

27 And say, Thus saith the king, [q,r]Put [s]this *fellow* in the prison, and feed him with [t]bread of affliction and with [u]water of affliction, until I come in peace.[Q]

28 And Mī-cā′iah said, If thou return at all in peace, the LORD hath not spoken by me. And he said, Hearken, O people, every one of you.

29 So the [g]king of Ĭş′ra-el and [h]Jĕ-hŏsh′a-phăt the king of Jū′dah went up to [d]Rā′-moth–gĭl′-e-ăd.

30 And the [g]king of Ĭş′ra-el said unto [h]Jĕ-hŏsh′a-phăt, I will disguise myself, and enter into the battle; but put thou on thy robes. And the king of Ĭş′ra-el disguised himself, and went into the battle.

31 But the king of [v]Sȳr′ĭ-ȧ commanded his thirty and two [w]captains that had rule over his [x]chariots, saying, Fight neither with small nor great, save[G] only with the king of Ĭş′ra-el.

32 And it came to pass, when the [w]captains of the [x]chariots saw [h]Jĕ-hŏsh′a-phăt, that they said, Surely it *is* the [g]king of Ĭş′ra-el. And they turned aside to fight against him: and Jĕ-hŏsh′a-phăt cried out.

33 And it came to pass, when the [w]captains of the [x]chariots perceived that it *was* not the king of Ĭş′ra-el, that they turned back from pursuing him.

34 ¶ And a *certain* man [y]drew a bow at a venture[G], and smote the king of Ĭş′ra-el between the joints of the [z]harness[G]: wherefore he said unto the driver of his chariot, Turn thine hand, and carry me out of the host; for I am wounded.

35 And the battle increased that day: and the [a]king was stayed up in his chariot against the Sȳr′ĭ-ans, and [b,c]died at even: and the blood ran out of the wound into the midst of the chariot.

36 And there went a proclamation throughout the host about the going down of the sun, saying, Every man to his city, and every man to his own country.

37 So the [a]king died, and was brought to [d]Sȧ-mā′rĭ-ȧ; and they [e]buried the king in Sȧ-mā′rĭ-ȧ.

38 And *one* washed the [f]chariot in the [g]pool of Sȧ-mā′rĭ-ȧ; and [h]the [i]dogs licked up his blood; [2]and they washed his armour; according unto the [c]word of the LORD which he spake.

39 Now the rest of the acts of [a]Ā′hăb, and all that he did, and the [j]ivory house which he made,

v.30–825 BC See footnote, *Time,* Rev. 10:6.

31
*v* *Syria,* 2 Kin. 6:23.
*w* *Captain,* Num. 31:48.
*x* *Chariot,* Josh. 11:4.

34
*y* *Archery,* Gen. 21:20.
*z* *Coat of Mail,* 1 Sam. 17:5.

35
*a* *Ahab,* 1 Kin. 16:29.
*b* *Death,* Num. 23:10.
*c* *Prophecies, fulfilled,* Dan. 9:24

37
*d* *Samaria,* 1 Kin. 16:24.
*e* *Burial,* Acts 8:2

38
*f* *Chariot,* Josh. 11:4.
*g* *Pool, of Samaria,* 2 Sam. 2:13.
*h* 1 Kin. 21:19.
*i* *Dog,* 1 Kin. 21:19.
2 R. V. (now the harlots washed themselves there;)

39
*j* *Ivory,* 2 Chr. 9:17.

**v.40–825 BC** See footnote, *Time*, Rev. 10:6.

*k Book*, Num. 5:23.
*l Israel, after the revolt*, 1 Kin. 12:1.

**41**
*m Jehoshaphat*, 2 Kin. 12:18.
*n Rulers, righteous, instances of*, Ex. 18:21.
**v.41–843 BC**
*o Asa*, 1 Kin. 15:8.
*p Judah, kingdom of*, 2 Chr. 11:17.

**42**
*q Jerusalem*, Judg. 19:10.
*r* 2 Chr. 20:31.
*s* 2 Chr. 20:31.

**43**
*t Influence, good*, 1 Cor. 7:14.
*u Parents, good influence of*, 2 Cor. 12:14.
*v High Places*, 1 Kin. 3:2.
*w Incense, offered in idolatrous worship*, Ex. 37:29.

**46**
*x Sodomites*, Gen. 19:25.

and all the cities that he built, *are* they not written in the[k]book of the chronicles of the kings of [l]Ĭs̩'ra-el?

40 So [a]Ā'hăb [b]slept[C] with his fathers; and †Ā-ha-zī'ah his son reigned in his stead.

41 ¶ And [m,n]Jē-hŏsh'a-phăt the son of [o]Ā'sȧ began to reign over [p]Jū'dah in the fourth year of Ā'hăb king of Ĭs̩'ra-el.

42 [m]Jē-hŏsh'a-phăt *was* thirty and five years old when he began to reign; and he reigned twenty and five years in [q]Jē-ru̩'sȧ-lĕm. And his mother's name *was* [r]Ā-zū'bah the daughter of [s]Shĭl'hī.

43 And he walked [t]in all the ways of Ā'sȧ his [u]father; he turned not aside from it, doing *that which was* right in the eyes of the LORD: nevertheless the [v]high places were not taken away; *for* the people offered and burnt [w]incense yet in the high places.

44 And [m]Jē-hŏsh'a-phăt made peace with the king of Ĭs̩'ra-el.

45 Now the rest of the acts of [m]Jē-hŏsh'a-phăt, and his might that he shewed, and how he warred, *are* they not written in the book of the chronicles of the kings of [p]Jū'dah?

46 And the remnant of the [x]sodomites, which remained in the days of his father [o]Ā'sȧ, he took out of the land.

47 *There was* then no king in [y]Ē'dom: [z]a ‡deputy *was* king.

48 [a]Jē-hŏsh'a-phăt made [b]ships of [c]Thär'shish to go to [d]Ō'phīr for [e]gold: but they went not; for the ships were broken at [f]Ē'zĭ-on–gē'bĕr.

49 Then said †Ā-ha-zī'ah the son of Ā'hăb unto [a]Jē-hŏsh'a-phăt, Let my servants go with thy servants in the [b]ships. But Jē-hŏsh'a-phăt would not.

50 ¶ And Jē-hŏsh'a-phăt [g]slept[C] with his fathers, and was buried with his fathers in the [h]city of Dā'vid his father: and ‖Jē-hō'-ram his son reigned in his stead.

51 ¶ †Ā-ha-zī'ah the son of Ā'hăb began to reign over Ĭs̩'ra-el in [i]Sā-mā'rĭ-ȧ the seventeenth year of [a]Jē-hŏsh'a-phăt king of [j]Jū'dah, and reigned two years over Ĭs̩'ra-el.

52 And he did evil in the sight of the LORD, and walked [k,l]in the way of his father, and [k,l]in the way of his mother, and in the way of [m]Jĕr-o-bō'am the son of Nē'băt, who made Ĭs̩'ra-el to sin:

53 For he [n]served [o]Bā'al, and worshipped him, and provoked to [p]anger the LORD God of Ĭs̩'ra-el, according[C] to all that his father had done.[s]

**v.46–843 BC**

**47**
*y Edomites*, 2 Kin. 8:21.
*z* 2 Kin. 15:5.

**48**
*a Jehoshaphat*, 2 Kin. 12:18.
*b Ship*, 2 Chr. 8:18.
*c* Or, *Tarshish*, 2 Chr. 20:36.
*d Ophir*, 1 Kin. 9:28.
*e Gold*, Ezek. 7:19.
*f Ezion-geber*, Num. 33:35.

**50**
*g Death, called sleep*, Num. 23:10.
**v.50–818 BC**
*h Jerusalem*, Judg. 19:10.

**51**
*i Samaria*, 1 Kin. 16:24.
**v.51–826 BC**
*j Judah, kingdom of*, 2 Chr. 11:17.

**52**
*k Influence, evil*, 1 Cor. 7:14.
*l Parents, evil influence of*, 2 Cor. 12:14.
*m Jeroboam*, 1 Kin. 14:5.

**53**
*n Idolatry*, 1 Sam. 15:23.
*o Baal*, 2 Kin. 17:16.
*p Anger of God*, 2 Kin. 13:3.

† **AHAZIAH.** *King of Israel*, 1 Kin. 22:40. *History of*, 1 Kin. 22:40, 49, 51–53; 2 Chr. 20:35–37; 2 Kin. 1. *Reigned two years*, 1 Kin. 22:51. *Idolatry of*, 1 Kin. 22:53. *Succeeded by Jehoram*, 2 Kin. 3:1.

‡ **DEPUTY.** *An officer who administers the functions of a superior in his absence*, 1 Kin. 22:47; Acts 13:7, 8; 18:12; 19:38.

‖ **JEHORAM** (*exalted by Jehovah*). *Called* JORAM, 2 Kin. 8:21, 23, 24. *King of Judah*, 1 Kin. 22:50; 2 Kin. 8:16; 2 Chr. 21:5. *Reigned eight years*, 2 Kin. 8:16, 17. *Marries Athaliah, whose wicked counsels influence his reign for evil*, 2 Kin. 8:18, 19; 2 Chr. 21:6–13. *Ancestor of Jesus*, Matt. 1:8.
*Slays his brothers to strengthen himself in his sovereignty*, 2 Chr. 21:4, 13. *Edom revolts from*, 2 Kin. 8:20–22; 2 Chr. 21:8–10. *Philistines and Arabians invade his territory*, 2 Chr. 21:16, 17. *Death of*, 2 Chr. 21:18–20; 2 Kin. 8:24. *Prophecy concerning*, 2 Chr. 21:12–15.

THE

# SECOND BOOK OF THE KINGS

v.1–825 BC
See footnote, *Time*, Rev. 10:6.

## CHAPTER 1

*Moab rebels. 2 Ahaziah sends to Baalzebub, but is answered by Elijah. 5 Fire from heaven consumes those sent to apprehend Elijah. 13 Those sent the third time are spared; and Elijah returns with them. 17 Jehoram succeeds Ahaziah.*

1
THEN [a]Mō'ab rebelled against
[b]Iș'ra-el after the death of
[c]Ā'hăb.

2
2 And [d]Ā-ha-zī'ah fell down
through a lattice in his upper
[e]chamber that *was* in [f]Să-mā'-
rĭ-ȧ, and was sick: and he sent
messengers, and said unto them,
Go, enquire of Bā'al-zē'bŭb the
god of [g]Ĕk'rŏn whether I shall
recover of this disease.

3
3 But the [h]angel of the LORD
said to [i]Ē-lī'jah the Tĭsh'bīte,
Arise, go up to meet the messengers
of the [d]king of [f]Să-mā'rĭ-ȧ,
and say unto them, *Is it* not because
*there is* not a God in Iș'-
ra-el, *that* ye go to enquire of
Bā'al-zē'bŭb the god of Ĕk'rŏn?
4 Now therefore thus saith the
LORD, Thou shalt not come
down from that bed on which
thou art gone up, but shalt surely
die. And [i]Ē-lī'jah departed.
5 ¶ And when the messengers
turned back unto him, he said
unto them, Why are ye now
turned back?

6
6 And they said unto him,
There came a man up to meet
us, and said unto us, Go, turn[G]
again unto the king that sent
you, and [j]say unto him, Thus
saith the LORD, *Is it* [1]not because
*there is* not a God in Iș'-
ra-el, *that* thou sendest to enquire
of Bā'al-zē'bŭb the god of
[g]Ĕk'rŏn? therefore thou shalt
not come down from that bed on
which thou art gone up, but
shalt surely die.
7 And he said unto them, What
manner[G] of man *was he* which
came up to meet you, and told
you these words?

8
8 And they answered him, *He
was* an hairy man, and girt with
a [k]girdle[G] of *leather about his
loins.[C] And he said, It *is* [i]Ē-lī'-
jah the Tĭsh'bīte.[Q]

9
9 Then the king sent unto him
a [l]captain of fifty with his fifty.
And he went up to him: and, behold,
he sat on the top of an hill.
And he spake unto him, Thou
man of God, the king hath said,
Come down.

10
10 [S]And [m]Ē-lī'jah answered
and said to the [l]captain of fifty,
If I *be* a man of God, then let
[n]fire come down from heaven,
and consume[G] thee and thy fifty.
And [o]there came down fire from
heaven, and consumed him and
his fifty.[Q]
11 Again also he sent unto him
another [l]captain of fifty with his
fifty. And he answered and said
unto him, O man of God, thus
hath the king said, Come down
quickly.
12 And [m]Ē-lī'jah answered and
said unto them, If I *be* a man of
God, let [n]fire come down from
heaven, and consume thee and
thy fifty. And [o]the fire of God
came down from heaven, and
consumed him and his fifty.[S]
13 And he sent again a [l]captain
of the third fifty with his
fifty. And the third captain of
fifty went up, and came and fell[C]
on his knees before Ē-lī'jah, and

---

*a* *Moab*, Num. 26:3.
*b* *Israel, after the revolt*, 1 Kin. 12:1.
*c* *Ahab* 1 Kin. 16:29.
*d* *Ahaziah*, 1 Kin. 22:40.
*e* *House, chambers of*, Esth. 8:1.
*f* *Samaria*, 1 Kin. 16:24.
*g* *Ekron*, Amos 1:8.
*h* *Angel*, Heb. 1:13.
*i* *Elijah*, 1 Kin. 17:1.
*j* *Reproof, faithfulness in*, Prov. 17:10.
1 R. V. *omits* not

v.6–825 BC
See footnote, *Time*, Rev. 10:6.

*k* *Girdle*, Prov. 31:24.
*l* *Captain, of fifties*, Num. 31:48
*m* *Elijah, miracles of*, 1 Kin. 17:1.
*n* *Fire, miracles connected with*, Ex. 12:8.
*o* *Miracles*, Luke 23:8.

***LEATHER.** *Girdles of*, 2 Kin. 1:8; Matt. 3:4; Mark 1:6 *Tanning of*, Acts 9:43, 10:5, 6.

v.13–825 BC
See footnote, *Time,*
Rev. 10:6.

13
*p* *Intercession, of man with man,* Jer. 27:18.

17
*q* *Prophecies, fulfilled,* Dan. 9:24.
*r* *Jehoram,* 1 Kin. 22:50.
*s* *Jehoshaphat,* 2 Kin. 12:18.
*t* *Judah, kingdom of,* 2 Chr. 11:17.

18
*u* *Book,* Num. 5:23.

1
*a* *Elijah,* **1 Kin.** 17:1.

[p]besought him, and said unto
him, O man of God, I pray thee,
let my life, and the life of these
fifty thy servants, be precious[G] in
thy sight.[G]
14 Behold, [o]there came [n]fire
down from heaven, and burnt up
the two captains of the former
fifties with their fifties: therefore
let my life now be precious in thy
sight.
15 And the [h]angel[G] of the LORD
said unto [i]Ē-lī′jah, Go down
with him: be not afraid of him.
And he arose, and went down
with him unto the king.[T]
16 And he [j]said unto him, Thus
saith the LORD, Forasmuch as
thou hast sent messengers to enquire of Bā′al-zē′bŭb the god of
[g]Ĕk′rŏn, *is it* [1]not because *there*
*is* no God in Iş′ra-el to enquire
of his word? therefore thou shalt
not come down off that bed on
which thou art gone up, but shalt
surely die.
17 ¶ So he died according to the
[q]word of the LORD which [i]Ē-lī′-
jah had spoken. And [†]Jē-hō′-
ram reigned in his stead in the
second year of [r]Jē-hō′ram the
son of [s]Jē-hŏsh′a-phăt king of
[t]Jū′dah; because he had no son.
18 Now the rest of the acts of
[d]Ā-ha-zī′ah which he did, *are*
they not written in the [u]book of
the chronicles[G] of the kings of
[b]Iş′ra-el?

## CHAPTER 2

*Elijah divides Jordan. 9 He grants Elisha his request, and is taken up by a fiery chariot into heaven. 12 Elisha is acknowledged his successor. 16 The young prophets seek for Elijah in vain. 19 Elisha heals the unwholesome waters at Jericho. 23 Bears destroy the children that mocked him.*

AND it came to pass, when
the LORD would [*]take
up [a]Ē-lī′jah into heaven by a
[b,c]whirlwind, that Ē-lī′jah went
with [d]Ē-lī′shȧ from [e]Gĭl′găl.
2 And [a]Ē-lī′jah said unto [d]Ē-lī′-
shȧ, Tarry here, I pray thee;
for the LORD hath sent me to
[f]Bĕth′-el. And Ē-lī′shȧ said *un-*
*to him,* [g]*As* the LORD liveth,
and *as* thy soul liveth, I will not
leave thee. So they went down
to Bĕth′-el.
3 And the [†,h]sons of the [i]proph-
ets that *were* at Bĕth′-el came
forth to Ē-lī′shȧ, and [j]said unto
him, Knowest thou that the
LORD will take away thy master
from thy head[G] to day? And he
said, Yea, I know *it;* hold ye
your peace.
4 And [a]Ē-lī′jah said unto him,
[d]Ē-lī′shȧ, tarry here, I pray thee;
for the LORD hath sent me to
[k]Jĕr′ĭ-chō. And he said, [g]*As* the
LORD liveth, and *as* thy soul liveth, I will not leave thee. So
they came to Jĕr′ĭ-chō.
5 And the [†,h]sons of the prophets that *were* at Jĕr′ĭ-chō came to
Ē-lī′shȧ, and [j]said unto him,
Knowest thou that the LORD
will take away thy master from
thy head to day? And he answered, Yea, I know *it;* hold[G] ye
your peace.
6 And Ē-lī′jah said unto him,
Tarry, I pray thee, here; for the
LORD hath sent me to [l]Jôr′dan.
And he said, [g]*As* the LORD liveth, and *as* thy soul liveth, I will
not leave thee. And they two
went on.
7 And fifty men of the [†]sons of
the prophets went, and stood to
view afar off: and they two stood
by [l]Jôr′dan.
8 And [a]Ē-lī′jah took his [m]man-
tle, and wrapped *it* together, and
smote the [l]waters, and they
[n]were divided hither[G] and thither,[G]

v.1–825 BC
See footnote, *Time*
Rev. 10:6.

*b* *Whirlwind,* Prov. 1:27.
*c* *Meteorology, phenomena of,* Matt. 16:2.
*d* *Elisha,* 1 Kin. 19:16.
*e* *Gilgal,* Josh. 4:19.

2
*f* *Beth-el,* Josh. 18:13.
*g* *Oath, a solemn qualification,* Num. 5:19.

3
*h* *School,* Acts 19:9.
*i* *Prophets,* Isa. 3:2.
*j* *Prophecies,* Dan 9:24.

4
*k* *Jericho,* Num. 22:1.

6
*l* *Jordan,* Gen. 32:10.

8
*m* *Mantle,* Ezra 9:3.
*n* *Miracles,* Luke 23:8.

† **JEHORAM**, called also JORAM. *King of Israel,* 2 Kin. 1:17. *King of Syria sends Naaman to, that he may be healed of his leprosy,* 2 Kin. 5:1–8. *Has war with the king of Syria,* 2 Kin. 6:8–33· 7: 8:28, 29; 2 Chr. 22:5, 6. *Inquires for the particulars concerning Elisha's miracles,* 2 Kin. 8:4, 5. *Slain by Jehu,* 2 Kin. 9:14–26. *Reigned twelve years,* 2 Kin. 3:1.

* **ASCENSION.** *Of Elijah,* 2 Kin. 2:1–18. *Of Jesus,* Mark 16:19, 20; Luke 24:50–53; Acts 1:2, 9–12.

† **STUDENTS.** *Poverty of,* 2 Kin. 4:1. *In state school,* Dan. 1. *In schools of the prophets,* 1 Sam. 19:20: 1 Kin. 20:35; 2 Kin. 2:2, 3, 5, 7, 15; 4:1. *In music,* 1 Chr. 25:7, 8. See footnotes: INSTRUCTION, Prov. 23:23; SCHOOL, Acts 19:9.

v.8–825 BC
See footnote, *Time*, Rev. 10:6.

so that they two went over on dry ground.[s]

9 ¶ And it came to pass, when they were gone over, that [a]Ē-lī'-jah said unto [d]Ē-lī'shȧ, Ask what I shall do for thee, before I be *taken away from thee. And Ē-lī'shȧ said, I pray thee, let a double portion of thy spirit be upon me.

10 And he said, Thou hast asked a hard thing: *nevertheless*, if thou see me *when I am* taken from thee, it shall be so unto thee; but if not, it shall not be *so*.

11 And it came to pass, as they still went on, and talked, that, behold, *there appeared* a [o]chariot of fire, and [p]horses of fire, and parted them both asunder;[G] and [a]Ē-lī'jah [*,q,r]went up by a [b,c]whirlwind into [s]heaven.[s Q]

12 And [d]Ē-lī'shȧ saw *it*, and he cried, My father, my father, the [o]chariot of Ĭs̤'ra-el, and the horsemen thereof. And he saw him no more: and he took hold of his own clothes, and [t,u]rent[G] them in two pieces.

13 [d]He took up also the [m]mantle of [a]Ē-lī'jah that fell from him, and went back, and stood by the bank of [l]Jôr'dan;

14 And [d]he took the [m]mantle of [a]Ē-lī'jah that fell from him, and smote the [l]waters, and said, Where *is* the LORD God of Ē-lī'-jah ? and when he also had smitten the waters, they [n]parted hither[G] and thither[G]: and Ē-lī'shȧ went over.[s]

15 And when the [†,h]sons of the prophets which *were* to[G] view at [k]Jĕr'ī-chō saw him, they said, The spirit of Ē-lī'jah doth rest on Ē-lī'shȧ. And they came to meet him, and [v]bowed[G] themselves to the ground before him.

16 And they said unto him, Behold now, there be with thy servants fifty strong men; let them go, we pray thee, and seek thy master: lest peradventure[G] the [1]Spirit of the LORD hath taken him up, and cast him upon some mountain, or into some valley. And he said, Ye shall not send.

17 And when they urged him till he was ashamed, he said, Send. They sent therefore fifty men; and they sought three days, but found him not.

18 And when they came again to him, (for he tarried at [k]Jĕr'ī-chō,) he said unto them, Did I not say unto you, Go not ?

19 ¶ [s]And the men of the city said unto Ē-lī'shȧ, Behold, I pray thee, the situation of this city *is* pleasant, as my lord seeth: but the water *is* naught,[G] and the ground barren.[G]

20 And he said, Bring me a new [w]cruse,[G] and put [‡]salt therein. And they brought *it* to him.[s]

21 And he went forth unto the spring of the waters, and cast the salt in there, and said, Thus saith the LORD, I have healed these [x]waters; there shall not be from thence[G] any more death or barren *land*.

22 So the [x]waters were healed unto this day, according to the saying of Ē-lī'shȧ which he spake.

23 ¶ And [d]he went up from thence[G] unto [f]Bĕth'–el: and as he was going up by the way, there came forth little [y]children[G] out of the city, and [z,a]mocked him, and [b]said unto him, Go[G] up, thou bald head; go up, thou bald head.

24 And [c]he turned back, and looked on them, and cursed[G] them in the name of the LORD. And there came forth two she

11
*o Chariot, symbolical*, Josh. 11:4.
*p Horse, symbolical*, Job 39:19.
*q Translation*, Heb. 11:5.
*r Death, exemption from*, Num. 23:10.
*s Heaven, the future home of the righteous*, Luke 18:22.

12
*t Rending of Garments*, 2 Chr. 34:27.
*u Mourning*, Lam. 2:5.

15
*v Salutations*, Luke 1:44.

v.16–825 BC
See footnote, *Time*, Rev. 10:6.

16
1 R. V. spirit

20
*w Cruse*, 1 Sam. 26:11.

21
*x Water, purified by Elisha*, 1 Kin. 17:10.

23
*y Children, wicked*, Mark 10:14.
*z Mocking*, 1 Kin. 18:27.
*a Persecution, instances of*, John 15:20.
*b Derision*, Job 30:1.

24
*c Elisha*, 1 Kin. 19:16.

‡ **SALT.** *Lot's wife turned into a pillar of*, Gen. 19:26. *The city of Salt*, Josh. 15:62. *The valley of salt*, 2 Sam. 8:13; 1 Chr. 18:12; 2 Kin. 14:7. *Salt sea*, Gen. 14:3; Num. 34:12; Deut. 3:17; Josh. 3:16; 12:3; 15:2. *Salt pits*, Zeph. 2:9.
*All sacrifices were required to be seasoned with*, Lev. 2:13; Ezra 6:9; Ezek. 43:24.
*Elisha casts, into pool at Jericho, to purify it*, 2 Kin. 2:20, 21.
**Emblematic:** *Of fidelity*, Num. 18:19; 2 Chr. 13:5. *Of barrenness and desolation*, Deut. 29:23; Judg. 9:45; Jer. 17:6; Zeph. 2:7
**Figurative:** *Of the saving efficacy of the church*, Matt. 5:13; Mark 9:50; Luke 14:34. *Of wise conversation*, Col. 4:6.

v.24–825 BC
See footnote, *Time*, Rev. 10:6.

*d Bear*, 2 Sam. 17:8.

25

*e Carmel*, Jer. 46:18.

*f Samaria*, 1 Kin. 16:24.

1

*a Jehoram*, 2 Kin. 1:17.

*b Ahab*, 1 Kin. 16:29.

*c Israel, after the revolt*, 1 Kin. 12:1.

*d Samaria*, 1 Kin. 16:24.

*e Jehoshaphat*, 2 Kin. 12:18.

*f Judah, kingdom of*, 2 Chr. 11:17.

2

*g Rulers, wicked, instances of*, Ex. 18:21.

*h Jezebel*, 1 Kin. 16:31.

*i Baal*, 2 Kin. 17:16.

1 R. V. pillar

3

*j Jeroboam*, 1 Kin. 14:5.

4

*k Moabites*, Gen. 19:37.

*l Sheep*, Deut. 32:14.

*m Tribute*, Ezra 4:13.

[d]bears out of the wood, and tare
forty and two children[G] of them.[S]
25 And he went from thence[G]
to mount [e]Cär′mel, and from
thence[G] he returned to [f]Să-mā′-
rĭ-ȧ.

## CHAPTER 3

*Jehoram's reign. 4 The war with Moab. 9 The distress of Jehoram and his allies for want of water. 12 They consult Elisha and obtain water, and promise of victory. 21 The Moabites, deceived by the appearance of the water, are overthrown.*

NOW [a]Jĕ-hō′ram the son of
[b]Ā′hăb began to reign over
[c]Ĭş′ra-el in [d]Să-mā′rĭ-ȧ the eighteenth year of [e]Jĕ-hŏsh′a-phăt
king of [f]Jū′dah, and reigned
twelve years.
2 And [a,g]he wrought evil in the
sight of the LORD; but not like
his [b]father, and like his [h]mother:
for he put away the [1]image[G] of
[i]Bā′al that his father had made.
3 Nevertheless he cleaved[G] unto
the sins of [j]Jĕr-o-bō′am the son
of Nē′băt, which made Ĭş′ra-el to
sin; he departed not therefrom.
4 ¶ And Mē′shȧ king of [k]Mō′ab
was a sheepmaster,[G] and rendered unto the king of Ĭş′ra-el an
hundred thousand [l,m]lambs, and
an hundred thousand rams, with
the [n]wool.
5 But it came to pass, when
[b]Ā′hăb was dead, that the king
of [k]Mō′ab rebelled against the
[a]king of Ĭş′ra-el.
6 ¶ And king [a]Jĕ-hō′ram went
out of [d]Să-mā′rĭ-ȧ the same time,
and [o]numbered[G] all Ĭş′ra-el.
7 And he went and sent to [e]Jĕ-
hŏsh′a-phăt the king of [f]Jū′dah,
saying, The king of [k]Mō′ab hath
rebelled against me: wilt thou go
with me against Mō′ab to battle?
And he said, [p]I will go up: I *am*
as thou *art*, my people as thy people, *and* my horses as thy horses.
8 And he said, [p]Which way
shall we go up? And he answered, The way through the
wilderness of Ē′dom.
9 So the [a]king of Ĭş′ra-el went,
and the [e]king of Jū′dah, and the
king of [q]Ē′dom: and they [1]fetch-
ed[G] a compass of seven days'
journey: and there was no water
for the [r]host, and for the cattle
that followed them.
10 And the [a]king of Ĭş′ra-el
said, Alas! that the LORD hath
called these three*kings together,

v.4–825 BC

*n Wool, tribute paid in*, Judg. 6:37.

6

*o Muster*, 2 Kin. 25:19.

7

*p Alliances, political*, Josh. 9:15.

9

*q Edomites*, 2 Kin. 8:21.

*r Armies, confederated*, Deut. 11:4.

1 R. V. made a circuit

*** KING.** *Called* KING OF KINGS, Ezra 7:12; Ezek. 26:7; Dan. 2:37. *Divinely authorized*, Deut. 17:15; 1 Sam. 9:16, 17; 1 Chr. 22:10; 2 Chr. 2:11, 12; Prov. 8:15; Dan. 2:21, 37; 4:17; Hos. 8:4; 13:11.

How chosen: *By divine appointment*, *Saul*, 1 Sam. 10:1; *David and the Davidic dynasty*, 1 Sam. 16:1–13. *By hereditary succession*, 2 Sam. 7:12–16; 1 Kin. 1:28–30; 2 Chr. 21:3, 4; Psa. 89:35–37; *not by hereditary succession*, 1 Chr. 1:43–51. *By lot*, 1 Sam. 10:20, 21.

Modes of induction into office: *By anointing*, Judg. 9:8, 15; *of Saul*, 1 Sam. 9:16; 10:1; 15:1; *of David*, 1 Sam. 16:3, 12, 13; 2 Sam. 2:4; 5:3; 12:7; 19:21; 1 Chr. 11:3; *of Solomon*, 1 Kin. 1:39; 1 Chr. 29:22; *of Jehu*, 1 Kin. 19:16; 2 Kin. 9:1–3, 6, 12; *of Hazael*, 1 Kin. 19:15; *of Joash*, 2 Kin. 11:12; 2 Chr. 23:11; *of Jehoahaz*, 2 Kin. 23:30; *of Cyrus*, Isa. 45:1. *By proclamation*, 2 Sam. 15:10; 1 Kin. 1:33, 34; 2 Kin. 9:13; 11: 12. *By an oath*, 2 Kin. 11:4.

Ceremonial recognition of: *By prostration*, 1 Sam. 25:41; 2 Sam. 9:6, 8; 1 Kin. 1:23, 31; *by obeisance*, 2 Sam. 9:6, 8; 1 Kin. 1:16; *by kneeling before*, Matt. 27:29; *by salutation to, O king, live forever*, Dan. 2:4; 6:6, 21.

*Drunkenness of, forbidden*, Prov. 31:4, 5. *Drunken, instances of*, Hos. 7:5; *Baasha*, 1 Kin. 16:9; *Ben-hadad*, 1 Kin. 20:16; *Belshazzar*, Dan. 5:1–4, 23; *Ahasuerus*, Esth. 1:7, 10.

*Prayer for*, Ezra 6:10. *Prayer for, enjoined*, 1 Tim. 2:1, 2.

*Decrees of, irrevocable*, Esth. 8:8; Dan. 6:8, 9, 12–15.

*Acts as judge*, 2 Sam. 8:15; 15:2; 1 Kin. 10:9; 2 Kin. 8:1–6; Psa. 72:1–4; 122:5; Acts 25:11, 12, 20, 21. *Precepts concerning*, Deut. 17:14–19; Prov. 31:4, 5; Ezek. 46:16–18.

*Obedience to, enjoined*, Eccl. 8:2–5.

*Rights and duties of*, Prov. 25:2; 29:4, 12, 14; Jer. 21:12. *Exercises executive clemency*, 1 Sam. 11:13; 2 Sam. 16:10; 19:13, 18–23.

*Constitutional restrictions of*, Deut. 17:18–20; 1 Sam. 10:24, 25; 2 Sam. 5:3; 2 Kin. 11:12, 17; 2 Chr. 23:11; Jer. 34:8–11; Dan. 6:12–15.

Influenced by popular opinion: *Saul*, 1 Sam. 14:45; 15:24; *Jehoshaphat*, 2 Chr. 20:21; *Hezekiah*, 2 Chr. 30:2; *Zedekiah*, Jer. 38:19, 24–27; *Herod*, Matt. 14:5; Acts 12:2, 3; *Pilate*, John 19:6–13.

*Religious duties of*, Ezek. 45:9–25; 46:2, 4–8. *Deification of*, Ezek. 28:2, 9; Acts 12:22, 23. *Loyalty to, enjoined*, Prov. 16:14, 15; Eccl. 10:20. *Respect due to*, Job 34:18; Isa. 8:21, Matt. 22:21; Mark 12:17.

Influence of queens over: *Bath-sheba*, 1 Kin. 1:28–34; *Jezebel*, 1 Kin. 18:4, 13 19:1–3; 21:5–16; *Esther*, Esth. 5:1–8.

Emoluments of: *Confiscated property*, 1 Kin. 21:1–16; *spoils*, 2 Sam. 12:30; 1 Chr. 26:26, 27; 2 Chr. 24:23; *tariff on imports, and internal revenue on merchandise*, 1 Kin. 10:15; 29; *tribute*, 2 Sam. 8:2; 20:24; 1 Kin. 10:25; 12:18; 2 Chr. 17:11; *poll tax*, Matt. 17:24–27; *presents*, 1 Sam. 10:27; 16:20; 2 Chr. 9:24.

*Commissary of*, 1 Kin. 4:7–19, 27, 28; 1 Chr. 27:25–31; 2 Chr. 26:10; 32:28, 29. *Extensive studs of*, 1 Kin. 1:33; 4: 26; 10:25; 2 Chr. 9:24, 25.

Chief officers of: *Captain of the host*, 2 Sam. 8:16; 1 Kin. 4:4; *recorder*, 2 Sam. 8:16; 20:24; 1 Kin. 4:3; *scribe*, 2 Sam. 8: 17; 20:25; 1 Kin. 4:3; *chief priests*, 2 Sam. 8:17; 20:25; 1 Kin. 4:2; *chief of the bodyguard*, 2 Sam. 8:18; 15:18 20:23; 1 Chr. 11:25; *collector of tribute*, 2 Sam. 20:24; *chief ruler*, 2 Sam. 20:26; 1 Kin. 4:5; Esth. 3:1, 2; 8:1, 2, 15; 10:3; *counselor*, 1 Kin. 4:5; *provincial governors*, Dan. 6:1–3.

Subordinate officers of: *Governor of the household*, 1 Kin. 4:6; 2 Chr. 28:7; *keeper of the wardrobe*, 2 Kin. 22:14; 2 Chr. 34:22.

*Chronicles of, kept*, 1 Kin. 11:41; 14:19; 2 Kin. 21:25; 1 Chr. 9:1; 27:24; 29:29; 2 Chr. 9:29; 12:15; 20:34; 26:22; 32:32; Ezra 5:17; Esth. 6:1.

*For the kings of Israel, before the revolt of the ten tribes*, see footnote, ISRAEL, Ex. 4:22; *after the revolt*, see footnote, ISRAEL, *After the revolt*, 1 Kin. 12:1.

*For the kings of Judah after the revolt*, see footnote, JUDAH, *Kingdom of*, 2 Chr. 11:17.

to deliver[C] them into the hand
of [k]Mō'ab!
11 But [e]Jĕ-hŏsh'a-phăt said,
*Is there* not here a prophet of the
LORD, that we may [s]enquire of
the LORD by him? And one of
the king of Ĭṣ'ra-el's servants answered and said, Here *is* [t]Ē-lī'-
shȧ the son of [u]Shā'phat, which
poured[C] water on the hands of
Ē-lī'jah.
12 And [e]Jĕ-hŏsh'a-phăt said,
The [v]word of the LORD is with
him. So the [a]king of Ĭṣ'ra-el
and Jĕ-hŏsh'a-phăt and the
king of Ē'dom went down to
him.
13 And [t]Ē-lī'shȧ [w]said unto the
king of Ĭṣ'ra-el, What have I to
do with thee? get thee to the
[x]prophets of thy father, and to
the prophets of thy mother. And
the king of Ĭṣ'ra-el said unto
him, Nay: for the LORD hath
called these three *kings together, to deliver them into the
hand of [k]Mō'ab.
14 And [t]Ē-lī'shȧ said, *As* the
LORD of hosts liveth, before
whom I stand, surely, were it not
that I regard the presence of
[e]Jĕ-hŏsh'a-phăt the king of [f]Jū'-
dah, I would not look toward
thee, nor see thee.
15 But now bring me a minstrel.[C] And it came to pass, when
the minstrel[C] played, that the
hand of the LORD [v]came upon
him.
16 And [v]he said, Thus saith the
LORD, Make this valley full of
ditches.
17 For thus saith the LORD, Ye
shall not see wind, neither shall
ye see rain; yet that valley shall
be filled with water, that ye may
drink, both ye, and your cattle,
and your beasts.
18 And this is *but* a light thing
in the sight of the LORD: [y,z]he
will deliver the [a]Mō'ab-ītes also
into your hand.
19 And ye shall smite every
fenced[C] city, and every choice
city, and shall fell every good
tree, and stop all wells of water,
and mar every good piece of land
with stones.
20 [s]And it came to pass in the
morning, when the meat[C] offering was offered[C] that, behold,
[b]there came water by the way
of Ē'dom, and the country was
filled with water.
21 ¶ And when all the [a]Mō'ab-
ītes heard that the kings were
come up to fight against them,
they gathered all that were able
to put on [c]armour, and upward,
and stood in the border.
22 And they rose up early in the
morning, and the sun shone upon the water, and the Mō'ab-ītes
saw the water on the other side
*as* red as blood:[s]
23 And they said, This *is* blood:
the kings are surely slain,[C] and
they have smitten one another:
now therefore, [a]Mō'ab, to the
[d]spoil.
24 And when they came to the
camp of Ĭṣ'ra-el, the Ĭṣ'ra-el-ītes
rose up and smote the [a]Mō'ab-
ītes, so that they fled before
them: but they went forward
smiting[C] the Mō'ab-ītes, even in
*their* country.
25 And [a,b]they beat down the
cities, and on every good piece of
land cast every man his stone,
and filled it; and they stopped
all the wells of water, and
felled all the good trees: only
in †Kĭr–hăr'a-sĕth left they
the stones thereof; howbeit the
slingers went about *it*, and
smote it.
26 ¶ And when the king of Mō'-
ab saw that the battle was too
sore[C] for him, he took with him

11
*s Armies, religious ceremonies in,* Deut. 11:4.
*t Elisha,* 1 Kin. 19:16.
*u* 1 Kin. 19:16; 2 Kin. 6:31.

12
*v Prophets, inspiration of,* Isa. 3:2.

13
*w Reproof, faithfulness in,* Prov. 17:10.
*x Idolatry, folly of,* 1 Sam. 15:23.

18
*y War, God in,* Judg. 3:2.
*z God, providence of,* Gen. 2:2.

*a Moabites,* Gen. 19:37.

20
*b Prophecies, fulfilled,* Dan. 9:24.

21
*c Armor,* 1 Sam. 17:54.

23
*d Spoils,* 1 Chr. 26:27.

† **KIR-HARASETH** (*city of the hill*), called also KIR-HARESH, KIR-HARESETH, and KIR-HERES. *A city of Moab,* 2 Kin. 3:25; Isa. 16:7, 11; Jer. 48:31, 36. *Called* KIR OF MOAB, Isa. 15:1.

seven hundred men that drew swords, to break through *even* unto the king of Ē'dom: but they could not.

27 Then he took his eldest son that should have reigned in his stead, and [e]offered [f]him *for* a burnt offering upon the wall. And there was great [g]indignation against Iș'ra-el: and they departed from him, and returned to *their own* land.

## CHAPTER 4

*Elisha multiplies the widow's oil. 8 He promises a son to the good Shunammite. 18 He restores her son to life. 38 At Gilgal he heals the deadly pottage. 42 He satisfies a hundred men with twenty loaves.*

NOW there cried a certain [a, b]woman of the wives of the sons of the [c]prophets unto [d]Ė-lī'shȧ, saying, Thy servant my husband is dead; and thou knowest that thy servant did [e]fear the LORD: and the [f]creditor is come to take unto him my two [g]sons to be [h]bondmen.[c]

2 And [d]Ė-lī'shȧ [i]said unto her, What shall I do for thee? tell me, what hast thou in the house? And she said, Thine handmaid hath not anything in the house, save a pot of [j]oil.

3 Then he said, Go, borrow thee vessels abroad of all thy neighbours, *even* empty vessels; borrow not a few.

4 And when thou art come in, thou shalt shut the door upon thee and upon thy sons, and shalt pour out into all those vessels, and thou shalt set aside that which is full.

5 So she went from him, and shut the door upon her and upon her sons, who brought *the vessels* to her; and [k]she poured out.

6 And it came to pass, when the vessels were full, that she said unto her son, Bring me yet a vessel. And he said unto her, *There is* not a vessel more. And the [j]oil stayed.[c]

7 Then she came and told the man of God. And he said, Go sell the [j]oil, and pay thy debt, and live thou and thy children of the rest.

8 ¶[Q]And it[c] fell on a day, that [d]Ė-lī'shȧ passed to [l]Shụ'nem, where *was* a great [m]woman; and she [n]constrained [o, p]him to eat bread.[c] And *so* it was, *that* as oft as he passed by, he turned in thither[c] to eat bread.[c]

9 And she said unto her husband, Behold now, I perceive that this *is* an holy man of God, which passeth by us continually.

10 Let us make a little [q]chamber, I pray thee, on the wall; and let us set for him there a bed, and a table, and a stool, and a candlestick[c]: and it shall be, when he cometh to us, that he shall turn in thither.[c]

11 And it fell on a day, that he came thither[c], and he turned into the [q]chamber, and lay there.

12 And he said to *Gē-hā'zī his servant, Call this [r]Shụ'nammīte. And when he had called her, she stood before him.

13 And [p]he said unto him, Say now unto her, Behold, [s]thou hast been careful[c] for us with all this care; what *is* to be done for thee? [t, u]wouldest thou be [v]spoken for to the king, or to the captain of the host? And she [w]answered, I dwell among mine own people.

14 And he said, What then *is* to be done for her? and *Gē-hā'zī answered, Verily she hath no child, and her husband is old.

15 And he said, Call her. And when he had called her, she stood in the door.

16 And [x]he said, About this

27
*e Idolatry, wicked practices of,* 1 Sam. 15:23.
*f Human Sacrifices,* Deut. 12:31.
*g Anger,* Psa. 37:8.

1
*a Widow,* 2 Sam. 14:5.
*b Debtor,* Luke 7:41.
*c Prophets, schools of,* Isa. 3:2.
*d Elisha, miracles of,* vs. 1–6; 1 Kin. 19:16.
*e Fear of God,* Acts 9:31.
*f Creditor, oppressions of,* Deut. 15:2.
*g Children, taken for debt,* Mark 10:14.
*h Servant,* Jer. 2:14.

2
*i Poor, kindness to,* vs. 1–7; Prov. 21:13.
*j Oil,* Deut. 12:17.

5
*k Miracles, of Elisha,* Luke 23:8.

8
*l Shunem,* Josh. 19:18.
*m Women, good,* Prov. 31:10.
*n Hospitality, instances of,* Rom. 12:13.
*o Minister, hospitality to,* Rom. 15:16.
*p Elisha,* 1 Kin. 19:16.

10
*q House, chambers in,* Esth. 8:1.

12
*r Shunammite,* 1 Kin. 1:3.

13
*s Thankfulness, of man to man,* Acts 24:3.
*t Minister, influential in public affairs,* Rom. 15:16.
*u Civil Service, influence in,* Dan. 1:5.
*v Mediation,* Gal. 3:19.
*w Contentment, instances of,* 1 Tim. 6:6.

16
*x Elisha, prophecies of,* v. 16; 1 Kin. 19:16.

***GEHAZI.** *Servant of Elisha,* 2 Kin. 4:12, 29, 31. 20–27. *Mentions to King Jehoram the miracles of Elisha, his master,* 2 Kin. 8:4, 5. *Covetousness of. and the judgment of leprosy upon,* 2 Kin. 5:

season, according to the time[G] of life, thou shalt embrace a son. And she said, Nay, my lord, *thou* man of God, do not lie unto thine handmaid.

17 And the woman conceived, and bare a son at that season that Ē-lī′shȧ had said unto her, according to the time[G] of life.

18 ¶ And when the child was grown, it fell on a day, that he went out to his father to the reapers.

19 And he said unto his father, My head, my head. And he said to [1]a lad, Carry him to his mother.

20 And when he had taken him, and brought him to his mother, he sat on her knees till noon, and *then* died.

21 And she went up, and laid him on the bed of the man of God, and shut *the door* upon him, and went out.

22 And she called unto her husband, and said, Send me, I pray thee, one of the young men, and one of the [y]asses, that I may run to the man of God, and come again.

23 And he said, Wherefore wilt thou go to him to day? *it is* neither [z]new moon, nor [a]sabbath. And she said, *It shall be* well.

24 Then she saddled an ass, and said to her servant, Drive, and go forward; slack not *thy* riding for me, except I bid thee.

25 So[Q] she went and came unto the man of God to mount [b]Cär′mel. And it came to pass, when the man of God saw her afar off, that he said to *Ḡē-hā′zī his servant, Behold, *yonder is* that [c]Shụ′nam-mīte:

26 Run now, I pray thee, to meet her, and say unto her, *Is it* well with thee? *is it* well with thy husband? *is it* well with the child? And she answered, [d]*It is* well.

27 And when she came to the man of God to the hill, she caught him by the feet: but *Ḡē-hā′zī came near to thrust her away. And the man of God said, Let her alone; for her soul *is* vexed[G] within her: and the LORD hath hid *it* from me, and hath not told me.

28 Then she said, Did I desire a son of my lord? did I not say, Do not deceive me?

29 Then he said to *Ḡē-hā′zī, Gird up thy loins, and take my staff in thine hand, and go thy way: if thou meet any man, salute[G] him not; and if any salute[G] thee, answer him not again: and lay my staff upon the face of the child.[Q]

30 And the mother of the child said, *As* the LORD liveth, and *as* thy soul liveth, I will not leave thee. And he arose, and followed her.

31 And *Ḡē-hā′zī passed on before them, and laid the staff upon the face of the child; but *there was* neither voice, nor hearing. Wherefore he went again to meet him, and told him, saying, The child is not awaked.

32 And when [e]Ē-lī′shȧ was come into the house, behold, the child was †dead, *and* laid upon his bed.

33 He went in therefore, and shut the door upon them twain,[G] and [f]prayed unto the LORD.[Q]

34 And he went up, and lay upon the child, and put his mouth upon his mouth, and his eyes upon his eyes, and his hands upon his hands: and he stretched himself upon the child;[G] and the flesh of the child waxed warm.

19
1 R. V. his servant,

22
y *Ass, domesticated*, 2 Chr. 28:15.

23
z *New Moon*, Amos 8:5.

a *Sabbath*, Ex. 16:23.

25
b *Carmel*, Jer. 46:18.
c *Shunammite*, 1 Kin. 1:3.

26
d *Resignation, exemplified*, Job 5:17.

32
e *Elisha, miracles of*, vs. 32–44; 1 Kin. 19:16.

33
f *Intercession, of man with God*, Jer. 27:18.

† **DEAD.** *Prepared for burial, by washing*, Acts 9:37; *by anointing*, Matt. 26:12; *by wrapping in linen*, Matt. 27:59. *Incense burnt for*, 2 Chr. 16:14; 21:19; Jer. 34:5.
**Raised to life.** INSTANCES OF: *Son of the widow of Zarephath*, 1 Kin. 17:17–23; *Shunammite's son*, 2 Kin. 4:32–37; *young man laid in Elisha's sepulchre*, 2 Kin. 13:21; *widow's son*, Luke 7:12–15; *Jairus' daughter*, Luke 8:49–55; *Lazarus*, John 11:43, 44; *Dorcas*, Acts 9:37–40; *Eutychus*, Acts 20:9–12; see also Heb. 11:35.
See footnote, DEATH, Num. 23:10.

35 Then he returned, and walked in the house to and fro; and went up, and stretched himself upon him: and the child sneezed seven times, and the [g]child [h]opened his eyes.

36 And he called *Gē-hā'zī, and said, Call this [c]Shu'nam-mīte. So he called her. And when she was come in unto him, he said, Take up thy son.[Q]

37 Then she went in, and fell at his feet, and bowed herself to the ground, and took up her son, and went out.[Q]

38 ¶ And [c]Ē-lī'shȧ came again to [i]Gĭl'găl: and *there was* a [j]dearth[C] in the land; and the sons of the [k]prophets *were* sitting before him: and he said unto his servant, Set on the great pot, and seethe[C] pottage[C] for the sons of the prophets.

39 And one went out into the field to gather herbs, and found a wild vine, and gathered thereof wild [l]gourds his lap full, and came and shred[C] *them* into the pot of pottage: for they knew *them* not.

40 So they poured out for the men to eat. And it came to pass, as they were eating of the pottage, that they cried out, and said, O *thou* man of God, *there is* death in the pot. And they could not eat *thereof*.

41 But he said, Then bring meal. And [e]he cast *it* into the pot; and he said, Pour out for the people, that they may eat. And [h]there was no harm in the pot.

42 ¶ And there came a man from [m]Bā'al-shăl'ĭ-shȧ, and brought the man of God [n,o]bread of the [p]firstfruits, twenty loaves of [q]barley, and [2]full ears of [r]corn[C] in [3]the husk thereof. And he said, Give unto the people, that they may eat.

43[Q] And his servitor[C] said, What, should I set this before an hundred men? [e]He said again, Give the people, that they may eat: for thus saith the LORD, They shall eat, and shall leave *thereof*.

44 So he set *it* before them, and [h]they did eat, and left *thereof* according to the word of the LORD.[Q]

35
*g* *Children, miracles in behalf of*, Mark 10:14.
*h* *Miracles*, Luke 23:8.

38
*i* *Gilgal*, Josh. 4:19.
*j* *Drought*, Gen. 31:40.
*k* *Prophets, schools of*, Isa. 3:2.

39
*l* Jonah 4:6-10.

42
*m* Or, *Shalisha*, 1 Sam. 9:4.
*n* *Bread*, Ezek. 4:13.
*o* *Prophets, emoluments of*, Isa. 3:2.
*p* *First Fruits*, Deut. 18:4.
*q* *Barley*, Ex. 9:31.
*r* *Corn*, Psa. 65:13.
2 R. V. fresh
3 R. V. his sack.

## CHAPTER 5

*Naaman's leprosy. 8 Elisha sends him to Jordan, and he is healed. 15 He refuses Naaman's gifts. 20 Gehazi by deception obtains a gift, and is smitten with leprosy.*

NOW [a]Nā'ȧ-man,[Q] [b]captain of the host of the king of [c]Sȳr'ĭ-ȧ, was a great man with his master, and honourable, because by him the LORD had given deliverance unto Sȳr'ĭ-ȧ: he was also a mighty man in valour,[C] *but he was* a [d]leper.

2 And the Sȳr'ĭ-ans had gone out by companies, and had brought away [e]captive out of the land of Ĭs'ra-el a little [f]maid; and [g]she waited[C] on Nā'ȧ-man's wife.

3 And [f,g]she said unto her mistress, Would God my lord *were* with the [h,i]prophet that *is* in [j]Sȧ-mā'rĭ-ȧ! for he would recover[C] him of his [d]leprosy.

4 And *one* went in, and told his lord, saying, Thus and thus said the maid that *is* of the land of Ĭs'ra-el.

5 And the king of [c]Sȳr'ĭ-ȧ said, Go[C] to, go, and I will send a letter unto the king of Ĭs'ra-el. And he departed, and took with him ten talents[C] of [k]silver, and six thousand *pieces* of [l]gold, and ten changes of [m]raiment.

6 And he brought the letter to the king of Ĭs'ra-el, saying, Now when this letter is come unto thee, behold, I have *therewith* sent [a]Nā'ȧ-man my servant to thee, [n]that thou mayest recover[C] him of his [d]leprosy.

7 And it came to pass, when the king of Ĭs'ra-el had read the let-

1
*a* Luke 4:27.
*b* *Captain*, Num. 31:48.
*c* *Syria*, 2 Kin. 6:23.
*d* *Leprosy*, Lev. 13:2.

2
*e* *Captive*, 1 Sam. 30:3.
*f* *Children, good*, Mark 10:14.
*g* *Servant, captives of war, made*, Jer. 2:14.

3
*h* *Elisha*, 1 Kin. 19:16.
*i* *Prophets*, Isa. 3:2.
*j* *Samaria*, 1 Kin. 16:24.

5
*k* *Silver*, 1 Chr. 28:14.
*l* *Gold*, Ezek. 7:1
*m* *Dress*, Zech. 3:

6
*n* *Intercession, of man with man*, Jer. 27:18.

ter, that he [o]rent[G] his clothes, and
said, *Am* I God, to kill and to
make alive, that this man doth
send unto me to recover[G] a man
of his [d]leprosy? wherefore consider, I pray you, and [p]see how
he seeketh a quarrel against me.
8 ¶ And it was *so*, when [h,q]Ė-lī′-
shȧ the man of God had heard
that the king of Ĭş′ra-el had
[o]rent[G] his clothes, that he sent to
the king, saying, Wherefore[G] hast
thou rent[G] thy clothes? let him
come now to me, and he shall
know that there is a prophet in
Ĭş′ra-el.
9 So [a]Nā′a-man came with his
[r]horses and with his [s]chariot,
and stood at the door of the
house of [h]Ė-lī′shȧ.
10 And [h]Ė-lī′shȧ sent a messenger unto him, saying, Go and
wash in [t]Jôr′dan [u]seven times,
and thy flesh shall come again to
thee, and thou shalt be clean.[G][Q]
11 But [a]Nā′a-man was [v]wroth,[G]
and [w]went away, and said, [x]Be-
hold, I thought, He will surely
come out to me, and stand, and
[y]call on the name of the LORD
his God, and [1]strike[G] his hand
over the place, and recover[G] the
[d]leper.
12 [z]*Are* not Ăb′a-nȧ and Phär′-
par, rivers of Dȧ-măs′cus, better
than all the waters of Ĭş′ra-el?
may I not wash in them, and be
clean? So he turned and went
away in a rage.
13 And his servants came near,
and spake unto him, and said,
My father, *if* the [a]prophet had
bid thee *do some* great thing,
wouldest thou not have done *it*?
how much rather then, when he
saith to thee, Wash, and be
clean?
14[S] Then went he down, and
dipped himself [b]seven times in
[c]Jôr′dan, according to the saying of the man of God: and his
flesh came again like unto the
flesh of a little child, and he was
[d]clean.[G][Q]
15 ¶ And he returned to the
[a]man of God, he and all his company, and came, and stood before him: and he said, Behold,
[e,f]now I know that *there is* no
God in all the earth, but in
Ĭş′ra-el: [g]now therefore, I pray
thee, take a [2,h]blessing of thy
servant.[S]
16 But he said, [i]*As* the LORD
liveth, before whom I stand, I
will receive none. And he urged
him to take [h]*it*; but he refused.
17 And [j]Nā′a-man said, Shall
there not then, I pray thee, be
given to thy servant two [k]mules'
burden of earth? for thy servant
will henceforth offer neither
[l]burnt offering nor sacrifice[G] unto
other gods, but unto the LORD.
18 In this thing the LORD pardon thy servant, *that* when my
master goeth into the [m]house of
Rĭm′mon to [n]worship there, and
he leaneth on my hand, and I
bow myself in the house of Rĭm′-
mon: when I bow down myself
in the house of Rĭm′mon, the
LORD pardon thy servant in this
thing.
19 And he said unto him, Go in
peace. So he departed from him
a little way.[Q]
20 ¶ But [o]Gē-hā′zī, the servant
of [a]Ė-lī′shȧ the man of God,
said, Behold, my master hath
spared [j]Nā′a-man this Sȳr′ĭ-an,
in not receiving at his hands that
which he brought: but, [i]*as* the
LORD liveth, [p]I will run after
him, and [q]take somewhat of him.
21 So [o,p]Gē-hā′zī followed after
[j]Nā′a-man. And when Nā′a-
man saw *him* running after him,
he lighted[G] down from the [r]char-
iot to meet him, and said, *Is* all
well?
22 And he said, All *is* well.
[s,t]My master hath sent me, saying, Behold, even now there be

**7**
o *Rending of Garments*, 2 Chr. 34:27.
p *Motive, misunderstood*, Psa. 106:8.

**8**
q *Prophets*, Isa. 3:2.

**9**
r *Horse*, Job 39:19.
s *Chariot*, Josh. 11:4.

**10**
t *Jordan*, Gen. 32:10.
u *Seven*, Gen. 7:2.

**11**
v *Anger*, Psa. 37:8.
w *Rashness, instances of*, 2 Sam. 6:7.
x *Pride, instances of*, Prov. 16:18.
y *Intercession, of man with God*, Jer. 27:18.
1 R. V. wave

**12**
z *Unbelief, instances of*, Heb. 3:12.

**13**
a *Elisha*, 1 Kin. 19:16.

**14**
b *Seven*, Gen. 7:2.
c *Jordan*, Gen. 32:10.

d *Leprosy, healed*, Lev. 13:2.

**15**
e *Miracles, convincing effect of*, Luke 23:8.
f *Faith*, Mark 11:22.
g *Thankfulness, of man to man*, Acts 24:3.
h *Presents*, Gen. 32:13.
2 R. V. present

**16**
i *Oath*, Num. 5:19.

**17**
j Luke 4:27.
k *Mule*, 2 Sam. 18:9.
l *Offerings, burnt*, Lev. 6:17.

**18**
m *Temple, idolatrous*, 1 Kin. 6:17.
n *Idolatry*, 1 Sam. 15:23.

**20**
o *Gehazi*, 2 Kin. 4:12.
p *Servant, wicked and unfaithful*, Jer. 2:14.
q *Covetousness, instances of*, Isa. 57:17.

**21**
r *Chariot*, Josh. 11:4.

**22**
s *Deception, instances of*, Josh. 9:4.
t *Falsehood, instances of*, Job 21:34.

come to me from mount Ē'phră-ĭm two young men of the sons of the prophets: give them, I pray thee, a talent[c] of [u]silver, and two changes of [v]garments.

23 And [i]Nā'a-man said, Be content, [w]take two talents.[c] And he urged him, and bound two talents of [u]silver in two bags, with two changes of [v]garments, and laid *them* upon two of his servants; and they bare *them* before him.

24 And when he came to the [3]tower, he took *them* from their hand, and bestowed[c] *them* in the house: and he let the men go, and they departed.

25 But [o,p]he went in, and stood before his master. And [a]Ė-lī'shȧ said unto him, Whence[c] *comest thou,* Gĕ-hā'zī? And he [l]said, Thy servant went no whither.[c]

26 [s]And he said unto him, Went not mine heart *with thee,* when the man turned again from his chariot to meet thee? [x]*Is it* a time to receive [y]money, and to receive garments, and oliveyards, and vineyards, and sheep, and oxen, and menservants, and maidservants?

27 [z]The [a,b]leprosy therefore of [c]Nā'a-man shall cleave[c] unto thee, and unto thy seed for ever. And he went out from his presence a leper *as white* as snow.[s]

u *Silver,* 1 Chr. 28:14.
v *Dress,* Zech. 3:3.

23
w *Generosity,* Gen. 20:14.

24
3 R. V. hill,

26
x *Reproof, faithfulness in,* Prov. 17:10.
y *Money,* Jer. 32:9.

27
z *Judgments,* Ex. 6:6.

a *Disease,* Ex. 15:26.
b *Leprosy, sent as a judgment,* Lev. 13:2.
c Luke 4:27.

## CHAPTER 6

*Elisha causes iron to swim. 8 He discloses the counsel of the king of Syria. 13 The Syrian army, sent to apprehend Elisha, is smitten with blindness. 19 Being led into Samaria, they are dismissed in peace. 24 The siege of Samaria, and the great famine consequent thereon 30 The king of Israel sends to slay Elisha.*

AND the [a]sons of the prophets said unto [b]Ė-lī'shȧ, Behold now, the [c]place where we dwell with thee is too strait[c] for us.

2 Let us go, we pray thee, unto [d]Jôr'dan, and take thence[c] every man a beam, and let us make us a place there, where we may dwell. And he answered, Go ye.

3 And one said, Be content, I pray thee, and go with thy servants. And he answered, I will go.

4 So he went with them. And when they came to [d]Jôr'dan, they cut down wood.

5 But as one was felling a beam, the [e]ax head fell into the water: and he cried, and said, Alas, master! for it was borrowed.

6 And the [f]man of God said, Where fell it? And he shewed him the place. And he cut down a stick, and cast *it* in thither;[c] and the [g]iron [h]did swim.[s]

7 Therefore said he, Take *it* up to thee. And he put out his hand, and took it.

8 ¶ Then the king of Sy̆r'ĭ-ȧ warred against [i]Ĭṣ'ra-el, and took counsel with his servants, saying, In such and such a place *shall be* my camp.

9 And the [b]man of God sent unto the [j]king of [i]Ĭṣ'ra-el, saying, Beware that thou pass not such a place; for thither the Sy̆r'ĭ-anṣ are come down.

10 And the [j]king of Ĭṣ'ra-el sent to the place which the man of God told him and warned him of, and saved himself there, not once nor twice.

11 Therefore the heart of the king of Sy̆r'ĭ-ȧ was sore[c] troubled for this thing; and he called his servants, and said unto them, Will ye not shew me which of us *is* for the king of Ĭṣ'ra-el?

12 And one of his servants said, None, my lord, O king: but [k]Ė-lī'shȧ, the prophet that *is* in Ĭṣ'ra-el, telleth the king of Ĭṣ'ra-el the words that thou speakest in thy bedchamber.[s]

13 And he said, Go and spy where he *is,* that I may send and fetch him. And it was told him, saying, Behold, *he is* in [l]Dō'than.

1
a *Students,* 2 Kin. 2:3.
b *Elisha,* 1 Kin. 19:16.
c *School, crowded attendance of,* Acts 19:9.

2
d *Jordan,* Gen. 32:10.

5
e *Ax,* Deut. 19:5.

6
f *Elisha, miracles of,* 1 Kin. 19:16.
g *Iron,* Prov. 27:17.
h *Miracles,* Luke 23:8.

8
i *Israel, after the revolt,* 1 Kin. 12:1.

9
j *Jehoram,* 2 Kin. 1:17.

12
k *Prophets, inspiration of,* Isa. 3:2.

13
l Gen. 37:17.

14 Therefore sent he thither
*m*horses, and *n*chariots, and a
great host: and they came by
night, and compassed the city
about.
15 And when the servant of the
man of God was risen early, and
gone forth, behold, an host compassed the city both with horses
and chariots. And his servant
said unto him, Alas, my master!
how shall we do?
16 And he answered, *o*Fear not:
for *p*they that *be* with us *are* more
than they that *be* with them.
17 And *b*Ê-lī'shȧ *q*prayed, and
said, LORD, I pray thee, open
his eyes, that he may see. And
the LORD *h*opened the eyes of
the young man; and he *r*saw:
and, behold, the mountain *was*
full of horses and *s*chariots of
fire round about Ê-lī'shȧ.
18 And when they came down
to him, *b*Ê-lī'shȧ *q*prayed unto
the LORD, and said, Smite this
people, I pray thee, with *blindness. And he smote them with
blindness according to the word
of Ê-lī'shȧ.
19 And Ê-lī'shȧ said unto them,
This *is* not the way, neither *is*
this the city: follow me, and I
will bring you to the man whom
ye seek. But he led them to
*t*Sā-mā'rĭ-ȧ.
20 And it came to pass, when
they were come into *t*Sā-mā'rĭ-ȧ,
that *b*Ê-lī'shȧ said, LORD, open
the eyes of these *men*, that they
may see. And the LORD opened
their eyes, and they saw; and,
behold, *they were* in the midst of
Sā-mā'rĭ-ȧ.
21 And the king of Ĭs'ra-el said
unto Ê-lī'shȧ, when he saw
them, My father, shall I smite
*them*? shall I smite *them*?
22 And he answered, *u*Thou
shalt not smite *them*: wouldest
thou smite those whom thou hast
taken captive with thy sword
and with thy bow? *v*set bread
and water before them, that they
may eat and drink, and go to
their master.
23 And *w*he prepared great provision for them: and when they
had eaten and drunk, he sent
them away, and they went to
their master. So the bands of
†Sўr'ĭ-ȧ came no more into the
land of Ĭs'ra-el.
24 ¶ And it came to pass after
this, that *x*Bĕn–hā'dăd king of
†Sўr'ĭ-ȧ gathered all his *y*host,
and went up, and *z*besieged *a*Sā-
mā'rĭ-ȧ.
25 And there was a great *b*famine in *a*Sā-mā'rĭ-ȧ: and, behold,
they *c*besieged it, until an *d*ass's
head was *sold* for fourscore
*pieces* of *e*silver, and the fourth
part of a *f*cab of dove's dung for
five *pieces* of silver.
26 ¶ And as the *g*king of Ĭs'-
ra-el was passing by upon the
wall, there cried a woman unto
him, saying, Help, my lord, O
king.

**14**
*m Horse*, Job 39:19.
*n Chariot*, Josh. 11:4.

**16**
*o Faith, instances of*, Mark 11:22.
*p God, preserver*, Gen. 2:2.

**17**
*q Prayer, answered*, Acts 6:4.
*r Vision*, Acts 9:10.
*s Chariot, figurative*, Josh. 11:4.

**19**
*t Samaria*, 1 Kin. 16:24.

**22**
*u Malice, forbidden*, Eph. 4:31.
*v Good for Evil*, Luke 6:27.

**23**
*w Hospitality, instances of*, Rom. 12:13.

**24**
*x Ben-hadad*, 1 Kin. 20:1.
*y Armies*, Deut. 11:4.
*z Siege, instances of*, Deut. 28:53.

*a Samaria*, 1 Kin. 16:24.

**25**
*b Famine, instances of*, 2 Kin. 8:1.
*c Siege, instances of*, Deut. 28:53.
*d Ass*, 2 Chr. 28:15.
*e Money*, Jer. 32:9.
*f Measure*, Deut. 25:15.

**26**
*g Jehoram*, 2 Kin. 1:17.

---

***BLINDNESS.** *Disqualified for priestly office*, Lev. 21:18. *Of animals, disqualified for sacrifice*, Lev. 22:22; Deut. 15:21; Mal. 1:8. *Miraculously inflicted, upon the Sodomites*, Gen. 19:11; *upon the Syrians*, 2 Kin. 6:18–20; *upon Saul of Tarsus*, Acts 9:8, 9; *upon Elymas*, Acts 13:11. *Sent as a judgment*, Deut. 28:28; Acts 13:11.

*Miraculous healing of*, Matt. 9:27–30; 11:5; 12:22; 21:14; *Bartimæus*, Matt. 20:30–34; Mark 10:46–52; *a man of Bethsaida*, Mark 8:22–25; *man born blind*, John 9:1–7.

**Instances of:** *Isaac*, Gen. 27:1. *Jacob*, Gen. 48:10. *Eli*, 1 Sam. 4:15. *Ahijah*, 1 Kin. 14:4.

**Figurative,** John 9:39–41; Rev. 3:17, 18. See footnote, SPIRITUAL BLINDNESS, 2 Cor. 4:4.

† **SYRIA,** highlands lying between the river Euphrates and the Mediterranean Sea. *Called* ARAM, Num. 23:7. *In the time of Abraham it seems to have embraced the region between the rivers Tigris and Euphrates*, Gen. 24:10; 25:20, *including Padan-aram*, Gen. 25:20; 28:5.

**Minor kingdoms within:** *Aram-zobah, called also* ZOBAH *and* ZOBA, 1 Sam. 41:47; 2 Sam. 8:3; 10:6, 8; 1 Kin. 11:23; 1 Chr. 18:5, 9; 19:6; *Geshur*, 2 Sam. 15:8; *Aram-rehob, called also* BETH-REHOB, 2 Sam. 10:6, 8; *Damascus*, 2 Sam. 8:5, 6; 1 Chr. 18:5, 6; *Hamath*, 2 Sam. 8:9, 10; Jer. 39:5.

Conquest of: *By David*, 2 Sam. 8:3–13; *by Jeroboam*, 2 Kin. 14:25, 28; *by Tiglath-pileser, king of Assyria*, 2 Kin. 16:7–9; 18:33, 34.

*People of, colonized in Samaria by the king of Assyria*, 2 Kin. 17:24. *Confederate with Nebuchadnezzar*, 2 Kin. 24:2; Jer. 39:5. *Damascus, the capital of*, Isa. 7:8. *Army of, fled from Samaria*, 2 Kin. 7:6, 7. *Idolatry of*, Judg. 10:6.

*Paul goes to, with letters to apprehend the Christians; is converted, and begins his evangelistic ministry in*, Acts 9:1–27.

*Paul preaches in*, Acts 15:41; 18:18; 21:3; Gal. 1:21.

*Prophecies concerning*, Isa. 7:8–16; 8:4–7; 17:1–3; Jer. 1:15; 49:23–27; Amos 1:3–5; Zech. 9:1.

**The Roman province of:** *Included the land of Canaan*, Luke 2:2, 3; *and Phenicia*, Mark 7:26; Acts 21:3. *The fame of Jesus extended over*, Matt. 4:24.

27 And he said, If the LORD do
not help thee, whence[C] shall I
help thee? out of the barnfloor,
or out of the winepress?
28 And the [g]king said unto her,
What aileth thee? And she answered, This woman said unto
me, [h]Give thy son, that we may
[i]eat him to day, and we will eat
my son to morrow.
29 So we boiled my son, and
did eat him: and I said unto her
on the next day, Give thy son,
that we may eat him: and she
hath hid her son.
30 And it came to pass, when
the [g]king heard the words of the
woman, that he [j]rent[C] his clothes;
and he passed by upon the wall,
and the people looked, and, behold, *he had* [k]sackcloth within
upon his flesh.
31 Then he said, [l]God do so and
more also to me, [m]if the head of
[n]Ĕ-lī'shȧ the son of [o]Shā'phat
shall stand on him this day.
32 But [n]Ĕ-lī'shȧ sat in his
house, and the elders sat with
him; and *the* [g]*king* sent a man
from before him: but ere[C] the
messenger came to him, he said
to the elders, See ye how this son
of a murderer hath sent to take
away mine head? look, when
the messenger cometh, shut the
door, and hold him fast at the
door: *is* not the sound of his
master's feet behind him?
33 And while he yet talked with
them, behold, the messenger
came down unto him: and [g]he
said, Behold, this [p]evil *is* of the
LORD; what[C] should I wait for
the LORD any longer?

## CHAPTER 7

*Elisha foretells plenty in Samaria. 3 Four lepers, going to the camp of the Syrians, bring back tidings of their flight. 12 The king spoils the tents of the Syrians. 17 The unbelieving lord is trodden to death in the press.*

THEN [a]Ĕ-lī'shȧ said, Hear
ye the word of the LORD;
Thus saith the LORD, To morrow about this time *shall* a
[b]measure[C] of fine flour *be sold* for
a shekel, and two measures[C] of
[c]barley for a shekel,[C] in the gate
of [d]Să-mā'rĭ-ȧ.
2 Then a lord on whose hand
the king leaned answered the
man of God, and said, [e]Behold,
*if* the LORD would make windows in heaven, might this thing
be? And he said, Behold, thou
shalt see *it* with thine eyes, but
shalt not eat thereof.
3 ¶ And there were four [f]lep-
rous men [g]at the entering in of
the gate: and they said one to
another, Why sit we here until
we die?
4 If we say, We will enter into
the city, then the [h]famine *is* in
the city, and we shall die there:
and if we sit still here, we die
also. Now therefore come, and
let us fall unto the [i]host of the
Sy̆r'ĭ-ans: if they save us alive,
we shall live; and if they kill us,
we shall but die.
5 And they rose up in the twilight, to go unto the camp of the
Sy̆r'ĭ-ans: and when they were
come to the uttermost[C] part of the
camp of [j]Sy̆r'ĭ-ȧ, behold, *there*
*was* no man there.
6 For the LORD [k]had made the
host of the Sy̆r'ĭ-ans to hear a
noise of chariots, and a noise of
horses, *even* the noise of a great
[i]host: and they said one to another, Lo, the king of Is̆'ra-el
hath hired against us the kings
of the [l]Hĭt'tītes, and the kings
of the [m]Ē-ġy̆p'tians, to come upon us.[s]
7 Wherefore [n]they arose and
[o]fled in the twilight, and left
their tents, and their horses, and
their asses, even the camp as it
*was*, and fled for their life.
8 And when these lepers came
to the uttermost[C] part of the
camp, they went into one tent,
and did eat and drink, and car-

28
h *War, evils of,* Judg. 3.2.
i *Cannibalism,* Lam. 2:20.

30
j *Rending of Garments,* 2 Chr. 34:27.
k *Sackcloth,* Isa. 15:3.

31
l *Malice, instances of,* Eph. 4:31.
m *Persecution, instances of,* John 15:20.
n *Elisha,* 1 Kin. 19:16.
o 1 Kin. 19:16.

33
p *Adversity, dispensation from God,* Psa. 10:6.

1
a *Elisha, prophecies of,* 1 Kin. 19:16.
b *Measure, dry,* Deut. 25:15.
c *Barley,* Ex. 9:31.
d *Samaria,* 1 Kin. 16:24.

2
e *Unbelief, instances of,* Heb. 3:12.

3
f *Leprosy, instances of,* Lev. 13:2.
g *Sanitation and Hygiene, isolation,* Num. 31:23.

4
h *Famine, instances of,* 2 Kin. 8:1.
i *Armies,* Deut. 11:4.

5
j *Syria,* 2 Kin. 6:23.

6
k *Miracles,* Luke 23:8.
l *Hittites,* Judg. 1:26.
m *Egyptians,* Gen. 50:3.

7
n *Armies, panics,* Deut. 11:4.
o *Panic,* Judg. 7:22.

ried thence[G] [p]silver, and [p]gold,
and [p]raiment, and went and hid
*it;* and came again, and entered into another tent, and carried thence[G] *also,* and went and
hid *it.*
9 Then they said one to another, [q]We do not well: this day
*is* a day of good tidings, and we
hold our peace: if we tarry till
the morning light, [1]some mischief will come upon us: [r]now
therefore come, that we may go
and tell the king's household.
10 [r]So they came and called
unto the [s]porter of the city: and
they told them, saying, We came
to the camp of the Sўr'ĭ-anș,
and, behold, *there was* no man
there, neither voice of man, but
horses tied, and asses tied, and
the tents as they *were.*
11 And he called the [s]porters;
and they told *it* to the king's
house within.
12 ¶ And the king arose in the
night, and said unto his servants, I will now shew you what
the Sўr'ĭ-anș have done to us.
They know that we *be* hungry;
therefore are they gone out of the
camp to hide themselves in the
field, saying, When they come
out of the city, we shall catch
them alive, and get into the
city.
13 And one of his servants answered and [t]said, Let *some* take,
I pray thee, five of the [u]horses
that remain, which are left in the
city, (behold, they *are* as all the
multitude of Ĭș'ra-el that are
left in it: behold, I *say,* they *are*
even as all the multitude of the
Ĭș'ra-el-ītes that are consumed[G]:)
and let us send and see.
14 They took therefore two
[2]chariot horses; and the king
sent after the host of the Sўr'ĭ-
anș, saying, Go and see.
15 And they went after them
unto [v]Jôr'dan: and, lo, all the

8
*p Spoils,* 1 Chr. 26:27.

9
*q Conscience, guilty,* Acts 23:1.
*r Patriotism, instances of,* Psa. 137:1.
1 R. V. punishment will overtake us:

10
*s Porters,* 2 Sam. 18:26.

13
*t Prudence, instances of,* 2 Chr. 2:12.
*u Horse,* Job 39:19.

14
2 R. V. chariots with

15
*v Jordan,* Gen. 32:10.

way *was* full of garments and
vessels, which the Sўr'ĭ-anș had
cast away in their haste. And
the messengers returned, and
told the king.
16 And the people went out,
and spoiled[G] the tents of the Sўr'-
ĭ-anș. So a measure of fine flour
was *sold* for a shekel, and two
measures of barley for a shekel,
according to the [w]word of the
LORD.
17 ¶ And the king appointed the
[3]lord on whose hand he leaned
to have the charge of the [x]gate:
and the people trode[G] upon him
in the gate, and he died, [w]as the
man[G] of God had said, who spake
when the king came down to
him.
18 And [w]it came to pass as the
man of God had spoken to the
king, saying, Two measures of
barley for a shekel, and a measure of fine flour for a shekel,
shall be to morrow about this
time in the gate of Sā-mā'rĭ-ȧ:
19 And that [3]lord answered the
man of God, and said, Now,
behold, *if* the LORD should
make windows in heaven, might
such a thing be? And he said,
Behold, thou shalt see it with
thine eyes, but shalt not eat
thereof.
20 And [w]so it fell out unto him:
for the people trode upon him in
the gate, and he died.

## CHAPTER 8

*The Shunammite, who had left her country, to avoid the famine, has her land restored by the king. 7 Hazael kills his master, and succeeds him. 16 Jehoram's wicked reign in Judah. 20 Edom and Libnah revolt. 23 Ahaziah succeeds Jehoram. 25 His wicked reign. 28 He visits Joram at Jezreel.*

[a]THEN spake [b]Ē-lī'shȧ unto
the woman, whose son
he had restored to life, saying,
Arise, and go thou and thine
household, and sojourn[G] wheresoever thou canst sojourn: for
the LORD hath called for a

16
*w Prophecies, fulfilled,* Dan. 9:24.

17
*x Gates, guards at,* Deut. 3:5.
3 R. V. captain

1
*a Kindness, instances of,* Acts 28:2.
*b Elisha, prophecies of,* 1 Kin. 19:16.

*famine; and it shall also come
upon the land [c]seven years.
2 And the woman arose, and
did after the saying of the man of
God: and she went with her
household, and sojourned in the
land of the [d]Phĭ-lĭs′tĭneṣ [c]seven
years.
3 And it came to pass at the
[c]seven years' end, that the
woman returned out of the land
of the [d]Phĭ-lĭs′tĭneṣ: and she
went forth to [e]cry[G] unto the king
for her house and for her [f]land.
4 And the [g]king talked with
[h]Gē-hā′zī the servant of the man
of God, saying, Tell me, I pray
thee, all the great things that
[i]Ē-lī′shȧ hath done.
5 And it came to pass, as [h]he
was telling the king how [i]he had
[j]restored a [k]dead body to life,
that, behold, the woman, whose
son he had restored to life, [e]cried[G]
to the king for her house and for
her [f]land. And Gē-hā′zī said,
My lord, O king, this *is* the
woman, and this *is* her son,
whom [i]Ē-lī′shȧ restored to life.
6 And when the [g]king asked the
woman, she told him. So the
[l]king appointed[G] unto her a certain officer, saying, Restore [f]all
that *was* her's, and all the fruits
of the field since the day that
she left the land, even until
now.
7 ¶ And Ē-lī′shȧ came to [m]Dȧ-
măs′cus; and [n]Bĕn–hā′dăd the
king of [o]Sȳr′ĭ-ȧ was sick; and it
was told him, saying, The man
of God is come hither.[G]
8 And the king said unto [p]Hăz′-
a-el, Take a [q, r]present in thine
hand, and go, meet the man of
God, and enquire of the LORD
by him, saying, Shall I recover
of this disease?
9 So [p]Hăz′a-el went to meet
him, and took a [q, r]present with
him, even of every good thing of
[m]Dȧ-măs′cus, forty [s]camels' burden, and came and stood before
him, and said, Thy son [n]Bĕn-
hā′dăd king of [o]Sȳr′ĭ-ȧ hath sent
me to thee, saying, Shall I recover of this disease?
10 And [i]Ē-lī′shȧ said unto him,
Go, say unto him, Thou mayest
certainly recover: howbeit the
LORD hath shewed me that he
shall surely die.
11 And he settled[G] his countenance stedfastly, until he was
ashamed: and the man of God
wept.
12 And [p]Hăz′a-el said, Why
weepeth my lord? And [b]he answered, Because [t]I know the
evil that [u]thou wilt do unto the
children of Ĭṣ′ra-el: their strong
holds wilt thou set on fire, and
their young men wilt thou slay
with the sword, and wilt dash
their children, and rip up their
[v]women with child.
13 And [p]Hăz′a-el said, But
what, *is* thy servant a [w]dog, that
he should do this great thing?
And Ē-lī′shȧ answered, The
LORD hath [x]shewed me that
thou *shalt be* king over [o]Sȳr′ĭ-ȧ.
14 So he departed from Ē-lī′-
shȧ, and came to his master; who
said to him, What said Ē-lī′shȧ
to thee? And he answered, He
told me *that* thou shouldest
surely recover.
15 And it came to pass on the
morrow, that [p]he took a thick
cloth, and dipped *it* in water,
and [y]spread *it* on his face, so that

c *Seven, years,* Gen. 7:2.

2
d *Philistines,* Gen. 26:14.

3
e *Petition, right of,* Esth. 5:6.
f *Property, in real estate,* Lev. 27:15.
**B.C. 885?**

4
g *Jehoram,* 2 Kin. 1:17.
h *Gehazi,* 2 Kin. 4:12.
i *Elisha, miracles of,* 1 Kin. 19:16.

5
j *Miracles,* Luke 23:8.
k *Dead,* 2 Kin. 4:32.

6
l *Judge, kings as,* Judg. 2:18.

7
m *Damascus,* Isa. 8:4.
n *Ben-hadad,* 1 Kin. 20:1.
o *Syria,* 2 Kin. 6:23.

8
p *Hazael,* 2 Kin. 9:14.
q *Presents,* Gen. 32:13.
r *Prophets, emoluments of,* Isa. 3:2.

9
s *Camel,* 1 Sam. 30:17.

12
t *Reproof, faithfulness in,* Prov. 17:10.
u *Rulers, wicked,* Ex. 18:21.
v *Captive,* 1 Sam. 30:3.

13
w *Dog,* 1 Kin. 21:19.
x *Prophets, inspiration of,* Isa. 3:2.

15
y *Regicide,* 2 Sam. 1:10.

***FAMINE.** *Pharaoh forewarned of, in dreams,* Gen. 41. *Described,* Deut. 28:53–57; Isa. 5:13; 9:20, 21; 17:4, 11; Jer. 14:1–6; 48:33; Lam. 1:11, 19; 2:11–22; 4:4–10; Joel 1:17–20. *Sent as a judgment,* Lev. 26:19–29; Deut. 28:23, 24, 38–42; 2 Sam. 21:1; 1 Kin. 17:1; 2 Kin. 8:1; 1 Chr. 21:12; Psa. 105:16; 107:33, 34; Isa. 3:1–8; 14:30; Jer. 14:15–22; 19:9; 29:17, 19; Lam. 5:4, 5, 10; Ezek. 4:16, 17; 5:16, 17; 14:13; Joel 1:15, 16; Amos 4:6–9; 5:16, 17; Hag. 1:9–11; Matt. 24:7; Luke 21:11; Rev. 6:5–8. *Cannibalism in,* Deut. 28:53; 2 Kin. 6:28. *Righteous delivered from,* Job 5:0; Psa. 33:19; 37:19.

**Instances of:** *In Canaan,* Gen. 12:10; 26:1; 42:1, 2, 5; Ruth 1:1; 2 Sam. 21:1; 1 Kin. 17; 18:1; 2 Kin. 6:25–29; 7:4; Neh. 5:3. *In Egypt,* Gen. 41:53–57. *Universal,* Gen. 41:56, 57; Acts 11:28. *In Jerusalem, from siege,* 2 Kin. 25:3; Jer. 52:6.

**Figurative,** Amos 8:11.

16
[z] *Ahab*, 1 Kin. 16:29.
[a] *Israel, after the revolt*, 1 Kin. 12:1.
[b] *Jehoshaphat*, 2 Kin. 12:18.
[c] *Judah, kingdom of*, 2 Chr. 11:17.
[d] *Jehoram*, 1 Kin. 22:50.
**v.16–821 BC**
17
[e] *Jerusalem*, Judg. 19:10.
18
[f] *Rulers, wicked, instances of*, Ex. 18:21.
[g] *Influence, evil*, 1 Cor. 7:14.
[h] *Athaliah*, 2 Kin. 11:1.
19
[i] *Intercession, intercessional influence of the righteous*, Jer. 27:18.
[j] *God, faithfulness of*, Gen. 2:2.
[k] *Children, of the righteous, blessed of God*, Mark 10:14.
21
[l] *Chariot*, Josh. 11:4.
23
[m] *Book*, Num. 5:23.
24
[n] *Death, called sleep*, Num. 23:10.

he died: and Hăz′a-el reigned in
his stead.
16 ¶ And in the fifth year of
Jō′ram the son of [z]Ā′hăb king of
[a]Ĭs̱′ra-el, [b]Jė-hŏsh′a-phăt *being*
then king of [c]Jū′dah, [d]Jė-hō′-
ram the son of Jė-hŏsh′a-phăt
king of Jū′dah began to reign.
17 Thirty and two years old
was he when he began to reign;
and he reigned eight years in
[e]Jė-ru̱′sȧ-lĕm.
18 And [f]he walked [g]in the way
of the kings of Ĭs̱′ra-el, as did the
house of Ā′hăb: for the [h]daugh-
ter of Ā′hăb was his wife: and he
did evil in the sight of the LORD.
19 Yet the LORD would not
destroy [c]Jū′dah for Dā′vid his
servant's [i]sake, as [j]he promised
him to give him alway a light,
*and* to his [k]children.[S]
20 ¶ In his days Ē′dom revolted
from under the hand of Jū′dah,
and made a king over themselves.
21 So [d]Jō′ram went over to
Zā′ĭr, and all the [l]chariots with
him: and he rose by night, and
smote the †Ē′dom-ītes which
compassed him about, and the
captains of the chariots: and
the people fled into their tents.
22 Yet Ē′dom revolted from
under the hand of Jū′dah unto
this day. Then Lĭb′nah revolted
at the same time.
23 And the rest of the acts of
[d]Jō′ram, and all that he did, *are*
they not written in the [m]book of
the chronicles[C] of the kings of
[c]Jū′dah?
24 And [d]Jō′ram [n]slept with his
fathers, and was buried with his
fathers in the [e]city of Dā′vid:
and ‡Ā-ha-zī′ah his son reigned
in his stead.
25 ¶ In the twelfth year of [o]Jō′-
ram the son of [p]Ā′hăb king of
[a]Ĭs̱′ra-el did ‡Ā-ha-zī′ah the son
of [d]Jė-hō′ram king of [c]Jū′dah
begin to reign.
26 Two and twenty years old
*was* ‡Ā-ha-zī′ah when he began
to reign; and he reigned one year
in [e]Jė-ru̱′sȧ-lĕm. And his mother's name *was* [h]Ăth-a-lī′ah, the
daughter of Ŏm′rī king of Ĭs̱′ra-el.
27 And he walked [g]in the way
of the house of [p,q]Ā′hăb, and did
evil in the sight of the LORD, as
*did* the house of Ā′hăb: for he
*was* the son in law of the house
of Ā′hăb.
28 ¶ [r]And he went with [o]Jō′-
ram the son of [p]Ā′hăb to the war
against [s]Hăz′a-el king of [t]Sўr′ĭ-ȧ
in [u]Rā′moth–gĭl′e-ăd; and the
Sўr′ĭ-ans̱ wounded Jō′ram.
29 And king [o]Jō′ram went back
to be healed in [v]Jĕz′re-el of the
wounds which the Sўr′ĭ-ans̱ had
given him at [u]Rā′mah, when he
fought against [s]Hăz′a-el king
of [t]Sўr′ĭ-ȧ. And ‡Ā-ha-zī′ah the
son of [d]Jė-hō′ram king of [c]Jū′-
dah [r]went down to see Jō′ram
the son of Ā′hăb in Jĕz′re-el, because he was sick.

## CHAPTER 9

*Elisha sends a young prophet to anoint Jehu at Ramoth-gilead. 11 Jehu, being made king, kills Joram in the field of Naboth. 27 Ahaziah is slain at Gur, and buried at Jerusalem. 30 Jezebel is thrown out of a window, and eaten by dogs.*

AND [a,b]Ė-lī′shȧ the prophet
called one of the children
of the [c]prophets, and said unto

**v.24–814 BC** See footnote, *Time*, Rev. 10:6.
25
[o] Or, *Jehoram*, 2 Kin. 1:17.
[p] *Ahab*, 1 Kin. 16:29.
27
[q] *Parents, evil influence of*, 2 Cor. 12:14.
28
[r] *Friendship, instances of*, Prov. 22:24.
[s] *Hazael*, 2 Kin. 9:14.
[t] *Syria* 2 Kin. 6:23.
[u] *Ramoth–gilead*, Josh. 20:8.
**v.28–814 BC**
29
[v] *Jezreel*, 1 Kin. 18:45.
1
[a] *Elisha*, 1 Kin. 19:16.
[b] *Church and State, ecclesiastical power superior to civil*, 1 Sam. 16:1.
[c] *Prophets, schools of*, Isa. 3:2.

† **EDOMITES**, called also EDOM. *Descendants of Esau*, Gen. 36. *Kings of*, Gen. 36:31–39; Num. 20:14; 1 Chr. 1:43–50; Ezek. 32:29; Amos 2:1. *Dukes of*, Gen. 36:9–31, 40–43; Ex. 15:15; 1 Chr. 1:51–54. *Land of*, Gen. 32:3; Deut. 2:4, 5, 12.

*Protected by divine command, from desolation by the Israelites*, Deut. 2:4–6; *from being held in abhorrence by the Israelites*, Deut. 23:7. *Refuse to the Israelites passage through their country*, Num. 20:18–21.

*Saul makes war against*, 1 Sam. 14:47. *David, makes conquest of*, 1 Kin. 11:14–16; 1 Chr. 18:11–13; *garrisons*, 2 Sam. 8:14; 1 Chr. 18:13; *writes battle songs concerning his conquest of*, Psa. 60:8, 9; 108:9, 10. *Become confederates of Jehoshaphat*, 2 Kin. 3:9, 26. *Ruled by a deputy king*, 1 Kin. 22:47. *Destruction of the army of*, 2 Chr. 20:20, 23. *Revolt in the days of Joram*, 2 Kin. 8:20–22; 2 Chr. 21:8–10. *Amaziah, king of Judah, invades the territory of*, 2 Kin. 14:5–7, 10; 2 Chr. 25:11, 12; 28:17. *Join Babylon in war against the Israelites*, Ezek. 35:5; Amos 1:9–11; Obad. 8, 11–16. *Imprecation against*, Psa. 137:7. *A Jewish prophet in Babylon denounces*, Ezek. 25:12–14; 35:3–10. *Children of the third generation might be received into the congregation of Israel*, Deut. 23:8.

*Prophecies concerning*, Gen. 25:23; Num. 24:18; Isa. 11:14; 21:11, 12; 3:5–17; 63:1–4; Jer. 9:25, 26; 27:1–11; 49:7–22; Lam. 4:21, 22; Ezek. 25:12–14; 32:29, 30; 35; 36:5; Joel 3:19; Amos 1:11, 12; 9:12; Obad. 1–21; Mal. 1:2–5.

‡ **AHAZIAH**, king of Judah, *Called* AZARIAH *and* JEHOAHAZ, 2 Chr. 21:17; 25:23. *History of*, 2 Kin. 8:25–29; 9:16–29. *Gifts of, to the temple*, 2 Kin. 12:18. *Brethren of, slain*, 2 Kin. 10:13, 14. *Reigned one year*, 2 Kin. 8:25, 26. *Succeeded by Athaliah*, 2 Chr. 22:10–12.

v.1–814 BC
See footnote, *Time*, Rev. 10:6.

*d Oil*, Deut. 12:17.
*e Ramoth-gilead*, Josh. 20:8.

2
*f Jehu*, 2 Chr. 22:8.

3
*g Government, God in*, Isa. 22:21.
*h Anointing*, Lev. 8:12.
*i Rulers, appointed by God*, Ex. 18:21.

5
*j Captain*, Num. 31:48.

6
*k Call, personal*, Phil. 3:14.

7
*l Agency*, Mark 1:17.
*m Jezebel*, 1 Kin. 16:31.

8
*n Ahab*, 1 Kin. 16:29.
*o Judgments, denounced against Ahab*, Ex. 6:6.
1 R. V. every man child, and him that is shut up and him that is left at large in Israel.

9
*p Jeroboam*, 1 Kin. 14:5.
*q Baasha*, 1 Kin. 15:16.
*r* 1 Kin. 15:27, 33.

him, Gird up thy loins, and take this box[G] of [d]oil in thine hand, and go to [e]Rā′moth–gĭl′e-ăd:[Q]

2 And when thou comest thither[G], look[G] out there [f]Jē′hū the son of Jĕ-hŏsh′a-phăt the son of Nĭm′shī, and go in, and make him arise up from among his brethren, and carry[G] him to an inner chamber;

3 Then take the box[G] of [d]oil, and pour *it* on his head, and say, Thus saith the LORD, [g]I have [h]anointed [i]thee king over Ĭṣ′ra-el. Then open the door, and flee, and tarry not.

4 So the young man, *even* the young man the [c]prophet, went to [e]Rā′moth–gĭl′e-ăd.

5 And when he came, behold, the [j]captains of the host *were* sitting; and he said, I have an errand to thee, O captain. And [f]Jē′hū said, Unto which of all us? And he said, To thee, O captain.

6 And he arose, and went into the house; and he poured the [d]oil on his head, and said unto him, Thus saith the LORD God of Ĭṣ′ra-el, [g]I have [h]anointed [i,k]thee king over the people of the LORD, *even* over Ĭṣ′ra-el.

7 And [l]thou shalt smite[G] the house of Ā′hăb thy master, that I may avenge the blood of my servants the prophets, and the blood of all the servants of the LORD, at the hand of [m]Jĕz′e-bĕl.[Q]

8 For the whole house of [n]Ā′hăb [o]shall perish: and I will cut off from Ā′hăb [1]him that pisseth[G] against the wall, and him that is shut up and left in Ĭṣ′ra-el:

9 And I will make the house of [n]Ā′hăb like the house of [p]Jĕr-o-bō′am the son of Nē′băt, and like the house of [q]Bā′a-shȧ the son of [r]Ā-hī′jah:

10 [s]And the dogs shall eat [m]Jĕz′e-bĕl in the portion of [t]Jĕz′re-el, and *there shall be* none to [u]bury *her*. And he opened the door, and fled.

11 ¶ Then [f]Jē′hū came forth to the servants of his lord: and *one* said unto him, *Is* all well? wherefore[G] came this mad *fellow* to thee? And he said unto them, Ye know the man, and his communication[G].

12 And they said, *It is* false; tell us now. And he said, Thus and thus spake he to me, saying, Thus saith the LORD, [g]I have [h]anointed [i,k]thee king over Ĭṣ′ra-el.

13 Then they hasted, and took every man his garment, and put *it* under him on the top of the stairs, and blew with [v]trumpets, saying, [f]Jē′hū is [w]king.[Q]

14 So [f]Jē′hū the son of Jĕ-hŏsh′a-phăt the son of Nĭm′shī [x]conspired against [y]Jō′ram. (Now Jō′ram had kept [e]Rā′moth–gĭl′e-ăd, he and all Ĭṣ′ra-el, because of *Hăz′a-el king of [z]Sȳr′ĭ-ȧ.

15 But king [a]Jō′ram was returned to be healed in [b]Jĕz′re-el of the wounds which the Sȳr′ĭ-anṣ had given him, when he fought with *Hăz′a-el king of [c]Sȳr′ĭ-ȧ.) And [d]Jē′hū said, If it be your minds[G], *then* let none go forth *nor* escape out of the city to go to tell *it* in Jĕz′re-el.

16 So [d]Jē′hū rode in a [e]chariot, and went to [b]Jĕz′re-el; for [a]Jō′ram lay there. And [f]Ā-ha-zī′ah king of [g]Jū′dah [h]was come down to see Jō′ram.

17 And there stood a [i]watchman on the [j]tower in [b]Jĕz′re-el, and he spied[G] the company of [d]Jē′hū as he came, and said, I see a company. And [a]Jō′ram said, Take an horseman, and

v.10–814 BC
See footnote, *Time*, Rev. 10:6.

10
*s Prophecies*, Dan. 9:24.
*t Jezreel*, 1 Kin. 18:45.
*u Burial*, Acts 8:2.

13
*v Trumpet*, Josh. 6:4.
*w King*, 2 Kin. 3:10.

14
*x Conspiracy, instances of*, vs. 14–26; 1 Kin. 16:9.
*y* Or, *Jehoram*, 2 Kin. 1:17.
*z Syria*, 2 Kin. 6:23.

15
*a* Or, *Jehoram*, 2 Kin. 1:17.
*b Jezreel*, 1 Kin. 18:45.
*c Syria*, 2 Kin. 6:23.
*d Jehu*, 2 Chr. 22:8.

16
*e Chariot*, Josh. 11:4.
*f Ahaziah*, 2 Kin. 8:25.
*g Judah, kingdom of*, 2 Chr. 11:17.
*h Friendship, instances of*, Prov. 22:24.

17
*i Watchman*, 2 Sam. 18:24.
*j Tower*, 2 Chr. 26:9.

* **HAZAEL**, king of Syria. *Anointed king by Elijah*, 1 Kin. 19:15. *Conquests by*, 2 Kin. 8:28, 29; 9:14; 10:32, 33; 12:17, 18; 13:3, 22; 2 Chr. 22:5, 6. *Conspires against, murders, and succeeds to the throne of Ben-hadad*, 2 Kin. 8:8–15. *Death of*, 2 Kin. 13:24.

v.17–814 BC
See footnote, *Time*, Rev. 10:6.

*k Peace*, Jer. 29:7.

send to meet them, and let him say, *Is*[G] *it* [k]peace?

18 So there went one on horseback to meet him, and said, Thus saith the king, *Is it* [k]peace? And [d]Jē'hū said, What hast thou to do with peace? turn[G] thee behind me. And the [i]watchman told, saying, The messenger came to them, but he cometh not again.

19 Then he sent out a second on horseback, which came to them, and said, Thus saith the king, *Is it* [k]peace? And [d]Jē'hū answered, What hast thou to do with peace? turn thee behind me.

20 And the [i]watchman told, saying, He came even unto them, and cometh not again: and the driving *is* like the driving of [d]Jē'hū the son of Nĭm'shī; for he driveth furiously.

21 And [a]Jō'ram said, Make ready. And his [e]chariot was made ready. And Jō'ram king of Ĭs'ra-el and [f]Ā-ha-zī'ah king of Jū'dah went out, each in his chariot, and they went out against [d]Jē'hū, and met him in the portion of [l]Nā'bŏth the Jĕz're-el-īte.

22 And it came to pass, when [a]Jō'ram saw [d]Jē'hū, that he said, *Is*[G] *it* [k]peace, Jē'hū? And he answered, What peace, so long as the whoredoms[G] of thy mother Jĕz'e-bĕl and her [m]witchcrafts *are so* many?[Q]

23 And [a]Jō'ram turned his hands, and fled, and said to [f]Ā-ha-zī'ah, *There is* †treachery,[G] O Ā-ha-zī'ah.

24 And [d]Jē'hū [n]drew a bow with his full strength, and [o]smote [a]Jė-hō'ram between his arms, and the arrow went out at his heart, and he sunk down in his [e]chariot.

25 Then said [d]*Je'hu* to Bĭd'kär his [p]captain, Take up, *and* cast him in the portion of the field of [l]Nā'bŏth the Jĕz're-el-īte: for remember how that, when I and thou rode together after Ā'hăb his father, the LORD laid this burden[G] upon him;

26 Surely I have seen yesterday the blood of [l]Nā'bŏth, and the blood of his sons, saith the LORD; and I will requite thee in this plat,[G] saith the LORD. Now therefore take *and* cast [q]him into the plat[G] *of ground*, according to the word of the LORD.

27 ¶ But when [f]Ā-ha-zī'ah the king of [g]Jū'dah saw *this*, he fled by the way of the garden house.[G] And [d]Jē'hū followed after him, and said, Smite him also in the [e]chariot. *And they* [o]*did so* at the going[G] up to Gûr, which *is* by [r]Ĭb'le-ăm. And he fled to [s]Mė-gĭd'dŏ, and died there.[Q]

28 And his servants carried him in a [e]chariot to [t]Jē-ru'sā-lĕm, and [u]buried him in his sepulchre[G] with his fathers in the city of Dā'vid.

29 And in the eleventh year of [a]Jō'ram the son of [v]Ā'hăb began [f]Ā-ha-zī'ah to reign over [g]Jū'dah.

30 ¶ And when [d]Jē'hū was come to [b]Jĕz're-el, [w,x]Jĕz'e-bĕl heard *of it*; and she ‡painted her face, and tired[G] her head, and looked out at a window.

31 And as [d]Jē'hū entered in at the gate, she said, *Had* [y,z]Zĭm'rī peace, who slew his master?

32 And [a]he lifted up his face to the window, and said, Who *is* on

21 *i* 1 Kin. 21:1–19.

22 *m Sorcery*, Isa. 47:9.

24 *n Archery*, Gen. 21:20.
*o Regicide*, 2 Sam. 1:10.

v.24–814 BC
See footnote, *Time*, Rev. 10:6.

25 *p Captain*, Num. 31:48.

26 *q Rulers, wicked*, Ex. 18:21.

27 *r* Or, *Gath-rimmon*, Josh. 21:25.
*s Megiddo*, Josh. 17:11.

28 *t Jerusalem*, Judg. 19:10.
*u Burial*, Acts 8:2.

29 *v Ahab*, 1 Kin. 16:29.
v.29–815 BC

30 *w Jezebel*, 1 Kin. 16:31.
*x Women, wicked*, Prov. 31:10.

31 *y* 1 Kin. 16:9–20.
*z Servant, wicked and unfaithful*, Jer. 2:14.
v.31–814 BC

32 *a Jehu*, 2 Chr. 22:8.

† **TREACHERY**, Jer. 9:8. *Of Simeon and Levi towards the Shechemites*, Gen. 34:13–31. *Of Rahab to her people*, Josh. 2. *Of the man of Beth-el*, Judg. 1:24, 25. *Of Jael*, Judg. 4: 18–21; 5:24–27. *Of Abimelech*, Judg. 9:1–5. *Of Shechemites*, Judg. 9:23. *Of Joab, toward Abner*, 2 Sam. 3:26, 27; *toward Amasa*, 2 Sam. 20:9, 10. *Of Baanah and Rechab*, 2 Sam. 4:6. *Of David toward Uriah*, 2 Sam. 11. *Of Absalom*, 2 Sam. 15: 6. *Of Ahithophel*, 2 Sam. 15:31. *Of Jehu*, 2 Kin. 10:18–28. *Of the enemies of Nehemiah*, Neh. 6. *Of Judas*, Matt. 26:47–50; Mark 54:43–45; Luke 22:47, 48; John 18:2–5; Acts 1: 16, 17.
See footnotes: CONSPIRACY, 1 Kin. 16:9; TREASON, 2 Kin. 11:14.

‡ **PAINTING**. *Around the eyes, to enlarge their appearance*, 2 Kin. 9:30; Jer. 4:30; Ezek. 23:40. *Of rooms*, Jer. 22: 14. *Of portraits*, Ezek. 23:14.

v.32–814 BC
See footnote, *Time,* Rev. 10:6.

my side? who? And there looked out to him two *or* three eunuchs.

33 And he said, Throw [b]her down. So they [c]threw her down: and *some* of her blood was sprinkled on the wall, and on the horses: and he trode her under foot.

34 And when he was come in, he did eat and drink, and said, Go, see now this cursed [d]*woman,* and bury her: for she *is* a king's daughter.

35 And they went to bury her: but they found no more of her than the skull, and the feet, and the palms of *her* hands.

36 Wherefore they came again, and told him. And he said, This *is* the [e]word of the LORD, which he spake by his servant [f]Ē-lī'jah the Tĭsh'bīte, saying, In the portion of [g]Jĕz're-el shall dogs eat the flesh of [b]Jĕz'e-bĕl:

37 And the carcase of [b]Jĕz'e-bĕl shall be as dung upon the face of the field in the portion of [g]Jĕz're-el; *so* that they shall not say, This *is* Jĕz'e-bĕl.

## CHAPTER 10

*Jehu causes seventy of Ahab's children to be beheaded. 8 He justifies the act by the prophecy of Elijah. 12 He slays two and forty of Ahaziah's brethren. 15 He takes Jehonadab into his company. 18 He destroys all the worshipers of Baal. 29 He follows Jeroboam's sins. 32 Hazael oppresses Israel. 35 Jehoahaz succeeds Jehu.*

AND [a]Ā'hăb had seventy sons in [b]Să-mā'rĭ-ȧ. And [c]Jē'hū wrote letters, and sent to Să-mā'rĭ-ȧ, unto the [d]rulers of [e]Jĕz're-el, to the elders, and to [f]them that brought up Ā'hăb's [g]*children,* saying,

2 Now as soon as this letter cometh to [f]you, seeing your [a]master's sons *are* with you, and *there are* with you chariots and horses, a fenced city also, and armour;

3 Look even out the best and meetest of your master's sons, and set *him* on his father's throne, and fight for your master's house.

4 But they were exceedingly afraid, and said, Behold, two kings stood not before him: how then shall we stand?

5 And he that *was* over the house, and he that *was* over the city, the [d]elders also, and the [f]bringers up *of the children,* sent to [c]Jē'hū, saying, We *are* thy servants, and will do all that thou shalt bid us; we will not make any king: do thou *that which is* good in thine eyes.

6 Then [c]he wrote a letter the second time to them, saying, If ye *be* mine, and *if* ye will hearken unto my voice, take ye the heads of the men your master's sons, and come to me to [e]Jĕz're-el by to morrow this time. Now the king's sons, *being* seventy persons, *were* with the [f]great men of the city, which brought them up.

7 And it came to pass, when the letter came to them, that they took the king's sons, and [h,i]slew seventy persons, and put their heads in [j]baskets, and sent him *them* to [e]Jĕz're-el.

8 And there came a messenger, and told him, saying, They have brought the heads of the king's sons. And he said, Lay ye them in two heaps at the entering in of the [k]gate until the morning.

9 And it came to pass in the morning, that he went out, and stood, and said to all the people, Ye *be* righteous: behold, I [l]conspired against my master, and [h]slew him: but who slew all these?

10 Know now that there shall fall unto the earth nothing of the word of the LORD, which the LORD spake concerning the house of Ā'hăb: for the LORD

**33**
*b* *Jezebel,* 1 Kin. 16:31.
*c* *Homicide, instances of,* Deut. 5:17.

**34**
*d* *Women, wicked,* Prov. 31:10.

**36**
*e* *Prophecies, fulfilled,* Dan. 9:24.
*f* *Elijah, prophecies of,* 1 Kin. 17:1.
*g* *Jezreel,* 1 Kin. 18:45.

**1**
*a* *Ahab,* 1 Kin. 16:29.
*b* *Samaria,* 1 Kin. 16:24.
*c* *Jehu,* 2 Chr. 22:8.
*d* *Government, municipal,* Isa. 22:21.
*e* *Jezreel,* 1 Kin. 18:45.
*f* *Tutor,* Gal. 4:2.
*g* *Children, tutors and governors for,* Mark 10:14.

v.3–814 BC
See footnote, *Time,* Rev. 10:6.

**7**
*h* *Homicide, instances of,* Deut. 5:17.
*i* *Massacre, instances of,* Esth. 3:13.
*j* *Basket,* Ex. 29:3.

**8**
*k* *Gates,* Deut. 3:5.

**9**
*l* *Conspiracy, instances of,* 1 Kin. 16:9.

v.10–814 BC
See footnote, *Time*, Rev. 10:6.

10
m *Prophecies, fulfilled*, Dan. 9:24.
n *Prophets, inspiration of*, Isa. 3:2.

11
1 R. V. familiar friends,

13
o *Ahaziah*, 2 Kin. 8:25.
p *Judah, kingdom of*, 2 Chr. 11:17.

15
q Or, *Jonadab*, Jer. 35:5–10, 16–19.
r *Friendship, instances of*, Prov. 22:24.
s *Hand, clasping of, a token of friendship*, Ezra 10:19.
t *Chariot*, Josh. 11:4.

16
u *Zeal*, 2 Cor. 7:11.

18
v *Baal*, 2 Kin. 17:16.

hath done [m]*that* which he [n]spake
by his servant Ē-lī′jah.
11 So [c]Jē′hū slew all that remained of the house of [a]Ā′hăb
in [e]Jĕz′re-el, and all his great
men, and his [1]kinsfolks, and his
priests, until he left him none
remaining.
12 ¶ And [c]he arose and departed, and came to [b]Să-mā′rĭ-ȧ.
*And* as he *was* at the shearing
house in the way,
13 [c]Jē′hū met with the brethren
of [o]Ā-ha-zī′ah king of [p]Jū′dah,
and said, Who *are* ye? And they
answered, We *are* the brethren
of Ā-ha-zī′ah; and we go down
to salute[C] the children of the king
and the children of the queen.
14 And he said, Take them
alive. And they took them alive,
and [h,i]slew them at the pit of the
shearing house, *even* two and
forty men; neither left he any of
them.
15 ¶ And when he was depart-
ed thence[C], he lighted[C] on [q]Jē-
hŏn′a-dăb the son of *Rē′chăb
*coming* to meet him: and he saluted[C] him, and said to him, [r]Is
thine heart right, as my heart *is*
with thy heart? And Jē-hŏn′a-
dăb answered, It is. If it be, give
*me* thine [s]hand. And he gave
*him* his hand; and he took him
up to him into the [t]chariot.
16 And he said, Come with me,
and see my [u]zeal for the LORD.
So they made him ride in his
chariot.
17 And when he came to [b]Să-
mā′rĭ-ȧ, he slew all that remained unto Ā′hăb in Să-mā′-
rĭ-ȧ, till he had destroyed him,
according to the [m]saying of the
LORD, which he [n]spake to
Ē-lī′jah.
18 ¶ And [c]Jē′hū gathered all
the people together, and said unto them, Ā′hăb served [v]Bā′al a
little; [w]*but* Jē′hū shall serve him
much.
19 Now therefore call unto me
all the prophets of [v]Bā′al, all his
servants, and all his priests; let
none be wanting[C]: for I have a
great sacrifice *to do* to Bā′al;
whosoever shall be wanting[C], he
shall not live. But [c]Jē′hū did *it*
in [x]subtilty, to the intent that he
might destroy the worshippers of
Bā′al.
20 And [c]Jē′hū said, Proclaim
a solemn assembly for [v]Bā′al.
And they proclaimed *it*.
21 And Jē′hū sent through all
Ĭș′ra-el: and all the worshippers
of [v]Bā′al came, so that there was
not a man left that came not.
And they came into the [y]house
of Bā′al; and the house of Bā′al
was full from one end to another.
22 And he said unto him that
*was* over the vestry, Bring forth
[z]vestments for all the worshippers of Bā′al. And he brought
them forth vestments.
23 And [a]Jē′hū went, and [b]Jē-
hŏn′a-dăb the son of *Rē′chăb,
into the [c]house of [d]Bā′al, and
said unto the worshippers of
Bā′al, Search, and look[C] that
there be here with you none of
the servants of the LORD, but
the worshippers of Bā′al only.
24 And when they went in to
offer sacrifices and [e]burnt offerings, Jē′hū appointed fourscore
men without, and said, [f]*If* any of
the men whom I have brought
into your hands escape, *he that
letteth him go*, his life *shall be* for
the life of him.
25 And it came to pass, as soon
as he had made an end of offering the [e]burnt offering, that [a]Jē′-
hū said to the guard and to the
captains, Go in, *and* slay them;
let none come forth. And they
[g,h,i]smote[C] them with the edge of

v.18–814 BC
See footnote, *Time*, Rev. 10:6.

w *Falsehood, instances of*, Job 21:34.

19
x *Deception, instances of*, Josh. 9:4.

21
y *Temple, idolatrous*, 1 Kin. 6:17.

22
z *Dress, uniform vestments kept in store for worshipers of Baal*, Zech. 3:3.

23
a *Jehu*, 2 Chr. 22:8.
b Or, *Jonadab*, Jer. 35:5–10, 16–19.
c *Temple, idolatrous*, 1 Kin. 6:17.
d *Baal*, 2 Kin. 17:16.

24
e *Offerings, burnt, offered in idolatrous worship*, Lev. 6:17.
f *Intolerance*, vs. 24–28; Num. 11:28.

25
g *Confidence, betrayed*, Mic. 7:5.
h *Treachery*, 2 Kin. 9:23.
i *Massacre, instances of*, Esth. 3:13.

* **RECHAB.** *Father of Jehonadab*, 2 Kin. 10:15, 23; 1 Chr. 2:55; Jer. 35:6, 8, 16, 19. *Ancestor of the Rechabites, distinguished for their total abstinence from the use of intoxicating wine*, Jer. 35.

v.25–814 BC
See footnote, *Time*, Rev. 10:6.

the sword; and the guard and
the captains cast *them* out, and
went to the city of the house of
[d]Bā'al.
26 And they brought forth
the [2]images out of the house of
[d]Bā'al, and [j]burned them.
27 And they [j]brake down the
[3]image of [d]Bā'al, and brake down
the house of Bā'al, and made it
a draught house unto this day.
28 Thus [a]Jē'hū destroyed
[d]Bā'al out of Ĭs'ra-el.
29 Howbeit *from* the sins of
[k,l]Jĕr-o-bō'am the son of Nē'-
băt, who [m]made Ĭs'ra-el to sin,
[a]Jē'hū departed not from after
them, *to wit*, the golden [n]calves
that *were* in [o]Bĕth'-el, and that
*were* in [p]Dăn.
30 And the LORD said unto
[a]Jē'hū, Because [q]thou hast done
well in executing *that which is*
right in mine eyes, *and* hast done
unto the house of Ā'hăb according to all that *was* in mine heart,
[r]thy children of the fourth *gene-*
*ration* shall sit on the throne of
Ĭs'ra-el.
31 But [a]Jē'hū [s]took no heed
to walk in the law of the LORD
God of Ĭs'ra-el with all his heart:
for he departed not from the sins
of [k]Jĕr-o-bō'am, which [m]made
Ĭs'ra-el to sin.
32 ¶ In those days the [t]LORD
began to [u]cut [v]Ĭs'ra-el short: and
[w]Hăz'a-el smote them in all the
coasts of Ĭs'ra-el;
33 From [x]Jôr'dan eastward, all
the land of [y]Gĭl'e-ăd, the [z]Găd'-
ītes, and the [a]Reu'ben-ītes, and
the [b]Mā-năs'sītes, from [c]Ăr'ŏ-ĕr,
which *is* by the [4]river [d]Ăr'nŏn,
even Gĭl'e-ăd and [e]Bā'shăn.
34 Now the rest of the acts of
[f]Jē'hū, and all that he did, and
all his might, *are* they not written in the [g]book of the chronicles
of the kings of [h]Ĭs'ra-el?
35 And Jē'hū [i]slept with his fathers: and they [j]buried him in
[k]Sā-mā'rĭ-ȧ. And [l]Jė-hō'a-hăz
his son reigned in his stead.
36 And the time that [f]Jē'hū
reigned over [h]Ĭs'ra-el in [j]Sȧ-
mā'rĭ-ȧ *was* twenty and eight
years.

## CHAPTER 11

*Athaliah destroys the seed royal. 2 Jehoash is hid six years in the house of God. 4 In the seventh year he is brought forth and made king. 13 Athaliah is slain. 17 Jehoiada restores the worship of God.*

AND when *,[a]Ăth-a-lī'ah the
mother of [b]Ā-ha-zī'ah saw
that her son was dead, she arose
and [c,d]destroyed all the seed
royal.
2 But [e]Jė-hŏsh'e-bȧ, the daughter of king [f]Jō'ram, sister of
[b]Ā-ha-zī'ah, took †Jō'ăsh the
son of Ā-ha-zī'ah, and stole him
from among the king's sons
*which were* slain; and they hid
him, *even* [g]him and his [h]nurse, in
the bedchamber from *Ăth-a-
lī'ah, so that he was not slain.
3 And †he was with her hid in
the [i,j]house of the LORD six
years. And *,[k]Ăth-a-lī'ah [l]did
reign over the [m]land.
4 ¶ [n]And the seventh year
[o,p,q]Jė-hoi'a-dȧ sent and fetched
the rulers over hundreds, with
the [r]captains and the guard, and
brought them to him into the
[i,j]house of the LORD, and [s]made
a covenant with them, and took
an [t]oath of them in the house of
the LORD, and shewed them the
king's †son.
5 And [o,p]he commanded them,

26
j *Iconoclasm*, Num. 33:52.
2 R. V. pillars that were in

27
3 R. V. pillar

29
k *Jeroboam*, 1 Kin. 14:5.
l *Rulers, wicked, instances of*, Ex. 18:21.
m *Temptation, leading into*, Luke 11:4.
n *Calf, images of*, Mic. 6:6.
o *Beth-el*, Josh. 18:13.
p *Dan*, Judg. 18:29.

30
q *Agency, in executing judgments*, Mark 1:17.
r *Prophecies*, Dan. 9:24.

31
s *Disobedience to God*, Eph. 5:6.

32
t *Government, God in*, Isa. 22:21.
u *Judgments*, Ex. 6:6.
v *Israel, after the revolt*, 1 Kin. 12:1.
w *Hazael*, 2 Kin. 9:14.

33
x *Jordan*, Gen. 32:10.
y *Gilead*, Deut. 3:13.
z *Gad, tribe of*, Deut. 33:20.
a *Reubenites*, Josh. 22:1.
b *Manasseh, tribe of*, Gen. 46:20.
c *Aroer*, Deut. 4:48.
d *Arnon*, Num. 22:36.
e *Bashan*, Num. 32:33.
4 R. V. valley of

v.34–814 BC
See footnote, *Time*, Rev. 10:6.

34
f *Jehu*, 2 Chr. 22:8.
g *Book*, Num. 5:23.
h *Israel, after the revolt*, 1 Kin. 12:1.

35
i *Death*, Num. 23:10.
j *Burial*, Acts 8:2.
k *Samaria*, 1 Kin. 16:24.
l 2 Kin. 13:1–9; 2 Chr. 25:17.

1
a *Women, wicked*, Prov. 31:10.
b *Ahaziah*, 2 Kin. 8:25.
c *Homicide, felonious*, Deut. 5:17.
d *Massacre, instances of*, Esth. 3:13.

2
e Or, *Jehoshabeath*, 2 Chr. 22:11.
f Or, *Jehoram*, 2 Kin. 1:17.
g *Children, nurses for*, Mark 10:14.
h *Nurse*, 2 Chr. 22:11.

3
i *Temple, Solomon's*, 1 Kin. 6:17.
j *Church, called house of the Lord*, 1 Kin. 9:3.
k *Women, as rulers*, Prov. 31:10.
l *Usurpation of political functions*, 2 Sam. 15:1.
m *Judah, kingdom of*, 2 Chr. 11:17.

4
n *Loyalty, instances of*, Eccl. 8:2.
o *Jehoiada*, 2 Kin. 12:2.
p *Minister, influential in public affairs*, Rom. 15:16.
q *Citizens, loyal*, Luke 15:15.
r *Captain*, Num. 31:48.
s *Conspiracy, instances of*, 1 Kin. 16:9.
t *Oath*, Num. 5:19.
v.4–807 BC

* **ATHALIAH** (*afflicted by Jehovah*). *Wife of Jehoram, king of Judah*, 2 Kin. 8:18, 26; 11:1–3; 2 Chr. 22:10–12. *Reigned over Judah six years*, 2 Kin. 11:3; 2 Chr. 22:12. *Overthrown by Jehoiada, the high priest, by the aid of the army; is slain*, 2 Kin. 11:12–16, 20; 2 Chr. 23:12–15, 21.

† **JOASH**, son of Ahaziah and king of Judah, called also JEHOASH. *Saved from his grandmother by Jehosheba, his aunt, and hidden for six years*, 2 Kin. 11:1–3; 2 Chr. 22:11, 12. *Anointed king*, 2 Kin. 11:12–21; 2 Chr. 23. *Reigned forty years*, 2 Kin. 12:1; 2 Chr. 24:1. *Righteousness of, under influence of Jehoiada*, 2 Kin. 12:2; 2 Chr. 24:2. *Repaired the temple*, 2 Kin. 12:4–16; 2 Chr. 24:4–14, 27. *Wickedness of, after Jehoiada's death*, 2 Chr. 24:17–22. *Procured peace from Hazael, king of Syria, by gift of dedicated treasures from the temple*, 2 Kin. 12:17, 18; 2 Chr. 24:23, 24. *Prophecy against*, 2 Chr. 24:19, 20. *Put Jehoiada's son to death*, 2 Chr. 24:20–22; Matt. 23:35. *Diseases of*, 2 Chr. 24:25. *Conspired against and slain*, 2 Kin. 12:20, 21; 2 Chr. 24:25, 26.

v.5—807 BC
See footnote, *Time*, Rev. 10:6.

**5**
u *Sabbath*, Ex. 16:23.
v *Watchman*, 2 Sam. 18:24.

**6**
w *Gates*, Deut. 3:5.
1 R. V. and be a barrier.

**8**
**2 R. V. ranks.**

**9**
x *High Priest*, Lev. 21:10.

**10**
y *Shield*, 1 Kin. 14:27.
z *Church, temple*, 1 Kin. 9:3.

a *Armory, temple used for*, Neh. 3:19.
b *Temple, Solomon's*, 1 Kin. 6:17.

saying, This *is* the thing that ye shall do; A third part of you that enter in on the [u]sabbath shall even be [v]keepers of the watch of the king's house;

6 And a third part *shall be* at the [w]gate of Sûr; and a third part at the gate behind the guard: so shall [v]ye keep the watch of the house, [1]that it be not broken down.

7 And two parts of all you that go forth on the [u]sabbath, even [v]they shall keep the watch of the [i,j]house of the LORD about the †king.

8 And ye shall compass the king round about, every man with his weapons in his hand: and he that cometh within the [2]ranges, let him be slain: and be ye with the king as he goeth out and as he cometh in.

9 And the [r]captains over the hundreds did according to all *things* that [o,p]Jĕ-hoi'a-dȧ the [x]priest commanded: and they took every man his men that were to come in on the [u]sabbath, with them that should go out on the sabbath, and came to Jĕ-hoi'a-dȧ the priest.

10 And to the [r]captains over hundreds did the [o,p]priest give king Dā'vid's ‡spears and [y]shields, that *were* in the [z,a,b]temple of the LORD.

11 And the guard stood, every man with his weapons in his hand, round about the king, from the right corner of the [b]temple to the left corner of the temple, *along* by the altar and the temple.

12 And [c,d]he brought forth the king's son, and [e]put the [f]crown upon him, and *gave him* the [g,h]testimony; and they made him king, and [i]anointed him; and they clapped their hands, and said, God save the king.

13 ¶ And when *Ăth-a-lī'ah heard the noise of the guard *and* of the people, she came to the people into the [b]temple of the LORD.

14 And when *she looked, behold, the †king stood by a pillar, as the manner *was*, and the princes and the trumpeters by the king, and all the people of the land rejoiced, and blew with [j]trumpets: and Ăth-a-lī'ah [k]rent her clothes, and cried, ‖Treason, Treason.

15 But [c,d]Jĕ-hoi'a-dȧ the [l]priest commanded the [m]captains of the hundreds, the officers of the [n]host, and said unto them, Have her forth [3]without the ranges: and him that followeth her kill with the sword. For the priest had said, Let her not be slain in the [b]house of the LORD.

16 And they laid hands on her; and she went by the way by the which the horses came into the king's house: and there was she [o]slain.

17 ¶ And [c,d]Jĕ-hoi'a-dȧ made a [p,q]covenant between the LORD and the king and the people, that they should be the LORD's people; between the king also and the people.

18 And [r]all the people of the land went into the [s]house of [t]Bā'al, and [u]brake it down; his

v.12—807 BC
See footnote, *Time*, Rev. 10:6.

**12**
c *Jehoiada*, 2 Kin. 12:2.
d *Minister, influential in public affairs*, Rom. 15:16.
e *King, modes of induction into office*, 2 Kin. 3:10.
f *Crown*, Ex. 29:6.
g *Law, of Moses*, Deut. 33:2.
h *King, constitutional restrictions of*, 2 Kin. 3:10.
i *Anointing, of kings*, Lev. 8:12.

**14**
j *Trumpet*, Josh. 6:4.
k *Rending of Garments*, 2 Chr. 34:27.

**15**
l *High Priest*, Lev. 21:10.
m *Captain*, Num. 31:48.
n *Armies*, Deut. 11:4.
3 R. V. between the ranks;

**16**
o *Homicide*, Deut. 5:17.

**17**
p *King, constitutional restrictions of*, 2 Kin. 3:10.
q *Covenant, of man with God*, Deut. 29:1.

**18**
r *Zeal*, 2 Cor. 7:11.
s *Temple, idolatrous*, 1 Kin. 6:17.
t *Baal*, 2 Kin. 17:16.
u *Iconoclasm*, Num. 33:52.

‡ **SPEAR.** Spears and javelins differed in weight and size, but had similar uses. *An implement of war*, 2 Kin. 11:10; Neh. 4:13. *Goliath's*, 1 Sam. 17:7. *Saul's*, 1 Sam. 18:10, 11. *Stored in the temple*, 2 Chr. 23:9. *To be changed into pruning hooks*, Isa. 2:4; Mic. 4:3. *Pruning hooks to be beaten into*, Joel 3:10. *Thrust into Jesus' side*, John 19:34; 20:27 (with Zech. 12:10); Rev. 1:7.

‖ **TREASON.** *Jesus falsely accused of*, Matt. 27:11, 29; Luke 23:2, 3, 38; John 19:12, 14, 15, 19. *Paul falsely accused of*, Acts 17:7.

*David's amnesty of the traitors, Shimei*, 2 Sam. 19:16–23; *Amasa*, 2 Sam. 19:13.

*Death penalty for*, Esth. 2:21–23.

**Instances of:** *Aaron and Miriam against Moses*, Num. 12:1–11. *Korah, Dathan, and Abiram against Moses and Aaron*, Num. 16:1–33. *Rahab against Jericho*, Josh. 2. *The betrayer of Beth-el*, Judg. 1:24, 25. *The Shechemites against Abimelech*, Judg. 9:22–25. *The Ephraimites against Jephthah*, Judg. 12:1–4. *The Israelites, against Saul*, 1 Sam. 10:27; *against Rehoboam*, 1 Kin. 12:16–19. *The Egyptian servant against the Amalekites*, 1 Sam. 30:15, 16. *Abner against Ish-bosheth*, 2 Sam. 3:6–21. *Absalom against David*, 2 Sam. chapters 15–17; 18:1–15. *Ahithophel against David*, 2 Sam. 17:1–4. *Sheba against David*, 2 Sam. 20:1–22. *Zimri against Elah*, 1 Kin. 16:2, 9, 20. *Jehoiada against Athaliah*, 2 Kin. 11:14–16; 2 Chr. 23:13. *Judas against Jesus*, Matt. 26:14–16, 47–49; Mark 14:10, 11, 43–45; Luke 6:16; 22:3–6, 47, 48; John 13:2; 18:2–5. See footnote, CONSPIRACY, 1 Kin. 16:9.

v.18–807 BC
See footnote, *Time*, Rev. 10:6.

*v* 2 Chr. 23:17.

altars and his images[c] [u]brake
they in pieces thoroughly, and
slew [v]Măt′tan the priest of
Bā′al before the altars. And
the [c,l]priest appointed officers
over the [b]house of the LORD.
19 And [c,d]he took the rulers
over hundreds, and the captains,
and the guard, and all the people
of the land; and they brought
down the king from the [b]house
of the LORD, and came by the
way of the gate of the guard to
the king's [w]house. And he sat on
the [x]throne of the kings.
20 And all the people of the
land rejoiced, and the city was
in quiet: and they slew Ăth-a-
lī′ah with the sword *beside* the
king's house.
21 Seven years old *was* Jĕ-hō′-
ăsh when he began to reign.

19
*w* *Palace*, 1 Kin. 21:1.
*x* *Throne*, 1 Kin. 2:19.

## CHAPTER 12

*Jehoash reigns well all the days of Jehoiada. 4 He gives orders to repair the temple. 17 Hazael is diverted from Jerusalem by a present of the hallowed treasures. 19 Jehoash is slain by his servants; and Amaziah succeeds him.*

1
IN the seventh year of [a]Jē′hū
[b]Jĕ-hō′ăsh began to reign;
and forty years reigned he in
[c]Jĕ-ru̦′să-lĕm. And his mother's
name *was* [d]Zĭb′ī-ah of [e]Bē′er-
shē′bȧ.
2 And [b]Jĕ-hō′ăsh [f]did *that*
*which was* right in the sight of
the LORD all his days wherein
*Jĕ-hoi′a-dȧ the [g]priest instruct-
ed him.
3 But the [h]high places were not
taken away: the people still [i]sac-
rificed and burnt incense in the
high places.
4 ¶ And [b]Jĕ-hō′ăsh said to the
priests, All the [j]money of the
dedicated[c] things that is brought
into the [k]house of the LORD,
[1]*even* the money of every one
that passeth *the account*, the
money that every man is set[c] at,
*and* all the money that cometh
[l]into any man's heart to bring
into the house of the LORD,
5 Let the priests take *it* to them
every man of his acquaintance:
and let them repair the breaches[c]
of the [k]house, wheresoever any
breach shall be found.
6 But it was *so, that* in the three
and twentieth year of king [b]Jĕ-
hō′ăsh the [m]priests had not repaired the breaches of the house.
7 Then king [b]Jĕ-hō′ăsh called
for *Jĕ-hoi′a-dȧ the priest, and
the *other* priests, and [n]said unto
them, Why repair ye not the
breaches of the house? now
therefore receive no *more* [j]money
of your acquaintance, but deliver
it for the breaches of the house.
8 And the priests consented to
receive no *more* [j]money of the
people, neither to repair the
breaches of the house.
9 But *Jĕ-hoi′a-dȧ the priest
took a [o]chest, and bored a hole
in the lid of it, and set it beside
the altar, on the right side as one
cometh into the [k]house of the
LORD: and the priests that kept
the door put therein all the [j]mon-
ey *that was* brought into the
house of the LORD.[Q]
10 And it was *so*, when they
saw that *there was* much [j]money
in the [o]chest, that the king's
[p]scribe[c] and the [q]high priest came
up, and they put up in bags, and
told[c] the money that was found
in the [k]house of the LORD.
11 And they gave the [j]money,
being told[c], into the hands of
them that did the work, that had
the oversight of the house[c] of the
LORD: and they laid it out to the
†carpenters and builders, that

1
*a* *Jehu*, 2 Chr. 22:8.
*b* Or, *Joash*, 2 Kin. 11:2.
*c* *Jerusalem*, Judg. 19:10.
*d* 2 Chr. 24:1.
*e* *Beer-sheba*, Judg. 20:1.
2
*f* *Zeal, instances of*, 2 Cor. 7:11.
*g* *Minister, influential in public affairs*, Rom. 15:16.
3
*h* *High Places*, 1 Kin. 3:2.
*i* *Idolatry*, 1 Sam. 15:23.
4
*j* *Money*, Jer. 32:9.
*k* *Temple, Solomon's*, 1 Kin. 6:17.
**1** R. V. in current money, the money of the persons for whom each man is rated,

*l* *Liberality, instances of*, 1 Tim. 6:18.
6
*m* *Minister, false and corrupt*, Rom. 15:16.
**v.6–785 BC**
7
*n* *Reproof, faithfulness in*, Prov. 17:10.
9
*o* 2 Chr. 24:8–11.
10
*p* *Scribe*, 1 Kin. 4:3.
*q* *High Priest, duties of*, Lev. 21:10.

* **JEHOIADA,** a high priest. *Overthrows Athaliah, the usurping queen of Judah, and establishes Jehoash upon the throne*, 2 Kin. 11:4–21; 2 Chr. 23. *Salutary influence of, over Jehoash*, 2 Kin. 12:2; 2 Chr. 24:2, 22. *Directs the repairs of the temple*, 2 Kin. 12:4–16; 2 Chr. 24:4–14. *Death of*, 2 Chr. 24:15, 16.

† **CARPENTRY,** Jer. 24:1. *Building, the ark*, Gen. 6:14–16; *the tabernacle, and furniture*, Ex. 31:2–9; *David's palace*, 2 Sam. 5:11; *the temple*, 2 Kin. 12:11; 22:6. *Making idols*, Isa. 41:7; 44:13.
**Instances of carpenters:** *Joseph*, Matt. 13:55; *Jesus*, Mark 6:3.

v.11–785 BC

**12**
*r* *Mason,* 2 Sam. 5:11.
*s* *Stones, hewn,* Ex. 24:12.

**13**
*t* *Silver,* 1 Chr. 28:14.
*u* *Snuffers,* 1 Kin. 7:50.
*v* *Basin,* 1 Kin. 7:50.
*w* *Trumpet,* Josh. 6:4.
*x* *Gold,* Ezek. 7:19.

**14**
*y* *Wages,* Gen. 31:7.

**15**
*z* *Honesty, instances of,* Rom. 13:13.

*a* *Integrity, instances of,* Job 2:3.
*b* *Faithfulness, instances of,* Luke 16:10.

**16**
*c* *Money, atonement,* Jer. 32:9.
*d* *Temple, Solomon's,* 1 Kin. 6:17.
*e* *Priest, emoluments of,* Lev. 1:5.

**17**
*f* *Hazael,* 2 Kin. 9:14.
*g* *Syria,* 2 Kin. 6:23.
*h* *Gath,* Josh. 11:22.
*i* *Jerusalem,* Judg. 19:10.

**18**
*j* Or, *Joash,* 2 Kin. 11:2.
*k* *Judah, kingdom of,* 2 Chr. 11:17.
*l* *Sacrilege,* Lev. 19:8.
*m* *Jehoram,* 1 Kin. 22:50.
*n* *Ahaziah,* 2 Kin. 8:25.
*o* *Gold,* Ezek. 7:19.
*p* *Palace,* 1 Kin. 21:1.
*q* *Diplomacy, instances of,* 2 Kin. 16:7.

wrought upon the house of the LORD.

12 And to [r]masons, and hewers of [s]stone, and to buy timber and hewed stone to repair the breaches of the [k]house of the LORD, and for all that was laid out for the house to repair *it.*

13 Howbeit there were not made for the [k]house of the LORD bowls of [t]silver, [u]snuffers, [v]basons, [w]trumpets, any vessels of [x]gold, or vessels of silver, of the [j]money *that was* brought into the house of the LORD:

14 But they gave [y]that to the workmen, and repaired therewith the house of the LORD.

15 Moreover they reckoned[G] not with the men, into whose hand they delivered the money to be bestowed on workmen: for they [z,a]dealt [b]faithfully.

16 The trespass [c]money and sin money was not brought into the [d]house of the LORD: [e]it was the priests'.

17 ¶ Then [f]Hăz'a-el king of [g]Sȳr'ĭ-ȧ went up, and fought against [h]Găth, and took it: and Hăz'a-el set his face to go up to [i]Jĕ-rṳ'sȧ-lĕm.

18 And [j]Jĕ-hō'ăsh king of [k]Jū'dah [l]took all the hallowed things that ‡Jĕ-hŏsh'a-phăt, and [m]Jĕ-hō'ram, and [n]Ā-ha-zī'ah, his fathers, kings of Jū'dah, had dedicated, and his own hallowed things, and all the [o]gold *that was* found in the treasures[G] of the [d]house of the LORD, and in the king's [p]house, and [q]sent *it* to [f]Hăz'a-el king of [g]Sȳr'ĭ-ȧ: and he went away from [i]Jĕ-rṳ'sȧ-lĕm.

19 ¶ And the rest of the acts of [j]Jō'ăsh, and all that he did, *are* they not written in the [r]book of the chronicles of the kings of [k]Jū'dah?

20 And his [s,t]servants arose, and made a [u]conspiracy, and [v,w,x]slew [j]Jō'ăsh in the house of [y]Mĭl'lō, which goeth down to Sĭl'lȧ.

21 For [z]Jŏz'a-chär the son of [a]Shĭm'e-ăth, and [a]Jĕ-hŏz'a-băd the son of [b]Shō'mĕr, his [c]servants, [d]smote[G] him, and he died; and they [e]buried him with his fathers in the [f]city of Dā'vid: and [g]Ăm-a-zī'ah his son reigned in his stead.

## CHAPTER 13

*The wicked reign of Jehoahaz. 3 Israel is delivered from the Syrians in answer to prayer. 8 Joash succeeds Jehoahaz. 10 His wicked reign. 12 Jeroboam succeeds him. 14 Elisha foretells to Joash three victories over the Syrians. 20 The death of Elisha 22 Hazael oppresses Israel. 25 Joash gains three victories over Ben-hadad.*

IN the three and twentieth year of [a]Jō'ăsh the son of [b]Ā-ha-zī'ah king of [c]Jū'dah [d,e]Jĕ-hō'a-hăz the son of [f]Jē'hū began to reign over [g]Ĭs'ra-el in [h]Sȧ-mā'-rĭ-ȧ, *and reigned* seventeen years.

2 And [d,e]he [i]did *that which was* evil in the sight of the LORD, and followed the sins of [j]Jĕr-o-bō'am the son of Nē'băt, [k]which made Ĭs'ra-el to sin; he departed not therefrom.

3 And the *anger of the LORD was kindled against [g]Ĭs'ra-el, and he [l]delivered[G] them into the

**2** *i* *Disobedience to God,* Eph. 5:6. *j* *Jeroboam,* 1 Kin. 14:5. *k* *Influence, evil,* 1 Cor. 7:14.
**3** *l* *Judgments,* Ex. 6:6.

v.18–895 BC

**19**
*r* *Book,* Num. 5:23.

**20**
*s* *Servant, wicked and unfaithful,* Jer. 2:14.
*t* *Citizens, wicked and treasonable,* Luke 15:15.
*u* *Conspiracy,* 1 Kin. 16:9.
*v* *Assassination, instances of,* Deut. 27:24.
*w* *Homicide, instances of,* Deut. 5:17
*x* *Regicide,* 2 Sam. 1:10.
*y* *Millo,* 2 Sam. 5:9.

v.21–767 BC

**21**
*z* Or, *Zabad,* 2 Chr. 24:26.

*a* 2 Chr. 24:26.
*b* Or, *Shimrith,* 2 Chr. 24:26.
*c* *Servant, wicked and unfaithful,* Jer. 2:14.
*d* *Assassination, instances of,* Deut. 27:24.
*e* *Burial,* Acts 8:2.
*f* *Jerusalem,* Judg. 19:10.
*g* *Amaziah,* 2 Kin. 14:1.

v.1–785 BC
See footnote, *Time,* Rev. 10:6.

**1**
*a* *Joash,* 2 Kin. 11:2.
*b* *Ahaziah,* 2 Kin. 8:25.
*c* *Judah, kingdom of,* 2 Chr. 11:17.
*d* 2 Kin. 10:35; 2 Chr. 25:17.
*e* *Rulers, wicked, instances of,* Ex. 18:21.
*f* *Jehu,* 2 Chr. 22:8.
*g* *Israel, after the revolt,* 1 Kin. 12:1.
*h* *Samaria,* 1 Kin. 16:24.

‡ **JEHOSHAPHAT,** king of Judah. *Succeeds Asa as king of Judah,* 1 Kin. 15:24; 22:41; 1 Chr. 3:10; 2 Chr. 17:1. *Strengthens himself against Israel,* 2 Chr. 17:2. *Inaugurates a system of public instruction in the law,* 2 Chr. 17:7–9. *His wise reign,* 1 Kin. 22:43; 2 Chr. 17:7–9; 19:3–11. *Receives tribute,* 2 Chr. 17:11. *Military forces and armament of,* 2 Chr. 17:12–19. *Joins Ahab in an invasion of Ramoth-gilead,* 1 Kin. 22:1–36; 2 Chr. 18. *Rebuked by the prophet Jehu,* 2 Chr. 19:2, 3. *The allied forces of the Amorites, Moabites, and other tribes invade his territory, and are defeated by,* 2 Chr. 20:1–30. *Builds ships for commerce with Tarshish; ships are destroyed,* 1 Kin. 22:48, 49; 2 Chr. 20:35–37. *Joins Jehoram, king of Israel, in an invasion of the land of Moab; defeats the Moabites,* 2 Kin. 3:4–27. *Makes gifts to the temple,* 2 Kin. 12:18. *Death of,* 1 Kin. 22:50; 2 Chr. 21:1. *Reigned twenty-five years,* 1 Kin. 22:42.
*Religious zeal of,* 1 Kin. 22:43, 46; 2 Chr. 17:1–9; 19; 20: 1–32; 22:9. *Prosperity of,* 1 Kin. 22:45, 48; 2 Chr. chapters 17–20. *Bequests of, to his children,* 2 Chr. 21:2, 3. *Ancestor of Jesus,* Matt. 1:8.

* **ANGER OF GOD,** Psa. 7:11; 74:1; 90:11; Isa. 30:27; Jer. 17:4; 23:20; Hos. 13:11; Rom. 1:18; Rev. 15:1, 7. *Invoked against enemies,* Psa. 69:24.
Provoked: *By disobedience,* Josh. 7:1, 26; 1 Sam. 28:18; 2 Sam. 6:7; 1 Kin. 16:2–13; 2 Kin. 22:13; Isa. 5:24, 25; 9:17, 19, 21; Eph. 5:6; Col. 3:6; *by obduracy,* Ex. 32:9, 10; 33:5; Num. 32:10, 11; Deut. 6:14, 15; 9:13, 14; Rom. 2:5; *by murmuring,* Num. 11:1, 10, 33; Psa. 106:32; *by sedition,* Num. 12:1–9; *by idolatry,* Num. 25:3; Deut. 32:21, 22; Josh. 23:16; Judg. 2:12; 3:7, 8; 10:7; 1 Kin. 11:9; Psa. 106:28, 29.
Appeased: *By intercession of the righteous,* Deut. 9:18–19, 20; Psa. 106:23; *by prayer,* Jer. 36:7; *by putting away evil,* Num. 25:6–11; *by penitence,* Jer. 4:4, 8.
*Prayer for averting of,* Dan. 9:16. *Turned away in mercy,* Psa.

*m Hazael, conquests by*, 2 Kin. 9:14.
*n Syria*, 2 Kin. 6:23.
*o* Amos 1:4.

**4**
*p Repentance, instances of*, Mark 1:4.
*q Prayer, answered*, Acts 6:4.
*r Oppression*, Eccl. 5:8.

**5**
*s God, preserver*, Gen. 2:2.
*t Oppression, national, relieved*, vs. 1–25; Eccl. 5:8.

**6**
*u Ingratitude, of man to God*, Rom. 1:21.
*v Groves*, Judg. 6:28.

**7**
*w Cavalry*, 1 Sam. 13:5.
*x Chariot*, Josh. 11:4.
*y* 1 Sam. 8:11.

**8**
*z Book*, Num. 5:23.

*a Israel, after the revolt*, 1 Kin. 12:1.

**9**
*b* 2 Kin. 10:35; 2 Chr. 25:17.
*c Death*, Num. 23:10.
*d Samaria*, 1 Kin. 16:24.
**v.9–768 BC**

**10**
*e Joash*, 2 Kin. 11:2.
*f Judah, kingdom of*, 2 Chr. 11:17.
**v.10–771 BC**

**11**
*g Rulers, wicked*, Ex. 18:21.
*h Disobedience to God*, Eph. 5:6.
*i Jeroboam*, 1 Kin. 14:5.

hand of [m]Hăz′a-el king of [n]Sȳr′ĭ-ȧ, and into the hand of [o]Bĕn-hā′dăd the son of Hăz′a-el, all *their* days.[s]

4 And [d]Jē-hō′a-hăz [p]besought the LORD, and the LORD [q]hearkened unto him: for he saw the [r]oppression of Ĭş′ra-el, because the king of [n]Sȳr′ĭ-ȧ oppressed them.

5 (And the [s]LORD gave Ĭş′ra-el a saviour, [t]so that they went out from under the hand of the Sȳr′ĭ-anş: and the children of Ĭş′ra-el dwelt in their tents, as beforetime.

6 Nevertheless [u]they departed not from the sins of the house of [i]Jĕr-o-bō′am, [k]who made Ĭş′ra-el sin, *but* walked therein: and there remained the [v]grove[c] also in [h]Să-mā′rĭ-ȧ.)

7 Neither did he leave of the people to [d]Jē-hō′a-hăz but fifty [w]horsemen, and ten [x]chariots, and ten thousand [y]footmen; for the king of [n]Sȳr′ĭ-ȧ had destroyed them, and had made them like the dust by threshing.

8 ¶ Now the rest of the acts of [d]Jē-hō′a-hăz, and all that he did, and his might, *are* they not written in the [z]book of the chronicles[c] of the kings of [a]Ĭş′ra-el?

9 And [b]Jē-hō′a-hăz [c]slept[c] with his fathers; and they buried him in [d]Să-mā′rĭ-ȧ: and Jō′ăsh his son reigned in his stead.

10 ¶ In the thirty and seventh year of [e]Jō′ăsh king of [f]Jū′dah began †Jē-hō′ăsh the son of [b]Jē-hō′a-hăz to reign over [a]Ĭş′ra-el in [d]Să-mā′rĭ-ȧ, *and reigned* sixteen years.

11 And [g]he [h]did *that which was* evil in the sight of the LORD; he departed not from all the sins of [i]Jĕr-o-bō′am the son of Nē′băt, who made Ĭş′ra-el sin: *but* he walked[c] therein.

12 And the rest of the acts of †Jō′ăsh, and all that he did, and his might wherewith he fought against [j]Ăm-a-zī′ah king of [f]Jū′dah, *are* they not written in the [k]book of the chronicles[c] of the kings of [a]Ĭş′ra-el?

13 And †Jō′ăsh [l]slept[c] with his fathers; and [m]Jĕr-o-bō′am sat upon his throne: and Jō′ăsh was buried in [d]Să-ma′rĭ-ȧ with the kings of Ĭş′ra-el.

14 ¶ Now [n]Ē-lī′shȧ was fallen sick of his sickness whereof he died. And †Jō′ăsh the king of Ĭş′ra-el came down unto him, and wept over his face, and said, O my father, my father, the chariot of Ĭş′ra-el, and the horsemen thereof.

15 And [n]Ē-lī′shȧ said unto him, Take bow and [o]arrows. And he took unto him bow and arrows.

16 And [n]he said to the †king of Ĭş′ra-el, Put thine hand upon the bow. And he put his hand *upon it*: and [n]Ē-lī′shȧ put his hands upon the king's hands.

17 And he said, Open the window eastward. And he opened *it*. Then Ē-lī′shȧ said, Shoot. And he shot. And he said, The arrow of the LORD's deliverance, and the arrow of deliverance from [p]Sȳr′ĭ-ȧ: for [q]thou shalt smite[c] the Sȳr′ĭ-anş in Ā′phek, till thou have consumed *them*.

18 And he said, Take the [o]arrows. And he took *them*. And he said unto the †king of Ĭş′ra-el, Smite[c] upon the ground. And he smote thrice, and stayed.[c]

19 And the man of God was wroth[c] with him, and said, Thou shouldest have smitten five or

**v.11–771 BC**
See footnote, *Time*, Rev. 10:6.

**12**
*j Amaziah*, 2 Kin. 14:1.
*k Book*, Num. 5:23.

**13**
*l Death*, Num. 23:10.
*m Jeroboam*, 1 Chr. 5:17.
**v.13–753 BC**

**14**
*n Elisha*, 1 Kin. 19:16.

**15**
*o Arrow*, 1 Sam. 20:20.

**17**
*p Syria*, 2 Kin. 6:23.
*q Elisha, prophecies of*, 1 Kin. 19:16.

78:21, 38; 85:3; 103:8, 9; Isa. 12:1; 57:16, 17; Jer. 3:12; 32:37; Hos. 11:8, 9; 14:4. *Deliverance from*, Rom. 5:9; 1 Thess. 1:10. *Destroys the wicked*, Ex. 22:24; Num. 16:20, 21, 45; 25:4; 32:13; 2 Sam. 22:8, 9; 2 Kin. 13:3; 17:18; Psa. 76:7; 78:49, 50; Isa. 13:9, 13; 42:25; 63:3, 4, 6; 66:15; Jer. 4:22, 26; 7:20; 10:10; 21:5, 6; 25:15–17, 37, 38; 30:23, 24; 33:5; 42:18; 44:6; 51:45; Lam. 2:1, 3, 6; 4:11; Ezek. 5:13, 15; 25:14–17; Nah. 1: 2, 3, 6; Matt. 22:7; Heb. 3:11; Rev. 14:10, 11; 16:19; 19:15.

† **JEHOASH** (*Jehovah given*), called also JOASH. *Successor of Jehoahaz*, 2 Kin. 13:10–25. *Defeats Amaziah*, 2 Kin. 13: 12; 14:8–15; 2 Chr. 25:17–24. *Reigned over Israel sixteen years*, 2 Kin. 13:10. *Death of*, 2 Kin. 13:13; 14:16.

six times; then hadst thou smitten [p]Sȳr'ĭ-ȧ till thou hadst consumed *it*: whereas now [q]thou
shalt smite Sȳr'ĭ-ȧ *but* thrice.
20 ¶ And [n]Ė-lī'shȧ [l]died, and
they buried him. And the bands
of the [r]Mō'ab-ītes invaded the
land at the coming in of the year.
21 And it came to pass, as they
were burying a man, that, behold, they spied[c] a band *of men*;
and they cast the man into the
sepulchre of [n]Ė-lī'shȧ: and when
the man was let down, and
touched the bones of Ė-lī'shȧ,
[s]he [t]revived, and stood up on
his feet.[s]
22 ¶ But [u]Hăz'a-el king of
[p]Sȳr'ĭ-ȧ [v]oppressed [a]Iṣ'ra-el all
the days of Jė-hō'a-hăz.
23 And the [w]LORD was gracious unto them, and had [x]com-
passion on them, and had respect unto them, because of
his [y]covenant with Ā'bră-hăm,
Ī'ṣaac, and Jā'cob, and would
not destroy them, neither cast
he them from his presence as yet.[s]
24 So [u]Hăz'a-el king of [p]Sȳr'ĭ-ȧ
died; and [z]Bĕn–hā'dăd his son
reigned in his stead.
25 And [†]Jė-hō'ăsh the son of
Jė-hō'a-hăz took again out of the
hand of [z]Bĕn–hā'dăd the son of
[u]Hăz'a-el the cities, which he
had taken out of the hand of Jė-
hō'a-hăz his father by war.
Three times did Jō'ăsh beat him,
and recovered the cities of Īṣ'-
ra-el.

20
*r* *Moabites*, Gen. 19:37.

21
*s* *Dead, raised to life*, 2 Kin. 4:32.
*t* *Miracles*, Luke 23:8.

22
*u* *Hazael*, 2 Kin. 9:14.
*v* *Oppression, instances of*, Eccl. 5:8.

23
*w* *God, faithfulness of*, Gen. 2:2.
*x* *God, mercy of*, Gen. 2:2.
*y* *Covenant, of God with men*, Deut. 29:1.

24
*z* Amos 1:4.

## CHAPTER 14

*Amaziah's good reign. 5 He punishes the murderers of his father. 7 His victory over Edom. 8 Amaziah, challenging Jehoash, is overcome and spoiled. 16 Jeroboam succeeds Jehoash. 17 Amaziah slain by a conspiracy. 21 Azariah succeeds him. 23 Jeroboam's wicked reign. 29 Zachariah succeeds him.*

IN the second year of [a]Jō'ăsh
son of Jė-hō'a-hăz king of [b]Īṣ'-
ra-el reigned *Ăm-a-zī'ah the
son of [c]Jō'ăsh king of [d]Jū'dah.
2 He was twenty and five years
old when he began to reign, and
reigned twenty and nine years in
[e]Jė-rṳ'sȧ-lĕm. And his mother's
name *was* [f]Jē-hō-ăd'dan of Jė-
rṳ'sȧ-lĕm.
3 And he did *that which was*
right in the sight of the LORD,
yet not like [g]Dā'vid his father:
he did according to all things [h]as
[c]Jō'ăsh his father did.
4 Howbeit the [i]high places were
not taken away: as yet the people [j]did sacrifice and burnt incense on the high places.
5 ¶ And it came to pass, as soon
as the kingdom was confirmed[c] in
his hand, that he [k]slew[c] his [l]serv-
ants which had slain the king
his father.
6 But the [m,n]children of the
murderers he slew not: according unto that which is written in
the book of the [o]law of Mō'ṣeṣ,
wherein the LORD commanded,
saying, [p]The fathers shall not be
put to death for the children,
[q]nor the children be put to death
for the fathers; but every man
shall be put to death for his own
sin.
7 He [r]slew of Ē'dom in the valley of [s]salt ten thousand, and
took [t]Sē'lah by [u]war, and called
the name of it Jŏk'the-el unto
this day.
8 ¶ Then *Ăm-a-zī'ah sent
[v]messengers to [a]Jė-hō'ăsh, the
son of Jė-hō'a-hăz son of [w]Jē'hū,
king of [b]Īṣ'ra-el, saying, Come,
let us look one another in the
face.
9 And Jė-hō'ăsh the king of
Īṣ'ra-el sent to *Ăm-a-zī'ah king
of [d]Jū'dah, saying, [x,y]The [z]this-
tle that *was* in Lĕb'a-non sent to
the [a]cedar that *was* in Lĕb'a-
non, saying, Give thy daughter
to my son to[c] wife: and there
passed by a wild beast that *was*

1
*a* Or, *Jehoash*, 2 Kin. 13:10.
*b* *Israel, after the revolt*, 1 Kin. 12:1.
*c* *Joash*, 2 Kin. 11:2.
*d* *Judah, kingdom of*, 2 Chr. 11:17.

v.2–767 BC
See footnote, *Time*, Rev. 10:6.

2
*e* *Jerusalem*, Judg. 19:10.
*f* 2 Chr. 25:1.

3
*g* *David*, 1 Sam. 16:13.
*h* *Influence, good*, 1 Cor. 7:14.

4
*i* *High Places*, 1 Kin. 3:2.
*j* *Idolatry*, 1 Sam. 15:23.

5
*k* *Homicide, punishment of*, Deut. 5:17.
*l* *Citizens, wicked and treasonable*, Luke 15:15.

6
*m* *Children, not punished on account of sins of parents*, Mark 10:14.
*n* *Innocent, shall not suffer for the guilty*, Deut. 24:16.
*o* *Law, of Moses*, Deut. 33:2.
*p* Deut. 24:16.
*q* *Sin, consequences of, not entailed on children*, Rom. 5:12.

7
*r* *Massacre, instances of*, Esth. 3:13.
*s* *Salt, valley of*, 2 Kin. 2:20.
*t* Isa. 16:1.
*u* *War*, Judg. 3:2.

8
*v* *Ambassadors*, Josh. 9:4.
*w* *Jehu*, 2 Chr. 22:8.

9
*x* *Parables*, Ezek. 20:49.
*y* *Sarcasm*, Judg. 10:14.
*z* *Thistle, parables of*, Hos. 10:8.
*a* *Cedar*, Isa. 9:10.

***AMAZIAH**, king of Judah. *Reigned twenty-nine years*, 2 Kin. 12:21; 13:12; 14:1, 2; 2 Chr. 25:1. *Slain in Lachish*, 2 Kin. 14:17–19; 2 Chr. 25:27. *Buried in Jerusalem*, 2 Kin. 14:20; 2 Chr. 25:28. *History of*, 2 Kin. 14:1–22; 2 Chr. 25.

in Lĕb′a-non, and trode down
the thistle.
10 Thou hast indeed smitten
[b]Ē′dom, and thine heart hath
[c]lifted thee up: glory *of this*, and
tarry at home: for why shouldest
thou meddle to *thy* hurt,[C] that
thou shouldest fall, *even* thou,
and [d]Jū′dah with thee?
11 But *Ăm-a-zī′ah would not
hear. Therefore [e]Jē-hō′ăsh king
of Ĭṣ′ra-el went up; and he and
Ăm-a-zī′ah king of Jū′dah looked one another in the face at
[f]Bĕth–shē′mesh, which *belongeth*
to Jū′dah.
12 And [d]Jū′dah was put[C] to the
worse before [g]Ĭṣ′ra-el; and they
fled every man to their tents.
13 And [e]Jē-hō′ăsh king of Ĭṣ′-
ra-el took *Ăm-a-zī′ah king of
Jū′dah, the son of Jē-hō′ăsh the
son of Ā-ha-zī′ah, at [f]Bĕth–shē′-
mesh, and came to [h]Jē-rṳ′sȧ-
lĕm, and brake down the wall of
Jē-rṳ′sȧ-lĕm from the [i]gate of
Ē′phrā-ĭm unto the corner gate,
four hundred cubits.[C]
14 And he took [j]all the gold and
silver, and all the vessels that
were found in the [k]house of the
LORD, and in the treasures[C] of
the king's [l]house, and [m]hostages,
and returned to [n]Sȧ-mā′rĭ-ȧ.
15 ¶ Now the rest of the acts of
[e]Jē-hō′ăsh which he did, and his
might, and how he fought with
*Ăm-a-zī′ah king of Jū′dah, *are*
they not written in the book of
the chronicles[C] of the kings of
Ĭṣ′ra-el?
16 And [e]Jē-hō′ăsh [o]slept[C] with
his fathers, and was [p]buried in
[n]Sȧ-mā′rĭ-ȧ with the kings of Ĭṣ′-
ra-el; and [q]Jĕr-o-bō′am his son
reigned in his stead.
17 ¶ And *Ăm-a-zī′ah the son
of [r]Jō′ăsh king of Jū′dah lived
after the death of [e]Jē-hō′ăsh son
of Jē-hō′a-hăz king of [g]Ĭṣ′ra-el
fifteen years.
18 And the rest of the acts of

10
b *Edomites*, 2 Kin. 8:21.
c *Pride*, Prov. 16:18.
d *Judah, kingdom of*, 2 Chr. 11:17.

11
e *Jehoash*, 2 Kin. 13:10.
f *Beth-shemesh*, Josh. 21:16.

12
g *Israel, after the revolt*, 1 Kin. 12:1.

13
h *Jerusalem*, Judg. 19:10.
i *Jerusalem, gates of*, Judg. 19:10.

14
j *Spoils*, 1 Chr. 26:27.
k *Temple, Solomon's, pillaged*, 1 Kin. 6:17.
l *Palace*, 1 Kin. 21:1.
m 2 Chr. 25:24.
n *Samaria*, 1 Kin. 16:24.

v.16–753 BC
16
o *Death*, Num. 23:10.
p *Burial*, Acts 8:2.
q *Jeroboam*, 1 Chr. 5:17.

17
r *Joash*, 2 Kin. 11:2.

*Ăm-a-zī′ah, *are* they not written in the [s]book of the chronicles
of the kings of [d]Jū′dah?
19 Now [t]they made a [u]con-
spiracy against him in [v]Jē-rṳ′-
sȧ-lĕm: and he fled to [w]Lā′chish;
but they sent after him to Lā′-
chish, and [x]slew him there.
20 And they brought him on
horses: and he was [p]buried at
[v]Jē-rṳ′sȧ-lĕm with his fathers in
the city of Dā′vid.
21 ¶ And all the people of Jū′-
dah took [y]Ăz-a-rī′ah, which *was*
sixteen years old, and made him
king instead of his father Ăm-
a-zī′ah.
22 [y]He built [z]Ē′lăth, and restored it to Jū′dah, after that
the king slept[C] with his fathers.
23 ¶ In the fifteenth year of
*Ăm-a-zī′ah the son of [a]Jō′ăsh
king of [b]Jū′dah [c]Jĕr-o-bō′am the
son of [d]Jō′ăsh king of Ĭṣ′ra-el
began to reign in [e]Sȧ-mā′rĭ-ȧ,
*and reigned* forty and one
years.
24 And [f]he did *that which was*
evil in the sight of the LORD: he
departed not from all the sins of
[g]Jĕr-o-bō′am the son of Nē′băt,
who made Ĭṣ′ra-el to sin.
25 He restored the coast[C] of Ĭṣ′-
ra-el from the entering of [h]Hā′-
math unto the [i]sea of the plain,
according to the [j]word of the
LORD God of Ĭṣ′ra-el, which he
spake by the hand of his servant
[k]Jō′nah, the son of [l]Ā-mĭt′ta-ī,
the prophet, which *was* of Găth–
hē′phēr.
26 For the LORD saw the [m]af-
fliction of Ĭṣ′ra-el, *that it was*
very bitter: for *there was* not any
shut up, nor any left, nor any
helper for Ĭṣ′ra-el.
27 And the LORD said not that
[n]he would blot out the name of
Ĭṣ′ra-el from under heaven: but
[o]he saved them by the hand of
Jĕr-o-bō′am the son of Jō′ăsh.
28 ¶ Now the rest of the acts of

v.19–739 BC
See footnote, *Time*, Rev. 10:6.

18
s *Book*, Num. 5:23.

19
t *Citizens, wicked and treasonable*, Luke 15:15.
u *Conspiracy, instances of*, 1 Kin. 16:9.
v *Jerusalem*, Judg. 19:10.
w *Lachish*, Josh. 10:5.
x *Regicide*, 2 Sam. 1:10.

21
y Or, *Uzziah*, 2 Chr. 26:1.

22
z *Elath*, Deut. 2:8.

23
a *Joash*, 2 Kin. 11:2.
b *Judah, king of*, 2 Chr. 11:17.
c *Jeroboam*, 1 Chr. 5:17.
d Or, *Jehoash*, 2 Kin. 13:10.
e *Samaria*, 1 Kin. 16:24.

24
f *Rulers, wicked, instances of*, Ex. 18:21.
g *Jeroboam*, 1 Kin. 14:5.

25
h *Hamath*, 1 Chr. 18:3.
i *Dead Sea*, Gen. 14:3.
j *Prophecies, fulfilled*, Dan. 9:24
k *Jonah*, Jonah 1:1.
l Jonah 1:1.

26
m *Afflictions*, Psa. 34:19.

27
n *God, mercy of*, Gen. 2:2.
o *God, preserver*, Gen. 2:2.

v.29–713 BC
See footnote, *Time*, Rev. 10:6.

28
*p* *Damascus*, Isa. 8:4.
*q* *Book*, Num. 5:23.
*r* *Israel, after the revolt*, 1 Kin. 12:1.

29
*s* *Death*, Num. 23:10.
*t* 2 Kin. 15:8–12.

v.1–727 BC
See footnote, *Time*, Rev. 10:6.

1
*a* *Jeroboam*, 1 Chr. 5:17.
*b* Or, *Uzziah*, 2 Chr. 26:1.
*c* *Amaziah*, 2 Kin. 14:1.
*d* *Judah, kingdom of*, 2 Chr. 11:17.

2
*e* *Jerusalem*, Judg. 19:10.
*f* 2 Chr. 26:3.

3
*g* *Influence, good*, 1 Cor. 7:14.
*h* *Parents, good influence of*, 2 Cor. 12:14.

4
*i* *High Places*, 1 Kin. 3:2.
*j* *Idolatry*, 1 Sam. 15:23.

5
*k* *Adversity, dispensation from God*, Psa. 10:6.
*l* *Leprosy*, Lev. 13:2.
*m* *Sanitation and Hygiene: isolation*, Num. 31:23.
*n* 1 Kin. 22:47.

6
*o* *Book*, Num. 5:23.

[c]Jĕr-o-bō′am, and all that he
did, and his might, how he
warred, and how he recovered
[p]Dȧ-măs′cus, and [h]Hā′math,
*which belonged* to Jū′dah, for
Ĭș′ra-el, *are* they not written in
the [q]book of the chronicles of the
kings of [r]Ĭș′ra-el?
29 And Jĕr-o-bō′am [s]slept with
his fathers, *even* with the kings
of Ĭș′ra-el; and [t]Zăch-a-rī′ah his
son reigned in his stead.

## CHAPTER 15

*Azariah's good reign. 5 He dies a leper; and Jonathan succeeds him. 8 Zachariah, the last of Jehu's race, is slain by Shallum. 13 Shallum, reigning a month, is slain by Menahem. 16 Menahem strengthens himself. 21 Pekahiah succeeds him; 23 and is slain by Pekah. 27 Pekah is oppressed by Tiglath-pileser, and slain by Hoshea. 32 Jotham's good reign. 36 Ahaz succeeds him.*

IN the twenty and seventh year
of [a]Jĕr-o-bō′am king of Ĭș′-
ra-el began [b]Ăz-a-rī′ah son of
[c]Ăm-a-zī′ah king of [d]Jū′dah to
reign.
2 Sixteen years old was he when
he began to reign, and he reigned
two and fifty years in [e]Jĕ-ru̧′sȧ-
lĕm. And his mother's name *was*
[f]Jĕch-o-lī′ah of Jĕ-ru̧′sȧ-lĕm.
3 And he did *that which was*
right in the sight of the LORD,
[g]according to all that his [h]father
Ăm-a-zī′ah had done;
4 Save[G] that the [i]high places
were not removed: the people
[j]sacrificed and burnt incense
still on the high places.
5 ¶ And [k]the LORD smote the
king, so that he was a [l]leper unto
the day of his death, and [m]dwelt
in a several[G] house. And *Jō′-
tham the king's son *was* [n]over
the house, judging the people of
the land.
6 And the rest of the acts of
[b]Ăz-a-rī′ah, and all that he did,
*are* they not written in the [o]book
of the chronicles[G] of the kings of
[d]Jū′dah?

7 So [b]Ăz-a-rī′ah [p]slept[G] with his
fathers; and they [q]buried him
with his fathers in the [e]city of
Dā′vid: and *Jō′tham his son
reigned in his stead.
8 ¶ In the thirty and eighth
year of [b]Ăz-a-rī′ah king of [d]Jū′-
dah did [r]Zăch-a-rī′ah the son of
[a]Jĕr-o-bō′am reign over Ĭș′ra-el
in [s]Sȧ-mā′rĭ-ȧ six months.
9 And [t]he did *that which was*
evil in the sight of the LORD,
[u]as his fathers had done: he
departed not from the sins of
Jĕr-o-bō′am the son of Nē′băt,
who made Ĭș′ra-el to sin.
10 And [v]Shăl′lum the son of
Jā′besh [w]conspired against him,
and [x, y]smote[G] him before[G] the people, and slew him, and [z]reigned
in his stead.
11 And the rest of the acts of
[a]Zăch-a-rī′ah, behold, they *are*
written in the [b]book of the
chronicles of the kings of [c]Ĭș′-
ra-el.
12 This *was* the word of the
LORD which he spake unto
[d]Jē′hū, saying, Thy sons shall
sit on the throne of Ĭș′ra-el unto
the fourth *generation*. And so
[e]it came to pass.
13 ¶ Shăl′lum the son of Jā′-
besh began to reign in the nine
and thirtieth year of [f]Ŭz-zī′ah
king of [g]Jū′dah; and he reigned
a full month in [h]Sȧ-mā′rĭ-ȧ.
14 For Mĕn′a-hĕm the son of
Gā′dī went up from [i]Tĭr′zah,
and came to [h]Sȧ-mā′rĭ-ȧ, and
[j, k]smote[G] Shăl′lum the son of
Jā′besh in Sȧ-mā′rĭ-ȧ, and slew
him, and [l]reigned in his stead.
15 And the rest of the acts of
Shăl′lum, and his conspiracy
which he made, behold, they *are*
written in the [b]book of the
chronicles of the kings of [c]Ĭș′-
ra-el.
16 Then Mĕn′a-hĕm [m]smote

v.7–676 BC
See footnote, *Time*, Rev. 10:6.

7
*p* *Death*, Num. 23:10.
*q* *Burial*, Acts 8:2.

8
*r* 2 Kin. 14:29; 10:30.
*s* *Samaria*, 1 Kin. 16:24.

v.8–690 BC

9
*t* *Rulers, wicked, instances of*, Ex. 18:21.
*u* *Influence, evil*, 1 Cor. 7:14.

10
*v* *Citizens, wicked*, Luke 15:15.
*w* *Conspiracy, instances of*, 1 Kin. 16:9.
*x* *Homicide, felonious, instances of*, Deut. 5:17.
*y* *Regicide*, 2 Sam. 1:10.
*z* *Usurpation, of political functions*, 2 Sam. 15:1.

11
*a* 2 Kin. 14:29.
*b* *Book*, Num. 5:23.
*c* *Israel, after the revolt*, 1 Kin. 12:1.

12
*d* *Jehu*, 2 Chr. 22:8.
*e* *Prophecies, fulfilled*, Dan. 9:24.

13
*f* *Uzziah, king of Judah*, 2 Chr. 26:1.
*g* *Judah, kingdom of*, 2 Chr. 11:17.
*h* *Samaria*, 1 Kin. 16:24.

14
*i* *Tirzah*, 1 Kin. 14:17.
*j* *Regicide*, 2 Sam. 1:10.
*k* *Homicide, felonious*, Deut. 5:17.
*l* *Usurpation, of political functions*, 2 Sam. 15:1.

16
*m* *Massacre, instances of*, Esth. 3:13.

***JOTHAM.** *Son of Azariah, king of Judah*, 2 Kin. 15: 5–7, 32–38; 1 Chr. 3:12; 2 Chr. 26:21–23. *Reigned sixteen years*, 2 Kin. 15:32, 33. *Piety of* 2 Chr. 27:1, 2, 6. *The moral condition of Israel during his reign*, **Hos. 4.** *Ancestor of Jesus*, Matt. 1:9.

v.17–689 BC
ee footnote, *Time*, Rev. 10:6.

*Captive, cruelty to*, 1 Sam. 30:3.
*Cruelty, instances of*, Psa. 27:12.

18
*Influence, evil*, 1 Cor. 7:14.
*Jeroboam*, 1 Kin. 14:5.

19
1 Chr. 5:26.
*Assyria*, Gen. 25:18.
*Alliances, instances of*, Josh. 9:15.

20
*Money*, Jer. 32:9.
*Tribute, from conquered nations*, Ezra 4:13.
*Tax*, Neh. 10:32.

22
*Death*, Num. 23:10.

v.23–678 BC

24
*Rulers, wicked, instances of*, Ex. 18:21.

Tĭph′sah, and all that *were*
therein, and the coasts[c] thereof
from [i]Tĭr′zah: because they
opened not *to him*, therefore he
smote *it*; *and* all the [n]women
therein that were with child he
[o]ripped up.
17 ¶ In the nine and thirtieth
year of [f]Ăz-a-rī′ah king of [g]Jū′-
dah began Mĕn′a-hĕm the son of
Gā′dī to reign over Ĭş′ra-el, *and*
*reigned* ten years in [h]Să-mā′rĭ-ȧ.
18 And he did *that which was*
evil in the sight of the LORD: he
departed not all his days from
the [p]sins of [q]Jĕr-o-bō′am the
son of Nē′băt, who made Ĭş′-
ra-el to sin.
19 *And* [r]Pŭl the king of [s]Ăs-
sy̆r′ĭ-ȧ came against the land:
and Mĕn′a-hĕm gave Pŭl a thousand talents[c] of silver, [t]that his
hand might be with him to confirm[c] the kingdom in his hand.
20 And Mĕn′a-hĕm exacted[c] the
[u,v]money of Ĭş′ra-el, *even* of all
the mighty men of wealth, of
each man [w]fifty shekels[c] of silver,
to give to the king of Ăs-sy̆r′ĭ-ȧ.
So the king of Ăs-sy̆r′ĭ-ȧ turned
back, and stayed not there in the
land.
21 ¶ And the rest of the acts of
Mĕn′a-hĕm, and all that he did,
*are* they not written in the [b]book
of the chronicles of the kings of
[c]Ĭş′ra-el?
22 And Mĕn′a-hĕm [x]slept with
his fathers; and Pĕk-a-hī′ah his
son reigned in his stead.
23 ¶ In the fiftieth year of [f]Ăz-
a-rī′ah king of [g]Jū′dah Pĕk-a-
hī′ah the son of Mĕn′a-hĕm began to reign over Ĭş′ra-el in [h]Să-
mā′rĭ-ȧ, *and reigned* two years.
24 And [y]he did *that which was*
evil in the sight of the LORD: he
departed not from the [p]sins of
[q]Jĕr-o-bō′am the son of Nē′băt,
who made Ĭş′ra-el to sin.
25 But [z,a]Pē′kah the son of
†Rĕm-a-lī′ah, a [b]captain of his,
[c]conspired against him, and
smote[c] him in [d]Să-mā′rĭ-ȧ, in the
[e]palace of the king's house, with
Ăr′gŏb and Ă-rī′eh, and with
him fifty men of the Gĭl′e-ăd-
ītes: and he [f]killed him, and
[g]reigned in his room[c].
26 And the rest of the acts of
Pĕk-a-hī′ah, and all that he did,
behold, they *are* written in the
[h]book of the chronicles of the
kings of [i]Ĭş′ra-el.
27 ¶ In the two and fiftieth year
of [j]Ăz-a-rī′ah king of [k]Jū′dah
[a]Pē′kah the son of †Rĕm-a-lī′ah
began to reign over Ĭş′ra-el in
[d]Să-mā′rĭ-ȧ, *and reigned* twenty
years.
28 And he did *that which was*
evil in the sight of the LORD: he
departed not from the [l]sins of
[m]Jĕr-o-bō′am the son of Nē′băt,
who made Ĭş′ra-el to sin.
29 In the days of [a]Pē′kah king
of Ĭş′ra-el came [n]Tĭg′lath–pĭ-lē′-
şer king of [o]Ăs-sy̆r′ĭ-ȧ, and took
[p]Ī′jon, and ‡Ā′bel–bĕth–mā′a-
chah, and Jă-nō′ah, and [q]Kē′-
desh, and [r]Hā′zôr, and [s]Gĭl′e-
ăd, and [t]Găl′ĭ-lee, all the land of
[u]Năph′ta-lī, and carried them
captive to Ăs-sy̆r′ĭ-ȧ.
30 And ‖,[v]Hō-shē′ȧ the son
of [w]Ē′lah made a [c]conspiracy
against [a]Pē′kah the son of †Rĕm-
a-lī′ah, and smote[c] him, and
[f]slew him, and reigned in his
stead, in the twentieth year of
*Jō′tham the son of [j]Ŭz-zī′ah.
31 And the rest of the acts of
[a]Pē′kah, and all that he did, behold, they *are* written in the
[h]book of the chronicles of the
kings of [i]Ĭş′ra-el.

v.24–678 BC
See footnote, *Time* Rev. 10:6.

25
z *Citizens, wicked, instances of*, Luke 15:15.
v.25–677 BC

a *Pekah*, Isa. 7:1.
b *Captain*, Num. 31:48.
c *Conspiracy, instances of*, 1 Kin. 16:9.
d *Samaria*, 1 Kin. 16:24.
e *Palace*, 1 Kin. 21:1.
f *Regicide*, 2 Sam. 1:10.
g *Usurpation, of political functions*, 2 Sam. 15:1.

26
h *Book*, Num. 5:23.
i *Israel, after the revolt*, 1 Kin. 12:1.

27
j Or, *Uzziah*, 2 Chr. 26:1.
k *Judah, kingdom of*, 2 Chr. 11:17.

28
l *Influence, evil*, 1 Cor. 7:14.
m *Jeroboam*, 1 Kin. 14:5.

29
n *Tiglath-pileser*, 2 Chr. 28:20.
o *Assyria*, Gen. 25:18.
p 2 Chr. 16:4.
q *Kedesh*, Josh. 21:32.
r *Hazor*, Josh. 11:1.
s *Gilead*, Deut. 3:13.
t *Galilee*, Mark 6:21.
u *Naphtali, tribe of*, Num. 1:42.

30
v *Citizens, wicked*, Luke 15:15.
w 2 Kin. 17:1.

† **REMALIAH.** *Father of Pekah, king of Israel*, 2 Kin. 15:25, 27, 30; 16:1, 5; 2 Chr. 28:6; Isa. 7:1, 4; 8:6.

‡ **ABEL-BETH-MAACHAH** (*the meadow of the house of Maachah*), called also ABEL-MAIM, a city in the N. of Palestine. *Sheba slain in*, 2 Sam. 20:14–22. *Taken, by Ben-hadad*, 1 Kin. 15:20; 2 Chr. 16:4; *by Tiglath-pileser*, 2 Kin. 15:29.

‖ **HOSHEA**, king of Israel. *Assassinates Pekah and usurps the throne*, 2 Kin. 15:30. *Evil reign of*, 2 Kin. 17:1, 2. *Becomes subject to Assyria*, 2 Kin. 17:3. *Conspires against Assyria, and is imprisoned*, 2 Kin. 17:4. *Reigned nine years*, 2 Kin. 17:6. *Last king of Israel*, 2 Kin. 17:6; 18:9–12; Hos. 10:3, 7.

v.32–675 BC
See footnote, *Time*, Rev. 10:6.

32 ¶ In the second year of [a]Pē'kah the son of †Rĕm-a-lī'ah king of Ĭṣ'ra-el began *Jō'tham the son of [j]Ŭz-zī'ah king of [k]Jū'dah to reign.

33 Five and twenty years old was he when he began to reign, and he reigned sixteen years in [x]Jĕ-rṳ'să-lĕm. And his mother's name *was* [y]Jĕ-rṳ'shȧ, the daughter of [y]Zā'dŏk.

34 And he did *that which was* right in the sight of the LORD: he did [z]according to all that his [a]father [b]Ŭz-zī'ah had done.

35 Howbeit the [c]high places were not removed: the people [d]sacrificed and burned incense still in the high places. He built the higher gate of the [e]house of the LORD.

36 ¶ Now the rest of the acts of *Jō'tham, and all that he did, *are* they not written in the [f]book of the chronicles[c] of the kings of [g]Jū'dah?

37 In those days the LORD began to [h]send against [g]Jū'dah §Rē'zin the king of [i]Sy̆r'ĭ-ȧ, and [j]Pē'kah the son of †Rĕm-a-lī'ah.

38 And *Jō'tham [k]slept[c] with his fathers, and was [l]buried with his fathers in the [m]city of Dā'vid his father: and +Ā'hăz his son reigned in his stead.[c]

33

*x* *Jerusalem*, Judg. 19:10.

*y* 2 Chr. 27:1.

34

*z* *Influence, good*, 1 Cor. 7:14.

*a* *Parents, good influence of*, 2 Cor. 12:14.

*b* *Uzziah*, 2 Chr. 26:1.

35

*c* *High Places*, 1 Kin. 3:2.

*d* *Idolatry*, 1 Sam. 15:23.

*e* *Temple, Solomon's*, 1 Kin. 6:17.

36

*f* *Book*, Num. 5:23.

*g* *Judah, kingdom of*, 2 Chr. 11:17.

37

*h* *Judgments*, Ex. 6:6.

*i* *Syria*, 2 Kin. 6:23.

*j* *Pekah*, Isa. 7:1.

38

*k* *Death*, Num. 23:10.

*l* *Burial*, Acts 8:2.

*m* *Jerusalem*, Judg. 19:10.

## CHAPTER 16

*The wicked reign of Ahaz. 5 He, assailed by Rezin and Pekah, hires Tiglath-pileser against them. 10 He goes to Damascus, and sends thence the pattern of an altar for the temple. 17 He spoils the temple. 20 Hezekiah succeeds him.*

v.1–660 BC
See footnote, *Time*, Rev. 10:6.

IN the seventeenth year of [a]Pē'kah the son of [b]Rĕm-a-lī'ah [c]Ā'hăz the son of [d]Jō'tham king of [e]Jū'dah began to reign.

2 Twenty years old *was* [c]Ā'hăz when he began to reign, and reigned sixteen years in [f]Jĕ-rṳ'să-lĕm, and [g]did not *that which was* right in the sight of the LORD his God, like Dā'vid his father.

3 But [h]he walked in the way of the kings of Ĭṣ'ra-el, yea, and [i]made his [j]son to pass through the [k]fire, according to the abominations of the heathen[c], whom the LORD cast out from before the children of Ĭṣ'ra-el.

4 And he [l]sacrificed and burnt incense in the [m]high places, and on the hills, and under every green tree.

5 ¶ [n]Then [o]Rē'zin king of [p]Sy̆r'ĭ-ȧ and [a]Pē'kah son of [b]Rĕm-a-lī'ah king of [q]Ĭṣ'ra-el came up to [r]Jĕ-rṳ'să-lĕm to war: and they [s]besieged [c]Ā'hăz, but could not overcome *him*.

6 At that time [o]Rē'zin king of [p]Sy̆r'ĭ-ȧ recovered [t]Ē'lăth to Sy̆r'ĭ-ȧ, and drave the [u]Jews from Ē'lăth: and the Sy̆r'ĭ-ans came to Ē'lăth, and dwelt there unto this day.

7 So [c]Ā'hăz *sent [v]messengers to [w]Tĭg'lath-pĭ-lē'ṣer king of [x]Ăs-sy̆r'ĭ-ȧ, saying, I *am* thy servant and thy son: come up, and save[c] me out of the hand of the [o]king of [p]Sy̆r'ĭ-ȧ, and out of the hand of the [a]king of [q]Ĭṣ'ra-el, which rise up against me.

8 And Ā'hăz took the silver and gold that was found in the [y]house of the LORD, and in the treasures[c] of the king's [z]house, and sent *it for* a [a]present to the [b]king of [c]Ăs-sy̆r'ĭ-ȧ.

1

*a* *Pekah*, Isa. 7:1.

*b* *Remaliah*, 2 Kin. 15:25.

*c* *Ahaz*, 2 Kin. 15:38.

*d* *Jotham*, 2 Kin. 15:5.

*e* *Judah, kingdom of*, 2 Chr. 11:17.

v.2–660 BC
See footnote, *Time*, Rev. 10:6.

2

*f* *Jerusalem*, Judg. 19:10.

*g* *Disobedience to God*, Eph. 5:6.

3

*h* *Rulers, wicked, instances of*, Ex. 18:21.

*i* *Idolatry, wicked practices of*, 1 Sam. 15:23.

*j* *Children, caused to pass through fire*, Mark 10:14.

*k* *Fire*, Ex. 12:8.

4

*l* *Idolatry, customs of*, 1 Sam. 15:23.

*m* *High Places*, 1 Kin. 3:2.

5

*n* *Alliances*, Josh. 9:15.

*o* *Rezin*, 2 Kin. 15:37.

*p* *Syria*, 2 Kin. 6:23.

*q* *Israel, after the revolt*, 1 Kin. 12:1.

*r* *Jerusalem, besieged*, Judg. 19:10.

*s* *Siege, instances of*, Deut. 28:53.

6

*t* *Elath, conquest of*, Deut. 2:8.

*u* *Jews*, Neh. 4:2.

7

*v* *Ambassadors*, Josh. 9:4.

*w* *Tiglath-pileser*, 2 Chr. 28:20.

*x* *Assyria*, Gen. 25:18.

8

*y* *Temple, Solomon's*, 1 Kin. 6:17.

*z* *Palace*, 1 Kin. 21:1.

*a* *Presents*, Gen. 32:13.

*b* *Tiglath-pileser*, 2 Chr. 28:20.

*c* *Assyria*, Gen. 25:18.

§ **REZIN.** *A king of Syria who harassed the kingdom of Judah*, 2 Kin. 15:37; 16:5–9. *Prophecy against*, Isa. 7:1–9; 8:4–8; 9:11.

+ **AHAZ** (*possessor*). *King of Judah, son and successor of Jotham*, 2 Kin. 15:38; 16:1; 2 Chr. 27:9; 28:1. *Reigned sixteen years*, 2 Kin. 16:2. *Idolatrous abominations of*, 2 Kin. 16:3, 4; 2 Chr. 28:2–4, 22–25. *Kingdom of, invaded by the kings of Syria and Samaria*, 2 Kin. 16:5, 6; 2 Chr. 28:5–8. *Robs the temple to purchase aid from the king of Assyria*, 2 Kin. 16:7–9, 17, 18; 2 Chr. 28:21; 29:19. *Visits Damascus, obtains a novel pattern of an altar, which he substitutes for the altar in the temple in Jerusalem, and otherwise perverts the forms of worship*, 2 Kin. 16:10–16. *Sun dial of*, 2 Kin. 20:11; Isa. 38:8.

*Prophets in the reign of*, Isa. 1:1; Hos. 1:1; Mic. 1:1. *Prophecy concerning*, Isa. 7:13–25. *Succeeded by Hezekiah*, 2 Kin. 16:20.

*Ancestor of Jesus*, Matt. 1:9.

* **DIPLOMACY.** *Of Abimelech*, Gen. 21:22, 23; 26:26–31. *Of the Gibeonites, in securing a league with the Israelites through deception*, Josh. 9:3–16. *Of Jephthah, with the king of Moab, unsuccessful*, Judg. 11:12–28. *Of Abigail*, 1 Sam. 25:23–31. *Of David, in propitiating the friends of Abner by denouncing Joab, who slew Abner*, 2 Sam. 3:28–32. *Of Toi, to promote the friendship of David*, 2 Sam. 8:10. *Of Absalom winning the people*, 2 Sam. 15:2–6. *Of David, in sending Hushai to Absalom's court*, 2 Sam. 15:32–37; 16:15–19; 17:1–14. *Of the wise woman of Abel*, 2 Sam. 20:16–22. *Of Solo-*

9 And the [b]king of [c]Ăs-sȳr′ĭ-ȧ
hearkened unto him: for the
king of Ăs-sȳr′ĭ-ȧ went up
against [d]Dȧ-măs′cus, and took[G]
it, and [e]carried *the people of* it
captive to †Kĭr, and slew [f]Rē′-
zin.
10 ¶ And king [g]Ā′hăz went to
[d]Dȧ-măs′cus to meet [b]Tĭg′lath-
pĭ-lē′ṣer king of [c]Ăs-sȳr′ĭ-ȧ, and
saw an [h]altar that *was* at Dȧ-
măs′cus: and [i]king Ā′hăz sent to
[j]U-rī′jah the priest the fashion[G] of
the altar, and the pattern of it,
according to all the workmanship thereof.
11 And [j]U-rī′jah the priest
built an [k]altar according to all
that king Ā′hăz had sent from
[d]Dȧ-măs′cus: so U-rī′jah the
priest made *it* against[G] king
[g]Ā′hăz came from Dȧ-măs′cus.
12 And when the [g]king was
come from [d]Dȧ-măs′cus, the
king saw the altar: and the king
approached to the altar, and
[i,l]offered[G] thereon.[G]
13 And he burnt his [m]burnt offering and his [1,n]meat[G] offering,
and poured his [o]drink offering,
and sprinkled the [p]blood of his
[q]peace offerings, upon the altar.
14 And he brought also the
brasen[G] [r]altar, which *was* before[G]
the LORD, from the forefront of
the [s]house, from between the
[k]altar and the house of the
LORD, and put it on the north
side of the altar.
15 And king [g]Ā′hăz com-
manded [j]U-rī′jah the priest, saying, Upon the great [k]altar burn
the morning [m]burnt offering,
and the evening [1,n]meat[G] offering,
and the king's burnt sacrifice,
and his [1]meat[G] offering, with the
burnt offering of all the people of
the land, and their [1]meat[G] offering, and their [o]drink offerings;
and sprinkle upon it all the
[p]blood of the burnt offering, and
all the blood of the sacrifice: and
the brasen[G] [r]altar shall be for me
to enquire[G] *by*.
16 Thus did [j]U-rī′jah the
priest, according to all that king
[g]Ā′hăz commanded.
17 ¶ And king [g]Ā′hăz cut off
the borders of the bases, and removed the [t]laver from off them;
and took down the sea from off
the brasen[G] oxen that *were* under
it, and put it upon a pavement
of stones.
18 And the [2]covert for the sabbath that they had built in the
house, and the king's entry without,[G] turned he [3]from the [s,u]house
of the LORD for the king of
Ăs-sȳr′ĭ-ȧ.
19 ¶ Now the rest of the acts of
[g]Ā′hăz which he did, *are* they
not written in the [v]book of the
chronicles of the kings of [w]Jū′-
dah?
20 And [g]Ā′hăz [x]slept with his
fathers, and was [y]buried with
his fathers in the [z]city of Dā′vid:
and ‡Hĕz-e-kī′ah his son reigned
in his stead.

**9**
d *Damascus*, Isa. 8:4.
e *Colonization*, 2 Kin. 17:6.
f *Rezin*, 2 Kin. 15:37.

**10**
g *Ahaz*, 2 Kin. 15:38.
h *Altar, used in idolatrous worship*, Gen. 8:20.
i *Church and State, civil power superior to ecclesiastical*, vs. 11–18; 1 Sam. 16:1.
j *Probably same as Uriah*, Isa. 8:2.

**11**
k *Altar, in Solomon's temple*, Gen. 8:20.

**12**
l *Usurpation, in ecclesiastical affairs*, 2 Sam. 15:1.

**13**
m *Offerings, burnt*, Lev. 6:17.
n *Offerings, meat*, Lev. 6:17.
o *Offerings, drink*, Lev. 6:17.
p *Jesus, atoning blood of, typified*, Matt. 1:21.
q *Offerings, peace*, Lev. 6:17.
1 R. V. meal

**14**
r *Altar, called brazen altar*, Gen. 8:20.
s *Temple, Solomon's*, 1 Kin. 6:17.

**17**
t *Laver*, Ex. 30:18.

**18**
u *Church, called house of the Lord*, 1 Kin. 9:3.
2 R. V. covered way
3 R. V. unto

**19**
v *Book*, Num. 5:23.
w *Judah, kingdom of*, 2 Chr. 11:17.

**20**
x *Death*, Num. 23:10.
y *Burial*, Acts 8:2.
z *Jerusalem*, Judg. 19:10.
v.20–646 BC

---

*mon, in his alliance with Hiram*, 1 Kin. 5:1–12; 9:10–14, 26, 27; 10:11; *by intermarriage with other nations*, 1 Kin. 11:1–5. *Of ambassadors from Ben-hadad to Ahab*, 1 Kin. 20:31–34. *Jehoash purchases peace from Hazael*, 2 Kin. 12:18. *Ahaz purchases aid from the king of Assyria*, 2 Kin. 16:7–9. *Of Rab-shakeh, in trying to induce Jerusalem to capitulate by bombastic harangue and letter*, 2 Kin. 18:17–37; 19:1–14; Isa. 36:11–22; 37:1–14. *Of Sanballat and others, in an attempt to prevent the rebuilding of Jerusalem by Nehemiah*, Neh. 6.
*Of the people of Tyre and Sidon, in securing the favor of Herod*, Acts 12:20–22. *Of Paul, in arraying the Pharisees and Sadducees against each other at his trial*, Acts 23:6–10.

**Ecclesiastical:** *Of Paul, in winning souls to Christ*, 1 Cor. 9:20–23; *in circumcising Timothy*, Acts 16:3; *in performing certain temple services to placate the Jews*, Acts 21:20–25; Gal. 6:12.

**Corrupt practices in:** *Of the officers of Nebuchadnezzar's court, to secure the destruction of Daniel*, Dan. 6:4–15.

See footnotes: PRUDENCE, 2 Chr. 2:12; TACT, Prov. 15:1.

† **KIR** (*a well, a walled place*), Isa. 22:6. *The inhabitants of Damascus, carried into captivity to, by the king of Assyria*, 2 Kin. 16:9; *delivered from captivity in*, Amos 9:7. *Prophecy concerning*, Amos 1:5.

‡ **HEZEKIAH** (*Jehovah strengthens*). *King of Judah*, 2 Kin. 16:20; 1 Chr. 3:13. *Religious zeal of*, 2 Chr. 29; 30; 31. *Purges the nation of idolatry*, 2 Kin. 18:4; 2 Chr. 31:1; 33:3. *Restores the true forms of worship*, 2 Chr. 31:2–21. *His piety*, 2 Kin. 18:3, 5, 6; 2 Chr. 29:2; 31:20, 21; 32:32; Jer. 26:19. *Military operations of*, 2 Kin. 18:19; 1 Chr. 4:39–43; 2 Chr. 32:1–23. *Sickness and restoration of*, 2 Kin. 20:1–11; 2 Chr. 32:24; Isa. 38:1–8, 21, 22. *His psalm of thanksgiving*, Isa. 38:9–20. *His lack of wisdom in showing his resources to commissioners of Babylon*, 2 Kin. 20:12–19; 2 Chr. 32:25, 26, 31; Isa. 39. *Prospered of God*, 2 Kin. 18:7; 2 Chr. 32:27–30. *Conducts the brook Gihon into Jerusalem*, 2 Kin. 18:17; 20:20; 2 Chr. 32:4, 30; Isa. 7:3; 22:9–11; 36:2. *Scribes of*, Prov. 25:1. *Reigned twenty-nine years*, 2 Kin. 18:1, 2; 2 Chr. 29:1. *Death and burial of*, 2 Kin. 20:21; 2 Chr. 32:33. *Ancestor of Jesus*, Matt. 1:9. *Prophecies concerning*, 2 Kin. 20:5, 6, 16–18; Isa. 38:5–8; 39:5–7.

v.1–648 BC
See footnote, *Time*, Rev. 10:6.

1
*a* *Ahaz*, 2 Kin. 15:38.
*b* *Judah, kingdom of*, 2 Chr. 11:17.
*c* *Hoshea*, 2 Kin. 15:30.
*d* 2 Kin. 15:30.
*e* *Samaria*, 1 Kin. 16:24.
*f* *Israel, after the revolt*, 1 Kin. 12:1.

2
*g* *Rulers, wicked, instances of*, Ex. 18:21.

3
*h* 2 Kin. 18:9–11.
*i* *Assyria*, Gen. 25:18.
*j* *Tribute*, Ezra 4:13.

4
*k* *Conspiracy*, 1 Kin. 16:9.
*l* *Ambassadors*, Josh. 9:4.
*m* *Egypt*, Gen. 41:8.

5
*n* *Samaria*, 1 Kin. 16:24.
*o* *Siege*, Deut. 28:53.
v.5–642 BC

6
*p* *Captivity, of the ten tribes*, Isa. 5:13.
*q* *Sin, punishment of*, Rom. 5:12.
*r* *Judgments*, Ex. 6:6.
*s* 2 Kin. 18:11; 1 Chr. 5:26.
*t* 2 Kin. 18:11; 1 Chr. 5:26.
*u* *Medes*, Dan. 5:28.
v.6–640 BC

7
*v* *Pharaoh, at the time of the exodus*, Ex. 3:10.
*w* *Idolatry*, 1 Sam. 15:23.

8
1 R.V. nations,

## CHAPTER 17

*Hoshea's wicked reign. 3 Being subdued by Shalmaneser, he conspires against him with So king of Egypt. 5 The ten tribes, for their sins, are subdued and carried into captivity. 24 The strange nations which were transplanted to Samaria. 25 Being plagued with lions, they partially introduce the worship of the true God.*

IN the twelfth year of [a]Ā'hăz
king of [b]Jū'dah began [c]Hō-
shē'ȧ the son of [d]Ē'lah to reign
in [e]Sȧ-mā'rĭ-ȧ over [f]Ĭṣ'ra-el nine
years.
2 And [g]he did *that which was*
evil in the sight of the LORD, but
not as the kings of Ĭṣ'ra-el that
were before him.
3 Against him came up [h]Shăl-
man-ē'ṣēr king of [i]Ăs-sy̆r'ĭ-ȧ;
and [c]Hō-shē'ȧ became his servant, and gave him [j]presents.
4 And the [h]king of [i]Ăs-sy̆r'ĭ-ȧ
found [k]conspiracy in [c]Hō-shē'ȧ:
for he had sent [l]messengers to
Sō king of [m]Ē'ġy̆pt, and brought
no [j]present[C] to the king of Ăs-
sy̆r'ĭ-ȧ, as *he had done* year by
year: therefore the king of Ăs-
sy̆r'ĭ-ȧ shut him up, and bound
him in prison.
5 Then the [h]king of [i]Ăs-sy̆r'ĭ-ȧ
came up throughout all the land,
and went up to [n]Sȧ-mā'rĭ-ȧ, and
[o]besieged it three years.
6 In the ninth year of [c]Hō-shē'ȧ
the [h]king of [i]Ăs-sy̆r'ĭ-ȧ took [n]Sȧ-
mā'rĭ-ȧ, and [p,q,r]carried [f]Ĭṣ'ra-el
away into Ăs-sy̆r'ĭ-ȧ, and *placed
them in [s]Hā'lah and in [t]Hā'bôr
*by* the river of †Gō'zan, and in
the cities of the [u]Mēdeṣ.
7 For *so* it was, that the children of [f]Ĭṣ'ra-el had sinned
against the LORD their God,
which had brought them up out
of the land of [m]Ē'ġy̆pt, from under the hand of [v]Phā'raōh king
of Ē'ġy̆pt, and had [w]feared other
gods,
8 And walked in the statutes of
the [1]heathen[C], whom the LORD
cast out from before the children
of Ĭṣ'ra-el, and of the kings of
Ĭṣ'ra-el, which they had made.
9 And the children of [f]Ĭṣ'ra-el
did secretly *those* things that
*were* not right against the LORD
their God, and they built them
[x]high places in all their cities,
from the tower of the [y]watch-
men to the fenced[C] [z]city.
10 And they [a]set them up [2]im-
ages[C] and [b]groves[C] in every high
hill, and under every green tree:
11 And there they burnt [c]in-
cense in all the [d]high places, as
*did* the [1]heathen[C] whom the LORD
carried away before them; and
wrought wicked things to provoke the LORD to [e]anger:[S]
12 For they [a]served idols,
whereof the LORD had said unto
them, Ye shall not do this thing.
13 Yet the LORD testified
against Ĭṣ'ra-el, and against Jū'-
dah, by all the prophets, *and by*
all the seers, saying, [f]Turn ye
from your evil ways, and keep my
commandments *and* my statutes,
according to all the [g]law which
I commanded your fathers, and
which I [h]sent to you by my servants the prophets.
14 Notwithstanding[C] they[C]
[i]would not hear, but [j]hardened
their necks, like to the neck of
their fathers, that did [k]not believe in the LORD their God.
15 And [j]they rejected his statutes[C], and his [l]covenant that he
made with their fathers, and his
testimonies which he testified
against them; and they [m]fol-
lowed vanity, and became vain,[C]
and [n]went after the [1]heathen
that *were* round about them, *concerning* whom the LORD had
charged them, that they should
not do like them.
16 And they left all the com-

v.8–640 BC
See footnote, *Time*, Rev. 10:6.

9
*x* *High Places*, 1 Kin. 3:2.
*y* *Watchman*, 2 Sam. 18:24.
*z* *Cities, fortified*, Num. 35:8.

10
*a* *Idolatry*, 1 Sam. 15:23.
*b* *Groves*, Judg. 6:28.
2 R. V. pillars and Asherim upon every

11
*c* *Incense, offered in idoaltrous worship*, Ex. 37:29.
*d* *High Places*, 1 Kin. 3:2.
*e* *Anger of God*, 2 Kin. 13:3.

13
*f* *Commandment, enjoining obedience*, Deut. 8:2.
*g* *Word of God, inspiration of*, Psa. 119:9.
*h* *Prophets, inspiration of*, Isa. 3:2

14
*i* *Impenitence, instances of*, Rom. 2:5.
*j* *Self-will*, Gen. 49:6.
*k* *Unbelief, instances of*, Heb. 3:12

15
*l* *Covenant, of God with men*, Deut. 29:1.
*m* *Idolatry, folly of*, 1 Sam. 15:23.
*n* *Fellowship, with the wicked*, 1 Cor. 1:9.

* **COLONIZATION**, of conquered countries and people. *People of Damascus deported to Kir*, 2 Kin. 16:9. *Israelites deported to Halah and Habor*, 2 Kin. 17:6; 18:11. *Mixed people colonized in Samaria*, Ezra 4:9, 10.

† **GOZAN**, one of the central districts of Mesopotamia. *The ten tribes of Israel, after the revolt, taken in captivity to, by the king of Assyria, after the conquest of Samaria*, 2 Kin. 17:6; 18:11; 19:12; 1 Chr. 5:26; Isa. 37:12.

v.16–640 BC
See footnote, *Time*, Rev. 10:6.

16
o *Idolatry, objects of*, 1 Sam. 15:23.
p *Calf*, Mic. 6:6.
q *Stars*, Judg. 5:20.
3 R. V. an Asherah.

17
r *Wicked, described*, Psa. 73:3.
s *Idolatry, wicked practices of*, 1 Sam. 15:23.
t *Human Sacrifices*, Deut. 12:31.
u *Children, caused to pass through fire*, Mark 10:14.
v *Fire, children caused to pass through*, Ex. 12:8.

18
w *Divine Chastisement*, Job 33:19.
x *Judah, kingdom of*, 2 Chr. 11:17.

19
y *Disobedience to God*, Eph. 5:6.

20
z *Judgments*, Ex. 6:6.

21
a *Influence, evil*, 1 Cor. 7:14.

23
b *God, providence of*, Gen. 2:2.
c *Captivity, of the ten tribes*, Isa. 5:13.
d *Assyria*, Gen. 25:18.

24
e *Babylon*, Ezra 5:12.
f Or, *Cuth*, v. 30.
g Or, *Ivah*, 2 Kin. 18:34; 19:13; Isa. 37:13.
h *Hamath*, 1 Chr. 18.3.

mandments of the LORD their God, and made them [o]molten images, *even* two [p]calves, and made [3]a [b]grove, and worshipped all the [q]host of heaven, and served [‡]Bā'al.

17 And [r]they [s]caused their [t,u]sons and their daughters to pass through the [v]fire, and used divination and enchantments, and sold themselves to do evil in the sight of the LORD, to provoke him to [e]anger.

18 Therefore the LORD was very [e]angry with Ĭs'ra-el, and [w]removed them out of his sight: there was none left but the tribe of [x]Jū'dah only.

19 Also [x]Jū'dah [y]kept not the commandments of the LORD their God, but walked in the statutes of Ĭs'ra-el which they made.

20 And the LORD rejected all the seed of Ĭs'ra-el, and afflicted them, and [z]delivered them into the hand of spoilers, until he had cast them out of his sight.

21 For he rent Ĭs'ra-el from the house of Dā'vid; and they made Jĕr-o-bō'am the son of Nē'băt king: and Jĕr-o-bō'am drave Ĭs'ra-el from following the LORD, and [a]made them sin a great sin.

22 For the children of Ĭs'ra-el walked in all the [a]sins of Jĕr-o-bō'am which he did; they departed not from them;

23 Until the LORD [b]removed Ĭs'ra-el out of his sight, as he had said by all his servants the prophets. So was Ĭs'ra-el [c]carried away out of their own land to [d]Ăs-sўr'ĭ-ȧ unto this day.

24 ¶ And the king of [d]Ăs-sўr'ĭ-ȧ brought *men* from [e]Băb'ў-lon, and from [f]Cū'thah, and from [g]Ā'vȧ, and from [h]Hā'math, and from [||]Sĕph-ar-vā'im, and *placed *them* in the cities of [i]Să-mā'rĭ-ȧ instead of the children of [j]Ĭs'ra-el: and they possessed Să-mā'rĭ-ȧ, and dwelt in the cities thereof.

25 And *so* it was at the beginning of their dwelling there, *that* they feared not the LORD: therefore the [k]LORD sent [l]lions among them, which slew *some* of them.

26 Wherefore they spake to the king of [d]Ăs-sўr'ĭ-ȧ, saying, The nations which thou hast removed, and placed in the cities of [i]Să-mā'rĭ-ȧ, know not the manner of the God of the land: therefore [k]he hath sent [l]lions among them, and, behold, they slay them, because they know not the manner of the God of the land.

27 Then the king of [d]Ăs-sўr'ĭ-ȧ commanded, saying, Carry thither one of the [m]priests whom ye brought from thence; and [n]let them go and dwell there, and let him [o]teach them the manner of the God of the land.

28 Then one of the priests whom they had carried away from [i]Să-mā'rĭ-ȧ came and dwelt in [p]Bĕth'-el, and [o]taught them how they should [q]fear the LORD.

29 Howbeit every nation [r]made gods of their own, and put *them* in the houses of the [s]high places which the Să-măr'ĭ-tans had made, every nation in their cities wherein they dwelt.

30 And the men of [e]Băb'ў-lon made Sŭc'coth–bē'noth, and the men of [f]Cŭth made Nēr'gal, and the men of [h]Hā'math made Ăsh'ĭ-mȧ,

31 And the Ā'vites made Nĭb'-

i *Samaria*, Isa. 7:9.
j *Israel, after the revolt*, 1 Kin. 12:1.

25
k *Judgments*, Ex. 6:6.
l *Lion*, Mic. 5:8.

27
m *Minister, duties of*, Rom. 15:16.
n *Missions*, Matt. 28:19.
o *Instruction, in religion*, Prov. 23:23.

28
p *Beth-el*, Josh. 18:13.
q *Fear of God*, Acts 9:31.

29
r *Idolatry*, 1 Sam. 15:23.
s *High Places*, 1 Kin. 3:2.

‡ **BAAL**, god of the sun, an idol of the Phenicians. *Worshiped, by the Israelites in the time of the judges*, Judg. 2:10–23; 1 Sam. 7:3, 4; 1 Kin. 16:31–33; 18:18; 19:18; 2 Kin. 3:2; *after the revolt of the ten tribes*, 2 Kin. 17:16; Jer. 23:13; Hos. 1; 2; 11:2; 13:1; *by the Jews*, 2 Kin. 21:3; 2 Chr. 24:7; 28:2; 33:3. *Jeremiah expostulates against the worship of*, Jer. 2:8, 23; 7:9. *Altars of, destroyed, by Gideon*, Judg. 6:25–32; *by Jehoiada*, 2 Kin. 11:18; 2 Chr. 23:17. *Vessels for the worship of, destroyed by Josiah*, 2 Kin. 23:4, 5.
*Prophets of, slain by Elijah*, 1 Kin. 18:40. *Worshipers of, destroyed by Jehu*, 2 Kin. 10:18–25.

|| **SEPHARVAIM.** *An Assyrian city, from which the king of Assyria colonized Samaria*, 2 Kin. 17:24, 31; 18:34; 19:13; Isa. 36:19; 37:13.

hăz and Tär′tăk, and the Sĕph′ar-vītes [t]burnt their [u,v]children in [w]fire to Ȧ-drăm′mē-lĕch and Ȧ-năm′me-lĕch, the gods of ‖Sĕph-ar-vā′im.

32 So they feared the LORD, and made unto [4]themselves of the lowest of them priests of the [s]high places, which [r]sacrificed for them in the [x]houses of the high places.

33 They feared the LORD, and served their own gods, [y]after the manner of the nations whom they carried away from thence.[c]

34 Unto this day they do after the former manners: they fear not the LORD, neither do they after their statutes, or after their ordinances, or after the law and commandment which the LORD commanded the children of Jā′cob, whom he named [z]Ĭṣ′ra-el;

35 With whom the LORD had made a [a]covenant,[c] and charged them, saying, [b]Ye shall not fear other gods, nor bow yourselves to them, nor serve them, nor sacrifice to them:

36 But the [c]LORD, who brought you up out of the land of [d]Ē′gȳpt with great power and a stretched[c] out arm, [e]him shall ye [f]fear,[c] and him shall ye [g]worship, and to him shall ye do sacrifice.[c]

37 And the statutes, and the ordinances, and the law, and the commandment, which he wrote for you, [h,i]ye shall observe to do for evermore; and [b]ye shall not fear[c] other gods.

38 And the [a]covenant that I have made with you ye shall not forget; [b]neither shall ye fear[c] other gods.

39 But [j]the LORD your God ye shall [f]fear; and [c,k]he shall deliver you out of the hand of all your enemies.

40 Howbeit they [l]did not hearken, but they did after their former manner.

41 So these nations feared the LORD, and served their graven[c] images, both their [m]children, and their children's children: [n]as did their fathers, so do they unto this day.

## CHAPTER 18

*Hezekiah's good reign. 4 He destroys idolatry, and prospers. 9 The ten tribes are carried away captive for their sins. 13 Sennacherib invading Judah is pacified by a tribute. 17 Rab-shakeh, sent by Sennacherib, reviles Hezekiah, and exhorts the people to revolt.*

NOW it came to pass in the third year of [a]Hȯ-shē′ȧ son of [b]Ē′lah king of [c]Ĭṣ′ra-el, *that* [d]Hĕz-e-kī′ah the son of [e]Ā′hăz king of [f]Jū′dah began to reign.

2 Twenty and five years old was [d]he when he began to reign; and he reigned twenty and nine years in [g]Jē-ru̧′să-lĕm. His mother's name also *was* [h]Ā′bī, the daughter of [i]Zăch-a-rī′ah.

3 And [j]he did *that which was* right in the sight of the LORD, according to all that Dā′vid his father did.

4 He removed the [k]high places, and [l]brake the [1]images,[c] and cut down the [2,m]groves,[c] and brake in pieces the *brasen[c] serpent that [n]Mō′şeş had made: for unto those days the children of Ĭṣ′ra-el [o]did burn [p]incense to it: and he called it Nē-hŭsh′tan.

5 He [q]trusted in the LORD God of Ĭṣ′ra-el; so that after him was none like him among all the kings of [f]Jū′dah, nor *any* that were before him.

6 For he [r]clave[c] to the LORD, *and* departed not from following him, but [s]kept[c] his [t]commandments, which the LORD commanded [n]Mō′şeş.

7 And the [u]LORD was with [d]him; *and* he [v]prospered whith-

---

**31**
t *Idolatry, wicked practices of,* 1 Sam. 15:23.
u *Children, sacrificed,* Mark 10:14.
v *Human Sacrifices,* Deut. 12:31.
w *Fire, children caused to pass through,* Ex. 12:8.

**32**
x *Temple, idolatrous,* 1 Kin. 6:17.
4 R. V. them from among themselves priests

**33**
y *Influence, evil,* 1 Cor. 7:14.

**34**
z *Israel,* Gen. 32:28.

**35**
a *Covenant, of God with men,* Deut. 29:1.
b *Commandment, forbidding idolatry,* Deut. 8:2.

**36**
c *God, providence of,* Gen. 2:2.
d *Egypt,* Gen. 41:8.
e *Commandment, enjoining fear of God, and worship,* Deut. 8:2.
f *Fear of God, enjoined,* Acts 9:31.
g *Worship, enjoined,* Gen. 22:5.

**37**
h *Commandment, enjoining obedience to God's law,* v. 38; Deut. 8:2.
i *Obedience, enjoined,* Heb. 5:8.

**39**
j *Commandment, enjoining fear of God,* Deut. 8:2.
k *Promise, to the obedient, of deliverance from enemies,* 2 Cor. 1:20.

**40**
l *Disobedience to God,* Eph. 5:6.

**41**
m *Children, wicked,* Mark 10:14.
n *Influence, evil,* 1 Cor. 7:14.

**v.1–646 BC**
See footnote, *Time,* Rev. 10:6.

**1**
a *Hoshea,* 2 Kin. 15:30.
b 2 Kin. 15:30.
c *Israel, after the revolt,* 1 Kin. 12:1.
d *Hezekiah,* 2 Kin. 16:20.
e *Ahaz,* 2 Kin. 15:38.
f *Judah, kingdom of,* 2 Chr. 11:17.

**2**
g *Jerusalem,* Judg. 19:10.
h Or, *Abijah,* 2 Chr. 29:1.
i 2 Chr. 29:1.

**3**
j *Rulers, righteous,* Ex. 18:21.

**4**
k *High Places,* 1 Kin. 3:2.
l *Iconoclasm,* Num. 33:52.
m *Groves, destroyed,* Judg. 6:28.
n *Moses,* Ex. 2:10.
o *Idolatry,* 1 Sam. 15:23.
p *Incense, offered in idolatrous worship,* Ex. 37:29.
1 R. V. pillars,
2 R. V. Asherah:

**5**
q *Faith, instances of,* Mark 11:22.

**6**
r *Faithfulness, instances of,* Luke 16:10.
s *Obedience, instances of,* Heb. 5:8.
t *Law, of Moses,* Deut. 33:2.

**7**
u *God, providence of,* Gen. 2:2.
v *Temporal Blessings, from God,* Psa. 103:2.

---

*** BRAZEN SERPENT.** *Made by Moses for the healing of the Israelites,* Num. 21:9. *Worshiped by Israelites,* 2 Kin. 18:4. *A symbol of Christ,* John 3:14, 15.

ersoever he went forth: and he
rebelled against the king of [w]Ăs-
sӯr'ĭ-ȧ, and served him not.
8 He smote the [x]Phĭ-lĭs'tĭneș,
*even* unto [y]Gā'zȧ, and the borders thereof, from the [z]tower[G]
of the [a]watchmen to the fenced
[b]city.
9 ¶ And it came to pass in the
fourth year of king [c]Hĕz-e-kī'ah,
which *was* the seventh year of
[d]Hȯ-shē'ȧ son of [e]Ē'lah king
of [f]Ĭș'ra-el, *that* [g]Shăl-man-ē'șĕr
king of [h]Ăs-sӯr'ĭ-ȧ came up
against [i]Sȧ-mā'rĭ-ȧ, and [j]be-
sieged it.
10 And at the end of three years
they took it: *even* in the sixth
year of [c]Hĕz-e-kī'ah, that *is* the
ninth year of [d]Hȯ-shē'ȧ king of
[f]Ĭș'ra-el, [i]Sȧ-mā'rĭ-ȧ was taken.
11 And the king of [h]Ăs-sӯr'ĭ-ȧ
did [k]carry away Ĭș'ra-el unto
Ăs-sӯr'ĭ-ȧ, and [l]put them in
[m]Hā'lah and in [m]Hā'bôr *by* the
river of [n]Gō'zan, and in the
cities of the [o]Mēdeș:
12 Because they [p]obeyed not
the voice of the LORD their God,
but transgressed his [q]covenant,
*and* all that [r]Mō'șeș the servant
of the LORD commanded, and
would not hear *them*, nor do
*them*.
13 ¶ Now in the fourteenth
year of king [t]Hĕz-e-kī'ah did
[s]Sĕn-năch'e-rĭb king of [h]Ăs-
sӯr'ĭ-ȧ come up against all the
fenced[G] [b]cities of [t]Jū'dah, and
took them.
14 And [c]Hĕz-e-kī'ah king of
[t]Jū'dah sent to the [s]king of [h]Ăs-
sӯr'ĭ-ȧ to [u]Lā'chish, saying, I
have offended[G]; return[G] from me:
[v]that which thou puttest on me
will I bear. And the king of Ăs-
sӯr'ĭ-ȧ appointed unto Hĕz-e-
kī'ah king of Jū'dah three hundred talents[G] of sĭlver and thirty
talents[G] of gold.
15 And [c]Hĕz-e-kī'ah gave *him*
all the silver that was found in
the [w]house of the LORD, and
in the treasures[G] of the king's
[x]house.
16 At that time did [c]Hĕz-e-
kī'ah cut off *the gold from* the
doors of the [w]temple of the
LORD, and *from* the [y]pillars
which Hĕz-e-kī'ah king of Jū'-
dah had overlaid, and gave it
to the king of Ăs-sӯr'ĭ-ȧ.
17 And the [s]king of [h]Ăs-sӯr'ĭ-ȧ
sent [z]Tär'tan and Răb'–sa-rĭs
and †Răb'–sha-keh from [a]Lā'-
chish to king [b]Hĕz-e-kī'ah with
a great [c]host against [d]Jĕ-ru̥'sȧ-
lĕm. And they went up and
came to Jĕ-ru̥'sȧ-lĕm. And when
they were come up, they came
and stood by the conduit of the
[e]upper pool, which *is* in the
highway of the [f]fuller's field.
18 And when they [g]had called
to the king, there came out to
them ‡,[h]Ē-lī'a-kĭm the son of
[i]Hĭl-kī'ah, which *was* over the
household, and ‖,[h]Shĕb'nȧ the
[j]scribe[G], and [h,k]Jō'ah the son of
[k]Ā'saph the recorder.
19 And †Răb'–sha-keh [l]said
unto [h]them, Speak ye now to
[b]Hĕz-e-kī'ah, Thus saith the
great [m]king, the king of [n]Ăs-
sӯr'ĭ-ȧ, What confidence *is* this
wherein thou trustest?
20 Thou sayest, (but *they are*
*but* vain[G] words,) I *have* counsel
and strength for the [o]war. Now
on whom dost thou trust, that
thou rebellest against me?
21 Now, behold, thou trustest
upon the staff of this bruised
[p]reed, *even* upon [q]Ē'gӯpt, on
which if a man lean, it will go
into his hand, and pierce it: so

*w Assyria*, Gen. 25:18.

**8**

*x Philistines*, Gen. 26:14.
*y Gaza*, Gen. 10:19.
*z Tower*, 2 Chr. 26:9.

*a Watchman*, 2 Sam. 18:24.
*b Cities, fortified*, Num. 35:8.

**9**

*c Hezekiah*, 2 Kin. 16:20.
*d Hoshea*, 2 Kin. 15:30.
*e* 2 Kin. 15:30.
*f Israel, after the revolt*, 1 Kin. 12:1.
*g* 2 Kin. 17:3–6.
*h Assyria*, Gen. 25:18.
*i Samaria*, 1 Sam. 16:24.
*j Siege, instances of*, Deut. 28:53.
**v.10–640 BC**

**11**

*k Captivity, of the ten tribes*, Isa. 5:13.
*l Colonization*, 2 Kin. 17:6.
*m* 2 Kin. 17:6; 1 Chr. 5:26.
*n Gozan*, 2 Kin. 17:6.
*o Medes*, Dan. 5:28.

**12**

*p Disobedience to God*, Eph. 5:6.
*q Law, of Moses*, Deut. 33:2.
*r Moses*, Ex. 2:10.

**13**

*s Sennacherib*, 2 Chr. 32:1.
*t Judah, kingdom of*, 2 Chr. 11:17.
**v.13–632 BC**

**14**

*u Lachish*, Josh. 10:5.
*v Tribute*, Ezra 4:13.

**B.C. 713?**
See footnote, *Time*, Rev. 10:6.

**15**

*w Temple, treasures of*, 1 Kin. 6:17.
*x Palace*, 1 Kin. 21:1.

**16**

*y Pillar*, Gen. 28:18.

**17**

*z* Isa. 20:1.

*a Lachish*, Josh. 10:5.
*b Hezekiah*, 2 Kin. 16:20.
*c Armies*, Deut. 11:4.
*d Jerusalem*, Judg. 19:10.
*e Pool, of Jerusalem*, 2 Sam. 2:13.
*f* Isa. 7:3; 36:2.
**B.C. 710?**

**18**

*g Diplomacy*, vs. 18–35; 2 Kin. 16:7.
*h Ambassadors*, Josh. 9:4.
*i* Isa. 22:20; 36: 3, 22.
*j Scribe*, 1 Kin. 4:3.
*k* Isa. 36:3, 22.

**19**

*l Boasting, instances of*, vs. 19–35; Prov. 25:14.
*m Sennacherib*, 2 Chr. 32:1.
*n Assyria*, Gen. 25:18.

**20**

*o War*, Judg. 3:2.

**21**

*p Reed, figurative*, Ezek. 40:3.
*q Egypt*, Gen. 41:8.

† **RAB-SHAKEH** (*chief cupbearer*), an Assyrian officer. *Sent by Sennacherib against Jerusalem; undertakes by a speech in the Jews' language to cause disloyalty to Hezekiah and a surrender of the city*, 2 Kin. 18:17–36. *Blasphemes God*, 19:4, 8–14. *His army visited by deadly scourge; he withdraws, and returns to Nineveh*, Isa. 36; 37:4, 8–14.

‡ **ELIAKIM.** *Son of Hilkiah, deputy of Hezekiah*, 2 Kin. 18:18; 19:2; Isa. 36:3, 11, 22; 37:2. *Prophecy concerning*, Isa. 22:20–24.

‖ **SHEBNA.** *A scribe of Hezekiah*, 2 Kin. 18:18, 26 37; 19:2; Isa. 36:3, 11, 22; 37:2. *Prophecy concerning*, Isa 22: 15–19.

B.C. 710?
See footnote, *Time*, Rev. 10:6.

*is* Phā′raōh king of Ē′ġўpt unto
all that trust on him.
22 But if ye say unto me, We
trust in the [r]LORD our God: *is*
not that he, whose high[G] places
and whose altars [b]Hĕz-e-kī′ah
hath taken away, and hath said
to Jū′dah and Jē-rṳ′sȧ-lĕm, Ye
shall worship before this altar in
Jē-rṳ′sȧ-lĕm?
23 Now therefore, [†]I pray thee,
give pledges[G] to my lord the [m]king
of [n]Ăs-sўr′ĭ-ȧ, and I will deliver
thee two thousand [s]horses, [t]if
thou be able on thy part to set
riders upon them.
24 How then wilt thou turn
away the face of one captain of
the least of my master's servants,
and put thy trust on Ē′ġўpt for
[u]chariots and for [v]horsemen?
25 Am I now come up without
the LORD against this place to
destroy it? [w]The LORD said to
me, Go up against this land, and
destroy it.
26 Then said [‡]Ē-lī′a-kĭm the
son of [i]Hĭl-kī′ah, and [‖]Shĕb′-
nȧ, and [k]Jō′ah, unto [†]Răb′-sha-
keh, Speak, I pray thee, to thy
servants in the Sўr′ĭ-an [x]lan-
guage; for we understand *it*: and
talk not with us in the [y]Jews̩'
language in the ears of the people that *are* on the wall.
27 But [†]Răb′-sha-keh said unto them, Hath my master sent
me to thy master, and to thee, to
speak these words? *hath he* not
*sent me* to the men which sit on
the wall, that they may eat their
own dung[G], and drink their own
[3]piss[G] with you?
28 ¶ Then [†]Răb′-sha-keh stood
and cried with a loud voice in the
[y]Jews̩' [x]language, and spake,
saying, Hear the word of the great
king, the [m]king of [n]Ăs-sўr′ĭ-ȧ:
29 Thus saith the king, Let not
Hĕz-e-kī′ah deceive you: for he
shall not be able to deliver you
out of his hand:

30 [z]Neither let Hĕz-e-kī′ah
make you trust in the LORD,
saying, The LORD will surely
deliver us, and this city shall not
be delivered into the hand of the
king of Ăs-sўr′ĭ-ȧ.
31 Hearken not to [a]Hĕz-e-kī′-
ah: for thus saith the [b]king of
[c]Ăs-sўr′ĭ-ȧ, Make [3]*an agreement*
with me by a present, and come
out to me, and *then* eat ye every
man of his own [d]vine, and every
one of his [e]fig tree, and drink ye
every one the waters of his
[f]cistern:
32 Until I come and take you
away to a land like your own
land, a land of [g]corn[G] and [h]wine,
a land of bread and [d]vineyards,
a land of [i]oil olive and of [j]honey,
that ye may live, and not die:
and hearken not unto [a]Hĕz-e-
kī′ah, when he persuadeth[G] you,
saying, The LORD will deliver
us.
33 Hath any of the gods of the
nations delivered at all his land
out of the hand of the king of
[c]Ăs-sўr′ĭ-ȧ?
34 Where *are* the gods of
[k]Hā′math, and of [l]Ār′pad?
where *are* the gods of [m]Sĕph-
ar-vā′im, [n]Hē′nȧ, and [o]Ī′vah?
have they delivered [p]Sȧ-mā′rĭ-ȧ
out of mine hand?
35 Who *are* they among all
the gods of the countries, that
have delivered their country out
of mine hand, that the LORD
should deliver [q]Jē-rṳ′sȧ-lĕm out
of mine hand?
36 But the people held their
peace, and answered him not a
word: for the king's commandment was, saying, Answer him
not.
37 Then came [‡]Ē-lī′a-kĭm the
son of [r]Hĭl-kī′ah, which *was* over
the household, and [‖]Shĕb′nȧ the
[s]scribe, and [t]Jō′ah the son of
[t]Ā′saph the recorder, to [a]Hĕz-e-
kī′ah with *their* clothes [u]rent[G],

22
r *God, preserver*, Gen. 2:2.

23
s *Horse, used for cavalry*, Job 39:19.
t *Sarcasm, instances of*, Judg. 10:14.

24
u *Chariot*, Josh. 11:4.
v *Cavalry*, 1 Sam. 13:5.

25
w *Falsehood*, Job 21:34.

26
x *Language*, Dan. 3:29.
y *Jews*, Neh. 4:2.

27
3 R. V. water

B.C. 710?
See footnote, *Time*, Rev. 10:6.

30
z *Temptation, leading into*, Luke 11:4.

31
a *Hezekiah*, 2 Kin. 16:20.
b *Sennacherib*, 2 Chr. 32:1.
c *Assyria*, Gen. 25:18.
d *Grape*, Lev. 25:5.
e *Fig Tree*, Luke 13:6.
f *Cistern*, Isa. 36:16.
3 R. V. your peace with me.

32
g *Corn*, Psa. 65:13.
h *Wine*, Prov. 23:31.
i *Oil*, Deut. 12:17.
j *Honey*, Prov. 25:27.

34
k *Hamath*, 1 Chr. 18:3.
l 2 Kin. 19:13; or, *Arphad*, Isa. 36:19.
m *Sepharvaim*, 2 Kin. 17:24.
n Isa. 37:13.
o 2 Kin. 19:13; Isa. 37:13; or, *Ava*, 2 Kin. 17:24.
p *Samaria*, 1 Kin. 16:24.

35
q *Jerusalem*, Judg. 19:10.

37
r Isa. 22:20; 36:3, 22.
s *Scribe*, 1 Kin. 4:3.
t Isa. 36:3, 22.
u *Rending of Garments*, 2 Chr. 34:27.

B.C. 710?
See footnote, *Time*, Rev. 10:6.

and told him the words of
[†]Răb′-sha-keh.

## CHAPTER 19

*Hezekiah sends to Isaiah to pray for deliverance. 6 Isaiah comforts him. 8 Sennacherib sends a blasphemous letter to Hezekiah. 14 Hezekiah's prayer. 20 Isaiah foretells the destruction of Sennacherib, and the safety of Zion. 35 An angel slays the Assyrians. 36 Sennacherib is slain at Nineveh by his own sons.*

AND it came to pass, when
king [a]Hĕz-e-kī′ah heard
*it*, that he [b,c]rent his clothes, and
covered himself with [d]sackcloth,
and went into the [e,f]house of the
LORD.
2 And he sent [g]Ē-lī′a-kĭm,
which *was* over the household,
and [h]Shĕb′nȧ the [i]scribe, and the
elders of the priests, [c]covered
with [d]sackcloth, to [j]Ī-ṣā′iah the
prophet the son of [k]Ā′mŏz.
3 And they said unto [j]him,
Thus saith [a]Hĕz-e-kī′ah, This
day *is* a day of trouble, and
of rebuke, and [1]blasphemy: for
the children are come to the
birth, and *there is* not strength
to bring forth.
4 It may be the LORD thy God
will hear all the words of [l]Răb′-
sha-keh, whom the [m]king of [n]Ăs-
sy̆r′ĭ-ȧ his master hath sent to
reproach the living God; and
will reprove the words which the
LORD thy God hath heard:
wherefore [o]lift up *thy* prayer
for the remnant that are left.
5 So the servants of king [a]Hĕz-
e-kī′ah came to [j]Ī-ṣā′iah.
6 ¶ And [j]Ī-ṣā′iah said unto
them, Thus shall ye say to your
master, Thus saith the LORD,
[p]Be not afraid of the words
which thou hast heard, with
which the servants of the king of
Ăs-sy̆r′ĭ-ȧ have [q]blasphemed me.
7 Behold, [r]I will [2]send a [s]blast
upon him, and he shall hear a
rumour, and shall return to his
own land; and I will cause him
to fall by the sword in his own
land.
8 ¶ So [l]Răb′-sha-keh returned,
and found the [m]king of [n]Ăs-
sy̆r′ĭ-ȧ warring against [t]Lĭb′nah:
for he had heard that he was departed from [u]Lā′chish.
9 And when he heard say
of [v]Tĭr′ha-kah king of [w]Ē-thĭ-
ō′pĭ-ȧ, Behold, he is come out
to fight against thee: he [x]sent
[y]messengers again unto [z]Hĕz-e-
kī′ah, saying,
10 Thus shall ye speak to [z]Hĕz-
e-kī′ah king of [a]Jū′dah, [b]saying,
Let not thy God in whom thou
trustest deceive thee, saying, [c]Jĕ-
ru̦′sȧ-lĕm shall not be delivered
into the hand of the king of
[d]Ăs-sy̆r′ĭ-ȧ.
11 [b,e]Behold, thou hast heard
what the kings of Ăs-sy̆r′ĭ-ȧ have
done to all lands, by destroying
them utterly: and shalt thou be
delivered?
12 [e]Have the gods of the nations delivered them which my
fathers have destroyed; *as* [f]Gō′-
zan, and [g]Hā′ran, and [h]Rē′zeph,
and the children of [i]Ē′dĕn which
*were* in [j]Thē-lā′sar?
13 Where *is* the king of [k]Hā′-
math, and the king of [l]Är′pad,
and the king of the city of
[m]Sĕph-ar-vā′im, of [n]Hē′nȧ, and
[o]Ī′vah?
14 ¶ And Hĕz-e-kī′ah re-
ceived the [p]letter of the hand of
the [q]messengers, and read it:
and Hĕz-e-kī′ah went up into the
[r]house of the LORD, and spread
it before the LORD.
15 And Hĕz-e-kī′ah [s]prayed
before the LORD, and said, O
LORD God of Ĭṣ′ra-el, which
[t]dwellest *between* the cherubims,
thou art the [u]God, *even* thou
alone, of all the kingdoms of the
earth; [v]thou hast made [w]heaven
and [x]earth.
16 [s,y]LORD, bow down thine
ear, and hear: open, LORD,
thine eyes, and see: and hear the
[z]words of [a]Sĕn-năch′e-rĭb, which

---

1
*a* *Hezekiah*, 2 Kin. 16:20.
*b* *Rending of Garments*, 2 Chr. 34:27.
*c* *Mourning*, Lam. 2:5.
*d* *Sackcloth*, Isa. 15:3.
*e* *Temple, Solomon's*, 1 Kin. 6:17.
*f* *Church, called house of the Lord*, 1 Kin. 9:3.
2
*g* *Eliakim*, 2 Kin. 18:18.
*h* *Shebna*, 2 Kin. 18:18.
*i* *Scribe*, 1 Kin. 4:3.
*j* *Isaiah*, Isa. 1:1.
*k* 2 Kin. 20:1; Isa. 1:1; 13:1.
3
1 R. V. of contumely:
4
*l* *Rab-shakeh*, 2 Kin. 18:17.
*m* *Sennacherib*, 2 Chr. 32:1.
*n* *Assyria*, Gen. 25:18.
*o* *Intercession, solicited*, Jer. 27:18.
6
*p* *Faith, enjoined in time of public danger*, Mark 11:22.
*q* *Blasphemy, instances of*, 2 Sam. 12:14.
7
*r* *God, providence of*, Gen. 2:2.
*s* *Blas ing*, 1 Kin. 8:37.
2 R. V. put a spirit in him.

B.C. 710?
See footnote, *Time*, Rev. 10:6.
8
*t* *Libnah*, Josh. 10:29.
*u* *Lachish*, Josh. 10:5.
9
*v* Isa. 37:9.
*w* *Ethiopia*, Isa. 18:1.
*x* *Diplomacy*, 2 Kin. 16:7.
*y* *Ambassadors*, Josh. 9:4.
*z* *Hezekiah*, 2 Kin 16:20.
10
*a* *Judah, kingdom of*, 2 Chr. 11:17.
*b* *Diplomacy*, 2 Kin. 16:7.
*c* *Jerusalem*, Judg. 19:10.
*d* *Assyria*, Gen. 25:18.
11
*e* *Boasting*, Prov. 25:14.
12
*f* *Gozan*, 2 Kin. 17:6.
*g* *Haran*, Gen. 11:31.
*h* Isa. 37:12.
*i* Isa. 37:12; Ezek. 27:23; Amos 1:5.
*j* Or, *Telassar*, Isa. 37:12.
13
*k* *Hamath*, 1 Chr. 18:3.
*l* 2 Kin. 18:34; or, *Arphad*, Isa. 36:19.
*m* *Sepharvaim*, 2 Kin. 17:24.
*n* *Hena*, Isa. 37:13.
*o* 2 Kin. 18:34; Isa. 37:13; or, *Ava*, 2 Kin. 17:24.
14
*p* *Letters*, Isa. 37:14.
*q* *Ambassadors*, Josh. 9:4.
*r* *Temple, Solomon's*, 1 Kin. 6:17.
15
*s* *Prayer, in adversity*, Acts 6:4.
*t* *Shekinah*, Lev. 16:2.
*u* *God, sovereign*, Gen. 2:2.
*v* *God, creator*, Gen. 2:2.
*w* *Heavens, physical*, Psa. 8:3
*x* *Earth*, Prov. 8:23.
16
*y* *Adversity, prayer in*, Psa. 10:6.
*z* *Blasphemy, instances of*, 2 Sam. 12:14
*a* *Sennacherib*, 2 Chr. 32:1.

B.C. 710?
See footnote, *Time*, Rev. 10:6.

17
b *Assyria*, Gen. 25:18.

18
c *Idol*, 1 Kin. 15:12.
d *Stone, idols made of*, Ex. 24:12.

19
e *Prayer, pleas offered in*, Acts 6:4.

20
f *Isaiah*, Isa. 1:1.
g *Prophets, inspiration of*, Isa. 3:2.
h *Hezekiah*, 2 Kin. 16:20
i *Prayer, answered*, Acts 6:4.

21
j *Zion*, 2 Sam. 5:7.
k *Jerusalem*, Judg. 19:10.

22
l *Blasphemy*, 2 Sam. 12:14.
m *God*, Gen. 2:2.

23
n *Ambassadors*, Josh. 9:4.
o *False Confidence, instances of*, Psa. 30:6.
p *Lebanon*, Deut. 1:7.
3 R. V. his farthest lodging place, the forest of his fruitful field.

24
4 R. V. Egypt.

hath sent him to reproach[G] the
living God.
17 Of a truth, LORD, the kings
of [b]Ăs-sȳr′ĭ-ȧ have destroyed the
nations and their lands,
18 And have cast their [c]gods
into the fire: for they *were* no
gods, but the work of men's
hands, wood and [d]stone: therefore they have destroyed them.
19 Now therefore, O LORD our
God, I beseech thee, save thou
us out of his hand, [e]that all the
kingdoms of the earth may know
that thou *art* the LORD God,
*even* thou only.
20 ¶ Then [f,g]Ī-ṣā′iah the son
of Ā′mŏz sent to [h]Hĕz-e-kī′ah,
saying, Thus saith the LORD
God of Ĭṣ′ra-el, *That* which thou
hast prayed to me against [a]Sĕn-
năch′e-rĭb king of Ăs-sȳr′ĭ-ȧ [i]I
have heard.
21 This *is* the word that the
LORD hath spoken concerning
him; The virgin the daughter of
[j]Zī′ŏn[G] hath despised thee, *and*
laughed thee to scorn; the
daughter of [k]Jė-rụ′sȧ-lĕm hath
shaken her head at thee.
22 Whom hast thou reproached
and [l]blasphemed? and against
whom hast thou exalted *thy*
voice, and lifted up thine eyes on
high? *even* against the [m]Holy
*One* of Ĭṣ′ra-el.
23 By thy [n]messengers thou hast
reproached[G] the LORD, and hast
[o]said, With the multitude of my
chariots I am come up to the
height of the mountains, to the
sides of [p]Lĕb′a-non, and will cut
down the tall cedar trees thereof,
*and* the choice fir trees thereof:
and I will enter into [3]the lodg-
ings of his borders, *and into* the
forest of his Cär′mel.
24 I have digged and drunk
strange waters, and with the sole
of my feet have I dried up all the
rivers of [4]besieged places.[T]
25 Hast thou not heard long
ago *how* I have done it, *and* of
ancient times that I have formed
it? now have I brought it to
pass, that [q]thou shouldest be to
lay waste fenced[G] [r]cities *into* ruinous heaps.
26 Therefore their inhabitants
were of small power, they were
dismayed and confounded; they
were *as* the grass of the field, and
*as* the green herb, *as* the grass on
the house tops, and *as corn*[G] blasted[G] before it be grown up.
27 But [s]I know thy abode, and
thy going out, and thy coming
in, and thy rage against me.[S]
28 Because thy rage against
me and [5]thy tumult is come up
into mine ears, therefore [t]I will
put my hook in thy nose, and
my [u]bridle in thy lips, and I will
turn thee back by the way by
which thou camest.
29 And this *shall be* a sign unto
thee, Ye shall eat this year such
things as grow of themselves, and
in the second year that which
springeth of the same; and in
the third year [v]sow ye, and
reap, and plant vineyards, and
eat the fruits thereof.
30 And the remnant that is escaped of the house of [w]Jū′dah
shall yet again take root downward, and bear fruit upward.
31 For out of [k]Jė-rụ′sȧ-lĕm
shall go forth a remnant, and
they that escape out of mount
[j]Zī-ŏn: the zeal of the LORD *of
hosts* shall do this.
32 Therefore thus saith the
LORD concerning the king of
[b]Ăs-sȳr′ĭ-ȧ, He shall not come
into [k]this city, nor shoot an [x]ar-
row there, nor come before it
with [y]shield, nor cast[G] a bank[G]
against it.
33 By the way that he came, by
the same shall he return, and
shall not come into [k]this city,
saith the LORD.
34 For [z]I will defend [a]this

B.C. 710?
See footnote, *Time*, Rev. 10:6.

25
q *Agency, in executing judgments*, Mark 1:17.
r *Cities, walled*, Num. 35:8.

27
s *God, knowledge of*, Gen. 2:2.

28
t *Divine Chastisement*, Job 33:19.
u *Bridle*, Psa. 32:9.
5 R. V. for that thine arrogancy is come

29
v *Agriculture*, Gen. 3:23.

30
w *Judah, kingdom of*, 2 Chr. 11:17.

32
x *Arrow*, 1 Sam. 20:20.
y *Shield*, 1 Kin. 14:27.

34
z *God, preserver*, Gen. 2:2.
a *Jerusalem*, Judg. 19:10.

B.C. 710?
See footnote, *Time*, Rev. 10:6.

*b Intercession, influence of the righteous*, Jer. 27:18.

35
*c Prophecies, fulfilled*, vs. 7, 20–37; Dan. 9:24.
*d Angel, functions of*, Heb. 1:13.
*e Judgments*, Ex. 6:6.
*f Miracles*, Luke 23:8.

36
*g Sennacherib*, 2 Chr. 32:1.
*h Assyria*, Gen. 25:18.
*i Nineveh*, Jonah 1:2.

37
*j* Isa. 37:38.
*k* Isa. 37:38.
*l Children, wicked, instances of*, Mark 10:14.
*m Assassination, instances of*, Deut. 27:24.
*n Regicide*, 2 Sam. 1:10.
*o* Or, *Ararat*, Gen. 8:4.
6 R. V. Ararat.

city, to save it, for mine own
sake, and for my servant Dā'-
vid's [b]sake.
35 ¶ And [c]it came to pass
that night, that the [d]angel of the
LORD went out, and [e,f]smote
in the camp of the Ăs-sўr'ĭ-anș
an hundred fourscore and five
thousand: and when they arose
early in the morning, behold,
they *were* all dead corpses.
36 So [g]Sĕn-năch'e-rĭb king of
[h]Ăs-sўr'ĭ-à departed, and went
and returned, and dwelt at
[i]Nĭn'e-veh.
37 And [c]it came to pass, as [g]he
was worshipping in the house of
[j]Nĭs'rŏch his god, that [k]Ă-drăm'-
me-lĕch and [k]Shă-rē'zĕr his [l]sons
*,[m,n]smote him with the sword:
and they escaped into the land of
[6,o]Är-mē'nĭ-à. And †Ē'sar–hăd'-
don his son reigned in his stead.

## CHAPTER 20

*Hezekiah, in answer to prayer, has his life lengthened. 8 The sun goes ten degrees backward for a sign to him. 12 The king of Babylon sends to congratulate Hezekiah. 14 Isaiah foretells the Babylonian captivity. 20 Manasseh succeeds Hezekiah.*

B.C. 713?
See footnote, *Time*, Rev. 10:6.

1
*a Hezekiah*, 2 Kin. 16:20.
*b Disease*, Ex. 15:26.
*c Prophets, inspiration of*, Isa. 3:2.
*d Isaiah*, Isa. 1:1.
*e* 2 Kin. 19:2; Isa. 1:1; 13:1.
*f Death, preparation for*, Num. 23:10.

2
*g Prayer, exemplified*, Acts 6:4.

3
*h Adversity, prayer in*, Psa. 10:6.
*i Rulers, righteous*, Ex. 18:21.
*j Obedience, exemplified*, Heb. 5:8.
*k Truth*, John 18:37.
*l Integrity*, Job 2:3.
*m Weeping, instances of*, Ezra 3:13.

4
*n House, architecture of*, Esth. 8:1.
1 R. V. part of the city.

IN those days was [a]Hĕz-e-kī'-
ah [b]sick unto death. And
the [c]prophet [d]Ī-șā'iah the son of
[e]Ā'mŏz came to him, and said
unto him, Thus saith the LORD,
[f]Set thine house in order; for
thou shalt die, and not live.
2 Then he turned his face to
the wall, and [g]prayed unto the
LORD, saying,
3 [h]I beseech thee, O LORD,
remember now how [i]I [j]have
walked before thee in [k]truth and
[l]with a perfect heart, and have
done *that which is* good in thy
sight. And Hĕz-e-kī'ah [m]wept
sore.
4 And it came to pass, afore
[d]Ī-șā'iah was gone out into the
middle [1,n]court, that [c]the word of
the LORD came to him, saying,
5 Turn again, and tell [a]Hĕz-e-
kī'ah the [o]captain of my people,
Thus saith the LORD, the God
of Dā'vid thy father, [p]I have
heard thy prayer, I have seen
thy tears: behold, [q,r]I will [s,t]heal
thee: on the third day thou shalt
go up unto the [u]house of the
LORD.
6 And I will add unto thy days
fifteen years; and [v]I will deliver
[w]thee and [x]this city out of the
hand of the king of [y]Ăs-sўr'ĭ-à;
and [v]I will defend this city for
mine own sake, and for my servant Dā'vid's [z]sake.
7 And [a]Ī-șā'iah said, Take a
lump of [b]figs. And they took and
laid *it* on the [c,d]boil, and he
recovered.
8 ¶ And [e]Hĕz-e-kī'ah said unto
[a]Ī-șā'iah, [f]What *shall be* the sign
that the LORD will heal me, and
that I shall go up into the [g]house
of the LORD the third day?
9 And [a]Ī-șā'iah said, This
[h]sign shalt thou have of the
LORD, that the LORD will do
the thing that he hath spoken:
shall the [i]shadow go forward
ten [2]degrees, or go back [2]ten
degrees?
10 And [e]Hĕz-e-kī'ah answered,
It is a light thing for the shadow
to go down ten [2]degrees: nay,
but let the shadow return backward ten [2]degrees.
11 And [a]Ī-șā'iah the prophet
cried unto the LORD: and [j]he
[k]brought the [i]shadow ten [2]de-
grees backward, by which it had
gone down in the [k]dial of [l]Ā'hăz.
12 ¶ At that time [m]Bĕ-rō'dăch–
băl'a-dăn, the son of Băl'a-dăn,
king of [n]Băb'ў-lon, [o]sent [p]let-
ters and a [q]present unto [e]Hĕz-
e-kī'ah: for he had heard that
Hĕz-e-kī'ah had been sick.
13 And [e]Hĕz-e-kī'ah [r]heark-
ened unto them, and shewed

B.C. 713?
See footnote, *Time*, Rev. 10:6.

5
*o Captain*, Num. 31:48.
*p Prayer, answered*, Acts 6:4.
*q God, preserver*, Gen. 2:2.
*r Temporal Blessings, from God*, Psa. 103:2.
*s Disease, healing of*, Ex. 15:26.
*t Healing, in answer to prayer*, Acts 4:22.
*u Temple, Solomon's*, 1 Kin. 6:17.

6
*v God, providence of*, Gen. 2:2.
*w Hezekiah, prophecies concerning*, 2 Kin. 16:20.
*x Jerusalem*, Judg. 19:10.
*y Assyria*, Gen. 25:18.
*z Intercession, influence of the righteous*, Jer. 27:18.

7
*a Isaiah*, Isa. 1:1.
*b Fig*, Mark 11:13.
*c Boil*, Ex. 9:9.
*d Disease*, Ex. 15:26.

8
*e Hezekiah*, 2 Kin. 16:20.
*f Faith, strengthened by miracles*, vs. 8–11; Mark 11:22.
*g Church, called house of the Lord*, 1 Kin. 9:3.

9
*h Miracles*, Luke 23:8.
*i Time*, Rev. 10:6.
2 R. V. steps.

11
*j Prayer, answered*, Acts 6:4.
*k* Isa. 38:8.
*l Ahaz*, 2 Kin. 15:38.

12
*m* Or, *Merodach-baladan*, Isa. 39:1.
*n Babylon, empire of*, Ezra 5:12.
*o Condolence*, 2 Sam. 10:2.
*p Letters*, Isa. 37:14.
*q Presents*, Gen. 32:13.

B.C. 712?

13
*r Temptation, yielding to*, Luke 11:4.

* **PARRICIDE.** *Sennacherib slain by his sons*, 2 Kin. 19:37; 2 Chr. 32:21; Isa. 37:38.

† **ESAR-HADDON,** king of Assyria. *Succeeds Sennacherib*, 2 Kin. 19:37; Isa. 37:38. *Called* ASNAPPER, Ezra 4:2, 10.

B.C. 712?
See footnote, *Time*, Rev. 10:6.

*s Silver*, 1 Chr. 28:14.
*t Gold*, Ezek. 7:19.
*u Spices*, 1 Kin. 10:2.
*v Ointment*, Eccl. 7:1.
*w Armory*, Neh. 3:19.
3 R. V. oil,

16
*x Reproof, faithfulness in*, Prov. 17:10.

17
*y Judah, prophecies concerning*, 2 Chr. 11:17.
*z Prophecies*, Dan. 9:24.

18
*a Eunuchs*, Matt. 19:12.
*b Palace*, 1 Kin. 21:1.
*c Babylon, empire of*, Ezra 5:12.

19
*d Resignation, exemplified*, Job 5:17.
*e Hezekiah*, 2 Kin. 16:20.

20
*f Water*, 1 Kin. 17:10.
*g Jerusalem*, Judg. 19:10.
B.C. 710?

them all the house of his precious things, the [s]silver, and the [t]gold, and the [u]spices, and the precious [3, v]ointment, and *all* the [w]house of his armour, and all that was found in his treasures: there was nothing in his house, nor in all his dominion, that Hĕz-e-kī'ah shewed them not.

14 ¶ Then came [a]Ī-ṣā'iah the prophet unto king [e]Hĕz-e-kī'ah, and said unto him, What said these men? and from whence came they unto thee? And Hĕz-e-kī'ah said, They are come from a far country, *even* from [n]Băb'ȳ-lon.

15 And he said, What have they seen in thine house? And Hĕz-e-kī'ah answered, All *the things* that *are* in mine house have they seen: there is nothing among my treasures that I have not shewed them.

16 And [a]Ī-ṣā'iah [x]said unto [e]Hĕz-e-kī'ah, Hear the word of the LORD.

17 [y, z]Behold, the days come, that all that *is* in thine house, and that which thy fathers have laid up in store unto this day, shall be carried into [n]Băb'ȳ-lon: nothing shall be left, saith the LORD.

18 [z]And of thy sons that shall issue from thee, which thou shalt beget, shall they take away; and they shall be [a]eunuchs in the [b]palace of the king of [c]Băb'ȳ-lon.

19 Then [d]said [e]Hĕz-e-kī'ah unto Ī-ṣā'iah, Good *is* the word of the LORD which thou hast spoken. And he said, *Is it* not *good*, if peace and truth be in my days?

20 ¶ And the rest of the acts of [e]Hĕz-e-kī'ah, and all his might, and how he made a pool, and a conduit, and brought [f]water into the [g]city, *are* they not written in the [h]book of the chronicles of the kings of [i]Jū'dah?

21 And [e]Hĕz-e-kī'ah [j]slept with his fathers: and Mȧ-năs'seh his son reigned in his stead.

## CHAPTER 21

*Manasseh's great idolatry. 10 His wickedness brings judgments upon Judah. 17 Amon succeeds him. 19 His wicked reign. 23 He is slain by his servants; and Josiah is made king.*

*MȦ-NĂS'SEH *was* twelve years old when he began to reign, and reigned fifty and five years in [a]Jĕ-ru̥'sȧ-lĕm. And his mother's name *was* Hĕph'-zī–bah.

2 And [b]he did *that which was* evil in the sight of the LORD, after the abominations of the heathen, whom the LORD cast out before the children of Ĭṣ'ra-el.

3 For he built up again the [c]high places which [d]Hĕz-e-kī'ah his father had destroyed; and he reared up altars for [e]Bā'al, and made [1]a [f]grove, as did [g]Ā'hăb king of Ĭṣ'ra-el; and worshipped all the [h, i]host of heaven, and served them.

4 And he built [j]altars in the [k]house of the LORD, of which the LORD said, In Jĕ-ru̥'sȧ-lĕm will I put my name.

5 And he built [j]altars for all the [h, i]host of heaven in the two courts of the house of the LORD.

6 And he [l]made his [m]son pass through the fire, and [2]observe times, and used [n]enchantments, and dealt with [3, o]familiar spirits and wizards: he wrought much wickedness in the sight of the LORD, to provoke *him* to [p, q]anger.

7 And he set a [h]graven image of [1]the [f]grove that he had made in the [k]house, of which the LORD said to Dā'vid, and to Sŏl'o-mon his son, In this house,

B.C. 710?
See footnote, *Time*, Rev. 10:6.

*h Book*, Num. 5:23.
*i Judah, kingdom of*, 2 Chr. 11:17.

21
*j Death*, Num. 23:10.

B.C. 698?
See footnote, *Time*, Rev. 10:6.

1
*a Jerusalem*, Judg. 19:10.

2
*b Rulers, wicked, instances of*, Ex. 18:21.

3
*c High Places*, 1 Kin. 3:2.
*d Hezekiah*, 2 Kin. 16:20.
*e Baal*, 2 Kin. 17:16.
*f Groves*, Judg. 6:28.
*g Ahab*, 1 Kin. 16:29.
*h Idolatry, objects of*, 1 Sam. 15:23.
*i Stars, worshiped*, Judg. 5:20.
1 R. V. an Asherah,

4
*j Altar, used in idolatrous worship*, Gen. 8:20.
*k Temple, Solomon's*, 1 Kin. 6:17.

6
*l Idolatry, wicked practices of*, 1 Sam. 15:23.
*m Human Sacrifices*, Deut. 12:31.
*n Sorcery*, Isa. 47:9.
*o Familiar Spirits*, Deut. 18:11.
*p Anger of God*, 2 Kin. 13:3.
*q Anthropomorphisms*, Gen. 11:5.
2 R. V. practised augury,
3 R. V. them that had familiar

* **MANASSEH.** *King of Judah*, 2 Kin. 20:21. *Reigned fifty-five years*, 2 Kin. 21:1; 2 Chr. 33:1. *Idolatry of*, 2 Kin. 21:1–7; 2 Kin. 23:12, 26; 2 Chr. 33:1–7. *Deported to Babylon*, 2 Chr. 33:11. *Repentance of*, 2 Chr. 33:12, 13. *Death of* 2 Kin. 21:18; 2 Chr. 33:20. *Ancestor of Jesus*, Matt. 1:10.

B.C. 698?
See footnote, *Time*, Rev. 10:6.

8
r *Blessings, contingent upon obedience*, Deut. 11:26.
s *Obedience*, Heb. 5:8.
t *Law, of Moses*, Deut. 33:2.

9
u *Influence, evil, of Manasseh*, 1 Cor. 7:14.
v *Temptation, leading into*, Luke 11:4.

10
w *Prophets, inspiration of*, Isa. 3:2.

11
x *Judah, kingdom of*, 2 Chr. 11:17.
y *Amorites, wickedness of*, Gen. 14:13.

12
z *God, providence of*, Gen. 2:2.

a *Judgments*, Ex. 6:6.
b *Jerusalem*, Judg. 19:10.
c *Judah, prophecies concerning*, 2 Chr. 11:17.

13
d *God, providence of*, Gen. 2:2.
e *Samaria*, Isa. 7:9.
f *Ahab*, 1 Kin. 16:29.

15
g *Sin, repugnant to God*, Rom. 5:12.
h *Anger of God*, 2 Kin. 13:3.
i *Anthropomorphisms*, Gen. 11:5.

and in [a]Jĕ-ru̇′să-lĕm, which I
have chosen out of all tribes of
Ĭṣ′ra-el, will I put my name for
ever:[s]
8 Neither will I make the feet
of Ĭṣ′ra-el move any more out
of the land which I gave their
fathers; only [r]if they will observe [s]to do according to all that
I have commanded them, and
according to all the [t]law that
my servant Mō′ṣeṣ commanded
them.
9 But they hearkened not: and
*Mă-năs′seh [u,v]seduced them to
do more evil than did the nations whom the LORD destroyed
before the children of Ĭṣ′ra-el.
10 ¶ And the LORD [w]spake
by his servants the prophets,
saying,
11 Because *Mă-năs′seh king of
[x]Jū′dah hath done these abominations, *and* hath done wickedly above all that the [y]Ăm′ôr-ītes
did, which *were* before him, and
hath [u,v]made Jū′dah also to sin
with his idols:
12 Therefore thus saith the
LORD God of Ĭṣ′ra-el, Behold,
[z]I *am* bringing *such* [a]evil upon
[b]Jĕ-ru̇′să-lĕm and [c]Jū′dah, that
whosoever heareth of it, both his
ears[G] shall tingle.
13 And [d]I will stretch over
[b]Jĕ-ru̇′să-lĕm the line of [e]Să-
mā′rĭ-ȧ, and the plummet[G] of the
house of [f]Ā′hăb: and I will wipe
Jĕ-ru̇′să-lĕm as *a man* wipeth a
dish, wiping *it*, and turning *it*
upside down.
14 And [d]I will forsake the remnant of mine inheritance[G], and
[a]deliver them into the hand of
their enemies; and they shall become a prey and a spoil[G] to all
their enemies;
15 Because they have done *that*
*which was* [g]evil in my sight, and
have provoked me to [h,i]anger,
since the day their fathers came
forth out of [j]Ē′ġy̆pt, even unto
this day.[s]
16 Moreover *,[k]Mă-năs′seh
[l]shed innocent blood very much,
till he had filled [b]Jĕ-ru̇′să-lĕm
from one end to another; beside
his [m]sin wherewith he made Jū′-
dah to sin, in doing *that which*
*was* evil in the sight of the LORD.
17 ¶ Now the rest of the acts of
*Mă-năs′seh, and all that he
did, and his sin that he sinned,
*are* they not written in the [n]book
of the chronicles of the kings of
[o]Jū′dah?
18 And *Mă-năs′seh [p]slept[G]
with his fathers, and was buried
in the [q]garden of his own house,
in the garden of Ŭz′ză: and
†Ā′mon his son reigned in his
stead.
19 ¶ †Ā′mon *was* twenty and
two years old when he began
to reign, and he reigned two
years in [b]Jĕ-ru̇′să-lĕm. And his
mother's name *was* Mĕ-shŭl′-
le-mĕth, the daughter of Hā′-
ruz of [r]Jŏt′bah.
20 And [k]he did *that which was*
evil in the sight of the LORD,
[m]as his [s]father *Mă-năs′seh did.
21 And [t]he walked [m]in all the
way that his [s]father walked in,
and [u]served the idols that his father served, and worshipped
them:
22 And [v]he forsook the LORD
God of his fathers, and [w]walked
not in the way of the LORD.
23 And the [x,y]servants of
†Ā′mon [z]conspired against him,
and [a,b]slew the king in his own
house.
24 And the people of the land
slew all them that had conspired
against king †Ā′mon; and the
people of the land made [c]Jō-
sī′ah his son king in his stead.
25 Now the rest of the acts of

B.C. 698?
See footnote, *Time*, Rev. 10:6.

j *Egypt*, Gen. 41:8.

16
k *Rulers, wicked, instances of*, Ex. 18:21.
l *Homicide*, Deut. 5:17.
m *Influence, evil*, 1 Cor. 7:14.

17
n *Book*, Num. 5:23.
o *Judah, kingdom of*, 2 Chr. 11:17.

18
p *Death*, Num. 23:10.
q *Burying Places*, Gen. 23:4.

B.C. 643?

19
r Or, *Jotbath*, Deut. 10:7.

20
s *Parents, evil influence of*, 2 Cor. 12:14.

21
t *Children, wicked, instances of*, Mark 10:14.
u *Idolatry*, 1 Sam. 15:23.

22
v *Backsliders, instances of*, Jer. 3:22.
w *Disobedience to God*, Eph. 5:6.

23
x *Citizens, wicked*, Luke 15:15.
y *Servant, wicked and unfaithful*, Jer. 2:14.
z *Conspiracy, instances of*, 1 Kin. 16:9.

a *Regicide*, 2 Sam. 1:10.
b *Assassination, instances of*, Deut. 27:24.

B.C. 641?

24
c *Josiah*, 1 Kin. 13:2.

† **AMON.** *King of Judah*, 2 Kin. 21:18–26; 2 Chr. 33:21–25; Zeph. 1:1. *Reigned two years*, 2 Kin. 21:19; 2 Chr. 33:21. *Ancestor of Jesus*, Matt. 1:10.

B.C. 641?
See footnote, *Time*, Rev. 10:6.

25
*d* *Book*, Num. 5:23.
*e* *King, chronicles of*, 2 Kin. 3:10.
*f* *Judah, kingdom of*, 2 Chr. 11:17.
26
*g* *Burying Places*, Gen. 23:4.

[†]Ā′mon which he did, *are* they not written in the [d]book of the chronicles of the [e]kings of [f]Jū′dah?

26 And he was buried in his sepulchre in the [g]garden of Ŭz′zȧ: and Jō-sī′ah his son reigned in his stead.

## CHAPTER 22

*Josiah's good reign. 3 He provides for the repair of the temple. 8 Hilkiah finds the book of the law in the temple. 12 Josiah sends to Huldah to inquire of the Lord. 15 Huldah foretells the destruction of Jerusalem, to take place after the death of Josiah.*

1
*a* *Josiah*, 1 Kin. 13:2.
*b* *Jerusalem*, Judg. 19:10.
*c* Or, *Bozkath*, Josh. 15:39.
2
*d* *Rulers, righteous*, Ex. 18:21.
*e* *Obedience, instances of*, Heb. 5:8.
*f* *Influence, good, of David*, 1 Cor. 7:14.
*g* *Faithfulness, instances of*, Luke 16:10.
3
*h* *Shaphan*, 2 Chr. 34:8.
*i* 2 Chr. 34:8.
*j* *Scribe*, 1 Kin. 4:3.
v.3–542 BC
4
*k* *Hilkiah, high priest*, Jer. 29:3.
*l* *High Priest, duties of*, Lev. 21:10.
*m* *Liberality, instances of*, 1 Tim. 6:18.
*n* *Treasure Houses, Solomon's temple used for*, Ezra 5:17.
*o* *Porters*, 2 Sam. 18:26.
6
*p* *Carpentry*, 2 Kin. 12:11.
*q* *Mason*, 2 Sam. 5:11.
*r* *Stones, hewn*, Ex. 24:12.

[a]JŌ-SĪ′AH *was* eight years old when he began to reign and he reigned thirty and one years in [b]Jē-rụ′sā-lĕm. And his mother's name *was* Jē-dī′dah, the daughter of Ăd-a-ī′ah of [c]Bŏs′cath.

2 And [d]he [e]did *that which was* right in the sight of the LORD, and walked [f]in all the way of Dā′vid his father, and [g]turned not aside to the right hand or to the left.

3 ¶ And it came to pass in the eighteenth year of king [a]Jō-sī′ah, *that* the king sent [h]Shā′phan the son of [i]Ăz-a-lī′ah, the son of Mē-shŭl′lam, the [j]scribe, to the house of the LORD, saying,

4 Go up to [k]Hĭl-kī′ah the [l]high priest, that he may sum[C] the silver which is [m]brought into the [n]house of the LORD, which the [o]keepers of the door have gathered of the people:

5 And let them deliver it into the hand of the doers of the work, that have the oversight of the house of the LORD: and let them give it to the doers of the work which *is* in the house of the LORD, to repair the breaches of the house,

6 Unto [p]carpenters, and builders, and [q]masons, and to buy timber and hewn [r]stone to repair the house.

7 Howbeit there was no reckoning made with them of the [s]money that was delivered into their hand, because they [t,u]dealt faithfully.[C]

8 ¶ And [k]Hĭl-kī′ah the [l]high priest said unto [h]Shā′phan the [j]scribe, I have found the [v]book of the [w]law in the house of the LORD. And Hĭl-kī′ah gave the book to Shā′phan, and he read it.

9 And [h]Shā′phan the [j]scribe came to the king, and brought the king word again, and said, Thy servants have gathered[C] the [s]money that was found in the [n]house, and have delivered it into the hand of them that do the work, that have the oversight of the house of the LORD.

10 And [h]Shā′phan the [j]scribe[C] shewed the king, saying, [k]Hĭl-kī′ah the [l]priest hath delivered me a [v]book. And Shā′phan read it before the king.

11 And it came to pass, when the king had heard the [x]words of the book of the law, that he [y,z,a]rent[C] his clothes.

12 And the king commanded [b]Hĭl-kī′ah the [c]priest, and *Ā-hī′kam the son of [d]Shā′phan, and [e]Ăch′bôr the son of [f]Mī-chā′iah, and [g]Shā′phan the [h]scribe, and [i]Ā-sa-hī′ah a servant of the king's, saying,

13 Go ye, [j]enquire[C] of the LORD for me, and for the people, and for all [k]Jū′dah, concerning the [l]words of this [m]book that is found: for great *is* the [n]wrath of the LORD that is kindled against us, because our fathers have not hearkened unto the words of this book, to do according unto all that which is written concerning us.[S]

14 So [b]Hĭl-kī′ah the [c]priest, and *Ā-hī′kam, and [e]Ăch′bôr,

v.7–542 BC
See footnote, *Time*, Rev. 10:6.

7
*s* *Money*, Jer. 32:9.
*t* *Integrity, instances of*, Job 2:3.
*u* *Honesty, instances of*, Rom. 13:13.
8
*v* *Book, law of Moses written in*, Num. 5:23.
*w* *Law, of Moses*, Deut. 33:2.
11
*x* *Word of God*, Psa. 119:9.
*y* *Mourning*, Lam. 2:5.
*z* *Rending of Garments*, 2 Chr. 34:27.
*a* *Repentance, instances of*, Mark 1:4.
12
*b* *Hilkiah*, Jer. 29:3.
*c* *High Priest*, Lev. 21:10.
*d* *Shaphan*, 2 Chr. 34:8.
*e* Or, *Abdon*, 2 Chr. 34:20.
*f* Or, *Micah*, 2 Chr. 34:20.
*g* 2 Chr. 34:14–20.
*h* *Scribe*, 1 Kin. 4:3.
*i* 2 Chr. 34:20–28.
13
*j* *Intercession, solicited*, Jer. 27:18.
*k* *Judah, kingdom of*, 2 Chr. 11:17.
*l* *Law, of Moses*, Deut. 33:2.
*m* *Book, law of Moses written in*, Num. 5:23.
*n* *Anger of God*, 2 Kin. 13:3.

***AHIKAM.** *Son of Shaphan*, 2 Kin. 22:12–14; 25:22; 2 Chr. 34:20; Jer. 26:24; 39:14; 40:5–16; 41:1–18; 43:6.

v.14–542 BC
See footnote, *Time,* Rev. 10:6.

and [g]Shā′phan, and [i]Ā-sa-hī′-
ah, went unto [o,p]Hŭl′dah the
[q]prophetess, the wife of [r]Shăl′-
lum the son of [r]Tĭk′vah, the son
of [s]Här′has, keeper of the wardrobe; (now she dwelt in [t]Jĕ-ru̇′-
sȧ-lĕm in the [1]college;) and they
communed[C] with her.
15 And [o,p]she said unto them,
Thus saith the LORD God of
Ĭs̤′ra-el, Tell the man that sent
you to me,
16 Thus saith the LORD, Behold, I will bring [u]evil upon this
place, and upon the [v]inhabit-
ants thereof, *even* all the words
of the [m]book which the king of
[k]Jū′dah hath read:
17 Because they have forsaken
me, and have [w]burned [x]incense
unto other gods, that they might
provoke me to [n]anger with all
the works of their hands; therefore my wrath shall be kindled
against this place, and shall not
be quenched.[S]
18 But to the king of [k]Jū′-
dah which sent you to [j]enquire
of the LORD, thus shall ye
say to him, [y]Thus saith the
LORD God of Ĭs̤′ra-el, *As touching* the words which thou
hast heard;
19 [y]Because thine [z]heart was
tender, and thou hast [a]humbled
thyself before the LORD, when
thou heardest what I spake
against this place, and against
the inhabitants thereof, that they
should become a desolation and
a curse, and hast rent[G] thy
clothes, and wept before me;
[b,c]I also have heard [d]*thee,* saith
the LORD.[T]
20 Behold therefore, [b,c]I will
[e]gather[G] thee unto thy fathers,
and thou shalt be gathered into
thy grave in peace; and thine
eyes shall not see all the evil
which I will bring upon this
place. And they brought the
[f]king word again.

**14**
*o* 2 Chr. 34:22–28.
*p* *Women, as prophets,* Prov. 31:10.
*q* *Prophetess,* Judg. 4:4.
*r* 2 Chr. 34:22.
*s* Or, *Hasrah,* 2 Chr. 34:22.
*t* *Jerusalem,* Judg. 19:10.
1 R. V. second quarter;

**16**
*u* *Judgments,* Ex. 6:6.
*v* *Judah, kingdom of,* 2 Chr. 11:17.

**17**
*w* *Idolatry,* 1 Sam. 15:23.
*x* *Incense, offered in idolatrous worship,* Ex. 37:29.

**18**
*y* *Afflictions, consolation in,* Psa. 34:19.

**19**
*z* *Heart,* Psa. 44:21.
*a* *Humility, instances of,* Prov. 22:4.
*b* *Prayer, answered,* Acts 6:4.
*c* *Promise, or ground of assurance, to the penitent, of divine favor,* 2 Cor. 1:20.
*d* *Penitent, promises to,* Psa. 51:17.

**20**
*e* *Death, of the righteous,* Num. 23:10.
*f* *Josiah,* 1 Kin. 13:2.

## CHAPTER 23

*Josiah causes the book of the law to be read in a solemn assembly. 3 He renews the covenant of the Lord. 4 He destroys idolatry. 15 He burns dead men's bones upon the altar at Beth-el. 21 He keeps a solemn passover. 24 He puts away wizards and all abominations. 26 God's wrath against Judah. 29 Josiah, going against Pharaoh-nechoh, is slain at Megiddo. 31 Jehoahaz, succeeding him, is imprisoned by Pharaoh-nechoh, who makes Jehoiakim king. 36 Jehoiakim's wicked reign.*

AND the [a,b]king sent, and
they gathered unto him all
the [c]elders of [d]Jū′dah and of
[e]Jĕ-ru̇′sȧ-lĕm.
2 And the [a,f]king went up into
the [g,h]house of the LORD, and
all the men of [d]Jū′dah and all
the inhabitants of [e]Jĕ-ru̇′sȧ-lĕm
with him, and the [i]priests, and
the [j]prophets, and all the people,
both small and great: and [f]he
[k]read in their ears all the [l]words
of the [m]book of the [n]covenant
which was found in the house of
the LORD.
3 And the [a,b]king stood[C] by a
pillar, and [o]made a [p]covenant[G]
before the LORD, to walk after
the LORD, and to keep his commandments and his testimonies
and his statutes with all *their*
heart and all *their* soul, to perform the words of this [n]covenant
that were written in this [m]book.
And [q]all the people stood[C] to the
covenant.
4 And the [a,b]king commanded
[r]Hĭl-kī′ah the [s]high priest, and
the priests of the second order,
and the [t]keepers of the door, to
bring forth out of the [g]temple of
the LORD all the vessels that
were made for [u]Bā′al, and for
the grove[G], and for all the [v]host
of heaven: and he [w]burned
them without[G] [e]Jĕ-ru̇′sȧ-lĕm in
the fields of [x]Kĭd′ron, and carried the ashes of them unto
[y]Bĕth′–el.
5 And he put down the idolatrous [z]priests, whom the kings of
Jū′dah had ordained to burn
[a]incense in the [b]high[G] places in

v.1–542 BC
See footnote, *Time,* Rev. 10:6.

**1**
*a* *Josiah,* 1 Kin. 13:2.
*b* *Rulers, righteous,* vs. 1–25; Ex. 18:21.
*c* *Senate,* Num. 11:16.
*d* *Judah, kingdom of,* 2 Chr. 11:17.
*e* *Jerusalem,* Judg. 19:10.

**2**
*f* *Zeal, instances of,* 2 Cor. 7:11.
*g* *Temple, Solomon's,* 1 Kin. 6:17.
*h* *Church, called house of the Lord,* 1 Kin. 9:3.
*i* *Priests,* Lev. 1:5.
*j* *Prophets,* Isa. 3:2.
*k* *Instruction, in religion,* Prov. 23:23.
*l* *Word of God, to be read publicly,* Psa. 119:9.
*m* *Book,* Num. 5:23.
*n* *Law, of Moses,* Deut. 33:2.

**3**
*o* *Decision, instances of,* Isa. 50:7.
*p* *Covenant, of man with God,* Deut. 29:1.
*q* *Religious Revivals, instances of,* Hab. 3:2.

**4**
*r* *Hilkiah, high priest,* Jer. 29:3.
*s* *High Priest,* Lev 21:10.
*t* *Porters,* 2 Sam. 18:26.
*u* *Baal, altars of, destroyed,* 2 Kin. 17:16.
*v* *Idolatry, objects of,* 1 Sam. 15:23.
*w* *Iconoclasm,* Num. 33:52.
*x* *Kidron,* 1 Kin. 2:37.
*y* *Beth-el,* Josh. 18:13.

**5**
*z* *Priest, idolatrous,* Lev. 1:5.
*a* *Incense, offered in idolatrous worship,* Ex. 37:29.
*b* *High Places,* 1 Kin. 3:2.

the cities of [c]Jū′dah, and in the
places round about [d]Jė-ru̱′sȧ-
lĕm; them also that burned incense unto [e]Bā′al, to the [f]sun,
and to the [f]moon, and to the
[f]planets, and to all the [f]host of
heaven.
6 And [g]he brought out the
[h]grove[G] from the [i]house of the
LORD, without[G] [d]Jė-ru̱′sȧ-lĕm,
unto the brook [j]Kĭd′ron, and
[k]burned it at the brook Kĭd′ron,
and stamped *it* small to powder,
and cast the powder thereof upon the graves of the [1]children of
the people.
7 And [g]he [k]brake down the
[l]houses of the [m,n]sodomites, that
*were* [2]by the [i]house of the LORD,
where the [o]women [p]wove [q]hang-
ings for the grove.[G]
8 And he brought all the
[r]priests out of the cities of [c]Jū′-
dah, and defiled[G] the [b]high[G] places
where the priests had burned
[a]incense, from [s]Gē′bȧ to [t]Bē′er-
shē′bȧ, and [k]brake down the
high places of the gates that *were*
in the entering in of the [u]gate of
Jŏsh′u-ȧ the governor of the city,
which *were* on a man's left hand
at the gate of the city.
9 Nevertheless the [r]priests of
the [b]high places came not up to
the [v]altar of the LORD in [d]Jė-
ru̱′sȧ-lĕm, but they did eat of the
unleavened bread among their
brethren.
10 And he defiled[G] *Tō′pheth,
which *is* in the valley of the children of [w]Hĭn′nom, that no man
might [l]make his [x]son or his
[x]daughter to pass through the
fire to [y]Mō′lech.
11 And he took away the
[z]horses that the kings of [a]Jū′dah
had given to the [b]sun, at the entering in of the [c,d]house of the
LORD, by the chamber of Nā′-
than–mē′lech the †chamberlain,[G]
which *was* in the suburbs,[G] and
[e]burned the chariots of the sun
with fire.
12 And the [f]altars[G] that *were* on
the top of the upper [g]chamber of
[h]Ā′hăz, which the kings of [a]Jū′-
dah had made, and the altars
which [i]Mȧ-năs′seh had made in
the two courts of the [c]house of
the LORD, did the king [e]beat[G]
down, and brake *them* down
from thence,[G] and cast the dust
of them into the [j]brook [k]Kĭd′-
ron.
13 And the [l]high places that
*were* before [m]Jė-ru̱′sȧ-lĕm, which
*were* on the right hand of the
[n]mount of corruption,[G] which
[o]Sŏl′o-mon the king of Ĭs̱′ra-el
had builded for [p]Ăsh′to-rĕth
the abomination[G] of the [q]Zī-dō′-
nĭ-ans̱, and for [r]Chē′mŏsh the
abomination of the [s]Mō′ab-ītes,
and for [t]Mĭl′com the abomination of the [u]children of Ăm′mŏn,
did the king defile.[G]
14 And he [e]brake in pieces the
[3,v]images, and cut down the
[w]groves,[G] and filled their places
with the bones of men.
15 ¶ Moreover the [f]altar[G] that
*was* at [x]Bĕth′–el, *and* the [l]high
place which [y]Jĕr-o-bō′am the
son of Nē′băt, who made Ĭs̱′-
ra-el to sin, had made, both that
altar and the high place he
[e]brake down, and burned the
high place, *and* stamped *it* small
to powder, and burned the
[w]grove.[G]
16 And as [z]Jō-sī′ah turned himself, he spied[G] the [a]sepulchres
that *were* there in the mount,
and sent, and took the bones out
of the sepulchres, and [b]burned
*them* upon the altar, and polluted it, according to the [c]word
of the LORD which the man of

v.5–542 BC See footnote, *Time*, Rev. 10:6.

c *Judah, kingdom of*, 2 Chr. 11:17.
d *Jerusalem*, Judg. 19:10.
e *Baal*, 2 Kin. 17:16.
f *Idolatry, objects of*, 1 Sam. 15:23.

6
g *Josiah*, 1 Kin. 13:2.
h *Groves, destroyed by Josiah*, Judg. 6:28.
i *Temple, Solomon's*, 1 Kin. 6:17.
j *Kidron*, 1 Kin. 2:37.
k *Iconoclasm*, Num. 33:52.
1 R. V. common people.

7
l *Idolatry, wicked practices of*, 1 Sam. 15:23.
m *Sodomites*, Gen. 19:25.
n *Sodomy*, Lev. 18:22.
o *Women, wicked*, Prov. 31:10.
p *Weaving*, Isa. 38:12.
q *Tapestry*, Prov. 7:16.
2 R. V. in

8
r *Priest, idolatrous*, Lev. 1:5.
s *Geba*, Josh. 21:17.
t *Beer-sheba*, Judg. 20:1.
u *Jerusalem, gates of*, Judg. 19:10.

9
v *Altar, of burnt offerings*, Gen. 8:20.

10
w *Hinnom*, Jer. 7:31.
x *Human Sacrifices*, Deut. 12:31.
y *Molech*, 1 Kin. 11:7.

11
z *Horse*, Job 39:19.

a *Judah, kingdom of*, 2 Chr. 11:17.
b *Sun*, Josh. 10:12.
c *Temple, Solomon's*, 1 Kin. 6:17.
d *Church, called house of God*, 1 Kin. 9:3.

v.11–542 BC See footnote, *Time*, Rev. 10:6.

e *Iconoclasm*, Num. 33:52.

12
f *Altar, used in idolatrous worship*, Gen. 8:20.
g *House, architecture of*, Esth. 8:1.
h *Ahaz*, 2 Kin. 15:38.
i *Manasseh*, 2 Kin. 21:1.
j *Brook, Kidron*, Deut. 8:7.
k *Kidron*, 1 Kin. 2:37.

13
l *High Places*, 1 Kin. 3:2.
m *Jerusalem*, Judg. 19:10.
n *Mount of Olives*, Mark 11:1.
o *Solomon*, 2 Sam. 12:24.
p *Ashtoreth*, 1 Kin. 11:5.
q *Zidon*, Ezek. 28:21.
r *Chemosh*, Judg. 11:24.
s *Moabites*, Gen. 19:37.
t Or, *Molech*, 1 Kin. 11:7.
u *Ammonites*, Deut. 2:20.

14
v *Idolatry, objects of*, 1 Sam. 15:33.
w *Groves*, Judg. 6:28.
3 R. V. pillars,

15
x *Beth-el*, Josh. 18:13.
y *Jeroboam*, 1 Kin. 14:5.

16
z *Josiah*, 1 Kin. 13:2.

a *Burying Places*, Gen. 23:4.
b *Cremation*, Josh. 7:25.
c *Prophecies, fulfilled*, Dan. 9:24.

* **TOPHETH**, called also TOPHET. *A place in the valley of the sons of Hinnom*, 2 Kin. 23:10. *Jewish children passed through the fire to Molech in*, 2 Kin. 23:10; 2 Chr. 28:3; 33:6; Jer. 7:31, 32; 19:6, 11–14; 32:35. *Destroyed by Josiah*, 2 Kin. 2 3:10. **Figurative**: *Of divine judgment*, Isa. 30:33.

† **CHAMBERLAIN**. *An officer of a king*, 2 Kin. 23:11; Esth. 1:10–15; 2:3–23; 4:4, 5; Acts 12:20. *Erastus the* [R.V. treasurer], Rom. 16:23.

v.16–542 BC
See footnote, *Time*, Rev. 10:6.

**17**
d *Prophets*, Isa. 3:2.
e *Judah, kingdom of*, 2 Chr. 11:17.
f *Altar, used in idolatrous worship*, Gen. 8:20.
g *Beth-el*, Josh. 18:13.
4 R. V. monument

**18**
h *Samaria*, Isa. 7:9.

**19**
i *High Places*, 1 Kin. 3:2.
j *Anger of God*, 2 Kin. 13:3.
k *Anthropomorphisms*, Gen. 11:5.
l *Josiah*, 1 Kin. 13:2.

**20**
m *Zeal, in punishing the wicked*, 2 Cor. 7:11.
n *Jerusalem*, Judg. 19:10.

**21**
o *Passover*, Num. 9:5.
p *Book*, Num. 5:23.
q *Law, of Moses*, Deut. 33:2.

**22**
r *Judge, of Israel*, Judg. 2:16.
s *Israel, under the judges*, Ex. 4:22.

v.23–542 BC

**24**
t *Familiar Spirits*, Deut. 18:11.
u *Sorcery*, Isa. 47:9.
v *Idolatry, objects of*, 1 Sam. 15:23.
5 R. V. teraphim,

God proclaimed, who proclaimed these words.

17 Then he said, What [4]title *is* that that I see? And the men of the city told him, *It is* the [a]sepulchre of the [d]man of God, which came from [e]Jū′dah, and [c]proclaimed these things that thou hast done against the [f]altar of [g]Bĕth′-el.

18 And he said, Let him alone; let no man move his bones. So they let his bones alone, with the bones of the prophet that came out of [h]Să-mā′rĭ-ȧ.

19 And all the houses[C] also of the [i]high[C] places that *were* in the cities of [h]Să-mā′rĭ-ȧ, which the kings of Ĭṣ′ra-el had made to provoke *the* LORD to [j,k]anger, [l]Jō-sī′ah took away, and did to them according to all the acts that he had done in [g]Bĕth′-el.[S]

20 And [m]he slew all the priests of the [i]high places that *were* there upon the [f]altars, and [b]burned men's bones upon them, and returned to [n]Jē-rṳ′să-lĕm.

21 ¶ And the [l]king commanded all the people, saying, Keep the [o]passover unto the LORD your God, as *it is* written in the [p]book of this [q]covenant.

22 Surely there was not holden such a [o]passover from the days of the [r]judges that judged [s]Ĭṣ′ra-el, nor in all the days of the kings of Ĭṣ′ra-el, nor of the kings of Jū′dah;

23 But in the eighteenth year of king [l]Jō-sī′ah, *wherein* this [o]passover was holden to the LORD in [n]Jē-rṳ′să-lĕm.

24 ¶ Moreover the *workers with* [t]familiar[C] spirits, and the [u]wizards, and the [5,v]images[C], and the idols, and all the abominations that were spied in the land of [e]Jū′dah and in [n]Jē-rṳ′să-lĕm, did [l]Jō-sī′ah [w]put away, that he might perform the words of the [q]law which were written in the [p]book that [x]Hĭl-kī′ah the [y]priest found in the [z]house of the LORD.

25 And like unto [a]him was there no king before him, that turned to the LORD with all his heart, and with all his soul, and with all his might, according to all the [b]law of Mō′ṣeṣ; neither after him arose there *any* like him.

26 Notwithstanding the LORD turned not from the fierceness of his great [c,d]wrath, wherewith his anger was kindled against [e]Jū′dah, because of all the [f]provocations that [g]Mă-năs′seh had provoked him withal.[S]

27 And the LORD said, I will [h]remove [i]Jū′dah also out of my sight, as I have removed Ĭṣ′ra-el, and will cast off this city [j]Jē-rṳ′să-lĕm which I have chosen, and the [k]house of which I said, My name shall be there.

28 Now the rest of the acts of [l]Jō-sī′ah, and all that he did, *are* they not written in the [m]book of the chronicles of the kings of [i]Jū′dah?

29 In his days [‡]Phā′raōh-nē′choh king of [n]Ē′ġy̆pt went up against the king of [o]Ăs-sy̆r′ĭ-ȧ to the river [p]Eū-phrā′tēṣ: and king [l]Jō-sī′ah went against him; and he slew him at [q]Mē-ġĭd′dō, when he had seen him.[Q]

30 And his servants carried him in a [r]chariot dead from [q]Mē-ġĭd′dō, and brought him to [j]Jē-rṳ′să-lĕm, and buried him in his own [s]sepulchre. And the [e]people of the land took [‖]Jē-hō′a-hăz the son of [l]Jō-sī′ah, and [t]anointed him, and made him king in his father's stead.

v.24–542 BC
See footnote, *Time*, Rev. 10:6.

w *Obedience, instances of*, Heb. 5:8.
x *Hilkiah, the high priest*, Jer. 29:3.
y *High Priest*, Lev. 21:10.
z *Temple, Solomon's*, 1 Kin. 6:17.

**25**
a *Rulers, righteous*, Ex. 18:21.
b *Law, of Moses*, Deut. 33:2.

**26**
c *Anger of God*, 2 Kin. 13:3.
d *Anthropomorphisms*, Gen. 11:5.
e *Judah, kingdom of*, 2 Chr. 11:17.
f *Sin, repugnant to God*, Rom. 5:12.
g *Manasseh, king of Judah*, 2 Kin. 21:1.

**27**
h *Judgments*, Ex. 6:6.
i *Judah, prophecies concerning*, 2 Chr. 11:17.
j *Jerusalem*, Judg. 19:10.
k *Temple, Solomon's*, 1 Kin. 6:17.

**28**
l *Josiah*, 1 Kin. 13:2.
m *Book*, Num. 5:23.

**29**
n *Egyptians*, Gen. 50:3.
o *Assyria*, Gen. 25:18.
p *Euphrates*, Gen. 15:18.
q *Megiddo*, Josh. 17:11.
v.29–529 BC

**30**
r *Chariot*, Josh. 11:4.
s *Burying Places*, Gen. 23:4.
t *Anointing, of kings*, Lev. 8:12.

‡ **PHARAOH-NECHOH.** *His invasion of Assyria; Josiah's death*, 2 Kin. 23:29–35; 24:7; 2 Chr. 35:20–24; 36:3, 4; Jer. 46:2; 47:1.

‖ **JEHOAHAZ,** called also SHALLUM. *King of Judah, and successor of Josiah*, 2 Kin. 23:30; 1 Chr. 3:15; Jer. 22:11. *Wicked reign of*, 2 Kin. 23:32. *Pharaoh-nechoh, king of Egypt, invades the kingdom of; defeats him, and takes him captive to Egypt*, 2 Kin. 23:33–35; 2 Chr. 36:3, 4. *Reigned three months*, 2 Kin. 23:31; 2 Chr. 36:1, 2. *Prophecies concerning*, Jer. 22:10, 11, 12.

v.31–529 BC
See footnote, *Time*, Rev. 10:6.

**31**
*u* 2 Kin. 24:18; Jer. 52:1.
*v* *Libnah*, Josh. 10:29.

**32**
*w* *Rulers, wicked*, Ex. 18:21.

**33**
*x* *Riblah*, Num. 34:11.
*y* *Hamath*, 1 Chr. 18:3.
*z* *Tribute*, Ezra 4:13.

*a* *Talent*, Ex. 38:25.

**34**
*b* 2 Chr. 36:4.
*c* *Josiah*, 1 Kin. 13:2.
*d* *Jehoiakim*, Jer. 26:1.
*e* *Egypt*, Gen. 41:8.
*f* *Death*, Num. 23:10.

**35**
*g* *Tribute*, Ezra 4:13.
*h* *Tax*, Neh. 10:32.
*i* *Money*, Jer. 32:9.

**36**
*j* *Jerusalem*, Judg. 19:10.

**37**
*k* *Rulers, wicked*, Ex. 18:21.

31 ¶ ‖Jē-hō'a-hăz *was* twenty and three years old when he began to reign; and he reigned three months in [j]Jē-rṳ'sȧ-lĕm. And his mother's name *was* [u]Hȧ-mū'tal, the daughter of [u]Jĕr-e-mī'ah of [v]Lĭb'nah.

32 And [w]he did *that which was* evil in the sight of the LORD, according to all that his fathers had done.

33 And ‡Phā'raōh–nē'choh put him in bands[c] at [x]Rĭb'lah in the land of [y]Hā'math, that he might not reign in [j]Jē-rṳ'sȧ-lĕm; and put the land to a [z]tribute[c] of an hundred [a]talents[c] of silver, and a talent[c] of gold.

34 And ‡Phā'raōh–nē'choh made [b]Ē-lī'a-kĭm the son of [c]Jō-sī'ah king in the room[c] of Jō-sī'ah his father, and turned[c] his name to [d]Jē-hoi'a-kĭm, and took ‖Jē-hō'a-hăz away: and he came to [e]Ē'ġy̆pt, and [f]died there.

35 And [d]Jē-hoi'a-kĭm gave the [g]silver and the [g]gold to ‡Phā'-raōh; but he [h]taxed the land to give the [i]money according to the commandment of Phā'raōh: he exacted[c] the silver and the gold of the people of the land, of every one according to his taxation[c], to give *it* unto Phā'raōh–nē'-choh.

36 ¶ [d]Jē-hoi'a-kĭm *was* twenty and five years old when he began to reign; and he reigned eleven years in [j]Jē-rṳ'sȧ-lĕm. And his mother's name *was* Ze-bū'dah, the daughter of Pē-dā'iah of Rṳ'mah.

37 And [k]he did *that which was* evil in the sight of the LORD, according to all that his fathers had done.

## CHAPTER 24

*Jehoiakim, subdued by Nebuchadnezzar, rebels against him to his own ruin. 6 Jehoiachin succeeds him. 8 His evil reign. 10 Jerusalem is taken, and the chief of the people carried away captive into Babylon. 17 Zedekiah is made king in Jerusalem. 19 His wicked reign.*

IN his days [a]Nĕb-u-chad-nĕz'-zar king of [b]Băb'y̆-lon came up, and [c]Jē-hoi'a-kĭm became his servant three years: then he turned and rebelled against him.

2 And the [d]LORD [e]sent against him bands of the [f]Chăl'dees, and bands of the [g]Sy̆r'ĭ-ans, and bands of the [h]Mō'ab-ītes, and bands of the [i]children of Ăm'mŏn, and sent them against [j]Jū'dah to destroy it, according to the word of the LORD, which he [k]spake by his servants the prophets.

3 Surely at the commandment of the LORD [e,l]came *this* upon [j]Jū'dah, to remove *them* out of his sight, for the sins of [m]Mȧ-năs'-seh, according to all that he did;

4 And also for the innocent [n]blood that he shed: for he filled [o]Jē-rṳ'sȧ-lĕm with innocent blood; [p]which the LORD would not pardon.

5 ¶ Now the rest of the acts of [c]Jē-hoi'a-kĭm, and all that he did, *are* they not written in the [q]book of the chronicles of the kings of [j]Jū'dah?

6 So [c]Jē-hoi'a-kĭm slept with his fathers: and *Jē-hoi'a-chĭn his son reigned in his stead.

7 And the [r]king of [s]Ē'ġy̆pt came not again any more out of his land: for the [a]king of [b]Băb'y̆-lon had taken from the river of [t]Ē'ġy̆pt unto the river [u]Eū-phrā'tēs all that pertained to the king of Ē'ġy̆pt.

8 ¶ *Jē-hoi'a-chĭn *was* eighteen years old when he began to reign,

**1**
*a* *Nebuchadnezzar*, Dan. 2:1.
*b* *Babylon, empire of*, Ezra 5:12.
*c* *Jehoiakim*, Jer. 26:1.

**2**
*d* *God, providence of*, Gen. 2:2.
*e* *Judgments*, Ex. 6:6.
*f* *Chaldea*, Isa. 23:13.
*g* *Syria*, 2 Kin. 6:23.
*h* *Moabites*, Gen. 19:37.
*i* *Ammonites*, Deut. 2:20.
*j* *Judah, kingdom of*, 2 Chr. 11:17.
*k* *Prophets, inspiration of*, Isa 3:2.

**3**
*l* *Sin, punishment of*, Rom. 5:12.
*m* *Rulers, wicked, instances of*, Ex. 18:21.

**4**
*n* *Homicide, instances of*, Deut. 5:17.
*o* *Jerusalem*, Judg. 19:10.
*p* *Unpardonable Sin*, Matt. 12:31.

**5**
*q* *Book*, Num. 5:23.

v.6–518 BC

**7**
*r* *Pharaoh-nechoh*, 2 Kin. 23:29.
*s* *Egypt*, Gen. 41:8.
*t* *Egypt, brook of*, Gen. 15:18.
*u* *Euphrates*, Gen. 15:18.

* **JEHOIACHIN** (*appointed of Jehovah*). *King of Judah and successor to Jehoiakim*, 2 Kin. 24:6–8; 2 Chr. 36:8. *Called*, JECONIAH, 1 Chr. 3:16; Jer. 24:1; CONIAH, Jer. 22:24; 37:1. *Reigned about three months*, 2 Kin. 24:8; 2 Chr. 36:9. *Wicked reign of*, 2 Kin. 24:9; 2 Chr. 36:9. *Nebuchadnezzar invades his kingdom; takes him captive to Babylon*, 2 Kin. 24: 10–16; 2 Chr. 36:10; Esth. 2:6; Jer. 27:20; 29:1, 2; Ezek. 1:2. *Confined in prison thirty-seven years*, 2 Kin. 25:27. *Released from prison by Evil-merodach, and promoted above other kings and honored until death*, 2 Kin. 25:27–30; Jer. 52:31–34. *Prophecies concerning*, Jer. 22:24–30; 28:4. *Sons of*, 1 Chr. 3:17, 18. *Ancestor of Jesus*, Matt. 1:12.

and he reigned in [o]Jē-ru̧′sȧ-lĕm
three months. And his mother's name *was* Nē-hŭsh′tȧ, the
daughter of [v]Ĕl′na-thăn of Jē-
ru̧′sȧ-lĕm.
9 And [m]he did *that which was* evil
in the sight of the LORD, according to all that his father had done.
10 ¶ At that time the servants of [a]Nĕb-u-chad-nĕz′zar king
of [b]Băb′ȳ-lon came up against
[o]Jē-ru̧′sȧ-lĕm, and the city was
[w]besieged.
11 And [a]Nĕb-u-chad-nĕz′zar
king of [b]Băb′ȳ-lon came against
the [o]city, and his servants did
[w]besiege it.
12 [Q] And *Jē-hoi′a-chĭn the king
of [j]Jū′dah went out to the [a]king
of [b]Băb′ȳ-lon, he, and his mother, and his servants, and his
princes, and his officers: and the
king of Băb′ȳ-lon took him in
the eighth year of his reign.
13 And [x]he carried out thence[G]
all the treasures of the [y]house of
the LORD, and the treasures of
the king's [z]house, and cut in
pieces all the vessels of gold
which Sŏl′o-mon king of Ĭs′ra-el
had made in the temple of the
LORD, as the LORD had said.
14 And [x]he carried away all
Jē-ru̧′sȧ-lĕm, and all the princes,
and all the mighty men of valour,[G]
*even* ten thousand [a]captives, and
all the [b]craftsmen and [c]smiths:
none remained, save[G] the poorest
sort of the people of the land.
15 And he carried away *Jē-
hoi′a-chĭn to [d]Băb′ȳ-lon, and the
king's mother, and the king's
[e]wives, and his officers, and the
mighty of the land, *those* carried
he into [a]captivity from [f]Jē-ru̧′sȧ-
lĕm to Băb′ȳ-lon.
16 And all the men of might,
*even* seven thousand, and [b]crafts-
men and [c]smiths a thousand, all
*that were* strong *and* apt[G] for war,
even them the king of [d]Băb′ȳ-
lon brought captive to Băb′ȳ-lon.[Q]
17 And the [g]king of [d]Băb′ȳ-lon
made Măt-ta-nī′ah his father's
brother king in his stead, and
changed his name to [h]Zĕd-e-
kī′ah.
18 ¶ [h]Zĕd-e-kī′ah *was* twenty
and one years old when he began
to reign, and he reigned eleven
years in [f]Jē-ru̧′sȧ-lĕm. And his
mother's name *was* [i]Hȧ-mū′tal,
the daughter of [i]Jĕr-e-mī′ah of
[j]Lĭb′nah.
19 And [k,h]he did *that which
was* evil in the sight of the
LORD, according to all that [l]Jē-
hoi′a-kĭm had done.
20 For through the [m,n]anger of
the LORD it came to pass in [f]Jē-
ru̧′sȧ-lĕm and [o]Jū′dah, until he
had cast them out from his presence, that [h]Zĕd-e-kī′ah rebelled
against the [g]king of [d]Băb′ȳ-lon.

## CHAPTER 25

*Jerusalem is besieged by Nebuchadnezzar. 4 Zedekiah is taken, his sons slain, and his eyes put out. 8 Nebuzar-adan destroys the city, carries away all the people, except the poor of the land, into captivity; 13 and takes away the treasures. 18 The nobles are slain at Riblah. 22 Gedaliah is set over the land. 25 He is slain, and the people flee into Egypt. 27 Evil-merodach advances Jehoiachin in his court.*

AND it came to pass in the
ninth year of his reign, in
the tenth [a]month, in the tenth
*day* of the month, *that* [b]Nĕb-u-
chad-nĕz′zar king of [c]Băb′ȳ-
lon came, he, and all his host,
against [d]Jē-ru̧′sȧ-lĕm, and pitched against it; and they built
[e]forts against it round about.
2 And the [d]city was [f]besieged
unto the eleventh year of king
+Zĕd-e-kī′ah.

v.8–518 BC See footnote, *Time*, Rev. 10:6.

**8**
v Jer. 26:22; 36:12, 25.

**10**
w *Siege*, Deut. 28:53.

**13**
x *Prophecies, fulfilled*, vs. 10–16; Dan. 9:24.
y *Temple, Solomon's*, 1 Kin. 6:17.
z *Palace*, 1 Kin. 21:1.

**14**
a *Captivity, of Judah*, Isa. 5:13.
b *Artisans, skillful*, 1 Chr. 29:5.
c *Smith*, Isa. 54:16.

**15**
d *Babylon*, Ezra 5:12.
e *Polygamy*, Deut. 17:17.
f *Jerusalem*, Judg. 19:10.

v.16–518 BC See footnote, *Time*, Rev. 10:6.

**17**
g *Nebuchadnezzar*, Dan. 2:1.
h *Zedekiah*, 2 Kin. 25:2.

**18**
i 2 Kin. 23:31; Jer. 52:1.
j *Libnah*, Josh. 10:29.

v.18–518 BC

**19**
k *Rulers, wicked*, Ex. 18:21.
l *Jehoiakim*, Jer. 26:1.

**20**
m *Anger of God*, 2 Kin. 13:3.
n *Anthropomorphisms*, Gen. 11:5.
o *Judah, kingdom of*, 2 Chr. 11:17.

v.1–509 BC See footnote, *Time*, Rev. 10:6.

**1**
a *Month*, Ex. 12:2.
b *Nebuchadnezzar*, Dan. 2:1.
c *Babylon, empire of*, Ezra 5:12.
d *Jerusalem*, Judg. 19:10.
e *Fortification*, Ezek. 17:17.

**2**
f *Siege*, Deut. 28:53.

**+ZEDEKIAH.** *Made king of Judah by Nebuchadnezzar*, 2 Kin. 24:17, 18; 1 Chr. 3:15; 2 Chr. 36:10; Jer. 37:1. *Throws off his allegiance to Nebuchadnezzar*, 2 Kin. 24:20; 2 Chr. 36:13; Jer. 52:3; Ezek. 17:12–21. *Forms an alliance with the king of Egypt*, Ezek. 17:11–18. *The rebellion denounced, by Jeremiah*, 2 Chr. 36:12; Jer. 21: 24:8–10; 27:12–22; 32:3–5; 34; 37:7–10, 17; 38:14–28; *by Ezekiel*, Ezek. 12:10–16; 17:12–21. *Imprisons Jeremiah on account of his denunciations*, Jer. 32: 2, 3; 37:15–21; 38:5–28. *Seeks the intercession of Jeremiah with God in his behalf*, Jer. 21:1–3; 37:3. *Wicked reign of*, 2 Kin. 24:19, 20; 2 Chr. 36:12, 13; Jer. 37:2; 38:5, 19, 24–26; 52:2. *Reigned eleven years*, 2 Kin. 24:18; 2 Chr. 36:11. *Nebuchadnezzar besieges Jerusalem, destroys the city and temple, takes him captive to Babylon, blinds his eyes, and slays his sons*, 2 Kin. 25:1–10; 2 Chr. 36:17–20; Jer. 1:3; 39:1–10; 51:59; 52:4–30.

3 And on the ninth *day* of the *fourth* [a]month the [g]famine prevailed in the city, and there was no bread for the people of the land.

4 And the [d]city was broken[G] up, and all the men of war *fled* by night by the way of the gate between two [h]walls, which *is* by the king's garden: (now the [i]Chăl′deeș *were* against the city round about:) and *the king* went the way toward the plain.

5 And the army of the [i]Chăl′deeș pursued after the +king, and overtook him in the plains of [j]Jĕr′ī-chō: and all his army were scattered from him.

6 So they took the +king, and brought him up to the [b]king of [c]Băb′ȳ-lon to [k]Rĭb′lah; and they gave judgment[G] upon him.

7 And they [l]slew the sons of +Zĕd-e-kī′ah before his eyes, and [m,n]put out the eyes of Zĕd-e-kī′ah, and bound him with [o]fetters of [p]brass, and carried him to [q]Băb′ȳ-lon.

8 ¶ And in the fifth [a]month, on the seventh *day* of the month, which *is* the nineteenth year of king [b]Nĕb-u-chad-nĕz′zar king of [c]Băb′ȳ-lon, came †Nĕb′u-zär-ā′dan, [r]captain of the guard, a servant of the king of Băb′ȳ-lon, unto Jĕ-ru̇′să-lĕm:

9 And he [s]burnt the [t,u]house of the LORD, and the king's [v]house, and all the houses of [d]Jĕ-ru̇′să-lĕm, and every great *man's* house burnt he with fire.

10 And all the army of the [i]Chăl′deeș, that *were with* the †captain of the guard, brake down the [h]walls of [d]Jĕ-ru̇′să-lĕm round about.

11 [w]Now the rest of the people *that were* left in the city, and the fugitives that fell away to the [b]king of [c]Băb′ȳ-lon, with the remnant of the multitude, did †Nĕb′u-zär-ā′dan the [r]captain of the guard [x]carry away.

12 But the †[r]captain of the guard left of the poor of the [y]land *to be* vinedressers and husbandmen[G].

13 And the [z]pillars of [a]brass[G] that *were* in the house of the LORD, and the bases, and the brasen[G] [b]sea that *was* in the [c]house of the LORD, did the [d]Chăl′deeș break in pieces, and carried the brass[G] of them to [e]Băb′ȳ-lon.

14 And the pots, and the [f]shovels, and the [g]snuffers, and the [h]spoons, and all the vessels of [a]brass wherewith they ministered, took they away.

15 And the [i]firepans, and the [j]bowls, *and* such things as *were* of [k]gold, *in* gold, and of [l]silver, *in* silver, the †[m]captain of the guard took away.

16 The two [n]pillars, one [b]sea, and the bases which Sŏl′o-mon had made for the [c]house of the LORD; the [a]brass[G] of all these vessels was without[G] weight.

17 The height of the one [n]pillar *was* eighteen [o]cubits[G], and the [p]chapiter[G] upon it *was* [a]brass[G]: and the height of the chapiter[G] three cubits[G]; and the wreathen[G] work, and [q]pomegranates upon the chapiters round about, all of brass[G]: and like unto these had the second pillar with wreathen[G] work.

18 ¶ And the †[m]captain of the guard took [r]Sĕr-a-ī′ah the chief [s]priest, and [t]Zĕph-a-nī′ah the second priest, and the three [u]keepers of the door:

19 And out of the city he took an officer that was set over the men of war, and five men of them that were in the king's presence, which were found in the city, and the principal [v]scribe

v.3–507 BC
See footnote, *Time*, Rev. 10:6.

3
g *Famine*. 2 Kin. 8:1.

4
h *Walls*, 1 Sam. 20:25.
i *Chaldea*, Isa. 23:13.

5
j Jer. 52:8.

6
k *Riblah*, Num. 34:11.

7
l *Captive, put to death*, 1 Sam. 30:3.
m *Cruelty, instances of*, Psa. 27:12.
n *Captive, cruelty to*, 1 Sam. 30:3.
o *Fetters*, Mark 5:4.
p *Brass*, Job 28:2.
q *Babylon, city of*, Ezra 5:12.

8
r *Captain*, Num. 31:48.

9
s *Arson, instances of*, 2 Sam. 14:30.
t *Temple, Solomon's, destroyed*, 1 Kin. 6:17.
u *Church, called house of the Lord*, 1 Kin. 9:3.
v *Palace*, 1 Kin. 21:1.

11
w *Prophecies, fulfilled*, Dan. 9:24.

v.11–507 BC
See footnote, *Time*, Rev. 10:6.

x *Captivity, of Judah*, Isa. 5:13.

12
y *Judah, kingdom of*, 2 Chr. 11:17.

13
z *Pillar*, Gen. 28:18.
a *Brass*, Job 28:2.
b *Laver*, Ex. 30:18.
c *Temple, Solomon's*, 1 Kin. 6:17.
d *Chaldea*, Isa. 23:13.
e *Babylon, city of*, Ezra 5:12.

14
f *Shovel*, Num. 4:14.
g *Snuffers*, 1 Kin. 7:50.
h *Spoons*, Num. 4:7.

15
i *Censer*, Lev. 16:12.
j *Bowl*, Ex. 25:29.
k *Gold*, Ezek. 7:19.
l *Silver*, 1 Chr. 28:14.
m *Captain*, Num. 31:48.

16
n *Pillar, of Solomon's temple*, Gen. 28.18.

17
o *Cubit*, Ex. 36:9.
p *Chapiter*, 1 Kin. 7:16.
q *Pomegranate*, Num. 13:23.

18
r Jer. 52:24-27.
s *High Priest*, Lev. 21:10.
t *Zephaniah*, Jer. 21:1.
u *Porters*, 2 Sam. 18:26.

19
v *Scribe*, 1 Kin. 4:3.

† **NEBUZAR-ADAN**, captain of the guard of king Nebuchadnezzar. *Commands the Assyrian army which besieges Jerusalem and carries the inhabitants captive to Babylon*, 2 Kin. 25:8-21; Jer. 39:9, 10; 43:6; 52:12-30. *Protects Jeremiah*, Jer. 39:11-14; 40:1-5.

v.19–507 BC
See footnote, *Time*, Rev. 10:6.

of the host, which ‡mustered the
people of the land, and threescore men of the people of the
land *that were* found in the
city:
20 And †Nĕb-u-zär-ā′dan
[m]captain of the guard took these,
and brought them to the [w]king
of [x]Băb′ȳ-lon to [y]Rĭb′lah:
21 And the [w]king of [x]Băb′ȳ-
lon smote them, and [z]slew them
at [y]Rĭb′lah in the land of [a]Hā′-
math. So [b]Jū′dah [c,d]was carried away out of their land.
22 ¶ And *as for* the people that
remained in the land of [b]Jū′dah,
whom [e]Nĕb-u-chad-nĕz′zar king
of [f]Băb′ȳ-lon had left, even over
them he made ‖Gĕd-a-lī′ah the
son of [g]Ā-hī′kam, the son of
[h]Shā′phan, ruler.
23 And when all the [i]captains
of the [j]armies, they and their
men, heard that the [e]king of
[f]Băb′ȳ-lon had made ‖Gĕd-a-lī′-
ah governor, there came to Gĕd-
a-lī′ah to [k]Mĭz′pah, even [l]Ĭsh′-
ma-el the son of [m]Nĕth-a-nī′ah,
and §Jō-hā′nan the son of [n]Că-
rē′ah, and [o]Sĕr-a-ī′ah the son
of [o]Tăn′hu-mĕth the Nē-tŏph′-
a-thīte, and [p]Jā-ăz-a-nī′ah the
son of a Mā-ăch′a-thīte, they
and their men.
24 And ‖Gĕd-a-lī′ah sware to
them, and to their men, and said
unto them, Fear not [1]to be the
servants of the [q]Chăl′deeș: dwell
in the land, and serve the [e]king
of [f]Băb′ȳ-lon; and it shall be
well with you.
25 But it came to pass in the
seventh [r]month, that [l]Ĭsh′ma-el
the son of [m]Nĕth-a-nī′ah, the son
of [s]Ē-lĭsh′a-mȧ of the seed royal,
came, and ten men with him,
and [t]smote [C] ‖Gĕd-a-lī′ah, that
he died, and the [u]Jews and the
[q]Chăl′deeș that were with him
at [k]Mĭz′pah.
26 And all the people, both
small and great, and the [i]cap-
tains of the [j]armies, arose, and
came to [v]Ē′ġȳpt: for they were
afraid of the [q]Chăl′deeș.
27 ¶ And it came to pass in
the seven and thirtieth year of
the [c]captivity of [w]Jē-hoi′a-chĭn
king of [b]Jū′dah, in the twelfth
[r]month, on the seven and twentieth *day* of the month, *that*
[x]Ē′vĭl-mē-rō′dach king of [f]Băb′-
ȳ-lon in the year that he began to
reign did lift [C] up the head of [y]Jē-
hoi′a-chĭn king of Jū′dah out of
prison;
28 And he [z]spake kindly to
him, and set his [a]throne above
the throne of the kings that *were*
with him in Băb′ȳ-lon;
29 And changed his prison garments: [b]and he did eat bread [C]
continually [C] before him all the
days of his life.
30 [b]And his allowance *was* a
continual [C] allowance given him of
the king, a daily rate for every
day, all the days of his life.

**20**
*w Nebuchadnezzar*, Dan. 2:1.
*x Babylon*, Ezra 5:12.
*y Riblah*, Num. 34:11.
**21**
*z Captive, put to death*, 1 Sam. 30:3.
*a Hamath*, 1 Chr. 18:3.
*b Judah, kingdom of*, 2 Chr. 11:17.
*c Captivity, of Judah*, Isa. 5:13.
*d Prophecies, fulfilled*, Dan. 9:24.
**22**
*e Nebuchadnezzar*, Dan. 2:1.
*f Babylon, empire of*, Ezra 5:12.
*g Ahikam*, 2 Kin. 22:12.
*h Shaphan*, 2 Chr. 34:8.
**23**
*i Captain*, Num. 31:48.
*j Armies*, Deut. 11:4.
*k Mizpah*, Josh. 18:26.
*l Ishmael*, Jer. 40:8.
*m* Jer. 40:8, 14, 15; 41:1, 2, 6–12.
*n* Or, *Kareah*, Jer. 40:8.
*o* Jer. 40:8.
*p* Or, *Jezaniah*, Jer. 40:8; 42:1.
**24**
*q Chaldeans*, Dan. 1:4.
1 R. V because of

v.24–507 BC
See footnote, *Time*, Rev. 10:6.

**25**
*r Month*, Ex. 12:2.
*s* Jer. 41:1.
*t Homicide, felonious*, Deut. 5:17.
*u Jews*, Neh. 4:2.
**26**
*v Egypt*, Gen. 41:8.
**27**
*w Jehoiachin*, 2 Kin. 24:6.
*x* Jer. 52:31–34.
*y Captive, kindness to*, 1 Sam. 30:3.
v.27–482 BC
**28**
*z Kindness, instances of*, Acts 28:2.
*a Throne*, 1 Kin. 2:19.
**29**
*b Hospitality, instances of*, Rom. 12:13.

‡ **MUSTER.** *Of troops*, 2 Sam. 20:4; 1 Kin. 20:26; 2 Kin. 25:19. *Of Israel's military forces, at Sinai*, Num. 1:1–50; *after the plague*, Num. 26; *by Saul*, 1 Sam. 11:8; *by David*, 2 Sam. 18:1, 2; 24:1–9; 1 Chr. 21:5, 6; *by Ahab*, 1 Kin. 20:15; *by Amaziah*, 2 Chr. 25:5. *For absentees*, 1 Sam. 14:17.
See footnote, ARMIES, Deut. 11:4.
**Figurative**, Isa. 13:4.

‖ **GEDALIAH.** *Governor of Judea, appointed by Nebuchadnezzar after carrying the Jews into captivity*, 2 Kin. 25:22–24. *Jeremiah committed to the care of*, Jer. 39:14; 40:5, 6. *Warned of the conspiracy of Ishmael by Johanan, and the captains of his army*, Jer. 40:13–16. *Slain by Ishmael*, 2 Kin. 25:25, 26; Jer. 41:1–10.

§ **JOHANAN.** *A Jewish captain*, 2 Kin. 25:22–24. *Warns Gedaliah against Ishmael*, Jer. 40:13–16. *Ishmael defeated by*, Jer. 41:11–15. *Besought Jeremiah to make intercession in behalf of the remnant of the Jews who were left in Judea*, Jer. 42:2, 3. *Disobeyed Jeremiah and took him to Egypt*, Jer. 43:1–7.

THE FIRST BOOK OF THE

# CHRONICLES

## CHAPTER 1

*Adam's line to Noah. 5 Sons of Japheth. 8 Sons of Ham. 17 Sons of Shem. 24 Shem's line to Abraham. 29 Ishmael's sons. 32 Sons of Keturah. 34 Posterity of Abraham by Esau. 43 Kings of Edom. 51 Dukes of Edom.*

[a, b] ADĂM,[Q] [c]Shĕth, [d]Ē'nosh,
2 [e]Kē'nan, [f]Mă-hā'la-
lē-el, [g]Jē'red,
3 [h]Hē'nŏch, [i]Mĕ-thu'se-lah,
[j]Lā'mech,
4 [k]Nō'ah, [l]Shĕm, [m]Hăm, and
[n]Jā'pheth.[Q]
5 ¶ [a]The sons of [n]Jā'pheth;
[o]Gō'mĕr, and *Mā'gŏg, and
[p]Măd'a-ī, and [q]Jā'văn, and
[p]Tu'bal, and [p]Mē'shech, and
[p]Tī'ras.
6 [a]And the sons of [o]Gō'mĕr;
[r]Ăsh'che-năz, and [s]Rī'phăth, and
[t]Tō-găr'mah.
7 [a]And the sons of [q]Jā'văn;
[u]Ē-lī'shah, and [v]Tăr'shish, [w]Kĭt'-
tim, and [v]Dō'da-nĭm.
8 ¶ The sons of [x]Hăm; [y]Cŭsh,
and [z]Mĭz'ra-ĭm, [a]Pŭt, and [b]Cā'-
năan.
9 And the sons of [c]Cŭsh; [d]Sē'-
bȧ, and [d]Hăv'i-lah, and [d]Săb'tȧ,
and [d]Rā'a-mah, and [d]Săb'te-
chȧ. And the sons of Rā'a-mah;
[d]Shē'bȧ, and [d]Dē'dan.
10 And [c]Cŭsh begat [e]Nĭm'rŏd:
he began to be mighty upon the
earth.
11 And [f]Mĭz'ra-ĭm begat [g]Lu'-
dim, and [g]Ăn'a-mĭm, and [g]Lē'-
hā-bĭm, and [g]Năph'tu-hĭm.
12 And [h]Păth-ru'sim, and
[h]Căs'lu-hĭm, (of whom came
the [i]Phĭ-lĭs'tĭnes,) and [j]Căph'-
thō-rĭm.
13 And [b]Cā'năan begat [k]Zī'-
dŏn his firstborn, and [l]Hĕth,
14 The [m]Jĕb'u-site also, and
the [n]Ăm'ôr-īte, and the [o]Gĭr'ga-
shīte,
15 And the [p]Hī'vīte, and the
[q]Ărk'īte, and the [q]Sĭn'īte,
16 And the [r]Ăr'vad-īte, and
the [s]Zĕm'a-rīte, and the [t]Hā'-
math-īte.
17 ¶ The sons of [u]Shĕm;
Ē'lăm, and [v]Ăs'shur, and [w]Ăr-
phăx'ad, and [x]Lŭd, and [x]Ā'ram,
and [y]Ŭz, and [y]Hŭl, and [y]Gē'-
thĕr, and Mē'shech.
18 And [w]Ăr-phăx'ad begat
[z]Shē'lah, and Shē'lah begat
[a]Ē'bĕr.
19 And unto [a]Ē'bĕr were born
two sons: the name of the one
*was* [b]Pē'lĕg; because in his days
the [c]earth was divided: and his
brother's name *was* [d]Jŏk'tan.
20 And [d]Jŏk'tan begat [e]Ăl-
mō'dăd, and [e]Shē'leph, and [e]Hā-
zar-mā'veth, and [e]Jē'răh,
21 [f]Hā-dō'ram also, and [f]Ū'zal,
and [f]Dĭk'lah,
22 And Ē'bal, and [g]Ā-bĭm'a-el,
and [g]Shē'bȧ,
23 And [h]Ō'phīr, and [h]Hăv'i-
lah, and [h]Jō'băb. All these *were*
the sons of [Q][d]Jŏk'tan.
24 ¶ [i]Shĕm, [j]Ăr-phăx'ad, [k]Shē'-
lah,
25 [a]Ē'bĕr, [b]Pē'lĕg, [l]Rē'u,
26 [m]Sē'rug, [n]Nā'hôr, [o]Tē'rah,
27 [p]Ā'brăm; the same *is* Ā'bră-
hăm.[Q]
28 The sons of [p]Ā'bră-hăm;
[q]Ī'saac, and [r]Ĭsh'ma-el.[Q]
29 ¶ These *are* their generations: The firstborn of [r]Ĭsh'-
ma-el, [s]Nē-bā'ioth; then [t]Kē'dăr,
and [t]Ăd'bē-el, and [t]Mĭb'sam,
30 [u]Mĭsh'mȧ, and [v]Dū'mah,
[u]Măs'sȧ, [w]Hā'dăd, and [u]Tē'mȧ,

**1**
a *Genealogy*, vs. 1–42; 1 Chr. 5:1.
b *Adam*, Gen. 2:19.
c Or, *Seth*, Gen. 4:25.
d Or, *Enos*, Gen. 4:26; 5:6–11; Luke 3:38.
**2**
e Or, *Cainan*, Gen. 5:9.
f *Mahalaleel*, Gen. 5:12.
g Or, *Jared*, Gen. 5:15.
**3**
h Or, *Enoch*, Gen. 5:18.
i Gen. 5:21–27.
j *Lamech*, Gen. 5:25.
**4**
k *Noah*, Gen. 5:29.
l *Shem*, Gen. 6:10.
m *Ham*, Gen. 5:32.
n *Japheth*, Gen. 7:13.
**5**
o Gen. 10:2, 3.
p Gen. 10:2.
q Gen. 10:2, 4.
**6**
r Or, *Ashkenaz*, Gen. 10:3.
s Gen. 10:3.
t Gen. 10:3; Ezek. 27:14; 38:6.
**7**
u *Elishah*, Gen. 10:4.
v Gen. 10:4.
w Or, *Chittim*, Dan. 11:30.
**8**
x *Ham*, Gen. 5:32.
y Gen. 10:6–8.
z Gen. 10:6, 13.

a Or, *Phut*, Gen. 10:6.
b *Canaan*, Gen. 9:18.
**9**
c Gen. 10:6–8.
d Gen. 10:7.
**10**
e Gen. 10:8, 9.
**11**
f Gen. 10:6, 13.
g Gen. 10:13.
**12**
h Gen. 10:14.
i *Philistines*, Gen. 26:14.
j Or, *Caphtorim*, Deut. 2:23.
**13**
k Or, *Sidon*, Gen. 10:15.
l Gen. 10:15.
**14**
m *Jebusites*, Deut. 7:1.

n *Amorites*, Gen. 14:13.
o *Girgashites*, Neh. 9:8.
**15**
p *Hivites*, Gen. 10:17.
q Gen. 10:17.
**16**
r *Arvadites*, Gen. 10:18.
s Gen. 10:18.
t *Hamath*, 1 Chr. 18:3.
**17**
u *Shem*, Gen. 6:10
v Gen. 10:11, 22.
w *Arphaxad*, Gen. 10:22.
x Gen. 10:22.
y Gen. 10:23.
**18**
z Or, *Salah*, Gen. 10:24.

a *Eber*, Gen. 10:21.
**19**
b *Peleg*, Gen. 10:25.
c *Earth, early divisions of*, Prov. 8:23.
d Gen. 10:25, 26, 29.
**20**
e Gen. 10:26.
**21**
f Gen. 10:27.
**22**
g Gen. 10:28.
**23**
h Gen. 10:29.
**24**
i *Shem*, Gen. 6:10
j *Arphaxad*, Gen. 10:22.
k Or, *Salah*, Gen. 10:24.
**25**
l *Reu*, Gen. 11:18.
**26**
m *Serug*, Gen. 11:20.
n *Nahor*, Gen. 11:22.
o *Terah*, Gen. 11:24.
**27**
p *Abraham*, Gen. 17:5.
**28**
q *Isaac*, Gen. 21:3.
r *Ishmael*, Gen. 16:11.
**29**
s Or, *Nebajoth*, Gen. 25:13.
t Gen. 25:13.
**30**
u Gen. 25:14.
v *Dumah*, Gen. 25:14.
w Or, *Hadar*, Gen 25:15.

* **MAGOG.** *Son of Japheth*, Gen. 10:2; 1 Chr. 1:5. *Prophecy concerning*, Ezek. 38:2; 39:6. *Symbolical of the enemies of God*, Rev. 20:8.

**31**
x Gen. 25:15.
**32**
y Gen. 25:1–4.
z *Concubinage*, 2 Sam. 21:11.

a Gen. 25:2.
b Gen. 25:2, 3.
c Gen. 25:2, 4.
d Gen. 25:3.
**33**
e *Ephah*, Gen. 25:4.
f Gen. 25:4.
g Or, *Hanoch*, Gen. 25:4.
h Gen. 25:1–4.
**34**
i *Abraham*, Gen. 17:5.
j *Isaac*, Gen. 21:3.
k *Esau*, Gen. 25:25.
l *Jacob*, Gen. 27:11.
**35**
m Gen. 36:4, 10–16.
n Gen. 36:4, 10, 13, 17.
o Gen. 36:5, 14, 18.
**36**
p Gen. 36:11, 15, 42.
q Gen. 36:11, 15.
r Or, *Zepho*, Gen. 36:11, 15.
s Gen. 36:11, 16.
t *Amalek*, Gen. 36:12.
**37**
u Gen. 36:13, 17.
**38**
v Gen. 36:20, 21.
w Gen. 36:20, 23, 29.
x Gen. 36:20, 24, 29.
y Gen. 36:21, 30.
z Gen. 36:21, 27, 30.

**39**
a Gen. 36:22, 30.
b Or, *Hemam*, Gen. 36:22.
c Gen. 36:22.
**40**
d Gen. 36:20, 23, 29.
e Or, *Alvan*, Gen. 36:23.
f Gen. 36:23.
g Or, *Shepho*, Gen. 36:23.
h Gen. 36: 20, 24, 29.
i Or, *Ajah*, Gen. 36:24.
**41**
j Gen. 36:25.
k Gen. 36:26.

31 [x]Jē′tŭr, [x]Nā′phish, and [x]Kĕd′e-mah. These are the sons of [r]Ĭsh′ma-el.

32 ¶ Now the sons of [y]Kĕ-tū′rah, [p]Ā′brā-hăm's [z]concubine: she bare [a]Zĭm′ran, and [b]Jŏk′shan, and [a]Mē′dan, and [c]Mĭd′ĭ-an, and [a]Ĭsh′băk, and [a]Shu̇′ah. And the sons of Jŏk′shan; [d]Shē′bȧ, and [d]Dē′dan.

33 And the sons of [c]Mĭd′ĭ-an; [e]Ē′phah, and [f]Ē′phĕr, and [g]Hē′nŏch, and [f]Ȧ-bī′dȧ, and [f]Ĕl′da-ah. All these *are* the sons of [h]Kĕ-tū′rah.

34 And [i]Ā′brā-hăm begat [j]Ī′ṣaac. The sons of Ī′ṣaac; [k]Ē′ṣau and [l]Ĭṣ′ra-el.

35 ¶ The sons of [k]Ē′ṣau; [m]Ĕl′i-phăz, [n]Reu̇′el, and [o]Jē′ŭsh, and [o]Jȧ-ā′lam, and [o]Kō′rah.

36 The sons of [m]Ĕl′i-phăz; [p]Tē′man, and [q]Ō′mar, [r]Zē′phī, and [s]Gā′tam, [q]Kē′năz, and Tĭm′nȧ, and [t]Ăm′a-lĕk.

37 The sons of [n]Reu̇′el; [u]Nā′hăth, [u]Zē′rah, [u]Shăm′mah, and [u]Mĭz′zah.

38 And the sons of [v]Sē′ĭr; Lō′tan, and [w]Shō′bal, and [x]Zĭb′e-on, and [x]Ā′nah, and [y]Dī′shon, and [z]Ē′zar, and [y]Dī′shan.

39 And the sons of Lō′tan; [a]Hō′rī, and [b]Hō′mam: and [c]Tĭm′nȧ *was* Lō′tan's sister.

40 The sons of [d]Shō′bal; [e]Ȧ-lī′an, and [f]Măn′a-hăth, and [f]Ē′bal, [g]Shē′phī, and [f]Ō′nam. And the sons of [h]Zĭb′e-on; [i]Ȧ-ī′ah, and Ā′nah.

41 The sons of Ā′nah; [j]Dī′shon. And the sons of Dī′shon; Ăm′răm, and [k]Ĕsh′ban, and [k]Ĭth′ran, and [k]Chē′ran.

42 The sons of [l]Ē′zĕr; [m]Bĭl′han, and [n]Zā′van, *and* [o]Jā′kan. The sons of Dī′shan; [p]Ūz, and [p]Ā′răn.

43 ¶ Now these *are* the [q]kings that reigned in the land of [r]Ē′dom before *any* king reigned over the children of Ĭṣ′ra-el; [s]Bē′lȧ the son of [t]Bē′or: and the name of his city *was* [t]Dĭn′ha-bah.

44 And when [s]Bē′lȧ was dead [u]Jō′băb the son of [v]Zē′rah of [w]Bŏz′rah reigned in his stead.

45 And when [u]Jō′băb was dead, [x]Hū′sham of the land of the Tē′man-ītes reigned in his stead.

46 And when [x]Hū′sham was dead, [y]Hā′dăd the son of Bē′dăd, which smote Mĭd′ĭ-an in the field of Mō′ab, reigned in his stead: and the name of his city *was* [y]Ā′vĭth.

47 And when [y]Hā′dăd was dead, [z]Săm′lah of [a]Măs′re-kah reigned in his stead.

48 And when Săm′lah was dead, [b]Shā′ul of [c]Rē-hō′both by the river reigned in his stead.

49 And when [b]Shā′ul was dead, [d]Bā′al–hā′nan the son of [e]Ăch′bôr reigned in his stead.

50 And when [d]Bā′al–hā′nan was dead, [f]Hā′dăd reigned in his stead: and the name of his city *was* [g]Pā′ī; and his wife's name *was* [e]Mĕ-hĕt′a-bĕl, the daughter of [e]Mā′tred, the daughter of [e]Mĕz′a-hăb.

51 [f]Hā′dăd died also. And the [h]dukes of [i]Ē′dom were; duke [j]Tĭm′nah, duke [k]Ȧ-lī′ah, duke [j]Jē′theth,

52 Duke [l]Ȧ-hŏl-i-bā′mah, duke [l]Ē′lah, duke [l]Pī′non,

53 Duke [m]Kē′năz, duke [n]Tē′man, duke [m]Mĭb′zar,

54 Duke [o]Măg′dĭ-el, duke [o]Ī′ram. These *are* the [h]dukes of [i]Ē′dom.

## CHAPTER 2

*The sons of Israel. 3 The posterity of Judah by Tamar. 13 The children of Jesse. 18 The posterity of Caleb the son of Hezron. 21 Hezron's posterity by the daughter of Machir. 25 Jerahmeel's posterity. 34 Sheshan's posterity. 42 Another branch of Caleb's posterity. 50 The posterity of Caleb the son of Hur.*

[a]THESE *are* the sons of [b]Ĭṣ′ra-el; [c]Reu̇′ben, [d]Sĭm′e-on, [e]Lē′vī, and [f]Jū′dah, [g]Ĭs′sa-char, and [h]Zĕb′u-lŭn,

2 [i]Dăn, [j]Jō′ṣeph, and [k]Bĕn′ja-

**42** l Gen. 36:21, 27, 30. m Gen. 36:27. n Or, *Zaavan*, Gen. 36:27. o Or, *Akan*, Gen. 36:27. p Gen. 36:28. **43** q *King*, 2 Kin. 3:10. r *Edomites*, vs. 43–50; 2 Kin. 8:21.

s Gen. 36:32, 33.
t Gen. 36:32.
**44**
u Gen. 36:33, 34.
v Gen. 36:33.
w *Bozrah*, Gen. 36:33.
**45**
x Gen. 36:34, 35.
**46**
y Gen. 36:35.
**47**
z Gen. 36:36, 37.

a Gen. 36:36.
**48**
b Or, *Saul*, Gen. 36:37, 38.
c Gen. 36:37.
**49**
d Gen. 36:38, 39.
e Gen. 36:39.
**50**
f Or, *Hadar*, Gen. 36:39.
g Or, *Pau*, Gen. 36:39.
**51**
h *Duke*, vs. 51–54; Gen. 36:15.
i *Edomites*, 2 Kin. 8:21.
j Gen. 36:40.
k Or, *Alvah*, Gen. 36:40.
**52**
l Gen. 36:41.
**53**
m Gen. 36:42.
n Gen. 36:11, 15, 42.
**54**
o Gen. 36:43.

**1**
a *Genealogy*, vs. 1–55; 1 Chr. 5:1.
b Or, *Jacob*, Gen. 27:11.
c *Reuben*, Gen. 35:22.
d *Simeon*, Gen. 29:33.
e *Levi*, Gen. 29:34.
f *Judah*, Gen. 37:26.
g *Issachar*, Gen. 30:18.
h *Zebulun*, Gen. 30:20.
**2**
i *Dan*, Gen. 30:6.
j *Joseph*, Gen. 33:2.
k *Benjamin*, Gen. 35:18.

mĭn, [l]Năph′ta-lī, [m]Găd, and [n]Ăsh′ēr.

3 ¶ The sons of [i]Jū′dah; [o]Ēr, and [p]Ō′nan, and [q]Shē′lah: *which* three were born unto him of [1]the daughter of [r]Shụ′ȧ the [s]Cā′năan-īt-ess. And Ēr, the [t]firstborn of Jū′dah, was evil in the sight of the LORD; and he [u]slew him.

4 [v]And [w]Tā′mar his daughter in law bare him [x]Phā′rĕz and [y]Zē′rah. All the sons of [i]Jū′dah *were* five.

5 The sons of [x]Phā′rĕz; *Hĕz′rŏn, and [z]Hā′mŭl.

6 And the sons of [y]Zē′rah; Zĭm′rī, and Ē′than, and [a]Hē′man, and [a]Căl′cŏl, and [b]Dā′rȧ: five of them in all.

7 And [c]the sons of [d]Cär′mī; [e]Ā′chär, the troubler of Ĭṣ′ra-el, who transgressed in the [2]thing [f]accursed.

8 And the sons of Ē′than; Ăz-a-rī′ah.

9 The sons also of *Hĕz′rŏn, that were born unto him; Jē-räh′me-el, and [g]Răm, and [h]Chē-lū′bāi.

10 And [g]Răm begat [i]Ăm-mĭn′-a-dăb; and Ăm-mĭn′a-dăb begat [j]Näh′shŏn, prince of the children of [k]Jū′dah;

11 And [j]Näh′shŏn begat [l]Săl′mȧ, and Săl′mȧ begat [m]Bō′ăz,

12 And [m]Bō′ăz begat [n]Ō′bed, and Ō′bed begat [o]Jĕs′se,

13 And [o]Jĕs′se begat his [p]firstborn [q]Ē-lī′ab, and [r]Ă-bĭn′a-dăb the second, and [s]Shĭm′mȧ the third,

14 Nē-thăn′e-el the fourth, Răd′da-ī the fifth,

15 Ō′zem the sixth, [t]Dā′vid the seventh:

16 Whose sisters *were* †Zĕr-u-ī′-ah, and [u]Ăb′ĭ-gail. And the sons of Zĕr-ụ-ī′ah; [v]Ă-bĭsh′a-ī, and [w]Jō′ăb, and [x]Ā′sa-hĕl, three.

17 And [u]Ăb′ĭ-gail bare [y]Ăm′-a-sȧ: and the father of Ăm′a-sȧ *was* [z]Jē′thēr the Ĭsh′me-el-īte.

18 ¶ [a]And [b]Cā′leb the son of *Hĕz′rŏn begat *children* of Ȧ-zū′bah *his* wife, and of Jē′rĭ-ŏth: her sons *are* these; Jē′shēr, and Shō′băb, and Är′dŏn.

19 And when Ȧ-zū′bah was dead, [b]Cā′leb took unto him [c]Ĕph′răth, which bare him [d]Hûr.

20 And [d]Hûr begat [e]Ū′rī, and Ū′rī begat [f]Bē-zăl′e-el.

21 And afterward *Hĕz′rŏn went in to the daughter of [g]Mā′chĭr the father of [h]Gĭl′-e-ăd, whom he married when he *was* threescore years old; and she bare him Sē′gụb.

22 And Sē′gub begat [i]Jā′ĭr, who had three and twenty cities in the land of [j]Gĭl′e-ăd.

23 And [3]he took [k]Gē′shŭr, and Ā′ram, with the towns of [i]Jā′ĭr, from them, with [l]Kē′năṭh, and the towns thereof, *even* threescore cities. All these [4]*belonged to* the sons of [g]Mā′chĭr the father of [h]Gĭl′e-ăd.

24 And after that *Hĕz′rŏn was dead in Cā′leb–ĕph′ra-tah, then Ȧ-bī′ah Hĕz′rŏn's wife bare him [m]Ăsh′ŭr the father of [m]Tĕkō′ȧ.

25 ¶ [a]And the sons of Jē-räh′-me-el the firstborn of *Hĕz′rŏn were, Răm the firstborn, and Bū′nah, and Ō′ren, and Ō′zem, *and* Ȧ-hī′jah.

26 Jē-räh′me-el had also [n]another wife, whose name *was* Ăt′-a-rah; she *was* the mother of Ō′nam.

27 And the sons of Răm the firstborn of Jē-räh′me-el were, Mā′ăz, and Jā′min, and Ē′kēr.

28 And the sons of Ō′nam were, Shăm′ma-ī, and Jā′dȧ. And the sons of Shăm′ma-ī; Nā′dăb and Ăb′i-shụr.

29 And the name of the wife

*l* *Naphtali*, Gen. 30:8.
*m* *Gad*, Gen. 30:11.
*n* *Asher*, Gen. 30:13.

**3**
*o* *Er*, Gen. 38:3.
*p* *Onan*, Gen. 38:8.
*q* *Shelah*, Gen. 38:5.
*r* Gen. 38:2, 12.
*s* *Canaanites*, Ex. 23:28.
*t* *Firstborn*, Zech. 12:10.
*u* *Sin, punishment*, Rom. 5:12.
1 R. V. Bath-shua

**4**
*v* *Incest*, Lev. 18:6.
*w* *Tamar*, Gen. 38:6.
*x* *Pharez*, Gen. 38:29.
*y* Or, *Zarah*, Gen. 38:30.

**5**
*z* Gen. 46:12; Num. 26:21.

**6**
*a* 1 Kin. 4:31.
*b* Or, *Darda*, 1 Kin. 4:31.

**7**
*c* *Genealogy*, vs. 7–18; 1 Chr. 5:1.
*d* Josh. 7:1, 18.
*e* Or, *Achan*, Josh. 7:1.
*f* *Accursed*, Deut. 21:23.
2 R. V. devoted thing.

**9**
*g* *Ram*, Ruth 4:19.
*h* Or, *Caleb*, vs. 18, 19, 42, 46–49; or, *Carmi*, 1 Chr. 4:1.

**10**
*i* *Amminadab*, Num. 2:3.
*j* *Nahshon*, Num. 7:12.
*k* *Judah, tribe of*, Num. 10:14.

**11**
*l* *Salma*, Ruth 4:20.
*m* *Boaz*, Ruth 2:1.

**12**
*n* *Obed*, Ruth 4:17.
*o* *Jesse*, Ruth 4:17.

**13**
*p* *Firstborn*, Zech. 12:10.
*q* *Eliab*, 1 Sam. 16:6.
*r* 1 Sam. 16:8; 17:13.
*s* Or, *Shammah*, 1 Sam. 16.9.

**15** *t* *David*, 1 Sam. 16:13. **16** *u* 2 Sam. 17:25. *v* *Abishai*, 2 Sam. 3:30. *w* *Joab*, 2 Sam. 20:23. *x* *Asahel*, 2 Sam. 2:18.

**17**
*y* *Amasa*, 2 Sam. 17:25.
*z* 1 Kin. 2:5, 32; or, *Ithra*, 2 Sam. 17:25.

**18**
*a* *Genealogy*, vs. 18–51; 1 Chr. 5:1.
*b* Or, *Chelubai*, v. 9; or, *Carmi*, 1 Chr. 4:1.

**19**
*c* Or, *Ephratah*, 1 Chr. 4:4.
*d* *Hur*, Ex. 31:2.

**20**
*e* *Uri*, Ex. 35:30.
*f* *Bezaleel*, Ex. 31:2.

**21**
*g* *Machir*, Gen. 50:23.
*h* *Gilead*, Num. 26:29.

**22**
*i* *Jair*, Josh. 13:30.
*j* *Gilead*, Deut. 3:13.

**23**
*k* *Geshur*, 2 Sam. 3:3.
*l* Num. 32:42.
3 R.V. Geshur and Aram took the towns
4 R. V. were the sons

**24**
*m* 1 Chr. 4:5.

**26**
*n* *Polygamy*, Deut. 17:17.

* **HEZRON.** *Son of Pharez*, Gen. 46:12; Ruth 4:18; Num. 26:6, 21; 1 Chr. 2:5, 9, 18, 21, 24. *Ancestor of Jesus*, Matt. 1:3; Luke 3:33.

† **ZERUIAH.** *Sister of David*, 1 Chr. 2:16. *Mother of three of David's great soldiers*, 1 Chr. 2:16; 11:39; 18:15; 26:28; 27:24; 2 Sam. 2:18; 3:39; 16:9–11; 17:25.

of Ăb′i-shụr *was* Ăb-i-hā′il, and
she bare him Äh′băn, and Mō′lid.
30 And the sons of Nā′dăb;
Sē′lĕd, and Ăp′pa-ĭm: but Sē′lĕd
died without children.
31 And the sons of Ăp′pa-ĭm;
Ī′shī. And the sons of Ī′shī;
Shē′shan. And the children of
Shē′shan; Äh′lāi.
32 And the sons of Jā′dȧ the
brother of Shăm′ma-ī; Jē′thēr,
and Jŏn′a-than: and Jē′thēr
died without children.
33 And the sons of Jŏn′a-than;
Pē′leth, and Zā′zȧ. These were
the sons of Jė-räh′me-el.
34 ¶ Now Shē′shan had no
sons, but daughters. And Shē′-
shan had a [o]servant, an Ė-ġy̆p′-
tian, whose name *was* Jär′hȧ.
35 And Shē′shan gave his
daughter to Jär′hȧ his servant to
wife; and she bare him Ăt′tāi.
36 And Ăt′tāi begat Nā′than,
and Nā′than begat Zā′băd,
37 And Zā′băd begat Ĕph′lăl,
and Ĕph′lăl begat Ō′bed,
38 And Ō′bed begat Jē′hū, and
Jē′hū begat Ăz-a-rī′ah,
39 And Ăz-a-rī′ah begat Hē′-
lez, and Hē′lez begat Ė-lē′a-sah,
40 And Ė-lē′a-sah begat Sĭ-
săm′a-ī, and Sĭ-săm′a-ī begat
Shăl′lum,
41 And Shăl′lum begat Jĕk-a-
mī′ah, and Jĕk-a-mī′ah begat
Ė-lĭsh′a-mȧ.
42 ¶ [a]Now the sons of [b]Cā′leb
the brother of Jė-räh′me-el *were,*
Mē′shȧ his firstborn, which *was*
the father of Zīph; and the sons
of Mā-rē′shah the father of Hē′-
bron.
43 And the sons of Hē′bron;
Kō′rah, and Tăp′pụ-ah, and
Rē′kem, and Shē′mȧ.
44 And Shē′mȧ begat Rā′hăm,
the father of Jôr′ko-ăm: and
Rē′kem begat Shăm′ma-ī.
45 And the son of Shăm′ma-ī
*was* Mā′on: and Mā′on *was* the
father of [p]Bĕth′–zûr.

46 And Ē′phah, [b]Cā′leb′s [q]con-
cubine, bare Hā′ran, and Mō′zȧ,
and Gā′zĕz: and Hā′ran begat
Gā′zĕz.
47 And the sons of Jäh′da-ī;
Rē′ḡĕm, and Jō′tham, and Ḡē′-
shăm, and Pē′let, and Ē′phah,
and Shā′ăph.
48 Mā′a-chah, [b]Cā′leb′s [q]con-
cubine, bare Shē′bēr, and Tĭr′-
ha-nah.
49 She bare also Shā′ăph the
father of Măd-măn′nah, Shē′vȧ
the father of Măch′be-nah, and
the father of Ḡĭb′e-ȧ: and the
daughter of [b]Cā′leb *was* [r]Ăch′sȧ.
50 ¶ These were the sons of
Cā′leb the son of [s]Hûr, the firstborn of [s]Ĕph′ra-tah; Shō′bal the
father of [t]Kĭr′jath–jē′a-rĭm,
51 Săl′mȧ the father of Bĕth′–
lĕ-hĕm, Hā′reph the father of
[u]Bĕth–gā′dēr.
52 And Shō′bal the father
of [t]Kĭr′jath–jē′a-rĭm had sons;
[v]Hăr′o-eh, *and* half of the Mȧ-
nā′heth-ītes.
53 And the families of [t]Kĭr′-
jath–jē′a-rĭm; the [w]Ĭth′rītes, and
the Pū′hītes, and the Shụ′math-
ītes, and the Mĭsh′ra-ītes; of
them came the Zā′re-ath-ītes,
and the Ĕsh′ta-ụl-ītes.
54 The sons of Săl′mȧ; Bĕth′–
lĕ-hĕm, and the Nė-tŏph′a-
thītes, [4]Ăt′a-rŏth, the house of
[x]Jō′ăb, and half of the Mȧ-nā′-
heth-ītes, the Zō′rītes.
55 And the families of the
scribes which dwelt at Jā′bĕz;
the Tī′rath-ītes, the Shĭm′e-ath-
ītes, *and* Sū′chath-ītes. These
*are* the [y]Kĕn′ītes that came of
Hē′math, the father of the
[z]house of [a]Rē′chăb.

## CHAPTER 3

*The sons of David. 10 The royal line to Zedekiah. 17 The posterity of Jeconiah.*

NOW [a]these were the sons of
[b]Dā′vid, which were born
unto him in [c]Hē′bron; the firstborn [d]Ăm′nŏn, of [e]Ă-hĭn′o-ăm

34
*o* *Servant,* Jer. 2:14.

45
*p* Neh. 3:16.

46
*q* *Concubinage,* 2 Sam. 21:11.

49
*r* Or, *Achsah,* Josh. 15:16.

50
*s* 1 Chr. 4:4.
*t* *Kirjath-jearim,* Josh. 15:9.

51
*u* See footnote, *Beth-gader,* p. 363.

52
*v* Or, *Reaiah,* 1 Chr. 4:2.

53
*w* 1 Chr. 11:40; 2 Sam. 23:38.

54
*x* *Joab,* 2 Sam. 20:23.
4 R. V. Atroth-beth-Joab,

55
*y* *Kenites,* 1 Sam. 15:6.
*z* *Rechabites,* Jer. 35:2.
*a* *Rechab,* 2 Kin. 10:15.

1
*a* *Genealogy,* vs. 1–24; 1 Chr. 5:1.
*b* *David,* 1 Sam. 16:13.
*c* *Hebron,* Gen. 23:2.
*d* 2 Sam. 3:2.
*e* *Ahinoam,* 1 Sam. 25:43.

the Jĕz′re-el-īt-ess; the second
[f]Dăn′iel, of [g]Ăb′ĭ-gail the Cär′-
mel-īt-ess:
2 The third, [h]Ăb′sa-lŏm the son
of [i]Mā′a-chah the daughter of
[i]Tăl′māi king of [j]Gē′shŭr: the
fourth, [k]Ăd-o-nī′jah the son of
[l]Hăg′gĭth:
3 The fifth, [m]Shĕph-a-tī′ah of
[m]Ăb′ĭ-tăl: the sixth, [n]Ĭth′re-ăm
by [n]Ĕg′lah his wife.
4 *These* six were born unto
him in [c]Hē′bron; and there he
reigned seven years and six
months: and in [o]Jė-ru̍′să-lĕm he
reigned thirty and three years.
5 And these were born unto
him in [o]Jė-ru̍′să-lĕm; [p]Shĭm′e-ȧ,
and [q]Shō′băb, and [q]Nā′than,
and [r]Sŏl′o-mon, four, of [s]Băth′-
shu̍-ȧ the daughter of [t]Ăm′-
mĭ-el:
6 [u]Ĭb′här also, and [v]Ė-lĭsh′a-
mȧ, and [w]Ė-lĭph′e-lĕt,
7 And [x]Nō′gah, and [y]Nē′pheg,
and [y]Jȧ-phī′ȧ,
8 And [z]Ė-lĭsh′a-mȧ, and [a]Ė-lī′-
a-dȧ, and [b]Ė-lĭph′e-lĕt, nine.
9 *These were* all the sons of
[c]Dā′vid, beside the sons of the
concubines, and [d]Tā′mar their
sister.
10 ¶ [Q] And [e]Sŏl′o-mon's son
*was* [f]Rē-ho-bō′am, [g]Ȧ-bī′ȧ his
son, [h]Ā′sȧ his son, [i]Jė-hŏsh′a-
phăt his son,
11 [j]Jō′ram his son, [k]Ā-ha-zī′ah
his son, [l]Jō′ăsh his son,
12 [m]Ăm-a-zī′ah his son, [n]Āz-a-
rī′ah his son, [o]Jō′tham his son,
13 [p]Ā′hăz his son, [q]Hĕz-e-kī′ah
his son, [r]Mȧ-năs′seh his son,
14 [s]Ā′mon his son, [t]Jŏ-sī′ah his
son.[Q]
15 [Q] And the sons of [t]Jŏ-sī′ah
*were*, the firstborn Jŏ-hā′nan,
the second [u]Jė-hoi′a-kĭm, the
third [v]Zĕd-e-kī′ah, the fourth
[w]Shăl′lum.

16 And the sons of [u]Jė-hoi′a-
kĭm: [x]Jĕc-o-nī′ah his son, Zĕd-
e-kī′ah his son.[Q]
17 ¶ And the sons of [x]Jĕc-o-
nī′ah; [1]Ăs′sĭr, [y]Să-lā′thĭ-el his
son,[Q]
18 Măl-chī′ram also, and Pĕ-
dā′iah, and Shĕ-nā′zar, Jĕc-a-
mī′ah, Hŏsh′a-mȧ, and Nĕd-a-
bī′ah.
19 And the sons of Pė-dā′iah
*were*, Zė-rŭb′ba-bĕl, and Shĭm′-
e-ī: and the sons of Zė-rŭb′-
ba-bĕl; Mĕ-shŭl′lam, and Hăn-
a-nī′ah, and Shĕl′o-mĭth their
sister:[Q]
20 And Hȧ-shu̍′bah, and Ō′hel,
and Bĕr-e-chī′ah, and Hăs-a-dī′-
ah, Jū′shăb–hē′sed, five.
21 And the sons of Hăn-a-
nī′ah; Pĕl-a-tī′ah, and Jĕ-sā′iah:
the sons of Rĕph-a-ī′ah, the sons
of Är′nan, the sons of Ō-ba-
dī′ah, the sons of Shĕch-a-nī′ah.
22 And the sons of Shĕch-a-
nī′ah; Shĕm-a-ī′ah: and the sons
of Shĕm-a-ī′ah; Hăt′tush, and
Ĭg′e-ăl, and Bȧ-rī′ah, and Nē-a-
rī′ah, and Shā′phat, six.
23 And the sons of Nē-a-rī′ah;
Ė-lĭ-o-ē′na-ī, and Hĕz-e-kī′ah,
and Ăz′rĭ-kăm, three.
24 And the sons of Ė-lĭ-o-ē′na-ī
*were*, Hŏd-a-ī′ah, and Ė-lī′a-
shĭb, and Pĕl-a-ī′ah, and Ăk′-
kŭb, and Jŏ-hā′nan, and Dăl-a-
ī′ah, and Ăn-ā′nī, seven.

## CHAPTER 4

*The posterity of Judah,* 5 *and of Ashur.* 9 *The prayer of Jabez.* 11 *The posterity of Chelub.* 21 *The posterity of Shelah.* 24 *The posterity and cities of Simeon.* 39 *Their conquest of Gedor, and of the Amalekites in mount Seir.*

THE [a]sons of [b]Jū′dah; [c]Phā′-
rĕz, [d]Hĕz′rŏn, and [e]Cär′-
mī, and [f]Hûr, and Shō′bal.
2 And [g]Rē-a-ī′ah the son of
Shō′bal begat Jā′hăth; and Jā′-
hăth begat Ȧ-hū′ma-ī, and Lā′-
hăd. These *are* the families of
the Zō′rath-ītes.
3 And these *were of* the father
of Ē′tăm; Jĕz′re-el, and Ĭsh′mȧ,

*f* Or, *Chileab*, 2 Sam. 3:3.
*g* *Abigail*, 1 Sam. 25:3.
2
*h* *Absalom*, 2 Sam. 3:3.
*i* 2 Sam. 3:3.
*j* *Geshur*, 2 Sam. 3:3.
*k* *Adonijah*, 1 Kin. 1:5.
*l* 2 Sam. 3:4; 1 Kin. 1:5, 11; 2:13.
3
*m* 2 Sam. 3:4.
*n* 2 Sam. 3:5.
4
*o* *Jerusalem*, Judg. 19:10.
5
*p* Or, *Shammuah*, 2 Sam. 5:14.
*q* 1 Chr. 14:4; 2 Sam. 5:14.
*r* *Solomon*, 2 Sam. 12:24.
*s* Or, *Bath-sheba*, 1 Kin. 1:11.
*t* Or, *Eliam*, 2 Sam. 11:3.
6
*u* 1 Chr. 14:5; 2 Sam. 5:15.
*v* Or, *Elishua*, 1 Chr. 14:5.
*w* Or, *Elpalet*, 1 Chr. 14:5.
7
*x* 1 Chr. 14:6.
*y* 2 Sam. 5:15; 1 Chr. 14:6.
8
*z* 1 Chr. 14:7; 2 Sam. 5:16.
*a* 2 Sam. 5:16; or, *Beeliada*, 1 Chr. 14:7.
*b* Or, *Eliphalet*, 2 Sam. 5:16; 1 Chr. 14:7.
9
*c* *David*, 1 Sam. 16:13.
*d* 2 Sam. 13:1–32.
10
*e* *Solomon*, 2 Sam. 12:24.
*f* *Rehoboam*, 1 Kin. 11:43.
*g* Or, *Abijam*, 1 Kin. 15:1.
*h* *Asa*, 1 Kin. 15:8.
*i* *Jehoshaphat*, 2 Kin. 12:18.
11
*j* Or, *Jehoram*, 1 Kin. 22:50.
*k* *Ahaziah*, 2 Kin. 8:25.
*l* *Joash*, 2 Kin. 11:2.
12
*m* *Amaziah*, 2 Kin. 14:1.
*n* Or, *Uzziah*, 2 Chr. 26:1.

*o* *Jotham*, 2 Kin. 15:5. **13** *p* *Ahaz*, 2 Kin. 15:38. *q* *Hezekiah*, 2 Kin. 16:20. *r* *Manasseh*, 2 Kin. 21:11. **14** *s* *Amon*, 2 Kin. 21:18. *t* *Josiah*, 1 Kin. 13:2. **15** *u* *Jehoiakim*, Jer. 26:1. *v* *Zedekiah*, 2 Kin. 25:2. *w* Or, *Jehoahaz*, 2 Kin. 23:30.

16
*x* Or, *Jehoiachin*, 2 Kin. 24:6.
17
*y* Or, *Shealtiel*, Ezra 3:2.
1 R. V. the captive; Shealtiel

1
*a* *Genealogy*, vs. 1–27; 1 Chr. 5:1.
*b* *Judah*, Gen. 37:26.
*c* *Pharez*, Gen. 38:29.
*d* *Hezron*, 1 Chr. 2:5.
*e* Or, *Chelubai*, 1 Chr. 2:9.
*f* *Hur*, Ex. 31:2.
2
*g* Or, *Haroeh*, 1 Chr. 2:52.

and Ĭd'băsh: and the name of
their sister *was* Hăz'e-lĕl-pō'nī:
4 And Pē-nū'el the father of
Ḡē'dôr, and Ē'zēr the father of
Hū'shah. These *are* the sons
of [h]Hûr, the firstborn of [i]Ĕph'-
ra-tah, the father of [j]Bĕth'–lĕ-
hĕm.
5 ¶ And [k]Ăsh'ŭr the father of
[k]Tē-kō'ȧ had [l]two wives, Hē'lah
and Nā'a-rah.
6 And Nā'a-rah bare him
Ȧ-hū'zam, and Hē'phēr, and
Tĕm'e-nī, and Hā-a-hăsh'ta-rī.
These *were* the sons of Nā'a-
rah.
7 And the sons of Hē'lah *were,*
Zē'reth, and Jē-zō'ar, and Ĕth'-
nan.
8 And Cŏz begat Ā'nụb, and
Zō-bē'bah, and the families of
Ȧ-här'hel the son of Hā'rum.
9 ¶ And Jā'bĕz was more honourable than his brethren: and
his mother called his name Jā'-
bĕz, saying, Because I bare him
with sorrow.
10 And Jā'bĕz called on the
God of Ĭṣ'ra-el, [m]saying, Oh that
thou wouldest bless me indeed,
and enlarge my [1]coast,[c] and that
thine hand might be with me,
and that thou wouldest keep *me*
from evil, that it may not grieve
me! And God [n]granted him that
which he requested.
11 ¶ And Chē'lŭb the brother
of Shụ'ah begat Mē'hīr, which
*was* the father of Ĕsh'ton.
12 And Ĕsh'ton begat Bĕth-
rā'phȧ, and Pȧ-sē'ah, and Tē-
hĭn'nah the father of Ĭr-nā'-
hăsh. These *are* the men of
Rē'chah.
13 And the sons of [o]Kē'năz;
[p]Ŏth'nī-el, and Sĕr-a-ī'ah: and
the sons of Ŏth'nī-el; Hā'thăth.
14 And Mē-ŏn'o-thāi begat
Ŏph'rah: and Sĕr-a-ī'ah begat
Jō'ăb, the father of the valley
of Chăr'a-shĭm; for they were
[q]craftsmen.[c]

**4**
*h* 1 Chr. 2:50.
*i* Or, *Ephrath,* 1 Chr. 2:19, 50.
*j* *Beth-lehem,* Gen. 48:7.

**5**
*k* 1 Chr. 2:24.
*l* *Polygamy,* Deut. 17:17.

**10**
*m* *Temporal Blessings, prayer for,* Psa. 103:2.
*n* *Prayer, answered,* Acts 6:4.
1 R. V. border

**13**
*o* *Kenaz,* Judg. 1:13.
*p* *Othniel,* Josh. 15:17.

**14**
*q* *Artisans,* 1 Chr. 29:5.

15 And the sons of [r]Cā'leb the
son of Jē-phŭn'neh; Ī'rụ, Ē'lah,
and Nā'am: and the sons of
Ē'lah, even Kē'năz.
16 And the sons of Jē'ha-lē'-
le-el; Zĭph, and Zī'phah, Tĭr'ī-ȧ,
and Ȧ-sā'rē-el.
17 And the sons of Ĕz'rȧ *were,*
Jē'thēr, and Mē'red, and Ē'-
phēr, and Jā'lon: and she bare
Mĭr'ī-am, and Shăm'ma-ī, and
Ĭsh'bah the father of Ĕsh-te-
mō'ȧ.
18 And his wife [2]Jē-hū-dī'jah
bare Jē'red the father of Ḡē'dôr,
and Hē'bēr the father of Sō'chō,
and Jē-kū'thī-el the father of Zȧ-
nō'ah. And these *are* the sons of
Bĭth'ī-ah the daughter of Phā'-
raōh, which Mē'red took.
19 And the sons of *his* wife Hō-
dī'ah the sister of Nā'ham, the
father of Kē-ī'lah the Gär'mīte,
and Ĕsh-te-mō'ȧ the Mȧ-ăch'a-
thīte.
20 And the sons of Shī'mon
*were,* Ăm'nŏn, and Rĭn'nah,
Bĕn–hā'nan, and Tī'lon. And
the sons of Ī'shī *were,* Zō'hĕth,
and Bĕn–zō'hĕth.
21 ¶ The sons of [s]Shē'lah the
son of [b]Jū'dah *were,* Ēr the father of Lē'cah, and Lā'a-dah the
father of Mȧ-rē'shah, and the
families of the house of them
that wrought fine linen, of the
house of Ăsh-bē'ȧ,
22 And Jō'kim, and the men of
[t]Chō-zē'bȧ, and Jō'ăsh, and Sā'-
răph, who had the dominion in
[u]Mō'ab, and Jăsh'ụ-bī–lē'hĕm.
And [3]*these are* ancient things.
23 These *were* the potters, and
[4]those that dwelt among plants
and hedges: there they dwelt
with the king for his work.
24 ¶ The sons of [v]Sĭm'e-on
*were,* [w]Nē-mū'el, and [x]Jā'min,
[y]Jā'rib, [z]Zē'rah, *and* [a]Shā'ul:
25 [b]Shăl'lum his son, Mĭb'sam
his son, Mĭsh'mȧ his son.
26 And the sons of Mĭsh'mȧ;

**15**
*r* *Caleb,* Num. 14:6.

**18**
2 R. V. the Jewess

**21**
*s* *Shelah,* Gen. 38:5.

**22**
*t* Or, *Chezib,* Gen 38:5.
*u* *Moab,* Num. 26:3.
3 R. V. the records are ancient.

**23**
4 R.V. the inhabitants of Netaim and Gederah:

**24**
*v* *Simeon,* Gen. 29:33.
*w* Num. 26:12.
*x* *Jamin,* Gen. 46:10.
*y* Or, *Jachin,* Num. 26:12.
*z* Num. 26:13.

*a* *Shaul,* Ex. 6:15.

**25**
*b* *Genealogy,* 1 Chr. 5:1.

Hā-mū'el his son, Zăc'chur his
son, Shĭm'e-ī his son.
27 And Shĭm'e-ī had sixteen
sons and six daughters; but his
brethren had not many children, neither did all their family multiply, like to the children
of [c]Jū'-dah.
28 And they dwelt at [d]Bē'er-
shē'bȧ, and Mŏl'a-dah, and
[e]Hā'zar-shu̥'al,
29 And at Bĭl'hah, and at
[f]Ē'zĕm, and at [g]Tō'lăd,
30 And at [h]Bĕth-u̥'el, and at
[i]Hôr'mah, and at [j]Zĭk'lăg,
31 And at [k]Bĕth-mär'ca-bŏth,
and [l]Hā'zar-sū'sim, and at
[m]Bĕth-bĭr'e-ī, and at [n]Shā-a-rā'-
im. These *were* their cities unto
the reign of [o]Dā'vid.
32 And their villages *were*,
Ē'tăm, and [p]Ā'in, [q]Rĭm'mon, and
Tō'chen, and [r]Ā'shan, five cities:
33 And all their villages that
*were* round about the same
cities, unto +Bā'al. These *were*
their habitations[G], and their
[b]genealogy.
34 [b]And Mē-shō'băb, and Jăm'-
lech, and Jō'shah the son of
Ăm-a-zī'ah,
35 And Jō'el, and Jē'hū the
son of Jŏs-ĭ-bī'ah, the son of
Sĕr-a-ī'ah, the son of Ā'sĭ-el,
36 And Ē-lĭ-o-ē'na-ī, and Jā-
ăk'o-bah, and Jĕsh-o-hā'iah, and
Ā-sa-ī'ah, and Ā'dĭ-el, and Jĕ-
sĭm'ĭ-el, and Bē-nā'iah,
37 And Zī'zȧ the son of Shī'-
phī, the son of Ăl'lŏn, the son
of Jĕ-dā'iah, the son of Shĭm'rī,
the son of Shĕm-a-ī'ah;
38 These mentioned by *their*
names *were* princes[G] in their families: and the house of their fathers increased greatly.

**27**
c *Judah*, Gen. 37:26.
**28**
d *Beer-sheba*, Judg. 20:1.
e Josh. 15:28; 19:3; Neh. 11:27.
**29**
f Or, *Azem*, Josh. 15:29; 19:3.
g Or, *Eltolad*, Josh. 15:30.
**30**
h Or, *Bethul*, Josh. 19:4.
i *Hormah*, Deut. 1:44.
j *Ziklag*, Josh. 15:31.
**31**
k *Beth-marcaboth*, Josh. 19:5.
l Or, *Hazar-susah*, Josh. 19:5.
m Or, *Beth-lebaoth*, Josh. 19:6.
n Or, *Shilhim*, Josh. 15:32; or, *Sharuhen*, Josh. 19:6.
o *David*, 1 Sam. 16:13.
**32**
p *Ain*, Josh. 19:7.
q *Rimmon*, Zech. 14:10.
r Josh. 15:42; 19:7.

39 ¶ And they went to the
entrance of Gē'dôr, *even* unto
the east side of the valley, to
seek pasture for their flocks.
40 And they found fat[G] pasture
and good, and the land *was*
wide, and quiet, and peaceable;
for *they* of [s]Hăm had dwelt there
of old.
41 And these written by name
came in the days of [t]Hĕz-e-kī'ah
king of [u]Jū'dah, and smote[G] their
tents, and the [5]habitations that
were found there, and destroyed
them utterly unto this day, and
dwelt in their [6]rooms[G]: because
*there was* pasture there for their
flocks.
42 And *some* of them, *even* of
the sons of [v]Sĭm'e-on, five hundred men, went to mount [w]Sē'ïr,
having for their [x]captains Pĕl-a-
tī'ah, and Nē-a-rī'ah, and Rĕph-
a-ī'ah, and Ŭz'zī-el, the sons of
Ī'shī.
43 And they smote[G] the rest of
the [y]Ăm'a-lĕk-ītes that were
escaped, and dwelt there unto
this day.

## CHAPTER 5

*The line of Reuben unto the captivity. 11 The chief men of Gad, and their dwelling places. 18 The war of Reuben, Gad, and the half tribe of Manasseh, with the Hagarites. 23 The dwelling places and chief men of the half tribe of Manasseh. 25 Their captivity.*

NOW the sons of [a]Reu̥'ben
the [b]firstborn of [c]Is̥'ra-el,
(for he *was* the firstborn; but,
forasmuch as he defiled[G] his father's bed, his [d]birthright was
given unto the sons of [e]Jō'se̥ph
the son of Is̥'ra-el: and the *genealogy is not to be reckoned after
the birthright.
2 For [f]Jū'dah prevailed above
his brethren, and of him *came*

**40**
s Psa. 78:51; 105:23, 27; 106:22.
**41**
t *Hezekiah*, 2 Kin. 16:20.
u *Judah, kingdom of*, 2 Chr. 11:17.
5 R. V. Meunim that
6 R. V. stead:
**42**
v *Simeon, tribe of*, Num. 2:12.
w *Seir*, Deut. 1:2.
x *Captain*, Num. 31:48.
**43**
y *Amalekites*, Num. 13:29.
**1**
a *Reuben*, Gen. 35:22.
b *Firstborn, birthright of, set aside*, Zech. 12:10.
c Or, *Jacob*, Gen. 27:11.
d *Birthright*, 2 Chr. 21:3.
e *Joseph*, Gen. 33:2.
**2**
f *Judah*, Gen. 37:26.

**+BAAL.** *A city in the tribe of Simeon*, 1 Chr. 4:33. *Called also*, BAALAH, Josh. 15:29; BALAH, Josh. 19:3; BILHAH, 1 Chr. 4:29; BIZJOTHJAH, Josh. 15:28; BAALATH-BEER, Josh. 19:8.
***GENEALOGY,** Num. 1:18; 2 Chr. 12:15; Ezra 2:59; Neh. 7:5; Heb. 7:3. *Of no spiritual significance*, 1 Tim. 1:4; Tit. 3:9.
*From Adam to Noah*, Gen. 4:16–22; 5; 1 Chr. 1:1–4; Luke 3:36–38. *From Noah to Abraham*, Gen. 11:10–32; 1 Chr. 1:4–27; Luke 3:34–38. *From Abraham to Joseph*, Matt. 1:1–16; Luke 3:23–34.
*Of the descendants of Noah*, Gen. 10. *Of Nahor*, Gen. 22:20–24. *Of Abraham, by his wife Keturah*, Gen. 25:1–4; 1 Chr. 1:32, 33. *Of Ishmael*, Gen. 25:12–16; 1 Chr. 1:28–31. *Of Esau*, Gen. 36; 1 Chr. 1:35–54.
*Of Jacob and his descendants*, Gen. 35:23–26; Ex. 1:5; 6:14–27; Num. 26; 1 Chr. chapters 2–9. *Of Pharez to David*, Ruth 4:18–22. *Of the Jews who returned from the captivity*, Ezra 7:1–5; 8:1–15; Neh. 7:5–64; 12:1–26.
*Of the ancestors of Joseph*, Matt. 1:1–16; Luke 3:23–38.

3
*g* *Hanoch*, Ex. 6:14.
*h* Or, *Phallu*, Gen. 46:9.
*i* Gen. 46:9; Ex. 6:14.

6
*j* *Tilgath-pilneser*, 2 Chr. 28:20.
*k* *Assyria*, Gen. 25:18.
*l* *Reubenites*, Josh. 22:1.

8
*m* *Aroer*, Deut. 4:48.
*n* *Nebo*, Num. 32:3.
*o* *Baal-meon*, Num. 32:38.

9
*p* *Euphrates*, Gen. 15:18.
*q* *Cattle*, Ex. 12:29.
*r* *Gilead*, Deut. 3:13.

10
*s* *Saul*, 1 Sam. 9:2.
*t* Or, *Ishmeelites*, Gen. 39:1.

11
*u* *Gad, tribe of*, Deut. 33:20.
*v* *Bashan*, Num. 32:33.
*w* Or, *Salchah*, Deut. 3:10.

the chief ruler; but the birthright[C] *was* [e]Jō'ṣeph's:)[Q]

3 The sons, *I say*, of [a]Reu̇'ben the [b]firstborn of [c]Ĭṣ'ra-el *were*, [g]Hā'nŏch, and [h]Păl'lu, [i]Hĕz'rŏn, and [i]Cär'mī.

4 *The sons of Jō'el; Shĕm-a-ī'ah his son, Gŏg his son, Shĭm-e-ī his son,

5 Mī'cah his son, Rē-a-ī'ȧ his son, Bā'al his son,

6 Bē-ē'rah his son, whom [j]Tĭl'gath-pĭl-nē'ṣer king of [k]Ăs-sy̆r'ĭ-ȧ carried away *captive*: he *was* prince of the [l]Reu̇'ben-ītes.

7 And his brethren by their families, when the *genealogy of their generations was reckoned, *were* the chief, Jē-ī'el, and Zĕch-a-rī'ah,

8 *And Bē'lȧ the son of Ā'zăz, the son of Shē'mȧ, the son of Jō'el, who dwelt in [m]Ăr'ŏ-ēr, even unto [n]Nē'bō and [o]Bā'al-mē'on:

9 And eastward he inhabited unto the entering in of the wilderness from the river [p]Eū-phrā'tēṣ: because their [q]cattle were multiplied in the land of [r]Ḡĭl'e-ăd.

10 And in the days of [s]Ṣaul they made war with the [t]Hā'gar-ītes, who fell by their hand: and they dwelt in their tents throughout all the east *land* of [r]Ḡĭl'e-ăd.

11 ¶ And the children of [u]Găd dwelt over against them, in the land of [v]Bā'shăn unto [w]Săl'cah:

12 Jō'el the chief, and Shā'pham the next, and Jȧ-ā'nāi, and Shā'phat in [v]Bā'shăn.

13 And their brethren of the house of their fathers *were*, Mī'chaĕl, and Mē-shŭl'lam, and Shē'bȧ, and Jō'rāi, and Jā'chan, and Zī'ȧ, and Hē'bēr, seven.

14 These *are* the children of Ăb-i-hā'il the son of Hū'rī, the son of Jȧ-rō'ah, the son of Ḡĭl'e-ăd, the son of Mī'chaĕl, the son of Jĕ-shĭsh'a-ī, the son of Jăh'dō, the son of Bŭz;

15 Ā'hī the son of Ăd'dĭ-el, the son of Gū'nī, chief of the house of their fathers.

16 And they dwelt in [r]Ḡĭl'e-ăd in [v]Bā'shăn, and in her towns, and in all the suburbs[C] of Shâr'on upon their borders.

17 All these were reckoned by *genealogies in the days of [x]Jō'tham king of [y]Jū'dah, and in the days of †Jĕr-o-bō'am king of [z]Ĭṣ'ra-el.

18 ¶ *The sons of [a]Reu̇'ben, and the [b]Găd'ītes, and half the tribe of [c]Mȧ-năs'seh, of valiant[C] men, men able to bear buckler[C] and sword, and to shoot with bow, and skilful in war, *were* four and forty thousand seven hundred and threescore, that went out to the war.

19 And they made war with the Hā'gar-ītes, with Jē'tŭr, and Nē'phish, and Nō'dăb.

20 And they were helped against them, and the Hā'gar-ītes were delivered into their hand, and all that *were* with them: for they [d]cried to God in the battle, and [e]he was intreated[C] of them; because they put their [f]trust in him.

21 And they took away their [g]cattle; of their [h]camels fifty thousand, and of [i]sheep two hundred and fifty thousand, and of [j]asses two thousand, and of men an hundred thousand.

22 For there fell down many slain, because the [k]war *was* of God. And they dwelt in their steads[C] until the [l]captivity.

23 ¶ And the children of the half tribe of [c]Mȧ-năs'seh dwelt in the land: they increased from [m]Bā'shăn unto [n]Bā'al-hēr'mon and Sē'nir, and unto mount [o]Hēr'mon.

17
*x* *Jotham*, 2 Kin. 15:5.
*y* *Judah, kingdom of*, 2 Chr. 11:17.
*z* *Israel, after the revolt*, 1 Kin. 12:1.

18
*a* *Reubenites*, Josh. 22:1.
*b* *Gad, tribe of*, Deut. 33:20.
*c* *Manasseh, tribe of*, Gen. 46:20.

20
*d* *Adversity, prayer in*, Psa. 10:6.
*e* *Prayer, answered*, Acts 6:4.
*f* *Faith, instances of*, Mark 11:22.

21
*g* *Cattle*, Ex. 12:29.
*h* *Camel*, 1 Sam. 30:17.
*i* *Sheep*, Deut. 32:14.
*j* *Ass, domesticated*, 2 Chr. 28:15.

22
*k* *War, as a judgment*, Judg. 3:2.
*l* *Captivity, of the Israelites*, Isa. 5:13.

23
*m* *Bashan*, Num. 32:33.
*n* Or, *Baal-gad*, Josh. 11:17.
*o* *Hermon*, Deut. 4:48.

† **JEROBOAM II.** *King of Israel*, Amos 1:1. *Successor of Jehoash*, 2 Kin. 14:16, 23. *Makes conquest of Hamath and Damascus*, 2 Kin. 14:25–28. *Reigns forty-one years*, 2 Kin. 14:23. *Wicked reign of*, 2 Kin. 14:24. *Prophecies concerning*, Amos 7:7–13. *Death of*, 2 Kin. 14:29. *Genealogies written during his reign*, 1 Chr. 5:17.

24 And these *were* the heads of
the house of their fathers, even
Ē′phĕr, and Ĭ′shī, and Ė-lī′el,
and Ăz′rĭ-el, and Jĕr-e-mī′ah,
and Hŏd-a-vī′ah, and Jăh′dĭ-el,
mighty men of valour,[c] famous
men, *and* heads of the house of
their fathers.
25 ¶ And they [p]transgressed
against the God of their fathers,
and went a[c] whoring after the
gods of the people of the land,
whom God destroyed before
them.
26 And the [q]God of Ĭs̱′ra-el
stirred up the spirit of [r]Pŭl king
of [s]Ăs-sȳr′ĭ-ȧ, and the spirit of
[t]Tĭl′gath–pĭl-nē′s̱er king of Ăs-
sȳr′ĭ-ȧ, and he carried them away,
even the [a]Reu̇′ben-ītes, and the
[b]Găd′ītes, and the half tribe of
[c]Mȧ-năs′seh, and brought them
unto [u]Hā′lah, and [u]Hā′bôr, and
Hā′rȧ, and to the river [v]Gō′zan,
unto this day.

## CHAPTER 6

*The sons of Levi. 4 The line of the priests unto the captivity. 16 The families of Gershom, Kohath, and Merari. 49 The office of Aaron, and his line unto Ahimaaz. 54 The cities of the priests and Levites.*

THE *,[a]sons of [b]Lē′vī; [c]Gēr′-
shŏn, [d]Kō′hăth, and [e]Mė-
rā′rī.
2 [a]And the sons of [d]Kō′hăth;
[f]Ăm′răm, [g]Ĭz′hār, and [h]Hē′-
bron, and Ŭz′zĭ-el.
3 And the children of [f]Ăm′-
răm; [i]Aâr′on, and [j]Mō′s̱es̱, and
[k]Mĭr′ĭ-am. The sons also of
Aâr′on; [l]Nā′dăb, and [m]Ȧ-bī′hū,
[n]Ē-le-ā′zar, and [o]Ĭth′a-mär.
4 [n]Ē-le-ā′zar begat [p]Phĭn′e-has,
Phĭn′e-has begat [q]Ȧ-bĭsh′u-ȧ,
5 And [q]Ȧ-bĭsh′u-ȧ begat [r]Bŭk′-
kī, and Bŭk′kī begat [r]Ŭz′zī,
6 And [r]Ŭz′zī begat [r]Zĕr-a-
hī′ah, and Zĕr-a-hī′ah begat
[s]Mė-rā′ioth,
7 [s]Mė-rā′ioth begat Ăm-a-rī′ah,
and Ăm-a-rī′ah begat Ȧ-hī′-
tub,
8 And Ȧ-hī′tub begat Zā′dŏk,
and Zā′dŏk begat Ȧ-hĭm′a-ăz,
9 And Ȧ-hĭm′a-ăz begat Ăz-a-
rī′ah, and Ăz-a-rī′ah begat Jȯ-
hā′nan,
10 And Jȯ-hā′nan begat Ăz-a-
rī′ah, (he *it is* that executed[c]
the priest's office in the [t]temple
that [u]Sŏl′o-mon built in [v]Jė-
ru̇′sȧ-lĕm:)
11 And Ăz-a-rī′ah begat [w]Ăm-
a-rī′ah, and Ăm-a-rī′ah begat
[x]Ȧ-hī′tub,
12 And [x]Ȧ-hī′tub begat [x]Zā′-
dŏk, and Zā′dŏk begat [y]Shăl′-
lum,
13 And [y]Shăl′lum begat [z]Hĭl-
kī′ah, and Hĭl-kī′ah begat [a]Ăz-
a-rī′ah,
14 And [a]Ăz-a-rī′ah begat Sĕr-a-
ī′ah, and Sĕr-a-ī′ah begat [b]Jė-
hŏz′a-dăk,
15 And [b]Jė-hŏz′a-dăk went *into captivity*, when the LORD
[c]carried away [d]Jū′dah and Jė-
ru̇′sȧ-lĕm by the hand of [e]Nĕb-u-
chad-nĕz′zar.
16 ¶ The [f,g]sons of Lē′vī;
[h]Gēr′shŏm, [i]Kō′hăth, and [j]Mė-
rā′rī.
17 And these *be* the names of
the [k]sons of Gēr′shŏm; [l]Lĭb′nī,
and [m]Shĭm′e-ī.
18 And the [n]sons of Kō′hăth
*were*, [o]Ăm′răm, and [p]Ĭz′hār, and
[q]Hē′bron, and [r]Ŭz′zĭ-el.
19 The [s]sons of Mė-rā′rī; [t]Măh′-
lī, and [u]Mū′shī. And [g]these *are*
the families of the [f]Lē′vītes according to their fathers.
20 Of [k]Gēr′shŏm; [l]Lĭb′nī his
son, Jā′hăth his son, Zĭm′mah
his son,
21 [v]Jō′ah his son, Ĭd′dō his son,
Zē′rah his son, Jė-ăt′e-rāi his
son.
22 [g]The [w]sons of Kō′hăth; Ăm-

25
p *Backsliding, of Israel,* Hos. 11:7.

26
q *God, providence of,* Gen. 2:2.
r 2 Kin. 15:19.
s *Assyria,* Gen. 25:18.
t *Tilgath-pilneser,* 2 Chr. 28:20.
u 2 Kin. 17:6; 18:11.
v *Gozan,* 2 Kin. 17:6.

1
a *Genealogy,* vs. 1–53; 1 Chr. 5:1.
b *Levi,* Gen. 29:34.
c *Gershon,* Gen. 46:11.
d *Kohath,* Num. 26:58.
e *Merari,* Gen. 46:11.

2
f *Amram,* Ex. 6:18.
g 1 Chr. 23:12, 18; Ex. 6:18, 21.
h *Hebron,* Num. 3:19.

3
i *Aaron,* Ex. 6:20.
j *Moses,* Ex. 2.10.
k *Miriam,* Ex. 15:20.
l *Nadab,* Ex. 24:1.
m *Abihu,* Ex. 6:23.
n *Eleazar,* Num. 3:2.
o *Ithamar,* Ex. 38:21.

4
p *Phinehas,* Num. 25:7.
q *Abishua,* Ezra 7:5.

5
r Ezra 7:4.

6
s Ezra 7:3.

10
t *Temple, Solomon's,* 1 Kin. 6:17.
u *Solomon,* 2 Sam. 12:24.
v *Jerusalem,* Judg. 19:10.

11
w Ezra 7:3.
x Ezra 7:2.

12
y Ezra 7:2; or, *Meshullam,* 1 Chr. 9:11; Neh. 11:11.

13
z *Hezekiah,* Jer. 29:3.

a 1 Chr. 9:11; Ezra 7:1; or, *Seriah,* Neh. 11:11.

14
b Or, *Jozadak,* Neh. 12:26.

15
c *Captivity, of Judah,* Isa. 5:13.
d *Judah, kingdom of,* 2 Chr. 11:17.
e *Nebuchadnezzar,* Dan. 2:1.

16
f *Levites,* Deut. 10:8.
g *Genealogy,* 1 Chr. 5:1.
h *Gershon,* Gen. 46:11.
i *Kohath,* Num. 26:58.
j *Merari,* Gen. 46:11.

17
k *Gershonites,* Num. 4:27.
l *Libni,* Ex. 6:17.
m *Shimei,* Ex. 6:17.

18
n *Kohathites,* Num. 3:27.
o *Amram,* Ex. 6:18.
p 1 Chr. 23:12, 18; Ex. 6:18, 21.
q *Hebron,* Num. 3:19.
r *Uzziel,* Num. 3:19.

19
s *Merarites,* Num. 26:57.
t Num. 3:20; Ezra 8:18; or, *Mahali,* Ex. 6:19.
u 1 Chr. 23:21; Ex. 6:19; Num. 3:20.

21
v 2 Chr. 29:12.

22
w *Kohathites,* Num. 3:27.

*[In order to publish this Bible in one volume with its numerous and diversified marginal notes and footnotes it has been necessary to avoid elaborate discussions of subjects, such, for instance, as would be necessary to point out the difficulties in connection with some of the names in genealogical lists. These difficulties grow out of errors of copyists, differences in the spelling of the same name and the fact that individuals and places are mentioned under different names in different chapters. Where the identity of persons or places is doubtful in the following lists, and where no note-

mĭn′a-dăb his son, Kō′rah his
son, [x]Ăs′sĭr his son,
23 [x]Ĕl′kă-nah his son, and
[y]Ĕ-bī′a-săph his son, and Ăs′sĭr
his son,
24 Tā′hăth his son, Ū′rĭ-el his
son, Ŭz-zī′ah his son, and Shā′ul
his son.
25 And [a]the sons of Ĕl′kă-nah;
Ă-măs′a-ī, and Ă-hī′mŏth.
26 *As for* Ĕl′kă-nah: the sons of
Ĕl′kă-nah; [z]Zō′phāi his son, and
[a]Nā′hăth his son,
27 [b]Ĕ-lī′ab his son, [c]Jĕr′o-hăm
his son, [c]Ĕl′kă-nah his son.
28 And the sons of [d]Săm′u-el;
the firstborn [e]Văsh′nī, and [f]Ă-
bī′ah.
29 [g]The [h]sons of Mė-rā′rī;
[i]Mäh′lī, Lĭb′nī his son, Shĭm′e-ī
his son, Ŭz′zȧ his son,
30 Shĭm′e-ȧ his son, Hăg′gī′ah
his son, [j]Ă-sa-ī′ah his son.
31 And these *are* [k]*they* whom
[l]Dā′vid set over the service of
song in the [m]house of the LORD,
after that the [n]ark had rest.
32 And [k]they ministered before
the dwelling place of the [m]taber-
nacle of the congregation with
singing, until [o]Sŏl′o-mon had
built the [p]house of the LORD
in [q]Jė-ru̧′să-lĕm: and *then* they
waited[c] on their office according
to their order.
33 And [g]these *are* they that
waited[c] with their children. Of
the sons of the [r]Kō′hath-ītes:
*Hē′man a singer, the son of
[e]Jō′el, the son of [d]Shė-mū′el,
34 The son of [c]Ĕl′kă-nah, the
son of [c]Jĕr′o-hăm, the son of
[b]Ĕ-lī′el, the son of [a]Tō′ah,
35 The son of [s]Zŭph, the son of
Ĕl′kă-nah, the son of [t]Mă′hăth,
the son of Ă-măs′a-ī,
36 The son of Ĕl′kă-nah, the
son of Jō′el, the son of Ăz-a-rī′-
ah, the son of Zĕph-a-nī′ah,
37 The son of Tā′hăth, the son
of Ăs′sĭr, the son of [u]Ĕ-bī′a-
săph, the son of Kō′rah,
38 The son of Ĭz′här, the son of
[v]Kō′hăth, the son of [w]Lē′vī, the
son of [x]Ĭș′ra-el.
39 And his brother [y]Ā′saph,
who stood on his right hand,
*even* Ā′saph the son of [z]Bĕr-a-
chī′ah, the son of Shĭm′e-ȧ,
40 [a]The son of Mī′chaĕl, the
son of Bā-a-sē′iah, the son of
Măl-chī′ah,
41 [a]The son of Ĕth′nī, the son
of Zē′rah, the son of Ăd-a-ī′ah,
42 The son of Ē′than, the son
of [b]Zĭm′mah, the son of Shĭm′e-ī,
43 The son of Jā′hăth, the son
of [c]Gĕr′shŏm, the son of [d]Lē′vī.
44 And their brethren the [e]sons
of Mė-rā′rī *stood* on the left
hand: [f]Ē′than the son of [g]Kĭsh′ī,
the son of Ăb′dī, the son of Măl′-
luch,
45 The son of Hăsh-a-bī′ah, the
son of Ăm-a-zī′ah, the son of
[h]Hĭl-kī′ah,
46 The son of Ăm′zī, the son of
Bā′nī, the son of Shā′mĕr,
47 The son of [i]Mäh′lī, the son
of [j]Mū′shī, the son of [k]Mė-rā′rī,
the son of [d]Lē′vī.
48 Their brethren also the [l]Lē′-
vītes *were* appointed unto all
manner of service of the tabernacle of the house of God.
49 ¶ But [m,n]Aâr′on and his
[n]sons offered upon the [o]altar of
the [p]burnt offering, and on the
[q]altar of incense, *and were appointed* for all the work of the
*place* most holy, and to make an
atonement for Ĭș′ra-el, according to all that [r]Mō′șeș the servant of God had commanded.
50 And [a]these *are* the sons of
[m]Aâr′on; [s]Ē-le-ā′zar his son,
[t]Phĭn′e-has his son, [u]Ă-bĭsh′u-ȧ
his son,
51 [v]Bŭk′kī his son, [v]Ŭz′zī his
son, [v]Zĕr-a-hī′ah his son,

x Ex. 6:24.
23
y 1 Chr. 9:19; or, *Abiasaph*, Ex. 6:24; or, *Asaph*, 1 Chr. 26:1.
26
z Or, *Zuph*, 1 Sam. 1:1.

a Or, *Toah*, v. 34; or, *Tohu*, 1 Sam. 1:1.
27
b Or, *Eliel*, v. 34; or, *Elihu*, 1 Sam. 1:1.
c 1 Sam. 1:1.
28
d *Samuel*, 1 Sam. 3:1.
e Or, *Joel*, 1 Sam. 8:2; 1 Chr. 15:17.
f 1 Sam. 8:1–5.
29
g *Genealogy*, vs. 29-40; 1 Chr. 5:1.
h *Merarites*, Num. 26:57.
i Num. 3:20; Ezra 8:18; or, *Mahali*, Ex. 6:19.
30
j 1 Chr. 15:6, 11.
31
k *Choir*, 1 Chr. 15:16.
l *David*, 1 Sam. 16:13.
m *Tabernacle*, Ex. 27:9.
n *Ark*, Ex. 25:10.
32
o *Solomon*, 2 Sam. 12:24.
p *Temple, Solomon's*, 1 Kin. 6:17.
q *Jerusalem*, Judg. 19:10.
33
r *Kohathites*, Num. 3:27.
35
s 1 Sam. 1:1.
t 2 Chr. 29:12.

37
u 1 Chr. 9:19; or, *Abiasaph*, Ex. 6:24; or, *Asaph* 1 Chr. 26:1.
38
v *Kohath*, Num. 26:58.
w *Levi*, Gen. 29:34
x Or, *Jacob*, Gen. 27:11.
39
y *Asaph*, 1 Chr. 15:17.
z 1 Chr. 15:17, 23.

40
a *Genealogy*, vs. 40–47; 1 Chr. 5:1.
42
b 2 Chr. 29:12.
43
c Or, *Gershon*, Gen. 46:11.
d *Levi*, Gen. 29:34.
44
e *Merarites*, Num. 26:57.
f Or, *Jeduthun*, 1 Chr. 16:38.
g Or, *Kushaiah*, 1 Chr. 15:17.
45
h 1 Chr. 26:11.
47
i 1 Chr. 23:23; 24:30.
j Ex. 6:19; 1 Chr. 23:21.
k *Merari*, Gen. 46:11.
48
l *Levites*, Deut. 10:8.
49
m *Aaron*, Ex. 6:20.
n *Priest, duties of*, Lev. 1:5.
o *Altar, of burnt offerings*, Gen. 8:20.
p *Offerings, burnt*, Lev. 6:17.
q *Altar, of incense*, Ex. 30:1.
r *Moses*, Ex. 2:10.
50
s *Eleazar*, Num. 3:2.
t *Phinehas*, Num. 25:7.
u Ezra 7:5.
51
v Ezra 7:4.

worthy fact is known concerning them, no mention of the name is made in either the margins or footnotes.]

*** HEMAN.** *The singer, a chief Levite, and musician*, 1 Chr. 6:33; 15:17, 19; 16:41; 2 Chr. 5:12. *The King's seer*, 1 Chr. 25:5. *His sons and daughters were temple musicians*, 1 Chr. 25:1–6.

52
w Ezra 7:3.
x Ezra 7:2.
53
y *Ahimaaz*, 2 Sam. 15:27.
54
z *Priest, cities of*, vs. 54–81; Lev. 1:5.

a *Aaron*, Ex. 6:20.
b *Kohathites, cities of*, Num. 3:27.
1 R. V. according to their encampments in
55
c *Hebron*, Gen. 23:2.
d *Judah, tribe of*, Num. 10:14.
56
e *Caleb*, Num. 14:6.
57
f *Cities, of refuge*, Num. 35:8.
g *Libnah*, Josh. 10:29.
h Josh. 15:48; 21:14; 1 Sam. 30:27.
i *Eshtemoa*, 1 Sam. 30:28.
2 R. V. refuge, Hebron; Libnah also with
58
j Or, *Holen*, Josh. 15:51.
k *Debir*, Josh. 15:15.
59
l Or, *Ain*, Josh. 19:7.
m *Beth-shemesh*, Josh. 21:16.
60
n *Bejamin, tribe of*, Num. 1:37.
o *Geba*, Josh. 21:17.
p Or, *Almon*, Josh. 21:18.
q *Anathoth*, Jer. 1:1.
61
r *Manasseh, tribe of*, Gen. 46:20.
s *Lot*, Esth. 3:7.
62
t Or, *Gershonites*, Num. 4:27.
u *Issachar, tribe of*, Num. 1:28.
v *Asher, tribe of*, Num. 1:40.
w *Naphtali, tribe of*, Num. 1:42.
x *Bashan*, Num. 32:33.
63
y *Merarites*, Num. 26:57.
z *Reubenites*, Josh. 22:1.

52 [w]Mē-rā′ioth his son, [w]Ăm-a-
rī′ah his son, [x]Ă-hī′tub his son,
53 [x]Zā′dŏk his son, [y]Ă-hĭm′a-
ăz his son.
54 ¶ Now these *are* their [z]dwell-
ing places [1]throughout their castles in their coasts, of the sons of
[a]Aâr′on, of the families of the
[b]Kō′hath-ītes: for their's was the
lot.
55 And they gave them [c]Hē′-
bron in the land of [d]Jū′dah,
and the suburbs thereof round
about it.
56 But the fields of the city, and
the villages thereof, they gave to
[e]Cā′leb the son of Jĕ-phŭn′neh.
57 And to the sons of [a]Aâr′on
they gave the cities of [2,d]Jū′dah,
*namely*, [c]Hē′bron, *the* [f]*city* of
refuge, and [g]Lĭb′nah with her
suburbs, and [h]Jăt′tĭr, and [i]Ĕsh-
te-mō′ȧ, with their suburbs,
58 And [j]Hī′len with her suburbs, [k]Dē′bīr with her suburbs,
59 And [l]Ā′shan with her suburbs, and [m]Bĕth-shē′mesh with
her suburbs:
60 And out of the tribe of
[n]Bĕn′ja-mĭn; [o]Gē′bȧ with her
suburbs, and [p]Ăl′e-mĕth with
her suburbs, and [q]Ăn′a-thŏth
with her suburbs. All their cities
throughout their families *were*
thirteen cities.
61 And unto the [b]sons of Kō′-
hăth, *which were* left of the family of that tribe, *were cities given*
out of the half tribe, *namely*, *out
of* the half *tribe* of [r]Mȧ-năs′seh,
by [s]lot, ten cities.
62 And to the [t]sons of Gēr′shŏm
throughout their families out of
the tribe of [u]Ĭs′sa-char, and out
of the tribe of [v]Ăsh′ēr, and out
of the tribe of [w]Năph′ta-lī, and
out of the tribe of [r]Mȧ-năs′seh in
[x]Bā′shăn, thirteen cities.
63 Unto the [y]sons of Mĕ-rā′rī
*were given* by [s]lot, throughout
their families, out of the [z]tribe of
Reu′ben, and out of the tribe
of [a]Găd, and out of the tribe of
[b]Zĕb′u-lŭn, twelve cities.
64 And the children of Ĭs′ra-el
gave to the Lē′vītes [c]*these* cities
with their suburbs.
65 And they gave by [d]lot out of
the tribe of the children of [e]Jū′-
dah, and out of the tribe of the
children of [f]Sĭm′e-on, and out of
the tribe of the children of [g]Bĕn′-
ja-mĭn, these cities, which are
called by *their* names.
66 And *the residue* of the families of the sons of Kō′hăth had
[h]cities of their coasts out of the
tribe of [i]Ē′phrā-ĭm.
67 And they gave unto them, *of*
the [j]cities of refuge, [k]Shē′chem
in mount [l]Ē′phrā-ĭm with her
suburbs; *they gave* also [m]Gē′zēr
with her suburbs,
68 And Jŏk′me-ăm with her
suburbs, and [n]Bĕth-hō′rŏn with
her suburbs,
69 And [o]Āij′a-lŏn with her suburbs, and [p]Găth-rĭm′mon with
her suburbs:
70 And out of the half tribe of
[q]Mȧ-năs′seh; Ā′nēr with her
suburbs, and Bĭl′e-ăm with her
suburbs, for the family of the
remnant of the [h]sons of Kō′hăth.
71 Unto the [r]sons of Gēr′shŏm
*were given*, out of the family of
the half tribe of [q]Mȧ-năs′seh,
[s]Gō′lan in [t]Bā′shăn with her
suburbs, and [u]Ăsh′ta-rŏth with
her suburbs:
72 And out of the tribe of
[v]Ĭs′sa-char, [w]Kē′desh with her
suburbs, [x]Dăb′e-răth with her
suburbs,
73 And Rā′moth with her suburbs, and Ā′nem with her suburbs:
74 And out of the tribe of
[y]Ăsh′ēr, [z]Mā′shal with her
suburbs, and [a]Ăb′dŏn with her
suburbs,
75 And [b]Hū′kŏk with her suburbs, and [c]Rē′hŏb with her suburbs:

a *Gad, tribe of*, Deut. 33:20.
b *Zebulun, tribe of*, Gen. 49:13.
64
c *Levites, emoluments of*, Deut. 10:8.
65
d *Lot*, Esth. 3:7.
e *Judah, tribe of*, Num. 10:14.
f *Simeon, tribe of*, Num. 2:12.
g *Benjamin, tribe of*, Num. 1:37.
66
h *Kohathites, cities of*, Num. 3:27.
i *Ephraim, tribe of*, Gen. 41:52.
67
j *Cities, of refuge*, Num. 35:8.
k *Shechem*, Josh. 20:7.
l *Ephraim, mount of*, Josh. 17:15.
m *Gezer*, Josh. 10:33.
68
n *Beth-horon*, Josh. 10:10.
69
o *Aijalon*, Josh. 21:24.
p *Gath-rimmon*, Josh. 21:25.
70
q *Manasseh, tribe of*, Gen. 46:20.
71
r Or, *Gershonites*, Num. 4:27.
s *Golan*, Deut. 4:43.
t *Bashan*, Num. 32:33.
u *Ashtaroth*, Deut. 1:4.
72
v *Issachar, tribe of*, Num. 1:28.
w *Kedesh*, Josh. 12:22.
x Josh. 19:12; or *Dabareh*, Josh. 21:28.
74
y *Asher, tribe of*, Num. 1:40.
z Or, *Misheal*, Josh. 19:26; or, *Mishal*, Josh. 21:30.

a Josh. 21:30.
75
b Or, *Helkath*, Josh. 19:25.
c *Rehob*, Josh. 19:30.

76 And out of the tribe of [d]Năph′ta-lī; [e]Kē′desh in [f]Găl′ĭ-lee[G] with her suburbs[G], and [g]Hăm′mŏn with her suburbs[G], and Kĭr-jath-ā′im with her suburbs[G].

77 Unto the rest of [3]the [h]children of Mė-rā′rī *were given* out of the tribe of [i]Zĕb′u-lŭn, [j]Rĭm′mon with her suburbs[G], [k]Tā′bôr with her suburbs[G]:

78 And on the other side [l]Jôr′dan by [m]Jĕr′ĭ-chō, on the east side of Jôr′dan, *were given them* out of the [n]tribe of Reu′ben, [o]Bē′zēr, in the wilderness with her suburbs[G], and [p]Jăh′zah with her suburbs[G],

79 [q]Kĕd′e-mŏth also with her suburbs[G], and [r]Mĕph′a-ăth with her suburbs[G]:

80 And out of the tribe of [s]Găd; [t]Rā′moth in Gĭl′e-ăd with her suburbs[G], and [u]Mā-hȧ-nā′im with her suburbs[G],

81 And [v]Hĕsh′bŏn with her suburbs[G], and [w]Jā′zēr with her suburbs[G].

## CHAPTER 7

*The sons of Issachar, 6 of Benjamin, 13 of Naphtali, 14 of Manasseh, 20 and of Ephraim. 28 Ephraim's habitations. 30 The sons of Asher.*

NOW [a]the sons of [b]Ĭs′sa-char *were*, [c]Tō′lȧ, and [d]Pū′ah, [e]Jăsh′ŭb, and [f]Shĭm′rŏm, four.

2 And the sons of [c]Tō′lȧ; Ŭz′zī, and Rĕph-a-ī′ah, and Jē′rĭ-el, and Jăh′ma-ī, and Jĭb′sam, and Shė-mū′el, heads of their father's house, *to wit*, of Tō′lȧ: *they were* valiant men of might in their generations; whose [g]number *was* in the days of Dā′vid two and twenty thousand and six hundred.

3 And the sons of Ŭz′zī; Ĭz-ra-hī′ah: and the sons of Ĭz-ra-hī′ah; Mī′chaĕl, and Ō-ba-dī′ah, and Jō′el, Ī-shī′ah, five: all of them chief men.

4 And with them, by their generations, after the house of their fathers, *were* bands of soldiers for war, [g]six and thirty thousand *men*: for they had many wives and sons.

5 And their brethren among all the families of [b]Ĭs′sa-char *were* valiant[G] men of might, reckoned in all by their [a]genealogies [g]fourscore and seven thousand.

6 ¶ *The sons* of [h]Bĕn′ja-mĭn; [i]Bē′lȧ, and [j]Bē′chēr, and Jė-dī′a-el, three.

7 And the sons of [i]Bē′lȧ; Ĕz′bŏn, and Ŭz′zī, and Ŭz′zĭ-el, and Jĕr′ĭ-mŏth, and Ī′rī, five; heads of the house of *their* fathers, mighty men of valour; and were reckoned by their [a]genealogies [g]twenty and two thousand and thirty and four.

8 And the sons of [j]Bē′chēr; Ze-mī′rȧ, and Jō′ăsh, and Ė-li-ē′zēr, and Ĕ-lī-o-ē′na-ī, and Ŏm′rī, and Jĕr′ĭ-mŏth, and Ȧ-bī′ah, and Ăn′a-thŏth, and Ăl′a-mĕth. All these *are* the sons of Bē′chēr.

9 And the number of them, after their [a]genealogy by their generations[G], heads of the house of their fathers, mighty men of valour, *was* [g]twenty thousand and two hundred.

10 The sons also of Jė-dī′a-el; Bĭl′han: and the sons of Bĭl′han; Jē′ŭsh, and Bĕn′ja-mĭn, and Ē′hŭd, and Chĕ-nā′a-nah, and Zē′-than, and Thär′shish, and Ȧ-hĭsh′a-här.

11 All these the sons of Jė-dī′a-el, by the heads of their fathers, mighty men of valour, *were* [g]seventeen thousand and two hundred *soldiers*, fit to go out for war *and* battle.

12 Shŭp′pim also, and [k]Hŭp′pim, the children of Īr, *and* Hū′shim, the sons of [l]Ā′hēr.

13 ¶ The sons of [m]Năph′ta-lī; [n]Jăh′zĭ-el, and [o]Gū′nī, and [o]Jē′zēr, and [p]Shăl′lum, the sons of [q]Bĭl′hah.

---

76
d *Naphtali, tribe of*, Num. 1:42.
e *Kedesh*, Josh. 21:32.
f *Galilee*, Mark 6:21.
g Or, *Hammoth-dor*, Josh. 21:32.

77
h *Merarites*, Num. 26:57.
i *Zebulun, tribe of*, Gen. 49:13.
j Or, *Remmon-methoar*, Josh. 19:13.
k Or, *Chisloth-tabor*, Josh. 19:12.
3 R. V. the Levites, the sons of

78
l *Jordan*, Gen. 32:10.
m *Jericho*, Num. 22:1.
n *Reubenites*, Josh. 22:1.
o *Bezer*, Deut. 4:43.
p Or, *Jahaz*, Judg. 11:20.

79
q *Kedemoth*, Josh. 13:18.
r *Mephaath*, Josh. 13:18.

80
s *Gad, tribe of*, Deut. 33:20.
t *Ramoth-gilead*, Josh. 20:8.
u *Mahanaim*, Gen. 32:2.

81
v *Heshbon*, Isa. 16:8.
w *Jazer*, Josh. 13:25.

1
a *Genealogy*, 1 Chr. 5:1.
b *Issachar, tribe of*, Num. 1:28.
c Gen. 46:13; Num. 26:23.
d Or, *Phuvah*, Gen. 46:13.
e Num. 26:24; or, *Job*, Gen. 46:13.
f Gen. 46:13; Num. 26:24.

2
g *Armies, enumeration of*, Deut. **11:4.**

6
h *Benjamin, tribe of*, Num. 1:37.
i *Bela*, Num. 26:38.
j Gen. 46:21.

12
k Gen. 46:21.
l Or, *Ehud*, 1 Chr 8:6.

13
m *Naphtali, tribe of*, Num. 1:42.
n Or, *Jahzeel*, Gen. 46:24; Num. 26:48.
o Gen. 46:24.
p Or, *Shillem*, Gen. 46:24; Num. 26:49.
q *Bilhah*, Gen. 29:29.

14 ¶ The sons of [r]Mȧ-năs′seh; [s]Ăsh′rĭ-el, whom she bare: (*but* his [t]concubine the Ā′ram-ĭt-ess bare [u]Mā′chĭr the father of [v]Ḡĭl′e-ăd:

15 And [u]Mā′chĭr took to wife *the sister* of [k]Hŭp′pim and Shŭp′pim, whose sister's name *was* Mā′a-chah;) and the name of the second *was* [w]Zė-lō′phe-hăd: and Zė-lō′phe-hăd had daughters.

16 And Mā′a-chah the wife of [u]Mā′chĭr bare a son, and she called his name Pē′resh; and the name of his brother *was* Shē′resh; and his sons *were* Ū′lam and Rā′kem.

17 And the sons of Ū′lam; Bē′dăn. These *were* the sons of [v]Ḡĭl′e-ăd, the son of Mā′chĭr, the son of Mȧ-năs′seh.

18 And his sister Hăm-mŏl′e-kĕth bare Ī′shŏd, and [x]Ā-bĭ-ē′zēr, and Mȧ-hā′lah.

19 And the sons of [y]Shė-mī′dah were, Ā-hī′an, and Shē′chem, and Lĭk′hī, and Ā′ni-ăm.

20 ¶ And the sons of [z]Ē′phrā-ĭm; [a]Shu̧′the-lah, and [b]Bē′red his son, and Tā′hăth his son, and Ĕl′a-dah his son, and Tā′hăth his son,

21 And Zā′băd his son, and Shu̧′the-lah his son, and Ē′zēr, and Ē′le-ăd, whom the men of [c]Găth *that were* born in *that* land slew,[c] because they came down to take away their cattle.

22 And [d]Ē′phrā-ĭm their father mourned many days, and his brethren came to comfort him.

23 ¶ And when he went in to his wife, she conceived, and bare a son, and he called his name Bė-rī′ah, because it went evil with his house.

24 (And his [e]daughter *was* Shē′rah, who built [f]Bĕth-hō′rŏn the nether,[c] and the upper, and Ŭz′zen-shē′rah.)

14 *r* *Manasseh, tribe of*, Gen. 46:20. *s* Or, *Asriel*, Josh. 17:2. *t* *Concubinage*, 2 Sam. 21:11. *u* *Machir*, Gen. 50:23. *v* *Gilead*, Num. 26:29.

15 *w* *Zelophehad*, Num. 27:1.

18 *x* *Abiezer*, Josh. 17:2.

19 *y* Or, *Shemida*, Num. 26:32; Josh. 17:2.

20 *z* *Ephraim, tribe of*, Gen. 41:52.

*a* Num. 26:35, 36. *b* Or, *Becher*, Num. 26:35.

21 *c* *Gath*, Josh. 11:22.

22 *d* *Ephraim*, Gen. 41:52.

24 *e* *Women, in business*, Prov.31:10. *f* *Beth-horon*, Josh. 10:10.

25 And Rē′phah *was* his son, also Rē′sheph, and Tē′lah his son, and Tā′hăn his son,

26 Lā′a-dăn his son, [g]Ăm-mī′hŭd his son, [h]Ė-lĭsh′a-mȧ his son,

27 Nŏn his son, [i]Jė-hŏsh′u-ah his son.

28 ¶ And [j]their possessions and habitations *were*, [k]Bĕth′-el and the towns thereof, and eastward Nā′a-răn, and westward [l]Ḡē′zēr, with the towns thereof; [m]Shē′chem also and the towns thereof, unto [n]Gā′zȧ and the towns thereof:

29 And by the borders of the children of [o]Mȧ-năs′seh, [p]Bĕth-shē′an and her towns, [q]Tā′a-năch and her towns, [r]Mė-gĭd′dō and her towns, [s]Dôr and her towns. In these dwelt the [j,o]children of Jō′şeph the son of Ĭş′ra-el.

30 ¶ The sons of [t]Ăsh′ēr; Ĭm′nah, and [u]Ĭs′u-ah, and [v]Ĭsh′u-āi, and [w]Bė-rī′ah, and [x]Sē′rah their sister.

31 And the sons of [w]Bė-rī′ah, [y]Hē′bēr, and [y]Măl′chĭ-el, who *is* the father of Bĭr′za-vĭth.

32 And Hē′bēr begat Jăph′let, and Shō′mēr, and Hō′tham, and Shu̧′ȧ their sister.

33 And the sons of Jăph′let; Pā′sach, and Bĭm′hăl, and Ăsh′văth. These *are* the children of Jăph′let.

34 And the sons of Shā′mēr; Ā′hī, and Rōh′gah, Jė-hŭb′bah, and Ā′ram.

35 And the sons of his brother Hē′lem; Zō′phah, and Ĭm′nȧ, and Shē′lesh, and Ā′măl.

36 The sons of Zō′phah; Sū′ah, and Här′ne-phēr, and Shu̧′al, and Bē′rī, and Ĭm′rah,

37 Bē′zēr, and Hŏd, and Shăm′mȧ, and Shĭl′shah, and Ĭth′ran, and Bė-ē′rȧ.

38 And the sons of Jē′thēr;

26 *g* Num. 2:18. *h* Num. 1:10.

27 *i* *Joshua*, Josh. 1:1.

28 *j* *Ephraim, tribe of*, Gen. 41:52. *k* *Beth-el*, Josh. 18:13. *l* *Gezer*, Josh. 10:33. *m* *Shechem*, Josh. 20:7. *n* *Gaza*, Judg. 6:4.

29 *o* *Manasseh, tribe of*, Gen. 46:20. *p* *Beth-shean*, Josh. 17:11. *q* *Taanach*, Josh. 12:21. *r* *Megiddo*, Josh. 17:11. *s* *Dor*, Josh. 11:2.

30 *t* *Asher, tribe of*, Num. 1:40. *u* Or, *Ishuah*, Gen. 46:17. *v* Or, *Isui*, Gen. 46:17; or, *Jesui*, Num. 26:44. *w* Gen. 46:17; Num. 26:44, 45. *x* Gen. 46:17: or, *Sarah*, Num. 26:46.

31 *y* Gen. 46:17; Num. 26:45.

Jĕ-phŭn′neh, and Pĭṣ′pah, and
Ā′rȧ.
39 And the sons of Ŭl′lȧ; Ā′rah,
and Hăn′ĭ-el, and Rē-zī′ȧ.
40 All these *were* the children of
[t]Ăsh′ẽr, heads of *their* father's
house, choice *and* mighty men
of valour, chief of the princes.
And the number throughout
the [z]genealogy of them that
were apt to the war *and* to
battle *was* twenty and six thousand men.

## CHAPTER 8

*The sons and chief men of Benjamin.* 33 *The family of Saul and Jonathan.*

NOW *[a,b]Bĕn′ja-mĭn begat
[c]Bē′lȧ his firstborn, [d]Ăsh′-
bĕl the second, and Ȧ-hăr′ah the
third,
2 Nō′hah the fourth, and Rā′-
phȧ the fifth.
3 And the sons of [c]Bē′lȧ were,
Ăd′där, and [e]Gē′rȧ, and Ȧ-bī′-
hụd,
4 And Ȧ-bĭsh′u-ȧ, and [f]Nā′a-
man, and Ȧ-hō′ah,
5 And [e]Gē′rȧ, and Shĕ-phū′-
phan, and Hū′ram.
6 And [a]these *are* the sons of
†Ē′hŭd: these are the heads of
the fathers of the inhabitants
of [g]Gē′bȧ, and they removed
them to Măn′a-hăth:
7 And Nā′a-man, and †Ȧ-hī′-
ah, and [e]Gē′rȧ, he removed
them, and begat Ŭz′zȧ, and Ȧ-
hī′hụd.
8 And Shā-ha-rā′im begat *children* in the country of Mō′ab,
after he had sent them away;
Hū′shim and Bā′a-rȧ *were* his
wives.
9 And he begat of Hō′desh his
wife, Jō′băb, and Zĭb′ĭ-ȧ, and
Mē′shȧ, and Măl′cham,
10 And Jē′ŭz, and Shȧ-chī′ȧ,
and Mīr′mȧ. These *were* his
sons, heads of the fathers.
11 And of Hū′shim he begat
Ȧb′ĭ-tŭb, and Ĕl′pā-al.
12 The sons of Ĕl′pā-al; Ē′bẽr,
and Mī′sham, and Shā′mĕd, who
built ‡Ō′nō, and ‖Lŏd, with the
towns thereof:
13 [a]Bē-rī′ah also, and Shē′mȧ,
who *were* heads of the fathers
of the inhabitants of [h]Ăij′a-lŏn,
who drove away the inhabitants
of [i]Găth:
14 And Ȧ-hī′ō, Shā′shăk, and
Jĕr′e-mŏth,
15 And Zĕb-a-dī′ah, and Ā′răd,
and Ā′dẽr,
16 And Mī′chaĕl, and Ĭs′pah,
and Jō′hȧ, the sons of Bē-rī′ah;
17 And Zĕb-a-dī′ah, and Mē-
shŭl′lam, and Hĕz′e-kī, and
Hē′bẽr,
18 Ĭsh′me-rāi also, and Jĕz-lī′-
ah, and Jō′băb, the sons of Ĕl′-
pā-al;
19 And Jā′kim, and Zĭch′rī,
and Zăb′dī,
20 And Ē-lī-ē′na-ī, and Zĭl′-
thāi, and Ē-lī′el,
21 And Ăd-a-ī′ah, and Bĕr-a-
ī′ah, and Shĭm′răth, the sons of
Shĭm′hī;
22 And Ĭsh′păn, and Hē′bẽr,
and Ē-lī′el,
23 And Ăb′dŏn, and Zĭch′rī,
and Hā′nan,
24 And Hăn-a-nī′ah, and Ē′-
lăm, and Ăn-to-thī′jah,
25 And Ĭph-e-dē′iah, and Pē-
nū′el, the sons of Shā′shăk;
26 And Shăm-she-rā′ī, and
Shē-ha-rī′ah, and Ăth-a-lī′ah,
27 And Jăr-e-sī′ah, and Ē-lī′ah,
and Zĭch′rī, the sons of Jĕr′o-
hăm.

40
z *Genealogy*, 1 Chr. 5:1.

1
a *Genealogy*, 1 Chr. 5:1.
b *Benjamin, tribe of*, vs. 1–40; Num. 1:37.
c *Bela*, Num. 26:38.
d *Ashbel*, Gen. 46:21.

3
e *Gera*, Judg. 3:15.

4
f Num. 26:40.

6
g *Geba*, Josh. 21:17.

13
h *Aijalon*, Josh. 21:24.
i *Gath*, Josh. 11:22.

*[In order to publish this Bible in one volume with its numerous and diversified marginal notes and footnotes it has been necessary to avoid elaborate discussions of subjects, such, for instance, as would be necessary to point out the difficulties in connection with some of the names in genealogical lists. These difficulties grow out of errors of copyists, differences in the spelling of the same name, and the fact that individuals and places are mentioned under different names in different chapters. Where the identity of persons and places is doubtful in the following lists, and when no noteworthy fact is known concerning them, no mention of the name is made in either the margins or footnotes.]

† **EHUD.** *Called* EHI, Gen. 46:21. *Probably identical with* AHIRAM, *mentioned in* Num. 26:38; *and* AHARAH, 1 Chr. 8:1; *and* AHIAH, v. 7; *and* AHER, 1 Chr. 7:12.

‡ **ONO.** *A town of Benjamin*, 1 Chr. 8:12; Ezra 2:33; Neh. 7:37; *situated in valley of same name*, Neh. 6:2; 11:35.

‖ **LOD.** *A city of Benjamin*, 1 Chr. 8:12; Ezra 2:33; Neh. 7:37; 11:35; *called* LYDDA, Acts 9:32, 35, 38.

28 [a]These *were* heads of the fathers, by their generations, chief *men*. These dwelt in [k]Jė-ru̦'sȧ-lĕm.

29 And at [l]Ḡĭb'e-on dwelt the father of Ḡĭb'e-on; whose wife's name *was* [m]Mā'a-chah:

30 And his firstborn son [n]Ăb'dŏn, and [n]Zûr, and [n]Kĭsh, and [n]Bā'al, and [n]Nā'dăb,

31 And [o]Ḡē'dôr, and [o]Ȧ-hī'ō, and [p]Zā'chēr.

32 And [q]Mĭk'loth begat [r]Shĭm'e-ah. And these also dwelt with their brethren in [k]Jė-ru̦'sȧ-lĕm, over against them.

33 ¶ And [s]Nēr begat [t]Kĭsh, and Kĭsh begat [u]Sa̦ul, and Sa̦ul begat [v]Jŏn'a-than, and [w]Măl'chī-shū'ȧ, and [x]Ȧ-bĭn'a-dăb, and [y]Ĕsh–bā'al.

34 And the son of [v]Jŏn'a-than *was* [z]Mĕr'ib–bā'al; and Mĕr'ib-bā'al begat [a]Mī'cah.

35 And the sons of [a]Mī'cah *were*, [b]Pī'thon, and [b]Mē'lech, and [b]Tā're-ȧ, and [b]Ā'hăz.

36 And [b]Ā'hăz begat Jė-hō'a-dah; and Jė-hō'a-dah begat [c]Ăl'e-mĕth, and [c]Ăz'ma-vĕth, and [c]Zĭm'rī; and Zĭm'rī begat [c]Mō'zȧ,

37 And [c]Mō'zȧ begat [d]Bĭn'e-ȧ: [e]Rā'phȧ *was* his son, [d]Ė-lē'a-sah his son, [d]Ā'zĕl his son:

38 And [d]Ā'zĕl had six sons, whose names *are* these, [f]Ăz'rĭ-kăm, [f]Bŏch'e-ru̦, and [f]Ĭsh'ma-el, and [f]Shē-a-rī'ah, and [f]Ō-ba-dī'ah, and [f]Hā'nan. All these *were* the sons of Ā'zĕl.

39 And the sons of Ē'shĕk his brother *were*, Ū'lam his firstborn, Jē'hŭsh the second, and Ė-lĭph'e-lĕt the third.

40 And the sons of Ū'lam were mighty men of valour, [g]archers, and had many sons, and sons' sons, an hundred and fifty. All these *are* of the [h]sons of Bĕn'ja-mĭn.

## CHAPTER 9

*The recorded genealogies of Israel and of Judah. 2 The first inhabitants in Jerusalem after the captivity. 17 The charge of certain Levites. 35 The family of Saul and Jonathan.*

SO all [a]Ĭs̩'ra-el were reckoned by [b]genealogies; and, behold, they *were* written in the [c]book of the [d]kings of Ĭs̩'ra-el and [e]Jū'dah, *who* were carried away to [f]Băb'y̆-lon for their transgression.

2 ¶ Now the first inhabitants that *dwelt* in their possessions in their cities *were*, the Ĭs̩'ra-el-ītes, the [g]priests, [h]Lē'vītes, and the [i]Nĕth'ĭ-nĭms̩.

3 And in [j]Jė-ru̦'sȧ-lĕm dwelt of the children of [k]Jū'dah, and of the children of [l]Bĕn'ja-mĭn, and of the children of [m]Ē'phrā-ĭm, and [n]Mȧ-năs'seh;

4 Ū'tha-ī the son of Ăm-mī'hŭd, the son of Ŏm'rī, the son of Ĭm'rī, the son of Bā'nī, of the children of [o]Phā'rĕz the son of [p]Jū'dah.

5 And of the [q]Shī'lo-nītes; Ā-sa-ī'ah the firstborn, and his sons.

6 And of the sons of [r]Zē'rah; Jė-ū'el, and their brethren, six hundred and ninety.

7 And of the sons of [l]Bĕn'ja-mĭn; [s]Săl'lu the son of Mė-shŭl'lam, the son of Hŏd-a-vī'ah, the son of Hăs-e-nū'ah,

8 And Ĭb-nē'iah the son of Jĕr'o-hăm, and Ē'lah the son of Ŭz'zī, the son of Mĭch'rī, and Mė-shŭl'lam the son of Shĕph-a-thī'ah, the son of Reu̦'el, the son of Ĭb-nī'jah;

9 [b]And their brethren, according to their generations, nine hundred and fifty and six. All these men *were* chief of the fathers in the house of their fathers.

10 ¶ And of the [t]priests; [u]Jė-dā'iah, and [v]Jė-hoi'a-rĭb, and [w]Jā'chin,

11 And [x]Ăz-a-rī'ah the son of [y]Hĭl-kī'ah, the son of [z]Mė-shŭl'-

**28** k *Jerusalem*, Judg. 19:10.
**29** l *Gibeon*, Jer. 41:16. m 1 Chr. 9:35.
**30** n 1 Chr. 9:36.
**31** o 1 Chr. 9:37. p Or, *Zechariah*, 1 Chr. 9:37.
**32** q 1 Chr. 9:37, 38. r Or, *Shimeam*, 1 Chr. 9:38.
**33** s 1 Chr. 9:39; 1 Sam. 14:50. t *Kish*, 1 Sam. 9:1. u *Saul*, 1 Sam. 9:2. v *Jonathan*, 1 Sam. 14:1. w Or, *Melchi-shua*, 1 Sam. 14:49. x *Abinadab*, 1 Sam. 31:2. y Or, *Ish-bosheth*, 2 Sam. 2:8.
**34** z Or, *Mephibosheth*, 2 Sam. 9:6.
a 1 Chr. 9:40, 41; or, *Micha*, 2 Sam. 9:12.
**35** b 1 Chr. 9:41.
**36** c 1 Chr. 9:42.
**37** d 1 Chr. 9:43. e Or, *Rephaiah*, 1 Chr. 9:43.
**38** f 1 Chr. 9:44.
**40** g *Archery*, Gen. 21:20. h *Benjamin, tribe of*, Num. 1:37.

**1** a *Israel, divided into families*, Ex. 4:22. b *Genealogy*, vs. 1-44; 1 Chr. 5:1. c *Book*, Num. 5:23. d *King*, 2 Kin. 3:10. e *Judah, captivity of*, 2 Chr. 11:17. f *Babylon, empire, of*, Ezra 5:12.
**2** g *Priest*, Lev. 1:5. h *Levites*, Deut. 10:8. i *Nethinim*, Ezra 8:20.
**3** j *Jerusalem, dwellers in*, vs. 3-44; Judg. 19:10. k *Judah, tribe of*, Num. 10:14. l *Benjamin, tribe of*, Num. 1:37. m *Ephraim, tribe of*, Gen. 41:52. n *Manasseh, tribe of*, Gen. 46:20.
**4** o *Pharez*, Gen. 38:29. p *Judah*, Gen. 37:26.
**5** q Or, *Shelanites*, Num. 26:20.
**6** r Or, *Zarah*, Gen. 38:30.
**7** s Neh. 11:7.
**10** t *Priest*, Lev. 1:5. u Ezra 2:36; Neh. 7:39. v Neh. 11:10; 12:6, 19. w Neh. 11:10.
**11** x 1 Chr. 6:13; Ezra 7:1; or, *Seraiah*, Neh. 11:11. y *Hilkiah*, Jer. 29:3. z Neh. 11:11; or, *Shallum*, 1 Chr. 6:12; Ezra 7:2.

*a* Neh. 11:11.
*b* *Church, called house of God,* 1 Kin. 9:3.

**12**
*c* Neh. 11:12.
*d* Or, *Malchiah*, Neh. 11:12; Jer. 38:1; or, *Melchiah*, Jer. 21:1.
*e* Ezra 2:37; 10:20; Neh. 7:40; 11:13.

**13**
*f* *Temple, the Second*, 1 Kin. 6:17.

**14**
*g* *Levites*, Deut. 10:8.
*h* Neh. 11:15.
*i* Neh. 11:15.
*j* *Merarites*, Num. 26:57.

**16**
*k* Or, *Shammua*, Neh. 11:17.
*l* Neh. 11:17.
*m* *Jeduthun*, 1 Chr. 16:38.

**17**
*n* *Porters*, 2 Sam. 18:26.

**18**
*o* *Jerusalem, gates of*, Judg. 19:10.

**19**
*p* 1 Chr. 26:1.
*q* 1 Chr. 6:23, 37; or, *Asaph*, 1 Chr. 26:1.
*r* *Korah*, Num. 16:1.

lam, the son of [a]Zā′dŏk, the son
of [a]Mĕ-rā′ioth, the son of [a]Ȧ-hī′-
tub, the ruler of the [b]house of
God;
12 And [c]Ăd-a-ī′ah the son of
[c]Jĕr′o-hăm, the son of *Păsh′ŭr,
the son of [d]Măl-chī′jah, and
Mȧ-ăs′ĭ-āi the son of Ā′dĭ-el, the
son of Jăh′ze-rah, the son of Mė-
shŭl′lam, the son of Mė-shĭl′le-
mĭth, the son of [e]Ĭm′mĕr;
13 And their brethren, heads
of the house of their fathers, a
thousand and seven hundred
and threescore; very able men
for the work of the service of
the [f]house of God.
14 ¶ And of the [g]Lē′vītes;
[h]Shĕm-a-ī′ah the son of [h]Hăs′-
shub, the son of [i]Ăz′rĭ-kăm, the
son of [i]Hăsh-a-bī′ah, of the [j]sons
of Mė-rā′rī;
15 And Băk-băk′kar, Hē′resh,
and Gā′lăl, and †Măt-ta-nī′ah
the son of ‡Mī′cah, the son of
‖Zĭch′rī, the son of Ā′saph;
16 And Ō-ba-dī′ah the son
of [k]Shĕm-a-ī′ah, the son of [l]Gā′-
lăl, the son of [m]Jĕd′ụ-thŭn, and
Bĕr-e-chī′ah the son of Ā′sȧ, the
son of Ĕl′kă-nah, that dwelt in
the villages of the Nė-tŏph′a-
thītes.
17 And the [n]porters *were*, Shăl′-
lum, and §Ăk′kŭb, and +Tăl′-
mon, and Ȧ-hī′man, and their
brethren: Shăl′lum *was* the
chief;
18 Who hitherto *waited* in the
[o]king's gate eastward: they *were*
[n]porters in the companies of the
[q]children of Lē′vī.
19 And Shăl′lum the son of
[p]Kō′rė, the son of [q]Ė-bī′a-săph,
the son of [r]Kō′rah, and his
brethren, of the house of his father, the Kō′rah-ītes, *were* over
the work of the service, [n]keepers
of the gates of the [s]tabernacle:
and their fathers, *being* over the
host of the LORD, *were* keepers
of the entry.
20 And [t,u]Phĭn′e-has the son
of [v]Ē-le-ā′zar was the ruler
over [g]them in time past, *and*
the LORD *was* with him.
21 *And* [w]Zĕch-a-rī′ah the son of
[x]Mė-shĕl-e-mī′ah *was* [n]porter of
the door of the [s]tabernacle of the
congregation.
22 All these *which were* chosen to be [n]porters in the gates
*were* two hundred and twelve.
These were reckoned by their
[y]genealogy in their villages,
whom [z]Dā′vid and [a]Săm′u-el
the [b]seer did ordain in their
set office.
23 So they and their children
*had* the oversight of the gates of
the house of the LORD, *namely*,
the house of the tabernacle, by
wards.
24 In four quarters were the
[c]porters, toward the east, west,
north, and south.
25 And their brethren, *which*
*were* in their villages, *were* to
come after seven days from time
to time with them.
26 For these [d]Lē′vītes, the four
chief [c]porters, were in *their* set
office, and were over the [e]cham-
bers and treasuries of the house
of God.
27 And they lodged round
about the house of God, because
the charge *was* upon them, and
the opening thereof every morning *pertained* to [d]them.
28 And *certain* of [d]them had the
charge of the ministering vessels,

*s* *Tabernacle*, Ex. 27:9.

**20**
*t* *Phinehas*, Num. 25:7.
*u* *High Priest, duties of*, Lev. 21:10.
*v* *Eleazar*, Num. 3:2.

**21**
*w* 1 Chr. 26:2, 14.
*x* 1 Chr. 26:1, 2, 9.

**22**
*y* *Genealogy*, 1 Chr. 5:1.
*z* *David*, 1 Sam. 16:13.
*a* *Samuel*, 1 Sam. 3:1.
*b* *Prophets*, Isa. 3:2.

**24**
*c* *Porters*, 2 Sam. 18:26.

**26**
*d* *Levites, functions of*, Deut. 10:8.
*e* *Treasure Houses*, Ezra 5:17.

* **PASHUR.** *A priest, son of Malchiah,* 1 Chr. 9:12. *An influential man and ancestor of an influential family,* Ezra 2:38; 10:22; Neh. 7:41; 10:3; 11:12; Jer. 21:1; 38:1.

† **MATTANIAH.** *A Levite, descendant of Asaph, whose family dwelt in Jerusalem,* 1 Chr. 9:15; 2 Chr. 20:14; Neh. 11: 17, 22; 12:8, 25, 35.

‡ **MICAH.** *A Levite, descendant of Asaph,* 1 Chr. 9:15. *Called* MICHA, Neh. 10:11; 11:17, 22; *and* MICAIAH, Neh. 12: 35, 41.

‖ **ZICHRI.** *A Levite, son of Asaph,* 1 Chr. 9:15. *Called* ZABDI, Neh. 11:17, *and* ZACCUR, 1 Chr. 25:2, 10; Neh. 10:12; 12:35.

§ **AKKUB,** a returned exile. *A porter of the temple,* 1 Chr. 9:17; Ezra 2:42; Neh. 7:45; 8:7; 11:19; 12:25.

+ **TALMON.** *A porter of the temple,* 1 Chr. 9:17. *Family of, return from captivity with Zerubbabel,* Ezra 2:42; Neh. 7: 45; 11:19; 12:25.

that they should bring them in
and out by tale.
29 *Some* of [d]them also *were*
appointed to oversee the vessels, and all the instruments of
the [f]sanctuary, and the fine
flour, and the [g]wine, and the
[h]oil, and the ⊙frankincense, and
the [i]spices.
30 And *some* of the sons of the
priests made the [h]ointment of
the [i]spices.
31 And Măt-tĭ-thī′ah, *one* of the
Lē′vītes, who *was* the firstborn
of Shăl′lum the Kō′rah-īte, had
the set office over the things that
were [1]made in the pans.
32 And *other* of their brethren,
of the sons of the [j]Kō′hath-ītes,
*were* over the [k]shewbread, to
prepare *it* every [l]sabbath.
33 And these *are* the [m,n]sing-
ers, chief of the fathers of the
Lē′vītes, *who remaining* in the
chambers *were* free: for they
were employed in *that* work day
and night.
34 These chief fathers of the
[o]Lē′vītes *were* chief throughout
their generations; these dwelt at
[p]Jė-ru′sȧ-lĕm.
35 ¶ And in [q]Gĭb′e-on dwelt
the father of Gĭb′e-on, Jė-hī′el,
whose wife's name *was* [r]Mā′a-
chah:
36 And his firstborn son [s]Ăb′-
dŏn, then [s]Zûr, and [s]Kĭsh, and
[s]Bā′al, and [t]Nēr, and [s]Nā′-
dăb,
37 And [u]Gē′dôr, and [u]Ȧ-hī′ō,
and [v]Zĕch-a-rī′ah, and [w]Mĭk′-
loth.
38 And [w]Mĭk′loth begat [w]Shĭm′-
e-ăm. And they also dwelt
with their brethren at [p]Jė-ru′-
sȧ-lĕm, over against their brethren.
39 And [t]Nēr begat [x]Kĭsh; and
Kĭsh begat [y]Saul; and Saul
begat [z]Jŏn′a-than, and [a]Măl′-
chĭ-shū′ȧ, and [b]Ȧ-bĭn′a-dăb, and
[c]Ĕsh-bā′al.
40 And the son of [d]Jŏn′a-than
*was* [e]Mĕr′ib-bā′al: and Mĕr′-
ib-bā′al begat [f]Mī′cah.
41 And the sons of [f]Mī′cah
*were*, [g]Pī′thon, and [g]Mē′lech,
and [h]Tăh′re-ȧ, *and* [g]*A′haz*.
42 And [g]Ā′hăz begat Jā′rah;
and Jā′rah begat [i]Ăl′e-mĕth,
and [i]Ăz′ma-vĕth, and [i]Zĭm′rī;
and Zĭm′rī begat [i]Mō′zȧ;
43 And [i]Mō′zȧ begat [j]Bĭn′e-ȧ;
and [k]Rĕph-a-ī′ah his son, [j]Ė-lē′-
a-sah his son, [j]Ā′zĕl his son.
44 And [j]Ā′zĕl had six sons,
whose names *are* these, [l]Ăz′rĭ-
kăm, [l]Bŏch′e-ru, and [l]Ĭsh′ma-
el, and [l]Shē-a-rī′ah, and [l]Ō-ba-
dī′ah, and [l]Hā′nan: these *were*
the sons of Ā′zĕl.

## CHAPTER 10

*Saul's overthrow and death. 8 The Philistines triumph over Saul. 11 The kindness of the men of Jabesh-gilead toward Saul and his sons. 13 The sin for which the kingdom was transferred from Saul to David.*

NOW the [a]Phĭ-lĭs′tīneş fought
against [b]Ĭş′ra-el; and the
men of Ĭş′ra-el fled from before
the Phĭ-lĭs′tīneş, and fell down
slain in mount [c]Gĭl-bō′ȧ.
2 And the [a]Phĭ-lĭs′tīneş followed hard after [d]Saul, and after his sons; and the Phĭ-lĭs′tīneş
slew [e]Jŏn′a-than, and [f]Ȧ-bĭn′a-
dăb, and [g]Măl′chĭ-shū′ȧ, the
sons of Saul.
3 And the battle went sore
against [d]Saul, and the [h]archers
[1]hit him, and he was [2]wounded
of the archers.
4 Then said [d]Saul to his [i]ar-
mourbearer, Draw thy sword,
and thrust me through therewith; lest these uncircumcised
come and abuse me. But his
armourbearer would not; for he

29
f *Church, called sanctuary*, 1 Kin. 9:3.
g *Wine*, Prov. 23:31.
h *Oil, sacred*, Deut. 12:17.
i *Spices*, 1 Kin. 10:2.

31
1 R. V. baked

32
j *Kohathites, duties of*, Num. 3:27.
k *Shewbread*, Ex. 35:13.
l *Sabbath*, Ex. 16:23.

33
m *Choir, sang morning and evening*, 1 Chr. 15:16.
n *Music*, 2 Chr. 5:13.

34
o *Levites*, Deut. 10:8.
p *Jerusalem*, Judg. 19:10.

35
q *Gibeon*, Jer. 41:16.
r 1 Chr. 8:29.

36
s 1 Chr. 8:30.
t 1 Chr. 8:33; 1 Sam. 14:50.

37
u 1 Chr. 8:31.
v Or, *Zacher*, 1 Chr. 8:31.
w 1 Chr. 8:32.

39
x *Kish*, 1 Sam. 9:1.
y *Saul*, 1 Sam. 9:2.
z *Jonathan*, 1 Sam. 14:1.
a Or, *Melchi-shua*, 1 Sam. 14:49.
b *Abinadab*, 1 Sam. 31:2.
c Or, *Ish-bosheth*, 2 Sam. 2:8.

40
d *Jonathan*, 1 Sam. 14:1.
e Or, *Mephibosheth*, 2 Sam. 9:6.
f 1 Chr. 8:34.

41
g 1 Chr. 8:35.
h Or, *Tarea*, 1 Chr. 8:35.

42
i 1 Chr. 8:36.

43
j 1 Chr. 8:37.
k Or, *Rapha*, 1 Chr. 8:37.

44
l 1 Chr. 8:38.

v.1–984 BC
See footnote, *Time*, Rev. 10:6.

1
a *Philistines*, Gen. 26:14.
b *Israel, under the kings*, Ex. 4:22.
c 1 Sam. 28:4.

2
d *Saul*, 1 Sam. 9:2.
e *Jonathan*, 1 Sam. 14:1.
f *Abinadab*, 1 Sam. 31:2.
g Or, *Melchi-shua*, 1 Sam. 14:49.

3
h *Archery*, Gen. 21:20.
1 R. V. overtook
2 R. V. distressed by reason of

4
i *Armor-bearer*, Judg. 9:54.

⊙ **FRANKINCENSE.** *A perfume*, Song 3:6; 4:6. *Commerce in*, Rev. 18:11–13. *Used as an incense*, Isa. 43:23; 60:6; 66:3; Jer. 6:20. *Gift of*, Matt. 2:11.
*An ingredient of the sacred perfume*, Ex. 30:34. *Used, with shewbread*, Lev. 24:7; *with meat* (R. V. meal) *offerings*, Lev. 2:1, 2, 15, 16; 6:15; Neh. 13:9. *Prohibited, in sin offerings when they consisted of turtle doves or pigeons*, Lev. 5:11; *in making an offering of memorial*, Num. 5:15.

v.4–984 BC
See footnote, *Time*, Rev. 10:6.

*f* *Suicide, instances of*, 1 Kin. 16:18.

was sore[G] afraid. So [f]Sa̤ul took a sword, and fell upon it.

5 And when his [i]armourbearer saw that [d]Sa̤ul was dead, [j]he fell likewise on the sword, and died.

6 So [d]Sa̤ul died, and his [e,f,g]three sons, and all his house died together.

7 And when all the men of [b]Ĭṣ′ra-el that *were* in the valley saw that they fled, and that Sa̤ul and his sons were dead, then they forsook their cities, and fled: and the [a]Phĭ-lĭs′tĭneṣ came and dwelt in them.

8 ¶ And it came to pass on the morrow[G], when the [a]Phĭ-lĭs′tĭneṣ came to strip[G] the slain, that they found [d]Sa̤ul and his sons fallen in mount [c]Gĭl-bō′ȧ.

9 And when they had stripped[G] him, they took his head, and his armour, and sent into the land of the Phĭ-lĭs′tĭneṣ round about, to carry tidings unto their [k]idols, and to the people.

10 And they put his [l]armour in the [m]house of their gods, and fastened his [l]head in the temple of [n]Dā′gon.

11 ¶ And when all [o]Jā′besh–gĭl′e-ăd heard all that the [a]Phĭ-lĭs′tĭneṣ had done to [d]Sa̤ul,

12 They arose, all the valiant men, and took away the body of [d]Sa̤ul, and the bodies of his [e,f,g]sons, and brought them to [o]Jā′besh, and buried their bones [p]under the oak in Jā′besh, and [q]fasted [r]seven days.

13 ¶ So [d,s]Sa̤ul [t,u]died for his transgression which he committed against the LORD, *even* against the word of the LORD, which he kept not, and also for asking *counsel* of *one that had* a [v,w]familiar[G] spirit, to enquire *of it*;

14 And enquired not of the LORD: therefore he [u]slew him, and turned the kingdom unto [x]Dā′vid the son of [y]Jĕs′se.

9
*k* *Idolatry*, 1 Sam. 15:23.

10
*l* *Trophies*, 1 Sam. 21:9.
*m* *Temple, idolatrous*, 1 Kin. 6:11.
*n* *Dagon, temple of*, Judg. 16:23.

11
*o* *Jabesh-gilead*, Judg. 21:8.

12
*p* *Burying Places*, Gen. 23:4.
*q* *Fasting, in times of bereavement*, Zech. 8:19.
*r* *Seven, days*, Gen. 7:2.

13
*s* *Wicked, punishment of*, Psa. 73:3.
*t* *Death, as a judgment*, Num. 23:10.
*u* *Judgments*, Ex. 6:6.
*v* *Familiar Spirits*, Deut. 18:11.
*w* *Sorcery*, Isa. 47:9.

14
*x* *David*, 1 Sam. 16:13.
*y* *Jesse*, Ruth 4:17.

## CHAPTER 11

*David is made king at Hebron. 4 He takes the castle at Zion from the Jebusites. 10 A catalogue of David's mighty men.*

THEN all [a]Ĭṣ′ra-el gathered themselves to [b]Dā′vid unto [c]Hē′bron, saying, Behold, we *are* thy bone and thy flesh.

2 And moreover in time past, even when [d]Sa̤ul was king, thou *wast* he that leddest out and broughtest in Ĭṣ′ra-el: and the LORD thy God said unto thee, Thou shalt feed my people Ĭṣ′ra-el, and thou shalt be ruler over my people Ĭṣ′ra-el.[Q]

3 Therefore came all the [e]elders of Ĭṣ′ra-el to the king to [c]Hē′bron; and [b]Dā′vid [f]made a [g]covenant[G] with them in Hē′bron before the LORD; and they [h]anointed[G] Dā′vid [i]king over [a]Ĭṣ′ra-el, according to the [j]word of the LORD by [k]Săm′u-el.

4 ¶ And [b]Dā′vid and all [a]Ĭṣ′ra-el went to [l]Jė-ru̧′sȧ-lĕm, which *is* Jē′bus; where the [m]Jĕb′u-sītes *were*, the inhabitants of the land.

5 And the inhabitants of [l]Jē′bus said to [b]Dā′vid, Thou shalt not come hither.[G] Nevertheless Dā′vid took the [1]castle[G] of [n]Zī′ŏn, which *is* the city of Dā′vid.

6 And [b]Dā′vid said, [o]Whosoever smiteth[G] the [m]Jĕb′u-sītes first shall be chief[G] and [p]captain. So [q]Jō′ăb the son of [r]Zĕr-u̧-ī′ah went first up, and [s]was chief.

7 And [b]Dā′vid dwelt in the [1]castle[G]; therefore they called it the [l,t]city of Dā′vid.

8 And he built the [t]city round about, even from [u]Mĭl′lō round about: and [q]Jō′ăb repaired the rest of the city.

9 So [b]Dā′vid waxed[G] greater and greater: for the LORD of hosts [v]*was* with him.

10 ¶ These also *are* the chief of the mighty men whom [b]Dā′vid had, who strengthened themselves with him in his kingdom,

v.1–976 BC
See footnote, *Time*, Rev. 10:6.

1
*a* *Israel, under the kings*, Ex. 4:22.
*b* *David*, 1 Sam. 16:13.
*c* *Hebron*, Gen. 23:2.

2
*d* *Saul*, 1 Sam. 9:2.

3
*e* *Senate*, Num. 11:16.
*f* *Constitution*, Dan. 6:12.
*g* *Covenant, of men with men*, Deut. 29:1.
*h* *Anointing*, Lev. 8:12.
*i* *King*, 2 Kin. 3:10.
*j* *Prophets, inspiration of*, Isa. 3:2.
*k* *Samuel*, 1 Sam. 3:1.

4
*l* *Jerusalem*, Judg. 19:10.
*m* *Jebusites*, Deut. 7:1.

5
*n* *Zion*, 2 Sam. 5:7.
1 R. V. strong hold

6
*o* *Armies, rewards in*, Deut. 11:4.
*p* *Captain*, Num. 31:48.
*q* *Joab*, 2 Sam. 20:23.
*r* *Zeruiah, sister of David*, 1 Chr. 2:16.
*s* *Promotion*, Psa. 75:6.

7
*t* *Cities, royal*, Num. 35:8.

8
*u* *Millo*, 2 Sam. 5:9.

9
*v* *God, dwells with the righteous*, 1 Kin. 6:13.

v.10—976 BC
See footnote, *Time*, Rev. 10:6.

**11**
*w* 1 Chr. 27:2; 2 Sam. 23:8.
*x* *Spear*, 2 Kin. 11:10.
2 R. V. the son of a
3 R. V. thirty;

**12**
*y* 2 Sam. 23:9, 10, 13.
*z* 2 Sam. 23:9; or, *Dodai*, 1 Chr. 27:4.

**13**
*a* *David*, 1 Sam. 16:13.
*b* Or, *Ephes-dammim*, 1 Sam. 17:1.
*c* *Philistines*, Gen. 26:14.
*d* *Barley*, Ex. 9:31.

**14**
*e* *God, preserver*, Gen. 2:2.

**15**
*f* *Captain*, Num. 31:48.
*g* *Cave*, Judg. 6:2.
*h* *Adullam*, 1 Sam. 22:1.

**16**
*i* *Garrison*, 1 Sam. 13:3.
*j* *Beth-lehem*, Gen. 48:7.

**18**
*k* *Love, of man for man*, 1 John 4:7.
*l* *Courage, instances of*, Deut. 31:7.
*m* 2 Sam. 23:16.
*n* *Consecration, instances of*, Lev. 7:37.

*and* with all Ĭṣ′ra-el, to make
him king, according to the word
of the LORD concerning Ĭṣ′ra-el.
11 And this *is* the number of
the mighty men whom Dā′vid
had; [w]Jā-shō′be-ăm, [2]an Hăch′-
mō-nīte, the chief of the [3,p]cap-
tains: he lifted up his [x]spear
against three hundred slain *by*
*him* at one time.
12 And after him *was* [y]Ē-le-ā′-
zar the son of [z]Dō′dō, the Ā-hō′-
hīte, who *was one* of the three
mighties.
13 He was with [a]Dā′vid at
[b]Păs–dăm′mim, and there the
[c]Phĭ-lĭs′tĭneṣ were gathered together to battle, where was a
parcel of ground full of [d]barley;
and the people fled from before
the Phĭ-lĭs′tĭneṣ.
14 And they set themselves in
the midst of *that* parcel, and
delivered it, and slew the [c]Phĭ-
lĭs′-tĭneṣ; and the LORD [e]saved
*them* by a great deliverance.
15 Now three of the thirty [f]cap-
tains went down to the rock to
[a]Dā′vid, into the [g]cave of [h]Ā-
dŭl′lăm; and the host of the
[c]Phĭ-lĭs′tĭneṣ encamped in the
valley of *Rĕph′a-ĭm.
16 And [a]Dā′vid *was* then in
the [g]hold, and the [c]Phĭ-lĭs′tĭneṣ′
[i]garrison *was* then at [j]Bĕth′–lĕ-
hĕm.
17 And [a]Dā′vid longed, and
said, Oh that one would give
me drink of the water of the
well of [j]Bĕth′–lĕ-hĕm, that *is* at
the gate!
18 And the [k]three [l]brake
through the host of the [c]Phĭ-
lĭs′tĭneṣ, and drew water out of
the well of [j]Bĕth′–lĕ-hĕm, that
*was* by the gate, and took *it*, and
[m]brought *it* to Dā′vid: but Dā′-
vid would not drink *of* it, but
[n]poured it out to the LORD,
19 And said, My God forbid it
me, that I should do this thing:
shall I drink the blood of these
men that have put their lives in
jeopardy? for with *the jeopardy*
*of* their lives they brought it.
Therefore he would not drink it.
These things did these three
mightiest.
20 And [o]Ā-bĭsh′a-ī the brother
of [p]Jō′ăb, he was chief of the
three: for lifting up his [q]spear
against three hundred, he slew
*them*, and had a name among
the three.
21 Of the three, he was more
honourable than the two; for
[r]he was [4]their [f]captain: howbeit
he attained not to the *first*
three.
22 [s]Bē-nā′iah the son of [t]Jē-
hoi′a-dȧ, the son of a valiant
man of [u]Kăb′ze-el, who had
done many acts; he slew [5]two
lionlike [v]men of Mō′ab: also he
went down and slew a [w]lion in a
pit in a snowy day.
23 And he slew an [x]Ē-ġy̆p′tian,
a man of *great* stature, five [y]cu-
bits high; and in the Ē-ġy̆p′-
tian′s hand *was* a [q]spear like a
[z]weaver′s beam; and he went
down to him with a staff, and
plucked the spear out of the
Ē-ġy̆p′tian′s hand, and slew him
with his own spear.
24 These *things* did [s]Bē-nā′-
iah the son of [t]Jē-hoi′a-dȧ, and
had the name among the three
mighties.
25 Behold, he was honourable
among the thirty, but attained
not to the *first* three: and Dā′vid
set him over his guard.
26 Also the valiant men of the
armies *were*, [a]Ā′sa-hĕl the brother of [b]Jō′ăb, [c]Ĕl-hā′nan the son
of [c]Dō′dō of [d]Bĕth′–lĕ-hĕm,
27 [e]Shăm′moth the Hā′ro-rīte,
[f]Hē′lez the [g]Pĕl′o-nīte,
28 [h]Ī′rȧ the son of [h]Ĭk′kĕsh the

**20**
*o* *Abishai*, 2 Sam. 3:30.
*p* *Joab*, 2 Sam. 20:23.
*q* *Spear*, 2 Kin. 11:10.

**21**
*r* *Promotion*, Psa. 75:6.
4 R. V. made their captain:

**22**
*s* *Benaiah*, 1 Kin. 4:4.
*t* 2 Sam. 8:18.
*u* Josh. 15:21; 2 Sam. 23:20.
*v* *Moabites*, Gen. 19:37.
*w* *Lion*, Mic. 5:8.
5 R. V. the two sons of Ariel of Moab:

**23**
*x* *Egyptians*, Gen. 50:3.
*y* *Cubit*, Ex. 36:9.
*z* *Weaving*, Isa. 38:12.

**26**
*a* *Asahel*, 2 Sam. 2:18.
*b* *Joab*, 2 Sam. 20:23.
*c* 2 Sam. 23:24.
*d* *Beth-lehem*, Gen. 48:7.

**27**
*e* Or, *Shammah*, 2 Sam. 23:25.
*f* 1 Chr. 27:10; 2 Sam. 23:26.
*g* 1 Chr. 27:10; or, *Paltite*, 2 Sam. 23:26.

**28**
*h* 1 Chr. 27:9; 2 Sam. 23:26.

* **REPHAIM.** *Boundary between Judah and Benjamin*, Josh. 15:8 [R. V.]; 18:16 [R. V.]. *Battle ground of David and the Philistines*, 2 Sam. 5:18, 22; 23:13; 1 Chr. 11:15; 14:9. *Productiveness of*, Isa. 17:5.

Tē-kō'īte, [i]Ā'bĭ-ē'zēr the Ăn'-
toth-īte,
29 [j]Sĭb'be-cāi the Hū'shath-īte,
Ī'lāi the Ă-hō'hīte,
30 [k]Mă-hăr'a-ī the Nē-tŏph'a-
thīte, [l]Hē'led the son of [m]Bā'a-
nah the Nē-tŏph'a-thīte,
31 [n]Ĭth'a-ī the son of [m]Rī'bāi of
[o]Ğĭb'e-ah, *that pertained* to the
children of Bĕn'ja-mĭn, [p]Bē-nā'-
iah the [q]Pĭr'a-thon-īte,
32 Hū'rāi of the [r]brooks of
Gā'ăsh, [s]Ā-bī'el the Är'bath-īte,
33 [t]Ăz'ma-vĕth the Bă-hā'rum-
īte, [u]Ē-lī'ah-bȧ the Shă-ăl'bo-
nīte,
34 The sons of Hā'shem the
Ğī'zo-nīte, [u]Jŏn'a-than the son
of Shā'ğē the Hā'ra-rīte,
35 [v]Ā-hī'am the son of [w]Sā'căr
the Hā'ra-rīte, [x]Ĕl'ī-phăl the son
of [y]Ûr,
36 Hē'phēr the Mē-chē'rath-
īte, [z]Ā-hī'jah the Pĕl'o-nīte,
37 [a]Hĕz'rō the Căr'mel-īte,
[b]Nā'a-rāi the son of Ĕz'ba-ī,
38 [c]Jō'el the brother of Nā'-
than, Mĭb'hăr the son of Hăğ'-
ge-rī,
39 [d]Zē'lek the [e]Ăm'mon-īte,
[d]Nă-hăr'a-ī the Bē'roth'īte, the
[f]armourbearer of [g]Jō'ăb the son
of [h]Zĕr-u-ī'ah,
40 [i]Ī'rȧ the Ĭth'rīte, Gā'rĕb the
Ĭth'rīte,
41 [j]U-rī'ah the [k]Hĭt'tīte, Zā'-
băd the son of Äh'lāi,
42 Ăd'ī-nȧ the son of Shī'zȧ the
Reu'ben-īte, a captain of the
[l]Reu'ben-ītes, and thirty with
him,
43 Hā'nan the son of Mā'-
a-chah, and Jŏsh'a-phăt the
Mĭth'nīte,
44 Ŭz-zī'ȧ the Ăsh'te-rath-īte,
Shā'mȧ and Jē-hī'el the sons of
Hō'than the Ăr'o-ēr-īte,
45 Jē-dī'a-el the son of Shĭm'-
rī, and Jō'hȧ his brother, the
Tī'zīte,
46 Ē-lī'el the Mā'ha-vīte, and
Jĕr'ī-bāi, and Jŏsh-a-vī'ah, the
sons of Ĕl'na-ăm, and Ĭth'mah
the [m]Mō'ab-īte,
47 Ē-lī'el, and Ō'bed, and Jā'-
sī-el the Mē-sō'ba-īte.

## CHAPTER 12

*The companies that came to David at Ziklag.*
*23 The armies that came to him at Hebron.*

NOW these *are* they that came
to [a]Dā'vid to [b]Zĭk'lăg, while
he yet kept himself close[c] because of [c]Saul the son of
[d]Kĭsh: and they *were* among
the mighty men, helpers of the
war.
2 *They were* armed with bows,
and could use both the right
hand and the left in [e]*hurling*
stones and [f]*shooting* arrows out
of a bow, *even* of [c]Saul's brethren of [g]Bĕn'ja-mĭn.
3 The chief *was* Ā-hī-ē'zēr, then
Jō'ăsh, the sons of Shē-mā'ah
the Ğĭb'e-ath-īte; and Jē'zī-el,
and Pē'let, the sons of Ăz'ma-
vĕth; and Bĕr'a-chah, and Jē'-
hū the [h]Ăn'toth-īte,
4 And Ĭs-ma-ī'ah the Ğĭb'e-on-
īte, a mighty man among the
thirty, and over the thirty; and
Jĕr-e-mī'ah, and Jă-hā'zī-el, and
Jō-hā'nan, and Jŏs'a-băd the
Ğĕd'e-rath-īte,
5 Ē-lū'za-ī, and Jĕr'ī-mŏth, and
Bē-a-lī'ah, and Shĕm-a-rī'ah,
and Shĕph-a-tī'ah the Hăr'u-
phīte,
6 Ĕl'kă-nah, and Jē-sī'ah, and
Ā-zăr'e-el, and Jō-ē'zēr, and Jă-
shō'be-ăm, the Kôr'hītes,
7 And Jō-ē'lah, and Zĕb-a-
dī'ah, the sons of Jĕr'o-hăm of
Ğē'dôr.
8 And of the [i]Găd'ītes there
separated[c] themselves unto [a]Dā'-
vid into the [j,k]hold[c] to[c] the wilderness [1]men of might, *and*
men of war *fit* for the battle,
that could handle [l]shield and
[2]buckler, whose faces *were like*
the faces of [m]lions, and *were* as
swift as the [n]roes upon the
mountains;

28
i 1 Chr. 27:12; 2 Sam. 23:27.
29
j 1 Chr. 27:11; or, *Sibbechai*, 1 Chr. 20:4; 2 Sam. 21:18.
30
k 1 Chr. 27:13; 2 Sam. 23:28.
l Or, *Heldai*, 1 Chr. 27:15; or, *Heleb*, 2 Sam. 23:29.
m 2 Sam. 23:29.
31
n Or, *Ittai*, 2 Sam. 23:29.
o *Gibeah*, Hos. 9:9.
p 1 Chr. 27:14; 2 Sam. 23:30.
q *Pirathon*, Judg. 12:15.
32
r *Brook, Gaash*, Deut. 8:7.
s Or, *Abi-albon*, 2 Sam. 23:31.
33
t 2 Sam. 23:31.
u 2 Sam. 23:32.
35
v 2 Sam. 23:33.
w Or, *Sharar*, 2 Sam. 23:33.
x Or, *Eliphelet*, 2 Sam. 23:34.
y Or, *Ahasbai*, 2 Sam. 23:34.
36
z Or, *Eliam*, 2 Sam. 23:34.

37
a Or, *Hezrai*, 2 Sam. 23:35.
b Or, *Paarai*, 2 Sam. 23:35.
38
c Or, *Igal*, 2 Sam. 23:36.
39
d 2 Sam. 23:37.
e *Ammonites*, Deut. 2:20.
f *Armor-bearer*, Judg. 9:54.
g *Joab*, 2 Sam. 20:23.
h *Zeruiah*, 1 Chr. 2:16.
40
i 2 Sam. 23:38.
41
j *Uriah*, 2 Sam. 11:3.
k *Hittites*, Judg. 1:26.
42
l *Reubenites*, Josh. 22:1.

46
m *Moabites*, Gen. 19:37.
1
a *David*, 1 Sam. 16:13.
b *Ziklag*, Josh. 15:31.
c *Saul*, 1 Sam. 9:2.
d *Kish*, 1 Sam. 9:1.
2
e *Sling, dexterous use of*, 1 Sam. 17:40.
f *Archery*, Gen. 21:20.
g *Benjamin, tribe of*, Num. 1:37.
3
h *Anathoth*, Jer. 1:1.
8
i *Gad, tribe of*, Deut. 33:20.
j *Cave*, Judg. 6:2.
k *Adullam*, 1 Sam. 22:1.
l *Shield*, 1 Kin. 14:27.
m *Lion*, Mic. 5:8.
n *Deer*, Deut. 14:5.
1 R. V. mighty men of valour, men trained for war,
2 R. V. spear;

9 Ē'zēr the first, Ō-ba-dī'ah the
second, Ē-lī'ab the third,
10 Mĭsh-măn'nah the fourth,
Jĕr-e-mī'ah the fifth,
11 Ăt'tāi the sixth, Ē-lī'el the
seventh,
12 Jō-hā'nan the eighth, Ĕl'za-
băd the ninth,
13 Jĕr-e-mī'ah the tenth, Măch'-
ba-nāi the eleventh.
14 These *were* of the [t]sons of
Găd, [o]captains of the [p]host: one
of the least *was* [3]over an hundred, and the greatest [4]over a
thousand.
15 These *are* they that went
over [q]Jôr'dan in the [r]first
[s]month, when it had overflown
all his banks; and they put to
flight all *them* of the valleys, *both*
toward the east, and toward the
west.
16 And there came of the children of [g]Bĕn'ja-mĭn and [t]Jū'dah
to the hold[C] unto Dā'vid.
17 And [a]Dā'vid went out to
meet them, and answered and
said unto them, If ye be come
peaceably unto me to help me,
mine heart shall be knit unto
you: but if *ye be come* to betray
me to mine enemies, seeing *there*
*is* no wrong in mine hands, the
God of our fathers look *thereon*,
and rebuke *it*.
18 Then the spirit came upon
Ā-măs'a-ī, *who was* chief of the
[5]captains, *and he said*, Thine *are*
*we*, [a]Dā'vid, and on thy side,
thou son of [u]Jĕs'se: peace, peace
*be* unto thee, and peace *be* to
thine helpers; for thy God helpeth thee. Then Dā'vid received
them, and made them captains
of the band.[T]
19 And there fell *some* of
[v]Mā-năs'seh to [a]Dā'vid, when
he came with the [w]Phĭ-lĭs'tĭneş
against [c]Saul to battle: but they
helped them not: for the lords
of the Phĭ-lĭs'tĭneş upon advisement[C] sent him away, saying, He
will fall to his master[C] Saul to *the*
*jeopardy*[C] *of* our heads.
20 As he went to [b]Zĭk'lăg, there
fell to him of [v]Mā-năs'seh, Ăd'-
nah, and Jŏz'a-băd, and Jē-dī'a-
el, and Mī'chaĕl, and Jŏz'a-băd,
and Ē-lī'hū, and Zĭl'thāi, [o]cap-
tains of the thousands that *were*
of Mā-năs'seh.
21 And they helped [a]Dā'vid
against the band *of the rovers*:
for they *were* all mighty men of
valour, and were [o]captains in the
[p]host.
22 For at *that* time day by day
there came to Dā'vid to help
him, until *it was* a great host[C],
like the host of God.
23 ¶ And these *are* the numbers
of the [x]bands[C] *that were* ready
armed to the war, *and* came to
[a]Dā'vid to [y]Hē'bron, to turn the
kingdom of Saul to him, according to the word of the LORD.
24 The children of [t]Jū'dah that
bare [l]shield and [z]spear *were* six
thousand and eight hundred,
ready armed to the war.
25 Of the children of [a]Sĭm'e-on,
mighty men of valour for the
war, seven thousand and one
hundred.
26 Of the [b]children of Lē'vī
four thousand and six hundred.
27 And [c]Jē-hoi'a-dā *was* the
leader of the Aâr'on-ītes, and
with him *were* three thousand
and seven hundred.
28 And Zā'dŏk, a young man
mighty of valour, and of his father's house twenty and two
[d]captains.
29 And of the children of [e]Bĕn'-
ja-mĭn, the [6]kindred of [f]Saul,
three thousand: for hitherto[C] the
greatest part of them had kept
[7]the ward[C] of the house of Saul.
30 And of the children of [g]Ē'-
phrā-ĭm twenty thousand and
eight hundred, mighty men of
valour, famous throughout the
house of their fathers.

**14**
*o Captain*, Num. 31:48.
*p Armies*, Deut. 11:4.
3 R. V. was equal to
4 R. V. to

**15**
*q Jordan*, Gen. 32:10.
*r Abib (April)*, Ex. 13:4.
*s Month, Abib*, Ex. 12:2.

**16**
*t Judah, tribe of*, Num. 10:14.

**18**
*u Jesse*, Ruth 4:17.
5 R. V. thirty,

**19**
*v Manasseh, tribe of*, Gen. 46:20.
*w Philistines*, Gen. 26:14.
**B.C. 1056?**

**23**
*x Armies*, Deut. 11:4.
*y Hebron*, Gen. 23:2.
**v.23–976 BC**

**24**
*z Spear*, 2 Kin. 11:10.

**25**
*a Simeon, tribe of*, Num. 2:12.

**26**
*b Levites*, Deut. 10:8.

**27**
*c Priest*, Lev. 1:5.

**28**
*d Captain*, Num. 31:48.

**29**
*e Benjamin, tribe of*, Num. 1:37.
*f Saul*, 1 Sam. 9:2.
6 R. V. brethren
7 R. V. their allegiance to the

**30**
*g Ephraim, tribe of*, Gen. 41:52.

v.31–976 BC
See footnote, *Time,* Rev. 10:6.

31
*h Manasseh, tribe of,* Gen. 46:20.
*i David,* 1 Sam. 16:13.

32
*j Issachar, tribe of,* Num. 1:28.
*k Wisdom, worldly,* Prov. 2:2.
*l Israel, under the kings,* Ex. 4:22.

33
*m Zebulun tribe of,* Gen. 49:13.
*n Armies,* Deut. 11:4.
*o Sincerity, exemplified,* 1 Cor. 5:8.
*p Heart,* Psa. 44:21.

34
*q Naphtali, tribe of,* Num. 1:42.
*r Shield,* 1 Kin. 14:27.
*s Spear,* 2 Kin. 11:10.

35
*t Dan, tribe of,* Gen. 30:6.

36
*u Asher, tribe of,* Num. 1:40.

37
*v Jordan,* Gen. 32:10.
*w Reubenites,* Josh. 22:1.
*x Gad, tribe of,* Deut. 33:20.

38
*y Hebron,* Gen. 23:2.
*z David,* 1 Sam. 16:13.
8 R. V. order the battle array,

40
*a Issachar, tribe of,* Num. 1:28.
*b Zebulun, tribe of,* Gen. 49:13.
*c Naphtali, tribe of,* Num. 1:42.
*d Bread,* Ezek. 4:13.
*e Ass, domesticated,* 2 Chr. 28:15.
*f Camel,* 1 Sam. 30:17.
*g Mule,* 2 Sam. 18:9.
*h Bullock,* Ex. 29:3.
*i Fig,* Mark 11:13.
*j Raisins,* 1 Sam. 25:18.
9 R. V. victual of meal,

31 And of the half tribe of
[h]Mā-năs′seh eighteen thousand,
which were expressed by name,
to come and make [i]Dā′vid king.
32 And of the children of [j]Ĭs′-
sa-char, *which were men* that
had [k]understanding of the times,
to know what [l]Ĭs̱′ra-el ought to
do; the heads of them *were* two
hundred; and all their brethren
*were* at their commandment.
33 Of [m]Zĕb′u-lŭn, [n]such as
went forth to battle, expert in
war, with all instruments of war,
fifty thousand, which could keep
rank: *they* [o]*were* not of double
[p]heart.
34 And of [q]Năph′ta-lī a thousand [d]captains, and with them
with [r]shield and [s]spear thirty
and seven thousand.
35 And of the [t]Dăn′ītes expert
in war twenty and eight thousand and six hundred.
36 And of [u]Ăsh′ēr, such as went
forth to battle, expert in war,
forty thousand.
37 And on the other side of
[v]Jôr′dan, of the [w]Reu̱′ben-ītes,
and the [x]Găd′ītes, and of the
half tribe of [h]Mā-năs′seh, with
all manner of instruments of war
for the battle, an hundred and
twenty thousand.
38 All these men of war, that
could [8]keep rank, came with a
perfect[G] heart[G] to [y]Hē′bron, to
make [z]Dā′vid king over all Ĭs̱′-
ra-el: and all the rest also of Ĭs̱′-
ra-el *were* of one heart to make
Dā′vid king.
39 And there they were with
[z]Dā′vid three days, eating and
drinking: for their brethren had
prepared for them.
40 Moreover they that were
nigh[G] them, *even* unto [a]Ĭs′sa-char
and [b]Zĕb′u-lŭn and [c]Năph′ta-lī,
brought [d]bread on [e]asses, and on
[f]camels, and on [g]mules, and on
[h]oxen, [9]*and* meat, meal, cakes of
[i]figs, and bunches of [j]raisins,
and [k]wine, and [l]oil, and oxen,
and [m]sheep abundantly: for
*there was* [n]joy in Ĭs̱′ra-el.

## CHAPTER 13

*David fetches the ark with great solemnity from Kirjath-jearim. 9 Uzza being smitten, the ark is left at the house of Obed-edom.*

AND [a]Dā′vid [b,c]consulted with
the [d]captains of thousands
and hundreds, *and* with every
leader.
2 And [a]Dā′vid said unto all the
congregation of [e]Ĭs̱′ra-el, If *it*
*seem* good unto you, and *that it*
*be* of the LORD our God, let us
send abroad unto our brethren
every where, *that are* left in all
the land of Ĭs̱′ra-el, and with
them *also* to the [f]priests and
[g]Lē′vītes *which are* in their cities
*and* suburbs[G], that they may
gather themselves unto us:
3 And let us bring again the
[h]ark of our God to us: for we enquired not at it in the days of
[i]Sa̱ul.
4 And all the congregation said
that they would do so: for the
thing was right in the eyes of all
the people.
5 So [a]Dā′vid gathered all [e]Ĭs̱′-
ra-el together, from [j]Shī′hôr of
[k]Ē′ġypt even unto the entering
of [l]Hē′math, to bring the [h]ark of
God from [m]Kĭr′jath–jē′a-rĭm.
6 And [a]Dā′vid went up, and
all Ĭs̱′ra-el, to Bā′al-ah, *that is,*
to [m]Kĭr′jath–jē′a-rĭm, which *be-*
*longed* to [n]Jū′dah, to bring up
thence[G] the [h]ark of God the
LORD, that [1]dwelleth [o]*between*
the [p]cherubims, whose name[G] is
called *on it.*
7 And they carried the [h]ark of
God in a new [q]cart out of the
house of [r]Ȧ-bĭn′a-dăb: and [s]Ŭz′-
zȧ and [t]Ȧ-hī′ō drave the cart.
8 And [a]Dā′vid and all Ĭs̱′-
ra-el played before God with all
*their* might, and with [u,v]sing-
ing, and with [w]harps, and with
[x]psalteries, and with [y]timbrels,

v.40–976 BC
See footnote, *Time,* Rev. 10:6.
*k Wine,* Prov. 23:31.
*l Oil,* Deut. 12:17.
*m Sheep,* Deut. 23:14.
*n Joy, instances of,* Psa. 5:11.

1
*a David,* 1 Sam. 16:13.
*b Tact,* Prov. 15:1.
*c War, councils of,* Judg. 3:2.
*d Captain,* Num. 31:48.

2
*e Israel, under the kings,* Ex. 4:22.
*f Priest,* Lev. 1:5.
*g Levites,* Deut. 10:8.

3
*h Ark, in house of Abinadab,* Ex. 25:10.
*i Saul,* 1 Sam. 9:2.

5
*j* Or, *Sihor,* Josh. 13:3.
*k Egypt,* Gen. 41:8.
*l* Or, *Hamath,* 1 Chr. 18:3.
*m Kirjath-jearim,* Josh. 15:9.

6
*n Judah, tribe of,* Num. 10:14.
*o Shekinah,* Lev. 16:2.
*p Cherubim,* Ex. 37:7.
1 R. V. sitteth upon the cherubim, which is called by the Name.

7
*q* 1 Sam. 6:7–14; 2 Sam. 6:3.
*r Abinadab,* 1 Sam. 7:1.
*s* Or, *Uzzah,* 2 Sam. 6:3, 6–8.
*t* 2 Sam. 6:3, 4.

8
*u Joy, instances of,* Psa. 5:11.
*v Music,* 2 Chr. 5:13.
*w Harp,* Dan. 3:10.
*x Psaltery,* 1 Chr 16:5.
*y Timbrel,* Ex 15:20.

and with *cymbals, and with [z]trumpets.

9 ¶ And when they came unto the threshingfloor of [a]Chī′don, [b]Ŭz′zȧ put forth his hand to hold the [c]ark; for the oxen stumbled.

10 And the [d]anger of the LORD was kindled against [b]Ŭz′zȧ, and he [e]smote[c] him, because he put his hand to the [c]ark: and there he died before God.

11 And [f]Dā′vid was displeased, because the LORD had made a breach[c] upon [b]Ŭz′zȧ: wherefore that place is called [g]Pē′rez–ŭz′zȧ to this day.

12 And Dā′vid was afraid of God that day, saying, How shall I bring the [c]ark of God *home* to me?

13 So Dā′vid brought not the ark *home* to himself to the [h]city of Dā′vid, but carried it aside into the house of [i]Ō′bed–ē′dom the [j]Gĭt′tīte.

14 And the [c]ark of God remained with the †family of [i]Ō′bed–ē′dom in his house three months. And the LORD blessed the house of Ō′bed–ē′dom, and all that he had.

## CHAPTER 14

*Hiram's kindness to David. 3 David's family. 8 His victories over the Philistines.*

NOW [a]Hī′ram king of [b]Tȳre sent messengers to [c]Dā′vid, and timber of [d]cedars, with [e]masons and [f]carpenters, to build him an house.

2 And [c]Dā′vid perceived that the [g]LORD had confirmed him [h]king over [i]Ĭş′ra-el, for his kingdom was lifted[c] up on high, because of his people Ĭş′ra-el.

3 ¶ And [c]Dā′vid [j]took more wives at [k]Jē-rṳ′sȧ-lĕm: and Dā′vid begat more sons and daughters.

4 Now these *are* the names of *his* children which he had in [k]Jē-rṳ′sȧ-lĕm; [l]Shăm-mū′ȧ, and [m]Shō′băb, [m]Nā′than, and [n]Sŏl′-o-mon,

5 And [o]Ĭb′här, and [p]Ĕl-ĭ-shṳ′ȧ, and [q]Ĕl′pa-lĕt,

6 And [r]Nō′gah, and [s]Nē′pheg, and [s]Jȧ-phī′ȧ,

7 And [t]Ē-lĭsh′a-mȧ, and [u]Bē-ĕl-ī′a-dȧ, and Ē-lĭph′a-lĕt.

8 ¶ And when the [v]Phĭ-lĭs′-tĭneş heard that [c]Dā′vid was [w]anointed[c] king over all [i]Ĭş′ra-el, all the Phĭ-lĭs′tĭneş went up to seek Dā′vid. And Dā′vid heard of *it*, and went out against them.

9 And the [v]Phĭ-lĭs′tĭneş came and [1]spread themselves in the valley of [x]Rĕph′a-ĭm.

10 And [c]Dā′vid [y,z]enquired of God, saying, Shall I go up against the [v]Phĭ-lĭs′tĭneş? And wilt thou deliver them into mine hand? And [a]the LORD said unto him, Go up; for [b]I will [c]deliver them into thine hand.

11 So they came up to [d]Bā′al–pĕr′a-zĭm; and [e]Dā′vid smote them there. Then Dā′vid said, [c]God hath broken in upon mine enemies by mine hand like the breaking forth of waters: therefore they called the name of that place Bā′al–pĕr′a-zĭm.

12 And when they had left their gods[c] there, Dā′vid gave a

---

z *Trumpet*, Josh. 6:4.

9
a Or, *Nachon*, 2 Sam. 6:6, 7.
b Or, *Uzzah*, 2 Sam. 6:3, 6–8.
c *Ark*, Ex. 25:10.

10
d *Anger of God*, 2 Kin. 13:3.
e *Judgments*, Ex. 6:6.

11
f *David*, 1 Sam. 16:13.
g 2 Sam. 6:8.

13
h *Jerusalem*, Judg. 19:10.
i *Obed-edom*, 2 Sam. 6:10.
j *Gath*, Josh. 11:22.

1
a *Hiram*, 2 Sam. 5:11.
b *Tyre*, 1 Kin. 5:1.
c *David*, 1 Sam. 16:13.
d *Cedar*, Isa. 9:10.
e *Mason*, 2 Sam. 5:11.
f *Carpentry*, 2 Kin. 12:11.

2
g *Government, God in*, Isa. 22:21.
h *Rulers, ordained of God*, Ex. 18:21.
i *Israel, under the kings*, Ex. 4:22.

3
j *Polygamy*, Deut. 17:17.
k *Jerusalem*, Judg. 19:10.

4
l 2 Sam. 5:14; or, *Shimea*, 1 Chr. 3:5.
m 1 Chr. 3:5; 2 Sam. 5:14.
n *Solomon*, 2 Sam. 12:24.

5
o 1 Chr. 3:6; 2 Sam. 5:15.
p 2 Sam. 5:15; or, *Elishama*, 1 Chr. 3:6.
q Or, *Eliphelet*, 1 Chr. 3:6; 2 Sam. 5:16.

6
r 1 Chr. 3:7.
s 1 Chr. 3:7; 2 Sam. 5:15.

7
t 1 Chr. 3:8; 2 Sam. 5:16.
u Or, *Eliada*, 1 Chr. 3:8; 2 Sam. 5:16.

8
v *Philistines*, Gen. 26:14.
w *Anointing, of kings*, Lev. 8:12.

9
x *Rephaim*, 1 Chr. 11:15.
1 R. V. made a raid

10
y *Armies, religious ceremonies in*, Deut. 11:4.
z *Prayer, for guidance*, Acts 6:4.
a *Guidance, prayer for, answered*, Psa. 48:14.
b *War, God in*, Judg. 3:2.
c *God, providence of*, Gen. 2:2.

11
d 2 Sam. 5:20; or, *Perazim*, Isa. 28:21.
e *David*, 1 Sam. 16:13.

---

***CYMBAL**, a musical instrument. *Of brass*, 1 Chr. 15:19, 28; 1 Cor. 13:1. *Used, in the tabernacle service*, 1 Chr. 16:5, 42; *in removal of the ark*, 2 Sam. 6:5; 1 Chr. 13:8; 15:16, 19, 28; *in the temple service*, 2 Chr. 5:12, 13; *on the day of atonement*, 2 Chr. 29:25; *at the laying of the foundation of the Second temple*, Ezra 3:10, 11; *at the dedication of the wall*, Neh. 12:27, 36.

† **FAMILY.** *Instituted*, Gen. 2:23, 24. *Love for*, Ex. 21:5, 6. *Government of*, Gen. 3:16; 18:19; Esth. 1:20, 22; 1 Cor. 11:3, 7–9; Eph. 5:22–24; Col. 3:18; 1 Tim. 3:2, 4, 5, 12; 1 Pet. 3:1, 6. *Duty to*, Isa. 58:7.
*Husband should provide for*, Gen. 30:30; 1 Tim. 5:8.
*Persian customs in*, Esth. 1:10–22.
*Idolatrous*, Jer. 7:18.

**Infelicity in:** *Caused, by indiscreetness*, Prov. 12:4; 14:1; 30:21, 23; *by hatred*, Prov. 15:17; *by contention*, Prov. 19:13; 21:9, 19; 25:24; 27:15.

**Instances of infelicity in the:** *Of Abraham*, Gen. 16:5; 21:10, 11. *Of Isaac*, Gen. 27:5–46. *Of Jacob*, Gen. 29:30–34; 30:1–25. *Of Moses*, Ex. 4:25, 26. *Of Elkanah*, 1 Sam. 1:4–7. *Of David*, 2 Sam. 6:16, 20–23. *Of Ahasuerus*, Esth. 1:10–22.

**Religion in the**, Gen. 18:19; Job 1:5; Psa. 101:2; 2 Thess. 1:5. *Manifested, in observance of religious rites*, Gen. 17:12–14; 35:2–4, 7; Luke 2:21; Acts 10:2, 47, 48; 16:15, 25–34; 1 Cor. 1:16; *in religious instruction of children*, Deut. 4:9, 10; 11:19, 20; *in household consecration*, Deut. 12:5–12; Josh. 24:15; Acts 10:1, 2; 18:8.

commandment, and they were [f]burned with fire.

13 And the [g]Phĭ-lĭs′tīneș yet again [1]spread themselves abroad in the [h]valley.

14 Therefore [e]Dā′vid [i,j]enquired again of God; and God [a]said unto him, Go not up after them; turn away from them, and come upon them over against the [k]mulberry trees.

15 And it shall be, when thou shalt hear a sound of [2]going in the tops of the [k]mulberry trees, *that* then thou shalt go out to battle: for [b]God is gone forth before thee to [c]smite the host of the [g]Phĭ-lĭs′tīneș.

16 [e]Dā′vid therefore did as God commanded him: and they smote the host of the [g]Phĭ-lĭs′tīneș from [l]Gĭb′e-on even to [m]Gā′zēr.

17 And the fame of [e]Dā′vid went out into all lands; and the LORD brought the [n]fear of him upon all nations.

## CHAPTER 15

*David, having prepared a place for the ark, 3 assembles the people to bring it from the house of Obed-edom. 11 He orders the priests and Levites to bear the ark. 25 David and his chief men unite in the solemnity with great joy. 29 Michal despises him.*

AND [a]*Da′vid* made him houses in the [b]city of Dā′vid, and prepared a place for the [c]ark of God, and pitched for it a [d]tent.

2 Then [a]Dā′vid said, None ought to carry the [c]ark of God but the [e]Lē′vītes: for them hath the LORD chosen to carry the ark of God, and to minister unto him for ever.

3 And Dā′vid gathered all [f]Ĭș′ra-el together to [b]Jē-ru′sā-lĕm, to bring up the [c]ark of the LORD unto his place, which he had prepared for it.

4 And Dā′vid assembled the [g]children of Aâr′on, and the [e]Lē′vītes:

12 [f] *Iconoclasm*, Num. 33:52.
13 [g] *Philistines*, Gen. 26:14.
[h] *Rephaim*, 1 Chr. 11:15.
14 [i] *Prayer, for guidance*, Acts 6:4.
[j] *Armies, religious ceremonies in*, Deut. 11:4.
[k] 2 Sam. 5:23, 24.
15 [2] R. V. marching
16 [l] *Gibeon*, Jer. 41:16.
[m] 2 Sam. 5:25.
17 [n] *Temporal Blessings, from God*, Psa. 103:2.
1 [a] *David*, 1 Sam. 16:13.
[b] *Jerusalem*, Judg. 19:10.
[c] *Ark, transferred to Jerusalem*, vs. 2–28; Ex. 25:10.
[d] *Tabernacle*, Ex. 27:9.
2 [e] *Levites*, Deut. 10:8.
3 [f] *Israel, under the kings*, Ex. 4:22.
4 [g] *Priest*, Lev. 1:5.

5 Of the [h]sons of Kō′hăth; Ū′rĭ-el the chief, and his brethren an hundred and twenty:

6 Of the [i]sons of Mē-rā′rī; [j]Ā-sa-ī′ah the chief, and his brethren two hundred and twenty:

7 Of the [k]sons of Gēr′shŏm; Jō′el the chief, and his brethren an hundred and thirty:

8 Of the sons of [l]Ē-lĭz′a-phăn; Shĕm-a-ī′ah the chief, and his brethren two hundred:

9 Of the sons of [m]Hē′bron; Ē-lī′el the chief, and his brethren fourscore:

10 Of the sons of [n]Ŭz′zĭ-el; Ăm-mĭn′a-dăb the chief, and his brethren an hundred and twelve.

11 And [a]Dā′vid called for [o]Zā′-dŏk and [p]Ā-bī′a-thär the [g]priests, and for the [e]Lē′vītes, for Ū′rĭ-el, [j]Ā-sa-ī′ah, and Jō′el, Shĕm-a-ī′ah, and Ē-lī′el, and Ăm-mĭn′a-dăb,

12 And said unto them, Ye *are* the chief of the fathers of the [e]Lē′vītes: sanctify yourselves, *both* ye and your brethren, that ye may bring up the [c]ark of the LORD God of Ĭș′ra-el unto *the place that* I have prepared for it.

13 For because ye [q]*did it* not at the first, the LORD our God [r]made a breach upon [s]us, for that we sought him not after the due order.

14 So the [g]priests and the [e]Lē′vītes [t,u]sanctified themselves to bring up the [c]ark of the LORD God of Ĭș′ra-el.

15 And the children of the [e]Lē′vītes bare the [c]ark of God upon their shoulders with the staves thereon, as Mō′șeș commanded according to the [v]word of the LORD.

16 And [a]Dā′vid spake to the chief of the Lē′vītes to appoint their brethren *to be* the *,[w]singers with instruments of [x]musick,

5 [h] *Kohathites*, Num. 3:27.
6 [i] *Merarites*, Num. 26:57.
[j] 1 Chr. 6:30.
7 [k] Or, *Gershonites*, Num. 4:27.
8 [l] Num. 3:30; or, *Elzaphan*, Ex. 6:22; Lev. 10:4.
9 [m] *Hebron*, 1 Chr. 2:42, 43.
10 [n] *Uzziel*, Num. 3:19.
11 [o] *Zadok*, 2 Sam. 19:11.
[p] *Abiathar*, 1 Sam. 22:20.
13 [q] *Disobedience to God*, Eph. 5:6.
[r] *Judgments*, Ex. 6:6.
[s] *Wicked, punishment of*, Psa. 73:3.
14 [t] *Purification*, Num. 19:19.
[u] *Holiness, typified*, Ex. 39:30.
15 [v] *Law, of Moses*, Deut. 33:2.
16 [w] *Art*, 2 Chr. 16:14.
[x] *Music*, 2 Chr. 5:13.

* **CHOIR.** *Leaders of*, 1 Chr. 25:2, 3, 5, 6; Neh. 12:42. *Presided over by chief musician*, title to Psa. 4; Hab. 31:9. *Instructed by teachers*, 1 Chr. 15:22, 27; 25:7, 8. *In the tabernacle*, 1 Chr. 6:31–47. *Composed of singers and instrumentalists*, 1 Chr. 15:16–21; 25:1–7; 2 Chr. 5:12, 13; 23:13; Isa. 38:20. *Mixed choirs*, 2 Chr. 35:15, 25; Ezra 2:64.

[y]psalteries and [z]harps and [a]cym-
bals, sounding, by lifting up the
voice with [b]joy.
17 So the [c]Lē′vītes appointed
[d]Hē′man the son of [e]Jō′el; and of
his brethren, †Ā′saph the son of
[f]Bĕr-e-chī′ah; and of the [g]sons of
Mē-rā′rī their brethren, [h]Ē′than
the son of [i]Kụ-shā′iah;
18 And with them their brethren of the second *degree*, [j]Zĕch-a-
rī′ah, Bĕn, and Jā-ā′zī-el, and
[j]Shē-mĭr′a-mŏth, and [j]Jē-hī′el,
and Ŭn′nī, [j]Ē-lī′ab, and [j]Bē-
nā′iah, and Mā-a-sē′iah, and
[j]Măt-tĭ-thī′ah, and Ē-lĭph′e-leh,
and Mĭk-nē′iah, and [k]Ō′bed–ē′-
dom, and [j]Jē-ī′el, the [l]porters.
19 So the *singers, [d]Hē′man,
†Ā′saph and [h]Ē′than, *were appointed* to sound with [a]cymbals
of brass;
20 And [j]Zĕch-a-rī′ah, and Ā′zī-
el, and [j]Shē-mĭr′a-mŏth, and
[j]Jē-hī′el, and Ŭn′nī, and [j]Ē-lī′-
ab, and Mā-a-sē′iah, and [j]Bē-
nā′iah, with [m]psalteries [1]on [n]Ăl′-
a-mŏth;
21 And [j]Măt-tĭ-thī′ah, and
Ē-lĭph′e-leh, and Mĭk-nē′iah,
and [k]Ō′bed–ē′dom, and [j]Jē-ī′el,
and Ăz-a-zī′ah, with [o]harps [1]on
the [n]Shĕm′ĭ-nĭth to [2]excel.
22 And [p]Chĕn-a-nī′ah, chief[c] of
the [c]Lē′vītes, *was* for song: he
[q]instructed about the *song, because he *was* skilful.
23 And [f]Bĕr-e-chī′ah and Ĕl′-
kă-nah *were* [l]doorkeepers for the
[r]ark.
24 And Shĕb-a-nī′ah, and Jē-
hŏsh′a-phăt, and Nē-thăn′e-el,
and Ā-măs′a-aī, and Zĕch-a-rī′-
ah, and Bē-nā′iah, and Ē-li-ē′-
zĕr, the priests, did blow with
the [s]trumpets before the [r]ark of
God: and [k]Ō′bed–ē′dom and Jē-

y *Psaltery*, 1 Chr. 16:5.
z *Harp*, Dan. 3:10.

a *Cymbal*, 1 Chr. 13:8.
b *Joy, instances of*, Psa. 5:11.

17
c *Levites*, Deut. 10:8.
d *Heman*, 1 Chr. 6:33.
e 1 Chr. 6:33; 1 Sam. 8:2; or, *Vashni*, 1 Chr. 6:28.
f Or, *Berachiah*, 1 Chr. 6:39.
g *Merarites*, Num. 26:57.
h Or, *Jeduthun*, 1 Chr. 16:38.
i Or, *Kishi*, 1 Chr. 6:44.

18
j 1 Chr 16:5.
k *Obed-edom*, 2 Sam. 6:10.
l *Porters*, 2 Sam. 18:26.

20
m *Psaltery*, 1 Chr. 16:5.
n *Music, symbols used in*, 2 Chr. 5:13.
1 R. V. set to

21
o *Harp*, Dan. 3:10.
2 R. V. lead.

22
p *Music, teachers of*, 2 Chr. 5:13.
q *Instruction, in music*, Prov. 23:23.

23
r *Ark*, Ex. 25:10.

24
s *Trumpet*, Josh. 6:4.

hī′ah *were* [l]doorkeepers for the
ark.
25 ¶ So [t]Dā′vid, and the [u]eld-
ers of Ĭṣ′ra-el, and the [v]captains
over thousands, went to bring
up the [r]ark of the covenant of
the LORD out of the house of
[k]Ō′bed–ē′dom with joy.
26 And it came to pass, when
God helped the [w]Lē′vītes that
bare the [r]ark of the covenant
of the LORD, that they offered
seven [x]bullocks and seven rams.
27 And [t, y]Dā′vid *was* clothed
with a robe of fine linen, and all
the [w]Lē′vītes that bare the [r]ark,
and the *singers, and [p]Chĕn-a-
nī′ah the master of the song with
the singers: Dā′vid also *had* upon him an [z]ephod[c] of linen.
28 Thus all Ĭṣ′ra-el brought up
the ark of the covenant of the
LORD with [a]shouting, and with
sound of the cornet, and with
[b]trumpets, and with [c]cymbals,
making a noise with [d]psalteries
and [e]harps.
29 And it came to pass, *as* the
ark of the covenant of the LORD
came to the city of Dā′vid, that
[f]Mī′chal the daughter of Saul
looking out at a window saw
king Dā′vid [g]dancing and playing: and she despised[c] him in her
heart.

## CHAPTER 16

*David's sacrifices and offerings. 4 He appoints a choir to sing the praises of God. 7 The psalm of thanksgiving. 37 He appoints ministers, porters, priests, and musicians, to attend continually on the ark.*

SO they brought the [a]ark of
God, and set it in the
midst of the [b]tent that [c]Dā′vid
had pitched[c] for it: and they offered [d]burnt sacrifices and
[e]peace offerings before God.
2 And when Dā′vid had made

25
t *David*, 1 Sam. 16:13.
u *Senate*, Num. 11:16.
v *Captain*, Num. 31:48.

26
w *Levites, duties of*, Deut. 10:8.
x *Offerings*, Lev. 6:17.

27
y 2 Sam. 6:14–16.
z *Ephod*, Ex. 28:6.

28
a *Shouting*, 2 Chr. 15:14.
b *Trumpet*, Josh. 6:4.
c *Cymbal*, 1 Chr. 13:8.
d *Psaltery*, 1 Chr. 16:5.
e *Harp*, Dan. 3:10.

29
f *Michal*, 1 Sam. 18:27.
g *Dancing*, Eccl. 3:4.

1
a *Ark*, Ex. 25:10.
b *Tabernacle*, Ex. 27:9.
c *David*, 1 Sam. 16:13.
d *Offerings, burnt*, Lev. 6:17.
e *Offerings, peace*, Lev. 6:17.

65. *Sang, every morning and evening*, 1 Chr. 9:33; 23:5, 30; *during offering of sacrifices*, 1 Chr. 16:41, 42; 2 Chr. 29:27, 28; *at restoration of the temple*, Ezra 2:41; 3:10, 11; *at the dedication of the wall of Jerusalem*, Neh. 12:27–30. *Detailed from the army to sing praises to God as a military stratagem*, 2 Chr. 20:21.
See footnote, MUSIC, 2 Chr. 5:13.

† **ASAPH**, son of Berachiah. *One of the three leaders of music in David's organization of the tabernacle service*, 1 Chr 15:16–19; 16:5–7; 25:1–9; 2 Chr. 5:12; 35:15; Neh. 12:46. *A composer of sacred lyrics*, 2 Chr. 29:30; see also titles to Psa. 50 and 73–83, inclusive. *Descendants of, in the temple choir*, 1 Chr. 25:1–9; 2 Chr. 20:14; 29:13; Ezra 2:41; 3:10; Neh. 7:44; 11:22.

an end of offering the [d]burnt offerings and the [e]peace offerings,
he [f]blessed the people in the
name of the LORD.
3 And [g]he dealt[C] to every one of
[h]Ĭṣ′ra-el, both man and woman,
to every one a loaf of bread, and
a good piece of flesh,[C] and a
[1]flagon[C] *of wine.*
4 ¶ And he appointed *certain* of
the [i]Lē′vītes to minister before
the [a]ark of the LORD, and to [2]re-
cord,[C] and to [j]thank and [k]praise
the LORD God of Ĭṣ′ra-el:
5 [l]Ā′saph the chief, and next to
him [m]Zĕch-a-rī′ah, [m]Jė-ī′el, and
[m]Shė-mĭr′a-mŏth, and [m]Jė-hī′el,
and [m]Măt-tĭ-thī′ah and [m]Ē-lī′-
ab, and [m]Bė-nā′iah, and [n]Ō′bed-
ĕ′dom: and [m]Jė-ī′el with *psalteries and with [o]harps[C]; but Ā′saph
made a sound with [p]cymbals;
6 [q]Bė-nā′iah also and Jă-hā′-
zĭ-el the [r]priests with [s]trumpets
continually before the [a]ark of the
covenant of God.
7 ¶ Then on that day [3,c]Dā′vid
delivered first *this psalm* to
[t]thank the LORD into the hand
of [l]Ā′saph and his brethren.
8 [u,v]Give [w]thanks unto the
LORD, call upon his name,
[x]make known his deeds among
the people.
9 [v,w,y]Sing unto him, sing
psalms unto him, [x]talk ye of all
his wondrous works.
10 [v,w]Glory ye in his [z]holy
name: let the heart of them rejoice that seek the LORD.[S]
11 [a,b]Seek the LORD and his
strength, seek his face [c]contin-
ually.
12 [d]Remember his marvellous
[e]works that he hath done, his
[f]wonders, and the judgments[C] of
his mouth;
13 O ye seed of Ĭṣ′ra-el his
servant, ye children of [g]Jā′cob,
his chosen ones.
14 He *is* the [h]LORD our God;
his [i]judgments *are* in all the
earth.
15 [j,k]Be ye mindful always of
his [l]covenant[C]; the [m]word *which*
he commanded to a thousand
generations;
16 *Even of the* [l]*covenant* which
he made with [n]Ā′bră-hăm, and
of his oath unto [o]Ī′ṣaac;
17 And hath confirmed the
same to [p]Jā′cob for a law, *and*
to [q]Ĭṣ′ra-el *for* an everlasting
[l]covenant,
18 Saying, Unto thee will I give
the land of [r]Cā′năan, the lot[C] of
your inheritance;
19 When ye were but few, even
a few, and strangers[C] in it.
20 And *when* they went from
nation to nation, and from *one*
kingdom to another people;
21 [s]He suffered no man to do
them wrong: yea, he reproved
kings for their sakes,
22 *Saying,* Touch not mine
anointed, and do my [t]prophets
no harm.
23 [u,v]Sing unto the LORD, all
the earth; shew forth from day
to day his [w]salvation.[C]
24 [u,v,x]Declare his [y]glory
[z]among the [4]heathen[C]; his marvellous [a]works among all nations.[C]
25 For great *is* the LORD, and
greatly to be [b]praised: he also *is*
to be [c]feared above all gods.[S]
26 For all [d]the gods of the people *are* idols: but the LORD
[e]made the [f]heavens.
27 Glory and honour *are* in his
presence; strength and [g]gladness
*are* in his place.
28 Give unto the LORD, ye
kindreds of the people, [h]give
unto the LORD glory and
strength.
29 [h,i]Give unto the LORD the
glory *due* unto his name: bring

2
*f Benedictions,* Deut. 21:5.
3
*g Liberality, instances of,* 1 Tim. 6:18.
*h Israel, under the kings,* Ex. 4:22.
1 R. V. cake of raisins.
4
*i Levites, duties of,* Deut. 10:8.
*j Thankfulness, ministers appointed to offer in public,* Acts 24:3.
*k Music,* 2 Chr. 5:13.
2 R. V. celebrate
5
*l Asaph,* 1 Chr. 15:17.
*m* 1 Chr. 15:18.
*n Obed-edom,* 2 Sam. 6:10.
*o Harp,* Dan. 3:10.
*p Cymbal,* 1 Chr. 13:8.
6
*q* 1 Chr. 15:24.
*r Priest,* Lev. 1:5.
*s Trumpet,* Josh. 6:4.
7
*t Thankfulness, cultivated by songs,* vs. 7–36; Acts 24:3.
3 R. V. did David first ordain to give thanks unto the LORD, by the hand
8
*u Poetry, didactic,* vs. 8–36; Acts 17:28.
*v Commandment, enjoining thanksgiving,* Deut. 8:2.
*w Praise,* Psa. 150:1.
*x Religious Testimony,* 2 Thess. 1:10.
9
*y Music,* 2 Chr. 5:13.
10
*z God, holiness of,* Gen. 2:2.

11
*a Commandment, enjoining seeking the Lord,* Deut. 8:2.
*b Seekers,* Isa. 55:6.
*c Perseverance, enjoined,* Eph. 6:18.
12
*d Commandment, enjoining remembrance of God's providences,* Deut. 8:2.
*e Works of God,* Psa. 40:5.
*f Miracles,* Luke 23:8.
13
*g Jacob,* Gen. 27:11.

14
*h God, sovereign,* Gen. 2:2.
*i Judgments,* Ex. 6:6.
15
*j Commandment, enjoining remembrance of God's law,* Deut. 8:2.
*k Obedience, enjoined,* Heb. 5:8.
*l Covenant, of God with men,* Deut. 29:1.
*m Word of God,* Psa. 119:9.
16
*n Abraham,* Gen. 17:5.
*o Isaac,* Gen. 21:3.
17
*p Jacob,* Gen. 27:11.
*q Israel,* Ex. 4:22.
18
*r Canaan, land of,* Gen. 37:1.
21
*s God, preserver,* Gen. 2:2.
22
*t Prophets,* Isa. 3:2.
23
*u Commandment, enjoining thanksgiving,* Deut. 8:2
*v Praise,* Psa. 150:1.
*w Salvation,* Acts 16:17.
24
*x Religious Testimony,* 2 Thess. 1:10.
*y God, glory of,* Gen. 2:2.
*z Missions,* Matt. 28:19.

*a Miracles,* Luke 23:8.
4 R. V. nations,
25
*b Praise,* Psa. 150:1.
*c Fear of God,* Acts 9:31.
26
*d Idolatry,* 1 Sam. 15:23.
*e God, creator,* Gen. 2:2.
*f Heavens, physical,* Psa. 8:3.
27
*g Joy,* Psa. 5:11.
28
*h Glorifying God,* Luke 5:25.
29
*i Duty, of man to God,* Eccl. 12:13.

* **PSALTERY,** a harp. *Used, in religious services,* 2 Sam. 6:5; 1 Chr. 13:8; 16:5; 25:1, 5, 6; 2 Chr. 29:25; Psa. 33:2; 71:22; 81:2; 92:3; 108:2; 144:9; 150:3; *at the dedication of the new wall of Jerusalem, when the captivity returned,* Neh. 12:27 *in idolatrous worship,* Dan. 3:5, 7, 10, 15.
See footnote, MUSIC, *Instruments of,* 2 Chr. 5:13.

an offering, and come before
him: [j]worship the LORD in the
[k]beauty of [l]holiness.
30 [c,m]Fear[G] before him, all the
earth: the world also shall be
stable, that it be not moved.
31 [b]Let the [l]heavens be glad,
and let the [n]earth rejoice: and
let *men* say among the nations,
The [o]LORD reigneth.
32 [b]Let the [p]sea roar, and the
fulness thereof: let the fields rejoice, and all that *is* therein.
33 Then shall the trees of the
wood sing out at the presence of
the LORD, because he cometh to
[q]judge the earth.[S T]
34 O [r]give [s]thanks unto the
LORD; for *he is* [t]good; for his
[u]mercy *endureth* for ever.[S]
35 And say ye, Save us, O God
of our [v]salvation, and gather us
together, and deliver us from the
[4]heathen,[G] [s]that we may give
thanks to thy holy name, *and*
glory in thy [b]praise.[Q]
36 [b]Blessed *be* the LORD God
of Ĭs̩′ra-el for ever and ever.
And all the people said, Ā-mĕn′,
and [b]praised the LORD.[S]
37 ¶ So [w]he left there before
the [x]ark of the covenant of the
LORD [y]Ā′saph and his brethren,
to minister[G] before the ark continually, as every day's work required:
38 And [z]Ō′bed–ē′dom with
their brethren, threescore and
eight; Ō′bed–ē′dom also the son
of †Jĕd′ụ-thŭn and [a]Hō′sah *to
be* [5,b]porters:[G]
39 And [c]Zā′dŏk the [d]priest, and
his brethren the [e]priests, before
the [f]tabernacle of the LORD
in the high[G] place that *was* at
[g]Gĭb′e-on,
40 [d,e]To offer burnt offerings
unto the LORD upon the [h]altar
of the burnt offering [i]contin-
ually morning and evening, and

*j Worship, enjoined,* Gen. 22:5.
*k Beauty, spiritual,* Psa. 45:11.
*l Holiness,* Ex. 39:30.
**30**
*m Commandment, enjoining the fear of God,* Deut. 8:2.
**31**
*n Earth,* Prov. 8:23.
*o God, sovereign,* Gen. 2:2.
**32**
*p Sea,* Jer. 5:22.
**33**
*q God, judge,* Gen. 2:2.
**34**
*r Commandment, enjoining thanksgiving,* Deut. 8:2.
*s Thankfulness, to God,* Acts 24:3.
*t God, goodness of,* Gen. 2:2.
*u God, mercy of,* Gen. 2:2.
**35**
*v Salvation,* Acts 16:17.
**37**
*w David,* 1 Sam. 16:13.
*x Ark,* Ex. 25:10.
*y Asaph,* 1 Chr. 15:17.
**38**
*z Obed-edom,* 2 Sam. 6:10.

a 1 Chr. 26:10, 11.
*b Porters,* 2 Sam. 18:26.
5 R. V. door-keepers:
**39**
*c Zadok,* 2 Sam. 19:11.
*d High Priest, duties of,* Lev. 21:10.
*e Priest, duties of,* Lev. 1:5.
*f Tabernacle,* Ex. 27:9.
*g Gibeon,* Jer. 41:16.
**40**
*h Altar, of burnt offerings,* Gen. 8:20.
*i Offerings, daily,* Lev. 6:17.

*to do* according to all that is written in the [j]law of the LORD,
which he commanded Ĭs̩′ra-el;
41 And with them [k]Hē′man
and †Jĕd′ụ-thŭn, and the [l]rest
that were chosen, who were expressed by name, [m]to give thanks
to the LORD, because his [n]mer-
cy *endureth* for ever;
42 And with them [k]Hē′man
and †Jĕd′ụ-thŭn with [o]trumpets
and [p]cymbals for those that
should make [q]a sound, and with
[6]**musical instruments** of God.
And the sons of Jĕd′ụ-thŭn
*were* [b]**porters.**
43 And all the people departed
every man to his house: and
[r]Dā′vid returned to bless his
house.

## CHAPTER 17

*Nathan approves the purpose of David to build a house for God. 3 Afterward by the command of God he forbids him; 11 but promises blessings to his seed. 16 David's prayer and thanksgiving.*

NOW[Q] it came to pass, as
[a]Dā′vid sat in his house,
that Dā′vid said to [b]Nā′than the
prophet, Lo, I dwell in an [c]house
of cedars, but the [d]ark of the
covenant of the LORD *remaineth*
under curtains.[G]
2 Then [b]Nā′than said unto
[a]Dā′vid, Do all that *is* in thine
heart; for God *is* with thee.
3 ¶ And it came to pass the
same night, that the word of
God [e]came to [b]Nā′than, saying,
4 Go and tell [a]Dā′vid my servant, Thus saith the LORD, Thou
shalt not build me an house to
dwell in:
5 For I have not dwelt[G] in an
house since the day that I
brought up Ĭs̩′ra-el unto this
day; but have gone from [f]tent to
tent, and from *one* tabernacle *to
another.*
6 Wheresoever I have walked
with all Ĭs̩′ra-el, spake I a word

*j Law, of Moses,* Deut. 33:2.
**41**
*k Heman,* 1 Chr. 6:33.
*l Choir,* 1 Chr. 15:16.
*m Thankfulness, to God,* Acts 24:3.
*n God, mercy of,* Gen. 2:2.
**42**
*o Trumpet,* Josh. 6:4.
*p Cymbal,* 1 Chr. 13:8.
*q Music,* 2 Chr. 5:13.
6 R.V. instruments for the songs of God: and the sons of Jeduthun to be at the gate.
**43**
*r David,* 1 Sam. 16:13.
**1**
*a David,* 1 Sam. 16:13.
*b Nathan,* 2 Sam. 7:2.
*c Palace,* 1 Kin. 21:1.
*d Ark,* Ex. 25:10.
**3**
*e Prophets, inspiration of,* Isa. 3:2.
**5**
*f Tabernacle,* Ex. 27:9.

† **JEDUTHUN** *(he who praises). Called* ETHAN, 1 Chr. 6:44; 15:17. *A musician of the tabernacle,* 1 Chr. 9:16; 16:38, 41; 25:1, 3, 6; 2 Chr. 5:12. See also titles to Psa. 39, 62, 77.

6
g *Judge, of Israel,* Judg. 2:16.
h *Israel, under the judges,* Ex. 4:22.
7
i *God, providence of,* Gen. 2:2.
j *Rulers, appointed by God,* Ex. 18:21.
k *Temporal Blessings, from God,* Psa. 103:2.
8
l *God, dwells with the righteous,* Gen. 2:2.
m *Grace of God,* Rom. 4:16.
11
n 2 Sam. 7:12–16.
o *Death,* Num. 23:10.
p *David, promises to,* 1 Sam. 16:13.
q *Covenant, of God with men,* Deut. 29:1.
r *Solomon, prophecies concerning,* 2 Sam. 12:24.
12
s *Temple, Solomon's,* 1 Kin. 6:17.
t *Government, God in,* Isa. 22:21.
u *Messianic Hope,* Gen. 49:10.
v *Throne, figurative,* 1 Kin. 2:19.
13
w *Spiritual Adoption,* Rom. 8:15.
x *God, mercy of,* Gen. 2:2.
y *Holy Spirit, withdrawn,* Acts 1:2.

to any of the [g]judges of [h]Is′ra-el,
whom I commanded to feed my
people, saying, Why have ye not
built me an house of cedars?
7 Now therefore [e]thus shalt
thou say unto my servant [a]Dā′-
vid, Thus saith the LORD of
hosts, [i]I took [j]thee from the
sheepcote, *even* from following
the sheep, that thou [k]shouldest
be ruler over my people Is′ra-el:
8 And [l]I [m]have been with thee
whithersoever thou hast walked,
and have cut[G] off all thine enemies from before thee, and have
made thee a name like the name
of the great men that *are* in the
earth.
9 Also [i]I will ordain[G] a place
for my people Is′ra-el, and will
plant[G] them, and they [k]shall dwell
in their place, and shall be
moved no more; neither shall
the children of wickedness waste[G]
them any more, as at the beginning,
10 And since the time that I
commanded [g]judges *to be* over
my people [h]Is′ra-el. Moreover
I will [i]subdue all thine enemies.
Furthermore I tell thee that the
LORD will build thee an house.
11 And it shall come to pass,
[n]when thy days be expired that
thou must [o]go[G] *to be* with thy fathers, that [p,q]I will raise up thy
[r]seed after thee, which shall be
of thy sons; and I will establish
his kingdom.[Q]
12 [r]He shall build me an [s]house,
and [t]I will stablish[G] [u]his [v]throne
for ever.
13 I will be his father, and [w]he
shall be my son: and I will not
take my [x]mercy away from him,
[y]as I took *it* from *him* that was
before thee:[Q]
14 But I will settle him in mine
house and in my kingdom for
ever: and [u]his [v]throne shall be
established for evermore.[Q]
15 According to all these
words, and according to all this
[z]vision, so did [a]Nā′than speak
unto [b]Dā′vid.
16 ¶ And [b]Dā′vid the king
came and sat before the LORD,
and [c]said, [d]Who *am* I, O LORD
God, and what *is* mine house,
that thou hast brought me hitherto[G]?
17 And *yet* this was a small
thing in thine eyes, O God; for
thou hast *also* spoken of thy
servant's house for a great while
to come, and hast regarded me
according to the estate of a man
of high degree, O LORD God.
18 What can Dā′vid *speak*
more to thee for the honour of
thy servant? for thou [e]knowest
thy servant.
19 O LORD, for thy servant's
sake, and according to [f]thine
own heart, hast thou done all
this greatness, in making known
all *these* great things.
20 O [g]LORD, *there is* none like
thee, neither *is there any* God
beside thee, according to all that
we have heard with our ears.
21 And what one nation in the
earth *is* like thy people [h]Is′ra-el,
whom [i]God went to redeem *to
be* his own people, to make thee
a name of greatness and terribleness, by driving out nations from
before thy people, whom thou
hast redeemed out of [j]E′gypt?
22 For thy people Is′ra-el didst
thou make thine own people for
ever; and thou, LORD, becamest
their God.
23 Therefore now, LORD, [k]let
the thing that thou hast spoken
concerning thy servant and [l]con-
cerning his house be established
for ever, and do as thou hast
said.
24 [k]Let it even be established,
that thy name may be magnified
for ever, saying, The LORD of
hosts *is* the God of Is′ra-el, *even*
a God to Is′ra-el: and [l]*let* the

15
z *Vision,* Acts 9:10.
a *Nathan,* 2 Sam. 7:2.
b *David,* 1 Sam. 16:13.
16
c *Prayer, exemplified,* vs. 16–27; Acts 6:4.
d *Humility, instances of,* Prov. 22:4.
18
e *God, knowledge of,* Gen. 2:2.
19
f *God, goodness of,* Gen. 2:2.
20
g *God, sovereign,* Gen. 2:2.
21
h *Israel,* Ex. 4:22.
i *God, love of, exemplified,* Gen. 2:2.
j *Egypt,* Gen. 41:8.
23
k *Temporal Blessings, prayer for,* Psa. 103:2.
l *Prayer, intercessory,* Acts 6:4.

25
*m Prayer, pleas offered in*, Acts 6:4.

26
*n God, faithfulness of*, Gen. 2:2.

house of Dā′vid thy servant *be* established before thee.

25 For [m]thou, O my God, hast told thy servant that thou wilt build him an house: therefore thy servant hath found *in his heart* to pray before thee.

26 And now, LORD, thou art [n]God, and hast promised this [k]goodness unto thy servant:

27 Now therefore let it please thee to bless the house of thy servant, that it may be before thee for ever: for thou blessest, O LORD, and *it shall be* blessed for ever.

## CHAPTER 18

*David subdues the Philistines and the Moabites. 3 He smites Hadarezer and the Syrians. 9 Tou sends his son to him with presents. 11 The presents and the spoil David dedicates to God. 13 He puts garrisons in Edom. 14 David's officers.*

1
*a David*, 1 Sam. 16:13.
*b Philistines*, Gen. 26:14.
*c Gath*, Josh. 11:22.

2
*d Moabites*, Gen. 19:37.
*e Tribute*, Ezra 4:13.

3
*f* Or, *Hadadezer*, 2 Sam. 8:3.
*g Zobah*, 1 Sam. 14:47.
*h Euphrates*, Gen. 15:18.

4
*i Chariot*, Josh. 11:4.
*j Cavalry*, 1 Sam. 13:5.
*k Horses*, Job 39: 19.
*l Animals, cruelty to*, Jer. 27:5.

5
*m Syria*, 2 Kin. 6:23.
*n Damascus*, Isa. 8:4.

6
*o Garrison*, 1 Sam. 13:3.

NOW after this it came to pass, that [a]Dā′vid smote the [b]Phĭ-lĭs′tīneṣ, and subdued them, and took [c]Găth and her towns out of the hand of the Phĭ-lĭs′tīneṣ.

2 And he smote Mō′ab; and the [d]Mō′ab-ītes became Dā′vid's servants, *and* brought [e]gifts.

3 ¶ And [a]Dā′vid smote [f]Hăd-är-ē′zēr king of [g]Zō′bah unto *Hā′math, as he went to stablish his dominion by the river [h]Eū-phrā′tēṣ.

4 And [a]Dā′vid took from him a thousand [i]chariots, and seven thousand [j]horsemen, and twenty thousand footmen: Dā′vid also houghed all the chariot [k,l]*horses*, but reserved of them an hundred chariots.

5 And when the [m]Sўr′ĭ-anṣ of [n]Dă-măs′cus came to help [f]Hăd-är-ē′zēr king of [g]Zō′bah, [a]Dā′vid slew of the Sўr′ĭ-anṣ two and twenty thousand men.

6 Then Dā′vid put [o]*garrisons* in Sўr′ĭ-ă–dă-măs′cus; and the Sўr′ĭ-anṣ became Dā′vid's servants, *and* brought [e]gifts. Thus the LORD [p]preserved Dā′vid whithersoever he went.

7 And [a]Dā′vid took the [q]shields of [r]gold that were on the servants of [f]Hăd-är-ē′zēr, and brought them to [s]Jē-ru̥′să-lĕm.

8 Likewise from Tĭb′hăth, and from Chŭn, cities of [f]Hăd-är-ē′zēr, brought Dā′vid very much [t]brass, wherewith [u]Sŏl′o-mon made the brasen [v]sea, and the [w]pillars, and the vessels of brass.

9 ¶ Now when [x]Tō′ū king of *Hā′math heard how Dā′vid had smitten all the host of [f]Hăd-är-ē′zēr king of [g]Zō′bah;

10 He [y]sent [z]Hă-dō′ram his son to king Dā′vid, to enquire of his welfare, and to congratulate him, because he had fought against Hăd-är-ē′zēr, and smitten him; (for Hăd-är-ē′zēr had war with Tō′ū;) and *with him* all manner of vessels of [a]gold and [b]silver and [c]brass.

11 Them also king [d,e]Dā′vid [f]dedicated unto the LORD, with the [b]silver and the [a]gold that he brought from all *these* nations; from [g]Ē′dom, and from [h]Mō′ab, and from the [i]children of Ăm′mŏn, and from the [j]Phĭ-lĭs′tīneṣ, and from [k]Ăm′a-lĕk.

12 Moreover [l]Ă-bĭsh′a-ī the son of [m]Zĕr-u̥-ī′ah slew of the [g]Ē′dom-ītes in the valley of [n]salt eighteen thousand.

13 And he put [o]garrisons in Ē′dom; and all the [g]Ē′dom-ītes became [d]Dā′vid's servants. Thus the [p]LORD preserved Dā′vid whithersoever he went.

14 ¶ So [d,q]Dā′vid reigned over all [r]Ĭṣ′ra-el, and executed judg-

*p God, providence of*, Gen. 2:2.

7
*q Shield*, 1 Kin. 14:27.
*r Gold*, Ezek. 7:19.
*s Jerusalem*, Judg. 19:10.

8
*t Brass*, Job 28:2.
*u Solomon*, 2 Sam. 12:24.
*v Laver*, Ex. 30:18.
*w Pillar*, Gen. 28: 18.

9
*x* Or, *Toi*, 2 Sam. 8:9, 10.

10
*y Diplomacy, instances of*, 2 Kin. 16:7.
*z* Or, *Joram*, 2 Sam. 8:10.

*a Gold*, Ezek. 7:19.
*b Silver*, 1 Chr. 28:14.
*c Brass*, Job 28:2.

11
*d David*, 1 Sam. 16:13.
*e Zeal, instances of*, 2 Cor. 7:11.
*f Liberality, instances of*, 1 Tim. 6:18.
*g Edomites*, 2 Kin. 8:21.
*h Moabites*, Gen. 19:37.
*i Ammonites*, Deut. 2:20.
*j Philistines*, Gen. 26:14.
*k Amalekites*, Num. 13:29.

12
*l Abishai*, 2 Sam. 3:30.
*m Zeruiah*, 1 Chr. 2:16.
*n Salt*, 2 Kin. 2:20.

13
*o Garrison*, 1 Sam. 13:3.
*p God, providence of*, Gen. 2:2.

14
*q Rulers, righteous*, Ex. 18:21.
*r Israel, under the kings*, Ex. 4:22.

* **HAMATH** (*fortress, citadel*), called also HEMATH. *The name of a country and of the chief city of the country in upper Syria*, Num. 13:21; 34:8; Josh. 13:5; 1 Kin. 8:65; 1 Chr. 18: 3; Ezek. 47:16. *Prosperity of*, Amos 6:2. *David receives gifts from king of*, 2 Sam. 8:9, 10; 1 Chr. 18:9, 10. *Solomon builds store cities in*, 2 Chr. 8:4. *Conquest of, by Jeroboam*, 2 Kin. 14:25, 28. *Riblah, a city of, sixty-five miles north of Damascus; strategic headquarters, of Pharaoh-nechoh*, 2 Kin. 23:33; *of Nebuchadnezzar, during siege of Jerusalem*, 2 Kin. 25:20, 21. *Israelites taken captive to*, Isa. 11:11. *Prophecy concerning*, Jer. 49:23.

ment and [s]justice among all his people.

15 And [t]Jō'ăb the son of [m]Zĕr-ụ-ī'ah *was* over the host; and [u]Jĕ-hŏsh'a-phăt the son of [v]Ă-hī'lụd, recorder.

16 And [w]Zā'dŏk the son of [x]Ă-hī'tub, and [y]Ă-bĭm'e-lĕch the son of [z]Ă-bī'a-thär, *were* the [a]priests; and [b]Shăv'shȧ was [c]scribe;

17 And [d]Bĕ-nā'iah the son of [e]Jĕ-hoi'a-dȧ *was* over the [f]Chĕr'-e-thītes and the [g]Pĕl'e-thītes; and the sons of [h]Dā'vid *were* chief about[G] the king.

## CHAPTER 19

*David's messengers, sent to comfort Hanun, are shamefully treated. 6 The Ammonites, strengthened by the Syrians, are overcome by Joab and Abishai. 16 The Syrians are again defeated.*

[a]NOW it came to pass after this, that [b]Nā'hăsh the king of the [c]children of Ăm'mŏn died, and his son reigned in his stead.

2 And [d]Dā'vid said, I will shew [e]kindness[G] unto [f]Hā'nŭn the son of [b]Nā'hăsh, because his father shewed kindness to me. And Dā'vid sent messengers to comfort him concerning his father. So the servants of Dā'vid came into the land of the [c]children of Ăm'mŏn to Hā'nŭn, to comfort him.

3 But the princes of the [c]children of Ăm'mŏn [g]said to [f]Hā'-nŭn, Thinkest thou that [d]Dā'vid doth honour thy father, that he hath sent comforters unto thee? [h,i]are not his servants come unto thee for to search, and to overthrow, and to spy out the land?

4 Wherefore [f,j]Hā'nŭn took Dā'vid's servants, and [k,l]shaved them, and cut off their garments in the midst hard[G] by their buttocks, and sent them away.

5 Then there went *certain*, and told [d]Dā'vid how the men were served. And he sent to meet them: for the men were greatly ashamed. And the king said, Tarry at [m]Jĕr'ĭ-chō until your beards be grown, and *then* return.

6 ¶ And when the [c]children of Ăm'mŏn saw that they had made themselves odious[G] to [d]Dā'-vid, [f]Hā'nŭn and the children of Ăm'mŏn sent a thousand [n]talents[G] of [o]silver to [p]hire them [q]chariots and [r]horsemen out of [s]Mĕs-o-pŏ-tā'mĭ-ȧ, and out of [t]Sy̆r'ĭ-ȧ–mā'a-chah, and out of [u]Zō'bah.

7 So they [p]hired thirty and two thousand [q]chariots, and the king of [v]Mā'a-chah and his people; who came and pitched[G] before [w]Mĕd'e-bȧ. And the [c]children of Ăm'mŏn gathered themselves together from their cities, and came to battle.

8 And when [d]Dā'vid heard *of it*, he sent [x]Jō'ăb, and all the host of the mighty men.

9 And the [c]children of Ăm'mŏn came out, and put the battle[G] in array[G] before the gate of the city: and the kings that were come *were* by themselves in the field.

10 Now when [x]Jō'ăb saw that the battle was set against him before and behind, he chose out of all the choice of [y]Ĭṣ'ra-el, and put *them* in array against the [t]Sy̆r'ĭ-anṣ.

11 And the rest of the people [x]he delivered unto the hands of [z]Ă-bĭsh'a-ī his brother, and they set *themselves* in array[G] against the children of Ăm'mŏn.

12 And [x]he said, If the Sy̆r'ĭ-anṣ be too strong for me, then thou shalt help me: but if the [c]children of Ăm'mŏn be too strong for thee, then I will help thee.

13 [a,b]Be of good courage, and let us behave ourselves valiantly[G]

---

s *Justice*, Deut. 33:21.

15
t *Joab*, 2 Sam. 20:23.
u 2 Sam. 8:16.
v 2 Sam. 8:16; 20:24; 1 Kin. 4:3, 12.

16
w *Zadok*, 2 Sam. 19:11.
x 2 Sam. 8:17.
y Or, *Abiathar*, 1 Sam. 22:20.
z Or *Ahimelech*, 1 Sam. 21:1.

a *High Priest*, Lev. 21:10.
b Or, *Seraiah*, 2 Sam. 8:17.
c *Scribe*, 1 Kin. 4:3.

17
d *Benaiah*, 1 Kin. 4:4.
e 2 Sam. 8:18.
f *Cherethites*, 1 Sam. 30:14.
g *Pelethites*, 2 Sam. 20:7.
h *David*, 1 Sam. 16:13.

1
a 2 Sam. 10:1-19.
b *Nahash*, 1 Sam. 11:1.
c *Ammonites*, Deut. 2:20.

2
d *David*, 1 Sam. 16:13.
e *Kindness*, Acts 28:2.
f 2 Sam. 10.

3
g *Uncharitableness, instances of*, Matt. 7:1.
h *False Accusation*, 2 Tim. 3:3.
i *Motive, misunderstood*, Psa. 106:8.

4
j *Rulers, wicked*, Ex. 18:21.
k *Beard, shaven*, 1 Sam. 21:13.
l *Evil for Good*, Psa. 35:12.

5
m *Jericho*, Num. 22:1.

6
n *Talent*, Ex. 38:25.
o *Silver*, 1 Chr. 28:14.
p *Armies, mercenaries*, Deut. 11:4.
q *Chariot*, Josh. 11:4.
r *Cavalry*, 1 Sam. 13:5.
s *Mesopotamia*, Gen. 24:10.
t Or, *Syria*, 2 Kin. 6:23.
u *Zobah*, 1 Sam. 14:47.

7
v Or, *Maachathi*, Deut. 3:14; or, *Maacah*, 2 Sam. 10:6, 8.
w *Medeba*, Num. 21:30.

8
x *Joab*, 2 Sam. 20:23.

10
y *Israel, under the kings*, Ex. 4:22.

11
z *Abishai*, 2 Sam. 3:30.

13
a *Courage, enjoined*, Deut. 31:7.
b *Faith, exemplified*, Mark, 11:22.

for our people, and for the cities
of our God: and [c]let the LORD do
*that which is* good in his sight.
14 So [d]Jō′ăb and the people
that *were* with him drew nigh
before the Sy̆r′ĭ-anṣ unto the
battle; and they [e]fled before him.
15 And when the [f]children of
Ăm′mŏn saw that the Sy̆r′ĭ-anṣ
were [e]fled, they likewise fled before [g]Ȧ-bĭsh′a-ī his brother, and
entered into the city. Then [d]Jō′-
ăb came to [h]Jē-ru̧′sȧ-lĕm.
16 ¶ And when the [i]Sy̆r′ĭ-anṣ
saw that they were put to the
worse before [j]Ĭṣ′ra-el, they sent
messengers, and drew forth the
Sy̆r′ĭ-anṣ that *were* beyond the
river: and [k]Shō′phăch the [l]cap-
tain of the host of [m]Hăd-är-ē′-
zēr *went* before them.
17 And it was told Dā′vid; and
he gathered all [j]Ĭṣ′ra-el, and
passed over [n]Jôr′dan, and came
upon them, and set *the battle* in
array against them. So when
Dā′vid had put the battle in array against the Sy̆r′ĭ-anṣ, they
fought with him.
18 But the Sy̆r′ĭ-anṣ [e]fled before Iṣ′ra-el; and Dā′vid slew
of the Sy̆r′ĭ-anṣ seven thousand
*men which fought in* [o]chariots,
and forty thousand footmen, and
killed [k]Shō′phăch the [l]captain
of the host.
19 And when the servants of
[m]Hăd-är-ē′zēr saw that they
were put to the worse before Ĭṣ′-
ra-el, they made peace with Dā′-
vid, and became his servants:
neither would the Sy̆r′ĭ-anṣ help
the [f]children of Ăm′mŏn any
more.

## CHAPTER 20

*Rabbah is besieged by Joab, spoiled by David, and the people thereof put to death. 4 Three giants are slain in three several battles with the Philistines.*

AND it came to pass, that
after the year was ex-
pired, at the time that kings go
out *to battle*, [a]Jō′ăb led forth the
power of the [b]army, and wasted
the country of the [c]children of
Ăm′mŏn, and came and [d]be-
sieged [e]Răb′bah. But [f]Dā′vid
tarried at [g]Jē-ru̧′sȧ-lĕm. And
Jō′ăb smote Răb′bah, and destroyed it.
2 [h]And Dā′vid took the [i]crown
of their king from off his head,
and found it to weigh a [j]talent
of [k]gold, and *there were* [l]precious
stones in it; and it was set upon
Dā′vid's head: and he brought
also exceeding much [m]spoil out
of the city.
3 And he brought out the peo-
ple that *were* in it, and [n]cut [o]*them*
with [p]saws, and with [q]harrows
of [r]iron, and with [s]axes. Even
so dealt [f]Dā′vid with all the cities of the [c]children of Ăm′mŏn.
And Dā′vid and all the people
returned to [g]Jē-ru̧′sȧ-lĕm.
4 ¶ And it came to pass after
this, that there arose war at
[t]Ġē′zēr with the [u]Phĭ-lĭs′tīneṣ;
at which time [v]Sĭb′be-chāi the
Hū′shath-īte slew [w]Sĭp′pāi, *that
was* of the children of [x]the giant:
and they were subdued.
5 And there was war again with
the [u]Phĭ-lĭs′tīneṣ; and [y]Ĕl-hā′-
nan the son of Jā′ïr slew [y]Läh′-
mī the brother of [z]Gō-lī′ath the
[a]Ġĭt′tīte, whose [b]spear staff *was*
like a [c]weaver's beam.
6 And yet again there was war
at [a]Găth, where was a man of
*great* stature, whose fingers and
[d]toes *were* four and twenty, six
*on each hand*, and six *on each
foot*: and he also was the son of
[e]the giant.
7 But when he [f]defied [g]Ĭṣ′ra-el,
[h]Jŏn′a-than the son of [i]Shĭm′e-ȧ
Dā′vid's brother slew him.
8 These were born unto [e]the
giant in [a]Găth; and they fell by
the hand of Dā′vid, and by the
hand of his servants.

c *Resignation, exemplified*, Job 5:17.

14
d *Joab*, 2 Sam. 20:23.
e *Panic*, Judg. 7:22.

15
f *Ammonites*, Deut. 2:20.
g *Abishai*, 2 Sam. 3:30.
h *Jerusalem*, Judg. 19:10.

16
i *Syria*, 2 Kin. 6:23.
j *Israel, under the kings*, Ex. 4:22.
k Or, *Shobach*, 2 Sam. 10:16, 18.
l *Captain*, Num. 31:48.
m Or, *Hadadezer*, 2 Sam. 8:3.

17
n *Jordan, fords of*, Gen. 32:10.

18
o *Chariot*, Josh. 11:4.

1
a *Joab*, 2 Sam. 20:23.
b *Armies*, Deut. 11:4.
c *Ammonites*, Deut. 2:20.
d *Siege, instances of*, Deut. 28:53.
e *Rabbah*, Deut. 3:11.
f *David*, 1 Sam. 16:13
g *Jerusalem*, Judg. 19:10.

2
h 2 Sam. 12:30, 31.
i *Crown*, Ex. 29:6.
j *Talent*, Ex. 38:25.
k *Gold*, Ezek. 7:19.
l *Precious Stones*, Ex. 39:10.
m *Spoils*, 1 Chr. 26:27.

3
n *Cruelty, instances of*, Psa. 27:12.
o *Captive, cruelty to*, 1 Sam. 30:3.
p *Saw*, 2 Sam. 12:31.
q 2 Sam. 12:31.
r *Iron*, Prov. 27:17.
s *Ax*, Deut. 19:5.

4
t *Gezer*, Josh. 10:33.
u *Philistines*, Gen. 26:14.
v 2 Sam. 21:18; or, *Sibbecai*, 1 Chr. 11:29; 27:11.
w Or, *Saph*, 2 Sam. 21:18.
x *Rephaim*, Gen. 14:5.

5
y 2 Sam. 21:19.
z *Goliath*, 1 Sam. 17:4.

a *Gath*, Josh. 11:22.
b *Spear*, 2 Kin. 11:10.
c *Weaving*, Isa. 38:12.

6
d *Toe*, Lev. 14:14.
e *Rephaim*, Gen. 14:5.

7
f *Championship*, 1 Sam. 17:23.
g *Israel, under the kings*, Ex. 4:22.
h 2 Sam. 21:21.
i Or, *Shammah*, 1 Sam. 16:9.

## CHAPTER 21

*David's sin in numbering the people. 8 His confession thereof. 9 Of the three judgments offered him, he chooses the three days' pestilence. 14 The destroying angel is stayed, and Jerusalem spared. 18 David buys Ornan's threshingfloor, erects an altar, and offers a sacrifice unto the Lord. 28 He continues to offer sacrifice in the same place.*

AND [a]Sā'tan stood up against [b]Ĭs̩'ra-el, and [1,c]provoked [d]Dā'vid to [e,f]number Ĭs̩'ra-el.

2 And [d]Dā'vid said to [g]Jō'ăb and to the rulers of the people, [h]Go, [e]number [b]Ĭs̩'ra-el from [i]Bē'er–shē'bȧ even to [j]Dăn; and bring the number of them to me, that I may know *it*.

3 And [g]Jō'ăb [k]answered, The LORD make his people an hundred times so many more as they *be*: but, my lord the king, *are* they not all my lord's servants? why then doth my lord require this thing? why will he be a cause of trespass to Ĭs̩'ra-el?

4 Nevertheless the king's word prevailed against [g]Jō'ăb. Wherefore Jō'ăb departed, and went throughout all Ĭs̩'ra-el, and came to [l]Jē-ru̇'sȧ-lĕm.

5 And [g]Jō'ăb gave the [e,f]sum of the number of the people unto [d]Dā'vid. And all *they of* [b]Ĭs̩'ra-el were a thousand thousand and an hundred thousand men that drew *sword: and [m]Jū'dah *was* four hundred threescore and ten thousand men that drew sword.

6 But [n]Lē'vī and [o]Bĕn'ja-mĭn counted he not among them: for the king's word was abominable to [g]Jō'ăb.

7 And God was [p]displeased with this thing; therefore he [q]smote Ĭs̩'ra-el.

8 And [d]Dā'vid said unto God, [r]I have sinned greatly, because I have done this thing: but now, I beseech thee, do away the iniquity of thy servant; for I have done very foolishly.

9 ¶ And the LORD [s,t]spake unto [u]Găd, [d]Dā'vid's seer, saying,

10 [s]Go and tell Dā'vid, saying, Thus saith the LORD, [v]I offer thee three *things*: choose thee one of them, that I may do *it* unto thee.

11 So [w]Găd came to [d]Dā'vid, and said unto him, Thus saith the LORD, [w]Choose thee.

12 Either three years' [x]famine; [y]or three months to be destroyed before thy foes, while that the *sword of thine enemies overtaketh *thee*; or else three days the sword of the LORD, even the [z]pestilence, in the land, and the angel of the LORD destroying throughout all the coasts of Ĭs̩'ra-el. Now therefore advise thyself what word I shall bring again to him that sent me.

13 And [a]Dā'vid said unto [b]Găd, I am in a great strait: let me fall now into the hand of the LORD; for very great *are* his [c]mercies: but let me not fall into the hand of man.

14 ¶ So the LORD sent [d,e]pestilence upon [f]Ĭs̩'ra-el: and there fell of Ĭs̩'ra-el seventy thousand men.

15 And God sent an [g]angel unto [h]Jē-ru̇'sȧ-lĕm [e]to destroy it: and as he was destroying, the LORD beheld, and he [i,j]repented him of the evil, and said to the angel that destroyed, It is enough, stay now thine hand. And the angel of the LORD stood by the threshingfloor of [k]Ôr'nan the [l]Jĕb'u-sīte.

16 And [a]Dā'vid lifted up his

1
a *Satan*, Matt. 4:10.
b *Israel, under the kings*, Ex. 4:22.
c *Temptation, yielding to*, Luke 11:4.
d *David*, 1 Sam. 16:13.
e *Census*, 2 Sam. 24:1.
f *Armies, enumeration of*, Deut. 11:4.
1 R. V. moved

2
g *Joab*, 2 Sam. 20:23.
h 2 Sam. 24.
i *Beer-sheba*, Judg. 20:1.
j *Dan*, Judg. 18:29.

3
k *Reproof, faithfulness in*, Prov. 17:10.

4
l *Jerusalem*, Judg. 19:10.

5
m *Judah, tribe of*, Num. 10:14.

6
n *Levites*, Deut. 10:8.
o *Benjamin, tribe of*, Num. 1:37.

7
p *Anger of God*, 2 Kin. 13:3.
q *Divine Chastisement*, Job 33:19.

8
r *Conscience, guilty*, Acts 23:1.

9
s *Inspiration, of prophets*, Job 32:8.
t *Prophets, inspiration of*, Isa. 3:2.
u *Gad*, 2 Sam. 24:11.

10
v *Sin, punishment of*, Rom. 5:12.

11
w *Choice, between judgments*, 2 Sam. 24:12.

12
x *Famine*, 2 Kin. 8:1.
y *War*, Judg. 3:2.
z *Plague*, Ex. 11:1.

13
a *David*, 1 Sam. 16:13.
b *Gad*, 2 Sam. 24:11.
c *God, mercy of*, Gen. 2:2.

14
d *Plague*, Ex. 11:1.
e *Judgments*, Ex. 6:6.
f *Israel, under the kings*, Ex. 4:22.

15
g *Angel, functions of*, Heb. 1:13.
h *Jerusalem*, Judg. 19:10.
i *Repentance, attributed to God*, Mark 1:4.
j *Anthropomorphisms*, Gen. 11:5.
k 2 Chr. 3:1; or, *Araunah*, 2 Sam. 24:16–25.
l *Jebusites*, Deut. 7:1.

* **SWORD.** *Used, by Gideon*, Judg. 7:20; *by Goliath*, 1 Sam. 21:9; *by Peter*, Matt. 26:51; John 18:10. *David's army equipped with*, 1 Chr. 21:5. *Jews equipped with, at rebuilding of the temple*, Neh. 4:13. *Two-edged*, Heb. 4:12. *To be beaten into plowshares*, Isa. 2:4; Mic. 4:3. *Plowshares to be converted into*, Joel 3:10.

**Figurative:** *Of war*, Gen. 27:40; Lev 26:25, 33; 1 Chr. 21:12. *Of judgments*, Deut. 32:41; 1 Chr. 21:12, 16, 27, 30; 2 Chr. 20:9; Psa. 17:13; Hos. 11:6; Zech. 13:7. *Of the malicious tongue*, Psa. 57:4; Prov. 25:18. *In John's vision*, Rev. 1:16; 2:12.
**Symbolical**, Gen. 3:24; Josh. 5:13.

**16**
*m Vision,* Acts 9:10.
*n Senate,* Num. 11:16.
*o Sackcloth,* Isa. 15:3.

**17**
*p Repentance, exemplified,* Mark 1:4.
*q Sin, confession of,* Rom. 5:12.
*r Sheep, figurative,* Deut. 32:14.
*s Unselfishness, instances of,* 1 Cor. 10:24.
*t Intercession, instances of,* Jer. 27:18.

**18**
*u Inspiration, of prophets,* Job 32:8.
*v Altar,* Gen. 8:20.

**21**
*w Salutations,* Luke 1:44.

**23**
*x Liberality, instances of,* 1 Tim. 6:18.

eyes, and [m]saw the angel of the LORD stand between the earth and the heaven, having a drawn *sword in his hand stretched out over [h]Jē-ru̧'sā-lĕm. Then Dā'vid and the [n]elders *of Is'ra-el, who were* clothed in [o]sackcloth, fell upon their faces.

17 And Dā'vid said unto God, *Is it* not I *that* commanded the people to be numbered? even [p,q]I it is that have sinned and done evil indeed; but *as for* these [r]sheep, what have they done? [s]let thine hand, I pray thee, O LORD my God, be on me, and on my father's house; [t]but not on thy people, that they should be plagued.

18 ¶ Then the [g]angel of the LORD [u]commanded [b]Găd to say to [a]Dā'vid, that Dā'vid should go up, and set up an [v]altar unto the LORD in the †threshingfloor of [k]Ôr'nan the [l]Jĕb'u-sīte.

19 And Dā'vid went up at the saying of [b]Găd, which he spake in the name of the LORD.

20 And [k]Ôr'nan turned back, and saw the angel; and his four sons with him hid themselves. Now Ôr'nan was †threshing wheat.

21 And as [a]Dā'vid came to [k]Ôr'nan, Ôr'nan looked and saw Dā'vid, and went out of the threshingfloor, and [w]bowed himself to Dā'vid with *his* face to the ground.

22 Then Dā'vid said to Ôr'nan, Grant me the place of *this* †threshingfloor, that I may build an [v]altar therein unto the LORD: thou shalt grant it me for the full price[G]: that the [d]plague[G] may be stayed[G] from the people.

23 And [k]Ôr'nan said unto Dā'vid, [x]Take *it* to thee, and let my lord the king do *that which is* good in his eyes: lo, I give *thee* the oxen *also* for [y]burnt offerings, and the †threshing instruments for wood, and the wheat for the [2,z]meat[C] offering; I give it all.

24 And king Dā'vid said to Ôr'nan, Nay; but I will verily buy it for the full price: for I will not take *that* which *is* thine for the LORD, nor offer [y]burnt offerings without cost.

25 So [a]Dā'vid gave to Ôr'nan for the place six hundred [b,c]shekels[G] of [d]gold by weight.

26 And Dā'vid built there an [e]altar unto the LORD, and offered [f]burnt [g]offerings and [h]peace offerings, and called upon the LORD; and he answered him from [i]heaven by [j]fire upon the altar of burnt offering.

27 And the LORD commanded the [k]angel; and he put up his *sword again into the sheath thereof.

28 ¶ At that time when [a]Dā'vid saw that the LORD had answered him in the †threshingfloor of Ôr'nan the [l]Jĕb'u-sīte, then he sacrificed[C] there.

29 For the [m]tabernacle of the LORD, which [n]Mō'şeş made in the wilderness, and the [e]altar of the [f]burnt offering, *were* at that season in the high place at [o]Ğĭb'e-on.

30 But [a]Dā'vid could not go before it to enquire[C] of God: for [p]he was afraid because of the *sword of the angel of the LORD.

## CHAPTER 22

*David prepares abundantly for the building of the temple. 6 His charge to Solomon respecting the same. 17 He commands the princes to assist his son.*

THEN [a]Dā'vid [l]said, This *is* the [b]house of the LORD God, and this *is* the

*y Offerings, burnt,* Lev. 6:17.
*z Offerings, meat,* Lev. 6:17.
2 R. V. meal

**25**
*a David,* 1 Sam. 16:13.
*b Shekel,* Ex. 30:13.
*c Money,* Jer. 32:9.
*d Gold,* Ezek. 7:19.

**26**
*e Altar,* Gen. 8:20.
*f Offerings, burnt,* Lev. 6:17.
*g Jesus, typified in offerings,* Matt. 1:21.
*h Offerings, peace,* Lev. 6:17.
*i Heaven, God's dwelling place,* Luke 18:22.
*j Fire, miracles connected with,* Ex. 12:8.

**27**
*k Angel, functions of,* Heb. 1:13.

**28**
*l Jebusites,* Deut. 7:1.

**29**
*m Tabernacle,* Ex. 27:9.
*n Moses,* Ex. 2:10.
*o Gibeon,* Jer. 41:16.

**30**
*p Conviction of Sin,* John 16:8.

**1**
*a David,* 1 Sam. 16:13.
*b Church, called house of the Lord,* 1 Kin. 9:3.

† **THRESHING.** *By beating,* Ruth 2:17. *By treading,* Deut. 25:4; Hos. 10:11; 1 Cor. 9:9; 1 Tim. 5:18. *With instruments, of wood,* 2 Sam. 24:22; 1 Chr. 21:23; *of iron,* Amos 1:3. *With a cart wheel,* Isa. 28:27, 28. *Floors for,* Gen. 50:10, 11; Judg. 6:37; Ruth 3:2–14; 1 Sam. 23:1; 2 Sam. 6:6; 2 Kin. 6:27; Hos. 9:2; Joel 2:24. *Floor of Araunah bought by David for a place of sacrifice,* 2 Sam. 24:16, 18–25; 1 Chr. 21:18–28.

[c]altar of the burnt offering for Ĭs̱′ra-el.

2 And Dā′vid commanded to gather together the strangers[G] that *were* in the land of Ĭs̱′ra-el; and he set [d]masons to hew wrought [e]stones to build the [f]house of God.

3 And [a]Dā′vid [g]prepared [h]iron in abundance for the [i]nails for the doors of the gates, and for the joinings; and [j]brass[G] in abundance without[G] weight;

4 Also [k]cedar trees in abundance: for the [l]Zĭ-dō′nĭ-ans̱ and they of [m]Tȳre brought much cedar wood to Dā′vid.

5 And [a]Dā′vid said, [n]Sŏl′o-mon my son *is* young and tender, and the [f]house *that is* to be builded for the LORD *must be* exceeding[G] magnifical,[G] of fame and of glory throughout all countries: I will *therefore* now make preparation for it. So Dā′vid [g]prepared abundantly before his death.

6 ¶ Then he called for [n]Sŏl′o-mon his son, and [o]charged him to build an [f]house for the LORD God of Ĭs̱′ra-el.

7 And [a]Dā′vid [o]said to [n]Sŏl′o-mon, My son, as for me, [p]it was in my mind to build an [f]house unto the name of the LORD my God:

8 But the word of the LORD came to me, saying, Thou hast shed blood abundantly, and hast made great [q]wars: thou shalt not build an house unto my name, because thou hast shed much blood upon the earth in my sight.

9 Behold, a [r]son shall be born to thee, who shall be a man of rest; and I will give him [s,t]rest[G] from all his enemies round about: for his name shall be [n]Sŏl′o-mon, and I will give [t,u]peace and quietness unto Ĭs̱′ra-el in his days.[s]

10 He shall build an [f]house for my name; and [v]he shall be my son, and [w]I *will be* his father; and [s]I will establish the [x]throne of [y]his kingdom over Ĭs̱′ra-el for ever.

11 Now, my son, [z,a]the LORD be with thee; and prosper thou, and build the house of the LORD thy God, as he hath said of thee.

12 Only the LORD give thee [b]wisdom and understanding, and give thee charge concerning Ĭs̱′ra-el, that thou mayest [c]keep[G] the [d]law of the LORD thy God.

13 [e]Then shalt thou prosper, [f]if thou takest heed to [c]fulfil the [d]statutes and judgments[G] which the LORD charged Mō′s̱es̱ with concerning Ĭs̱′ra-el: be strong, and of good [g]courage; dread not, nor be dismayed.[s]

14 Now, behold, in my trouble I have prepared for the [h]house of the LORD an hundred thousand [i]talents[G] of [j]gold, and a thousand thousand talents[G] of [k]silver; and of [l]brass and [m]iron without[G] weight; for it is in abundance: [n]timber also and stone have I prepared; and thou mayest add thereto.

15 Moreover *there are* workmen with thee in abundance, hewers and workers of [o]stone and timber,[G] and all manner of cunning men for every manner of [p]work.

16 Of the [j]gold, the [k]silver, and the [l]brass, and the [m]iron, *there is* no number. Arise *therefore,* and be doing, and the LORD be with thee.

17 ¶ Dā′vid also commanded all the princes of Ĭs̱′ra-el to help [q]Sŏl′o-mon his son, *saying,*

18 *Is* not the LORD your God with you? and [r]hath he *not* given you [s]rest[G] on every side? for he hath given the inhabitants of the land into mine hand; and the land is subdued[G] before the LORD, and before his people.

c *Altar, of burnt offerings,* Gen. 8:20.

2

d *Mason,* 2 Sam. 5:11.

e *Stones,* Ex. 24:12.

f *Temple, Solomon's,* 1 Kin. 6:17.

3

*Liberality, instances of,* 1 Tim. 6:18.

h *Iron,* Prov. 27:17.

i *Nail,* Isa. 41:7.

j *Brass,* Job 28:2.

4

k *Cedar,* Isa. 9:10.

l *Zidon,* Ezek. 28:21.

m *Tyre,* 1 Kin. 5:1.

5

n *Solomon,* 2 Sam. 12:24.

6

o *Children, counsel of parents to,* Mark 10:14.

7

p 1 Chr. 28:2–10.

8

q *War, repugnant to God,* Judg. 3:2.

9

r *Children, the gift of God,* Mark 10:14.

s *God, providence of,* Gen. 2:2.

t *Nation, promises of peace to,* Isa. 2:4.

u *Temporal Blessings, from God,* Psa. 103:2.

10

v *Spiritual Adoption,* Rom. 8:15.

w *God, fatherhood of,* Gen. 2:2.

x *Throne, figurative,* 1 Kin. 2:19.

y *Messianic Hope,* Gen. 49:10.

11

z *Prayer, intercessory,* Acts 6:4.

a *Parents, prayers of, in behalf of children,* v. 12; 2 Cor. 12:14.

12

b *Wisdom, spiritual, from God,* Prov. 2:2.

c *Obedience,* Heb. 5:8.

d *Law,* Deut. 33:2.

13

e *Blessings, contingent upon obedience,* Deut. 11:26.

f *Children, counsel of parents to,* Mark 10:14.

g *Courage, enjoined,* Deut. 31:7.

14

h *Temple, Solomon's,* 1 Kin. 6:17.

i *Talent,* Ex. 38:25.

j *Gold,* Ezek. 7:19.

k *Silver,* 1 Chr. 28:14.

l *Brass,* Job 28:2.

m *Iron,* Prov. 27:17.

n *Cedar,* Isa. 9:10.

15

o *Stones, hewers of,* Ex. 24:12.

p *Art,* 2 Chr. 16:14

17

q *Solomon,* 2 Sam. 12:24.

18

r *God, providence of,* Gen. 2:2.

s *Nation, peace given to, by God,* Isa. 2:4.

19 Now [t]set your heart and your soul to [u]seek the LORD your God; arise therefore, and build ye the [v]sanctuary of the LORD God, to bring the [w]ark of the covenant of the LORD, and the holy vessels of God, into the [h]house that is to be built to the name of the LORD.

## CHAPTER 23

*David makes Solomon king. 2 Number and distribution of the Levites. 7 Sons of Gershon, 12 of Kohath, 21 and of Merari. 24 Office of the Levites.*

SO when [a]Dā'vid was [b]old and full of days, he made [c]Sŏl'o-mon his son king over [d]Ĭṣ'ra-el.

2 ¶ And he gathered together all the princes of Ĭṣ'ra-el, with the [e]priests and the Lē'vītes.

3 Now the [f]Lē'vītes were numbered from the age of thirty years and upward: and their number by their polls[C], man by man, was thirty and eight thousand.

4 Of which, twenty and four thousand *were* [g]to set[C] forward the work of the [h,i]house of the LORD; and six thousand *were* officers and [j]judges:

5 Moreover four thousand *were* [k]porters[C]; and four thousand [l]praised the LORD with the [m]instruments which I [n]made, *said Da'vid*, to praise *therewith*.

6 And [a]Dā'vid divided them into courses[C] among the sons of Lē'vī, *namely*, [o]Ḡēr'shŏn, [p]Kō'hăth, and [q]Mė-rā'rī.

7 ¶ Of the [r]Ḡēr'shon-ītes *were*, [s]Lā'a-dăn, and [t]Shĭm'e-ī.

8 The sons of [s]Lā'a-dăn; the chief *was* [u]Jė-hī'el, and Zē'tham, and Jō'el, three.

9 The sons of [u]Shĭm'e-ī; Shĕl'o-mĭth, and Hā'zī-el, and Hā'ran, three. These *were* the chief[C] of the fathers of Lā'a-dăn.

10 And the sons of [u]Shĭm'e-ī *were*, Jā'hăth, Zī'nȧ, and Jē'ŭsh, and Bė-rī'ah. These four *were* the sons of Shĭm'e-ī.

11 And Jā'hăth was the chief, and Zī'zah the second: but Jē'ŭsh and Bė-rī'ah had not many sons; therefore they were in one reckoning[C], according to *their* father's house.

12 ¶ The [v]sons of Kō'hăth; [w]Ăm'răm, [x]Ĭz'här, [y]Hē'bron, and [z]Ŭz'zī-el, four.

13 The sons of [a]Ăm'răm; [b]Aâr'on and [c]Mō'ṣeṣ: and [d]Aâr'on was separated, that [e]he should sanctify the most holy things, he and his sons for ever, to burn incense before the LORD, to minister unto him, and to [f]bless in his name for ever.

14 Now *concerning* [c]Mō'ṣeṣ the man of God, his sons were named of the [g]tribe of Lē'vī.

15 The sons of [c]Mō'ṣeṣ *were*, [h]Ḡēr'shŏm, and [i]Ė-li-ē'zēr.

16 Of the sons of [h]Ḡēr'shŏm, [j]Shĕb'u-el *was* the chief.

17 And the sons of [i]Ė-li-ē'zēr *were*, [k]Rē-ha-bī'ah the chief. And Ė-li-ē'zēr had none other sons; but the sons of Rē-ha-bī'ah were very many.

18 Of the sons of [l]Ĭz'här; [m]Shĕl'o-mĭth the chief.

19 Of the sons of [n]Hē'bron; [o]Jė-rī'ah the first, [p]Ăm-a-rī'ah the second, [p]Jȧ-hā'zī-el the third, and [p]Jĕk-a-mē'am the fourth.

20 Of the sons of [q]Ŭz'zī-el; [r]Mī'cah the first, and Jė-sī'ah the second.

21 ¶ The [s]sons of Mė-rā'rī; [t]Māh'lī, and [u]Mū'shī. The sons of Māh'lī; [v]Ė-le-ā'zar, and [w]Kĭsh.

22 And [v]Ė-le-ā'zar died, and had no sons, but daughters: and their brethren[C] the sons of [w]Kĭsh [x]took them.

23 The sons of [u]Mū'shī; [y]Māh'lī, and [z]Ē'dēr, and [z]Jĕr'e-mŏth, three.

24 ¶ These *were* the sons of Lē'vī after the house of their fathers; *even* the chief[C] of the fa-

**19**
t *Diligence*, Rom. 12:8.
u *Seekers*, Isa. 55:6.
v *Church, called sanctuary*, 1 Kin. 9:3.
w *Ark*, Ex. 25:10.

v.1–944 BC

**1**
a *David*, 1 Sam. 16:13.
b *Old Age*, Isa. 46:4.
c *Solomon*, 2 Sam. 12:24.
d *Israel, under the kings*, Ex. 4:22.

**2**
e *Priest*, Lev. 1:5.

**3**
f *Levites, age of, when inducted into office*, Deut. 10:8.

**4**
g *Levites, duties of*, Deut. 10:8.
h *Church, called house of the Lord*, 1 Kin. 9:3.
i *Temple, Solomon's*, 1 Kin. 6:17.
j *Judge, priests and Levites as*, Judg. 2:18.

**5**
k *Porters*, 2 Sam. 18:26.
l *Choir*, 1 Chr. 15:16.
m *Music, instruments of*, 2 Chr. 5:13.
n *Invention*, 2 Chr. 26:15.

**6**
o *Gershon*, Gen. 46:11.
p *Kohath*, Num. 26:58.
q *Merari*, Gen. 46:11.

**7**
r *Gershonites*, Num. 4:27.
s Or, *Libni*, Ex. 6:17.
t *Shimei*, Ex. 6:17.

**8**
u 1 Chr. 29:8; or, *Jehieli*, 1 Chr. 26:21, 22.

**12**
v *Kohathites*, Num. 3:27.
w *Amram*, Ex. 6:18.
x 1 Chr. 6:2, 18, 38; Ex. 6:18, 21.
y *Hebron*, Num. 3:19.
z *Uzziel*, Num. 3:19.

**13**
a *Amram*, Ex. 6:18.
b *Aaron*, Ex. 6:20.
c *Moses*, Ex. 2:10.
d *Minister, call of*, Rom. 15:16
e *High Priest, duties of*, Lev. 21:10.
f *Benedictions*, Deut. 21:5.

**14**
g *Levites*, Deut. 10:8.

**15**
h *Gershom*, Ex. 2:22.
i 1 Chr. 26:25; Ex. 18:4.

**16**
j 1 Chr. 26:24; or, *Shubael*, 1 Chr. 24:20.

**17**
k 1 Chr. 24:21; 26:25.

**18**
l 1 Chr. 6:2, 18, 38; Ex. 6:18, 21.
m Or, *Shelomoth*, 1 Chr. 24:22.

**19**
n *Hebron*, Num. 3:19.
o 1 Chr. 24:23; or, *Jerijah*, 1 Chr. 26:31.
p 1 Chr. 24:23.

**20**
q *Uzziel*, Num. 3:19.
r Or, *Michah*, 1 Chr. 24:24, 25.

**21**
s *Merarites*, Num. 26:57.
t 1 Chr. 6:19; Num. 3:20; or, *Mahali*, Ex. 6:19.
u 1 Chr. 6:19; Ex. 6:19; Num. 3:20.
v 1 Chr. 24:28.
w 1 Chr. 24:29.

**22**
x *Marriage*, Gen. 34:9.

**23**
y 1 Chr. 6:47: 24:30.
z 1 Chr. 24:30.

thers, as they were counted by number of names by their polls, that did the work for the service of the house of the LORD, [a]from the age of twenty years and upward.

25 For [b]Dā'vid said, The LORD God of Is'ra-el [c]hath given rest unto his people, that they may dwell in [d]Jē-ru'sā-lĕm for ever:

26 And also unto the Lē'vītes; they shall no *more* carry the [e]tabernacle, nor any vessels of it for the service thereof.

27 For by the last words of [b]Dā'vid the [a]Lē'vītes *were* numbered from twenty years old and above:

28 Because [f]their office *was* to wait on the [g]sons of Aâr'on for the service of the [e]house of the LORD, in the courts, and in the chambers, and in the purifying of all holy things, and the work of the service of the house of God;

29 Both for the [h]shewbread, and for the fine flour for [1,i]meat offering, and for the unleavened cakes, and for *that which is baked in* the pan, and for that which is [2]fried, and for all manner of measure and size;

30 And to stand every morning to [j]thank and [k]praise the LORD, and likewise at even;

31 And to offer all [l]burnt sacrifices unto the LORD in the [m]sabbaths, in the new [n]moons, and on the set [o]feasts, by number, according to the order commanded unto them, continually before the LORD:

32 And that they should keep the charge of the [p]tabernacle of the congregation, and the charge of the [q]holy *place*, and the charge of the sons of Aâr'on their brethren, in the service of the house of the LORD.

24
*a Levites, age of, when inducted into office,* Deut. 10:8.

25
*b David,* 1 Sam. 16:13.
*c Nation, peace given to, by God,* Isa. 2:4.
*d Jerusalem,* Judg. 19:10.

26
*e Tabernacle,* Ex. 27:9.

28
*f Levites, duties of,* Deut. 10:8.
*g Priest,* Lev. 1:5.

29
*h Shewbread,* Ex. 35:13.
*i Offerings, meat,* Lev. 6:17.
1 R. V. a meal
2 R. V. soaked,

30
*j Thankfulness, in public worship,* Acts 24:3.
*k Praise,* Psa. 150:1.

31
*l Offerings, burnt,* Lev. 6:17.
*m Sabbath, offerings prescribed for,* Ex. 16:23.
*n New Moon, feast of,* Amos 8:5.
*o Annual Feasts,* Num. 15:3.

32
*p Tabernacle,* Ex. 27:9.
*q Holy Place,* Ex. 26:33.

## CHAPTER 24

*The division of the sons of Aaron by lot into four and twenty orders. 20 The Kohathites, 27 and the Merarites divided by lot.*

NOW *these are* the divisions of the [a]sons of Aâr'on. The sons of Aâr'on; [b]Nā'dăb, and [c]Ă-bī'hū, [d]Ē-le-ā'zar, and [e]Ĭth'a-mär.

2 But [b]Nā'dăb and [c]Ă-bī'hū died before their father, and had no children: therefore [d]Ē-le-ā'zar and [e]Ĭth'a-mär executed the priest's office.

3 And [f]Dā'vid distributed [g]them, both [h]Zā'dŏk of the sons of [d]Ē-le-ā'zar, and [i]Ă-hĭm'e-lĕch of the sons of [e]Ĭth'a-mär, according to their offices in their service.

4 And there were more chief men found of the sons of [d]Ē-le-ā'zar than of the sons of [e]Ĭth'a-mär; and *thus* were they divided. Among the sons of Ē-le-ā'zar *there were* sixteen chief men of the house of *their* fathers, and eight among the sons of Ĭth'a-mär according to the house of their fathers.

5 Thus were they divided by [j]lot, one sort with another; [1]for the governors of the [k]sanctuary, and governors *of the house* of God, were of the sons of [d]Ē-le-ā'zar, and of the sons of [e]Ĭth'a-mär.

6 And Shĕm-a-ī'ah the son of Nĕ-thăn'e-el the [l]scribe, *one* of the [m]Lē'vītes, wrote them before the king, and the princes, and [h]Zā'dŏk the priest, and [i]Ă-hĭm'e-lĕch the son of [n]Ă-bī'a-thär, and *before* the chief of the fathers of the priests and Lē'vītes: one principal household being taken for Ē-le-ā'zar, and *one* taken for Ĭth'a-mär.

7 Now the first [j]lot came forth to Jĕ-hoi'a-rĭb, the second to Jĕ-dā'iah,

8 The third to Hā'rim, the fourth to Sĕ-ō'rim,

1
*a Aaron, children of,* Ex. 6:20.
*b Nadab,* Ex. 24:1.
*c Abihu,* Ex. 6:23.
*d Eleazar,* Num. 3:2.
*e Ithamar,* Ex. 38:21.

3
*f David,* 1 Sam. 16:13.
*g Priest, courses of,* vs. 3-19; Lev. 1:5.
*h Zadok,* 2 Sam. 19:11.
*i* Or, *Abiathar,* 1 Sam. 22:20.

5
*j Lot,* Esth. 3:7.
*k Sanctuary,* Lev. 4:6.
1 R. V. there were princes of the sanctuary, and princes of God, both of the sons

6
*l Scribe,* 1 Kin. 4:3.
*m Levites,* Deut. 10:8.
*n* Or, *Ahimelech,* 1 Sam. 21:1.

9 The fifth to *Măl-chī′jah, the
sixth to Mĭj′a-mĭn,
10 The seventh to Hăk′kŏz,
the eighth to Ȧ-bī′jah,[Q]
11 The ninth to Jĕsh′u-ah, the
tenth to Shĕc-a-nī′ah,
12 The eleventh to Ē-lī′a-shĭb,
the twelfth to Jā′kim,
13 The thirteenth to Hŭp′pah,
the fourteenth to Jė-shĕb′e-ăb,
14 The fifteenth to Bĭl′gah, the
sixteenth to Ĭm′mẽr,
15 The seventeenth to Hē′zīr,
the eighteenth to Ăph′sēș,
16 The nineteenth to Pĕth-a-hī′-
ah, the twentieth to Jė-hĕz′e-kĕl,
17 The one and twentieth to
Jā′chin, the two and twentieth
to Gā′mŭl,
18 The three and twentieth to
Dĕl-a-ī′ah, the four and twentieth to Mā-a-zī′ah.
19 These *were* the orderings of
[g]them in their service to come
into the house of the LORD,
according to their manner,[G] under [a]Aâr′on their father, as the
LORD God of Ĭș′ra-el had commanded him.
20 ¶ And the rest of the [m]sons
of Lē′vī *were these*: Of the
sons of [o]Ăm′răm; [p]Shu̇′ba-el:
of the sons of Shu̇′ba-el; Jeh-
dē′iah.
21 Concerning [q]Rē-ha-bī′ah: of
the sons of Rē-ha-bī′ah, the first
*was* Ĭs-shī′ah.
22 Of the [r]Ĭz′hăr-ītes; [s]Shĕl′o-
mŏth: of the sons of Shĕl′o-
mŏth; Jā′hăth.
23 And the sons *of* [t]*He′bron;*
[u]Jė-rī′ah *the first,* [v]Ăm-a-rī′ah
the second, [v]Jā-hā′zĭ-el the third,
[v]Jĕk-a-mē′am the fourth.
24 *Of* the sons of [w]Ŭz′zĭ-el;
[x]Mī′chah: of the sons of Mī′-
chah; Shā′mĭr.
25 The brother of [x]Mī′chah
*was* Ĭs-shī′ah: of the sons of Ĭs-
shī′ah; [y]Zĕch-a-rī′ah.
26 The [z]sons of Mė-rā′rī *were*
[a]Mäh′lī and [b]Mū′shī: the sons
of Jā-a-zī′ah; Bē′nō.
27 The sons of Mė-rā′rī by Jā-
a-zī′ah; Bē′nō, and Shō′hăm,
and Zăc′cur, and Ĭb′rī.
28 Of Mäh′lī *came* [c]Ē-le-ā′zar,
who had no sons.
29 Concerning [c]Kĭsh: the son
of Kĭsh *was* Jė-räh′me-el.
30 The sons also of [b]Mū′shī;
[d]Mäh′lī, and [e]Ē′dẽr, and [e]Jĕr′ī-
mŏth. These *were* the sons of the
[f]Lē′vītes after the house of their
fathers.
31 These likewise cast [g]lots over
against their brethren the sons
of Aâr′on in the presence of
[h]Dā′vid the king, and [i]Zā′dŏk,
and [j]Ȧ-hĭm′e-lĕch, and the chief
of the fathers of the priests and
Lē′vītes, even the principal fathers over[G] against their younger
brethren.

## CHAPTER 25

*The number and offices of the singers. 8 Their division by lot into four and twenty orders.*

MOREOVER *[a,b]Dā′vid and
the [c]captains of the host
separated[G] to the service of the
sons of [d]Ā′saph, and of [e]Hē′-
man, and of [f]Jĕd′u̇-thŭn, [g]who
should prophesy[G] with [h,i]harps,
with [j]psalteries, and with [k]cym-
bals: and the number of the workmen according to their service
was:
2 Of the sons of [d]Ā′saph; [l]Zăc′-
cur, and Jō′șeph, and Nĕth-a-
nī′ah, and Ăs-a-rē′lah, the sons
of Ā′saph under the hands of
[d,m]Ā′saph, which prophesied[G] according to the order of the king.
3 Of [f]Jĕd′u̇-thŭn: the sons of
Jĕd′u̇-thŭn; Gĕd-a-lī′ah, and
[n]Zē′rī, and Jė-shā′iah, Hăsh-a-

**20**
o *Amram*, Ex. 6:18.
p Or, *Shebuel*, 1 Chr. 23:16; 26:24.

**21**
q 1 Chr. 23:17; 26:25.

**22**
r 1 Chr. 6:2; 23:12, 18; Ex. 6:18, 21.
s Or, *Shelomith*, 1 Chr. 23:18.

**23**
t *Hebron*, Num. 3:19.
u 1 Chr. 23:19; or, *Jerijah*, 1 Chr. 26:31.
v 1 Chr. 23:19.

**24**
w *Uzziel*, Num. 3:19.
x Or, *Micah*, 1 Chr. 23:20.

**25**
y 2 Chr. 34:12.

**26**
z *Merarites*, Num. 26:57.

a 1 Chr. 6:19; or, *Mahali*, Ex. 6:19.
b 1 Chr. 23:21; Ex. 6:19.

**28**
c 1 Chr. 23:21, 22.

**30**
d 1 Chr. 6:47; 23:23.
e 1 Chr. 23:23.
f *Levites*, Deut. 10:8.

**31**
g *Lot*, Esth. 3:7.
h *David*, 1 Sam. 16:13.
i *Zadok*, 2 Sam. 19:11.
j Or, *Abiathar*, 1 Sam. 22:20.

**1**
a *David*, 1 Sam. 16:13.
b *Church and State, civil power superior to ecclesiastical*, vs. 1–3; 1 Sam. 16:1.
c *Captain*, Num. 31:48.
d *Asaph*, 1 Chr. 15:17.
e *Heman*, 1 Chr. 6:33.
f *Jeduthun*, 1 Chr. 16:38.
g *Choir*, 1 Chr. 15:16.
h *Harp*, Dan. 3:10.
i *Music*, vs. 2–31; 2 Chr. 5:13.
j *Psaltery*, 1 Chr. 16:5.
k *Cymbal*, 1 Chr. 13:8.

**2**
l Neh. 12:35.
m *Choir, leaders of*, vs. 1–31; 1 Chr. 15:16.

**3**
n Or, *Izri*, v. 11.

*[In order to publish this Bible in one volume with its numerous and diversified marginal notes and footnotes it has been necessary to avoid elaborate discussions of subjects, such, for instance, as would be necessary to point out the difficulties in connection with some of the names in genealogical lists. These difficulties grow out of errors of copyists, differences in the spelling of the same name, and the fact that individuals and places are mentioned under different names in different chapters. Where the identity of persons or places is doubtful in the following lists, and when no noteworthy fact is known concerning them, no mention of the name is made in either the margins or footnotes.]

bī'ah, and Măt-tĭ-thī'ah, six, under the hands of their father [m]Jĕd'u̇-thŭn, who prophesied with a [h]harp, to give [o]thanks and to [p]praise the LORD.

4 Of [e]Hē'man: the sons of Hē'man; Bŭk-kī'ah, Măt-ta-nī'ah, Ŭz'zī-el, [q]Shĕb'u-el, and Jĕr'ĭ-mŏth, Hăn-a-nī'ah, Hā-nā'nī, Ė-lī'a-thah, Ğĭd-dăl'tī, and Rō-măm'tī-ē'zĕr, Jŏsh-bĕk'a-shah, Măl'lo-thī, Hō'thīr, *and* Mā-hā'-zī-ŏth:

5 All these *were* the sons of [e]Hē'man the king's seer in the words of God, to lift up the [r]horn. And God gave to Hē'man fourteen [s]sons and three [s]daughters.

6 All [g]these *were* under the hands of their [m]father for song *in* the [t]house of the LORD, with [k]cymbals, [j]psalteries, and [h]harps, for the service of the house of God, according to the king's order to [d]Ā'saph, [f]Jĕd'u̇-thŭn, and [e]Hē'man.

7 So the number of [g,u]them, with their brethren that were [v]instructed in the songs of the LORD, *even* all that were cunning,[c] was two hundred fourscore and eight.

8 ¶ And they cast [w]lots, [1]ward[c] against *ward*,[c] as well the small as the great, the [†]teacher as the [u]scholar.

9 Now the first [w]lot came forth for [d]Ā'saph to Jō'şeph: the second to Ğĕd-a-lī'ah, who with his brethren and sons *were* twelve:

10 The third to [l]Zăc'cur, *he*, his sons, and his brethren, *were* twelve:

11 The fourth to [x]Ĭz'rī, *he*, his sons, and his brethren, *were* twelve:

12 The fifth to Nĕth-a-nī'ah, *he*, his sons, and his brethren, *were* twelve:

13 The sixth to Bŭk-kī'ah, *he*, his sons, and his brethren, *were* twelve:

14 The seventh to Jė-shăr'e-lah, *he*, his sons, and his brethren, *were* twelve:

15 The eighth to Jė-shā'iah, *he*, his sons, and his brethren, *were* twelve:

16 The ninth to Măt-ta-nī'ah, *he*, his sons, and his brethren, *were* twelve:

17 The tenth to Shĭm'e-ī, *he*, his sons, and his brethren, *were* twelve:

18 The eleventh to Ā-zăr'e-el, *he*, his sons, and his brethren, *were* twelve:

19 The twelfth to Hăsh-a-bī'ah, *he*, his sons, and his brethren, *were* twelve:

20 The thirteenth to [y]Shu̇'ba-el, *he*, his sons, and his brethren, *were* twelve:

21 The fourteenth to Măt-tĭ-thī'ah, *he*, his sons, and his brethren, *were* twelve:

22 The fifteenth to Jĕr'e-mŏth, *he*, his sons, and his brethren, *were* twelve:

23 The sixteenth to Hăn-a-nī'-ah, *he*, his sons, and his brethren, *were* twelve:

24 The seventeenth to Jŏsh-bĕk'a-shah, *he*, his sons, and his brethren, *were* twelve:

25 The eighteenth to Hā-nā'nī, *he*, his sons, and his brethren, *were* twelve:

26 The nineteenth to Măl'lo-thī, *he*, his sons, and his brethren, *were* twelve:

27 The twentieth to Ė-lī'a-thah, *he*, his sons, and his brethren, *were* twelve:

28 The one and twentieth to Hō'thīr, *he*, his sons, and his brethren, *were* twelve:

29 The two and twentieth to

o *Thankfulness, in public worship,* Acts 24:3.
p *Praise,* Psa. 150:1.

4
q Or, *Shubael,* v. 20.

5
r *Trumpet,* Josh. 6:4.
s *Children, the gift of God,* Mark 10:14.

6
t *Tabernacle,* Ex. 27:9.

7
u *Students,* 2 Kin. 2:3.
v *Music, teachers of,* 2 Chr. 5:13.

8
w *Lot,* Esth. 3:7.
1 R. V. for their charges, all alike,

11
x Or, *Zeri,* v. 3.

20
y Or, *Shebuel,* v. 4.

† **TEACHERS.** *Itinerant,* 2 Chr. 17:7–9. *Samuel, head of school of prophets,* 1 Sam. 19:20. *Elisha, head of, at Gilgal,* 2 Kin. 4:38. *Of public assemblies,* Neh. 8:1–8, 13, 18. *Should receive compensation,* Gal. 6:6. See footnotes: INSTRUCTION, Prov. 23:23; JESUS, *Teacher,* Matt. 1:21.

Ğĭd-dăl′tī, *he,* his sons, and his
brethren, *were* twelve:
30 The three and twentieth to
Mă-hā′zī-ŏth, *he,* his sons, and
his brethren, *were* twelve:
31 The four and twentieth to
Rō-măm′tĭ-ē′zēr, *he,* his sons,
and his brethren, *were* twelve.

## CHAPTER 26

*The divisions of the porters. 13 The gates assigned by lot. 20 The Levites that had charge of the treasures. 29 Officers and judges.*

CONCERNING the divisions
of the [a]porters[G]: Of the Kôr′-
hītes *was* [b]Mē-shĕl-e-mī′ah the
son of [c]Kō′rē, of the sons of
[d]Ā′saph.
2 And the sons of [b]Mē-shĕl-
e-mī′ah *were,* [e]Zĕch-a-rī′ah the
firstborn, Jē-dī′a-el the second,
Zĕb-a-dī′ah the third, Jăth′nĭ-el
the fourth,
3 Ē′lăm the fifth, Jē-hō-hā′-
nan the sixth, Ĕ-lĭ-o-ē′na-ī the
seventh.
4 Moreover the sons of [f]Ō′bed-
ē′dom *were,* Shĕm-a-ī′ah the
firstborn, Jē-hŏz′a-băd the second, Jō′ah the third, and Sā′cär
the fourth, and Nē-thăn′e-el the
fifth,
5 Ăm′mĭ-el the sixth, Ĭs′sa-
char the seventh, Pē-ŭl′thāi the
eighth: for God blessed him.
6 Also unto Shĕm-a-ī′ah his
son were sons born, that ruled
throughout the house of their father: for they *were* mighty men
of valour.
7 The sons of Shĕm-a-ī′ah;
Ŏth′nī, and Rē′pha-el, and Ō′-
bed, Ĕl′za-băd, whose brethren
*were* strong men, Ē-lī′hū, and
Sĕm-a-chī′ah.
8 All these of the sons of
[f]Ō′bed-ē′dom: they and their
sons and their brethren, able
men for strength for the service,
*were* threescore and two of Ō′-
bed-ē′dom.
9 And [b]Mē-shĕl-e-mī′ah had
sons and brethren, strong men,
eighteen.
10 Also [g]Hō′sah, of the [h]chil-
dren of Mē-rā′rī, had sons; Sĭm′-
rī the chief, ([i]for *though* he was
not the [j]firstborn, yet his father
made him the chief;)
11 [k]Hĭl-kī′ah the second, Tĕb-
a-lī′ah the third, Zĕch-a-rī′ah the
fourth: all the sons and brethren
of [g]Hō′sah *were* thirteen.
12 Among these *were* the divisions of the [a]porters[G], *even* among
the chief men, *having* [1]wards[G]
one against another, to minister
in the [l,m]house of the LORD.
13 ¶ And [a]they cast [n]lots, as
well the small as the great, according to the house of their fathers, for every gate.
14 And the [n]lot eastward fell to
[b]Shĕl-e-mī′ah. Then for [e]Zĕch-
a-rī′ah his son, a wise counsellor,
they cast lots; and his lot came
out northward.
15 To [f]Ō′bed-ē′dom southward; and to his sons the [2]house
of Ă-sŭp′pim.
16 To Shŭp′pim and [g]Hō′sah
*the lot came forth* westward, with
the [o]gate Shăl′le-chĕth, by the
causeway of the going up, ward[G]
against ward[G].
17 Eastward *were* six [p]Lē′-
vītes, northward four a day,
southward four a day, and [3]to-
ward Ă-sŭp′pim two *and* two.
18 At Pär′bar westward, four
at the causeway, *and* two at
Pär′bar.
19 These *are* the divisions of
the [a]porters[G] among the sons
of [4,c]Kō′rē, and among the [h]sons
of Mē-rā′rī.
20 ¶ And of the [p]Lē′vītes,
Ă-hī′jah *was* over the [q]treasures[G]
of the [l,m]house of God, and over
the treasures of the dedicated[G]
things.
21 *As concerning* the sons of
[r]Lā′a-dăn; the sons of the [s]Gēr′-
shon-īte Lā′a-dăn, chief fathers,

**1**
a *Porters,* 2 Sam. 18:26.
b 1 Chr. 9:21.
c 1 Chr. 9:19.
d Or, *Ebiasaph,* 1 Chr. 6:23, 37; 9:19.

**2**
e 1 Chr. 9:21.

**4**
f *Obed-edom,* 2 Sam. 6:10.

**10**
g 1 Chr. 16:38.
h *Merarites,* Num. 26:57.
i *Birthright, set aside,* 2 Chr. 21:3.
j *Firstborn, birthright of, set aside,* Zech. 12:10.

**11**
k 1 Chr. 6:45.

**12**
l *Tabernacle,* Ex. 27:9.
m *Church, called house of the Lord,* 1 Kin. 9:3.
1 R. V. charges like as their brethren,

**13**
n *Lot,* Esth. 3:7.

**15**
2 R. V. storehouse.

**16**
o *Jerusalem, gates of,* Judg. 19:10.

**17**
p *Levites,* Deut. 10:8.
3 R. V. for the storehouse two and two.

**19**
4 R. V. the Korahites,

**20**
q *Treasure Houses,* Ezra 5:17.

**21**
r Or, *Libni,* Ex. 6:17.
s *Gershonites,* Num. 4:27.

even of Lā'a-dăn the Gēr'shon-
īte, *were* [t]Jĕ-hī'e-lī.
22 The sons of [t]Jĕ-hī'e-lī; Zē'-
tham, and Jō'el his brother,
*which were* over the [q]treasures of
the [l,m]house of the LORD.
23 Of the [u]Ăm'ram-ītes, *and*
the [v]Ĭz'hār-ītes, the [w]Hē'bron-
ītes, *and* the [x]Ŭz'zĭ-el-ītes:
24 And [y]Shĕb'u-el the son of
[z]Gēr'shŏm, the son of [a]Mō'ṣeṣ,
*was* ruler of the [b]treasures.
25 And his brethren by [c]Ĕ-li-ē'-
zēr; [d]Rē-ha-bī'ah his son, and
Jĕ-shā'iah his son, and Jō'ram
his son, and [e]Zĭch'rī his son, and
Shĕl'o-mĭth his son.
26 Which Shĕl'o-mĭth and his
brethren *were* over all the [b]trea-
sures of the [f]dedicated things,
which [g]Dā'vid the king, and
the chief fathers, the [h]captains
over thousands and hundreds,
and the captains of the host,
had dedicated.
27 Out of the *spoils won in
battles did they dedicate to
[5]maintain the [i]house of the
LORD.
28 And all that [j]Săm'u-el the
seer, and [k]Saul the son of [l]Kĭsh,
and [m]Ăb'nēr the son of [n]Nēr,
and [o]Jō'ăb the son of [p]Zĕr-u-ī'-
ah, had [f]dedicated; *and* whosoever had dedicated *any thing, it
was* under the hand of Shĕl'o-
mĭth, and of his brethren.
29 ¶ Of the Ĭz'hār-ītes, Chĕn-
a-nī'ah and his sons *were* for the
outward business over Ĭṣ'ra-el,
for officers and [q]judges.
30 *And* of the [r]Hē'bron-ītes,
[s]Hăsh-a-bī'ah and his brethren, men of valour, a thousand
and seven hundred, *were* officers
among them of Ĭṣ'ra-el on this
side [t]Jôr'dan westward in all the
business of the LORD, and in the
service of the king.
31 Among the [r]Hē'bron-ītes *was*
[u]Jĕ-rī'jah the chief, *even* among
the Hē'bron-ītes, according to
the generations of his fathers.
In the fortieth year of the reign
of Dā'vid they were sought for,
and there were found among
them mighty men of valour at
[v]Jā'zēr, of [w]Gĭl'e-ăd.
32 And his brethren, men of
valour, *were* two thousand and
seven hundred chief fathers,
whom king Dā'vid made rulers
over the [x]Reu'ben-ītes, the
[y]Găd'ītes, and the half tribe of
[z]Mă-năs'seh, for every matter
pertaining to God, and affairs of
the king.

Or, *Jehiel*, 1 Chr. 23:8; 29:8.
23 *u* *Amram*, Ex. 6:18. *v* 1 Chr. 6:2, 18; Ex. 6:18, 21. *w* *Hebronites*, Num. 3:27. *x* *Uzziel*, Num. 3:19.
24 *y* 1 Chr. 23:16; or, *Shubael*, 1 Chr. 24:20. *z* *Gershom*, Ex. 2:22.
*a* *Moses*, Ex. 2:10. *b* *Treasure Houses*, Ezra 5:17.
25 *c* 1 Chr. 23:15; Ex. 18:4. *d* 1 Chr. 23:17; 24:21. *e* 1 Chr. 27:16.
26 *f* *Dedication*, Ezra 6:17. *g* *David*, 1 Sam. 16:13. *h* *Captain*, Num. 31:48.
27 *i* *Tabernacle*, Ex. 27:9. 5 R. V. repair
28 *j* *Samuel*, 1 Sam. 3:1. *k* *Saul*, 1 Sam. 9:2. *l* *Kish*, 1 Sam. 9:1. *m* *Abner*, 1 Sam. 14:50. *n* 1 Sam. 14:50. *o* *Joab*. 2 Sam. 20:23. *p* *Zeruiah*, 1 Chr. 2:16.
29 *q* *Court, civil*, vs. 29–32; Ex. 18:26.
30 *r* *Hebronites, duties of*, vs. 31–32; Num. 3:27. *s* 1 Chr. 27:17. *t* *Jordan*, Gen. 32:10.

v.31–944 BC See footnote, *Time*, Rev. 10:6.
31 *u* Or, *Jeriah*, 1 Chr. 23:19; 24:23. *v* *Jazer*, Josh. 13:25. *w* *Gilead*, Deut. 3:13.
32 *x* *Reubenites*, Josh. 22:1. *y* *Gad, tribe of*, Deut. 33:20. *z* *Manasseh, tribe of*, Gen. 46:20.

## CHAPTER 27

*Twelve captains, one for each month.* 16 *The princes of the twelve tribes.* 23 *The numbering of the people is hindered.* 25 *David's officers.*

NOW the [a]children of Ĭṣ'-
ra-el after their number,
*to wit*, the chief fathers and
[b]captains of thousands and hundreds, and their officers that
served the king in any matter
of the courses, which came in
and went out [c]month by month
throughout all the months of the
year, of every course *were* twenty
and four thousand.
2 Over the first course for the
[d]first [c]month *was* [e]Jă-shō'be-ăm
the son of Zăb'dī-el: and in his
course *were* twenty and four
thousand.
3 Of the children of [f]Pē'rĕz *was*
the chief of all the captains of the
host for the first month.
4 And over the course of the
second [c]month *was* [g]Dō'da-ī an
Ā-hō'hīte, and of his course *was*
Mĭk'loth also the ruler: in his
course likewise *were* twenty and
four thousand.
5 The third [b]captain of the host
for the third [c]month *was* [h]Bĕ-
nā'iah the son of [i]Jĕ-hoi'a-dā, a

1 *a* *Armies, standing*, Deut. 11:4. *b* *Captain*, Num. 31:48. *c* *Month*, Ex. 12:2.
2 *d* *Abib*, Ex. 13:4. *e* 1 Chr. 11:11; 2 Sam. 23:8.
3 *f* Or, *Pharez*, Gen. 38:29.
4 *g* Or, *Dodo*, 1 Chr. 11:12; 2 Sam. 23:9.
5 *h* *Benaiah*, 1 Kin. 4:4. *i* 1 Chr. 11:22; 2 Sam. 8:18.

*** SPOILS.** *Of war*, Gen. 14:11, 12; Num. 31:9, 10; Deut. 2:35. *Divided between the combatants and non-combatants of the Israelites, including priests and Levites*, Num. 31:25–54; 1 Sam. 30:24. *Dedicated to the Lord*, Josh. 6:19; 1 Sam. 15:15; 1 Chr. 26:27; 2 Chr. 15:11. See footnote, WAR, Judg. 3:2.

chief priest: and in his course[c] *were* twenty and four thousand.

6 This *is that* [h]Bē-nā'iah, *who was* mighty *among* the thirty, and above the thirty: and in his course *was* Ăm-mĭz'a-băd his son.

7 The fourth [b]*captain* for the fourth [c]month *was* [j]Ā'sa-hĕl the brother of [k]Jō'ăb, and Zĕb-a-dī'ah his son after him: and in his course[G] *were* twenty and four thousand.

8 The fifth [b]captain for the fifth [c]month *was* Shăm'hŭth the Ĭz'ra-hīte: and in his course *were* twenty and four thousand.

9 The sixth [b]*captain* for the sixth [c]month *was* [l]Ī'râ the son of [l]Ĭk'kĕsh the Tē-kō'īte: and in his course *were* twenty and four thousand.

10 The seventh [b]*captain* for the seventh [c]month *was* [m]Hē'lez the [n]Pĕl'o-nīte, of the [o]children of Ē'phră-ĭm: and in his course[G] *were* twenty and four thousand.

11 The eighth [b]*captain* for the eighth [c]month *was* [p]Sĭb'be-cāi the Hū'shath-īte, of the Zär'-hītes: and in his course *were* twenty and four thousand.

12 The ninth [b]*captain* for the ninth [c]month *was* [q]Ā-bĭ-ē'zēr the Ăn-e-tŏth'īte, of the [r]Bĕn'ja-mītes: and in his course[G] *were* twenty and four thousand.

13 The tenth [b]*captain* for the tenth [c]month *was* [s]Mâ-hăr'a-ī the Nē-tŏph'a-thīte, of the Zär'-hītes: and in his course *were* twenty and four thousand.

14 The eleventh [b]*captain* for the eleventh [c]month *was* [t]Bē-nā'iah the [u]Pĭr'a-thon-īte, of the children of [o]Ē'phră-ĭm: and in his course *were* twenty and four thousand.

15 The twelfth [b]*captain* for the twelfth [c]month *was* [v]Hĕl'da-ī the Nē-tŏph'a-thīte, of [w]Ŏth'nĭ-el: and in his course *were* twenty and four thousand.

16 ¶ Furthermore over the tribes of Ĭş'ra-el: the ruler of the [x]Reu'ben-ītes *was* Ĕ-li-ē'zēr the son of [y]Zĭch'rī: of the [z]Sim'e-on-ītes, Shĕph-a-tī'ah the son of Mā'a-chah:

17 Of the [a]Lē'vītes, [b]Hăsh-a-bī'ah the son of Kĕ-mū'el: of the [c]Aâr'on-ītes, [d]Zā'dŏk:

18 Of [e]Jū'dah, [f]Ē-lī'hū, *one* of the brethren of [g]Dā'vid: of [h]Ĭs'sa-char, Ŏm'rī the son of Mī'chaĕl:

19 Of [i]Zĕb'u-lŭn, Ĭsh-ma-ī'ah the son of Ō-ba-dī'ah: of [j]Năph'-ta-lī, Jĕr'ĭ-mŏth the son of Ăz'-rĭ-el:

20 Of the children of [k]Ē'phră-ĭm, Hō-shē'â the son of Ăz-a-zī'ah: of the half tribe of [l]Mâ-năs'seh, Jō'el the son of Pĕ-dā'-iah:

21 Of the half *tribe* of [l]Mâ-năs'seh in [m]Gĭl'e-ăd, Ĭd'dō the son of Zĕch-a-rī'ah: of [n]Bĕn'ja-mĭn, Jâ-ā'sĭ-el the son of [o]Ăb'nēr:

22 Of [p]Dăn, Â-zăr'e-el the son of Jĕr'o-hăm. These *were* the princes of the tribes of Ĭş'ra-el.

23 ¶ But [g]Dā'vid took not the [q,r]number of them from twenty years old and under: because the LORD had said he would increase [s]Ĭş'ra-el like to the stars of the heavens.

24 [t]Jō'ăb the son of [u]Zĕr-u-ī'ah began to [q,r]number, but he finished not, because there fell [v]wrath for it against Ĭş'ra-el; neither was the number put in the account of the [w]chronicles of king [g]Dā'vid.

25 ¶ And over the king's [x]treasures[G] *was* Ăz'ma-vĕth the son of Ā'dĭ-el: and over the [y]storehouses in the fields, in the cities, and in the villages, and in the castles[G], *was* Jē-hŏn'-a-than the son of Ŭz-zī'ah:

7
j *Asahel*, 2 Sam. 2:18.
k *Joab*, 2 Sam. 20:23.

9
l 1 Chr. 11:28; 2 Sam. 23:26.

10
m 1 Chr. 11:27; 2 Sam. 23:26.
n 1 Chr. 11:27; or, *Palite*, 2 Sam. 23:26.
o *Ephraim, tribe of*, Gen. 41:52.

11
p 1 Chr. 11:29; or, *Sibbechai*, 1 Chr. 20:4; 2 Sam. 21:18.

12
q 1 Chr. 11:28; 2 Sam. 23:27.
r *Benjamin, tribe of*, Num. 1:37.

13
s 1 Chr. 11:30; 2 Sam. 23:28.

14
t 1 Chr. 11:31; 2 Sam. 23:30.
u *Pirathon*, Judg. 12:15.

15
v Or, *Heled*, 1 Chr. 11:30; or, *Heleb*, 2 Sam. 23:29.
w *Othniel*, Josh. 15:17.

16
x *Reubenites*, Josh. 22:1.
y 1 Chr. 26:25.
z *Simeon, tribe of*, Num. 2:12.

17
a *Levites*, Deut. 10:8.
b 1 Chr. 26:30.
c *Priest*, Lev. 1:5.
d *Zadok*, 2 Sam. 19:11.

18
e *Judah, tribe of*, Num. 10:14.
f Or, *Eliab*, 1 Sam. 16:6.
g *David*, 1 Sam. 16:13.
h *Issachar, tribe of*, Num. 1:28.

19
i *Zebulun, tribe of*, Gen. 49:13.
j *Naphtali, tribe of*, Num. 1:42.

20
k *Ephraim, tribe of*, Gen. 41:52.
l *Manasseh, tribe of*, Gen. 46:20.

21
m *Gilead*, Deut. 3:13.
n *Benjamin, tribe of*, Num. 1:37.
o *Abner*, 1 Sam. 14:50.

22
p *Dan, tribe of*, Gen. 30:6.

23
q *Census*, 2 Sam. 24:1.
r *Israel, number of*, Ex. 4:22.
s *Descendants, of Abraham*, Gen. 22:17.

24
t *Joab*, 2 Sam. 20:23.
u *Zeruiah*, 1 Chr. 2:16.
v *Judgments*, Ex. 6:6.
w *Book, chronicles kept in*, Num. 5:23.

25
x *Treasure Houses*, Ezra 5:17.
y *Storehouses*, 2 Chr. 32:28.

26 And over them that did the
[z]work of the field for tillage of
the ground *was* Ĕz′rī the son of
Chē′lŭb:
27 And over the [a]vineyards *was*
Shĭm′e-ī the Rā′math-īte: over
the increase of the vineyards for
the [b]wine cellars *was* Zăb′dī the
Shĭph′mīte:
28 And over the [c]olive trees and
the [d]sycomore trees that *were* in
the low plains *was* Bā′al–hā′nan
the Gĕd′e-rīte: and over the cellars of [e]oil *was* Jō′ăsh:
29 And over the herds that
fed in ‖Shâr′on *was* Shĭt′ra-ī
the Shâr′on-īte: and over the
herds *that were* in the valleys
*was* Shā′phat the son of Ăd′la-ī:
30 Over the [f]camels also *was*
Ō′bĭl the [g]Ĭsh′ma-el-īte: and
over the asses *was* Jeh-dē′iah
the Mē-rŏn′o-thīte:
31 And over the flocks *was*
Jā′zĭz the Hā′gēr-īte. All these
*were* the rulers of the [h]substance which *was* king Dā′vid's.
32 [i]Also Jŏn′a-than [j]Dā′vid's
uncle was a [k]counsellor, a wise
man, and a [l]scribe[C]: and Jē-hī′el
the son of Hăch′mō-nī *was* with
the king's sons:
33 [i]And [m]Ă-hĭth′o-phĕl *was* the
king's [k]counsellor: and [n]Hū′-
shāi the Är′chīte *was* the king's
companion:
34 And after [m]Ă-hĭth′o-phĕl
*was* [o]Jē-hoi′a-dȧ the son of [p]Bē-
nā′iah, and [q]Ă-bī′a-thär: and the
[r]general of the king's army *was*
[s]Jō′ăb.

## CHAPTER 28

*David, in a solemn assembly, exhorts the people to fear God. 9 His charge to Solomon. 11 He gives him patterns for the temple, and gold and silver for the furniture thereof. 20 He encourages him to proceed with the work.*

AND [a]Dā′vid assembled all
the princes of Ĭs′ra-el, the
princes of the tribes, and the
[b]captains of the companies that
ministered to the king by course[C],
and the [c]captains over the thousands, and captains over the
hundreds, and the [d]stewards
over all the substance and possession of the king, and of his
sons, with the officers[C], and with
the mighty men, and with all the
valiant men, unto [e]Jē-ru′sȧ-lĕm.
2 Then [a]Dā′vid the king stood
up upon his feet, and said, Hear
me, my brethren, and my people: *As for me,* [f,g]I *had* in mine
heart to build an house of rest
for the [h]ark of the covenant[C] of
the LORD, and for the *footstool of our God, and had made
ready for the building:
3 But God said unto me, Thou
shalt not build an house for
my name, because thou *hast been*
a man of [i]war, and hast shed
blood.
4 Howbeit the [j]LORD God of
Ĭs′ra-el [k]chose me before all the
house of my father to be king
over Ĭs′ra-el for ever: for he hath
chosen [l]Jū′dah *to be* the ruler;
and the house of Jū′dah, the
house of my father; and among
the sons of my father he liked[C] me
to make *me* king over all Ĭs′ra-el:
5 And of all my sons, (for
the LORD hath given me many
sons,) he hath [k]chosen [m]Sŏl′o-
mon my son to sit upon the
throne of the kingdom of the
LORD over Ĭs′ra-el.
6 And he said unto me, [m]Sŏl′o-
mon thy son, he shall build my
[n]house and my courts: for [o]I
have [p]chosen him *to be* my son,
and [q]I will be his father.
7 Moreover [j]I will establish
[r,s]his kingdom for ever, [t]if he be
constant to [u]do my commandments and my judgments[C], as at
this day.
8 Now therefore in the sight of
all Ĭs′ra-el the congregation of

26
z *Agriculture, practised by David,* vs. 26–31; Gen. 3:23.

27
a *Vineyard,* Isa. 1:8.
b *Wine,* Prov. 23:31.

28
c *Olive,* Deut. 6:11.
d *Sycomore,* 2 Chr. 1:15.
e *Oil,* Deut. 12:17.

30
f *Camel,* 1 Sam. 30:17.
g Or, *Ishmeelites,* Gen. 39:1.

31
h *King, emoluments of,* 2 Kin. 3:10.

32
i *Cabinet,* Ezra 7:14.
j *David,* 1 Sam. 16:13.
k *Counselor,* Prov. 11:14.
l *Scribe,* 1 Kin. 4:3.

33
m *Ahithophel,* 2 Sam. 15:12.
n 2 Sam. 16:16.

34
o *By error in transcribing, Jehoiada is made to appear in this passage to be the son of Benaiah, while in fact he was the father of Benaiah,* See 1 Chr. 18:17; 2 Sam. 8:18.
p *Benaiah,* 1 Kin. 4:4.
q *Abiathar,* 1 Sam. 22:20.
r *Captain,* Num. 31:48.
s *Joab,* 2 Sam. 20:23.

1
a *David,* 1 Sam. 16:13.
b *Captain,* Num. 31:48.

v.1–944 BC
See footnote, *Time,* Rev. 10:6.

c *Armies, how officered,* Deut. 11:4.
d *Steward,* Gen. 43:19.
e *Jerusalem,* Judg. 19:10.

2
f 1 Chr. 22:7–13.
g *Liberality, instances of,* 1 Tim. 6:18.
h *Ark,* Ex. 25:10.

3
i *War, repugnant to God,* Judg. 3:2.

4
j *Government, God in,* Isa. 22:21.
k *Rulers, appointed by God,* Ex. 18:21.
l *Judah, tribe of,* Num. 10:14.

5
m *Solomon,* 2 Sam. 12:24.

6
n *Temple, Solomon's,* 1 Kin. 6:17.
o *Spiritual Adoption,* Rom. 8:15.
p *Call, personal,* Phil. 3:14.
q *God, fatherhood of,* Gen. 2:2.

7
r *Solomon, prophecies concerning,* 2 Sam. 12:24.
s *Messianic Hope,* Gen. 49:10.
t *Blessings, contingent upon obedience,* Deut. 11:26.
u *Obedience, rewarded,* Heb. 5:8.

‖ **SHARON** (*even the plain*), the maritime slope of Palestine north of Joppa. Song 2:1; Isa. 33:9; 35:2; 65:10. *David's herds in,* 1 Chr. 27:29. *Called* SARON, Acts 9:35.

* **FOOTSTOOL. Figurative:** *Of the earth,* Isa. 66:1; Matt. 5:35; Acts 7:49. *Of complete subjugation,* Psa. 110:1; Mark 12:36; Luke 20:43; Acts 2:35; Heb. 1:13.

v.8–944 BC
See footnote, *Time*, Rev. 10:6.

8
v *Commandment, enjoining obedience to God's word*, Deut. 8:2.
w *Obedience, enjoined*, Heb. 5:8.
x *Canaan*, Gen. 37:1.

9
y *Commandment, enjoining wholehearted service*, Deut. 8:2.
z *Perfection*, Heb. 6:1.

a *Heart*, Psa. 44:21.
b *God, knowledge of*, Gen. 2:2.
c *Evil Imagination*, Gen. 6:5.
d *Seekers, promises to*, Isa. 55:6.
e *Penitent, promises to*, Psa. 51:17.
f *Promise, to seekers*, 2 Cor. 1:20.
g *Prayer, answer to, promised*, Acts 6:4.
h *Apostasy*, Acts 1:25.
i *Wicked, punishment of*, Psa. 73:3.

10
j *Call, personal*, Phil. 3:14.
k *Sanctuary*, Lev. 4:6.

11
l *David*, 1 Sam. 16:13.
m *Solomon*, 2 Sam. 12:24.
n *Pattern, of the temple*, Ex. 25:40.
o *Treasure Houses*, Ezra 5:17.
p *Mercy Seat*, Ex. 25:17.

12
q *Holy Spirit, inspiration of*, Acts 1:2.
r *Court, of the temple*, Ex. 38:9.
s *Temple, Solomon's*, 1 Kin. 6:17.

13
t *Priest*, Lev. 1:5.
u *Levites*, Deut. 10:8.

the LORD, and in the audience[G]
of our God, [v,w]keep and seek for
all the commandments of the
LORD your God: [t]that ye may
possess this good [x]land, and
leave *it* for an inheritance for
your children after you for ever.[S]
9 ¶ And thou, [m]Sŏl′o-mon my
son, know thou the God of thy
father, and [w,y]serve him with a
[z]perfect [a]heart and with a willing
mind: for the LORD searcheth
all hearts, and [b]understand-
eth all the [c]imaginations of the
thoughts: if [d,e]thou seek him,
[f,g]he will be found of thee; but if
thou [h]forsake him, he will [i]cast
thee off for ever.
10 Take heed now; for the
LORD hath [j]chosen thee to build
an house for the [k]sanctuary: be
strong, and do *it*.
11 ¶ Then [l]Dā′vid gave to
[m]Sŏl′o-mon his son the [n]pattern
of the porch, and of the houses
thereof, and of the [o]treasuries
thereof, and of the upper chambers thereof, and of the inner
parlours thereof, and of the
place of the [p]mercy seat,
12 And the [n]pattern of all that
he had by the [q]spirit, of the
[r]courts of the [s]house of the
LORD, and of all the chambers
round about, of the [o]treasuries
of the house of God, and of
the treasuries of the dedicated
things:[T]
13 Also for the courses of the
[t]priests and the [u]Lē′vītes, and
for all the work of the service
of the [s]house of the LORD, and
for all the vessels of service in
the house of the LORD.

14 *He gave* of [v]gold by weight
for [1]*things* of gold, for all [1]in-
struments[G] of all manner of service; [†]*silver also* for all [1]instru-
ments[G] of silver by weight for all
[1]instruments[G] of every kind of
service:
15 Even the weight for the
[w]candlesticks[G] of [v]gold, and for
their lamps of gold, by weight
for every candlestick[G], and for
the lamps thereof: and for the
candlesticks[G] of silver by weight,
*both* for the candlestick[G], and *also*
for the lamps thereof, according
to the use of every candlestick.[G]
16 And by weight *he gave* [v]gold
for the [x]tables of shewbread, for
every table; and *likewise* [†]silver
for the tables of silver:
17 Also pure [v]gold for the
[y]fleshhooks, and the [z]bowls, and
the cups: and for the golden
[a]basons *he gave gold* by weight
for every bason; and *likewise*
[†]*silver* by weight for every bason
of silver:
18 And for the [b]altar of incense [‡]refined [c]gold by weight;
and gold for the pattern of the
[d]chariot of the [e]cherubims, that
spread out *their wings*, and covered the [f]ark of the covenant of
the LORD.
19 All *this, said* [g]*Da′vid,* the
LORD [h]made me understand in
writing by *his* hand upon me,
*even* all the works of this [i]pat-
tern.
20 And [g]Dā′vid said to [j]Sŏl′o-
mon his son, [k]Be strong and [l]of
good courage, and do *it*: fear
not, nor be dismayed: for [m,n]the
LORD God, *even* my God, [o]*will*

v.20–944 BC
See footnote, *Time*, Rev. 10:6.

14
v *Gold*, Ezek. 7:19.
1 R. V. vessels

15
w *Candlestick*, Ex. 25:31.

16
x *Shewbread, table of*, Ex. 35:13.

17
y *Fleshhook*, Ex. 27:3.
z *Bowl*, Ex 25:29.

a *Basin*, 1 Kin. 7:50.

18
b *Altar, of incense*, Ex. 30:1.
c *Gold*, Ezek. 7:19.
d *Chariot*, Josh. 11:4.
e *Cherubim*, Ex. 37:7.
f *Ark*, Ex. 25:10.

19
g *David*, 1 Sam. 16:13.
h *Inspiration*, Job 32:8.
i *Pattern, of the temple*, Ex. 25:40.

20
j *Solomon*, 2 Sam. 12:24.
k *Commandment, enjoining courage and obedience*, Deut. 8:2.
l *Courage, enjoined*, Deut. 31:7.
m *Righteous, promises to*, Psa. 64:10.
n *Promise, to the righteous, of God's help*, 2 Cor. 1:20.
o *Faith, instances of*, Mark 11:22.

† **SILVER.** *From Tarshish*, Ezek. 27:12. *Refining of*, Prov. 17:3; Jer. 6:29, 30; Ezek. 22:18–22; Zech. 13:9; Mal. 3:3. *Used for money*, Gen. 20:16; 23:13–16; Amos 8:6; Matt. 10:9; 26:15; Mark 14:11; Acts 19:19. *Used for ornamentation; and in the manufacture of the utensils, for the tabernacle*, Ex. 26:19; 27:17; 35:24, 36:24; 38:25; Num. 7:13, 19, 25, 31, 37, 43, 49, 55, 61, 67, 73, 79, 85; 2 Sam. 8:10; *for the temple*, 2 Sam. 8:10; 1 Kin. 10:25; 2 Kin. 12:13; 1 Chr. 18:10; 28:14; 29:2–5; 2 Chr. 24:14; Ezra 1:6; 5:14; 6:5; 8:26; Dan. 5:2; 11:8.

*Abundance of*, 1 Kin. 10:27; 1 Chr. 22:14; 29:2–7; 2 Chr. 1:15; Eccl. 2:8; Isa. 2:7. *Dross from*, Prov. 25:4; 26:23. *Reprobate*, Jer. 6:30. *Workers in*, 2 Chr. 2:14; Acts 19:24.

ARTICLES MADE OF: *Cups*, Gen. 44:2; 2 Kin. 12:13; *trumpets*, Num. 10:2; *chains*, Isa. 40:19; *shrines*, Acts 19:24; *idols*, Ex. 20:23; Isa. 30:22; Hos. 13:2; *baskets* [R. V.], or, *filigree* [marg., R. V.], Prov. 25:11; *jewels*, Song 1:11.

**Figurative,** 1 Cor. 3:12.

**Symbolical,** Dan. 2:32, 35.

‡ **REFINING.** *Of gold*, 1 Chr. 28:18. *Of silver*, 1 Chr. 29:4. *Of wine*, Isa. 25:6.

**Figurative:** *Of the corrective judgments of God*, Isa. 1:25; 48:10; Jer. 9:7; Zech. 13:9; Mal. 3:2, 3. *Of the purity of the word of God*, Psa. 18:30.

v.20–944 BC
See footnote, *Time*, Rev. 10:6.

*p God, faithfulness of*, Gen. 2:2.

21
*q Priest*, Lev. 1:5.
*r Levites*, Deut. 10:8.
*s Temple, Solomon's*, 1 Kin. 6:17.

1
*a David*, 1 Sam. 16:13.
*b Solomon*, 2 Sam. 12:24.
*c Rulers, appointed by God*, Ex. 18:21.
*d Temple, Solomon's*, 1 Kin. 6:17.

2
*e Liberality, instances of*, 1 Tim. 6:18.
*f Gold*, Ezek. 7:19.
*g Silver*, 1 Chr. 28:14.
*h Brass*, Job 28:2.
*i Iron*, Prov. 27:17.
*j Onyx*, Ezek. 28:13.
*k Precious Stones*, Ex. 39:10.
1 R. V. stones for inlaid work,

3
*l Church, holy*, 1 Kin. 9:3.
2 R. V. seeing that I have a treasure of mine own of gold

be with thee; [p]he will not fail
thee, nor forsake thee, until thou
hast finished all the work for the
service of the house of the LORD.[S]
21 And, behold, the courses of
the [q]priests and the [r]Lē′vītes,
*even they shall be with thee* for
all the service of the [s]house of
God: and *there shall be* with thee
for all manner of workmanship
every willing skilful man, for
any manner of service: also the
princes and all the people *will be*
wholly at thy commandment.

## CHAPTER 29

*David, by his example and entreaty, causes the princes and people to offer willingly. 10 His thanksgiving and prayer. 20 The people, having blessed God, and sacrificed, make Solomon king. 27 David's reign and death.*

FURTHERMORE [a]Dā′vid
the king said unto all the
congregation, [b]Sŏl′o-mon my
son, whom alone God hath [c]cho-
sen, *is yet* young and tender,[G] and
the work *is* great: for the [d]palace
*is* not for man, but for the LORD
God.
2 Now [e]I have prepared with
all my might for the [d]house of
my God the [f]gold for *things to be*
*made* of gold, and the [g]silver for
*things* of silver, and the [h]brass
for *things* of brass, the [i]iron for
*things* of iron, and wood for
*things* of wood; [j]onyx stones,
and *stones* to be set, [1]glistering[G]
stones, and of divers[G] colours, and
all manner of [k]precious stones,
and *marble stones in abundance.
3 Moreover, because I have set
my affection to the [d]house of my
God, [2]I have of mine own proper[G]
good,[G] of [f]gold and [g]silver, *which*
[e]I have given to the house of
my God, over and above all
that I have prepared for the
[l]holy house,

4 *Even* three thousand [m]talents[G]
of [f]gold, of the [n]gold of [o]Ō′phĭr,
and seven thousand talents[G] of
[p]refined [g]silver, to overlay the
walls of the houses *withal*:
5 The [f]gold for *things* of gold,
and the [g]silver for *things* of silver, and for all manner of work
*to be made* by the hands of †artif-
icers.[G] And who *then* is willing
to consecrate [3]his service this
day unto the LORD?
6 ¶ Then the chief[G] of the fathers and princes of the tribes
of Ĭş′ra-el, and the [q]captains of
[r]thousands and of hundreds,
with the rulers of the king's
work, [e]offered willingly,
7 And [e]gave for the service of
the [d]house of God of [f]gold five
thousand [m]talents[G] and ten thousand ‡drams,[G] and of [g]silver ten
thousand talents,[G] and of [h]brass
eighteen thousand talents,[G] and
one hundred thousand talents[G]
of [i]iron.
8 And they with whom [k]*precious* stones were found [e]gave
*them* to the [s]treasure[G] of the house
of the LORD, by the hand of [t]Jē-
hī′el the [u]Gēr′shon-īte.
9 Then the people [v]rejoiced,
for that they [e]offered willingly,
because with perfect[G] heart they
offered willingly to the LORD:
and Dā′vid the king also rejoiced with great [w]joy.
10 ¶ Wherefore [x]Dā′vid [y]bless-
ed the LORD before all the
congregation: and Dā′vid said,
Blessed *be* thou, LORD God of
Ĭş′ra-el our father, [z]for ever and
ever.[S T]
11[S] Thine, O LORD, *is* the
greatness, and the [a]power, and
the [b]glory, and the victory, and
the majesty: for all *that is* in the
heaven and in the earth *is thine*;
thine *is* the kingdom, O LORD,

v.4–944 BC
See footnote, *Time*, Rev. 10:6.

4
*m Talent*, Ex. 38:25.
*n Imports*, 1 Kin. 10:11.
*o Ophir*, 1 Kin. 9:28.
*p Refining*, 1 Chr. 28:18.

5
3 R. V. himself this day

6
*q Captain*, Num. 31:48.
*r Armies, how officered*, Deut. 11:4.

8
*s Treasure*, Luke 12:33.
*t* 1 Chr. 23:8; or, *Jehieli*, 1 Chr. 26:21, 22.
*u Gershonites*, Num. 4:27.

9
*v Thankfulness*, Acts 24:3.
*w Joy, instances of*, Psa. 5:11.

10
*x David, devoutness of*, 1 Sam. 16:13.
*y Praise*, Psa. 150:1.
*z God, eternity of*, Gen. 2:2.

11
*a God, power of*, Gen. 2:2.
*b God, glory of*, Gen. 2:2.

*** MARBLE.** *In the temple*, 1 Chr. 29:2. *Pillars of*, Esth. 1:6; Song 5:15. *Merchandise of*, Rev. 18:12. *Mosaics of*, Esth. 1:6.

**† ARTISAN. Skillful:** *Jubal*, Gen. 4:21. *Tubal-cain*, Gen. 4:22. *Bezaleel and Aholiab, divinely inspired to build the tabernacle*, Ex. 31:2–11; 35:30–35. *Hiram, an expert workman for the temple*, 1 Kin. 7:13–51; 2 Chr. 2:13, 14. See footnote, ART, 2 Chr. 16:14.

**‡ DRAM** (R. V. daric). *A Persian coin of differently estimated value*, 1 Chr. 29:7; Ezra 2:69; 8:27; Neh. 7:70–72 and [c]thou art exalted as head above all.[Q]

12 Both [d]riches and honour *come* of thee, and [c]thou reignest over all; and in thine hand *is* [a]power and might; and [e]in thine hand *it is* to [d]make great, and to [d]give strength unto all.[S]

13 Now therefore, our God, we [f]thank thee, and [g]praise thy glorious name.

14 But[S] [h]who *am* I, and what *is* my people, that we should be able to offer so willingly after this sort? for all things *come* of thee, and of thine own have we given thee.

15 For we *are* strangers before thee, and sojourners,[C] as *were* all our fathers: [i]our days on the earth *are* as a shadow, and *there is* none abiding.[C][Q]

16 O LORD our God, all this store[C] that we have prepared to build thee an [j]house for thine holy name *cometh* of thine hand, and *is* all thine own.[S]

17 I know also, my God, that [k]thou triest[C] the [l]heart, and hast pleasure in [m]uprightness. As for me, in the uprightness of mine heart [n]I have willingly [o]offered all these things: and now have I seen with [f,p]joy thy people, which are present here, to offer willingly unto thee.[S]

18 O LORD God of [q]Ā'bră-hăm, [r]Ī'ṣaac, and of [s]Ĭṣ'ra-el, our fathers, [t]keep this for ever in the imagination of the thoughts of the heart of thy people, and prepare[C] their heart unto thee:

19 And [t]give unto [u]Sŏl'o-mon [v]my son a [w]perfect [l]heart, to keep thy commandments, thy testimonies, and thy statutes, and to do all *these things,* and to build the [j]palace, *for* the which I have made provision.

20 ¶ And Dā'vid said to all the congregation, Now bless the LORD your God. And all the congregation [g]blessed the LORD God of their fathers, and bowed down their heads, and worshipped the LORD, and the king.

21 And they sacrificed sacrifices unto the LORD, and offered [x]burnt [y]offerings unto the LORD, on the morrow[C] after that day, *even* a thousand bullocks, a thousand rams, *and* a thousand lambs, with their [z]drink offerings, and sacrifices in abundance for all Ĭṣ'ra-el:

22 And did eat and drink before the LORD on that day with great [a]gladness. And they made [b]Sŏl'o-mon the son of [c]Dā'vid king the second time, and [d]anointed *him* unto the LORD *to be* the chief[C] governor, and [e]Zā'dŏk *to be* [f]priest.

23 Then [b]Sŏl'o-mon sat on the [g]throne of the LORD as king instead of [c]Dā'vid his father, and prospered; and all Ĭṣ'ra-el obeyed him.

24 And all the princes, and the mighty men, and all the sons likewise of king Dā'vid, submitted themselves unto Sŏl'o-mon the king.

25 And the LORD [h]magnified [b]Sŏl'o-mon exceedingly in the sight of all Ĭṣ'ra-el, and bestowed upon him *such* royal majesty as had not been on any king before him in Ĭṣ'ra-el.

26 ¶ Thus [c]Dā'vid the son of [i]Jĕs'se reigned over all Ĭṣ'ra-el.

27 And the time that he reigned over [j]Ĭṣ'ra-el *was* forty years; seven years reigned he in [k]Hē'-bron, and thirty and three *years* reigned he in [l]Jē-rụ'să-lĕm.

28 And he [m]died in a good [n]old age, full of days, [h]riches, and honour: and [b]Sŏl'o-mon his son reigned in his stead.[C]

29 Now the acts of [c]Dā'vid the [o]king, first and last, behold, they *are* written in the [p]book of [q]Săm'u-el the [r]seer, and in the

v.11–944 BC
See footnote, *Time,* Rev. 10:6.

c *God, sovereign,* Gen. 2:2.

12
d *Temporal Blessings, from God,* Psa. 103:2.
e *God, providence of,* Gen. 2:2.

13
f *Thankfulness, to God, instances of,* Acts 24:3.
g *Praise,* Psa. 150:1.

14
h *Humility,* Prov. 22:4.

15
i *Life, brevity and uncertainty of,* Eccl. 8:15.

16
j *Temple, Solomon's,* 1 Kin. 6:17.

17
k *God, knowledge of,* Gen. 2:2.
l *Heart,* Psa. 44:21.
m *Integrity,* Job 2:3.
n *Zeal,* 2 Cor. 7:11.
o *Liberality, instances of,* 1 Tim. 6:18.
p *Joy, instances of,* Psa. 5:11.

18
q *Abraham,* Gen. 17:5.
r *Isaac,* Gen. 21:3.
s *Israel,* Ex. 4:22.
t *Intercession, exemplified,* Jer. 27:18.

19
u *Children, prayers in behalf of,* Mark 10:14.
v *Parents, prayers of, in behalf of children,* 2 Cor. 12:14.
w *Perfection,* Heb. 6:1.

v.20–944 BC
See footnote, *Time,* Rev. 10:6.

21
x *Offerings, burnt,* Lev. 6:17.
y *Jesus, typified in offerings,* Matt. 1:21.
z *Offerings, drink,* Lev. 6:17

22
a *Joy, instances of,* Psa. 5:11.
b *Solomon,* 2 Sam. 12:24.
c *David,* 1 Sam. 16:13.
d *Anointing, of kings,* Lev. 8:12.
e *Zadok,* 2 Sam. 19:11.
f *High Priest,* Lev. 21:10.

23
g *Throne,* 1 Kin. 2:19.

25
h *Temporal Blessings, from God,* Psa. 103:2.

26
i *Jesse,* Ruth 4:17.

27
j *Israel, under the kings,* Ex. 4:22.
k *Hebron,* Gen. 23:2.
l *Jerusalem,* Judg. 19:10.

28
m *Death,* Num. 23:10.
n *Old Age,* Isa. 46:4.

29
o *King, chronicles of,* 2 Kin. 3:10.
p *Book,* Num. 5:23.
q *Samuel,* 1 Sam. 3:1.
r *Prophets,* Isa. 3:2.

book of [s]Nā′than the [r]prophet, and in the book of [t]Găd the seer,

30 With all his reign and his might, and the times that went over him, and over Ĭş′ra-el, and over all the kingdoms of the countries.

v.29–944 BC

s *Nathan*, 2 Sam. 7:2.

t *Gad*, 2 Sam. 24:11.

v.30–944 BC
See footnote, *Time*, Rev. 10:6.

---

THE SECOND BOOK OF THE

# CHRONICLES

## CHAPTER 1

*The solemn offering of Solomon at Gibeon. 7 His choice of wisdom is blessed by God. 13 Solomon's power and wealth.*

AND [a]Sŏl′o-mon the son of [b]Dā′vid was [c]strengthened in his kingdom, and the LORD his God *was* with him, and magnified him exceedingly.

2 Then [a]Sŏl′o-mon spake unto all [d]Ĭş′ra-el, to the [e]captains of [f]thousands and of hundreds, and to the [g]judges, and to every governor in all Ĭş′ra-el, the chief of the fathers.

3 So [a]Sŏl′o-mon, and all the congregation with him, went to the [h]high place that *was* at [i]Gĭb′-e-on; for there was the [1,j]tabernacle of the congregation of God, which [k]Mō′şeş the servant of the LORD had made in the wilderness.

4 But the [l]ark of God had [b]Dā′vid brought up from [m]Kĭr′jath-jē′a-rĭm to *the place which* Dā′vid had prepared for it: for he had pitched a [j]tent for it at [n]Je-ru̥′sā-lĕm.

5 Moreover the brasen [o]altar, that [p]Bē-zăl′e-el the son of [q]Ū′rī, the son of [r]Hûr had made, he put before the [j]tabernacle of the LORD: and [a]Sŏl′o-mon and the congregation sought unto it.

6 And [a]Sŏl′o-mon went up thither to the brasen [o]altar before the LORD, which *was* at the [1,j]tabernacle of the congregation, and offered a thousand [s]burnt [t]offerings upon it.

7 ¶ In that night did God [u]appear unto [a]Sŏl′o-mon, and [v]said unto him, Ask what I shall give thee.

8 And [a]Sŏl′o-mon [v]said unto God, Thou hast shewed great mercy unto [b]Dā′vid my father, and [w]hast made me to reign in his stead.

9 Now, O LORD God, let thy promise unto Dā′vid my father be established: for thou hast made me king over a people like the dust of the earth in multitude.

10 [x,y]Give me now [z]wisdom and knowledge, that I may go out and come in before this people: for who can judge this thy people, *that is so* great?

11 And God [v]said to Sŏl′o-mon, Because this was in thine heart, and thou hast not asked riches, wealth, or honour, nor the life of thine enemies, neither yet hast asked long life; but hast asked [z]wisdom and knowledge for thyself, that thou mayest judge my people, over whom I have made thee king:

12 [x]Wisdom and knowledge *is* granted unto thee; and I will [a]give thee [b]riches, and [b]wealth, and [b]honour, such as none of the kings have had that *have been* before thee, neither shall there any after thee have the like.

13 ¶ Then [c]Sŏl′o-mon came *from his journey* to the [d]high place that *was* at [e]Gĭb′e-on to [f]Jē-ru̥′sā-lĕm, from before the [1,g]tabernacle of the congregation, and reigned over [h]Ĭş′ra-el.

14 [i]And [c]Sŏl′o-mon gathered [j]chariots and [k,l]horsemen: and

v.1–943 BC
See footnote, *Time*, Rev. 10:6.

1

a *Solomon*, 2 Sam. 12:24.

b *David*, 1 Sam. 16:13.

c *Temporal Blessings, from God*, Psa. 103:2.

2

d *Israel, under the kings*, Ex. 4:22.

e *Captain*, Num. 31:48.

f *Armies, how officered*, Deut. 11:4.

g *Judge*, Judg. 2:18.

3

h *High Places*, 1 Kin. 3:2.

i *Gibeon*, Jer. 41:16.

j *Tabernacle*, Ex. 27:9.

k *Moses*, Ex. 2:10.

1 R. V. tent of meeting

4

l *Ark*, Ex. 25:10.

m *Kirjath-jearim*, Josh. 15:9.

n *Jerusalem*, Judg. 19:10.

5

o *Altar*, Gen. 8:20.

p *Bezaleel*, Ex. 31:2.

q *Uri*, Ex. 35:30.

r *Hur*, Ex. 31:2.

6

s *Offerings, burnt*, Lev. 6:17.

t *Jesus, typified in offerings*, Matt. 1.21.

7

u *God, appearances of*, Gen. 2:2.

v *Communion, with God*, 2 Cor. 13:14.

v.7–943 BC
See footnote, *Time*, Rev. 10:6.

8

w *Government, God in*, Isa. 22:21.

10

x *Prayer, answer to, exceeds petition*, vs. 10–12; Acts 6:4.

y *Humility*, Prov. 22:4.

z *Wisdom, prayer for*, Prov. 2:2.

12

a *God, providence of*, Gen. 2:2.

b *Temporal Blessings, from God*, Psa. 103:2.

13

c *Solomon*, 2 Sam. 12:24.

d *High Places*, 1 Kin. 3:2.

e *Gibeon*, Jer. 41:16.

f *Jerusalem*, Judg. 19:10.

g *Tabernacle*, Ex. 27:9.

h *Israel, under the kings*, Ex. 4:22.

14

i 1 Kin. 10:26–29

j *Chariot*, Josh. 11:4.

k *Armies*, Deut. 11:4.

l *Cavalry*, 1 Sam. 13:5.

he had a thousand and four hundred chariots, and twelve thousand horsemen, which he placed in the chariot [m]cities, and with the king at [l]Jĕ-rṳ′să-lĕm.

15 And the king made [n]silver and [o]gold at [l]Jĕ-rṳ′să-lĕm *as plenteous* as stones, and [p]cedar trees made he as the *sycomore trees that *are* in the [2]vale for abundance.

16 And [c]Sŏl′o-mon had[q, r]horses brought out of [3, s]Ē′ġy̆pt, and linen yarn: the king's [t]merchants received the linen yarn at a price.

17 And they [r]fetched up, and brought forth out of [s]Ē′ġy̆pt a [j]chariot for six hundred [u]*shekels*[c] of [n]silver, and an [q]horse for an hundred and fifty: and so brought they out *horses* for all the kings of the [v]Hĭt′tītes, and for the kings of [w]Sy̆r′ĭ-ȧ, by their means.

## CHAPTER 2

*Solomon's laborers for the building of the temple. 3 His message to Huram for workmen and timber. 11 Huram's kind answer.*

AND [a]Sŏl′o-mon determined to build an [b]house for the name of the LORD, and an [c]house for his kingdom.

2 And [a]Sŏl′o-mon told[c] out threescore and ten thousand men to bear burdens, and fourscore thousand to hew[c] in the mountain, and three thousand and six hundred to oversee[c] them.

3 ¶ And [a]Sŏl′o-mon sent to [d]Hū′ram the king of [e]Ty̆re, saying, As thou didst deal with [f]Dā′vid my father, and didst send him [g]cedars to build him an house to dwell therein, *even so deal with me.*

4 Behold, I build an [b]house to the name of the LORD my God, to dedicate *it* to him, *and* to burn before him [1]sweet [h]incense, and for the continual [i]shewbread, and for the [j]burnt offerings morning and evening, on the [k]sabbaths, and on the [l]new moons, and on the [2]solemn [m]feasts of the LORD our God. This *is an ordinance* for ever to Ĭṣ′ra-el.

5 And the [b]house which I build *is* great: for great *is* our God above all gods.

6 But who is able to build him an house, seeing the [n]heaven and heaven of heavens [o]cannot contain [p]him? [q]who *am* I then, that I should build him an house, save[c] only to burn [3]sacrifice[c] before him?[s]

7 Send me now therefore a [r]man cunning[c] to work in gold, and in silver, and in brass, and in iron, and in [s]purple, and [s]crimson, and [s]blue, and that can skill[c] to grave[c] with the cunning[c] men that *are* with me in [t]Jū′dah and in [u]Jĕ-rṳ′să-lĕm, whom Dā′vid my father did provide.

8 Send me also [g]cedar trees, [v]fir trees, and [w]algum trees, out of [x]Lĕb′a-non: for I know that thy servants can skill[c] to cut timber in Lĕb′a-non; and, behold, my servants *shall be* with thy servants.

9 Even to prepare me timber in abundance: for the [b]house which I am about to build *shall be* wonderful great.

10 And, behold, I will give to thy servants, the hewers that cut timber, twenty thousand [y]measures[c] of beaten[c] [z]wheat, and twenty thousand measures of [a]barley, and twenty thousand [b]baths[c] of [c]wine, and twenty thousand baths of [d]oil.

11 ¶ Then [e]Hū′ram the king of [f]Ty̆re answered in writing, which he sent to [g]Sŏl′o-mon,

m *Cities*, Num. 35:8.

15
n *Silver*, 1 Chr. 28:14.
o *Gold*, Ezek. 7:19.
p *Cedar*, Isa. 9:10.
2 R. V. lowland,

16
q *Horse*, Job 39:19.
r *Imports*, 1 Kin. 10:11.
s *Egypt*, Gen. 41:8.
t *Merchant*, Neh. 3:32.
3 R. V. Egypt; the king's merchants received them in droves, each drove at a price.

17
u *Shekel*, Ex. 30:13.
v *Hittites*, Judg. 1:26.
w *Syria*, 2 Kin. 6:23.

1
a *Solomon*, 2 Sam. 12:24.
b *Temple, Solomon's*, 1 Kin. 6:17.
c *Palace*, 1 Kin. 21:1.

3
d Or, *Hiram*, 2 Sam. 5:11.
e *Tyre*, 1 Kin. 5:1.
f *David*, 1 Sam. 16:13.
g *Cedar*, Isa. 9:10.

4
h *Incense*, Ex. 37:29.
1 R. V. incense of sweet spices,
i *Shewbread*, Ex. 35:13.
j *Offerings, daily*, Lev. 6:17.
k *Sabbath, offerings prescribed for*, Ex. 16:23.
l *New Moon, feast of*, Amos 8:5.
m *Annual Feasts*, Num. 15:3.
2 R. V. set

6
n *Heavens, physical*, Psa. 8:3.
o *God, infinite*, Gen. 2:2.
p *God, omnipresent*, Gen. 2:2.
q *Humility*, Prov. 22:4.
3 R. V. incense

7
r *Goldsmith*, Neh. 3:8.
s *Colors*, Ezek. 16:16.
t *Judah, kingdom of*, 2 Chr. 11:17.
u *Jerusalem*, Judg. 19:10.

8
v *Fir Tree*, 2 Sam. 6:5.
w 2 Chr. 9:10, 11; or, *almug*, 1 Kin. 10:11, 12.
x *Lebanon*, Deut. 1:7.

10
y *Measure, dry*, Deut. 25:15.
z *Wheat*, Ezra 6:9.
a *Barley*, Ex. 9:31.
b *Measure, liquid*, Deut. 25:15.
c *Wine*, Prov. 23:31.
d *Oil*, Deut. 12:17.

11
e Or, *Hiram*, 2 Sam. 5:11.
f *Tyre*, 1 Kin. 5:1.
g *Solomon*, 2 Sam. 12:24.

* **SYCOMORE**, or SYCAMORE, a fruit tree of the genus to which the fig tree belongs, and differing essentially from the sycamore tree of America. *Abundant in the lowlands of Canaan*, 1 Kin. 10:27; 2 Chr. 1:15; 9:27; Isa. 9:10. *Groves of*, 1 Chr. 27:28. *Destroyed by frost*, Psa. 78:47. *Care of*, Amos 7:14 [R. V.]. *Zacchæus climbs into*, Luke 19:4.

*h* *Government, God in,* Isa. 22:21.
*i* *King, divinely authorized,* 2 Kin. 3:10.
12
¶ *Thankfulness, to God,* Acts 24:3.
*k* *God, creator,* Gen. 2:2.
*l* *Heavens, physical,* Psa. 8:3.
*m* *Earth,* Prov. 8:23.
*n* *David,* 1 Sam. 16:13.
*o* *Temple, Solomon's,* 1 Kin. 6:17.
*p* *Palace,* 1 Kin. 21:1.
13
*q* *Artisan,* 1 Chr. 29:5.
*r* *Master Workman,* 1 Cor. 3:10.
*s* Or, *Hiram,* 1 Kin. 7:13.
14
*t* *Dan, tribe of,* Gen. 30:6.
*u* *Genius,* Ex. 28:3.
*v* *Gold,* Ezek. 7:19.
*w* *Silver,* 1 Chr. 28:14.
*x* *Brass,* Job 28:2.
*y* *Iron,* Prov. 27:17.
*z* *Stones,* Ex. 24:12.
*a* *Colors,* Ezek. 16:16.
15
*b* *Wheat,* Ezra 6:9.
*c* *Barley,* Ex. 9:31.
*d* *Oil,* Deut. 12:17.
*e* *Wine,* Prov. 23:31.
16
*f* *Cedar,* Isa. 9:10.
*g* *Lebanon,* Deut. 1:7.
*h* *Jerusalem,* Judg. 19:10.

Because the LORD hath loved
his people, [h]he hath made thee
[i]king over them.
12 [e]Hū'ram said moreover,
[j]Blessed *be* the LORD God of
Ĭṣ'ra-el, [k]that made [l]heaven and
[m]earth, who hath given to [n]Dā'-
vid the king a wise son, endued
with *prudence and understanding, that might build an [o]house
for the LORD, and an [p]house for
his kingdom.
13 And now I have sent a [q,r]cun-
ning man, endued with understanding, of [s]Hū'ram my father's,
14 The [s]son of a woman of the
daughters of [t]Dăn, and his father *was* a man of [f]Tȳre, [u]skilful
to work in [v]gold, and in [w]silver,
in [x]brass, in [y]iron, in [z]stone, and
in timber, in [a]purple, in [a]blue,
and in fine linen, and in [a]crim-
son; also to grave any manner of
graving, and to find out every
device which shall be put to him,
with thy cunning men, and with
the cunning men of my lord
Dā'vid thy father.
15 Now therefore the [b]wheat,
and the [c]barley, the [d]oil, and the
[e]wine, which my lord hath spoken of, let him send unto his
servants:
16 And we will cut [f]wood out
of [g]Lĕb'a-non, as much as thou
shalt need: and we will bring it
to thee in flotes by sea to †Jŏp'-
pȧ; and thou shalt carry it up to
[h]Jē-ru̥'sȧ-lĕm.

17 ¶ And [i]Sŏl'o-mon numbered
all the [j]strangers that *were* in the
land of Ĭṣ'ra-el, after the numbering wherewith Dā'vid his father had numbered them; and
they were found an hundred and
fifty thousand and three thousand and six hundred.
18 And he set threescore and
ten thousand of them *to be* bearers of burdens, and fourscore
thousand *to be* hewers in the
[4]mountain, and three thousand
and six hundred overseers to set
the people a work.

## CHAPTER 3

*The place, and time of building the temple. 3 The measure and ornaments of the house. 10 The cherubim. 14 The vail and pillars.*

[a]THEN [b]Sŏl'o-mon began to
build the [c]house of the
LORD at [d]Jē-ru̥'sȧ-lĕm in mount
[e]Mō-rī'ah, where *the* LORD appeared unto [f]Dā'vid his father,
in the place that Dā'vid had
prepared in the [g]threshingfloor
of [h]Ôr'nan the [i]Jĕb'u-sīte.
2 And he began to build in the
second *day* of the second [j]month,
in the fourth year of his reign.
3 ¶ Now these *are the* [1]*things*
*wherein* [b]Sŏl'o-mon was instructed for the building of the
[c]house of God. The length by
[k]cubits after the first measure
*was* threescore cubits, and the
breadth twenty cubits.
4 And the [l]porch that *was* in the
front *of the house,* the length *of*

17
*i* *Solomon,* 2 Sam. 12:24.
*j* *Foreigners,* Deut. 23:20.
18
4 R. V. mountains.
**v.1–940 BC**
See footnote, *Time,* Rev. 10:6.
1
*a* 1 Kin. 6:7, 15–51.
*b* *Solomon,* 2 Sam. 12:24.
*c* *Temple, Solomon's,* 1 Kin. 6:17.
*d* *Jerusalem,* Judg. 19:10.
*e* Gen. 22:2.
*f* *David,* 1 Sam. 16:13.
*g* *Threshing, floors for,* 1 Chr. 21:20.
*h* 1 Chr. 21:15, 25, 28; or, *Araunah,* 2 Sam. 24:16–25.
*i* *Jebusites,* Deut. 7:1.
2
*j* *Month, Zif,* Ex. 12:2.
3
*k* *Cubit,* Ex. 36:9.
1 R. V. foundations which Solomon laid for
4
*l* *Temple, Solomon's, porch of,* 1 Kin. 6:17.

* **PRUDENCE,** Prov. 12:16, 23; 13:16; 14:8, 15, 18; 16:21; 18:15; 22:3; 27:12; Hos. 14:9; Matt. 7:6.
*In restraining speech,* Psa. 39:1; Prov. 21:23; 23:9; 26:4; 29:11; Amos 5:13. *In heeding counsel,* Prov. 15:5; 20:18. *In restraining appetite,* Prov. 23:1, 2. *In avoiding strife,* Prov. 25:8–10; 29:8. *In avoiding litigation,* Matt. 5:25, 26. *In refraining from suretyship,* Prov. 6:1, 2.
**Instances of:** *Abraham, in refusing gifts from king of Sodom,* Gen. 14:22, 23. *Jacob, toward Esau,* Gen. 32:3–21; *toward his sons, after Dinah's defilement,* Gen. 34:5. *Joseph in the affairs of Egypt,* Gen. 41:33–57. *Jethro's advice to Moses,* Ex. 18:17–23. *The Israelites, in the threatened war with the two and one-half tribes,* Josh. 22:10–34. *Saul, in not slaying the Jabesh-gileadites,* 1 Sam. 11:13. *David, in his conduct with Saul,* 1 Sam. 18:5–30; *in overthrowing Ahithophel's counsel,* 2 Sam. 15:33–37. *Abigail, in averting David's wrath,* 1 Sam. 25:18–31. *Achish, in dismissing David,* 1 Sam. 29. *Elijah, in his flight from Jezebel,* 1 Kin. 19:3, 4. *Rehoboam's counselors,* 1 Kin. 12:7. *Jehoram, in suspecting a Syrian stratagem,* 2 Kin. 7:12–14. *Nehemiah, in conduct of affairs at Jerusalem,* Neh. 2:12–16; 4:13–23. *Daniel,* Dan. 1:8–14. *Certain elders of Israel,* Jer. 26:17–23. *Joseph, in his conduct toward Mary,* Matt. 1:19; *in his flight to Egypt to save the life of Jesus,* Matt. 2:13–15. *Jesus, in charging those who were healed not to advertise his miracles,* Matt. 8:4; 9:30; Mark 1:44; 3:12; 5:43; 7:36; Luke 5:14; 8:56; *in going to the feast secretly,* John 7:10; *in avoiding his enemies,* Matt. 12:14–16; Mark 3:7; John 11:47–54; 12:36. *Peter, in escaping from Herod,* Acts 12:17. *Paul, in circumcising Timothy,* Acts 16:3; *in performing temple rites,* Acts 21:20–26; *in setting the Jewish sects on each other,* Acts 23:6; *in avoiding suspicion in administering the gifts of the churches,* 2 Cor. 8:20. *Paul and Barnabas, in escaping persecution,* Acts 14:6. *Paul and Silas, in escaping from Berea,* Acts 17:10–15. *The town clerk of Ephesus, in averting a riot,* Acts 19:29–41.
*Paul's lack of, in his persistence in going to Jerusalem despite the warnings of the Holy Spirit and his friends,* Acts 20:22–25, 37, 38; 21:10–14.
See footnotes: DIPLOMACY, 2 Kin. 16:7; TACT, Prov. 15:1.

† **JOPPA.** *A seaport,* Josh. 19:46; 2 Chr. 2:16; Ezra 3:7. *Passenger traffic from,* Jonah 1:3. *Peter, performs a miracle at,* Acts 9:36–43; *has a vision of a sheet let down from heaven at,* Acts 10:5, 8–18.

v.4–940 BC
See footnote, *Time*, Rev. 10:6.

m *Gold*, Ezek. 7:19.

**5**
n *Fir Tree*, 2 Sam. 6:5.
o *Palm Tree*, Song 7:7.
p *Chains*, Dan. 5:7.
2 R. V. wrought

**6**
q *Precious Stones*, Ex. 39:10.

**7**
r *Cherubim*, Ex. 37:7.
3 R. V. thresholds,

**8**
s *Holy of Holies*, Ex. 26:33.
t *Talent*, Ex. 38:25.

**9**
u *Nail*, Isa. 41:7.
v *Shekel*, Ex. 30:13.

*it was* according to the breadth of the house, twenty [k]cubits,[C] and the height *was* an hundred and twenty: and he overlaid it within with pure [m]gold.

5 And the greater house he cieled[C] with [n]fir tree, which he overlaid with fine [m]gold, and [2]set thereon [o]palm trees and [p]chains.

6 And he garnished[C] the house with [q]precious stones for beauty: and the [m]gold *was* gold of Pär-vā'im.

7 He overlaid also the house, the beams, the [3]posts, and the walls thereof, and the doors thereof, with [m]gold; and graved[C] [r]cherubims on the walls.

8 And he made the [s]most holy house, the length whereof *was* according to the breadth of the house, twenty [k]cubits,[C] and the breadth thereof twenty cubits:[C] and he overlaid it with fine [m]gold, *amounting* to six hundred [t]talents.

9 And the weight of the [u]nails *was* fifty [v]shekels[C] of gold. And he overlaid the upper chambers with [m]gold.

10 And in the [s]most holy house he made two [r]cherubims of image[C] work, and overlaid them with [m]gold.

11 And the wings of the [r]cherubims *were* twenty [k]cubits[C] long: one wing *of the one cherub was* five cubits,[C] reaching to the wall of the house: and the other wing *was likewise* five cubits, reaching to the wing of the other cherub.

12 And *one* wing of the other cherub *was* five [k]cubits, reaching to the wall of the house: and the other wing *was* five cubits *also*, joining to the wing of the other cherub.

13 The wings of these [r]cherubims spread themselves forth twenty cubits:[C] and they stood on their feet, and their faces *were* [4]inward.

14 And he made the *,[w]vail *of* [x]blue, and [x]purple, and [x]crimson, and fine [y]linen, and wrought [r]cherubims thereon.

15 Also he made before the [l]house two [z]pillars of thirty and five [a]cubits[C] high, and the [b]chapiter[C] that *was* on the top of each of them *was* five cubits.

16 And he made [c]chains, *as* in the oracle,[C] and put *them* on the heads of the [d]pillars; and made an hundred [e]pomegranates, and put *them* on the chains.

17 And he reared up the [d]pillars before the [f]temple, one on the right hand, and the other on the left; and called the name of that on the right hand [g]Jā'chin, and the name of that on the left [g]Bō'ăz.

## CHAPTER 4

*The altar of brass. 2 The molten sea upon twelve oxen. 6 The ten lavers, candlesticks, and tables. 9 The courts, and the instruments of brass. 19 The instruments of gold.*

[a]MOREOVER [b]he made an [c]altar of brass,[C] twenty [d]cubits[C] the length thereof, and twenty cubits[C] the breadth thereof, and ten cubits[C] the height thereof.

2 ¶ Also he made a molten[C] [e]sea of ten [d]cubits[C] from brim to brim, round in compass, and five cubits the height thereof; and a line of thirty cubits did compass[C] it round about.

3 And under [e]it *was* the similitude[C] of [f]oxen, which did compass it round [1]about: ten in a cubit, compassing the sea round about. Two rows of oxen *were* cast, when it was cast.

4 [e]It stood upon twelve [f]oxen, three looking toward the north, and three looking toward the

v.13–940 BC
See footnote, *Time*, Rev. 10:6.

**13**
4 R. V. toward the house.

**14**
w *Types, of the Savior*, Heb. 10:1.
x *Colors*, Ezek. 16:16.
y *Linen*, Ezek. 27:16.

**15**
z *Pillar*, Gen. 28:18.
a *Cubit*, Ex. 36:9.
b *Chapiter*, 1 Kin. 7:16.

**16**
c *Chains*, Dan. 5:7.
d *Pillar*, Gen. 28:18.
e *Pomegranate*, Num. 13:23.

**17**
f *Temple, Solomon's*, 1 Kin. 6:17.
g 1 Kin. 7:21.

**1**
a 1 Kin. 6; 7: 15–51.
b *Solomon*, 2 Sam. 12:24.
c *Altar, of burnt offerings*, Gen. 8:20.
d *Cubit*, Ex. 36:9.

**2**
e *Laver, brazen*, Ex. 30:18.

**3**
f *Bullock*, Ex. 29:3.
1 R. V. about, for ten cubits, compassing

* **VAIL.** *Of the temple*, 2 Chr. 3:14. *Rent at the time of the crucifixion of Jesus*, Matt. 27:51; Mark 15:38; Luke 23:45
See footnotes: VAIL, *Of the tabernacle*, Ex. 26:31; VAIL, *Of the Ark*, Ex. 35:12.
**Figurative,** Heb. 6:19. *A symbol of the body of Christ*, Heb. 10:20.

v.4–940 BC
See footnote, *Time,* Rev. 10:6.

west, and three looking toward
the south, and three looking toward the east: and the sea[G] *was*
*set* above upon them, and all
their hinder[G] parts *were* inward.
5 And the thickness of it *was* an
[g,h]handbreadth[G], and the brim
of it like the work of the brim
of a cup, with flowers of [i]lilies;
*and* it received and held three
thousand [j,k]baths[G].
6 ¶ He made also ten lavers,
and put five on the right hand,
and five on the left, to [l]wash in
them: such things as [2]they offered for the [m]burnt offering they
[l]washed in them; but the sea *was*
for the priests to wash in.
7 And he made ten [n]candlesticks[G]
of [o]gold according to [3]their form,
and set *them* in the [p]temple, five
on the right hand, and five on
the left.
8 He made also ten [q]tables, and
placed *them* in the [p]temple, five
on the right side, and five on the
left. And he made an hundred
[r]basons[G] of [o]gold.
9 ¶ Furthermore he made
the [s]court of the [t]priests, and the
great court, and doors for the
court, and overlaid the doors of
them with [u]brass.
10 And he set the [e]sea on the
right side of the [4]east end, over
against the south.
11 ¶ And [v,w]Hū'ram made
the pots, and the [x]shovels, and
the [r]basons[G]. And Hū'ram finished the work that he was to
make for king [b]Sŏl'o-mon for
the [p]house of God;
12 *To wit,* the two [y]pillars, and
the [G][5]pommels[G], and the [z]chapi-
ters *which were* on the top of the
two pillars, and the two [6]wreaths[G]
to cover the two pommels[G] of the
chapiters[G] which *were* on the top
of the pillars;
13 And four hundred [a]pome-
granates on the two [6]wreaths[G];
two rows of pomegranates on
each wreath[G], to cover the two
[5]pommels[G] of the chapiters[G] which
*were* upon the pillars.
14 He made also bases, and
lavers[G] made he upon the bases;
15 One [b]sea, and twelve oxen
under it.
16 The pots also, and the [c]shov-
els, and the [d]fleshhooks, and all
their instruments, did [e]Hū'ram
his father make to king [f]Sŏl'o-
mon for the [g]house of the LORD
of bright [h]brass.
17 In the plain of [i]Jôr'dan did
the king [j]cast[G] them, in the clay
ground between [k]Sŭc'coth and
Zē-rĕd'a-thah.
18 Thus [f]Sŏl'o-mon made all
these vessels in great abundance:
for the weight of the [h]brass could
not be found out.
19 ¶ And [f]Sŏl'o-mon made all
the vessels that *were for* the
[g]house of God, the [l]golden altar
also, and the tables whereon the
[m]shewbread *was set;*
20 Moreover the [n]candlesticks[G]
with their lamps, that they
should burn after the manner[G]
before the oracle[G], of pure [o]gold;
21 And the flowers, and the
lamps, and the [p]tongs, *made*
*he of* [o]gold, *and* that perfect[G]
gold;
22 And the [q]snuffers, and the
[r]basons[G], and the [s]spoons, and
the [7,t]censers[G], *of* pure [o]gold: and
the entry of the house, the inner
doors thereof for the most [u]holy
*place,* and the doors of the house
of the [g]temple, *were of* gold.

## CHAPTER 5

*The dedicated treasures. 2 The ark is brought into the most holy place. 11 God gives a visible sign of his presence.*

THUS all the work that [a]Sŏl'-
o-mon made for the [b]house
of the LORD was finished: and
Sŏl'o-mon brought in *all* the
things that [c]Dā'vid his father
had dedicated; and the [d]silver,
and the [e]gold, and all the [1]instru-

5
g *Handbreadth,* 1 Kin. 7:26.
h *Measure, linear,* Deut. 25:15.
i *Lily,* Matt. 6:28.
j *Bath,* 1 Kin. 7:26.
k *Measure, liquid,* Deut. 25:15.

6
l *Ceremonial Washing,* Ex. 19:10.
m *Offerings, burnt,* Lev. 6:17.
2 R. V. belonged to the

7
n *Candlestick,* Ex. 25:31.
o *Gold,* Ezek. 7:19
p *Temple, Solomon's,* 1 Kin. 6:17.
3 R. V. the ordinance concerning them;

8
q *Table,* Judg. 1:7.
r *Basin,* 1 Kin. 7:50.

9
s *Court, of the temple,* Ex. 38:9.
t *Priests,* Lev. 1:5.
u *Brass,* Job. 28:2.

10
4 R. V. house eastward, toward

11
v Or, *Hiram,* 1 Kin. 7:13.
w *Master Workman,* 1 Cor. 30:1.
x *Shovel,* Num. 4:14.

12
y *Pillar,* Gen. 28:18.
z *Chapiter,* 1 Kin. 7:16.
5 R. V. bowls,
6 R. V. networks

13
a *Pomegranate,* Num. 13:23.

v.13–940 BC
See footnote, *Time,* Rev. 10:6.

15
b *Laver, brazen,* Ex. 30:18.

16
c *Shovel,* Num. 4:14.
d *Fleshhook,* Ex. 27:3.
e Or, *Hiram,* 1 Kin. 7:13.
f *Solomon,* 2 Sam. 12:24.
g *Temple, Solomon's,* 1 Kin. 6:17.
h *Brass,* Job 28:2.

17
i *Jordan, plain of,* Gen. 32:10.
j *Molding,* 1 Kin. 7:16.
k *Succoth,* Judg. 8:5.

19
l *Altar, of incense,* Ex. 30:1.
m *Shewbread, table of,* Ex. 35:13.

20
n *Candlestick,* Ex. 25:31.
o *Gold,* Ezek. 7:19

21
p *Tongs,* Ex. 25:38.

22
q *Snuffers,* 1 Kin. 7:50.
r *Basin,* 1 Kin. 7:50.
s *Spoons,* Num. 4:7.
t *Censer,* Lev. 16:12.
u *Holy Place,* Ex. 26:33.
7 R. V. firepans,

v.1–933 BC
See footnote, *Time,* Rev. 10:6.

1
a *Solomon,* 2 Sam. 12:24.
b *Temple, Solomon's,* 1 Kin. 6:17.
c *David,* 1 Sam. 16:13.
d *Silver,* 1 Chr. 28:14.
e *Gold,* Ezek. 7:19.
1 R. V. vessels,

B.C. 1005?
See footnote, *Time*, Rev. 10:6.

ments, put he among the treasures of the house of God.
2 ¶ Then [a]Sŏl′o-mon assembled the [f]elders of Ĭş′ra-el, and
all the heads of the tribes, the
chief of the fathers of the children of Ĭş′ra-el, unto [g]Jē-ru̥′să-
lĕm, to bring up the [h]ark of the
covenant of the LORD out of the
city of Dā′vid, which *is* [i]Zī′ŏn.
3 Wherefore all the men of Ĭş′-
ra-el assembled themselves unto
the king in the [j]feast which *was*
in the seventh [k]month.
4 And all the [f]elders of Ĭş′ra-el
came; and the [l]Lē′vītes took up
the [h]ark.
5 And they brought up the [h]ark,
and the [2,m]tabernacle of the congregation, and all the holy vessels that *were* in the [3]tabernacle,
these did the [n]priests *and* the
[l]Lē′vītes bring up.
6 Also king [a]Sŏl′o-mon, and all
the congregation of Ĭş′ra-el that
were assembled unto him before
the [h]ark, sacrificed [o]sheep and
[p]oxen, which could not be told
nor numbered for multitude.
7 And the [n]priests brought in
the [h]ark of the covenant of the
LORD unto his place, to the
[q]oracle of the [b]house, into the
most [r]holy *place*, *even* under
the wings of the [s]cherubims:
8 For the [s]cherubims spread
forth *their* wings over the place
of the [h]ark, and the cherubims
covered the ark and the staves
thereof above.
9 And they drew out the staves
*of the* [h]*ark*, that the ends of the
staves were seen from the ark
before the [q]oracle; but they were
not seen without. And there it
is unto this day.
10 *There was* nothing in the
[t]ark save the two [u]tables which
[v]Mō′şeş put *therein* at [w]Hō′reb,
when the LORD made *a* [x]*covenant* with the children of [y]Ĭş-
ra-el, when they came out of
[z]Ē′ġy̆pt.
11 ¶ And it came to pass, when
the priests were come out of the
[a]holy *place*: (for all the priests
*that were* present were [b]sancti-
fied, *and* did not *then* wait by
course:
12 Also the [c]Lē′vītes *which
were* the [d]singers, all of them of
[e]Ā′saph, of [f]Hē′man, of [g]Jĕd′u̥-
thŭn, with their sons and their
brethren, *being* arrayed in [h]white
linen, having [i]cymbals and [j]psal-
teries and [k]harps, stood at the
east end of the altar, and with
them an hundred and twenty
priests sounding with [l]trump-
ets:)
13 It came even to pass, as the
[l]trumpeters and [d]singers *were* as
one, to make one sound to be
heard in [m]praising and [n]thank-
ing the LORD; and when they
lifted up *their* voice with the
trumpets and [i]cymbals and instruments of *musick, and
praised the LORD, *saying*, For
*he is* [o]good; for his [p]mercy *en-*

**2**
*f Senate*, Num. 11:16.
*g Jerusalem*, Judg. 19:10.
*h Ark*, Ex. 25:10.
*i Zion*, 2 Sam. 5:7.

**3**
*j Tabernacles, feast of*. Deut. 16:13.
*k Month*, Ex. 12:2.

**4**
*l Levites*, Deut. 10:8.

**5**
*m Tabernacle*, Ex. 27:9.
*n Priests*, Lev. 1:5.
2 R. V. tent of meeting,
3 R. V. Tent:

**6**
*o Sheep*, Deut. 32:14.
*p Bullock*, Ex. 29:3.

**7**
*q Oracle*, 1 Kin. 6:5.
*r Holy of Holies*, Ex. 26:33.
*s Cherubim*, Ex. 37:7.

**10**
*t Ark, contents of*, Ex. 25:10.
*u Table, of testimony*, Ex. 31:18.
*v Moses*, Ex. 2:10.
*w Horeb*, Ex. 3:1.
*x Covenant, of God with men*, Deut. 29:1.
*y Israel*, Ex. 4:22.
*z Egypt*, Gen. 41:8.

**11**
*a Holy Place*, Ex. 26:33.
*b Purification*, Num. 19:19.

**12**
*c Levites*, Deut. 10:8.
*d Choir*, 1 Chr. 15:16.
*e Asaph*, 1 Chr. 15:17.
*f Heman*, 1 Chr. 6:33.
*g Jeduthun*, 1 Chr 16:41.
*h Colors, symbolical*, Ezek. 16:16.
*i Cymbal*, 1 Chr. 13:8.
*j Psaltery*, 1 Chr. 16:5.
*k Harp*, Dan. 3:10.
*l Trumpet*, Josh. 6:4.

**13**
*m Praise*, Psa. 150:1.
*n Thankfulness, to God, of the Levites*, Acts 24:3.
*o God, goodness of*, Gen. 2:2.
*p God, mercy of*, Gen. 2:2.

---

***MUSIC.** *Used, at the crowning of kings*, 1 Kin. 1:39, 40; 2 Chr. 23:13, 18; *in national triumphs*, Ex. 15:1–21; Judg. 5:1–31; 11:34; 1 Sam. 18:6, 7; *in worship*, 1 Chr. 6:31, 32; 15:16–22, 24, 27, 28; 16:4–36, 42; 23:5; 25:1–7; 2 Chr. 5:12, 13; 20:19, 21, 22, 28; 29:25–30; 35:15; Ezra 2:64, 65; 3:10, 11; Neh. 12:27–47; Psa. 33:1–3; 68:4, 25, 26, 32; 81:1–3; 87:7; 92:1–3; 95:1, 2; 98:1–8; 104:33; 105:2; 135:1–3; 144:9; 149:1–3, 6; 150:1–6; Mark 14:26; 1 Cor. 14:15; Eph. 5:19; Col. 3:16; Heb. 2:12; *at the offering of sacrifices*, 2 Chr. 29:27, 28; *in idolatrous worship*, Dan. 3:4–7, 10, 15; *for dancing*, Matt. 11:17; *in mirth*, Gen. 31:27; 2 Sam. 19:35; Job 21:12; Eccl. 2:8; Isa. 5:12; *in revelry*, Amos 6:5; *in mourning*, 2 Chr. 35:25; *in preparing for funerals*, Matt. 9:23.

*Refrained from in sorrow*, Prov. 25:20; Isa. 16:10; 24:8, 9; Ezek. 26:13; Rev. 18:22. *Captive Jews refrained from*, Psa. 137:1–4.

*Teachers of*, 1 Chr. 15:22; 25:7, 8. *Physical effect of, on man*, 1 Sam. 16:15, 16, 23; Ezek. 33:32. *Chief musician*, Neh. 12:42; Hab. 3:19. *Chambers for musicians in the temple*, Ezek. 40:44.

**Instruments of:** *Invented, by Jubal*, Gen. 4:21; *by David*, 1 Chr. 23:5; 2 Chr. 7:6; 29:26; Amos 6:5. *Made, by Solomon*, 1 Kin. 10:12; 2 Chr. 9:11; *by Tyrians*, Ezek. 28:13.

*Cornet*, Dan. 3:5, 7, 10; see footnote, TRUMPET, Josh. 6:4. *Cymbal*, 1 Chr. 15:19, 28; 1 Cor. 13:1. *Dulcimer, a double pipe*, Dan. 3:5, 10, 15. *Flute*, Dan. 3:5, 7, 10, 15. *Gittith, a stringed instrument*, title to Psa. 8; 81; 84. *Harp*, 1 Sam. 10:5; 16:16, 23; 1 Chr. 16:5. *Organ, probably composed of pipes furnishing a number of notes*, Gen. 4:21; Job 21:12; 30:31; Psa. 150:4. *Pipe*, 1 Sam. 10:5; Isa. 30:29. *Psaltery*, see footnote, PSALTERY, 1 Chr. 16:5. *Sackbut, a harp*, Dan. 3:5, 7, 10, 15. *Tabret*, see footnote, TIMBREL, Ex. 15:20. *Timbrel, a tambourine*, see footnote, TIMBREL, Ex. 15:20. *Trumpet*, see footnote, TRUMPET, Josh. 6:4. *Viol, a lyre*, Isa. 5:12; 14:11; Amos 5:23; 6:5.

**Allegorical**, Rev. 5:8, 9; 14:2, 3; 15:2, 3.

**Symbols used in:** ALAMOTH, literally *virgins*. A musical term which appears in 1 Chr. 15:20 and in the title of Psa. 46. It seems to indicate the rendering of the song by female voices, possibly soprano.

*q Temple, Solomon's,* 1 Kin. 6:17.
14
*r God, glory of,* Gen. 2:2.
*s Church, called house of God,* 1 Kin. 9:3.
1
*a* 1 Kin. 8:12–50.
*b Solomon,* 2 Sam. 12:24.
*c God, unsearchable,* Gen. 2:2.
*d Darkness, figurative,* Gen. 1:2.
2
*e Temple, Solomon's,* 1 Kin. 6:17.
3
*f Benedictions, instances of,* Deut. 21:5.
4
*g Thankfulness, to God,* Acts 24:3.
*h God, faithfulness of,* Gen. 2:2.
5
*i God, providence of,* Gen. 2:2.
*j Egypt,* Gen. 41:8.
6
*k Foreordination,* Rom. 8:30.
*l Jerusalem,* Judg. 19:10.

*dureth* for ever: that *then* the
[q]house was filled with a cloud,
*even* the house of the LORD;
14 So that the priests could not
stand to minister[G] by reason of
the cloud: for the [r]glory of the
LORD had filled the [q,s]house of
God.[Q]

## CHAPTER 6

*Solomon's blessing and declaration. 12 His prayer at the consecration of the temple.*

[a]THEN said [b]Sŏl′o-mon, The
LORD hath said that [c]he
would dwell in the thick [d]dark-
ness.[S]
2 But I have built an [e]house of
habitation for thee, and a place
for thy dwelling for ever.[Q]
3 And the [b]king turned his face,
and [f]blessed the whole congregation of Ĭş′ra-el: and all the congregation of Ĭş′ra-el stood.
4 And he said, [g]Blessed *be* the
LORD God of Ĭş′ra-el, who hath
with his hands [h]fulfilled *that*
which he spake with his mouth
to my father Dā′vid, saying,
5 Since the day that [i]I brought
forth my people out of the land
of [j]Ē′ġy̆pt I chose no city among
all the tribes of Ĭş′ra-el to build
an house in, that my name
might be there; neither chose I
any man to be a ruler over my
people Ĭş′ra-el:
6 But I have [k]chosen [l]Jĕ-ru′-
să-lĕm, that my name might be
there; and [m]have chosen [n]Dā′vid
to be over my people Ĭş′ra-el.[S]
7 Now[Q] it was in the heart of
[n]Dā′vid my father to build an
[o]house for the name[G] of the LORD
God of Ĭş′ra-el.
8 But[S] the LORD said to [n]Dā′-
vid my father, Forasmuch as it
was in thine heart to build an
house for my name, thou didst
well in that it was in thine heart:[Q]
9 Notwithstanding thou shalt
not build the house; but thy son
which shall come forth out of thy
loins, he shall build the house
for my name.
10 The LORD therefore hath
performed his word that he hath
spoken: for I am risen up in the
room[G] of Dā′vid my father, and
am set on the [p]throne of Ĭş′ra-el,
as the LORD promised, and have
built the [e]house for the name of
the LORD God of Ĭş′ra-el.[Q]
11 And in it have I put the
[q]ark, wherein *is* the [r]covenant[G] of
the LORD, that he made with the
children of Ĭş′ra-el.[S]
12 ¶ And he stood before the
altar of the LORD in the presence of all the congregation of
Ĭş′ra-el, and spread forth his
hands:
13 For [b]Sŏl′o-mon had made a
brasen[G] [s]scaffold,[G] of five [t]cubits[G]

*m Government, God in,* Isa. 22:21.
*n David,* 1 Sam. 16:13.
7
*o Church, place of worship,* 1 Kin. 9:3.
10
*p Throne, figurative,* 1 Kin. 2:19.
11
*q Ark,* Ex. 25:10.
*r Covenant, of God with men,* Deut. 29:1.
13
*s* Neh. 8:4.
*t Cubit,* Ex. 36:9.

AL-TASCHITH. It appears in the titles of Psa. 57, 58, 59, 75, and seems to have been used to indicate the kind of ode, or the kind of melody in which the ode should be sung.

HIGGAION. In Psa. 92:3; according to Gesenius, it signifies the murmuring tone of a harp, and hence that the music should be rendered in a plaintive manner. In Psa. 9:16, combined with "Selah," it may have been intended to indicate a pause in the vocal music while the instruments rendered an interlude. In Psa. 19:14, Mendelssohn translates it "meditation, thought"; hence that the music was to be rendered in a mode to promote devout meditation.

MAHALATH, MASCHIL, LEANNOTH. These terms are found in the titles of Psalm 53 and 88. Authorities grope in darkness as to their signification. They may indicate the instruments to be played or the melodies to be sung.

MASCHIL. This musical sign occurs in the titles of Psalms 32, 42, 44, 45, 52, 53, 54, 55, 74, 78, 88, 89, 142. The meaning is obscure. But its signification where it occurs elsewhere than in the titles of Psalms is equivalent to the English word "instruction," or to become wise by instruction; hence Psa. 47:7, "Sing ye praises with understanding."

MICHTAM. A musical term in the titles of Psalms 16, 56, 57, 58–60. Luther interprets as "golden," that is, precious. Ewald interprets it as signifying a plaintive manner.

MUTH-LABBEN, in the title of Psalm 9. Authorities, ancient and modern, differ as to the probable signification. Gesenius and De Wette interpret it, "with the voice of virgins, by boys." Others derive the word from a different Hebrew root, and interpret it as indicating that the Psalm was a funeral ode.

NEGINAH and NEGINOTH appear in the titles of Psalms 4, 54, 55, 61, 67, and Hab. 3:19. Their use seems to have been to indicate that the song should be accompanied by stringed instruments.

NEHILOTH, in the title of Psalm 5. It seems to indicate, according to Gesenius, that when this Psalm was sung it was to be accompanied by wind instruments.

SELAH. This term appears frequently in the Psalms. Its use is not known. Possibly it signified a pause in the vocal music while an instrumental interlude or finale was rendered; or, as some think, it was an equivalent to *forte* or *fortissimo*.

SHEMINITH, in the titles of Psalms 6 and 12, translated "eighth," probably indicates the measure, movement, or pitch.

SHIGGAION, in the title of Psalm 7, and its plural, SHIGIONOTH, in the title of Hab. 3, are supposed to have been musical terms to guide in rendering the song. At the close of the chapter the author refers the ode "to the chief musician, on my stringed instruments." The term may suggest the movement in interpreting the music set to it.

SHOSHANNIM and SHUSHAN-EDUTH, in the titles of Psalms 45, 60, 69, 80, seem to indicate the manner in which these Psalms were to be rendered. Kimchi, Tremellius, and Eichhorn render it "hexachorda," that is, that in singing these Psalms instruments of six strings were to accompany.

u *Court, of the temple*, Ex. 38:9.
v *Prayer, postures in*, Acts 6:4.

**14**

w *Prayer, exemplified*, vs. 14–42; Acts 6:4.
x *God, faithfulness of*, Gen. 2:2.
y *God, mercy of*, Gen. 2:2.
z *Obedience, rewarded*, Heb. 5:8.

**15**

a *Covenant, of God with men*, Deut. 29:1.

**16**

b *Blessings, contingent upon obedience*, Deut. 11:26.

**18**

c *Heavens, physical*, Psa. 8:3.
d *God, infinite*, Gen. 2:2.
e *Temple, Solomon's*, 1 Kin. 6:17.

long, and five cubits broad, and three cubits[C] high, and had set it in the midst of the [u]court: and upon it he stood, and [v]kneeled down upon his knees before all the congregation of Is'ra-el, and spread forth his hands toward heaven,

14 And [w]said, O LORD God of Is'ra-el, *there is* no God like thee in the heaven, nor in the earth; which [x]keepest [r]covenant, and *shewest* [y]mercy unto thy servants, [z]that walk before thee with all their hearts:

15 Thou which hast kept with thy servant Dā'vid my father [a]that which thou hast promised him; and spakest with thy mouth, and hast fulfilled *it* with thine hand, as *it is* this day.

16 Now therefore, O LORD God of Is'ra-el, keep with thy servant Dā'vid my father [a]that which thou hast promised him, saying, There shall not fail thee a man in my sight to sit upon the throne of Is'ra-el; [b]yet so that thy children take heed to their way to walk in my law, as thou hast walked before me.

17 Now then, O LORD God of Is'ra-el, let thy word be verified, which thou hast spoken unto thy servant Dā'vid.

18 But will God in[C] very deed dwell with men on the earth? behold, [c]heaven and the heaven of heavens cannot contain [d]thee; how much less this [e]house which I have built! [S] [Q]

19 Have respect therefore to the prayer of thy servant, and to his supplication, O LORD my God, to hearken unto the cry and the prayer which thy servant prayeth before thee:

20 That thine eyes may be open upon this [e]house day and night, upon the place whereof thou hast said that thou wouldest put thy name there; to hearken unto the prayer which thy servant prayeth toward[C] this place.

21 Hearken therefore unto the supplications of thy servant, and of thy people Is'ra-el, which they shall make toward this place: hear thou from thy dwelling place, *even* from [f]heaven; and when thou hearest, forgive.

22 ¶ [g,h]If [S] a man sin against his neighbour, and an [i]oath be laid upon him to make him [j]swear,[G] and the oath come before thine altar in this [e]house;

23 [g,h]Then hear thou from [f]heaven, and do, and [k]judge thy servants, by requiting the [l]wicked, by recompensing his way upon his own head; and by justifying the righteous, by giving him according to his righteousness.[S]

24 ¶ [g,h]And if thy people Is'ra-el be [m]put[C] to the worse before the enemy, because they have sinned against thee; and [n]shall return and confess thy name, and [o]pray and make supplication before thee in this house;

25 [g,h]Then hear thou from the [f]heavens, and [p]forgive the sin of thy people Is'ra-el, and bring them again unto the [q]land which thou gavest to them and to their fathers.

26 ¶ [m]When the heaven is [r]shut up, and there is [s]no rain, because they have sinned against thee; [g,h]*yet* if they pray toward this place, and confess thy name, and [t]turn from their sin, when thou dost afflict them;

27 [g,h]Then hear thou from [f]heaven, and [p]forgive the sin of thy servants, and of thy people Is'ra-el, when thou hast taught them the good way, wherein they should walk; and send [u,v]rain upon thy [q]land, which thou hast given unto thy people for an inheritance.

28 ¶ If there be [1,w]dearth[G] in

**21**

f *Heaven, God's dwelling place*, Luke 18:22.

**22**

g *Prayer, intercessory*, Acts 6:4.
h *Intercession, of man with God*, Jer. 27:18.
i *Oath*, Num. 5:19.
j *Self-crimination*, Josh. 7:20.

**23**

k *God, judge*, Gen. 2:2.
l *Wicked, punishment of*, Psa. 73:3.

**24**

m *Divine Chastisement, corrective*, Job 33:19.
n *Adversity, design of*, vs. 24–39; Psa. 10:6.
o *Prayer, in adversity*, Acts 6:4.

**25**

p *Sin, forgiveness of*, Rom. 5:12.
q *Canaan*, Gen. 37:1.

**26**

r *Judgments*, Ex. 6:6.
s *Drought*, Gen. 31:40.
t *Repentance*, Mark 1:4.

**27**

u *Rain, prayer for*, 2 Sam. 1:21.
v *Temporal Blessings, prayer for*, Psa. 103:2.

**28**

w *Famine*, 2 Kin. 8:1.
1 R. V. in the land famine.

*x* *Plague*, Ex. 11:1.
*y* *Blasting*, 1 Kin. 8:37.
*z* *Locust*, Nah. 3:17.

*a* *Caterpillar*, 1 Kin. 8:37.

**29**
*b* *Afflictions, benefits of*, Psa. 34:19.
*c* *Sin, confession of*, Rom. 5:12.
*d* *Prayer, confession in*, Acts 6:4.
2 R. V. toward

**30**
*e* *Intercession, of man with God*, Jer. 27:18.
*f* *Heaven, God's dwelling place*, Luke 18:22.
*g* *Sin, forgiveness of*, Rom. 5:12.
*h* *Heart*, Psa. 44:21.
*i* *God, knowledge of*, Gen. 2:2.

**31**
*j* *Fear of God*, Acts 9:31.
*k* *Obedience*, Heb. 5:8.

**32**
*l* *Foreigners*, Deut. 23:20.
*m* *Arm, figurative*, Psa. 89:13.

**33**
*n* *Temple, Solomon's*, 1 Kin. 6:17.
3 R. V. heaven,

**34**
4 R. V. battle

the land, if there be [x]pestilence,
if there be [y]blasting[c], or mildew,
[z]locusts, or [a]caterpillers; if their
enemies besiege them in the cities of their land; whatsoever sore[c]
or whatsoever sickness *there be*:
29 *Then* what prayer *or* what
supplication soever shall be
made of any man, or of all thy
people Ĭṣ′ra-el, when every one
[b]shall know his own sore[c] and his
own grief, and [c,d]shall spread
forth his hands [2]in this house:
30 [e]Then hear thou from [f]heav-
en thy dwelling place, and [g]for-
give, and render unto every man
according unto all his ways,
whose [h]heart thou [i]knowest; (for
thou only knowest the hearts of
the children of men:)[s]
31 That they may [j]fear thee,
to [k]walk in thy ways, so long as
they live in the land which thou
gavest unto our fathers.
32 ¶ [e]Moreover concerning the
[l]stranger[c], which is not of thy people Ĭṣ′ra-el, but is come from a
far country for thy great name's
sake, and thy mighty hand, and
thy stretched[c] out [m]arm; if they
come and pray [2]in this house;
33 [e]Then hear thou from [3]the
[f]heavens, *even* from thy dwelling place, and do according to
all that the [l]stranger[c] calleth to
thee for; that all people of the
earth may know thy name, and
fear thee, as *doth* thy people Ĭṣ′-
ra-el, and may know that this
[n]house[c] which I have built is
called by thy name.
34 ¶ [e]If thy people go out to
[4]war against their enemies by the
way that thou shalt send them,
and they pray unto thee toward
this city which thou hast chosen,
and the [n]house which I have
built for thy name;
35 [e]Then hear thou from the
[f]heavens their prayer and their
supplication, and maintain[c] their
cause[c].
36 ¶ [e]If they sin against thee,
(for [o,p]*there is* no man which
sinneth not,) and thou be [q]angry
with them, and deliver them
over before *their* enemies, and
they carry them away captives
unto a land far off or near;[s]
37 Yet *if* they bethink[c] themselves in the land whither they
are carried captive, and [r]turn
and [d]pray unto thee in the land
of their captivity, [c]saying, We
have sinned, we have done
[5]amiss, and have dealt wickedly;
38 If they [r]return to thee with
all their heart and with all their
soul in the land of their captivity, whither they have carried
them captives, and pray toward
their land, which thou gavest unto their fathers, and *toward* the
[s]city which thou hast chosen,
and toward the [n]house which I
have built for thy name:
39 [e]Then hear thou from [3]the
[f]heavens, *even* from thy dwelling
place, their prayer and their supplications, and maintain their
cause, and [g]forgive thy people
which have sinned against thee.
40 Now, my God, let, I beseech
thee, thine [t]eyes be open, and
*let* thine [t]ears *be* attent[c] unto the
prayer *that is made* in this place.
41 Now therefore arise, O
LORD God, into thy resting
place, thou, and the [u]ark of thy
strength: [v]let thy [w,x]priests, O
LORD God, be [y]clothed with
[z]salvation[c], and let thy saints rejoice in goodness.
42 O LORD God, turn not away
the face of thine anointed: remember the mercies of Dā′vid
thy servant.

## CHAPTER 7

*God's testimony to Solomon. 4 Solomon's sacrifice. 8 He dismisses the people. 12 God appears to Solomon and gives him gracious promises.*

NOW when [a]Sŏl′o-mon had
made an end of praying,
the [b]fire [c]came down from heav-

**36**
*o* *Sinfulness, universal*, Rom. 3:23.
*p* *Depravity*, Job 15:14.
*q* *Anger of God*, 2 Kin. 13:3.

**37**
*r* *Repentance, tribulation leads to*, Mark 1:4.
5 R. V. perversely,

**38**
*s* *Jerusalem*, Judg. 19:10.

**40**
*t* *Anthropomorphisms*, Gen. 11:5.

**41**
*u* *Ark*, Ex. 25:10.
*v* *Prayer, intercessory*, Acts 6:4.
*w* *Minister, character and qualifications of*, Rom. 15:16.
*x* *Minister, prayer for, exemplified*, Rom. 15:16.
*y* *Dress, figurative*, Zech. 3:3.
*z* *Salvation*, Acts 16:17.

**1**
*a* *Solomon*, 2 Sam. 12:24.
*b* *Fire, miracles connected with* Ex. 12:8.
*c* *Miracles*, Luke 23:8.

d *Offerings, burnt,* Lev. 6:17.
e *God, glory of,* Gen. 2:2.
f *Temple, Solomon's,* 1 Kin. 6:17.

2
g *Priest,* Lev. 1:5.

3
h *Prayer, postures in,* Acts 6:4.
i *Worship,* Gen. 22:5.
j *Praise,* Psa. 150:1.
k *God, goodness of,* Gen. 2:2.
l *God, mercy of,* Gen. 2:2.

4
m 1 Kin. 8:62–66.
n *Offerings,* Lev. 6:17.

5
o *Bullock,* Ex. 29:3.
p *Sheep,* Deut. 32:14.
q *Dedication,* Ezra 6:17.

6
r *Levites,* Deut. 10:8.
s *Music,* 2 Chr. 5:13.
t *David,* 1 Sam. 16:13.
u *Invention,* 2 Chr. 26:15.
v *Praise,* Psa. 150:1.
w *God, mercy of,* Gen. 2:2.
x *Trumpet,* Josh. 6:4.
1 R. V. stood, according to their

7
y *Court, of the temple,* Ex. 38:9.
z *Offerings, peace,* Lev. 6:17.

a *Altar, of burnt offerings,* Gen. 8:20.
b *Offerings, meat,* Lev. 6:17.
2 R. V. meal

8
c *Solomon,* 2 Sam. 12:24.
d *Dedication, feast of,* Ezra 6:17.

en, and consumed the [d]burnt offering and the sacrifices; and the
[e]glory of the LORD filled the
[f]house.
2 And the [g]priests could not
enter into the [f]house of the
LORD, because the [e]glory of the
LORD had filled the LORD's
house.
3 And when all the children
of Iṣ'ra-el saw how the [b]fire
came down, and the [e]glory of
the LORD upon the house, they
[h]bowed themselves with their
faces to the ground upon the
pavement, and [i]worshipped, and
[j]praised the LORD, *saying,* For
*he is* [k]good; for his [l]mercy *endureth* for ever.
4 ¶ [m]Then the [a]king and all the
people offered [n]sacrifices before
the LORD.
5 And king [a]Sŏl'o-mon offered
a [n]sacrifice of twenty and two
thousand [o]oxen, and an hundred
and twenty thousand [p]sheep: so
the king and all the people [q]dedi-
cated the [f]house of God.
6 And the [g]priests [1]waited on
their offices: the [r]Lē'vītes also
with instruments of [s]musick of
the LORD, which [t]Dā'vid the
king [u]had made to [v]praise the
LORD, because his [w]mercy *endureth* for ever, when Dā'vid
praised by their ministry; and
the priests sounded [x]trumpets
before them, and all Iṣ'ra-el
stood.
7 Moreover Sŏl'o-mon hal-
lowed the middle of the [y]court
that *was* before the [f]house of
the LORD: for there he offered
burnt offerings, and the fat of
the [z]peace offerings, because the
brasen [a]altar which Sŏl'o-mon
had made was not able to receive the burnt offerings, and the
[2,b]meat offerings, and the fat.
8 ¶ Also at the same time [c]Sŏl'-
o-mon kept the [d]feast seven
days, and all Iṣ'ra-el with him,
a very great congregation, from
the entering in of [e]Hā'math unto
the [3]river of [f]Ē'ġy̆pt.
9 And in the eighth day they
made a solemn assembly: for
they kept the [d]dedication of the
altar seven days, and the feast
seven days.
10 And on the three and twentieth day of the seventh [g]month
he sent the people away into
their tents, glad and merry in
heart for the [h]goodness that the
LORD had shewed unto Dā'vid,
and to Sŏl'o-mon, and to Iṣ'ra-el
his people.
11 Thus [c]Sŏl'o-mon finished
the [i]house of the LORD, and the
[j]king's house: and all that came
into Sŏl'o-mon's heart to make
in the house of the LORD, and in
his own house, he prosperously
effected.
12 ¶ And the LORD [k]appeared
to [c]Sŏl'o-mon by night, and said
unto him, [l]I have heard thy
prayer, and have chosen [i]this
place to myself for an house of
sacrifice.
13 If I [m,n]shut up heaven that
there be [o]no rain, or if I command the [p]locusts to devour the
land, or if I send [q]pestilence
among my people;
14 If my people, which [r]are
called by my name, [s]shall humble themselves, and pray, and
seek my face, and [t]turn from
their wicked ways; [u,v]then will
I hear from [w]heaven, and will
[x]forgive their sin, and will heal
their land.
15 Now mine [y]eyes shall be
open, and mine ears attent unto
the prayer *that is made* in this
place.
16 For now have I chosen and
sanctified [i]this house, that my
name may be there for ever:
and mine eyes and mine heart
shall be there perpetually.
17 And as for thee, [z,a]if thou

e *Hamath,* 1 Chr. 18:3.
f *Egypt, brook of,* Gen. 15:18.
3 R. V. brook

10
g *Month,* Ex. 12:2.
h *God, goodness of,* Gen. 2:2.

11
i *Temple, Solomon's,* 1 Kin. 6:17.
j *Palace,* 1 Kin. 21:1.

12
k *God, appearances of,* Gen. 2:2.
l *Prayer, answered,* Acts 6:4.

13
m *Adversity, design of,* v. 14; Psa. 10:6.
n *Divine Chastisement, corrective,* v. 14; Job 33:19.
o *Drought, as a judgment,* Gen. 31:40.
p *Locust, devastation by,* Nah. 3:17.
q *Plague,* Ex. 11:1.

14
r *Spiritual Adoption,* Rom. 8:15.
s *Nation, penitent, promises to,* Isa. 2:4.
t *Repentance,* Mark 1:4.
u *Prayer, answer to, promised,* Acts 6:4.
v *Promise, to the penitent,* 2 Cor. 1:20.
w *Heaven, God's dwelling place,* Luke 18:22.
x *Sin, forgiveness of,* Rom. 5:12.

15
y *Anthropomorphisms,* Gen. 11:5.

17
z *Blessings, contingent upon obedience,* Deut. 11:26.

a *Contingencies in Divine Government,* 1 Kin. 3:14.

18
*b God, providence of*, Gen. 2:2.

19
*c Backsliders*, Jer. 3:22.
*d Idolatry*, 1 Sam. 15:23.

20
*e Judgments*, Ex. 6:6.
*f Temple, Solomon's*, 1 Kin. 6:17.

22
*g Disobedience to God*, Eph. 5:6.
*h Egypt*, Gen. 41:8.

v.1–920 BC
See footnote, *Time*, Rev. 10:6.

1
*a Solomon*, 2 Sam. 12:24.
*b Temple, Solomon's*, 1 Kin. 6:17.
*c Palace*, 1 Kin. 21:1.

2
*d* Or, *Hiram*, 2 Sam. 5:11.
1 R. V. given

wilt walk before me, as Dā′vid
thy father walked, and do according to all that I have commanded thee, and shalt observe
my statutes and my judgments;[G]
18 Then will [b]I stablish[G] the
throne of thy kingdom, according as I have covenanted with
Dā′vid thy father, saying, There
shall not fail thee a man *to be*
ruler in Ĭş′ra-el.[S]
19 But if [c]ye turn away, and
forsake my statutes and my commandments, which I have set before you, and shall go and [d]serve
other gods, and worship them;
20 Then will I [e]pluck them
up by the roots out of my land
which I have given them; and
[f]this house, which I have sanctified[G] for my name, will I cast out
of my sight, and will make it
*to be* a proverb and a byword[G]
among all nations.
21 And [f]this house[G], which is
high[G], shall be an astonishment
to every one that passeth by it;
so that he shall say, Why hath
the LORD done thus unto this
land, and unto this house?
22 And it shall be answered, Because [c]they [g]forsook the LORD
God of their fathers, [b]which
brought them forth out of the
land of [h]Ē′ġȳpt, and laid[G] hold
on other gods, and worshipped
them, and served them: therefore hath he brought all this [e]evil
upon them.

## CHAPTER 8

*The houses and cities built by Solomon. 7 Tribute of service levied by him on the Canaanites, but not on the Israelites. 12 Solomon's solemn sacrifices thrice a year. 14 He appoints the priests and Levites to their places. 17 His navy fetches gold from Ophir.*

AND it came to pass at the end
of twenty years, wherein
[a]Sŏl′o-mon had built the [b]house
of the LORD, and his own [c]house,
2 That the cities which [d]Hū′-
ram had [1]restored[G] to Sŏl′o-
mon, Sŏl′o-mon built them, and
caused the children of Ĭş′ra-el to
dwell there.
3 And [a]Sŏl′o-mon went to
[e]Hā′math–zō′bah, and prevailed
against it.
4 And he built [f]Tăd′môr in the
wilderness, and all the [g]store[G] cities, which he built in [h]Hā′math.
5 Also he built [i]Bĕth–hō′rŏn
the upper, and Bĕth–hō′rŏn the
nether[G], fenced[G] [j]cities, with [k]walls,
[l]gates, and bars;
6 And [m]Bā′al-ăth, and all the
[g]store[G] cities that [a]Sŏl′o-mon had,
and all the [n]chariot cities, and
the cities of the [o]horsemen, and
all that Sŏl′o-mon desired to
[2]build in [p]Jė-rụ′să-lĕm, and in
[q]Lĕb′a-non, and throughout all
the land of his dominion.
7 ¶ *As for* all the people *that*
*were* left of the [r]Hĭt′tītes, and
the [s]Ăm′ôr-ītes, and the [t]Pĕr′ĭz-
zītes, and the [u]Hī′vītes, and the
[v]Jĕb′u-sītes, which *were* not of
Ĭş′ra-el,
8 *But* of their children, who
were left after them in the land,
whom the children of Ĭş′ra-el
consumed not, them did [a]Sŏl′o-
mon [3]make to pay [w]tribute until
this day.
9 But of the children of Ĭş′ra-el
did Sŏl′o-mon make no servants
for his work; but they *were* [x]men
of war, and chief of his [y]cap-
tains, and captains of his [n]char-
iots and [o]horsemen.
10 And these *were* the chief of
king Sŏl′o-mon's officers, *even*
two hundred and fifty, that bare
rule over the people.
11 ¶ And Sŏl′o-mon brought
up the daughter of [z]Phā′raōh
out of the [a]city of Dā′vid unto
the house that he had built for
her: for he said, My wife shall
not dwell in the house of [b]Dā′-
vid king of Ĭş′ra-el, because *the*
*places are* holy[G], whereunto the
[c]ark of the LORD hath come.
12 ¶ Then [d]Sŏl′o-mon offered

v.2–920 BC
See footnote, *Time*, Rev. 10:6.

3
*e* Or, *Zobah*, 1 Sam. 14:47.

4
*f* 1 Kin. 9:18.
*g Treasure Cities*, Ex. 1:11.
*h Hamath*, 1 Chr. 18:3.

5
*i Beth-horon*, Josh 10:10.
*j Cities, fortified*, Num. 35:8.
*k Walls*, 1 Sam. 20:25.
*l Gates*, Deut. 3:5

6
*m* Josh. 19:44; 1 Kin. 9:18.
*n Chariot*, Josh. 11:4.
*o Cavalry*, 1 Sam. 13:5.
*p Jerusalem*, Judg. 19:10.
*q Lebanon*, Deut. 1:7.
2 R. V. build for his pleasure in

7
*r Hittites*, Judg. 1:26.
*s Amorites*, Gen. 14:13.
*t Perizzites*, Gen. 15:20.
*u Hivites*, Gen. 10:17.
*v Jebusites*, Deut. 7:1.

8
*w Tribute*, Ezra 4:13.
3 R. V. raise a levy of bondservants unto this day.

9
*x Soldiers*, Ezra 8:22.
*y Captain*, Num. 31:48.

11
*z Pharaoh, at the time of Solomon*, 1 Kin. 3:1.
*a Jerusalem*, Judg. 19:10.
*b David*, 1 Sam. 16:13.
*c Ark*, Ex. 25:10.

12
*d Solomon*, 2 Sam. 12:24.

[e]burnt offerings unto the LORD
on the [f]altar of the LORD, which
he had built before the porch,
13 Even after a certain rate[G]
[g]every day, offering according
to the [h]commandment of Mō′-
şeş, on the sabbaths, and on the
[i]new moons, and on the solemn
[j]feasts, three times in the year,
*even* in the [k]feast of unleavened
bread, and in the [l]feast of weeks,
and in the feast of [m]tabernacles.
14 And he appointed, according
to the order of [b]Dā′vid his father, the courses[G] of the [n]priests
to their service[G], and the [o]Lē′vītes
to their charges[G], to praise and
minister before the priests, as the
duty of every day required: the
[4,p]porters also by their courses
at every gate: for so had Dā′vid
the man of God commanded.
15 And they departed not from
the commandment of the king
unto the priests and Lē′vītes concerning any matter, or concerning the treasures[G].
16 Now all the work of [q]Sŏl′o-
mon was prepared unto[G] the day
of the foundation of the [r,s]house
of the LORD, and until it was
finished. *So* the house of the
LORD was perfected[G].
17 ¶ Then went [q]Sŏl′o-mon to
[t]Ē′zĭ-on-ġē′bẽr, and to [u]Ē′lŏth, at
the sea side in the land of [v]Ē′dom.
18 And [w]Hū′ram sent him by
the hands of his servants [†]ships,
and [x]servants that had knowledge of the sea; and they went
with the servants of [q]Sŏl′o-mon
to [y]Ō′phĩr, and [z]took thence[G]
four hundred and fifty [a]talents[G]
of [b]gold, and brought *them* to
king Sŏl′o-mon.

*e Offerings, burnt*, Lev. 6:17.
*f Altar, of burnt offerings*, Gen. 8:20.

13

*g Offerings, daily*, Lev. 6:17.
*h Law, of Moses*, Deut. 33:2.
*i New Moon*, Amos 8:5.
*j Annual Feasts*, Num. 15:3.
*k Passover*, Num. 9:5.
*l Pentecost*, Acts 2:1.
*m Tabernacles, feast of*, Deut. 16:13.

14

*n Priest, duties of*, Lev. 1:5.
*o Levites, duties of*, Deut. 10:8.
*p Porters*, 2 Sam. 18:26.
4 R. V. doorkeepers

16

*q Solomon*, 2 Sam. 12:24.
*r Temple, Solomon's*, 1 Kin. 6:17.
*s Church, called house of the Lord*, 1 Kin. 9:3.

17

*t* Or, *Ezion-gaber*, Num. 33:35.
*u* Or, *Elath*, Deut. 2:8.
*v Edom*, Obad. 1.

18

*w* Or, *Hiram*, 2 Sam. 5:11.
*x Mariner*, Ezek. 27:27.
*y Ophir*, 1 Kin. 9:28.
*z Commerce*, 1 Kin. 10:15.

*a Talent*, Ex. 38:25.
*b Gold*, Ezek. 7:19.

## CHAPTER 9

*The queen of Sheba admires the wisdom of Solomon. 13 Solomon's gold and the use made of it. 23 The presents received by him. 25 His chariots and horsemen. 29 His reign and death.*

[a]AND[Q] when the [b,c]queen of
[d]Shē′bȧ heard of the fame
of [e]Sŏl′o-mon, she came to prove[G]
Sŏl′o-mon with hard questions
at [f]Jē-rụ′sȧ-lĕm, with a very
great company, and [g]camels that
bare [h]spices, and [i]gold in abundance, and [j]precious stones: and
when she was come to Sŏl′o-
mon, she communed[G] with him
of all that was in her heart.
2 And [e]Sŏl′o-mon told[G] her all
her questions: and there was
nothing hid from Sŏl′o-mon
which he told her not.
3 [Q]And when the [b]queen of
[d]Shē′bȧ had seen the [k]wisdom
of Sŏl′o-mon, and the house that
he had built,
4 And the meat[G] of his table, and
the sitting of his servants, and
the attendance of his *ministers,
and their apparel; his [l]cupbear-
ers also, and their apparel; and
his ascent by which he went up
into the [m]house of the LORD;
there was no more spirit in
her.
5 And [b]she said to the king, *It*
*was* a true report which I heard
in mine own land of thine acts,
and of thy [k]wisdom:
6 Howbeit I believed not their
words; until I came, and mine
eyes had seen *it*: and, behold, the
one half of the greatness of thy
[k]wisdom was not told me: *for*
thou exceedest the fame that I
heard.[Q]
7 Happy *are* thy men, and
happy *are* these thy servants,

1

*a* 1 Kin. 10:1-25.
*b Queen, of Sheba*, 1 Kin. 11:19.
*c Women, as rulers*, Prov. 31:10.
*d Sheba*, 1 Kin. 10:1.
*e Solomon*, 2 Sam. 12:24.
*f Jerusalem*, Judg. 19:10.
*g Camel*, 1 Sam. 30:17.
*h Spices*, 1 Kin. 10:2.
*i Gold*, Ezek. 7:19.
*j Precious Stones*, Ex. 39:10.

3

*k Wisdom, of Solomon*, Prov. 2:2.

4

*l Cupbearer*, 1 Kin. 10:5.
*m Temple, Solomon's*, 1 Kin. 6:17.

† **SHIP.** *Built, by Noah*, Gen. 6:13–22; *by Solomon*, 1 Kin. 9:26; *by Jehoshaphat*, 1 Kin. 22:48; 2 Chr. 20:35, 36. *Built, of gopher wood*, Gen. 6:14; *of bulrushes* (R. V. papyrus), Isa. 18:2. *Sealed with pitch*, Gen. 6:14.

*Equipped, with helm*, Jas. 3:4; *with rudder*, Acts 27:40; *with tackling*, Isa. 33:23; Acts 27:19; *with sails*, Isa. 33:23; Acts 27:40; *with masts*, Isa. 33:23; Ezek. 27:5; *with oars*, Jonah 1:13; Mark 6:48; *with figurehead*, Acts 28:11; *with anchor*, Acts 27:29, 30, 40; *with lifeboats*, Acts 27:30, 32. *Sails of, embroidered*, Ezra 47:7. *Used, in commerce*, Acts 21:3; 27:10, 18, 38; *in commerce, with Tarshish*, 1 Kin. 22:48; Isa. 60:9; Jonah 1:3; *with Ophir*, 1 Kin. 10:11; 2 Chr. 8:18; *with Adramyttium*, Acts 27:2. *Used, for passenger traffic*, Isa. 60:9; Jonah 1:3; Acts 20:13; 27:2, 37; 28:11; *for ferriage*, 2 Sam. 19:18. *Repaired by calking*, Ezek. 27:9. *Wrecked, at Ezion-geber*, 1 Kin. 22:48; 2 Chr. 20:35–37; *at Melita*, Acts 27:14, 44. *Navy of*, 1 Kin. 10:11, 22; 2 Chr. 8:18. *Warships used by Chittim*, Num. 24:24; Dan. 11:30. See footnote, MARINERS, Ezek. 27:27.

* **MINISTER,** an officer in civil government. *Joseph*, Gen. 41:40–44. *Joshua*, Josh. 1:1. *Ira*, 2 Sam. 20:26. *Ahithophel*, 1 Chr. 27:33. *Zebadiah*, 2 Chr. 19:11. *Elkanah*, 2 Chr. 28:7. *Haman*, Esth. 3:1. *Mordecai*, Esth. 10:3, with chapters 8, 9. *Daniel*, Dan. 2:48; 6:1–3.
See footnote, CABINET, Ezra 7:14.

which stand continually before
thee, and hear thy [k]wisdom.
8 Blessed be the LORD thy
God, which delighted in [n]thee
[o]to set thee on his [p]throne, *to be*
king for the LORD thy God: because thy God loved Is'ra-el, to
establish them for ever, therefore made he thee king over
them, to do judgment[C] and justice.[C]
9 And [b]she [q]gave the [e]king an
hundred and twenty [r]talents[C] of
[i]gold, and of [h]spices great abundance, and [j]precious stones: neither was there any such spice as
the queen of [d]Shē'bȧ gave king
Sŏl'o-mon.
10 And the servants also of
[s]Hū'ram, and the servants of
[e]Sŏl'o-mon, which brought [i]gold
from [t]Ō'phĭr, brought [u]algum
trees and [j]precious stones.
11 And the king made *of* the
[u]algum trees terraces to the
[m]house of the LORD, and to
the king's [v]palace, and [w,x]harps
and [y]psalteries for [z]singers: and
there were none such seen before
in the land of Jū'dah.
12 And king [a]Sŏl'o-mon gave
to the [b]queen of [c]Shē'bȧ all her
desire, whatsoever she asked, beside *that* which she had brought
unto the king. So she turned,
and went away to her own land,
she and her servants.[Q]
13 ¶ Now the weight of [d]gold
that came to [a]Sŏl'o-mon in one
year was six hundred and threescore and six [e]talents[C] of gold;
14 Beside *that which* chapmen[C]
and [f]merchants brought. And
all the kings of †Ā-rā'bĭ-ȧ and
governors of the country brought
[d,g]gold and [g,h]silver to Sŏl'o-
mon.
15 ¶ And king [a]Sŏl'o-mon
made two hundred targets[C] *of*
beaten [d]gold: six hundred [i]*shekels*[C] of beaten gold went to one
target.[C]
16 And three hundred [j]shields
*made he of* beaten gold: three
hundred [i]*shekels*[C] of gold went to
one shield. And the king put
them in the [k]house of the forest
of [l]Lĕb'a-non.
17 ¶ Moreover the king made
a great [m]throne of ‡ivory, and
overlaid it with pure [d]gold.
18 And *there were* six steps to
the [m]throne, with a footstool of
[d]gold, *which were* fastened to the
throne, and stays[C] on each side of
the sitting place, and two lions
standing by the stays:
19 And twelve lions stood there
on the one side and on the other
upon the six steps. There was
not the like made in any kingdom.
20 ¶ And all the drinking vessels of king [a]Sŏl'o-mon *were of*
[d]gold, and all the vessels of the
[k]house of the forest of [l]Lĕb'a-
non *were of* pure gold: none *were
of* [h]silver; it was *not* any thing
accounted of in the days of Sŏl'-
o-mon.
21 For the king's ships [n]went
to [o]Tär'shish with the servants
of [p]Hū'ram: every three years
once came the ships of Tär'-
shish [q]bringing [d]gold, and [h]sil-
ver, ‡ivory, and [r]apes, and [s]pea-
cocks.
22 And king Sŏl'o-mon passed
all the kings of the earth in
[t]riches and [u]wisdom.
23 ¶ And all the kings of the
earth sought the presence of
Sŏl'o-mon, to hear his [u]wisdom,
that God had put in his heart.
24 And they brought every man
his [v,w]present, vessels of [h]sil-

**8**
*n* *Rulers, righteous*, Ex. 18:21.
*o* *Rulers, ordained of God*, Ex. 18:21.
*p* *Throne, figurative*, 1 Kin. 2:19.

**9**
*q* *Liberality, instances of*, 1 Tim. 6:18.
*r* *Talent*, Ex. 38:25.

**10**
*s* Or, *Hiram*, 2 Sam. 5:11.
*t* *Ophir*, 1 Kin. 9:28.
*u* 2 Chr. 2:8; or, *almug*, 1 Kin. 10:11, 12.

**11**
*v* *Palace*, 1 Kin. 21:1.
*w* *Harp*, Dan. 3:10.
*x* *Music, instruments of*, 2 Chr. 5:13.
*y* *Psaltery*, 1 Chr. 16:5.
*z* *Choir*, 1 Chr. 15:16.

**12**
*a* *Solomon*, 2 Sam. 12:24.
*b* *Queen, of Sheba*, 1 Kin. 11:19.
*c* *Sheba*, 1 Kin. 10:1.

**13**
*d* *Gold*, Ezek. 7:19.
*e* *Talent*, Ex. 38:25.

**14**
*f* *Merchant*, Neh. 3:32.
*g* *Tribute*, Ezra 4:13.
*h* *Silver*, 1 Chr. 28:14.

**15**
*i* *Shekel*, Ex. 30:33.

**16**
*j* *Shield*, 1 Kin. 14:27.
*k* *Armory*, Neh. 3:19.
*l* *Lebanon*, Deut. 1:7.

**17**
*m* *Throne*, 1 Kin. 2:19.

**21**
*n* *Commerce*, 1 Kin. 10:15.
*o* *Tarshish*, 2 Chr. 20:36.
*p* Or, *Hiram*, 2 Sam. 5:11.
*q* *Imports*, 1 Kin. 10:11.
*r* 1 Kin. 10:22.
*s* 1 Kin. 10:22.

**22**
*t* *Riches*, Eccl. 4:8.
*u* *Wisdom, of Solomon*, Prov. 2:2.

**24**
*v* *Tribute*, Ezra 4:13.
*w* *King, emoluments of*, 2 Kin. 3:10.

† **ARABIA.** *Tributary, to Solomon*, 2 Chr. 9:14; *to Jehoshaphat*, 2 Chr. 17:11. *Exports of*, Ezek. 27:21. *Prophecies against*, Isa. 21:13; Jer. 25:24. *Paul visits*, Gal. 1:17. See footnote, ARABIANS, 2 Chr. 17:11.

‡ **IVORY,** Song 5:14; 7:4; Ezek. 27:15. *Exported, from Tarshish*, 1 Kin. 10:22; 2 Chr. 9:21; *from Chittim*, Ezek. 27:6. *Ahab's palace made of*, 1 Kin. 22:39. *Other houses made of*, Psa. 45:8; Amos 3:15. Various articles made of: *Thrones*, 1 Kin. 10:18; 2 Chr. 9:17; *benches*, Ezek. 27:6; *beds*, Amos 6:4; *vessels*, Rev. 18:12.

ver, and vessels of [d]gold, and
raiment, [1]harness,[C] and [x]spices,
[y]horses, and [z]mules, a rate[C] year
by year.
25 ¶ And [a]Sŏl′o-mon had four
thousand stalls for [b]horses and
[c]chariots, and twelve thousand
[d]horsemen; whom he bestowed[C]
in the chariot [e]cities, and with
the king at [f]Jė-ru̦′sȧ-lĕm.
26 ¶ And he reigned over all the
kings [g]from the [h]river even unto
the land of the [i]Phĭ-lĭs′tĭne̦s, and
to the border of [j]Ē′ġy̆pt.
27 And the king made [k]silver in
[f]Jė-ru̦′sȧ-lĕm as stones, and [l]ce-
dar trees made he as the [m]syco-
more trees that *are* in the low
plains in abundance.
28 And they brought unto Sŏl′-
o-mon [b,n]horses out of [j]Ē′ġy̆pt,
and out of all lands.
29 ¶ Now the rest of the acts of
[a,o]Sŏl′o-mon, first and last, *are*
they not written in the [p]book
of [q]Nā′than the [r]prophet, and
in the prophecy[C] of [s]Ȧ-hī′jah the
Shī′lo-nīte, and in the visions of
[t]Ĭd′dō the seer[C] [2]against [u]Jĕr-o-
bō′am the son of Nē′bȧt?
30 And Sŏl′o-mon reigned in
[f]Jė-ru̦′sȧ-lĕm over all [v]Ĭs̩′ra-el
forty years.
31 And Sŏl′o-mon [w]slept with
his fathers, and he was buried
in the [f]city of Dā′vid his father: and [x]Rē-ho-bō′am his son
reigned in his stead.

## CHAPTER 10

*The people, assembled at Shechem to crown Rehoboam, through Jeroboam ask of him a redress of grievances. 6 He refuses their request, and answers them roughly. 16 Ten tribes revolt and kill Hadoram.*

[a] AND [b]Rē-ho-bō′am went to
[c]Shē′chem: for to Shē′-
chem were all [d]Ĭs̩′ra-el come to
make him king.
2 And it came to pass, when
[e]Jĕr-o-bō′am the son of Nē′bȧt,
who *was* in [f]Ē′ġy̆pt, whither[C] he
had [g]fled from the presence of
[h]Sŏl′o-mon the king, heard *it*,
that Jĕr-o-bō′am returned out of
Ē′ġy̆pt.
3 And they sent and called him.
So [e]Jĕr-o-bō′am and all [d]Ĭs̩′ra-el
came and spake to [b]Rē-ho-bō′-
am, [i]saying,
4 [i]Thy [j]father made our [k,l]yoke
grievous: now therefore ease
thou somewhat the grievous
[1]servitude of thy father, and his
heavy yoke that he put upon us,
and we will serve thee.
5 And he said unto them, Come
again unto me after three days.
And the people departed.
6 ¶ And king [b]Rē-ho-bō′am
took [m]counsel[C] with the old men
that had stood before [j]Sŏl′o-mon
his father while he yet lived, saying, What counsel give ye *me* to
return answer to this people?
7 And they spake unto him,
saying, If [n]thou be kind to this
people, and please them, and
speak good words to them, they
will be thy servants for ever.
8 But [b]he [o,p]forsook the counsel which the old men gave
him, and took counsel with the
[q]young men that were brought
up with him, that stood before
him.
9 And he said unto them, What
[m]advice give ye that we may return answer to this people, which
have spoken to me, saying, Ease
somewhat the [k,l]yoke that thy
father did put upon us?
10 And the [q]young men that
were brought up with him spake
unto him, saying, Thus shalt
thou answer the people that
spake unto thee, saying, Thy father made our [k,l]yoke heavy, but
make thou *it* somewhat lighter
for us; thus shalt thou say unto
them, My little *finger* shall[C] be
thicker than my father's loins.[C]
11 For whereas my father put
a heavy [k,l]yoke upon you, I
will put more to your yoke:
my father [r]chastised you with

x *Spices*, 1 Kin. 10:2.
y *Horse*, Job 39:19.
z *Mule*, 2 Sam. 18:9.
1 R. V. armour,

**25**
a *Solomon*, 2 Sam. 12:24.
b *Horse*, Job 39:19.
c *Chariot*, Josh. 11:4.
d *Cavalry*, 1 Sam. 13:5.
e *Cities*, Num. 35:8.
f *Jerusalem*, Judg. 19:10.

**26**
g *Canaan, in Solomon's time*, Gen. 37:1.
h *Euphrates*, Gen. 15:18.
i *Philistines*, Gen. 26:14.
j *Egypt*, Gen. 41:8.

**27**
k *Silver*, 1 Chr. 28:14.
l *Cedar*, Isa. 9:10.
m *Sycomore*, 2 Chr. 1:15.

**28**
n *Imports*, 1 Kin. 10:11.

**29**
o *King, chronicles of*, 2 Kin. 3:10.
p *Book*, Num. 5:23.
q *Nathan*, 2 Sam. 7:2.
r *Prophets*, Isa. 3:2.
s *Ahijah*, 1 Kin. 11:29.
t 2 Chr. 12:15; 13:22.
u *Jeroboam*, 1 Kin. 14:5.
2 R. V. concerning

**30**
v *Israel, under the kings*, Ex. 4:22.

**31**
w *Death*, Num. 23:10.
x *Rehoboam*, 1 Kin. 11:43.
v.31–903 BC

**1**
a 1 Kin. 12:1–19.
b *Rehoboam*, 1 Kin. 11:43.
c *Shechem*, Josh. 20:7.
d *Israel, after the revolt*, 1 Kin. 12:1.

**2**
e *Jeroboam*, 1 Kin. 14:5.
f *Egypt*, Gen. 41:8.
g *Fugitives*, Judg. 12:4.
h *Solomon*, 2 Sam. 12:24.

v.2–903 BC
See footnote, *Time*, Rev. 10:6.

**3**
i *Petition, right of*, Esth. 5:6.

**4**
j *Solomon, oppression of*, 2 Sam. 12:24.
k *Yoke, figurative*, 1 Sam. 6:7.
l *Oppression*, Eccl. 5:8.
1 R. V. service

**6**
m *Counsel*, Prov. 12:15.

**7**
n *Rulers, character and qualifications of*, Ex. 18:21.

**8**
o *Rashness, instances of*, 2 Sam. 6:7.
p *Counsel, rejected*, Prov. 12:15.
q *Young Men*, Prov. 1:4.

**11**
r *Scourging, figurative*, Acts 22:24.

v.11–903 BC
See footnote, *Time*, Rev. 10:6.

s 1 Kin. 12:11.
t *Scorpion, figurative*, Luke 10:19.

13
u *Rulers, wicked, instances of*, Ex. 18:21.

15
v *Government, God in*, Isa. 22:21.
w *God, providence of*, Gen. 2:2.
x *Ahijah*, 1 Kin. 11:29.

16
y *Citizens, treasonable, instances of*, Luke 15:15.
z *David*, 1 Sam. 16:13.

a *Jesse*, Ruth 4:17.
b *Treason, instances of*, 2 Kin. 11:14.
c *Tent*, Gen. 13:5.

17
d *Judah, kingdom of*, 2 Chr. 11:17.
e *Rehoboam*, 1 Kin. 11:43.

18
f Or, *Adoniram*, 1 Kin. 5:14.
g *Tax*, Neh. 10:32.
h *King, emoluments of*, 2 Kin. 3:10.
i *Homicide, felonious*, Deut. 5:17.
j *Chariot*, Josh. 11:4.
k *Jerusalem*, Judg. 19:10.
2 R. V. levy;

19
l *Israel, after the revolt*, 1 Kin. 12:1.

[s]whips, but I *will chastise you*
with [t]scorpions.[G]
12 ¶ So [e]Jĕr-o-bō′am and all
the people came to [b]Rē-ho-bō′-
am on the third day, as the king
bade,[G] saying, Come again to me
on the third day.
13 And the [b,u]king answered
them roughly; and king Rē-ho-
bō′am forsook the [p]counsel[G] of
the old men,
14 And answered them after
the advice of the [q]young men,
saying, My [i]father made your
[k,l]yoke heavy, but [u]I will add
thereto: my father [r]chastised you
with [s]whips, but I *will chastise*
*you* with [t]scorpions.[G]
15 So the king hearkened not
unto the people: [v]for the cause
was of [w]God, that the LORD
might perform his word, which
he spake by the hand of [x]Ā-hī′-
jah the Shī′lo-nīte to Jĕr-o-bō′-
am the son of Nē′băt.
16 And when all Ĭṣ′ra-el *saw*
that the king would not heark-
en unto them, the [y]people answered the king, saying, What
portion have we in [z]Dā′vid? and
*we have* none inheritance in the
son of [a]Jĕs′se: [b]every man to
your [c]tents, O Ĭṣ′ra-el: *and* now,
Dā′vid, see to thine own house.
So all Ĭṣ′ra-el went to their tents.
17 But *as for* the children of
Ĭṣ′ra-el that dwelt in the cities of
[d]Jū′dah, [e]Rē-ho-bō′am reigned
over them.
18 Then king [e]Rē-ho-bō′am
sent [f]Hă-dō′ram that *was* over
the [2,g,h]tribute;[G] and the children
of Ĭṣ′ra-el [i]stoned him with
stones, that he died. But king
Rē-ho-bō′am made speed to get
him up to *his* [j]chariot, to flee to
[k]Jē-ru′sā-lĕm.
19 And [l]Ĭṣ′ra-el rebelled against
the house of Dā′vid unto this
day.

## CHAPTER 11

*Rehoboam is forbidden to war against Israel. 5 He strengthens his kingdom. 13 The priests and Levites, and such as feared God, forsaken by Jeroboam, strengthen the kingdom of Judah. 18 The wives and children of Rehoboam.*

[a]AND when [b]Rē-ho-bō′am was
come to [c]Jē-ru′sā-lĕm, he
gathered of the house of [d]Jū′dah
and [e]Bĕn′ja-mĭn an hundred
and fourscore thousand chosen
*men*, which were warriors, to
fight against Ĭṣ′ra-el, that he
might bring the kingdom again
to Rē-ho-bō′am.
2 But the word of the LORD
came to [f]Shĕm-a-ī′ah the man of
God, saying,
3 Speak unto [b]Rē-ho-bō′am the
son of [g]Sŏl′o-mon, king of [h]Jū′-
dah, and to all Ĭṣ′ra-el in Jū′dah
and Bĕn′ja-mĭn, saying,
4 Thus saith the LORD, Ye
shall not go up, nor fight against
your brethren: return every man
to his house: for [i]this thing is
done of [j]me. And they obeyed
the words of the LORD, and returned from going against Jĕr-
o-bō′am.
5 ¶ And [b]Rē-ho-bō′am dwelt
in [c]Jē-ru′sā-lĕm, and built cities
for defence in Jū′dah.
6 He built even [k]Bĕth′–lĕ-hĕm,
and Ē′tăm, and [l]Tē-kō′ā.
7 And [m]Bĕth′–zûr, and [n]Shō′-
cō, and *Ā-dŭl′lăm,
8 And [o]Găth, and [p]Mā-rē′shah,
and [q]Zĭph,
9 And Ăd-o-rā′im, and [r]Lā′-
chish, and [s]Ā-zē′kah,
10 And [t]Zō′rah, and [u]Āij′a-lŏn,
and [v]Hē′bron, which *are* in [d]Jū′-
dah and in [e]Bĕn′ja-mĭn, fenced[G]
[w]cities.
11 And he fortified the [x]strong
holds, and put [y]captains in
them, and store[G] of victual,[G] and
of oil and wine.
12 [z]And in every several city *he*
*put* [a]shields and [b]spears, and

v.1–903 BC
See footnote, *Time*, Rev. 10:6.

1
a 1 Kin. 12:21–24.
b *Rehoboam*, 1 Kin. 11:43.
c *Jerusalem*, Judg. 19:10.
d *Judah, tribe of*, Num. 10:14.
e *Benjamin, tribe of*, Num. 1:37.

2
f *Shemaiah*, 1 Kin. 12:22.

3
g *Solomon*, 2 Sam. 12:24.
h *Judah, kingdom of*, 2 Chr. 11:17.

4
i *Government, God in*, Isa. 22:21.
j *God, providence of*, Gen. 2:2.

6
k *Beth-lehem*, Gen. 48:7.
l *Tekoa*, Jer. 6:1.

7
m 1 Chr. 2:45; Neh. 3:16.
n Or, *Shochoh*, 1 Sam. 17:1.

8
o *Gath*, Josh. 11:22.
p *Mareshah*, Josh. 15:44.
q Josh. 15:24, 55.

9
r *Lachish*, Josh. 10:5.
s *Azekah*, Josh. 10:10.

10
t *Zorah*, Josh. 19:41.
u *Aijalon*, Josh. 21:24.
v *Hebron*, Gen. 23:2.
w *Cities, fortified*, Num 35:8.

11
x *Fortification*, Ezek. 17:17.
y *Captain*, Num. 31:48.

12
z *Armory*, Neh. 3:19.

a *Shield*, 1 Kin. 14:27.
b *Spear*, 2 Kin. 11:10.

* **ADULLAM.** *An ancient city of Canaan*, Gen. 38:1; Josh. 12:15; 15:35; 2 Chr. 11:7; Neh. 11:30; Mic. 1:15. *A cave by the same name supposed to be near to*, 1 Sam. 22:1; 24:3.

1 R. V. And Judah and Benjamin belonged to him.

**13**

*c Priest*, Lev. 1:5.
*d Levites*, Deut. 10:8.
2 R. V. border.

**14**

*e Jerusalem*, Judg. 19:10.
*f Jeroboam*, 1 Kin. 14:5.
*g Rulers, wicked*, Ex. 18:21.

made them exceeding[G] strong,
[1]having Jū′dah and Bĕn′ja-mĭn
on his side.
13 And the [c]priests and the
[d]Lē′vītes that *were* in all Ĭs′ra-el
resorted[G] to him out of all their
[2]coasts[G].
14 For the [d]Lē′vītes left their
suburbs[G] and their possession,
and came to Jū′dah and [e]Jē-ru′-
sā-lĕm: for [f,g]Jĕr-o-bō′am and
his sons had cast them off from
executing[G] the priest's office unto
the LORD:
15 And [h]he ordained[G] him
priests for the [i]high places, and
for the [3]devils[G], and for the calves
which he had made.
16 And after them out of all the
tribes of Ĭs′ra-el [j]such as [k]set
their hearts to seek the LORD
God of Ĭs′ra-el came to [e]Jē-ru′-
sā-lĕm, to sacrifice unto the
LORD God of their fathers.
17 So they strengthened the
kingdom of †Jū′dah, and made
[l]Rē-ho-bō′am the son of [m]Sŏl′-
o-mon strong, three years: for

**15**

*h National Religion*, Gal. 1:13.
*i High Places*, 1 Kin. 3:2.
3 R. V. he-goats.

**16**

*j Seekers*, Isa. 55:6.
*k Decision, instances of*, Isa. 50:7.

**17**

*l Rehoboam*, 1 Kin. 11:43.
*m Solomon*, 2 Sam. 12:24.

---

† **JUDAH, KINGDOM OF.** Composed of the tribes of Judah and Benjamin, after the revolt of the ten tribes under the reign of Rehoboam.

Circumstances foreshadowing the separation of the Israelites into two nations: *Disagreement after Saul's death*, 2 Sam. 2; 1 Chr. 12:23–40; 13; *lukewarmness of the ten tribes, and zeal of Judah for David in Absalom's rebellion*, 2 Sam. 19:41–43; *the rebellion of Sheba*, 2 Sam. 20. *The two factions are distinguished as Israel and Judah during David's reign*, 2 Sam. 21:2.

*Revolt consummated under Rehoboam, son and successor of Solomon*, 1 Kin. 12; 2 Chr. 10.

In the historical books of the Kings and the Chronicles the nation is called JUDAH, but in the prophecies it is frequently referred to as ISRAEL, as in Isa. 8:14; 49:7, and as JEWS, in 2 Kin. 16:6; 25:25; Matt. 2:2; 27:11.

List of rulers and the periods of time during which they reigned:

1. *Rehoboam, seventeen years*, 1 Kin. 11:43.
2. *Abijah*, or *Abijam, three years*, 1 Kin. **15:1.**
3. *Asa, forty-one years*, 1 Kin. 15:8.
4. *Jehoshaphat, twenty-five years*, 2 Kin. **12:18.**
5. *Jehoram, eight years*, 1 Kin. 22:50.
6. *Ahaziah, one year*, 2 Kin. 8:25.
7. *Athaliah's usurpation, six years*, 2 Kin. **11:1.**
8. *Joash*, or *Jehoash, forty years*, 2 Kin. 11:2.
9. *Amaziah, twenty-nine years*, 2 Kin. 14:1.
10. *Uzziah*, or *Azariah, fifty-two years*, **2 Chr. 26:1.**
11. *Jotham, sixteen years*, 2 Kin. 15:5.
12. *Ahaz, sixteen years*, 2 Kin. 15:38.
13. *Hezekiah, twenty-nine years*, 2 Kin. **16:20.**
14. *Manasseh, fifty-five years*, 2 Kin. 21:1.
15. *Amon, two years*, 2 Kin. 21:18.
16. *Josiah, thirty-one years*, 1 Kin. 13:2.
17. *Jehoahaz, Josiah's son, three months*, 2 Kin. **23:30.**
18. *Jehoiakim, Josiah's son, eleven years*, Jer. 26:22.
19. *Jehoiachin*, or *Jeconiah, Jehoiakim's son, three months*, 2 Kin. 24:6.
20. *Zedekiah*, or *Mattaniah, Josiah's son, eleven years*, 2 Kin. 25:2.

*Rehoboam succeeds Solomon; in consequence of his arbitrary policy ten tribes rebel*, 1 Kin. 12. *Other circumstances of his reign*, 1 Kin. 14:21–31; 2 Chr. 10; 11; 12. *Death of Rehoboam*, 1 Kin. 14:31; 2 Chr. 12:16.

*Abijah's wicked reign*, 1 Kin. 15:1–8; 2 Chr. 13. *Asa's good reign*, 1 Kin. 15:9–24; 2 Chr. chapters 14–16. *Asa makes a league with Ben-hadad, king of Syria, to make war against Israel*, 1 Kin. 15:16–24; 2 Chr. 16.

*Jehoshaphat succeeds Asa*, 1 Kin. 15:24; 2 Chr. chapters 17–20; 21:1; *joins Ahab against the king of Syria*, 1 Kin. 22. *Jehoram, called also* JORAM, *reigns in the stead of his father, Jehoshaphat*, 1 Kin. 22:51; 2 Kin. 8:16–24; 2 Chr. 21. *Edom revolts*, 2 Kin. 8:20–22. *Ahaziah, called also* AZARIAH, 2 Chr. 22:6, *and* JEHOAHAZ, 2 Chr. 21:17; 25:23, *succeeds Jehoram*, 2 Kin. 8:24–29; 2 Chr. 22; *slain by Jehu*, 2 Kin. 9:27–29; 2 Chr. 22:8, 9. *Athaliah, his mother, succeeds him*, 2 Kin. 11:1–16; 2 Chr. 22:10–12; 23:1–15.

*Jehoash, called also* JOASH, *succeeds Athaliah*, 2 Kin. 11:21; 12:1–21; 2 Chr. 24. *The temple repaired*, 2 Kin. 12. *Amaziah reigns, and Judah is invaded by the king of Israel; Jerusalem is taken and the sacred things of the temple carried away*, 2 Kin. 13:21; 14:1–20; 2 Chr. 25. *Azariah, called also* UZZIAH, *succeeds him*, 2 Kin. 14:21, 22; 15:1–7; 2 Chr. 26. *Jotham succeeds Uzziah*, 2 Kin. 15:7, 32–38; 2 Chr. **27.** ***Rezin, king of Syria, invades Judah***, 2 Kin. 15:37.

*Jotham is succeeded by Ahaz*, 2 Kin. 16:1; 2 Chr. 28. *Judah is invaded by kings of Samaria and Syria; Ahaz hires the king of Assyria to make war on the king of Syria*, 2 Kin. 16: 5–9. *Ahaz changes the use of the altar*, 2 Kin. 16:14, 15. *Makes another altar after the pattern of one in Damascus*, 2 Kin. 16:10–18.

*Hezekiah succeeds Ahaz*, 2 Kin. 16:20; 2 Chr. chapters 29–32. *His good reign*, 2 Kin. 18:1–8. *He revolts from the sovereignty of the king of Assyria*, 2 Kin. 18:7. *King of Assyria invades Judah, and blasphemes the God of Judah; his army overthrown*, 2 Kin. 18:13–37; 19; 2 Chr. 32:1–22; Isa. 36; 37. *Hezekiah's sickness and miraculous restoration*, 2 Kin. 20; Isa. 38:1–21; 39:1. *Succeeded by Manasseh*, 2 Kin. 20:21; 2 Chr. 32:33. *Manasseh's wicked reign*, 2 Kin. 21:1–18; 2 Chr. 33:1–20. *Amon succeeds Manasseh on the throne*, 2 Kin. 21:18–26; 2 Chr. 33:20–25.

*Josiah succeeds Amon; the temple is repaired; the book of the law recovered; religious revival follows; and the king dies*, 2 Kin. 22; 23:1–30; 2 Chr. 34; 35. *Josiah is succeeded by Jehoahaz, who reigns three months, is dethroned by the king of Egypt, and the land put under tribute*, 2 Kin. 23:30–35; 2 Chr. 36:1–3.

*Jehoiakim is elevated to the throne; becomes tributary to Nebuchadnezzar for three years; rebels; is conquered and carried to Babylon*, 2 Kin. 24:1–6; 2 Chr. 36:4–8. *Jehoiachin is made king; suffers invasion, and is carried to Babylon*, 2 Kin. 24:8–16; 2 Chr. 36:9, 10.

*Zedekiah is made king by Nebuchadnezzar; rebels; Nebuchadnezzar invades Judah, takes Jerusalem, and carries the people to Babylon, despoiling the temple*, 2 Kin. 24:17–20; 25; 2 Chr. 36:11–21. *The poorest of the people are left to occupy the country, and are joined by fragments of the army of Judah, the dispersed Israelites in other lands, and the king's daughters*, 2 Kin. 25:12, 22, 23; Jer. 39:10; 40:7–12; 52:16. *Gedaliah appointed governor of*, 2 Kin. 25:22; Jer. 40:5–7. *His administration favorable to the people*, 2 Kin. 25:23, 24; Jer. 40: 7–12. *Conspired against and slain by Ishmael*, 2 Kin. 25:25; Jer. 40:13–16; 41:1–3. *Ishmael seeks to betray the people to the Ammonites*, Jer. 41:1–18. *The people, in fear, take refuge in Egypt*, 2 Kin. 25:26; Jer. 41:14–18; 42:13–18.

**Captivity of the people of:** *Great wickedness the cause of their adversity*, Ezek. chapters 5–7; 16; 23:22–44. *Dwell, in Babylon*, Jer. 52:28–30; Dan. 5:13; 6:13; *by the river Chebor*, Ezek. 1:1; 10:15. *Patriotism of*, Psa. 137. *Plotted against, by Haman*, Esth. 3. *Are saved by Esther*, Esth. chapters 4–9.

**After the captivity:** *Cyrus, decrees their restoration*, 2 Chr. 36:22, 23; Ezra 1:1–4; *directs the rebuilding of the temple, and the restoration of the vessels which had been carried to Babylon*, 2 Chr. 36:23; Ezra 1:3–11. *Proclamation renewed by Darius and Artaxerxes*, Ezra 6:1–14. *Ezra's lists of the captives who returned to Jerusalem*, Ezra 2; 8:1–30. *Nehemiah's list*, Neh. 7:6–67. *Temple rebuilt and dedicated*, Ezra chapters 3–6. *Artaxerxes issues proclamation to restore the temple service*, Ezra **7.** *Priests and Levites authorized to return*, Ezra 8. *Corruptions among the returned captives; their reform*, Ezra 9; 10.

*Nehemiah is commissioned to lead the captives back to Canaan*, Neh. 2; 7:5–67. *Wall of Jerusalem rebuilt and dedicated*, Neh. chapters 2–6; 12. *The law read and expounded*, Neh. 8. *Solemn feast is kept; priests are purified; the covenant sealed*, Neh. chapters 8–10. *One-tenth of the people, to be determined by lot, volunteer to dwell in Jerusalem, and the remaining nine parts dwell in other cities*, Neh. 11. *Catalogue of the priests and Levites who came up with Zerubbabel*, Neh. 12. *Nehemiah reforms various abuses*, Neh. 13.

*Expect a Messiah*, Luke 3:15. *Many accept Jesus as the Christ*, John 2:23; 10:42; 11:45; 12:11; Acts 21:20.

**Prophecies concerning:** *Their rejection of the Messiah*, Isa. 8:14, 15; 49:5, 7; 53:1–3 (with John 12:38); Zech. 11; Matt. 21:33–44; 22:1–14.

*War and other judgments*, 2 Kin. 20:17, 18; 21:12–15; 22: 16, 17; 23:26, 27; Isa. 1:1–24; 3; 5; 7:17–25; 8:14–22; 30:1–17; 31:1–3; 32:9–14; Jer. 1:11–16; 4:5–31; 6; 7:8–34; 8; 9:9–26;

three years they walked in the
way of Dā′vid and Sŏl′o-mon.
18 ¶ And [l]Rē-ho-bō′am [n,o]took
him Mā′ha-lăth the daughter of
Jĕr′ĭ-mŏth the son of [p]Dā′vid to[G]
wife, *and* [o]Ăb-i-hā′il the daughter
of [q]Ē-lī′ab the son of [r]Jĕs′se;
19 Which bare him [4]children;
Jē′ŭsh, and Shăm-a-rī′ah, and
Zā′ham.
20 And after her he [n,o]took
[s]Mā′a-chah the daughter of
[t]Ăb′sa-lŏm; which bare him [u]Ă-
bī′jah, and Ăt′tāi, and Zī′zȧ, and
Shĕl′o-mĭth.
21 And [l]Rē-ho-bō′am loved
[s]Mā′a-chah the daughter of
[t]Ăb′sa-lŏm above all his wives
and his [v]concubines: (for he
[o,w]took eighteen wives, and
threescore concubines; and begat twenty and eight sons, and
threescore daughters.)
22 And [l]Rē-ho-bō′am made
[u]Ă-bī′jah the son of [s]Mā′a-chah
the chief, *to be* ruler among his
brethren: for *he thought* to make
him king.
23 And he dealt wisely, and
dispersed of all his [4]children
throughout all the countries of
[x]Jū′dah and [y]Bĕn′ja-mĭn, unto
every fenced[G] [z]city: and he gave
them victual[C] in abundance. And
he [5]desired many wives.

## CHAPTER 12

*Rehoboam, forsaking the Lord, is punished by Shishak. 5 He and the princes, humbling themselves, are delivered from destruction. 13 The reign and death of Rehoboam.*

AND it came to pass, when
[a]Rē-ho-bō′am had estab-
lished the [b]kingdom, and had
strengthened himself, [c]he [d,e]for-
sook the law of the LORD, and
all Ĭṣ′ra-el with him.
2 And it came to pass, *that* in
the fifth year of king [a]Rē-ho-
bō′am [f]Shī′shăk king of [g]Ē′ġўpt
[h]came up against [i]Jĕ-ru̇′sȧ-lĕm,
because they had transgressed
against the LORD,
3 With twelve hundred [j]char-
iots, and threescore thousand
[k]horsemen: and the people *were*
without number that came with
him out of [g]Ē′ġўpt; the [l]Lu̇′-
bĭmṣ, the Sŭk′kĭ-ĭmṣ, and the
Ē-thĭ-ō′pĭ-anṣ.
4 And he took the fenced[C] [m]cit-
ies which *pertained* to [b]Jū′dah,
and came to [i]Jĕ-ru̇′sȧ-lĕm.
5 Then came [n]Shĕm-a-ī′ah the
[o]prophet to [a]Rē-ho-bō′am, and
*to* the princes of Jū′dah, that
were gathered together to [i]Jĕ-
ru̇′sȧ-lĕm because of [f]Shī′shăk,
and [p]said unto them, Thus saith
the LORD, Ye have forsaken me,
and therefore have I also [q]left
you in the hand of Shī′shăk.
6 Whereupon the princes of
Ĭṣ′ra-el and the king [r,s]humbled
themselves; and they said, The
LORD *is* [t]righteous.
7 And when the LORD saw that
they [r,s]humbled themselves, the
word of the LORD [u]came to
[n]Shĕm-a-ī′ah, saying, They have
humbled themselves; *therefore*
[v]I will not destroy them, but I
will grant them some deliverance; and my wrath shall not
be poured out upon [i]Jĕ-ru̇′sȧ-
lĕm by the hand of [f]Shī′shăk.
8 Nevertheless they [w]shall be
his servants; that they may know
my service, and the service of the
kingdoms of the countries.
9 So [f]Shī′shăk king of [g]Ē′ġўpt
came up against [i]Jĕ-ru̇′sȧ-lĕm,
and took away the treasures of
the [x]house of the LORD, and the
treasures of the [y]king's house;

18
n *Marriage*, Gen. 34:9.
o *Polygamy*, Deut. 17:17.
p *David*, 1 Sam. 16:13.
q *Eliab*, 1 Sam. 16:6.
r *Jesse*, Ruth 4:17.
19
4 R. V. sons;
20
s 2 Chr. 15:16; 1 Kin. 15:2, 10–13; or, *Michaiah*, 2 Chr. 13:2.
t *Absalom*, 2 Sam. 3:3.
u Or, *Abijam*, 1 Kin. 15:1.
21
v *Concubinage*, 2 Sam. 21:11.
w *Lasciviousness*, 1 Pet. 4:3.
23
x *Judah, tribe of* Num. 10:14.
y *Benjamin, tribe of*, Num. 1:37.
z *Cities, fortified*, Num. 35:8.
5 R. V. sought for them many wives.
1
a *Rehoboam*, 1 Kin. 11:43.
b *Judah, kingdom of*, 2 Chr. 11:17.
c *Backsliders, instances of*, Jer. 3:22.
d *Character, instability of*, Phil. 2:15.
e *Ingratitude, of man to God*, Rom. 1:21.

v.2–899 BC
See footnote, *Time*, Rev. 10:6.
2
f *Shishak*, 1 Kin. 11:40.
g *Egypt*, Gen. 41:8.
h *War, as a judgment*, Judg. 3:2.
i *Jerusalem*, Judg. 19:10.
3
j *Chariot*, Josh. 11:4.
k *Cavalry*, 1 Sam. 13:5.
l 2 Chr. 16:8.
4
m *Cities, fortified*, Num. 35:8.
5
n *Shemaiah*, 1 Kin. 12:22.
o *Prophets*, Isa. 3:2.
p *Reproof, faithfulness in*, Prov. 17:10.
q *Judgments*, Ex. 6:6.
6
r *Humility, instances of*, Prov. 22:4.
s *Repentance, instances of*, Mark 1:4.
t *God, righteousness of*, Gen. 2:2.
7
u *Inspiration*, Job 32:8.
v *God, mercy of*, Gen. 2:2.
8
w *Divine Chastisement*, Job 33:19.
9
x *Temple, Solomon's*, 1 Kin. 6:17.
y *Palace*, 1 Kin. 21:1.

11:9–23; 13:9–27; 14:14–18; 15:1–14; 16; 17:1–4; 18:15–17; 19; 20:4–6; 21:4–7, 10; 22:24–30; 25:8–38; 28:14; 34; 37; 38: 1–3; 42:13–22; 43; 44; 45; Ezek. 4; 5; 11:7–12; 12; 15; 16:27, 37–43; 17; 22:13–22; 23:22–35; 24; 33:21–29; Dan. 9:26, 27; Joel 2:1–17; Amos 2:4, 5; Mic. 2:10; 3:4, 6, 12; 4:10; Hab. 1: 6–11; Zeph. 1; Zech. 11; 14:1–3.
*Dispersion of*, Deut. 28:64; Jer. 9:16; Ezek. 4:13; 5:10, 12; 20:23; 36:19; Dan. 9:7; Joel 3:6.

*Blessing and restoration of*, Isa. 1:25–27; 2:1–5; 11:11–13; 26:1, 2, 12–19; 27:13; 29:18–24; 30:18–26; 32:15–20; 37:31, 32; 40:2, 9; 44; 49:13–23; 51; 52:1–12; 60; 61:4–9; 62; 66:5–22; Jer. 3:14–18; 12:14–16; 23:3; 24:1–7; 29:1–14; 30:3–22; 32: 36–44; 33; Ezek. 16:60–63; 20:40, 41; 36:1–38; 37:12, 21; Dan. 12:1; Joel 3; Amos 9:9–15; Obad. 17–21; Mic. 2:12, 13; Zeph. 2:7; Zech. 1:14–21; 2; 8; 10:5–12; 12:1–14; 13; 14:3–21; Mal. 3:4.

he took all: he carried away also the [z]shields of [a]gold which [b]Sŏl′-o-mon had made.

10 Instead of which king [c]Rē-ho-bō′am made [d]shields of [e]brass, and committed *them* to the hands of the chief[G] of the guard, that kept the entrance of the king's house.

11 And when the king entered into the [f]house of the LORD, the guard came and fetched them, and brought them again into the guard chamber.

12 And when he [g,h]humbled himself, the wrath of the LORD turned from him, that he would not destroy *him* altogether: and also in [i]Jū′dah [1]things went well.

13 ¶ So king [c]Rē-ho-bō′am strengthened himself in [j]Jĕ-ru′să-lĕm, and reigned: for Rē-ho-bō′am *was* one and forty years old when he began to reign, and he reigned seventeen years in Jĕ-ru′să-lĕm, the city which the LORD had chosen out of all the tribes of Ĭs′ra-el, to put his name there. And his mother's name *was* [k]Nā′a-mah an [l]Ăm′mon-īt-ess.

14 And he did evil, because he [m]prepared not his [n]heart to seek the LORD.

15 Now the acts of [c,o]Rē-ho-bō′am, first and last, *are* they not written in the [p]book of [q]Shĕm-a-ī′ah the [r]prophet, and of [s]Ĭd′-dō the seer concerning [t]genealogies? And *there were* [u]wars between Rē-ho-bō′am and [v]Jĕr-o-bō′am continually.

16 And [c]Rē-ho-bō′am [w]slept with his fathers, and was buried in the [j]city of Dā′vid: and [x]Ă-bī′-jah his son reigned in his stead.

## CHAPTER 13

*Abijah's reign. 2 His war with Jeroboam. 4 He declares the righteousness of his cause. 13 Trusting in God, he overcomes Jeroboam. 21 The wives and children of Abijah.*

NOW in the eighteenth year of king [a]Jĕr-o-bō′am began [b]Ă-bī′jah to reign over [c]Jū′dah.

2 He reigned three years in [d]Jĕ-ru′să-lĕm. His mother's name also *was* [e]Mī-chā′iah the daughter of Ū′rĭ-el of Gĭb′e-ah. And there was [f]war between [b]Ă-bī′jah and [a]Jĕr-o-bō′am.

3 And [b]Ă-bī′jah set the battle in array[G] with an army of valiant [g]men of war, *even* four hundred thousand chosen men: [a]Jĕr-o-bō′am also set the battle in array[G] against him with eight hundred thousand chosen men, *being* mighty men of valour[G].

4 ¶ And [b]Ă-bī′jah stood up upon mount[G] Zĕm-a-rā′im, which *is* in [1]mount[G] [h]Ē′phră-ĭm, and [i]said, Hear me, thou [a]Jĕr-o-bō′am, and all Ĭs′ra-el;

5 [i]Ought ye not to know that the LORD God of Ĭs′ra-el gave the kingdom over Ĭs′ra-el to [j]Dā′vid for ever, *even* to him and to his sons by a [k]covenant of [l]salt?

6 [i]Yet [a]Jĕr-o-bō′am the son of [m]Nē′băt, the servant of [n]Sŏl′o-mon the son of [j]Dā′vid, is risen up, and hath rebelled against his lord.

7 And there are gathered unto him vain[G] men, the children of Bē′lĭ-al[G], and have strengthened themselves against [o]Rē-ho-bō′-am the son of [n]Sŏl′o-mon, when Rē-ho-bō′am was young and tenderhearted, and could not withstand them.

8 [i]And now ye think to withstand the [p]kingdom of the LORD in the hand of the sons of [j]Dā′-vid; and ye *be* a great multitude, and *there are* with you golden [q]calves, which Jĕr-o-bō′am made you for [r]gods.

9 Have ye not cast out the [s]priests of the LORD, the sons of Aâr′on, and the [t]Lē′vītes, and have made you priests after the manner of the nations of *other* lands? so that whosoever cometh to consecrate[G] himself with a

---

v.9–899 BC See footnote, *Time*, Rev. 10:6.

z *Shield*, 1 Kin. 14:27.

a *Gold*, Ezek. 7:19.
b *Solomon*, 2 Sam. 12:24.

**10**
c *Rehoboam*, 1 Kin. 11:43.
d *Shield*, 1 Kin. 14:27.
e *Brass*, Job 28:2.

**11**
f *Temple, Solomon's*, 1 Kin. 6:17.

**12**
g *Humility, instances of*, Prov. 22:4.
h *Repentance, instances of*, Mark 1:4.
i *Judah, kingdom of*, 2 Chr. 11:17.
1 R. V. there were good things found.

**13**
j *Jerusalem*, Judg. 19:10.
k 1 Kin. 14:21, 31.
l *Ammonites*, Deut. 2:20.

**14**
m *Wicked, described*, Psa. 73:3.
n *Heart*, Psa. 44:21.

**15**
o *King, chronicles of*, 2 Kin. 3:10.
p *Book*, Num. 5:23.
q *Shemaiah*, 1 Kin. 12:22.
r *Prophets*, Isa. 3:2.
s 2 Chr. 9:29; 13:22.
t *Genealogy*, 1 Chr. 5:1.
u *War*, Judg. 3:2.
v *Jeroboam*, 1 Kin. 14:5.

**16**
w *Death*, Num. 23:10.
x Or, *Abijam*, 1 Kin. 15:1.

v.1–886 BC See footnote, *Time*, Rev. 10:6.

**1**
a *Jeroboam*, 1 Kin. 14:5.
b Or, *Abijam*, 1 Kin. 15:1.
c *Judah, kingdom of*, 2 Chr. 11:17.

**2**
d *Jerusalem*, Judg 19:10.
e Or, *Maachah*, 2 Chr. 11:20–23; 15:16; 1 Kin. 15:2, 10–13.
f *War*, Judg. 3:2.

**3**
g *Soldiers*, Ezra 8:22.

**4**
h *Ephraim*, Josh. 17:15.
i *Reproof, faithfulness in*, Prov. 17:10.
1 R. V. the hill country of

**5**
j *David*, 1 Sam. 16:13.
k *Covenant, of God with men*, Deut. 29:1.
l *Salt, emblematic*, 2 Kin. 2:20.

**6**
m 1 Kin. 11:26; 12:2.
n *Solomon*, 2 Sam. 12:24.

**7**
o *Rehoboam*, 1 Kin. 11:43.

**8**
p *Theocracy*, Judg. 8:23.
q *Calf*, Mic. 6:6.
r *Idolatry*, 1 Sam. 15:23.

**9**
s *Priest*, Lev. 1:5.
t *Levites*, Deut. 10:8.

young bullock and seven rams, *the same* may be a priest of *them that are* no gods.[Q]

10 But as for us, [u]the LORD *is* our God, and [v]we have not forsaken him; and the [w]priests, which minister unto the LORD, *are* the sons of Aâr′on, and the Lē′vītes *wait*[G] upon *their* business:

11 And [w]they burn unto the LORD every morning and every evening [x]burnt sacrifices and sweet [y]incense: the shewbread also *set they in order* upon the pure [z]table; and the [a]candlestick[G] of [b]gold with the lamps thereof, to burn every evening: for we keep[G] the charge[G] of the LORD our God; but ye have forsaken him.

12 And, behold, God himself *is* with us for *our* captain, and his [c,d]priests with sounding [e]trumpets to cry alarm against you. O children of Ĭṣ′ra-el, fight ye not against the LORD God of your fathers; for ye shall not prosper.

13 ¶ But [f]Jĕr-o-bō′am [g]caused an [h]ambushment to come about behind them: so they were before Jū′dah, and the ambushment[G] *was* behind them.

14 And when Jū′dah looked back, behold, the battle *was* before and behind: and they cried unto the LORD, and the [c,d]priests sounded with the [e]trumpets.

15 Then the men of [i]Jū′dah gave a [j]shout: and as the men of Jū′dah shouted, it came to pass, [k]that [l,m]God smote [f]Jĕr-o-bō′am and all [n]Ĭṣ′ra-el before [o]Ă-bī′jah and Jū′dah.

16 And the children of Ĭṣ′ra-el fled before Jū′dah: and God [m]delivered them into their hand.

17 And [o]Ă-bī′jah and his people slew them with a great slaughter: so there fell down slain of Ĭṣ′ra-el five hundred thousand chosen men.

18 Thus the children of [n]Ĭṣ′ra-el were brought under at that time, and the children of [i]Jū′dah prevailed, because they [p]relied upon the LORD God of their fathers.

19 And [o]Ă-bī′jah pursued after [f]Jĕr-o-bō′am, and took cities from him, [q]Bĕth′–el with the towns thereof, and Jĕsh′a-nah with the towns thereof, and [r]Ē′phră-ĭn with the towns thereof.

20 Neither did [f]Jĕr-o-bō′am recover strength again in the days of [o]Ă-bī′jah: and [s]the LORD [t]struck him, and he died.

21 ¶ But [o]Ă-bī′jah waxed[G] mighty, and married [u]fourteen wives, and begat twenty and two sons, and sixteen daughters.

22 And the rest of the acts of [o]Ă-bī′jah, and his ways, and his sayings, *are* written in the [2,v]story of the [w]prophet [x]Ĭd′dō.

## CHAPTER 14

*Asa's reign. 3 He destroys idolatry. 6 Having peace, he strengthens his kingdom. 9 Calling on God, he overthrows Zerah, and spoils the Ethiopians.*

SO [a]Ă-bī′jah [b]slept with his fathers, and they [c]buried him in the [d]city of Dā′vid: and [e]Ā′sȧ his son reigned in his stead. In his days the [f]land was quiet ten years.

2 And [e,g]Ā′sȧ [h]did *that which was* good and right in the eyes of the LORD his God:

3 For he took away the [1]altars of the strange[G] *gods,* and the [i]high places, and [j]brake down the [2]images, and cut down the [3,k]groves[G]:

4 And commanded Jū′dah to seek the LORD God of their fathers, and to do the [l]law and the commandment.

5 Also he took away out of all the cities of [f]Jū′dah the [i]high places and the [4]images[G]: and the kingdom was quiet before him.

6 ¶ And he built fenced[G] [m]cities

**10**
u *Faith, instances of,* Mark 11:22.
v *Faithfulness, instances of,* Luke 16:10.
w *Priest, duties of,* Lev. 1:5.

**11**
x *Offerings, burnt, daily,* Lev. 6:17.
y *Incense,* Ex. 37:29.
z *Shewbread, table of,* Ex. 35:13.

a *Candlestick,* Ex. 25:31.
b *Gold,* Ezek. 7:19.

**12**
c *Priest, sound trumpets in battle,* Lev. 1:5.
d *Minister, in war,* Rom. 15:16.
e *Trumpet,* Josh. 6:4.

**13**
f *Jeroboam,* 1 Kin. 14:5.
g *Armies, stratagems,* Deut. 11:4.
h *Ambush, instances of,* Josh. 8:2.

**15**
i *Judah, kingdom of,* 2 Chr. 11:17.
j *Shouting, in battle,* 2 Chr. 15:14.
k *Prayer, answered, instances of,* v. 14; Acts 6:4.
l *War, God in,* Judg. 3:2.
m *God, providence of, instances of,* Gen. 2:2.
n *Israel, after the revolt,* 1 Kin. 12:1.
o Or, *Abijam,* 1 Kin. 15:1.

**18**
p *Faith, instances of,* Mark 11:22.

**19**
q *Beth-el,* Josh. 18:13.
r *Possibly identical with Ephraim,* John 11:54.

**20**
s *Disease, sent from God,* Ex. 15:26.
t *Judgments,* Ex. 6:6.

**21**
u *Polygamy,* Deut. 17:17.

**22**
v *Book,* Num. 5:23.
w *Prophets,* Isa. 3:2.
x 2 Chr. 9:29; 12:15.
2 R. V. commentary

**v.1–884 BC**
See footnote, *Time,* Rev. 10:6.

**1**
a Or, *Abijam,* 1 Kin. 15:1.
b *Death,* Num. 23:10.
c *Burying Places,* Gen. 23:4.
d *Jerusalem,* Judg. 19:10.
e *Asa,* 1 Kin. 15:8.
f *Judah, kingdom of,* 2 Chr. 11:17.

**2**
g *Rulers, righteous,* Ex. 18:21.
h *Obedience, instances of,* Heb. 5:8.

**3**
i *High Places,* 1 Kin. 3:2.
j *Iconoclasm,* Num. 33:52.
k *Groves,* Judg. 6:28.
1 R. V. strange altars, and the
2 R. V. pillars,
3 R. V. Asherim;

**4**
l *Law, of Moses,* Deut. 33:2.

**5**
4 R. V. sun-images:

**6**
m *Cities, fortified,* Num. 35:8.

in [l]Jū′dah: for the land had
[n]rest[G], and he had no war in those
years; because the [o]LORD had
given him rest.

7 Therefore he said unto [l]Jū′-
dah, Let us build these [m]cities,
and make about *them* [p]walls,
and [q]towers, [r]gates, and bars,
*while* the land *is* yet before us;
because [s]we have sought the
LORD our God, we have sought
*him*, and he hath given us [n]rest
on every side. So they built and
prospered.

8 And [e]Ā′sȧ had an army *of*
*men* that bare [5,t]targets[G] and
[t,u]spears, out of [v]Jū′dah three
hundred thousand; and out of
[w]Běn′ja-mĭn, that bare [t,x]shields
and [y]drew [t]bows, two hundred
and fourscore thousand: all
these *were* mighty men of [z]val-
our.

9 ¶ And there came out against
them Zē′rah the Ē-thĭ-ō′pĭ-an
with an [a]host of a thousand
thousand, and three hundred
[b]chariots; and came unto [c]Mȧ-
rē′shah.

10 Then [d]Ā′sȧ went out against
him, and they set the [e]battle in
array in the valley of Zĕph′a-
thah at [c]Mȧ-rē′shah.

11 And [d]Ā′sȧ [f]cried unto the
LORD his God, and said, LORD,
[6]*it is* nothing with thee to help,
whether with many, or with
them that have no power: [g]help
us, O LORD our God; [h]for we
[i]rest on thee, and in thy name
we go against this multitude. O
LORD, thou *art* our God; let not
man prevail[G] against thee.

12 So [j]the LORD smote[G] the
[k]Ē-thĭ-ō′pĭ-anș before [d]Ā′sȧ, and
before [l]Jū′dah; and the Ē-thĭ′ō-
pĭ-anș fled.

13 And [d]Ā′sȧ and the people
that *were* with him pursued them
unto [m]Gē′rär: and [7]the [k]Ē-thĭ-
ō′pĭ-anș were overthrown, that
they could not recover themselves; for [j]they were destroyed
before the LORD, and before his
host; and they carried away very
much [n]spoil[G].

14 And they smote[G] all the cities
round about [m]Gē′rär; for the
[o]fear of the LORD came upon
them: and they spoiled[G] all the
cities; for there was exceeding
much [n]spoil[G] in them.

15 They smote also the [p]tents
of cattle, and carried away sheep
and camels in abundance, and
returned to [q]Jē-ru̧′sȧ-lĕm.

## CHAPTER 15

*Asa with Judah and many of Israel make a solemn covenant with God. 16 He removes Maachah his mother for her idolatry. 18 He brings dedicated things into the house of God, and enjoys a long peace.*

AND the [1,a]Spirit of God
[b]came upon Ăz-a-rī′ah the
son of Ō′ded:

2 And he went out to meet
[c]Ā′sȧ, and [d]said unto him, Hear
ye me, Ā′sȧ, and all [e]Jū′dah and
Běn′ja-mĭn; The LORD *is* with
you, while ye be with him; and
[f]if [g]ye seek him, [h]he will be
found of you; but if ye forsake
him, he [i]will forsake you.[S]

3 Now for a long season [e]Ĭș′-
ra-el *hath been* without the true
God, and without a [j]teaching
[k]priest, and without [l]law.

4 But when [m]they in their
[n]trouble did turn unto the LORD
God of Ĭș′ra-el, and sought him,
he was found of them.

5 And in those times *there was*
no peace to him that went out,
nor to him that came in, but
great vexations[G] *were* upon all the
inhabitants of the countries.

6 And [2,o]nation was destroyed
of nation, and city of city: for
God did vex[G] them with all [p]ad-
versity.[Q]

7 [q]Be ye strong therefore, and
let not your hands be [3]weak: [r]for
your work shall be rewarded.[Q]

8 ¶ And when [c]Ā′sȧ heard
these words, and the prophecy[G] of

n *Temporal Blessings, from God*, Psa. 103:2.
o *God, providence of*, Gen. 2:2.

**7**
p *Walls*, 1 Sam. 20:25.
q *Tower*, 2 Chr. 26:9.
r *Gates*, Deut. 3:5.
s *Seekers*, Isa. 55:6.

**8**
t *Armor*, 1 Sam. 17:54.
u *Spear*, 2 Kin. 11:10.
v *Judah, tribe of*, Num. 10:14.
w *Benjamin, tribe of*, Num. 1:37.
x *Shield*, 1 Kin. 14:27.
y *Archery*, Gen. 21:20.
z *Courage*, Deut. 31:7.
5 R. V. bucklers

**9**
a *Armies*, Deut. 11:4.
b *Chariot*, Josh. 11:4.
c *Mareshah*, Josh. 15:44.

**10**
d *Asa*, 1 Kin. 15:8.
e *Battle*, 1 Sam. 17:20.

**11**
f *Adversity, prayer in*, Psa. 10:6.
g *God, preserver*, Gen. 2:2.
h *Prayer, pleas offered in*, Acts 6:4.
i *Faith, instances of*, Mark 11:22.
6 R. V. there is none beside thee to help, between the mighty and him that hath no strength:

**12**
j *War, God in*, Judg. 3:2.
k *Ethiopia*, Isa. 18:1.
l *Judah, kingdom of*, 2 Chr. 11.17.

**13**
m *Gerar*, Gen. 20:1.
7 R. V. there fell of the Ethiopians so many that

n *Spoils*, 1 Chr. 26:27.

**14**
o *Fear of God*, Acts 9:31.

**15**
p *Tent*, Gen. 13:5.
q *Jerusalem*, Judg. 19:10.

**1**
a *Holy Spirit, inspiration of*, Acts 1:2.
b *Prophets, inspiration of*, Isa. 3:2.
1 R. V. spirit

**2**
c *Asa*, 1 Kin. 15:8.
d *Reproof, faithfulness in*, vs. 2–7; Prov. 17:10.
e *Judah, kingdom of*, 2 Chr. 11:17.
f *Contingencies in Divine Government*, 1 Kin. 3:14.
g *Seekers*, Isa. 55:6.
h *Promise, to seekers*, 2 Cor. 1:20.
i *Wicked, punishment of*, Psa. 73:3.

**3**
j *Instruction*, Prov. 23:23.
k *Minister, duties of, to teach*, Rom. 15:16.
l *Word of God*, Psa. 119:9.

**4**
m *Backsliders*, Jer. 3:22.
n *Afflictions, benefits of*, Psa. 34:19.

**6**
o *War*, Judg. 3:2.
p *Adversity, dispensation from God*, Psa. 10:6.
2 R. V. they were broken in pieces, nation against nation, and city against city:

**7**
q *Faith, enjoined*, Mark 11:22
r *Righteous, promises to*, Psa. 64:10.
3 R. V. slack:

8
s *Repentance, instances of*, Mark 1:4.
t *Ephraim*, Josh. 17:15.
u *Altar*, Gen. 8:20.
v *Temple, Solomon's, porch of*, 1 Kin. 6:17.
4 R. V. abominations
5 R. V. the hill country of

9
w *Foreigners*, Deut. 23:20.
x *Ephraim, tribe of*, Gen. 41:52.
y *Manasseh, tribe of*, Gen. 46:20.
z *Simeon, tribe of*, Num. 2:12.

a *Israel, after the revolt*, 1 Kin. 12:1.

10
b *Jerusalem*, Judg. 19:10.
c *Month, Sivan*, Ex. 12:2.
d *Asa*, 1 Kin. 15:8.

11
e *Spoils, dedicated to the Lord*, 1 Chr. 26:27.

12
f *Decision, instances of*, Isa. 50:7.
g *Covenant, of men with men*, Deut. 29:1.
h *Spiritual Desire*, Psa. 42:1.

13
i *Intolerance, of idolatrous religions*, Num. 11:28.
6 R. V. And

14
j *Oath*, Num. 5:19.
k *Trumpet*, Josh. 6:4.

15
l *Joy, instances of*, Psa. 5:11.
m *Prayer, answered, instances of*, Acts 6:4.
n *Temporal Blessings, from God*, Psa. 103:2.

16
o 2 Chr. 11:20; 1 Kin. 15:2; **or**, *Michaiah*, 2 Chr. 13:2.

Ō′ded the prophet, he took courage, and [s]put away the [4]abominable[C] idols out of all the land of [e]Jū′dah and Bĕn′ja-mĭn, and out of the cities which he had taken from [5]mount[C] [t]Ē′phră-ĭm, and renewed the [u]altar of the LORD, that *was* before the [v]porch of the LORD.

9 And he gathered all [e]Jū′dah and Bĕn′ja-mĭn, and the [w]strangers[C] with them out of [x]Ē′phră-ĭm and [y]Mă-năs′seh, and out of [z]Sĭm′e-on: for they fell to him out of [a]Ĭş′ra-el in abundance, when they saw that the LORD his God *was* with him.

10 So they gathered themselves together at [b]Jē-ru̥′sā-lĕm in the third [c]month, in the fifteenth year of the reign of [d]Ā′sȧ.

11 And they offered unto the LORD[C] the same time, of the [e]spoil[C] *which* they had brought, seven hundred oxen and seven thousand sheep.

12 And they [f]entered into a [g]covenant to [h]seek the LORD God of their fathers with all their heart and with all their soul;

13 [6]That whosoever would not seek the LORD God of Ĭş′ra-el [i]should be put to death, whether small or great, whether man or woman.

14 And they [j]sware unto the LORD with a loud voice, and with *shouting, and with [k]trumpets, and with cornets.

15 And all Jū′dah [l]rejoiced at the [j]oath: for they had sworn with all their heart, and [h]sought him with their whole desire; and [m]he was found of them: and the LORD gave them [n]rest[C] round about.

16 ¶ And also *concerning* [o]Mā′a-chah the mother of [d]Ā′sȧ the king, he removed her from *being* queen, because she had [p]made an [7]idol in a [q]grove: and Ā′sȧ [r]cut down her [8]idol, and stamped *it*, and burnt *it* at the [s]brook Kĭd′ron.

17 But the [t]high places were not taken away out of Ĭş′ra-el: nevertheless the [u]heart of [d,v]Ā′sȧ was [w]perfect all his days.

18 And he brought into the [x]house of God the things that his father had [y]dedicated, and [z]that he himself had dedicated, [a]silver, and [b]gold, and vessels.

19 And [c]there was no *more* war unto the five and thirtieth year of the reign of Ā′sȧ.

## CHAPTER 16

*Asa, by the aid of the Syrians, diverts Baasha from building Ramah. 7 Being reproved by Hanani, he puts him in prison. 12 When smitten with disease, he seeks not to God, but to the physicians. 13 His death and burial.*

IN the six and thirtieth year of the reign of [a]Ā′sȧ [b,c]Bā′a-shȧ king of [d]Ĭş′ra-el came up against [e]Jū′dah, and built [f]Rā′mah, to the intent that he might let none go out or come in to Ā′sȧ king of Jū′dah.

2 Then [a]Ā′sȧ brought out [g]silver and [h]gold out of the treasures[C] of the [i]house of the LORD and of the [j]king's house, and sent to [k]Bĕn–hā′dăd king of [l]Sўr′ĭ-ȧ, that dwelt at [m]Dă-măs′cus, saying,

3 *There is* a [n]league[C] between me and thee, as *there was* between my father and thy father: behold, I have sent thee [g]silver and [h]gold; go, break thy [o]league with [b]Bā′a-shȧ king of [d]Ĭş′ra-el, that he may depart from me.

4 And [k]Bĕn–hā′dăd hearkened unto king [a]Ā′sȧ, and sent the [p]captains of his [q]armies against the cities of [d]Ĭş′ra-el; and they smote [r]Ī′jon, and [s]Dăn, and

p *Idolatry*, 1 Sam. 15:23.
q *Groves*, Judg. 6:28.
r *Iconoclasm*, Num. 33:52.
s *Brook*, Deut. 8:7.
7 R. V. abominable image for an Asherah;
8 R. V. image.

17
t *High Places*, 1 Kin. 3:2.
u *Heart*, Psa. 44:21.
v *Rulers, righteous*, Ex. 18:21.
w *Perfection*, Heb. 6:1.

18
x *Temple, Solomon's*, 1 Kin. 6:17.
y *Dedication*, Ezra 6:17.
z *Liberality*, 1 Tim. 6:18.

a *Silver*, 1 Chr. 28:14.
b *Gold*, Ezek. 7:19.

19
c *Nation, peace of*, Isa. 2:4.

v.1–848 BC
See footnote, *Time*, Rev. 10:6.

1
a *Asa*, 1 Kin. 15:8.
b *Baasha*, 1 Kin. 15:16.
c 1 Kin. 15:17–22.
d *Israel, after the revolt*, 1 Kin. 12:1.
e *Judah, kingdom of*, 2 Chr. 11:17.
f *Ramah*, Judg. 19:13.

2
g *Silver*, 1 Chr. 28:14.
h *Gold*, Ezek. 7:19.
i *Temple, Solomon's*, 1 Kin. 6:17.
j *Palace*, 1 Kin. 21:1.
k 1 Kin. 15:18–20.
l *Syria*, 2 Kin. 6:23.
m *Damascus*, Isa. 8:4.

3
n *Treaty, between Judah and Syria*, 1 Kin. 5:12.
o *Alliances*, Josh. 9:15.

4
p *Captain*, Num. 31:48.
q *Armies, confederated*, Deut. 11:4.
r 1 Kin. 15:20; 2 Kin. 15:29.
s *Dan*, Judg. 18:29.

* **SHOUTING.** *In joy and praise*, 1 Chr. 15:28; 2 Chr. 15:12–14; Ezra 3:11–13; Psa. 5:11; 47:1; Isa. 12:6; Luke 17:15; 19:37–41; Acts 3:8, 9; Rev. 5:12–14.
*In battle*, Josh. 6:20; Judg. 7:18; 1 Sam. 17:20, 52; 2 Chr. 13:15.

v.4–848 BC See footnote, *Time*, Rev. 10:6.

*t* Or, *Abel-beth-maachah*, 2 Kin. 15:29.
*u* *Treasure Cities*, Ex. 1:11.
*v* *Cities*, Num. 35:8.
*w* *Naphtali, tribe of*, Num. 1:42.

6
*x* *Geba*, Josh. 21:17.
*y* *Mizpah*, Josh. 18:26.
1 R. V. had builded;

7
*z* *Prophets*, Isa. 3:2.

*a* *Asa*, 1 Kin. 15:8.
*b* *Judah, kingdom of*, 2 Chr. 11:17.
*c* *Reproof, faithfulness in*, Prov. 17:10.
*d* *False Confidence, instances of*, Psa. 30:6.
*e* *Syria*, 2 Kin. 6:23.

v.7–848 BC

8
*f* *Ethiopia*, Isa. 18:1.
*g* 2 Chr. 12:3.
*h* *Chariot*, Josh. 11:4.
*i* *Cavalry*, 1 Sam. 13:5.
*j* *God, providence of*, Gen. 2:2.

9
*k* *Promise, implied, to the righteous*, 2 Cor. 1:20.
*l* *Anthropomorphisms*, Gen. 11:5.
*m* *Righteous, promises to*, Psa. 64:10.
*n* *Perfection*, Heb. 6:1.

10
*o* *Rulers, wicked, instances of*, Ex. 18:21.
*p* *Anger, instances of*, Psa. 37:8.
*q* *Persecution, instances of*, John 15:20.
*r* *Minister, persecution of*, Rom. 15:16.
*s* *Reproof, despised*, Prov. 17:10.
*t* *Oppression*, Eccl. 5:8.

11
*u* *Book*, Num. 5:23.

[t]Ā′bel–mā′im, and all the [u]store[G]
[v]cities of [w]Năph′ta-lī.
5 And it came to pass, when
[b]Bā′a-shȧ heard *it*, that he left
off building of [f]Rā′mah, and let
his work cease.
6 Then [a]Ā′sȧ the king took all
Jū′dah; and they carried away
the stones of [f]Rā′mah, and the
timber thereof, wherewith [b]Bā′-
a-shȧ [1]was building; and he
built therewith [x]Gē′bȧ and
[y]Mĭz′pah.
7 ¶ And at that time Hȧ-nā′nī
the [z]seer came to [a]Ā′sȧ king of
[b]Jū′dah, and [c]said unto him, Because thou [d]hast relied on the
king of [e]Sўr′ĭ-ȧ, and not relied
on the LORD thy God, therefore
is the host of the king of Sўr′ĭ-ȧ
escaped out of thine hand.
8 Were not the [f]Ē-thĭ-ō′pĭ-ans
and the [g]Lu′bĭms a huge host,
with very many [h]chariots and
[i]horsemen? yet, because thou
didst rely on the LORD, [j]he delivered them into thine hand.
9 [k]For the [l]eyes of the LORD
run to and fro throughout the
whole earth, to shew himself
strong in the behalf of [m]*them*
whose heart *is* [n]perfect toward
him. [c]Herein thou hast done
foolishly: therefore from henceforth thou shalt have wars.[S]
10 Then [a,o]Ā′sȧ was [p]wroth[G]
with the seer, and [q,r]put him in
a prison house; for [s]*he was* in a
rage with him because of this
*thing*. And Ā′sȧ [t]oppressed *some*
of the people the same time.
11 ¶ And, behold, the acts of
[a]Ā′sȧ, first and last, lo, they *are*
written in the [u]book of the kings
of [b]Jū′dah and Ĭs′ra-el.

12 And [a]Ā′sȧ in the thirty and
ninth year of his reign was diseased in his feet, until his [v]dis-
ease *was* exceeding[G] *great*: yet [w]in
his disease he sought[G] not to the
LORD, but to the *physicians.
13 And [a]Ā′sȧ [x]slept with his fathers, and died in the one and
fortieth year of his reign.
14 And they buried him in his
own [y]sepulchres[G], which he had
[2]made for himself in the [z]city
of Dā′vid, and [a]laid him in the
bed which was filled with sweet
odours and divers[G] kinds *of*
[b]*spices* prepared by the [c]apothe-
caries[G]′ †art: and they made a
very great [d]burning for him.

## CHAPTER 17

*Jehoshaphat, succeeding Asa, reigns well, and prospers. 7 He sends Levites with the princes to teach in Judah. 10 His enemies bring him presents and tribute. 12 His greatness, and his captains and armies.*

AND [a]Jĕ-hŏsh′a-phăt his son
reigned in his stead, and
strengthened himself against
[b]Ĭs′ra-el.
2 And he placed forces[G] in all the
fenced[G] [c]cities of [d]Jū′dah, and set
[e]garrisons in the land of Jū′dah,
and in the cities of Ē′phră-ĭm,
which [f]Ā′sȧ his father had taken.
3 And the [g]LORD was with
[a,h]Jĕ-hŏsh′a-phăt, because he
[i]walked [j]in the first ways of his
father [k]Dā′vid, and sought[G] not
unto [l]Bā′al-ĭm;
4 But sought[G] to the *LORD* God
of his father, and [m]walked in his
commandments, and not after
the doings of Ĭs′ra-el.
5 Therefore the [n]LORD [o]stab-
lished[G] the kingdom in his hand;
and all [d]Jū′dah brought to
[a]Jĕ-hŏsh′a-phăt [o]presents[G]; and

v.12–845 BC See footnote, *Time*, Rev. 10:6.

12
*v* *Disease*, Ex. 15:26.
*w* *Afflictions, impenitence in*, Psa. 34:19.

13
*x* *Death*, Num. 23:10.

v.13–843 BC

14
*y* *Burying Places*, Gen. 23:4.
*z* *Jerusalem*, Judg. 19:10.

*a* *Burial*, Acts 8:2.
*b* *Spices*, 1 Kin. 10:2.
*c* *Apothecary*, Neh. 3:8.
*d* *Dead, incense burnt for*, 2 Kin. 4:32.
2 R. V. hewn out

1
*a* *Jehoshaphat*, 2 Kin. 12:18.
*b* *Israel, after the revolt*, 1 Kin. 12:1.

2
*c* *Cities, fortified*, Num. 35:8.
*d* *Judah, kingdom of*, 2 Chr. 11:17.
*e* *Garrison*, 1 Sam. 13:3.
*f* *Asa*, 1 Kin. 15:8.

3
*g* *God, providence of*, Gen. 2:2.
*h* *Rulers, righteous*, Ex. 18:21.
*i* *Obedience, instances of*, Heb. 5:8.
*j* *Influence, good*, 1 Cor. 7:14.
*k* *David*, 1 Sam. 16:13.
*l* Or, *Baal*, 2 Kin. 17:16.

4
*m* *Faithfulness, instances of*, Luke 16:10.

5
*n* *Government, God in*, Isa. 22:21.
*o* *Presents*, Gen. 32:13.

* **PHYSICIAN,** Gen. 50:2; 2 Chr. 16:12; Mark 5:26; Luke 8:43. *Proverbs about*, Matt. 9:12; Mark 2:17; Luke 4:23; 5:31. *Luke, a physician*, Col. 4:14.
See footnote, DISEASE, Ex. 15:26.
**Figurative,** Job 13:4; Jer. 8:22.

† **ART.** *Invention of musical instruments, and instruments of iron and copper (or brass, according to the text, the accuracy of which is doubtful)*, Gen. 4:21, 22. *Carpentry*, Gen. 6:14–16. *Of the apothecary or perfumer*, Ex. 30:25, 35. *Of the armorer*, 1 Sam. 8:12. *Of the baker*, Gen. 40:1; 1 Sam. 8:13. *Of the brickmaker*, Gen. 11:3; Ex. 5:7, 8, 18. *Of the calker*, Ezek. 27:9, 27. *Of the goldsmith*, Isa. 40:19. *Of the mariner*, Ezek. 27:8, 9. *Of the mason*, 2 Sam. 5:11; 2 Chr. 24:12. *Of the musician*, 1 Sam. 18:6; 1 Chr. 15:16. *Of the potter*, Isa. 64:8; Jer. 18:3; Lam. 4:2; Zech. 11:13. *Of the stonecutter*, Ex. 20:25; 1 Chr. 22:15. *Of the shipbuilder*, 1 Kin. 9:26. *Of the smelter of metals*, Job 28:2. *Of the spinner*, Ex. 35:25; Prov. 31:19. *Of the tailor*, Ex. 28:3. *Of the tanner*, Acts 9:43; 10:6. *Of the tentmaker*, Gen. 4:20; Acts 18:3. *Of the weaver*, Ex. 35:35; John 19:23.
See footnote, ARTISANS, 1 Chr. 29:5.

*p Temporal Blessings, from God,* Psa. 103:2.

**6**

*q Iconoclasm,* Num. 33:52.

*r High Places,* 1 Kin. 3:2.

*s Groves,* Judg. 6:28.

1 R. V. the Asherim

**7**

*t School, state,* Acts 19:9.

*u Teachers, itinerant,* 1 Chr. 25:8.

*v Instruction, in religion,* Prov. 23:23.

v.7–840 BC

**8**

*w Levites,* Deut. 10:8.

*x Priest,* Lev. 1:5.

**9**

*y Word of God,* Psa. 119:9.

*z Law, of Moses, expounded,* Deut. 33:2.

**10**

*a Fear of God,* Acts 9:31.

*b Judah, kingdom of,* 2 Chr. 11:17.

*c Jehoshaphat,* 2 Kin. 12:18.

**11**

*d Philistines,* Gen. 26:14.

*e Presents,* Gen. 32:13.

*f Tribute,* Ezra 4:13.

*g King, emoluments of,* 2 Kin. 3:10.

*h Sheep,* Deut. 32:14.

*i Goat,* Deut. 14:4.

**12**

*i Cities, treasure,* Num. 35:8.

**13**

*k Armies, standing,* Deut. 11:4.

*l Courage,* Deut. 31:7.

*m Jerusalem,* Judg. 19:10.

2 R. V. many works

he had [p]riches and [p]honour in abundance.

6 And his heart was lifted up in the ways of the LORD: moreover he [q]took away the [r]high places and [1,s]groves[C] out of [d]Jū'dah.

7 ¶ [t]Also in the third year of his reign he sent to his [u]princes, *even* to Bĕn–hā'il, and to Ō-ba-dī'ah, and to Zĕch-a-rī'ah, and to Nē-thăn'e-el, and to Mī-chā'-iah, to [v]teach in the cities of Jū'dah.

8 And with them *he sent* [u,w]Lē'vītes, *even* Shĕm-a-ī'ah, and Nĕth-a-nī'ah, and Zĕb-a-dī'ah, and Ā'sa-hĕl, and Shē-mĭr'a-mŏth, and Jė-hŏn'a-than, and Ăd-o-nī'jah, and Tō-bī'jah, and Tŏb'–ăd-o-nī'jah, Lē'vītes; and with them Ē-lĭsh'a-mȧ and Jė-hō'ram, [u,x]priests.

9 And they [v]taught in Jū'dah, and *had* the book of the [y,z]law of the LORD with them, and went about throughout all the cities of Jū'dah, and taught the people.

10 ¶ And the [a]fear of the LORD fell upon all the kingdoms of the lands that *were* round about [b]Jū'dah, so that they made no war against [c]Jė-hŏsh'a-phăt.

11 Also *some* of the [d]Phĭ-lĭs'-tĭneș brought [c]Jė-hŏsh'a-phăt [e]presents, and [f,g]tribute silver; and the *Ā-rā'bĭ-anș brought him flocks, seven thousand and seven hundred [h]rams, and seven thousand and seven hundred he [i]goats.

12 ¶ And [c]Jė-hŏsh'a-phăt waxed[C] great exceedingly; and he built in Jū'dah castles,[C] and [i]cities of store.[C]

13 And he had [2]much business in the cities of [b]Jū'dah: and the [k]men of war, mighty men of [l]valour, *were* in [m]Jė-ru'sȧ-lĕm.

14 And these *are* the numbers of them according to the house of their fathers: Of [n]Jū'dah, the [o]captains of thousands; Ăd'nah the chief, and with him mighty men of [l]valour three hundred thousand.

15 And next to him *was* [p]Jė-hō-hā'nan the [o]captain, and with him two hundred and fourscore thousand.

16 And next him *was* Ăm-a-sī'ah the son of Zĭch'rī, who willingly offered himself unto the LORD; and with him two hundred thousand mighty men of [l]valour.

17 And of [q]Bĕn'ja-mĭn; Ē-lī'a-dȧ a mighty man of [l]valour, and with him armed men with [r]bow and [s]shield two hundred thousand.

18 And next him *was* Jė-hŏz'a-băd, and with him an hundred and fourscore thousand ready prepared for the war.

19 These waited on the king, beside *those* whom the king put in the fenced[C] [t]cities throughout all Jū'dah.

## CHAPTER 18

*Jehoshaphat and Ahab go up against Ramoth-gilead. 4 Ahab's false prophets assure him of victory. 8 Micaiah, being sent for, prophesies. 28 Jehoshaphat's escape. 33 Ahab is slain.*

NOW [a]Jė-hŏsh'a-phăt had [b]riches and honour in abundance, and [c]joined affinity[C] with [d]Ā'hăb.

2 [e]And after *certain* years he went down to [d]Ā'hăb to [f]Sȧ-mā'-rī-ȧ. [g]And Ā'hăb killed sheep and oxen for him in abundance, and for the people that *he had* with him, and persuaded him to go[C] up *with him* to [h]Rā'moth–gĭl'e-ăd.

3 And [d]Ā'hăb king of [i]Iș'ra-el said unto [a]Jė-hŏsh'a-phăt king of [j]Jū'dah, Wilt thou go with me

**14**

*n Judah, tribe of,* Num. 10:14.

*o Captain,* Num. 31:48.

**15**

*p* 2 Chr. 23:1.

**17**

*q Benjamin, tribe of,* Num. 1:37.

*r Archery,* Gen. 21.20.

*s Shield,* 1 Kin. 14:27.

**19**

*t Cities, fortified,* Num. 35:8.

**1**

*a Jehoshaphat,* 2 Kin. 12:18.

*b Riches,* Eccl. 4:8.

*c Alliances, instances of,* Josh. 9:15.

*d Ahab,* 1 Kin. 16:29.

**2**

*e* 1 Kin. 22:2–35.

*f Samaria,* 1 Kin. 16:24.

*g Feasts,* Mark 12:39.

*h Ramoth-gilead,* Josh. 20:8.

**3**

*i Israel, after the revolt,* 1 Kin. 12:1.

*j Judah, kingdom of,* 2 Chr. 11:17.

* **ARABIANS.** *Pay tribute, to Solomon,* 2 Chr. 9:14; *to Jehoshaphat,* 2 Chr. 17:11. *Invade and defeat Judah,* 2 Chr. 21:16, 17; 22:1. *Defeated by Uzziah,* 2 Chr. 26:7. *Oppose Nehemiah's rebuilding the walls of Jerusalem,* Neh. 2:19; 4:7. *Commerce of,* Ezek. 27:21. *Gospel preached to,* Acts 2:11; Gal. 1:17. *Prophecies concerning,* Isa. 21:13–17; 42:11; 60:7; Jer. 25:24. See footnote, ARABIA, 2 Chr. 9:14.

k *Armies, confederated,* Deut. 11:4.

4

l *Guidance, prayer for,* Psa. 48:14.
m *Armies, religious ceremonies in,* Deut. 11:4.

5

n *Prophets, false,* Isa. 3:2.

7

o *Hatred,* Prov. 15:17.
p 1 Kin. 22:8–28.

9

q *Throne,* 1 Kin. 2:19.
r *Gates,* Deut. 3:5.
1 R. V. an open

10

s *Zedekiah,* 1 Kin. 22:11.
t 1 Kin. 22:11, 24.
u *Horn, symbolical,* 1 Kin. 1:39.
v *Syria,* 2 Kin. 6:23.

to [h]Rā-moth–gĭl′e-ăd? And he answered him, I *am* as thou *art,* and my people as thy people; and [c,k]*we will be* with thee in the war.

4 ¶ And [a]Jē-hŏsh′a-phăt said unto the [d]king of [i]Ĭş′ra-el, [l,m]Enquire,[C] I pray thee, at the word of the LORD to day.

5 Therefore the [d]king of [i]Ĭş′-ra-el gathered together of [n]prophets four hundred men, and said unto them, Shall we go to [h]Rā′moth–gĭl′e-ăd to battle, or shall I forbear? And they said, Go up; for God will deliver *it* into the king's hand.

6 ¶ But [a]Jē-hŏsh′a-phăt said, *Is there* not here a prophet of the LORD besides, that we might enquire of him?

7 And the king of [i]Ĭş′ra-el said unto [a]Jē-hŏsh′a-phăt, *There is* yet one man, by whom we may enquire of the LORD: but I [o]hate him; for he never prophesied good unto me, but always evil: the same *is* [p]Mī-cā′iah the son of Ĭm′lȧ. And Jē-hŏsh′-a-phăt said, Let not the king say so.

8 And the [d]king of [i]Ĭş′ra-el called for one *of his* officers,[C] and said, Fetch quickly [p]Mī-cā′iah the son of Ĭm′lȧ.

9 And the king of Ĭş′ra-el and [a]Jē-hŏsh′a-phăt king of [j]Jū′dah sat either of them on his [q]throne, clothed in *their* robes, and they sat in [1]a void[C] place at the entering in of the [r]gate of [f]Să-mā′rĭ-ȧ; and all the [n]prophets prophesied before them.

10 And [s]Zĕd-e-kī′ah the son of [t]Chĕ-nā′a-nah had made him [u]horns of iron, and said, Thus saith the LORD, With these thou shalt push [v]Sȳr′ĭ-ȧ until they be consumed.

11 And all the [n]prophets prophesied so, saying, Go up to [h]Rā′moth–gĭl′e-ăd, and prosper: for the LORD shall deliver *it* into the hand of the king.

12 And the messenger that went to call [p]Mī-cā′iah spake to him, saying, [w]Behold, the words of the [n]prophets *declare* good to the king with one[C] assent; [x]let thy word therefore, I pray thee, be like one of their's, and speak thou good.

13 And [p,y]Mī-cā′iah said, *As* the LORD liveth, even what my God [z]saith, that will I speak.

14 And when he was come to the king, the king said unto him, [a]Mī-cā′iah, shall we go to [b]Rā′-moth–gĭl′e-ăd to battle, or shall I forbear? And he said, [c]Go ye up, and prosper, and they shall be delivered into your hand.

15 And the king said to him, How many times shall I adjure[C] thee that thou say nothing but the truth to me in the name of the LORD?

16 Then he [d]said, I did [e]see all Ĭş′ra-el scattered upon the mountains, as sheep that have no shepherd: and the LORD said, These have no master; let them return *therefore* every[Q] man to his house in peace.

17 And the [f]king of Ĭş′ra-el said to [g]Jē-hŏsh′a-phăt, Did I not tell thee *that* he would not prophesy[C] good unto me, but evil?

18 Again he said, Therefore hear the word of the LORD; I [e]saw the LORD sitting upon his [h]throne, and all the [i]host of heaven standing on his right hand and *on* his left.[Q]

19 And the LORD said, Who shall entice [f]Ā′hăb king of Ĭş′-ra-el,[C] that he may go up and fall at [b]Rā′moth–gĭl′e-ăd? And one spake saying after this manner, and another saying after that manner.

20 Then there came out a spirit, and stood before the LORD, and

12

w *Influence, evil,* 1 Cor. 7:14.
x *Temptation, leading into,* Luke 11:4.

13

y *Minister, faithful,* Rom. 15:16.
z *Inspiration,* Job 32:8.

14

a 1 Kin. 22:22–28.
b *Ramoth-gilead,* Josh. 20:8.
c *Irony,* Mark 12:14.

16

d *Reproof, faithfulness in,* Prov. 17:10.
e *Vision,* vs. 16–22; Acts 9:10.

17

f *Ahab,* 1 Kin. 16:29.
g *Jehoshaphat,* 2 Kin. 12:18.

18

h *Throne, figurative,* 1 Kin. 2:19.
i *Angel,* Heb. 1:13.

said, I will entice him. And the
LORD said unto him, Wherewith[C]?
21 [s]And he said, I will go out,
and be a [j]lying spirit in the
mouth of all his [k]prophets. And
*the* LORD said, Thou shalt entice *him*, and thou shalt also prevail: go out, and do *even* so.
22 Now therefore, behold, the
LORD hath put a [j]lying spirit in
the mouth of these thy [k]proph-
ets, and the LORD hath spoken
evil against thee.[s]
23 ¶ Then [l]Zĕd-e-kī'ah the son
of [m]Chĕ-nā'a-nah came near,
and [n,o]smote[C] [a]Mī-cā'iah upon
the cheek, and [p]said, Which way
went the [2]Spirit of the LORD
from me to speak unto thee?
24 And [a]Mī-cā'iah said, Behold, thou shalt see on that day
when thou shalt go into an [q]in-
ner chamber to hide thyself.
25 [Q]Then the [f]king of Īṣ'ra-el
said, Take ye [a]Mī-cā'iah, and
carry him back to [r]Ā'mon the
governor of the city, and to [r]Jō'-
ăsh the king's son;
26 And say, [s]Thus saith the
king, [n,t]Put [u]this *fellow* in the
[v]prison, and feed him with
[w]bread of affliction and with
[x]water of affliction, until I return in peace.[Q]
27 And [a]Mī-cā'iah said, If thou
certainly return in peace, *then*
hath not the LORD spoken by
me. And he said, Hearken[C], all
ye people.
28 So the [f]king of Īṣ'ra-el and
[g]Jĕ-hŏsh'a-phăt the king of
Jū'-dah went up to [b]Rā'moth-
gĭl'e-ăd.
29 And the [f]king of Īṣ'ra-el
said unto [g]Jĕ-hŏsh'a-phăt, I will
disguise myself, and will go to
the battle; but put thou on thy
robes. So the king of Īṣ'ra-el
disguised himself; and they went
to the battle.
30 Now the king of [y]Sȳr'ĭ-ȧ had
commanded the [z]captains of the
[a]chariots that *were* with him,
saying, Fight ye not with small
or great, save[C] only with the king
of Īṣ'ra-el.
31 And it came to pass, when
the captains of the [a]chariots saw
[b]Jĕ-hŏsh'a-phăt, that they said,
It *is* the king of Īṣ'ra-el. Therefore they [3]compassed[C] about him
to fight: but Jĕ-hŏsh'a-phăt
[c]cried out, and the LORD helped
him; and God moved them *to*
*depart* from him.
32 For it came to pass, that,
when the [d]captains of the [a]char-
iots perceived that it was not the
king of Īṣ'ra-el, they turned back
again from pursuing him.
33 And a *certain* man [e]drew a
bow at a venture[C], and smote the
[f]king of Īṣ'ra-el between[C] the
joints of the [g]harness: therefore
he said to his chariot man, Turn
thine hand, that thou mayest
carry me out of the host; for I
am wounded.
34 And the battle increased
that day: howbeit[C] the [f]king of
Īṣ'ra-el stayed[C] *himself* up in *his*
[a]chariot against the [h]Sȳr'ĭ-anṣ
until the even: and about the
time of the sun going down he
[i]died.

## CHAPTER 19

*Jehoshaphat is reproved by Jehu the prophet. 5 His instructions to the judges, 8 and to the priests and Levites.*

AND [a]Jĕ-hŏsh'a-phăt the king
of [b]Jū'dah returned to his
house in peace to [c]Jĕ-ru'sȧ-lĕm.
2 [T]And [d]Jē'hū the son of [d]Hȧ-
nā'nī the seer went out to meet
him, and [e]said to king [a]Jĕ-hŏsh'-
a-phăt, Shouldest thou [f]help the
[1,g]ungodly[C], and [h]love them that
hate the LORD? therefore *is*
wrath upon thee from before the
LORD.
3 Nevertheless there are good
things found in thee, in that
thou hast [i]taken away the
[2,j]groves[C] out of the land, and

**21**
*j Evil Spirit*, 1 Sam. 18:10.
*k Prophets, false*, Isa. 3:2.

**23**
*l Zedekiah*, 1 Kin. 22:11.
m 1 Kin. 22:11, 24.
*n Persecution, of the righteous*, John 15:20.
*o Presumption*, Psa. 19:13.
*p Mocking*, 1 Kin. 18:27.
2 R. V. spirit

**24**
*q House, architecture of*, Esth. 8:1.

**25**
r 1 Kin. 22:26.

**26**
*s Government, monarchical, tyranny in*, Isa. 22:21.
*t Revenge, exemplified*, Ezek. 25:15.
*u Prisoners*, Psa. 79:11.
*v Prison*, Gen. 39:20.
*w Bread, of affliction*, Ezek. 4:13.
*x Water, of affliction*, 1 Kin. 17:10.

**30**
*y Syria*, 2 Kin. 6:23.

*z Captain*, Num. 31:48.
*a Chariot*, Josh. 11:4.

**31**
*b Jehoshaphat*, 2 Kin. 12:18.
*c Prayer, answered, instances of*, Acts 6:4.
3 R. V. turned about to fight against him:

**32**
*d Captain*, Num. 31:48.

**33**
*e Archery*, Gen. 21:20.
*f Ahab*, 1 Kin. 16:29.
*g Coat of Mail*, 1 Sam. 17:5.

**34**
*h Syria*, 2 Kin. 6:23.
*i Death*, Num. 23:10.

**1**
*a Jehoshaphat*, 2 Kin. 12:18.
*b Judah, kingdom of*, 2 Chr. 11:17.
*c Jerusalem*, Judg. 19:10.

**2**
d 2 Chr. 20:34; 1 Kin. 16:1, 7.
*e Reproof, faithfulness in*, Prov. 17:10.
*f Alliances*, Josh. 9:15.
*g Evil Company*, Prov. 13:20.
*h Fellowship, with the wicked*, 1 Cor. 1:9.
1 R. V. wicked,

**3**
*i Iconoclasm*, Num. 33:52.
*j Groves*, Judg. 6:28.
2 R. V. Asheroth

k *Heart*, Psa. 44: 21.

4

l *Rulers, righteous, instances of*, Ex. 18:21.

m *Beer-sheba*, Judg. 20:1.

n *Ephraim*, Josh. 17:15.

3 R. V. the hill country of

5

o *Court*, Ex. 18:26.

p *Cities, fortified*, Num. 35:8.

6

q *Judge, must be righteous*, Judg. 2:18.

r *God, judge*, Gen. 2:2.

7

s *Fear of God*, Acts 9:31.

t *Watchfulness, enjoined*, Matt. 24: 42.

u *God, holiness of*, Gen. 2:2.

v *Holiness, attribute of God*, Ex. 39:30.

w *Respect, of persons*, Prov. 24: 23.

8

x *Levites, duties of*, Deut. 10:8.

y *Priest, duties of*, Lev. 1:5.

z *Court, civil*, Ex. 18:26.

a *Judge, priests and Levites as*, Judg. 2:18.

9

b *Faithfulness, exhortation to*, Luke 16:10.

c *Fear of God*, Acts 9:31.

d *Integrity*, Job 2:3.

10

4 R. V. whensoever any controversy shall

5 R. V. from

11

e *Minister, an officer of civil government*, 2 Chr. 9:4.

hast prepared thine [k]heart to seek God.

4 And [a,l]Jē-hŏsh'a-phăt dwelt at [c]Jē-rụ'să-lĕm: and he went out again through the people from [m]Bē'er–shē'bȧ to [3]mount [n]Ē'phră-ĭm, and brought them back unto the LORD God of their fathers.

5 And he set [o]judges in the land throughout all the fenced[G] [p]cities of [b]Jū'dah, city by city,

6 And said to the [q]judges, Take heed what ye do: for ye judge not for man, but for the LORD, who *is* with you in the [r]judgment.

7 Wherefore now let the [s]fear of the LORD be upon you; [t]take heed and do *it*: for *there is* [u,v]no iniquity with the LORD our God, nor [w]respect of persons, nor taking of gifts.[G Q]

8 Moreover in Jē-rụ'să-lĕm did Jē-hŏsh'a-phăt set of the [x]Lē'vītes, and *of* the [y]priests, and of the chief[G] of the fathers of Ĭṣ'ra-el, for the [z,a]judgment of the LORD, and for controversies, when they returned to Jē-rụ'-să-lĕm.

9 And he charged them, saying, [b]Thus shall ye do in the [c]fear of the LORD, faithfully, and [d]with a perfect[G] heart.

10 And [4]what cause soever shall come to you [5]of your brethren that dwell in their cities, between blood and blood, between law and commandment, statutes and judgments,[G] ye shall even warn them that they trespass[G] not against the LORD, and *so* wrath come upon you, and upon your brethren: this do, and ye shall not trespass.[G T]

11 And, behold, Ăm-a-rī'ah the chief priest *is* over you in all matters of the LORD; and [e]Zĕb-a-dī'ah the son of Ĭsh'ma-el, the ruler of the house of Jū'dah, for all the king's matters: also the [f]Lē'vītes *shall be* officers before you. [b,g]Deal courageously, and [h]the LORD shall be with the good.

## CHAPTER 20

*Moab and Ammon invade Judah. 3 Jehoshaphat proclaims a fast. 5 His prayer. 14 The prophecy of Jahaziel. 20 Jehoshaphat exhorts the people to trust in the Lord. 22 The great overthrow of the enemy. 26 The people return in triumph. 31 Jehoshaphat's reign. 35 His ships broken at Ezion-gaber.*

IT came to pass after this also, *that* the [a]children of Mō'ab, and the [b]children of Ăm'mŏn, and [c]with them *other* beside the Ăm'mon-ītes, came against [d]Jē-hŏsh'a-phăt to [e]battle.

2 Then there came some that told [d]Jē-hŏsh'a-phăt, saying, There cometh a great multitude against thee from beyond the [f]sea [1]on this side [g]Sȳr'ĭ-ȧ; and, behold, they *be* in Hăz'a-zon–tā'mar, which *is* *Ĕn–gē'dī.

3 And [d,h]Jē-hŏsh'a-phăt feared, and set himself to [i,j]seek the LORD, and proclaimed a [k]fast throughout all [l]Jū'dah.

4 And [l]Jū'dah gathered themselves together, to [m,n,o]ask *help* of the LORD: even out of all the cities of Jū'dah [i]they came to seek the LORD.

5 ¶ And [d]Jē-hŏsh'a-phăt stood in the congregation of Jū'dah and [p]Jē-rụ'să-lĕm, in the [q]house of the LORD, before the new [r]court,

6 And [m]said, O LORD God of our fathers, *art* not thou God in [s]heaven? and [t]rulest *not* thou over all the kingdoms of the [2]heathen[G]? and in thine hand *is there not* [u]power and might, so that none is able to withstand thee?[S]

7 *Art* not thou our God, [v]*who* didst drive out the inhabitants of this land before thy people Ĭṣ'-

f *Levites, duties of*, Deut. 10:8.

g *Courage*, Deut. 31:7.

h *Promise, to the righteous*, 2 Cor. 1:20.

1

a *Moabites*, Gen. 19:37.

b *Ammonites*, Deut. 2:20.

c *Armies, confederated*, Deut. 11:4.

d *Jehoshaphat*, 2 Kin. 12:18.

e *War*, Judg. 3:2.

2

f *Dead Sea*, Gen. 14:3.

g *Syria*, 2 Kin. 6:23.

1 R. V. from Syria.

3

h *Rulers, righteous, instances of*, Ex. 18:21.

i *Seekers*, Isa. 55:6.

j *Repentance, instances of*, Mark 1:4.

k *Fasting, instances of*, Zech. 8:19.

l *Judah, kingdom of*, 2 Chr. 11:17.

4

m *Prayer, in adversity*, Acts 6:4.

n *Adversity, prayer in*, Psa. 10:6.

o *Battle, prayer before*, 1 Sam. 17: 20.

5

p *Jerusalem*, Judg. 19:10.

q *Temple, Solomon's*, 1 Kin. 6:17.

r *Court, of the temple*, Ex. 38:9.

6

s *Heaven, God's dwelling place*, Luke 18:22.

t *God, sovereign*, Gen. 2:2.

u *God, power of*, Gen. 2:2.

2 R. V. nations?

7

v *God, providence of*, Gen. 2:2.

* **EN-GEDI** (*fountain of the kid*), called HAZEZON-TAMAR. *A city allotted to Judah*, Josh. 15:62. *Built by the Amorites*, Gen. 14:7; 2 Chr. 20:2. *Famous for its vineyards*, Song 1:14. Wilderness of, in the vicinity of the Dead Sea. *David uses as a stronghold*, 1 Sam. 23:29; 24. *Cave of*, 1 Sam. 24:3.

ra-el, and gavest it to the seed of [w]Ā′brā-hăm thy friend for ever?[Q]

8 And they dwelt therein, and have built thee a [x,y]sanctuary therein for thy name, saying,

9 If, *when* evil cometh upon us, *as* the [z]sword, [a]judgment, or [b]pestilence, or [c]famine, we stand before [d]this house, and in thy presence, (for thy name *is* in this house,) and [e]cry unto thee in our [f]affliction, then [g]thou wilt hear and [h]help.

10 And now, behold, the children of [i]Ăm′mŏn and [j]Mō′ab and mount [k]Sē′īr, whom thou wouldest not let Ĭs′ra-el invade, when they came out of the land of [l]Ē′ġy̆pt, but they turned from them, and destroyed them not;

11 Behold, *I say, how* they reward us, to come to cast us out of thy possession, which [m]thou hast given us to inherit.

12 O our God, wilt thou not [n]judge them? for we have no might against this great company that cometh against us; neither know we what to do: but [h]our eyes *are* upon thee.[T]

13 And all [o]Jū′dah [p]stood before the LORD, with their little ones, their wives, and their [q]children.

14 Then upon Jă-hā′zĭ-el the son of Zĕch-a-rī′ah, the son of Bĕ-nā′iah, the son of Jĕ-ī′el, the son of [r]Măt-ta-nī′ah, a [s]Lē′vīte of the sons of [t]Ā′saph, [u]came the [3,v]Spirit of the LORD in the midst of the congregation;

15 And[S] he said, Hearken ye, all [o]Jū′dah, and ye inhabitants of [w]Jĕ-ru′să-lĕm, and thou king [x]Jĕ-hŏsh′a-phăt, Thus saith the LORD unto you, [y]Be not afraid nor dismayed by reason of this great multitude; for [z]the battle *is* not your's, but God's.

16 To morrow go ye down against them: behold, they come up by the cliff of Zīz; and ye shall find them at the end of the [4]brook, before the wilderness of Jĕr′u-el.[S]

17 Ye shall not *need* to fight in this *battle*: set yourselves, stand ye *still*, and see the [z]salvation of the LORD with you, O Jū′dah and Jĕ-ru′să-lĕm: [y]fear not, nor be dismayed; to morrow go out against them: for [z]the LORD *will be* with you.[S]

18 And [a]Jĕ-hŏsh′a-phăt [b]bowed his head with *his* face to the ground: and all [c]Jū′dah and the inhabitants of [d]Jĕ-ru′să-lĕm fell before the LORD, [e]worshipping the LORD.

19 And the [f]Lē′vītes, of the children of the [g]Kō′hath-ītes, and of the children of the Kôr′hītes, stood up to [h,i]praise the LORD God of Ĭs′ra-el with a loud voice on high.

20 ¶ And they rose early in the morning, and went forth into the wilderness of [j]Tē-kō′ȧ: and as they went forth, [a]Jĕ-hŏsh′a-phăt stood and said, Hear me, O Jū′dah, and ye inhabitants of [d]Jĕ-ru′să-lĕm; [k,l]Believe in the LORD your God, so shall ye be established; believe his prophets, so shall ye prosper.[S]

21 And when he had [m]consulted with the people, he appointed [f]singers unto the LORD, and that should [h]praise the beauty of [n]holiness, as they went out before the [o]army, and to say, Praise the LORD; for his [p]mercy *endureth* for ever.[S]

22 ¶ And when [f]they began to [i]sing and to [h]praise, the LORD [q]set [r]ambushments[G] against the [s]children of Ăm′mŏn, [t]Mō′ab, and mount [u]Sē′īr, which were come against [c]Jū′dah; and they were smitten.[G]

23 For the [s]children of Ăm′mŏn and [t]Mō′ab stood up against the inhabitants of mount [u]Sē′īr, utterly to slay and destroy *them*:

w *Abraham*, Gen. 17:5.

**8**

x *Sanctuary*, Lev. 4:6.
y *Church, called sanctuary*, 1 Kin. 9:3.

**9**

z *Sword, figurative*, 1 Chr. 21:5.
a *Judgments*, Ex. 6:6.
b *Plague*, Ex. 11:1.
c *Famine*, 2 Kin. 8:1.
d *Temple, Solomon's*, 1 Kin. 6:17.
e *Prayer, in adversity*, Acts 6:4.
f *Adversity, prayer in*, Psa. 10:6.
g *Faith*, Mark 11:22.
h *God, preserver*, Gen. 2:2.

**10**

i *Ammonites*, Deut. 2:20.
j *Moabites*, Gen. 19:37.
k *Seir*, Deut. 1:2.
l *Egypt*, Gen. 41:8.

**11**

m *God, providence of*, Gen. 2:2.

**12**

n *God, judge*, Gen. 2:2.

**13**

o *Judah, kingdom of*, 2 Chr. 11:17.
p *Worship*, Gen. 22:5.
q *Children, attend divine worship*, Mark 10:14.

**14**

r *Mattaniah*, 1 Chr. 9:15.
s *Levites*, Deut. 10:8.
t *Asaph*, 1 Chr. 15:17.
u *Inspiration*, Job 32:8.
v *Holy Spirit, inspiration of*, Acts 1:2.
3 R. V. spirit

**15**

w *Jerusalem*, Judg. 19:10.
x *Jehoshaphat*, 2 Kin. 12:18.
y *Faith, enjoined*, vs. 17, 20; Mark 11:22.
z *God, preserver*, Gen. 2:2.

**16**

4 R. V. valley.

**18**

a *Jehoshaphat*, 2 Kin. 12:18.
b *Prayer, postures in*, Acts 6:4.
c *Judah, kingdom of*, 2 Chr. 11:17.
d *Jerusalem*, Judg. 19:10.
e *Worship*, Gen. 22:5.

**19**

f *Choir*, 1 Chr. 15:16.
g *Kohathites*, Num. 3:27.
h *Praise*, Psa. 150:1.
i *Music*, 2 Chr. 5:13.

**20**

j *Tekoa*, Jer. 6:1.
k *Commandment, enjoining faith*, Deut. 8:2.
l *Faith, enjoined*, Mark 11:22.

**21**

m *King, influenced by popular opinion*, 2 Kin. 3:10.
n *Holiness*, Ex. 39:30.
o *Armies, religious ceremonies in*, Deut. 11:4.
p *God, mercy of*, Gen. 2:2.

**22**

q *Armies, stratagems*, Deut. 11:4.
r *Ambush, instances of*, Josh. 8:2.
s *Ammonites*, Deut. 2:20.
t *Moabites*, Gen. 19:37.
u *Seir*, Deut. 1:2.

23
*v Panic, from God,* Judg. 7:22.

25
*w Spoils,* 1 Chr. 26:27.

26
*x Thankfulness, to God,* Acts 24:3.

27
*y Joy,* Psa. 5:11.

28
*z Armies, religious ceremonies in,* Deut. 11:4.

*a Jerusalem,* Judg. 19:10.
*b Psaltery,* 1 Chr. 16:5.
*c Music,* 2 Chr. 5:13.
*d Harp,* Dan. 3:10.
*e Trumpet,* Josh. 6:4.
*f Temple, Solomon's,* 1 Kin. 6:17.

29
*g Fear of God,* Acts 9:31.
*h War, God in,* Judg. 3:2.

30
*i Jehoshaphat,* 2 Kin. 12:18.
*j God, providence of,* Gen. 2:2.
*k Temporal Blessings, from God,* Psa. 103:2.

31
*l Judah, kingdom of,* 2 Chr. 11:17.

and when they had made an end of the inhabitants of Sē'îr, [v]every one helped to destroy another.

24 And when Jū'dah came toward the watch tower in the wilderness, they looked unto the multitude, and, behold, they *were* dead bodies fallen to the earth, and none escaped.

25 And when [a]Jē-hŏsh'a-phăt and his people came to take away the [w]spoil of them, they found among them in abundance both riches with the dead bodies, and precious jewels, which they stripped off for themselves, more than they could carry away: and they were three days in gathering of the spoil, it was so much.

26 And on the fourth day they assembled themselves in the valley of Bĕr'a-chah; for there they [h,x]blessed the LORD: therefore the name of the same place was called, The valley of Bĕr'a-chah, unto this day.

27 Then they returned, every man of Jū'dah and Jē-rṳ'sā-lĕm, and Jē-hŏsh'a-phăt in the forefront[G] of them, to go again to Jē-rṳ'sā-lĕm with [y]joy; for the LORD had made them to rejoice over their enemies.

28 [z]And they came to [a]Jē-rṳ'sā-lĕm with [b,c]psalteries and [d]harps[G] and [e]trumpets unto the [f]house of the LORD.

29 And the [g]fear[G] of God was on all the kingdoms of *those* countries, when they had heard that [h]the LORD fought against the enemies of Ĭs'ra-el.

30 So the realm of [i]Jē-hŏsh'a-phăt was quiet: for his [j]God gave him [k]rest[G] round about.

31 ¶ And [i]Jē-hŏsh'a-phăt reigned over [l]Jū'dah: *he was* thirty and five years old when he began to reign, and he reigned twenty and five years in [a]Jē-rṳ'-sā-lĕm. And his mother's name *was* [m]Ȧ-zū'bah the daughter of [m]Shĭl'hī.

32 And [n]he walked [o]in the way of Ā'sȧ his father, and departed not from it, [p,q]doing *that which was* right in the sight of the LORD.

33 Howbeit the [r]high[G] places were not taken away: for as yet the people had not prepared their hearts unto the God of their fathers.

34 Now the rest of the acts of [i]Jē-hŏsh'a-phăt, first and last, behold, they *are* written in the [5,s]book of [t]Jē'hū the son of [t]Hă-nā'nī, [6]who *is* mentioned in the book of the kings of Ĭs'ra-el.

35 ¶ And after this did [i]Jē-hŏsh'a-phăt king of [l]Jū'dah [u]join himself with [v]Ā-ha-zī'ah king of [w]Ĭs'ra-el, who did very wickedly:

36 And he [u]joined himself with him to make [x]ships to go to †Tär'shish: and they made the ships in [y]Ē'zĭ-on–gā'bĕr.

37 Then Ē-li-ē'zēr the son of Dō'da-vah of [z]Mă-rē'shah prophesied against [a]Jē-hŏsh'a-phăt, saying, Because thou hast [b]joined thyself with [c]Ā-ha-zī'ah, the LORD hath broken thy works. And the [d]ships were broken, that they were not able to go to †Tär'shish.

## CHAPTER 21

*Jehoram's reign. 4 He slays his brethren. 5 His wickedness. 8 Edom and Libnah revolt. 12 The prophecy of Elijah against him. 16 The Philistines and Arabians oppress him. 18 His sickness, death, and unhonored burial.*

NOW [a]Jē-hŏsh'a-phăt [b]slept with his fathers, and was buried with his fathers in the [c]city of Dā'vid. And [d]Jē-hō'ram his son reigned in his stead.

2 And he had brethren the sons

*m* 1 Kin. 22:42.

32
*n Rulers, righteous,* Ex. 18:21.
*o Influence, good,* 1 Cor. 7:14.
*p Obedience, instances of,* Heb. 5:8.
*q Integrity,* Job 2:3.

33
*r High Places,* 1 Kin. 3:2.

34
*s Book,* Num. 5:23.
*t* 2 Chr. 19:2; 1 Kin. 16:1, 7.
5 R. V. history
6 R. V. which is inserted

35
*u Alliances,* Josh. 9:15.
*v Ahaziah,* 1 Kin. 22:40.
*w Israel, after the revolt,* 1 Kin. 12:1.

36
*x Ship,* 2 Chr. 8:18.
*y Ezion-gaber,* Num. 33:35.

37
*z Mareshah,* Josh. 15:44.

*a Jehoshaphat,* 2 Kin. 12:18.
*b Alliances,* Josh. 9:15.
*c Ahaziah,* 1 Kin. 22:40.
*d Ship,* 2 Chr. 8:18.

v.1–818 BC
See footnote, *Time,* Rev. 10:6.

1
*a Jehoshaphat,* 2 Kin. 12:18.
*b Death,* Num. 23:10.
*c Jerusalem,* Judg. 19:10.
*d Jehoram,* 1 Kin. 22:50.

† **TARSHISH,** probably Spain, a land noted for its valuable minerals and other commercial resources; called also THARSHISH. *Solomon makes valuable imports from,* 1 Kin. 10:22; 2 Chr. 9:21. *Commerce and wealth of,* 1 Kin. 10:22; 22:48; 2 Chr. 9:21; 20:36; Psa. 48:7; Isa. 2:16; 23:1–14; 60:9; Jer. 10:9; Ezek. 27:12, 25; 38:13. *Jonah would flee to,* Jonah 1:3; 4:2. *Prophecies concerning,* Psa. 72:10; Isa. 2:16; 23:1–14; 60:9; 66:19.

of [a]Jė-hŏsh′a-phăt, Ăz-a-rī′ah, and Jė-hī′el, and Zĕch-a-rī′ah, and Ăz-a-rī′ah, and Mī′chaĕl, and Shĕph-a-tī′ah: all these *were* the sons of Jė-hŏsh′a-phăt king of Ĭṣ′ra-el.

3 And their father gave them great gifts of [e]silver, and of [f]gold, and of precious things, with fenced[G] [g]cities in [h]Jū′dah: but the *,[i]kingdom gave he to [d,j]Jė-hō′-ram; because he *was* the [k]firstborn.

4 Now when [d]Jė-hō′ram was risen up to the kingdom of his father, he strengthened himself, and [l,m,n]slew all his brethren with the sword, and *divers*[G] also of the princes of Ĭṣ′ra-el.

5 ¶ [d]Jė-hō′ram *was* thirty and two years old when he began to reign, and he reigned eight years in [c]Jė-rụ′sā-lĕm.

6 And [d]he walked [o]in the way of the kings of Ĭṣ′ra-el, like as did the house of [p]Ā′hăb: for he had the [q]daughter of [r]Ā′hăb to wife: and he wrought *that which was* evil in the eyes of the LORD.

7 Howbeit[G] the [s]LORD would not destroy the house of [t]Dā′vid, because of the [u]covenant that he had made with Dā′vid, and as he promised to give a [1]light to him and to his sons for ever.

8 ¶ In his days the [v]Ē′dom-ītes revolted from under the dominion[G] of [h]Jū′dah, and made themselves a king.

9 Then [d]Jė-hō′ram went forth with his princes, and all his [w]chariots with him: and he [x,y]rose up by night, and smote the [v]Ē′dom-ītes which compassed[G] him in, and the [z]captains of the chariots.

10 So the [a]Ē′dom-ītes revolted from under the hand of [b]Jū′dah unto this day. The same time *also* did [c]Lĭb′nah revolt from under his hand; because he had forsaken the LORD God of his fathers.

11 Moreover he made [d]high places in the mountains of Jū′dah, and [e]caused the inhabitants of [f]Jė-rụ′sā-lĕm to commit fornication[G], and compelled Jū′dah *thereto*[G].

12 ¶ And there came a writing to [g]him from [h]Ē-lī′jah the prophet, saying, Thus saith the LORD God of Dā′vid thy father, Because [i]thou hast not walked in the ways of [j]Jė-hŏsh′a-phăt thy father, nor in the ways of [k]Ā′sȧ king of [b]Jū′dah,

13 But hast walked in the way of the kings of [l]Ĭṣ′ra-el, and hast [m]made [b]Jū′dah and the inhabitants of [f]Jė-rụ′sā-lĕm to go a[G] whoring, like to the whoredoms[G] of the house of [n]Ā′hăb, and also hast [o]slain thy brethren of thy father's house, *which were* better than thyself:

14 Behold, with a great [p]plague will the LORD smite thy people, and thy children, and thy wives, and all thy goods:

15 And thou *shalt have* great sickness by [q]disease of thy [r]bowels[G], until thy bowels[G] fall out by reason of the sickness day by day.

16 ¶ Moreover the [s]LORD stirred up against [g]Jė-hō′ram the spirit of the [t]Phĭ-lĭs′tīneṣ, and of the [u]Ā-rā′bĭ-anṣ, that *were* near the [v]Ē-thĭ-ō′pĭ-anṣ:

17 And they came up into [b]Jū′dah, and brake into it, and carried away all the substance[G] that was found in the [w]king's house, and his sons also, and his wives; so that there was never[G] a son left him, save [x]Jė-hō′a-hăz, the youngest of his sons.

v.2-818 BC

3
*e* *Silver*, 1 Chr. 28:14.
*f* *Gold*, Ezek. 7:19.
*g* *Cities, fortified*, Num. 35:8.
*h* *Judah, kingdom of*, 2 Chr. 11:17.
*i* *Inheritance*, Num. 27:7.
*j* *King, hereditary succession of*, 2 Kin. 3:10.
*k* *Firstborn, birthright of*, Zech. 12:10.

4
*l* *Fratricide, instances of*, Gen. 4:8.
*m* *Homicide, felonious, instances of*, Deut. 5:17.
*n* *Government, monarchical, tyranny in*, Isa. 22:21.

6
*o* *Influence, evil*, 1 Cor. 7:14.
*p* *Ahab*, 1 Kin. 16:29.
*q* *Women, wicked*, Prov. 31:10.
*r* *Parents, evil influence of*, 2 Cor. 12:14.

7
*s* *God, faithfulness of*, Gen. 2:2.
*t* *David*, 1 Sam. 16:13.
*u* *Covenant, of God with men*, Deut. 29:1.
1 R. V. lamp

8
*v* *Edomites*, 2 Kin. 8:21.

9
*w* *Chariot*, Josh. 11:4.
*x* *Army, tactics of*, Deut. 11:4.
*y* *Strategy*, Judg. 7:16.
*z* *Captain*, Num. 31:48.

10
*a* *Edomites*, 2 Kin. 8:21.
*b* *Judah, kingdom of*, 2 Chr. 11:17.
*c* *Libnah*, Josh. 10:29.

11
*d* *High Places*, 1 Kin. 3:2.
*e* *Idolatry, wicked practices of*, 1 Sam. 15:23.
*f* *Jerusalem*, Judg. 19:10.

12
*g* *Jehoram*, 1 Kin. 22:50.
*h* *Elijah, prophecies of*, 1 Kin. 17:1.
*i* *Rulers, wicked*, Ex. 18:21.
*j* *Jehoshaphat*, 2 Kin. 12:18.
*k* *Asa*, 1 Kin. 15:8.

13
*l* *Israel, after the revolt*, 1 Kin. 12:1.
*m* *Temptation, leading into*, Luke 11:4.
*n* *Ahab*, 1 Kin. 16:29.
*o* *Homicide, felonious*, Deut. 5:17.

14
*p* *Plague*, Ex. 11:1.

15
*q* *Disease*, Ex. 15:26.
*r* *Bowels, diseased*, 1 Kin. 3:26.

16
*s* *God, providence of*, Gen. 2:2.
*t* *Philistines*, Gen. 26:14.
*u* *Arabians*, 2 Chr. 17.11.
*v* *Ethiopia*, Isa. 18:1.

17
*w* *Palace*, 1 Kin. 21:1.
*x* Or, *Ahaziah*, 2 Kin. 8:25.

***BIRTHRIGHT.** *Entitled the firstborn, to a double portion of inheritance*, Deut. 21:15–17; *to royal succession*, 2 Chr. 21:3. *Sold by Esau*, Gen. 25:29–34; 27:36 (with 25:33); Heb. 12:16. Set aside: *Reuben's, as a punishment*, Gen. 49:3, 4; 1 Chr. 5:1, 2; *Manasseh's*, Gen. 48:15–20; *Adonijah's*, 1 Kin. 2:15; *Hosah's son's*, 1 Chr. 26:10.
See footnote, FIRSTBORN, Zech. 12:10.

18 And after all this the LORD smote [g]him in his [r]bowels with an incurable [q]disease.

19 And it came to pass, that in process of time, after the end of two years, his [r]bowels fell out by reason of his sickness: so he died of sore[C] [q]diseases. [y]And his people made no burning for him, like the burning[C] of his fathers.

20 Thirty and two years old was [g]he when he began to reign, and he reigned in [f]Jē-ru'sā-lĕm eight years, and departed without being desired.[C] Howbeit they buried him in the city of Dā'vid, but not in the [z]sepulchres of the kings.

## CHAPTER 22

*Ahaziah's wicked reign. 5 Through his confederacy with Joram the son of Ahab, he is slain by Jehu. 10 Athaliah usurps the kingdom; and destroys all the seed royal, save Joash.*

AND the inhabitants of [a]Jē-ru'sā-lĕm made [b]Ā-ha-zī'ah his youngest son king in his stead: for the band of men that came with the [c]Ā-rā'bĭ-ans to the camp had slain all the eldest. So Ā-ha-zī'ah the son of [d]Jē-hō'-ram king of [e]Jū'dah reigned.

2 Forty and two years old *was* [b]Ā-ha-zī'ah when he began to reign, and he reigned one year in [a]Jē-ru'sā-lĕm. His mother's name also *was* [f]Ăth-a-lī'ah the daughter of [g]Ŏm'rī.

3 [b]He also walked [h]in the ways of the house of [i]Ā'hăb: for his [j,k]mother was his counsellor[C] to do wickedly.

4 Wherefore [b,l]he did evil in the sight of the LORD like the house of [i]Ā'hăb: for they were his counsellors after the death of his father to his destruction.

5 [b]He walked also after their counsel,[C] and went with [m]Jē-hō'-ram the son of [i]Ā'hăb king of [n]Ĭs'ra-el to war against [o]Hăz'a-el king of [p]Sўr'ĭ-ȧ at [q]Rā'moth-gĭl'e-ăd: and the Sўr'ĭ-ans smote[C] Jō'ram.

6 And he returned to be healed in [r]Jĕz're-el because of the wounds which were given him at [q]Rā'mah, when he fought with [o]Hăz'a-el king of [p]Sўr'ĭ-ȧ. And [b]Ăz-a-rī'ah the son of [d]Jē-hō'-ram king of [e]Jū'dah went down to see [m]Jē-hō'ram the son of [i]Ā'hăb at Jĕz're-el, because he was sick.

7 And the [s]destruction of [b]Ā-ha-zī'ah [t]was of God by coming to [m]Jō'ram: for when he was come, he went out with Jē-hō'-ram against *Jē'hū the son of Nĭm'shī, [u]whom the [v]LORD had anointed to [s]cut[C] off the house of [i]Ā'hăb.

8 And it came to pass, that, when *Jē'hū [u]was executing judgment upon the house of [i]Ā'hăb, and found the princes of [e]Jū'dah, and the sons of the brethren of [b]Ā-ha-zī'ah, that ministered to Ā-ha-zī'ah, he slew them.

9 And he sought [b]Ā-ha-zī'ah: and they caught him, (for he was hid in [w]Sā-mā'rĭ-ȧ,) and brought him to *Jē'hū: and when they had slain him, they buried him: Because, said they, he *is* the son of [x]Jē-hŏsh'a-phăt, [y]who sought the LORD with all his heart. So the house of Ā-ha-zī'ah had no power to keep[C] still the kingdom.

10 ¶ But when Ăth-a-lī'ah the mother of Ā-ha-zī'ah saw that her son was dead, [z]she arose and destroyed all the seed[C] royal of the house of Jū'dah.

11 But [a]Jē-hō-shăb'e-ăth, the daughter of the king, [b,c]took

19
y *Dead, incense burnt for,* 2 Kin. 4:32.

20
z *Burying Places,* Gen. 23:4.

1
a *Jerusalem,* Judg. 19:10.
b *Ahaziah,* 2 Kin. 8:25.
c *Arabians,* 2 Chr. 17:11.
d *Jehoram,* 1 Kin. 22:50.
e *Judah, kingdom of,* 2 Chr. 11:17.

2
f *Athaliah,* 2 Kin. 11:1.
g 2 Kin. 8:26.

3
h *Influence, evil,* vs. 3–5; 1 Cor. 7:14.
i *Ahab,* 1 Kin. 16:29.
j *Women, wicked,* Prov. 31:10.
k *Parents, evil influence of,* 2 Cor. 12:14.

4
l *Rulers, wicked,* Ex. 18:21.

5
m *Jehoram,* 2 Kin. 1:17.

v.5–814 BC
See footnote, *Time,* Rev. 10:6.

n *Israel, after the revolt,* 1 Kin. 12:1.
o *Hazael,* 2 Kin. 9:14.
p *Syria,* 2 Kin. 6:23.
q *Ramoth-gilead,* Josh. 20:8.

6
r *Jezreel,* 1 Kin. 18:45.

7
s *Judgments,* Ex. 6:6.
t *Foreordination,* Rom. 8:30.
u *Agency, in executing judgments,* Mark 1:17.
v *Government, God in,* Isa. 22:21.

9
w *Samaria,* 1 Kin. 16:24.
x *Jehoshaphat, religious zeal of,* 2 Kin. 12:18.
y *Zeal,* 2 Cor. 7:11.

10
z *Women, wicked, instances of,* Prov. 31:10.

11
a Or, *Jehosheba,* 2 Kin. 11:2.
b *Kindness, instances of,* Acts 28:2.
c *Love,* 1 John 4:7.

* **JEHU,** king of Israel. *Son of Jehoshaphat,* 2 Kin. 9:1–14. *Called son, more accurately should have been called grandson, of Nimshi,* 1 Kin. 19:16; 2 Kin. 9:20. *Religious zeal of, in slaying idolaters,* 2 Kin. 9:14–37; 10:1–28; 2 Chr. 22:8, 9. *His territory invaded by Hazael, king of Syria,* 2 Kin. 10:32, 33. *Prophecies concerning,* 1 Kin. 19:17; 2 Kin. 10:30; 15:12; Hos. 1:4. *Reigned twenty-eight years,* 2 Kin. 10:36. *Death of,* 2 Kin. 10:35.

v.11–814 BC
See footnote, *Time*, Rev. 10:6.

*d Joash*, 2 Kin. 11:2.
*e Ahaziah*, 2 Kin. 8:25.
*f Jehoram*, 1 Kin. 22:50.
*g Jehoiada*, 2 Kin. 12:2.
*h Priest*, Lev. 1:5.
*i Athaliah*, 2 Kin. 11:1.

12
*j Temple, Solomon's*, 1 Kin. 6:17.

v.1–807 BC
See footnote, *Time*, Rev. 10:6.

1
*a Jehoiada*, 2 Kin. 12:2.
*b Captain*, Num. 31:48.
*c* 2 Chr. 17:15.
*d Covenant, of men with men*, Deut. 29:1.

2
*e Judah, kingdom of*, 2 Chr. 11:17.
*f Levites*, Deut. 10:8.
*g Jerusalem*, Judg. 19:10.

3
*h Constitution*, Dan. 6:12.
*i King, by hereditary succession*, 2 Kin. 3:10.

4
*j Sabbath*, Ex. 16:23.
*k Priest*, Lev. 1:5.
*l Porters*, 2 Sam. 18:26.

5
*m Palace*, 1 Kin. 21:1.
*n Court, of temple*, Ex. 38:9.
*o Temple, Solomon's*, 1 Kin. 6:17.

[d]Jō'ăsh the son of [e]Ā-ha-zī'ah, and stole him from among the king's sons that were slain, and put him and his †nurse in a bedchamber. So Jė-hō-shăb'e-ăth, the daughter of king [f]Jė-hō'ram, the wife of [g]Jė-hoi'a-dȧ the [h]priest, (for she was the sister of Ā-ha-zī'ah,) hid him from [i]Ăth-a-lī'ah, so that she slew him not.

12 And [d]he was with them hid in the [j]house of God six years: and [i]Ăth-a-lī'ah reigned over the land.

## CHAPTER 23

*Jehoiada makes Joash king. 12 Athaliah is slain. 16 Jehoiada restores the worship of God.*

AND in the seventh year [a]Jė-hoi'a-dȧ strengthened himself, and took the [b]captains of hundreds, Ăz-a-rī'ah the son of Jĕr'o-hăm, and Ĭsh'ma-el the son of [c]Jė-hō-hā'nan, and Ăz-a-rī'ah the son of Ō'bed, and Mā-a-sē'iah the son of Ăd-a-ī'ah, and Ė-lĭsh'a-phăt the son of Zĭch'rī, into [d]covenant[C] with him.

2 And they went about in [e]Jū'dah, and gathered the [f]Lē'vītes out of all the cities of Jū'dah, and the chief[C] of the fathers of Ĭṣ'ra-el, and they came to [g]Jė-ru-sā'lĕm.

3 And all the congregation made a [d,h]covenant[C] with the king in the house of God. And he said unto them, Behold, [i]the king's son shall reign, as the LORD hath said of the sons of Dā'vid.

4 This *is* the thing that ye shall do; A third part of you entering on the [j]sabbath, of the [k]priests and of the [f]Lē'vītes, *shall be* [l]porters[C] of the doors;

5 And a third part *shall be* at the [m]king's house; and a third part at the gate of the foundation: and all the people *shall be* in the [n]courts of the [o]house of the LORD.

6 But let none come into the house of the LORD, save[C] the [h]priests, and they that minister of the [f]Lē'vītes; they shall go in, for [p]they *are* holy: but all the people shall keep[C] the watch of the LORD.

7 And the [f]Lē'vītes shall compass the [q]king round about, every man with his weapons in his hand; and whosoever *else* cometh into the house, [1]he shall be put to death: but be ye with the king when he cometh in, and when he goeth out.

8 So the [f]Lē'vītes and all [e]Jū'dah did according to all things that [a]Jė-hoi'a-dȧ the [k]priest had commanded, and took every man his men that were to come in on the [j]sabbath, with them that were to go *out* on the sabbath: for Jė-hoi'a-dȧ the priest dismissed not the [r]courses.

9 Moreover [a]Jė-hoi'a-dȧ the [k]priest delivered to the [b]captains of hundreds [s,t]spears, and bucklers, and [s,u]shields, that *had been* king [v]Dā'vid's, which *were* in the [o]house of God.

10 And he set all the people, every man having his weapon in his hand, from the right side of the [o]temple to the left side of the temple, along by the [w]altar and the temple, by the king round about.

11 Then they brought out the king's [q]son, and put upon him the [x]crown, and *gave him* the [y,z,a]testimony, and made him king. And [b]Jė-hoi'a-dȧ and his sons [c]anointed him, and said, God save[C] the king.

12 ¶ Now when [d,e]Ăth-a-lī'ah heard the noise of the people running and praising the king, she came to the people into the [f]house of the LORD:

13 And [d]she looked, and, behold, the king stood at his pil-

v.6–807 BC
See footnote, *Time*, Rev. 10:6.

6
*p Ministers, character of*, Rom. 15:16.

7
*q Joash*, 2 Kin. 11:2.
1 R. V. let him be slain:

8
*r Priest, courses of*, Lev. 1:5.

9
*s Armor*, 1 Sam. 17:54.
*t Spear*, 2 Kin. 11:10.
*u Shield*, 1 Kin. 14:27.
*v David*, 1 Sam. 16:13.

10
*w Altar*, Gen. 8:20.

11
*x Crown*, Ex. 29:6.
*y Constitution*, Dan. 6:12.
*z Law, of Moses*, Deut. 33:2.
*a King, constitutional restrictions of*, 2 Kin. 3:10.
*b Jehoiada*, 2 Kin. 12:2.
*c Anointing, of kings*, Lev. 8:12.

12
*d Athaliah*, 2 Kin. 11:1.
*e Women, wicked*, Prov. 31:10.
*f Temple, Solomon's*, 1 Kin. 6:17.

† **NURSE,** Gen. 24:59; 35:8; Ex. 2:7; Ruth 4:16; 2 Kin. 11:2; 1 Thess. 2:7. *Careless*, 2 Sam. 4:4.

v.13–807 BC
See footnote, *Time*,
Rev. 10:6.

13
*g* *Trumpet*, Josh. 6:4.
*h* *Joy*, Psa. 5:11.
*i* *Choir*, 1 Chr. 15:16.
*j* *Music*, 2 Chr. 5:13.
*k* *Rending of Garments*, 2 Chr. 34:27.

14
*l* *Captain*, Num. 31:48.
1 R. V. between the ranks;

15
*m* *Jerusalem, gates of*, Judg. 19:10.
*n* *Palace*, 1 Kin. 21:1.
2 R. V. made way for

16
*o* *Religious Revivals, instances of*, Hab. 3:2.
*p* *Covenant, of men with men*, Deut. 29:1.

17
*q* *Zeal, exemplified*, 2 Cor. 7:11.
*r* *Baal*, 2 Kin. 17:16.
*s* *Iconoclasm*, Num. 33:52.
*t* 2 Kin. 11:18.

18
*u* *Priest, duties of*, Lev. 1:5.
*v* *David*, 1 Sam. 16:13.
*w* *Offerings, burnt*, Lev. 6:17.
*x* *Law, of Moses*, Deut. 33:2.

19
*y* *Porters*, 2 Sam. 18:26.
*z* *Defilement*, Lev. 5:2.

*a* *Sin, typified*, Rom. 5:12.

20
*b* *Captain*, Num. 31:48,

lar at the entering in, and the
princes and the [g]trumpets by
the king: and all the people of
the land [h]rejoiced, and sounded
with trumpets, also the [i]singers
with instruments of [j]musick, and
such as taught to sing praise.
Then [d]Ăth-a-lī'ah [k]rent[C] her
clothes, and said, Treason,
Treason.
14 Then [b]Jē-hoi'a-dȧ the priest
brought out the [l]captains of hundreds that were set over the host,
and said unto them, Have her
forth [1]of the ranges[C]: and whoso
followeth her, let him be slain
with the sword. For the priest
said, Slay her not in the [j]house
of the LORD.
15 So they [2]laid hands on her;
and when she was come to the
entering of the [m]horse gate by
the [n]king's house, they slew
her there.
16 ¶ [o]And [b]Jē-hoi'a-dȧ made a
[p]covenant[C] between him, and between all the people, and between the king, that they should
be the LORD's people.
17 Then [q]all the people went to
the house of [r]Bā'al, and [s]brake
it down, and [s]brake his altars
and his images in pieces, and
slew [t]Măt'tan the priest of Bā'al
before the altars.
18 Also [b]Jē-hoi'a-dȧ appointed[C]
the offices of the [j]house of the
LORD by the hand of the [u]priests
the Lē'vītes, whom [v]Dā'vid had
distributed in the house of the
LORD, to offer the [w]burnt offerings of the LORD, as *it is* written
in the [x]law of Mō'ṣeṣ, with [h]re-
joicing and with [j]singing, *as it*
*was ordained* by Dā'vid.
19 And he set the [y]porters at
the gates of the [j]house of the
LORD, that none *which was*
[z,a]unclean in any thing should
enter in.
20 And he took the [b]captains of
hundreds, and the nobles, and
the governors of the people,
and all the people of the land,
and brought down the king
from the [c]house of the LORD:
and they came through the
[3,d]high gate into the king's
house, and set the king upon
the [e]throne of the kingdom.
21 And all the people of the
land [f]rejoiced: and the city was
quiet, after that they had slain
[g]Ăth-a-lī'ah with the sword.

## CHAPTER 24

*Joash reigns well all the days of Jehoiada. 4 He gives orders to repair the temple. 15 Jehoiada's death and honorable burial. 17 Joash falls into idolatry. 20 Being reproved by Zechariah the son of Jehoiada, he slays him. 23 Jerusalem is spoiled by the Syrians; and Joash, slain by his servants. 27 Amaziah succeeds him.*

[a]JŌ'ĂSH *was* seven years old
when he began to reign,
and he reigned forty years in
[b]Jē-ru'sā-lĕm. His mother's
name also *was* [c]Zĭb'ī-ah of [d]Bē'-
er–shē'bȧ.
2 And [a,e]Jō'ăsh did *that which*
*was* right in the sight of the
LORD all the days of [f]Jē-hoi'a-
dȧ the [g]priest.
3 And Jē-hoi'a-dȧ took for him
[h]two wives; and he begat sons
and daughters.
4 ¶ And it came to pass after
this, *that* [a,i]Jō'ăsh was minded to
[1]repair the [j]house of the LORD.
5 And he gathered together the
[k]priests and the [l]Lē'vītes, and
said to them, Go out unto the
cities of [m]Jū'dah, and gather of
all Ĭṣ'ra-el [n]money to repair the
[j]house of your God from year to
year, and see that ye hasten the
matter. Howbeit the [o]Lē'vītes
hastened *it* not.
6 And the king called for [f]Jē-
hoi'a-dȧ the [g]chief, and said unto him, Why hast thou not required of the Lē'vītes to bring
in out of [m]Jū'dah and out of
[b]Jē-ru'sā-lĕm the [2,p]collection,
*according to the commandment*
of [q]Mō'ṣeṣ the servant of the

v.20–807 BC
See footnote, *Time*,
Rev. 10:6.

*c* *Temple, Solomon's*, 1 Kin. 6:17.
*d* *Jerusalem, gates of*, Judg. 19:10.
*e* *Throne*, 1 Kin. 2:19.
3 R. V. upper

21
*f* *Joy*, Psa. 5:11.
*g* *Athaliah*, 2 Kin. 11:1.

1
*a* *Joash*, 2 Kin. 11:2.
*b* *Jerusalem*, Judg. 19:10.
*c* 2 Kin. 12:1.
*d* *Beer-sheba*, Judg. 20:1.

2
*e* *Rulers, righteous*, Ex. 18:21.
*f* *Jehoiada*, 2 Kin. 12:2.
*g* *High Priest*, Lev. 21:10.

3
*h* *Polygamy*, Deut. 17:17.

4
*i* *Zeal*, 2 Cor. 7:11.
*j* *Temple, Solomon's*, 1 Kin. 6:17.
1 R. V. restore

5
*k* *Priest*, Lev. 1:5.
*l* *Levites*, Deut. 10:8.
*m* *Judah, kingdom of*, 2 Chr. 11:17.
*n* *Money*, Jer. 32:9.
*o* *Minister, false and corrupt*, Rom. 15:16.

6
*p* *Tax*, Neh. 10:32.
*q* *Moses*, Ex. 2:10.
2 R. V. tax of Moses

*r Tabernacle*, Ex. 27:9.
3 R. V. tent of the testimony?
7
*s Athaliah*, 2 Kin. 11:1.
*t Women, wicked*, Prov. 31:10.
*u Sacrilege*, Lev. 19:8.
*v* Or, *Baal*, 2 Kin. 17:16.
9
*w Israel*, Ex. 4:22.
4 R. V. tax
11
*x Scribe*, 1 Kin. 4:3.
5 R. V. chief
12
*y Mason*, 2 Sam. 5:11.
*z Carpentry*, 2 Kin. 12:11.

*a Iron*, Prov. 27:17.
*b Brass*, Job 28:2.
13
*c Church, called House of God*, 1 Kin. 9:3.
*d Temple, Solomon's*, 1 Kin. 6:17.
14
*e Money*, Jer. 32:9.
*f Joash*, 2 Kin. 11:2.
*g Jehoiada*, 2 Kin. 12:2.

LORD, and of the congregation
of Ĭṣ′ra-el, for the [3,r]tabernacle
of witness?
7 For the sons of [s]Ăth-a-lī′ah,
that wicked [t]woman, had [u]bro-
ken up the [j]house of God; and
also all the dedicated things of
the house of the LORD [u]did they
bestow[G] upon [v]Bā′al-ĭm.
8 And at the king's commandment they made a chest, and set
it without[G] at the gate of the
[j]house of the LORD.
9 And they made a procla-
mation through [m]Jū′dah and
[b]Jĕrụ′sā-lĕm, to bring in to
the LORD the [4,p]collection *that*
[q]Mō′ṣeṣ the servant of God *laid*
upon [w]Ĭṣ′ra-el in the wilderness.
10 And all the princes and all
the people rejoiced, and brought
in, and cast into the chest, until
they had made an end.
11 Now it came to pass, that
at what time the chest was
brought unto the king's office by
the hand of the [l]Lē′vītes, and
when they saw that *there was*
much [n]money, the king's [x]scribe
and the [5,g]high priest's officer
came and emptied the chest, and
took it, and carried it to his place
again. Thus they did day by
day, and gathered money in
abundance.
12 And the king and Jĕ-hoi′a-
dȧ gave it to such as did the work
of the service of the [j]house of the
LORD, and hired [y]masons and
[z]carpenters to [1]repair the house
of the LORD, and also such as
wrought [a]iron and [b]brass to
mend the house of the LORD.
13 So the workmen wrought,
and the work was perfected[G] by
them, and they set the [c,d]house
of God in his state[G], and strengthened it.
14 And when they had finished
[d]*it*, they brought the rest of the
[e]money before the [f]king and [g]Jĕ-
hoi′a-dȧ, whereof were made
vessels for the house of the
LORD, *even* vessels to minister,
and to offer *withal*, and [h]spoons,
and vessels of [i]gold and [j]silver.
And they offered [k]burnt offerings in the house of the LORD
continually all the days of [g]Jĕ-
hoi′a-dȧ.
15 ¶ But [g]Jĕ-hoi′a-dȧ waxed[G]
old, and was full of days when
he died; [l]an hundred and thirty
years old *was he* when he died.
16 And they buried him in
the [m]city of Dā′vid [n]among the
kings, because he [o]had done
good in Ĭṣ′ra-el, both toward
God, and toward his house.
17 Now after the death of
[g]Jĕ-hoi′a-dȧ came the princes
of [p]Jū′dah, and made obeisance[G]
to the [f]king. Then the [q]king
hearkened unto them.
18 And they left the [d]house of
the LORD God of their fathers,
and [r]served [6,s]groves[G] and idols:
and [t]wrath came upon [p]Jū′dah
and [m]Jĕ-rụ′sā-lĕm for this their
trespass.
19 Yet [u]he sent [v]prophets to
them, to bring them again unto
the LORD; and they [w]testified
against them: but they [x]would
not give ear.
20 And[Q] the [7,y]Spirit of God
[z]came upon [a]Zĕch-a-rī′ah the
son of [b]Jĕ-hoi′a-dȧ the priest,
which stood above the people,
and [c]said unto them, Thus saith
God, Why transgress ye the
commandments of the LORD,
that ye cannot prosper? because
ye have forsaken the LORD, [d]he
hath also forsaken you.
21 And they [e]conspired against
him, and [f,g]stoned him with
stones at the commandment of
the [h]king in the [i]court of the
[j]house of the LORD.[Q]
22 Thus [h,k]Jō-ăsh the king
[l]remembered not the kindness
which [b]Jĕ-hoi′a-dȧ his father[G]
had done to him, but slew his

*h Spoons*, Num. 4:7.
*i Gold*, Ezek. 7:19.
*j Silver*, 1 Chr. 28:14.
*k Offerings, burnt*, Lev. 6:17.
15
*l Longevity, instances of*, Psa. 91:16.
16
*m Jerusalem*, Judg. 19:10.
*n Burying Places*, Gen. 23:4.
*o Obedience, exemplified*, Heb. 5:8.
17
*p Judah, kingdom of*, 2 Chr. 11:17.
*q Rulers, wicked, instances of*, Ex. 18:21.
18
*r Idolatry*, 1 Sam. 15:23.
*s Groves*, Judg. 6:28.
*t Anger of God*, 2 Kin. 13:3.
6 R. V. the Asherim
19
*u God, mercy of*, Gen. 2:2.
*v Prophets*, Isa. 3:2.
*w Reproof*, Prov. 17:10.
*x Impenitence, instances of*, Rom. 2:5.
20
*y Holy Spirit, inspiration of*, Acts 1:2.
*z Inspiration, of prophets*, Job 32:8.

*a Possibly identical with Zacharias* in Matt. 23:35; Luke 11:51.
*b Jehoiada*, 2 Kin. 12:2.
*c Reproof, faithfulness in*, Prov. 17:10.
*d Backsliders, punished*, Jer. 3:22.
7 R. V. spirit
21
*e Conspiracy, instances of*, 1 Kin. 16:9.
*f Persecution, instances of*, John 15:20.
*g Martyrdom, instances of*, Rev. 17:6.
*h Rulers, wicked*, Ex. 18:21.
*i Court, of the temple*, Ex. 38:9.
*j Temple, Solomon's*, 1 Kin. 6:17.
22
*k Joash*, 2 Kin. 11:2.
*l Ingratitude, of man to man*, Rom. 1:21.

son. And when he [m]died, he
said, The LORD look upon *it*,
and require *it*.
23 ¶ And it came to pass at the
end of the year, *that* the host of
[n]Sȳr'ĭ-ȧ [o]came up against [k]him:
and they came to Jū'dah and
Jė-rṳ'să-lĕm, and destroyed all
the princes of the people from
among the people, and sent all
the [p,q]spoil[c] of them unto the
king of [r]Dă-măs'cus.
24 For the army of the Sȳr'ĭ-anș
came with a small company of
men, and the [s]LORD [t]delivered
a very great host into their hand,
because [u]they had forsaken the
LORD God of their fathers. So
they executed judgment against
[k]Jō'ăsh.
25 And when they were de-
parted from him, (for they left
him in great [v]diseases,) his own
servants [e]conspired against him
for the blood of the sons of Jė-
hoi'a-dȧ the priest, and [w]slew
him on his bed, and he died: and
they buried him in the [x]city of
Dā'vid, but they buried him not
in the [y]sepulchres of the kings.
26 And these are they that conspired against him; [z]Zā'băd the
son of [a]Shĭm'e-ăth an [b]Ăm'mon-
ĭt-ess, and [a]Jė-hŏz'a-băd the son
of [c]Shĭm'rĭth a [d]Mō'ab-ĭt-ess:
27 Now *concerning* his sons,
and the greatness of the burdens
*laid* upon [e]him, and the [8]repair-
ing of the [f]house of God, behold,
they *are* written in the [9]story of
the [g]book of the kings. And
[h]Ăm-a-zī'ah his son reigned in
his stead.

## CHAPTER 25

*Amaziah's reign. 3 He punishes the murderers of his father. 5 His war with the Edomites. 11 His victory over them. 14 He serves the gods of Edom, and despises the admonitions of the prophet. 17 He challenges Joash, and is overcome. 27 He is slain by conspiracy.*

[a]AM-A-ZĪ'AH *was* twenty and
five years old *when* he
began to reign, and he reigned
twenty and nine years in [b]Jė-
rṳ'să-lĕm. And his mother's
name *was* [c]Jē-hō-ăd'dan of Jė-
rṳ'să-lĕm.
2 And he did *that which was*
right in the sight of the LORD,
but not with a perfect[c] heart.
3 Now it came to pass, when
the kingdom was established to
him, that he [d]slew his servants
that had killed the king his
father.
4 But he slew not their children, but *did* as *it is* written in
the [e]law in the book of Mō'șeș,
where the LORD commanded,
saying, [f]The fathers shall not
die for the children, [g,h]neither
shall the children die for the fathers, but every man shall die
for his own sin.
5 ¶ Moreover [a]Ăm-a-zī'ah
gathered Jū'dah together, and
made them [i]captains over thousands, and [j]captains over hundreds, according to the houses
of *their* fathers, throughout [k]all
Jū'dah and Bĕn'ja-mĭn: and he
numbered them from twenty
years old and above, and found
them three hundred thousand
choice *men, able* to go forth to
war, that could handle [l]spear
and [m]shield.
6 He hired also an hundred
thousand mighty [n]men of valour
out of [o]Ĭș'ra-el for an hundred
[p]talents[c] of [q]silver.
7 But there came a [r]man of
God to him, saying, O king, let
not the army of Ĭș'ra-el go with
thee; for the LORD *is* not with
Ĭș'ra-el, *to wit, with* all the children of Ē'phră-ĭm.
8 But if thou wilt go, [1]do *it*, be
strong for the battle: God shall
make thee fall before the enemy:
for God hath [s]power to [t]help,
and to cast down.
9 And [a]Ăm-a-zī'ah said to the
[r]man of God, But what shall we
do for the hundred [p]talents[c]

m *Death*, Num. 23:10.

23

n *Syria*, 2 Kin. 6:23.
o *War*, Judg. 3:2.
p *Spoils*, 1 Chr. 26:27.
q *King, emoluments of*, 2 Kin. 3:10.
r *Damascus*, Isa. 8:4.

24

s *God, providence of*, Gen. 2:2.
t *Judgments*, Ex. 6:6.
u *Backsliders, instances of*, Jer. 3:22.

25

v *Disease*, Ex. 15:26.
w *Regicide*, 2 Sam. 1:10.
x *Jerusalem*, Judg. 19:10.
y *Burying Places*, Gen. 23:4.

26

z Or, *Jozachar*, 2 Kin. 12:21.

a 2 Kin. 12:21.
b *Ammonites*, Deut. 2:20.
c Or, *Shomer*, 2 Kin. 12:21.
d *Moabites*, Gen. 19:37.

27

e *Joash*, 2 Kin. 11:2.
f *Temple, Solomon's*, 1 Kin. 6:17.
g *Book*, Num. 5:23.
h *Amaziah*, 2 Kin. 14:1.
8 R. V. rebuilding
9 R. V. commentary

1

a *Amaziah*, 2 Kin. 14:1.

v.1–767 BC
See footnote, *Time*. Rev. 10:6.

b *Jerusalem*, Judg. 19:10.
c 2 Kin. 14:2.

3

d *Government, monarchical, tyranny in*, Isa. 22:21.

4

e *Law, of Moses*, Deut. 33:2.
f *Innocent, shall not suffer for the guilty*, Deut. 24:16.
g *Punishment, not entailed on children*, Lev. 26:41.
h *Sin, guilt of, not entailed on children*, Rom. 5:12.

5

i *Armies, how officered*, Deut. 11:4.
j *Captain*, Num. 31:48.
k *Judah, kingdom of*, 2 Chr. 11:17.
l *Spear*, 2 Kin. 11:10.
m *Shield*, 1 Kin. 14:27.

6

n *Armies, mercenaries*, Deut. 11:4.
o *Israel, after the revolt*, 1 Kin. 12:1.
p *Talent*, Ex. 38:25.
q *Silver*, 1 Chr. 28:14.

7

r *Prophets*, Isa. 3:2.

8

s *God, power of*, Gen. 2:2.
t *God, preserver*, Gen. 2:2.
1 R. V. do valiantly.

which I have given to the [n]army of [o]Iș′ra-el? And the man of God answered, [u]The LORD is able to give thee much more than this.

10 Then [a]Ăm-a-zī′ah separated them, *to wit*, [n]the army that was to come to him out of Ē′phră-ĭm, to go home again: wherefore their [v]anger was greatly kindled against [k]Jū′dah, and they returned home in great anger.

11 And [a]Ăm-a-zī′ah [2]strengthened himself, and led forth his people, and went to the valley of [w]salt, and smote of the [x]children of [y]Sē′ĭr ten thousand.

12 And *other* ten thousand *left* alive did the children of Jū′dah carry away captive, and brought them unto the top of the rock, and [z]cast [a]them down from the top of the rock, that they all were broken in pieces.

13 But the soldiers of the army which [b]Ăm-a-zī′ah sent back, that they should not go with him to battle, fell upon the cities of Jū′dah, from [c]Sā-mā′rĭ-ȧ even unto [d]Bĕth–hō′rŏn, and smote three thousand of them, and took much [e]spoil.

14 ¶ Now it came to pass, after that [b,f]Ăm-a-zī′ah was come from the slaughter of the [g]Ē′dom-ītes, that he brought the [h]gods of the children of [i]Sē′ĭr, and [j]set them up *to be* his gods, and [k]bowed down himself before them, and burned [l]incense unto them.

15 Wherefore the [m]anger of the LORD was kindled against [b]Ăm-a-zī′ah, and he sent unto him a [n]prophet, which [o]said unto him, Why hast thou [k]sought after the gods of the people, which could not deliver their own people out of thine hand?

16 And it came to pass, as he talked with him, that *the* [b]*king* said unto him, [p]Art thou made of the king's counsel? forbear; why shouldest thou be smitten? Then the prophet forbare, and said, I know that God hath determined to [q]destroy thee, because thou hast done this, and hast not hearkened unto my counsel.

17 ¶ Then [b]Ăm-a-zī′ah king of [r]Jū′dah took advice, and sent to [s]Jō′ăsh, the son of [t]Jē-hō′a-hăz, the son of [u]Jē′hū, king of [v]Iș′ra-el, saying, Come, let us see one another in the face.

18 And [s]Jō′ăsh king of [v]Iș′ra-el sent to [b]Ăm-a-zī′ah king of [r]Jū′dah, saying, [w, x]The [y]thistle that *was* in [z]Lĕb′a-non sent to the [a]cedar that *was* in Lĕb′a-non, saying, Give thy daughter to my son to wife: and there passed by a wild beast that *was* in Lĕb′a-non, and trode down the thistle.

19 Thou sayest, [b]Lo, thou hast smitten the [c]Ē′dom-ītes; and thine heart [d]lifteth thee up to [e]boast: abide now at home; why shouldest thou meddle to *thine* hurt, that thou shouldest fall, *even* thou, and Jū′dah with thee?

20 But [f]Ăm-a-zī′ah would not hear; for [g]it *came* of God, that he might deliver them into the hand *of their enemies*, because they [h]sought after the gods of Ē′dom.

21 So [i]Jō-ăsh the king of [j]Iș′ra-el went up; and they saw one another in the face, *both* he and [f]Ăm-a-zī′ah king of [k]Jū′dah, at [l]Bĕth–shē′mesh, which *belongeth* to Jū′dah.

22 And [k]Jū′dah was put to the worse before [j]Iș′ra-el, and they fled every man to his tent.

23 And [i]Jō′ăsh the king of [j]Iș′ra-el took [f]Ăm-a-zī′ah king of [k]Jū′dah, the son of [m]Jō′ăsh, the son of [n]Jē-hō′a-hăz, at [l]Bĕth–shē′mesh, and brought him to [o]Jē-ru′să-lĕm, and brake down the wall of Jē-ru′să-lĕm from the

---

9
u *Faith, exemplified,* Mark 11:22.

10
v *Anger, instances of,* Psa. 37:8.

11
w *Salt, valley of,* 2 Kin. 2:20.
x *Edomites,* 2 Kin. 8:21.
y *Seir,* Deut. 1:2.
2 R. V. took courage.

12
z *Massacre,* Esth. 3:13.
a *Captive, cruelty to,* 1 Sam. 30:3.

13
b *Amaziah,* 2 Kin. 14:1.
c *Samaria,* 1 Kin. 16:24.
d *Beth-horon,* Josh. 10:10.
e *Spoils,* 1 Chr. 26:27.

14
f *Rulers, wicked,* Ex. 18:21.
g *Edomites,* 2 Kin. 8:21.
h *Idol,* 1 Kin. 15:12.
i *Seir,* Deut. 1:2.
j *Apostasy, instances of,* Acts 1:25.
k *Idolatry,* 1 Sam. 15:23.
l *Incense, offered in idolatrous worship,* Ex. 37:29.

15
m *Anger of God,* 2 Kin. 13:3.
n *Prophets,* Isa. 3:2.
o *Reproof, faithfulness in,* Prov. 17:10.

16
p *Impenitence, instances of,* Rom. 2:5.
q *Wicked, punishment of,* Psa. 73:3.

17
r *Judah, kingdom of,* 2 Chr. 11:17.
s Or, *Jehoash,* 2 Kin. 13:10.
t 2 Kin. 10:35; 13:1-9.
u *Jehu,* 2 Chr. 22:8.
v *Israel, after the revolt,* 1 Kin. 12:1.

18
w *Pride,* Prov. 16:18.
x *Sarcasm, instances of,* v. 19; Judg. 10:14.
y *Thistle, parable of,* Hos. 10:8.
z *Lebanon,* Deut. 1:7.
a *Cedar,* Isa. 9:10.

19
b *Sarcasm,* Judg. 10:14.
c *Edomites,* 2 Kin. 8:21.
d *Pride,* Prov. 16:18.
e *Boasting, instances of,* Prov. 25:14.

20
f *Amaziah,* 2 Kin. 14:1.
g *Foreordination,* Rom. 8:30.
h *Idolatry, punishment for,* 1 Sam. 15:23.

21
i Or, *Jehoash,* 2 Kin. 13:10.
j *Israel, after the revolt,* 1 Kin. 12:1.
k *Judah, kingdom of,* 2 Chr. 11:17.
l *Beth-shemesh,* Josh. 21:16.

23
m *Joash,* 2 Kin. 11:2.
n Or, *Ahaziah,* 2 Kin. 8:25.
o *Jerusalem,* Judg. 19:10.

[p]gate of Ē′phră-ĭm to the corner
gate, four hundred [q]cubits.[C]
24 And *he took* all the gold
and the silver, and all the vessels that were found in the
[r]house of God with [s]Ō′bed-ē′dom, and the treasures of the
[t]king's house, the [u]hostages also, and returned to [v]Sā-mā′rĭ-ȧ.
25 ¶ And [f]Ăm-a-zī′ah the son
of [m]Jō′ăsh king of [k]Jū′dah lived
after the death of [i]Jō′ăsh son of
[w]Jē-hō′a-hăz king of [j]Ĭş′ra-el fifteen years.
26 Now the rest of the acts of
[f]Ăm-a-zī′ah, first and last, behold, *are* they not written in the
[x]book of the kings of [k]Jū′dah
and Ĭş′ra-el?
27 ¶ Now after the time that
[f]Ăm-a-zī′ah did turn away from
following the LORD they made a
[y]conspiracy against him in [o]Jē-rụ′sȧ-lĕm; and he fled to [z]Lā′chish: but they sent to Lā′chish
after him, and [a]slew him there.
28 And they brought him upon
horses, and [b]buried him with his
fathers in the [c]city of Jū′dah.

## CHAPTER 26

*Uzziah's reign and prosperity. 16 Waxing proud, he invades the priest's office, and is smitten with leprosy. 22 He dies, and Jotham succeeds him.*

THEN all the people of [a]Jū′dah took *Ŭz-zī′ah, who
*was* sixteen years old, and made
him king in the room of his father [b]Ăm-a-zī′ah.
2 He built [c]Ē′lŏth, and restored
it to Jū′dah, after that the king
[d]slept with his fathers.
3 Sixteen years old *was* *Ŭz-zī′ah when he began to reign,
and he reigned fifty and two
years in [e]Jē-rụ′sȧ-lĕm. His
mother's name also *was* [f]Jĕc-o-lī′ah of Jē-rụ′sȧ-lĕm.
4 And he [g]did *that which was*
right in the sight of the LORD,
according to all that his father
[b]Ăm-a-zī′ah did.
5 And [h]he sought God in the
days of Zĕch-a-rī′ah, who had
[i]understanding in the [j]visions of
God: and [k,l]as long as he
[m]sought the LORD, [n]God made
him to [o]prosper.
6 And *he went forth and
warred against the [p]Phĭ-lĭs′tĭneş,
and brake down the wall of
[q]Găth, and the wall of Jăb′neh,
and the wall of [r]Ăsh′dŏd, and
built cities about Ăsh′dŏd, and
among the Phĭ-lĭs′tĭneş.
7 And God [n]helped him against
the [p]Phĭ-lĭs′tĭneş, and against the
[s]Ȧ-rā′bĭ-anş that dwelt in Gûr-bā′al, and the [t]Mē-hū′nimş.
8 And the [u]Ăm′mon-ītes gave
[v]gifts to *Ŭz-zī′ah: and his name
spread abroad *even* to the entering in of [w]Ē′ġy̆pt; for he strengthened *himself* exceedingly.
9 Moreover *Ŭz-zī′ah built
†, [x]towers in Jē-rụ′sȧ-lĕm at the
corner [y]gate, and at the [y]valley
gate, and at the turning *of the
wall*, and fortified them.
10 Also he built †, [x]towers in
the desert, and digged many
[1,z]wells: for he had much cattle,
both in the low country, and in
the plains: husbandmen *also*,
and [a]vine dressers in the mountains, and in [2,] ‡Cär′mel: for he
loved [b]husbandry.[C]

p *Jerusalem, gates of*, Judg. 19:10.
q *Cubit*, Ex. 36:9.
**24**
r *Temple, Solomon's*, 1 Kin. 6:17.
s *Obed-edom*, 2 Sam. 6:10.
t *Palace*, 1 Kin. 21:1.
u 2 Kin. 14:14.
v *Samaria*, 1 Kin. 16:24.
**25**
w 2 Kin. 10:35.
**26**
x *Book*, Num. 5:23.
**27**
y *Conspiracy, instances of*, 1 Kin. 16:9.
z *Lachish*, Josh. 10:5.

a *Homicide, felonious, instances of*, Deut. 5:17.
v.27–739 BC
**28**
b *Burial*, Acts 8:2.
c *Jerusalem*, Judg. 19:10.
**1**
a *Judah, kingdom of*, 2 Chr. 11:17.
b *Amaziah*, 2 Kin. 14:1.
**2**
c Or, *Elath*, Deut. 2:8.
d *Death*, Num. 23:10.

v.3–727 BC
See footnote, *Time*, Rev. 10:6.
**3**
e *Jerusalem*, Judg. 19:10.
f Or, *Jecholiah*, 2 Kin. 15:2.
**4**
g *Obedience, instances of*, Heb. 5:8.
**5**
h *Seekers*, Isa. 55:6.
i *Prophets, inspiration of*, Isa. 3:2.
j *Vision*, Acts 9:10.
k *Contingencies, in divine government of man*, 1 Kin. 3:14.
l *Blessings, contingent upon obedience*, Deut. 11:26.
m *Obedience, rewarded*, Heb. 5:8.
n *God, providence of*, Gen. 2:2.
o *Temporal Blessings, from God*, Psa. 103:2.
**6**
p *Philistines*, Gen. 26:14.
q *Gath*, Josh. 11:22.
r *Ashdod*, 1 Sam. 6:17.
**7**
s *Arabians*, 2 Chr. 17:11.
t See *Maon*, Josh. 15:55.
**8**
u *Ammonites*, Deut. 2:20.
v *Tribute*, Ezra 4:13.
w *Egypt*, Gen. 41:8.
**9**
x *Fortification*, Ezek. 17:17.
y *Jerusalem, gates of*, Judg. 19:10.
**10**
z *Wells*, Gen. 21:19.

a *Grape*, Lev. 25:5.
b *Agriculture*, Gen. 3:23.
1 R. V. cisterns,
2 R. V. the fruitful fields;

* **UZZIAH,** Isa. 1:1; 6:1. *Called*, AZARIAH, 2 Kin. 14:21; OZIAS, Matt. 1:8, 9. *King of Judah*, 2 Kin. 14:21; 2 Chr. 26:1, 3. *Reigned fifty-two years*, 2 Kin. 15:1, 2. *Rebuilds Elath*, 2 Kin. 14:22; 2 Chr. 26:2. *Reigns righteously*, 2 Kin. 15:3; 2 Chr. 26:4, 5. *Defeats the Philistines*, 2 Chr. 26:6, 7. *Takes tribute from the Ammonites; strengthens the kingdom*, 2 Chr. 26:8. *Strengthens the fortifications of Jerusalem*, 2 Chr. 26:9. *Promotes cattle raising and agriculture*, 2 Chr. 26:10. *Military establishment of*, 2 Chr. 26:11–15. *Is presumptuous in burning incense; stricken with leprosy; quarantined*, 2 Kin. 15:5; 2 Chr. 26:16–21. *Jotham, regent during quarantine of*, 2 Kin. 15:5; 2 Chr. 26:21. *Death of*, 2 Kin. 15:7; 2 Chr. 26:23. *History of, written by Isaiah*, 2 Chr. 26:22. *Earthquake in the reign of*, Amos 1:1; Zech. 14:5.

† **TOWER.** *Of Babel*, Gen. 11:1–9. *Of Edar*, Gen. 35:21. *Of Penuel*, Judg. 8:8, 9, 17. *Of Shechem*, Judg. 9:46, 49. *Of Meah*, Neh. 3:1; 12:39. *Of Hananeel*, Neh. 3:1; 12:39; Jer. 31:38; Zech. 14:10. *Of Ophel*, Neh. 3:25–27. *Of David*, Song 4:4. *Of Syene*, Ezek. 29:10. *Of Siloam*, Luke 13:4. *In the walls of Jerusalem*, 2 Chr. 26:9; 32:5; Neh. 12:38, 39. *Of other cities*, 2 Chr. 14:7.
*In the desert*, 2 Chr. 26:10. *For watchmen or sentinels*, 2 Kin. 9:17; 17:9; 18:8. *As fortress*, Matt. 21:33.
*Parable of*, Luke 14:28, 29.
**Figurative:** *Of divine protection*, 2 Sam. 22:3; Psa. 18:2; 61:3; 144:2, Prov. 18:10.

‡ **CARMEL.** *A city of Judah*, Josh. 15:55. *Saul erects a memorial at*, 1 Sam. 15:12. *Nabal's possessions at*, 1 Sam. 25:2. *King Uzziah, who delighted in agriculture, had vineyards at*, 2 Chr. 26:10.

11 ¶ Moreover *Ŭz-zī′ah had an host of fighting men, that went out to war by bands, according to the number of their account by the hand of Jĕ-ī′el the [c]scribe and Mā-a-sē′iah the [3]ruler, under the hand of Hăn-a-nī′ah, *one* of the king's [d]captains.

12 The whole number of the chief[G] of the fathers of the mighty men of valour *were* two thousand and six hundred.

13 And under their hand *was* [4]an army, three hundred thousand and seven thousand and five hundred, that made war with mighty power, to help the king against the enemy.

14 And *Ŭz-zī′ah prepared for them throughout all the host [e]shields, and [f]spears, and [g]helmets, and [5,h]habergeons,[G] and [i]bows, and [6,j]slings *to cast* stones.

15 And he made in [k]Jĕ-ru′să-lĕm [l]engines, ‖invented by cunning[G] men, to be on the [†,m]towers and upon the [n]bulwarks,[G] to [i]shoot arrows and great stones withal. And his name spread far abroad; [o]for he was marvellously helped, till he was strong.

16 ¶ But when he [o]was strong, [p]his [q]heart was lifted up [7]to *his* destruction: for [r,s]he transgressed against the LORD his God, and went into the [t]temple of the LORD [u,v,w]to burn [x]incense upon the [y]altar of incense.

17 And Ăz-a-rī′ah the [z,a]priest went in after him, and with him fourscore priests of the LORD, *that were* valiant[G] men:

18 And they withstood *Ŭz-zī′ah the king, and [b]said unto him, [c]*It appertaineth* not unto thee, Ŭz-zī′ah, to burn [d]incense unto the LORD, [e]but to the [f]priests the sons of [g]Aâr′on, that are consecrated to burn incense: go out of the [h]sanctuary; for thou hast trespassed; neither *shall it be* for thine honour from the LORD God.

19 Then *Ŭz-zī′ah was [i]wroth,[G] and *had* a [j]censer in his hand to burn [d]incense: and while he was wroth with the priests, the [k,l]leprosy even rose up in his forehead before the priests in the [m]house of the LORD, from beside the incense [n]altar.

20 And Ăz-a-rī′ah the [a]chief priest, and all the priests, looked upon him, and, behold, he *was* [k,l]leprous in his forehead, and they thrust him out from thence;[G] yea, himself hasted[G] also to go out, because the LORD had [o]smitten[G] him.

21 And *Ŭz-zī′ah the king was a [k]leper unto the day of his death, and [p]dwelt in a several[G] house, *being* a leper; for he was [q]cut off from the [m]house of the LORD: and [r]Jō′tham his son *was* over the king's house, judging the people of the land.

22 ¶ Now the rest of the acts of *Ŭz-zī′ah, first and last, did [s]Ī-ṣā′iah the [t]prophet, the son of [u]Ā′mŏz, write.

23 So *Ŭz-zī′ah [v]slept with his fathers, and they buried him with his fathers in the [w]field of the burial which *belonged* to the kings; for they said, He *is* a leper: and [r]Jō′tham his son reigned in his stead.

## CHAPTER 27

*Jotham's reign.* 5 *He subdues the Ammonites.* 7 *His acts.* 9 *Ahaz succeeds him.*

[a]JŌ′THAM *was* twenty and five years old when he began to reign, and he reigned sixteen years in [b]Jĕ-ru′să-lĕm. His

11
c *Scribe*, 1 Kin. 4:3.
d *Captain*, Num. 31:48.
3 R. V. officer,

13
4 R. V. a trained army,

14
e *Shield*, 1 Kin. 14:27.
f *Spear*, 2 Kin. 11:10.
g *Helmet*, Jer. 46:4.
h *Coat of Mail*, 1 Sam. 17:5.
i *Archery*, Gen. 21:20.
j *Sling*, 1 Sam. 17:40.
5 R. V. coats of mail,
6 R. V. stones for slinging.

15
k *Jerusalem*, Judg. 19:10.
l Ezek. 26:9.
m *Fortification*, Ezek. 17:17.
n *Bulwark*, Deut. 20:20.
o *Prosperity*, Eccl. 7:14.

16
p *Pride*, Prov. 16:18.
q *Heart*, Psa. 44:21.
r *Ingratitude, of man to God*, Rom. 1:21.
s *Rulers, wicked*, Ex. 18:21.
t *Temple, Solomon's*, 1 Kin. 6:17.
u *Usurpation, in ecclesiastical affairs*, 2 Sam. 15:1.
v *Sacrilege*, Lev. 19:8.
w *Presumption*, Psa. 19:13.
x *Incense*, Ex. 37:29.
y *Altar, of incense*, Ex. 30:1.
7 R. V. so that he did corruptly, and he

17
z *Minister, faithful*, Rom. 15:16.
a *High Priest*, Lev. 21:10.

18
b *Reproof, faithfulness in*, Prov. 17:10.
c *Usurpation, in ecclesiastical affairs*, 2 Sam. 15:1.
d *Incense*, Ex. 37:29.

e *Church and State, ecclesiastical power superior to civil*, 1 Sam. 16:1.
f *Priest*, Lev. 1:5.
g *Aaron*, Ex. 6:20.
h *Sanctuary*, Lev. 4:6.

19
i *Anger*, Psa. 37:8.
j *Censer*, Lev. 16:12.
k *Leprosy*, Lev. 13:2.
l *Disease, as a judgment*, Ex. 15:26.
m *Temple, Solomon's*, 1 Kin. 6:17.
n *Altar, of incense*, Ex. 30:1.

20
o *Judgments*, Ex. 6:6.

21
p *Sanitation and Hygiene, isolation*, Num. 31:23.
q *Disfellowship*, Num. 15:31.
r *Jotham*, 2 Kin. 15:5.

22
s *Isaiah*, Isa. 1:1.
t *Prophets*, Isa. 3:2.
u 2 Kin. 19:2; 20:1; Isa. 1:1; 13:1.

23
v *Death*, Num. 23:10.
w *Burying Places*, Gen. 23:4.

v. 1–675 BC
See footnote, *Time*, Rev. 10:6.

1
a *Jotham*, 2 Kin. 15:5.
b *Jerusalem*, Judg. 19:10.

‖ **INVENTION**, Prov. 8:12. Of musical instruments: *By Jubal*, Gen. 4:21; *by David*, 1 Chr. 23:5; 2 Chr. 7:6; 29:26; Amos 6:5. *The use of metals*, Gen. 4:22. *Engines of war*, 2 Chr. 26:15.

mother's name also *was* [c]Jē-ru'-
shah, the daughter of [c]Zā'dŏk.
2 And [d]he [e]did *that which was*
right in the sight of the LORD,
[f]according to all that his father
[g]Ŭz-zī'ah did: howbeit he entered not into the [h]temple of the
LORD. And the people did yet
corruptly.
3 He built the [1]high gate of the
[h]house of the LORD, and on the
wall of [i,j]Ō'phel he built much.
4 Moreover he built cities in the
[2]mountains of [k]Jū'dah, and in
the forests he built castles[G] and
[l]towers.
5 He fought also with the king
of the [m]Ăm'mon-ītes, and prevailed against them. And the
children of Ăm'mŏn gave him
the same year an [n]hundred [o]tal-
ents[G] of [p]silver, and [n]ten thousand [q]measures[G] of [r]wheat, and
[n]ten thousand of [s]barley. So
much did the children of Ăm'-
mŏn pay unto him, both the
second year, and the third.
6 So [a]Jō'tham [t,u]became
mighty, because he [3]prepared his
ways before the LORD his God.
7 ¶ Now the rest of the acts of
[a]Jō'tham, and all his wars, and
his ways, lo, they *are* written in
the [v]book of the kings of [w]Ĭş'-
ra-el and [k]Jū'dah.
8 He was five and twenty years
old when he began to reign, and
reigned sixteen years in [b]Jē-ru'-
să-lĕm.
9 And Jō'tham [x]slept with his
fathers, and they [y]buried him in
the city of Dā'vid: and [z]Ā'hăz
his son reigned in his stead.

## CHAPTER 28

*Ahaz, reigning wickedly, is afflicted by the Syrians. 8 The Israelites, by the counsel of Oded the prophet, send home the captives taken from Judah. 16 Ahaz sends for aid to Assyria. 22 In his distress he grows more idolatrous. 26 Hezekiah succeeds him.*

[a]A'HĂZ *was* twenty years old
when he began to reign,
and he reigned sixteen years in
[b]Jē-ru'să-lĕm: but [c]he [d]did not
*that which was* right in the sight
of the LORD, like [e]Dā'vid his
father:
2 For [a,c]he walked in the ways
of the kings of Ĭş'ra-el, and made
also molten[G] [f]images for [g]Bā'-
al-ĭm.
3 Moreover [a,c]he burnt [h]in-
cense in the valley of the son of
[i]Hĭn'nom, and [j]burnt his [k]chil-
dren in the fire, after the abominations of the heathen[G] whom
the LORD had cast out before
the children of Ĭş'ra-el.
4 [a,c]He sacrificed also and
burnt [h]incense in the [l]high[G]
places, and on the hills, and
under every green tree.
5 Wherefore the LORD his
[m]God [n]delivered him into the
hand of the king of [o]Sўr'ĭ-ȧ; and
they smote[G] him, and carried
away a great multitude of them
captives, and brought *them* to
[p]Dȧ-măs'cus. And he was also
delivered into the hand of the
king of [q]Ĭş'ra-el, who smote
him with a great slaughter.
6 For [r]Pē'kah the son of [s]Rĕm-
a-lī'ah [n]slew in [t]Jū'dah an hundred and twenty thousand in one
day, *which were* all valiant[G] men;
because they had forsaken the
LORD God of their fathers.
7 And Zĭch'rī, a mighty man
of [u]Ē'phră-ĭm, slew Mā-a-sē'iah
the king's son, and Ăz'rĭ-kăm
the governor of the house, and
[v]Ĕl'kă-nah *that was* next to the
king.
8 And the children of [q]Ĭş'ra-el
carried away captive of their
brethren two hundred thousand,
women, sons, and daughters,
and took also away much [w]spoil[G]
from them, and brought the
spoil to [x]Sȧ-mā'rĭ-ȧ.
9 But a [y]prophet of the LORD
was there, whose name *was*
Ō'ded: and he went out before
the host that came to [x]Sȧ-mā'-

v.1–675 BC
See footnote, *Time*, Rev. 10:6.

c 2 Kin. 15:33.

2
d *Rulers, righteous*, Ex. 18:21.
e *Obedience, instances of*, Heb. 5:8.
f *Example, good*, John 13:15.
g *Uzziah*, 2 Chr. 26:1.
h *Temple, Solomon's*, 1 Kin. 6:17.

3
i *Jerusalem, gates of*, Judg. 19:10.
j *Jerusalem, towers of*, Judg. 19:10.
1 R. V. upper

4
k *Judah, kingdom of*, 2 Chr. 11:17.
l *Tower*, 2 Chr. 26:9.
2 R. V. hill country of

5
m *Ammonites*, Deut. 2:20.
n *Tribute*, Ezra 4:13.
o *Talent*, Ex. 38:25.
p *Silver*, 1 Chr. 28:14.
q *Measure, dry*, Deut. 25:15.
r *Wheat*, Ezra 6:9.
s *Barley*, Ex. 9:31.

6
t *Temporal Blessings, from God*, Psa. 103:2.
u *Blessings, contingent upon obedience*, Deut. 11:26.
3 R. V. ordered

7
v *Book*, Num. 5:23.
w *Israel, after the revolt*, 1 Kin. 12:1.

9
x *Death*, Num. 23:10.
y *Burial*, Acts 8:2.
z *Ahaz*, 2 Kin. 15:38.

v.9–660 BC

v.1–660 BC
See footnote, *Time*, Rev. 10:6.

1
a *Ahaz*, 2 Kin. 15:38.

v.1–660 BC
See footnote, *Time*, Rev. 10:6.

b *Jerusalem*, Judg. 19:10.
c *Rulers, wicked*, Ex. 18:21.
d *Disobedience to God*, Eph. 5:6.
e *David*, 1 Sam. 16:13.

2
f *Idol*, 1 Kin. 15:12.
g Or, *Baal*, 2 Kin. 17:16.

3
h *Incense, offered in idolatrous worship*, Ex. 37:29.
i *Hinnom*, Jer. 7:31.
j *Idolatry, wicked practices of*, 1 Sam. 15:23.
k *Human Sacrifices*, Deut. 12:31.

4
l *High Places*, 1 Kin. 3:2.

5
m *God, providence of*, Gen. 2:2.
n *Nation, punishment of*, Isa. 2:4.
o *Syria*, 2 Kin. 6:23.
p *Damascus*, Isa. 8:4.
q *Israel, after the revolt*, 1 Kin. 12:1.

6
r *Pekah*, Isa. 7:1.
s *Remaliah*, 2 Kin 15:25.
t *Judah, kingdom of*, 2 Chr. 11:17.

7
u *Ephraim, tribe of*, Gen. 41:52.
v *Minister*, 2 Chr. 9:4.

8
w *Spoils*, 1 Chr. 26:27.
x *Samaria*, 1 Kin. 16:24.

9
y *Prophets*, Isa. 3:2.

*z Reproof, faithfulness in*, vs. 9–11; Prov. 17:10.

*a Anger of God*, 2 Kin. 13:3.
*b Judah, kingdom of*, 2 Chr. 11:17.
*c Nation, punishment of*, Isa. 2:4.

10
*d Jerusalem*, Judg. 19:10.
*e Servant, captives of war made*, Jer. 2:14.

13
*f Israel, after the revolt*, 1 Kin. 12:1.
1 R. V. ye purpose that which will bring upon us a trespass against the Lord, to add unto

14
*g Spoils*, 1 Chr. 26:27.

15
*h Captive, kindness to*, 1 Sam. 30:3.
*i Anointing, of captives*, Deut. 28:40.

rĭ-ȧ, and [z]said unto them, Behold,
hold, because the LORD God of
your fathers was [a]wroth with
[b]Jū′dah, he hath [c]delivered
them into your hand, and ye
have slain them in a rage *that*
reacheth up unto heaven.
10 And now ye purpose to keep
under the children of [b]Jū′dah
and [d]Jē-ru̧′sā-lĕm for [e]bondmen
and [e]bondwomen unto you: *but
are there* not with you, even with
you, sins against the LORD your
God?
11 Now hear me therefore, and
deliver the captives again, which
ye have taken captive of your
brethren: for the fierce [a]wrath of
the LORD *is* upon you.
12 Then certain of the heads of
the children of Ē′phrā-ĭm, Ăz-a-
rī′ah the son of Jō̇-hā′nan, Bĕr-
e-chī′ah the son of Mē̇-shĭl′le-
mōth, and Jē-hĭz-kī′ah the son
of Shăl′lum, and Ăm′a-sȧ the
son of Hăd′la-ī, stood up against
them that came from the war,
13 And said unto them, Ye
shall not bring in the captives
hither: for [1]whereas we have offended
fended against the LORD *already*,
*ready*, ye intend to add *more* to
our sins and to our trespass: for
our trespass is great, and *there is*
fierce wrath against [f]Ĭş′ra-el.
14 So the armed men left the
captives and the [g]spoil before the
princes and all the congregation.
15 And the men which were expressed
pressed by name rose up, and
took the [h]captives, and with the
[g]spoil clothed all that were naked
ked among them, and arrayed
them, and shod them, and gave
them to eat and to drink, and
[i]anointed them, and carried all
the feeble of them upon *asses,
and brought them to [j]Jĕr′ĭ-chō,
the city of palm trees, to their
brethren: then they returned to
[k]Sȧ-mā′rĭ-ȧ.
16 ¶ At that time did king
[l]Ā-hăz send unto the kings of
[m]Ăs′sy̆r′ĭ-ȧ to help him.
17 For again the [n]Ē′dom-ītes
had come and smitten [c]Jū′dah,
and carried away captives.
18 The [o]Phĭ-lĭs′tĭneş also had
invaded the cities of the low
country, and of the south of
[b]Jū′dah, and had taken [p]Bĕth-
shē′mesh, and [q]Ăj′a-lŏn, and
[r]Gē̇-dē′roth, and [s]Shō′chō̇ with
the villages thereof, and [t]Tĭm′-
nah with the villages thereof,
Gĭm′zō̇ also and the villages
thereof: and they dwelt there.
19 For the [u]LORD [c]brought
[b]Jū′dah low because of [l,v]Ā′hăz
king of Ĭş′ra-el; for he [2]made
Jū′dah naked, and transgressed
sore against the LORD.
20 And †Tĭl′gath-pĭl-nē′şer
king of [m]Ăs-sy̆r′ĭ-ȧ came unto
him, and distressed him, but
strengthened him not.
21 For [l,v]Ā′hăz took away a
portion *out* of the [w]house of the
LORD, and *out* of the [x]house of
the king, and of the princes, and
gave *it* unto the king of [m]Ăs-sy̆r′-
ĭ-ȧ: but [3]he helped him not.
22 And in the time of his [y]distress
tress did he trespass yet more
against the LORD: this *is that*
king [l]Ā′hăz.
23 For he [z]sacrificed unto
the gods of [a]Dȧ-măs′cus, which
smote him: and he said, Because
the gods of the kings of Sy̆r′ĭ-ȧ
help them, *therefore* will I sacrifice
fice to them, that they may help

*j Jericho*, Num. 22:1.
*k Samaria*, 1 Kin. 16:24.

16
*l Ahaz*, 2 Kin. 15:38.
*m Assyria*, Gen. 25:18.

17
*n Edomites*, 2 Kin. 8:21.

18
*o Philistines*, Gen. 26:14.
*p Beth-shemesh*, Josh. 21:16.
*q* Or, *Aijalon*, Josh. 21:24.
*r* Josh. 15:41.
*s* Or, *Shochoh*, 1 Sam. 17:1.
*t* Josh. 15:10.

19
*u God, providence of*, Gen. 2:2.
*v Rulers, wicked*, Ex. 18:21.
2 R. V. had dealt wantonly in Judah,

21
*w Temple, Solomon's*, 1 Kin. 6:17.
*x Palace*, 1 Kin. 21:1.
3 R. V. it

22
*y Adversity, impenitence in*, Psa. 10:6.

23
*z Idolatry*, 1 Sam. 15:23.
*a Damascus*, Isa. 8:4.

* **ASS. Domesticated:** *Herds of*, Gen. 12:16; 24:35; 32:5; 34:28; Num. 31:34, 45; 1 Chr. 5:21; Ezra 2:67; Neh. 7:69. *Used, for riding*, Gen. 22:3; Num. 22:21–33; Josh. 15:18; Judg. 1:14; 5:10; 1 Sam. 25:23; 2 Chr. 28:15; Zech. 9:9; *by Jesus*, Matt. 21:2, 5; John 12:14, 15; *for carrying burdens*, Gen. 42:26; 2 Sam. 16:1; Isa. 30:6; *for food*, 2 Kin. 6:25. *Not to be yoked with an ox*, Deut. 22:10. *Entitled to rest on Sabbath*, Ex. 23:12. *Bridles for*, Prov. 26:3. *Balaam's, reproves him*, Num. 22:28–30; 2 Pet. 2:15, 16. *Jawbone of, used by Samson with which to slay Philistines*, Judg. 15:15–17. *Firstlings of, redeemed*, Ex. 13:13; 34:20.
**Wild**, Job 6:5; 24:5; 39:5; Psa. 104:11; Isa. 32:14; Jer. 2:24; 14:6; Hos. 8:9.

† **TILGATH-PILNESER**, king of Assyria, called also TIGLATH-PILESER. *Invades Israel; carries part of the people captive to Assyria*, 2 Kin. 15:29; 1 Chr. 5:6, 26. *Forms an alliance with Ahaz; captures Damascus*, 2 Kin. 16:7–10; 2 Chr. 28:19–21.

**24**
*b* *Ahaz,* 2 Kin. 15:38.
*c* *Temple, Solomon's,* 1 Kin. 6:17.
*d* *Sacrilege,* Lev. 19:8.
*e* *Altar, used in idolatrous worship,* Gen. 8:20.
*f* *Jerusalem,* Judg. 19:10.

**25**
*g* *High Places,* 1 Kin. 3:2.
*h* *Incense, offered in idolatrous worship,* Ex. 37:29.
*i* *Anger of God,* 2 Kin. 13:3.

**26**
*j* *Book,* Num. 5:23.

**27**
*k* *Death,* Num. 23:10.
*l* *Burying Places,* Gen. 23:4.
*m* *Hezekiah,* 2 Kin. 16:20.
v.27–643 BC

**1**
*a* *Hezekiah,* 2 Kin. 16:20.
*b* *Jerusalem,* Judg. 19:10.
*c* Or, *Abi,* 2 Kin. 18:2.
*d* 2 Kin. 18:2.

**2**
*e* *Obedience, instances of,* Heb. 5:8.
*f* *Influence, good,* 1 Cor. 7:14.

**3**
*g* *Temple, Solomon's,* 1 Kin. 6:17.

**4**
*h* *Priest,* Lev. 1:5.
*i* *Levites,* Deut. 10:8.
*j* *Jerusalem, streets of,* Judg. 19:10.
1 R. V. broad place on the east,

me. But they were the ruin of
him, and of all Ĭş′ra-el.
24 And [b]Ā′hăz gathered together the vessels of the [c]house
of God, and [d]cut in pieces the
vessels of the house of God, and
shut up the doors of the house of
the LORD, and he made him
[e]altars[C] in every corner of [f]Jē-
ru̧′sā-lĕm.
25 And in every several[C] city
of Jū′dah he made [g]high places
to burn [h]incense unto other
gods, and provoked to [i]anger
the LORD God of his fathers.
26 ¶ Now the rest of his acts
and of all his ways, first and last,
behold, they *are* written in the
[j]book of the kings of Jū′dah and
Ĭş′ra-el.
27 And [b]Ā′hăz [k]slept with his
fathers, and they buried him in
the city, *even* in [f]Jē-ru̧′sā-lĕm:
but they brought him not into
the [l]sepulchres of the kings of
Ĭş′ra-el: and [m]Hĕz-e-kī′ah his
son reigned in his stead.

## CHAPTER 29

*Hezekiah's good reign. 3 He restores the worship of God. 5 His exhortation to the Levites. 12 They sanctify themselves, and cleanse the house of God. 20 Hezekiah and the rulers of the city offer solemn sacrifices to the Lord.*

[a]HĔZ-E-KĪ′AH began to
reign *when he was* five
and twenty years old, and he
reigned nine and twenty years in
[b]Jē-ru̧′sā-lĕm. And his mother's
name *was* [c]Ā-bī′jah, the daughter of [d]Zĕch-a-rī′ah.
2 And he [e]did *that which was*
right in the sight of the LORD,
[f]according to all that Dā′vid his
father had done.
3 ¶ He in the first year of his
reign, in the first month, opened
the doors of the [g]house of the
LORD, and repaired them.
4 And he brought in the [h]priests
and the [i]Lē′vītes, and gathered
them together into the [1,j]east
street,
5 And said unto them, Hear
me, ye [i]Lē′vītes, [k]sanctify now
yourselves, and sanctify the
[g,l]house of the LORD God of
your fathers, and carry forth
the filthiness out of the [m]holy
*place.*
6 [n]For our fathers have trespassed,[C] and done *that which was*
evil in the eyes of the LORD our
God, and have [o]forsaken him,
and have turned away their
faces from the habitation[C] of the
LORD, and turned *their* backs.
7 Also they have shut up the
doors of the [p]porch, and put out
the lamps, and have not burned
[q]incense nor offered [r]burnt offerings in the [m]holy *place* unto the
God of Ĭş′ra-el.
8 Wherefore the [s]wrath of the
LORD was upon Jū′dah and
Jē-ru̧′sā-lĕm, and he hath [t]deliv-
ered them to [2]trouble, to astonishment, and to hissing, as ye
see with your eyes.
9 For, lo, our fathers have [t]fal-
len by the sword, and our sons
and our daughters and our wives
*are* in [u]captivity for this.
10 Now [v]*it is* in mine heart
to make a [w]covenant with the
LORD God of Ĭş′ra-el, that his
fierce [s]wrath may turn away
from us.
11 My sons, [x]be not now negligent: for the LORD hath chosen
you [y]to stand before him, to
serve him, and that ye should
minister unto him, and burn
[q]incense.
12 ¶ Then the [i]Lē′vītes arose,
[z]Mā′hăth the son of Ā-măs′a-ī,
and Jō′el the son of Ăz-a-rī′ah,
of the sons of the [a]Kō′hath-ītes:
and of the [b]sons of Mē-rā′rī,
Kĭsh the son of Ăb′dī, and Ăz-a-
rī′ah the son of Jē-hăl′e-lĕl: and
of the [c]Gēr′shon-ītes; [d]Jō′ah the
son of [e]Zĭm′mah, and Ē′dĕn the
son of Jō′ah:
13 And of the sons of Ē-lĭz′a-
phăn; Shĭm′rī, and Jē-ī′el: and

v.5–643 BC
See footnote, *Time,* Rev. 10:6.

**5**
*k* *Sanctification,* 1 Pet. 1:2.
*l* *Church, called house of the Lord,* 1 Kin. 9:3.
*m* *Holy Place,* Ex. 26:33.

**6**
*n* *Sin, confession of,* Rom. 5:12.
*o* *Backsliding,* Hos. 11:7.

**7**
*p* *Temple, Solomon's, porch of,* 1 Kin. 6:17.
*q* *Incense,* Ex. 37:29.
*r* *Offerings, burnt,* Lev. 6:17.

**8**
*s* *Anger of God,* 2 Kin. 13:3.
*t* *Nation, punishment of,* Isa. 2:4.
2 R. V. be tossed to and fro, to be an astonishment, and an hissing,

**9**
*u* *Captivity, as a judgment,* Isa. 5:13.

**10**
*v* *Decision, instances of,* Isa. 50:7.
*w* *Covenant, of man with God,* Deut. 29:1.

**11**
*x* *Minister, character and qualifications of,* Rom. 15:16.
*y* *Minister, duties of,* Rom. 15:16.

**12**
*z* 1 Chr. 6:35.
*a* *Kohathites, duties of,* vs. 12–15; Num. 3:27.
*b* *Merarites, duties of,* vs. 12–15; Num. 26:57.
*c* *Gershonites,* Num. 4:27.
*d* 1 Chr. 6:21.
*e* 1 Chr. 6:42.

v.13–643 BC
See footnote, *Time*, Rev. 10:6.

13
f *Asaph*, 1 Chr. 15:17.

14
g *Heman*, 1 Chr. 6:33.
h *Jeduthun*, 1 Chr. 16:41.

15
i *Sanctification*, 1 Pet. 1:2.
j *Temple, Solomon's*, 1 Kin. 6:17.

16
k *Priest*, Lev. 1:5.
l *Levites*, Deut. 10:8.
m *Brook*, Deut. 8:7.
n *Kidron*, 1 Kin. 2:37.

17
o *Month*, Ex. 12:2.

18
p *Hezekiah*, 2 Kin. 16:20.
q *Altar, of burnt offerings*, Gen. 8:20.
r *Shewbread, table of*, Ex. 35:13.
3 R. V. within the palace, and said,

19
s *Ahaz*, 2 Kin. 15:38.

of the sons of [f]Ā′saph; Zĕch-a-
rī′ah, and Măt-ta-nī′ah:
14 And of the sons of [g]Hē′man;
Jē-hī′el, and Shĭm′e-ī: and of
the sons of [h]Jĕd′ụ-thŭn; Shĕm-
a-ī′ah, and Ŭz′zī-el.
15 And they gathered their
brethren, and [i]sanctified themselves, and came, according to
the commandment of the king,
by the words of the LORD, to
[i]cleanse the [j]house of the LORD.
16 And the [k]priests went into
the inner part of the [j]house of
the LORD, to [i]cleanse *it*, and
brought out all the uncleanness
that they found in the temple
of the LORD into the court of
the house of the LORD. And
the [l]Lē′vītes took *it*, to carry *it*
out abroad into the [m]brook
[n]Kĭd′ron.
17 Now they began on the first
*day* of the first [o]month to [i]sanc-
tify,[C] and on the eighth day of the
month came they to the porch of
the LORD: so they sanctified the
[j]house of the LORD in eight
days; and in the sixteenth day of
the first month they made an
end.
18 Then they went in to [p]Hĕz-
e-kī′ah the king, [3]and said, We
have cleansed all the [j]house of
the LORD, and the [q]altar of
burnt offering, with all the vessels[C] thereof, and the [r]shewbread
table, with all the vessels thereof.
19 Moreover all the vessels,
which king [s]Ā′hăz in his reign
did cast away in his transgression, have we prepared and
[i]sanctified,[C] and, behold, they *are*
before the [q]altar of the LORD.
20 ¶ Then [p]Hĕz-e-kī′ah the
king rose early, and gathered the
rulers of the city, and went up to
the [j]house of the LORD.
21 And they brought seven bullocks, and seven rams, and seven
lambs, and seven he goats, for a
[t]sin [u]offering for the [v]kingdom,
and for the [w]sanctuary, and for
[v]Jū′dah. And he commanded
the [k]priests the sons of Aâr′on to
offer *them* on the [q]altar of the
LORD.
22 So they [x]killed the bullocks,
and the priests received the
[y,z]blood, and sprinkled *it* on the
[q]altar: likewise, when they had
[x]killed the rams, they sprinkled
the [y,z]blood upon the altar: they
[x]killed also the lambs, and they
sprinkled the [y,z]blood upon the
altar.
23 And they brought forth the
he goats *for* the [a]sin [b]offering before the king and the congregation; and they laid their [c]hands
upon them:
24 And the priests [d]killed them,
and they made [4]reconciliation[C]
with their [e,f]blood upon the [g]al-
tar, to make an [h,i]atonement for
all [j]Ĭş′ra-el: for the king commanded *that* the [k]burnt [b]offering
and the [a]sin [b]offering *should be
made* for all Ĭş′ra-el.
25 And he set the [l]Lē′vītes in
the [m]house of the LORD with
[n,o]cymbals, with [n,p]psalteries,
and with [n,q]harps,[C] according to
the commandment of [r]Dā′vid,
and of [s]Găd the king's seer, and
[t]Nā′than the prophet: for *so was*
the commandment of the LORD
by his [u]prophets.
26 And the [l]Lē′vītes stood with
the [n]instruments of [r]Dā′vid, and
the [v]priests with the [w]trumpets.
27 And [x]Hĕz-e-kī′ah commanded to offer the [k]burnt offering upon the [g]altar. And when
the burnt offering began, [y]the
song of the LORD began *also*
with the [w]trumpets, and with the
[n]instruments *ordained* by [r]Dā′-
vid king of Ĭş′ra-el.
28 And all the congregation
[z]worshipped, and the [y]singers
sang, and the [w]trumpeters
sounded: *and* all *this continued*

v.21–643 BC

21
t *Offerings, sin*, Lev. 6:17.
u *Jesus, typified in offerings*, Matt. 1:21.
v *Nation, atonement made for*, Isa. 2:4.
w *Temple, atonement made for*, 1 Kin. 6:17.

22
x *Jesus, vicarious death of, typified*, Matt. 1:21.
y *Blood, sacrificial*, Heb. 9:19.
z *Jesus, atoning blood of, typified*, Matt. 1:21.

23
a *Offerings, sin*, Lev. 6:17.
b *Jesus, typified in offerings*, Matt. 1:21.
c *Hand, imposition of*, Ezra 10:19.

24
d *Jesus, vicarious death of, typified*, Matt. 1:21.
e *Blood, sacrificial*, Heb. 9:19.
f *Jesus, atoning blood of, typified*, Matt. 1:21.
g *Altar, of burnt offerings*, Gen. 8:20.
h *Atonement, made by animal sacrifices*, Lev. 17:11.
i *Jesus, atonement by, typified*, Matt. 1:21.
j *Nation, atonement made for*, Isa. 2:4.
k *Offerings, burnt*, Lev. 6:17.
4 R. V. a sin offering

25
l *Levites, duties of*, Deut. 10:8.
m *Temple, Solomon's*, 1 Kin. 6:17.
n *Cymbal*, 1 Chr. 13:8.
o *Music, instruments of*, 2 Chr. 5:13.
p *Psaltery*, 1 Chr. 16:5.
q *Harp*, Dan. 3:10.
r *David*, 1 Sam. 16:13.
s *Gad*, 2 Sam. 24:11.
t *Nathan*, 2 Sam. 7:2.
u *Prophets*, Isa. 3:2.

26
v *Priest, duties of*, Lev. 1:5.
w *Trumpets*, Josh. 6:4.

27
x *Hezekiah*, 2 Kin. 16:20.
y *Choir*, 1 Chr. 15:16.

28
z *Worship*, Gen. 22:5.

v.28–643 BC
See footnote, *Time*, Rev. 10:6.

*a Offerings, burnt*, Lev. 6:17.

29

*b Prayer, postures in*, Acts 6:4.

*c Worship*, Gen. 22:5.

30

*d Hezekiah*, 2 Kin. 16:20.

*e Levites*, Deut. 10:8.

*f Praise*, Psa. 150:1.

*g David*, 1 Sam. 16:13.

*h Asaph*, 1 Chr. 15:17.

*i Joy, instances of*, Psa. 5:11.

31

*j Rulers, righteous*, Ex. 18:21.

*k Priest, consecration of*, Lev. 1:5.

*l Offerings, thank*, Lev. 6:17.

*m Temple, Solomon's*, 1 Kin. 6:17.

*n Religious Revivals*, Hab. 3:2.

*o Liberality, instances of*, 1 Tim. 6:18.

5 R. V. willing

34

*p Priests, duties of*, Lev. 1:5.

*q Minister, false and corrupt*, Rom. 15:16.

*r Sanctification*, 1 Pet. 1:2.

35

*s Offerings, peace*, Lev. 6:17.

*t Offerings, drink*, Lev. 6:17.

until the [a]burnt offering was finished.

29 And when they had made an end of offering, the king and all that were present with him [b]bowed themselves, and [c]worshipped.

30 Moreover [d]Hĕz-e-kī′ah the king and the princes commanded the [e]Lē′vītes to sing [f]praise unto the LORD with the words of [g]Dā′vid, and of [h]Ā′saph the seer. And they sang praises with [i]gladness, and they bowed their heads and [c]worshipped.

31 Then [d,j]Hĕz-e-kī′ah answered and said, Now ye have [k]consecrated yourselves unto the LORD, come near and bring sacrifices and [l]thank offerings into the [m]house of the LORD. [n]And the congregation brought in sacrifices and thank offerings; and [o]as many as were of a [5]free heart burnt offerings.[Q]

32 And the number of the [a]burnt offerings, which the congregation brought, was threescore and ten bullocks, an hundred rams, *and* two hundred lambs: all these *were* for a burnt offering to the LORD.

33 And the consecrated things *were* six hundred oxen and three thousand sheep.

34 But the [p]priests were too few, so that they could not flay[C] all the [a]burnt offerings: wherefore their brethren the [e]Lē′vītes did help them, till the work was ended, and until the *other* [q]priests had [r]sanctified themselves: for the Lē′vītes *were* more upright in heart to sanctify themselves than the priests.

35 And also the [a]burnt offerings *were* in abundance, with the fat of the [s]peace offerings, and the [t]drink offerings for *every* burnt offering. So the service[C] of the [m]house of the LORD was set in order.

36 And [d]Hĕz-e-kī′ah [i]rejoiced, and all the people, that God had prepared the people: for the thing was *done* suddenly.

## CHAPTER 30

*Hezekiah proclaims a solemn passover in the second month for Judah and Israel. 13 The assembly destroy the altars of idolatry. 15 They keep the feast fourteen days. 27 The priests and Levites bless the people.*

AND [a,b,c]Hĕz-e-kī′ah sent to all [d]Ĭș′ra-el and [e]Jū′dah, and wrote [f]letters also to [g]Ē′phră-ĭm and [h]Mă-năs′seh, that they should come to the [i]house of the LORD at [j]Jĕ-ru̥′să-lĕm, to keep the [k]passover unto the LORD God of Ĭș′ra-el.

2 For the [l]king had taken counsel, and his princes, and all the congregation in [j]Jĕ-ru̥′să-lĕm, to keep the [k]passover in the second [m]month.

3 For they could not keep it at that time, because the [n]priests had not sanctified themselves [1]sufficiently, neither had the people gathered themselves together to [j]Jĕ-ru̥′să-lĕm.

4 And the thing pleased the king and all the congregation.

5 So they established a decree to make [o]proclamation throughout all Ĭș′ra-el, from [p]Bē′er-shē′bă even to [q]Dăn, that they should come to keep the [k]passover unto the LORD God of Ĭș′ra-el at [j]Jĕ-ru̥′să-lĕm: for they had not [2]done *it* of a long *time in such sort* as it was written.

6 So the [r]posts[G] went with the [f]letters from the king and his princes throughout all Ĭș′ra-el and Jū′dah, and according to the commandment of the king, saying, Ye children of Ĭș′ra-el, [s]turn again unto the LORD God of [t]Ā′bră-hăm, [u]Ī′șaac, and [v]Ĭș′ra-el, and he will return to the remnant of you, that are escaped out of the hand of the kings of [w]Ăs-sy̆r′ĭ-ă.

7 And be not ye like your

v.36–643 BC
See footnote, *Time*, Rev. 10:6.

1

*a Hezekiah*, 2 Kin. 16:20.

*b Rulers, righteous*, Ex. 18:21.

*c Zeal, instances of*, 2 Cor. 7:11.

*d Israel, after the revolt*, 1 Kin. 12:1.

*e Judah, kingdom of*, 2 Chr. 11:17.

*f Letters*, Isa. 37:14.

*g Ephraim, tribe of*, Gen. 41:52.

*h Manasseh, tribe of*, Gen. 46:20.

*i Temple, Solomon's*, 1 Kin. 6:17.

*j Jerusalem*, Judg. 19:10.

*k Passover*, Num. 9:5.

2

*l King, influenced by popular opinion*, 2 Kin. 3:10.

*m Month, Zif*, Ex 12:2.

3

*n Minister, false and corrupt*, Rom. 15:16.

1 R. V. in sufficient number,

5

*o Proclamation*, 1 Kin. 15:22.

*p Beer-sheba*, Judg. 20:1.

*q Dan*, Judg. 18:29.

2 R. V. kept it in great numbers in such

6

*r Post*, Job 9:25.

*s Repentance, enjoined*, Mark 1:4

*t Abraham*, Gen. 17:5.

*u Isaac*, Gen. 21:3.

*v Or, Jacob*, Gen. 27:11.

*w Assyria*, Gen. 25:18.

v.7–643 BC
See footnote, *Time*, Rev. 10:6.

**7**

*x Example, bad*, John 13:15.
*y Nation, punishment of*, Isa. 2:4.

**8**

*z Self-will*, Gen. 49:6.

*a Commandment, enjoining submission to God*, Deut. 8:2.
*b Church, called sanctuary*, 1 Kin. 9:3.
*c Anger of God*, 2 Kin. 13:3.

**9**

*d Blessings, contingent upon obedience*, Deut. 11:26.
*e Backsliders, promises to penitent, of temporal prosperity*, Jer. 3:22.
*f Grace of God*, Rom. 4:16.
*g God, mercy of*, Gen. 2:2.

**10**

*h Post*, Job 9:25.
*i Ephraim, tribe of*, Gen. 41:52.
*j Manasseh, tribe of*, Gen. 46:20.
*k Zebulun, tribe of*, Gen. 49:13.
*l Scoffing, instances of*, Hab. 1:10.
*m Derision, instances of*, Job 30:1.

**11**

*n Asher, tribe of*, Num. 1:40.
*o Repentance, instances of*, Mark 1:4.
*p Jerusalem*, Judg. 19:10.

**13**

*q Passover*, Num. 9:5.
*r Annual Feasts*, Num. 15:3.
*s Month, Zif*, Ex. 12:2.

**14**

*t Iconoclasm*, Num. 33:52.
*u Altar, used in idolatrous worship*, Gen. 8:20.
*v Brook*, Deut. 8:7.
*w Kidron*, 1 Kin. 2:37.

**15**

*x Jesus, vicarious death of, typified*, Matt. 1:21.

fathers, and like your brethren, [x]which trespassed[C] against the LORD God of their fathers, *who* therefore [y]gave them up to desolation, as ye see.

8 Now be ye not [z]stiffnecked, as your fathers *were, but* [a]yield yourselves unto the LORD, and enter into his [b]sanctuary, which he hath sanctified[C] for ever: and serve the LORD your God, that the fierceness of his [c]wrath may turn away from you.

9 For [d]if [e]ye turn again unto the LORD, your brethren and your children *shall find* compassion before them that lead them captive, so that they shall come again into this land: for the LORD your God *is* [f]gracious and [g]merciful, and will not turn away *his* face from you, if ye return unto him.[S]

10 So the [h]posts passed from city to city through the country of [i]Ē′phră-ĭm and [j]Mă-năs′seh even unto [k]Zĕb′u-lŭn: but they [l,m]laughed them to scorn,[G] and mocked them.

11 Nevertheless divers of [n]Ăsh′ēr and [j]Mă-năs′seh and of [k]Zĕb′u-lŭn [o]humbled themselves, and came to [p]Jē-ru̇′să-lĕm.

12 Also in Jū′dah the hand of God was to give them one heart to do the commandment of the king and of the princes, by the word of the LORD.

13 ¶ And there assembled at [p]Jē-ru̇′să-lĕm much[C] people to keep the [q,r]feast of unleavened bread in the second [s]month, a very great congregation.

14 And they arose and [t]took away the [u]altars that *were* in [p]Jē-ru̇′să-lĕm, and all the altars for incense took they away, and cast *them* into the [v]brook [w]Kĭd′ron.

15 Then they [x]killed the [q]passover on the fourteenth *day* of the second [s]month: and the [y,z]priests and the Lē′vītes were ashamed,[C] and [a]sanctified[C] themselves, and [b]brought in the [c]burnt offerings into the [d]house of the LORD.

16 And they stood in their place after their manner,[C] according to the [e]law of Mō′ṣeṣ the man of God: the priests sprinkled the [f,g]blood, *which they received* of the hand of the Lē′vītes.

17 For *there were* many in the congregation that were not sanctified:[C] therefore the [a]Lē′vītes had the charge of the killing of the [h]passovers for every one *that was* not clean, to sanctify *them* unto the LORD.[Q]

18 For a multitude of the people, *even* many of [i]Ē′phră-ĭm, and [j]Mă-năs′seh, [k]Ĭs′sa-char, and [l]Zĕb′u-lŭn, had not cleansed themselves, yet did they eat the [h]passover otherwise than it was written. But [m]Hĕz-e-kī′ah [n,o]prayed for them, saying, The good LORD pardon every one

19 *That* prepareth his [p]heart to [q]seek God, the LORD God of his fathers, though *he be* not *cleansed* according to the purification of the sanctuary.

20 And the LORD [r,s]hearkened to [m]Hĕz-e-kī′ah, and healed the people.

21 And the children of Ĭṣ′ra-el that were present at [t]Jē-ru̇′să-lĕm, kept the [h,u]feast of unleavened bread seven days with great [v]gladness: and the Lē′vītes and the priests [w]praised the LORD day by day, [x]*singing* with loud instruments unto the LORD.

22 And [m]Hĕz-e-kī′ah spake comfortably[G] unto all the [a]Lē′vītes that [3]taught the good knowledge of the LORD: and they did eat throughout the [h,u]feast seven days, offering

v.15–643 BC
See footnote, *Time*, Rev. 10:6.

*y Priests*, Lev. 1:5.
*z Minister, false and corrupt*, Rom. 15:16.

*a Sanctification*, 1 Pet. 1:2.
*b Levites, duties of*, Deut. 10:8.
*c Offerings, burnt*, Lev. 6:17.
*d Temple, Solomon's*, 1 Kin. 6:17.

**16**

*e Law, of Moses*, Deut. 33:2.
*f Blood, sacrificial*, Heb. 9:19.
*g Jesus, atoning blood of, typified*, Matt. 1:21.

**17**

*h Passover*, Num. 9:5.

**18**

*i Ephraim, tribe of*, Gen. 41:52.
*j Manasseh, tribe of*, Gen. 46:20.
*k Issachar, tribe of*, Num. 1:28.
*l Zebulun, tribe of*, Gen. 49:13.
*m Hezekiah*, 2 Kin. 16:20.
*n Prayer, intercessory*, Acts 6:4.
*o Intercession*, Jer. 27:18.

**19**

*p Heart*, Psa. 44:21.
*q Seekers*, Isa. 55:6.

**20**

*r God, mercy of*, Gen. 2:2.
*s Prayer, answered*, Acts 6:4.

**21**

*t Jerusalem*, Judg. 19:10.
*u Annual Feasts*, Num. 15:3.
*v Joy, instances of*, Psa. 5:11.
*w Praise*, Psa. 150:1.
*x Music*, 2 Chr. 5:13.

**22**

3 R. V. were well skilled in the service of the Lord.

[y]peace offerings, and making
[z]confession to the LORD God
of their fathers.
23 And the whole assembly
took counsel to keep other seven
days: and they kept *other* seven
days with [v]gladness.
24 For [a]Hĕz-e-kī′ah king of
[b]Jū′dah [c]did give to the congregation a thousand bullocks and
seven thousand sheep; and the
princes gave to the congregation
a thousand bullocks and ten
thousand sheep: and a great
number of priests [d]sanctified[C]
themselves.
25 And all the congregation of
Jū′dah, with the priests and the
Lē′vītes, and all the congregation that came out of Īṣ′ra-el,
and the [e]strangers[C] that came out
of the land of Īṣ′ra-el, and that
dwelt in [b]Jū′dah, [f]rejoiced.
26 So there was great [f]joy in
[g]Jē-rṳ′sȧ-lĕm: for since the time
of [h]Sŏl′o-mon the son of [i]Dā′vid
king of [j]Īṣ′ra-el *there was* not the
like in Jē-rṳ′sȧ-lĕm.
27 Then the [k]priests the Lē′-
vītes arose and [l]blessed the people: and their voice was heard,
and their [m]prayer came *up* to his
holy dwelling place, *even* unto
[n]heaven.

## CHAPTER 31

*The people destroy idol worship. 2 Hezekiah orders the courses of the priests and Levites, and provides for their work and maintenance. 5 The forwardness of the people in offerings and tithes. 11 Hezekiah appoints officers to dispose of the tithes. 20 His sincerity.*

NOW when all this was finished, all Īṣ′ra-el that were
present [a]went out to the cities
of [b]Jū′dah, and [c]brake the [1]im-
ages in pieces, and cut down the
[2,d]groves[C], and threw down the
[e]high places and the altars out
of all Jū′dah and Bĕn′ja-mĭn,
in [f]Ē′phrȧ-ĭm also and [g]Mȧ-
năs′seh, until they had utterly
destroyed them all. Then all
the children of Īṣ′ra-el returned,
every man to his possession, into their own cities.
2 ¶ And [h,i,j]Hĕz-e-kī′ah appointed the courses[C] of the
[k]priests and the [l]Lē′vītes after
their courses, every man according to his service, the priests and
Lē′vītes for [m]burnt offerings and
for [n]peace offerings, to minister, and to give [o]thanks, and to
praise in the gates of the tents of
the LORD.
3 *He appointed* [p]also the king's
portion[C] of his substance for the
burnt offerings, *to wit*, for the
[q]morning and evening burnt offerings, and the burnt offerings
for the [r]sabbaths, and for the
[s]new moons, and for the set
[t]feasts, as *it is* written in the
[u]law of the LORD.
4 Moreover he commanded the
people that dwelt in [v]Jē-rṳ′sȧ-
lĕm to give the [w,x]portion[C] of
the priests and the Lē′vītes,
that they might [3]be encouraged
in the law of the LORD.
5 And as soon as the commandment came abroad, the children
of Īṣ′ra-el brought in abundance
the [y]firstfruits of corn[C], wine, and
oil, and honey, and of all the
increase of the field; and the
[z]tithe of all *things* brought they
in abundantly.
6 And *concerning* the children of Īṣ′ra-el and Jū′dah,
that dwelt in the cities of Jū′-
dah, they also brought in the
[z]tithe of oxen and sheep, and the
tithe of [4]holy things which were
consecrated unto the LORD
their God, and laid *them* by
heaps[C].
7 In the third [a]month they began to lay the foundation of the
heaps[C], and finished *them* in the
seventh month.
8 And when [b]Hĕz-e-kī′ah and
the princes came and saw the
heaps, they [c]blessed the LORD,
and his people Īṣ′ra-el.

v.22–643 BC
See footnote, *Time*, Rev. 10:6.

y *Offerings, peace*, Lev. 6:17
z *Sin, confession of*, Rom. 5:12.

24
a *Hezekiah*, 2 Kin. 16:20.
b *Judah, kingdom of*, 2 Chr. 11:17.
c *Liberality, instances of*, 1 Tim. 6:18.
d *Sanctification*, 1 Pet. 1:2.

25
e *Foreigners*, Deut. 23:20.
f *Joy, instances of*, Psa. 5:11.

26
g *Jerusalem*, Judg. 19:10.
h *Solomon*, 2 Sam. 12:24.
i *David*, 1 Sam. 16:13.
j *Israel, under the kings*, Ex. 4:22.

27
k *Priest, duties of*, Lev. 1:5.
l *Benedictions*, Deut. 21:5.
m *Prayer*, Acts 6:4.
n *Heaven, God's dwelling place*, Luke 18:22.

1
a *Zeal*, 2 Cor. 7:11.
b *Judah, kingdom of*, 2 Chr. 11:17.
c *Iconoclasm*, Num. 33:52.
d *Groves, destroyed*, Judg. 6:28.
e *High Places*, 1 Kin. 3:2.
f *Ephraim, tribe of*, Gen. 41:52.
g *Manasseh, tribe of*, Gen. 46:20.
**1 R. V. pillars,**
**2 R. V. Asherim,**

v.1–643 BC
See footnote, *Time*, Rev. 10:6.

2
h *Hezekiah*, 2 Kin. 16:20.
i *Rulers, righteous*, Ex. 18:21.
j *Church and State, civil power superior to ecclesiastical*, 1 Sam. 16:1.
k *Priest*, Lev. 1:5.
l *Levites*, Deut. 10:8.
m *Offerings, burnt*, Lev. 6:17.
n *Offerings, peace*, Lev. 6:17.
o *Thankfulness*, Acts 24:3.

3
p *Liberality, instances of*, 1 Tim. 6:18.
q *Offerings, daily*, Lev. 6:17.
r *Sabbath*, Ex. 16:23.
s *New Moon, feast of*, Amos 8:5.
t *Annual Feasts*, Num. 15:3.
u *Law, of Moses*, Deut. 33:2.

4
v *Jerusalem*, Judg. 19:10.
w *Priest, emoluments of*, Lev. 1:5.
x *Levites, emoluments of*, Deut. 10:8.
**3 R. V. give themselves to the**

5
y *First Fruits*, Deut. 18:4.
z *Tithes*, Num. 18:24.

6
**4 R. V. dedicated**

7
a *Month*, Ex. 12:2.

8
b *Hezekiah*, 2 Kin. 16:20.
c *Praise*, Psa. 150:1.

v.9–643 BC
See footnote, *Time*, Rev. 10:6.

**9**
*d Priest*, Lev. 1:5.
*e Levites*, Deut. 10:8.

**10**
*f* 1 Chr. 6:13.
*g High Priest*, Lev. 21:10.
*h Zadok*, 2 Sam. 19:11.
*i Temple, Solomon's*, 1 Kin. 6:17.
*j God, providence of*, Gen. 2:2.
*k Temporal Blessings, from God*, Psa. 103:2.

**12**
*l Tithes, stored in the temple*, Num. 18:24.
*m* 2 Chr. 35:9.

**14**
*n Porter*, 2 Sam. 18:26.
*o Offerings, free will*, Lev. 6:17.
*p Levites, duties of*, Deut. 10:8.
4 R. V. at the east gate,
5 R. V. at the east gate,

**15**
*q Cities, priestly*, Num. 35:8.

**16**
*r Genealogy*, 1 Chr. 5:1.

9 Then [b]Hĕz-e-kī'ah questioned with the [d]priests and the [e]Lē'vītes concerning the heaps.

10 And [f]Ăz-a-rī'ah the [g]chief priest of the house of [h]Zā'dŏk answered him, and said, Since *the people* began to bring the offerings into the [i]house of the LORD, we have had enough to eat, and have left plenty: for the [j]LORD hath [k]blessed his people; and that which is left *is* this great store.[s]

11 ¶ Then [b]Hĕz-e-kī'ah commanded to prepare chambers[G] in the [i]house of the LORD; and they prepared *them*,

12 And brought in the offerings and the [l]tithes and the dedicated *things* faithfully: over which [m]Cŏn-o-nī'ah the Lē'vīte *was* ruler, and Shĭm'e-ī his brother *was* the next.

13 And Jĕ-hī'el, and Ăz-a-zī'ah, and Nā'hăth, and Ā'sa-hĕl, and Jĕr'ĭ-mŏth, and [m]Jŏz'a-băd, and Ĕ-lī'el, and Ĭs-ma-chī'ah, and Mā'hăth, and Bĕ-nā'iah, *were* overseers under the hand of [m]Cŏn-o-nī'ah and Shĭm'e-ī his brother, at the commandment of [b]Hĕz-e-kī'ah the king, and Ăz-a-rī'ah the ruler of the [i]house of God.

14 And Kō'rē the son of Ĭm'nah the Lē'vīte, the [n]porter[G] [5]toward the east, *was* over the [o]freewill offerings of God, to [p]distribute the oblations[G] of the LORD, and the most holy things.

15 And next him *were* Ē'dĕn, and Mĭn'ĭ-a-mĭn, and Jĕsh'u-ȧ, and Shĕm-a-ī'ah, Ăm-a-rī'ah, and Shĕc-a-nī'ah, in the [q]cities of the priests, in *their* set[G] office, to give to their brethren by courses, as well to the great as to the small:

16 Beside their [r]genealogy of males, from three years old and upward, *even* unto every one that entereth into the [i]house of the LORD, his daily portion[G] for their service in their charges according to their courses[G];

17 Both to the [r]genealogy of the [d]priests by the house of their fathers, and the [e]Lē'vītes from twenty years old and upward, in their charges by their courses;

18 And to the [r]genealogy of all their little ones, their wives, and their sons, and their daughters, through all the congregation: for in their set office they [s]sanctified themselves in holiness[G]:

19 Also of the sons of Aâr'on the priests, *which were* in the fields of the suburbs[G] of their cities, in every several[G] city, the men that were expressed by name, to give portions to all the males among the [d]priests, and to all that were reckoned by [r]genealogies among the [e]Lē'vītes.

20 ¶ And thus did [b,t]Hĕz-e-kī'ah throughout all [u]Jū'dah, and [v]wrought *that which was* good and right and [6]truth before the LORD his God.

21 And in every work that he began in the service of the [i]house of God, and in the law, and in the commandments, [w]to seek his God, he [x]did *it* with all his heart, and prospered.

## CHAPTER 32

*Sennacherib invades Judah. 2 Hezekiah fortifies himself, and encourages his people. 9 The blasphemy of Sennacherib, 20 Hezekiah and Isaiah pray. 21 An angel destroys the host of the Assyrians. 24 Hezekiah's sickness. 25 His pride is humbled. 27 His wealth and works. 32 Manasseh succeeds him.*

AFTER these things, and [1]the establishment thereof, *Sĕn-năch'e-rĭb king of [a]Ăs-sy̆r'ĭ-ȧ came, and entered into [b]Jū'dah, and [c]encamped

v.16–643 BC
See footnote, *Time*, Rev. 10:6.

**18**
*s Sanctification*, 1 Pet. 1:2.

**20**
*t Rulers, righteous*, Ex. 18:21.
*u Judah, kingdom of*, 2 Chr. 11:17.
*v Faithfulness, instances of*, Luke 16:10.
6 R. V. faithful

**21**
*w Seekers, instances of*, Isa. 55:6.
*x Diligence, exemplified*, Rom. 12:8.

v.1–632 BC
See footnote, *Time*, Rev. 10:6.

**1**
*a Assyria*, Gen. 25:18.
*b Judah, kingdom of*, 2 Chr. 11:17.
*c Siege, instances of*, Deut. 28:53.
1 R. V. this faithfulness,

* **SENNACHERIB**, king of Assyria. *Invades Judah and takes all fortified cities*, 2 Kin. 18:13; Isa. 36:1. *Lays siege to Jerusalem; 185,000 of his army miraculously destroyed by the angel of the Lord; he abandons the country and returns to Assyria*, 2 Kin. 18:17–37; 19:8, 35, 36; 2 Chr. 32:1–23; Isa. 36:37. *Death of*, 2 Kin. 19:37; 2 Chr. 32:21; Isa. 37:38.

against the fenced[C] [d]cities, and
thought to win them for himself.
2 And when [e]Hĕz-e-kī′ah saw
that *Sĕn-năch′e-rĭb was come,
and that he was purposed to
fight against [f]Jē-ru̥′să-lĕm,
3 He took counsel with his
princes and his mighty men [g]to
stop the waters of the fountains
which *were* without the city: and
they did help him.
4 So there was gathered much
people together, who [g]stopped
all the fountains, and the [h]brook
that ran through the midst of the
land, saying, Why should the
kings of [a]Ăs-sy̆r′ĭ-ȧ come, and
find much water?
5 Also he [2]strengthened himself, and built up all the [i]wall
that was broken, and raised *it* up
to the [j]towers, and another wall
without, and [3]repaired [k]Mĭl′lō
*in* the city of Dā′vid, and made
darts and [l]shields in abundance.
6 And he set [m]captains of war
over the people, and gathered
them together to him in the
[4]street of the gate of the city, and
spake comfortably[C] to them,
saying,
7 [n]Be strong and [o]courageous,
be not afraid nor dismayed for
the king of [a]Ăs-sy̆r′ĭ-ȧ, nor for
all the multitude that *is* with
him: for [p]*there* [5]*be* more with us
than with him:
8 With him *is* an arm of flesh;
but [p]with us *is* the LORD our
[q]God to help us, and to fight our
battles. And the people rested[C]
themselves upon the words of
[e]Hĕz-e-kī′ah king of [b]Jū′dah.
9 ¶ After this did *Sĕn-năch′e-
rĭb king of [a]Ăs-sy̆r′ĭ-ȧ send his
servants to [f]Jē-ru̥′să-lĕm, (but he
[6]*himself laid* [c]*siege* against [r]Lā′-
chish, and all his power with
him,) unto [e]Hĕz-e-kī′ah king
of [b]Jū′dah, and unto all Jū′dah
that *were* at Jē-ru̥′să-lĕm, saying,
10 Thus saith *Sĕn-năch′e-rĭb
king of [a]Ăs-sy̆r′ĭ-ȧ, Whereon[G] do
ye trust, that ye abide in the
[c]siege in [f]Jē-ru̥′să-lĕm?
11 Doth not [e]Hĕz-e-kī′ah persuade you to give over yourselves to die by [s]famine and by
thirst, saying, The LORD our
God shall deliver us out of
the hand of the king of Ăs-
sy̆r′ĭ-ȧ?
12 Hath not the same [e]Hĕz-
e-kī′ah taken away his [t]high[G]
places and his altars, and commanded Jū′dah and Jē-ru̥′să-
lĕm, saying, Ye shall worship
before one [u]altar, and burn [v]in-
cense upon it?
13 [w]Know ye not what I and
my fathers have done unto all
the people of *other* lands? were
the gods of the nations of those
lands any ways able to deliver
their lands out of mine hand?
14 [w]Who *was there* among all
the gods of those nations that
my fathers utterly destroyed,
that could deliver his people
out of mine hand, that your
God should be able to deliver
you out of mine hand?
15 Now therefore let not [e]Hĕz-
e-kī′ah deceive you, nor persuade you on this manner, neither yet believe him: [w]for no god
of any nation or kingdom was
able to deliver his people out of
mine hand, and out of the hand
of my fathers: how much less
shall your God deliver you out
of mine hand.[T]
16 And his servants spake yet
*more* against the LORD God,
and against his servant [e]Hĕz-e-
kī′ah.
17 He wrote also [x]letters to
[y]rail[C] on the LORD God of Ĭs′-
ra-el, and to speak against him,
[w]saying, As the gods of the nations of *other* lands have not delivered their people out of mine
hand, so shall not the God of

v.1–632 BC See footnote, *Time*, Rev. 10:6.
d *Cities, fortified*, Num. 35:8.
2
e *Hezekiah*, 2 Kin. 16:20.
f *Jerusalem*, Judg. 19:10.
3
g *Strategy*, v. 4; Judg. 7:16.
4
h *Brook*, Deut. 8:7.
5
i *Walls*, 1 Sam. 20:25.
j *Tower*, 2 Chr. 26:9.
k *Millo*, 2 Sam. 5:9.
l *Shield*, 1 Kin. 14:27.
2 R. V. took courage,
3 R. V. strengthened
6
m *Captain*, Num. 31:48.
4 R. V. broad place at the
7
n *Faith, enjoined in time of public danger*, Mark 11:22.
o *Courage, enjoined*, Deut. 31:7.
p *Faith, instances of*, Mark 11:22.
5 R. V. is a greater with
8
q *God, providence of*, Gen. 2:2.
9
r *Lachish*, Josh. 10:5.
6 R. V. was before Lachish,
v.9–632 BC

v.10–632 BC See footnote, *Time*, Rev. 10:6.
11
s *Famine*, 2 Kin. 8:1.
12
t *High Places*, 1 Kin. 3:2.
u *Altar*, Ex. 30:1.
v *Incense*, Ex. 37:29.
13
w *Boasting*, Prov. 25:14.
17
x *Letters*, Isa. 37:14.
y *Blasphemy*, 2 Sam. 12:14.

v.17–632 BC
See footnote, *Time*, Rev. 10:6.

18
z *Jews*, Neh. 4:2.

19
a *Blasphemy*, 2 Sam. 12:14.
b *Idol*, 1 Kin. 15:12.

20
c *Hezekiah*, 2 Kin. 16:20.
d *Prophets*, Isa. 3:2.
e *Isaiah*, Isa. 1:1.
f 2 Kin. 19:2, 20; 20:1; Isa. 1:1; 13:1.
g *Prayer, answered*, Acts 6:4.

21
h *Angel, functions of*, Heb. 1:13.
i *Assyria*, Gen. 25:18.
j *Children, wicked*, Mark 10:14.
k *Parricide*, 2 Kin. 19:37.

22
l *God, preserver*, Gen. 2:2.
m *Jerusalem*, Judg. 19:10.
n *God, guide*, Gen. 2:2.

23
o *Presents*, Gen. 32:13.
p *Judah, kingdom, of*, 2 Chr. 11:17.
7 R. V. precious things to

24
q *Afflictions*, Psa. 34:19.
v.24–632 BC

25
r *Ingratitude, of man to God*, Rom. 1:21.
s *Pride*, Prov. 16:18.

Hĕz-e-kī'ah deliver his people
out of mine hand.
18 Then they cried with a loud
voice in the [z]Jews' speech unto
the people of Jĕ-ru'să-lĕm that
*were* on the wall, to affright[G]
them, and to trouble them; that
they might take the city.
19 And they [a]spake against the
God of Jĕ-ru'să-lĕm, as against
the [b]gods of the people of the
earth, *which were* the work of
the hands of man.
20 And for this *cause* [c]Hĕz-e-
kī'ah the king, and the [d]prophet
[e]Ī-sā'iah the son of [f]Ā'mŏz,
[g]prayed and cried to heaven.
21 And [g]the LORD sent an [h]an-
gel, which cut off all the mighty
men of valour, and the leaders
and captains in the camp of the
*king of [i]Ăs-sy̆r'ĭ-ȧ. So he re-
turned with shame of face to his
own land. And when he was
come into the house of his god,
[j]they that came forth of his own
bowels[G] [k]slew him there with the
sword.
22 Thus the [l]LORD saved [c]Hĕz-
e-kī'ah and the inhabitants of
[m]Jĕ-ru'să-lĕm from the hand of
*Sĕn-năch'e-rĭb the king of [i]Ăs-
sy̆r'ĭ-ȧ, and from the hand of all
*other*, and [n]guided them on every
side.
23 And many brought gifts unto the LORD to Jĕ-ru'sa-lĕm,
and [7,o]presents to [c]Hĕz-e-kī'ah
king of [p]Jū'dah: so that he was
magnified in the sight of all nations from thenceforth.
24 ¶ In those days [c]Hĕz-e-kī'-
ah was [q]sick to the death, and
prayed unto the LORD: and he
spake unto him, and he gave
him a sign[G].
25 But [c]Hĕz-e-kī'ah [r]rendered
not again according to the benefit *done* unto him; for his heart[G]
was [s]lifted up: therefore there
was [t]wrath upon him, and upon
[p]Jū'dah and [m]Jĕ-ru'să-lĕm.
26 Notwithstanding [c]Hĕz-e-kī'-
ah [u]humbled himself for the
[s]pride of his heart, *both* he and
the inhabitants of [m]Jĕ-ru'să-lĕm,
so that the wrath of the LORD
came not upon them in the days
of Hĕz-e-kī'ah.
27 ¶ And [c]Hĕz-e-kī'ah had exceeding[G] much [v]riches and honour: and he made himself [w]treas-
uries for [x]silver, and for [y]gold,
and for [z]precious stones, and for
[a]spices, and for [b]shields, and for
all manner of [8]pleasant jewels;
28 †Storehouses also for the increase of [c]corn[G], and [d]wine, and
[e]oil; and stalls for all manner of
beasts, and [9]cotes[G] for flocks.
29 Moreover he provided him
cities, and possessions of flocks
and herds in abundance: for
[f]God had given him [g]substance[G]
very much.
30 This same [h]Hĕz-e-kī'ah also
stopped the upper watercourse
of [i]Gī'hon, and brought it
straight down to the west side of
the [j]city of Dā'vid. And Hĕz-e-
kī'ah [g]prospered in all his works.
31 Howbeit in *the business of*
the [k,l]ambassadors of the princes
of [m]Băb'y̆-lon, who sent unto
him to enquire of the wonder
that was *done* in the land, God
left him, [n]to try[G] him, that he
might know all *that was* in his
heart.
32 ¶ Now the rest of the acts of
[h]Hĕz-e-kī'ah, and his goodness,
behold, they *are* written in the
[o]vision of [p]Ī-sā'iah the prophet
the son of Ā'mŏz, *and* in the
[q]book of the kings of Jū'dah and
Īș'ra-el.
33 And [h]Hĕz-e-kī'ah [r]slept with
his fathers, and they buried him
in the [10]chiefest of the [s]sepul-
chres of the sons of Dā'vid: and

v.25–632 BC
See footnote, *Time*, Rev. 10:6.
t *Nation, punishment of*, Isa. 2:4.

26
u *Repentance, instances of*, Mark 1:4.

27
v *Riches*, Eccl. 4:8.
w *Treasure Houses*, Ezra 5:17.
x *Silver*, 1 Chr. 28:14.
y *Gold*, Ezek. 7:19.
z *Precious Stones*, Ex. 39:10.
a *Spices*, 1 Kin. 10:2.
b *Shield*, 1 Kin. 14:27.
8 R. V. goodly vessels;

28
c *Corn*, Psa. 65:13.
d *Wine*, Prov. 23:31.
e *Oil*, Deut. 12:17.
9 R. V. flocks in folds.

29
f *God, providence of*, Gen. 2:2.
g *Temporal Blessings, from God*, Psa. 103:2.

30
h *Hezekiah*, 2 Kin. 16:20.
i *Gihon*, 1 Kin. 1:33.
j *Jerusalem*, Judg. 19:10.

31
k *Ambassadors*, Josh. 9:4.
l *Interpreter, of languages*, Gen. 40:8.
m *Babylon*, Ezra 5:12.
n *Temptation, a test*, Luke 11:4.
v.31–632 BC

32
o *Vision*, Acts 9:10.
p *Isaiah*, Isa. 1:1.
q *Book*, Num. 5:23.

33
r *Death*, Num. 23:10.
s *Burying Places*, Gen. 23:4.
10 R. V. ascent
v.33–617 BC

† **STOREHOUSES**, Gen. 41:56; Deut. 28:8; 1 Chr. 27:25; 2 Chr. 32:28; Psa. 33:7; Mal. 3:10; Luke 12:24. See footnote, TREASURE HOUSES, Ezra 5:17.

v.33–617 BC
See footnote, *Time*, Rev. 10:6.

*t Manasseh*, 2 Kin. 21:1.

all Jū′dah and the inhabitants of
Jē-ru̦′să-lĕm did him honour at
his death. And [t]Mă-năs′seh his
son reigned in his stead.

## CHAPTER 33

*Manasseh's wicked reign. 3 He restores idolatry. 11 He is carried captive to Babylon. 12 Upon repentance, he is restored to his kingdom. 15 He puts down idolatry. 18 His acts. 20 Amon succeeds him. 21 He reigns wickedly, and is slain by his servants. 25 Josiah succeeds him.*

**1**
*a Manasseh*, 2 Kin. 21:1.
*b Jerusalem*, Judg. 19:10.

**2**
*c Disobedience to God*, Eph. 5:6.
*d Rulers, wicked, instances of*, Ex. 18:21.
*e Canaanites*, Ex. 23:28.

**3**
*f High Places*, 1 Kin. 3:2.
*g Hezekiah*, 2 Kin. 16:20.
*h Altar, used in idolatrous worship*, Gen. 8:20.
*i* Or, *Baal*, 2 Kin. 17:16.
*j Groves*, Judg. 6:28.
*k Idolatry, objects of*, 1 Sam. 15:23.
1 R. V. Asheroth,

**4**
*l Temple, Solomon's*, 1 Kin. 6:17.

**5**
*m Court, of the temple*, Ex. 38:9.

**6**
*n Idolatry, wicked practices of*, 1 Sam. 15:23.
*o Hinnom*, Jer. 7:31.
*p Sorcery*, Isa. 47:9.
*q Witchcraft*, Ex. 22:18.
*r Familiar Spirits*, Deut. 18:11.
*s Anger of God*, 2 Kin. 13:3.
2 R. V. practised augury,
3 R. V. them that had familiar spirits,

**7**
*t Profanation, of the house of God*, Lev. 22:32.
*u Idol*, 1 Kin. 15:12.
*v David*, 1 Sam. 16:13.
*w Solomon*, 2 Sam. 12:24.

[a]MĂ-NĂS′SEH *was* twelve
years old when he began
to reign, and he reigned fifty and
five years in [b]Jē-ru̦′să-lĕm:
2 But [c,d]did *that which was* evil
in the sight of the LORD, like
unto the abominations[G] of the
[e]heathen[G], whom the LORD had
cast out before the children of
Is̱′ra-el.[s]
3 For he built again the [f]high
places which [g]Hĕz-e-kī′ah his father had broken down, and he
reared up [h]altars for [i]Bā′al-ĭm,
and made [1,j]groves[G], and worshipped all the [k]host of heaven,
and served them.
4 Also he built [h]altars in the
[l]house of the LORD, whereof the
LORD had said, In [b]Jĕr-u̦′să-
lĕm shall my name be for ever.
5 And he built [h]altars for all
the [k]host of heaven in the two
[m]courts of the [l]house of the
LORD.
6 And he [n]caused his children
to pass through the fire in the
valley of the son of [o]Hĭn′nom:
also he [2]observed times, and
used [p]enchantments, and used
[q]witchcraft[G], and dealt with [3]a
[r]familiar[G] spirit, and with wizards: he wrought much evil in
the sight of the LORD, to provoke him to [s]anger.
7 And he [t]set a carved [u]image,
the idol which he had made, in
the [l]house[G] of God, of which God
had said to [v]Dā′vid and to [w]Sŏl′-
o-mon his son, In this house[G], and
in [b]Jē-ru̦′să-lĕm, which I have
chosen before all the tribes of
Is̱′ra-el, will I put my name for
ever:
8 Neither will I any more remove the foot of Is̱′ra-el from
out of the land which I have appointed for your fathers; [4,x]so
that they will take heed to do all
that I have commanded them,
according to the whole [y]law and
the statutes and the ordinances
by the hand of Mō′s̱es̱.
9 So Mă-năs′seh [z]made Jū′dah
and the inhabitants of Jē-ru̦′să-
lĕm to err, *and* to do worse than
the [5]heathen, whom the LORD
had destroyed before the children of Is̱′ra-el.
10 ¶ And the LORD spake to
[a]Mă-năs′seh, and to his people:
but they [b]would not hearken[G].
11 Wherefore the [c]LORD
brought upon [d]them the [e]cap-
tains of the host of the king
of [f]Ăs-sȳr′ĭ-ȧ, which took [a]Mă-
năs′seh [6]among the thorns, and
bound him with [g]fetters, and
carried him to [h]Băb′ȳ-lon.
12 And when he was in [i]af-
fliction[G], he [j]besought the LORD
his God, and [k]humbled himself
greatly before the God of his
fathers,[s]
13 And prayed unto him:
and he was [l]intreated of him,
and heard his supplication, and
brought him again to [m]Jē-ru̦′să-
lĕm into his kingdom. Then
[a]Mă-năs′seh knew that the
LORD he *was* God.
14 ¶ Now after this he built
a wall without the [m]city of Dā′-
vid, on the west side of [n]Ḡī′hon,
in the valley, even to the entering in at the [o]fish gate, and
compassed about [p]Ō′phel, and
raised it up a very great height,
and put captains of war in all the
fenced[G] [q]cities of Jū′dah.
15 And he [r]took away the
strange[G] gods, and the idol out of
the [s]house of the LORD, and all

**8**
*x Blessings, contingent upon obedience*, Deut. 11:26.
*y Law, of Moses*, Deut. 33:2.
4 R. V. if only they will observe to do

**9**
*z Influence, evil*, 1 Cor. 7:14.
5 R. V. nations,

**10**
*a Manasseh*, 2 Kin. 21:1.
*b Impenitence*, Rom. 2:5.

**11**
*c God, providence of*, Gen. 2:2.
*d Nation, punishment of*, Isa. 2:4.
*e Captain*, Num. 31:48.
*f Assyria*, Gen. 25:18.
*g Fetters*, Mark 5:4.
*h Babylon, empire of*, Ezra 5:12.
6 R. V. in chains,

**12**
*i Adversity, prayer in*, v. 13; Psa. 10:6.
*j Prayer, in adversity*, Acts 6:4.
*k Repentance, instances of*, Mark 1:4.

**13**
*l Prayer, answered*, Acts 6:4.
*m Jerusalem*, Judg. 19:10.

**14**
*n Gihon*, 1 Kin. 1:33.
*o Jerusalem, gates of*, Judg. 19:10.
*p Jerusalem, towers of*, Judg. 19:10.
*q Cities, fortified*, Num. 35:8.

**15**
*r Iconoclasm*, Num. 33:52.
*s Temple, Solomon's*, 1 Kin. 6:17.

the [t]altars that he had built in the mount of the house of the LORD, and in [m]Jē-rṳ'sā-lĕm, and cast *them* out of the city.

16 And he repaired the [u]altar of the LORD, and sacrificed thereon [v]peace offerings and [w]thank offerings, and commanded [x]Jū'dah to serve the LORD God of Ĭs̤'ra-el.

17 Nevertheless the people did sacrifice still in the [y]high places, *yet* unto the LORD their God only.

18 ¶ Now the rest of the acts of Mȧ-năs'seh, and his [z]prayer unto his God, and the words of the seers that spake to him [a]in the name of the LORD God of Ĭs̤'ra-el, behold, they *are written* in the [b]book of the kings of Ĭs̤'ra-el.

19 His prayer also, and *how God* [c]was intreated of him, and all his sins, and his trespass, and the places wherein he built [d]high places, and set up [7,e]groves and graven [f]images, before he was humbled: behold, they *are* written [8]among the sayings of the seers.

20 So [g]Mȧ-năs'seh [h]slept with his fathers, and they buried him in his own [i]house: and [j]Ā'mon his son reigned in his stead.

21 ¶ [j]Ā'mon *was* two and twenty years old when he began to reign, and reigned two years in [k]Jē-rṳ'sā-lĕm.

22 But [l]he did *that which was* evil in the sight of the LORD, [m]as did [g]Mȧ-năs'seh his father: for [j]Ā'mon [n]sacrificed unto all the carved images which Mȧ-năs'seh his father had made, and served them;

23 And [o]humbled not himself before the LORD, [o]as [g]Mănăs'seh his father had humbled himself; but [j]Ā'mon trespassed more and more.

24 And his servants [p]conspired against him, and [q,r]slew him in his own house.

25 But the people of the land slew all them that had [p]conspired against king [j]Ā'mon; and the people of the land made [s]Jō-sī'ah his son king in his stead.

## CHAPTER 34

*Josiah's good reign. 3 He destroys idolatry. 8 He provides for the repair of the temple. 14 Hilkiah finds the book of the law in the temple. 20 Josiah sends to Huldah to inquire of the Lord. 23 Huldah foretells the destruction of Jerusalem, to take place after the death of Josiah. 28 Josiah causes the book to be read in a solemn assembly, and renews the covenant with God.*

[a]JŌ-SĪ'AH *was* eight years old when he began to reign, and he reigned in [b]Jē-rṳ'sā-lĕm one and thirty years.

2 And [c,d]he did *that which was* right in the sight of the LORD, and walked [e]in the ways of [f]Dā'vid his father, and declined *neither* to the right hand, nor to the left.

3 For in the eighth year of his reign, while he was yet [g]young, [h]he began to [i]seek after the God of [f]Dā'vid his father: and in the twelfth year he began to purge [j]Jū'dah and [b]Jē-rṳ'sā-lĕm from the [k]high places, and the [1,l]groves, and the carved [m]images, and the molten images.

4 And they [n]brake down the [o]altars of [p]Bā'al-ĭm in his presence; and the [2]images, that *were* on high above them, he cut down; and the [1,l]groves, and the carved [m]images, and the molten images, he brake in pieces, and made dust *of them*, and strowed *it* upon the graves of them that had sacrificed unto them.

5 And he [q]burnt the bones of the priests upon their altars, and cleansed [j]Jū'dah and [b]Jē-rṳ'sā-lĕm.

6 And *so did he* in the cities of [r]Mȧ-năs'seh, and [s]Ē'phrȧ-ĭm, and [t]Sĭm'e-on, even unto [u]Năph'ta-lī, [3]with their mattocks round about.

t *Altar, used in idolatrous worship*, Gen. 8:20.

16

u *Altar, of burnt offerings*, Gen. 8: 20.
v *Offerings, peace*, Lev. 6:17.
w *Offerings, thank*, Lev. 6:17.
x *Judah, kingdom of*, 2 Chr. 11:17.

17

y *High Places*, 1 Kin. 3:2.

18

z *Prayer, exemplified*, Acts 6:4.

a *Prophets, inspiration of*, Isa. 3:2.
b *Book*, Num. 5:23.

19

c *Prayer, answered*, Acts 6:4.
d *High Places*, 1 Kin. 3:2.
e *Groves*, Judg. 6:28.
f *Idol*, 1 Kin. 15:12.
7 R. V. the Asherim
8 R. V. in the history of Hozai.

20

g *Manasseh*, 2 Kin. 21:1.
h *Death*, Num. 23:10.
i *Burying Places*, Gen. 23:4.
j *Amon*, 2 Kin. 21:18.

21

k *Jerusalem*, Judg. 19:10.

22

l *Rulers, wicked*, Ex. 18:21.
m *Influence, evil*, 1 Cor. 7:14.
n *Idolatry*, 1 Sam. 15:23.

23

o *Impenitence, instances of*, Rom. 2:5.

24

p *Conspiracy, instances of*, 1 Kin. 16:9.

**v.24–560 BC**
See footnote, *Time*, Rev. 10:6.

q *Homicide, felonious, instances of*, Deut. 5:17.
r *Regicide*, 2 Sam. 1:10.

25

s *Josiah*, 1 Kin. 13:2.

**v.1–560 BC**

1

a *Josiah*, 1 Kin. 13:2.
b *Jerusalem*, Judg. 19:10.

2

c *Rulers, righteous instances of*, Ex. 18:21.
d *Children, good*, Mark 10:14.
e *Influence, good*, 1 Cor. 7:14.
f *David*, 1 Sam. 16:13.

3

g *Young Men*, Prov. 1:4.
h *Zeal, instances of*, 2 Cor. 7:11.
i *Seekers, instances of*, Isa. 55:6.
j *Judah, kingdom of*, 2 Chr. 11:17.
k *High Places*, 1 Kin. 3:2.
l *Groves*, Judg. 6:28.
m *Idol*, 1 Kin. 15:12.
1 R. V. Asherim,

**v.4–548 BC**

4

n *Iconoclasm*, Num. 33:52.
o *Altar, used in idolatrous worship*, Gen. 8:20.
p Or, *Baal*, 2 Kin. 17:16.
2 R. V. sun-images,

5

q *Cremation*, Josh. 7:25.

6

r *Manasseh, tribe of*, Gen. 46:20.
s *Ephraim, tribe of*, Gen. 41:52.
t *Simeon, tribe of*, Num. 2:12.
u *Naphtali, tribe of*, Num. 1:42.
3 R. V. in their ruins round about.

v.7–548 BC
See footnote, *Time*, Rev. 10:6.

7 And when he had [n]broken down the [o]altars and the [1,l]groves[G], and had beaten the graven[G] [v,m]images[G] into powder, and cut down all the [2]idols throughout all the land of Ĭṣ ra-el, he returned to [b]Jĕ-rụ să-lĕm.

8 ¶ Now in the eighteenth year of his reign, when he had purged the land, and the [v]house, he sent *Shā′phan the son of [w]Ăz-a-lī′-ah, and Mā-a-sē′iah the [x]governor of the city, and Jō′ah the son of Jō′a-hăz the recorder, to repair the house of the LORD his God.

9 And when they came to [y]Hĭl-kī′ah the [z]high priest, they delivered the [a]money that was [b]brought into the [c]house of God, which the [d]Lē′vītes that kept the doors had gathered of the hand of [e]Mă-năs′seh and [f]Ē′phră-ĭm, and of all the remnant of Ĭṣ′ra-el, and of all [g]Jū′dah and [h]Bĕn′-ja-mĭn; and they returned to [i]Jĕ-rụ′să-lĕm.

10 And they put [a]*it* in the hand of the workmen that had the oversight of the [c]house of the LORD, and they gave it to the workmen that wrought in the house of the LORD, to repair and amend[G] the house:

11 Even to the artificers[G] and [j]builders gave they [a]*it*, to buy hewn [k]stone, and timber for couplings, and to [4]floor the houses which the kings of [l]Jū′dah had destroyed.

12 And the men did the work [m]faithfully: and the overseers of them *were* Jā′hăth and Ō-ba-dī′ah, the [n]Lē′vītes, of the [o]sons of Mĕ-rā′rī; and Zĕch-a-rī′ah and Mĕ-shŭl′lam, of the sons of the [p]Kō′hath-ītes, to set[G] *it* forward; and *other of* the Lē′vītes, all that could skill[G] of [q]instruments of musick.

13 Also *they were* over the bearers of burdens, and *were* overseers of all that wrought the work in any manner of service: and of the [r]Lē′vītes *there were* [s]scribes, and officers, and [d]porters.

14 ¶ And when they brought out the [a]money that was brought into the [c]house of the LORD, Hĭl-kī′ah the [t]priest found [5,u]a book of the [v]law of the LORD *given* by Mō′ṣeṣ.

15 And Hĭl-kī′ah answered and said to *Shā′phan the [s]scribe, I have found the [5,u]book of the [v]law in the [c]house of the LORD. And Hĭl-kī′ah delivered the book to Shā′phan.

16 And *Shā′phan carried the [u]book to the [w,x]king, and brought the king word back again, saying, All that was committed to thy servants, [m]they do *it*.

17 And they have [6]gathered together the [a]money that was found in the [c]house of the LORD, and have delivered it into the hand of the overseers, and to the hand of the workmen.

18 Then *Shā′phan the [s]scribe told the [w,x]king, saying, Hĭl-kī′ah the priest hath given me a [u]book. And Shā′phan read it before the king.

19 And it came to pass, when the [w,x]king had heard the words of the [v]law, that he rent[G] his clothes.

20 And the [w]king commanded Hĭl-kī′ah, and [y]Ă-hī′kam the son of *Shā′phan, and [z]Ăb′dŏn the son of [a]Mī′cah, and Shā′-phan the [b]scribe, and [c]Ā-sa-ī′ah a servant of the king's, saying,

21 Go, [d]enquire of the LORD for me, and for them that are left in Ĭṣ′ra-el and in Jū′dah,

8
*v* *Temple, Solomon's*, 1 Kin. 6:17.
*w* 2 Kin. 22:3.
*x* *Government, municipal*, Isa. 22:21.
v.8–542 BC

9
*y* *Scribe*, 1 Kin. 4:3.
*z* *High Priest, duties of*, Lev. 21:10.
*a* *Money*, Jer. 32:9.
*b* *Liberality, instances of*, 1 Tim. 6:18.
*c* *Temple, Solomon's*, 1 Kin. 6:17.
*d* *Porters*, 2 Sam. 18:26.
*e* *Manasseh, tribe of*, Gen. 46:20.
*f* *Ephraim, tribe of*, Gen. 41:52.
*g* *Judah, tribe of*, Num. 10:14.
*h* *Benjamin, tribe of*, Num. 1:37.
*i* *Jerusalem*, Judg. 19:10.

11
*j* *Carpentry*, 2 Kin. 12:11.
*k* *Stones, hewn*, Ex. 24:12.
*l* *Judah, kingdom of*, 2 Chr. 11:17.
4 R. V. make beams for the houses

12
*m* *Faithfulness, instances of*, Luke 16:10.
*n* *Levites*, Deut. 10:8.
*o* *Merarites, duties of*, Num. 26:57.
*p* *Kohathites, duties of*, Num. 3:27.
*q* *Music, instruments of*, 2 Chr. 5:13.

v.13–542 BC
See footnote, *Time*, Rev. 10:6.

13
*r* *Levites, duties of*, Deut. 10:8.
*s* *Scribe*, 1 Kin. 4:3.

14
*t* *High Priest*, Lev. 21:10.
*u* *Book*, Num. 5:23.
*v* *Law, of Moses*, Deut. 33:2.
5 R. V. the book

16
*w* *King*, 2 Kin. 3:10.
*x* *Josiah*, 1 Kin. 13:2.

17
6 R. V. emptied out

20
*y* *Ahikam*, 2 Kin. 22:12.
*z* Or, *Achbor*, 2 Kin. 22:12.
*a* Or, *Michaiah*, 2 Kin. 22:12.
*b* *Scribe*, 1 Kin. 4:3.
*c* Or, *Asahiah*, 2 Kin. 22:12–20.

21
*d* *Guidance, prayer for*, Psa. 48:14.

* **SHAPHAN.** *A scribe at the time of the reign of Josiah, king of Judah*, 2 Kin. 22:3–14; 25:22; 2 Chr. 34:8–20. *Probably identical with the Shaphan mentioned in* Jer. 26:24; 39:14; 40:5, 9, 11; 41:2; 43:6.

concerning the words of the [e]book that is found: for great *is* the [f]wrath of the LORD that is poured out upon us, because our fathers have not kept the [g]word of the LORD, to do after all that is written in this book.[T]

22 And [h]Hĭl-kī′ah, and *they* that the king *had appointed,* went to [i]Hŭl′dah the [j,k]prophetess, the wife of [l]Shăl′lum the son of [m]Tĭk′văth, the son of [n]Hăs′rah, keeper of the wardrobe; (now she dwelt in [o]Jē-ru′să-lĕm in the [7]college[G]:) and they spake to her to that *effect.*

23 And [j,k]she answered them, Thus saith the LORD God of Ĭs′ra-el, Tell ye the man that sent you to me,

24 Thus saith the LORD, Behold, I will [f]bring evil upon this place, and upon the inhabitants thereof, *even* all the curses that are written in the [e,g]book which they have read before the king of Jū′dah:

25 Because they have [p]forsaken me, and have [q]burned [r]incense[G] unto other gods, that they might provoke me to anger with all the works of their hands; therefore my [f]wrath shall be poured out upon this place, and shall not be quenched.

26 And as for the [s]king of [t]Jū′dah, who sent you to [d]enquire of the LORD, so shall ye say unto him, Thus saith the LORD God of Ĭs′ra-el *concerning* the words which thou hast heard;

27 Because thine heart was tender, and thou didst [u]humble thyself before God, when thou heardest his words against this place, and against the inhabitants thereof, and humbledst thyself before me, and didst [†]rend[G] thy clothes, and weep before me; I have even [v]heard *thee* also, saith the LORD.

28 Behold, I will gather thee to thy fathers, and thou shalt be gathered to thy grave in peace, neither shall thine eyes see all the [f]evil that I will bring upon this place, and upon the inhabitants of the same. So they brought the king word again.

29 ¶ Then the [s]king sent and gathered together all the [w]elders of Jū′dah and Jē-ru′să-lĕm.

30 And [x]the king went up into the [y]house of the LORD, and all the men of Jū′dah, and the inhabitants of Jē-ru′să-lĕm, and the [z]priests, and the [a]Lē′vītes, and all the people, great and small: and he [b]read in their ears all the words of the [c]book of the covenant that was found in the house of the LORD.

31 And the [d]king stood in his place, and [e]made a [f]covenant before the LORD, to walk after the LORD, and to keep his commandments, and his testimonies, and his statutes, with all his heart, and with all his soul, to perform the words of the covenant which are written in this [c]book.

32 And he [g]caused all that were present in Jē-ru′să-lĕm and [h]Bĕn′ja-mĭn to stand *to it.* And the inhabitants of Jē-ru′să-lĕm did according to the covenant of God, the God of their fathers.

33 And Jō-sī′ah took away all the abominations[G] out of all the countries that *pertained* to the children of Ĭs′ra-el, and [g]made all that were present in Ĭs′ra-el to serve, *even* to serve the LORD their God. *And* all his days they departed not from following the LORD, the God of their fathers.

**v.21–542 BC** See footnote, *Time,* Rev. 10:6.

e *Book,* Num. 5:23.
f *Nation, punishment of,* Isa. 2:4.
g *Law, of Moses,* Deut. 33:2.

**22**
h *Hilkiah,* Jer. 29:3.
i 2 Kin. 22:14–20.
j *Prophetess,* Judg. 4:4.
k *Women, as prophets,* Prov. 31:10.
l 2 Kin. 22:14.
m Or, *Tikvah,* 2 Kin. 22:14.
n Or, *Harhas,* 2 Kin. 22:14.
o *Jerusalem,* Judg. 19:10
7 R. V. second quarter;

**25**
p *Backsliding, of Israel,* Hos. 11:7.
q *Idolatry,* 1 Sam. 15:23.
r *Incense, offered in idolatrous worship,* Ex. 37:29.

**26**
s *Josiah,* 1 Kin. 13:2.
t *Judah, kingdom of,* 2 Chr. 11:17.

**27**
u *Humility, instances of,* Prov. 22:4.

**v.27–542 BC** See footnote, *Time,* Rev. 10:6.

v *Prayer, answered,* Acts 6:4.

**29**
w *Senate,* Num. 11:16.

**30**
x *Rulers, righteous,* Ex. 18:21.
y *Temple, Solomon's,* 1 Kin. 6:17.
z *Priest,* Lev. 1:5.
a *Levites,* Deut. 10:8.
b *Instruction, in religion,* Prov. 23:23.
c *Word of God,* Psa. 119:9.

**31**
d *Josiah,* 1 Kin. 13:2.
e *Decision, instances of,* Isa. 50:7.
f *Covenant, of man with God,* Deut. 29:1.

**32**
g *Influence, good,* 1 Cor. 7:14.
h *Benjamin, tribe of,* Num. 1:37.

† **RENDING OF GARMENTS.** *A token, of affliction.* Gen. 37:29, 34; 44:13; Num. 14:6; Judg. 11:35; 2 Sam. 1:2, 11; 3:31; 13:19, 31; 15:32; 2 Kin. 2:12; 5:7; 6:30; 11:14; 19:1; 22:11, 19; Ezra 9:3, 5; Job 1:20; 2:12; Isa. 36:22; 37:1; Jer. 41:5; *of indignation,* Matt. 26:65; *of surprise,* Acts 14:14.
**Figurative,** Joel 2:13. *Symbolical, by Samuel,* 1 Sam. 15:27, 28; *by Ahijah,* 1 Kin. 11:30–32.

## CHAPTER 35

*Josiah keeps a solemn passover. 20 He, going against Pharaoh-nechoh, is slain at Megiddo. 25 Lamentations for Josiah.*

MOREOVER[a,b] Jō-sī′ah [c]kept
a [d]passover unto the LORD
in [e]Jē-ru̥′sā-lĕm: and they [f]killed
the passover on the fourteenth
*day* of the first [g]month.
2 And [b,h]he set the [i]priests in
their charges[G], and encouraged
them to the service of the [j]house
of the LORD,
3 And [h]said unto the [k]Lē′vītes
that [l]taught all Ĭs̱′ra-el, which
were [m]holy unto the LORD, Put
the holy [n]ark in the [o]house
which [p]Sŏl′o-mon the son of
[q]Dā′vid king of [r]Ĭs̱′ra-el did
build; *it shall* not *be* a burden[G]
upon *your* shoulders: serve now
the LORD your God, and his
people Ĭs̱′ra-el,
4 [h]And prepare *yourselves* by
the houses[G] of your fathers, after
your courses[G], according to the
writing of Dā′vid king of Ĭs̱′-
ra-el, and according to the writing of Sŏl′o-mon his son.
5 And stand in the [s]holy *place*
according to the divisions of the
families of the fathers of your
brethren the people, and *after*
the division of the families of the
Lē′vītes.
6 So kill the [d]passover, and
[t]sanctify yourselves, and prepare
your brethren, that *they* may do
according to the [u]word of the
LORD by the hand of Mō′s̱ĕs̱.
7 And [a]Jō-sī′ah [v]gave to the
[1]people, of the flock, lambs and
kids, all for the [d]passover offerings, for all that were present, to
the number of thirty thousand,
and three thousand [w]bullocks:
these *were* of the king's substance[G].
8 And his princes [v]gave [2]will-
ingly unto the people, to the
priests, and to the Lē′vītes: [x]Hĭl-
kī′ah and Zĕch-a-rī′ah and Jē-
hī′el, rulers of the [o]house of God,
gave unto the priests for the
passover offerings two thousand
and six hundred *small cattle*[G], and
three hundred [w]oxen.
9 [y]Cŏn-a-nī′ah also, and Shĕm-
a-ī′ah and Nē-thăn′e-el, his
brethren, and Hăsh-a-bī′ah and
Jē-ī′el and [z]Jŏz′a-băd, chief of
the Lē′vītes, [v]gave unto the Lē′-
vītes for passover offerings five
thousand *small cattle*, and five
hundred oxen.
10 So the service was prepared,
and the [a]priests stood in their
place, and the [b]Lē′vītes in their
courses[G], according to the king's
commandment.
11 And [a]they [c]killed the [d]pass-
over, and the priests sprinkled
*the* [e,f]*blood* [3]from their hands,
and the [b]Lē′vītes flayed[G] *them*.
12 And they removed the
[g]burnt offerings, that they might
give according to the divisions of
the families of the people, to offer unto the LORD, as *it is* written in the [h]book of Mō′s̱ĕs̱. And
so *did they* with the [i]oxen.
13 And they roasted the [d]pass-
over with fire according to the
ordinance[G]: but the *other* holy *offerings* sod[G] they in pots, and in
[j]caldrons, and in pans, and divided *them* speedily among all
the people.
14 And afterward they made
ready for themselves, and for the
priests: because the [a]priests the
sons of Aâr′on *were busied* in offering of [g]burnt offerings and the
fat until night; therefore the [b]Lē′-
vītes prepared for themselves,
and for the priests the sons of
Aâr′on.
15 And the [k]singers the sons of
[l]Ā′saph *were* in their place, according to the commandment of
[m]Dā′vid, and Ā′saph, and [n]Hē′-
man, and [o]Jĕd′u̥-thŭn the king's
seer; and the [p]porters[G] *waited* at
every gate; they might not de-

v.1–541 BC
See footnote, *Time*, Rev. 10:6.

**1**
a *Josiah*, 1 Kin. 13:2.
b *Rulers, righteous*, Ex. 18:21.
c *Religious Revivals*, Hab. 3:2.
d *Passover*, Num. 9:5.
e *Jerusalem*, Judg. 19:10.
f *Jesus, vicarious death of, typified*, Matt. 1:21.
g *Month, Abib*, Ex. 12:2.

**2**
h *Church and State, civil power superior to ecclesiastical*, 1 Sam. 16:1.
i *Priest, duties of*, Lev. 1:5.
j *Temple, Solomon's*, 1 Kin. 6:17.

**3**
k *Levites, duties of*, Deut. 10:8.
l *Instruction, in religion*, Prov. 23:23.
m *Holiness*, Ex. 39:30.
n *Ark*, Ex. 25:10.
o *Temple, Solomon's*, 1 Kin. 6:17.
p *Solomon*, 2 Sam. 12:24.
q *David*, 1 Sam. 16:13.
r *Israel, under the kings*, Ex. 4:22.

**5**
s *Holy Place*, Ex. 26:33.

**6**
t *Sanctification*, 1 Pet. 1:2.
u *Law, of Moses*, Deut. 33:2.

**7**
v *Liberality, instances of*, 1 Tim. 6:18.
w *Bullock*, Ex. 29:3.
1 R. V. children of the people,

**8**
x *Hilkiah*, Jer. 29:3.
2 R. V. for a freewill offering

v.8–541 BC
See footnote, *Time*, Rev. 10:6.

**9**
y Or, *Cononiah*, 2 Chr. 31:12, 13.
z 2 Chr. 31:13.

**10**
a *Priest, duties of*, Lev. 1:5.
b *Levites, duties of*, Deut. 10:8.

**11**
c *Jesus, vicarious death of, typified*, Matt. 1:21.
d *Passover*, Num. 9:5.
e *Blood, sacrificial*, Heb. 9:19.
f *Jesus, atoning blood of, typified*, Matt. 1:21.
3 R. V. which they received of their hand,

**12**
g *Offerings, burnt*, Lev. 6:17.
h *Law, of Moses*, Deut. 33:2.
i *Bullock*, Ex. 29:3.

**13**
j *Caldron*, 1 Sam. 2:14.

**15**
k *Choir*, 1 Chr. 15:16.
l *Asaph*, 1 Chr. 15:17.
m *David*, 1 Sam. 16:13.
n *Heman*, 1 Chr. 6:33.
o *Jeduthun*, 1 Chr. 16:41.
p *Porters*, 2 Sam. 18:26.

v.15–541 BC
See footnote, *Time*, Rev. 10:6.

16
*q Altar*, Gen. 8:20.
*r Josiah*, 1 Kin. 13:2.

18
*s Samuel*, 1 Sam. 3:1.
*t Jerusalem*, Judg. 19:10.

20
*u Temple, Solomon's*, 1 Kin. 6:17.
*v* Or, *Pharaoh-nechoh*, 2 Kin. 23:29.
*w Egypt*, Gen. 41:8.
*x* Isa. 10:9; Jer. 46:2.
*y Euphrates*, Gen. 15:18.

v.20–529 BC

21
*z Ambassadors*, Josh. 9:4.

*a Judah, kingdom of*, 2 Chr. 11:17.
*b War, God in*, Judg. 3:2.

22
*c Josiah*, 1 Kin. 13:2.
*d Self-will, exemplified*, Gen. 49:6.
*e Rashness*, 2 Sam. 6:7.
*f* Or, *Pharaoh-nechoh*, 2 Kin. 23:29.
*g Megiddo*, Josh. 17:11.

23
*h Archery*, Gen. 21:20.

part from their service; for their
brethren the [b]Lē′vītes prepared
for them.
16 So all the service of the
LORD was prepared the same
day, to keep the [d]passover, and
to offer [q]burnt offerings upon the
[q]altar of the LORD, according
to the commandment of king
[r]Jȯ-sī′ah.
17 And the children of Ĭṣ′ra-el
that were present kept the [d]pass-
over at that time, and the feast
of unleavened bread seven days.
18 And there was no [d]passover
like to that kept in Ĭṣ′ra-el from
the days of [s]Săm′u-el the prophet; neither did all the kings of
Ĭṣ′ra-el keep such a passover as
[r]Jȯ-sī′ah kept, and the priests,
and the Lē′vītes, and all Jū′-
dah and Ĭṣ′ra-el that were present, and the inhabitants of [t]Jė-
rṳ′sȧ-lĕm.
19 In the eighteenth year of the
reign of [r]Jȯ-sī′ah was this [d]pass-
over kept.
20 ¶ After all this, when [r]Jȯ-
sī′ah had prepared the [u]temple,
[v]Nē′chȯ king of [w]Ē′ġypt came
up to fight against [x]Chär′che-
mĭsh by [y]Eū-phrā′tēṣ: and Jȯ-
sī′ah went out against him.
21 But he sent [z]ambassadors to
him, saying, What have I to do
with thee, thou king of [a]Jū′dah?
*I come* not against thee this day,
but against the house[G] wherewith
I have war: for [b]God commanded me to make haste: forbear
thee from *meddling with* God,
who *is* with me, that he destroy
thee not.
22 Nevertheless [c]Jȯ-sī′ah
[d,e]would not turn his face from
him, but disguised himself, that
he might fight with him, and
hearkened not unto the words of
[f]Nē′chȯ from the mouth of God,
and came to fight in the valley of
[g]Mė-ġĭd′dȯ.
23 And the [h]archers shot at
king [c]Jȯ-sī′ah; and the king said
to his servants, Have[G] me away;
for I am sore[G] wounded.
24 His servants therefore took
him out of that [i]chariot, and put
him in the second chariot that he
had; and they brought him to
[j]Jė-rṳ′sȧ-lĕm, and he [k]died, and
was buried in *one of* the [l]sep-
ulchres of his fathers. And
all [a]Jū′dah and Jė-rṳ′sȧ-lĕm
mourned for [c]Jȯ-sī′ah.
25 And [m]Jĕr-e-mī′ah lamented
for [c]Jȯ-sī′ah: and all the [n]singing
men and the [n]singing women
spake of Jȯ-sī′ah in their [o]lamen-
tations to this day, and made
them an ordinance in Ĭṣ′ra-el:
and, behold, they *are* written in
the lamentations.
26 Now the rest of the acts of
[c]Jȯ-sī′ah, and his [4]goodness, according to *that which was* written in the [p]law of the LORD,
27 And his deeds, first and last,
behold, they *are* written in the
[q]book of the kings of Ĭṣ′ra-el and
Jū′dah.

## CHAPTER 36

*Jehoahaz, made king, is deposed by Pharaoh-nechoh, and carried into Egypt. 5 Jehoiakim's evil reign; he is carried bound to Babylon. 9 Jehoiachin's evil reign; he is brought to Babylon. 11 Zedekiah's evil reign; he rebels against Nebuchadnezzar. 14 For the transgressions of the priests and the people, Jerusalem is wholly destroyed. 22 The proclamation of Cyrus.*

THEN the people of the land
took [a]Jė-hō′a-hăz the son
of [b]Jȯ-sī′ah, and made him king
in his father's stead in [c]Jė-rṳ′-
sȧ-lĕm.
2 [a]Jė-hō′a-hăz *was* twenty and
three years old when he began
to reign, and he reigned three
months in [c]Jė-rṳ′sȧ-lĕm.
3 And the [d]king of [e]Ē′ġÿpt [1]put
him down at [c]Jė-rṳ′sȧ-lĕm and
[2,f]condemned[C] the land in an
hundred [g]talents[G] of [h]silver and a
talent[C] of [i]gold.
4 And the [d]king of [e]Ē′ġÿpt
made Ė-lī′a-kĭm his brother
king over [j]Jū′dah and [c]Jė-rṳ′-

v.23–529 BC
See footnote, *Time*, Rev. 10:6.

24
*i Chariot*, Josh. 11:4.
*j Jerusalem*, Judg. 19:10.
*k Death*, Num. 23:10.
*l Burying Places*, Gen. 23:4.

25
*m Jeremiah*, Jer. 1:1.
*n Choir*, 1 Chr. 15:16.
*o Mourning*, Lam. 2:5.

26
*p Law, of Moses*, Deut. 33:2.
4 R. V. good deeds,

27
*q Book*, Num. 5:23.

1
*a Jehoahaz*, 2 Kin. 23:30.
*b Josiah*, 1 Kin. 13:2.
*c Jerusalem*, Judg. 19:10.

3
*d Pharaoh-nechoh*, 2 Kin. 23:29.
*e Egypt*, Gen. 41:8.
*f Tribute*, Ezra 4:13.
*g Talent*, Ex. 38:25.
*h Silver*, 1 Chr. 28:14.
*i Gold*, Ezek. 7:19.
1 R. V. deposed him at
2 R. V. amerced

4
*j Judah, kingdom of*, 2 Chr. 11:17.

v.4–529 BC See footnote, *Time*, Rev. 10:6.
k *Jehoiakim*, Jer. 26:1.
l *Captive*, 1 Sam. 30:3.

sā-lĕm, and turned his name to
[k]Jĕ-hoi′a-kĭm. And [d]Nē′chō
took [a]Jĕ-hō′a-hăz his brother,
and [l]carried him to [e]Ē′ġy̆pt.
5 ¶ [k]Jĕ-hoi′a-kĭm *was* twenty
and five years old when he began
to reign, and he reigned eleven
years in [c]Jĕ-ru̥′sā-lĕm: and [m]he
did *that which was* evil in the
sight of the LORD his God.
6 Against him came up [n]Nĕb-
u-chad-nĕz′zar king of [o]Băb′y̆-
lon, and bound him in [p]fetters,
to [l]carry him to [q]Băb′y̆-lon.
7 [n]Nĕb-u-chad-nĕz′zar also carried of the vessels of the [r]house
of the LORD to [q]Băb′y̆-lon, and
put them in his [s]temple at Băb′-
y̆-lon.
8 Now the rest of the acts of
[k]Jĕ-hoi′a-kĭm, and his abominations which he did, and that
which was found in him, behold,
they *are* written in the [t]book
of the kings of Ĭs′ra-el and Jū′-
dah: and [u]Jĕ-hoi′a-chĭn his son
reigned in his stead.
9 ¶ [u]Jĕ-hoi′a-chĭn *was* eight
years old when he began to reign,
and he reigned three months
and ten days in [c]Jĕ-ru̥′sā-lĕm:
and [m]he did *that which was*
evil in the sight of the LORD.
10 And when the year was expired, king [n]Nĕb-u-chad-nĕz′zar
sent, and [l]brought him to [q]Băb′-
y̆-lon, with the goodly vessels of
the [r]house of the LORD, and
made [v]Zĕd-e-kī′ah his brother
king over [j]Jū′dah and [c]Jĕ-ru̥′-
sā-lĕm.
11 ¶ [v]Zĕd-e-kī′ah *was* one and
twenty years old when he began to reign, and reigned eleven
years in [c]Jĕ-ru̥′sā-lĕm.
12 And [m]he did *that which was*
evil in the sight of the LORD his
God, *and* [w]humbled not himself
before [x]Jĕr-e-mī′ah the prophet
*speaking* [y]from the mouth of the
LORD.
13 And he also [z]rebelled against

5
m *Rulers, wicked*, Ex. 18:21.
6
n *Nebuchadnezzar*, Dan. 2:1.
o *Babylon, empire of*, Ezra 5:12.
p *Fetters*, Mark 5:4.
q *Babylon, city of*, Ezra 5:12.
v.6–526 BC
7
r *Temple, Solomon's*, 1 Kin. 6:17.
s *Temple, idolatrous*, 1 Kin. 6:17.
8
t *Book*, Num. 5:23.
u *Jehoiachin*, 2 Kin. 24:6.
v.8–518 BC
10
v *Zedekiah*, 2 Kin. 25:2.
12
w *Impenitence, instances of*, Rom. 2:5.
x *Jeremiah*, Jer. 1:1.
y *Prophets, inspiration of*, Isa. 3:2.
13
z *Perjury*, 1 Tim. 1:10.

king [a]Nĕb-u-chad-nĕz′zar, who
had made him [b]swear by God:
but he [c,d]stiffened his neck, and
[e]hardened his heart from turning
unto the LORD God of Ĭs̥′ra-el.
14 Moreover all the chief of the
[f]priests, and the people, transgressed very much after all the
abominations of the heathen;
and [g]polluted the [h]house of the
LORD which he had hallowed in
Jĕ-ru̥′sā-lĕm.
15 And the LORD God of their
fathers sent to them by his messengers, rising up betimes, and
sending; because he had [i]com-
passion on his people, and on his
dwelling place:
16 But they [j,k]mocked the [l]mes-
sengers of God, and [m]despised
his words, and [3]misused his
prophets, until the [n]wrath of the
LORD arose against his people,
till *there was* no remedy.
17 Therefore he [o]brought upon
them the king of the [p]Chăl′dees̥,
who slew their young men with
the sword in the [h]house of their
sanctuary, and had no compassion upon young man or maiden,
old man, or him that stooped for
age: he gave *them* all into his
hand.
18 And all the vessels of the
[h]house of God, great and small,
and the treasures of the house of
the LORD, and the treasures of
the king, and of his princes; all
*these* he brought to [q]Băb′y̆-lon.
19 And they burnt the [h]house
of God, and brake down the
wall of [r]Jĕ-ru̥′sā-lĕm, and burnt
all the [s]palaces thereof with fire,
and destroyed all the goodly vessels thereof.
20 And them that had escaped
from the sword [o,t]carried he
away to [q]Băb′y̆-lon; where they
were [u]servants to him and his
sons until the reign of the kingdom of [v]Pēr′s̥iȧ:
21 To [w]fulfil the word of the

a *Nebuchadnezzar*, Dan. 2:1.
b *Oath*, Num. 5:19.
c *Self-will*, Gen. 49:6.
d *Obduracy*, Prov. 29:1.
e *Heart, hardened*, Psa. 44:21.
14
f *Priest*, Lev. 1:5.
g *Profanation, of the house of God*, Lev. 22:32.
h *Temple, Solomon's*, 1 Kin. 6:17.
15
i *God, mercy of*, Gen. 2:2.
16
j *Scoffing*, Hab. 1:10.
k *Persecution, of the prophets*, John 15:20.
l *Prophets, persecutions of*, Isa. 3:2.
m *Impenitence*, Rom. 2:5.
n *Anger of God*, 2 Kin. 13:3.
3 R. V. scoffed at
17
o *Nation, punishment of*, Isa. 2:4.
p *Chaldea*, Isa. 23:13.
18
q *Babylon, city of*, Ezra 5:12.
v.18–507 BC
19
r *Jerusalem*, Judg. 19:10.
s *Palace*, 1 Kin. 21:1.
20
t *Captive*, 1 Sam. 30:3.
u *Servant*, Jer. 2:14.
v *Persia*, Esth. 1:3.
21
w *Prophecies, fulfilled*, Dan. 9:24.

v.21–507 BC
*x Jeremiah*, Jer. 1:1.
*y Sabbath*, Ex. 16:23.
22
*z Persia*, Esth. 1:3.

*a Prophecies, fulfilled*, v. 23; Dan. 9:24.
*b Jeremiah*, Jer. 1:1.
*c God, providence of*, Gen. 2:2.
*d Church and State, state favorable to religion*, 1 Sam. 16:1.
*e Proclamation*, 1 Kin. 15:22.
v.22–457 BC

Lord by the mouth of [x]Jĕr-e-mī′ah, until the land had enjoyed her [y]sabbaths: *for* as long as she lay desolate she kept sabbath, to fulfil threescore and ten years.

22 ¶ Now in the first year of +Çȳ′rus king of [z]Pēr′ṣiȧ, that the [a]word of the Lord *spoken* by the mouth of [b]Jĕr-e-mī′ah might be accomplished, the Lord [c]stirred up the spirit of Çȳ′rus king of Pēr′ṣiȧ, that [d]he made a [e]proclamation throughout all his kingdom, and *put it* also in writing, saying,

23 Thus [e]saith +Çȳ′rus king of [f]Pēr′ṣiȧ, All the kingdoms of the earth hath the Lord God of heaven given me; and he hath charged me to build him an house in [g]Jē-ru̧′sȧ-lĕm, which *is* in [h]Jū′dah. Who *is there* among you of all his people? The Lord his God *be* with him, and let him go up.

v.22–457 BC
See footnote, *Time*, Rev. 10:6.

23
*f Persia*, Esth. 1:3.
*g Jerusalem*, Judg. 19:10.
*h Judah, kingdom of*, 2 Chr. 11:17.

# EZRA

v.1–457 BC
See footnote, *Time*, Rev. 10:6.

1
*a Cyrus*, 2 Chr. 36:22.
*b Rulers, righteous*, Ex. 18:21.
*c Persia*, Esth. 1:3.
*d Prophecies, fulfilled*, Dan. 9:24.
*e Jeremiah*, Jer. 1:1.
*f Prophets, inspiration of*, Isa. 3:2.
*g God, providence of*, Gen. 2:2.
*h Church and State, state favorable to religion*, 1 Sam. 16:1.
*i Proclamation*, vs. 1–4; 1 Kin. 15:22.
*j Emancipation*, vs. 1–4; Deut. 15:12.
2
*k Temple, Second*, 1 Kin. 6:17.
*l Jerusalem*, Judg. 19:10.
*m Judah, kingdom of*, 2 Chr. 11:17.
1 A.R.V. Jehovah, the
3
*n Servant, emancipated*, Jer. 2:14.
2 R. V. is God,
4
*o Liberality, enjoined*, 1 Tim. 6:18.
*p Silver*, 1 Chr. 28:14.
*q Gold*, Ezek. 7:19.

## CHAPTER 1

*The proclamation of Cyrus for the rebuilding of the temple. 5 The people provide for their return. 7 Cyrus restores the vessels of the temple.*

NOW in the first year of [a,b]Çȳ′rus king of [c]Pēr′ṣiȧ, that the [d]word of the Lord by the mouth of [e,f]Jĕr-e-mī′ah might be fulfilled, the [g]Lord stirred up[C] the spirit of Çȳ′rus king of Pēr′ṣiȧ, that [h]he made a [i,j]proclamation throughout all his kingdom, and *put it* also in writing, saying,

2 Thus saith [a]Çȳ′rus king of [c]Pēr′ṣiȧ, [h]The [1]Lord God of heaven hath given me all the kingdoms of the earth; and he hath charged me to build him an [k]house at [l]Jē-ru̧′sȧ-lĕm, which *is* in [m]Jū′dah.

3 Who *is there* among you of all his people? his God be with him, and let [n]him go up to [l]Jē-ru̧′sȧ-lĕm, which *is* in [m]Jū′dah, and build the [k]house of the Lord God of Ĭṣ′ra-el, (he [2]*is* the God,) which *is* in Jē-ru̧′sȧ-lĕm.

4 And whosoever remaineth in any place where he sojourneth, let the men of his place[C] [o]help him with [p]silver, and with [q]gold, and with goods, and with beasts, beside the [r]freewill offering for the [k]house of God that *is* in [l]Jē-ru̧′sȧ-lĕm.

5 ¶ Then rose up the chief[G] of the fathers of [s]Jū′dah and [t]Bĕn′ja-mĭn, and the [u]priests, and the [v]Lē′vītes, with all *them* whose spirit God had raised, to go up to build the [k]house of the Lord which *is* in [l]Jē-ru̧′sȧ-lĕm.

6 And all they that *were* about them [w]strengthened[G] their hands[G] with vessels of [p]silver, with [q]gold, with goods, and with beasts, and with precious things, beside all *that* was [r]willingly offered.

7 ¶ Also [a]Çȳ′rus the king brought forth the vessels of the [x]house[G] of the Lord, which [y]Nĕb-u-chad-nĕz′zar had brought forth out of [l]Jē-ru̧′sȧ-lĕm, and had put them in the [z]house of his gods;

8 Even those did [a]Çȳ′rus king of [b]Pēr′ṣiȧ bring forth by the hand of Mĭth′re-dăth the treasurer, and numbered[G] them unto [c]Shĕsh-băz′zar, the prince of [d]Jū′dah.

9 And this *is* the number of them: thirty *chargers of [e]gold, a

v.4–457 BC
See footnote, *Time*, Rev. 10:6.
*r Offerings, free will*, Lev. 6:17.
5
*s Judah, tribe of*, Num. 10:14.
*t Benjamin, tribe of*, Num. 1:37.
*u Priest*, Lev. 1:5.
*v Levites*, Deut. 10:8.
6
*w Liberality, instances of*, 1 Tim. 6:18.
7
*x Temple, Solomon's*, 1 Kin. 6:17.
*y Nebuchadnezzar*, Dan. 2:1.
*z Treasure Houses*, Ezra 5:17.
8
*a Cyrus*, 2 Chr. 36:22.
*b Persia*, Esth. 1:3.
*c* Or, *Zerubbabel*, Ezra 3:2.
*d Judah, tribe of*, Num. 10:14.
9
*e Gold*, Ezek. 7:19.

+ **CYRUS**, king of Persia. *Issues a decree for the emancipation of the Jews and rebuilding of the temple*, 2 Chr. 36:22, 23; Ezra 1; 3:7; 4:3; 5:13, 14; 6:3. *Prophecies concerning*, Isa. 13:17–22; 21:2; 41:2; 44:28; 45:1–4, 13; 46:11.

* **CHARGER**, a dish. *Dedicated to the tabernacle*, Num. 7:13, 19, 25, 31, 37, 43, 49, 55, 61, 67, 73, 79, 84, 85. *Returned to the temple*, Ezra 1:9. *John the Baptist's head carried on*, Matt. 14:8, 11; Mark 6:25, 28.

v.9–457 BC
See footnote, *Time*, Rev. 10:6.

*f* *Silver*, 1 Chr. 28:14.
*g* *Knife*, Gen. 22:6.

10
*h* *Basin*, 1 Kin. 7:50.

11
*i* *Captivity*, Isa. 5:13.
*j* *Babylon*, Ezra 5:12.
*k* *Jerusalem*, Judg. 19:10.

thousand chargers[G] of [f]silver, nine
and twenty [g]knives,
10 Thirty [h]basons of [e]gold, [f]sil-
ver basons of a second *sort* four
hundred and ten, *and* other vessels a thousand.
11 All the vessels of [e]gold and
of [f]silver *were* five thousand and
four hundred. All *these* did
[c]Shĕsh-băz′zar bring up with
*them of* the [i]captivity that were
brought up from [j]Băb′ȳ-lon unto [k]Jē-rṳ′sȧ-lĕm.

## CHAPTER 2

*The number that return, of the people,* 36 *of the priests,* 40 *of the Levites,* 43 *of the Nethinim,* 55 *of Solomon's servants,* 62 *and of the priests who could not shew their pedigree.* 64 *The whole number.* 68 *Their oblations.*

1
*a* *Captivity*, Isa. 5:13.
*b* *Judah, tribe of*, Num. 10:14.
*c* *Nebuchadnezzar*, Dan. 2:1.
*d* *Babylon, empire of*, Ezra 5:12.
*e* *Jerusalem*, Judg. 19:10.

2
*f* *Zerubbabel*, Ezra 3:2.
*g* *Israel, number of, after the captivity*, vs. 2–64; Ex. 4:22.

NOW these *are* the children
of the province that went
up out of the [a]captivity, of [b]those
which had been carried away,
whom [c]Nĕb-u-chad-nĕz′zar the
king of [d]Băb′ȳ-lon had carried
away unto Băb′ȳ-lon, and came
again unto [e]Jē-rṳ′sȧ-lĕm and
Jū′dah, every one unto his
city;
2 Which came with *,[f]Zē-rŭb′-
ba-bĕl: †Jĕsh′u-ȧ, Nē-he-mī′ah,
Sĕr-a-ī′ah, Rē-el-ā′iah, Môr′de-
cāi, Bĭl′shăn, Mĭz′pär, Bĭg′va-ī,
Rē′hum, Bā′a-nah. The number of the men of the people of
[g]Iș′ra-el:
3 The children of Pā′rŏsh, [g]two
thousand an hundred seventy
and two.
4 The children of Shĕph-a-tī′-
ah, [g]three hundred seventy and
two.
5 The children of Ā′rah, [g]seven
hundred seventy and five.
6 The children of Pā′hath-
mō′ab, of the children of Jĕsh′-
u-ȧ *and* Jō′ăb, [g]two thousand
eight hundred and twelve.
7 The children of Ē′lăm, [g]a
thousand two hundred fifty and
four.
8 The children of Zăt′tu, [g]nine
hundred forty and five.
9 The children of Zăc′ca-ī,
[g]seven hundred and threescore.
10 The children of Bā′nī, [g]six
hundred forty and two.
11 The children of Bĕb′a-ī, [g]six
hundred twenty and three.
12 The children of Ăz′găd, [g]a
thousand two hundred twenty
and two.
13 The children of Ȧ-dŏn′ĭ-
kăm, [g]six hundred sixty and six.
14 The children of Bĭg′va-ī,
[g]two thousand fifty and six.
15 The children of Ā′dĭn, [g]four
hundred fifty and four.
16 The children of Ā′tĕr of
Hĕz-e-kī′ah, [g]ninety and eight.
17 The children of Bē′zāi,
[g]three hundred twenty and
three.
18 The children of Jō′rah, [g]an
hundred and twelve.
19 The children of Hā′shum,
[g]two hundred twenty and three.
20 The children of Gĭb′bar,
[g]ninety and five.
21 The children of [h]Bĕth′–lĕ-
hĕm, [g]an hundred twenty and
three.
22 The men of ‡Nē-tō′phah,
[g]fifty and six.
23 The men of [i]Ăn′a-thŏth, an
hundred twenty and eight.
24 The children of Ăz′ma-vĕth,
[g]forty and two.
25 The children of [j]Kĭr′jath-
ā′rim, [k]Chē-phī′rah, and [k]Bē-

v.6–457 BC
See footnote, *Time*, Rev. 10:6.

21
*h* *Beth-lehem*, Gen. 48:7.

23
*i* *Anathoth*, Jer. 1:1.

25
*j* Or, *Kirjath-jearim*, Josh. 15:9.
*k* Josh. 9:17; 18:26.

*[In order to publish this Bible in one volume with its numerous and diversified marginal notes and footnotes it has been necessary to avoid elaborate discussions of subjects, such, for instance, as would be necessary to point out the difficulties in connection with some of the names in genealogical lists. These difficulties grow out of errors of copyists, differences in the spelling of the same name, and the fact that individuals and places are mentioned under different names in different chapters. Where the identity of persons or places is doubtful in this chapter, or when no noteworthy fact is known concerning them, no mention of the name is made in either the margins or footnotes.]

† **JESHUA.** 1. *A priest who accompanied Zerubbabel from Babylon*, Ezra 2:2; Neh. 7:7; 12:1, 7. *Son of Josedech*, or *Jozadak*, Hag. 1:1, 12–14; 2:2, 4. *Rebuilds, the altar*, Ezra 3:2; *the temple*, Ezra 3:8–13. *Contends with those who sought to defeat the rebuilding*, Ezra 4:1–3; 5:1, 2. *Zechariah's vision concerning*, Zech. 3; 6:11.

2. *A Levitical house with successive heads, that returned from Babylon to Jerusalem*, Ezra 3:9; Neh. 8:7; 9:4.

‡ **NETOPHAH,** a town due south of Jerusalem, on the road to Bethlehem. *Inhabited by priests*, 1 Chr. 9:16. *Birthplace of two of David's valiant men*, 2 Sam. 23:28, 29; *and of Seraiah*, 2 Kin. 25:23; Jer. 40:8.

v.25–457 BC
See footnote, *Time*, Rev. 10:6.

26
*l Ramah*, Judg. 19:13.
*m* Josh. 18:24; Neh. 7:30.

27
*n* Or, *Michmash*, 1 Sam. 14:5.

28
*o Beth-el*, Josh. 18:13.
*p Ai*, Josh. 7:2.

33
*q Lod*, 1 Chr. 8:12.

34
*r Jericho*, Num. 22:1.

36
*s Priest*, Lev. 1:5.

38
*t Pashur*, 1 Chr. 9:12.

40
*u Levites*, Deut. 10:8.

41
*v Choir*, 1 Chr. 15:16.
*w Asaph*, 1 Chr. 15:17.

42
*x Porters*, 2 Sam. 18:26.
*y Talmon*, 1 Chr. 9:17.
*z Akkub*, 1 Chr. 9:17.

*a Israel, number of, after the captivity*, Ex. 4:22.

ē′roth, [g]seven hundred and forty
and three.
26 The children of [l]Rā′mah
and [m]Gā′bȧ, [g]six hundred twenty and one.
27 The men of [n]Mĭch′mas, [g]an
hundred twenty and two.
28 The men of [o]Bĕth′-el and
[p]Ā′ī, [g]two hundred twenty and
three.
29 The children of Nē′bō, [g]fifty
and two.
30 The children of Măg′bĭsh,
[g]an hundred fifty and six.
31 The children of the other
Ē′lăm, [g]a thousand two hundred fifty and four.
32 The children of Hā′rim,
[g]three hundred and twenty.
33 The children of [q]Lŏd, Hā′-
dĭd, and Ō′nō, [g]seven hundred
twenty and five.
34 The children of [r]Jĕr′ĭ-chō,
[g]three hundred forty and five.
35 The children of Sē-nā′ah,
[g]three thousand and six hundred
and thirty.
36 ¶ The [s]priests: the children
of Jē-dā′iah, of the house of
Jĕsh′u-ȧ, [g]nine hundred seventy
and three.
37 The children of Ĭm′mēr, [g]a
thousand fifty and two.
38 The children of [t]Păsh′ŭr, [g]a
thousand two hundred forty and
seven.
39 The children of Hā′rim, a
thousand and seventeen.
40 ¶ The [u]Lē′vītes: the children of Jĕsh′u-ȧ and Kăd′mĭ-el,
of the children of Hŏd-a-vī′ah,
seventy and four.
41 ¶ The [v]singers: the children
of [w]Ā′saph, [g]an hundred twenty
and eight.
42 ¶ The children of the [x]por-
ters:[c] the children of Shăl′lum,
the children of Ā′tēr, the children of [y]Tăl′mon, the children
of [z]Ăk′kŭb, the children of Hăt′-
ĭ-tȧ, the children of Shō′ba-ī, *in*
all [a]an hundred thirty and nine.

43 ¶ The [b]Nĕth′ĭ-nĭmș: the
children of Zī′hȧ, the children
of Hȧ-sū′phȧ, the children of
Tăb′ba-ōth,
44 The children of Kē′rŏs, the
children of Sī′a-hȧ, the children
of Pā′dọn,
45 The children of Lĕb′a-nah,
the children of Hăg′a-bah, the
children of Ăk′kŭb,
46 The children of Hā′găb, the
children of Shăl′ma-ī, the children of Hā′nan,
47 The children of Ḡĭd′del, the
children of Gā′här, the children
of Rē-a-ī′ah,
48 The children of Rē′zin, the
children of Nē-kō′dȧ, the children of Găz′zam,
49 The children of Ŭz′zȧ, the
children of Pȧ-sē′ah, the children of Bē′sāi,
50 The children of Ăs′nah, the
children of Mē-hū′nim, the children of Nē-phū′sim,
51 The children of Băk′bŭk,
the children of Hȧ-kū′phȧ, the
children of Här′hûr,
52 The children of Băz′lŭth,
the children of Mē-hī′dȧ, the
children of Här′shȧ,
53 The children of Bär′kŏs, the
children of Sĭs′e-rȧ, the children
of Thā′mah,
54 The children of Nē-zī′ah,
the children of Hăt′ĭ-phȧ.
55 The children of Sŏl′o-mon's
servants: the children of Sō′ta-ī,
the children of Sŏph′e-rĕth, the
children of Pē-rụ′dȧ,
56 The children of Jȧ-ā′lah, the
children of Där′kon, the children
of Ḡĭd′del,
57 The children of Shĕph-a-
tī′ah, the children of Hăt′til, the
children of Pŏch′e-rĕth of Ze-
bā′im, the children of Ā′mī.
58 All the [b]Nĕth′ĭ-nĭmș, and
the children of Sŏl′o-mon's servants, *were* [a]three hundred ninety
and two.
59 And these *were* they which

v.43–457 BC
See footnote, *Time*, Rev. 10:6.

43
*b Nethinim*, Ezra 8:20.

v.59–457 BC
See footnote. *Time*, Rev. 10:6.

59
c *Genealogy*, 1 Chr. 5:1.

61
d *Priest*, Lev. 1:5.

63
e *Urim and Thummim*, Lev. 8:8.

65
f *Servant*, Jer. 2:14.
g *Choir*, 1 Chr. 15:16.
h *Music*, 2 Chr. 5:13.

66
i *Horse*, Job 39:19.
j *Mule*, 2 Sam. 18:9.

67
k *Camel*, 1 Sam. 30:17.
l *Ass, domesticated*, 2 Chr. 28:15.

went up from Tĕl–mē′lah, Tĕl–här′sȧ, Chē′rub, Ăd′dăn, *and* Ĭm′mēr: but they could not shew their father's [c]house, and their seed,[C] whether they *were* of Ĭṣ′ra-el:

60 The children of Dĕl-a-ī′ah, the children of Tō-bī′ah, the children of Nē-kō′dȧ, [a]six hundred fifty and two.

61 And of the children of the [d]priests: the children of Hȧ-bā′iah, the children of Kŏz, the children of Bär-zĭl′la-ī; which took a wife of the daughters of Bär-zĭl′la-ī the Ġĭl′e-ăd-īte, and was called after their name:

62 These sought their register[C] *among* those that were reckoned by [c]genealogy, but they were not found: therefore were they, as polluted,[C] put from the priesthood.

63 And the Tĭr′sha-thȧ[C] said unto them, that they should not eat of the most holy things, till there stood up a [d]priest with [e]Ū′rim and with Thŭm′mim.

64 ¶ The whole congregation together *was* [a]forty and two thousand three hundred *and* threescore,

65 Beside their [f]servants and their maids, of whom *there were* [a]seven thousand three hundred thirty and seven: and *there were* among them [g]two hundred [h]singing men and singing women.

66 Their [i]horses *were* seven hundred thirty and six; their [j]mules, two hundred forty and five;

67 Their [k]camels, four hundred thirty and five; *their* [l]asses, six thousand seven hundred and twenty.

68 ¶ And *some* of the chief[C] of the fathers, when they came to the [m]house of the LORD which *is* at [n]Jē-ru̟′sā-lĕm, [o]offered freely for the [p]house of God to set it up in his place:

69 They [o]gave after their ability unto the treasure[C] of the work threescore and one thousand [q,r]drams[C] of [s]gold, and five thousand pound[C] of [t]silver, and one hundred priests' [u]garments.

70 So the [d]priests, and the [v]Lē′vītes, and *some* of the people, and the [g]singers, and the [w]porters, and the [x]Nĕth′ĭ-nĭmṣ, dwelt in their cities, and all Ĭṣ′ra-el in their cities.

## CHAPTER 3

*The altar is set up, and the sacrifices renewed. 8 The foundation of the temple is laid.*

AND when the seventh [a]month was come, and the children of Ĭṣ′ra-el *were* in the cities, the [b]people gathered themselves together as one man to [c]Jē-ru̟′sȧ-lĕm.

2 Then stood up [d]Jĕsh′u-ȧ the son of [e]Jŏz′a-dăk, and his brethren the [f]priests, and *Zē-rŭb′ba-bĕl the son of †Shē-ăl′tĭ-el, and his brethren, and [g]builded the [h]altar of the God of Ĭṣ′ra-el, to offer burnt offerings thereon, as *it is* written in the [i]law of Mō′ṣeṣ the man of God.[Q]

3 And they set the [h]altar upon his bases; for fear *was* upon them because of the people of those countries: and they [j]offered [k]burnt [l]offerings thereon unto the LORD, *even* burnt offerings [m]morning and evening.

4 They kept also the [n]feast of [o]tabernacles, as *it is* written, and *offered* the [m]daily burnt offerings by number, according to the custom, as the duty of every day required;

v.68–457 BC
See footnote. *Time*, Rev. 10:6.

68
m *Temple, Solomon's*, 1 Kin. 6:17.
n *Jerusalem*, Judg. 19:10.
o *Liberality, instances of*, 1 Tim. 6:18.
p *Temple, Second*, 1 Kin. 6:17.

69
q *Dram*, 1 Chr. 29:7.
r *Weight*, Lev. 19:35.
s *Gold*, Ezek. 7:19.
t *Silver*, 1 Chr. 28:14.
u *Priest, vestments of*, Lev. 1:5.

70
v *Levites*, Deut. 10:8.
w *Porters*, 2 Sam. 18:26.
x *Nethinim*, Ezra 8:20.

1
a *Month, Ethanim* (October), Ex. 12:2.
b *Jews*, Neh. 4:2.
c *Jerusalem*, Judg. 19:10.

2
d *Jeshua*, Ezra 2:2.
e *Jozadak*, Neh. 12:26.
f *Priest*, Lev. 1:5.
g *Liberality, instances of*, 1 Tim. 6:18.
h *Altar, of burnt offerings*, Gen. 8:20.
i *Law, of Moses*, Deut. 33:2.

3
j *Worship*, Gen. 22:5.
k *Offerings, burnt*, Lev. 6:17.
l *Jesus, typified in offerings*, Matt. 1:21.
m *Offerings, daily*, Lev. 6:17.

4
n *Annual Feasts*, Num. 15:3.
o *Tabernacles, feast of*, Deut. 16:13.

* **ZERUBBABEL.** *Called* SHESHBAZZAR, Ezra 1:8, 11; 5:14, 16. *Called* ZOROBABEL *in the genealogy of Joseph*, Matt. 1:12; Luke 3:27. *Directs the rebuilding of the altar and temple after his return from captivity in Babylon*, Ezra 3:2–8; 4:2, 3; 5:2, 14–16; Hag. 1:12–14. *Leads the emancipated Jews back from Babylon*, Ezra 1:8–11; 2; Neh. 12. *Prophecies relating to*, Hag. 2:2; Zech. 4:6–10.

†**SHEALTIEL** (*asked of God*), called also SALATHIEL. *Father of Zerubbabel and ancestor of Joseph*, 1 Chr. 3:17; Ezra 3:2, 8; 5:2; Neh. 12:1; Hag. 1:1, 12, 14; 2:2, 23; Matt. 1:12; Luke 3:27.

v.5–457 BC
See footnote, *Time*, Rev. 10:6.

5
*p New Moon, feast of*, Amos 8:5.
*q Offerings, free will*, Lev. 6:17.

6
*r Temple, Second*, 1 Kin. 6:17.

7
*s Money*, Jer. 32:9.
*t Wages*, Gen. 31:7.
*u Mason*, 2 Sam. 5:11.
*v Carpentry*, 2 Kin. 12:11.
*w Zidon*, Ezek. 28:21.
*x Tyre, city of*, Josh. 19:29.
*y Cedar*, Isa. 9:10.
*z Lebanon*, Deut. 1:7.

*a Mediterranean Sea*, Ex. 23:31.
*b Joppa*, 2 Chr. 2:16.
*c Cyrus*, 2 Chr. 36:22.
*d Persia*, Esth. 1:3.

8
*e Jerusalem*, Judg. 19:10.
*f Month, Zif* (May), Ex. 12:2.
*g Jeshua*, Ezra 2:2.
*h Jozadak*, Neh. 12:26.
*i Priests*, Lev. 1:5.
*j Levites*, Deut. 10:8.
*k Captivity, of Judah*, Isa. 5:13.
*l Temple, Second*, 1 Kin. 6:17.

v.8–456 BC

5 And afterward *offered* the continual burnt offering, both of the [p]new moons, and of all the set feasts of the LORD that were consecrated, and of every one that [q]willingly offered a [q]freewill offering unto the LORD.

6 From the first day of the seventh [a]month began they to offer [k]burnt offerings unto the LORD. But the foundation of the [r]temple of the LORD was not *yet* laid.

7 [g]They gave [s,t]money also unto the [u]masons, and to the [v]carpenters; and meat,[c] and drink, and oil, unto them of [w]Zī'dŏn, and to them of [x]Tȳre, to bring [y]cedar trees from [z]Lĕb'a-non to the [a]sea of [b]Jŏp'pȧ, according to the grant that they had of [c]Çȳ'rus king of [d]Pĕr'ṣi̤ȧ.

8 ¶ Now in the second year of their coming unto the house of God at [e]Jē-ru̥'sā-lĕm, in the second [f]month, began *Zē-rŭb'ba-bĕl the son of †Shē-ăl'tĭ-el, and [g]Jĕsh'u-ȧ the son of [h]Jŏz'a-dăk, and the remnant of their brethren the [i]priests and the [j]Lē'vītes, and all they that were come out of the [k]captivity unto Jē-ru̥'sā-lĕm; and appointed the Lē'vītes, from twenty years old and upward, to set forward the work of the [l]house of the LORD.

9 Then stood [g]Jĕsh'u-ȧ *with* his sons and his brethren, Kăd'mĭ-el and his sons, the sons of Jū'dah, together, to set forward the workmen in the [l]house of God: the sons of Hĕn'a-dăd, *with* their sons and their brethren the [j]Lē'vītes.

10 And when the builders laid the foundation of the [l]temple of the LORD, they set the [i]priests in their apparel with [m]trumpets, and the [j,n]Lē'vītes the sons of [o]Ā'saph with [p,q]cymbals, to [r]praise the LORD, after the ordinance of [s]Dā'vid king of Ĭṣ'ra-el.

11 And [n]they [q]sang together by course in [r]praising and [t]giving thanks unto the LORD; because *he is* good, for his [u]mercy *endureth* for ever toward Ĭṣ'ra-el. And all the people [v,w]shouted with a great shout, when they praised the LORD, because the foundation of the [l]house of the LORD was laid.

12 But many of the [i]priests and [j]Lē'vītes and chief of the fathers,[c] *who were* [x]ancient men, that had seen the [y]first house, when the foundation of [l]this house was laid before their eyes, ‡wept with a loud voice; and many [v]shouted aloud for [w]joy:

13 So that the people could not discern the noise of the [v]shout of [w]joy from the noise of the ‡weeping of the people: for the people shouted with a loud shout, and the noise was heard afar off.

## CHAPTER 4

*The adversaries endeavor to hinder the building of the temple. 7 Their letter to Artaxerxes. 17 His decree. 23 The work ceases.*

NOW when the adversaries of [a,b]Jū'dah and [a,c]Bĕn'ja'mĭn heard that the children of the [d]captivity builded the [e,f]temple unto the LORD God of Ĭṣ'ra-el;

2 Then they came to [g]Zē-rŭb'ba-bĕl, and to the chief[c] of the fathers, and said unto them, Let us build with you: for we seek your God, as ye *do*; and we do

v.10–456 BC
See footnote, *Time*, Rev. 10:6.

10
*m Trumpet*, Josh. 6:4.
*n Choir*, 1 Chr. 15:16.
*o Asaph*, 1 Chr. 15:17.
*p Cymbal*, 1 Chr. 13:8.
*q Music*, 2 Chr. 5:13.
*r Praise*, Psa. 150:1.
*s David*, 1 Sam. 16:13.

11
*t Thankfulness, to God*, Acts 24:3.
*u God, mercy of*, Gen. 2:2.
*v Shouting, in joy and praise*, 2 Chr. 15:14.
*w Joy, instances of*, Psa. 5:11.

12
*x Old Age*, Isa. 46:4.
*y Temple, Solomon's*, 1 Kin. 6:17.

1
*a Jews, after the captivity*, Neh. 4:2.
*b Judah, tribe of*, Num. 10:14.
*c Benjamin, tribe of*, Num. 1:37.
*d Captivity, of Judah*, Isa. 5:13.
*e Temple, Second*, 1 Kin. 6:17.
*f Church, called temple*, 1 Kin. 9:3.

2
*g Zerubbabel*, Ezra 3:2.

‡ **WEEPING**, Psa. 126:5, 6; 1 Cor. 7:30. *A time for*, Eccl. 3:4.
*Penitential*, Jer. 50:4; Joel 2:12 *Instances of penitential, the Israelites*, Judg. 2:4, 5; *Peter*, Matt. 26:75; Mark 14:72; Luke 22:62.
*For others*, Jer. 9:1. *With others, enjoined*, Rom. 12:15. *On account of tribulation*, Jer. 22:10; Amos 5:16, 17.
*In perdition*, Matt. 8:12; 22:13; 24:51; 25:30. *None in heaven*, Rev. 7:17.
**Instances of**: *Abraham for Sarah*, Gen. 23:2. *Esau*, Gen. 27:38. *Jacob and Esau*, Gen. 33:4. *Jacob*, Gen. 29:11; 37:35. *Joseph*, Gen. 42:24; 43:30; 45:2, 14, 15; 46:29; 50:1, 4, 17. *Hannah*, 1 Sam. 1:7. *Jonathan and David*, 1 Sam. 20:41. *David*, 2 Sam. 1:12; 3:32; 13:36; 15:23, 30; 18:33; 19:1. *Hezekiah*, 2 Kin. 20:3; Isa. 38:3. *Jesus, over Jerusalem*, Luke 19:41; *at the grave of Lazarus*, John 11:35. *Mary, when she washed the feet of Jesus*, Luke 7:38; John 11:2, 33. *Mary Magdalene*, John 20:11. *Paul*, Acts 20:19, 31; Phil. 3:18.

h *Esar-haddon*, 2 Kin. 19:37.
i Or, *Assyria*, Gen. 25:18.

3
j *Jeshua*, Ezra 2:2.
k *Cyrus*, 2 Chr. 36:22.
l *Persia, rulers of*, Esth. 1:3.
1 R. V. Lord, the

4
m *Malice, instances of*, Eph. 4:31.
n *Persecution, instances of*, John 15:20.

5
o *Darius*, Ezra 5:5.

6
p *Ahasuerus*, Esth. 1:1.
q *False Accusation*, 2 Tim. 3:3.
r *Jerusalem*, Judg. 19:10.
v.6—450 BC

7
s *Artaxerxes*, Ezra 7:1.
t *Letters*, Isa. 37:14.
u *Language*, Dan. 3:29.

8
v *Scribe*, 1 Kin. 4:3.
w *Government, provincial*, Isa. 22:21.

9
x *Babylon, empire of*, Ezra 5:12.

sacrifice[c] unto him since the days
of [h]Ē′sar-hăd′don king of [i]Ăs′-
sur, which brought us up hither.
3 But [g]Zĕ-rŭb′ba-bĕl, and
[j]Jĕsh′u-ȧ, and the rest of the
chief of the fathers of Ĭs̩′ra-el,
said unto them, Ye have nothing to do with us to build an
house unto our God; but we
ourselves together will build
unto the [1]LORD[c] God of Ĭs̩′ra-el,
as king [k]Çȳ′rus the king of
[l]Pĕr′s̩iȧ hath commanded us.[Q]
4 Then the people of the land
[m]weakened the hands[c] of the people of Jū′dah, and [n]troubled
them in building,
5 And hired counsellors against
them, to frustrate their purpose,
all the days of [k]Çȳ′rus king of
[l]Pĕr′s̩iȧ, even until the reign of
[o]Dȧ-rī′us king of Pĕr′s̩iȧ.
6 And in the reign of [p]Ȧ-hăs̩-
ū-ē′rŭs, in the beginning of his
reign, wrote they *unto him* an
[q]accusation against the [a]inhabit-
ants of Jū′dah and [r]Jĕ-ru̥′să-lĕm.
7 And in the days of [s]Är-tăx̣-
ērx′ēs̩ wrote Bĭsh′lăm, Mĭth′re-
dăth, Tā′be-el, and the rest of
their companions, unto Är-tăx̣-
ērx′ēs̩ king of [l]Pĕr′s̩iȧ; and the
writing of the [t]letter *was* written
in the Sȳr′ĭ-an tongue, and interpreted in the Sȳr′ĭ-an [u]tongue.
8 Rē′hum the chancellor and
Shĭm′shāi the [v]scribe[c] wrote a
[t]letter against [r,w]Jĕ-ru̥′să-lĕm to
[s]Är-tăx̣-ērx′ēs̩ the king in this sort:
9 Then *wrote* Rē′hum the chancellor, and Shĭm′shāi the [v]scribe,
and the rest of their companions; the Dī′na-ītes, the Ȧ-phär′-
sath-chītes, the Tär′pel-ītes, the
Ȧ-phär′sītes, the Är′che-vītes,
the [x]Băb-ȳ-lō′nĭ-ans̩, the Su̥′san-
chītes, the Dĕ-hā′vītes, *and* the
Ē′lam-ītes,
10 And the rest of the nations
whom the great and noble Ăs-
năp′pĕr brought over, and [y]set
in the cities of [z]Să-mā′rĭ-ȧ, and
the rest *that are* [2]on this side the
river, and at such a time.
11 ¶ This *is* the copy of the
[a]letter that they sent unto him,
*even* unto [b]Är-tăx̣-ērx′ēs̩ the
king; Thy servants the men [2]on
this side the river, and at such
a time.
12 [c]Be it known unto the king,
that the [d]Jews̩ which came up
from thee to us are come unto
[e]Jĕ-ru̥′să-lĕm, building the rebellious and the bad city, and
have set up the walls *thereof*, and
joined the foundations.
13 [c]Be it known now unto the
king, that, if this city be builded,
and the walls set up *again*, *then*
will they not pay toll, *tribute,
and custom[c], and *so* thou shalt
endamage [c] the revenue of the
kings.
14 Now because we [3]have
maintenance from *the king's* palace, and it was not meet[c] for us to
see the king's dishonour, therefore have we sent and certified[c]
the king;
15 That search may be made
in the [f]book of the records of thy
fathers: so shalt thou find in the
book of the records, and know
[c]that this [e]city *is* a rebellious
city, and hurtful unto kings and
provinces, and that they have
moved sedition within the same
of[c] old time: for which cause was
this city destroyed.
16 We certify[c] the king that, if
this city be builded *again*, and
the walls thereof set up, by this
means thou shalt have no portion[c] on this side the river.
17 ¶ *Then* sent the king an [a]an-

10
y *Colonization*, 2 Kin. 17:6.
z *Samaria*, Isa. 7:9.
2 R. V. beyond the river, and so forth.

11
a *Letters*, Isa. 37:14.
b *Artaxerxes*, Ezra 7:1.

12
c *False Accusation*, 2 Tim. 3:3.
d *Jews, after the captivity*, Neh. 4:2.
e *Jerusalem*, Judg. 19:10.

14
3 R. V. eat the salt of the palace.

15
f *Book*, Num. 5:23.

* **TRIBUTE.** *From conquered nations*, 2 Kin. 15:19, 20; 23:33, 35. *By Moabites to David*, 2 Sam. 8:2; 1 Chr. 18:2. *By Syrians to David*, 2 Sam. 8:6; 1 Chr. 18:6. *By Arabians to Solomon*, 2 Chr. 9:14. *By Arabians and Philistines to Jehoshaphat*, 2 Chr. 17:11. *By Ammonites to Jotham*, 2 Chr. 27:5. *Collectors of, called publicans*, Matt. 9:9; Mark 2:14; Luke 5:27; *abhorred*, Matt. 11:19; 21:31; Luke 18:11; *stoned*, 2 Chr. 10:18. *Teaching, of Jesus concerning*, Matt. 22:17–21; Mark 12:14–17; Luke 20:22–25; *of Paul concerning*, Rom. 13:6, 7. *Jesus falsely accused of forbidding*, Luke 23:2.

swer unto Rē′hum the chancellor, and *to* Shĭm′shāi the [g]scribe,
and *to* the rest of their companions that dwell in [h]Să-mā′rĭ-ȧ,
and *unto* the rest beyond the
river, Peace, and [4]at such a time.
18 The [a]letter which ye sent
unto us hath been plainly read
before me.
19 And I commanded, and
search hath been made, and it is
found that this [e]city of [c]old time
hath made insurrection against
kings, and *that* rebellion and sedition have been made therein.
20 There have been mighty
kings also over [e]Jē-ru′ṣă-lĕm,
which have ruled over all *countries* beyond the river; and toll,
*tribute, and custom, was paid
unto them.
21 Give ye now commandment
to cause these men to cease, and
that this city be not builded, until *another* commandment shall
be given from me.
22 Take heed [5]now that ye fail
not to do this: why should damage grow to the hurt of the
kings?
23 ¶ Now when the copy of
king [b]Är-tăx-ērx′ēṣ′ [a]letter *was*
read before Rē′hum, and Shĭm′-
shāi the [g]scribe, and their companions, they went up in haste to
[e]Jē-ru′să-lĕm unto the [d]Jewṣ,
and made them to cease by force
and power.
24 Then ceased the work of
the [i]house of God which *is* at
[e]Jē-ru′să-lĕm. So it ceased unto
the second year of the reign of
[j]Dā-rī′us king of [k]Pĕr′ṣiȧ.

## CHAPTER 5

*The building of the temple is resumed. 3 Tatnai and others strive to hinder the work. 6 Their letter to Darius against the Jews.*

THEN the [a]prophets, [b]Hăg′-
ga-ī the prophet, and
[c]Zĕch-a-rī′ah the son of [d]Ĭd′dō,
prophesied unto the [e]Jewṣ that
*were* in [f]Jū′dah and [g]Jē-ru′să-
lĕm in the name of the God of
Ĭṣ′ra-el, *even* unto them.
2 Then rose up [h]Zē-rŭb′ba-
bĕl the son of [i]Shē-ăl′tĭ-el, and
[j]Jĕsh′u-ȧ the son of [k]Jŏz′a-dăk,
and began to build the [l]house of
God which *is* at [g]Jē-ru′să-lĕm:
and with them *were* the prophets
of God [m]helping them.
3 ¶ At the same time came to
them [n]Tăt′na-ī, [o]governor on
this side the river, and [n]Shē′-
thär–bŏz′na-ī, and their companions, and said thus unto
them, Who hath commanded
you to build this house, and to
make up this wall?
4 Then said we unto them after this manner, What are the
names of the men that make this
building?
5 But the [p]eye of their [q]God
was upon the [r]elders of the Jewṣ,
that they could not cause them
to cease, till the matter came to
*Dā-rī′us: and then they re-
turned answer by [s]letter concerning this *matter.* [s]
6 ¶ The copy of the [s]letter that
[n]Tăt′na-ī, [o]governor [1]on this side
the river, and [n]Shē′thär–bŏz′-
na-ī, and his companions the
Ā-phär′sach-ītes, which *were* [1]on
this side the river, sent unto
*Dā-rī′us the king:
7 They sent a [s]letter unto him,
wherein was written thus; [t]Unto
*Dā-rī′us the [u]king, all peace.
8 Be it known unto the king,
that we went into the province of
Jū-dē′ȧ, to the [l,v]house [c]of the
great God, which is builded with
great [c]stones, and timber is laid
in the walls, and this work goeth
fast on, and prospereth in their
hands.
9 Then asked we those [r]elders,
*and* said unto them thus, Who

---

17
*g Scribe,* 1 Kin. 4:3.
*h Samaria,* Isa. 7:9.
4 R. V. so forth.

22
5 R. V. that ye be not slack herein:

24
*i Temple, Second,* 1 Kin. 6:17.
*j Darius,* Ezra 5:5.
*k Persia,* Esth. 1:3.
v.24–441 BC

1
*a Prophets,* Isa. 3:2.
*b Haggai,* Hag. 1:1.
*c Zechariah,* Zech. 1:1.
*d* Ezra 6:14; Zech. 1:1, 7.

v.1–441 BC
See footnote, *Time,* Rev. 10:6.

*e Jews,* Neh. 4:2.
*f Judah, after the captivity,* 2 Chr. 11:17.
*g Jerusalem,* Judg. 19:10.

2
*h Zerubbabel,* Ezra 3:2.
*i Shealtiel,* Ezra 3:2.
*j Jeshua,* Ezra 2:2.
*k Jozadak,* Neh. 12:26.
*l Temple, Second,* 1 Kin. 6:17.
*m Liberality, instances of,* 1 Tim. 6:18.

3
*n* Ezra 6:6, 13.
*o Government, provincial,* Isa. 22:21.

5
*p Anthropomorphisms,* Gen. 11:5.
*q God, providence of,* Gen. 2:2.
*r Senate,* Num. 11:16.
*s Letters,* Isa. 37:14.

6
1 R. V. beyond

7
*t Salutations, by letter,* Luke 1:44.
*u King,* 2 Kin. 3:10.

8
*v Church, called house of God,* 1 Kin. 9:3.

---

* **DARIUS.** *King of Persia,* Ezra 4:5, 24. *Letter of Tatnai and other adversaries of the Jews to, protesting against the rebuilding of the temple,* Ezra 5:6–17. *His reply, forbidding interference and commanding Tatnai to aid in restoring the temple,* Ezra 6:1–12. *Temple in Jerusalem finished in the sixth year of the reign of,* Ezra 6:15. *Referred to by Nehemiah,* Neh. 12:22.

11

*w Courage, instances of*, Deut. 31:7.

*x Faith, instances of*, Mark 11:22.

*y God, sovereign*, Gen. 2:2.

*z Solomon*, 2 Sam. 12:24.

12

*a Anger of God*, 2 Kin. 13:3.

*b Nebuchadnezzar*, Dan. 2:1.

*c Chaldea*, Isa. 23:13.

*d Captivity, as a judgment*, Isa. 5:13.

13

*e Cyrus*, 2 Chr. 36:22.

*f Proclamation*, 1 Kin. 15:22.

14

*g Gold*, Ezek. 7:19.

*h Silver*, 1 Chr. 28:14.

*i Temple, Solomon's*, 1 Kin. 6:17.

*j Jerusalem*, Judg. 19:10.

*k Temple, idolatrous*, 1 Kin. 6:17.

*l Liberality, instances of*, 1 Tim. 6:18.

*m* Or, *Zerubbabel*, Ezra 3:2.

*n Government, provincial*, Isa. 22:21.

commanded you to build this house, and to make up these walls?

10 We asked their names also, to certify [C]thee, that we might write the names of the men that *were* the chief of them.

11 And thus [w]they returned us answer, [x]saying, We are the servants of the [y]God of heaven and earth, and build the house[C] that was builded these many years ago, which [z]a great king of Ĭs̤′ra-el builded and set up.

12 But after that our fathers had provoked the God of heaven unto [a]wrath, he gave them into the hand of [b]Nĕb-u-chad-nĕz′-zar the king of †Băb′ȳ-lon, the [c]Chăl-dē′an, who destroyed this house,[C] and [d]carried the people away into Băb′ȳ-lon.[T]

13 But in the first year of [e]Çȳ′-rus the king of †Băb′ȳ-lon *the same* king Çȳ′rus made a [f]decree to build this house[C] of God.

14 And the vessels also of [g]gold and [h]silver of the house of God, which [b]Nĕb-u-chad-nĕz′zar took out of the [i]temple that *was* in [j]Jĕ-rṳ′sā-lĕm, and brought them into the [k]temple of Băb′ȳ-lon, [l]those did [e]Çȳ′rus the king take out of the temple of Băb′ȳ-lon, and they were delivered unto *one*, whose name *was* [m]Shĕsh-băz′zar, whom he had made [n]governor;

15 And [l]said unto him, Take these vessels, go, carry them into the temple that *is* in [j]Jĕ-rṳ′sā-lĕm, and let the [o]house of God be builded in his place.

16 Then came the same [m]Shĕsh-băz′zar, *and* laid the foundation of the [o]house[C] of God which *is* in [j]Jĕ-rṳ′sā-lĕm: and since that time even until now hath it been in building, and *yet* it is not finished.

17 Now therefore, if *it seem* good to the *,[p]king, let there be search made in the king's ‡treasure house, which *is* there at †Băb′ȳ-lon, whether it be *so*, that a [f]decree was made of [e]Çȳ′rus the king to build [o]this house of God at [j]Jĕ-rṳ′sā-lĕm, and let the king send his pleasure to us concerning this matter.

## CHAPTER 6

*The decree of Cyrus being found, Darius makes a new decree for the completion of the temple. 14 The work is finished. 15 The feast of the dedication is kept, 19 and the passover.*

THEN [a,b]Dā-rī′us the king made a decree, and search was made in the [c]house of the [1,d]rolls,[C] where the treasures were laid up in Băb′ȳ-lon.

2 And there was found at Ăch′-me-thā, in the [e]palace that *is* in the province of the [f]Mēdes̤, a [d]roll,[C] and therein *was* a record thus written:

3 In the first year of [g]Çȳ′rus the king *the same* Çȳ′rus the king made a [h]decree *concerning* the

15

*o Temple, Second*, 1 Kin. 6:17.

17

*p King*, 2 Kin. 3:10.

1

*a Darius*, Ezra 5:5.

*b Church and State, state favorable to religion*, 1 Sam. 16:1.

*c Treasure Houses*, Ezra 5:17.

*d Book*, Num. 5:23.

1 R. V. archives.

2

*e Palace*, 1 Kin. 21:1.

*f Medes*, Dan. 5:28.

3

*g Cyrus*, 2 Chr. 36:22.

*h Proclamation*, 1 Kin. 15:22.

† **BABYLON** (*confusion*). **City of:** *Built by Nimrod*, Gen. 10:10. *In the land of Shinar*, Gen. 10:10; 11:2. *Tower of*, Gen. 11:1–9. *Capital of the empire of Babylon*, Dan. 4:30; 2 Kin. 25:13; 2 Chr. 36:6, 7, 10, 18, 20. *Gates of*, Isa. 45:1, 2; Jer. 51:58. *Wall of*, Jer. 51:44, 58. *Splendor of*, Isa. 14:4.

*Peter writes from*, 1 Pet. 5:13.

*Prophecies concerning*, Isa. 13; 14:4–23; 21:1–10; 46:1, 2; 47; 48:14, 20; Jer. 21:4–10; 25:12–14; 27:1–11; 28:14; 32:28; 34:2, 3; 42:11, 12; 43:10–13; 46:13, 25, 26; 49:28–30; 50; 51; Ezek. 21:19; 26:7–12; 29:17–20; 30:10, 24, 25; 32:11; Dan. 2:31–38; 4:10–26; 5:25–29; 7:2–4; Hab. 1:5–11; Zech. 2:7–9.

FIGURATIVE, Rev. 14:8; 16:19; 17; 18.

**Empire of:** *Called*, LAND OF SHINAR, Gen. 10:10; 11:2; 14:1, 9; Isa. 11:11; Dan. 1:2; Zech. 5:11; SHESHACH, Jer. 25:26; 51:41; MERATHAIM, Jer. 50:21. *Called also* CHALDEA, see footnote, CHALDEA, Isa. 23:13.

*Divisions of*, 2 Kin. 17:24; 24:7; Dan. 3:1. *Extent of, at the time, of Nebuchadnezzar*, 2 Kin. 24:7; Dan. 2:37, 38; *of Ahasuerus*, Esth. 1:1; 8:9; 9:30.

*Armies of, invade, ancient Canaan*, Gen. 14; *Samaria*, 2 Kin. 17:5–24; *Judah*, 2 Kin. 24: 1–16; Jer. 32:2. *Jews carried captive to, after the conquest of Jerusalem by Nebuchadnezzar*, 2 Kin. 24:14–16; 25; 1 Chr. 9:1; 2 Chr. 33:11; 36:17–21; Jer. 39:52. *Colonists from, sent to Samaria*, Ezra 4:9, 10, with 2 Kin. 17:29–32. *Conquest of Egypt by*, 2 Kin. 24:7.

*Prophecies of conquests by*, 2 Kin. 20:16–19; Jer. 21; 22:20–26; 25:1–11; chapters 27–29; 32:28, 29; 34; 36:29; 38:17, 18; 43:8–13; 46:13–26; Ezek. chapters 12, 17, 19, 21, 24, 26; 29:18–20; 30; 32.

*Prophetic denunciations against*, Psa. 137:8, 9; Isa. 13; 14:21–23; 43:14–17; 47; Jer. 50; 51.

Government of: *A limited monarchy*, Esth. 1:13–19; 8:8; Dan. 6:8, 14, 17; *tyrannical*, Esth. 3:7–15; Dan. 3.

Sovereigns of: See footnotes: CYRUS, 2 Chr. 36:22; DARIUS, Ezra 5:5; NEBUCHADNEZZAR, Dan. 2:1.

‡ **TREASURE HOUSES.** *Of kings*, 2 Kin. 20:13; 1 Chr. 27:25; 2 Chr. 32:27, 28; Ezra 1:7, 8; Esth. 3:9. *Records preserved in*, Ezra 5:17; 6:1. *Treasurers in charge of*, Ezra 1:8; 7:20, 21.

*Heathen temples used for*, Ezra 1:7, 8; Dan. 1:2.

*Tabernacle used for*, Num. 31:54; Josh. 6:19, 24. *Temple used for*, 1 Kin. 7:51; 2 Kin. 12:4–14, 18; 22:4, 5; 1 Chr. 28:11, 12; Matt. 27:6; Mark 12:41, 43; Luke 21:1; John 8:20. *Under the charge of the Levites*, 1 Chr. 26:20. *Chambers provided in the temple for various kinds of treasure*, Neh. 10:38, 39; 13:5, 9, 12; Mal. 3:10. *Priests and Levites in charge of*, 1 Chr. 9:26; 26:20–28; Neh. 12:44; 13:13.

*i Temple, Second,* 1 Kin. 6:17.
*j Jerusalem,* Judg. 19:10.
*k House,* Esth. 8:1.
*l Offerings,* Lev. 6:17.
*m Cubit,* Ex. 36:9.

4
*n Stones,* Ex. 24:12.
*o Liberality, instances of,* 1 Tim. 6:18.

5
*p Gold,* Ezek. 7:19.
*q Silver,* 1 Chr. 28:14.
*r Nebuchadnezzar,* Dan. 2:1.
*s Temple, Solomon's,* 1 Kin. 6:17.
*t Babylon, city of,* see footnote on opposite page.

6
*u* Ezra 5:3, 6.
*v Government, provincial,* Isa. 22:21.

7
*w Church and State, state favorable to religion,* vs. 7–12; 1 Sam. 16:1.
*x Jews,* Neh. 4:2.
*y Senate,* Num. 11:16.

8
*z Tribute,* Ezra 4:13.

9
*a Liberality, instances of,* 1 Tim. 6:18.
*b Offerings, burnt,* Lev. 6:17.
*c Salt,* 2 Kin. 2:20.
*d Wine,* Prov. 23:31.
*e Oil,* Deut. 12:17.
*f Priest,* Lev. 1:5.
*g Jerusalem,* Judg. 19:10.

[i]house of God at [j]Jē-ru̥'sā-lĕm,
Let the [k]house be builded, the
place where they offered [l]sacri-
fices, and let the foundations
thereof be strongly laid; the
height thereof threescore [m]cu-
bits,[c] *and* the breadth thereof
threescore cubits;
4 *With* three rows of great
[n]stones, and a row of new timber: and [o]let the expences be
given out of the king's house:
5 And [o]also let the [p]golden and
[q]silver vessels of the house[c] of
God, which [r]Nĕb-u-chad-nĕz'-
zar took forth out of the [s]temple
which *is* at [j]Jē-ru̥'sā-lĕm, and
brought unto [t]Băb'ȳ-lon, be restored, and brought again unto
the [i]temple which *is* at Jē-ru̥'sā-
lĕm, *every one* to his place, and
place *them* in the house of God.
6 Now *therefore,* [u]Tăt'na-ī,
[v]governor beyond the river,
[u]Shē'thär-bŏz'na-ī, and your
companions the Ă-phär'sach-
ītes, which *are* beyond the
river, be ye far from thence:
7 [w]Let the work of this [i]house
of God alone; let the [v]governor
of the [x]Jews and the [y]elders of
the Jews build this house of God
in his place.
8 [w]Moreover I make a decree
what ye shall do to the [y]elders of
these [x]Jews for the building of
this [i]house of God: that [o]of the
king's goods, *even* of the [z]tribute
beyond the river, forthwith expences be given unto these men,
that they be not hindered.
9 [w]And [a]that which they have
need of, both young bullocks,
and rams, and lambs, for the
[b]burnt offerings of the God of
heaven, *wheat, [c]salt, [d]wine, and
[e]oil, according to the appointment of the [f]priests which
*are* at [g]Jē-ru̥'sā-lĕm, let it be
given them day by day without
fail:
10 [h]That they may offer sacrifices of sweet savours unto the
God of heaven, and [i,j]pray for
the life of the [k]king, and of his
sons.
11 Also I have made a decree,
that whosoever shall alter this
word, let timber be pulled down
from his house, and being set up,
let him be hanged[c] thereon; and
let his house be made a dunghill for this.
12 And the God that hath
caused his name to dwell there
destroy all kings and people,
that shall put to[c] their hand to
alter *and* to destroy this [l]house
of God which *is* at [g]Jē-ru̥'sā-
lĕm. I [m]Dā-rī'us have made a
decree; let it be done with
speed.
13 ¶ Then [n]Tăt'na-ī, [o]governor
on this side the river, [n]Shē'thär-
bŏz'na-ī, and their companions,
according to that which [m]Dā-
rī'us the king had sent, so they
did speedily.
14 And the [p]elders of the Jews
builded, and they prospered
through the prophesying of
[q]Hăg'ga-ī the prophet and
[r]Zĕch-a-rī'ah the son of [s]Ĭd'dō.
And they builded, and finished
[l]*it*, according to the commandment of the God of Ĭs'ra-el, and
according to the commandment
of [t]Çȳ'rus, and [m]Dā-rī'us, and
[u]Är-tăx-ērx'ēs king of [v]Pēr'sia.
15 And [l]this house was finished
on the third day of the [w]month
[x]Ā'där, which was in the sixth
year of the reign of [m]Dā-rī'us the
king.
16 ¶ And the children of Ĭs'-
ra-el, the [f]priests, and the [y]Lē'-
vītes, and the rest of the children
of the captivity, kept the dedi-

10
*h Church and State, state favorable to religion,* 1 Sam 16:1.
*i Citizens, duties of,* Luke 15:15.
*j Intercession, solicited,* Jer. 27:18.
*k King, prayer for* 2 Kin. 3:10.

12
*l Temple, Second.* 1 Kin. 6:17.
*m Darius,* Ezra 5:5

13
*n* Ezra 5:3, 6.
*o Government, provincial,* Isa. 22:21.

14
*p Senate,* Num. 11:16.
*q Haggai,* Hag. 1:1.
*r Zechariah,* Zech. 1:1.
*s* Ezra 5:1; Zech. 1:1, 7.
*t Cyrus,* 2 Chr. 36:22.
*u Artaxerxes,* Ezra 7:1.
*v Persia,* Esth. 1:3.

15
*w Month, Adar,* Ex. 12:2.
*x* Esth. 3:7; 8:12; 9:1.

**v.15–437 BC**

16
*y Levites,* Deut. 10:8.

* **WHEAT,** Luke 16:7. *Grown, in Egypt,* Ex. 9:32; *in Palestine,* 1 Kin. 5:11; 2 Chr. 2:10, 15. *Offerings of,* Num. 18:12. *Prophecy of the sale of a measure of, for a penny,* Rev. 6:6. *Ground in a mortar,* Prov. 27:22. *Growth of, figurative of vicarious death,* John 12:24. *Parable of,* Matt. 13:24–30. **Figurative,** Jer. 12:13. *Of God's mercy,* Psa. 81:16; 147:14. *Of the righteous,* Matt. 3:12; Luke 3:17.

v.16–437 BC
See footnote, *Time*, Rev. 10:6.

*z Joy, instances of*, Psa. 5:11.

**17**
*a Offerings, sin*, Lev. 6:17.
*b Jesus, typified in offerings*, Matt. 1:21.

**18**
*c Priest*, Lev. 1:5.
*d Levites*, Deut. 10:8.
*e Worship*, Gen. 22:5.
*f Jerusalem*, Judg. 19:10.
*g Law, of Moses*, Deut. 33:2.

**19**
*h Passover*, Num. 9:5.
*i Abib*, Ex. 13:4.
*j Month*, Ex. 12:2.

**20**
*k Priest, duties of*, Lev. 1:5.
*l Levites, functions of*, Deut. 10:8.

**21**
*m Repentance*, Mark 1:4.
*n Fellowship, with the wicked*, 1 Cor. 1:9.
*o Seekers*, Isa. 55:6.

**22**
*p Annual Feasts*, Num. 15:3.
*q Joy*, Psa. 5:11.
*r God, providence of*, Gen. 2:2.
*s Assyria*, Gen. 25:18.

cation of this house[C] of God with
[z]joy,
17 And offered at the [+]dedi-
cation of this house[C] of God an
hundred bullocks, two hundred
rams, four hundred lambs; and
for a [a]sin [b]offering for all Ĭṣ'-
ra-el, twelve he goats, according
to the number of the tribes of
Ĭṣ'ra-el.
18 And they set the [c]priests in
their divisions, and the [d]Lē'vītes
in their courses[C], for the [e]service
of God, which *is* at [f]Jē-rṳ'sā-
lĕm; as it is written in the [g]book
of Mō'ṣeṣ.
19 ¶ And the children of the
captivity kept the [h]passover upon the fourteenth *day* of the
[i]first [j]month.
20 For the [k]priests and the
[l]Lē'vītes were purified together,
all of them *were* pure, and killed
the [h]passover for all the children
of the captivity, and for their
brethren the priests, and for
themselves.
21 And the children of Ĭṣ'ra-el,
which were come again out of
captivity, and all such as had
[m]separated themselves unto
them [n]from the filthiness[C] of the
heathen [C]of the land, to [o]seek
the LORD God of Ĭṣ'ra-el, did
eat,
22 And kept the [p]feast of unleavened bread seven days with
[q]joy: for the [r]LORD had made
them joyful, and turned the
heart of the king of [s]Ăs-sy̆r'ĭ-ȧ
unto them, to strengthen their
hands in the work of the house
of God, the God of Ĭṣ'ra-el.

## CHAPTER 7

*Ezra goes up to Jerusalem. 11 The gracious commission of Artaxerxes to him. 27 Ezra blesses God for his favor.*

NOW after these things, in
the reign of *Är-tăx-ērx'ēṣ
king of [a]Pĕr'ṣiȧ, [†]Ĕz'rȧ [b]the son
of [c]Sĕr-a-ī'ah, the son of Ăz-a-
rī'ah, the son of [d]Hĭl-kī'ah,
2 The son of Shăl'lum, the son
of Zā'dŏk, the son of Ȧ-hī'tub,
3 The son of Ăm-a-rī'ah, the
son of Ăz-a-rī'ah, the son of Mē-
rā'ioth,
4 The son of Zĕr-a-hī'ah, the
son of Ŭz'zī, the son of Bŭk'kī,
5 The son of Ȧ-bĭsh'u-ȧ, the
son of [e]Phĭn'e-has, the son of
[f]Ē-le-ā'zar, the son of [g]Aâr'on
the [h]chief priest:
6 This [†,i]Ĕz'rȧ went up from
[j]Băb'y̆-lon; and he *was* a ready[C]
[k]scribe[C] in the [l]law of Mō'ṣeṣ,
which the LORD God of Ĭṣ'-
ra-el had given: and the [*,m]king
granted him all his request, according to the hand of the LORD
his God upon him.
7 And there went up *some* of the
children of Ĭṣ'ra-el, and of the
[n]priests, and the [o]Lē'vītes, and
the [p]singers, and the [q]porters,
and the [r]Nĕth'ĭ-nĭmṣ, unto [s]Jē-
rṳ'sā-lĕm, in the seventh year of
*Är-tăx-ērx'ēṣ the [t]king.
8 And he came to [s]Jē-rṳ'sā-lĕm
in the fifth [u]month, which *was*
in the seventh year of the [t]king.
9 For upon the first *day* of the
[v]first month began he to go up
from [j]Băb'y̆-lon, and on the first
*day* of the fifth [u]month came he
to [s]Jē-rṳ'sā-lĕm, according to the

v.1–436 BC
See footnote, *Time*, Rev. 10:6.

**1**
*a Persia, rulers of*, Esth. 1:3.
*b Genealogy*, 1 Chr. 5:1.
*c* 2 Kin. 25:18–21; Jer. 52:24–27.
*d Hilkiah*, Jer. 29:3.

**5**
*e Phinehas*, Num. 25:7.
*f Eleazar*, Num. 3:2.
*g Aaron*, Ex. 6:20.
*h High Priest*, Lev. 21:10.

**6**
*i Priest, duties of*, Lev. 1:5.
*j Babylon*, Ezra 5:12.
*k Scribe*, 1 Kin. 4:3.
*l Law, of Moses*, Deut. 33:2.
*m Rulers, righteous*, Ex. 18:21.

**7**
*n Priest*, Lev. 1:5.
*o Levites*, Deut. 10:8.
*p Choir*, 1 Chr. 15:16.
*q Porters*, 2 Sam. 18:26.
*r Nethinim*, Ezra 8:20.
*s Jerusalem*, Judg. 19:10.
*t King*, 2 Kin. 3:10.

**8**
*u Month*, Ex. 12:2.

**9**
*v Abib*, Ex. 13:4.

**+ DEDICATION**, 1 Chr. 26:26, 27. *Law concerning dedicated things*, Lev. 27; Num. 18:14. *Things offered in, must be without blemish*, Lev. 22:18–23; Mal. 1:14; *not redeemable*, Lev. 27:28, 29; *must be voluntary*, Lev. 1:3; 22:19.
*Of the altar of the tabernacle*, Num. 7. *Of Solomon's temple*, 1 Kin. 8; 2 Chr. 7:5. *Of the Second temple*, Ezra 6:16, 17. *Of the wall of Jerusalem*, Neh. 12:27–43. *Of houses*, Deut. 20:5. *Of Samuel by his mother*, 1 Sam. 1:11, 22; 2:20.
*For instances of liberality in dedicated things*, see footnote, LIBERALITY, *Instances of*, 1 Tim. 6:18.
*Feast of*, John 10:22.
**Of Self:** See footnote, CONSECRATION, *Personal*, Lev. 7:37.

*** ARTAXERXES** (*the great warrior*, or, *king*), king of Persia. *Letter to, from the enemies of the Jews, opposing the rebuilding of Jerusalem*, Ezra 4:7–16. *His reply, forbidding the building of the temple*, Ezra 4:17–22. *Decrees of, in behalf of the Jews*, Ezra 7; Neh. 2; 5:14.

**† EZRA.** *A famous scribe and priest*, Ezra 7:1–6, 10–12, 21; Neh. 12:36. *Appoints a fast*, Ezra 8:21. *Commissioned by Artaxerxes to rebuild the temple; returns to Jerusalem with a large company of Jews*, Ezra 7; 8. *Is persecuted by Tatnai, the governor*, Ezra 6:3–17. *Darius renews the decree of Cyrus for rebuilding the temple; rebuilding of, completed*, Ezra 6:1–15. *His charge to the priests*, Ezra 8:29. *Exhorts people to put away their heathen wives*, Ezra 10:1–17. *Reads the law*, Neh. 8. *Reforms corruptions*, Ezra 10; Neh. 13. *Participates in the dedication of the wall of Jerusalem*, Neh. 12:27–43.

v.9–436 BC
See footnote, *Time*, Rev. 10:6.

*w God, providence of*, Gen. 2:2.

10

*x Minister, character and qualifications of*, Rom. 15:16.
*y Heart*, Psa. 44:21.
*z Law, of Moses*, Deut. 33:2.

*a Obedience*, Heb. 5:8.
*b Instruction*, Prov. 23:23.
*c Minister, duties of*, Rom. 15:16.

11

*d Letters*, Isa. 37:14.
*e Scribe*, 1 Kin. 4:3.
*f Word of God*, Psa. 119:9.

12

*g King*, 2 Kin. 3:10.

13

*h Church and State, state favorable to religion*, vs. 13–26; 1 Sam. 16:1.
*i Proclamation*, vs. 13–26; 1 Kin. 15:22.
*j Priest*, Lev. 1:5.
*k Levites*, Deut. 10:8.
*l Jerusalem*, Judg. 19:10.

14

*m Seven*, Gen. 7:2.
*n Judah, after the captivity*, 2 Chr. 11:17.

15

*o Silver*, 1 Chr. 28:14.
*p Gold*, Ezek. 7:19.
*q Liberality, instances of*, 1 Tim. 6:18.

16

*r Babylon*, Ezra 5:12.
*s Offerings, free will* Lev. 6:17.
*t Temple, Second*, 1 Kin. 6:17.

17

*u Money*, Jer. 32:9.
*v Offerings, meat*, Lev. 6:17.
*w Offerings, drink*, Lev. 6:17.
1 R. V. meal

good hand of his [w]God upon
him.
10 For [†,x]Ĕz′rȧ had prepared
his [y]heart to seek the [z]law of
the LORD, and to [a]do *it*, and to
[b,c]teach in Ĭs′ra-el statutes and
judgments.[C]
11 ¶ Now this *is* the copy of
the [d]letter that the king *Är-
tăx-ērx′ēs gave unto †Ĕz′rȧ the
priest, the [e]scribe, *even* a scribe
of the [f]words of the commandments of the LORD, and of his
statutes to Ĭs′ra-el.
12 *Är-tăx-ērx′ēs, [g]king of
kings, unto †Ĕz′rȧ the priest, a
[e]scribe of the law of the God of
heaven, perfect *peace*, and at
such a time.
13 [h]I make a [i]decree, that all
they of the people of Ĭs′ra-el,
and *of* his [j]priests and [k]Lē′vītes,
in my realm, which are minded
of their own freewill to go up to
[l]Jē-ru′sȧ-lĕm, go with thee.
14 Forasmuch as thou art sent
of the [g]king, and of his [m]seven
‡counsellors, to enquire concerning [n]Jū′dah and [l]Jē-ru′sȧ-
lĕm, according to the law of thy
God, which *is* in thine hand;
15 [h]And to carry the [o]silver and
[p]gold, which the [g]king and his
‡counsellors have [q]freely offered
unto the God of Ĭs′ra-el, whose
habitation *is* in [l]Jē-ru′sȧ-lĕm,
16 And [q]all the [o]silver and
[p]gold that thou canst find in all
the province of [r]Băb′y̆-lon, with
the [s]freewill offering of the people, and of the priests, offering willingly for the [t]house[C] of
their God which *is* in [l]Jē-ru′sȧ-
lĕm:
17 That thou mayest buy
speedily with this [u]money bullocks, rams, lambs, with their
[1,v]meat[C] offerings and their [w]drink
offerings, and offer them upon
the [x]altar of the house of your
God which *is* in [l]Jē-ru′sȧ-lĕm.
18 [h]And whatsoever shall seem
good to thee, and to thy brethren, to do with the rest of the
[o]silver and the [p]gold, that do
after the will of your God.
19 [h]The vessels also that are
given thee for the service of the
[t,y]house of thy God, *those* deliver
thou before the God of [l]Jē-ru′-
sȧ-lĕm.
20 And whatsoever more shall
be needful for the [t,y]house of thy
God, which thou shalt have occasion to bestow, bestow *it* out
of the king's [z]treasure house.
21 And [a]I, *even* I *Är-tăx-
ērx′ēs the king, do make a decree to all the treasurers which
*are* beyond the [b]river,[C] that whatsoever †Ĕz′rȧ the priest, the
[c]scribe of the law of the God
of heaven, shall require of you,
it be done speedily,
22 Unto an hundred [d]talents[C] of
[e]silver, and to an hundred [f]meas-
ures[C] of [g]wheat, and to an hundred [h,i]baths[C] of [j]wine, and to an
hundred baths of [k]oil, and [l]salt
without prescribing *how much*.
23 Whatsoever is commanded
by the God of heaven, [m]let it be
[2]diligently done for the house[C] of
the God of heaven:[C] for why
should there be wrath against
the realm of the king and his
sons?
24 Also [a]we certify[C] you, that
touching any of the [n]priests
and [o]Lē′vītes, [p]singers, [q]porters,[C]
[r]Nĕth′ĭ-nĭms, or ministers of
this house of God, it shall not be
lawful to impose [s]toll, tribute, or
custom, upon them.
25 And thou, †Ĕz′rȧ, after the
[t,u]wisdom of thy God, that *is* in
thine hand, set ‖magistrates
and [v]judges, which may judge

v.17–436 BC
See footnote, *Time*, Rev. 10:6.

*x Altar, of burnt offerings*, Gen. 8:20.

19

*y Church, called house of God*, 1 Kin. 9:3.

20

*z Treasure Houses*, Ezra 5:17.

21

*a Church and State, state favorable to religion*, vs. 21–26; 1 Sam. 16:1.
*b Euphrates*, Gen. 15:18.
*c Scribe*, 1 Kin. 4:3.

22

*d Talent*, Ex. 38:25.
*e Silver*, 1 Chr. 28:14.
*f Measure, dry*, Deut. 25:15.
*g Wheat*, Ezra 6:9.
*h Bath*, 1 Kin. 7:26.
*i Measure, liquid*, Deut. 25:15.
*j Wine*, Prov. 23:31.
*k Oil*, Deut. 12:17.
*l Salt*, 2 Kin. 2:20.

23

*m Zeal*, 2 Cor. 7:11.
2 R. V. exactly

24

*n Priest*, Lev. 1:5.
*o Levites*, Deut. 10:8.
*p Choir*, 1 Chr. 15:16.
*q Porters*, 2 Sam. 18:26.
*r Nethinim*, Ezra 8:20.
*s Tax, priests exempt from*, Neh. 10:32.

25

*t Wisdom*, Prov. 2:2.
*u God, wisdom of*, Gen. 2:2.
*v Judge*, Judg. 2:18.

‡ **CABINET,** heads of departments in government. *Of David*, 2 Sam. 8:15–18; 15:12; 20:23–26; 1 Chr. 27:32–34. *Of Solomon*, 1 Kin. 4:1–7. *Of Hezekiah*, Isa. 36:3. *Of Artaxerxes*, Ezra 7:14.

See footnote, MINISTER, 2 Chr. 9:4.
‖ **MAGISTRATE.** *An officer of civil law*, Judg. 18:7; Ezra 7:25; Luke 12:11, 58; Acts 16:20, 22, 35, 38. *Obedience to, enjoined*, Tit. 3:1. *Not to be reviled*, Ex. 22:28.

v.25–436 BC
See footnote, *Time*, Rev. 10:6.

*w Rulers, character and qualifications of*, Ex. 18:21.
*x Instruction, in religion*, Prov. 23:23.
26
*y Disobedience to God*, Eph. 5:6.
*z Citizens, duties of*, Luke 15:15.
*a Ruler, loyalty to, enjoined*, Ex. 18:21.
*b Criminals*, Matt. 27:15.
*c Death, penalty*, Num. 23:10.
*d Confiscation*, Ezra 10:8.
*e Prison*, Gen. 39:20.
27
*f Thankfulness, exemplified*, Acts 24:3.
*g God, providence of*, Gen. 2:2.
*h Heart*, Psa. 44:21.
*i Temple, Second*, 1 Kin. 6:17.
*j Church, called house of the Lord*, 1 Kin. 9:3.
*k Jerusalem*, Judg. 19:10.
28
*l Temporal Blessings, from God*, Psa. 103:2.

all the people that *are* beyond
the river, all [w]such as know the
laws of thy God; and [x]teach ye
them that know *them* not.[s]
26 And whosoever will [y]not [z]do
the law of thy God, and the law
of the [a]king, let judgment be
executed speedily upon [b]him,
whether *it be* unto [c]death, or to
[§]banishment, or to [d]confiscation
of goods, or to [e]imprisonment.
27 ¶ [f]Blessed *be* the LORD God
of our fathers, which [g]hath put
*such a thing* as this in the king's
[h]heart, to beautify the [i,j]house of
the LORD which *is* in [k]Jē-ru̥'să-
lĕm:
28 And [g]hath extended mercy
unto [†]me before the king, and
his [‡]counsellors, and before all
the king's mighty princes. And
I was [l]strengthened as the hand
of the LORD my God *was* upon
me, and I gathered together out
of Iș'ra-el chief men to go up
with me.

## CHAPTER 8

*Ezra's companions from Babylon. 15 He sends to Iddo for ministers for the temple. 21 He keeps a fast. 24 He commits the treasures to the custody of the priests. 31 He and his company come to Jerusalem. 33 The treasure is weighed in the temple. 36 They deliver the king's commissions to his officers.*

1
*a Genealogy*, 1 Chr. 5:1.
*b Babylon*, Ezra 5:12.
*c Artaxerxes*, Ezra 7:1.
2
*d Phinehas*, Num. 25:7.
*e Ithamar*, Ex. 38:21.
*f David*, 1 Sam. 16:13.

THESE *are* now the chief [c]of
their fathers, and *this is*
the [a]genealogy of them that went
up with me from [b]Băb'y̆-lon, in the
reign of [c]Är-tăx̣-ērx'ēș the king.
2 Of the sons of [d]Phĭn'e-has;
Gēr'shŏm: of the sons of [e]Ĭth'a-
mär; Dăn'iel: of the sons of
[f]Dā'vid; Hăt'tush.
3 Of the sons of Shĕch-a-nī'ah,
of the sons of Phā'rŏsh; Zĕch-a-
rī'ah: and with him were reckoned by [a]genealogy of the males
an hundred and fifty.
4 Of the sons of Pā'hath–mō'-
ab; Ė-lī-ho-ē'na-ī the son of Zĕr-
a-hī'ah, and with him two hundred males.
5 Of the sons of Shĕch-a-nī'ah;
the son of Jă-hā'zī-el, and with
him three hundred males.
6 Of the sons also of Ā'dĭn;
Ē'bed the son of Jŏn'a-than, and
with him fifty males.
7 And of the sons of Ē'lăm; Jĕ-
shā'iah the son of Ăth-a-lī'ah,
and with him seventy males.
8 And of the sons of Shĕph-
a-tī'ah; Zĕb-a-dī'ah the son of
Mī'-chaĕl, and with him fourscore males.
9 Of the sons of Jō'ăb; Ō-ba-
dī'ah the son of Jĕ-hī'el, and
with him two hundred and
eighteen males.
10 And of the sons of Shĕl'o-
mĭth; the son of Jŏs-ĭ-phī'ah,
and with him an hundred and
threescore males.
11 And of the sons of Bĕb'a-ī;
Zĕch-a-rī'ah the son of Bĕb'a-ī,
and with him twenty and eight
males.
12 And of the sons of Ăz'găd;
Jŏ-hā'nan the son of Hăk'ka-
tăn, and with him an hundred
and ten males.
13 And of the last sons of
Ă-dŏn'ĭ-kăm, whose names *are*
these, Ė-lĭph'e-lĕt, Jĕ-ī'el, and
Shĕm-a-ī'ah, and with them
threescore males.
14 Of the sons also of Bĭg'va-ī;
Ū'tha-ī, and Zăb'bud, and with
them seventy males.
15 ¶ And [g]I gathered them together to the river that runneth
to Ă-hā'vȧ; and there abode we
in tents three days: and I viewed
the people, and the [h]priests, and
found there none of the [i]sons of
Lē'vī.
16 Then sent I for Ė-lī-ē'zēr,
for Ā'rī-el, for Shĕm-a-ī'ah, and
for Ĕl'na-thăn, and for Jā'rib,
and for Ĕl'na-thăn, and for Nā'-
than, and for Zĕch-a-rī'ah, and
for Mĕ-shŭl'lam, chief men; also

v.5–436 BC
See footnote, *Time*, Rev. 10:6.

15
*g Ezra*, Ezra 7:1.
*h Priest*, Lev. 1:5.
*i Levites*, Deut. 10:8.

§ **BANISHMENT.** *As a penalty*, Ezra 7:26. *Of Adam and Eve, from Eden*, Gen. 3:22–24. *Of Cain, to be a fugitive and a vagabond*, Gen. 4:12, 14. *Of Jews, from Rome*, Acts 18:2.

v.16–436 BC
See footnote, *Time*, Rev. 10:6.

16
1 R. V. which were teachers.

17
*j* *Zeal, instances of*, 2 Cor. 7:11.
*k* *Minister*, Rom. 15:16.
*l* *Temple, Second*, 1 Kin. 6:17.
*m* *Church, called house of God*, 1 Kin. 9:3.

18
*n* *God, providence of*, Gen. 2:2.
*o* *Levi*, Gen. 29:34.
*p* Or, *Jacob*, Gen. 27:11.

19
*q* *Merarites, sons of Merari*, Num. 26:57.

20
*r* *David*, 1 Sam. 16:13.

21
*s* *Fasting*, Zech. 8:19.
*t* *Humility, instances of*, Prov. 22:4.
*u* *Prayer*, Acts 6:4.
*v* *Temporal Blessings, from God*, Psa. 103:2.
*w* *Children*, Mark 10:14.
2 R. V. humble

22
*x* *Courage, instances of*, Deut. 31:7.
*y* *Promise, implied, to seekers*, 2 Cor. 1:20.
*z* *Faith, instances of*, Mark 11:22.

*a* *God, providence of*, Gen. 2:2.
*b* *Righteous, promises to*, Psa. 64:10.
*c* *Seekers*, Isa. 55:6.
*d* *God, power of*, Gen. 2:2.
*e* *Backsliders, punishment of*, Jer. 3:22.

23
*f* *Fasting*, Zech. 8:19.

for Joi′a-rĭb, and for Ĕl′na-thăn, [1]men of understanding.

17 And [g,j]I sent them with commandment unto Ĭd′dō the chief at the place Că-sĭph′ĭ-ȧ, and I told them what they should say unto Ĭd′dō, *and* to his brethren the *Nĕth′ĭ-nĭmṣ, at the place Că-sĭph′ĭ-ȧ, that they should bring unto us [k]ministers for the [l,m]house of our God.

18 And by the good hand of our [n]God upon us they brought us a man of understanding, of the sons of Măh′lī, the son of [o]Lē′vī, the son of [p]Ĭṣ′ra-el; and Shĕr-e-bī′ah, with his sons and his brethren, eighteen;

19 And Hăsh-a-bī′ah, and with him Jė-shā′iah of the [q]sons of Mė-rā′rī, his brethren and their sons, twenty;

20 Also of the *Nĕth′ĭ-nĭmṣ, whom [r]Dā′vid and the princes had appointed for the service of the [i]Lē′vītes, two hundred and twenty Nĕth′ĭ-nĭmṣ: all of them were expressed by name.

21 ¶ Then [g]I proclaimed a [s]fast there, at the river of Ȧ-hā′vȧ, that we might [2,t]afflict[c] ourselves before our God, to [u]seek of him a [v]right way for us, and for our [w]little ones, and for all our substance.

22[s] [x]For [g]I was ashamed to require of the king a band of †soldiers and horsemen to help us against the enemy in the way: because we had spoken unto the king, saying, [y,z]The [a]hand of our God *is* upon [b]all them for good that [c]seek him; but his [d]power and his wrath *is* against all them that [e]forsake him.

23 So we [f]fasted and besought our God for this: and he was [g]intreated of us.[s]

24 ¶ Then I separated twelve of the chief of the [h]priests, Shĕr-e-bī′ah, Hăsh-a-bī′ah, and ten of their brethren with them,

25 And weighed unto them the [i]silver, and the [j]gold, and the vessels, *even* the offering of the [k]house of our God, which the king, and his counsellors, and his lords, and all Ĭṣ′ra-el *there* present, [l]had offered:

26 I even weighed unto their hand six hundred and fifty [m]talents[c] of [i]silver, and silver vessels[c] an hundred talents,[c] *and* of [j]gold an hundred talents;[c]

27 Also twenty [n]basons of [j]gold, of a thousand [3,o]drams;[c] and two vessels of fine [4,p]copper, precious as gold.

28 And I said unto them, Ye *are* holy[c] unto the LORD; the vessels *are* holy also; and the [i]silver and the [j]gold *are* a [l]freewill offering unto the LORD God of your fathers.

29 Watch ye, and keep *them*, until ye weigh *them* before the chief[c] of the [q]priests and the [r]Lē′vītes, and chief of the fathers of Ĭṣ′ra-el, at [s]Jė-ru̥′sȧ-lĕm, in the chambers of the [k]house of the LORD.

30 So took the [q]priests and the [r]Lē′vītes the weight of the [i]silver, and the [j]gold, and the vessels, to bring *them* to [s]Jė-ru̥′sȧ-lĕm unto the [k,t]house of our God.

31 ¶ Then we departed from the river of Ȧ-hā′vȧ on the twelfth *day* of the [u]first [v]month, to go unto [s]Jė-ru̥′sȧ-lĕm: and the hand of our God was upon

v.23–436 BC
See footnote, *Time*, Rev. 10:6.
*g* *Prayer, answered*, Acts 6:4.

24
*h* *Priest*, Lev. 1:5.

25
*i* *Silver*, 1 Chr. 28:14.
*j* *Gold*, Ezek. 7:19.
*k* *Temple, Second*, 1 Kin. 6:17.
*l* *Liberality, instances of*, 1 Tim. 6:18.

26
*m* *Talent*, Ex. 38:25.

27
*n* *Basin*, 1 Kin. 7:50.
*o* *Dram*, 1 Chr. 29:7.
*p* *Brass*, Job 28:2.
3 R. V. darics;
4 R. V. bright brass,

29
*q* *Priest, duties of*, Lev. 1:5.
*r* *Levites, duties of*, Deut. 10:8.
*s* *Jerusalem*, Judg. 19:10.

30
*t* *Church, called house of God*, 1 Kin. 9:3.

31
*u* *Abib*, Ex. 13:4.
*v* *Month*, Ex. 12:2.

* **NETHINIM.** *Servants of the, Levites* Ezra 8:20. *Return from the captivity*, 1 Chr. 9:2; Ezra 2:43, 58, 70; 7:7, 24; 8:17; Neh. 3:26, 31; 7:46, 60, 73; 10:28; 11:3, 21.

† **SOLDIERS.** *Military enrollment of Israel, in the wilderness of Sinai*, Num. 1; 2; *in the plains of Moab*, Num. 26. *Levies of, in the ratio of one man to ten subject to duty*, Judg. 20:10. *Cowards excused from duty*, Deut. 20:8; Judg. 7:3. *Others exempt from service*, Deut. 20:5–9; 24:5.
*Garrisoned in cities*, Acts 21:31–33; 22:24–28. *Come to John*, Luke 3:14. *Mock Jesus*, Matt. 27:27–31; Mark. 15:16–20; Luke 23:11, 36, 37. *Crucify Jesus*, Matt. 27:27, 31–37; Mark 15:16–24; John 19:23, 24. *Guard the sepulchre*, Matt. 27:65; 28:11–15. *Guard prisoners*, Acts 12:4–6; 28:16. *Quell riots*, Acts 21:31–35; 22:24–28. *Their duty as sentinels*, Acts 12:18, 19. *Perform escort duty*, Acts 23:23, 31–33; 27:1, 31, 42, 43; 28:16.
*Officers concerned in the betrayal of Jesus*, Luke 22:4.
See footnote, ARMIES, Deut. 11:4.

v.31–436 BC
See footnote, *Time*, Rev. 10:6.

*w God, preserver*, Gen. 2:2.

**35**

*x Captivity, of Judah*, Isa. 5:13.
*y Offerings, burnt*, Lev. 6:17.
*z Jesus, typified in offerings*, Matt. 1:21.

*a Offerings, sin*, Lev. 6:17.
*b Jesus, typified in offerings*, Matt. 1:21.

**36**

*c Government, provincial*, Isa. 22:21.
*d Temple, Second*, 1 Kin. 6:17.
5 R. V. satraps,
6 R. V. beyond

**1**

*a Zeal, instances of*, 2 Cor. 7:11.
*b Ezra*, Ezra 7:1.
*c Priest*, Lev. 1:5.
*d Minister, false and corrupt*, Rom. 15:16.
*e Levites*, Deut. 10:8.
*f Fellowship, with the wicked*, 1 Cor. 1:9.
*g Canaanites*, Ex. 23:28.
*h Hittites*, Judg. 1:26.

us, and he [w]delivered us from the hand of the enemy, and of such as lay in wait by the way.

32 And we came to [s]Jĕ-rṳ'sā-lĕm, and abode there three days.

33 ¶ Now on the fourth day was the [i]silver and the [j]gold and the vessels weighed in the [k,l]house of our God by the hand of Mĕr'e-mŏth the son of U-rī'ah the priest; and with him *was* Ē-le-ā'zar the son of Phĭn'e-has; and with them *was* Jŏz'a-băd the son of Jĕsh'u-ȧ, and Nō-a-dī'ah the son of Bĭn'nu̧-ī, [r]Lē'-vītes;

34 By number *and* by weight of every one: and all the weight was written at that time.

35 *Also* the children of those that had been carried away, which were come out of the [x]captivity, offered [y]burnt [z]offerings unto the God of Ĭs̡'ra-el, twelve bullocks for all Ĭs̡'ra-el, ninety and six rams, seventy and seven lambs, twelve he goats *for* a [a]sin [b]offering: all *this was* a burnt offering unto the LORD.

36 And they delivered the king's commissions unto the king's [5]lieutenants, and to the [c]governors [6]on[G] this side the river: and they furthered[G] the people, and the [d]house[G] of God.

## CHAPTER 9

*The princes complain to Ezra of the intermarriages of the people with the heathen. 3 His distress on account of them. 5 His confession and prayer to God.*

NOW[Q] when these things were done, [a]the princes came to [b]me, saying, The people of Ĭs̡'ra-el, and the [c,d]priests, and the [e]Lē'vītes, [f]have not separated themselves from the people of the lands, *doing* according to their abominations, *even* of the [g]Cā'năan-ītes, the [h]Hĭt'tītes, the [i]Pĕr'ĭz-zītes, the [j]Jĕb'u-sītes, the [k]Ăm'mon-ītes, the [l]Mō'ab-ītes, the [m]Ē-ġy̆p'tians̡, and the [n]Ăm'-ôr-ītes.

2 For [o]they have [p,q]taken of their daughters for themselves, and for their sons: so that the holy seed have mingled[G] themselves with the people of *those* lands: yea, the hand of the princes and rulers hath been chief[G] in this trespass.[G]

3 And when I heard this thing, I [r,s]rent my garment and my *mantle, and plucked off the hair of my head and of my [t]beard, and sat down astonied.[Q] [G]

4 Then were assembled unto me every one that trembled at the words of the God of Ĭs̡'ra-el, because of the transgression of those that had been [u]carried away; and I sat astonied until the evening [v]sacrifice.

5 ¶ And at the evening [v]sacrifice I arose up from my [1]heaviness; and having [r]rent[G] my garment and my mantle, I [w]fell upon my knees, and spread out my hands unto the LORD my God,

6 And [x,y]said, O my God, I am ashamed and [z]blush to lift up my face to thee, my God: for [a]our [b]iniquities are increased over *our* head, and our [2]trespass[G] is grown up unto the heavens.

7 Since the days of our fathers *have* we *been* [3]in a great trespass unto this day; and for our [c]iniquities have we, our kings, *and* our priests, [d]been delivered into the hand of the kings of the lands, to the sword, to [e]captivity, and to a spoil, and to confusion[G] of face, as *it is* this day.[Q]

8 And [f]now for a little space[G] [g]grace hath been *shewed* from the LORD our God, to leave us a

v.1–436 BC
See footnote, *Time*, Rev. 10:6.

*i Perizzites*, Gen. 15:20.
*j Jebusites*, Deut. 7:1.
*k Ammonites*, Deut. 2:20.
*l Moabites*, Gen. 19:37.
*m Egyptians*, Ex. 50:3.
*n Amorites*, Gen. 14:13.

**2**

*o Israel, marriage of, with Canaanites*, Ex. 4:22.
*p Miscegenation, instances of*, Josh. 23:12.
*q Marriage*, Gen. 34:9.

**3**

*r Rending of Garments*, 2 Chr. 34:27.
*s Mourning*, Lam. 2:5.
*t Beard*, 1 Sam. 21:13.

**4**

*u Captivity, of Judah*, Isa. 5:13.
*v Offerings, daily*, Lev. 6:17.

**5**

*w Prayer, postures in*, Acts 6:4.
1 R. V. humiliation,

**6**

*x Nation, in adversity, prayer for*, vs. 6–15; Isa. 2:4.
*y Adversity, prayer in*, vs. 6–15; Psa. 10:6.
*z* Jer. 6:15; 8:12.

*a Prayer, confession in*, vs. 6–15; Acts 6:4.
*b Sin, confession of*, Rom. 5:12.
2 R. V. guiltiness

**7**

*c Sin, punishment of*, Rom. 5:12.
*d Judgments*, Ex. 6:6.
*e Captivity, as a judgment*, Isa. 5:13.
3 R. V. exceeding guilty

**8**

*f Thankfulness, to God*, Acts 24:3.
*g Grace of God*, Rom. 4:16.

* **MANTLE**, a robe of office, probably. *Worn by Samuel, the prophet, and rent by him as a symbol of the rending of the kingdom from Saul*, 1 Sam. 15:27. *Worn by Elijah*, 1 Kin. 19:13. *Cast by Elijah upon Elisha, as a sign of Elisha's call to the prophetic office*, 1 Kin. 19:19. *Elijah smites the waters of Jordan with, and the waters are divided*, 2 Kin. 2:2. *Elijah's, recovered by Elisha, with which he divides Jordan*, 2 Kin. 2:13, 14.

An article of dress, an extra wrap. *Babylonian, hidden by Achan*, Josh. 7:21, 24. *Rending of, a token of surprise and grief*, Job 1:20; 2:12.

See footnote, DRESS, Zech. 3:3.

v.8–436 BC
See footnote, *Time*, Rev. 10:6.

*h* *Nail, figurative*, Isa. 41:7.
*i* *Bondage*, Ex. 1:14.

9
*j* *God, faithfulness of*, Gen. 2:2.
*k* *Persia*, Esth. 1:3.
*l* *Temple, Second*, 1 Kin. 6:17.
*m* *Judah, kingdom of*, 2 Chr. 11:17.
*n* *Jerusalem*, Judg. 19:10.

10
*o* *Backsliders*, Jer. 3:22.
*p* *Disobedience to God*, Eph. 5:6.
*q* *Law, of Moses*, Deut. 33:2.

11
*r* *Prophets, inspiration of*, Isa. 3:2.
*s* *Defilement*, Lev. 5:2.
*t* *Wicked, described*, Psa. 73:3.

12
*u* *Fellowship, with the wicked, forbidden*, 1 Cor. 1:9.
*v* *Blessings, contingent upon obedience*, Deut. 11:26.

13
*w* *Divine Chastisement*, Job 33:19.
*x* *Humility*, Prov. 22:4.
4 R. V. guilt,
5 R. V. a remnant, (*omitting* as this;)

14
*y* *Evil Company*, Prov. 13:20.
*z* *Anger of God*, 2 Kin. 13:3.
6 R. V. Shall

remnant to escape, and to give us a [h]nail[G] in his holy place, that our God may lighten our eyes, and give us a little reviving in our [i]bondage.

9 For we *were* bondmen[G]; [j]yet our God [j]hath not forsaken us in our [i]bondage, but hath extended mercy unto us in the sight of the kings of [k]Pĕr′ṣiȧ, to give us a reviving, to set up the [l]house of our God, and to repair the desolations[G] thereof, and to give us a wall in [m]Jū′dah and in [n]Jė-rụ′sȧ-lĕm.[S]

10 And now, O our God, what shall we say after this? for [a,b]we have [o,p]forsaken thy [q]commandments,

11 Which thou hast [r]commanded by thy servants the prophets, saying, The land, unto which ye go to possess it, is an [s]unclean land with the filthiness of the [t]people of the lands, with their abominations,[G] which have filled it from one end to another with their uncleanness.

12 Now therefore [u]give not your daughters unto their sons, neither take their daughters unto your sons, nor seek their peace or their wealth for ever: [v]that ye may be strong, and eat the good of the land, and leave *it* for an inheritance to your children for ever.

13 [f]And after [c,d]all that is come upon us for our evil deeds, and for our great [4]trespass, seeing that [w]thou our God hast punished us [x]less than our iniquities *deserve*, and hast given us *such* [5]deliverance as this;

14 [6]Should we again [p]break thy commandments, and join in affinity[G] with [y]the people of these abominations? wouldest not thou be [z]angry with us till thou hadst consumed[G] *us*, so that *there should be* no remnant nor escaping?

15 O Lord God of Ĭṣ′ra-el, thou *art* [a]righteous: for we remain yet escaped, as *it is* this day: behold, [b]we *are* before thee in our trespasses: for we cannot stand before thee because of this.

## CHAPTER 10

*Ezra is encouraged to begin the work of reform. 6 He assembles and exhorts the people. 9 They confess their sins, and promise amendment. 18 The names of those who had married strange wives.*

NOW [1]when [a,b,c]Ĕz′rȧ had [d]prayed, and when he had confessed, [e]weeping and casting himself down before the [f]house of God, there assembled unto him out of Ĭṣ′ra-el a very great congregation of men and women and children: for [g,h]the people wept very sore.[T G]

2 And Shĕch-a-nī′ah the son of Jė-hī′el, *one* of the sons of Ē′lăm, answered and said unto [a]Ĕz′rȧ, [g,i]We have trespassed[G] against our God, and have [j,k]taken strange[G] wives of the people of the land: yet now there is hope in Ĭṣ′ra-el concerning this thing.

3 [g]Now therefore let us make a covenant[G] with our God to put away all the wives, and such as are born of them, according to the counsel[G] of my lord, and of [l]those that [m]tremble at the commandment of our God; and let it be done according to the law.

4 Arise; for *this* matter *belongeth* unto thee: we also *will be* with thee: be of good courage, and do *it*.

5 Then arose [a]Ĕz′rȧ, and made the chief [n]priests, the [o]Lē′vītes, and all Ĭṣ′ra-el, to swear[G] that they should do according to this word. And they [p]sware.

6 Then [a]Ĕz′rȧ rose up from before the [f]house of God, and went into the chamber of Jō-hā′nan the son of Ė-lī′a-shĭb: and *when* he came thither, he did [q]eat no

v.15–436 BC
See footnote, *Time*, Rev. 10:6.

15
*a* *God, righteousness of*, Gen. 2:2.
*b* *Sin, confession of*, Rom. 5:12.

1
*a* *Ezra*, Ezra 7:1.
*b* *Zeal, instances of*, 2 Cor. 7:11.
*c* *Influence, good*, 1 Cor. 7:14.
*d* *Prayer*, Acts 6:4.
*e* *Weeping*, Ezra 3:13.
*f* *Temple, Second*, 1 Kin. 6:17.
*g* *Repentance, instances of*, Mark 1:4.
*h* *Backsliders, return of*, Jer. 3:22.
1 R. V. while

2
*i* *Sin, confession of*, Rom. 5:12.
*j* *Marriage*, Gen. 34:9.
*k* *Israel, marriage of, with Canaanites*, Ex. 4:22.

3
*l* *Righteous, described*, Psa. 64:10.
*m* *Fear of God*, Acts 9.31.

5
*n* *Priest*, Lev. 1:5.
*o* *Levites*, Deut. 10:8.
*p* *Oath*, Num. 5:19.

6
*q* *Fasting, instances of*, Zech. 8:19.

v.6–436 BC
See footnote, *Time*, Rev. 10:6.

r *Captivity, of Judah*, Isa. 5:13.

**7**

s *Judah, kingdom of*, 2 Chr. 11:17.
t *Jerusalem*, Judg. 19:10.
u *Citizens, duties of*, Luke 15:15.

**8**

v *Senate*, Num. 11:16.
w *Church, rules of discipline in*, Matt. 16:18.

**9**

x *Judah, tribe of*, Num. 10:14.
y *Benjamin, tribe of*, Num. 1:37.
z *Month*, Ex. 12:2.

a *Jerusalem, streets of*, Judg. 19:10.
b *Rain*, 2 Sam. 1:21.
2 R. V. broad place before the

**10**

c *Ezra*, Ezra 7:1.
d *Reproof, faithfulness in*, Prov. 17:10.
e *Miscegenation*, Josh. 23:12.
3 R. V. guilt

**11**

f *Sin, confession of*, Rom. 5:12.
g *Fellowship, with the wicked*, 1 Cor. 1:9.
h *Divorce*, Matt. 19:7.

**12**

i *Decision, instances of*, Isa. 50:7.

bread, nor drink water: for he
mourned because of the transgression[c] of them that [r]had been
carried away.
7 And they made proclamation
throughout [s]Jū′dah and [t]Jē-ru̥′-
sā-lĕm unto all the children of
the captivity, that [u]they should
gather themselves together unto
Jē-ru̥′sā-lĕm;
8 And that [u]whosoever would
not come within three days, according to the counsel of the
princes and the [v]elders, [w]all his
substance should be *forfeited,
and [w]himself separated from the
congregation of those that had
been carried away.
9 ¶ Then all the [u]men of [x]Jū′-
dah and [y]Bĕn′ja-mĭn gathered
themselves together unto Jē-ru̥′-
sā-lĕm within three days. It *was*
the ninth [z]month, on the twentieth *day* of the month; and all
the people sat in the [2,a]street
of the house of God, trembling
because of *this* matter, and for
the great [b]rain.
10 And [c]Ĕz′rȧ the priest stood
up, and [d]said unto them, Ye
have transgressed, and have [e]tak-
en strange[c] wives, to increase
the [3]trespass of Ĭs̡′ra-el.
11 [d]Now therefore make [f]con-
fession unto the LORD God of
your fathers, and do his pleasure: and separate yourselves
from the [g]people of the land, and
[h]from the strange[c]wives.
12 Then all the congregation
answered and said with a loud
voice, As thou hast said, [i]so
must we do.
13 But the people *are* many,
and *it is* a time of much [b]rain,
and we are not able to stand
without,[c] neither *is this* a work
of one day or two: for we [4]are
many that have transgressed[c]in
this thing.
14 Let now our [5]rulers of all the
congregation stand, and let all
them which have taken strange[c]
wives in our cities come at appointed times, and with them the
[j]elders of every city, and the
[j]judges thereof, until the fierce
[k]wrath of our God for this matter be turned [f]from us.
15 Only Jŏn′a-than the son
of Ā′sa-hĕl and Jȧ-hȧ-zī′ah the
son of Tĭk′vah were employed
about this *matter*: and Mē-shŭl′-
lam and Shăb′be-thāi the Lē′-
vīte helped them.
16 And the [l]children of the captivity did so. And [c]Ĕz′rȧ the
priest, *with* certain chief[c]of the
fathers, after the house of their
fathers, and all of them by *their*
names, were separated, and
sat down in the first day of the
tenth [m]month to examine the
matter.
17 And they made an end with
all the men that had [e]taken
strange[c]wives by the first day of
the first [m]month.
18 ¶ And among the [n]sons of
the [o]priests there were found
that had [e]taken strange[c]wives:
*namely*, of the sons of [†,p]Jĕsh′-
u-ȧ the son of [q]Jŏz′a-dăk, and
his brethren; Mā-a-sē′iah, and
Ē-li-ē′zēr, and Jā′rib, and Gĕd-
a-lī′ah.
19 And they [r]gave their [‡]hands
that they would [h]put away their

v.13–436 BC
See footnote, *Time*, Rev. 10:6.

**13**

4 R. V. have greatly transgressed in this matter.

**14**

j *Government, municipal*, Isa. 22:21.
k *Anger of God*, 2 Kin. 13:3.
5 R. V. princes be appointed for all the congregation, and let

**16**

l *Jews, after the captivity*, Neh. 4:2.
m *Month*, Ex. 12:2.

**18**

n *Minister, false and corrupt*, Rom. 15:16.
o *Priest*, Lev. 1:5.
p *Jeshua*, Ezra 2:2.
q *Jozadak*, Neh. 12:26.

v.18–435 BC

**19**

r *Covenant, of men with men*, Deut. 29:1.

* **CONFISCATION.** Of property: *By David, that of Mephibosheth*, 2 Sam. 16:4; *by Ahab, of Naboth's vineyard*, 1 Kin. 21:7–16; *by Ahasuerus, of Haman's house*, Esth. 8:1. *As a penalty*, Ezra 7:26; 10:8.

† [In order to publish this Bible in one volume with its numerous and diversified marginal notes and footnotes it has been necessary to avoid elaborate discussions of subjects, such, for instance, as would be necessary to point out the difficulties in connection with some of the names in genealogical lists. These difficulties grew out of errors of copyists, differences in the spelling of the same name, and the fact that individuals and places are mentioned under different names in different chapters. Where the identity of persons or places is doubtful in this chapter, or when no noteworthy fact is known concerning them, no mention of the name is made in either the margins or footnotes.]

‡ **HAND.** *Imposition of hands*, Heb. 6:2; Ex. 29:10, 15, 19; Lev. 1:4; 3:2, 8, 13; 4:4, 15, 24, 33; 8:14; 16:21; Num. 8:12; *in ordaining the Levites*, Num. 8:10, 11; *in ordaining Joshua*, Num. 27:18–23; Deut. 34:9; *in ordaining deacons*, Acts 6:6; *in ordaining Timothy*, 1 Tim. 4:14; 2 Tim. 1:6; *in ordaining Barnabas and Saul*, Acts 13:3; *in healing*, Mark 6:5; 7:32; 16:18; Luke 4:40; Acts 28:8; *in blessing children*, Gen. 48:14; Matt. 19:13; Mark 10:16; *in solemnizing testimony*, Lev. 24:14; *preceding the gift of the Holy Spirit*, **Acts 8:17; 9:17; 19:6.**

v.19–435 BC
See footnote, *Time*, Rev. 10:6.

s *Offerings, trespass*, Lev. 6:17.
t *Jesus, typified in offerings*, Matt. 1:21.
6 R. V. guilt.

wives; and *being* guilty, *they offered* a [s,t]ram of the flock for
their [6]trespass.[C]
20 And of the sons of Ĭm'mēr;
Hă-nā'nī, and Zĕb-a-dī'ah.
21 And of the sons of Hā'rim;
Mā-a-sē'iah, and Ē-lī'jah, and
Shĕm-a-ī'ah, and Jĕ-hī'el, and
Ŭz-zī'ah.
22 And of the sons of [u]Păsh'ŭr;
Ē-lĭ-o-ē'na-ī, Mā-a-sē'iah, Ĭsh'ma-el, Nĕ-thăn'e-el, Jŏz'a-băd,
and Ĕl'a-sah.
23 Also of the [v]Lē'vītes; Jŏz'a-băd, and Shĭm'e-ī, and Kĕ-lā'iah, (the same *is* Kĕl'ĭ-tȧ,) Pĕth-a-hī'ah, Jū'dah, and Ē-li-ē'zĕr.
24 Of the [w]singers also;[C] Ē-lī'a-shĭb: and of the [x]porters; Shăl'lum, and Tē'lem, and Ū'rī.
25 Moreover of Ĭs'ra-el: of
the sons of Pā'rŏsh; Rȧ-mī'ah,
and Jĕ-zī'ah, and Măl-chī'ah,
and Mī'a-mĭn, and Ē-le-ā'zar,
and Măl-chī'jah, and Bĕ-nā'iah.
26 And of the sons of Ē'lăm;
Măt-ta-nī'ah, Zĕch-a-rī'ah, and
Jĕ-hī'el, and Ăb'dī, and Jĕr'e-mŏth, and Ē-lī'ah.
27 And of the sons of Zăt'tu;
Ē-lĭ-o-ē'na-ī, Ē-lī'a-shĭb, Măt-ta-nī'ah, and Jĕr'e-mŏth, and
Zā'băd, and Ȧ-zī'zȧ.
28 Of the sons also of Bĕb'a-ī; Jē-hō-hā'nan, Hăn-a-nī'ah,
Zăb'bāi, *and* Ăth'lāi.
29 And of the sons of Bā'nī;
Mĕ-shŭl'lam, Măl'luch, and Ăd-a-ī'ah, Jăsh'ŭb, and Shē'al, and
Rā'moth.

22
u *Pashur*, 1 Chr. 9:12.

23
v *Levites*, Deut. 10.8.

24
w *Choir*, 1 Chr. 15:16.
x *Porters*, 2 Sam. 18:26.

30 And of the sons of Pā'hath–mō'ab; Ăd'nȧ, and Chē'lăl, Bĕ-nā'iah, Mā-a-sē'iah,
Măt-ta-nī'ah, Bĕ-zăl'e-el, and
Bĭn'nụ-ī, and Mȧ-năs'seh.
31 And *of* the sons of Hā'rim;
Ē-li-ē'zĕr, Ī-shī'jah, Măl-chī'ah,
Shĕm-a-ī'ah, Shĭm'e-on,
32 Bĕn'ja-mĭn, Măl'luch, *and*
Shĕm-a-rī'ah.
33 Of the sons of Hā'shum;
Măt-te-nā'ī, Măt'ta-thah, Zā'băd, Ē-lĭph'e-lĕt, Jĕr'e-māi, Mȧ-năs'seh, *and* Shĭm'e-ī.
34 Of the sons of Bā'nī; Mȧ-ăd'āi, Ăm'răm, and Ū'el,
35 Bĕ-nā'iah, Bĕ-dē'iah, Chĕl'lụh,
36 Vȧ-nī'ah, Mĕr'e-mŏth, Ē-lī'a-shĭb,
37 Măt-ta-nī'ah, Măt-te-nā'ī,
and Jā'a-sạu,
38 And Bā'nī, and Bĭn'nụ-ī, Shĭm'e-ī,
39 And Shĕl-e-mī'ah, and Nā'than, and Ăd-a-ī'ah,
40 Măch-na-dē'bāi, Shăsh'a-ī,
Shăr'a-ī,
41 Ȧ-zăr'e-el, and Shĕl-e-mī'ah,
Shĕm-a-rī'ah,
42 Shăl'lum, Ăm-a-rī'ah, *and*
Jō'ṣeph.
43 Of the sons of Nē'bō; Jĕ-ī'el, Măt-tĭ-thī'ah, Zā'băd, Ze-bī'nȧ, Jȧ-dā'u, and Jō'el, Bĕ-nā'iah.
44 All these had [e]taken strange[C]
wives: and *some* of them had
wives by whom they had children.[Q]

v.30–435 BC
See footnote, *Time*, Rev. 10:6.

*Lifting up of, in taking an oath*, Gen. 14:22; Psa. 106:26; *in benediction*, Lev. 9:22; Luke 24:50; *in prayer*, Lam. 3:41; 1 Tim. 2:8.
*Ceremonial washing of*, Matt. 15:2; Mark 7:2–5. *Washing of, a symbol of innocency*, Deut. 21:6; Matt. 27:24.
*Clasping of, in token, of contract*, Ezra 10:19; Prov. 6:1; 17:18; Lam. 5:6; Ezek. 17:18; *of friendship*, 2 Kin. 10:15; Job 17:3.
***Right, a symbol of power*, Isa. 23:11; 41:10. *At the right, a place of honor*,** Psa. 45:9; 80:17; Acts 7:55. *Clean, symbolical of righteousness*, Job 17:9.
**Figurative:** *Of source of temptation*, Matt. 5:30; 18:8; Mark 9:43.
Anthropomorphic use of: *Of God, waxed short*, Num. 11:23; *is mighty*, Josh. 4:24; *was heavy*, 1 Sam. 5:6; *was against the Philistines*, 1 Sam. 7:13; *was on Elijah*, 1 Kin. 18:46; *is not shortened*, Isa. 59:1; *was with the early Christians*, Acts 11:21. **See footnote, ANTHROPOMORPHISMS, Gen. 11:5.**

THE

# BOOK OF NEHEMIAH

v.1–423 BC
See footnote, *Time*, Rev. 10:6.

1

*a* Neh. 10:1.
*b* *Month*, Ex. 12:2.
*c* *Shushan*, Esth. 1:2.
*d* *Palace, at Shushan*, 1 Kin. 21:1.

2

*e* Neh. 7:2.
*f* *Judah, kingdom of*, 2 Chr. 11:17.
*g* *Patriotism, instances of, Jewish exiles*, Psa. 137:1.
*h* *Jews*, Neh. 4:2.
*i* *Captivity, of Judah*, Isa. 5:13.
*j* *Jerusalem*, Judg. 19:10.

3

*k* *Adversity*, Psa. 10:6.
*l* *Gates*, Deut. 3:5.

4

*m* *Weeping*, Ezra 3:13.
*n* *Mourning*, Lam. 2:5.
*o* *Fasting*, Zech. 8:19.
*p* *Prayer, importunity in*, Acts 6:4.
*q* *Nation, in adversity, prayer for*, Isa. 2:4.

5

*r* *God, faithfulness of*, Gen. 2:2.
*s* *Covenant, of God with men*, Deut. 29:1.
*t* *Love, of man for God*, 1 John 4:19.
*u* *Obedience*, Heb. 5:8.
1 R. V. the God

6

*v* *Intercession, instances of*, Jer. 27:18.

## CHAPTER 1

*Nehemiah, hearing from Hanani of the deplorable condition of Jerusalem, mourns, fasts, and prays.* 5 *His prayer.*

THE words of *Nē-he-mī′ah the son of [a]Hăch-a-lī′ah. And it came to pass in the [b]month Chĭs′leū, in the twentieth year, as I was in [c]Shu̥′shan the [d]palace,

2 That [e]Hă̊-nā′nī, one of my brethren, came, he and *certain* men of [f]Jū′dah; and *·[g]I asked them concerning the [h]Jewș that had escaped, which were left of the [i]captivity, and concerning [j]Jē̊-ru̥′să̊-lĕm.

3 And they said unto me, The remnant that are left of the [i]captivity there in the province *are* in great [k]affliction[C] and reproach: the wall of [j]Jē̊-ru̥′să̊-lĕm also *is* broken down, and the [l]gates thereof are burned with fire.

4 ¶ And it came to pass, when I heard these words, that I sat down and [m]wept, and [n]mourned *certain* days, and [o]fasted, and [p,q]prayed before the God of heaven,

5 And [p,q]said, *I beseech thee, O LORD [1]God of heaven, the great and terrible[C] God, [r]that keepeth [s]covenant[C] and mercy for them that [t]love him and [u]observe[C] his commandments:[S]

6 Let thine ear now be attentive, and thine eyes open, that thou mayest hear the prayer of thy servant, which I pray before thee now, day and night, [v]for the children of Ĭș′ra-el thy servants, and [w]confess the [x]sins of the children of Ĭș′ra-el, which we have sinned against thee: [y]both I and my father's house have sinned.

7 [x,y]We have dealt very corruptly against thee, and [z]have not kept the [a]commandments, nor the statutes, nor the judgments,[C] which thou commandedst thy servant Mō′șeș.

8 Remember, I beseech thee, the word that thou commandedst thy servant Mō′șeș, saying, *If* ye transgress, [b]I will scatter you abroad among the nations:[C]

9 But [c]*if* ye [d]turn unto me, and keep my commandments, and do them; though there were of you cast out unto the uttermost part of the heaven, *yet* [e]will I gather them from thence,[C] and [f]will bring them unto the place that I have[S] chosen to set my name there.

10 Now these *are* thy servants and thy people, whom thou hast redeemed by thy great [g]power, and by thy strong hand.

11 O LORD, *I beseech thee, let now thine ear be attentive to the prayer of thy servant, and to the prayer of thy servants, who [2]desire to fear thy name: and [h]prosper, I pray thee, thy servant this day, and grant him mercy in the sight of this man. For I was the [i]king's [j]cupbearer.

v.6–423 BC
See footnote, *Time*, Rev. 10:6.

*w* *Prayer, confession in*, Acts 6:4.
*x* *Sin, confession of*, Rom. 5:12.
*y* *Repentance, exemplified*, Mark 1:4.

7

*z* *Disobedience to God*, Eph. 5:6.
*a* *Law, of Moses*, Deut. 33:2.

8

*b* *Divine Chastisement*, Job 33:19.

9

*c* *Blessings, contingent upon obedience*, Deut. 11:26.
*d* *Repentance, condition of divine favor*, Mark 1:4.
*e* *Promise, to penitents*, 2 Cor. 1:20.
*f* *God, mercy of*, Gen. 2:2.

10

*g* *God, power of*, Gen. 2:2.

11

*h* *Temporal Blessings, from God*, Psa. 103:2.
*i* *King*, 2 Kin. 3:10.
*j* *Cupbearer*, 1 Kin. 10:5.
2 R. V. delight

* **NEHEMIAH** (*whom Jehovah comforts*). *Son of Hachaliah*, Neh. 1:1. *Cupbearer of Artaxerxes*, Neh. 1:11; 2:1. *Is grieved over the desolation of his country*, Neh. 1. *Is sent by the king to rebuild Jerusalem*, Neh. 2:1–8. *Register, of the people whom he led from Babylon*, Neh. 7; *of the priests and Levites*, Neh. 12:1–22. *Rebuilds Jerusalem*, Neh. chapters 2–6. *His administration as ruler of the people*, Neh. chapters 5, 6, 8–11, 13.

v.1–423 BC
See footnote, *Time*, Rev. 10:6.

1
*a* *Month, Abib*, Ex. 12:2.
*b* *Artaxerxes*, Ezra 7:1.
*c* *Wine*, Prov. 23:31.
*d* *Nehemiah*, Neh. 1:1.
*e* *Cupbearer*, 1 Kin. 10:5.

2
*f* *Countenance*, Prov. 15:13.

3
*g* *Patriotism, instances of*, Psa. 137:1.
*h* *Jerusalem*, Judg. 19:10.

4
*i* *Petition, right of*, Esth. 5:6.
*j* *Temporal Blessings, prayer for*, Psa. 103:2.

6
*k* *Queen*, 1 Kin. 11:19.
*l* *Women*, Prov. 31:10.

7
*m* *Letters*, Isa. 37:14.
*n* *Government, provincial*, Isa. 22:21.
*o* *Euphrates*, Gen. 15:18.
1 R. V. let me pass through

## CHAPTER 2

*Nehemiah is sent by Artaxerxes to repair the walls of Jerusalem. 9 His arrival there is a source of grief to the enemies of the Jews. 12 He views by night the ruins of the walls. 17 His exhortation to the people.*

AND it came to pass in the
[a]month Nī′san, in the
twentieth year of [b]Är-tăx̣-ērx′ēṣ
the king, *that* [c]wine *was* before
him: and [d,e]I took up the wine,
and gave *it* unto the king. Now
I had not been *beforetime* sad
in his presence.
2 Wherefore the [b]king said unto me, Why *is* thy [f]countenance
sad, seeing thou *art* not sick?
this *is* nothing *else* but sorrow of
heart. Then I was very sore[C]
afraid,
3 And said unto the king, Let
the king live for ever: [g]why
should not my countenance be
sad, when the [h]city, the place
of my fathers' sepulchres, *lieth*
waste, and the gates thereof are
consumed with fire?
4 Then the king said unto me,
For what dost thou make [i]re-
quest? So I [j]prayed to the God
of heaven.
5 And I said unto the king, If it
please the king, and if thy servant have found favour in thy
sight, that thou wouldest send
me unto Jū′dah, unto the [h]city
of my fathers' sepulchres, [g]that
I may build it.
6 And the [b]king said unto me,
(the [k,l]queen[C] also sitting by
him,) For how long shall thy
journey be? and when wilt thou
return? So it pleased the king
to send me; and I set him a time.
7 Moreover I said unto the
king, If it please the king, let
[m]letters be given me to the [n]gov-
ernors beyond the [o]river, that
they may [1]convey me over till I
come into Jū′dah;
8 And a [m]letter unto Ā′saph the
keeper of the king's forest, that
he may give me timber to make
beams for the gates of the palace
which *appertained*[C] to the house,
and for the [p]wall of the city, and
for the house that I shall enter
into. And the king granted me,
according to the good hand of
my [q]God upon me.
9 ¶ Then I came to the [n]gov-
ernors beyond the [o]river, and
gave them the king's [m]letters.
Now the king had sent [r]cap-
tains of the army and [s]horsemen
with me.
10 When *Săn-băl′lat the
[t]Hŏr′o-nīte, and †Tō-bī′ah the
servant, the [u]Ăm′mon-īte, heard
*of it*, [v]it grieved them exceedingly that there was come a man
to seek the welfare of the children of Iṣ′ra-el.
11 ¶ So [d]I came to [h]Jē-ru′să-
lĕm, and was there three days.
12 And I arose in the night, I
and some few men with me;
[w]neither told I *any* man what
my God had put in my heart to
do at [h]Jē-ru′să-lĕm: neither *was
there any* beast with me, save[C] the
beast that I rode upon.
13 And I went out by night by
the [x]gate of the valley, even before the dragon well, and to the
dung port,[C] and viewed the [p]walls
of Jē-ru′să-lĕm, which were broken down, and the gates thereof
were consumed[C] with fire.
14 Then I went on to the [x]gate
of the fountain, and to the king's
[y]pool: but *there was* no place
for the beast *that was* under me
to pass.
15 Then went I up in the night
by the [z,a]brook, and viewed the
[b]wall, and turned back, and entered by the [c]gate of the valley,
and *so* returned.

v.8–423 BC
See footnote, *Time*, Rev. 10:6.

8
*p* *Jerusalem, walls of*, Judg. 19:10.
*q* *God, providence of*, Gen. 2:2.

9
*r* *Captain*, Num. 31:48.
*s* *Cavalry*, 1 Sam. 13:5.

10
*t* Neh. 13:28.
*u* *Ammonites*, Deut. 2:20.
*v* *Malice*, Eph. 4:31.

12
*w* *Prudence*, 2 Chr. 2:12.

13
*x* *Jerusalem, gates of*, Judg. 19:10.

14
*y* *Pool*, 2 Sam. 2:13.

15
*z* *Brook*, Deut. 8:7.
*a* *Kidron*, 1 Kin. 2:37.
*b* *Jerusalem, walls of*, Judg. 19:10.
*c* *Jerusalem, gates of*, Judg. 19:10.

* **SANBALLAT.** *An enemy of the Jews after the captivity*, Neh. 2:10, 19; 4:1–3, 7, 8; 6:1–14. *Father-in-law of Joiada, a priest*, Neh. 13:28.

† **TOBIAH,** an enemy of the Jews in the time of Nehemiah. *Opposes the rebuilding of the walls of Jerusalem*, Neh. 2:10, 19; 4:3, 7, 8. *Conspires to injure and intimidate Nehemiah*, Neh. 6:1–14, 19. *Subverts nobles of Judah*, Neh. **6:17**, 18. *Allies himself with Eliashib, the priest*, Neh. **13:4–9.**

v.16–423 BC
See footnote, *Time*, Rev. 10:6.

**16**
*d Jews*, Neh. 4:2.
*e Priest*, Lev. 1:5.

**17**
*f Patriotism, instances of*, Psa. 137:1.

**18**
*g God, providence of*, Gen. 2:2.

**19**
*h* Neh. 13:28.
*i Ammonites*, Deut. 2:20.
*j* Neh. 6:1–6.
*k Arabians*, 2 Chr. 17:11.
*l Faith, instances of trial of*, Mark 11:22.

**20**
*m Faith*, Mark 11:22.
*n Jerusalem*, Judg. 19:10.

**1**
*a* Vs. 20, 21; Neh. 12:10, 22, 23; 13:4–9, 28.
*b High Priest*, Lev. 21:10.
*c Priest*, Lev. 1:5.
*d Patriotism*, Psa. 137:1.
*e Jerusalem, walls of, restored*, vs. 1–32; Judg. 19:10.
*f Jerusalem, gates of*, Judg. 19:10.
*g Tower*, 2 Chr. 26:9.
*h Jerusalem, towers of*, Judg. 19:10.

**2**
*i Jericho*, Num. 22:1.

16 And the rulers knew not whither[C] I went, or what I did; neither had I as yet told *it* to the [d]Jews, nor to the [e]priests, nor to the nobles, nor to the rulers, nor to the rest that did the work.

17 Then said I unto them, Ye see the distress that we *are* in, how Jē-ru̥′sā-lĕm *lieth* waste, and the [c]gates thereof are burned with fire: come, and [f]let us build up the [b]wall of Jē-ru̥′sā-lĕm, that we be no more a reproach.[C]

18 Then I told them of the hand of my [g]God which was good upon me: as also the king's words that he had spoken unto me. And they said, Let us rise up and build. So they strengthened their hands for *this* good *work*.

19 But when Săn-băl′lat the [h]Hŏr′o-nīte, and Tō-bī′ah the servant, the [i]Ăm′mon-īte, and [j]Gē′shem the [k]Ā-rā′bĭ-an, heard *it*, they [l]laughed us to scorn, and despised us, and said, What *is* this thing that ye do? will ye rebel against the king?

20 Then answered I them, and said unto them, The God of heaven, [m]he will prosper us; therefore we his servants will arise and build: but ye have no portion, nor right, nor memorial, in [n]Jē-ru̥′sā-lĕm.

## CHAPTER 3

*The names of those who built the wall, and the order of the work.*

THEN [a]Ē-lī′a-shĭb the [b]high priest rose up with his brethren the [c]priests, and [d]they [e]builded the [f]sheep gate; they sanctified it, and set up the doors of it; even unto the [g,h]tower of Mē′ah they sanctified it, unto the [g,h]tower of Hā-năn′e-el.

2 And next unto him builded the men of [i]Jĕr′ī-chō. And next to them builded Zăc′cur the son of Ĭm′rī.

3 But the [j]fish gate did the sons of Hăs-se-nā′ah build, who *also* laid the beams thereof,[C] and set up the doors thereof, the [1,j]locks thereof,[C] and the bars thereof.[C]

4 And next unto them [e]repaired Mĕr′e-mŏth the son of U-rī′jah, the son of Kŏz. And next unto them repaired Mē-shŭl′lam the son of Bĕr-e-chī′ah, the son of Mē-shĕz′a-beel. And next unto them repaired Zā′dŏk the son of Bā′a-nȧ.

5 And next unto them the [k]Tē-kō′ītes [e]repaired; but their nobles [l]put not their necks to the work of their [2]Lord.

6 Moreover the [f]old gate [e]repaired Jē-hoi′a-dȧ the son of Pā-sē′ah, and Mē-shŭl′lam the son of Bĕs-o-dē′iah; they laid the beams thereof,[C] and set up the doors thereof, and the [j]locks thereof, and the bars thereof.

7 And next unto them [e]repaired Mĕl-a-tī′ah the Gĭb′e-on-īte, and Jā′dŏn the Mē-rŏn′o-thīte, the men of Gĭb′e-on, and of [m]Mĭz′pah, unto the throne of the [n]governor on this side the river.

8 Next unto him repaired Ŭz′zī-el the son of Här-ha-ī′ah, of the *goldsmiths. Next unto him also repaired Hăn-a-nī′ah the son of *one of* the †apothecaries,[C] and they fortified Jē-ru̥′sā-lĕm unto the [e]broad wall.

9 And next unto them [e]repaired Rĕph-a-ī′ah the son of Hûr, the [o,p]ruler of the half part of Jē-ru̥′sā-lĕm.

10 And next unto them [e]repaired Jē-dā′iah the son of Hā-ru̥′maph, even over[C] against his house. And next unto him repaired Hăt′tush the son of Hăsh-ab-nī′ah.

11 Măl-chī′jah the son of Hā′-

v.2–423 BC
See footnote, *Time*, Rev. 10:6.

**3**
*j* Judg. 3:23–25.
1 R. V. bolts

**5**
*k Tekoa*, Jer. 6:1.
*l Lukewarmness*, Rev. 3:16.
2 R. V. lord.

**7**
*m Mizpah*, Josh. 18:26.
*n Government, provincial*, Isa. 22:21.

**9**
*o Cities, government of, by rulers*, Num. 35:8.
*p Government, municipal*, Isa. 22:21.

* **GOLDSMITH**, 2 Chr. 2:7, 14. *Repair the walls of Jerusalem after the captivity*, Neh. 3:8, 31, 32. *Make idols*, Isa. 40:19; 41:7; 46:6.

† **APOTHECARY**, Eccl. 10:1. *A compounder of drugs* (according to A. V.), *but more accurately, a perfumer* (according to Am. R. V.), Ex. 30:25, 35; 37:29; 2 Chr. 16:14; Neh. 3:8.

v.11–423 BC
See footnote, *Time*, Rev. 10:6.

rim, and Hā′shub the son of Pā′hath–mō′ab, [e]repaired the other piece, and the tower of the furnaces.

12 And next unto him repaired Shăl′lum the son of Hă-lō′hesh, the ruler of the half part of Jĕ-ru̇′să-lĕm, he and his daughters.

13 The [l]valley gate repaired Hā′nŭn, and the inhabitants of [q]Ză-nō′ah; they built it, and set up the doors thereof, the [j]locks thereof, and the bars thereof, and a thousand cubits[G] on the wall unto the dung gate.

14 But the [l]dung gate repaired Măl-chī′ah the son of Rē′chăb, the ruler of part of [r]Bĕth–hăc′çe-rĕm; he built it, and set up the doors thereof, the locks thereof, and the bars thereof.

15 But the [l]gate of the fountain repaired Shăl′lun the son of Cŏl–hō′zeh, the ruler of part of [m]Mĭz′pah; he built it, and covered it, and set up the doors thereof, the [j]locks thereof, and the bars thereof, and the wall of the [s]pool of [t]Sĭ-lō′ah by the king's garden, and unto the [u]stairs that go down from the city of Dā′vid.

16 After him repaired Nē-he-mī′ah the son of Ăz′bŭk, the ruler of the half part of [v]Bĕth′–zûr, unto *the place* over against the [w]sepulchres[G] of Dā′vid, and to the pool that was made, and unto the house of the mighty.

17 After him repaired the [x]Lē′vītes, Rē′hum the son of Bā′nī. Next unto him repaired Hăsh-a-bī′ah, the ruler of the half part of [y]Kēi′lah, in his part.

18 After him repaired their brethren, Băv′a-ī the son of Hĕn′a-dăd, the ruler of the half part of [y]Kēi′lah.

19 And next to him repaired Ē′zēr the son of Jĕsh′u-ȧ, the ruler of [m]Mĭz′pah, another piece over[G]against the going up to the [‡]armoury at the turning *of the wall.*

20 After him Bā′ru̇ch the son of Zăb′bāi earnestly repaired the other piece, from the turning *of the wall* unto the door of the house of Ē-lī′a-shĭb the high [z]priest.

21 After him repaired Mĕr′e-mŏth the son of U-rī′jah the son of Kŏz another piece, from the door of the house of Ē-lī′a-shĭb even to the end of the house of Ē-lī′a-shĭb.

22 And after him repaired the [a]priests, the men of the plain.

23 After him repaired Bĕn′ja-mĭn and Hā′shub over[G]against their house. After him repaired Ăz-a-rī′ah the son of Mā-a-sē′iah the son of Ăn-a-nī′ah by his house.

24 After him repaired Bĭn′nu̇-ī the son of Hĕn′a-dăd another piece, from the house of Ăz-a-rī′ah unto the turning *of the* [b]*wall*, even unto the corner.

25 Pā′lal the son of Ū′za-ī, over[G] against the turning *of the* [b]*wall*, and the [c,d]tower which lieth out[G] from the king's high[G] house, that *was* by the court of the [3]prison.[G] After him Pē-dā′iah the son of Pā′rŏsh.

26 Moreover the [e]Nĕth′ĭ-nĭms dwelt in [f]Ō′phel, unto *the place* over[G]against the [g]water gate toward the east, and the tower that lieth out.

27 After them the [h]Tē-kō′ītes repaired another piece, over[G] against the great tower that lieth out, even unto the wall of [f]Ō′phel.

28 From above the [g]horse gate repaired the [a]priests, every one over against his house.

29 After them repaired Zā′dŏk

13
q Neh. 11:30; Josh. 15:34.

14
r Jer. 6:1.

15
s *Pool*, 2 Sam. 2:13.
t Or, *Siloam*, John 9:11.
u Neh. 12:37.

16
v Josh. 15:58; 1 Chr. 2:45; 2 Chr. 11:7.
w *Burying Places*, Gen. 23:4.

17
x *Levites*, Deut. 10:8.
y *Keilah*, 1 Sam. 23:1.

v.19–423 BC
See footnote, *Time*, Rev. 10:6.

20
z *High Priest*, Lev. 21:10.

22
a *Priest*, Lev. 1:5.

24
b *Jerusalem, walls of, restored*, Judg. 19:10.

25
c *Tower*, 2 Chr. 26:9.
d *Jerusalem, towers of*, Judg. 19:10.
3 R. V. guard.

26
e *Nethinim*, Ezra 8:20.
f Neh. 11:21.
g *Jerusalem, gates of*, Judg. 19:10.

27
h *Tekoa*, Jer. 6:1.

‡ **ARMORY.** *A place for the storage of armor*, 2 Kin. 20:13; Neh. 3:19; Song 4:4; Isa. 22:8; 39:2. *In different parts of the kingdom*, 1 Kin. 10:17; 2 Chr. 9:16; 11:12. *Temple used for*, 2 Kin. 11:10; 2 Chr. 23:9. *Figurative*, Jer. 50:25.

v.29—423 BC
See footnote, *Time*, Rev. 10:6.

**29**
*i Porters*, 2 Sam. 18:26.

the son of Ĭm′mēr over[G] against
his house. After him repaired
also Shĕm-a-ī′ah the son of
Shĕch-a-nī′ah, the [i]keeper of the
[g]east gate.
30 After him repaired Hăn-a-
nī′ah the son of Shĕl-e-mī′ah,
and Hā′nŭn the sixth son of Zā′-
laph, another piece. After him
repaired Mĕ-shŭl′lam the son of
Bĕr-e-chī′ah over[G] against his
chamber.[G]
31 After him repaired Măl-
chī′ah the goldsmith's son unto
the place of the [e]Nĕth′ĭ-nĭmș,
and of the ‖merchants, over[G]
against the [g]gate Mĭph′kăd, and
to the going up of the corner.
32 And between the going up of
the corner unto the [g]sheep gate
repaired the goldsmiths and the
‖merchants.

## CHAPTER 4

*While the enemy scoff, Nehemiah prays and continues the work. 7 Knowing the secret design of the enemy, he sets a watch. 13 He arms the laborers, 19 and gives them directions how to act.*

**1**
*a Sanballat*, Neh. 2:10.
*b Patriotism*, vs. 1-23; Psa. 137:1.
*c Nehemiah*, Neh. 1:1.
*d Jerusalem, walls of*, Judg. 19:10.

BUT it came to pass, that
when [a]Săn-băl′lat heard
that [b,c]we builded the [d]wall, he
was wroth,[G] and took great indignation, and [e,f,g]mocked the
*Jewș.
2 And he spake before his
brethren and the army of [h]Să-
mā′rĭ-ȧ, and said, [g]What do
these feeble *Jewș? [i]will they
[j]fortify themselves? will they
sacrifice[G]? will they make an
end in a day? will they revive
the stones out of the heaps
of the rubbish which are
burned?
3 Now [k]Tō-bī′ah the Ăm′mon-
īte *was* by him, and he said,
Even that which they build, if a
[l]fox go up, he shall even break
down their [m]stone [d]wall.
4 [n]Hear, O our God; for we
are despised: and turn their reproach[G] upon their own head,
and give them for a prey[G] in the
land of captivity:
5 And cover not their iniquity,
and let not their sin be blotted
out from before thee: for they
have provoked *thee* to [o]anger before the builders.
6 So built we the [d]wall; and
all the wall was joined together
unto the half thereof: for the
people [b,p]had a mind to work.

v.1—423 BC
See footnote, *Time*, Rev. 10:6.

*e Malice, instances of*, Eph. 4:31.
*f Persecution, instances of*, John 15:20.
*g Scoffing, instances of*, Hab. 1:10.

**2**
*h Samaria*, Isa. 7:9.
*i Sarcasm, instances of*, Judg. 10:14.
*j Fortification*, Ezek. 17:17.

**3**
*k Tobiah*, Neh. 2:10.
*l Fox*, Psa. 63:10.
*m Cities, fortified*, Num. 35:8.

**4**
*n Adversity, prayer in*, Psa. 10:6.

**5**
*o Anger of God*, 2 Kin. 13:3.

**6**
*p Diligence, exemplified*, Rom. 12:8.

---

‖ **MERCHANTS**, 1 Kin. 10:15; 2 Chr. 1:16; 9:14; Neh. 3:32; Job 41:6; Song 3:6; Isa. 23:2; 47:15; Ezek. 17:4; 27:17, 18, 21-36; 38:13; Nah. 3:16; Rev. 18:3, 11, 23. *Determine standards of money value*, Gen. 23:16. *Buyers, of slaves*, Gen. 37:28; Ezek. 27:13; *of horses*, 1 Kin. 10:28; *of pearls*, Matt. 13:45, 46. *Dishonest*, Hos. 12:7. *Sabbath profaned by*, Neh. 13:15-20.

* **JEWS.** A corrupted form, doubtless, of Judah, and applied to the people of the kingdom of Judah and Benjamin, 2 Kin. 16:6; 25:25; 2 Chr. 32:18. After the dissolution of the kingdom of Israel, the name was applied to all Israelites as well as to those of the two tribes.

*Wickedness of*, Isa. 1:4-25; 2:6-10; 3:9; 59:2-15; 65:2-7; Jer. 5:1; 6:21-28; 44:1-3; Ezek. 5:6; 12:2; 16:2, 15-47, 57-63. *The book of Jeremiah deals chiefly with the wickedness of, and prophecies of the corrective judgments of God to be inflicted upon*, which see.

*Captive in Babylon*, 2 Kin. 24:1-20; 25:1, 21. *Haman's plot against*, Esth. 3:6-15. *Feast of Purim instituted to commemorate their deliverance from Haman's plot*, Esth. 9:26-32. *The proclamation of Cyrus authorizing their return to the land of Canaan*, 2 Chr. 36:22, 23; Ezra 1:2-4; *and of Artaxerxes*, Ezra 7:11-26.

**After the captivity:** *Return from Babylon*, Ezra 7:1-9; 8:31, 32. *Lists of those who returned from Babylon*, Ezra 2:1-67; 8:1-20; Neh. 7:6-69; 12:1-21. *Rebuild the temple*, Ezra 3:8-13. *Rebuilding suspended during the reign of Artaxerxes*, Ezra 4:1-24. *Resumption of the rebuilding interfered with by Tatnai, governor of the province, by protest followed by a letter to Darius*, Ezra 5. *Darius' reply to Tatnai, authorizing the rebuilding of the temple; temple completed*, Ezra 6:1-15.

*Vessels of the temple, that were taken to Babylon by Nebuchadnezzar, returned by command of Cyrus*, Ezra 1:7-11, 13, 14; 6:5. *Liberality of Artaxerxes toward the temple*, Ezra 7:14-23.

*Make marriages among the Canaanites; Ezra institutes reforms*, Ezra 10. *Rebuild the walls of Jerusalem under proclamation of Artaxerxes*, Neh. chapters 2-4, 6. *Walls dedicated*, Neh. 12:27-43.

*Mission of Jesus to*, Matt. 10:5, 6; 15:24; Mark 7:27. *Disbelieve in Jesus*, Matt. 13:5-8; John 5:38, 40, 43; 6:36; 12:37. *Reject Jesus*, Luke 13:34; 17:25; John 1:11. *Crucify Jesus*, see footnote, CRUCIFIXION, Mark 16:13. *Some accept Jesus*, John 2:23; 10:42; 11:45; 12:11; Acts 21:20. *Devout, among them*, Acts 2:5. *Spurned Paul's preaching*, Acts 13:46; 18:5, 6; 28:24-27. *Persecuted Paul*, Acts 9:22, 23; 13:50; 20:3, 19; 23:12-30; 2 Cor. 11:24. *Entrusted with the oracles of God*, Acts 7:38; Rom. 3:1, 2.

**Prophecies concerning:** *Of their rejection of the Messiah*, Isa. 49:5, 7; 52:14; 53:1-3; Zech. 13; Matt. 21:33-39; 22:1-5.

*Of war and other judgments*, Isa. 3; 4:1; 5; 6:9-13; 7:17-25; 8:14-22; 10:12; 22:1-14; 28:14-22; 29:1-10; 30:1-17; 31:1-3; 32:9-14; Jer. 1:11-16; 4:5-31; 6; 7:8-34; 8; 9:9-26; 10:17-22; 11:9-23; 13:9-27; 14:14-18; 15:1-14; 16; 17:1-4; 18:15-17; 19; 20:5; 21:4-7; 22:24-30; 25:8-38; chapters 28, 34, 37; 38:1-3; 42:13-22; chapters 43-45; Lam. 5:6; Ezek. 4; 5; 11:7-12; chapters 12, 15-17, 19; 22:13-22; 23:22-35; 24; 33:21-29; Dan. 9:26, 27; Joel 2:1-17; Amos 2:4, 5; Mic. 3; 4:8-10; Hab. 1:6-11; Zeph. 1; Zech. 14:1-3; Mal. 4:1; Matt. 21:33-45; 23:35-38; 24:2, 14-42; Mark 13:1-13; Luke 13:34, 35; 19:43, 44; 21:5-25; 23:28-31; Rev. 1:7.

*Dispersion of*, Isa. 24:1; Jer. 9:16; Hos. 9:17; Joel 3:6, 20; Amos 9:9; Ezek. 4:13; 5:10, 12; 20:23; 36:19; Dan. 9:7.

*Blessing and restoration of*, Isa. 1:25-27; 2:1-5; 4:2-6; 11:11-13; 25; 26:1, 2, 12-19; 27:13; 29:18-24; 30:18-26; 32:15-20; 33:13-24; 35; 37:31, 32; 40:2, 9; 41:27; 44; 49:13-23; 51; 52:1-12; 60; 61:4-9; 62; 66:5-22; Jer. 3:14-18; 4:3-18; 12:14-16; 23:3; 24:1-7; 30:3-22; 32:36-44; 33; 44:28; Ezek. 14:22, 23; 16:60-63; 20:40, 41; 36:1-38; 37:12, 21; Dan. 11:30-45; 12:1; Joel 3; Amos 9:9-15; Obad. 17-21; Mic. 2:12, 13; 5:3; Zeph. 2:7; Zech. 1:14-21; 2; 8; 10:5-12; 12:1-14; 13; 14:3-21; Mal. 3:4; Rom. 11.

See footnote, JUDAH, *Kingdom of*, 2 Chr. 11:17.

7 ¶ But it came to pass, *that* when [a]Săn-băl'lat, and [k]Tō-bī'-ah, and the [q]Ā-rā'bĭ-anș, and the [r]Ăm'mon-ītes, and the [s]Ăsh'-dod-ītes, heard that the [1,d]walls of Jė-ru̧'să-lĕm [2]were made up, *and* that the breaches[C] began to be stopped, then they were very [t]wroth,[C]

8 And [u]conspired all of them together to come *and* to fight against Jė-ru̧'să-lĕm, and to hinder it.

9 [v]Nevertheless we made our [w]prayer unto our God, and [x,y]set a [z]watch against them day and night, because of them.

10 And *Jū'dah [a]said, The strength of the bearers of burdens is decayed,[C] and *there is* much rubbish; so that we are not able to build the [b]wall.

11 And our adversaries said, They shall not know, neither see, till we come in the midst among them, and slay them, and cause the work to cease.

12 ¶ And it came to pass, that when the *Jewș which dwelt by them came, they said unto us ten times, From all places whence[C] ye shall return unto us *they will be upon you.*

13 Therefore set I in the lower places behind the [b]wall, *and* on the [3]higher places, I even [c]set the people after[C] their families with their [d]swords, their [e]spears, and their [f]bows.

14 And I looked, and rose up, and said unto the nobles, and to the rulers, and to the rest of the people, [g]Be not ye afraid of them: remember the Lord, *which is* great and terrible,[C] and fight for your brethren, your sons, and your daughters, your wives, and your houses.

15 And it came to pass, when our enemies heard that it was known unto us, and God had [h]brought their counsel to nought,[C] that [i]we returned all of us to the [b]wall, every one unto his work.

16 And it came to pass from that time forth, [c]*that* the half of my servants wrought in the work, and [c]the other half of them held both the [e]spears, the [j]shields, and the [f]bows, and the [k]habergeons[C]; and the rulers *were* behind all the house of Jū'dah.

17 They which builded on the [b]wall, and they that bare burdens, with those that laded,[C] *every one* [c]with one of his hands wrought in the work and with the other *hand* held a weapon.

18 For the builders, every one [c]had his sword girded by his side, and *so* builded. And he that sounded the [l]trumpet *was* by me.

19 And I said unto the nobles, and to the rulers, and to the rest of the people, The work *is* great and large, and we are separated upon the [b]wall, one far from another.

20 In what place *therefore* ye hear the sound of the [l]trumpet, resort ye thither[C] unto us: [m]our [h]God shall fight for us.

21 So [i]we laboured in the work: and half of them held the spears from the rising of the morning till the stars appeared.

22 Likewise at the same time said I unto the people, Let every one with his servant lodge within Jė-ru̧'să-lĕm, that in the night they may be a guard to us, and labour on the day.

23 [i]So neither I, nor my brethren, nor my servants, nor the men of the guard which followed me, none of us put off our clothes, [4]*saving*[C] *that* every one put them off for washing.

v.7–423 BC See footnote. *Time*, Rev. 10:6.

**7**

q *Arabians*, 2 Chr. 17:11.
r *Ammonites*, Deut. 2:20.
s *Ashdod*, 1 Sam. 6:17.
t *Anger*, Psa. 37:8.
1 R. V. repairing of the
2 R. V. went forward,

**8**

u *Conspiracy, instances of*, 1 Kin. 16:9.

**9**

v *Temptation, instances of those who resisted*, Luke 11:4.
w *Prayer, in adversity*, Acts 6:4.
x *Prudence, instances of*, vs. 9–22; 2 Chr. 2:12.
y *Watchfulness, with prayer*, Matt. 24:42.
z *Watchman*, 2 Sam. 18:24.

**10**

a *Despondency*, Eccl. 2:20.
b *Jerusalem, walls of*, Judg. 19:10.

**13**

c *Prudence, instances of*, 2 Chr. 2:12.
d *Sword*, 1 Chr. 21:5.
e *Spear*, 2 Kin. 11:10.
f *Archery*, Gen. 21:20.
3 R. V. open

**14**

g *Faith, enjoined, in time of public danger*, Mark 11:22.

v.15–423 BC See footnote, *Time* Rev. 10:6.

**15**

h *God, providence of*, Gen. 2:2.
i *Patriotism*, vs. 15–23; Psa. 137:1.

**16**

j *Shield*, 1 Kin. 14:27.
k *Coat of Mail*, 1 Sam. 17:5.

**18**

l *Trumpet*, Josh. 6:4.

**20**

m *Faith, instances of*, Mark 11:22.

**23**

4 R. V. every one went with his weapon to the water.

v.1—423 BC
See footnote, *Time*, Rev. 10:6.

**1**
*a Jews*, Neh. 4:2.

**3**
*b Debtor*, Luke 7:41.
*c Land mortgaged for debt*, Ruth 4:3.
*d Vineyard*, Isa. 1:8.
*e House*, Esth. 8:1.
*f Famine*, 2 Kin. 8:1.
1 R. V. are mortgaging

**4**
*g Borrowing*, Ex. 22:14.
*h Debt*, 1 Sam. 22:2.
*i Money*, Jer. 32:9.
*j Tax*, Neh. 10:32.

**5**
*k Poor, oppressions of*, Prov. 21:13.
*l Children, sold for debt*, Mark 10:14.
*m Creditor, oppressions of*, Deut. 15:2.

**6**
*n Nehemiah*, Neh. 1:1.
*o Anger*, Psa. 37:8.

**7**
*p Rulers, righteous*, Ex. 18:21.
*q Reproof, faithfulness in*, Prov. 17:10.
*r Rich, oppressive*, Jas. 5:1.
*s Rulers, wicked*, Ex. 18:21.
*t Covetousness*, Isa. 57:17.
*u Interest*, Ex. 22:25.

**8**
*v Liberality, instances of*, 1 Tim. 6:18.
*w Example, good*, John 13:15.
*x Kindness, instances of*, Acts 28:2.
*y Servant, redeemed*, Jer. 2:14.

## CHAPTER 5

*Certain Jews complain of their hardships. 6 Nehemiah rebukes the usurers, and causes them to make restitution. 14 His good example.*

AND there was a great cry
of the people and of their
wives against their brethren the
[a]Jews.
2 For there were that said, We,
our sons, and our daughters, *are*
many: therefore we take[G] up corn[G]
*for them*, that we may eat, and
live.
3 *Some* also there were that
said, [b]We [1]have mortgaged our
[c]lands, [d]vineyards, and [e]houses,
that we might buy corn,[G] because
of the [f]dearth.[G]
4 There were also that said, We
have [g,h]borrowed [i]money for the
king's [j]tribute,[G] *and that upon* our
[c]lands and [d]vineyards.
5 Yet now our flesh *is* as the
flesh of our brethren, our children as their children: and, lo,
[k]we bring in to bondage our
[l]sons and our daughters to be
servants, and [k]*some* of our
daughters are brought unto
bondage *already*: neither *is it*
in our power *to redeem them*;
for [m]other men have our [c]lands
and [d]vineyards.
6 ¶ And [n]I was very [o]angry
when I heard their cry and these
words.
7 Then [n,p]I consulted with myself, and I [q]rebuked the [r]nobles,
and the [s]rulers, and said unto
them, [t]Ye exact [u]usury,[G] every
one of his brother. And I set a
great assembly against them.
8 And I [q]said unto them,
[v]We after our ability [w,x]have
redeemed our [y]brethren the
Jews, which were sold unto
the heathen; and will ye even
sell your brethren? or shall
they be sold unto us? Then
held they their peace, and
found nothing *to answer*.
9 Also I [q]said, It *is* not good
that ye do: ought ye not to walk
in the [z]fear of our God because
of the reproach[G] of the heathen[G]
our enemies?
10 I likewise, *and* my brethren,
and my servants, [2]might exact[G] of
them [a]money and [b]corn[G]: [c]I pray
you, [d]let us leave off this usury.[G]
11 Restore, I [e]pray you, to
them, even this day, their [f]lands,
their [g]vineyards, their oliveyards, and their [h]houses, also the
hundredth *part* of the [a]money,
and of the [b]corn,[G] the [i]wine, and
the [j]oil, that ye exact[G] of them.
12 Then said they, [k]We will restore *them*, and will require nothing of them; so will we do as
thou sayest. Then I called the
[l]priests, and took an [m]oath of
them, that they should do according to this [n]promise.
13 Also I shook my lap, and
said, So God shake out every
man from his house, and from
his labour, that performeth not
this promise, even thus be he
shaken out, and emptied. And
all the congregation said, Ā-
mĕn′, and praised the LORD.
And the people did according to
this [n]promise.
14 ¶ Moreover from the time
that I was appointed to be their
[o]governor in the land of Jū′dah,
from the twentieth year even
unto the two and thirtieth year
of [p]Är-tăx-ërx′ēs the king, *that*
*is*, twelve years, [c]I and my brethren [q,r,s]have not eaten the bread[G]
of the governor.
15 But the former [t]governors
that *had been* before me were
chargeable[G] unto the people, and
had taken of them [u]bread[G] and
[i]wine, beside forty [v]shekels[G] of
[w]silver; yea, even their servants
bare rule over the people: but
[r,s,x]so did not I, because of the
[y]fear of God.
16 Yea, [s]also I continued in
the work of this [z]wall, neither

v.9—423 BC
See footnote, *Time*, Rev. 10:6.

**9**
*z Fear of God*, Acts 9:31.

**10**
*a Money*, Jer. 32:9.
*b Corn*, Psa. 65:13.
*c Rulers, righteous*, Ex. 18:21.
*d Interest, exaction of, rebuked*, Ex. 22:25.
2 R. V. do lend them money and corn on usury. I pray you,

**11**
*e Intercession, of man with man*, Jer. 27:18.
*f Land, mortgaged for debt*, Ruth 4:3.
*g Vineyard*, Isa. 1:8.
*h House*, Esth. 8:1.
*i Wine*, Prov. 23:31.
*j Oil*, Deut. 12:17.

**12**
*k Repentance*, Mark 1:4.
*l Priest*, Lev. 1:5.
*m Oath*, Num. 5:19.
*n Covenant, of men with men*, Deut. 29:1.

**14**
*o Government, provincial*, Isa. 22:21.
*p Artaxerxes*, Ezra 7:1.
*q Unselfishness, instances of*, 1 Cor. 10:24.
*r Integrity, instances of*, Job 2:3.
*s Patriotism*, vs. 14–19; Psa. 137:1.

**15**
*t Rulers, wicked*, Ex. 18:21.
*u Bread*, Ezek. 4:13.
*v Shekels*, Ex. 30:13.
*w Silver*, 1 Chr. 28:14.
*x Civil Service, reform in*, Dan. 1:5.
*y Fear of God, instances of*, Acts 9:31.

**16**
*z Jerusalem, walls of*, Judg. 19:10.

v.16–423 BC
See footnote, *Time*, Rev. 10:6.

17
*a Hospitality*, Rom. 12:13.
*b Jews*, Neh. 4:2.

18
*c Bullock*, Ex. 29:3.
*d Sheep, used for food*, Deut. 32:14.
*e Wine*, Prov. 23:31.
*f Integrity, instances of*, Job 2:3.
*g Unselfishness*, 1 Cor. 10:24.
*h Patriotism*, Psa. 137:1.

19
*i Works, good*, 2 Tim. 1:9.

1
*a Sanballat*, Neh. 2:10.
*b Tobiah*, Neh. 2:10.
*c Gashmu*, in v. 6; Neh. 2:19.
*d Nehemiah*, Neh. 1:1.
*e Jerusalem, walls of*, Judg. 19:10.

2
*f Diplomacy, instances of*, 2 Kin. 16:7.
*g Ono*, 1 Chr. 8:12.
*h Malice, instances of*, Eph. 4:31.

3
*i Patriotism*, Psa. 137:1.
*j Decision, instances of*, Isa. 50:7.
*k Fellowship, with the wicked, avoided*, 1 Cor. 1:9.

bought we any land: and all my
servants *were* gathered thither[c]
unto the work.
17 Moreover [a]*there were* at my
table an hundred and fifty of the
[b]Jews and rulers, [a]beside those
that came unto us from among
the heathen[c] that *are* about us.
18 Now *that* which was prepared *for me* daily *was* one [c]ox
*and* six choice [d]sheep; also fowls
were prepared for me, and once
in ten days store of all sorts of
[e]wine: yet for all this [f,g]required
not I the bread[c] of the governor,
[h]because the bondage was heavy
upon this people.
19 Think upon me, my God,
for good, *according* to [i]all that I
have done for this people.

## CHAPTER 6

*The insidious attempts of Sanballat to hinder the rebuilding of the wall.* 15 *The work finished.* 17 *Secret correspondence kept up between the nobles of Judah and Tobiah.*

NOW it came to pass, when
[a]Săn-băl'lat, and [b]Tō-bī'-
ah, and [c]Gē'shem the Ā-rā'bĭ-
an, and the rest of our enemies,
heard that [d]I had builded the
[e]wall, and *that* there was no
breach[c] left therein; (though at
that time I had not set up the
doors upon the gates;)
2 That [a]Săn-băl'lat and [c]Gē'-
shem [f]sent unto me, saying,
Come, let us meet together in
*some one of* the villages in the
plain of [g]Ō'nō. But they
[h]thought to do me mischief.
3 And I sent messengers unto them, saying, [i]I *am* doing a
great work, so that [j,k]I cannot
come down: why should the
work cease, whilst I leave it,
and come down to you?
4 Yet they sent unto me four
times after this sort; and [k]I answered them after the same
manner.
5 ¶ Then sent [a]Săn-băl'lat his
servant unto me in like manner
the fifth time with an open [l]letter
in his hand;
6 Wherein *was* written, [m]It is
reported among the [1]heathen,[c]
and [c]Găsh'mū saith *it*, [n]*that*
thou and the Jews think to rebel: for which cause thou buildest the wall, that thou mayest be
their king, according to these
words.
7 And [n]thou hast also appointed [o]prophets to preach of thee at
Jē-rụ'sā-lĕm, saying, *There is* a
king in [p]Jū'dah: and now shall
it be reported to the king according to these words. Come
now therefore, and let us take
counsel together.
8 Then I sent unto him, saying, There are no such things
done as thou sayest, but thou
[q]feignest[c] them out of thine own
heart.
9 For they all made us afraid,
saying, Their hands shall be
weakened from the work, that
it be not done. Now therefore, [r]*O God*, [s]strengthen my
hands.
10 ¶ Afterward [d]I came unto
the house of Shĕm-a-ī'ah the son
of Dĕl-a-ī'ah the son of Mē-hĕt'-
a-beel, who *was* shut up; and he
said, Let us meet together in the
[t]house of God, within the [u]temple, and [v]let us shut the doors of
the temple: for they will come to
slay thee; yea, in the night will
they come to slay thee.
11 And I [w]said, Should such a
man as I flee? and who *is there*,
that, *being* as I *am*, would go into the temple to save his life? I
will not go in.
12 And, lo, I perceived that
God had not sent him; but that
[x,y]he pronounced this prophecy[c]
against me: for Tō-bī'ah and
Săn-băl'lat had [z]hired him.
13 Therefore *was* he hired,
[a]that I should be afraid, and do
so, and sin, and *that* they might

v.5–423 BC
See footnote, *Time*, Rev. 10:6.

5
*l Letters*, Isa. 37:14.

6
*m Falsehood, instances of*, Job 21:34.
*n False Accusation*, 2 Tim. 3:3.
1 R. V. nations,

7
*o Prophets*, Isa. 3:2.
*p Judah, kingdom of*, 2 Chr. 11:17.

8
*q Deception, instances of*, Josh. 9:4.

9
*r Adversity, prayer in*, Psa. 10:6.
*s Temporal Blessings, prayer for*, Psa. 103:2.

10
*t Church, called house of God*, 1 Kin. 9:3.
*u Temple, Second*, 1 Kin. 6:17.
*v Cowardice instances of*, Lev. 26:36.

11
*w Courage, instances of*, Deut. 31:7.

12
*x Prophets, false*, Isa. 3:2.
*y Treachery*, 2 Kin. 9:23.
*z Bribery, instances of*, 1 Sam. 8:3.

13
*a Temptation, leading into*. Luke 11:4.

v.13–423 BC
See footnote, *Time*, Rev. 10:6.

**14**
b *Prayer, imprecatory*, Acts 6:4.
c *Tobiah*, Neh. 2:10.
d *Sanballat*, Neh. 2:10.
e *Prophetess*, Judg. 4:4.
f *Women, as prophets*, Prov. 31:10.

**15**
g *Jerusalem, walls of*, Judg. 19:10.
h *Month, Elul*, Ex. 12:2.

**16**
i *Temporal Blessings, from God*, Psa. 103:2.
j *God, providence of*, Gen. 2:2.

**17**
k *Jews*, Neh. 4:2.
l *Treachery*, 2 Kin. 9:23.
m *Letters*, Isa. 37:14.

**18**
n *Oath*, Num. 5:19.

**1**
a *Jerusalem, walls of*, Judg. 19:10.
b *Nehemiah*, Neh. 1:1.
c *Porters*, 2 Sam. 18:26.
d *Choir*, 1 Chr. 15:16.
e *Levites*, Deut. 10:8.

have *matter* for an evil report, that they might reproach me.

14 [b]My God, think thou upon [c]Tō-bī′ah and [d]Săn-băl′lat according to these their works, and on the [e,f]prophetess Nō-a-dī′ah, and the rest of the prophets, that would have put me in fear.

15 ¶ So the [g]wall was finished in the twenty and fifth *day* of *the* [h]*month* Ē′lŭl, in fifty and two days.

16 And it came to pass, that when all our enemies heard *thereof*, and all the heathen[C] that *were* about us saw *these things*, they were much cast down in their own eyes: for they perceived that [i]this work was wrought[C] of our [j]God.

17 ¶ Moreover in those days the [k]nobles of Jū′dah [l]sent many [m]letters unto [c]Tō-bī′ah, and *the letters* of Tō-bī′ah came unto them.

18 For *there were* many in [k]Jū′dah [l,n]sworn unto him, because he *was* the son in law of Shĕch-a-nī′ah the son of Ā′rah; and his son Jō-hā′nan had taken the daughter of Mē-shŭl′lam the son of Bĕr-e-chī′ah.

19 Also they reported his good deeds before me, and [l]uttered my words to him. *And* [c]Tō-bī′ah sent [m]letters to put me in fear.

## CHAPTER 7

*Nehemiah commits the charge of Jerusalem to Hanani and Hananiah. 5 A register of those who first came from Babylon, 8 of the people, 39 of the priests, 43 of the Levites, 46 of the Nethinim, 57 of Solomon's servants, 63 and of the priests who could not find their pedigree. 66 The whole number of them. 70 Their oblations.*

NOW it came to pass, when the [a]wall was built, and [b]I had set up the doors, and the [c]porters[C] and the [d]singers and the [e]Lē′vītes were appointed,

2 That [b]I [f]gave my brother [g]Hā-nā′nī, and Hăn-a-nī′ah the ruler of the [h]palace, [i]charge over [j]Jē-rṳ′sā-lĕm: for he *was* a [k]faithful man, and [l]feared God above many.

3 And I said unto them, Let not the [m]gates of [j]Jē-rṳ′sā-lĕm be opened until the sun be hot; and while they stand [1]by, let them shut the doors, and bar *them*: and appoint [n]watches[C] of the inhabitants of Jē-rṳ′sā-lĕm, every one in his watch, and every one *to be* over[C] against his house.

4 ¶ Now the [j]city *was* large and great: but the people *were* few therein, and the houses *were* not builded.

5 And my God put into mine heart to gather together the nobles, and the rulers, and the people, that they might be reckoned by [o]genealogy. And I found [2]a register[C] of the genealogy of them which came up at the first, and found written therein,

6 These *are* the children of the province, that went up out of the [p]captivity, of those that had been carried away, whom [q]Nĕb-u-chad-nĕz′zar the king of [r]Băb′ȳ-lon had carried away, and came again to [j]Jē-rṳ′sā-lĕm and to Jū′dah, every one unto his city;

7 Who came with *,[s]Zē-rŭb′ba-bĕl, [t]Jĕsh′u-ȧ, Nē-he-mī′ah, Ăz-a-rī′ah, Rā-a-mī′ah, Nā-hăm′a-nī, Môr′de-cāi, Bĭl′shăn, Mĭs′pe-rĕth, Bĭg′va-ī, Nē′hum, Bā′a-nah. The [u]number, *I say*, of the men of the people of Ĭṣ′ra-el *was this*;

8 The children of Pā′rŏsh, [u]two thousand an hundred seventy and two.

9 The children of Shĕph-a-tī′ah, [u]three hundred seventy and two.

v.2–423 BC
See footnote, *Time*, Rev. 10:6.

**2**
f *Nepotism*, Gen. 47:11.
g Neh. 1:2.
h *Palace*, 1 Kin. 21:1.
i *Cities, government of*, Num. 35:8.
j *Jerusalem*, Judg. 19:10.
k *Faithfulness, instances of*, Luke 16:10.
l *Fear of God, instances of*, Acts 9:31.

**3**
m *Gates*, Deut. 3:5.
n *Watchman*, 2 Sam. 18:24.
1 R. V. on guard,

**5**
o *Genealogy*, vs. 5–66; 1 Chr. 5:1.
2 R. V. the book

**6**
p *Captivity, of Judah*, Isa. 5:13.
q *Nebuchadnezzar*, Dan. 2:1.
r *Babylon*, Ezra 5:12.

**7**
s *Zerubbabel*, Ezra 3:2.
t *Jeshua*, Ezra 2:2.
u *Israel, number of, after the captivity*, vs. 7–67; Ex. 4:22.

* [In order to publish this Bible in one volume with its numerous and diversified marginal notes and footnotes it has been necessary to avoid elaborate discussions of subjects, such, for instance, as would be necessary to point out the difficulties in connection with some of the names in genealogical lists. These difficulties grow out of errors of copyists, differences in the spelling of the same name, and the fact that individuals and places are mentioned under different names in different chapters. Where the identity of persons or places is doubtful in the following lists, or when no noteworthy fact is known concerning them, no mention of the name is made in either the margins or footnotes.]

10 The children of Ā′rah, [u]six hundred fifty and two.

11 The children of Pā′hath-mō′ab, of the children of Jĕsh′-u-ȧ and Jō′ăb, [u]two thousand and eight hundred *and* eighteen.

12 The children of Ē′lăm, [u]a thousand two hundred fifty and four.

13 The children of Zăt′tu, [u]eight hundred forty and five.

14 The children of Zăc′ca-ī, [u]seven hundred and threescore.

15 The children of Bĭn′nụ-ī, [u]six hundred forty and eight.

16 The children of Bĕb′a-ī, [u]six hundred twenty and eight.

17 The children of Ăz′găd, [u]two thousand three hundred twenty and two.

18 The children of Ȧ-dŏn′ĭ-kăm, [u]six hundred threescore and seven.

19 The children of Bĭg′va-ī, [u]two thousand threescore and seven.

20 The children of Ā′dĭn, [u]six hundred fifty and five.

21 The children of Ā′tĕr of Hĕz-e-kī′ah, [u]ninety and eight.

22 The children of Hā′shum, [u]three hundred twenty and eight.

23 The children of Bē′zāi, [u]three hundred twenty and four.

24 The children of Hā′riph, [u]an hundred and twelve.

25 The children of Ğĭb′e-on, [u]ninety and five.

26 The men of [v]Bēth′-lĕ-hĕm and [w]Nĕ-tō′phah, [u]an hundred fourscore and eight.

27 The men of [x]Ăn′a-thŏth, [u]an hundred twenty and eight.

28 The men of Bĕth–ăz′ma-vĕth, [u]forty and two.

29 The men of [y]Kĭr′jath–jē′a-rĭm, [z]Chĕ-phī′rah, and [a]Bĕ-ē′-roth, [b]seven hundred forty and three.

30 The men of [c]Rā′mah and [d]Gā′-bȧ, six hundred twenty and one.

31 The men of [e]Mĭch′mas, [b]an hundred and twenty and two.

32 The men of [f]Bĕth′–el and [g]Ā′ī, an hundred twenty and three.

33 The men of the other Nē′bō, [b]fifty and two.

34 The children of the other Ē′lăm, [b]a thousand two hundred fifty and four.

35 The children of Hā′rim, [b]three hundred and twenty.

36 The children of [h]Jĕr′ĭ-chō, [b]three hundred forty and five.

37 The children of [i]Lŏd, Hā′-dĭd, and Ō′nō, [b]seven hundred twenty and one.

38 The children of Sĕ-nā′ah, [b]three thousand nine hundred and thirty.

39 ¶ The [j]priests: the children of Jĕ-dā′iah, of the house of Jĕsh′u-ȧ, [b]nine hundred seventy and three.

40 The children of Ĭm′mĕr, [b]a thousand fifty and two.

41 The children of [k]Păsh′ŭr, [b]a thousand two hundred forty and seven.

42 The children of Hā′rim, [b]a thousand and seventeen.

43 ¶ The [l]Lē′vītes: the children of Jĕsh′u-ȧ, of Kăd′mĭ-el, *and* of the children of Hŏ-dē′vah, [b]seventy and four.

44 ¶ The [m]singers: the children of [n]Ā′saph, [b]an hundred forty and eight.

45 ¶ The [o]porters: the children of Shăl′lum, the children of Ā′tĕr, the children of [p]Tăl′-mon, the children of [q]Ăk′kŭb, the children of Hăt′ĭ-tȧ, the children of Shō′ba-ī, [b]an hundred thirty and eight.

46 ¶ The [r]Nĕth′ĭ-nĭmș: the children of Zī′hȧ, the children of Hȧ-shụ′phȧ, the children of Tăb′ba-ŏth,

47 The children of Kē′rŏs, the children of Sī′ȧ, the children of Pā′don,

**26**
*v* *Beth-lehem,* Gen. 48:7.
*w* *Netophah,* Ezra 2:22.

**27**
*x* *Anathoth,* Jer. 1:1.

**29**
*y* *Kiriath-jearim,* Josh. 15:9.
*z* Ezra 2:25; Josh. 18:26.
*a* *Beeroth,* Josh. 9:17.
*b* *Israel, number of, after the captivity,* vs. 30–66; Ex. 4:22.

**30**
*c* *Ramah,* Judg. 19:13.
*d* Josh. 18:24; Ezra 2:26.

**31**
*e* Or, *Michmash,* 1 Sam. 14:5.

**32**
*f* *Beth-el,* Josh. 18:13.
*g* *Ai,* Josh. 7:2.

**36**
*h* *Jericho,* Num. 22:1.

**37**
*i* *Lod,* 1 Chr. 8:12.

**39**
*j* *Priest,* Lev. 1:5.

**41**
*k* *Pashur,* 1 Chr. 9:12.

**43**
*l* *Levites,* Deut. 10:8.

**44**
*m* *Choir,* 1 Chr. 15:16.
*n* *Asaph,* 1 Chr. 15:17.

**45**
*o* *Porters,* 2 Sam. 18:26.
*p* *Talmon,* 1 Chr. 9:17.
*q* *Akkub,* 1 Chr. 9:17.

**46**
*r* *Nethinim,* Ezra 8:20.

48 The children of Lĕb′a-nȧ,
the children of Hăg′a-bȧ, the
children of Shăl′ma-ī,
49 The children of Hā′nan, the
children of Ḡĭd′del, the children
of Gā′här,
50 The children of Rē-a-ī′ah,
the children of Rē′zin, the children of Nė-kō′dȧ,
51 The children of Găz′zam,
the children of Ŭz′zȧ, the children of Phȧ-sē′ah,
52 The children of Bē′sai, the
children of Mė-ū′nim, the children of Nė-phĭsh′e-sĭm,
53 The children of Băk′bŭk,
the children of Hȧ-kū′phȧ, the
children of Här′hûr,
54 The children of Băz′lith, the
children of Mȧ-hī′dȧ, the children of Här′shȧ,
55 The children of Bär′kŏs, the
children of Sĭs′e-rȧ, the children
of Tā′mah,
56 The children of Nė-zī′ah,
the children of Hăt′ĭ-phȧ.
57 The children of Sŏl′o-mon′s
servants: the children of Sō′ta-ī,
the children of Sŏph′e-rĕth, the
children of Pė-rī′dȧ,
58 The children of Jȧ-ā′lȧ, the
children of Där′kon, the children of Ḡĭd′del,
59 The children of Shĕph-a-
tī′ah, the children of Hăt′til, the
children of Pŏch′e-rĕth of Ze-
bā′im, the children of Ā′mon.
60 All the [r]Nĕth′ĭ-nĭmș, and
the children of Sŏl′o-mon′s servants, *were* [b]three hundred ninety
and two.
61 And these *were* they which
went up *also* from Tĕl–mē′lah,
Tĕl′–hȧ-rē′shȧ, Chē′rub, Ăd′-
dŏn, and Ĭm′mēr: but they
could not shew their father′s
[s]house, nor their seed, whether
they *were* of Ĭș′ra-el.
62 The children of Dĕl-a-ī′ah,
the children of Tō-bī′ah, the
children of Nė-kō′dȧ, [b]six hundred forty and two.

63 ¶ And of the [j]priests: the
children of Hȧ-bā′iah, the children of Kŏz, the children of
Bär-zĭl′la-ī, which took *one* of
the daughters of Bär-zĭl′la-ī the
Ḡĭl′e-ăd-īte to wife, and was
called after their name.
64 These sought their register[c]
*among* those that were reckoned
by [s]genealogy, but it was not
found: therefore were they, as
polluted, put from the priesthood.
65 And the Tĭr′sha-thȧ said unto them, that they should not eat
of the most holy things, till there
stood *up* a [j]priest with [t]Ū′rim
and Thŭm′mim.
66 ¶ The whole congregation
together *was* [b]forty and two
thousand three hundred and
threescore,
67 Beside their [u]manservants
and their [u]maidservants, of
whom *there were* seven thousand
three hundred thirty and seven:
and they had [v]two hundred forty
and five singing men and singing [w]women.
68 Their [x]horses, seven hundred thirty and six: their [y]mules,
two hundred forty and five:
69 *Their* [z]camels, four hundred thirty and five: six thousand seven hundred and twenty
[a]asses.
70 ¶ And some of the chief[c] of
the fathers [b]gave unto the work.
The Tĭr′sha-thȧ gave to the
treasure[c] a thousand [1,c,d]drams
of [e]gold, fifty [f]basons, five hundred and thirty priests′ [g]gar-
ments.
71 And *some* of the chief[c] of the
fathers [b]gave to the treasure[c]
of the work twenty thousand
[1,c,d]drams[c] of [e]gold, and two thousand two hundred pound[c] of
[h]silver.
72 And *that* which the rest of
the people [b]gave *was* twenty
thousand [1,c,d]drams[c] of [e]gold, and

**61**
s *Genealogy*, 1 Chr. 5:1.

**65**
t *Urim and Thummim*, Lev. 8:8.

**67**
u *Servant*, Jer. 2:14.
v *Choir*, 1 Chr. 15:16.
w *Women*, Prov. 31:10.

**68**
x *Horse*, Job 39:19.
y *Mule*, 2 Sam. 18:9.

**69**
z *Camel*, 1 Sam. 30:17.

a *Ass, domesticated*, 2 Chr. 28:15.

**70**
b *Liberality, instances of*, 1 Tim. 6:18.
c *Dram*, 1 Chr. 29:7.
d *Weight*, Lev. 19:35.
e *Gold*, Ezek. 7:19.
f *Basin*, 1 Kin. 7:50.
g *Priests, vestments of*, Lev. 1:5.
1 R. V. darics

**71**
h *Silver*, 1 Chr. 28:14.

73
i Priest, Lev. 1:5.
j Levites, Deut. 10:8.
k Porters, 2 Sam. 18:26.
l Choir, 1 Chr. 15:16.
m Nethinim, Ezra 8:20.
n Jews, Neh. 4:2.
o Month, Ex. 12:2.

v.1–423 BC
See footnote, *Time*, Rev. 10:6.

1
a *Jerusalem, gates of*, Judg. 19:10.
b *Gates*, Deut. 3:5.
c *Ezra*, Ezra 7:1.
d *Scribe*, 1 Kin. 4:3.
e *Word of God*, Psa. 119:9.
f *Law, of Moses*, Deut. 33:2.
1 R. V. broad place

2
g *Priest, duties of*, Lev. 1:5.
h *Instruction, in religion*, Prov. 23:23.
i *Trumpets, feast of*, Lev. 23:24.
j *Month*, Ex. 12:2.

4
k 2 Chr. 6:13.

two thousand pound[c] of [h]silver,
and threescore and seven priests'
[g]garments.
73 So the [i]priests, and the [j]Lē'-
vītes, and the [k]porters,[c] and the
[l]singers, and *some* of the people,
and the [m]Nĕth'ĭ-nĭms, and all
[n]Ĭs'ra-el, dwelt in their cities;
and when the seventh [o]month
came, the children of Ĭs'ra-el
*were* in their cities.

## CHAPTER 8

*The public reading and expounding of the law. 9 The people comforted. 13 Their forwardness to hear and be instructed. 16 They keep the feast of tabernacles.*

AND all the people gathered
themselves together as one
man into the [1]street that *was* before the [a]water [b]gate; and they
spake unto [c]Ĕz'rȧ the [d]scribe
to bring the book of the [e,f]law
of Mō'ṣeṣ, which the LORD
had commanded to Ĭs'ra-el.
2 And [c]Ĕz'rȧ the [g]priest
[h]brought the [e,f]law before the
congregation both of men and
women, and all that could hear
with understanding, upon the
[i]first day of the seventh [j]month.
3 And [c,d]he [h]read therein before the street that *was* before
the [a]water [b]gate from the morning until midday, before the men
and the women, and those that
could understand; and the ears
of all the people *were attentive*
unto the book of the [e,f]law.
4 And [c]Ĕz'rȧ the [d]scribe stood
upon a [k]pulpit of wood, which
they had made for the purpose;
and beside him stood Măt-tĭ-
thī'ah, and Shē'mȧ, and Ăn-a-
ī'ah, and U-rī'jah, and Hĭl-kī'ah,
and Mā-a-sē'iah, on his right
hand; and on his left hand, Pĕ-
dā'iah, and Mĭsh'a-el, and Măl-
chī'ah, and Hā'shum, and Hăsh-
băd'a-nȧ, Zĕch-a-rī'ah, *and* Mĕ-
shŭl'-lam.
5 And [c,d]Ĕz'rȧ opened the book
in the sight of all the people; (for
he was above all the people;) and
when he opened it, all the people
stood up:
6 And [c,d]Ĕz'rȧ blessed the
LORD, the great God. And all
the people answered, Amen,
Amen, with lifting up their
hands: and they bowed their
heads, and [l]worshipped the
LORD with *their* faces to the
ground.
7 Also Jĕsh'u-ȧ, and Bā'nī, and
Shĕr-e-bī'ah, Jā'min, [m]Ăk'kŭb,
Shăb'be-thāi, Hō-dī'jah, Mā-a-
sē'iah, Kĕl'ī-tȧ, Ăz-a-rī'ah, Jŏz'-
a-bād, Hā'nan, Pĕl-a-ī'ah, and
the [n]Lē'vītes, [h]caused the people
to understand the [e,f]law: and
the people *stood* in their place.
8 So they read in the book in
the [e,f]law of God distinctly, and
gave the sense, and [h]caused *them*
to understand the reading.
9 ¶ And [o]Nē-he-mī'ah, which
*is* the Tĭr'sha-thȧ, and [c]Ĕz'rȧ
the [g]priest the [d]scribe,[c] and the
[n]Lē'vītes that [h]taught the people, said unto all the people,
[p]This day *is* holy unto the LORD
your God; mourn not, nor weep.
For all [q]the people wept, when
they heard the [e]words of the law.
10 Then he said unto them, Go
your way, eat the fat, and drink
the sweet, and [r]send [s]portions
unto [t]them for whom nothing is
prepared: for [p]*this* day *is* holy
unto our Lord: neither be ye
sorry; for the [u]joy of the LORD
is your [v]strength.
11 So the [n]Lē'vītes stilled all
the people, saying, Hold your
peace, for the day *is* holy; neither be ye grieved.
12 [p]And all the people went
their way to eat, and to drink,
and [w]to send [s]portions, and to
make great mirth, because they
had understood the [e,f]words that
were declared unto them.
13 ¶ And on the second day
were gathered together the chief
of the fathers of all the people,

v.5–423 BC
See footnote, *Time*, Rev. 10:6.

6
l *Worship*, Gen. 22:5.

7
m *Akkub*, 1 Chr. 9:17.
n *Levites*, Deut. 10:8.

9
o *Nehemiah*, Neh. 1:1.
p *Annual Feasts, kept with rejoicing*, Num. 15:3
q *Repentance, instances of*, Mark 1:4.

10
r *Liberality, enjoined*, 1 Tim. 6:18.
s *Presents*, Gen. 32:13.
t *Poor*, Prov. 21:13.
u *Joy*, Psa. 5:11.
v *Spiritual Blessings, from God*, Eph. 1:3.

12
w *Liberality, instances of*, 1 Tim. 6:18.

v.13–423 BC
See footnote, *Time*, Rev. 10:6.

14
*x Prophets, inspiration of*, Isa. 3:2.
*y Moses*, Ex. 2:10.
*z Booth*, Lev. 23:42.

*a Tabernacles, feast of*, Deut. 16:13.
*b Month, Ethanim*, Ex. 12:2.

15
*c Jerusalem*, Judg. 19:10.
*d Olive*, Deut. 6:11.
*e* Isa. 41:19; 55:13.
*f Palm Tree*, Song 7:7.
*g Booth*, Lev. 23:42.
2 R. V. branches of wild olive,

16
*h House*, Esth. 8:1.
*i Temple, Second*, 1 Kin. 6:17.
*j Jerusalem, streets of*, Judg. 19:10.
*k Jerusalem, gates of*, Judg. 19:10.

17
*l Captivity, of Judah*, Isa. 5:13.
*m* Or, *Joshua*, Josh. 1:1.
*n Joy, instances of*, Psa. 5:11.
3 R. V. dwelt in

18
*o Instruction, in religion*, Prov. 23:23.
*p Law, of Moses*, Deut. 33:2.
*q Word of God*, Psa. 119:9.
*r Tabernacles, feast of*, Deut. 16:13.

1
*a Month, Ethanim*, Ex. 12:2.

the priests, and the Lē′vītes, unto [c]Ĕz′rȧ the [d]scribe, even to
understand the [e]words of the
law.
14 And they found written in
the [f]law which the LORD had
[x]commanded by [y]Mō′ṣeṣ, that
the children of Ĭṣ′ra-el should
dwell in [z]booths in the [a]feast of
the seventh [b]month:
15 And that they should publish and proclaim in all their
cities, and in [c]Jē-ru′să-lĕm, saying, Go forth unto the mount,
and fetch [d]olive branches, and
[2]pine branches, and [e]myrtle
branches, and [f]palm branches,
and branches of thick trees, to
make [g]booths, as *it is* written.
16 So the people went forth,
and brought *them*, and made
themselves [g]booths, every one
upon the roof of his [h]house,
and in their courts, and in the
courts of the [i]house of God,
and in the [j]street of the [k]water
gate, and in the street of the
[k]gate of Ē′phră-ĭm.
17 And all the congregation of
them that were come again out
of the [l]captivity made [g]booths,
and [3]sat under the booths: for
since the days of [m]Jĕsh′u-ȧ the
son of Nŭn unto that day had
not the children of Ĭs′ra-el done
so. And there was very great
[n]gladness.
18 Also day by day, from the
first day unto the last day, he
[o]read in the book of the [p,q]law
of God. And they kept the
[r]feast seven days; and on the
eighth day *was* a solemn assembly, according unto the manner.[C]

## CHAPTER 9

*The solemn fast and confession of the people.* 4 *The prayer and confession of the Levites.* 38 *They make a covenant.*

NOW in the twenty and
fourth day of this [a]month
the children of Ĭṣ′ra-el were assembled [b]with [c]fasting, and with
[d]sackclothes, and [e]earth upon
them.
2 And the seed of Ĭṣ′ra-el separated themselves from all strangers,[C] and stood and [f]confessed
their [g]sins, and the iniquities of
their fathers.
3 And they stood up in their
place, and read in the book of
the [h]law of the LORD their God
*one* fourth part of the day; and
*another* fourth part they [f,g]con-
fessed, and [i]worshipped the
LORD their God.
4 Then stood up upon the
stairs, of the [j]Lē′vītes, Jĕsh′u-ȧ,
and Bā′nī, Kăd′mĭ-el, Shĕb-a-
nī′ah, Bŭn′nī, Shĕr-e-bī′ah, Bā′-
nī, *and* Chĕn′a-nī, and cried with
a loud voice unto the LORD
their God.
5 Then the [j]Lē′vītes, Jĕsh′u-ȧ,
and Kăd′mĭ-el, Bā′nī, Hăsh-ab-
nī′ah, Shĕr-e-bī′ah, Hȯ-dī′jah,
Shĕb-a-nī′ah, *and* Pĕth-a-hī′ah,
said, Stand up *and* [k]bless the
LORD your God for ever and
ever: and blessed be thy glorious
name, which is exalted above all
blessing and [l]praise.[S]
6 [l]Thou, *even* thou, *art* [m]LORD
alone; thou hast [n]made [o]heaven,
the heaven of heavens, with all
their [p]host, the [q]earth, and all
*things* that *are* therein, the seas,
and all that *is* therein, and thou
[r]preservest them all; and the
[s]host of heaven [t]worshippeth
thee.[S T Q]
7[S]Thou *art* the LORD the God,
who didst [u]choose [v]Ā′brăm, and
broughtest him forth out of
[w]Ûr of the [x]Chăl′deeṣ, and
gavest him the name of Ā′bră-
hăm;
8 And foundest his [y]heart
[z,a]faithful before thee, and
madest a [b]covenant with him to
give the [c]land of the [d]Cā′năan-
ītes, the [e]Hĭt′tītes, the [f]Ăm′ŏr-
ītes, and the [g]Pĕr′ĭz-zītes, and

·423 BC
See footnote, *Time*, Rev. 10:6.

*b Repentance, instances of*, Mark 1:4.
*c Fasting*, Zech. 8:19.
*d Sackcloth*, Isa. 15:3.
*e Dust*, Eccl. 3:20.

2
*f Prayer, confession in*, vs. 6–38; Acts 6:4.
*g Sin, confession of*, Rom. 5:12.

3
*h Law, of Moses*, Deut. 33:2.
*i Worship*, Gen. 22:5.

4
*j Levites*, Deut. 10:8.

5
*k Thankfulness, to God*, Acts 24:3.
*l Praise*, Psa. 150:1.

6
*m God, sovereign*, Gen. 2:2.
*n God, creator*, Gen. 2:2.
*o Heavens, physical*, Psa. 8:3.
*p Stars*, Judg. 5:20.
*q Earth*, Prov. 8:23.
*r God, preserver*, Gen. 2:2.
*s Angel*, Heb. 1:13.
*t Praise, in heaven*, Psa. 150:1.

7
*u Call, personal*, Phil. 3:14.
*v Abraham, divine call of*, Gen. 17:5.
*w Ur*, Gen. 11:28.
*x Chaldea*, Isa. 23:13.

8
*y Heart*, Psa. 44:21.
*z Faithfulness*, Luke 16:10.

*a Abraham, piety of*, Gen. 17:5.
*b Covenant, of God with men*, Deut. 29:1.
*c Canaan*, Gen. 37:1.
*d Canaanites*, Ex. 23:28.
*e Hittites*, Judg. 1:26.
*f Amorites*, Gen. 14:13.
*g Perizzites*, Gen. 15:20.

v.8—423 BC
See footnote, *Time,* Rev. 10:6.

*h Jebusites,* Deut. 7:1.
*i God, faithfulness of,* Gen. 2:2.

**9**
*j Adversity, prayer in,* Psa. 10:6.
*k Israel,* Ex. 4:22.
*l Egypt,* Gen. 41:8.
*m Prayer, answered,* Acts 6:4.
*n Red Sea,* Ex. 10:19.

**10**
*o Miracles,* Luke 23:8.
*p Pharaoh,* Ex. 3:10.
*q Egyptians, visited by plagues,* Gen. 50:3.
*r God, knowledge of,* Gen. 2:2.

**11**
*s God, preserver,* Gen. 2:2.
1 R. V. pursuers

**12**
*t God, guide,* Gen. 2:2.
*u Pillar of Cloud and Fire,* Ex. 13:21.

**13**
*v God, sovereign,* Gen. 2:2.
*w Sinai,* Ex. 16:1.
*x Law, of Moses,* Deut. 33:2.

**14**
*y Sabbath, holy,* Ex. 16:23.

**15**
*z Manna,* Ex. 16:31.

*a Temporal Blessings, from God,* Psa. 103:2.
*b Water, miraculously supplied,* 1 Kin. 17:10.
*c Meribah,* Ex. 17:7.
2 R. V. commandedst

the [h]Jĕb′u-sītes, and the *Gĭr′-
ga-shītes, to give *it, I say,* to his
seed, and [i]hast performed thy
words; for thou *art* righteous:[s]
9 And didst see the [j]affliction[G] of
our [k]fathers in [l]Ē′ġȳpt, and
[m]heardest their cry by the [n]Red
sea;
10 And shewedst [o]signs and
wonders upon [p]Phā′raōh, and
on all his servants, and on all
the [q]people of his land: for thou
[r]knewest that they dealt proudly
against them. So didst thou get
thee a name, as *it is* this day.[s]
11 And [s]thou didst [o]divide the
[n]sea before [k]them, so that they
went through the midst of the
sea on the dry land; and their
[1]persecutors thou threwest into
the deeps, as a stone into the
mighty waters.
12 Moreover thou [t]leddest
[k]them in the day by a cloudy
[u]pillar; and in the night by a
pillar of fire, to give them light
in the way wherein they should
go.
13 [v]Thou camest down also upon mount [w]Sī′nāi, and spakest
with them from heaven, and
gavest them right judgments,[G]
and true [x]laws, good statutes
and commandments:
14 And madest known unto
[k]them thy holy [y]sabbath, and
commandedst them [x]precepts,
statutes, and laws, by the hand
of Mō′ṣeṣ thy servant:
15 And gavest [k]them [z,a]bread
from heaven for their †hunger,
and broughtest forth [a,b]water
for them out of the [c]rock for
their thirst, and [2]promisedst
them that they should go in to
possess the land which thou
hadst sworn to give them.[Q]

16 But [d]they and our fathers
dealt proudly, and [e,f]hardened
their necks, and [g]hearkened not
to thy commandments,
17 And [g]refused to obey, neither were mindful of thy [h]won-
ders that thou didst among
them; but [e,f]hardened their
necks, and in their rebellion appointed a captain to return to
their bondage: but thou *art* a
God ready to pardon, [i]gracious
and [3,j]merciful, slow to anger,
and [4]of great kindness, and for-
sookest them not.[s]
18 Yea, when [d]they had [k]made
them a molten[G] [l]calf, and said,
This *is* thy god that brought
thee up out of [m]Ē′ġȳpt, and had
wrought[G] great provocations;
19 [s]Yet thou in thy manifold
[j]mercies [n]forsookest [d]them not
in the wilderness: the pillar of
the cloud departed not from
them by day, to [o,p]lead them in
the way; neither the pillar of fire
by night, to shew them light,
and the way wherein they should
go.
20 Thou gavest also thy good
[q]spirit to [r]instruct [d]them, and
withheldest not thy [a,s]manna
from their mouth, and gavest
them [a,b]water for their thirst.[S T]
21 Yea, [t]forty years didst thou
[n]sustain [d]them in the wilderness,
*so that* they lacked nothing;
their [u]clothes waxed[G] not old, and
their feet swelled not.
22 Moreover thou gavest them
kingdoms and [5]nations, and didst
divide them into corners: so they
possessed the land of [v]Sī′hŏn,
and the land of the king of
[w]Hĕsh′bŏn, and the land of [x]Ŏg
king of [y]Bā′shăn.
23 Their [z]children also multi-

v.16—423 BC
See footnote, *Time,* Rev. 10:6.

**16**
*d Israel,* Ex. 4:22.
*e Self-will,* Gen. 49:6.
*f Impenitence, instances of,* Rom. 2:5.
*g Disobedience to God,* Eph. 5:6.

**17**
*h Miracles,* Luke 23:8.
*i Grace of God,* Rom. 4:16.
*j God, mercy of,* Gen. 2:2.
3 R. V. full of compassion,
4 R. V. plenteous in mercy,

**18**
*k Idolatry,* 1 Sam. 15:23.
*l Calf, golden,* Mic. 6:6.
*m Egypt,* Gen. 41:8.

**19**
*n God, faithfulness of,* Gen. 2:2.
*o God, guide,* Gen. 2:2.
*p Guidance, by pillar of cloud and fire,* Psa. 48:14.

**20**
*q Holy Spirit, wisdom and strength from,* Acts 1:2.
*r Wisdom, spiritual,* Prov. 2:2.
*s Manna,* Ex. 16:31.

**21**
*t Forty, years,* Jonah 3:4.
*u Dress,* Zech. 3:3.

**22**
*v Sihon,* Num. 21:26.
*w Heshbon,* Isa. 16:8.
*x Og,* Num. 21:33.
*y Bashan,* Num. 32:33.
5 R. V. peoples, which thou didst allot after their portions:

**23**
*z Children, the gift of God,* Mark 10:14.

* **GIRGASHITES.** *Land of, given to Abraham and his descendants,* Gen. 15:21; Deut. 7:1; Josh. 3:10; Neh. 9:8. *Delivered to the children of Israel,* Josh. 24:11.

† **HUNGER,** Deut. 8:3; Matt. 21:18; Mark 11:12. *Labor excites,* Prov. 16:26. *A source of temptation,* Gen. 25:29–34 (with Heb. 12:16); Ex. 16:2, 3. *An occasion of the temptation of Jesus,* Matt. 4:3, 4; Luke 4:2, 3. *Of an enemy, an opportunity for good works,* Prov. 25:21, 22; Rom. 12:20. *Endured, by Jesus during his temptation in the wilderness,* Matt. 4:2–4; Luke 4:2–4; John 4:8, 31–34; *by Paul for Christ's sake,* 1 Cor. 4:11. *Foretold as a judgment upon the Israelites,* Isa. 8:21; 9:20.

**Figurative:** *Of spiritual desire,* Psa. 107:9; Isa. 55:1, 2; Amos 8:11–13; Matt. 5:6; Luke 1:53; 6:21; John 6:35; 1 Pet. 2:2.

See footnotes: APPETITE, Prov. 23:2; FAMINE, 2 Kin. 8:1.

v.23–423 BC
See footnote, *Time*, Rev. 10:6.

*a God, providence of*, Gen. 2:2.
*b Canaan*, Gen. 37:1.
*c God, faithfulness of*, Gen. 2:2.

**24**
*d Canaanites*, Ex. 23:28.

**25**
*e God, goodness of*, Gen. 2:2.
6 R. V. fenced

**26**
*f Disobedience to God*, Eph. 5:6.
*g Backsliding*, Hos. 11:7.
*h Persecution, of the righteous*, John 15:20.

**27**
*i Divine Chastisement*, Job 33:19.
*j Adversity, prayer in*, vs. 27–37; Psa. 10:6.
*k Prayer, answered*, Acts 6:4.
*l Heaven, God's dwelling place*, Luke 18:22.
*m God, mercy of*, Gen. 2:2.

**28**
*n Repentance*, Mark 1:4.
*o God, longsuffering of*, Gen. 2:2.

pliedst thou as the stars of heaven, and [a]broughtest them into the [b]land, concerning which thou hadst [c]promised to their fathers, that they should go in to possess *it*.

24 So the children went in and possessed the [b]land, and thou [a]subduedst before them the inhabitants of the land, the [d]Cā′năan-ītes, and gavest them into their hands, with their kings, and the people of the land, that they might do with them as they would.[C]

25 And they took [6]strong cities, and a fat[C] land, and possessed houses full of all goods, wells digged, vineyards, and oliveyards, and fruit trees in abundance: so they did eat, and were filled, and became fat, and delighted themselves in thy great [e]goodness.[s]

26 Nevertheless they were [f]disobedient, and [g]rebelled against thee, and [g]cast thy law behind their backs, and [h]slew thy prophets which testified[C] against them to turn them to thee, and they wrought great provocations.

27 Therefore thou [i]deliveredst them into the hand of their enemies, who vexed[C] them: and in the time of their trouble, when they [j]cried unto thee, thou [k]heardest *them* from [l]heaven; and according to thy manifold [m]mercies thou gavest them saviours, who saved them out of the hand of their enemies.

28 But after they had rest, they did evil again before thee: therefore leftest thou them in the hand of their enemies, so that they had the dominion over them: yet when they [n]returned, and cried unto thee, thou [k]heardest *them* from [l]heaven; and [o]many times didst thou deliver them according to thy mercies;

29 And testifiedst against them, that thou mightest bring them again unto thy law: yet they dealt proudly, and hearkened not unto thy commandments, but sinned against thy judgments,[C] (which if a man do, he shall live in them;) and withdrew[C] the shoulder, and [p]hardened their neck, and would not hear.

30[s] [o]Yet many years didst thou forbear them, and testifiedst against them by [q]thy spirit in thy prophets: yet would they not give[C] ear: therefore [i]gavest thou them into the hand of the people of the lands.

31 Nevertheless for thy great [m]mercies' sake thou didst not utterly consume them, nor forsake them; for thou *art* a gracious and merciful God.[s]

32 Now therefore, our God, the great, the mighty, and the terrible[C] [r]God, who [c]keepest covenant[C] and [m]mercy, let not all the [7,j]trouble seem little before thee, that hath come upon us, on our kings, on our princes, and on our priests, and on our prophets, and on our fathers, and on all thy people, since the time of the kings[s] of [s]Ăs-sy̆r′ĭ-ȧ unto this day.[s]

33 [t]Howbeit [u]thou *art* just in [i]all that is brought upon us; for thou hast done right,[s] but [n,v]we have done wickedly:

34 [j,v]Neither have our [w]kings, our princes, our priests, nor our fathers, kept thy law, nor hearkened unto thy commandments and thy testimonies, wherewith thou didst testify[C] against them.

35 For [w]they [l]have not served thee in their kingdom, and in thy great [e]goodness that thou gavest them, and in the large and fat[C] land which thou gavest before them, neither turned they from their wicked works.

v.29–423 BC
See footnote, *Time*, Rev. 10:6.

**29**
*p Obduracy*, Prov. 29:1.

**30**
*q Prophets, inspiration of*, Isa. 3:2.

**32**
*r God, sovereign*, Gen. 2:2.
*s Assyria*, Gen. 25:18.
7 R. V. travail

**33**
*t Resignation, exemplified*, Job 5:17.
*u God, judge*, Gen 2:2.
*v Sin, confession of*, Rom. 5:12.

**34**
*w Rulers, wicked*, Ex. 18:21.

v.36–423 BC
See footnote, *Time*, Rev. 10:6.

36
x *Sin, punishment of*, Rom. 5:12.
y *Prophecies, fulfilled*, Dan. 9:24.

38
z *Faithfulness, instances of*, Luke 16:10.

a *Covenant, of man with God*, Deut. 29:1.
b *Seal*, 1 Kin. 21:8.
8 R. V. yet for all

36 Behold, [x,y]we *are* servants this day, and *for* the land that thou gavest unto our fathers to eat the fruit thereof and the good thereof, behold, [x]we *are* servants in it: [Q]

37 And [x,y]it yieldeth much increase unto the kings whom thou hast set over us because of our sins: also they have dominion over our bodies, and over our cattle, at their pleasure, and we *are* in great distress.

38 And [8]because of all this [z]we make a sure [a]*covenant*, and write *it*; and our princes, Lē′vītes, *and* priests, [b]seal unto it.

## CHAPTER 10

*The names of those who sealed the covenant.*
*28 The agreement and oath of the rest.*

1
a *Seal*, 1 Kin. 21:8.
b *Covenant, of man with God*, Deut. 29:1.
c *Decision, instances of*, Isa. 50:7.
d *Nehemiah*, Neh. 1:1.

3
e *Pashur*, 1 Chr. 9:12.

9
f *Levites*, Deut. 10:8.

NOW those that [*,a,b,c]sealed *were*, [d]Nē-he-mī′ah, the Tĭr′sha-thȧ, the son of Hăch-a-lī′ah, and Zĭd-kī′jah,

2 Sĕr-a-ī′ah, Ăz-a-rī′ah, Jĕr-e-mī′ah,

3 [e]Păsh′ŭr, Ăm-a-rī′ah, Măl-chī′jah,

4 Hăt′tush, Shĕb-a-nī′ah, Măl′luch,

5 Hā′rim, Mĕr′e-mŏth, Ō-ba-dī′ah,

6 Dăn′iel, Gĭn′ne-thŏn, Bā′ruch,

7 Mė-shŭl′lam, Ȧ-bī′jah, Mĭj′a-mĭn,

8 Mā-a-zī′ah, Bĭl′ga-ī, Shĕm-a-ī′ah: these *were* the priests.

9 And the [f]Lē′vītes: both Jĕsh′u-ȧ the son of Ăz-a-nī′ah, Bĭn′nu-ī of the sons of Hĕn′a-dăd, Kăd′mī-el;

10 And their brethren, Shĕb-a-nī′ah, Hō-dī′jah, Kĕl′ī-tȧ, Pĕl-a-ī′ah, Hā′nan,

11 Mī′chȧ, Rē′hŏb, Hăsh-a-bī′ah,

12 Zăc′cur, Shĕr-e-bī′ah, Shĕb-a-nī′ah,

13 Hō-dī′jah, Bā′nī, Bĕn′ī-nū.

14 The chief of the people; Pā′rŏsh, Pā′hath–mō′ab, Ē′lăm, [k]Zăt′thu, Bā′nī,

15 Bŭn′nī, Ăz′găd, Bĕb′a-ī,

16 Ăd-o-nī′jah, Bĭg′va-ī, Ā′dĭn,

17 Ā′tĕr, Hĭz-kī′jah, Ăz′zŭr,

18 Hō-dī′jah, Hā′shum, Bē′zāi,

19 Hā′riph, Ăn′a-thŏth, Nĕb′a-ī,

20 Măg′pī-ăsh, Mė-shŭl′lam, Hē′zīr,

21 Mė-shĕz′a-beel, Zā′dŏk, Jăd-dū′ȧ,

22 Pĕl-a-tī′ah, Hā′nan, Ăn-a-ī′ah,

23 Hō-shē′ȧ, Hăn-a-nī′ah, Hā′shub,

24 Hăl-lō′hesh, Pĭl′e-hȧ, Shō′bek,

25 Rē′hum, Hā-shăb′nah, Mā-a-sē′iah,

26 And Ȧ-hī′jah, Hā′nan, Ā′nan,

27 Măl′luch, Hā′rim, Bā′a-nah.

28 ¶ And the rest of the people, the [g]priests, the [f]Lē′vītes, the [h]porters,[c] the [i]singers, the [j]Nĕth′ī-nĭmș, and all they that had separated themselves from the people of the lands unto the law of God, their wives, their sons, and their daughters, every one having knowledge, and having understanding;

29 They [k]clave to their brethren, their nobles, and entered into a curse, and into an [l,m]oath, to walk in God's [n]law, which was given by Mō′șeș the servant of God, and to observe and do all the commandments of the LORD our Lord, and his judgments[c] and his statutes;

30 And that we would not [o,p]give our daughters unto the

v.12–423 BC
See footnote, *Time*, Rev. 10:6.

28
g *Priest*, Lev. 1:5.
h *Porters*, 2 Sam. 18:26.
i *Choir*, 1 Chr. 15:16.
j *Nethinim*, Ezra 8:20.

29
k *Fellowship, instances of*, 1 Cor. 1:9.
l *Oath*, Num. 5:19.
m *Covenant, of men with men*, Deut. 29:1.
n *Law, of Moses*, Deut. 33:2.

30
o *Marriage, wives of Israelites must be Israelites*, Gen. 34:9.
p *Miscegenation*, Josh. 23:12.

* [In order to publish this Bible in one volume with its numerous and diversified marginal notes and footnotes it has been necessary to avoid elaborate discussions of subjects, such, for instance, as would be necessary to point out the difficulties in connection with some of the names in genealogical lists. These difficulties grow out of errors of copyists, differences in the spelling of the same name, and the fact that individuals and places are mentioned under different names in different chapters. Where the identity of persons or places is doubtful in the following lists, or when no noteworthy fact is known concerning them, no mention of the name is made in either the margins or footnotes.

v.30–423 BC
See footnote, *Time*, Rev. 10:6.

**31**
*q* *Sabbath, profanation of*, Ex. 16:23.
*r* *Creditor*, Deut. 15:2.
*s* *Sabbatic Year*, Lev. 25:2.
1 R. V. a holy day:

**32**
*t* *Liberality, instances of*, 1 Tim. 6:18.
*u* *Shekel*, Ex. 30:13.
*v* *Temple, Second*, 1 Kin. 6:17.

**33**
*w* *Shewbread*, Ex. 35:13.
*x* *Offerings, meat*, Lev. 6:17.
*y* *Offerings, burnt*, Lev. 6:17.
*z* *Sabbath*, Ex. 16:23.

*a* *New Moon, feast of*, Lev. 17:11.
*b* *Annual Feasts*, Num. 15:3.
*c* *Offerings, sin*, Lev. 6:17.
*d* *Atonement*, Lev. 17:11.
*e* *Temple, Second*, 1 Kin. 6:17.
2 R. V. meal

**34**
*f* *Lot*, Esth. 3:7.
*g* *Priest, duties of*, Lev. 1:5.
*h* *Levites*, Deut. 10:8.
*i* *Offerings, wood*, Lev. 6:17.
*j* *Altar*, Gen. 8:20.
*k* *Law, of Moses*, Deut. 33:2.

**35**
*l* *First Fruits*, Deut. 18:4.
*m* *Priest, emoluments of*, Lev. 1:5.

**36**
*n* *Firstborn*, Zech. 12:10.

people of the land, nor take their
daughters for our sons:
31 And *if* the people of the land
bring ware[G] or any victuals[G] on the
[q]sabbath day to sell, *that* we
would not buy it of them on the
sabbath, or on [1]the holy day:
and *that* [r]we would leave[G] the
[s]seventh year, and the exaction
of every debt.
32 Also we made ordinances[G]
for us, [t]to charge ourselves yearly with the *third part of a
[u]shekel[G] for the service of the
[v]house of our God;
33 For the [w]shewbread, and for
the continual [2,x]meat offering,
and for the continual [y]burnt offering, of the [z]sabbaths, of the
[a]new moons, for the set [b]feasts,
and for the holy *things*, and for
the [c]sin offerings to make an
[d]atonement for Ĭṣ′ra-el, and *for*
all the work of the [e]house of our
God.
34 And we cast the [f]lots among
the [g]priests, the [h]Lē′vītes, and
the people, for the [i]wood offering, to bring *it* into the [e]house of
our God, after the houses of our
fathers, at times appointed year
by year, to burn upon the [j]altar
of the LORD our God, as *it is*
written in the [k]law:
35 And to bring the [l,m]first-
fruits of our ground, and the
[l,m]firstfruits of all fruit of all
trees, year by year, unto the
[e]house of the LORD:
36 Also the [n]firstborn of our
sons, and of our cattle, as *it is*
written in the [k]law, and the
[m]firstlings of our herds and of
our flocks, to bring to the [e]house
of our God, unto the priests that
minister in the house of our God:
37 And *that* we should bring the
[l,m]firstfruits of our dough, and
our [3,o]offerings, and the fruit of
all manner of trees, of [p]wine and
of [q]oil, unto the priests, to the
chambers[G] of the [e]house[G] of our
God; and the [r,s]tithes of our
ground unto the Lē′vītes, that
the same Lē′vītes might have the
[s]tithes in all the cities of our
tillage.[Q]
38 And the [g]priest the son of
Aâr′on shall be with the Lē′vītes,
when the Lē′vītes take [r,s]tithes:
and the Lē′vītes shall bring up
the [t]tithe of the tithes unto the
house of our God, to the chambers,[G] into the [u]treasure house.
39 For the children of Ĭṣ′ra-el
and the children of Lē′vī shall
bring the [o]offering of the [v]corn,
of the new [p]wine, and the [q]oil,
unto the chambers, where *are*
the vessels of the [w]sanctuary,
and the priests that minister,
and the [x]porters, and the [y]sing-
ers: and we will not forsake the
[e]house of our God.

## CHAPTER 11

*The rulers and the tenth part of the people dwell at Jerusalem. 3 A catalogue of their names. 20 The residue dwell in other cities.*

AND the rulers of the people
dwelt at [a]Jē-ru̧′sā̤-lĕm: the
rest of the people also cast [b]lots,
to bring one of ten to dwell in
Jē-ru̧′sā̤-lĕm the holy city, and
nine parts *to dwell* in *other* cities.[Q]
2 And the people blessed all
the men, that willingly [c]offered
themselves to dwell at [a]Jē-ru̧′-
sā̤-lĕm.
3 ¶ Now these *are* the chief of
the province that dwelt in [a]Jē-
ru̧′sā̤-lĕm: but in the cities of
Jū′dah dwelt every one in his
possession in their cities, *to wit*,
Ĭṣ′ra-el, the [d]priests, and the
[e]Lē′vītes, and the [f]Nĕth′ĭ-nĭmṣ,

v.37–423 BC
See footnote, *Time*, Rev. 10:6.

**37**
*o* *Offerings*, Lev. 6:17.
*p* *Wine*, Prov. 23:31.
*q* *Oil*, Deut. 12:17.
*r* *Tithes*, Num. 18:24.
*s* *Levites, emoluments of*, Deut. 10:8.
3 R. V. heave offerings,

**38**
*t* *Tithes, tithe of tithes for priests*, Num. 18:24.
*u* *Treasure Houses*, Ezra 5:17.

**39**
*v* *Corn*, Psa. 65:13.
*w* *Sanctuary*, Lev. 4:6.
*x* *Porters*, 2 Sam. 18:26.
*y* *Choir*, 1 Chr. 15:16.

**1**
*a* *Jerusalem*, Judg. 19:10.
*b* *Lot*, Esth. 3:7.

**2**
*c* *Patriotism*, Psa. 137:1.

**3**
*d* *Priest, emoluments of*, Lev. 1:5.
*e* *Levites*, Deut. 10:8.
*f* *Nethinim*, Ezra 8:20.

* **TAX.** *Pol'*, Ex. 30:11–16; 38:26; 2 Chr. 24:6, 9, 10; Neh. 10:32. *Jesus pays*, Matt. 17:24–27.
*Land*, Gen. 41:34, 48; 2 Kin. 23:35. *Land mortgaged for*, Neh. 5:3, 4. *Priests exempted from*, Gen. 47:26; Ezra 7:24. *Paid, in provisions*, 1 Kin. 4:7–28; *in levies of men*, 1 Kin. 5:13; 9:15.
*Personal*, 2 Kin. 15:19, 20. *Resisted by Israelites*, 1 Kin. 12:18; 2 Chr. 10:18.
**Collectors of,** 2 Sam. 20:24; 1 Kin. 4:6; Isa. 33:18; Mark 2:14; Luke 3:13; 5:27. *Stoned by the Israelites*, 2 Chr. 10:18. *Unpopular among the Jews*, Matt. 9:11; 11:19; 18:17; 21:31; Luke 18:11.

v.3–423 BC
See footnote, *Time*,
Rev. 10:6.

4
*g Judah, tribe of*, Num 10:14.
*h Benjamin, tribe of*, Num. 1:37.
*i* Or, *Pharez*, Gen. 38:29.

7
*j* 1 Chr. 9:7.

10
*k* 1 Chr. 9:10.
*l* Or, *Jehoiarib*, 1 Chr. 9:10.

11
*m* Or, *Azariah*, 1 Chr. 6:13, 14; 9:11; Ezra 7:1.
*n* 1 Chr. 9:11; or, *Shallum*, 1 Chr. 6:12, 13; Ezra 7:2.
*o* 1 Chr. 9:11.
*p Temple, Second*, 1 Kin. 6:17.
*q Church, called house of God*, 1 Kin. 9:3.

12
*r Genealogy*, vs. 12–19; 1 Chr. 5:1.
*s* 1 Chr. 9:12.
*t Pashur*, 1 Chr. 9:12.
*u* Or, *Malchijah*, 1 Chr. 9:12.

and the children of Sŏl′o-mon′s
servants.
4 And at [a]Jė-rṳ′să-lĕm dwelt
*certain* of the children of [g]Jū′-
dah, and of the children of
[h]Bĕn′ja-mĭn. Of the children
of Jū′dah; Ăth-a-ī′ah the son of
Ŭz-zī′ah, the son of Zĕch-a-rī′ah,
the son of Ăm-a-rī′ah, the son of
Shĕph-a-tī′ah, the son of Mā-
hā′la-lē-el, of the children of
[i]Pē′rĕz;
5 And Mā-a-sē′iah the son of
Bā′rṳch, the son of Cŏl–hō′zeh,
the son of Hā-zā′iah, the son of
Ăd-a-ī′ah, the son of Joi′a-rĭb,
the son of Zĕch-a-rī′ah, the son
of Shī-lō′nī.
6 All the sons of [i]Pē′rĕz that
dwelt at [a]Jė-rṳ′să-lĕm *were* four
hundred threescore and eight
valiant[C] men.
7 And these *are* the sons of
[h]Bĕn′ja-mĭn; [j]Săl′lu the son of
Mė-shŭl′lam, the son of Jō′ed,
the son of Pė-dā′iah, the son of
Kŏl-a-ī′ah, the son of Mā-a-sē′-
iah, the son of Ĭth′ĭ-el, the son of
Jė-să′iah.
8 And after him Găb′ba-ī, Săl′-
la-ī, nine hundred twenty and
eight.
9 And Jō′el the son of Zĭch′rī
*was* their overseer: and Jū′dah
the son of Sĕ-nū′ah *was* second
over the city.
10 Of the priests: [k]Jė-dā′iah
the son of [l]Joi′a-rĭb, [k]Jā′chin.
11 [m]Sĕr-a-ī′ah the son of Hĭl-
kī′ah, the son of [n]Mė-shŭl′lam,
the son of [o]Zā′dŏk, the son of
[o]Mė-rā′ioth, the son of [o]Ā-hī′-
tub, *was* the ruler of the [p,q]house
of God.
12 And their brethren that did
the work of the [p]house *were*
eight hundred twenty and two:
[r]and [s]Ăd-a-ī′ah the son of [s]Jĕr′-
o-hăm, the son of Pĕl-a-lī′ah, the
son of Ăm′zī, the son of Zĕch-a-
rī′ah, the son of [t]Păsh′ŭr, the son
of [u]Măl-chī′ah,
13 And his brethren, chief[C] of
the fathers, two hundred forty
and two: [r]and Ā-măsh′a-ī the
son of Ā-zăr′e-el, the son of Ā-
hăs′a-ī, the son of Mė-shĭl′le-
mŏth, the son of [s]Ĭm′mĕr,
14 And their brethren, mighty
men of valour[C], an hundred twenty and eight: and their overseer
*was* Zăb′dĭ-el, the son of [1]*one of*
the great men.
15 Also of the [e]Lē′vītes:
[v]Shĕm-a-ī′ah the son of [v]Hā′-
shub, the son of [v]Ăz′rĭ-kăm, the
son of [v]Hăsh-a-bī′ah, the son of
Bŭn′nī;
16 And Shăb′be-thāi and Jŏz′-
a-băd, of the chief of the [e]Lē′-
vītes, *had* the oversight of the
outward business of the [p]house[C]
of God.
17 And [w]Măt-ta-nī′ah the son
of [x]Mī′chȧ, the son of [y]Zăb′dī,
the son of [z]Ā′saph, *was* the principal[C] to begin the [a]thanksgiving
in prayer: and Băk-bŭk-ī′ah the
second among his brethren, and
Ăb′dȧ the son of [b]Shăm-mū′ȧ,
the son of Gā′lăl, the son of
[c]Jĕd′ṳ-thŭn.
18 All the [d]Lē′vītes in the [e]holy
city *were* two hundred fourscore
and four.
19 Moreover the [f]porters, [g]Ăk′-
kŭb, [h]Tăl′mon, and their brethren that kept the gates, *were* an
hundred seventy and two.
20 ¶ And the residue[C] of Ĭs̱′ra-
el, of the [i]priests, *and* the [d]Lē′-
vītes, *were* in all the cities of Jū′-
dah, every one in his inheritance.
21 But the [j]Nĕth′ĭ-nĭms̱ dwelt
in [k]Ō′phel: and Zī′hȧ and Ḡĭs′-
pȧ *were* over the Nĕth′ĭ-nĭms̱.
22 The overseer also of the
[d]Lē′vītes at [e]Jė-rŭ′să-lĕm *was*
Ŭz′zī the son of Bā′nī, the son of
Hăsh-a-bī′ah, the son of [l]Măt-
ta-nī′ah, the son of [m]Mī′chȧ. Of
the sons of [n]Ā′saph, the [o]singers
*were* over the business of the
[p]house of God.

v.13–423 BC
See footnote, *Time*,
Rev. 10:6.

14
1 R. V. Haggedolim.

15
*v* 1 Chr. 9:14.

17
*w Mattaniah*, 1 Chr. 9:15.
*x* Or, *Micah*, 1 Chr 9:15.
*y* Or, *Zichri*, 1 Chr. 9:15.
*z Asaph*, 1 Chr. 15:17.
*a Thankfulness*, Acts 24:3.
*b* Or, *Shemaiah*, 1 Chr. 9:16.
*c Jeduthun*, 1 Chr. 16:38.

18
*d Levites*, Deut. 10:8.
*e Jerusalem*, Judg. 19:10.

19
*f Porters*, 2 Sam. 18:26.
*g Akkub*, 1 Chr. 9:17.
*h Talmon*, 1 Chr. 9:17.

20
*i Priest*, Lev. 1:5.

21
*j Nethinim*, Ezra 8:20.
*k* Neh. 3:26, 27.

22
*l Mattaniah*, 1 Chr. 9:15.
*m* Or, *Micah*, 1 Chr 9:15.
*n Asaph*, 1 Chr. 15:17.
*o Choir*, 1 Chr. 15:16.
*p Temple, Second*, 1 Kin. 6:17.

v.23–423 BC
See footnote, *Time*, Rev. 10:6.

23 For *it was* the king's commandment concerning them,
that a certain portion should be
for the [o]singers, due for every
day.
24 And Pěth-a-hī′ah the son of
Mė-shĕz′a-beel, of the children
of [q]Zē′rah the son of Jū′dah,
*was* at the king's hand in all
matters concerning the people.
25 And for the villages, with
their fields, *some* of the children
of Jū′dah dwelt at [r]Kĭr′jath–
är′bȧ, and *in* the villages thereof, and at Dī′bŏn, and *in* the
villages thereof, and at Jė-kăb′-
ze-el, and *in* the villages thereof,
26 And at Jĕsh′u-ȧ, and at
*Mŏl′a-dah, and at [s]Bĕth–phē′-
let,
27 And at [t]Hā′zar–shụ′al, and
at [u]Bē′er–shē′bȧ, and *in* the villages thereof,
28 And at [v]Zĭk′lăg, and at
Mĕk′o-nah, and in the villages
thereof,
29 And at Ĕn–rĭm′mon, and at
[w]Zā′re-ah, and at †Jär′mŭth,
30 [x]Zȧ-nō′ah, [y]Ȧ-dŭl′lăm, and
*in* their villages, at [z]Lā′chish,
and the fields thereof, at [a]Ȧ-zē′-
kah, and *in* the villages thereof.
And they dwelt from [b]Bē′er-
shē′bȧ unto the valley of [c]Hĭn′-
nom.
31 The children also of [d]Bĕn′-
ja-mĭn from [e]Gē′bȧ *dwelt* at
[f]Mĭch′mash, and [g]Ȧ-ī′jȧ, and
[h]Bĕth–el, and *in* their villages,
32 *And* at [i]Ăn′a-thŏth, ‡Nŏb,
Ăn-a-nī′ah,
33 [j]Hā′zôr, [k]Rā′mah, [l]Gĭt′-
ta-ĭm,
34 [m]Hā′dĭd, [n]Ze-bō′im, Nė-
băl′lat,
35 [o]Lŏd, and [p]Ō′nŏ, the valley
of craftsmen.
36 And of the [q]Lē′vītes *were*
divisions *in* [r]Jū′dah, *and* in
[s]Bĕn′ja-mĭn.

## CHAPTER 12

*The priests, 8 and the Levites, who came up with Zerubbabel. 10 The succession of high priests. 22 Certain chief Levites. 27 The dedication of the wall. 44 The offices of priests and Levites appointed in the temple.*

NOW these *are* the +,[a]priests
and the [b]Lē′vītes that went
up with [c]Zė-rŭb′ba-bĕl the son
of Shė-ăl′tĭ-el, and [d]Jĕsh′u-ȧ:
Sĕr-a-ī′ah, Jĕr-e-mī′ah, Ĕz′rȧ,
2 Ăm-a-rī′ah, Măl′luch, Hăt′-
tush,
3 Shĕch-a-nī′ah, Rē′hum, Mĕr′-
e-mŏth,
4 Ĭd′dŏ, Gĭn′ne-thō, Ȧ-bī′jah,
5 Mī′a-mĭn, Mȧ-a-dī′ah, Bĭl′-
gah,
6 Shĕm-a-ī′ah, and Joi′a-rĭb,
Jė-dā′iah,
7 Săl′lu, Ā′mok, Hĭl-kī′ah, Jė-
dā′iah. These *were* the chief of
the [a]priests and of their brethren
in the days of [d]Jĕsh′u-ȧ.
8 Moreover the [b]Lē′vītes:
Jĕsh′u-ȧ, Bĭn′nụ-ī, Kăd′mī-el,
Shĕr-e-bī′ah, Jū′dah, *and* Măt-
ta-nī′ah, *which was* over the
thanksgiving, he and his brethren.
9 Also Băk-bŭk-ī′ah and Ŭn′-
nī, their brethren, *were* over[G]
against them in the watches.[G]
10 ¶ And [d]Jĕsh′u-ȧ begat Joi′a-
kĭm, Joi′a-kĭm also begat [e]Ė-lī′-
a-shĭb, and Ė-lī′a-shĭb begat
[f]Joi′a-dȧ,
11 And [f]Joi′a-dȧ begat Jŏn′-
a-than, and Jŏn′a-than begat
Jăd-dū′ȧ.
12 And in the days of Joi′a-

**24**
*q* Or, *Zarah*, Gen. 38:30.
**25**
*r* Or, *Hebron*, Gen. 23:2.
**26**
*s* Or, *Beth-palet*, Josh. 15:27.
**27**
*t* Josh. 15:28; 1 Chr. 4:28.
*u* *Beer-sheba*, Judg. 20:1.
**28**
*v* *Ziklag*, Josh. 15:31.
**29**
*w* Or, *Zorah*, Josh. 19:41.
**30**
*x* Neh. 3:13; Josh. 15:34.
*y* *Adullam*, 2 Chr. 11:7.
*z* *Lachish*, Josh. 10:5.
*a* *Azekah*, Josh. 10:10.
*b* *Beer-sheba*, Judg. 20:1.
*c* *Hinnom*, Jer. 7:31.
**31**
*d* *Benjamin, tribe of*, Num. 1:37.
*e* *Geba*, Josh. 21:17.
*f* *Michmash*, 1 Sam. 14:5.
*g* Or, *Ai*, Josh. 7:2.
*h* *Beth-el*, Josh. 18:13.
**32**
*i* *Anathoth*, Jer. 1:1.
**33**
*j* *Hazor*, Josh. 11:1.
*k* *Ramah*, Judg. 19:13.
*l* 2 Sam. 4:3.
**34**
*m* Ezra 2:33.
*n* 1 Sam. 13:18.

v.35–423 BC
See footnote, *Time*, Rev. 10:6.

**35**
*o* *Lod*, 1 Chr. 8:12.
*p* *Ono*, 1 Chr. 8:12.
**36**
*q* *Levites*, Deut. 10:8.
*r* *Judah, tribe of*, Num. 10:14.
*s* *Benjamin, tribe of*, Num. 1:37.

**1**
*a* *Priest*, Lev. 1:5.
*b* *Levites*, Deut. 10:8.
*c* *Zerubbabel*, Ezra 3:2.
*d* *Jeshua*, Ezra 2:2.

**10**
*e* Neh. 3:1, 20, 21; 13:4-9, 28.
*f* Neh. 13:28.

* **MOLADAH**, a city in the S. W. of Judah. *Allotted to the tribe of Simeon*, Josh. 15:26; 19:2; 1 Chr. 4:28; Neh. 11:26.

† **JARMUTH**, a city in Judah. *King of, confederates with other kings against the Israelites, and is defeated*, Josh. 10:3, 5, 23; 12:11. *Allotted to Judah*, Josh. 15:35. *People of, return from Babylon*, Neh. 11:29.

‡ **NOB.** *A city of Benjamin*, Neh. 11:31, 32. *Called the city of the priests*, 1 Sam. 22:19. *Abode of Ahimelech, the priest*, 1 Sam. 21:1; 22:11. *Probable seat of the tabernacle in Saul's time*, 1 Sam. 21:4, 6, 9. *David flees to, and is aided by Ahimelech*, 1 Sam. 21:1-9; 22:9, 10. *Destroyed by Saul*, 2 Sam. 22:19. *Prophecy concerning*, Isa. 10:32.

+ [In order to publish this Bible in one volume with its numerous and diversified marginal notes and footnotes it has been necessary to avoid elaborate discussions of subjects, such, for instance, as would be necessary to point out the difficulties in connection with some of the names in genealogical lists. These difficulties grow out of errors of copyists, differences in the spelling of the same name, and the fact that individuals and places are mentioned under different names in different chapters. Where the identity of persons or places is doubtful in the following lists, or when no noteworthy fact is known concerning them, no mention of the name is made in either the margins or footnotes.]

kĭm were priests, the chief of the
fathers: of Sĕr-a-ī′ah, Mĕr-a-ī′-
ah; of Jĕr-e-mī′ah, Hăn-a-nī′ah;
13 Of Ēz′rȧ, Mĕ-shŭl′lam; of
Ăm-a-rī′ah, Jē-hō-hā′nan;
14 Of Mĕl′ĭ-cū, Jŏn′a-than; of
Shĕb-a-nī′ah, Jō′ṣeph;
15 Of Hā′rim, Ăd′nȧ; of Mĕ-
rā′ioth, Hĕl′ka-ī;
16 Of Ĭd′dō, Zĕch-a-rī′ah; of
Gĭn′ne-thŏn, Mĕ-shŭl′lam;
17 Of Ȧ-bī′jah, Zĭch′rī; of
Mĭn′ĭ-a-mĭn, of Mō-a-dī′ah, Pĭl′-
tāi;
18 Of Bĭl′gah, Shăm-mū′ȧ; of
Shĕm-a-ī′ah, Jē-hŏn′a-than;
19 And of Joi′a-rĭb, Măt-te-
nā′ī; of Jē-dā′iah, Ŭz′zī;
20 Of Săl′la-ī, Kăl′la-ī; of
Ā′mok, Ē′bĕr;
21 Of Hĭl-kī′ah, Hăsh-a-bī′ah;
of Jē-dā′iah, Nē-thăn′e-el.
22 ¶ The [g]Lē′vītes in the days
of [e]Ē-lī′a-shĭb, [f]Joi′a-dȧ, and
Jō-hā′nan, and Jăd-dū′ȧ, *were*
recorded chief of the fathers: also the priests, to the reign of
[h]Dā-rī′us the [i]Pĕr′ṣian.
23 The [g]sons of Lē′vī, the chief
of the fathers, *were* written in the
book of the chronicles, even until the days of Jō-hā′nan the son
of Ē-lī′a-shĭb.
24 And the chief of the [g]Lē′-
vītes: Hăsh-a-bī′ah, Shĕr-e-bī′-
ah, and Jĕsh′u-ȧ the son of
Kăd′mĭ-el, with their brethren
over against them, to [j]praise *and*
to give [k]thanks, according to the
commandment of [l]Dā′vid the
man of God, ward over against
ward.
25 Măt-ta-nī′ah, and Băk-bŭk-
ī′ah, Ō-ba-dī′ah, Mē-shŭl′lam,
Tăl′mon, Ăk′kŭb, *were* [m]porters
keeping the ward at the [1]thresh-
olds of the [n]gates.
26 These *were* in the days of
Joi′a-kĭm the son of [o]Jĕsh′u-ȧ,
the son of *Jŏz′a-dăk, and in the
days of [p]Nē-he-mī′ah the [q]gov-
ernor, and of [r]Ēz′rȧ the priest,
the [s]scribe.
27 ¶ And at the [t]dedication of
the [u]wall of Jē-ru′sā-lĕm they
sought the [v]Lē′vītes out of all
their places, to bring them to Jē-
ru′sā-lĕm, to keep the dedication with gladness, both with
[k]thanksgivings, and with [w]sing-
ing, *with* [x]cymbals, [y]psalteries,
and with [z]harps.
28 And the sons of the [a]singers
gathered themselves together,
both out of the plain country
round about [b]Jē-ru′sā-lĕm, and
from the villages of Nē-tŏph′-
a-thī;
29 Also from [2]the house of
[c]Gĭl′găl, and out of the fields of
[d]Gē′bȧ and Ăz′ma-vĕth: for the
[a]singers had builded them villages round about [b]Jē-ru′sā-lĕm.
30 And the [e]priests and the
[f]Lē′vītes [g]purified themselves,
and purified the people, and the
[h]gates, and the [i]wall.
31 Then I brought up the princes of Jū′dah upon the [i]wall, and
appointed two great *companies*
[3]*of them that gave* thanks, *where-*
*of one* went on the right hand
upon the wall toward the [h]dung
gate:
32 And after them went Hŏsh-
a-ī′ah, and half of the princes of
Jū′dah,
33 And Ăz-a-rī′ah, Ēz′rȧ, and
Mē-shŭl′lam,
34 Jū′dah, and Bĕn′ja-mĭn, and
Shĕm-a-ī′ah, and Jĕr-e-mī′ah,
35 And *certain* of the priests'
sons with [j]trumpets; *namely,*
Zĕch-a-rī′ah the son of Jŏn′a-
than, the son of Shĕm-a-ī′ah, the
son of Măt-ta-nī′ah, the son of
Mī-chā′iah, the son of Zăc′cur,
the son of [k]Ā′saph:
36 And his brethren, Shĕm-a-
ī′ah, and Ȧ-zăr′a-el, Mĭl-a-lā′ī,

22
g *Levites,* Deut. 10:8.
h *Darius,* Ezra 5:5.
i *Persia, rulers of,* Esth. 1:3.

24
j *Music,* 2 Chr. 5:13.
k *Thankfulness, of man to God,* Acts 24:3.
l *David,* 1 Sam. 16:13.

25
m *Porters,* 2 Sam. 18:26.
n *Gates,* Deut. 3:5.
1 R. V. storehouses

26
o *Jeshua,* Ezra 2:2.
p *Nehemiah,* Neh. 1:1.
q *Government, provincial,* Isa. 22:21.
r *Ezra,* Ezra 7:1.
s *Scribe,* 1 Kin. 4:3.

27
t *Dedication,* Ezra 6:17.
u *Jerusalem, walls of,* Judg. 19:10.
v *Choir,* 1 Chr. 15:16.
w *Music,* 2 Chr. 5:13.
x *Cymbal,* 1 Chr. 13:8.
y *Psaltery,* 1 Chr. 16:5.
z *Harp,* Dan. 3:10.
**v.28–423 BC**

28
a *Choir,* 1 Chr. 15:16.
b *Jerusalem,* Judg. 19:10.

29
c *Gilgal,* Josh. 4:19.
d *Geba,* Josh. 21:17.
2 R. V. Beth-gilgal,

30
e *Priest,* Lev. 1:5.
f *Levites,* Deut. 10:8.
g *Purification,* Num. 19:19.
h *Jerusalem, gates of,* Judg. 19:10.
i *Jerusalem, walls of,* Judg. 19:10.

31
3 R. V. that gave thanks and went in procession; whereof one went

35
j *Trumpet,* Josh. 6:4.
k *Asaph,* 1 Chr. 15:17.

* **JOZADAK,** called also JOSEDECH and JEHOZADAK. *A priest of the exile,* 1 Chr. 6:14, 15; Ezra 3:2, 8; 5:2; 10:18; Neh. 12:26; Hag. 1:1, 12, 14; 2:2, 4; Zech. 6:11.

v.36–423 BC
See footnote, *Time*, Rev. 10:6.

36
*l* *Music, instruments of*, 2 Chr. 5:13.
*m* *David*, 1 Sam. 16:13.
*n* *Ezra*, Ezra 7:1.

37
*o* Neh. 3:15.
*p* *Palace*, 1 Kin. 21:1.

38
*q* *Thankfulness, of man to God*, Acts 24:3.
*r* *Nehemiah*, Neh. 1:1.
*s* *Tower*, 2 Chr. 26:9.
*t* *Jerusalem, towers of*, Judg. 19:10.

39
4 R. V. Hammeah,
5 R. V. gate of the guard.

41
*u* *Trumpet*, Josh. 6:4.

42
*v* *Choir*, 1 Chr. 15:16.
*w* *Music, chief musician*, 2 Chr. 5:13.

43
*x* *Offerings*, Lev. 6:17.
*y* *Joy, instances of*, Psa. 5:11.
*z* *Children, attend divine worship*, Mark 10:14.
6 R V. women

44
*a* *Treasure Houses*, Ezra 5:17.
*b* *Offerings*, Lev. 6:17.
*c* *First Fruits*, Deut. 18:4.

Gĭl'a-lāi, Mā-ā'ī, Nē-thăn'e-el,
and Jū'dah, Hā-nā'nī, with the
musical [l]instruments of [m]Dā'vid
the man of God, and [n]Ĕz'rȧ the
scribe before them.
37 And at the [h]fountain gate,
which was over[G] against them,
they went up by the [o]stairs of the
city of Dā'vid, at the going up of
the [i]wall, above the [p]house of
Dā'vid, even unto the [h]water
gate eastward.
38 And the other *company of*
*them that gave* [q]thanks went over
against *them*, and [r]I after them,
and the half of the people upon
the [i]wall, from beyond the
[s,t]tower of the furnaces even
unto the broad wall;
39 And from above the [h]gate of
Ē'phră-ĭm, and above the [h]old
gate, and above the [h]fish gate,
and the [s]tower of [t]Hā-năn'e-el,
and the [s]tower of [4,t]Mē'ah, even
unto the [h]sheep gate: and they
stood still in the [5,h]prison gate.
40 So stood the two *companies*
*of them that gave* [q]thanks in the
house of God, and [r]I, and the
half of the rulers with me:
41 And the [e]priests; Ē-lī'a-
kĭm, Mā-a-sē'iah, Mĭn'ī-a-mĭn,
Mī-chā'iah, Ē-lī-o-ē'na-ī, Zĕch-
a-rī'ah, *and* Hăn-a-nī'ah, with
[u]trumpets;
42 And Mā-a-sē'iah, and Shĕm-
a-ī'ah, and Ē-le-ā'zar, and Ŭz'zī,
and Jē-hō-hā'nan, and Măl-chī'-
jah, and Ē'lăm, and Ē'zĕr. And
the [v]singers sang loud, with
[w]Jĕz-ra-hī'ah *their* overseer.
43 Also that day they offered
great [x]sacrifices, and rejoiced:
for God had made them rejoice
with great [y]joy: the [6]wives also
and the [z]children rejoiced: so
that the joy of Jē-ru'sā-lĕm was
heard even afar off.
44 ¶ And at that time were
some appointed over the [a]cham-
bers[G] for the treasures, for the
[b]offerings, for the [c]firstfruits,
and for the [d]tithes, to gather into
them out of the fields of the
cities the [e,f]portions of the law
for the priests and Lē'vītes: for
[g]Jū'dah rejoiced for the priests
and for the Lē'vītes that waited.[G]
45 And both the [h]singers and
the [i]porters[G] kept the ward[G] of
their God, and the ward[G] of
the purification, according to the
commandment of [j]Dā'vid, *and*
of [k]Sŏl'o-mon his son.
46 For in the days of [j]Dā'vid
and [l]Ā'saph of old *there were*
chief[G] of the [h]singers, and [m]songs
of [n]praise and thanksgiving unto
God.
47 And all Īs'ra-el in the days
of [o]Zē-rŭb'ba-bĕl, and in the
days of [p]Nē-he-mī'ah, gave the
portions of the [h]singers and the
[i]porters, every day his portion:
and they sanctified[G] [e,f]*holy things*
unto the Lē'vītes; and the Lē'-
vītes sanctified *them* unto the
children of Aâr'on.

## CHAPTER 13

*The mixed multitude is separated from Israel. 4 Nehemiah causes the chambers of the temple to be cleansed. 10 He corrects the abuses in the house of God. 15 He restrains the violation of the sabbath, 23 and intermarriages with the heathen.*

ON that day they [a]read in the
[b]book of Mō'ṣeṣ in the
audience[G] of the people; and
therein was found written, that
the [c]Ăm'mon-īte and the [d]Mō'-
ab-īte should not come into the
congregation of God for ever;
2 Because they met not the
children of [e]Īs'ra-el with bread
and with water, but hired [f]Bā'-
laam against them, that he
should curse them: howbeit our
God [g]turned the curse into a
blessing.
3 Now it came to pass, when
they had heard the [b]law, that
[h]they separated from [i]Īs'ra-el all
the mixed multitude.
4 ¶ And before this, [j]Ē-lī'a-
shĭb the [k,l]priest, having the
oversight of the chamber of the

v.44–423 BC
See footnote, *Time*, Rev. 10:6.

*d* *Tithes*, Num. 18.24.
*e* *Priest, emoluments of*, Lev. 1:5.
*f* *Levites, emoluments of*, Deut. 10:8.
*g* *Jews*, Neh. 4:2.

45
*h* *Choir*, 1 Chr. 15:16.
*i* *Porters*, 2 Sam. 18:26.
*j* *David*, 1 Sam. 16:13.
*k* *Solomon*, 2 Sam. 12:24.

46
*l* *Asaph*, 1 Chr. 15:17.
*m* *Song*, Psa. 77:6.
*n* *Praise*, Psa. 150:1.

47
*o* *Zerubbabel*, Ezra 3:2.
*p* *Nehemiah*, Neh. 1:1.

1
*a* *Instruction, in religion*, Prov. 23:23.
*b* *Law, of Moses*, Deut. 33:2.
*c* *Ammonites*, Deut. 2:20.
*d* *Moabites*, Gen. 19:37.

2
*e* *Israel*, Ex. 4:22.
*f* *Balaam*, Deut. 23:4.
*g* *God, providence of*, Gen. 2:2.

3
*h* *Obedience*, Heb. 5:8.
*i* *Jews*, Neh. 4:2.

4
*j* Neh. 3:1; 12:10, 22, 23.
*k* *High Priest, corrupt*, Lev. 21:10.
*l* *Minister, false and corrupt*, Rom. 15:16.

m Temple, Second, 1 Kin. 6:17.
n Tobiah, Neh. 2:10.
5
o Treasure Houses, Ezra 5:17.
p Offerings, meat, Lev. 6:17.
q Frankincense, 1 Chr. 9:29.
r Tithes, Num. 18:24.
s Levites, emoluments of, Deut. 10:8.
t Choir, 1 Chr. 15:16.
u Porters, 2 Sam. 18:26.
v Priest, emoluments of, Lev. 1:5.
1 R. V. meal
2 R. V. heave offerings
6
w Nehemiah, Neh. 1:1.
x Jerusalem, Judg. 19:10.
y Artaxerxes, Ezra 7:1.
z Babylon, Ezra 5:12.
**v.6–411 BC**

7
a Nehemiah, Neh. 1:1.
b Zeal, instances of, 2 Cor. 7:11.
c Jerusalem, Judg. 19:10.
d Profanation, of the house of God, Lev. 22:32.
e Neh. 3:1; 12:10, 22, 23.
f Tobiah, Neh. 2:10.
g Treasure Houses, Ezra 5:17.
h Temple, Second, 1 Kin. 6:17.
8
i Sin, repugnant to the righteous, Rom. 5:12.
9
j Purification, Num. 19:19.
k Offerings, meat, Lev. 6:17.
l Frankincense, 1 Chr. 9:29.
10
m Levites, emoluments of, Deut. 10:8.
n Choir, 1 Chr. 15:16.
11
o Reproof, faithfulness in, Prov. 17:10.
12
p Liberality, instances of, 1 Tim. 6:18.
q Jews, Neh. 4:2.
r Tithes, Num. 18:24.
s Treasure Houses, Ezra 5:17.

[m]house of our God, *was* allied
unto [n]Tō-bī′ah:
5 And he had prepared for him
a [o]great chamber,[c] where aforetime[c] they laid the [1,p]meat[c] offerings, the [q]frankincense, and the
vessels, and the [r,s]tithes of the
corn,[c] the new wine, and the oil,
which was commanded *to be giv-
en* to the Lē′vītes, and the [t]sing-
ers, and the [u]porters[c]; and the
[2,v]offerings of the priests.
6 But in all this *time* was not
[w]I at [x]Jē-ru̥′sā-lĕm: for in the
two and thirtieth year of [y]Är-
tăx̣-ērx′ēṣ king of [z]Băb′ȳ-lon
came I unto the king, and after
certain days obtained I leave[c] of
the king:
7 And [a,b]I came to [c]Jē-ru̥′sā-
lĕm, and understood of the [d]evil
that [e]Ē-lī′a-shĭb did for [f]Tō-bī′-
ah, in preparing him a [g]chamber
in the courts of the [h]house[c] of
God.
8 And [i]it grieved me sore:[c]
therefore I cast forth all the
household stuff of [f]Tō-bī′ah out
of the chamber.
9 Then I commanded, and they
[j]cleansed the [g]chambers: and
thither[c] brought I again the vessels of the [h]house of God, with
the [1,k]meat[c] offering and the
[l]frankincense.
10 ¶ And I perceived that the
[m]portions of the Lē′vītes had not
been given *them*: for the Lē′vītes
and the [n]singers, that did the
work, were fled every one to his
field.
11 Then [o]contended I with the
rulers, and said, Why is the
[h]house of God forsaken? And I
gathered them together, and set
them in their place.
12 Then [p]brought all [q]Jū′dah
the [r]tithe of the corn[c] and the new
wine and the oil unto the [s]treas-
uries.
13 And I made treasurers over
the [s]treasuries, Shĕl-e-mī′ah the
[t]priest, and Zā′dŏk the [u]scribe,
and of the [v]Lē′vītes, Pē-dā′iah:
and next to them *was* Hā′nan
the son of Zăc′cur, the son of
Măt-ta-nī′ah: for they were
counted [w,x]faithful, and their
office *was* to distribute unto
their brethren.
14 Remember me, O my God,
concerning this, and wipe not
out my [y,z]good deeds that I have
done for the house of my God,
and for the offices[c] thereof.
15 ¶ In those days saw [a]I in
Jū′dah [b]*some* [c]treading [d]wine
presses on the [e]sabbath, and
[f]bringing in sheaves,[c] and lading[c]
asses; as also [g]wine, [h]grapes, and
[i]figs, and all *manner of* burdens,
which [j]they brought into [k]Jē-
ru̥′sā-lĕm on the sabbath day:
and I testified *against them* in
the day wherein they sold victuals.[c]
16 There dwelt men of [l]Tȳre
also therein, which brought
[m]fish, and all manner[c] of ware,[c]
and sold on the [e]sabbath unto
the [b]children of Jū′dah, and in
[k]Jē-ru̥′sā-lĕm.
17 Then I [b,n]contended with the
nobles of Jū′dah, and said unto
them, What evil thing *is* this
that ye do, and [c]profane the sabbath day?
18 Did not your fathers thus,
and did not our God bring all
this [o]evil upon us, and upon this
city? yet ye bring more wrath
upon Iṣ′ra-el by [c]profaning the
sabbath.
19 And it came to pass, that
when the [p]gates of [k]Jē-ru̥′sā-
lĕm began to be dark before
the sabbath, I commanded that
the [3]gates should be shut, and
charged that they should not be
opened till after the sabbath:
and *some* of my [q]servants set I at
the gates, *that* there should no
burden be brought in on the
[e]sabbath day.

**v.13–409 BC**
See footnote, *Time*, Rev. 10:6.

13
t Priest, duties of, Lev. 1:5.
u Scribe, 1 Kin. 4:3.
v Levites, duties of, Deut. 10:8.
w Faithfulness, instances of, Luke 16:10.
x Honesty, instances of, Rom. 13:13.
14
y Works, good, 2 Tim. 1:9.
z Zeal, instances of, 2 Cor. 7:11.

15
a Nehemiah, Neh. 1:1.
b Jews, wickedness of, Neh. 4:2.
c Profanation, of the Sabbath, Lev. 22:32.
d Wine-press, Isa. 5:2.
e Sabbath, profanation of, Ex.16:23.
f Harvest, Ex. 34:21.
g Wine, Prov. 23:31.
h Grape, Lev. 25:5.
i Fig, Mark 11:13.
j Merchant, Neh. 3:32.
k Jerusalem, Judg. 19:10.
16
l Tyre, Josh. 19:29.
m Fish, traffic in, Matt. 17:27.
17
n Reproof, faithfulness in, Prov. 17:10.
18
o Judgments, Ex. 6:6.
19
p Gates, Deut. 3:5.
q Porters, 2 Sam. 18:26.
3 R. V. doors

20 So the [l]merchants and sellers of all kind of ware[G] lodged[G] without[G] [k]Jė-rṳ'sȧ-lĕm once or twice.

21 Then [r]I testified[G] against them, and [n]said unto them, Why lodge[G] ye about[G] the wall? if ye do *so* again, I will lay hands on you. From that time forth came they no *more* on the sabbath.

22 And I commanded the [s]Lē'vītes that they should [t]cleanse themselves, and *that* they should come *and* keep the [p]gates, to sanctify[G] the sabbath day. Remember me, O my God, *concerning* this also, and spare me according to the greatness of thy [u]mercy.

23 ¶ In those days also saw I [v]Jews *that* had [w, x]married wives of [y]Ăsh'dŏd, of [z]Ăm'mŏn, *and* of [a]Mō'ab:

24 And their children spake half in the speech of Ăsh'dŏd, and could not speak in the Jews' [b]language, but according to the language of each people.

25 And [c]I contended with them, and cursed[G] them, and smote certain of them, and plucked off their hair, and made them [d]swear by God, *saying*, [e]Ye shall not give your daughters unto their sons, nor take their daughters unto your sons, or for yourselves.

26 Did not [f]Sŏl'o-mon king of [g]Ĭṣ'ra-el sin by these things? yet among many nations was there no king like him, who was [h]beloved of his God, and [i,j]God made him king over all Ĭṣ'ra-el: nevertheless even [k]him did [4]outlandish[G] [l,m]women [n]cause to sin.[S]

27 Shall we then hearken unto you to do all this great [o]evil, to transgress against our God in [e]marrying strange[G] wives?

28 And *one* of the sons of [p]Joi'-a-dȧ, the son of [q]Ė-lī'a-shĭb the [r]high priest, *was* son in law to [s]Săn-băl'lat the [t]Hŏr'-o-nīte: therefore I chased him from me.

29 Remember [u]them, O my God, because they have defiled the priesthood, and the [v]covenant[G] of the priesthood, and of the [w]Lē'vītes.

30 Thus cleansed I them from all strangers,[G] and appointed the wards[G] of the [x]priests and the [w]Lē'vītes, every one in his business;

31 And for the [y]wood offering, at times appointed, and for the firstfruits. Remember me, O my God, for good.

v.20–409 BC
See footnote, *Time*, Rev. 10:6.

21
r *Rulers, righteous*, Ex. 18:21.

22
s *Levites*, Deut. 10:8.
t *Purification*, Num. 19:19.
u *God, mercy of*, Gen. 2:2.

23
v *Jews, wickedness of*, Neh. 4:2.
w *Marriage*, Gen. 34:9.
x *Miscegenation*, Josh. 23:12.
y *Ashdod*, 1 Sam. 6:17.
z *Ammonites*, Deut. 2:20.
a *Moabites*, Gen. 19:37.

24
b *Language*, Dan. 3:29.

25
c *Rulers, righteous*, Ex. 18:21.
d *Oath*, Num. 5:19.
e *Miscegenation*, Josh. 23:12.

v.25–409 BC
See footnote, *Time*, Rev. 10:6.

26
f *Solomon*, 2 Sam. 12:24.
g *Israel, under the kings*, Ex. 4:22.
h *God, love of*, Gen. 2:2.
i *Government, God in*, Isa. 22:21.
j *Rulers, appointed by God*, Ex. 18:21.
k *Backsliders, instances of*, Jer. 3:22.
l *Women, wicked*, Prov. 31:10.
m *Wife, idolatrous*, Prov. 5:18.
n *Temptation, yielding to*, Luke 11:4.
4 R. V. strange

27
o *Sin, repugnant to the righteous*, Rom. 5:12.

28
p Neh. 12:10, 11, 22.
q Neh. 3:1, 20, 21.
r *High Priest*, Lev. 21:10.
s *Sanballat*, Neh. 2:10.
t Neh. 2:10, 19.

29
u *Minister, false and corrupt*, Rom. 15:16.
v *Covenant, of God with men*, Deut. 29:1.
w *Levites*, Deut. 10:8.

30
x *Priest*, Lev. 1:5.

31
y *Offerings, wood*, Lev. 6:17.

THE

# BOOK OF ESTHER

## CHAPTER 1

*Ahasuerus makes a feast. 10 He sends for Vashti, who refuses to come. 13 The king is counseled to put her away. 21 His decree.*

NOW it came to pass in the days of *Ȧ-hăṣ-ū-ē'rŭs, (this *is* Ȧ-hăṣ-ū-ē'rŭs which [a]reigned, [b]from [c]Ĭn'dĭ-ȧ even unto [d]Ė-thĭ-ō'pĭ-ȧ, *over* an hundred and seven and twenty provinces:)

2 *That* in those days, when the king *Ȧ-hăṣ-ū-ē'rŭs sat on the [e]throne of his kingdom, which *was* in †Shṳ'shan the [f]palace,

3 In the third year of his reign, he made a [g]feast unto all his princes and his servants; the power of ‡Pĕr'ṣiȧ and [h]Mē'dĭ-ȧ, the nobles and princes of the provinces, *being* before him:

v.1–440 BC
See footnote, *Time*, Rev. 10:6.

1
a *Government, imperial*, Isa. 22:21.
b *Babylon, empire of*, Ezra 5:12.
c Esth. 8:9.
d *Ethiopia*, Isa. 18:1.

v.2–440 BC
See footnote, *Time*, Rev. 10:6.

2
e *Throne*, 1 Kin. 2:19.
f *Palace*, 1 Kin. 21:1.

3
g *Feasts*, Mark 12:39.
h *Medes*, Dan. 5:28.
v.3–440 BC

* **AHASUERUS.** *Dominions of*, Esth. 1:1. *Power of*, Esth. 10:1, 2. *Degrades Vashti, his wife*, Esth. 1:10–22. *Makes Esther queen*, Esth. 2:17. *Decrees the destruction of the Jews*, Esth. 3:9–15. *Exalts Mordecai, the Jew*, Esth. 6:10, 11. *Decrees the death of Haman*, Esth. 7:9, 10. *Reverses the decree of death to the Jews*, Esth. 8:5–12.

† **SHUSHAN** (a lily). *Capital of the Medo-Persian empire*, Esth. 1:2, 3; 8:15. *King's palace at*, Neh. 1:1; Esth. 1:2, 5; 2:5, 8; 4:8, 16; 8:14, 15; 9:11, 15.

‡ **PERSIA.** *An empire which extended from India to Ethiopia, comprising one hundred and twenty-seven provinces*, Esth. 1:1; Dan. 6:1. *Government of, restricted by constitutional limi-*

v.4—440 BC
See footnote, *Time*, Rev. 10:6.

4
i *Riches*, Eccl. 4:8.

5
j *Seven, days*, Gen. 7:2.
k *House*, Esth. 8:1.

6
l *Curtains*, Ex. 26:1.
m *Tapestry*, Prov. 7:16.
n *Silver*, 1 Chr. 28:14.
o *Pillar*, Gen. 28:18.
p *Marble*, 1 Chr. 29:2.
q *Bed*, Amos 6:4.
r *Gold*, Ezek. 7:19.
1 R. V. yellow,

7
s *Wine*, Prov. 23:31.
2 R. V. bounty

8
3 R. V. could

9
t Esth. 2:1, 4, 17.
u *Queen*, 1 Kin. 11:19.

10
v *Drunkenness, instances of*, Luke 21:34.
w *Feasts, drunkenness at*, Mark 12:39.
x *Wine, intoxication from*, Prov. 23:31.
y Esth. 7:9.
z *Chamberlain*, 2 Kin. 23:11.

11
a Esth. 2:1, 4, 17.
b *Queen*, 1 Kin. 11:19.
c *Crown*, Ex. 29:6.

4 When he shewed the [i]riches
of his glorious kingdom and the
honour of his excellent majesty
many days, *even* an hundred and
fourscore days.
5 And when these days were
expired, the king made a [g]feast
unto all the people that were
present in †Shu̱′shan the [j]palace,
both unto great and small, [j]seven
days, in the court of the garden
of the king's [k]palace;
6 *Where were* white, green, and
blue [l,m]*hangings*, fastened with
cords of fine linen and purple to
[n]silver rings and [o]pillars of [p]marble:
the [q]beds[c] *were of* [r]gold and
silver, upon a pavement of red,
and [1]blue, and white, and black,
marble.
7 And they gave *them* drink in
vessels of [r]gold, (the vessels being
diverse[c] one from another,)
and royal [s]wine in abundance,
according to the [2]state of the
king.
8 And the drinking *was* according
to the law; none [3]did compel:
for so the king had appointed
to all the officers of his house,
that they should do according
to every man's pleasure.
9 Also [t]Văsh′tī the [u]queen
made a [g]feast for the women *in*
the royal house which *belonged*
to king *Ȧ-hăs̱-ū-ē′rŭs.
10 ¶ On the seventh day, when
the heart of the king was
[v,w]merry with [x]wine, he commanded
Mė-hū′man, Bĭz′thȧ,
[y]Här-bō′-nȧ, Bĭg′thȧ, and Ȧ-băg′thȧ,
Zē′thär, and Cär′cas,
the seven [z]chamberlains[c] that
served in the presence of *Ȧ-hăs̱-ū-ē′rŭs
the king,
11 To bring [a]Văsh′tī the [b]queen
before the king with the [c]crown
royal, to shew the people and the
princes her [d]beauty: for she *was*
fair to look on.
12 But the [b,e]queen [a]Văsh′tī
[f]refused to come at the king's
commandment by *his* [g]chamberlains:
therefore was the king
very [h]wroth,[c] and his anger
burned in him.
13 ¶ Then the *king said to
the wise men, which knew the
times, (for so *was* the king's
manner toward all that knew
law and judgment:
14 And the next unto him *was*
Cär-shē′nȧ, Shē′thär, Ăd′ma-thȧ,
Tär′shish, Mē′rēs̱, Mär′-se-nȧ,
*and* Mė-mū′can, the seven
princes of ‡Pēr′s̱iȧ and [i]Mē′dĭ-ȧ,
which saw the king's face, *and*
which sat the first in the kingdom;)
15 What shall we do unto the
queen [a]Văsh′tī according to law,
because she hath not performed
the commandment of the king
*Ȧ-hăs̱-ū-ē′rŭs by the [g]chamberlains?
16 And Mė-mū′can answered
before the king and the princes,
[a]Văsh′tī the [b]queen hath not
done wrong to the king only, but
also to all the princes, and to all
the people that *are* in all the provinces
of the king *Ȧ-hăs̱-ū-ē′rŭs.
17 For *this* deed of the queen
shall come abroad[c] unto all
women, so that they shall despise[c]
their [j]husbands in their eyes,
when it shall be reported, The
king Ȧ-hăs̱-ū-ē′rŭs commanded
Văsh′tī the queen to be brought
in before him, but she came not.
18 *Likewise* shall the [4]ladies of
‡Pēr′s̱iȧ and [i]Mē′dĭ-ȧ say this
day unto all the king's princes,
which have heard of the deed

v.11—440 BC
See footnote, *Time*, Rev. 10:6.
d *Beauty, instances of*, Prov. 6:25.

12
e *Women, good, instances of*, Prov. 31:10.
f *Modesty, instances of*, 1 Tim. 2:9.
g *Chamberlain*, 2 Kin. 23:11.
h *Anger, instances of*, Psa. 37:8.

14
i *Medes*, Dan. 5:28.

17
j *Husband*, Num. 30:6.

18
4 R. V. princesses

---

*tations*, Esth. 8:8; Dan. 6:8–12. *Municipalities in, provided with dual governors*, Neh. 3:9, 12, 16–18. *The princes of, advisory in matters of administration*, Dan. 6:1–7.
Status of women in: *Queen sat on the throne with the king*, Neh. 2:6. *Vashti divorced for refusing to appear before the king's courtiers*, Esth. 1:10–22; 2:4.
*Jews captive in*, 2 Chr. 36:20, 22, 23. *Men of, in the Tyrian army*, Ezek. 27:10.

Rulers of: *Ahasuerus*, Esth. 1:1, 3; *Darius*, Ezra 4:5, 24; Dan. 5:31; 6; 9:1; *possibly, Darius II*, Hag. 1:1, 15; 2:10; *Artaxerxes*, Ezra 4:7–24; 7; Neh. 2; 5:14; *Cyrus*, 2 Chr. 36:22, 23; Ezra 1; 3:7; 4:3; 5:13, 14, 17; 6:3; Isa. 44:28; 45:1–4, 13. *Princes of*, Esth. 1:14.
*System of justice in*, Ezra 7:25. *Prophecies concerning*, Isa. 13:17; 21:1–10; Ezek. 38:5; Dan. 2:31–45; 5:28; 8; 11:1–4.
See footnotes: BABYLON, Ezra 5:12; CHALDEA, Ezek. 11:24.

v.18–440 BC
See footnote, *Time*, Rev. 10:6.

19
*k* *Proclamation*, 1 Kin. 15:22.
*l* *Divorce*, Matt. 19:7.

20
*m* *Family, government of*, 1 Chr. 13:14.

22
*n* *Letters*, Isa. 37:14.

1
*a* *Anger*, Psa. 37:8.
*b* *Ahasuerus*, Esth. 1:1.
*c* Esth. 1:9–22.
*d* *Government, monarchical, tyranny in*, Isa. 22:21.

2
*e* *Virgin*, Isa. 62:5.

of the queen. Thus *shall there arise* too much contempt and wrath.

19 If it please the king, let there go a royal [k]commandment from him, and let it be written among the laws of the Pĕr′ṣianṣ and the Mēdeṣ, that it be not altered, [l]That [a,b]Văsh′tī come no more before king Ă-hăṣ-ū-ē′rus; and let the king give her royal estate[c] unto another that is better than she.

20 And when the king's decree which he shall make shall be published throughout all his empire, (for it is great,) all the wives [m]shall give to their husbands honour, both to great and small.

21 And the saying pleased the king and the princes; and the king did according to the word of Mē-mū′can:

22 For he sent [k,n]letters into all the king's provinces, into every province according to the writing thereof, and to every people after their language, that every man should bear rule in his own house, and that *it* should be published according to the language of every people.

## CHAPTER 2

*A queen to be chosen instead of Vashti. 8 Esther is preferred. 15 She is made queen. 21 Mordecai's service to the king recorded.*

AFTER these things, when the [a]wrath of king [b]Ă-hăṣ-ū-ē′rŭs was appeased, he remembered [c]Văsh′tī, and what she had done, and what was [d]decreed against her.

2 Then said the king's servants that ministered unto him, Let there be fair young [e]virgins sought for the king:

3 And let the king appoint officers in all the [f]provinces of his kingdom, that they may gather together all the fair young [e]virgins unto [g]Shụ′shan the [h]palace, to the house of the women, unto the custody of Hē′gē the king's [i]chamberlain[c], keeper of the women; and let their things for purification[c] be given *them*:

4 And let the maiden which pleaseth the king be [j]queen instead of [c]Văsh′tī. And the thing pleased the king; and he did so.

5 ¶ *Now* in [g]Shụ′shan the [h]palace there was a certain [k]Jew, whose name *was* *Môr′de-cāi, the son of Jā′īr, the son of Shĭm′e-ī, the son of Kĭsh, a [l]Bĕn′ja-mīte;

6 Who had been carried away from [m]Jĕ-rụ′să-lĕm with the [n]captivity[c] which had been carried away with [o]Jĕc-o-nī′ah king of Jū′dah, whom [p]Nĕb-u-chad-nĕz′zar the king of [q]Băb′y̆-lon had carried away.

7 And he [r]brought up Hă-dăs′-sah, that *is*, †Ĕs′thēr, his uncle's daughter: for [s]she had neither father nor mother, and the maid *was* [t]fair and beautiful; whom *Môr′de-cāi, when her father and mother were dead, [u]took for his own daughter.

8 ¶ So it came to pass, when the king's [v]commandment and his decree was heard, and when many maidens were gathered together unto [g]Shụ′shan the [h]palace, to the custody of Hĕg′a-ī, that †Ĕs′thēr was brought also unto the king's house, to the custody of Hĕg′a-ī, keeper of the women.

9 And the maiden pleased him, and she obtained kindness of

3
*f* *Government, provincial*, Isa. 22:21.
*g* *Shushan*, Esth. 1:2.
*h* *Palace*, 1 Kin. 21:1.
*i* *Chamberlain*, 2 Kin. 23:11.

4
*j* *Queen*, 1 Kin. 11:19.

5
*k* *Jews*, Neh. 4:2.
*l* *Benjamin, tribe of*, Num. 1:37.

6
*m* *Jerusalem*, Judg. 19:10.
*n* *Captivity, of Judah*, Isa. 5:13.
*o* Or, *Jehoiachin*, 2 Kin. 24:6.
*p* *Nebuchadnezzar*, Dan. 2:1.
*q* *Babylon*, Ezra 5:12.

7
*r* *Kindness, instances of*, Acts 28:2.
*s* *Orphan, instances of*, Lam. 5:3.
*t* *Beauty, instances of*, Prov. 6:25.
*u* *Adoption, of children*, Gen. 48:5.

8
*v* *Proclamation*, 1 Kin. 15:22.

* **MORDECAI.** *A Jewish captive in Persia, of the tribe of Benjamin*, Esth. 2:5, 6. *Foster father of Esther*, Esth. 2:7. *Informs Ahasuerus of a conspiracy against his life, and is rewarded*, Esth. 2:21–23; 6:1–11. *Promoted in Haman's place*, Esth. 8:1, 2, 15; 10:1–3. *Intercedes with Ahasuerus for the Jews; festival of Purim established in commemoration of their deliverance*, Esth. chapters 8, 9.

† **ESTHER** (*star*), an orphan Jewess of the captivity; called also HADASSAH. *Cousin of Mordecai*, Esth. 2:7, 15. *Selected for the harem of Ahasuerus*, Esth. 2:7–16. *Chosen queen*, Esth. 2:17. *Tells the king of the plot against his life*, Esth. 2:22. *Fasts on account of the decree to destroy the Israelites; diplomatic tact of; accuses Haman to the king; intercedes for, and saves, her people*, Esth. chapters 4–9.

9
*w Women, separate apartments for,* Prov. 31:10.

10
*x Tact,* Prov. 15:1.

12
*y Anointing, of the body,* Deut. 28:40.
*z Ointment,* Eccl. 7:1.

*a Myrrh,* Ex. 30:23.

13
*b Ahasuerus,* Esth. 1:1.
*c Women, separate apartments for,* Prov. 31:10.

14
*d Chamberlain,* 2 Kin. 23:11.
*e Concubinage,* 2 Sam. 21:11.

15
*f* Esth. 9:29.
*g Adoption, of children,* Gen. 48:5.

him; and he speedily gave her her things for purification,[G] with such things as belonged to her, and seven maidens, *which were* meet[G] to be given her, out of the king's house: and he preferred[G] her and her maids unto the best *place* of the [w]house of the women.

10 †Ĕs′thēr [x]had not shewed[G] her [k]people nor her kindred: for *Môr′de-cāi had charged her that she should not shew[G] *it.*

11 And *Môr′de-cāi walked every day before the court of the [w]women's house, to know how †Ĕs′thēr did, and what should become of her.

12 ¶ Now when every maid's turn was come to go in to king Ā-hăṣ-ū-ē′rŭs, after that she had been twelve months, according to the manner[G] of the women, (for so were the days of their purifications[G] accomplished, *to wit,*[G] six months with [y,z]oil of [a]myrrh, and six months with sweet odours, and with *other* things for the purifying of the women;)

13 Then thus came *every* maiden unto the [b]king; whatsoever she desired was given her to go with her out of the [c]house of the women unto the king's house.

14 In the evening she went, and on the morrow[G] she returned into the second [c]house of the women, to the custody of Shā-ăsh′găz, the king's [d]chamberlain[G], which kept the [e]concubines[G]: she came in unto the [b]king no more, except the king delighted in her, and that she were called by name.

15 ¶ Now when the turn of †Ĕs′thēr, the daughter of [f]Ăb-i-hā′il the uncle of *Môr′de-cāi, who had [g]taken her for his daughter, was come to go in unto the [b]king, she required nothing but what Hĕg′a-ī the king's [d]chamberlain, the keeper of the women, appointed.[G] And Ĕs′thēr obtained favour in the sight of all them that looked upon her.

16 So †Ĕs′thēr was taken unto king [b]Ā-hăṣ-ū-ē′rŭs into his house royal in the tenth [h]month, which *is* the month [i]Tē′beth, in the seventh year of his reign.

17 And the [b]king loved †Ĕs′thēr above all the women, and she obtained grace and favour[G] in his sight more than all the [j]virgins; so that he set the royal [k]crown upon her head, and [l]made her [m]queen instead of [n]Văsh′tī.

18 Then the king made a great [o]feast unto all his princes and his servants, *even* †Ĕs′thēr's feast; and he made a release to the provinces, and gave gifts, according to the [1]state of the king.

19 And when the [j]virgins were gathered together the second time, then *Môr′de-cāi sat in the king's gate.

20 †Ĕs′thēr [p]had not *yet* shewed[G] her kindred nor her [q]people; as *Môr′de-cāi had charged her: for Ĕs′thēr did the commandment of Môr′de-cāi, like as when she was brought up with him.

21 ¶ In those days, while *Môr′de-cāi sat in the king's gate, two of the king's [d]chamberlains[G], [r,s]Bĭg′thăn and [s,t]Tē′resh, of [u]those which kept the door, were wroth,[G] and [v]sought to lay hand on the king [b]Ā-hăṣ-ū-ē′rŭs.

22 And the thing was known to *Môr′de-cāi, [w]who [x]told *it* unto †Ĕs′thēr the [m]queen; and Ĕs′thēr certified[G] the king *thereof* in Môr′de-cāi's name.

23 And when inquisition was made of the matter, [y]it was found out; therefore they were both [y]hanged on a [z]tree: and it was written in the [a]book of the chronicles before the king.

v.15–436 BC
See footnote, *Time,* Rev. 10:6.

16
*h Month,* Ex. 12:2.
*i* Ezek. 29:1.

17
*j Virgin,* Isa. 62:5.
*k Crown,* Ex. 29:6.
*l Captive, advanced,* 1 Sam. 30:3.
*m Queen,* 1 Kin. 11:19.
*n* Esth. 1:9–22.

18
*o Feasts,* Mark 12:39.
1 R. V. bounty

20
*p Tact,* Prov. 15:1.
*q Jews,* Neh. 4:2.

21
*r* Or, *Bigthana,* Esth. 6:2.
*s Citizens, wicked,* Luke 15:15.
*t* Esth. 6:2.
*u Porters,* 2 Sam. 18:26.
*v Treason,* 2 Kin. 11:14.

22
*w Citizens, loyal,* Luke 15:15.
*x Loyalty,* Eccl. 8:2.

23
*y Punishment, death penalty,* Lev. 26:41.
*z Gallows,* Esth. 5:14.

*a Book,* Num. 5:23.

## CHAPTER 3

*Haman's promotion. 2 Mordecai refuses to do him reverence. 5 Haman seeks revenge. 8 He obtains a decree of the king to destroy the Jews.*

AFTER these things did king
[a]Ā-hăș-ū-ē′rŭs promote
*Hā′man the son of [b]Hăm-mĕd′-
a-thȧ the Ā′găg-īte, and advanced him, and set his seat
above all the [c]princes that *were*
with him.
2 And all the king's servants,
that *were* in the king's gate,
[d]bowed, and reverenced[c] *Hā′-
man: for the king had so commanded concerning him. But
[e]Môr′de-cāi bowed not, nor did
*him* reverence.[c]
3 Then the king's servants,
which *were* in the king's gate,
said unto [e]Môr′de-cāi, Why
transgressest thou the king's
commandment?
4 Now it came to pass, when
they spake daily unto him, and
he hearkened not unto them,
that they told *Hā′man, to see
whether [e]Môr′de-cāi's matters[c]
would stand: for he had told
them that he *was* a [f]Jew.
5 And when *Hā′man saw that
[e]Môr′de-cāi bowed not, nor did
him [d]reverence,[c] then was Hā′-
man full of [g,h]wrath.
6 And he [h,i]thought[c] scorn[c] to
lay hands on [e]Môr′de-cāi alone;
for they had shewed[c] him the
people of Môr′de-cāi: wherefore
*Hā′man sought to destroy all
the [f]Jews that *were* throughout
the whole kingdom of [a]Ā-hăș-ū-
ē′rŭs, *even* the people of Môr′-
de-cāi.
7 ¶ In the [j]first [k]month, that
*is*, the month Nī′san, in the
twelfth year of king [a]Ā-hăș-ū-
ē′rŭs, they cast Pûr, that *is*,
the [†]lot, before *Hā′man from
day to day, and from month to
month, *to* the twelfth *month*,
that *is*, the month Ā′där.
8 ¶ And *Hā′man said unto
king [a]Ā-hăș-ū-ē′rŭs, There is a
[l]certain people scattered abroad
and dispersed among the people
in all the provinces of thy kingdom; and their laws *are* diverse[c]
from all people; [l]neither keep
they the king's laws: therefore it
*is* not for the king's profit to
suffer[c] them.
9 If it please the [a]king, let it
be written that they may be
destroyed: and [m]I [n]will pay ten
thousand [o]talents[c] of [p]silver to the
hands of those that have the
charge of the business, to bring
*it* into the king's [q]treasuries.
10 And the [a]king took his [r]ring
from his hand, and gave it unto
*Hā′man the son of [b]Hăm-mĕd′-
a-thȧ the Ā′găg-īte, the [f]Jews'
enemy.
11 And the [s]king said unto
*Hā′man, The [p]silver *is* given to
thee, the people also, to [t]do with
them as it seemeth good to thee.
12 Then were the king's
[u]scribes[c] called on the thirteenth
day of the first [k]month, and
there was written according to
all that *Hā′man had commanded unto the king's [1]lieutenants,
and to the governors that *were*
over every province, and to the
rulers of every people of every
province according to the writing thereof, and *to* every people
after their language; in the name
of king [a]Ā-hăș-ū-ē′rŭs was [v]it
written, and sealed with the
king's [r]ring.
13 And the [v,w]letters were sent
by [x]posts[c] into all the king's prov-

**1**
*a Ahasuerus*, Esth. 1:1.
*b* Esth. 8:5; 9:10, 24.
*c King, chief officers of*, 2 Kin. 3:10.

**2**
*d Homage*, Acts 10:25.
*e Mordecai*, Esth. 2:5.

**4**
*f Jews*, Neh. 4:2.

**5**
*g Anger, instances of*, Psa. 37:8.
*h Malice, instances of*, Eph. 4:31.

**6**
*i Pride, instances of*, Prov. 16:18.

**7**
*j Abib*, Ex. 13:4.
*k Month*, Ex. 12:2.

v.7–431 BC
See footnote, *Time*, Rev. 10:6.

**8**
*l Falsehood, instances of*, Job 21:34.

**9**
*m Statecraft, corruption in*, Prov. 28:2.
*n Bribery, instances of*, 1 Sam. 8:3.
*o Talent*, Ex. 38:25.
*p Silver*, 1 Chr. 28:14.
*q Treasure Houses.* Ezra 5:17.

**10**
*r Ring*, Gen. 41:42.

**11**
*s Rulers, wicked*, Ex. 18:21.
*t Babylon, government of, tyrannical*, Ezra 5:12.

**12**
*u Scribe, king's secretary*, 1 Kin. 4:3.
*v Proclamation*, 1 Kin. 15:22.
1 R. V. satraps,

**13**
*w Letters*, Isa. 37:14.
*x Post*, Job 9:25.

* **HAMAN.** *Prime minister of Ahasuerus*, Esth. 3:1. *Plotted against Esther and the Jews; thwarted by Esther and Mordecai; hanged*, Esth. chapters 3–9.

† **LOT**, Prov. 16:33; 18:18; Isa. 34:17; Joel 3:3. *The scapegoat chosen by*, Lev. 16:8–10.
*The land of Canaan divided among the tribes by*, Num. 26:55, 56; Josh. 15; 18:10; 19:51; Ezek. 45:1; 47:22; 48:29. *The Levitical cities designated by*, Josh. 21; 1 Chr. 6:61, 64, 65. *Saul chosen king by*, 1 Sam. 10:20, 21. *Priests and Levites designated by, for sanctuary service*, 1 Chr. 24:5–31; 25; 26:13; Neh. 10:34; Luke 1:9. *Used to determine who of the people after the captivity should dwell in Jerusalem*, Neh. 11:1. *An apostle chosen by*, Acts 1:26.
Guilt ascertained by: *Of Achan*, Josh. 7:14–18; *of Jonathan*, 1 Sam. 14:41, 42; *of Jonah*, Jonah 1:7. *Used to fix the time for the execution of condemned persons*, Esth. 3:7; 9:24.
*The garments of Jesus divided by*, Psa. 22:18; Matt. 27:35; Mark 15:24; John 19:23, 24.

v.13–431 BC
See footnote, *Time*, Rev. 10:6.

inces, to ‡destroy, to kill, and
to cause to perish, all Jews, both
young and old, little children
and women, in one day, *even*
upon the thirteenth *day* of the
twelfth [k]month, which *is* the
month Ā′där, and *to take* the
spoil[C] of them for a prey.[C]
14 The copy of the [v]writing for
a commandment to be given in
every province was published
unto all people, that they should
be ready against that day.
15 The [x]posts[C] went out, being
hastened by the king's commandment, and the [v]decree was
given in [y]Shu′shan the [z]palace.
And the king and Hā′man sat
down to drink; but the city Shu′-
shan was perplexed.

15
*y Shushan*, Esth. 1:2.
*z Palace*, 1 Kin. 21:1.

## CHAPTER 4

*The lamentation of Mordecai and the Jews. 4 Esther inquires the cause thereof. 7 Mordecai makes it known to her, and urges her to intercede with the king for her people. 15 She consents, and appoints a fast.*

WHEN [a]Môr′de-cāi per-
ceived all that was done,
Môr′de-cāi [b]rent[C] his clothes,
and put on [c]sackcloth with
[d]ashes, and went out into the
midst of the city, and [e]cried
with a loud and a bitter cry;[Q]
2 And came even before the
king's gate: for none *might* enter
into the king's gate clothed with
[c]sackcloth.
3 And in every province, whithersoever[C] the king's commandment and his decree came, *there*
*was* great [e]mourning among the
[f]Jews, and [g]fasting, and [h]weep-
ing, and wailing; and many lay
in [c]sackcloth and [d]ashes.
4 ¶ So [i]Ĕs′thēr's maids and her
[j]chamberlains[C] came and told *it*
her. Then was the [k]queen exceedingly grieved; and she sent
raiment to clothe [a]Môr′de-cāi,
and to take away his [c]sackcloth
from him: but he received[C] *it* not.
5 Then called [i]Ĕs′thēr for Hā′-
tăch, *one* of the king's [j]chamber-
lains,[C] whom he had appointed to
attend upon her, and gave him a
commandment to [a]Môr′de-cāi,
to know[C] what it *was*, and why
it *was*.
6 So Hā′tăch went forth to
[a]Môr′de-cāi unto the [1]street of
the city, which *was* before the
king's gate.
7 And [a]Môr′de-cāi told him of
all that had happened unto him,
and of the sum of the [l]money
that [m]Hā′man had promised to
[n]pay to the king's [o]treasuries for
the [f]Jews, to destroy them.
8 Also he gave him the copy of
the writing of the decree that
was given at [p]Shu′shan to destroy them, to shew *it* unto [i]Ĕs′-
thēr, and to declare *it* unto her,
and to charge her that she should
go in unto the king, to make
[q]supplication unto him, and to
make request before him for her
[f]people.
9 And Hā′tăch came and told
[i]Ĕs′thēr the words of [a]Môr′de-
cāi.
10 ¶ Again [i]Ĕs′thēr spake unto
Hā′tăch, and gave him commandment unto [a]Môr′de-cāi;
11 All the king's servants, and
the people of the king's provinces, do know, that whosoever,
whether man or woman, shall
come unto the king into the inner court, who is not called,
*there is* one law of his to put *him*
to death, except such to whom
the king shall hold out the
golden *sceptre, that he may
live: but I have not been called

1
*a Mordecai*, Esth. 2:5.
*b Rending of Garments*, 2 Chr. 34:27.
*c Sackcloth*, Isa. 15:3.
*d Ashes, a symbol of mourning*, Num. 19:9.
*e Mourning*, Lam. 2:5.

3
*f Jews*, Neh. 4:2.
*g Fasting*, Zech. 8:19.
*h Weeping*, Ezra 3:13.

4
*i Esther*, Esth. 2:7.
*j Chamberlain*, 2 Kin. 23:11.
*k Queen*, 1 Kin. 11:19.

v.4–431 BC
See footnote, *Time*, Rev. 10:6.

6
1 R. V. broad place

7
*l Money*, Jer. 32:9
*m Haman*, Esth. 3:1.
*n Bribery*, 1 Sam. 8:3.
*o Treasure Houses*, Ezra 5:17.

8
*p Shushan*, Esth. 1:2.
*q Intercession, of man with man*, Jer. 27:18.

‡ **MASSACRE.** *Authorized by Moses*, Deut. 20:13, 16. *Decree to destroy the Jews*, Esth. 3.
**Instances of:** *The inhabitants, of Heshbon*, Deut. 2:34; *of Bashan*, Deut. 3:3–6; *of Ai*, Josh. 8:24–26; *of Hazor*, Josh. 11:11, 12; *of the cities of the seven kings*, Josh. 10:28–40; *of Tiphsah*, 2 Kin. 15:16. *The Midianites*, Num. 31:7, 8. *The prophets of Baal*, 1 Kin. 18:40. *The worshipers of Baal*, 2 Kin. 10:18–28. *The sons of Ahab*, 2 Kin. 10:1–8. *The seed royal by Athaliah*, 2 Kin. 11:1. *The Edomites*, 2 Kin. 14:7. *The Babylonians*, Esth. 9:14–16. *The infants in Judea by Herod*, Matt. 2:16.

* **SCEPTER.** *A symbol of authority*, Num. 24:17; Isa. 14:5. *Used by kings to signify favor or disfavor to those who desired audience*, Esth. 5:2; 8:4. *Made of gold*, Esth. 4:11. *Of iron, figurative of severity in executive administration*, Psa. 2:9; Rev. 2:27; 12:5.
**Figurative,** Gen. 49:10; Psa. 45:6.

v.11–431 BC
See footnote, *Time*, Rev. 10:6.

14
*r* *Faith, instances of*, Mark 11:22.

15
*s* *Women, good*, Prov. 31:10.

16
*t* *Fasting*, Zech. 8:19.
*u* *Adversity, resignation in, exemplified*, Psa. 10:6.
*v* *Self Denial, instances of*, Mark 8:34.
*w* *Resignation, exemplified*, Job 5:17.

1
*a* *Esther*, Esth. 2:7.
*b* *Dress*, Zech. 3:3.
*c* *Courage, instances of*, Deut. 31:7.
*d* *Palace*, 1 Kin. 21:1.
*e* *Ahasuerus*, Esth. 1:1.

to come in unto the king these thirty days.

12 And they told to [a]Môr′de-cāi [i]Ĕs′thĕr's words.

13 Then [a]Môr′de-cāi commanded to answer [i]Ĕs′thĕr, Think not with thyself that thou shalt escape in the king's house, more than all the [l]Jews.

14 For if thou altogether holdest thy peace at this time, *then* [r]shall there enlargement[c] and deliverance arise to the [l]Jews from another place; but thou and thy father's house shall be destroyed: and who knoweth whether thou art come to the kingdom for *such* a time as this?

15 ¶ Then [i,s]Ĕs′thĕr bade[c] *them* return Môr′de-cāi *this answer*,

16 Go, gather together all the [l]Jews that are present in [p]Shu′shan, and [t]fast ye for me, and neither eat nor drink three days, night or day: I also and my maidens will fast likewise; and [u]so will I go in unto the king, which *is* not according to the law: and [v,w]if I perish, I perish.

17 So Môr′de-cāi went his way, and did according to all that Ĕs′thĕr had commanded him.

## CHAPTER 5

*Esther, venturing to go to the king, obtains his favor, and invites the king and Haman to a banquet. 6 She, being encouraged by the king, invites them to another banquet the next day. 9 Haman repines at the contempt of Mordecai. 13 He builds a gallows for him.*

NOW it came to pass on the third day, that [a]Ĕs′thĕr put on *her* [b]royal *apparel*, and [c]stood in the inner court of the [d]king's house, over[c] against the king's house: and the [e]king sat upon his royal throne in the royal house, over[c] against the gate of the house.

2 And it was so, when the [e]king saw [a]Ĕs′thĕr the queen standing in the court, *that* she obtained favour in his sight: and the king held out to Ĕs′thĕr the golden [f]sceptre that *was* in his hand. So Ĕs′thĕr drew near, and touched the top of the sceptre.

3 Then said the king unto her, What wilt thou, queen [a]Ĕs′thĕr? and what *is* thy request? it shall be even given thee to the half of the kingdom.[Q]

4 And [a]Ĕs′thĕr answered, If *it seem* good unto the king, let the king and [g]Hā′man come this day unto the [h]banquet that I have prepared for him.

5 Then the king said, Cause [g]Hā′man to make haste, that he may do as [a]Ĕs′thĕr hath said. So the king and Hā′man came to the [h]banquet that Ĕs′thĕr had prepared.

6 ¶ And the king said unto [a]Ĕs′thĕr at the [h]banquet of [i]wine, What *is* thy *petition? and it shall be granted thee: and what *is* thy request? even to the half of the kingdom it shall be performed.[Q]

7 Then answered Ĕs′thĕr, and said, My *petition and my request *is*;

8 If I have found favour in the sight of the king, and if it please the king to grant my *petition, and to perform my request, let the king and [g]Hā′man come to the [h]banquet that I shall prepare for them, and I will do to morrow as the king hath said.

9 ¶ Then went [g]Hā′man forth that day [j]joyful and with a glad heart: but when Hā′man saw [k]Môr′de-cāi in the king's gate, that he stood not up, nor moved for him, he was [1]full of [l]indignation against Môr′de-cāi.

10 Nevertheless [g]Hā′man refrained himself: and when he came home, he sent and called

v.2–431 BC
See footnote, *Time*, Rev. 10:6.

2
*f* *Scepter*, Esth. 4:11.

4
*g* *Haman*, Esth. 3:1.
*h* *Feasts*, Mark 12:39.

6
*i* *Wine*, Prov. 23:31.

9
*j* *Ambition, instances of*, Hab. 2:5.
*k* *Mordecai*, Esth. 2:5.
*l* *Malice*, Eph. 4:31.
1 R. V. filled with wrath

***PETITION. Right of, recognized:** *By David*, 1 Kin. 1:15–21. *For redress of public wrongs, by Pharaoh*, Ex. 5:15–18; *by Rehoboam*, 1 Kin. 12:1–17; 2 Chr. 10; *by Ahasuerus*, Esth. 7:3, 4; *by Herod*, Acts 12:20, 21. *For redress of private wrong, by Jehoram*, 2 Kin. 8:3, 6. *For private rights, by Israel*, Num. 27:1–5; 32:1–5; 36:1–5; Josh. 17:4, 14, 16; 21:1, 2.

for his friends, and [m]Zē′resh his wife.

11 And [g]Hā′man [n]told them of the glory of his [o]riches, and the multitude of his children, and all *the things* wherein the king had promoted him, and how he had advanced him above the princes and servants of the king.

12 [g]Hā′man [n]said moreover, Yea, [a]Ĕsthēr the queen did let no man come in with the king unto the [h]banquet that she had prepared but myself; and to morrow am I invited unto her also with the king.

13 Yet all this availeth me nothing, [l]so long as I see [k]Môr′-de-cāi the [p]Jew sitting at the king's gate.

14 Then said [m,q]Zē′resh his wife and all his [r]friends unto him, Let a †gallows be made of fifty [s]cubits[G] high, and to morrow speak thou unto the king that [k]Môr′de-cāi may be hanged thereon: then go thou in merrily with the king unto the [h]banquet. And the thing pleased Hā′man; and he caused the gallows to be made.

## CHAPTER 6

*Ahasuerus, reading in the chronicles of the good service done by Mordecai, provides for his reward. 4 Haman, coming to ask that Mordecai may be hanged, unawares gives counsel how the king may do Mordecai honor. 12 When Haman complains of his misfortune, his friends predict his fall.*

ON that night [a]could not the [b]king sleep, and he commanded to bring the [c]book of records of the [d]chronicles; and they were read before the king.

2 And it was found written, that [e,f]Môr′de-cāi [g]had told of [h]Bĭg′tha-nȧ and [i]Tē′resh, two of the king's chamberlains, the [j]keepers of the door, [k]who sought to lay hand on the king [b]Ă-hăș-ū-ē′rŭs.

3 And the [b]king said, What honour and dignity hath been done to [e]Môr′de-cāi for this? Then said the king's servants that ministered unto him, There is nothing done for him.

4 And the [b]king said, Who *is* in the court? Now [l]Hā′man was come into the outward court of the [m]king's house, [n]to speak unto the king to hang [e]Môr′de-cāi on the [o]gallows that he had prepared for him.

5 And the [b]king's servants said unto him, Behold, [l]Hā′man standeth in the court. And the king said, Let him come in.

6 So [l]Hā′man came in. And the [b]king said unto him, What shall be done unto the man whom the king delighteth to honour? Now Hā′man [p,q]thought in his heart, To whom would the king delight to do honour more than to myself?

7 And Hā′man answered the king, For the man whom the king delighteth to honour,

8 Let the [r]royal apparel be brought which the king *useth* to wear, and the horse that the king rideth upon, and [1]the [s]crown royal which is set upon his head:

9 And let this [r]apparel and horse be delivered to the hand of one of the king's most noble princes, that they may array[G] the man *withal* whom the king delighteth to honour, and bring him on horseback through the street of the city, and proclaim before him, Thus shall it be done to the man whom the king delighteth to honour.

10 Then the king said to [l]Hā′man, Make haste, *and* take the apparel[G] and the horse, as thou hast said, and do even so to [e]Môr′de-cāi the [t]Jew, that sitteth at the king's gate: let nothing fail of all that thou hast spoken.

v.10–431 BC
See footnote, *Time*, Rev. 10:6.

10
m Esth. 6:13.

11
n *Pride, instances of*, Prov. 16:18.
o *Riches*, Eccl. 4:8.

13
p *Jews*, Neh. 4:2.

14
q *Women, wicked*, Prov. 31:10.
r *Friends*, Ex. 33:11.
s *Cubit*, Ex. 36:9.

1
a *Insomnia, instances of*, Dan. 6:18.
b *Ahasuerus*, Esth. 1:1.
c *Book*, Num. 5:23.
d *King, chronicles of*, 2 Kin. 3:10.

2
e *Mordecai*, Esth. 2:5.
f *Citizens, loyal*, Luke 15:15.
g *Loyalty, instances of*, Eccl. 8:2.
h Or, *Bigthan*, Esth. 2:21–23.
i Esth. 2:21–23.
j *Porters*, 2 Sam. 18:26.
k *Citizens, wicked*, Luke 15:15.

v.3–431 BC
See footnote, *Time*, Rev. 10:6.

4
l *Haman*, Esth. 3:1.
m *Palace*, 1 Kin. 21:1.
n *Malice, instances of*, Eph. 4:31.
o *Gallows*, Esth. 5:14.

6
p *Ambition, disappointed*, vs. 6–13; Hab. 2:5.
q *Pride, instances of*, Prov. 16:18.

8
r *Dress*, Zech. 3:3.
s *Crown*, Ex. 29:6.
1 R. V. on the head of which a crown royal is set:

10
t *Jews*, Neh. 4:2.

† **GALLOWS.** *Used for execution, of criminals*, Gen. 40:19, 22; Deut. 21:22, 23; Josh. 8:29; Esth. 2:23; 5:14; 6:4; 7:9, 10; 8:7; 9:13, 25; *of captives of war*, Josh. 10:26, 27. *To be hanged on, a reproach*, Gal. 3:13. See footnote, PUNISHMENT, Lev. 26:41.

v.11–431 BC
See footnote, *Time*, Rev. 10:6.

11 Then took [l]Hā′man the apparel and the horse, and arrayed [e]Môr′de-cāi, and brought him on horseback through the street of the city, and proclaimed before him, Thus shall it be done unto the man whom the king delighteth to honour.

12 ¶ And [e]Môr′de-cāi came again to the king's gate. [p]But [l]Hā′man hasted to his house [u]mourning, and having his head covered.

13 And [l,p]Hā′man told [v]Zē′resh his wife and all his friends every *thing* that had befallen him. Then said his wise men and Zē′resh his wife unto him, If [e]Môr′de-cāi *be* of the seed of the [t]Jews, before whom thou hast begun to fall, thou shalt not prevail against him, but shalt surely fall before him.

14 And while they *were* yet talking with him, came the king's chamberlains,[c] and hasted to bring [l]Hā′man unto the [w]banquet that [x]Ĕs′thēr had prepared.

12
*u* *Mourning, for calamities*, Lam. 2:5.

13
*v* Esth. 5:10-14.

14
*w* *Feasts*, Mark 12:39.
*x* *Esther*, Esth. 2:7.

## CHAPTER 7

*Esther, entertaining the king and Haman, pleads for her own life and for that of her people. 5 She accuses Haman. 7 The king in his anger commands that Haman be hanged on the gallows made for Mordecai.*

SO the [a]king and [b]Hā′man came to [c]banquet[c] with [d]Ĕs′thēr the [e]queen.

2 And the king said again unto [d]Ĕs′thēr on the second day at the [c]banquet of [f]wine, What *is* thy [g]petition, queen Ĕs′thēr? and it shall be granted thee: and what *is* thy request? and it shall be performed, *even* to the half of the kingdom.[Q]

3 Then [d]Ĕs′thēr the [e]queen answered and [h]said, If I have found favour in thy sight, O king, and if it please the king, let my life be given me at my [g]petition, and [i]my people at my request:

4 For we are sold, I and my people, to be destroyed, to be [j]slain, and to perish. But if we had been sold for bondmen[c] and bondwomen,[c] I had held my [1]tongue, although the enemy could not countervail[c] the king's damage.

5 ¶ Then the king [a]Ā-hăş-ū-ē′-rŭs answered and said unto [d]Ĕs′thēr the [e]queen, Who is he, and where is he, that durst[c] presume in his heart to do so?

6 And [d]Ĕs′thēr said, The adversary and enemy *is* this wicked [b]Hā′man. Then Hā′man was afraid before the king and the queen.

7 ¶ And the king arising from the [c]banquet of [f]wine in his [k]wrath *went* into the [l]palace garden: and [b]Hā′man stood up to make request for his life to [d]Ĕs′thēr the [e]queen; for he saw that there was evil determined against him by the king.

8 Then the king returned out of the [l]palace garden into the place of the banquet of wine; and [b]Hā′man was fallen upon the bed[c] whereon [d]Ĕs′thēr *was*. Then said the king, Will he force[c] the queen also before[c] me in the house? As the word went out of the king's mouth, they covered Hā′man's face.

9 And [m]Här-bō′nah, one of the chamberlains,[c] said before the king, Behold also, the [n]gallows fifty [o]cubits[c] high, which [b]Hā′man had made for [p]Môr′de-cāi, who had spoken good for the king, standeth in the house of Hā′man. Then the [a]king said, Hang him thereon.

10 So they [q,r]hanged Hā′man on the [n]gallows that he had prepared for [p]Môr′de-cāi. Then was the king's [k]wrath pacified.

1
*a* *Ahasuerus*, Esth. 1:1.
*b* *Haman*, Esth. 3:1.
*c* *Feasts*, Mark 12:39.
*d* *Esther*, Esth. 2:7.
*e* *Queen*, 1 Kin. 11:19.

2
*f* *Wine*, Prov. 23:31.
*g* *Petition*, Esth. 5:6.

3
*h* *Tact*, Prov. 15:1.

v.3–431 BC
See footnote, *Time*, Rev. 10:6.

*i* *Intercession, of man with man*, Jer. 27:18.

4
*j* *Massacre*, Esth. 3:13.
1 R. V. peace, although the adversary could not have compensated for the king's damage.

7
*k* *Anger, instances of*, Psa. 37:8.
*l* *Palace*, 1 Kin. 21:1.

9
*m* Esth. 1:10.
*n* *Gallows*, Esth. 5:14.
*o* *Cubit*, Ex. 36:9
*p* *Mordecai*, Esth 2:5.

10
*q* *Hanging*, Josh. 8:29.
*r* *Death, penalty*, Num. 23:10.

v.1–431 BC
See footnote, *Time*, Rev. 10:6.

1
a *Ahasuerus*, Esth. 1:1.
b *Confiscation*, Ezra 10:8.
c *Haman*, Esth. 3:1.
d *Esther*, Esth. 2:7.
e *Queen*, 1 Kin. 11:19.
f *Mordecai*, Esth. 2:5.

2
g *Ring*, Gen. 41:42.
h *Civil Service, appointment in*, Dan. 1:5.
i *Captive, advanced*, 1 Sam. 30:3.

3
j *Intercession, of man with man*, Jer. 27:18.
k *Jews*, Neh. 4:2.

4
l *Scepter*, Esth. 4:11.

5
m *Tact*, Prov. 15:1.
n Esth. 3:1, 10; 9:10, 24.

## CHAPTER 8

*Mordecai is promoted. 3 Esther makes suit to the king to reverse Haman's letters. 7 Ahasuerus gives the Jews permission to defend themselves. 15 The honor shown to Mordecai, and the joy of the Jews.*

ON that day did the king
[a]Ā-hăș-ū-ē′rŭs [b]give the
*house of [c]Hā′man the Jewș′
enemy unto [d]Ĕs′thĕr the [e]queen.
And [f]Môr′de-cāi came before
the king; for Ĕs′thĕr had told
what he *was* unto her.
2 And the king took off his
[g]ring, which he had taken from
[c]Hā′man, and gave it unto [f]Môr′-
de-cāi. And [d]Ĕs′thĕr [h]set [i]Môr′-
de-cāi over the *house of Hā′man.
3 ¶ And [d]Ĕs′thĕr spake yet
again before the king, and fell
down at his feet, and [j]besought[c]
him with tears to put away the
mischief of Hā′man the Ā′găg-
īte, and his device[c] that he had
devised against the [k]Jewș.
4 Then the king held out the
golden [l]sceptre toward Ĕs′thĕr.
So Ĕs′thĕr arose, and stood before the king,
5 And said, [m]If it please the
king, and if I have found favour
in his sight, and the thing *seem*
right before the king, and I *be*
pleasing in his eyes, let it be
written to reverse the letters devised by [c]Hā′man the son of
[n]Hăm-mĕd′a-thȧ the Ā′găg-īte,
which he wrote to destroy the
[k]Jewș which *are* in all the king's
provinces:
6 For how can I endure to see
the evil that shall come unto my
people? or how can I endure to
see the destruction of my kindred?
7 ¶ Then the king [a]Ā-hăș-ū-
ē′rŭs said unto [d]Ĕs′thĕr the
queen and to [f]Môr′de-cāi the
Jew, Behold, I have given Ĕs′-
thĕr the *house of Hā′man, and
him they have [o]hanged upon the
gallows, because he laid his hand
upon the [k]Jewș.
8 Write ye also for the [k]Jewș,
as it liketh[c] you, in the king's
name, and [p]seal *it* with the
king's [g]ring: for the writing
which is written in the king's
name, and sealed with the king's
ring, [q]may no man reverse.
9 Then were the king's [r]scribes
called at that time in the third
[s]month, that *is*, the month Sī′-
van, on the three and twentieth
*day* thereof; and [t]it was written
according to all that [f]Môr′de-cāi
commanded unto the [k]Jewș, and
to the [1]lieutenants, and the deputies and rulers of the [u]provinces
which *are* [v]from [w]Ĭn′dĭ-ȧ unto
[x]Ē-thĭ-ō′pĭ-ȧ, an hundred twenty
and seven provinces, unto every
province according to the writing thereof, and unto every
people after their [y]language,
and to the Jewș according to
their writing, and according to
their language.
10 And he wrote in the king [a]Ā-
hăș-ū-ē′rŭs′ name, and [p]sealed
[t]*it* with the king's [g]ring, and
sent letters by [z]posts[c] on horseback, [2]*and* riders on mules, camels, *and* young dromedaries:
11 [a]Wherein the [b]king granted
the [c]Jewș which *were* in every
city to gather themselves together, and to stand[c] for their life, to
destroy, to slay, and to cause to
perish, all the power of the peo-

v.7–431 BC
See footnote, *Time*, Rev. 10:6.

7
o *Hanging*, Josh. 8:29.

8
p *Seal*, 1 Kin. 21:8.
q *King, decrees of, irrevocable*, 2 Kin. 3:10.

9
r *Scribe*, 1 Kin. 4:3.
s *Month, Sivan*, Ex. 12:2.
t *Proclamation, imperial*, 1 Kin. 15:22.
u *Government, provincial*, Isa. 22:21.
v *Babylon, empire of*, Ezra 5:12.
w Esth. 1:1.
x *Ethiopia*, Isa. 18:1.
y *Language*, Dan. 3:29.
1 R. V. satraps,

10
z *Post*, Job 9:25.
2 R. V. riding on swift steeds that were used in the king's service, bred of the stud:

11
a *Proclamation, imperial*, 1 Kin. 15:22.
b *Ahasuerus*, Esth. 1:1.
c *Jews*, Neh. 4:2.

* **HOUSE**, Neh. 5:3. *Built of stone*, Lev. 14:40–45; Amos 5:11. *Built into city walls*, Josh. 2:15. *How treated for leprosy*, Lev. 14:34–53.
*Used for worship*, Acts 1:13, 14; 12:12; Rom. 16:5; 1 Cor. 16:19; Col. 4:15; Philemon 2.
*As a home, was protected from invasion by creditors*, Deut. 24:10, 11.
*Painted*, Jer. 22:14. *Mural paintings of*, Ezek. 8:10, 12. *Chimneys of*, Hos. 13:3. *Texts of scripture on doorposts of*, Deut. 6:9. *Laws regarding sale of*, Lev. 25:29–33. *Dedicated*, Deut. 20:5; title to Psa. 30.
**Architecture of:** *Foundations of stone*, 1 Kin. 7:9; Ezra 6:3, 4; Jer. 51:26.
*Porches of*, Judg. 3:23; 1 Kin. 7:6, 7. *Courts of*, Esth. 1:5. *Summer apartment of*, Judg. 3:20; Amos 3:15. *Inner chamber of*, 1 Kin. 22:25. *Chambers of*, Gen. 43:30; 2 Sam. 18:33; 1 Kin. 17:19; 2 Kin. 1:2; 4:10; Acts 1:13; 9:37; 20:8. *Guest chamber of*, Mark 14:14. *Pillars of*, Judg. 16:29. *Lattice of*, Judg. 5:28; 2 Kin. 1:2. *Windows of*, Josh. 2:15; Judg. 5:28; 1 Sam. 19:12; Acts 20:9. *Ceiled and plastered*, Dan. 5:5.
**Roofs of, and their uses**, Josh. 2:6; Judg. 16:27; 1 Sam. 9:25; 2 Sam. 11:2; 16:22; Isa. 15:3; Matt. 24:17. *Battlements for, required in Mosaic law*, Deut. 22:8. *Used as place to sleep*, Josh. 2:8. *Prayer on*, Acts 10:9. *Altars on*, 2 Kin. 23:12; Jer. 19:13; 32:29; Zeph. 1:5. *Booths on*, Neh. 8:16.
**Figurative**, Psa. 23:6; 36:8; John 14:2; **2 Cor. 5:1; Eph.** 2:20–22.

v.11–431 BC
See footnote, *Time*, Rev. 10:6.

12
*d Month, Adar,* Ex. 12:2.

14
*e Post,* Job 9:25.
*f Shushan,* Esth. 1:2.
3 R.V. swift steeds that were used in the king's service went out,

15
*g Mordecai,* Esth. 2:5.
*h Colors, symbolical,* Ezek. 16:16.
*i Crown,* Ex. 29:6.
*j Gold,* Ezek. 7:19.
*k Linen,* Ezek. 27:16.

16
*l Joy, instances of,* Psa. 5:11.

17
*m Feasts,* Mark 12:39.

ple and province that would assault them, *both* little ones and
women, and *to take* the spoil[C] of
them for a prey,[C]
12 Upon one day in all the
provinces of king [b]Ā-hăș-ū-ē′-
rŭs, *namely,* upon the thirteenth
*day* of the twelfth [d]month, which
*is* the month Ā′där.
13 The copy of the [a]writing for
a commandment to be given in
every province *was* published
unto all people, and that the
[c]Jews should be ready against
that day to avenge themselves on
their enemies.
14 *So* the [e]posts[C] that rode upon
[3]mules *and* camels went out, being hastened and pressed on[C] by
the king's commandment. And
the [a]decree was given at [f]Shu′-
shan the palace.
15 ¶ And [g]Môr′de-cāi went out
from the presence of the [b]king
in royal apparel of [h]blue[C] and
[h]white, and with a great [i]crown
of [j]gold, and with a garment of
fine [k]linen and [h]purple: and the
city of [f]Shu′shan rejoiced and
was glad.
16 The [c]Jews had light, and
gladness, and [l]joy, and honour.
17 And in every province, and
in every city, whithersoever[C] the
king's [a]commandment and his decree came, the [c]Jews had [l]joy and
gladness, a [m]feast and a good
day. And many of the people of
the land became Jews; for the
fear of the Jews fell upon them.

## CHAPTER 9

*The Jews (the rulers abetting) destroy their enemies. 12 Ahasuerus, at the request of Esther, grants another day of slaughter, and the destruction of Haman's sons. 20 The festival of Purim established.*

v.1–431 BC
See footnote, *Time*, Rev. 10:6.

1
*a Month, Adar,* Ex. 12:2.
*b Ahasuerus,* Esth. 1:1.
*c Proclamation, imperial,* 1 Kin. 15:22.

NOW in the twelfth [a]month,
that *is,* the month Ā′där,
on the thirteenth day of the
same, when the [b]king's [c]com-
mandment and his decree drew
near to be put in execution, in
the day that the enemies of the
[d]Jews hoped to have power over
them, (though it was turned to
the contrary, that the Jews had
rule over them that hated them;)
2 The [d]Jews gathered themselves together in their cities
throughout all the provinces of
the king [b]Ā-hăș-ū-ē′rŭs, to lay
hand on such as sought their
hurt:[C] and no man could withstand them; for the fear of them
fell upon all people.
3 And all the rulers of the
[e]provinces, and the lieutenants,
and the deputies, and officers of
the king, helped the [d]Jews; because the fear of [f]Môr′de-cāi fell
upon them.
4 For [f]Môr′de-cāi *was* great in
the king's house, and his fame
went out throughout all the
provinces: for this man Môr′de-
cāi waxed[C] greater and greater.
5 Thus the [d]Jews [g]smote all
their enemies with the stroke of
the sword, and slaughter, and
destruction, and did what they
would unto those that hated
them.
6 And in [h]Shu′shan the [i]palace
the Jews [g]slew and [j]destroyed
five hundred men.
7 And Pär-shăn′da-thȧ, and
Dăl′phon, and Ăs′pa-thȧ,
8 And Pŏr′a-thȧ, and Ăd-a-
lī′ȧ, and Ȧ-rĭd′a-thȧ,
9 And Pär-măsh′tȧ, and Ȧ-rĭs′-
a-ī, and Ȧ-rĭd′a-ī, and Vȧ-jĕz′a-
thȧ,
10 The ten sons of [k]Hā′man the
son of [l]Hăm-mĕd′a-thȧ, the enemy of the [d]Jews, [g]slew they; but
on the spoil[C] laid they not their
hand.
11 On that day the number of
those that were slain in [h]Shu′-
shan the [i]palace was brought before the king.
12 ¶ And the king said unto
[m]Ĕs′thēr the queen, The [d]Jews
have [j]slain and destroyed five
hundred men in [h]Shu′shan the

v.1–431 BC
See footnote, *Time*, Rev. 10:6.
*d Jews,* Neh. 4:2.

3
*e Government, provincial,* Isa. 22:21.
*f Mordecai,* Esth. 2:5.

5
*g Retaliation, instances of,* Deut. 19:19.

6
*h Shushan,* Esth. 1:2.
*i Palace,* 1 Kin. 21:1.
*j Massacre,* Esth. 3:13.

10
*k Haman,* Esth. 3:1.
*l* Esth. 3:1, 10; 8:5.

12
*m Esther,* Esth. 2:7.

v.12–431 BC
See footnote, *Time*, Rev. 10:6.

*n Petition*, Esth. 5:6.

13
*o Gallows*, Esth. 5:14.

17
*p Annual Feasts, Purim*, Num. 15:3.
*q Joy, instances of*, Psa. 5:11.

19
*r Presents*, Gen. 32:13.

[i]palace, and the ten sons of
[k]Hā′man; what have they done
in the rest of the king's provinces? now what *is* thy [n]peti-
tion? and it shall be granted
thee: or what *is* thy request further? and it shall be done.
13 Then said [m]Ĕs′thēr, If it
please the king, let it be granted
to the [d]Jews which *are* in [h]Shu′-
shan to do to morrow also according unto this day's decree,
and let [k]Hā′man's ten sons be
hanged upon the [o]gallows.
14 And the king commanded it
so to be done: and the decree was
given at [h]Shu′shan; and they
[g]hanged [k]Hā′man's ten sons.
15 For the [d]Jews that *were* in
[h]Shu′shan gathered themselves
together on the fourteenth day
also of the [a]month Ā′där, and
[i]slew three hundred men at
Shu′shan; but on the prey[c] they
laid not their hand.
16 But the other [d]Jews that
*were* in the king's [e]provinces
gathered themselves together,
and stood[c] for their lives, and had
rest from their enemies, and
[i]slew of their foes seventy and
five thousand, but they laid not
their hands on the prey,[c]
17 On the thirteenth day of the
[a]month Ā′där; and on the fourteenth day of the same rested
they, and made it a day of
[p]feasting and [q]gladness.
18 But the [d]Jews that *were* at
[h]Shu′shan assembled together on
the thirteenth *day* thereof, and
on the fourteenth thereof; and
on the fifteenth *day* of the same
they rested, and made it a day of
[p]feasting and [q]gladness.
19 Therefore the [d]Jews of the
villages, that dwelt in the unwalled towns, made the fourteenth day of the [a]month Ā′där
*a day of* gladness and feasting,
and a good day, and of sending
[r]portions[c] one to another.

20 ¶ And [l]Môr′de-cāi wrote
these things, and sent [s]letters
unto all the [d]Jews that *were* in all
the provinces of the king [b]Ȧ-hăs-
ū-ē′rŭs, *both* nigh[c] and far,
21 To stablish[c] *this* among
them, that they should keep the
fourteenth day of the [a]month
Ā′där, and the fifteenth day of
the same, yearly,
22 As the days wherein the
[d]Jews rested from their enemies,
and the [a]month which was turned unto them from sorrow to
[q]joy, and from mourning into a
good day: that they should make
them days of [p]feasting and [q]joy,
and of sending [r]portions[c] one to
another, and [r]gifts to the [t]poor.
23 And the [d]Jews undertook to
do as they had begun, and as
[l]Môr′de-cāi had written unto
them;
24 Because [k]Hā′man the son of
[l]Hăm-mĕd′a-thȧ, the Ā′găg-īte,
the enemy of all the [d]Jews, had
devised[c] against the Jews to destroy them, and had cast Pûr,
that *is*, the [u]lot, to consume[c]
them, and to destroy them;
25 But when [1]*Es′ther* came
before the king, he commanded
by [s]letters that his wicked device,[c] which he devised against
the Jews, [v]should return upon
his own head, and that he and
his sons should be [w]hanged on
the [o]gallows.
26 Wherefore they called these
days [p]Pū′rim after the name of
Pûr. Therefore for all the words
of this letter, and *of that* which
they had seen concerning this
matter, and which had come unto them,
27 The [d]Jews ordained, and
took upon them, and upon their
seed, and upon all such as joined
themselves unto them, so as it
should not fail, that they would
keep [p]these two days according
to their writing, and according

v.20–431 BC
See footnote, *Time*, Rev. 10:6.

20
*s Letters*, Isa. 37:14.

22
*t Poor, kindness to*, Prov. 21:13.

24
*u Lot*, Esth. 3:7.

25
*v Sin, retroactive*, Rom. 5:12.
*w Punishment, death penalty*, Lev. 26:41.
1 R. V. the matter

v.27–431 BC
See footnote, *Time*,
Rev. 10:6.

to their *appointed* time every year;

28 And *that* these days *should be* remembered and kept throughout every generation, every family, every province, and every city; and *that* these days of [p]Pū′rim should not fail from[c] among the [d]Jews̩, nor the memorial of them perish from their seed.

29
*x* Esth. 2:15.

29 Then [m]Ĕs′thēr the queen, the daughter of [x]Ăb-i-hā′il, and [l]Môr′de-cāi the Jew, wrote with all authority, to confirm this second letter of [p]Pū′rim.

30
*y* *Babylon, empire of,* Ezra 5:12.

30 And he sent the [s]letters unto all the Jews̩, to the hundred twenty and seven [e]provinces of the [y]kingdom of [b]Ȧ-hăs̩-ū-ē′rŭs, *with* words of peace and truth,

31 To confirm these days of [p]Pū′rim in their times *appointed*, according as [l]Môr′de-cāi the Jew and [m]Ĕs′thēr the queen had enjoined them, and as they had decreed for themselves and for their seed, the matters of the [z]fastings and their cry.

32 And the decree of [m]Ĕs′thēr confirmed these matters of [p]Pū′rim; and it was written in the book.

v.31–431 BC
See footnote, *Time*,
Rev. 10:6.

31
*z* *Fasting,* Zech. 8:19.

## CHAPTER 10

*The greatness of Ahasuerus, 3 and of Mordecai.*

AND the king [a]Ȧ-hăs̩-ū-ē′rŭs laid a [b]tribute upon the land, and *upon* the isles of the sea.

2 And all the acts of his power and of his might, and the declaration of the greatness of [c]Môr′de-cāi, whereunto the king advanced [d]him, *are* they not written in the [e]book of the chronicles of the kings of [f]Mē′dĭ-ȧ and [g]Pēr′s̩iȧ?

3 For [c,h]Môr′de-cāi the Jew *was* [d]next unto king [a]Ȧ-hăs̩-ū-ē′rŭs, and great among the [i]Jews̩, and accepted of the multitude of his brethren, seeking the [1]wealth[c] of his people, and speaking [j]peace to all his seed.

v.1–431 BC
See footnote, *Time*,
Rev. 10:6.

1
*a* *Ahasuerus,* Esth. 1:1.
*b* *Tax,* Neh. 10:32.

2
*c* *Mordecai,* Esth. 2:5.
*d* *Captive, advanced,* 1 Sam. 30:3.
*e* *Book,* Num. 5:23.
*f* *Medes,* Dan. 5:28.
*g* *Persia,* Esth. 1:3.

3
*h* *Minister,* 2 Chr. 9:4.
*i* *Jews,* Neh. 4:2.
*j* *Peace,* Jer. 29:7.
1 R. V. good

# THE BOOK OF JOB

1
*a* Jer. 25:20; Lam. 4:21.
*b* *Perfection, ascribed to Job,* Heb. 6:1.
*c* *Righteousness,* Psa. 15:2.
*d* *Integrity,* Job 2:3.
*e* *Fear of God,* Acts 9:31.
*f* *Sin, repugnant to the righteous,* Rom. 5:12.

2
*g* *Children,* Mark 10:14.

## CHAPTER 1

*The piety and prosperity of Job. 6 Satan obtains leave to afflict him. 13 Job's loss of his substance, 18 and of his children. 20 His patience in his afflictions.*

THERE was a man in the land of [a]Ŭz, whose name *was* *Jōb; and that man was [b]perfect[c] and [c,d]upright, and one that [e]feared God, and [f]eschewed[c] evil.[Q]

2 And there were born unto him seven [g]sons and three [g]daughters.

3 His substance[c] also was seven thousand sheep, and three thousand camels, and five hundred yoke of oxen, and five hundred she ăs̈ses, and a very great household; so that this man was the greatest of all the men of the east.

4 And his sons went and [h]feasted *in their* houses, every one his day; and sent and called for their three sisters to eat and to drink with them.

5 And it was so, when the days of *their* [h]feasting were gone about, that *Jōb [i]sent and [j]sanctified them, and rose up early in the morning, and [k,l]offered [m]burnt offerings *according* to the number of them all: for Jōb said, It may be that my sons

4
*h* *Feasts,* Mark 12:39.

5
*i* *Parents, affection of, exemplified,* 2 Cor. 12:14.
*j* *Sanctification,* 1 Pet. 1:2.
*k* *Intercession, of man with God,* Jer. 27:18.
*l* *Family Worship,* 1 Sam. 1:19.
*m* *Offerings, burnt,* Lev. 6:17.

* **JOB** (*presented*). *Dwelt in Uz,* Job 1:1. *Righteous,* Job **1**:1, 5, 8; 2:3; Ezek. 14:14, 20. *Rich,* Job 1:3. *Trial of, by affliction from Satan,* Job 1:13–19; 2:7–10. *Fortitude of,* Job **1**:20–22; 2:10; Jas. 5:11. *Visited by Eliphaz, Bildad, and Zophar, as comforters,* Job 2:11–13. *Complaints of, and the replies of his three friends to,* Job chapters 3–37. *God replies to the complaints of,* Job chapters 38–41. *Submission of, to God,* Job 40:3–5; 42:1–6. *God reproves the three friends,* Job 42:7–9. *Job intercedes for his friends,* Job 42:9. *Later prosperity of,* Job 42:10–16. *Death of,* Job 42:16,17.

*n Blasphemy,* 2 Sam. 12:14.
*o Perseverance,* Eph. 6:18.
1 R. V. renounced

6
*p Angel,* Heb. 1:13.
*q Satan,* Matt. 4:10.
2 *That is,* the Adversary,

9
*r False Accusation,* 2 Tim. 3:3.
*s Motive, impugned,* Psa. 106:8.
*t Innuendo,* Prov. 6:13.

10
*u God, providence of,* Gen. 2:2.
*v Prosperity, from God,* Eccl. 7:14.
*w Temporal Blessings, from God,* Psa. 103:2.

11
*x Blasphemy* 2 Sam. 12:14.
3 R. V. renounce

12
*y God, providence of, mysterious,* Gen. 2:2.

13
*z Wine,* Prov. 23:31.

14
*a Plow,* Deut. 22:10.
*b Ass, domesticated,* 2 Chr. 28:15.

15
*c Sabeans,* Isa. 45:14.
*d Robbers,* Hos. 6:9.
*e Servant,* Jer. 2:14.

have sinned, and [1,n]cursed[C] God
in their hearts. [o]Thus did Jōb
continually.
6 ¶ Now there was a day when
the [p]sons of God came to present themselves before the
LORD, and [2,q]Sā′tan[C] came also
among them.
7 And the LORD said unto
[q]Sā′tan, Whence[C] comest thou?
Then Sā′tan answered the
LORD, and said, From going to
and fro in the earth, and from
walking up and down in it.
8 And the LORD said unto [q]Sā′-
tan, Hast thou considered my
servant *Jōb, that *there is* none
like him in the earth, a [b]perfect[C]
and an [c,d]upright man, one that
[e]feareth God, and [f]escheweth[C]
evil?[Q]
9[Q] Then [q]Sā′tan answered the
LORD, and said, [r,s,t]Doth *Jōb
[e]fear God for nought[C]?
10 Hast not thou [u]made an
hedge about *him, and about
his house, and about all that he
hath on every side? thou hast
[v]blessed the work of his hands,
and his [w]substance[C] is increased
in the land.[S]
11 [t]But put forth thine hand
now, and touch all that he hath,
and *he will [3,x]curse thee to thy
face.[Q]
12 And the LORD said unto
[q]Sā′tan, Behold, [y]all that he
hath *is* in thy power; only upon
himself put not forth thine hand.
So Sā′tan went forth from the
presence of the LORD.[S]
13 ¶ And there was a day when
*his sons and his daughters *were*
[h]eating and drinking [z]wine in
their eldest brother's house:
14 And there came a messenger
unto *Jōb, and said, The oxen
were [a]plowing, and the [b]asses
feeding beside them:
15 And the [c,d]Sā-bē′ans fell *upon them,* and took them away;
yea, they have slain the [e]servants with the edge of the [f]sword;
and I only am escaped alone to
tell thee.
16 While he *was* yet speaking,
there came also another, and
said, The [g]fire of God is fallen
from heaven, and hath burned
up the [h]sheep, and the [e]servants,
and consumed[C] them; and I only
am escaped alone to tell thee.
17 While he *was* yet speaking,
there came also another, and
said, The [i]Chăl-dē′ans [j]made
out three bands, and fell[C] upon
the [k]camels, and have carried
them away, yea, and slain the
servants with the edge of the
[f]sword; and I only am escaped
alone to tell thee.
18 While he *was* yet speaking,
there came also another, and
said, Thy sons and thy daughters *were* [l]eating and drinking
wine in their eldest brother's
house:
19 And, behold, there came a
great [m,n]wind from the wilderness, and smote[C] the four corners
of the house, and it fell upon
the young men, and they are
dead; and I only am escaped
alone to tell thee.
20 Then *Jōb arose, and
[o,p]rent[C] his [q]mantle[C], and [r]shaved
his head, and fell down upon the
ground, and [s]worshipped,[Q]
21 And said, [t]Naked came I out
of my mother's womb, and naked shall I return thither[C]: the
LORD [u]gave, and the LORD
[v,w]hath taken away; [x,y,z]blessed
be the name of the LORD.[Q]
22 In all this *Jōb [a]sinned not,
nor charged[C] God [4]foolishly.

## CHAPTER 2

*Satan obtains further leave to afflict Job. 7 He smites him with sore boils. 9 Job's wife moves him to curse God; he rebukes her. 11 His three friends condole with him.*

AGAIN there was a day
when the [a]sons of God
came to present themselves be-

*f Sword,* 1 Chr. 21:5.

16
*g Lightning,* Job 28:26.
*h Sheep,* Deut. 32:14.

17
*i Chaldeans,* Dan. 1:4.
*j Armies, tactics of,* Deut. 11:4.
*k Camel,* 1 Sam. 30:17.

18
*l Feasts,* Mark 12:39.

19
*m Wind,* Job 37:17.
*n Meteorology,* Matt. 16:2.

20
*o Rending of Garments,* 2 Chr. 34:27.
*p Mourning,* Lam. 2:5.
*q Mantle,* Ezra 9:3.
*r Shaving,* Ezek. 44:20.
*s Worship,* Gen. 22:5.

21
*t* 1 Tim. 6:7.
*u Children, the gift of God,* Mark 10:14.
*v Adversity, dispensation from God,* Psa. 10:6.
*w Death,* Num. 23:10.
*x Praise,* Psa. 150:1.
*y Faith,* Mark 11:22.
*z Resignation, exemplified,* Job 5:17.

22
*a Sinlessness,* 1 John 5:18.
4 R. V. with foolishness.

1
*a Angel,* Heb. 1:13.

fore the LORD, and [b]Sā′tan
came also among them to present himself before the LORD.
2 And the LORD said unto
[b]Sā′tan, From whence[C] comest
thou? And Sā′tan answered the
LORD, and said, From going to
and fro in the earth, and from
walking up and down in it.
3 And the LORD said unto
[b]Sā′tan, Hast thou considered
my servant [c]Jōb, that *there is*
none like him in the earth, a
[d]perfect[C] and an [e]upright man,
one that [f]feareth God, and [g]es-
cheweth[C] evil? and still he holdeth fast his *integrity, although
thou movedst me against him,
to destroy him without cause.[Q]
4 And Sā′tan answered the
LORD, and said, [h,i]Skin for
skin, yea, all that a man hath
will he give for his life.
5 [j]But put forth thine hand
now, and touch his bone and his
flesh, and he will [1,k]curse thee
to thy face.
6 And the LORD [l]said unto
[b]Sā′tan, Behold, he *is* in thine
hand; but save his life.[S Q]
7 ¶ So went [b]Sā′tan forth from
the presence of the LORD, and
smote [c]Jōb with sore[C] [m,n]boils
from the sole of his foot unto his
crown.
8 And he took him a [o]potsherd
to scrape himself withal[C]; and he
sat down among the [p]ashes.
9 ¶ Then [q]said his [r]wife unto
him, Dost thou still retain thine
*integrity? [1,k]curse[C] God, and
die.
10 But he said unto her, Thou
[s]speakest as one of the foolish
women speaketh. [t]What? shall
we receive good at the hand of
God, and shall we not receive
[u]evil? In all this[S] did not [c]Jōb
sin with his lips.
11 ¶ Now when [c]Jŏb's three
[v]friends heard of all this evil that
was come upon him, [w]they came
every one from his own place;
[x]Ĕl′i-phăz the Tē′man-īte, and
[y]Bĭl′dăd the Shu′hīte, and [z]Zō′-
phar the Nā′a-math-īte: for they
had made an appointment together to come to [a]mourn with
him and to [b]comfort him.
12 And [c]when they lifted up
their eyes afar off, and knew[C] him
not, [d]they [a]lifted up their voice,
and [e]wept; and they [f]rent[C] every
one his [g]mantle, and sprinkled
[h]dust upon their heads toward
heaven.[Q]
13 So [c]they [d]sat down [a]with
him upon the ground seven days
and seven nights, and none
spake a word unto him: for they
saw that *his* grief was very great.

## CHAPTER 3

*Job's complaint; he curses the day of his birth; 11 wishes he had died from the womb; 13 then would he have been at rest; 20 and asks why life is given to the miserable.*

AFTER this opened [a]Jōb his
mouth, and [b,c,d]cursed
his day.
2 And Jōb spake, and [c,d]said,
3 [c,d]Let the [e]day perish wherein
I was born, and the night *in
which* it was said, There is a
man[C] child conceived.
4 [c,d]Let that [e]day be darkness;
let not God regard it from above,

b *Satan*, Matt. 4:10.

3
c *Job*, Job 1:1.
d *Perfection*, Heb. 6:1.
e *Righteousness*, Psa. 15:2.
f *Fear of God*, Acts 9:31.
g *Sin, repugnant to the righteous*, Rom. 5:12.

4
h *False Accusation*, 2 Tim. 3:3.
i *Motive, impugned*, Psa. 106:8.

5
j *Innuendo*, Prov. 6:13.
k *Blasphemy*, 2 Sam. 12:14.
1 R. V. renounce

6
l *God, providence of, mysterious*, Gen. 2:2.

7
m *Boil*, Ex. 9:9.
n *Afflictions, from Satan*, Psa. 34:19.

8
o Isa. 45:9.
p *Ashes*, Num. 19:9.

9
q *Temptation, leading into*, Luke 11:4.
r *Women, wicked*, Prov. 31:10.

10
s *Speech, evil*, Col. 4:6.
t *Resignation, exemplified*, Job 5:17.
u *Adversity, resignation in*, Psa. 10:6.

11
v *Friends*, Ex. 33:11.
w *Friendship, instances of*, Prov. 22:24.
x Job 4; 5; 22; 42: 7–9.
y Job 8; 18; 25; 42: 7–9.
z Job 11; 20; 42: 7–9.

a *Sympathy*, 1 Pet. 3:8.
b *Condolence, instances of*, 2 Sam. 10:2.

12
c *Friends*, Ex. 33:11.
d *Friendship, instances of*, Prov. 22:24.
e *Mourning*, Lam. 2:5.
f *Rending of Garments*, 2 Chr. 34:27.
g *Mantle*, Ezra 9:3.
h *Dust*, Eccl. 3:20.

1
a *Job*, Job 1:1.
b *Afflictions, despondency in*, vs. 1–26; Psa. 34:19.
c *Murmuring, instances of*, vs. 1–26; Num. 14:2.
d *Presumption, instances of*, vs. 1–10; Psa. 19:13.

3
e *Birthday*, Gen. 40:20.

* **INTEGRITY**, Ex. 18:21; Luke 16:10; 2 Cor. 8:21.
*Enjoined*, Deut. 16:19, 20; Prov. 4:25–27; Isa. 56:1; Mic. 6:8; Zech. 7:9; Luke 3:13, 14; 6:31; 11:42; Eph. 6:6; Phil. 4:8; Col. 3:22, 23; 1 Tim. 3:9; Tit. 1:7, 8. *Rewards of*, 2 Sam. 12:21; Psa. 15:1–5; 18:20; 24:3–5; Prov. 10:9; 20:7; 28:20; Isa. 33:15, 16; Jer. 7:5, 7; Ezek. 18:5, 7–9. *Proverbs concerning*, Prov. 11:3, 5; 20:7; 21:3; 28:6.
**Instances of:** *Pharaoh, when he learned that Sarah was Abraham's wife*, Gen. 12:18–20. *Abimelech, when warned of God that the woman he had taken into his household was Isaac's wife*, Gen. 26:9–11. *Joseph, in resisting Potiphar's wife*, Gen. 39:8–12; *in his innocence of the charge on which he was cast into the dungeon*, Gen. 40:15. *Moses, in taking nothing from the Israelites in consideration of his services*, Num. 16:15. *Samuel, in exacting nothing from the people on account of services*, 1 Sam. 12:4, 5. *Workmen, who repaired the temple*, I Kin. 12:15; 22:7. *Priests, who received the offerings of gold and other gifts for the renewing of the temple under Ezra*, Ezra 2:24–30, 33, 34. *Nehemiah, reforming the civil service, and receiving no compensation for his own services*, Neh. 5:14–19. *Job*, Job 1:8; 2:3; 10:7; 13:15; 16:17; 27:4–6; 29:14; 31:1–40. *The psalmist*, Psa. 7:3–5, 8; 17:3; 26:1–3; 119:121. *The Rechabites, in keeping the Nazirite vows*, Jer. 35:12–19. *Daniel, in maintaining uprightness of character*, Dan. 6:4. *The three Hebrews, who refused to worship Nebuchadnezzar's idol*, Dan. 3:16–21, 28. *Joseph, the husband of Mary, in not jealously accusing her of immorality*, Matt. 1:19. *Zacchæus, in the administration of his wealth*, Luke 19:8. *Nathanael, in whom was no guile*, John 1:47. *Joseph, a counselor*. Luke 23:50, 51. *Peter, when offered money by Simon Magus*, Acts 8:18–23. *Paul and Barnabas*, Acts 14:12–15. *Paul*, Acts 23:1; 24:16; Rom. 9:1; 2 Cor. 4:2; 5:11; 7:2; 1 Thess. 2:4.

neither let the light shine upon
it.[T]
5 Let darkness and the shadow
of death [1]stain [e]it; let a cloud
dwell upon it; let the blackness
of the day terrify it.
6 *As for* that night, let darkness
seize upon it; let it not be joined
unto the days of the year, let it
not come into the number of the
months.
7 Lo, let that night be [2]solitary,
let no joyful voice come therein.
8 Let them curse it that curse
the day, who are ready to [3]raise
up their mourning.
9 Let the [f]stars of the twilight
thereof be dark; let it look for
light, but *have* none; neither let
it [4]see the dawning of the day:
10 Because it shut not up the
doors of my *mother's* womb, nor
hid sorrow from mine eyes.
11 [c,d]Why died I not from the
womb? *why* did I *not* give up
the ghost[G] when I came out of
the belly[G]?
12 [c,d]Why did the knees [5]pre-
vent me? or why the breasts that
I should suck?
13 For now should I have lain
still and been quiet, I should
have [g]slept: then had I been at
rest,
14 With [h]kings and [i]counsel-
lors of the earth, which built
[6]desolate places for themselves;
15 Or with princes that had
[j]gold, who filled their houses
with [k]silver:
16 Or as an hidden untimely[G]
birth I had not been; as infants
*which* never saw light.
17 [g]There the wicked cease
*from* troubling; and there the
weary be at rest.
18 [g]*There* the prisoners rest together; they hear not the voice of
the [7]oppressor.
19 The small and great are
[g]there; and the servant *is* free
from his master.
20 Wherefore is light given to
him that is in misery, and life
unto the bitter *in* soul;
21 Which long for [l]death, but
it *cometh* not; and dig for it more
than for hid treasures;[Q]
22 Which rejoice exceedingly,
*and* are glad, when they can find
the [l,m]grave?
23 [c,d]*Why is light given* to a
man whose way is hid, and
whom God hath hedged in?[T]
24 For my sighing cometh before I eat, and my roarings[G] are
poured out like the waters.
25 For the thing which I
[8]greatly feared is come upon
me, and that which I was afraid
of is come unto me.
26 I [9]was not in safety, neither
had I rest, neither was I quiet;
yet trouble came.

## CHAPTER 4

*The speech of Eliphaz; he calls in question Job's uprightness; 7 and teaches that the judgments of God fall only on the wicked. 12 His night vision.*

THEN [a]Ĕl′ĭ-phăz the Tē′man-
ite answered and said,
2 *If* we assay[G] to commune[G] with
thee, wilt thou be grieved? but
who can withhold himself from
speaking?
3 [b,c]Behold, thou hast instructed many, and thou hast
strengthened the weak hands.
4 [b,c]Thy words have upholden
him that was falling, and thou
hast strengthened the feeble
knees.
5 But [d]now [e]it is come upon
thee, and thou [f]faintest; it toucheth thee, and thou art troubled.
6 [d]*Is* not [1]*this* thy fear, thy confidence, thy hope, and the uprightness of thy ways?
7 [b,c]Remember, I pray thee,
who *ever* perished, being innocent? or where were the [g]right-
eous cut off?[S]
8 Even as I have seen, they that
plow iniquity, and [h]sow wickedness, [i,j]reap the same.

**5**
1 R. V. claim it for their own;

**7**
2 R. V. barren;

**8**
3 R. V. rouse up leviathan.

**9**
*f* *Stars*, Judg. 5:20.
4 R. V. behold the eyelids of the morning:

**12**
5 R. V. receive me?

**13**
*g* *Death*, Num. 23:10.

**14**
*h* *King*, 2 Kin. 3:10.
*i* *Counselor*, Prov. 11:14.
6 R. V. up waste places

**15**
*j* *Gold*, Ezek. 7:19.
*k* *Silver*, 1 Chr. 28:14.

**18**
7 R. V. taskmaster.

**21**
*l* *Death, desired*, Num. 23:10.

**22**
*m* *Grave*, 2 Sam. 3:32.

**25**
8 R. V. fear cometh upon me, And that which I am afraid of cometh unto me.

**26**
9 R. V. am not at ease, neither am I quiet, neither have I rest: But trouble cometh.

**1**
*a* Job 2:11; 5; 22; 42:7–9.

**3**
*b* *Condolence*, 2 Sam. 10:2.
*c* *Sympathy*, Jas. 1:27.

**5**
*d* *Reproof, faithfulness in*, Prov. 17:10.
*e* *Adversity, despondency in*, Psa. 10:6.
*f* *Despondency*, Eccl. 2:20.

**6**
1 R. V. thy fear of God thy confidence, And thy hope the integrity of thy ways?

**7**
*g* *Righteous, promises to, implied*, Psa. 64:10.

**8**
*h* *Sower, figurative*, Matt. 13:3.
*i* *Sin, fruits of*, Rom. 5:12.
*j* *Wicked, punishment of*, Psa 73:3.

9
2 R. V. breath
k *Blasting, figurative.* 1 Kin. 8:37.
l *Anger of God,* 2 Kin. 13:3.
3 R. V. blast
m *Breath, figurative,* Gen 7:15.
4 R. V. anger

10
n *Lion,* Mic. 5:8.

13
o *Vision,* vs. 12–16; Acts 9:10.

17
p *God, justice of,* Gen. 2:2.
q *God, holiness of,* Gen. 2:2.

18
r *Angel,* Heb. 1:13.

19
s *Body,* 1 Cor. 6:19.
t *Clay, figurative,* Job 33:6.
u *Ground, man made from,* Gen. 3:17.
v *Life, brevity and uncertainty of,* Eccl. 8:15.

21
5 R. V. Is not their tent-cord plucked up within them?

9 By the [2,k,l]blast of God they perish, and by the [3,m]breath of his [4]nostrils are they consumed.[Q]

10 The roaring[G] of the [n]lion, and the voice of the fierce lion, and the teeth of the young lions, are broken.

11 The old lion perisheth for lack of prey, and the stout[G] lion's whelps are scattered abroad.

12 Now a thing was secretly brought to me, and mine ear received a little thereof.

13 In thoughts from the [o]visions of the night, when deep sleep falleth on men,

14 Fear came upon me, and trembling, which made all my bones to shake.

15 Then a spirit passed before my face; the hair of my flesh stood up:

16 It stood still, but I could not discern the form thereof: an image *was* before mine eyes, *there was* silence, and I heard a voice, *saying,*

17 Shall mortal *man be more just than [p]God? shall a man be more [q]pure than his maker?[S]

18 Behold, he put no trust in his servants; and his [r]angels he charged[C] with folly:

19 How much less *in* them that dwell in [s]houses of [t]clay, whose foundation *is* in the [u]dust, *which* are [v]crushed before the †moth?[Q]

20 [v]They are destroyed from morning to evening: they perish for ever without any regarding *it.*

21 [5]Doth not their excellency *which is* in them go away? they [v]die, even without wisdom.

## CHAPTER 5

*Eliphaz teaches that evil awaits the wicked; 6 that afflictions are from God; 8 urges Job to commit his cause to God; 17 and shows the happy fruits of God's correction.*

CALL now, if there be any that will answer thee; and to which of the [1]saints[C] wilt thou turn?

2 For [a]wrath [b]killeth the foolish man, and [c]envy slayeth the silly[G] one.

3 [d]I have seen the [e]foolish taking root: but suddenly I cursed his habitation.

4 His [f]children are far from safety, and they are crushed in the gate, neither *is there* any to deliver *them.*

5 Whose harvest the hungry eateth up, and taketh it even out of the thorns, and the [2]robber swalloweth up their substance.[C]

6 Although [g]affliction cometh not forth of the dust, neither doth trouble spring out of the ground;

7 Yet man is born unto trouble, as the sparks fly upward.

8 [3,h]I would seek unto God, and unto God would I commit my[S] cause:

9 [i,j]Which [k]doeth great things and unsearchable; marvellous things without number:

10 Who giveth [l]rain upon the earth, and sendeth waters upon the fields:

11 [m]To set up on high those that be low; that those which mourn may be exalted to safety.[Q]

12 He [4,n]disappointeth the devices of the crafty, so that their hands cannot perform *their* enterprise.[G]

13 [o]He taketh the [p]wise in their

1
1 R. V. holy ones

2
a *Anger,* Psa. 37:8.
b *Sin, fruits of,* Rom. 5:12.
c *Envy,* v. 3; Prov. 14:30.

3
d Job 2:11; 4; 22; 42.7–9.
e *Wicked, prosperity of,* Psa. 73:3.

4
f *Children, involved in guilt of parents,* Mark 10:14.

5
2 R. V. snare gapeth for

6
g *Adversity,* Psa. 10:6.

8
h *Faith, in adversity,* Mark 11:22.
3 R. V. But as for me, I would seek unto God,

9
i *Philosophy,* vs. 9–20; Col. 2:8.
j *God, dissertations on,* vs. 9–20; Gen. 2:2.
k *God, power of,* Gen. 2:2.

10
l *Temporal Blessings, from God,* Psa. 103:2.

11
m *Humility, rewards of,* Prov. 22:4.

12
n *God, providence of,* Gen. 2:2.
4 R. V. frustrateth

13
o 1 Cor. 3:19.
p *Wisdom, worldly,* Prov. 2.2.

* **MAN.** *Created,* Gen. 1:26, 27; 2:7; 5:1, 2; Deut. 4:32; Job 4:17; 10:2, 3, 8, 9; 31:15; 33:4; 34:19; 35:10; 36:3; Psa. 100:3; 119:73; 138:8; 139:14, 15; Eccl. 7:29; Isa. 17:7; 42:5; 45:12; 64:8; Jer. 27:5; Zech. 12:1; Mal. 2:10; Matt. 19.4; Mark 10:6. *Created, in the image of God,* Gen. 1:26, 27; 9:6; 1 Cor. 11:7; Jas. 3:9; *a little lower, than the angels,* Heb. 2:7, 8; *than God* (R. V.), Psa. 8:5.

*Design of the creation of, to have dominion over all the animate creation,* Psa. 8:6–8; *for the glory of God,* Isa. 43:7.

*A spirit,* Job 14:10; 32:8; Psa. 31:5; Prov. 20:27; Isa. 26:9; Zech. 12:1; Matt. 4:4; 10:28; 26:41; Acts 7:59; Rom. 1:9; 2:29; 7:14–25; 1 Cor. 2:11; 7:34; 14:14; 2 Cor. 4:6, 7, 16; Eph. 3:16; 1 Thess. 5:23; Heb. 4:12; Jas. 2:26. *Mortal,* Job 4:17; Eccl. 2:14, 15; 3:20; 1 Cor. 15:21, 22; Heb. 9:27.

*All men equal,* Job 21:26; Prov. 22:2; Matt. 23:8–11; Acts 10:28, 34, 35; 17:26; *under the gospel,* Gal. 3:28.

*Dominion of,* Gen. 1:26, 28; 2:19, 20; 9:2, 3; Psa. 8:6–8; Jer. 27:6; 28:14; Heb. 2:7, 8; Jas. 3:7. *Insignificance of,* Gen. 6:3; 18:27; Job 4:18, 19; 7:17; 15:14; 22:2–5; 25:4–6; 35:2–8; Psa. 8:3, 4; 78:39; 144:3, 4. *Above other creatures,* Matt. 10:31; 12:12.

† **MOTH.** *An insect,* Job 4:19; 27:18; Psa. 39:11. *Destructive of garments,* Job 13:28, Isa. 50:9; 51:8; Hos. 5:12. **Figurative,** Matt. 6:19, 20; Jas. 5:2.

14
*q Spiritual Blindness*, 2 Cor. 4:4.
15
*r God, preserver*, Gen. 2:2.
*s Poor, God's care of*, v. 16; Prov. 21:13.
5 R. V. from the sword of their mouth, even the needy from the hand
17
*t Righteous, happiness of*, vs. 17–27; Psa. 64:10.
*u Divine Chastisement a blessing*, Job 33:19.
*v Adversity, resignation in*, Psa. 10:6.
19
*w Promise, to the righteous*, vs. 19–26; 2 Cor. 1:20.
20
*x Famine, righteous delivered from*, 2 Kin. 8:1.
*y War*, Judg. 3:2.
21
*z Scoffing*, Hab. 1:10.

22
*a Righteous, promises to*, Psa. 64:10.
*b Famine*, 2 Kin. 8:1.
23
*c Peace*, Jer. 29:7.
24
6 R. V. tent is in peace;
7 R. V. fold, and shalt miss nothing.
25
*d Children, promised to the righteous*, Mark 10.14.
26
*Longevity*, Psa. 91.16.

own craftiness: and the counsel of
the froward[c] is carried headlong.[Q]
14 They meet with [q]darkness in
the daytime, and grope in the
noonday as in the night.
15 But he [r]saveth [5]the [s]poor
from the sword, from their
mouth, and from the hand of
the mighty.
16 So the poor hath hope, and
iniquity stoppeth her mouth.
17 Behold, [t]happy *is* the man
whom God [u]correcteth: therefore *·[v]despise not thou the
chastening of the Almighty:
18 For he [n]maketh sore, and
bindeth up: he [n]woundeth, and
his hands make whole.
19 [w]He shall deliver thee in six
troubles: yea, in seven there shall
no evil touch thee.
20 [w]In [x]famine he shall redeem
thee from death: and in [y]war
from the power of the sword.
21 [w]Thou shalt be hid from the
[z]scourge of the tongue: neither
shalt thou be afraid of destruction when it cometh.
22 [a]At destruction and [b]famine
thou shalt laugh: neither shalt
thou be afraid of the beasts of
the earth.
23 For thou shalt be in league
with the stones of the field: and
the beasts of the field shall be at
[c]peace with thee.
24 And [a]thou shalt know that
thy [6]tabernacle *shall be* in peace;
and thou shalt visit thy [7]habita-
tion, and shalt not sin.
25 Thou shalt know also that
thy [d]seed *shall be* great, and
thine offspring as the grass of the
earth.
26 [a]Thou shalt come to *thy*
grave in a [e]full age, like as a
shock of corn[c] cometh in in his
season.
27 Lo this, we have searched it,
so it *is*; hear it, and [f]know thou
*it* for thy good.[s]

## CHAPTER 6

*Job's answer to Eliphaz; he justifies his complaints; 8 longs for death; 14 reproves his friends for their unkindness; 24 and urges them to consider his case.*

BUT [a]Jōb answered and
[b]said,
2 [b]Oh that my grief were
throughly[c] weighed, and my
[c]calamity laid in the [d]balances[G]
together!
3 [b]For now it would be heavier
than the sand of the sea: therefore [1]my words are swallowed
up.
4 [b]For the [e,f]arrows of the Almighty *are* within me, the poison
whereof [2]drinketh up my spirit:
the terrors of God do set themselves in array[G] against me.
5 Doth the wild [g]ass bray when
he hath grass? or loweth the ox
over his fodder?
6 Can that which is unsavoury[G]
be eaten without [h]salt? or is
there *any* taste in the white of an
egg?
7 The things *that* my soul refused to touch *are* as [3]my sorrowful meat.
8 [b]Oh that I might have my request; and that God would grant
*me* the [i]thing that I long for!
9 Even that it would please
God to [i]destroy me; that he
would let loose his hand, and
cut me off!
10 Then should I yet have comfort; [4]yea, I would harden myself in sorrow: let him not spare;
for I have not concealed the
words of the [j]Holy One.[S]
11 [b,k]What *is* my strength, that
I should hope? and what *is* mine
end, that I should [5]prolong my
life?

27
*f Wisdom, spiritual*, Prov. 2:2
1
*a Job*, Job 1:1.
*b Murmuring, instances of*, vs. 1–30; Num. 14:2.
2
*c Afflictions*, Psa. 34:19.
*d Balances, figurative*, Prov. 11:1.
3
1 R. V. have my words been rash.
4
*e Arrow, figurative*, 1 Sam. 20:20.
*f Afflictions, from God*, Psa. 34:19.
2 R. V. my spirit drinketh up:
5
*g Ass, wild*, 2 Chr. 28:15.
6
*h Salt*, 2 Kin. 2:20.
7
3 Am. R. V. loathsome food to me.
8
*i Death, desired*, Num. 23:10.
10
*i God, holiness of*, Gen. 2:2.
4 Am. R. V. Yea, let me exult in pain that spareth not, That I have not denied the words
11
*k Despondency*, Eccl. 2:20.
5 R. V. be patient?

* **RESIGNATION.** **Enjoined,** Rom. 12.12; 1 Pet. 4:12, 13, 19. *Under chastisements*, Job 5:17; Prov. 3:11; Lam. 3:39; Mic. 6:9; 1 Thess. 3:3; Heb. 12:5, 9. *Under bereavement*, 1 Thess. 4:13–18.
**Exemplified:** *By Aaron*, Lev. 10:1–3. *By David*, 2 Sam. 12:23. *By the Shunammite*, 2 Kin. 4:26. *By Hezekiah*, 2 Kin. 20:19. *By Nehemiah*, Neh. 9:33. *By Esther*, Esth. 4:16. *By Job*, Job 1:13–22. *By Jesus*, Matt. 26:39; Mark 14:36; Luke 22:42; John 18:11. *By Stephen*, Acts 7:59, 60. *By Paul*, Rom. 5:3–5; 2 Cor. 6:4–10; 7:4; Phil. 1:20–24, 2 Tim. 4:6. *By Paul and Silas*, Acts 16:25. *By Hebrew Christians*, Heb. 10:34.

**13**
6 R. V. Is it not that I have no help in me, And that effectual working is driven quite from me?

**14**
*l* *Afflicted, sympathy with,* Job 34:28.
*m* *Pity, enjoined,* Job 19:21.
*n* *Sympathy, enjoined,* Jas. 1:27.
*o* *Friendship,* Prov. 22:24.
7 R. V. ready to faint kindness

**15**
*p* *Friends, false,* Ex. 33:11.
*q* *Deception, instances of,* Josh. 9:4.

**16**
*r* Job 38:29; Psa. 147:17.
*s* *Snow,* Jer. 18:14.

**18**
8 R. V. caravans that travel by the way of them turn aside;
9 R.V. up into the waste, and perish.

**19**
*t* Isa. 21:14; Jer. 25:23.
*u* *Sheba,* 1 Kin. 10:1.
10 R. V. caravans

**21**
11 R. V. a terror, and are afraid.

**22**
*v* *Sarcasm,* Judg. 10:14.

**23**
12 R. V. oppressors?

**25**
*w* *Words,* Luke 4:22.

**27**
*x* *Orphan,* Lam. 5:3.
13 R. V. would cast lots upon the fatherless, and make merchandise of your friend.

**28**
14 R. V. pleased to look upon me; for surely I shall not lie to your face.

12 *Is* my strength the strength of stones? or *is* my flesh of brass?

13 [6,k]*Is* not my help in me? and is wisdom driven quite from me?

14 To [l]him that is [7]afflicted [m,n]pity *should be shewed* from his [o]friend; but he forsaketh the fear of the Almighty.

15 My [p]brethren have [q]dealt deceitfully as a brook, *and* as the stream of brooks they pass away;

16 Which are blackish by reason of the [r]ice, *and* wherein the [s]snow is hid:

17 What time they wax warm, they vanish: when it is hot, they are consumed out of their place.

18 The [8]paths of their way are turned aside; they go [9]to nothing, and perish.

19 The [10]troops of [t]Tē′mȧ looked, the companies of [u]Shē′bȧ waited for them.

20 They were confounded because they had hoped; they came thither, and were ashamed.

21 For now [p]ye are nothing; ye see [11]*my* casting down, and are afraid.

22 [v]Did I say, Bring unto me? or, Give a reward for me of your substance?

23 [v]Or, Deliver me from the enemy's hand? or, Redeem me from the hand of the [12]mighty?

24 Teach me, and I will hold my tongue: and cause me to understand wherein I have erred.

25 How forcible are right [w]words! but what doth your arguing reprove?

26 Do ye imagine to reprove [w]words, and the speeches of one that is desperate, *which are* as wind?

27 Yea, ye [13]overwhelm the [x]fatherless, and ye dig *a pit* for your friend.

28 Now therefore be [14]content, look upon me; for *it is* evident unto you if I lie.

29 Return, I pray you, let [15]it not be iniquity; yea, return again, my righteousness *is* in it.

30 Is there iniquity in my tongue? cannot my taste discern perverse things?

## CHAPTER 7

*Job excuses his desire for death; 12 complains to God of his dealings with him.*

[a]IS *there* not [1]an appointed time to man upon earth? *are not* his [b]days also like the days of an [c,d]hireling?

2 As a [e]servant earnestly desireth the shadow, and as an [c,d]hireling looketh for [2]*the reward of* his work:

3 [a]So am I made to possess months of vanity, and wearisome nights are appointed to me.

4 [a]When I lie down, I say, When shall I arise, [3]and the night be gone? and I am full of tossings to and fro unto the dawning of the day.

5 My flesh is [f]clothed with worms and clods of dust; my skin [4]is broken, and become loathsome.

6 [b]My days are swifter than a [g]weaver's shuttle, and are spent without hope.

7 O remember that my [b]life *is* wind: mine eye shall no more see good.

8 [b]The eye of him that hath seen me shall see me no *more*: thine eyes *are* upon me, and I *am* not.

9 *As* the cloud is consumed and vanisheth away: so he that goeth down to [5]the [h]grave shall come up no *more*.

10 He shall return no more to his house, neither shall his place know him any more.

11 Therefore I will not refrain my mouth; I will speak in the [i]anguish of my spirit; I will

**29**
15 R.V. there be no injustice; yea, return again, my cause is righteous.

**1**
*a* *Murmuring,* Num. 14:2.
*b* *Life, brevity and uncertainty of,* Eccl. 8:15.
*c* *Hired Servant,* Lev. 25:40.
*d* *Employee,* Deut. 24:14.
1 R. V. a warfare to man

**2**
*e* *Servant,* **Jer.** 2:14.
2 R. V. his wages:

**4**
3 R. V. but the night is long;

**5**
*f* *Disease,* **Ex.** 15:26.
4 R. V. closeth up and breaketh out afresh.

**6**
*g* *Weaving,* **Isa.** 38:12.

**9**
*h* *Hell,* **Mark 9:43.**
4 **R. V. Sheol**
5 R. V. Sheol

**11**
*i* *Afflictions,* **Psa.** 34:19.

[a]complain in the bitterness of my soul.

12 [j]*Am* I a sea, or a [6,k]whale, that thou settest a watch over me?

13 When I say, My bed shall comfort me, my couch shall ease my [i]complaint;

14 Then thou scarest me with [l]dreams, and terrifiest me through [m]visions:

15 So that my soul chooseth strangling, *and* [n]death rather than [7]my life.

16 I loathe [8]*it;* I [n]would not live alway: let me alone; for my days *are* [o]vanity.

17 What *is* [p]man, that thou shouldest magnify[c] him? and that thou shouldest set thine heart upon him?[s]

18 And *that* thou shouldest visit him every morning, *and* try[c] him every moment?

19 How long wilt thou not depart from me, nor let me alone till I swallow down my spittle?

20 [9]I have sinned; what shall I do unto thee, O thou preserver of men? why hast thou set me as a mark [10]against thee, so that I am a burden to myself?

21 And why dost thou not [q]pardon my transgression, and take away mine iniquity? for now shall I [r]sleep[c] in the dust; and thou shalt seek me [11]in the morning, but I *shall* not *be.*

## CHAPTER 8

*The speech of Bildad; he shows the justice of God in his dealings with men; 8 the miserable condition of the wicked; 20 and the safety of the righteous.*

THEN answered [a]Bĭl′dăd the Shu′hīte, and [b]said,

2 [b]How long wilt thou speak these *things*? and *how long shall* the [c]words of thy mouth *be like* a strong wind?

3 [b]Doth God pervert judgment? or doth the Almighty pervert [d]justice?[s]

4 If thy children have sinned against him, and he have [1,e]cast them away for their transgression;

5 If thou wouldest [f]seek unto God betimes[c], and make thy [g]supplication to the Almighty;

6 If[s] [b]thou *wert* pure and upright; [h]surely now he would awake[c] for thee, and make the habitation of thy righteousness [i]prosperous.

7 Though thy beginning was small, yet thy latter end should greatly increase.[s]

8 For [j]enquire[c], I pray thee, of the former age, and [2]prepare thyself to the search of their fathers:

9 (For we *are but of* yesterday, and [k]know nothing, because our [l]days upon earth *are* a shadow:)

10 Shall not they teach thee, *and* tell thee, and utter words out of their heart?

11 Can the rush grow up without mire? can the flag grow without water?

12 Whilst it *is* yet in his greenness, *and* not cut down, it withereth before any *other* herb.

13 So *are* the paths of *all that forget God; and the [3]hypocrite's [m,n]hope shall perish:

14 Whose [m,n]hope shall be cut off, and whose trust *shall be* a [o]spider's web.

15 He shall [p]lean upon his house, but it shall not stand: he shall hold it fast, but it shall not endure.

16 He *is* green before the sun, and his branch shooteth forth in his garden.

17 His roots are wrapped about the heap, *and* seeth the place of stones.

**12**
j *Sarcasm*, Judg. 10:14.
k *Dragon*, Deut. 32:33.
6 R. V. sea-monster,

**14**
l *Dream*, Dan. 1:17.
m *Vision*, Acts 9:10.

**15**
n *Death, desired*, Num. 23:10.
7 R. V. these my bones.

**16**
o *Vanity*, Eccl. 1:2.
8 R. V. my life; .

**17**
p *Man, insignificance of*, Job 4:17.

**20**
9 R. V. If I have sinned, what do I unto thee, O thou watcher of men?
10 R. V. for thee,

**21**
q *Sin, forgiveness of*, Rom. 5:12.
r *Death*, Num. 23:10.
11 R. V. diligently, but

**1**
a Job 2:11; 18; 25; 42:7–9.
b *Reproof, faithfulness in*, vs. 2–20; Prov. 17:10.

**2**
c *Words*, Luke 4:22.

**3**
d *God, justice of*, Gen. 2:2.

**4**
e *Divine Chastisement*, Job 33:19.
1 R. V. delivered them into the hand of their transgression:

**5**
f *Seekers*, Isa. 55:6.
g *Prayer*, Acts 6:4.

**6**
h *Faith, exemplified*, Mark 11:22.
i *Spiritual Blessings, from God*, Eph. 1:3.

**8**
j *Wisdom, spiritual*, vs. 8–20; Prov. 2:2.
2 R. V. apply thyself to that which their fathers have searched out:

**9**
k *Ignorance*, Acts 3:17.
l *Life, brevity and uncertainty of*, Eccl. 8:15.

**13**
m *Wicked, hope of*, Psa. 73:3.
n *Hope, of the wicked*, Prov. 13:12.
3 R. V. hope of the godless man shall perish:

**14**
o *Spider*, Isa. 59:5.

**15**
p *False Confidence*, Psa. 30:6.

* **GODLESS.** Described as: *Destitute of the love of God*, John 5:42, 44; *forgetting God*, Psa. 50:22; Isa. 17:10; Jer. 2:32; *ignoring God*, Job 35:10; Psa. 52:7; 53:2, 3; 54:3; 55:19; 86:14; Isa. 5:12; 22:11; 30:1; 31:1; Hos. 7:2–4; *forsaking God*, Deut. 32:15; *despising God*, 1 Sam. 2:30; Psa. 36:1; Prov. 14:2; John 15:23–25; *loving deceits*, Isa. 30:9–11; *devoid of understanding*, Psa. 14:2, 3; 53:4; Isa. 1:3; Rom. 1:21, 22; 3:11; Eph. 4:18; *rebellious*, Psa. 2:2; Isa. 30:2; Dan. 5:23; *enemies to God*, Col. 1:21; Jas. 4:4; *impugning God's justice*, Ezek. 33:17–20; Mal 2:17; *atheistical*, Psa. 10:4 [R. V.].

18 If he destroy him from his
place, then *it* shall deny him,
*saying*, I have not seen thee.
19 Behold, this *is* the joy of his
way, and out of the earth shall
others grow.
20 Behold, [q]God will not cast
away a perfect *man*, neither will
he [4]help the evil doers:
21 [5]Till he fill thy mouth with
laughing, and thy lips with [6]re-
joicing.
22 They that hate thee shall be
clothed with shame; and the
[7]dwelling place of the wicked
shall come to nought.

## CHAPTER 9

*Job's answer to Bildad; he acknowledges the justice and power of God; 22 but contends that man's outward estate determines not his true character.*

THEN [a]Jōb answered and
said,
2 [b]I know *it is* so of a truth: but
[c]how should man be just with
[d,e]God?
3 [b,d]If he will contend with him,
he cannot answer him one of a
thousand.
4 [d]*He is* [f]wise in heart, and
mighty in [g]strength: [b]who hath
hardened *himself* against him,
and hath prospered?
5 [d]Which [h]removeth the [i]moun-
tains, and they know not: which
overturneth them in his [j,k]anger.
6 [d]Which [h]shaketh the [l]earth
out of her place, and the pillars
thereof tremble.
7 [d]Which [g]commandeth the
[m,n]sun, and it riseth not; and
sealeth up the [n,o]stars.
8 [d]Which alone [p]spreadeth out
the [q]heavens, and [g]treadeth upon the waves of the [r]sea.
9 [d]Which [p]maketh [1,n,s]Ärc-tū'-
rus, [n,t]Ō-rī'ŏn, and [n,t]Plē'ia-dēs,
and the chambers of the south.
10 [d]Which [g]doeth [u]great things
[v]past finding out; yea, and wonders without number.

**20**
q *Righteous, promises to*, Psa. 64:10.
4 R. V. uphold
**21**
5 R. V. He will yet fill
6 R. V. shouting.
**22**
7 R. V. tent
**1**
a *Job*, Job 1:1.
**2**
b *Philosophy*, vs. 2–35; Col. 2:8.
c *Depravity*, Job 15:14.
d *God, dissertations on*, vs. 2–35; Gen. 2:2.
e *God, holiness of*, Gen. 2:2.
**4**
f *God, wisdom of*, Gen. 2:2.
g *God, power of*, Gen. 2:2.
**5**
h *Earthquakes*, Isa. 29:6.
i *Mountain*, Mic. 7:12.
j *Anger of God*, 2 Kin. 13:3.
k *Anthropomorphisms*, Gen. 11:5.
**6**
l *Earth, ancient notions concerning*, Prov. 8:23.
**7**
m *Sun*, Josh. 10:12.
n *Astronomy*, Isa. 13:10.
o *Stars*, Judg. 5:20.
**8**
p *God, creator*, Gen. 2:2.
q *Heavens, physical*, Psa. 8:3.
r *Sea*, Jer. 5:22.
**9**
s Job 38:32.
t Job 38:31; Amos 5:8.
1 R. V. the Bear,
**10**
u *Works of God*, Psa. 40:5.
v *God, unsearchable*, Gen. 2:2.

11 Lo, he goeth by me, and I
[w]see *him* not: he passeth on also,
but I perceive him not.
12 Behold, he [2,x]taketh away,
[y]who can hinder him? who will
say unto him, What doest
thou?
13 *If* God will not withdraw
his [j,k]anger, the [3]proud helpers
do stoop under him.
14 [z]How much less shall I answer him, *and* choose out my
[a]words *to reason* with him?
15 Whom, though I were righteous, *yet* would I not answer, *but*
I would make supplication to
[4]my judge.
16 If I had called, and he had
answered me; [b]*yet* would I [c]not
believe that he had hearkened
unto my voice.
17 [b]For he breaketh me with
a tempest, and multiplieth my
wounds without cause.
18 [d,e]He will not suffer me to
take my breath, but filleth me
with bitterness.
19 If *I speak* of strength, lo, *he*
*is* strong: and if of judgment,
who shall set me a time *to*
*plead*?
20 [5]If I justify myself, *mine
own mouth shall condemn me:
[6]*if I say*, I *am* [f]perfect, it shall
also prove me perverse.
21 [7]*Though* I *were* [f]perfect, *yet*
would I not know my soul: I
would despise my life.
22 [8]This *is* one *thing*, therefore
I said *it*, He destroyeth the perfect and the wicked.
23 [d,e]If the [g]scourge slay suddenly, he will [9]laugh at the trial
of the innocent.
24 [d,e]The earth is given into
the hand of the wicked: he covereth the faces of the judges
thereof; if not, where, *and* who
*is* he?
25 Now my [h]days are swifter

**11**
w *God, invisible*, Gen. 2:2.
**12**
x *Adversity, dispensation from God*, Psa. 10:6.
y *God, sovereign*, Gen. 2:2.
2 R. V. seizeth the prey,
**13**
3 R. V. helpers of Rahab do stoop
**14**
z *Humility*, v. 15; Prov. 22:4.
a *Words*, Luke 4:22.
**15**
4 R. V. mine adversary.
**16**
b *Despondency*, vs. 16–35; Eccl. 2:20.
c *Doubting*, Rom. 14:23.
**18**
d *Murmuring*, Num. 14:2.
e *Afflictions, despondency in*, Psa. 34:19.
**20**
f *Perfection*, Heb. 6:1.
5 R. V. Though I be righteous,
6 R. V. Though I be perfect,
**21**
7 R. V. I am perfect; I regard not myself; I despise my life.
**22**
8 R. V. It is all one; therefore I say, He
**23**
g *Scourging*, Acts 22:24.
9 R. V. mock
**25**
h *Life, brevity and uncertainty of*, Eccl. 8:15.

* **SELF-CONDEMNATION,** 2 Sam. 24:17; Job 9:20; Prov. 5:12, 13; Matt. 23:31; 25:24–27 (with Luke 19:21, 22); Mark 12:1–12 (with Matt. 21:33–41); John 8:9; Rom. 2:1; 1 John 3:20, Rev. 1:7. INSTANCES OF: *Achan*, Josh. 7:19–25. *David*, 2 Sam. 12:5–7. *Ahab*, 1 Kin. 20:39–42. *Jonah*, Jonah 1:12.

than a †post: they flee away,
they see no good.
26 [h]They are passed away as
the swift [i]ships: as the [j]eagle
*that* [10]hasteth to the prey.
27 If I say, I will forget my
complaint, I will leave off my
heaviness, and comfort *myself*:
28 [d,e]I am afraid of all my sorrows, I know that [k]thou wilt not
hold me innocent.
29 [11]*If* I be wicked, why then
labour I in vain?
30 If I wash myself with [l]snow
water, and make my hands never
so [m]clean;
31 Yet shalt thou plunge me in
the ditch, and mine own clothes
shall abhor me.
32 For *he is* not a man, as I *am*,
*that* I should answer him, *and*
we should come together in judgment.
33 Neither is there any [n]days-
man betwixt us, *that* might lay
his hand upon us both.
34 Let him take his [o]rod away
from me, and let not his fear
terrify me:
35 *Then* would I speak, and
not fear him; [12]but *it is* not so
with me.

26
*i* *Ship*, 2 Chr. 8:18.
*j* *Eagle*, Lev. 11:13.
10 R. V. swoopeth on

28
*k* *God, judge*, Gen. 2:2.

29
11 R. V. I shall be condemned; why

30
*l* *Snow*, Jer. 18:14.
*m* *Spiritual Purification*, Psa. 51:2.

33
*n* *Mediation*, Gal. 3:19.

34
*o* *Divine Chastisement*, Job 33:19.

35
12 R.V For I am not so in myself.

## CHAPTER 10

*Job expostulates with God because of his afflictions; 18 complains of life; 20 and craves a little comfort before death.*

[a]MY soul is weary of my [b]life;
[c]I will [1]leave my complaint upon myself; I will speak
in the bitterness of my soul.
2 I will [d]say unto God, Do not
condemn me; shew me wherefore thou contendest with me.
3 [a,e]*Is it* good unto thee that
thou shouldest oppress, that thou
shouldest despise [f,g]the work of
thine hands, and shine upon the
counsel of the wicked?
4 [e]Hast thou eyes of flesh? or
seest thou as man seeth?
5 [e]*Are* thy days as the days of
man? *are* thy years as man's
days,
6 [a,e]That thou enquirest after
mine iniquity, and searchest after my sin?
7 [e]Thou [h]knowest that I am
[i]not wicked; and *there is* none
that can deliver out of thine
hand.
8 [e]Thine hands have [g]made
me and fashioned me together
round about; yet thou dost [j]de-
stroy me.
9 [e]Remember, I beseech thee,
that thou hast made me as the
clay; and [a,k]wilt thou bring me
into dust again?
10 Hast thou not poured me
out as *milk, and curdled me
like [l]cheese?
11 Thou hast clothed me †with
skin and flesh, and hast [2]fenced
me with bones and sinews.
12 Thou hast granted me life
and [m]favour, and thy [n]visitation
hath preserved my spirit.
13 And these *things* hast thou
hid in thine heart: I know that
this *is* with thee.
14 [a]If I sin, then [o]thou markest
me, and thou [p]wilt not acquit me
from mine iniquity.
15 [a]If I be wicked, woe unto
me; and *if* I be righteous, *yet*
will I not lift up my head. [3]*I am*
full of confusion; therefore see
thou mine affliction;
16 [4,a]For it increaseth. Thou
huntest me as a fierce lion: and
again thou shewest thyself marvellous upon me.

1
*a* *Murmuring*, vs. 1–22; Num. 14:2.
*b* *Life, weary of*, Eccl. 8:15.
*c* *Job*, Job 1:1.
1 R. V. give free course to my complaint;

2
*d* *Adversity, prayer in*, Psa. 10:6.

3
*e* *Reasoning, with God*, Job 13:6.
*f* *Man, created*, Job 4:17.
*g* *God, creator*, v. 8; Gen. 2:2.

7
*h* *God, knowledge of*, Gen. 2:2.
*i* *Integrity*, Job 2:3.

8
*j* *Afflictions, from God*, Psa. 34:19.

9
*k* *Life, brevity and uncertainty of*, Eccl. 8:15.

10
*l* 1 Sam. 17:18; 2 Sam. 17:29.

11
2 R. V. knit me together with

12
*m* *Grace of God*, Rom. 4:16.
*n* *God, providence of*, Gen. 2:2.

14
*o* *Sin, known to God*, Rom. 5:12.
*p* *Wicked, punishment of*, v. 15; Psa. 73:3.

15
3 R. V. Being filled with ignominy and looking upon mine affliction.

16
4 R. V. And if my head exalt itself, thou huntest me as a lion:

† **POST.** *A bearer of messages*, Job 9:25; Jer. 51:31. *Of Hezekiah*, 2 Chr. 30:6, 10. *Of Ahasuerus*, Esth. 3:13, 15; 8:10, 14.

* **MILK.** *Of goats*, Prov. 27:27. *Of sheep*, Deut. 32:14; Isa. 7:21, 22. *Of camels*, Gen. 32:15. *Of cows*, Deut. 32:14; 1 Sam. 6:7, 10. *Used for food*, Gen. 18:8; Judg. 4:19; Song 5:1; Ezek. 25:4; 1 Cor. 9:7. *Churned*, Prov. 30:33. *Kid not to be boiled in its mother's*, Ex. 23:19; 34:26; Deut. 14:21.

**Figurative**, Ex. 3:8, 17; 13:5; 33:3; Num. 13:27; Deut. 11:9; 26:9, 15; Isa. 55:1; 60:16; Jer. 11:5; 32:22; Ezek. 20:6; Joel 3:18; 1 Cor. 3:2; Heb. 5:12, 13; 1 Pet. 2:2.

† **PHYSIOLOGY.** The following citations contain references to the human body which for the convenience of the student are grouped under the topic physiology. No other term would serve the purpose so well as the one adopted, but its use must not be understood as implying that the scriptures teach the science of physiology. Job 10:11; Psa. 139:14–16; Prov. 14:30.

See footnote, SANITATION, Num. 31:23.

*Human body, with its many related members, a figure of the mutual relations of believers*, Eph. 4:16; Col. 2:19.

17 Thou renewest thy witnesses
against me, and increasest thine
indignation upon me; changes
and war *are* against me.
18 [a]Wherefore then hast thou
brought me forth out of the
womb ?[G] [b]Oh that I had given up
the ghost, and no eye had seen me!
19 I should have been as
though I had not been; I should
have been carried from the
womb to the grave.
20 *Are* not my [k]days few ? cease
*then, and* let me alone, that I
may take comfort a little,
21 Before I go *whence* I shall not
return, *even* to the [q]land of darkness and the shadow of death;
22 A [q]land of darkness, as
darkness *itself*; *and* of the
shadow of death, without any
order, and *where* the light *is* as
darkness.

## CHAPTER 11

*The speech of Zophar; he reproves Job for justifying himself; 5 shows that God's ways are unsearchable; 13 and exhorts Job to repentance.*

THEN answered [a]Zō'phar the
Nā'a-math-īte, and [b]said,
2 [b]Should not the multitude of
words be answered ? and should
a man full of talk be justified ?
3 [b,c]Should thy [1]lies make men
hold[G] their peace ? and when thou
mockest, shall no man make
thee ashamed ?
4 For thou hast [d]said, My doctrine *is* pure, and I am clean in
thine eyes.
5 [b]But oh that God would
speak, and open his lips against
thee;
6 And that he would shew
thee the secrets of [e]wisdom,
[2]that *they are* double to that
which is! Know therefore that
[f]God exacteth[G] of thee *less* than
thine iniquity *deserveth.*
7[S] Canst thou by searching find
out [g,h]God ? canst thou find out
the Almighty unto perfection ?
8 *It is* as high as heaven; what
canst thou do ? deeper than
[3,i]hell;[G] [j]what canst thou know ?
9 The measure thereof *is* longer
than the earth, and broader than
the sea.[S]
10 If he [4,k]cut off, and shut up,
[5]or gather together, then [l]who
can hinder him ?[S]
11 For he [m,n]knoweth [o,p]vain
men: he [q]seeth wickedness also;
[6]will he not then consider *it* ?[S]
12 For [o,p]vain man [7]would be
wise, though man be born *like* a
wild ass's colt.
13 If thou prepare thine heart,
and [r,s]stretch out thine hands
toward him;
14 If iniquity *be* in thine hand,
[t]put it far away, and let not wickedness dwell in thy tabernacles.[G] [S]
15 For then shalt thou lift up thy
face without spot; yea, [u]thou shalt
be stedfast, and shalt not fear:
16 Because thou shalt forget
*thy* [v]misery, *and* remember *it* as
waters *that* pass away:
17[S] And [u]*thine* age[G] shall be
clearer than the noonday; [8]thou
shalt shine forth, thou shalt be
as the morning.
18 And [u]thou shalt be secure,[G]
because there is hope; yea, thou
shalt dig *about thee, and* thou
shalt take thy rest in safety.[S]
19 Also [u]thou shalt lie down,
and none shall make *thee* afraid;
yea, many shall make suit unto
thee.[S]
20 But [w]the eyes of the wicked
shall fail, and they shall not escape, and their [x]hope *shall be as*
the giving up of the ghost.[G]

## CHAPTER 12

*Job's answer to Zophar; he censures the arrogance of his friends; 6 shows that the wicked often prosper in this world; 9 and discourses concerning the wisdom and power of God.*

AND [a]Jōb answered and
said,
2 [b]No doubt but [c]ye *are* the
people, and [d]wisdom shall die
with you.

---

**21**
q *Death, described,* Num. 23:10.

**1**
a Job 2:11; 20; 42: 7–9.
b *Reproof,* vs. 2–14; Prov. 17:10.

**3**
c *Uncharitableness,* Matt. 7:1.
1 R. V. boastings

**4**
d *Self-righteousness,* Luke 18:11.

**6**
e *Wisdom, spiritual,* Prov. 2:2.
f *God, mercy of,* Gen. 2:2.
2 Am. R. V. For he is manifold in understanding,

**7**
g *God, incomprehensible,* vs. 7–9; Gen. 2:2.
h *God, unsearchable,* vs. 7–9; Gen. 2:2.

**8**
i *Hell,* Mark 9:43.
j *Ignorance,* Acts 3:17.
3 R. V. Sheol;

**10**
k *Afflictions, from God,* Psa. 34:19.
l *God, power of,* Gen. 2:2.
4 R. V. pass through,
5 R. V. And call unto judgment,

**11**
m *Heart, known to God,* Psa. 44:21.
n *God, knowledge of,* Gen. 2:2.
o *Vanity,* Eccl. 1:2.
p *Pride,* Prov. 16:18.
q *Sin, known to God,* Rom. 5:12.
6 R. V. even though he consider it not.

**12**
7 R. V. is void of understanding, Yea, man is born

**13**
r *Prayer, of the wicked not heard,* Acts 6:4.
s *Prayer, in adversity,* Acts 6:4.

**14**
t *Repentance,* Mark 1:4.

**15**
u *Promise, to the righteous,* vs. 15–19; 2 Cor. 1:20.

**16**
v *Afflictions, consolation in,* Psa. 34:19.

**17**
8 R. V. Though there be darkness, it shall be

**20**
w *Wicked, punishment of,* Psa. 73:3.
x *Hope, of the wicked, shall perish,* Prov. 13:12.

**1**
a *Job,* Job 1:1.

**2**
b *Irony, instances of,* Mark 12:14.
c *Self-righteousness,* Luke 18:11.
d *Wisdom, worldly* Prov. 2:2.

3 But [e]I have understanding as well as you; I *am* not inferior to you: yea, who knoweth not such things as these?

4 I am *as* one [1]mocked of his neighbour, who calleth upon God, and he answereth him: the just upright *man is* laughed to scorn.

5 [2]He that is ready to [f]slip with *his* feet *is as* a lamp despised in the thought of him that is [g]at ease.

6 The tabernacles of [h,i]robbers prosper, and they that provoke God are secure; into whose hand God [j]bringeth *abundantly.*

7 But [k,l]ask now the [m]beasts, and they shall teach thee; and the fowls of the air, and they shall tell thee:

8 [k,l]Or speak to the earth, and it shall teach thee: and the fishes of the sea shall declare unto thee.

9 [n]Who knoweth not in all these that the hand of the LORD hath [j,o]wrought this?

10 In [n,p]whose hand *is* the soul of every living thing, and the breath of all mankind.

11 Doth not the ear try words? [3]and the mouth taste his meat?

12 With [4]the [q]ancient *is* wisdom; and in length of days understanding.

13 With [n]him *is* [r]wisdom and [s]strength, he hath counsel and understanding.

14 Behold, [n]he [s]breaketh down, and it cannot be built again: [t]he shutteth up a man, and there can be no opening.

15 Behold, he [u]withholdeth the waters, and they dry up: also he [v]sendeth them out, and they overturn the earth.

16 With [n]him *is* [s]strength and [5,r]wisdom: the deceived and the deceiver *are* his.

17 [n]He leadeth [w]counsellors away spoiled, and maketh the [x]judges fools.

18 [n]He looseth the bond of [y]kings, and girdeth their loins with a girdle.

19 [n]He leadeth [6]princes away spoiled, and overthroweth the mighty.

20 [n]He removeth away the speech of the trusty, and taketh away the understanding of the aged.

21 [n]He poureth contempt upon princes, and weakeneth the strength of the mighty.

22 [n]He discovereth deep things out of darkness, and bringeth out to light the shadow of death.

23 [n]He [z]increaseth the nations, and destroyeth them: he enlargeth the nations, and straiteneth them *again.*

24 He taketh away the heart of the chief of the people of the earth, and causeth them to wander in a wilderness *where there is* no way.

25 They grope in the dark without light, and he maketh them to stagger like *a* [a]drunken *man.*

## CHAPTER 13

*Job reproves his friends for their partiality; 14 professes his confidence in God; 20 and entreats to know his sins, and God's purpose in afflicting him.*

LO, [a]mine eye hath seen all *this,* mine ear hath heard and understood it.

2 What ye know, *the same* do I know also: [b]I *am* not inferior unto you.

3 Surely I would speak to the Almighty, and I desire to reason with God.

4 But ye *are* forgers of [c]lies, ye *are* all [d]physicians of no value.

5 O that ye would altogether hold your peace! and it should be your wisdom.

6 Hear now my *reasoning,

3
e *Conceit,* Prov. 26:5.

4
1 Am. R. V. that is a laughing-stock to his neighbor, I who called upon God, and he answered: The just, the perfect man is a laughing-stock.

5
f *Adversity,* Psa. 10:6.
g *Prosperity,* Eccl. 7:14.
2 R. V. In the thought of him that is at ease there is contempt for misfortune; It is ready for them whose foot slippeth.

6
h *Robbers,* Hos. 6:9.
i *Wicked, prosperity of,* Psa. 73:3.
j *God, providence of,* Gen. 2:2.

7
k *Reasoning,* Job 13:6.
l *Natural Religion,* vs. 7–15; Psa. 19:1.
m *Animals, habits of,* Jer. 27:5.

9
n *God, dissertations on,* vs. 7–25; Gen. 2:2.
o *God, creator,* vs. 7–9; Gen. 2:2.

10
p *God, sovereign,* Gen. 2:2.

11
3 Am. R. V. Even as the palate tasteth its food?

12
q *Old Age,* Isa. 46:4.
4 R. V. aged men is wisdom,

13
r *God, wisdom of,* Gen. 2:2.
s *God, power of,* Gen. 2:2.

14
t *Adversity, dispensation from God,* Psa. 10:6.

15
u *Drought,* Gen. 31:40.
v *Flood,* Gen. 6:17.

16
5 R. V. effectual working;

17
w *Counselor,* Prov. 11:14.
x *Judge,* Judg. 2:18.

18
y *King,* 2 Kin. 3:10.

19
6 R. V. priests

23
z *Temporal Blessings, from God,* Psa. 103:2.

25
a *Drunkard,* Psa. 69:12.

1
a *Job,* Job 1:1.

2
b *Conceit,* Prov. 26:5.

4
c *Falsehood,* Job 21:34.
d *Physician, figurative,* 2 Chr. 16:12.

* **REASONING.** *With God,* Job 13:3, 17–28; 14. *God reasons with men,* Ex. 4:11; 20:5, 11; Isa. 1:18; 5:3, 4; 43:26; Hos. 4:1; Mic. 6:2.

*Natural understanding,* Dan. 4:36. *To be applied to religion,* 1 Cor. 10:15; 1 Pet. 3:15. *Not a sufficient guide in human affairs,* Deut. 12:8; Prov. 3:5; 14:12. *Of the Pharisees,* Luke 5:21, 22; 20:5. *Of Paul, from the Scriptures,* Acts 17:2; 18:4, 19; 24:25. *The gospel cannot be explained by,* 1 Cor. 1:18–28; 2:1–14.

See footnote, PHILOSOPHY, Col. 2:8.

and hearken to the pleadings of my lips.

7 Will ye speak wickedly for God? and talk deceitfully for him?

8 Will ye accept[C] his person? will ye contend for God?

9 Is it good that he should search you out? or as one [1]man mocketh another, do ye *so* mock him?

10 He will surely reprove[C] you, if ye do secretly accept persons.

11 Shall not his [2,e]excellency make you afraid? and his dread fall upon you?[S]

12 Your [3]remembrances *are* like unto ashes, your bodies to bodies of clay.

13 Hold your peace, let me alone, that I may speak, and let come on me what *will*.

14 Wherefore[C] do I take my flesh in my teeth, and put my life in mine hand?

15 [4]Though he slay me, [f]yet will I [g]trust in him: but I will maintain[C] mine own ways before him.

16 [5]He also *shall be* my [h]salvation[C]: [6]for an hypocrite shall not come before him.[S Q]

17 Hear diligently my *speech, and my declaration with your ears.

18 Behold now, I have ordered *my* cause; I know that I shall be justified.

19 Who *is* he *that* will [7]plead with me? for now, [8]if I hold my tongue, I shall give up the ghost.[C]

20 Only do not two *things* unto me: then will I not hide myself from thee.

21 Withdraw thine hand far from me: and let not thy dread make me afraid.

22 Then call thou, and I will answer: or let me speak, and answer thou me.

23 How many *are* mine iniquities and sins? make me to know my transgression and my sin.

24 *Wherefore[C] hidest thou thy face, and holdest me for thine enemy?

25 *Wilt thou [9]break a leaf driven to and fro? and wilt thou pursue the dry stubble?

26 For thou writest bitter things against me, and makest me to possess the [i]iniquities of my [j]youth.

27 Thou puttest my feet also in the †stocks, and lookest narrowly[C] unto all my paths; thou settest [10]a print upon the heels of my feet.

28 [11]And he, as a rotten thing, consumeth, as a garment that is [k]moth eaten.

## CHAPTER 14

*Job entreats God for a respite from his sufferings in view of the shortness of life, 7 and because the dead return not; 14 yet waits submissively for his change. 16 By reason of sin the creature is subject to corruption.*

[a]MAN *that is* born of a woman *is* of [b]few days, and full of [c]trouble.

2 He cometh forth like a flower, and is [b,d]cut down: he fleeth also as a shadow, and [b]continueth not.

3 And dost thou open thine eyes upon such an [e]one, and bringest me into judgment with thee?

4 [f,g]Who can bring a clean *thing* out of an [h]unclean? not one.[S]

5 Seeing his [b]days *are* determined, the number of his months *are* with thee, [i]thou hast appointed his[S] bounds that he cannot pass;

6 Turn from him, that he may rest, till he shall accomplish, as an [j]hireling, his day.

7 For there is hope of a tree, if it be cut down, that it will

---

**9**
1 R. V. deceiveth a man, will ye deceive him?

**11**
e *God, glory of,* Gen. 2:2.
2 Am. R. V. majesty

**12**
3 R. V. memorable sayings are proverbs of ashes, Your defences are defences of clay.

**15**
f *Resignation, exemplified* (according to A.V.), Job 5:17.
g *Faith, exemplified* (according to A. V.), Mark 11:22.
4 Am. R. V. Behold, he will slay me; I have no hope:

**16**
h *Salvation,* Acts 16:17.
5 R. V. This also
6 Am. R. V. that a godless man shall not

**19**
7 R. V. contend
8 R. V. shall I hold my peace and give up the ghost.

**25**
9 R. V. harass a driven leaf?

**26**
i *Sin, fruits of,* Rom. 5:12.
j *Children, wicked,* Mark 10:14.

**27**
10 Am. R. V. a bound to the soles of my feet:

**28**
k *Moth,* Job 4:19.
11 R. V. Though I am like a rotten thing that consumeth,

**1**
a *Man, mortal,* Job 4:17.
b *Life, brevity and uncertainty of,* Eccl. 8:15.
c *Adversity,* Psa. 10:6.

**2**
d *Death,* Num. 23:10.

**3**
e *Man, insignificance of,* Job 4:17.

**4**
f *Depravity,* Job 15:14.
g *Heredity,* Ezek. 18:2.
h *Wicked, described,* Psa. 73:3.

**5**
i *God, sovereign,* Gen. 2:2.

**6**
j *Hired Servant,* Lev. 25:40.

---

**† STOCKS.** *Feet fastened in, as a punishment,* Job 13:27; 33:11; Prov. 7:22. *In prisons,* Jer. 20:2; Acts 16:24.

10
[k] *Man, a spirit,* Job 4:17.

12
[l] *Heavens, physical, destruction of,* Psa. 8:3.
[m] *Sleep, a symbol of death,* Psa. 127:2.
[n] *Death, called sleep,* Num. 23:10.
1 R. V. roused

13
[o] *Murmuring, against God,* Num. 14:2.
[p] *Hell,* Mark 9:43.
[q] *Immortality,* vs. 13–15; 1 Cor. 15:54.
2 R. V. Sheol.

14
[r] *Afflictions, resignation in,* Psa. 34:19.
3 R. V. warfare would I wait, Till my release should come.

15
[s] *Faith, exemplified,* Mark 11:22.

16
[t] *Sin, known to God,* Rom. 5:12.

18
[u] *Mountain,* Mic. 7:12.

19
4 R. V. The overflowings thereof wash away the dust

20
[v] *God, power of,* Gen. 2:2.

sprout again, and that the
tender branch thereof will not
cease.
8 Though the root thereof wax[C]
old in the earth, and the stock
thereof die in the ground;
9 *Yet* through the scent of
water it will bud, and bring
forth boughs like a plant.
10 But man [d]dieth, and wasteth
away: yea, man giveth up the
[k]ghost,[C] and where *is* he?
11 *As* the waters fail from the
sea, and the flood decayeth and
drieth up:
12 So man lieth down, and
riseth not: till the [l]heavens *be* no
more, they shall not awake, nor
be [1]raised[C] out of their [m,n]sleep.
13 [o]O that thou wouldest hide
me in [2]the [p]grave,[C] that thou
wouldest keep me secret,[C] until
thy wrath be past, that thou
wouldest [q]appoint me a set
time, and remember me!
14 If a man [d]die, shall he live
*again?* [r]all the days of my [3]appointed time will I wait, till my
change come.
15 [s]Thou shalt call, and I will
answer thee: thou wilt have a desire to the work of thine hands.
16 For now thou numberest my
steps: dost thou not [t]watch over
my sin?
17 My transgression *is* sealed
up in a bag, and thou sewest up
mine iniquity.
18 And surely the [u]mountain
falling cometh to nought,[C] and the
rock is removed out of his place.
19 The waters wear the stones:
[4]thou washest away the things
which grow *out* of the dust of the
earth; and thou destroyest the
hope of man.
20 Thou [v]prevailest for ever
against him, and he passeth:
thou changest his countenance,
and sendest him away.

21 His sons come to honour,
and he knoweth *it* not; and they
are brought low, but he perceiveth *it* not of them.
22 But his flesh upon him shall
have *pain, and his soul within
him shall mourn.

## CHAPTER 15

*The reply of Eliphaz; he reproves Job for impiety in what he had uttered; 17 and shows the misery that comes upon the wicked.*

THEN answered [a]Ĕl'ĭ-phăz
the Tē'man-īte, and said,
2 Should a wise man utter vain
knowledge, and fill his belly with
the east wind?
3 Should he reason with
unprofitable [b]talk? or with
[b]speeches wherewith he can do
no good?
4 Yea, thou castest off [c]fear,
and [d]restrainest prayer before
God.
5 For [1]thy mouth uttereth
thine iniquity, and thou choosest
the tongue of the crafty.
6 Thine own mouth condemneth thee, and not I: yea, thine
own lips testify against thee.
7 [e]*Art* thou the first man *that*
was born? or wast thou made
before the hills?
8 [e,f]Hast thou heard the secret
of God? and dost thou restrain[C]
wisdom to thyself?[S Q]
9 What knowest thou, that we
know not? *what* understandest
thou, which *is* not in us?
10 With us *are* both the grayheaded and very [g]aged men,
much elder[G] than thy father.
11 [e]*Are* the consolations of God
[2]small with thee? is there any
secret thing with thee?
12 [e]Why doth thine heart carry
thee away? and [3]what do thy
eyes wink at,
13 That thou turnest thy spirit
against God, and lettest *such*
[h]words go out of thy mouth?

1
[a] Job 2:11; 4; 5; 22; 42:7–9.

3
[b] *Speech, foolish,* Col. 4:6.

4
[c] *Fear of God,* Acts 9:31.
[d] *Prayerlessness,* Job 21:15.

5
1 R. V. thine iniquity teacheth thy mouth,

7
[e] *Mocking,* 1 Kin. 18:27.

8
[f] *God, incomprehensible,* Gen. 2:2.

10
[g] *Old Age,* Isa. 46:4.

11
2 Am. R. V. too small for thee, even the word that is gentle toward thee?

12
3 Am. R. V. why do thine eyes flash?

13
[h] *Murmuring,* Num. 14:2.

* **PAIN,** Job 14:22; 30:17, 18; Rev. 16:10. *Chastens,* Job 33:19. *None in heaven,* Rev. 21:4. See footnote, AFFLICTIONS, Psa. 34:19.

14 i Man, insignificance of, Job 4:17.

15 j God, holiness of, Gen. 2:2.
k Heavens, physical, Psa. 8:3.
4 R. V. holy ones;

16 l Wicked, described, Psa. 73:3.
m Sin, love of, Rom. 5:12.

20 n Wicked, punishment of, Psa. 73:3.
o Fear of God, guilty, Acts 9:31.
5 R. V. Even
6 R. V. that are laid up for

21 p Conscience, guilty, v. 24; Acts 23:1.
q Wicked, happiness of, is short, Psa. 73:3.

24 r Cowardice, Lev. 26:36.

25 s Presumption, Psa. 19:13.
t Infidelity, 2 Cor. 6:15.
7 R. V. behaveth himself proudly against

26 u Shield, 1 Kin. 14:27.
8 R. V. with a stiff neck, with the

14 *What *is* [i]man, that he
should be clean? and *he which*
*is* born of a woman, that he
should be righteous?
15 Behold, he putteth no trust
in his [4]saints; yea, [j]the [k]heavens
are not clean in his sight.
16 How much more *abominable and filthy *is* [l]man, [l]which
drinketh [m]iniquity like water?
17 I will shew thee, hear me;
and that *which* I have seen I
will declare;
18 Which wise men have told
from their fathers, and have not
hid *it*:
19 Unto whom alone the earth
was given, and no stranger
passed among them.
20 The [n]wicked man [o]travaileth with pain all *his* days, [5]and
the number of years [6]is hidden
to the oppressor.
21 A [p]dreadful sound *is* in his
ears: [q]in prosperity the destroyer
shall come upon him.
22 He believeth not that he
shall return out of darkness,
and he is waited for of the
sword.
23 He wandereth abroad for
bread, *saying*, Where *is it*? he
knoweth that the day of darkness is ready at his hand.
24 Trouble and anguish shall
make him [p, r]afraid; they shall
prevail against him, as a king
ready to the battle.
25 For he [s, t]stretcheth out
his hand against God, and
[7]strengtheneth himself against
the Almighty.
26 He [s]runneth upon him,
[8]*even* on *his* neck, upon the
thick bosses of his [u]bucklers:
27 Because he covereth his face
with his fatness, and maketh collops of fat on *his* flanks.
28 And he dwelleth in desolate
cities, *and* in houses which no
man inhabiteth, which are ready
to become heaps.
29 [n]He shall not be rich, [q]neither shall his substance continue,
neither shall [9]he prolong the perfection thereof upon the earth.
30 He shall not depart out of
darkness; the flame shall dry up
his branches, and by the [v]breath
of his mouth shall he go away.
31 [w]Let not him that is deceived
trust in vanity: for vanity shall
be his recompence.
32 It shall be accomplished before his time, and his branch
shall not be green.
33 He shall shake off his unripe
[x]grape as the vine, and shall cast
off his flower as the [y]olive.
34 For the [10]congregation of
hypocrites *shall be* desolate, and
fire shall consume the tabernacles of [z]bribery.
35 They [a]conceive mischief,
and bring forth [11]vanity, and
their belly prepareth [b]deceit.

## CHAPTER 16

*Job's answer; he reproves his friends for their want of sympathy; 7 shows the greatness of his sufferings; 17 and asserts his integrity.*

THEN [a]Jōb answered and
said,
2 I have heard many such
things: miserable comforters *are*
ye all.
3 Shall [b]vain words have an
end? or what [1]emboldeneth thee
that thou answerest?
4 I also could speak as ye *do*:
if your soul were in my soul's
stead, I could heap up words
against you, and shake mine
head at you.
5 *But* I would [c]strengthen you
with my [d]mouth, and the [2]moving of my lips should asswage
*your grief*.
6 [e]Though I speak, my [f]grief is
not asswaged: and *though* I forbear, what am I eased?

29 9 Am. R. V. their possessions be extended on the earth.

30 v Breath, figurative, Gen. 7:15.

31 w False Confidence, warning against, Psa. 30:6.

33 x Grape, figurative, Lev. 25:5.
y Olive, Deut. 6:11.

34 z Bribery, denunciation against, 1 Sam. 8:3.
10 R. V. company of the godless shall be barren,

35 a Malice, devises mischief, Eph. 4:31.
b Deceit, the wicked practise, Psa. 36:3.
11 R. V. iniquity.

1 a Job, Job 1:1.

3 b Speech, foolish, Col. 4:6.
1 R. V. provoketh

5 c Afflictions, consolation in, Psa. 34:19.
d Speech, wise, Col. 4:6.
2 R. V. solace

6 e Murmuring, vs. 6–14; Num. 14:2.
f Afflictions, Psa. 34:19.

* **DEPRAVITY**, Gen. 6:5; 8:21; Job 15:14–16; 25:4–6; Psa. 5:9; 51:5; 53:1–3; 58:1–5; Eccl. 9:3; Isa. 1:5, 6; Jer. 13:23; 16:12; 17:9; Matt. 7:17; 12:34, 35; Rom. 1:21–32; 7:5, 11, 13–15, 18–25; 8:5–8, 13; Gal. 5:17, 19–21; 1 John 2:16. *Universal*, Gen. 6:11–13; 2 Chr. 6:36; Psa. 14:1–3; 143:2; Eccl. 7:20; Isa. 64:6; Mic. 7:2–4; Rom. 3:9–19, 23.

7 [e]But now he hath made me weary: thou hast made desolate all my company.

8 [e]And thou hast [3]filled me with wrinkles, *which* is a witness *against me*: and my leanness rising up in me beareth witness to my face.

9 He teareth *me* in his [g]wrath, who hateth me: he *gnasheth upon me with his teeth; mine enemy sharpeneth his eyes upon me.[Q]

10 [e]They have gaped upon me with their mouth; they have [f]smitten me upon the cheek reproachfully; they have gathered themselves together against me.

11 [e]God [h]hath delivered me to the ungodly, and turned me over into the hands of the wicked.

12 I was at ease, but he [h]hath broken me asunder: he hath also taken *me* by my neck, and shaken me to pieces, and set me up for his mark.[G]

13 [h]His archers compass[G] me round about, he cleaveth my reins[G] asunder,[G] and doth not spare; he poureth out my †gall upon the ground.

14 [e]He [h]breaketh me with breach upon breach, he runneth upon me like a giant.

15 I have sewed [i]sackcloth upon my skin, and defiled my horn[G] in the dust.

16 My face is foul with weeping, and on my eyelids *is* the shadow of death;

17 [4]Not for *any* injustice in mine hands: also my prayer *is* pure.

18 O earth, cover not thou my blood, and let my cry have no place.

19 Also now, behold, [j]my witness *is* in heaven, and [5]my record *is* on high.

20 My [k]friends scorn me: *but* mine eye [l]poureth out *tears* unto God.[6]

21 [7]O that one might plead for a man with God, as a man *pleadeth* for his neighbour!

22 When a few years are come, then I shall [m]go the way *whence* I shall not return.

## CHAPTER 17

*Job complains of the conduct of his friends: 11 and declares that his hope is not in life, but in death.*

MY [1,a,b]breath[G] is corrupt, my [c]days are extinct, the graves *are ready* for me.

2 *Are there* not mockers with me? and doth not mine eye continue in their provocation?

3 Lay down now, put me in a surety with thee; who *is* he *that* will strike[G] [d]hands with me?

4 For thou hast hid their heart from understanding: therefore shalt thou not exalt *them*.

5 He that [2]speaketh flattery to *his* friends, even the eyes of his children shall fail.

6 He hath made me also a byword[G] of the people; and [3]aforetime[G] I was as a tabret.[G]

7 [a,b]Mine eye also is dim by reason of sorrow, and all my members *are* as a shadow.

8 Upright *men* shall be astonied[G] at this, and the innocent shall stir up himself against the [4]hypocrite.

9 The righteous also [e]shall hold on his way, and he that hath clean [f]hands shall be stronger and stronger.

10 But as for you all, do ye return, and come now: for I cannot find *one* wise *man* among you.

---

**8**
3 R. V. laid fast hold on me.

**9**
*g Anger of God,* 2 Kin. 13:3.

**11**
*h Divine Chastisement,* Job 33:19.

**15**
*i Sackcloth,* Isa. 15:3.

**17**
4 R. V. Although there is no violence in mine hands, And my prayer is pure.

**19**
*j Faith, in affliction,* Mark 11:22.

5 R. V. he that voucheth for me is on high.

**20**
*k Friends, false,* Ex. 33:11.
*l Adversity, prayer in,* Psa. 10:6.
6 (R.V. has a semicolon at the end of v. 20.)

**21**
7 R. V. That he would maintain the right of a man with God, And of a son of man with his neighbor!

**22**
*m Death,* Num. 23:10.

**1**
*a Despondency,* Eccl. 2:20.
*b Affliction, despondency in,* Psa. 34:19.
*c Life, brevity and uncertainty of,* Eccl. 8:15.
1 R. V. spirit is consumed,

**3**
*d Hand, clasping of, in token of friendship,* Ezra 10:19.

**5**
2 R. V. denounceth his friends for a prey,

**6**
3 Am. R. V. they spit in my face.

**8**
4 R. V. godless.

**9**
*e Perseverance,* Eph. 6:18.
*f Hand, figurative,* Ezra 10:19.

---

***GNASHING OF TEETH.** *In malicious anger,* Job 16:9; Psa. 35:16; 37:12; 112:10; Lam. 2:16.
*Of the lost, from anguish of spirit,* Matt. 8:12; 13:42; 22:13; 24:51; 25:30; Luke 13:28.

**† GALL.** *Any bitter or poisonous substance, such, as bile,* Job 16:13; *as venom of serpents,* Job 20:14. *A bitter decoction given to Jesus,* Psa. 69:21; Matt. 27:34.
**Figurative:** *Of moral corruption,* Deut. 29:18; 32:32; Job 20:14; Acts 8:23. *Of oppression,* Amos 6:12. *Of divine judgments,* Jer. 8:14; 9:15; 23:15; Lam. 3:5, 19.

11 [a,c]My days are past, [b]my
purposes are broken off, *even*
the thoughts of my heart.
12 They change the night into
day: the light *is* short because of
darkness.
13 [a,b]If I [5]wait, the [c,g]grave[C] *is*
mine house: I have made my
bed in the darkness.
14 [6]I have said to *,[h]corruption,[C]
Thou *art* my father: to the
worm, *Thou art* my mother, and
my sister.
15 [7]And [a,b]where *is* now my
hope? as for my hope, who shall
see it?
16 [8]They shall go down to the
bars of [9]the pit,[C] when *our* rest
together *is* in the dust.

## CHAPTER 18

*The reply of Bildad; he reproves Job for his pride and arrogance; 5 and shows the calamities which come upon the wicked.*

THEN answered [a]Bĭl'dăd the
Shu'hīte, and said,
2 How long *will* [1]*it be ere* ye
make an end of [b]words? mark,
and afterwards we will speak.
3 Wherefore[C] are we counted as
beasts, *and* reputed vile in your
sight?
4 [2]He teareth himself in his
[c]anger: shall the earth be forsaken
for thee? and shall the
rock be removed out of his
place?
5 Yea, [d]the light of the wicked
shall be put out, and the spark
of his fire shall not shine.
6 [d]The light shall be dark in his
tabernacle,[C] and his [e]candle[C] shall
be put out with him.
7 [d]The steps of his strength
shall be straitened,[C] and his own
counsel shall cast him down.
8 For [d]he is cast into a [f]net by
his own feet, and he walketh
upon a [g]snare.
9 [d]The gin[C] shall take *him* by
the heel, *and* [3]the robber shall
prevail against him.
10 The snare *is* laid for him in
the ground, and a [h]trap for him
in the way.
11 [d]Terrors shall make [i]him
[j,k]afraid on every side, and shall
drive him to his feet.
12 [d]His strength shall be hungerbitten,
and destruction *shall*
*be* ready at his side.
13 [4,d]It shall devour the strength
of his skin: *even* the firstborn of
death shall devour his [5]strength.
14 [6]His [l]confidence shall be
rooted out of his tabernacle,[C] and
it shall bring him to the [m]king of
terrors.
15 [7]It shall dwell in his tabernacle,
because *it is* none of
his: [n]brimstone shall be scattered
upon his habitation.
16 [d]His roots shall be dried up
beneath, and above shall his
branch be cut off.
17 [d]His remembrance shall perish
from the earth, and he shall
have no name in the street.
18 [d]He shall be driven from
light into darkness, and chased
out of the world.
19 [d]He shall neither have son nor
[8]nephew[C] among his people, nor
any remaining in his dwellings.
20 They that come after *him*
shall be astonied[C] at his day,[C] as
they that went before were
affrighted.[C]
21 Surely such *are* the dwellings
of the wicked, and this *is* the
place *of him that* knoweth not
God.

## CHAPTER 19

*Job's answer; he complains of the unkindness of his friends; 5 confesses that God had overthrown him; 21 entreats their pity; 23 and is confident that God will yet vindicate his cause.*

THEN [a]Jōb answered and
said,
2 How long will ye vex my soul,

**13**
g *Hell,* Mark 9:43.
5 R. V. look for Sheol as mine house: If I

**14**
h *Body, corruptible,* 1 Cor. 6:19.
6 R. V. If I

**15**
7 R. V. Where then is my hope? And as

**16**
8 R. V. It
9 R. V. Sheol, When once there is rest in the dust.

**1**
a Job 8; 25; 42: 7-9.

**2**
b *Words,* Luke 4:22.
1 R. V. ye lay snares for words?

**4**
c *Anger,* Psa. 37:8.
2 R. V. Thou that tearest thyself in thine anger,

**5**
d *Wicked, punishment of,* vs. 5-21; Psa. 73:3.

**6**
e *Lamp, figurative,* Ex. 27:20.

**8**
f *Net, figurative,* Isa. 51:20.
g *Snare, figurative,* Amos 3:5.

**9**
3 R. V. a snare shall lay hold on

**10**
h Josh. 23:13; Jer. 5:26.

**11**
i *Wicked, dread God,* Psa. 73:3.
j *Fear of God, guilty,* Acts 9:31.
k *Cowardice, caused by adversity,* Lev. 26:36.

**13**
4 Am. R. V. The members of his body shall be devoured,
5 R. V. members.

**14**
l *False Confidence,* Psa. 30:6.
m *Death, described as king of terrors,* Num. 23:10.
6 R. V. He shall be rooted out of his tent wherein he trusteth; And he shall be brought to

**15**
n *Brimstone, figurative,* Deut. 29:23.
7 R. V. There shall dwell in his tent that which is none of his:

**19**
8 R. V. son's son

**1**
a *Job,* **Job 1:1.**

*__CORRUPTION.__ **Physical decomposition,** Lev. 22:25. *After death,* Gen. 3:19; Job 17:14; 21:26; 34:15; Psa. 16:10; 49:9; 104:29; Eccl. 3:20; 12:7; Jonah 2:6; Acts 2:27, 31; 13:34–37; 1 Cor. 15:42, 50. **Figurative:** *Of annihilation,* Isa. 38:17. *Of sin,* Rom. 8:21. *Of the consequences of sin,* Gal. 6:8. *Of the evil existing in the world,* 2 Pet. 1:4; 2:19. *Mount of, where Solomon built a high place for idolatrous worship,* 2 Kin. 23:13, with 1 Kin. 11:7.

**3**
1 R. V. deal hardly with me.

**6**
*b Murmuring, against God*, vs. 7–20; Num. 14:2.
*c Afflictions, from God*, Psa. 34:19.
*d Net, figurative*, Isa. 51:20.
2 R. V. subverted me in my cause.

**7**
*e Adversity*, vs. 7–20; Psa. 10:6.

**11**
*f Anger of God*, 2 Kin. 13:3.
*g Anthropomorphisms*, Gen. 11:5.

**14**
*h Friends, false*, Ex. 33:11.

**15**
*i Servant, wicked*, Jer. 2:14.

and break me in pieces with words?

3 These ten times have ye reproached[c] me: ye are not ashamed *that* ye [1]make yourselves strange[c] to me.

4 And be it indeed *that* I have erred, mine error remaineth with myself.

5 If indeed ye will magnify[c] *yourselves* against me, and plead against me my reproach[c]:

6 [b]Know now that God [c]hath [2]overthrown me, and hath compassed me with his [d]net.[T]

7 [b]Behold, I cry out of [e]wrong, but I am not heard: I cry aloud, but *there is* no judgment.[c]

8 [b]He hath fenced[c] up my way that I cannot pass, and he hath set darkness in my paths.

9 [b]He hath stripped me of my glory, and taken the crown *from* my head.

10 [b]He hath destroyed me on every side, and I am gone: and mine hope hath he removed like a tree.

11 [b]He hath also kindled his [f,g]wrath against me, and he counteth me unto him as *one of* his enemies.

12 His troops come together, and raise up their way against me, and encamp round about my tabernacle[c].

13 [b]He hath put my brethren far from me, and mine acquaintance are verily estranged from me.

14 My kinsfolk have failed, and my familiar [h]friends have forgotten me.

15 They that dwell in mine house, and my [i]maids, count me for a stranger: I am an alien in their sight.

16 I called my [i]servant, and he gave *me* no answer; I intreated him with my mouth.

17 My breath is strange[c] to my [j]wife, [3]though I intreated for the children's *sake* of mine own body.

18 Yea, young [k]children despised me; I arose, and they [l]spake against me.

19 All my inward[c] [h]friends abhorred me: and they whom I loved are turned against me.

20 [m]My bone cleaveth to my skin and to my flesh, and I am escaped with the skin of my teeth.

21 Have pity upon me, have *pity upon me, O ye my friends; for [b]the hand of God hath touched me.[T]

22 Why do ye persecute me as God, and are not satisfied with my flesh?

23 Oh that my words were now written! oh that they were printed in a [n]book!

24 That they were graven[c] with an [o]iron [p]pen and [q]lead in the rock for ever!

25 For I [r,s]know *that* my redeemer liveth, and *that* he shall stand at the latter *day* upon the earth:[T Q]

26 [r,s]And [4]*though* after my skin *worms* destroy this *body*, yet in my flesh shall I see God:[T]

27 [r,s]Whom I shall see for myself, and mine eyes shall behold, and not another; *though* my reins[c] be consumed within me.[T Q]

28 But ye should say, Why persecute we him, seeing the root of the matter is found in me?

29 Be ye afraid of the [t,u]sword: for wrath *bringeth* the punishments of the sword, that ye may know *there is* a judgment.

**17**
*j Women, wicked, instances of*, Prov. 31:10.
3 Am. R. V. And my supplication to the children of mine own mother.

**18**
*k Children, wicked*, Mark 10:14.
*l Speech, evil*, Col. 4:6.

**20**
*m Disease*, Ex. 15:26.

**23**
*n Book*, Num. 5:23.

**24**
*o Iron*, Prov. 27:17.
*p Pen*, Jer. 8:8.
*q Lead*, Ezek. 22:18.

**25**
*r Assurance*, Heb. 10:22.
*s Faith, in afflictions*, Mark 11:22.

**26**
4 Am. R. V. after my skin, even this body, is destroyed, then without my flesh

**29**
*t Sword, figurative*, 1 Chr. 21:5.
*u War, as a judgment*, Judg. 3:2.

***PITY.** *Enjoined*, Job 6:14; 1 Pet. 3:8. *For the poor*, Prov. 19:17; 28:8. *Forbidden, to Canaanites*, Deut. 7:16; *to idolatrous proselytizers*, Deut. 13:8; *to murderers*, Deut. 19:13; *to false witnesses*, Deut. 19:21; *to amazons*, Deut. 25:12. *Withholding of, from Jesus, prefigured in David*, Psa. 69:20. *Of God*, Psa. 103:13; Isa. 63:9; Joel 2:18; Jas. 5:11. *Of God withheld from reprobate sinners*, Jer. 13:14; 21:7; Ezek. 5:11; 7:4; 8:18; 9:5, 10; Zech. 11:6.
See footnotes: GOD, *Mercy of*, Gen. 2:2; JESUS, *Compassion of*, Matt. 1:21; MERCY, Deut. 5:10.

**1**
*a* Job 2:11; 11; 42: 7–9.

**3**
1 R. V. reproof which putteth me to shame,
2 R. V. answereth me.

**5**
*b* *Wicked, prosperity of, brief,* vs. 5–29; Psa. 73:3.
*c* *Joy, of the wicked,* Psa. 5:11.
*d* *Wicked, happiness of, brief,* Psa. 73:3.
3 R. V. godless

**8**
*e* *Dream,* Dan. 1:17.

**10**
4 R. V. the favour of the
5 R. V. give back his wealth.

**11**
6 R. V. of his youth, But it shall

**12**
*f* *Sin, love of,* Rom. 5:12.

**14**
*g* *Sin, fruits of,* Rom. 5:12.
*h* *Gall, figurative,* Job 16:13.

## CHAPTER 20

*The reply of Zophar; he assigns the reason of his speaking; 4 and shows the state and portion of the wicked.*

THEN answered [a]Zō'phar the Nā'a-math-īte, and said,

2 Therefore do my thoughts cause me to answer, and for *this* I make haste.

3 I have heard the [1]check[c] of my reproach[c], and the spirit of my understanding [2]causeth me to answer.

4 Knowest thou *not* this of old, since man was placed upon earth,

5 That the [b]triumphing of the wicked *is* short, and the [c,d]joy of the [3]hypocrite *but* for a moment?

6 [b]Though his excellency mount up to the heavens, and his head reach unto the clouds;

7 *Yet* [b,d]he shall perish forever like his own dung: they which have seen him shall say, Where *is* he?

8 [b,d]He shall fly away as a [e]dream, and shall not be found: yea, he shall be chased away as a vision of the night.

9 [b,d]The eye also *which* saw him shall *see him* no more; neither shall his place any more behold him.

10 His children shall seek [4]to please the poor, and his hands shall [5]restore their goods.

11 His bones are full [6]*of the sin* of his youth, which shall lie down with him in the dust.

12 Though [f]wickedness be sweet in his mouth, *though* he hide it under his tongue;

13 *Though* he spare it, and forsake it not; but [f]keep it still within his mouth:

14 *Yet* [b,d]his meat[c] in his bowels[c] [g]is turned, *it is* the [h]gall of *asps within him.

15 He hath [i]swallowed down riches, and [b,d]he shall vomit them up again: God shall cast them out of his belly.

16 [b,d]He shall suck the [j]poison of *asps: the [k]viper's tongue shall slay him.

17 He shall not see the rivers, the floods, the brooks of [l]honey and [m]butter.

18 [b,d]That which he laboured for shall he restore, and shall not swallow[c] *it* down: according to *his* substance [7]*shall* the restitution *be,* and he shall not rejoice *therein.*

19 Because [n]he hath oppressed *and* hath forsaken the [o,p]poor; *because* he hath violently [i]taken away an house which he builded not;

20 [8]Surely he shall not feel quietness in his belly, he shall not save of that [9]which he desired.

21 There [10]shall none of his meat[c] be left; therefore shall no man look for his goods.

22 In the fulness of his sufficiency[c] he shall be in straits[c]: [11]every hand of the wicked shall come upon him.

23 [b,d]*When* he is about to fill his belly, *God* shall cast the fury of his [q]wrath upon him, and shall rain *it* upon him while he is eating.

24 He shall flee from the [r]iron weapon, *and* the [s]bow of [12]steel[c] shall strike him through.

25 It is drawn, and cometh out of the body; yea, the glittering [13]sword cometh out of his gall: terrors *are* upon him.

26 All darkness [14]*shall be* hid in his secret places: a fire[c] not blown shall consume him; it shall [15]go ill with him that is left in his tabernacle.[c]

**15**
*i* *Covetousness,* Isa. 57:17.

**16**
*j* *Serpent, venom of, figurative,* Num. 21:6.
*k* *Viper, figurative,* Isa. 30:6.

**17**
*l* *Honey, figurative,* Prov. 25:27.
*m* *Butter,* Gen. 18:8.

**18**
7 R. V. that he hath gotten, he

**19**
*n* *Creditor, oppressions by,* Deut. 15:2.
*o* *Poor, oppressions of,* Prov. 21:13.
*p* *Debtor, oppressed,* Luke 7:41.

**20**
8 R. V. Because he knew no quietness within him,
9 R. V. wherein he delighteth.

**21**
10 R. V. was nothing left that he devoured not; Therefore his prosperity shall not endure.

**22**
11 R. V. The hand of every one that is in misery shall come upon him.

**23**
*q* *Judgments,* Ex. 6:6.

**24**
*r* *Iron,* Prov. 27: 17.
*s* *Bow,* 2 Sam. 1:18.
12 R. V. brass

**25**
13 R. V. point

**26**
14 R. V. is laid up for his treasures:
15 R. V. consume that which is left in his tent.

* **ASP.** *A venomous serpent,* Deut. 32:33; Job 20:14, 16; Isa. 11:8; Rom. 3.13. *Venom of, figurative, of the speech of the wicked,* Psa. 140: 3; Rom. 3:13, *of the injurious effects of wine,* Deut. 32:33; Prov. 23:32. *Deprived of venom, figurative of the peaceful conditions of Messiah's Kingdom,* Isa. 11:8, 9.

27
[t] *Sin, known to God,* Rom. 5:12.

27 The heaven shall [t]reveal his iniquity; and the earth shall rise up against him.
28 The increase of his house shall depart, *and his goods* shall flow away in the day of his wrath.
29 This *is* the portion of a wicked man from God, and the heritage appointed[c] unto him by God.

## CHAPTER 21

*Job's answer; he entreats his friends to hear him diligently; 7 shows that the wicked often prosper and despise God; 16 that destruction often comes upon them; 22 that all are alike in death; 27 and that the wicked are reserved unto the day of wrath.*

1
a *Job,* Job 1:1.

BUT [a]Jōb answered and said,
2 Hear diligently my speech, and let this be your consolations.

3
b *Mocking,* 1 Kin. 18:27.

3 Suffer[c] me that I may speak; and after that I have spoken, [b]mock on.

4
1 R. V. why should I not be impatient?

4 As for me, *is* my complaint to man? and [1]if *it were so,* why should not my spirit be troubled?
5 Mark me, and be astonished, and lay *your* hand upon *your* mouth.

6
2 R. V. horror

6 Even when I remember I am afraid, and [2]trembling taketh hold on my flesh.

7
c *God, providence of, mysterious,* Gen. 2:2.
d *Wicked, prosperity of,* vs. 7–13; Psa. 73:3.

7 [c]Wherefore do the [d]wicked live, become old, yea, are mighty in power?
8 [d]Their seed[c] is established in their sight with them, and their offspring before their eyes.
9 [d]Their houses *are* safe from fear, neither *is* the rod of God upon them.
10 Their bull gendereth[c], and faileth not; their cow calveth, and casteth[c] not her calf

11
e *Children, amusements of,* Mark 10:14.
f *Dancing, of children,* Eccl. 3:4.
g *Worldly Pleasure,* Eccl. 2:1.

11 They send forth their little ones like a flock, and their [e]children [f,g]dance.

12
h *Wicked, happiness of,* Psa. 73:3.
i *Timbrel,* Ex. 15:20.
j *Music, instruments of,* 2 Chr. 5:13.

12 [h]They take the [i,j]timbrel and [j,k]harp, and rejoice at the sound of the [3]organ[c].

k *Harp,* Dan. 3:10.
3 R. V. pipe.

13
l *Worldliness,* 1 John 2:15.
m *Riches,* Eccl. 4:8.
n *Death, of the wicked,* Num. 23:10.
o *Hell,* Mark 9:43.
4 R. V. Sheol.

13 They [l]spend their days in [m]wealth, and in a moment [n]go down to the [4,o]grave.[c]

14
p *Spiritual Blindness,* 2 Cor. 4:4.
q *Infidelity,* 2 Cor. 6:15.

14 Therefore they say unto God, [p]Depart from us; for [q]we desire not the knowledge of thy ways.

15
r *Skepticism,* Psa. 53:1.
s *Scoffing,* Hab. 1:10.
t *Prayer, disbelief in,* Acts 6:4.

15 [q,r]What *is* the Almighty, that we should serve him? and *,[s]what profit should we have, if we [t]pray unto him?

16
u *Sin, repugnant to the righteous,* Rom. 5:12.

16 Lo, their good *is* not in their hand: the [u]counsel of the wicked is far from me.

17
v *Wicked, prosperity of, brief,* Psa. 73:3.
w *Wicked, punishment of,* Psa. 73:3.
x *Afflictions, from God,* Psa. 34:19.
y *Anger of God,* 2 Kin. 13:3.

17 How oft is the candle[c] of the [v]wicked [w]put out! and *how oft* cometh their destruction upon them! *God* distributeth [x]sorrows in his [y]anger.

18
z *Wicked, compared to chaff,* Psa. 73:3.
a *Stubble,* Isa. 5:24.
b *Chaff,* Hos. 13:3.

18 [z]They are as [a]stubble before the wind, and as [b]chaff that the storm carrieth away.

19
c *Sin, consequences of, entailed upon children,* Rom. 5:12.
d *Heredity,* Ezek. 18:2.

19 God layeth up his [c]iniquity [d]for his children: he rewardeth him, and he shall know *it.*

20
e *Wicked, punishment of,* Psa. 73:3.

20 [e]His eyes shall see his destruction, and he shall drink of the wrath of the Almighty.
21 For what pleasure *hath* he in his house after him, when the number of his months is cut off in the midst?

22
f *God, knowledge of,* Gen. 2:2.
g *God, judge,* Gen. 2:2.

22 Shall *any* teach God [f]knowledge? seeing he [g]judgeth those that are high.[s]

23
h *Death,* Num. 23:10.

23 One [h]dieth in his full strength, being wholly at ease and quiet.
24 His breasts are full of milk, and his bones are moistened with marrow.
25 And another [h]dieth in the bitterness of his soul, and never eateth with pleasure.

26
i *Man, all men equal,* Job 4:17.
j *Corruption,* Job 17:14.

26 They shall lie down [i]alike in the dust, and [j]the worms shall cover them.
27 Behold, I know your

* **PRAYERLESSNESS,** Josh. 9:14; Job 15:4; 21:14, 15; Psa. 14:4; 53:4; 79:6; Isa. 43:22; 64:7; Jer. 10:21, 25; Dan. 9:13; Hos. 7:7; Jonah 1:6; Zeph. 1:6. See footnote, PRAYER, Acts 6:4.

thoughts, and the devices[c] *which* ye wrongfully imagine against me.

28 For ye say, Where *is* the house of the prince? and where *are* the dwelling places of the wicked?

29 Have ye not asked them that go by the way? and do ye not know their tokens,[c]

30 That the wicked is reserved to the day of destruction? they shall be brought forth to the day of wrath.

31 Who shall declare his way to his face? and who shall repay him *what* he hath done?

32 Yet shall he be brought to the grave, and shall [5]remain in the tomb.

33 The clods of the valley shall be sweet unto him, and every man shall draw after him, as *there are* innumerable before him.

34 How then comfort ye me in vain, seeing in your answers there remaineth †falsehood?

32
5 R. V. keep watch over the tomb.

## CHAPTER 22

*Eliphaz replies again; he teaches that man's goodness can not profit God; 5 accuses Job of divers sins; 15 refers him to the case of those who had perished in the flood; 21 and exhorts him to repentance.*

THEN [a]Ĕl′i-phăz the Tē′man-īte answered and said,

2 Can a [b]man be profitable unto God, [1]as he that is wise may be profitable unto himself?

3 *Is it* any pleasure to the Almighty, that thou art righteous? or *is it* gain *to him*, that thou makest thy ways perfect?

4 [2]Will he reprove thee for fear of thee? will he enter with thee into judgment?

5 *Is* not [c]thy [d]wickedness great? [3]and thine iniquities infinite?[s]

6 For [e]thou hast taken a pledge from thy [f]brother for nought,[c] and stripped the naked of their [g]clothing.

1
a Job 2:11; 4; 5; 15; 42:7–9.

2
b *Man, insignificance of*, Job 4:17.
1 R. V. Surely he that is wise is profitable

4
2 R. V. Is it for thy fear of him that he reproveth thee, That he entereth

5
c *Wicked*, Psa. 73:3.
d *Sin, sinfulness of*, Rom. 5:12.
3 R. V. Neither is there any end to thine iniquities.

6
e *Creditor, oppressions by*, Deut. 15:2.
f *Poor, oppressions of*, Prov. 21:13.
g *Debt, security for*, 1 Sam, 22:2.

---

† **FALSEHOOD,** Job 13:4; Psa. 116:11; Prov. 10:18, 31; 12:17, 19, 20; 17:4; 19:22; 20:17; Isa. 28:15. *Forbidden*, Ex. 23:1; Lev. 19:11, 12, 16; Psa. 34:13 (with 1 Pet. 3:10); Prov. 3:3; 17:7; Eccl. 5:6; Zeph. 3:13; Eph. 4:25, 29; Col. 3:9; 1 Tim. 1:9, 10. *Destructive*, Prov. 11:9; 26:18, 19, 24–26, 28; Isa. 32:7. *An abomination to the Lord*, Psa. 5:6, 9; Prov. 6:12, 13, 16–19; 12:22. *Abhorred by the righteous*, Psa. 31:18; 59:12; 101:5, 7; 119:29, 69, 163; 120:2–4; 144:8, 11; Prov. 13:5.

*Refrained from by the righteous*, Job 27:4; 31:5, 6, 33; 36:4; Isa. 63:8.

*Practiced by the wicked*, Psa. 10:7; 28:3; 36:3; 50:19, 20; 58:3; 62:4; 109:2; Prov. 2:12–15; Isa. 57:11; 59:3, 4, 12, 13; Jer. 7:8, 28; 9:3, 5, 6, 8; 12:6; Hos. 4:1, 2; Obad. 7; Mic. 6:12; Nah. 3:1; John 8.44, 45; 1 Tim. 4:2; 1 Pet. 3:16.

*Atonement for*, Lev. 6:2–7. *Punishment for*, Psa. 12:2, 3; Prov. 19:5, 9; Rev. 21:8, 27; 22:15.

**Instances of:** *Satan, in deceiving Eve*, Gen. 3:4, 5; *in impugning Job's motives for being righteous*, Job 1:9, 10; 2:4, 5; *in his false pretensions to Jesus*, Matt. 4:8, 9; Luke 4:6, 7. *Adam and Eve, in attempting to evade responsibility*, Gen. 3:12, 13. *Cain, in denying knowledge of his brother*, Gen. 4:9. *Abraham, in denying that Sarah was his wife*, Gen. 12:11–19; 20:2. *Sarah, to the angels, denying her derisive laugh of unbelief*, Gen. 18:15; *in denying to the king of Gerar, that she was Abraham's wife*, Gen. 20:5, 16. *Isaac, denying that Rebekah was his wife*, Gen. 26:7–10. *Rebekah and Jacob, in the conspiracy against Esau*, Gen. 27:6–24, 46. *Jacob's sons, in the scheme to destroy the Shechemites by first having them circumcised*, Gen. 34:13–16, 25, 26.

*Joseph's brethren, in deceiving their father into a belief that Joseph was killed by wild beasts*, Gen. 37:31–35. *Potiphar's wife, in falsely accusing Joseph*, Gen. 39:14–17. *Joseph, in the deception he carried on with his brethren*, Gen. chapters 42–44. *Pharaoh, in dealing deceitfully with the Israelites*, Ex. chapters 7–12.

*Aaron, in attempting to shift responsibility for the making of the golden calf*, Ex. 32:1–24. *Rahab, in denying that the spies were in her house*, Josh. 2:4–6. *The Gibeonites, in the deception they perpetrated upon Joshua and the elders of Israel in leading the latter to believe that they came from a distant region, when in fact they dwelt in the immediate vicinity*, Josh. 9. *Ehud, in pretending to bear secret messages to Eglon, king of Moab, while his object was to assassinate him*, Judg. 3:16–23. *Sisera, who instructed Jael to mislead his pursuers*, Judg. 4:20. *Saul, in professing to Samuel to have obeyed the commandment to destroy all spoils of the Amalekites, when in fact he had not obeyed*, 1 Sam. 15:1–26; *in accusing Ahimelech of conspiring with David against himself*, 1 Sam. 22:11–16. *David, to Ahimelech, professing to have a mission from the king, in order that he might obtain provisions and armor*, 1 Sam. 21:1–9; *in feigning madness*, 1 Sam. 21:13–15; *in telling Achish that he had raided Judah*, 1 Sam. 27:8–12.

*Michal, in the false statement that David was sick, in order to save him from Saul's violence*, 1 Sam. 19:12–17. *The Amalekite who claimed to have slain Saul*, 2 Sam. 1:10–12. *Hushai, in false professions to Absalom*, 2 Sam. 16:16–19; *in his deceitful counsel to Absalom*, 2 Sam. 17:7–14.

*The wife of the Bahurimite, who saved the lives of Hushai's messengers sent to apprise David of the movements of Absalom's army*, 2 Sam. 17:15–22. *The murder, under false pretense, of Adonijah*, 1 Kin. 2:23; *of Shimei*, 1 Kin. 2:42, 43; *of Jeroboam's wife*, 1 Kin. 14:2. *The old prophet of Beth-el, who misguided the prophet of Judah*, 1 Kin. 13:11–22. *Jeroboam's wife, feigning herself another woman*, 1 Kin. 14:5, 6.

*The conspirators against Naboth*, 1 Kin. 21:7–13. *Gehazi, who told Naaman that Elisha wanted a talent of silver and two changes of raiment*, 2 Kin. 5:20–24. *Hazael, misstating the prophet Elisha's message in regard to the king's recovery*, 2 Kin. 8:7–15. *Jehu, to the worshipers of Baal in order to gain advantage over them, and destroy them*, 2 Kin. 10:18–28. *Zedekiah, in violating his oath of allegiance to Nebuchadnezzar*, 2 Chr. 36:13; Ezek. 16:59; 17:15–20. *Samaritans, in their efforts to hinder the rebuilding of the temple*, Ezra 4. *Sanballat and others, in trying to obstruct the rebuilding of Jerusalem*, Neh. 6. *Haman, in his conspiracy against the Jews*, Esth. 3:8. *Jeremiah's adversaries, in accusing him of joining the Chaldeans*, Jer. 37: 13–15. *Princes of Israel, when they went to Jeremiah for a vision from the Lord*, Jer. 42:20.

*Herod, to the wise men, in professing to desire to worship Jesus*, Matt. 2:8.

*Jews, in accusing Jesus of being gluttonous and a winebibber*, Matt. 11:19; *in refusing to bear truthful testimony concerning John the Baptist*, Matt. 21:24:27.

*Peter, in denying Jesus*, Matt. 26:69–75; Mark 14:68–72; Luke 22:56–62; John 18:25–27. *The Roman soldiers, who said the disciples stole the body of Jesus*, Matt. 28:13, 15.

*The disobedient son, who promised to work in the vineyard, but did not*, Matt. 21:30. *Ananias and Sapphira falsely stating that they had sold their land for a given sum*, Acts 5:1–10.

*Stephen's accusers, who falsely accused him of blaspheming Moses and God*, Acts 6:11–14. *Paul's traducers, falsely accusing him of treason to Cæsar*, Acts 16:20, 21; 17:5–7; 24:5; 25:7, 8. *The Cretians*, Tit. 1:12.

7 [c]Thou hast not given water to the weary to drink, and thou hast withholden bread from the hungry.

8 But *as for* the mighty man, he had the earth; and the honourable man dwelt in it.

9 [c]Thou has sent [h]widows away empty, and the arms of the [i]fatherless have been broken.

10 Therefore [j]snares *are* round about thee, and sudden fear troubleth thee;

11 Or darkness, *that* thou canst not see; and abundance of waters cover thee.

12 *Is* not God in the height of [k]heaven? and behold the height of the stars, how high they are!

13 And thou sayest, [l]How doth God [m]know? can he [n]judge through the [4]dark cloud?

14 Thick clouds *are* a covering to him, that he seeth not; and he walketh [5]in the circuit of heaven.

15 [6]Hast thou marked the old way which wicked men have trodden?

16 Which were cut down out of time, whose foundation was overflown with a [o]flood:

17 Which said unto God, Depart from us: and [p]what can the Almighty do for [7]them?

18 Yet he [q]filled their houses with [r]good *things*: but the [s]counsel of the wicked is far from me.

19 The righteous see *it*, and are glad: and the innocent laugh them to scorn.

20 [8]Whereas our substance is not cut down, but the remnant of them the fire consumeth.

21 Acquaint now thyself with him, and be at [t]peace: thereby [u]good shall come unto thee.

22 Receive, I pray thee, the [v]law from his mouth, and [w]lay up his words in thine heart.

**9**
*h* *Widow*, 2 Sam. 14:5.
*i* *Orphan*, Lam. 5:3.

**10**
*j* *Snare, figurative*, Amos 3:5.

**12**
*k* *Heaven, God's dwelling place*, Luke 18:22.

**13**
*l* *Infidelity, exemplified, by impugning God's knowledge*, 2 Cor. 6:15.
*m* *God, knowledge of*, Gen. 2:2.
*n* *God, judge*, Gen. 2:2.
4 R. V. thick darkness?

**14**
5 Am. R. V. on the vault of

**15**
6 R. V. Wilt thou keep the old

**16**
*o* *Flood*, Gen. 6:17.

**17**
*p* *Skepticism*, Psa. 53:1.
7 R. V. us?

**18**
*q* *God, providence of*, Gen. 2:2.
*r* *Temporal Blessings, from God*, Psa. 103:2.
*s* *Sin, repugnant to the righteous*, Rom. 5:12.

**20**
8 R. V. Saying, Surely they that did rise up against us are cut off, And the

**21**
*t* *Spiritual Peace*, Gal. 1:3.
*u* *Righteous, promises to*, vs. 27–30; Psa. 64:10.

**22**
*v* *Word of God*, Psa. 119:9.
*w* *Wisdom, spiritual, from God*, Prov. 2:2.

23 If [x]thou [y]return to the Almighty, [z]thou shalt be [a]built up, thou shalt put away iniquity far from thy tabernacles.

24 Then shalt thou lay up [b]gold as dust, and the *gold* of [c]Ō′phĭr as the stones of the brooks.

25 Yea, the [d]Almighty shall be thy defence, and thou shalt have plenty of [e]silver.

26 For then shalt thou have thy [f]delight in the Almighty, and shalt lift up thy face unto God.

27 Thou shalt make thy prayer unto him, and he [g]shall hear thee, and thou shalt pay thy [h]vows.

28 Thou shalt also decree a thing, and it shall be established unto thee: and the light shall shine upon thy ways.

29 When [9]*men* are [i]cast down, then thou shalt say, *There is* lifting up; and he shall save the [j]humble person.

30 He shall deliver [10]the island of the innocent: and it is delivered by the pureness of thine hands.

## CHAPTER 23

*Job's answer; he longs to plead his cause before God, 8 but can not find him. 10 He comforts himself in the omniscience of God. 11 He is innocent. 13 But is troubled at the presence of him whose purpose is immutable.*

THEN [a]Jōb answered and said,

2 [b]Even to day *is* my complaint [1]bitter: my stroke is heavier than my groaning.

3 [b]Oh that I knew where I might find him! *that* I might come *even* to his seat!

4 I would order *my* cause before him, and fill my mouth with arguments.

5 I would know the words *which* he would answer me, and understand what he would say unto me.

6 [2]Will he plead against me with *his* great power? No; but [c]he would [3,d]put *strength* in me.

**23**
*x* *Backsliders, promises to*, vs. 23–30; Jer. 3:22.
*y* *Repentance, condition of forgiveness*, Mark 1:4.
*z* *Penitent, promises to, of mercy*, vs. 23–29; Psa. 51:17.

*a* *Prosperity*, Eccl. 7:14.

**24**
*b* *Gold*, Ezek. 7:19.
*c* *Ophir*, 1 Kin. 9:28.

**25**
*d* *God, providence of*, Gen. 2:2.
*e* *Silver*, 1 Chr. 28:14.

**26**
*f* *Joy*, Psa. 5:11.

**27**
*g* *Prayer, answer to, promised*, Acts 6:4.
*h* *Vows*, Num. 30:2.

**29**
*i* *Afflicted, help for*, Job 34:28.
*j* *Humility*, Prov. 22:4.
9 R. V. they cast thee down,

**30**
10 R. V. even him that is not innocent: Yea, he shall be delivered through the cleanness of thine hands.

**1**
*a* *Job*, Job 1:1.

**2**
*b* *Murmuring, instances of*, Num. 14:2.
1 R. V. rebellious:

**6**
*c* *Faith, instances of*, Mark 11:22.
*d* *God, mercy of*, Gen. 2:2.
2 R. V. Would he contend with me in the greatness of his power?
3 R. V. give heed unto me.

7 There the righteous might [4]dispute with him; so should I be delivered for ever from my [e]judge.[s]

8 [b]Behold, I go forward, but he *is* not *there*; and backward, but I [f]cannot perceive him:

9 On the left hand, where he doth work, but I cannot behold *him*: he hideth himself on the right hand, that I cannot see *him*:

10 But he [g]knoweth the way that I take: *when* he hath [h]tried[G] me, I shall come forth as gold.[S][Q]

11 My foot [i]hath held his steps, his way have I [j]kept, and not declined.

12 Neither have I gone back from the [k]commandment of his lips; I have esteemed the words of his mouth more than my necessary *food*.[T]

13 But [l]he *is* in one *mind*, and who can turn him? and *what* his soul desireth, even *that* he doeth.[S]

14 For he performeth *the thing that is* [m]appointed for me: and many such *things are* with him.

15 Therefore am I troubled at his presence: when I consider, I am afraid of him.

16 For God maketh my [n]heart soft, and the Almighty [o]troubleth me:

17 Because I was not cut off before the darkness, *neither* hath he covered the darkness from my face.

## CHAPTER 24

*Job shows that the wicked often go unpunished in this world; 23 but that they shall be brought low and cut off.*

WHY, [1]seeing times are not hidden from the [a]Almighty, do they that know him [b]not see his days?

2 [c]*Some* [d]remove the [e]landmarks; they violently take away flocks, and feed *thereof*.

3 [c,f]They drive away the ass of the [g]fatherless, they take the [h]widow's ox for a *pledge.

4 [c,f] They turn the [i]needy out of the way: the poor of the earth hide themselves together.

5 Behold, *as* wild [j,k]asses in the desert, go [i]they forth to their work; [2]rising betimes[G] for a prey: the wilderness *yieldeth* food for them *and* for *their* children.

6 [i]They [l]reap *every one* his corn[G] in the field: and they gather the vintage of the wicked.

7 They [3]cause the naked to lodge[G] without clothing, that *they have* no covering in the cold.

8 They are wet with the showers of the mountains, and embrace the rock for want of a shelter.

9 [c,f]They pluck the [m]fatherless from the breast, and take a *,[n]pledge of the poor.

10 [4]They cause *him* to go naked without clothing, and [5]they take away the sheaf *from* the hungry;

11 *Which* make oil within their walls, *and* tread *their* winepresses, and suffer thirst.

12 Men groan from out of the city, and the soul of the wounded crieth out: yet [b]God layeth not folly *to them*.

13 [c]They are of those that rebel against the light; they know not the ways thereof, nor abide in the paths thereof.

14 The murderer rising with the light [o]killeth the poor and needy, and in the night is as a [p]thief.[S]

15 The eye also of the [q]adulterer waiteth for the twilight, saying, No eye shall see me: and disguiseth *his* face.

**7**
e *God, judge,* Gen. 2:2.
4 R. V. reason

**8**
f *God, invisible,* Gen. 2:2.

**10**
g *God, knowledge of,* Gen. 2:2.
h *Afflictions, benefits of,* Psa. 34:19.

**11**
i *Integrity,* Job 2:3.
j *Faithfulness, instances of,* Luke 16:10.

**12**
k *Word of God,* Psa. 119:9.

**13**
l *God, immutable,* Gen. 2:2.

**14**
m *Foreordination,* Rom. 8:30.

**16**
n *Heart,* Psa. 44:21.
o *Afflictions, from God,* Psa. 34:19.

**1**
a *God, omnipotent,* Gen. 2:2.
b *God, providence of, mysterious,* Gen. 2:2.
1 Am. R. V. are times not laid up by the Almighty? And why do not they that know him see his days?

**2**
c *Wicked, described,* vs. 2–21; Psa. 73:3.
d *Dishonesty,* Ezek. 22:13.
e *Landmarks,* Deut. 19:14.

**3**
f *Creditor, oppressions by.* Deut. 15:2.
g *Orphan,* Lam. 5:3.
h *Widow,* 2 Sam. 14:5.

**4**
i *Poor, oppression of,* Prov. 21:13.

**5**
j *Ass, wild,* 2 Chr. 28:15.
k *Animals, abodes of,* Jer. 27:5.
2 Am. R. V. seeking diligently for food;

**6**
l *Harvest, figurative,* Ex. 34:21.

**7**
3 R. V. lie all night naked without

**9**
m *Children, sold for debt,* Mark 10:14.
n *Debt, security for,* 1 Sam. 22:2.

**10**
4 R. V. So that they go about naked
5 Am. R. V. being hungry they carry the sheaves;

**14**
o *Homicide, felonious,* Deut. 5:17.
p *Thieves,* Deut. 24:7.

**15**
q *Adultery,* Lev. 20:10.

***PAWN.** *Of widow's raiment forbidden,* Deut. 24:17. *Of mill-stones forbidden,* Deut. 24:6. *Raiment given as, to be returned before night,* Ex. 22:26; Deut. 24:12, 13. *Creditor forbidden to invade debtor's home to receive,* Deut. 24:10, 11. *Mercilessly exacted,* Job 24:3. *Unlawfully retained,* Ezek. 18:12; Amos 2:8. *Restoration of, required of the righteous* Ezek. 18:5, 7; 33:15.
See footnote, SURETY, Gen. 44:32.

16 In the dark [p]they dig
through houses, [6]*which* they had
marked for themselves in the
day time: they know not the
light.
17 For the morning *is* to them
even as the shadow of death: if
*one* know *them, they are in* the
terrors of the shadow of death.
18 [c]He *is* swift [7]as the waters;
their portion is cursed in the
earth: he beholdeth not the way
of the vineyards.
19 [r]Drought and heat consume
the snow waters: [s]*so doth* [8]the
[t]grave[G] *those which* have sinned.
20 The womb shall forget him;
[s,u]the worm shall feed sweetly
on him; he shall be no more remembered; and wickedness shall
be broken as a tree.
21 [c]He evil entreateth[G] the [v]bar-
ren *that* beareth not: and doeth
not good to the [h]widow.
22 [w]He draweth also the
mighty with his power: he riseth
up, and no *man* is sure of life.
23 [9,w]*Though* it be given him *to*
*be* in safety, whereon he resteth;
yet his eyes *are* upon their ways.[S]
24 [x]They are exalted[G] for a little
while, but are gone and brought
low; they are taken out of the
way as all *other*[G], and cut off as
the tops of the ears of corn.[C]
25 And if *it be* not *so* now, who
will make me a liar, and make
my speech nothing worth?

## CHAPTER 25

*Bildad replies again; he shows that man cannot be justified before God.*

THEN answered [a]Bĭl′dăd the
Shu′hite, and said,
2 Dominion and fear *are* with
[b]him, he maketh peace in his
high places.
3 Is there any number of his
armies? and upon whom doth
not his [c]light arise?[S]
4 How then can [d]man be [1]jus-
tified with [e]God? or [f]how can
he be clean *that is* born of a
woman?
5 Behold even to the [g]moon,
and it shineth not; yea, the
[h]stars are not pure in [e]his sight.[S]
6 How much less man, *that is*
a [i]worm? and the son of man,
*which is* a worm?

## CHAPTER 26

*Job's answer; he reproves Bildad; 5 and speaks of the infinite power and majesty of God.*

BUT [a]Jōb answered and
said,
2 [b]How hast thou helped *him*
*that is* without power? *how* savest thou the arm *that hath* no
strength?
3 [b]How hast thou counselled
*him that hath* no wisdom? and
*how* hast thou plentifully declared the thing as it is?
4 [b]To whom hast thou uttered
words? and whose spirit came
from thee?
5 [1]Dead *things* are formed from
under the waters, and the inhabitants thereof.
6 [2,c]Hell[G] *is* naked before [d]him,
and [3]destruction hath no covering.[S Q]
7 [e,f]He stretcheth out the north
over the empty place, *and* [g]hang-
eth the [h]earth upon nothing.
8 [e,i]He bindeth up the waters
in his thick clouds; and the
cloud is not rent[G] under them.
9 [e,j]He holdeth back the face
of his throne, *and* spreadeth his
cloud upon it.[S]
10 [e]He hath compassed the
[k]waters with bounds,[C] until the
day and night come to an end.
11 [l]The pillars of heaven tremble and are astonished at his
reproof.
12 He [4]divideth the [k]sea with
his [l]power, and by his understanding he smiteth through [5]the
proud.
13 By his spirit he hath garnished[G] the heavens; his hand

---

16
6 R. V. They shut themselves up in

18
7 R. V. upon the face of the waters;

19
r *Drought*, Gen. 31:40.
s *Death, of the wicked*, Num. 23:10.
t *Hell*, Mark 9:43.
8 R. V. Sheol

20
u *Corruption*, Job 17:14.

21
v *Barrenness*, Deut. 7:14.

22
w *God, providence of, mysterious*, Gen. 2:2.

23
9 R. V. God giveth them to be in security, and they rest thereon; And his

24
x *Wicked, prosperity of, brief*, Psa. 73:3.

1
a Job 2:11; 8; 18; 42:7–9.

2
b *God, sovereign*, Gen. 2:2.

3
c *God, glory of*, Gen. 2:2.

4
d *Man, insignificance of*, vs. 4–6; Job 4:17.
e *God, holiness of*, Gen. 2:2.
f *Depravity, of man*, vs. 4–6; Job 15:14.
1 R. V. just

5
g *Moon, darkening of*, Song 6:10.
h *Stars*, Judg. 5:20.

6
i *Worm, figurative*, Jonah 4:7.

1
a *Job*, Job 1:1.

2
b *Sarcasm*, vs. 2–4; Judg. 10:14.

5
1 R. V. They that are deceased tremble Beneath the waters

6
c *Hell*, Mark 9:43.
d *God, knowledge of*, Gen. 2:2.
2 R. V. Sheol
3 R. V. Abaddon

7
e *God, dissertations on*, vs. 6–14; Gen. 2:2.
f *God, creator*, Gen. 2:2.
g *Astronomy*, Isa. 13:10.
h *Earth*, Prov. 8:23.

8
i *Meteorology*, Matt. 16:2.

9
j *God, unsearchable*, Gen. 2:2.

10
k *Sea*, Jer. 5:22.

11
l *God, power of*, Gen. 2:2.

12
4 R. V. stirreth up
5 R. V. Rahab.

13
6 R. V. pierced the swift serpent.

14
m *Thunder*, 1 Sam. 7:10.

1
a *Job*, Job 1:1.

2
b *Afflictions, from God*, Psa. 34:19.

3
c *Life, from God*, Eccl. 8:15.

4
d *Integrity*, Job 2:3.
e *Falsehood, refrained from by the righteous*, Job 21:34.
f *Deceit, the righteous free from*, Psa. 36:3.

5
g *Honesty*, Rom. 13:13.

6
h *Righteousness*, Psa. 15:2.
i *Conscience, approving*, Acts 23:1.

7
j *Prayer, imprecatory*, Acts 6:4.

8
k *Hope, of the wicked*, Prov. 13:12.
l *Death, of the wicked*, Num. 23:10.
1 R. V. godless,

9
m *Wicked, prayer of*, Psa. 73:3.

11
n *Instruction, in religion*, Prov. 23: 23.

hath [6]formed the crooked[c] serpent.[T]
14 Lo, these *are* parts of his
ways: but [j]how little a portion is
heard of him ? but the [m]thunder
of his [l]power who can understand ?[s]

## CHAPTER 27

*Job purposes to hold fast his integrity; 7 and shows the groundless hope of the hypocrite; 11 and the miserable end of the wicked.*

MOREOVER [a]Jōb continued
his parable, and said,
2 *As* God liveth, *who* hath
taken[G] away my judgment; and
the Almighty, *who* [b]hath vexed
my[s] soul;
3 All the while my breath *is*
in me, and the [c]spirit of God
*is* in my nostrils;[T]
4 My lips [d]shall not speak
[e]wickedness, nor my tongue
utter [f]deceit.
5 God forbid that I should justify you: till I die I will not remove mine [d,g]integrity from
me.
6 My [h]righteousness I hold
fast, and will not let it go: my
[i]heart shall not reproach *me* so
long as I live.[s]
7 [j]Let mine enemy be as the
wicked, and he that riseth up
against me as the unrighteous.
8 For what *is* the [k]hope of
the [1]hypocrite, though he hath
gained, when God [l]taketh away
his soul ?
9 Will God hear his [m]cry when
trouble cometh upon him ?
10 Will he delight himself in
the Almighty ? will he always
call upon God ?
11 I will [n]teach you by the
hand of God: *that* which *is* with
the Almighty will I not conceal.
12 Behold, all ye yourselves
have seen *it*; why then are ye
thus altogether vain ?

13 This *is* the portion of a
[o]wicked man with God, and the
heritage of [p]oppressors, *which*
they shall receive of the Almighty.
14 If his children be multiplied, [o]*it is* for the sword: and
his offspring shall not be satisfied with bread.
15 Those that remain of him
[o]shall be buried in death: and
his widows shall not weep.
16 Though he heap up [q]silver
as the dust, and prepare [r]rai-
ment as the clay;
17 He may prepare *it*, but [o]the
just shall put *it* on, and the innocent shall divide the [q]silver.
18 He buildeth his house as a
[s]moth, and as a [t]booth *that* the
keeper maketh.
19 The [u]rich man shall lie
down, but he shall not be gathered: he openeth his eyes, and
he *is* not.
20 [o]Terrors take hold on him
as waters, a [v]tempest stealeth
him away in the night.
21 [v]The east [w]wind carrieth
him away, and he departeth:
and as a storm hurleth him out
of his place.
22 For *God* shall [o]cast upon
him, and not spare: he would
fain[G] flee out of his hand.
23 [o]*Men* shall clap their hands
at him, and shall hiss him out
of his place.

## CHAPTER 28

*Job shows that man may gain some knowledge of natural things; 12 but that he can not understand the secret counsels of God.*

SURELY there is a vein for
the [a]silver, and a place for
[b]gold *where* they fine[G] *it*.
2 [c]Iron is taken out of the earth,
and *brass[G] *is* [d]molten[G] *out of* the
stone.
3 [1]He setteth an end to dark-

13
o *Wicked, punishment of*, Psa. 73:3.
p *Oppression*, Eccl. 5:8.

16
q *Silver*, 1 Chr. 28:14.
r *Dress*, Zech. 3:3.

18
s *Moth*, Job 4:19.
t *Booth*, Lev. 23.42.

19
u *Rich*, Jas. 5:1.

20
v *Meteorology*, Matt. 16:2.

21
w *Wind, east*, Job 37:17.

1
a *Silver*, 1 Chr. 28:14.
b *Gold*, Ezek. 7:19.

2
c *Iron*, Prov. 27:17.
d *Art, of the smelter of metals*, 2 Chr. 16:14.

3
1 R .V. man

*** BRASS**, or more probably COPPER. *A mineral, of Canaan*, Deut. 8:9; Josh. 22:8; *of Syria* 2 Sam. 8:8. *Abundance of, for the temple*, 1 Kin. 7:47; 1 Chr. 22:14. *Smelted*, Ezek. 22:20; Job 28:2. *Tyrians traded in*, Ezek. 27:13.

Articles made of: *Royal vessels*, 2 Sam. 8:10; *altar, vessels, and other articles of the tabernacle and temple*, Ex 38:28–31; 1 Kin. 7:14–47; Ezra 8:27; *cymbals*, 1 Chr. 15:19; *trumpets*, 1 Cor. 13:1; *armor*, 1 Sam. 17:5, 6; *shields*, 1 Kin. 14:27;

ness, and searcheth out [2]all perfection: the stones of darkness,
and the shadow of death.
4 [3]The flood breaketh out from
the inhabitant; *even the waters*
forgotten of the foot: they are
dried up, they are gone away
from men.
5 *As for* the earth, out of it
cometh bread: and under it is
turned up as it were fire.
6 The stones of it *are* the place
of †sapphires: and it hath dust
of [b]gold.
7 [4]*There is* a path which no
fowl knoweth, and which the
vulture's eye hath not seen:
8 The [5,e]lion's whelps have not
trodden it, nor the fierce lion
passed by it.
9 He putteth forth his hand
upon the rock; he overturneth
the [f]mountains by the roots.
10 He cutteth out rivers among
the rocks; and his eye seeth
every precious thing.
11 He bindeth the floods from
overflowing; and *the thing that
is* hid bringeth he forth to
light.
12 But where shall [g]wisdom be
found? and where *is* the place
of understanding?
13 Man knoweth not the price
thereof; neither is [g]it found in
the land of the living.
14 The depth saith, [g]It *is* not
in me: and the sea saith, *It is* not
with me.
15 [g]It cannot be gotten for
[b]gold, neither shall [a,h]silver be
weighed *for* the price thereof.
16 [g]It cannot be valued with
the [b]gold of [i]Ō'phīr, with the
precious [j]onyx, or the †sap-
phire.
17 The [b]gold and the [6,k]crystal
cannot equal it: and the exchange of it *shall not be for*
jewels of fine gold.
18 No mention shall be made
of [l]coral, or of [7]pearls: for the
price of [g]wisdom *is* above
[m]rubies.
19 The [n]topaz of [o]Ē-thĭ-ō'pĭ-ȧ
shall not equal it, neither shall it
be valued with pure [b]gold.
20 Whence then cometh [g]wis-
dom? and where *is* the place of
understanding?
21 Seeing [g]it is hid from the
eyes of all living, and kept close
from the fowls of the air.
22 Destruction and death say,
We have heard the fame thereof
with our ears.
23 God [p]understandeth the way
thereof, and he knoweth the
place thereof.
24 For he [p]looketh to the ends
of the earth, *and* seeth under the
whole heaven;
25 To make the weight for
the winds; and he weigheth the
waters by measure.
26 When he made a decree
for the rain, and a way for
the ‡lightning of the thunder:
27 Then did he see it, and declare it; he prepared it, yea, and
searched it out.
28 And unto man he said, Behold, the [q]fear of the Lord, that
*is* [g]wisdom; and [r]to depart from
evil *is* understanding.

## CHAPTER 29

*Job describes his former prosperity and honorable condition; 14 his care for the poor; 18 and his expectation of continued happiness.*

MOREOVER [a]Jōb continued
his parable, and said,
2 Oh that I were as *in* months

---

2 R. V. to the furthest bound The stones of thick darkness

**4**
3 Am. R. V. He breaketh open a shaft away from where men sojourn; They are forgotten of the foot; They hang afar from men, they swing to and fro.

**7**
4 R. V. That path no bird of prey knoweth, Neither hath the falcon's eye seen it:

**8**
e *Lion,* Mic. 5:8.
5 R. V. proud beasts

**9**
f *Mountain,* Mic. 7:12.

**12**
g *Wisdom, spiritual,* Prov. 2:2.

**15**
h *Money, weighed,* Jer. 32:9.

**16**
i *Ophir, gold of,* 1 Kin. 9:28.
j *Onyx,* Ezek. 28:13.

**17**
k Rev. 21:18.
6 R. V. glass

**18**
l Ezek. 27:16.
m Prov. 20:15; 31:10; Lam. 4:7.
7 R. V. crystal:

**19**
n *Topaz,* Ezek. 28:13.
o *Ethiopia,* Isa. 18:1.

**23**
p *God, knowledge of,* Gen. 2:2.

**28**
q *Fear of God,* Acts 9:31.
r *Holiness,* Ex. 39:30.

**1**
a *Job,* Job 1:1.

---

2 Chr. 12:10; *bows* (R. V.), 2 Sam. 22:35; Job 20:24; Psa. 18:34; *fetters,* Judg. 16:21; *gates,* Psa. 107:16; Isa. 45:2; *bars,* 1 Kin. 4:13; *idols,* Dan. 5:4; Rev. 9:20; *mirrors,* Ex. 38:8; *household vessels,* Mark 7:4; *money,* Matt. 10:9.
Workers in: *Tubal-cain,* Gen. 4:22; *Hiram,* 1 Kin. 7:14; *Alexander,* 2 Tim. 4:14.
**Figurative,** Deut. 33:25; Isa. 48:4; Jer. 1:18; Zech. 6:1.
**Symbolical,** Dan. 2:32, 39; 7:19; Zech. 6:1.
† **SAPPHIRE.** *A precious stone,* Job 28:6, 16; Isa. 54:11; Ezek. 1:26; 28:13. *Set in the breastplate,* Ex. 28:18. *Seen in the foundation of the New Jerusalem in John's apocalyptic vision,* Rev. 21:19.
‡ **LIGHTNING,** Job 28:26; 37:3; 38:25, 35; Psa. 18:14; 97:4; 135:7; 144:6; Jer. 10:13; 51:16; Ezek. 1:13, 14; Dan. 10:6; Nah. 2:4; Zech. 9:14; 10:1; Matt. 24:27; 28:3; Luke 10:18. *In John's vision,* Rev. 4:5; 8:5; 11:19; 16:18.
*Plague of, sent upon Egypt,* Ex. 9:23; Psa. 77:18; 78:48; 105:32.

2
*b* *God, preserver,* Gen. 2.2.
3
*c* *Lamp, figurative,* Ex. 27:20.
*d* *Temporal Blessings, from God,* Psa. 103:2.
4
1 R. V. ripeness of my days,
6
*e* *Rock,* Psa. 78:15.
8
*f* *Manners,* Gen. 18:2.
12
*g* *Liberality, instances of,* 1 Tim. 6:18.
*h* *Kindness,* Acts 28:2.
*i* *Poor, kindness to,* Prov. 21:13.
*j* *Orphan,* Lam. 5:3.
13
*k* *Widow,* 2 Sam. 14:5.
14
*l* *Righteousness, figuratively described as a garment,* Psa. 15:2.
2 R. V. justice
16
3 R.V.of him that I
17
4 R. V. prey

past, as *in* the days *when* God
[b]preserved me;
3[s] When his [c]candle[C] [d]shined upon my head, *and when* by his
[d]light I walked *through* darkness;
4 As I was in the [1]days of my
youth, when the secret of God
*was* upon my tabernacle[C];
5 When the Almighty *was* yet
with me, *when* my [d]children *were*
about me;[s]
6 [d]When I washed my steps
with butter, and the [e]rock poured me out rivers of oil;
7 [d]When I went out to the gate
through the city, *when* I prepared my seat in the street!
8 The young men saw me, and
hid themselves: and [f]the aged
arose, *and* stood up.
9 [f]The princes refrained talking, and laid *their* hand on their
mouth.
10 [f]The nobles held their peace,
and their tongue cleaved to the
roof of their mouth.
11 When the ear heard *me,*
then it blessed me; and when the
eye saw *me,* it gave witness to
me:
12 Because I [g,h]delivered the
[i]poor that cried, and the [j]father-
less, and *him that had* none to
help him.
13 The blessing of him that
was ready to perish came upon
me: and I [h]caused the [k]widow's
heart to sing for joy.
14 I put on [l]righteousness, and
it clothed me: my [2]judgment
*was* as a robe and a diadem.
15 [h]I was eyes to the blind,
and feet *was* I to the lame.
16 [h]I *was* a father to the [i]poor:
and the cause [3]*which* I knew not
I searched out.
17 And I brake the jaws of the
wicked, and plucked the [4]spoil[C]
out of his teeth.
18 Then I said, I shall die in
my nest, and I shall multiply *my*
days as the sand.
19[s] My root *was* spread out by
the waters, and the dew lay all
night upon my branch.
20 My glory *was* fresh in me,
and my bow was renewed in my
hand.[s]
21 Unto me *men* gave ear, and
waited, and kept silence at my
counsel.
22 After my words they spake
not again; and my speech
dropped upon them.
23 And they waited for me as
for the rain; and they opened
their mouth wide *as* for the latter rain.
24 *If* I laughed on them, they
believed *it* not; and the light of
my [m]countenance they cast not
down.
25 I chose out their way, and
sat chief, and dwelt as a king in
the army, as one *that* comforteth
the mourners.

## CHAPTER 30

*Job bemoans his altered state; 15 and shows the greatness of his sufferings.*

BUT now *they that are* younger
than [a]I have me in *,[b]deri-
sion[C], whose fathers [1]I would have
disdained to have set with the
[c]dogs of my flock.
2 Yea, whereto *might* the
strength of their hands *profit* me,
in whom old age was perished?
3 [2]For want and [d]famine *they
were* solitary; fleeing into the
wilderness in former time desolate and waste.
4 [3]Who cut up mallows by the
bushes, and [4]juniper roots *for*
their meat.[C]
5 They were driven forth from
among *men,* (they cried after
them as *after* a [e]thief;)
6 To dwell in the [5]cliffs of the
valleys, *in* caves of the earth,
and *in* the rocks.

24
*m* *Countenance.* Prov. 15:13.
1
*a* *Job,* Job 1:1.
*b* *Mocking,* 1 Kin. 18:27.
*c* *Dog,* 1 Kin. 21:19.
1 R. V. I disdained to set
3
*d* *Famine,* 2 Kin. 8:1.
2 R. V. They are gaunt with want and famine; They gnaw the dry ground, in the gloom of wasteness and desolation.
4
3 R. V. They pluck salt-wort by the bushes;
4 Am. R. V. the roots of the broom are their food.
5
*e* *Thieves,* Deut. 24:7.
6
5 R. V. clefts

* **DERISION.** *The obdurately wicked held in, by God,* Psa. 2:4; Prov. 1:26. **Instances of:** *Sarah, when the angels gave her the promise of a child,* Gen. 18:12. *The evil children of Beth-el deride Elisha,* 2 Kin. 2:23. *The people of Israel scoff at Hezekiah,* 2 Chr. 30:1-10. See footnote, MOCKING, 1 Kin. 18:27.

**7**
*f* *Nettles, figurative*, Prov. 24:31.

**8**
6 R. V. scourged out of the land.

**11**
7 R. V. cast off

**12**
8 R. V. rabble;

**14**
9 R. V. As through a wide breach they come:

**15**
10 R. V. chase mine honour

**16**
*g* *Afflictions*, Psa. 34:19.
11 R. V. within

**17**
*h* *Pain*, Job 14:22.
12 R. V. the pains that gnaw me take

**18**
*i* *Disease*, Ex. 15:26.

**20**
*j* *Prayer, answer to, withheld*, Acts 6:4.

**21**
*k* *Murmuring, against God*, Num. 14:2.

7 Among the bushes they brayed; under the [f]nettles they were gathered together.

8 *They were* children of fools, yea, children of base men: they were [6]viler than the earth.

9 And [b]now am I their song, yea, I am their byword.

10 They abhor me, they flee far from me, and spare not to spit in my face.

11 Because he hath loosed my cord, and afflicted me, they have [7]also let loose the bridle before me.

12 Upon *my* right *hand* rise the [8]youth; they push away my feet, and they raise up against me the ways of their destruction.

13 They mar my path, they set forward my calamity, they have no helper.

14 [9]They came *upon me* as a wide breaking in *of waters*: in the desolation they rolled themselves *upon me*.

15 Terrors are turned upon me: they [10]pursue my soul as the wind: and my welfare passeth away as a cloud.

16 And now my soul is poured out [11]upon me; the days of [g]affliction have taken hold upon me.

17 My bones are [h]pierced in me in the night season: and [12]my sinews take no rest.

18 By the great force *of my* [i]*disease* is my garment changed: it bindeth me about as the collar of my coat.

19 He hath cast me into the mire, and I am become like dust and ashes.

20 I cry unto thee, and [j]thou dost not hear me: I stand up, and thou regardest me *not*.

21 [k]Thou art become cruel to me: with thy strong hand thou opposest thyself against me.

22 [k]Thou liftest me up to the wind; thou causest me to ride *upon it*, and dissolvest [13]my substance.

23 For I know *that* thou wilt bring me *to* [l]death, and *to* the house appointed for all living.

24 [14]Howbeit he will not stretch out *his* hand to the grave, though they cry in his destruction.

25 Did not I [m]weep for him that was in trouble? was *not* my soul [m]grieved for the [n]poor?

26 When I looked for good, then evil came *unto me*: and when I waited for light, there came darkness.

27 My [o]bowels boiled, and rested not: the days of [g]affliction [15]prevented me.

28 I went mourning without the sun: I stood up, *and* I cried in the congregation.

29 I am a brother to [16]dragons, and a companion to [17,p]owls.

30 My skin is black upon me, and my bones are burned with [q]heat.

31 My [r,s]harp also is *turned* to mourning, and my [18]organ into the voice of them that weep.

## CHAPTER 31

*Job makes a solemn protestation of his integrity in several duties.*

[a,b]I MADE a *,[c]covenant with mine eyes; why then should I [d]think upon a maid?

2 For what portion of God *is there* from above? and *what* inheritance of the Almighty from on high?

3 *Is* not [e]destruction to the wicked? and a strange *punishment* to the workers of iniquity?

4 Doth not [f]he see [g]my ways, and count all my steps?

5 If I have walked with [h]vanity, or if my foot hath hasted to [i]deceit;

6 Let me be weighed in an even

**22**
13 R. V. me in the storm.

**23**
*l* *Death, inevitable*, Num. 23:10.

**24**
14 R. V. Surely against a ruinous heap he will not put forth his hand; Though it be in his destruction, one may utter a cry because of these things.

**25**
*m* *Sympathy*, Jas. 1:27.
*n* *Poor*, Prov. 21:13.

**27**
*o* *Bowels, figurative*, 1 Kin. 3:26.
15 R. V. are come upon me.

**29**
*p* *Ostriches*, Lam. 4:3.
16 R. V. jackals.
17 R. V. ostriches.

**30**
*q* *Fever*, Deut. 28:22.

**31**
*r* *Harp, used in mourning*, Dan. 3:10.
*s* *Music, instruments of*, 2 Chr. 5:13.
18 R. V. pipe

**1**
*a* *Job*, Job 1:1.
*b* *Integrity*, vs. 1–40; Job 2:3.
*c* *Vows, instances of*, Num. 30:2.
*d* *Temptation, instances of those who resisted*, Luke 11:4.

**3**
*e* *Wicked, punishment of*, Psa. 73:3.

**4**
*f* *God, knowledge of*, Gen. 2:2.
*g* *Heart, known to God*, Psa. 44:21.

**5**
*h* *Falsehood, refrained from, by the righteous*, Job 21:34.
*i* *Deceit*, Psa. 36:3.

* **CHASTITY**, Rev. 14:4. *Enjoined*, Ex. 20:14; Prov. 5:3–21; 6:24–35; 7; 31:3; Matt. 5:27–32; Acts 15:20; Rom. 13:13; 1 Cor. 6:13–19; 7:1, 2, 7–9; Eph. 5:3; Col. 3:5; 1 Thess. 4:3, 7. **Instances of:** *Joseph*, Gen. 39:7–20. *Boaz*, Ruth 3:6–13. *Job*, Job 31:1, 9–12.
See footnote, CONTINENCE, Matt. 19:12.

**6**
*j* *Balances, figurative*, Prov. 11:1.

**8**
1 R. V. the produce of my field

**9**
*k* *Lust, sinful*, 2 Pet. 1:4.
*l* *Adultery*, Lev. 20:10.
2 R. V. enticed unto

**13**
*m* *Employer*, Deut. 24:14.
*n* *Master, good, instances of*, Col. 4:1.
*o* *Injustice*, Isa. 26:10.
*p* *Servant, kindness to, exemplified*, Jer. 2:14.
*q* *Servant, rights of*, Jer. 2:14.

**14**
*r* *God, judge*, Gen. 2:2.

**15**
*s* *Man, equality of*, Job 4:17.
*t* *God, creator of man*, Gen. 2:2.
*u* *Man, created*, Job 4:17.

**16**
*v* *Liberality*, 1 Tim. 6:18.
*w* *Poor, kindness to*, Prov. 21:13.
*x* *Widow, kindness to*, 2 Sam. 14:5.

**17**
*y* *Orphan, kindness to*, Lam. 5:3.

**20**
*z* *Sheep*, Deut. 32:14.

[j]balance,[C] that God may know mine [b]integrity.

7 If my step hath turned out of the way, and mine heart walked after mine eyes, and if any blot hath cleaved to mine hands;

8 *Then* let me sow, and let another eat; yea, let [1]my offspring be rooted out.

9 If mine [k]heart have been [2]deceived by a woman, or *if* I have [l]laid wait at my neighbour's door;

10 *Then* let my wife grind[C] unto another, and let others bow[C] down upon her.

11 For [k,l]this *is* an heinous crime; yea, it *is* an iniquity *to be punished by* the judges.

12 For [k,l]it *is* a fire *that* consumeth to destruction, and would root out all mine increase.

13[S] If [m,n]I did [o]despise the cause of my [p]manservant or of my [p]maidservant, [q]when they contended with me;

14 What then shall I do when [r]God riseth up? and when he visiteth, what shall I answer him?

15 [s]Did not he that [t]made [u]me in the womb make him? and did not one fashion us in the womb?[S]

16 [v]If I have withheld the [w]poor from *their* desire, or have caused the eyes of the [x]widow to fail;

17 [v]Or have eaten my morsel myself alone, and the [y]fatherless hath not eaten thereof;

18 (For from my youth [w,y]he was brought up with me, as *with* a father, and I have guided [x]her from my mother's womb;)

19 [v]If I have seen [w]any perish for want of clothing, or any poor without covering;

20 If his loins have not blessed me, and *if* he were *not* warmed with the fleece of my [z]sheep;

21 If I have lifted up my hand against the [y]fatherless, when I saw my help in the gate:

22 *Then* let [3]mine arm fall from my shoulder blade, and mine arm be broken from the bone.

23 For destruction *from* God *was* a terror to me, and by reason of his highness[C] I could not endure.

24 If I [a]have made [b]gold my [c]hope, or have said to the fine gold, *Thou art* my confidence;

25 If [d]I rejoiced because my [e]wealth *was* great, and because mine hand had gotten much;

26 If I [f]beheld the [g]sun when it shined, or the [h]moon walking *in* brightness;

27 And my heart hath been [f]secretly enticed, or my mouth hath [f]kissed my hand:

28 [f]This also *were* an iniquity *to be punished by* the judge: for I should have [4]denied the God *that is* above.

29 If I [i]rejoiced at the destruction of [j]him that hated me, or lifted up myself when evil found him:

30 Neither have I suffered my mouth to sin by [5]wishing a curse to his soul.

31 If the men of my tabernacle[C] said not, [6]Oh that we had of his flesh! we cannot be satisfied.

32 The stranger[C] did not lodge in the street: *but* I [k]opened my doors to the traveller.

33 If I covered my transgressions as [l]Ăd'ăm, by [m]hiding mine iniquity in my bosom:

34 [7]Did I fear a great multitude, or did the contempt of families terrify me, that I kept silence, *and* went not out of the door?

35 Oh that one would hear me! [8]behold, my desire *is, that* the Almighty would answer me, and *that* mine adversary had written a book.[S]

36 Surely I would take it upon

**22**
3 R. V. my shoulder

**24**
*a* *Covetousness*, Isa. 57:17.
*b* *Gold*, Ezek. 7:19.
*c* *Hope, of the wicked*, Prov. 13:12.

**25**
*d* *Rich*, Jas. 5:1.
*e* *Riches, a snare*, Eccl. 4:8.

**26**
*f* *Idolatry*, 1 Sam. 15:23.
*g* *Sun, worshiped*, Josh. 10:12.
*h* *Moon, worshiped*, Song 6:10.

**28**
4 R. V. lied to God

**29**
*i* *Malice, Job's freedom from*, Eph. 4:31.
*j* *Enemy*, Prov. 24:17.

**30**
5 R. V. asking his life with a curse;

**31**
6 Am. R. V. Who can find one that hath not been filled with his meat?

**32**
*k* *Hospitality*, Rom. 12:13.

**33**
*l* *Adam, temptation and sin of*, Gen. 2:19.
*m* *Hypocrisy*, Jas. 3:17.

**34**
7 Am. R. V. Because I feared the great multitude, And the contempt of families terrified me, So that I kept silence, and went not out of the door—

**35**
8 R. V. (Lo, here is my signature, let the Almighty answer me;) And that I had the indictment which mine adversary hath written!

my shoulder, *and* bind it *as* a
crown to me.
37 I would declare unto him the
number of my steps; as a prince
would I go near unto him.
38 If my land cry against
me, or that the furrows likewise thereof complain;
39 If I have eaten the fruits
thereof without [n]money, or have
[o]caused the owners thereof to
lose their life:
40 Let [p]thistles grow instead of
[q]wheat, and cockle[C] instead of
[r]barley. The words of [s]Jōb are
ended.

39
*n Money*, Jer. 32:9.
*o Homicide*, Deut. 5:17.

40
*p Thistle*, Hos. 10:8.
*q Wheat*, Ezra 6:9.
*r Barley*, Ex. 9:31.
*s Job*, Job 1:1.

## CHAPTER 32

*The speech of Elihu; he is angry with Job and his friends; 6 he gives his reasons for speaking; 11 and reproves the friends of Job for not answering his argument. 16 His zeal for speaking.*

SO these three men ceased to
answer [a]Jōb, because he
*was* [b]righteous in his own eyes.
2 Then was kindled the [c]wrath
of [d]Ē-lī′hū the son of Băr′a-
chĕl the Bū′zīte, of the kindred
of Răm: against [a]Jōb was his
wrath kindled, because he [b]jus-
tified himself rather than God.
3 Also against his three friends
was his [c]wrath kindled, because
they had found no answer, and
*yet* had condemned [a]Jōb.
4 Now [d]Ē-lī′hū had [e,f]waited
till Jōb had spoken, because
they *were* [g]elder[C] than he.
5 When [d]Ē-lī′hū saw that *there*
*was* no answer in the mouth of
*these* three men, then his [c]wrath
was kindled.

1
*a Job*, Job 1:1.
*b Self-righteousness*, Luke 18:11.

2
*c Anger, instances of*, Psa. 37:8.
*d* Job 33; 34; 35; 36.

4
*e Modesty, instances of*, 1 Tim. 2:9.
*f Reverence, for the aged*, Lev. 19:30.
*g Old Age*, Isa. 46:4.

6 And [d]Ē-lī′hū the son of Băr′-
a-chĕl the Bū′zīte answered and
said, I *am* young, and ye *are*
very old; wherefore [e]I was
afraid, and [f]durst[C] not shew you
mine opinion.
7 I said, [g]Days should speak,
and multitude of years should
teach [h]wisdom.
8 But *there is* a [i]spirit in man:
and the *inspiration of the Almighty giveth them understanding.
9 Great men are not *always*
wise: neither do the aged understand judgment.
10 Therefore I said, Hearken
to me; I also will shew mine
opinion.
11 Behold, I [e]waited for your
words; I gave ear to your [j]rea-
sons, whilst ye searched out
what to say.
12 Yea, I attended unto you,
and, behold, *there was* none of
you that convinced[C] [a]Jōb, *or* that
answered his words:
13 Lest ye should say, We have
found out wisdom: God thrusteth him down, not man.
14 Now he hath not directed
*his* [j]words against me: neither
will I answer him with your
speeches.
15 They were amazed, they
answered no more: they left off
speaking.
16 When I had waited, (for
they spake not, but stood still,
*and* answered no more;)
17 *I said*, I will answer also

7
*h Wisdom, spiritual*, Prov. 2:2.

8
*i Man, a spirit*, Job 4:17.

11
*j Reasoning*, Job 13:6.

---

* **INSPIRATION**, 1 Kin. 13:20; 2 Chr. 33:18; 36:15; Neh. 9:30; Job 33:14–16; Isa. 51:16; Jer. 7:25; 17:16; Dan. 9:6, 10; Hos. 12:10; Joel 2:28; Amos 3:7, 8; Zech. 7:12; Luke 1:70; Acts 3:18; Rom. 1:1, 2; 1 Cor. 12:7–11; 2 Tim. 3:16; Heb. 1:1; 2 Pet. 1:21; Rev. 10:7; 22:6, 8. *Of Enoch*, Jude 14. *Of Joseph*, Gen. 40:8; 41:16, 38, 39. *Of Moses*, Ex. 3:14, 15; 4:12, 15, 27; 6:13, 29; 7:2; 19:9–19; 24:16; 25:22; 33:9, 11; Lev. 1:1; Num. 1:1; 7:8, 9; 9:8–10; 11:17, 25; 12:6–8; 16:28, 29; Deut. 1:5, 6; 5:4, 5, 31; 34:10, 11; Psa. 103:7. *Of Aaron*, Ex. 6:13; 12:1. *Of the tabernacle workmen*, Ex. 28:3; 31:3, 6; 35:31; 36:1. *Of the seventy elders*, Num. 11:16, 17, 24, 25. *Of Eldad and Medad*, Num. 11:26–29. *Of Balaam*, Num. 23:5, 16, 20, 26; 24:2–4, 15, 16. *Of Joshua*, Deut. 34:9; Josh. 4:15. *Of Samuel*, 1 Sam. 3:1, 4–10, 19–21; 9:6, 15–20; 15:16. *Of Saul*, 1 Sam. 10:6, 7, 10–13; 19:23, 24. *Of messengers of Saul*, 1 Sam. 19:20, 23. *Of David*, 2 Sam. 23:2, 3; 1 Chr. 28:19; Mark 12:36. *Of Nathan*, 2 Sam. 7:3, 4, 8. *Of Gad*, 2 Sam. 24:11. *Of Ahijah*, 1 Kin. 14:5. *Of Elijah*, 1 Kin. 17:1, 24; 19:15; 2 Kin. 10:10. *Of Micaiah*, 1 Kin. 22:14, 28; 2 Chr. 18:27. *Of Elisha*, 2 Kin. 2:9; 3:11, 12, 15; 15:8; 6:8–12, 32. *Of Jahaziel*, 2 Chr. 20:14. *Of Azariah*, 2 Chr. 15:1, 2. *Of Zechariah, the son of Jehoiada*, 2 Chr. 24:20; 26:5. *Of Isaiah*, 2 Kin. 20:4; Isa. 6:1–9; 8:11; 44:26; Acts 28:25. *Of Jeremiah*, 2 Chr. 26:12; Jer. 1:9; 2:1; 7:1; 11:1, 18; 13:1–3; 16:1; 18:1; 20:9; 23:9; 24:4; 25:3; 26:1, 2, 12; 27:1, 2; 29:30; 33:1; 34:1; 42:4, 7; Dan. 9:2. *Of Ezekiel*, Ezek. 1:1, 3; 2:1, 2, 4, 5; 3:10–12, 14, 16, 17, 22, 24, 27; 8:1; 11:1, 4, 5, 24; 33:22; 37:1; 40:1; 43:5, 6. *Of Daniel*, Dan. 2:19; 7:16; 8:16; 9:22; 10:7–9. *Of Hosea*, Hos. 1:1, 2. *Of Joel*, 1:1. *Of Amos*, 3:7, 8; 7:14, 15. *Of Obadiah*, Obad. 1. *Of Jonah*, Jonah 1:1; 3:1, 2. *Of Micah*, Mic. 1:1; 3:8. *Of Habakkuk*, Hab. 1:1. *Of Haggai*, Hag. 1:13. *Of Zechariah, the son of Iddo*, Zech. 2:9; 7:8. *Of Elisabeth*, Luke 1:41. *Of Zacharias*, Luke 1:67. *Of Simeon*, Luke 2:26, 27. *Of disciples*, Matt. 10:19; Mark 13:11; Luke 12:11, 12; 21:14, 15; Acts 21:4. *Of the apostles*, Acts 2:4. *Of Philip*, Acts 8:29. *Of Agabus*, Acts 11:28; 21:10, 11. *Of John the apostle*, Rev. 1:10, 11. See footnote, WORD OF GOD, *Inspired*, Psa. 119:9.

my part, I also will shew mine opinion.

18 For I am full of [1]matter, the spirit within me constraineth me.[S]

19 Behold, my [2]belly *is* as [k]wine *which* hath no vent; it is ready to burst like new [l]bottles.[C]

20 I will speak, that I may be refreshed: I will open my lips and answer.

21 Let me not, I pray you, accept[C] any man's person, neither let me give [m]flattering titles unto man.

22 For I know not to give [m]flattering titles; *in so doing* my maker would soon take me away.

## CHAPTER 33

*Elihu bespeaks Job's attention; 8 reproves him for reflecting upon the justice of God; 12 and shows him the design of God in his dealings with men; 14 that God calls men to repentance by visions, 19 by afflictions, 23 and by his ministry.*

WHEREFORE, [a]Jōb, I pray thee, hear my speeches, and hearken to all my words.

2 Behold, now [b]I have opened my mouth, my tongue hath spoken in my mouth.

3 My words *shall be of* the [c]uprightness of my heart: and [1]my lips shall utter knowledge clearly.

4 The spirit of God hath [d]made [e]me, and the [f]breath of the Almighty hath given me life.[S T]

5 If thou canst answer me, set *thy words* in order before me, stand up.

6 Behold, I *am* [2]according to thy wish in God's stead: I also am formed out of the [*, g]clay.

7 Behold, my terror shall not make thee afraid, neither shall my hand be heavy upon thee.

8 Surely thou hast spoken in mine hearing, and I have heard the voice of *thy* words, [h]*saying*,

9 [h, i]I am clean without transgression, I *am* innocent; neither *is there* iniquity in me.

10 [h]Behold, he findeth occasions against me, he counteth me for his enemy,

11 [h]He [j]putteth my feet in the [k]stocks, he marketh all my paths.

12 Behold, *in* this thou art not just: I will answer thee, that [l]God is greater than man.

13 [l]Why dost thou [h]strive[C] against him? for [m, n]he giveth not account of any of his matters.

14 For God speaketh [o]once, yea [o]twice, *yet* [p]*man* perceiveth it not.

15 In a [q]dream, in a vision of the night, when deep sleep falleth upon men, in slumberings upon the bed;

16[S] Then he [r]openeth the ears of men, and sealeth their instruction,

17 That he may withdraw man *from his* purpose, and hide pride from man.

18 He [s]keepeth back his soul from the pit, and his life from perishing by the sword.

19 He is [†]chastened also with [t, u]pain upon his bed, and [3]the multitude of his bones with strong *pain*:[S]

20 So that his life abhorreth bread, and his soul dainty [4]meat.

21 His flesh is consumed away, that it cannot be seen; and his bones *that* were not seen stick out.

22 Yea, his soul draweth near unto the grave,[C] and his life to the destroyers.

**18**
1 R. V. words;

**19**
k *Wine*, Prov. 23:31.
l *Bottle, made of skins*, Gen. 21:14.
2 Am. R. V. breast

**21**
m *Flattery*, Prov. 6:24.

**1**
a *Job*, Job 1:1.

**2**
b Job 32; 34; 35; 36.

**3**
c *Integrity*, Job 2:3.
1 R. V. that which my lips know they shall speak sincerely.

**4**
d *God, creator of man*, Gen. 2:2.
e *Man, created*, Job 4:17.
f *Breath, of God*, Gen. 7:15.

**6**
g *Ground*, Gen. 3:17.
2 R. V. toward God even as thou art:

**8**
h *Murmuring, against God*, Num. 14:2.

**9**
i *Self-righteousness*, Luke 18:11.

**11**
j *Adversity*, Psa. 10:6.
k *Stocks*, Job 13:27.

**12**
l *God, dissertations on*, Gen. 2:2.

**13**
m *God, providence of, mysterious*, Gen. 2:2.
n *God, sovereign*, Gen. 2:2.

**14**
o *God, mercy of*, Gen. 2:2.
p *Wicked, God's mercy to*, vs. 14–30; Psa. 73:3.

**15**
q *Dream*, Dan. 1:17.

**16**
r *Wisdom, spiritual*, Prov. 2:2.

**18**
s *God, preserver*, Gen. 2:2.

**19**
t *Pain*, Job 14:22.
u *Afflictions*, Psa. 34:19.
3 R. V. with continual strife in his bones:

**20**
4 Am. R. V. food.

* **CLAY.** *Man formed from*, Job 33:6. *Used by potter*, Isa. 29:16; 41:25; 45:9; Jer. 18:6; Rom. 9:21. *Blind man's eyes anointed with*, John 9:6.
**Figurative**, Job 4:19; Psa. 40:2; Isa. 45:9; 64:8.
SYMBOLICAL, Dan. 2:33–45.

† **DIVINE CHASTISEMENT.** *A blessing*, Job 5:17; Psa. 94:12, 13; Heb. 12:11.
*Corrective*, Deut. 11:2–9; 2 Sam. 7:14, 15; 2 Chr. 6:24–31; 7:13, 14; Job 33:19; 34:31; Psa. 118:18; 119:67, 75; Isa. 57:16–18; Jer. 24:5, 6; 46:28; 1 Cor. 11:32.
*Inflicted for sins*, Lev. 26:28; Psa. 89:32; 107:10–12, 17; Isa. 40:2; Jer. 30:14; Lam. 1:5; Hos. 7:12; 10:10; Amos 4:6.
*Administered in love*, Deut. 8:5; Prov. 3:11, 12; Heb. 12:5–10; Rev. 3:19.
*Penitence under*, Psa. 106:43, 44; 107:10–13, 17–19; Isa. 26:16; Jer. 31:18, 19. *Impenitence under*, Isa. 42:25; Jer. 2:30; Hag. 2:17.
*Prayer to be spared from*, Psa. 6:1; 38:1.
*Vicariously borne by Jesus*, Isa. 53:4, 5.
See footnote, PUNISHMENT, Lev. 26:41.

23[s] If there be [5]a messenger with him, an interpreter, one among a thousand, to shew unto man [6]his uprightness:

24 Then he is gracious unto him, and [s]saith, Deliver him from going down to the pit: I have found a [v]ransom.

25 His flesh shall be fresher than a child's: he shall return to the days of his youth:

26 He shall pray unto God, and [w, x]he will be favourable unto him: and he shall see his face with [y]joy: for he will render unto man his [z]righteousness.

27 He [7]looketh upon men, and *if any* say, I have sinned, and perverted *that which was* right, and it profited me not;

28 He [8]will deliver his soul from going into the pit, and [9]his life shall see the light.

29 Lo, all these *things* worketh God oftentimes with man,

30 To bring back his soul from the pit, to be enlightened with the light of the living.[s]

31 Mark well, O Jōb, hearken unto me: hold thy peace, and I will speak.

32 If thou hast any thing to say, answer me: speak, for I desire to justify thee.

33 If not, hearken unto me: hold thy peace, and I shall teach thee wisdom.

## CHAPTER 34

*Elihu addresses the friends of Job; calls their attention to what Job had uttered;* 10 *and shows that God can not be charged with injustice.* 34 *He reproves Job.*

FURTHERMORE [a]Ē-lī'hū answered and said,

2 Hear my words, O ye wise *men*; and give ear unto me, ye that have knowledge.

3 For the ear trieth[c] words, as the [1]mouth tasteth meat.[c]

4 Let us choose [2]to us judgment: let us know among ourselves what *is* good.

5 For [b]Jōb hath [c]said, I am righteous: and God hath taken[c] away my [3]judgment.

6 [4]Should I lie against my right? my wound *is* incurable [5]without transgression.[c]

7 What man *is* like [b]Jōb, *who* drinketh up [d]scorning like water?

8 Which goeth in company with the workers of iniquity, and walketh with wicked men.

9 For he hath said, It profiteth a man nothing that he should delight himself with God.

10 Therefore hearken unto me, ye men of understanding: far be it from God, [e]*that he should do* wickedness; and *from* the Almighty, [e]*that he should commit* iniquity.[s]

11 For the work of a man shall [f]he render unto him, and [g]cause every man to find according to *his* ways.[s]

12 Yea, surely [e]God will not do wickedly, [h]neither will the Almighty pervert[c] judgment.

13 Who hath given [i]him a charge over the earth? or who hath disposed the whole world?

14 If he set his heart upon man, *if* he [j]gather unto himself his spirit and his breath;

15 All flesh shall [j]perish together, and man shall turn again unto dust.

16 If now *thou hast* understanding, hear this: hearken to the voice of my words.

17[s] Shall even he that hateth right govern? and wilt thou condemn him that is [h]most just?

18 [k]*Is it fit* to say to a [l]king, *Thou art* [6]wicked? *and* to princes, *Ye are* ungodly?

19 *How much less to* [m, n]*him* that [o]accepteth not the persons of princes, nor regardeth the rich more than the [p]poor? for [q]they all *are* the [r]work of his hands.[s Q]

20 In a moment shall they [j]die,

**23**
5 R. V. with him an angel,
6 R. V. what is right for him;

**24**
*v* *Ransom, figurative,* Ex. 21:30.

**26**
*w* *Prayer, answer to, promised,* Acts 6:4.
*x* *Penitent, promises to, of mercy,* vs. 26–28; Psa. 51:17.
*y* *Joy,* Psa. 5:11.
*z* *Righteousness, fruits of,* Psa. 15:2.

**27**
7 R. V. singeth before men, and saith, I have sinned,

**28**
8 R. V. hath redeemed my
9 R. V. my

**1**
*a* Job 32; 33; 35; 36.

**3**
1 Am. R. V. palate tasteth food.

**4**
2 R. V. for us that which is right:

**5**
*b* *Job,* Job 1:1.
*c* *Self-righteousness,* Luke 18:11.

3 R. V. right:

**6**
4 R. V. Notwithstanding my right I am accounted a liar;
5 R. V. though I am without

**7**
*d* *Scoffing,* Hab. 1:10.

**10**
*e* *God, holiness of,* Gen. 2:2.

**11**
*f* *God, judge,* Gen. 2:2.
*g* *Judgment, according to opportunity and works,* 1 Pet. 1:17.

**12**
*h* *God, justice of,* Gen. 2:2.

**13**
*i* *God, sovereign,* Gen. 2:2.

**14**
*j* *Death,* Num. 23:10.

**18**
*k* *Citizens, duties of, to honor rulers,* Luke 15:15.
*l* *King, respect due to,* 2 Kin. 3:10.
6 R. V. vile?

**19**
*m* *God, righteousness of,* Gen. 2:2.
*n* *God, impartial,* Gen. 2:2.
*o* *Respect of Persons,* Prov. 24:23
*p* *Poor, God's care of,* Prov. 21:13.
*q* *Man, created,* Job 4:17.
*r* *God, creator of man,* Gen. 2:2.

and the people shall be troubled at midnight, and pass away: and the mighty shall be taken away without hand.

21 For [s]his [t]eyes *are* upon the [u]ways of man, and he seeth all his goings.

22 [v]*There is* no darkness, nor shadow of death, where the workers of iniquity may hide themselves.[s]

23 For he [7]will not lay upon man more *than right*; that he should enter into judgment[G] with God.[s]

24 [w]He shall break in pieces mighty men [8]without[G] number, and set others in their stead.

25 Therefore he [s]knoweth their works, and he [x]overturneth *them* in the night, so that they are destroyed.[s]

26 He striketh them as wicked men in the open sight of others;

27 Because they [y]turned back from him, and would not consider any of his ways:

28 So that they cause the cry of the poor to come unto him, and [z]he heareth the cry of the *afflicted.

29 When he giveth quietness, who then can [9]make trouble? and when he hideth *his* face, who then can behold him? whether *it be done* against a nation, or against a man only:[s]

30 That the [10]hypocrite reign not, lest the people be ensnared.

31 [11]Surely it is meet[G] to be said unto God, [a]I have borne [b,c]*chastisement*, [d]I will not offend *any more*:

32 [e]*That which* I see not teach thou me: if I have done iniquity, I will do no more.

33 [12]*Should it be* according to thy mind? he will recompense it, whether thou refuse, or whether thou choose; and not I: therefore speak what thou knowest.

34 Let men of understanding tell me, and let a wise man hearken unto me.

35 [f]Jōb hath spoken without knowledge, and his words *were* without wisdom.

36 My desire *is that* Jōb may be tried[G] unto the end because of *his* answers for[G] wicked men.

37 For he addeth rebellion unto his sin, he clappeth *his hands* among us, and [g]multiplieth his words against God.

## CHAPTER 35

*Elihu rebukes Job for selfrighteousness; 4 and shows that God can not be affected by man's acts. 9 The cry of the oppressed is not heard for their want of faith.*

[a]E-LĪ'HŪ spake moreover, and said,

2 Thinkest thou this to be right, *that* thou saidst, [b]My righteousness *is* more than God's?

3 For thou [c]saidst, What advantage will it be unto thee? *and*, What profit shall I have, [1]*if I be cleansed* from my sin?

4 I will answer thee, and thy companions with thee.

5 Look unto the heavens, and see; and behold the clouds *which* are higher than [d]thou.

6 [s]If thou sinnest, what [2]doest thou against him? or *if* thy transgressions be multiplied, what doest thou unto him?

7 If thou be righteous, what givest thou him? or what receiveth he of thine hand?[s]

8 Thy wickedness *may hurt* a man as thou *art*; and thy righteousness *may profit* the son of man.

9 By reason of the multitude of [e]oppressions they make *the oppressed* to cry: they cry out by reason of the arm of the mighty.

10 But [f]none saith, Where *is* [g]God [h]my maker, who giveth songs in the night;

11 Who [i]teacheth us more than

---

**21**
s *God, knowledge of*, Gen. 2:2.
t *Eye, figurative*, Matt. 6:22.
u *Heart, known to God*, Psa. 44:21.

**22**
v *Punishment, no escape from*, Lev. 26:41.

**23**
7 R. V. needeth not further to consider a man, That he should go before God in judgment.

**24**
w *God, providence of, mysterious*, Gen. 2:2.
8 R. V. in ways past finding out.

**25**
x *Wicked, punishment of*, Psa. 73:3.

**27**
y *Backsliders*, Jer. 3:22.

**28**
z *Prayer, answered*, Acts 6:4.

**29**
9 R. V. condemn?

**30**
10 R. V. godless man

**31**
a *Resignation*, Job 5:17.
b *Divine Chastisement, corrective*, Job 33:19.
c *Afflictions, resignation in*, Psa. 34:19.
d *Repentance*, Mark 1:4.
11 R. V. For hath any said unto God,

**32**
e *Wisdom, prayer for spiritual*, Prov. 2:2.

**33**
12 R. V. Shall his recompence be as thou wilt, that thou refuseth it? For thou must choose, and

**35**
f *Job*, Job 1:1.

**37**
g *Murmuring, against God*, Num. 14:2.

**1**
a Job 32: 34; 36; 37.

**2**
b *Self-righteousness*, Luke 18:11.

**3**
c *Infidelity*, 2 Cor. 6:15.
1 R. V. more than if I had sinned?

**5**
d *Man, insignificance of*, Job 4:17.

**6**
2 Am. R. V. effect est thou against him?

**9**
e *Oppression*, Eccl. 5:8.

**10**
f *Godless, described*, Job 8:13
g *God, creator*, Gen. 2:2.
h *Man, created*, Job 4:17.

**11**
i *Wisdom, spiritual*, Prov. 2:2.

---

* **AFFLICTED.** *Exhorted to pray*, Jas. 5:13. *Intercessory prayer for*, Jas. 5:14, 15. *Sympathy with*, Job 6:14; Matt. 25:34–40. *Help for*, Job 22:29; Isa. 58:6, 7; Luke 10:30–37; 1 Tim. 5:10. *Rewards of service to*, Isa. 53:10; Matt. 25:34–45. See footnotes: ADVERSITY, Psa. 10:6; AFFLICTIONS, Psa. 34:19.

the [j]beasts of the earth, and maketh us wiser than the fowls of heaven?

12 There [k]they cry, but none giveth answer, because of the [l]pride of evil men.

13 Surely God will not hear vanity, neither will the Almighty regard it.[s]

14 [3]Although thou sayest thou shalt not see him, *yet* judgment *is* before him; therefore trust thou in him.[s]

15 But now, because [4]*it is* not *so*, he hath visited in his [m]anger; yet he knoweth *it* not in great extremity:

16 Therefore doth [n]Jōb open his mouth in [5]vain; he multiplieth words without knowledge.

## CHAPTER 36

*Elihu shows that God is just in all his ways; 15 that he deals gently with the humble; and that Job's sins prevented his dealing thus with him; 18 and exhorts him to repentance. 26 God's infinite power.*

[a]E-LĪ'HŪ also proceeded, and said,

2 Suffer[C] me a little, and I will shew thee that *I have* yet to [b]speak on [c]God's behalf.

3 I will fetch my knowledge from afar, and will ascribe [d]righteousness to my Maker.[s]

4 For truly my words *shall* not *be* false: [c]he that is perfect in [e]knowledge *is* with thee.[s]

5 Behold, [c]God *is* [f]mighty, and [g]despiseth not *any*: *he is* mighty in strength *and* [h]wisdom.[s]

6 [c]He preserveth not the life of the wicked: but [i]giveth right to the [j]poor.

7 [k,l]He withdraweth not his eyes from the righteous: but with kings *are they* on the throne; yea, he doth establish them for ever, and they are exalted.[s]

8 And if *they be* [m]bound in fetters, *and* be holden in cords of affliction;[C]

9 [m]Then [c]he sheweth them their work, and their transgressions that they have [1]exceeded.[C]

10 [c]He [m]openeth also their ear to [2]discipline,[C] and commandeth that they [n]return from iniquity.

11 [o]If they [p]obey and serve *him*, [l,q]they shall spend their days in prosperity, and their years in pleasures.[s]

12 But if they [r]obey not, [s]they shall [t]perish by the sword, and they shall die without knowledge.

13 But [3]the [u]hypocrites in heart heap up wrath: they cry [4]not when he bindeth them.

14 [u]They die in youth, and their life *is* among the unclean.

15 [c]He [k,v]delivereth the [5,j]poor in his affliction, and openeth their ears in oppression.

16 Even so would [c]he have removed thee out of the strait[C] *into* a broad place, where *there is* no straitness;[C] and that which should be set on thy table *should be* full of fatness.[s]

17 But thou hast fulfilled the judgment of the wicked: judgment and justice take hold *on thee*.

18 [6]Because *there is* wrath, *beware* lest he take thee away with *his* stroke: then a great [w]ransom cannot deliver thee.

19 Will [7]he esteem thy [x]riches? *no*, not gold, nor all the forces of strength.[s]

20 Desire not the night, when people are cut off in their place.

21 Take heed, [y]regard not iniquity: for this hast thou chosen rather than affliction.

22 Behold, God exalteth by his [z]power: who [a,b]teacheth like him?

23 Who hath enjoined[C] him his way? or who can say, [c]Thou hast wrought iniquity?[s]

24 Remember that thou [d]magnify his work, [8]which men behold.

j *Animals, instincts of*, Jer. 27:5.

**12**

k *Wicked, prayer of, not heard*, Psa. 73:3.

l *Pride*, Prov. 16:18.

**14**

3 R. V. How much less when thou sayest thou beholdest him not, The cause is before him, and thou waitest for him!

**15**

m *Anger of God*, 2 Kin. 13:3.

4 R. V. he hath not visited in his anger, Neither doth he greatly regard arrogance;

**16**

n *Job*, Job 1:1.

5 R. V. vanity;

**1**

a Job 32; 33; 35; 37.

**2**

b *Reasoning*, vs. 2–33; Job 13:6.

c *God, dissertations on*, vs. 2–33; Gen. 2:2.

**3**

d *God, righteousness of*, Gen. 2:2.

**4**

e *God, knowledge of*, Gen. 2:2.

**5**

f *God, power of*, Gen. 2:2.

g *God, impartial*, Gen. 2:2.

h *God, wisdom of*, Gen. 2:2.

**6**

i *God, justice of*, Gen. 2:2.

j *Afflicted*, Job 34:28.

**7**

k *God, preserver*, Gen. 2:2.

l *Righteous, promises to*, Psa. 64:10.

**8**

m *Adversity, design of*, Psa. 10:6.

1 R. V. behaved themselves proudly.

**10**

n *Repentance, enjoined*, Mark 1:4.

2 R. V. instruction,

**11**

o *Blessings, contingent upon obedience*, Deut. 11:26.

p *Obedience, rewarded, by prosperity*, Heb. 5:8.

q *Righteousness, fruits of*, Psa. 15:2.

**12**

r *Adversity, obduracy in*, Psa. 10:6.

s *Wicked, punishment of*, Psa. 73:3.

t *Death, of the wicked, a judgment*, Num. 23:10.

**13**

u *Godless*, Job 8:13.

3 R. V. they that are godless in heart lay up anger:

4 R. V. not for help when

**15**

v *Afflictions, consolation in*, Psa. 34:19.

5 R. V. afflicted by his affliction,

**18**

w *Ransom*, Ex. 21:30.

6 Am. R. V. For let not wrath stir thee up against chastisements; Neither let the greatness of the ransom turn thee aside.

**19**

x *Riches*, Eccl. 4:8.

7 R. V. thy riches suffice thee, that thou be not in distress, Or all the forces of thy strength?

**21**

y *Holiness, enjoined*, Ex. 39:30.

**22**

z *God, power of*, Gen. 2:2.

a *God, teacher*, Gen. 2:2.

b *Wisdom, spiritual*, Prov. 2:2.

**23**

c *God, holiness of*, Gen. 2:2.

**24**

d *Praise*, Psa. 150:1.

8 R. V. Whereof men have sung.

25 Every man may see it, man
may behold *it* afar off.
26 Behold, God *is* great, and
we [e]know[G] *him* not, neither can
the [f]number of his years be
[g]searched out.[S]
27 For he [9,h]maketh small the
drops of water: they pour down
rain according to the vapour
thereof:
28 [h]Which the clouds do drop
*and* distil upon man abundantly.
29 Also can *any* understand the
[h]spreadings of the clouds, *or* the
noise of his tabernacle?
30[T] Behold, he spreadeth his
light upon it, and covereth the
bottom of the sea.
31 For by them [i]judgeth he the
people; he [j]giveth [10,k]meat[G] in
abundance.
32 [11]With clouds he covereth
the [h,l]light; and commandeth it
*not to shine* by *the cloud* that
cometh betwixt.[G T]
33 The noise thereof sheweth
concerning [12]it, the cattle also
concerning the [13]vapour.

## CHAPTER 37

*Elihu speaks of the power and incomprehensible wisdom of God as seen in his works; 23 and urges men to fear him.*

AT this also [a]my heart trembleth, and is moved out
of his place.
2 [b]Hear attentively the noise
of his voice, and the sound *that*
goeth out of his mouth.
3[S] [b]He directeth it under the
whole heaven, and his [c]lightning
unto the ends of the earth.
4 After it a voice roareth: he
thundereth with the voice of his
[1,d]excellency; and he will not
stay[G] them when his voice is
heard.
5 [b]God thundereth marvellously with his voice; [e]great
things doeth he, [f]which we cannot comprehend.[S]
6 For [b,g]he saith to the
[h,i,j]snow, Be thou *on* the earth;
likewise to the small [j,k]rain, and
to the great rain of his strength.
7 [b]He sealeth[G] up the hand of
every man; that all men [2]may
know his work.[S]
8 Then the [l]beasts go into dens,
and remain in their places.
9 Out of the [3]south cometh the
[m]whirlwind: and cold out of the
north.
10 By the [n]breath of God frost
is given: and the breadth of the
waters is straitened.[G]
11 Also by watering he wearieth
the thick cloud: he scattereth his
bright cloud:
12 And it is turned round about
by his counsels: that they may
do whatsoever he commandeth
them upon the face of the world
in the earth.
13 [b]He causeth it to come,
whether for correction, or for his
land, or for mercy.
14 Hearken unto this, O [o]Jōb:
stand still, and consider the wondrous [e,p]works of God.
15 Dost thou know when God
disposed them, and caused the
[c]light of his cloud to shine?[T]
16 Dost thou know the balancings of the clouds, the wondrous
[e,p]works of him which is perfect
in [q]knowledge?[S]
17 How thy garments *are* warm,
when he quieteth the earth by
the south **wind*?
18 Hast thou with him spread
out the [r]sky, *which is* strong,
*and* as a molten [†]looking glass?[S]
19 Teach us what we shall say
unto him; *for* we cannot order

**26**
*e* *Ignorance, concerning God,* Acts 3:17.
*f* *God, eternity of,* Gen. 2:2.
*g* *God, unsearchable,* Gen. 2:2.
**27**
*h* *Meteorology,* Matt. 16:2.
9 R. V. draweth up the drops of water, Which distil in rain from his vapour:
**31**
*i* *God, judge,* Gen. 2:2.
*j* *God, providence of,* Gen. 2:2.
*k* *Food, from God,* Psa. 136:25.
10 Am. R. V. food
**32**
*l* *Lightning,* Job 28:26.
11 R. V. He covereth his hands with the lightning; And giveth it a charge that it strike the mark.
**33**
12 R. V. him,
13 R. V. storm that cometh up.
**1**
*a* Job 32; 33; 35; 36.
**2**
*b* *God, dissertations on,* vs. 2–24; Gen. 2:2.
**3**
*c* *Lightning,* Job 28:26.
**4**
*d* *God, glory of,* Gen. 2:2.
1 R. V. majesty:

**5**
*e* *Works of God,* Psa. 40:5.
*f* *God, unsearchable,* Gen. 2:2.
**6**
*g* *God, providence of,* Gen. 2:2.
*h* *Snow,* Jer. 18:14.
*i* *Meteorology,* Matt. 16:2.
*j* *Temporal Blessings, from God,* Psa. 103:2.
*k* *Rain, sent by God,* 2 Sam. 1:21.
**7**
2 R. V. whom he hath made may know it.
**8**
*l* *Animals, habits of,* Jer. 27:5.
**9**
*m* *Whirlwind,* Prov. 1:27.
3 R. V. chamber of the south cometh the storm:
**10**
*n* *Breath, figurative,* Gen. 7:15.
**14**
*o* *Job,* Job 1:1.
*p* *God, creator,* Gen. 2:2.
**16**
*q* *God, knowledge of,* Gen. 2:2.
**18**
*r* *Heavens, physical,* Psa. 8:3.

* **WIND,** Job 37:21. *Mysterious,* John 3:8. *Miraculous,* Ex. 10:13, 19: 14:21. *Tempestuous, on the Mediterranean Sea,* Acts 27:14; *in Uz,* Job 27:21.
**East:** *Hot and blasting, in Egypt,* Gen. 41:6; *in the valley of the Euphrates,* Ezek. 19:12; *in Canaan,* Hos. 13:15; Luke 12:55; *at Nineveh,* Jonah 4:8.
**North:** *Brings rain* (R. V.), Prov. 25:23.
**South:** *Soothing,* Job 37:17. *Tempestuous,* Job 37:9. *Purifying,* Job 37:21.
**Figurative,** Hos. 4:19. *Of the judgments of God,* Jer. 22:22; Hos. 13:15. *Of adversity,* Matt. 7:25, 27. *Of heresy,* Eph. 4:14.
† **MIRROR.** *Of polished metal,* Job 37:18; Jas. 1:23, 24. *Given by the Israelitish women to be melted for the laver,* Ex. 38:8.
**Figurative,** 1 Cor. 13:12; 2 Cor. 3:18.

our speech by reason of darkness.
20 Shall it be told him that I
speak? if a man speak, surely he
shall be swallowed up.
21 And now *men* see not the
bright light which *is* in the
clouds: but the *,[i]wind passeth,
and [4]cleanseth them.
22 [5,i]Fair weather cometh out
of the north: with God *is* terrible [s]majesty.
23 *Touching* the Almighty, [t]we
cannot find him out: *he is* excellent in [u]power, and in [v]judg-
ment, and in plenty of [w]justice:
he will not afflict.
24 Men do therefore [x]fear him:
he [y]respecteth not any *that are*
[z]wise of heart.

21
4 Am. R. V. cleareth

22
s God, glory of, Gen. 2:2.
5 R. V. Out of the north cometh golden splendour:

23
t God, unsearchable, Gen. 2:2.
u God, power of, Gen. 2:2.
v God, judge, Gen. 2:2.
w God, justice of, Gen. 2:2.

24
x Fear of God, Acts 9:31.
y God, impartial, Gen. 2:2.
z Wisdom, worldly, Prov. 2:2.

## CHAPTER 38

*God calls upon Job to answer; 4 and by his mighty works convinces him of ignorance, 31 and of weakness.*

THEN the LORD [a]answered
[b]Jōb out of the [c]whirl-
wind, and said,
2 Who *is* this that darkeneth
counsel by [d,e]words [f]without
knowledge?
3 Gird up now thy loins like a
man; for I will demand of thee,
and answer thou me.
4 Where wast thou when I
[g,h]laid the [i]foundations of the
[j]earth? declare, if thou hast understanding.
5 Who hath laid the measures
thereof, if thou knowest? or who
hath stretched the line upon it?
6 Whereupon are the [i]founda-
tions thereof fastened? or who
laid the corner stone thereof;
7 When the morning stars sang
together, and all the sons of God
[k]shouted for joy?
8 Or *who* [l]shut up the [m]sea
with doors, when it brake forth,
*as if* it had issued out of the
womb?

1
a God, condescension of, Gen. 2:2.
b Job, Job 1:1.
c Whirlwind, Prov. 1:27.

2
d Words, Luke 4:22.
e Speech, foolish, Col. 4:6.
f Ignorance, Acts 3:17.

4
g God, creator, Gen. 2:2.
h Creation, of the earth, Mark 13:19.
i Geology, vs. 4–18; Psa. 104:5.
j Earth, created by God, Prov. 8:23.

7
k Praise, in heaven, Psa. 150:1.

8
l God, power of, Gen. 2:2.
m Sea, Jer. 5:22.

9 When I [g]made the cloud
the garment thereof, and
thick [n]darkness a [o]swaddling-
band for it,
10 And [1]brake up for it my decreed *place,* and set bars and
doors,
11 And said, Hitherto shalt
thou come, but no further: and
here shall thy proud waves be
stayed?
12 Hast thou commanded the
morning since thy days; *and*
caused the dayspring to know
his place;
13 That it might take hold of
the ends of the earth, that the
wicked might be shaken out
of it?
14 It is [2]turned as [p]clay *to* the
seal; and they stand as a garment.
15 And from the wicked their
light is withholden, and the high
arm shall be broken.
16 Hast thou entered into the
springs of the [m]sea? or hast thou
walked in the search of the
depth?
17 Have the [q]gates of [r]death
been opened unto thee? or hast
thou seen the doors of the shadow of death?
18 Hast thou perceived the
breadth of the [j]earth? declare if
thou knowest it all.
19 Where *is* the way *where* light
dwelleth? and *as for* darkness,
where *is* the place thereof,
20 That thou shouldest take it
to the bound thereof, and that
thou shouldest know the paths
*to* the house thereof?
21 Knowest thou *it,* because
thou wast then born? or *because*
the number of thy days *is* great?
22 Hast thou entered into the
treasures of the [s,t]snow? or hast
thou seen the treasures of the
*hail,

9
n Darkness, over the face of the earth, Gen. 1:2.
o Ezek. 16:4; Luke 2:7, 12.

10
1 Am. R. V. marked out for it my bound,

14
p Clay, Job 33:6.
2 R. V. changed as clay under the seal; And all things stand forth as a garment:

17
q Gates, figurative, Deut. 3:5.
r Death, Num. 23:10.

22
s Snow, Jer. 18:14.
t Meteorology, Matt. 16:2.

* **HAIL,** Job 38:22; Hag. 2:17. *Plague of, in Egypt,* Ex. 9:18–34; Psa. 78:47, 48; 105:32. *Destroys army of the Amorites* Josh. 10:11. **Figurative,** Rev. 8:7; 11:19; 16:21.

23
*u* *God, providence of*, Gen. 2:2.

24
3 R. V. Or the east wind scattered upon the earth?

25
*v* *Lightning*, Job 28:26.

26
*w* *Rain*, 2 Sam. 1:21.

27
4 R. V. tender grass to spring forth?

29
*x* Job 6:16; Psa. 147:17.

31
*y* *Astronomy*, Isa. 13:10.
*z* Job 9:9; Amos 5:8.
5 R. V. cluster of the

32
*a* Job 9:9.
6 Am. R. V. the Mazzaroth in their
7 R. V. the Bear with her train?

33
*b* *Heavens, physical*, Psa. 8:3.
*c* *Earth*, Prov. 8:23.

35
*d* *Lightning*, Job 28:26.
*e* *Meteorology*, Matt. 16:2.

36
*f* *Wisdom*, Prov. 2:2.

23 Which I have [u]reserved
against the time of trouble,
against the day of battle and
war?
24 By what way is the light
parted, [3]*which* scattereth the
east [t]wind upon the earth?
25 Who [u]hath divided a watercourse for the overflowing of
waters, or a way for the [t,v]light-
ning of thunder;
26 To cause it to [t,w]rain on the
earth, *where* no man *is*; *on* the
wilderness, wherein *there is* no
man;
27 To satisfy the desolate and
waste *ground*; and to cause the
[4]bud of the tender herb to spring
forth?
28 Hath the rain a father? or who
hath begotten the drops of dew?[T]
29 Out of whose womb came
the [x]ice? and the hoary frost of
heaven, who hath gendered[C] it?
30 The waters are hid as *with*
a stone, and the face of the deep
is frozen.
31 [y]Canst thou bind the [5]sweet[C]
influences of [z]Plē′ia-dēș, or loose
the bands of [z]Ō-rī′ŏn?
32 Canst thou bring forth
[6]Măz′za-rŏth in his season? or
canst thou guide [7,a]Är-tū′rus
with his sons?
33 Knowest thou the ordinan-
ces[C] of [b]heaven? canst thou set the
dominion thereof in the [c]earth?
34 Canst thou lift[C] up thy voice
to the clouds, that abundance of
waters may cover thee?
35 Canst thou send [d,e]light-
nings, that they may go, and say
unto thee, Here we *are*?
36 Who hath put [f]wisdom in the
inward parts? or who hath given
understanding to the heart?
37 Who can number the clouds
in wisdom? or who can stay[C] the
bottles[C] of heaven,
38 When the dust groweth into
hardness, and the clods cleave
fast together?
39 [g]Wilt thou hunt the prey for
the lion? or fill the appetite of
the young lions,
40 When they couch[C] in *their*
dens, *and* abide in the covert[C] to
lie in wait?
41 [g,h]Who provideth for the
[†,i]raven his food? when his
young ones cry unto God, [8]they
wander for lack of meat.[C]

## CHAPTER 39

*God's power and providence illustrated in the **wild** goats and hinds; 5 in the wild ass; 9 in the unicorn; 13 in the peacock, stork, and ostrich; 19 in the horse; 26 in the hawk; 27 and in the eagle.*

KNOWEST thou the time
when the wild [a]goats of
the rock bring forth? *or* canst
thou mark when the hinds do
calve?
2 [a]Canst thou number the
months *that* they fulfil? or knowest thou the time when they
bring forth?
3 They bow themselves, they
bring forth their young ones,
they cast out their sorrows.
4 Their young ones are in good
liking[C], they grow up [1]with corn;
they go forth, and return not
unto them.
5 [b]Who hath sent out the wild
[c]ass free? or who hath loosed the
bands of the wild ass?
6 Whose house I have made the
wilderness, and the [2]barren land
his dwellings.
7 He scorneth the multitude of
the city, neither regardeth he the
crying of the driver.
8 [a]The range of the mountains
*is* his pasture, and he [a]searcheth
after every green thing.
9 Will the [3,*]unicorn be willing
to serve thee, or abide by thy
[d]crib[C]?

39
*g* *Animals, God's care of*, Jer. 27:5.

41
*h* *God, providence of*, Gen. 2:2.
*i* *Birds, divine care of*, Eccl. 12:4.
8 Am. R. V. And wander for lack of food?

1
*a* *Animals, habits of*, Jer. 27:5.

4
1 R. V. in the open field;

5
*b* *God, providence of*, Gen. 2:2.
*c* *Ass, wild*, 2 Chr. 28:15.

6
2 R. V. salt

9
*d* Prov. 14:4; Isa. 1:3.
3 R. V. wild-ox

† **RAVEN.** *A black, carnivorous bird*, Prov. 30:17; Song 5:11. *Forbidden as food*, Lev. 11:15; Deut. 14:14. *Preserved by Noah in the ark*, Gen. 8:7. *Fed Elijah*, 1 Kin. 17:4-6. *God's care for*, Luke 12:24.

* **UNICORN** (R. V. wild ox). *Intractable*, Job 39:9-12. *Horned*, Deut. 33:17; Psa. 22:21; 92:10. *Great strength of* Num. 23:22; 24:8; Job 39:10, 11. *Agile*, Psa. 29:6. **Figurative:** *Of the judgments of God*, Isa. 34:7.

10 Canst thou bind the [3,*]unicorn with his band in the furrow? or will he harrow the valleys after thee?
11 Wilt thou trust him, because his strength *is* great? or wilt thou leave thy labour to him?
12 Wilt thou [4]believe him, that he will bring home thy seed, and gather [5]*it into* thy barn?
13 [6]*Gavest thou* the goodly wings unto the peacocks? or wings and feathers unto the [e]ostrich?
14 [f]Which leaveth her eggs in the earth, and warmeth them in dust,
15 And forgetteth that the foot may crush them, or that the wild beast may [7]break them.
16 [f]She is hardened against her young ones, as though *they were* not her's: her labour is in vain without fear;
17 Because God hath deprived her of wisdom, neither hath he imparted to her understanding.
18 What time she lifteth up herself on high, [f]she scorneth the †horse and his rider.
19 Hast thou given the †horse strength? hast thou clothed his neck with [8]thunder?
20 Canst thou make him [9]afraid as a [g]grasshopper? the glory of his [10]nostrils *is* terrible.[C]
21 He paweth in the valley, and rejoiceth in *his* strength: he goeth on to meet the armed men.
22 He mocketh at fear, and is not affrighted[C]; neither turneth he back from the sword.
23 The quiver rattleth against him, the glittering [h]spear and the [11]shield.
24 He swalloweth the ground with fierceness and rage: neither believeth he that *it is* the sound of the [i]trumpet.
25 He saith among the [i]trumpets, Ha, ha; and he smelleth the [j]battle afar off, the thunder of the [k]captains, and the [l]shouting.
26 Doth the [m]hawk fly by thy wisdom, *and* stretch her wings toward the south?
27 Doth the [n]eagle mount up at thy command, and make her nest on high?
28 [12,f]She dwelleth and abideth on the rock, upon the crag of the rock, and the strong place.
29 [f]From thence she [13]seeketh the prey, *and* her eyes behold afar off.
30 [f]Her young ones also suck up blood: and where the slain *are*, there *is* she.[Q]

## CHAPTER 40

*God rebukes Job for his presumption. 3 Job humbles himself, and will not reply. 6 God's power and majesty as displayed in his judgments, 15 and also in the behemoth.*

MOREOVER the LORD answered [a]Jōb, and said,
2 Shall he that [1]contendeth with the Almighty instruct *him*? he that [2]reproveth God, let him answer it.
3 ¶ Then [a]Jōb answered the LORD, and said,
4 Behold, [b]I am [3]vile; what shall I answer thee? [4]I will lay mine hand upon my mouth.
5 Once have I spoken; [b]but I will not answer: yea, twice; but I will proceed no further.
6 ¶ Then answered the LORD unto [a]Jōb out of the [c]whirlwind, and said,
7 Gird up thy loins now like a man: I will demand of thee, and declare thou unto me.[Q]
8 Wilt thou also disannul[C] my

**12**
4 R. V. confide in
5 Am. R. V. the grain of thy threshing-floor?
**13**
*e Ostriches*, Lam. 4:3.
6 Am. R. V. The wings of the ostrich wave proudly; But are they the pinions and plumage of love?
**14**
*f Birds, habits of*, Eccl. 12:4.
**15**
7 R. V. trample
**19**
8 R. V. the quivering mane?
**20**
*g Locust*, Nah. 3:17.
9 R. V. to leap as a locust?
10 R. V. snorting
**23**
*h Spear*, 2 Kin. 11:10.
11 R. V. javelin.

**24**
*i Trumpet*, Josh. 6:4.
**25**
*j Battle*, 1 Sam. 17:20.
*k Captain*, Num. 31:48.
*l Shouting, in battle*, 2 Chr. 15:14.
**26**
*m* Lev. 11:16; Deut. 14:15.
**27**
*n Eagle*, Lev. 11:13.
**28**
12 Am. R. V. On the cliff she dwelleth, and maketh her home, Upon the point of the cliff, and the stronghold.
**29**
13 R. V. spieth out
**1**
*a Job*, Job 1:1.
**2**
1 R. V. cavilleth contend with the Almighty?
2 R. V. argueth with God,
**4**
*b Humility*, Prov. 22:4.
3 R. V. of small account;
4 R. V. I lay
**6**
*c Whirlwind*, Prov. 1:27.

† **HORSE.** *Great strength of*, Job 39:19–25; Psa. 33:17. *Swifter than eagles*, Jer. 4:13. *Snorting and neighing of*, Jer. 8:16. *A vain thing for safety*, Psa. 33:17. *Egypt famous for*, 1 Kin. 10:28, 29; Isa. 31:1, 3; Ezek. 17:15. *Used, by the Egyptians in war*, Ex. 14:9; 15:19; *by the Israelites*, 1 Kin. 22:4. *Used for cavalry*, 2 Kin. 18:23; Prov. 21:31; Jer. 47:3; 51:21. *Multiplying forbidden to kings of Israel*, Deut. 17:16. *Hamstrung, by Joshua*, Josh. 11:6, 9; *by David*, 2 Sam. 8:4; 1 Chr. 18:4. *Israel reproved for keeping*, Isa. 2:7; 31:1; Ezek. 17:15; Hos. 14:3. *Exported from Egypt*, 1 Kin. 10:28, 29; 2 Chr. 9:25, 28. *Brought by returning exiles from Babylon*, Ezra 2:66; Neh. 7:68. *Commerce in*, Rev. 18:13. *Bits for*, Jas. 3:3. *Bells for*, Zech. 14:20. *Harness for*, Jer. 46:4. *Color of*, Zech. 1:8. *Dedicated to idolatrous uses*, 2 Kin. 23:11.
**Allegorical representations of**, Zech. 1:8; Rev. 6:2–8; 9:17; 19:11–21.

judgment? wilt thou condemn me, that thou mayest be [5]righteous?

9 [d]Hast thou an arm like God? or canst thou thunder with a voice like him?

10 Deck thyself now *with* majesty and excellency; and array thyself with glory and beauty.

11 Cast abroad the rage of thy wrath: and behold every one *that is* [e]proud, and abase him.

12 Look on every one *that is* [e]proud, *and* bring him low; and tread down the wicked in their place.

13 Hide them in the dust together; *and* bind their faces in secret.

14 Then will I also confess unto thee that thine own right hand can save thee.

15 ¶ Behold now behemoth, which I made [6]with thee; he eateth grass as an ox.

16 Lo now, his strength *is* in his loins, and his force *is* in the [7]navel of his belly.

17 He moveth his tail like a cedar: the sinews of his [8]stones are wrapped together.

18 His bones *are as* [9]strong pieces of brass; his [10]bones *are* like bars of iron.

19 He *is* the chief of the ways of God: [11]he that made him can make his sword to approach *unto him*.

20 Surely the mountains bring him forth food, where all the beasts of the field play.

21 He lieth under the [12]shady trees, in the covert of the reed, and fens.

22 The [12]shady trees cover him *with* their shadow; the willows of the brook compass him about.

23 Behold, [13]he drinketh up a river, *and* hasteth not: he trusteth that he can draw up [f]Jôr′dan into his mouth.

**8**
5 R. V. justified?

**9**
*d* *God, power of,* Gen. 2:2.

**11**
*e* *Pride,* Prov 16:18.

**15**
6 Am. R. V. as well as thee;

**16**
7 R. V. muscles

**17**
8 R. V. thighs are knit

**18**
9 R. V. tubes of brass;
10 R. V. limbs

**19**
11 Am. R. V. He only that made him giveth him his sword.

**21**
12 R. V. lotus

**23**
*f* Jordan, Gen. 32:10.
13 R. V. if a river overflow, he trembleth not: He is confident, though Jordan swell even to his mouth.

24 [14]He taketh it with his eyes: *his* nose pierceth through snares.

## CHAPTER 41

*God's power and majesty as seen in the leviathan.*

[a]CANST [b]thou draw out leviathan with an hook? or [1]his tongue with a cord *which* thou lettest down?

2 Canst thou put an hook into his nose? or bore his jaw through with a [2]thorn?

3 Will he make many supplications unto thee? will he speak soft *words* unto thee?

4 Will he make a covenant with thee? wilt thou take him for a servant for ever?

5 Wilt thou play with him as *with* a [c]bird? or wilt thou bind him for thy maidens?

6 Shall the [3]companions make a banquet of him? shall they part him among the [d]merchants?

7 Canst thou fill his skin with barbed [e]irons? or his head with [f]fish spears?

8 Lay thine hand upon him, remember the battle, do no more.

9 Behold, the hope of him is in vain: shall not *one* be cast down even at the sight of him?

10 None *is so* fierce that dare stir him up: [g]who then is able to stand before me?

11 Who hath [4]prevented me, that I should repay *him*? *whatsoever is* under the whole heaven is [h]mine.

12 I will not conceal his parts, nor his power, nor his comely proportion.

13 Who can [5]discover the face of his garment? *or* who can come *to him* with his double bridle?

14 Who can open the doors of his face? his teeth *are* terrible round about.

15 *His* scales *are his* pride, shut up together *as with* a close seal.

16 One is so near to another,

**24**
14 R. V. Shall any take him when he is on the watch, Or pierce through his nose with a snare?

**1**
*a* *God, condescension of,* Gen. 2:2.
*b* *Job,* Job 1:1.
1 R. V. Or press down his tongue with a cord?

**2**
2 R. V. hook?

**5**
*c* *Birds,* Eccl. 12:4

**6**
*d* *Merchant,* Neh. 3:32.
3 R. V. bands of fishermen make traffic of him?

**7**
*e* *Iron, articles made of,* Prov. 27:17.
*f* *Fish,* Matt. 17:27.

**10**
*g* *God, power of,* Gen. 2:2.

**11**
*h* *God, sovereign,* Gen. 2:2.
4 R. V. first given unto me,

**13**
5 R. V. strip off his outer garment? Who shall come within his double bridle?

that no air can come between them.

17 They are joined one to another, they stick together, that they cannot be sundered.[G]

18 [6]By his neesings[G] a light doth shine, and his eyes *are* like the eyelids of the morning.

19 Out of his mouth go burning lamps, *and* sparks of fire leap out.

20 Out of his nostrils goeth smoke, [7]as *out* of a seething[G] pot or caldron.

21 His breath kindleth coals, and a flame goeth out of his mouth.

22 In his neck remaineth strength, and [8]sorrow is turned into joy before him.

23 The flakes[G] of his flesh are joined together: they are firm in themselves; they cannot be moved.

24 His heart is as firm as a stone; yea, as hard as a piece of the nether[G] [i]*millstone*.

25 When he raiseth up himself, the mighty are afraid: by reason of [9]breakings[G] they purify themselves.

26 The [j]sword of him that layeth[G] at him cannot hold: the [k]spear, the [l]dart, nor the [10]habergeon.[G]

27 He esteemeth [m]iron as straw, *and* [n]brass as rotten wood.

28 The [o]arrow cannot make him flee: slingstones are turned with him into stubble.

29 [11]Darts are counted as stubble: he laugheth at the shaking of a [k]spear.

30 [12]Sharp stones *are* under him: he spreadeth sharp pointed things upon the mire.

31 He maketh the deep to boil like a pot: he maketh the sea like a pot of ointment.

32 He maketh a path to shine after him; *one* would think the deep *to be* hoary

**18**
6 Am. R. V. His sneezings flash forth light.

**20**
7 Am. R. V. As of a boiling pot and burning rushes.

**22**
8 R. V. terror danceth before him.

**24**
*i* *Millstone*, Judg. 9:53.

**25**
9 R. V. consternation they are beside themselves.

**26**
*j* *Sword*, 1 Chr. 21:5.
*k* *Spear*, 2 Kin. 11:10.
*l* *Dart*, 2 Sam. 18:14.
10 R. V. pointed shaft.

**27**
*m* *Iron*, Prov. 27:17.
*n* *Brass*, Job 28:2.

**28**
*o* *Arrow*, 1 Sam. 20:20.

**29**
11 R. V. Clubs

**30**
12 R. V. His underparts are like sharp potsherds: He spreadeth as it were a threshing wain upon the mire.

33 Upon earth there is not his like, who is made without fear.

34 He beholdeth all high *things*: he *is* a king over all the children of pride.

## CHAPTER 42

*Job humbles himself before God. 7 His friends are condemned for their wrong speaking. 10 Job's prosperity. 16 His age and death.*

THEN [T] [a]Jōb answered the LORD, and said,

2 I [b]know that thou canst [c]do every *thing*, and *that* no [1]thought can be withholden from thee.[S Q]

3 Who *is* he that hideth counsel without knowledge? therefore have I uttered that I understood not; things too wonderful for me, which I knew not.

4 Hear, I beseech thee, and I will speak: I will demand of thee, and declare thou unto me.

5 I have heard of thee by the hearing of the ear: but now [d]mine eye seeth thee.

6 Wherefore [e,f]I abhor[G] *myself*, and [g]repent in [h]dust and [i]ashes.[T]

7 ¶ And it was *so*, that after the LORD had spoken these words unto [a]Jōb, the LORD said to [j]Ĕl'i-phăz the Tē'man-īte, My [k]wrath is kindled against thee, and against thy two friends: for ye have not spoken of me *the thing that is* right, as my servant Jōb *hath*.

8 Therefore take unto you now seven bullocks and seven rams, and go to my servant [a]Jōb, and offer up for yourselves a [l]burnt offering; and my servant Jōb shall [m]pray [n]for you: for him will I accept: lest I deal with you *after your* folly, in that ye have not spoken of me *the thing which is* right, like my servant Jōb.

9 ¶ So [j]Ĕl'i-phăz the Tē'man-īte and [o]Bĭl'dăd the Shu'hīte *and* [p]Zō'phar the Nā'a-math-īte went, and did according as the

**1**
*a* *Job*, Job 1:1.

**2**
*b* *Faith, exemplified*, Mark 11:22.
*c* *God, power of*, Gen. 2:2.
1 R. V. purpose of thine can be restrained.

**5**
*d* *Wisdom, spiritual*, Prov. 2:2.

**6**
*e* *Conviction of Sin*, John 16:8.
*f* *Humility, exemplified*, Prov. 22:4.
*g* *Repentance, instances of*, Mark 1:4.
*h* *Dust*, Eccl. 3:20.
*i* *Ashes*, Num. 19:9.

**7**
*j* Job 2:11; 4: 5; 22.
*k* *Anger of God*, 2 Kin. 13:3.

**8**
*l* *Offerings, burnt*, Lev. 6:17.
*m* *Prayer, intercessory*, Acts 6:4.
*n* *Intercession, of man with God*, Jer. 27:18.

**9**
*o* Job 2:11; 8; 18; 25.
*p* Job 2:11; 11; 20.

Lord commanded them: the
Lord also accepted[c] [a]Jōb.
10 And the [q]Lord turned the
captivity[c] of [a]Jōb, when he
[m]prayed [n]for his friends: also
the Lord [r]gave Jōb twice as
much as he had before.
11 Then came there unto him
all his brethren, and all his sisters,
and all they that had been
of his acquaintance before, and
did eat bread with him in his
house: and [s]they bemoaned him,
and comforted him over all
the [t]evil that the Lord had
brought upon him: every man
also gave him a [u]piece of money,
and every one [2]an earring of
gold.
12 So the Lord [q]blessed the
latter end of [a]Jōb more than his
beginning: for [r]he had fourteen
thousand sheep, and six thousand
camels, and a thousand
yoke of oxen, and a thousand
she asses.
13 He had also seven sons and
three daughters.
14 And he called the name of
the first, Jĕ-mī′mȧ; and the
name of the second, Kĕ-zī′ȧ;
and the name of the third,
Kĕr′en–hăp′pụch.
15 And in all the land were no
women found *so* fair as the
daughters of Jōb: and their
father gave [v]them [w]inheritance
among their brethren.
16 After this lived [a]Jōb [x]an
hundred and forty years, and saw
his sons, and his sons' sons, *even*
four generations.
17 So [a]Jōb died, *being* [x]old and
full of days.

**10**

*q God, providence of,* Gen. 2:2.

*r Temporal Blessings, from God,* Psa. 103:2.

**11**

*s Sympathy,* Jas. 1:27.

*t Adversity, dispensation from God,* Psa. 10:6.

*u Presents,* Gen. 32:13.

2 R. V. a ring

**15**

*v Women, property rights of,* Prov. 31:10.

*w Inheritance,* Num. 27:7.

**16**

*x Longevity,* Psa. 91:16.

# THE PSALMS

## *PSALM 1

*The blessedness of the righteous. 4 The misery of the ungodly.*

[a,b] BLESSED *is* the [c]man that [d]walketh not in the [e]counsel of the [f]ungodly, nor standeth in the way of sinners, nor sitteth in the seat of the [g]scornful.

2 But [c,h]his delight *is* in the [i]law of the LORD; and in his law doth he [j]meditate [k]day and [l]night.

3 And [a,c]he shall be like a [m]tree planted by the rivers of water, that bringeth forth his [n]fruit in his season; his leaf also shall not wither; and whatsoever he doeth shall [o]prosper.

4 The [p]ungodly *are* not so: but *are* like the [q]chaff which the [r]wind driveth away.

5 Therefore the [s]ungodly shall not stand in the judgment, nor sinners in the [t]congregation of the righteous.

6 For the LORD [u]knoweth the [v]way of the righteous: but the way of the [s]ungodly shall perish.

**1**
*a Promise, to the obedient, of prosperity,* vs. 1–3; 2 Cor. 1:20.
*b Spiritual Peace,* Gal. 1:3.
*c Righteous, described,* Psa. 64:10.
*d Fellowship, with the wicked, forbidden,* 1 Cor. 1:9.
*e Counsel,* Prov. 12:15.
*f Evil Company,* Prov. 13:20.
*g Scoffing,* Hab. 1:10.
**2**
*h Obedience, exemplified,* Heb. 5:8.
*i Word of God, called law of the Lord,* Psa. 119:9.
*j Meditation, on the law of the Lord,* Psa. 49:3.
*k Day,* Gen. 1:5.
*l Night,* Gen. 1:5.
**3**
*m Tree, figurative,* Rev. 22:14.
*n Righteousness, fruits of,* Psa. 15:2.
*o Prosperity,* Eccl. 7:14.
**4**
*p Wicked, contrasted with the righteous,* vs. 1–6; Psa. 73:3.
*q Chaff,* Hos. 13:3.
*r Wind,* Job 37:17.
**5**
*s Wicked, punishment of,* Psa. 73:3.
*t Church,* Matt. 16:18.
**6**
*u God, knowledge of,* Gen. 2:2.
*v Heart, known to God,* Psa. 44:21.

## PSALM 2

*The kingdom of the Messiah. 10 Kings exhorted to serve him.*

A Messianic Psalm in which the poet describes the jealousies of the petty kings of the nations toward the king of Israel, and unconsciously, no doubt, under divine inspiration and in measures of an exalted, poetic imagination, describes the sovereignty of the Messiah and his universal kingdom of righteousness.

[a] WHY do the [1,b]heathen rage, and the people imagine a vain thing?

2 [c,d]The [e]kings of the earth set themselves, and the rulers take [f]counsel together, against the LORD, and against his anointed, *saying,*

3 Let us break their bands asunder, and cast away their cords from us.

4 He that sitteth in the [g]heavens shall [h]laugh: the LORD shall have them in [i]derision.

5 Then shall he speak unto [j]them in his [k]wrath, and vex them in his sore displeasure.

6 Yet have I set my king upon my holy hill of Zī'ŏn.

7 I will declare the decree: the LORD hath said unto me, [l,m,n]Thou *art* my [2]Son; this day have I begotten thee.

8 Ask of me, and [o]I shall give [p,q]*thee* the [1,r]heathen *for* thine inheritance, and the uttermost parts of the earth *for* thy possession.

9 [s]Thou shalt break them with a rod of [t]iron; thou shalt dash them in pieces like a [u]potter's vessel.

10 Be [v]wise now therefore, O ye [w]kings: be instructed, ye [x]judges of the earth.

11 Serve the LORD with [y]fear, and [z]rejoice with trembling.

12 Kiss the [2,l]Son, lest he be angry and ye perish *from* the way, [3]when his wrath is kindled

**1**
a Acts 4:25, 26.
*b Heathen,* Lam. 1:10.
1 R. V. nations

**2**
*c Prophecies, concerning the Messiah and their fulfillment,* vs. 1–9; Gen. 12 3.
*d Persecution, of Jesus, foretold,* vs. 1–3; John 15:20
*e Rulers,* Ex. 18:21.
*f Counsel,* Prov. 12:15.
**4**
*g Heaven, God's dwelling place,* Luke 18:22.
*h Anthropomorphisms,* Gen. 11:5.
*i Derision,* Job 30:1.
**5**
*j Wicked, punishment of,* Psa. 73:3.
*k Anger of God,* 2 Kings 13:3.
**7**
*l Jesus, divine sonship of,* Matt. 1:21.
m Acts 13:33; Heb. 1:5; 5:5.
*n Jesus, divinity of,* Matt. 1:21.
2 R. V. son;
**8**
*o Church, prophecies concerning prosperity of,* Matt. 16:18.
*p Jesus, exaltation of,* Matt. 1:21.
*q Jesus, prophecies concerning kingdom of,* Matt. 1:21.
*r Gentiles, prophecies of the conversion of,* Acts 10:45.
**9**
*s Jesus, power of,* Matt. 1:21.
*t Iron,* Prov. 27:17.
*u Pottery,* Jer. 18:3.
**10**
*v Wisdom, spiritual,* Prov. 2:2.
*w Rulers, character and qualifications of,* Ex. 18:21. *x Judge,* Judg. 2:18.
**11** *y Fear of God, enjoined,* Acts 9:31. *z Joy,* Psa. 5:11.
**12** 3 R. V. For his wrath will soon be kindled.

***PSALMS.** *Concerning adversity,* Psa. 3; 4; 5; 7; 11; 13; 16; 17; 22; 26; 27; 28; 31; 35; 41; 42; 43; 44; 54; 55; 56; 57; 59; 60; 61; 62; 63; 64; 69; 70; 71; 74; 77; 79; 80; 83; 84; 86; 88; 89; 94; 102; 109; 120; 123; 129; 137; 140; 141; 142; 143.
*Didactic,* Psa. 1; 5; 7; 9; 11; 12; 14; 15; 17; 24; 25; 32; 34; 36; 37; 39; 49; 50; 52; 53; 58; 73; 75; 82; 84; 90; 91; 92; 94; 101; 112; 119; 121; 125; 127; 128; 131; 133.
*Historical,* Psa. 78; 105; 106.
*Intercessional,* Psa. 20; 67; 122; 132; 144.
*Messianic,* Psa. 2; 21; 22; 45; 67; 68; 69; 72; 87; 89; 96; 110; 132
*Penitential,* Psa. 6; 25; 32; 38; 51; 102; 130; 143.
*Praise,* Psa. 8; 19; 24; 29; 33; 47; 50; 65; 66; 67; 76; 77; 93; 95; 96; 97; 99; 104; 111; 113; 114; 115; 134; 139; 147; 148; 150.
*Prophetic,* Psa. 2; 16; 22; 40; 45; 68; 69; 72; 87; 97; 110; 118.
*Thanksgiving, for God's goodness to Israel,* Psa. 21; 46; 48; 66; 68; 76; 81; 85; 98; 105; 124; 126; 129; 135; 136; 149; *for God's goodness to good men,* Psa. 23; 34; 36; 91; 100; 103; 107; 117; 121; 145; 146; *for God's mercies to individuals,* Psa. 9; 18; 30; 34; 40; 75; 103; 108; 116; 118; 138; 144.

*a Faith in Christ,* John 6:69.

1

*a Prayer, in adversity,* Acts 6:4.
*b Persecution, of the righteous,* John 15:20.

2

*c Infidelity, exemplified in doubting God's help,* 2 Cor. 6:15.

3

*d Faith, instances of,* Mark 11:22.
*e God, preserver,* Gen. 2:2.
*f Shield, figurative,* 1 Kin. 14:27.

4

*g Prayer, answered,* Acts 6:4.

5

*h Sleep,* Psa. 127:2.

6

*i Assurance, of saints,* Heb. 10:22.

7

*j Wicked, punishment of,* Psa. 73:3.

8

*k Salvation,* Acts 16:17.
*l God, savior,* Gen. 2:2.

---

*a Music,* 2 Chr. 5:13.

1

*b Prayer, in adversity,* Acts 6:4.

2

*c Vanity, the wicked love,* Eccl. 1:2.
1 R. V. falsehood?

3

*d God, love of, exemplified,* Gen. 2:2.

but a little. Blessed *are* all they that put their [a]trust in him.[T]

## PSALM 3

*The psalmist's confidence in God's protection.*

A Psalm of David, when he fled from Absalom his son.

[a]LORD, how are they increased that [b]trouble me! many *are* they that rise up against me.

2[S] Many *there be* which say of my soul, [c]*There is* no help for him in God. [Sē´lah.[C]

3 But [d]thou, O LORD, *art* a [e,f]shield for me; my glory, and the lifter up of mine head.[S]

4 I cried unto the LORD with my voice, and he [g]heard me out of his holy hill.[S] [Sē´lah.

5 I laid me down and [h]slept; I awaked; for the LORD [e]sustained me.

6 [i]I will not be afraid of ten thousands of people, that have set *themselves* against me round about.

7 Arise, O LORD; save me, O my God: for thou hast smitten all mine enemies *upon* the cheek bone; thou hast broken the teeth of the [j]ungodly.

8 [k]Salvation[C] *belongeth* unto the [l]LORD: thy blessing *is* upon thy people.[S] [Sē´lah.

## PSALM 4

*The psalmist prays to be heard. 2 He reproves his enemies, 4 and exhorts them to obedience. 6 Man's happiness is in God's favor.*

To the chief Musician on [a]Neginoth, A Psalm of David.

HEAR me when I [b]call, O God of my righteousness: thou hast enlarged[C] me *when I was* in distress; have mercy upon me, and hear my prayer.

2 O ye sons of men, how long *will ye turn* my glory into shame? *how long* will ye love [c]vanity, *and* seek after [1]leasing[C]? [Sē´lah.[C]

3 But know that the [d]LORD hath set apart him that is [e]godly for himself: [f,g]the LORD will hear when I call unto him.[S]

4 Stand in [h]awe, and [i]sin not: [j,k]commune with your own [l]heart upon your bed, and be still.[Q] [Sē´lah.

5 Offer the sacrifices of righteousness, and put your [m]trust in the LORD.

6 *There be* many that say, [n]Who will shew us *any* good? LORD, lift thou up the light of thy [o]countenance upon us.

7 Thou hast put [p]gladness in my [l]heart, more than in the time *that* their [q]corn[C] and their [r]wine increased.

8 [f]I will both lay me down in [s]peace, and [t]sleep: for thou, LORD, only [u]makest me dwell in safety.[T]

## PSALM 5

*The psalmist, imploring help from God, 3 professes his constancy in prayer, 8 and pleads especially for guidance, 10 for the destruction of his enemies, 11 and for the preservation of the righteous.*

To the chief Musician upon [a]Nehiloth, A Psalm of David.

[b]GIVE ear to [c]my words, O LORD, consider my meditation.

2 Hearken unto the voice of my cry, my King, and my God: for unto thee will I [b]pray.

3 My [d]voice shalt thou hear in the morning, O LORD; in the morning will I direct *my prayer* unto thee, and will look up.

4 For thou *art* not a God that hath pleasure in [e]wickedness: neither shall evil dwell with thee.

5 The [1,f]foolish shall not stand in thy sight: thou [g]hatest all [h]workers of iniquity.

6 Thou shalt destroy [i]them that speak [2,i]leasing[C]: the LORD will abhor the bloody and [j]deceitful man.

7 But as for me, I will come *into* thy house in the multitude of thy mercy: *and* in thy [k]fear will I [l]worship toward thy [m]holy temple.

*e Righteous, described,* Psa. 64:10.
*f Faith, instances of,* Mark 11:22.
*g Righteous, promises to,* Psa. 64:10.

4

*h Fear of God, enjoined,* Acts 9:31.
*i Holiness, enjoined,* Ex. 39:30.
*j Meditation,* Psa. 49:3.
*k Self-examination,* 2 Cor. 13:5.
*l Heart,* Psa. 44:21.

5

*m Faith, enjoined,* Mark 11:22.

6

*n Infidelity,* 2 Cor. 6:15.
*o Countenance,* Prov. 15:13.

7

*p Joy,* Psa. 5:11.
*q Corn,* Psa. 65:13.
*r Wine,* Prov. 23:31.

8

*s Spiritual Peace,* Gal. 1:3.
*t Sleep,* Psa. 127:2.
*u God, preserver,* Gen. 2:2.

---

*a Music,* 2 Chr. 5:13.

1

*b Prayer, in adversity,* vs. 1–12; Acts 6:4.
*c David,* 1 Sam. 16:13.

3

*d Prayer, morning* Acts 6:4.

4

*e Sin, repugnant to God,* Rom. 5:12.

5

*f Wicked, punishment of,* Psa. 73:3.
*g Hatred, of God,* Prov. 15:17.
*h Wicked, God is angry with,* Psa. 73:3.
1 R. V. arrogant

6

*i Falsehood, an abomination,* Job 21:34.
*j Deceit, the Lord abhors,* Psa. 36:3.
2 R. V. lies:

7

*k Fear of God,* Acts 9:31.
*l Worship,* Gen. 22:5.
*m Church, called holy temple,* 1 Kin. 9:3.

8 [n]Lead me, O [o]LORD, in thy [p]righteousness [q]because of mine enemies; make thy way straight before my face.

9 For *there is* [r,s]no [t]faithfulness in their mouth; their inward part *is* [u]very wickedness; [v]their throat *is* an open sepulchre[G]; they [w]flatter with their tongue.[Q]

10 [3, x]Destroy thou them, O God; let them fall by their own counsels; cast them out in the multitude of their transgressions; for they have rebelled against thee.

11 But let all those that put their [y]trust in thee rejoice: let them ever [z]shout for *joy, because thou [a]defendest them: let them also that [b]love thy name be joyful in thee.

12 For thou, LORD, wilt bless the [c]righteous; with [d]favour wilt thou compass[G] him as *with* a [e]shield.[S]

8
*n Guidance, prayer for,* Psa. 48:14.
*o God, guide,* Gen. 2:2.
*p God, righteousness of.* Gen. 2:2.
*q Adversity, prayer in,* Psa. 10:6.
9
*r Hypocrisy,* Jas. 3:17.
*s Wicked, described,* Psa. 73:3.
*t Sincerity, the wicked devoid of,* 1 Cor. 5:8.
*u Depravity,* Job 15:14.
*v* Rom. 3:13.
*w Flattery,* Prov. 6:24.
10
*x Prayer, imprecatory,* Acts 6:4.
3 R. V. Hold them guilty,
11
*y Faith, rewards of,* Mark 11:22.
*z Shouting,* 2 Chr. 15:14.

*a God, preserver,* Gen. 2:2.
*b Love, of man for God,* 1 John 4:19.
12
*c Promise, to the righteous,* 2 Cor. 1:20.
*d Grace of God,* Rom. 4:16.
*e Shield, figurative,* 1 Kin. 14:27.

## PSALM 6

*The psalmist's prayer in affliction. 8 His supplication is heard.*

To the chief Musician on [a]Neginoth upon [a]Sheminith, A Psalm of David.

[b, c]O LORD, rebuke me not in thine [d]anger, neither [e]chasten me in thy hot displeasure.

2 [b, c]Have [f]mercy upon me, O LORD; for I *am* weak: O LORD, heal me; for my bones are vexed.[G]

3 My soul is also sore[G] vexed:[G] but thou, O LORD, how long?[Q]

4 [b]Return, O LORD, deliver my soul: oh save me for thy [f]mercies' sake.

5 For in [g]death *there is* no remembrance of thee: in [1]the [h]grave[G] who shall give thee thanks?

6 I am weary with my [c]groaning; all the night make I my bed to swim; I water my couch with my †tears.

7 Mine eye is consumed[G] because of grief; it waxeth[G] old because of all mine enemies.

8 Depart from me, all ye [i]workers of iniquity; for [j]the LORD [k]hath heard the voice of my weeping.[Q]

9 The LORD hath heard my [k]supplication; the LORD will receive my prayer.

10 Let all mine enemies be ashamed and sore[G] vexed:[G] let them return *and* be ashamed suddenly.

*a Music,* 2 Chr. 5:13.
1
*b Prayer, in adversity,* Acts 6:4.
*c Afflictions, prayer in,* Psa. 34:19.
*d Anger of God,* 2 Kin. 13:3.
*e Divine Chastisement, prayer to be spared from,* Job 33:19.
2
*f God, mercy of,* Gen. 2:2.
5
*g Death,* Num. 23:10.
*h Hell,* Mark 9:43.
1 R. V. Sheol
8
*i Evil Company, the righteous shun,* Prov. 13:20.
*j Faith, instances of,* Mark 11:22.
*k Prayer, answered,* Acts 6:4.

## PSALM 7

*The psalmist prays to be delivered from his enemies. 10 He trusts in God, who saves the upright, 12 and will punish the wicked.*

[a]Shiggaion of David, which he sang unto the Lord, concerning the words of Cush the Benjamite.

[b]O LORD my God, in thee do I put my [c]trust: save me from all them that [d]persecute[G] me, and deliver me:

2 Lest he tear my soul like a [e]lion, rending[G] *it* in pieces, while *there is* none to deliver.

3 [b]O LORD my God, if I have

*a Music,* 2 Chr. 5:13.
1
*b Prayer, in adversity,* Acts 6:4.
*c Faith, instances of,* Mark 11:22.
*d Adversity, prayer in,* Psa. 10:6.
2
*e Lion,* Mic. 5:8.

* **JOY,** Psa. 30:5, 11; 33:21; 97:11; 132:16; Prov. 29:6. *From God,* Eccl. 2:26; Rom. 15:13. *In the Lord,* Psa. 9:2; 104:34; Isa. 9:3; 29:19; 41:16; 61:10; Luke 1:47; Rom. 5:11. *In Christ,* Phil. 3:3; 4:4; 1 Pet. 1:8. *In the word of God,* Psa. 19:8; 119:14, 16, 111, 162; Jer. 15:16. *In worship,* 2 Chr. 7:10; Ezra 6:22; Neh. 12:43; Psa. 42:4; 43:4; 71:23; Isa. 56:7; Zeph. 3:14; Zech. 2:10; 9:9. *A fruit of the Spirit,* Gal. 5:22; Eph. 5:18, 19. *For salvation,* Psa. 13:5; 20:5; 21:1, 6; 35:9; Isa. 12:2, 3; 25:9; 35:1, 2, 10; 55:12; Rom. 5:2; 14:17. *On account of a good conscience,* 2 Cor. 1:12. *Over a sinner's repentance,* Luke 15:6–10, 22–32.

*Under adversity,* Psa. 126:5, 6; Isa. 61:3; Matt. 5:12; Acts 5:41; 2 Cor. 6:10; 7:4; 8:2; 12:10; Col. 1:11; 1 Thess. 1:6; Heb. 10:34; Jas. 1:2; 1 Pet. 4:13.

*Fullness of,* Psa. 16:11; 36:8; 63:5; John 15:11; 16:24; Acts 2:28; 1 John 1:4.

*Everlasting,* Isa. 51:11; 61:7.

*In heaven,* Matt. 25:21; Luke 15:7, 10.

*Attributed to God,* Deut. 28:63; 30:9; Jer. 32:41.

*Of the wicked, short,* Job 20:5.

**Enjoined,** Deut. 12:18; Neh. 8:10; Psa. 2:11; 5:11; 32:11; 68:3; 97:12; 100:1, 2; 105:3, 43; 149:2, 5; Joel 2:23; Luke 2:10; 6:23; 10:20; Rom. 12:12; 1 Thess. 5:16.

**Instances of:** *Of Moses and the Israelites, when Pharaoh and his army were destroyed,* Ex. 15:1–21. *Of Deborah and the Israelites, when Sisera was overthrown,* Judg. 5.

Of the Israelites: *When Saul was presented as their king,* 1 Sam. 10:24; *when David slew Goliath,* 1 Sam. 18:6, 7; *when they kept the dedication of the temple, and the feast of tabernacles under Ezra,* Ezra 6:16, 22.

Of the Jews: *After hearing, anew, the word of God,* Neh. 8:9–18; *when they turned from idolatry,* 2 Chr. 15:14, 15; 23:18, 21; 29:30, 36; 30:21, 23, 26; *when the wall of Jerusalem was dedicated,* Neh. 12:43; *when the foundation of the second temple was laid,* Ezra 3:11–13.

*Of Zacharias, when John was born,* Luke 1:67–79. *Of the shepherds, when they saw the infant Jesus,* Luke 2:20. *Of the Magi,* Matt. 2:10. *Of Simeon, when Jesus was presented in the temple,* Luke 2:28–32.

*Of angels, when sinners repent,* Luke 15:7, 10. *Of the disciples, when Jesus triumphantly entered Jerusalem,* Matt. 21:8, 9; Mark 11:8–10; *after the resurrection of Jesus,* Luke 24:41. *Of the impotent man, healed by Peter,* Acts 3:8. *Of Paul and Silas, in the jail at Philippi,* Acts 16:25. *Of Paul, in tribulation,* 2 Cor. 7:4.

† **TEARS,** Psa. 6:6; 39:12; 42:3. *Observed by God,* Psa.

done this; if there be iniquity in my hands;

4 If I have rewarded [f]evil unto him that was at peace with me; (yea, I have delivered him that without cause is mine enemy:)

5 Let the enemy persecute my soul, and take *it*; yea, let him tread down my life upon the earth, and lay mine honour in the dust. [Sē′lah.

6 [b,d]Arise, O LORD, in thine [g]anger, lift up thyself because of the rage of mine enemies: and awake for me *to* the judgment *that* thou hast commanded.

7 So shall the congregation of the people compass[G] thee about: for their sakes therefore return thou on high.

8 The LORD shall [h]judge the people: judge me, O LORD, according to my righteousness, and according to mine [i]integrity *that is* in me.[T]

9 [b]Oh let the wickedness of the wicked come to an end; but establish the just: for the [j]righteous God [h]trieth[G] the [k]hearts and reins.[G S Q]

10 [c]My defence *is* of God, which [l]saveth the upright in heart.[S]

11 [1]God [h]judgeth the righteous, and God is [g]angry *with the wicked* every day.

12 If he [m]turn not, he will whet[G] his sword; he hath bent[Q] his bow, and made it ready.[Q]

13 He hath also prepared for him the instruments of death; [2]he ordaineth his [n]arrows against the persecutors.

14 Behold, he travaileth with iniquity, and hath [o]conceived mischief, and brought forth [p]falsehood.

15 He made a *pit, and digged it, and [q]is fallen into the ditch *which* he made.

16 His [q]mischief shall return upon his own head, and his violent dealing shall come down upon his own pate.[G]

17 I will [r]praise the LORD according to his [j]righteousness: and will sing praise to the name of the LORD most high.[T]

## PSALM 8

*God's glory manifested in his works, 4 and in his goodness to man.*

To the chief Musician upon [a]Gittith, A Psalm of David.

O LORD our Lord, [b]how excellent *is* thy name in all the earth! who hast set thy glory [1]above the heavens.[S]

2 [c]Out of the mouth of †babes and sucklings hast thou ordained strength because of thine enemies, that thou mightest still the enemy and the [d]avenger.[Q]

3 When I consider thy [‡,e]heavens, the [f]work of thy fingers, the [g]moon and the [h]stars, which [i,j]thou hast ordained;[S]

4[Q] [k]What is [l]man, that thou art mindful of him? and the son of man, that thou visitest him?

5 For [m]thou hast [i]made [n]him [2]a little lower than the angels, and hast crowned him with glory and honour.

6 Thou [i]madest [o]him to have dominion over the [f]works of thy hands; [p]thou hast put all *things* under his feet:[Q]

---

**4**
f *Evil for Good,* Psa. 35:12.

**6**
g *Anger of God,* 2 Kin. 13:3.

**8**
h *God, judge,* Gen. 2:2.
i *Integrity,* Job 2:3.

**9**
j *God, righteousness of,* Gen. 2:2.
k *Heart,* Psa. 44:21.

**10**
l *God, preserver,* Gen. 2:2.

**11**
1 **R. V. God is a righteous judge, Yea, a God that hath indignation every day.**

**12**
m *Impenitence, judgments denounced against,* Rom. 2:5.

**13**
n *Arrow,* 1 Sam. 20:20.
2 R. V. He maketh his arrows fiery shafts.

**14**
o *Malice,* Eph. 4:31.
p *Falsehood,* Job 21:34.

**15**
q *Sin, retroactive,* Rom. 5:12.

**17**
r *Praise,* Psa. 150:1.

a *Music,* 2 Chr. 5:13.

**1**
b *Praise,* Psa. 150:1.
1 R. V. upon

**2**
c Matt. 21:16.
d *Avenger of Blood, figurative,* Deut. 19:6.

**3**
e *Astronomy,* Isa. 13:10.
f *Works, of God,* vs. 3–5; Psa. 40:5.
g *Moon,* Song 6:10.
h *Stars,* Judg. 5:20.
i *God, creator,* Gen. 2:2.
j *God, power of,* Gen. 2:2.

**4**
k Heb. 2:6.
l *Man, insignificance of,* Job 4:17.

**5**
m Heb. 2:7.
n *Man, created a little lower than the angels,* Job 4:17.
2 R. V. but little lower than God, And crownest him

**6**
o *Man, dominion of,* Job 4:17.
p 1 Cor. 15:27.

---

56:8; Isa. 38:3–5. *Wiped away,* Rev. 7:17. *None in heaven,* Rev. 21:4.

**Figurative,** Psa. 80:5.

***PIT.** *Joseph cast into,* Gen. 37:23, 24. *Benaiah slew a lion in,* 2 Sam. 23:20. *Absalom buried in,* 2 Sam. 18:17.

**Figurative,** Psa. 9:15; 35:7; 55:23; Prov. 22:14; 28:10. *Of the dead,* Psa. 28:1; 30:3; 143:7. *Of guilt,* Psa. 40:2; Isa. 38:17.

**†BABES.** *In the mouth of, is praise perfected,* Psa. 8:2; Matt. 21:16. *Righteous compared to,* Matt. 11:25; 18:2–6; Mark 10:15; Luke 10:21; 18:17.

**Figurative:** *Of weak Christians,* Rom. 2:20; 1 Cor. 3:1; Heb. 5:13; 1 Pet. 2:2.

See footnotes: CHILDREN, Mark 10:14; PARENTS, 2 Cor. 12:14.

**‡ HEAVENS, PHYSICAL,** Gen. 1:1; 2 Chr. 2:6; 6:18; Job 38:31–33; Psa. 19:1; 50:6; 68:33; 89:29; 103:11; 113:4; 115:16; 136:5; Jer. 31:37; Ezek. 1:1; Matt. 24:29, 30; Acts 2:19, 20.

**Created,** Gen. 1:1; 2:1; Ex. 20:11; 1 Chr. 16:26; 2 Chr. 2:12; Neh. 9:6; Job 9:8; Psa. 8:3; 19:1; 33:6, 9; 148:4–6; Prov. 8:27; Isa. 37:16; 40:22; 42:5; 45:12, 18; Jer. 10:12; 32:17, 51:15; Acts 4:24; 14:15; Heb. 1:10; Rev. 10:6; 14:7.

**Destruction of,** Job 14:12; Psa. 102:25, 26; Isa. 51:6; Matt. 5:18; 24:35; Heb. 1:10–12; 2 Pet. 3:10, 12; Rev. 6:12–14; 20:11; 21:1, 4.

**Figurative:** *Of divine judgments,* Isa. 34:4.

7 All [q]sheep and [r]oxen, yea, and the beasts of the field;
8 The [s]fowl of the air, and the [t]fish of the sea, *and whatsoever* passeth through the paths of the seas.
9 O LORD our Lord, how excellent[C] *is* thy name in all the earth![S T]

## PSALM 9

*The psalmist praises God for maintaining his cause. 7 His trust in God, 13 and prayer for help. 15 The destruction of the wicked.*

To the chief Musician upon [a]Muth-labben, A Psalm of David.

I WILL [b,c]praise *thee*, O LORD, with my whole [d]heart; I will shew[C] forth all thy marvellous works.
2 I will be [e]glad and rejoice in thee: I will sing [c]praise to thy name, O thou most High.
3 When mine enemies are turned back, they shall fall and perish at thy presence.
4 For thou hast maintained my right and my cause; thou satest in the [f]throne [g]judging right.[S]
5 Thou hast rebuked the [1]heathen,[C] thou hast [h]destroyed the [i]wicked, thou hast put out their name for ever and ever.
6 [2]O thou enemy, destructions are come to a perpetual end: and thou hast [h]destroyed cities; their memorial is perished with them.
7[T] But the LORD [3]shall [j]endure for ever: he hath prepared his [g]throne for judgment.[S]
8 And he shall [f]judge the world in [k]righteousness, he shall minister judgment to the people in uprightness.[S T Q]
9 The [l]LORD also will be a [4]refuge for the [m]oppressed, a [4,n]refuge in times of trouble.[S]
10 And they that know thy name will put their [o]trust in thee: for thou, LORD, [p]hast not forsaken them that [q]seek thee.[S]
11 Sing [c]praises to the LORD, which dwelleth in [r]Zī'ŏn: [s]declare among the people his doings.
12 When he maketh inquisition[C] for [t]blood, he remembereth them: [p]he forgetteth not the cry of the [5,u]humble.[C]
13 Have [v]mercy upon me, O LORD; consider my [w]trouble *which I suffer* of them that hate me, thou that [l]liftest me up from the [x]gates of [y]death:
14 That I may shew[C] forth all thy praise in the gates of the daughter[C] of [r]Zī'ŏn: I will rejoice in thy [z]salvation.
15 The [1]heathen[C] [a]are sunk down in the [b]pit *that* they made: in the [c]net which they hid is their own foot taken.
16 [6]The LORD is known *by* the [d]judgment *which* he executeth: the wicked [a]is snared[C] in the work of his own hands. [[e]Hĭg-gā'ion. Sē'lah.[C]
17 The [f]wicked shall [7]be turned into [g]hell,[C] *and* all the [h]nations that [i]forget God.[S]
18 For [j]the [k]needy shall not alway be forgotten: [j]the [l]expectation of the poor shall *not* perish for ever.
19 Arise, O LORD; let not man prevail: let the [1]heathen[C] be judged in thy sight.
20 Put them in fear, O LORD: *that* the nations may know themselves *to be but* men. [Sē'lah.

## PSALM 10

*The psalmist complains to God of the outrage of the wicked. 12 His prayer for help, 16 and his confidence in God.*

WHY standest thou afar off, O LORD? *why* hidest thou *thyself* in times of [a]trouble?
2 The wicked in *his* [b]pride doth persecute the [c]poor: let them [d]be taken in the devices that they have imagined.
3 For the wicked [e,f]boasteth of his heart's desire, [1]and blesseth the [g]covetous, *whom* the LORD abhorreth.

---

7
q *Sheep*, Deut. 32:14.
r *Bullock*, Ex. 29:3.
8
s *Birds*, Eccl. 12:4.
t *Fish*, Matt. 17:27.

a *Music*, 2 Chr. 5:13.
1
b *Thankfulness, exemplified*, Acts 24:3.
c *Praise*, Psa. 150:1.
d *Heart*, Psa. 44:21.
2
e *Joy*, Psa. 5:11.
4
f *Throne, figurative*, 1 Kin. 2:19.
g *God, judge*, Gen. 2:2.
5
h *Judgments*, Ex. 6:6.
i *Wicked, punishment of*, Psa. 73:3.
1 R. V. nations,
6
2 R. V. The enemy are come to an end, they are desolate for ever;
7
j *God, eternity of*, Gen. 2:2.
3 R. V. sitteth as king
8
k *God, righteousness of*, Gen. 2:2.
9
l *God, preserver*, Gen. 2:2.
m *Oppression*, Eccl. 5:8.
n *Adversity, consolation in*, Psa. 10:6.
4 R. V. high tower
10
o *Faith*, Mark 11:22.
p *God, faithfulness of*, Gen. 2:2.
q *Seekers*, Isa. 55:6.
11
r *Zion*, 2 Sam. 5:7.
s *Religious Testimony*, 2 Thess. 1:10.

12
t *Homicide*, Deut. 5:17.
u *Poor, God's care of*, Prov. 21:13.
5 R. V. poor.
13
v *God, mercy of*, Gen. 2:2.
w *Adversity, prayer in*, Psa. 10:6.
x *Gates, figurative*, Deut. 3:5.
y *Death*, Num. 23:10.
14
z *Salvation*, Acts 16:17.

15
a *Sin, retroactive*, Rom. 5:12.
b *Pit, figurative*, Psa. 7:15.
c *Net, figurative*, Isa. 51:20.
16
d *Judgments*, Ex. 6:6.
e *Music*, 2 Chr. 5:13.
6 R. V. The Lord hath made himself known, he hath executed judgment:
17
f *Wicked, punishment of*, Psa. 73:3.
g *Hell, the future abode of the wicked*, Mark 9:43.
h *Nation*, Isa. 2:4.
i *The Godless, described*, Job 8:13.
7 R. V. return to Sheol,
18
j *Promise, to the poor*, 2 Cor. 1:20.
k *Poor, God's care of*, Prov. 21:13.
l *Hope*, Prov. 13:12.

1
a *Afflictions, prayer in*, Psa. 34:19.
2
b *Pride*, Prov. 16:18.
c *Poor, oppression of*, Prov. 21:13.
d *Sin, retroactive*, Rom. 5:12.
3
e *Boasting*, Prov. 25:14.
f *Impenitence*, Rom. 2:5.
g *Covetousness*, Isa. 57:17.
1 R. V. And the covetous renounceth, yea, contemneth the Lord.

**4**
h *Wicked, described,* Psa. 73:3.
i *Countenance,* Prov. 15:13.
j *False Confidence,* Mic. 7:5.
k *Atheism,* Psa. 14:1.
2 R. V. saith, He will not require it. All his thoughts are, There is no God.

**5**
l *God, providence of, mysterious,* Gen. 2:2.
3 R. V. firm at all times:

**6**
m *Spiritual Blindness, manifested in presumption,* 2 Cor. 4:4.
n *Delusion,* 2 Thess. 2:11.

**7**
o Rom. 3:14.
p *Speech, evil,* Col. 4:6.
q *Deceit,* Psa. 36:3.
r *Dishonesty,* Ezek. 22:13.

**8**
s *Homicide,* Deut. 5:17.

**9**
t *Lion,* Mic. 5:8.
u *Net, figurative,* Isa. 51:20.

**11**
v *Blasphemy,* 2 Sam. 12:14.
w *Infidelity,* 2 Cor. 6:15.

4 The [h]wicked, through the
[b]pride of his [i]countenance,
[2,j]will not seek *after God:* [k]God
*is* not in all his thoughts.
5 [h]His ways are [3]always grievous; [l]thy judgments *are* far
above out of his sight: *as for* all
his enemies, he puffeth[G] at them.
6 [h,m]He hath said in his heart,
[j,n]I shall not be moved: for *I*
*shall* never *be* in *adversity.
7 [h,o]His mouth is full of [p]curs-
ing and [q]deceit and [r]fraud: under his tongue *is* mischief and
vanity.[Q]
8 [h]He sitteth in the lurking
places of the villages: in the secret places doth he [s]murder the
innocent: his eyes are privily[G] set
against the [c]poor.
9 [h]He lieth in wait secretly as a
[t]lion in his den: he lieth in wait
to catch the [c]poor: he doth catch
the poor, when he draweth him
into his [u]net.
10 [h]He croucheth[G], *and* humbleth himself, that the poor may
fall by his strong ones.
11 [h]He hath said in his heart,
[v,w,n]God hath forgotten: he hideth his face; he will never see *it.*
12 Arise, O LORD; O God, lift
up thine hand: forget not the
humble.
13 Wherefore doth the wicked
contemn[G] God? [4]he hath said in his
heart, [x]Thou wilt not require[G] *it.*
14 Thou hast seen *it*; for thou
beholdest mischief and spite, to
requite[G] *it* with thy hand: the
[y]poor committeth himself unto
thee; [z]thou art the helper of the
[a,b]fatherless.
15 Break thou the arm of the
[c]wicked and the evil *man*: seek
out his wickedness *till* thou find
none.
16 The [d]LORD *is* King for ever
and ever: the [4]heathen[G] are perished out of his land.[Q]
17[S] LORD, thou hast heard the
desire of the humble: thou wilt
prepare their [e]heart, thou wilt
cause thine [f]ear to hear:
18 To [g]judge the [a]fatherless
and the [h]oppressed, that the man
of the earth may no more oppress.[S]

## PSALM 11

*The psalmist's reply to those who advised him to flee for safety.*

To the chief Musician, A Psalm of David.

IN the LORD put I my [a]trust:
how say ye to my soul, Flee
*as* a bird to your mountain?

**13**
x *Delusion,* 2 Thess. 2:11.
4 R. V. and say in his heart,

**14**
y *Poor, God's care of,* Prov. 21:13.
z *God, preserver,* Gen. 2:2.

a *Orphan, God, the friend of,* Lam. 5:3.
b *Children, God's care of,* Mark 10:14.

**15**
c *Wicked, punishment of,* Psa. 73:3.

**16**
d *God, sovereign,* Gen. 2:2.
4 R. V. nations

**17**
e *Heart,* Psa. 44:21.
f *Ear, figurative,* Lev. 8:23.

**18**
g *God, judge,* Gen. 2:2.
h *Oppression,* Eccl. 5:8.

**1**
a *Faith, instances of,* Mark 11:22.

* **ADVERSITY,** Job 19:7–20; Psa. 31:9–13; 77:2–4; 109:22–24; John 16:33; 2 Cor. 1:8, 9; 4:7–12, 16, 17; 6:4–10; 11:23–30; 1 Pet. 5:9.

**Benefits of,** Psa. 94:12, 13; 107:4–6; Isa. 19:20, 22; 26:9; Jer. 2:27; 22:22, 23; Ezek. 20:37, 43 (with 6:9); Hos. 5:15; Rom. 5:3, 4; 8:17, 28; 2 Cor. 4:17; Phil. 1:12–14, 19; Jas. 1:2–4, 12; 1 Pet. 1:7; 4:14.

**Benefits of, illustrated,** Gen. 32:11 (with vs. 9–31); 42:21; Ex. 9:27, 28; 10:7, 16, 17; Ex. 12:31–33; Num. 21:7; Judg. 10:6–8, 10; 1 Sam. 12:9, 10; Ezra 9:13 (with vs. 5–15); Psa. 66:12; Jonah 2:1–10; Luke 15:17 (with vs. 11–24).

**Consolation in,** Gen. 21:17 (with vs. 12–21, and 16:7–13); 26:24 (with vs. 17–33); 31:42; Ex. 3:7, 8, 16, 17; 14:13, 14; Deut. 33:27; Psa. 9:9; 27:5, 6; 31:7; 34:4, 19, 20; 37:33; 46:1; 50:15; 68:6; 140:12; Isa. 25:4; 41:17; 43:2; 58:10; 66:5; Nah. 1:7; Matt. 5:10–12; Luke 6:21–23; John 15:18, 20; Acts 12:5; Rom. 8:28, 35–39; 12:12; 2 Cor. 1:3, 4; 4:8, 9, 16, 17; 7:6; 2 Thess. 1:7; 2 Tim. 4:17; Heb. 13:3, 5, 6; Jas. 1:27.

**Despondency in,** Job 4:5; Psa. **22:1, 2;** Prov. **24:10;** Mark 15:34 (with Matt. 27:46).

**Design of,** Deut. 8:2, 16; 30:1–3; 31:17; Judg. 2:21, 22; 1 Kin. 8:33–48; 2 Chr. 6:24–31; 7:13, 14; Job 33:11, 16–21, 36:8–10; Psa. 106:43, 44; 107:10–14, 17–21, 23–31; Eccl. 7:14; Isa. 52:5, 6; Dan. 4:25; Amos 4:6; Mic. **6:9;** 4:17; 12:7; Phil. 1:29, 30; 2 Thess. 1:4, 5; Rev. 2:10.

*For correction,* Deut. 8:5; 2 Sam. 7:14; Job 5:**6, 7, 17, 18;** Psa. 66:10–12.

*As a judgment,* Gen. 3:16, 17; Lev. 26:14–39; **Deut. 28:** 15–68; 29:20–28; 32:19–43; 1 Kin. 9:7.

**Dispensation from God,** Deut. 28:20 (with vs. 15–68); 32:39; Ruth 1:20, 21; 1 Sam. 2:6, 7; 2 Kings 6:33; 15:5; 2 Chr. **7:13** (with vs. 12–22); Job 1:21; 5:17, 18; 9:12; Psa. 66:**11; 71:20; 78:**31–34; 80:5–7, 16; 89:38–45; 90:7, 15; 102:10, 23; Isa. 30:20; Lam. 1:5; 3:1; Dan. 4:24, 25; Amos **3:6;** Jonah 2:3; 2 Cor. 12:7.

**Obduracy in,** Job 36:12, 13; Rev. 9:20, 21; 16:9–11, 21. *Of Pharaoh,* Ex. 7:21, 22; 8:12–15, 19, 31, 32; 9:6, 7, 10–12, 33–35; 10:19–28; 12:29; 14:4–8. *Of Israelites,* Psa. 78:31, 32; Hos. 7:9, 10, 14; Amos 4:6–11. *Of Jews,* Isa. 8:21; 22:12, 13; 42:25; 57:17; Jer. 5:3; Dan. 9:13; Zeph. 3:2, 7; Hag. 2:17.

**Prayer in,** Gen. 43:14; Ex. 14:10; 17:4; 2 Sam. 15:31; 2 Chr. 33:12, 13; Psa. 3:1, 2, 7; 5:8; 9:13; 22:1, 11, 19–21; 28:1; 30:9, 10; 38:1, 2, 9, 10, 16; 57:1, 2; 60:1–3, 11; 61:1, 2; 74:1–3, 11, 19–23; 77:1, 2, 7–9; 79:1, 5, 11; 80:3–5, 14; Isa. 64:9–12; Jer. 14:8, 9, 19–21; Lam. 1:20; 5:1, 19–22; Dan. 6:10; Joel 1:19; Jonah 1:14; 2:1–7; Hab. 1:12, 13; Matt. 8:25; 14:30; 15:22–28; 26:39, 42, 44 (with Mark 14:36; Luke 22:42); 27:46; Mark 15:34; Luke 23:46; John **11:3;** Acts 4:29, 30; 7:59, 60; 2 Cor. 12:8; Jas. 5:13–15.

*For deliverance from enemies,* Gen. 32:11; Judg. 3:9; 2 Sam. 22:7; 2 Kin. 19:16, 19; Neh. 4:4, 5, 9; Psa. 7:1, 2, 6; 13:1–4; 17:1, 6–9, 13; 25:2, 16–19; 27:11, 12; 31:1–4, 9, 14, 15; 35:1–3, 17, 19, 22–25; 42:9; 43:1, 2; 54:1–3; 55:1–3; 56:1, 2; 59:1–4; 64:1, 2; 69:13–19; 70:1–3; 71:1–4; 106:47; 108:6, 12; 109:1, 2, 26–28; 120:2; 142:5–7; Jer. 15:15.

*For deliverance from oppression,* Ex. **2:23;** Num. 20:16; Psa. 44:24–26.

*For victory in battle,* 1 Chr. 5:20; 2 Chr. **14:11;** 20:12.

**Resignation in,** Job 5:17; 13:15; Matt. 26:39; Rom. 5:3; 12:12; 2 Cor. 12:9; 1 Thess. 3:3, 4; 2 Thess. 1:4; 2 Tim. 4:5; Heb. 10:34; 12:3–12); 1 Pet. 1:6; 2:20; 4:12, 13, 19.

**Resignation in, exemplified,** 1 Sam. 3:18; 2 Sam. 12:23; 16:10, 12; 24:14; 2 Kin. 4:26; 20:19 (with Isa. 39:8); Neh. 9:33; Job 1:21, 22; 2:10; 13:15; Psa. 39:9; 119:75; Lam. 3:39; Dan. 9:14; Mic. 7:9; Acts 5:41; Rom. **5:3, 4, 2** Cor. **6:4–10;** 7:4; 2 Thess. 1:4.

**2**
*b* *Wicked,* Psa. 73:3.
*c* *Arrow, figurative,* 1 Sam. 20:20.
*d* *Persecution, of the righteous,* John 15:20.
1 R. V. may shoot in darkness
**3**
*e* *Righteous,* Psa. 64:10.
**4**
*f* *Church, called holy temple,* 1 Kin. 9:3.
*g* *Throne, figurative,* 1 Kin. 2:19.
*h* *Heaven, God's dwelling place,* Luke 18:22.
*i* *God, knowledge of,* Gen. 2:2.
*j* *Anthropomorphisms,* Gen. 11:5.
*k* *God, judge,* Gen. 2:2.
**5**
*l* *Hatred, of God,* Prov. 15:17.
**6**
*m* *Wicked, punishment of,* Psa. 73:3.
*n* *Fire, figurative,* Ex. 12:8.
*o* *Brimstone, figurative,* Deut. 29:23.
*p* *Cup, figurative,* Matt. 20:22.
2 R. V. burning wind shall be
**7**
*q* *God, righteousness of,* Gen. 2:2.
3 R. V. The upright shall behold his face.

---

*a* *Music,* 2 Chr. 5:13.
**1**
*b* *Church, backslidden,* Matt. 16:18.
*c* *Faithfulness,* Luke 16:10.
**2**
*d* *Vanity,* Eccl. 1:2.
*e* *Flattery,* Prov. 6:24.
*f* *Falsehood,* Job 21:34.
*g* *Heart,* Psa. 44:21.
**3**
*h* *Speech, evil,* Col. 4:6.
*i* *Presumption,* Psa. 19:13.
**4**
*j* *Boasting,* Prov. 25:14.
**5**
*k* *Oppression, the Lord a refuge from,* Eccl. 5:8.
*l* *Injustice,* Isa. 26:10.
*m* *God, preserver,* Gen. 2:2.
*n* *Poor, God's care of,* Prov. 21:13.
1 R. V. at whom they puff.
**6**
*o* *Word of God,* Psa. 119:9.
*p* *Purity,* 1 Tim. 4:12.

2 For, lo, the [b]wicked bend *their* bow, they make ready their [c]arrow upon the string, that they [1]may privily[C] [d]shoot at the upright in heart.

3 If the foundations be destroyed, what can the [e]righteous do?

4 The LORD *is* in his [f]holy temple, the LORD'S [g]throne *is* in [h]heaven: [i]his [j]eyes behold, his eyelids [k]try,[C] the children of men.[S]

5 The LORD trieth[C] the righteous: but the wicked and him that loveth violence his soul [l]hateth.

6 Upon the [m]wicked he shall rain snares, [n]fire and [o]brimstone, and [2]an horrible tempest: *this shall be* the portion of their [p]cup.[Q]

7 For the [q]righteous LORD loveth righteousness; [3]his countenance doth behold the upright.[S]

## PSALM 12

*The psalmist craves help of God. 3 He is confident that God will punish the wicked, and protect the righteous.*

To the chief Musician upon [a]Sheminith, A Psalm of David.

HELP, LORD; for [b]the godly man ceaseth; for the [c]faithful fail from among the children of men.

2 They speak [d]vanity[C] every one with his neighbour: *with* [e,f]flattering lips *and* with a double [g]heart do they speak.

3 The LORD shall cut off all [e,f]flattering lips, *and* the tongue that [h,i]speaketh proud things:

4 Who have said, [i,j]With our tongue will we prevail; our lips *are* our own: who *is* lord over us?

5 For the [k,l]oppression of the poor, for the sighing of the needy, now will I arise, saith the LORD; [m]I will set [n]*him* in safety [1]*from him that* puffeth[C] at him.

6 The [o]words of the LORD *are* [p]pure words: *as* silver tried[C] in a [q]furnace of earth, purified seven times.

7 Thou shalt [m]keep them, O LORD, thou shalt preserve them from this generation for ever.[S]

8 The wicked walk on every side, [2]when the vilest men are exalted.

## PSALM 13

*The psalmist's complaint to God. 3 His prayer for help, 5 and trust in the mercy of the Lord.*

To the chief Musician, A Psalm of David.

[a]HOW long wilt thou forget me, O LORD? for ever? how long wilt thou hide thy face from me?

2 [a]How long shall I take counsel in my soul, *having* sorrow in my heart daily? how long shall mine enemy be exalted over me?

3 [a]Consider *and* hear me, O LORD my God: lighten[C] mine eyes, [b]lest I sleep the *sleep of* [c]death;

4 Lest mine enemy say, I have prevailed against him; *and* those that trouble me rejoice when I am moved.

5 But I have [d]trusted in thy [e]mercy; my heart shall [f]rejoice in thy [g]salvation.

6 [h]I will sing unto the LORD, because [i]he hath dealt bountifully with me.

## PSALM 14

*The psalmist describes the corruption of men; 4 shews the workers of iniquity their guilt; 7 and longs for the salvation of Israel.*

To the chief Musician, A Psalm of David.

THE[Q] [a]fool hath said in his heart, [*,b,c]*There is* no God. [d]They are corrupt, they have done abominable works, [e]*there is* none that doeth good.

2 [S]The LORD [f]looked down from [g]heaven upon the children of men, to see if there were any that did [h]understand, *and* [i]seek God.

3 They are all gone aside, they are *all* together become filthy:[C]

*q* *Furnace, figurative,* Prov. 17:3.
**8**
2 R. V. When vileness is exalted among the sons of men.

**1**
*a* *Adversity, prayer in,* Psa. 10:6.
**3**
*b* *Despondency,* Eccl. 2:20.
*c* *Death,* Num. 23:10.
**5**
*d* *Faith, instances of,* Mark 11:22.
*e* *God, mercy of,* Gen. 2:2.
*f* *Joy,* Psa. 5:11
*g* *Salvation,* Acts 16:17.
**6**
*h* *Thankfulness, exemplified,* Acts 24:3.
*i* *God, goodness of,* Gen. 2:2.

**1**
*a* *Fool, atheistic,* Prov. 18:2.
*b* *Spiritual Blindness,* 2 Cor. 4:4.
*c* *Infidelity,* 2 Cor. 6:15.
*d* Rom. 3:10-12.
*e* *Depravity,* Job 15:14.
**2**
*f* *Anthropomorphisms,* Gen. 11:5.
*g* *Heaven, God's dwelling place,* Luke 18:22.
*h* *Spiritual Understanding,* Luke 8:8.
*i* *Seekers,* Isa. 55:6.

---

* **ATHEISM,** Psa. 10:4; 14:1; 53:1. *Arguments against,* Job 12:7-25; Rom. 1:19, 20.

[e]*there is* none that doeth good,
no, not one.
4 Have all the workers of iniquity [b]no knowledge? who eat
up my people *as* they eat bread,
and [j]call not upon the LORD.
5 There were they in great fear:
for God *is* in the generation of
the righteous.
6 Ye have shamed the counsel
of the [k]poor, because the [l]LORD
*is* his refuge.
7 Oh that the salvation of Ĭș'-
ra-el *were come* out of Zī'ŏn!
when the LORD bringeth back
the captivity of his people, Jā'-
cob shall [m]rejoice, *and* Ĭș'ra-el
shall be glad.

## PSALM 15

*The psalmist describes a citizen of Zion.*

A Psalm of David.

LORD, who shall abide in
thy [a]tabernacle? who shall
dwell in thy holy hill?
2 [b]He that walketh [c]uprightly,
and worketh *righteousness, and
speaketh the [d]truth in his heart.
3 [b]*He that* [e]backbiteth not with
his tongue, nor doeth evil to his
[f]neighbour, nor taketh up a reproach against his neighbour.
4 [b]In whose eyes a [g]vile person
is contemned; but he honoureth
them that [h]fear the LORD. [b,i]*He*
*that* [c,j,k]sweareth to *his own*
hurt, and changeth not.
5 [b]*He that* putteth not out his
[l]money to [m]usury, nor taketh reward against the innocent. [n]He
that doeth these *things* shall
never be moved.

## PSALM 16

*The psalmist's trust in God and hatred of idolatry. 5 His portion and goodly heritage. 8 His hope of future blessedness.*

[a]Michtam of David.

[b]PRESERVE me, O God: for
in thee do I put my [c]trust.
2 *O my soul*, thou hast said unto the LORD, Thou *art* my Lord:
[1]my goodness *extendeth* not to
thee;
3 *But* to the [d]saints that *are* in
the earth, and *to* the excellent,
in whom *is* all my delight.
4 Their sorrows shall be multiplied [2]*that* [e]hasten *after* another
*god*: their drink offerings of
blood will I not offer, nor take
up their names into my lips.
5 [f]The LORD *is* the portion of
mine inheritance and of my cup:
thou maintainest my lot.
6 [g]The lines are fallen unto me
in pleasant *places*; yea, I have a
goodly heritage.
7 I will bless the LORD, [h]who
hath given me [i]counsel: my reins
also instruct me in the night
seasons.
8 [j]I have set the LORD always
before me: because [k]*he is* at my
right hand, I shall not be moved.
9 Therefore my heart is [l]glad,
and my glory rejoiceth: my flesh
also shall [3]rest in [m]hope.
10 For thou [n,o]wilt not leave
[p,q]my soul [4]in [r]hell; [s]neither wilt
thou suffer thine [5]Holy One to
see [t]corruption.
11 [c]Thou wilt [u]shew me the
[v]path of life: in thy presence *is*
fulness of [l]joy; at thy right hand
*there are* pleasures for evermore.

## PSALM 17

*The psalmist pleads for God's protection; 10 shews the wickedness of his enemies; 13 and entreats deliverance from them.*

A Prayer of David.

[a]HEAR the right, O LORD,
attend unto my cry, give
ear unto my prayer, *that goeth*
not out of feigned lips.
2 [b]Let my sentence come forth
from thy presence; let thine eyes
behold the things that are equal.
3 Thou hast proved mine heart;
thou hast visited *me* in the night;

4
j *Prayerlessness*, Job 21:15.

6
k *Poor, God's care of*, Prov. 21:13.
l *God, preserver*, Gen. 2:2.

7
m *Joy*, Psa. 5:11.

1
a *Church, called tabernacle*, 1 Kin. 9:3.

2
b *Righteous, described*, Psa. 64:10.
c *Integrity*, Job 2:3.
d *Truth*, John 18:37.

3
e *Slander*, Prov. 10:18.
f *Neighbor*, Luke 10:29.

4
g *Evil Company*, Prov. 13:20.
h *Fear of God*, Acts 9:31.
i *Witness, incorruptible*, Num. 35:30.
j *Oath*, Num. 5:19.
k *Honesty*, Rom. 13:13.

5
l *Money*, Jer. 32:9.
m *Interest*, Ex. 22:25.
n *Righteous, promises to*, Psa. 64:10.

a *Music*, 2 Chr. 5:13.

1
b *Prayer*, Acts 6:4.
c *Faith*, Mark 11:22.

2
1 R. V. I have no good beyond thee.

3
d *Righteous*, Psa. 64:10.

4
e *Idolatry*, 1 Sam. 15:23.
2 R. V. that exchange the LORD for another god

5
f *Religious Testimony*, 2 Thess. 1:10.

6
g *Contentment, instances of*, 1 Tim. 6:6.

7
h *Communion, with God*, 2 Cor. 13:14.
i *Wisdom, spiritual, from God*, Prov. 2:2.

8
j Acts 2:25–28.
k *God, preserver*, Gen. 2:2.

9
l *Joy*, Psa. 5:11.
m *Hope*, Prov. 13:12.
3 R. V. dwell in safety.

10
n *Resurrection*, 1 Cor. 15:12.
o *Immortality*, 1 Cor. 15:54.
p *Jesus, resurrection of*, Matt. 1:21.
q *Jesus, prophecies concerning*, Matt. 1:21.
r *Hell, the unseen state*, Mark 9:43.
s Acts 13:35.
t *Corruption*, Job 17:14.
4 R. V. to Sheol;
5 R. V. holy one

11
u *God, guide*, Gen. 2:2.
v *Way, figurative*, Isa. 35:8.

1
a *Prayer, in adversity*, Acts 6:4.

2
b *God, justice of*, Gen. 2:2.

* **RIGHTEOUSNESS**, Psa. 15:1–5; 24:3–5; 106:3; Prov. 11:5, 6, 18, 30; Hos. 10:12; Matt. 5:20; Luke 1:75; John 16:8, 10; Rom. 6:19–22; 8:4; Eph. 4:24; Jas. 1:27. *Figuratively described as a garment*, Job 29:14; Isa. 61:10; Zech. 3:4; Matt. 22:11–14; Rev. 6:11; 7:9; 19:8. *Required*, Isa. 28:17; Hos. 10:12; Mic. 6:8; Zech. 7:9, 10; 8:16, 17; Mal. 3:3; Matt. 5:20; 23:23; Luke 3:10–14; 13:6–9; Rom. 6:19–22; 7:4–6; 8:4; 14:17–19; 2 Tim. 2:22; 1 John 3:10. *Enjoined in official administration*, Jer. 22:3, 6. *Imputed, on account of obedience*, Deut. 6:25; Psa. 106:31;

3
*c Integrity,* Job 2:3.
*d Decision, instances of,* Isa. 50:7.
*e Obedience, exemplified,* Heb. 5:8.
4
*f Word of God,* Psa. 119:9.
*g Temptation, resistance to,* Luke 11:4.
5
1 R. V. My steps have held fast to thy paths, My feet have not slipped.
6
*h Faith, instances of,* Mark 11:22.
*i Ear, figurative,* Lev. 8:23.
7
*j God, goodness of,* Gen. 2:2.
*k God, preserver,* vs. 8–14; Gen. 2:2.
9
*l Wicked,* Psa. 73:3.
*m Oppression,* Eccl. 5:8.
*n Adversity, prayer in,* Psa. 10:6.
12
*o Lion,* Mic. 5:8.
13
*p God, providence of,* Gen. 2:2.
*q Sword, figurative,* 1 Chr. 21:5.
2 R. V. by thy sword;
14
*r Wicked, happiness of,* Psa. 73:3.
3 R. V. by thy hand,
4 R. V. satisfied with

thou hast tried[G] me, *and* [c]shalt
find nothing[G]; I am [d]purposed
*that* my mouth shall [e]not transgress.
4 Concerning the works of men,
by the [f]word of thy lips [g]I have
kept *me from* the paths of the
destroyer.
5 [1]Hold up my goings in thy
paths, *that* my footsteps slip not.
6 I have [a]called upon thee, for
[h]thou wilt hear me, O God: incline thine [i]ear unto me, *and*
*hear* my speech.
7 Shew thy marvellous [j]loving-
kindness, O thou that [k]savest by
thy right hand them which put
their [h]trust *in thee* from those
that rise up *against them.*[S]
8 [a]Keep me as the apple of the
eye, hide me under the shadow
of thy wings,
9 [a]From the [l]wicked that [m,n]op-
press me, *from* my deadly enemies, *who* compass[G] me about.
10 [l]They are inclosed in their
own fat: with their mouth they
speak proudly.
11 [l]They have now compassed
us in our steps: they have set
their eyes bowing down to the
earth;
12 Like as a [o]lion *that* is greedy
of his prey, and as it were a
young lion lurking in secret
places.
13 [a]Arise, O LORD, disap-
point him, cast him down: [p]de-
liver my soul from the wicked,
[2]*which is* thy [q]sword:
14 From men [3]*which are* thy
hand, O LORD, from [r]men of the
world, *which have* their portion
in *this* life, and whose belly thou
fillest with thy hid *treasure*: they
are [4]full of children, and leave
the rest of their *substance* to
their babes.

15 As for me, [s]I [h]will behold
thy face in righteousness: I shall
be [t]satisfied, when I awake, with
thy [u]likeness.[Q]

## PSALM 18

*The psalmist praises God for his wonderful deliverances.*

To the chief Musician, A Psalm of David, the servant of the Lord, who spake unto the Lord the words of this song in the day *that* the Lord delivered him from the hand of all his enemies, and from the hand of Saul: And he said,

I WILL [a]love thee, O LORD,
my strength.[S]
2 [b]The LORD *is* my [c]rock, and
my fortress, and my [d]deliverer;
my God, my strength, in whom
I will [e]trust; my [f]buckler,[G] and
the horn[G] of my [g]salvation, *and*
my high [h]tower.[Q]
3 I will [i]call upon the LORD,
[b]*who is worthy* to be [j]praised: so
shall I be saved from mine enemies.
4 The [k]sorrows of death compassed[G] me, and the floods of ungodly men made me afraid.[Q]
5 The [1]sorrows of [l]hell[G] compassed me about: the snares of
death prevented[G] me.
6 In my distress I called upon
the LORD, and cried unto my
God: he [m]heard my voice out of
his temple, and my cry came before him, *even* into his ears.[Q]
7 Then the earth [n]shook and
trembled; the foundations also
of the [2]hills moved and were
shaken, because he was [o]wroth.[G]
8 There went up a smoke out
of his nostrils, and fire out of
his mouth devoured: coals were
kindled by it.
9 He bowed the heavens also,
and came down: and [p]darkness
*was* under his feet.
10 And he rode upon a cherub,
and did fly: yea, he did fly upon
the wings of the wind.

15
*s Assurance,* Heb. 10:22.
*t Spiritual Peace,* Gal. 1:3.
*u Image, figurative,* 1 Cor. 11:7.
1
*a Love, of man for God,* 1 John 4:19.
2
*b Religious Testimony, exemplified,* 2 Thess. 1:10.
*c Rock, figurative,* Psa. 78:15.
*d God, preserver,* Gen. 2:2.
*e Faith, instances of,* Mark 11:22.
*f Shield, figurative,* 1 Kin. 14:27.
*g Salvation,* Acts 16:17.
*h Tower, figurative,* 2 Chr. 26:9.
3
*i Prayer,* Acts 6:4.
*j Praise,* Psa. 150:1.
4
*k Adversity,* Psa. 10:6.
5
*l Hell, the unseen state,* Mark 9:43.
1 R. V. cords of Sheol
6
*m Prayer, answered,* Acts 6:4.
7
*n Earthquakes,* Isa. 29:6.
*o Anger of God,* 2 Kin. 13:3.
2 R. V. mountains
9
*p Darkness, figurative,* Gen. 1:2.

Ezek. 18:9; *on account of faith,* Gen. 15:6; Rom. 4:3, 5, 9, 11, 13, 20, 22, 24; Gal. 3:6; Jas. 2:23. *Proof of regeneration,* 1 John 2:29. *Exalts a nation,* Prov. 14:34. *Safeguards life,* Prov. 10:2, 16; 11:19; 12:28; 13:6. *Winning others to, rewarded,* Dan. 12:3.

**Fruits of,** Psa. 1:3; Matt. 7:16–18; 12:35; Luke 6:43; John 15:4–8; 2 Cor. 9:10; Gal. 5:22, 23; Phil. 1:11; Col. 3:12–15; 1 Thess. 1:3; Titus 2:2–6, 11, 12; 1 Pet. 3:8–14; 2 Pet. 1:5–8; 1 John 3:7. *Liberality,* Acts 11:29. *Peace,* Isa. 32:17; Jas. 3:8.

**Symbolized,** Ezek. 47:12; Rev. 22:2.

**Of God,** see footnote, GOD, *Righteousness of,* Gen. 2:2.

**Of Jesus,** see footnote, JESUS, *Holiness of,* Matt. 1:21.

11
q *God, incomprehensible,* Gen. 2:2.
r *God, invisible,* Gen. 2:2.
s *Symbols and Similitudes,* Heb. 9:9.

14
t *Arrow, figurative,* 1 Sam. 20:20.
u *Lightning,* Job 28:26.

15
v *Geology,* Psa. 104:5.
w *Breath, figurative,* Gen. 7:15.

16
x *God, providence of,* Gen. 2:2.
y *God, preserver,* Gen. 2:2.

19
z *Grace of God,* Rom. 4:16.

---

20
a *God, justice of,* Gen. 2:2.
b *Integrity,* Job 2:3.
c *Righteousness,* Psa. 15:2.

11 [q,r]He made [p,s]darkness his
secret place; his pavilion round
about him *were* dark waters *and*
thick clouds of the skies.
12 At the brightness *that was*
before him his thick clouds
passed, hail *stones* and coals of
fire.
13 The LORD also thundered
in the heavens, and the Highest
gave his voice; hail *stones* and
coals of fire.
14 Yea, he sent out his [t]arrows,
and scattered them; and he shot
out [u]lightnings, and discomfited[C]
them.
15 Then [v]the channels of waters were seen, and the foundations of the world were discovered[C] at thy rebuke, O LORD, at
the blast of the [w]breath of thy
nostrils.
16 He sent from above, he [x]took
me, he [y]drew me out of many
waters.
17 He [y]delivered me from my
strong enemy, and from them
which hated me: for they were
too strong for me.[S]
18 They prevented[C] me in the
day of my calamity: but the
LORD was my [y]stay.
19 He [y]brought me forth also
into a large[C] place; he [y]deliv-
ered me, because [z]he delighted
in me.[S]
20 The LORD [a]rewarded me
according to my [b,c]righteous-
ness; according to the cleanness
of my hands hath he recompensed me.
21 For I [b]have kept the ways of
the LORD, and have not wickedly departed from my God.
22 For all his judgments[C] *were*
before me, and I [b]did not put
away his statutes from me.
23 I was also [b]upright before
him, and I kept myself from
mine iniquity.
24 Therefore hath the LORD
[a]recompensed me according to
my [b,c]righteousness, according
to the cleanness of my hands in
his eyesight.
25 With the [d]merciful [e,f]thou
wilt shew thyself merciful; with
an upright man thou wilt shew
thyself upright;[S]
26 With the [g]pure thou wilt
shew thyself pure; and with the
[3,h]froward[C] thou wilt shew thyself froward.[C]
27 For thou wilt [i]save the [j]af-
flicted people; but wilt bring
down [k]high looks.[S]
28 For thou wilt light my candle[C]: the LORD my God will enlighten my darkness.
29 For [l]by thee I have run
through a troop; and by my God
have I leaped over a wall.
30 *As for* God, his way *is* [m]per-
fect: the [n]word of the LORD is
tried:[C] he *is* a [o]buckler[C] to all
those that trust in him.[S]
31 For who *is* God save the
LORD? or who *is* a [p]rock save
our God?[T]
32 *It is* God that girdeth me
with [q]strength, and maketh my
way [r]perfect.
33 He maketh my feet like
hinds' *feet,* and setteth me upon
my high places.
34 He teacheth my hands to
[s]war, [4]so that a [t]bow of steel[C] is
broken by mine arms.
35 Thou hast also given me the
[o]shield of thy [u]salvation: and thy
right hand hath holden[C] me up,
and thy [v]gentleness hath made
me great.
36 Thou hast enlarged[C] my steps
under me, that my feet did not
slip.
37 I have pursued mine enemies, and overtaken them: neither did I turn again till they
were consumed.
38 I have wounded them that
they were not able to rise: they
are fallen under my feet.
39 For thou hast girded me

25
d *Mercy,* Deut. 5:10.
e *God, judge,* Gen. 2:2.
f *God, mercy of,* Gen. 2:2.

26
g *Purity,* 1 Tim. 4:12.
h *Wicked, punishment of,* Psa. 73:3.
3 R. V. perverse

27
i *God, preserver,* Gen. 2:2.
j *Afflicted,* Job 34:28.
k *Pride,* Prov. 16:18.

29
l *Faith,* Mark 11:22.

30
m *God, righteousness of,* Gen. 2:2.
n *Word of God,* Psa. 119:9.
o *Shield, figurative,* 1 Kin. 14:27.

31
p *Rock, figurative,* Psa. 78:15.

32
q *Spiritual Blessings,* Eph. 1:3.
r *Perfection,* Heb. 6:1.

34
s *War,* Judg. 3:2.
t *Bow,* 2 Sam. 1:18.
4 R. V. So that mine arms do bend a bow of brass.

35
u *Salvation,* Acts 16:17.
v *Gentleness, of God,* 2 Cor. 10:1

with strength unto the battle: thou hast subdued under me those that rose up against me.

40 Thou hast also given me the necks of mine enemies; that I might destroy them that hate me.

41 They cried, but *there was* none to save *them*: *even* unto the LORD, but he [w]answered them not.

42 Then did I beat them small as the dust before the wind: I did cast them out as the dirt in the streets.

43 Thou hast [x]delivered me from the strivings of the people; *and* thou hast made [y]me the head of the [5]heathen[G]: a people *whom* I have not known shall serve me.

44 As soon as they hear of me, they shall obey me: the strangers[G] shall submit themselves unto me.

45 The strangers[G] shall fade away, and be afraid out of their close[G] places.

46 The LORD liveth; and [z]blessed *be* my [a]rock; and let the God of my [b]salvation be exalted.[T]

47 *It is* God that avengeth me, and subdueth the people under me.

48 He delivereth me from mine enemies: yea, thou liftest me up above those that rise up against me: thou hast delivered me from the violent man.

49 [c]Therefore [d]will I give [e]thanks unto thee, O LORD, among the [5]heathen[G], and sing [f]praises unto thy name.[Q]

50 Great deliverance giveth he to his king; and sheweth mercy to his [g]anointed, to [h]Dā'vid, and to his seed for evermore.

41
w *Wicked, prayer of, not heard*, Psa. 73: 3.

43
x *God, providence of*, Gen. 2:2.
y *David, a type of Christ*, 1 Sam. 16: 13.
5 R. V. nations:

46
z *Praise*, Psa. 150:1.

a *Rock, figurative*, Psa. 78:15.
b *Salvation*, Acts 16:17.

49
c Rom. 15:9.
d *Religious Testimony*, 2 Thess. 1:10.
e *Thankfulness*, Acts 24:3.
f *Praise*, Psa. 150:1.

50
g *Anointing*, Lev. 8:12.
h *David*, 1 Sam. 16: 13.

## PSALM 19

*The creation shews God's glory. 7 The excellency of his laws. 12 The psalmist prays for grace.*

To the chief Musician, A Psalm of David.

THE [a, b]heavens declare[G] the [c]glory of God; and the [d]firmament sheweth [e]his [f]handywork.[S Q G]

2 Day unto day uttereth *speech, and night unto night sheweth [g]knowledge.

3 *There is* no speech nor language, [1]*where* their voice is not heard.

4 [h]Their line is gone out through all the earth, and their *words to the end of the world. In them hath he set a tabernacle for the sun,[S Q]

5 Which *is* as a bridegroom coming out of his chamber, *and* rejoiceth as a strong man to run [2]a †race.

6 His going forth *is* from the end of the heaven, and his circuit unto the ends of it: and there is nothing hid from the heat thereof.

7 The [i, j]law of the LORD *is* perfect, [3]converting the soul: the testimony of the LORD *is* sure, making [g]wise the simple.[S T]

8 The [i, j]statutes of the LORD *are* right, [k]rejoicing the heart: the commandment of the LORD *is* [l]pure, [g]enlightening the eyes.[T]

9 The [m]fear of the LORD *is* clean[C], enduring for ever: the judgments[G] of the [n]LORD *are* true *and* righteous altogether.[Q S T]

10 More to be desired *are they* than gold, yea, than much fine gold: sweeter also than honey and the honeycomb.

11 Moreover by them is thy servant warned: *and* in [o]keeping of them *there is* great reward.

12 [p]Who can understand *his* errors? [q, r, s]cleanse thou me from secret [t]*faults*.

1
a *Astronomy*, Isa. 13:10.
b *Heavens, physical*, Psa. 8:3.
c *God, glory of*, Gen. 2:2.
d *Firmament*, Gen. 1:6.
e *God, creator*, Gen. 2:2.
f *Works of God*, Psa. 40:5.

2
g *Wisdom, spiritual, from God*, Prov. 2:2.

3
1 R. V. Their voice cannot be heard.

4
h Rom. 10:18.

5
2 R. V. his course.

7
i *Law*, Deut. 33:2.
j *Word of God*, Psa. 119:9.
3 R. V. restoring

8
k *Spiritual Peace*, Gal. 1:3.
l *Purity*, 1 Tim. 4:12.

9
m *Fear of God*, Acts 9:31.
n *God, justice of*, Gen. 2:2.

11
o *Obedience, rewarded*, Heb. 5:8.

12
p *Self-examination*, 2 Cor. 13: 5.
q *Spiritual Purification*, Psa. 51:2.
r *Sin, forgiveness of*, Rom. 5:12.
s *Sin, confession of*, Rom. 5:12.
t *Sin, secret*, Rom. 5:12.

* **NATURAL RELIGION,** Job 12:7-16; 37:1-24; Psa. 8:1-9; 19:1-6; Acts 14:17; 17:23-28; Rom. 1:18-20; 10:16-18.

† **FOOT RACE.** Figurative, Eccl. 9:11; 1 Cor. 9:24; Gal. 5:7; Phil. 2:16; Heb. 12:1, 2.

14
*u Meditation*, Psa. 49:3.
*v God, preserver*, Gen. 2:2.
*w God, savior*, Gen. 2:2.
4 R. V. rock,

13 Keep back thy servant also from ‡presumptuous[G] *sins*; let them not have dominion over me: then shall I be upright, and I shall be innocent from the great transgression.

14 Let the words of my mouth, and the [u]meditation of my heart, be acceptable in thy sight, O LORD, my [4,v]strength, and my [w]redeemer.[S T]

## PSALM 20

*A prayer for the king in the day of trouble. 6 Confidence in God's protection.*

To the chief Musician, A Psalm of David.

1
*a God, preserver*, Gen. 2:2.

2
*b Church, called sanctuary*, 1 Kin. 9:3.
*c Zion*, 2 Sam. 5:7.

3
*d Offerings, burnt*, Lev. 6:17.

5
*e Faith, instances of*, Mark 11:22.
*f Joy*, Psa. 5:11.
*g Salvation*, Acts 16:17.
*h Standard, figurative*, Num. 1:52.

6
*i Anointing*, Lev. 8:12.
*j Heaven, God's dwelling place*, Luke 18:22.

7
*k False Confidence*, Psa. 30:6.
*l Chariot*, Josh. 11:4.
*m Horse*, Job 39:19.

THE [a]LORD hear[G] thee in the day of trouble; the name of the God of Jā′cob defend thee;

2 Send thee help from the [b]sanctuary, and strengthen thee out of [c]Zī′ŏn;

3 Remember all thy offerings, and accept thy [d]burnt sacrifice;[G] [Sē′lah.

4 Grant thee according to thine own heart, and fulfil all thy counsel.[G]

5 [e]We will [f]rejoice in thy [g]salvation, and in the name of our God we will set up *our* [h]banners: the LORD fulfil all thy petitions.

6 Now [e]know I that the LORD saveth his [i]anointed; he will hear him from his holy [j]heaven with the saving strength of his right hand.

7 Some [k]*trust* in [l]chariots, and some in [m]horses: but we will remember the name of the LORD our God.

8 They are brought down and fallen: but we are risen, and stand upright.

9 Save, [a]LORD: let the king hear us when we call.

## PSALM 21

*A thanksgiving for victory. 7 Confidence of further success.*

To the chief Musician, A Psalm of David.

A Messianic Psalm, which while extolling the king must be understood in a broader sense as extolling the Messiah, the hope of Israel. The Chaldee Targum makes the opening of this Psalm to read "O Lord, the king Messiah shall rejoice in thy strength." Rashi, a Jewish commentator, admits that the older Hebrew doctors expounded this Psalm as referring to the Messiah; but that, in order to avoid agreement with Christian interpretation, later Jewish doctors confine its application to David. The church, however, has signified its faith in its Messianic character by appointing its use in the festival of Christ's ascension.

THE king shall [a]joy[G] in thy strength, O LORD; and in thy [b]salvation how greatly shall he rejoice!

2 Thou hast given him his heart's desire, and hast not withholden the [c]request of his lips. [Sē′lah.[G]

3[S] For [d]thou preventest[G] him with the [e]blessings of goodness: thou settest a [f]crown of pure [g]gold on his head.

4 He asked life of thee, *and* thou [c]gavest *it* him, *even* [h]length of days for ever and ever.[T]

5 His glory *is* great in thy [b]salvation: honour and majesty hast thou laid upon him.[S]

6 For thou hast made him most blessed for ever: thou hast made him exceeding [a]glad with [1]thy countenance.[G]

7 For the king [i]trusteth[G] in the LORD, and through the [j]mercy of the most High he shall not be moved.[G]

8 Thine hand shall find out all thine enemies: thy right hand shall find out those that hate thee.

9 Thou shalt make [k]them as a fiery [2,l]oven in the time of thine [m]anger: the LORD shall swallow them up in his wrath, and the fire shall devour them.[T Q]

1
*a Joy*, Psa. 5:11.
*b Salvation*, Acts 16:17.

2
*c Prayer, answered*, Acts 6:4.

3
*d God, providence of*, Gen. 2:2.
*e Spiritual Blessings*, Eph. 1:3.
*f Crown*, Ex. 29:6.
*g Gold*, Ezek. 7:19.

4
*h Longevity*, Psa. 91:16.

6
1 R. V. joy in thy presence.

7
*i Faith, instances of*, Mark 11:22.
*j God, mercy of*, Gen. 2:2.

9
*k Wicked, punishment of*, Psa. 73:3.
*l Oven, figurative*, Ex. 8:3.
*m Anger of God*, 2 Kin. 13:3.
2 R. V. furnace

‡ **PRESUMPTION,** Deut. 29:19, 20; Psa. 10:6; 19:13; 73:8, 9. *Admonitions against*, Prov. 25:6, 7; Luke 14:7-11.
Sins of: *Of the self-righteous*, Isa. 65:5; Luke 18:11, 12; *of the selfish rich, in forgetting God*, Luke 12:18-20. *Temptation to*, Matt. 4:5-7; Luke 4:9-11.
*In ignoring God*, Isa. 10:15; 29:16; 37:23-25; Rom. 9:20, 21, Jas. 4:13-15. *In impeaching God's righteousness*, Isa. 58:3; Rom. 9:20, 21. *In defying God*, Job 15:25; Psa. 94:7; Isa. 5:18-25; 14:13, 14; 28:14-18, 22; 29:15, 16, 20; 40:27; 45:9, 10; Rom. 1:32; 9:20, 21; 2 Thess. 2:3. *In reviling God's prophet*, 1 Kin. 22:24. *In despising the lordship of Christ, and the authority of the church*, 2 Pet. 2:10, 11.
*Warning against*, 1 Cor. 10:9-12. *Excommunication for*, Num. 15:30.
**Instances of:** *Satan, when he said to Eve, Ye shall not surely die*, Gen. 3:1-5. *Pharaoh*, Ex. 5:2. *Moses, in upbraiding Jehovah*, Num. 11:11-15, 21, 22. *Nadab and Abihu*, Lev. 10:1, 2. *Israelites, in going to war contrary to*

11
*n Malice*, Eph.4:31.

12
*o Arrow, figurative*, 1 Sam.20:20.

13
*p Praise*, Psa. 150:1.
*q God, power of*, Gen. 2:2.

*a Music*, 2 Chr. 5:13.

1
*b* Matt. 27:46; Mark 15:34.
*c Adversity, prayer in*, Psa. 10:6
*d Prayer, in adversity*, Acts 6:4
*e Despondency*, Eccl. 2:20.

10 Their fruit[C] shalt thou destroy
from the earth, and their seed
from among the children of men.
11 For they [n]intended[C] evil
against thee: they imagined a
mischievous device, *which* they
are not able to *perform*.
12 Therefore shalt thou make
them turn their back, *when* thou
shalt make ready *thine* [o]*arrows*
upon thy strings against the face
of them.
13 Be thou exalted, LORD, in
thine own strength: *so* will we
sing and [p]praise thy [q]power.[S]

## PSALM 22

*The psalmist's complaint in distress, and prayer for help. 22 His purpose to praise God. 27 All nations shall praise him.*

To the chief Musician upon [a]Aijeleth Shahar, A Psalm of David.

A Messianic Psalm. The introduction to this Psalm in a commentary issued by Cambridge University for schools and colleges begins with the following sentence: "The first and greatest of the 'Passion Psalms' consecrated for us by our Lord's appropriation of it to himself." The Apostle Paul also quotes from it in his reference to the Lord, Heb. 2:12. The opening words of the Psalm are used by Jesus on the cross and it is thought, with much probability, that this Psalm was the subject of meditation in his dying agony. It, no doubt, has an historical basis in a suffering saint, the poetic delineation of whom, under divine inspiration and guidance, was made to describe, in type, the sufferings of our Lord. The description of the persecution, "They pierced my hands and my feet," v. 16; "They look and stare upon me; they part my garments among them; they cast lots upon my vesture," vs. 17, 18; the mockery of the bystanders, vs. 7, 8 describe with surprising accuracy the sufferings of our Lord. At v. 24 the scenes change from the sufferings to the compassion of the Messiah; and vs. 27, 28 describe the triumph of his kingdom when all the earth shall turn to him as the governor among the nations. The purpose of the Holy Spirit was twofold in inspiring the poet. While primarily he describes a suffering but triumphant hero, the dominant theme of the poem is *to describe the crucified but risen and glorified King of kings*.

[b,c,d,e]MY God[Q], my God, why hast
thou forsaken me? *why*
*art thou so* far from helping
me, *and from* the words of my
roaring[G]?
2 O my God, I [e]cry in the daytime,
[f]but thou hearest not; and
in the night season, and am not
silent.
3 But [g]thou *art* holy, O *thou*
that inhabitest the [h]praises of
Is'ra-el.[S]
4 Our fathers [i]trusted in thee:
they trusted, and thou didst [j]deliver
them.
5 [k]They [l]cried unto thee, and
were delivered: they [i]trusted in
thee, and were not confounded.[Q][G]
6 But I *am* a worm, and no
man; a reproach of men, and
despised of the people.[S]
7 All[Q] they that see me [m]laugh
me to scorn: they shoot[C] out the
lip, they shake the head, *saying*,
8 He [i]trusted[C] on the LORD *that*
he would deliver him: let him
deliver him, seeing he delighted
in him.[Q]
9 But thou *art* he that took me
out of the womb: thou didst
make me hope *when I was* upon
my mother's breasts.
10 I was cast upon thee from
the womb: thou *art* my God
from my mother's belly.[C]
11 Be not far from me; for
[c]trouble *is* near; for *there is* none
to help.
12 Many bulls have compassed
me: strong *bulls* of Bā'shăn have
beset[C] me round.
13 They gaped upon me *with*
their mouths, *as* a ravening and
a roaring [n]lion.
14 [e]I am poured out like water,
and all my bones are out of joint:
my heart is like wax; it is melted
in the midst of my [o]bowels.[C]

2
*f Doubting*, Rom. 14:23.

3
*g God, holiness of*, Gen. 2:2.
*h Praise*, Psa. 150:1.

4
*i Faith, instances of*, Mark 11:22.
*j God, preserver*, Gen. 2:2.

5
*k Nation, in adversity, prayer of*, Isa. 2:4.
*l Prayer, answered*, Acts 6:4.

7
*m Malice*, Eph. 4:31.

13
*n Lion*, Mic. 5:8.

14
*o Bowels, figurative*, 1 Kin. 3:26.

---

*the divine command*, Num. 14:44, 45; Deut. 1:43; *in murmuring*, Ex. 15:11, 12; 17:2, 7; Num. 21:5; 1 Cor. 10:9–12; *in reviling God* Mal. 1:6, 7, 12; 3:7, 8, 13. *Korah, Dathan, and Abiram*, Num. 16:3. *Saul, in offering sacrifices*, 1 Sam. 13:8–14; *in sparing the Amalekites*, 1 Sam. 15:3, 9–23. *Men of Beth-shemesh*, 1 Sam. 6:19. *Uzzah, in steadying the ark*, 2 Sam. 6:6, 7. *David's anger at Uzzah's death*, 2 Sam. 6:8. *David, in numbering Israel*, 2 Sam. 24:1–17. *Jeroboam*, 1 Kin. 13:4. *Ben-hadad*, 1 Kin. 20:10. *Zedekiah*, 1 Kin. 22: 24, 25; 2 Chr 18:23, 24. *Uzziah*, 2 Chr. 26:16. *Sennacherib*, 2 Kin. 19:22; 2 Chr. 32:13, 14; Isa. 37:23–25. *The Syrians in limiting the sovereignty of Jehovah*, 1 Kin. 20:23, 28. *Job, in cursing the day of his birth*, Job 3:2–19. *Jonah*, Jonah 4:1–8. *Peter, in objecting to Jesus' statement that he must be killed*, Matt. 16:21–23; Mark 8:32; *in objecting to Jesus washing his feet*, John 13:8; *in asking Jesus, What shall this man do?* John 21:20–22. *The disciples, in rebuking those who brought little children to Jesus*, Matt. 19:13; Mark 10:13, 14; Luke 18:15; *in their indignation at the anointing of Jesus*, Matt. 26:8, 9; Mark 14:4, 5; John 12:5. *The brothers of Jesus*, John 7:3–5. *James and John, in desiring to call down fire on the Samaritans*, Luke 9:54. *Those who reviled Jesus*, Matt. 27:42, 43; Mark 15:29–32. *Theudas*, Acts 5:36. *Sons of Sceva*, Acts 19:13, 14.

15 [e]My strength is [p]dried up like a potsherd; and my tongue cleaveth to my jaws; and thou hast brought me into the dust of death.

16 For dogs have compassed me: the assembly of the wicked have inclosed me: they pierced my hands and my feet.

17 I may tell all my bones: they look *and* stare upon me.

18 [q,r]They part my garments among them, and cast [s]lots upon my vesture.

19 But be not thou far from me, O LORD: O my strength, haste thee to help me.

20 Deliver my soul from the sword; my darling from the power of the dog.

21 Save me from the [n]lion's mouth: [1]for thou hast [l]heard me from the horns of the [t]unicorns.

22 [u]I will [v]declare thy name unto my [w]brethren: in the midst of the congregation will I [h]praise thee.

23 Ye that [x]fear the LORD, [h]praise him; all ye the seed of Jā'cob, [y]glorify him; and fear him, all ye the seed of Īs'ra-el.

24 For he hath not despised nor abhorred the affliction of the afflicted; neither hath he hid his face from him; but when he [l]cried unto him, he heard.

25 My [h]praise *shall be* of thee in the great congregation: I will pay my [z]vows before them that [x]fear him.

26 The [a]meek shall eat and be satisfied: they shall praise the LORD that [b]seek him: your heart shall live for ever.

27 [c,d]All the ends of the world shall remember and [e]turn unto the LORD: and all the kindreds of the nations shall [f]worship before thee.

28 For the kingdom *is* the [g]LORD's: and [h]he *is* the governor among the nations.

29 All *they that be* fat upon earth shall eat and [f]worship: all they that [i]go down to the dust shall bow before him: and none can keep alive his own soul.

30 A seed shall serve him; [2]it shall be accounted to the LORD for a generation.

31 They shall come, and shall declare his [j]righteousness unto a people that shall be born, that he hath done *this*.

## PSALM 23

*The psalmist's confidence in God's grace.*

A Psalm of David.

[a]THE [b,c]LORD *is* my [d]shepherd; [e]I shall not want.

2 He maketh me to lie down in green pastures: [f]he leadeth me beside the still waters.

3 He [g]restoreth my soul: [f]he [1]leadeth me in the paths of righteousness for his name's sake.

4 Yea, though I walk through the valley of [2]the shadow of death, [h]I will fear no evil: for [i,j]thou *art* with me; thy rod and thy staff they comfort me.

5 [c]Thou preparest a table before me in the presence of mine enemies: thou anointest my head with [k]oil; my [l]cup runneth over.

6 [e]Surely [m]goodness and [n]mercy shall follow me all the days of my life: and I will dwell in the [o]house of the LORD for ever.

## PSALM 24

*God's dominion in the world. 3 Who shall stand in his holy place. 7 An exhortation to receive the King of glory.*

A Psalm of David.

[a]THE earth *is* the [b]LORD's, and the fulness thereof; the world, and they that dwell therein.

2 [c]For he hath [d]founded it upon the seas, and established it upon the floods.

3 Who shall ascend into the hill of the LORD? or who shall [e]stand in his [f]holy place?

---

15
p *Fever*, Deut. 28:22.

18
q Matt. 27:35; Luke 23:34; John 19:24.
r *Prophecies, concerning the Messiah, and their fulfillment*, Gen. 12:3.
s *Lot*, Esth. 3:7.

21
t *Unicorn*, Job 39:9.
1 R. V. Yea, from the horns of the wild-oxen thou hast answered me.

22
u Heb. 2:12.
v *Religious Testimony*, 2 Thess. 1:10.
w *Fraternity*, Zech. 11:14.

23
x *Fear of God*, Acts 9:31.
y *Glorifying God, enjoined*, Luke 5:25.

25
z *Vows*, Num. 30:2.

26
a *Meekness*, Psa. 45:4.
b *Seekers*, Isa. 55:6.

27
c *Gentiles, prophecies of the conversion of*, vs. 27–31; Acts 10:45.
d *Church, prophecies concerning its mission*, Matt. 16:18.
e *Repentance*, Mark 1:4.
f *Worship*, Gen. 22:5.

28
g *God, sovereign*, v. 29; Gen. 2:2.
h *Government, God in*, Isa. 22:21.

29
i *Life, brevity and uncertainty of*, Eccl. 8:15.

30
2 R. V. It shall be told of the Lord unto the next generation.

31
j *Righteousness*, Psa. 15:2.

1
a *Religious Testimony, exemplified*, vs. 1–6; 2 Thess. 1:10.
b *God, preserver*, Gen. 2:2.
c *God, providence of*, Gen. 2:2.
d *Shepherd, figurative*, Jer. 31:10.
e *Faith, instances of*, Mark 11:22.

2
f *God, guide*, Gen. 2:2.

3
g *Spiritual Blessings, from God*, Eph. 1:3.
1 R. V. guideth

4
h *Assurance*, Heb. 10:22.
i *God, presence of*, Gen. 2:2.
j *Afflictions, consolation in*, Psa. 34:19.
2 *Or*, deep darkness

5
k *Oil sacred*, Deut. 12:17.
l *Cup, figurative*, Matt. 20:22.

6
m *God, goodness of*, Gen. 2:2.
n *God, mercy of*, Gen. 2:2.
o *House, figurative*, Esth. 8:1.

1
a 1 Cor. 10:26.
b *God, sovereign*, Gen. 2:2.

2
c *Geology*, Psa. 14:5.
d *God, creator*, Gen. 2:2.

3
e *Worship*, Gen. 2:5.
f *Church, called holy place*, 1 Kin. 8:3.

4
*g Righteous, described*, Psa. 64:10.
*h Integrity*, Job 2:3.
*i Purity*, 1 Tim. 4:12.
*j Holiness*, Ex. 39:30.
*k Heart*, Psa. 44:21.
*l Vanity*, Eccl. 1:2.
*m Honesty*, Rom. 13:13.
*n Deceit*, Psa. 36:3.
5
*o Righteous, promises to*, Psa. 64:10.
*p Righteousness*, Psa. 15:2.
*q Salvation*, Acts 16:17.
6
*r Seekers*, Isa. 55:6.
*s Spiritual Desire*, Psa. 42:1.
7
*t Gates*, Deut. 3:5.
8
*u God, glory of*, Gen. 2:2.

4 [g]He that hath [h]clean hands,
and a [i,j]pure [k]heart; who hath
not lifted up his soul unto [l]van-
ity, [h,m]nor sworn [n]deceitfully.[S] [Q]
5 [o]He shall receive the blessing
from the LORD, and [p]righteous-
ness from the God of his [q]salva-
tion.[S]
6 This *is* the generation of
[r]them that [s]seek him, that seek
thy face, O Jā′cob. [Sē′lah.[G]
7[Q] Lift up your heads, O ye
[t]gates; and be ye lift up, ye everlasting doors; and the King of
[u]glory shall come in.
8 Who *is* this King of [u]glory?
The LORD strong and mighty,
the LORD mighty in battle.
9 Lift up your heads, O ye
[t]gates; even lift *them* up, ye everlasting doors; and the King of
[u]glory shall come in.
10 Who is this King of [u]glory?
The LORD of hosts, he *is* the King
of glory.[Q] [Sē′lah.

## PSALM 25

*The psalmist's trust in God. 4 His prayer for direction, 7 for the pardon of sin, 16 and for deliverance from all his troubles.*

A Psalm of David.

2
*a Faith, instances of*, Mark 11:22.
*b Adversity, prayer in*, Psa. 10:6.
3
1 R. V. that deal treacherously
4
*c Wisdom, prayer for spiritual*, Prov. 2:2.
5
*d Spiritual Desire*, Psa. 42:1.
*e Guidance, prayer for*, Psa. 48:14.
*f God, guide*, Gen. 2:2.
*g God, savior*, Gen. 2:2.
6
*h Prayer, pleas offered in*, Acts 6:4.
*i God, mercy of*, Gen. 2:2.
7
*j Sin, forgiveness of*, Rom. 5:12.
*k God, goodness of*, Gen. 2:2.

UNTO thee, O LORD, do I
lift up my soul.
2 O my God, I [a]trust in thee:
let me not be ashamed, [b]let not
mine enemies triumph over me.
3 Yea, let none that wait on thee
be ashamed: let them be ashamed
[1]which transgress without cause.
4 [c]Shew me thy ways, O LORD;
teach me thy paths.
5 [d,e,f]Lead me in thy truth, and
teach me: for thou *art* the God
of my [g]salvation; on thee do I
wait all the day.
6 [h]Remember, O LORD, thy
tender [i]mercies and thy lovingkindnesses; for they *have been*
ever of old.
7 Remember not the [j]sins of my
youth, nor my transgressions:
according to thy [i]mercy remember thou me for [k]thy goodness'
sake, O LORD.

8 [k]Good and upright *is* the
LORD: therefore will he [l]teach
sinners in the way.[S]
9 [m]The [n,o]meek will [f]he guide
in judgment:[G] and the meek will
he teach his way.[S]
10 [m]All the paths of the [p]LORD
*are* [i]mercy and [q]truth unto [o]such
as [r]keep[G] his covenant[G] and his
testimonies.[S] [T]
11 For thy name's sake, O
LORD, [j]pardon mine iniquity;
for [s]it *is* great.[Q]
12 What man *is* he that [t]feareth
the LORD? him shall he [l]teach
in the way *that* he shall choose.[S]
13 [o]His soul shall dwell [u]at
ease; and his seed shall inherit
the earth.
14 The secret of the LORD *is*
with them that [t]fear him; and he
will shew them his covenant.[S]
15 Mine eyes *are* ever toward
the LORD; for [v]he shall pluck
my feet out of the [w]net.
16 Turn thee unto me, and
[x]have mercy upon me; for I *am*
desolate and [b]afflicted.
17 The [b]troubles of my heart
are enlarged: [x]O bring thou me
out of my distresses.
18 [x]Look upon mine [b]affliction
and my pain; and [j]forgive all
my sins.
19 Consider mine enemies; for
they are many; and they hate me
with cruel [y]hatred.[Q]
20 [z]O keep my soul, and deliver me: let me not be ashamed;
for I put my [z]trust in thee.[Q]
21 Let [a]integrity and uprightness
preserve me; for I wait[G] on thee.[Q]
22 [b]Redeem[G] Iṣ′ra-el, O God,
out of all his troubles.

## PSALM 26

*The psalmist's appeal to God, 4 and profession of his integrity. 9 His prayer to be delivered from the death of the wicked.*

A Psalm of David.

[a]JUDGE me, O LORD; for I
have walked in mine [b]in-
tegrity: I have [c]trusted also in

8
*l Wisdom, spiritual, from God*, Prov. 2:2.
9
*m Promise, to the righteous*, 2 Cor. 1:20.
*n Meekness*, Psa. 45:4.
*o Righteous, promises to*, Psa. 64:10.
10
*p God, faithfulness of*, Gen. 2:2.
*q God, truth*, Gen. 2:2.
*r Obedience*, Heb. 5:8.
11
*s Sin, sinfulness of*, Rom. 5:12.
12
*t Fear of God*, Acts 9:31.
13
*u Spiritual Peace*, Gal. 1:3.
15
*v God, preserver*, Gen. 2:2.
*w Net, figurative*, Isa. 51:20.
16
*x Prayer, in adversity*, Acts 6:4.
19
*y Hatred*, Prov. 15:17.
20
*z Faith, instances of*, Mark 11:22.
21
*a Integrity*, Job 2:3.
22
*b Intercession, instances of*, Jer. 27:18.
1
*a God, judge*, Gen 2:2.
*b Integrity*, Job 2:3.
*c Faith, instances of*, Mark 11:22.

1 R. V. without wavering.
2
*d Faith, trial of,* Mark 11:22.
3
*e God, love of,* Gen. 2:2.
*f Obedience, exemplified,* Heb. 5:8.
*g Truth, attribute of God,* John 18:37.
4
*h Fellowship, with the wicked,* 1 Cor. 1:9.
*i Evil Company,* Prov. 13:20.
*j Dissembling,* Josh. 7:11.
5
*k Sin, repugnant to the righteous,* Rom. 5:12.
6
*l Decision, instances of,* Isa. 50:7.
*m Ablution, of the hands as a token of innocency,* Judg. 19:21.
*n Purification, figurative,* Num. 19:19.
*o Ceremonial Washing,* Ex. 19:10.
*p Worship,* vs. 6–8; Gen. 22:5.
7
*q Thankfulness, exemplified,* Acts 24:3.
*r Works of God,* Psa. 40:5.
10
*s Bribery,* 1 Sam. 8:3.
12
*t Praise,* Psa. 150:1.
1
*a Religious Testimony, exemplified,* 2 Thess. 1:10.
*b Faith, instances of,* Mark 11:22.
*c Light, figurative,* Matt. 5:14.
*d God, savior,* Gen. 2:2.

the LORD; [1]*therefore* I shall not
slide.[G S]
2 Examine me, O LORD, and
[d]prove me; try[C] my reins[C] and my
heart.
3 For thy [e]lovingkindness *is* before mine eyes: and I have
[f]walked in thy [g]truth.[T]
4 I have not [h]sat with [i]vain persons, neither will I go in with
[j]dissemblers.
5 I have [k]hated the congregation of evil doers; and [i]will not
sit with the wicked.
6 [l]I will [m,n,o]wash mine hands
in *innocency: so will I [p]com-
pass thine altar, O LORD:[Q]
7 That I may publish[C] with the
voice of [q]thanksgiving, and tell
of all thy wondrous [r]works.
8 LORD, I have loved the habitation of thy house, and the place
where thine honour dwelleth.[Q]
9 Gather not my soul with sinners, nor my life with bloody men:
10 In whose hands *is* mischief,
and their right hand is full of
[s]bribes.
11 But as for me, I will walk in
mine [b]integrity: redeem me, and
be merciful unto me.
12 My foot standeth in an even
place: in the congregations will I
[t]bless the LORD.

## PSALM 27

*The psalmist's confidence in God's protection, 7 and prayer to be delivered from his enemies.*

A Psalm of David.

[a, b]THE LORD *is* my [c]light and
my [d]salvation; whom shall
I fear? the LORD *is* the strength
of my life; of whom shall I be
afraid?[T]
2 When the wicked, *even* mine
enemies and my foes, came upon
me to eat up my flesh, they
stumbled and fell.
3 Though an host should encamp against me, [b]my [e]heart
shall not fear: though [f]war
should rise against me, in this
*will* I *be* confident.
4 One *thing* have I [g]desired of
the LORD, that will I seek after;
that I may dwell in the [h,i]house of
the LORD all the days of my life,
to behold the [j]beauty of the LORD,
and to [k]enquire in his temple.
5 For [b]in the time of [l]trouble he
shall hide me in his pavilion: in
the secret of his [i]tabernacle shall
he hide me; he shall set me up
upon a rock.
6 And now shall mine head be
lifted up above mine enemies
round about me: therefore will I
offer in his [i]tabernacle sacrifices
of joy; I will sing, yea, I will sing
[m]praises unto the LORD.
7 Hear, O LORD, *when* I [n]cry
with my voice: have [o]mercy[C] also
upon me, and answer me.
8 *When thou saidst,* Seek ye my
face; my [e]heart said unto thee,
[g]Thy face, LORD, will I seek.
9 [n]Hide not thy face *far* from
me; put not thy servant away in
[p]anger: [q]thou hast been my help;
leave me not, neither forsake me,
O God of my [d]salvation.
10 When my *father and my
mother forsake me, then the
LORD will take [r]me up.
11 [s,t]Teach me thy [u]way, O
LORD, and [v,w,x]lead me in a plain
path, because of mine enemies.[S]
12 [x]Deliver me not over unto
the will of mine enemies: for
[y]false[C] witnesses are risen up
against me, and such as breathe
out †cruelty.

3
*e Heart,* Psa. 44:21.
*f War,* Judg. 3:2.
4
*g Spiritual Desire,* Psa. 42:1.
*h Church, called house of the Lord,* 1 Kin. 9:3.
*i Tabernacle,* Ex. 27:9.
*j Beauty, spiritual,* Psa. 45:11.
*k Worship, loved by God's people,* Gen. 22:5.
5
*l Adversity, consolation in,* Psa. 10:6.
6
*m Praise,* Psa. 150:1.
7
*n Prayer, in adversity,* Acts 6:4.
*o God, mercy of,* Gen. 2:2.
9
*p Anger of God,* 2 Kin. 13:3.
*q God, preserver,* Gen. 2:2.
10
*r Children, God's care of,* Mark 10:14.
11
*s Wisdom, prayer for spiritual,* Prov. 2:2.
*t Prayer, in adversity,* Acts 6:4.
*u Way,* Isa. 35:8.
*v God, guide,* Gen. 2:2.
*w Guidance, prayer for,* Psa. 48:14.
*x Adversity, prayer in,* Psa. 10:6.
12
*y False Witness, innocent suffer from,* Matt. 19:18.

* **INNOCENCY.** *Signified by washing the hands,* Deut. 21:6; Psa. 26:6; Matt. 27:24. *Found, in Daniel,* Dan. 6:22; *in Jesus,* Luke 23:4, 13–15, 22; John 18:38; Acts 13:28. *Professed by Pilate,* Matt. 27:24.
*Contrasted with guilt,* compare Gen. 2:25; 3:7–11.

* **FATHER.** *To be revered,* Ex. 20:12; 21:15, 17; Lev. 18:7; 19:3; Deut. 5:16; Matt. 15:4; Mark 7:10; 10:19; Luke 18:20; Eph. 6:2, 3. *To be obeyed,* **Deut. 21:18; Prov. 1:8; 6:20; 23:22; Eph. 6:1.** *Cursing of, forbidden,* Lev. 20:9; Prov. 20:20.
**Duty of:** *To chasten and admonish children,* Prov. 13:24; Eph. 6:4; Heb. 12:7. *To provide for family,* Gen. 30:30; 1 Tim. 5:8. ***To govern his household,*** **Gen. 18:19; 1 Tim. 3:4.**
**Fatherhood of God,** see footnote, GOD, *Fatherhood of,* Gen. 2:2.

† **CRUELTY.** *Of the wicked,* Psa. 25:19; 27:12; 74:20; Prov. 11:17; 12:10; Jer. 6:23; 50:42. *In war,* Isa. 13:16, 18.
**Instances of:** *Sarah, to Hagar,* Gen. 16:6; 21:9–14. *Sim-*

13 *I had fainted*, unless I had
[z]believed to see the [a]goodness of
the LORD in the land of the
living.
14 [b]Wait[G] on the LORD: [1]be of
good courage, and he shall
[c]strengthen thine [d]heart: wait, I
say, on the LORD.

## PSALM 28

*The psalmist implores God to have compassion on him in distress. 6 He blesses God, 9 and prays for the people.*

A Psalm of David.

UNTO thee will I [a, b]cry, O
LORD my [c]rock; be not
silent to me: lest, *if* thou be silent to me, I become like them
that go down into the [d]pit.
2 [a]Hear the voice of my [b]sup-
plications, when I cry unto thee,
when I lift up my hands toward
thy [e]holy [f]oracle.
3 Draw me not away with the
[g]wicked, and with the workers of
iniquity, which [h]speak peace to
their neighbours, but mischief[G] *is*
in their [i]hearts.
4 [j]Give [k]them according to
their deeds, and according to the
wickedness of their [1]endeavours:
give them after the work of their
hands; render to them their
desert.[Q]
5 Because [l]they regard[G] not the
works of the LORD, nor the
operation of his hands, he shall
destroy [k]them, and not build
them up.
6 [m]Blessed *be* the LORD, because he hath [n]heard the voice of
my supplications.
7 The [o]LORD *is* my [p]strength
and my [q]shield: my heart [r]trust-
ed in him, and I am helped:
therefore [s]my heart greatly [t]re-
joiceth; and with my song will I
[m]praise him.
8 [u]The LORD *is* their [p]strength,
and he *is* the [v]saving strength of
his anointed.[S]
9 [w, x]Save thy people, and bless
thine inheritance: feed them also, and lift them up for ever.

## PSALM 29

*An exhortation to give glory to God, who is the strength and security of his people.*

A Psalm of David.

[a]GIVE unto the LORD, O ye
mighty, give unto the LORD
[b]glory and strength.
2 Give unto the LORD the
[b]glory due unto his name; [c]wor-
ship the LORD in the [d]beauty of
holiness.
3 The voice of the LORD *is* upon the waters: the God of [b]glory
thundereth: the LORD *is* upon
many waters.[Q]
4 The voice of the [e]LORD *is*
powerful; the voice of the LORD
*is* full of majesty.[S]
5 The voice of the [e]LORD
breaketh the cedars; yea, the
LORD breaketh the [f]cedars of
Lĕb′a-non.
6 He maketh them also to skip
like a calf; [f]Lĕb′a-non and [g]Sĭr′-
i-ŏn like a young [1, h]unicorn.
7 The voice of the LORD divideth the flames of fire.
8 The voice of the LORD shaketh the wilderness; the LORD
shaketh the wilderness of [i]Kā′-
desh.
9 The voice of the LORD [j]mak-
eth the [k]hinds to calve, and [2]dis-
covereth[G] the forests: and in his
[l]temple doth every [3]one speak of
*his* [b]glory.
10 The LORD [4]sitteth upon the
flood; yea, the LORD sitteth
[m]King for ever.
11 The LORD will give
[n]strength unto his people; the
LORD will bless [o]his people with
[p]peace.[S]

---

**13**
*z Faith, instances of*, Mark 11:22.

*a God, goodness of*, Gen. 2:2.
**14**
*b Faith, enjoined*, Mark 11:22.
*c Spiritual Blessings, from God*, Eph. 1:3.
*d Heart*, Psa. 44:21.
1 R. V. Be strong, and let thine heart take courage.

**1**
*a Adversity, prayer in*, Psa. 10:6.
*b Prayer, in adversity*, Acts 6:4.
*c Rock, figurative*, Psa. 78:15.
*d Pit, figurative*, Psa. 7:15.
**2**
*e Church, called holy oracle*, 1 Kin. 9:3.
*f Oracle*, 1 Kin. 6:5.
**3**
*g Evil Company, shunned by the righteous*, Prov. 13:20.
*h Hypocrisy*, Jas. 3:17.
*i Heart, the unregenerate*, Psa. 44:21.
**4**
*j Prayer, imprecatory*, Acts 6:4.
*k Wicked, punishment of*, Psa. 73:3.
1 R. V. doings:
**5**
*l Godless, described*, Job 8:13.
**6**
*m Praise*, Psa. 150:1.
*n Prayer, answered*, Acts 6:4.
**7**
*o God, preserver*, Gen. 2:2
*p Spiritual Blessings, from God*, Eph. 1:3.
*q Shield, figurative*, 1 Kin. 14:27.
*r Faith, instances of*, Mark 11:22.
*s Thankfulness, exemplified*, Acts 24:3.
*t Joy*, Psa. 5:11.
**8**
*u Righteous, promises to*, Psa. 64:10.

*v God, savior*, Gen. 2:2.
**9**
*w Intercession, instances of*. Jer. 27:18.
*x Prayer, intercessory*, Acts 6:4.

**1**
*a Praise*, Psa. 150:1.
*b God, glory of*, Gen. 2:2.
**2**
*c Worship, enjoined*, Gen. 22:5.
*d Spiritual Beauty*, Psa. 45:11.
**4**
*e God, power of*, Gen. 2:2.
**5**
*f Lebanon, cedars of*, Deut. 1:7.
**6**
*g* Or, *Hermon*, Deut. 4:48.
*h Unicorn*, Job 39:9.
1 R. V. wild-ox.
**8**
*i Kadesh*, Gen. 14:7.
**9**
*j Abortion*, Ex. 21:22.
*k Animals*, Jer. 27:5.
*l Church, called temple*, 1 Kin. 9:3.
2 R. V. strippeth the forests bare:
3 R.V. thing saith, Glory.
**10**
*m God, sovereign*, Gen. 2:2.
4 R. V. sat as king at the Flood;
**11**
*n Spiritual Blessings, from God*, Eph. 1:3.
*o Righteous, promises to*, Psa. 64:10.
*p Spiritual Peace, from God*, Gal. 1:3.

---

*eon and Levi, to the Shechemites*, Gen. 34:25; 49:5, 7. *Joseph's brethren, to Joseph*, Gen. 37:24, 28. *Egyptians, to Israelites*, Ex. 5:6-18. *Joshua, to the kings of the Amorites*, Josh. 10:24, 26. *Samuel, to Agag*, 1 Sam. 15:32, 33. *The tribe of Judah, to Adonibezek*, Judg. 1:6, 7. *Abimelech, to his brother*, Judg. 9:5. *The Philistines, to Samson*, Judg. 16:21. *Peninnah, to Hannah*, 1 Sam. 1:4-7. *David, to the Ammonites*, 2 Sam. 12:31; 1 Chr. 20:3. *Athaliah, to the royal sons*, 2 Kin. 11:1. *Menahem, to the inhabitants of Tiphsah*, 2 Kin. 15:16. *Zedekiah, to Jeremiah*, Jer. 38:6. *Nebuchadnezzar, to Zedekiah*, 2 Kin. 25:7; Jer. 39:7. *Herod, to the Jews in slaying their children*, Matt. 2:16. *Jews, to Jesus*, Matt. 26:67. *Soldiers, to Jesus*, Matt. 27:28-31, 34; Luke 22:63, 64; John 19:3.

1
a *Thankfulness, exemplified,* Acts 24:3.
b *Praise,* Psa. 150:1.
2
c *Prayer, answered,* Acts 6:4.
d *Healing, from God,* Acts 4:22.
3
e *God, preserver,* Gen. 2:2.
f *Life, from God,* Eccl. 8:15.
g *Death,* Num. 23:10.
h *Pit, figurative,* Psa. 7:15.
1 R. V. Sheol:
4
i *Thankfulness, enjoined,* Acts 24:3.
j *God, holiness of,* Gen. 2:2.
2 R. V. to his holy name.
5
k *Anger of God,* 2 Kin. 13:3.
l *Grace of God,* Rom. 4:16.
m *God, mercy of,* Gen. 2:2.
n *Weeping,* Ezra 3:13.
o *Afflictions, consolation in,* Psa. 34:19.
p *Joy,* Psa. 5:11.
6
q *Delusion,* 2 Thess. 2:11.
8
r *Prayer, in adversity,* Acts 6:4.
9
s *God, truth,* Gen. 2:2.
11
t *Mourning,* Lam. 2:5.
u *Dancing, figurative of joy,* Eccl. 3:4.
v *Sackcloth,* Isa. 15:3.

## PSALM 30

*The psalmist praises God for his deliverance. 4 He exhorts others also to praise him.*

A Psalm *and* Song *at* the dedication of the house of David.

[a]I WILL [b]extol[G] thee, O LORD;
for thou hast lifted me up,
and hast not made my foes to rejoice over me.
2 O LORD my God, I [c]cried unto thee, and thou hast [d]healed
me.
3 O LORD, thou hast [d]brought
up my soul from [1]the grave[G]:
[e]thou hast kept me [f]alive, that I
should not [g]go down to the [h]pit.
4 [b]Sing unto the LORD, O ye
saints of his, and give [i]thanks [2]at
the remembrance of his [j]holi-
ness.[S]
5 For his [k]anger *endureth but* a
moment; in his [l,m]favour *is* [f]life:
[n,o]weeping may endure for a
night, but [p]joy *cometh* in the
morning.
6 And in my prosperity I said,
*,[q]I shall never be moved.
7 LORD, by thy [l]favour thou
hast made my mountain to stand
strong: thou didst hide thy face,
*and* I was troubled.[S]
8 I [r]cried to thee, O LORD; and
unto the LORD I made supplication.
9 What profit *is there* in my
blood, when I [g]go down to the
[h]pit? Shall the dust praise thee?
shall it declare thy [s]truth?[T]
10 [r]Hear, O LORD, and have
[m]mercy upon me: LORD, be
[e]thou my helper.
11 Thou hast turned for me my
[t]mourning into [u]dancing: thou
hast put off my [v]sackcloth, and
girded me with [p]gladness;
12 To the end that *my* glory
may sing [b]praise to thee, and not
be silent. O LORD my God, I
will give [a]thanks unto thee for
ever.

## PSALM 31

*The psalmist expresses his confidence in God and craves his help. 19 God's goodness to them that fear him.*

To the chief Musician, A Psalm of David.

IN thee, O LORD, do I put
my [a]trust; let me never be
ashamed: [b]deliver me in thy
[c]righteousness.
2 [d]Bow down thine ear to me;
[a]deliver me speedily: be thou my
strong [e]rock, for an house of defence to save me.
3 For thou *art* my [e]rock and
my [f]fortress; therefore [g]for thy
name's sake [h,i]lead me, and
guide me.[S]
4 [b,j]Pull me out of the [k]net that
they have laid privily[G] for me: for
[l]thou *art* my [1]strength.
5 [m]Into thine hand I commit
my [n]spirit: [o]thou hast redeemed
me, O LORD [p]God of truth.[S T Q]
6 I have hated [q]them that regard lying [r]vanities[G]: but I [b]trust
in the LORD.[S]
7 [s]I will be glad and rejoice in
thy [t]mercy: for thou hast considered my [u]trouble; thou hast
known my soul in adversities;
8 And hast not shut[G] me up into
the hand of the enemy: [l]thou
hast set my feet in a large
room.[C]
9 [b]Have [t]mercy upon me, O
LORD, for I am in [j]trouble: mine
eye is consumed with grief, *yea*,
my soul and my [2]belly.[G]
10 [v]For my life is spent with
grief, and my years with sighing:

1
a *Faith, instances of,* Mark 11:22.
b *Prayer, in adversity,* Acts 6:4.
c *God, righteousness of,* Gen. 2:2.
2
d *Anthropomorphisms,* Gen. 11:5.
e *Rock, figurative,* Psa. 78:15.
3
f *Fortification, figurative,* Ezek. 17:17.
g *Prayer, pleas offered in,* Acts 6:4.
h *God, guide,* Gen. 2:2.
i *Guidance, prayer for,* Psa. 48:14.
4
j *Adversity, prayer in,* Psa. 10:6.
k *Net, figurative,* Isa. 51:20.
l *God, providence of,* Gen. 2:2.
1 R. V. strong hold.
5
m Luke 23:46.
n *Man, spirit,* Job 4:17.
o *God, savior,* Gen. 2:2.
p *God, truth,* Gen. 2:2.
6
q *Evil Company, shunned by the righteous,* Prov. 13:20.
r *Vanity,* Eccl. 1:2.
7
s *Thankfulness, exemplified,* Acts 24:3.
t *God, mercy of,* Gen. 2:2.
u *Adversity, consolation in,* Psa. 10:6.
9
2 R. V. body.
10
v *Remorse, instances of,* Matt. 27:3.

* **FALSE CONFIDENCE.** *Of the apostate,* Deut. 29:18, 19. *Of the infidel,* Ezek. 8:12; Zeph. 1:12. *Of the self-righteous,* John 5:45; Rom. 2:3. *Of the spiritually blind,* Psa. 36:2; Prov. 16:25; Isa. 9:9, 10; 28:15, 18; 30:10, 15, 16; 47:7, 8, 10; 56:12; Jer. 2:18, 22, 23, 37; 6:14; 7:8; 8:11; 23:17; Ezek. 13:10, 11; Amos 9:10; Mic. 3:11; Gal. 6:7, 8; 1 Thess. 5:3.

*In riches,* Psa. 30:6; 49:6, 7; 52:7; Prov. 11:28; Mark 10:24; 1 Tim. 6:17. *In worldly success,* Job 29:18; Psa. 10:6; 20:7, 8; Prov. 18:11; Obad. 3; Luke 12:19, 20. *In worldly wisdom,* Isa. 22:11; Jas. 4:13–15. *In worldly help,* Psa. 108:12; 118:8, 9; 146:3, 4; Isa. 20:5; 30:1, 2, 5, 7; 31:1–3; 36:6; 57:13; Jer. 3:23; 5:17; Lam. 4:17; Ezek. 29:6, 7; 30:8; Hos. 5:13; 7:9, 11–16; 10:13. *In worldly security,* Luke 17:26–30.

*In self-sufficiency,* Job 18:14; Prov. 14:16; 26:12; 28:26; Isa. 5:21; Jer. 21:13; 48:7, 11; Zeph. 2:15; Zech. 4:6; Matt. 26:33–35; Mark 14:29–31; Luke 18:9–14; 22:33, 34; John 13:37, 38; Rev. 18:7, 8.

*Warning against,* 1 Kin. 20:11; Job 15:31; Psa. 33:16, 17; 62:10; Prov. 23:4; Jer. 17:5; Luke 11:35; Rom. 12:16; 1 Cor. 3:21; 2 Cor. 1:9.

**Instances of:** *Builders of Babel,* Gen. 11:4. *Sennacherib,* 2 Kin. 19:23. *Asa,* 2 Chr. 16:7–9. *Hezekiah,* Isa.

my strength faileth because of mine [w]iniquity, and my bones are consumed.

11 [3]I was a reproach among all mine enemies, but especially among my neighbours, and a fear to mine acquaintance: they that did see me without [x]fled from me.

12 I am forgotten as a [y]dead man out of mind: I am like a broken vessel.

13 For I have heard the [4,z]slander of many: fear *was* on every side: while they [a]took counsel together against me, they devised to take away my life.

14 But I [b]trusted in thee, O LORD: I said, Thou *art* my God.

15 My times *are* in thy hand: deliver me from the hand of mine enemies, and from them that [a]persecute me.

16 Make thy face to shine upon thy servant: save me for thy [c]mercies' sake.

17 Let me not be ashamed, O LORD; for I have called upon thee: [d]let the wicked be ashamed, *and* let them be silent in [5]the [e]grave.

18 [d]Let the [f]lying lips be put to silence; which speak grievous things proudly and contemptuously against the righteous.

19 *Oh* how great *is* thy [g]goodness, which thou hast laid up for them that [h]fear thee; *which* thou hast wrought for them that trust in thee before the sons of men!

20 [i]Thou shalt hide them in the secret of thy presence from the [6]pride of man: thou shalt keep them secretly in a pavilion from the [j]strife of tongues.

21 [k]Blessed *be* the LORD: for he hath shewed me his marvellous [g]kindness in a strong city.

22 For I [l]said in my haste, [m]I am cut off from before thine eyes: nevertheless [n]thou heardest the voice of my supplications when I cried unto thee.

23 O [o,p]love the LORD, all ye his saints: *for* the [i]LORD preserveth the [q]faithful, and plentifully rewardeth the [r]proud doer.

24 [7,s]Be of good [t]courage, and he shall [u]strengthen your heart, all ye that [v]hope in the LORD.

## PSALM 32

*The blessedness of the man whose sin is pardoned. 3 The psalmist's own experience. 8 The safety of the righteous.*

A Psalm of David, Maschil.

[a,b]BLESSED *is he whose* transgression *is* [c]forgiven, *whose* sin *is* covered.

2 [b]Blessed *is* the man unto whom the [d]LORD [e]imputeth not [f]iniquity, and in whose spirit *there is* [g,h]no [i]guile.

3 [j]When I kept silence, [k]my bones waxed old through my roaring all the day long.

4 For day and night [l]thy hand was heavy upon me: my moisture is turned into the [m]drought of [n]summer. [Sē'lah.

5 I [o,p]acknowledge my sin unto thee, and mine iniquity have I not hid. I said, I will confess my transgressions unto the LORD; and [d]thou [c]forgavest the iniquity of my sin. [Sē'lah.

6 [q]For this shall every one that is godly pray unto thee in a time when thou mayest be found: surely in the floods of great waters they shall not come nigh unto him.

7 Thou *art* my hiding place; [r]thou shalt [s]preserve me from trouble; thou shalt compass me about with songs of deliverance. [Sē'lah.

8 I will [t]instruct thee and teach thee in the [u]way which thou

w *Conviction, of sin,* John 16:8.

**11**

x *Afflictions, forsaken by friends in,* Psa. 34:19.

3 R. V. Because of all mine adversaries I am become a reproach,

**12**

y *Dead,* 2 Kin. 4:32.

**13**

z *Slander, instances of,* Prov. 10:18.

a *Persecution, instances of,* John 15:20.

4 R. V. defaming

**14**

b *Faith, instances of,* Mark 11:22.

**16**

c *God, mercy of,* Gen. 2:2.

**17**

d *Prayer, imprecatory,* Acts 6:4.

e *Hell,* Mark 9:43.

5 R. V. Sheol.

**18**

f *Falsehood, abhorred by the righteous,* Job 21:34.

**19**

g *God, goodness of,* Gen. 2:2.

h *Fear of God,* Acts 9:31.

**20**

i *God, preserver,* Gen. 2:2.

j *Strife,* Prov. 20:3.

6 R. V. plottings

**21**

k *Praise,* Psa. 150:1.

**22**

l *Doubting,* Rom. 14:23.

m *Despondency,* Eccl. 2:20.

n *Prayer, answered,* Acts 6:4.

**23**

o *Love, of man for God,* 1 John 4:19.

p *Duty, of man to God,* Eccl. 12:13.

q *Faithfulness,* Luke 16:10.

r *Pride,* Prov. 16:18.

**24**

s *Faith, enjoined,* Mark 11:22.

t *Courage,* Deut. 31:7.

u *Spiritual Blessings, from God,* Eph. 1:3.

v *Hope, in God,* Prov. 13:12.

7 R. V. Be strong, and let your heart take courage,

**1**

a Rom. 4:7.

b *Spiritual Peace,* Gal. 1:3.

c *Sin, forgiveness of,* Rom. 5:12.

**2**

d *God, mercy of,* Gen. 2:2.

e *Justification,* Rom. 4:25.

f *Sin, not imputed,* Rom. 5:12.

g *Holiness,* Ex. 39:30.

h *Sincerity,* 1 Cor. 5:8.

i *Deceit,* Psa. 36:3.

**3**

j *Prayer, confession in,* Acts 6:4.

k *Conscience, guilty,* Acts 23:1.

**4**

l *Afflictions, dispensation of God,* Psa. 34:19.

m *Drought, figurative,* Gen. 31:40.

n *Summer, drought of,* Isa. 28:4.

**5**

o *Repentance, instances of,* Mark 1:4.

p *Sin, confession of,* Rom. 5:12.

**6**

q *Promise, or ground of assurance,* 2 Cor. 1:20.

**7**

r *Faith, instances of,* Mark 11:22.

s *God, preserver,* Gen. 2:2.

**8**

t *Wisdom, spiritual, from God,* Prov. 2:2.

u *Way, figurative,* Isa. 35:8.

22:11. *Jonah,* Jonah 1:3-5. *Peter,* Matt. 26:33-35; Luke 22:33, 34.

See footnotes: CONCEIT, Prov. 26:5; SPIRITUAL BOASTING, Rom. 3:27.

shalt go: [v]I will [1]guide thee with
mine eye.[S]
9 Be ye not [w]as the [x]horse, *or* as
the mule, *which* have no understanding: whose mouth must be
held in with [y]bit and *bridle,
[2]lest they come near unto thee.
10 Many sorrows *shall be* to the
[z]wicked: but [a]he that [b]trusteth
in the LORD, [c]mercy shall compass him about.[T]
11 [d]Be glad in the LORD, and
rejoice, ye righteous; and shout
for [e]joy, all *ye that are* upright
in heart.[T]

## PSALM 33

*An exhortation to praise God for his goodness, 6 for his power, 12 and for his providence. 20 The Lord is the help of his people.*

[a]REJOICE in the LORD, O
ye righteous: *for* [b]praise
is comely[G] for the upright.
2 [Q] [b,c]Praise the LORD with
[d,e]harp: sing unto him with the
[f]psaltery[G] *and* an instrument of
ten strings.
3 [b,e]Sing unto him a new [g]song;
play skilfully with a loud noise.[Q]
4 For the [h]word of the [i]LORD
*is* right; and all his [j]works *are*
*done* in [1,k]truth.[S T]
5 He loveth righteousness and
[l]judgment[G]: the earth is full of
the [m]goodness of the LORD.[S]
6 [S] By the word of the [n]LORD
were the [o]heavens [p]made; and
all the [q]host of them by the
[r,s]breath of his mouth.[T Q]
7 He gathereth the waters of the
[t]sea together as an heap: he layeth up the depth in storehouses.
8 Let all the earth [u]fear the
LORD: let all the inhabitants of
the world stand in awe of him.
9 For [n,v]he spake, and it was
*done*; he commanded, and it
stood fast.[S T Q G]
10 The [w]LORD bringeth the
counsel of the [2]heathen[G] to
nought: he maketh the devices
of the people of none effect.[S]
11 The counsel of the [x,y]LORD
standeth for ever, the thoughts
of his heart to all generations.[S T]
12 Blessed *is* the [z]nation whose
[a]God *is* the LORD; *and* the people *whom* he [b]hath chosen for
his own inheritance.[S]
13 [S] The [c]LORD [d]looketh from
[e]heaven; he beholdeth all the
sons of men.
14 From the [e]place of his habitation he [d]looketh upon all the
inhabitants of the earth.
15 [f]He [3]fashioneth their hearts
alike; he considereth all their
works.[S]
16 [g]There is no king saved by
the multitude of an [h]host: a
mighty man is not delivered by
much strength.
17 [g]An [i]horse *is* a vain[G] thing
for safety: neither shall he deliver *any* by his great strength.
18 Behold, the [j]eye of the
LORD *is* upon [k]them that [l]fear
him, upon them that [m,n]hope in
his [o]mercy;
19 To [a,p]deliver their soul from
death, and to keep them alive in
[q]famine.
20 Our soul [r]waiteth for the
LORD: [s]he *is* our help and our
[t]shield.
21 For our heart shall [u]rejoice
in him, because we have [s]trusted
in his holy name.
22 Let thy [o]mercy, O LORD, be
upon us, according as we [m]hope
in thee.

## PSALM 34

*The psalmist praises the Lord. 3 He exhorts others to exalt his name; 11 and teaches them the fear of the Lord. 18 Blessing on the penitent; 19 on the righteous.*

A Psalm of David, when he changed his behavior before Abimelech; who drove him away, and he departed.

I WILL [a,b]bless the LORD at
all times: his praise *shall*
continually *be* in my mouth.
2 My soul shall make her [c]boast

v *God, guide,* Gen. 2:2.
1 R. V. counsel thee with mine eye upon thee.
9
w *Self-will, illustrated,* Gen. 49:6.
x *Animals,* Jer. 27:5.
y Jas. 3:3.
2 R. V. Else they will not come near unto thee.
10
z *Wicked, punishment of,* Psa. 73:3.

a *Promise, to the righteous,* 2 Cor. 1:20.
b *Faith,* Mark 11:22.
c *God, mercy of,* Gen. 2:2.
11
d *Praise,* Psa. 150:1.
e *Joy,* Psa. 5:11.

1
a *Joy,* Psa. 5:11.
b *Praise,* Psa. 150:1.
2
c *Thankfulness, enjoined,* Acts 24:3.
d *Harp,* Dan. 3:10.
e *Music,* 2 Chr. 5:13.
f *Psaltery,* 1 Chr. 16:5.
3
g *Song,* Psa. 77:6.
4
h *Word of God,* Psa. 119:9.
i *God, righteousness of,* Gen. 2:2.
j *Works of God,* Psa. 40:5.
k *God, truth,* Gen. 2:2.
1 R. V. faithfulness.
5
l *God, justice of,* Gen. 2:2.
m *God, goodness of,* Gen. 2:2.
6
n *God, creator,* Gen. 2:2.
o *Physical Heavens, created,* Psa. 8:3.
p *Creation, by God's word,* Mark 13:19.
q *Stars, created by God,* Judg. 5:20.
r *Breath, figurative,* Gen. 7:15.
s *Anthropomorphisms,* Gen. 11:5.
7
t *Sea,* Jer. 5:22.
8
u *Fear of God,* Acts 9:31.
v *God, power of,* Gen. 2:2.
10
w *God, providence of,* Gen. 2:2.
2 R. V. nations

11
x *God, eternity of,* Gen. 2:2.
y *God, immutable,* Gen. 2:2.
12
z *Nation,* Isa. 2:4.
a *God, providence of,* Gen. 2:2.
b *Foreordination, according to purpose of grace,* Rom. 8:30.
13
c *God, knowledge of,* Gen. 2:2.
d *Anthropomorphisms,* Gen. 11:5.
e *Heaven, God's dwelling place,* Luke 18:22.
15
f *God, creator of man,* Gen. 2:2.
3 R. V. that fashioneth the hearts of them all,
16
g *False Confidence, warning against,* Psa. 30:6.
h *Armies,* Deut. 11:4.
17
i *Horse,* Job 39:19.
18
j *Anthropomorphisms,* Gen. 11:5.
k *Righteous, promises to,* Psa. 64:10.
l *Fear of God,* Acts 9:31.
m *Hope,* Prov. 13:12.
n *Faith,* Mark 11:22.
o *God, mercy of,* Gen. 2:2.
19
p *God, savior,* Gen. 2:2.
q *Famine, righteous delivered from,* 2 Kin. 8:1.
20
r *Spiritual Desire,* Psa. 42:1.
s *Faith, instances of,* Mark 11:22.
t *Shield, figurative,* 1 Kin. 14:27.
21
u *Joy,* Psa. 5:11.

1
a *Praise,* Psa. 150:1.
b *Glorifying God,* Luke 5:25.
2
c *Religious Testimony,* 2 Thess. 1:10.

*** BRIDLE,** Psa. 32:9; Prov. 26:3; Rev. 14:20. | **Figurative,** 2 Kin. 19:28; Psa. 39:1; Jas. 1:26.

in the LORD: the [1,d]humble shall
hear *thereof* and be glad.
3 O [a,b]magnify the LORD with
me, and let us exalt his [e]name
together.
4 [f]I sought the LORD, and [g,h]he
heard me, and delivered me
from all my fears.
5 They looked unto him, and
were lightened: and their faces
were not ashamed.
6 This [i]poor man [g]cried, and
the LORD heard *him*, and [j]saved
him out of all his [h]troubles.
7 The [k]angel of the LORD [l]en-
campeth round about them that
[m]fear him, and [j,n]delivereth
them.
8 O taste and see that the
LORD *is* [o]good: [p]blessed *is* the
man *that* [q]trusteth in him.
9 O [r]fear the LORD, ye his
saints: [s]for *there is* no want to
them that fear him.
10 The young lions do lack,
and suffer hunger: but [s]they that
[f]seek the LORD shall not want
[t]any good *thing*.

11 Come, ye [u]children, hearken
unto me: I will [v]teach you the
[m]fear of the LORD.
12 [w]What man *is he that* desireth life, *and* loveth [x]*many*
days, that he may see good?
13 [y]Keep thy tongue from [z]evil,
and thy lips from [z]speaking
[a]guile.
14 [b]Depart from [c]evil, and do
good; seek [e]peace, and pursue it.
15 The [f]eyes of the LORD *are*
upon the [g]righteous, and [h]his
ears *are open* unto their cry.
16 The face of the LORD *is*
against [i]them that do [c]evil, to
cut off the remembrance of them
from the earth.
17 *The* [g]*righteous* [j]cry, and the
LORD heareth, and [k]delivereth
them out of all their troubles.
18 [l]The LORD *is* nigh unto
them that are of a [m]broken heart;
and [n]saveth [o]such as be of a contrite spirit.
19 Many *are* the *afflictions of

*d Meekness*, Psa. 45:4.
1 R. V. meek

**3**
*e God, name of, to be praised*, Gen. 2:2.

**4**
*f Seekers*, Isa. 55:6.
*g Prayer, answered*, Acts 6:4.
*h Adversity, consolation in*, Psa. 10:6.

**6**
*i Poor, God's care of*, Prov. 21:13.
*j God, preserver*, Gen. 2:2.

**7**
*k Angel*, Heb. 1:13.
*l Armies, figurative*, Deut. 11:4.
*m Fear of God*, Acts 9:31.
*n God, providence of*, Gen. 2:2.

**8**
*o God, goodness of*, Gen. 2:2.
*p Spiritual Peace*, Gal. 1:3.
*q Faith*, Mark 11:22.

**9**
*r Fear of God, enjoined*, Acts 9:31.
*s Promises, to the righteous*, 2 Cor. 1:20.

**10**
*t Temporal Blessings, from God*, Psa. 103:2.

**11**
*u Children, instruction of*, Mark 10:14.
*v Instruction, of children*, Prov. 23:23.

**12**
*w* 1 Pet. 3:10–12.
*x Longevity*, Psa. 91:16.

**13**
*y Guilelessness, enjoined*, John 1:47.
*z Speech, evil*, Col. 4:6.

*a Falsehood, forbidden*, Job 21:34.

**14**
*b Holiness, enjoined*, Ex. 39:30.
*c Evil*, 1 Thess. 5:22.
*d Works, good*, 2 Tim. 1:9.
*e Social Peace, enjoined*, Jer. 29:7.

**15**
*f Eye, anthropomorphic uses of*, Matt. 6:22.
*g Righteous, promises to*, Psa. 64:10.
*h Prayer, answer to, promised*, Acts 6:4.

**16**
*i Wicked, punishment of*, Psa. 73:3.

**17**
*j Prayer, answered*, Acts 6:4.
*k God, preserver*, Gen. 2:2. **18** *l Promise, or ground of assurance*, 2 Cor. 1:20. *m Repentance*, Mark 1:4. *n God, savior*, Gen. 2:2. *o Penitent, promises to*, Psa. 51:17.

* **AFFLICTIONS,** Job 5:6, 7; Rom. 8:28.

**Benefits of:** *Corrective*, Job 5:17; Psa. 78:31–34; 94:12, 13; 119:67; Prov. 3:11, 12; Isa. 27:9; Jer. 24:5; 46:28; Lam. 3:27, 28; Ezek. 14:10, 11; 1 Cor. 11:32; Heb. 12:5–11; Rev. 3:19.

*Lead, to repentance*, Deut. 4:30; 30:1, 2; 31:17; 1 Kin. 8:33, 35, 47–49, 53; 2 Chr. 6:28–31; Jer. 22:22; 31:19; Ezek. 6:9; 20:37, 43; Hos. 2:6, 7; *to prayer*, Neh. 9:27; Psa. 107:4–6, 10–13, 17–19; Isa. 19:20, 22; Jer. 2:27; *to remembrance of past mercies*, Lam. 1:7; *to knowledge of God*, Isa. 52:5, 6; Ezek. 6:10; Dan. 4:24–37; *to knowledge of God's law*, Psa. 119:71; *to righteousness*, Isa. 26:9; *to furtherance of the gospel*, Phil. 1:12–14; *to development of character*, Rom. 5:3, 4; Jas. 1:2–4.

*Work eternal glory*, Rom. 8:17; 2 Cor. 4:17; Jas. 1:12; 1 Pet. 1:7.

**Benefits of, illustrated:** *In humiliation, of Jacob*, Gen. 32:9–31; *of Joseph's brethren*, Gen. 42:21; *of Pharaoh*, Ex. 9:27, 28; 10:7, 16, 17; 12:30–33.

*In sending Joseph to Egypt*, Gen. 42:5, 7, 8. *In Israel*, Deut. 8:3–5; Psa. 78:34, 35; *when scourged by serpents*, Num. 21:7; *when oppressed by enemies*, Judg. 10:6–10; 1 Sam. 12:9, 10; 2 Chr. 15:4.

*In king Jeroboam, when his hand was withered*, 1 Kin. 13:4–6. *In Josiah*, 2 Kin. 22:19. *In Hezekiah*, 1 Kin. 20:1–11; 2 Chr. 32:24–26. *In Manasseh when carried captive to Babylon*, 2 Chr. 33:12, 13. *In Jeremiah*, Lam. 3:19, 20. *In the Psalmist*, Psa. 18:4–6; 66:10–12; 119:67, 71. *In God's people when in trouble*, Isa. 26:16; Hos. 6:1; Jer. 31:18, 19; Hos. 6:1. *In Jonah when cast into the sea*, Jonah 2:1–9.

**Consolation in:** *Absence of*, Psa. 69:20; Eccl. 4:1; Rom. 8:28.

FROM GOD, 2 Cor. 1:4. *Through his word*, Psa. 119:50, 52, 54, 92, 143. *By his presence*, Gen. 16:7–13; 21:12–21; 31:42; Psa. 23:4; Isa. 43:2; Acts 23:11. *By promises of deliverance*, Ex. 3:7, 8, 16, 17; 6:6–8; 14:13–16; 2 Sam. 22:28; Job 5:19 21; Psa. 27:5, 6; 50:15; Isa. 66:13, 14; Jer. 39:16–18; 1 Cor. 10:13; Heb. 2:14, 15; Rev. 3:10. *In assurance of his care*, Luke 21:16–18; Rom. 8:28, 38, 39; 1 Pet. 5:7, 9. *In his help*, Psa. 9:9, 10; 41:3; 46:1; 55:22; 69:33; 71:20; 94:17–19; 138:3, 7, 8; 140:12; 145:14; 147:3; Isa. 26:4; 30:19; 40:29; 41:10, 13, 14, 17; 50:7, 9; Hos. 6:1–3; Zeph. 3:18, 19; Matt. 11:28; 2 Cor. 12:9; 2 Tim. 4:17, 18; Heb. 13:5, 6. *In his justice*, Psa. 140:12; 1 Pet. 2:21–24. *In his compassion*, Psa. 112:4; Isa. 49:13; 61:1–3; 63:9; Lam. 3:31–33; Luke 7:13; Jonah 15:18, 20; Heb. 4:15, 16.

*Through ministration of friends*, 2 Cor. 7:6. *By the Holy Spirit*, John 14:16, 17; Phil. 1:19.

*By promises of reward*, Matt. 5:4, 10–12; Luke 6:20–23; John 16:20, 22, 33; Rom. 8:18; Cor. 4:8–10, 16, 17; 2 Tim. 2:12; Jas. 1:12; 1 Pet. 4:12–14; Rev. 2:10; 7:14–17.

FROM MEN: *In sympathy*, Job 16:5; Isa. 50:4; Acts 14:22; Rom. 12:13, 15; 2 Cor. 1:3–6; Heb. 10:34; 13:3. *In help*, Job 31:19–22; Isa. 58:10; Gal. 6:2; Jas. 1:27. *In intercessory prayer*, Acts 12:5.

**Design of,** Psa. 119:71. *To prove*, Deut. 8:2, 16; Judg. 2:21, 22; Psa. 66:10; 106:43, 44; Prov. 17:3; Eccl. 7:14; Phil. 1:29, 30; 2 Thess. 1:4, 5; 1 Pet. 1:6, 7; Rev. 2:10. *To lead to repentance*, Lev. 26:21–39; Deut. 30:1–3; 31:17; 1 Kin. 8:33–48; 2 Chr. 6:24–31; 7:13, 14; Job 33:11, 16–30; 36:8–10; Psa. 39:11; 107:10–12, 17–19; Dan. 4:25–27, 34; Hos. 5:15; Mic. 6:9. *To humble*, 2 Cor. 12:7. *To sanctify*, Isa. 1:25–27; 4:34; Mal. 3:3; John 15:2; 2 Cor. 4:11, 17. *To glorify God*, John 9:2, 3; 11:4; 21:19. *To perfect Christ as author of salvation*, Heb. 2:10, 18; 5:8, 9.

**Despondency in,** Job 4:5; 7:3–6; 9:16–35; 17:7; Psa. 6:6; 22:1, 2; 55:4–7; 69:1–3, 20; 88:3–6; Prov. 24:10; Lam. 3:39; Matt. 27:46; Mark 15:34; Luke 18:1.

**From God,** 2 Sam. 7:14; 12:14; Job 10:8; 11:10; 12:14–25; 19:6, 21; 21:17; 23:16; 27:2; 30:11; Psa. 66:11; 71:20; 80:5, 6; 88:6, 7, 16; 89:30–32, 38–45; 90:7, 15; 102:10, 23; 119:75; Isa. 9:13; 30:20; Jer. 45:3; Lam. 1:5, 12; 3:1; Ezek. 20:37; Amos 3:6; Nah. 1:12, 13; Mark 9:49; 1 Cor. 11:32; 2 Cor. 12:7; Heb. 12:5–10; Rev. 3:19.

*Physical*, Gen. 3:16; Ex. 4:11; Deut. 32:39; 2 Kin. 15:5; Job 5:17, 18; 6:4; Psa. 38:3.

*Temporal adversity*, Gen. 3:17; Deut. 28:15–68; 1 Sam. 2:6, 7; 2 Sam. 16:10; 2 Kin. 6:33; 2 Chr. 7:12–22; Job 9:12, 22.

*Bereavement*, Ruth 1:20, 21; Job 1:21. *Divine judgments*, Num. 14:29–35; Job 21:17; Isa. 24:1–6.

**From Satan,** Job 2:7; Matt. 4:24; 8:16, 28, 33; 9:32; 12:22; 15:22; 17:18; Mark 1:32; 5:15, 16; 7:29, 30; Luke 4:33, 35; 8:27–36; 9:42; 11:14; 13:16; Acts 10:38.

**20**

*p Bones,* Ezek. 37:1.

*q Jesus, prophecies concerning,* Matt. 1:21.

**22**

*r Faith,* Mark 11:22.

**1**

*a Adversity, prayer in,* Psa. 10:6.

*b Prayer, in adversity,* Acts 6:4.

**2**

*c Shield,* 1 Kin. 14:27.

**3**

*d Spear,* 2 Kin. 11:10.

*e Persecution, of the righteous,* John 15:20.

*f God, preserver,* Gen. 2:2.

**4**

*g Prayer, imprecatory,* Acts 6:4.

**5**

*h Chaff,* Hos. 13:3.

*i Angel,* Heb. 1:13.

**7**

*j Net, figurative,* Isa. 51:20.

*k Pit, figurative,* Psa. 7:15.

the righteous: but the [k]LORD
delivereth him out of them[Q] all.[s]
20 He keepeth all his [p]bones:
[q]not one of them is broken.[Q]
21 [c]Evil shall slay the [i]wicked:
and they that hate the righteous
shall be desolate.
22 The [n]LORD redeemeth the
soul of his servants: and [l]none of
them that [r]trust in him shall be
desolate.[s]

## PSALM 35

*The psalmist prays for the confusion of his enemies. 11 He describes their conduct; 22 and pleads to be delivered from them. 28 Will praise the Lord.*

A Psalm of David.

[a,b]PLEAD *my cause,* O LORD,
with them that strive with
me: fight against them that fight
against me.
2 Take hold of [c]shield[G] and
buckler,[G] and stand up for mine
help.
3 Draw out also the [d]spear, and
stop *the way* against them that
[e]persecute me: say unto my soul,
[f]I *am* thy salvation.
4 [g]Let them be confounded[G] and
put to shame that seek after my
soul: let them be turned back
and brought to confusion that
devise my hurt.
5 [g]Let them be as [h]chaff before
the wind: and let the [i]angel of
the LORD chase *them.*
6 [g]Let their way be dark and
slippery: and let the [i]angel of the
LORD persecute them.
7 For without cause have they
hid for me their [j]net *in* a [k]pit,
*which* without cause they have
digged for my soul.
8 [g]Let destruction come upon
him at unawares;[G] and let his [j]net
that he hath hid catch himself:
[1]into that very destruction let
him fall.[Q]
9 And [l]my soul shall be [m]joyful in the LORD: it shall rejoice
in his [n]salvation.
10 All my bones shall say,
[o]LORD who *is* like unto thee,
which deliverest the [p]poor from
him that is too strong for him,
yea, the poor and the needy from
him that spoileth him?
11 [e,q]False[G] witnesses[G] did [r]rise
up; [2]they laid to my charge
*things* that I knew not.
12 They [s]rewarded me * evil for
good *to* the [3]spoiling of my soul.
13 But [t]as for me, when they
were sick, my clothing *was*
[u]sackcloth: I humbled my soul
with [v]fasting; and my prayer returned into mine own bosom.[Q]
14 [t]I behaved myself as though
*he had been* my friend *or* brother:
I bowed down heavily,[G] as one
that mourneth *for his* mother.
15 But in mine adversity [w]they
[x]rejoiced, and gathered themselves together: *yea,* the abjects[G]
gathered themselves together
against me, and I knew *it* not;
they did tear *me,* and ceased not:
16 [4]With hypocritical [y]mockers in feasts, they [z]gnashed upon
me with their teeth.[Q]
17 [a]LORD, how long wilt thou
look on? rescue my soul from
their destructions, my darling[G]
from the lions.
18 I will [b]give thee [c]thanks in
the great congregation: I will
[d]praise thee among much[G] people.
19 Let not them that are mine
enemies wrongfully rejoice over

**8**

1 R. V. With destruction let him fall therein.

**9**

*l Thankfulness, exemplified,* Acts 24:3.

*m Joy,* Psa. 5:11.

*n Salvation,* Acts 16:17.

**10**

*o Faith, instances of,* Mark 11:22.

*p Poor, God's care of,* Prov. 21:13.

**11**

*q False Witness,* Matt. 19:18.

*r Conspiracy,* 1 Kin. 16:9.

2 R. V. They ask me of things that I know not.

**12**

*s Ingratitude, of man to man,* Rom. 1:21.

3 R. V. bereaving

**13**

*t Friendship, faithfulness in,* Prov. 22:24.

*u Sackcloth,* Isa. 15:3.

*v Fasting, instances of,* Zech. 8:19.

**15**

*w Friends, false, instances of,* Ex. 33:11.

*x Malice,* Eph. 4:31.

**16**

*y Scoffing, instances of,* Hab. 1:10.

*z Gnashing of Teeth,* Job 16:9.

4 R. V. Like the profane

**17**

*a Prayer, in adversity,* Acts 6:4.

**18**

*b Worship,* Gen. 22:5.

*c Thankfulness,* Acts 24:3.

*d Praise,* Psa. 150:1.

**Forsaken by friends in:** INSTANCES OF, Job 2:9; 19: 13–19. *David,* Psa. 31:11, 12; 41:9; 88:8, 18. *Jesus,* Matt. 26:56. *Paul,* 2 Tim. 4:16.

**Impenitence in,** Psa. 78:31, 32; Isa. 8:21; 9:13; 22:12, 13; 57:17; Jer. 2:30, 35; 3:3; 5:3; Dan. 9:13; Hos. 7:9, 10, 14; Amos 4:6–11; Zeph. 3:2, 7; Hag. 2:17.

**Prayer in,** Psa. 9:13; 31:9; 77:2; 87:9; 90:15; 119:28, 107, 121, 134, 153, 154, 170; 2 Cor. 12:7, 8. *For healing of disease,* 2 Sam. 12:22; 2 Kin. 20:3; Isa. 38:2, 3; Matt. 15: 22–28; Jas. 5:13–16. *For deliverance from,* Psa. 6:1–6; 18: 4–6; 39:12, 13; 59:7, 8, 9; 80:4–7; 116:3, 4; 123:3, 4; 130:1–8.

**Resignation in:** *Enjoined,* 2 Tim. 2:3; 4:5; 1 Pet. 2:20. *Under chastening, enjoined,* Job 5:17; Prov. 3:11; Rom. 12:12; Heb. 12:3–11. *Inspiring to others,* 2 Thess. 1:4. *Exhortation to,* 1 Pet. 4:12, 13, 19.

*Exemplified,* 1 Sam. 3:18; 2 Sam. 12:23; 15:26; 16:10, 12; 24:14; 2 Kin. 4:26; 20:19; Neh. 9:33; Esth. 4:16; Job 1:21, 22; 2:10; 13:15; 14:14; Psa. 39:9; 119:75; Isa. 39:8; Jer. 10:19; Lam. 1:18; Dan. 9:14; Mic. 7:9; Luke 23:40, 41; Acts 21:13, 14; Rom. 5:3, 4; 2 Cor. 6:4–10; 7:4; Jas. 5:11.

*** EVIL FOR GOOD,** Psa. 7:4, 5; 35:12; 109:5.

**Instances of:** *Joseph accuses his brethren of rendering,* Gen. 44:4. *Israelites render to Moses,* Ex. 5:21; 14:11; 15: 24; 16:2, 3; 17:3, 4. *Nabal, to David,* 1 Sam. 25:21. *Saul, to David,* 1 Sam. 19:1, 4, 5, 10. *David, to Uriah,* 2 Sam. 11.

See footnote, GOOD FOR EVIL, Luke 6:27.

19
*e Innuendo*, Prov. 6:13.
*f* Psa. 69:4; John 15:25.
*g Hatred*, Prov. 15:17.
20
*h Deceit, the wicked practise*, Psa. 36:3.
21
*i Slander, instances of*, Prov. 10:18.
*j Evil Speech*, Col. 4:6.
22
*k Prayer, importunity in*, Acts 6:4.
24
*l God, judge*, Gen. 2:2.
*m God, righteousness of*, Gen. 2:2.
26
*n Prayer, imprecatory*, Acts 6:4.
28
*o Religious Testimony*, 2 Thess. 1:10.
1
*a Wicked, described*, Psa. 73:3.
*b* Rom. 3:18.

me: *neither* let them [e]wink with the eye that [f,g]hate me without a cause.[Q]

20 For they speak not peace: but they devise [h]deceitful matters against *them that are* quiet in the land.

21 Yea, they [i,j]opened their mouth wide against me, *and* said, Aha, aha, our eye hath seen *it*.

22 *This* thou hast seen, [k]O LORD: keep not silence: O LORD, be not far from me.

23 [k]Stir up thyself, and awake to my judgment, *even* unto my cause, my God and my LORD.

24 [k,l]Judge me, O LORD my God, according to thy [m]righteousness; and let them not rejoice over me.

25 Let them not say in their hearts, Ah, so would we have it: let them not say, We have swallowed him up.

26 [n]Let them be ashamed and brought to confusion[C] together that rejoice at mine hurt: let them be clothed with shame and dishonour that magnify *themselves* against me.

27 Let them shout for joy, and be glad, that favour my righteous cause: yea, let them say continually, Let the LORD be magnified, which hath pleasure in the prosperity of his servant.

28 And my tongue shall [o]speak of thy [m]righteousness *and* of thy [d]praise all the day long.

## PSALM 36

*The transgression of the wicked, 5 and the mercy of the Lord contrasted. 10 A prayer for the continuance of God's lovingkindness to the upright.*

To the chief Musician, A Psalm of David, the servant of the Lord.

THE transgression of the wicked saith within my heart, *that* [a]*there is* [b]no fear of God before his eyes.[Q]

2 [a]For he [c]flattereth himself in his own eyes, [1]until his iniquity be found to be hateful.

3 [a]The words of his mouth *are* iniquity and *,[d]deceit: [a]he hath left[C] off to be wise, *and* to do good.

4 [a]He [e]deviseth mischief upon his bed; [a]he setteth himself in a way *that is* not good; [a]he abhorreth not evil.

5 Thy [f]mercy, O LORD, *is* in the heavens; *and* thy [g]faithfulness *reacheth* unto the clouds.

6 Thy [h]righteousness *is* like [2]the great mountains; thy judgments *are* a great deep: O LORD,[i]thou [j]preservest man and [k]beast.[S]

7 How excellent *is* thy [l]lovingkindness, O God! therefore the children of men [3]put their [m]trust under the shadow of thy wings.[S]

8 [n]They shall be abundantly satisfied with the fatness of thy [o]house; and thou shalt make [p]them drink of the [q,r]river of thy pleasures.

9 For with [s]thee *is* the [t]fountain of life: in thy [u]light shall we see [v]light.[S T Q]

10 [w]O continue thy [x]lovingkindness unto them that know thee; and thy [h]righteousness to the upright in heart.

11 [y]Let not the foot of pride come against me, and let not the hand of the wicked remove me.

12 There are the workers of iniquity fallen: [z]they are cast down, and shall not be able to rise.

## PSALM 37

*An exhortation to patience and confidence in God, in view of the different estate of the righteous and the wicked.*

A Psalm of David.

FRET not thyself because of evildoers, [a]neither be thou [b]envious against the workers of iniquity.

2
*c False Confidence*, Psa. 30:6.
1 R. V. That his iniquity shall not be found out and be hated.
3
*d Falsehood, practised by the wicked*, Job 21:34.
4
*e Malice*, Eph. 4:31.
5
*f God, mercy of*, Gen. 2:2.
*g God, faithfulness of*, Gen. 2:2.
6
*h God, righteousness of*, Gen. 2:2.
*i God, providence of*, Gen. 2:2.
*j Temporal Blessings, from God*, Psa. 103:2.
*k Animals, God's care of*, Jer. 27:5.
2 R. V. the mountains of God;
7
*l God, goodness of*, Gen. 2:2.
*m Faith*, Mark 11:22.
3 R. V. take refuge
8
*n Promise, to the righteous*, 2 Cor. 1:20.
*o Church, privileges of*, Matt. 16:18.
*p Righteous, happiness of*, Psa. 64:10.
*q River, figurative*, Psa. 46:4.
*r Salvation*, Acts 16:17.
9
*s God, savior*, Gen. 2:2.
*t Fountain, figurative*, Zech. 13:1.
*u Light, figurative*, Matt. 5:14.
*v Wisdom, spiritual, from God*, Prov. 2:2.
10
*w Prayer, intercessory*, Acts 6:4.
*x God, love of*, Gen. 2:2.
*y Prayer, in adversity*, Acts 6:4.
12
*z Wicked, punishment of*, Psa. 73:3.
1
*a Commandment, forbidding envy*, Deut. 8:2.
*b Envy, forbidden*, Prov. 14:30.

* **DECEIT,** Jer. 17:9; Mark 7:21, 22; Rom. 1:29. *Admonitions against*, 1 Pet. 2:1; 3:10. *Forbidden*, Prov. 24:28. *The psalmist's aversion to workers of*, Psa. 101:7; 120:2. *The righteous free from*, Job 27:4; Psa. 24:4, 5; 32:2; Isa. 53:9; Zeph. 3:13; 1 Pet. 2:22. *The wicked practise*, Job 15:35; Psa. 10:7; 35:20; 36:3; 38:12; 43:1; Prov. 11:18; 12:5, 17; 14:8, 25; 26:24–26; 27:6; Jer. 5:27; 9:5, 6, 8; 14:14; Rom. 3:13; 2 Cor. 11:13; 2 Tim. 3:13; 2 John 7. *The Lord abhors workers of*, Psa. 5:6. *Punishment for*, Psa. 55:23; 119:118; Prov. 20:17.

**2**
c *Wicked, death of,* Psa. 73:3.
d *Death, of the wicked,* Num. 23:10.

**3**
e *Faith, enjoined,* Mark 11:22.
f *Commandment, enjoining trust,* Deut. 8:2.
1 Am. R. V. Dwell in the land, and feed on his faithfulness.

**4**
g *Love, of man for God,* 1 John 4:19.
h *Righteous, promises to,* Psa. 64: 10.
i *Promise, to the righteous,* vs. 4–6; 2 Cor. 1:20.
j *Spiritual Desire,* Psa. 42:1.
k *Prayer, answer to, promised,* Acts 6:4.

**5**
l *Anxiety, remedy for,* 1 Pet. 5:7.

**6**
m *Righteousness,* Psa. 15:2.

**7**
n *Contentment, enjoined,* 1 Tim. 6:6.
o *Patience, enjoined,* Luke 8:15.

**8**
p *Commandment, enjoining restraint of temper,* Deut. 8:2.
2 R. V. it tendeth only to evil-doing.

**9**
q *Wicked, punishment of,* Psa. 73:3.

**11**
r *Meekness,* Psa. 45:4.
s Matt. 5:5.
t *Spiritual Peace, assured to the righteous,* Gal. 1:3.

**12**
u *Wicked, described,* Psa. 73:3.
v *Conspiracy,* 1 Kin. 16:9.

**13**
w *Anthropomorphisms,* Gen. 11:5.

2 For [c]they shall soon be [d]cut
down like the grass, and wither
as the green herb.
3 [s] [e,f]Trust in the LORD, and
do good; [1]*so* shalt thou dwell in
the land, and verily thou shalt
be fed.
4 [g]Delight thyself also in the
LORD; and [h,i]he shall give thee
the [j,k]desires of thine heart.[Q]
5 [l]Commit thy way unto the
LORD; [e,f]trust also in him; and
he shall bring *it* to pass.
6 And he shall bring forth thy
[m]righteousness as the light, and
thy judgment[C] as the noonday.
7 [f,l,n]Rest in the LORD, and
[o]wait patiently for him: fret not
thyself because of him who
prospereth in his way, because
of the man who bringeth
wicked devices to pass.
8 [p]Cease from *anger, and forsake wrath: fret not thyself [2]in
any wise[C] to do evil.
9 For evildoers [q]shall be cut[C]
off: but [h,i]those that wait upon
the LORD, they shall inherit the
earth.[s]
10 For yet a little while, and
the [q]wicked *shall* not *be*: yea,
thou shalt diligently consider his
place, and it *shall* not *be*.
11 But [h,i]the [r,s]meek shall inherit the earth; and shall delight themselves in the abundance of [t]peace.[Q]
12 The [u]wicked [v]plotteth
against the just, and gnasheth
upon him with his teeth.[Q]
13 The LORD shall [w]laugh at
him: for he seeth that his day is
coming.

14 The wicked have drawn out
the sword, and have bent their
bow, to [x]cast down the poor and
needy, *and* to slay such as be [3]of
upright conversation.[C]
15 Their sword shall enter into
their own heart, and their bows
shall be broken.
16 A [y]little that a righteous man
hath *is* better than the [z]riches of
many wicked.
17 For the arms of the wicked
shall be [a]broken: but the LORD
[b,c]upholdeth the righteous.[s]
18 The LORD [d]knoweth the
days of the upright: and their
inheritance shall be for ever.[s]
19[s] They shall not be ashamed
in the evil time: and in the days
of [e]famine they shall be satisfied.
20 But the wicked shall [a]perish,
and the enemies of the LORD
*shall be* as the [4]fat of lambs:
they shall consume; into smoke
shall they consume away.
21 The wicked [f]borroweth, and
[g]payeth not again: but the righteous sheweth mercy,[C] and giveth.
22 For *such as be* [h]blessed of
him shall inherit the earth; and
*they that be* cursed of him shall
be [c]cut off.[s]
23 [5,i,j]The steps of a *good* man
are ordered by the LORD: and
he delighteth in his way.[s]
24 [i,j]Though he fall, he shall
not be utterly cast down: for the
LORD [b,c]upholdeth *him with* his
hand.[s]
25 I have been young, and *now*
am old; yet have I not seen the
righteous forsaken, nor his seed
[k]begging bread.[s]

**14**
x *Poor, oppression of,* Prov. 21:13.
3 R. V. upright in the way:

**16**
y *Poverty,* Prov. 30:8.
z *Riches,* Eccl. 4:8.

**17**
a *Wicked, punishment of,* Psa. 73:3.
b *God, preserver,* Gen. 2:2.
c *Spiritual Blessings, from God,* Eph. 1:3.

**18**
d *God, knowledge of,* Gen. 2:2.

**19**
e *Famine, righteous delivered from,* 2 Kin. 8:1.

**20**
4 R. V. excellency of the pastures:

**21**
f *Borrowing,* Ex. 22:14.
g *Dishonesty, in not paying debts,* Ezek. 22:13.

**22**
h *God, providence of,* v. 23; Gen. 2:2.

**23**
i *Promise, or ground of assurance, to the righteous,* 2 Cor. 1:20.
j *Righteous, promises to,* vs. 23–26; Psa. 64:10.
5 Am. R. V. A man's goings are established of Jehovah;

**25**
k *Beggars,* Luke 16:20.

* **ANGER,** Psa. 55:3; Prov. 15:1, 10; 29:9, 22; 30:33; Amos 1:11; Gal. 5:19–21.
*Described,* Prov. 14:17, 29; 16:14; 19:12; 27:3, 4.
*Forbidden,* Psa. 37:8; Prov. 17:14; 22:24, 25; Eccl. 7:9; Jonah 4:4; 2 Cor. 12:20; Eph. 4:31; Col. 3:8; 1 Tim. 2:8; Tit. 1:7.
*Restraint of,* Prov. 16:32; 19:11; 29:11; Eph. 4:26; Jas. 1: 19, 20. *Punished,* Prov. 19:19; Matt. 5.22.
**Instances of:** *Cain, toward Abel,* Gen. 4:5–8. *Simeon and Levi, on account of the humbling of their sister, Dinah,* Gen. 49: 5–7. *Pharaoh, toward Moses,* Ex. 10:11, 28. *Moses, toward Pharaoh,* Ex. 11:8; *toward Israel,* Ex. 32:19; Num. 20:10, 11; *toward the sons of Aaron,* Lev. 10:16. *Ephraimites, toward Gideon, for not soliciting their aid against the Midianites,* Judg. 8:1. *Jonathan, on account of Saul's persecution of David,* 1 Sam. 20: 34. *Saul, toward Ammonites,* 1 Sam. 11:6; *toward Jonathan,* 1 Sam. 20:30–34. *Ahab, because Naboth would not sell his vineyard,* 1 Kin. 21:4. *Naaman, because Elisha directed him to wash in the Jordan,* 2 Kin. 5:12. *Asa, because the prophet reproved him,* 2 Chr. 16:10. *Ephraimites, toward Judah,* 2 Chr. 25:10. *Uzziah, toward Azariah, the priest, because of his reproof,* 2 Chr. 26:19. *Ahasuerus, toward Vashti,* Esth. 1:12. *Haman, because Mordecai did not salute him,* Esth. 3:5. *Elihu, toward Job and his three friends, because Job had beaten his friends in argument,* Job 32:2, 3. *Nebuchadnezzar, on account of the insubordination of the three Hebrews who refused to worship his idol,* Dan. 3:13, 19. *Jonah, at the mercy of God in saving Nineveh, and because the gourd withered,* Jonah 4:1–11. *Herod, toward the wise men who deceived him,* Matt. 2:16. *People of Nazareth, toward Jesus,* Luke 4:28. *Jews, toward Stephen,* Acts 7:54–58.

26 [l]*He is* ever [m]merciful, and [n]lendeth; and his [o]seed[G] *is* blessed.[S]

27 [p,q]Depart from [r]evil, and [s]do good; and dwell for evermore.[S]

28 For the LORD loveth judgment,[G] and [i,j,t]forsaketh not his saints; [i,j]they are preserved for ever: but the [u]seed of the wicked shall be cut off.[S]

29 [i,j]The righteous shall inherit the land, and dwell therein for ever.

30 The mouth of the righteous [v]speaketh wisdom, and his tongue talketh of judgment.[G]

31 [w]The [x]law of his God *is* in his heart; none of his steps shall slide.[G]

32[S] The wicked watcheth the righteous, and [y]seeketh to [z]slay him.

33 [a]The LORD will not leave him in his hand, nor condemn him when he is judged.

34 Wait on the LORD, and [b]keep his way, and [a]he shall exalt thee to inherit the land: when the wicked are [c]cut off, thou shalt see *it*.[S]

35 I have seen the [d]wicked in great power, and spreading himself like a green [6]bay tree.

36 [7]Yet he passed away, and, lo, he *was* not: yea, I sought him, but he could not be found.

37 Mark the perfect *man*, and behold the upright: for the [e]end of *that* man *is* peace.

38 But the transgressors shall be [c]destroyed together: the end of the wicked shall be cut off.

39 But the [f]salvation of the righteous *is* of the [g]LORD: [h]*he is* their [8,i]strength in the time of trouble.[S]

40 And [a,h]the LORD shall [j]help them, and deliver them: he shall deliver them from the wicked, and save them, because they [k]trust in him.

**26**
l *Righteous, described*, Psa. 64:10.
m *Mercy, a grace of the godly*, Deut. 5:10.
n *Lending*, Deut. 15:2.
o *Children, of the righteous, blessed of God*, Mark 10:14.
**27**
p *Commandment, enjoining abstinence from evil*, Deut. 8:2.
q *Holiness, enjoined*, Ex. 39:30.
r *Evil, to be eschewed*, 1 Thess. 5:22.
s *Works, good*, 2 Tim. 1:9.
**28**
t *God, faithfulness of* Gen. 2:2.
u *Children, involved in sins of parents*, Mark 10:14.
**30**
v *Speech, wise*, Col. 4:6.
**31**
w *Righteous, described*, Psa. 64:10.
x *Word of God*, Psa. 119:9.
**32**
y *Persecution, of the righteous*, John 15:20.
z *Homicide, felonious*, Deut. 5:17.

**33**
a *Promise, to the righteous*, 2 Cor. 1:20.
**34**
b *Commandment, enjoining obedience*, Deut. 8:2.
c *Wicked, punishment of*, Psa. 73:3.
**35**
d *Wicked, prosperity of*, Psa. 73:3.
6 R. V. tree in its native soil.
**36**
7 R. V. But one passed by, and,
**37**
e *Death, of the righteous*, Num. 23:10.
**39**
f *Salvation*, Acts 16:17.
g *God, savior*, Gen. 2:2.
h *Righteous, promises to*, Psa. 64:10.
i *Spiritual Blessings, from God*, Eph. 1:3.
8 R. V. strong hold
**40**
j *God, preserver*, Gen. 2:2.
k *Faith*, Mark 11:22.

## PSALM 38

*The psalmist, in sore distress of body and mind, confesses his sins, and implores help of God.*

A Psalm of David, to bring to remembrance.

[a]O LORD, rebuke me not in thy [b]wrath: neither [c]chasten me in thy hot displeasure.

2 [a]For thine [d]arrows stick fast[G] in me, and thy hand presseth me sore.[G]

3 [a]*There is* [e]no soundness in my flesh because of thine [b]anger; neither *is there any* [1]rest in my bones because of my [f]sin.

4 [g,h]For mine iniquities are gone over mine head: [i]as an heavy burden they are too heavy for me.

5 [h]My wounds stink *and* are corrupt because of my foolishness.

6 [h,i]I am troubled; I am bowed down greatly; I go mourning all the day long.

7 For my loins are filled with [2]a loathsome [j]*disease*: and *there is* no soundness in my flesh.

8 [a]I am feeble and sore broken: I have roared[G] by reason of the disquietness of my heart.

9 [a]Lord, all my desire *is* before thee; and my groaning [k]is not hid from thee.[S]

10 [a]My heart panteth, my strength faileth me: as for the light of mine eyes, it also is gone from me.

11 My lovers and my friends [l]stand aloof from my sore; and my kinsmen stand afar off.[Q]

12 They also that [m]seek after my life lay snares *for me*: and they that seek my hurt [n]speak mischievous things, and imagine [o]deceits all the day long.

13 But I, as a deaf *man*, heard not; and *I was* as a dumb man *that* [p]openeth not his mouth.

14 Thus I was as a man that heareth not, and [p]in whose mouth *are* no reproofs.

**1**
a *Prayer, in adversity*, vs. 1–22; Acts 6:4.
b *Anger of God*, 2 Kin. 13:3.
c *Divine Chastisement*, Job 33:19.
**2**
d *Arrow, figurative*, 1 Sam. 20:20.
**3**
e *Afflictions, from God*, Psa. 34:19.
f *Sin, confession of*, Rom. 5:12.
1 R. V. health
**4**
g *Prayer, confession in*, Acts 6:4.
h *Repentance, instances of*, Mark 1:4.
i *Remorse, instances of*, Matt. 27:3.
**7**
j *Disease*, Ex. 15:26.
2 R. V. burning;
**9**
k *God, knowledge of*, Gen. 2:2.
**11**
l *Selfishness*, 2 Tim. 3:2.
**12**
m *Malice*, Eph. 4:31.
n *Slander*, Prov. 10:18.
o *Deceit*, Psa. 36:3
**13**
p *Meekness, instances of*, Psa. 45:4.

15
q *Hope*, Prov. 13:12.
r *Faith, exemplified*, Mark 11:22.

18
s *Conviction of Sin*, John 16:8.

19
t *Hatred*, Prov. 15:17.

20
u *Persecution, of the righteous*, John 15:20.
v *Evil for Good*, Psa. 35:12.

22
w *God, preserver*, Gen. 2:2.

a *Jeduthun*, 1 Chr. 16:38.

1
b *Watchfulness, over the tongue*, Matt. 24:42.
c *Prudence, in restraining speech*, 2 Chr. 2:12.
d *Bridle, figurative*, Psa. 32:9.

3
e *Meditation*, Psa. 49:3.

4
f *Prayer, in adversity*, Acts 6:4.
g *Wisdom, prayer for spiritual*, Prov. 2:2.
h *Death, preparation for*, Num. 23:10.
i *Life, brevity and uncertainty of*, Eccl. 8:15.

5
j *Handbreadth*, 1 Kin. 7:26.
k *Measure*, Deut. 25:15.

15 [a]For in thee, O LORD, do I [q]hope: [r]thou wilt hear, O Lord my God.

16 For I said, *Hear me*, lest *otherwise* they should [m]rejoice over me: when my foot slippeth, they magnify *themselves* against me.

17 For I *am* ready to halt,[G] and my sorrow *is* continually before me.

18 For [s]I will [f]declare mine iniquity; I will [h]be sorry for my sin.[T]

19 But mine enemies *are* lively,[G] *and* they are strong: and they that [t]hate me wrongfully are multiplied.

20 They also that [u]render [v]evil for good are mine adversaries; because I follow *the thing that* good *is*.

21 [a]Forsake me not, O LORD: O my God, be not far from me.

22 Make haste to help me, O Lord [w]my salvation.

## PSALM 39

*The psalmist's purpose to take heed to his ways. 4 He prays for a sense of the brevity of life; 7 for pardon; 10 for deliverance from God's judgments.*

To the chief Musician, *even* to [a]Jeduthun, A Psalm of David.

I SAID, I will [b]take heed to my ways, that I sin not with my tongue: I will [c]keep my mouth with a [d]bridle, while the wicked is before me.[Q]

2 [c]I was dumb with silence, I held[G] my peace, *even* from good; and my sorrow was stirred.

3 My heart was hot within me, while I was [e]musing[G] the fire burned: *then* spake I with my tongue,

4 [f]LORD, [g]make me to know mine [h]end, and the measure of my days, what it *is*; *that* I may know [i]how frail I *am*.

5 Behold, thou hast made my [i]days *as* an [j,k]handbreadth; and mine age *is* as nothing before thee: verily every man at his best state *is* altogether vanity. [Sē'lah.

6 Surely every man walketh in a vain shew: surely they are [l]disquieted in vain: he heapeth up [m]*riches*, and knoweth not who shall gather them.

7 And now, Lord, what wait I for? my [n,o]hope *is* in thee.

8 [f,p,q]Deliver me from all my transgressions: make me not the reproach of the foolish.

9 [r]I was dumb, I opened not my mouth, because thou didst *it*.

10 [f]Remove thy [s]stroke away from me: I am consumed by the blow of thine hand.

11 When thou with rebukes dost [t]correct man for iniquity, thou makest his [u]beauty to consume away like a [v]moth: surely every man *is* vanity. [Sē'lah.

12 [w]Hear my prayer, O LORD, and give [x]ear unto my cry; hold not thy peace at my [y]tears: for I *am* a stranger with thee, *and* a sojourner, as all my fathers *were*.[Q]

13 [w]O spare me, that I may recover strength, before I go hence, and be no more.

## PSALM 40

*The psalmist's acknowledgment of God's goodness. 6 His purpose to do God's will. 11 His prayer for help in trouble.*

To the chief Musician, A Psalm of David.

[a,b]I [c,d]WAITED patiently for the LORD; and he inclined unto me, and [e]heard my cry.

2 [a,f]He brought me up also out of an horrible [g]pit, out of the [h]miry [i]clay, and set my feet upon a [j]rock, *and* established my goings.

3 And [a,f]he hath put a new [k]song in my mouth, *even* [l]praise unto our God: many shall see *it*, and fear, and shall [m]trust in the LORD.[Q]

4 [n]Blessed *is* that man that maketh the LORD his [m]trust,

6
l *Anxiety*, 1 Pet. 5:7.
m *Riches*, Eccl. 4:8.

7
n *Faith, instances of*, Mark 11:22.
o *Hope, in God*, Prov. 13:12.

8
p *Repentance*, Mark 1:4.
q *Sin, forgiveness of*, Rom. 5:12.

9
r *Afflictions, resignation in, exemplified*, Psa. 34:19.

10
s *Afflictions, from God*, Psa. 34:19

11
t *Divine Chastisement*, Job 33:19.
u *Beauty, vanity of*, Prov. 6:25.
v *Moth*, Job 4:19.

12
w *Prayer, importunity in*, Acts 6:4.
x *Ear, figurative*, Lev. 8:23.
y *Tears*, Psa. 6:6.

1
a *Religious Testimony, exemplified*, 2 Thess. 1:10.
b *Spiritual Desire*, Psa. 42:1.
c *Adversity, prayer in*, Psa. 10:6.
d *Prayer, in adversity*, Acts 6:4.
e *Prayer, answered*, Acts 6:4.

2
f *Thankfulness, to God, exemplified*, Acts 24:3.
g *Pit, figurative*, Psa. 7:15.
h Psa. 69:2.
i *Clay, figurative*, Job 33:6.
j *Rock, figurative*, Psa. 78:15.

3
k *Song*, Psa. 77:6.
l *Praise*, Psa. 150:1.
m *Faith*, Mark 11:22.

4
n *Spiritual Peace*, Gal. 1:3.

*o Pride,* Prov. 16:18.
*p Falsehood,* Job 21:34.

**5**
*q God, providence of,* Gen. 2:2.

**6**
*r* Heb. 10:5–7.
*s Obedience better than Sacrifice,* vs. 6–9; 1 Sam. 15: 22.
*t Ear, figurative of the understanding,* Lev. 8:23.
*u Offerings, burnt,* Lev. 6:17.
*v Offerings, sin,* Lev. 6:17.
1 R. V. hast no delight in;

**7**
*w Jesus, prophecies concerning* (according to many interpreters), Matt. 1:21.
*x Word of God,* Psa. 119:9.

**8**
*y Zeal, exemplified,* 2 Cor. 7:11.
*z Obedience, exemplified,* Heb. 5:8.
*a Will of God,* Mark 3:35.

**9**
*b Religious Testimony,* 2 Thess. 1:10.
*c Instruction, in religion,* Prov. 23:23.
*d Righteousness,* Psa. 15:2.

**10**
*e God, righteousness of,* Gen. 2:2.
*f God, faithfulness of,* Gen. 2:2.
*g God, mercy of,* Gen. 2:2.
*h God, truth,* Gen. 2:2.

**12**
*i Conscience, guilty,* Acts 23:1.
*j Repentance, instances of,* Mark 1:4.
*k Sin, confession of,* Rom. 5:12.

**13**
*l Prayer, in adversity,* Acts 6:4.

**14**
*m Prayer, imprecatory,* Acts 6:4.

and respecteth not the [o]proud, nor such as turn aside to [p]lies.

5 Many, O LORD my God, *are* thy [q]wonderful *works *which* thou hast done, and thy thoughts *which are* to us-ward: they cannot be reckoned up in order unto thee: *if* I would declare and speak *of them,* they are more than can be numbered.

6 [r,s]Sacrifice and offering thou [1]didst not desire; mine [t]ears hast thou opened: [u]burnt offering and [v]sin offering hast thou not required.

7 [r]Then said [w]I, Lo, I come: in the volume of the [x]book *it is* written of me,

8 [r]I [y]delight to [z]do thy [a]will, O my God: yea, thy law *is* within my heart.

9 I have [b,c]preached [d]righteousness in the great congregation: lo, I have not refrained my lips, O LORD, thou knowest.

10 I have not hid thy [e]righteousness within my heart; I have [b]declared thy [f]faithfulness and thy salvation: I have not concealed thy [g]lovingkindness and thy [h]truth from the great congregation.

11 Withhold not thou thy tender [g]mercies from me, O LORD: let thy lovingkindness and thy [h]truth continually preserve me.

12 For innumerable evils have compassed me about: [i,j]mine [k]iniquities have taken hold upon me, so that I am not able to look up; they are more than the hairs of mine head: therefore my heart faileth me.

13 [l]Be pleased, O LORD, to deliver me: O LORD, make haste to help me.

14 [m]Let them be ashamed and confounded together that seek after my soul to destroy it; let them be driven backward and put to shame that [2]wish me evil.

15 [m]Let them be desolate [3]for a reward of their shame that say unto me, Aha, aha.

16 Let all those that [n]seek thee [o]rejoice and be glad in thee: let such as love thy salvation say continually, [p]The LORD be magnified.

17 But [q]I *am* poor and needy; [r]*yet* the LORD thinketh upon me: [s]thou *art* my help and my deliverer; make no tarrying, O my God.

## PSALM 41

*The blessedness of the man who cares for the poor. 4 The psalmist complains of the malice of enemies and the treachery of friends. 10 His prayer for succor. 13 Praise to God.*

To the chief Musician, A Psalm of David.

[a]BLESSED *is* he that [b,c]considereth the [d]poor: [e,f]the LORD will [g]deliver him in time of trouble.

2 [e,f]The LORD will [g]preserve him, and keep him alive; *and* he shall be blessed upon the earth: and thou wilt not deliver him unto the will of his enemies.

3 The LORD will [h]strengthen him upon the bed of languishing: thou wilt make all his bed in his sickness.

4 I said, LORD, be merciful unto me: heal my soul; for [i,j]I have sinned against thee.

5 Mine enemies [k,l,m,n]speak evil of me, When shall he die, and his name perish?

6 And if he come to see *me,* he [n]speaketh vanity: his heart gathereth iniquity to itself; *when* he goeth abroad, he [m]telleth *it.*

7 All that [o]hate me whisper together against me: against me do they devise my hurt.

8 An evil [p]disease, *say they,* cleaveth fast unto him: and *now* that he lieth he shall rise up no more.

2 R. V. delight in my hurt.

**15**
3 R. V. by reason of

**16**
*n Seekers,* Isa. 55:6.
*o Joy,* Psa. 5:11.
*p Praise,* Psa. 150:1.

**17**
*q Humility,* Prov. 22:4.
*r Faith, exemplified,* Mark 11:22.
*s God, preserver,* Gen. 2:2.

**1**
*a Righteous, happiness of,* Psa. 64: 10.
*b Liberality,* vs. 1–3; 1 Tim. 6:18.
*c Mercy,* Deut. 5:10.
*d Poor, duty to,* Prov. 21:13.
*e Promise, to the merciful,* vs. 1–3; 2 Cor. 1:20.
*f Righteous, promises to,* Psa. 64: 10.
*g God, preserver,* Gen. 2:2.

**3**
*h Afflictions, consolation in,* Psa. 34:19.

**4**
*i Repentance, instances of,* Mark 1:4.
*j Sin, confession of,* Rom. 5:12.

**5**
*k False Accusation,* 2 Tim. 3:3.
*l Malice,* Eph. 4:31.
*m Slander, instances of,* Prov. 10: 18.
*n Speech, evil,* Col. 4:6.

**7**
*o Hatred,* Prov. 15:17.

**8**
*p Disease,* Ex. 15:26.

* **WORKS OF GOD.** *In creation,* Job 9:8, 9; Psa. 8:3–5; 89:11; 136:5–9; 139:13, 14; 148:4, 5; Eccl. 3:11; Jer. 10:12; *good,* Gen. 1:10, 18, 21, 25. *Faithful,* Psa. 33:4. *Wonderful,* Psa. 26:7; 40:5. *Incomparable,* Psa. 86:8. *In his overruling providence in the affairs of men,* Psa. 26:7; 40:5; 66:3; 75:1; 111:2, 4, 6; 118:17; 145:4–17.

9
q *Friends, false,* Ex. 33:11.
r John 13:18.
s *Infidelity, of friends,* 2 Cor. 6:15.
t *Ingratitude, of man to man,* Rom. 1:21.
10
u *Prayer, in adversity,* Acts 6:4.
11
v *Faith, exemplified,* Mark 11:22.
w *Grace of God,* Rom. 4:16.
12
x *Integrity,* Job 2:3.
13
y *Praise,* Psa. 150:1.
z *God, eternity of,* Gen. 2:2.
1
a *Brook,* Deut. 8:7.
b *Seekers,* Isa. 55:6.
2
c *Zeal,* 2 Cor. 7:11.
d *Thirst, figurative,* John 4:14.
3
e *Tears,* Psa. 6:6.
f *Persecution, of the righteous,* John 15:20.
g *Infidelity,* 2 Cor. 6:15.
h *Scoffing,* Hab. 1:10.
4
i *Church, called house of God,* 1 Kin. 9:3.
j *Worship,* Gen. 22:5.
k *Joy,* Psa. 5:11.
l *Praise,* Psa. 150:1.
5
m *Doubting,* Rom. 14:23.
n *Despondency,* Eccl. 2:20.
o *Hope,* Prov. 13:12.
p *Afflictions, consolation in,* Psa. 34:19.
q *Faith, exemplified,* Mark 11:22.
6
r *Afflictions, prayer in,* Psa. 34:19.

9 Yea, mine own familiar
[q]friend, in whom I trusted,
[r]which did eat of my bread, hath
[s,t]lifted up *his* heel against me.[Q]
10 [u]But thou, O LORD, be
merciful unto me, and raise me
up, that I may requite them.
11 [v]By this I know that thou
[w]favourest me, because mine enemy doth not triumph over me.[S]
12 And as for me, [v]thou up-
holdest me in mine [x]integrity,
and settest me before thy face
for ever.[S]
13 [y]Blessed *be* the LORD God
of Ĭş'ra-el from [z]everlasting,
and to everlasting. Amen, and
Amen.[S Q]

## PSALM 42

*The psalmist ardently desires to worship in the temple. 5 He encourages himself to trust in God.*

To the chief Musician, Maschil, for the sons of Korah.

AS the hart panteth after the
water [a]brooks, so *,[b]pant-
eth my soul after thee, O God.
2 *,[c]My soul [d]thirsteth for God,
for the living God: when shall I
come and appear before God?[Q]
3 My [e]tears have been my meat[G]
day and night, while they continually [f]say unto me, [g,h]Where
*is* thy God?
4 When I remember these
*things,* I pour out my soul in me:
for I had gone with the multitude, I went with them to the
[i]house of God, [j]with the voice of
[k]joy and [l]praise, with a multitude that kept holyday.[G]
5 Why art thou [m,n]cast[G] down,
O my soul? and *why* art thou
disquieted in me? [o]hope thou in
God: [p,q]for I shall yet praise him
*for* the help of his countenance.[Q]
6 [r]O my God, my soul[G] is [n]cast
down within me: therefore will I
remember thee from the land of
Jôr'dan, and of the Hēr'mon-
ītes, from the hill Mī'zar.
7 Deep calleth unto deep at the
noise of thy waterspouts: all thy
waves and thy billows are gone
over me.
8 [q]*Yet* the LORD will command
his [s]lovingkindness in the daytime, and in the night his song
*shall be* with me, *and* my prayer
unto the God of my life.[S]
9 I will say unto God my [t]rock,
[u]Why hast thou forgotten me?
why go I mourning because of
the [v]oppression of the enemy?
10 *As* with a sword in my
bones, mine enemies reproach
me; while they [f]say daily unto
me, [g,h]Where *is* thy God?
11 Why art thou [m,n]cast[G] down,
O my soul? and why art thou
disquieted within me? [o]hope
thou in God: [p,q]for I shall yet
praise him, *who is* the health[G] of
my [w]countenance[G], and my God.[Q]

## PSALM 43

*The psalmist prays to be restored to the temple, 5 and upbraids himself for his despondency.*

[a,b]JUDGE me, O God, and
plead my cause against
an ungodly nation: [c]O deliver
me from the [d]deceitful and [e]un-
just man.
2 [a,c]For thou *art* the God of my
strength: why dost thou cast me
off? why go I mourning because
of the [f]oppression of the enemy?
3 O send out thy [g]light and thy
[h]truth: [i]let them lead me; let
them bring me unto thy holy
hill, and to thy tabernacles.[S T]
4 Then will I go unto the [j]altar
of God, unto God my exceeding[G]
[k]joy: yea, upon the [l]harp will I
[m]praise thee, O God my God.

8
s *God, love of,* Gen. 2:2.
9
t *Rock, figurative,* Psa. 78:15.
u *Adversity, prayer in,* Psa. 10:6.
v *Oppression,* Eccl. 5:8.
11
w *Countenance,* Prov. 15:13.
1
a *Prayer, in adversity,* Acts 6:4.
b *God, judge,* Gen. 2:2.
c *Adversity, prayer in,* Psa. 10:6.
d *Deceit,* Psa. 36:3.
e *Injustice,* Isa. 26:10.
2
f *Oppression,* Eccl. 5:8.
3
g *Wisdom, prayer for,* Prov. 2:2.
h *God, truth,* Gen. 2:2.
i *Guidance, prayer for,* Psa. 48:14.
4
j *Altar,* Gen. 8:20.
k *Joy,* Psa. 5:11.
l *Harp,* Dan. 3:10.
m *Praise,* Psa. 150:1.

* **SPIRITUAL DESIRE.** *For divine pity,* Psa. 17:1; 51:1-4, 7-13; 119:82; Hab. 3:2. *For divine fellowship,* Psa. 62:1; 63:1, 8. *For divine help,* Psa. 25:5, 15; 68:28; 119:77, 116, 117.

*Exhortations concerning,* Psa. 70:4; 105:4; Isa. 55:1-3, 6; Hos. 10:12.

*For God,* Psa. 24:6; 27:8; 33:20; 40:1; 42; 69:3; 73:26; 119:10, 12, 19, 20, 25, 40, 81, 88, 123, 131, 132, 135, 136, 149, 156, 174; 123:1, 2; 130:5, 6; 143:6-12; Isa. 8:17, 19; 26:8, 9; Matt. 13:17; Luke 10:42; Phil. 3:12-14; 1 Pet. 1:10. *For his holy courts,* Psa. 84:2.

*Reward of,* Deut. 4:29; Psa. 34:10; 37:4, 9, 34; 107:9; 119:2; Prov. 2:3-5; Isa. 40:31; Jer. 29:13; Matt. 5:6; Luke 1:53; 6:21; John 6:35.

See footnotes: SPIRITUAL HUNGER, Matt. 5:6; THIRST, *Figurative,* John 4:14.

5
*n Despondency*, Eccl. 2:20.
*o Hope*, Prov. 13:12.
*p Faith, exemplified*, Mark 11:22.
*q Afflictions consolation in*, Psa. 34:19.
*r Countenance*, Prov. 15:13.

*a Music, symbols used in*, 2 Chr. 5:13.

1
*b Instruction, in religion*, Prov. 23:23.
*c God, providence of*, Gen. 2:2.

2
1 R. V. nations

3
*d Canaan*, Gen. 37:1.
*e Temporal Blessings, from God*, Psa. 103:2.
*f Grace of God*, Rom. 4:16.

4
*g God, sovereign*, Gen. 2:2.

5
*h Faith, exemplified*, Mark 11:22.

7
*i God, preserver*, Gen. 2:2.
*j Hatred*, Prov. 15:17.

8
*k Thankfulness, to God, exemplified*, Acts 24:3.

9
*l Murmuring, against God*, Num. 14:2.
2 R. V. now thou hast cast us off,

5 Why art thou [n]cast down, O my soul? and why art thou disquieted within me? [o]hope in God: [p,q]for I shall yet praise him, *who is* the health of my [r]countenance, and my God.

## PSALM 44

*The people of God remember his former mercies; 9 but complain of present evils. 17 Their profession of integrity, 23 and prayer for help.*

To the chief Musician for the sons of Korah, [a]Maschil.

WE have heard with our ears, O God, our fathers have [b]told us, *what* [c]work thou didst in their days, in the times of old.

2 *How* [c]thou didst drive out the [1]heathen with thy hand, and plantedst them; *how* thou didst afflict the people, and cast them out.

3 For they got not the [d,e]land in possession by their own sword, neither did their own arm save them: but [c]thy right hand, and thine arm, and the light of thy countenance, because thou hadst a [f]favour unto them.

4 Thou art my [g]King, O God: command deliverances for Jā′cob.

5 [h]Through thee will we push down our enemies: through thy name will we tread them under that rise up against us.

6 For I will not trust in my bow, neither shall my sword save me.

7 But [c]thou hast [i]saved us from our enemies, and hast put them to shame that [j]hated us.

8 In God we boast all the day long, and [k]praise thy name for ever. [Sē′lah.

9 [2,l]But thou hast cast off, and put us to shame; and goest not forth with our [m]armies.

10 [l]Thou makest us to turn back from the enemy: and they which hate us spoil for themselves.

11 [l]Thou hast given us like sheep *appointed* for meat: and hast [n]scattered us among the [1]heathen.

12 [l]Thou sellest thy people for nought, and dost not increase *thy wealth* by their price.

13 [l]Thou [n]makest us a reproach to our neighbours, a scorn and a derision to them that are round about us.

14 [l]Thou [n]makest us a byword among the [1]heathen, a shaking of the head among the people.

15 [3,l]My confusion *is* continually before me, and the shame of my face hath covered me,

16 For the voice of him that reproacheth and blasphemeth; by reason of the enemy and [o]avenger.

17 All this is come upon us; [p]yet have we not forgotten thee, neither have we dealt falsely in thy covenant.

18 [p]Our heart is not turned back, neither have our steps declined from thy way;

19 Though thou hast sore [n]broken us in the place of [4]dragons, and covered us with the shadow of death.

20 If we have [q]forgotten the name of our God, or [r]stretched out our hands to a strange god;

21 Shall not God search this out? for he [s]knoweth the secrets of the *heart.

22 Yea, [t]for thy sake are we [u]killed all the day long; we

*m Armies*, Deut. 11:4.

11
*n Adversity, dispensation from God*, Psa. 10:6.

15
3 R. V. All the day long is my dishonour before me,

16
*o Avenger of Blood*, Deut. 19:6.

17
*p Faithfulness*, Luke 16:10.

19
4 R. V. jackals,

20
*q Backsliders*, Jer. 3:22.
*r Idolatry*, 1 Sam. 15:23.

21
*s God, knowledge of*, Gen. 2:2.

22
*t* Rom. 8:36.
*u Persecution, of the righteous*, John 15:20.

* **HEART.** *Seat of the affections, and source of action*, Prov. 4:23; Matt. 12:33, 35; 15:18–20; 23:26; Mark 7:21–23. *Is known to God*, 1 Sam. 16:7; 1 Kin. 8:39; 2 Chr. 6:30; Psa. 44:21; 139:1–12; Prov. 21:2; Luke 16:15; Acts 1:24; 15:8; Rom. 8:27; 1 Cor. 3:20; *to Christ*, Rev. 2:23.
*Changed*, 1 Sam. 10:9; 1 Kin. 3:12.
*Hardening of, forbidden*, Heb. 3:8, 15; 4:7.
*Of the heathen, taught of God*, Rom. 2:14–16.
**Hardened:** INSTANCES OF: *Of Pharaoh*, Ex. 4:21; 7:3, 13, 22; 8:15, 32; 9:12, 35; 10:1; 14:8. *Of Hivites*, Josh. 11:19, 20.
**Regenerate:** *Is penitent*, Psa. 34:18; 51:10, 17; 147:3. *Is renewed*, Deut. 30:6; Psa. 51:10; Ezek. 11:19, 20; 18:31; 36:26; John 3:3, 7; Eph. 4:22–24; Col. 3:9, 10; Heb. 10:22; Jas. 4:8. *Is pure*, Psa. 24:4; 66:18; Prov. 20:9; Matt. 5:8; 2 Tim. 2:22; 1 Pet. 3:15. *Is enlightened*, 2 Cor. 4:6. *Is established*, Psa. 57:7; 108:1; 112:7, 8; 1 Thess. 3:13. *Is refined by affliction*, Prov. 17:3.
**Unregenerate:** *Is depraved*, Gen. 6:5; 8:21; Eccl. 9:3; Jer. 17:9; Acts 8:21–23; Rom. 1:21. *Is under the wrath of God*, Rom. 1:18, 19, 31; 2:5, 6.

are counted as sheep for the slaughter.[Q]

23 [v]Awake, why [w]sleepest thou, O Lord? arise, cast *us* not off for ever.

24 [x]Wherefore hidest[G] thou thy face,[G] *and* forgettest our [y]affliction and our [z]oppression?

25 For our soul is [a]bowed down to the dust: our [b]belly cleaveth unto the earth.

26 Arise for our help, and [c]redeem us for thy [d]mercies' sake.

## PSALM 45

*The majesty and grace of the Messiah. 10 The duties and honors of Zion.*

To the chief Musician upon Shoshannim, for the sons of Korah, [a]Maschil, A Song of loves.

A Messianic Psalm. The poet is celebrating the marriage of his king to a royal bride. The king is a warrior. He goes forth in majesty and with sword of conquest. He conquers and reigns in righteousness. The bride is glorious in person and apparel, and the people rejoice in her. The poet's lofty and inspired numbers describe the Messiah and the church, his royal bride. The conquest of the world to truth and righteousness and the marriage of the militant Prince of righteousness to his glorious bride, described by St. John (Rev. 19:7-9), is the true theme of the inspired Song.

MY heart [1]is inditing[G] a good matter: I speak of the things which I have made touching the king: my tongue *is* the [b]pen of a ready writer.

2 [c]Thou art fairer than the children of men: [d]grace is poured into thy lips: therefore God hath blessed thee for ever.[T Q]

3 Gird[G] thy sword upon *thy* thigh, O *most* mighty, [d]with thy glory and thy majesty.

4 And [d]in thy majesty ride prosperously because of [e]truth and *meekness *and* [f]righteousness; and thy right hand shall teach thee terrible[G] things.[T]

5 Thine [g]arrows *are* sharp [2]in the heart of the king's enemies; *whereby* the people fall under thee.

6 [h,i,j]Thy[T Q] [k]throne, O God, *is* for ever and ever: [3]the [l]sceptre of thy kingdom *is* a right[G] sceptre.

7 Thou lovest [f]righteousness, and [m]hatest wickedness: therefore God, thy God, hath [n]anointed thee with the oil of gladness above thy fellows.[T Q]

8 All thy garments *smell* of [o]myrrh, and †aloes, *and* [p]cassia, out of the [q]ivory palaces, [4]whereby they have made thee glad.

9 King's daughters *were* among thy honourable women: upon thy right [r]hand did stand the queen in [s]gold of [t]Ō'phĭr.

10 Hearken, O [u]daughter, and consider, and incline[G] thine ear; forget also thine own people, and thy father's house;

11 So shall the king greatly desire thy ‡beauty: for he *is* thy LORD; and worship thou him.

12 And the daughter of [v]Tȳre *shall be there* with a [w]gift; *even* the rich among the people shall intreat thy favour.[G]

13 The king's [u]daughter [5]*is* all glorious within: her clothing *is* [6]of wrought [s]gold.

14 She shall be brought unto the king in raiment of [x]needlework: the [y]virgins her companions that follow her shall be brought unto thee.

15 With [z]gladness and rejoicing shall they be brought: they shall enter into the king's palace.

**23**
*v* *Prayer, importunity in*, Acts 6:4.
*w* *Anthropomorphisms*, Gen. 11:5.

**24**
*x* *Prayer, answer to, delayed*, Acts 6:4.
*y* *Adversity, prayer in*, Psa. 10:6.
*z* *Oppression, prayer for deliverance from*, Eccl. 5:8.

**25**
*a* *Despondency*, Eccl. 2:20.
*b* *Belly*, Prov. 20:27.

**26**
*c* *God, preserver*, Gen. 2:2.
*d* *God, mercy of*, Gen. 2:2.

*a* *Music, symbols used in*, 2 Chr. 5:13.

**1**
*b* *Pen*, Jer. 8:8.
1 R. V. overfloweth with a goodly matter:

**2**
*c* *Jesus, perfections of*, Matt. 1:21.
*d* *Jesus, prophecies concerning*, Matt. 1:21.

**4**
*e* *Truth*, John 18:37.
*f* *Righteousness*, Psa. 15:2.

**5**
*g* *Arrow, figurative*, 1 Sam. 20:20.
2 R. V. The peoples fall under thee; They are in the heart of the king's enemies.

**6**
*h* Heb. 1:8, 9.
*i* *Prophecies, concerning the Messiah, and their fulfillment*, Gen. 12:3.
*j* *Jesus, prophecies concerning*, vs. 7–17; Matt. 1:21.
*k* *Throne, figurative*, 1 Kin. 2:19.
*l* *Scepter, figurative*, Esth. 4:11.
3 R. V. A sceptre of equity is the sceptre of thy kingdom.

**7**
*m* *Hatred*, Prov. 15:17.
*n* *Anointing, figurative*, Deut. 28:40.

**8**
*o* *Myrrh*, Ex. 30:23.
*p* *Cassia*, Ezek. 27:19.
*q* *Ivory*, 2 Chr. 9:17.
4 R. V. stringed instruments have

**9**
*r* *Hand, right hand, place of honor*, Ezra 10:19.
*s* *Gold*, Ezek. 7:19.
*t* *Ophir*, 1 Kin. 9:28.

**10**
*u* *Bride, figurative*, vs. 10–17; Isa. 49:18.

**12**
*v* *Tyre*, Josh. 19:29.
*w* *Marriage, bridal presents*, Gen. 34:9.

**13**
5 R. V. within the palace is all glorious:
6 R. V. inwrought with gold.

**14**
*x* *Embroidery*, Ezek. 26:16.
*y* *Virgin*, Isa. 62:5.

**15**
*z* *Joy*, Psa. 5:11.

* **MEEKNESS,** Psa. 25:9; Prov. 14:29; 15:1, 18; 19:11; 1 Cor. 13:4, 5, 7. *Advantageous*, Eccl. 7:8; 10:4. *Honorable*, Prov. 20:3. *Potent*, Prov. 25:15.
*Enjoined*, Zeph. 2:3; Matt. 5:38–41 (with Luke 6:29); 11:29; Rom. 12:14, 18; 14:19; 1 Cor. 6:7; 7:15; 2 Cor. 13:11; Gal. 6:1; Eph. 4:1, 2; Phil. 2:14, 15; Col. 3:12, 13; 1 Thess. 5:14, 15; 1 Tim. 3:3; 6:11; 2 Tim. 2:24, 25; Tit. 2:2, 9; 3:2; Heb. 10:36; 12:14; Jas. 1:4, 19, 21; 3:13; 1 Pet. 2:18–23; 3:4, 11, 15.
*A fruit of the Spirit*, Gal. 5:22, 23, 26.
*Rewards of*, Psa. 22:26; 37:11; 76:8, 9; 147:6; 149:4; Isa. 29:19; Matt. 5:5; 11:29.
**Instances of:** *Abraham*, Gen. 13:8, 9. *Isaac*, Gen. 26:20–22. *Moses*, Ex. 16:7, 8; 17:2–7; Num. 12:3; 16:4–11. *Gideon*, Judg. 8:2, 3. *Hannah*, 1 Sam. 1:13–16. *Saul*, 1 Sam. 10:27. *David*, 1 Sam. 17:29; 2 Sam. 16:9–14; Psa. 38:13, 14. *The Psalmist*, Psa. 120:5–7. *Jesus*, Isa. 11:4; 42:1–4; 53:7; Lam. 3:28–30; Matt. 11:29; 26:47–54; 27:13, 14; Mark 15:4, 5; Luke 23:34; 2 Cor. 10:1; 1 Pet. 2:21–23; see footnote, JESUS, *Humility of; Meekness of*, Matt. 1:21. *Stephen*, Acts 7:60. *Paul*, 1 Cor. 4:12, 13; 2 Cor. 12:10; 2 Tim. 4:16. *The Thessalonians*, 2 Thess. 1:4. *Job*, Jas. 5:11. *The angel*, Jude 9.
See footnotes: KINDNESS, Acts 28:2; PATIENCE, Luke 8:15.

†**ALOES.** *Used, as perfume*, Psa. 45:8; Prov. 7:17; Song 4:14; *in embalming the dead*, John 19:39. *Lign-aloes*, Num. 24:6.

‡ **BEAUTY. Spiritual,** 1 Chr. 16:29; Psa. 27:4; 29:2; 45:11; 90:17; 110:3; Isa. 52:7; Ezek. 16:14; Zech. 9:17.

16 Instead of thy fathers shall be thy children, whom thou mayest make princes in all the earth.

17 I will make [a]thy name to be remembered in all generations: therefore shall the people praise thee for ever and ever.

## PSALM 46

*Zion's confidence in God. 8 An exhortation to behold the works of the Lord.*

To the chief Musician for the sons of Korah, A Song upon Alamoth.

[a]GOD *is* our [b]refuge and strength, [c]a very present help in trouble.

2 Therefore [d]will not we fear, though the earth [1]be removed, and though the mountains be carried into the midst of the sea;

3 *Though* the waters thereof roar *and* be troubled, *though* the mountains [e]shake with the swelling thereof. [Sē'lah.

4 *There is* a *river, the streams whereof shall make [f]glad the [g]city of God, the holy *place* of the tabernacles of the most High.

5 God *is* in the midst of her; she shall not be moved: God shall help her, *and that* right early.

6 The [2]heathen raged, the kingdoms were moved: [h]he uttered his voice, the earth melted.

7 [a]The LORD of hosts *is* with us; [a]the God of Jā'cob *is* our [i]refuge. [Sē'lah.

8 Come, behold the works of the LORD, what [j]desolations he hath made in the earth.

9 [k]He [l]maketh [m]wars to cease unto the end of the earth; he breaketh the [n]bow, and cutteth the [o]spear in sunder; he burneth the [p]chariot in the fire.

10 Be still, and know that I *am* God: I will be exalted among the [2,q]heathen, I will be exalted in the earth.

**17**
*a Jesus, prophecies concerning,* Matt. 1:21.

**1**
*a Faith, exemplified,* Mark 11:22.
*b God, preserver,* Gen. 2:2.
*c Adversity, consolation in,* Psa. 10:6.

**2**
*d Assurance,* Heb. 10:22.
1 R. V. do change,

**3**
*e Earthquakes,* Isa. 29:6.

**4**
*f Joy,* Psa. 5:11.
*g Church, prophecies concerning. prosperity,* Matt. 16:18.

**6**
*h God, power of,* Gen. 2:2.
2 R. V. nations

**7**
*i God, preserver,* Gen. 2:2.

**8**
*j Judgments,* Ex. 6:6.

**9**
*k Jesus, kingdom of, prophecies concerning,* Matt. 1:21.
*l Peace,* Jer. 29:7.
*m War, to cease,* Judg. 3:2.
*n Bow,* 2 Sam. 1:18.
*o Spear,* 2 Kin. 11:10.
*p Chariot,* Josh. 11:4.

**10**
*q Gentiles, prophecies of the conversion of,* Acts 10:45.

11 [a]The LORD of hosts *is* with us; [a]the God of Jā'cob *is* our [i]refuge. [Sē'lah.

## PSALM 47

*The nations exhorted to praise God.*

To the chief Musician, A Psalm for the sons of Korah.

[a]O CLAP your hands, all ye people; [b]shout unto God with the voice of triumph.

2 For the LORD [1]most high *is* terrible; *he is* a great [c]King over all the earth.

3 [d]He shall subdue the people under us, and the nations under our feet.

4 He shall choose our inheritance for us, the excellency of Jā'cob whom he [e]loved. [Sē'lah.

5 God is gone up with a shout, the LORD with the sound of a trumpet.

6 Sing [a]praises to God, sing praises: sing praises unto our [c]King, sing praises.

7 For God *is* the [c]King of all the earth: sing ye [a]praises with understanding.

8 [c]God reigneth over the [2]heathen: God sitteth upon the [f]throne of his holiness.

9 The princes of the people are gathered together, *even* the people of the God of Ā'brā-hăm: for the shields of the earth *belong* unto God: he is greatly exalted.

## PSALM 48

*A song of thanksgiving to God for his protection of Zion.*

A Song *and* Psalm for the sons of Korah.

GREAT *is* the LORD, and greatly to be [a]praised in the city of our God, *in* [1]the mountain of his holiness.

2 Beautiful for situation, the joy of the whole earth, *is* mount [b]Zī'ŏn, *on* the sides of the north, the [c]city of the great King.

3 God is known in her palaces for a [d]refuge.

**1**
*a Praise,* Psa. 150:1.
*b Shouting,* 2 Chr. 15:14.

**2**
*c God, sovereign,* Gen. 2:2.
1 R. V. Most High

**3**
*d Faith, exemplified,* Mark 11:22.

**4**
*e God, love of,* Gen. 2:2.

**8**
*f Throne, figurative,* 1 Kin. 2:19.
2 R. V. nations:

**1**
*a Praise,* Psa. 150:1.
1 R. V. his holy mountain.

**2**
*b Zion,* 2 Sam. 5:7.
*c Jerusalem,* Judg. 19:10.

**3**
*d God, preserver,* Gen. 2:2.

* **RIVER,** Isa. 32:2. **Figurative:** *Of salvation,* Psa. 36:8; 46:4; Ezek. 47:1–12; Rev. 22:1, 2. *Of grief,* Psa. 119:136; Lam. 3:48.

4 For, lo, the kings were assembled,[C] they passed by together.[Q]

5 They saw *it, and* so they marvelled; they were troubled, *and* hasted away.

6 Fear took hold upon them there, *and* pain, as of a woman in *travail.[C]

7 Thou breakest the [e]ships of [f]Tär'shish with an east [g]wind.

8 As we have heard, so have we seen in the [c]city of the LORD of hosts, in the city of our God: [h]God will establish it for ever. [Sē'lah.[C]

9 We have [i]thought of thy [j]lovingkindness, O God, in the midst of thy [k]temple.

10 According to thy name, O God, so *is* thy [a]praise unto the ends of the earth: thy right hand is full of [l]righteousness.

11 [m]Let mount [b]Zī'ŏn rejoice, let the daughters[C] of Jū'dah be glad, because of thy judgments.

12 Walk about [b]Zī'ŏn, and go round about her: tell[C] the towers thereof.

13 Mark[C] ye well her [n]bulwarks, consider her palaces; that ye may tell *it* to the generation following.

14 For this God is our God for ever and ever: he will be our †,[o]guide *even* unto [p]death.[S]

## PSALM 49

*The psalmist calls upon all men to hear. 6 He shews the vanity of trusting in wealth. 16 Worldly prosperity is not to be envied.*

To the chief Musician, A Psalm for the sons of Korah.

HEAR this, all *ye* people; give ear, all *ye* inhabitants of the world:

2 Both low and high, rich and poor,[C] together.

3 My mouth shall speak of [a]wisdom; and the +meditation of my heart *shall be* of understanding.

4 I will incline mine ear to a parable: I will open my dark saying upon the [b]harp.

5 Wherefore should I [c]fear in the days of evil, *when* [1]the iniquity of my heels shall compass[C] me about?

6 They that [d]trust in their [e]wealth, and [f]boast themselves in the multitude of their riches;

7 [g]None *of them* can by any means redeem his brother, nor give to God a [h]ransom for him:

8 (For the redemption of their [2]soul *is* precious,[C] and it ceaseth for ever:)

9 That he should still live for ever, *and* not see [i,j]corruption.[C]

10 For he seeth *that* wise men [j]die, likewise the fool and the brutish[C] person perish, and leave their wealth to others.

11 [d,k]Their inward thought *is, that* their houses *shall continue* for ever, *and* their dwelling places to all generations; they call *their* lands after their own names.

12 Nevertheless man *being* in honour abideth[C] not: he is like the [l]beasts *that* perish.

13 This their way *is* their folly: yet [3]their posterity approve their sayings.[C] [Sē'lah.

14 [4]Like sheep [m]they are [g]laid in the [n]grave; death shall feed on them; and the upright shall have dominion over them in the morning; and their [o]beauty

**7**
*e Ship,* 2 Chr. 8:18.
*f Tarshish,* 2 Chr. 20:36.
*g Meteorology,* Matt. 16:2.

**8**
*h Faith, exemplified,* Mark 11:22.

**9**
*i Worship,* Gen. 22:5.
*j God, love of,* Gen. 2:2.
*k Church, called temple,* 1 Kin. 9:3.

**10**
*l God, righteousness of,* Gen. 2:2.

**11**
*m Thankfulness, to God, enjoined,* Acts 24:3.

**13**
*n Bulwark, figurative,* Deut. 20:20.

**14**
*o God, guide,* Gen. 2:2.
*p Death,* Num. 23:10.

**3**
*a Wisdom,* Prov. 2:2.

**4**
*b Harp, used in worship,* Dan. 3:10.

**5**
*c Doubting,* Rom. 14:23.
1 R. V. iniquity at my heels compasseth me about?

**6**
*d False Confidence,* Psa. 30:6.
*e Riches,* Eccl. 4:8.
*f Boasting,* Rom. 3:27.

**7**
*g Death, of the wicked,* Num. 23:10.
*h Ransom, of a man's life,* Ex. 21:30.

**8**
2 Am. R. V. life is costly, And it faileth for ever:

**9**
*i Corruption,* Job 17:14.
*j Death,* Num. 23:10.

**11**
*k Delusion,* 2 Thess. 2:11.

**12**
*l Animals,* Jer. 27:5.

**13**
3 R. V. after them men approve

**14**
*m Wicked, death of,* Psa. 73:3.
*n Hell,* Mark 9:43.
*o Beauty,* Prov. 6:25.
4 R. V. They are appointed as a flock for Sheol; Death shall be their shepherd:

---

***BIRTH.** *Pangs in giving,* Psa. 48:6; Isa. 13:8; 21:3; Jer. 4:31; 6:24; 30:6; 31:8. *Giving of, ordained to be in sorrow,* Gen. 3:16.

**† GUIDANCE,** Gen. 12:1; Ex. 15:13; 33:13–15; Num. 10:33; Deut. 32:10, 12; 2 Sam. 22:29; 2 Chr. 32:22; Neh. 9:20; Psa. 23:23; 25:9; 48:14; 78:52; 80:1; 107:7; 139:9, 10; Isa. 55:4; Jer. 3:4; John 10:3, 4.

*By pillar of cloud and fire,* Ex. 13:21; Neh. 9:19. *By counsel,* Psa. 73:24. *By the Holy Spirit,* John 16:13.

**Prayer for,** Judg. 1:1; 18:5; 20:18, 28; 1 Sam. 22:10; 1 Kin. 22:5; 2 Chr. 18:4; 34:21; Psa. 5:8; 25:5; 27:11; 31:3; 61:2; 139:24. *Answered,* 1 Sam. 30:8; 2 Sam. 2:1; 1 Chr. 14:10, 14. *Not heard,* 1 Sam. 28:6.

**Promised,** Psa. 32:8; Isa. 40:11; 42:16; 48:17; 57:18; 58:11; Luke 1:79.

**+ MEDITATION.** *On the Lord,* Psa. 63:5, 6; 104:34; 139:17, 18. *On the law of the Lord,* Psa. 1:2; 19:14; 49:3; 119:11, 15, 16, 23, 48, 55, 59, 78, 97–99, 148. *On the law, enjoined,* Josh. 1:8.

*On the works of the Lord,* Psa. 77:10–12; 143:5.

**Instances of:** *Isaac,* Gen. 24:63. *The Psalmist,* Psa. 4:4; 39:3. *The Psalmist concerning the wicked,* Psa. 73:12–22.

5 R. V. be for Sheol to consume, that there be no habitation for it.

15

*p Death, of the righteous,* Num. 23:10.

6 R. V. Sheol:

16

*q Rich,* Jas. 5:1.

20

*r Rulers, wicked,* Ex. 18:21.

*s Wicked, described,* Psa. 73:3.

1

*a God, sovereign,* Gen. 2:2.

*b God, power of,* Gen. 2:2.

1 Am. R. V. Mighty One, God, Jehovah, hath spoken,

2

*c Church, described,* Matt. 16:18.

4

*d God, judge,* Gen. 2:2.

5

*e Covenant, of man with God,* Deut. 29:1.

*f Offerings,* Lev. 6:17.

6

*g God, righteousness of,* Gen. 2:2.

7

2 R. V. unto thee:

shall [5]consume in the grave from
their dwelling.
15 But God will redeem my
soul from the [p]power of [6]the
[n]grave:[G] for he shall receive
me. [Sē′lah.[G]
16 Be not thou afraid when one
is made [q]rich, when the glory of
his house is increased;
17 For when he [j]dieth he shall
carry nothing away: his glory
shall not descend after him.
18 Though while he lived he
blessed his soul:[G] and *men* will
praise thee, when thou doest
well to thyself.
19 [g]He shall go to the generation
of his fathers; they shall
never see light.
20 [r]Man *that is* in honour, and
[s]understandeth not, is like the
beasts *that* perish.

## PSALM 50

*The majesty of God in Zion. 5 His order to gather his saints together. 7 His pleasure is not in ceremonies, 14 but in sincere obedience.*

A Psalm of Asaph.

THE [1,a,b]mighty God, *even* the
LORD, hath spoken, and
called the earth, from the rising
of the sun unto the going down
thereof.
2 Out of Zī′ŏn, the [c]perfection
of beauty, God hath shined.
3 Our God shall come, and
shall not keep silence: a fire
shall devour before him, and it
shall be very tempestuous round
about him.
4 [S]He[T] shall call to the heavens
from above, and to the earth,
that he may [d]judge his people.
5 Gather my saints together unto
me; those that have made a
[e]covenant with me by [f]sacrifice.
6 And the heavens shall declare
his [g]righteousness: for God
*is* [d]judge himself.[S T Q] [Sē′lah.[G]
7 Hear, O my people, and I
will speak; O Is′ra-el, and I will
testify [2]against thee: I *am* [a]God,
*even* thy God.

8 I will not reprove[G] thee for thy
[f]sacrifices [3]or thy burnt offerings,
*to have been* continually before
me.
9 I will take no bullock out of
thy house, *nor* he goats out of
thy folds.
10 For every [h]beast of the forest
*is* [a]mine, *and* the cattle upon a
thousand hills.[S]
11 I know all the fowls of the
mountains: and the wild [h]beasts
of the field *are* [a]mine.
12 If I were hungry, I would
not tell thee: for the [i]world *is*
[a]mine, and the fulness thereof.[Q S]
13 Will I eat the flesh of bulls,
or drink the blood of goats?
14 Offer unto God [j]thanksgiving;
and pay thy [k]vows unto
the [a]most High:[Q]
15 And [l]call upon me in the day
of [m]trouble: [n,o,p]I will [q]deliver
[r]thee, and thou shalt [s]glorify me.[S]
16 [Q]But unto the [t]wicked God
saith, [u]What hast thou to do to
declare my statutes,[G] or *that* thou
shouldest take my covenant[G] in
thy mouth?
17 Seeing thou [v]hatest [w]instruction,
and castest my [x]words behind
thee.
18 When thou sawest a [y]thief,
then thou [z,a]consentedst with
him, and hast been [b]partaker[G]
with [c]adulterers.
19 Thou givest thy mouth to
[d]evil, and thy tongue frameth
[e]deceit.
20 Thou sittest *and* [f]speakest
against thy brother; thou [g]slanderest
thine own mother's son.
21 These *things* hast thou done,
and I [h,i]kept silence; thou
[j,k,l,m]thoughtest that I was altogether
*such an one* as thyself:
*but* I will [n]reprove[G] thee, and set
*them* in order before thine eyes.[Q]
22 Now consider this, [o]ye that

8

3 R. V. And thy burnt offerings are continually before me.

10

*h Animals,* Jer. 27:5.

12

*i Earth, is the Lord's,* Prov. 8:23.

14

*j Thankfulness, to God, enjoined,* Acts 24:3.

*k Vows,* Num. 30:2.

15

*l Commandment, enjoining prayer,* Deut. 8:2.

*m Adversity, prayer in,* Psa. 10:6.

*n Promise, to the prayerful,* 2 Cor. 1:20.

*o Prayer, answer to, promised,* Acts 6:4.

*p Adversity, consolation in,* Psa. 10:6.

*q God, preserver,* Gen. 2:2.

*r Righteous, promises to,* Psa. 64:10.

*s Glorifying God,* Luke 5:25.

16

*t Wicked, worship of, offensive to God,* Psa. 73:3.

*u Hypocrisy, abhorred of God,* Jas. 3:17.

17

*v Impenitence,* Rom. 2:5.

*w Instruction, hatred of,* Prov. 23:23.

*x Word of God, disbelief in,* Psa. 119:9.

18

*y Evil Company,* Prov. 13:20.

*z Complicity,* Prov. 29:24.

*a Dishonesty, in collusion with thieves,* Ezek. 22:13.

*b Fellowship, with the wicked,* 1 Cor. 1:9.

*c Adultery,* Lev. 20:10.

19

*d Falsehood,* Job 21:34.

*e Deceit,* Psa. 36:3.

20

*f Gossip,* Lev. 19:16.

*g Slander,* Prov. 10:18.

**21** *h God, longsuffering of,* Gen. 2:2. *i Punishment, delayed,* Lev 26: 41. *j Blasphemy,* 2 Sam. 12:14. *k Infidelity,* 2 Cor. 6:15. *l False Confidence,* Psa. 30:6. *m Delusion,* 2 Thess. 2:11. *n Judgments,* Ex. 6:6.
**22** *o Godless,* Job 8:13.

*p Wicked, punishment of,* Psa. 73:3.

**23**

*q Praise,* Psa. 150:1.

*r Glorifying God,* Luke 5:25.

*s Speech, wise,* Col. 4:6.

*t God, savior,* Gen. 2:2.

**1**

*a Prayer, penitential,* vs. 1–17; Acts 6:4.

*b Spiritual Desire,* Psa. 42:1.

*c Repentance, instances of,* Mark 1:4.

*d Mercy,* Deut. 5:10.

*e God, love of,* Gen. 2:2.

*f Conviction of Sin,* John 16:8.

**2**

*g Sin, defiles,* Rom. 5:12.

**3**

*h Prayer, confession in,* Acts 6:4.

*i Sin, confession of,* Rom. 5:12.

*j Conscience, guilty,* Acts 23:1.

*k Remorse, instances of,* Matt. 27:3.

**4**

*l* Rom. 3:4.

*m God, judge,* Gen. 2:2.

**5**

*n Depravity,* Job 15:14.

*o Heredity,* Ezek. 18:2.

**6**

*p Truth,* John 18:37.

*q Wisdom, spiritual, from God,* Prov. 2:2.

**7**

*r Purification, figurative,* Num. 19:19.

*s Hyssop, figurative,* Ex. 12:22.

*t Purity,* 1 Tim. 4:12.

*u Righteous, described,* Psa. 64:10.

*v Washing, figurative,* Matt. 27:24.

*w Colors, figurative,* Ezek. 16:16.

*x Snow,* Jer. 18:14.

**8**

*y Joy,* Psa. 5:11.

**9**

*z Sin, forgiveness of,* Rom. 5:12.

forget God, lest I [p]tear *you* in pieces, and *there be* none to deliver.

23 Whoso offereth [q]praise [r]glorifieth me: and to him that ordereth *his* [+,s]conversation[G] *aright* will I shew the [t]salvation of God.[Q]

## PSALM 51

*The psalmist confesses his sin, and prays to be forgiven, and restored to God's favor. 13 His purpose to serve God, 18 and his prayer for Zion.*

To the chief Musician, A Psalm of David, when Nathan the prophet came unto him, after he had gone in to Bath-sheba.

[a,b] [c] HAVE[T] [d]mercy upon me, O God, according to thy [e]lovingkindness: according unto the multitude of thy tender mercies blot out my [f]transgressions.[Q]

2 [*,b]Wash me throughly[G] from mine iniquity, and cleanse me from my [c,g]sin.

3 For [a]I [c,h,i]acknowledge my transgressions: and [j,k]my sin *is* ever before me.[T]

4 [a]Against thee, thee only, have I sinned, and done *this* evil in thy sight: [l]that thou mightest be justified when thou speakest, *and* be clear[G] when thou [m]judgest.[Q S]

5 Behold, I was [n]shapen in iniquity; and [o]in sin did my mother conceive me.[S T Q]

6 Behold, thou desirest [p]truth in the inward parts: and in the hidden *part* thou shalt make me to know [q]wisdom.

7 [a,b,r]Purge me with [s]hyssop, and I shall be [t,u]clean: [*,v]wash me, and I shall be [u,w]whiter than [x]snow.

8 [a,b]Make me to hear [y]joy and gladness; *that* the bones *which* thou hast broken may rejoice.

9 [z]Hide thy face from my sins, and [z]blot out all mine iniquities.

10 [a,b]Create[T] in me a [*,c]clean [d]heart, O God; and [c]renew a right spirit within me.[S]

11 Cast me not away from thy presence; and take not thy [e]holy spirit from me.

12 Restore unto me the [f,g]joy of thy [h]salvation; and uphold me *with thy* free[G] spirit.[T]

13 *Then* [i]will I [j]teach transgressors thy ways; and sinners shall be [c]converted unto thee.[S]

14 [a]Deliver me from [k]bloodguiltiness,[G] O God, thou God of my [h]salvation: *and* my tongue shall sing aloud of thy [l]righteousness.

15 O Lord, open thou my lips; and my mouth shall shew forth thy [m]praise.

16 [n]For thou [1]desirest not sacrifice; else would I give *it*: thou [2]delightest not in [o]burnt offering.

17 The [p,q,r]sacrifices of God *are* a [s]broken spirit: [†]a broken and a contrite [d]heart, O God, thou wilt not despise.

18 [t]Do good in thy good pleasure unto [u]Zī′ŏn: [v]build thou the walls of Jĕ-ru̦′să-lĕm.

19 Then shalt thou be pleased with the [q]sacrifices of righteousness, with [o]burnt offering and whole burnt offering: then shall they [w]offer bullocks upon thine altar.[T]

## PSALM 52

*The psalmist expostulates with his enemy, 4 and foretells his destruction. 6 He shews the joy of the righteous thereat, 8 and gives thanks to God.*

To the chief Musician, [a]Maschil, *A Psalm* of David, when Doeg the Edomite came and told Saul, and said unto him, David is come to the house of Ahimelech.

WHY [b]boastest [c]thou thyself in mischief, O mighty man? the [d]goodness of God *endureth* continually.[S]

**10**

*a Prayer, penitential,* Acts 6:4.

*b Spiritual Desire,* Psa. 42:1.

*c Regeneration, spiritual cleansing,* Tit. 3:5.

*d Heart,* Psa. 44:21.

**11**

*e Holy Spirit,* Acts 1:2.

**12**

*f Joy,* Psa. 5:11.

*g Spiritual Peace,* Gal. 1:3.

*h Salvation,* Acts 16:17.

**13**

*i Zeal, exemplified,* 2 Cor. 7:11.

*j Religious Testimony,* 2 Thess. 1:10.

**14**

*k Homicide,* Deut. 5:17.

*l God, righteousness of,* Gen. 2:2.

**15**

*m Praise,* Psa. 150:1.

**16**

*n Obedience better than Sacrifice,* 1 Sam. 15:22.

*o Offerings, burnt,* Lev. 6:17.

1 R. V. delightest not in

2 R. V. hast no pleasure in

**17**

*p Consecration,* Lev. 7:37.

*q Sacrifices, figurative,* Rom. 12:1.

*r Offerings, figurative,* Lev. 6:17.

*s Repentance,* Mark 1:4.

**18**

*t Prayer, intercessory,* Acts 6:4.

*u Church,* Matt. 16:18.

*v Patriotism,* Psa. 137:1.

**19**

*w Worship,* Gen. 22:5.

*a Music, symbols used in,* 2 Chr. 5:13.

**1**

*b Impenitence,* Rom. 2:5.

*c Wicked, described,* vs. 1–4; Psa. 73:3.

*d God, goodness of,* Gen. 2:2.

---

**+ CONVERSATION.** *Profane, forbidden,* Matt. 5:37; Jas. 5:12. *Corrupt, forbidden,* Eph. 4:29; Col. 3:8.
*Edifying, enjoined,* Eph. 4:29; Col. 4:6.
*Men shall be judged by,* Matt. 12:36, 37.
See footnote, SPEECH, Col. 4:6.

*** SPIRITUAL PURIFICATION,** **Psa. 65:3; 73:1;** **Prov.** 20:9; John 13: 8, 9.
*By corrective judgments,* Isa. 4:3, 4. *By mercy and truth,* Prov. 16:6. *By the Holy Spirit,* 1 Cor. 6:11; Tit. 3:5, 6. *By the blood of Christ,* Heb. 1:3; 9:14; 2 Pet. 1:9; 1 John 1:7; Rev. 1:5; 7:14.
*Of the church,* Eph. 5:26.
*Enjoined,* Isa. 1:16; Matt. 23:26; Acts 22:16; 1 Cor. 5:7; 2 Cor. 7:1; Heb. 10:22; Jas. 4:8.
*Promised,* Isa. 1:18; Jer. 33:8; Ezek. 36:25; Dan. 12:10; Zech. 13:1; 1 John 1:9. *Prayer for,* Psa. 51:2, 7; 79:9.

**† PENITENT. Promises to:** *Of mercy,* Job 22:23–29; 33:26–28; Psa. 145:18, 19; 147:3; Matt. 5:4; 7:7–11 (with Luke

2
e *Falsehood*, Job 21:34.
f *Speech, evil*, Col. 4:6.

4
g *Hypocrisy*, Jas. 3:17.

5
h *Wicked, punishment of*, Psa. 73:3.

6
i *Righteous*, Psa. 64:10.
j *Fear of God*, Acts 9:31.

7
k *Godless, described*, Job 8:13.
l *False Confidence*, Psa. 30:6.
m *Pride*, Prov. 16:18.
n *Riches*, Eccl. 4:8.

8
o *Church, called house of God*, 1 Kin. 9:3.
p *Faith, exemplified*, Mark 11:22.
q *God, mercy of*, Gen. 2:2.

9
r *Praise*, Psa. 150:1.

a *Music, symbols used in*, 2 Chr. 5:13.

1
b *Fool, atheistic*, vs. 1–6; Prov. 18:2.
c *Atheism*, Psa. 14:1.
d *Wicked, described*, vs. 1–5; Psa. 73:3.
e *Depravity*, vs. 1–3; Job 15:14.

2
f *Anthropomorphisms*, Gen. 11:5.
g *Heaven, God's dwelling place*, Luke 18:22.
h *Spiritual Understanding*, Luke 8:8.
i *Seekers*, Isa. 55:6.

3
j *Infidelity, exemplified*, 2 Cor. 6:15.

2 [c]Thy tongue deviseth [e]mischiefs; like a sharp razor, working [f]deceitfully.

3 Thou [c]lovest evil more than good; *and* [e,f]lying rather than to speak righteousness. [Sē′lah.[C]

4 Thou [c]lovest all devouring words, O *thou* [g]deceitful tongue.

5 God shall likewise [h]destroy thee for ever, he shall take thee away, and pluck thee out of *thy* dwelling place, and root thee out of the land of the living. [Sē′lah.

6 The [i]righteous also shall see, and [j]fear, and shall laugh at him:

7 Lo, *this is* the man *that* [k]made not God his strength; but [l,m]trusted in the abundance of his [n]riches, *and* [b]strengthened himself in his wickedness.

8 But I *am* like a green olive tree in the [o]house of God: I [p]trust in the [q]mercy of God for ever and ever.

9 I will [r]praise thee for ever, because thou hast done *it*: and I will wait on thy name; for *it is* good before thy saints.

## PSALM 53

*The psalmist describes the corruption of men; 4 shews the workers of iniquity their guilt; 6 and longs for the salvation of Israel.*

To the chief Musician upon [a]Mahalath, [a]Maschil, *A Psalm* of David.

THE[Q] [b]fool hath said in his heart, *,[c]*There is* no God. [d]Corrupt are they, and have done abominable iniquity: [e]*there is* none that doeth good.

2 God [f]looked down from [g]heaven upon the children of men, to see if there were *any* that did [h]understand, that did [i]seek God.

3 Every one of them [j]is gone back: [d]they are altogether become filthy; [e]*there is* none that doeth good, no, not one.[Q]

4 Have the [d]workers of iniquity no knowledge? who eat up my people *as* they eat bread: [k]they [l]have not called upon God.

5 There were they in great fear, *where* no fear was: for God [m]hath scattered the bones of him that encampeth *against* thee: thou hast put *them* to shame, because God hath [1]despised them.

6 Oh that the salvation of Ĭş′ra-el *were come* out of Zī′ŏn! When God bringeth back the captivity of his people, Jā′cob shall [n]rejoice, *and* Ĭş′ra-el shall be glad.

## PSALM 54

*The psalmist prays for deliverance from his enemies.*

To the chief Musician on [a]Neginoth, [a]Maschil, *A Psalm* of David, when the Ziphims came and said to Saul, Doth not David hide himself with us?

[b]SAVE me, O God, by thy name, and judge me by thy strength.

2 Hear my [b]prayer, O God; give ear to the words of my mouth.

3 For strangers are [c]risen up against me, and oppressors seek after my soul: [d]they have not set God before them. [Sē′lah.[C]

4 Behold, [e]God *is* mine [f]helper: the Lord *is* with them that uphold my soul.

5 He shall [1]reward evil unto mine enemies: cut[C] them off in thy truth.[T]

6 [2,g]I will freely sacrifice unto thee: [h]I will praise thy name, O LORD; for *it is* good.

7 For he hath [f]delivered me out of all trouble: and mine eye hath seen *his desire* upon mine enemies.

4
k *Godless, described*, Job 8:13.
l *Prayerlessness*, Job 21:15.

5
m *Judgments*, Ex. 6:6.
1 R. V. rejected

6
n *Joy*, Psa. **5:11.**

a *Music, symbols used in*, 2 Chr. 5:13.

1
b *Prayer, in adversity*, Acts 6:4.

3
c *Adversity, prayer in*, vs. 1–3; Psa. 10:6.
d *Godless, described*, Job 8:13.

4
e *Faith, exemplified*, Mark 11:22.
f *God, providence of*, Gen. 2:2.

5
1 R. V. requite the

6
g *Thankfulness, to God, exemplified*, Acts 24:3.
h *Religious Testimony*, 2 Thess. 1:10.
2 R. V. With a freewill offering will I sacrifice unto thee:

11:9–13); 12:20. *Of forgiveness*, Psa. 32:5, 6; 34:18; 51:17; 86:5; Isa. 55:7; Ezek. 18:21–23; 33:10–16; Matt. 11:28–30; Luke 15:4–32 (with Matt. 18:12–14); 18:10–14; John 6:37; Acts 13:38, 39; 1 John 1:9. *Of salvation*, Rom. 10:9–13; Heb. 7:25. *Of divine favor*, Isa. 66:2.

See footnotes: REPENTANCE, Mark 1:4; SEEKERS, Isa. 55:6.
* **SKEPTICISM,** Job 21:15; 22:17; Psa. 14:1; Zeph. 1:12; Mal. 3:14. *Of Pharaoh*, Ex. 5:2. *Of Thomas, concerning the resurrection of Jesus*, John 20:25–28.
See footnote, UNBELIEF, Heb. 3:12.

*a Music, symbols used in,* 2 Chr. 5:13.

1
*b Prayer, in adversity,* Acts 6:4.

3
*c Adversity, prayer in,* vs. 1–3; Psa. 10:6.
*d Malice,* Eph. 4:31.
*e Anger,* Psa. 37:8.
*f Hatred,* Prov. 15:17.
1 R. V. anger they persecute me.

4
*g Despondency,* Eccl. 2:20.

9
*h Prayer, imprecatory,* Acts 6:4.
*i Strife,* Prov. 20:3.

10
2 R. V. Iniquity also and mischief are in

11
*j Deception,* Josh. 9:4.
3 R. V. Oppression

12
*k Friends, false,* Ex. 33:11.

13
4 R.V. companion, and my familiar friend.

14
*l Communion, of saints,* 1 Cor. 10:16.
*m Fellowship, of the righteous,* 1 Cor. 1:9.
*n Church, called house of God,* 1 Kin. 9:3.
5 R. V. in the house of God with the throng.

## PSALM 55

*The psalmist, in his distress, cries unto God, 9 and prays against his enemies. 16 He comforts himself in God's protection.*

To the chief Musician on [a]Neginoth, [a]Maschil, *A Psalm* of David.

GIVE ear to my [b]prayer, O
God; and hide not thyself
from my supplication.
2 [b]Attend unto me, and hear
me: I mourn in my complaint,
and make a noise;
3 Because of the voice of the
enemy, because of the [c]oppression
of the wicked: for they
[d]cast iniquity upon me, and in
[1,e]wrath they [f]hate me.
4 My heart is sore pained within
me: and [g]the terrors of death
are fallen upon me.
5 [g]Fearfulness and trembling
are come upon me, and horror
hath overwhelmed me.
6 And I said, Oh that I had
wings like a dove! *for then* would
I fly away, and be at rest.
7 Lo, *then* would I wander far
off, *and* remain in the wilderness.
[Sē'lah.
8 I would hasten my escape from
the windy storm *and* tempest.
9 [h]Destroy, O Lord, *and* divide
their tongues: for I have seen
violence and [i]strife in the city.
10 Day and night they go about
it upon the walls thereof: [2]mischief
also and sorrow *are* in the
midst of it.
11 Wickedness *is* in the midst
thereof: [3]deceit and [j]guile depart
not from her streets.
12 For *it was* not an [k]enemy
*that* reproached me; then I could
have borne *it*: neither *was it* he
that [f]hated me *that* did magnify
*himself* against me; then I would
have hid myself from him:
13 But *it was* [k]thou, a man
mine equal, my [4]guide, and
mine acquaintance.
14 We took [l,m]sweet counsel
together, *and* walked [5]unto the
[n]house of God in company.
15 [h]Let death seize upon them,
*and* let them go down [6]quick
into [o]hell: for wickedness *is*
in their dwellings, *and* among
them.
16 As for me I will [b]call upon
God; and [p]the LORD shall
[q]save me.
17 [r]Evening, and morning, and
at noon, will I [7,b]pray, and cry
aloud: and [p]he shall hear my
voice.
18 He hath [q]delivered my soul
in peace from the battle *that*
*was* against me: for there were
many [8]with me.
19 God shall hear, and [9]afflict
them, even he that [s]abideth
of old. Sē'lah. Because they
have no changes, therefore [t]they
fear not God.
20 He hath put forth his hands
against such as be at peace with
him: he hath [10]broken his [u]covenant.
21 [v]*The* [w]*words* of his mouth
were smoother than butter, [x]but
war *was* in his heart: his words
were softer than oil, [x]yet *were*
they drawn swords.
22 [y,z]Cast thy burden upon
the LORD, and [a,b]he [c]shall sustain
thee: [d]he shall never suffer
the righteous to be moved.
23 But thou, O God, shalt
bring them down into the [e]pit of
destruction: [f]bloody and [g]deceitful
men [h]shall not live out
half their days; but I [i]will trust
in thee.

## PSALM 56

*The psalmist complains of the malice of his enemies; but declares his purpose to trust in God, and to praise him.*

To the chief Musician upon Jonath-elem-rechokim, [a]Michtam of David, when the Philistines took him in Gath.

[b]BE [c]merciful unto me, O God:
for man would swallow
me up; he fighting daily [d]oppresseth
me.
2 [b]Mine [e]enemies would daily
swallow *me* up: for *they be* many

15
*o Hell,* Mark 9:43.
6 Am. R. V. alive into Sheol;

16
*p Faith, in adversity,* Mark 11:22.
*q God, preserver,* Gen. 2:2.

17
*r Prayer, thrice, daily,* Acts 6:4.
7 R. V. complain, and moan:

18
8 R. V. that strove with me.

19
*s God, eternity of,* Gen. 2:2.
*t Godless, described,* Job 8:13.
9 R. V. answer

20
*u Covenant, of men with men,* Deut. 29:1.
10 R. V. profaned

21
*v Falsehood,* Job 21:34.
*w Words, of the hypocrite,* Luke 4:22.
*x Hypocrisy,* Jas. 3:17.

22
*y Faith, enjoined,* Mark 11:22.
*z Anxiety, remedy for,* 1 Pet. 5:7.

---

*a Promise, to the righteous,* 2 Cor. 1:20.
*b Afflictions, consolation in,* Psa. 34:19.
*c Spiritual Blessings, from God,* Eph. 1:3.
*d Righteous, promises to,* Psa. 64:10.

23
*e Pit, figurative,* Psa. 7:15.
*f Wicked, punishment of,* Psa. 73:3.
*g Deceit, punishment for,* Psa. 36:3.
*h Death, of the wicked,* Num. 23:10.
*i Faith, in adversity,* Mark 11:22.

---

*a Music, symbols used in,* 2 Chr. 5:13.

1
*b Prayer, in adversity,* vs. 1–13; Acts 6:4.
*c God, mercy of,* Gen. 2:2.
*d Adversity, prayer in,* Psa. 10:6.

2
*e Enemy,* Prov. 24:17.

[d]that fight against me, O thou most High.[S]

3 What[C] time I am afraid, I will [f]trust in thee.

4 In God I will [g]praise his [h]word, in God I have put my [f]trust; I will not fear what flesh can do unto me.

5 Every day [e]they [i]wrest[C] my words: all their thoughts *are* against me for evil.

6 [e,i]They gather themselves together, they hide themselves, they mark[C] my steps, when they wait for my soul.

7 Shall they escape by iniquity? in *thine* [j]anger [k]cast down the people, O God.

8 Thou tellest[C] my wanderings: put thou my [l]tears into thy [m]bottle: *are they* not in thy [n]book?

9 When I [b,d]cry *unto thee,* then shall mine [e]enemies turn back: this I know; for [f]God *is* for me.

10 In God will I [g]praise *his* [h]word: in the LORD will I praise *his* word.

11 In God have I put my [f]trust: I will not be afraid what man can do unto me.

12 Thy [o]vows[C] *are* upon me, O God: [p]I will render [g]praises unto thee.

13 For thou hast [q]delivered my soul from death: *wilt* not *thou deliver* my feet from falling, that I may walk before God in the light of the living?

## PSALM 57

*The psalmist's refuge in calamity. 7 His determination to praise God for his mercy and truth.*

To the chief Musician, [a]Al-taschith, [a]Michtam of David, when he fled from Saul in the cave.

[b]BE [c]merciful unto me, O God, be merciful unto me: for my soul [1,d]trusteth in thee: yea, in the shadow of thy wings will I make my refuge, until *these* [e]calamities be overpast.[C]

2 I will [b]cry unto God most high; unto God that [f]performeth *all things* for me.

3 [d]He shall send from [g]heaven, and save me *from* the reproach of him that would swallow[C] me up. Sē'lah.[C] God shall send forth his [c]mercy and his [h]truth.[S T]

4 My soul *is* among [i,j]lions: *and* I lie *even among* them that are set on fire, *even* the sons of men, whose teeth *are* spears and [k]arrows, and [l]their tongue a sharp [m]sword.

5 Be thou exalted, O God, above the heavens; *let* thy [n]glory *be* above all the earth.[S]

6 [l]They have prepared a [o]net for my steps; my soul is bowed down: they have digged a [p]pit before me, into the midst whereof they are fallen *themselves.* [Sē'lah.

7 [q,r]My [s]heart [t]is fixed, O God, my heart is fixed: I will sing and give [u]praise.

8 Awake up, my glory; awake, [v]psaltery and [w]harp: I *myself* will awake early.

9 [x]I will [u]praise thee, O Lord, among the people: I will sing unto thee among the nations.

10 For thy [c]mercy *is* great unto the heavens, and thy [h]truth unto the clouds.[S T]

11 Be thou exalted, O God, above the heavens: *let* thy [n]glory *be* above all the earth.[S]

## PSALM 58

*The psalmist describes the conduct of the wicked, 6 and prays that their power may be broken; 10 whereat the righteous shall rejoice.*

To the chief Musician, [a]Al-taschith, [a]Michtam of David.

DO ye indeed speak righteousness, O congregation? do [b]ye judge uprightly, O ye sons of men?

2 Yea, in heart [b,c]ye work wickedness; ye weigh[C] the violence of your hands in the earth.

3 The [d]wicked are estranged[C] [e]from the womb: they [f]go astray

3
f *Faith, in adversity,* Mark 11:22.

4
g *Praise,* Psa. 150:1.
h *Word of God,* Psa. 119:9.

5
i *Malice,* Eph. 4:31.

7
j *Anger of God,* 2 Kin. 13:3.
k *Prayer, imprecatory,* Acts 6:4.

8
l *Tears,* Psa. 6:6.
m *Bottle,* Gen. 21:14.
n *Book, of remembrance,* Psa. 139:16.

12
o *Vows,* Num. 30:2.
p *Thankfulness, to God, exemplified,* Acts 24:3.

13
q *God, providence of,* Gen. 2:2.

a *Music, symbols used in,* 2 Chr. 5:13.

1
b *Prayer, in adversity,* Acts 6:4.
c *God, mercy of,* Gen. 2:2.
d *Faith, in adversity,* Mark 11:22.
e *Adversity, prayer in,* Psa. 10:6.
1 R. V. taketh refuge

2
f *God, faithfulness of,* Gen. 2:2.

3
g *Heaven, God's dwelling place,* Luke 18:22.
h *Truth, attribute of God,* John 18:37.

4
i *Lion, figurative,* Mic. 5:8.
j *Enemy,* Prov. 24:17.
k *Arrow, figurative,* 1 Sam. 20:20.
l *Malice,* Eph. 4:31.
m *Sword, figurative,* 1 Chr. 21:5.

5
n *God, glory of,* Gen. 2:2.

6
o *Net, figurative,* Isa. 51:20.
p *Pit, figurative,* Psa. 7:15.

7
q *Decision, instances of,* Isa. 50:7.
r *Religious Testimony, exemplified,* vs. 7–9; 2 Thess. 1:10.
s *Heart,* Psa. 44:21.
t *Character, stability of,* Phil. 2:15.
u *Praise,* Psa. 150:1.

8
v *Psaltery,* 1 Chr. 16:5.
w *Harp,* Dan. 3:10.

9
x *Thankfulness, to God,* Acts 24:3.

a *Music, symbols used in,* 2 Chr. 5:13.

1
b *Judge, must judge righteously,* Judg. 2:18.

2
c *Rulers, wicked,* Ex. 18:21.

3
d *Wicked, described,* Psa. 73:3.
e *Heredity,* Ezek. 18:2.
f *Depravity,* Job 15:14.

*g Falsehood*, Job 21:34.

4

*h Serpent, venom of*, Num. 21:6.

*i Adder*, Gen. 49:17.

5

*j Charmers*, Isa. 19:3.

6

*k Prayer, imprecatory*, Acts 6:4.

*l Lion, figurative*, Mic. 5:8.

7

*m Arrow, figurative*, 1 Sam. 20:20.

9

*n Thorn*, Hos. 2:6.

*o Death, of the wicked*, Num. 23:10.

1 R. V. the green and the burning alike.

10

*p Blood, figurative*, Gen. 9:4.

11

*q God, judge*, Gen. 2:2.

*a Music, symbols used in*, 2 Chr. 5:13.

1

*b Prayer, in adversity*, vs. 1–17; Acts 6:4.

*c Adversity, prayer in*, Psa. 10:6.

3

*d Malice*, Eph. 4:31.

as soon as they be born, speaking [g]lies.[s]
4 Their poison *is* like the [h]poi-
son of a serpent: *they are* like the
deaf [i]adder *that* stoppeth her
ear;
5 Which will not hearken to
the voice of [j]charmers, charming
never so wisely.
6 [k]Break their teeth, O God,
in their mouth: break out the
great teeth of the young [l]lions,
O LORD.
7 [k]Let them melt away as waters *which* run continually: *when*
he bendeth *his bow to shoot* his
[m]arrows, let them be as cut in
pieces.
8 As a snail *which* melteth,
[k]let *every one of them* pass away:
*like* the untimely birth of a woman, *that* they may not see the sun.
9 Before your pots can feel the
[n]thorns, he shall [o]take them
away as with a whirlwind, [1]both
living, and in *his* wrath.
10 The righteous shall rejoice
when he seeth the vengeance: he
shall wash his feet in the [p]blood
of the wicked.
11 So that a man shall say,
Verily *there is* a reward for the
righteous: verily he is a God[s]
that [q]judgeth in the earth.

## PSALM 59

*The psalmist complains of the workers of iniquity, and prays for their overthrow. 16 His purpose to sing of the power and mercy of God.*

To the chief Musician, [a]Al-taschith, [a]Michtam of David; when Saul sent, and they watched the house to kill him.

[b]DELIVER me from mine
enemies, O my God: de-
fend me from them that [c]rise up
against me.
2 [b,c]Deliver me from the workers of iniquity, and save me from
bloody men.
3 For, lo, they [d]lie in wait for
my soul: the mighty are gathered against me; not *for* my
transgression, nor *for* my sin,
O LORD.

4 They run and prepare themselves without[c] *my* fault: [e]awake
to [f]help me, and behold.
5 Thou therefore, O LORD
God of hosts, the God of Is'ra-el,
[e]awake to visit all the heathen[c]:
[g]be not merciful to any wicked
transgressors. [Sē'lah.[c]
6 They return at evening: they
make a noise like a [h]dog, and go
round about the city.
7 Behold, they belch out with
their mouth: [i]swords *are* in their
lips: [j]for who, *say they*, doth
hear?
8 But thou, O LORD, shalt
[e]laugh at them; thou shalt have
all the heathen[c] in derision.
9 [1,k]*Because of* his strength will
I wait upon thee: for God *is* my
[f]defence.
10 The God of my mercy shall
prevent[c] me: God shall let me see
*my desire* upon mine enemies.
11 Slay them not, lest my people forget: [g]scatter them by thy
[l]power; and bring them down,
O Lord our [m]shield.[T]
12 *For* the sin of their mouth
*and* the [n]words of their lips [g]let
them even be taken in their
[o]pride: and for cursing and [p]ly-
ing *which* they speak.
13 [g]Consume *them* in wrath,
consume *them*, that they *may* not
*be*: and let them know that [q]God
ruleth in Jā'cob unto the ends
of the earth.[T] [Sē'lah.
14 And at evening let them return; *and* let them make a noise
like a [h]dog, and go round about
the city.
15 Let them wander up and
down for meat[c], and [2]grudge[c] if
they be not satisfied.
16 But [r]I will [s]sing of thy
[l]power; yea, I will sing aloud of
thy [t]mercy in the morning: for
thou hast been my [f]defence and
refuge in the day of my trouble.
17 Unto thee, O my strength,

4

*e Anthropomorphisms*, Gen. 11:5.

*f God, preserver*, Gen. 2:2.

5

*g Prayer, imprecatory*, Acts 6:4.

6

*h Animals, instincts of*, Jer. 27:5.

7

*i Sword, figurative*, 1 Chr. 21:5.

*j Infidelity*, 2 Cor. 6:15.

9

*k Faith, in adversity*, Mark 11:22.

1 R. V. O my strength, I will wait upon thee: For God is my high tower.

11

*l God, power of*, Gen. 2:2.

*m Shield, figurative*, 1 Kin. 14:27.

12

*n Speech, evil*, Col. 4:6.

*o Pride*, Prov. 16:18.

*p Falsehood*, Job 21:34.

13

*q God, sovereign*, Gen. 2:2.

15

2 R. V. tarry all night if

16

*r Thankfulness, to God, exemplified*, Acts 24:3.

*s Praise*, Psa. 150:1.

*t God, mercy of*, Gen. 2:2.

will I [s]sing: for God *is* my [3,t]defence, *and* the God of my mercy.

## PSALM 60

*The psalmist laments the afflictions of Israel, and prays for deliverance. 6 He recalls God's promises, 9 and trusts in them.*

To the chief Musician upon [a]Shushan-eduth, [a]Michtam of David, to teach; when he strove with Aram-naharaim and with Aram-zobah, when Joab returned, and smote of Edom in the valley of salt twelve thousand.

[b]O GOD, thou hast [c]cast us off, thou hast [1]scattered us, thou hast been displeased; O turn thyself to us again.

2 [b]Thou hast made the earth to [d]tremble; thou hast broken it: heal the breaches thereof; for it shaketh.

3 [b]Thou hast shewed thy people hard things: thou hast made us to drink the [e]wine of [2]astonishment.

4 Thou hast given a [f]banner to them that [g]fear thee, that it may be displayed because of the truth. [Sē′lah.

5 [b]That thy beloved may be delivered; save *with* thy right hand, and hear me.

6 God hath spoken in his [h]holiness; I will rejoice, I will divide [i]Shē′chem, and mete out the valley of [j]Sŭc′coth.

7 [k]Gĭl′e-ăd *is* mine, and [l]Mă-năs′seh *is* mine; [m]Ē′phră-ĭm also *is* the [3]strength of mine head; [n]Jū′dah *is* my [4]lawgiver;

8 [o]Mō′ab *is* my washpot; over [p]Ē′dom will I cast out my shoe: [q]Phĭ-lĭs′tiȧ, triumph thou because of me.

9 Who will bring me *into* the strong city? who will lead me into [p]Ē′dom?

10 *Wilt* not thou, O God, *which* hadst cast us off? and *thou*, O God, *which* didst not go out with our armies?

11 [b]Give us help from trouble: for [r]vain *is* the help of man.

12 [s]Through God we shall do valiantly: for he *it is that* shall [t]tread down our enemies.

## PSALM 61

*The psalmist, in view of former mercies, cries unto God. 4 He vows perpetual service to him because of his promises.*

To the chief Musician upon Neginah, *A Psalm* of David.

HEAR my [a]cry, O God; attend unto my prayer.

2 From the end of the earth will I [a]cry unto thee, [b]when my heart is overwhelmed: [c]lead me to the [d]rock *that* is higher than I.

3 For thou hast been a [e]shelter for me, *and* a strong [f]tower from the enemy.

4 [g]I will abide in thy [h]tabernacle for ever: I will [1]trust in the covert of thy wings. [Sē′lah.

5 For thou, O God, hast heard my [i]vows: thou hast given *me* the heritage of those that [j]fear thy name.

6 Thou wilt [k]prolong the king's life: *and* his years as many generations.

7 He shall abide before God for ever: O prepare [l]mercy and [m]truth, *which* may preserve him.

8 So will I sing [n]praise unto thy name for ever, that I may daily perform my [i]vows.

## PSALM 62

*The psalmist trusts in God, and rebukes his enemies. 8 He exhorts the people to trust in God. 11 Power and mercy belong to him.*

To the chief Musician, to [a]Jeduthun, A Psalm of David.

TRULY my soul [b]waiteth upon God: [c]from him *cometh* my salvation.

2 [d,e]He only *is* my [f]rock and my [g]salvation; *he is* my defence; I shall not be greatly moved.

3 How long will ye [1,h]imagine mischief against a man? ye shall be slain all of you: as a bowing wall *shall ye be, and as* a tottering *fence.

---

17
3 R. V. high tower, the

a *Music, symbols used in*, 2 Chr. 5:13.

1
b *Prayer, intercessory*, Acts 6:4.
c *Adversity, prayer in*, vs. 1–3, 11; Psa. 10:6.
1 R. V. broken us down; Thou hast been angry; O restore us again.

2
d *Earthquakes*, Isa. 29:6.

3
e *Wine, figurative*, Prov. 23:31.
2 R. V. staggering.

4
f *Standard, figurative*, Num. 1:52.
g *Fear of God*, Acts 9:31.

6
h *God, holiness of*, Gen. 2:2.
i *Shechem*, Josh. 20:7.
j *Succoth*, Judg. 8:5.

7
k *Gilead*, Deut. 3:13.
l *Manasseh, tribe of*, Gen. 46:20.
m *Ephraim, tribe of*, Gen. 41:52.
n *Judah, tribe of*, Num. 10:14.
3 R. V. defence
4 R. V. sceptre.

8
o *Moab*, Num. 26:3.
p *Edom*, Obad. 1.
q Psa. 87:4; 108:9.

11
r *False Confidence*, Psa. 30:6.

12
s *Faith, exemplified*, Mark 11:22.
t *God, providence of*, Gen. 2:2.

1
a *Prayer, in adversity*, Acts 6:4.

2
b *Adversity, prayer in*, Psa. 10:6.
c *God, guide*, Gen. 2:2.
d *Rock, figurative*, Psa. 78:15.

3
e *God, preserver*, Gen. 2:2.
f *Tower, figurative*, 2 Chr. 26:9.

4
g *Faith, in adversity*, Mark 11:22.
h *Church, called tabernacle*, 1 Kin. 9:3.
1 R. V. take refuge

5
i *Vows*, Num. 30:2.
j *Fear of God*, Acts 9:31.

6
k *God, providence of*, Gen. 2:2.

7
l *Mercy*, Deut. 5:10.
m *Truth*, John 18:37.

8
n *Praise*, Psa. 150:1.

a *Jeduthun*, 1 Chr. 16:38.

1
b *Spiritual Desire*, Psa. 42:1.
c *Afflictions, consolation in*, Psa. 34:19.

2
d *Religious Testimony, exemplified*, 2 Thess. 1:10.
e *Faith, exemplified*, Mark 11:22.
f *Rock, figurative*, Psa. 78:15.
g *God, savior*, Gen. 2:2.

3
h *Malice*, Eph. 4:31.
1 Am. R. V. set upon a man, That ye may slay him, all of you, Like a leaning wall, like a tottering fence?

---

***FENCE.** *Consisting, of stone walls*, Num. 22:24; Psa. 62:3; Prov. 24:30, 31; Mic. 7:11; *of hedge*, Eccl. 10:8; Isa. 5:5; Nah. 3:17; Prov. 15:19; Hos. 2:6; Matt. 21:33.

4

*i Enemy*, Prov. 24:17.
*j Falsehood*, Job 21:34.
*k Hypocrisy*, Jas. 3:17.

8

*l Faith, enjoined*, Mark 11:22.
*m Righteous, promises to*, Psa. 64:10.
*n God, preserver*, Gen. 2:2.

9

*o Vanity*, Eccl. 1:2.
*p Balances, figurative*, Prov. 11:1.

10

*q Oppression*, Eccl. 5:8.
*r Dishonesty, forbidden*, Ezek. 22:13.
*s Theft*, Mark 7:22.
*t Riches*, Eccl. 4:8.
*u False Confidence, warnings against*, Psa. 30:6.

11

*v God, power of*, Gen. 2:2.

12

*w God, mercy of*, Gen. 2:2.
*x God, justice of*, Gen. 2:2.
*y Judgment, according to opportunity and works*, 1 Pet. 1:17.

1

*a Love, of man for God*, 1 John 4:19.
*b Worship*, Gen. 22:5.
*c Seekers*, Isa. 55:6.
*d Spiritual Desire*, Psa. 42:1.
*e Thirst, figurative*, John 4:14.
1 R. V. weary

2

*f God, power of*, Gen. 2:2.
*g God, glory of*, Gen. 2:2.
*h Church, called sanctuary*, 1 Kin. 9:3.

4 [i]They only consult to cast *him* down from his excellency: they delight in [j]lies: they bless[C] with their mouth, [k]but they curse inwardly. [Sē'lah.[C]

5 My soul, [b]wait[C] thou only upon God; for my expectation *is* from him.

6 [d,e]He only *is* my [f]rock and my [g]salvation: *he is* my defence; I shall not be moved.

7 In God *is* my [g]salvation and my glory: the [f]rock of my strength, *and* my refuge, *is* in God.

8 [l]Trust in him at all times; ye people, pour out your heart before him: [e,m]God *is* a [n]refuge for us. [Sē'lah.

9 Surely men of low degree *are* [o]vanity, *and* men of high degree *are* a lie: to be laid in the [p]balance, they *are* altogether *lighter* than vanity.

10 Trust not in [q]oppression, and [r]become not vain in [s]robbery: if [t]riches increase, [u]set not your heart *upon them*.[Q]

11 God hath spoken once; twice have I heard this; that [v]power *belongeth* unto God.[S]

12 Also unto thee, O Lord, *belongeth* [w]mercy: for thou [x,y]renderest to every man according to his work.[S Q]

## PSALM 63

*The psalmist's thirst for God. 4 His manner of blessing God. 9 His confidence of his enemies' destruction, and his own safety.*

A Psalm of David, when he was in the wilderness of Judah.

O GOD, [a]thou *art* my God; early will [b,c]I seek thee: my soul [d,e]thirsteth for thee, my flesh longeth for thee in a dry and [1]thirsty land, where no water is;

2 To see thy [f]power and thy [g]glory, so *as* I have seen thee in the [h]sanctuary.

3 [a]Because thy [i]lovingkindness *is* better than life, my lips shall [j]praise thee.[S]

4 [a]Thus will I [b]bless[C] thee while I live: I will lift up my hands in thy name.

5 [a]My soul shall be [k]satisfied as *with* marrow[C] and fatness; and my mouth shall praise *thee* with [l]joyful lips:

6 When I [a]remember thee upon my bed, *and* [m]meditate on thee in the [n]*night* watches.

7 Because [o]thou hast been my help, therefore in the shadow of thy wings will I [l]rejoice.[S]

8 My soul [c,d]followeth hard[C] after thee: thy right hand upholdeth me.

9 But those *that* seek my soul, to destroy *it*, shall go into the lower parts of the earth.

10 They shall fall by the sword: they shall be a portion for *foxes.

11 But the king shall rejoice in God; every one that sweareth by him shall glory: but the mouth of them that speak [p]lies shall be stopped.

## PSALM 64

*The psalmist prays for deliverance from his enemies. He foretells their destruction; 10 at which the righteous shall rejoice.*

To the chief Musician. A Psalm of David.

HEAR my voice, O God, in my [a]prayer: preserve my life from fear of the enemy.

2 Hide me from the [b,c]secret counsel of the wicked; from the [1]insurrection of the workers of iniquity:

3 Who whet[C] their tongue like a sword, *and* bend *their bows to shoot* their [d]arrows, *even* bitter [e]words:

4 That they may shoot in secret at the perfect: suddenly do they shoot at him, and fear not.

5 They encourage themselves *in* an evil matter: they commune[C]

3

*i God, love of*, Gen. 2:2.
*j Praise*, Psa. 150:1.

5

*k Righteous, happiness of*, Psa. 64:10.
*l Joy*, Psa. 5:11.

6

*m Meditation*, Psa. 49:3.
*n Night*, Gen. 1:5.

7

*o Faith, exemplified*, Mark 11:22.

11

*p Falsehood*, Job 21:34.

1

*a Prayer, in adversity*, Acts 6:4.

2

*b Adversity, prayer in*, Psa. 10:6.
*c Malice*, Eph. 4:31.
1 R. V. tumult

3

*d Arrow, figurative*, 1 Sam. 20:20.
*e Speech, evil*, Col. 4:6.

* **FOX.** *Dens of*, Matt. 8:20; Luke 9:58. *Samson uses, to burn the field of the Philistines*, Judg. 15:4. *Depredations of*, Psa. 63:10; Song 2:15. *Illustrative of unfaithful prophets*, Ezek. 13:4. *Figurative of craftiness*, Luke 13:32.

**5**
*f Infidelity,* 2 Cor. 6:15.

**6**
2 R. V. We have accomplished, say they, a diligent search: And the inward thought of every one, and the heart, is deep.

**7**
*g Wicked, punishment of,* v. 8; Psa. 73:3.

**8**
*h Sin, retroactive,* Rom. 5:12.
3 R. V. be made to stumble, their own tongue being against them:
4 R. V. wag the head.

**9**
*i Fear of God,* Acts 9:31.

**10**
*j Joy,* Psa. 5:11.
*k Faith,* Mark 11:22.

of laying snares privily[C]; [f]they
say, Who shall see them?
6 They search out iniquities[C];
[2]they accomplish a diligent
search: both the inward *thought*
of every one *of them,* and the
heart, *is* deep.
7 But God shall [g]shoot at them
*with* an [d]arrow; suddenly shall
they be wounded.
8 So they shall [3]make their own
[e]tongue to [h]fall upon themselves:
all that see them shall [4]flee
away.
9 And all men shall [i]fear, and
shall declare the work of God;
for they shall wisely consider of
his doing.
10 The *righteous shall be
[j]glad in the LORD, and shall
[k]trust in him; and all the upright in heart shall glory.

## PSALM 65

*The psalmist praises God for his grace.* 4
*The blessedness of his chosen people.* 6
*God's power;* 9 *and goodness.*

To the chief Musician, A Psalm *and* Song of David.

[a]PRAISE waiteth for thee, O
God, in Sī'ŏn: and unto
thee shall the [b]vow be performed.
2 O thou [c]that hearest prayer,
unto thee shall [d]all flesh come.[Q]
3 Iniquities prevail against me:
*as for* our transgressions, [e]thou
shalt [f,g,h]purge them away.
4 [i]Blessed[C] *is the man whom*
thou choosest, and causest to
[j]approach *unto thee, that* he may
dwell in thy courts: we shall be
satisfied with the goodness of thy
house, *even* of thy holy temple.[S]
5 *By* terrible[C] things in righteousness wilt thou answer us, O
[k]God of our [l]salvation; *who art*

**1**
*a Praise,* Psa. 150:1.
*b Vows,* Num. 30:2.

**2**
*c Faith, exemplified,* Mark 11:22.
*d Prayer, answered,* Acts 6:4.

**3**
*e God, mercy of,* Gen. 2:2.
*f Spiritual Purification,* Psa. 51:2.
*g Purity, of heart,* 1 Tim. 4:12.
*h Sin, forgiveness of,* Rom. 5:12.

**4**
*i Spiritual Peace,* Gal. 1:3.
*j Access to God,* Eph. 3:12.

**5**
*k God, savior,* Gen. 2:2.
*l Salvation,* Acts 16:17.

* **RIGHTEOUS.** *Compared, to the sun,* Judg. 5:31; Matt. 13:43; *to stars,* Dan. 12:3; *to lights,* Matt. 5:14; Phil. 2:15; *to treasure,* Ex. 19:5; Psa. 135:4; *to jewels* [R. V. peculiar treasure], Mal. 3:17; *to gold,* Job 23:10; Lam. 4:2; *to children,* Matt. 18:3; 1 Cor. 14:20; *to obedient children,* 1 Pet. 1:14; *to soldiers,* 2 Tim. 2:3, 4; *to runners in a race,* 1 Cor. 9:24; Heb. 12:1; *to fruitful trees,* Psa. 1:3; Jer. 17:8; *to salt,* Matt. 5:13.

**Contrasted with the wicked,** Psa. 1:1–6; 11:5; 17:14, 15; 32:10; 37:17–22, 37, 38; 73:1–28; 75:10; 91:7, 8; Prov. 2:21, 22; 3:32, 33; 4:16–19; 10:3, 6, 9, 11, 16, 20, 21, 23–25, 28–32; 11:3, 5, 6, 8–11, 18–21, 23, 31; 12:2, 3, 5–7, 10, 12, 13, 21, 26; 13:5, 6, 9, 17, 21, 22, 25; 14:2, 11, 19, 22, 32; 15:6, 8, 9, 28, 29; 21:15, 18, 26, 29; 22:5, 8, 9; 24:16; 28:1, 4, 5, 13, 14, 18; 29:2, 6, 7, 27; Isa. 32:1–8; 65:13, 14; Rom. 2:7–10; Eph. 2:12–14; Phil. 2:15; 1 Thess. 5:5–8; Tit. 1:15; 1 Pet. 4:17, 18; 1 John 3:3–17.

**Described,** Psa. 1:1–3; 15:1–5; 24:3–5; 37:26, 30, 31; 84:7; 112:1–9; 119:1–3; Isa. 33:15, 16; 51:1; 62:12; 63:8; Jer. 17:7, 8; 31:12–14, 33, 34; Ezek. 18:5–9; Zech. 3:2, 7, 8.

*As, dead to sin,* Rom. 6:2, 11; Col. 3:3; *freed from sin,* Rom. 6:7, 18, 22; 1 John 3:6, 9; *good,* Luke 6:45; *pure,* Matt. 5:8; 1 John 3:3; 2 Tim. 2:21, 22; *holy,* Deut. 7:6; Eph. 1:4; 4:24; Col. 1:22; 3:12; 1 Pet. 1:15; 2 Tim. 2:19; Heb. 3:1; *sanctified,* 1 Cor. 1:2; 6:11; *godly,* Psa. 4:3; 2 Pet. 2:9; *wise,* Psa. 37:30; Prov. 2:9–12; *faithful,* Matt. 24:45; 25:21, 23; Luke 19:17; Eph. 1:1; Col. 1:2; Rev. 17:14; *merciful,* Matt. 5:7; *meek,* Matt. 5:5; 2 Tim. 2:25; *industrious,* Eph. 4:28; 2 John 9; *stable,* Matt. 7:24–27; Eph. 4:14; *saved,* Acts 2:47; *saints,* Rom. 1:7; 1 Cor. 1:2; Eph. 1:1; *chosen,* 1 Pet. 2:9; Rev. 17:14; *spotless,* Jas. 1:27; *separate,* Ex. 33:16; *obedient,* Matt. 12:50; John 15:14; 1 John 2:3, 5; *new creature,* 2 Cor. 5:17; Eph. 2:10; 4:23, 24; Col. 3:9, 10; *spiritually minded,* Rom. 8:4, 6; *servants of Christ,* Eph. 6:6; *servants of righteousness,* Rom. 6:19; *children of light,* 1 Thess. 5:5; *sons of God,* Rom. 8:14, 16; John 3:2; *a temple of God,* 2 Cor. 6:16; *beloved of God,* Rom. 1:7; *poor in spirit,* Matt. 5:3; *hungering and thirsting after righteousness,* Matt. 5:6; *growing in grace,* Psa. 84:7; Eph. 4:13; *imitators of Christ,* 1 Pet. 4:1, 2; 1 John 2:6; *salt of the earth,* Matt. 5:13; *city set on a hill,* Matt. 5:14; *led by the spirit,* Rom. 8:14; Gal. 5:18; *filled with goodness and knowledge,* Rom. 15:14; Col. 1:9–13; *grounded in love,* Eph. 3:17; *following Christ,* Matt. 10:38; 16:24; Mark 8:34; Luke 9:23; *rooted in Christ,* Col. 2:7; *patient, longsuffering, joyful,* Col. 1:11; 1 Thess. 1:3; *peaceful, meek, gentle, patient,* 2 Tim. 2:21–25; *blameless, harmless and without blemish,* Eph. 1:4; Phil. 2:15; *kind, tender-hearted, forgiving,* Eph. 4:32; *hating falsehood,* Prov. 13:5; *abhorring wickedness,* Psa. 101:3, 4; *having renounced dishonesty,* 2 Cor. 4:2; *without bitterness, wrath, anger, clamor, evil speaking, malice,* Eph. 4:31; *grieved by the wickedness of the wicked,* Psa. 119:158; Acts 17:16; 2 Pet. 2:7, 8.

**Happiness of,** Job 5:17–27; Prov. 3:13–18; 16:20; Matt. 5:3–12. *Satisfying,* Psa. 36:8; 63:5.

*Under fiery trials,* 1 Pet. 4:12, 13. *Under persecution,* Matt. 5:10–12.

**Promises to, and Grounds of Assurance and Comfort of:** *Of deliverance, from temptation,* 1 Cor. 10:13; 2 Pet. 2:9; *from trouble,* Job 5:19–24; 34:15, 17; 50:15; 91:15; 97:10, 11; Prov. 3:25, 26; Isa. 41:10–13; 43:2. *Of refuge in adversity,* Psa. 33:18, 19; 62:8; 91:1–15; Prov. 14:26; Nah. 1:7. *Of strength in adversity,* Psa. 29:11. *Of security,* Psa. 32:6, 7; 84:11; 121:3–8; Isa. 33:16. *Of providential care,* Gen. 15:1; Ex. 23:22; Lev. 26:5, 6, 10; Deut. 33:27; 1 Sam. 2:9; 2 Chr. 16:9; Ezra 8:22; Job 5:15; Psa. 34:9, 10; 125:1–3; 145:19, 20; Prov. 1:33; 2:7; 3:6; 10:3; 16:7; Isa. 49:9–11; 65:13, 14; Ezek. 34:11–17, 22–31; Luke 12:7, 32; 21:18; 1 Pet. 5:7. *Of overruling providence,* Rom. 8:28; 2 Cor. 4:17. *Of answer to prayer,* Prov. 15:29; Mark 11:23, 24; John 14:13, 14; Acts 10:4; 1 Pet. 3:12; 1 John 3:22. *Of temporal blessings,* Lev. 25:18, 19; 26:5; Deut. 28:1–13; Psa. 37:9; 128:1–6; Prov. 2:21; 3:1–4, 7–10; Matt. 6:26–33; Mark 10:30; Luke 18:29, 30. *Of blessings upon their children,* Psa. 103:17; 112:2, 3.

*Of comfort in tribulation,* Isa. 25:8; 66:13, 14; Matt. 5:4; John 14:16–18; Rev. 21:4. *Of joy,* Isa. 35:10; 51:11. *Of spiritual enlightenment,* Isa. 2:3; John 8:12. *Of peace,* Isa. 26:3; Rom. 2:10. *Of seeing God,* Matt. 5:8. *Of inconceivable spiritual blessings,* Isa. 64:4; 1 Cor. 2:9. *Of the rest of faith,* Heb. 4:9. *Of wisdom,* Jas. 1:5. *Of divine help,* Psa. 55:22; Isa. 41:10–13; Heb. 13:5, 6. *Of divine guidance,* Psa. 25:12; 32:8; 37:23, 24; 48:14; 73:24; Prov. 3:5, 6. *Of divine mercy,* Psa. 32:10; 103:17, 18; Mal. 3:17. *Of the divine presence* Gen. 26:3, 24; 28:15; 31:3; Ex. 33:14; Deut. 31:6, 8; Josh. 1:5; 1 Kin. 6:13; Hag. 1:13; 2:4, 5; Matt. 28:20; John 14:17, 23; 2 Cor. 6:16; 13:11; Phil. 4:9; Heb. 13:5; Jas. 4:8; Rev. 21:3. *Of the divine likeness,* 1 John 3:2. *Of the ministry of angels,* Heb. 1:14. *Of dwelling with Christ,* John 14:2, 3, Col. 3:4; 1 Thess. 4:17; 5:10. *Of everlasting remembrance,* Psa. 112:6. *Of having names written in heaven,* Luke 10:20. *Of resurrection,* John 5:29; 1 Cor. 15:48–57; 2 Cor. 4:14; 1 Thess. 4:16. *Of future glory,* Rom. 8:18; Col. 3:4; 2 Tim. 2:10; 1 Pet. 5:4. *Of inheritance,* Matt. 25:34; Acts 20:32; 26:18; Col. 1:12; 3:24; Tit. 3:7; Heb. 9:15; Jas. 2:5; 1 Pet. 1:4. *Of heavenly reward,* Matt. 5:12; 13:43; 2 Tim. 4:8; Heb. 11:16; Jas. 1:12; 2 Pet. 1:11; Rev. 2:7, 10; 22:5, 12, 14. *Of eternal life,* Dan. 12:2, 3; Matt. 19:29; 25:46; Mark 10:29, 30; Luke 18:29, 30; John 3:15, 16, 36; 4:14; 5:24, 29; 6:39, 40; 10:28; 12:25; Rom. 2:7; 6:22, 23; Gal. 6:8; 1 Thess. 4:15–17; 1 Tim. 1:16; 4:8; Titus 1:2; 1 John 2:25; 5:13; Rev. 7:14–17.

CONTINGENT UPON PERSEVERANCE, Heb. 10:36; Rev. 2:7, 10, 11, 17, 26–28; 3:4, 5, 10, 12, 21; 21:7.

**Union of, with God,** 1 John 3:24; 4:13, 15, 16; 2 John 9.

**Union of, with Christ,** John 6:51–58; 14:20; 15:1–11, 17:21–23, 26; Rom. 8:1; 12:5; 1 Cor. 6:13–20; 10:16; 2 Cor. 13:5; Gal. 2:20; Col. 1:27; 2:6, 7; 1 John 2:6, 24, 28; 3:6, 24; 5:12, 20; 2 John 9; see footnotes: ADOPTION, Rom. 8:15; FELLOWSHIP, *With Christ,* 1 Cor. 1:9.

[m] *Mariner* Ezek. 27:27.

6

[n] *God, power of,* Gen. 2:2.

9

[o] *God, providence of,* vs. 9–12; Gen. 2:2.

[p] *Temporal Blessings, from God,* Psa. 103:2.

[q] *Rain,* 2 Sam. 1:21.

10

1 R. V. her furrows abundantly;

1

[a] *Praise,* vs. 1–12; Psa. 150:1.

3

[b] *Works of God,* Psa. 40:5.

[c] *God, power of,* Gen. 2:2.

1 R. V. are thy works!

the confidence of all the ends of
the earth, and of [m]them that are
afar off *upon* the sea:
6 Which by [n]his strength setteth fast[G] the mountains; *being*
girded with power:[s]
7 [n]Which stilleth the noise of
the seas, the noise of their waves,
and the tumult of the people.[Q]
8 They also that dwell in the
uttermost parts are afraid at thy
tokens[G]: thou makest the outgoings[G] of the morning and evening
to rejoice.
9 [s]Thou [o]visitest[G] the earth, and
[p,q]waterest it: thou greatly en-
richest it with the river of God,
*which* is full of water: thou preparest them *corn[G], when thou
hast so provided for it.
10 [o]Thou [p]waterest [1]the ridges
thereof abundantly: thou settlest
the furrows thereof: thou makest it soft with [q]showers: thou
blessest the springing thereof.
11 [o]Thou crownest the year
with thy goodness; and thy paths
drop fatness.
12 They drop *upon* the pastures
of the wilderness: and the little
hills rejoice on every side.
13 The pastures are clothed
with flocks; the valleys also are
covered over with *corn; they
shout for joy, they also sing.[s]

## PSALM 66

*An exhortation to praise God, in view of his great works,* 8 *and gracious benefits.* 13 *The psalmist's purpose to fulfill his vows,* 16 *and to declare what God hath done for his soul.*

To the chief Musician, A Song or Psalm.

[a]MAKE a joyful noise unto
God, all ye lands:
2 [a]Sing forth the honour of his
name: make his praise glorious.
3 Say unto God, How terrible[G]
[1]*art thou in* thy [b]works! through
the greatness of thy [c]power shall
thine enemies submit themselves
unto thee.[s]
4 [a,d,e]All the earth shall [f]wor-
ship thee, and shall sing unto thee; they shall sing *to* thy
name. [Sē′lah.[G]
5 Come and see the [b]works of
God: *he is* terrible[G] *in his* doing
toward the children of men.
6 [a]He turned the [g]sea into dry
*land*: [h]they went through the
[2]flood on foot: there did we rejoice in him.
7 He [i]ruleth by his [c]power for
ever; his eyes [j]behold the nations: let not the rebellious exalt
themselves.[s] [Sē′lah.
8 [a]O [k]bless[G] our God, ye [3]peo-
ple, and make the voice of his
praise to be heard:
9 [l]Which [m]holdeth our soul in
life, and [m]suffereth not our feet
to be moved.
10 For thou, O God, hast
[n,o]proved[G] us: thou hast tried us,
as silver is tried.[Q]
11 Thou broughtest us into the
[p]net; thou laidst [q]affliction upon
our loins.
12 [r]Thou hast caused men to
ride over our heads; we went
through fire and through water:
[s]but thou broughtest us out into
a wealthy *place*.
13 [k]I will go into thy house
[l]with [t]burnt offerings: I will pay
thee my [u]vows,
14 [u]Which my lips have uttered, and my mouth hath spoken,
when I was in trouble.
15 [k]I will offer unto thee [t]burnt
[4]sacrifices of fatlings, with the
incense of rams; I will offer bullocks with goats. [Sē′lah.
16 [k]Come *and* hear, all ye that
[v]fear God, and I will [w]declare
what he hath done for my soul.
17 I cried unto him with my
mouth, and he was [x]extolled
with my tongue.
18 [y]If I regard iniquity in my

4

[d] *Church, prophecies concerning its prosperity,* Matt. 16:18.

[e] *Gentiles, prophecies of the conversion of,* Acts 10:45.

[f] *Worship,* Gen. 22:5.

6

[g] *Red Sea, Israelites cross,* Ex. 10:19.

[h] *Israel, passes through the Red Sea,* Ex. 4:22.

2 R. V. river

7

[i] *God, sovereign,* Gen. 2:2.

[j] *God, knowledge of,* Gen. 2:2.

8

[k] *Thankfulness, to God, exemplified,* Acts 24:3.

3 R. V. peoples,

9

[l] *Faith, exemplified,* Mark 11:22.

[m] *God, preserver,* Gen. 2:2.

10

[n] *Adversity, design of,* Psa. 10:6.

[o] *Temptation, a test,* Luke 11:4.

11

[p] *Net, figurative,* Isa. 51:20.

[q] *Adversity, dispensation from God,* Psa. 10:6.

12

[r] *God, providence of, mysterious,* Gen. 2:2.

[s] *Adversity, benefits of,* Psa. 10:6.

13

[t] *Offerings, burnt,* Lev. 6:17.

[u] *Vows,* Num. 30:2.

15

4 R. V. offerings

16

[v] *Fear of God,* Acts 9:31.

[w] *Religious Testimony, exemplified,* 2 Thess. 1:10.

17

[x] *Praise,* Psa. 150:1.

18

[y] *Wicked, prayers of, not answered,* Psa. 73:3.

* **CORN,** a general term applied to cereals, such as wheat, barley and rye *or* spelt, etc. *Product, of Egypt,* Gen. 41:47–49; 42:1–5, 25–27; *of Palestine,* Deut. 33:28; Ezek. 27:17. *Parched,* Ruth 2:14; 1 Sam. 17:17; 25:18; 2 Sam. 17:28. *Ground,* 2 Sam. 17:19. *Eaten by the Israelites,* Josh. 5:11, 12. *Shocks of, burnt,* Judg. 15:5. *Heads of, plucked by Christ's disciples,* Matt. 12:1; Mark 2:23–28; Luke 6:1–5. *Mosaic laws concerning,* Ex. 22:6; Deut. 23:25.
**Figurative,** Psa. 72:16. *Symbolical,* Gen. 41:5.
See footnotes: BARLEY, Ex. 9:31; WHEAT, Ezra 6:9.

*z Heart*, Psa. 44:21.

19

*a Prayer, answered*, Acts 6:4.

20

*b Praise*, Psa. 150:1.

*c God, mercy of*, Gen. 2:2.

1

*a Prayer*, Acts 6:4.

*b God, mercy of*, Gen. 2:2.

3

*c Praise*, Psa. 150:1.

1 R. V. peoples

4

*d Joy*, Psa. 5:11.

*e God, judge*, Gen. 2:2.

*f God, sovereign*, Gen. 2:2.

6

*g God, providence of*, Gen. 2:2.

*h Faith, exemplified*, Mark 11:22.

2 R. V. The earth hath yielded her increase:

7

*i Fear of God*, Acts 9:31.

[z]heart, the Lord will not hear
*me*:
19 *But* verily God hath [a]heard
*me*; he hath attended to the voice
of my prayer.
20 [b]Blessed *be* God, which hath
not turned away my prayer, nor
his [c]mercy from me.

## PSALM 67

*A prayer for the enlargement of God's kingdom, 3 and for the joy of his people.*

To the chief Musician on Neginoth, A Psalm *or* Song.

A Messianic Psalm. The opening theme of the poem is the mission and message of Israel to the world, namely, "that thy way may be known upon the earth, thy salvation among all nations." The inspired vision of the prophet bursts the restrictions of national exclusiveness that forbade Israel's fellowship with the nations of the world, and reveals the coming of all the peoples of the earth into one spiritual kingdom, when all the ends of the earth shall fear God. The theme of the psalm sung in the tabernacle of old is the theme of the Gospel that inspires our faith as we sing in Christian assemblies of this day:

"From all that dwell below the skies,
Let the Creator's praise arise;
Let the Redeemer's name be sung
Through every land by every tongue."

The fulfillment of the Messianic hope expressed in both the ancient and modern song is approaching its realization in the glorious kingdom of the world's triumphing Messiah.

[a]GOD be [b]merciful unto us,
and bless us; *and*
cause his face to shine upon
us; [Sē'lah.
2 That thy way may be known
upon earth, thy saving health
among all nations.
3 Let the [1]people [c]praise thee,
O God; let all the people praise
thee.
4 O let the nations be glad
and sing for [d]joy: for thou shalt
[e]judge the people righteously,
and [f]govern the nations upon
earth. [Sē'lah.
5 Let the [1]people [c]praise thee,
O God; let all the people praise
thee.
6 [2,g]*Then* shall the earth yield
her increase; *and* [h]God, *even* our
own God, shall bless us.
7 [h]God shall bless us; and
all the ends of the earth shall
[i]fear him.

## PSALM 68

*A prayer for the overthrow of God's enemies, and the joy of the righteous. 4 An exhortation to praise him for his mercies, 7 for his care of Israel, 19 and for his great benefits.*

To the chief Musician, A Psalm *or* Song of David.

LET God arise, [a]let his enemies be scattered: let them
also that hate him flee before
him.
2 [a]As smoke is driven away,
*so* drive [b]*them* away: as wax
melteth before the fire, *so* let the
wicked perish at the presence of
God.
3 But let the righteous be [c]glad:
let them rejoice before God: yea,
let them exceedingly rejoice.
4 Sing unto God, sing [d]praises
to his name: [1]extol him that
rideth upon the heavens by
his name JÄH, and [c]rejoice before him.
5 A [e]father of the [f,g]fatherless,
and a judge of the [h]widows, *is*
God in his holy habitation.
6 [i,j]God [k]setteth the solitary in
families: he [l]bringeth out [2]those
which are bound with chains:
but the [m]rebellious dwell in a
dry *land*.
7 O God, when thou [n]wentest
forth before thy people, when
thou didst march through the
wilderness; [Sē'lah:
8 The earth [o]shook, the heavens also dropped at the presence
of God: [3]*even* [p]Sī'nāi itself *was*
*moved* at the presence of God,
the God of [q]Iṣ'ra-el.
9 Thou, O God, didst [l]send a
plentiful [k]rain, whereby thou
didst confirm thine inheritance,
when it was weary.
10 Thy congregation hath
dwelt therein: thou, O God, hast
prepared of thy [r]goodness for
the [s]poor.
11 The Lord gave the word:
[4]great *was* the company of [t]those
that published *it*.
12 [u]Kings of [v]armies did [w]flee

1

*a Prayer, imprecatory*, Acts 6:4.

2

*b Wicked, punishment of*, Psa. 73:3.

3

*c Joy*, Psa. 5:11.

4

*d Praise*, Psa. 150:1.

1 Am. R. V. Cast up a highway for him that rideth through the deserts; His name is Jehovah; and exult ye before him.

5

*e God, fatherhood of*, Gen. 2:2.

*f Orphan*, Lam. 5:3.

*g Children, God's care of*, Mark 10:14.

*h Widow*, 2 Sam. 14:5.

6

*i Adversity, consolation in*, Psa. 10:6.

*j God, preserver*, Gen. 2:2.

*k Temporal Blessings, from God*, Psa. 103:2.

*l God, providence of*, Gen. 2:2.

*m Wicked, contrasted with the righteous*, Psa. 73:3.

2 R. V. the prisoners into prosperity:

7

*n God, guidance of*, Gen. 2:2.

8

*o Earthquakes*, Isa. 29:6.

*p Sinai*, Ex. 16:1.

*q Israel*, Ex. 4:22.

3 Am. R. V. That Sinai trembled at

10

*r God, goodness of*, Gen. 2:2.

*s Poor, God's care of*, Prov. 21:13.

11

*t Women*, Prov. 31:10.

4 R. V. The women that publish the tidings are a great host.

12

*u King*, 2 Kin. 3:10.

*v Armies*, Deut. 11:4.

*w Panic*, Judg. 7:22.

*x Spoils*, 1 Chr. 26:27.

**13**

5 Am. R. V. When ye lie among the sheepfolds, It is as the wings

6 R. V. pinions

**14**

*y* Or, *Zalmon*, Judg. 9:48.

7 R. V. as when it snoweth in Zalmon.

**16**

8 R. V. Why look ye askance, ye high mountains, At the mountain which God hath desired for his abode?

**17**

*z Armies, figurative*, Deut. 11:4.

*a Chariot, figurative*, Josh. 11:4.

*b Sinai*, Ex. 16:1.

*c Sanctuary*, Lev. 4:6.

9 R. V. upon thousands:

10 R. V. sanctuary.

**18**

*d* Eph. 4:8–10.

*e Jesus, exaltation of*, Matt. 1:21.

*f Prophecies, concerning the Messiah, and their fulfillment*, Gen. 12:3.

*g Captivity, figurative*, Isa. 5:13.

11 R. V. among

**19**

*h Thankfulness, to God, exemplified*, Acts 24:3.

*i God, goodness of*, Gen. 2:2.

*j Spiritual Blessings, from God*, Eph. 1:3.

*k God, savior*, Gen. 2:2.

12 R. V. beareth our burden,

**20**

*l Death, God's power over*, Num. 23:10.

13 R. V. Jehovah

**21**

*m Enemy*, Prov. 24:17.

*n Impenitence, judgment denounced against*, Rom. 2:5.

14 R. V. guiltiness.

apace: and she that tarried at
home divided the [x]spoil.
13 [5]Though ye have lien[c] among
the pots,[c] *yet shall ye be as* the
wings of a dove covered with
silver, and her [6]feathers with
yellow gold.
14 When the Almighty scattered kings in it, it was [7]*white*
as snow in [y]Săl′mŏn.
15 The hill of God *is as* the hill
of Bā′shăn; an high hill *as* the
hill of Bā′shăn.
16 [8]Why leap ye, ye high
hills? *this is* the hill *which*
God desireth to dwell in; yea,
the LORD will dwell *in it* for
ever.[s]
17 [T][z]The [a]chariots of God *are*
twenty thousand, *even* thousands [9]of angels: the Lord *is*
among them, *as in* [b]Sī′nāi, in the
[10,c]holy *place*.
18 [d,e,f]Thou hast ascended
on high, thou hast led [g]cap-
tivity captive: thou hast received gifts [11]for men; yea,
[11]*for* the rebellious also, that
the LORD God might dwell
*among them*.[T] [Q]
19 [h]Blessed *be* the Lord, [i]*who*
daily [12]loadeth us *with* [j]*benefits*,
*even* the God of our [k]salva-
tion.[s] [Sē′lah.
20 *He that is* our God *is* the
God of [k]salvation; and unto
[13]GOD the Lord *belong* the issues[c]
from [l]death.
21 But God shall wound the
head of his [m]enemies, *and* the
hairy scalp of such an one
as [n]goeth on still in his [14]tres-
passes.
22 The Lord said, I will bring
again from Bā′shăn, I will bring
*my people* again from the depths
of the sea:[s]
23 That thy foot may be dipped
in the blood of *thine* enemies,
*and* the tongue of thy dogs in the
same.
24 They have seen thy goings,
O God; *even* the goings[G] of my
God, my [o]King, in the [p]sanc-
tuary.
25 The [q]singers went before,
the [15,q]players on instruments
*followed* after; among *them were*
the damsels playing with [r]tim-
brels.
26 [h,s]Bless[G] ye God in the
congregations, *even* the Lord,
[16]from the fountain of Ĭs′-
ra-el.
27 There *is* little [t]Bĕn′ja-mĭn
*with* their ruler, the princes of
[u]Jū′dah *and* their council,[c] the
princes of [v]Zĕb′u-lŭn, *and* the
princes of [w]Năph′ta-lī.
28 Thy God hath commanded
thy strength: [x]strengthen, O
God, that which thou hast
wrought for us.
29 Because of thy [y]temple at
[z]Jē-ru′sā-lĕm shall kings bring
[a]presents unto thee.
30 Rebuke the [17]company of
spearmen, the multitude of the
bulls, with the calves of the people, [18]*till every one* submit himself with pieces of silver: scatter
thou the people *that* delight in
war.
31 [b,c]Princes shall come out
of [d]Ē′ġўpt; [e]Ē-thĭ-ō′pĭ-ȧ shall
[19]soon stretch out her hands unto
God.
32 [f]Sing unto God, ye kingdoms of the earth; O sing praises
unto the Lord; [Sē′lah:
33 To him that rideth upon the
[g]heavens of heavens, *which were*
of old; lo, he doth send out
his voice, *and that* a mighty
voice.[s]
34 Ascribe ye [h]strength unto
God: his excellency *is* over Ĭs′-
ra-el, and his [h]strength *is* in the
clouds.
35 O God, *thou art* terrible[c]
out of thy holy places: the God
of Ĭs′ra-el *is* he that giveth
[i]strength and power unto *his*
people. [f]Blessed *be* God.[Q]

**24**

*o God, sovereign*, Gen. 2:2.

*p Church, called sanctuary*, 1 Kin. 9:3.

**25**

*q Music*, 2 Chr. 5:13.

*r Timbrel*, Ex. 15:20.

15 R. V. minstrels

**26**

*s Praise*, Psa. 150:1.

16 R. V. ye that are of the fountain of Israel.

**27**

*t Benjamin, tribe of*, Num. 1:37.

*u Judah, tribe of*, Num. 10:14.

*v Zebulun, tribe of*, Gen. 49:13.

*w Naphtali, tribe of*, Num. 1:42.

**28**

*x Spiritual Desire*, Psa. 42:1.

**29**

*y Temple, Second*, 1 Kin. 6:17.

*z Jerusalem*, Judg. 19:10.

*a Presents*, Gen. 32:13.

**30**

17 R. V. wild beast of the reeds,

18 R. V. Trampling under foot the pieces of silver; He hath scattered the peoples

**31**

*b Church, prophecies concerning its prosperity*, Matt. 16:18.

*c Gentiles, prophecies of the conversion of*, Acts 10:45.

*d Egypt*, Gen. 41:8.

*e Ethiopia*, Isa. 18:1.

19 R. V. haste to stretch

**32**

*f Praise*, Psa. 150:1.

**33**

*g Heavens, physical*, Psa. 8:3.

**34**

*h God, power of*, Gen. 2:2.

**35**

*i Spiritual Blessings*, Eph. 1:3.

## PSALM 69

*The psalmist complains of his affliction. 13 He prays for deliverance. 22 He devotes his enemies to destruction. 30 And praises God with thanksgiving.*

To the chief Musician upon Shoshannim, *A Psalm* of David.

A Messianic Psalm. This Psalm is frequently quoted in the New Testament. The experience of the psalmist, which is graphically described herein, is frequently referred to as typical of the sufferings of Jesus, and the causeless hatred of the Jews. Compare v. 4 with John 15:25. The zeal of Jesus is typified in v. 9, as shown in John 2:17. The rest of this verse is applied by Paul to Jesus (see Romans 15:3). Verse 25 seems to have been combined with Psalm 109:8 in Acts 1:20 describing the doom of the traitor. Verses 22, 23 are applied by Paul in Romans 11:9 to the rejection of apostate Israel. The physical sufferings of the psalmist described in v. 21 foreshadow the sufferings of Jesus (see John 19:25). While Matthew does not quote this verse, it seems to have been in his mind (see Matt. 27:34, 48) as descriptive of the sufferings of Jesus. Verses 12, 20 are descriptive of the mockery endured by the psalmist, which prefigures the mockery of the Savior described in Matt. 27:27. Verse 26, in the light of Isa. 53 and Zech. 13:7, foreshadows the sufferings of the Savior. The Psalm cannot be interpreted as wholly Messianic, for the almost shocking imprecations against the psalmist's enemies, as for instance, vs. 22-25, 27, 28, are inconsistent with the meekness of Jesus, who, while "He was reviled, reviled not again" (1 Pet. 2:23). Nevertheless, it must be recognized that the strong similitudes in the persecutions endured by the psalmist foreshadow the sufferings of the Savior of men.

[a]SAVE me, O God; for [b]the
waters are come in unto
*my* soul.
2 [b]I sink in deep [c]mire, where
*there is* no standing: I am come
into deep waters, where the
floods overflow me.
3 [b]I am weary of my crying: my
throat is dried: mine eyes fail
while I [d]wait for my God.
4 [e]They that [f,g]hate me without
a cause are more than the hairs
of mine head: they that would
destroy me, *being* mine [h]enemies
wrongfully, are mighty: then I
restored *that* which I took not
away.
5 [b,i]O God, thou [j]knowest my
foolishness: and [k]my sins are not
hid from thee.
6 [l]Let not them that wait on
thee, O Lord GOD of hosts, [m]be
ashamed for my sake: let not
those that [d]seek thee be [1,m]confounded for my sake, O God of
Is'ra-el.
7 Because [n]for thy sake [o]I have
borne reproach; shame hath
covered my face.
8 [o]I am become a stranger unto
my brethren, and an alien unto
my mother's children.
9 For [p]the [q]zeal of thine house
hath eaten me up; and [r]the [s]reproaches of them that reproached thee are fallen upon me.
10 When I [t]wept, *and chastened*
my soul with [u]fasting, that was
to my reproach.
11 I made [v]sackcloth also my
garment; and I became a [w]proverb to them.
12 They that sit in the [x]gate
[y]speak against me; and I *was*
the song of the *,[z]drunkards.
13 But as for me, [a]my [b]prayer
*is* unto thee, O LORD, *in* an acceptable time: O God, in the
multitude of thy [c]mercy hear me,
in the [d]truth of thy [e]salvation.
14 [b]Deliver me out of the [f]mire,
and let me not sink: let me be delivered from [g]them that [h]hate
me, and out of the deep waters.
15 [b]Let not the waterflood overflow me, neither let the deep
swallow me up, and let not the
[i]pit shut her mouth upon me.
16 [b]Hear me, O LORD; [j]for thy
[k,l]lovingkindness *is* good: turn
unto me according to the multitude of thy tender [c]mercies.
17 And [b]hide not thy face from
thy servant; for I am in trouble:
hear me speedily.
18 [b]Draw nigh unto my soul,
*and* redeem it: deliver me because of mine enemies.
19 [m]Thou hast [n]known my reproach, and my shame, and my

**1**
a *Prayer, in adversity*, vs. 1–36; Acts 6:4.
b *Afflictions, despondency in*, Psa. 34:19.
**2**
c Psa. 40:2.
**3**
d *Spiritual Desire*, Psa. 42:1.
**4**
e John 15:25.
f *Hatred*, Prov. 15:17.
g *Malice*, Eph. 4:31.
h *Enemy*, Prov. 24:17.
**5**
i *Prayer, confession in*, Acts 6:4.
j *God, knowledge of*, Gen. 2:2.
k *Sin, confession of*, Rom. 5:12.
**6**
l *Unselfishness, instances of*, 1 Cor. 10:24.
m *Stumbling, figurative*, Isa. 8:14.
1 R. V. brought to dishonour through me,
**7**
n *Zeal, exemplified*, 2 Cor. 7:11.
o *Jesus, sufferings of, typified*, vs. 7–9, 20; Matt. 1:21.
**9**
p John 2:17.
q *Jesus, zeal of, typified*, Matt. 1:21.
r Rom. 15:3.
s *Persecution, of the righteous*, John 15:20.
**10**
t *Weeping*, Ezra 3:13.
u *Fasting*, Zech. 8:19.
**11**
v *Sackcloth*, Isa. 15:3.
w *Proverbs*, 1 Sam. 24:13.
**12**
x *Gates, open square of, a place for idlers*, Deut. 3:5.
y *Speech, evil*, Col. 4:6.
z *Drunkenness, mockery in*, Luke 21:34.
**13**
a *Decision*, Isa. 50:7.
b *Adversity, prayer in*, Psa. 10:6.
c *God, mercy of*, Gen. 2:2.
d *Truth*, John 18:37.
e *Salvation*, Acts 16:17.
**14**
f Psa. 40:2.
g *Enemy*, Prov. 24:17.
h *Hatred*, Prov. 15:17.
**15**
i *Pit, figurative*, Psa. 7:15.
**16**
j *Prayer, pleas offered in*, Acts 6:4.
k *God, goodness of*, Gen. 2:2.
l *God, love of*, Gen. 2:2.
**19**
m *Faith, exemplified*, Mark 11:22.
n *God, knowledge of*, Gen. 2:2.

* **DRUNKARD**, Joel 1:5; Nah. 1:10. *Described*, Prov. 23:29, 30. *The psalmist mocked by*, Psa. 69:12. *Temporal adversity of*, Prov. 23:21; Isa. 28:1, 3. *Insatiable appetite of*, Hab. 2:5, 6. *Fellowship with, forbidden by Paul*, 1 Cor. 5:11. *Punishment of*, Deut. 21:20, 21. *Excluded from kingdom of God*, 1 Cor. 6:9, 10.
See footnotes: DRUNKENNESS, Luke 21:34; WINE, Prov. 23:31. See also TEMPERANCE, 2 Pet. 1:6; TOTAL ABSTINENCE, Lev. 10:9.

**20**
o *Despondency,* Eccl. 2:20.
p *Afflictions, consolation in,* Psa. 34:19.

**21**
q *Jesus, prophecies concerning,* Matt. 1:21.
r Matt. 27:34, 48; Mark 15:23; John 19:29.
s *Gall,* Job 16:13.

**22**
t Rom. 11:9, 10.
2 R. V. And when they are in peace,

**24**
u *Anger of God, invoked,* 2 Kin. 13:3.

**26**
v *Prophecies, concerning the Messiah, and their fulfillment,* Gen. 12:3.
w Matt. 27:30.
3 R. V. tell of the sorrow of

**27**
x *God, righteousness of,* Gen. 2:2.

**28**
y *Book, figurative,* Psa. 139:16.
z *Righteous,* Psa. 64:10.
4 R. V. life,

**29**
a *Salvation,* Acts 16:17.

**30**
b *Praise,* Psa. 150:1.
c *Thankfulness, to God, exemplified,* Acts 24:3.

**31**
d *Obedience better than Sacrifice,* 1 Sam. 15:22.

**32**
e *Meekness,* Psa. 45:4.
f *Joy,* Psa. 5:11.
g *Spiritual Desire,* Psa. 42:1.
5 R. V. meek

**33**
h *Prayer, answer to, promised,* Acts 6:4.
i *Poor, God's care of,* Prov. 21:13.

dishonour: mine adversaries *are* all before thee.[S]

20 Reproach hath broken my heart; and I am [o]full of heaviness: and I looked *for some* to [p]take pity, but *there was* none; and for comforters, but I found none.

21 [q,r]They gave me also [s]gall for my meat; and in my thirst they gave me vinegar to drink.

22 [t]Let their table become a snare before them: [2]and *that which should have been* for *their* welfare, *let it become* a trap.

23 Let their eyes be darkened, that they see not; and make their loins continually to shake.

24 Pour out thine indignation upon them, and let thy wrathful [u]anger take hold of them.

25 Let their habitation be desolate; *and* let none dwell in their tents.

26 [v]For they persecute [q]*him* whom thou hast [w]smitten; and they [3]talk to the grief of those whom thou hast wounded.

27 Add iniquity unto their iniquity: and let them not come into [x]thy righteousness.

28 Let them be blotted out of the [y]book of [4]the living, and not be written with the [z]righteous.

29 But I *am* poor and sorrowful: let thy [a]salvation, O God, set me up on high.

30 I will [b]praise the name of God with a song, and will magnify him with [c]thanksgiving.

31 [d]*This* also shall please the LORD better than an ox *or* bullock that hath horns and hoofs.

32 The [5,e]humble shall see *this, and* be [f]glad: and your heart shall live that [g]seek God.

33 For [h]the LORD heareth the [i]poor, and despiseth not his prisoners.

34 Let the heaven and earth [b]praise him, the seas, and every thing that moveth therein.

35 For God will [j]save [k]Zī′ŏn, and will [l]build the cities of Jū′-dah: that they may dwell there, and have it in possession.

36 The seed also of his servants shall inherit it: and they that [m]love his name shall dwell therein.

## PSALM 70

*The psalmist prays for speedy deliverance from his enemies.*

To the chief Musician, *A Psalm* of David, to bring to remembrance.

[a,b]MAKE *haste,* O God, to [c]deliver me; make haste to help me, O LORD.

2 [d]Let them be ashamed and confounded that [e]seek after my soul: let them be turned backward, and [1]put to confusion, that desire my hurt.

3 [d]Let them be turned back [2]for a reward of their shame that [f]say, Aha, aha.

4 Let all [g]those that [h]seek thee rejoice and be [i]glad in thee: and let such as love thy [j]salvation say continually, [k]Let God be magnified.

5 [b]But I *am* poor and needy: [l]make haste unto me, O God: [m]thou *art* my [n]help and my deliverer; O LORD, make no tarrying.

## PSALM 71

*The psalmist entreats to be rescued from his enemies. 6 He acknowledges God's goodness to him from his youth, 9 and prays that he may not be cast off in his old age. 14 His confidence in God's help, 22 and purpose to praise him.*

[a,b]IN thee, O LORD, do I put my [c]trust: let me never be put to confusion.

2 [a,b]Deliver me in thy righteousness, and cause me to escape: incline thine ear unto me, and save me.

3 Be thou [1]my strong habitation, whereunto I may continually resort: [c]thou hast given commandment to [d]save me; for [c]thou *art* my [e]rock and my [f]fortress.

**35**
j *God, providence of,* Gen. 2.2.
k *Church, prophecies concerning its prosperity,* Matt. 16:18.
l *Temporal Blessings, from God,* v. 36; Psa. 103:2.

**36**
m *Love, of man for God,* 1 John 4:19.

**1**
a *Adversity, prayer in,* vs. 9, 12; Psa. 10:6.
b *Prayer, in adversity,* Acts 6:4.
c *Persecution, prayer for deliverance from,* John 15:20.

**2**
d *Prayer, imprecatory,* Acts 6:4.
e *Malice,* v. 3; Eph. 4:31.
1 R. V. brought to dishonour

**3**
f *Speech, evil,* Col. 4:6.
2 R. V. by reason

**4**
g *Seekers,* Isa. 55:6.
h *Spiritual Desire,* Psa. 42:1.
i *Joy,* Psa. 5:11.
j *Salvation,* Acts 16:17.
k *Praise,* Psa. 150:1.

**5**
l *Prayer, importunity in,* Acts 6:4.
m *Faith, exemplified,* Mark 11:22.
n *God, preserver,* Gen. 2:2.

**1**
a *Adversity, prayer in,* vs. 1–24; Psa. 10:6.
b *Prayer, in adversity,* vs. 1–24; Acts 6:4.
c *Faith, exemplified,* Mark 11:22.

**3**
d *God, preserver,* Gen. 2:2.
e *Rock, figurative,* Psa. 78:15.
f *Fortification, figurative,* Ezek. 17: 17.
1 R. V. to me a rock of habitation,

4 [a,b]Deliver me, O my God, out of the hand of the wicked, out of the hand of the unrighteous and cruel man.

5 [c]For thou *art* my [g]hope, O Lord GOD: *thou art* my trust from my [h]youth.

6 [S]By thee have I been [i]holden up from the womb: thou art he that took me out of my mother's bowels: [j]my [k]praise *shall be* continually of thee.

7 I am as a wonder unto many; but [c]thou *art* my strong [d]refuge.[S]

8 [j]Let my mouth be filled *with* thy [k]praise *and with* thy honour all the day.

9 [a,b]Cast me not off in the time of [l]old age; forsake me not when my strength faileth.

10 For mine [m]enemies [n]speak against me; and they that [n]lay[G] wait for my soul[G] take counsel[G] together,

11 Saying, God hath forsaken him: [n]persecute[G] and take him; for *there is* none to deliver *him*.

12 [a,b]O God, be not far from me: O my God, make haste for my help.

13 [o]Let them be confounded *and* consumed that are adversaries to my soul; let them be covered *with* reproach and dishonour that seek my hurt.

14 But I will [g]hope continually, and will yet [k]praise thee more and more.

15 [j]My mouth shall shew forth thy [p]righteousness *and* thy [q,r]salvation all the day; for I know not the numbers *thereof*.[S]

16 [s]I will [2]go in the strength of the Lord GOD: I will [t]make mention of thy righteousness, *even* of thine only.[S]

17 O God, thou hast [u]taught me from my youth: and hitherto have I [t,v]declared thy wondrous works.

18 Now also [w]when I am [x]old and greyheaded, O God, forsake me not; until I have [t]shewed thy [r]strength unto *this* generation, *and* thy [y]power to every one *that* is to come.

19 Thy [p]righteousness also, O God, *is* very high, who hast done great things: O God, who *is* like unto thee![S T]

20 *Thou*, which hast shewed me great and sore[G] [z]troubles, [a]shalt quicken[G] me again, and shalt bring me up again from the depths of the earth.

21 [3,a]Thou shalt [b]increase my greatness, and comfort me on every side.

22 I will also [c]praise thee with the [d]psaltery, *even* thy [e]truth, O my God: unto thee will I sing with the [f]harp, O thou Holy One of Is'ra-el.[S T]

23 [g]My lips shall greatly [h]rejoice when I [c]sing [4]unto thee; and my soul, which thou hast redeemed.

24 My tongue also shall [i]talk of thy [j]righteousness all the day long: for they are confounded,[G] for they are brought unto shame, that [k]seek my hurt.

## PSALM 72

*The psalmist, praying for the king, foretells his prosperous and glorious reign.*

*A Psalm* for Solomon.

A Messianic Psalm in which the poet by divine inspiration describes under the type of Solomon and his vast empire and incomparable prosperity and glory the sovereignty or lordship of Christ and the growth, peace and glory of his kingdom.

[a]GIVE the [b,c]king thy [d,e]judgments, O God, and thy [f,g]righteousness unto the king's son.

2 [b,c]He[Q] shall [d]judge thy people with [e,g,h]righteousness, and thy [i]poor with judgment.[G]

3 The mountains shall bring peace to the [j]people, and the little hills, by [h]righteousness.

4 [b,c]He shall judge the [i]poor of the people, he shall [k]save the [l]children of the needy, and shall break in pieces the [m]oppressor.[Q T]

---

5
g *Hope*, Prov. 13:12.
h *Children, good*, v. 17; Mark 10:14.
6
i *God, providence of*, Gen. 2:2.
j *Thankfulness, to God*, Acts 24:3.
k *Praise*, Psa. 150:1.
9
l *Old Age*, Isa. 46:4.
10
m *Enemy*, Prov. 24:17.
n *Malice*, Eph. 4:31.
13
o *Prayer, imprecatory*, Acts 6:4.
15
p *God, righteousness of*, Gen. 2:2.
q *Salvation*, Acts 16:17.
r *God, savior*, Gen. 2:2.
16
s *Faith, exemplified*, Mark 11:22.
t *Religious Testimony*, 2 Thess. 1:10.
2 Am. R. V. come with the mighty acts of the Lord Jehovah:
17
u *Wisdom, spiritual, from God*, Prov. 2:2.
v *Zeal, exemplified*, 2 Cor. 7:11.
18
w *Prayer, pleas offered in*, Acts 6:4.
x *Old Age*, Isa. 46:4.

y *God, power of*, Gen. 2:2.
20
z *Adversity, dispensation from God*, Psa. 10:6.
a *Faith, exemplified*, Mark 11:22
21
b *God, providence of*, Gen. 2:2.
3 R. V. Increase thou my greatness, And turn again and comfort me.
22
c *Praise*, Psa. 150:1.
d *Psaltery*, 1 Chr. 16:5.
e *Truth, attribute of God*, John 18:37.
f *Harp*, Dan. 3:10.
23
g *Thankfulness, to God*, Acts 24:3.
h *Joy*, Psa. 5:11.
4 R. V. praises unto
24
i *Religious Testimony*, 2 Thess. 1:10.
j *God, righteousness of*, Gen. 2:2.
k *Malice*, Eph. 4:31.
1
a *Prayer*, Acts 6:4.
b *King, acts as judge*, 2 Kin. 3:10.
c *Jesus, king, typified in Solomon*, vs. 1–19; Matt. 1:21.
d *Judge, character of, and precepts relating to*, Judg. 2:18.
e *Rulers, character and qualifications of*, Ex. 18:21.
f *God, righteousness of*, Gen. 2:2.
g *Justice*, Deut. 33:21.
2
h *Righteousness*, Psa. 15:2.
i *Poor*, Prov. 21:13.
3
j *Nation, promises of peace to*, Isa. 2:4.
4
k *Jesus, savior*, vs. 12–14; Matt. 1:21.
l *Children*, Mark 10:14.
m *Oppression*, Eccl. 5:8.

5 They shall [n]fear [c,o]thee as
long as the sun and moon endure, throughout all generations.
6 [p]He shall come down like
[q]rain upon the [r]mown [s]grass:
as showers *that* water the earth.
7 In [o]his days shall the [t]right-
eous flourish; and abundance of
[u,v]peace so long as the moon
endureth.
8 [c,o,w]He shall have dominion
also from sea to sea, and from the
river unto the ends of the earth.
9 They that dwell in the wilderness shall bow before [c,o]him;
and his enemies shall lick the
dust.
10 The[Q] kings of [x]Tär′shish and
of the isles shall bring [y]presents:
the kings of [z]Shē′bȧ and [a]Sē′bȧ
shall offer gifts.
11 Yea, [b,c]all kings shall fall
down before him: all [d]nations
shall serve him.[Q]
12 For he shall [e]deliver the
needy when he crieth; the [f]poor
also, and *him* that hath no
helper.
13 He shall spare the [f]poor and
needy, and shall [e]save the souls
of the needy.
14 [g]He shall [e]redeem their soul
from [1,h]deceit and violence: and
[i]precious shall their blood be in
his sight.[S Q]
15 And he shall live, and to
him shall be given of the [j]gold
of [k]Shē′bȧ: [l]prayer also shall
be made for him continually;
*and* daily shall he be praised.[Q]
16[S] There shall be [2]an handful
of [m]corn[G] in the earth upon the
top of the mountains; the fruit
thereof shall shake like [n]Lĕb′a-
non: and *they* of the city shall
flourish like [o]grass of the earth.
17 [c]His name shall [p]endure for
ever: his name shall be continued as long as the sun: and *men*
shall be blessed in him: all [d]na-
tions shall call him blessed.
18 [q]Blessed *be* the LORD God,
the God of Is̱′ra-el, who only
doeth wondrous things.[S Q]
19 And [q]blessed *be* his glorious [r]name for ever: and let
the whole earth be filled *with*
his [s]glory; Amen, and Amen.[S]
20 The prayers of [t]Dā′vid the
son of [u]Jĕs′se are ended.

## PSALM 73

*The psalmist, strongly tempted by the prosperity of the wicked, 16 finds relief, in the sanctuary, in view of the end of the wicked, and the salvation of the righteous.*

A Psalm of Asaph.

1 TRULY God *is* [a]good to Is̱′-
ra-el, *even* to such as are
of a [b]clean [c]heart.[S]
2 But as for me, [d]my feet were
almost gone; my steps had well[G]
nigh slipped.
3 For [d]I was [e]envious at the
[1]foolish, *when* I saw the prosperity of the *wicked.[S]
4 For *there are* no bands[G] in

5
n *Fear of God*, Acts 9:31.
o *Jesus, prophecies concerning*, Matt. 1:21.
6
p *Spiritual Blessings, from God*, Eph. 1:3.
q *Rain*, 2 Sam. 1:21.
r Amos 7:1.
s *Grass*, Isa. 40:7.
7
t *Church, prophecies concerning its prosperity*, Matt. 16:18.
u *Spiritual Peace*, Gal. 1:3.
v *Peace*, Jer. 29:7.
8
w *Gentiles, prophecies concerning the conversion of*, vs. 8–11; Acts 10:45.
10
x *Tarshish*, 2 Chr. 20:36.
y *King, emoluments of*, 2 Kin. 3:10.
z *Sheba*, 1 Kin. 10:1.
a Isa. 43:3.
11
b *Jesus, king, typified in Solomon*, Matt. 1:21.
c *Jesus, kingdom of, prophecies concerning*, Matt. 1:21.
d *Gentiles, prophecies of the conversion of*, Acts 10:45.
12
e *Jesus, savior*, Matt. 1:21.
f *Poor*, Prov. 21:13.
14
g *Rulers, righteous*, Ex. 18:21.
h *Deceit*, Psa. 36:3.
i *Jesus, love of*, Matt. 1:21.
1 R. V. oppression
15 j *Gold, exported from Sheba*, Ezek. 7:19.

k *Sheba, rich in gold*, 1 Kin. 10:1.
l *Prayer, intercessory*, Acts 6:4.
16
m *Corn, figurative*, Psa. 65:13.
n *Lebanon*, Deut. 1:7.
o *Grass*, Isa. 40:7.
2 R. V. abundance
17
p *Jesus, eternity of*, Matt. 1:21.
18
q *Praise*, Psa. 150:1.
19
r *God, name of, to be praised*, Gen. 2:2.
s *God, glory of*, Gen. 2:2.
20
t *David*, 1 Sam. 16:13.
u *Jesse*, Ruth 4:17.

1
a *God, goodness of*, Gen. 2:2.
b *Holiness*, Ex. 39:30.
c *Heart*, Psa. 44:21.
2
d *Spiritual Blindness*, vs. 2–28; 2 Cor. 4:4.
3
e *Envy*, Prov. 14:30.
1 R. V. arrogant,

* **WICKED.** Compared to: *Tares*, Matt. 13:38; *chaff*, Job 21:18; Psa. 1:4; Matt. 3:12; *dross*, Ezek. 22:18, 19; *reprobate silver*, Jer. 6:30; *corrupt trees*, Luke 6:43; *wells without water*, 2 Pet. 2:17; *troubled sea*, Isa. 57:20; *whited sepulchres*, Matt. 23:27; *fools building upon sand*, Matt. 7:26; *deaf adders*, Psa. 58:4; *scorpions*, Ezek. 2:6; *serpents*, Psa. 58:4; Matt. 23:33; *dogs*, Prov. 26:11; Matt. 7:6; 2 Pet. 2:22; *goats*, Matt. 25:32; *swine*, Matt. 7:6; 2 Pet. 2:22.

*God is angry with*, Psa. 5:5, 6; 1 Cor. 10:5. *Spirit of God is withdrawn from*, Gen. 6:3; Hos. 4:17–19; Rom. 1:24, 26, 28. *Hate the righteous*, Matt. 5:11, 12; Luke 6:22, 23. *Worship of, offensive to God*, Psa. 50:16, 17; Isa. 1:10–15.

**Contrasted with the righteous,** Psa. 1:1–6; 11:5; 17:14, 15; 32:10; 37:17–22, 37, 38; 73:1–28; 75:10; 91:7, 8; Prov. 2:21, 22; 3:32, 33; 4:16–19; 10:3, 6, 9, 11, 16, 20, 21, 23–25, 28–32; 11:3, 5, 6, 8–11, 18–21, 23, 31; 12:2, 3, 5–7, 10, 12, 13, 21, 26; 13:5, 6, 9, 17, 21, 22, 25; 14:2, 11, 19, 22, 32; 15:6, 8, 9, 28, 29; 21:15, 18, 26, 29; 22:5, 8, 9; 24:16; 28:1, 4, 5, 13, 14, 18; 29:2, 6, 7, 27; Isa. 32:1–8; 65:13, 14; Mal. 3:18; Rom. 2:7–10; Eph. 2:12–14; Phil. 2:15; 1 Thess. 5:5–8; Tit. 1:15; 1 Pet. 4:17, 18; 1 John 1:6, 7; 3:3–17.

**Described,** Job 8:13–17; 15:16, 20–35; Psa. 10:4–11; 36:1–4; 73:4–12; Isa. 59:2–8; Jer. 2:22–25. *As blind*, Ezek. 12:2. *As carnal*, Rom. 8:5, 7, 8; 9:8. *As children of the devil*, John 8:44; Acts 13:10; 1 John 3:10. *As perverse*, Jer. 9:6; Rom. 1:21; 2:4, 5; Phil. 2:15. *As despising God*, Job 21:14; Rom. 11:28. *As contentious*, Rom. 2:8. *As corrupt*, Psa. 53:1; 73:8; Isa. 59:3; Jer. 2:22; Ezek. 16:47; 20:16; Mic. 7:2–4; Tit. 1:15. *As loving darkness*, John 3:19, 20. *As dead in sin*, Eph. 2:1–3; 1 John 3:14. *As delighting, in lies*, Psa. 62:4; *in frowardness*, Prov. 2:13–19. *As defiled*, Tit. 1:15, 16. *As depraved*, Isa. 1:4–6; Jer. 17:9; 30:12–15; Rom. 1:20–32; 3:10–18; 1 Tim. 1:9, 10; 2 Tim. 3:2–9, 13; Tit. 3:3; 2 Pet. 2:10, 12–19; Jude 12, 13. *As destitute, of faithfulness*, Psa. 5:9; *of the love of God*, John 5:42. *As devilish*, 1 John 3:8. *As devisers of mischief*, Psa. 52:1–4; 64:3–6; Prov. 4:16; 6:12–15; 10:23; Isa. 32:6, 7; Jer. 4:22.

*As uncircumcised*, Isa. 52:1; Jer. 6:10; Ezek. 28:10; 31:18; 32:19–32. *As uncircumcised, of heart*, Lev. 26:41; Ezek. 44:7; Acts 7:51; *of lips*, Ex. 6:12.

*As disobedient*, Jer. 11:8; Tit. 1:16. *As alienated from God*, Col. 1:21. *As full of gall and venom*, Deut. 32:32, 33; Psa. 58:3–5. *As grievous sinners*, Gen. 13:13; 18:20; Job 22:5; Isa. 1:4–6.

*As hating, correction*, Prov. 15:10; Amos 5:10; *instruction*, Psa. 50:17; Prov. 1:29, 30; *the light*, John 3:20.

*As being in moral darkness*, Matt. 4:16; 6:23; Luke 1:79; Eph. 4:17, 18. *As not knowing the way of the Lord*, Jer. 5:4.

**4**
*f Death, of the wicked,* Num. 23:10.
**6**
*g Pride,* Prov. 16:18.
*h Chains, figurative,* Dan. 5:7.
**7**
*i Rich,* Jas. 5:1.
**8**
*j Speech, evil,* Col. 4:6.
2 R. V. scoff, and in wickedness utter oppression:
**9**
*k Blasphemy,* 2 Sam. 12:14.
**10**
*l Cup, figurative,* Matt. 20:22.
3 Am. R. V. drained by them.
**11**
*m Infidelity,* 2 Cor. 6:15.
*n Scoffing,* Hab. 1:10.
*o God, knowledge of,* Gen. 2:2.
**12**
*p Riches,* Eccl. 4:8.
4 R. V. And, being always at ease, they
**13**
*q Murmuring, against God,* Num. 14:2.
*r Doubting,* Rom. 14:23.
*s Spiritual Purification,* Psa. 51:2.
*t Ablution, of hands, a token of innocency,* Judg. 19:21.

*their [f]death: but their strength
*is* firm.
5 *They *are* not in trouble *as*
*other* men; neither are they
plagued like *other* men.
6 Therefore [g]pride compasseth
them about as a [h]chain; violence
covereth them *as* a garment.
7 *Their eyes stand out with
fatness: they [i]have more than
heart could wish.
8 *They [2]are corrupt, and
[j]speak wickedly *concerning* oppression: they speak loftily.
9 *They [k]set their mouth
against the heavens, and their
tongue walketh through the
earth.
10 Therefore his people return
hither: and waters of a full [l]*cup*
are [3]wrung out to them.
11 And they [k,m,n]say, How
doth God [o]know? and is there
knowledge in the most High?
12 Behold, these *are* the *ungodly, [4]who prosper in the world;
[i]they increase *in* [p]riches.
13 [q,r]Verily I have [s]cleansed
my heart *in* vain, and [t]washed
my hands in innocency.
14 For all the day long have I
been [u]plagued, and chastened
every morning.
15 If I say, I will speak thus;
behold, I [5]should offend *against*
the generation of thy children.
16 When I [v]thought to know
this, it *was* too painful for me;
17 Until I went into the [w]sanc-
tuary of God; [6]*then* understood
I their end.
18 Surely thou didst [x]set *them
in slippery places: thou castedst
them down into destruction.
19 How are *they *brought* into desolation, as in a moment!
they are utterly consumed with
terrors.
20 As a dream when *one*
awaketh; *so,* O Lord, when
thou awakest, thou shalt despise their image.
21 [y,z]Thus my heart was
grieved, and I was [a]pricked in
my reins.
22 [b]So [7]foolish *was* I, and ignorant: I was *as* a beast before thee.
23 Nevertheless I *am* continually with thee: [c]thou hast
[d,e]holden *me* by my right hand.

**14**
*u Divine Chastisement,* Job 33:19.
**15**
5 R. V. had dealt treacherously with the
**16**
*v Meditation,* Psa. 49:3.
**17**
*w Church, called sanctuary,* 1 Kin. 9:3.
6 R. V. And considered their latter end.
**18**
*x God, providence of,* Gen. 2:2.
**21**
*y Repentance,* Mark 1:4.
*z Sin, confession of,* Rom. 5:12.

*a Conscience, guilty,* Acts 23:1.
**22**
*b Humility, exemplified,* Prov. 22:4.
7 R. V. brutish was I,
**23**
*c Faith, exemplified,* Mark 11:22.
*d God, preserver,* Gen. 2:2.
*e Spiritual Blessings, from God,* Eph. 1:3.

*As lost,* Luke 19:10. *As loving wickedness,* Psa. 7:14; Jer. 14:10; Hos. 4:8; Mic. 3:2. *As malicious toward the righteous,* Psa. 37:12; 94:3, 8; 140:9. *As obdurate,* Psa. 10:4–11; Prov. 1:29, 30; Isa. 26:10, 11; Ezek. 3:7. *As past feeling,* Eph. 4:19. *As progressing in wickedness,* Isa. 30:1, 10, 11; Jer. 9:3; 2 Tim. 3:13. *As rebellious,* Deut. 9:24. *As sensual,* Phil. 3:19; Jude 19. *As servants of sin,* John 8:34. *As shameless,* Jer. 6:15; 8:12; Zeph. 3:5. *As unscrupulous,* Job 24:2–4; Psa. 10:4–10; Isa. 5:18–23; Jer. 5:26–28; 9:2–6. *As sold to work iniquity,* 1 Kin. 21:20. *As stiff-necked,* Deut. 9: 13; Acts 7:51. *As under condemnation,* John 3:18, 19.

**Happiness of:** *Sensual,* Isa. 22:13; 56:12. *Limited to this life,* Luke 16:25. *Ends suddenly,* Job 21:12, 13; Luke 12:19, 20.

**Hope of:** *Shall perish,* Job 8:13; 11:20; 27:8; Prov. 10:28.

**Miscellany concerning:** *Hate reproof,* 1 Kin. 22:8; 2 Chr. 18:7. *God's mercy to,* Job 33:14–30. *God's love for,* Deut. 5: 29; 32:29; Matt. 18:12–14; John 3:16, 17; Rom. 5:8; 1 John 4:9, 10.

*Gospel invitation to, illustrated by the parables of the householder,* Matt. 20:1–16; *and marriage supper,* Matt. 22:1–14.

*Terrors of, at the judgment,* Rev. 1:7. *Death of,* Psa. 49: 14; 73:3, 4, 17–19.

**Prayers of:** *Abominable to God,* Prov. 15:8, 29; 28:9. *Not answered,* Deut. 1:45; 1 Sam. 28:6; 2 Sam. 22:42; Job 27:9; 35: 12, 13; Psa. 18:41; 66:18; Prov. 1:24–28; Isa. 1:15; 59:2; Jer. 11:11; 14:12; Lam. 44; Ezek. 8:18; 20:3, 31; Hos. 5:6; Mic. 3:4; Zech. 7:13; Jas. 4:3.

**Prosperity of,** Job 12:6; 21:7–13; Psa. 73:3–12; Jer. 12:1, 2; Mal. 3:15. *Brief,* Job 5:3–5; 15:21, 23, 27, 29; 20:5, 22, 23; 21: 17, 18; 24:24; Psa. 37:35, 36; 49:10–14; 73:18, 19; 92:7; Eccl. 8:12, 13.

**Punishment of,** Job 18:5–21; 27:13–23; Psa. 37:1, 2, 9, 10, 17, 20, 22, 34–38; 73:18–20, 27; Prov. 10:3, 6–8, 14, 24, 25, 27–31; 11:3, 5–8, 19, 21, 23, 31; 16:4, 5; Isa. 3:11; 26:21; Jer. 21:14; 36:31; Lam. 3.39; Ezek. 3:18–20; 18:1–32; 33: 7–20; Hos. 14:9; Amos 3:2; Rom. 2:5, 8, 9; 1 Thess. 1:10; 2 Pet. 2:3–9, 12–17; Jude 5–7; Rev. 14:10, 11.

*By chastisements,* Psa. 89:32; 1 Cor. 5:5; 1 Tim. 1:20. *By judgments,* Ex. 32:35; Lev. 26:14–39; Deut. 11:26–28; 28:15–68; 30:15, 18, 19; Job 20:5–29; Psa. 11:6; 21:9, 10; 39:11; 75:8; 78:49–51; Isa. 13:9, 11, 14–22; 28:18–22; 65:12–15; Jer. 5:25; 44:2–14, 23–29; Ezek. 5:4, 8–17; 9:5–7, 10; Luke 12:46; 1 Cor. 10:5–11; Heb. 10:26–31. *By sorrow,* Gen. 3:16–19; Job 15:20–24; Psa. 32:10; Eccl. 2:26; Isa. 50:11. *By trouble,* Isa. 48:22; 57:20, 21. *By being rejected of the Lord,* 1 Chr. 28:9; Matt. 10: 33; Luke 13:27, 28 (with Matt. 7:23); John 8:21; Heb. 6:8. *By being excluded from the kingdom of heaven,* 1 Cor. 6:9, 10; Gal. 5: 19–21; Eph. 5:5; Rev. 21:27; 22:19. *By being blotted from God's book,* Ex. 32:33. *By destruction,* Deut. 7:9, 10; 1 Sam. 12: 25; 1 Chr. 10:13, 14; Job 4:8, 9; 31:3; Psa. 2:9; 7:11–13; 9:5, 17; 34:16, 21; 55:19, 23; 92:7, 9; 145:20; Prov. 2:22; 12:7; 21:12, 15, 16; 24:20; Isa. 11:4; Matt. 3:10, 12; (with Luke 3: 17); 7:13, 19; 10:28 (with Luke 12:4, 5); 21:41, 44 (with Mark 12:1–9; Luke 20:16, 18); 24:50, 51; Luke 9:24, 25 (with Matt. 16:26; Mark 8:36); 19:27; John 5:29; Acts 3:23; Rom. 2:12; 9:22; 1 Cor. 3:17; Phil. 3:19; 1 Thess. 5:3. *By sudden destruction,* Prov. 6:15; 24:22; 28:18; 29:1. *By everlasting destruction,* 2 Thess. 1:9. *By everlasting contempt,* Dan. 12:2. *By everlasting fire,* Matt. 18:8, 9; 25:41; Mark 9:43; Rev. 20:15; 21:8. *By death,* Gen. 2:17; Rom. 6:16, 21; 8:2, 6, 13; Jas. 1:15; 5:20. *By the second death,* Rev. 21:8. *By the damnation of hell,* Matt. 23:33. *By being cast into outer darkness,* Matt. 8:12; 22:13; 25:30.

*Everlasting,* Matt. 25:46; Rev. 14:10, 11; 20:10.

*Degrees in,* Matt. 10:15; 11:22, 24; Mark 12:40.

*No escape from,* Job 34:22; 1 Thess. 5:3; Heb. 2:3.

Set forth in parables: *Of the tares,* Matt. 13:24–30, 38–42, 49, 50; *of the talents,* Matt. 25:14–30; *of the barren fig tree,* Luke 13:6–9; *of the man who built his house on the sand,* Matt. 7:26, 27; Luke 6:49; *of Lazarus and the rich man,* Luke 16: 22–28. *Woes denounced against,* Isa. 5:8, 11, 18–23; Matt. 26:24; Mark 14:21; Luke 11:52; 17:1, 2; 22:22; Jude 11.

*God has no pleasure in the death of,* Ezek. 18:23; 33:11. See footnote, PUNISHMENT, Lev. 26:41.

**Warned,** Jer. 7:13–15, 23–25; 25:4–6; 26:2–7, 12, 13; 29: 17–19; Ezek. 33:8; Dan. 4:4–27; 5:4–29; Zeph. 2:1, 2; Luke 3:7–9; 1 Cor. 10:11; Rev. 3:1–3, 16–19.

**24**
*f Promise, implied, of divine guidance*, 2 Cor. 1:20.
*g Guidance*, Psa. 48:14.
*h God, guidance of*, Gen. 2:2.
**25**
*i Love, of man for God*, 1 John 4:19.
*j Spiritual Desire*, Psa. 42:1.
**26**
*k Afflictions, consolation in*, Psa. 34:19.
*l Spiritual Peace*, Gal. 1:3.
**27**
*m Apostasy*, Acts 1:25.
**28**
*n Access to God*, Eph. 3:12.
*o Religious Testimony*, 2 Thess. 1:10.

---

*a Music, symbols used in*, 2 Chr. 5:13.
**1**
*b Prayer, in adversity*, vs. 1–23; Acts 6:4.
*c Adversity, prayer in*, Psa. 10:6.
*d Nation, in adversity, prayer for*, vs. 1–23; Isa. 2:4.
*e Anger of God*, 2 Kin. 13:3.
*f Sheep, figurative*, Deut. 32:14.
**2**
*g God, love of*, Gen. 2:2.
*h Zion*, 2 Sam. 5:7.
1 R. V. Which thou hast redeemed to be the tribe of thine inheritance; And mount
**3**
*i Church, called sanctuary*, 1 Kin. 9:3.
**4**
*j Standard*, Num. 1:52.
**5**
*k Ax*, Deut. 19:5.
2 R. V. They seemed as men that lifted
**6**
*l Carving*, Ex. 35:33.
**7**
*m Arson*, 2 Sam. 14:30.
3 R. V. set thy sanctuary on fire; They have profaned the dwelling place of thy name even to the ground.
**8**
*n Persecution, of the righteous*, John 15:20.

24 [c,f]Thou shalt [g,h]guide me
with thy counsel, and afterward
receive me *to* glory.[s]
25 [i]Whom have I in heaven *but*
*thee*? and *there is* none upon
earth *that* I [j]desire beside thee.[T]
26 My flesh and my heart faileth:[G]
*but* [k]God *is* the [d,l]strength
of my heart, and my portion
for ever.
27 For, lo, *they that are far
from thee shall perish: thou hast
destroyed all them that [m]go a[C]
whoring from thee.
28 But *it is* good for me to
[n]draw near to God: I have put
my [c]trust in the Lord GOD, that
I may [o]declare all thy works.

## PSALM 74

*The psalmist complains of the desolations of Zion; and pleads with God to interpose, as of old, in behalf of his suffering people.*

[a]Maschil of Asaph.

[b,c]O GOD, why hast thou cast
[d]*us* off for ever? *why*
doth thine [e]anger smoke against
the [f]sheep of thy pasture?
2 Remember thy congregation,
*which* [g]thou hast purchased of
old; [1]the rod of thine inheritance,
*which* thou hast redeemed;
this mount [h]Zī'ŏn, wherein thou
hast dwelt.[T Q]
3 Lift up thy feet unto the perpetual
desolations; *even* all *that*
the enemy hath done wickedly
in the [i]sanctuary.
4 Thine enemies roar in the
midst of thy congregations; they
set up their [j]ensigns[G] *for* signs.
5 [2]*A man* was famous according
as he had lifted up [k]axes
upon the thick trees.
6 But now they break down the
[l]carved work thereof at once
with [k]axes and hammers.
7 They have [3,m]cast fire into
thy [i]sanctuary, they have defiled
*by casting down* the dwelling
place of thy name to the ground.
8 They said in their hearts, Let
us [n]destroy them together: they
have burned up all the [o]synagogues
of God in the land.
9 We see not our signs: *there is*
no more any [p]prophet: neither
*is there* among us any that knoweth
how long.
10 [q]O God, how long shall the
adversary reproach[G]? shall the
enemy [r]blaspheme[G] thy name
for ever?
11 Why withdrawest thou thy
[s,t]hand, even thy right hand?
pluck *it* out of thy bosom.[4]
12 For [u]God *is* my [v]King of
old, working [w]salvation in the
midst of the earth.
13[S] Thou didst divide the [x]sea
by thy [y]strength: thou brakest
the heads of the [z]dragons in
the waters.
14 Thou [y]brakest the heads of
leviathan in pieces, *and* gavest
him *to be* meat[G] to the people inhabiting
the wilderness.
15 [y]Thou didst cleave[G] the fountain
and the flood: thou driedst
up mighty rivers.
16 The [a]day *is* thine, the [b]night
also *is* thine: thou hast [c]prepared
the [d]light and the [e]sun.[T]
17 Thou hast [c]set all the borders
of the earth: thou hast made
[f]summer and [g]winter.[S]
18 Remember this, *that* the enemy
hath reproached, O LORD,
and *that* [5]the foolish people have
[h]blasphemed[G] thy name.
19 [i]O deliver not the soul of thy
turtledove[G] unto the [6]multitude *of*
*the wicked*: forget not the [7]congregation
of thy poor for ever.
20 [i]Have respect unto the covenant:
for the dark places of the
earth are full of the habitations
of cruelty.
21 [j]O let not the oppressed return
ashamed: let the [k]poor and
needy [l]praise thy name.
22 Arise, O God, plead thine
own cause: remember how the
foolish man reproacheth[G] thee
daily.

*o Synagogue*, Matt. 12:9.
**9**
*p Prophets*, Isa. 3:2.
**10**
*q Prayer*, Acts 6:4.
*r Blasphemy*, 2 Sam. 12:14.
**11**
*s Anthropomorphisms*, Gen. 11:5.
*t Hand, figurative*, Ezra 10:19.
4 R. V. *adds*, and consume them.
**12**
*u Faith, exemplified*, Mark 11:22.
*v God, sovereign*, Gen. 2:2.
*w God, savior*, Gen. 2:2.
**13**
*x Red Sea, divided*, Ex. 10:19.
*y God, power of*, Gen. 2:2.
*z Dragon*, Deut. 32:33.

---

**16**
*a Day*, Gen. 1:5.
*b Night*, Gen. 1:5.
*c God, creator*, Gen. 2:2.
*d Light, created*, Gen. 1:3.
*e Sun, created*, Josh. 10:12.
**17**
*f Summer*, Isa. 28:4.
*g Winter*, Gen. 8:22.
**18**
*h Blasphemy*, 2 Sam. 12:14.
5 R. V. a foolish people
**19**
*i Prayer, in adversity*, Acts 6:4.
6 R. V. wild beast:
7 R. V. life of
**21**
*j Prayer, intercessory*, Acts 6:4.
*k Poor, God's care of*, Prov. 21:13.
*l Praise*, Psa. 150:1.

23 Forget not the voice of thine enemies: the tumult of those that rise up against thee [8]increaseth continually.

## PSALM 75

*The psalmist praises God. 4 The proud rebuked. 9 A promise to praise God, and to execute justice.*

To the chief Musician, [a]Al-taschith, A Psalm *or* Song of Asaph.

UNTO thee, O God, do we give [b, c]thanks, *unto thee* do we give thanks: for [1]*that* thy name is near thy wondrous [d]works declare.

2 When I shall [2]receive the congregation I will judge uprightly.

3 The earth and all the inhabitants thereof are dissolved: I bear up the pillars of it. [Sē′lah.

4 I said unto the [3]fools, Deal not [4, e]foolishly: and to the wicked, Lift not up the horn:

5 Lift not up your horn on high: speak *not with* a [f]stiff neck.

6 For *promotion *cometh* neither from the east, nor from the west, nor from the south.

7 But God *is* the [g]judge: [h]he putteth down one, and setteth up another.

8 For in the [i]hand of the LORD *there is* a [j]cup, and the [k]wine [5]is red; it is full of mixture; and he poureth out of the same: but the [l]dregs thereof, all the [m]wicked of the earth shall [6]wring *them* out, *and* drink *them.*

9 But I will [n]declare for ever; I will sing [c]praises to the God of Jā′cob.

10 All the horns of the [o]wicked also will I [m]cut off; *but* the horns of the righteous shall be exalted.

## PSALM 76

*A declaration of God's majesty in Zion. 11 An exhortation to serve him.*

To the chief Musician on Neginoth, A Psalm *or* Song of Asaph.

[a]IN [b]Jū′dah *is* God known: his name *is* great in [c]Iṣ′ra-el.

2 In [d]Sā′lem also is his [e]tabernacle, and his dwelling place in [f]Zī′ŏn.

3 [g]There brake he the arrows of the bow, the shield, and the sword, and the battle. [Sē′lah.

4 Thou *art* more [h]glorious *and* excellent than the mountains of prey.

5 The stouthearted are spoiled, they have slept their [i]sleep: and none of the men of might have found their hands.

6 At [j]thy rebuke, O God of Jā′cob, both the chariot and horse are cast into a dead sleep.

7 Thou, *even* thou, *art* to be [k]feared: and who may stand in thy sight when once thou art [l]angry?

8 Thou didst cause [m]judgment to be heard from heaven; the earth [k]feared, and was still,

9 When God arose to [m]judgment, to [n]save all the [o]meek of the earth. [Sē′lah.

10 Surely the [p]wrath of man shall praise thee: the remainder of wrath shalt thou [1]restrain.

11 [q]Vow, and [r]pay unto the [s]LORD your God: let all that be round about him [t]bring presents unto him that ought to be [k]feared.

12 He shall [u]cut off the spirit of princes: *he is* terrible to the kings of the earth.

## PSALM 77

*The psalmist troubled, 7 and tempted to distrust God. 10 He encourages himself in God by remembering his works of old, 15 and especially his deliverance of Israel.*

To the chief Musician, to [a]Jeduthun, A Psalm of Asaph.

I [b]CRIED unto God with my voice, *even* unto God with my voice; and he gave [c]ear unto me.

2 In the day of my [d]trouble I sought the LORD: [1]my sore ran in the night, and ceased not: my soul refused to be comforted.

---

**74:23**
8 R. V. ascendeth continually.

**75**
a *Music, symbols used in,* 2 Chr. 5:13.

**1**
b *Thankfulness,* Acts 24:3.
c *Praise, for God's goodness,* Psa. 150:1.
d *Works of God,* Psa. 40:5.
1 R. V. thy name is near: Men tell of thy wondrous works.

**2**
2 R. V. find the set time, I will

**4**
e *Pride,* Prov. 16:18.
3 R. V. arrogant,
4 R. V. arrogantly:

**5**
f *Self-will, forbidden,* Gen. 49:6.

**7**
g *God, judge,* Gen. 2:2.
h *God, sovereign,* Gen. 2:2.

**8**
i *Anthropomorphisms,* Gen. 11:5.
j *Cup, figurative,* Matt. 20:22.
k *Wine, figurative,* Prov. 23:31.
l Isa. 25:6; Jer. 48:11; Zeph. 1:12.
m *Wicked, punishment of,* Psa. 73:3.
5 R. V. foameth;
6 Am. R. V. drain them, and

**9**
n *Religious Testimony,* 2 Thess. 1:10.

**10**
o *Wicked, contrasted with the righteous,* Psa. 73:3.

**76:1**
a *Praise, for God's goodness to Israel,* Psa. 150:1.
b *Judah, kingdom of,* 2 Chr. 11:17.
c *Israel,* vs. 1–12; Ex. 4:22.

**2**
d *Jerusalem, called Salem,* Judg. 19:10.
e *Church, called tabernacle,* 1 Kin. 9:3.
f *Zion,* 2 Sam. 5:7.

**3**
g *War, God inflicts defeat in,* Judg. 3:2.

**4**
h *God, glory of,* Gen. 2:2.

**5**
i *Death, called sleep,* Num. 23:10.

**6**
j *God, power of,* Gen. 2:2.

**7**
k *Fear of God,* Acts 9:31.
l *Anger of God,* 2 Kin. 13:3.

**8**
m *God, judge,* Gen. 2:2.

**9**
n *God, savior,* Gen. 2:2.
o *Meekness,* Psa. 45:4.

**10**
p *Anger,* Psa. 37:8.
1 R. V. gird upon thee.

**11**
q *Vows,* Num. 30:2.
r *Faithfulness,* Luke 16:10.
s *God, sovereign,* Gen. 2:2.
t *Liberality, enjoined,* 1 Tim. 6:18.

**12**
u *Wicked, punishment of,* Psa. 73:3.

**77**
a *Jeduthun,* 1 Chr. 16:38.

**1**
b *Prayer, answered,* Acts 6:4.
c *Ear, figurative,* Lev. 8:23.

**2**
d *Adversity, prayer in,* vs. 1–20; Psa. 10:6.
1 R. V. My hand was stretched out in

---

* **PROMOTION,** Psa. 75:6, 7; 78:70, 71; 113:7, 8. *As a reward of merit,* 1 Chr. 11:6. *Unselfish seeking of, for others, enjoined,* Rom. 12:10.
**Instances of:** *Joseph, from imprisoned slave to prince,* Gen. 41:1–45. *Moses, from exile to lawgiver,* Ex. 3:10; 19. *Saul, from obscurity to a scepter,* 1 Sam. 9. *David, from shepherd to throne,* Psa. 78:70, 71 (with 1 Sam. 16). *Jeroboam, from servant to throne,* 1 Kin. 11:26–35. *Baasha, out of the dust to throne,* 1 Kin. 16:1, 2. *Daniel, from captive to premier,* Dan. 2:48. *Shadrach, Meshach, and Abed-nego,* Dan. 3:30.

**3**
e *Doubting*, Rom. 14:23.
f *Murmuring, against God*, Num. 14:2.

**6**
g *Night, meditation in*, Gen. 1:5.
h *Self-examination*, 2 Cor. 13:5.
i *Heart*, Psa. 44:21.
j *Diligence*, Rom. 12:8.

**7**
k *Despondency*, Eccl. 2:20.

**8**
l *God, mercy of*, Gen. 2:2.

**9**
m *Anger of God*, 2 Kin. 13:3.

**10**
n *Faith, exemplified*, Mark 11:22.

**12**
o *Meditation*, Psa. 49:3.
2 R. V. muse on

**13**
p *Church, called sanctuary*, 1 Kin. 9:3.
3 R. V. a great god like unto God?

**14**
q *God, power of*, Gen. 2:2.
4 R. V. peoples.

**15**
r *Arm, figurative*, Psa. 89:13.

**17**
s *Arrow, figurative*, 1 Sam. 20:20.

3 I remembered God, and [e]was troubled: I [f]complained, and my spirit was overwhelmed.[C] [Sē′lah.

4 Thou holdest mine eyes waking: I am so troubled that I cannot speak.

5 I have considered the days of old, the years of ancient times.

6 I call to remembrance my *song in the [g]night: I [h]commune with mine own [i]heart: and my spirit made [j]diligent search.

7 [k]Will the LORD cast off for ever? and will he be favourable no more?

8 [e]Is his [l]mercy clean[C] gone for ever? [e]doth *his* promise fail for evermore?

9 Hath God forgotten to be [l]gracious? hath he in [m]anger shut up his tender mercies? [Sē′lah.

10 And I said, This *is* my infirmity: *but* [n]*I will remember* the years of the right hand of the most High.

11 [n]I will remember the works of the LORD: surely I will remember thy wonders of old.

12 I will [o]meditate also of all thy work, and [2]talk of thy doings.

13 Thy way, O God, *is* in the [p]sanctuary: who *is* [3]*so* great a God as *our* God?

14 Thou *art* the God that [q]doest wonders: thou hast declared thy strength among the [4]people.[S]

15 Thou hast with *thine* [r]arm redeemed thy people, the sons of Jā′cob and Jō′ṣeph. [Sē′lah.

16 The waters saw thee, O God, the waters saw thee; they were afraid: the depths also were troubled.[S]

17 The clouds poured out water: the skies sent out a sound: thine [s]arrows also went abroad.

18 The voice of thy [t]thunder *was* in the [5]heaven: the [u]lightnings lightened the world: the earth [v]trembled and shook.

19 Thy way *is* in the sea, and thy path in the great waters, and [w]thy footsteps are not known.[S]

20 Thou leddest [x]thy people like a flock by the hand of [y]Mō′ṣeṣ and [z]Aâr′on.

## PSALM 78

*The people exhorted to hear. 5 The object of establishing a testimony in Jacob. 9 God's dealings with unbelieving and disobedient Israel. 67 The other tribes being rejected, God chose Judah. He chose also Zion and David.*

[a]Maschil of Asaph.

GIVE ear, O my[C] people, *to* my law: incline your ears to the words of my mouth.

2 [b]I will open my mouth in a parable: I will utter dark sayings of old:[Q]

3 Which we have heard and known, and our fathers have told us.

4 We will not hide *them* from their children, [c]shewing to the generation to come the [d]praises of the LORD, and his [e]strength, and his wonderful [f]works that he hath done.[Q]

5 For he [l]established a [g,h]testimony in Jā′cob, and appointed a law in Ĭṣ′ra-el, which he commanded our [i]fathers, that they should [j]make them known to their [k]children:

6 That the generation to come might know *them, even* the children *which* should be born; *who* should arise and [k]declare *them* to their children:

7 That they might set their [l]hope in God, and not forget the works of God, but [m]keep his commandments:

8 And might not be as their fathers, a [n,o]stubborn and rebel-

**18**
t *Thunder*, 1 Sam. 7:10.
u *Lightning*, Job 28:26.
v *Earthquakes*, Isa. 29:6.
5 R. V. whirlwind;

**19**
w *God, unsearchable*, Gen. 2:2.

**20**
x *Israel*, Ex. 4:22.
y *Moses*, Ex. 2:10.
z *Aaron*, Ex. 6:20.

a *Music, symbols used in*, 2 Chr. 5:13.

**2**
b Matt. 13:35.

**4**
c *Religious Testimony*, 2 Thess. 1:10.
d *Praise*, Psa. 150:1.
e *God, power of*, Gen. 2:2.
f *God, providence of*, Gen. 2:2.

**5**
g *Law, of Moses*, Deut. 33:2.
h *Word of God, inspiration of*, Psa. 119:9.
i *Parents, duty of, to instruct children in righteousness*, 2 Cor. 12:14.
j *Instruction, of children*, Prov. 23:23.
k *Children, instruction of*, Mark 10:14.

**7**
l *Hope*, Prov. 13:12.
m *Obedience*, Heb. 5:8.

**8**
n *Obduracy*, Prov. 29:1.
o *Self-will*, Gen. 49:6.

* **SONG.** *Sung at the passover*, Matt. 26:30; Mark 14:26. *Didactic*, Deut. 31:19–22; 32:1–45. *Of Moses*, Ex. 15:1–19. *Of Deborah and Barak*, Judg. 5. *Of Hannah*, 1 Sam. 2:1–10. *Of David*, 2 Sam. 22:2–51; 23:1–7. *Of Mary*, Luke 1:46–55. *Of Moses and the Lamb*, Rev. 15:3, 4. *New*, Psa. 33:3; 40:3. *Of redemption*, Rev. 5:9, 10. *Of the redeemed*, Rev. 14:2–5. *Solomon wrote one thousand and five*, 1 Kin. 4:32. *Spiritual, singing of, enjoined*, Eph. 5:19; Col. 3:16. See footnotes: MUSIC, 2 Chr. 5:13; POETRY, Acts 17:28; PRAISE, Psa. 150:1; PSALMS, Psa. 1:1.

p *Instability,* Jas. 1:8.

**9**
q *Ephraim, tribe of,* Gen. 41:52.
r *Cowardice, instances of,* Lev. 26:36.

**10**
s *Disobedience to God,* Eph. 5:6.
t *Backsliding, of Israel,* Hos. 11:7.
u *Covenant, of man with God,* Deut. 29:1.

**11**
v *Miracles,* Luke 23:8.

**12**
w *God, power of,* Gen. 2:2.
x *Egypt,* Gen. 41:8.
y *Zoan,* Isa. 30:4.

**13**
z *Red Sea, divided,* Ex. 10:19.

a *Israel,* Ex. 4:22.

**14**
b *Pillar of Cloud and Fire, a guide to Israel,* Ex. 13:21.
c *Symbols and Similitudes, of divine presence,* Heb. 9:9.

**15**
d *Meribah,* Ex. 17:7.
e *Temporal Blessings, from God,* Psa. 103:2.

**17**
f *Ingratitude, of man to God,* Rom. 1:21.
1 R. V. Yet went they on still to sin against him, To rebel against the Most High in the desert.

**18**
g *Appetite,* Prov. 23:2.

**19**
h *Infidelity* 2 Cor. 6:15.
i *Unbelief,* Heb. 3:12.

**21**
j *Anger of God,* 2 Kin. 13:3.

lious generation; a generation
*that* set not their heart aright,
and whose spirit was [p]not stedfast with God.[Q]
9 The children of [q]Ē'phră-ĭm,
*being* armed, *and* carrying bows,
[r]turned back in the day of battle.
10 They [s,t]kept not the [u]cove-
nant of God, and [n,o]refused to
walk in his [g]law;
11 And [t]forgat his [f]works, and
his [v]wonders that he had shewed
them.
12 [v]Marvellous things did [w]he
in the sight of their fathers, in
the land of [x]Ē'ġȳpt, *in* the field
of [y]Zō'an.
13 He divided the [z]sea, and
caused [a]them to pass through;
and he made the waters to stand
as an heap.
14 In the daytime also he led
[a]them with a [b,c]cloud, and all
the night with a light of fire.
15 He clave[C] the *,[d]rocks in
the wilderness, and gave [a]*them*
[e]drink as *out of* the great depths.[Q]
16 He brought [e]streams also
out of the *,[d]rock, and caused
waters to run down like rivers.
17 [1]And [a,f]they sinned yet more
against him by provoking the
most High in the wilderness.
18 And [a]they tempted[C] God in
their heart by asking meat[C] for
their [g]lust.[C]
19[T] Yea, [a]they [h]spake against
God; they [i]said, Can God furnish a table in the wilderness?
20 Behold, he smote the
*,[d]rock, that the waters gushed
out, and the streams overflowed;
[h,i]can he give bread also? can
he provide flesh for his people?
21 Therefore the LORD heard
*this,* and was [j]wroth[C]: so a fire
was kindled against Jā'cob, and
anger also came up against Ĭṣ'-
ra-el;[S T]
22 Because [a]they [h,i]believed not
in God, and trusted not in his
[k]salvation:
23 Though he had command-
ed the clouds from above, and
opened the doors of heaven,
24 And[Q] had rained down [e,l]man-
na upon them to eat, and had
given them of the [e]corn[C] of heaven.
25 Man did eat [2]angels' food:
he sent them [e,m]meat[C] to the full.
26 He caused an east [n]wind to
blow in the heaven: and by his
[o]power he brought in the south
wind.[S]
27 He rained [e,m]flesh also upon [a]them as dust, and feathered
fowls like as the sand of the
sea:
28 And he let *it* fall in the midst
of their camp, round about their
habitations.
29 So they did eat, and were
[p]well filled: for he gave them
their own desire;[Q]
30 They were not estranged[C]
from their [g]lust.[C] But [q]while
their [m]meat[C] *was* yet in their
mouths,
31 The [j]wrath of God came upon [a]them, and [r]slew the fattest of
them, and smote down the [3]cho-
sen *men* of Ĭṣ'ra-el.[Q]
32 For all this [a]they [s,t]sinned
still, and [i]believed not for his
wondrous [u]works.
33 Therefore their days [v]did he
consume in [w]vanity, and their
years in [4]trouble.
34 When [v]he [x]slew them, then
they [y,z]sought him: and they returned and enquired early after
God.
35 [x]And they remembered that
God *was* their *rock, and the
high God their redeemer.[T]
36 Nevertheless they did [a]flat-
ter him with their mouth, and
they [b]lied unto him with their
tongues.
37 For [c]their heart was not

**22**
k *Salvation,* Acts 16:17.

**24**
l *Manna,* Ex. 16:31.

**25**
m *Quail,* Ex. 16:13.
2 R. V. the bread of the mighty:

**26**
n *Meteorology,* Matt. 16:2.
o *God, power of,* Gen. 2:2.

**29**
p *Gluttony, instances of,* Prov. 30:22.

**30**
q Num. 11:33.

**31**
r *Wicked, punishment of,* Psa. 73:3.
3 R. V. young men

**32**
s *Obduracy,* Prov. 29:1.
t *Impenitence,* Rom. 2:5.
u *Miracles, design of,* Luke 23:8.

**33**
v *Adversity, dispensation from God,* Psa. 10:6.
w *Vanity,* Eccl. 1:2.
4 R. V. terror.

**34**
x *Afflictions, benefits of,* Psa. 34:19.
y *Repentance,* Mark 1:4.
z *Seekers,* Isa. 55:6.

**36**
a *Hypocrisy,* Jas. 3:17.
b *Falsehood,* Job 21:34.

**37**
c *Israel,* Ex. 4:22.

* **ROCK.** *Smitten by Moses for water,* Deut. 8:15; Psa. 78:15, 16, 20. *House built upon,* Matt. 7:24, 25. *Name of God,* Deut. 32:4, 18, 30, 31. **Figurative,** Deut. 32:13; 2 Sam. 22:3, 32, 47; 23:3; Job 29:6; Psa. 18:2; 31:2, 3; 40:2; 61:2; 62:2; 71:3; Isa. 17:10; 32:2; 44:8; Matt. 16:18; 1 Cor. 10:4.

right with him, [d]neither were
they stedfast[G] in his [e]covenant.[GQ]
38 But he, *being* full of [f]com-
passion, [g]forgave *their* iniquity,
and destroyed *them* not: yea,
many a time [j]turned he his [h]an-
ger away, and did not stir up all
his wrath.[S]
39 For he remembered that
[i]they *were but* flesh; [j]a wind that
passeth away, and cometh not
again.
40[T] How oft did [c]they [5]provoke
him in the wilderness, *and* grieve
him in the desert!
41 Yea, [c,k]they turned back
and tempted[G] God, and [6]limited
the Holy One of Iṣ′ra-el.[T]
42 They [l]remembered not his
hand, *nor* the day when he [m]de-
livered them from the enemy.
43 How he had wrought his
[n]signs in [o]Ē′ġy̆pt, and his wonders in the field of [p]Zō′an:
44 And had turned their rivers
into [q]blood; and their floods,[G]
that they could not drink.[Q]
45 He sent divers[G] sorts of [r]flies
among [o]them, which devoured
them; and [s]frogs, which destroyed them.
46 He gave also their increase[G]
unto the [t]caterpiller, and their
labour unto the [u]locust.
47 He destroyed their [v]vines
with [w]hail, and their [x]sycomore
trees with frost.
48 He gave up their cattle also
to the [w]hail, and their flocks to
hot [y]thunderbolts.
49[S] He cast upon [o]them the
fierceness of his [h]anger, wrath,
and indignation, and trouble, [7]by
sending evil angels *among them*.
50 He made a way to his [h]an-
ger; he spared not their soul
from [z]death, but gave their life
over to the [a]pestilence;[S]
51 And smote all the [b]first-
born in [c]Ē′ġy̆pt; the chief of
*their* strength in the tabernacles
of [d]Hăm:
52[S] But [e]made [f]his own people to go forth like sheep, and
[g,h]guided them in the wilderness
like a flock.
53 And [h]he [g]led them on [f]safely,
so that they feared not: but the
[i]sea overwhelmed their enemies.
54 And he [g,h]brought them
to the border of his [j]sanctuary,
*even to* this [k]mountain, *which*
his right hand had purchased.
55 He [f]cast out the [8,l]heathen[G]
also before them, and divided
them [9]an inheritance by line,
and made the tribes of [m]Iṣ′ra-el
to dwell in their tents.[S]
56 Yet [n]they tempted[G] and provoked the most high God, and
[o]kept not his testimonies:
57 But [p]turned back, and dealt
[10]unfaithfully like their fathers:
they were turned aside like a
deceitful [q]bow.
58 For they provoked him to
[r,s]anger with their [t]high places,
and moved him to [†,s]jealousy
with their graven[G] [u]images.
59 When God heard [v]*this*, he
was [r]wroth,[G] and greatly abhorred [m]Iṣ′ra-el:
60 So that he [w]forsook the [x]tab-
ernacle of [y]Shī′lōh, the tent
*which* he placed among men;
61 And delivered his [z]strength
into captivity, and his glory into
the enemy's hand.
62 He [a]gave his people over
also unto the sword; and was
[b]wroth[G] with his inheritance.
63 The fire consumed their
young men; and their [c]maidens
[11]were not given to [d]marriage.

d *Instability*, Jas. 1:8.
e *Law, of Moses*, Deut. 33:2.
**38**
f *God, mercy of*, Gen. 2:2.
g *Sin, forgiveness of*, Rom. 5:12.
h *Anger of God*, 2 Kin. 13:3.
**39**
i *Man, insignificance of*, Job 4:17.
j *Life, brevity and uncertainty of*, Eccl. 8:15.
**40**
5 R. V. rebel against him
**41**
k *Backsliders*, Jer. 3:22.
6 R. V. provoked
**42**
l *Ingratitude, of man to God*, Rom. 1:21.
m *God, providence of*, Gen. 2:2.
**43**
n *Miracles*, Luke 23:8.
o *Egyptians, visited by plagues*, Gen. 50:3.
p *Zoan*, Isa. 30:4.
**44**
q *Blood, plague of*, Gen. 9:4.
**45**
r *Flies, plague of*, Eccl. 10:1.
s *Frogs, plague of*, Ex. 8:2.
**46**
t *Caterpillar*, 1 Kin. 8:37.
u *Locust*, Nah. 3:17.
**47**
v *Egypt, productions of*, Gen. 41:8.
w *Hail, plague of, in Egypt*, Job 38:22.
x *Sycomore*, 2 Chr. 1:15.
**48**
y *Lightning*, Job 28:26.
**49**
7 R. V. A band of angels of evil.
**50**
z *Death, of the wicked, a judgment*, Num. 23:10.

a *Plague*, Ex. 11:1.

**51**
b *First-born, of Egyptians, slain*, Zech. 12:10.
c *Egyptians, visited by plagues*, Gen. 50:3.
d 1 Chr. 4:40; Psa. 105:23, 27; 106:22.
**52**
e *God, preserver*, Gen. 2:2.
f *Shepherd, figurative of God's care*, Jer. 31:10.
g *Guidance*, Psa. 48:14.
h *God, guidance of*, Gen. 2:2.
**53**
i *Red Sea, Pharaoh's army drowned in*, Ex. 10:19.
**54**
j *Canaan*, Gen. 37:1.
k *Zion*, 2 Sam. 5:7.
**55**
l *Canaanites, destroyed*, Ex. 23:28.
m *Israel*, Ex. 4:22.
8 R. V. nations
9 R. V. for an
**56**
n *Ingratitude, of man to God*, Rom. 1:21.
o *Disobedience to God*, Eph. 5:6.
**57**
p *Backsliding of Israel*, Hos. 11:7.
q *Bow, figurative*, 2 Sam. 1:18.
10 R.V. treacherously
**58**
r *Anger of God*, 2 Kin. 13:3.
s *Anthropomorphisms*, Gen. 11:5.
t *High Places*, 1 Kin. 3:2.
u *Idol*, 1 Kin. 15:12.
**59**
v *Sin, repugnant to God*, Rom. 5:12.
**60**
w *Sin, separates from God*, Rom. 5:12.
x *Tabernacle*, Ex. 27:9.
y *Shiloh, tabernacle at*, Judg. 21:12.
**61**
z *Ark, captured by the Philistines*, Ex. 25:10.

**62**
a *Judgments*, Ex. 6:6.
b *Anger of God*, 2 Kin. 13:3. **63** c *Women, not to be given in marriage considered a calamity*, Prov. 31:10. d *Marriage*, Gen. 34:9.
11 R. V. had no marriage-song.

† **JEALOUSY,** Prov. 6:34; 27:4; Eccl. 4:4; Song 8:6. *Illustrated in the brother of the prodigal*, Luke 15:25–32. *Law concerning, when husband is jealous of his wife*, Num. 5:12–31. *Image of*, Ezek. 8:3, 4. *Forbidden*, Rom. 13:13 [R. V.].
*Attributed to God*, Ex. 20:5; 34:13, 14; Num. 25:11; Deut. 29:20; 32:16, 21; 1 Kin. 14:22; Psa. 78:58; 79:5; Isa. 30:1, 2; 31:1, 3; Ezek. 16:42; 23:25; 36:5, 6; 38:19; Zeph. 1:18; 3:8; Zech. 1:14; 8:2; 1 Cor. 10:22.
**Instances of:** *Cain, of Abel*, Gen. 4:5, 6, 8. *Sarah, of Hagar*, Gen. 16:5. *Joseph's brethren, of Joseph*, Gen. 37:4–11, 18–28. *Saul, of David*, 1 Sam. 18:8–30; 19:8–24; 20:24–34. *Joab, of Abner*, 2 Sam. 3:24–27. *Sectional, between Israel and the tribe of Judah*, 2 Sam. 19:41–43.

64 Their [e]priests fell by the sword; and their [f]widows made no lamentation.

65 Then the Lord [g]awaked as one out of sleep, *and* like a mighty man that shouteth by reason of wine.

66 And he [a]smote his enemies in the hinder parts: he put them to a perpetual reproach.

67 Moreover he refused the [h]tabernacle of Jō′ṣeph, and [i]chose not the tribe of [j]Ē′phrā-ĭm:

68 But chose the tribe of [k]Jū′dah, the mount [l]Zī′ŏn which he [m]loved.

69 And he built his [n]sanctuary like [12]high *palaces,* like the [o]earth which he hath [p]established for ever.

70 [q]He [i]chose Dā′vid also his servant, and [r]took [s]him from the sheepfolds:

71 From following the ewes great with young he brought him to feed Jā′cob his people, and Iṣ′ra-el his inheritance.

72 So he fed them according to the [t]integrity of his heart; and [u]guided them by the skilfulness of his hands.

## PSALM 79

*The psalmist complains of the desolation of Jerusalem. 8 He prays for deliverance, 13 and promises to give thanks to God.*

A Psalm of Asaph.

[a,b]O GOD, the heathen are come into thine inheritance; thy [c]holy [d]temple have they defiled; they have laid [e]Jē-ru̥′sā-lĕm on heaps.

2 [f]The dead bodies of thy servants have they given *to be* meat unto the fowls of the heaven, the flesh of thy saints unto the beasts of the earth.

3 [f]Their blood have they shed like water round about [e]Jē-ru̥′sā-lĕm; and *there was* none to bury *them.*

4 [g]We are become a reproach to our neighbours, a scorn and derision to them that are round about us.

5 [a,b]How long, LORD? wilt thou be [h,i]angry for ever? shall thy [i,j]jealousy burn like fire?

6 [k]Pour out thy wrath upon the [l]heathen that have [m]not known thee, and upon the kingdoms that have [n]not called upon thy name.

7 For they have devoured Jā′cob, and laid waste his dwelling place.

8 [a,b]O [o]remember not against [g]us [1]former iniquities: let thy tender [p]mercies speedily [2]prevent us: for we are brought very low.

9 [a,b]Help us, O God of our salvation, for the glory of thy name: and deliver us, and [o,q]purge away our sins, for thy name's sake.

10 [r]Wherefore should the [l]heathen [s]say, Where *is* their God? [3,k]let him be known among the heathen in our sight *by* the revenging of the blood of thy servants *which is* shed.

11 Let the sighing of the *prisoner come before thee; according to the greatness of thy [t]power preserve thou those that are appointed to die;

**64**
*e* *Priest,* Lev. 1.5.
*f* *Widow,* 2 Sam. 14:5.

**65**
*g* *Anthropomorphisms,* Gen. 11:5.

**67**
*h* *Tabernacle,* Ex. 27:9.
*i* *Foreordination, according to purpose of grace,* Rom. 8:30.
*j* *Ephraim, tribe of,* Gen. 41:52.

**68**
*k* *Judah, tribe of,* Num. 10:14.
*l* *Zion,* 2 Sam. 5:7.
*m* *God, love of,* Gen. 2:2.

**69**
*n* *Church, called sanctuary,* 1 Kin. 9:3.
*o* *Earth, perpetuity of,* Prov. 8:23.
*p* *God, creator,* Gen. 2:2.
12 R V. the heights,

**70**
*q* *David, chosen of God,* 1 Sam. 16:13.
*r* *Promotion, instances of,* v. 71; Psa. 75:6.
*s* *Shepherd,* Jer. 31:10.

**72**
*t* *God, faithfulness of,* Gen. 2:2.
*u* *God, guidance of,* Gen. 2:2.

**1**
*a* *Prayer, in adversity,* vs. 1–13; Acts 6:4.
*b* *Adversity, prayer in,* vs. 1–13; Psa. 10:6.
*c* *Church, called holy temple,* 1 Kin. 9:3.
*d* *Temple, Solomon's,* 1 Kin. 6:17.
*e* *Jerusalem,* Judg. 19:10.

**2**
*f* *War, evils of,* Judg. 3:2.

**4**
*g* *Israel,* Ex. 4:22.

**5**
*h* *Anger of God,* 2 Kin. 13:3.
*i* *Anthropomorphisms,* Gen. 11:5.
*j* *Jealousy, attributed to God,* Psa. 78:58.

**6**
*k* *Prayer, imprecatory,* Acts 6:4.
*l* *Heathen,* Lam. 1:10.
*m* *Spiritual Blindness,* 2 Cor. 4:4.
*n* *Prayerlessness,* Job 21:15.

**8**
*o* *Sin, forgiveness of,* Rom. 5:12.
*p* *God, mercy of,* Gen. 2:2.
1 R. V. iniquities of our forefathers:
2 Am. R. V. meet us;

**9**
*q* *Spiritual Purification,* Psa. 51:2.

**10**
*r* *Prayer, pleas offered in,* Acts 6:4.
*s* *Scoffing,* Hab. 1:10.
3 R. V. Let the revenging of the blood of thy servants which is shed Be known among the heathen in our sight.

**11**
*t* *God, power of,* Gen. 2:2.

---

*** PRISONERS.** *Joseph,* Gen. 39:20–23; 40; 41:1–44. *Jeremiah,* Jer. 38:6–28; 39:14. *John the Baptist,* Matt. 4:12; 11:2; 14:3–12; Mark 6:17; Luke 3:20. *Jesus,* Matt. 26:47–75; 27:1–50; Mark 14:43–72; 15:1–37; Luke 22:47–71; 23:1–46; John 18:3–40; 19:1–30. *Apostles,* Acts 5:17–42. *Peter,* Acts 12:3–19. *Paul,* Acts 16:19–40; 21:27–40; chapters 22–28. *Silas,* Acts 16:19–40.

*Required to labor,* Judg. 16:21. *Kept on bread and water of affliction,* 1 Kin. 22:27. *Bound, in chains,* Acts 12:6; *in fetters,* Prov. 7:22; *in shackles,* Jer. 29:26. *Confined in stocks,* Acts 16:24.

*Confined, in court of the palace,* Jer. 32:2; *in house of the scribe,* Jer. 37:15; *in house of captain of the guard,* Gen. 40:3. *Visited by friends,* Matt. 11:2; Acts 24:23. *Bound to soldiers,* Acts 12:6, 7. *Keepers responsible for,* Acts 12:18, 19. *Permitted to make defense before courts,* Acts 24:10; 25:8, 16; 26:1; 2 Tim. 4:16.

*Cruelty to,* Jer. 38:6; 52:11; Lam. 3:53, 54. *Tortured to extort self-criminating testimony,* Acts 22:24. *Scourged,* Matt. 27:26; Mark 15:15; Acts 16:23, 33; 2 Cor. 6:5; 11:23, 24.

KINDNESS TO: *To Jeremiah,* Jer. 37:20, 21; 38:7–28. *To Paul, by Philippian jailer,* Acts 16:33; *by Felix,* Acts 24:23; *by the centurion,* Acts 27:1, 3; *by authorities at Rome,* Acts 28:16, 30, 31; *by Onesiphorus,* 2 Tim. 1:16–18. *To be visited and ministered to,* Matt. 25:35–46. *Released at feasts,* Matt. 27:15–17; Mark 15:6; John 18:39. *Joyful, Paul and Silas,* Acts 16:25. *Consolations for,* Psa. 69:33; 79:11; 102:19, 20; 146:7.

See footnotes: CAPTIVE, 1 Sam. 30:3; IMPRISONMENT, Acts 12:4.

**Figurative,** Isa. 61:1; Luke 4:18.

12 [k]And render unto our neighbours sevenfold into their bosom their reproach, wherewith they have reproached thee, O Lord.

13 So [g]we thy people and [u]sheep of thy pasture will give thee [v]thanks for ever: we will shew forth thy [w]praise to all generations.

## PSALM 80

*The psalmist cries to God for Israel in distress. 8 The vine brought out of Egypt. 14 God entreated to return.*

To the chief Musician upon [a]Shoshannim-Eduth, A Psalm of Asaph.

[b]GIVE [c]ear, O [d]Shepherd of [e]Ĭṣ′ra-el, thou that [f, g]leadest Jō′ṣeph like a flock; thou that dwellest [h]*between* the cherubims, shine forth.[s]

2 Before [i]Ē′phră-ĭm and [j]Bĕn′ja-mĭn and [k]Mā-năs′seh stir up thy strength, and come *and* save us.

3 [l, m]Turn[G] [e, n]us again, O God, and cause thy face to shine; and we shall be saved.[s]

4 O LORD God of hosts, how long wilt thou be [o]angry against the prayer of thy people?

5 [p]Thou feedest them with the bread of tears; and givest them tears to drink in great measure.

6 Thou makest us a [q]strife unto our neighbours: and our enemies laugh among themselves.

7 [b]Turn[G] [e, n]us again, O God of hosts, and cause thy face to shine; and we shall be saved.[s]

8 [r, s]Thou hast brought a [e, t]vine out of [u]Ē′ġÿpt: thou hast cast out the [1, v]heathen,[G] and planted it.

9 Thou [r]preparedst *room* before [e, t]it, and didst cause it to take deep root, and it filled the [w]land.

10 The hills were covered with the shadow of it, and the boughs thereof *were like* the [2]goodly[G] cedars.

11 She sent out her boughs unto the sea, and her branches unto the [3, x]river.

12 Why hast thou *then* broken down her hedges, so that all they which pass by the way do pluck her?

13 The [y]boar out of the wood[G] doth waste[G] it, and the wild beast of the field doth devour it.

14 [z]Return, we beseech thee, O God of hosts: look down from heaven, and behold, and visit this vine;

15 And the vineyard which thy right hand hath planted, and the [a]branch *that* thou madest strong for thyself.

16 *It is* burned with fire, *it is* cut down: they perish at the rebuke of thy countenance.

17 Let thy hand be upon the man of thy right hand, upon the son of man *whom* thou madest strong for thyself.

18 So will not we go back from thee: quicken[G] us, and we will call upon thy name.

19 [b, c]Turn[G] [d]us again, O LORD God of hosts, cause thy face to shine; and we shall be saved.[s]

## PSALM 81

*An exhortation to praise God. 8 Israel's ingratitude set forth. 13 What God would have done for them, if they had been obedient.*

To the chief Musician upon [a]Gittith, *A Psalm* of Asaph.

[b]SING aloud unto God our strength: make a joyful noise unto the God of Jā′cob.

2 Take a psalm, and bring hither the [c]timbrel, the pleasant[G] [d]harp with the [e]psaltery.[G]

3 Blow up the [f]trumpet in the [g]new moon, [1]in the time appointed, on our solemn [h]feast day.

4 For this *was* a statute for [i]Ĭṣ′ra-el, *and* a law of the God of Jā′cob.

5 This he ordained in Jō′ṣeph *for* a testimony, when he went out through the land of [j]Ē′ġÿpt: *where* I heard a [k]language *that* I understood not.

---

13
*Sheep, figurative,* Deut. 32:14.
*Thankfulness, to God, exemplified,* Acts 24:3.
w *Praise,* Psa. 150:1.

a *Music, symbols used in,* 2 Chr. 5:13.

1
b *Prayer, intercessory,* vs. 1–3; Acts 6:4.
c *Ear, figurative,* Lev. 8:23.
d *Shepherd, figurative, of God's care,* Jer. 31:10.
e *Israel,* Ex. 4:22.
f *God, guidance of,* Gen. 2:2.
g *God, preserver,* Gen. 2:2.
h *Shekinah,* Lev. 16:2.

2
i *Ephraim, tribe of,* Gen. 41:52.
j *Benjamin, tribe of,* Num. 1:37.
k *Manasseh, tribe of,* Gen. 46:20.

3
l *Adversity, prayer in,* vs. 3–5, 14; Psa. 10:6.
m *Backsliding, prayer for help against,* vs. 14–19; Hos. 11:7.
n *Backsliders, return of,* Jer. 3:22.

4
o *Anger of God,* 2 Kin. 13:3.

5
p *Adversity, dispensation from God,* Psa. 10:6.

6
q *Strife,* Prov. 20:3.

8
r *God, providence of,* Gen. 2:2.
s *Parables,* Ezek. 20:49.
t *Vine, parables of,* vs. 8–14; Judg. 13:14.
u *Egypt,* Gen. 41:8.
v *Canaanites,* Ex. 23:28.
1 R. V. nations,

9
w *Canaan,* Gen. 37:1.

10
2 R. V. cedars of God.

11
x *Euphrates,* Gen. 15:18.
3 R. V. River.

---

13
y *Swine,* Lev. 11:7.

14
z *Prayer, intercessory,* Acts 6:4.

15
a *Branch, figurative,* Dan. 4:14.

19
b *Adversity, prayer in,* Psa. 10:6.
c *Backsliding, prayer for help against,* Hos. 11:7.
d *Backsliders, return of,* Jer. 3:22.

a *Music, symbols used in,* 2 Chr. 5:13.

1
b *Praise,* Psa. 150:1.

2
c *Timbrel,* Ex. 15:20.
d *Harp,* Dan. 3:10.
e *Psaltery,* 1 Chr. 16:5.

3
f *Trumpet,* Josh. 6:4.
g *New Moon, feast of,* Amos 8:5.
h *Annual Feasts,* Num. 15:3.
1 R. V. At the full moon,

4
i *Israel,* Ex. 4:22.

5
j *Egypt,* Gen. 41:8.
k *Language,* Dan. 3:29.

6
*l God, providence of*, Gen. 2:2.
2 R. V. basket.
7
*m Prayer, answered*, Acts 6:4.
*n Faith, trial of*, Mark 11:22.
*o Meribah*, Ex. 17:7.
9
*p Idolatry, denounced*, 1 Sam. 15:23.
11
*q Impenitence, judgment denounced against*, v. 12; Rom. 2:5.
12
*r Reprobates*, 1 Cor. 9:27.
*s Delusion*, 2 Thess. 2:11.
3 R. V. let them go after the stubbornness of their heart, That they might walk in
13
*t God, love of, exemplified*, Gen. 2:2.
*u Backsliders, God's solicitude for*, Jer. 3:22.
14
*v Temporal Blessings, from God*, Psa. 103:2.
16
*w Wheat*, Ezra 6:9.
*x Honey*, Prov. 25:27.
1
*a God, sovereign*, Gen. 2:2.
*b God, judge*, Gen. 2:2.
1 R. V. God;
2
*c Judge, character of, and precepts relating to*, vs. 2–13; Judg. 2:18.
*d Injustice, in civil judgments*, Isa. 26:10.

6 I [l]removed his shoulder from
the burden: his hands were delivered from the [2]pots.
7 Thou calledst in trouble, and
I [m]delivered thee; I answered
thee in the secret place of thunder: I [n]proved[C] thee at the waters
of [o]Mĕr′i-bah. [Sē′lah.[C]
8 Hear, O my people, and I
will testify unto thee: O [i]Iṣ′ra-el,
if thou wilt hearken unto me;
9 [p]There shall no strange[C] god
be in thee; neither shalt thou
worship any strange god.
10 I *am* the LORD thy God,
which [l]brought thee out of the
land of [j]Ē′gȳpt: open thy mouth
wide, and I will [l]fill it.
11[S] But my people would [q]not
hearken to my voice; and Iṣ′-
ra-el would none of me.
12 So I [3]gave [r]them up unto
their own hearts' lust[C]: *and* they
[s]walked in their own counsels.[S]
13[S] [t]Oh that my [i,u]people had
hearkened unto me, *and* Iṣ′ra-el
had walked in my ways!
14 I should soon have [l,v]sub-
dued their enemies, and turned
my hand against their adversaries.
15 The haters of the LORD
should have submitted themselves unto him: but their time
should have endured for ever.
16 He should have [l]fed them
also with the finest of the
[v,w]wheat: and with [v,x]honey out
of the rock should I have satisfied thee.[S]

## PSALM 82

*The psalmist reproves the judges for their negligence, 8 and prays God to judge.*

A Psalm of Asaph.

[a]GOD standeth in the congregation of [1]the mighty; he
[b]judgeth[C] among the gods[C].
2 How long will ye [c]judge [d]un-
justly, and [e]accept the persons of
the wicked? [Sē′lah.[C]
3 [2]Defend the [f]poor and [g]fa-
therless: do [h]justice to the [i]af-
flicted and needy.
4 Deliver the [f]poor and needy:
rid *them* out of the hand of the
wicked.
5 They know not, [j,k]neither
will they understand; they walk
on in [k]darkness: all the foundations of the earth are out of
course[C].
6 I have said, [l]Ye *are* gods[C]; and
all of you *are* children of the
most High.[Q]
7 But ye shall die like men, and
fall like one of the princes.
8 Arise, O God, [b]judge[C] the
earth: for thou shalt inherit all
nations.[S T]

## PSALM 83

*The psalmist complains to God of a conspiracy against his people, 9 and prays for the destruction of their enemies.*

A Song *or* Psalm of Asaph.

[a,b]KEEP not thou silence, O
[c]God: hold not thy peace,
and be not still, O God.
2 [d]For, lo, thine enemies make
a tumult: and they that hate thee
have lifted[C] up the head.
3 They have taken *crafty
counsel against thy people, and
consulted against thy hidden
ones.
4 [e]They have said, Come, and
let us cut them off from *being* a
nation; that the name of Iṣ′ra-el
may be no more in remem-
brance.
5 For they have consulted together with one consent[C]: they
are confederate[C] against thee:
6 The tabernacles[C] of [e]Ē′dom,
and the [f]Ish′ma-el-ītes; of [g]Mō′-
ab, and the Hā′gar-ēneṣ;
7 Gē′bal, and [h]Ăm′mŏn, and

*e Respect of Persons*, Prov. 24:23.
3
*f Poor*, Prov. 21:13.
*g Orphan, justice to, required*, Lam. 5:3.
*h Justice, enjoined*, Deut. 33:21.
*i Afflicted*, Job 34:28.
2 R. V. Judge
5
*j Obduracy*, Prov. 29:1.
*k Spiritual Blindness*, 2 Cor. 4:4.
6
*l* John 10:34.
1
*a Adversity, prayer in*, vs. 1–18; Psa. 10:6.
*b Intercession, instances of*, vs. 1–18; Jer. 27:18.
*c Persecution, prayer for deliverance from*, vs. 1–18; John 15:20.
2
*d Prayer, pleas offered in*, Acts 6:4.
6
*e Edomites*, 2 Kin 8:21.
*f Ishmeelites*, Gen. 39:1.
*g Moabites*, Gen. 19:37.
7
*h Ammonites*, Deut. 2:20.

* **CRAFTINESS. Instances of:** *Satan, in the temptation of Eve*, Gen. 3:1–5. *Jacob, in purchase of Esau's birthright*, Gen. 25:31–33; *in obtaining Isaac's blessing*, Gen. 27:6–29, 35; *in management of Laban's flocks and herds*, Gen. 30:31–43. *Gibeonites, in deceiving Joshua and the Israelites into a treaty*, Josh. 9:3–15. *Saul, in deceiving David*, 1 Sam. 18:25. *David, in sending Hushai to Absalom*, 2 Sam. 15:32–37. *Sanballat, in trying to inveigle Nehemiah into a conference*, Neh. 6. *Jews, in seeking to entangle Jesus by questions, of public policy*, Matt. 22:15–17, 24–28; Mark 12:13, 14; Luke 20:19–34; *of the future life*, Mark 12:18–22; *in seeking to slay Jesus secretly*, Matt. 26:4; Mark 14:1.

*i* *Amalekites*, Num. 13:29.
*j* *Philistines*, Gen. 26:14.
*k* *Tyre*, Josh. 19:29.

**8**

*l* Or, *Assyria*, Gen. 25:18.
*m* *Lot*, Gen. 11:27.

**9**

*n* *Prayer, imprecatory*, Acts 6:4.
*o* *Midianites*, Gen. 37:28.
*p* *Sisera*, Judg. 4:2.
*q* Josh. 11:1; Judg. 4:2.
*r* Or, *Brook*, Deut. 8:7.
*s* Or, *Kishon*, Judg. 4:7.

**10**

*t* *Endor*, 1 Sam. 28:7.

**11**

*u* Judg. 7:25; 8:3.
*v* Judg. 8:5-21.

**13**

*w* *Stubble*, Isa. 5:24.
1 R. V. the whirling dust;

**16**

*x* *Judgments, design of*, Ex. 6:6.
*y* *Seekers*, Isa. 55:6.

**18**

*z* *God, name of*, Gen. 2:2.

---

*a* *God, sovereign*, Gen. 2:2.
2 R. V. Most High

---

*a* *Music, symbols used in*, 2 Chr. 5:13.

**1**

*b* *Church, love for*, Matt. 16:18.

**2**

*c* *Spiritual Desire*, Psa. 42:1.
*d* *Church, called courts*, 1 Kin. 9:3.
*e* *Worship, loved by God's people*, Gen. 22:5.
*f* *Heart*, Psa. 44:21.

[i]Ăm′a-lĕk; the [j]Phĭ-lĭs′tīnes with
the inhabitants of [k]Tȳre;
8 [l]Ăs′sur also is joined with
them: they have holpen[c] the children of [m]Lŏt. [Sē′lah.[c]
9 [n]Do unto them as *unto* the
[o]Mĭd′ĭ-an-ītes; as *to* [p]Sĭs′e-rȧ,
as *to* [q]Jā′bin, at the [r]brook of
[s]Kī′son:
10 *Which* perished at [t]Ĕn′-dôr: they became *as* dung[c] for
the earth.
11 Make their nobles like [u]Ō′-reb, and like [u]Zē′eb: yea, all
their princes as [v]Zē′bah, and as
[v]Zăl-mŭn′nȧ:
12 Who said, Let us take to
ourselves the houses of God in
possession.
13 [n]O my God, make them like
[1]a wheel; as the [w]stubble before
the wind.
14 As the fire burneth a wood,[c]
and as the flame setteth the
mountains on fire;
15 [n]So persecute them with thy
tempest, and make them afraid
with thy storm.
16 [n]Fill their faces with shame;
[x]that they may [y]seek thy name,
O LORD.
17 [n]Let them be confounded
and troubled for ever; yea, let
them be put to shame, and
perish:
18 That *men* may know that
thou, whose [z]name alone *is* JĔ-HŌ′VAH,[c] *art* the [2,a]most high
over all the earth.[s]

## PSALM 84

*The psalmist longs for the communion of the sanctuary; 4 shews how blessed are they that dwell therein. 8 He prays to be restored unto it.*

To the chief Musician upon [a]Gittith, A Psalm for the sons of Korah.

HOW [b]amiable[c] *are* thy tabernacles, O LORD of hosts!
2 My soul [c]longeth, yea, even
fainteth for the [d,e]courts of the
LORD: my [f]heart and my
flesh [c]crieth out for the living
God.
3 Yea, the *sparrow hath found
an house, and the †swallow a
nest for herself, where she may
lay her young, *even* thine altars,
O LORD of hosts, my [g]King,
and my God.
4 [h]Blessed *are* they that dwell
in thy house: they will be still
[e,i]praising thee. [Sē′lah.[c]
5 [h]Blessed *is* the man whose
[j]strength *is* in thee; in whose
heart *are* the [1]ways *of them*.
6 [2]*Who* passing through the
valley of Bā′cȧ make it a well;
the rain also filleth the pools.
7 They [k]go from strength to
strength, *every one of them* in
Zī′ŏn appeareth before God.
8 O LORD God of hosts, hear
my prayer: give [l]ear, O God of
Jā′cob. [Sē′lah.
9 Behold, O God our [m]shield,
and look upon the face of thine
anointed.
10 For a day in thy [d,e]courts *is*
better than a thousand. I had
rather be a [n]doorkeeper in the
[o]house of my God, than to
dwell in the [p]tents of [q]wickedness.
11 For the LORD God *is* a
[r,s]sun and [r,m]shield: [t,u]the LORD
will give [v]grace and glory: no
good *thing* will he withhold from
them that walk uprightly.[s]
12 O LORD of hosts, blessed *is*
the man that [w]trusteth in thee.

## PSALM 85

*The psalmist praises God for his goodness to Israel, 4 and prays for the continuance thereof. 8 His confidence in the truth and faithfulness of God.*

To the chief Musician, A Psalm for the sons of Korah.

[a,b]LORD,[T] thou hast been favourable unto thy land:
thou hast brought back the captivity of [c]Jā′cob.
2 Thou hast [d,e]forgiven the in-

**3**

*g* *God, sovereign*, Gen. 2:2.

**4**

*h* *Spiritual Peace*, Gal. 1:3.
*i* *Praise*, Psa. 150:1.

**5**

*j* *Spiritual Blessings, from God*, Eph. 1:3.
1 R. V. high ways to Zion.

**6**

2 R. V. Passing through the valley of Weeping they make it a place of springs; Yea, the early rain covereth it with blessings.

**7**

*k* *Growth in Grace*, 2 Pet. 3:18.

**8**

*l* *Ear, figurative*, Lev. 8:23.

**9**

*m* *Shield, figurative*, 1 Kin. 14:27.

**10**

*n* *Porters*, 2 Sam. 18:26.
*o* *Church, called house of God*, 1 Kin. 9:3.
*p* *Evil Company*, Prov. 13:20.
*q* *Sin, repugnant to the righteous*, Rom. 5:12.

**11**

*r* *God, preserver*, Gen. 2:2.
*s* *Sun, figurative*, Josh. 10:12.
*t* *Promise, implied, of divine help*, 2 Cor. 1:20.
*u* *Righteous, promises to*, Psa. 64:10.
*v* *Grace of God*, Rom. 4:16.

**12**

*w* *Faith*, Mark 11:22.

**1**

*a* *Patriotism, instances of*, vs. 1-13; Psa. 137:1.
*b* *Praise, for God's goodness*, Psa. 150:1.
*c* *Jews*, Neh. 4:2.

**2**

*d* *God, mercy of*, Gen. 2:2.
*e* *Sin, forgiveness of*, Rom. 5:12.

---

* **SPARROW**, Psa. 102:7. *Nests of*, Psa. 84:3. *Two sold for a farthing*, Matt. 10:29; Luke 12:6. *God's providential care of*, Matt. 10:29; Luke 12:6.

† **SWALLOW**. *Builds its nest in the sanctuary*, Psa. 84:3. *Chattering of, figurative of the mourning of the afflicted*, Isa. 38:14. *Migration of*, Jer. 8:7.

3
[f] *Anger of God*, 2 Kin. 13:3.
4
[g] *Backsliding, prayer for help against*, Hos. 11:7.
5
[h] *Adversity, prayer in*, Psa. 10:6.
6
[i] *Joy*, Psa. 5:11.
7
[j] *Nation, prayer for*, Isa. 2:4.
8
[k] *Peace*, Jer. 29:7.
[l] *Backsliding, admonitions against*, Hos. 11:7.
9
[m] *Righteous, promises to*, Psa. 64:10.
[n] *God, savior*, Gen. 2:2.
[o] *Fear of God*, Acts 9:31.
10
[p] *Mercy*, Deut. 5:10.
[q] *Truth*, John 18:37.
[r] *Righteousness*, Psa. 15:2.
12
[s] *God, providence of*, Gen. 2:2.
[t] *Temporal Blessings, from God*, Psa. 103:2.
13
1 R. V. make his footsteps a way to walk in.

iquity of thy people, thou hast
covered all their sin. [Sē'lah.[C]
3 Thou hast [d]taken away all thy
[f]wrath: thou hast turned *thyself*
from the fierceness of thine anger.[S]
4 [g]Turn us, O God of our salvation, and cause thine [f]anger
toward us to cease.[S]
5 [h]Wilt thou be angry with us
for ever? wilt thou draw out
thine [f]anger to all generations?
6 Wilt thou not revive us again:
that thy people may [i]rejoice in
thee?
7 [h,j]Shew us thy [d]mercy, O
LORD, and grant us thy salvation.
8 I will hear what God the
LORD will speak: for he will
speak [k]peace unto his people,
and to his saints: but let them
[l]not turn again to folly.[C]
9 [m]Surely his [n]salvation *is* nigh[G]
them that [o]fear him; that glory
may dwell in our land.
10 [p]Mercy and [q]truth are met
together; [r]righteousness and
[k]peace have kissed *each other*.[S]
11 [q]Truth shall spring out of
the earth; and [r]righteousness
shall look down from heaven.[T]
12 Yea, the LORD shall [s]give
[t]*that which is* good; and our land
shall yield her increase.[S]
13 [r]Righteousness shall go before him; and shall [1]set *us* in the
way of his steps.

## PSALM 86

*The psalmist entreats God to preserve him; 11 to teach him his way; 16 and to shew him a token for good, that his enemies may see it and be ashamed.*

A Prayer of David.

1
[a] *Afflictions, prayer in*, Psa. 34:19.
[b] *Prayer, pleas offered in*, Acts 6:4.
[c] *Humility*, Prov. 22:4.
2
[d] *Faith, exemplified*, Mark 11:22.
1 R. V. godly:
3
[e] *Prayer, importunity in*, Acts 6:4.

[a]BOW down thine ear, O
LORD, hear me: [b]for [c]I
*am* poor and needy.[S]
2 [a]Preserve my soul; for I *am*
[1]holy: O thou my God, save thy
servant that [d]trusteth[C] in thee.
3 [a]Be merciful unto me, O
Lord: for [e]I cry unto thee daily.
4 [a]Rejoice the soul of thy servant: for unto thee, O Lord, do
I [f]lift up my soul.
5 For thou, Lord, *art* [g]good,
and ready to forgive; and plenteous in [h]mercy unto all [i]them that
call upon thee.[S]
6 [a]Give ear, O LORD, unto my
prayer; and attend to the voice
of my supplications.
7 [j]In the day of my trouble I
will [a]call upon thee: for [d]thou
wilt answer me.
8 Among the gods *there is* none
like unto thee, O Lord; neither
*are there any* [k]*works* like unto
thy works.
9 [l,m]All [n]nations whom thou
hast [o]made shall come and worship before thee, O Lord; and
shall [p]glorify thy name.[S Q]
10 For thou *art* great, and
doest [k]wondrous things: [q]thou
*art* God alone.[T]
11 [l,r]Teach me thy [s]way, O
LORD; [t]I will walk in thy [u]truth:
unite my heart to [v]fear[G] thy name.[T S]
12 I will [w]praise thee, O Lord
my God, with all my heart: and
I will [p]glorify thy [x]name for
evermore.
13 For great *is* thy [h]mercy toward me: and thou hast [y]deliv-
ered[G] my soul from the lowest
[1,z]hell.[C]
14 [a]O God, the proud are [b]ris-
en against me, and the [2]assem-
blies of violent *men* have sought
after my soul; and [c]have not set
thee before them.
15 But thou, O Lord, *art* a
God full of compassion, and
gracious, [3,d]longsuffering, and
plenteous in [e]mercy and [f]truth.[T S]
16 [g]O turn unto me, and
have mercy[G] upon me; give thy
strength unto thy servant, and
save the son of thine handmaid.
17 Shew me a *token[G] for good;

[e] *God, mercy of*, Gen. 2:2. [f] *Truth, attribute of God*, John 18:37
3 R. V. Slow to anger,
16 [g] *Adversity, prayer in*, Psa. 10:6.

4
[f] *Spiritual Desire*, Psa. 42:1.
5
[g] *God, goodness of*, Gen. 2:2.
[h] *God, mercy of*, Gen. 2:2.
[i] *Seekers*, Isa. 55:6.
7
[j] *Prayer, in adversity*, Acts 6:4.
8
[k] *Works of God*, Psa. 40:5.
9
[l] *Church, prophecies concerning its prosperity*, Matt. 16:18.
[m] *Messianic Hope*, Gen. 49:10.
[n] *Gentiles, prophecies of the conversion of*, Acts 10:45.
[o] *God, creator*, Gen. 2:2.
[p] *Glorifying God*, Luke 5:25.
10
[q] *God, sovereign*, Gen. 2:2.
11
[r] *Wisdom, prayer for spiritual*, Prov. 2:2.
[s] *Will of God*, Mark 3:35.
[t] *Decision*, Isa. 50:7.
[u] *Truth*, John 18:37.
[v] *Fear of God*, Acts 9:31.
12
[w] *Praise*, Psa. 150:1.
[x] *God, name of, praised*, Gen. 2:2.
13
[y] *Salvation*, Acts 16:17.
[z] *Hell*, Mark 9:43.
1 R. V. pit.
14
[a] *Prayer, in adversity*, Acts 6:4.
[b] *Malice*, Eph. 4:31.
[c] *Godless, described*, Job 8:13.
2 R. V. congregation
15
[d] *God, longsuffering of*, Gen. 2:2.

*** TOKEN.** *A sign*, Ex. 3:12. *The mark of Cain*, Gen. 4:15. *Rainbow, that the world shall not again be destroyed by flood*, Gen. 9:12–17 *Circumcision, of the covenant of Abraham*, Gen. 17:11. *Presents, of covenant obligation*, Gen. 21:27, 30. *Miracles of Moses, of the divine authority of his mission*, Ex. 4:1–9. *Blood of the paschal lamb*, Ex. 12:13. *The Pass-*

that they which hate me may see *it,* and be ashamed: because thou, LORD, hast [h]holpen[C] me, and comforted me.

## PSALM 87

*The security of Zion. 3 Her glory and increase.*

A Psalm *or* Song for the sons of Korah.

A Messianic Psalm foreshadowing the union of all peoples in the universal Zion or Church of Christ, the use of whose inspiring numbers in public worship awakened, with other similar Messianic psalms, the expectation of one universal kingdom that finds its fulfillment in the Kingdom of Christ.

[a]HIS foundation *is* in the holy mountains.

2 The LORD loveth the gates of [b]Zī′ŏn more than all the dwellings of Jā′cob.

3 Glorious things are spoken of thee, O city of God. [Sē′lah.[C]

4 [c]I will make mention of [d]Rā′hăb and [e]Băb′ȳ-lon to them that know me: behold [f]Phĭ-lĭs′tiȧ, and [g]Tȳre, with [h]Ē-thĭ-ō′pĭ-ȧ; this *man* was born there.

5 And of [b]Zī′ŏn it shall be said, This and that man was born in her: and the [1]highest himself shall [i,j]establish her.[S]

6 The LORD shall count, when he [k]writeth up the people, *that* this *man* was born there. [Sē′lah.

7 [2]As well the [l]singers as the players on instruments *shall be there*: all my springs *are* in thee.

## PSALM 88

*The psalmist complains to God of his sore afflictions.*

A Song *or* Psalm for the sons of Korah, to the chief Musician upon [a]Mahalath [a]Leannoth, [a]Maschil of Heman the Ezrahite.

[b]O LORD God of my [c]salvation, I have [d]cried day *and* night before thee:

2 [b]Let my prayer come before thee: incline[C] thine ear unto my cry;

3 For [e]my soul is full of troubles: and my life[C] draweth nigh[C] unto [1]the grave.[C]

4 [e]I am counted with them that go down into the pit[C]: I am as a man *that hath* no [2]strength:

5 Free among the dead, like the slain that lie in the grave, whom thou rememberest no more: and they are cut off from thy hand.

6 [e]Thou hast [f]laid me in the lowest pit, in darkness, in the deeps.

7 [e,g]Thy wrath lieth hard upon me, and thou hast afflicted *me* with all thy waves. [Sē′lah.[C]

8 [f,g]Thou hast [h]put away mine [i]acquaintance far from me; thou hast made me an abomination unto them: *I am* shut up, and I cannot come forth.[Q]

9 Mine eye [3]mourneth by reason of affliction: LORD, I have [d,j]called daily upon thee, I have stretched out my hands unto thee.

10 Wilt thou shew wonders to the [k]dead? shall the dead arise *and* praise thee? [Sē′lah.

11 Shall thy [l]lovingkindness be declared in the [m]grave? *or* thy [n]faithfulness in destruction?

12 Shall thy wonders be known in the dark? and thy [o]righteousness in the land of forgetfulness?

13 But unto thee have I [b]cried, O LORD; and in the [i]morning shall my prayer [4]prevent[C] thee.

14 [e]LORD, why castest thou off my soul? *why* hidest thou thy face from me?

15 [e]I *am* afflicted and ready to die from *my* youth up: *while* I suffer thy terrors I am distracted.

16 [f,g]Thy fierce wrath goeth over me; thy terrors have cut me off.

17 They came round about me daily like water; they compassed me about together.

18 [h]Lover[C] and [i]friend hast thou put far from me, *and* mine acquaintance into darkness.

---

**17**
*h God, preserver,* Gen. 2:2.

**1**
*a Jesus, kingdom of, prophecies concerning,* vs. 1-5; Matt. 1:21.

**2**
*b Zion,* 2 Sam. 5:7.

**4**
*c Church, prophecies concerning its prosperity,* Matt. 16:18.
*d* Or, *Egypt,* Gen. 41:8.
*e Babylon, prophecies concerning,* Ezra 5:12.
*f* Psa. 60:8; 108:9.
*g Tyre, prophecies relating to,* Josh. 19:29.
*h Ethiopia, prophecies concerning the conversion of,* Isa. 18:1.

**5**
*i God, preserver, Gen.* 2:2.
*j God, providence of,* Gen. 2:2.
1 R. V. Most High

**6**
*k Book, figurative,* Psa. 139:16.

**7**
*l Music,* 2 Chr. 5:13.
2 R. V. They that sing as well as they that dance shall say, All my fountains are in thee.

---

*a Music, symbols used in,* 2 Chr. 5:13.

**1**
*b Afflictions, prayer in,* Psa. 34:19.
*c God, savior,* Gen. 2:2.
*d Prayer, importunity in,* Acts 6:4.

**3**
*e Despondency,* Eccl. 2:20.
1 R. V. Sheol.

**4**
2 R. V. help:

**6**
*f Adversity, dispensation from God,* Psa. 10:6.

**7**
*g Divine Chastisement,* Job 33:19.

**8**
*h Afflictions, forsaken by friends in,* Psa. 34:19.
*i Friends, false,* Ex. 33:11.

**9**
*j Prayer, daily,* Acts 6:4.
3 R. V. wasteth away

**10**
*k Dead,* 2 Kin. 4:32.

**11**
*l God, love of,* Gen. 2:2.
*m Hell,* Mark 9:43.
*n God, faithfulness of,* Gen. 2:2.

**12**
*o God, righteousness of,* Gen. 2:2.

**13**
4 R. V. come before

---

*over,* Ex. 13:9. *Consecration of the firstborn,* Ex. 13:14-16. *The Sabbath,* Ex. 31:13, 17. *A fringe,* Num. 15:38-40. *Cover of the altar,* Num. 16:38-40. *Aaron's rod,* Num. 17:10. *Scarlet thread,* Josh. 2:18, 21. *Memorial stones,* Josh. 4:2-9. *Dew on Gideon's fleece,* Judg. 6:36-40. *Prayer for tokens of mercy,* Psa. 86:17. See footnote, MIRACLES, Luke 23:8.

## PSALM 89

*The psalmist recounts the mercy and faithfulness of God in his covenant made with David; 38 but complains that he had cast off his anointed. 46 and implores him to have mercy.*

[a]Maschil of Ethan the Ezrahite.

A Messianic Psalm in which the inspired poet rehearses the covenant of God with David that *his seed* should be established upon the throne of universal and everlasting empire, vs. 3, 4, 29, 34–37. This promised seed, the glorious King, is the "first-born, higher than the kings of the earth," v. 27. The angel Gabriel in his message to Mary concerning Jesus says, "He shall be great, and shall be called the son of the Most High, and the Lord God shall give unto him the throne of his father David, and he shall reign over the house of Jacob for ever: and of his kingdom there shall be no end." (Luke 1:32, 33.) Messianic psalms such as this one arose, by divine inspiration, above the themes of the occasion of their writing, to the sublime theme of which the occasion was a type, and the poet set in musical measures the more glorious truths of the Messiah's Kingdom of which there shall be no end.

[b]I WILL [c]sing[S T] of the [d]mercies
of the LORD for ever: with
my mouth will I make known
thy [e]faithfulness to all generations.
2 For I have said, [f]Mercy shall
be built up for ever: thy [e]faithfulness
shalt thou establish in
the very heavens.[S T]
3 I have[T Q] made a [g]covenant with
my chosen, I have sworn unto
[h]Dā'vid my servant,
4 [i]Thy seed will I establish for
ever, and build up thy throne to
all generations.[S T Q] [Sē'lah.[C]
5 And the heavens shall [j]praise
thy wonders, O LORD: thy
[e]faithfulness also in the congregation
of the [1]saints.[S]
6 For who in the heaven can be
compared unto the LORD? *who*
among the sons of the mighty
can be likened unto the LORD?
7 [2]God is greatly to be feared
in the assembly of the saints,
and to be had in reverence of all
*them that are* about him.[Q]
8 O LORD God of hosts, who *is*
a [k]strong LORD like unto thee?
or to thy [e]faithfulness round
about thee?[S]
9[S] [k]Thou rulest the [3]raging of
the sea: when the waves thereof
arise, thou stillest them.
10 Thou hast broken [l,m]Rā'hăb
in pieces, as one that is slain;
thou hast scattered thine enemies
with thy strong *arm.[Q]
11 The heavens *are* [n]thine, the
earth also *is* thine: *as for* the
world and the fulness thereof,
thou hast [o]founded them.[Q]
12 The north and the south
thou hast [o]created them: [p]Tā'bôr
and [q]Hēr'mon shall rejoice
in thy name.[T]
13 Thou hast a [k]mighty *arm:
strong is thy hand,[C] *and* high is
thy right hand.[G S T]
14 [4,r]Justice and [s]judgment *are*
the [5]habitation of thy [t]throne:
[u,v]mercy and [w]truth shall go before
thy face.[S T]
15 Blessed *is* the [x]people that
know the joyful sound: they
shall walk, O LORD, in the light
of thy countenance.
16 In thy name shall they [y]rejoice
all the day: and in thy
[r]righteousness shall they be exalted.
17 For thou *art* the glory of
their [z]strength: and in thy [a]favour
our [b]horn shall be exalted.
18 [6]For the LORD *is* our [c]defence;
and the Holy One of Iṣ'ra-el
*is* our [d]king.
19 Then thou spakest in [e]vision
to thy [7]holy one, and saidst,
[f]I have laid help upon *one that
is* mighty; I have [g]exalted *one*
chosen out of the people.[S Q]
20 I have found [h]Dā'vid my
servant; with my holy oil have I
[i]anointed him:[T Q]
21 With whom my hand shall
be established: mine *arm also
shall strengthen him.
22 The enemy shall not exact
upon him; nor the son of wickedness
afflict him.
23 And I will beat down his

---

a *Music, symbols used in*, 2 Chr. 5:13.

**1**
b *Thankfulness, to God*, Acts 24:3.
c *Religious Testimony, exemplified*, 2 Thess. 1:10.
d *God, mercy of*, Gen. 2:2.
e *God, faithfulness of*, Gen. 2:2.

**2**
f *Mercy*, Deut. 5:10.

**3**
g *Covenant, of God with men*, Deut. 29:1.
h *David*, 1 Sam. 16:13.

**4**
i *Jesus, prophecies concerning*, Matt. 1:21.

**5**
j *Praise*, Psa. 150:1.
1 R. V. holy ones.

**7**
2 R. V. A God very terrible in the council of the holy ones, And to be feared above all

**8**
k *God, power of*, Gen. 2:2.

**9**
3 R. V. pride

**10**
l Or, *Egypt*, Gen. 41:8.
m *Wicked, punishment of*, Psa. 73:3.

**11**
n *God, sovereign*, Gen. 2:2.
o *God, creator*, Gen. 2:2.

**12**
p *Tabor*, Judg. 8:18.
q *Hermon*, Deut. 4:48.

**14**
r *God, righteousness of*, Gen. 2:2.
s *God, justice of*, Gen. 2:2.
t *Throne, figurative*, 1 Kin. 2:19.
u *Mercy*, Deut. 5:10.
v *God, mercy of*, Gen. 2:2.
w *Truth*, John 18:37.
4 R. V. Righteousness
5 R. V. foundation

**15**
x *Nation, peace of*, Isa. 2:4.

**16**
y *Joy*, Psa. 5:11.

**17**
z *Spiritual Blessings, from God*, Eph. 1:3.

a *Grace of God*, Rom. 4:16.
b *Horn, figurative of power*, 1 Kin. 1:39.

**18**
c *God, preserver*, Gen. 2:2.
d *God, sovereign*, Gen. 2:2.
6 Am. R. V. For our shield belongeth unto Jehovah; And our king to the Holy One of Israel.

**19**
e *Vision*, Acts 9:10.
f *Government, God in*, Isa. 22:21.
g *Rulers, appointed by God*, Ex. 18:21.
7 R. V. saints,

**20**
h *David*, 1 Sam. 16:13.
i *Anointing, of kings*, Lev. 8:12.

---

*** ARM. Figurative:** *Of divine providence*, Ex. 6:6; 15:16; Deut. 4:34; 5:15; 7:19; 9:29; 26:8; 1 Kin. 8:42; Psa. 77:15; 89:10, 21; 98:1; Isa. 33:2; 40:10, 11; 51:5, 9; 52:10; 53:1; 59:16; 62:8; 63:5, 12; Jer. 21:5; 27:5; 32:17; Luke 1:51; Acts 13:17.

foes before his face, and plague them that hate him.

24 But my [j]faithfulness and my [k]mercy *shall be* with him: and in my name shall his [b]horn be exalted.[S]

25 I will set his hand also in the sea, and his right hand in the rivers.

26[T] [l]He shall cry unto me, Thou *art* [m]my father, my God, and the [n]rock of my salvation.[Q]

27 Also [o]I will make him *my* [p]firstborn, higher than the kings of the earth.[Q]

28 My [k]mercy will I keep for him for evermore, and my [q]covenant shall stand fast with him.[S]

29 His [r]seed also will I make *to endure* for ever, and his [s]throne as the days[G] of heaven.[T]

30 If his children [t]forsake my law, and walk not in my judgments;[G]

31 If they break my statutes,[G] and [u]keep[G] not my commandments;

32 Then will I [v]visit[G] their transgression[G] with the rod, and their iniquity with stripes.

33 [S] Nevertheless my [k]lovingkindness will I not utterly take from him, nor suffer[G] my [j]faithfulness to fail.

34 My [q]covenant [j]will I not break, nor alter the thing that is gone out of my lips.[S] [T]

35 Once have I [w]sworn by my [x]holiness that I will not lie unto Dā′vid.[S]

36 His [r]seed shall endure for ever, and his [s]throne as the sun before me.[Q]

37 It shall be established for ever as the moon, and *as* a faithful witness in heaven.[Q] [Sē′lah.

38 But thou hast [y]cast off and [8]abhorred, thou hast been wroth[G] with thine anointed.[G]

39 Thou hast [9]made void the covenant of thy servant: thou hast profaned his [z]crown *by casting it* to the ground.

40 Thou hast [y]broken down all his hedges; thou hast brought his strong holds to ruin.

41 All that pass by the way spoil[G] him: he is a reproach to his neighbours.

42 Thou hast [y]set up the right hand of his adversaries; thou hast made all his enemies to rejoice.

43 Thou hast also turned the edge of his sword, and hast not made him to stand in the battle.

44 Thou hast [y]made his glory to cease, and cast his throne down to the ground.

45 [v]The days of his youth hast thou shortened: thou hast covered him with shame. [Sē′lah.

46 [a]How long, LORD? wilt thou hide thyself for ever? shall thy wrath burn like fire?

47 Remember how short my [b]time is: [c]wherefore[G] hast thou made all men in vain?

48 What man *is he that* liveth, and shall not see [d]death? shall he deliver his soul from the [10]hand[G] of the [e]grave[G]? [Sē′lah.

49 Lord, [f]where *are* thy former lovingkindnesses, *which* thou swarest unto [g]Dā′vid in thy [11]truth?[T]

50[Q] [a]Remember, Lord, the reproach of thy servants; *how* I do bear in my bosom *the reproach of* all the mighty people;

51 Wherewith thine enemies have reproached, O LORD; wherewith they have reproached the footsteps of thine anointed.[Q]

52 [h]Blessed *be* the LORD for evermore. Amen, and Amen.[T]

## PSALM 90

*The psalmist, setting forth God's eternity,* 3 *complains of human frailty,* 7 *of divine chastisements,* 10 *and of the brevity of life.* 12 *He prays for the return of God's favour.*

A prayer of Moses the man of God.

LORD,[S] [a]thou hast been our dwelling place in all generations.

---

**24**
j *God, faithfulness of,* Gen. 2:2.
k *God, mercy of,* Gen. 2:2.

**26**
l *Spiritual Adoption,* Rom. 8:15.
m *God, fatherhood of,* Gen. 2:2.
n *Rock, figurative,* Psa. 78:15.

**27**
o *Jesus, typified in Solomon,* Matt. 1:21.
p *Firstborn, figurative,* Zech. 12:10.

**28**
q *Covenant, of God with men,* Deut. 29:1.

**29**
r *Jesus, prophecies concerning,* Matt. 1:21.
s *Throne, figurative,* 1 Kin. 2:19.

**30**
t *Backsliders,* Jer. 3:22.

**31**
u *Disobedience to God,* Eph. 5:6.

**32**
v *Divine Chastisement,* Job 33:19.

**35**
w *Oath, attributed to God,* Num. 5:19.
x *God, holiness of,* Gen. 2:2.

**38**
y *Adversity, dispensation from God,* Psa. 10:6.
8 R. V. rejected.

**39**
9 R. V. abhorred

z *Crown, figurative,* Ex. 29:6.

**46**
a *Adversity, prayer in,* Psa. 10:6.

**47**
b *Life, brevity and uncertainty of,* Eccl. 8:15.
c *God, providence of, mysterious and misinterpreted,* Gen. 2:2.

**48**
d *Death, inevitable,* Num. 23:10.
e *Hell,* Mark 9:43.
10 R. V. power of Sheol?

**49**
f *Prayer, pleas offered in,* Acts 6:4.
g *David,* 1 Sam. 16:13.
11 R. V. faithfulness?

**52**
h *Praise,* Psa. 150:1.

**1**
a *Faith, exemplified,* Mark 11:22.

**2**
b *God, creator,* Gen. 2:2.
c *Earth, created by God,* Prov. 8:23.
d *God, eternity of,* Gen. 2:2.

**3**
e *God, sovereign,* Gen. 2:2.
f *Death,* Num. 23:10.

**4**
g *Year,* Lev. 25:29.

**5**
h *Life, brevity and uncertainty of,* Eccl. 8:15.
i *Flood,* Gen. 6:17.
j *Grass,* Isa. 40:7.

**7**
k *Adversity, dispensation from God,* Psa. 10:6.
l *Anger of God,* 2 Kin. 13:3.

**8**
m *God, judge,* Gen. 2:2.
n *Sin, attempt to cover, vain,* Rom. 5:12.

**9**
1 R. V. bring our years to an end as

**10**
o *Longevity,* Psa. 91:16.
p *Old Age,* Isa. 46:4.
2 R. V. pride but labor and sorrow;

**11**
q *Fear of God,* Acts 9:31.
3 R. V. And thy wrath according to the fear that is due unto thee?

**12**
r *Instruction, sought,* Prov. 23:23.
s *Spiritual Desire,* Psa. 42:1.
t *Wisdom, prayer for spiritual,* Prov. 2:2.
4 Am. R. V. get us a heart of wisdom.

**13**
u *Repentance, attributed to God,* Mark 1:4.
v *Anthropomorphisms,* Gen. 11:5.

**14**
w *God, mercy of,* Gen. 2:2.
5 R. V. in the morning with thy mercy;

**15**
x *Adversity, prayer in,* Psa. 10:6.

2 Before the mountains were brought forth, or ever thou hadst [b]formed the [c]earth and the world, even from [d]everlasting to everlasting, thou *art* God.

3 Thou [e]turnest man to [f]destruction; and sayest, Return, ye children of men.

4 For a thousand [g]years in thy sight *are but* as yesterday when it is past, and *as* a watch in the night.

5 Thou [h]carriest them away as with a [i]flood; they are *as* a sleep: in the morning *they are* like [j]grass *which* groweth up.

6 In the morning [h,j]it flourisheth, and groweth up; in the evening it is cut down, and withereth.

7 For we are [k]consumed by thine [l]anger, and by thy wrath are we troubled.

8 Thou hast [m]set our [n]iniquities before thee, our secret *sins* in the light of thy countenance.

9 For all our [h]days are passed away in thy wrath: we [1]spend our years as a tale *that is told.*

10 The days of our years *are* [o,p]threescore years and ten; and if by reason of strength *they be* fourscore years, yet *is* their [2]strength labour and sorrow; for [h]it is soon cut off, and we fly away.

11 Who knoweth the power of thine [l]anger? [3]even according to thy [q]fear, *so is* thy wrath.

12 So [r,s]teach *us* to number our days, that we may [4]apply *our* hearts unto [t]wisdom.

13 Return, O LORD, how long? and let it [u,v]repent thee concerning thy servants.

14 O satisfy us [5]early with thy [w]mercy; that we may rejoice and be glad all our days.

15 [x]Make us glad according to the days *wherein* thou hast afflicted us, *and* the years *wherein* we have seen evil.

16 Let thy work appear unto thy servants, and thy [y]glory unto their children.

17 And let the [z]beauty of the LORD our God be upon us: and establish thou the [a]work of our hands upon us; yea, the work of our hands establish thou it.

## PSALM 91

*The safety of the righteous at all times. 11 Their final triumph over all their enemies.*

[a]HE that dwelleth in the secret place of the most High [b,c]shall abide under the shadow of the Almighty.

2 I will [d]say of the LORD, *He is* my refuge and my [e]fortress: my God; in him will I [a]trust.

3 Surely [a,c]he shall [f]deliver thee from the snare of the fowler, *and* from the noisome pestilence.

4 [a,b,c]He shall cover thee with his feathers, and under his wings shalt thou [1]trust: his [g,h]truth *shall be thy* [i]shield and buckler.

5 Thou shalt not be afraid for the terror by night; *nor* for the [j]arrow *that* flieth by day;

6 *Nor* for the [k]pestilence *that* walketh in darkness; *nor* for the destruction *that* wasteth at noonday.

7 [l]A thousand shall fall at thy side, and ten thousand at thy right hand; *but* [c,l]it shall not come nigh thee.

8 Only with thine eyes shalt thou behold and see the [m]reward of the wicked.

9 Because thou hast made the LORD, *which is* my refuge, *even* the most High, thy habitation;

10 [b,c]There shall no evil befall thee, neither shall any plague come nigh thy dwelling.

11 For [b,c,n]he shall give his [o]angels charge over thee, to keep thee in all thy ways.

12 [b,c,o]They shall bear thee up in *their* hands, lest thou dash thy foot against a stone.

13 Thou shalt tread upon the

**16**
y *God, glory of,* Gen. 2:2.

**17**
z *Beauty, spiritual,* Psa. 45:11.

a Works, 2 Tim. 1:9.

**1**
a *Faith, exemplified,* vs. 1–16; Mark 11:22.
b *Righteous, promises to,* vs. 1–16; Psa. 64:10.
c *Promise, implied, of divine protection,* vs. 1–16; 2 Cor. 1:20.

**2**
d *Religious Testimony, exemplified,* 2 Thess. 1:10.
e *Fortification, figurative,* Ezek. 17:17.

**3**
f *Temporal Blessings, from God,* Psa. 103:2.

**4**
g *God, truth,* Gen. 2:2.
h *Truth,* John 18:37.
i *Shield, figurative,* 1 Kin. 14:27.
1 R.V. take refuge:

**5**
j *Arrow, figurative,* 1 Sam. 20:20.

**6**
k *Plague,* Ex. 11:1.

**7**
l *Wicked, contrasted with the righteous,* Psa. 73:3.

**8**
m *Wicked, punishment of,* Psa. 73:3.

**11**
n Matt. 4:6; Luke 4:10, 11.
o *Angel, functions of,* Heb. 1:13.

**13**
*p Lion*, Mic. 5:8.
*q Adder*, Gen. 49:17.
*r Dragon*, Deut. 32:33.
2 R. V. serpent
**14**
*s Love, of man for God*, 1 John 4:19.
**15**
*t Prayer, answer to, promised*, Acts 6:4.
*u God, preserver*, Gen. 2:2.
**16**
*v Salvation*, Acts 16:17.
**1**
*a Thankfulness, to God*, Acts 24:3.
*b Music*, 2 Chr. 5:13.
*c Praise*, Psa. 150:1.
**2**
*d Prayer, morning and evening*, Acts 6:4.
*e God, love of*, Gen. 2:2.
*f God, faithfulness of*, Gen. 2:2.
**3**
*g Psaltery*, 1 Chr. 16:5.
*h Harp*, Dan. 3:10.
**5**
*i God, unsearchable*, Gen. 2:2.
**7**
*j Wicked, prosperity of*, Psa. 73:3.
*k Wicked, punishment of*, Psa. 73:3.
*l Death, of the wicked*, Num. 23:10.

[p]lion and [q]adder: the young lion and the [2,r]dragon shalt thou trample under feet.[Q]

14 [b,c]Because [s]he hath set his love upon me, therefore will I deliver him: I will set him on high, because he hath known my name.

15 He shall call upon me, and [t]I will answer him: [u]I *will be* with him in trouble; I will [u]deliver him, and honour him.

16 With *,[f]long life will I satisfy him, and shew him my [v]salvation.[T]

## PSALM 92

*The psalmist exhorts to praise God, 4 for his great works, 6 for his judgments on the wicked, 10 and for his goodness to the righteous.*

A Psalm *or* Song for the sabbath day.

IT *is a* good *thing* to give [a]thanks unto the LORD, and to [b]sing [c]praises unto thy name, O most High:

2 [d]To shew[G] forth thy [e]lovingkindness in the morning, and thy [f]faithfulness every night.[S]

3 Upon an [b]instrument of ten strings, and upon the [g]psaltery; upon the [h]harp with a solemn sound.

4 For thou, LORD, hast made me glad through thy work: I will triumph in the works of thy hands.

5 O LORD, how great are thy works! *and* thy [i]thoughts are very deep.[S Q]

6 A brutish[G] man knoweth not; neither doth a fool understand this.

7 When the wicked [j]spring as the grass, and when all the workers of iniquity [j]do flourish; *it is* that they shall be [k,l]destroyed for ever:

8 But thou, LORD, *art most* high [m]for evermore.[S]

9 For, lo, thine enemies, O LORD, for, lo, thine enemies shall perish; all the workers of iniquity shall be [k]scattered.

10 But [n]my [o]horn[G] shalt thou exalt like *the horn of* [1]an [p]unicorn: I shall be [q]anointed with fresh oil.

11 Mine eye also shall see *my desire* on mine enemies, *and* mine ears shall hear *my desire* of the wicked that rise up against me.

12 [r]The righteous shall flourish like the [s]palm tree: he shall grow like a [t]cedar in [u]Lĕb′a-non.

13 Those that be planted in the [v]house of the LORD shall flourish in the courts of our God.

14 [r]They shall still bring forth fruit in [w]old age; they shall be [2]fat and flourishing;

15 To shew[G] that the LORD *is* [x]upright: *he is* my [y]rock, and *there is* [z]no unrighteousness in him.[S]

## PSALM 93

*The majesty, power, and holiness of God.*

[a]THE LORD [b]reigneth, he is clothed with majesty; the LORD is clothed with [c]strength, *wherewith* he hath girded himself: the world also is stablished,[G] that it cannot be moved.[G Q]

2 Thy [d]throne *is* established of old: [e]thou *art* from everlasting.[S]

3 The floods have lifted up, O LORD, the floods have lifted up their voice; the floods lift up[T] their waves.

4 The LORD on high *is* [c]mightier than the noise of many

**8**
*m God, eternity of*, Gen. 2:2.
**10**
*n Faith, exemplified*, Mark 11:22.
*o Horn, figurative of power*, 1 Kin. 1:39.
*p Unicorn*, Job 39:9.
*q Anointing*, Deut. 28:40.
1 R. V. the wild-ox:
**12**
*r Righteous, promises to*, Psa. 64:10.
*s Palm Tree*, Song 7:7.
*t Cedar*, Isa. 9:10.
*u Lebanon*, Deut. 1:7.
**13**
*v Church*, 1 Kin. 9:3.
**14**
*w Old Age*, Isa. 46:4.
2 R. V. full of sap and green:
**15**
*x God, righteousness of*, Gen. 2:2.
*y Rock, figurative*, Psa. 78:15.
*z God, holiness of*, Gen. 2:2.
**1**
*a Praise, for God's attributes*, Psa. 150:1.
*b God, sovereign*, Gen. 2:2.
*c God, power of*, Gen. 2:2.
**2**
*d Throne, figurative*, 1 Kin. 2:19.
*e God, eternity of*, Gen. 2:2.

* **LONGEVITY**, Gen. 6:3; Psa. 90:10. *Promised, to the obedient*, Ex. 20:12; Deut. 4:40; 22:7; *to the righteous*, Job 5:26; Psa. 21:4; 34:11–13; 91:16; Prov. 3:2, 16; 9:11; 10:27; Isa. 65:20; 1 Pet. 3:10, 11; *to Solomon*, 1 Kin. 3:11–14.
**Instances of:** *Adam*, 930 *years*, Gen. 5:5. *Seth*, 912 *years*, Gen. 5:8. *Enos*, 905 *years*, Gen. 5:11. *Cainan*, 910 *years*, Gen. 5:14. *Mahalaleel*, 895 *years*, Gen. 5:17. *Jared*, 962 *years*, Gen. 5:20. *Enoch*, 365 *years*, Gen. 5:23. *Methuselah*, 969 *years*, Gen. 5:27. *Lamech*, 777 *years*, Gen. 5:31. *Noah*, 950 *years*, Gen. 9:29. *Shem*, Gen. 11:11. *Arphaxad*, Gen. 11:13. *Salah*, Gen. 11:15. *Eber*, Gen. 11:17. *Peleg*, Gen. 11:19. *Reu*, Gen. 11:21. *Serug*, Gen. 11:23. *Nahor*, Gen. 11:25. *Terah*, 205 *years*, Gen. 11:32. *Sarah*, 127 *years*, Gen. 23:1. *Abraham*, 175 *years*, Gen. 25:7. *Isaac*, 180 *years*, Gen. 35:28. *Jacob*, 147 *years*, Gen. 47:28. *Joseph*, 110 *years*, Gen. 50:26. *Amram*, 137 *years*, Ex. 6:20. *Aaron*, 123 *years*, Num. 33:39. *Moses*, 120 *years*, Deut. 31:2; 34:7. *Joshua*, 110 *years*, Josh. 24:29. *Eli*, 98 *years*, 1 Sam. 4:15. *Barzillai*, 80 *years*, 2 Sam. 19:32. *Job*, Job 42:16. *Jehoiada*, 130 *years*, 2 Chr. 24:15. *Anna*, Luke 2:36, 37. *Paul*, Philemon 9.
See footnote, OLD AGE, Isa. 46:4.

5
*f* *Word of God*, Psa. 119:9.
*g* *Holiness*, Ex. 39:30.

1
*a* *Afflictions, prayer in*, Psa. 34:19.
1 R.V. shine forth.
2
*b* *God, judge*, Gen. 2:2.
*c* *Prayer, imprecatory*, Acts 6:4.
2 R. V. to the proud their desert.
4
*d* *Wicked, described*, Psa. 73:3.
*e* *Boasting, of the wicked*, Prov. 25:14.
3 R.V. They prate, they speak arrogantly:
5
*f* *Persecution, of the righteous*, John 15:20.
6
*g* *Homicide, felonious*, Deut. 5:17.
*h* *Widow*, 2 Sam. 14:5.
*i* *Orphan*, Lam. 5:3.
7
*j* *Spiritual Blindness*, 2 Cor. 4:4.
*k* *Presumption, in defying God*, Psa. 19:13.
*l* *Infidelity, exemplified*, 2 Cor. 6:15.
8
*m* *Wisdom, spiritual*, Prov. 2:2.
9
*n* *God, creator*, Gen. 2:2.
*o* *Anthropomorphisms*, Gen. 11:5.
10
*p* *Divine Chastisement*, Job 33:19.
4 R. V. nations,
11
*q* 1 Cor. 3:20.
*r* *God, knowledge of*, Gen. 2:2.
*s* *Heart, known to God*, Psa. 44:21.
*t* *Vanity*, Eccl. 1:2.
12
*u* *Adversity, benefits of*, Psa. 10:6.
*v* *Wisdom, spiritual, from God*, Prov. 2:2.
*w* *Word of God*, Psa. 119:9.

waters, *yea, than* the mighty
waves of the sea.
5 Thy [f]testimonies are very
sure: [g]holiness becometh thine
house, O LORD, for ever.

## PSALM 94

*The psalmist calls for justice upon the wicked. 8 He rebukes them, 12 and shews the blessedness of affliction. 16 God is the defender of the afflicted.*

[a]O LORD God, to whom
*vengeance belongeth; O
God, to whom vengeance belongeth, [1]shew thyself.
2 Lift up thyself, thou [b]judge of
the earth: [c]render [2]a reward to
the proud.
3 LORD, how long shall the
wicked, how long shall the
wicked triumph?
4 [3]*How long* shall [d]they utter
*and* speak hard things? *and* all
the workers of iniquity [e]boast
themselves?
5 [d]They [f]break in pieces thy
people, O LORD, and afflict
thine heritage.
6 [d]They [g]slay the [h]widow and
the stranger, and murder the
[i]fatherless.
7 Yet they [j,k,l]say, The LORD
shall not see, neither shall the
God of Jā'cob regard *it*.
8 Understand, ye brutish among
the people: and *ye* fools, when
will ye be [m]wise?
9 He that [n]planted the ear,
shall he not [o]hear? he that
[n]formed the eye, shall he not
[o]see?
10 He that [p]chastiseth the
[4]heathen, shall not he correct?
he that teacheth man knowledge,
*shall not he know*?
11 [q]The LORD [r]knoweth the
[s]thoughts of man, that they *are*
[t]vanity.
12 [u]Blessed *is* the man whom
thou [p]chastenest, O LORD, and
[v]teachest him out of thy [w]law;
13 That thou mayest give him
[x]rest from the days of adversity,
until the [y]pit be digged for the
wicked.
14 For [z,a]the LORD [b]will not
cast off his people, [b]neither will
he forsake his inheritance.
15 But judgment shall return
unto [c]righteousness: and all the
upright in heart shall follow it.
16 Who will rise up for me
against the evil doers? *or* who
will stand up for me against the
workers of iniquity?
17 [d]Unless the LORD *had been*
my [e]help, my soul had [5]almost
dwelt in [f]silence.
18 When I said, [g]My foot slippeth; [h]thy [i]mercy, O LORD, held
me up.
19 In the multitude of my
thoughts within me [d]thy comforts delight my soul.
20 Shall [j]the throne of [k]iniquity
have fellowship with thee, which
frameth mischief by a law?
21 [j]They gather themselves together against the soul of the
righteous, and condemn the innocent blood.
22 But the LORD is my [6,e]de-
fence; and my God *is* the [l]rock
of my refuge.
23 And he shall [m,n]bring upon
them their own iniquity, and
shall cut them off in their own
wickedness; *yea*, the LORD our
God shall cut them off.

## PSALM 95

*An exhortation to praise God, 3 for his greatness, 6 and for his goodness, 8 and not to tempt him, as did Israel.*

[a]O COME, let us [b]sing unto
the LORD: let us make a
joyful noise to the [c]rock of our
[d]salvation.
2 [e]Let us come before his presence with [f]thanksgiving, and
make a joyful noise unto him
with psalms.
3 For the LORD *is* a great God,

13
*x* *God, preserver*, Gen. 2:2.
*y* *Wicked, punishment of*, Psa. 73:3.
14
*z* *Faith, exemplified*, Mark 11:22.
*a* *Promise, implied to the righteous*, 2 Cor. 1:20.
*b* *God, faithfulness of*, Gen. 2:2.
15
*c* *Righteousness*, Psa. 15:2.
17
*d* *Afflictions, consolation in*, Psa. 34:19.
*e* *God, preserver*, Gen. 2:2.
*f* *Death, described*, Num. 23:10.
5 R. V. soon
18
*g* *Temptation*, Luke 11:4.
*h* *Faith, exemplified*, Mark 11:22.
*i* *God, mercy of*, Gen. 2:2.
20
*j* *Rulers, wicked*, Ex. 18:21.
*k* *Sin, separates from God*, Rom. 5:12.
22
*l* *Rock, figurative*, Psa. 78:15.
6 R. V. high tower;
23
*m* *Judgments*, Ex. 6:6.
*n* *Sin, fruits of*, Rom. 5:12.
1
*a* *Praise*, Psa. 150:1.
*b* *Music*, 2 Chr. 5:13.
*c* *Rock, figurative*, Psa. 78:15.
*d* *Salvation*, Acts 16:17.
2
*e* *Duty, of man to God*, Eccl. 12:13
*f* *Thankfulness, to God*, Acts 24:3.

* **VENGEANCE.** *Belongs to God*, Deut. 32:35, 36; Luke 18:7, 8; Rom. 12:19; 2 Thess. 1:6; Heb. 10:30; Rev. 6:10. **Instance of:** *Sons of Jacob, on Hamor and Shechem*, Gen 34:20–31. See footnote, REVENGE, Ezek. 25:15.

and a great [g]King above all
gods.[G]
4[S] In his hand *are* the deep
places of the earth: the [1]strength
of the hills *is* his also.
5 [h]The [i]sea *is* his, and he [j]made
it: and his hands formed the dry
*land*.[S]
6 O [T]come, let us [k]worship and
bow down: let us [l]kneel before
the LORD our [j]maker.
7 F[Q]or he *is* our God; and we *are*
the people of [m]his pasture, and
the [n]sheep of [o]his hand. [p]To day
if ye will hear his voice,
8 [q,r]Harden not your [s]heart, as
[2]in the [t]provocation, *and* as *in*
the day of [3]temptation in the
wilderness:[Q]
9 When your fathers tempted[G]
me, proved[G] me, and saw my
work.
10 [u]Forty years long was I
[v]grieved with *this* generation,
and said, It *is* a [w]people that
do err in their [x]heart, and they
[y]have not known my ways:
11 Unto [z]whom I [a,b]sware in
my [c,d]wrath that they should not
enter into my rest.[T Q]

## PSALM 96

*An exhortation to praise God, 4 for his goodness, 8 and for the establishment of his kingdom in the world.*

A Messianic Psalm. The inspired poet, rising above the horizon common to ethnic religions and breaking over the disciplinary customs and traditions of the narrow Mosaic régime, sees, with a divinely exalted faith, and in his inspired numbers describes the widening cycles of the true religion, embracing all nations of the earth. The Jehovah of the psalmist becomes the triumphing Messiah or Christ of the Gospel. The heathen shall see his wonders (v. 3), and all the kindreds of the earth shall give glory to his name (v. 7) and worship him in the beauty of holiness (v. 9). It was from these lofty and inspiring psalms of praise that the Messianic hope of Israel grew to the widespread expectation that prepared Zachariah and Elisabeth and Mary and Simeon and Anna for the coming of our Lord.

[a]O SING unto the LORD a
new [b]song: sing unto the
LORD, all the earth.[Q]
2 Sing unto the LORD, [a]bless[G]
his name; [c,d]shew forth his [e,f]sal-
vation from day to day.
3 [c,d,g]Declare his [h]glory among
the [1]heathen,[G] his wonders among
all people.
4 For the LORD *is* great, and
greatly to be [a]praised: he *is* to be
[i]feared above all gods.[G S]
5 For all the gods of the [2]na-
tions *are* [j]idols:[G] but the LORD
[k]made the heavens.[S]
6 Honour and majesty *are* before him: strength and beauty
*are* in his [l]sanctuary.
7 Give[G] unto the LORD, O ye
kindreds of the [2]people, give unto the LORD [h]glory and strength.
8 Give unto the LORD the
glory *due unto* his name: bring an
offering, and come into his [l]courts.
9 O [m]worship the LORD in the
beauty of holiness: [i]fear before
him, all the earth.
10 [c,d]S[T]ay among the [1]heathen[G]
*that* the LORD [n]reigneth: the
world also shall be established
that it shall not be moved:[G] he
shall [o]judge the [2]people [p]right-
eously.[S]
11 [a]Let the heavens rejoice, and
let the earth be glad; let the sea
roar, and the fulness thereof.[Q]
12 [a]Let the field be joyful, and
all that *is* therein: then shall all
the trees of the wood[G] rejoice
13 Before the LORD: for he
cometh, for he cometh to [o]judge
the earth: he shall judge the
world with [p]righteousness, and
the [2]people with his [q]truth.[S T Q]

## PSALM 97

*The majesty and power of God. 7 The confusion of idolaters, and the joy of Zion thereat. 10 An exhortation to hate evil and to rejoice in the Lord.*

[a]THE LORD [b]reigneth; let the
earth rejoice; let the multitude of isles be glad *thereof*.[S Q]
2 [c,d,e]Clouds and [f]darkness *are*
round about him: [g]righteousness
and judgment[G] *are* the [1]habita-
tion of his [h]throne.[S]
3[S] A fire goeth before him, and
[i]burneth up his enemies round
about.[Q]

---

**3**
g *God, sovereign,* Gen. 2:2.
**4**
1 R. V. heights
**5**
h *Geology,* Psa. 104:5.
i *Sea,* Jer. 5:22.
j *God, creator,* Gen. 2:2.
**6**
k *Worship,* Gen. 22:5.
l *Prayer, postures in,* Acts 6:4.
**7**
m *Shepherd, figurative, of God's care,* Jer. 31:10.
n *Sheep, figurative,* Deut. 32:14.
o *God, love of, exemplified,* Gen. 2:2.
p Heb. 3:7–11.
**8**
q *Impenitence, admonitions against,* Rom. 2:5.
r *Obduracy,* Prov. 29:1.
s *Heart,* Psa. 44:21.
t *Meribah,* Ex. 17:7.
2 R. V. at Meribah,
3 R. V. Massah
**10**
u *Forty, years,* Jonah 3:4.
v *Sin, repugnant to God,* Rom. 5:12.
w *Reprobates,* 1 Cor. 9:27.
x *Heart, unregenerate,* Psa. 44:21.
y *Spiritual Blindness,* 2 Cor. 4:4.
**11**
z *Unbelieving Israelites Destroyed,* Num. 14:11.

a Heb. 3:11; 4:3, 5–11.
b *Oath, attributed to God,* Num. 5:19.
c *Anger of God,* 2 Kin. 13:3.
d *Anthropomorphisms,* Gen. 11:5.

**1**
a *Praise,* vs. 1–13; Psa. 150:1.
b *Missions, missionary hymn,* vs. 1–13; Matt. 28:19.
**2**
c *Religious Testimony,* 2 Thess. 1:10.
d *Zeal, enjoined,* 2 Cor. 7:11.
e *Salvation,* Acts 16:17.
f *God, savior,* Gen. 2:2.

**3**
g *Missions,* Matt. 28:19.
h *God, glory of,* Gen. 2:2.
1 R. V. nations,
**4**
i *Fear of God, enjoined,* Acts 9:31.
**5**
j *Idolatry,* 1 Sam. 15:23.
k *God, creator,* Gen. 2:2.
2 R. V. peoples
**6**
l *Church,* 1 Kin. 9:3.
**9**
m *Worship,* Gen. 22:5.
**10**
n *God, sovereign,* Gen. 2:2.
o *God, judge,* Gen. 2:2.
p *God, righteousness of,* Gen. 2:2.
**13**
q *Truth,* John 18:37.

**1**
a *Praise,* vs. 1–12; Psa. 150:1.
b *God, sovereign,* Gen. 2:2.
**2**
c *God, incomprehensible,* Gen. 2:2.
d *God, invisible,* Gen. 2:2.
e *God, unsearchable,* Gen. 2:2.
f *Darkness, figurative,* Gen. 1:2.
g *God, righteousness of,* Gen. 2:2.
h *Throne, figurative,* 1 Kin. 2:19.
1 R. V. foundation
**3**
i *Wicked, punishment of,* Psa. 73:3.

**4**
*j Lightning*, Job 28:26.

**6**
*k God, glory of*, Gen. 2:2.
2 R. V. peoples

**7**
*l Idolatry, denounced*, 1 Sam. 15:23.
*m Idol*, 1 Kin. 15:20.
*n Worship, enjoined*, Gen. 22:5.
3 R. V. Ashamed be

**10**
*o Love, of man for God*, 1 John 4:19.
*p Hatred*, Prov. 15:17.
*q Holiness, enjoined*, Ex. 39:30.
*r Evil, to be abhorred*, 1 Thess. 5:22.
*s Sin, repugnant to the righteous*, Rom. 5:12.
*t Promise, implied, to the righteous*, 2 Cor. 1:20.
*u Righteous, promises to*, Psa. 64:10.
*v God, preserver*, Gen. 2:2.
*w God, providence of*, Gen. 2:2.

**11**
*x Joy*, Psa. 5:11.
*y Heart*, Psa. 44:21.

**12**
*z Thankfulness, to God*, Acts 24:3.

---

*a God, holiness of*, Gen. 2:2.
4 Am. R. V. to his holy memorial name.

**1**
*a Praise*, Psa. 150:1.
*b Music*, 2 Chr. 5:13.
*c Thankfulness, to God*, Acts 24:3.
*d God, holiness of*, Gen. 2:2.
*e Arm, figurative*, Psa. 89:13.
1 R. V. wrought salvation for him.

**2**
*f Salvation*, Acts 16:17.
*g God, savior*, Gen. 2:2.
*h God, righteousness of*, Gen. 2:2.
2 R. V. nations.

**3**
*i God, faithfulness of*, Gen. 2:2.
*j God, mercy of*, Gen. 2:2.
3 R. V. faithfulness

4 His [j]lightnings enlightened the world: the earth saw, and trembled.

5 The hills melted like wax at the presence of the LORD, at the presence of the [b]Lord of the whole earth.[S]

6 The heavens declare his [g]righteousness, and all the [2]people see his [k]glory.[S]

7 [3,l]Confounded be all they that serve graven[G] [m]images, that boast themselves of idols: [n]worship him, all *ye* gods.[S Q]

8 Zī′ŏn heard, and was glad; and the daughters of Jū′dah rejoiced because of thy judgments, O LORD.

9 For thou, LORD, *art* [b]high above all the earth: thou art [b]exalted far above all gods.[Q]

10 Ye that [o]love the LORD, [p,q,r]hate [s]evil: [t,u]he [v]preserveth the souls of his saints; he [w]delivereth them out of the hand of the wicked.[S]

11 [t]Light is sown for the righteous, and [x]gladness for the upright in [y]heart.

12 Rejoice in the LORD, ye righteous; and give [z]thanks [4]at the remembrance of his [a]holiness.

## PSALM 98

*An exhortation to praise God for his salvation.*

A Psalm.

[a]O [b,c]SING unto the LORD a new song; for he hath done marvellous things: his right hand, and his [d]holy [e]arm, hath [1]gotten him the victory.[S Q]

2 The LORD hath made known his [f,g]salvation: his [h]righteousness hath he openly shewed in the sight of the [2]heathen.[S]

3 He hath [i]remembered his [j]mercy and his [3]truth toward the house of Ĭş′ra-el: all the ends of the earth have seen the [f,g]salvation of our God.[S T Q]

4 Make a joyful noise unto the LORD, all the earth: make a loud noise, and rejoice, and [b]sing [a]praise.

5 [a,b]Sing unto the LORD with the [k]harp; with the harp, and the voice of [4]a psalm.

6 With [l]trumpets and sound of cornet make a joyful noise before the LORD, the [m]King.

7 [a]Let the sea roar, and the fulness thereof; the world, and they that dwell therein.

8 [a]Let the floods clap *their* hands: let the hills be joyful together

9 Before the LORD; for he cometh to [n]judge the earth: with [h]righteousness shall he judge the world, and the people with [o]equity.[G S T Q]

## PSALM 99

*God's majesty in Zion. 5 An exhortation to worship God at his holy hill.*

THE LORD [a]reigneth; let the people [b]tremble: he sitteth [c]*between* the [d]cherubims; let the earth be moved.[S Q]

2 The LORD *is* great in [e]Zī′ŏn; and he *is* high above all the people.

3 Let them [f]praise thy great and terrible[G] [g]name; [1]*for* it *is* [h]holy.[S]

4 The king's[G] strength also loveth judgment;[G] thou dost establish [i]equity,[G] thou executest judgment and righteousness in Jā′cob.[S]

5 [f]Exalt[G] ye the LORD our God, and [j]worship at his [k]footstool; *for* he *is* [h]holy.[S]

6 [l]Mō′şeş and [m]Aâr′on among his priests, and [n]Săm′u-el among them that call[G] upon his name;[G] they called upon the LORD, and he [o]answered them.

7 He spake unto them in the cloudy [p]pillar: they [q]kept his [r]testimonies, and the ordinance[G] *that* he gave them.

8 Thou answeredst them, O LORD our God: thou wast a God

**5**
*k Harp*, Dan. 3:10.
4 R. V. melody.

**6**
*l Trumpet*, Josh. 6:4.
*m God, sovereign*, Gen. 2:2.

**9**
*n God, judge*, Gen. 2:2.
*o God, justice of*, Gen. 2:2.

**1**
*a God, sovereign*, Gen. 2:2.
*b Fear of God*, Acts 9:31.
*c Shekinah*, Lev. 16:2.
*d Cherubim*, Ex. 37:7.

**2**
*e Zion*, 2 Sam. 5:7.

**3**
*f Praise*, vs. 1–9; Psa. 150:1.
*g God, name of, to be praised*, Gen. 2:2.
*h God, holiness of*, Gen. 2:2.
1 R. V. Holy is he.

**4**
*i God, justice of*, Gen. 2:2.

**5**
*j Worship, enjoined*, Gen. 22:5.
*k Footstool, figurative*, 1 Chr. 28:2.

**6**
*l Moses*, Ex. 2:10.
*m Aaron, priesthood of*, Ex. 6:20.
*n Samuel*, 1 Sam. 3:1.
*o Prayer, answered*, Acts 6:4.

**7**
*p Pillar of Cloud and Fire*, Ex. 13:21.
*q Obedience, exemplified*, Heb. 5:8.
*r Word of God, inspired*, Psa. 119:9.

**8**
*s* *God, mercy of,* Gen. 2:2.
*t* *Sin, forgiveness of,* Rom. 5:12.
*u* *Vengeance,* Psa. 94:1.
2 R. V. doings.

**1**
*a* *Praise,* vs. 1–5; Psa. 150:1.
*b* *Joy,* Psa. 5:11.
**2**
*c* *Worship,* Gen. 22:5.
*d* *Music,* 2 Chr. 5:13.
**3**
*e* *God, creator,* Gen. 2:2.
*f* *Man, created,* Job 4:17.
*g* *Sheep, figurative,* Deut. 32:14.
*h* *Shepherd, figurative of God's care,* Jer. 31:10.
1 R. V. we are his;
**4**
*i* *Thankfulness, to God, enjoined,* Acts 24:3.
*j* *Church, called courts,* 1 Kin. 9:3.
**5**
*k* *God, goodness of,* Gen. 2:2.
*l* *God, mercy of,* Gen. 2:2.
*m* *God, faithfulness of,* Gen. 2:2.
2 R. V. faithfulness

**1**
*a* *Mercy,* Deut. 5:10.
*b* *Justice,* Deut. 33:21.
**2**
*c* *Decision, instances of,* Isa. 50:7.
*d* *Example, good,* John 13:15.
*e* *Family, religion in the,* 1 Chr. 13:14.
*f* *Perfection,* Heb. 6:1.
**3**
*g* *Hatred,* Prov. 15:17.
*h* *Sin, repugnant to the righteous,* Rom. 5:12.
1 R. V. base
**4**
*i* *Evil Company,* Prov. 13:20.
*j* *Fellowship, with the wicked avoided,* 1 Cor. 1:9.
2 R. V. know no evil thing.
**5**
*k* *Slander,* Prov. 10:18.
*l* *Falsehood,* Job 21:34.
*m* *Pride,* Prov. 16:18.

that [s,t]forgavest them, though
thou tookest [u]vengeance of their
[2]inventions.
9 [f]Exalt the LORD our God,
and worship at his holy hill; for
the LORD our God *is* [h]holy.

## PSALM 100

*All lands exhorted to praise God.*

A Psalm of praise.

[a]MAKE a [b]joyful noise unto
the LORD, all ye lands.
2 Serve the LORD with gladness: [c]come before his presence
with [d]singing.
3 Know ye that the LORD he
*is* God: *it is* he *that* hath [e]made
[f]us, and [1]not we ourselves; *we
are* his people, and the [g]sheep of
[h]his pasture.
4 Enter into his gates with
[i]thanksgiving, *and* into his
[j]courts with [a]praise: be thankful
unto him, *and* bless his name.
5 For the LORD *is* [k]good; his
[l]mercy *is* everlasting; and his
[2,m]truth *endureth* to all generations.

## PSALM 101

*The psalmist's vow and profession of godliness.*

A Psalm of David.

I WILL sing of [a]mercy and
[b]judgment: unto thee, O
LORD, will I sing.
2 [c]I will behave myself wisely
in a perfect way. O when wilt
thou come unto me? [d]I will walk
[e]within my house with a [f]perfect
heart.
3 I will set no [1]wicked thing
before mine eyes: I [g]hate the
[h]work of them that turn aside;
[h]*it* shall not cleave to me.
4 A [i]froward heart [j]shall depart from me: I will [2]not know
a wicked *person.*
5 Whoso privily [k,l]slandereth
his neighbour, [j]him will I cut off:
him that hath an high look and a
[m]proud heart will not I suffer.
6 Mine eyes *shall be* upon the
[n]faithful of the land, that they
may dwell with me: he that
walketh in a [f]perfect way, he
shall serve me.
7 [i]He that worketh [o]deceit shall
not dwell within my house: he
that telleth [l]lies shall not [3]tarry
in my sight.
8 [4,p]I will early [q]destroy all the
wicked of the land; that I may
cut off all wicked doers from the
city of the LORD.

## PSALM 102

*The prophet makes a grievous complaint.*
*12 He takes comfort in the eternity and mercy of God.*

A Prayer of the afflicted, when he is overwhelmed, and pours out his complaint before the LORD.

HEAR my [a,b]prayer, O LORD,
and let my cry come unto thee.
2 [a]Hide not thy face from me in
the day *when* I am in [b]trouble;
incline thine ear unto me: in
the day *when* I call answer me
speedily.
3 For [b]my days are consumed
like smoke, and my bones are
burned as [1]an hearth.
4 [b]My heart is smitten, and
withered like grass; so that I
forget to eat my bread.
5 By reason of the voice of
my groaning my bones cleave
to my [2]skin.
6 I am like a [c]pelican of the
wilderness: I am like an [d]owl
of the desert.
7 I [e]watch, and am as a [f]sparrow alone upon the house top.
8 Mine [g]enemies [h,i]reproach
me all the day; *and* they that
are mad against me [3]are sworn
against me.
9 For I have eaten ashes like
bread, and mingled my drink
with weeping,
10 Because of thine [j]indignation and thy wrath: for thou
hast lifted me up, and [k]cast me
down.
11 My days *are* like a [l]shadow

**6**
*n* *Citizens, loyal,* Luke 15:15.
**7**
*o* *Deceit,* Psa. 36:3.
3 R. V. be established before mine eyes.
**8**
*p* *Zeal, exemplified,* 2 Cor. 7:11.
*q* *Wicked, punishment of,* Psa. 73:3.
4 R. V. Morning by morning will I destroy

**1**
*a* *Prayer, in adversity,* vs. 1–11; Acts 6:4.
*b* *Afflictions, prayer in,* vs. 1–11; Psa. 34:19.
**3**
1 R. V. a firebrand.
**5**
2 R. V. flesh.
**6**
*c* Lev. 11:18.
*d* *Owl,* Lev. 11:17.
**7**
*e* *Watchfulness,* Matt. 24:42.
*f* *Sparrow,* Psa. 84:3.
**8**
*g* *Enemy,* Prov. 24:17.
*h* *Speech, evil,* Col. 4:6.
*i* *Malice,* Eph. 4:31.
3 R. V. do curse by me.
**10**
*j* *Anger of God,* 2 Kin. 13:3.
*k* *Afflictions, from God,* Psa. 34:19.
**11**
*l* *Life, brevity and uncertainty of,* Eccl. 8:15.

**12**
*m God, eternity of,* vs. 24, 27; Gen. 2:2.
4 Am. R. V. memorial name

**13**
*n Faith, exemplified,* Mark 11:22.
*o Church, prophecies concerning its prosperity,* Matt. 16:18.
5 R. V. it is time to have pity upon her,

**14**
*p Church, loved by believers,* Matt. 16:18.
6 R. V. have pity upon her dust.

**15**
*q Gentiles, prophecies of the conversion of,* Acts 10:45.
*r God, glory of,* Gen. 2:2.
7 R. V. nations

**17**
*s Promise, of answer to prayer,* 2 Cor. 1:20.
*t Prayer, answer to, promised,* Acts 6:4.
*u Poor, God's care of,* Prov. 21:13.

**18**
*v Praise,* Psa. 150:1.

**19**
*w Heaven, God's dwelling place,* Luke 18:22.

**20**
*x God, mercy of,* Gen. 2:2.
*y Prisoners,* Psa. 79:11.
*z Death,* Num. 23:10.

**21**
*a Jerusalem,* Judg. 19:10.

that declineth; and I am withered like grass.[Q]
12 But thou, O LORD, [m]shalt
endure for ever; and thy [4]re-
membrance unto all generations.[S]
13 [n]Thou shalt arise, *and* have
mercy upon [o]Zī'ŏn: for [5]the time
to favour her, yea, the set time,
is come.[S]
14 For thy servants [p]take pleasure in her stones, and [6]favour
the dust thereof.
15 So the [7,q]heathen[G] shall fear
the name of the LORD, and all
the kings of the earth thy [r]glory.
16 When the LORD shall build
up [o]Zī'ŏn, he shall appear in his
[r]glory.[S]
17 [s,t]He will regard the prayer
of the [u]destitute, and not despise
their prayer.
18 This shall be written for the
generation to come: and the people which shall be created shall
[v]praise the LORD.[T]
19 For he hath looked down
from the height of his sanctuary;
from [w]heaven did the LORD behold the earth;[S]
20 [x]To hear the groaning of the
[y]prisoner; to loose those that are
appointed to [z]death;
21 To declare the name of the
LORD in Zī'ŏn, and his praise in
[a]Jĕ-ru̦'sā-lĕm;[S]
22 When the people are gathered together, and the kingdoms,
to serve the LORD.[S]

23 He weakened my strength in
the[S] way; he shortened my days.
24 I [b]said, O my God, take me
not away in the midst of my
days: thy years *are* throughout
all generations.
25 [b]Of[Q] old hast [c]thou [d]laid the
foundation of the [e]earth: and the
[f]heavens *are* the [d]work of thy
hands.[S]
26 They shall perish, but thou
[g]shalt endure: yea, all of them
shall wax[G] old like a garment;
as a vesture shalt thou change
them, and they shall be changed:[Q T S]
27 But thou *art* [h]the same, and
[g]thy years shall have no end.[S]
28 The [i]children of thy servants shall continue,[G] and their
seed shall be established before
thee.

## PSALM 103

*An exhortation to bless God for his mercy,* 15 *and for the constancy thereof.*

*A Psalm* of David.

[a]BLESS[G] the LORD, O my soul:
and all that is within me,
*bless*[G] his holy name.
2 [a]Bless[S G] the LORD, O my soul,
and forget not all his [*,b]benefits:
3 Who [c,d]forgiveth all thine iniquities; who [e,f]healeth all thy
[g]diseases;[S Q]
4 Who [f]redeemeth thy life from
destruction; who crowneth thee
with [h]lovingkindness and tender
[d]mercies;[S T]
5 Who [b]satisfieth thy mouth

**24**
*b Prayer, in affliction.* Acts 6:4.

**25**
*c* Heb. 1:10–12.
*d God, creator,* Gen. 2:2.
*e Earth, created by God,* Prov. 8:23.
*f Heavens, physical,* Psa. 8:3.

**26**
*g God, eternity of,* Gen. 2:2.

**27**
*h God, immutable,* Gen. 2:2.

**28**
*i Children, of the righteous, blessed of God,* Mark 10:14.

**1**
*a Praise, for God's goodness,* vs. 1–22; Psa. 150:1.

**2**
*b God, providence of,* Gen. 2:2.

**3**
*c Sin, forgiveness of,* Rom. 5:12.
*d God, mercy of,* Gen. 2:2.
*e Healing, the Lord, the healer,* Acts 4:22.
*f God, preserver,* Gen. 2:2.
*g Disease, healing of, from God,* Ex. 15:26.

**4**
*h God, love of,* Gen. 2:2.

* **TEMPORAL BLESSINGS. From God,** Psa. 136:25.
*Rain,* Deut. 11:14; 28:12; Job 37:6; 38:25–27; Psa. 68:9; 135:7; 147:8; Jer. 10:13; 14:22; 51:16; Joel 2:23; Amos 4:7; Zech. 10:1; Matt. 5:45; Acts 14:17.
*Seed time and harvest,* Gen. 8:22; Lev. 25:20–22; 26:4, 5; Psa. 107:35–38; Isa. 55:10; Jer. 5:24; Ezek. 36:30; Mal. 3:11; Acts 14:17.
*Food and raiment,* Gen. 9:1–3; 28:20, 21; Deut. 8:3–4; 10:18; 29:5; Ruth 1:6; 2 Chr. 31:10; Psa. 65:9; 68; 81:16; 104:14, 15, 27, 28; 111:5; 132:15; 145:15, 16; 146:7; Eccl. 2:24; 3:13; Isa. 33:15, 16; Joel 2:26; Matt. 6:26, 30–33; Luke 12:22–31; John 6:31.
*Preservation of life,* Deut. 4:4, 40; 5:33; 7:15; Psa. 21:4; 36:6; 91:16; 103:2–5; Dan. 6:20, 22.
*Children,* Psa. 113:9; 127:3–5.
*Prosperity,* Gen. 24:56; 26:24; 49:24, 25; Num. 10:29; Deut. 8:7–10, 18; 1 Sam. 2:7, 8; 1 Chr. 29:12, 14, 16; 2 Chr. 1:12; Ezra 8:22; Psa. 147:13, 14; Eccl. 5:19; Isa. 30:23; Hos. 2:8.
*Social Peace,* Lev. 26:6; 1 Chr. 22:9.
*Worldly honors,* 2 Sam. 7:8, 9; 1 Chr. 17:7, 8. *Victory over enemies,* Ex. 23:22; Lev. 26:6–9; Deut. 28:7; Psa. 44:3. *National greatness,* Gen. 22:17; 26:3, 4; Deut. 1:10; 7:13, 14; 15:4, 6; 26:18, 19; 32:13, 14; Job 12:23; Psa. 69:35, 36; Isa. 51:2; Jer. 30:19; Ezek. 36:36–38; Dan. 5:18.
EXEMPLIFIED TO: *Noah, at the time of the flood,* Gen. 7:1. *Abraham,* Gen. 24:1. *Isaac,* Gen. 26:12–24, 28. *Jacob,* Gen. 35:9–15. *The Israelites, in Egypt,* Ex. 11:3; *in the wilderness, supplying water,* Ex. 17:1–7; Num. 20:10, 11; Psa. 78:15–20; 105:41; *supplying manna,* Ex. 16:14, 15, 31; Num. 11:7–9; Neh. 9:15; Psa. 78:23, 24; *supplying quails,* Num. 11:31–33; Psa. 78:23–30; 105:40. *David,* 1 Chr. 14:17. *Obed-edom,* 2 Sam. 6:11. *Solomon,* 1 Kin. 3:13; 1 Chr. 29:25; 2 Chr. 1:1. *Elijah fed, by ravens,* 1 Kin. 17:2–7; *by an angel,* 1 Kin. 19:5–8. *The widow of Zarephath,* 1 Kin. 17:12–16. *Hezekiah prospered,* 2 Kin. 18:6, 7; 2 Chr. 32:29; *and restored to health,* 2 Kin. 20:1–7. *Asa,* 2 Chr. 14:6, 7. *Jehoshaphat,* 2 Chr. 17:3–5; 20:30. *Uzziah,* 2 Chr. 26:5–15. *Jotham,* 2 Chr. 27:6. *Job,* Job 1:10; 42:10, 12. *Daniel,* Dan. 1:9.
**Prayer for:** *Rain,* 1 Kin. 8:36; 2 Chr. 6:27. *Plentiful harvests,* Gen. 27:28; Deut. 26:15; 33:13–16. *Daily bread,* Matt. 6:11; Luke 11:3. *Prosperity,* Gen. 28:3, 4; 1 Chr. 4:10; Neh. 1:11; 3 John 2. *Providential guidance,* Gen. 24:12–14, 42–44; Rom. 1:10; 1 Thess. 3:11.
**Instances of Prayer for:** *By Abraham,* Gen. 15:2–4. *By Abraham's servant,* Gen. 24:12. *By Laban and Bethuel,* Gen. 24:60. *By Isaac,* Gen. 25:21. *By Hannah,* 1 Sam. 1:11. *By Elijah,* 1 Kin. 17:20, 21; 18:42; Jas. 5:17, 18. *By Ezra,* Ezra 8:21–23. *By Nehemiah,* Neh. 1:11; 2:4; 6:9.
See footnotes: SPIRITUAL BLESSINGS, Eph. 1:3; BLESSINGS, *Contingent upon obedience,* Deut. 11:26.

5
[i] *Food, from God,* Psa. 136:25.
[j] *Eagle,* Lev. 11:13.
6
[k] *God, justice of,* Gen. 2:2.
[l] *Oppression,* Eccl. 5:8.
7
[m] *Prophets, inspiration of,* Isa. 3:2.
[n] *Law, of Moses, divine authority for,* Deut. 33:2.
8
[o] *God, longsuffering of,* Gen. 2:2.
[p] *Anger of God,* 2 Kin. 13:3.
1 R. V. full of compassion and
11
[q] *Heavens, physical,* Psa. 8:3.
[r] *Earth,* Prov. 8:23.
[s] *Promise, implied, to the righteous,* vs. 12, 13; 2 Cor. 1:20.
[t] *Righteous, promises to,* Psa. 64:10.
[u] *Fear of God,* Acts 9:31.
12
[v] *Sin, forgiveness of,* Rom. 5:12.
13
[w] *Parents, love of,* 2 Cor. 12:14.
[x] *Pity, of God,* Job 19:21.
14
[y] *God, knowledge of,* Gen. 2:2.
15
[z] *Life, brevity and uncertainty of,* v. 16; Eccl. 8:15.

17
[a] *Promise, implied, to the righteous,* 2 Cor. 1:20.
[b] *Righteous, promises to,* Psa. 64:10.
[c] *God, mercy of,* Gen. 2:2.
[d] *Parents, covenant benefits of, entailed upon children,* 2 Cor. 12:14.
[e] *Children, of the righteous, blessed of God,* Mark 10:14.

with [i]good *things*; *so that* thy
youth is renewed like the [j]eagle's.
6 The LORD executeth [k]right-
eousness and judgment for all
that are [l]oppressed.
7 He [m]made known his [n]ways
unto Mō′ṣeṣ, his acts unto the
children of Is̱′ra-el.
8 The LORD *is* [1,h]merciful and
gracious, [o]slow to [p]anger, and
plenteous in [d]mercy.
9 He [d]will not always chide:
neither will he keep *his* [p]*anger*
for ever.
10 He [d]hath not dealt with
us after our sins; [d]nor rewarded
us according to our iniquities.
11 For as the [q]heaven is high
above the [r]earth, [s,t]*so* great is
his [d]mercy toward them that
[u]fear him.
12 As far as the east is from the
west, *so* far [v]hath he removed
our transgressions from us.
13 [s,t]Like as a father [w]pitieth
*his* children, *so* the LORD [x]piti-
eth them that [u]fear him.
14 For he [y]knoweth our frame;
he remembereth that we *are*
dust.
15 *As for* man, his [z]days *are* as
grass: as a flower of the field, so
he flourisheth.
16 For the wind passeth over
it, and it is gone; and the place
thereof shall know it no more.
17 But [a,b]the [c]mercy of the
LORD *is* from everlasting to
everlasting upon them that fear
him, and his righteousness unto
[d]children's [e]children;
18 To such as [f]keep his covenant, and to those that remember
his commandments to do them.
19 The [g]LORD hath prepared
his [h]throne in the [i]heavens; and
[g]his kingdom ruleth over all.
20 [j]Bless the LORD, ye his [k]an-
gels, that excel in strength, that
do his commandments, hearkening unto the voice of his word.
21 [j]Bless ye the LORD, all *ye*
his hosts; *ye* ministers of his, that
do his pleasure.
22 [j]Bless the LORD, all his
[l,m]works in all places of his
dominion: bless the LORD, O
my soul.

18 [f] *Obedience, rewarded,* Heb. 5:8. 19 [g] *God, sovereign,* Gen. 2:2. [h] *Throne, figurative,* 1 Kin. 2:19. [i] *Heaven, God's dwelling place,* Luke 18:22. 20 [j] *Praise, in heaven,* Psa. 150:1. [k] *Angel,* Heb. 1:13.

## PSALM 104

*An exhortation to bless the Lord for his mighty power, and wonderful providence. 27 The dependence of all creatures upon God. 31 His glory is eternal. 33 The psalmist's purpose to praise him.*

[a]BLESS the LORD, O my soul.
O LORD my God, thou
art very great; thou art clothed
with honour and majesty.
2 [b]Who coverest *thyself* with
light as *with* a garment: who
[c,d]stretchest out the [e]heavens
like a curtain:
3 [b]Who layeth the beams of his
chambers in the waters: who
maketh the clouds his [f]chariot:
who walketh upon the wings of
the wind:
4 [b,g]Who maketh [1]his angels
spirits; his ministers a flaming
fire:
5 [b]*Who* [c]laid the *foundations
of the [h]earth, *that* it should not
be removed for ever.
6 [b]Thou coveredst it with the
[i]deep as *with* a garment: the
waters stood above the mountains.
7 At thy [j]rebuke they fled; at
the voice of thy thunder they
hasted away.
8 They go up by the moun-
tains; they go down by the valleys unto the place which thou
hast founded for them.
9 [b]Thou hast set a bound that
they may not pass over; that
they turn not again to cover the
earth.
10 He [k]sendeth the springs into

22
[l] *Works of God,* Psa. 40:5.
[m] *God, creator,* Gen. 2:2.
1
[a] *Praise, for God's attributes,* vs. 1–35; Psa. 150:1.
2
[b] *God, dissertations on,* vs. 3–32; Gen. 2:2.
[c] *God, creator,* Gen. 2:2.
[d] *Works of God,* Psa. 40:5.
[e] *Firmament,* Gen. 1:6.
3
[f] *Chariot, figurative,* Josh. 11:4.
4
[g] Heb. 1:7.
1 R. V. winds his messengers;
5
[h] *Earth,* Prov. 8:23.
6
[i] *Sea,* Jer. 5:22.
7
[j] *God, power of,* Gen. 2:2.
10
[k] *God, providence of,* Gen. 2:2.

* **GEOLOGY.** The scriptures grouped under this subject are not cited with a view of teaching the science of geology, but for the reason that the facts mentioned therein come within the scope of that science. Gen. 1:9, 10; 1 Sam. 2:8; 2 Sam. 22:16; Job 28:9–11; Psa. 18:15; 24:1, 2; 104:5–13; 136:6; Prov. 30:4; Jer. 31–37; Hab. 3:9; 2 Pet. 3:5–7.

11
*l Animals, God's care of,* v. 21; Jer. 27:5.
*m Ass, wild,* 2 Chr. 28:15.
12
*n Birds,* Eccl. 12:4.
14
*o Grass,* Isa. 40:7.
*p Temporal Blessings, from God,* Psa. 103:2.
*q Animals, food of,* Jer. 27:5.
*r Food, from God,* Psa. 136:25.
15
*s Wine,* Prov. 23:31.
*t Oil,* Deut. 12:17.
*u Bread,* Ezek. 4:13.
16
*v Lebanon, cedars of,* Deut. 1:7.
2 R. V. satisfied;
17
*w Birds,* Eccl. 12:4.
*x Stork,* Lev. 11:19.
18
*y Goat,* Deut. 14:4.
*z Coney,* Lev. 11:5.

19
*a God, dissertations on,* Gen. 2:2.
*b Moon, seasons of,* Song 6:10.
*c Seasons,* Dan. 2:21.
*d Sun,* Josh. 10:12.
20
*e Animals, habits of,* Jer. 27:5.
24
*f Works of God,* Psa. 40:5.
*g God, wisdom of,* Gen. 2:2.
*h God, creator,* Gen. 2:2.
25
*i Sea,* Jer. 5:22.
*j Creeping Things,* Rom. 1:23.

the valleys, *which* run among
the hills.
11 They give drink to every
[l]beast of the field: the wild
[m]asses quench their thirst.
12 By them shall the [n]fowls of
the heaven have their habitation,
*which* sing among the branches.
13 [b]He watereth the hills from
his chambers: the earth is satisfied with the fruit of thy
works.
14 [b]He [k]causeth the [o,p]grass
to grow for the [q]cattle, and
[p]herb for the service of man:
that he may [k]bring forth [r]food
out of the earth;
15 [k]And [p,s]wine *that* maketh
glad the heart of man, *and* [p,t]oil
to make *his* face to shine, and
[p,r,u]bread *which* strengtheneth
man's heart.
16 The trees of the LORD are
[2]full *of sap*; the cedars of [v]Lĕb'-
a-non, which he hath planted;
17 Where the [w]birds make their
nests: *as for* the [x]stork, the fir
trees *are* her house.
18 The high hills *are* a refuge
for the wild [y]goats; *and* the rocks
for the [z]conies.
19 [a]He appointed the [b]moon for
[c]seasons: the [d]sun knoweth his
going down.
20 [a]Thou makest darkness, and
it is night: wherein all the [e]beasts
of the forest do creep *forth*.
21 The young [e]lions roar after
their prey, and seek their meat
from God.
22 The sun ariseth, [e]they
gather themselves together, and
lay them down in their dens.
23 Man goeth forth unto his
work and to his labour until the
evening.
24 [a]O LORD, how manifold
are thy [f]works! in [g]wisdom hast
thou [h]made them all: the earth
is full of thy riches.
25 *So is* this great and wide
[i]sea, wherein *are* things [j]creep-
ing innumerable, both small and
great beasts.
26 There go the [k]ships: *there is*
that leviathan, *whom* thou hast
made to play therein.
27 These wait all upon [a]thee;
that thou mayest give *them* their
meat in due season.
28 [l]*That* thou givest them they
gather: thou openest thine hand,
they are filled with good.
29 Thou hidest thy face, they
are troubled: thou takest away
their breath, they [m]die, and [n]re-
turn to their dust.
30 Thou sendest forth thy spirit,
[o]they are [h]created: and thou renewest the face of the earth.
31 The [p]glory of the LORD
shall endure for ever: the LORD
shall rejoice in his [f]works.
32 He looketh on the earth, and
it [q]trembleth: he toucheth the
hills, and they smoke.
33 I will [r]sing unto the LORD
as long as I live: I will sing
[s]praise to my God while I have
my being.
34 My [t]meditation of him shall
be sweet: I will be [u]glad in the
LORD.
35 Let the sinners [v]be consumed out of the earth, and let
the wicked be no more. Bless
thou the LORD, O my soul.
[s]Praise ye the LORD.

## PSALM 105

*An exhortation to praise God for his goodness to his people, from the covenant made with Abraham to their deliverance from Egypt and settlement in Canaan.*

O [a]GIVE [b]thanks unto the
LORD; call upon his
name: make known his deeds
among the people.
2 [c]Sing unto him, sing psalms
unto him: talk ye of all his
wondrous [d]works.
3 Glory ye in his [e]holy name:
let the heart of [f]them [g]rejoice
that seek the LORD.
4 [f,h]Seek the LORD, and his

26
*k Ship,* 2 Chr. 8:18.
28
*l Temporal Blessings, from God,* Psa. 103:2.
29
*m Death,* Num. 23:10.
*n Corruption,* Job 17:14.
30
*o Life, from God,* Eccl. 8:15.
31
*p God, glory of,* Gen. 2:2.
32
*q Earthquakes,* Isa. 29:6.
33
*r Music,* 2 Chr. 5:13.
*s Praise, for God's attributes,* Psa. 150:1.
34
*t Meditation,* Psa. 49:3.
*u Joy,* Psa. 5:11.
35
*v Wicked, punishment of,* Psa. 73:3.

1
*a Thankfulness, to God, enjoined,* Acts 24:3.
*b Praise,* vs. 1–5; *for God's goodness to Israel,* Psa. 150:1.
2
*c Music,* 2 Chr. 5:13.
*d Works of God,* Psa. 40:5.
3
*e God, holiness of,* Gen. 2:2.
*f Seekers,* Isa. 55:6.
*g Joy,* Psa. 5:11.
4
*h Spiritual Desire,* Psa. 42:1.

[i]strength: seek his face evermore.

5 Remember his marvellous [d]works that he hath done; his wonders, and the judgments of his mouth;

6[T] O ye seed of [j]Ā′brā-hăm his servant, ye children of [k]Jā′cob his chosen.

7 He *is* the LORD our God: [l]his judgments *are* in all the earth.

8[Q] He hath [m]remembered his [n]covenant[G] for ever, the word *which* he commanded to a thousand generations.[S]

9 Which [n]*covenant* he made with [o]Ā′brā-hăm, and his [p]oath unto [q]Ī′ṣaac;[Q]

10 And confirmed the [n]same unto [r]Jā′cob for a law, *and* to Iṣ′ra-el *for* an everlasting covenant:

11 Saying, Unto thee will I give the land of [s]Cā′năan, the lot of your inheritance:[T]

12 When they were *but* a few men in number; yea, very few, and strangers[G] in it.

13 When they went from one nation to another, from *one* kingdom to another people;

14[S] He [t]suffered[G] no man to do them wrong: yea, he reproved[G] [u,v]kings for their sakes;

15 *Saying*, Touch not mine [w]anointed,[G] and do my [x]prophets no harm.[S]

16 Moreover he called for a [y]famine upon the land: he brake[G] the whole staff of bread.

17[S] He [t,z]sent a man before them, *even* [a]Jō′ṣeph, *who* was sold for a servant:

18 [b]Whose feet they hurt with [c]fetters: he was laid in [d]iron:

19 Until the time that his word came: the word of the LORD tried[G] him.

20 The [e]king sent and loosed him; *even* the ruler of the people, and let him go free.

21 [e]He made [a]him lord of his house, and ruler of all his substance:[G Q]

22 To bind his princes at his pleasure; and teach his [f]senators[G] [g]wisdom.[S]

23 [h]Iṣ′ra-el also came into [i]Ē′ġўpt; and Jā′cob sojourned in the land of [j]Hăm.

24[T] And he [k,l]increased his [m]people greatly; and made them stronger than their enemies.

25 He [k]turned their heart to hate his people, to deal subtilly with his servants.[S]

26 He [k,n]sent [o]Mō′ṣeṣ his servant; *and* [p]Aâr′on whom he had chosen.[S T]

27 [o,p]They shewed his [q]signs among them, and wonders[G] in the land of [j]Hăm.

28 He [k]sent [r,s]darkness, and made it dark; and they rebelled not against his word.

29 He turned their waters into [s,t]blood, and slew their [u]fish.

30 Their land brought forth [s,v]frogs in abundance, in the chambers[G] of their kings.

31 He spake, and there came [1]divers[G] sorts of [s,w]flies, *and* [s,x]lice in all their coasts.[G]

32 He gave them [s,y]hail for rain, *and* flaming [s,z]fire in their land.

33 He [a]smote their vines also and their [b]fig trees; and brake[G] the trees of their coasts.[G]

34 He spake, and the [a,c]locusts came, and [2,a]caterpillers, and that without number,

35 And did eat up all the herbs in their land, and devoured the fruit of their ground.

36 He [a]smote also all the [d]firstborn in [e]their land, the chief of all their strength.

37 He [f]brought [g]them forth also with [h,i]silver and [j]gold: and *there was* not one feeble *person* among their tribes.

38 Ē′ġўpt was glad when they departed: for the fear of them fell upon them.[Q]

i *Spiritual Blessings*, Eph. 1:3.

**6**
j *Abraham*, Gen. 17:5.
k *Jacob*, Gen. 27:11.

**7**
l *God, sovereign*, Gen. 2:2.

**8**
m *God, faithfulness of*, Gen. 2:2.
n *Covenant, of God with men*, Deut. 29:1.

**9**
o *Abraham, Canaan given to*, vs. 10, 11; Gen. 17:5.
p *Oath, attributed to God*, Num. 5:19.
q *Isaac, Abrahamic covenant confirmed in*, Gen. 21:3.

**10**
r *Jacob, prophecies concerning*, Gen. 27:11.

**11**
s *Canaan, promised to Abraham and his seed*, Gen. 37:1.

**14**
t *God, providence of*, Gen. 2:2.
u Gen. 12:14–17.
v Gen. 20:3–9.

**15**
w *Anointing*, Lev. 8:12.
x *Prophets*, Isa. 3:2.

**16**
y *Famine*, 2 Kin. 8:1.

**17**
z *Foreordination, of Joseph's mission in Egypt*, Rom. 8:30.

a *Joseph*, Gen. 33:2.

**18**
b *Prisoners, cruelty to*, Psa. 79:11.
c *Fetters*, Mark 5:4.
d *Iron*, Prov. 27:17.

**20**
e *Pharaoh*, Gen. 37:36.

**22**
f *Senate*, Num. 11:16.
g *Wisdom*, Prov. 2:2.

**23**
h Or, *Jacob, removes to Egypt*, Gen. 27:11.
i *Egypt*, Gen. 41:8.
j 1 Chr. 4:40; Psa. 78:51; 106:22.

**24**
k *God, providence of*, Gen. 2:2.
l *Temporal Blessings, from God*, Psa. 103:2.
m *Israel, number of, who went into Egypt*, Ex. 4:22.

**26**
n *Call, to special religious duty*, Phil. 3:14.
o *Moses*, Ex. 2:10.
p *Aaron*, Ex. 6:20.

**27**
q *Miracles, design of*, Luke 23:8.

**28**
r *Darkness, miraculous*, Gen. 1:2.
s *Plague, as a judgment on the Egyptians*, Ex. 11:1.

**29**
t *Blood, plague of*, Gen. 9:4.
u *Fish*, Matt. 17:27.

**30**
v *Frogs, plague of*, Ex. 8:2.

**31**
w *Flies, plague of*, Eccl. 10:1.
x *Lice, plague of*, Ex. 8:16–19.
1 R. V. swarms of

**32**
y *Hail, plague of*, Job 38:22.
z *Lightning, plague of*, Job 28:26.

**33**
a *Plague, as a judgment on the Egyptians*, Ex. 11:1.
b *Fig Tree*, Luke 13:6.

**34**
c *Locust, plague of*, Nah. 3:17.
2 Am. R. V. the grasshopper,

**36**
d *Firstborn, of Egyptians, slain*, Zech. 12:10.
e *Egyptians, firstborn of, destroyed*, Gen. 50:3.

**37**
f *God, providence of*, Gen. 2:2.
g *Israel, borrowed jewels from the Egyptians*, Ex. 4:22.
h Ex. 12:35, 36.
i *Silver*, 1 Chr. 28:14.
j *Gold*, Ezek. 7:19.

**39**
k *Pillar of Cloud and Fire*, Ex. 13:21.
**40**
l *Quail*, Ex. 16:13.
m *Temporal Blessings, from God*, Psa. 103:2.
n *Manna*, Ex. 16:31.
**41**
o *Meribah*, Ex. 17:7.
**42**
p *God, faithfulness of*, Gen. 2:2.
q *Abraham*, Gen. 17:5.
r *Intercession, influence of the righteous*, Jer. 27:18.
**43**
3 R. V. singing.
**44**
s *Canaanites*, Ex. 23:28.
4 R. V. nations;
**45**
t *Law, of Moses*, Deut. 33:2.
u *Praise*, Psa. 150:1.
**1**
a *Praise*, Psa. 150:1.
b *Thankfulness, to God, enjoined*, Acts 24:3.
c *God, goodness of*, Gen. 2:2.
d *God, mercy of*, Gen. 2:2.
**3**
e *Spiritual Peace*, Gal. 1:3.
f *Righteous, described*, Psa. 64:10.
g *Righteousness*, Psa. 15:2.
**6**
h *Prayer, confession in*, Acts 6:4.
i *Sin, confession of*, Rom. 5:12.

39 He [l]spread a [k]cloud for a covering; and fire to give light in the night.
40 *The people* asked, and he [l]brought [l,m]quails, and satisfied them with the [m,n]bread of heaven.[Q]
41 He [l]opened the [o]rock, and the [m]waters gushed out; they ran in the dry places *like* a river.
42 [T]For he [p]remembered his holy promise, *and* [q,r]Ā'bră-hăm his servant.[S]
43 And he [l]brought forth his people with joy, *and* his chosen with [3]gladness:
44 And gave them the lands of the[4,s]heathen[G]: and they inherited the labour of the people;
45 That they might observe his statutes, and keep his [t]laws. [u]Praise ye the LORD.[T]

## PSALM 106

*The psalmist exhorts men to praise God. 3 The blessedness of the righteous, and his desire to share in their joy. 7 The history of Israel's rebellion and God's mercy. 47 Prayer and praise.*

[a]PRAISE ye the LORD. O [b]give thanks unto the LORD; for *he is* [c]good: for his [d]mercy *endureth* for ever.[S]
2 Who can utter the mighty acts of the LORD? *who* can shew forth all his [a]praise?
3 [e]Blessed *are* [f]they that keep[G] judgment[G], *and* [f]he that doeth [g]righteousness at all times.
4 Remember me, O LORD, with the favour *that thou bearest unto* thy people: O visit[G] me with thy salvation;
5 That I may see the good of thy chosen, that I may rejoice in the gladness of thy nation, that I may glory with thine inheritance.[S]
6 [h,i]We have sinned with our fathers, we have committed iniquity, we have done wickedly.
7 Our fathers [j]understood not thy [k]wonders in [l]E'gȳpt; [m]they remembered not the multitude of thy [d]mercies; but [1]provoked *him* at the sea, *even* at the [n]Red sea.
8 Nevertheless he [d]saved them *for his name's sake, [o]that he might make his mighty [p]power to be known.[S]
9 He rebuked the [n]Red sea also, and it was [o]dried up: so he led them through the depths, as through the wilderness.
10 And he [d]saved them from the hand of him that [q]hated *them*, and redeemed them from the hand of the enemy.[Q]
11 And the waters [o]covered their [r]enemies: there was not one of them left.
12 [o]Then believed they his words; they sang his [a]praise.
13 [s]They soon [t]forgat his works; they waited not for his counsel:
14 But [u]lusted exceedingly in[G] the wilderness, and tempted God in the desert.[Q]
15 And he gave them their [v]request; but sent leanness into their soul.
16 They [w]envied [x]Mō'ṣeṣ also in the camp, *and* [y]Aâr'on the saint[G] of the LORD.
17 The earth opened and swallowed up [z]Dā'than, and covered the company of [a]Ā-bī'ram.
18 And a fire was kindled in their company; the flame [b]burned up the wicked.
19 They made a [c]calf in [d]Hō'-reb, and [e]worshipped the molten[G] image.
20 Thus they changed their glory into the [e]similitude of an ox that eateth grass.[Q]
21 They [f,g]forgat God their [h]saviour, which had done great [i]things in [j]E'gȳpt;[T]

**7**
j *Unbelief*, Heb. 3:12.
k *Miracles*, Luke 23:8.
l *Egypt*, Gen. 41:8.
m *Ingratitude, of man to God*, Rom. 1:21.
n *Red Sea*, Ex. 10:19.
1 R. V. were rebellious at
**8**
o *Miracles, design of*, vs. 8–12; Luke 23:8.
p *God, power of*, Gen. 2:2.
**10**
q *Hatred*, Prov. 15:17.
**11**
r *Egyptians*, Gen. 50:3.
**13**
s *Instability, instances of*, Jas. 1:8.
t *Backsliding*, Hos. 11:7.
**14**
u *Lust, of Israelites*, 2 Pet. 1:4.
**15**
v *Prayer, answer to, different from request*, Acts 6:4.
**16**
w *Envy*, Prov. 14:30.
x *Moses*, Ex. 2:10.
y *Aaron*, Ex. 6:20.
**17**
z *Dathan*, Num. 16:1.
a *Abiram*, Num. 16:1.
**18**
b *Wicked, punishment of*, Psa. 73:3.
**19**
c *Calf, made by Aaron*, Mic. 6:6.
d *Horeb*, Ex. 3:1.
e *Idolatry*, 1 Sam. 15:23.
**21**
f *Instability*, Jas. 1:8.
g *Backsliding*, Hos. 11:7.
h *God, preserver*, Gen. 2:2.
i *Miracles*, Luke 23:8.
j *Egypt*, Gen. 41:8.

* **MOTIVE.** *Ascribed to God*, Psa. 106:8; Ezek. 36:21, 22, 32. *Right, required*, Matt. 6:1–18; Eph. 6:7; Col. 3:23. *Sinful, illustrated by Cain*, Gen. 4:7; 1 John 3:12. *Impugned*, Job 1:9–11; 2:4, 5.
**Misunderstood:** *Of the tribes of Reuben and Gad, in asking inheritance E. of Jordan*, Num. 32:1–33; *when they built the memorial*, Josh. 22:9–34. *David's, by King Hanun*, 2 Sam. 10:2, 3; 1 Chr. 19:3, 4. *The king of Syria's, in sending presents to the king of Israel by Naaman when Naaman came to the prophet to be healed of leprosy*, 2 Kin. 5:5–7.

22 Wondrous [i]works in the land
of [k]Hăm, *and* [i]terrible[C] things by
the [l]Red sea.
23 Therefore he said that he
would [b]destroy them, had not
[m]Mō′ṣeṣ his chosen [n]stood before him in the breach, to turn
away his [o]wrath, lest he should
destroy *them.*[S]
24 Yea, they despised the pleasant
land, they [p]believed not his word:
25[Q] But [q]murmured in their
tents, *and* [r]hearkened not unto
the voice of the LORD.
26 Therefore he [b]lifted up his
hand [2]against [s]them, to overthrow them in the wilderness:
27 To [b]overthrow their seed
also among the nations, and to
scatter them in the lands.[Q]
28 They joined themselves also
unto [t]Bā′al–pē′or, and ate the
sacrifices of the dead.
29 Thus they provoked *him*
to [u]anger with their [3]inventions:
and the [v,w]plague brake[C] in upon
them.[S]
30 Then [x]stood up [y]Phĭn′e-has,
and [z]executed judgment: and *so*
the [v]plague was stayed.[C]
31 And that was counted unto
him for [a]righteousness unto all
generations for evermore.
32 They angered *him* also at the
[b]waters of strife, so that it went
ill with Mō′ṣeṣ for their sakes:[S]
33 Because they [4]provoked his
spirit, so that he spake unadvisedly[C] with his lips.
34 They [c]did not destroy the
nations, concerning whom the
LORD commanded them:
35 But were [d]mingled among
the [e]heathen,[C] and learned their
works.
36 And they [f]served their idols:
which were a snare[C] unto them.
37 Yea, they [g]sacrificed their
[h]sons and their [h]daughters unto
[5,i]devils,[CQ]
38 And shed innocent blood,
*even* the blood of their [h]sons
and of their [h]daughters, whom
they [g]sacrificed unto the idols of
Cā′năan: and the land was polluted with blood.
39 Thus were they defiled[C] with
their own works, and went a[C]
whoring with their own [6]inven-
tions.
40 [j]Therefore was the wrath of
the LORD kindled against his
people, insomuch that he abhorred his own inheritance.
41 And he [k]gave them into the
hand of the [7]heathen;[C] and they
that hated them ruled over
them.
42 Their enemies also [l]op-
pressed them, and they were
brought into subjection under
their hand.
43 Many times did he [m,n]de-
liver them; but they [8]provoked
*him* with their counsel, and were
[o]brought low for their iniquity.
44 Nevertheless he regarded
[p]their [q]affliction, when he [r]heard
their cry:
45[Q] And he [s]remembered for
them his [t]covenant, and [s,u]re-
pented according to the multitude of his mercies.
46 He made them also to be
pitied of all those that carried
them [v]captives.[Q]
47 [q]Save [p]us, O LORD our God,
and gather us from among the
[7]heathen,[C] to give thanks unto thy
holy name, *and* to triumph in
thy [w]praise.
48 [w]Blessed *be* the LORD God
of Ĭṣ′ra-el from everlasting to
everlasting: and let all the people say, Amen. Praise ye the
LORD.[Q]

## PSALM 107.

*The redeemed are exhorted to praise God for his goodness in gathering them from their dispersions.* 4 *Their deliverance represented under various aspects of his providence over men.*

[a]O[S] [b]GIVE thanks unto the
LORD, for *he is* [c]good: for
his [d]mercy *endureth* for ever.

22
k 1 Chr. 4:40; Psa. 78:51; 105:23,27.
l *Red Sea*, Ex. 10:19.
23
m *Moses*, Ex. 2:10.
n *Intercession, answered*, Jer. 27:18.
o *Anger of God, appeased*, 2 Kin. 13:3.
24
p *Unbelief*, Heb. 3:12.
25
q *Murmuring*, Num. 14:2.
r *Disobedience to God*, Eph. 5:6.
26
s *Unbelieving Israelites Destroyed*, Num. 14:11.
2 R. V. unto them, That he would overthrow
28
t *Baal-peor*, Num. 25:3.
29
u *Anger of God*, vs. 32, 40; 2 Kin. 13:3.
v *Plague*, Ex. 11:1.
w *Judgments*, Ex. 6:6.
3 R. V. doings;
30
x *Zeal, instances of*, 2 Cor. 7:11.
y *Phinehas*, Num. 25:7.
z *Obedience, exemplified*, Heb. 5:8.
31
a *Righteousness, imputed on account of obedience*, Psa. 15:2.
32
b *Meribah*, Ex. 17:7.
33
4 R. V. were rebellious against his
34
c *Disobedience to God*, Eph. 5:6.
35
d *Fellowship, with the wicked, punishment of*, vs. 35–41; 1 Cor. 1:9.
e *Evil Company*, Prov. 13:20.
36
f *Idolatry*, 1 Sam. 15:23.
37
g *Idolatry, wicked practices of*, 1 Sam. 15:23.
h *Human Sacrifices*, Deut. 12:31.
i *Demons, worship of*, Matt. 4:24.
5 R. V. demons,

39
6 R. V. doings.
40
j *Sin, repugnant to God*, Rom. 5:12.
41
k *Divine Chastisement*, Job 33:19.
7 R. V. nations;
42
l *Oppression*, Eccl. 5:8.
43
m *God, mercy of*, Gen. 2:2.
n *God, providence of*, Gen. 2:2.
o *Adversity, design of*, v. 44; Psa. 10:6.
8 R. V. were rebellious in their
44
p *Nation, in adversity prayer of*, Isa. 2:4.
q *Adversity, prayer in*, Psa. 10:6.
r *Prayer, answered*, Acts 6:4.
45
s *Anthropomorphisms*, Gen. 11:5.
t *Covenant, of God with men*, Deut. 29:1.
u *Repentance, attributed to God*, Mark 1:4.
46
v *Captive, kindness to*, 1 Sam. 30:3.
47
w *Praise*, Psa. 150:1.
1
a *Praise, for God's goodness*, vs. 1–43; Psa. 150:1.
b *Thankfulness, to God, enjoined*, Acts 24:3.
c *God, goodness of*, Gen. 2:2.
d *God, mercy of*, Gen. 2:2.

2 Let the redeemed of the LORD say *so*, whom he hath redeemed from the hand of the enemy;

3 And gathered them out of the lands, from the east, and from the west, from the north, and from the south.[Q]

4 They wandered in the wilderness in a [1]solitary way; they found no city to dwell in.

5 [e,f,g]Hungry and thirsty, their soul [h]fainted in them.

6 [f,g]Then they [i]cried unto the LORD in their trouble, *and* he [c,d]delivered them out of their distresses.

7 And [j]he [k]led them forth by the right way, that they might go to a city of habitation.

8 Oh that *men* would [a]praise the LORD *for* his [c]goodness, and *for* his wonderful works to the children of men![S]

9 For he satisfieth the longing soul, and filleth the hungry soul with goodness.[T Q]

10 Such as sit in [f,g]darkness and in the shadow of death, *being* [l]bound in affliction and iron;

11 Because they rebelled against the words of God, and contemned[G] the counsel of the most High:

12 Therefore he [f,g]brought down their heart with labour; they fell down, and *there was* none to help.

13 [f,g]Then [m]they [i]cried unto the LORD in their trouble, *and* he [c,d]saved them out of their distresses.

14 He [c,d]brought them out of darkness and the shadow of death, and brake[G] their bands[G] in sunder.[G]

15 Oh that *men* would [a]praise the LORD *for* his [c]goodness, and *for* his wonderful [n]works to the children of men!

16 For he hath broken the [o]gates of [p]brass[G], and cut the bars of [q]iron in sunder.[S]

17 [r]Fools because of their transgression, and because of their iniquities, are [l,s,t]afflicted.

18 Their soul[G] abhorreth all manner of meat; and they draw near unto the gates of [u]death.

19[S] [t]Then they [i]cry unto the LORD in their trouble, *and* he [c,d]saveth them out of their distresses.

20 He sent his word, and [v]healed them, and [n]delivered *them* from their destructions.[T Q]

21 Oh that *men* would [a]praise the LORD *for* his [c]goodness, and *for* his wonderful [n]works to the children of men![S]

22 And let them [w]sacrifice the sacrifices of thanksgiving, and [x]declare his works with rejoicing.

23 [y]They that go down to the sea in [z]ships, that do [a]business in great waters;

24 [b]These see the works of the LORD, and his wonders in the deep.[G]

25 For he [c]commandeth, and raiseth the stormy [d]wind, which lifteth up the waves thereof.[S]

26 [b]They mount up to the heaven, they go down again to the depths: their soul is melted because of trouble.

27 [b]They reel to and fro, and stagger like a [e]drunken man, and are at their wit's[G] end.

28[S] Then [b]they [f]cry unto the LORD in their trouble, and he [f]bringeth them out of their distresses.

29 He [c]maketh the storm a calm, so that the waves thereof are still.[S]

30 Then are they glad because they be quiet; so he [g]bringeth them unto their desired haven.

31 Oh that *men* would [h]praise the LORD *for* his [i]goodness, and *for* his [j]wonderful works to the children of men![S]

---

**4**
1 R. V. desert

**5**
*e Hunger*, Neh. 9:15.
*f Adversity, benefits of*, vs. 6, 7, 10–14; Psa. 10:6.
*g Adversity, design of*, vs. 6, 7, 10–14; Psa. 10:6.
*h Despondency*, Eccl. 2:20.

**6**
*i Prayer, answered*, vs. 7, 13–28; Acts 6:4.

**7**
*j God, guidance of*, Gen. 2:2.
*k Guidance*, Psa. 48:14.

**10**
*l Divine Chastisement*, Job 33:19.

**13**
*m Nation, in adversity, prayer of*, Isa. 2:4.

**15**
*n God, providence of*, Gen. 2:2.

**16**
*o Gates*, Deut. 3:5.
*p Brass*, Job 28:2.
*q Iron*, Prov. 27:17.

**17**
*r Fool*, Prov. 18:2.
*s Wicked, punishment of*, Psa. 73:3.
*t Afflictions, benefits of*, vs. 17–19; Psa. 34:19.

**18**
*u Death*, Num. 23:10.

**20**
*v Disease, healing of, from God*, Ex. 15:26.

**22**
*w Worship*, Gen. 22:5.
*x Religious Testimony*, 2 Thess. 1:10.

**23**
*y Mariner*, Ezek. 27:27.
*z Ship*, 2 Chr. 8:18.

*a Commerce, carried on by means of ships*, 1 Kin. 10:15.

**24**
*b Mariner*, Ezek. 27:27.

**25**
*c God, power of*, Gen. 2:2.
*d Meteorology*, Matt. 16:2.

**27**
*e Drunkenness*, Luke 21:34.

**28**
*f Prayer, answered*, Acts 6:4.

**30**
*g God, preserver*, Gen. 2:2.

**31**
*h Praise*, Psa. 150:1.
*i God, goodness of*, Gen. 2:2.
*j God, providence of*, Gen. 2:2.

32 [k]Let them exalt him also in
the congregation of the people,
and [h]praise him in the assembly
of the elders.
33 [l]He turneth rivers into a
wilderness, and the watersprings
into dry ground;
34 [l]A fruitful land into [2]bar-
renness, for the wickedness of
them that dwell therein.
35 He [i,j]turneth the wilderness
into a standing [m]water, and dry
ground into watersprings.
36 And there [i,j]he maketh the
hungry to dwell, that they
may prepare a city for habitation;
37 And sow the fields, and plant
[n]vineyards, which may yield
fruits of increase.
38 He [i,j]blesseth them also, so
that they are [o]multiplied greatly;
and [m]suffereth[c] not their cattle to
decrease.
39 Again, they are minished[c]
and brought low through [p]op-
pression, [q]affliction, and sorrow.
40 He poureth contempt upon
princes, and causeth them to
wander in the wilderness, *where*
*there is* no way.
41 [r]Yet setteth he the poor on
high from affliction, and maketh
*him* [o]families like a flock.[s]
42 The righteous shall see *it*,
and rejoice: and all iniquity shall
stop her mouth.
43 Whoso *is* [s]wise, and will observe these *things*, even they shall
understand the [t]lovingkindness
of the LORD.[s]

## PSALM 108

*The psalmist's purpose to praise God. 5 He recalls his promises, 10 and trusts in his help.*

A Psalm *or* Song of David.

O GOD, [a]my [b]heart is [c]fixed; I
will sing and give [d]praise,
even with my glory.
2 Awake, [e,f]psaltery and [f,g]harp:
I *myself* will awake early.

32
*k Worship, enjoined*, Gen. 22:5.

33
*l Famine, sent as a judgment*, 2 Kin. 8:1.

34
2 R. V. a salt desert,

35
*m Temporal Blessings, from God*, Psa. 103:2.

37
*n Vineyard*, Isa. 1:8.

38
*o Children, the gift of God*, v. 41; Mark 10:14.

39
*p Oppression*, Eccl. 5:8.
*q Adversity*, Psa. 10:6.

41
*r Poor, God's care of*, Prov. 21:13.

43
*s Wisdom, spiritual*, Prov. 2:2.
*t God, mercy of*, Gen. 2:2.

1
*a Decision, instances of*, Isa. 50:7.
*b Heart*, Psa. 44:21.
*c Character, stability of*, Phil. 2:15.
*d Praise, for God's goodness*, Psa. 150:1.

2
*e Psaltery*, 1 Chr. 16:5.
*f Music*, 2 Chr. 5:13.
*g Harp*, Dan. 3:10.

3 I will [d]praise thee, O LORD,
among the people: and I will
sing praises unto thee among the
nations.
4 For thy [h]mercy *is* great
above the heavens: and thy
[i]truth *reacheth* unto the clouds.[T][s]
5 [d]Be thou exalted, O God,
above the heavens: and thy
[j]glory above all the earth;
6 That thy beloved may be
delivered: [k]save *with* thy right
hand, and answer me.
7 God hath spoken in his [l]holi-
ness; I will rejoice, I will divide
[m]Shē′chem, and mete[c] out the
valley of [n]Sŭc′coth.
8 [o]Gĭl′e-ăd *is* mine; [p]Mă-năs′-
seh *is* mine; [q]Ē′phră-ĭm also
*is* the [1]strength of mine head;
[r]Jū′dah *is* my [2]lawgiver;
9 [s]Mō′ab *is* my washpot[c]; over
[t]Ē′dom will I cast out my shoe;
over [u]Phĭ-lĭs′tiȧ will I triumph.
10 Who will bring me into the
[3]strong city? who will lead me
into [t]Ē′dom?
11 [4]*Wilt* not *thou*, O God, *who*
hast cast us off? and wilt not
thou, O God, go forth with our
hosts?
12 [v]Give us help from trouble: for [w]vain *is* the help of
man.
13 [x]Through God we shall do
valiantly[c]: for he *it is that* shall
[y]tread down our enemies.

## PSALM 109

*The psalmist complains of his slanderous enemies, 6 and prays for God's judgments upon them. 22 He pleads for help, 30 and promises to give thanks.*

To the chief Musician, A Psalm of David.

[a]HOLD not thy peace, O
God of my praise;
2 For the mouth of the [b]wicked
and the mouth of the deceitful
are [c]opened against me: they
have spoken [1]against me with
a [d,e]lying tongue.
3 They compassed me about
also with words of [c,f]hatred;

4
*h God, mercy of*, Gen. 2:2.
*i God, truth*, Gen. 2:2.

5
*j God, glory of*, Gen. 2:2.

6
*k Prayer, in adversity*, Acts 6:4.

7
*l God, holiness of*, Gen. 2:2.
*m Shechem*, Josh. 20:7.
*n Succoth*, Judg. 8:5.

8
*o Gilead*, Deut. 3:13.
*p Manasseh, tribe of*, Gen. 46:20.
*q Ephraim, tribe of*, Gen. 41:52.
*r Judah, tribe of*, Num. 10:14.
1 R. V. defence
2 R. V. sceptre,

9
*s Moabites*, Gen. 19:37.
*t Edomites*, 2 Kin. 8:21.
*u* Psa. 60:8; 87:4.

10
3 R. V. fenced

11
4 R. V. Hast not thou cast us off, O God? And thou goest not forth, O God, with our hosts.

12
*v Adversity, prayer in*, Psa. 10:6.
*w False Confidence, in worldly help*, Psa. 30:6.

13
*x Faith, exemplified*, Mark 11:22.
*y God, providence of*, Gen. 2:2.

1
*a Prayer, in adversity*, vs. 2–4; Acts 6:4.

2
*b Enemy*, Prov. 24:17.
*c Malice*, Eph. 4:31.
*d Falsehood*, Job 21:34.
*e Slander*, Prov. 10:18.
1 R. V. unto me

3
*f Hatred*, Prov. 15:17.

and fought against me without a cause.[Q]

4 [g]For my [h]love [i]they are my adversaries: but I [j]*give myself unto* prayer.

5 And they have rewarded me [g]evil for good, and [f]hatred for my [h]love.

6 [k]Set thou a wicked man over him: and let [2]Sā'tan stand at his right hand.

7 When he shall be judged, [k]let him be condemned: and let his [l]prayer become sin.[Q]

8 [k]Let his days be few; *and* [m]let another take his office.[GQ]

9 [k]Let his children be [n]fatherless, and his wife a [o]widow.

10 [k]Let his children be [3]continually vagabonds,[G] and beg: let them seek *their bread* also out of their desolate places.

11 [k]Let the [p]extortioner catch all that he hath; and let the strangers spoil his labour.

12 [k]Let there be none to extend [q]mercy unto him: neither let there be any to [4]favour his fatherless children.

13 [k]Let his posterity be cut off; *and* in the generation following let their name be blotted out.

14 [k]Let the iniquity of his fathers be remembered with the LORD; and let not the sin of his mother be blotted out.

15 Let them be before the LORD continually, that he may cut off the memory of them from the earth.

16 Because that he remembered not to shew mercy, but persecuted the poor and needy man, that he might even slay the broken in heart.

17 [k]As he loved cursing, so let it come unto him: as he delighted not in blessing, so let it be far from him.

18 [k]As he clothed himself with cursing like as with his garment,[G] so let it come into his bowels like water, and like oil into his bones.

19 [k]Let it be unto him as the garment *which* covereth him, and for a girdle wherewith he is girded continually.

20 [k]*Let* this *be* the reward of mine adversaries from the LORD, and of them that speak evil against my soul.

21 But [r]do thou for me, O GOD the Lord, [s]for thy name's sake: because thy [t]mercy *is* good, deliver thou me.

22 [s]For I *am* poor and needy, and my heart is wounded within me.

23 I am gone like the shadow when it declineth: I am tossed up and down as the locust.

24 My knees are weak through [u]fasting; and my flesh faileth of fatness.

25 I became also a reproach[G] unto them: *when* they looked upon me they shaked their heads.[Q]

26 [v]Help me, O LORD my God: O save me according to thy [t]mercy:

27 [s]That they may know that this *is* thy hand; *that* thou, LORD, hast done it.

28 Let them curse, but bless[G] thou: when they arise, let them be ashamed;[G] but let thy servant rejoice.[Q]

29 [k]Let mine adversaries be clothed with shame, and let them cover themselves with their own confusion, as with a mantle.

30 I will greatly [w]praise the LORD with my mouth; yea, I will [x]praise him among the multitude.

31 For he shall stand at the right hand of the [y]poor, to save *him* from those that [5]condemn his soul.

**4**
g *Evil for Good,* Psa. 35:12.
h *Love, of man for man,* 1 John 4:7.
i *Ingratitude, of man to man,* Rom. 1:21.
j *Prayerfulness, exemplified,* 1 Tim. 5:5.

**6**
k *Prayer, imprecatory,* vs. 7–20, 28, 29; Acts 6:4.
2 R. V. an adversary

**7**
l *Prayer, of the wicked,* Acts 6:4.

**8**
m Acts 1:20.

**9**
n *Orphan,* Lam. 5:3.
o *Widow,* 2 Sam. 14:5.

**10**
3 R. V. *omits* continually.

**11**
p *Extortion,* Isa. 16:4.

**12**
q *Mercy,* Deut. 5:10.
4 R. V. have pity on

**21**
r *Adversity, prayer in,* vs. 22–24; Psa. 10:6.
s *Prayer, pleas offered in,* Acts 6:4.
t *God, mercy of,* Gen. 2:2.

**24**
u *Fasting,* Zech. 8:19.

**26**
v *Prayer, in adversity,* Acts 6:4.

**30**
w *Praise,* Psa. 150:1.
x *Religious Testimony,* 2 Thess. 1:10.

**31**
y *Poor, God's care of,* Prov. 21:13.
5 R. V. judge

1

*a* *Prophecies, concerning the Messiah and their fulfillment*, Gen. 12:3.
*b* *Jesus, king*, Matt. 1:21.
*c* *Jesus, relation of, to the Father*, Matt. 1:21.
*d* *Church, prophecies concerning its prosperity*, vs. 1–7; Matt. 16:18.
*e* *Footstool, figurative*, 1 Chr. 28:2.

3

*f* *Jesus, power of*, Matt. 1:21.
*g* *Beauty, spiritual*, Psa. 45:11.
*h* *Holiness*, Ex. 39:30.
*i* *Dew, figurative*, Dan. 4:15.
1 R. V. offer themselves willingly in

4

*j* *God, immutable*, Gen. 2:2.
*k* Heb. 5:6.
*l* *Jesus, priesthood of*, Matt. 1:21.
*m* *Jesus, mediation of*, Matt. 1:21.
*n* *Melchizedek*, Gen. 14:18.

6

*o* *Jesus, judge*, Matt. 1:21.
2 R. V. nations,
3 R. V. strike through the head in many countries.

1

*a* *Poetry, acrostic*, vs. 1–10; Acts 17:28.
*b* *Praise, for God's attributes*, vs. 1–10; Psa. 150:1.
*c* *Church*, Matt. 16:18.
1 R. V. council

## PSALM 110

*The kingdom, 4 the priesthood, 5 and the triumphs of the Messiah.*

A Psalm of David.

A Messianic Psalm in which David, under the inspiration of the Holy Spirit, writes a song in celebration of the sovereign and priestly offices of the future Messiah, who, according to the divine covenant, will establish an everlasting throne in Zion. In poetic measures he describes the glad offering of the people to Him who shall come in the beauties of holiness (v. 3) to an everlasting mediatorship (v. 4), to universal dominion (v. 5), and as judge among the nations (v. 6). The identity of the Messiah described in this psalm with Jesus is certified to by Jesus himself in Matt. 22:41–45; Mark 12:35–37; Luke 20:41–44.

[a]THE [Q] LORD said unto my [b,c]Lord, Sit thou at my *right hand, [d]until I make thine enemies thy [e]footstool.[T]

2 The LORD shall send the rod of thy strength out of Zī′ŏn: [d]rule thou in the midst of thine enemies.[S T Q]

3 [d]Thy people [1]*shall be* willing[G] in the day of thy [f]power, in the [g]beauties of [h]holiness from the womb of the morning: thou hast the [i]dew of thy youth.[S]

4 The LORD hath sworn, and [j]will not repent, [k,l]Thou *art* a [m]priest for ever after the order of [n]Mĕl-chĭz′e-dĕk.[T Q]

5 The Lord at thy right hand shall strike[C] through kings in the day of his wrath.[S Q]

6 He shall [o]judge among the [2]heathen[C], he shall fill *the places* with the dead bodies; he shall [3]wound the heads[G] over many countries.[T Q]

7 He shall drink of the brook in the way: therefore shall he lift up the head.

## PSALM 111

*The psalmist exhorts men to praise God for his wonderful works. 10 The fear of the Lord is the beginning of wisdom.*

[a,b]PRAISE ye the LORD. I will praise the LORD with *my* whole heart, in the [1,c]assembly of the upright, and *in* the congregation.

2 The [d]works of the LORD *are* great, sought out of all them that have pleasure therein.[Q]

3 His [d]work *is* honourable and glorious: and his [e]righteousness endureth for ever.[S]

4 He hath made his wonderful [d]works to be remembered: the [f]LORD *is* gracious and full of compassion.[Q]

5 [T]He hath [g]given [h,i]meat[G] unto them that [j]fear him: he will [k]ever be mindful of his [l]covenant.[S]

6 He hath shewed his people the [m]power of his [d]works, that he may give them the heritage of the [2]heathen[C].

7 The works of his hands *are* [n]verity[G] and [o]judgment[G]; all his [p]commandments *are* sure.[S]

8 They stand fast for ever and ever, *and are* done in [n]truth and [q]uprightness.[S]

9 He sent [r]redemption unto his people: he hath commanded his [l]covenant for ever: [s]holy and reverend[G] *is* his [t]name.[S Q]

10 The [u]fear of the LORD *is* the beginning of [v]wisdom: a good understanding have all they that [w]do *his commandments*: his [b]praise endureth for ever.[T]

## PSALM 112

*The blessedness of the man that fears the Lord. 10 The desire of the wicked shall perish.*

[a]PRAISE ye the LORD. [b,c]Blessed *is* the [d]man *that* [e]feareth the LORD, *that* [f]delighteth greatly in his [g]commandments.

2 His [h]seed shall be mighty upon earth: the generation of the upright shall be blessed.

3 [i]Wealth[C] and riches *shall be* in his house: and his [j]righteousness endureth for ever.

4 Unto the upright there ariseth

2

*d* *Works of God*, Psa. 40:5.

3

*e* *God, righteousness of*, Gen. 2:2.

4

*f* *God, mercy of*, Gen. 2:2.

5

*g* *God, providence of*, Gen. 2:2.
*h* *Food, from God*, Psa. 136:25.
*i* *Temporal Blessings, from God*, Psa. 103:2.
*j* *Fear of God*, Acts 9:31.
*k* *God, faithfulness of*, Gen. 2:2.
*l* *Covenant, of God with men*, Deut. 29:1.

6

*m* *God, power of*, Gen. 2:2.
2 R. V. nations.

7

*n* *Truth*, John 18:37.
*o* *God, judge*, Gen. 2:2.
*p* *Word of God*, Psa. 119:9.

8

*q* *Righteousness*, Psa. 15:2.

9

*r* *God, savior*, Gen. 2:2.
*s* *God, holiness of*, Gen. 2:2.
*t* *God, name of, to be reverenced* Gen. 2:2.

10

*u* *Fear of God*, Acts 9:31.
*v* *Wisdom, spiritual*, Prov. 2:2.
*w* *Obedience*, Heb. 5:8.

1

*a* *Praise*, Psa. 150:1.
*b* *Promise, to the righteous*, vs. 1–9; 2 Cor. 1:20.
*c* *Spiritual Peace*, Gal. 1:3.
*d* *Righteous, described*, vs. 1–10; Psa. 64:10.
*e* *Fear of God*, Acts 9:31.
*f* *Obedience*, Heb. 5:8.
*g* *Word of God*, Psa. 119:9.

2

*h* *Children, of the righteous, blessed of God*, Mark 10:14.

3

*i* *Riches*, Eccl. 4:8.
*j* *Righteousness*, Psa. 15:2.

* **SOVEREIGNTY OF THE MESSIAH,** Psa. 110:1; Matt. 22:44; Mark 12:36; Luke 20:42, 43; Acts 2:34, 35; 1 Cor. 15:25; Eph. 1:20; Col. 3:1; Heb. 1:3, 13; 8:1; 10:12, 13; 12:2.

[k]light in the [l]darkness: [d]*he is*
[m]gracious, and full of [m,n,o]com-
passion, and righteous.
5 [1]A [d]good man sheweth [m,n,o]fa-
vour, and lendeth: he will guide
his affairs with discretion.
6 Surely [p]he shall not be moved
for ever: the righteous shall be
in everlasting remembrance.
7 He shall not be afraid of
evil tidings: his [q]heart is [r]fixed,
[s]trusting in the LORD.
8 His [q]heart *is* [r]established, he
shall not be afraid, until he see
*his desire* upon his enemies.
9 [d,t]He hath [u]dispersed, he hath
given to the [v]poor; his [j]righteous-
ness endureth for ever; his [w]horn
shall be exalted with honour.
10 The wicked shall see *it*, and
[x]be grieved; he shall [y]gnash with
his teeth, and melt away: the
desire of the wicked shall perish.

## PSALM 113.

*An exhortation to praise God for his excellency and his mercy.*

[a]PRAISE ye the LORD. Praise,
O ye servants of the LORD,
praise the [b]name of the LORD.
2 [a]Blessed be the [b]name of the
LORD from this time forth and
for evermore.
3 From the rising of the sun
unto the going down of the
same the LORD's [b]name *is* to
be [a]praised.
4 The LORD *is* [c]high above all
nations, *and* his [d]glory above the
[e]heavens.
5 Who *is* like unto the LORD
our God, who dwelleth on high,
6 Who [f]humbleth *himself* to
behold *the things that are* in
heaven, and in the earth!
7 He [g]raiseth up the [h]poor out
of the dust, *and* lifteth the needy
out of the dunghill;
8 That he may [i]set *him* with
princes, *even* with the princes of
his people.
9 He [j]maketh the barren
woman to keep house, *and to*
*be* a joyful mother of children.
[a]Praise ye the LORD.

## PSALM 114

*The psalmist recounts the mighty works of God in behalf of Israel.*

WHEN [a]Iṣ'ra-el went out of
[b]Ē'ġy̆pt, the house of Jā'cob
from a people of strange [c]lan-
guage;
2 Jū'dah was his sanctuary,
*and* Iṣ'ra-el his dominion.
3 The [d]sea saw *it*, and fled:
[e]Jôr'dan was driven back.
4 The mountains skipped like
rams, *and* the little hills like
lambs.
5 What *ailed* thee, O thou [d]sea,
that thou fleddest? thou [e]Jôr'-
dan, *that* thou wast driven back?
6 Ye mountains, *that* ye skipped like rams; *and* ye little hills,
like lambs?
7 Tremble, thou earth, at the
[f]presence of the Lord, at the
presence of the God of Jā'cob;
8 Which turned the [g]rock *into* a
[1]standing [h]water, the [i]flint into
a fountain of waters.

## PSALM 115

*God's name is to be glorified. 4 The vanity of idols. 9 Israel exhorted to trust in God. 12 He will bless those who fear him.*

NOT unto us, O LORD, not
unto us, but unto thy
name give [a]glory, for thy [b]mercy,
*and* for thy [c]truth's sake.
2 Wherefore should the [1]heath-
en say, Where *is* now their God?
3 But our [d]God *is* in the heavens: [e]he hath done whatsoever
he hath pleased.
4 Their [f]idols *are* [g]silver and
[h]gold, the work of men's hands.
5 [f]They have mouths, but they
speak not: eyes have they, but
they see not:
6 They have ears, but they hear
not: noses have they, but they
smell not:
7 They have hands, but they
handle not: feet have they, but

---

**4**
k *Righteousness, fruits of*, Psa. 15:2.
l *Afflictions, consolation in*, Psa. 34:19.
m *Christian Graces*, Gal. 5:22.
n *Kindness, of good men*, Acts 28:2.
o *Love, of man for man*, 1 John 4:7.

**5**
1 R. V. Well is it with the man that dealeth graciously and lendeth; He shall maintain his cause in judgment.

**6**
p *Righteous, promises to*, Psa. 64:10.

**7**
q *Heart*, Psa. 44:21.
r *Character, stability of*, Phil. 2:15.
s *Faith*, Mark 11:22.

**9**
t 2 Cor. 9:9.
u *Liberality*, 1 Tim. 6:18.
v *Poor, liberality to*, Prov. 21:13.
w *Horn, figurative*, 1 Kin. 1:39.

**10**
x *Envy*, Prov. 14:30.
y *Gnashing of Teeth*, Job 16:9.

**1**
a *Praise*, Psa. 150:1.
b *God, name of, praised*, Gen. 2:2.

**4**
c *God, sovereign*, Gen. 2:2.
d *God, glory of*, Gen. 2:2.
e *Heavens, physical*, Psa. 8:3.

**6**
f *God, condescension of*, Gen. 2:2.

**7**
g *God, providence of*, Gen. 2:2.
h *Poor, God's care of*, Prov. 21:13.

**8**
i *Promotion*, Psa. 75:6.

**9**
j *Temporal Blessings, from God*, Psa. 103:2.

**1**
a *Israel*, Ex. 4:22.
b *Egypt*, Gen. 41:8.
c *Language*, Dan. 3:29.

**3**
d *Red Sea, divided*, Ex. 10:19.
e *Jordan, waters of, miraculously separated*, Gen. 32:10.

**7**
f *God, presence of*, Gen. 2:2.

**8**
g *Meribah*, Ex. 17:7.
h *Water, miraculously supplied to Israelites*, 1 Kin. 17:10.
i *Flint*, Deut. 8:15.
1 R. V. pool of

**1**
a *Praise*, Psa. 150:1.
b *God, mercy of*, Gen. 2:2.
c *God, truth*, Gen. 2:2.

**2**
1 R. V. nations

**3**
d *God, sovereign*, Gen. 2:2.
e *God, power of*, Gen. 2:2.

**4**
f *Idol, of gold*, vs. 4-7; 1 Kin. 15:12.
g *Silver*, 1 Chr. 28:14.
h *Gold*, Ezek. 7:19.

they walk not: neither speak they through their throat.[Q]

8 They that make them [2]are like unto them; *so is* every one that [i]trusteth in them.

9[S] O [j]Iṣ′ra-el, [k]trust thou in the LORD: he *is* their [l]help and their [m]shield.

10 O [n]house of Aâr′on, [k]trust in the LORD: he *is* their [l]help and their [m]shield.

11 Ye that [o]fear the LORD, [k]trust in the LORD: he *is* their [l]help and their [m]shield.

12 The LORD hath been mindful of us: [p]he will bless[G] *us*; he will bless[G] the house of [j]Iṣ′ra-el; he will bless the [n]house of Aâr′on.

13 [p,q]He will bless[G] them that [o]fear the LORD, *both* small and great.[Q]

14 [3]The LORD shall increase you more and more, you and your children.

15 Ye *are* blessed of the LORD which [r]made [s]heaven and [t]earth.[S]

16 The [s]heaven, *even* the heavens, *are* the LORD's: but the [t,u]earth hath he given to the children of men.[S]

17 The [v]dead praise not the LORD, neither any that go down into [w]silence.

18 But we will bless[G] the LORD from this time forth and for evermore. Praise the LORD.

## PSALM 116

*The psalmist declares his love to God. He studies to be thankful.* 12

[a]I[S] [b]LOVE the LORD, because he hath [c]heard my voice *and* my supplications.

2 Because he hath inclined[G] his [d]ear unto me, therefore will I [e]call upon *him* as long as I live.

3 The [1]sorrows of death compassed me, and the pains of [2,f]hell[G] gat hold upon me: [g]I found trouble and sorrow.[Q]

4 Then [g]called I upon the name of the LORD; O LORD, I beseech thee, deliver my soul.

5 Gracious *is* the LORD, and [h]righteous; yea, our God *is* [i]merciful.

6 [j]The LORD [k]preserveth the simple: I was brought low, and he [l]helped me.

7 Return unto thy rest, O my soul; for the LORD hath dealt bountifully with thee.

8 For thou hast [k,l]delivered my soul from death, mine eyes from tears, *and* my feet from falling.

9 [m]I will walk before the LORD in the land of the living.

10 [n]I [3,j]believed, therefore have I spoken: I was greatly afflicted:[Q]

11 I said in my [o]haste, All men *are* [4,p]liars.[Q]

12 [q,r]What shall I render[G] unto the LORD *for* all his benefits toward me?

13 I will take the [s]cup of salvation, and [t]call upon the name of the LORD.

14 I will pay my [u]vows unto the LORD [5]now in the presence of all his people.

15 Precious in the sight of the LORD *is* the [v]death of his saints.[S]

16 O LORD, truly I *am* thy [w]servant; I *am* thy servant, *and* the son of thine handmaid: thou hast [k,l]loosed my bonds.

17 I will offer to thee the [x]sacrifice of [r]thanksgiving, and will [t]call upon the name of the LORD.

18 I will pay my [u]vows unto the LORD [5]now in the presence of all his people,

19 In the courts of the [y]LORD's house, in the midst of thee, O [z]Jē-ru̇′sā-lĕm. [q]Praise ye the LORD.

## PSALM 117

*An exhortation to praise God.*

O [a,b]PRAISE the LORD, all ye nations: praise him, all ye people.[Q]

2 For his [c]merciful kindness is great toward us: and the [d]truth

---

8
- [i] *Idolatry, folly of,* 1 Sam. 15:23.
- 2 R. V. shall be like

9
- j *Israel,* Ex. 4:22.
- k *Faith, enjoined,* Mark 11:22.
- l *God, preserver,* Gen. 2:2.
- m *Shield, figurative,* 1 Kin. 14:27.

10
- n *Priest,* Lev. 1:5.

11
- o *Fear of God,* Acts 9:31.

12
- p *Faith, exemplified,* Mark 11:22.

13
- q *Righteous, promises to,* Psa. 64:10.

14
- 3 Am. R. V. Jehovah increase you

15
- r *God, creator,* Gen. 2:2.
- s *Heavens, physical,* Psa. 8:3.
- t *Earth,* Prov. 8:23.

16
- u *Temporal Blessings, from God,* Psa. 103:2.

17
- v *Dead,* 2 Kin. 4:32.
- w *Death, described,* Num. 23:10.

1
- a *Religious Testimony, exemplified,* 2 Thess. 1:10.
- b *Love, of man for God,* 1 John 4:19.
- c *Prayer, answered,* Acts 6:4.

2
- d *Anthropomorphisms,* Gen. 11:5.
- e *Prayerfulness,* 1 Tim. 5:5.

3
- f *Hell,* Mark 9:43.
- g *Afflictions, prayer in,* v. 4; Psa. 34:19.
- 1 R. V. cords
- 2 R. V. Sheol

5
- h *God, righteousness of,* Gen. 2:2.
- i *God, mercy of,* Gen. 2:2.

6
- j *Faith, exemplified,* Mark 11:22.
- k *God, preserver,* Gen. 2:2.
- l *Disease, healing of, in answer to prayer,* vs. 3–8; Ex. 15:26.

9
- m *Decision, instances of,* Isa. 50:7.

10
- n 2 Cor. 4:13.
- 3 R. V. believe, for I will speak:

11
- o *Rashness,* 2 Sam. 6:7.
- p *Falsehood,* Job 21:34.
- 4 R. V. a lie.

12
- q *Praise,* Psa. 150:1.
- r *Thankfulness, to God,* Acts 24:3.

13
- s *Cup, figurative,* Matt. 20:22.
- t *Worship,* Gen. 22:5.

14
- u *Vows,* Num. 30:2.
- 5 R. V. Yea,

15
- v *Death, of the righteous,* Num. 23:10.

16
- w *Servant, figurative,* Jer. 2:14.

17
- x *Sacrifices, figurative,* Rom. 12:1.

19
- y *Church,* 1 Kin. 9:3.
- z *Jerusalem,* Judg. 19:10.

1
- a Rom. 15:11.
- b *Praise, for God's goodness,* Psa. 150:1.

2
- c *God, mercy of,* Gen. 2:2.
- d *God, truth,* Gen. 2:2.

of the LORD *endureth* for ever. [b]Praise ye the LORD.[S T]

## PSALM 118

*The psalmist exhorts to praise God and to trust in him. 19 His determination to enter the sanctuary, and to praise God with thankfulness and joy*

O [a,b]GIVE thanks unto the LORD; for *he is* good: because his [c]mercy *endureth* for ever.

2 Let [d]Is'ra-el now say, that his [c]mercy *endureth* for ever.

3 Let the [e]house of Aâr'on now say, that his [c]mercy *endureth* for ever.

4 Let them now that [f]fear the LORD say, that his [c]mercy *endureth* for ever.

5[S] I called upon the LORD in distress: the LORD [g]answered me, *and* [h]*set me* in a large[G] place.

6 [i]The [j]LORD *is* on my side; I will not fear: what can man do unto me?[S Q]

7 [i]The [j]LORD taketh my part with them that help me: therefore shall I see *my desire* upon them that hate me.

8 *It is* better to [k]trust in the LORD than to put [l]confidence in man.

9 *It is* better to [k]trust in the LORD than to put [l]confidence in princes.

10 All nations compassed[G] me about: but [i]in the name of the LORD will I destroy them.

11 They compassed me about; yea, they compassed me about: but [i]in the name of the LORD I will destroy them.

12 They compassed me about like [m]bees; they are quenched as the fire of [n]thorns: for [i]in the name of the LORD I will destroy them.[S]

13 Thou hast thrust sore[G] at me that I might fall: but the LORD [j]helped me.

14 The LORD *is* my [o]strength and song,[S] and is become my salvation.

15 The voice of [b]rejoicing and salvation *is* in the tabernacles of the righteous: the right [p,q]hand of the LORD doeth valiantly.[G]

16 The right hand of the LORD is exalted: the right [p,q]hand of the LORD doeth valiantly.

17 I shall not die, but live, and [r]declare the [s]works of the LORD.

18 The LORD hath [t]chastened me sore[G]: but he hath not given me over unto [u]death.[Q]

19 Open to me the [v]gates of [w]righteousness: I will go into them, *and* I will [b,x]praise the LORD:

20 This [v]gate of the LORD, into which the [y]righteous shall enter.[Q]

21 I will [b,x]praise thee: for thou hast heard me, and art become my [o]salvation.

22[Q] [z]The [a,b]stone *which* the builders [c]refused[G] is become the [d]head *stone* of the corner.

23 This is the LORD's doing; it *is* marvellous in our eyes.[Q]

24 This *is* the day *which* the LORD hath made; we will rejoice and be glad in it.

25[Q] Save now, I beseech thee, O LORD: O LORD, I beseech thee, send now prosperity.

26 [e,f]Blessed *be* he that cometh in the name of the LORD: we have blessed you out of the [g]house of the LORD.[Q]

27 [1]God *is* the LORD, which hath shewed us light: bind the sacrifice with cords, *even* unto the horns of the [h]altar.[T]

28 Thou *art* my God, and I will [i]praise thee: *thou art* my God, I will exalt thee.

29 O give [j]thanks unto the LORD; for *he is* [k]good: for his [l]mercy *endureth* for ever.[S]

## PSALM 119

*The psalmist shews the excellence of God's word, and prays for grace to profit by it.*

ALEPH

[a,b]BLESSED *are* [1]the [c,d,e]undefiled in the way, who walk in the [f]law of the LORD.

---

1
*a Thankfulness, to God, enjoined,* Acts 24:3.
*b Praise, for God's goodness,* vs. 1–29; Psa. 150:1.
*c God, mercy of,* Gen. 2:2.
2
*d Israel,* Ex. 4:22.
3
*e Priest,* Lev. 1:5.
4
*f Fear of God,* Acts 9:31.
5
*g Prayer, answered,* Acts 6:4.
*h God, providence of,* Gen. 2:2.
6
*i Faith, exemplified,* Mark 11:22.
*j God, preserver,* Gen. 2:2.
8
*k Faith, enjoined,* Mark 11:22.
*l False Confidence,* Psa. 30:6.
12
*m Bee,* Deut. 1:44.
*n Thorn,* Hos. 2:6.
14
*o God, savior,* Gen. 2:2.

15
*p Anthropomorphisms,* Gen. 11:5.
*q God, power of,* Gen. 2:2.
17
*r Religious Testimony,* 2 Thess. 1:10.
*s Works of God,* Psa. 40:5.
18
*t Divine Chastisement,* Job 33:19.
*u Death,* Num. 23:10.
19
*v Gates, figurative,* Deut. 3:5.
*w Righteousness,* Psa. 15:2.
*x Worship,* Gen. 22:5.
20
*y Righteous,* Psa. 64:10.
22
*z Prophecies, concerning the Messiah and their fulfillment,* Gen. 12:3.

*a Corner Stone, figurative,* Psa. 144:12.
*b Jesus, typified in the corner stone,* Matt. 1:21.
*c Jesus, rejected,* Matt. 1:21.
*d Church, Christ head of,* Matt. 16:18.
26
*e* Matt. 21:9; 23:39; Mark 11:9; Luke 13:35; 19:38; John 12:13.
*f Prophecies, concerning the Messiah and their fulfillment,* Gen. 12:3.
*g Church, called house of the Lord,* 1 Kin. 9:3.
27
*h Altar, of burnt offerings,* Gen. 8:20.
1 Am. R. V. Jehovah is God, and he hath given us
28
*i Praise,* Psa. 150:1.
29
*j Thankfulness, to God, enjoined,* Acts 24:3.
*k God, goodness of,* Gen. 2:2.
*l God, mercy of,* Gen. 2:2.
1
*a Poetry, acrostic,* Acts 17:28.
*b Spiritual Peace,* Gal. 1:3.
*c Righteous, described,* vs. 1–3; Psa. 64:10.
*d Holiness,* Ex. 39:30.
*e Perfection,* Heb. 6:1.
*f Law,* Deut. 33:2.
1 R. V. they that are perfect in

**2**
g *Obedience, rewarded*, Heb. 5:8.
h *Commandments*, Deut. 8:2.
i *Seekers*, Isa. 55:6.
j *Spiritual Desire, reward of*, Psa. 42:1.
**3**
k *Sinlessness*, 1 John 5:18.
**4**
l *Obedience, enjoined*, Heb. 5:8.
m *Diligence, required*, Rom. 12:8.
**5**
2 R. V. established To observe
**7**
n *Praise*, Psa. 150:1.
**8**
o *Decision*, Isa. 50:7.
**9**
p *Young Men*, Prov. 1:4.
q *Watchfulness, enjoined upon young men*, Matt. 24:42.
**10**
r *Love, of man for God, exemplified*, vs. 10–20; 1 John 4:19.
s *Heart*, Psa. 44:21.
t *Spiritual Desire, exemplified*, Psa. 42:1.
**11**
3 R. V. laid up in
**12**
u *Wisdom, prayer for spiritual*, Prov. 2:2.
**13**
v *Religious Testimony, exemplified*, 2 Thess. 1:10.

2 [b]Blessed *are* [c]they that [g]keep
his [h]testimonies, *and that* [i,j]seek
him with the whole heart.
3 [c]They also [d,k]do no iniquity:
they [g]walk in his ways.
4 Thou hast commanded *us* to
[l]keep thy [h]precepts [m]diligently.
5 O that my ways were [2]direct-
ed to keep thy [h]statutes!
6 Then shall I not be ashamed,
when I have respect unto all thy
[h]commandments.
7 I will [n]praise thee with uprightness of heart, when I shall
have learned thy righteous judgments.
8 [o]I will keep thy [h]statutes: O
forsake me not utterly.

BETH

9 Wherewithal shall a [p]young
man cleanse his way? by [q]tak-
ing heed *thereto* according to thy
*word.
10 [r]With my whole [s]heart have
I [t]sought thee: O let me not wander from thy [h]commandments.
11 [r]Thy word have I [3]hid in
mine [s]heart, that I might not sin
against thee.
12 Blessed *art* thou, O LORD:
[t,u]teach me thy statutes.
13 With my lips have I [v]de-
clared all the judgments of thy
mouth.
14 [r]I have rejoiced in the way
of thy [h]testimonies, as *much as*
in all riches.
15 I will [w]meditate in thy [h]pre-
cepts, and have respect unto thy
ways.
16 [r]I will delight myself in thy
[h]statutes: I will not forget thy
*word.

GIMEL

17 Deal bountifully with thy
servant, *that* I may live, and
[r]keep thy *word.
18 [t,u]Open thou mine eyes, that
I may behold wondrous things
out of thy [l]law.
19 I *am* a [4]stranger in the
earth: hide not thy [h]command-
ments from me.
20 [r]My soul breaketh for the
[t,x]longing *that it hath* unto thy
judgments at all times.
21 Thou hast [y]rebuked the
proud *that are* cursed, which [z]do
err from thy [a]commandments.
22 [b]Remove from me reproach
and contempt; for I have [c]kept
thy [a]testimonies.
23 Princes also did sit *and*
speak against me: *but* thy servant did [d]meditate in thy [a]statutes.

**15**
w *Meditation, on the law of the Lord*, Psa. 49:3.
**19**
4 R. V. sojourner
**20**
x *Love, for God's word*, 1 John 4:19.
**21**
y *Wicked, punishment of*, Psa. 73:3.
z *Disobedience to God*, Eph. 5:6.

a *Commandments*, Deut. 8:2.
**22**
b *Adversity, prayer in*, Psa. 10:6.
c *Faithfulness, exemplified*, Luke 16:10.
**23**
d *Meditation, on the law of the Lord*, Psa. 49:3.

* **WORD OF GOD.** Called: *Book*, Psa. 40:7; Rev. 22:19; *Book of the Lord*, Isa. 34:16; *Book of the Law*, Neh. 8:3; Gal. 3:10; *Good Word of God*, Heb. 6:5; *Holy Scriptures*, Rom. 1:2; 2 Tim. 3:15; *Law of the Lord*, Psa. 1:2; Isa. 30:9; *Oracles of God*, Rom. 3:2; 1 Pet. 4:11; *Scriptures*, 1 Cor. 15:3; *Scriptures of Truth*, Dan. 10:21; *Sword of the Spirit*, Eph. 6:17; *The Word*, Jas. 1:21–23; 1 Pet. 2:2; *Word of God*, Luke 11:28; Heb. 4:12; *Word of Christ*, Col. 3:16; *Word of Life*, Phil. 2:16; *Word of Truth*, Prov. 22:21; Eph. 1:13; 2 Tim. 2:15; Jas. 1:18.

Compared to: *A lamp*, Psa. 119:105; Prov. 6:23; *fire*, Jer. 23:29; *seed*, Matt. 13:3–8, 18–23, 37, 38; Mark 4:3–20, 26–32; Luke 8:5–15.

*Is, wonderful*, Psa. 119:129; *pure*, Psa. 12:6; 19:8; 119:140; *perfect*, Psa. 19:7; *living*, Heb. 4:12; *effective*, Isa. 55:11; *comforting*, Psa. 119:28, 50, 52, 76, 82, 92; *edifying*, Psa. 19:98, 99, 104, 130; Rom. 15:4; *quickening*, Psa. 119:93; 1 Pet. 1:23; *restraining*, Psa. 17:4; 119:11; *sanctifying*, John 15:3; 17:17, 19; Eph. 5:26; 1 Tim. 4:5; *enduring*, Psa. 119:152; Isa. 40:8; Mark 13:31; 1 Pet. 1:23–25. *Is truth*, Psa. 119:142, 151, 160.

*Is inspired*, Ex. 34:27, 32; Deut. 4:5, 10, 14; 2 Kin. 17:13; 2 Chr. 33:18; Zech. 7:12; Acts 1:16; 28:25; Rom. 3:1, 2; Eph. 6:17; 1 Thess. 2:13; 2 Tim. 3:16, 17; Heb. 1:1, 2; 3:7, 8; 2 Pet. 1:21; 3:2, 15; Rev. 1:1, 2; 2:7.

*Is, trustworthy*, Psa. 93:5; 11:7, 8; 119:86; *more to be desired than gold*, Psa. 119:72, 127.

*Is the delight of the righteous*, Job 23:12; Psa. 1:2; 119:16, 24, 35, 77, 103, 143, 162, 174.

*Is, loved*, Psa. 119:47, 48, 70, 97, 111, 113, 119, 159; *revered*, Psa. 119:161.

*Is spirit and life*, John 6:63. *Is part of the Christian armor*, Eph. 6:17. *Is the standard of righteousness*, Psa. 119:144, 172; Isa. 8:20. *Bears the test of criticism and experience*, 2 Sam. 22:31; Psa. 18:30.

*Is, for admonition*, 1 Cor. 10:11; *for instruction*, 2 Tim. 3:16, 17. *Searching of*, Acts 17:11. *Searching of, enjoined*, Isa. 34:16; John 7:52.

*To be in the heart*, Deut. 30:11–14; Job 22:22; Psa. 37:31; 40:8; 119:11; Rom. 10:6–8. *To be meditated upon*, Josh. 1:8; Psa. 1:2; 119:15, 23, 48, 78, 97, 99, 148. *To be worn on the hand and forehead*, Deut. 6:8; 11:18. *To be posted in public places*, Deut. 6:9; 27:2, 3, 8; Josh. 8:32. *To be studied by rulers*, Deut. 17:18, 19; Josh. 1:8. *To be taught to children*, Deut. 6:7; 11:19; 31:12, 13. *To be read in public assemblies*, Deut. 31:11. *To be taught in psalms*, Deut. 31:19, 21; Psa. 119:54.

*Convicts of sin*, 2 Kin. 22:9–13; 2 Chr. 17:7–10; 34:14–33. *Makes free*, Psa. 119:45; John 8:32. *Makes wise*, 2 Tim. 3:15. *Works salvation*, 1 Thess. 2:13; 1 Pet. 1:23. *Rejoices the heart*, Psa. 119:111; Jer. 15:16. *Testifies of Jesus*, John 5:39; 20:31; Acts 18:28; 1 Cor. 15:3.

*The world to be judged by*, John 12:48; Rom. 2:16.

*Not to be added to, nor taken from*, Deut. 4:2; 12:32; Prov. 30:6; Rev. 22:18, 19. *Not to be handled deceitfully*, 2 Cor. 4:2. *Obedience to, enjoined*, Deut. 4:5, 6; Psa. 78:1, 7; Luke 11:28; 2 Thess. 2:14, 15; 2 Pet. 3:1, 2; Jude 3; Rev. 1:3.

*Longing for*, Psa. 119:20, 131; Amos 8:11–13. *Walking after*, Psa. 119:30.

*Public instruction in*, Ex. 24:7; Deut. 31:9–13; Josh. 8:33–35; 2 Kin. 23:2; 2 Chr. 17:7–9; Neh. 8:1–8, 13, 18; Isa. 2:3; Jer. 36:6. *Instruction in, desired*, Psa. 119:18, 19.

*Expounded, by Jesus*, Luke 4:16–28; 24:27, 45; John 2:22; *by the apostles*, Acts 2:16–47; 8:32, 35; 17:2; 28:23.

*Ignorance of*, Matt. 22:29; Mark 12:24. *Rejected by the wicked*, Prov. 13:13; Isa. 28:13; 30:9; Jer. 8:9; Hos. 8:12; Mark 7:9, 13; Acts 13:46. *Disbelief in*, Psa. 50:16, 17; Isa. 30:9; Jer. 6:10; Luke 16:31; 24:25; John 5:46, 47; 8:37; 2 Tim. 4:3, 4; 1 Pet. 2:8; 2 Pet. 3:15, 16.

24 Thy *,[a]testimonies also *are* my delight *and* my counsellors.[G]

DALETH

25 My soul cleaveth[G] unto the dust: quicken[G] thou me according to thy word.

26 I have declared my ways, and thou [e]heardest me: [f]teach me thy [a]statutes.

27 [f]Make me to understand the way of thy [a]precepts[G]: so shall I [5,d]talk of thy [g]wondrous works.

28 My soul melteth[G] for heaviness[G]: [j]strengthen thou me according unto thy *word.

29 Remove from me the way of [h]lying: and [f]grant me thy law graciously.

30 I have [i]chosen the way of [6]truth: thy judgments[G] have I laid *before me.*

31 I [7]have [j]stuck unto thy [a,]*testimonies: O LORD, put me not to shame.

32 I will run the way of thy [a]commandments, when thou shalt [k]enlarge my heart.[Q]

HE

33 [f,l]Teach me, O LORD, the way of thy [a]statutes; and I shall keep it *unto* the end.

34 [f,l]Give me understanding, and I shall keep thy [m]law; yea, I shall observe it with *my* whole heart.

35 [f,l]Make me to go in the path of thy [a]commandments; for therein do I delight.

36 Incline my heart unto thy [a]testimonies, and not to [n]covetousness.

37 [o]Turn away mine eyes from beholding vanity; *and* [f,l]quicken[G] thou me in thy way.[S]

38 [8]Stablish[G] thy word unto thy servant, who *is devoted* to thy [p]fear.

39 Turn away my reproach which I fear: for thy judgments[G] *are* good.

40 Behold, I have [l]longed after thy precepts[G]: quicken[G] me in thy [q]righteousness.

VAU

41 Let thy [r]mercies come also unto me, O LORD, *even* thy [s]salvation, according to thy *word.[S]

42 So shall I have wherewith[G] to answer him that reproacheth me: for I [t]trust in thy *word.

43 And take not the word of truth utterly out of my mouth; for I have [f,u]hoped in thy judgments.[G]

44 So shall I keep thy [m]law continually for ever and ever.

45 And I will walk at [v]liberty: for I [l]seek thy [a]precepts.[G]

46 I will [w]speak of thy testimonies also before kings, and will not be ashamed.[Q]

47 And I will delight myself in thy *commandments, which I have [x]loved.

48 My hands also will I lift up unto thy commandments, which I have [x]loved; and I will meditate in thy statutes.

ZAIN

49 Remember the word unto thy servant, upon which thou hast caused me to [f,u]hope.

50 [y]This *is* my comfort in my affliction: for thy *word hath quickened[G] me.

51 The proud [z]have had me greatly in derision: *yet* have I [a]not declined from thy *,[b]law.

52 I remembered thy judgments[G] of old, O LORD; and have [c]comforted myself.

53 [9]Horror hath taken hold upon me because of the wicked that forsake thy *,[b]law.

54 Thy [d]statutes have been my songs in the house of my pilgrimage.

55 I have [e]remembered thy name, O LORD, in the night, and have [f]kept thy [b]law.

56 This I had, because I [f]kept thy precepts.[G]

---

**26**
e *Prayer, answered,* Acts 6:4.
f *Wisdom, spiritual, prayer for,* Prov. 2:2.

**27**
g *God, providence of,* Gen. 2:2.
5 R. V. meditate

**29**
h *Falsehood,* Job 21:34.

**30**
i *Decision,* Isa. 50:7.
6 R. V. faithfulness:

**31**
j *Faithfulness, exemplified,* Luke 16:10.
7 R. V. cleave unto

**32**
k *Spiritual Blessings, from God,* Eph. 1:3.

**33**
l *Spiritual Desire,* Psa. 42:1.

**34**
m *Law, of God,* Deut. 33:2.

**36**
n *Covetousness,* Isa. 57:17.

**37**
o *Sin, repugnant to the righteous,* Rom. 5:12.

**38**
p *Fear of God,* Acts 9:31.
8 Am. R. V. Confirm unto thy servant thy word, Which is in order unto the fear of thee.

**40**
q *God, righteousness of,* Gen. 2:2.

**41**
r *God, mercy of,* Gen. 2:2.
s *God, savior,* Gen. 2:2.

**42**
t *Faith, exemplified,* Mark 11:22.

**43**
u *Hope,* Prov. 13:12.

**45**
v *Liberty, spiritual,* Lev. 25:10.

**46**
w *Religious Testimony,* 2 Thess. 1:10.

**47**
x *Love, for God's word,* 1 John 4:19.

**50**
y *Afflictions, consolation in,* Psa. 34:19.

**51**
z *Persecution, of the righteous,* John 15:20.

a *Faithfulness, exemplified,* Luke 16:10.
b *Law, of God,* Deut. 33:2.

**52**
c *Afflictions, consolation in,* Psa. 34:19.

**53**
9 R. V. Hot indignation hath

**54**
d *Commandments,* Deut. 8:2.

**55**
e *Prayer, in the night,* Acts 6:4.
f *Obedience,* Heb. 5:8.

CHETH

57 [10,g]*Thou art* my portion, O LORD: I have said that I would [f]keep thy *words.

58 I [h]intreated thy favour[G] with *my* whole heart: be [i]merciful unto me according to thy *word.

59 I [j]thought on my ways, and turned my feet unto thy [d,]*testimonies.[s]

60 I made haste, and [a]delayed not to [f]keep[G] thy [d]commandments.

61 [11]The bands of the wicked have robbed me: *but* I [a,k]have not forgotten thy *,[b]law.

62 At [e]midnight I will rise to give [l]thanks unto thee because of thy righteous judgments.

63 I *am* a [m]companion of all *them* that [n]fear thee, and of them that [f]keep thy [d]precepts.[G]

64 The earth, O LORD, is full of thy [i]mercy[G]: [o,p]teach me thy [d]statutes.[s]

TETH

65 Thou hast [q]dealt well with thy servant, O LORD[s], according unto thy *word.

66 [o,p]Teach me good judgment and [r]knowledge: for I have [g]believed thy [d]commandments.

67 Before I was [s]afflicted I went astray: [t]but now have I kept thy word.

68 Thou *art* [u]good, and doest[s] good; [o,p]teach me thy statutes.[G]

69 The proud have forged a [v]lie against me: *but* [w]I will [f]keep thy precepts with *my* whole heart.

70 Their heart is as fat as grease; *but* [x]I delight in thy *law.

71 [t]*It is* good for me that I have been [s]afflicted; that I[s] might learn thy statutes.

72 The *law of thy mouth *is* better unto me than thousands of [y]gold and [z]silver.[T]

JOD.

73 Thy hands have [a]made [b]me and fashioned me: [c,d]give me understanding, that I may [c,d]learn thy [e]commandments.[s]

74 They that [f]fear thee will be glad when they see me; because I have [g,h]hoped in thy *word.

75 [i]I know, O LORD, that thy judgments *are* [12,j]right, and *that* thou in faithfulness [k]hast afflicted me.[T]

76 Let, I pray thee, thy [13,l]merciful kindness be for my comfort, according to thy word unto thy servant.[s]

77 [d]Let thy tender [l]mercies[G] come unto me, that I may live: for thy [m]law *is* my [n]delight.

78 [o]Let the proud be ashamed; for they [14,p]dealt perversely with me without a cause: *but* I will [q]meditate in thy [e]precepts.[G]

79 Let those that [f]fear[G] thee turn unto me, and those that have known thy [e]testimonies.

80 Let my heart be [15]sound in thy *,[e]statutes; that I be not ashamed.

CAPH

81 My soul [d]fainteth for thy salvation: *but* I [g]hope in thy *word.

82 [d]Mine eyes fail for thy *word, saying, When wilt thou comfort me?

83 For I am become like a [r]bottle[G] in the smoke; *yet* do I not forget thy [e]statutes.

84 How many *are* the days of thy servant? when wilt thou execute judgment on them that [s]persecute me?

85 The [t]proud have [p]digged [u]pits for me, which *are* not after thy [m]law.

86 All thy [e]commandments *are* faithful: they [s]persecute me wrongfully; [v]help thou me.[T]

87 They had almost consumed me upon earth; but I [w]forsook not thy [e]precepts.[G]

88 Quicken[G] me after [l]thy lov-

**57**
g *Faith, exemplified,* Mark 11:22.
10 R. V. The Lord is my portion:

**58**
h *Prayer, importunity in,* Acts 6:4.
i *God, mercy of,* Gen. 2:2.

**59**
j *Self-examination,* 2 Cor. 13:5.

**61**
k *Temptation, resisted,* Luke 11:4.
11 R. V. The cords of the wicked have wrapped me round;

**62**
l *Praise,* Psa. 150:1.

**63**
m *Fellowship, of the righteous,* 1 Cor. 1:9.
n *Fear of God,* Acts 9:31.

**64**
o *Wisdom, spiritual, prayer for,* Prov. 2:2.
p *Spiritual Desire,* Psa. 42:1.

**65**
q *God, faithfulness of,* Gen. 2:2.

**66**
r *Knowledge, desire for,* Luke 11:52.

**67**
s *Divine Chastisement,* Job 33:19.
t *Afflictions, benefits of,* Psa. 34:19.

**68**
u *God, goodness of,* Gen. 2:2.

**69**
v *Falsehood,* Job 21:34.
w *Decision,* Isa. 50:7.

**70**
x *Word of God, love for,* see footnote, p. 894.

**72**
y *Gold,* Ezek. 7:19.
z *Silver,* 1 Chr. 28:14.

**73**
a *God, creator,* Gen. 2:2.
b *Man, created,* Job 4:17.
c *Wisdom, spiritual, prayer for,* Prov. 2:2.
d *Spiritual Desire,* Psa. 42:1.
e *Commandments,* Deut. 8:2.

**74**
f *Fear of God,* Acts 9:31.
g *Hope,* Prov. 13:12.
h *Faith, exemplified,* Mark 11:22.

**75**
i *Adversity, resignation in, exemplified,* Psa. 10:6.
j *God, justice of,* Gen. 2:2.
k *Divine Chastisement,* Job 33:19.
12 R. V. righteous,

**76**
l *God, love of,* Gen. 2:2.
13 R. V. lovingkindness

**77**
m *Law,* Deut. 33:2.
n *Word of God, love for,* see footnote, p. 894.

**78**
o *Prayer, imprecatory,* Acts 6:4.
p *Malice,* Eph. 4:31.
q *Meditation, on the law of the Lord,* Psa. 49:3.
14 R. V. have overthrown me wrongfully:

**80**
15 R. V. perfect

**83**
r *Bottle,* Gen. 21:14.

**84**
s *Persecution, of the righteous,* John 15:20.

**85**
t *Pride,* Prov. 16:18.
u *Pit, figurative,* Psa. 7:15.

**86**
v *Prayer, in adversity,* Acts 6:4.

**87**
w *Faithfulness, exemplified,* Luke 16:10.

ingkindness; so shall I keep the
testimony of thy mouth.

LAMED

89 For ever, O LORD, thy word
is [x]settled in heaven.[S]
90 [x]Thy [y]faithfulness *is* unto
all generations: thou hast [z]estab-
lished the earth, and it abideth.[GS]
91 They continue this day according to [a]thine ordinances[G]: for
all [16]*are* thy servants.[S]
92 Unless thy law *had been* my
[b]delights, I should then have
perished in mine [c]affliction.
93 I will never forget thy [d]pre-
cepts[G]: for with them thou hast
quickened[G] me.
94 I *am* thine, save me; for I
have [e]sought thy [d]precepts[G].
95 [f]The wicked have [g]waited
for me to destroy me: *but* I will
consider thy [d]testimonies.
96 I have seen an end of all
perfection: *but* thy *commandment *is* exceeding broad.[T]

MEM

97 O how [b]love I thy law! it *is*
my [h]meditation all the day.
98 Thou through thy [d]com-
mandments hast made me [i]wiser
than mine enemies: for they *are*
ever with me.
99 I have more [i]understanding
than all my teachers: for thy [d]tes-
timonies *are* my [h]meditation.
100 I [i]understand more than
the [17]ancients, because I [j]keep
thy [d]precepts.
101 [k]I have [l]refrained[G] my feet
from every evil way, that I might
[j]keep thy word.
102 [k]I have not departed from
thy [d]judgments[G]: for thou hast
[m]taught me.
103 [b]How sweet are thy *words
unto my taste! *yea, sweeter* than
honey to my mouth!
104 Through thy [d]precepts I
get [i]understanding: therefore I
[n]hate every false way.

NUN

105 Thy *word *is* a [o]lamp unto
my feet, and a [p]light unto my
path.[T]
106 [q]I have sworn, and I will
perform *it*, that I will [j]keep thy
righteous [d]judgments.
107 I am afflicted very much:
quicken[G] me, O LORD, according
unto thy word.
108 Accept, I beseech thee, the
freewill [r,s]offerings of my mouth,
O LORD, and [m,t]teach me thy
[d]judgments[G].
109 My soul *is* continually in
my hand: yet do I not forget thy
[d]law.
110 The wicked have [f,g]laid a
snare for me: yet I [k,l]erred not
from thy precepts[G].
111 Thy [d]testimonies have I
[q]taken as an heritage for ever:
for they *are* the [b]rejoicing of my
heart.
112 I have inclined mine [u]heart
to perform thy statutes[G] alway,
*even unto* the end.

SAMECH

113 I [n]hate [18]*vain* thoughts: but
thy law do I [b]love.
114 [v]Thou *art* my hiding place
and my shield: I [w]hope in thy
*word.
115 [x]Depart from me, ye [y]evil-
doers: [19]for I will keep the commandments of my God.
116 Uphold me according unto
thy *word, that I may live: and let
me not be ashamed of my [w]hope.
117 [v]Hold thou me up, and I
shall be safe: and I will have
respect[G] unto thy statutes continually.
118 Thou hast [20,z]trodden[G]
down all them that err from
thy statutes: for their deceit
*is* [a]falsehood.
119 Thou [b]puttest away all the
wicked of the earth *like* [c]dross[G]:
therefore I [d]love thy [e]testimo-
nies[G].
120 My flesh trembleth for [f]fear
of thee; and I am afraid of thy
[g]judgments.

**89**
x *God, immutable,* Gen. 2:2.

**90**
y *God, faithfulness of, confidence in,* Gen. 2:2.
z *God, creator,* Gen. 2:2.

**91**
a *God, sovereign,* Gen. 2:2.
16 R. V. things are

**92**
b *Word of God, love for,* see footnote, p. 894.
c *Afflictions, consolation in,* Psa. 34:19.

**93**
d *Commandments,* Deut. 8:2.

**94**
e *Spiritual Desire,* Psa. 42:1.

**95**
f *Malice,* Eph. 4:31.
g *Persecution, of the righteous,* John 15:20.

**97**
h *Meditation, on the law of the Lord,* Psa. 49:3.

**98**
i *Wisdom, spiritual,* Prov. 2:2.

**100**
j *Obedience,* Heb. 5:8.
17 R. V. aged,

**101**
k *Integrity,* Job 2:3.
l *Temptation, resistance to,* Luke 11:4.

**102**
m *God, teacher,* Gen. 2:2.

**104**
n *Sin, repugnant to the righteous,* Rom. 5:12.

**105**
o *Lamp, figurative,* Ex. 27:20.

p *Light, figurative,* Matt. 5:14.

**106**
q *Decision,* Isa. 50:7.

**108**
r *Prayer,* Acts 6:4.
s *Worship,* Gen. 22:5.
t *Wisdom, spiritual, prayer for,* Prov. 2:2.

**112**
u *Heart,* Psa. 44:21.

**113**
18 R. V. them that are of a double mind;

**114**
v *God, preserver,* Gen. 2:2.
w *Faith, exemplified,* Mark 11:22.

**115**
x *Fellowship, with the wicked, avoided,* 1 Cor. 1:9.
y *Evil Company, the righteous shun,* Prov. 13:20.
19 R. V. That I may keep

**118**
z *Wicked, punishment of,* Psa. 73:3.
a *Falsehood,* Job 21:34.
20 R. V. set at nought

**119**
b *Wicked, punishment of,* Psa. 73:3.
c Prov. 25:4; 26:23; Isa. 1:22; Ezek. 22:18, 19.
d *Word of God, love for,* see footnote, p. 894.
e *Commandments,* Deut. 8:2.

**120**
f *Fear of God,* Acts 9:31.
g *Judgments,* Ex. 6:6.

**121**
*h Integrity*, Job 2:3.
*i Oppression, prayer against*, Eccl. 5:8.

**124**
*j God, mercy of*, Gen. 2:2.
*k God, teacher*, Gen. 2:2.
*l Wisdom, spiritual, prayer for*, Prov. 2:2.

**126**
*m Law*, Deut. 33:2.

**127**
*n Gold*, Ezek. 7:19.

**128**
*o Sin, repugnant to the righteous*, Rom. 5:12.

**129**
*p Obedience*, Heb. 5:8.

**130**
*q Wisdom, spiritual, from God*, Prov. 2:2.
21 R. V. opening of

**131**
*r Spiritual Desire*, Psa. 42:1.

**132**
*s Righteous, described*, Psa. 64:10.

**136**
*t Tears*, Psa. 6:6.
*u Disobedience to God*, Eph. 5:6.

AIN

121 [h]I have done judgment and
justice: [i]leave me not to mine
oppressors.
122 Be surety for thy servant
for good: [i]let not the proud oppress me.
123 Mine eyes fail for thy salvation, and for the *word of thy
righteousness.
124 Deal with thy servant according unto thy [j]mercy, and
[k,l]teach me thy statutes.
125 I *am* thy servant; [l]give me
understanding, that I may know
thy testimonies.
126 *It is* time for *thee*, LORD, to
work: *for* they have made void
thy [m]law.
127 Therefore I [d]love thy [e]commandments above [n]gold; yea,
above fine gold.
128 Therefore I esteem all *thy*
precepts *concerning* all *things to
be* right; *and* [o]I hate every false
way.

PE

129 Thy [e]testimonies *are* wonderful: therefore doth my soul
[p]keep them.
130 The [21]entrance of thy
words giveth [q]light; it giveth
[q]understanding unto the simple.
131 I opened my mouth, and
panted: for I [r]longed for thy
[e]commandments.
132 Look thou upon me, and be
[j]merciful unto me, as thou usest
to do unto those that [s]love thy
name.
133 Order my steps in thy
word: and let not any iniquity
have dominion over me.
134 [i]Deliver me from the oppression of man: so will I [p]keep
thy [e]precepts.
135 Make thy face to shine upon thy servant; and [k,r]teach me
thy statutes.
136 [t]Rivers of waters run down
mine eyes, because they [u]keep
not thy [m]law.

TZADDI

137 [v]Righteous *art* thou, O
LORD, and [w]upright *are* thy
judgments.
138 [22]Thy testimonies *that*
thou hast commanded *are* [v]righteous and very [x]faithful.
139 My [y]zeal hath consumed
me, because mine enemies have
forgotten thy *words.
140 Thy *word *is* very pure:
therefore thy servant loveth it.
141 I *am* small and despised:
*yet* do not I forget thy precepts.
142 Thy [v]righteousness *is* an
everlasting righteousness, and
thy law *is* the [z]truth.
143 Trouble and anguish have
taken hold on me: *yet* thy [a]commandments *are* my delights.
144 The righteousness of thy
[a]testimonies *is* everlasting:
[b,c]give me understanding, and I
shall live.

KOPH

145 I [d]cried with *my* whole
heart; hear me, O LORD: [e]I will
keep thy [a],*statutes.
146 I [d]cried unto thee; save
me, and [e]I shall keep thy [a],*testimonies.
147 I [23]prevented the dawning
of the morning, and [d]cried: I
[f]hoped in thy *word.
148 Mine eyes [23]prevent the
[g]*night* watches, that I might
[h]meditate in thy *word.
149 Hear my voice according
unto thy [i]lovingkindness: O
LORD, [c]quicken me according to
thy judgment.
150 They draw nigh that [j]follow after mischief: they are far
from thy [k]law.
151 Thou *art* near, O LORD;
and all thy [a]commandments *are*
[l]truth.
152 Concerning thy [a]testimonies, I have known of old that
thou hast founded them for ever.

RESH

153 Consider mine [m]affliction,

**137**
*v God, righteousness of*, Gen. 2:2.
*w God, justice of*, Gen. 2:2.

**138**
*x God, faithfulness of*, Gen. 2:2.
22 R. V. Thou hast commanded thy testimonies in righteousness And very faithfulness.

**139**
*y Zeal, exemplified*, 2 Cor. 7:11.

**142**
*z Truth*, John 18:37.

**143**
*a Commandments*, Deut. 8:2.

**144**
*b Wisdom, spiritual, prayer for*, Prov. 2:2.
*c Spiritual Desire*, Psa. 42:1.

**145**
*d Prayer, importunity in*, Acts 6:4.
*e Decision*, Isa. 50:7.

**147**
*f Hope*, Prov. 13:12.
23 Am. R. V. anticipated

**148**
*g Night, divided into watches*, Gen. 1:5.
*h Meditation, on the law of the Lord*, Psa. 49:3.

**149**
*i God, love of*, Gen. 2:2.

**150**
*j Wicked, described*, Psa. 73:3.
*k Law*, Deut. 33:2.

**151**
*l Truth*, John 18:37.

**153**
*m Afflictions, prayer in*, Psa. 34:19.

and deliver me: for I do not forget thy [k]law.

154 Plead my cause, and deliver me: [c]quicken me according to thy *word.

155 Salvation *is* far from the [j]wicked: for they seek not thy [a]statutes.

156 Great *are* thy [i]tender mercies, O LORD: [c]quicken me according to thy [a]judgments.

157 Many *are* my [n]persecutors and mine enemies; *yet* do [o]I not decline from thy [a]testimonies.

158 I beheld the [24]transgressors, and was [p,q]grieved; because they [r]kept not thy *word.

159 Consider how I [s]love thy [a]precepts: [c]quicken me, O LORD, according to thy loving-kindness.

160 [25]Thy *word *is* [l]true *from* the beginning: and every one of thy righteous judgments *endureth* for ever.

SCHIN

161 Princes have [n]persecuted me without a cause: but my heart standeth in awe of thy word.

162 I [t]rejoice at thy word, as one that findeth great spoil.

163 I [q]hate and abhor [u]lying: *but* thy *,[k]law do I [s]love.

164 Seven times a day do I [v,w]praise thee because of thy righteous judgments.

165 Great [x]peace have they which [s]love thy *law: [26]and nothing shall [y]offend them.

166 LORD, I have [z]hoped for thy salvation, and [a]done thy [b]commandments.

167 My soul hath [a]kept thy [b]testimonies; and I [c]love them exceedingly.

168 I have [a]kept thy [b]precepts and thy testimonies: for all my ways *are* [d]before thee.

TAU

169 Let my [e]cry come near before thee, O LORD: [f,g]give me understanding according to thy *word.

170 Let my [e]supplication come before thee: deliver me according to thy *word.

171 My lips shall utter [h]praise, when thou hast taught me thy [b]statutes.

172 My tongue shall [i]speak of thy *word: for all thy [b]commandments *are* righteousness.

173 Let thine hand help me; for [j]I have chosen thy [b]precepts.

174 I have [g]longed for thy salvation, O LORD; and thy [k]law *is* my delight.

175 Let my soul live, and it shall [h]praise thee; and let thy judgments help me.

176 [l]I have gone astray like a lost sheep; seek thy servant; for I do not forget thy [b]commandments.

## PSALM 120

*The psalmist prays for deliverance from lying lips; 5 and complains of his necessary sojourn with the wicked.*

A Song of degrees.

IN my distress I cried unto the LORD, and he [1,a]heard me.

2 [b,c]Deliver my soul, O LORD, from [d,e]lying lips, *and* from a [f]deceitful tongue.

3 What shall be given unto thee? or what shall be done unto thee, thou [f]false tongue?

4 Sharp [g]arrows of the mighty, with coals of [h]juniper.

5 Woe is me, that I sojourn in Mē'sech, *that* I dwell in the tents of [i]Kē'där!

6 My soul hath long dwelt with him that hateth [j]peace.

7 I *am for* [j]peace: but when I speak, they *are* for war.

## PSALM 121

*The safety of those who trust in God's protection.*

A Song of degrees.

I WILL lift up mine eyes unto the [1]hills, from whence cometh my help.

2 [a]My help *cometh* from the

---

157

n *Persecution, of the righteous,* John 15:20.

o *Integrity,* Job 2:3.

158

p *Righteous, grieved on account of wickedness of the wicked,* Psa. 64:10.

q *Sin, repugnant to the righteous,* Rom. 5:12.

r *Disobedience to God,* Eph. 5:6.

24 R. V. treacherous dealers,

159

s *Word of God, love for,* see footnote, p. 894.

160

25 R. V. The sum of thy word is truth;

162

t *Joy,* Psa. 5:11.

163

u *Falsehood,* Job 21:34.

164

v *Praise,* Psa. 150:1.

w *Thankfulness, to God,* Acts 24:3.

165

x *Spiritual Peace,* Gal. 1:3.

y *Stumbling, figurative,* Isa. 8:14.

26 R. V. And they have none occasion of stumbling.

166

z *Hope,* Prov. 13:12.

---

a *Obedience,* Heb. 5:8.

b *Commandments,* Deut. 8:2.

167

c *Word of God, love for,* see footnote, p. 894.

168

d *God, knowledge of,* Gen. 2:2.

169

e *Prayer, importunity in,* Acts 6:4.

f *Wisdom, spiritual, prayer for,* Prov. 2:2.

g *Spiritual Desire,* Psa. 42:1.

---

171

h *Praise,* Psa. 150:1.

172

i *Religious Testimony,* 2 Thess. 1:10.

173

j *Decision,* Isa. 50:7.

174

k *Law,* Deut. 33:2.

176

l *Prayer, confession in,* Acts 6:4.

1

a *Prayer, answered,* Acts 6:4.

1 R. V. answered

2

b *Prayer, in adversity,* Acts 6:4.

c *Adversity, prayer in,* Psa. 10:6.

d *Falsehood,* Job 21:34.

e *Speech, evil,* Col. 4:6.

f *Deceit,* vs. 2–4; Psa. 36:3.

4

g *Arrow, figurative,* 1 Sam. 20:20.

h 1 Kin. 19:4.

5

i *Kedar,* Jer. 49:28.

6

j *Peace,* Jer. 29:7.

1

1 R.V. mountains: From whence shall my help come?

2

a *Faith, exemplified,* Mark 11:22.

LORD, which [b]made heaven and earth.

3 [c,d]He will not suffer thy foot to be moved: he that [e]keepeth thee [f]will not slumber.

4 Behold, he that [e]keepeth Is′ra-el [f]shall neither slumber nor sleep.

5 The LORD *is* thy [e]keeper: the LORD *is* thy shade upon thy right hand.

6 The [g]sun shall not smite thee by day, nor the [h]moon by night.

7 The LORD shall [e]preserve thee from all evil: he shall preserve thy soul.

8 The LORD shall [e]preserve thy going out and thy coming in from this time forth, and even for evermore.

## PSALM 122

*The psalmist's delight in Jerusalem, 6 and prayer for the peace thereof.*

A Song of degrees of David.

I WAS glad when they said unto me, Let us go into the [a]house of the LORD.

2 Our feet shall stand within thy gates, O [b]Jē-ru′sā-lĕm.

3 [b]Jē-ru′sā-lĕm is builded as a city that is compact together:

4 [c]Whither the tribes go up, the tribes of the LORD, unto the testimony of Is′ra-el, to give [d]thanks unto the name of the LORD.

5 For there are set thrones of judgment, the thrones of the house of Dā′vid.

6 [e]Pray for the [f]peace of [b]Jē-ru′sā-lĕm: they shall prosper that love thee.

7 [e,f]Peace be within thy walls, *and* prosperity within thy palaces.

8 For my brethren and companions' sakes, I will now say, [f]Peace *be* within thee.

9 Because of the [a]house of the LORD our God I will seek thy good.

b *God, creator,* Gen. 2:2.

3

c *Promise, to the righteous,* vs. 4–8: 2 Cor. 1:20.

d *Righteous, promises to,* Psa. 64:10.

e *God, preserver,* vs. 3–8; Gen. 2:2.

f *God, faithfulness of,* Gen. 2:2.

6

g *Sun,* Josh. 10:12.

h *Moon,* Song 6:10.

1

a *Church, called house of the Lord,* 1 Kin. 9:3.

2

b *Jerusalem,* Judg. 19:10.

4

c *Annual Feasts,* Num. 15:3.

d *Thankfulness, to God,* Acts 24:3.

6

e *Patriotism,* Psa. 137:1.

f *Peace,* Jer. 29:7.

## PSALM 123

*The psalmist's confidence in God, and prayer to be delivered from contempt.*

A Song of degrees.

[a]UNTO thee lift I up mine eyes, O thou that dwellest in the [b]heavens.

2 Behold, as the eyes of [c]servants *look* unto the hand of their masters, *and* as the eyes of a maiden unto the hand of her mistress; so [d]our eyes [a]*wait* upon the LORD our God, until that he have [e]mercy upon us.

3 [f]Have [e]mercy upon us, O LORD, have mercy upon us: for we are exceedingly filled with [g]contempt.

4 [f]Our soul is exceedingly filled with the [g]scorning of those that are at ease, *and* with the contempt of the proud.

## PSALM 124

*Israel blesses God for a miraculous deliverance.*

A Song of degrees of David.

[a]IF *it had not been* the LORD who was [b]on our side, now may [c]Is′ra-el say;

2 If *it had not been* the LORD who [b]was on our side, when men [d]rose up against us:

3 Then they had swallowed us up quick, when their [e]wrath was kindled against us:

4 Then the waters had overwhelmed us, the stream had gone over our soul:

5 Then the proud waters had gone over our soul.

6 [f]Blessed *be* the LORD, [b]who hath not given us *as* a prey to their teeth.

7 Our soul is escaped as a bird out of the snare of the fowlers: the snare is broken, and we are escaped.

8 [a]Our help *is* in the name of the LORD, who [g]made [h]heaven and [i]earth.

1

a *Spiritual Desire, exemplified,* Psa. 42:1.

b *Heaven, God's dwelling place,* Luke 18:22.

2

c *Servant,* Jer. 2:14.

d *Faith, exemplified,* Mark 11:22.

e *God, mercy of,* Gen. 2:2.

3

f *Adversity, prayer in,* Psa. 10:6.

g *Scoffing,* Hab. 1:10.

1

a *Faith, exemplified,* Mark 11:22.

b *God, preserver,* Gen. 2:2.

c *Israel,* Ex. 4:22.

2

d *Persecution, of the righteous,* John 15:20.

3

e *Anger,* Psa. 37:8.

6

f *Praise,* Psa. 150:1.

8

g *God, creator,* Gen. 2:2.

h *Heavens, physical,* Psa. 8:3.

i *Earth, created,* Prov. 8:23.

**1**
*a* *Faith*, Mark 11:22.
*b* *Christian Graces, faith*, Gal. 5:22.
*c* *Promise, implied, to the righteous*, 2 Cor. 1:20.

**2**
*d* *Jerusalem*, Judg. 19:10.
*e* *Promise, to the righteous*, 2 Cor. 1:20.
*f* *Righteous, promises to*, Psa. 64:10.
*g* *God, preserver*, Gen. 2:2.

**3**
1 R. V. sceptre of wickedness

**4**
*h* *Prayer, intercessory*, Acts 6:4.

**5**
*i* *Wicked, contrasted with the righteous*, Psa. 73:3.
*j* *Backsliders, described*, Jer. 3:22.
*k* *Spiritual Peace*, Gal. 1:3.

## PSALM 125

*The safety of such as trust in God. 4 A prayer for the upright in heart.*

A Song of degrees.

THEY that [a,b]trust in the LORD [c]*shall be* as mount Zī'ŏn, *which* cannot be removed, *but* abideth for ever.

2 *As* the mountains *are* round about [d]Jĕ-ru'să-lĕm, so [e,f]the LORD *is* [g]round about his people from henceforth even for ever.

3 For the [1]rod of the wicked shall not rest upon the lot of the righteous; lest the righteous put forth their hands unto iniquity.

4 [h]Do good, O LORD, unto *those that be* good, and to *them that are* upright in their hearts.

5 As for [i]such as [j]turn aside unto their crooked ways, the LORD shall lead them forth with the workers of iniquity: *but* [k]peace *shall be* upon Iș'ra-el.

**1**
*a* *God, preserver*, Gen. 2:2.
*b* *Jews, after the captivity*, vs. 1–6; Neh. 4:2.

**2**
*c* *Music*, 2 Chr. 5:13.
*d* *Praise*, Psa. 150:1.
1 R. V. nations,

**3**
*e* *Thankfulness, to God*, Acts 24:3.

**4**
*f* *Adversity, prayer in*, Psa. 10:6.

**5**
*g* *Sower, figurative*, Matt. 13:3.
*h* *Weeping*, Ezra 3:13.
*i* *Promise, or ground of assurance, to the righteous*, 2 Cor. 1:20.
*j* *Reaping, figurative*, 1 Sam. 6:13.
*k* *Joy*, Psa. 5:11.

**6**
2 R. V. Though he goeth on his way weeping, bearing forth the seed; He shall come again with joy,

## PSALM 126

*The people of God celebrate their return from captivity, 4 and pray for further success.*

A Song of degrees.

WHEN the LORD [a]turned again the [b]captivity of Zī'ŏn, we were like them that dream.

2 Then was our mouth filled with laughter, and our tongue with [c,d]singing: then said they among the [1]heathen, The LORD hath done great things for them.

3 The LORD hath done great things for us; *whereof* we are [e]glad.

4 [f]Turn again our captivity, O LORD, as the streams in the south.

5 They that [g]sow in [h]tears [i]shall [j]reap in [k]joy.

6 [2]He that goeth forth and [h]weepeth, bearing precious seed, [g]shall doubtless come again with rejoicing, [j]bringing his sheaves *with him.*

## PSALM 127

*The vanity of human endeavors without God's blessing. 3 Children are his gift.*

A Song of degrees for Solomon.

[a,b]EXCEPT the LORD [c]build the house, they [d]labour in vain that build it: except the LORD keep the city, the [e]watchman waketh *but* in vain.

2 [f,g]*It is* vain for you to rise up early, to sit up late, to eat the [h]bread of sorrows: *for* so he [c]giveth his beloved [*,b]sleep.

3 Lo, [b,i]children *are* an heritage of the LORD: *and* the fruit of the womb *is his* reward.

4 As [j]arrows *are* in the hand of a mighty man; so *are* children of the youth.

5 Happy *is* the man that hath his quiver full of [k]them: they shall not be ashamed, but they shall speak with the enemies in the gate.

## PSALM 128

*The blessedness of the man that fears the Lord.*

A Song of degrees.

[a]BLESSED *is* [b]every one that [c]feareth the LORD; that walketh in his ways.

2 For [d,e]thou shalt eat the labour of thine hands: [f]happy *shalt* thou *be*, and *it shall be* well with thee.

3 [d,e]Thy wife *shall be* as a fruitful vine [1]by the sides of thine house: thy children like [g]olive plants round about thy table.

4 Behold, that [d,e]thus shall the man be [h]blessed that [c]feareth the LORD.

5 [d,e]The LORD shall bless thee out of Zī'ŏn: and thou shalt see the good of [i]Jĕ-ru'să-lĕm all the days of thy life.

6 Yea, thou shalt see thy chil-

**1**
*a* *Prosperity, from God*, Eccl. 7:14.
*b* *Temporal Blessings, from God*, vs. 1–5; Psa. 103:2.
*c* *God, providence of*, Gen. 2:2.
*d* *Works, insufficiency of*, 2 Tim. 1:9.
*e* *Watchman*, 2 Sam. 18:24.

**2**
*f* *Anxiety, unavailing*, 1 Pet. 5:7.
*g* *Worldliness*, 1 John 2:15.
*h* *Bread, figurative*, Ezek 4:13.

**3**
*i* *Children, the gift of God*, Mark 10:14.

**4**
*j* *Arrow*, 1 Sam. 20:20.

**5**
*k* *Children, a blessing*, Mark 10:14.

**1**
*a* *Spiritual Peace*, Gal. 1:3.
*b* *Righteous, happiness of*, Psa. 64:10.
*c* *Fear of God*, Acts 9:31.

**2**
*d* *Promise, to the righteous*, 2 Cor. 1:20.
*e* *Righteous, promises to*, Psa. 64:10.
*f* *Prosperity, from God*, Eccl. 7:14.

**3**
*g* *Olive, figurative*, Deut. 6:11.
1 R. V. in the innermost parts of thine house:

**4**
*h* *Temporal Blessings, from God*, Psa. 103:2.

**5**
*i* *Jerusalem*, Judg. 19:10.

* **SLEEP.** *From God*, Gen. 2:21; 1 Sam. 26:12; Psa. 127:2. *Of a laboring man, sweet*, Eccl. 5:12. *Of the sluggard*, Prov. 6:9, 10. *Of Jesus*, Matt. 8:24; Mark 4:38; Luke 8:23. *A symbol of death*, Job 14:12; Matt. 9:24; Mark 5:39; Luke 8:52; John 11:11–14; 1 Thess. 4:14. See footnote, DEATH, Num. 23:10.

6
i *Peace*, Jer. 29:7.
k *Nation, promises of peace to*, Isa. 2:4.

1
a *Enemy*, Prov. 24:17.
b *Persecution, of the righteous*, John 15:20.
c *Israel*, Ex. 4:22.

4
d *God, righteousness of*, Gen. 2:2.
e *Wicked, punishment of*, Psa. 73:3.
5
f *Prayer, imprecatory*, Acts 6:4.
g *Church*, Matt. 16:18.
6
h *Grass*, Isa. 40:7.

7
i Psa. 72:6; 90:6; Amos 7:1.
j *Reaping*, 1 Sam. 6:13.

8
k *Salutations*, Luke 1:44.

1
a *Afflictions, prayer in*, Psa. 34:19.
b *Repentance, exemplified*, vs. 1–4; Mark 1:4.
c *Prayer, importunity in*, Acts 3.4.
3
d *Prayer, confession in*, Acts 6:4.
e *Sin, confession of*, Rom. 5:12.
f *God, mercy of*, Gen. 2:2.
g *Sinfulness, universal*, Rom 3:23.
4
h *Sin, forgiveness of*, Rom 5:12.
i *Fear of God*, Acts 9:31.
5
j *Spiritual Desire, exemplified*, Psa. 42:1.
k *Word of God*, Psa. 119:9.
l *Hope*, Prov. 13:12.
m *Faith, exemplified*, Mark 11:22.

dren's children, *and* [i]peace upon [k]Īṣ'ra-el.[S Q]

## PSALM 129

*Israel's deliverances, 5 and prayer that the haters of Zion may be confounded.*

A Song of degrees.

MANY a time have [a]they [b]afflicted me from my youth, may [c]Īṣ'ra-el now say:

2 Many a time have [a]they [b]afflicted[C] me from my youth: yet they have not prevailed against me.

3 The plowers plowed upon my back: they made long their furrows.

4 The LORD *is* [d]righteous: he hath [e]cut asunder the cords of the wicked.[S]

5 [f]Let them all be confounded and turned back that hate [g]Zī'ŏn.

6 Let them be as the [h]grass *upon* the housetops, which withereth afore[C] it groweth up:

7 Wherewith the [i]mower filleth not his hand; nor he that [j]bindeth sheaves his bosom.

8 Neither do they which go by say, [k]The blessing of the LORD *be* upon you: we bless[C] you in the name of the LORD.

## PSALM 130

*The psalmist's confidence in God, 7 and exhortation to Israel to hope in him.*

A Song of degrees.

OUT of the [a,b]depths have I [c]cried unto thee, O LORD.

2 [b]Lord, hear my voice: let thine ears be attentive to the voice of my supplications.

3 [b,d,e]If thou, LORD, shouldest [f]mark iniquities, O Lord, [g]who shall stand?[S]

4 But *there is* [h]forgiveness with thee, that thou mayest be [i]feared.[S]

5 I [j]wait for the LORD, my soul doth wait, and in his [k]word do I [l,m]hope.

6 My soul [j]*waiteth* for the Lord more than they that watch for the morning: *I say, more than* they that watch for the morning.

7 [n]Let Īṣ'ra-el [l]hope in the LORD: for with the LORD *there is* [f]mercy,[C] and with him *is* plenteous [o]redemption.[S]

8 And he shall [o]redeem Īṣ'ra-el from all his iniquities.[Q]

## PSALM 131

*The psalmist professes his humility, and exhorts Israel to hope in God.*

A Song of degrees of David.

LORD, [a]my heart is not haughty,[C] nor mine eyes lofty:[C] neither do I exercise[C] myself in great matters, or in things too high[C] for me.

2 Surely I have [1]behaved and quieted myself, as a child that is [b]weaned of his mother: my soul *is* even as a weaned child.

3 [c]Let Īṣ'ra-el [d]hope in the LORD from henceforth and for ever.

## PSALM 132

*David's zeal for the house of God commended. 8 A prayer at the removing of the ark. 11 God's promises to David, 13 and to Zion.*

A Song of degrees.

A Messianic Psalm, in three parts, probably used responsively in the tabernacle service. The first part, vs. 1–5, was probably a solo by the leader. The second part, vs. 6–10, was sung by the whole choir. The third, vs. 11–17, was a solo, probably, impersonating Jehovah answering the prayer. The opening solo rehearses David's zeal for a temple (1 Sam. 7:1–13), then the people rejoice in divine worship (v. 7), and pray for priests and people (v. 9), and that the anointed, the Messianic hope, be not taken away; that is, that the covenant promise to David that the Messiah shall establish an everlasting kingdom shall not be forfeited in this time of Zion's desolation. The poem closes with the promise from Jehovah to keep his covenant (vs. 11, 12), to dwell in Zion (the church) (vs. 13, 14), to clothe her priests (ministers) with salvation, and fill the saints with joy and establish the Messiah with a kingly crown, who shall flourish and, according to the covenant, have a kingdom of which there will be no end (1 Chr. 17:11–14). The sublime imagery in the Psalm finds its fulfillment in the spiritual kingdom of Christ and its wonderful conquest of the world to the knowledge and worship of the true God.

[a]LORD, remember [b]Dā'vid, *and* all his afflictions:

2 How he [c]sware unto the LORD, *and* [d]vowed unto the [1]mighty *God* of Jā'cob;

7
n *Faith, enjoined*, Mark 11:22.
o *Redemption, of our souls*, Eph. 1:7.

1
a *Humility*, Prov. 22:4.

2
b *Children, weaning of*, Mark 10:14.
1 R. V. stilled

3
c *Faith, enjoined*, Mark 11:22.
d *Hope*, Prov. 13:12.

1
a *Adversity, prayer in*, Psa. 10:6.
b *David, desires to build a temple*, vs. 1-5; 1 Sam. 16:13.
2
c *Oath*, Num 5:19.
d *Vows*, vs. 2-5; Num. 30:2.
1 R. V. Mighty One

3
*e Self-denial*, Mark 8:34.

4
*f Sleep*, Psa. 127:2.

5
*g Zeal*, 2 Cor. 7:11.
2 R. V. A tabernacle

7
*h Church*, 1 Kin. 9:3.
*i Worship*, Gen. 22:5.
*j Footstool, figurative*, 1 Chr. 28:2.

8
*k Ark, in the tabernacle*, Ex. 25:10.

9
*l Prayer, intercessory*, Acts 6:4.
*m Minister, character and qualifications of*, Rom. 15:16.
*n Joy*, Psa. 5:11.

10
*o Prayer, pleas offered in*, Acts 6:4.
*p Intercession, influence of the righteous*, Jer. 27:18.

11
*q Prophecies, concerning the Messiah and their fulfillment*, Gen. 12:3.
*r Oath, attributed to God*, Num. 5:19.
*s Covenant, of God with men*, Deut. 29:1.
*t God, faithfulness of*, Gen. 2:2.
*u* Acts 2:30.
*v Solomon, prophecies concerning*, 2 Sam. 12:24.
*w Throne*, 1 Kin. 2:19.

12
*x Blessings, contingent upon obedience*, Deut. 11:26.

13
*y Zion*, 2 Sam. 5:7.

14
*z Church, God dwells in*, Matt. 16:18.

15
*a Church, prophecies concerning its prosperity*, Matt. 16:18.
*b Poor, God's care of*, Prov. 21:13.
*c Temporal Blessings*, Psa. 103:2.

3 Surely [e]I will not come into
the tabernacle of my house, nor
go up into my bed;
4 [e]I will not give [f]sleep to mine
eyes, *or* slumber to mine eyelids,
5 [g]Until [b]I find out a place for
the LORD, [2]an habitation for the
[1]mighty *God* of Jā′cob.[Q]
6 Lo, we heard of it at Ĕph′ra-
tah: we found it in the fields of
the wood.
7 We will go into his [h]taber-
nacles: we will [i]worship at his
[j]footstool.
8 Arise, O LORD, into thy
rest; thou, and the [k]ark of thy
strength.
9 [l]Let thy priests [m]be clothed
with righteousness; and let thy
saints shout for [n]joy.[S]
10 [o]For thy servant Dā′vid's
[p]sake turn not away the face of
thine anointed.
11 [q]The LORD hath [r,s]sworn *in*
truth unto Dā′vid; [t]he will not
turn from it; [u]Of the [v]fruit of
thy body will I set upon thy
[w]throne.[S T Q]
12 [x]If thy children will keep my
covenant and my testimony that
I shall teach them, their children
shall also sit upon thy [w]throne
for evermore.
13[S] For the LORD hath chosen
[y]Zī′ŏn; he hath desired *it* for his
habitation.
14 This *is* my rest for ever:
[z]here will I dwell; for I have desired it.[S]
15 [a]I will abundantly bless[G] her
provision: I will satisfy her [b]poor
with [c]bread.
16 [a]I will also clothe her priests
with [d,e]salvation: and her saints
shall shout aloud for [f]joy.
17 [g,h]There will I make the
[i]horn[G] of Dā′vid to bud: I
have ordained a lamp for mine
anointed.[Q]
18 [h]His enemies will I clothe
with shame: but upon himself
shall his crown flourish.

## PSALM 133

*The communion of saints, delightful.*

A Song of degrees of David.

BEHOLD, how good and
how pleasant *it is* for
[a,b,c]brethren to [d]dwell together
in *,[e]unity!
2 *It is* like the precious [1,f]oint-
ment upon the head, that ran
down upon the [g]beard, *even*
Aâr′on's beard: that went down
to the skirts of his garments;
3 As the [h]dew of [i]Hĕr′mon, *and*
*as the dew* that [h]descended upon
the mountains of Zī′ŏn: for there
the LORD commanded the blessing, *even* life for evermore.

## PSALM 134

*An exhortation to bless God.*

A Song of degrees.

BEHOLD, [a]bless[G] ye the LORD,
all *ye* servants of the LORD,
which by [b]night stand in the
[c]house of the LORD.[Q]
2 [a]Lift up your hands [1]*in* the
[c]sanctuary, and bless[G] the LORD.
3 [d]The LORD that [e]made
heaven and earth [f]bless[G] thee
out of Zī′ŏn.

## PSALM 135

*God's people exhorted to praise him for his mercy,* 5 *for his power,* 8 *and for his judgments.* 15 *The vanity of idols.* 19 *An exhortation to bless God.*

[a]PRAISE ye the LORD. Praise
ye the name of the LORD;
praise *him*, O [b]ye servants of
the LORD.[Q]
2 Ye that stand in the [c]house of
the LORD, in the courts of the
house of our God,
3 [a]Praise the LORD; for the
LORD *is* [d]good: [e]sing praises unto his name; for *it is* pleasant.

1
*a Church, fellowship in*, Matt. 16:18.
*b Fraternity*, Zech. 11:14.
*c Righteous, happiness of*, Psa. 64:10.
*d Fellowship, of the righteous*, 1 Cor. 1:9.
*e Peace*, Jer. 29:7.

2
*f Anointing, of priests*, Lev. 8:12.
*g Beard*, 1 Sam. 21:13.
1 R. V. oil

3
*h Meteorology*, Matt. 16:2.
*i Hermon*, Deut. 4:48.

1
*a Praise, enjoined*, Psa. 150:1.
*b Night, worship in*, Gen. 1:5.
*c Church*, 1 Kin. 9:3.

2
1 R. V. to

3
*d Prayer, intercessory*, Acts 6:4.
*e God, creator*, Gen. 2:2.
*f Benedictions*, Deut. 21:5.

1
*a Praise, enjoined*, Psa. 150:1.
*b Righteous, described*, Psa. 64:10.

2
*c Church*, 1 Kin. 9:3.

3
*d God, goodness of*, Gen. 2:2.
*e Music*, 2 Chr. 5:13.

**16** *d Salvation*, Acts 16:17. *e Spiritual Blessings, from God*, Eph. 1:3. *f Joy*, Psa. 5:11.
**17** *g* Luke 1:69. *h Jesus, prophecies concerning*, Matt. 1:21. *i Horn, figurative of power*, 1 King 1:39.

* **UNITY.** *Advantages of*, Prov. 15:22; Eccl. 4:9-12. *Fraternal*, Matt. 23:8. *Of the righteous*, Psa. 133:1; Isa. 52:8; Acts 4:32. *Enjoined among Christians*, 1 Cor. 1:10; Eph. 4:3; Phil. 1:27; 2:2. *Christ's prayer for, of the church*, John 17:11, 21-23. See footnote, FELLOWSHIP, 1 Cor. 1:9.

4 For the LORD hath [f]chosen Jā′cob unto himself, *and* [g]Ĭṣ′[S]-ra-el for his peculiar[G] treasure.

5 For I know that the LORD *is* great, and *that* our [h]Lord *is* above all gods.

6 Whatsoever the [h]LORD pleased, *that* [i]did he in [j]heaven, and in [k]earth, in the [l]seas, and all deep places.[S]

7 He [i]causeth the [m]vapours to ascend from the ends of the earth; he maketh [n]lightnings for the [o,p]rain; he bringeth the [q]wind out of his treasuries.

8 [i]Who [r]smote the [s]firstborn of [t]Ē′ġy̆pt, both of man and beast.

9 *Who* [i]sent [u]tokens[G] and wonders into the midst of thee, O [t]Ē′ġy̆pt, upon [v]Phā′raōh, and upon all his servants.

10 Who [i]smote great nations, and slew mighty kings;

11 [w]Sī′hŏn king of the [x]Ăm′ôr-ītes, and [y]Ŏg king of [z]Bā′shăn, and all the kingdoms of [a]Cā′-năan:

12 And gave [a]their land *for* an heritage, an heritage unto [b]Ĭṣ′-ra-el his people.

13 Thy name, O LORD, [c]*endureth* for ever; *and* thy [1]memorial, O LORD, throughout all generations.[S]

14 For the LORD will [d]judge his people, and [e]he will [f,g]repent[G] himself concerning his servants.[Q T S]

15[Q] The [h]idols of the [2]heathen[G] *are* [i]silver and [j]gold, the work of men's hands.

16 [h]They have mouths, but they speak not; eyes have they, but they see not;

17 [h]They have ears, but they hear not; neither is there *any* breath in their mouths.[Q]

18 They that make [h]them are like unto them: *so is* every one that [k]trusteth[G] in them.

19 [l]Bless[G] the LORD, O house of [b]Ĭṣ′ra-el: bless[G] the LORD, O [m]house of Aâr′on:

**4**
*f* *God, love of, exemplified,* Gen. 2:2.
*g* *Israel, a holy people,* Ex. 4:22.
**5**
*h* *God, sovereign,* Gen. 2:2.
**6**
*i* *God, providence of,* Gen. 2:2.
*j* *Heavens, physical,* Psa. 8:3.
*k* *Earth,* Prov. 8:23.
*l* *Sea,* Jer. 5:22.
**7**
*m* *Meteorology, phenomena of,* Matt. 16:2.
*n* *Lightning,* Job 28:26.
*o* *Rain,* 2 Sam. 1:21.
*p* *Temporal Blessings, from God,* Psa. 103:2.
*q* *Wind,* Job 37:17.
**8**
*r* *Plague,* Ex. 11:1.
*s* *Firstborn, of Egyptians, slain,* Zech. 12:10.
*t* *Egyptians, visited by plagues,* Gen. 50:3.
**9**
*u* *Miracles,* Luke 23:8.
*v* *Pharaoh, at the time of the Exodus,* Ex. 3:10.
**11**
*w* *Sihon,* Num. 21:21.
*x* *Amorites,* Gen. 14:13.
*y* *Og,* Num. 21:33.
*z* *Bashan,* Num. 32:33.

*a* *Canaanites, land of, given to the Israelites,* Ex. 23:28.
**12**
*b* *Israel,* Ex. 4:22.
**13**
*c* *God, eternity of,* Gen. 2:2.
1 Am. R. V. memorial name,
**14**
*d* *God, judge,* Gen. 2:2.
*e* *God, mercy of,* Gen. 2:2.
*f* *Repentance, attributed to God,* Mark 1:4.
*g* *Anthropomorphisms,* Gen. 11:5.
**15**
*h* *Idol,* 1 Kin. 15:12.
*i* *Silver,* 1 Chr. 28:14.
*j* *Gold,* Ezek. 7:19.
2 R. V. nations
**18**
*k* *Idolatry, folly of,* 1 Sam. 15:23.
**19**
*l* *Praise, enjoined,* Psa. 150:1.
*m* *Priest,* Lev. 1:5.

20 [l]Bless[G] the LORD, O [n]house of Lē′vī: ye that [o]fear the LORD, bless[G] the LORD.

21 [l]Blessed be the LORD out of Zī′ŏn, which dwelleth at [p]Jē-ru̧′sâ-lĕm. Praise ye the LORD.[T]

## PSALM 136

*The psalmist exhorts men to praise God as the creator of all things, 10 as the deliverer of Israel from Egypt, 17 and as the conqueror of their enemies.*

[a]O GIVE [b]thanks unto the LORD; for *he is* [c]good: for his [1,d]mercy *endureth* for ever.[S]

2 [a]O give [b]thanks unto the [e]God of gods: for his [1,d]mercy *endureth* for ever.

3 [a]O give [b]thanks to the [e]Lord of lords: for his [1,d]mercy *endureth* for ever.

4 To him who alone doeth great wonders: for his [1,d]mercy *endureth* for ever.

5[S] To him that by [f]wisdom [g]made the [h]heavens: for his [1,d]mercy *endureth* for ever.

6[S] To him that [g]stretched out the [i]earth above the waters: for [1,d]his mercy *endureth* for ever.

7 To him that made great [j,k,l]lights: for his [1,d]mercy *endureth* for ever:

8 The [j]sun to rule by day: for his [1,d]mercy *endureth* for ever:

9 The [k]moon and [l]stars to rule by night: for his [1,d]mercy *endureth* for ever.[S]

10 To him that smote [m]Ē′ġy̆pt in their [n]firstborn: for his [1,d]mercy *endureth* for ever:

11 And [o]brought out [p]Ĭṣ′ra-el from among them: for his [1,d]mercy *endureth* for ever:

12 With a [q]strong hand, and with a stretched[G] out [r]arm: for his [1,d]mercy *endureth* for ever.

13 To him which divided the [s]Red sea into parts: for his [1,d]mercy *endureth* for ever:

14 And made [t]Ĭṣ′ra-el to pass through the midst of it: for his [1,d]mercy *endureth* for ever:

15 But overthrew [u]Phā′raōh

**20**
*n* *Levites,* Deut. 10:8.
*o* *Fear of God,* Acts 9:31.
**21**
*p* *Jerusalem,* Judg. 19:10.

**1**
*a* *Praise, enjoined,* vs. 1–25; Psa. 150:1.
*b* *Thankfulness, to God,* Acts 24:3.
*c* *God, goodness of,* Gen. 2:2.
*d* *God, mercy of,* Gen. 2:2.
1 Am. R.V. loving-kindness
**2**
*e* *God, sovereign,* Gen. 2:2.
**5**
*f* *God, wisdom of,* Gen. 2:2.
*g* *God, creator,* Gen. 2:2.
*h* *Heavens, physical created,* Psa. 8:3.
**6**
*i* *Geology,* Psa. 104:5.
**7**
*j* *Sun,* Josh. 10:12.
*k* *Moon,* Song 6:10.
*l* *Stars,* Judg. 5:20.
**10**
*m* *Egyptians, firstborn of, destroyed,* Gen. 50:3.
*n* *Firstborn, of Egyptians, slain,* Zech. 12:10.
**11**
*o* *God, providence of,* Gen. 2:2.
*p* *Israel, led of God,* Ex. 4:22.
**12**
*q* *God, power of,* Gen. 2:2.
*r* *Arm, figurative,* Psa. 89:13.
**13**
*s* *Red Sea,* Ex. 10:19.
**14**
*t* *Israel, passes through the Red Sea,* Ex. 4:22.
**15**
*u* *Pharaoh, at the time of the Exodus,* Ex. 3:10.

16
v God, guideance of, Gen. 2:2.
w Guidance, Psa. 48:14.
19
x Sihon, Num. 21:21.
y Amorites, Gen. 14:13.
20
z Og, Num. 21:33.
a Bashan, Num. 32:33.
b God, mercy of, Gen. 2.2.
21
c Canaanites, land of, given to the Israelites, Ex. 23:28.
22
d Israel, Ex. 4:22.
23
e God, preserver, Gen. 2:2.
25
f God, providence of, Gen. 2:2.
g Temporal Blessings, from God, Psa. 103:2.
26
h Praise, Psa. 150:1.
i Thankfulness, to God, Acts 24:3.
1
a Babylon, Ezra 5:12.
b Judah, captivity of, 2 Chr. 11:17.
c Weeping, Ezra 3:13.
d Church, love for, Matt. 16:18.
e Zion, 2 Sam. 5:7.
2
f Harp, Dan. 3:10.
g Lev. 23:40; Isa. 44:4; Ezek. 17:5.

and his host in the [s]Red sea: for
his [1,d]mercy *endureth* for ever.
16 To him which [o,v,w]led his
[p]people through the wilderness:
for his [1,d]mercy *endureth* for
ever.
17 To him which smote great
kings: for his [1,d]mercy *endureth*
for ever:
18 And slew famous kings: for
his [1,d]mercy *endureth* for ever:
19 [x]Sī′hŏn king of the [y]Ăm′-
ôr-ītes: for his [1,d]mercy *endureth*
for ever:
20 And [z]Ŏg the king of [a]Bā′-
shăn: for his [1,b]mercy *endureth*
for ever:
21 And gave [c]their land for an
heritage: for his [1,b]mercy *endureth* for ever:
22 *Even* an heritage unto [d]Is′-
rael his servant: for [b]his [1]mercy
*endureth* for ever.
23 [e]Who remembered us in our
low estate: for [b]his [1]mercy *endureth* for ever:
24 And hath [e]redeemed us from
our enemies: for [b]his [1]mercy *endureth* for ever.
25 [f]Who giveth *,[g]food to all
flesh: for [b]his [1]mercy *endureth*
for ever.[S]
26 [h]O give [i]thanks unto the
God of heaven: for [b]his [1]mercy
*endureth* for ever.

## PSALM 137

*The afflictions of the Jews in captivity. 5 Their remembrance of Jerusalem, 7 and prayer for the punishment of their oppressors.*

+BY the rivers of [a]Băb′ȳ-lon,
there [b]we sat down, yea,
we [c]wept, when we remembered
[d,e]Zī′ŏn.
2 We hanged[G] our [f]harps upon
the [g]willows in the midst thereof.
3 For there they that carried
[b]us away captive required of us
a [h]song; and they that wasted
us *required of us* mirth, *saying,*
Sing us *one* of the songs of [e]Zī′ŏn.
4 How shall we sing the LORD'S
song in a strange[G] land?
5 [i,j]If I forget thee, O [k]Jĕ-ru′-
să-lĕm, [l]let my right hand forget
*her cunning*.[G]
6 [i]If I do not remember thee,
[l]let my tongue cleave to the [k]roof
of my mouth; if I prefer[C] not
[k]Jĕ-ru′să-lĕm above my chief
joy.
7 [m]Remember, O LORD, the
[n]children of Ē′dom in the day
of [k]Jĕ-ru′să-lĕm; who said, Rase[G]
*it*, rase[G] *it*, *even* to the foundation
thereof.
8 O daughter of [o]Băb′ȳ-lon,
who art to be destroyed; happy
*shall he be*, that [p]rewardeth thee
as thou hast served us.[Q]
9 Happy *shall he be*, that taketh and [q]dasheth thy little ones
against the stones.[Q]

## PSALM 138.

*The psalmist praises God for his faithfulness, 4 and declares that the kings of the earth shall praise him. 7 His confidence in God.*

*A Psalm* of David.

[a]I WILL [b]praise thee with my
whole heart: before[C] the
gods[G] will I sing praise unto thee.
2 I will [c]worship toward thy
[d]holy temple, and [b]praise thy
[e]name for thy [f]lovingkindness
and for thy [g]truth: for thou hast
magnified thy [h]word above all
thy name.[S T]
3 In the day when I cried thou
[i]answeredst me, *and* [j,k]strength-
enedst me *with* strength in my
soul.

3
h Music, 2 Chr. 5:13.
5
i Zeal, 2 Cor. 7:11.
j Church, love for, Matt. 16:18.
k Jerusalem, beloved, Judg. 19:10.
l Decision, Isa. 50:7.
7
m Prayer, imprecatory, Acts 6:4.
n Edomites, 2 Kin. 8:21.
8
o Babylon, city of, prophecies concerning, Ezra 5:12.
p Retaliation, Deut. 19:19.
9
q War, evils of, Judg. 3:2.
1
a Thankfulness, to God, Acts 24:3.
b Praise, Psa. 150:1.
2
c Worship, Gen. 22:5.
d Church, called holy temple, 1 Kin. 9:3.
e God, name of, to be praised, Gen. 2:2.
f God, love of, Gen. 2:2.
g God, truth, Gen. 2:2.
h Word of God, Psa. 119:9.
3
i Prayer, answered, instances of, Acts 6:4.
j Afflictions, consolation in, Psa. 34:19.
k Spiritual Blessings, from God, Eph. 1:3.

***FOOD.** *From God*, Gen. 1:29, 30; 9:3; 48:15; Job 36:31; Psa. 103:5; 104:14, 15; 111:5; 136:25; 145:15; 146:7; 147:9; Prov. 30:8; Isa. 3:1; Matt. 6:11; Acts 14:17; 1 Tim. 4:3–5.

Articles of: *Milk*, Prov. 27:27; *butter*, Deut. 32:14; 2 Sam. 17:29; *cheese*, 1 Sam. 17:18; Job 10:10; *bread*, Gen. 18:5; 1 Sam. 17:17; *parched corn*, Ruth 2:14; 1 Sam. 17:17; *flesh*, 2 Sam. 6:19; *fish*, Matt. 7:10; Luke 24:42; *vegetables*, Prov. 15:17; Rom. 14:2; Heb. 6:7; *fruit*, 2 Sam. 16:2; *dried fruit*, 1 Sam. 25:18; 30:12; *honey*, Song 5:1; Isa. 7:15; *oil*, Deut. 12:17; Prov. 21:17; Ezek. 16:13; *vinegar*, Num. 6:3; Ruth 2:14; *wine*, John 2:3, 10.

*Things prohibited as*, Ex. 22:31; Lev. 11:4–8, 10–20, 41, 42; 17:10–15; Deut. 14:3, 7, 8, 10, 12–19, 21. *Peter's vision concerning*, Acts 10:10–16. *Flesh unwarrantedly forbidden as*, 1 Tim. 4:3, 4. *Paul's teaching concerning the eating of flesh offered to idols*, Rom. 14:2–23; 1 Cor. 8:4–13; 10:18–32.

*Prepared by women*, Gen. 27:9, 14, 17; 1 Sam. 8:13; Prov. 31:15. *Thanks given before taking*, Mark 8:6; Acts 27:35. *A hymn sung after taking*, Matt. 26:30. *Men and women did not partake of, together*, Gen. 18:8, 9; Esth. 1:3, 9.

**+PATRIOTISM.** *Exhortation concerning*, 2 Sam. 10:12

5
*l Joy*, Psa. 5:11.
*m God, glory of*, Gen. 2:2.

6
*n God, condescension of*, Gen. 2:2.
*o Humility, rewards of*, Prov. 22:4.
*p Pride*, Prov. 16:18.

7
*q Faith, exemplified*, Mark 11:22.
*r God, preserver*, Gen. 2:2.

8
*s God, mercy of*, Gen. 2:2.
*t Man, created*, Job 4:17.

1
*a God, knowledge of*, vs. 1–24; Gen. 2:2.

2
*b Heart, known to God*, Psa. 44:21.

3
1 R. V. searchest out

6
*c God, unsearchable*, Gen. 2:2.
*d Ignorance, concerning God*, Acts 3:17.

7
*e God, omnipresent*, Gen. 2:2.
*f God, presence of*, Gen. 2:2.

4 All the kings of the earth shall [b]praise thee, O LORD, when they hear the words of thy mouth.

5 Yea, they shall [l]sing in the ways of the LORD: for great *is* the [m]glory of the LORD.

6 Though the LORD *be* high, yet hath he [n]respect[c] unto the [o]lowly: but the [p]proud he knoweth afar off.

7 [i]Though I walk in the midst of trouble, [q]thou wilt [r]revive me: thou shalt stretch forth thine hand against the wrath of mine enemies, and thy right hand shall save me.

8 The LORD will perfect[c] *that which* concerneth me: thy [s]mercy, O LORD, *endureth* for ever: forsake not the [t]works of thine own hands.[s]

## PSALM 139.

*The psalmist sets forth God's omniscience and omnipresence. 19 His hatred of the wicked, 23 and prayer to God.*

To the chief Musician, A Psalm of David.

O[s] LORD, thou hast [a]searched me, and known *me*.[Q]

2 Thou [a]knowest my downsitting and mine uprising, thou understandest my [b]thought afar off.

3 Thou [1]compassest my path and my lying down, and art [a]acquainted *with* all my ways.

4 For *there is* not a word in my tongue, *but*, lo, O LORD, thou [a]knowest it altogether.

5 Thou hast beset me behind and before, and laid thine hand upon me.

6 [c,d]*Such* [a]knowledge *is* too wonderful for me; it is high, I cannot *attain* unto it.

7[T] [e]Whither shall I go from thy spirit? or whither shall I flee from thy [f]presence?

8 If I ascend up into heaven, thou *art* [e,f]there: if I make my bed in [2,g]hell, behold, thou *art* [e,f]*there*.

9 *If* I take the wings of the morning, *and* dwell in the uttermost parts of the sea;

10 Even [e,f]there shall thy hand [h]lead me, and thy right hand shall hold me.

11 If I say, Surely the darkness shall cover me; [3]even the night shall be light about me.

12 [4]Yea, [e,f]the darkness hideth not from thee; but the night shineth as the day: the darkness and the light *are* both alike *to thee*.

13 For [i]thou hast possessed my reins: thou hast covered me in my mother's womb.

14 [j]I will praise thee; for I am fearfully *and* wonderfully [k,l]made: marvellous *are* thy [m]works; and *that* my soul knoweth right well.[Q]

15 My substance [a]was not hid from thee, when I was [k]made in secret, *and* [l]curiously[G] wrought in the lowest parts of the earth.

16 Thine eyes [a]did see my substance, yet being unperfect; and in thy *book all *my* [l]*members* were written, *which* in continuance were fashioned, when *as yet there was* none of them.

17 [n]How precious also are thy thoughts unto me, O God! how great is the sum of them!

18 *If* I should count them, they are more in number than the sand: when I awake, I am still with thee.

19 Surely thou wilt [o]slay the wicked, O God: [p]depart from me therefore, [q]ye [5]bloody men.

20 For they [r]speak against thee

8
*g Hell*, Mark 9:43.
2 R. V. Sheol,

10
*h God, guidance of*, Gen. 2:2.

11
3 R. V. And the light about me shall be night;

12
4 R. V. Even

13
*i God, creator*, Gen. 2:2.

14
*j Thankfulness, to God*, Acts 24:3.
*k Man, created*, Job 4:17.
*l Physiology*, vs. 14–16; Job 10:11.
*m Works of God*, Psa. 40:5.

17
*n Meditation*, Psa. 49:3.

19
*o Wicked, punishment of*, Psa. 73:3.
*p Sin, repugnant to the righteous*, Rom. 5:12.
*q Evil Company, the righteous shun*, Prov. 13:20.
5 R. V. bloodthirsty

20
*r Blasphemy, in reproaching God*, 2 Sam. 12:14.

*Religious ceremonial for the fostering of, enjoined*, Deut. 26:1–11. *Appealed to, in battle*, 2 Sam. 10:12.

**Instances of:** *Deborah and Barak*, Judg. 4:5. *The tribes of Zebulun and Naphtali*, Judg. 5:18–20. *Eli*, 1 Sam. 4:17, 18. *Phinehas' wife*, 1 Sam. 4:19–22. *Joab*, 2 Sam. 10:12. *Uriah*, 2 Sam. 11:11. *The Psalmist*, Psa. 51:18; 85:1–13. *Hadad*, 1 Kin. 11:21,22. *The lepers of Samaria*, 2 Kin. 7:9. *Jewish exiles*, Neh. 1:1–11; 2:1–20; Psa. 137:1–6. *Nehemiah*, Neh. 1:2, 4–11; 2:3. *The Jews in public defense*, Neh. 2:3; 4:1–23. *Jeremiah*, Jer. 8:11, 21, 22; 9:1, 2; Lam. 5:1–22.

**Lack of:** *The tribes of Reuben, Asher, and Dan, and inhabitants of Meroz in Deborah's campaign against Sisera*, Judg. 5:15–17, 23. *The inhabitants of Succoth and Penuel in Gideon's campaign against the kings of Midian*, Judg. 8:4–17.

*** BOOK. Figurative:** OF LIFE: *Names, of righteous written in*, Ex. 32:32; Dan. 12:1; Luke 10:20; Phil. 4:3; Heb. 12:23; Rev. 3:5; 21:27; *of wicked blotted out of*, Ex. 32:33; Rev. 22:18, 19; *of wicked not written in*, Rev. 13:8; 17:8.

OF REMEMBRANCE, Psa. 56:8; 139:16; Mal. 3:16; Rev. 20:12. See footnote, BOOK, p. 224.

s *Profanation, of God's name,* Lev. 22:32.
t *God, name of, not to be profaned,* Gen. 2:2.

21
u *Zeal,* 2 Cor. 7:11.

23
v *Spiritual Desire,* Psa. 42:1.

24
w *Guidance, prayer for,* Psa. 48:14.
x *Wisdom, prayer for spiritual,* Prov. 2:2.

1
a *Prayer, in adversity,* Acts 6:4.
b *Adversity, prayer in,* Psa. 10:6.

2
c *Evil Imagination,* Gen. 6:5.
d *Heart, unregenerate,* Psa. 44:21.

3
e *Falsehood,* Job 21:34.
f *Slander,* Prov. 10:18.
g *Speech, evil,* Col. 4:6.
h *Serpent, venom of,* Num. 21:6.
i *Adder,* Gen. 49:17.
j Rom. 3:13.

4
1 R V. thrust aside my steps.

5
k *Snare, figurative,* Amos 3:5.
l *Rope, figurative,* 1 Kin. 20:31.
m *Net, figurative,* Isa. 51:20.

6
n *Faith, exemplified,* Mark 11:22.

7
o *God, preserver,* Gen. 2:2.

wickedly, *and* thine enemies [s]take *thy* [t]*name* in vain.

21 [p,u]Do not I hate them, O LORD, that hate thee? and [p,u]am not I grieved with those that rise up against thee?[Q]

22 I [u]hate them with perfect[G] hatred: I count them mine enemies.

23 [v]Search me, O God, and know my heart: try me, and know my thoughts:

24 And see if *there be any* wicked way in me, and [v,w,x]lead me in the way everlasting.[S]

## PSALM 140.

*The psalmist entreats to be delivered from the hands of the wicked; 8 and prays against them. 12 His confidence in God.*

To the chief Musician, A Psalm of David.

[a,b]DELIVER me, O LORD, from the evil man: preserve me from the violent man;

2 Which [c]imagine mischiefs[G] *in their* [d]heart; continually are they gathered together *for* war.

3 They have sharpened their [e,f,g]tongues like a [h]serpent; [i,j]adders' poison *is* under their lips.[Q] [Sē'lah.[G]

4 [a,b]Keep me, O LORD, from the hands of the wicked; preserve me from the violent man; who have purposed to [1]overthrow my goings.

5 The proud have hid a [k]snare for me, and [l]cords; they have spread a [m]net by the wayside; they have set gins[G] for me. [Sē'lah.

6 I said unto the LORD, [n]Thou *art* my God: [a,b]hear the voice of my supplications, O LORD.

7 O GOD the Lord, the [o]strength of my salvation, thou hast covered my head in the day of battle.

8 [a,b]Grant not, O LORD, the desires of the wicked: further not his wicked device; *lest* they exalt themselves. [Sē'lah.

9 *As for* the head of those that compass me about, [p]let the mischief of their own lips cover them.

10 [p]Let burning coals fall upon them: let them be cast into the fire; into deep pits, that they rise not up again.

11 [2]Let not an [f,g]evil speaker be established in the earth: evil shall hunt the violent man to overthrow *him.*

12 [n,q]I know that the LORD will maintain the cause of the [r]afflicted, *and* the right of the [s]poor.

13 Surely the righteous shall give [t,u]thanks unto thy name: the upright shall dwell in thy presence.

## PSALM 141.

*The psalmist prays that God would hear him; 3 that he would keep him from the power of temptation, 8 and from the snares of the wicked.*

A Psalm of David.

LORD, I [a,b]cry unto thee: make haste unto me; give ear unto my voice, when I cry unto thee.

2 Let my [a]prayer be set forth before thee *as* [c]incense; *and* the lifting up of my hands *as* the evening [d]sacrifice.[Q]

3 Set a [e]watch, O LORD, before my mouth; [f]keep the door of my lips.[Q]

4 Incline not my heart to *any* evil thing, to practise wicked works with [g]men that work iniquity: and let me not eat of their dainties.

5 [h]Let the righteous smite me; *it shall be* a kindness: and let him [i]reprove me; *it shall be* [1]an excellent oil, *which* shall not break my head: for yet my prayer also *shall be* in their calamities.

6 When their [j]judges are overthrown in stony places, they shall hear my words; for they are sweet.

9
p *Prayer, imprecatory,* Acts 6:4.

11
2 R. V. An evil speaker shall not be established

12
q *Adversity, consolation in,* Psa. 10:6.
r *Afflicted,* Job 34:28.
s *Poor, God's care of,* Prov. 21:13.

13
t *Praise,* Psa. 150:1.
u *Thankfulness, to God,* Acts 24:3.

1
a *Prayer, importunity in,* Acts 6:4.
b *Adversity, prayer in,* Psa. 10:6.

2
c *Incense, figurative,* Ex. 37:29.
d *Offerings, daily,* Lev. 6:17.

3
e *Watchfulness, over the tongue,* Matt. 24.42.
f *Speech, wise,* Col. 4:6.

4
g *Evil Company, the righteous shun,* Prov. 13:20.

5
h *Humility,* Prov. 22:4.
i *Reproof,* Prov. 17:10.
1 R. V. as oil upon the head: Let not my head refuse it: For even in their wickedness shall my prayer continue.

6
j *Judge, corrupt,* Judg. 2:18.

7 Our bones are scattered at
the grave's mouth, as when one
[2]cutteth and cleaveth *wood* upon
the earth.
8 But mine eyes *are* unto thee,
O GOD the Lord: in thee is my
[k]trust; leave not my soul destitute.
9 Keep me from the [l]snares
*which* they have laid for me,
and the gins[C] of the workers of
iniquity.
10 [m]Let the wicked [n]fall into
their own [o]nets, whilst that I
withal[C] escape.

## PSALM 142.

*The psalmist shews that, in his trouble, God was his refuge and portion.*

[a]Maschil of David; A Prayer when he was in the cave.

I [b,c]CRIED unto the LORD
with my voice; with my
voice unto the LORD did I make
my supplication.
2 I [c]poured out my complaint
before him; I shewed before him
my [b]trouble.
3 When my spirit was overwhelmed within me, then thou
[d]knewest my path. In the
way wherein I walked have
they [e]privily[C] laid a [f]snare for
me.[S]
4 I looked on *my* right hand,
and beheld, but *there was* no
man that would know me: refuge failed me; [g]no man cared
for my soul.
5 I [c]cried unto thee, O LORD:
I said, [h]Thou *art* my refuge
*and* my portion in the land of
the living.
6 [b, c] Attend unto my cry;
for I am brought very low:
deliver me from my [i]persecu-
tors; for they are stronger
than I.
7 Bring my soul out of prison,
that I may [j]praise thy [k]name:
the righteous shall compass me
about; for thou shalt deal bountifully with me.

7
2 R. V. ploweth and cleaveth the earth,

8
k *Faith, exemplified,* Mark 11:22.

9
l *Snare, figurative,* Amos. 3:5.

10
m *Prayer, imprecatory,* Acts 6:4.
n *Sin, retroactive,* Rom. 5:12.
o *Net, figurative,* Isa. 51:20.

a *Music, symbols used in,* 2 Chr. 5:13.

1
b *Adversity, prayer in,* Psa. 10:6.
c *Prayer, importunity in,* Acts 6:4.

3
d *God, knowledge of,* Gen. 2:2.
e *Malice,* Eph. 4:31.
f *Snare, figurative,* Amos 3:5.

4
g *Despondency,* Eccl. 2:20.

5
h *Faith, exemplified,* Mark 11:22.

6
i *Persecution, prayer for deliverance from,* John 15:20.

7
j *Praise,* Psa. 150:1.
k *God, name of, to be praised,* Gen. 2:2.

## PSALM 143

*The psalmist prays for mercy; 3 laments his distress; 5 and prays for deliverance from his enemies, 10 and for spiritual guidance.*

A Psalm of David.

HEAR my [a]prayer, O LORD,
give ear to my supplica-
tions: in thy [b]faithfulness answer me, *and* in thy [c]righteous-
ness.
2 And enter not into judgment
with thy servant: [d,e]for in [f]thy
sight shall no man living be
justified.[S T Q]
3 [a]For the enemy hath [g,h]perse-
cuted my soul; he hath smitten
my life down to the ground; he
hath made me to dwell in [i]dark-
ness, as those that have been
long dead.
4 [j]Therefore is my spirit overwhelmed within me; my heart
within me is desolate.
5 I remember the days of old; I
[k]meditate on all thy [1]works; I
muse[C] on the work of thy hands.
6 I stretch forth my hands
unto thee: my soul [l,m]*thirst-
eth* after thee, as a [2]thirsty
land. [Se'lah.[C]
7 [a]Hear me speedily, O LORD:
my spirit faileth: hide not thy
face from me, lest I be like unto
them that go down into the
pit.[C]
8 Cause me to hear thy lovingkindness in the morning; for in
thee do I [n]trust: [l,o]cause me to
know the [p]way wherein I should
walk; for I lift up my soul unto
thee.
9 [a]Deliver me, O LORD, from
mine enemies: I flee unto thee
to hide me.
10 [l,o]Teach me to do thy will;
for thou *art* my God: thy spirit
*is* [q]good; lead me into the land
of uprightness.[T]
11 Quicken[C] me, O LORD, [r]for
thy name's sake: [3,a]for thy
[c]righteousness' sake bring my
soul out of trouble.
12 And of thy [s]mercy [t]cut off

1
a *Adversity, prayer in,* Acts 6:4.
b *God, faithfulness of,* Gen. 2:2.
c *God, righteousness of,* Gen. 2:2.

2
d *Depravity,* Job 15:14.
e *Sinfulness, universal,* Rom. 3:23.
f *God, holiness of,* Gen. 2:2.

3
g *Malice,* Eph. 4:31.
h *Persecution, of the righteous,* John 15:20.
i *Darkness, figurative,* Gen. 1:2.

4
j *Despondency,* Eccl. 2:20.

5
k *Meditation,* Psa. 49:3.
1 R. V. doings:

6
l *Spiritual Desire,* Psa. 42:1.
m *Thirst, figurative,* John 4:14.
2 R. V. weary

8
n *Faith, exemplified* Mark 11:22.
o *Wisdom, spiritual, prayer for,* Prov. 2:2.
p *Way, of holiness,* Isa. 35:8.

10
q *God, goodness of,* Gen. 2:2.

11
r *Prayer, pleas offered in,* Acts 6:4.
3 R. V. In thy righteousness bring

12
s *God, mercy of,* Gen. 2:2.
t *Prayer, imprecatory,* Acts 6:4.

mine enemies, and destroy all
them that afflict my soul: [r]for I
*am* thy servant.

## PSALM 144

*The psalmist blesses God for his mercy. 3 The vanity of man. 5 Prayer for deliverance from enemies.*

*A Psalm* of David.

[a]BLESSED *be* [1]the LORD my
strength, which teacheth
my hands to war, *and* my
fingers to fight:
2 My goodness, and my [b]fortress;
my high [c]tower, and my
[d]deliverer; my [e]shield, and *he*
in whom I [f]trust; who subdueth
my people under me.
3 LORD, [g]what *is* [h]man, that
[i]thou takest knowledge of him!
*or* the son of man, that thou
makest account of him!
4 [h]Man is like to vanity: his
[j]days *are* as a shadow that
passeth away.
5 [k]Bow thy heavens, O LORD,
and come down: [l]touch the
mountains, and they shall
smoke.
6 [m]Cast forth lightning, and
scatter them: shoot out thine
arrows, and destroy them.
7 [k]Send thine hand from above;
[2]rid me, and deliver me out of
great waters, from the hand of
strange children;
8 Whose mouth [n]speaketh vanity,
and their right hand *is* a
right hand of [o]falsehood.
9 I will [p]sing a new song unto
thee, O God: upon a [q]psaltery
[3]*and* an instrument of ten
strings will I sing [a]praises unto
thee.
10 *It is he* that giveth salvation
unto kings: who [d]delivereth
[r]Dā'vid his servant from the
hurtful sword.
11 [2,k]Rid me, and deliver me
from the hand of strange children,
whose mouth speaketh
vanity, and their right hand *is* a
right hand of [o]falsehood:
12 [4]That our sons *may be* as
plants grown up in their youth;
[5]*that* our daughters *may be* as
*corner stones, polished *after* the
similitude of a palace:
13 [4]*That* our garners *may be*
full, affording all manner of
store: [6]*that* our sheep may bring
forth thousands and ten thousands
in our [7]streets:
14 [8]*That* our oxen *may be*
strong to labour; *that there be* no
breaking in, nor going out; that
*there be* no complaining in our
streets.
15 [s]Happy *is that* people, that
is in such a case: *yea*, happy *is*
*that* people, whose God *is* the
LORD.

## PSALM 145

*The psalmist praises God for his greatness, 8 for his goodness, 11 for the glory of his kingdom, 14 and for his saving mercy.*

David's *Psalm* of praise.

[a]I WILL [b]extol thee, my God,
O king; and I will bless thy
name for ever and ever.
2 Every day will I [c]bless thee;
and I will [b]praise thy name for
ever and ever.
3 Great *is* the LORD, and
greatly to be praised; and his
greatness *is* [d]unsearchable.
4 One generation shall [b]praise
thy [e]works to another, and shall
[f]declare thy mighty acts.
5 I will [f]speak of the [g]glorious
honour of thy majesty, and of
thy wondrous [e]works.
6 And *men* shall speak of the
might of thy terrible acts: and I
will [f]declare thy [h]greatness.
7 They shall abundantly utter
the memory of thy great [i]goodness,
and shall sing of thy [j]righteousness.
8 The LORD *is* gracious, and
full of compassion; [k]slow to
anger, and of great [l]mercy.

---

1
*a* *Praise*, Psa. 150:1.
1 Am. R. V. Jehovah my rock,
2
*b* *Fortification, figurative*, Ezek. 17:17.
*c* *Tower, figurative*, 2 Chr. 26:9.
*d* *God, preserver*, Gen. 2:2.
*e* *Shield, figurative*, 1 Kin. 14:27.
*f* *Faith, exemplified*, Mark 11:22.
3
*g* *Humility*, Prov. 22:4.
*h* *Man, insignificance of*, Job 4:17.
*i* *God, goodness of*, Gen. 2:2.
4
*j* *Life, brevity and uncertainly of*, Eccl. 8:15.
5
*k* *Adversity, prayer in*, Psa. 10:6.
*l* *God, power of*, Gen. 2:2.
6
*m* *Prayer, imprecatory*, Acts 6:4.
7
2 R. V. Rescue
8
*n* *Speech, evil*, Col. 4:6.
*o* *Falsehood*, Job 21:34.
9
*p* *Music*, 2 Chr. 5:13.
*q* *Psaltery*, 1 Chr. 16:5.
3 R. V. *omits* and an instrument.
10
*r* *David*, 1 Sam. 16:13.

12
4 R. V. When our
5 R. V. And our daughters as corner stones hewn after the fashion of a palace;
13
6 R. V. And
7 R. V. fields;
14
8 R. V. When our oxen are well laden; When there is no breaking in, and no going forth, And no outcry in our streets:
*s* *Righteous, happiness of*, Psa. 64:10.

1
*a* *Poetry, acrostic*, vs. 1–21; Acts 17:28.
*b* *Praise*, Psa. 150:1.
2
*c* *Thankfulness, to God*, Acts 24:3.
3
*d* *God, unsearchable*, Gen. 2:2.
4
*e* *God, providence of*, Gen. 2:2.
*f* *Religious Testimony*, 2 Thess. 1:10.
5
*g* *God, glory of*, Gen. 2:2.
6
*h* *God, power of*, v. 16; Gen. 2:2.
7
*i* *God, goodness of*, Gen. 2:2.
*j* *God, righteousness of*, Gen. 2:2.
8
*k* *God, longsuffering of*, Gen. 2:2.
*l* *God, mercy of*, Gen. 2:2.

---

***CORNERSTONE.** **Figurative**, Psa. 144:12; Isa. 28:16. *Of Christ*, Psa. 118:22; Isa. 28:16; Matt. 21:42; Mark 12:10; Luke 20:17; Acts 4:11; Eph. 2:20; 1 Pet. 2:6–8.

9 The LORD *is* [i]good to all: and his tender [l]mercies *are* over all his works.[S]

10 All thy [m]works shall praise thee, O LORD; and thy saints shall bless[G] thee.

11[S] They shall [l]speak of the glory of thy kingdom, and talk of thy power;

12 To [l]make known to the sons of men his [h]mighty acts, and the [g]glorious majesty of his kingdom.[S]

13 Thy kingdom *is* an [n]everlasting kingdom, and thy dominion [n]*endureth* throughout all generations.[S]

14 [o,p]The[S] LORD [q]upholdeth all that fall, and raiseth up all *those that be* bowed down.

15 The eyes of all wait[G] upon thee; and [p]thou [e]givest them their [r,s]meat[G] in due season.

16 [e]Thou openest thine hand, and [s]satisfiest the desire of every living thing.[S]

17 The LORD *is* [j]righteous in all his ways, and [1,t]holy[G] in all his works.[S Q]

18 [u,v]The LORD *is* [w]nigh[G] unto all [x,y]them that [z]call upon him, to all that call upon him in [a]truth.[Q]

19[S] He will fulfil the desire of them that [b]fear him: he also will hear their cry, and will [c]save them.

20 The LORD [c]preserveth all them that love him: but all the wicked will he [d]destroy.[S]

21 My mouth shall speak the [e]praise of the LORD: and let all flesh bless[G] his [f]holy name for ever and ever.

## PSALM 146

*The psalmist vows perpetual praises to God. 3 He exhorts not to trust in man. 5 God, for his power, justice, mercy, and kingdom, is only worthy to be trusted.*

[a]PRAISE ye the LORD. Praise the LORD, O my soul.

2 While [b]I live will I [a]praise the LORD: I will sing praises unto my God while I have any being.

3 Put not your [c]trust in princes, *nor* in the son of man, in whom *there is* no help.

4 His [d]breath goeth forth, he returneth to his earth; in that very day his thoughts perish.

5 [e,f]Happy *is he* that *hath* the God of Jā′cob for his [g]help, whose [h]hope *is* in the LORD his God:[S]

6 Which [i]made [j]heaven, and [k]earth, the [l]sea, and all that therein *is*: which [m]keepeth [n,o]truth for ever:[S T Q]

7 Which [p]executeth judgment[G] for the [q]oppressed: which [r]giveth [s]food to the [t]hungry. The LORD looseth the [u]prisoners:

8 The LORD openeth *the eyes of* the [v]blind: the LORD raiseth them that are bowed down: the LORD [w]loveth the [x]righteous:

9 The LORD [p]preserveth the [y]strangers;[G] he [1]relieveth the [z]fatherless and [a]widow: but the way of the wicked he [b]turneth upside down.

10 The [c]LORD shall reign for ever, *even* thy God, O Zī′ŏn, unto all generations. Praise ye the LORD.[S]

## PSALM 147

*The psalmist exhorts to praise God for his care of the church, his power, his goodness, his mercy; 19 and for his statutes and judgments to his chosen people.*

[a]PRAISE ye the LORD: for *it is* good to sing praises unto our God; for *it is* pleasant; *and* praise is comely.[G]

2 The LORD doth [b]build up [c]Jē-rṳ′să-lĕm: he gathereth together the outcasts of [d]Ĭṣ′ra-el.

3 [e,f]He healeth the [g,h]broken in [i]heart, and bindeth up their wounds.[S G]

4[S] He [j]telleth the number of the [k]stars; he calleth them all by *their* names.

10
m *Works of God,* Psa. 40:5.

13
n *God, eternity of,* Gen. 2:2.

14
o *Afflictions, consolation in,* Psa. 34:19.
p *Promise, or ground of assurance, in adversity,* 2 Cor. 1:20.
q *God, preserver,* Gen. 2:2.

15
r *Food, from God,* Psa. 136:25.
s *Temporal Blessings, from God,* Psa. 103:2.

17
t *God, righteousness of,* Gen. 2:2.
1 R. V. gracious

18
u *Promise, to seekers,* 2 Cor. 1:20.
v *Righteous, promises to,* Psa. 64:10.
w *God, access to,* Gen. 2:2.
x *Penitent, promises to,* v. 1; Psa. 51:17.
y *Seekers,* Isa. 55:6.
z *Prayer, answer to, promised,* Acts 6:4.

a *Truth,* John 18:37.

19
b *Fear of God,* Acts 9:31.
c *God, preserver,* Gen. 2:2.

20
d *Wicked, punishment of,* Psa. 73:3.

21
e *Praise,* Psa. 150:1.
f *God, holiness of,* Gen. 2:2.

1
a *Praise,* vs. 1–10; Psa. 150:1.

2
b *Decision,* Isa. 50:7.

3
c *False Confidence,* Psa. 30:6.

4
d *Death,* Num. 23:10.

5
e *Spiritual Peace,* Gal. 1:3.
f *Righteous, happiness of,* Psa. 64:10.
g *Spiritual Blessings, from God,* Eph. 1:3.
h *Hope,* Prov. 13:12.

6
i *God, creator,* Gen. 2:2.
j *Heavens, physical,* Psa. 8:3.
k *Earth,* Prov. 8:23.
l *Sea,* Jer. 5:22.
m *God, faithfulness of,* Gen. 2:2.
n *Truth,* John 18:37.
o *God, truth,* Gen. 2:2.

7
p *God, mercy of,* Gen. 2:2.
q *Oppression,* Eccl. 5:8.
r *God, providence of,* Gen. 2:2.
s *Food, from God,* Psa. 136:25.
t *Poor, God's care of,* Prov. 21:13.
u *Prisoners, consolations for,* Psa. 79:11.

8
v *Spiritual Blindness,* 2 Cor. 4:4.
w *God, love of,* Gen. 2:2.
x *Righteous,* Psa. 64:10.

9
y *Foreigners,* Deut. 23:20.
z *Orphan,* Lam. 5:3.

a *Widow,* 2 Sam. 14:5.
b *Wicked, punishment of,* Psa. 73:3.
1 R. V. upholdeth

10
c *God, eternity of,* Gen. 2:2.

1
a *Praise, for God's attributes,* vs. 1–20; Psa. 150:1.

2
b *God, preserver,* Gen. 2:2.
c *Jerusalem,* Judg. 19:10.
d *Israel,* Ex. 4:22.

3
e *Afflictions, consolation in,* Psa. 34:19.
f *Promise, to penitents,* 2 Cor. 1:20.
g *Penitent, promises to,* Psa 51:17.
h *Repentance,* Mark 1:4.
i *Heart,* Psa. 44:21.

4
j *God, knowledge of,* Gen. 2:2.
k *Stars,* Judg. 5:20.

5 Great *is* our Lord, and of great [l]power: his [m,n]understanding *is* [o]infinite.[S]

6 The LORD [1,b]lifteth up the [p]meek: he [q]casteth the wicked down to the ground.

7 [r]Sing unto the LORD with [s]thanksgiving; sing praise upon the [t]harp unto our God:

8 Who [u]covereth the heaven with [v]clouds, who prepareth [w]rain for the earth, who maketh grass to grow upon the mountains.[Q]

9 He giveth to the [x]beast his [y]food, *and* to the young ravens which cry.[Q]

10 He delighteth not in the strength of the horse: he taketh not pleasure in the legs of a man.

11 The LORD taketh pleasure in them that [z]fear him, in those that [a]hope in his [b]mercy.

12 [c]Praise the LORD, O [d]Jē-ru̧'sā-lĕm; praise thy God, O Zī'ŏn.

13 For he hath strengthened the bars of thy gates; he hath blessed thy children within thee.

14 He maketh [e]peace *in* [f]thy borders, *and* filleth thee with the finest of the [g]wheat.

15 He sendeth forth his [h]commandment *upon* earth: his word runneth very swiftly.

16 He giveth [i]snow like [j]wool: he scattereth the hoarfrost like ashes.

17 He casteth forth his [k]ice like morsels: who can stand before his cold?

18[T] He sendeth out his word, and melteth them: he causeth his [l]wind to blow, *and* the waters flow.[Q]

19 He[Q] sheweth his [h]word unto Jā'cob, his statutes and his judgments[G] unto [m]Ĭs̨'ra-el.

20 He hath not dealt so with any nation: and *as for his* judgments,[G] they have not known them. [c]Praise ye the LORD.[T Q]

5
*l God, power of,* Gen. 2:2.
*m God, wisdom of,* Gen. 2:2.
*n Anthropomorphisms,* Gen. 11:5.
*o God, infinite,* Gen. 2:2.
6
*p Meekness,* Psa. 45:4.
*q Wicked, punishment of,* Psa. 73:3.
1 R. V. upholdeth
7
*r Music,* 2 Chr. 5:13.
*s Thankfulness, to God,* Acts 24:3.
*t Harp,* Dan. 3:10.
8
*u God, providence of,* Gen. 2:2.
*v Meteorology,* Matt. 16:2.
*w Temporal Blessings, from God,* Psa. 103:2.
9
*x Animals, God's care of,* Jer. 27:5.
*y Food, from God,* Psa. 136:25.
11
*z Fear of God,* Acts 9:31.

*a Hope,* Prov. 13:12.
*b God, mercy of,* Gen. 2:2.
12
*c Praise,* Psa. 150:1.
*d Jerusalem,* Judg. 19:10.
14
*e Peace,* Jer. 29:7.
*f Nation, peace given to, by God,* Isa. 2:4.
*g Wheat, figurative,* Ezra 6:9.
15
*h Word of God,* Psa. 119:9.
16
*i Snow,* Jer. 18:14.
*j Wool,* Judg. 6:37.
17
*k* Job 6:16; 38:29.
18
*l Meteorology,* Matt. 16:2.
19
*m Israel,* Ex. 4:22.

## PSALM 148

*The psalmist exhorts the celestial, 7 the terrestrial, 11 and rational creatures to praise God.*

[a]PRAISE ye the LORD. Praise ye the LORD from the heavens: praise him in the heights.

2 [b,c]Praise ye him, all his [d]angels: praise ye him, all his hosts.

3 [a]Praise ye him, sun and moon: praise him, all ye stars of light.

4 [a]Praise him, ye [e]heavens of heavens, and ye [f]waters that *be* above the heavens.

5 Let them praise the [g]name of the LORD: for he [h]commanded, and they were created.[S T]

6 He hath also [h]stablished[G] them for ever and ever: he hath made a decree which shall not pass.[S]

7 [a]Praise the LORD from the earth, ye [i]dragons, and all deeps:

8 [j]Fire, and hail; snow, and vapours; stormy wind fulfilling his word:[S T]

9 Mountains, and all hills; fruitful trees, and all cedars:

10 Beasts, and all cattle; creeping things, and flying fowl:

11 [k]Kings of the earth, and all people; princes, and all [l]judges of the earth:

12 Both [m]young men, and maidens; [n]old men, and [o]children:

13 Let them [a]praise the name of the LORD: for his name alone is [1]excellent;[G] his glory *is* above the earth and heaven.

14 He also exalteth the [p]horn of his people, the praise of all his saints; *even* of the children of Ĭs̨'ra-el, a people near unto him. [a]Praise ye the LORD.

## PSALM 149

*The psalmist exhorts to praise God for his love to Zion, 5 and for that power which he has given to the saints.*

[a]PRAISE ye the LORD. [b,c]Sing unto the LORD a new song, *and* his praise in the [d]congregation of saints.[Q]

2 Let [e]Ĭs̨'ra-el rejoice in him

1
*a Praise,* vs. 1–14; Psa. 150:1.
2
*b Praise, in heaven,* Psa. 150:1.
*c Worship,* Gen. 22:5.
*d Angel,* Heb. 1:13.
4
*e Heavens, physical,* Psa. 8:3.
*f Water,* 1 Kin. 17:10.
5
*g God, name of, to be praised,* Gen. 2:2.
*h God, creator,* Gen. 2:2.
7
*i Dragon,* Deut. 32:33.
8
*j Meteorology,* Matt. 16:2.
11
*k Rulers,* Ex. 18:21.
*l Judge,* Judg. 2:18.
12
*m Young Men,* Prov. 1:4.
*n Old Age,* Isa. 46:4.
*o Children,* Mark 10:14.
13
1 R. V. exalted:
14
*p Horn, figurative,* 1 Kin. 1:39.

1
*a Praise,* v. 1–9; Psa. 150:1.
*b Music,* 2 Chr. 5:13.
*c Worship,* Gen. 22:5.
*d Church,* Matt. 16:18.
2
*e Israel,* Ex. 4:22.

*f* *God, creator of man*, Gen. 2:2.
*g* *Zion*, 2 Sam. 5:7.
*h* *Joy*, Psa. 5:11.

3
*i* *Dancing, as a religious ceremony*, Eccl. 3:4.
*j* *Timbrel*, Ex. 15:20.
*k* *Harp*, Dan. 3:10.

4
*l* *God, love of*, Gen. 2:2.
*m* *Beauty, spiritual*, Psa. 45:11.
*n* *Meekness*, Psa. 45:4.
*o* *Salvation*, Acts 16:17.

5
1 R. V. for joy

6
*p* *Sword, figurative of judgments*, 1 Chr. 21:5.

7
2 R. V. nations,

8
*q* *King*, 2 Kin. 3:10.
*r* *Chains*, Dan. 5:7.
*s* *Fetters*, Mark 5:4.
*Iron*, Prov. 27:17.

that [f]made him: let the children of [g]Zī′ŏn be [h]joyful in their King.

3 Let them [a]praise his name in the [i]dance: let them [b,c]sing praises unto him with the [j]timbrel and [k]harp.

4 For the LORD taketh [l]pleasure in his people: he will [m]beautify the [n]meek with [o]salvation.

5 Let the saints be [h]joyful in glory: let them [b,c]sing [1]aloud upon their beds.

6 *Let* the high [a]*praises* of God *be* in their mouth, and a two-edged [p]sword in their hand;

7 To execute vengeance upon the [2]heathen, *and* punishments upon the people;

8 To bind their [q]kings with [r]chains, and their nobles with [s]fetters of [t]iron;

9 To execute upon them the judgment written: this honour have all his saints. Praise ye the LORD.

## PSALM 150

*An exhortation to praise God with instruments.*

*PRAISE ye the LORD. Praise God in his [a]sanctuary: praise him in the firmament of his power.

2 *Praise him for his mighty acts: praise him according to his excellent greatness.

3 *Praise him with the [b]sound of the [c]trumpet: praise him with the [d]psaltery and [e]harp.

4 *Praise him with the [f]timbrel and [g]dance: praise him with stringed instruments and [1]organs.

5 *Praise him upon the loud [h]cymbals: praise him upon the high sounding cymbals.

6 Let every thing that hath breath praise the LORD. Praise ye the LORD.

1
*a* *Church, called sanctuary*, 1 Kin. 9:3.

3
*b* *Music*, 2 Chr. 5:13.
*c* *Trumpet*, Josh. 6:4.
*d* *Psaltery*, 1 Chr. 16:5.
*e* *Harp*, Dan. 3:10.

4
*f* *Timbrel*, Ex. 15:20.
*g* *Dancing*, Eccl. 3:4.
1 R. V. the pipe.

5
*h* *Cymbal*, 1 Chr. 13:8.

* **PRAISE.** *Exemplified*, Psa. 7:17; 22:22, 23; 28:6, 7; 32:11; 34:1–3; 41:1–3; 42:4; 51:15; 65:1; 71:8, 14, 15; 75:1; 79:13; 81:1; 84:4; 86:12; 89:95; 104:33, 34; 109:30; 113:1, 2; 115:18; 118:15; 140:13; 145:1–21; 146:1–10; 148; 149; 150; Isa. 24:15, 16; 25:1; 35:10; 38:19; 43:21; 49:13; 51:3; 52:7–10; Jer. 31:7; Rom. 11:36; 16:27; 1 Cor. 15:57; Eph. 3:20, 21; Heb. 2:12; Jude 25; Rev. 1:6; 14:7.

*With music*, Psa. 33:2, 3; 43:3, 4; 47:1, 6, 7; 57:7–9 (with 108:1–3); 66:1, 2, 4; 67:4; 68:4, 32–34; 69:30; 71:22; 81:1; 92:1–3; 95:1, 2; 98:4–6; 104:33; 144:9; 149:2, 3; 150:3–5; Jas. 5:13.

*Daily*, 1 Chr. 23:30; Psa. 92:1, 2; 145:2. *In the night*, Psa. 42:8; 63:5, 6; 77:6; 92:1–3; 119:62; 134:1; 149:5; Acts 16:25. *Seven times a day*, Psa. 119:164.

*Congregational*, Psa. 22:22; 26:12; 68:26; 111:1; 116:18, 19; 134:1, 2; 135:2; 149:1.

*For God's goodness and mercy*, Psa. 13:6· 63:3–6; 100:5; 101:1; 106:1, 48; 107:8, 9, 15, 21, 31; 117:2; 118:29; 136:1–26; 138:2; 144:1, 2; 145:7–9, 14–21; 146:7–9; Isa. 12:1–6; Jer. 33:11. *For God's greatness*, Psa. 48:1; 145:3, 10–12; 147:1–20; Isa. 24:14. *For God's holiness*, Psa. 99:3, 5, 9. *For God's works*, Psa. 9:1, 2; 107:8, 9, 15, 21, 31, 32; 145:4–6, 10–13; 147:12–18; 150:2.

*For deliverance from enemies*, Gen. 14:20; Psa. 44:7, 8; 54:6, 7; 69:16.

*For salvation*, Isa. 61:3.

*Enjoined*, Deut. 8:10; Psa. 9:11; 30:4; 32:11; 33:1–3; 69:34; 70:4; 95:1, 2, 6, 7; 96:1–4, 7–9; 97:12; 100:1–5; 105:1–5; 117:1; 134:1, 2; 135:1–3, 19–21; Isa. 42:10–12; Eph. 5:19; Heb. 13:15; 1 Pet. 4:11; 5:11. *All nations to praise God*, Psa. 69:34; 103:22; 148:1–14. *Angels exhorted to*, Psa. 103:20, 21; 148:2. *In heaven*, Neh. 9:6; Job 38:7; Psa. 103:20, 21; 148:2–4; Isa. 6:3; Ezek. 3:12; Luke 2:13, 14; 15:7, 10.

**Songs of:** *Of Moses, after the passage of the Red Sea*, Ex. 15:1–19. *Of Miriam*, Ex. 15:21. *Of Deborah, after defeating the Canaanites*, Judg. 5. *Of Hannah*, 1 Sam. 2:1–10. *Of David, celebrating his deliverance from the hand of Saul*, 2 Sam. 22; *on bringing the ark to Zion*, 1 Chr. 16:8–36.

**Psalms of:** *For God's goodness to Israel*, Psa. 46, 48, 65, 66, 68, 76, 81, 85, 98, 105, 124, 126, 129, 135, 136. *For God's goodness to righteous men*, Psa. 23, 34, 36, 91, 100, 103, 107, 117, 121. *For God's goodness to individuals*, Psa. 9, 18, 22, 30, 40, 75, 103, 108, 116, 118, 138, 144. *For God's attributes*, Psa. 8, 19, 22, 24, 29, 33, 47, 50, 65, 66, 76, 77, 92, 93, 95, 96, 97, 98, 99, 104, 111, 113, 114, 115, 139, 147, 148, 150.

See footnote, THANKFULNESS, Acts 24:3.

**Instances of:** *Israelites*, 2 Chr. 7:2, 3; Neh. 9:5, 6. *The chorus when Solomon brought the ark into the temple*, 2 Chr. 5:13. *Daniel*, Dan. 2:20, 23. *Nebuchadnezzar*, Dan. 4:37 *Jonah*, Jonah 2:9. *Mary*, Luke 1:46–55. *Shepherds*, Luke 2:20. *The leper*, Luke 17:15. *Jesus and his disciples*, Matt. 26:30; Mark 14:26. *Disciples*, Acts 2:46, 47; 4:24. *Paul and Silas, in prison*, Acts 16:25.

# THE PROVERBS

## CHAPTER 1

*The design of the book. 7 An exhortation to fear God, 10 and to avoid the enticements of the wicked. 20 Wisdom reproves the simple; 24 and solemnly warns despisers.*

THE [a]proverbs of [b,c]Sŏl′o-
mon the son of [d]Dā′vid,
king of [e]Is̱′ra-el;
2 To know [f]wisdom and [g]in-
struction; to perceive the words
of understanding;
3 To receive [1]the [g]instruction
of [h]wisdom, [i]justice, and judgment, and [j]equity;
4 To give subtilty to the simple, to the *young man [k]knowl-
edge and [h]discretion.
5 A wise *man* will hear, and
will increase [l]learning; and a
man of understanding shall attain unto wise [l]counsels:
6 To understand a [a]proverb,
and [2]the interpretation; the
words of the wise, and their
[m]dark sayings.
7 ¶ The [n]fear of the LORD *is*
the beginning of [k]knowledge:
*but* [3,o]fools [p]despise [f]wisdom
and [g]instruction.
8 My *,[q]son, [r]hear the [g]in-
struction of thy [s]father, and
forsake not the law of thy
[t]mother:
9 For they *shall be* [4]an ornament of grace unto thy head,
and [u]chains about thy neck.
10 ¶ My *,[q]son, if [v,w]sinners
[x]entice thee, [y,z]consent thou not.
11 If they [a]say, Come with us,
let us [b]lay wait for blood, let
us lurk privily for the innocent
without cause:
12 Let us swallow them up
alive as [5]the [c]grave; and whole,
as those that go down into the
pit:
13 [d]We shall find all precious
substance, we shall fill our
houses with spoil:
14 [a]Cast in thy lot [e]among us;
let us all have one purse:
15 My *son, [f,g]walk not thou
in the way with [h]them; refrain
thy foot from their path:
16 For their feet run to evil,
and make haste to [b]shed blood.
17 [i]Surely in vain the [j]net is
[k]spread in the sight of any bird.
18 And they lay wait for their
*own* blood; they lurk privily for
their *own* lives.
19 So *are* the ways of every one
that is [l]greedy of gain; *which*
[b]taketh away the life of the
owners thereof.
20 ¶ [m]Wisdom crieth [6]with-
out; she uttereth her voice in
the [7]streets:
21 [m]She crieth in the chief
place of concourse, in the openings of the [n]gates: in the city she
uttereth her [o]words, *saying*,
22 [o]How long, ye simple ones,
will ye love simplicity? and the
[p]scorners delight in their [q]scorn-
ing, and [r]fools [s]hate [t]knowledge?
23 [u]Turn you at my [o]reproof:

**1** *a Proverbs, written by Solomon,* 1 Sam. 24:13. *b Solomon,* 2 Sam. 12:24. *c Rulers,* Ex. 18:21. *d David,* 1 Sam. 16:13. *e Israel, under the kings,* Ex. 4:22.
**2** *f Wisdom,* Prov. 2:2. *g Instruction,* Prov. 23:23.
**3** *h Prudence,* 2 Chr. 2:12. *i Righteousness,* Psa. 15:2. *j Justice,* Deut. 33:21. 1 R. V. instruction in wise dealing, In righteousness and judgment
**4** *k Knowledge,* Luke 11:52.
**5** *l Counsel,* Prov. 12:15.
**6** *m* Judg. 14:12; Ezek. 17:2. 2 R. V. a figure;
**7** *n Fear of God,* Acts 9:31. *o Fool,* Prov. 18:2. *p Spiritual Blindness,* 2 Cor. 4:4. 3 R. V. the foolish
**8** *q Children, commandments to,* Mark 10:14. *r Commandment, enjoining heed to instruction,* Deut. 8:2. *s Father,* Psa. 27:10. *t Mother,* 1 Kin. 2:20.
**9** *u Chains, figurative,* Dan. 5:7. 4 R. V. a chaplet **10** *v Wicked,* Psa. 73:3. *w Evil Company, forbidden,* Prov. 13:20. *x Temptation, leading into* Luke 11:4. *y Commandment, warning against temptation,* v. 15; Deut. 8:2. *z Temptation, admonitions against yielding to,* Luke 11:4.

**11** *a Temptation, leading into,* Luke 11:4. *b Homicide, felonious,* Deut. 5:17.
**12** *c Hell,* Mark 9:43. 5 R. V. Sheol,
**13** *d Robbers,* Hos. 6:9.
**14** *e Fellowship, with the wicked,* 1 Cor. 1:9.
**15** *f Children, commandments to,* Mark 10:14. *g Temptation, admonitions against yielding to,* Luke 11:4. *h Evil Company, forbidden,* Prov. 13:20.
**17** *i Proverbs,* 1 Sam. 24:13. *j Net,* Isa. 51:20. *k Hunting, fowling,* Gen. 27:5.
**19** *l Covetousness,* Isa. 57:17.
**20** *m Wisdom, personified,* Prov. 2:2. 6 R. V. aloud in the street; 7 R. V. broad places;
**21** *n Gates, place for public concourse,* Deut. 3:5. *o Reproof,* Prov. 17:10.
**22** *p Scorners, admonitions to,* Prov. 19:25. *q Scoffing,* Hab. 1:10. *r Fool,* Prov. 18:2. *s Spiritual Blindness,* 2 Cor. 4:4. *t Knowledge, fools hate,* Luke 11:52. **23** *u Repentance, exhortations to,* Mark 1:4.

* **YOUNG MEN.** *Wise, exemplified in Moses' wise choice,* Heb. 11:24–26. *Wise, a comfort to parents,* Prov. 10:1; 15:20; 29:3. *Foolish, a sorrow to parents,* Prov. 10:1; 17:25; 19:13, 26; 28:7. *Wise and foolish, contrasted,* Prov. 10:1; 13:1; 15:20. **Admonitions to,** Prov. 3:1–5; 4:20–27; 6:1–5, 20–25; 19:27; 22:15–23, 25, 26; 24:1–12, 15–34. *Against lust,* 2 Tim. 2:22, 23. *Against wine,* Prov. 23:20, 21, 29–35. *Against loving the world,* 1 John 2:13–17. *Against the snares of the harlot,* Prov. 5:3–14; 6:24–35; 7:1–27; 23:27, 28; 31:1–3. *Against the enticements of sinners,* Prov. 1:10–16. *Against evil companions,* Prov. 2:12–15; 4:14, 15; 24:1, 2.

**Exhortations to:** *To be sober-minded,* Tit. 2:6. *To be an example of piety,* 1 Tim. 4:12. *To keep the heart with all diligence,* Prov. 4:23. *To take heed to their ways,* Psa. 119:9. *To seek wisdom,* Prov. 2:1–8; 3:13–23; 4:5–13; 24:13, 14. *To obey parents,* Prov. 6:20–23; 23:22–26. *To obey the Lord,* Prov. 3:5–12. *To praise the Lord,* Psa. 148:12, 13. **Folly of:** *Exemplified, by Esau,* Gen. 25:31–34; Heb. 12:16, 17; *by Rehoboam's counselors,* 1 Kin. 12:8–11; *by Rehoboam,* 1 Kin. 12:13, 14; *by the rich young ruler,* Matt. 19:16–22; Mark 10:17–22; Luke 18:18–23; *by the prodigal,* Luke 15:11–32.

*v Wisdom, spiritual, from God,* Prov. 2:2.

**24**
*w God, longsuffering of, abused,* Gen. 2:2.
*x Call, personal,* Phil. 3:14.
*y Opportunity, spurned,* Gal. 6:10.
*z Impenitence,* Rom. 2:5.

*a Self-will,* Gen. 49:6.

**25**
*b Reprobates,* 1 Cor. 9:27.
*c Counsel, rejected,* Prov. 12:15.

**26**
*d Adversity,* Psa. 10:6.
*e Mocking,* 1 Kin. 18:27.
*f Remorse,* Matt. 27:3.
8 R. V. in the day of your

**27**
*g Afflictions,* Psa. 34:19.
9 R. V. a storm,
10 R. V. calamity

**28**
*h Wicked, prayer of, not heard,* Psa. 73:3.
*i Opportunity, lost,* Gal. 6:10.
11 R. V. diligently,

**29**
*j Wicked, described,* Psa. 73:3.
*k Spiritual Blindness,* 2 Cor. 4:4.
*l Knowledge, fools hate,* Luke 11:52.
*m Fear of God,* Acts 9:31.

behold, I will pour out my [v]spir-
it unto you, I will make known
my words unto you.
24 ¶ Because [w]I have [x]called,
and [y]ye [z,a]refused; I have
stretched out my hand, and no
man regarded;
25 But [b]ye have [c]set at nought
all my counsel, and would none
of my reproof:
26 I also will laugh [8]at your
[d]calamity; I will [e]mock when
your [f]fear cometh;
27 When your [f]fear cometh as
[9]desolation, and your [10]destruc-
tion cometh as a[†]whirlwind; when
[g]distress and anguish cometh
upon you.
28 Then shall they [h]call upon
me, [i]but I will not answer; they
shall seek me [11]early, but they
shall not find me:
29 For that [b,j]they [k]hated
[l]knowledge, and did not choose
the [m]fear of the LORD:
30 [b]They would none of my
[c]counsel: they despised all my
reproof.
31 Therefore shall [n]they eat of
the fruit of their own way, and
[o]be filled with their own devices.
32 For the [12]turning away of
the simple shall slay them, and
the prosperity of fools shall destroy them.

**31** *n Sin, fruits of,* Rom. 5:12. *o Sin, retroactive,* Rom. 5:12.
**32** 12 R. V. backsliding

33 But [p,q]whoso [r]hearkeneth
unto me shall dwell safely, and
shall be quiet from fear of evil.

## CHAPTER 2

*How to obtain wisdom. 10 The blessings thereof.*

MY [a]son, if [b]thou wilt receive
my words, and [1]hide my
commandments with thee;
2 So that [b]thou incline thine
ear unto *wisdom, *and* apply
thine heart to understanding;
3 Yea, if [b]thou [c,d,e]criest after
[2,f]knowledge, *and* liftest up thy
voice for *understanding;
4 If [b]thou [c,d,e]seekest her as
silver, and searchest for her as
*for* hid treasures;
5 [g]Then shalt thou [i,h]under-
stand the [i]fear of the LORD,
and find the *knowledge of
God.
6 For the LORD giveth *[j,k]wis-
dom: out of his mouth *cometh*
[f]knowledge and understanding.
7 [l]He layeth up sound *[j,k]wis-
dom for the righteous: [l]*he is* a
[m,n]buckler to them that walk
uprightly.
8 He keepeth the paths of
judgment, and [l,m]preserveth the
way of his saints.
9 [g]Then shalt thou understand
[o]righteousness, and judgment,
and [p]equity; *yea,* every good
path.
10 ¶ When *[j,k]wisdom entereth into thine heart, and

**33**
*p Promise, to the righteous,* 2 Cor. 1:20.
*q Righteous, promises to,* Psa. 64:10.
*r Obedience, rewarded,* Heb. 5:8.

**1**
*a Young Men,* Prov. 1:4.
*b Righteous, described,* vs. 1–9; Psa. 64:10.
1 R. V. lay up

**3**
*c Seekers,* Isa. 55:6.
*d Spiritual Desire,* Psa. 42:1.
*e Zeal,* 2 Cor. 7:11.
*f Knowledge,* Luke 11:52.
2 R. V. discernment,

**5**
*g Promise, to seekers,* 2 Cor. 1:20.
*h Righteousness, fruits of,* Psa. 15:2.
*i Fear of God,* Acts 9:31.

**6**
*j Spiritual Gifts, from God,* 1 Cor. 12:4.
*k Christian Graces,* Gal. 5:22.

**7**
*l Righteous, promises to,* Psa. 64:10.
*m God, preserver,* Gen. 2:2.
*n Shield, figurative,* 1 Kin. 14:27.

**9**
*o Righteousness,* Psa. 15:2.
*p Justice,* Deut. 33:21.

† **WHIRLWIND.** *Destructive,* Prov. 1:27. *From the south, in the land of Uz,* Job 37:9; *in the valley of the Euphrates,* Isa. 21:1; *in the land of Canaan,* Zech. 9:14. *From the north,* Ezek. 1:4. *Elijah translated in,* 2 Kin. 2:1, 11. *God answered Job in,* Job 38:1.
See footnote, METEOROLOGY, Matt. 16:2.
**Figurative:** *Of the judgment of God,* Jer. 23:19; 30:23. *Of the fruits of unrighteousness,* Hos. 8:7.

* **WISDOM,** Psa. 2:10; 90:12; Prov. 2:2; 7:4; 9:1–6; 10:13, 21, 23; 12:1; 15:33; 19:8, 20; Luke 1:17; 21:15; Jas. 1:5.
*Commended,* Prov. 3:13–26; 24:3–7; Eccl. 7:11, 12, 19; 10:10. *Is above value,* Job 28:12–19; Prov. 3:13–15; 16:16.
*Of, Joseph,* Gen. 41:16, 25–39; Acts 7:10; *Moses,* Acts 7:22; *Bezaleel,* Ex. 31:3–5; 35:31–35; 36:1; *Aholiab,* Ex. 31:6; 35:34, 35; 36:1; *other skilled artisans,* Ex. 36:2; *women,* Ex. 35:26; *Hiram,* 1 Kin. 7:14; 2 Chr. 2:14; *Solomon,* 1 Kin. 3:12, 16–28; 4:29–34; 5:12; 10:4–9, 24; 2 Chr. 9:3–8, 23; *Ethan, Heman, Chalcol, and Darda,* 1 Kin. 4:31; *the princes of Issachar,* 1 Chr. 12:32; *Ezra,* Ezra 7:25; *Daniel,* Dan. 1:17; 5:14; *Paul,* 2 Pet. 3:15; *the magi,* Matt. 2:1–12.
**Personified,** Prov. 1:20–33; 8:1–36; 9:1–18.
**Spiritual,** Deut. 32:29. *The fear of the Lord is the beginning of,* Psa. **111:10; Prov. 1:7; 9:10.** *Is revealed to the obedient,* **1 Cor. 2:6–16.**
*Exhortations to attain to,* Prov. 4:4–13; 22:17–21; 23:12, 19, 23; Rom. 16:19; Eph. 5:15–17; 2 Pet. 3:18.
*Prayer for,* Num. 27:21; Judg. 20:18, 23, 26–28; 1Kin. 3:7–9; 2 Chr. 1:10; Job 34:32; Psa. 119:18, 26, 27, 33, 34, 66, 68, 73, 80, 124, 125, 135, 144, 169; Col. 2:2. *To be possessed in humility,* Jer. 9:23, 24; Jas. 3:13. *Opportunity to obtain, forfeited,* Prov. 1:24–31.
*From God,* Ex. 4:12; Deut. 4:35, 36; 1 Chr. 22:12; Neh. 9:20; Job 11:5, 6; 22:21, 22; 28:20–28; 32:7, 8; 33:16; 36:22; Psa. 25:8, 9, 12, 14; 32:8; 51:6; 71:17; 94:12; 119:130; Prov. 2:6, 7; Eccl. 2:26; Isa. 2:3; 48:17; 54:13; Jer. 24:7; Dan. 1:17; 2:21–23; Matt. 16:17; John 6:45; 1 Cor. 2:12, 13; 12:8; 2 Cor. 4:6; Phil. 3:15; Jas. 3:17; 1 John 2:20, 27.
*Shall become universal,* Isa. 11:9; Jer. 31:34.
ILLUSTRATED: *By parable of virgins,* Matt. 25:1–13.
**Worldly:** *Desired by Eve,* Gen. 3:6, 7. *Misleading,* Isa. 47:10. *Increases sorrow,* Eccl. 1:18. *Shall perish,* Isa. 29:14. *Heavenly things not discerned by,* Matt. 11:25; Luke 10:21. *Gospel not to be preached with,* 1 Cor. 1:17–26; 2:1–14. *To be renounced in order to attain spiritual wisdom,* 1 Cor. 3:18–20.
*Admonitions against,* Col. 2:8; 1 Tim. **6:20, 21.** *Admonitions against glorying in,* Jer. 9:23, 24.

[f,k]knowledge is pleasant unto thy soul;

11 [q,r]Discretion shall preserve thee, *understanding shall keep thee:

12 [s]To deliver thee from the way of the [t]evil *man*, from the man that [u]speaketh froward things;

13 [t]Who leave the paths of uprightness, to walk in the ways of darkness;

14 [t]Who [v]rejoice to do evil, *and* delight in the frowardness of the wicked;

15 [t]Whose ways *are* crooked, and *they* froward in their paths:

16 [s,w,x]To deliver thee from the strange [y,z]woman, *even* from the stranger *which* [a]flattereth with her words;

17 Which [b]forsaketh the [3]guide of her youth, and [b]forgetteth the covenant of her God.

18 For her house inclineth unto [c]death, and her paths unto the dead.

19 None that go unto her return again, neither take they hold of the paths of [d]life.

20 That [e]thou mayest walk in the way of good *men*, and keep the paths of the righteous.

21 For [f,g]the upright shall dwell in the land, and the [h]perfect shall remain in it.

22 But the wicked shall be [i,j]cut off from the [4]earth, and the transgressors shall be rooted out of it.

## CHAPTER 3

*An exhortation to obedience, 5 to trust in God, 7 to fear him, 9 to honor him with our substance, 11 and to be patient in affliction. 13 The happiness secured by wisdom. 27 An exhortation to charitableness, 30 peaceableness, 31 and contentedness. 33 The miserable state of the wicked.*

MY [a,b]son, forget not my [c]law; but [d]let thine heart [e]keep my commandments:

2 [f]For [g,h,i]length of days, and [j]long life, and [k]peace, shall they add to thee.

3 [a,l]Let not [m]mercy and [n]truth forsake thee: bind them about thy neck; write them upon the table of thine heart:

4 [f,g]So shalt thou find [o]favour and good understanding in the sight of God and man.

5 ¶ [a,p,q]Trust in the LORD with all thine [r]heart; and [s]lean not [1]unto [t]thine own [u]understanding.

6 [a,d]In all thy ways acknowledge him, [f]and [v]he shall [w]direct thy paths.

7 [t,x]Be not [y]wise in thine own eyes: [z]fear the LORD, and [a]depart from evil.

8 [b]It shall be health to thy navel, and marrow to thy bones.

9 [c,d,e]Honour the LORD with thy substance, and with the [f]firstfruits of all thine increase:

10 [d,g,h]So shall thy *barns be filled with plenty, and thy [2,i]presses shall burst out with new wine.

11 ¶ [j]My [k]son, despise not the [l,m]chastening of the LORD; [n,o]neither be weary of his [3]correction:

12 For whom the LORD [p]loveth he [4,l]correcteth; even as a [q]father the son *in whom* he delighteth.

13 ¶ [r,s]Happy *is* the man *that* findeth [t]wisdom, and the man *that* getteth understanding.

14 For the merchandise of it *is* better than the merchandise of [u]silver, and the gain thereof than fine [v]gold.

---

**11**
*q Promise, to the righteous*, vs. 10–21: 2 Cor. 1:20.
*r Prudence*, 2 Chr. 2:12.
**12**
*s Evil Company, warnings against*, Prov. 13:20.
*t Wicked, described*, Psa. 73:3.
*u Speech, evil*, Col. 4:6.
**14**
*v Sin, love of*, Rom. 5:12.
**16**
*w Adultery*, Lev. 20:10.
*x Lasciviousness*, 1 Pet. 4:3.
*y Harlot*, Prov. 7:10.
*z Women, wicked*, Prov. 31:10.
*a Flattery*, Prov. 6:24.
**17**
*b Backsliders, described*, Jer. 3.22.
3 R. V. friend
**18**
*c Death*, Num. 23:10.
**19**
*d Life*, Eccl. 8:15.
**20**
*e Righteous, described*, Psa. 64:10.
**21**
*f Promise, to the righteous*, 2 Cor. 1:20.
*g Righteous, promises to*, Psa. 64: 10.
*h Perfection*, Heb. 6:1.
**22**
*i Wicked, punishment of*, Psa. 73:3.
*j Death, of the wicked, a judgment*, Num. 23: 10.
4 R. V. land, And they that deal treacherously
**1**
*a Children, commandments to*, Mark 10:14.
*b Young Men*, Prov. 1:4.
*c Word of God*, Psa. 119:9.
*d Commandment, enjoining obedience*, Deut. 8:2.
*e Obedience, enjoined*, Heb. 5:8.

**2**
*f Blessings, contingent upon obedience*, Deut. 11:26.
*g Promise, to the obedient, of long life*, 2 Cor. 1:20.
*h Righteous, promises to*, Psa. 64: 10.
*i Children, promises and assurances to*, Mark 10:14.
*j Longevity*, Psa. 91:16.
*k Spiritual Peace*, Gal. 1:3.
**3**
*l Commandment, enjoining mercy and truth*, Deut. 8:2.
*m Mercy*, Deut. 5:10.
*n Truth*, John 18:37.
**4**
*o Grace of God*, Rom. 4:16.
**5**
*p Commandment, enjoining faith, and forbidding self-confidence*, Deut. 8:2.
*q Faith, enjoined*, Mark 11:22.
*r Heart*, Psa. 44:21.
*s False Confidence*, Psa. 30:6.
*t Conceit, warnings against*, Prov. 26:5.
*u Reasoning*, Job 13:6.
1 R. V. upon
**6**
*v Promise, to the righteous, of guidance*, 2 Cor. 1:20.
*w God, guidance of*, Gen. 2:2.
**7**
*x Commandment, forbidding self-confidence, and enjoining the fear of God*, Deut. 8:2.
*y Wisdom, worldly*, Prov. 2:2.
*z Fear of God, enjoined*, Acts 9:31.
*a Evil, to be eschewed*, 1 Thess. 5:22.
**8**
*b Promise, to the righteous*, 2 Cor. 1:20.

**9** *c Commandment, enjoining liberality*, Deut. 8:2. *d Liberality, rewards for*, 1 Tim. 6:18. *e Thankfulness, enjoined*, Acts 24:3. *f First Fruits*, Deut. 18:4. **10** *g Blessings, contingent upon obedience*, Deut. 11: 26. *h Promise, to the liberal, of prosperity*, 2 Cor. 1:20. *i Wine-press*, Isa. 5:2. 2 Am. R. V. vats shall overflow **11** *j* Heb. 12:5, 6. *k Young Men*, Prov. 1:4. *l Divine Chastisement*, Job 33:19. *m Afflictions, resignation in*, Psa. 34:19. *n Commandment, enjoining patience under affliction*, Deut. 8:2. *o Resignation, enjoined*, Job 5:17. 3 R. V. reproof: **12** *p God, love of*, Gen. 2:2. *q Father*, Psa. 27:10. 4 R. V. reproveth; **13** *r Spiritual Peace*, Gal. 1:3. *s Righteous, happiness of*, Psa 64:10. *t Wisdom*, Prov. 2:2. **14** *u Silver*, 1 Chr. 28:14. *v Gold*, Ezek. 7:19.

***BARN**, 2 Kin. 6:27; Prov. 3:10; Joel 1:17; Hag. 2:19; Matt. 6:26; 13:30; Luke 12:18, 24.

15 [t]She *is* more precious than [w]rubies: and all the things thou canst desire are not to be compared unto her.

16 [x]Length of days *is* in her right hand; *and* in her left hand [y]riches and honour.

17 Her ways *are* ways of pleasantness, and all her paths *are* [r]peace.

18 [t]She *is* a tree of [z]life to them that lay hold upon her: and happy *is every one* that retaineth her.

19 The LORD by [a]wisdom hath [b,c,d]founded the [e]earth; by understanding hath he established the [f]heavens.

20 By his [g]knowledge the depths are broken up, and the clouds drop down the [h]dew.

21 ¶ My [i]son, let not them depart from thine eyes: [j]keep sound [k]wisdom and [l]discretion:

22 [m,n,o]So shall they be life unto thy soul, and grace to thy neck.

23 [m,n,o]Then shalt thou walk in thy way safely, and thy foot shall not stumble.

24 When thou liest down, [m,o]thou shalt not be afraid: yea, thou shalt lie down, and thy [p]sleep shall be sweet.

25 [q,r]Be not afraid of sudden fear, neither of the desolation of the wicked, when it cometh.

26 For [m,o]the LORD shall be thy confidence, and shall [s]keep thy foot from being taken.

27 ¶ [t,u]Withhold not [v]good from them to whom it is due, when it is in the power of thine hand to do *it*.

28 Say not unto thy [w]neighbour, Go, and come again, and to morrow I will give; when thou hast it by thee.

29 [x]Devise not evil against thy [w]neighbour, seeing he dwelleth securely by thee.

30 [y,z]Strive not with a man without cause, if he have done thee no harm.

31 ¶ [a,b,c]Envy thou not the [5]oppressor, and choose none of his ways.

32 For the [d]froward *is* [e]abomination to the LORD: but [f]his secret *is* with the righteous.

33 The [g]curse of the LORD *is* in the house of the wicked: but [h]he [i]blesseth the habitation of the just.

34 Surely he [6]scorneth the [j,k]scorners: but [l]he giveth [m]grace unto the [n]lowly.

35 [h]The [o]wise shall inherit glory: but [g]shame shall be the promotion of [p]fools.

## CHAPTER 4

*Solomon persuades the young to obedience by reference to the instruction of his parents; 5 exhorts them to get wisdom; 14 to shun the path of the wicked; 23 and to keep the heart with all diligence.*

[a]HEAR, ye [b]children, the [c]instruction of a [d]father, and attend to know understanding.

2 For I give you good doctrine, forsake ye not my law.

3 For I was my [d]father's son, tender and only *beloved* in the sight of my [e]mother.

4 He taught me also, and said unto me, Let thine heart retain my words: keep my commandments, and live.

5 [b,f]Get [g,h]wisdom, get understanding: forget *it* not; neither decline from the words of my mouth.

6 Forsake her not, and she shall preserve thee: love her, and she shall keep thee.

7 [g]Wisdom *is* the principal thing; *therefore* [f]get wisdom: and with all thy getting get understanding.

8 Exalt [g]her, and she shall promote thee: she shall bring thee to honour, when thou dost embrace her.

9 [g]She shall give to thine head

---

**15**
w Prov. 20:15; 31:10; Job 28:18; Lam. 4:7.
**16**
x *Longevity*, Psa. 91:16.
y *Riches*, Eccl. 4:8.
**18**
z *Life, tree of*, Eccl. 8:15.
**19**
a *God, wisdom of*, Gen. 2:2.
b *God, creator*, Gen. 2:2.
c *Creation*, Mark 13:19.
d *Works of God*, Psa. 40:5.
e *Earth, creation of*, Prov. 8:23.
f *Heavens, physical, created*, Psa. 8:3.
**20**
g *God, knowledge of*, Gen. 2:2.
h *Dew*, Dan. 4:15.
**21**
i *Young Men*, Prov. 1:4.
j *Commandment, enjoining wisdom*, Deut. 8:2.
k *Wisdom, spiritual*, Prov. 2:2.
l *Prudence*, 2 Chr. 2:12.
**22**
m *Promise, to the righteous*, vs. 23-26; 2 Cor. 1:20.
n *Blessings, contingent upon obedience*, Deut. 11:26.
o *Righteous, promises to*, Psa. 64:10.
**24**
p *Sleep, from God*, Psa. 127:2.
**25**
q *Commandment, enjoining faith*, Deut. 8:2.
r *Faith, enjoined*, Mark 11:22.
**26**
s *God, preserver*, Gen. 2:2.
**27**
t *Commandment, enjoining kindness*, v. 28; Deut. 8:2.
u *Liberality, enjoined*, 1 Tim. 6:18.
v *Kindness*, Acts 28:2.
**28**
w *Neighbor, benevolence toward, enjoined*, Luke 10:29.
**29**
x *Commandment, forbidding evil to a neighbor*, Deut. 8:2.

**30**
y *Strife*, Prov. 20:3.
z *Commandment, forbidding causeless strife*, Deut. 8:2.
**31**
a *Commandment, forbidding envy*, Deut. 8:2.
b *Envy, forbidden*, Prov. 14:30.
c *Children, commandments to*, Mark 10:14.
5 R. V. man of violence.
**32**
d *Sin, repugnant to God*, Rom. 5:12.
e *Abomination*, Lev. 18:27.
f *Communion with God*, 2 Cor. 13:14.
**33**
g *Wicked, punishment of*, Psa. 73:3.
h *Promise, to the righteous*, 2 Cor. 1:20.
i *Temporal Blessings, from God*, Psa. 103:2.
**34**
j *Scoffing*, Hab. 1:10.
k *Pride*, Prov. 16:18.
l Jas. 4:6; 1 Pet. 5:5.
m *Grace of God*, Rom. 4:16.
n *Humility, rewards of*, Prov. 22:4.
6 Am. R. V. scoffeth at the scoffers.
**35**
o *Wisdom, spiritual*, Prov. 2:2.
p *Fool*, Prov. 18:2.

**1**
a *Commandment, enjoining reverence for parents*, Deut. 8:2.
b *Children, commandments to*, Mark 10:14.
c *Instruction, receiving, enjoined*, Prov. 23:23.
d *Father*, Psa. 27:10.
**3**
e *Mother*, 1 Kin. 2:20.
**5**
f *Commandment, enjoining wisdom*, Deut. 8:2.
g *Wisdom*, Prov. 2:2.
h *Christian Graces*, Gal. 5:22.

[1]an ornament of grace: a crown
of [2]glory shall she deliver to thee.
10 [i]Hear, O my [j]son, and receive my sayings; and [k]the years
of thy life shall be [l]many.
11 I have taught thee in the
way of [g]wisdom; I have led thee
in right paths.
12 [k]When thou goest, thy steps
shall not be straitened[c]; and
when thou runnest, thou shalt
not stumble.
13 [f,c]Take fast hold of instruction; let *her* not go[T]: keep her;
for she *is* thy life.
14 ¶ [m,n,o,p]Enter not into the
path of the wicked, and go not
in the way of evil *men*.
15 [m,n,o,p]Avoid it, pass not by
it, turn from it, and pass away.
16 For [q,r]they sleep not, except
they have done mischief; and
their sleep is taken away, unless
they cause *some* to fall.
17 For [q]they eat the bread of
[s]wickedness, and drink the [t]wine
of violence.
18 But [u]the path of the just *is*
as the shining light, that shineth
more and more unto the perfect
day.
19 [q]The way of the wicked *is*
as [v]darkness: they know not at
what they stumble.
20 ¶ My [i]son, [i]attend to my
words; incline thine ear unto my
sayings.
21 [i]Let them not depart from
thine eyes; keep them in the
midst of thine heart.
22 For [k]they *are* life unto those
that find them, and health to all
their flesh.
23 ¶ [w,x]Keep thy [y]heart with
all [z]diligence; for out of it *are*
the issues of life.
24 [a]Put away from thee a [b]fro-
ward[c] mouth, and perverse[c] lips
put far from thee.
25 [c]Let thine eyes look right
on, and let thine eyelids look
straight before thee.

**9**
1 R. V. a chaplet
2 R. V. beauty
**10**
*i Commandment, enjoining obedience,* Deut. 8:2.
*j Young Men,* Prov. 1:4.
*k Promise, to the obedient,* v. 12; 2 Cor. 1:20.
*l Longevity,* Psa. 91:16.
**14**
*m Commandment, forbidding fellowship with the wicked,* Deut. 8:2.
*n Temptation, admonitions against yielding to,* Luke 11:4.
*o Fellowship, with the wicked forbidden,* 1 Cor. 1:9.
*p Evil Company, warnings against,* Prov. 13:20.
**16**
*q Wicked, described,* Psa. 73:3.
*r Malice,* Eph. 4:31.
**17**
*s Sin, love of,* Rom. 5:12.
*t Wine, intoxicates,* Prov. 23:31.
**18**
*u Righteous, described,* Psa. 64:10.
**19**
*v Spiritual Blindness,* 2 Cor. 4:4.
**23**
*w Watchfulness, enjoined,* Matt. 24:42.
*x Commandment, enjoining watchfulness,* Deut. 8:2.
*y Heart,* Psa. 44:21.
*z Diligence, in keeping the heart,* Rom. 12:8.
**24**
*a Commandment, forbidding evil speech,* Deut. 8:2.
*b Speech, evil,* Col. 4:6.
**25**
*c Commandment, enjoining right conduct,* Deut. 8:2.

26 [3,c]Ponder the path of thy
feet, and let all thy ways be established.[Q]
27 [c]Turn[c] not to the right hand
nor to the left: [d]remove thy foot
from evil.

## CHAPTER 5

*An exhortation to attend to wisdom;* 3 *to avoid the snare of the strange woman;* 15 *and to be chaste.* 22 *The end of the wicked.*

MY [a]son, [b]attend unto my
[c]wisdom, *and* bow thine
ear to my understanding:
2 That thou mayest [1]regard
[d]discretion, and *that* thy lips
may keep [e]knowledge.
3 ¶ [f,g]For the lips of a strange
[h,i]woman drop *as* an honeycomb,
and her [j]mouth *is* smoother
than oil:
4 But her end is bitter as
[k]wormwood, sharp as a two-
edged [l]sword.
5 Her feet [m]go down to [n]death;
her steps take hold on [2,o]hell[c].
6 [3]Lest thou shouldest ponder
the path of life, her ways are
[4]moveable, *that* thou canst not
know *them*.
7 Hear me now therefore, O
ye [a]children, and [p,q]depart not
from the words of my mouth.
8 [r,s]Remove thy way far from
her, and come not nigh[c] the door
of her house:
9 Lest thou give thine honour
unto others, and thy years unto
the cruel:
10 Lest strangers be filled with
thy [5]wealth; and thy labours *be*
in the house of a [6]stranger[c];
11 And thou [t]mourn at the last,
when thy flesh and thy body are
consumed,
12 And [u]say, How have I hated
[v]instruction, and my heart despised reproof;
13 [u]And have not obeyed the
[v]voice of my teachers, nor inclined mine ear to them that instructed me!
14 [u]I was almost in all evil in

**26**
3 R. V. Make level
**27**
*d Evil, to be eschewed,* 1 Thess. 5:22.
**1**
*a Young Men,* Prov. 1:4.
*b Commandment, enjoining wisdom,* Deut. 8:2.
*c Wisdom, spiritual,* Prov. 2:2.
**2**
*d Prudence,* 2 Chr. 2:12.
*e Knowledge,* Luke 11:52.
1 R. V. preserve
**3**
*f Adultery,* vs. 5–22; Lev. 20:10.
*g Lasciviousness,* 1 Pet. 4:3.
*h Women, wicked,* Prov. 31:10.
*i Harlot, to be shunned,* Prov. 7:10.
*j Flattery,* Prov. 6:24.
**4**
*k Wormwood,* Deut. 29:18.
*l Sword,* 1 Chr. 21:5.
**5**
*m Wicked, punishment of,* Psa. 73:3.
*n Death,* Num. 23:10.
*o Hell,* Mark 9:43.
2 R. V. Sheol;
**6**
3 R. V. So that she findeth not the level path
4 R. V. unstable and she knoweth it not.
**7**
*p Obedience, enjoined,* Heb. 5:8.
*q Commandment, enjoining obedience,* v. 8; Deut. 8:2.
**8**
*r Temptation, admonitions against yielding to,* Luke 11:4.
*s Evil Company, warnings against,* Prov. 13:20.
**10**
5 R. V. strength;
6 R. V. alien;
**11**
*t Remorse, of the lascivious,* Matt. 27:3.
**12**
*u Self-condemnation,* Job 9:20.
*v Instruction, hatred of,* Prov. 23:23.

15
*w Chastity, enjoined*, Job 31:1.
*x Commandment, enjoining chastity*, vs. 16–19; Deut. 8:2.
*y Water, figurative*, 1 Kin. 17:10.
*z Husband, chastity of*, vs. 15–20; Num. 30:6.

16
7 R. V. Should thy springs be

20
*a Chastity, enjoined*, Job 31:1.
*b Young Men*, Prov. 1:4.
*c Adultery*, Lev. 20:10.
*d Harlot, to be shunned*, Prov. 7:10.

21
*e God, knowledge of*, Gen. 2:2.
8 R. V. maketh level all his paths.

22
*f Sin, fruits of*, Rom. 5:12.
*g Sin, retroactive*, Rom. 5:12.
*h Wicked, punishment of*, Psa. 73:3.

23
*i Death, of the wicked*, Num. 23:10.
9 R. V. for lack of

1
*a Young Men*, Prov. 1:4.
*b Surety*, Gen. 44:32.
*c Hand, clasping of*, Ezra 10:19.
1 R. V. hands for a

2
*d Contracts, binding*, Matt. 20:2.

the midst of the congregation
and assembly.
15 ¶ [w,x]Drink [y]waters out of
[z]thine own cistern, and running
waters out of thine own well.
16 [7]Let thy fountains be dispersed abroad, *and* rivers of
waters in the streets.
17 Let them be only thine own,
and not strangers' with thee.
18 Let thy fountain be blessed:
and rejoice with the *wife of
thy youth.
19 Let *her be as the loving
hind and pleasant roe; [w,x]let her
breasts satisfy thee at all times;
and be thou ravished[G] always with
her love.
20 And [a]why wilt thou, my
[b]son, be [c]ravished with a strange
[d]woman, and embrace the bosom
of a stranger[G]?
21 For the ways of man *are* before the eyes of the [e]LORD, and
he [8]pondereth all his goings.[S]
22 His own [f]iniquities [g,h]shall
take the wicked himself, and he
shall be holden[G] with the cords
of his sins.
23 He shall [i]die [9]without instruction; and in the greatness
of his folly he shall go astray.

## CHAPTER 6

*Cautions against suretyship, 6 idleness, 12 and evil doing. 16 Seven things hateful to God. 20 An exhortation to filial obedience, 24 and to avoid the evils of lewdness.*

MY [a]son, if thou be [b]surety[G]
for thy friend, *if* thou
hast stricken[G] thy [1,c]hand with
a stranger,
2 Thou art [d]snared with the
words of thy mouth, thou art
taken[G] with the words of thy
mouth.
3 Do this now, my [a]son, and
deliver thyself, [2]when thou art
come into the hand of thy
friend; go, humble thyself, and
make[G] sure thy friend.
4 Give not [e]sleep to thine eyes,
nor slumber to thine eyelids.
5 Deliver thyself as a [f]roe from
the hand *of the hunter*, and as a
bird from the hand of the fowler.
6 ¶ Go to the [g,h]ant, thou [i]slug-
gard; [j]consider her ways, and be
wise:
7 [g]Which having no [3]guide,
overseer, or ruler,
8 [g]Provideth her meat[G] in the
[k]summer, *and* gathereth her food
in the harvest.
9 [l]How long wilt thou [e]sleep, O
sluggard? when wilt thou [m]arise
out of thy sleep?
10 [l]*Yet* a little [e]sleep, a little
slumber, a little folding of the
hands to sleep:
11 So shall thy [n]poverty come
as [4]one that travelleth, and thy
want as an armed man.
12 ¶ A [5,o]naughty[G] person, a
wicked man, walketh with a
[p]froward[G] mouth.
13 [o]He *winketh with his eyes,
he speaketh with his feet, he
[6]teacheth with his fingers;
14 [p]Frowardness[G] *is* in his
[q]heart, he [r]deviseth mischief continually; he soweth [s]discord.
15 Therefore shall [t]his [u]ca-
lamity come suddenly; suddenly shall he be broken without remedy.
16 ¶ These six [v]*things* doth the

3
2 R. V. Seeing thou art come into the hand of thy neighbour: Go, humble thyself, and importune thy neighbour.

4
*e Sleep*, Psa. 127:2.

5
*f Deer*, Deut. 14:5.

6
*g Animals, instinct of*, Jer. 27:5.
*h* Prov. 30:25.
*i Idleness*, Eccl. 10:18.
*j Commandment, enjoining industry*, Deut. 8:2.

7
3 R. V. chief,

8
*k Summer*, Isa. 28:4.

9
*l Laziness*, Prov. 19:15.
*m Rising, late*, Gen. 19:2.

11
*n Poverty, caused by laziness*, Prov. 30:8.
4 R. V. a robber, And

12
*o Wicked, described*, Psa. 73:3.
*p Falsehood*, Job 21:34.
5 R. V. worthless

13
6 R. V. maketh signs

14
*q Heart, unregenerate*, Psa. 44:21.
*r Malice*, Eph. 4:31.
*s Strife*, Prov. 20:3.

15
*t Wicked, punishment of*, Psa. 73:3.
*u Afflictions*, Psa. 34:19.

16
*v Sin, repugnant to God*, Rom. 5:12.

*** WIFE,** Prov. 30:23.
Called: *Help*, Gen. 2:18, 20; *desire of the eyes*, Ezek. 24:16. *Compared to fruitful vine*, Psa. 128:3.
*Contentious*, Prov. 19:13; 21:9, 19; 25:24. *Instances of, Zipporah*, Ex. 4:25.
*Unfaithful*, Num. 5:12–31. *Instances of, Potiphar's*, Gen. 39:7; *Bath-sheba*, 2 Sam. 11:2–5.
*Tactful, Abigail*, 1 Sam. 25:3, 14–34; *Esther*, Esth. 5:5–8; 7:1–4.
*Prudent*, Prov. 19:14. *Loyal, Jacob's*, Gen. 31:14–16. *Virtuous*, Prov. 12:4; 31:10–12. *Incorruptible, Vashti*, Esth. 1:10–12.
*Taking of, commended*, Prov. 18:22; 1 Cor. 7:2. *Bought*, Gen. 29:18–30; 31:41; Ex. 21:7–11; Ruth 4:10. *Obtained by kidnapping*, Judg. 21:21.
*Duty of husband to*, 1 Cor. 7:2–5, 27; Eph. 5:25, 28, 31, 33; Col. 3:19; 1 Pet. 3:7. *Relation of, to husband*, Gen. 2:18, 23, 24; 1 Cor. 7:2–5, 10, 11, 13, 39; 11:3, 8, 9, 11, 12.
Duty of, to husband: *To be obedient*, Eph. 5:22, 24; Col. 3:18; Tit. 2:5; 1 Pet. 3:1, 6; *to be affectionate*, Tit. 2:4.
*Vows of*, Num. 30:6–16.
**Instances of evil influence of, upon husbands:** *Eve*, Gen. 3:6, 12. *Solomon's wives*, 1 Kin. 11:1–8; Neh. 13:26. *Jezebel*, 1 Kin. 21:25. *Haman's*, Esth. 5:14. *Herodias*, Matt. 14:3, 6–11; Mark 6:17, 24–28.
See footnotes: MARRIAGE, Gen. 34:9; WOMEN, Prov. 31:10.

*** INNUENDO.** *A malicious and covert word or act imputing a damaging charge against its object*, Psa. 35:19; Prov. 6:13; 10:10.
See footnote, FALSE ACCUSATION, 2 Tim. 3:3.

w *Abomination*, Lev. 18:27.

**17**

x *Pride*, Prov. 16:18.

y *Speech, evil*, Col. 4:6.

z *Homicide, felonious*, Deut. 5:17.

**18**

a *Heart, unregenerate*, Psa. 44:21.

b *Evil Imagination*, Gen. 6:5.

**19**

c *False Witness*, Matt. 19:18.

d *Falsehood*, Job 21:34.

e *Slander*, Prov. 10:18.

f *Strife*, Prov. 20:3.

**20**

g *Young Men*, Prov. 1:4.

h *Commandment, enjoining obedience*, Deut. 8:2.

i *Father*, Psa. 27:10.

j *Mother*, 1 Kin. 2:20.

**22**

k *Promise, to the obedient*, 2 Cor. 1:20.

7 R. V. watch over thee;

**23**

l *Lamp, figurative*, Ex. 27:20.

m *Light, figurative*, Matt. 5:14.

n *Life*, Eccl. 8:15.

**24**

o *Chastity, enjoined*, Job 31:1.

p *Adultery*, Lev. 20:10.

q *Temptation, admonitions against yielding to*, Luke 11:4.

r *Women, subtle and deceitful*, Prov. 31:10.

s *Harlot*, Prov. 7:10.

**25**

t *Lust, forbidden*, 2 Pet. 1:4.

u *Commandment, forbidding association with harlots*, Deut. 8:2.

**29**

8 R. V. unpunished.

**30**

v *Thieves*, Deut. 24:7.

LORD hate: yea, seven *are* an [w]abomination unto him:

17 A [x]proud look, a [p,y]lying tongue, and hands that [z]shed innocent blood,

18 An [a]heart that deviseth wicked [b]imaginations, feet that be swift in running to mischief,

19 A [c]false[G] witness *that* speaketh [d,e]lies, and he that soweth [f]discord among brethren.

20 ¶ My [g]son, [h]keep thy [i]father's commandment, and forsake not the law of thy [j]mother:

21 [h]Bind them continually upon thine heart, *and* tie them about thy neck.

22 [k]When thou goest, it shall lead thee; when thou sleepest, it shall [7]keep thee; and *when* thou awakest, it shall talk with thee.

23 For the commandment *is* a [l]lamp; and the law *is* [m]light; and reproofs of instruction *are* the way of [n]life:[T]

24 [o,p,q]To keep thee from the evil [r,s]woman, from the †flattery of the tongue of a strange[G] woman.

25 [t,u]Lust not after her ‡beauty in thine heart; neither let her take thee with her eyelids.

26 For [p]by means of a [s]whorish woman *a man is brought* to a piece of bread: and the adulteress will hunt for the precious life.

27 [q]Can a man take fire in his bosom, and his clothes not be burned?

28 [q]Can one go upon hot coals, and his feet not be burned?

29 So he that [p]goeth in to his neighbour's wife; whosoever toucheth her shall not be [8]innocent.

30 *Men* do not despise a [v]thief, if he [w]steal to satisfy his soul when he is [x]hungry;

31 But *if* [v]he be found, he shall [y]restore [z]sevenfold; he shall [a]give all the substance of his house.

32 *But* whoso committeth [b]adultery with a woman lacketh understanding: he *that* doeth it [b]destroyeth his own soul.

33 [b,c]A wound and dishonour shall he get; and his reproach shall not be wiped away.

34 For [d]jealousy *is* the rage of a man: therefore he will not spare in the day of vengeance.

35 He will not regard[G] any [e]ransom; neither will he rest content, though thou givest many gifts.

## CHAPTER 7

*An exhortation to keep the law, and thus avoid the enticements of the strange woman. 6 An instance of a young man led astray. 24 The young exhorted to avoid such snares.*

MY [a]son, [b,c]keep my words, and lay up my commandments with thee.

2 [b,c]Keep my commandments, and [d]live; and my law as the apple of thine eye.

3 [b,c]Bind them upon thy fingers, write them upon the table of thine heart.[Q]

4 Say unto [e]wisdom, Thou *art* my sister; and call understanding *thy* kinswoman:

5 That they may keep thee from [f]the strange [g]woman, from the stranger[G] *which* [h]flattereth with her words.

6 ¶ For at the window of my [i]house I looked through my casement,

7 And beheld among the simple[G] ones, I discerned among the youths, a [a]young man [j,k,l]void of understanding,

w *Theft*, Mark 7:22.

x *Hunger*, Neh. 9:15.

**31**

y *Restitution, to be made for theft*, Ex. 22:3.

z *Fine, for theft*, Ex. 22:1.

a *Damages and Compensation*, Ex. 21:19.

**32**

b *Adultery, fatal consequences of*, Lev. 20:10.

**33**

c *Wicked, punishment of*, Psa. 73:3.

**34**

d *Jealousy*, Psa. 78:58.

**35**

e *Ransom, of a man's life*, Ex. 21:30.

**1**

a *Young Men*, Prov. 1:4.

b *Obedience, enjoined*, Heb. 5:8.

c *Commandment, enjoining obedience*, vs. 2–4; Deut. 8:2.

**2**

d *Blessings, contingent upon obedience*, Deut. 11:26.

**4**

e *Wisdom, spiritual*, Prov. 2:2.

**5**

f *Adultery*, Lev. 20:10.

g *Women, wicked*, Prov. 31:10.

h *Flattery*, Prov. 6:24.

**6**

i *House*, Esth. 8:1.

**7**

j *Fool*, Prov. 18:2.

k *Spiritual Blindness*, 2 Cor. 4:4.

l *Ignorance*, Acts 3:17.

† **FLATTERY**, Job 32:21, 22; Psa. 5:8, 9; 12:2, 3; 78:36; Prov. 2:16; 5:3; 6:24; 7:5, 21; 24:24: 26:28; 27:14; 28:23; 29:5; Dan. 11:21, 34; Rom. 16:18; Gal. 1:10.
**Instances of:** *By Jacob*, Gen. 33:10. *By Gideon*, Judg. 8:1–3. *By woman of Tekoah*, 2 Sam. 14:17–20. *By Absalom*, 2 Sam. 15:2–6. *By Darius's courtiers*, Dan. 6:7. *By Herodians*, Luke 20:21. *By Tyrians*, Acts 12:22. *Tertullus flatters Felix*, Acts 24:2–4.

‡ **BEAUTY.** *Vanity of*, Psa. 39:11; Prov. 31:30; Isa. 3. 24; Ezek. 16:14; 28:17. *Transient*, Psa. 39:11; 49:14.
**Instances of:** *Sarah*, Gen. 12:11. *Rebekah*, Gen. 24:16. *Rachel*, Gen. 29:17. *Joseph*, Gen. 39:6. *Moses*, Ex. 2:2; Heb. 11:23. *David*, 1 Sam. 16:12, 18. *Abigail*, 1 Sam. 25:3. *Bath-sheba*, 2 Sam. 11:2. *Tamar*, 2 Sam. 13:1. *Absalom*, 2 Sam. 14:25. *Abishag*, 1 Kin. 1:4. *Vashti*, Esth. 1:11. *Esther*, Esth. 2:7.

8 Passing through the street
near [g]her corner; and [a,i]he went
the way to her [i]house,
9 In the twilight, in the evening, in the black and dark
night:
10 And, behold, there met him
a [g]woman *with* the attire of an
*harlot, and [m]subtil of [n]heart.
11 (*,[g]She *is* [1]loud and [o]stub-
born; her feet abide not in her
house:
12 Now *is* *,[g]*she* [2]without, now
in the [3]streets, and lieth in wait
at every corner.)
13 So *she [p]caught him, and
[q]kissed him, *and* with an impudent face [r]said unto him,
14 **I have* [s]peace offerings
with me; this day have I payed
my vows.
15 Therefore came *,[g]I forth
to [p]meet thee, diligently to seek
thy face, and I have found thee.
16 I have [4]decked my [t]bed
with coverings of †tapestry, with
carved *works*, with fine [u]linen of
[v]E'gypt.
17 *I have [w]perfumed my [t]bed
with [x]myrrh, [y]aloes, and [z]cinna-
mon.
18 [a]Come, [b]let us take our fill
of love until the morning: let us
solace ourselves with loves.
19 For the goodman *is* not at
home, he is gone a long journey:
20 He hath taken a bag of
[c]money with him, *and* will come
home at the [5]day appointed.
21 With her much fair [d]speech
*,[e]she caused him to [f]yield, with
the [g]flattering of her lips she
forced him.
22 [f]He goeth after her straightway, as an ox goeth to the
slaughter, or as [6]a [h,i]fool to the
correction of the [j]stocks;
23 Till a dart strike through his
[k]liver; as a bird hasteth to the
snare, and knoweth not that it
*is* for his life.
24 ¶ [l]Hearken unto me now
therefore, O ye [m]children, and
attend to the words of my
mouth.
25 Let not thine heart decline
to *her ways, go not astray in
her paths.
26 For *she hath cast down many
wounded: yea, [7]many strong *men*
have been slain by her.
27 [n]Her house *is* the way to
[8,o]hell, going down to the chambers of [p]death.

## CHAPTER 8

*A commendation of wisdom, in which is shown its nature, power, and excellence. 32 The blessedness it secures.*

DOTH not [a]wisdom cry? and
understanding put forth
her voice?
2 [a]She standeth in the top of
high places, by the way in the
places of the paths.
3 [a]She [b]crieth at the [c]gates, at
the entry of the city, at the coming in at the doors.
4 Unto you, O men, [a]I [b]call; and
my voice *is* to the sons of man.
5 [d]O ye [e]simple, understand
wisdom: and, ye [f]fools, be ye of
an understanding heart.
6 Hear; for [a]I will speak of excellent things; and the opening
of my lips *shall be* right things.
7 For my mouth shall speak
truth; and wickedness *is* an
[g]abomination to my lips.
8 All the words of my mouth *are*
in righteousness; *there is* nothing
froward or perverse in them.
9 They *are* all plain to him that
understandeth, and right to them
that find knowledge.
10 Receive my [h]instruction, and
not silver; and [i]knowledge rather
than choice gold.
11 For [j]wisdom *is* better than

10
m *Hypocrisy*, Jas. 3:17.
n *Heart, unregenerate*, Psa. 44:21.
11
o *Self-will*, Gen. 49:6.
1 R. V. clamorous
12
2 R. V. in the streets,
3 R. V. broad places,
13
p *Temptation, leading into*, Luke 11:4.
q *Lasciviousness*, 1 Pet. 4:3.
r *Speech, evil*, Col. 4:6.
14
s *Offerings, peace, by harlots*, Lev. 6:17.
16
t *Bed*, Amos 6:4.
u *Linen*, Ezek. 27:16.
v *Egypt, productions of*, Gen. 41:8.
4 R. V. I have spread my couch with carpets of tapestry, With striped cloths of the yarn of Egypt.
17
w *Perfume*, Prov. 27:9.
x *Myrrh*, Ex. 30:23.
y *Aloes*, Psa. 45:8.
z *Cinnamon*, Song 4:14.
18
a *Temptation, leading into*, Luke 11:4.
b *Lasciviousness*, 1 Pet. 4:3.
20
c *Money*, Jer. 32:9.
5 R. V. full moon.
21
d *Speech, evil*, Col. 4:6.
e *Women, wicked*, Prov. 31:10.
f *Temptation, yielding to*, Luke 11:4.
g *Flattery*, Prov. 6:24.
22
h *Fool*, Prov. 18:2.
i *Prisoners*, Psa. 79:11.
j *Stocks*, Job 13:27.
6 Am. R. V. one in fetters to the correction of the fool;
23
k *Liver*, Lev. 3:4.

24
l *Commandment, enjoining obedience*, Deut. 8:2.
m *Young Men*, Prov. 1:4.
26
7 R. V. all her slain are a mighty host.
27
n *Adultery, fatal consequences of*, Lev. 20:10.
o *Hell*, Mark 9:43.
p *Death*, Num. 23:10.
8 R. V. Sheol,
1
a *Wisdom, personified*, Prov. 2:2.
3
b *Call, personal*, Phil. 3:14.
c *Gates, place for public concourse*, Deut. 3:5.
5
d *Commandment, enjoining wisdom*, Deut. 8:2.
e *Ignorance*, Acts 3:17.
f *Fool*, Prov. 18:2.
7
g *Abomination*, Lev. 18:27.
10
h *Instruction*, Prov. 23:23.
i *Knowledge*, Luke 11:52.
11
j *Wisdom*, Prov. 2:2.

* **HARLOT**, Gen. 38:14-26. *Shamelessness of*, Prov. 2:16; 7:11-27; 9:13-18. *Wiles of*, Prov. 7:10; 9:14-17; Isa. 23:15, 16; Hos. 2:13. *To be shunned*, Prov. 5:3-20; 7:25-27. *Hire of, not to be received at the temple*, Deut. 23:18. *Punishment of*, Lev. 21:9. *Rahab*, Josh. 2:1-21; 6:17, 23, 25; Heb. 11:31; Jas. 2:25. See footnote, ADULTERY, Lev. 20:10.

† **TAPESTRY**, Prov. 7:16; 31:22. *Of the tabernacle*, Ex. 26:1-14, 31-37; 27:9-17; 36:8-18. *In palaces*, Esth. 1:6; Song 1:5. See footnote, EMBROIDERY, Ezek. 26:16.

rubies; and all the things that
may be desired are not to be
compared to it.
12 [a]I wisdom [1]dwell with prudence, and find out knowledge
[2]of witty[G] inventions.[S]
13 The [k]fear of the LORD *is* to
[l,m,n]hate evil: [o]pride, and [p]ar-
rogancy, and the evil way, and
the [q]froward[G] mouth, do I hate.
14 Counsel *is* [a]mine, and sound
[j]wisdom: I *am* understanding; I
have strength.
15 By [a]me [r,s]kings reign, and
princes decree justice.[Q]
16 By [a]me [s]princes rule, and
nobles, *even* all the judges of the
earth.
17 [a]I love them that love me;
and [t,u]those that [v]seek me [3]early
shall find me.
18 Riches and honour *are* with
[a]me; *yea*, durable riches and
[w]righteousness.
19 My fruit *is* better than gold,
yea, than fine [x]gold; and my revenue than choice silver.
20 [a]I lead in the way of [w]right-
eousness, in the midst of the
paths of judgment[G]:[S]
21 [u]That [a]I may cause those
that love me to inherit substance[G];
and [4]I will fill their treasures[G].
22 The[S] LORD[T Q] possessed [a]me in
the beginning of his way, before
his works of old.
23[T] [a]I was set up from everlasting, from the beginning, or ever[G]
the *earth was.
24 When *there were* no depths,
[a]I was brought forth; when *there*
*were* no fountains abounding
with water.
25 Before the mountains were
settled, before the hills was [a]I
brought forth:[S Q]
26[S] While as yet he had not
[y]made the *earth, nor the fields,
nor the [5]highest part of the dust
of the world.
27[S] When he [y,z]prepared the
[a]heavens, [b]I *was* there: when he
set a [6]compass upon the face of
the depth:
28 When he[c,d]established the
clouds above: when he strengthened the fountains of the deep:
29 When [c]he gave to the [e]sea his
decree, that the waters should
not pass his commandment:
when he appointed the [f]founda-
tions of the earth:[S]
30 Then [b]I was by [c]him, *as*
[7,g]one brought up *with him*:
and I was daily *his* delight, rejoicing always before him;[T]
31 Rejoicing in the habitable
part of his *earth; and my delights *were* with the sons of men.[T S]
32 Now therefore hearken unto
[b]me, O ye [h]children: for [i,j]blessed
*are they that* keep my ways.
33 Hear instruction, and [k]be
wise, and refuse it not.
34 [i,j]Blessed *is* the man that
heareth [b]me, [l]watching daily at
my gates, waiting at the posts of
my doors.
35 For [j]whoso findeth me findeth life, and shall obtain [m]favour
of the LORD.[T]
36 But he that [n]sinneth against
[b]me wrongeth his own soul: all
they that hate me love death.[T]

## CHAPTER 9

*Wisdom's feast. 4 Her invitation to the simple. 7 Her instruction. 13 The way of a foolish woman.*

[a]WISDOM hath builded her
house, she hath hewn out
her seven pillars:
2 [a]She hath killed her beasts;

**12**
1 R. V. have made subtilty my dwelling,
2 R. V. and discretion.
**13**
k *Fear of God*, Acts 9:31.
l *Holiness*, Ex. 39:30.
m *Sin, repugnant to the righteous*, Rom. 5:12.
n *Evil, to be abhorred*, 1 Thess. 5:22.
o *Pride*, Prov. 16:18.
p 1 Sam. 2:3; Isa. 13:11.
q *Speech, evil*, Col. 4:6.
**15**
r *King*, 2 Kin. 3:10.
s *Rulers*, Ex. 18:21.
**17**
t *Seekers*, Isa. 55:6.
u *Promise, to seekers*, 2 Cor. 1:20.
v *Spiritual Desire*, v. 34; Psa. 42:1.
3 R. V. diligently
**18**
w *Righteousness*, Psa. 15:2.
**19**
x *Gold, refined*, Ezek. 7:19.
**21**
4 R. V. that I may fill their treasuries.

**26**
y *God, creator*, Gen. 2:2.
5 R. V. beginning of the
**27**
z *Creation*, Mark 13:19.
a *Heavens, physical*, Psa. 8:3.
b *Wisdom, personified*, Prov. 2:2.
6 R. V. circle
**28**
c *God, creator*, Gen. 2:2.
d *Creation*, Mark 13:19.
**29**
e *Sea*, Jer. 5:22.
f *Geology*, Psa. 104:5.
**30**
g *Master Workman*, 1 Cor. 3:10.
7 R. V. a master workman:
**32**
h *Young Men*, Prov. 1:4.
i *Blessings, contingent upon obedience*, Deut. 11:26.
j *Promise, to the righteous*, 2 Cor. 1:20.
**33**
k *Commandment, enjoining wisdom*, Deut. 8:2.
**34**
l *Watchfulness*, Matt. 24:42.
**35**
m *Grace of God*, Rom. 4:16.
**36**
n *Sin, fruits of*, Rom. 5:12.
**1**
a *Wisdom, personified*, Prov. 2:2.

* **EARTH.** *Created, by God*, Gen. 1:1; Ex. 20:11; 2 Kin. 19:15; 2 Chr. 2:12; Neh. 9:6; Job 38:4; Psa. 90:2; 102:25; 115:15; 124:8; 146:6; Prov. 8:22–26; Isa. 37:16; 45:18; Jer. 10:12; 27:5; 32:17; 51:15; 2 Pet. 3:5; Rev. 10:6; 14:7; *by Christ*, John 1:3; Heb. 1:10.
*Is the Lord's*, Ex. 9:29; 19:5; Deut. 10:14; Psa. 24:1; 50:12; 1 Cor. 10:26. *Primordial condition of*, Gen. 1:2; Job 26:7; Psa. 104:5–9; Jer. 4:23. *Created for habitation*, Isa. 45:18. *Ancient notions concerning*, 1 Sam. 2:8; Job 9:6; Rev. 7:1. *Cursed of God*, Gen. 3:17, 18; Rom. 8:19–22. *Circle of*, Isa. 40:22. *God's footstool*, Isa. 66:1. *Given to man*, Psa. 115:16. *Early divisions of*, Gen. chapters 10, 11; Deut. 32:8. *Perpetuity of*, Gen. 49:26; Deut. 33:15; Psa. 78:69; 104:5; Eccl. 1:4; Hab. 3:6.
*Destruction of, foretold*, Psa. 102:25, 26 (with Heb. 1:10 12); Isa. 24:19, 20; 51:6; Matt. 5:18; 24:6, 14, 29–39; Mark 13:24–37; 2 Pet. 3:10–13.
*A new earth*, Isa. 65:17; 66:22; 2 Pet. 3:13; Rev. 21:1.

she hath mingled her [b]wine; she hath also furnished her table.

3 [a]She hath sent forth her maidens: she crieth upon the highest places of the city,

4 Whoso *is* simple, let him turn in hither: *as for* him that wanteth understanding, she saith to him,

5 Come, eat of [a]my bread, and drink of the [b]wine *which* I have mingled.

6 [1,c,d]Forsake the [e,f]foolish, and live; and go in the way of understanding.

7 He that [g]reproveth a [h]scorner getteth to himself shame: and he that rebuketh a wicked *man getteth* himself a blot.

8 [g]Reprove not a [h]scorner, lest he hate thee: rebuke a wise man, and he will love thee.

9 Give [i]*instruction* to a wise *man,* and he will be yet wiser: teach a just *man,* and he will increase in learning.

10 The [j]fear of the LORD *is* the beginning of [k]wisdom: and the knowledge of the [2,l,m]holy *is* understanding.

11 For by [a]me thy days shall be [n]multiplied, and the years of thy life shall be [n]increased.

12 If thou be [k]wise, thou shalt be wise for thyself: [3]but *if* thou [o]scornest, [p]thou alone shalt bear *it.*

13 ¶ A foolish [q]woman *is* [r]clamorous: *she is* simple, and knoweth nothing.

14 For [s]she sitteth at the door of her house, on a seat in the high places of the city,

15 [s]To [t]call [4]passengers who go right on their ways:

16 Whoso *is* [e]simple, let him turn in hither: and *as for* him that wanteth understanding, she [s,t]saith to him,

17 [t,u]Stolen waters are sweet, and bread *eaten* in secret is pleasant.

18 But he knoweth not that the dead *are* there; *and that* her guests *are* in the depths of [5,v]hell.

**2**
b *Wine, figurative,* Prov. 23:31.

**6**
c *Repentance, exhortations to,* Mark 1:4.
d *Fellowship, with the wicked, forbidden,* 1 Cor. 1:9.
e *Fool,* Prov. 18:2.
f *Evil Company, warnings against,* Prov. 13:20.
1 R. V. Leave off, ye simple ones,

**7**
g *Reproof,* Prov. 17:10.
h *Scorners,* Prov. 19:25.

**9**
i *Counsel, the wise profit by,* Prov. 12:15.

**10**
j *Fear of God,* Acts 9:31.
k *Wisdom, spiritual,* Prov. 2:2.
l *God, holiness of,* Gen. 2:2.
m *Holiness, attribute of God,* Ex. 39:30.
2 R. V. Holy One is understanding.

**11**
n *Longevity,* Psa. 91:16.

**12**
o *Scoffing,* Hab. 1:10.
p *Responsibility, personal,* Ezek. 18:20.
3 R. V. And if

**13**
q *Women, wicked,* Prov. 31:10.
r *Harlot, shamelessness of,* Prov. 7:10.

**14**
s *Harlot, wiles of,* Prov. 7:10.

**15**
t *Temptation, leading into,* Luke 11:4.
4 R. V. to them that pass by, who

**17**
u *Lust,* 2 Pet. 1:4.

## CHAPTER 10

*The Proverbs of Solomon; extending to the seventeenth verse of the twenty-second chapter, and containing sundry observations, maxims, and precepts of wisdom.*

THE [a]proverbs of [b]Sŏl′o-mon. A [c]wise [d]son maketh a glad [e]father: but a [f,g]foolish [d]son *is* the heaviness of his [h]mother.

2 [i]Treasures of wickedness profit nothing: but [j]righteousness delivereth from death.

3 [k,l]The [m]LORD will not suffer the soul of the righteous to famish: but he [1]casteth away the substance of the [n]wicked.

4 He becometh [o]poor that [p]dealeth *with* a [q]slack hand: but the hand of the [r]diligent maketh rich.

5 He that [r]gathereth in [s]summer *is* a [c]wise [d]son: *but* he that [q,t]sleepeth in [u]harvest *is* a [f]son that causeth shame.

6 [k,l]Blessings *are* upon the head of the just: [v]but violence covereth the mouth of the wicked.

7 [j]The memory of the just *is* blessed: [v]but the name of the wicked shall rot.

8 The [w]wise in [x]heart will [y]receive commandments: but a [z]prating [a]fool shall fall.

9 He that [b]walketh uprightly walketh surely: [c]but he that perverteth his ways shall be known.

10 He that [d,e]winketh with the eye causeth sorrow: but a [f]prating [a]fool shall fall.

11 The [g]mouth of a righteous *man is* a well of life: [c]but violence covereth the [h]mouth of the wicked.

12 [i]Hatred stirreth up [j]strifes: but *,[k,l]love covereth all sins.

**18**
v *Hell,* Mark 9:43.
5 R. V. Sheol.

**1**
a *Proverbs,* 1 Sam. 24:13.
b *Solomon,* 2 Sam. 12:24.
c *Children, good,* Mark 10:14.
d *Young Men,* Prov. 1:4.
e *Father,* Psa. 27:10.
f *Fool,* Prov. 18:2.
g *Children, wicked,* Mark 10:14.
h *Mother, grieves over wayward children,* 1 Kin. 2:20.

**2**
i *Riches, fraudulently gotten,* Eccl. 4:8.
j *Righteousness, fruits of,* Psa. 15:2.

**3**
k *Promise, to the righteous,* 2 Cor. 1:20.
l *Righteous, promises to,* Psa. 64:10.
m *God, preserver,* Gen. 2:2.
n *Wicked, punishment of,* Psa. 73:3.
1 R. V. thrusteth away the desire

**4**
o *Poverty, caused by laziness,* Prov. 30:8.
p *Idleness, poverty from,* Eccl. 10:18.
q *Laziness,* Prov. 19:15.
r *Diligence, rewarded,* Rom. 12:8.

**5**
s *Summer,* Isa. 28:4.
t *Sleep,* Psa. 127:2
u *Harvest,* Ex. 34:21.

**6**
v *Wicked, contrasted with the righteous,* Psa. 73:3.

**8**
w *Wisdom, spiritual,* Prov. 2:2.
x *Heart,* Psa. 44:21.
y *Humility,* Prov. 22:4.
z *Speech, foolish,* Col. 4:6.

a *Fool,* Prov. 18:2.

**9** b *Integrity, rewards of,* Job 2:3. c *Wicked, contrasted with the righteous,* Psa. 73:3. **10** d *Connivance,* Lev. 20:4. e *Innuendo,* Prov. 6:13. f *Speech, foolish,* Col. 4:6. **11** g *Speech, wise,* Col. 4:6. h *Speech, evil,* Col. 4:6. **12** i *Hatred,* Prov. 15:17. j *Strife,* Prov. 20:3. k *Love, of man for man,* 1 John 4:7. l *Christian Graces,* Gal. 5:22.

* **CHARITABLENESS,** Prov. 10:12; 17:9. *Enjoined,* Matt. 5:23, 24; 7:1, 3–5; 18:21, 22; Luke 6:36–42; 17:3, 4; John 7:24; Rom. 14:1–23; 15:1, 2; 1 Cor. 4:5; 10:28–33; 16:14; 2 Cor. 2:7; Gal. 6:1; Eph. 4:32; Col. 3:13; Jas. 4:11, 12; 1 Pet. 3:9. *Covers sins,* Prov. 10:12; 17:9; 19:11; 1 Pet. 4:8. *Pleases God,* Matt. 6:14, 15; 18:23–35. *Described,* 1 Cor. 13.

**13**
*m Wisdom*, Prov. 2:2.
**14**
2 R. V. a present destruction.
**15**
*n Riches*, Eccl. 4:8.
*o Poor*, Prov. 21:13.
*p Poverty*, Prov. 30:8.
**16**
*q Righteousness, fruits of*, Psa. 15:2.
3 R. V. increase of
**17**
*r Counsel*, Prov. 12:15.
*s Pride*, Prov. 16:18.
*t Reproof, hated*, Prov. 17:10.
4 R. V. heedeth correction:
**18**
*u Falsehood*, Job 21:34.
**19**
*v Words*, Luke 4:22.
**21**
*w Spiritual Blindness*, 2 Cor. 4:4.
**22**
*x God, providence of*, Gen. 2:2.
**23**
*y Sin, love of*, Rom. 5:12.
5 R. V. wickedness: And so is wisdom to a man of understanding.
**24**
*z Wicked, punishment of*, Psa. 73:3.

*a Wicked, contrasted with the righteous*, Psa. 73:3.
*b Fear of God, guilty*, Acts 9:31.
*c Promise, to the righteous*, 2 Cor. 1:20.
*d Righteous, promises to*, Psa. 64:10.
*e Spiritual Desire*, Psa. 42:1.
*f Prayer, answer to, promised*, Acts 6:4.
**25**
*g Wicked, punishment of*, Psa. 73:3.
*h Death, of the wicked, sudden*, Num. 23:10.

13 In the lips of him that hath
understanding [m]wisdom is found:
but a rod *is* for the back of [a]him
that is void of understanding.
14 Wise *men* lay up [m]knowl-
edge: but the [l]mouth of the foolish *is* [2]near destruction.
15 The rich man's [n]wealth *is*
his strong city: the destruction
of the [o]poor *is* their [p]poverty.
16 The labour of the [q]righteous
*tendeth* to life: [c]the [3]fruit of the
wicked to sin.
17 He *is in* the way of life that
[4]keepeth [r]instruction: but he
that [s]refuseth [t]reproof erreth.
18 He that hideth [i]hatred *with*
[u]lying lips, and he that uttereth
a †slander, *is* a [a]fool.
19 In the multitude of [v]words
there wanteth not sin: but he
that refraineth his lips *is*
wise.
20 The [q]tongue of the just *is as*
choice silver: [c]the heart of the
wicked *is* little worth.
21 The [q]lips of the righteous
feed many: but [a]fools die for
[w]want of [m]wisdom.
22 The [x]blessing of the LORD,
it maketh rich, and he addeth
no sorrow with it.
23 [y]*It is* as sport to a fool to do
[5]mischief: but a man of understanding hath [m]wisdom.
24 [z,a]The [b]fear of the wicked, it
shall come upon him: but [c,d]the
[e]desire of the righteous shall be
[f]granted.
25 As the whirlwind passeth,
[g,h]so *is* the wicked no *more*: but
the righteous *is* an everlasting
foundation.
26 As vinegar to the teeth, and
as smoke to the eyes, so *is*
the [i]sluggard to them that send
him.
27 [c]The [j]fear of the LORD [k]pro-
longeth days: [a]but the years of
the wicked shall be [h]shortened.
28 The [l]hope of the righteous
*shall be* [m]gladness: [a]but the [n]ex-
pectation of the wicked [g]shall
perish.
29 [c]The way of the LORD *is*
[6]strength to the upright: [a]but
[g]destruction *shall be* to the workers of iniquity.
30 [c]The righteous shall never
be removed: [a]but the wicked
shall not inhabit the earth.
31 The [o]mouth of the just
bringeth forth wisdom: [a]but
the [p]froward tongue shall be
cut out.
32 The [o]lips of the righteous
know what is acceptable: [a]but
the mouth of the wicked [p]*speaketh* frowardness.

## CHAPTER 11

*Sundry Proverbs.*

A [a]FALSE *,[b]balance *is*
[c]abomination to the LORD:
but a [d]just [e]weight *is* his delight.
2 *When* [f]pride cometh, then
cometh shame: but with the
[g]lowly *is* wisdom.
3 The [h]integrity of the upright shall guide them: [i]but the
[j,k]perverseness of [1]transgressors
shall [l]destroy them.
4 [m]Riches profit not in the day
of wrath: but [n]righteousness delivereth from death.
5 The [n]righteousness of the [o]per-
fect shall direct his way: but the
wicked [l]shall fall by his own
[k]wickedness.
6 The [n]righteousness of the

**26**
*i Laziness*, Prov. 19:15.
**27**
*j Fear of God*, Acts 9:31.
*k Longevity*, Psa. 91:16.
**28**
*l Hope*, Prov. 13:12.
*m Joy*, Psa. 5:11.
*n Hope, of the wicked*, Prov. 13:12.
**29**
6 R. V. a strong hold to
**31**
*o Speech, wise*, Col. 4:6.
*p Speech, evil*, Col. 4:6.

**1**
*a Dishonesty*, Ezek. 22:13.
*b Measure*, Deut. 25:15.
*c Abomination, unjust weights and measures*, Lev. 18:27.
*d Honesty*, Rom. 13:13.
*e Weights, must be just*, Lev. 19:35.
**2**
*f Pride*, Prov. 16:18.
*g Humility*, Prov. 22:4.
**3**
*h Integrity*, Job 2:3.
*i Wicked, contrasted with the righteous*, Psa. 73:3.
*j Impenitence, judgments denounced against*, Rom. 2:5.
*k Sin, fruits of*, Rom. 5:12.
*l Wicked, punishment of*, Psa. 73:3.
1 R. V. the treacherous
**4**
*m Riches*, Eccl. 4:8.
*n Righteousness*, Psa. 15:2.
**5**
*o Perfection*, Heb. 6:1.

† **SLANDER,** Psa. 50:20; Prov. 10:18; 11:9; Jer. 6:28; Ezek. 22:9; Matt. 5:11; Rom. 3:8; 1 Cor. 4:13; 2 Cor. 6:8.
*Forbidden*, Ex. 23:1; 1 Tim. 3:11; Tit. 2:3; 3:2; Jas. 4:11; 1 Pet. 2:1.
*Benevolence under*, 1 Cor. 4:13. *Separates friends*, Prov. 16:28. *Punished by fines*, Deut. 22:13–19.
**Instances of:** *Joseph by Potiphar's wife*, Gen. 39:14–19. *Mephibosheth by Ziba*, 2 Sam. 16:3; 19:24–30. *David by his enemies*, 1 Sam. 24:9. *Naboth by Jezebel*, 1 Kin. 21:9–14. *Jeremiah by the Jews*, Jer. 18:18. *Jesus by the Jews who charged him, with being a winebibber*, Matt. 11:19; *with blaspheming*, Mark 14:64; John 5:18; *with having a devil*, John 8:48, 52; 10:20; *with being seditious*, Luke 22:65; 23:5; *with saying that he was a king*, Luke 23:2; John 18:33–37; 19:1–5. *Christians*, 1 Pet. 3:16. *Paul*, see footnote, PAUL, Acts 13:9.
See footnotes: FALSE ACCUSATION, 2 Tim. 3:3; FALSE WITNESS, Matt. 19:18; SPEECH, *Evil*, Col. 4:6.

* **BALANCES.** *Used for weighing*, Job 31:6; Isa. 40:12, 15; Ezek. 5:1. *Money weighed with*, Isa. 46:6; Jer. 32:10. *Must be just*, Lev. 19:36; Prov. 16:11; Ezek. 45:10. *False, used*, Hos. 12:7; Amos 8:5; Mic. 6:11. *False, an abomination*, Prov. 11:1; 20:23.
**Figurative**, Job 6:2; 31:6; Psa. 62:9; Isa. 40:12; Dan. 5:27; Rev. 6:5.

upright shall deliver them: [i]but [2]transgressors [l]shall be taken in *their own* [3,k]naughtiness.

7 When a wicked man [p]dieth, *his* [q]expectation [l]shall perish: and the [q]hope of [4]unjust *men* perisheth.

8 The [r]righteous is delivered out of [s]trouble, and [i]the [l]wicked cometh in his stead.

9 [5]An hypocrite with *his* [t,u]mouth destroyeth his neighbour: but through [v]knowledge shall the just be delivered.

10 When it goeth well with the righteous, the city rejoiceth: and when the wicked [l]perish, *there is* shouting.

11 By the blessing of the upright the city is exalted: but it is overthrown by the [w]mouth of the wicked.

12 [6,x]He that is void of [v]wisdom despiseth his neighbour: but a man of [y]understanding holdeth his peace.

13 [7]A [†]talebearer [z]revealeth secrets: but he that is of a [y,a]faithful spirit concealeth the matter.

14 Where no [b]counsel *is*, the people fall: but in the multitude of [‡]counsellors *there is* safety.

15 He that is [c,d]surety for a stranger shall smart *for it*: and he that [e]hateth suretiship is sure.

16 A gracious [f]woman retaineth honour: and [8]strong *men* retain riches.

17 The [g]merciful man doeth good to his own soul: but *he that is* [h]cruel [i]troubleth his own flesh.

18 [j]The wicked [9]worketh a deceitful work: but [k,l]to [m]him that soweth [n]righteousness *shall be* a sure reward.

19 [10]As [n]righteousness *tendeth* to life: [j]so he that pursueth evil *pursueth it* [o]to his own death.

20 [j]They that are of a [p]froward [q]heart *are* [r]abomination to the LORD: but *such as are* [n]upright in *their* way *are* his delight.

21 *Though* hand *join* in hand, [s,j]the [o]wicked shall not be unpunished: but [k,l]the [t]seed of the righteous shall be delivered.

22 *As* a jewel of gold in a [u]swine's snout, *so is* a fair [f]woman which is without [e]discretion.

23 The desire of the righteous *is* only good: [j]*but* the [v]expectation of the wicked *is* wrath.

24 There is that [w]scattereth, and yet increaseth; and *there is* that [x]withholdeth more than is meet, but *it tendeth* to [y]poverty.

25 [z]The [w]liberal soul shall be made fat: and he that watereth shall be watered also himself.

26 He that [a,b]withholdeth corn, the people shall curse him: but blessing *shall be* upon the head of him that [c]selleth *it*.

27 He that [d]diligently seeketh good [11]procureth favour: but he that seeketh mischief, it shall come unto him.

28 [e]He that [f]trusteth in his [g]riches shall fall: but [h,i]the righteous [j]shall flourish as a [k]branch.

29 He that troubleth his own house shall inherit the wind: and the [l]fool *shall be* servant to the wise of heart.

30 The fruit of the righteous *is* a tree of life; and he that [12,m]winneth souls *is* wise.

31 Behold, [h,i]the righteous shall be recompensed in the earth:

6
2 R. V. they that deal treacherously
3 R. V. mischief.

7
*p Death, of the wicked,* Num. 23:10.
*q Hope, of the wicked, shall perish,* Prov. 13:12.
4 R. V. iniquity perisheth.

8
*r Righteous, grounds of assurances to,* Psa. 64:10.
*s Adversity,* Psa. 10:6.

9
*t Falsehood,* Job 21:34.
*u Slander,* Prov. 10:18.
*v Wisdom, spiritual,* Prov. 2:2.
5 R. V. With his mouth the godless man destroyeth

11
*w Speech, evil,* Col. 4:6.

12
*x Fool,* Prov. 18:2.
*y Prudence, in restraining speech,* 2 Chr. 2:12.
6 R. V. He that despiseth his neighbour is void of wisdom:

13
*z Gossip,* Lev. 19:16.

*a Friendship,* Prov. 22:24.
7 R. V. He that goeth about as a

14
*b Counsel, wisdom in,* Prov. 12:15.

15
*c Surety,* Gen. 44:32.
*d Debt, security for,* 1 Sam. 22:2.
*e Prudence,* 2 Chr. 2:12.

16
*f Women,* Prov. 31:10.
8 R. V. violent

17
*g Mercy,* Deut. 5:10.
*h Cruelty,* Psa. 27:12. *i Sin, fruits of,* Rom. 5:12.

**18** *j Wicked, contrasted with the righteous,* Psa. 73:3. *k Promise, to the righteous,* 2 Cor. 1:20. *l Righteous, promises to,* Psa. 64:10. *m Sower, figurative,* Matt. 13:3. 9 R. V. earneth deceitful wages:

*n Righteousness,* Psa. 15:2.

19
*o Wicked, punishment of,* Psa. 73:3.
10 R. V. He that is stedfast in righteousness shall attain unto life: And

20
*p Sin, repugnant to God,* Rom. 5:12.
*q Heart, unregenerate,* Psa. 44:21.
*r Abomination,* Lev. 18:27.

21
*s Punishment, no escape from,* Lev. 26:41.
*t Children, of the righteous, blessed of God,* Mark 10:14.

22
*u Swine,* Lev. 11:7.

23
*v Hope, of the wicked,* Prov. 13:12.

24
*w Liberality,* 1 Tim. 6:18.
*x Covetousness,* Isa. 57:17.
*y Poverty,* Prov. 30:8.

25
*z Promise, to the liberal,* 2 Cor. 1:20.

26
*a Selfishness,* 2 Tim. 3:2.
*b Monopoly, of food,* Isa. 5:8.
*c Commerce,* 1 Kin. 10:15.

27
*d Diligence,* Rom. 12:8.
11 R. V. seeketh

28
*e Rich, deluded,* Jas. 5:1.
*f False Confidence,* Psa. 30:6.
*g Riches, delusive,* Eccl. 4:8.
*h Promise, to the righteous,* 2 Cor. 1:20.
*i Righteous, promises to,* Psa. 64:10.
*j Prosperity, promised to the righteous,* Eccl. 7:14.
*k Branch, figurative,* Dan. 4:14. **29** *l Fool,* Prov. 18:2.

**30** *m Zeal,* 2 Cor. 7:11. 12 R. V. is wise winneth souls.

† **TALEBEARING,** the pernicious vice, too frequently indulged by otherwise well disposed persons, of repeating damaging reports, either true or false, Prov. 11:13; 20:19. *Separates friends,* Prov. 16:28. *Causes strife,* Prov. 26:20. *Is forbidden,* Lev. 19:16; 1 Tim. 5:11. 13. See footnotes: BUSYBODY, 2 Thess. 3:11; SLANDER, Prov. 10:18.

‡ **COUNSELOR.** *An adviser in public affairs, in law and diplomacy,* 1 Chr. 27:32, 33. *Moses, to Israel,* Ex. 18:13–16. *Jethro, to Moses,* Ex. 18:13–26. *Ahithophel, to David,* 1 Chr. 27:33; 2 Sam. 16:23; *to Absalom,* 2 Sam. 16:23. *Was member of the Sanhedrin at Jerusalem,* Mark 15:43; Luke 23:50, 51. *A title of Christ,* Isa. 9:6.

[n]much more the wicked and the sinner.[S Q]

## CHAPTER 12

*Sundry Proverbs.*

WHOSO loveth [1]instruction loveth [a]knowledge: but he that hateth [b]reproof *is* brutish.[G]

2 A good *man* obtaineth [c]favour of the LORD: [d]but a man of wicked devices will he condemn.[S]

3 A [d]man shall not be established by wickedness: but [e]the root of the righteous shall not be moved.[S]

4 A virtuous [f,g]woman *is* a crown to her husband: but [h]she that maketh ashamed *is* as rottenness in his bones.

5 The thoughts of the righteous *are* right: *but* [d]the [i]counsels[G] of the wicked *are* [j]deceit.

6 [d]The [i]words of the wicked *are* to [k]lie in wait for blood: but [e]the [l]mouth of the upright shall deliver them.

7 [d]The wicked are [m]overthrown, and *are* not: but [e]the [n]house of the righteous shall stand.

8 A man shall be commended according to his [o]wisdom: [d]but he that is of a perverse [p]heart shall be despised.

9 [2]*He that is* despised, and hath a [q]servant, *is* better than he that [r]honoureth himself, and [s]lacketh bread.

10 A righteous *man* [t,u]regardeth the life of his beast: [d]but the tender mercies of the wicked *are* [v]cruel.

11 He that [w]tilleth his land shall be satisfied with bread: but he that [x]followeth [y]vain *persons is* void of understanding.

12 The wicked desireth the [z]net of evil *men*: but the root of the righteous yieldeth *fruit*.

13 [a]The wicked is snared by the transgression of *his* lips: but [b,c]the just shall come out of [d]trouble.[S]

14 A man shall be satisfied with good by the fruit of *his* [e]mouth: and [f,g]the [3]recompence of a man's hands shall be rendered unto him.

15 The way of a [h]fool [i,j]*is* right in his own eyes: but he that [k]hearkeneth unto *counsel *is* wise.

16 A [h]fool's [4,l]wrath is presently known: but a [m]prudent *man* [5]covereth shame.

17 *He that* speaketh [n]truth sheweth forth righteousness: but a [o]false[G] witness [p]deceit.

18 There is that speaketh [6]like the piercings of a sword: but the [e]tongue of the wise *is* health.

19 The lip of [n]truth shall be established for ever: but a [q]lying tongue *is* but for a moment.

20 [p,r]Deceit *is* in the heart of them that [7]imagine evil: but to the counsellors of [s]peace *is* joy.

21 [b,c]There shall no evil happen to the just: [r]but the wicked shall be filled with mischief.[G S]

22 [q]Lying lips *are* [t]abomination[G] to the LORD: but they that deal [u,v]truly *are* his delight.

23 A [m]prudent man concealeth knowledge: but the [w]heart of [h]fools [x]proclaimeth foolishness.

24 The hand of the [y,z]diligent shall bear rule: but the [a]slothful shall be [8]under tribute.[G]

25 [b]Heaviness in the heart of man maketh it stoop: but a [c]good word maketh it glad.

26 The righteous *is* [9]more excellent than his neighbour: [d]but the [e]way of the wicked [10]seduceth them.

27 The [a]slothful *man* roasteth not that which he took in hunt-

**31** *n Wicked, punishment of,* Psa. 73:3.

**1** *a Knowledge, desire for,* Luke 11:52. *b Reproof, hated,* Prov. 17:10. 1 R. V. correction

**2** *c Grace of God,* Rom. 4:16. *d Wicked, contrasted with the righteous,* Psa. 73:3.

**3** *e Righteous, promises to,* Psa. 64:10.

**4** *f Women, good,* Prov. 31:10. *g Wife,* Prov. 5:18. *h Family, infelicity in,* 1 Chr. 13:14.

**5** *i Speech, evil,* Col. 4:6. *j Deceit,* Psa. 36:3.

**6** *k Homicide, felonious,* Deut. 5:17. *l Speech, wise,* Col. 4:6.

**7** *m Wicked, punishment of,* Psa. 73:3. *n Children, of the righteous, blessed of God,* Mark 10:14.

**8** *o Prudence,* 2 Chr. 2:12. *p Heart, unregenerate,* Psa. 44:21.

**9** *q Servant,* Jer. 2:14. *r Pride,* Prov. 16:18. *s Poverty,* Prov. 30:8. 2 R. V. Better is he that is lightly esteemed, and hath a servant,

**10** *t Mercy,* Deut. 5:10. *u Animals, kindness to,* Jer. 27:5. *v Cruelty,* Psa. 27:12.

**11** *w Industry,* 1 Kin. 11:28. *x Fellowship, with the wicked,* 1 Cor. 1:9. *y Evil Company,* Prov. 13:20.

**12** *z Net, figurative,* Isa. 51:20.

**13** *a Sin, fruits of,* Rom. 5:12. *b Promise, to the righteous,* 2 Cor. 1:20. *c Righteous, promises to,* Psa. 64:10. *d Adversity, consolation in,* Psa. 10:6.

**14** *e Speech, wise,* Col. 4:6. *f Judgment, according to opportunity,* 1 Pet. 1:17. *g Punishment, according to deeds,* Lev. 26:41. 3 R. V. doings of

**15** *h Fool,* Prov. 18:2. *i Conceit,* Prov. 26:5. *j Self-righteousness,* Luke 18:11. *k Humility,* Prov. 22:4.

**16** *l Anger,* Psa. 37:8. *m Prudence,* 2 Chr. 2:12. 4 R. V. vexation 5 R. V. concealeth

**17** *n Truth,* John 18:37. *o False Witness,* Matt. 19:18. *p Deceit,* Psa. 36:3.

**18** 6 R. V. *inserts* rashly

**19** *q Falsehood,* Job 21:34.

**20** *r Wicked, contrasted with the righteous,* Psa. 73:3. *s Peace,* Jer. 29:7. 7 R. V. devise

**22** *t Abomination,* Lev. 18:27. *u Honesty,* Rom. 13:13. *v Integrity,* Job 2:3.

**23** *w Heart, unregenerate,* Psa. 44:21. *x Speech, foolish,* Col. 4:6.

**24** *y Diligence,* Rom. 12:8. *z Industry,* 1 Kin. 11:28. —*a Laziness,* Prov. 19:15. 8 R. V. put under taskwork.

**25** *b Despondency,* Eccl. 2:20. *c Kindness,* Acts 28:2.

**26** *d Wicked, contrasted with the righteous,* Psa. 73:3. *e Sin,* Rom. 5:12. 9 R. V. a guide to his 10 R. V. causeth them to err.

***COUNSEL.** *Wisdom in,* Ex. 18:14-23; Prov. 11:14; 15:22; 19:20; 20:18; 24:6. *The wise profit by,* Prov. 9:9; 12:15; 27:9. *Rejected,* 1 Kin. 12:8-16; Matt. 19:22. *Consequences of rejecting divine,* Prov. 1:24-32.

ing: but the [11]substance of a [f]dil-
igent man *is* precious.
28 In the way of [g]righteousness
*is* life; and *in* the pathway *thereof*
*there is* no death.

## CHAPTER 13

*Sundry Proverbs.*

A WISE [a]son *heareth* his [b]fa-
ther's [c]instruction: [d]but a
[e]scorner heareth not rebuke.
2 A man shall eat good by the
fruit of *his* [f]mouth: [d]but [g]the
soul of the [1]transgressors *shall*
*eat* violence.
3 He that [f]keepeth his mouth
keepeth his life: [d]*but* [g]he that
[h]openeth wide his lips shall have
destruction.
4 The soul of the [i]sluggard
desireth, and *hath* nothing: but
the soul of the [j,k]diligent shall
be made [l]fat.
5 A righteous *man* [m]hateth [n]ly-
ing: [d]but a wicked *man* is loathsome, and [o]cometh to shame.
6 [p]Righteousness keepeth *him*
*that is* upright in the way: [d]but
wickedness [o]overthroweth the
sinner.
7 [q]There is that [r]maketh himself [s]rich, yet *hath* nothing: *there*
*is* that [t]maketh himself [u]poor,
yet *hath* great [v]riches.
8 The [w]ransom of a man's life
*are* his riches: but the [u]poor
heareth [2]not rebuke.
9 The [x]light of the righteous
rejoiceth: but the [y]lamp of the
wicked shall be [z]put out.

**27**
*f* *Diligence*, Rom. 12:8.
11 R. V. precious substance of men is to the diligent.
**28**
*g* *Righteousness, fruits of*, Psa. 15:2.
**1**
*a* *Young Men*, Prov. 1:4.
*b* *Father*, Psa. 27:10.
*c* *Counsel*, Prov. 12:15.
*d* *Wicked, contrasted with the righteous*, Psa. 73:3.
*e* *Scorners*, Prov. 19:25.
**2**
*f* *Speech, wise*, Col. 4:6.
*g* *Wicked, punishment of*, Psa. 73:3.
1 R. V. treacherous
**3**
*h* *Speech, foolish*, Col. 4:6.
**4**
*i* *Idleness*, Eccl. 10:18.
*j* *Diligence*, Rom. 12:8.
*k* *Industry, brings prosperity*, 1 Kin. 11:28.
*l* *Prosperity*, Eccl. 7:14.
**5**
*m* *Righteous, described*, Psa. 64:10.
*n* *Falsehood*, Job 21:34.
*o* *Sin, fruits of*, Rom. 5:12.
**6**
*p* *Righteousness*, Psa. 15:2.
**7**
*q* *Paradox*, 2 Cor. 12:4.
*r* *Covetousness*, Isa. 57:17.
*s* *Rich*, Jas. 5:1.

*t* *Liberality, rewards for*, 1 Tim. 6:18. *u* *Poor*, Prov. 21:13. *v* *Riches, liberality with*, Eccl. 4:8. **8** *w* *Ransom, of a man's life*, Ex. 21:30. 2 R. V. no threatening. **9** *x* *Righteous, happiness of*, Psa. 64:10. *y* *Wicked, happiness of*, Psa. 73:3. *z* *Wicked, punishment of*, Psa. 73:3.

10 [3]Only by [a]pride cometh [b]con-
tention: but with the well advised
*is* [c]wisdom.
11 [d]Wealth *gotten* by [e]vanity
shall be diminished: but he that
gathereth by [f]labour shall increase.
12 *Hope deferred maketh the
heart [g]sick: but *when* the desire
cometh, *it is* a tree of [h]life.
13 Whoso despiseth the [i]word
[4]shall be destroyed: but he that
[j]feareth the commandment shall
be rewarded.
14 The law of the [k]wise *is* a
fountain of life, to depart from
the [l]snares of death.
15 Good understanding giveth
favour: but the way of [5]trans-
gressors *is* hard.
16 Every [m]prudent *man* dealeth with knowledge: but a [n]fool
layeth open *his* folly.
17 [o]A wicked [p]messenger falleth into mischief: but a [q]faithful
[p]ambassador *is* health.
18 [r]Poverty and shame *shall*
*be to* him that [s]refuseth [6]instruc-
tion: but he that regardeth [t]re-
proof shall be honoured.
19 The desire accomplished is
sweet to the soul: but *it is* abomination to [n]fools to depart from
evil.
20 He that walketh with wise
*men* shall be wise: but a companion of †fools shall [7]be destroyed.
21 Evil pursueth [o]sinners: but
[8]to the righteous good shall be
repayed.
22 A good [u]*man* leaveth an in-

**10**
*a* *Pride*, Prov. 16:18.
*b* *Strife*, Prov. 20:3.
*c* *Wisdom*, Prov. 2:2.
3 R. V. By pride cometh only contention:
**11**
*d* *Riches*, Eccl. 4:8.
*e* *Dishonesty*, Ezek. 22:13.
*f* *Diligence*, Rom. 12:8.
**12**
*g* *Despondency*, Eccl. 2:20.
*h* *Life, tree of*, Eccl. 8:15.
**13**
*i* *Word of God*, Psa. 119:9.
*j* *Fear of God*, Acts 9:31.
4 R. V. bringeth destruction on himself:
**14**
*k* *Wisdom, spiritual*, Prov. 2:2.
*l* *Temptation*, Luke 11:4.
**15**
5 R. V. the treacherous is rugged.
**16**
*m* *Prudence*, 2 Chr. 2:12.
*n* *Fool*, Prov. 18:2.
**17**
*o* *Wicked, contrasted with the righteous*, Psa. 73:3.
*p* *Ambassadors*, Josh. 9:4.
*q* *Faithfulness*, Luke 16:10.
**18**
*r* *Wicked, punishment of*, Psa. 73:3.
*s* *Spiritual Blindness*, 2 Cor. 4:4.
*t* *Reproof*, Prov. 17:10.
6 R. V. correction:

**20** 7 R. V. smart for it.
**21** 8 R. V. the righteous shall be recompensed with good.
**22** *u* *Parents*, 2 Cor. 12:14.

---

***HOPE**, Job 31:24, 28; Psa. 9:18; 16:9; 119:116; Prov. 14:32; 23:18, 22; 24:14; Lam. 3:21, 24, 26; Hos. 2:15; Zech. 9:12; Rom. 4:18; 5:3–5; 15:13; 1 Cor. 13:13; 2 Cor. 3:12; Gal. 5:5; Eph. 2:12; Phil. 1:20; 2 Thess. 21:16; Heb. 6:11; 1 Pet. 3:15.
*In God*, Psa. 31:24; 33:22; 38:15; 39:7; 43:5; 71:5, 14; 78:7; 130:7; 146:5; Jer. 17:7; 1 Pet. 1:21. *A helmet*, 1 Thess. 5:8. *An anchor*, Heb. 6:18, 19.
Grounds of: *God's word*, Psa. 119:74, 81; Rom. 15:4; *God's mercy*, Psa. 33:18; *Jesus Christ*, 1 Thess. 1:3; 1 Tim. 1:1.
*Joy in*, Prov. 10:28; Rom. 5:2; 12:12; Heb. 3:6.
*Of God's calling*, Eph. 1:18; 4:4. *Of eternal life*, Col. 1:5, 6, 23, 27; Tit. 1:2; 2:13; 3:7; 1 Pet. 1:3, 13; 1 John 3:3. *Of the resurrection*, Acts 23:6; 24:14, 15; 26:6, 7; 28:20.
*Deferred*, Prov. 13:12. *Of wicked shall perish*, Job 8:13; 11:20; 27:8; Prov. 10:28; 11:7, 23.

† **EVIL COMPANY**, Prov. 29:24; 2 Pet. 2:7, 8. *Seductive*, Prov. 12:26; 16:29; Matt. 24:12; 1 Cor. 15:33; 2 Pet. 2:18.
*Warnings against*, Prov. 2:11, 12, 16, 19; 4:14, 15; 5:8; 20:19; 22:5, 24, 25; 23:6, 20; 24:1; 28:7, 19.
*Forbidden*, Ex. 23:2, 32, 33; 34:12–15; Deut. 7:2–4; 12:30; Josh. 23:6–13; Prov. 1:10–15; Isa. 8:11, 12; Jer. 51:6, 45; Rom. 16:17, 18; 1 Cor. 5:6, 9–11; 2 Cor. 6:14, 15, 17; Eph. 5:6, 7, 11; 2 Thess. 3:6; 1 Tim. 5:22; 2 Tim. 3:4, 5; 2 John 10, 11; Rev. 18:4.
*Perils of*, Gen. 19:14, 15; Num. 16:21–26; 33:55; Judg. 2:1–3; 2 Chr. 19:2; Ezra 9:14; 106:35, 36.
*Shunned by the righteous*, Psa. 6:8; 26:4, 5; 28:3; 31:6; 84:10; 101:7; 119:115; 139:19, 21, 22; 141:4; Jer. 9:2; Rev. 2:2.
See footnotes: EXAMPLE, John 13:15; INFLUENCE, *Evil*, 1 Cor. 7:14.

heritance to his children's children: and the wealth of the sinner *is* laid up for the just.

23 Much food *is in* the tillage of the poor: but there is *that is* destroyed [9]for want of judgment.

24 He that spareth his rod hateth his son: but he that loveth him [v]chasteneth him betimes.

25 The righteous eateth to the satisfying of his soul: [o]but the belly of the wicked shall want.

## CHAPTER 14

*Sundry Proverbs.*

EVERY [a]wise woman buildeth her house: but the [b,c]foolish plucketh it down with her hands.

2 He that walketh in his [d]uprightness [e]feareth the LORD: but [f]*he that is* perverse in his ways despiseth him.

3 In the [g]mouth of the foolish *is* a rod of pride: but the [h]lips of the wise shall preserve them.

4 Where no [i]oxen *are*, the [j]crib *is* clean: but much increase *is* by the strength of the ox.

5 A faithful witness will not [k]lie: but a [l]false witness will [m]utter lies.

6 A [n]scorner seeketh [o]wisdom, and *findeth it* not: but [p]knowledge *is* easy unto him that understandeth.

7 Go [1]from the presence of a [b]foolish man, when thou perceivest not *in him* the lips of knowledge.

8 The [o]wisdom of the [q]prudent is to understand his way: but the folly of [b]fools *is* [r,s]deceit.

9 [b]Fools make a [t]mock at [u]sin: but among the righteous *there is* favour.

10 The heart knoweth his own bitterness; and a stranger doth not intermeddle with his joy.

11 [v]The house of the wicked shall be overthrown: but the tabernacle of the upright shall flourish.

12 [w]There is a way which [x,y]seemeth right unto a man, but the end thereof *are* the [z]ways of [a]death.

13 Even in [b]laughter the heart is sorrowful; and the end of that [c]mirth *is* heaviness.

14 The [d]backslider in heart shall be filled with his own ways: and a good man *shall be* [e,f]*satisfied* from himself.

15 The [g]simple believeth every word: but the [h]prudent *man* looketh well to his going.

16 A [h]wise *man* [i]feareth, and departeth from evil: but the [g]fool [2]rageth, and is [j]confident.

17 *He that is* soon [k]angry dealeth foolishly: and a man of wicked devices is hated.

18 The [g]simple inherit folly: but the [h]prudent are crowned with [l]knowledge.

19 The evil bow before the good; and the wicked at the gates of the righteous.

20 The [m]poor is hated even of his own neighbour: but the [n]rich *hath* many [o,p]friends.

21 [q]He that despiseth his neighbour sinneth: [r]but he that hath [3,s,t,u]mercy on the [v]poor, [w]happy *is* he.

22 [q]Do they not err that devise evil? but [s]mercy and [x]truth *shall be* to them that devise good.

23 In all [y]labour there is profit: but the [z]talk of the lips *tendeth* only to [a]penury.

24 The crown of the wise *is* their riches: *but* the foolishness of [b]fools *is* folly.

25 A true [c]witness delivereth souls: but [4]a [d]deceitful *witness* speaketh [e]lies.

26 In the [f]fear of the LORD *is* strong [g]confidence: and [h,i]his children shall have a place of refuge.

---

**23**
9 R. V. by reason of injustice.

**24**
v *Children, punishment of*, Mark 10:14.

**1**
a *Women, good*, Prov. 31:10.
b *Fool*, Prov. 18:2.
c *Women, wicked*, Prov. 31:10.

**2**
d *Integrity*, Job 2:3.
e *Fear of God*, Acts 9:31.
f *The Godless*, Job 8:13.

**3**
g *Speech, foolish*, Col. 4:6.
h *Speech, wise*, Col. 4:6.

**4**
i *Bullock*, Ex. 29:3.
j Job 39:9; Isa. 1:3.

**5**
k *Falsehood*, Job 21:34.
l *False Witness*, Matt. 19:18.
m *Perjury*, 1 Tim. 1:10.

**6**
n *Scorner*, Prov. 19:25.
o *Wisdom*, Prov. 2:2.
p *Knowledge*, Luke 11:52.

**7**
1 R. V. Go into the presence of a foolish man, And thou shalt not perceive in him the lips of knowledge.

**8**
q *Prudence*, 2 Chr. 2:12.
r *Deceit*, Psa. 36:3.
s *Hypocrisy*, Jas. 3:17.

**9**
t *Wicked, described*, Psa. 73:3.
u *Sin, fools mock at*, Rom. 5:12.

**11**
v *Sin, consequences of, entailed upon children*, Rom. 5:12.

**12**
w *Spiritual Blindness*, 2 Cor. 4:4.
x *Delusion*, 2 Thess. 2:11.
y *Self-righteousness*, Luke 18:11.
z *Wicked, punishment of*, Psa. 73:3.

a *Spiritual Death*, 1 John 3:14.

**13**
b *Joy*, Psa. 5:11.
c *Worldly Pleasure*, Eccl. 2:1.

**14**
d *Backsliders*, Jer. 3:22.
e *Contentment*, 1 Tim. 6:6.
f *Spiritual Peace*, Gal. 1:3.

**15**
g *Fool*, Prov. 18:2.
h *Prudence*, 2 Chr. 2:12.

**16**
i *Fear of God*, Acts 9:31.
j *False Confidence*, Psa. 30:6.
2 R. V. beareth himself insolently, and is confident.

**17**
k *Anger*, Psa. 37:8.

**18**
l *Knowledge*, Luke 11:52.

**20**
m *Poor*, Prov. 21:13.
n *Rich*, Jas. 5:1.
o *Friends, false*, Ex. 33:11.
p *Flattery*, Prov. 6:24.

**21**
q *Wicked, contrasted with the righteous*, Psa. 73:3.
r *Righteous, contrasted with the wicked*, Psa. 64:10.
s *Mercy*, Deut. 5:10.
t *Liberality*, 1 Tim. 6:18.
u *Kindness*, Acts 28:2.
v *Poor, compassion toward*, Prov. 21:13.
w *Righteous, happiness of*, Psa. 64:10.
3 R. V. pity

**22** x *Truth* John 18:37. **23** y *Labor*, Luke 10:7. z *Idleness, poverty from*, Eccl. 10:18.—a *Poverty*, Prov. 30:8. **24** b *Fool*, Prov. 18:2. **25** c *Witness*, Num. 35:30. d *Deceit*, Psa. 36:3. e *Falsehood*, Job 21:34. 4 R. V. he that uttereth lies causeth deceit. **26** f *Fear of God*, Acts 9:31. g *Boldness, of the righteous*, Phil. 1:20. h *Righteous, promises to*, Psa. 64:10. i *Spiritual Adoption*, Rom. 8:15.

27 The [j]fear of the LORD *is* a
fountain of life, to depart from
the [j]snares of death.
28 In the multitude of people
*is* the king's honour: but in the
want of people *is* the destruction
of the prince.
29 *He that is* [k,l]slow to [m]wrath
*is* of great [n]understanding: but
*he that is* [o]hasty of spirit exalteth folly.
30 A sound [p]heart *is* the life of
the flesh: but [+]envy the rottenness of the bones.
31 He that [q]oppresseth the
[r]poor reproacheth his Maker:
but he that [5]honoureth him hath
[s]mercy on the poor.
32 [t]The wicked is [6,u]driven
away in his wickedness: but
the righteous hath [v]hope in his
[w]death.
33 Wisdom resteth in the [p]heart
of him that hath understanding:
but *that which is* in the [7]midst
of [b]fools is made known.
34 [x]Righteousness exalteth a
[y]nation: but [z]sin *is* a reproach
to any people.[s]
35 The king's favour *is* toward
a [8]wise servant: but his wrath is
*against* him that causeth shame.

## CHAPTER 15

*Sundry Proverbs.*

A [*,a,b,c]SOFT answer turneth
away [d]wrath: but [e]griev-
ous words stir up anger.
2 The tongue of the [f]wise
[*]useth knowledge aright: but
the mouth of [g]fools [h]poureth out
foolishness.
3 The [i]eyes of the LORD *are* in
every place, [1,j]beholding the evil
and the good.[s]
4 A [c]wholesome tongue *is* a tree
of life: but [e]perverseness therein
*is* a [2]breach in the spirit.
5 A [g,k]fool despiseth his [l]fath-
er's [3]instruction: but [m]he that
[b]regardeth [n]reproof [4]is [o]pru-
dent.
6 In the house of the righteous
*is* much [p]treasure: [q]but in the
revenues of the wicked is trouble.[s]
7 The lips of the [f]wise [c]disperse
knowledge: [q]but the heart of the
[g]foolish *doeth* not so.[s]
8 [q]The [r,s]sacrifice of the
[t]wicked *is* an [u]abomination to
the LORD: but the prayer of the
upright *is* his delight.
9 [q]The [v]way of the wicked *is* an
[u]abomination unto the LORD:
but he [w]loveth [x]him that followeth after righteousness.[s]
10 [5,y]Correction *is* grievous
unto him that forsaketh the
way: *and* he that [z]hateth [a]re-
proof shall die.
11 [6,b]Hell and destruction *are*
[c]before the LORD: how much
more then the [d]hearts of the
children of men?[s]
12 A [7,e]scorner loveth not one
that [a]reproveth him: neither
will he go unto the wise.

**27**
*j Temptation*, Luke 11:4.
**29**
*k Patience*, Luke 8:15.
*l Meekness*, Psa. 45:4.
*m Anger*, Psa. 37:8.
*n Wisdom*, Prov. 2:2.
*o Rashness*, 2 Sam. 6:7.
**30**
*p Heart*, Psa. 44:21.
**31**
*q Oppression*, Eccl. 5:8.
*r Poor*, Prov. 21:13.
*s Mercy*, Deut. 5:10.
5 R. V. hath mercy on the needy honoureth him.
**32**
*t Wicked, contrasted with the righteous*, Psa. 73:3.
*u Death, of the wicked*, Num. 23:10.
*v Hope*, Prov. 13:12.
*w Death, of the righteous*, Num. 23:10.
6 R. V. thrust down
**33**
7 R. V. inward part of
**34**
*x Righteousness*, Psa. 15:2.
*y Nation, righteousness exalts*, Isa. 2:4.
*z Sin*, Rom. 5:12.
**35**
8 R. V. servant that dealeth wisely:

**1**
*a Christian Graces, meekness*, Gal. 5:22.
*b Meekness*, Psa. 45:4.
*c Speech, wise*, Col. 4:6.
*d Anger*, Psa. 37:8.
*e Speech, evil*, Col. 4:6. **2** *f Wisdom, spiritual*, Prov. 2:2.

*g Fool*, Prov. 18:2.
*h Speech, foolish*, Col. 4:6.
**3**
*i Anthropomorphisms*, Gen. 11:5.
*j God, knowledge of*, Gen. 2:2.
1 R. V. Keeping watch upon the
**4**
2 R. V. breaking of the spirit.
**5**
*k Children, wicked*, Mark 10:14.
*l Father*, Psa. 27:10.
*m Children, good*, Mark 10:14.
*n Reproof, profitable*, Prov. 17:10.
*o Prudence, in heeding counsel*, 2 Chr. 2:12.
3 R. V. correction:
4 R. V. getteth prudence.
**6**
*p Riches*, Eccl. 4:8.
*q Wicked, contrasted with the righteous*, Psa. 73:3.
**8**
*r Prayer, of the wicked*, Acts 6:4.
*s Hypocrisy, abhorred of God*, Jas. 3:17.
*t Wicked, prayer of*, Psa. 73:3.
*u Abomination*, Lev. 18:27.
*v Sin, repugnant to God*, Rom. 5:12.
**9**
*w God, love of*, Gen. 2:2.
*x Righteous*, Psa. 64:10.
**10**
*y Wicked, described*, Psa. 73:3.
*z Impenitence, judgments denounced against*, Rom. 2:5. 5 R. V. There is grievous correction for him—*a Reproof*, Prov. 17:10.
**11** *b Hell*, Mark 9:43. *c God, knowledge of*, Gen. 2:2. 6 R. V. Sheol and Abaddon are *d Heart, known to God*, Psa. 44:21.
**12** *e Scorners*, Prov. 19:25. 7 Am. R. V. scoffer loveth not to be reproved:

**+ ENVY,** Psa. 73:3; Prov. 14:30; Eccl. 4:4; Rom. 1:29; 1 Cor. 13:4; Gal. 5:19–21, 26; 1 Tim. 6:4; Tit. 3:3; Jas. 4:5.
*Forbidden*, Psa. 37:1; Prov. 3:31; 23:17; 24:1, 19; Rom. 13:13 [R. V. jealousy]; 1 Pet. 2:1.
*Punishment for*, Ezek. 35:11.
**Instances of:** *Cain, of Abel*, Gen. 4:4–8. *Sarah, of Hagar*, Gen. 16:5, 6; 21:9, 10. *Philistines, of Isaac*, Gen. 26:14. *Rachel, of Leah*, Gen. 30:1. *Leah, of Rachel*, Gen. 30:15. *Laban's sons, of Jacob*, Gen. 31:1. *Joseph's brethren, of Joseph*, Gen. 37:4–11, 18–20; Acts 7:9. *Miriam and Aaron, of Moses*, Num. 12:1–10. *Korah, Dathan, and Abiram, of Moses*, Num. 16:3; Psa. 106:16–18. *Saul, of David*, 1 Sam. 18:8, 9, 29; 1 Sam. 20:31. *The princes of Babylon, of Daniel*, Dan. 6:4. *Priests, of Jesus*, Matt. 27:18; Mark 15:10; John 11:47. *Jews, of Paul and Barnabas*, Acts 13:45; 17:5.
*** TACT,** Prov. 15:1; 25:15; Eccl. 10:4. *In preaching*, 1 Cor. 9:19–22; 2 Cor. 12:6. *Of Gideon*, Judg. 8:1–3. *Of Saul, in managing malcontents*, 1 Sam. 10:27; 11:7, 12–15. *Of Nabal's wife*, 1 Sam. 25:18–35.

In David's popular methods: *In organizing the temple music*, 1 Chr. 15:16–24; *in securing popular consent to bringing the ark to Jerusalem*, 1 Chr. 13:1–4.
*Joab's trick in obtaining David's consent to the return of Absalom*, 2 Sam. 14:1–22. *The wise woman of Abel*, 2 Sam. 20:16–22. *Solomon, in judging between the harlots*, 1 Kin. 3:24–28.
*Esther, in concealing her nationality*, Esth. 2:10; *in placating the king*, Esth. 5:1–8; 7.
*Jesus, in charging those who were healed not to advertise his miracles*, Matt. 8:4; 9:30; Mark 1:44; 3:12; 5:43; 7:36; Luke 5:14; 8:56; *in going to the feast secretly*, John 7:10; *in avoiding his enemies*, Matt. 12:14–16; Mark 3:7; John 11:47–54; 12:36; *in evading captious questions by asking questions*, Luke 20:34.
*Paul, in circumcising Timothy*, Acts 16:3; *in stimulating benevolent giving*, 2 Cor. 8:1–8; 9:1–5; *in arraying the two religious factions of the Jews against each other*, Acts 23:6–10.
*The town clerk of Ephesus*, Acts 19:35–41. *The church council at Jerusalem*, Acts 21:20–25.

13 A merry heart maketh a cheerful †countenance: but by sorrow of the heart the spirit is broken.

14 The heart of him that hath understanding seeketh [f]knowledge: but the mouth of [g]fools feedeth on foolishness.

15 All the days of the [h]afflicted *are* evil: but he that is of a merry heart *hath* a continual feast.

16 Better *is* [i]little with the [j]fear of the LORD than great [k]treasure and trouble therewith.

17 Better *is* a dinner of [l]herbs where [m,n]love is, than a stalled[C] [o]ox and ‡,[p,q]hatred therewith.

18 A wrathful man stirreth up [r]strife: but *he that is* [s,t]slow to [u]anger appeaseth strife.

19 The way of the [v,w]slothful *man is* as an [x,y]hedge of thorns: but the way[S] of the righteous *is* made plain.

20 A [z]wise son maketh a glad [a]father: but a [b,c]foolish man despiseth his [d]mother.

21 [e]Folly *is* [f]joy to [b,c]*him that is* destitute of [g]wisdom: but a man of understanding walketh [h]uprightly.

22 Without [i]counsel purposes are disappointed: but [j]in the multitude of counsellors they are established.

23 A man hath joy by the [k]answer of his mouth: and a [l]word *spoken* in *due season, how good *is it*!

24 [8]The way of life *is* above to the wise, that he may depart from [9,m]hell[C] beneath.

25 The LORD will [n]destroy the house of the [o]proud: but he will [n]establish the border of the [p]widow.

26 [10]The [q]thoughts of the [r]wicked *are* an [s]abomination to the LORD: but [11]*the* [k]*words* of the pure *are* pleasant words.

27 He that is [t]greedy of gain troubleth his own house; but he that hateth [u]gifts[C] shall live.

28 The heart of the righteous [v]studieth to [k]answer: [r]but the mouth of the wicked [w]poureth out evil things.

29 [r]The LORD *is* far from the wicked: [x]but he [y]heareth the prayer of the righteous.[Q]

30 The light of the eyes rejoiceth the heart: *and* [12]a [z]good report maketh the bones fat.

31 The ear that heareth the [a]reproof of life abideth among the wise.

32 He that refuseth [b]instruction despiseth his own soul: but he that heareth[C] [a]reproof getteth understanding.

33 The [c]fear of the LORD *is* the instruction of [d]wisdom; and before honour *is* [e]humility.

## CHAPTER 16

*Sundry Proverbs.*

THE preparations of the [a]heart [1]in man, and the answer of the tongue, *is* from the LORD.

2 All the ways of a man *are* [b]clean in his own eyes; but the LORD [c,d]weigheth the [e]spirits.[C S]

3 [f]Commit thy works unto the LORD, and thy thoughts shall be established.[S]

4 The LORD hath [g]made [2]all

**14**
*f Knowledge, desire for*, Luke 11:52.
*g Fool*, Prov. 18:2.
**15**
*h Afflictions*, Psa. 34:19.
**16**
*i Poverty, better than unrighteous wealth*, Prov. 30:8.
*j Fear of God*, Acts 9:31.
*k Riches*, Eccl. 4:8.
**17**
*l Food, vegetables*, Psa. 136:25.
*m Love, of man for man*, 1 John. 4:7.
*n Peace*, Jer. 29:7.
*o Cattle, stall-fed*, Ex. 12:29.
*p Family, infelicity in*, 1 Chr. 13:14.
*q Malice*, Eph. 4:31.
**18**
*r Strife*, Prov. 20:3.
*s Patience*, Luke 8:15.
*t Christian Graces*, Gal. 5:22.
*u Anger*, Psa. 37:8.
**19**
*v Idleness*, Eccl. 10:18.
*w Laziness*, Prov. 19:15.
*x Hedge*, Isa. 5:5.
*y Fence*, Psa. 62:3.
**20**
*z Children, good*, Mark 10:14.

*a Father*, Psa. 27:10.
*b Fool*, Prov. 18:2.
*c Children, wicked*, Mark 10:14.
*d Mother*, 1 Kin. 2:20.
**21**
*e Worldly Pleasure*, Eccl. 2:1.
*f Joy, of the wicked*, Psa. 5:11.
*g Wisdom*, Prov. 2:2.
*h Integrity*, Job 2:3.
**22**
*i Counsel, wisdom in*, Prov. 12:15
*j Unity, advantages of*, Psa. 133:1.
**23** *k Speech, wise*, Col. 4:6. *l Words, of the wise*, Luke 4:22. **24** *m Hell*, Mark 9:43. 8 R. V. To the wise the way of life goeth upward, 9 R. V. Sheol. **25** *n God, providence of*, Gen. 2:2.

*o Pride*, Prov. 16:18.
*p Widow*, 2 Sam. 14:5.
**26**
*q Sin, repugnant to God*, Rom. 5:12.
*r Wicked, contrasted with the righteous*, Psa. 73:3.
*s Abomination*, Lev. 18:27.
10 R. V. Evil devices are
11 R. V. pleasant words are pure.
**27**
*t Covetousness*, Isa. 57:17.
*u Bribery*, 1 Sam. 8:3.
**28**
*v Prudence*, 2 Chr. 2:12.
*w Speech, evil*, Col. 4:6.
**29**
*x Righteous, promises to*, Psa. 64:10.
*y Prayer, answer to, promised*, Acts 6:4.
**30**
*z* Prov. 25:25.
12 R. V. good tidings

**31**
*a Reproof, profitable*, Prov. 17:10.
**32**
*b Counsel*, Prov. 12:15.
**33**
*c Fear of God*, Acts 9:31.
*d Wisdom, spiritual*, Prov. 2:2.
*e Humility*, Prov. 22:4.

**1**
*a Heart*, Psa. 44:21.
1 R. V. belong to man: But the answer of the tongue is

**2**
*b Self-righteousness*, Luke 18:11.
*c God, judge*, Gen. 2:2.
*d God, knowledge of*, Gen. 2:2.
*e Heart, known to God*, Psa. 44:21.
**3** *f Faith, enjoined*, Mark 11:22.
**4** *g God, creator*, Gen. 2:2. 2 R. V. every thing for its own end:

† **COUNTENANCE,** Psa. 4:6; 42:11; 43:5; 44:3; Prov. 27:17. *Angry*, Prov. 25:23. *Cheerful*, Job 29:24; Prov. 15:13. *Fierce*, Deut. 28:50; Dan. 8:23. *Guilty*, Gen. 4:5; Isa. 3:9. *Health indicated in*, Psa. 42:11; 43:5; Dan. 1:15. *Pride in*, Psa. 10:4. *Reading of*, Gen. 31:2, 5. *Sad*, 1 Sam. 1:18; Neh. 2:2, 3; Eccl. 7:3; Ezek. 27:35; Dan. 5:6; Matt. 6:16.
Transfigured: *Of Moses*, Ex. 34:29–35 (with 2 Cor. 3:7, 13); *of Jesus*, Matt. 17:2; Mark 9:3; Luke 9:29; *of the one seen by John in his vision*, Rev. 1:16.
See footnote, FACE, Ex. 34:29.
‡ **HATRED,** Prov. 15:17; 26:24–26; 1 John 2:9, 11. *A work of the flesh*, Gal. 5:19, 20. *A bar to loving God*, 1 John 4:20. *Produces strife*, Prov. 10:12. *Is, unforgiving*, Matt. 6:15; *murderous*, 1 John 3:15.
*Toward the righteous*, Psa. 25:19; 35:19; Matt. 10:22; John 15:18, 19, 23–25; 17:14.
*Forbidden*, Eph. 4:31; Col. 3:8. *Toward a brother, forbidden*, Lev. 19:17. *Toward an enemy, forbidden*, Matt. 5:43, 44.
*Against iniquity, justified*, Psa. 97:10; 101:3; 119:104, 128, 163; 139:21, 22.
*Of God, against iniquity*, Psa. 5:5; 45:7; Isa. 61:8; Mal. 2:16.

*h Wicked, punishment of*, Psa. 73:3.

**5**

*i Abomination*, Lev. 18:27.

*j Punishment, no escape from*, Lev. 26:41.

**6**

*k Mercy*, Deut. 5:10.

*l Christian Graces*, Gal. 5:22.

*m Truth*, John 18:37.

*n Spiritual Purification*, Psa. 51:2.

*o Fear of God, a motive to obedience*, Acts 9:31.

*p Holiness*, Ex. 39:30.

3 Am. R. V. *marg.* atoned for:

**7**

*q Promise, to the righteous*, 2 Cor. 1:20.

*r Righteous, promises to*, Psa. 64:10.

*s Blessings, contingent upon obedience*, Deut. 11:26.

*t God, providence of*, Gen. 2:2.

*u Peace*, Jer. 29:7.

**8**

*v Poverty*, Prov. 30:8.

*w Riches*, Eccl. 4:8.

**9**

*x God, preserver*, Gen. 2:2.

**10**

*y Rulers, character and qualifications of*, Ex. 18:21.

4 R. V. shall not transgress in judgment.

**11**

*z Honesty*, Rom. 13:13.

*a Integrity*, Job 2:3.

*b Weights, must be just*, Lev. 19:35.

*c Balances, must be just*, Prov. 11:1.

*things* for himself: yea, even the
wicked for the [h]day of evil.[S T Q]
5 Every one *that is* *proud in
heart *is* an [i]abomination to the
LORD: *though* hand *join* in
hand, [j]he shall not be unpunished.
6 By [k,l]mercy and [l,m]truth iniquity is [3,n]purged:[C] and by the
[o]fear of the LORD *men* [p]depart
from evil.
7 [q,r,s]When a man's ways please
the LORD, he [t]maketh even his
enemies to be at [u]peace with
him.[S]
8 Better *is* a [v]little with righteousness than great [w]revenues
without right.
9 A man's heart deviseth[C] his
way: but the LORD [x]directeth
his steps.[S]
10 A divine sentence[G] *is* in the
lips of the king: [y]his mouth
[4]transgresseth not in judgment.
11 A [z,a]just [b]weight and [c]bal-
ance[C] *are* the LORD's: all the
weights of the bag *are* his work.[C]
12 [d]*It is* an abomination to
kings to commit wickedness: for
the throne is established by
righteousness.
13 [d]Righteous [e]lips *are* the delight of kings; and they love him
that speaketh right.
14 The [f]wrath of a king *is as*
messengers of death: but a wise
[g]man will [h]pacify it.
15 In the light of the king's
countenance *is* life; and his favour *is* as a cloud of the latter
rain.
16 How much better *is it* to
get [i]wisdom than gold! and to
get understanding rather to be
chosen than silver!
17 The [j]highway of the upright
*is* to [k]depart from evil: he that
[l]keepeth his way preserveth his
soul.[S]
18 *Pride *goeth* before destruction, and an haughty spirit before a fall.
19 Better *it is to be* of an [m]hum-
ble spirit with the lowly, than
to divide the spoil with the
[*,n]proud.
20 He that [5]handleth a matter wisely shall find good: and
[o]whoso [p]trusteth in the LORD,
happy *is* he.
21 The [i]wise in heart shall be
called [q]prudent: and the [e]sweet-
ness of the lips increaseth learning.
22 [i]Understanding *is* a wellspring[C] of life unto him that hath
it: but the [6]instruction of fools
*is* folly.
23 The heart of the [i]wise
teacheth his mouth, and addeth
learning to his lips.
24 [r]Pleasant words *are as* an
honeycomb, sweet to the soul,
and health to the bones.
25 [s]There is a way that [t]seem-
eth right unto a man, but the end
thereof *are* the ways of [u]death.
26 [7]He that [v]laboureth laboureth for himself; for his mouth
[w]craveth it of him.
27 [8]An ungodly man diggeth
up evil: and in his [x]lips *there is*
as a burning fire.
28 A froward[C] man soweth
[y]strife: and a [z,a]whisperer separateth chief [b]friends.

**16**

*i Wisdom*, Prov. 2:2.

**17**

*j Highways, figurative*, Deut. 2:27.

*k Holiness*, Ex. 39:30.

*l Watchfulness*, Matt. 24:42.

**19**

*m Humility*, Prov. 22:4.

*n Evil Company*, Prov. 13:20.

**20**

*o Righteous, happiness of*, Psa. 64:10.

*p Faith*, Mark 11:22.

5 R. V. giveth heed unto the word shall find good:

**21**

*q Prudence*, 2 Chr. 2:12.

**22**

6 R. V. correction of fools is their folly.

**24**

*r Kindness*, Acts 28:2.

**25**

*s Spiritual Blindness, consequences of*, 2 Cor. 4:4.

*t Delusion*, 2 Thess. 2:11.

*u Spiritual Death*, 1 John 5:14.

**26**

*v Industry*, 1 Kin. 11:28.

*w Hunger, a stimulus to work*, Neh. 9:15.

7 R. V. The appetite of the labouring man laboureth for him;

**27**

*x Speech, evil*, Col. 4:6.

8 R. V. A worthless man deviseth mischief:

**28**

*y Strife*, Prov. 20:3.

*z Slander*, Prov. 10:18.

*a Talebearing*, Prov. 11:13.

*b Friends*, Ex. 33:11.

**12** *d Rulers, character and qualifications of*, Ex. 18:21.
**13** *e Speech, wise*, Col. 4:6.
**14** *f Anger*, Psa. 37:8. *g Citizens*, Luke 15:15. *h Tact*, Prov. 15:1.

* **PRIDE,** Psa. 10:2–6; 21:4, 24; 73:6, 8; 119:21, 69, 78; Prov. 16:19; 20:6; 27:2; 30:12, 13; Jer. 49:4, 16; 1 Cor. 1:29; 8:1; Gal. 6:3; 1 John 2:16.

*Admonitions against*, Deut. 8:11–14, 17–20; Jer. 9:23; Matt. 23:5–7; Luke 14:8, 9; 20:46, 47; Rom. 11:17–21, 25; 12:3, 16; 1 Cor. 4:6–8, 10; 5:2, 6; 10:12; Eph. 4:17; Phil. 2:3; 1 Tim. 2:9; 6:3, 4, 17; 1 Pet. 5:3, 5; Rev. 3:17, 18.

*Rebuked*, 2 Kin. 14:9, 10; 2 Chr. 25:18, 19; Job 12:2; Jer. 13:9, 15, 17; Hab. 2:4, 5, 9.

*Repugnant to God*, Job 37:24; Psa. 12:3; 18:27; 31:23; 101:5; 138:6; Prov. 6:16, 17; 8:13; 16:5; Jer. 50:21, 32; Luke 1:51; Jas. 4:6.

*Proceeds from the carnal mind*, Mark 7:21, 22. *Leads, to strife*, Prov. 13:10; 28:25; *to destruction*, Prov. 15:25; 16:18; 17:19; 18:11, 12; Isa. 14:12–16; 26:5; 28:3; Dan. 11:45; Mal. 4:1; 1 Tim. 3:6; Rev. 18:7, 8.

*Shall be humbled*, Prov. 11:2; Isa. 2:11–17; 3:16–26; 5:15; 13:11; 47:7–11; Dan. 4:37; Obad. 3, 4; Matt. 23:12; Luke 1:52; 18:14; Rev. 18:7, 8.

*Prevented by divine discipline*, 2 Cor. 12:7.

**Instances of:** *Pharaoh*, Ex. chapters 7–11; 12:29–36; 14. *Ahithophel*, 2 Sam. 17:23. *Naaman*, 2 Kin. 5:11–13. *Hezekiah*, 2 Kin. 20:13; 2 Chr. 32:25, 26, 31; Isa. 39:2. *Uzziah*, 2 Chr. 26:16–19. *Nebuchadnezzar*, Dan. 4:30–34: 5:20. *Belshazzar*, Dan. 5:22, 23. *Haman*, Esth. 3:5; 5:11, 13; 6:6; 7:10. *The scribes and Pharisees*, Matt. 23:6–8, 10, 11; Mark 12:38; Luke 11:43; 20:45–47. *Herod*, Acts 12:21–23.

29 A [c]violent man [d]enticeth his
neighbour, and leadeth him into
the way *that is* not good.
30 He shutteth his eyes to [e]de-
vise froward things: [9]moving his
lips he bringeth evil to pass.
31 The [f]hoary head *is* a crown
of glory, [10]*if* it be found in the
way of [g]righteousness.
32 *He that is* [h,i]slow to [j]anger
*is* better than the mighty; and
he that [j]ruleth his spirit than he
that taketh a city.
33 The [k]lot is cast into the lap;
but the whole disposing thereof
*is* of the [l]LORD.

## CHAPTER 17

*Sundry Proverbs.*

BETTER *is* a dry morsel,
and [a]quietness therewith,
than an house full of [1]sacrifices
*with* [b]strife.
2 A [c,d]wise [e]servant shall have
rule over a [f,g]son that causeth
shame, and shall have part of
the [h]inheritance among the
brethren.
3 The fining pot *is* for [i]silver,
and the *furnace for [j]gold: but
the [k]LORD [l,m]trieth the [n]hearts.
4 A wicked doer giveth heed to
[o]false lips; *and* a liar giveth ear
to a [p]naughty tongue.
5 Whoso [q]mocketh the [r]poor
[s]reproacheth his Maker: *and* he
that is [t]glad at calamities shall
not be unpunished.
6 Children's [u]children *are* the
crown of [v]old men; and the glory
of children *are* their fathers.
7 [w]Excellent speech becometh
not a [x]fool: much less do [o]lying
lips a [y]prince.
8 A gift *is as* a precious stone
in the eyes of him that hath it:
whithersoever it turneth, it prospereth.
9 He that [z]covereth a transgression seeketh [a,b]love; but he
that [2]repeateth a matter separateth [3]*very* [c]friends.
10 A †reproof entereth more
into a wise man than an hundred [d]stripes into a [e]fool.
11 An [f]evil *man* seeketh only
rebellion: [g]therefore a cruel messenger shall be sent against him.
12 Let a [h]bear robbed of her
whelps meet a man, rather than
a [e]fool in his folly.
13 Whoso [i]rewardeth [j]evil for
good, [k]evil shall not depart from
his house.
14 The beginning of [l]strife *is*
*as* when one letteth out water:
therefore [m,n]leave off contention,
before [4]it be meddled with.

**29** *c Evil Company,* Prov. 13:20. *d Temptation,* Luke 11:4. **30** *e Malice, devises mischief,* Eph. 4:31. 9 R. V. He that compresseth his lips bringeth **31** *f Old Age,* Isa. 46:4. *g Righteousness,* Psa. 15:2. 10 R. V. It shall be found **32** *h Patience,* Luke 8:15. *i Christian Graces,* Gal. 5:22. *j Anger, restraint of,* Psa. 37:8. **33** *k Lot,* Esth. 3:7. *l God, providence of,* Gen. 2:2.

**1** *a Peace,* Jer. 29:7. *b Strife,* Prov. 20:3. 1 R. V. feasting with strife. **2** *c Wisdom, worldly,* Prov. 2:2. *d Prudence,* 2 Chr. 2:12. *e Servant,* Jer. 2:14. *f Children, wicked, disgrace parents,* Mark 10:14. *g Young Men,* Prov. 1:4. *h Inheritance,* Num. 27:7. **3** *i Silver, refining of,* 1 Chr. 28:14. *j Gold, refined,* Ezek. 7:19. *k God, judge,* Gen. 2:2. *l Temptation, a test,* Luke 11:4. *m Afflictions, design of,* Psa. 34:19. *n Heart, regenerate,* Psa. 44:21. **4** *o Falsehood,* Job 21:34. *p Speech, evil,* Col. 4:6.

**5** *q Mocking,* 1 Kin. 18:27. *r Poor, oppressions of,* Prov. 21:13. *s Blasphemy,* 2 Sam. 12:14. *t Malice, punishment for,* Eph. 4:31. **6** *u Children, a blessing,* Mark 10:14. *v Old Age,* Isa. 46:4. **7** *w Speech, wise,* Col. 4:6. *x Fool,* Prov. 18:2. *y Rulers, character and qualifications of,* Ex. 18:21. **9** *z Charitableness,* Prov. 10:12. *a Love, of man for man,* 1 John 4:7. *b Friendship,* Prov. 22:24. *c Friends,* Ex. 33:11. 2 R. V. harpeth on a matter 3 R. V. chief friends. **10** *d Punishment, minor offenses,* Lev. 26:41. *e Fool,* Prov. 18:2. **11** *f Citizens, wicked,* Luke 15:15. *g Loyalty, enforced,* Eccl. 8:2. **12** *h Bear,* 2 Sam. 17:8. **13** *i Ingratitude, of man to man,* Rom. 1:21. *j Evil for Good,* Psa. 35:12. *k Sin, fruits of,* Rom. 5:12. **14** *l Strife,* Prov. 20:3. *m Litigation, to be avoided,* Matt. 5:25. *n Anger, forbidden,* Psa. 37:8. 4 R. V. there be quarrelling.

* **FURNACE.** *For refining, silver,* Psa. 12:6; Ezek. 22:22; *gold,* Prov. 17:3. *For melting lead and tin,* Ezek. 22:20. *Shadrach, Meshach, and Abed-nego cast into, by Nebuchadnezzar,* Dan. 3:6–26.

**Figurative:** *Of affliction,* Deut. 4:20; 1 Kin. 8:51; Isa. 48:10; Jer. 11:4 *Of lust,* Hos. 7:4. *Of judgment,* Mal. 4:1; Matt. 13:42, 50.

† **REPROOF.** *Enjoined,* Lev. 19:17; Psa. 141:5; Prov. 10:17; Matt. 18:15–17; Luke 17:3; Eph. 5:11; 1 Thess. 5:14; 1 Tim. 5:20; 2 Tim. 4:2; Tit. 1:13.

*Of seniors, forbidden,* 1 Tim. 5:1, 2.

*Profitable,* Prov. 13:18; 15:5, 31, 32; 27:5, 6; 28:23; Eccl. 7:5. *Wise profit by,* Prov. 17:10; 19:25.

*Hated,* Prov. 12:1; 10:17; Amos 5:10; John 7:7; Gal. 4:16; *by Ahab,* 1 Kin. 22:8; *by Asa,* 2 Chr. 16:10; *by Herodias,* Mark 6:18, 19; *by the people of Nazareth,* Luke 4:28, 29; *by the Jews,* Acts 5:33; 7:54.

**Faithfulness in:** INSTANCES OF: *Moses, of Pharaoh,* Ex. 10:29; 11:8; *of the Israelites,* Ex. 16:6–10; 32:19–30; Num. 14:41; 20:10; 32:14; Deut. 1:12, 26–43; 9:16–24; 29:2–4; 31:27–29; 32:15–18; *of Eleazar and Ithamar,* Lev. 10:16–18; *of Korah,* Num. 16:8–11. *Israelites, of the two and one-half tribes,* Josh. 22:15–20; *of the tribe of Benjamin,* Judg. 20:12, 13. *Samuel, of Saul,* 1 Sam. 15:14–35. *Jonathan, of Saul,* 1 Sam. 19:4, 5. *Nathan, of David,* 2 Sam. 12:1–14. *Joab, of David,* 2 Sam. 19:1–7; 24:3; 1 Chr. 21:3. *The prophet Gad, of David,* 2 Sam. 24:13. *Shemaiah, of Rehoboam,* 2 Chr. 12:5. *A prophet of Judah, of Jeroboam,* 1 Kin. 13:1–10. *Abijah, of Jeroboam,* 2 Chr. 13:8–11. *Elijah, of Ahab and Israel,* 1 Kin. 18:17–21; *of Ahab and Jezebel,* 1 Kin. 21:20–24; *of Ahaziah,* 2 Kin. 1:2–17. *Micaiah, of Ahab,* 1 Kin. 22:14–28. *Elisha, of Jehoram,* 2 Kin. 3:13, 14; *of Gehazi,* 2 Kin. 5:26, 27; *of Joash,* 2 Kin. 13:19. *Isaiah, of Hezekiah,* 2 Kin. 20:14–18. *Jehoash, of Jehoiada and other priests,* 2 Kin. 12:7. *Azariah, of Uzziah,* 2 Chr. 26:17, 18. *Hanani, of Asa,* 2 Chr. 16:7–9. *Jehu, of Jehoshaphat,* 2 Chr. 19:2. *Zechariah, of Judah and Jerusalem,* 2 Chr. 24:20. *Obed, of the people of Samaria,* 2 Chr. 28:9–11. *Jeremiah, of the cities of Judah,* Jer. 26:2–15. *Ezra, of the men of Judah and Benjamin,* Ezra 10:9, 10. *Nehemiah, of the Jews,* Neh. 5:6–13; 13:10–28. *Daniel, of Nebuchadnezzar,* Dan. 4:27; *of Belshazzar,* Dan. 5:17–24. *Amos, of the Israelites,* Amos 7:12–17.

Jesus, of the Jews: *When Pharisees and Sadducees came to him desiring a sign,* Matt. 16:1–4; Mark 8:11, 12; *the scribes and Pharisees,* Matt. 23; *the Pharisees,* Luke 11:37–44; 16; *the lawyers,* Luke 11:42–52; *when they brought to him the woman taken in adultery,* John 8:7. *In his parables, of the king's feast,* Luke 14:16–24; *of the two sons,* Matt. 21:28–32; *of the vineyard,* Matt. 21:33–46; Mark 12:1–12; Luke 20:9–19; *of the barren fig tree,* Luke 13:3–9.

*John the Baptist, of the Jews,* Matt. 3:7–12; Luke 3:7–9; *of Herod,* Matt. 14:4; Mark 6:18; Luke 3:19, 20. *Peter, of Simon, the sorcerer,* Acts 8:20–23. *Stephen, of the Jews,* Acts 7:51–53. *Paul, of Elymas, the sorcerer,* Acts 13:9–11; *of the*

15 [o,p]He that [q]justifieth the wicked, and he that [q]condemneth the just, even they both *are* [r]abomination to the LORD.[T]

16 Wherefore[G] *is there* a price in the hand of a fool to get [s]wisdom, seeing *he hath* [t]no heart *to it*?

17 A [c]friend [a,b]loveth at all times, and a [u]brother is born for adversity.

18 A man void[G] of understanding [v]striketh [w]hands, *and* becometh [x]surety in the presence of his friend.

19 He loveth transgression that loveth [l]strife: *and* he that [y]exalteth his gate seeketh destruction.

20 He that hath a froward[G] [z]heart findeth no good: and he that hath a [a]perverse tongue falleth into mischief.

21 He that begetteth a [b,c]fool *doeth it* to his sorrow: and the father of a fool hath no joy.

22 A merry heart [5]doeth good *like* a [‡]medicine: but a [d]broken spirit drieth the bones.

23 A wicked *man* taketh a [e]gift[G] out of the bosom to pervert the ways of judgment.[G]

24 [f]Wisdom *is* before him that hath understanding; but the eyes of a [b]fool *are* in the ends of the earth.

25 A [b]foolish [c,g]son *is* a grief to his father, and bitterness to her that bare him.

26 Also to [h]punish[G] the just *is* not good, *nor* to strike princes for equity.

27 He that [6]hath knowledge spareth his words: *and* a man of understanding is of an excellent spirit.

28 Even a fool, when he [i]holdeth his peace, is counted wise: *and* he that [i]shutteth his lips *is* *esteemed* [7]a man of understanding.

## CHAPTER 18

*Sundry Proverbs.*

[1]THROUGH desire a man, having separated himself, seeketh *and* intermeddleth[G] with all [a]wisdom.

2 A *fool hath no delight in understanding, but that his heart may discover itself.

3 [b]When the wicked cometh, *then* cometh also contempt, and with ignominy reproach.

4 The [c]words of a man's mouth *are as* deep waters, *and* the wellspring[G] of [a]wisdom *as* a flowing brook.[Q]

5 *It is* not good to accept the person of the wicked, to [d]overthrow the righteous in judgment.

6 A *fool's [e]lips enter into [f]contention, and his mouth calleth for strokes.

7 A *fool's [e]mouth *is* his destruction, and his [e]lips *are* the snare of his soul.

8 The [e,g]words of a [2,h]talebearer[G] *are* as wounds, and they go down into the innermost parts of the belly.

9 He also that is [3,i,j]slothful in his work is brother to him that is a [4]great waster.

10 The name of the LORD *is* a strong [k,l]tower: the righteous runneth into it, and is safe.

11 The [m]rich man's wealth *is* his strong city, and as an high wall in his own [n,o]conceit.[G]

12 Before destruction the [p]heart of man is [o]haughty, and before honour *is* [q]humility.

13 He that [r]answereth a matter before he heareth *it*, it *is* folly and shame unto him.

14 The [s]spirit of a man will

15
*o* *Rulers, wicked,* Ex. 18:21.
*p* *Court, corrupt,* Ex. 18:26.
*q* *Injustice,* Isa. 26:10.
*r* *Abomination,* Lev. 18:27.

16
*s* *Wisdom,* Prov. 2:2.
*t* *Spiritual Blindness,* 2 Cor. 4:4.

17
*u* *Brother, love of,* Prov. 18:24.

18
*v* *Contracts, modes of ratifying,* Matt. 20:2.
*w* *Hand, clasping of, in token of contract,* Ezra 10:19.
*x* *Surety,* Gen. 44:32.

19
*y* *Pride,* Prov. 16:18.

20
*z* *Heart, unregenerate,* Psa. 44:21.

*a* *Speech, evil,* Col. 4:6.

21
*b* *Fool, causes sorrow,* Prov. 18:2.
*c* *Children, wicked,* Mark 10:14.

22
*d* *Despondency,* Eccl. 2:20.
5 R. V. is a good medicine:

23
*e* *Bribery, perverts justice,* 1 Sam. 8:3.

24
*f* *Wisdom, spiritual,* Prov. 2:2.

25
*g* *Young Men,* Prov. 1:4.

26
*h* *Injustice,* Isa. 26:10.

27
6 R. V. spareth his words hath knowledge: And he that is of a cool spirit is a man of understanding.

28
*i* *Prudence,* 2 Chr. 2:12.

7 R. V. as prudent.

1
*a* *Wisdom,* Prov. 2:2.
1 R. V. He that separateth himself seeketh his own desire, And rageth against all sound wisdom.

3
*b* *Sin, fruits of,* Rom. 5:12.

4
*c* *Speech, wise,* Col. 4:6.

5
*d* *Injustice,* Isa. 26:10.

6
*e* *Speech, evil,* Col. 4:6.
*f* *Strife,* Prov. 20:3.

8
*g* *Slander,* Prov. 10:18.
*h* *Talebearing,* Prov. 11:13.
2 R. V. whisperer are as dainty morsels,

9
*i* *Laziness,* Prov. 19:15.
*j* *Idleness,* Eccl. 10:18.
3 R. V. slack
4 R. V. destroyer.

10
*k* *Tower, figurative,* 2 Chr. 26:9.
*l* *Fortification, figurative,* Ezek. 17:17.

11
*m* *Rich, deluded,* Jas. 5:1.
*n* *False Confidence,* Psa. 30:6.
*o* *Pride,* Prov. 16:18.

12
*p* *Heart,* Psa. 44:21.
*q* *Humility,* Prov. 22:4.

13
*r* *Speech, foolish,* Col. 4:6.

14
*s* *Courage,* Deut. 31:7.

*magistrates of Philippi,* Acts 16:37–39; *of Ananias, the high priest,* Acts 23:3.

‡ **MEDICINE,** Isa. 38:21; Luke 10:34.

**Figurative,** Prov. 17:22; Isa. 1:6; Jer. 8:22; 30:13; 46:11; 51:8, 9.

**Allegorical,** Rev. 22:2.

* **FOOL.** *One, who is lacking in understanding,* Prov. 3:35; 9:21; 10:13; 15:21; 26:1, 3–12; Eccl. 7:4–6; or, *is of uncontrolled temper,* Eccl. 7:9; or, *is deficient in conscience,* Prov. 10:23; or, *is willful, disregarding wise counsels and lessons from experience,* Prov. 1:7; 27:22.

Described as: *Idle,* Eccl. 4:5; *wasteful,* Prov. 21:20; *loquacious,* Prov. 10:8, 10; 29:11; Eccl. 10:12–14; *meddlesome,* Prov. 20:3; *contentious,* Prov. 18:6; 29:9; *unfilial,* Prov. 15:20; *despising wisdom,* Prov. 1:7, 22; 18:2; *atheistic,* Psa. 14:1; 53:1. *Causes sorrow,* Prov. 14:13.

**Parables concerning:** *The foolish virgins,* Matt. 25:1–13. *The rich fool,* Luke 12:16–20.

sustain[G] his infirmity; but a
[5,t]wounded spirit who can bear?
15 The heart of the [u]prudent
getteth [v]knowledge; and the ear
of the wise [v]seeketh knowledge.
16 A man's [w,x]gift maketh room
for him, and bringeth him before
great men.
17 *He that* [6]*is* first in his own
cause *seemeth* just; but his neighbour cometh and [7]search[G]eth him.
18 The [y]lot causeth [t]conten-
tions to cease, and parteth between the mighty.
19 A †brother offended *is harder
to be won* than a strong city:
and [8]*their* [t]contentions *are* like
the bars of a castle.
20 A man's [z]belly shall be satisfied with the fruit of his mouth;
*and* with the increase of his lips
shall he be filled.
21 Death and life *are* in the
power of the tongue: and they
that love it shall eat the fruit
thereof.
22 *Whoso* [a]findeth a [b]wife findeth a good *thing*, and obtaineth
favour of the LORD.
23 The [c]poor useth intreaties;
but the [d]rich [e]answereth roughly.
24 [9]A man *that hath* [f,g]friends
must shew himself friendly: and
there is a friend *that* sticketh
closer than a †brother.

t *Despondency*, Eccl. 2:20.
5 R. V. broken

15
u *Prudence*, 2 Chr. 2:12.
v *Knowledge, desire for*, Luke 11:52.

16
w *Presents*, Gen. 32:13.
x *Bribery*, 1 Sam. 8:3.

17
6 R. V. pleadeth his cause first seemeth
7 R. V. searcheth him out.

18
y *Lot*, Esth. 3:7.

19
8 R. V. such

20
z *Belly*, Prov. 20:27.

22
a *Marriage, commended*, Gen. 34:9.
b *Wife*, Prov. 5:18.

23
c *Poor*, Prov. 21:13.
d *Rich*, Jas. 5:1.
e *Speech, evil*, Col. 4:6.

24
f *Friends*, Ex. 33:11.
g *Friendship*, Prov. 22:24.
9 R. V. He that maketh many friends doeth it to his own destruction:

## CHAPTER 19

*Sundry Proverbs.*

BETTER *is* the [a]poor that
walketh in his [b]integrity,
than *he that is* [c]perverse[G] in his
lips, and is a fool.
2 Also, *that* the soul *be* [d]without
knowledge, *it is* not good; and he
that hasteth with *his* feet sinneth.
3 The foolishness of man [1]per-
verteth his way: and his heart
[e]fretteth against the LORD.
4 [f,g]Wealth maketh many
[h,i]friends; but the [j]poor is separated from his neighbour.
5 A [k]false[G] witness shall not be
unpunished, and *he that* speaketh [l]lies shall not escape.
6 Many will intreat the favou[G]r
of the [2]prince: and every man *is*
a [h]friend to him that [m]giveth
gifts.
7 All the brethren of the [j]poor
do [n]hate him: how much more
do his [o]friends go far from him?
he pursueth *them with* words,
[3]*yet* they *are* wanting[G] *to him*.
8 He that getteth [p]wisdom loveth his own soul: he that keepeth
understanding shall find good.
9 A [k]false[G] witness shall not be
unpunished, and *he that* speaketh [l]lies shall perish.
10 [4]Delight is not seemly[G] for a
fool; much less for a [q]servant to
have rule over princes.
11 The discretion of a man
[5,r,s]deferreth his [t]anger; and *it
is* his glory to [u,v]pass over a
transgression.
12 The [w]king's wrath *is* as the
roaring of a [x]lion; but his favour
*is* as dew upon the grass.
13 A [y,z]foolish [a]son *is* the calamity of his father: and [b]the
[c]contentions of a [d,e]wife *are* a
continual dropping.
14 House and riches *are* the [f]in-
heritance of fathers: and a prudent [d]wife *is* from the LORD.
15 *Slothfulness casteth into a

1
a *Poor*, Prov. 21:13.
b *Integrity*, Job 2:3.
c *Speech, evil*, Col. 4:6.

2
d *Ignorance*, Acts 3:17.

3
e *Murmuring, against God*, Num. 14:2.
1 R. V. subverteth

4
f *Riches*, Eccl. 4:8.
g *Rich, have many friends*, Jas. 5:1.
h *Friends*, Ex. 33:11.
i *Flattery*, Prov. 6:24.
j *Poor, friendlessness of*, Prov. 21:13.

5
k *False Witness*, Matt. 19:18.
l *Falsehood*, Job 21:34.

6
m *Liberality*, 1 Tim. 6:18.
2 R. V. liberal man:

7
n *Hatred*, Prov. 15:17.
o *Friends, false*, Ex. 33:11.
3 R. V. but they are gone.

8
p *Wisdom*, Prov. 2:2.

10
q *Servant*, Jer. 2:14.
4 R. V. Delicate living is not

11
r *Patience*, Luke 8:15.
s *Meekness*, Psa. 45:4.
t *Anger, restraint of*, Psa. 37:8.
u *Charitableness*, Prov. 10:12.
v *Forgiveness, honorable*, Matt. 18:21.
5 R. V. maketh him slow to anger;

12
w *Rulers*, Ex. 18:21.
x *Lion*, Mic. 5:8.

**13** y *Fool, causes sorrow*, Prov. 18:2. z *Children, wicked, disgrace parents*, Mark 10:14.—a *Young Men*, Prov. 1:4. b *Family, infelicity in*, 1 Chr. 13:14. c *Strife*, Prov. 20:3. d *Wife*, Prov. 5:18. e *Women*, Prov. 31:10. **14** f *Inheritance*, Num. 27:7.

† **BROTHER,** Gen. 9:5. *Avenger of murder*, Gen. 9:5. *Love of*, Prov. 17:17; 18:24; Song 8:1. *Estranged*, Gen. 27:35, 36. *Reconciled*, Gen. 33:4. *Reuben's love for Joseph*, Gen. 37:21, 22, 29, 30; *Joseph's, for his brethren*, Gen. 43:30–34; 45:1–15; 50:19–25; *Judah's, for Benjamin*, Gen. 44:18–34.

*Brother's widow, law concerning levirate marriage of*, Deut. 25:5–10; Matt. 22:24; Mark 12:19; Luke 20:28.

*Signifying, a relative*, Gen. 14:16; 29:12, *any Israelite*, Neh. 5:7; Jer. 34:9; Obad. 10; *mankind*, 1 Kin. 20:32, 33; Matt. 5:22–24; 18:35; 1 John 3:15; *companion*, 2 Sam. 1:26; 1 Kin. 13:30.

Expressive of fraternity: *Used, among Israelites*, Lev. 19:17; Deut. 22:1–4; *by Christ*, Matt. 12:50; 25:40; Heb. 2:11, 12; *by disciples*, Acts 9:17; 21:20; Rom. 16:23; 1 Cor. 7:12; 2 Cor. 2:13; 1 Pet. 1:22.

* **LAZINESS,** Prov. 12:27; 18:9; 19:24; 21:25; 22:13; 26:13, 14–16.

*Brings, adversity*, Prov. 12:24; Eccl. 10:18; *destitution*, Prov. 13:4; 19:15; 20:4; 23:21; 24:30–34.

*Admonitions against*, Prov. 6:6–11; 10:4, 5, 26; 15:19.

*Denounced*, Matt. 25:26, 27. *Of ministers, denounced*, Isa. 56:10.

*Forbidden*, Rom. 12:11; Heb. 6:12.

See footnote, IDLENESS, Eccl. 10:18.

**15**
*g Idleness*, Eccl. 10:18.
*h Hunger*, Neh. 9:15.

**16**
*i Obedience, rewarded*, Heb. 5:8.
*j Wicked, punishment of*, Psa. 73:3.
6 R. V. is careless of his

**17**
*k Pity, for the poor*, Job 19:21.
*l Poor, liberality to*, Prov. 21:13.
*m Lending*, Deut. 15:2.

**18**
*n Children, punishment of*, Mark 10:14.
7 R. V. seeing there is hope; And set not thy heart on his destruction.

**19**
*o Anger, punished*, Psa. 37:8.

**20**
*p Commandment, enjoining heed to instruction*, Deut. 8:2.
*q Counsel*, Prov. 12:15.

**21**
*r God, immutable*, Gen. 2:2.

**22**
*s Kindness*, Acts 28:2.
*t Poor*, Prov. 21:13.
*u Falsehood*, Job 21:34.
8 Am. R. V. That which maketh a man to be desired is his kindness:

**23**
*v Fear of God*, Acts 9:31.

deep sleep; and an [g]idle soul
shall suffer [h]hunger.
16 He that [i]keepeth the commandment keepeth his own soul;
*but* he that [6]despiseth his ways
[j]shall die.
17 He that hath [k]pity upon the
[l]poor [m]lendeth unto the LORD;
and that which he hath given
will he pay him again.[Q]
18 Chasten thy [n]son [7]while
there is hope, and let not thy
soul spare for his crying.[Q]
19 A man of great [o]wrath shall
suffer punishment: for if thou
deliver *him*, yet thou must do it
again.
20 [p]Hear [q]counsel, and receive
instruction, that thou mayest be
wise in thy latter end.
21 *There are* many devices in
a man's heart; nevertheless the
counsel of the [r]LORD, that shall
stand.[S T]
22 [8]The desire of a man *is* his
[s]kindness: and a [t]poor man *is*
better than a [u]liar.
23 The [v]fear of the LORD *tendeth* to life: and *he that hath it*
shall abide satisfied; [w]he shall
not be visited with evil.
24 A [9,g]slothful *man* hideth
his hand in *his* bosom, and will
not so much as bring it to his
mouth again.
25 [x]Smite[†]a scorner,[G] and the simple[G] will beware: and [y]reprove one
that hath understanding, *and* he
will understand knowledge.

*w Righteous, promises to*, Psa. 64:10.
**24** 9 R. V. The sluggard burieth his hand in the dish,
**25** *x Punishment, design of*, Lev. 26:41. *y Reproof, wise profit by*, Prov. 17:10.

26 He that [10]wasteth *his* [z]fa-
ther, *and* chaseth away *his*
[a]mother, *is* a [b,c]son that causeth
shame, and bringeth reproach.
27 [d]Cease, my [b,c]son, to hear
[11]the instruction *that causeth* to
err from the words of knowledge.
28 [12]An [e]ungodly witness[†]scorn-
eth[G] judgment[G]: and the mouth of
the wicked devoureth iniquity.
29 Judgments are prepared for
[†]scorners,[G] and [f]stripes for the
back of fools.

## CHAPTER 20

*Sundry Proverbs.*

WINE *is* a mocker, strong
drink [1]*is* raging: and [a]who-
soever [2]is deceived thereby is not
wise.
2 The fear of a [b]king *is* as the
roaring of a [c]lion: [d]*whoso* provoketh him to [e]anger [f]sinneth
*against* his own [3]soul.
3 [g]*It is* an honour for a man to
[4,h]cease from *strife: but every
[i]fool will be [5]meddling.
4 The sluggard will [j,k]not plow
by reason of the [6,l]cold; *therefore* shall he [m]beg in [n]harvest,
and *have* nothing.
5 Counsel in the heart of man *is
like* deep water; but a man of
understanding will draw it out.
6 Most men will proclaim every
one his own [7]goodness: but a
[o]faithful man who can find?
7 The just *man* walketh in
his [p]integrity: his [q]children *are*
blessed after him.

**26**
*z Father*, Psa. 27:10.
*a Mother*, 1 Kin. 2:20.
*b Children, wicked*, Mark 10:14.
*c Young Men*, Prov. 1:4.
10 *Heb.* doeth violence to

**27**
*d Commandment, warning against temptation*, Deut. 8:2.
11 R. V. instruction Only to err

**28**
*e False Witness*, Matt. 19:18.
12 R. V. A worthless

**29**
*f Punishment*, Lev. 26:41.

**1**
*a Wine, admonitions against the use of*, Prov. 23:31.
1 R. V. a brawler;
2 R. V. erreth thereby

**2**
*b Rulers*, Ex. 18:21.
*c Lion*, Mic. 5:8.
*d Citizens, wicked*, Luke 15:15.
*e Anger*, Psa. 37:8.
*f Sin*, Rom. 5:12.
3 R. V. life.

**3**
*g Meekness, honorable*, Psa. 45:4.
*h Peace*, Jer. 29:7.
*i Fool*, Prov. 18:2.
4 R. V. keep aloof
5 R.V. quarrelling.

**4**
*j Laziness*, Prov. 19:15.
*k Idleness*, Eccl. 10:18.
*l Winter*, Gen. 8:22.

*m Beggars*, Luke 16:20. *n Harvest*, Ex. 34:21. 6 R. V. winter; **6** *o Faithfulness*, Luke 16:10. 7 R. V. kindness: **7** *p Integrity*, Job 2:3. *q Children, of the righteous, blessed of God*, Mark 10:14.

† **SCORNERS,** Psa. 1:1; Prov. 9:12; 13:1; 14:6; 21:11, 24; 22:10. *An abomination*, Prov. 24:9. *Admonitions to*, Prov 1:22, 23. *Punishment of*, Prov. 19:29; Isa. 29:20.

* **STRIFE,** Prov. 26:21; 27:15; 28:25; Jas. 4:1, 2.

*Domestic*, Prov. 19:13; 21:19; 25:24.

*Caused, by busybodies*, Prov. 26:20; *by perversity*, Prov. 16:28; *by hatred*, Prov. 10:12; *by pride*, Prov. 13:10; *by scornfulness*, Prov. 22:10; *by wrath*, Prov. 15:18; 29:22; 30:33; *by excessive indulgence in the use of intoxicating liquors*, Prov. 23:29, 30.

*Destructive to those who are involved therein*, Matt. 12:25; Mark 3:24, 25; Luke 11:17.

*Exhortations against*, Gen. 13:8; 45:24; Prov. 3:30; 17:14; 25:8; Matt. 5:25, 39–41; Rom. 12:18; 13:13; 14:1, 19, 21; 16:17, 18; 2 Cor. 12:20; Gal. 5:15, 20; Phil. 2:3, 14, 15; 1 Tim. 6:3–5; 2 Tim. 2:14, 23–25; Tit. 3:1–3, 9; Jas. 3:14–16.

*Abstinence from, honorable*, Prov. 20:3.

**Instances of:** *Between Abraham's and Lot's herdmen*, Gen. 13:6, 7. *Between Abraham and Abimelech*, Gen. 21:25. *Between Isaac's herdmen and those of Gerar*, Gen. 26:20–22. *Between Laban and Jacob*, Gen. 31:36. *Among Israelites*, Deut. 1:12. *Between Jephthah and his brethren*, Judg. 11:2; *and Ephraimites*, Judg. 12:1–6. *Between Israel and Judah, about David*, 2 Sam. 19:41–43. *Among disciples, over question who should be greatest*, Mark 9:34; Luke 22:24. *Among Jews, concerning Jesus*, John 10:19. *Among Christians at Antioch, about circumcision*, Acts 15:2. *Between Paul and Barnabas, about Mark*, Acts 15:38, 39. *Between Pharisees and Sadducees, concerning the resurrection*, Acts 23:7–10. *In the churches, at Corinth*, 1 Cor. 1:10–12; 3:3, 4; 6:1–7; 11:16–21; *at Philippi*, Phil. 1:15–17.

See footnotes: ANGER, Psa. 37:8; ENVY, Prov. 14:30; JEALOUSY, Psa. 75:58; MALICE, Eph. 4:31.

8 A [r,s]king that sitteth in the
[t]throne of judgment scattereth
away all evil with his eyes.
9 Who can say, I have made
my [u]heart [v]clean, I am [w]pure
from my sin? [S]
10 [x]Divers[C] [y]weights, *and* divers[C]
[z]measures, both of them *are* alike
[a]abomination to the LORD.
11 Even a child is known by
his doings, whether his work *be*
pure, and whether *it be* right.
12 The hearing ear, and the
seeing eye, the LORD hath [b]made
even both of them.
13 Love not [c]sleep, lest thou
come to [d]poverty; [e]open thine
eyes, *and* thou shalt be satisfied
with bread.
14 [f]*It is* naught,[C] *it is* naught,[C]
saith the buyer: but when he is
gone his way, then he [g]boasteth.
15 There is [h]gold, and a multitude of [i]rubies: but the [j]lips[C] of
knowledge *are* a precious [k]jewel.
16 Take his garment that is
[l]surety *for* a stranger: and [8]take
a [m]pledge of him for a strange[C]
woman.
17 Bread of [n,o]deceit *is* sweet
to a man; but afterwards his
mouth shall be filled with gravel.
18 [p]*Every* purpose is established by [q]counsel: and with
good [r]advice make war.
19 He that goeth about *as*
a [s]talebearer revealeth secrets:
therefore [t]meddle not with him
that [9,u]flattereth with his lips.
20 [v]Whoso curseth his [w]father
or his [x]mother, his [y]lamp shall
be put out in obscure [z]darkness.
21 An [a]inheritance *may be* gotten hastily at the beginning; but
the end thereof shall not be
blessed.
22 [b]Say[S] not thou, I will [c]recom-
pense[C] [d]evil; *but* [e]wait on the
LORD, and [f,g]he shall [h]save thee.[Q]
23 [i]Divers[C] [j]weights *are* an
[k]abomination unto the LORD;
and a false [l]balance *is* not good.
24 [m]Man's goings *are* of the
LORD; how can a man then understand his own way? [S]
25 *It is* a snare to [10]the man *who*
devoureth *that which is* holy, and
after [n]vows to make enquiry.
26 A wise [o]king [11]scattereth
the wicked, and bringeth the
[12,p]wheel over them.
27 The spirit of [q]man *is* the
candle[C] of the LORD, searching
all the inward parts of the †belly.[Q]
28 [13,r]Mercy and [s]truth preserve the king: and his throne is
upholden[C] by [13]mercy.
29 The glory of [t]young men *is*
their strength: and the beauty of
[u]old men *is* the grey head.
30 [14]The blueness of a wound
cleanseth away evil: so *do*
[v]stripes the inward parts of
the †belly.

## CHAPTER 21

*Sundry Proverbs.*

THE [a]king's heart *is* [b]in the
hand of the LORD, *as* the
rivers of water: he turneth it
whithersoever he will.[S]
2 [c]Every[S] way of a man *is* [d]right
in his own eyes: but the LORD
[1,e]pondereth the [f]hearts.
3 To [g]do [h]justice and [i]judg-
ment *is* more acceptable to the
LORD than [j]sacrifice.[S]
4 An high look, and a [k]proud
heart, *and* the [2]plowing of the
wicked, *is* sin.

**8**
r *Rulers, character and qualifications of*, Ex. 18:21.
s *Judge, kings as*, Judg. 2:18.
t *Throne*, 1 Kin. 2:19.

**9**
u *Heart*, Psa. 44:21.
v *Spiritual Purification*, Psa. 51:2.
w *Purity, of heart*, 1 Tim. 4:12.

**10**
x *Dishonesty, forbidden*, Ezek. 22:13.
y *Weights, must be just*, Lev. 19:35.
z *Measure, false, an abomination*, Deut. 25:15.

a *Abomination*, Lev. 18:27.

**12**
b *God, creator*, Gen. 2:2.

**13**
c *Laziness*, Prov. 19:15.
d *Poverty, caused by laziness*, Prov. 30:8.
e *Industry, brings prosperity*, 1 Kin. 11:28.

**14**
f *Hypocrisy*, Jas. 3:17.
g *Boasting, deceitful*, Prov. 25:14.

**15**
h *Gold*, Ezek. 7:19.
i Prov. 3:15; 31:10; Job 28:18.
j *Speech, wise*, Col. 4:6.
k *Jewels, figurative*, Gen. 24:53.

**16**
l *Surety*, Gen. 44:32.
m *Pawn*, Job 24:3.
8 R. V. hold him in pledge that is surety for strangers.

**17**
n *Deceit*, Psa. 36:3. o *Falsehood*, Job 21:34. **18** p *Prudence, in heeding counsel*, 2 Chr. 2:12. q *Counsel, wisdom in*, Prov. 12:15. r *War, councils of*, Judg. 3:2. **19** s *Talebearing*, Prov. 11:13. t *Evil Company, warnings against*, Prov. 13:20. u *Gossip, forbidden*, Lev. 19:16. 9 R. V. openeth wide **20** v *Children, wicked, punishment of*, Mark 10:14. w *Father, cursing of, forbidden*, Psa. 27:10. x *Mother, dishonoring of, to be punished*, 1 Kin. 2:20. y *Lamp, figurative*, Ex. 27:20. z *Darkness, figurative of judgments*, Gen. 1:2. **21**—a *Inheritance*, Num. 27:7.

**22**
b *Malice, forbidden*, Eph. 4:31.
c *Retaliation, malicious, forbidden*, Deut. 19:19.
d *Evil*, 1 Thess. 5:22.
e *Commandment, enjoining faith in God*, Deut. 8:2.
f *Promise, to the righteous*, 2 Cor. 1:20.
g *Righteous, promises to*, Psa. 64:10.
h *God, preserver*, Gen. 2:2.

**23**
i *Dishonesty*, Ezek. 22:13.
j *Weights*, Lev. 19:35.
k *Abomination*, Lev. 18:27.
l *Balances, false, an abomination*, Prov. 11:1.

**24**
m *God, providence of*, Gen. 2:2.

**25**
n *Vows* Num. 30:2.
10 R. V. a man rashly to say, It is holy,

**26**
o *King*, 2 Kin. 3:10.
p *Wheel, figurative*, Eccl. 12:6.
11 R. V winnoweth
12 R. V. threshing wheel

**27**
q *Man, spirit*, Job 4:17.

**28**
r *Mercy*, Deut. 5:10.
s *Truth*, John 18:37.
13 Am. R. V. Kindness

**29**
t *Young Men*, Prov. 1:4.
u *Old Age*, Isa. 46:4.

**30**
v *Punishment*, Lev. 26:41.
14 Am. R. V. Stripes that wound cleanse away evil: And strokes reach the innermost parts of the body.

**1**
a *Rulers*, Ex. 18:21.
b *God, providence of*, Gen. 2:2.

**2** c Prov. 16:2. d *Self-righteousness*, Luke 18:11. e *God, knowledge of*, Gen. 2:2. f *Heart, known to God*, Psa. 44:21. 1 R. V. weigheth **3** g *Obedience, better than sacrifice*, 1 Sam. 15:22. h *Righteousness*, Psa. 15:2. i *Integrity*, Job 2:3. j *Offerings, unavailing, when not accompanied by piety*, Lev. 6:17. **4** k *Pride*, Prov. 16:18. 2 R. V. lamp

† **BELLY.** *Figurative, of the soul*, **Psa. 44:25; Prov. 18:20; 20:27, 30;** *of the nervous system*, **Hab. 3:16;** *of the sanctified heart*, **John 7:38.**

5 The thoughts of the [l]diligent *tend* only to plenteousness; but of every one *that is* [m]hasty only to want.

6 The getting of [n]treasures by a [o]lying tongue *is* a [3]vanity tossed to and fro of them that seek [p]death.

7 The [4]robbery of the wicked shall destroy them; because they refuse to do judgment.

8 [q]The way of [5]man *is* froward and strange: but *as for* the [r,s]pure, his work *is* right.

9 [t,u]*It is* better to dwell in a corner of the [v]housetop, than with a [w]brawling [x,y]woman in a wide house.

10 The soul of the wicked [z]desireth evil: his neighbour findeth no favour in his eyes.

11 When the [6,a]scorner is [b]punished, the simple is made [c]wise: and when the wise is instructed, he receiveth knowledge.

12 The righteous *man* wisely considereth the house of the wicked: [7]*but God* [d]overthroweth the wicked for *their* wickedness.

13 Whoso stoppeth his ears at the cry of the *poor, [e]he also shall [f]cry himself, but shall not be heard.

14 A [g]gift in secret pacifieth [h]anger: and a [8]reward in the bosom strong wrath.

15 *It is* joy to the [i]just to do judgment: but [d]destruction *shall be* to the workers of iniquity.

16 The man that wandereth out of the way of understanding [j]shall remain in the congregation of the [k]dead.

17 He that loveth [l]pleasure *shall be* a poor man: he that [m]loveth [n]wine and [o]oil shall not be rich.

18 The wicked *shall be* a ransom for the righteous, and the [9]transgressor for the upright.

19 [p]*It is* better to dwell in the wilderness, than with a [q]contentious and [10]an angry [r]woman.

20 *There is* treasure to be desired and [o]oil in the dwelling of the [s,t]wise; but a [u]foolish man [11]spendeth it up.

21 [v,w]He that followeth after [x]righteousness and [y]mercy findeth life, righteousness, and honour.

22 A wise *man* scaleth the city of the mighty, and casteth down the strength of the confidence thereof.

23 Whoso [z]keepeth his [a]mouth

**5**
*l Industry, brings prosperity,* 1 Kin. 11:28.
*m Rashness,* 2 Sam. 6:7.

**6**
*n Riches,* Eccl. 4:8.
*o Falsehood,* Job 21:34.
*p Spiritual Death,* 1 John 3:14.
3 R. V. vapour driven to and fro; they that seek them seek death.

**7**
4 R. V. The violence of the wicked shall sweep them away;

**8**
*q Wicked, described,* Psa. 73:3.
*r Purity, of heart,* 1 Tim. 4:12.
*s Holiness,* Ex. 39:30.
5 R. V. him that is laden with guilt is exceeding crooked:

**9**
*t Family, infelicity in,* 1 Chr. 13:14.
*u Marriage, unhappiness in,* Gen. 34:9.
*v House, roofs of,* Esth. 8:1.
*w Strife,* Prov. 20:3.
*x Women,* Prov. 31:10.
*y Wife,* Prov. 5:18.

**10**
*z Malice, the wicked filled with,* Eph. 4:31.

**11**—*a Scorners,* Prov. 19:25. *b Punishment, design of,* Lev. 26:41. *c Wisdom, spiritual,* Prov. 2:2. 6 Am. R. V. scoffer **12** *d Wicked, punishment of,* Psa. 73:3. 7 R. V. How the wicked are overthrown to their ruin. **13** *e Wicked, prayer of, not heard,* Psa. 73:3. *f Prayer, of the wicked, not heard,* Acts 6:4.

**14**
*g Presents, to obtain favor,* Gen. 32:13.
*h Anger,* Psa. 37:8.
8 R. V. present

**15**
*i Righteous,* Psa. 64:10.

**16**
*j Sin, fruits of,* Rom. 5:12.
*k Death, of the wicked,* Num. 23:10.

**17**
*l Worldly Pleasure,* Eccl. 2:1.
*m Appetite,* Prov. 23:2.
*n Wine, admonitions against the use of,* Prov. 23:31.
*o Oil, used for food,* Deut. 12:17.

**18**
9 R. V. treacherous cometh in the stead of the upright.

**19**
*p Family, infelicity in,* 1 Chr. 13:14.
*q Strife,* Prov. 20:3.
*r Women,* Prov. 31:10.
10 R. V. fretful

**20**
*s Wisdom, worldly,* Prov. 2:2.
*t Frugality,* Matt. 14:20.
*u Fool,* Prov. 18:2.
11 R. V. swalloweth it up.

**21** *v Promise, to the righteous,* 2 Cor. 1:20. *w Righteous, promises to,* Psa. 64:10. *x Righteousness,* Psa. 15:2. *y Mercy,* Deut. 5:10.
**23** *z Prudence, in restraining speech,* 2 Chr. 2:12.—*a Speech, wise,* Col. 4:6.

***POOR,** Prov. 10:15; 13:7, 8, 23; 17:5; 18:23; 19:17; 22:2; 28:6, 8, 11; Eccl. 6:8; Isa. 29:19; Matt. 26:11; Mark 12:43, 44; 14:7; John 12:8; 2 Cor. 6:10.

*God's care of,* 1 Sam. 2:7, 8; Job 5:15, 16; Psa. 9:18; 10:14; 12:5; 14:6; 34:6; 35:10; 68:10; 69:33; 102:17; 107:9, 36, 41; 109:31; 113:7, 8; 132:15; 140:12; 146:5, 7; Prov. 22:2, 22, 23; Isa. 11:4; 14:30; 25:4; 29:19; 41:17; Jer. 20:13. See footnotes: GOD, *Goodness of,* Gen. 2:2; GOD, *Providence of,* Gen. 2:2.

*Friendlessness of,* Prov. 14:20; 19:4, 7. *Wisdom of, despised,* Eccl. 9:15, 16.

*Warning against neglect of,* Prov. 21:13; 22:16; Ezek. 16:49. *Neglect of, by the disciples,* Acts 6:1–6. *Neglect of, denounced,* Matt. 25:42–45.

*Righteous treatment of, required,* Psa. 82:3, 4; Prov. 22:22; 31:9; Isa. 1:17; *rewarded,* Prov. 29:14; Jer. 22:16; Ezek. 18:7, 16, 17; Dan. 4:27. *Compassion toward,* Job 30:25; Prov. 14:21; 29:7; Heb. 13:3; Jas. 1:27.

*Liberality to,* Prov. 31:20; Isa. 58:7; Matt. 5:42 (with Luke 6:30); Luke 3:11; 19:8; Rom. 12:8, 13, 20; 1 Cor. 13:3; 16:1, 2; 2 Cor. 9:1–15; Gal. 2:10; Eph. 4:28; 1 Tim. 5:9, 10, 16; Jas. 2:15, 16; 1 John 3:17. *Liberality to, rewarded,* Prov. 19:17; 22:9; 28:27; Psa. 112:9; Matt. 19:21; 25:34–36; Luke 12:33; 18:22; Acts 20:35.

**Kindness to:** *Enjoined,* Neh. 8:10, 12. *Rewarded,* Psa. 41:1–3; Isa. 58:10; Luke 14:12–14.

INSTANCES OF: *By Ruth, to Naomi,* Ruth 2:2, 11. *By Boaz, to Ruth,* Ruth 2:8–16; 3:15. *By Elijah, to the widow of Zarephath,* 1 Kin. 17:12–24. *By Elisha, to the prophet's widow,* 2 Kin. 4:1–7. *By the Jews,* Esth. 9:22. *By Job,* Job 29:11–17; 31:16–22, 38–40. *By the Temaites,* Isa. 21:14. *By Nebuzar-adan,* Jer. 39:10. *By the good Samaritan,* Luke 10:33–35. *By Zacchæus,* Luke 19:8. *By Dorcas,* Acts 9:36. *By Cornelius,* Acts 10:2, 4. *By Christian church, at Jerusalem,* Acts 6:1; *at Antioch,* Acts 11:29, 30. *By churches of Macedonia and Achaia,* Rom. 15:25, 26; 2 Cor. 8:1–5.

**Oppression of,** Neh. 5:1–13; Job 20:19–21; 22:6, 7; 24:4, 7–12; Psa. 37:14; 109:16; Prov. 14:31; 22:7, 16; 28:3, 15; 30:14; Eccl. 5:8; Isa. 3:14, 15; 10:1, 2; 32:6, 7; Ezek. 18:12; 22:29; Amos 2:6; 4:1; 5:11, 12; 8:4–6; Hab. 3:14; Jas. 2:6; 5:4. *Forbidden,* Deut. 24:14; Zech. 7:10.

INSTANCES OF OPPRESSION OF, 2 Kin. 4:1; Neh. 5:1–5.

**Mosaic laws concerning:** *Atonement money of, must be uniform with that of the rich,* Ex. 30:15. *Inexpensive offerings authorized for,* Lev. 5:7; 12:8; 14:21, 22.

*Discrimination, in favor of, forbidden,* Ex. 23:3; Lev. 19:15; *against, forbidden,* Ex. 23:6; Jas. 2:2–9. *Exactions of interest from, forbidden,* Ex. 22:25; Lev. 25:35–37. *Raiment of, taken in pledge, to be restored,* Ex. 22:26; Deut. 24:12, 13. *To participate triennially in the tithes,* Deut. 14:28, 29; 26:12, 13. *Gleanings reserved for,* Lev. 19:9, 10; 23:22; Deut. 24:19–21. *To share the products of the land in the sabbatic year,* Ex. 23:11. *To be released from debt in sabbatic year,* Deut. 15:7–11. *To be released from servitude, in sabbatic year,*

**24**
*b Pride,* Prov. 16:18.
*c Scorners,* Prov. 19:25.
12 Am. R. V. The proud and haughty man, scoffer is his name, He worketh in the arrogance of pride.
**25**
*d Idleness,* Eccl. 10:18.
*e Laziness,* Prov. 19:15.
**26**
*f Wicked, contrasted with the righteous,* Psa. 73:3.
*g Covetousness, insatiable,* Isa. 57:17.
*h Liberality,* 1 Tim. 6:18.
13 R. V. withholdeth
**27**
*i Sin, repugnant to God,* Rom. 5:12.
*j Hypocrisy,* Jas. 3:17.
*k Abomination,* Lev. 18:27.
*l Offerings, unavailing when not accompanied by piety,* Lev. 6:17.
**28**
*m False Witness,* Matt. 19:18.
*n Falsehood,* Job 21:34.
14 Am. R. V. shall speak so as to endure.
**29**
*o Impenitence,* Rom. 2:5.
**31**
*p Horse,* Job 39:19.
*q Victories, from God,* Deut. 28:7.
15 Am. R. V. victory is of Jehovah.

**1**
*a Character, good,* Phil. 2:15.
*b* Eccl. 7:1.

and his tongue keepeth his soul from troubles.

24 [12,b]Proud *and* haughty [c]scorner[G] *is* his name, who dealeth in proud wrath.

25 The desire of the [d,e]slothful killeth him; for his hands refuse to labour.

26 [f]He [g]coveteth greedily all the day long: but the righteous [h]giveth and [13]spareth not.

27 [i]The [j]sacrifice of the wicked *is* [k]abomination: how much more, *when* he bringeth [l]it with a wicked mind?

28 A [m,n]false[G] witness shall perish: but the man that heareth [14]speaketh constantly.

29 [o]A wicked man [o]hardeneth his face: but *as for* the upright, he directeth his way.

30 *There is* no wisdom nor understanding nor counsel against the LORD.

31 The [p]horse *is* prepared against[G] the day of battle: but [15,q]safety *is* of the LORD.[S]

## CHAPTER 22

*Sundry Proverbs. 17 The words of the wise.*

[a] A [b]GOOD *name *is* rather to be chosen than great riches, *and* loving favour rather than silver and gold.

2 [c]The [d]rich and [e]poor meet together: the LORD *is* the [f]maker of them all.[S]

3 A [g]prudent *man* foreseeth the evil, and hideth himself: but the [h]simple[G] pass on, and [1]are punished.

4 [2]By †humility *and* the [i]fear of the LORD *are* riches, and honour, and life.[S]

5 [j,k]Thorns *and* [l]snares *are* in the way of the froward[G]: he that doth keep his soul shall be far from them.

6 [m,n]Train up a [o]child in the way he should go: and when he is old, he will not depart from it.[Q]

7 The rich ruleth over the [p]poor, and the [q]borrower *is* servant to the [r]lender.

8 [s]He that soweth iniquity shall reap [3]vanity: and the rod of his anger shall fail.[Q]

9 He that hath a [t]bountiful[G] eye shall be blessed; for he giveth of his bread to the [u]poor.[Q]

10 Cast out the [4,v]scorner[G], and [w]contention shall go out; yea, strife and reproach shall cease.

11 He that loveth [x]pureness of heart, *for* the [y]grace of his lips the king *shall be* his [z]friend.

12 The eyes of the [a]LORD preserve [5]knowledge, and he overthroweth the words of the [6]transgressor.[S]

13 The [b,c]slothful *man* saith, *There is* a [d]lion without[G], I shall be slain in the streets.

14 The [e]mouth of strange [f,g]women *is* a deep pit: he that

*h Ignorance,* Acts 3:17.
1 R. V. suffer for it.
**4**
*i Fear of God,* Acts 9:31.
2 R. V. The reward of
**5**
*j Thorn, figurative,* Hos. 2:6.
*k Wicked, contrasted with the righteous,* Psa. 73:3
*l Temptation,* Luke 11:4.
**6**
*m Parents, duty of, to instruct children in righteousness,* 2 Cor. 12:14.
*n Instruction, of children,* Prov. 23:23.
*o Children, instruction of,* Mark 10:14.
**7**
*p Poor, oppression of,* Prov. 21:13.
*q Borrowing,* Ex. 22:14.
*r Lending,* Deut. 15:2.
**8**
*s Sin, fruits of,* Rom. 5:12.
3 R. V. calamity:
**9**
*t Liberality, rewards for,* 1 Tim. 6:18.
*u Poor, liberality to,* Prov. 21:13.
**10**
*v Scorners,* Prov. 19:25.
*w Strife,* Prov. 20:3.
4 Am. R. V. scoffer,
**11**

**2** *c Man, equality of,* Job. 4:17. *d Rich,* Jas. 5:1. *e Poor,* Prov. 21:13. *f God, creator,* Gen. 2:2.
**3** *g Prudence,* 2 Chr. 2:12.

*x Purity, of heart,* 1 Tim. 4:12. *y Speech, wise,* Col. 4:6. *z Friends,* Ex. 33:11. **12**—*a God, providence of,* Gen. 2:2. 5 R. V. him that hath knowledge, 6 R. V. treacherous man. **13** *b Idleness,* Eccl. 10:18. *c Laziness,* Prov. 19:15. *d Lion,* Mic. 5:8. **14** *e Temptation,* Luke 11:4. *f Harlot,* Prov. 7:10. *g Women, wicked,* Prov. 31:10.

---

Deut. 15:12; *in jubilee,* Lev. 25:39–4. *Alienated lands of, to be restored in jubilee,* Lev. 25:25–28.
See footnotes: ALMS, Matt. 6:2; LIBERALITY, 1 Tim. 6:18; ORPHAN, Lam. 5:3; WIDOWS, 2 Sam. 14:5.

***NAME.** *Signifying prestige,* 1 Kin. 1:47. *Value of a good,* Prov. 22:1; Eccl. 7:1.
*New, given, to persons who have spiritual adoption,* Isa. 62:2; *to Abraham,* Gen. 17:5; *to Sarah,* Gen. 17:15; *to Jacob,* Gen. 32:27, 28; *to Paul,* Acts 13:9.
*Intercessional influence of the name of Jesus,* see footnote, NAME OF JESUS, John 14:13.
**Symbolical,** Hos. 1:3, 4, 6, 9; 2:1.

**† HUMILITY,** Psa. 51:17; 69:32; 138:6; Prov. 3:34; 11:2; 12:15; 16:19; Isa. 57:15; 66:2; Luke 10:21; 2 Cor. 7:6; Gal. 6:14; Jas. 4:6.
*Enjoined,* Deut. 15:15; Prov. 25:6, 7; 27:2; 30:32; Eccl. 5:2; Jer. 45:5; Mic. 6:8; Matt. 18:2–4; 20:26, 27; Mark 9:33–37; 10:43, 44; Luke 9:46–48; 14:10; 17:10; 22:24–27; John 13:14–16; Rom. 11:18–20, 25; 12:3, 10, 16; 1 Cor. 3:18; 4:6; 10:12; Gal. 5:26; Eph. 4:1, 2; 5:21; Phil. 2:3–11; Col. 3:12; Jas. 1:9, 10; 4:10; 1 Pet. 5:3, 5, 6.
*Feigned, forbidden,* Col. 2:18–23.
*Rewards of,* Job 5:11; 22:29; Psa. 138:6; Prov. 15:33; 18:12; 22:4; 29:23; Matt. 5:3; 23:12; Luke 1:52; 14:11; 18:13, 14.
Exemplified in: *Abraham,* Gen. 18:27, 32; *Jacob,* Gen. 32:10; *Joseph,* Gen. 41:16; *Moses,* Ex. 3:11; 4:10; *David,* 1 Sam. 18:18–23; 24:14; 26:20; 2 Sam. 7:18–20; 1 Chr. 17:16–18; 29:14; *the psalmist,* Psa. 8:3, 4; 73:22; 131:1–2; 141:5; 144:3; *Solomon,* 1 Kin. 3:7; 2 Chr. 1:10; 2:6; *Mephibosheth,* 2 Sam. 9:8; *Ahab,* 1 Kin. 21:29; *kings and princes of Israel,* 2 Chr. 12:6, 7, 12; *Josiah,* 2 Kin. 22:18, 19; 2 Chr. 34:26, 27; *Job,* Job 7:17, 18; 9:14, 15; 40:4, 5; 42:2–6; *Elihu,* Job 32:4–7; 33:6; *Ezra,* Ezra 9:13, 15; *Agur,* Prov. 30:2, 3; *Isaiah,* Isa. 6:5; *Hezekiah,* Isa. 38:15; *Jeremiah,* Jer. 1:6; 10:23, 24; *Daniel,* Dan. 2:30; *Ezra and the Jews,* Ezra 8:21, 23; *Elisabeth,* Luke 1:43; *John the Baptist,* Matt. 3:14; Mark 1:7; Luke 3:16; John 1:27; 3:29, 30; *Jesus,* Matt. 11:29; 13:4–16; *women of Canaan,* Matt. 15:27; *the righteous,* Matt. 25:37–40; *the publican,* Luke 18:13; *centurion,* Matt. 8:8; Luke 7:6, 7;

is abhorred of the LORD shall
fall therein.
15 Foolishness *is* bound in the
[h]heart of a child; *but* the rod[C] of
[i]correction[C] shall drive it far
from him.
16 [j,k]He that [l,m]oppresseth the
[n,o]poor [p]to increase his [7]*riches*,
*and* he that [q]giveth to the rich,
*shall* surely *come* to want.
17 ¶ [r]Bow down thine ear, and
hear the [s]words of the [t]wise,
and apply thine heart unto my
knowledge.
18 For *it is* a pleasant thing
if thou keep them within thee;
they shall withal be fitted in thy
lips.
19 That thy [u]trust may be in
the LORD, I have made known
to thee this day, even to thee.
20 Have not I written to thee
excellent things in counsels and
knowledge,
21 That I might make thee
know the certainty of the [v]words
of truth; that thou mightest answer the words of truth to them
that send unto thee?
22 [w]Rob not the [x]poor, because
he *is* poor: neither oppress the
afflicted in the [y]gate:
23 For [z]the LORD will plead
their cause, and [8,a]spoil the soul
of those that spoiled them.
24 [b]Make no ‡friendship with
[9]an [c]angry man; and with a furious man thou shalt not go:
25 [d]Lest thou learn [e]his ways,
and get a snare to thy soul.
26 Be not thou *one* of them that
[f]strike[C] hands, *or* of them that are
[g]sureties for [h]debts.
27 If thou hast nothing to pay,
why should he take away thy
[i,j]bed from under thee?
28 [k]Remove not the ancient
[l]landmark, which thy fathers
have set.
29 Seest thou a man [m,n]diligent
in his business? he shall stand
before kings; he shall not stand
before mean[C] *men*.

## CHAPTER 23

*The words of the wise.*

[a,b]WHEN thou sittest to eat
with a ruler, [c,d]consider
diligently what *is* before thee:
2 And *,[e,f]put a knife to thy
throat, if thou *be* a man given to
†appetite.
3 *,[c,e,f]Be not desirous of his
dainties: for they *are* deceitful
meat.[C]
4 [1,g,h]Labour not to be [i]rich:
[j,k]cease from thine own wisdom.[Q]
5 Wilt thou [h]set thine eyes upon
that which is not? for *riches* certainly make themselves wings;
they fly away as an eagle toward
heaven.
6 [l,m]Eat thou not the bread of
*him that hath* an evil eye, *,[f]neither desire thou his [2]dainty
meats:[C]

**15** *h Heart*, Psa. 44:21. *i Children, punishment of*, Mark 10:14.
**16** *j Employer*, Deut. 24:14. *k Master*, Col. 4:1. *l Oppression*, Eccl. 5:8. *m Extortion*, Isa. 16:4. *n Poor, oppression of*, Prov. 21:13. *o Employee, oppressions of*, Deut. 24:14. *p Covetousness*, Isa. 57:17. *q Presents, to obtain favor*, Gen. 32:13. 7 R. V. gain,
**17** *r Commandment, enjoining heed to instruction*, Deut. 8:2. *s Instruction*, Prov. 23:23. *t Wisdom, spiritual*, Prov. 2:2.
**19** *u Faith*, Mark 11:22.
**21** *v Word of God*, Psa. 119:9.
**22** *w Commandment, forbidding robbery and oppression*, Deut. 8:2. *x Poor, oppression of, forbidden*, Prov. 21:13. *y Gates*, Deut. 3:5.
**23** *z Poor, God's care of*, Prov. 21:13.

*a Wicked, punishment of*, Psa. 73:3. 8 R. V. despoil of life those that despoil them. **24** *b Evil Company, warnings against*, Prov. 13:20. *c Anger*, Psa. 37:8. 9 R. V. a man that is given to anger;

**25** *d Influence, evil*, 1 Cor. 7:14. *e Example, bad*, John 13:15.
**26** *f Contracts, modes of ratifying*, Matt. 20:2. *g Surety*, Gen. 44:32. *h Debt, security for*, 1 Sam. 22:2.
**27** *i Bed*, Amos 6:4. *j Property, personal*, Lev. 27:15.
**28** *k Commandment, forbidding removal of landmarks*, Deut. 8:2. *l Landmarks*, Deut. 19:14.
**29** *m Diligence*, Rom. 12:8. *n Industry*, 1 Kin. 11:28.
**1** *a Manners, rules for guests*, Gen. 18:2. *b Guest, rules for conduct of*, Zeph. 1:7. *c Commandment, enjoining prudence in guests*, Deut. 8:2. *d Prudence*, 2 Chr. 2:12.
**2** *e Temperance, in eating*, 2 Pet. 1:6. *f Self-denial*, Mark 8:34.
**4** *g Commandment, forbidding haste for riches*, Deut. 8:2. *h Covetousness, gains of, unstable*, Isa. 57:17.

*i Riches*, Eccl. 4:8. *j False Confidence, warnings against*, Psa. 30:6. *k Conceit, warnings against*, Prov. 26:5. 1 R. V. Weary not thyself to be rich; **6** *l Commandment, warning against evil company*, Deut. 8:2. *m Evil Company, warnings against*, Prov. 13:20. 2 R. V. dainties:

*Peter*, Acts 3:12; *Paul*, Acts 20:19; Rom. 7:18; 1 Cor. 2:1–3; 15:9, 16; 2 Cor. 3:5; 11:30; 12:5–12; Eph. 3:8; Phil. 3:12, 13; 4:12; 1 Tim. 1:15.

‡ **FRIENDSHIP**, Amos 3:3. *Value of*, Eccl. 4:9–12.
*Promoted, by fidelity*, Prov. 11:13; *by sympathy*, Job 6:14, 15; *by not wearing out one's welcome*, Prov. 25:17, 19.
*Faithfulness in*, Psa. 35:13, 14; Prov. 17:9, 17; 27:6, 9, 10, 14, 17, 19.
*Temptations growing out of*, Deut. 13:6–9; Prov. 22:24–27.
*Jesus calls his disciples friends*, Luke 12:4; John 15:14, 15.
**Instances of:** *Abraham and Lot*, Gen. 4:14–16. *Ruth and Naomi*, Ruth 1:16, 17. *Samuel and Saul*, 1 Sam. 15:35; 16:1. *David and Jonathan*, 1 Sam. 18:1–4; 19:2–7; 20; 23:16–18; 2 Sam. 1:17–27; 9:1–13. *David and Abiathar*, 1 Sam. 22:23. *David and Nahash*, 2 Sam. 10:2. *David and Hiram*, 1 Kin. 5:1. *David and Mephibosheth*, 2 Sam. 9. *David and Hushai*, 2 Sam. 15:32–37; 16:16–19; 17:1–22. *David and Ittai*, 2 Sam. 15:19–21. *Nathan and Bath-sheba*, 1 Kin. 1:11–28. *David and Barzillai*, 2 Sam. 19:33, 37–39. *Joram and Ahaziah*, 2 Kin. 8:28, 29; 9:16. *Jehu and Jehonadab*, 2 Kin. 10:15–27. *Job and his three friends*, Job 2:11–13; 42:7–10. *Daniel and his three companions*, Dan. 2:49.
*Mary, Martha, and Lazarus, for Jesus*, Luke 10:38–42; John 11:1–46. *The Marys and Joseph of Arimathea, for Jesus*, Matt 27:55–61; 28:1–8; Luke 24:10; John 20:11–18. *Luke and Theophilus*, Luke 1:3; Acts 1:1. *Paul and his nephew*, Acts 23:16. *Paul, Priscilla, and Aquila*, Rom. 16:3, 4. *Paul, Timothy, and Epaphroditus*, Phil. 2:19, 20, 22, 25. *Paul and his fellow workers*, Col. 4:7–11.
See footnote, FRIENDS, Ex. 33:11.

* **ABSTEMIOUSNESS**, Prov. 23:1–3.
**Instances of:** *Daniel and his Hebrew companions*, Dan. 1:8–16. *John the Baptist*, Matt. 11:18.
See footnotes: TOTAL ABSTINENCE, Lev. 10:9; TEMPERANCE, 2 Pet. 1:6.

† **APPETITE**, Eccl. 8:15; Luke 12:19. *Gluttonous*, Prov. 23:20, 21; Titus 1:12. *Insatiable*, Eccl. 6:7. *An occasion of temptation*, Gen. 3:6; Matt. 4:2–4. *A source of temptation*, Gen. 25:29–34 (with Heb. 12:16); Num. 11:4, 5. *A god of the wicked*, Phil. 3:19.

7 For as he thinketh in his heart, so *is* he: Eat and drink, saith he to thee; [n,o]but his heart *is* not with thee.

8 The morsel *which* thou hast eaten shalt thou vomit up, and lose thy sweet words.

9 [p]Speak not in the ears of a [q]fool: for he will despise the wisdom of thy words.

10 [r]Remove not the old [s]landmark; and enter not into the fields of the [t]fatherless:

11 For their redeemer *is* mighty; he shall plead their cause with thee.[T]

12 [u]Apply thine heart unto ‡instruction, and thine ears to the words of [v]knowledge.

13 [w]Withhold not correction[G] from the child: for *if* thou beatest him with the rod, he shall not die.

14 [w]Thou shalt beat him with the rod, and shalt deliver his soul from [3,x]hell.[G]

15 My [y,z]son, if thine [a]heart be [b]wise, my heart shall rejoice, even mine.

16 Yea, my reins[G] shall rejoice, when thy lips speak right things.

17 [c,d]Let not thine heart envy sinners: but [e]*be thou* in the fear of the LORD all the day long.

18 For surely there is [4]an end; and thine [f]expectation shall not be cut off.

19 Hear thou, my son, and be [b]wise, and guide thine [a]heart in the way.

20 *,[g,h,i]Be not among[G] [j]winebibbers;[G] among [5]riotous eaters of flesh:

21 For the [k]drunkard and the [l]glutton shall come to [m]poverty: and [n]drowsiness shall clothe *a man* with rags.

22 [o,p]Hearken[G] unto thy [q]father that begat thee, and despise not thy [r]mother when she is old.

23 [s]Buy the [t]truth, and sell *it* not; *also* [b]wisdom, and ‡instruction, and understanding.

24 The [q]father of the righteous shall greatly rejoice: and he that begetteth a wise [u]*child* shall have joy of him.

25 [u]Thy [q]father and thy [r]mother shall be glad, and she that bare thee shall rejoice.

26 My son, [v,w]give me thine [x]heart, and let thine eyes [6]observe my ways.

27 For a [y,z]whore[G] *is* a deep ditch; and a strange[G] woman *is* a narrow [a]pit.

28 She also [b]lieth in wait as [7]*for*

**7** *n Hypocrisy,* Jas. 3:17. *o Deceit,* Psa. 36:3.
**9** *p Commandment, enjoining wisdom in speech,* Deut. 8:2. *q Fool,* Prov. 18:2.
**10** *r Commandment, forbidding removal of landmarks,* Deut. 8:2. *s Landmarks,* Deut. 19:14. *t Orphan,* Lam. 5:3.
**12** *u Commandment, enjoining wisdom,* v. 19; Deut. 8:2. *v Wisdom,* Prov. 2:2.
**13** *w Children, punishment of,* Mark 10:14.
**14** *x Hell,* Mark 9:43. 3 R. V. Sheol.
**15** *y Young Men,* Prov. 1:4. *z Children, promises to,* Mark 10:14.

*a Heart,* Psa. 44:21. *b Wisdom,* Prov. 2:2.
**17** *c Commandment, forbidding envy, and enjoining fear of God,* Deut. 8:2. *d Envy, forbidden,* Prov. 14:30. *e Fear of God, enjoined,* Acts 9:31.
**18** 4 R. V. a reward; And thy hope shall

*f Hope,* Prov. 13:12.
**20** *g Commandment, forbidding company with winebibbers,* Deut. 8:2. *h Total Abstinence, from intoxicating beverages,* Lev. 10:9. *i Drunkenness, forbidden,* Luke 21:34. *j Evil Company,* Prov. 13:20. 5 R. V. gluttonous
**21** *k Drunkard,* Psa. 69:12. *l Gluttony, impoverishes,* Prov. 30:22. *m Poverty, caused by drunkenness,* Prov. 30:8. *n Idleness, poverty from,* Eccl. 10:18.
**22** *o Commandment, enjoining reverence for parents,* Deut. 8:2. *p Children, commandments to,* Mark 10:14. *q Father,* Psa. 27:10. *r Mother,* 1 Kin. 2:20.
**23** *s Commandments,* Deut. 8:2. *t Truth,* John 18:37.
**24** *u Children, good,* Mark 10:14.

**26** *v Duty, of man to God,* Eccl. 12:13. *w Commandment, enjoining love to God,* Deut. 8:2. *x Love, of man for God, enjoined,* 1 John 4:19. 6 R. V. delight in my ways. **27** *y Harlot,* Prov. 7:10. *z Women, wicked,* Prov. 31:10.—*a Pit, figurative,* Psa. 7:15. **28** *b Temptation, leading into,* Luke 11:4. 7 R. V. a robber,

*To be restrained,* Prov. 21:17; 23:2. *Restrained,* 1 Cor. 9:27; *for conscience' sake,* Dan. 1:8–16; *for a brother's sake,* Rom. 14:21; 1 Cor. 8:13.

See footnote, HUNGER, Neh. 9:15.

‡ **INSTRUCTION,** Matt. 5:2–48; Luke 4:16–21; 24:27; John 7:14; 8:2.

*Provision for, made by the state,* 2 Chr. 17:7–9; Dan. 1:3–5, 17–20.

*Precept upon precept, precept upon precept; line upon line, line upon line,* Isa. 28:10.

*Sought,* Psa. 90:12; 119:12; 143:8, 10. *Giving heed to, enjoined,* Prov. 4:1, 2, 10, 13, 20; 5:1, 2; 22:17; 23:12, 23.

*Lack of,* 2 Chr. 15:3; Prov. 24:30–34. *Hated,* Psa. 50:17; Prov. 1:29, 30; 5:12, 13; Jer. 32:33; Luke 20:1, 2.

*From Nature,* Prov. 24:30–34; Eccl. 1:13–18; 3; 4:1; Matt. 6:25–30. *From the study of human nature,* Eccl. chapters 3–12.

**In religion,** Ex. 24:12; Lev. 10:11; Deut. 24:8; 27:14–26; 31:9–13; 33:10; 2 Chr. 17:8, 9; 35:3; Neh. 8:7–13; Mal. 2:6, 7.

*By means, of the law,* Deut. 27:1–26; Rom. 2:18; Gal. 3:24, 25; *of proverbs,* Prov. 1:1–6, 20–30; *of songs,* Deut. 31:19; 32:1–44.

*By priests,* Ezra 7:10; Mal. 2:7. *By Jesus,* Matt. 5:1, 2; Mark 6:2; 12:35; Luke 4:16; 19:47; 20:1–8; 21:37, 38; 24:27; John 7:14; 8:2. *By preachers,* Rom. 10:14; 1 Cor. 12:28, 29; Eph. 4:11; Col. 1:2, 8. *By teachers,* 2 Kin. 23:2; Neh. 8:7, 8; 1 Cor. 12:28, 29; Eph. 4:11.

*By symbols,* see footnote, SYMBOLS, Heb. 9:9.

*By parables,* see footnote, PARABLES, Ezek. 20:49.

*By inscriptions, on doors and gates,* Deut 11:20, 21; *on monuments,* Josh. 8:30–35.

*By the public reading of the law,* Deut. 31:9–13; Josh. 8:35; Neh. 8:2, 3.

**By object lessons:** *Passover feast,* Ex. 12:26, 27. *Dedication of firstlings,* Ex. 13:14–16. *Phylacteries,* Ex. 13:9, 16. *Legends,* Ex. 28:36; 39:30; Deut. 6:6–9; 11:18–20; Zech. 14:20; Matt. 27:37. *The pot of manna, a reminder of God's care,* Ex. 16:32. *The sacred oil, a symbol of holiness,* Ex. 30:31. *The pillar of twelve stones at the fords of the Jordan,* Josh. 4:7, 19–24. *Fringes on the borders of garments,* Num. 15:38, 39. *The garment rent in pieces,* 1 Kin. 11:30–32. *The symbolical wearing of sackcloth and the going barefoot,* Isa. 20:2, 3. *The linen girdle,* Jer. 13:1–11. *Potter's vessel,* Jer. 19:1–12. *Basket of figs,* Jer. 24. *Bonds and yokes,* Jer. 27:2–11; 28. *By stones being put in a brick kiln,* Jer. 3:8–10. *Illustrations on a tile,* Ezek. 4:1–3. *Lying on one side in public view for a long period,* Ezek. 4:4–8. *Eating bread baked with dung,* Ezek. 4:9–17. *Shaving the head,* Ezek. 5. *Moving household goods,* Ezek. 12:3–16. *Eating and drinking sparingly,* Ezek. 12:18–20. *Sighing,* Ezek. 21:6, 7. *The boiling pot,* Ezek. 24:1–14. *Widowhood,* Ezek. 24:16–27. *Two sticks joined together,* Ezek. 37:16–22.

**Of children:** *By parents, enjoined,* Ex. 10:2; Deut. 4:9, 10; 6:6–9; 11:18, 19; Psa. 78:5–8; Prov. 22:6; Isa. 38:19; Eph. 6:4.

**By types,** see footnotes: ABLUTION, Judg. 19:21; BLEMISH, Lev. 14:10; DEFILEMENT, Lev. 5:2; DISFELLOWSHIP, Num. 15:31. See also prefatory note to footnote, HOLINESS, Ex. 39:30.

a prey, and increaseth the [8]transgressors among men.

29 Who hath woe? who hath sorrow? who hath [c]contentions? who hath [9]babbling? who hath wounds without cause? who hath redness of eyes?

30 They that [d]tarry long at the ‖wine; they that go to seek mixed wine.

31 [e,f]Look not thou upon the ‖wine when it is red, when it giveth his colour in the cup, *when* it [10]moveth itself aright.[Q]

32 At the last ‖it biteth like a [g]serpent, and stingeth like an [h]adder.

33 Thine eyes shall behold strange[G] [11]women, and thine heart shall utter perverse things.

34 Yea, [d]thou shalt be as he that lieth down in the midst of the sea, or as he that lieth upon the top of a mast.

35 [d]They have stricken me, *shalt thou say, and* I was not [12]sick; they have beaten me, *and* I felt *it* not: when shall I awake? I will seek ‖it yet again.

## CHAPTER 24

*The words of the wise.*

[a]BE not [b]thou [c]envious against [d]evil men, neither desire to be with them.

2 For their [e]heart studieth [1]destruction, and their lips[G] [f]talk of mischief.

3 Through [g]wisdom is an house builded; and by understanding it is established:

4 And by [g,h]knowledge shall the chambers be filled with all precious and pleasant riches.

5 A wise man *is* strong; yea, a man of [g,h]knowledge increaseth strength.

6 For [i]by wise [j]counsel thou shalt make thy [k]war: and in multitude of counsellors *there is* safety.

7 [g]Wisdom *is* too high for a fool: he openeth not his mouth in the gate.

8 He that [l]deviseth to do evil shall be called a mischievous person.

9 The [m]thought of foolishness *is* sin: and the [2,n]scorner[G] *is* an [o]abomination to men.

10 *If* thou [p,q]faint in the day of [r]adversity, thy strength *is* small.

11 [s,t]If thou forbear to deliver *them that are* drawn unto death, and *those that are* ready to be slain;

12 If thou [u]sayest, Behold, we knew it not; doth not he that [3,v]pondereth the heart consider *it*? and he that keepeth thy soul, doth *not* he [v]know *it*? and shall *not* he [w,x]render to *every* man according to his works?[S Q]

13 My son, eat thou honey, because *it is* good; and the honeycomb, *which is* sweet to thy taste:

14 So *shall* the knowledge of [g]wisdom *be* unto thy soul: when

---

8 R. V. treacherous among men.

**29**
c *Strife*, Prov. 20:3.
9 R. V. complaining?

**30**
d *Drunkenness*, Luke 21:34.

**31**
e *Commandment, forbidding indulgence in wine*, Deut. 8:2.
f *Total Abstinence*, Lev. 10:9.
10 R. V. goeth down smoothly:

**32**
g *Serpent, venom of*, Num. 21:6.
h *Adder*, Gen. 49:17.

**33**

**35**
12 R. V. hurt;

**1**
a *Commandment, forbidding envy*, Deut. 8:2.
b *Young Men*, Prov. 1:4.
c *Envy, forbidden*, Prov. 14:30.
d *Evil Company, warnings against*, Prov. 13:20.

**2**
e *Heart*, Psa. 44:21.
f *Speech, evil*, Col. 4:6.
1 R. V. oppression,

**3**
g *Wisdom*, Prov. 2:2.

**4**
h *Knowledge, is power*, Luke 11:52.

**6**
i *Prudence*, 2 Chr. 2:12.
j *Counsel*, Prov. 12:15.
k *War*, Judg. 3:2.

**8**
l *Malice*, Eph. 4:31.

**9**
m *Sin, defined*, Rom. 5:12.
n *Scorners*, Prov. 19:25.
o *Abomination*, Lev. 18:27.
2 Am. R. V. scoffer

**10**
p *Doubting*, Rom. 14:23.
q *Despondency*, Eccl. 2:20.
r *Adversity, despondency in*, Psa. 10:6.

**11**
s *Commandment, enjoining assistance to the distressed*, Deut. 8:2.
t *Duty, of man to man*, Eccl. 12:13.

**12**
u *Excuses*, Luke 14:18.
v *God, knowledge of*, Gen. 2:2.
w *Judgment, according to opportunity and works*, 1 Pet. 1:17.
x *Punishment, according to deeds*, Lev. 26:41.
3 R. V. weigheth

---

‖ **WINE,** Isa. 25:6; Jer. 40:10, 12. *Made, from grapes*, Gen. 40:11; 49:11; *from pomegranates*, Song 8:2. *Kept, in bottles*, Jer. 13:12; 48:12; *in skins*, Josh. 9:4, 13; Job 32:19; Matt. 9:17; Luke 5:37, 38. *Storehouses for*, 2 Chr. 32:28. *Cellars for*, 1 Chr. 27:27.

*New*, Mark 2:22; Luke 5:37–39. *Old*, Luke 5:39.

*Fermented*, Lev. 10:9; Num. 6:3; 28:7; Deut. 14:26; 29:6; Prov. 23:31, 32; Mark 2:22. *Refined*, Isa. 25:6; Jer. 48:11. *Plentiful in Canaan*, Deut. 33:28; 2 Kin. 18:32.

*Offerings of*, Ex. 29:40; Lev. 23:13; Num. 15:5, 10; 18:12; 28:7, 14; Deut. 14:23; Neh. 10:39. *Given by Melchizedek to Abraham*, Gen. 14:18.

*Medicinal use of*, Prov. 31:6, 7. *Medicinal use of, recommended by Paul to Timothy*, 1 Tim. 5:23.

*Given to Jesus at the crucifixion*, Matt. 27:34, 48; Mark 15: 23; Luke 23:36; John 19:29.

*Drunk at meals*, Matt. 26:27–29; Mark 14:23. *Made by Jesus at the marriage feast in Cana*, John 2:9, 10.

*Sacramental use of*, Matt. 26:27–29; Luke 22:17–20.

*Admonitions, against the use of, as a beverage*, Lev. 10:9; Num. 6:3; Judg. 13:4; Prov. 20:1; 21:17; 23:29–32; 31:4, 5; Isa. 5:11, 22; 24:9; 28:1, 3, 7; 35:2–10, 14, 18, 19; Ezek. 44: 21; Hos. 4:11; Luke 1:15; Rom. 14:21; *against the immoderate use of*, Eph. 5:18; Tit. 2:3.

*Forbidden, to priests while on duty*, Lev. 10:9; Ezek. 44:21; *to kings*, Prov. 31:4; *to Nazirites*, Num. 6:2, 3.

*Abstinence from, by Daniel*, Dan. 1:5, 8, 16; 10:3; *by the Rechabites*, Jer. 35:6, 8, 14, 16; *by Timothy*, 1 Tim. 5:23. *Denied to the Israelites in the wilderness, that they might know, with other restrictions, that the Lord was God*, Deut. 29:6. *Samson's mother forbidden to use, during gestation*, Judg. 13:4, 5

*Inflames the eyes*, Gen. 49:12. *Intoxicates*, Psa. 60:3; Prov. 4:17; 31:6, 7; Jer. 23:9; Joel 1:5; Hab. 2:5; Zech. 10:7.

*Children sold for*, Joel 3:3. *Banquets of*, Esth. 5:6.

*Jesus accused of drinking*, Matt. 11:19; Luke 7:34. *Intoxication from, falsely charged against the apostles*, Acts 2:13.

**Instances of intoxication from:** *Noah*, Gen. 9:21. *Lot*, Gen. 19:32–35. *Nabal*, 1 Sam. 25:36. *Amnon*, 2 Sam. 13:28, 29. *Ahasuerus*, Esth. 1:10.

**Figurative:** *Of the divine judgments*, Psa. 60:3; 75:8; Jer. 51:7. *Of the joy of wisdom*, Prov. 9:2, 5. *Of the joys of religion*, Isa. 25:6; 55:1. *Of abominations*, Rev. 14:8; 16:19.

**Symbolical:** *Of the blood of Jesus*, Matt. 26:28; Mark 14: 23, 24; Luke 22:20.

thou hast found *it,* then there
shall be a reward, and thy [v]expectation shall not be cut off.
15 Lay not wait, O wicked
*man,* against the dwelling of the
righteous; spoil not his resting
place:
16 For a just *man* falleth seven
times, and riseth up again: but
the wicked [4,z]shall fall into mischief.
17 [a,b]Rejoice not when thine
*enemy falleth, and let not thine
heart be glad when he [5]stumbleth:
18 Lest the LORD see *it,* and it
displease him, and he turn away
his [c]wrath from him.
19 Fret not thyself because of
evil *men,* [d]neither be thou envious at the wicked;
20 For there shall be no reward
to the evil *man;* [e]the candle of
the wicked shall be put out.
21 My son, [f,g,h]fear [i]thou the
LORD and the [j]king: [k]*and* meddle not with [l]them that are given
to change:
22 For their [m]calamity shall rise
suddenly; and who knoweth the
ruin of them both?
23 These *things* also *belong* to
the wise. [n,o]*It is* not good to have
†respect of persons in judgment.
24 He that [p,q]saith unto the
[r]wicked, Thou *art* righteous; him
shall the people curse, nations
shall abhor him:
25 But to them that [s]rebuke
*him* shall be delight, and a good
blessing shall come upon them.
26 [6]*Every man* shall kiss *his*
lips that giveth a right answer.
27 Prepare thy work without,
and make it fit for thyself in the
field; and afterwards build thine
house.
28 [t]Be not a [u,v]witness against
thy neighbour without cause; and
[w]deceive *not* with thy lips.
29 [b]Say not, I will [x]do so to him
as [y]he hath done to me: I will
render to the man according to
his work.
30 I went by the field of the
[z,a]slothful, and by the [b]vineyard
of the man void of understanding;
31 And, lo, it was all grown
over with [c]thorns, *and* ‡nettles
had covered the face thereof,
and the stone [d]wall thereof was
broken down.
32 Then I saw, *and* considered
*it* well: I looked upon *it, and* received [e]instruction.
33 [a,f]*Yet* a little sleep, a little
slumber, a little folding of the
hands to sleep:
34 So shall thy [g]poverty come
*as* [7]one that travelleth; and thy
want as an armed man.

## CHAPTER 25

*Observations about kings, 8 and about avoiding causes of quarrels, and sundry causes thereof.*

THESE *are* also [a]proverbs of
[b]Sŏl′o-mon, which the men
of [c]Hĕz-e-kī′ah king of [d]Jū′dah
copied out.
2 *It is* the glory of [e]God to conceal a thing: but the honour of
kings *is* to search out a matter.
3 The heaven for height, and
the earth for depth, and the
heart of kings *is* unsearchable.
4 Take away the [f]dross from
the [g]silver, and there shall come
forth a vessel for the finer.
5 Take away the wicked *from*

14
v *Hope,* Prov. 13:12.
16
z *Wicked, punishment of,* Psa. 73:3.
4 R. V. are overthrown by calamity.
17
a *Commandment, forbidding uncharitableness,* Deut. 8:2.
b *Malice, forbidden,* Eph. 4:31.
5 R. V. is overthrown:
18
c *Anger of God,* 2 Kin. 13:3.
19
d *Envy, forbidden,* Prov. 14:30.
20
e *Wicked, punishment of,* Psa. 73:3.
21
f *Commandment, enjoining fear of God,* Deut. 8:2.
g *Fear of God, enjoined,* Acts 9:31.
h *Loyalty, enjoined,* Eccl. 8:2.
i *Citizens, duties of,* Luke 15:15.
j *Government, duty of citizens to,* Isa. 22:21.
k *Character, instability of,* Phil. 2:15.
l *Instability, warnings against,* Jas. 1:8.
22
m *Adversity,* Psa. 10:6.
23
n *Justice,* Deut. 33:21.
o *Judge, character and qualifications of,* Judg. 2:18.
24
p *Falsehood,* Job 21:34.
q *Flattery,* Prov. 6:24.
r *Rulers, wicked,* Ex. 18:21.
25
s *Reproof, faithfulness in,* Prov. 17:10.
26
6 R. V. He kisseth the lips That

28
t *Commandment, forbidding false witness,* Deut. 8:2.
u *False Witness, forbidden,* Matt. 19:18.
v *Evidence, false, forbidden,* Deut. 17:6.
w *Deceit, forbidden,* Psa. 36:3.
29
x *Revenge, forbidden,* Ezek. 25:15.
y *Retaliation, malicious, forbidden,* Deut. 19:19.
30
z *Idleness,* Eccl. 10:18.
a *Laziness,* Prov. 19:15.
b *Vineyard,* Isa. 1:8.
31
c *Thorn,* Hos. 2:6.
d *Fence, made of stones,* Psa. 62:3.
32
e *Instruction,* Prov. 23:23.
33
f *Rising, late,* Gen. 19:2.
34
g *Poverty, caused by laziness,* Prov. 30:8.
7 R. V. a robber;

1
a *Proverbs, of Solomon,* 1 Sam. 24:13.
b *Solomon,* 2 Sam. 12:24.
c *Hezekiah,* 2 Kin. 16:20.
d *Judah, kingdom of,* 2 Chr. 11:17.
2
e *God, unsearchable,* Gen. 2:2.
4
f *Dross,* Psa. 119:119.
g *Silver, refining of,* 1 Chr. 28:14.

* **ENEMY,** Job 31:29; Psa. 56:2, 5, 6; 57:4, 6; 62:4; 69:4; 71:10; 102:8; 109:2–5.
*Kindness to, enjoined,* Ex. 23:4, 5; Prov. 25:21, 22; Matt. 5:43–48; Luke 6:27–36; Rom. 12:14, 20.
*Rejoicing at destruction of, forbidden,* Prov. 24:17, 18.
**Forgiveness of:** *Enjoined,* Matt. 6:12–15; 18:21–35; Mark 11:25; Luke 17:3, 4; Eph. 4:31, 32; Col. 3:13; 1 Pet. 3:9.
INSTANCES OF FORGIVENESS OF: *Esau, of Jacob,* Gen. 33:4, 11. *Joseph, of his brethren,* Gen. 45:5–15; 50:19–21. *Moses, of Miriam and Aaron,* Num. 12:1–13. *David, of Saul,* 1 Sam. 24:10–12; 26:9, 23; 2 Sam. 1:14–17; *of Shimei,* 2 Sam. 16:9–13; 19:23, with 1 Kin. 2:8, 9; *of Absalom and his co-conspirators,* 2 Sam. 18:5, 12, 32, 33; 19:6, 12, 13. *The prophet of Judah, of Jeroboam,* 1 Kin. 13:3–6. *Jesus, of his enemies,* Luke 23:34. *Stephen, of his murderers,* Acts 7:60.
**Figurative,** Matt. 13:25, 28, 39.

† **RESPECT OF PERSONS,** Prov. 24:23; 28:21; Jas. 2:1–9. *God does not have,* Deut. 10:17; 2 Chr. 19:7; Job 31:13–15; 34:19; Acts 10:34; 15:9; Rom. 2:11, 12; 10:12; Col. 3:25; 1 Pet. 1:17.

‡ **NETTLE.** *An obnoxious plant,* Prov. 24:31; Isa. 34:13
**Figurative,** Job 30:7; Hos. 9:6; Zeph. 2:9.

before the [h,i]king, and his throne shall be established in righteousness.

6 [j,k,l]Put not forth [m]thyself in the presence of the king, and stand not in the place of great *men*:

7 For [l]better *it is* that it be said unto thee, Come up hither; than that thou shouldest be put lower in the presence of the prince whom thine eyes have seen.[Q]

8 [n,o]Go not forth [p]hastily to [q,r]strive, lest *thou know not* what to do in the end thereof, when thy neighbour hath put thee to shame.

9 [n,o,s]Debate thy cause with thy neighbour *himself*; and [1]discover[C] not a secret to another:

10 Lest he that heareth *it* [2]put thee to shame, and thine infamy turn not away.

11 A [t]word [u]fitly spoken *is like* apples of [v]gold in [3]pictures of [w]silver.

12 *As* an *earring of [v]gold, and an ornament of fine gold, *so is* a wise [x]reprover upon an obedient ear.

13 As the cold of [y]snow in the time of [z]harvest, *so is* a faithful [a]messenger to them that send him: for he refresheth the soul of his masters.

14 Whoso [†,b]boasteth himself of a false gift *is like* clouds and wind without rain.

15 By long [c]forbearing is a [4]prince persuaded, and a [d]soft tongue breaketh the bone.

16 Hast thou found honey? eat [e]so much as is sufficient for thee, lest thou be filled therewith, and vomit it.

17 [5]Withdraw thy foot from thy neighbour's house; lest he be weary of thee, and *so* hate thee.

18 A man that beareth [f]false[C] witness against his neighbour *is* a maul,[C] and a [g]sword, and a sharp [h]arrow.

19 Confidence in an unfaithful man in time of trouble *is like* a broken tooth, and a foot out of joint.

20 *As* he that taketh [6]away a garment in cold weather, *and as* [i]vinegar upon nitre,[C] so *is* he that singeth [j]songs to an heavy heart.

21 [k,l]If[Q] thine [m]enemy be [n]hungry, [o,p,q]give him bread to eat; and if he be thirsty, give him water to drink:

22 For thou shalt heap [r]coals of fire upon his head, and [s]the LORD shall reward thee.[Q]

23 The north [t]wind [7]driveth away [u]rain: so *doth* [8]an [v]angry countenance a [‡,w,x]backbiting tongue.

24 [y]*It is* better to dwell in the corner of the [z]housetop, than with a [9,a]brawling [b,c]woman and in a wide house.

25 *As* cold waters to a thirsty soul, so *is* [d]good news from a far country.

26 [10]A [e]righteous man [f]falling down before the wicked *is as* a troubled fountain, and a corrupt spring.

27 *It is* not good to eat much ‖honey: so *for men* to search their own glory *is not* glory.

28 He that *hath* no rule over

**5**
h *Rulers, corrupted by evil counselors,* Ex. 18:21.
i *Government, corruption in,* Isa. 22:21.
**6**
j *Presumption, admonitions against,* Psa. 19:13.
k *Respect, to rulers,* Isa. 22:11.
l *Humility, enjoined,* Prov. 22:4.
m *Citizens, duties of,* Luke 15:15.
**8**
n *Commandment, forbidding haste in litigation,* Deut. 2:8.
o *Prudence, in avoiding strife,* 2 Chr. 2:12.
p *Rashness,* 2 Sam. 6:7.
q *Strife,* Prov. 20:3.
r *Litigation,* Matt. 5:25.
**9**
s *Compromise, before litigation, enjoined,* Luke 12:58.
1 R. V. disclose not the secret of another:
**10**
2 R. V. revile thee,
**11**
t *Words,* Luke 4:22.
u *Speech, wise,* Col. 4:6.
v *Gold,* Ezek. 7:19.
w *Silver,* 1 Chr. 28:14.
3 Am. R. V. network
**12**
x *Reproof,* Prov. 17:10.
**13**
y *Snow,* Jer. 18:14.
z *Harvest,* Ex. 34:21.

a *Servant,* Jer. 2:14.
**14**
b *Pride,* Prov. 16:18.
**15**
c *Meekness,* Psa. 45:4.
d *Tact,* Prov. 15:1.
4 R. V. ruler
**16**
e *Temperance, in eating,* 2 Pet. 1:6.

**17**
5 R. V. Let thy foot be seldom in thy
**18**
f *False Witness,* Matt. 19:18.
g *Sword, figurative,* 1 Chr. 21:5.
h *Arrow, figurative,* 1 Sam. 20:20.
**20**
i *Vinegar,* Num. 6:3.
j *Music,* 2 Chr. 5:13.
6 R. V. off
**21**
k Rom. 12:20.
l *Good for Evil,* Luke 6:27.
m *Enemy, kindness to, enjoined,* Prov. 24:17.
n *Hunger,* Neh. 9:15.
o *Commandment, enjoining kindness to enemies,* Deut. 8:2.
p *Forgiveness, of enemies,* Matt. 18:21.
q *Liberality,* 1 Tim. 6:18.
**22**
r 2 Sam. 14:7; Isa. 6:6, 7.
s *Promise, to the merciful,* 2 Cor. 1:20.
**23**
t *Meteorology,* Matt. 16:2.
u *Rain,* 2 Sam. 1:21.
v *Countenance, angry,* Prov. 15:13.
w *Slander,* Prov. 10:18.
x *Speech, evil,* Col. 4:6.
7 R. V. bringeth forth
8 R. V. a backbiting tongue an angry countenance.
**24**
y *Family, infelicity in,* 1 Chr. 13:14.
z *House, roofs of,* Esth. 8:1.

—a *Strife,* Prov. 20:3. b *Women,* Prov. 31:10. c *Wife,* Prov. 5:18. 9 R. V. contentious **25** d Prov. 15:30. **26** e *Righteous,* Psa. 64:10. f *Temptation, yielding to,* Luke 11:4. 10 R. V. As a troubled fountain, and a corrupted spring, So is a righteous man that giveth way before the wicked.

* **EARRING,** Gen. 35:4. *Of gold,* Prov. 25:12. *Offering of, for the golden calf,* Ex. 32:2, 3; *for the tabernacle,* Ex. 35:22.

† **BOASTING,** Jas. 3:5. *Folly of,* Psa. 49:6–9; Prov. 27:1; Isa. 10:15; Jas. 4:16. *Deceitful,* Prov. 20:14; 25:14. *Of the wicked,* Psa. 52:1; 94:4; Rom. 1:30.

**Forbidden,** Jer. 9:23.

**Instances of:** *Goliath,* 1 Sam. 17:8–11, 23–26, 31–54. *Ben-hadad,* 1 Kin. 20:10. *Amaziah,* 2 Chr. 25:17–20. *Sennacherib,* 2 Kin. 18:19, 28–35; 19:8–13; Isa. 10:8–15. *The disciples,* Luke 10:17, with v. 20.

‡ **BACKBITING,** Psa. 15:1–3; Prov. 25:23; Rom. 1:30; 2 Cor. 12:20.

See footnotes: SPEECH, *Evil,* Col. 4:6; SLANDER, Prov. 10:18.

‖ **HONEY,** Ex. 16:31; 2 Sam. 17:29; Prov. 25:27; Song 4:11; Isa. 7:15; Matt. 3:4. *Not to be offered with sacrifices,* Lev. 2:11. *Found, in rocks,* Deut. 32:13; Psa. 81:16; *upon the ground,* 1 Sam. 14:25. *Samson's riddle concerning,* Judg. 14:14. *Sent as a present by Jacob to Egypt,* Gen. 43:11. *Plentiful, in Palestine,* Ex. 3:8; Lev. 20:24; Deut. 8:8; *in Assyria,* 2 Kin. 18:32. *An article of merchandise from Palestine,* Ezek. 27:17.

**Figurative,** Ex. 3:8, 17; 13:5; 33:3; Lev. 20:24; Num. 13:27; 14:8; 16:13, 14; Deut. 6:3; 11:9; 26:9, 15; 27:3; 31:20; Job 20:17; Isa. 7:15; Jer. 11:5; Ezek. 20:6.

his own spirit *is like* a city *that* *is* broken down, *and* without walls.

## CHAPTER 26

*Observations concerning fools, 13 sluggards, 17 and busybodies.*

AS [a]snow in [b]summer, and as [a]rain in [c]harvest, so honour is not seemly for a [d]fool.

2 As the [1]bird by wandering, as the swallow by flying, so the curse causeless shall not come.

3 A whip for the horse, a [e]bridle for the [f]ass, and a [g]rod for the [c]fool's back.

4 [h,i]Answer not a [d]fool according to his folly, [j]lest thou also be like unto him.

5 [k,l]Answer a [d]fool according to his folly, [j]lest he be wise in his own *conceit.

6 He that sendeth a message by the hand of a [d]fool cutteth off the feet, *and* drinketh damage.

7 The legs of the lame [2]are not equal: so *is* a parable in the mouth of [d]fools.

8 As he that bindeth [3]a stone in a sling, so *is* he that giveth honour to a fool.

9 *As* a thorn goeth up into the hand of a [m]drunkard, so *is* a parable in the mouth of [d]fools.

10 [4]The great *God* that formed all *things* both rewardeth the fool, and rewardeth transgressors.

11 [n]As a [o]dog returneth to his vomit, [5,p]*so* a [d]fool returneth to his folly.

12 Seest thou a man [q]wise in his own *conceit? *there is* more hope of a [d]fool than of him.

13 The [r,s]slothful *man* saith, *There is* a [t]lion in the way; a lion *is* in the streets.

14 *As* the door turneth upon his hinges, so *doth* the [r]slothful upon his bed.

15 The [6,r]slothful hideth his hand in *his* bosom; it grieveth him to bring it again to his mouth.

16 The sluggard *is* wiser in his own *conceit than [v]seven men that can render a reason.

17 [w]He that passeth by, *and* [7]meddleth with [x]strife *belonging* not to him, *is like* one that taketh a [o]dog by the ears.

18 As a †mad *man* who casteth firebrands, arrows, and death,

19 So *is* the man *that* deceiveth his neighbour, and saith, Am not I in sport?

20 Where no wood is, *there* the fire goeth out: so where *there is* no [8,y,z]talebearer, the [x]strife ceaseth.

21 *As* coals *are* to burning coals, and wood to fire; so *is* a contentious man to kindle [x]strife.

22 The [z]words of a [9,y] talebearer *are* as [10]wounds, and they go down into the innermost parts of the [11]belly.

23 [12]Burning lips and a wicked heart *are like* [13]a potsherd covered with [a]silver [b]dross.

24 He that [c]hateth [d,e]dissembleth with his lips, and layeth up [f]deceit within him;

25 When he speaketh fair, believe him not: for *there are* seven abominations in his heart.

26 [14]*Whose* [c]hatred is covered by [f]deceit, his wickedness shall be shewed before the *whole* congregation.

27 Whoso diggeth a [g]pit [h]shall fall therein: and he that rolleth a stone, it will return upon him.

28 A [i]lying tongue [c]hateth *those*

**1**
a *Meteorology*, Matt. 16:2.
b *Summer*, Isa. 28:4.
c *Harvest*, Ex. 34:21.
d *Fool*, Prov. 18:2.

**2**
1 R. V. sparrow in her wandering, as the swallow in her flying, So the curse that is causeless lighteth not.

**3**
e *Bridle*, Psa. 32:9.
f *Ass, domesticated*, 2 Chr. 28:15.
g *Punishment*, Lev. 26:41.

**4**
h *Commandment, enjoining wisdom in speech*, Deut. 8:2.
i *Speech, foolish*, Col. 4:6.
j *Prudence*, 2 Chr. 2:12.

**5**
k *Speech, wise*, Col. 4:6.
l *Reproof*, Prov. 17:10.

**7**
2 R. V. hang loose?

**8**
3 R. V. a bag of gems in a heap of stones, so

**9**
m *Drunkard*, Psa. 69:12.

**10**
4 R. V. As an archer that woundeth all, So is he that hireth the fool and he that hireth them that pass by.

**11**
n 2 Pet. 2:22.
o *Dog*, 1 Kin. 21:19.
p *Wicked, compared to dogs*, Psa. 73:3.
5 R. V. So is a fool that repeateth his folly.

**12**
q *False Confidence*, Psa. 30:6.

**13**
r *Laziness*, Prov. 19:15.
s *Idleness*, Eccl. 10:18.
t *Lion*, Mic. 5:8.

**15**
6 R. V. sluggard burieth his hand in the dish; It wearieth him

**16**
v *Seven*, Gen. 7:2.

**17**
w *Busybody*, 2 Thess. 3:11.
x *Strife*, Prov. 20:3.
7 R. V. vexeth himself with

**20**
y *Talebearing*, Prov. 11:13.
z *Speech, evil*, Col. 4:6.
8 R. V. whisperer, contention ceaseth.

**22**
9 R. V. whisperer
10 R. V. dainty morsels,
11 Am. R. V. body.

**23**
a *Silver*, 1 Chr. 28:14.
b *Dross*, Psa. 119:119.
12 R. V. Fervent
13 R. V. an earthen vessel overlaid

**24**
c *Hatred*, Prov. 15:17.
d *Dissembling*, Josh. 7:11.
e *Hypocrisy*, Jas. 3:17.
f *Deceit*, Psa. 36:3.

**26**
14 R. V. Though his hatred cover itself with guile,

**27**
g *Pit*, Psa. 7:15.
h *Sin, retroactive*, Rom. 5:12.

**28**
i *Falsehood*, Job 21:34.

* **CONCEIT.** *Of the foolish*, Prov. 12:15; 26:5, 12, 16; 28:26; Rom. 1:22. *Of the rich*, Prov. 28:11. *Of the self-righteous*, Psa. 36:2; Luke 18:11, 12.
*Warnings against*, Prov. 3:5, 7; 23:4; Isa. 5:21; Jer. 9:23; Rom. 11:25; 12:16; 1 Cor. 3:18; Gal. 6:3.
See footnote, SELF-EXALTATION, Luke 14:11.

† **INSANITY,** Prov. 26:18. *Feigned by David*, 1 Sam. 21:13–15. *Sent as a judgment from God*, Deut. 28:28; Zech. 12:4; *upon Nebuchadnezzar*, Dan. 4:32–34.
False accusations of: *Against Jesus*, Mark 3:21; John 10:20; *against Paul*, Acts 26:24, 25; 2 Cor. 5:13.
*Cured by Jesus*, Matt. 4:24.
*Demoniacal, of Saul*, 1 Sam. 16:14; 18:10, 11.
See footnote, DEMONS, *Possession by*, Matt. 4:24.

*that are* afflicted by it; and a [f]flat-
tering mouth worketh ruin.

## CHAPTER 27

*Sundry maxims and observations.*

[a,b]BOAST not thyself of to
morrow; for thou [c]know-
est not what a day may bring
forth.[Q]
2 [d,e]Let another man praise
thee, and not [f,g]thine own
mouth; a stranger, and not
thine own lips.
3 A stone *is* heavy, and the
sand weighty; but a fool's [1]wrath
*is* heavier than them both.
4 [h]Wrath *is* cruel, and anger *is*
outrageous; but who *is* able to
stand before [2,i,j]envy?
5 Open [k]rebuke *is* better than
secret love.
6 [l]Faithful *are* the wounds of
a [m]friend; but the [n,o]kisses of an
enemy *are* [3]deceitful.
7 The full soul loatheth an
honeycomb; but to the hungry
soul every bitter thing is sweet.
8 As a bird that wandereth
from her nest, so *is* a man that
[p,q]wandereth from his place.
9 [r]Ointment and [*]perfume rejoice the heart: so *doth* the
sweetness of a man's [l,m]friend
[4]by hearty[G] [s]counsel.[G]
10 [t]Thine own [m]friend, and
thy father's friend, forsake not;
neither go into thy [u]brother's
house in the day of thy calamity:
*for* better *is* a neighbour *that is*
near than a brother far off.
11 [v]My [w,x]son, be wise, and
make my heart glad, that I may
answer him that reproacheth
me.
12 A [y]prudent *man* [5]foreseeth
the evil, *and* hideth himself; *but*
the [z]simple[G] pass on, *and* [6]are
punished.
13 Take his garment that is
[a]surety[G] for a stranger, and [7]take
a pledge of him for a [b]strange[G]
[c]woman.
14 He that [d,e]blesseth his friend
with a [f]loud voice, rising early in
the morning, it shall be counted
a curse to him.
15 [g]A continual dropping in a
very rainy day and a contentious
[c]woman are alike.
16 [8,g]Whosoever hideth [c]her
hideth the wind, and the ointment of his right hand, *which*
bewrayeth[G] *itself*.
17 [†]Iron sharpeneth iron; [h]so
a man sharpeneth the [i]counte-
nance of his friend.
18 Whoso keepeth[G] the [j]fig tree
shall eat the fruit thereof: so [k]he
that waiteth on his master shall
be honoured.
19 As in water face *answereth*
to face, so the heart of man to
man.
20 [9,l]Hell[G] and destruction are
never full; so the [‡,m]eyes of man
are never satisfied.[Q]
21 [10]*As* the fining[G] pot for [n]sil-
ver, and the furnace for [o]gold;
[11]so *is* a man to his praise.
22 Though thou shouldest bray[G]
a fool in a [p]mortar among wheat
with a pestle, *yet* will not his
foolishness depart from him.
23 [q,r]Be thou [s,t]diligent to know

*Flattery*, Prov. 6:24.

**1**
a *Boasting*, Prov. 25:14.
b *Life, brevity and uncertainty of*, Eccl. 8:15.
c *Ignorance*, Acts 3:17.

**2**
d *Commandment, forbidding self-praise*, Deut. 8:2.
e *Humility, enjoined*, Prov. 22:4.
f *Pride*, Prov. 16:18.
g *Self-righteousness*, Luke 18:11.

**3**
1 R. V. vexation

**4**
h *Anger*, Psa. 37:8.
i *Envy*, Prov. 14:30.
j *Jealousy*, Psa. 78:58.
2 R. V. jealousy?

**5**
k *Reproof*, Prov. 17:10.

**6**
l *Friendship*, Prov. 22:24.
m *Friends*, Ex. 33:11.
n *Kiss, deceitful*, Ruth 1:14.
o *Deceit*, Psa. 36:3.
3 R. V. profuse.

**8**
p *Character, instability of*, Phil. 2:15.
q *Instability*, Jas. 1:8.

**9**
r *Ointment*, Eccl. 7:1.
s *Counsel*, Prov. 12:15.
4 R. V. that cometh of hearty counsel.

**10**
t *Commandment, enjoining faithfulness to friends*, Deut. 8:2.

**12**
y *Prudence*, 2 Chr. 2:12.
5 R. V. seeth
z *Fool*, Prov. 18:2.
6 R. V. suffer for it.

**13**
a *Surety*, Gen. 44:32.
b *Harlot*, Prov. 7:10.
c *Women, wicked*, Prov. 31:10.
7 R. V. And hold him in pledge that is surety for

**14**
d *Flattery*, Prov. 6:24.
e *Falsehood*, Job 21:34.
f *Hypocrisy*, Jas. 3:17.

**15**
g *Family, infelicity in*, 1 Chr. 13:14.

**16**
8 R. V. He that would restrain her restraineth the wind, And his right hand encountereth oil.

**17**
h *Friendship*, Prov. 22:24.
i *Countenance*, Prov. 15:13.

**18**
j *Fig Tree*, Luke 13:6.
k *Servant*, Jer. 2:14.

**20**
l *Hell*, Mark 9:43.
m *Eye, figurative*. Matt. 6:22.
9 R. V. Sheol and Abaddon

**21**
n *Silver*, 1 Chr. 28:14.
o *Gold, refined*, Ezek. 7:19.
10 R.V. The fining pot is for
11 R.V. And a man is tried by his praise.

**22**
p *Mortar*, Lev. 14:42.

u *Brother*, Prov. 18:24. **11** v *Commandment, enjoining wisdom*, Deut. 8:2. w *Children, commandments to*, Mark 10:14. x *Young Men*, Prov. 1:4.

**23** q *Commandment, enjoining diligence in business*, Deut. 8:2. r *Agriculture*, Gen. 3:23. s *Diligence*, Rom. 12:8. t *Industry, enjoined*, 1 Kin. 11:28.

---

[*] **PERFUME,** Prov. 27:9; Song 3:6; Isa. 57:9. *Used in the tabernacle*, Ex. 30:7; 35:28. *Beds perfumed with myrrh*, Prov. 7:17. *Bottles* ( A. V. tablets) *for*, Isa. 3:20.

[†] **IRON.** *First recorded use of*, Gen. 4:22. *Used in the temple*, 1 Chr. 22:3; 29:2, 7.
Articles made of: *Ax*, 2 Kin. 6:6; Eccl. 10:10; Isa. 10:34; *bedstead*, Deut. 3:11; *breastplate*, Rev. 9:9; *chariot*, Josh. 17:16, 18; Judg. 1:19; 4:3; *fetters*, Psa. 105:18; 107:10; 149:8; *file*, Prov. 27:17; *gate*, Acts 12:10; *harrow*, 2 Sam. 12:31; *horn*, 1 Kin. 22:11; 2 Chr. 18:10; Mic. 4:13; *idols*, Dan. 5:4, 23; *pans*, Ezek. 4:3; 27:19; *pen*, Job 19:24; Jer. 17:1; *pillars*, Jer. 1:18; *rods for scourging*, Psa. 2:9; Rev. 2:27; 12:5; 19:15; *threshing instruments*, Amos 1:3; *tools*, 1 Kin. 6:7; *vessels*, Josh. 6:24; *weapons*, Num. 35:16; 1 Sam. 17:7; Job 20:24; 41:7; *yokes*, Deut. 28:48; Jer. 28:13, 14.
*Stones of*, Deut. 8:9; Job 28:2.
**Figurative**, 2 Sam. 23:7; Jer. 15:12; 1 Tim. 4:2.
**Symbolical**, Dan. 2:33.

[‡] **CURIOSITY,** Prov. 27:20; Eccl. 7:21.
**Instances of:** *Eve*, Gen. 3:6. *The Israelites, to see God*, Ex. 19:21, 24. *Manoah, to know the name of an angel*, Judg. 13:17, 18. *The people of Beth-shemish, to see inside the ark*, 1 Sam. 6:19. *The Babylonians, to see Hezekiah's treasures*, 2 Kin. 20:13. *Herod, to see Jesus*, Luke 9:9; 23:8. *The Jews, to see Lazarus, after he was raised from the dead*, John 12:9. *The Athenians, to hear some new thing*, Acts 17:19–21.

24
*u Riches, transient,* Eccl. 4:8.

25
*v* Song 2:11–13.
*w* 1 Cor. 3:12.

26
*x Goat,* Deut. 14:4.

27
*y Milk,* Job 10:10.

1
*a Wicked, contrasted with the righteous,* Psa. 73:3.
*b Cowardice,* Lev. 26:36.
*c Conscience, guilty,* Acts 23:1.
*d Righteous, described,* Psa. 64:10.
*e Boldness, of the righteous,* Phil. 1:20.

3
*f Oppression,* Eccl. 5:8.
*g Poor, oppression of,* Prov. 21:13.
1 R. V. needy

4
*h Law,* Deut. 33:2.
*i Zeal, exemplified,* 2 Cor. 7:11.

5
*j Spiritual Blindness,* 2 Cor. 4:4.
*k Seekers,* Isa. 55:6.
*l Wisdom, spiritual,* Prov. 2:2.

6
*m Poor,* Prov. 21:13.
*n Integrity,* Job 2:3.
*o Rich, wicked,* Jas. 5:1.

7
*p Obedience,* Heb. 5:8.

the state of thy flocks, *and* look
well to thy herds.
24 For [u]riches *are* not for ever:
and doth the crown *endure* to
every generation?
25 [v]The [w]hay appeareth, and
the tender grass sheweth itself,
and herbs of the mountains are
gathered.
26 The lambs *are* for thy clothing, and the [x]goats *are* the price
of the field.
27 And *thou shalt have* goats'
[y]milk enough for thy food, for
the food of thy household, and
*for* the maintenance for thy
maidens.

## CHAPTER 28

*General observations concerning impiety and religious integrity.*

[a]THE wicked [b,c]flee when no
man pursueth: but the
[d]righteous are [e]bold as a lion.
2 For the transgression of a
land many *are* the princes thereof: but *by a man of understanding *and* knowledge the
state *thereof* shall be prolonged.
3 A [1]poor man that [f]oppresseth
the [g]poor *is like* a sweeping rain
which leaveth no food.
4 They that forsake the [h]law
praise the wicked: but such as
keep the law [i]contend with
them.
5 [j]Evil men understand not
judgment: but [k]they that seek
the LORD [l]understand all *things*.
6 Better *is* the [m]poor that walketh in his [n]uprightness, than *he*
*that is* perverse *in his* ways,
though he *be* [o]rich.
7 Whoso [p]keepeth the law *is*
a wise [q]son: but he that is a
companion of [2,r]riotous *men*
shameth his father.
8 [s]He that by [s,t]usury and [u]unjust gain increaseth his [v]substance, [w]he shall gather it for
him that will [x]pity the [y]poor.
9 He that turneth away his ear
from hearing the law, even [z]his
prayer *shall be* [a]abomination.
10 Whoso [b]causeth the righteous to go astray in an evil way,
[c]he shall fall himself into his
own [d]pit: [e,f]but the upright shall
have good *things* in possession.
11 The [g]rich man *is* wise in his
own [h,i]conceit; but the poor that
hath understanding searcheth
him out.
12 When [3]righteous *men* do rejoice, *there is* great glory: but
when the wicked rise, [4]a man is
hidden.
13 He that [j]covereth his sins
shall not prosper: but whoso
[k,l]confesseth and [m]forsaketh *them*
shall have [n]mercy.
14 Happy *is* the man that
[o]feareth alway: but he that
[j]hardeneth his [p]heart shall fall
into mischief.
15 *As* a roaring [q]lion, and a
ranging [r]bear; *so is* a wicked
[s]ruler over the [t]poor people.
16 The [s]prince that wanteth understanding *is* also a great [t]oppressor: *but* he that hateth covetousness shall prolong *his* days.
17 A man that [5,u]doeth violence to the blood of *any* person

*q Young Men,* Prov. 1:4.
*r Evil Company,* Prov. 13:20.
2 R. V. gluttonous

8
*s Interest,* Ex. 22:25.
*t Lending,* Deut. 15:2.
*u Injustice,* Isa. 26:10.
*v Riches,* Eccl. 4:8.
*w God, providence of,* Gen. 2:2.
*x Pity,* Job 19:21.
*y Poor, kindness to,* Prov. 21:13.

9
*z Wicked, prayer of, not heard,* Psa. 73:3.

*a Abomination,* Lev. 18:27.

10
*b Temptation, leading into,* Luke 11:4.
*c Sin, retroactive,* Rom. 5:12.
*d Pit, figurative,* Psa. 7:15.
*e Righteous, promises to,* Psa. 64:10.
*f Promise, to the righteous,* 2 Cor. 1:20.

11
*g Rich,* Jas. 5:1.
*h Conceit,* Prov. 26:5.
*i Pride,* Prov. 16:18.

12
3 R. V. the righteous triumph,
4 R. V. men hide themselves.

13
*j Impenitence, judgments denounced against,* Rom. 2:5.
*k Sin, confession of,* Rom. 5:12.
*l Prayer, confession in,* Acts 6:4.
*m Repentance, condition of forgiveness,* Mark 1:4.

*n Mercy,* Deut. 5:10. **14** *o Fear of God,* Acts 9:31. *p Heart,* Psa. 44:21. **15** *q Lion,* Mic. 5:8. *r Bear,* 2 Sam. 17:8. *s Rulers, wicked,* Ex. 18:21. *t Poor, oppression of,* Prov. 21:13. **17** *u Homicide, felonious,* Deut. 5:17. 5 R. V. is laden with the blood

* **STATECRAFT.** *Wisdom in,* Prov. 28:2. *School in,* Dan. 1:3–5.

Skilled in: *Joseph,* Gen. 41:38–41, 46–57; 47:13–26; *Saul,* 1 Sam. 11:12, 13; *Samuel,* 1 Sam. 11:14, 15; *David,* 2 Sam. 15:13–37; 19:8–40; 21:1–9, 14; 1 Kin. 1:28–35; 2:1–9; *Hushai,* 2 Sam. 17:5–16; *Solomon,* 1 Kin. 5; 9:10–14; *Jeroboam,* 1 Kin. 12:26–33; *Daniel,* Dan. 5:11.

**Ministers in:** *Samuel, in selecting a king,* 1 Sam. 9:15–27; 10:1; *in anointing a successor to Saul,* 1 Sam. 16:1–13. *Zadok and Abiathar the priests, partisans of David,* 2 Sam. 15:24–29, 35, 36; 17:15–17; 19:11. *Nathan, the prophet, influences the selection of David's successor,* 1 Kin. 1:11–40.

**Women in:** *The wise woman of Abel, who saved the city through diplomacy,* 2 Sam. 20:16–22. *Bath-sheba, in securing the crown for Solomon,* 1 Kin. 1:15–21. *Jezebel, in securing Naboth's vineyard for Ahab,* 1 Kin. 21:1–15. *The queen of Babylon, in commending to the king the wisdom of Daniel,* Dan. 5:9–13. *Herodias, in influencing the administration of Herod,* Matt. 14:3–11; Mark 6:17–28. *Pilate's wife,* Matt. 27:19. *Mother of Zebedee's children, in seeking favor for her sons,* Matt. 20:20–23.

**Influence in,** Neh. 6:17–19; Acts 12:20. *Bath-sheba's, sought,* 1 Kin. 2:13–18. *Proffered to the Shunammite woman by Elisha,* 2 Kin. 4:12, 13.

**Corruption in,** Psa. 12:8. *In the court, of Ahasuerus,* Esth. 3; *of Darius,* Dan. 6:4–15.

INSTANCES OF: *Absalom, electioneering for the throne,* 2 Sam. 15:2–6. *Pilate, condemning Jesus to gratify popular clamor,* Matt. 27:23–26; Mark 15:15; Luke 23:13–25; John 18:38, 39; 19:4–13. *Felix, who desired money from Paul,* Acts 24:26.

See footnotes: CIVIL SERVICE, Dan. 1:5; GOVERNMENT, Isa. 22:21.

18
v Wicked, punishment of, Psa. 73:3.
19
w Promise, to the diligent, 2 Cor. 1:20.
x Industry, 1 Kin. 11:28.
y Fellowship, with the wicked, impoverishing, 1 Cor. 1:9.
z Evil Company, Prov. 13:20.

a Poverty, Prov. 30:8.
20
b Promise, to the righteous, 2 Cor. 1:20.
c Righteous, promises to, Psa. 64:10.
d Faithfulness, rewards of, Luke 16:10.
e Integrity, rewards of, Job 2:3.
f Covetousness, Isa. 57:17.
6 R. V. unpunished.
21
g Respect of Persons, Prov. 24:23.
h Justice, Deut. 33:21.
i Bribery, perverts justice, 1 Sam. 8:3.
7 R. V. Neither that a man should transgress for a piece of bread.
22
8 R. V. hath an evil eye hasteth after riches, And knoweth not
23
j Reproof, profitable, Prov. 17:10.
k Flattery, Prov. 6:24.
24
l Father, Psa. 27:10.
m Mother, 1 Kin. 2:20.
25
n Strife, Prov. 20:3.
o Faith, Mark 11:22.
9 R. V. greedy spirit
26
p False Confidence, in self, Psa. 30:6.
27
q Promise, to the liberal, 2 Cor. 1:20.
r Liberality, rewards for, 1 Tim. 6:18.
s Poor, duty to, Prov. 21:13.
t Selfishness, 2 Tim. 3:2.

shall flee to the [d]pit; let no man
stay him.
18 [e,f]Whoso walketh uprightly
shall be saved: but *he that is* perverse *in his* ways shall [v]fall at once.
19 [w]He that [x]tilleth his land
shall have plenty of bread: but
he that [y]followeth after [z]vain *persons* shall have [a]poverty enough.
20 [b,c]A [d,e]faithful man shall
abound with blessings: but he
that [f]maketh haste to be rich
shall not be [6]innocent.
21 To have [g]respect of persons
*is* not [h]good: [7]for a [i]piece of
bread *that* man will transgress.
22 He that [8,f]hasteth to be rich
*hath* an evil eye, and considereth not that [a]poverty shall come
upon him.
23 He that [j]rebuketh a man
afterwards shall find more favour than he that [k]flattereth
with the tongue.
24 Whoso robbeth his [l]father
or his [m]mother, and saith, *It is*
no transgression; the same *is* the
companion of a destroyer.
25 He that is of a [9,f]proud
heart stirreth up [n]strife: but
[b,c]he that putteth his [o]trust in
the LORD shall be made fat.
26 He that [p]trusteth in his own
heart is a fool: but whoso walketh
wisely, [b,c]he shall be delivered.
27 [q]He that [r]giveth unto the
[s]poor shall not lack: but he that
[t]hideth his eyes shall have many
a curse.
28 When the wicked rise, men
hide themselves: but when they
perish, the righteous increase.

## CHAPTER 29

*Sundry maxims and observations.*

HE, that being often [a]re-
proved *,[b,c]hardeneth *his*
neck, shall suddenly be [1,d,e]de-
stroyed, and that without remedy.
2 When the [f]righteous are [2]in
authority, the people rejoice: but
when the [g]wicked beareth rule,
the people mourn.
3 [h,i]Whoso loveth [j]wisdom rejoiceth his father: but he that
[k]keepeth company with [l]harlots
[3]spendeth *his* substance.
4 The [m]king by judgment establisheth the land: but [n]he that
[4]receiveth [o]gifts overthroweth it.
5 A man that [p]flattereth his
neighbour spreadeth a [q]net for
his feet.
6 In the transgression of an
evil man *there is* a snare: but the
righteous doth sing and [r]rejoice.
7 The [f]righteous considereth
the cause of the [s]poor: [5,t]*but* the
wicked regardeth not to know *it*.
8 [6,u]Scornful men bring a city
into a snare: but [v]wise *men*
[w]turn away wrath.
9 *If* a wise man contendeth
with a [x]foolish man, whether he
[y]rage or laugh, *there is* no rest.
10 The bloodthirsty [z]hate the upright: [7]but the just seek his soul.
11 A [a]fool [b]uttereth all his
[8]mind: but a wise *man* [c,d]keep-
eth it [9]in till afterwards.
12 If a ruler hearken to [e]lies,
[f]all his servants *are* wicked.
13 The [g]poor and the [10]deceit-
ful man meet together: the LORD
lighteneth both their eyes.
14 The [h]king that [i]faithfully
judgeth the [g]poor, his throne
shall be established for ever.
15 [j]The rod and reproof give wisdom: but a child left *to himself*
[11]bringeth his [k]mother to shame.
16 When the wicked are multiplied, transgression increaseth:

2
f Righteous, Psa. 64:10.
g Rulers, wicked, Ex. 18:21.
2 R. V. increased,
3
h Children, promises to, Mark 10:14.
i Young Men, Prov. 1:4.
j Wisdom, Prov. 2:2.
k Evil Company, Prov. 13:20.
l Harlot, Prov. 7:10.
3 R. V. wasteth
4
m King, duties of, 2 Kin. 3:10.
n Rulers, corrupted by gifts, Ex. 18:21.
o Bribery, 1 Sam. 8:3.
4 R. V. exacteth
5
p Flattery, Prov. 6:24.
q Net, figurative, Isa. 51:20.
6
r Joy, Psa. 5:11
7
s Poor, duty to, Prov. 21:13.
t Wicked, contrasted with the righteous, Psa. 73:3.
5 R. V. The wicked hath not understanding to know it.
8
u Scorners, Prov. 19:25.
v Wisdom, Prov. 2:2.
w Prudence, in avoiding strife, 2 Chr. 2:12.
6 Am. R. V. Scoffing men set a city in a flame:
9
x Fool, Prov. 18:2.
y Anger, Psa. 37:8.
10
z Hatred, Prov. 15:17.
7 R. V. And as for the upright, they seek his life.

11
a Fool, Prov. 18:2.
b Speech, foolish, Col. 4:6.
c Prudence, in restraining speech, 2 Chr. 2:12.

**1** *a Reproof,* Prov. 17:10. *b Impenitence, judgments denounced against,* Rom. 2:5. *c Self-will,* Gen. 49:6. *d Wicked, punishment of,* Psa. 73:3. *e Punishment, no escape from,* Lev. 26:41. 1 R.V. broken, *d Anger, restraint of,* Psa. 37:8. 8 R. V. anger: 9 R. V. back and stilleth it. **12** *e Falsehood,* Job 21:34. *f Influence, evil,* 1 Cor. 7:14. **13** *g Poor,* Prov. 21:13. 10 R. V. oppressor meet **14** *h Rulers, righteous,* Ex. 18:21. *i Justice,* Deut. 33:21. **15** *j Children, punishment of,* Mark 10:14. *k Mother,* 1 Kin. 2:20. 11 R. V. causeth shame to his mother.

* **OBDURACY,** 2 Chr. 36:15, 16; Psa. 78:31, 32; Isa. 9:13; 57:17; Jer. 2:30; 3:3; 5:3; Rev. 9:20, 21.
*Warnings against,* Psa. 95:8–11; Heb. 3:8, 15; 4:7.
*Punishment for,* Lev. 26: 23–25; Prov. 1:24–31; 29:1; Amos 4:6–11.
**Instances of:** *The antediluvians,* Gen. 6:3, 5, 7. *Sodom*

but the righteous shall see [l]their
fall.
17 [m,i]Correct thy son, and he
shall give thee rest; yea, he shall
give delight unto thy soul.
18 Where *there is* no [n]vision,
the people [12]perish: but [o]he that
[p]keepeth the law, happy *is* he.
19 A [q]servant will not be corrected by words: for though he
understand he will not [13]answer.
20 Seest thou a man *that is*
[r]hasty in his [s,t]words? *there is*
more hope of a fool than of him.
21 [u]He that delicately bringeth up his [v]servant from a
child shall have him become
*his* son at the length.
22 An [w]angry man stirreth
up [x]strife, and a furious man
aboundeth in transgression.
23 A man's [y]pride shall bring
him low: [14]but honour shall uphold the [z]humble in spirit.[Q]
24 Whoso is [†,a]partner with a
thief hateth his own soul: he
heareth [15]cursing, and bewrayeth[G] *it* not.
25 The [b]fear of man bringeth a
snare[G]: but [c,d]whoso putteth his
[e]trust in the LORD shall be safe.
26 Many seek the ruler's favour; but *every* man's [f]judgment
*cometh* from the LORD.[S]
27 [g]An [h]unjust man *is* an
[i]abomination to the just: and
*he that is* upright in the way *is*
abomination to the wicked.

## CHAPTER 30

*Agur's confession. 7 His prayer. 11 Four wicked generations. 15 Four things insatiable. 17 Parents are not to be despised. 18 Four things hard to be known. 21 Four things intolerable. 24 Four things exceeding wise. 29 Four things stately. 32 Wrath is to be prevented.*

THE words of Ā'gûr the son
of Jā'keh, *even* the prophecy[G]: the man spake unto
Ĭth'ĭ-el, even unto Ĭth'ĭ-el and
Ū'cal,
2 [a]Surely I *am* more brutish[G]
than *any* man, and [b]have not
the understanding of a man.
3 [c]I neither learned [d]wisdom,
[b]nor have the knowledge of the
[1]holy.
4 Who hath ascended up into heaven, or descended? who
hath gathered the [e]wind in his
fists? who hath bound the
waters in a garment? who hath
[f,g]established all the ends of the
earth? what *is* [h]his name, and
what *is* his son's name, if thou
canst tell?[S Q]
5 Every [i]word of God *is* [2]pure:
[j]he *is* a [k,l]shield unto them that
put their trust in him.
6 Add thou not unto his [m]words,
lest he reprove thee, and thou be
found a [n]liar.
7 Two *things* have I required
of thee; deny me *them* not before I die:
8 Remove far from me vanity
and [n]lies: [o,p]give me neither
*poverty nor [q]riches; [o]feed me
with [3,r]food convenient[G] for me:[Q]
9 Lest I be full, and deny *thee*,
and [s]say, Who *is* the LORD? or
lest I be *poor, and [t]steal, and
[u]take the [v]name of my God *in*
*vain*.
10 [4,w]Accuse not a [x]servant
unto his master, lest he curse
thee, and thou be found guilty.
11 *There is* a [y]generation *that*
curseth their [z]father, and doth
not bless their [a]mother.
12 *There is* a generation *that*
*are* [b,c]pure in their own eyes,
and *yet* is not [d]washed from
their filthiness.

**16** *l* *Wicked, punishment of,* Psa. 73:3. **17** *m* *Commandment, to parents,* Deut. 8:2. **18** *n* *Vision,* Acts 9:10. *o* *Righteous, happiness of,* Psa. 64:10. *p* *Obedience,* Heb. 5:8. 12 R. V. cast off restraint: **19** *q* *Servant,* Jer. 2:14. 13 R. V. give heed. **20** *r* *Rashness,* 2 Sam. 6:7. *s* *Words,* Luke 4:22. *t* *Speech, foolish,* Col. 4:6. **21** *u* *Employer,* Deut. 24:14. *v* *Servant, kindness to,* Jer. 2:14. **22** *w* *Anger,* Psa. 37:8. *x* *Strife,* Prov. 20:3. **23** *y* *Pride,* Prov. 16:18. *z* *Humility,* Prov. 22:4. 14 R. V. But he that is of a lowly spirit shall obtain honour.

**24** *a* *Fellowship, with the wicked,* 1 Cor. 1:9. 15 R. V. the adjuration and uttereth nothing. **25** *b* *Cowardice,* Lev. 26:36. *c* *Promise, implied, to the truthful,* 2 Cor. 1:20. *d* *Righteous, promises to,* Psa. 64:10. *e* *Faith, rewards of,* Mark 11:22. **26** *f* *God, judge,* Gen. 2:2. **27** *g* *Sin, repugnant to the righteous,* Rom. 5:12. *h* *Injustice,* Isa. 26:10. *i* *Abomination,* Lev. 18:27.

**2** *a* *Humility,* Prov. 22:4. *b* *Spiritual Blindness,* 2 Cor. 4:4. **3** *c* *Ignorance,* Acts 3:17. *d* *Wisdom, spiritual,* Prov. 2:2. 1 R. V. Holy One. **4** *e* *Meteorology,* Matt. 16:2. *f* *Geology,* Psa. 104:5. *g* *God, creator,* Gen. 2:2. *h* *God, unsearchable,* Gen. 2:2. **5** *i* *Word of God,* Psa. 119:9. *j* *Faith, rewards of,* Mark 11:22. *k* *Shield, figurative,* 1 Kin. 14:27. *l* *God, preserver,* Gen. 2:2. 2 R. V. tried: **6** *m* *Word of God, not to be added to,* Psa. 119:9. *n* *Falsehood,* Job 21:34. **8** *o* *Contentment,* 1 Tim. 6:6. *p* *Temporal Blessings, prayer for,* Psa. 103:2. *q* *Riches, a snare,* Eccl. 4:8. *r* *Food, from God,* Psa. 136:25. 3 R. V. the food that is needful for me: **9** *s* *Blasphemy, reproaching God,* 2 Sam. 12:14. *t* *Theft,* Mark 7:22. *u* *Profanation, of God's name,* Lev. 22:32. *v* *God, name of, not to be profaned,* Gen. 2:2. **10** *w* *Commandment, forbidding slander,* Deut. 8:2. *x* *Servant,* Jer. 2:14. 4 R. V. Slander

**11** *y* *Children, wicked,* Mark 10:14. *z* *Father,* Psa. 27:10. —*a* *Mother,* 1 Kin. 2:20. **12** *b* *Self-righteousness,* Luke 18:11. *c* *Delusion,* 2 Thess. 2:11. *d* *Washing, figurative,* Matt. 27:24.

*ites,* Gen. 19:14. *Pharaoh,* Ex. 7:14, 22, 23; 8:15, 19, 32; 9:7, 12, 35; 10:20, 28; 11:10; 14:5–8. *Israelites,* Num. 14:22; Neh. 9:28, 29; Psa. 78:32; Isa. 9:13, 14; Jer. 5:3; Amos 4:6–12; Zech. 7:11, 12. *Sons of Eli,* 1 Sam. 2:22–25. *Brothers of the rich man,* Luke 16:31.
See footnote, IMPENITENCE, Rom. 2:5.

† **COMPLICITY,** Psa. 50:18; Prov. 29:24; 2 John 10, 11.
**Instances of:** *Sarah, in the deception practiced, upon Pharaoh,* Gen. 12:11–19; *upon Abimelech,* Gen. 20:2–5, 11–14. *Rebekah, in the deception practiced upon Isaac,* Gen. 27:5–17. *The elders and nobles of Jezreel, in stoning Naboth,* 1 Kin. 21:7–14. *Certain Jews, in opposing the rebuilding of the temple,* Neh. 6:10–19. *Paul, in the stoning of Stephen,* Acts 7:58.

* **POVERTY,** 1 Sam. 2:7. *Destructive,* Prov. 10:15. *A source of temptation,* Prov. 30:8, 9.
Caused: *By laziness,* Prov. 6:11; 20:13; 24:33, 34; *by drunkenness,* Prov. 23:21; *by evil association,* Prov. 28:19.

13 *There is* a generation, O how [e]lofty[C] are their eyes! and their eyelids are lifted up.

14 *There is* a generation, [f]whose teeth *are as* swords, and their jaw teeth *as* knives, [g]to [h]devour the [i]poor from off the earth, and the needy from *among* men.[T]

15 The horseleach hath two daughters, *crying*, [g]Give, give. There are three *things that* are never satisfied, *yea*, four *things* say not, *It is* enough:

16 [g]The [j]grave[C]; and the barren womb; the earth *that* is not filled with water; and the fire *that* saith not, *It is* enough.

17 The [k]eye *that* mocketh at *his* father, and despiseth to obey *his* mother, [l]the [m]ravens of the valley shall pick it out, and the young eagles shall eat it.

18 There be three *things which* are too wonderful for me, yea, four which I know not:

19 The way of an [n]eagle in the air; the way of a [o]serpent upon a rock; the way of a ship in the midst of the sea; and the way of a man with a maid.

20 Such *is* the way of an adulterous woman; she [p]eateth, and wipeth her mouth, and saith, [q,r]I have done no wickedness.

21 For three *things* the earth is disquieted, and for four *which* it cannot bear:

22 For a servant when he reigneth; and a fool when he [†]is filled with meat[C];

23 [s]For an odious [t]*woman* when she is married; and an handmaid that is heir to her mistress.

24 There be four *things which are* little upon the earth, but they *are* exceeding[C] wise:

25 The [u,v]ants *are* a people not strong, yet they [w]prepare their meat[C] in the [x]summer;

26 The [y]conies *are but* a feeble folk, yet make [u]they their houses in the rocks;

27 The [z]locusts have no king, yet [u]go they forth all of them by bands;

28 The [5,a]spider taketh hold with her hands, and is in kings' palaces.

29 There be three *things* which [6]go well, yea, four are comely[C] in going:

30 A [b]lion *which is* strongest among beasts, and turneth not away for any;

31 A [c]greyhound; an he goat also; and a king, against whom *there is* no rising up.

32 If thou hast done foolishly in lifting up thyself, or if thou hast thought evil, [d]*lay* thine hand upon thy mouth.

33 Surely the churning of [e]milk bringeth forth [f]butter, and the wringing of the nose bringeth forth blood: so the forcing of [g]wrath bringeth forth [h]strife.

## CHAPTER 31

*The words which king Lemuel's mother taught him. 10 The description of a virtuous woman.*

THE words of king Lĕm'-u-el, the [1]prophecy[C] that his mother taught him.

2 What, my son? and what, the son of my womb? and what, the son of my vows?

3 [a,b,c]Give not thy strength unto women, nor thy ways to [d]that which destroyeth kings.

4 [e,f]*It is* not for [g]kings, O Lĕm'u-el, *it is* not for kings to drink [h]wine; nor for princes strong drink:

5 Lest they drink, and forget the law, and [i]pervert[C] the judgment[C] of any of the afflicted[C].

6 [j]Give strong drink unto him that is ready to perish, and

**13**
e *Pride*, Prov. 16:18.

**14**
f *Malice*, Eph. 4:31.
g *Covetousness*, vs. 15, 16; Isa. 57:17.
h *Oppression*, Eccl. 5:8.
i *Poor, oppression of*, Prov. 21:13.

**16**
j *Hell*, Mark 9:43.

**17**
k *Children, wicked*, Mark 10:14.
l *Wicked, punishment of*, Psa. 73:3.
m *Raven*, Job 38:41.

**19**
n *Eagle*, Lev. 11:13.
o *Serpent*, Num. 21:6.

**20**
p *Sin, fruits of, moral insensibility*, Rom. 5:12.
q *Conscience, dead*, Acts 23:1.
r *Adultery, impenitence in*, Lev. 20:10.

**23**
s *Family, infelicity in*, 1 Chr. 13:14.
t *Wife*, Prov. 5:18.

**25**
u *Animals, instincts of*, Jer. 27:5.
v Prov. 6:6–8.
w *Industry*, 1 Kin. 11:28.
x *Summer*, Isa. 28:4.

**26**
y *Coney*, Lev. 11:5.

**27**
z *Locust*, Nah. 3:17.

**28**
a Job 8:14; Isa. 59:5.
5 R. V. lizard

**29**
6 R. V. are stately in their march, Yea, four which are stately in going:

**30**
b *Lion*, Mic. 5:8.

**31**
c *Dog*, 1 Kin. 21:19.

**32**
d *Prudence*, 2 Chr. 2:12.

**33**
e *Milk*, Job 10:10.
f *Butter*, Gen. 18:8.
g *Anger*, Psa. 37:8.
h *Strife*, Prov. 20:3.

**1**
1 R. V. oracle

**3**
a *Commandment, admonishing against lusts*, Deut. 8:2.
b *Chastity, enjoined*, Job 31:1.
c *Young Men, admonitions to*, Prov. 1:4.
d *Lasciviousness*, 1 Pet. 4:3.

**4**
e *Total Abstinence*, Lev. 10:9.
f *Drunkenness, forbidden*, Luke 21:34.
g *Rulers, character and qualifications of*, Ex. 18:21.
h *Wine, forbidden to kings*, Prov. 23:31.

**5**
i *Injustice*, Isa. 26:10.

**6**
j *Commandment, prescribing stimulants for the perishing*, Deut. 8:2.

† **GLUTTONY,** Deut. 21:20, 21; Prov. 30:21, 22.
*Impoverishes*, Prov. 23:21. *Deadens moral sensibilities*, Amos 6:4–7; Luke 12:19, 20, 45, 46; Phil. 3:19.
*Israel plagued for*, Num. 11:32, 33.
***Proverb relating to***, **Isa. 22:13; 1 Cor. 15:32.**
*Jesus falsely accused of*, Matt. 11:19; Luke 7:34.
*Warnings against*, Luke 21:34; Rom. 13:13, 14; 1 Pet. 4:2, 3.
**Instances of:** *Esau*, Gen. 25:30–34, **with Heb. 12:16, 17.** *Israelites*, Num. 11:4, 5, 32–35.

[k]wine unto [2]those that be of
heavy[G] hearts.
7 Let him drink, and forget his
[l]poverty, and remember his misery no more.
8 Open thy mouth for the
dumb in the cause of all such
as are [3]appointed to destruction.
9 Open thy mouth, [m]judge
righteously, and [4]plead the cause
of the [n]poor and needy.
10 ¶ [o]Who can find a virtuous
*,[p]woman? for her price *is* far
above [q]rubies.
11 The heart of *her husband
doth safely trust in [p]her, so that
he shall have no [5]need of spoil.
12 *,[p]She will do him good and
not evil all the days of her life.
13 *,[p]She seeketh [r]wool, and
[s]flax, and [t]worketh willingly
with her hands.
14 *,[p]She is like the [u]mer-
chants' ships; she bringeth her
food from afar.

k *Wine, medicinal use of,* Prov. 23:31.
2 R. V. the bitter in soul:
**7**
l *Poverty,* Prov. 30:8.
**8**
3 R. V. left desolate.
**9**
m *Rulers, required to judge justly,* Ex. 18:21.
n *Poor, duty to,* Prov. 21:13.
4 R. V. minister judgment to the
**10**
o *Poetry, acrostic,* Acts 17:28.

p *Wife,* Prov. 5:18.
q Prov. 20:15; Job 28:18; Lam. 4:7.
**11**
5 R. V. lack of gain.
**13**
r *Wool,* Judg. 6:37.
s *Flax,* Ex. 9:31.
t *Industry,* 1 Kin. 11:28.
**14**
u *Commerce, carried on by ships,* 1 Kin. 10:15.

---

* **WOMEN.** *Creation of,* Gen. 1:27; 2:21, 22. *Named,* Gen. 2:23. *Fall of, and curse upon,* Gen. 3:1–8, 12–16; 2 Cor. 11:3; 1 Tim. 2:14. *Relation of, to husband,* see footnote, WIFE, Prov. 5:18.

*Virtuous, held in high esteem,* Ruth. 3:11; Prov. 31:10–31. *Had separate dwelling places,* Gen. 24:67; 31:33; Esth. 2:9, 11. *Veiled the face,* Gen. 24:65. *Ornaments of,* Isa. 3:16–23; Jer. 2:32.

*Forbidden to wear men's costume,* Deut. 22:5. *Wore hair long,* 1 Cor. 11:5–15. *Rules for dress of Christian,* 1 Tim. 2:9, 10; 1 Pet. 3:3, 4.

*Took part, in worship,* Ex. 15:20, 21; *in choir,* 1 Chr. 25:5, 6; Ezra 2:65; Neh. 7:67. *Ministered in tabernacle,* Ex. 38:8; 1 Sam. 2:22. *Consecrated jewels to tabernacle,* Ex. 35:22; *also mirrors,* Ex. 38:8. *Required to attend the reading of the law,* Deut. 31:12; Josh. 8:35.

*Could not marry without consent of father,* Gen. 34:6–8; Ex. 22:17; Josh. 3:16, 17; 1 Sam. 17:25; 18:17–27. *Not to be given in marriage considered a calamity,* Judg. 11:37; Psa. 78:63; Isa. 4:1. *Taken captive,* Num. 31:9, 15, 17, 18, 35; Lam. 1:18; Ezek. 30:18. *Sold for husband's debts,* Matt. 18:25. *Weaker than men,* 1 Pet. 3:7.

*Punishment of, for fornication, when betrothed,* Deut. 22:23–27. *Penalty for seducing, when not betrothed,* Ex. 22:16, 17; Deut. 22:28, 29. *Protected during menstruation,* Lev. 18:19; 20:18. *Treated with cruelty in war,* Deut. 32:25; Lam. 2:21; 5:11.

Purifications of: *After menstruation,* Lev. 15:19–33; 2 Sam. 11:4; *after childbirth,* Lev. 12; Luke 2:22.

Social status of: *In Persia,* Esth. 1:10–22; Dan. 5:1, 2, 10–12; *in the Roman empire,* Acts 24:24; 25:13, 23; 26:30.

*Vows of,* Num. 30:3–16. *Guilt or innocence of, when charged by husband with infidelity, must be determined by trial in court,* Num. 5:12–31.

*In business,* 1 Chr. 7:24; Prov. 31:14–18, 24.

Property rights of: *In inheritance,* Num. 27:1–11; 36; Josh. 17:3–6; Job 42:15; *to sell real estate,* Ruth 4:3–9.

*Duties of,* Gen. 18:6; Prov. 31:15–19; Matt. 24:41; *to cook,* Gen. 18:6; *to spin,* Ex. 35:25, 26; Prov. 31:19; *to make garments,* 1 Sam. 2:19; Acts 9:39; *to glean,* Ruth. 2:7, 8, 15–23; *to keep vineyards,* Song 1:6; *to tend flocks and herds,* Gen. 24:11, 13, 14, 19, 20; 29:9; Ex. 2:16; *to work in fields,* Isa. 27:11; Ezek. 26:6, 8.

*First to sin,* Gen. 3:6. *First at the sepulchre,* Mark 15:46, 47; 16:1–6; Luke 23:55, 56; 24:1–10. *First to whom the risen Lord appeared,* Mark 16:9; John 20:14–18.

*Religious privileges of, among early Christians,* Acts 1:14; 12:12; 1 Cor. 11:5; 14:34; 1 Tim. 2:11.

*Converted by preaching of Paul,* Acts 16:14, 15; 17:4, 12, 34.

*Paul's precepts concerning,* 1 Cor. 14:34, 35; Eph. 5:22–24; Col. 3:18; 1 Tim. 2:9–12; 3:11; 5:1–16; Tit. 2:3–5.

*Mirthful,* Judg. 11:34; 21:21; Jer. 31:13.

Patriotic: *Miriam,* Ex. 15:20, 21; *Deborah,* Judg. 4:4–16; 5; *Jael,* Judg. 4:17–22; 5:22–27; *the women of Israel,* 1 Sam. 18:6; *the women of Thebez,* Judg. 9:53, 54; *the wise woman of Abel,* 2 Sam. 20:16–22; *Esther,* Esth. 4:4–17; 5:1–8; 7:1–6; 8:1–8.

Influential in public affairs: *Bath-sheba,* 1 Kin. 1:15–21; *Jezebel,* 1 Kin. 21:7–15, 25; *Athaliah,* 2 Kin. 11:1, 3; 2 Chr. 21:6; 22:3; *the queen of Babylon,* Dan. 5:9–13; *Pilate's wife,* Matt. 27:19.

As rulers, Isa. 3:12; *Deborah,* Judg. 4:4; *Athaliah,* 2 Kin. 11:1–16; 2 Chr. 22:2, 3, 10–12; 2 Chr. 23:1–15; *the queen of Sheba,* 1 Kin. 10:1–13; 2 Chr. 9:1–9, 12; *Candace,* Acts 8:27; *the Persian queen sat on throne with the king,* Neh. 2:6.

As poets: *Miriam,* Ex. 15:21; *Deborah,* Judg. 5; *Hannah,* 1 Sam. 2:1–10; *Mary,* Luke 1:46–55.

As prophets: *Miriam,* Ex. 15:20, 21; Mic. 6:4; *Deborah,* Judg. 4:4, 5; *Huldah,* 2 Kin. 22:14–20; 2 Chr. 34:22–28; *Noadiah,* Neh. 6:14; *Anna,* Luke 2:36–38; *Philip's daughters,* Acts 21:9. *False prophets,* Ezek. 13:17–23.

**Good,** Prov. 12:4; 31:10–31; 1 Tim. 2:9, 10; 3:11; 5:3–16; Tit. 2:3–5. *Affectionate,* 2 Sam. 1:26; *to offspring,* Isa. 49:15. *Illustrated by the five wise virgins,* Matt. 25:1–10.

INSTANCES OF: *Deborah, a judge, prophetess, and military leader,* Judg. 4; 5. *Mother of Samson,* Judg. 13:23. *Naomi,* Ruth 1; 2:1–3, 18–22; 3:1; 4:14–17. *Ruth,* Ruth 1.4–22; chapters 2–4. *Hannah, the mother of Samuel,* 1 Sam. 1:2–28. *Widow of Zarephath, who fed Elijah during the famine,* 1 Kin. 17:8–24. *The Shunammite, who gave hospitality to Elisha,* 2 Kin. 4:8–38. *Vashti,* Esth. 1:11, 12. *Esther,* Esth. 4:4–17; 5:1–8; 7:1–6; 8:1–8. *Mary,* Luke 1:26–38. *Elisabeth,* Luke 1:6, 41–45. *Anna,* Luke 2:37, 38. *The widow who cast her mite into the treasury,* Mark 12:41–44; Luke 21:2–4. *Mary and Martha,* Mark 14:3–9; Luke 10:38–42; John 11:1–5, 17–40. *Mary Magdalene,* Mark 16:1; Luke 8:2; John 20:1, 2, 11–18. *Dorcas,* Acts 9:36–39. *Lydia,* Acts 16:14, 15. *Priscilla,* Acts 18:26; Rom. 16:3, 4. *Phebe,* Rom. 16:1, 2. *Julia,* Rom. 16:15. *Mary,* Rom. 16:6. *Lois and Eunice,* 2 Tim. 1:5. *Of Philippi,* Phil. 4:3.

**Wicked,** 2 Kin. 23:7; Jer. 44:15–19, 25; Ezek. 8:14; 13:17–23; Rom. 1:26. *Zeal of, in licentious practices of idolatry,* Hos. 4:13, 14. *Careless,* Isa. 32:9–11. *Contentious,* Prov. 27:15, 16. *Idolatrous,* Num. 31:15, 16; 2 Kin. 23:7; Neh. 13:26; Jer. 7:18. *Tattling,* 1 Tim. 5:11–13. *Haughty and vain,* Isa. 3:16. *Odious,* Prov. 30:23. *Guileful and licentious,* Prov. 2:16–19; 5:3–6; 6:24–29; 7:6–27; Eccl. 7:26; Ezek. 16:32; Rom. 1:26. *Commit forgery,* 1 Kin. 21:8. *Illustrated by the five foolish virgins,* Matt. 25:1–12.

INSTANCES OF: *Eve, in yielding to temptation and seducing her husband,* Gen. 3:6; 1 Tim. 2:14. *Sarah, in her jealousy and malice toward Hagar,* Gen. 21:9–11, with vs. 12–21. *Lot's wife, in desiring to return to Sodom,* Gen. 19:26; Luke 17:32. *The daughters of Lot, in their incestuous lust,* Gen. 19:31–38. *Rebekah, in her partiality for Jacob and her sharp practice to secure for him Isaac's blessing,* Gen. 27:5–17. *Rachel, in her jealousy of Leah,* Gen. 30:1; *in stealing the images,* Gen. 31:19, 34. *Tamar, in her adultery,* Gen. 38:14–24. *Potiphar's wife, in her lascivious lust and slander against Joseph,* Gen. 39:7–20. *Miriam, in her sedition together with Aaron against Moses,* Num. 12. *Rahab, in her harlotry,* Josh. 2:1. *Delilah, in her conspiracy against Samson,* Judg. 16:4–20. *Peninnah, the wife of Elkanah, in her jealous taunting of Hannah,* 1 Sam. 1:4–8. *The Midianitish woman in the camp of Israel, taken in adultery,* Num. 25:6–8. *Michal, in her derision of David's religious zeal,* 2 Sam. 6:16, 20–23. *Bath-sheba, in her adultery and in becoming the wife of her husband's murderer,* 2 Sam. 11:4, 5, 27; 12:9, 10. *Solomon's wives, in their idolatrous and wicked influence over Solomon,* 1 Kin. 11:1–11; Neh. 13:26. *Jezebel, in her persecution and destruction of the prophets of the Lord,* 1 Kin. 18:4, 13; *in her persecution of Elijah,* 1 Kin. 19:2; *in her conspiracy against Naboth, to despoil him of his vineyard,* 1 Kin. 21:1–16; *in her evil counsels to, and influence over, Ahab,* 1 Kin. 21:25 (with vs. 17–27); 2 Kin. 9:30–37. *Athaliah, in destroying the royal household and usurping the throne,* 2 Kin. 11:1, 3, 13–16; 2 Chr. 22:10, 12; 23:12–15. *Noadiah, a false prophetess,* Neh. 6:14. *Zeresh, Haman's wife, in counseling him to hang Mordecai,* Esth. 5:14. *Job's wife, in counseling him to curse God,* Job 2:9. *The idolatrous wives of Hosea,* Hos. 1:2, 3. *Herodias, in her adulterous marriage with Herod,* Matt. 14:3, 4; Mark 6:17–28; Luke 3:19; *in compassing the death of John the Baptist,* Matt. 14:6–11; Mark 6:24–28. *Daughter of Herodias,* Matt. 14:8; Mark 6:24, 25. *The woman taken in adultery and brought to Jesus in the temple,* John 8:1–11. *Sapphira, in her falsehood,* Acts 5:2–10.

SYMBOLICAL: *Of wickedness,* Zech. 5:7, 8; Rev. 17; 19:2.

See footnotes: WIDOW, 2 Sam. 14:5; WIFE, Prov. 5:18.

15 *,[p]She [v]riseth also while it is yet night, and giveth [w]meat to her household, and [6]a portion to her maidens.

16 *,[p]She considereth a field, and buyeth it: with the fruit of her hands she planteth a vineyard.

17 *,[p]She girdeth her loins with strength, and strengtheneth her arms.

18 *,[p]She perceiveth that her merchandise *is* [7]good: her candle goeth not out by night.

19 *,[p]She [x,y]layeth her hands to the spindle, and her hands hold the distaff.

20 *,[p]She [z,a]stretcheth out her hand to the [b]poor; yea, she [a]reacheth forth her hands to the needy.

21 *,[c]She is not afraid of the snow for her household: for all her household *are* clothed with [d]scarlet.

22 She maketh herself coverings of [e]tapestry; her clothing *is* [8]silk and [d]purple.

23 *,[c]Her husband is known in the gates, when he sitteth among the [f]elders of the land.

24 *,[c]She maketh fine linen, and selleth *it*; and delivereth †girdles unto the merchant.

25 Strength and honour *are* her clothing; and she shall rejoice in time to come.

26 *,[c]She [g]openeth her mouth with wisdom; and in her tongue *is* the law of [h]kindness.

27 *,[c]She [i]looketh well to the ways of her [j]household, and [i]eateth not the bread of idleness.

28 *,[c,k]Her children arise up, and call her blessed; her husband *also*, and he praiseth her.

29 Many daughters have done virtuously, but thou excellest them all.

30 Favour *is* deceitful, and [l]beauty *is* vain: *but* a *woman *that* [m]feareth the LORD, she shall be praised.

31 Give *her of the fruit of her hands; and let her own works praise her in the gates.

**15**
- *v* *Rising, early,* Gen. 19:2.
- *w* *Food,* Psa. 136:25.
- 6 R. V. their task to her maidens.

**18**
- 7 R. V. profitable:

**19**
- *x* Ex. 35:25.
- *y* *Art, of the spinner,* 2 Chr. 16:14.

**20**
- *z* *Liberality,* 1 Tim. 6:18.
- *a* *Christian Graces, liberality,* Gal. 5:22.
- *b* *Poor, liberality to,* Prov. 2[illegible]:13.

**21**
- *c* *Wife,* Prov. 5:18.
- *d* *Colors,* Ezek. 16:16.

**22**
- *e* *Tapestry,* Prov. 7:16.
- 8 R. V. fine linen

**23**
- *f* *Senate,* Num. 11:16.

**26**
- *g* *Speech, wise,* Col. 4:6.
- *h* *Kindness,* Acts 28:2.

**27**
- *i* *Industry,* 1 Kin. 11:28.
- *j* *Family,* 1 Chr. 13:14.

**28**
- *k* *Mother,* 1 Kin. 2:20.

**30**
- *l* *Beauty,* Prov. 6:25.
- *m* *Fear of God,* Acts 9:31.

# ECCLESIASTES;

## OR, THE PREACHER.

### CHAPTER 1

*The Preacher declares the vanity of all human things.*

[a]THE words of the [b]Preacher, the son of [c]Dā′vid, [d,e]king in [f]Jĕ-ru′să-lĕm.

2 +Vanity of vanities, saith the [b]Preacher, vanity of vanities; all *is* vanity.

3 What profit hath a man of all his [g]labour which he taketh under the sun?

4 [h]*One* generation passeth away, and *another* generation cometh: but the [i]earth abideth for ever.

5 [j]The [k]sun also ariseth, and the sun goeth down, and hasteth to his place where he arose.

6 The [l]wind goeth toward the south, and turneth about unto the north; it whirleth about continually, and the wind returneth again according to his circuits.

7 All the rivers run into the

**1**
- *a* *Philosophy,* vs. 1–18; Col. 2:8.
- *b* *Preaching,* Matt. 9:35.
- *c* *David,* 1 Sam. 16:13.
- *d* *Rulers,* Ex. 18:21.
- *e* *King,* 2 Kin. 3:10.
- *f* *Jerusalem,* Judg. 19:10.

**3**
- *g* *Industry,* 1 Kin. 11:28.

**4**
- *h* *Life, brevity and uncertainty of,* Eccl. 8:15.
- *i* *Earth, perpetuity of,* Prov. 8:23.

**5**
- *j* *Astronomy,* Isa. 13:10.
- *k* *Sun,* Josh. 10:12

**6**
- *l* *Meteorology,* Matt. 16:2.

† **GIRDLE.** *Worn, by the high priest,* Ex. 28:4, 39; 39:29; Lev. 8:7; 16:4; *by other priests,* Ex. 28:40; 29:9; Lev. 8:13; *by women,* Isa. 3:24; *by warriors,* 1 Sam. 18:4; 2 Sam. 20:8.
*Embroidered,* Ex. 28:8, 27, 28; 29:5; Lev. 8:7. *Made of leather,* 2 Kin. 1:8; Matt. 3:4. *Traffic in,* Prov. 31:24. *Used to bear arms,* 1 Sam. 18:4; 2 Sam. 20:8; 2 Kin. 3:21.
**Figurative,** Isa. 11:5; 22:21.
**Symbolical,** Jer. 13:1–11; Acts 21:11; Rev. 15:6.

+ **VANITY,** Eccl. 1:2; 12:8. *Man is,* Psa. 39:5, 11; 62:9. *The thoughts of man,* Psa. 94:11. *All worldly things,* Eccl. 1:2. *Worldly pleasure,* Eccl. 2:1. *The strenuous pursuit of wealth,* Prov. 4:8. *Worldly possessions,* Eccl. 2:4–11; 6:2. *Love of riches,* Eccl. 5:10.
*Wealth gotten by, diminishes,* Prov. 13:11.
*The wicked love,* Psa. 4:2.
See footnote, FOOL, Prov. 18:2.

**7**
*m Sea*, Jer. 5:22.
1 R. V. whither the rivers go, thither they go again.
**8**
*n Man, spirit*, Job 4:17.
*o Eye, figurative*, Matt. 6:22.
**9**
2 R. V. hath been done
**11**
3 R. V. the former generations;
**12**
*p Israel, under the kings*, Ex. 4:22.
**13**
*q Wisdom*, Prov. 2:2.
*r Instruction*, vs. 13–18; Prov. 23:23.
**14**
*s Works, insufficiency of, for salvation*, 2 Tim. 1:9.
4 R. V. a striving after wind.
**16**
*t Knowledge*, Luke 11:52.
5 R. V. *omits* am come to great estate, and

[m]sea; yet the sea *is* not full; unto the place [1]from whence the rivers come, thither they return again.

8 All things *are* full of labour; [n]man cannot utter *it*: the [o]eye is not satisfied with seeing, nor the ear filled with hearing.

9 The thing that hath been, it *is that* which shall be; and that which [2]is done *is* that which shall be done: and *there is* no new *thing* under the sun.

10 Is there *any* thing whereof it may be said, See, this *is* new? it hath been already of old time, which was before us.

11 *There is* no remembrance of [3]former *things*; neither shall there be *any* remembrance of *things* that are to come with *those* that shall come after.

12 ¶ I the [b]Preacher was [e]king over [p]Is′ra-el in [f]Je-ru′sa-lem.

13 And I gave my heart to seek and †search out by [q,r]wisdom concerning all *things* that are done under heaven: this sore travail hath God given to the sons of man to be exercised therewith.

14 I have seen all the [s]works that are done under the sun; and, behold, all *is* +vanity and [4]vexation of spirit.

15 *That which is* crooked cannot be made straight: and that which is wanting cannot be numbered.[s]

16 I communed with mine own heart, saying, Lo, I [5]am come to great estate, and have gotten more [q]wisdom than all *they* that have been before me in [f]Je-ru′sa-lem: yea, my heart had great experience of wisdom and [t]knowledge.

17 And I gave my heart to ▲know [q]wisdom, and to know madness and folly: I perceived that [u]this also [6]is vexation of spirit.

18 For in much [q]wisdom *is* much grief: and he that increaseth [t]knowledge increaseth sorrow.

## CHAPTER 2

*The vanity of mirth, wealth, and greatness; 12 of wisdom, though far better than folly; 18 and of all the labors of a man. 24 A man should make a cheerful use of what he has.*

I SAID in mine heart, Go to now, I will prove thee with mirth, therefore enjoy *pleasure: and, behold, this also *is* vanity.

2 I said of laughter, *It is* mad: and of mirth, What doeth it?

3 I sought in mine heart [1]to give myself unto [a]wine, yet acquainting mine heart with [b]wisdom; and to lay hold on *folly, till I might see what *was* that good for the sons of men, which they should do under the heaven all the days of their life.

4 *I made me great works; I builded me houses; I [c]planted me [d]vineyards:

5 I made me gardens and [2]orchards, and I planted trees in them of all *kind of* fruits:

6 I made me [e]pools of water, †to water therewith the wood that bringeth forth trees:

7 I got *me* [f]servants and maidens, and had servants born in my house; also I had great [g]possessions of great and small cattle above all that were in [h]Je-ru′sa-lem before me:

8 I [g]gathered me also [i]silver and [j]gold, and the peculiar treasure of kings and of the provinces: I gat me men singers and women singers, and the delights of the

**17**
*u Worldly Pleasure*, Eccl. 2:1.
6 R. V. was a striving after wind.
**3**
*a Wine*, Prov. 23:31.
*b Wisdom*, Prov. 2:2.
1 R. V. how to cheer my flesh with wine, my heart yet guiding me with wisdom,
**4**
*c Agriculture*, Gen. 3:23.
*d Vineyard*, Isa. 1:8.
**5**
2 R. V. parks,
**6**
*e Pool*, 2 Sam. 2:13.
**7**
*f Servant*, Jer. 2:14.
*g Riches*, Eccl. 4:8.
*h Jerusalem*, Judg. 19:10.
**8**
*i Silver*, 1 Chr. 28:14.
*j Gold*, Ezek. 7:19.

▲ **INVESTIGATION.** *By Solomon into the nature and design of things*, Eccl. 1:13–18; 2:1–12; 7:25; 8:17; 12:9–14.

* **WORLDLY PLEASURE**, Job 20:12; Eccl. 7:4; Isa. 22:13; 2 Tim. 3:4; Tit. 3:3. *Eschewed by Moses*, Heb. 11:25. *To be eschewed by the righteous*, 1 Pet. 4:3, 4. *Brings poverty*, Prov. 21:17. *Chokes righteousness*, Luke 8:14. *Leads to suffering*, Isa. 47:8, 9; 2 Pet. 2:13; *to spiritual death*, 1 Tim. 5:6. *Denounced*, Isa. 5:11, 12; Jas. 5:5. *Folly of*, Eccl. 1:17; 2:1–13.
See footnote, WORLDLINESS, 1 John 2:15.

† **IRRIGATION.** Deut. 11:10; Eccl. 2:6; Isa. 58:11. **Figurative**, 1 Cor. 3:6, 8.

sons of men, [3]*as* musical instruments, and that of all sorts.

9 So I was great, and increased more than all that were before me in [h]Jė-ru̇'sȧ-lĕm: also my [b]wisdom remained with me.

10 And *whatsoever mine eyes desired I kept not from them, I withheld not my heart from any [k]joy; for my heart rejoiced in all my [l]labour: and this was my portion of all my labour.

11 Then I looked on all the works that my hands had wrought, and on the labour that I had [l]laboured to do: and, behold, *all *was* vanity and [4]vexation of spirit, and *there was* no profit under the sun.

12 ¶ And I turned myself to behold [b]wisdom, and madness, and folly: for what *can* the man *do* that cometh after the king? *even* that which hath been already done.

13 Then I saw that wisdom excelleth folly, as far as [m]light excelleth [n]darkness.

14 The [b]wise man's eyes *are* in his head; but the [o]fool walketh in [p]darkness: and I myself perceived also that [q]one event happeneth to [r]them all.

15 Then said I in my heart, As [q]it happeneth to the [o]fool, so it happeneth even to me; and why was I then more [b]wise? Then I said in my heart, that this also *is* vanity.

16 For *there is* no remembrance of the wise more than of the fool for ever; seeing that which now *is* in the days to come shall all be forgotten. And how dieth the wise *man*? as the fool.

17 Therefore I hated [s]life; [t]because the work that is wrought under the sun *is* grievous unto me: for all *is* vanity and [4]vexation of spirit.

18 ¶ Yea, [t]I hated all my labour which I had taken under the sun: because I should leave [u]it unto the [v]man that shall be after me.

19 And [t]who knoweth whether he shall be a [w]wise *man* or a [p]fool? yet shall [v]he have rule over all my [l]labour wherein I have laboured, and wherein I have shewed myself wise under the sun. This *is* also vanity.

20 Therefore I went about to cause my heart to ‡despair of all the labour which I took under the sun.

21 For [t]there is a man whose labour *is* in [w]wisdom, and in knowledge, and [5]in equity; [t]yet to a man that hath not laboured therein shall he leave [u]it *for* his portion. This also *is* vanity and a great evil.

22 For [t]what hath man of all his labour, and of the [6]vexation of his heart, wherein he hath laboured under the sun?

23 For all his days *are* [x]sorrows, and his travail grief; yea, his heart taketh not rest in the night. This is also vanity.

24 ¶ *There is* nothing better for a man, *than* that [y,z]he should eat and drink, and *that* he should make his soul enjoy good in his labour. This also I saw, that [a]it *was* from the hand of God.

25 For who can eat, or who else can hasten *hereunto*, more than I?

26 For *God* [b]giveth to a [c]man

3 Eng. R. V., and Am. R. V. *alternate reading*, concubines very many. *Am. Standard adheres to the King James translation, but agrees in footnote with Eng. and Am. R. V.*

**10**
*k* *Joy*, Psa. 5:11.
*l* *Industry*, 1 Kin. 11:28.

**11**
4 R. V. a striving after wind,

**13**
*m* *Light*, Gen. 1:3.
*n* *Darkness*, Gen. 1:2.

**14**
*o* *Fool*, Prov. 18:2.
*p* *Spiritual Blindness*, 2 Cor. 4:4.
*q* *Death, inevitable*, Num. 23:10.
*r* *Man, mortal*, Job 4:17.

**17**
*s* *Life, hated*, Eccl. 8:15.
*t* *Murmuring, instances of*, Num. 14:2.

**18**
*u* *Inheritance*, Num. 27:7.
*v* *Heir*, Gen. 15:3.

**19**
*w* *Wisdom*, Prov. 2:2.

**21**
5 R. V. with skilfulness;

**22**
6 R. V. striving

**23**
*x* *Afflictions*, Psa. 34:19.

**24**
*y* *Epicureans*, Acts 17:18.
*z* *Sensuality*, Jude 19.

*a* *Temporal Blessings, from God*, Psa. 103:2.

**26**
*b* *God, providence of*, Gen. 2:2.
*c* *Righteous, described*, Psa. 64:10.

‡ **DESPONDENCY**, Eccl. 2:20; Isa. 35:3, 4; Heb. 12:12, 13. *Caused, by corrective judgments*, Num. 17:12, 13; Deut. 28:65–67; Isa. 2:19; Hos. 10:8; Matt. 24:30; Luke 23:29, 30; Rev. 6:14–17; 9:5, 6; *by deferred hope*, Prov. 13:12; *by adversity*, Job 4:5; 9:16–35; 17:7–16.
*Lament in*, Job 3:1–26; 17:13–16; Psa. 6:6; 22:1, 2; 55:4–7; 77:7–9; 88:3–17; Jer. 8:20; Lam. 3:1–20; 5:15–22; Mic. 7:1–7.
**Instances of:** *Cain, when God pronounced judgment upon him*, Gen. 4:13, 14. *Hagar, when cast out of the household of Abraham*, Gen. 21:15, 16. *Moses, when sent on his mission to the Israelites*, Ex. 4:1, 10, 13; 6:12; *at the Red Sea*, Ex. 14:15; *when the people lusted for flesh*, Num. 11:15. *The Israelites, on account of the cruel oppressions of the Egyptians*, Ex. 6:9. *Joshua, over the defeat at Ai*, Josh. 7:7–9. *Elijah, when he fled from Jezebel to the wilderness and sat under the juniper tree, and wished to die*, 1 Kin. 19:4. *Jonah, after he had preached to the Ninevites*, Jonah 4:3, 8. *The mariners with Paul*, Acts 27:20.
See footnotes: AFFLICTIONS, *Despondency in*, Psa. 34:19; REMORSE, Matt. 27:3.

*d Wisdom,* Prov. 2:2.
*e Knowledge,* Luke 11:52.
*f Joy,* Psa. 5:11.
*g Wicked, punishment of,* Psa. 73:3.
*h Riches,* Eccl. 4:8.

that *is* good in his sight [d]wisdom, and [a,e]knowledge, and [a,f]joy: but to the sinner he giveth [g]travail, [h]to gather and to heap up, that he may give to *him that is* good before God. This also *is* vanity and [4]vexation of spirit.

## CHAPTER 3

*All things have their appointed time, 11 and are good in their season. 16 The perversion of justice and a future retribution. 18 The vanity of man as mortal.*

[a]TO every *thing there is* a season, and a time to every purpose under the heaven:

2 A time to be born, and a time to [b]die; a time to plant, and a time to pluck up *that which is* planted;

3 A time to kill, and a time to heal; a time to break down, and a time to build up;

4 A time to [c]weep, and a time to laugh; a time to mourn, and a time to *dance;

5 A time to cast away stones, and a time to gather stones together; a time to embrace, and a time to refrain from embracing;

6 A time to get, and a time to lose; a time to keep, and a time to cast away;

7 A time to rend, and a time to sew; a time to keep silence, and a time to speak;

8 A time to [d]love, and a time to [e]hate; a time of [f]war, and a time of [g]peace.

9 [h]What profit hath he that worketh in that wherein he laboureth?

10 [a]I have seen the travail, which God [i]hath given to the sons of men to be exercised in it.

11 [a]He hath [j,k]made every *thing* beautiful in his time: also he hath set the world in their heart, so that [l]no man can find out the [m]work that [n,o]God maketh from the beginning to the end.

12 [a,p]I know that *there is* [1]no good in them, but for *a* [q]*man* to rejoice, and to do good in his life.

13 [a]And also that every man should eat and drink, and enjoy the good of all his labour, [q,r]it *is* the [i]gift of God.

14 I know that, whatsoever God doeth, [s]it shall be for ever: nothing can be put to it, nor any thing taken from it: and God doeth *it,* that *men* should [t]fear before him.

15 That which hath been is now; and that which is to be hath already been; and God [2]requireth that which is past.

16 And moreover I saw under the sun [u]the place of judgment, *that* [v]wickedness *was* there; and the place of righteousness, *that* [v]iniquity *was* there.

17 I said in mine heart, God shall [w,x]judge the [y]righteous and the [z]wicked: for *there is* a time there for every purpose and for every work.

18 [a]I said in mine heart concerning the estate of the [b]sons of men, that God [3]might manifest them, and that they might see that they themselves are [4]beasts.

19 [a]For [c]that which befalleth the [b]sons of men befalleth beasts; even one thing befalleth them: as the one dieth, so dieth the other; yea, they have all one breath; so that a man hath no preeminence above a beast: for all *is* vanity.

20 [a]All go unto one place; [b]all are of the †,[d]dust, and [b]all turn to dust again.

21 Who knoweth the [e]spirit of man that [f]goeth upward, and

**1**
*a Philosophy,* vs. 1–22; Col. 2:8.

**2**
*b Death,* vs. 19–21; Num. 23:10.

**4**
*c Weeping,* Ezra. 3:13.

**8**
*d Love, of man for man,* 1 John 4:7.
*e Hatred,* Prov. 15:17.
*f War,* Judg. 3:2.
*g Peace,* Jer. 29:7.

**9**
*h Murmuring,* Num. 14:2.

**10**
*i God, providence of,* Gen. 2:2.

**11**
*j God, creator,* Gen. 2:2.
*k Creation,* Mark 13:19.
*l Ignorance, concerning God's works,* Acts 3:17.
*m Works of God,* Psa. 40:5.
*n God, incomprehensible,* Gen. 2:2.
*o God, unsearchable,* Gen. 2:2.

**12**
*p Contentment,* 1 Tim. 6:6.
*q Righteous, happiness of, from God,* Psa. 64:10.
1 R. V. nothing better for them, than to rejoice,

**13**
*r Temporal Blessings, from God,* Psa. 103:2.

**14**
*s God, immutable,* Gen. 2:2.
*t Fear of God,* Acts 9:31.

**15**
2 R. V. seeketh again that which is passed

**16**
*u Rulers, wicked,* Ex. 18:21.
*v Injustice,* Isa. 26:10.

**17**
*w God, judge,* Gen. 2:2.
*x Judgment, the general,* 2 Pet. 3:7.
*y Righteous,* Psa. 64:10.
*z Wicked,* Psa. 73:3.

**18**
*a Philosophy,* Col. 2:8.
*b Man, mortal,* Job 4:17.
3 R. V. may prove
4 R. V. but as beasts.

**19**
*c Death,* Num. 23:10.

**20**
*d Corruption,* Job 17:14.

**21**
*e Man, spirit,* Job 4:17.
*f Immortality,* 1 Cor. 15:54.

***DANCING.** *Of children,* Job 21:11. *Of women,* Ex. **15**:20; Judg. 11:34; 21:19–21, 1 Sam. 18:6; 21:11. *Of David,* **2** Sam. 6:14–16; 1 Chr. 15:29.
*In the market-place,* Matt. 11:16, **17**. *At feasts,* Matt. 14:6; Mark 6:22; Luke 15:23–25. *As a religious ceremony,* Psa. **149:3; 150:4.** *Idolatrous,* Ex. 32:19.
**Figurative:** *Of joy,* Psa. 30:11; Eccl. 3:4; Jer. 31:4, **13;** Lam. 5:15.

† **DUST.** *Man made from,* Gen. 2:7; 3:19, 23; Eccl. 3:20. *Shaken from feet, as a testimony,* Matt. 10:14; Luke 9:5; 10:11; Acts 13:51. *Put on the head in mourning,* Josh. **7:6;** 1 Sam. 4:12; 2 Sam. 1:2; 15:32; Job 2:12.

5 R. V. whether it goeth

22

6 R. V. *inserts* back

1

*a* *Oppression*, Eccl. 5:8.
*b* *Afflictions*, Psa. 34:19.
*c* *Life, vanity of*, Eccl. 8:15.
*d* *Rulers, wicked*, Ex. 18:21.

4

*e* *Envy*, Prov. 14:30.
*f* *Jealousy*, Psa. 78:58.
1 R. V. skilful
2 R. V. a striving after wind.

5

*g* *Fool*, Prov. 18:2.
*h* *Idleness*, Eccl. 10:18.

6

*i* *Contentment*, 1 Tim. 6:6.
*j* *Poverty*, Prov. 30:8.
*k* *Peace*, Jer. 29:7.

the spirit of the beast [5]that goeth
downward to the earth?
22 [a]Wherefore I perceive that
*there is* nothing better, than that
a man should rejoice in his own
works; for that *is* his portion:
for who shall bring him [6]to see
what shall be after him?

## CHAPTER 4

*The sorrows of the oppressed. 4 The evils of envy, 5 of idleness, 7 of covetousness, 9 and of solitariness. 13 The evil of a foolish king.*

SO I returned, and considered
all the [a,b]oppressions that
are done under the sun: and
[c]behold the tears of *such as were*
oppressed, and they had no comforter; and on the side of their
[d]oppressors *there was* power; but
they had no comforter.
2 Wherefore I praised the dead
which are already dead more
than the living which are yet
alive.
3 Yea, better *is he* than both
they, which hath not yet been,
who hath not seen the evil work
that is done under the sun.
4 ¶ Again, I considered all travail, and every [1]right work, that
for this a man is [e,f]envied of his
neighbour. This *is* also vanity
and [2]vexation of spirit.
5 ¶ The [g]fool [h]foldeth his hands
together, and eateth his own
flesh.
6 [i]Better *is* an [j]handful *with*
[k]quietness, than both the hands
full *with* travail and [2]vexation
of spirit.
7 ¶ Then I returned, and I saw
vanity under the sun.
8 There is one *alone*, and *there*
*is* not a second; yea, he hath
neither child nor brother: yet *is*
*there* no end of all his labour;
[l,m]neither is his eye satisfied with
*riches; neither *saith he*, For
whom do I labour, and [3]bereave
my soul of good? This *is* also
vanity, yea, it *is* a sore travail.
9 ¶ [n,o,p]Two *are* better than
one; because they have a good
reward for their labour.
10 For [p]if they fall, [o]the one
will lift up his fellow: but woe to
him *that is* alone when he falleth;
for *he hath* not another to help
him up.
11 Again, [p]if two lie together,
then they have heat: but how
can one be warm *alone*?
12 And if one prevail against
him, [p]two shall withstand him;
and a threefold cord is not
quickly broken.
13 ¶ Better *is* a poor and a wise
[4]child than an old and foolish
[q]king, who will no more be admonished.
14 For out of [r]prison he cometh
to [5]reign; whereas also *he that is*
born in his kingdom becometh
poor.
15 I considered all the living
which walk under the sun, [6]with
the second child that shall stand
up in his stead.
16 *There* [7]*is* no end of all the
people, *even* of all [8]that have
been before them: they also that
come after shall not rejoice in
him. Surely this also *is* vanity
and [2]vexation of spirit.

## CHAPTER 5

*How to behave in the house of God. 4 Concerning vows. 9 The vanity of riches. 18 Joy in them is the gift of God.*

[a]KEEP thy foot when thou
goest to the [b,c]house of
God, [1]and be more ready to
hear, than to give the sacrifice

8

*l* *Avarice, insatiable*, Eccl. 5:10.
*m* *Covetousness, insatiable*, Isa. 57:17.
3 R. V. deprive

9

*n* *Fellowship*, 1 Cor. 1:9.
*o* *Friendship*, Prov. 22:24.
*p* *Unity, advantages of*, vs. 9–12; Psa. 133:1.

13

*q* *King*, 2 Kin. 3:10.
4 R. V. youth

14

*r* *Prison*, Gen. 39:20.
5 R. V. be king, yea, even in his kingdom he was born poor.

15

6 R. V. that they were with the youth, the second, that stood up in his stead.

16

7 R. V. was
8 R. V. them over whom he was: yet they that come

1

*a* *Commandment, enjoining reverence for God's house*, Deut. 8:2.
*b* *Church, called house of God*, 1 Kin. 9:3.
*c* *Worship*, Gen. 22:5.
1 R. V. for to draw nigh to hear is better than

* **RICHES,** 1 Sam. 2:7; Psa. 37:16; 52:7; Prov. 11:4; Eccl. 4:8; 5:11–14; 6:1, 2; 7:11, 12; 10:19; Jer. 48:36. *Delusive*, Prov. 11:28; Luke 12:16–21. *Unstable*, Prov. 23:5; 27:24.
*Unsatisfying to the covetous*, Eccl. 5:10–12. *A snare*, Deut. 6:10–12; 8:7–17; 31:20; 32:15; Prov. 30:8, 9; Jer. 5:7, 8; Hos. 12:8; Matt. 13:22; 19:16–24; Mark 4:19; 10:17–25; Luke 16:19–26; 18:18–25; 1 Tim. 6:9–11, 17.
*Impotent in day of calamity*, Ezek. 7:17, 19; Zeph. 1:18.
*Fraudulently gotten, unprofitable*, Prov. 10:2; 21:6; 28:8; Jer. 17:11.
*Admonitions against the desire for*, Prov. 23:4; 28:20, 22; 1 Tim. 6:9–11, 17. *The heart not to be set upon*, Psa. 62:10; Matt. 6:19–21.
*Liberality with*, Prov. 13:7, 8. *Benevolent use of, required*, 1 John 3:17.
**Figurative**, Rev. 3:17, 18.
See footnotes: COVETOUSNESS, Isa. 57:17; RICH, Jas. 5:1.

of [d]fools: for they consider not that they do evil.

2 [e]Be not [f]rash with thy [g]mouth, and [h]let not thine heart be hasty to utter *any* thing before God: for God *is* in [i]heaven, and thou upon earth: therefore let thy [j]words be few.

3 For a [k]dream cometh through the multitude of business; and a fool's voice *is known* by [g]multitude of words.

4 When thou vowest a [l]vow unto God, [m]defer not to pay it; for *he hath* no pleasure in [d]fools: pay that which thou hast vowed.

5 Better *is it* that thou shouldest not [l]vow, than that thou shouldest vow and not pay.

6 [e]Suffer not thy mouth to cause thy flesh to sin; [n]neither say thou before the angel, that it *was* an error: wherefore should God be [o]angry at thy voice, and [p]destroy the work of thine hands?

7 For in the multitude of [k]dreams and [g]many words *there are* also *divers* vanities: but [q]fear thou God.

8 ¶ If thou seest the *oppression of the [r]poor, and violent [s]perverting of judgment and [t]justice in a province, marvel not at the matter: for [u]*he that is* higher than the [v]highest [w]regardeth; and *there be* higher than they.

9 ¶ Moreover [x]the profit of the [y]earth is for all: the [z]king *himself* is served by the field.

10 He that [†,a]loveth [b]silver shall not be satisfied with silver; nor he that loveth [b]abundance with increase: this *is* also vanity.

11 When [b]goods increase, they are increased that eat them: and what good *is there* to the owners thereof, saving the beholding *of them* with their eyes?

12 The [c]sleep of a [d]labouring man *is* sweet, whether he eat little or much: but the [2,b]abundance of the rich will not suffer him to sleep.

13 There is a sore evil *which* I have seen under the sun, *namely*, [b]riches kept for the [e]owners thereof to their hurt.

14 But those [b]riches perish by evil [3]travail: and [e]he begetteth a son, and *there is* nothing in his hand.

15 As he came forth of his mother's womb, naked shall he return to [f]go as he came, and shall take nothing of his labour, which he may carry away in his hand.

16 And this also *is* a sore evil, *that* in all points as he came, so shall he [f]go: and what profit hath he that hath laboured for the wind?

17 All his days also he eateth in darkness, and *he hath* much [g]sorrow and wrath with his sickness.

18 ¶ Behold *that* which I have seen: *it is* good and comely *for one* to eat and to drink, and to enjoy the good of all his labour that he taketh under the sun all the days of his life, which God giveth him: for it *is* his portion.

19 Every man also to whom God hath [h]given [i]riches and wealth, and hath given him power to eat thereof, and to take his portion, and to rejoice in his labour; [i]this *is* the gift of God.

20 For he shall not much remember the days of his life;

*d Fool*, Prov. 18:2.

**2**

*e Commandment, enjoining prudence in speech*, Deut. 8:2.

*f Rashness*, 2 Sam. 6:7.

*g Speech, foolish*, Col. 4:6.

*h Humility, enjoined*, Prov. 22:4.

*i Heaven, God's dwelling place*, Luke 18:22.

*j Prayer*, Acts 6:4.

**3**

*k Dream*, Dan. 1:17.

**4**

*l Vows*, Num. 30:2.

*m Commandment, enjoining fidelity to vows*, Deut. 8:2.

**6**

*n Falsehood, forbidden*, Job 21:34.

*o Anger of God*, 2 Kin. 13:3.

*p Judgments*, Ex. 6:6.

**7**

*q Fear of God, enjoined*, Acts 9:31.

**8**

*r Poor, oppression of*, Prov. 21:13.

*s Injustice, in civil administration*, Isa. 26:10.

*t Justice*, Deut. 33:21.

*u Poor, God's care of*, Prov. 21:13.

*v Rulers, wicked*, Ex. 18:21.

*w Sin, known to God*, Rom. 5:12.

**9**

*x Agriculture*, Gen. 3:23.

*y Land, products of, for all*, Ruth 4:3.

*z King*, 2 Kin. 3:10.

**10**

*a Covetousness, insatiable*, Isa. 57:17.

*b Riches*, Eccl. 4:8.

**12**

*c Sleep*, Psa. 127:2.

*d Labor*, Luke 10:7.

2 R. V. fulness

**13**

*e Rich*, Jas. 5:1.

**14**

3 R. V. adventure;

**15**

*f Death, inevitable*, Num. 23:10.

**17**

*g Afflictions*, Psa. 34:19.

**19**

*h God, providence of*, Gen. 2:2.

*i Temporal Blessings, from God*, Psa. 103:2.

* **OPPRESSION.** Psa. 62:10; 72:14; Prov. 14:31; 28:3; 30:14; Eccl. 4:1; 5:8; 7:7; Isa. 1:17; 58:6; Jer. 22:17; Ezek. 22:29; Amos 4:1; 5:11, 12; Mic. 2:1–3; Mal. 3:5; Jas. 2:6; 5:4. *Forbidden*, Ex. 22:21–24; Deut. 23:15, 16; 24:14, 15; Prov. 22:22; Zech. 7:10.

*Prayer for deliverance from*, Psa. 17:8, 9; 44:24; 74:21; 119:121, 134; Isa. 38:14. *The Lord, a refuge from*, Psa. 9:9; 12:5.

*Oppressors punished*, Job 27:13–23; Psa. 72:4; 103:6; Isa. 10.

*National, relieved*, Ex. 3:9; 12:30–39; Deut. 26:7, 8; Judg. 2:14, 16, 18; 6; 7; 8:1–22, 28; 10; 11:1–33; 2 Kin. 13:3–5.

**Instances of:** *Hagar, by Sarah*, Gen. 16:6. *Jacob, by Laban*, Gen. 31:39. *Israelites, by Egyptians*, Ex. 1:10–22; 5; *by Assyrians*, Isa. 52:4.

† **AVARICE.** *A root of all evil*, 1 Tim. 6:10. *Insatiable*, Eccl. 4:7, 8; 5:10, 11. *Forbidden in bishops*, 1 Tim. 3:2, 3; Tit. 1:7.

See footnote, COVETOUSNESS, Isa. 57:17.

1
a *Philosophy*, vs. 1–12; Col. 2:8.

2
b *Riches*, Eccl. 4:8.
c *Temporal Blessings, from God*, Psa. 103:2.
d *God, providence of, mysterious*, Gen. 2:2.
e *Life, vanity of*, vs. 1–12; Eccl. 8:15.

3
f *Old Age*, Isa. 46:4.
g *Burial*, Acts 8:2.

6
h *Death*, Num. 23:10.

7
i *Appetite*, Prov. 23:2.

9
2 R. V. a striving after wind.

because God answereth *him* in
the joy of his heart.

## CHAPTER 6

*The evil of riches without power to use them. 7 Sundry observations.*

[a]THERE is an evil which I
have seen under the sun,
and it *is* [1]common among men:
2 [a]A man to whom God hath
given [b,c]riches, wealth, and honour, so that he wanteth nothing
for his soul of all that he desireth, yet God [d]giveth him not
power to eat thereof, but a stranger eateth it: this *is* [e]vanity, and
it *is* an evil disease.
3 ¶ [a]If a man beget an hundred
*children*, and live many years, so
that the days of his years be
[f]many, and his soul be not filled
with good, and also *that* he have
no [g]burial; I say, *that* an untimely birth *is* better than he.
4 [a]For he cometh in with vanity, and departeth in darkness,
and [e]his name shall be covered
with darkness.
5 Moreover he hath not seen
the sun, nor known *any thing*:
this hath more rest than the
other.
6 [a]Yea, though he [e]live a thousand years twice *told*, yet hath he
seen no good: do not all [h]go to
one place?
7 [a]All the labour of man *is* for
his [i]mouth, and yet the appetite
is not filled.
8 [a]For what hath the wise more
than the fool? what hath the
poor, that knoweth to walk before the living?
9 [a]Better *is* the sight of the eyes
than the wandering of the desire:
this *is* also vanity and [2]vexation
of spirit.
10 ¶ That which hath been is
named already, and it is known
that it *is* man: neither may he
contend with him that is mightier than he.
11 [a]Seeing there be many
things that increase vanity, what
*is* man the better?
12 [e]For who knoweth what *is*
good for man in *this* life, all the
days of his vain [j]life which he
spendeth as a shadow? for who
can tell a man what shall be after
him under the sun?

## CHAPTER 7

*Sundry observations and admonitions. 11 A commendation of wisdom. 23 The difficulty in obtaining it.*

A GOOD [a,b]name *is* better
than precious *ointment;
[c]and the day of death than the
[d]day of one's birth.
2 ¶ *It is* better to [e]go to the
house of [f]mourning, than to go
to the house of feasting: for that
*is* the end of all men; and the
living will lay *it* to his heart.
3 [f]Sorrow *is* better than laughter: for by the sadness of the
[g]countenance the heart is made
[1]better.
4 The heart of the wise *is* in the
house of mourning; but the heart
of fools *is* in the [h]house of mirth.
5 *It is* better to hear the [i]rebuke
of the wise, than for a man to
hear the song of fools.
6 For as the crackling of thorns
under a pot, so *is* the [j]laughter of
the fool: this also *is* vanity.
7 ¶ Surely [2,k]oppression maketh a wise man [3]mad; and a [l]gift
destroyeth the [4]heart.
8 Better *is* the end of a thing
than the beginning thereof: *and*
the [m,n]patient in spirit *is* better
than the [o]proud in spirit.
9 [p]Be not [q]hasty in thy spirit to
be [r]angry: for anger resteth in
the bosom of fools.
10 Say not thou, [s]What is *the*
*cause* that the former days were
better than these? for thou dost

12
j *Life, brevity, and uncertainty of*, Eccl. 8:15.

1
a *Name, value of a good*, Prov. 22:1.
b *Character, good*, Phil. 2:15.
c *Life, vanity of*, Eccl. 8:15.
d *Birthday*, Gen. 40:20.

2
e *Sympathy*, Jas. 1:27.
f *Afflictions*, Psa. 34:19.

3
g *Countenance*, Prov. 15:13.

4
h *Worldly Pleasure*, Eccl. 2:1.

5
i *Reproof, profitable*, Prov. 17:10.

6
j *Wicked, happiness of*, Psa. 73:3.

7
k *Oppression*, Eccl. 5:8.
l *Bribery, corrupts conscience*, 1 Sam. 8:3.
2 R. V. extortion
3 R. V. foolish;
4 R. V. understanding.

8
m *Patience*, Luke 8:15.
n *Meekness*, Psa. 45:4.
o *Pride*, Prov. 16:18.

9
p *Commandment, enjoining restraint of temper*, Deut. 8:2.
q *Rashness*, 2 Sam. 6:7.
r *Anger, forbidden*, Psa. 37:8.

10
s *Murmuring*, Num. 14:2.

* **OINTMENT**, 2 Kin. 20:13; Esth. 2:12; Eccl. 7:1; 10:1; Song 1:3; 4:10; Amos 6:6; John 12:3–5. *The alabaster box of*, Matt. 26:7; Mark 14:3–5; Luke 7:37; John 12:5. **Sacred**: *Formula for*, Ex. 30:23–25. *Uses of*, Ex. 30:26–33. *Compounded by Bezaleel*, Ex. 37:1, 29. See footnote, OIL, *Sacred*, Deut. 12:17.

11
[t] *Wisdom,* Prov. 2:2.
[u] *Inheritance,* Num. 27:7.
5 R. V. as good as an inheritance: yea, more excellent is it for them
12
[v] *Money,* Jer. 32:9.
[w] *Knowledge,* Luke 11:52.
6 R. V. even as
7 R. V. preserveth the life of him that hath it.
13
[x] *God, immutable,* Gen. 2:2.
14
[y] *Thankfulness, enjoined,* Acts 24:3.
[z] *Adversity, design of,* Psa. 10:6.
8 R. V. not find out anything that shall be after him.

15
[a] *God, providence of, mysterious,* Gen. 2:2.
[b] *Righteous,* Psa. 64:10.
[c] *Righteousness,* Psa. 15:2.
[d] *Wicked,* Psa. 73:3.
[e] *Sin,* Rom. 5:12.
16
[f] *Commandment, enjoining wise self-restraint,* Deut. 8:2.
[g] *Prudence,* 2 Chr. 2:12.
[h] *Zeal, without knowledge,* 2 Cor. 7:11.
17
[i] *Wicked, punishment of,* Psa. 73:3.
18
[j] *Righteous, promises to,* Psa. 64:10.
[k] *Fear of God, secures divine blessing,* Acts 9:31.
19
[l] *Wisdom,* Prov. 2:2.
20
[m] *Depravity, universal,* Job 15:14.
[n] *Sinfulness, universal,* Rom. 3:23.
[o] *Sinlessness,* 1 John 5:18.
[p] *Perfection,* Heb. 6:1.

not enquire[C] wisely concerning
this.
11 ¶ [t]Wisdom *is* [5]good with
an [u]inheritance: and *by it there*
*is* profit to them that see the
sun.
12 For [t]wisdom *is* a defence,
[6]*and* [v]money *is* a defence: but
the excellency of [w]knowledge *is,*
*that* wisdom [7]giveth life to them
that have it.
13 Consider the work of God:
[x]for who can make *that* straight,
which he hath made crooked?[S]
14 In the day of †prosperity [y]be
joyful, but in the day of [z]ad-
versity consider: God also hath
set the one over against the other,
to the end that man should [8]find
nothing after him.
15 All *things* have I seen in the
days of my vanity: [a]there is a
[b]just *man* that perisheth in his
[c]righteousness, and there is a
[d]wicked *man* that prolongeth *his*
*life* in his [e]wickedness.[S]
16 [f,g]Be not righteous[C] [h]over
much; neither make thyself over
wise: why shouldest thou destroy
thyself?
17 Be not over much wicked,
neither be thou foolish: why
shouldest thou [i]die before thy
time?
18 *It is* good that thou shouldest take hold of this; yea, also
from this withdraw not thine
hand: for [j]he that [k]feareth God
shall come forth of them all.
19 [l]Wisdom strengtheneth the
wise more than ten mighty *men*
which are in the city.
20 For *there is* [m,n]not a [b]just
man upon earth, that doeth good,
and [o,p]sinneth not.[S Q]
21 Also [t]take no heed unto all
words that are spoken; lest thou
hear thy [q]servant [r]curse thee:
22 For oftentimes also [s]thine
own heart knoweth that thou thyself likewise hast [r]cursed others.
23 All this have I proved by
[l,t]wisdom: I said, I will be wise;
but it *was* far from me.
24 That which is far off, and exceeding deep, who can find it out?[S]
25 I applied mine [u]heart to
know, and to search, and to seek
out [l]wisdom, and the [t]reason *of*
*things,* and to know the wickedness of folly, even of foolishness
*and* madness:
26 And I find more bitter than
death the [v]woman, whose [u]heart
*is* [w]snares and [x]nets, *and* her
hands *as* bands: [y]whoso pleaseth
God shall escape from her; but
the sinner shall be taken by her.
27 Behold, this have I found,
saith the preacher, *counting* one
by one, to find out the account:
28 Which yet my soul seeketh,
but I find not: one man among a
thousand have I found; but a
woman among all those have I
not found.
29 Lo, this only have I found,
that God hath [z,a]made man upright; but they have sought out
many inventions.[GS]

## CHAPTER 8

*Obedience to rulers enjoined.* 6 *Man's misery from not knowing the future.* 9 *An evil work sure to be punished.* 12 *The end of the righteous and of the wicked.* 16 *God's works unsearchable.*

WHO *is* as the wise *man*? and
who knoweth the inter-
pretation of a thing? a man's
[a]wisdom maketh his face to
shine, and the [1]boldness of his
face shall be changed.
2 *I *counsel* [b]thee to keep the

21
[q] *Servant,* Jer. 2:14.
[r] *Speech, evil,* Col. 4:6.
22
[s] *Conscience, guilty,* Acts 23:1.
23
[t] *Philosophy,* Col. 2:8.
25
[u] *Heart,* Psa. 44:21.
26
[v] *Women, guileful and licentious,* Prov. 31:10.
[w] *Snare, figurative,* Amos 3:5.
[x] *Net, figurative,* Isa. 51:20.
[y] *Temptation,* Luke 11:4.
29
[z] *God, creator,* Gen. 2:2.

[a] *Man, created in the image of God,* Job 4:17.

1
[a] *Wisdom, spiritual,* Prov. 2:2.
1 R. V. hardness of his face is changed.
2
[b] *Citizens, duties of,* Luke 15:15.

† **PROSPERITY.** *From God,* Gen. 33:11; 49:24–26; Psa. 127:1; 128:1, 2. *Promised to the righteous,* Job 22:23–27; Prov. 11:28.

*Dangers from,* Deut. 8:10–18; 31:20; 32:15; Jer. 5:7; 22:21; Hos. 13:6.

**Evil effects of,** Hos. 4:7. *Pride,* 2 Chr. 32:25. *Forgetfulness of God,* 2 Chr. 26:16. *The prosperous despise the unfortunate,* Job 12:5.

See footnotes: RICHES, Eccl. 4:8; TEMPORAL BLESSINGS, **Psa. 103:2.**

* **LOYALTY.** *Enjoined,* Ex. 22:28; Num. 27:20; Ezra 6:10; 7:26; Prov. 24:21; Eccl. 8:2; 10:4; Rom. 13:1; Tit. 3:1.

See footnotes: CITIZENS, *Loyal,* Luke 15:15; PATRIOTISM, Psa. 137:1.

**Instances of:** *Israelites,* Josh. 1:16–18; 2 Sam. 15:23, 30; 18:3. *David,* 1 Sam. 24:6–10; 26:6–16; 2 Sam. 1:14. *Uriah,* 2 Sam. 11:9–11. *Ittai,* 2 Sam. 15:21. *Hushai,* 2 Sam. 17:15, 16. *David's soldiers,* 2 Sam. 18:12, 13; 23:15, 16. *Joab,* 2 Sam. 19:5, 6. *Abishai,* 2 Sam. 21:17. *Barzillai,* 2 Sam. 19:32. *Jehoiada,* 2 Kin. 11:4–12. *Mordecai,* Esth. 2:21–23.

c *King*, 2 Kin. 3:10.
d *Oath*, Num. 5:19.
**3**
e *Prudence*, 2 Chr. 2:12.
2 R. V. persist not
**5**
f *Obedience.* Heb. 5:8.
**8**
g *Death, inevitable*, Num. 23:10.
**9**
h *Rulers, wicked*, Ex. 18:21.
**10**
i *Death, of the wicked*, Num. 23:10.
3 R. V. withal I saw the wicked buried, and they came to the grave; and they that had done right went away from the holy place, and were forgotten in the city:

[c]king's commandment, and *that* in regard of the [d]oath of God.

3 [b,e]Be not hasty to go out of his sight: [2]stand not in an evil thing; for he doeth whatsoever pleaseth him.

4 Where the word of a [c]king *is, there is* power: and who may say unto him, What doest thou?

5 Whoso [f]keepeth the commandment shall feel[G] no evil thing: and a wise man's heart [e]discerneth both time and judgment.

6 Because to every purpose there is time and judgment, therefore the misery of man *is* great upon him.

7 For he knoweth not that which shall be: for who can tell him when it shall be?

8 *There is* no man that hath power over the spirit to retain the spirit; [g]neither *hath he* power in the day of death: and *there is* no discharge in *that* war; neither shall wickedness deliver those that are given to it.

9 All this have I seen, and applied my heart unto every work that is done under the sun: *there is* a time wherein one [h]man ruleth over another to his own hurt.

10 And [3,i]so I saw the wicked buried, who had come and gone from the place of the holy, and they were forgotten in the city where they had so done: this *is* also vanity.

11 [j,k]Because [l]sentence against an evil work is not executed speedily, therefore the [m]heart of the sons of men is [n]fully set in them to do evil.

12 [k,o]Though a sinner do evil an hundred times, and his *days* be prolonged, yet surely I know that [p]it shall be well with them that [q]fear God, which fear before him:

13 But [o,r]it shall not be well with the wicked, neither shall he prolong *his* days, *which are* as a shadow; because he feareth not before God.

14 There is a vanity which is done upon the earth; that [k]there be just *men*, unto whom it happeneth according to the work of the wicked; again, [k]there be wicked *men*, to whom it happeneth according to the work of the righteous: I said that this also *is* vanity.

15 [s]Then I commended mirth, because a man hath no better thing under the sun, [t]than to [u]eat, and to drink, and to be merry: for that shall abide with him of his labour the days of his [†]life, which God giveth him under the sun.

16 ¶ When I applied mine heart to know [v]wisdom, and to see the business that is done upon the earth: (for also *there is that* neither day nor night seeth sleep with his eyes:)

17 Then I beheld all the [w]work

**11**
j *God, longsuffering of, abused*, Gen. 2:2.
k *God, providence of, mysterious*, Gen. 2:2.
l *Punishment, delayed*, vs. 11–13; Lev. 26:41.
m *Heart, unregenerate*, Psa. 44:21
n *Depravity*, Job 15:14.
**12**
o *Wicked, contrasted with the righteous*, Psa. 73:3.
p *Promise, or ground of assurance, to the righteous*, 2 Cor. 1:20.
q *Fear of God*, Acts 9:31.
**13**
r *Wicked, punishment of*, Psa. 73:3.
**15**
s *Worldliness*, 1 John 2:15.
t *Sensuality*, Jude 19.
u *Appetite*, Prov. 23:2.
**16**
v *Wisdom*, Prov. 2:2.
**17**
w *Works of God*, Psa. 40:5.

† **LIFE.** *Breath of*, Gen. 2:7.

Weary of: *Job*, Job 3; 7:1–3; 10:18, 19; *Jeremiah*, Jer. 20:14–18; *Elijah*, 1 Kin. 19:1–4; *Jonah*, Jonah 4:8; *Paul*, Phil. 1:21–24.

*Hated*, Eccl. 2:17. *To be hated for Christ's sake*, Luke 14:26. *What shall a man give in exchange for*, Matt. 16:26; Mark 8:37. *He that loseth it for Christ's sake shall save it*, Matt. 10:39; 16:25, 26; Luke 9:24; John 12:25.

Long, promised, Gen. 6:3; Psa. 91:16; *to Solomon*, 1 Kin. 3:11–14; *to the wise*, Prov. 3:16; 9:11; *to the obedient*, Deut. 4:40; Prov. 3:1, 2; *to those who honor parents*, Ex. 20:12; Deut. 5:16; *to those who show kindness to animals*, Deut. 22:7; *given to those who fear God*, Prov. 10:27; Isa. 65:20. See footnote, LONGEVITY, Psa. 91:16.

Brevity of, Gen. 47:9; Job 10:9, 20, 21; Psa. 89:47, 48; 90:10. *Compared, to a shadow*, 1 Chr. 29:15; Job 8:9; 14:1, 2; Psa. 102:11; 144:3, 4; Eccl. 6:12; *to a weaver's shuttle*, Job 7:6–10; *to a courier*, Job 9:25, 26; *to a handbreadth*, Psa. 39:4, 5, 11; *to a wind*, Psa. 78:39; *to grass*, Psa. 90:3, 5, 6, 9, 10; 102:11; 103:14–16; Isa. 40:6, 7, 8, 24; 51:12; Jas. 1:10, 11; 1 Pet. 1:24; *to a leaf*, Isa. 64:6; *to a vapor*, Jas. 4:14.

*Uncertainty of*, 1 Sam. 20:3; Job 4:19–21; 17:1; Prov. 27:1; Luke 12:20.

*End of, certain*, 2 Sam. 14:14; Eccl. 1:4.

**From God**, Gen. 2:7; Deut. 8:3; 30:20; 32:39; 1 Sam. 2:6; Job 27:3; Psa. 30:3; Eccl. 12:7; Isa. 38:16; Acts 17:25, 28; Rom. 4:17; 1 Tim. 6:13; Jas. 4:15.

**Spiritual**, Deut. 8:3. *From Christ*, John 1:4; 6:27, 33, 35; 10:10; 17:2, 3; Rom. 6:11; 8:10; Col. 3:4. *Through faith*, John 3:14–16; 5:24–26, 40; 6:40, 47; 11:25, 26; 20:31; Gal. 2:19, 20. *Signified, in figure of new birth*, John 3:3–8; Tit. 3:5; *in figure of death, burial, and resurrection*, Rom. 6:4–8.

**Everlasting**, Isa. 25:8; Dan. 12:2; Matt. 19:16–21, 29 (with Mark 10:17–21, 29, 30; Luke 18:18–22, 29, 30); 25:46; Luke 18:30; 20:36; John 3:14–16, 36; 4:14; 5:24, 25, 29, 39; 6:27, 40, 47, 50–58, 68; 10:10, 27, 28; 12:25, 50; 17:2, 3; Acts 13:46, 48; Rom. 2:7; 5:21; 6:22, 23; 1 Cor. 15:53, 54; 2 Cor. 5:1; Gal. 6:8; 1 Tim. 1:16; 4:8; 6:12, 19; 2 Tim. 1:10, Tit. 1:2; 3:7; 1 John 2:25; 3:15; 5:11–13, 20; Jude 21; Rev. 1:18. See footnote, IMMORTALITY, 1 Cor. 15:54.

of God, that a man [x]cannot find out the work that is done under the sun: because though a man labour to seek *it* out, yet he shall not find *it*; yea farther; though a wise *man* think to know *it*, yet shall he not be able to find *it*.

## CHAPTER 9

*Like things happen to good and bad. 4 Death the end of worldly enjoyments. 11 God's providence over all. 13 Wisdom is better than strength.*

FOR all this I considered in my heart even to declare all this, that the righteous, and the wise, and their works, *are* in the hand of [a]God: [1]no man knoweth either love or hatred *by* all *that is* before them.

2 [b]All *things come* alike to all: *there is* one event to the righteous, and to the wicked; to the good and to the clean, and to the unclean; to him that sacrificeth, and to him that sacrificeth not: as *is* the good, so *is* the sinner; *and* he that sweareth, as *he* that feareth an oath.

3 This *is* an evil among all *things* that are done under the sun, that *there is* [c]one event unto all: yea, also the [d]heart of the sons of men is [e]full of evil, and madness *is* in their heart while they live, and after that *they go* to the dead.[s]

4 For to him that is joined to all the living there is hope: for a living [f]dog is better than a dead [g]lion.

5 For the living know that they shall [c]die: but the dead know not any thing, neither have they any more a reward; for the memory of them is forgotten.

6 Also their [h]love, and their [i]hatred, and their [j]envy, is now perished; neither have they any more a portion for ever in any *thing* that is done under the sun.

7 ¶ [k,l]Go thy way, eat thy bread with [m]joy, and drink thy [n]wine with a merry heart; for God now accepteth thy [o]works.

8 [k]Let thy garments be always [p]white; and let thy head lack no [q]ointment.

9 [k]Live joyfully with the [r]wife whom [s]thou lovest all the days of the life of thy vanity, which he hath given thee under the sun, all the days of thy vanity: for that *is* thy portion in *this* life, and in thy labour which thou takest under the sun.

10 Whatsoever thy hand findeth to do, [t,u,v]do *it* with *,[w]thy might; for [x]*there is* no work, nor device, nor knowledge, nor wisdom, in the grave[c], whither thou goest.

11 ¶ I returned, and saw under the sun, [y]that the [z]race *is* not to the swift, nor the battle to the strong, neither yet bread to the wise, nor yet riches to men of understanding, nor yet favour to men of skill; but time and chance happeneth to them all.

12 For man also knoweth not his time: as the [a]fishes that are taken in an evil [b]net, and as the birds that are [c]caught in the [d]snare; so *are* the sons of men snared in an evil time, when [e]it falleth suddenly upon them.

13 ¶ This [f]wisdom have I seen also under the sun, and it *seemed* great unto me:

14 *There was* a little city, and few men within it; and there came a great king against it, and [g]besieged it, and built great [h]bulwarks against it:

15 Now there was found in it a poor wise man, and he by his [i]wisdom delivered the city; yet [j]no man remembered that same [k]poor man.

16 Then said I, [f]Wisdom *is* better than strength: nevertheless

x *Ignorance, concerning God,* Acts 3:17.

**1**

a *God, sovereign,* Gen. 2:2.

1 R. V. whether it be love or hatred, man knoweth it not; all is before them.

**2**

b *God, providence of, mysterious,* Gen. 2:2.

**3**

c *Death,* Num. 23:10.

d *Heart,* Psa. 44:21.

e *Depravity,* Job 15:14.

**4**

f *Dog,* 1 Kin. 21:19.

g *Lion,* Mic. 5:8.

**6**

h *Love, of man for man,* 1 John 4:7.

i *Hatred,* Prov. 15:17.

j *Envy,* Prov. 14:30.

**7**

k *Commandment, enjoining cheerfulness,* Deut. 8:2.

l *Contentment, enjoined,* vs. 7–9; 1 Tim. 6:6.

m *Joy,* Psa. 5:11.

n *Wine,* Prov. 23:31.

o *Works, good,* 2 Tim. 1:9.

**8**

p *Colors, symbolical,* Ezek. 16:16.

q *Anointing, of the body,* Deut. 28:40.

**9**

r *Wife,* Prov. 5:18.

s *Husband,* Num. 30:6.

**10**

t *Commandment, enjoining diligence,* Deut. 8:2.

u *Diligence, required in business,* Rom. 12:8.

v *Industry, enjoined,* 1 Kin. 11:28.

w *Christian Graces, zeal,* Gal. 5:22.

x *Death, inevitable,* Num. 23:10.

**11**

y *God, providence of, mysterious,* Gen. 2:2.

z *Foot Race, figurative,* Psa. 19:5.

**12**

a *Fish,* Matt. 17:27.

b *Net,* Isa. 51:20.

c *Hunting,* Gen. 27:5.

d *Snare,* Amos 3:5.

e *Death, sudden,* Num. 23:10.

**13**

f *Wisdom,* Prov. 2:2.

**14**

g *Siege,* Deut. 28:53.

h *Bulwark,* Deut. 20:20.

**15**

i *War, wisdom required in,* Judg. 3:2.

j *Ingratitude, of man to man,* Rom. 1:21.

k *Poor, wisdom of, despised,* Prov. 21:13.

* **STRENUOUSNESS.** *Enjoined,* Eccl. 9:10; Rom. 12:11; Eph. 6:10–18; Heb. 12:1, 2. **Instances of:** *Hezekiah,* 2 Chr. 31:20, 21. *Isaiah,* Isa. 62:1. *Jesus,* John 4:34, 35; 9:4. *Paul,* Acts 20:27, 31; 26:19–29; 1 Cor. 9:16–27; 2 Cor. 5:11, 13, 14, 20; 6:3–10; 11:22–33; 12:10, 14, 15; Phil. 3:4–16; 1 Thess. 2:8–11; 2 Tim. 4:7.

17
*l* *Speech, wise,* Col. 4:6.
2 R. V. the wise spoken in quiet are heard more
18
*m* *Evil Company,* Prov. 13:20.

the [k]poor man's wisdom *is* despised, and his words are not
heard.
17 The [l]words of [2]wise *men are*
heard in quiet more than the cry
of him that ruleth among fools.
18 [l]Wisdom *is* better than weapons of war: but one [m]sinner
destroyeth much good.

## CHAPTER 10

*Reflections on wisdom and folly; 16 on riot, 18 slothfulness, 19 and money.*

1
*a* *Ointment,* Eccl. 7:1.
*b* *Apothecary,* Neh. 3:8.
*c* *Wisdom,* Prov. 2:2.
*d* *Prudence,* 2 Chr. 2:12.
1 R. V. outweigh wisdom and honour.
2
*e* *Fool,* Prov. 18:2.
4
*f* *Rulers,* Ex. 18:21.
*g* *Government, duty of citizens to,* Isa. 22:21.
*h* *Citizens, duties of,* Luke 15:15.
*i* *Loyalty, enjoined,* Eccl. 8:2.
*j* *Meekness,* Psa. 45:4.
*k* *Tact,* Prov. 15:1.
2 R. V. allayeth
5
*l* *Rulers, wicked,* Ex. 18:21.
8
*m* *Sin, retroactive,* Rom. 5:12.
*n* *Pit, figurative,* Psa. 7:15.
*o* *Fence, hedge,* Psa. 62:3.
*p* *Serpent,* Num. 21:6.
9
3 R. V. heweth out
10
*q* *Iron,* Prov. 27:17.

DEAD *flies cause the [a]oint-
ment of the [b]apothecary
to send forth a stinking savour:
*so doth* a little folly [1]him that is
in reputation for [c,d]wisdom *and*
honour.
2 A [c]wise man's heart *is* at his
right hand; but a [e]fool's heart at
his left.
3 Yea also, when he that is a
fool walketh by the way, his wisdom faileth *him,* and he saith to
every one *that* he *is* a fool.
4 If the spirit of the [f,g]ruler rise
up against thee, [h,i,j]leave not thy
place; for [k]yielding [2]pacifieth
great offences.
5 There is an evil *which* I
have seen under the sun, as an
error *which* proceedeth from the
[l]ruler:
6 Folly is set in great dignity,
and the rich sit in low place.
7 I have seen servants upon
horses, and princes walking as
servants upon the earth.
8 [m]He that diggeth a [n]pit shall
fall into it; and whoso breaketh
an [o]hedge, a [p]serpent shall bite
him.
9 Whoso [3]removeth stones shall
be hurt therewith; *and* he that
cleaveth wood shall be endan-
gered thereby.
10 If the [q]iron be blunt, and he
do not whet the edge, then must
he put to more strength: but
[c]wisdom *is* profitable to direct.
11 [4]Surely the [r]serpent will
bite without enchantment; and
a babbler is no better.
12 The [s]words of a [c]wise man's
mouth *are* gracious; but the [t]lips
of a [e]fool will swallow up himself.
13 The beginning of the [t]words
of his mouth *is* foolishness: and
the end of his [u]talk *is* mischievous madness.
14 A fool also is full of words: a
man cannot tell what shall be;
and what shall be after him, who
can tell him?
15 The labour of the [e]foolish
wearieth every one of them, because he knoweth not how to go
to the city.
16 ¶ Woe to thee, O land, when
thy king *is* a child, and thy
princes eat in the morning!
17 [5]Blessed *art* thou, O land,
when thy [v]king *is* the son of
nobles, and thy princes eat in
due season, for strength, and not
for drunkenness!
18 ¶ By much [w]slothfulness the
[6]building decayeth; and through
†idleness of the hands the house
[7]droppeth through.
19 ¶ A [x]feast is made for
laughter, and [y]wine maketh
merry: but [z,a]money answereth
all *things.*
20 ¶ [b,c,d]Curse not the [e,f]king,
no not in thy thought; and curse
not the rich in thy bedchamber:
for a bird of the air shall carry
the voice, and that which hath
wings shall tell the matter.

## CHAPTER 11

*An exhortation to works of charity. 7 Admonitions respecting death and judgment.*

[a,b]CAST thy bread upon the
waters: for [c]thou shalt find
it after many days.

11
*r* *Serpent, charming of,* Num. 21:6.
4 R. V. If the serpent bite before it be charmed, then is there no advantage in the charmer.
12
*s* *Speech, wise,* Col. 4:6.
*t* *Speech, foolish,* Col. 4:6.
13
*u* *Speech, evil,* Col. 4:6.
17
*v* *Rulers, character and qualifications of,* Ex. 18:21.
5 R. V. Happy
18
*w* *Laziness,* Prov. 19:15.
6 R. V. roof sinketh in;
7 R. V. leaketh.
19
*x* *Feasts,* Mark 12:39.
*y* *Wine,* Prov. 23:31.
*z* *Money,* Jer. 32:9
*a* *Riches,* Eccl. 4:8
20
*b* *Commandment, enjoining prudence in speech,* Deut. 8:2.
*c* *Speech, evil,* Col 4:6.
*d* *Reverence, for kings,* Lev. 19:30.
*e* *King, loyalty to, enjoined,* 2 Kin. 3:10.
*f* *Rulers, must not be reviled,* Ex. 18:21.
1
*a* *Commandment, enjoining liberality,* Deut. 8:2.
*b* *Faith, enjoined,* Mark 11:22.
*c* *Liberality, rewards for,* 1 Tim. 6:18.

* **FLIES**, Eccl. 10:1. *Plague of,* Ex. 8:21-31; Psa. 78:45; 105:31.
**Figurative**, Isa. 7:18.
† **IDLENESS**, Prov. 15:19; 18:9; 22:13; 26:13-16; Eccl. 4:5; Isa. 56:10; Matt. 20:6, 7; Acts 17:21. *Poverty from,* Prov. 6:6-11; 10:4, 5; 13:4; 14:23; 19:15; 20:4, 13; 23:21; 24:30-34; Eccl. 10:18.
*A sin of Sodom,* Ezek. 16:49.
*Denounced,* Luke 19:20-24; 2 Thess. 3:10, 11; 1 Tim. 5:13.
See footnote, LAZINESS, Prov. 19:15

2 [a]Give a portion to [d]seven, and also to eight; for thou knowest not what evil shall be upon the earth.

3 [e]If the clouds be full of rain, they empty *themselves* upon the earth: and if the tree fall toward the south, or toward the north, in the place where the tree falleth, there it shall be.

4 [f]He that observeth the [e]wind shall not [g]sow; and he that regardeth the [e]clouds shall not reap.

5 As thou knowest not what *is* the way of the [1]spirit, *nor* how the bones *do grow* in the womb of her that is with child: even so thou [h,i]knowest not the works of God who [j,k]maketh all.[S Q]

6 [l,m]In the morning sow thy [n]seed, and in the evening withhold not thine hand: for thou knowest not whether[G] shall prosper, either this or that, or whether they both *shall be* alike good.

7 ¶ Truly the light *is* sweet, and a pleasant *thing it is* for the eyes to behold the sun:

8 But if a man live many years, *and* rejoice in them all; yet let him remember the days of darkness; for they shall be many. All that cometh *is* vanity.

9 ¶ [o,p]Rejoice, O [q]young man, in thy youth; and let thy heart cheer thee in the days of thy youth, and walk in the ways of thine heart, and in the sight of thine eyes: but know thou, that for all these *things* [r]God will bring thee into judgment.[S]

10 Therefore [o]remove sorrow from thy heart, and put away evil from thy flesh: for [2]childhood and youth *are* vanity.

2 — *d Seven*, Gen. 7:2.

3 — *e Meteorology*, Matt. 16:2.

4 — *f Industry, enjoined*, 1 Kin. 11:28. *g Sower*, Matt. 13:3.

5 — *h Ignorance, concerning the works of God*, Acts 3:17. *i God, unsearchable*, Gen. 2:2. *j God, creator*, Gen. 2:2. *k Creation*, Mark 13:19. 1 R. V. wind.

6 — *l Commandment, enjoining diligence*, Deut. 8:2. *m Agriculture, requires diligence*, Gen. 3:23. *n Seed*, Lev. 19:19.

9 — *o Commandment, enjoining regulated pleasures*, Deut. 8:2. *p Worldly Pleasure*, Eccl. 2:1. *q Young Men*, Prov. 1:4. *r God, judge*, Gen. 2:2.

10 — 2 Am. R. V. youth and the dawn of life

## CHAPTER 12

*The young exhorted to remember their Creator. 9 The Preacher's care to edify. 13 The whole duty of man.*

[a]REMEMBER now [b,c]thy [d]Creator in the days of thy youth, while the [e]evil days come not, nor the years draw nigh[G], when thou shalt say, I have no pleasure in them;

2 While the [f]sun, or the light, or the [g]moon, or the [h]stars, be not darkened, nor the clouds return after the rain:

3 [e]In the day when the keepers of the house shall [i]tremble, and the strong men shall bow themselves, and the grinders[G] cease because they are few, and those that look out of the windows be darkened,

4 And the doors shall be shut in the streets, when the sound of the grinding is low, and he shall rise up at the voice of the *bird, and all the daughters of musick shall be brought low;

5 [j]Also *when* they shall be afraid of *that which is* high, and fears *shall be* in the way, and the [j]almond tree shall [1]flourish, and the grasshopper shall be a burden, and [2]desire shall fail: because man [k]goeth to his long home, and the [l]mourners go about the streets:

6 [k]Or ever the silver cord be loosed, or the [m]golden [n]bowl be broken, or the pitcher be broken at the fountain, or the †wheel broken at the [o]cistern.

7 [p]Then shall the [q]dust [r]return to the earth as it was: and the [s]spirit shall [t]return unto [d]God who gave [u]it.

1 — *a Commandment, enjoining remembrance of God*, Deut. 8:2. *b Children, commandments to*, Mark 10:14. *c Young Men*, Prov. 1:4. *d God, creator*, Gen. 2:2. *e Old Age*, Isa. 46:4.

2 — *f Sun*, Josh. 10:12. *g Moon*, Song 6:10. *h Stars*, Judg. 5:20.

3 — *i Infirmity, physical*, John 5:5.

5 — *j Almond, figurative*, Gen. 43:11. *k Death, described*, Num. 23:10. *l Mourning*, Lam. 2:5. 1 R. V. blossom. 2 R. V. the caperberry

6 — *m Gold, figurative*, Ezek. 7:19. *n Bowl, figurative*, Ex. 25:29. *o Cistern, figurative*, Isa. 36:16.

7 — *p Death, separates spirit and body*, Num. 23:10. *q Body*, 1 Cor 6:19. *r Corruption, physical*, Job 17:14. *s Man, spirit*, Job 4:17. *t Immortality*, 1 Cor. 15:54. *u Life, from God*, Eccl. 8:15.

*** BIRDS.** *Creation of, on the fifth creative day*, Gen. 1:20–30. *Man's dominion over*, Gen. 1:26, 28; 9:2, 3; Psa. 8:5–8; Dan. 2:38; Jas. 3:7. *Appointed for food*, Gen. 9:2, 3; Deut. 14:11–20. *Species of, forbidden as food*, Lev. 11:13–20; Deut. 14:12–19.

*Divine care of*, Job 38:41; Psa. 147:9. *Divine care of, used by the Savior as a ground of comfort to believers*, Matt. 10:29; Luke 12:6, 24. *Songs of*, Psa. 104:12; Eccl. 12:4; Song 2:12. *Domesticated*, Job 41:5; Jas. 3:7. *Solomon's proverbs about*, 1 Kin. 4:33. *Nests of*, Psa. 104:17; Matt. 8:20; 13:32. *Instincts of*, Prov. 1:17. *Habits of*, Job 39:13–18, 26–30. *Migrate*, Jer. 8:7.

*Mosaic law protected the mother, from being taken with the young*, Deut. 22:6, 7. *Cages for*, Jer. 5:27; Rev. 18:2.

*Used for sacrifice*, see footnotes: DOVE, Gen. 8:8; PIGEON, Gen. 15:9.

**Figurative**, Isa. 46:11; Jer. 12:9; Ezek. 39:4.

**† WHEEL.** *Potter's*, Jer. 18:3.

**Figurative**, Prov. 20:26; Eccl. 12:6.

**Symbolical**, Ezek. 1:15–21; 3:13; 10:9–19; 11:22.

8 ¶ Vanity of vanities, saith the
preacher; [v]all *is* vanity.
9 And moreover, because the
preacher was wise, he still
[w]taught the people [x]knowledge; yea, he [3]gave good heed,
and [y]sought out, *and* set in order many [z]proverbs.
10 The preacher [y]sought to find
out acceptable [a]words: and *that
which was* written *was* upright,
*even* words of truth.
11 The [a,b]words of the [c]wise
*are* as goads, and as nails [3]fastened *by* the masters of assemblies, *which* are given from one
shepherd.
12 And further, by these, my
[d]son, be admonished: of making
many [e]books *there is* no end; and
much study *is* a weariness of the
flesh.
13 ¶ [4]Let us hear the conclusion
of the whole matter: [f,g]Fear God,
and [h]keep his [i]commandments:
for this *is* the whole ‡*duty* of man.
14 For [j]God shall bring every
work into [k]judgment, with every
secret thing, whether [l]*it be* good,
or whether *it be* [m]evil.

8 v *Life, vanity of,* Eccl. 8:15.
9 w *Instruction,* Prov. 23:23. x *Knowledge,* Luke 11:52. y *Investigation,* Eccl. 1:13. z *Proverbs,* 1 Sam. 24:13. 3 R. V. pondered,
10 a *Speech, wise,* Col. 4:6.
11 b *Words, of the wise,* Luke 4:22. c *Wisdom.* Prov. 2:2. 3 R. V. well fastened are the words of the masters of assemblies,
12 d *Young Men,* Prov. 1:4. e *Book, numerous,* Num. 5:23.
13 f *Commandment, enjoining fear of God and obedience,* Deut. 8:2. g *Fear of God, enjoined,* Acts 9:31. h *Obedience, enjoined,* Heb. 5:8. i *Word of God,* Psa. 119:9. 4 R. V. This is the end of the matter: all hath been heard: fear
14 j *God, judge,* Gen. 2:2. k *Judgment, the general,* 2 Pet. 3:7. l *Works, good,* 2 Tim. 1:9. m *Sin, in secret,* Rom. 5:12.

THE

# SONG OF SOLOMON

## CHAPTER 1

*The bride commends her beloved, 7 and inquires where he feeds his flock. 8 His answer. 12 Their mutual love.*

1 THE song of songs, which *is*
[a]Sŏl′o-mon's.
2 Let him kiss me with the
kisses of his mouth: for thy [b]love
*is* better than wine.
3 [1]Because of the savour of thy
good ointments thy name *is as*
ointment poured forth, therefore
do the virgins love thee.
4 Draw me, we will run after
thee: the king hath brought me
into his chambers: we will be
glad and rejoice in thee, we will
[2]remember thy [b]love more than
wine: [3]the upright love thee.
5 ¶ I *am* black, but comely, O
ye daughters of Jē-ru̦′să-lĕm, as
the tents of [c]Kē′där, as the curtains of [a]Sŏl′o-mon.
6 Look not upon me, because I
*am* [4]black, because the sun hath
[5]looked upon me: my mother's
[6]children were angry with me;
they made me the keeper of the
[d]vineyards; *but* mine own vineyard have I not kept.
7 Tell me, O thou whom my
soul loveth, where [e]thou [7]feedest,
where thou makest *thy flock* to
rest at noon: for why should I be
as one that [8]turneth aside by the
flocks of thy companions?
8 ¶ If thou know not, O thou
fairest among women, go thy
way forth by the footsteps of the
flock, and feed thy kids beside
the shepherds' tents.
9 I have compared thee, O my
love, to a [9]company of horses in
[f]Phā′raōh's [g]chariots.
10 Thy cheeks are comely with
[10]rows *of* [h]*jewels,* thy neck with
chains *of gold.*
11 We will make thee [11]borders
of [i]gold with studs of [j]silver.

1 a *Solomon,* 2 Sam. 12:24.
2 b *Love,* chapters 1–8; 1 John 4:7.
3 1 Am. R. V. Thine oils have a goodly fragrance; Thy name is as oil poured
4 2 R. V. make mention of thy 3 R. V. Rightly do they love thee.
5 c *Kedar,* Jer. 49:28.
6 4 R. V. swarthy, d *Vineyard,* Isa. 1:8. 5 R. V. scorched 6 R. V. sons
7 e *Shepherd,* Jer. 31:10. 7 R. V. feedest thy flock, 8 R. V. is veiled Beside the
9 f *Pharaoh, at the time of Solomon,* 1 Kin. 3:1. g *Chariot,* Josh. 11:4. 9 R. V. steed in
10 h *Jewels,* Gen. 24:53. 10 R. V. plaits of hair, Thy neck with strings of jewels.
11 i *Gold,* Ezek. 7:19. j *Silver,* 1 Chr. 28:14. 11 R. V. plaits

‡ **DUTY.** *Escape from, sought, by Moses,* Ex. 3:11; 4:1, 10, 13; 6:12, 30; *by Jonah,* Jonah 1:1–15; *by Ananias,* Acts 9:13, 14.
**Of man to God:** *To love,* Deut. 11:1; 30:15–20; Josh. 23:11; Psa. 31:23; Jude 21; *with all the heart, with all the soul and with all the strength,* Deut. 6:15; Matt. 22:37; Luke 12:27. *To obey,* Deut. 10:12, 13; 30:15–20; Josh. 22:5; Prov. 23:26; Matt. 12:50; 22:21; 23:23; Luke 17:10; John 14:15, 21; 15:14; Acts 4:19, 20; 5:29. *To worship,* 1 Chr. 16:29; Psa. 29:1, 2; 95:2–7; Matt. 4:10; John 4:23; Rev. 22:9.
**Of man to man:** *To love,* Lev. 19:18; Matt. 19:19; 22:39; Mark 12:31; John 13:34; Rom. 13:8–10; Gal. 5:14; Jas. 2:8. *To help,* Isa. 58:6, 7; Matt. 25:34–46; Luke 10:25–36. *To forgive,* Matt. 18:21–35; Luke 17:3, 4; Eph. 4:32; Col. 3:13. *To practice the Golden Rule toward,* Matt. 7:12. *To respect a brother's conscience,* Rom. 14:1–23; 1 Cor. 8:1–13. *To restore a sinning brother,* Gal. 6:1, 2.

12 ¶ While the king sitteth at his table, my [k]spikenard sendeth forth [12]the smell thereof.

13 [13]A bundle of [l]myrrh *is* my well-beloved unto me; he shall lie all night betwixt my breasts.

14 My beloved *is* unto me *as* a cluster of [14,m]camphire in the [d]vineyards of [n]Ĕn-gē′dī.

15 Behold, thou *art* fair, my love; behold, thou *art* fair; [15]thou *hast* doves' eyes.

16 Behold, thou *art* fair, my beloved, yea, pleasant: also our bed *is* green.

17 The beams of our [o]house *are* [p]cedar, *and* our rafters of [q]fir.

**12**
*k Spikenard,* Song 4:13.
12 R. V. its fragrance.

**13**
*l Myrrh,* Ex. 30:23.
13 R. V. My beloved is unto me as a bundle of myrrh, That lieth betwixt

**14**
*m* Song 4:13.
*n En-gedi,* 2 Chr. 20:2.
14 R. V. henna-flowers

**15**
15 R. V. Thine eyes are as doves.

**17**
*o House,* Esth. 8:1.
*p Cedar,* Isa. 9.10.
*q Fir Tree,* 2 Sam. 6:5.

## CHAPTER 2

*The graces of the bride and her beloved, and their delight in each other. 8 He invites her to behold the beauties of spring. 14 His care of her. 16 Her trust in him.*

I AM the [a]rose of [b]Shâr′on, *and* the [c]lily of the valleys.

2 As the [c]lily among thorns, so *is* my love among the daughters.

3 As the apple tree among the trees of the wood, so *is* my beloved among the sons. I sat down under his shadow with great delight, and his fruit *was* sweet to my taste.

4 He brought me to the banqueting house, and his banner over me *was* [d]love.

5 Stay me with [1]flagons, comfort me with apples: for I *am* sick of love.

6 His left hand *is* under my head, and his right hand doth embrace me.

7 I [2]charge you, O ye daughters of Jĕ-rṳ′sā-lĕm, by the roes, and by the hinds of the field, that ye stir not up, nor [3]awake *my* love, till he please.

8 ¶ The voice of my beloved! behold, he cometh leaping upon the mountains, skipping upon the hills.

9 My beloved is like a roe or a young hart: behold, he standeth behind our wall, he looketh forth at the windows, shewing himself through the lattice.

10 My beloved spake, and said unto me, Rise up, my love, my fair one, and come away.

11 For, lo, the [e]winter is past, the [f]rain is over *and* gone;

12 The flowers appear on the earth; the time of the singing *of* [g]*birds* is come, and the voice of the turtle is heard in our land;

13 The [h]fig tree [4]putteth forth her green figs, and the vines [5]*with* the tender [i]grape give a *good* smell. Arise, my love, my fair one, and come away.

14 O my dove, *that art* in the clefts of the rock, in the [6]secret *places* of the stairs, let me see thy countenance, let me hear thy voice; for sweet *is* thy voice, and thy countenance *is* comely.

15 Take us the [j]foxes, the little foxes, that spoil the [7]vines: for our vines *have* tender [i]grapes.

16 ¶ My beloved *is* mine, and I *am* his: he [8]feedeth among the [c]lilies.

17 Until the day [9]break, and the shadows flee away, turn, my beloved, and be thou like a roe or a young hart upon the mountains of Bē′thēr.

**1**
*a* Isa. 35:1.
*b Sharon,* 1 Chr. 27:29.
*c Lily,* Matt. 6:28.

**4**
*d Love,* 1 John 4:7.

**5**
1 R. V. raisins,

**7**
2 R. V. adjure
3 R. V. awaken love, Until it please.

**11**
*e Winter,* Gen. 8:22.
*f Rain,* 2 Sam. 1:21.

**12**
*g Birds,* Eccl. 12:4.

**13**
*h Fig Tree,* Luke 13:6.
*i Grape,* Lev. 25:5.
4 R. V. ripeneth
5 R. V. are in blossom, They give forth their fragrance.

**14**
6 R. V. covert of the steep place,

**15**
*j Fox,* Psa. 63:10.
7 R. V. vineyards; For our vineyards are in blossom.

**16**
8 R. V. feedeth his flock

**17**
9 R. V. be cool,

## CHAPTER 3

*The bride's despondency. 6 The splendor of the beloved.*

BY night on my bed I sought him whom my soul loveth: I sought him, but I found him not.

2 I will rise now, and go about the city in the streets, and in the broad ways I will seek him whom my soul loveth: I sought him, but I found him not.

3 The [a]watchmen that go about the city found me: *to whom I said,* Saw ye him whom my soul loveth?

4 *It was* but a little that I passed from them, but I found him whom my soul loveth: I

**3**
*a Watchman,* 2 Sam. 18:24.

held him, and would not let him go, until I had brought him into my mother's house, and into the chamber[G] of her that conceived me.

5 I [1]charge you, O ye daughters of Jĕ-ru̥'sā-lĕm, by the roes, and by the hinds of the field, that ye stir not up, nor awake *my* love, till he please.

6 ¶ Who *is* this that cometh out of the wilderness like pillars of smoke, [b]perfumed with [c]myrrh and [d]frankincense, with all powders of the [e]merchant?

7 Behold [2]his bed, which *is* [f]Sŏl'o-mon's; threescore valiant men *are* about it, of the valiant of Ĭṣ'ra-el.

8 They all hold [g]swords, *being* expert in war: every man *hath* his sword upon his thigh because of fear in the night.

9 King [f]Sŏl'o-mon made himself a [3]chariot of the wood of [h]Lĕb'a-non.

10 He made the pillars thereof *of* [i]silver, the bottom thereof *of* [j]gold, the covering of it *of* [k]purple, the midst thereof being paved *with* love, for the daughters of Jĕ-ru̥'sā-lĕm.

11 Go forth, O ye daughters of Zī'ŏn, and behold king [f]Sŏl'o-mon with the crown wherewith his mother crowned him in the day of his espousals, and in the day of the gladness of his heart.

## CHAPTER 4

*The beloved sets forth the graces of the bride. 8 His love for her. 16 Her desire for his presence.*

BEHOLD, thou *art* fair, my love; behold, thou *art* fair; [1]thou *hast* doves' eyes within thy locks: thy hair *is* as a flock of goats, that [2]appear from mount *Gĭl'e-ăd.

2 Thy teeth *are* like a flock

5
1 R. V. adjure

6
*b* *Perfume,* Prov. 27:9.
*c* *Myrrh,* Ex. 30:23.
*d* *Frankincense,* 1 Chr. 9:29.
*e* *Merchant,* Neh. 3:32.

7
*f* *Solomon,* 2 Sam. 12:24.
2 R. V. it is the litter of Solomon;

8
*g* *Sword,* 1 Chr. 21:5.

9
*h* *Lebanon,* Deut. 1:7.
3 R. V. palanquin

10
*i* *Silver,* 1 Chr. 28:14.
*j* *Gold,* Ezek. 7:19.
*k* *Colors, symbolical,* Ezek. 16:16.

1
1 R. V. Thine eyes are as doves behind thy veil:
2 R. V. lie along the side of mount Gilead.

*of* [3]*sheep that are even* shorn, which came up from the washing; whereof every one bear twins, and none *is* [4]barren among them.

3 Thy lips *are* like a thread of scarlet, and thy speech *is* comely[C]: thy temples *are* like a piece of a [a]pomegranate [5]within thy locks.

4 Thy neck *is* like the [b]tower of Dā'vid builded for an [c]armoury, whereon there hang a thousand [d]bucklers, all shields of mighty men.

5 Thy two breasts *are* like two young roes that are twins, which feed among the lilies.

6 Until the day [6]break, and the shadows flee away, I will get me to the mountain of [e]myrrh, and to the hill of [f]frankincense.

7 Thou *art* all fair, my love; *there is* no spot in thee.

8 ¶ Come with me from [g]Lĕb'a-non, *my* [7]spouse, with me from Lĕb'a-non: look from the top of Ăm'a-nȧ, from the top of Shē'nir and [h]Hĕr'mon, from the lions' dens, from the mountains of the [†]leopards.

9 Thou hast ravished my heart, my sister, *my* [7]spouse; thou hast ravished my heart with one of thine eyes, with one chain of thy neck.

10 How fair is thy [i]love, my sister, *my* [7]spouse! how much better is thy love than wine! and the smell of thine [8]ointments[C] than all spices!

11 Thy lips, O *my* [7]spouse, drop *as* the honeycomb: honey and milk *are* under thy tongue; and the smell of thy garments *is* like the smell of [g]Lĕb'a-non.

12 A garden inclosed *is* my sister, *my* [7]spouse; a spring shut up, a fountain sealed.

13 Thy plants *are* an orchard of [a]pomegranates, with [9]pleasant

2
3 R. V. ewes that are newly
4 R. V. bereaved

3
*a* *Pomegranate,* Num. 13:23.
5 R. V. Behind thy veil.

4
*b* *Tower, of David* 2 Chr. 26:9.
*c* *Armory,* Neh. 3:19.
*d* *Shield,* 1 Kin. 14:27.

6
*e* *Myrrh,* Ex. 30:23.
*f* *Frankincense,* 1 Chr. 9:29.
6 R. V. be cool,

8
*g* *Lebanon,* Deut. 1:7.
*h* *Hermon,* Deut. 4:48.
7 R. V. bride,

10
*i* *Love,* 1 John 4:7.
8 Am. R. V. oils

13
9 R. V. precious

* **GILEAD.** *A mountain,* Judg. 7:3; Song 4:1; 6:5. *Laban overtakes Jacob at; good understanding is established, and a covenant is made between them,* Gen. 31:21–25.

† **LEOPARD,** Jer. 13:23; Song 4:8; Hos. 13:7; Hab. 1:8. **Figurative,** Jer. 5:6. *Taming of, of the triumph of the gospel,* Isa. 11:6. *Similitude of,* Dan. 7:6.

j Song 1:14.
10 R. V. Henna
**14**
k *Calamus*, Ezek. 27:19.
l *Aloes*, Psa. 45:8.
m *Spices*, 1 Kin. 10:2.

**1**
a *Myrrh*, Ex. 30:23.
b *Spices*, 1 Kin. 10:2.
c *Honey*, Prov. 25:27.
d *Wine*, Prov. 23:31.
e *Milk*, Job 10:10.
1 R. V. bride:

**3**
f *Ablution, of the feet*, Judg. 19:21.

**4**
g *Bowels, figurative*, 1 Kin. 3:26.
2 R. V heart was moved

**5**
3 R. V. liquid myrrh,
4 R. V. bolt.

fruits; [10,j]camphire, with ‡spike-
nard,
14 ‡Spikenard and saffron; [k]cal-
amus and ‖cinnamon, with all
trees of [f]frankincense; [e]myrrh
and [l]aloes, with all the chief
[m]spices:
15 A fountain of gardens, a
well of living waters, and streams
from [g]Lĕb′a-non.
16 ¶ Awake, O north wind; and
come, thou south; blow upon my
garden, *that* the [m]spices thereof
may flow out. Let my beloved
come into his garden, and eat his
[9]pleasant fruits.

## CHAPTER 5

*The beloved in his garden. 2 The bride's love for him. 9 His graces described.*

I AM come into my garden, my
sister, *my* [1]spouse: I have
gathered my [a]myrrh with my
[b]spice; I have eaten my honeycomb with my [c]honey; I have
drunk my [d]wine with my [e]milk:
eat, O friends; drink, yea, drink
abundantly, O beloved.
2 ¶ I sleep, but my heart
waketh: *it is* the voice of my
beloved that knocketh, *saying*,
Open to me, my sister, my love,
my dove, my undefiled: for my
head is filled with dew, *and* my
locks with the drops of the
night.
3 I have put off my coat; how
shall I put it on? I have [f]washed
my feet; how shall I defile them?
4 My beloved put in his hand
by the hole *of the door*, and my
[2,g]bowels were moved for him.
5 I rose up to open to my beloved; and my hands dropped
*with* myrrh, and my fingers *with*
[3]sweet smelling myrrh, upon the
handles of the [4]lock.
6 I opened to my beloved; but
my beloved had withdrawn himself, *and* was gone: my soul failed
when he spake: I sought him,
but I could not find him; I called
him, but he gave me no answer.
7 The [h]watchmen that went
about the city found me, they
smote me, they wounded me; the
keepers of the walls took away
my [5]veil from me.
8 I [6]charge you, O daughters of
Jĕ-rṳ′să-lĕm, if ye find my beloved, that ye tell him, that I *am*
sick of love.
9 ¶ What *is* thy beloved more
than *another* beloved, O thou
fairest among women? what *is*
thy beloved more than *another* beloved, that thou dost so
[6]charge us?
10 ¶ My beloved *is* white and
ruddy, the chiefest among ten
thousand.
11 His head *is as* the most fine
gold, his locks *are* bushy, *and*
black as a raven.
12 His eyes *are* [7]as *the eyes* of
doves by the rivers of waters,
washed with milk, *and* fitly set.
13 His cheeks *are* as a bed
of spices, *as* sweet flowers: his
lips *like* lilies, dropping [3]sweet
smelling myrrh.
14 His hands *are as* gold rings
set with the [i]beryl: his [8]belly *is*
*as* bright [j]ivory overlaid *with*
[k]sapphires.
15 His legs *are as* pillars of
[l]marble, set upon sockets of fine
gold: his [m]countenance *is* as
[n]Lĕb′a-non, excellent as the
[o]cedars.
16 His mouth *is* most sweet:
yea, he *is* altogether lovely. This
*is* my beloved, and this *is* my
[p]friend, O daughters of Jĕ-rṳ′-
să-lĕm.

## CHAPTER 6

*The bride's confidence in the beloved. 4 He sets forth her graces, 10 and his love for her.*

WHITHER is thy beloved
gone, O thou fairest among
women? whither is thy beloved

**7**
h *Watchman*, 2 Sam. 18:24.
5 R. V. mantle

**8**
6 R. V. adjure

**12**
7 R. V. like doves beside the water brooks;

**14**
i *Beryl*, Ezek. 1:16.
j *Ivory*, 2 Chr. 9:17.
k *Sapphire*, Job 28:6.
8 R. V. body is as ivory work

**15**
l *Marble*, 1 Chr. 29:2.
m *Countenance*, Prov. 15:13.
n *Lebanon*, Deut. 1:7.
o *Cedar*, Isa. 9:10.

**16**
p *Friends*, Ex. 33:11.

‡ **SPIKENARD.** *An aromatic plant*, Song 4:13, 14. *Perfume prepared from*, Song 1:12. *A fragrant oil from, used in anointing*, Mark 14:3; John 12:3.

‖ **CINNAMON.** *A spice*, Prov. 7:17; Song 4:14; Rev. 18:13. *An ingredient of the sacred oil used in the tabernacle and for anointing priests*, Ex. 30:23.

**2**
*a Spices*, 1 Kin. 10:2.
*b Lily*, Matt. 6:28.

**3**
1 R. V. his flock among

**4**
*c Jerusalem*, Judg. 19:10.
*d Armies*, Deut. 11:4.
*e Standard*, Num. 1:52.

**5**
*f Gilead*, Song 4:1.
2 R. V. lie along the side of

**6**
3 R. V. none is bereaved among them.

**7**
4 R. V. Behind thy veil.

**10**
*g Sun*, Josh. 10:12.

**11**
5 R. V. green plants
6 R. V. budded,
7 R. V. were in flower.

turned aside? that we may seek
him with thee.
2 ¶ My beloved is gone down
into his garden, to the beds of
[a]spices, to feed in the gardens,
and to gather [b]lilies.
3 I *am* my beloved's, and my
beloved *is* mine: he feedeth
[1]among the lilies.
4 ¶ Thou *art* beautiful, O my
love, as Tĭr′zah, comely as [c]Jĕ-
ru̇′să-lĕm, terrible as *an* [d]*army*
with [e]banners.
5 Turn away thine eyes from
me, for they have overcome me:
thy hair *is* as a flock of goats
that [2]appear from [f]Gĭl′e-ăd.
6 Thy teeth *are* as a flock of
sheep which go up from the
washing, whereof every one
beareth twins, and [3]*there is* not
one barren among them.
7 As a piece of a pomegranate
*are* thy temples [4]within thy locks.
8 There are threescore queens,
and fourscore concubines, and
virgins without number.
9 My dove, my undefiled is *but*
one; she *is* the *only* one of her
mother, she *is* the choice *one* of
her that bare her. The daughters saw her, and blessed her;
*yea*, the queens and the concubines, and they praised her.
10 ¶ Who *is* she *that* looketh
forth as the morning, fair as the
*moon, clear as the [g]sun, *and*
terrible as *an* [d]*army* with [e]ban-
ners?
11 I went down into the garden of nuts to see the [5]fruits of
the valley, *and* to see whether the
vine [6]flourished, *and* the pomegranates [7]budded.
12 Or ever I was aware, my
soul [8]made me *like* the chariots
of Ăm′mi-nā′dib.
13 Return, return, O Shu̇′lam-
īte; return, return, that we
may look upon thee. [9]What will
ye see in the Shu̇′lam-īte? As
it were the company of two
armies.

## CHAPTER 7

*The bride's graces further described. 12 Her invitation to the beloved.*

HOW beautiful are thy feet
[1]with shoes, O prince's
daughter! the joints of thy
thighs *are* like jewels, the work
of the hands of a cunning workman.
2 [2]Thy navel *is like* a round
goblet, *which* wanteth not liquor: thy belly *is like* an heap
of wheat set about with lilies.
3 Thy two breasts *are* like two
young roes *that are* twins.
4 Thy neck *is* as a tower of
[a]ivory; thine eyes *like* the fish-
pools in [b]Hĕsh′bŏn, by the gate
of Băth–răb′bim: thy nose *is* as
the tower of [c]Lĕb′a-non which
looketh toward [d]Dă-măs′cus.
5 Thine head upon thee *is* like
[e]Cär′mel, and the hair of thine
head like purple; the king *is* held
[3]in the galleries.
6 How fair and how pleasant
art thou, O love, for delights!
7 This thy stature is like to a
*palm tree, and thy breasts to
[4]clusters *of grapes*.
8 I said, I will [5]go up to the
*palm tree, I will take hold of
the boughs thereof: now also
thy breasts shall be as clusters
of the vine, and the smell of
thy [6]nose like apples;
9 And [7]the roof of thy mouth

**12**
8 R. V. set me Among the chariots of my princely people.

**13**
9 R. V. Why will ye look upon the Shulammite, As upon the dance of Mahanaim?

**1**
1 R. V. in sandals,

**2**
2 Am. R. V. Thy body is like a round goblet, Wherein no mingled wine is wanting: Thy waist is like

**4**
*a Ivory*, 2 Chr. 9:17.
*b Heshbon*, Isa. 16:8.
*c Lebanon*, Deut. 1:7.
*d Damascus*, Isa. 8:4.

**5**
*e Carmel*, Jer. 46:18.
3 R. V. captive in the tresses thereof.

**7**
4 Am. R. V. its clusters.

**8**
5 R. V. climb up into
6 R. V. breath

**9**
7 R. V. thy mouth like the best wine, That goeth down smoothly for my beloved, Gliding through the lips of those that are asleep.

* **MOON.** *Called queen of heaven*, Jer. 7:18; 44:17–19, 25. *Created by God*, Gen. 1:16; Psa. 8:3; 136:7–9. *Its light*, Gen. 1:14–17; Job 31:26; Eccl. 12:2; Song 6:10; Jer. 31:35; 1 Cor. 15:41. *Its influences*, Deut. 33:14; Psa. 121:6. *Seasons of* (months), Psa. 104:19. *Joseph's dream concerning*, Gen. 37:9. *Stands still*, Josh. 10:12, 13; Hab. 3:11. *Worship of, forbidden*, Deut. 4:19; 17:3. *Worshiped*, 2 Kin. 23:5; Job 31:26, 27; Jer. 7:18; 8:2; 44:17–19, 25. *No light of, in heaven*, Rev. 21:23.

*Darkening of, figurative of judgments*, Isa. 13:10; 24:23; Ezek. 32:7; Joel 2:10, 31; 3:15; Matt. 24:29; Mark 13:24; Luke 21:25; Acts 2:20; Rev. 6:12; 8:12.

SYMBOLICAL, Rev. 12:1.

**Feast of the new moon**, Num. 10:10; 28:11–15; 1 Chr. 23:31; 2 Chr. 31:3; Ezra 3:5. *Traffic at time of, prohibited*, Amos 8:5.

* **PALM TREE**, Psa. 92:12. *In Palestine*, Judg. 4:5. *Figures of, carved on walls and doors of the temple*, 1 Kin. 6:29, 32, 35; 2 Chr. 3:5. *In the temple seen in the vision of Ezekiel*, Ezek. 40:16; 41:18. *Branches of, used in making booths*, Neh. 8:15; *thrown in the way when Jesus made his triumphal entry into Jerusalem*, John 12:13. *Jericho was called the* CITY OF PALM TREES, Deut. 34:3.

*A symbol of victory*, Rev. 7:9.

like the best wine for my beloved, that goeth *down* sweetly,
causing the lips of those that
are asleep to speak.
10 ¶ I *am* my beloved's, and
his desire *is* toward me.
11 Come, my beloved, let us go
forth into the field; let us lodge
in the villages.
12 Let us get up early to the
vineyards; let us see [3]if the vine
flourish, *whether* the tender grape
appear, *and* the pomegranates
bud forth: there will I give thee
my loves.
13 The [f]mandrakes give a smell,
and at our gates *are* all manner
of pleasant *fruits*, new and old,
*which* I have laid up for thee, O
my beloved.

## CHAPTER 8

*The delight of the bride and her beloved in each other. 6 Love strong as death. 8 The bride's desire in behalf of her sister. 14 She longs for the coming of her beloved.*

O THAT thou *wert* as my
brother, that sucked the
breasts of my mother! *when* I
should find thee without, I would
kiss thee; yea, I should not be
despised.
2 I would lead thee, *and* bring
thee into my mother's house,
*who* would [a]instruct me: I
would cause thee to drink of
spiced [b]wine of the juice of my
[c]pomegranate.
3 His left hand *should be* under my head, and his right hand
should embrace me.
4 I [1]charge you, O daughters
of Jĕ-ru̥'să-lĕm, that ye stir not
up, nor awake *my* love, until he
please.
5 ¶ Who *is* this that cometh up
from the wilderness, leaning upon her beloved? I raised thee up
under the apple tree: there thy
mother brought thee forth: there
she brought thee forth *that* bare
thee.
6 Set me as a seal upon thine
heart, as a seal upon thine arm:
for [d]love *is* strong as [e]death;
[f,g]jealousy *is* cruel as the grave:
[2]the coals thereof *are* coals of
fire, *which hath* a most vehement flame.
7 Many waters cannot quench
[d]love, neither can the floods
drown it: if a man would give
all the substance of his house
for love, it would utterly be
contemned.
8 ¶ We have a little sister, and
she hath no breasts: what shall
we do for our sister in the day
when she shall be spoken for?
9 If she *be* a wall, we will build
upon her a [3]palace of silver: and
if she *be* a door, we will inclose
her with boards of cedar.
10 I *am* a wall, and my breasts
like towers: then was I in his
eyes as one that found favour.
11 Sŏl'o-mon had a vineyard
at Bā'al–hā'mon; he let out the
vineyard unto keepers; every one
for the fruit thereof was to bring
a thousand *pieces* of silver.
12 My vineyard, which *is* mine,
*is* before me: thou, O Sŏl'o-mon,
*must have* a thousand, and those
that keep the fruit thereof two
hundred.
13 Thou that dwellest in the
gardens, the companions heark-
en to thy voice: cause me to
hear *it*.
14 ¶ Make haste, my beloved,
and be thou like to a roe or to a
young hart upon the mountains
of spices.

---

12
3 R. V. whether the vine hath budded, and its blossom be open, And the pomegranates be in flower:

13
*f* Gen. 30:14-16.

2
*a Instruction,* Prov. 23:23.
*b Wine, made from pomegranates,* Prov. 23:31.
*c Pomegranate, wine made of,* Num. 13:23.

4
1 R. V. adjure

6
*d Love,* 1 John 4:7.
*e Death,* Num. 23:10.
*f Jealousy,* Psa 78:58.
*g Envy,* Prov. 14:30.
2 Am. R. V. The flashes thereof are flashes of fire, A very flame of Jehovah.

9
3 R. V. turret

THE

# BOOK OF ISAIAH

## CHAPTER 1

*The prophet mourns over the corruption of Judah. 5 Their chastisement. 10 Their hypocrisy rebuked. 16 An exhortation to repentance. 21 Severer judgments threatened. 25 The purification of Zion, and the destruction of the transgressors.*

1 THE [a,b]vision of *Ī-ṣā'iah the son of [c]Ā'mŏz, which he saw concerning [d]Jū'dah and [e]Jĕ-ru'-sȧ-lĕm in the days of [f]Ŭz-zī'ah, [g]Jō'tham, [h]Ā'hăz, *and* [i]Hĕz-e-kī'ah, [j]kings of Jū'dah.

2 ¶ [b]Hear, O heavens, and give ear, O earth: for the LORD hath spoken, [k]I have nourished and brought up children, and [l]they have rebelled against me.

3 The ox [m]knoweth his owner, and the [n]ass his master's [o]crib[G]: *but* Ĭṣ'ra-el doth [p,q]not know, my people [r]doth not consider.

4 Ah [s]sinful [t]nation, a people [u]laden with iniquity, a seed of evildoers, children that [1]are corrupters: [v]they have forsaken the LORD, they have [2]provoked the [w]Holy One of Ĭṣ'ra-el unto [x]anger, they are gone away backward.

5 Why should ye be stricken any more? ye will [t]revolt more and more: [u]the whole head is [z]sick, and the whole heart faint.

6 From the sole of the foot even unto the head *there is* [z]no soundness in it; *but* [a]wounds, and bruises, and putrifying sores: they have not been closed[G], neither bound up, neither [b]mollified with [3,c,d]ointment.

7 [e]Your country *is* desolate, your [f]cities *are* burned with fire: your land, [g]strangers[G] devour[G] it in your presence, and *it is* desolate, as overthrown by strangers.

8 And the [h]daughter of [i]Zī'ŏn is left as a [4]cottage in a †vineyard, as a lodge[G] in a garden of cucumbers, as a besieged city.

9 [j]Except the [k,l]LORD of hosts had left unto us a very small remnant, we should have been as [m]Sŏd'om, *and* we should have been like unto [n]Gŏ-mŏr'rah.[Q]

10 ¶ Hear the [o]word of the LORD, ye [p]rulers of [q]Sŏd'om; give ear unto the law of our God, ye people of Gŏ-mŏr'rah.[Q]

11 [r]To what purpose *is* the multitude of [s]your [t,u]sacrifices unto me? saith the LORD: I am full of the burnt offerings of rams, and the fat of fed beasts; and I delight not in the blood of bullocks, or of lambs, or of he goats.

12 When [s]ye come to [u]appear before me, who hath required

**1**
*a Vision,* Acts 9:10.
*b Prophecies,* Dan. 9:24.
*c* Isa. 13:1; 2 Kin. 19:2, 20; 20:1.
*d Judah, kingdom of, prophecies concerning,* 2 Chr. 11:17.
*e Jerusalem,* Judg. 19:10.
*f Uzziah,* 2 Chr. 26:1.
*g Jotham,* 2 Kin. 15:5.
*h Ahaz,* 2 Kin. 15:38.
*i Hezekiah,* 2 Kin. 16:20.
*j King,* 2 Kin. 3:10.

**2**
*k God, fatherhood of,* Gen. 2:2.
*l Backsliding, of Israel,* Hos. 11:7.

**3**
*m Animals, instincts of,* Jer. 27:5.
*n Ass,* 2 Chr. 28:15.
*o* Job 39:9; Prov. 14:4.
*p Ignorance,* Acts 3:17.
*q Spiritual Blindness,* 2 Cor. 4:4.
*r Ingratitude, of man to God,* Rom. 1:21.

**4**
*s Wicked, described,* Psa. 73:3. *t Nation,* Isa. 2:4. *u Depravity,* Job 15:14. *v Backsliders,* Jer. 3:22. *w God, holiness of,* Gen. 2:2. *x Anger of God,* 2 Kin. 13:3. 1 R. V. deal corruptly: 2 R. V. despised the Holy One of Israel, they are estranged and gone backward.
**5** *y Obduracy,* Prov. 29:1. *z Disease, figurative,* Ex. 15:26.

**6**
*a* Luke 10:34.
*b Disease, remedies used,* Ex. 15:26.
*c Anointing, the sick,* Deut. 28:40.
*d Medicine,* Prov. 17:22.
3 R. V. oil.

**7**
*e Judgments,* Ex. 6:6.
*f Cities,* Num. 35:8.
*g Foreigners,* Deut. 23:20.

**8**
*h Church,* Matt. 16:18.
*i Zion,* 2 Sam. 5:7.
4 R. V. booth

**9**
*j* Rom. 9:29.
*k God, preserver,* Gen. 2:2.
*l God, mercy of,* Gen. 2:2.
*m Sodom, destroyed,* Gen. 13:10.
*n Gomorrah, destroyed,* Gen. 13:10.

**10**
*o Word of God,* Psa. 119:9.
*p Rulers,* Ex. 18:21.
*q Sodom, figurative,* Gen. 13:10.

**11**
*r Hypocrisy, abhorred of God,* Jas. 3:17.
*s Wicked, worship of, offensive to God,* Psa. 73:3. *t Offerings, unavailing when not accompanied by piety,* Lev. 6:17. *u Worship, of hypocrites,* Gen. 22:5.

---

*** ISAIAH** (*salvation of Jehovah*). *Son of Amos,* Isa. 1:1. *Prophesies in the days of Uzziah, Jotham, Ahaz, and Hezekiah, kings of Judah,* Isa. 1:1; 6:1; 7:1, 3; 14:28; 36:1; 38:1; 39:1; *at the time of the invasion by Tartan, of Assyria,* Isa. 20:1. *Vision of,* Isa. 6:1–10. *Symbolically wears sackcloth, and walks barefoot, as a sign to Israel,* Isa. 20:2, 3. *Comforts and encourages Hezekiah and the people in the siege of Jerusalem by Rab-shakeh,* 2 Kin. 19:5–7, 20–34; Isa. 37:5–7. *Comforts Hezekiah in his affliction,* 2 Kin. 20:1–11; Isa. 38:1–8, 21. *Gives the sign of the returning shadow to confirm Hezekiah's faith,* 2 Kin. 20:8–11; Isa. 38:7, 8. *Reproves Hezekiah's folly in exhibiting his resources to the commissioners from Babylon,* 2 Kin. 20:12–19; Isa. 39. *Is chronicler of the times of Uzziah and Hezekiah,* 2 Chr. 26:22; 32:32.

*Foreshadows the person and the kingdom of the Messiah,* Isa. 9:1–7; chapters 32–35; 42; 49; 50:5–9; and chapters 52–55; 59:15–21; and chapters, 60–63; 65; 66:10–23. *Foretells the conversion of the Gentiles, and triumph of the gospel,* Isa. 45:5–25.

**† VINEYARD.** *Cottages or booths in,* Isa. 1:8. *Tower and wine press in,* Isa. 5:2; Matt. 21:33; Mark 12:1. *Leased,* Song 8:11, 12; Isa. 7:23; Matt. 21:33–41. *Of kings,* 1 Chr. 27:27. *Of Naboth taken by Ahab,* 1 Kin. 21:16. *Neglected,* Prov. 24:30, 31. *Plain of the,* Judg. 11:33.

*Parables of, to illustrate the church,* Isa. 5:1–7; 27:2, 3; Jer. 12:10; Matt. 20:1–16; 21:28–31, 33–41; Mark 12:1–9; Luke 13:6–9.

See footnotes: VINE, Judg. 13:14; WINE, Prov. 23:31.

this at your hand, to [5]tread[G] my
[v]courts?
13 [r,s,u]Bring no more vain [t]ob-
lations[G]; [w]incense is an [x]abomina-
tion unto me; the new [y]moons
and [z]sabbaths, the calling of assemblies, [6]I cannot away[G] with;
*it is* iniquity, even the solemn
meeting.
14 [t]Your new [y]moons and your
appointed [a]feasts my soul hateth: they are a trouble unto me;
I am weary to bear *them*.
15 And when ye [b]spread[G] forth
your hands, I will [c]hide mine
eyes from you: yea, when [d]ye
make many [e]prayers, I will not
hear: your hands are full of blood.[Q]
16[T] [f,g,h]Wash you, make you
[i]clean; [j]put away the [k]evil of
your doings from before mine
eyes; cease to do evil;[Q]
17 Learn to do well; seek [l]judg-
ment,[G] [m]relieve the [n]oppressed,
judge the [o]fatherless, plead for
the [p]widow.[T]
18 ¶ Come now, and let us
[q,r]reason together, saith the
LORD: [s]though your sins be as
[t,u]scarlet, [v,w]they shall be as
[x,y]white as [z]snow: though they
be [t,u]red like crimson, [v,w]they
shall be [y]as wool.[T]
19 [a]If ye be [b]willing and [c]obedi-
ent, [d,e]ye shall eat the good of
the land:
20 But if ye [f]refuse and rebel,
[g]ye shall be [h]devoured[G] with the
[i]sword: for the mouth of the
[j]LORD hath spoken *it*.
21 ¶ How is the faithful [k]city
[l]become an harlot! it was full of
judgment; [m]righteousness lodged
in it; but now [n]murderers.
22 Thy [m]silver is become [o]dross,
thy [p]wine mixed with water:
23 Thy [q]princes *are* rebellious,
and companions of [r,s]thieves:
every one [t]loveth [u]gifts[G], and
followeth after rewards: [v]they
judge not the [w]fatherless, neither
doth the cause of the [x]widow
come unto them.
24 Therefore saith the [j]LORD,
the LORD of hosts, the [y]mighty
One of Iṣ′ra-el, Ah, I will ease[G]
me of mine adversaries, and
avenge me of mine enemies:[S]
25 And I will turn my [z]hand
upon thee, and [7]purely [a]purge
away thy [b]dross, and take away
all thy tin:
26 And I will restore thy
[c]judges as at the first, and thy
counsellors as at the beginning:
afterward thou shalt be called,
The city of [d]righteousness, the
faithful city.
27 [e]Zī′ŏn shall be redeemed
with judgment[G], and her converts
with [d]righteousness.[S]
28 And the [f]destruction of the
transgressors and of the sinners
*shall be* together, and they that
[g]forsake the LORD shall be consumed.
29 For they shall be ashamed
of the oaks[G] which ye have desired, and ye shall be confounded[G]
for the gardens that ye have
chosen.
30 For ye shall be as an oak
whose leaf fadeth, and as a garden that hath no water.
31 And the [f]strong shall be as
[h]tow[G], and [8]the maker of it as a
spark, and they shall both burn
together, and none shall quench
*them*.

## CHAPTER 2

*The future prosperity of Zion. 6 The wickedness of the people the cause of God's forsaking them. 10 A warning in view of God's judgments.*

THE [a]word that [b]Ī-ṣā′iah the
son of [c]Ā′mŏz saw concerning [d]Jū′dah and [e]Jĕ-ru′sā-lĕm.
2 And it shall come to pass
in the last days, *that* the [f]moun-

---

**12**
v *Church, called courts,* 1 Kin. 9:3.
5 R. V. trample
**13**
w *Incense,* Ex. 37:29.
x *Abomination,* Lev. 18:27.
y *Moon, feast of the,* Song 6:10.
z *Sabbath,* Ex. 16:23.
6 R. V. I cannot away with iniquity and the solemn meeting.
**14**
a *Annual Feasts,* Num. 15:3.
**15**
b *Prayer, postures in,* Acts 6:4.
c *Anthropomorphisms,* Gen. 11:5.
d *Wicked, prayers of, not answered,* Psa. 73:3.
e *Prayer, of wicked not heard,* Acts 6:4.
**16**
f *Washing, figurative,* Matt. 27:24.
g *Spiritual Purification,* Psa. 51:2.
h *Commandment, enjoining holiness,* vs. 17, 18; Deut. 8:2.
i *Holiness,* Ex. 39:30.
j *Repentance, enjoined,* v. 17; Mark 1:4.
k *Sin, repugnant to God,* Rom. 5:12.
**17**
l *Justice,* Deut. 33:21.
m *Kindness, enjoined,* Acts 28:2.
n *Oppression,* Eccl. 5:8.
o *Orphan,* Lam. 5:3.
p *Widow,* 2 Sam. 14:5.
**18**
q *Reasoning,* Job 13:6.
r *Anthropomorphisms,* Gen. 11:5.
s *God, mercy of,* Gen. 2:2.
t *Colors, scarlet, symbol of iniquity,* Ezek. 16:16.
u *Sin, sinfulness of,* Rom. 5:12.
v *Promise, to penitents,* 2 Cor. 1:20.
w *Sin, forgiveness of,* Rom. 5:12.
x *Colors, symbol of holiness,* Ezek. 16:16. y *Purity, of heart,* 1 Tim. 4:12. z *Snow, illustrative,* Jer. 18:14. **19**—a *Blessings, contingent upon obedience,* Deut. 11:26. b *Faithfulness, rewards of,* Luke 16:10. c *Obedience, rewarded,* Heb. 5:8. d *Reward, a motive, to faithfulness,* Matt. 5:12. e *Promise, to the obedient,* 2 Cor. 1:20. **20** f *Disobedience to God,* Eph. 5:6. g *Fear of God,* Acts 9:31. h *Sin, punishment of,* Rom. 5:12. i *Judgments,* Ex. 6:6. j *God, sovereign,* Gen. 2:2. **21** k *Jerusalem,* Judg. 19:10. l *Backsliding,* Hos. 11:7. m *Righteousness,* Psa. 15:2. n *Homicide, felonious,* Deut. 5:17. **22** o Psa. 119:119. p *Wine, figurative,* Prov. 23:31.

**23**
q *Rulers, corrupted by gifts,* Ex. 18:21.
r *Thieves,* Deut. 24:7.
s *Evil Company,* Prov. 13:20.
t *Covetousness, reproof for,* Isa. 57:17.
u *Bribery, perverts justice,* 1 Sam. 8:3.
v *Court, corrupt,* Ex. 18:26.
w *Orphan,* Lam. 5:3.
x *Widow,* 2 Sam. 14:5.
**24**
y *God, omnipotent,* Gen. 2:2.
**25**
z *Divine Chastisement,* Job 33:19.
a *Refining, figurative,* 1 Chr. 28:18.
b Psa. 119:119.
7 R. V. thoroughly
**26**
c *Judge,* Judg. 2:18.
d *Righteousness,* Psa. 15:2.
**27**
e *Zion,* 2 Sam. 5:7.
**28**
f *Wicked, punishment of,* Psa. 73:3.
g *Apostasy,* Acts 1:25.
**31**
h Judg. 16:9.
8 R. V. his work as
**1**
a *Vision,* Acts 9:10.
b *Isaiah,* Isa. 1:1.
c Isa. 1:1; 2 Kin. 19:2, 20; 20:1.
d *Judah, prophecies concerning,* 2 Chr. 11:17.
e *Jerusalem,* Judg. 19:10.
**2**
f *Jesus, kingdom of, prophecies concerning,* Matt. 1:21.

tain of the [g]LORD's house shall
be established in the top of the
mountains, and shall be exalted
above the hills; and all [h]nations
shall flow unto it.
3 [i]And many people shall go
and [i]say, Come ye, and let us go
up to the [j]mountain of the LORD,
to the house of the God of Jā′-
cob; and [k]he will [l]teach us of his
[m]ways, and we will walk in his
paths: for out of [n]Zī′ŏn shall go
forth the law, and the [o]word of
the LORD from [e]Jė-rṳ′să-lĕm.[T Q]
4 [i]And he shall [p]judge among
the *nations, and shall rebuke
many people: and [q]they shall
beat their [r]swords into [s]plow-
shares, and their [t]spears into
[u]pruninghooks: [v]nation shall not
lift up sword against nation,
neither shall they learn [w]war
any more.[T Q]
5 ¶ O house of Jā′cob, come ye,
and let us walk in the [m, x]light of
the LORD.[T Q]
6 Therefore thou hast forsaken
thy [y]people the house of Jā′cob,
[z]because they be [1]replenished
from the east, and *are* [a]sooth-
sayers[G] like the [b]Phĭ-lĭs′tĭneș, and
they [2]please themselves in the
children of [c]strangers.[C]
7 Their land also is full of [d]sil-
ver and [e]gold, neither *is there any*
end of their [f]treasures; their land
is also full of [g]horses, neither *is
there any* end of their [h]chariots:
8 Their land also is full of idols;
they [i]worship the work of their
own hands, that which their own
fingers have made:
9 And the mean[C] man [3]boweth
down, and the great man [4]hum-
bleth himself: therefore forgive
them not.
10 ¶ Enter[Q] into the rock, and
hide thee in the dust, [5]for fear of
the LORD, and for the [j]glory of
his majesty.
11 The [k]lofty[C] looks of man
[l, m]shall be humbled, and the
haughtiness of men shall be
bowed down, and the LORD
alone shall be exalted in that
[n]day.[T Q]
12 For the [n]day of the LORD of
hosts [l, m]*shall be* upon every *one
that is* [k]proud and lofty, and upon every *one that is* lifted up; and
he shall be brought low:
13 And upon all the cedars of
[o]Lĕb′a-non, *that are* high and
lifted up, and upon all the oaks
of [p]Bā′shăn,
14 And upon all the high mountains, and upon all the hills *that
are* lifted up,
15 And upon every high tower,
and upon every fenced[C] wall,
16 And upon all the ships of
[q]Tär′shish, and upon all pleasant [6]pictures.
17 And the [k]loftiness of man
[l, m]shall be bowed down, and the
haughtiness of men shall be
made low: and the LORD alone
shall be exalted in that [n]day.
18 And [r]the idols [7]he shall utterly abolish.

g *Church, prophecies concerning its universality,* Matt. 16:18.
h *Gentiles, prophecies of the conversion of,* Acts 10:45.

3

i *Worship, summons to,* Gen. 22:5.
j *Church, its mission,* vs. 4, 5; Matt. 16:18.
k *Jesus, prophecies concerning,* Matt. 1:21.
l *Instruction, in religion,* Prov. 23:23.
m *Wisdom, spiritual,* Prov. 2:2.
n *Zion,* 2 Sam. 5:7.
o *Gospel, prophecies concerning,* vs. 4, 5; Mark 13:10.

4

p *Jesus, judge,* Matt. 1:21.
q *Zeal,* 2 Cor. 7:11.
r *Sword,* 1 Chr. 21:5.
s Joel 3:10; Mic. 4:3.
t *Spear,* 2 Kin. 11:10.
u *Hooks, for pruning,* Ex. 36:36.
v *Peace, promised,* Jer. 29:7.
w *War, to cease,* Judg. 3:2.

5

x *Light, figurative,* Matt. 5:14.

6

y *Backsliders, forsaken by God,* Jer. 3:22.
z *Sin, repugnant to God,* Rom. 5:12.

a *Sorcery,* Isa. 47:9.
b *Philistines,* Gen. 26:14.
c *Foreigners,* Deut. 23:20.
1 R. V. filled with customs from
2 R. V. strike hands with the

**7** d *Silver,* 1 Chr. 28:14. e *Gold,* Ezek. 7:19. f *Riches,* Eccl. 4:8. g *Horse,* Job 39:19. h *Chariot,* Josh. 11:4.

8

i *Idolatry, folly of,* 1 Sam. 15:23.

9

3 R. V. is bowed down,
4 R. V. is brought low:

10

j *God, glory of,* Gen. 2:2.
5 Am. R. V. from before the terror of Jehovah, and from the

11

k *Pride,* Prov. 16:18.
l *Wicked, punishment of,* Psa. 73:3.
m *Judgments,* Ex. 6:6.
n *Day, figurative,* Gen. 1:5.

13

o *Lebanon,* Deut. 1:7.
p *Bashan,* Num. 32:33.

16

q *Tarshish,* 2 Chr. 20:36.
6 R. V. imagery.

18

r *Idolatry, prophecies relating to,* 1 Sam. 15:23.
7 R. V. shall utterly pass away.

* **NATION.** *People divided into nations after the flood,* Gen. 10:1–32. *Ordained of God,* Acts 17:26. *Righteousness exalts,* Prov. 14:34.

*Involved in sins, of rulers,* Gen. 20:4, 9; 2 Sam. 24:10–17; 1 Kin. 15:26, 30, 34; 2 Kin. 24:3; 1 Chr. 21:7–17; Jer. 15:4; *of other individuals, as Achan,* Josh. 7:1, 11–26.

*Atonement made for,* 2 Chr. 29:21.

*Penitent, promises to,* Lev. 26:40–42; Deut. 4:29–31; 5:29; 30:1–10; 2 Chr. 7:13, 14; Jer. 3:22.

*In adversity, prayer of,* Judg. 6:7; 10:10; 21:2–4; Jer. 3:21; 31:18.

*In adversity, prayer for,* Ezra 9:6–15; Neh. 1:4–11; Psa. 74; 85:1–7; Isa. 63:7–19; Jer. 14:7, 20; Lam. 2:20–22; Dan. 9:3–21.

*Peace of,* Job 34:29; Psa. 33:12; 89:15–18. *Promises of peace to,* Lev. 26:6; 1 Chr. 22:9; Psa. 46:9; 72:3, 7; Isa. 2:4; 14:4–7; 60:17, 18; 65:25; Jer. 30:10; 50:34; Hos. 2:18; Mic. 4:3, 4; Zech. 1:11; 3:10; 8:4, 5; 9:10; 14:11. *Prayer for peace of,* Jer. 29:7; 1 Tim. 2:1, 2. *Peace given to, by God,* Josh. 21:44; 1 Chr. 22:18; 23:25; Psa. 46:9; 147:13, 14; Isa. 45:7. *Instances of peace of,* Josh. 14:15; Judg. 3:11, 30; 1 Kin. 4:24, 25.

*Chastisement of,* Lev. 18:24–30; 26:28; Deut. 11:2; 2 Chr. 6:24, 26, 28; 7:13, 14; Psa. 106:43; Jer. 2:30; 30:14; 31:18–20; 46:28; Lam. 1:5; Hos. 7:12; 10:10; Hag. 2:17.

*Judgments denounced against, on account of its unrighteousness,* Deut. 9:5; Psa. 9:17; Isa. 3:4–8; 14:24–27; 19:4; 59:1–15; 60:12; Jer. 2:19, 35–37; 5:6–29; 6; 9:7–26; 12:14, 17; 18:6–10; 25:12–33; 50:45, 46; 51; Ezek. 2:9, 10; 7; 22:13–31; 24:6–24; 33:25–29; Hos. 4:1–10; 7:12, 13, 16; 13; Amos 2; 3; 5; 9:8–10; Mic. 6:13–16; Zeph. 3:8.

Instances of punishment of: *The Canaanites,* Deut. 9:5. *The Sodomites,* Gen. 19:24, 25, 28, 29; Lam. 4:6. *The Egyptians,* Ex. chapters 7–11; 12:1–36; 14. *The Israelites,* 2 Sam. 21:1; 24:14–16; 2 Kin. 24:2–4, 20; 2 Chr. 28:1, 5–8, 16–19; 29:8, 9; 30:7; 36:16–20; Ezra 9:7; Neh. 9:36, 37; Jer. 2:15, 16; 5:3; 30:11–15; Lam. 1:3, 8, 14; Ezek. 36:16–20; 39:17–24; Joel 1:1–20; Amos 4:6–11.

19
s *Conscience, guilty*, Acts 23:1.

20
t *Idol*, 1 Kin. 15:12.
u Lev. 11:30.
v Lev. 11:19; Deut. 14:18.

22
w *False Confidence*, Psa. 30:6.

1
a *Famine, sent as a judgment*, 2 Kin. 8:1.
b *Judgments*, Ex. 6:6.
c *Jerusalem, prophecies against*, Judg. 19:10.
d *Judah, kingdom of, prophecies concerning*, vs. 1–26; 2 Chr. 11:17.

2
e *Soldiers*, Ezra 8:22.
f *Judge*, Judg. 2:18.

19 And [†,s]they shall go into the
holes of the rocks, and into the
caves of the earth, [5]for fear of
the LORD, and for the [j]glory of
his majesty, when he ariseth to
shake terribly the earth.[Q]
20 [r]In that [n]day a man shall
cast[C] his [t]idols of silver, and his
idols of gold, which they made
*each one* for himself to worship, to the [u]moles and to the
[v]bats;
21 [†,s]To go into the clefts of the
rocks,[C] and into the tops of the ragged rocks, [5]for fear of the LORD,
and for the [j]glory of his majesty,
when he ariseth to shake terribly the earth.[Q]
22 [w]Cease ye from man, whose
breath *is* in his nostrils: for
wherein is he to be accounted of?

## CHAPTER 3

*The calamities about to come upon Jerusalem and Judah for their sins. 12 The oppression and covetousness of the rulers. 16 Judgments threatened for the pride of the women.*

FOR, behold, the Lord, the
LORD of hosts, doth [a,b]take
away from [c]Jĕ-ru̍'să-lĕm and
from [d]Jū'dah the stay and the
staff, the whole stay of bread, and
the whole stay of water,
2 The mighty man, and the
[e]man of war, the [f]judge, and the
*prophet, and the [1]prudent, and
the ancient,
3 The [e,g]captain of [h]fifty, and
the honourable man, and the
[i]counsellor, and the cunning[C] artificer,[C] and the [2]eloquent orator.
4 And I will give children *to be*
their princes, and babes shall
rule over them.
5 And [j]the people shall be oppressed, every one by another,
and every one by his neighbour:
the [k]child shall behave himself
proudly against the ancient, and
the base against the honourable.
6 [j]When a man shall take hold
of his brother of the house of his
father, *saying*, Thou hast clothing, be thou our ruler, and *let*
this ruin *be* under thy hand:
7 [j]In that day shall he swear,[C]
saying, I will not be an healer;
for in my house *is* neither bread
nor clothing: make me not a
ruler of the people.
8 For [c]Jĕ-ru̍'să-lĕm is [l]ruined,
and [d]Jū'dah is fallen: because
their tongue and their doings *are*
against the LORD, to provoke
the eyes[C] of his glory.
9 [m,n]The shew of their [o]coun-
tenance doth witness against
them; and they declare their sin
as [p]Sŏd'om, they hide *it* not. Woe

1 R. V. diviner.

3
g *Captain*, Num. 31:48.
h *Armies*, Deut. 11:4.
i *Counselor*, Prov. 11:14
2 R. V. skilful enchanter.

5
j *Anarchy*, Jude 8.
k *Children, wicked*, Mark 10:14.

8
l *Nation, punishment of*, Isa. 2:4.

9
m *Sin, fruits of*, Rom. 5:12.
n *Character, revealed in countenance*, Phil. 2:15.
o *Countenance, guilty*, Prov. 15:13.
p *Sodom, wickedness of*, Gen. 13:10.

† **TERROR OF THE WICKED,** Isa. 2:10, 19; Hos. 10:8; Luke 23:30; Rev. 6:15, 16.

* **PROPHETS.** *Called* SEERS, 1 Sam. 9:19; 2 Sam. 15:27; 24:11; 2 Kin. 17:13; 1 Chr. 9:22; 29:29; 2 Chr. 9:29; 12:15; 29:30; Isa. 30:10; Mic. 3:7. *Schools for*, 1 Kin. 20:35; 2 Kin. 2:3, 5, 7, 15–18; 4:1, 38; 9:1. *Kept the chronicles*, 1 Chr. 29:29; 2 Chr. 9:29; 12:15. *Officiate at installation of kings*, 1 Kin. 1:32–35. *Counselors to kings*, 1 Kin. 22:6–28; 2 Kin. 6:9–12; Isa. 37:2, 3; Jer. 27:12–15. *Not honored in their own country*, Matt. 13:57; Luke 4:24–27; John 4:44. *Persecutions of*, 2 Chr. 36:16; Amos 2:12. *Martyrs*, Jer. 2:30; Matt. 23:37; Mark 12:5; Luke 13:34; 1 Thess. 2:15; Heb. 11:37; Rev. 16:6.

**Inspiration of**, 1 Kin. 13:20; 2 Chr. 33:18; 36:15; Neh. 9:30; Job 33:14–16; Jer. 7:25; Dan. 9:6, 10; Hos. 12:10; Joel 2:28; Amos 3:7, 8; Zech. 7:12; Luke 1:70; Acts 3:18; Rom. 1:1, 2; 1 Cor. 12:7–11; Heb. 1:1; 2 Pet. 1:21; Rev. 10:7; 22:6, 8. *Of Enoch*, Jude 14. *Of Joseph*, Gen. 40:8; 41:16, 38, 39. *Of Moses*, Ex. 3:14, 15; 4:12, 15, 27; 6:13, 29; 7:2; 19:9–19; 24:16; 25:22; 33:9, 11; Lev. 1:1; Num. 1:1; 7:8, 9; 9:8–10; 11:17, 25; 12:6–8; 16:28, 29; Deut. 1:5, 6; 5:4, 5, 31; 34:10, 11; Psa. 103:7. *Of Aaron*, Ex. 6:13; 12:1. *Of Eleazar*, Num. 26:1. *Of Balaam*, Num. 23:5, 16, 20, 26; 24:2–4, 15, 16. *Of Joshua*, Josh. 4:15. *Of Samuel*, 1 Sam. 3:1, 4–10, 19–21; 9:6, 15–20; 15:16. *Of Saul*, 1 Sam. 10:6, 7, 10–13; 19:23, 24. *Of messengers of Saul*, 1 Sam. 19:20, 23. *Of David*, 2 Sam. 23:2, 3; Mark 12:36. *Of Nathan*, 2 Sam. 7:3, 4, 8. *Of Gad*, 2 Sam. 24:11. *Of Ahijah*, 1 Kin. 14:5. *Of Elijah*, 1 Kin. 17:1, 24; 19:15; 2 Kin. 10:10. *Of Micaiah*, 1 Kin. 22:14, 28; 2 Chr. 18:27. *Of Elisha*, 2 Kin. 2:9; 3:11, 12, 15; 15:8; 6:8–12, 32. *Of Jahaziel*, 2 Chr. 20:14. *Of Azariah*, 2 Chr. 15:1, 2. *Of Zechariah, the son of Jehoiada*, 2 Chr. 24:20; 26:5. *Of Isaiah*, 2 Kin. 20:4; Isa. 6:1–9; 8:11; 44:26; Acts 28:25. *Of Jeremiah*, 2 Chr. 36:12; Jer. 1; 2:1; 7:1; 11:1, 18; 13:1–3; 16:1; 18:1; 20:9; 23:9; 24:4; 25:3; 26:1, 2, 12; 27:1, 2; 29:30; 33:1; 34:1; 42:4, 7; Dan. 9:2. *Of Ezekiel*, Ezek. 1:1, 3; 2:1, 2, 4, 5; 3:10–12, 14, 16, 17, 22, 24, 27; 8:1; 11:1, 4, 5, 24; 33:22; 37:1; 40:1; 43:5, 6. *Of Daniel*, Dan. 2:19; 7:16; 8:16; 9:22; 10:7–9. *Of Hosea*, Hos. 1:1, 2. *Of Joel*, 1:1. *Of Amos*, Amos 3:7, 8; 7:14, 15. *Of Obadiah*, Obad. 1:1. *Of Jonah*, Jonah 1:1; 3:1, 2. *Of Micah*, Mic. 1:1; 3:8. *Of Habakkuk*, Hab. 1:1. *Of Haggai*, Hag. 1:13. *Of Zechariah, the son of Berechiah*, Zech. 2:9; 7:8. *Of Elisabeth*, Luke 1:41. *Of Zacharias*, Luke 1:67. *Of Simeon*, Luke 2:26, 27. *Of John the Baptist*, Luke 3:2. *Of the apostles*, Acts 2:4. *Of Philip*, Acts 8:29. *Of Agabus*, Acts 11:28; 21:10, 11. *Of disciples at Tyre*, Acts 21:4. *Of John, the apostle*, Rev. 1:10, 11.

*Inspired by angels*, Zech. 1:9, 13, 14, 19; Acts 7:53; Gal. 3:19; Heb. 2:2.

**Emoluments of:** *Presents*, 1 Sam. 9:7, 8; 1 Kin. 14:3; 2 Kin. 4:42; 8:8, 9; Ezek. 13:19. *Presents refused by*, Num. 22:18; 1 Kin. 13:7, 8; 2 Kin. 5:5, 16.

**False**, Deut. 18:21, 22; 1 Kin. 13:18; Neh. 6:12; Jer. 23:16–27, 30–32; Lam. 2:14. *Warnings against*, Deut. 13:1–3; Matt. 24:5, 23, 24, 26; Mark 13:6, 21, 22; Luke 21:8. *Punishment of*, Deut. 18:20; Jer. 14:13–16; 20:6; 28:16, 17; 29:32; Zech. 13:3. *Drunken*, Isa. 28:7.

INSTANCES OF FALSE: *Noadiah*, Neh. 6:14; *four hundred in Samaria*, 1 Kin. 22:6–12; 2 Chr. 18:5; *Pashhur*, Jer. 20:6; *Hanani*, Jer. 28; Rom. 15:16.

**Idolatrous**, 1 Kin. 18:19, 22, 25–28, 40.

q *Sin, retroactive,* Rom. 5:12.

**10**

r *Righteous, promises to,* Psa. 64:10.

s *Promise, to the righteous,* 2 Cor. 1:20.

t *Judgment, according to opportunity and works,* 1 Pet. 1:17.

u *Reward, a motive, to faithfulness,* Matt. 5:12.

**11**

v *Wicked, punishment of,* Psa. 73:3.

**12**

w *Women, as rulers,* Prov. 31:10.

**13**

x *God, judge,* Gen. 2:2.

**14**

y *Rulers, wicked,* Ex. 18:21.

z *Oppression,* Eccl. 5:8.

a *Poor, oppressions of,* Prov. 21:13.

**15**

3 Am. R. V. Jehovah

**16**

b *Pride,* vs. 17–26; Prov. 16:18.

c *Women, ornaments of,* Prov. 31:10.

d *Feet, bells worn on,* 2 Sam. 4:4.

**17**

e *Divine Chastisement,* Job 33:19.

f *Scab,* Lev. 14:56.

g *Disease, as judgment,* Ex. 15:26.

4 R. V. lay bare

**18**

h Ezek. 24:17.

5 Am. R. V. beauty of their anklets, and the cauls, and the crescents;

**19**

i *Bracelet,* Gen. 24:22.

j *Dress,* Zech. 3:3.

6 R. V. pendants,

**20**

k *Turban,* Ex. 28:40.

l *Perfume,* Prov. 27:9.

7 R. V. The headtires, and the ankle chains, and the sashes, and the perfume boxes, and the amulets;

unto their soul! for they have rewarded [q]evil unto themselves.

10 Say ye to the [r]righteous, that [s]*it shall be* well *with him*: for [t,u]they shall eat the fruit of their doings.

11 Woe unto the wicked! [v]*it shall be* ill *with him*: [t]for the [m]reward of his hands shall be given him.

12 *As for* my people, children *are* their oppressors, and [w]women rule over them. O my people, they which lead thee cause *thee* to err, and destroy the way of thy paths.

13 ¶ [S]The LORD standeth up to plead, and standeth to [x]judge the people.

14 The LORD will enter into judgment with the ancients[G] of his people, and the [y]princes thereof: for ye have eaten up the vineyard; [z]the spoil of the [a]poor *is* in your houses.[S]

15 What mean ye *that* ye beat my people to pieces, and grind the faces of the [a]poor? saith the Lord [3]GOD of hosts.

16 ¶ Moreover the LORD saith, Because the daughters of Zī′ŏn are [b]haughty, and walk with stretched forth necks and wanton eyes, walking and mincing[G] *as* they go, and making a [c]tinkling with their [d]feet:

17 Therefore the Lord will [e]smite with a [f,g]scab the crown of the head of the daughters of Zī′ŏn, and the LORD will [4]discover[G] their secret parts.

18 In that day the Lord will take away the [5]bravery[G] of *their* tinkling [c]ornaments *about their* [d]*feet,* and *their* cauls[G], and *their* round [h]tires[G] like the moon,

19 The [6]chains, and the [i]bracelets, and the [j]mufflers[G],

20 The [7,k]bonnets[G], and the ornaments of the legs, and the headbands, and the [l]tablets[G], and the earrings,

21 The [m]rings, and nose jewels,

22 [8,j]The changeable[G] suits of apparel, and the mantles, and the [9]wimples[G], and the [10]crisping[G] pins,

23 The [11]glasses[G], and the fine [n]linen, and the [12,k]hoods, and the [o]vails.

24 And it shall come to pass, *that* instead of sweet [13]smell there shall be [14]stink; and instead of a [p]girdle a [15]rent; and instead of well set hair [q]baldness; and instead of a stomacher[G] a girding of [r]sackcloth[G]; [16]*and* burning instead of [s]beauty.

25 Thy men shall fall by the sword, and thy mighty in the [t]war.

26 [t]And her [u]gates shall lament and [v]mourn; and she *being* desolate shall sit upon the ground.

## CHAPTER 4

*The greatness of the coming distress.* 2 *The future prosperity of Zion.*

AND in that day [a]seven [b]women shall take hold of one man, saying, We will eat our own bread, and wear our own apparel: only let us [c,d]be called by thy name, to take away our reproach.

2 ¶ In[S] that day shall the [e]branch of the LORD be beautiful and glorious, and the fruit of the earth *shall be* excellent and comely[G] for them that are escaped of Iș′ra-el.[Q]

3 [f]And it shall come to pass, *that he that is* left in Zī′ŏn, and *he that* remaineth in [g]Jĕ-ru′sā-lĕm, shall be called [h]holy, *even* every one that is written among the living in Jĕ-ru′sā-lĕm:[T Q]

4 When the Lord shall have [i,j]washed away the filth of the daughters of Zī′ŏn, and shall have purged[G] the blood of [g]Jĕ-ru′sā-lĕm from the midst thereof by the spirit of [k]judgment[G], and by the spirit of burning.[S]

5 And the LORD will create up-

**21**

m *Ring,* Gen. 41:42.

**22**

8 R. V the festival robes,

9 R. V. shawls,

10 R. V. satchels;

**23**

n *Linen,* Ezek. 27:16.

o *Veil,* Gen. 24:65.

11 R. V. hand mirrors,

12 R. V. turbans,

**24**

p *Girdle,* Prov. 31:24.

q *Baldness, a judgment,* Lev. 21:5.

r *Sackcloth,* Isa. 15:3.

s *Beauty,* Prov. 6:25.

13 R. V. spices

14 R. V. rottenness;

15 R. V. rope;

16 R. V. branding

**25**

t *War, evils of,* Judg. 3:2.

**26**

u *Gates, figurative,* Deut. 3:5.

v *Mourning,* Lam. 2:5.

**1**

a *Seven,* Gen. 7:2.

b *Women,* Prov. 31:10.

c *Marriage,* Gen. 34:9.

d *Polygamy, sought by women,* Deut. 17:17.

**2**

e *Branch, figurative,* Dan. 4:14.

**3**

f *Judah, kingdom of, prophecies concerning,* 2 Chr. 11:17.

g *Jerusalem,* Judg. 19:10.

h *Holiness,* Ex. 39:30.

**4**

i *Washing, figurative,* Matt. 27:24.

j *Spiritual Purification,* Psa. 51:2.

k *Judgments,* Ex. 6:6.

on every dwelling place of mount Zī'ŏn, and upon her assemblies, a cloud and smoke by day, and the shining of a flaming fire by night: for upon all the glory *shall be* [1]a defence.[S]

6 And there shall be a tabernacle for a shadow in the daytime from the heat, and for a place of refuge, and for a covert[C] from storm and from rain.

## CHAPTER 5

*The parable of the vineyard and its application to Judah. 8 Woes denounced against covetousness, 11 revelry, 18 impiety, 20 and sundry other sins. 26 The executioners of judgments.*

[a]NOW will[S] I[Q] sing to my wellbeloved a song of my beloved touching his [b,c]vineyard. My wellbeloved hath a vineyard in a very fruitful hill:

2 And he [1]fenced [b]it, and gathered out the stones thereof, and planted it with the choicest vine, and built a [d]tower in the midst of it, and also [2]made a *winepress therein: and he looked[C] that it should bring forth [e,f]grapes, and [g,h]it brought forth wild grapes.

3 [i]And now, O inhabitants of Jĕ-ru̇'sȧ-lĕm, and men of Jū'dah, judge, I pray you, betwixt[C] me and my vineyard.

4 [i]What could have been done more to my vineyard, that I have not done in it? wherefore,[C] when I looked that it should bring forth [e,f]grapes, [g,h]brought it forth wild grapes?[S]

5 And now go to[C]; [j]I will tell you what I will do to my vineyard: [k]I will take away the †hedge thereof, and it shall be eaten up; *and* break down the wall thereof, and it shall be trodden[C] down:

6 And [j,k]I will lay it waste: it shall not be pruned, nor digged; but there shall come up [l]briers and [m]thorns: I will also command the clouds that they rain no rain upon it.[S]

7 For the [b]vineyard of the LORD of hosts *is* the house of Ĭs'ra-el, and the men of [a]Jū'dah his pleasant plant: and he looked for judgment,[C] but behold [n]oppression; for [f]righteousness, but behold a cry.[Q]

8 ¶ [o]Woe unto them that [p,q]join house to house, *that* ‡lay [r]field to field, till *there be* no [3]place, that they may be placed alone in the midst of the earth!

9 In mine ears *said* the LORD of hosts, Of a truth [s]many houses shall be desolate, *even* great and fair, without inhabitant.[Q]

10 Yea, ten [t]acres of vineyard shall yield one [u,v]bath,[C] and [4]the seed of an [w]homer[C] shall yield an [w]ephah.[C]

11 ¶ [x,y]Woe unto them that [z]rise up early in the morning, *that* they may follow [a]strong drink; that [5]continue until night, *till* wine inflame them!

12 And [b]the [c]harp, and the [6,c]viol, the [c]tabret,[C] and [c]pipe,[C] and wine, are in their [d]feasts: but [e]they regard not the work of the LORD, neither consider the operation of his hands.

13 Therefore my [f]people are [g]gone into ‖captivity, because *they have* [h,i]no knowledge: and their honourable men *are* [j]famished, and their multitude dried up with thirst.

14 Therefore [7,k]hell[C] hath enlarged [8]herself, and opened her

5
1 R. V. spread a canopy.

1
a *Judah, kingdom of, prophecies concerning,* vs. 1–7, 26–30; 2 Chr. 11:17.
b *Vineyard, parables of,* Isa. 1:8.
c *Parables, of the vineyard,* Ezek. 20:49.

2
d *Fortification,* Ezek. 17:17.
e *Grape, figurative,* Lev. 25:5.
f *Righteousness, fruits of,* Psa. 15:2.
g *Unfruitfulness,* Matt. 7:19.
h *Unfaithfulness,* Luke 16:11.
1 R. V. made a trench about
2 R. V. hewed out

3
i *Reasoning, God reasons with men,* Job 13:6.

5
j *Judgment, according to opportunity and works,* 1 Pet. 1:17.
k *Punishment, according to deeds,* Lev. 26:41.

6
l Isa. 55:13; Ezek. 2:6; 28:24.
m *Thorn, figurative,* Hos. 2:6.

7
n *Oppression,* Eccl. 5:8.

8
o *Rich, denounced,* Jas. 5:1.
p *Covetousness, denounced,* Isa. 57:17.
q *Ambition,* Hab. 2:5.
r *Land, monopoly of,* Ruth 4:3.
3 R. V. room, and ye be made to dwell alone

9
s *Wicked, punishment of,* Psa. 73:3.

10
t 1 Sam. 14:14.
u *Bath,* 1 Kin. 7:26.
v *Measure, liquid,* Deut. 25:15.
w *Measure, dry,* Deut. 25:15.
4 R. V a homer of seed shall yield

11
x *Drunkenness, woes denounced against,* Luke 21:34.
y *Worldly Pleasure, sensual,* v. 12; Eccl. 2:1.
z *Rising, early,* Gen. 19:2.

a *Wine, admonitions against the use of,* Prov. 23:31.
5 R. V. tarry late into the night,

12
b *Wicked, happiness of,* Psa. 73:3.
c *Music, instruments of,* 2 Chr. 5:13.
d *Feasts, music at,* Mark 12:39.
e *Backsliding, of Israel,* Hos. 11:7.
6 R. V. lute,

13
f *Nation, punishment of,* Isa. 2:4.
g *Judgments,* Ex. 6:6.
h *Ignorance,* Acts 3.17. i *Spiritual Blindness,* 2 Cor. 4:4. j *Famine,* 2 Kin. 8:1. **14** k *Hell,* Mark 9:43. 7 Am. R. V. Sheol 8 R. V. her desire,

* **WINE PRESS,** Num. 18:27, 30; Deut. 15:14; Judg. 6:11. *In vineyards,* Isa. 5:2; Matt. 21:33; Mark 12:1. *Trodden with joy and shouting,* Jer. 25:30; 48:33.
**Figurative,** Isa. 63:2, 3. *Of the judgments of God,* Lam. 1:15; Rev. 14:19, 20.

† **HEDGE.** *A fence,* Job 1:10; Isa. 5:5; Jer. 49:3; Ezek. 13:5; Hos. 2:6; Mic. 7:4; Mark 12:1; *of thorns,* Prov. 15:19. *People sheltered in,* Luke 14:23.

‡ **MONOPOLY.** *Of lands,* Isa. 5:8; *by Pharaoh,* Gen. 47:19–26. *Of food,* Prov. 11:26.

‖ **CAPTIVITY.** *Of the Israelites foretold,* Lev. 26:33; Deut. 28:36. *Of the ten tribes,* 2 Kin. 17:6, 23, 24; 18:9–12.
*Of Judah in Babylon, prophecies of,* Isa. 39:6; Jer. 13:19; 20:4; 25:8–11; 32:28; *fulfilled,* 2 Kin. 24:11–16; 25; 2 Chr. 36:5–23; Jer. 52:28–30. *Jews return from,* Ezra chapters 2, 8.
*As a judgment,* 1 Kin. 8:46; 2 Chr. 29:9; Ezra 5:12; 9:7; Isa. 5:13; Jer. 29:17–19; Lam. 1:3–5; Ezek. 39:23, 24.
**Figurative,** Isa. 61:1; Rom. 7:23; 1 Cor. 9:27; 2 Cor. 10:5; 2 Tim. 2:26; 3:6. *Captivity led captive,* Judg. 5:12; Psa. 68:18; Eph. 4:8.

**15**
9 R. V. is bowed
10 R. V. is
11 R. V. are

**16**
*l God, holiness of,* Gen. 2:2.
*m Holiness, attribute of God,* Ex. 39:30.
12 R. V. the Holy One is

**17**
13 R. V. as in their pasture,

**19**
*n Presumption, in defying God,* Psa. 19:13.
*o Scoffing,* Hab. 1:10.
*p Blasphemy, in reproaching God,* 2 Sam. 12:14.

**21**
*q Conceit,* Prov. 26:5.
*r False Confidence,* Psa. 30:6.

**22**
*s Drunkenness, woes denounced against,* Luke 21:34.

**23**
*t Judge, corrupt,* Judg. 2:18.
*u Rulers, wicked,* Ex. 18:21.
*v Bribery, perverts justice,* 1 Sam. 8:3.

**24**
*w Backsliders, punishment of,* Jer. 3:22.
*x Judgments,* Ex. 6:6.
*y Word of God, disbelief in,* Psa. 119:9.
14 R. V. as the dry grass sinketh down in the flame,

mouth without measure: and
[l]their glory, and their multitude,
and their pomp, and he that rejoiceth, shall descend into it.
15 And the mean man [9]shall be
brought down, and the mighty
man [10]shall be humbled, and the
eyes of the lofty [11]shall be humbled:
16 But the LORD of hosts shall
be exalted in judgment, and
[l]God [12]that is [m]holy shall be
sanctified in righteousness.
17 Then shall the lambs feed
[13]after their manner, and the
waste places of the fat ones shall
strangers eat.
18 ¶ Woe unto them that draw
iniquity with cords of vanity, and
sin as it were with a cart rope:
19 That [n,o,p]say, Let him make
speed, *and* hasten his work, that
we may see *it*: and let the counsel of the [l,m]Holy One of Iṣ′-
ra-el draw nigh and come, that
we may know *it*!
20 Woe unto them that call
evil good, and good evil; that
put darkness for light, and light
for darkness; that put bitter for
sweet, and sweet for bitter!
21 Woe unto *them that are* [q,r]wise
in their own eyes, and prudent
in their own sight!
22 [s]Woe unto *them that are*
mighty to drink [a]wine, and men of
strength to mingle strong drink:
23 [t,u]Which justify the wicked
for [v]reward, and take away the
righteousness of the righteous
from him!
24 Therefore as the fire devoureth the §stubble, and [14]the flame
consumeth the chaff, *so* [w,x]their
root shall be as rottenness, and
their blossom shall go up as dust:
because they have cast away the
law of the LORD of hosts, and
despised the [y]word of the [l]Holy
One of Iṣ′ra-el.

25 Therefore is the [z]anger of
the LORD kindled against his
people, and he hath [x]stretched
forth his hand against them, and
[a]hath smitten them: and the hills
did tremble, and their carcases
*were* [15]torn in the midst of the
streets. For all this his anger is
not turned away, but his hand *is*
stretched out still.
26 ¶ And he will lift up an [b]en-
sign to the nations from far, and
will hiss unto them from the end
of the earth: and, behold, [c]they
shall come with speed swiftly:
27 [c]None shall be weary nor
stumble among them; none shall
slumber nor sleep; neither shall
the girdle of their loins be loosed,
nor the latchet of their shoes be
broken:
28 Whose arrows *are* sharp,
and all their [d]bows bent, their
[e]horses' hoofs shall be counted
like flint, and their [f]wheels like
a whirlwind:
29 Their roaring *shall be* like a
[g]lion, they shall roar like young
lions: yea, they shall roar, and
lay hold of the prey, and shall
carry *it* away safe, and none
shall deliver *it*.
30 And in that day they shall
roar against them like the roaring of the sea: and if *one* look unto the land, behold darkness *and*
sorrow, and the light is darkened
in the heavens thereof.

## CHAPTER 6

*Isaiah's vision of the Lord in the temple.* 5 *His confession and preparation for his work.* 9 *His commission, and the predicted results of his labors.*

IN the year that king [a]Ŭz-zī′ah
died [b]I [c]saw also the [d,e]Lord
sitting upon a [f]throne, high and
lifted up, and his train filled the
temple.
2 Above it stood the seraphims:
each one had six wings; with
twain he covered his face, and

**25**
*z Anger of God,* 2 Kin. 13:3.
*a Nation, chastisement of,* Isa. 2:4.
15 R. V. as refuse in

**26**
*b Standard,* Num. 1:52.
*c Armies, forced marches of,* Deut. 11:4.

**28**
*d Bow,* 2 Sam. 1:18.
*e Horse,* Job 39:19.
*f Chariot,* Josh. 11:4.

**29**
*g Lion,* Mic. 5:8.

**v.1–676 BC**
See footnote, *Time,* Rev. 10:6.

**1**
*a Uzziah,* 2 Chr. 26:1.
*b Isaiah,* Isa. 1:1.
*c Vision,* Acts 9:10.
*d God, sovereign,* Gen. 2:2.
*e God, glory of,* Gen. 2:2.
*f Throne, figurative,* 1 Kin. 2:19.

§ **STUBBLE.** *Scattering of, illustrative of judgments upon the wicked,* Job 21:18; Isa. 40:24; 41:2; Jer. 13:24. *Destruction of, illustrative of the destruction of the wicked,* Ex. 15:7; Isa. 5:24; 47:14; Nah. 1:10; Mal. 4:1.

v.2–676 BC
See footnote, *Time*, Rev. 10:6.

**3**

g *Praise*, Psa. 150:1.
h *Holiness, attribute of God*, Ex. 39:30.
i *God, holiness of*, Gen. 2:2.
j *Holy Trinity*, Luke 3:22.

**4**

1 R. V. foundations of the thresholds were

**5**

k *Repentance, instances of*, Mark 1:4.
l *Self-condemnation*, Job 9:20.
m *Humility, exemplified*, Prov. 22:4.
n *Sin, conviction of*, Rom. 5:12.
o *Sin, confession of*, Rom. 5:12.
p *Speech, evil*, Col. 4:6.
q *Evil Company, perils of*, Prov. 13:20.

**6**

r *Fire, figurative*, Ex. 12:8.

**7**

s *God, mercy of*, Gen. 2:2.
t *Sin, forgiveness of*, Rom. 5:12.
u *Purity, of heart*, 1 Tim. 4:12.

**8**

v *Minister, call of*, Rom 15:16.
w *Zeal, exemplified*, 2 Cor. 7:11.

**9**

x Matt. 13:14, 15; Mark 4:12; Acts 28:25–27; Rom. 11:8.
y *Reprobates*, 1 Cor. 9:27.
z *Unbelief*, Heb. 3:12.

a *Moral Insensibility*, Luke 8:10.

**10**

b *Heart, unregenerate*, Psa. 44:21.
c *Deafness, figurative*, Matt. 11:5.
2 R. V. turn again,

**12**

3 R. V. the forsaken places be many in

with twain he covered his feet,
and with twain he did fly.
3 And one cried unto another,
and [g]said, [h,i,j]Holy, holy, holy,
*is* the LORD of hosts: the whole
earth *is* full of his [e]glory. [S T Q]
4 And the [1]posts of the door
moved at the voice of him that
cried, and the house was filled
with smoke.[Q]
5 Then [k]said I, [l]Woe *is* me!
for I am undone; because [m,n,o]I
*am* a man of [p]unclean lips, and I
dwell in the midst of a [q]people of
unclean lips: for mine eyes have
[c]seen the [d]King, the LORD of
hosts.[T]
6 Then flew one of the seraphims unto me, having a [r]live coal
in his hand, *which* he had taken
with the tongs from off the altar:
7 And he laid *it* upon my
mouth, and said, Lo, this hath
touched thy lips; and [s]thine iniquity[C] is [t]taken away, and thy sin
[u]purged.[G S]
8[T] Also I heard the voice of the
LORD, saying, [v]Whom shall I
send, and who will go for us?
Then [w]said I, Here *am* I; send
me.
9[Q] And he said, Go, and tell this
people, [x]Hear [y]ye indeed, but
[z,a]understand not; and see ye indeed, but [a]perceive not.[S T]
10 Make the [b]heart of this
people fat, and make their ears
[c]heavy, and shut their eyes; lest
they see with their eyes, and hear
with their ears, and understand
with their heart, and [2]convert,[C]
and be healed.[S Q]
11 Then said I, Lord, how
long? And he answered, Until
the cities be wasted without inhabitant, and the houses without
man, and the land be utterly
desolate,
12 And the LORD have re-
moved men far away, and [3]*there*
*be* a great forsaking in the midst
of the land.[S]
13 [4]But yet in it *shall be* a tenth,
and *it* shall return, and shall be
eaten: as a teil tree, and as an
oak, whose [4]substance *is* in them,
when they cast *their leaves*: *so* the
holy seed *shall be* the substance
thereof.

## CHAPTER 7

*The invasion of Judah by Rezin and Pekah. 3 The prophet assures Ahaz of safety. 10 Ahaz refuses to ask a sign. 14 The Lord promises Immanuel. 17 The evils to come upon Judah from Assyria.*

AND it came to pass in the
days of [a]Ā'hăz the son of
[b]Jō'tham, the son of [c]Ŭz-zī'ah,
king of [b]Jū'dah, *that* [e]Rē'zin the
king of [f]Sўr'ĭ-ȧ, and *Pē'kah the
son of [g]Rĕm-a-lī'ah, king of [h]Ĭș'-
ra-el, went up toward [i]Jĕ-rṳ'sā-
lĕm to war against it, but could
not prevail against it.
2 And it was told the house of
Dā'vid, saying, [f]Sўr'ĭ-ȧ is [j]con-
federate[C] with [k]Ē'phră-ĭm. And
his heart was moved, and the
heart of his people, as the trees
of the wood[G] are moved with the
wind.
3 Then said the LORD unto
[l]Ī-ṣā'iah, Go forth now to meet
[a]Ā'hăz, thou, and Shē'är-jā'-
shŭb thy son, at the end of the
conduit of the upper [m]pool in the
highway of the [n]fuller's field;
4 And say unto him, Take heed,
and be quiet; [o]fear not, neither
be faint-hearted for the two tails
of these smoking firebrands, for
the fierce anger of [e]Rē'zin with
[f]Sўr'ĭ-ȧ, and of the *son of Rĕm-
a-lī'ah.
5 [p]Because [f]Sўr'ĭ-ȧ, [k]Ē'phră-ĭm,
and the *son of [g]Rĕm-a-lī'ah,
have taken evil counsel[G] against
thee, saying,
6 Let us go up against [d]Jū'dah,
and vex[C] it, and let us make a
breach[C] therein for us, and set a

v.12–676 BC
See footnote, *Time*, Rev. 10:6.

**13**

4 R. V. And if there be yet a tenth in it, it shall again be eaten up: as a terebinth, and as an oak, whose stock remaineth, when they are felled; so the holy seed is the stock thereof.

**1**

a *Ahaz*, 2 Kin. 15:38.
b *Jotham*, 2 Kin. 15:5.
c *Uzziah*, 2 Chr. 26:1.
d *Judah, kingdom of*, 2 Chr. 11:17.
e *Rezin*, 2 Kin. 15:37.
f *Syria*, 2 Kin. 6:23.
g *Remaliah*, 2 Kin. 15:25.
h *Israel, after the revolt*, 1 Kin. 12:1.
i *Jerusalem*, Judg. 19:10.

**2**

j *Armies, confederated*, Deut. 11:4.
k *Ephraim, name applied to the ten tribes*, Gen. 41:52.

**3**

l *Isaiah*, Isa. 1:1.
m *Pool*, 2 Sam. 2:13.
n 2 Kin. 18:17; Isa. 36:2.

**4**

o *Courage, enjoined*, Deut. 31:7.

**5**

p *Alliances*, Josh. 9:15.

* **PEKAH,** son of Remaliah. *Captain of the army of Israel*, 2 Kin. 15:25. *Conspires against and assassinates king Pekahiah*, 2 Kin. 15:25. *Is made king of Israel*, 2 Kin. 15:27. *Victorious in war with Judah*, 2 Chr. 28:5, 6. *Reigns twenty years*, 2 Kin. 15:27. *Is plotted against and slain by Hoshea*, 2 Kin. 15:30, 31. *Prophecies against*, Isa. 7:1–9; 8:4–10.

**8**
*q Damascus,* Isa. 8:4.
*r Israel, after the revolt, prophecies concerning,* 1 Kin. 12:1.
v.8—659 BC

**9**
*s Unbelief,* Heb. 3:12.

**11**
*t Sign,* Mark 8:11.

**12**
*u Hypocrisy, instances of,* with vs. 17–25; Jas. 3:17.

**14**
*v* Matt. 1:23.
*w Prophecies concerning the Messiah, and their fulfillment,* Gen. 12:3.
*x Virgin,* Isa. 62:5.
*y Mary, prophecies concerning,* Luke 1:27.
*z Jesus, prophecies concerning,* Matt. 1:21.

*a Jesus, incarnation of,* Matt. 1:21.
*b Jesus, names of,* Matt. 1:21.

**15**
*c Butter,* Gen. 18:8.
*d Honey,* Prov. 25:27.
*e Temptation, resistance to,* Luke 11:4.

**16**
1 R. V. whose two kings thou abhorrest shall be forsaken.

**17**
*f Ephraim, name applied to the ten tribes,* Gen. 41:52.
*g Judah, kingdom of,* 2 Chr. 11:17.
*h Assyria, prophecies concerning,* vs. 18–25; Gen. 25:18.

king in the midst of it, *even* the
son of Tā'be-al:
7 Thus saith the Lord GOD, It
shall not stand, neither shall it
come to pass.
8 For the head of [f]Sy̆r'ĭ-ȧ *is*
[q]Dȧ-măs'cus, and the head of
Dȧ-măs'cus *is* [e]Rē'zin; and within threescore[G] and five years shall
[k,r]Ē'phră-ĭm be broken, that it
be not a people.
9 And the head of [h,k]Ē'phră-ĭm
*is* †Sȧ-mā'rĭ-ȧ, and the head of
Sȧ-mā'rĭ-ȧ *is* Rĕm-a-lī'ah's *son.
If ye will [s]not believe, surely ye
shall not be established.[S]
10 ¶ Moreover the LORD spake
again unto [a]Ā'hăz, saying,
11 Ask thee a [t]sign of the LORD
thy God; ask it either in the
depth, or in the height above.
12 But [a]Ā'hăz [u]said, I will not
ask, neither will I tempt[G] the
LORD.
13 And [l]he said, Hear ye now,
O house of Dā'vid; *Is it* a small
thing for you to weary men, but
will ye weary my God also?
14 Therefore the Lord himself
shall give you a [t]sign; [v,w]Behold,[G]
a [x,y]virgin shall conceive, and
bear a [z,a]son, and shall call his
name [b]Ĭm-măn'u-el.[G] [Q]
15 [c]Butter and [d]honey shall he
eat, that he may know to [e]refuse[G]
the evil, and choose the good.
16 For before the child shall
know to [e]refuse the evil, and
choose the good, the land [1]that
thou abhorrest[G] shall be forsaken
of both her kings.
17 ¶ The LORD shall bring upon thee, and upon thy people,
and upon thy father's house,
days that have not come, from
the day that [f]Ē'phră-ĭm departed from [g]Jū'dah; *even* the king
of [h]Ăs-sy̆r'ĭ-ȧ.

18 And it shall come to pass in
that day, *that* the LORD shall
hiss[G] for the fly that *is* in the
uttermost part of the rivers of
[i]Ē'gy̆pt, and for the bee that
*is* in the land of [h]Ăs-sy̆r'ĭ-ȧ.
19 And they shall come, and
shall rest all of them in the desolate valleys, and in the holes of
the rocks, and upon all thorns,
and upon all [2]bushes.
20 In the same day shall the
Lord shave with a razor that is
hired, *namely*, by them beyond
the river, by the king of Ăs-sy̆r'-
ĭ-ȧ, the head, and the hair of the
feet: and it shall also consume
the beard.
21 And it shall come to pass in
that day, *that* a man shall nourish a young cow, and two sheep;
22 And it shall come to pass, for
the abundance of [j]milk *that* they
shall give he shall eat [c]butter: for
butter and [d]honey shall every one
eat that is left in the land.
23 And it shall come to pass in
that day, *that* every place shall
be, where there were a thousand
vines at a thousand silverlings,[G] it
shall *even* be for briers and thorns.
24 With arrows and with [k]bows
shall *men* come thither[G]; because
all the land shall become briers
and thorns.
25 And *on* all hills that shall be
digged[G] with the [l]mattock, there
shall not come thither[G] the fear of
briers and thorns: but it shall be
for the sending forth of oxen, and
for the treading of [3]lesser[G] cattle.[G]

## CHAPTER 8

*Syria and Israel to be subdued by Assyria. 5 The like overthrow to come upon Judah. 19 The distress to come upon those that seek unto familiar spirits.*

MOREOVER the LORD [a]said
unto [b]me, Take thee a great
[c]roll, and write in it with a man's

**18**
*i Egypt,* Gen. 41:8.

**19**
2 R. V. pastures.

**22**
*j Milk,* Job 10:10.

**24**
*k Bow,* 2 Sam. 1:18.

**25**
*l* 1 Sam. 13:20, 21.
3 R. V. sheep.

**1**
*a Prophets, inspiration of,* Isa. 3:2.
*b Isaiah,* Isa. 1:1.
*c Book,* Num. 5:23.

† **SAMARIA.** *Country of,* Isa. 7:9. *Prophecies concerning,* Hos. chapters 3–13. *Famine in,* 1 Kin. 18:2. *Foreign colonies distributed among the cities of, by the king of Assyria,* 2 Kin. 17:24–41; Ezra 4:9, 10. *Roads through, from Judea into Galilee,* Luke 17:11; John 4:3–8. *Jesus, journeys through,* John 4:1–42; *heals lepers in,* Luke 17:11–19. *The good Samaritan from,* Luke 10:33–35. *No dealings between the Jews and the inhabitants of,* John 4:9. *People of, expect the Messiah,* John 4:25. *Disciples made among the inhabitants of,* John 4:39–42; Acts 8:5–8, 14–17, 25. *Jesus forbids the apostles to preach in the cities of,* Matt. 10:5.
See footnote, SAMARIA, *City of,* 1 Kin. 16:24.

[d]pen concerning Māh′ēr–shăl′-
al–hăsh′–băz.
2 And I took unto me faithful
[e]witnesses to record, [f]U-rī′ah the
priest, and Zĕch-a-rī′ah the son
of Jĕ-bĕr-e-chī′ah.
3 And I went[G] unto the prophetess; and she conceived, and bare
a son. Then said the LORD to
me, Call his name Mā′hēr–shăl′-
al–hăsh′–băz.[G]
4 For [g]before[G] the child shall
have knowledge to cry, My father, and my mother, the riches
of *,[h]Dă-măs′cus and the spoil
of [i]Să-mā′rĭ-ȧ shall be taken
away before the [j]king of [k]Ăs-
sỹr′ĭ-ȧ.
5 ¶ The LORD [a]spake also unto
me again, saying,
6 Forasmuch as [g]this people refuseth[G] the waters of Shĭ-lō′ah
that go softly, and rejoice in
[j]Rē′zin and [l]Rĕm-a-lī′ah's [m]son;
7 Now therefore, behold, the
LORD [n]bringeth up upon [g]them
the waters of the [o]river, strong
and many, *even* the [j]king of
[k]Ăs-sỹr′ĭ-ȧ, and all his glory:
and he shall come up over all
his channels, and go over all
his banks:
8 And he shall pass through
[p]Jū′dah; he shall overflow and
go over, he shall reach *even* to
the neck; and the stretching out
of his wings shall fill the breadth
of thy land, O Ĭm-măn′u-el.[Q]
9 ¶ [1]Associate yourselves, O ye
people, and ye shall be broken in
pieces; and give ear, all ye of far
countries: gird yourselves, and
ye shall be broken in pieces; gird
yourselves, and ye shall be broken in pieces.[S]
10 Take counsel together, and
it shall come to nought; speak
the word, and it shall not stand:
for [q]God *is* with us.[S Q]
11 For the LORD [a]spake thus to
[b]me with a strong hand, and instructed me that I should not
walk in the [r]way of this [s]people,
saying,
12[Q] Say ye not, A [2]confederacy,[G]
to all *them to* whom this people
shall say, A confederacy; neither
fear ye their fear, nor be afraid.
13 Sanctify[G] the LORD of hosts
himself; and [t]*let* him *be* your
[u]fear, and *let* him *be* your dread.[Q]
14[Q] And he shall be for a sanctuary;[G] but for a [v]stone of †stum-
bling and for a rock of offence to
both the houses of Ĭş′ra-el, for a
gin[G] and for a snare to the inhabitants of Jĕ-ru̧′să-lĕm.
15 And many among them shall
stumble, and fall, and be broken,
and be snared, and be taken.[Q]
16 Bind up the testimony,[G] seal
the law among my disciples.
17 And I [w]will wait[G] upon the
LORD, that hideth his face from
the house of Jā′cob, and I will
look for him.[Q]
18 Behold, [x]I and the children
whom the LORD hath given me
*are* for signs and for wonders in
Ĭş′ra-el from the LORD of hosts,
which dwelleth in mount Zī′ŏn.[Q T]
19 And when they shall [y]say
unto you, Seek unto them that
have [z]familiar[G] spirits, and unto
[a]wizards that peep,[G] and that
mutter: should not a people seek
unto their God? [3,b]for the living
to the dead?[Q]
20 To the law and to the testimony: if they speak not according to this word, *it is* because
*there is* no [4]light in them.
21 And they shall pass through
it, [c]hardly[G] bestead and hungry:

d *Pen*, Jer. 8:8.

2

e *Witness*, Num. 35:30.

f Probably identical with *Urijah*, 2 Kin. 16:10.

4

g *Israel, after the revolt, prophecies concerning*, vs. 4–8, 1 Kin. 12:1.

h *Syria*, 2 Kin. 6:23.

i *Samaria*, Isa. 7:9.

j *Rezin*, 2 Kin. 15:37.

k *Assyria, prophecies concerning*, Gen. 25:18.

6

l *Remaliah*, 2 Kin. 15:25.

m *Pekah*, Isa. 7:1.

7

n *Divine Chastisement*, Job 33:19.

o *Euphrates, symbolical*, Gen. 15:18.

8

p *Judah, kingdom of, prophecies concerning*, 2 Chr. 11:17.

9

1 R. V. Make an uproar,

10

q *Faith, exemplified*, Mark 11:22.

11

r *Example, bad, to be shunned*, John 13:15.

s *Evil Company, forbidden*, Prov. 13:20.

12

2 R. V. conspiracy, concerning all whereof this people shall say, A conspiracy;

13

t *Commandment, enjoining fear of God*, Deut. 8:2.

u *Fear of God*, Acts 9:31.

14

v *Stones, figurative*, Ex. 24:12.

17

w *Spiritual Desire*, Psa. 42:1.

18

x Heb. 2:13.

19

y *Temptation, leading into*, Luke 11:4.

z *Familiar Spirits*, Deut. 18:11.

a *Sorcery*, Isa. 47:9.

b *Necromancy*, Deut. 18:11.

3 R. V. on behalf of the living should they seek unto

20

4 R. V. morning for them.

21

c *Wicked, punishment of*, Psa. 73:3.

* **DAMASCUS.** *An ancient city*, Gen. 14:15; 15:2. *Capital of Syria*, 1 Kin. 20:34; Isa. 7:8; Jer. 49:23–29; Ezek. 47:16, 17. *Laid under tribute to David*, 2 Sam. 8:5, 6. *Ruled by Rezon*, 1 Kin. 11:23, 24. *Recovered by Jeroboam*, 2 Kin. 14:28. *Taken by king of Assyria*, 2 Kin. 16:9. *Walled*, Jer. 49:27; 2 Cor. 11:33. *Garrisoned*, 2 Cor. 11:32. *Luxury in*, Amos 3:12. *Paul's experiences in*, Acts 9:1–25, 27; 22:5–16; 26:12–20; 2 Cor. 11:32; Gal. 1:17. *Prophecies concerning*, Isa. 8:4; 17:1, 2; Jer. 49:23–29; Amos 1:3, 5; Zech. 9:1.

† **STUMBLING. Figurative**, Psa. 119:165. *Causes of*, Psa. 69:6. *Stone of*, Isa. 8:14; Rom. 9:32, 33; 1 Pet. 2:8. *Stumbling-block*, Lev. 19:14; Psa. 119:165; Isa. 57:14; Jer. 6:21; Ezek. 3:20; 7:19; 14:3, 4, 7; Zeph. 1:3; Rom. 11:9; 14:13; 1 Cor. 1:23; 8:9–13; Rev. 2:14.
See footnote, TEMPTATION, Luke 11:4.

5 R. V. by their king and by their God, and turn their faces upward:

22

*d Darkness, figurative,* Gen. 1:2.

1

*a* Matt. 4:15, 16.

*b Zebulun, tribe of,* Gen. 49:13.

*c Naphtali, tribe of,* Num. 1:42.

*d Jordan,* Gen. 32:10.

*e Galilee, prophecy concerning,* Mark 6:21.

1 R. V. But there shall be no gloom to her that was in anguish. In the former time he brought into contempt the land

2 R. V. but in the latter time hath he made it glorious, by

2

*f Prophecies concerning the Messiah, and their fulfillment,* Gen. 12:3.

*g Jesus, kingdom of, prophecies concerning,* Matt. 1:21.

*h Gentiles, prophecies of the conversion of,* Acts 10:45.

*i Darkness, figurative,* Gen. 1:2.

*j Spiritual Blindness,* 2 Cor. 4:4.

*k Light, figurative,* Matt. 5:14.

*l Gospel, prophecies concerning,* Mark 13:10.

3

*m Joy,* Psa. 5:11.

*n Harvest, celebrated with joy,* Ex. 34:21.

*o Spoils,* 1 Chr. 26:27.

4

*p Yoke, figurative,* 1 Sam. 6:7.

5

*q War, evils of,* Judg. 3:2.

3 R. V. all the armour of the armed man in the tumult, and the garments rolled in blood, shall even be for burning, for fuel of fire. **6** *r Jesus, prophecies concerning,* Matt. 1:21. *s Jesus, incarnation of,* Matt. 1:21. *t Jesus, king,* Matt. 1:21.

and it shall come to pass, that when they shall be hungry, they shall fret themselves, and curse [5]their king and their God, and look upward.

22 And they shall look unto the earth; and behold [c]trouble and [d]darkness, dimness of anguish; and *they shall be* driven to darkness.[Q]

## CHAPTER 9

*Some mitigation of distress promised.* 2 *The coming of the Messiah and the enlargement of his kingdom.* 8 *The judgments to come upon Israel for their pride* 13 *and impenitence.*

[1]NEVERTHELESS[Q] the dimness *shall* not *be* such as *was* in her vexation,[G] when at the first he lightly afflicted [a]the land of [b]Zĕb′u-lŭn and the land of [c]Năph′ta-lī, [2]and afterward did more grievously afflict *her by* the way of the sea, beyond [d]Jôr′dan, in [e]Găl′ĭ-lee of the nations.

2 [f,g]The [h]people that walked in [i,j]darkness have seen a great [k,l]light: they that dwell in the land of the shadow of death, upon them hath the light shined.[Q]

3 Thou hast multiplied the nation, *and* not[G] increased the [m]joy: they joy before thee according to the joy in [n]harvest, *and* as *men* rejoice when they divide the [o]spoil.

4 For thou hast broken the [p]yoke of his burden, and the staff of his shoulder, the rod of his oppressor, as in the day of Mĭd′ĭ-an.

5 For [3]every battle of the warrior *is* with confused noise, and [q]garments rolled in blood; but *this* shall be with burning *and* fuel of fire.

6 [f]For[T] unto us a [r,s]child is born, unto us a son is given: and [t]the government shall be upon his shoulder: and his name shall be called [u]Wonderful, [u,v]Counsellor, [u,w]The mighty God, [u]The everlasting Father, [w]The Prince of [x]Peace.[S Q]

7 [f]Of the increase of [t]*his* government and [x]peace *there shall be* no end, upon the [y]throne of [z]Dā′vid, and upon his kingdom, to order it, and to establish it with judgment[G] and with justice[G] from henceforth even for ever. The zeal of the LORD of hosts will perform this.[T Q]

8 ¶ The Lord sent a word into Jā′cob, and it hath lighted[G] upon Ĭş′ra-el.

9 And all the people shall know, *even* [a]Ē′phrā-ĭm and the inhabitant of [b]Să-mā′rĭ-ȧ, that say in the pride and [c]stoutness[G] of heart,

10 The [d]bricks are fallen down, but [e]we will build with hewn [f]stones: the [g]sycomores are cut down, but we will change *them into* *cedars.

11 Therefore the LORD [h]shall set up the adversaries of [i]Rē′zin against him, and join his enemies together;

12 The [j]Sy̆r′ĭ-anş before, and the [k]Phĭ-lĭs′tīneş behind; and they shall devour [l]Ĭş′ra-el with open mouth. For all this his [m]anger is not turned away, but his [h]hand *is* stretched out still.

13 ¶ For the [n]people [o]turneth not unto him that [h,p]smiteth[G] them, [o]neither do they seek the LORD of hosts.

14 Therefore the LORD will [h,n]cut off from [l]Ĭş′ra-el head and tail, branch and rush, in one day.

15 The ancient and honourable, he *is* the head; and the [q]prophet that teacheth lies, he *is* the tail.

16 For the leaders of this people [r]cause *them* to err; and

*u Jesus, names of,* Matt. 1:21.

*v Counselor,* Prov. 11:14.

*w Jesus, divinity of,* Matt. 1:21.

*x Peace,* Jer. 29:7.

7

*y Throne, of David,* 1 Kin. 2:19.

*z David,* 1 Sam. 16:13.

9

*a Ephraim, name applied to the ten tribes,* Gen. 41:52.

*b Samaria,* Isa. 7:9.

*c Obduracy,* Prov. 29:1.

10

*d Brick,* Gen. 11:3.

*e False Confidence,* Psa. 30:6.

*f Stones,* Ex. 24:12.

*g Sycomore,* 2 Chr. 1:15.

11

*h Divine Chastisement,* Job 33:19.

*i Rezin,* 2 Kin. 15:37.

12

*j Syria,* 2 Kin. 6:23.

*k Philistines,* Gen. 26:14.

*l Israel, after the revolt,* 1 Kin. 12:1.

*m Anger of God,* 2 Kin. 13:3.

13

*n Nation, punishment of,* Isa. 2:4.

*o Adversity, obduracy in,* Psa. 10:6.

*p Adversity, design of,* Psa. 10:6.

15

*q Prophets, false,* Isa. 3:2.

16

*r Influence, evil,* 1 Cor. 7:14.

***CEDAR.** *Lebanon famous for,* Judg. 9:15; Ezra 3:7; Psa. 92:12. *Valuable for building purposes,* Isa. 9:10. *Solomon's ample provision of, in Jerusalem, for the temple,* 2 Chr. 1:15; 2:3, 4, 8. *Furnished by Hiram, king of Tyre, for Solomon's temple,* 1 Kin. 5:6–10; 9:11. *Used, in rebuilding the temple,* Ezra 3:7; *in David's palace,* 2 Sam. 5:11; 1 Chr. 17:1; *in Solomon's palace,* 1 Kin. 7:2; *for masts of ships,* Ezek. 27:5; *in purifications,* Lev. 14:4, 6, 49–52; Num. 19:6.
**Figurative,** Isa. 2:13; 14:8; Jer. 22:7; Ezek. 31:3; Zech. 11:2.

*they that are* led of them *are* destroyed.
17 The[s]refore the Lord shall
have no joy in their [s]young men,
neither shall have mercy on their
[t]fatherless and [u]widows: for every one *is* [4]an hypocrite and an
evildoer, and every mouth
[v]speaketh folly. For all this his
[m]anger is not turned away, but
his hand *is* stretched out still.
18 ¶ For [w, x]wickedness burneth as the fire: it shall devour the
briers and thorns, and shall kindle in the thickets of the forest,
and they shall mount up *like* the
lifting up of smoke.
19 Through the [m]wrath of the
LORD of hosts is the land
[5, y]darkened, and the [n]people
shall be as the fuel of the fire:
no man shall spare his brother.
20 [z]And he shall snatch on the
right hand, and be [a]hungry; and
he shall eat on the left hand, and
they shall not be satisfied: they
shall eat every man the flesh of
his own arm:
21 [b]Mă-năs′seh, [c]Ē′phră-ĭm;
and Ē′phră-ĭm, Mă-năs′seh: *and*
they together *shall be* against
[d]Jū′dah. For all this his anger is
not turned away, but his hand *is*
stretched out still.[s]

**17**
*s Young Men,* Prov. 1:4.
*t Orphan,* Lam. 5:3.
*u Widow,* 2 Sam. 14:5.
*v Speech, foolish,* Col. 4:6.
4 R. V. profane

**18**
*w Sin, fruits of,* Rom. 5:12.
*x Sin, retroactive,* Rom. 5:12.

**19**
*y Judgments,* Ex. 6:6.
5 R. V. burnt up:

**20**
*z Famine,* 2 Kin. 8:1.
*a Hunger, as a judgment,* Neh. 9:15.

**21**
*b Manasseh, tribe of,* Gen. 46:20.
*c Ephraim, tribe of,* Gen. 41:52.
*d Judah, kingdom of,* 2 Chr. 11:17.

## CHAPTER 10

*A woe denounced upon tyrants. 5 The king of Assyria to be sent against Judah. 8 His confident boasting. 16 His overthrow predicted. 20 A remnant of Israel shall return. 24 God's people comforted with the promise of deliverance from Assyria.*

[a]WOE unto [b, c]them that decree unrighteous decrees,
and that write grievousness
*which* they have prescribed;
2 To turn aside the needy from
judgment,[c] and to take away the
right from the [d]poor of my people, that [e]widows may be their
prey, and *that* they may rob the
[f]fatherless!
3 And [g, h]what will ye do in the
day of visitation, and in the des-

**1**
*a Oppression, oppressors punished,* vs. 1–34; Eccl. 5:8.
*b Rulers, wicked,* Ex. 18:21.
*c Court, corrupt,* Ex. 18:26.

**2**
*d Poor,* Prov. 21:13.
*e Widow,* 2 Sam. 14:5.
*f Orphan,* Lam. 5:3.

**3**
*g Wicked, punishment of,* Psa. 73:3.
*h Punishment, no escape from,* Lev. 26:41.

olation *which* shall come from
far? [g, h]to whom will ye flee for
help? and where will ye leave
your glory?[Q]
4 [1]Without me [g]they shall bow
down under the prisoners, and
they shall fall under the slain.
For all this his [i]anger is not
turned away, but his [j]hand *is*
stretched out still.
5 ¶ O [k]Ăs-sȳr′ĭ-an, the [l]rod of
mine [i]anger, and the staff in
their hand is mine indignation.
6 [m]I will send him against [2]an
hypocritical nation, and against
the people of my wrath will I
give him a charge,[c] to take the
spoil, and to take the prey, and
to tread them down like the mire
of the streets.
7 Howbeit[c] he meaneth not so,
neither doth his heart think so;
but *it is* in his heart to destroy
and cut off nations not a few.
8 For he [n]saith, *Are* not my
princes altogether kings?
9 *Is* not Căl′nō as Cär′che-
mĭsh? *is* not Hā′math as Är′-
pad? *is* not Sȧ-mā′rĭ-ȧ as Dȧ-
măs′cus?
10 As my hand hath found
the kingdoms of the idols, and
whose graven[c] images did excel
them of Jĕ-ru̦′sȧ-lĕm and of Sȧ-
mā′rĭ-ȧ;
11 Shall I not, as I have done
unto Sȧ-mā′rĭ-ȧ and her idols,
[o]so do to Jĕ-ru̦′sȧ-lĕm and her
idols?
12 [p]Wherefore it shall come to
pass, *that* when the Lord hath
performed his whole [q]work upon
mount Zī′ŏn and on Jĕ-ru̦′sȧ-
lĕm, I will punish[c] the fruit of the
stout[c] heart of the king of [r]Ăs-
sȳr′ĭ-ȧ, and the glory of his [s]high
looks.
13 For he [n]saith, By the strength
of my hand I have done *it*, and
by my wisdom; for I am prudent:
and I have removed the bounds[c]
of the people, and have robbed

**4**
*i Anger of God,* 2 Kin. 13:3.
*j Judgments,* Ex. 6:6.
1 R. V. *omits* without me

**5**
*k Assyria,* Gen. 25:18.
*l Agency, in executing judgment,* Mark 1:17.

**6**
*m Nation, punishment of,* Isa. 2:4.
2 R. V. a profane

**8**
*n Boasting,* Prov. 25:14.

**11**
*o Idolatry, denounced,* 1 Sam. 15:23.

**12**
*p Judah, kingdom of, prophecies concerning,* 2 Chr. 11:17.
*q Divine Chastisement,* Job 33:19.
*r Assyria, prophecies concerning,* Gen. 25:18.
*s Pride,* Prov. 16:18.

their treasures, and I have [3]put down the inhabitants like a valiant[C] *man*:

14 [n]And my hand hath found as a nest the riches of the people: and as one gathereth eggs *that are* left, have I gathered all the earth, and there was none that moved the wing, or opened the mouth, or peeped.[C]

15 [t]Shall the ax [n]boast itself against him that heweth therewith? *or* shall the saw magnify itself against him that [4]shaketh it? as if the rod should [5]shake *itself* against them that lift it up, *or* as if the staff should lift up [6]*itself, as if it were* no wood.

16 Therefore shall the Lord, the Lord of hosts, [u]send among his fat ones leanness; and under his glory he shall kindle a burning like the burning of a fire.

17[S] And the light of Ĭş′ra-el shall be for a fire, and his Holy One for a flame: and it shall [u]burn and devour his thorns and his briers in one day;[T]

18 And shall [u]consume the glory of his forest, and of his fruitful field, both soul and body: and they shall be as when a standardbearer fainteth.[S]

19 And the rest of the trees of his forest shall be few, that a child may write them.

20 ¶ And it shall come to pass in that day, *that* the remnant of Ĭş′ra-el, and such as are escaped of the house of Jā′cob, shall no more again stay[G] upon him that smote them; but [v]shall stay[G] upon the LORD, the [w]Holy One of Ĭş′ra-el, in truth.

21 [v]The remnant shall [x]return, *even* the remnant of Jā′cob, unto the [y]mighty God.

22[Q] For [z]though thy people Ĭş′ra-el be as the sand of the sea, *yet* a remnant of them shall return: the consumption[G] decreed shall overflow with righteousness.

23 For the Lord GOD of hosts shall make a consumption,[G] even determined, in the midst of all the land.[Q]

24 ¶ Therefore thus saith the Lord [7]GOD of hosts, O my people that dwellest in Zī′ŏn, be not afraid of the [a]Ăs-sўr′ĭ-an: he shall smite thee with a rod, and shall lift up his staff against thee, after the manner of [b]Ē′ġўpt.

25 For yet a very little while, and the indignation shall [8]cease, and mine [c]anger in their destruction.

26 And the LORD of hosts shall stir up a scourge[G] for him according to the slaughter of [d]Mĭd′ĭ-an at the rock of [e]Ō′reb: and *as* his rod *was* upon the sea, so shall he lift it up after the manner of [b]Ē′ġўpt.

27 And it shall come to pass in that day, *that* his burden shall be taken away from off thy shoulder, and his [f]yoke from off thy neck, and the yoke shall be destroyed because of the anointing.[S]

28 He is come to Ā-ī′ath, he is passed to [g]Mĭg′rŏn; at [h]Mĭch′-mash he hath laid up his [9]carriages:[G]

29 They are gone over the passage:[G] they have taken up their lodging at [i]Gē′bȧ; [j]Rā′mah is afraid; [k]Ġĭb′e-ah of Saul is fled.

30 Lift up thy voice, O daughter of [l]Găl′lim: cause it to be heard unto Lā′ish, O poor Ăn′a-thŏth.

31 Măd-mē′nah is removed; the inhabitants of Ġē′bim gather themselves to flee.

32 As yet shall he remain at [m]Nŏb that day: he shall shake his hand *against* the mount of the daughter of Zī′ŏn, the hill of Jē-ru̧′sȧ-lĕm.

33 Behold, the Lord, the LORD of hosts, shall lop the bough with terror: and the high ones of stat-

**13**
3 R. V. brought down as a valiant man them that sit on thrones:

**15**
t *Presumption*, Psa. 19:13.
4 Am. R. V. wieldeth
5 Am. R. V. wield them
6 Am. R. V. him that is not wood.

**16**
u *Judgments*, Ex. 6:6.

**20**
v *Adversity, benefits of*, Psa. 10:6.
w *God, holiness of*, Gen. 2:2.

**21**
x *Repentance*, Mark 1:4.
y *God, power of*, Gen. 2:2.

**22**
z Rom. 9:27, 28.

**24**
a *Assyria*, Gen. 25:18.
b *Egypt*, Gen. 41:8.
7 Am. R. V. Jehovah

**25**
c *Anger of God*, 2 Kin. 13:3.
8 R. V. be accomplished,

**26**
d *Midianites*, Gen. 37:28.
e Judg. 7:25.

**27**
f *Yoke, figurative*, 1 Sam. 6:7.

**28**
g 1 Sam. 14:2.
h *Michmash*, 1 Sam. 14:5.
9 R. V. baggage

**29**
i *Geba*, Josh. 21:17.
j *Ramah*, Judg. 19:13.
k *Gibeah*, Hos. 9:9.

**30**
l 1 Sam. 25:44.

**32**
m *Nob*, Neh. 11:32.

ure *shall be* hewn down, and the
haughty shall be humbled.
34 And he shall cut down the
thickets of the forest with iron,
and Lĕb'a-non shall fall by a
mighty one.

## CHAPTER 11

*The coming and character of the Messiah, and of his kingdom. 10 The gathering in of the Gentiles, and the restoration of Israel.*

AND[T] [a, b, c]there shall come forth
a [1]rod out of the stem of
[d]Jĕs'se, and a [e]Branch shall grow
out of his roots:[Q]
2 And the spirit of the LORD
shall rest upon him, the spirit
of [f]wisdom and understanding,
the spirit of counsel[G] and might,
the spirit of knowledge and of
the fear of the LORD;[T Q]
3 And [2]shall make him of quick
understanding in the fear of the
LORD: and he shall not [g]judge
after the sight of his eyes, neither reprove after the hearing of
his ears:[Q]
4 But with [h, i]righteousness
shall he [g]judge the [j]poor, and reprove with equity[G] for the meek
of the earth: and [k]he shall smite
the earth with the rod of his
mouth, and with the breath of
his lips shall he slay[G] the [l]wicked.[Q]
5 And [h, i]righteousness shall be
the [m]girdle of his loins, and
[n]faithfulness the [m]girdle of his
reins.[G S Q]
6 [o, p, q]The [r]wolf also shall dwell
with the [s]lamb, and the [t]leopard
shall lie down with the kid; and
the calf and the young lion and
the fatling together; and a little
child shall lead them.
7 And the cow and the [u]bear
shall feed; their young ones shall
lie down together: and the lion
shall eat straw like the ox.
8 And the sucking child shall
play on the hole of the [v]asp, and
the weaned child shall put his
hand on the *cockatrice[G]' den.
9 They shall not hurt nor destroy in all my holy mountain:
for the earth shall be full of the
[w, x]knowledge of the LORD, as
the waters cover the sea.
10 And [y, z]in that day [a]there
shall be a root of [b]Jĕs'se, which
shall stand for an [c]ensign[G] of the
[3]people; to it shall the [d]Ġĕn'tīleṣ[G]
seek: and his rest shall be glorious.[Q]
11 And it shall come to pass in
that day, *that* the [e]Lord shall set
his hand again the second time
to recover the remnant of his
[f]people, which shall be left, from
[g]Ăs-sy̆r'ĭ-ȧ, and from [h]Ē'ġy̆pt,
and from †Păth'ros, and from
[i]Cŭsh, and from ‡Ē'lăm, and
from [j]Shī'när, and from [k]Hā'-
math, and from the islands of
the sea.[T]
12 And he shall set up an
[c]ensign[G] for the nations, and
shall assemble the outcasts of
[f]Ĭṣ'ra-el, and gather together the
[l]dispersed of [m]Jū'dah from the
four corners of the earth.
13 [n]The [o]envy also of [p]Ē'phră-
ĭm shall depart, and the adversaries of [q]Jū'dah shall be cut
off: Ē'phră-ĭm shall not envy
Jū'dah, and Jū'dah shall not
vex Ē'phră-ĭm.
14 But they shall fly upon the
shoulders of the [r]Phĭ-lĭs'tīneṣ toward the west; they shall spoil[G]
them of the east together: they
shall lay their hand upon [s]Ē'-
dom and Mō'ab; and the [u]chil-
dren of Ăm'mŏn shall obey them.
15 And the LORD shall ut-
terly [v]destroy the tongue of the
Ē-ġy̆p'tian sea; and with his
[4]mighty wind shall he shake his

**1**
a *Church, prophecies concerning its prosperity,* vs. 1–10; Matt. 16:18.
b *Jesus, prophecies concerning,* vs. 1–5; Matt. 1:21.
c Rom. 15:12.
d *Jesse,* Ruth 4:17.
e *Branch, figurative,* Dan. 4:14.
1 R. V. shoot out of the stock of Jesse, and a branch out of his roots shall bear fruit:

**2**
f *Wisdom, spiritual,* Prov. 2:2.

**3**
g *Jesus, judge,* Matt. 1:21.
2 R. V. his delight shall be in

**4**
h *Jesus, holiness of,* Matt. 1:21.
i *Jesus, perfections of,* Matt. 1:21.
j *Poor, God's care of,* Prov. 21:13.
k *Jesus, power of,* Matt. 1:21.
l *Wicked, punishment of,* Psa. 73:3.

**5**
m *Girdle, figurative,* Prov. 31:24.
n *Jesus, faithfulness of,* Matt. 1:21.

**6**
o *Allegory,* vs. 6–8; Gal. 4:24.
p *Peace, through Christ,* Jer. 29:7.
q *Spiritual Peace,* Gal. 1:3.
r *Wolf, figurative,* Jer. 5:6.
s *Lamb, figurative,* Num. 7:15.
*Leopard, figurative,* Song 4:8.

**7**
u *Bear, illustrative,* 2 Sam. 17:8.

**8**
v *Asp, figurative,* Job 20:14.

**9**
w *Knowledge,* Luke 11:52.
x *Wisdom, spiritual,* Prov. 2:2.

**10**
y *Jesus, prophecies concerning,* Matt. 1:21.
z *Prophecies concerning the Messiah, and their fulfillment,* Gen. 12:3.

a Rom. 15:12.
b *Jesse,* Ruth 4:17.
c *Standard, figurative,* Num. 1:52.
d *Gentiles, prophecies of the conversion of,* Acts 10:45.
3 R. V. peoples, unto him shall the nations seek; and his resting place shall be glorious.

**11**
e *God, providence of,* Gen. 2:2.
f *Israel, prophecies concerning,* Ex. 4:22.
g *Assyria,* Gen. 25:18.
h *Egypt,* Gen. 41:8.
i Or, *Ethiopia,* Isa. 18:1.
j Or, *Babylon, empire of,* Ezra 5:12.
k *Hamath,* 1 Chr. 18:3.

**12**
l *Dispersion, of the Jews,* Gen. 11:8.
m *Jews, prophecies concerning,* Neh. 4:2.

**13**
n *Peace, through Christ,* Jer. 29:7.
o *Envy,* Prov. 14:30.
p *Ephraim, name applied to the ten tribes,* Gen. 41:52.
q *Judah, kingdom of,* 2 Chr. 11:17.

**14**
r *Philistines,* Gen. 26:14.
s *Edomites,* 2 Kin. 8:21.
t *Moabites,* Gen. 19:37.
u *Ammonites,* Deut. 2:20.

**15**
v *Judgments,* Ex. 6:6.
4 R. V. scorching

* **COCKATRICE** (Am. R. V. adder).
**Figurative:** *Of the evil dispositions of the wicked that shall be subdued under the Gospel,* Isa. 11:8. *Of divine judgments,* Isa. 14:29; Jer. 8:17. *Of the evil devices of the wicked,* Isa. 59:5.

† **PATHROS.** *A part of Upper Egypt,* Ezek. 29:14. *Jewish captives in,* Isa. 11:11; Jer. 44:1, 15. *Prophecy against,* Ezek. 30:14.

‡ **ELAM.** *A district southeast of Babylon,* Gen. 14:1, 9; Dan. 8:2. *Prophecies concerning,* Isa. 11:11; 21:2; 22:6; Jer. 25:25; 49:34–39; Ezek. 32:24. *Jews from,* Acts 2:9.

5 R. V. into seven

**16**

*w Israel,* Ex. 4:22.

**1**

*a Praise,* Psa. 150:1.

*b Thankfulness, to God,* Acts 24:3.

*c Anger of God,* 2 Kin. 13:3.

*d God, mercy of,* Gen. 2:2.

*e Spiritual Peace,* Gal. 1:3.

**2**

*f Salvation,* Acts 16:17.

*g God, savior,* Gen. 2:2.

*h Faith, exemplified,* Mark 11:22.

**3**

*i Promise, to the righteous,* 2 Cor. 1:20.

*j Joy,* Psa. 5:11.

*k Wells, figurative,* Gen. 21:19.

**4**

*l Religious Testimony,* 2 Thess. 1:10.

**5**

*m Worship, enjoined,* Gen. 22:5.

1 R. V. let this be known

**6**

*n Shouting, in joy and praise,* 2 Chr. 15:14.

*o God, holiness of,* Gen. 2:2.

*p Holiness, attribute of God,* Ex. 39:30.

*q Church, God dwells in,* Matt. 16:18.

**1**

*a Burden, figurative,* Luke 11:46.

*b Babylon, empire of,* vs. 1–23; Ezra 5:12.

*c Isaiah,* Isa. 1:1.

*d* Isa. 1:1; 2 Kin. 19:2; 20:1.

hand over ‖the river, and shall
smite it [5]in the seven streams,
and make *men* go over dryshod.
16 And there shall be an highway for the remnant of his people, which shall be left, from
[g]Ăs-sȳr′ĭ-ȧ; like as it was to [w]Ĭs′-
ra-el in the day that he came up
out of the land of [h]Ē′ġy̆pt.

## CHAPTER 12

*A song of thanksgiving to God for his mercies unto his people.*

AND in that day thou shalt say,
O LORD, I will [a,b]praise
thee: though thou wast [c]angry
with me, [d]thine anger is turned
away, and thou [e]comfortedst me.
2 Behold, God *is* my [f,g]salva-
tion; I will [h]trust, and not be
afraid: for the LORD JĒ-HŌ′-
VAH *is* my strength and *my*
song; he also is become my salvation.
3 Therefore [i]with [j]joy shall ye
draw water out of the [k]wells of
[f]salvation.
4 And in that day shall ye say,
[a,b]Praise the LORD, call upon
his name, [l]declare his doings
among the people, make mention that his name is exalted.
5 [a,b,m]Sing unto the LORD; for
he hath done excellent things:
[1,l]this *is* known in all the earth.
6 [a,b,l]Cry out and [n]shout, thou
inhabitant of Zī′ŏn: for great *is*
the [o,p]Holy One of Ĭs′ra-el in
the midst of [q]thee.

## CHAPTER 13

*God musters the hosts of his wrath against Babylon. 6 Their work of slaughter described. 19 The desolation of Babylon.*

THE [a]burden of [b]Băb′y̆-lon,
which [c]Ī-sā′iah the son of
[d]Ā′mŏz did see.
2 Lift ye up a [e]banner upon the
high [f]mountain, exalt the voice
unto them, shake the hand, that
they may go into the gates of the
nobles.
3 I have commanded my [1]sanc-
tified ones, I have also called my
mighty ones for mine [g]anger,
*even* [2]them that rejoice in my
highness.
4 The noise of a multitude in
the mountains, like as of a great
people; a tumultuous noise of
the kingdoms of nations gathered together: the LORD of
hosts mustereth the host of the
battle.
5 [h]They come from a far country, from the end of heaven, *even*
the LORD, and the weapons of
his indignation, to destroy the
whole land.
6 ¶ Howl ye; for the [i,j]day of
the LORD *is* at hand; it shall
come as a destruction from the
Almighty.
7 Therefore shall all hands be
faint, and every man's heart shall
melt:
8 And they shall be afraid:
pangs and sorrows shall take
hold of them; they shall be in
pain as a woman that [k]travail-
eth: they shall be amazed one at
another; their faces *shall be as*
flames.
9 Behold, the [i,j]day of the
LORD cometh, cruel both with
[g]wrath and fierce anger, to lay
the land desolate: and he shall
destroy the [l]sinners thereof out
of it.
10 For *the [m]stars of heaven
and the constellations thereof
[n]shall not give their light: the

**2**

*e Standard,* Num. 1:52.

*f Mountain, signals from,* Mic. 7:12.

**3**

*g Anger of God,* 2 Kin. 13:3.

1 R. V. consecrated

2 R. V. my proudly exulting ones.

**5**

*h Agency, in executing judgments,* Mark 1:17.

**6**

*i Day, times of adversity called day of the Lord,* Gen. 1:5.

*j Judgments,* Ex. 6:6.

**8**

*k Birth, pangs in giving,* Psa. 48:6.

**9**

*l Wicked, punishment of,* Psa. 73:3.

**10**

*m Stars,* Judg. 5:20.

*n Celestial Phenomena,* Luke 23:44.

‖ **NILE.** *Called,* THE RIVER, Gen. 41:1, 17; Isa. 11:15; 19:5–8; Amos 8:8; SIHOR, Isa. 23:3; Jer. 2:18.

* **ASTRONOMY.** The phenomena mentioned in the following citations belong to the general field of astronomy. They are grouped here, not with a view of teaching the science of astronomy, but to enable the student to find the scriptures which mention astronomical phenomena.

**The Universe:** *God the creator of,* Job 9:6–9; 26:7, 13; Psa. 136:5–9; Isa. 40:22, 26. *God the ruler of,* Job 38:31–33; Amos 5:8. *Immeasurable,* Jer. 31:37; 33:22. *Laws of, permanent,* Eccl. 1:5; Jer. 31:35, 36. *Declares God's glory,* Psa. 19:1–6. *Destruction of,* Isa. 34:4; Matt. 24:35; 2 Pet. 3:10; Rev. 6:12–14.

**Extraordinary phenomena in:** *Staying of sun and moon,* Josh. 10:12–14. *Darkness, over Egypt,* Ex. 10:21–23; *at crucifixion,* Matt. 27:45; Luke 23:44. *Signs in sun, moon, and stars,* Isa. 13:10. *Foretold by Jesus as a sign of his second coming,* Matt. 24:29; Mark 13:24, 25; Luke 21:25; Acts 2:19, 20.

**Constellations,** Isa. 13:10. *The serpent,* Job 26:13. *Orion,* Job 9:9; 38:31; Amos 5:8. *Pleiades,* Job 9:9; 38:31; Amos 5:8.

o *Sun, darkening of*, Josh. 10:12.
p *Moon, darkening of*, Song 6:10.

**11**
q 1 Sam. 2:3; Prov. 8:13.
r *Pride*, Prov. 16:18.

**12**
s *Gold*, Ezek. 7:19.
t *Ophir, gold of*, 1 Kin. 9:28.
3 R. V. rare
4 R. V. pure gold

**13**
u *Earthquakes, as judgments*, Isa. 29:6.

**15**
v *War, evils of*, Judg. 3:2.
w *Massacre*, Esth. 3:13.
5 R. V. taken shall

**16**
x *Cruelty, in war*, Psa. 27:12.
y *Rape*, Deut. 22:25.

**17**
z *Medes*, Dan. 5:28.

---

a *Silver*, 1 Chr. 28:14.
b *Gold*, Ezek. 7:19.

**18**
c *War, evils of*, Judg. 3:2.
d *Cruelty, in war*, Psa. 27:12.

**19**
e *Babylon, prophecy concerning*, Ezra 5:12.
f *Judgments*, Ex. 6:6.
g *Sodom, destroyed*, Gen. 13:10.
h *Gomorrah, destroyed*, Gen. 13:10.
6 R. V. Chaldeans' pride,

[o]sun shall be [†]darkened in his going forth, and the [p]moon shall not cause her light to shine.[Q]

11 And I will [l]punish the world for *their* evil, and the wicked for their iniquity; and I will cause the [q]arrogancy of the [r]proud to cease, and will lay low the haughtiness of the terrible.

12 I will make a man more [3]precious[G] than fine [s]gold; even a man than the [4]golden wedge of [t]Ō′phĭr.

13 Therefore I will shake the heavens, and the earth shall [u]remove out of her place, in the [g]wrath of the LORD of hosts, and in the day of his fierce anger.[S]

14 And it shall be as the chased roe, and as a sheep that no man taketh up: they shall every man turn to his own people, and flee every one into his own land.

15 [v,w]Every one that is found shall be thrust through; and every one that is [5]joined *unto them* shall fall by the sword.

16 [v]Their children also shall be [x]dashed to pieces before their eyes; their houses shall be spoiled, and their wives [y]ravished.

17 Behold, I will stir up the [z]Mēdeș against them, which shall not regard [a]silver; and *as for* [b]gold, they shall not delight in it.

18 [c]*Their* bows also shall [d]dash the young men to pieces; and they shall have [d]no pity on the fruit of the womb; their eye shall not spare children.

19 And [e]Băb′y̆-lon, the glory of kingdoms, the beauty of the [6]Chăl′deeș′ excellency, shall be as when God [f]overthrew [g]Sŏd′-om and [h]Gō-mŏr′rah.

20 [e]It shall never be inhabited, neither shall it be dwelt in from generation to generation: neither shall the [i]Ā-rā′bĭ-an pitch tent there; neither shall the shepherds make their fold there.

21 But wild beasts of the desert shall lie there; and their houses shall be full of doleful[G] creatures; and [7,j]owls shall dwell there, and [‡]satyrs[G] shall dance there.[Q]

22 And [8]the wild beasts of the islands[G] shall cry in their desolate houses, and [k]dragons[G] in *their* pleasant palaces: and her time *is* near to come, and her days shall not be prolonged.

## CHAPTER 14

*The restoration of Israel. 4 Their triumphant song over the king of Babylon. 24 God's purpose against Assyria. 29 Palestine threatened.*

FOR the LORD will have [a]mercy on Jā′cob, and will yet choose [b]Ĭș′ra-el, and set them in their own land: and the strangers[G] shall be joined with them, and they shall cleave[G] to the house of Jā′cob.

2 And the people shall take them, and bring them to their place: and the house of Ĭș′ra-el shall possess them in the land of the LORD for servants and handmaids: and they shall take them captives, whose captives they were; and they shall rule over their oppressors.

3 And it shall come to pass in the day that the [c]LORD shall give thee [d]rest from thy sorrow, and from thy fear, and from the hard bondage[G] wherein thou wast made to serve,[S]

4 That thou shalt take up this [e]proverb[G] against the [f]king of [g]Băb′y̆-lon, and say, How hath the oppressor ceased! the golden city ceased!

5 The LORD hath broken the staff of the wicked, *and* the sceptre of the rulers.

**20**
i *Arabians*, 2 Chr. 17:11.

**21**
j *Owl*, Lev. 11:17.
7 R. V. ostriches

**22**
k *Dragon*, Deut. 32:33.
8 R. V. wolves shall cry in their castles, and jackals in the pleasant palaces:

**1**
a *God, mercy of*, Gen. 2:2.
b *Israel, after the revolt, prophecies concerning*, 1 Kin. 12:1.

**3**
c *God, preserver*, Gen. 2:2.
d *Temporal Blessings, from God*, Psa. 103:2.

**4**
e *Proverbs*, 1 Sam. 24:13.
f *Rulers, wicked*, Ex. 18:21.
g *Babylon*, Ezra 5:12.

---

See footnotes: CELESTIAL PHENOMENA, Luke 23:44; METEOROLOGY, Matt. 16:2.

† **ECLIPSE.** *Of the sun and moon*, Isa. 13:10; Ezek. 32:7, 8; Joel 2:10, 31; 3:15; Amos 8:9; Matt. 24:29; Mark 13:24; Acts 2:20; Rev. 6:12, 13; 8:12.

See footnotes: SUN, Josh. 10:12; MOON, Song 6:10. **Figurative**, Mic. 3:6.

‡ **SATYR.** *A mythological creature, represented as half man and half goat*, Lev. 17:7 [R. V. *margin*]; 2 Chr. 11:15 [R. V. *margin*]; Isa. 13:21; 34:14.

6 He who smote the people in wrath with a continual stroke, he that ruled the nations in anger, is persecuted, *and* none hindereth.

7 The whole earth is at rest, *and* is quiet: they break forth into singing.

8 Yea, the fir trees rejoice at thee, *and* the cedars of Lĕb′-a-non, *saying*, Since thou art laid down, no feller[G] is come up against us.

9 [h]Hell[G] from beneath is moved for thee to meet *thee* at thy coming: it stirreth up the dead for thee, *even* all the chief ones of the earth; it hath raised up from their thrones all the kings of the nations.

10 All they shall speak and say unto thee, Art thou also become weak as we? art thou become like unto us?

11 Thy pomp is brought down to [1]the grave[G], *and* the noise of thy [i]viols[G]: the worm is spread under thee, and the worms cover thee.

12 How art [j]thou fallen from heaven, O [2]Lụ′çĭ-fēr, son of the morning! *how* art thou cut down to the ground, which didst weaken the nations![Q]

13 For thou hast [k,l]said in thine heart, I will ascend into heaven, I will exalt my throne above the stars of God: I will sit also upon the mount of the congregation, in the sides of the north:[Q]

14 I will ascend above the heights of the clouds; I will be like the most High.[Q]

15 Yet thou shalt be [m]brought down to [h]hell[G], to the sides of the pit.

16 They that see thee shall narrowly[G] look upon thee, *and* consider thee, *saying*, *Is* this the man that made the earth to tremble, that did shake kingdoms;

17 *That* made the world as a wilderness, and destroyed the cities thereof; *that* opened not the house of his prisoners?

18 All the kings of the nations, *even* all of them, lie in glory, every one in his own house.

19 But thou art cast out of thy grave like an abominable branch, [3]*and as* the raiment of those that are slain, thrust through with a sword, that go down to the stones of the pit; as a carcase trodden[G] under feet.

20 Thou shalt not be joined with them in burial, because thou hast destroyed thy land, *and* slain thy people: [n]the [o]seed of evildoers shall never be renowned.

21 [p]Prepare slaughter for his [o]children for the iniquity[G] of their [q]fathers; that they do not rise, nor possess the land, nor fill the face of the world with cities.

22 For I will [m]rise up against them, saith the LORD of hosts, and cut off from [g]Băb′y̆-lon the name, and remnant, and son, and nephew, saith the LORD.

23 [m]I will also make it a possession for the [4,r]bittern, and pools of water: and I will sweep it with the besom[G] of destruction, saith the LORD of hosts.

24 ¶ The LORD of hosts hath [s]sworn, saying, Surely as I have thought, [t]so shall it come to pass; and as I have purposed, *so* shall it stand:[S]

25 That I will break the [u]Ăs-sy̆r′ĭ-an in my land, and upon my mountains tread him under foot: then shall his [v]yoke depart from off them, and his burden depart from off their shoulders.

26 This *is* the purpose that is purposed upon the whole earth: and this *is* the hand that is stretched out upon all the [w]nations.[S]

**9**
h *Hell,* Mark 9:43.

**11**
i *Music, instruments of,* 2 Chr. 5:13.
1 Am. R. V. Sheol,

**12**
j *Nebuchadnezzar,* Dan. 2:1.
2 R. V. day star,

**13**
k *Presumption, in defying God,* Psa. 19:13.
l *Ambition,* Hab. 2:5.

**15**
m *Judgments,* Ex. 6:6.

**19**
3 R. V. clothed with the slain, that are thrust

**20**
n *Heredity, results of,* Ezek. 18:2.
o *Children, involved in sins of parents,* Mark 10:14.

**21**
p *Sin, fruits of,* Rom. 5:12.
q *Parents, curses upon, entailed upon children,* 2 Cor. 12:14.

**23**
r Isa. 34:11; Zeph. 2:14.
4 R. V. porcupine,

**24**
s *Oath, attributed to God,* Num. 5:19.
t *God, immutable,* Gen. 2:2.

**25**
u *Assyria, prophecies concerning,* Gen. 25:18.
v *Yoke, figurative,* 1 Sam. 6:7.

**26**
w *Nation, chastisement of,* Isa. 2:4.

27 For the [t]LORD of hosts hath purposed, and who shall disannul *it*? and his hand *is* stretched out, and who shall turn it back?

28 ¶ In the year that king [x]Ā′hăz died was this [y]burden.

29 ¶ Rejoice not [5]thou, whole [z]Păl-es-tī′nȧ, because the rod of him that smote thee is broken: for out of the [a]serpent's root shall come forth a [6,b]cockatrice, and his fruit *shall be* a fiery flying serpent.

30 And the firstborn of the [c]poor shall feed, and the needy shall lie down in safety: and I will [d]kill thy root with [e]famine, and he shall slay thy remnant.

31 Howl, O gate; cry, O city; thou, [7]whole Păl-es-tī′nȧ, *art* dissolved: for there shall come from the north a smoke, and none *shall be* alone in his appointed times.

32 What shall *one* then answer the messengers of the nation? That the LORD hath founded [f]Zī′ŏn, and the poor of his people shall trust in it.

## CHAPTER 15

*The desolation of Moab.*

THE [a]burden of [b]Mō′ab. Because [c]in the night [d]Är of Mō′ab is [e,f]laid waste, *and* brought to silence; because in the night [g]Kīr of Mō′ab is laid waste, *and* brought to silence;

2 He is gone up to Bā′jith, and to [h]Dī′bŏn, the high places, to weep: [b]Mō′ab shall howl over [i]Nē′bō, and over [j]Mĕd′e-bȧ: on all their heads *shall be* baldness, *and* every beard cut off.

3 [e,f]In their streets they shall gird themselves with *sackcloth: on the [k]tops of their houses, and in their [1]streets, every one shall howl, weeping abundantly.

4 [e,f]And [l]Hĕsh′bŏn shall cry, and [m]Ē-le-ā′leh: their voice shall be heard *even* unto [n]Jā′hăz: therefore the armed soldiers of [b]Mō′ab shall cry out; his [2]life shall be grievous unto him.

5 My heart shall cry out for Mō′ab; [3]his fugitives *shall flee* unto [o]Zō′ar, an heifer of three years old: for by the mounting up of [p]Lu̦′hith with weeping shall they go it up; for in the way of [q]Hŏr-o-nā′im they shall raise up a cry of destruction.

6 For the waters of [r]Nĭm′rim shall be desolate: for the [4]hay is withered away, the [5]grass faileth, there is no green thing.

7 Therefore the abundance they have gotten, and that which they have laid up, shall they carry away to the brook of the willows.

8 For the cry is gone round about the borders of Mō′ab; the howling thereof unto Ĕg′la-ĭm, and the howling thereof unto Bē′er–ē′lim.

9 For the waters of Dī′mŏn shall be full of blood: for I will bring more upon Dī′mŏn, [s]lions upon him that escapeth of Mō′ab, and upon the remnant of the land.

## CHAPTER 16

*Moab is exhorted to renew his allegiance to the throne of David. 6 His pride, 7 and hence his desolation and distress. 13 The time of his calamity.*

SEND ye the lamb to the ruler of the land from [a]Sē′lȧ to the wilderness, unto the mount of the daughter of Zī′ŏn.

2 For it shall be, *that*, as [1]a wandering [b]bird cast out of the nest, *so* the daughters of [c]Mō′ab shall be at the fords of [d]Är′nŏn.

3 Take counsel, execute judgment; make thy shadow as the night in the midst of the noon-

---

**Chapter 14**

**28**
x *Ahaz,* 2 Kin. 15:38.
y *Burden, figurative,* Luke 11:46.

**29**
z *Philistines, prophecies against,* vs. 29–31; Gen. 26:14.
a *Serpent, figurative,* Num. 21:6.
b *Cockatrice, figurative,* Isa. 11:8.
5 R. V. O Philistia, all of thee, because
6 Am. R. V. an adder,

**30**
c *Poor, God's care of,* Prov. 21:13.
d *Judgments,* Ex. 6:6.
e *Famine, sent as a judgment,* 2 Kin. 8:1.

**31**
7 R. V. art melted away, O Philistia, all of thee; for

**32**
f *Zion,* 2 Sam. 5:7.

**Chapter 15**

**1**
a *Burden, figurative,* Luke 11:46.
b *Moabites,* vs. 1–9; Gen. 19:37.
c *Strategy, in war,* Judg. 7:16.
d Num. 21:15; Deut. 2:9, 18, 29.
e *Nation, chastisement of,* vs. 1–9; Isa. 2:4.
f *Judgments,* Ex. 6:6.
g Or, *Kir-haraseth,* 2 Kin. 3:25.

**2**
h *Dibon,* Num. 21:30.
i *Nebo,* Num. 32:3.
j *Medeba,* Num. 21:30.

**3**
k *House, roof of,* Esth. 8:1.
1 R. V. broad places,

**4**
l *Heshbon,* Isa. 16:8.
m Isa. 16:9; Num. 32:3, 37.
n *Jahaz,* Judg. 11:20.
2 R. V. soul trembleth within him.

**5**
o *Zoar,* Deut. 34:3.
p Jer. 48:5.
q Jer. 48:3, 5, 34.
3 R. V. her nobles flee unto Zoar, to Eglath-shelishiyah:

**6**
r Jer. 48:34.
4 R. V. grass
5 R. V. tender grass

**9**
s *Lion, figurative,* Mic. 5:8.

**Chapter 16**

**1**
a 2 Kin. 14:7.

**2**
b *Birds,* Eccl. 12:4.
c *Moabites,* Gen. 19:37.
d *Arnon, fords of,* Num. 22:36.
1 R. V. wandering birds, as a scattered nest,

---

* **SACKCLOTH.** *A symbol of mourning,* 1 Kin. 20:31, 32; Job 16:15; Isa. 15:3; Jer. 4:8; 6:26; 49:3; Lam. 2:10; Ezek. 7:18; Dan. 9:3; Joel 1:8. *Worn by Jacob when it was reported to him that Joseph had been devoured by wild beasts,* Gen. 37:34. *Animals covered with, at time of national mourning,* Jonah 3:8.

4
[e] *Oppression,* Eccl. 5:8.

5
[f] *Mercy,* Deut. 5:10.
[g] *Jesus, prophecies concerning* (as some interpret), Matt. 1:21.
[h] *Truth,* John 18:37.
2 R. V. swift to do righteousness.

6
[i] *Pride,* Prov. 16:18.
3 R. V. his boastings are nought.

7
[j] *Kir-haraseth,* 2 Kin. 3:25.
4 R. V. raisin-cakes

8
[k] Jer. 48:32.
[l] *Sibmah,* Josh. 13:19.
[m] *Jazer,* Josh. 13:25.

9
[n] Isa. 15:4; Num. 32:3, 37.
[o] *Harvest,* Ex. 34:21.
5 R. V. upon thy summer fruits and upon thy harvest the battle shout is fallen.

10
[p] *Joy,* Psa. 5:11.
[q] *Vineyard,* Isa. 1:8.
[r] *Music,* 2 Chr. 5:13.
[s] *Wine,* Prov. 23:31.

day; hide the outcasts; bewray[c]
not him that wandereth.
4 Let mine outcasts dwell with
thee, [c]Mō′ab; be thou a covert to
them from the face of the spoiler:
for the *extortioner is at an end,
the spoiler ceaseth, the [e]oppressors are consumed out of the
land.
5 And in [f]mercy shall the throne
be established: and [g]he shall sit
upon it in [h]truth in the tabernacle of Dā′vid, judging, and
seeking judgment[c], and [2]hasting
righteousness.
6 ¶ We have heard of the [i]pride
of Mō′ab; *he is* very proud: *even*
of his haughtiness, and his pride,
and his wrath: [3]*but* his lies *shall*
not *be* so.
7 Therefore shall [c]Mō′ab howl
for Mō′ab, every one shall howl:
for the [4]foundations of [j]Kĭr-hăr′e-sĕth shall ye mourn; surely
*they are* stricken.
8 For the fields of †Hĕsh′bŏn
languish, *and* [k]the vine of [l]Sĭb′-
mah: the lords of the heathen
have broken down the principal
plants thereof, they are come
*even* unto [m]Jā′zēr, they wandered *through* the wilderness:
her branches are stretched
out, they are gone over the
sea.
9 Therefore I will bewail with
the weeping of [m]Jā′zēr the vine
of Sĭb′mah: I will water thee
with my tears, O †Hĕsh′bŏn,
and [n]Ē-le-ā′leh: for [5]the shouting
for thy summer fruits and for thy
[o]harvest is fallen.
10 And gladness is taken away,
and [p]joy out of the plentiful field;
and in the [q]vineyards there shall
be no [r]singing, neither shall
there be shouting: the treaders
shall tread out no [s]wine in *their*
presses; I have made *their vintage* shouting to cease.
11 Wherefore my bowels[c] shall
sound like an harp for Mō′ab,
and mine inward parts for [l]Kĭr-hā′resh.
12 And it shall come to pass,
when it is seen that Mō′ab is
weary on the high place, that he
shall come to his sanctuary[c] to
pray; but he shall not prevail.
13 This *is* the word that the
LORD hath spoken concerning
[c]Mō′ab since that time.
14 But now the LORD hath spoken, saying, Within three years,
as the years of an hireling, and
the glory of [c,t]Mō′ab shall be
contemned[c], with all that great
multitude; and the remnant *shall*
*be* very small *and* feeble.

## CHAPTER 17

*The overthrow of Syria and Israel foretold. 6 Some shall forsake idolatry; 9 but the land shall be plagued for its impiety. 12 The enemies of Israel threatened.*

THE [a]burden of [b]Dā-măs′cus.
Behold, [c]Dā-măs′cus is taken away from *being* a city, and
it shall be a ruinous heap.
2 The cities of Ăr′ŏ-ēr *are* forsaken: they shall be for flocks,
which shall lie down, and none
shall make *them* afraid.
3 The fortress also shall cease
from [d]Ē′phră-ĭm, and the kingdom from [b]Dā-măs′cus, and the
remnant of [e]Sўr′ĭ-ȧ: they shall be
as the glory of the children
of Ĭș′ra-el, saith the LORD of
hosts.[s]
4 And in that day it shall come
to pass, *that* the glory of Jā′cob
shall be made thin, and the fatness of his flesh shall wax[c] lean.
5 And it shall be as when the
harvestman gathereth the corn[c],
and reapeth the ears with his
arm; and it shall be as he that

14
[t] *Nation, chastisement of,* Isa. 2:4.

1
[a] *Burden, figurative,* Luke 11:46.
[b] *Damascus, prophecies concerning,* Isa. 8:4.
[c] *Nation, chastisement of,* vs. 1–14; Isa. 2:4.

3
[d] *Ephraim, name applied to the ten tribes,* Gen. 41:52.
[e] *Syria, prophecies concerning,* 2 Kin. 6:23.

* **EXTORTION,** Psa. 109:11; Isa. 16:4; Matt. 23:25; Luke 18:11. *Warning against,* Prov. 22:16. *Forbidden,* Luke 3:13, 14. *Cruel,* Mic. 3:2, 3. *Cause for disfellowship,* 1 Cor. 5:10, 11. *Excludes from the kingdom of God,* 1 Cor. 6:10.
**Instances of:** *Jacob in demanding Esau's birthright for a mess of pottage,* Gen. 25:31. *Pharaoh in exacting of the Egyptians lands and persons for corn,* Gen. 47:13–26. *The Jews after the captivity,* Neh. 5:1–13.

† **HESHBON.** *A city of the Amorites,* Num. 21:25–35; Deut. 1:4; 29:7. *Built by Reuben,* Num. 32:37. *Allotted to Gad,* Josh. 21:38, 39. *Given to sons of Merari,* 1 Chr. 6:81. *Fish pools at,* Song 7:4. *Prophecies concerning,* Isa. 16:8; Jer. 48:2, 34, 35; 49:1–3.

gathereth ears in the valley of [f]Rĕph'a-ĭm.

6 [g]Yet [h]gleaning grapes shall be left in it, as the shaking of an [i]olive tree, two *or* three berries in the top of the uppermost bough, four *or* five in the outmost fruitful branches thereof, saith the LORD God of Ĭṣ'ra-el.

7 At that day shall a [j]man [k]look to his [l]Maker, and his eyes shall have respect to the [m]Holy One of Ĭṣ'ra-el.

8 And [n]he shall not look to the [o]altars, the work of his hands, neither shall respect *that* which his fingers have made, either the [1,p]groves, or the [q]images.

9 [r]In that day shall his strong cities be as [2]a forsaken bough, and an uppermost branch, which they left because of the children of Ĭṣ'ra-el: and there shall be desolation.

10 Because [r,s]thou hast forgotten the God of thy [t]salvation, and hast not been mindful of the [u]rock of thy strength, therefore shalt thou plant pleasant plants, and shalt set it with strange slips:

11 [r]In the day shalt thou make thy plant to grow, and in the morning shalt thou make thy seed to flourish: *but* the harvest *shall be* a heap in the day of grief and of desperate sorrow.

12 ¶ Woe to the multitude of many people, *which* make a noise like the noise of the seas; and to the rushing of nations, *that* make a rushing like the rushing of mighty waters!

13 The nations shall rush like the rushing of many waters: but [v]*God* shall rebuke [c]them, and they shall flee far off, and shall be chased as the [w]chaff of the mountains before the wind, and like a rolling thing before the whirlwind.

14 And behold at eveningtide trouble; *and* before the morning he *is* [x]not. This *is* the [y]portion of them that spoil us, and the lot of them that rob us.

## CHAPTER 18

*A woe denounced against the Ethiopians. 7 The happy result of the chastisement.*

1 WOE to the land shadowing with wings, which *is* beyond the rivers of *Ē-thĭ-ō'pĭ-ȧ:

2 That sendeth [a]ambassadors by the sea, even in [b]vessels of [2,c]bulrushes upon the waters, *saying*, Go, ye swift messengers, to a nation [3]scattered and peeled, to a people terrible from their beginning [4]hitherto; a nation [5]meted out and trodden down, whose land the rivers have spoiled!

3 All ye inhabitants of the world, and dwellers on the earth, see ye, when he lifteth up an [d]ensign on the [e]mountains; and when he bloweth a trumpet, hear ye.

4 For so the LORD said unto me, I will take my rest, and I will consider in my dwelling place like a clear heat [6]upon herbs, *and* like a cloud of dew in the heat of harvest.

5 For [f]afore the [g]harvest, when the [7]bud is perfect, and the sour grape is ripening in the flower, he shall both [h]cut off the sprigs with †pruning [i]hooks, and [h]take away *and* cut down the [j]branches.

6 They shall be [k,l]left together unto the fowls of the mountains, and to the beasts of the earth: and the fowls shall summer upon them, and all the beasts of the earth shall winter upon them.

**5**
*f Rephaim*, 1 Chr. 11:15.

**6**
*g God, mercy of*, Gen. 2:2.
*h Gleaning, figurative*, Lev. 23:22.
*i Olive*, Deut. 6:11.

**7**
*j Man, created*, Job 4:17.
*k Backsliders, return of*, Jer. 3:22.
*l God, creator*, Gen. 2:2.
*m God, holiness of*, Gen. 2:2.

**8**
*n Idolatry, prophecies relating to*, 1 Sam. 15:23.
*o Altar, used in idolatrous worship*, Gen. 8:20.
*p Groves*, Judg. 6:28.
*q Idol*, 1 Kin. 15:12.
1 R. V. Asherim, or the sun-images.

**9**
*r Backsliders, punishment of*, Jer. 3:22.
2 R. V. the forsaken places in the wood and on the mountain top, which were forsaken from before the children of Israel: and it shall be a desolation.

**10**
*s Godless, described as forgetting God*, Job 8:13.
*t God, savior*, Gen. 2:2.
*u Rock, figurative*, Psa. 78:15.

**13**
*v God, power of*, Gen. 2:2.
*w Chaff*, Hos. 13:3.

**14**
*x Death, of the wicked, sudden*, Num. 23:10.
*y Wicked, punishment of*, Psa. 73:3.

**1**
1 R. V. Ah, the land of the rustling of wings,

**2**
*a Ambassadors*, Josh. 9:4.
*b Ship*, 2 Chr. 8:18.
*c Bulrush*, Ex. 2:3.
2 R. V. papyrus
3 R. V. tall and smooth,
4 R. V. onward;
5 R. V. that meteth out and treadeth down, whose land the rivers divide!

**3**
*d Standard*, Num. 1:52.
*e Mountain, signals from*, Mic. 7:12.

**4**
6 R. V. in sunshine,

**5**
*f Agriculture*, Gen. 3:23.
*g Harvest*, Ex. 34:21.
*h Judgments*, Ex. 6:6.
*i Hooks, for pruning*, Ex. 36:36.
*j Branch, figurative*, Dan. 4:14.
7 R. V. blossom is over, and the flower becometh a ripening grape,

**6**
*k War, slain in, neglected*, Judg. 3:2.
*l War, evils of* Judg. 3:2.

* **ETHIOPIA** (*burned faces*), a region in Africa, inhabited by the descendants of Ham, called also CUSH. *The inhabitants of, black*, Jer. 13:23. *The Babylonian empire, extended to*, Esth. 1:1. *Rivers of*, Isa. 18:1. *Armies of*, Jer. 46:9; 2 Chr. 12:3; Ezek. 38:5; *defeated by Asa*, 2 Chr. 14:9–15; 16:8; *invade Syria*, 2 Kin. 19:9.
*Merchandise of*, Isa. 45:14. *Moses marries a woman of* [R. V. Cushite], Num. 12:1. *Ebed-melech, an Ethiopian, at the court of Babylon, treats Jeremiah kindly*, Jer. 38:7–13; 39:15–18. *Candace, queen of*, Acts 8:27. *A eunuch from, becomes a disciple under the preaching of Philip*, Acts 8:27–39. *Prophecies concerning the conversion of*, Psa. 68:31; Isa. 45:14. *Desolation of*, Isa. 20:2–6; 43:3; Ezek. 30:4–9; Hab. 3:7; Zeph. 2:12.

† **PRUNING**, Lev. 25:3, 4; Isa. 5:6; 18:5; John 15:2–6. *Pruning hook*, Isa. 2:4; 18:5; Joel 3:10; Mic. 4:3.

7 ¶ [m]In that time shall the present be brought unto the LORD of
hosts of a people [3]scattered and
peeled,[C] and from a people terrible from their beginning [4]hither-
to[C]; a nation [5]meted[C] out and trodden[C] under foot, whose land the
rivers have spoiled, to the place
of the name of the LORD of
hosts, the mount Zī′ŏn.

## CHAPTER 19

*Judgments upon Egypt. 11 The counsel of her princes, foolishness. 18 Many of her people shall turn unto the Lord. 23 The covenant of Egypt, Assyria, and Israel.*

THE [a]burden[C] of [b]Ē′ġy̆pt. Behold, the LORD rideth upon
a swift cloud, and shall come into
Ē′ġy̆pt: and [c]the idols of Ē′ġy̆pt
shall be moved at his presence,
and the heart of Ē′ġy̆pt shall
melt in the midst of it.[S Q]
2 And [d]I will [e,f]set the [g]Ē-ġy̆p′-
tians against the Ē-ġy̆p′tians:
and they shall fight every one
against his brother, and every
one against his neighbour;
city against city, *and* kingdom
against kingdom.[Q]
3 And the spirit of [b]Ē′ġy̆pt shall
fail in the midst thereof; and I
will destroy the counsel thereof:
and they shall seek to the idols,
and [h]to the *charmers, and to
them that have familiar[C] spirits,
and to the wizards.
4 And the [i]Ē′ġy̆p′tians will [j]I
give over into the hand of a cruel
lord; and a fierce king shall rule
over them, saith the Lord, the
LORD of hosts.
5 And the waters shall fail from
the sea, and the [k]river shall be
wasted and dried up.
6 And [1]they shall turn the rivers far away; *and* the brooks of
defence shall be emptied and
dried up: the [l]reeds and flags
shall wither.[T]
7 The [2]paper reeds by the
[k]brooks, by the mouth of the
brooks, and every thing sown
by the brooks, shall wither, be
driven away, and be no *more*.
8 The fishers also shall mourn,
and all they that cast angle[C] into
the [k]brooks shall lament, and
they that spread nets upon the
waters shall languish.
9 Moreover they that work in
fine [m,n]flax, and they that [o]weave
[3]networks, shall be confounded.[C]
10 And [4]they shall be broken in
the purposes thereof, all that
make sluices *and* ponds for fish.
11 Surely the princes of [p]Zō′an
*are* fools, the counsel of the wise
counsellors of [q]Phā′raōh is become brutish[C]: how say ye unto
Phā′raōh, I *am* the son of the
wise, the son of ancient kings?
12 Where *are* they? where *are*
thy wise *men*? and let them tell
thee now, and let them know
what the [d]LORD of hosts hath
purposed upon [b]Ē′ġy̆pt.[Q]
13 The princes of [p]Zō′an are
become fools, the princes of
†Nŏph are deceived; they have
also seduced Ē′ġy̆pt, *even they
that are* the [5]stay of the tribes
thereof.
14 The LORD hath mingled a
perverse spirit in the midst thereof: and they have caused Ē′ġy̆pt
to err in every work thereof, as a
[r]drunken *man* staggereth in his
vomit.
15 Neither shall there be *any*
work for [b]Ē′ġy̆pt, which the head
or tail, branch or rush, may do.
16 In that day shall [b]Ē′ġy̆pt be
like unto [s]women: and [i]it shall
be afraid and fear because of
the shaking of the [j]hand of the
LORD of hosts, which he shaketh over it.
17 And the land of Jū′dah shall
be a terror unto Ē′ġy̆pt, every
one that maketh mention thereof
shall be afraid in himself, be-

**7**
m *Gentiles, prophecies of the conversion of,* Acts 10:45.

**1**
a *Burden, figurative,* Luke 11:46.
b *Egypt, prophecies against,* vs. 1–25; Gen. 41:8.
c *Idolatry, prophecies relating to,* 1 Sam. 15:23.

**2**
d *God, providence of,* Gen. 2:2.
e *War, civil,* Judg. 3:2.
f *War, as a judgment,* Judg. 3:2.
g *Egypt, civil war in,* Gen. 41:8.

**3**
h *Sorcery, practiced by Egyptians,* Isa. 47:9.

**4**
i *Nation, chastisement of,* Isa. 2:4.
j *Judgments,* Ex. 6:6.

**5**
k *Nile,* Isa. 11:15.

**6**
l *Reed,* Ezek. 40:3.
1 Am. R. V. the rivers shall become foul; the streams of Egypt shall be diminished

**7**
2 R. V. The meadows by the Nile, by the brink of the Nile, and all that is sown by the Nile, shall become dry,

**9**
m *Flax,* Ex. 9:31.
n *Egypt, productions of,* Gen. 41:8.
o *Weaving,* Isa. 38:12.
3 R. V. white cloth,

**10**
4 R. V. her pillars shall be broken in pieces, all they that work for hire shall be grieved in soul.

**11**
p *Zoan,* Isa. 30:4.
q Isa. 30:2, 3; 36:6.

**13**
5 R. V. corner stone of

**14**
r *Drunkenness, consequences of,* Luke 21:34.

**16**
s *Women,* Prov. 31:10.

* **CHARMERS.** *Those who practiced enchantments by muttering, as snake charmers,* Isa. 19:3; Jer. 8:17. *Prohibited,* Deut. 18:10, 11. *Of serpents,* Psa. 58:4, 5; Jer. 8:17.

† **NOPH.** *Called also* MEMPHIS, Hos. 9:6. *A city of Egypt,* Jer. 2:16. *Prophecy against Jews in,* Jer. 44. *Prophecies against,* Isa. 19:13; Jer. 46:13–19; Ezek. 30:13, 16.

18
t *Language*, Dan. 3:29.

19
u *Pillar*, Gen. 28:18.

20
v *Adversity, benefits of*, Psa. 10:6.
w *Prayer, answer to promised*, Acts 6:4.
x *Oppression*, Eccl. 5:8.
6 R. V. defender,

21
y *Worship*, Gen. 22:5.

22
z *Divine Chastisement*, Job 33:19.

23
a *Peace*, Jer. 29:7.
b *Assyria, prophecies concerning*, Gen. 25:18.

24
c *Egypt*, Gen. 41:8.

25
d *Israel*, Ex. 4:22.

cause of the counsel of the LORD
of hosts, which he hath determined against it.
18 In that day shall five cities
in the land of Ē′ġȳpt speak the
[t]language of Cā′năan, and swear
to the LORD of hosts; one shall
be called, The city of destruction.
19 In that day shall there be an
altar to the LORD in the midst
of the land of [b]Ē′ġȳpt, and a
[u]pillar at the border thereof to
the LORD.
20 And it shall be for a sign and
for a witness unto the LORD of
hosts in the land of Ē′ġȳpt: for
[v]they shall [w]cry unto the LORD
because of the [x]oppressors, and
he shall send them a saviour, and
a [6]great one, and he shall deliver
them.
21 And the LORD shall be
known to Ē′ġȳpt, and the Ē-ġȳp′-
tians shall know the LORD in
that day, and shall [y]do sacrifice
and oblation; yea, they shall vow
a vow unto the LORD, and perform *it*.
22 And the LORD shall [z]smite
Ē′ġȳpt: he shall smite and heal
*it*: and [v]they shall return *even* to
the LORD, and he shall be intreated of them, and shall heal
them.
23 In that day shall [a]there be
a highway out of Ē′ġȳpt to
[b]Ăs-sȳr′ĭ-ȧ, and the Ăs-sȳr′ĭ-an
shall come into Ē′ġȳpt, and the
Ē-ġȳp′tian into Ăs-sȳr′ĭ-ȧ, and
the Ē-ġȳp′tians shall serve with
the Ăs-sȳr′ĭ-ans.
24 [a]In that day shall Ĭș′ra-el be
the third with [c]Ē′ġȳpt and with
[b]Ăs′sȳr′ĭ-ȧ, *even* a blessing in the
midst of the land:
25 Whom the LORD of hosts
shall bless, saying, Blessed *be*
[c]Ē′ġȳpt my people, and [b]Ăs-
sȳr′ĭ-ȧ the work of my hands,
and [d]Ĭș′ra-el mine inheritance.

## CHAPTER 20

*A sign prefiguring the captivity of Egypt and Ethiopia.*

IN the year that [a]Tär′tan came
unto [b]Ăsh′dŏd, (when Sär′-
gon the king of [c]Ăs-sȳr′ĭ-ȧ sent
him,) and fought against Ăsh′-
dŏd, and took it;
2 At the same time [d]spake the
LORD by [e]Ī-șā′iah the son of
Ā′mŏz, saying, [f]Go and loose the
[g]sackcloth from off thy loins, and
put off thy [h]shoe from thy foot.
And he did so, *walking naked
and barefoot.
3 And the LORD said, Like as
my servant [e]Ī-șā′iah hath walked
naked and barefoot three years
*for* a sign and wonder upon [i]Ē′-
ġȳpt and upon [j]Ē-thĭ-ō′pĭ-ȧ;
4 So shall the king of [c]Ăs-sȳr′ĭ-ȧ
lead away the [i]Ē-ġȳp′tians [k]pris-
oners, and the [j]Ē-thĭ-ō′pĭ-ans
[k]captives, young and old, naked
and barefoot, even with *their*
buttocks uncovered, to the
shame of Ē′ġȳpt.
5 And they shall be afraid and
ashamed of [j]Ē-thĭ-ō′pĭ-ȧ their
expectation, and of [i]Ē′ġȳpt their
glory.
6 And the inhabitant of this
[1]isle shall say in that day, Behold, such *is* our expectation,
whither we flee for help to be
delivered from the king of
[c]Ăs-sȳr′ĭ-ȧ: and how shall we
escape?

## CHAPTER 21

*The prophet sees in a vision the downfall of Babylon by the Medes and Persians. 11 The burden of Edom. 13 The burden of Arabia.*

THE burden of the desert of
the sea. As [a]whirlwinds in
the south pass through; *so* it
cometh from the desert, from a
terrible land.
2 A grievous vision is [b,c]de-
clared unto [d]me; the treacherous
dealer dealeth treacherously, and

v.1–632 BC

1
a 2 Kin. 18:17.
b *Ashdod*, 1 Sam. 6:17.
c *Assyria*, Gen. 25:18.

2
d *Prophets, inspiration of*, Isa. 3:2.
e *Isaiah*, Isa. 1:1.
f *Instruction, by object lessons*, Prov. 23:23.
g *Sackcloth*, Isa. 15:3.
h *Shoe*, Josh. 5:15.

3
i *Egypt, prophecies against*, Gen. 41:8.
j *Ethiopia, desolation of*, Isa. 18:1.

4
k *Captive*, 1 Sam. 30:3.

6
1 R. V. coastland

1
a *Whirlwind*, Prov. 1:27.

2
b *Inspiration*, Job 32:8.
c *Prophets, inspiration of*, Isa. 3:2.
d *Isaiah*, Isa. 1:1.

***PANTOMIME.** *Prophecies illustrated by, by Isaiah*, Isa. 20:2, 3; *by Jeremiah*, Jer. 43:8–10; *by Ezekiel*, Ezek. 4:1–8; 12:3–7, 18; 37:16–20; *by Agabus*, Acts 21:11.

the spoiler spoileth.[C] Go up, O
[e]Ē'lăm: besiege, O [f]Mē'dĭ-ȧ; all
the sighing thereof have I made
to cease.
3 Therefore are my loins filled
with pain: pangs have taken
hold upon me, as the pangs of a
woman that [g]travaileth: I [1]was
bowed down at the hearing *of*
*it*; I was dismayed at the seeing *of it*.[Q]
4 My heart panted, fearfulness
affrighted[C] me: the [2]night of my
pleasure hath he turned into fear
unto me.
5 [3]Prepare the table, [h]watch
in the watchtower, eat, drink:
arise, ye princes, *and* anoint the
shield.
6 For thus hath the Lord said
unto me, Go, set a [h]watchman,
let him declare what he seeth.
7 And [4]he saw a chariot *with* a
couple of horsemen, a chariot of
[i]asses, *and* a chariot of [j]camels;
and he hearkened diligently with
much heed:
8 And he cried, A lion: My
lord, I stand continually upon
the watchtower in the daytime,
and I am set in my ward[C] whole
nights:
9 And, behold, here cometh a
[5]chariot of men, *with* a couple of
horsemen. And he answered and
said, [k]Băb'y̆-lon is fallen, is fall-
en; and all the [l]graven[C] images[C] of
her gods he hath broken unto
the ground.[Q]
10 O my threshing, and the
corn[C] of my floor: that which [d]I
have [b,c]heard of the LORD of
hosts, the God of Ĭş'ra-el, have I
declared unto you.
11 ¶ The burden of [m]Dụ'mah.
He calleth to me out of [n]Sē'ĭr,
[h]Watchman, what of the night?
Watchman, what of the night?
12 The watchman said, The
morning cometh, and also the
night: if ye will enquire, enquire
ye: return, come.
13 ¶ The burden upon [o]Ȧ-rā'-
bĭ-ȧ. In the forest in Ȧ-rā'bĭ-ȧ
shall ye lodge, O ye travelling
[p]companies of Dĕd'a-nĭm.
14 [6]The inhabitants of the land
of [q]Tē'mȧ [r]brought water to him
that was thirsty, they prevented[C]
with their bread him that fled.
15 For they fled from the
[s]swords, from the drawn sword,
and from the bent [t]bow, and
from the grievousness of [u]war.
16 For thus hath the Lord
[b,c]said unto [d]me, Within a year,
according to the years of an hireling, and all the glory of [v]Kē'-
där shall fail:
17 And the residue[C] of the number of [w]archers, the mighty men
of the children of [v]Kē'där, shall
be diminished: for the LORD
God of Ĭş'ra-el hath [b]spoken *it*.

## CHAPTER 22

*A siege of Jerusalem foretold, and the prophet's grief in view of the impending calamity. 8 He rebukes the confidence of the people in their own wisdom. 15 He foretells the removal of Shebna from the office of treasurer, 20 and the promotion of Eliakim to his place.*

THE burden of the valley of
vision. What aileth thee
now, that thou art wholly gone
up to the housetops?
2 Thou that art full of stirs,[C] a
tumultuous city, a joyous city:
thy slain *men are* not slain with
the sword, nor dead in battle.
3 All thy rulers are fled together, they are bound by the
[a]archers: all that are found in
thee are bound together, *which*
have fled from far.
4 Therefore [b,c]said I, Look
away from me; I will weep bitterly, labour not to comfort me,
because of the spoiling[C] of the
daughter of my people.
5 [d]For *it is* a day of trouble,
and of treading[C] down, and of
perplexity by the Lord [1]GOD
of hosts in the valley of vision,
breaking down the walls, and of
crying to the mountains.

e *Elam, prophecies concerning,* Isa. 11:11.
f *Medes,* Dan. 5:28.

3
g *Birth,* Psa. 48:6.
1 R. V. am pained so that I cannot hear; I am dismayed so that I cannot see.

4
2 R. V. twilight that I desired hath been turned into trembling unto me.

5
h *Watchman,* 2 Sam. 18:24.
3 R. V. They prepare the table, they set the watch, they eat, they drink:

7
i *Ass,* 2 Chr. 28:15.
j *Camel,* 1 Sam. 30:17.
4 R. V. when he seeth a troop, horsemen in pairs, a troop of asses, a troop of camels, he shall hearken diligently

9
k *Babylon, prophecies concerning,* Ezra 5:12.
l *Idolatry, prophecies relating to,* 1 Sam. 15:23.
5 R. V. troop of men, horsemen in pairs.

11
m *Dumah,* Gen. 25:14.
n *Edomites, prophecies concerning,* 2 Kin. 8:21.

13
o *Arabia, prophecies against,* 2 Chr. 9:14.
p *Arabians, prophecies concerning,* 2 Chr. 17:11.

14
q Job 6:19; Jer. 25:23.
r *Liberality, instances of,* 1 Tim. 6:18.
6 R. V. Unto him that was thirsty they brought water; the inhabitants of the land of Tema did meet the fugitives with their bread.

15
s *Sword,* 1 Chr. 21:5.
t *Bow,* 2 Sam. 1:18.
u *War, evils of,* Judg. 3:2.

16
v *Kedar,* Jer. 49:28.

17
w *Archery,* Gen. 21:20.

3
a *Archery,* Gen. 21:20.

4
b *Patriotism,* Psa. 137:1.
c *Citizens, loyal,* Luke 15:15.

5
d *Nation, chastisement of,* Isa. 2:4.
1 Am. R. V. Jehovah

6 And [e]Ē′lăm bare the [f]quiver with chariots of men *and* horsemen, and [g]Kĭr uncovered the [h]shield.

7 And it shall come to pass, *that* thy choicest valleys shall be full of chariots, and the horsemen shall set themselves in array at the gate.

8 ¶ And he discovered[c] the covering of Jū′dah, and thou didst look in that day to the armour of the [i]house of the forest.

9 Ye have seen also the breaches of the [j]city of Dā′vid, that they are many: and ye gathered together the waters of the lower [k]pool.

10 And ye have numbered the houses of [j]Jē-ru̧′sā-lĕm, and the houses have ye broken down to fortify the [l]wall.

11 [m]Ye made also a ditch[c] between the two walls for the water of the old pool: but ye have not looked unto the maker thereof, neither had *respect unto him that fashioned it long ago.

12 And in that day did the Lord GOD of hosts [n]call to weeping, and to [o]mourning, and to [p]baldness, and to girding with [q]sackcloth:

13 And behold [r,s]joy and gladness, slaying oxen, and killing sheep, [t]eating flesh, and drinking wine: [u,v]let us eat and drink; for to morrow we shall die.[Q]

14 And it was [w,x]revealed in mine ears by the LORD of hosts, Surely this iniquity shall not be purged from [y]you till ye [z]die, saith the Lord [2]GOD of hosts.[S]

15 ¶ Thus saith the Lord [2]GOD of hosts, Go, get thee unto this treasurer, *even* unto Shĕb′nȧ, which *is* over the house, *and say*,

16 What hast thou here? and whom hast thou here, that thou hast hewed thee out a sepulchre here, *as* he that heweth him out a sepulchre on high, *and* that graveth[c] an habitation for himself in a rock?

17 Behold, [3]the LORD will [a]carry thee away with a mighty [b]captivity, and will surely cover thee.

18 He will surely violently turn and toss thee *like* a ball into a large country: there shalt thou die, and there [4]the chariots of thy glory *shall be* the shame of thy lord's house.

19 And I will drive thee from thy station, and from thy state shall he pull thee down.

20 ¶ And it shall come to pass in that day, that I will call my servant [c]Ē-lī′a-kĭm the son of [d]Hĭl-kī′ah:

21 And I will clothe him with thy robe, and strengthen him with thy [e]girdle, and I will commit thy †government into his hand: and he shall be a father to

6
*e* *Elam, prophecies concerning*, Isa. 11:11.
*f* Gen. 27:3.
*g* *Kir*, 2 Kin. 16:9.
*h* *Shield*, 1 Kin. 14:27.

8
*i* *Armory*, Neh. 3:19.

9
*j* *Jerusalem*, Judg. 19:10.
*k* *Pool, of Jerusalem*, 2 Sam. 2:13.

10
*l* *Walls*, 1 Sam. 20:25.

11
*m* *False Confidence*, Psa. 30:6.

12
*n* *Repentance, enjoined*, Mark 1:4.
*o* *Mourning*, Lam. 2:5.
*p* *Baldness, artificial*, Lev. 21:5.
*q* *Sackcloth*, Isa. 15:3.

13
*r* *Wicked, happiness of*, Psa. 73:3.
*s* *Worldly Pleasure*, Eccl. 2:1.
*t* *Sensuality*, Jude 19.
*u* 1 Cor. 15:32.
*v* *Epicureans*, Acts 17:18.

14
*w* *Inspiration*, Job 32:8.
*x* *Prophets, inspiration of*, Isa. 3:2.
*y* *Reprobates*, 1 Cor. 9:27.
*z* *Wicked, punishment of*, Psa. 64:10.
2 Am. R. V. Jehovah

17
*a* *Judgments*, Ex. 6:6.
*b* *Captivity, as a judgment*, Isa. 5:13.
3 Am. R. V. Jehovah will hurl thee away violently as a strong man; yea, he will wrap thee up closely.

18
4 R. V. shall be the chariots of thy glory, thou shame of

20
*c* *Eliakim*, 2 Kin. 18:18.
*d* Isa. 36:22; 2 Kin. 18:18, 26, 37.

21
*e* *Girdle, figurative*. Prov. 31:24.

---

* **RESPECT**, Isa. 22:11. *To the aged, enjoined*, Lev. 19:32. *To rulers*, Prov. 25:6. *To one another*, Rom. 12:10; Phil. 2:3; 1 Pet. 2:17.

† **GOVERNMENT.** *Paternal functions of*, Gen. 41:25–57. *Civil service school provided by*, Dan. 1:3–20. *Maintains a system of public instruction*, 2 Chr. 17:7–9.

**Constitutional:** It was provided in the law of Moses that in the event of the establishment of a monarchy a copy of the law of Moses should be made and that the king should be enjoined to study this law all the days of his life and conform his administration thereto, Deut. 17:18–20. This constituted the fundamental law and had its likeness to the constitution of modern governments. When David was crowned king of all Israel he made a league in the nature of a constitution which was a basis of good understanding between himself and the people, 2 Sam. 5:3. When Joash was enthroned a covenant, which must have been in the nature of a limitation of monarchical power, was made between him and the people, 2 Chr. 23:3, 11. In v. 11 this covenant is called a "testimony" and, no doubt, refers to the law of Moses, Deut. 17:18–20, which, it is quite probable, had been preserved sacredly by Jehoiada, the priest. Zedekiah made a covenant with the people proclaiming liberty, Jer. 34:8–11. That the king of the Medes and Persians was restricted by a constitution, which "altereth not," is evident from Dan. 6:12–15. See footnote, CONSTITUTION, Dan. 6:12.

**Corruption in,** 1 Kin. 21:5–13; Prov. 25:5; Mic. 3:1–4, 9–11.

INSTANCES OF CORRUPTION IN: *Pilate, in delivering Jesus to death to please the clamorous multitude*, Matt. 27:24; John 19:12–16. *Felix, who hoped for money from Paul*, Acts 24:26. See footnote, RULERS, *Wicked, instances of*, Ex. 18:21.

**Duty of Citizens to:** *To pay taxes*, Matt. 22:17–21; Luke 20:22–25. *To render obedience to civil authority*, Rom. 13:1–7; Tit. 3:1; 1 Pet. 2:13–17.

**God in,** 2 Chr. 22:7; Jer. 18:6; Ezek. 21:25–27; 29:19, 20. *In appointment of Saul as king*, 1 Sam. 9:15–17; 10:1. *In Saul's rejection*, 1 Sam. 15:26–28; Acts 13:22. *In appointment, of David*, 1 Sam. 16:1, 7, 13; 2 Sam. 7:13–16; Psa. 89:19–37; Acts 13:22; *of Solomon*, 1 Kin. 2:13–15. *In counseling Solomon*, 1 Kin. 9:2–9. *In magnifying Solomon*, 1 Chr. 29:25. *In reproving Solomon's wickedness*, 1 Kin. 11:9–13. *In raising adversaries against Solomon*, 1 Kin. 11:14, 23. *In rending the nation of Israel in twain*, 1 Kin. 11:13; 12:1–24; 2 Chr. 10:15; 11:4. *In blotting out the house of Jeroboam*, 1 Kin. 14:7–16; 15:27–30. *In appointment of kings*, 1 Kin. 14:14; 16:1, 2; 1 Chr. 28:4, 5; Dan. 2:20, 21, 37; 4:17; 5:18–23. *In destruction of nations*, Jer. 25:12–17; Amos 9:8; Hag. 2:22.

[f] *Jerusalem,* Judg. 19:10.
[g] *Judah, kingdom of,* 2 Chr. 11:17.

22
[h] *Key, a symbol,* Judg. 3:25.
[i] *David,* 1 Sam. 16:13.

23
[j] *Nail, figurative,* Isa. 41:7.

the inhabitants of [f]Jĕ-ru̥′sā-lĕm,
and to the house of [g]Jū′dah.
22 And the [h]key of the house of
[i]Dā′vid will I lay upon his shoulder; so he shall open, and none
shall shut; and he shall shut, and
none shall open.[S Q]
23 And I will fasten him *as* a
[j]nail in a sure place; and he shall
be for a glorious throne to his
father's house
24 And they shall hang upon
him all the glory of his father's
house, the offspring and the issue, all vessels of small quantity,
from the vessels of cups,[G] even to
all the vessels of flagons.[G]
25 In that day, saith the LORD
of hosts, shall the [j]nail that is
fastened in the sure place be removed, and be cut down, and
fall; and the burden that *was*
upon it shall be cut off: for the
LORD hath spoken *it.*

## CHAPTER 23

*The overthrow of Tyre;* 8 *God's purpose therein.* 15 *The time of her desolation.* 17 *Her restoration and devotion to the Lord.*

1
[a] *Tyre, prophecies relating to,* vs. 1–18; Josh. 19:29.
[b] *Tarshish,* 2 Chr. 20:36.

THE burden[Q] of [a]Tȳre. Howl,
ye ships of [b]Tär′shish; for
it is laid waste, so that there is
no house, no entering in: from
the land of [c]Chĭt′tim it is revealed to them.[S]
2 Be still, ye inhabitants of
the isle; thou whom the [d,e]mer-
chants of [f]Zī′dŏn, that pass over
the sea, have replenished.[G]
3 And by great waters the seed
of [g]Sī′hôr, the harvest of the
[h]river, *is* her revenue; and she is
a mart[G] of nations.
4 Be thou ashamed, O [f]Zī′dŏn:
for the sea hath spoken, *even* the
strength of the sea, saying, I
travail not, nor bring forth children, neither do I nourish up
young men, *nor* bring up virgins.
5 As at the report concerning
[i]Ē′ġȳpt, *so* shall they be sorely[G]
pained at the report of [a]Tȳre.
6 Pass ye over to [b]Tär′shish;
howl, ye inhabitants of the isle.
7 *Is* this your joyous [a]*city,*
whose antiquity *is* of ancient
days? her own feet shall carry
her afar off to sojourn.[G]
8 Who hath taken this counsel
against [a]Tȳre, the crowning *city,*
whose [d,j]merchants *are* princes,
whose traffickers[G] *are* the honourable of the earth?[Q]

[c] *Chittim,* Dan. 11:30.

2
[d] *Merchant,* Neh. 3:32.
[e] *Commerce, of Zidonians,* 1 Kin. 10:15.
[f] *Zidon,* Ezek. 28:21.

3
[g] *Sihor,* Josh. 13:3.
[h] *Nile,* Isa. 11:15.

5
[i] *Egypt,* Gen. 41:8.

8
[j] *Commerce, of Tyre,* 1 Kin. 10:15.

*Relation of God to,* Psa. 22:28; Prov. **8:15, 16; Jer. 18:6–10;** Ezek. 21:25–27.

**Mosaic:** *Administrative and judicial system,* Ex. 18: 13–26; Num. 11:16, 17, 24, 25; Deut. 1:9–17.

POPULAR GOVERNMENT, BY A NATIONAL ASSEMBLY, OR ITS REPRESENTATIVES: *Accepted the law given by Moses,* Ex. 19:7, 8; 24:3, 7; Deut. 29:10–15. *Refused to make conquest of Canaan,* Num. 14:1–10. *Chose, or ratified, the chief ruler,* 1 Sam. 10:24 (with 8:4–22); 11:14, 15; 2 Sam. 3:17–21; 5:1–3; 1 Chr. 29:22; 2 Chr. 23:3. *Possessed veto power over king's purposes,* 1 Sam. 14:44, 45. *Constituted the court in certain capital cases,* Num. 35:12, 24, 25.

DELEGATED, SENATORIAL COUNCIL: *Closely associated with Moses and subsequent leaders,* Ex. 3:16, 18; 4:29–31; 12:21; 17:5, 6; 18:12; 19:7, 8; 24:1, 14; Lev. 4:15; 9:1; Num. 11:16, 17, 30; 16:25; Deut. 1:13–15; 5:23; 27:1; 29:10–15; 31:9, 28; Josh. 7:6; 8:10, 32, 33; 23:2, 3, 6; 24:1, 24, 25; Judg. 21:16–25; Acts 5:17, 18, 21–41.

MISCELLANY OF FACTS RELATING TO THE SENATE: *Demands a king,* 1 Sam. 8:4–10, 19–22. *Saul pleads to be honored before,* 1 Sam. 15:30. *Chooses David as king,* 2 Sam. 5:3; 1 Chr. 11:3. *Closely associated with David,* 2 Sam. 12: 17; 1 Chr. 15:25; 21:16. *Joins Absalom in his usurpation,* 2 Sam. 17:4. *David upbraids,* 2 Sam. 19:11. *Assists Solomon at the dedication of the temple,* 1 Kin. 8:1–3; 2 Chr. 5:2–4. *Counsels king Rehoboam,* 1 Kin. 12:6–8, 13. *Counsels king Ahab,* 1 Kin. 20:7, 8. *Josiah assembles, to hear the law of the Lord,* 2 Kin. 23:1; 2 Chr. 34:29, 31.

*Legislates with Ezra in reforming certain marriages with the heathen,* Ezra 9:1; 10:8–14. *Legislates in later times,* Matt. 15:2, 7–9; Mark 7:1–13. *Sits as a court,* Jer. 26:10–24. *Constitutes, with priests and scribes, a court for the trial of both civil and ecclesiastical causes,* Matt. 21:23; 26:3–5, 57–68; 27: 1, 2; Mark 8:31; 14:43, 53–65; 15:1; Luke 22:52–54, 66–71; Acts 4:1–21; 6:9–15. *Unfaithful to the city,* Lam. 1:19. *Seeks counsel from prophets,* Ezek. 8:1; 14:1; 20:1, 3. *Corrupt,* 1 Kin. 21:8–14; Ezek. 8:11, 12; Matt. 26:14, 15, with 27:3, 4.

*A similar senate existed among the Egyptians,* Gen. 50:7; *and among the Midianites and Moabites,* Num. 22:4, 7; *and Gibeonites,* Josh. 9:11.

EXECUTIVE OFFICERS OF TRIBES AND CITIES, CALLED PRINCES OR NOBLES, MEMBERS OF THE NATIONAL ASSEMBLY, Num. 1:4–16, 44; 7:2, 3, 10, 11, 18, 24, 54, 84; 10:4; 16:2; 17:2, 6; 27:2; 31:13, 14; 32:2; 34:18–29; 36:1; Josh. 9:15–21; 17:4; 22:13–32; 1 Kin. 21:11–14; Neh. 3:9, 12, 16, 18, 19.

THE MOSAIC JUDICIAL SYSTEM, see footnotes: COURT, Ex. 18:26; JUDGE, Judg. 2:18.

**Ecclesiastical:** See footnotes: CHURCH, *Government of,* Matt. 16:18; CHURCH AND STATE, 1 Sam. 16:1.

**Imperial,** Gen. 14:1; Josh. 11:10; 1 Kin. 4:21; Esth. 1:1; Dan. 4:1; 6:1–3; Luke 2:1.

**Monarchical:** TYRANNY IN: *By Pharaoh,* Ex. 1:8–22; 2:23, 24; 3:7; 5:1–19. *By Saul,* 1 Sam. 22:6, 12–19. *By David,* 2 Sam. 11:14–17. *By Solomon,* 1 Kin. 2:23–25, 28–34, 36–46. *By Rehoboam,* 1 Kin. 12:1–16. *By Ahab and Jezebel,* 1 Kin. 21:7–16. *By Jehu,* 2 Kin. 10:1–14. *By Ahasuerus,* Esth. 1:11, 12, 19–22; 3:8–15; 8:8–13. *By Nebuchadnezzar,* Dan. 1:10; 2:5–13; 5:19. *By Herod,* Mark 6:27, 28.

**Municipal:** *Devolving on a local senate and executive officers,* Deut. 19:12; 21:2–8, 18–21; 22:13–21; 25:7–9; Josh. 20:4; Judg. 8:14–16; 11:5–11; Ruth 4:2–11; 1 Sam. 11:3; 16:4; 30:26; 1 Kin. 21:8–14; 2 Kin. 10:1–7; Ezra 10:8, 14; Neh. 3:9, 12, 16, 18, 19; Lam. 5:14.

**Patriarchal,** Gen. 27:29, 37.

**Provincial,** Ezra 4:8, 9; 5:3, 6; 6:6; 8:36; Neh. 2:7, 9; 5:14; Dan. 6:1–3; Matt. 27:2; 28:14; Luke 2:2; 3:1; Acts 24:1.

**Representative,** Deut. 1:13–15; Josh. 9:11. See DELEGATED, SENATORIAL COUNCIL, above.

**Theocratic,** Ex. 19:3–8; Deut. 26:16–19; **29:1–13; Judg. 8:23; 1 Sam. 8:6, 7; 10:19; 12:12; Isa. 33:22.**

9 The LORD of hosts hath purposed it, to stain the [k]pride of all glory, *and* to bring into contempt all the honourable of the earth.

10 Pass through thy land as a [h]river, O daughter of [b]Tär′shish: *there is* no [1]more strength.

11 [l]He stretched out his hand over the sea, he shook the kingdoms: the LORD hath given a commandment [2]against the merchant *city*, to destroy the strong holds thereof.

12 And he said, Thou shalt no more rejoice, O thou oppressed virgin, daughter of Zī′dŏn: arise, pass over to [c]Chĭt′tim; there also shalt thou have no rest.

13 Behold the land of the Chăl-dē′anṣ; this people was not, *till* the Ăs-sӯr′ĭ-an founded it for them that dwell in the wilderness: they set up [3]the towers thereof, they raised up the palaces thereof; *and* he brought it to ruin.

14 Howl, ye ships of [b]Tär′shish: for your strength is laid waste.

15 And it shall come to pass in that day, that [a]Tӯre shall be forgotten seventy years, according to the days of one king: after the end of seventy years [4]shall Tӯre sing as an [m]harlot.

16 Take an [n]harp, go about the city, thou harlot that hast been forgotten; make sweet [o]melody, sing many songs, that thou mayest be remembered.

17 ¶ And it shall come to pass after the end of seventy years, that the LORD will visit [a]Tӯre, and she shall turn to her hire, and shall commit fornication with all the kingdoms of the world upon the face of the earth.

18 And her merchandise and her hire shall be holiness to the LORD: it shall not be treasured nor laid up; for her merchandise shall be for them that dwell before the LORD, to eat sufficiently, and for durable clothing.

9
*k* *Pride*, Prov. 16:18.

10
1 Am. R. V. restraint any more.

11
*l* *God, power of*, Gen. 2:2.
2 R. V. concerning Canaan.

13
3 R. V. their towers, they overthrew the

15
*m* *Harlot*, Prov. 7:10.
4 R. V. it shall be unto Tyre as in the song of the harlot.

16
*n* *Harp*, Dan. 3:10.
*o* *Music*, 2 Chr. 5:13.

## CHAPTER 24

*God's judgments upon the land for its iniquities. 13 A remnant shall praise him. 16 By his judgments God will advance his kingdom.*

BEHOLD, the LORD [a]maketh the earth empty, and maketh it waste, and turneth it upside down, and scattereth abroad the inhabitants thereof.

2 And [b]it shall be, as with the people, so with the [c]priest; as with the [d]servant, so with his master; as with the maid, so with her mistress; as with the buyer, so with the seller; as with the [e]lender, so with the borrower; as with the taker of [f]usury, so with the giver of usury to him.

3 [a]The land shall be utterly emptied, and utterly spoiled: for the LORD hath spoken this word.

4 The earth mourneth *and* fadeth away, the world languisheth *and* fadeth away, the [g]haughty people of the earth do languish.

5 The earth also is defiled under the inhabitants thereof; because they have [h]transgressed the laws, [h]changed the [i]ordinance, [h]broken the everlasting [j]covenant.

6 [a, k]Therefore hath the curse devoured the earth, and they that dwell therein are [1]desolate: therefore the inhabitants of the earth are burned, and few men left.

7 The new wine mourneth, the vine languisheth, all the merryhearted do sigh.

8 The mirth of tabrets ceaseth, the noise of them that rejoice endeth, the joy of the [l, m]harp ceaseth.

9 They shall not [n]drink [o]wine with a song; strong drink shall be bitter to them that drink it.

1
*a* *Judgments*, Ex. 6:6.

2
*b* *Judgment, according to opportunity and works* 1 Pet. 1:17.
*c* *Priest*, Lev. 1:5.
*d* *Servant*, Jer. 2:14.
*e* *Lending*, Deut. 15:2.
*f* *Interest*, Ex. 22:25.

4
*g* *Pride*, Prov. 16:18.

5
*h* *Backsliding, of Israel*, Hos. 11:7.
*i* *Ordinance*, Num. 9:14.
*j* *Covenant, of man with God*, Deut. 29:1.

6
*k* *Wicked, punishment of*, Psa. 73:3.
1 R. V. found guilty:

8
*l* *Harp*, Dan. 3:10
*m* *Music, refrained from in sorrow*, 2 Chr. 5:13.

9
*n* *Drunkenness*, Luke 21:34.
*o* *Wine*, Prov. 23:31.

10 The city of confusion is broken down: every house is shut
up, that no man may come in.
11 *There is* a crying [2]for [o]wine
in the streets; all joy is darkened,
the mirth of the land is gone.
12 In the city is left desolation,
and the gate is smitten with destruction.
13 ¶ When thus it shall be
in the midst of the land among
the people, *there shall be* as the
shaking of an olive tree, *and* as
the gleaning grapes when the
vintage is done.
14 They shall [p]lift up their
voice, they shall sing for the
majesty of the LORD, they shall
cry aloud from the sea.
15 Wherefore [q]glorify ye the
LORD in the [3]fires,[G] *even* the
name of the LORD God of Ĭș'-
ra-el in the isles of the sea.[Q]
16 ¶ From the uttermost[G] part
of the earth have we heard songs,
*even* glory to the righteous. But
I said, [4]My leanness,[G] my leanness,[G] woc unto me! the treacherous dealers have dealt treacherously; yea, the treacherous dealers have dealt very treacherously.
17 [k]Fear, and the pit, and the
snare, *are* upon thee, O inhabitant of the earth.[Q]
18 And it shall come to pass,
*that* he who fleeth from the noise
of the fear shall [a]fall into the pit;
and he that cometh up out of the
midst of the pit shall be [a]taken in
the snare: for the windows from
on high are open, and the foundations of the earth do shake.
19 [a]The [r]earth is utterly broken down, the earth is clean[G] dissolved, the earth is [s]moved exceedingly.[Q]
20 The earth shall [s]reel to and
fro like a drunkard, and shall
be removed like a cottage; and
the transgression thereof shall be
heavy upon it; and it shall fall,
and not rise again.
21 And it shall come to pass in
that day, *that* the LORD shall
[k]punish the host of the high ones
*that are* on high, and the kings of
the earth upon the earth.[Q]
22 And they shall be gathered
together, *as* prisoners are gathered in the pit, and shall be shut
up in the prison, and after many
days shall they be visited.
23 Then the [t]moon shall be confounded, and the [u]sun ashamed,
when the [v]LORD of hosts shall
reign in mount Zī'ŏn, and in
[w]Jē-ru'sā-lĕm, and before his
ancients[G] gloriously.[Q]

## CHAPTER 25

*The prophet praises God for his judgments;*
*6 and declares the future glories of Zion.*

O LORD, thou *art* my God; I
will exalt thee, I will [a]praise
thy name; for thou hast done
wonderful *things*; *thy* counsels of
old *are* [b]faithfulness *and* [c,d]truth.[T][S]
2 For thou hast [e]made of a city
an heap; *of* a defenced[G] city a
ruin: a palace of strangers[G] to be
no city; it shall never be built.
3 Therefore shall the strong people [f]glorify thee, the city of the
terrible nations shall [g]fear thee.
4 For [h,i]thou hast been a
[1,j,k]strength to the [l]poor, a
[1]strength to the needy in his distress, a refuge from the storm, a
shadow from the heat, when the
blast of the terrible ones *is* as a
storm *against* the wall.[S]
5 [h]Thou shalt bring down the
noise of strangers, as the heat
in a dry place; *even* the heat
with the shadow of a cloud:
the [2]branch of the terrible ones
shall be brought low.
6 ¶ And in this [m,n]mountain
shall the LORD of hosts make
unto all people a feast of [o]fat
things, a feast of [p]wines on the
[q]lees,[G] of fat things full of marrow, of wines on the lees well
[r]refined.

11
2 R. V. in the streets because of the wine;

14
p *Praise*, Psa. 150:1.

15
q *Glorifying God*, Luke 5:25.
3 R. V. east,

16
4 R. V. I pine away, I pine away, woe is me!

19
r *Earth, destruction of*, Prov. 8:23.
s *Earthquakes, as judgments*, Isa. 29:6.

23
t *Moon, darkening of*, Song 6:10.
u *Sun, darkening of*, Josh. 10:12.
v *God, sovereign*, Gen. 2:2.
w *Jerusalem*, Judg. 19:10.

1
a *Praise*, Psa. 150:1.
b *God, faithfulness of*, Gen. 2:2.
c *God, truth*, Gen. 2:2.
d *Truth, attribute of God*, John 18:37.

2
e *Judgments*, Ex. 6:6.

3
f *Glorifying God*, Luke 5:25.
g *Fear of God*, Acts 9:31.

4
h *God, providence of*, Gen. 2:2.
i *Adversity, consolation in*, Psa. 10:6.
j *God, preserver*, Gen. 2:2.
k *Temporal Blessings, from God*, Psa. 103:2.
l *Poor, God's care of*, Prov. 21:13.
1 R. V. strong hold

m *Church, prophecies concerning its prosperity*, vs. 6–8; Matt. 16:18.
n *Jesus, kingdom of, prophecies concerning*, Matt. 1:21.
o *Fat, figurative*, Lev. 7:24.
p *Wine, figurative*, Prov. 23:31.
q Psa. 75:8; Jer. 48:11; Zeph. 1:12.
r *Refining, of wine*, 1 Chr. 28:18.

7 And he will destroy in this mountain the face of the covering cast over all people, and the vail that is spread over all nations.[Q]

8 [s,t]He [3]will [u]swallow up [v]death in victory; and the Lord GOD will wipe away tears from off all faces; and the rebuke of [w]his people shall he take away from off all the earth: for the LORD hath spoken *it*.[Q]

9 ¶ And it shall be [x]said in that day, Lo, [y]this *is* our God; we have [z]waited for him, and [a]he will [b]save us: this *is* the LORD; we have waited for him, we will be glad and [c]rejoice in his salvation.

10 For in this mountain shall the hand of the LORD rest, and [d]Mō'ab shall be [e]trodden[C] down under him, even as straw is trodden down for the dunghill.

11 And he shall spread forth his hands in the midst of them, as he that swimmeth spreadeth forth *his hands* to swim: and he shall [e]bring down their [f]pride together with the [4]spoils[C] of their hands.

12 And the fortress of the high fort of thy walls shall he bring down, lay low, *and* bring to the ground, *even* to the dust.

## CHAPTER 26

*A song of praise and of thanksgiving to God for the deliverance of his people. 20 An exhortation to wait on God.*

IN that day shall this [a]song be sung in the land of [b]Jū'dah; We have a strong city; [c,d]salvation will [e]God appoint *for* walls and [f]bulwarks.

2 Open ye the [g]gates, that the righteous nation which keepeth[C] the truth may enter in.

3 [h,i]Thou wilt keep [j]*him* in perfect [k,l]peace, *whose* mind *is* [m]stayed *on thee*:[S Q] because he trusteth in thee.

4 [n,o]Trust ye in the LORD for ever: for in the LORD JĔ-HŌ'-VAH[C] *is* [1,p]everlasting strength:[S]

5 ¶ For [q]he [r]bringeth down them that dwell on high; the lofty city, he layeth it low; he layeth it low, *even* to the ground; he bringeth it *even* to the dust.

6 The foot shall tread[C] it down, *even* the feet of the poor, *and* the steps of the needy.

7 The way of the just *is* uprightness: thou, most [s]upright, dost [2]weigh[C] the path of the just.[S]

8 Yea, in the way of [t]thy judgments, O LORD, have we waited for thee; [3]the [u]desire of [v]*our* soul *is* to thy name, and to the remembrance of thee.

9 With my soul have I [u]desired thee in the night; yea, with my [w]spirit within me will [v]I seek thee early: for when thy [x]judgments *are* in the earth, [y]the inhabitants of the world will learn righteousness.

10 Let favour be shewed to the wicked, *yet* [z]will he [a,b]not learn righteousness; in the land of uprightness will [c]he deal *unjustly, and [c]will not behold[C] the majesty of the LORD.[T]

11 LORD, *when* thy hand is lifted up, they will [a,b]not see: *but* they shall see, [4]and be ashamed for *their* envy at the people; yea, the fire of thine enemies shall devour them.[Q]

12 ¶ LORD, thou wilt ordain[C] peace for us: for thou also [d]hast wrought all our works [5]in us.

13 O LORD our God, [e]other lords beside thee have had dominion over us: *but* by thee only will we make mention of thy name.[Q]

14 *They are* [f]dead, they shall

**8**
s 1 Cor. 15:54.
t *Prophecies concerning the Messiah, and their fulfillment,* Gen. 12:3.
u *Immortality, implied in the abolition of death,* 1 Cor. 15:54.
v *Death, to be destroyed,* Num. 23:10.
w *Righteous, promises to,* Psa. 64:10.
3 R. V. hath swallowed up death for ever;

**9**
x *Religious Testimony,* 2 Thess. 1:10.
y *Faith, in adversity,* Mark 11:22.
z *Spiritual Desire,* Psa. 42:1.

a *Afflictions, consolation in,* Psa. 34:19.
b *God, savior,* Gen. 2:2.
c *Joy,* Psa. 5:11.

**10**
d *Moab,* Num. 26:3.
e *Judgments,* Ex. 6:6.

**11**
f *Pride,* Prov. 16:18.
4 R. V. craft

**1**
a *Praise,* Psa. 150:1.
b *Judah, kingdom of,* 2 Chr. 11:17.
c *Faith, instances of,* Mark 11:22.
d *Salvation,* Acts 16:17.
e *God, savior,* Gen. 2:2.
f *Bulwark, figurative,* Deut. 20:20.

**2**
g *Gates, figurative,* Deut. 3:5.

**3**
h *Promise, to believers,* 2 Cor. 1:20.
i *Faith, rewards of,* Mark 11:22.
j *Righteous, promises to,* Psa. 64:10.
k *Spiritual Peace,* Gal. 1:3.
l *Spiritual Blessings, from God,* Eph. 1:3.

m *Christian Graces, faith,* Gal. 5:22.

**4**
n *Commandment, enjoining faith,* Deut. 8:2.
o *Faith, enjoined,* Mark 11:22.
p *God, eternity of,* Gen. 2:2.
1 R.V. an everlasting rock.

**5**
q *God, providence of,* Gen. 2:2.
r *Judgments,* Ex. 6:6.

**7**
s *God, righteousness of,* Gen. 2:2.
2 R. V. direct

**8**
t *God, judge,* Gen. 2:2.
u *Spiritual Desire, exemplified,* Psa. 42:1.
v *Seekers,* Isa. 55:6.
3 Am. R. V. to thy name, even to thy memorial name, is the desire of our soul.

**9**
w *Man, spirit,* Job 4:17.
x *Judgments, design of,* Ex. 6:6.
y *Adversity, benefits of,* Psa. 10:6.

**10**
z *Wicked, described,* Psa. 73:3.

a *Spiritual Blindness,* 2 Cor. 4:4.
b *Impenitence,* Rom. 2:5.
c *Wicked, described,* Psa. 73:3.

**11**
4 Am. R. V. thy zeal for the people, and be put to shame; yea, fire shall devour thine adversaries.

**12**
d *God, providence of,* Gen. 2:2.
5 R. V. for

**13**
e *Sin, confession of,* Rom. 5:12.

**14**
f *Death, of the wicked, a judgment,* Num. 23:10.

* **INJUSTICE**, Job 31:13–15; Psa. 43:1; Prov. 17:15; 29:27; Eccl. 3:16; Zeph. 3:5. *In civil administration,* Psa. 82:2; Eccl. 5:8; Lam. 3:34–36. *Its gains, unstable,* Prov. 28:8; Amos 5:11, 12. **Forbidden:** *Toward the needy,* Ex. 22:21–24; Jer. 22:3–5. *In testimony,* Ex. 23:1; Luke 3:14. *In civil courts,* Ex. 23:2, 3, 6, 7; Lev. 19:15; Deut. 16:19, 20; 24:17, 18; 27:19; Prov. 31:4, 5. *In business transactions,* Lev. 19:35, 36.

not live; *they are* deceased, they
shall not rise: therefore hast thou
visited[c] and destroyed them, and
made all their memory to perish.
15 [d]Thou hast [g]increased the
nation, O LORD, thou hast increased the nation: thou art
glorified: thou hadst removed
*it* far *unto* all the ends of the
earth.[s]
16 LORD, in [h]trouble have they
visited thee, they poured out a
[i]prayer *when* thy [j]chastening
*was* upon them.
17 Like as a woman with child,
*that* draweth near the time of her
delivery, is in pain, *and* crieth
out in her pangs; so have we
been in thy sight, O LORD.[Q]
18 We have been with child, we
have been in pain, we have as
it were brought forth wind; we
have not wrought[c] any deliverance
in the earth; neither have the inhabitants of the world fallen.
19 Thy dead *men* shall [k]live,
[6]*together with* my dead body shall
they [l]arise. Awake and sing, ye
that dwell in dust: for thy [m]dew
*is as* the dew of herbs, and the
earth shall cast out the dead.
20 ¶ Come, my people, enter
thou into thy chambers, and
shut thy doors about thee: hide
thyself as it were for a little moment, until the [n]indignation be
overpast.[G][Q]
21 For, behold, the LORD cometh out of his place to [n,o]punish
the inhabitants of the earth for
their iniquity: the earth also shall
disclose her blood, and shall no
more cover her slain.

## CHAPTER 27

*God's care of his vineyard. 7 His chastisements differ from judgments. 12 The restoration of the scattered Jews.*

IN that day the LORD with his
sore[G] and great and strong
[a,b]sword shall punish leviathan
the [1]piercing serpent, even leviathan that crooked serpent; and
he shall slay the dragon that
*is* in the sea.
2 ¶ In that day sing ye unto
her, [c]A vineyard of red wine.
3 I the LORD do [d]keep[c] it; I will
water it every moment: lest *any*
hurt it, I will keep it night and
day.[s]
4 Fury *is* not in me: who
would set the briers *and* thorns
against me in battle? I would
go through them, I would burn
them together.
5 Or let him take hold of my
strength, *that* he may make
peace with me; *and* he shall
make peace with me.
6 [2]He shall cause them that
come of Jā'cob to take root:
Iș'ra-el shall blossom and bud,
and fill the face of the world
with fruit.
7 Hath he smitten him, as he
smote those that smote him?
*or* is he slain according to the
slaughter of them that are slain
by him?
8 In measure, when [3]it shooteth
forth, thou wilt debate with it:
he stayeth his rough wind in the
day of the east wind.
9 By this therefore shall the [e]in-
iquity of Jā'cob be purged; and
this *is* all the fruit to take away
his sin; when he maketh all the
stones of the [f]altar as chalk-
stones that are beaten in sunder,
[4,g]the [h]groves[G] and [i]images[G] shall
not stand up.[Q]
10 [5]Yet the defenced[G] city [b]*shall*
*be* desolate, *and* the habitation
forsaken, and left like a wilderness: there shall the calf feed,
and there shall he lie down, and
consume the branches thereof.
11 When the boughs thereof are
withered, they shall be broken
off: the [j]women come, *and* set
them on fire: for it *is* a people of
[k]no understanding: therefore he
that [l]made them will not have
mercy on them, and he that

15
g *Temporal Blessings, from God,* Psa. 103:2.

16
h *Adversity, benefits of,* Psa. 10:6.
i *Prayer, in adversity,* Acts 6:4.
j *Divine Chastisement, penitence under,* Job 33:19.

19
k *Immortality, implied, in the resurrection,* 1 Cor. 15:54.
l *Resurrection, prophecies concerning,* 1 Cor. 15:12.
m *Dew, figurative,* Dan. 4:15.
6 R. V. my dead bodies shall arise.

20
n *Judgments,* Ex. 6:6.

21
o *Wicked, punishment of,* Psa. 73:3.

1
a *Sword, figurative,* 1 Chr. 21:5.
b *Judgments,* Ex. 6:6.
1 R. V. swift

2
c *Parables, of the vineyard,* v. 3; Ezek. 20:49.

3
d *God, preserver,* Gen. 2:2.

6
2 **R. V. In days to come shall Jacob take root;**

8
3 **R. V. thou sendest her away, thou dost contend with her; he hath removed her with his rough blast in**

9
e *Sin, forgiveness of,* Rom. 5:12.
f *Altar, used in idolatrous worship,* Gen. 8:20.
g *Idolatry, prophecies relating to,* 1 Sam. 15:23.
h *Groves,* Judg. 6:28.
i *Idol,* 1 Kin. 15:12.
4 **R. V. so that the Asherim and the sun-images shall rise no more.**

10
5 **Am. R. V. For the fortified city is solitary,**

11
j *Women,* Prov. 31:10.
k *Spiritual Blindness,* 2 Cor. 4:4.
l *God, creator,* Gen. 2:2.

formed them will shew them no
favour.

12 And it shall come to pass in
that day, *that* the LORD shall
beat[C] off from the channel of the
[m]river unto the stream of [n]Ē'-
ġy̆pt, and ye shall be gathered
one by one, O ye children of
Ĭs'ra-el.

13 And it shall come to pass in
that day, *that* the great [o]trumpet
shall be blown, and they shall
come which were ready to perish in the land of [p]Ăs-sy̆r'ĭ-ȧ,
and the outcasts in the land
of Ē'ġy̆pt, and shall [q]worship
the LORD in the holy mount at
[r]Jē-ru'sā-lĕm.[Q]

12
m *Euphrates*, Gen. 15:18.
n *Egypt, brook of*, Gen. 15:18.

13
o *Trumpet, figurative*, Josh. 6:4.
p *Assyria*, Gen. 25:18.
q *Worship*, Gen. 22:5.
r *Jerusalem*, Judg. 19:10.

## CHAPTER 28

*A woe against the drunkards of Ephraim. 5 A promise to the residue of the people. 7 Yet they have erred, and deserve rebuke. 14 In contrast with the refuge of lies, God has laid in Zion a sure foundation. 23 His dealings with his people illustrated.*

[a]WOE to the crown of pride,
to the [b]drunkards of [c]Ē'-
phră-ĭm, whose glorious beauty
*is* a fading flower, which *are* on
the head of the fat[C] valleys of
them that are overcome with
[d]wine!

2 Behold, the Lord hath a
mighty and strong one, *which* as
a tempest of [e]hail *and* a destroying storm, as a flood of mighty
waters overflowing, shall [f]cast
down to the earth with the hand.

3 The crown of pride, the
[b]drunkards of [c]Ē'phră-ĭm, shall
be trodden[C] under feet:

4 And the glorious beauty,
which *is* on the head of the fat
valley, shall be a fading flower,
*and* as the [1]hasty fruit before the
*summer; which *when* he that
looketh upon it seeth, while it is
yet in his hand he eateth it up.

5 ¶ In that day shall the LORD
of hosts be for a [g]crown of [h]glory,
and for a diadem of beauty, unto
the residue of his [i]people,[S]

6 And for a [j]spirit of judgment[C]
to him that sitteth in judgment,[C]
and for strength to them that
turn the battle to the gate.

7 But they also have erred[C]
through [d]wine, and through
strong drink are out of the way;
the [k]priest and the [l]prophet have
erred[C] through strong drink, they
are swallowed up of wine, [m]they
are out of the way through strong
drink; [m]they err[C] in vision, they
stumble *in* judgment.

8 For all tables are full of vomit
*and* filthiness, *so that there is* no
place *clean*.

9 Whom shall he [n]teach knowledge? and whom shall he make
to understand [2]doctrine[C]? [o]*them
that are* weaned from the milk,
*and* drawn from the breasts.

10 [p]For precept *must be* upon
precept, precept upon precept;
line upon line, line upon line;
here a little, *and* there a little:

11 [3,q]For with stammering[C] lips
and another tongue will he speak
to this people.

12 To whom he said, This *is*
the rest [4]*wherewith* ye may cause
the weary to rest; and this *is* the
refreshing: yet they [r]would not
hear.[Q]

13 But the [s]word of the LORD
was [p]unto them precept[C] upon
precept,[C] precept[C] upon precept;[C]
line upon line, line upon line;
here a little, *and* there a little;
that [t,u]they might go, and fall
backward, and be broken, and
snared, and taken.[S]

14 ¶ Wherefore hear the word
of the LORD, [v]ye scornful [w]men,
that rule this people which *is* in
[x]Jē-ru'sā-lĕm.

15 Because ye have [y]said, We
have made a covenant with

1
a *Drunkenness, woes denounced against*, Luke 21:34.
b *Drunkard*, Psa. 69:12.
c *Ephraim, name applied to the ten tribes*, Gen. 41:52.
d *Wine, intoxication from*, Prov. 23:31.

2
e *Hail*, Job 38:22.
f *Judgments*, Ex. 6:6.

4
1 R. V. firstripe fig before

5
g *Crown, figurative*, Ex. 29:6.
h *God, glory of*, Gen. 2:2.
i *Church, prophecies concerning* (as some interpret), Matt. 16:18.

6
j *Rulers, character and qualifications of*, Ex. 18:21.

7
k *Priest, drunken*, Lev. 1:5.
l *Prophets, drunken*, Isa. 3:2.
m *Drunkenness, consequences of*, Luke 21:34.

9
n *Instruction, in religion*, Prov. 23:23.
o *Children, instruction of*, Mark 10:14.
2 R. V. the message?

10
p *Instruction*, Prov. 23:23.

11
q 1 Cor. 14:21.
3 R. V. Nay, but by men of strange lips and with another

12
r *Impenitence*, Rom. 2:5.
4 R. V. give ye rest to him that is weary;

13
s *Word of God*, Psa. 119:9.
t *Reprobates*, 1 Cor. 9:27.
u *Spiritual Blindness*, 2 Cor. 4:4.

14
v *Scorners*, Prov. 19:25.
w *Rulers, wicked*, Ex. 18:21.
x *Jerusalem*, Judg. 19:10.

15
y *False Confidence*, Psa. 30:6.

---

***SUMMER.** *Season of, promised while the earth remains*, Gen. 8:22. *Cool rooms for*, Judg. 3:20, 24. *Summer house*, Amos 3:15. *Fruits of*, 2 Sam. 16:1, 2; Isa. 16:9; Jer. 40:10, **12**; 48:32; Amos 8:1, 2; Mic. 7:1. *Drought of*, Psa. 32:4. *Given by God*, Psa. 74:17. *The time for labor and harvest*, Prov. 6:6–8; 10:5; 30:25; Jer. 8:20. *Snow in*, Prov. 26:1. *Approach of*, Matt. 24:32; Mark 13:28; Luke 21:30. **Figurative**, Jer. 8:20.

death, and with [z]hell[G] are we at
agreement; when the overflowing scourge shall pass through,
it shall not come unto us: for we
have made lies our refuge, and
under falsehood have we hid
ourselves:
16 Therefore thus saith the
Lord GOD, [a,b,c]Behold, I lay in
Zī′ŏn for a foundation a stone, a
tried[G] stone, a precious[G] [d,e]corner
*stone*, a sure foundation: [f]he that
[g]believeth shall not make[G] haste.[Q S]
17 Judgment[G] also will I lay to
the line, and [h]righteousness to
the [i]plummet[G]: and the hail shall
sweep away the refuge of lies,
and the waters shall overflow
the hiding place.[S]
18 And your covenant with
death shall be disannulled,[G] and
your agreement with [j]hell[G] shall
not stand; when the overflowing
scourge shall pass through, then
[k]ye shall be [l]trodden[G] down by it.
19 From the time that it goeth
forth it shall take you: for morning by morning shall it pass over,
by day and by night: and it shall
be [5]a vexation[G] only *to* understand
the report.
20 For the bed is shorter than
that *a man* can stretch himself
*on it*: and the covering nar-
rower than that he can wrap
himself *in it*.
21 For the LORD shall rise
up as *in* mount [m]Pĕr′a-zĭm, he
shall be [n]wroth[G] as *in* the valley
of [o]Gĭb′e-on, that he may do
his work, his strange work; and
bring to pass his act, his strange
act.[S]
22 Now therefore be ye not
[p]mockers, lest your bands[G] be
made strong: for I have heard
from the Lord GOD of hosts a
consumption,[G] even determined
upon the whole earth.
23 ¶ Give ye ear, and hear my
voice; hearken, and hear my
[q]speech.

z *Hell*, Mark 9:43.

**16**

a 1 Pet. 2:6.
b *Prophecies concerning the Messiah, and their fulfillment*, Gen. 12:3.
c *Jesus, prophecies concerning*, Matt. 1:21.
d *Corner Stone, figurative*, Psa. 144:12.
e *Jesus, typified in the corner stone*, Matt. 1:21.
f Rom. 10:11.
g *Faith in Christ*, John 6:69.

**17**

h *Righteousness*, Psa. 15:2.
i Amos 7:7, 8; Zech. 4:10.

**18**

j *Hell*, Mark 9:43.
k *Wicked, punishment of*, Psa. 73:3.
l *Judgments*, Ex. 6:6.

**19**

5 R. V. nought but terror to understand the message.

**21**

m Or, *Baal-Perazim*, 2 Sam. 5:20; 1 Chr. 14:11.
n *Anger of God*, 2 Kin. 13:3.
o *Gibeon*, Jer. 41:16.

**22**

p *Mocking*, 1 Kin. 18:27.

**23**

q *Parables, of the husbandman*, vs. 23–29; Ezek. 20:49.

24 [q,r,s]Doth the plowman plow
all day to sow? doth he open and
break the clods of his ground?
25 [r,s]When he hath made plain
the face thereof, doth [t]he not
cast abroad the [u]fitches, and
scatter the [v]cummin, and cast
in the principal[G] [w]wheat and the
appointed [x]barley and the [y]rie[G]
in their place?
26 For [r]his God doth [z,a]instruct
him to discretion, *and* doth teach
him.
27 [b]For the [c]fitches are not
[d]threshed with a threshing instrument, neither is a cart wheel
turned about upon the [e]cum-
min; but the fitches are beaten
out with a staff, and the cummin with a rod.
28 Bread *corn* is [6]bruised; because he will not ever be [d]thresh-
ing it, [7]nor break *it with* the wheel
of his cart, nor bruise[G] it *with* his
horsemen.
29 [f]This also cometh forth from
the LORD of hosts, *which* is wonderful in [g]counsel, *and* excellent
in working.[S T]

## CHAPTER 29

*God's judgments upon Jerusalem.* 7 *The hope of her enemies to be disappointed.* 9 *The stupidity and blindness of her people.* 13 *Their hypocrisy to be punished.* 17 *A promise of prosperity.*

WOE to [a]Ā′rĭ-el, to Ā′rĭ-el,
the city *where* Dā′vid dwelt!
add ye year to year; let them
kill sacrifices.
2 Yet I will [b]distress [a]Ā′rĭ-el,
and there shall be heaviness and
sorrow: and it shall be unto me
as Ā′rĭ-el.
3 And I will camp against thee
round about, and will lay [c]siege
against thee with a mount,[G] and I
will raise [d]forts against thee.
4 And thou shalt be brought
down, *and* shalt speak out of
the ground, and thy speech shall
be low out of the dust, and thy
voice shall be, as of one that
hath a [e]familiar[G] spirit, out of the

**24**

r *Agriculture, requires wisdom*, Gen. 3:23.
s *Wisdom, worldly*, Prov. 2:2.

**25**

t *Sower*, Matt. 13:3.
u Ezek. 4:9.
v Matt. 23:23.
w *Wheat*, Ezra 6:9.
x *Barley*, Ex. 9:31.
y Ex. 9:32.

**26**

z *God, teacher*, Gen. 2:2.
a *Wisdom, worldly*, Prov. 2:2.

**27**

b *Agriculture, requires wisdom*, Gen. 3:23.
c Ezek. 4:9.
d *Threshing*, 1 Chr. 21:20.
e Matt. 23:23.

**28**

6 R. V. ground;
7 R. V. and though the wheel of his cart and his horses scatter it, he doth not grind it.

**29**

f *God, guide*, Gen. 2:2.
g *God, wisdom of*, Gen. 2:2.

**1**

a Or, *Jerusalem*, Judg. 19:10.

**2**

b *Judgments*, Ex. 6:6.

**3**

c *Siege*, Deut. 28:53.
d *Fortification*, Ezek. 17:17.

**4**

e *Familiar Spirits*, Deut. 18:11.

ground, and thy speech shall
whisper out of the dust.
5 Moreover the multitude of
thy [1]strangers shall be like small
dust, and the multitude of the
terrible ones *shall be* as chaff
that passeth away: yea, it shall
be at an instant suddenly.
6 Thou shalt be [b]visited of the
LORD of hosts with [f]thunder,
and with *earthquake, and great
noise, with storm and tempest,
and the flame of devouring
fire.
7 And the multitude of all the
nations that fight against [a]Ā'-
rĭ-el, even all that fight against
her and her munition, and that
distress her, shall be as a [g]dream
of a night vision.
8 It shall even be as when an
hungry *man* [g]dreameth, and, behold, he eateth; but he awaketh, and his soul is empty: or as
when a thirsty man dreameth,
and, behold, he drinketh; but he
awaketh, and, behold, *he is* faint,
and his soul hath appetite: so
shall the multitude of all the
nations be, that fight against
mount Zī'ŏn.
9 ¶ [2]Stay [h]yourselves, and wonder; [3,i]cry ye out, and [j]cry: they
are drunken, but not with wine;
they stagger, but not with strong
drink.
10 For the LORD hath poured
out upon you the spirit of deep
sleep, and hath [j]closed your
eyes: the [k]prophets and your
rulers, the seers hath he [j]cov-
ered.
11 And the vision of all is become unto you as the words of a
[l]book that is sealed, which *men*
deliver to one that is learned,
saying, Read this, I pray thee:
and he saith, I cannot; for it *is*
sealed:
12 And the book is delivered to
him that is not learned, saying,
Read this, I pray thee: and he
saith, I am not learned.
13 ¶ Wherefore the Lord said,
[m]Forasmuch as [n]this people
[o,p]draw near *me* with their
mouth, and with their lips do
honour me, but have removed
their heart far from me, and
their [q]fear [4]toward me is taught
by the [r]precept of men:
14 Therefore, behold, I will
proceed to do a marvellous work
among this people, *even* a marvellous work and a wonder: for
[s]the [t]wisdom of their wise *men*
shall perish, and the understanding of their prudent *men* shall be
hid.
15 Woe unto them that [u]seek
deep to hide their counsel from
the LORD, and their works are
in the dark, and they [v]say, Who
seeth us? and who knoweth us?
16 [5]Surely your turning of
things upside down shall be esteemed as the potter's [w]clay: for
[x,y]shall the work say of him that
made it, He made me not? or
shall the thing framed say of him
that framed it, He had no understanding?
17 ¶ *Is* it not yet a very little
while, and [z]Lĕb'a-non shall be
turned into a fruitful field, and
the fruitful field shall be esteemed as a forest?
18 And [a,b]in that day shall the
[c]deaf hear the [d]words of the
book, and the eyes of the blind
shall see out of [e]obscurity, and
out of [e]darkness.
19 The [f]meek also shall increase
*their* [g]joy in the LORD, and the

**5**
1 R. V. foes

**6**
*f Thunder,* 1 Sam. 7:10.

**7**
*g Dream,* Dan. 1:17.

**9**
*h Reprobates,* 1 Cor. 9:27.
*i Worldliness,* 1 John 2:15.
*j Spiritual Blindness,* 2 Cor. 4:4.
2 R. V. Tarry ye
3 R. V. take your pleasure and be blind:

**10**
*k Prophets, false,* Isa. 3:2.

**11**
*l Book, sealed,* Num. 5:23.

**13**
*m Prophecies, miscellaneous,* Dan. 9:24.
*n* Matt. 15:8, 9; Mark 7:6, 7.
*o Worship, of hypocrites,* Gen. 22:5.
*p Hypocrisy, described,* Jas. 3:17.
*q Fear of God,* Acts 9:31.
*r Commandments of Men,* Mark 7:7.
4 R. V. of me is a commandment of men which hath been taught them:

**14**
*s* 1 Cor. 1:19.
*t Wisdom, worldly,* Prov. 2:2.

**15**
*u Sin, attempt to cover, vain,* Rom. 5:12.
*v Infidelity,* 2 Cor. 6:15.

**16**
*w Clay,* Job 33:6.
*x* Isa. 45:9; Rom. 9:20, 21.
*y Infidelity, arguments against,* 2 Cor. 6:15.
5 R. V. Ye turn things upside down! Shall the potter be counted as clay;

**17**
*z Lebanon, figurative,* Deut. 1:7.

**18**
*a Church, prophecies concerning its prosperity,* Matt. 16:18.
*b Jesus, kingdom of, prophecies concerning,* Matt. 1:21.
*c Deafness, figurative,* Matt. 11:5.
*d Gospel, prophecies concerning,* Mark 13:10.
*e Spiritual Blindness,* 2 Cor. 4:4.

**19**
*f Meekness, rewards of,* Psa. 15:1.
*g Joy,* Psa. 5:11.

* **EARTHQUAKES,** Job 9:6; Psa. 18:7; 46:2, 3; 104:32. *As judgments,* Psa. 18:15; 60:2; Isa. 13:13, 14; 24:19, 20; 29:6; Nah. 1:5. *Prophecies of,* Zech. 14:4; Matt. 24:7; Mark 13:8; Luke 21:11.
**Instances of:** *At Sinai,* Ex. 19:18; Psa. 68:8; 77:18; 114:4-7; Heb. 12:26. *When Korah, Dathan, and Abiram were swallowed up,* Num. 16:30-35. *When Jonathan and his armor-bearer attacked the garrison at Gibeah,* 1 Sam. 14:15. *When the Lord revealed himself to Elijah in the still small voice,* 1 Kin. 19:11, 12. *In Canaan, in the days of Uzziah, king of Judah,* Amos 1:1; Zech. 14:5.
*At the crucifixion of Jesus,* Matt. 27:51. *At the resurrection of Jesus,* Matt. 28:2. *When Paul and Silas were in prison at Philippi,* Acts 16:26.
**Figurative,** Psa. 60:2. *In John's vision,* Rev. 6:12-14; 11:13; 16:18, 20.

poor among men shall rejoice in
the [h,i]Holy One of Ĭş′ra-el.[S]
20 For the terrible one is
brought to nought,[C] and the
[j]scorner is consumed, and all
that watch for iniquity are cut
off:
21 That [k]make a man an offender [6]for a word, and [k]lay a
snare for him that reproveth in
the gate, and [k]turn aside the just
for a thing of nought.[C]
22 Therefore thus saith the
LORD, who redeemed [l]Ā′bră-
hăm, concerning the house of
Jā′cob, Jā′cob shall not now be
ashamed, neither shall his face
now wax[C] pale.
23 But when he seeth his children, the work of mine hands, in
the midst of him, they shall sanctify my name, and sanctify the
[h,i]Holy One of Jā′cob, and shall
[m]fear the God of Ĭş′ra-el.[S]
24 They also that [n]erred in spirit
shall come to [o]understanding,
and they that murmured[C] shall
learn [p]doctrine.[S]

## CHAPTER 30

*A woe upon the people for their confidence in Egypt. 8 A record to be made of their rebellious character and contempt of God's word. 18 God's mercies to Zion. 27 The destruction of Assyria.*

1 WOE to the [a]rebellious [b]chil-
dren, saith the LORD, that
[c]take counsel,[C] but not of me; and
that [c]cover[C] with a covering, but
not of my spirit, that they may
[d]add sin to sin:
2 That walk to go down into
[e]Ē′ġy̆pt, and have not [f]asked[C] at
my mouth; to [g]strengthen themselves in the strength of [h]Phā′-
raōh, and to [c]trust in the shadow
of Ē′ġy̆pt!
3 Therefore shall the strength
of [h]Phā′raōh be [b]your shame,
and the [c]trust in the shadow of
[e]Ē′ġy̆pt *your* confusion.

*h God, holiness of,* Gen. 2:2.
*i Holiness, attribute of God,* Ex. 39:30.

20
*j Scorners,* Prov. 19:25.

21
*k Temptation, leading into,* Luke 11:4.
6 R. V. in a cause,

22
*l Abraham,* Gen. 17:5.

23
*m Fear of God,* Acts 9:31.

24
*n Backsliders, return of,* Jer. 3:22.
*o Wisdom, spiritual,* Prov. 2:2.
*p Truth,* John 18:37.

1
*a Wicked, described,* vs. 9–11; Psa. 73:3.
*b Nation, punishment of,* Isa. 2:4.
*c False Confidence,* Psa. 30:6.
*d Sin, progressive,* Rom. 5:12.

2
*e Egyptians, alliances with,* Gen. 50:3.
*f Prayer, for guidance,* Acts 6:4.
*g Alliances,* Josh. 9:15.
*h* Isa. 19:11; 36:6.

4 For his princes were at *Zō′-
an, and his [i]ambassadors came
to Hā′nēş.
5 They were all ashamed of a
people *that* could not profit them,
nor be an help nor profit, but a
shame, and also a reproach.
6 The burden of the [j]beasts of
the south: into the land of trouble and anguish, from whence
*come* the [1]young and old lion,
the †viper and fiery flying [k]ser-
pent, they will [l]carry their riches
upon the shoulders of young
[m]asses, and their treasures upon
the bunches[C] of [n]camels, to a people *that* shall not profit *them.*
7 For [2]the [e]Ē-ġy̆p′tianş shall
help in vain, and to no purpose:
therefore have I [3]cried concerning this, Their strength *is* to sit
still.
8 ¶ Now go, write it before
them [4]in a table, and note it in a
book, that it may be for the time
to come for ever and ever:
9 That [o]this *is* a [a]rebellious
[b]people, [p]lying children, [q]chil-
dren *that* will not hear[C] the [r]law
of the LORD:
10 [s]Which say to the seers, See
not; and to the prophets, Prophesy[C] not unto us right things,
speak unto us smooth things,
prophesy[C] deceits:
11 [s]Get you out of the way,
turn aside out of the path, cause
the [t]Holy One of Ĭş′ra-el to cease
from before us.
12 Wherefore thus saith the
[t]Holy One of Ĭş′ra-el, Because
ye despise this [r]word, and [c]trust
in [u]oppression and perverseness,
and stay[C] thereon:
13 [v]Therefore this iniquity shall
be to you as a breach ready to
fall, swelling out in a high wall,
whose breaking cometh suddenly
at an instant.

4
*i Ambassadors,* Josh. 9:4.

6
*j Beasts, figurative,* Dan. 7:3.
*k Serpent,* Num. 21:6.
*l Commerce,* 1 Kin. 10:15.
*m Ass,* 2 Chr. 28:15.
*n Camel,* 1 Sam. 30:17.
1 R. V. lioness and the lion,

7
2 R. V. Egypt helpeth in vain,

8
4 R. V. on a tablet,

9
*o Reproof, faithfulness in,* Prov. 17:10.
*p Falsehood,* Job 21:34.
*q Backsliders,* Jer. 3:22.
*r Word of God, rejected,* Psa. 119:9.

10
*s Minister, discouragements of,* Rom. 15:16.

11
*t God, holiness of,* Gen. 2:2.

12
*u Oppression,* Eccl. 5:8.

13
*v Wicked, punishment of,* Psa. 73:3.

* **ZOAN,** a city in Egypt. *Built seven years after Hebron in the land of Canaan,* Num. 13:22. *Prophecies concerning,* Ezek. 30:14. *Wise men from, were counselors of Pharaoh,* **Isa. 19:11, 13.** *Princes of,* Isa. 30:4.

† **VIPER.** *A serpent,* Job 20:16; Isa. 30:6. *Fastens on Paul's hand,* Acts 28:3.
See footnote, SERPENT, Num. 21:6.
**Figurative,** Isa. 59:5; Matt. 3:7; 23:33; **Luke 3:7.**

14 And he [w]shall break it as the breaking of the [x]potters' vessel that is broken in pieces; he shall not spare: so that there shall not be found in the bursting of it a sherd[G] to take fire from the hearth, or to take water *withal* out of the [5]pit.

15 For thus saith the Lord GOD, the [t]Holy One of Ĭṣ′ra-el; [y]In returning and rest shall ye be saved; in quietness and in [z]confidence shall be your strength: and ye would not.

16 But ye said, No; for we will flee upon horses; therefore shall ye flee: and, We will ride upon the swift; therefore shall they that pursue you be swift.

17 [a]One thousand *shall flee* at the rebuke of one; at the rebuke of five shall ye flee: till ye be left as a [b,c]beacon upon the top of a [d]mountain, and as an [e]ensign on an hill.

18 And therefore will the LORD [f]wait, that he may be gracious unto you, and therefore will he be exalted, that he may have [g]mercy upon you: for the LORD *is* a God of [h]judgment[G]: blessed *are* all they that wait for him.[S]

19 ¶ For the people shall dwell in [i]Zī′ŏn at [j]Jē-rụ′sā-lĕm: [k]thou shalt weep no more: [k]he will be very [g]gracious unto thee at the voice of thy cry; when he shall hear it, [l]he will answer thee.

20 And *though* the Lord [m]give you the [n]bread of [o]adversity, and the [p]water of affliction[G], yet shall not thy [q]teachers be [6]removed into a corner any more, but thine eyes shall see thy teachers:

21 And thine ears shall hear a [r]word behind thee, saying, This *is* the way, walk ye in it, when ye turn[G] to the right hand, and when ye turn[G] to the left.[S]

22 Ye shall defile also the covering of thy graven[G] [s]images of [t]silver, and the ornament of thy molten[G] images of [u]gold: thou shalt cast them away as [7]a menstruous cloth; thou shalt say unto it, Get thee hence.

23 [S]Then shall [v]he give the [w,x]rain of thy seed, that thou shalt sow the ground withal; and bread of the increase of the earth, and it shall be fat and plenteous: in that day shall thy cattle feed in large pastures.

24 The oxen likewise and the young asses that [8]ear[G] the ground shall eat [9]clean provender[G], which hath been [y]winnowed with the shovel and with the [z]fan[G].

25 And there shall be upon every high mountain, and upon every high hill, rivers *and* streams of waters in the day of the great slaughter, when the towers fall.

26 Moreover the light of the moon shall be as the light of the sun, and the light of the sun shall be sevenfold, as the light of seven days, [a]in the day that the LORD bindeth up the breach of his people, and healeth the stroke of their wound.[S]

27 ¶ [S]Behold, the name of the LORD cometh from far, [b]burning *with* his [c]anger, and [10]the burden *thereof is* heavy: his lips are full of indignation, and his tongue as a devouring fire:

28 And his breath, as an overflowing stream, shall reach to the midst of the neck, to sift the nations with the [d]sieve of vanity: and *there shall be* a bridle in the jaws of the people, causing *them* to err.

29 Ye shall have a [e]song, as in the night [f]*when* a holy [11,g]solemnity is kept; and [h]gladness of heart, as when one goeth with a [i]pipe[G] to come into the mountain of the LORD, to the [12]mighty One of Ĭṣ′ra-el.

30 And the LORD shall cause his glorious voice to be heard,

14
*w Judgments*, Ex. 6:6.
*x Pottery*, Jer. 18:3.
5 R. V. cistern.

15
*y Backsliders, called to repentance*, Jer. 3:22.
*z Faith*, Mark 11:22.

17
*a Cowardice*, Lev. 26:36.
*b* Jer. 6:1.
*c Fire, used as a signal in war*, Ex. 12:8.
*d Mountain, signals from*, Mic. 7:12.
*e Standard*, Num. 1:52.

18
*f God, longsuffering of*, Gen. 2:2.
*g God, mercy of*, Gen. 2:2.
*h God, justice of*, Gen. 2:2.

19
*i Zion*, 2 Sam. 5:7.
*j Jerusalem*, Judg. 19:10.
*k Afflictions, consolation in*, Psa. 34:19.
*l Prayer, answer to, promised*, Acts 6:4.

20
*m Divine Chastisement*, Job 33:19.
*n Bread, figurative*, Ezek. 4:13.
*o Adversity, dispensation from God*, Psa. 10:6.
*p Water, of affliction*, 1 Kin. 17:10.
*q Minister, called teacher*, Rom. 15:16.
6 R. V. hidden any more,

21
*r Instruction*, Prov. 23:23.

22
*s Idol*, 1 Kin. 15:12.
*t Silver*, 1 Chr. 28:14.

*u Gold*, Ezek. 7:19.
7 R. V. an unclean thing;

23
*v God, providence of*, Gen. 2:2.
*w Rain*, 2 Sam. 1:21.
*x Temporal Blessings, from God*, Psa. 103:2.

24
*y Winnowing*, Ruth 3:2.
*z* Jer. 15:7; 51:2; Matt. 3:12.
8 R. V. till
9 R. V. savoury

26
*a Nation, promises of peace to*, Isa. 2:4.

27
*b Judgments*, Ex. 6:6.
*c Anger of God*, 2 Kin. 13:3.
10 R. V. in thick rising smoke:

28
*d* Amos 9:9; Luke 22:31.

29
*e Music*, 2 Chr. 5:13.
*f Worship, at night*, Gen. 22:5.
*g Annual Feasts, kept with rejoicing*, Num. 15:3.
*h Joy*, Psa. 5:11.
*i* 1 Sam. 10:5; 1 Kin. 1:40.
11 R. V. feast
12 R. V. Rock of Israel.

and shall shew the lighting down of his arm, with the [b]indignation of *his* [c]anger, and *with* the flame of a devouring fire, *with* [13]scattering, and tempest, and hailstones.[S][Q]

31 For through the voice of the LORD shall the [j]Ăs-sy̆r′ĭ-an be beaten down,[C] *which* smote with a rod.

32 And [14]*in* every place where the grounded staff shall pass, which the LORD shall lay upon[C] him, *it* shall be with tabrets and [k]harps: and in battles of shaking will he fight with it.[C]

33 For [b,l]Tō′phet *is* ordained of old; yea, for the [m]king it is prepared; he hath made *it* deep *and* large: the pile thereof *is* fire and much wood; the [n]breath of the LORD, like a stream of [o]brimstone, doth kindle it.[Q]

## CHAPTER 31

*The folly of forsaking God and trusting in Egypt. 6 An exhortation to turn unto God.*

WOE to them that [a]go down to [b]Ē′gy̆pt for help; and [c]stay[C] on [d]horses, and [c]trust in [e]chariots, because *they are* many; and in [f]horsemen, because they are very strong; but [g]they look not unto the [h]Holy One of Is′ra-el, neither seek the LORD!

2 Yet he also *is* [i]wise, and will bring evil, and [j]will not call back his words: but will arise against the house of the evildoers, and against the help[C] of them that work iniquity.[S]

3 Now the Ē-gy̆p′tians *are* men, and not God; and their horses flesh, and not spirit. When the [k]LORD shall stretch out his [l]hand, both he that helpeth shall fall, and he that is holpen[C] shall fall down, and they all shall fail together.

4 For thus hath the LORD spoken unto me, Like as the lion and the young lion roaring on his prey, when a multitude of shepherds is called forth against him, *he* will not be afraid of their voice, nor abase himself for the noise of them: so shall the LORD of hosts come down to [m,n]fight for mount Zī′ŏn, and for the hill thereof.

5 As birds flying, so will the LORD of hosts [m]defend [o]Jĕ-ru̇′sā-lĕm; defending also he will deliver *it*; *and* passing over he will [n]preserve *it*.[S]

6 ¶ [p,q]Turn ye unto *him from* whom the children of Is′ra-el have deeply revolted.[S]

7 For [r]in that day every man shall cast away his [s]idols of silver, and his idols of gold, which your own hands have made unto you *for* a sin.

8 Then shall the [t]Ăs-sy̆r′ĭ-an fall with the [l,u]sword, not of [1]a mighty man; and the sword, not of [2]a mean man, shall devour him: but he shall flee from the sword, and his young men shall [3]be discomfited.[C]

9 And [4]he shall pass over to his strong hold for fear, and his princes shall be afraid of the [v]ensign, saith the LORD, whose fire *is* in Zī′ŏn, and his furnace in [o]Jĕ-ru̇′sā-lĕm.[S]

## CHAPTER 32

*Blessings promised to Zion. 9 Judgments to come upon Israel and upon their enemies*

BEHOLD, [a]a [b]king shall reign in righteousness, and princes shall rule in judgment.[C][Q]

2 And a man shall be as an hiding place from the wind, and a covert[C] from the tempest; as [c]rivers of water in a dry place, as the shadow of a great rock in a weary land.[S]

3 And [a]the eyes of them that see shall [d]not be dim,[C] and the ears of them that hear [d]shall hearken.

4 [a]The heart also of the rash[C]

---

**30**
13 R. V. a blast,

**31**
j *Assyria, prophecies concerning*, vs. 27–33; Gen. 25:18.

**32**
k *Harp*, Dan. 3:10.
14 R. V. every stroke of the appointed staff, which

**33**
l Or, *Topheth, figurative*, 2 Kin. 23:10.
m *Rulers, wicked*, Ex. 18:21.
n *Breath, of God*, Gen. 7:15.
o *Brimstone, figurative*, Deut. 29:23.

**1**
a *Alliances, with idolaters forbidden*, Josh. 9:15.
b *Egypt, armies of*, Gen. 41:8.
c *False Confidence, in worldly help*, Psa. 30:6.
d *Horse*, Job 39:19.
e *Chariot*, Josh. 11:4.
f *Cavalry*, 1 Sam. 13:5.
g *God, jealous*, Gen. 2:2.
h *God, holiness of*, Gen. 2:2.

**2**
i *God, wisdom of*, Gen. 2:2.
j *God, immutable*, Gen. 2:2.

**3**
k *God, power of, irresistible*, Gen. 2:2.
l *Judgments*, Ex. 6:6.

**4**
m *God, providence of*, Gen. 2:2.
n *God, preserver*, Gen. 2:2.

**5**
o *Jerusalem*, Judg. 19:10.

**6**
p *Repentance, enjoined*, Mark 1:4.
q *Backsliders, called to repentance*, Jer. 3:22.

**7**
r *Idolatry, prophecies relating to*, 1 Sam. 15:23.
s *Idol*, 1 Kin. 15:12.

**8**
t *Assyria, prophecies concerning*, Gen. 25:18.
u *Sword, figurative*, 1 Chr. 21:5.
1 R. V. *omits* a mighty
2 R. V. men,
3 R. V. become tributary.

**9**
v *Standard*, Num. 1:52.
4 R. V. his rock shall pass away by reason of terror,

**1**
a *Church, prophecies concerning its prosperity*, vs. 1–20; Matt. 16:18.
b *Jesus, typified in Hezekiah*, Matt. 1:21.

**2**
c *River*, Psa. 46:4.

**3**
d *Wisdom, spiritual*, Prov. 2:2.

shall understand knowledge, and the tongue of the [e]stammerers shall be ready to [f]speak plainly.

5 The [g]vile person shall be no more called liberal, nor the churl said *to be* bountiful.

6 For the [g]vile person will [h]speak villany, and his heart will [i]work iniquity, to practise [1]hypocrisy, and to utter error against the LORD, to [j]make empty the soul of the hungry, and he will cause the drink of the thirsty to fail.

7 The instruments also of the churl *are* evil: he [i]deviseth wicked devices to destroy the [2]poor with [k]lying words, even when the needy speaketh right.

8 But the liberal deviseth [l]liberal things; and by liberal things shall he stand.

9 ¶ [m]Rise up, ye [n]women that are [o]at ease; hear my voice, [o]ye careless daughters; give ear unto my speech.

10 [3,m]Many days and years shall ye be troubled, ye [o]careless [n]women: for the vintage shall fail, the gathering shall not come.

11 [m]Tremble, ye [n]women that are [o]at ease; be troubled, ye [o]careless ones: strip you, and make you bare, and gird *sackcloth* upon *your* loins.

12 They shall [4]lament for the teats, for the pleasant fields, for the fruitful vine.

13 [p]Upon the land of my people shall come up thorns *and* briers; yea, upon all the houses of joy *in* the joyous city:

14 Because the palaces shall be forsaken; the multitude of the city shall be left; the forts and towers shall be for dens for ever, a joy of wild asses, a pasture of flocks;

15 [a,q]Until the [r]spirit be poured upon us from on high, and the wilderness be a fruitful field, and the fruitful field be counted for a forest.

16 Then judgment shall dwell in the wilderness, and [s]righteousness remain in the fruitful field.

17 And the work of righteousness shall be [t,u]peace; and the effect of righteousness [u]quietness and [5,u,v]assurance for ever.

18 And [u]my people shall dwell in a [t]peaceable habitation, and in sure dwellings, and in quiet resting places;

19 When it shall hail, [6]coming down on the forest; and the city shall be low in a low place.

20 Blessed *are* ye that sow beside all waters, that send forth *thither* the feet of the ox and the ass.

## CHAPTER 33

*A woe against the enemies of God's people. 13 The peace and security of Zion.*

WOE to thee that spoilest, and thou *wast* not spoiled; and dealest treacherously, and they dealt not treacherously with thee! when thou shalt cease to spoil, thou shalt be spoiled; *and* when thou shalt make an end to deal treacherously, they shall deal treacherously with thee.

2 [a]O LORD, be gracious unto us; [b]we have waited for thee: be thou their [c]arm every morning, our [d]salvation also in the time of trouble.

3 At the noise of the tumult the people fled; at the lifting up of thyself the nations were scattered.

4 And your spoil shall be gathered *like* the gathering of the caterpiller: as [1]the running to and fro of [e]locusts shall he run upon them.

5 The LORD is exalted; for he dwelleth on high: he hath filled Zī'ŏn with [f]judgment and [f]righteousness.

6 And [g]wisdom and [h]knowl-

**4**
e Ex. 4:10; Isa. 33:19.
f *Religious Testimony*, 2 Thess. 1:10.
g *Wicked, described*, Psa. 73:3.

**6**
h *Speech, evil*, Col. 4:6.
i *Malice*, Eph. 4:31.
j *Poor, oppressions of*, Prov. 21:13.
1 R. V. profaneness,

**7**
k *Falsehood*, Job 21:34.
2 R. V. meek

**8**
l *Liberality*, 1 Tim. 6:18.

**9**
m *Impenitence, admonitions against*, Rom. 2:5.
n *Women, wicked*, Prov. 31:10.
o *Worldliness*, 1 John 2:15.

**10**
3 R. V. For days beyond a year

**12**
4 R. V. smite upon the breasts for the pleasant

**13**
p *Jerusalem, prophecies against*, Judg. 19:10.

**15**
q *Jesus, kingdom of, prophecies concerning*, vs. 15–17; Matt. 1:21.
r *Holy Spirit, poured upon Israel*, Acts 1:2.

**16**
s *Righteousness*, Psa. 15:2.

**17**
t *Peace*, Jer. 29:7.
u *Righteousness, fruits of*, Psa. 15:2.
v *Assurance*, Heb. 10:22.
5 R. V. confidence

**19**
6 R. V. in the downfall of the forest; and the city shall be utterly laid low.

**2**
a *Prayer, in adversity*, Acts 6:4.
b *Faith, in adversity*, Mark 11:22.
c *Arm, figurative*, Psa. 89:13.
d *God, preserver*, Gen. 2:2.

**4**
e *Locust, devastation by*, Nah. 3:17.
1 Am. R. V. locusts leap shall men leap upon it.

**5**
f *Spiritual Blessings, from God*, Eph. 1:3.

**6**
g *Wisdom, spiritual*, Prov. 2:2.
h *Knowledge*, Luke 11:52.

edge shall be the stability of thy times, *and* strength of salvation: the [i]fear of the LORD *is* his treasure.

7 Behold, their valiant[C] ones shall cry without[C]: the [j]ambassadors of peace shall weep bitterly.

8 [k]The highways lie waste, the wayfaring[C] man ceaseth: he hath broken the covenant, he hath despised the cities, he regardeth no man.

9 [k]The earth mourneth *and* languisheth: [l]Lĕb′a-non is ashamed *and* hewn[C] down: [m]Shâr′on is like a wilderness; and [n]Bā′shăn and [o]Cär′mel shake off *their* [2]*fruits*.

10 ¶ Now will I rise, saith the LORD; now will I be exalted; now will I lift up myself.

11 [p]Ye shall conceive chaff, ye shall bring forth stubble: your breath, *as* fire, shall devour you.

12 And the [p]people shall be *as* the burnings of [q]lime: *as* thorns cut up shall they be burned in the fire.

13 ¶ Hear, ye *that are* far off, what I have done; and, ye *that are* near, acknowledge [r]my might.

14 [p]The sinners in Zī′ŏn are [s]afraid; fearfulness hath [3]surprised the hypocrites[C]. Who among us shall dwell with the devouring [t]fire? who among us shall dwell with everlasting burnings?[Q]

15 [u,v]He that walketh [w]righteously, and speaketh uprightly; he that [x]despiseth the gain of [y]oppressions, that [x]shaketh his hands from holding of [z]bribes, that [x]stoppeth his ears from hearing of blood, and [x]shutteth his eyes from seeing evil;

16 [a,b]He shall dwell on high: his place of defence *shall be* the [c]munitions[C] of rocks: [d]bread shall be given him; his waters *shall be* sure.[S]

17 Thine eyes shall see the king in his beauty: they shall behold the land that is very far off.[S Q]

18 Thine heart shall meditate terror. Where *is* [4]the scribe? where *is* the [e]receiver[C]? where *is* he that counted the towers?[Q]

19 Thou shalt not see a fierce people, a people of a deeper speech than thou canst perceive; of a [5,f]stammering[C] tongue, *that thou canst* not understand.

20 Look upon Zī′ŏn, the city of our solemnities: thine eyes shall see [g]Jē-ru̧′sȧ-lĕm a quiet habitation, a tabernacle *that* shall not be taken down; not one of the stakes thereof shall ever be removed, neither shall any of the cords thereof be broken.

21 But there the glorious LORD *will be* unto us a place of broad rivers *and* streams; wherein shall go no galley[C] with oars, neither shall gallant[C] ship pass thereby.[S]

22 For the LORD *is* our [h]judge, the LORD *is* our lawgiver, the LORD *is* our [i]king; he will [j]save us.[S T]

23 Thy tacklings are loosed; they could not well strengthen their mast, they could not spread the sail: then is the prey of a great spoil[C] divided; the lame take the prey.

24 And the inhabitant shall not say, I am sick: the people that dwell therein *shall be* [k]forgiven *their* iniquity.[Q]

## CHAPTER 34

*God's judgments upon the enemies of Zion. 11 The desolation of their lands. 16 The certainty of the prophecy.*

COME near, ye nations, to hear; and hearken, ye people: let the earth hear, and all that is therein; the world, and all things that come forth of it.

2 For the [a,b]indignation of the LORD *is* upon all nations, and *his* fury upon all their armies: he hath utterly destroyed them,

i *Fear of God*, Acts 9:31.

7

j *Ambassadors*, Josh. 9:4.

8

k *War, evils of*, Judg. 3:2.

9

l *Lebanon*, Deut. 1:7.
m *Sharon*, 1 Chr. 27:29.
n *Bashan*, Num. 32:33.
o *Carmel*, Jer. 46:18.
2 R. V. leaves.

11

p *Wicked, punishment of*, Psa. 73:3.

12

q Amos 2:1.

13

r *God, power of*, Gen. 2:2.

14

s *Fear of God, guilty*, Acts 9:31.
t *Fire, figurative of judgments*, Ex. 12:8.
3 Am. R. V. seized the godless ones.

15

u *Righteous, described*, Psa. 64:10.
v *Righteousness, fruits of*, Psa. 15:2.
w *Honesty*, Rom. 13:13.
x *Temptation, resistance to*, Luke 11:4.
y *Oppression*, Eccl. 5:8.
z *Bribery*, 1 Sam. 8:3.

16

a *Righteous, promises to*, Psa. 64:10.
b *Promise, to the righteous*, 2 Cor. 1:20.
c *Fortification*, Ezek. 17:17.
d *Temporal Blessings*, Psa. 103:2.

18

e *Tax, collectors of*, Neh. 10:32.
4 R. V. he that counted, where is he that weighed the tribute? where

19

f Isa. 32:4.
5 R. V. strange

20

g *Jerusalem*, Judg. 19:10.

22

h *God, judge*, Gen. 2:2.
i *God, sovereign*, Gen. 2:2.
j *God, preserver*, Gen. 2:2.

24

k *Sin, forgiveness of*, Rom. 5:12.

2

a *Judgments*, Ex. 6:6.
b *Nation, punishment of*, vs. 1–15; 2:4.

he hath delivered them to the
slaughter.
3 [a,b]Their slain also shall be
cast out, and their stink shall
come up out of their carcases,
and the mountains shall be melted with their blood.
4 And all the host of heaven
shall be dissolved, and the [c]heav-
ens shall be rolled together as a
scroll: and all their host shall
[1]fall down, as the leaf falleth off
from the vine, and as a falling *fig*
from the fig tree.[Q]
5 For my [a,d]sword [2]shall be
bathed in [c]heaven: behold, [b]it
shall come down upon [3,e]Ī-du-
mē'ȧ, and upon the people of my
curse, to judgment.
6 The [a,d]sword of the LORD is
filled with blood, it is made fat
with fatness, *and* with the blood
of lambs and goats, with the fat
of the kidneys of rams: for the
LORD hath a [f]sacrifice in [g]Bŏz'-
rah, and a great slaughter in the
land of [e]Ī-du-mē'ȧ.
7 And the [4,h]unicorns shall come
down with them, and the bullocks with the bulls; and [i]their
land shall be soaked with blood,
and their dust made fat with
fatness.
8 For *it is* the [j]day of the
LORD's [a]vengeance, *and* the
year of recompences for the
controversy of Zī'ŏn.
9 And [a]the streams thereof
shall be turned into *pitch, and
the dust thereof into brimstone,
and the land thereof shall become burning pitch.
10 [a]It shall not be quenched
night nor day; the smoke thereof
shall go up for ever: from generation to generation it shall lie
waste; none shall pass through
it for ever and ever.[Q]
11 But the [5,k]cormorant and
the [l]bittern shall possess it; the
[m]owl also and the raven shall
dwell in it: and he shall stretch
out upon it the line of confusion,[C] and the [6]stones of empti-
ness.[Q]
12 They shall call the nobles
thereof to the kingdom, but none
*shall be* there, and all her princes
shall be nothing.[Q]
13 [b]And thorns shall come
up in her palaces, [n]nettles and
[o]brambles in the fortresses thereof: and it shall be an habitation
of [7,p]dragons, *and* a court for
[8,m]owls.
14 [b]The wild [q]beasts of the desert shall also meet with the [9]wild
beasts of the island, and the
[r]satyr[C] shall cry to his fellow; the
[10]screech owl also shall rest there,
and find for herself a place of
rest.[Q]
15 [q]There shall the [11]great owl
make her nest, and lay, and
hatch, and gather under her
shadow: there shall the [12,s]vul-
tures also be gathered, every one
with her mate.
16 ¶ Seek ye out of the [t]book of
the LORD, and read: no one of
these shall fail, none shall want[C]
her mate: for my mouth it hath
commanded, and his spirit it
hath gathered them.
17 And he hath cast the [u]lot for
them, and his hand hath divided
it unto them by line: they shall
possess it for ever, from generation to generation shall they
dwell therein.

## CHAPTER 35

*The future prosperity of Zion described.*

[a,b,c]THE wilderness and the
[d]solitary place shall be
[e]glad for them; and the [d,f]desert
shall rejoice, and blossom as the
[g]rose.
2 [a,b,c]It shall blossom abundantly, and rejoice even with

4
c *Heavens, physical, destruction of,* Psa. 8:3.
1 R. V. fade away,

5
d *Sword, figurative,* 1 Chr. 21:5.
e Or, *Edomites, prophecies concerning,* 2 Kin. 8:21.
2 R. V. hath drunk its fill in
3 R. V. Edom,

6
f *Sacrifices, figurative,* Rom. 12:1.
g *Bozrah, prophecies concerning,* Gen. 36:33.

7
h *Unicorn, figurative,* Job 39:9.
i *War, evils of,* Judg. 3:2.
4 R. V. wild-oxen

8
j *Day, times of adversity called day of the Lord,* Gen. 1:5.

11
k *Cormorant,* Lev. 11:17.
l Isa. 14:23; Zeph. 2:14.
5 R. V. pelican and the porcupine
m *Owl,* Lev. 11:17.
6 R. V. plummet

13
n *Nettles,* Prov. 24:31.
o Judg. 9:14, 15; Luke 6:44.
p *Dragon,* Deut. 32:33.
7 R. V. jackals,
8 R. V. ostriches.

14
q *Animals, habits and abodes of,* Jer. 27:5.
r *Satyr,* Isa. 13:21
9 R. V. wolves,
10 R. V. night-monster

15
s Lev. 11:14; Deut. 14:13.
11 R. V. arrow-snake
12 R. V. kites

16
t *Word of God, inspired,* Psa. 119:9.

17
u *Lot,* Esth. 3:7.

1
a *Allegory,* vs. 1–10; Gal. 4:24.
b *Church, prophecies concerning, its prosperity,* vs. 1–10; Matt. 16:18.
c *Jesus, kingdom of, prophecies concerning,* Matt. 1:21.
d *Gentiles, prophecies of the conversion of,* vs. 1–10; Acts 10:45.
e *Joy,* Psa. 5:11.
f *Desert, figurative,* Lev. 16:22.
g Song 2:1.

* **PITCH.** *An opaque mineral used as a plaster and cement,* Isa. 34:9. *Used by Noah in the ark,* Gen. 6:14. *Used in making the ark in which Moses was hidden,* Ex. 2:3.

2
h *Lebanon,* Deut. 1:7.
i *Carmel,* Jer. 46:18.
j *Sharon,* 1 Chr. 27:29.
k *God, glory of,* Gen. 2:2.
3
l Heb. 12:12.
m *Despondency, comfort in,* Eccl. 2:20.
n *Weak, duty of strong to,* 1 Cor. 8:9.
4
o *Courage, enjoined,* Deut. 31:7.
p *God, savior,* Gen. 2:2.
5
q *Spiritual Blindness,* 2 Cor. 4:4.
r *Deafness, figurative,* Matt. 11:5.
6
s *Lameness,* Lev. 21:18.
t *Deer,* Deut. 14:5.
u *Dumb,* Ex. 4:11.
7
v *Reed,* Ezek. 40:3.
1 R. V. glowing sand
2 R. V. jackals,
8
w *Highways, figurative,* Deut. 2:27.
x *Holiness,* Ex. 39:30
9
y *Lion, figurative,* Mic. 5:8.
10
z *Promise, to the righteous,* 2 Cor. 1:20.

a *Ransom, figurative,* Ex. 21:30.
b *Righteous, promises to,* Psa. 64:10.
c *Zion,* 2 Sam. 5:7.
d *Praise,* Psa. 150:1.

[e]joy and singing: the glory of
[h]Lĕb′a-non shall be given unto
it, the excellency of [i]Cär′mel
and [j]Shâr′on, they shall see the
[k]glory of the LORD, *and* the excellency of our God.[S]
3 [l,m]Strengthen ye the [n]weak
hands, and confirm the feeble
knees.[Q]
4 Say to them *that are* of a fearful heart, Be strong, [o]fear not:
behold, your God will come *with*
vengeance, *even* God *with* a recompence; he will come and [p]save
you.[S]
5[Q] [b,c]Then the eyes of the
[q]blind shall be opened, and the
ears of the [r]deaf shall be un-
stopped.
6 [a,b,c]Then shall the [s]lame *man*
leap as an [t]hart, and the tongue
of the [u]dumb sing: for in the wilderness shall waters break out,
and streams in the desert.[Q]
7 [a,b,c]And the [1,d]parched
ground shall become a pool,
and the [d]thirsty land springs
of water: in the [d]habitation
of [2]dragons, where each lay,
*shall be* grass with [v]reeds and
rushes.
8 [b,c]And an [w]highway shall be
there, and a *way, and it shall be
called The way of [x]holiness; the
unclean shall not pass over it;
but it *shall be* for those: the wayfaring men, though fools, shall
not err *therein*.
9 No [y]lion shall be there, nor
*any* ravenous beast shall go up
thereon, it shall not be found
there; but the redeemed shall
walk *there*:[S]
10 And [z]the [a,b]ransomed of the
LORD shall return, and come to
[c]Zī′ŏn with [d]songs and everlasting joy upon their heads: they
shall obtain joy and gladness,
and sorrow and sighing shall flee
away.[Q]

## CHAPTER 36

*Sennacherib invades Judah. 2 Rabshakeh sent to Jerusalem. 3 His interview with Eliakim, Shebna, and Joah. 13 He solicits the people to revolt. 22 His words reported to Hezekiah.*

NOW it came to pass in the
fourteenth year of king
[a]Hĕz-e-kī′ah, *that* [b]Sĕn-năch′e-
rĭb king of [c]Ăs-sy̆r′ĭ-ȧ came up
against all the defenced[C] cities of
[d]Jū′dah, and took them.
2 And the [b]king of [c]Ăs-sy̆r′ĭ-ȧ
sent [e]Răb′sha-keh from [f]Lā′-
chish to [g]Jē-ru̧′sā-lĕm unto king
[a]Hĕz-e-kī′ah with a great army.
And he stood by the conduit of
the upper [h]pool in the highway
of the [i]fuller's field.
3 Then came forth unto him
[j,k]Ė-lī′a-kĭm, [l]Hĭl-kī′ah's son,
which was over the house, and
[k,m]Shĕb′nȧ the [n]scribe,[G] and
[k,o]Jō′ah, [p]Ā′saph's son, the recorder.
4 And [e]Răb′sha-keh [q]said unto
them, Say ye now to [a]Hĕz-e-kī′-
ah, Thus saith the great [b]king,
the king of [c]Ăs-sy̆r′ĭ-ȧ, What
confidence *is* this wherein thou
trustest?
5 I say, [1]*sayest thou*, (but *they
are but* vain[G] words) *I have* counsel and strength for war: [q]now on
whom dost thou trust, that thou
rebellest against me?
6 Lo, thou trustest in the staff
of this broken [r]reed, on [s]Ē′ġy̆pt;
whereon if a man lean, it will go
into his hand, and pierce it: so *is*
[t]Phā′raōh king of Ē′ġy̆pt to all
that trust in him.
7 But if thou say to me, We
[u]trust in the LORD our God: *is
it* not he, whose high places and
whose altars [a]Hĕz-e-kī′ah hath
taken away, and said to [d]Jū′dah
and to Jē-ru̧′sā-lĕm, Ye shall
worship before this altar?
8 Now therefore give pledges,
I pray thee, to my master the

v.1–632 BC
See footnote, *Time,* Rev. 10:6.
1
a *Hezekiah,* 2 Kin. 16:20.
b *Sennacherib,* 2 Chr. 32:1.
c *Assyria,* Gen. 25:18.
d *Judah, kingdom of,* 2 Chr. 11:17.
2
e *Rabshakeh,* 2 Kin. 18:17.
f *Lachish,* Josh. 10:5.
g *Jerusalem,* Judg. 19:10.
h *Pool,* 2 Sam. 2:13.
i Isa. 7:3; 2 Kin. 18:17.
v.2–632 BC
3
j *Eliakim,* 2 Kin. 18:18.
k *Cabinet,* Ezra 7:14.
l Isa. 22:20; 2 Kin. 18:18, 26, 37.
m *Shebna,* 2 Kin. 18:18.
n *Scribe,* 1 Kin. 4:3.
o 2 Kin. 18:18, 26.
p 2 Kin. 18:18, 37.
4
q *Boasting,* Prov. 25:14.
5
1 R. V. thy counsel and strength for the war are but vain words:
6
r *Reed, figurative of weakness,* Ezek. 40:3.
s *Egypt,* Gen. 41:8
t Isa. 19:11; 30: 2, 3.
7
u *Faith,* Mark 11:22.

* **WAY.** *Of holiness,* Psa. 16:11; Isa. 35:8, 9; Jer. 6:16; Hos. 14:9. *Of righteousness, narrow,* Matt. 7:14. *Of sin, broad,* Matt. 7:13. *Jesus the,* John 14:6; Heb. 9:8. *The doctrines to be believed and the life to be lived taught by Jesus called the,* Acts 9:2; 18:25, 26; 19:9, 23; 22:4; 24:14, 22.

v.8–632 BC
See footnote, *Time*, Rev. 10:6.

8
*v* *Sarcasm*, Judg. 10:14.

11
*w* *Tact*, Prov. 15:1.
*x* *Language*, Dan. 3:29.

12
2 R. V. water

15
*y* *Blasphemy, defying God*, 2 Sam. 12:14.

16
3 R. V. your peace with me, and

[b]king of [c]Ăs-sy̆r′ĭ-ȧ, and I will give thee two thousand horses, [v]if thou be able on thy part to set riders upon them.

9 [q]How then wilt thou turn away the face of one captain of the least of my master's servants, and put thy trust on [s]Ē′-ġy̆pt for chariots and for horsemen?

10 And am I now come up without the LORD against this land to destroy it? the LORD said unto me, Go up against this land, and destroy it.

11 Then [w]said [j]Ē-lī′a-kĭm and [m]Shĕb′nȧ and [o]Jō′ah unto [e]Răb′-sha-keh, Speak, I pray thee, unto thy servants in the Sy̆r′ĭ-an [x]language; for we understand *it*: and speak not to us in the Jews̱' language, in the ears of the people that *are* on the wall.

12 But [e]Răb′sha-keh said, Hath my master sent me to thy master and to thee to speak these words? *hath he* not *sent me* to the men that sit upon the wall, that they may eat their own dung,[C] and drink their own [2]piss[C] with you?

13 Then [e]Răb′sha-keh stood, and cried with a loud voice in the Jews̱' [x]language, and said, Hear ye the words of the great [b]king, the king of [c]Ăs-sy̆r′ĭ-ȧ.

14 Thus saith the king, Let not [a]Hĕz-e-kī′ah deceive you: for he shall not be able to deliver you.

15 [y]Neither let [a]Hĕz-e-kī′ah make you trust in the LORD, saying, The LORD will surely deliver us: the city shall not be delivered into the hand of the [b]king of [c]Ăs-sy̆r′ĭ-ȧ.

16 Hearken not to [a]Hĕz-e-kī′-ah: for thus saith the [b]king of [c]Ăs-sy̆r′ĭ-ȧ, Make [3]*an agreement* with me *by* a present, and come out to me: and eat ye every one of his vine, and every one of his [z]fig tree, and drink ye every one the waters of his own *cistern;

17 Until I come and take you away to a land like your own land, a land of corn[C] and wine, a land of bread and vineyards.

18 *Beware* lest Hĕz-e-kī′ah persuade you, saying, The LORD will deliver us. Hath any of the gods of the nations delivered his land out of the hand of the king of Ăs-sy̆r′ĭ-ȧ?

19 Where *are* the gods of [a]Hā′-math and [a]Är′phad? where *are* the gods of [b]Sĕph-ar-vā′im? and have they delivered [c]Să-mā′rĭ-ȧ out of my hand?

20 Who *are they* among all the gods of these lands, that have delivered their land out of my hand, that the LORD should deliver [d]Jē-ru̇′să-lĕm out of my hand?

21 But they held[C] their peace, and answered him not a word: for the king's commandment was, saying, Answer him not.

22 Then came [e]Ē-lī′a-kĭm, the son of [f]Hĭl-kī′ah, that *was* over the household, and [g]Shĕb′nȧ the scribe, and [h]Jō′ah, the son of Ā′saph, the recorder, to [i]Hĕz-e-kī′ah with *their* clothes [j]rent,[C] and told him the words of [k]Răb′-sha-keh.

## CHAPTER 37

*Hezekiah sends to Isaiah to pray for deliverance. 6 Isaiah comforts him. 8 Sennacherib sends a blasphemous letter to Hezekiah. 14 Hezekiah's prayer. 21 Isaiah foretells the destruction of Sennacherib, and the safety of Zion. 36 An angel slays the Assyrians. 37 Sennacherib is slain at Nineveh by his own sons.*

AND it came to pass, when king [a]Hĕz-e-kī′ah heard *it*, that he [b]rent[C] his clothes, and covered himself with [c]sackcloth, and went into the [d]house of the LORD.

2 And he sent [e]Ē-lī′a-kĭm, who *was* over the household, and [f]Shĕb′nȧ the [g]scribe, and the elders of the priests covered with

v.16–632 BC
See footnote, *Time*, Rev. 10:6.

*z* *Fig Tree, figurative*, Luke 13:6.

19
*a* Isa. 37:13.
*b* *Sepharvaim*, 2 Kin. 17:24.
*c* *Samaria*, 1 Kin. 16:24.

20
*d* *Jerusalem*, Judg. 19:10.

22
*e* *Eliakim*, 2 Kin. 18:18.
*f* Isa. 22:20; 2 Kin. 18:18, 26, 37.
*g* *Shebna*, 2 Kin. 18:18.
*h* 2 Kin. 18:18, 26, 37.
*i* *Hezekiah*, 2 Kin. 16:20.
*j* *Rending of Garments, a token of affliction*, 2 Chr. 34:27.
*k* *Rabshakeh*, 2 Kin. 18:17.

1
*a* *Hezekiah*, 2 Kin. 16:20.
*b* *Rending of Garments, a token of affliction*, 2 Chr. 34:27.
*c* *Sackcloth*, Isa. 15:3.
*d* *Church*, 1 Kin. 9:3.

2
*e* *Eliakim*, 2 Kin. 18:18.
*f* *Shebna*, 2 Kin. 18:18.
*g* *Scribe*, 1 Kin. 4:3.

***CISTERN**, 2 Kin. 18:31; Isa. 36:16. **Figurative**, Prov. 5:15; Eccl. 12:6; Jer. 2:13.

v.2–632 BC
See footnote, *Time*, Rev. 10:6.

*h Isaiah*, Isa. 1:1.
*i Prophet*, Isa. 3:2.

3
1 R.V. contumely:

4
*j Rabshakeh*, 2 Kin. 18:17.
*k Sennacherib*, 2 Chr. 32:1.
*l Assyria*, Gen. 25:18.
*m Blasphemy*, 2 Sam. 12:14.
*n Intercession, solicited*, Jer. 27:18.

6
*o Prophets, inspiration of*, Isa. 3:2.
*p Faith, enjoined*, Mark 11:22.
*q Adversity, consolation in*, Psa. 10:6.

7
*r God, providence of*, Gen. 2:2.
2 R.V. put a spirit in

8
*s Libnah*, Josh. 10:29.
*t Lachish*, Josh. 10:5.

9
*u* 2 Kin. 19:9.
*v Ethiopia*, Isa. 18:1.

10
*w Judah, kingdom of*, 2 Chr. 11:17.
*x Jerusalem*, Judg. 19:10.

[c]sackcloth, unto [h]Ī-ṣā'iah the
[i]prophet the son of Ā'mŏz.
3 And they said unto him,
Thus saith [a]Hĕz-e-kī'ah, This
day *is* a day of trouble, and of
rebuke, and of [1]blasphemy: for
the children are come to the
birth, and *there is* not strength
to bring forth.
4 It may be the LORD thy God
will hear the words of [j]Răb'-
sha-keh, whom the [k]king of [l]Ăs-
sўr'ĭ-ȧ his master hath sent to
[m]reproach the living God, and
will reprove[C] the words which
the LORD thy God hath heard:
wherefore [n]lift up *thy* prayer for
the remnant that is left.
5 So the servants of king [a]Hĕz-
e-kī'ah came to [h]Ī-ṣā'iah.
6 And [h]Ī-ṣā'iah said unto them,
Thus shall ye say unto your
master, [o]Thus saith the LORD,
[p,q]Be not afraid of the words
that thou hast heard, wherewith
the servants of the king of [l]Ăs-
sўr'ĭ-ȧ have [m]blasphemed me.
7 Behold, [r]I will [2]send a blast
upon him, and he shall hear a
rumour, and return to his own
land; and I will cause him to
fall by the sword in his own
land.
8 ¶ So [j]Răb'sha-keh returned,
and found the [k]king of [l]Ăs-
sўr'ĭ-ȧ warring against [s]Lĭb'-
nah: for he had heard that he
was departed from [t]Lā'chish.
9 And he heard[C] say concerning
[u]Tĭr'ha-kah king of [v]Ē-thĭ-ō'-
pĭ-ȧ, He is come forth to make
war with thee. And when he
heard *it*, he sent messengers to
[a]Hĕz-e-kī'ah, saying,
10 Thus shall ye speak to Hĕz-
e-kī'ah king of [w]Jū'dah, saying,
[m]Let not thy God, in whom thou
trustest, deceive thee, saying,
[x]Jĕ-ru̥'sȧ-lĕm shall not be given
into the hand of the king of [l]Ăs-
sўr'ĭ-ȧ.
11 [y]Behold, thou hast heard
what the kings of Ăs-sўr'ĭ-ȧ have
done to all lands by destroying
them utterly; and shalt thou be
delivered?
12 [y]Have the gods of the nations delivered them which my
fathers have destroyed, *as* [z]Gō'-
zan, and [a]Hā'ran, and [b]Rē'-
zeph, and the children of [c]Ē'-
dĕn which *were* in [d]Tē-lăs'sar?
13 Where *is* the king of [e]Hā'-
math, and the king of [e]Är'phad,
and the king of the city of [f]Sĕph-
ar-vā'im, [g]Hē'nȧ, and [h]Ī'vah?
14 ¶ And [i]Hĕz-e-kī'ah received
the *letter from the hand of the
messengers, and read it: and
Hĕz-e-kī'ah went up unto the
[j]house of the LORD, and spread
it before the LORD.
15 And [i]Hēz-e-kī'ah [k]prayed
unto the LORD, saying,
16 [k]O LORD of hosts, God of
Ĭṣ'ra-el, that [l]dwellest [m]*between*
the [n]cherubims, [o,p]thou *art* the
God, *even* thou alone, of all the
kingdoms of the earth: [q]thou
hast made [r]heaven and [s]earth.[S]
17 Incline thine ear, O LORD,
and hear; open thine eyes, O
LORD, and see: and hear all the
words of [t]Sĕn-năch'e-rĭb, which
hath sent to reproach the living
God.
18 Of a truth, LORD, the kings
of [u]Ăs-sўr'ĭ-ȧ have [v]laid waste
all the nations, and their countries,
19 And have cast their [w]gods into the fire: for [x]they *were* no gods,
but the work of men's hands,
wood and stone: therefore they
have destroyed them.[Q]
20 Now therefore, O LORD our
God, [y]save us from his hand,
[z]that all the kingdoms of the

v.10–632 BC
See footnote, *Time*, Rev. 10:6.

11
*y Boasting*, Prov. 25:14.

12
*z Gozan*, 2 Kin. 17:6.

*a Haran*, Gen. 11:31.
*b* 2 Kin. 19:12.
*c* 2 Kin. 19:12; Ezek. 27:23.
*d* Or, *Thelasar*, 2 Kin. 19:12.

13
*e* 2 Kin. 18:34.
*f Sepharvaim*, 2 Kin. 17:24.
*g* 2 Kin. 18:34; 19:13.
*h* 2 Kin. 18:34; 19:13; or, *Ava*, 2 Kin. 17:24.

14
*i Hezekiah*, 2 Kin. 16:20.
*j Temple, Solomon's*, 1 Kin. 6:17.

15
*k Prayer*, Acts 6:4.

16
*l Shekinah*, Lev. 16:2.
*m Mercy Seat*, Ex. 25:17.
*n Cherubim*, Ex. 37:7.
*o God, sovereign*, Gen. 2:2.
*p Faith, exemplified*, Mark 11:22.
*q God, creator*, Gen. 2:2.
*r Heavens, created*, Psa. 8:3.
*s Earth, created by God*, Prov. 8:23.

17
*t Sennacherib*, 2 Chr. 32:1.

18
*u Assyria*, Gen. 25:18.
*v War, evils of*, Judg. 3:2.

19
*w Idol*, 1 Kin. 15:12.
*x Idolatry, folly of*, 1 Sam. 15:23.

20
*y God, preserver*, Gen. 2:2.
*z Prayer, pleas offered in*, Acts 6:4.

***LETTERS.** *Written, by David to Joab*, 2 Sam. 11:14; *by king of Syria to king of Israel*, 2 Kin. 5:5, 6; *by king of Babylon to Hezekiah*, Isa. 39:1; *by Sennacherib to Hezekiah*, 2 Kin. 19:9–14; Isa. 37:9–14, 17; *by Elijah to Jehoram*, 2 Chr. 21:12–15; *by adversaries of the Jews to Artaxerxes, and his reply*, Ezra 4:6–23; *by Tatnai to Darius*, Ezra 5:6–17; *by Artaxerxes to Ezra*, Ezra 7:11–26; *and to Nehemiah*, Neh. 2:7–9; *by Sanballat to Nehemiah*, Neh. 6:5–7; *by Claudius Lysias to Felix*, Acts 23:25–30; *by Paul to Philemon in behalf of Onesimus*, Philemon 1. *Of commendation*, 2 Cor. 3:1.

v.20–632 BC
See footnote, *Time*, Rev. 10:6.

**21**
*a* *Isaiah*, Isa. 1:1.
*b* *Hezekiah*, 2 Kin. 16:20.
*c* *Sennacherib*, 2 Chr. 32:1.
*d* *Assyria, prophecies concerning*, vs. 21–35; Gen. 25:18.

**23**
*e* *Blasphemy*, 2 Sam. 12:14.
*f* *God, holiness of*, Gen. 2:2.

**24**
*g* *Boasting*, Prov. 25:14.
*h* *Lebanon*, Deut. 1:7.
3 R. V. his farthest height, the forest of his fruitful field.

**25**
4 R. V. Egypt.

**27**
5 Am. R. V. a field of grain before it be grown up.

**28**
*i* *God, knowledge of*, Gen. 2:2.

earth may know that thou *art* the LORD, *even* thou only.

21 ¶ Then [a]Ī-ṣā′iah the son of Ā′mŏz sent unto [b]Hĕz-e-kī′ah, saying, Thus saith the LORD God of Iṣ′ra-el, Whereas[C] thou hast prayed to me against [c]Sĕn-năch′e-rĭb king of [d]Ăs-sỹr′ĭ-ȧ:

22 This *is* the [d]word which the LORD hath spoken concerning him; The virgin, the daughter of Zī′ŏn, hath despised thee, *and* laughed thee to scorn; the daughter of Jē-ru̇′sā-lĕm hath shaken her head at thee.

23 Whom hast thou reproached and [e]blasphemed? and against whom hast thou exalted[C] *thy* voice, and lifted up thine eyes on high? *even* against the [f]Holy One of Iṣ′ra-el.

24 By thy servants hast thou [e]reproached the Lord, and hast [g]said, By the multitude of my chariots am I come up to the height of the mountains, to the sides of [h]Lĕb′a-non; and I will cut down the tall cedars thereof, *and* the choice fir trees thereof: and I will enter into [3]the height of his border, *and* the forest of his Cär′mel.

25 I have digged, and drunk water; and with the sole of my feet have I dried up all the rivers of [4]the besieged places.[T]

26 Hast thou not heard long ago, *how* I have done it; *and* of ancient times, that I have formed it? now have I brought it to pass, that thou shouldest be to lay[C] waste defenced[C] cities *into* ruinous heaps.

27 Therefore their inhabitants *were* of small power, they were dismayed and confounded: they were *as* the grass of the field, and *as* the green herb, *as* the grass on the housetops, and *as* [5]corn[C] blasted[C] before it be grown up.

28 But I [i]know thy abode[C], and thy going out, and thy coming in, and thy rage against me.[S]

29 [6]Because thy rage against me, and thy tumult, is come up into mine ears, therefore will I put my hook in thy nose, and my bridle in thy lips, and I will [j]turn thee back by the way by which thou camest.

30 And this *shall be* a sign unto thee, Ye shall eat *this* year such as groweth of itself; and the second year that which springeth of the same: and in the third year sow ye, and reap, and plant vineyards, and eat the fruit thereof.

31 And the remnant that is escaped of the house of [k]Jū′dah shall again take root downward, and bear fruit upward:

32 For out of [l]Jē-ru̇′sā-lĕm shall go forth a remnant, and they that escape out of mount Zī′ŏn: the zeal of the LORD of hosts shall do this.[S]

33 Therefore thus saith the LORD concerning the king of [d]Ăs-sỹr′ĭ-ȧ, He shall not come into this city, nor shoot an arrow there, nor come before it with shields, nor cast a bank[C] against it.

34 By the way that he came, by the same shall he return, and shall not come into this city, saith the LORD.

35 For I will defend this city to save it for mine own sake, and [m]for my servant [n]Dā′vid's sake.[S]

36 ¶ Then the [o]angel[C] of the LORD went forth, and [j,p]smote in the camp of the [q]Ăs-sỹr′ĭ-anṣ a hundred and fourscore[C] and five thousand: and when they arose early in the morning, behold, they *were* all dead corpses.[S]

37 So [c]Sĕn-năch′e-rĭb king of [q]Ăs-sỹr′ĭ-ȧ departed, and went and returned, and dwelt at [r]Nĭn′-e-veh.

38 And it came to pass, as he was worshipping in the house of

v.38–632 BC
See footnote, *Time*, Rev. 10:6.

**29**
*j* *Judgments*, Ex. 6:6.
6 R. V. Because of thy raging against me, and for that thine arrogancy is

**31**
*k* *Judah, kingdom of*, 2 Chr. 11:17.

**32**
*l* *Jerusalem*, Judg. 19:10.

**35**
*m* *Intercession, influence of the righteous*, Jer. 27:18.
*n* *David, his intercessional influence with God*, 1 Sam. 16:13.

**36**
*o* *Angel, functions of*, Heb. 1:13.
*p* *Miracles*, Luke 23:8.
*q* *Assyria*, Gen. 25:18.

**37**
*r* *Nineveh*, Jonah 1:2.

v.38–632 BC
See footnote, *Time*, Rev. 10:6.

**38**

s 2 Kin. 19:37.
t *Children, wicked*, Mark 10:14.
u *Parricide*, 2 Kin. 19:37.
v *Homicide, felonious*, Deut. 5:17.
w *Assassination*, Deut. 27:24.
x Or, *Ararat*, Gen. 8:4.
y *Esar-haddon*, 2 Kin. 19:37.

v.1–632 BC
See footnote, *Time*, Rev. 10:6.

**1**

a *Hezekiah*, 2 Kin. 16:20.
b *Isaiah*, Isa. 1:1.
c Isa. 1:1; 13:1; 2 Kin. 19:2.
d *Prophets, inspiration of*, Isa. 3:2.
e *Death, God's power over*, Num. 23:10.

**2**

f *Afflictions, prayer in*, Psa. 34:19.

**3**

g *Prayer, pleas offered in*, Acts 6:4.
h *Obedience, instances of*, Heb. 5:8.
i *Sincerity, exemplified*, 1 Cor. 5:8.
j *Weeping*, Ezra 3:13.

**5**

k *Hezekiah, prophecy concerning*, 2 Kin. 16:20.
l *Prayer, answered*, Acts 6:4.
m *Tears, observed by God*, Psa. 6:6.

**6**

n *God, preserver*, Gen. 2:2.
o *Assyria*, Gen. 25:18.

**8**

p *Sun*, Josh. 10:12.
q 2 Kin. 20:11.
r *Ahaz*, 2 Kin. 15:38.
1 R. V. steps,
2 R. V. on the dial whereon it was gone down.

[s]Nĭs′rŏch his god, that [s]Ā-drăm′-
me-lĕch and [s]Shă-rē′zĕr his [t]sons
[u,v,w]smote him with the sword;
and they escaped into the land of
[x]Är-mē′nĭ-ȧ: and [y]Ē′sar–hăd′-
don his son reigned in his stead.

## CHAPTER 38

*Hezekiah, in answer to prayer, has his life lengthened.* 8 *The sun goes ten degrees backward for a sign to him.* 9 *His song of thanksgiving.*

IN those days was [a]Hĕz-e-kī′ah
sick unto death. And [b]Ī-ṣā′-
iah the prophet the son of [c]Ā′-
mŏz came unto him, and said
unto him, [d]Thus saith the LORD,
Set thine house in order: for thou
shalt [e]die, and not live.
2 Then [a]Hĕz-e-kī′ah turned his
face toward the wall, and [f]prayed
unto the LORD,
3 And [g]said, Remember now,
O LORD, I beseech[G] thee, how
I have [h]walked before thee in
[i]truth and with a perfect heart,
and have done *that which is* good
in thy sight. And [a]Hĕz-e-kī′ah
[j]wept sore.[G]
4 Then [d]came the word of the
LORD to [b]Ī-ṣā′iah, saying,
5 Go, and [d]say to Hĕz-e-kī′ah,
[k]Thus saith the LORD, the God
of Dā′vid thy father, I have
heard thy [l]prayer, I have seen
thy [m]tears: behold, I will add unto thy days fifteen years.
6 And I will [n]deliver thee and
this city out of the hand of the
king of [o]Ăs-sȳr′ĭ-ȧ: and I will
defend this city.
7 And this *shall be* a sign unto
thee from the LORD, that the
LORD will do this thing that he
hath spoken;[S]
8 Behold, I will bring again the
shadow of the [1]degrees,[G] which
is gone down in the [p]sun [q]dial of
[r]Ā′hăz, ten [1]degrees[G] backward.
So the sun returned ten [1]degrees,[G]
[2]by which degrees[G] it was gone
down.

9 ¶ The writing of [a]Hĕz-e-kī′ah
king of [s]Jū′dah, when he had
been sick, and was [t]recovered of
his sickness:
10 I [u,v]said in the [3]cutting off of
my days, I shall go to the [w]gates
of the [4]grave[G]: I am deprived of
the residue of my years.[Q]
11 I [u]said, I shall not see the
LORD, *even* the LORD, in the
land of the living: I shall behold
man no more with the inhabitants of the world.
12 Mine [x]age is departed, and
is removed from me as a shepherd's [y]tent: I have [5]cut off like
a *weaver my life: he will cut me
off [6]with pining sickness: from
day *even* to night wilt thou make
an end of me.
13 I [7]reckoned[G] till morning,
*that*, as a [z]lion, so will he break
all my bones: from day *even* to
night wilt thou make an end of
me.
14 Like a [a]crane *or* a [b]swallow,
so did I chatter: I did mourn as
a [c]dove: mine eyes fail *with looking* upward: [d]O LORD, I am oppressed; [8]undertake[G] for me.
15 What shall I say? he hath
both spoken unto me, and himself hath done *it*: [e]I shall go
softly all my years in the bitterness of my soul.
16 O Lord, by these *things men*
live, and in all these *things is* the
life of my spirit: [f]so wilt thou recover me, and [g]make me to live.
17 Behold, for peace I had great
bitterness: but thou hast in [h]love
to my soul *delivered it* from
the pit of [i]corruption: for thou
hast [j]cast all my sins behind thy
back.
18 For the [k]grave[G] cannot praise
thee, [l]death can *not* celebrate
thee: they that go down into the
pit cannot [m]hope for thy [n]truth.[T]
19 The living, the living, he shall

v.9–632 BC
See footnote, *Time*, Rev. 10:6.

**9**

s *Judah, kingdom of*, 2 Chr. 11:17.
t *Disease, healing of*, Ex. 15:26.

**10**

u *Murmuring*, Num. 14:2.
v *Despondency*, Eccl. 2:20.
w *Gates, figurative*, Deut. 3:5.
3 R. V. noontide of
4 Am. R. V. Sheol:

**12**

x *Life, brevity of*, Eccl. 8:15.
y *Tent*, Gen. 13:5.
5 R. V. rolled up like
6 R. V. from the loom:

**13**

z *Lion*, Mic. 5:8.
7 R. V. quieted myself until morning; as

**14**

a Jer. 8:7.
b *Swallow*, Psa. 84:3.
c *Dove*, Gen. 8:8.
d *Afflictions, prayer in*, Psa. 34:19.
8 R. V. be thou my surety.

**15**

e *Humility, exemplified*, Prov. 22:4.

**16**

f *God, preserver*, Gen. 2:2.
g *Life, from God*, vs. 17–20; Eccl. 8:15.

**17**

h *God, love of*, Gen. 2:2.
i *Corruption, figurative*, Job 17:14.
j *Sin, forgiveness of*, Rom. 5:12.

**18**

k *Grave*, 2 Sam. 3:32.
l *Death*, Num. 23:10.
m *Hope*, Prov. 13:12.
n *Truth*, John 18:37.

* **WEAVING**, Isa. 19:9; 38:12. *Bezaleel and Aholiab skilled in*, Ex. 35:34, 35; 38:22, 23. *By women*, 2 Kin. 23:7. *Of the ephod*, Ex. 28:32; 39:22. *Of coats*, Ex. 39:27. *Weaver's shuttle*, Job 7:6; *beam*, Judg. 16:14; 2 Sam. 21:19; 1 Chr. 11:23.
See footnote, ART, 2 Chr. 16:14.

[o]praise thee, as I *do* this day: the [p]father to the [q]children shall [r]make known thy [n]truth.[T]

20 The LORD *was ready* to [l]save me: therefore we will [s,t]sing my songs to the stringed [u]instruments all the days of our life in the [v]house of the LORD.

21 For [w]Ī-ṣā'iah had said, Let them take a lump of [x,y]figs, and lay *it* for a plaister upon the [z]boil, and he shall recover.[S]

22 Hĕz-e-kī'ah also had said, What *is* the sign that I shall go up to the house of the LORD?

## CHAPTER 39

*The king of Babylon sends to congratulate Hezekiah upon his recovery. 3 Isaiah foretells the Babylonian captivity.*

AT that time [a]Mē-rō'dăch–băl'a-dăn, the son of Băl'a-dăn, king of [b]Băb-ȳ-lon, sent [c]letters and a present to [d]Hĕz-e-kī'ah: for he had heard that he had been sick, and was recovered.

2 And [d]Hĕz-e-kī'ah was glad of them, and [e]shewed [f]them the [g]house of his precious[G] things, the [h]silver, and the [i]gold, and the [j]spices, and the precious [1,k]ointment, and all the [l]house of his armour, and all that was found in his treasures[G]: there was nothing in his house, nor in all his dominion, that [d]Hĕz-e-kī'ah shewed them not.

3 ¶ Then came [m,n]Ī-ṣā'iah the prophet unto king [d]Hĕz-e-kī'ah, and said unto him, What said these men? and from whence came they unto thee? And Hĕz-e-kī'ah said, They are come from a far country unto me, *even* from [b]Băb'ȳ-lon.

4 Then said he, What have they seen in thine house? And [d]Hĕz-e-kī'ah answered, All that *is* in mine house have they seen: there is nothing among my treasures that I have not shewed them.

5 Then said [m,n]Ī-ṣā'iah to [d]Hĕz-e-kī'ah, [o]Hear the word of the LORD of hosts:

6 Behold, the days come, that all that *is* in thine house, and *that* which thy fathers have laid up in store until this day, shall be carried to [p]Băb'ȳ-lon: nothing shall be left, saith the LORD.

7 And of thy sons that shall issue from thee, which thou shalt beget, shall they [q]take away; and they shall be [r]eunuchs in the palace of the king of [p]Băb'ȳ-lon.

8 Then said [d]Hĕz-e-kī'ah to [m]Ī-ṣā'iah, [s,t]Good *is* the word of the LORD which thou hast spoken. He said moreover, For there shall be [u]peace and [v]truth in my days.

## CHAPTER 40

*God's command to comfort his people. 3 An exhortation to prepare the way of the Lord, 9 and to proclaim the glad tidings of his coming. 12 The power and wisdom of God. 18 The folly of likening him to any thing. 26 His perfections a sure ground of trust in him.*

[a]COMFORT ye, comfort ye [b]my people, saith your God.[Q]

2 [a]Speak ye comfortably[G] to [c]Jē-rụ'sā-lĕm, and cry unto her, that her warfare is accomplished, that her iniquity is [d]pardoned: for [e]she hath received of the LORD's hand [f]double for all her sins.[Q]

3 ¶[Q] [g]The voice of [h]him that crieth in the wilderness, [i,j]Prepare ye the way of the [k]LORD, make straight in the desert a [l]highway for our God.[T]

4 [m,n,o,p]Every valley shall be exalted, and every mountain and hill shall be made low: and the crooked shall be made straight,[G] and the rough places plain:

5 [n,o]And the [q]glory of the LORD shall be revealed, and [p]all flesh shall see *it* together: for the mouth of the LORD hath spoken *it*.[Q S]

6[T] The[Q] voice said, Cry. And he

---

**v.19—632 BC**
See footnote, *Time*, Rev. 10:6.

**19**
o *Praise*, Psa. 150:1.
p *Parents, duty of, to instruct children in righteousness*, 2 Cor. 12:14.
q *Children, instruction of*, Mark 10:14.
r *Instruction, of children*, Prov. 23:23.

**20**
s *Thankfulness, to God*, Acts 24:3.
t *Worship*, Gen. 22:5.
u *Music, instruments of*, 2 Chr. 5:13.
v *Church*, 1 Kin. 9:3.

**21**
w *Isaiah*, Isa. 1:1.
x *Fig, employed as a remedy*, Mark 11:13.
y *Disease, remedies used for*, Ex. 15:26.
z *Boil*, Ex. 9:9.

**v.1—632 BC**
See footnote, *Time*, Rev. 10:6.

**1**
a Or, *Berodach-baladan*, 2 Kin. 20:12.
b *Babylon*, Ezra 5:12.
c *Letters*, Isa. 37:14.
d *Hezekiah*, 2 Kin. 16:20.

**2**
e *Pride*, Prov. 16:18.
f *Ambassadors*, Josh. 9:4.
g *Treasure Houses*, Ezra 5:17.
h *Silver*, 1 Chr. 28:14.
i *Gold*, Ezek. 7:19.
j *Spices*, 1 Kin. 10:2.
k *Ointment*, Eccl. 7:1.
l *Armory*, Neh. 3:19.
1 R. V. oil,

**3**
m *Isaiah*, Isa. 1:1.
n *Minister, faithful*, vs. 3–7; Rom. 15:16.

**v.5—632 BC**
See footnote, *Time*, Rev. 10:6.

**5**
o *Prophets, inspiration of*, Isa. 3:2.

**6**
p *Babylon, prophecies concerning*, Dan. 4:30.

**7**
q *Captivity*, Isa. 5:13.
r *Eunuch*, Matt. 19:12.

**8**
s *Adversity, resignation in*, Psa. 10:6.
t *Resignation, exemplified*, Job 5:17.
u *Peace*, Jer. 29:7.
v *Truth*, John 18:37.

**1**
a *Minister, duties of*, Rom. 15:16.
b *Judah, kingdom of*, 2 Chr. 11:17.

**2**
c *Jerusalem*, Judg. 19:10.
d *Sin, forgiveness of*, Rom. 5:12.
e *Wicked, punishment of*, Psa. 73:3.
f *Divine Chastisement*, Job 33:19.

**3**
g Matt. 3:3; Luke 3:4; John 1:23.
h *John the Baptist, prophecies concerning*, Luke 1:63.
i *Prophecies concerning the Messiah, and their fulfillment*, Gen. 12:3.
j *Jesus, prophecies concerning*, Matt. 1:21.
k *Jesus, divinity of*, Matt. 1:21.
l *Highways, figurative*, Deut. 2:27.

**4**
m Luke 3:5.
n *Church, prophecies concerning its universality*, Matt. 16:18.
o *Jesus, kingdom of, prophecies concerning*, vs. 4–11; Matt. 1:21.
p *Gentiles, prophecies of the conversion of*, vs. 4–11; Acts 10:45.

**5**
q *God, glory of*, Gen. 2:2.

said, What shall I cry? [r,s]All
flesh *is* *grass, and all the goodliness[G] thereof *is* as the flower of
the field:
7 The *grass withereth, the
flower fadeth: because the [1]spirit
of the LORD bloweth upon it:
surely the people *is* grass.[T Q]
8 The *grass withereth, the
flower fadeth: but the [t]word of
our God shall stand for ever.[Q]
9 ¶ O [2,n,o,u]Zī′ŏn, that bringest
good tidings,[G] get thee up into the
high mountain; O [3]Jē-ru̥′să-lĕm,
that bringest good tidings,[G] lift up
thy voice with strength; lift *it* up,
be not afraid; say unto the cities
of [b]Jū′dah, Behold your God![Q]
10 Behold, the [v]Lord GOD will
come [4]with strong *hand*, and his
[w]arm shall rule for him: behold,
his [x]reward *is* with him, and his
[5]work before him.[Q]
11 [y]He shall [z]feed his flock like
a [a]shepherd: [b]he shall gather the
lambs with his arm, and carry
*them* in his bosom, *and* shall
gently [c,d]lead those that [6]are
with young.[Q S]
12 ¶ [e]Who[S] hath measured the
waters in the hollow of his hand,
and meted[G] out heaven with the
span, and comprehended[G] the dust
of the earth in a measure, and
weighed the mountains in scales,
and the hills in a balance?
13[T] [f,g]Who[Q] hath directed the
Spirit of the LORD, or *being* his
counsellor hath taught him?
14 With whom took he counsel,
and *who* instructed him, and
taught him in the path of judgment,[G] and taught him [g]knowl-
edge, and shewed to him the way
of understanding?[T Q]
15[S] Behold, the nations *are*
as a drop of a bucket, and are
counted as the small dust of
the balance: behold, he taketh
up the isles as a very little thing.
16 And [h]Lĕb′a-non *is* not sufficient to burn, nor the beasts
thereof sufficient for a [i]burnt offering.
17 All nations before him *are*
as nothing; and they are counted
to him less than nothing, and
vanity.
18 ¶[Q] To whom then will ye
liken God? or what likeness
will ye compare unto him?[S]
19 [j,k]The workman melteth a
graven[G] [l]image,[G] and the [m]gold-
smith spreadeth it over with
[n]gold, and casteth [o]silver chains.
20 [i]He that *is* so impover-
ished that he hath no oblation[G]
chooseth a tree *that* will not
rot; he seeketh unto him a
cunning[G] [k]workman to prepare
a graven[G] [l]image,[G] *that* shall not
be moved.[Q]
21[S] [p]Have ye not known? have
ye not heard? hath it not been
told you from the beginning?
have ye not understood from the
foundations of the earth?
22 *It is* [q]he that sitteth upon
the circle of the [r]earth, and the
[s]inhabitants thereof *are* as
[t]grasshoppers; that stretcheth
out the [u]heavens as a curtain,
and spreadeth them out as a
tent to dwell in:[S]
23 That bringeth the [v]princes
to nothing; he maketh the judges
of the earth as vanity.
24 Yea, they shall not be
planted; yea, they shall not be
sown: yea, their stock shall not
take root in the earth: and he
shall also blow upon them, and
they shall wither, and the whirlwind shall take them away as
[w]stubble.
25 To whom then will ye liken
me, or shall I be equal? saith
the [x]Holy One.
26 Lift up your eyes on high,
and behold who hath created

6
r Jas. 1:10; 1 Pet. 1:24, 25.
s *Life, brevity of,* Eccl. 8:15.

7
1 Am. R. V. breath of Jehovah

8
t *Word of God,* Psa. 119:9.

9
u *Zion,* 2 Sam. 5:7.
2 R. V. thou that tellest good tidings to Zion,
3 R. V. thou that tellest good tidings to Jerusalem, lift

10
v *God, power of,* Gen. 2:2.
w *Arm, figurative,* v. 1; Psa. 89:13.
x *Reward, a motive, to faithfulness,* Matt. 5:12.
4 R. V. as a mighty one,
5 R. V. recompence

11
y *God, preserver,* Gen. 2:2.
z *Spiritual Blessings, from God,* Eph. 1:3.

a *Shepherd,* Jer. 31:10.
b *Righteous, promises to,* Psa. 64:10.
c *Guidance,* Psa. 48:14.
d *God, guidance of,* Gen. 2:2.
6 R. V. give suck.

12
e *God, dissertations on,* vs. 12–29; Gen. 2:2.

13
f Rom. 11:34; 1 Cor. 2:16.
g *God, knowledge of,* Gen. 2:2.

16
h *Lebanon,* Deut. 1:7.
i *Offerings, burnt,* Lev. 6:17.

19
j *Idolatry, folly of,* 1 Sam. 15:23.
k *Art,* 2 Chr. 16:14.
l *Idol, manufacture of,* 1 Kin. 15:12.
m *Goldsmith,* Neh. 3:8.
n *Gold,* Ezek. 7:19.
o *Silver,* 1 Chr. 28:14.

21
p *Spiritual Blindness,* 2 Cor. 4:4.

22
q *God, sovereign,* Gen. 2:2.
r *Earth,* Prov. 8:23.
s *Man, insignificance of,* Job 4:17.
t Num. 13:33; Eccl. 12:5; Nah. 3:17.
u *Heavens, physical,* Psa. 8:3.

23
v *Rulers,* Ex. 18:21.

24
w *Stubble,* Isa. 5:24.

25
x *God, holiness of.* Gen. 2:2.

***GRASS.** *Created on the third creative day,* Gen. 1:11. *Mown,* Psa. 72:6. *God's care of,* Matt. 6:30; Luke 12:28. *On roofs of houses,* Psa. 129:6. *The brevity of human life compared to,* Psa. 90:5, 6; Jas. 1:10, 11; 1 Pet. 1:24. *The eternal word of God contrasted with,* Isa. 40:7. **Figurative:** *Of the brevity of human life,* Isa. 40:6.

these *things*, that bringeth out
their host by number: he calleth
them all by names by the greatness of his might, for that *he is*
strong in [y]power; not one faileth.[T]
27 [z]Why [a,b]sayest thou, O Jā'-
cob, and speakest, O Ĭṣ'ra-el,
My way is hid from the LORD,
and my judgment is passed over
from my God?
28 Hast thou not known? hast
thou not heard, *that* the [c]ever-
lasting God, the LORD, the [d]Cre-
ator of the ends of the earth,
fainteth not, neither is weary?
[e]*there is* no searching of his understanding.[S]
29 [f]He giveth [g,h]power to the
faint; and to *them that have* no
might he increaseth strength.[S]
30 Even the youths shall faint
and be weary, and the young
men shall utterly fall:
31 But [i,j]they that [k]wait[G] upon the LORD [l]shall renew *their*
strength; they shall mount up
with wings as eagles; they shall
run, and not be weary; *and* they
shall walk, and not faint.[S T]

## CHAPTER 41

*God calls upon idolaters to consider his power to aid his people. 8 His gracious assurance to Israel of protection. 21 The vanity of idols.*

KEEP silence before me, O
islands; and let the people
renew *their* strength: let them
come near; then let them speak:
let us come near together to judgment.
2 [a]Who raised up [1,b]the righteous *man* from the east, [2]called
him to his foot, gave the nations
before him, and made *him* rule
over kings? he gave *them* as the
dust to his sword, *and* as driven
stubble to his bow.[S Q]
3 He pursued them, *and* passed
safely; *even* by the way *that* he
had not gone with his feet.
4 [a]Who hath wrought and done
*it*, calling the generations from
the beginning? [a]I the [c]LORD,
the first, and with the last; I
*am* he.[S Q]
5 The isles saw *it*, and feared;
the ends of the earth were afraid,
drew near, and came.
6 They helped every one his
neighbour; and *every one* said to
his brother, Be of good courage.
7 So the [d]carpenter encouraged
the [e]goldsmith, *and* he that
smootheth *with* the [f]hammer him
that smote the anvil, saying, [3]It
*is* ready for the sodering: and he
fastened it with *nails, *that* it
should not be moved.
8[Q] But thou, Ĭṣ'ra-el, *art* my
servant, Jā'cob whom I have
chosen, the seed of [g]Ā'brā-hăm
my friend.[T]
9 *Thou* whom I have taken
from the ends of the earth, and
called thee from the [4]chief men
thereof, and said unto thee,
Thou *art* my servant; I have
chosen thee, and not cast thee
away.[Q]
10 ¶ [h,i]Fear thou not; for [j,k]I
*am* with thee: be not dismayed;
for I *am* thy God: [j,k]I will
[l,m]strengthen thee; yea, [j,l]I will
help thee; yea, [j]I will uphold
thee with the right [n,o]hand of
my [p]righteousness.[S Q]
11[S] Behold, [k]all they that were
incensed against thee shall be
ashamed and confounded: they
shall be as nothing; and they
that strive with thee shall perish.
12 Thou shalt seek them, and
shalt not find them, *even* them
that contended with thee: they
that war against thee shall be
as nothing, and as a thing of
nought.[S]
13 For [j,k]I the LORD thy God
will hold thy right hand, [h,i]say-

**26**
y *God, power of,* Gen. 2:2.

**27**
z *Doubting,* Rom. 14:23.

a *Presumption, in defying God,* Psa. 19:13.
b *Blasphemy, manifested in imputing ignorance to God,* 2 Sam. 12:14.

**28**
c *God, eternity of,* Gen. 2:2.
d *God, creator,* Gen. 2:2.
e *God, unsearchable,* Gen. 2:2.

**29**
f *Afflictions, consolation in,* Psa. 34:19.
g *Spiritual Power, from God,* Luke 24:49.
h *Spiritual Blessings, from God,* Eph. 1:3.

**31**
i *Righteous, promises to,* Psa. 64:10.
j *Promise, to the righteous,* 2 Cor. 1:20.
k *Spiritual Desire,* Psa. 42:1.
l *Worship, renews strength,* Gen. 22:5.

**2**
a *God, providence of,* Gen. 2:2.
b *Cyrus, prophecies concerning,* 2 Chr. 36:22.
1 R. V. one from
2 R. V. whom he calleth in righteousness to his foot? he giveth nations before him, and maketh him

**4**
c *God, eternity of,* Gen. 2:2.

**7**
d *Carpentry,* 2 Kin. 12:11.
e *Goldsmith,* Neh. 3:8.
f 1 Kin. 6:7.
3 R. V. of the soldering, It is good:

**8**
g *Abraham, friend of God,* Gen. 17:5.

**9**
4 R. V. corners thereof,

**10**
h *Faith, enjoined,* Mark 11:22.
i *Courage, enjoined,* Deut. 31:7.
j *Promise, to the righteous,* 2 Cor. 1:20.
k *Adversity, consolation in,* vs. 13–17; Psa. 10:6.
l *God, preserver,* Gen. 2:2.
m *Spiritual Blessings, from God,* Eph. 1:3.
n *Hand, symbol of power,* Ezra 10:19.
o *God, power of,* Gen. 2:2.
p *God, righteousness of,* Gen. 2:2.

***NAIL,** Isa. 41:7; Jer. 10:4. *Made, of iron,* 1 Chr. 22:3; *of gold,* 2 Chr. 3:9. *Jael kills Sisera with,* Judg. 4:21; 5:26. **Figurative,** Ezra 9:8; Isa. 22:23, 25; Zech. 10:4.

**14**

*q* *Man, insignificance of*, Job 4:17.
*r* *God, savior*, Gen. 2:2.
*s* *God, holiness of*, Gen. 2:2.
*t* *Holiness, attribute of God*, Ex. 39:30.

**15**

*u* *Agency, in executing judgments*, Mark 1:17.
*v* *Nation, punishment of*, Isa. 2:4.

**17**

*w* *Poor, God's care of*, Prov. 21:13.
*x* *God, faithfulness of*, Gen. 2:2.

**19**

*y* *Cedar*, Isa. 9:10.
*z* Or, *Acacia*, Ex. 26:15.

*a* Neh. 8:15; Isa. 55:13; Zech. 1:8.
*b* *Fir Tree*, 2 Sam. 6:5.
*c* Isa. 60:13.

**20**

*d* *God, holiness of*, Gen. 2:2.
*e* *God, creator*, Gen. 2:2.

**21**

*f* *Idolatry, folly of*, vs. 21–29; 1 Sam. 15:23.

ing unto thee, Fear not; [l]I will help thee.[S]

14 [h,i]Fear not, thou [q]worm Jā′cob, *and* ye men of Ĭṣ′ra-el; [j]I will help thee, saith the LORD, and thy [r]redeemer, the [s,t]Holy One of Ĭṣ′ra-el.[S T]

15 Behold, I will make thee a new sharp threshing instrument having teeth:[G] [u]thou shalt thresh the [v]mountains, and beat *them* small, and shalt make the [v]hills as chaff.

16 [v]Thou shalt fan[G] them, and the wind shall carry them away, and the whirlwind shall scatter them: and thou shalt rejoice in the LORD, *and* shalt glory in the [s t]Holy One of Ĭṣ′ra-el.

17 *When* the [w]poor and needy seek water, and *there is* none, *and* their tongue faileth for thirst, I the LORD will hear them, [l,x]*I* the God of Ĭṣ′ra-el will not forsake them.

18 [l,x]I will open rivers in high places, and fountains in the midst of the valleys: I will make the wilderness a pool of water, and the dry land springs of water.

19 I will plant in the wilderness the [y]cedar, the [z]shittah tree, and the [a]myrtle, and the oil tree; I will set in the desert the [b]fir tree, *and* the [c]pine, and the [c]box tree together:

20 That they may see, and know, and consider, and understand together, that the hand of the LORD hath done this, and the [d]Holy One of Ĭṣ′ra-el hath [e]created it.

21 ¶[T] [f]Produce your cause, saith the LORD; bring forth your strong *reasons*, saith the King of Jā′cob.

22 [f]Let them bring *them* forth, and shew us what shall happen: let them shew the former things, what they *be*, that we may consider them, and know the latter end of them; or declare us things for to come.

23 [f]Shew the things that are to come hereafter, that we may know that ye *are* gods: yea, do good, or do evil, that we may be dismayed, and behold *it* together.

24 [f]Behold, ye *are* of nothing, and your work of nought:[G] an abomination *is he that* chooseth you.

25 [g]I have raised up [h]*one* from the north, and he shall come: from the rising[G] of the sun shall he call upon my name: and he shall come upon princes as *upon* morter, and as the potter treadeth clay.[Q]

26 Who hath declared from the beginning, that we may know? and beforetime, that we may say, *He is* righteous? yea, *there is* none that sheweth, yea, *there is* none that declareth, yea, *there is* none that heareth your words.[T]

27 The first *shall say* to [i]Zī′ŏn, Behold, behold them: and I will give to [j]Jē-rụ′sā-lĕm one that bringeth good tidings.

28 For I beheld, and *there was* no man; even among them, and *there was* no counsellor, that, when I asked of them, could answer a word.

29 Behold, they *are* all vanity; their works *are* nothing: [f]their molten[G] images *are* wind and confusion.

## CHAPTER 42

*The servant of Jehovah. 2 His character. 5 God's promise unto him. 10 An exhortation to praise God for his salvation. 17 His rebuke of Israel for their unbelief.*

[a,b,c]BEHOLD[T Q] my servant, whom I uphold, [1]mine elect, *in whom* my soul delighteth; I have put my [d]spirit upon him: [e,f]he shall bring forth judgment[G] to the [g]Gĕn′tīleṣ.[G S]

2 [h]He shall not cry, nor lift up, nor cause his voice to be heard in the street.[T]

**25**

*g* *God, providence of*, Gen. 2:2.
*h* *Cyrus, prophecies concerning*, 2 Chr. 36:22.

**27**

*i* *Zion*, 2 Sam. 5:7.
*j* *Jerusalem*, Judg. 19:10.

**1**

*a* Matt. 12:18–21.
*b* *Jesus, kingdom of, prophecies concerning*, vs. 2–21; Matt. 1:21.
*c* *Prophecies concerning the Messiah, and their fulfillment*, Gen. 12:3.
*d* *Holy Spirit*, Acts 1:2.
*e* *Jesus, prophecies concerning*, vs. 1–9; Matt. 1:21.
*f* *Church, prophecies concerning its prosperity*, vs. 1–12; Matt. 16:18.
*g* *Gentiles, prophecies of the conversion of*, Acts 10:45.
1 R. V. my chosen.

**2**

*h* *Jesus, meekness of*, Matt. 1:21.

3
[i] *Jesus, love of,* Matt. 1:21.
[j] *Penitent, promises to,* Psa. 51:17.
[k] *Reed, figurative,* Ezek. 40:3.
[l] *Flax, figurative,* Ex. 9:31.

5
[m] *God, creator,* Gen. 2:2.
[n] *Heavens, physical,* Psa. 8:3.
[o] *Man, created,* Job 4:17.

6
[p] Luke 2:32.
[q] *Jesus, mission of,* Matt. 1:21.
[r] *Light, figurative,* Matt. 5:14.
[s] *Wisdom, spiritual, from God,* Prov. 2:2.

7
[t] Luke 4:17, 18.
[u] *Spiritual Blindness,* 2 Cor. 4:4.
[v] *Darkness, figurative,* Gen. 1:2.

9
[w] *God, foreknowledge of,* Gen. 2:2.

10
[x] *Praise,* Psa. 150:1.
[y] *Mariner,* Ezek. 27:27.

11
[z] *Kedar,* Jer. 49:28.

12
[a] *Glorifying God, enjoined,* Luke 5:25.
[b] *Praise, enjoined,* Psa. 150:1.

3 [i,j]A bruised [k]reed shall he not break, and the smoking [l]flax shall he not quench: he shall bring forth judgment[G] unto truth.[T]

4 [b,j]He shall not fail nor be discouraged, till he have set judgment[G] in the earth: and the isles shall wait for his law.[T Q]

5 ¶ Thus saith God the LORD, he that [m]created the [n]heavens, and stretched them out; he that spread forth the earth, and that which cometh out of it; he that giveth breath unto the [o]people upon it, and spirit to them that walk therein:[S T Q]

6 I the LORD have called thee in righteousness, and will hold thine hand, and will keep thee, and give thee for a covenant of the people, [p,q]for a [r,s]light of the [g]Gĕn'tīleṣ;[G T Q]

7 [s,t]To open the [u]blind eyes, to bring out the prisoners from the prison, *and* them that sit in [u,v]darkness out of the prison house.[T Q]

8 I *am* the LORD: that *is* my name: and my glory will I not give to another, neither my praise to graven[G] images.[G T]

9 Behold, the former things are come to pass, and new things do I declare: before they spring forth [w]I tell you of them.[S]

10 ¶ Sing unto the LORD a new song, *and* his [x]praise from the end of the earth, [y]ye that go down to the sea, and all that is therein; the isles, and the inhabitants thereof.[Q]

11 Let the wilderness and the cities thereof lift up *their voice,* the villages *that* [z]Kē'där doth inhabit: let the inhabitants of the rock sing, let them shout from the top of the mountains.

12 [a]Let them give glory unto the LORD, and [b]declare his praise in the islands.[Q]

13 The LORD shall go forth as a mighty man, he shall stir up jealousy like a man of war: he shall cry, yea, roar; he shall prevail against his enemies.[S]

14 I have long time holden[G] my peace; I have been still, *and* refrained[G] myself: *now* will I cry like a travailing woman; I will [2]destroy and devour at once.

15 I will make waste mountains and hills, and dry up all their herbs; and I will make the rivers islands, and I will dry up the pools.

16 [c]And I will bring the [d]blind by a way *that* they knew not; I will [e]lead them in paths *that* they have not known: I will make [f]darkness light before them, and crooked things straight. These things will I do unto them, and [g]not forsake them.[S T Q]

17 They shall be turned back, they shall be greatly ashamed, that [h]trust in graven[G] images,[G] that say to the molten[G] images,[G] Ye *are* our gods.

18 ¶ Hear, ye [i]deaf; and look, ye [d]blind, that ye may see.[Q]

19 Who *is* blind, but my servant? or deaf, as my messenger *that* I sent? who *is* blind as *he that is* [3]perfect, and blind as the LORD's servant?

20 Seeing many things, but thou observest not; opening the ears, but he heareth not.

21 The LORD is well pleased for his [j]righteousness' sake; he will magnify the law, and make *it* honourable.[S Q]

22 But this *is* a [k]people [l]robbed and spoiled[G]; *they are* all of them snared in holes, and they are hid in prison houses: they are for a prey, and none delivereth; for a spoil, and none saith, Restore.

23 Who among you will give ear to this? *who* will hearken[G] and hear for the time to come?

24 Who [l]gave Jā'cob for a spoil,[G] and Iṣ'ra-el to the robbers?

14
2 R. V. gasp and pant together.

16
[c] *Wisdom, spiritual, from God,* Prov. 2:2.
[d] *Spiritual Blindness,* 2 Cor. 4:4.
[e] *God, guidance of,* Gen. 2:2.
[f] *Darkness, figurative,* Gen. 1:2.
[g] *God, faithfulness of,* Gen. 2:2.

17
[h] *Idolatry, folly of,* 1 Sam. 15:23.

18
[i] *Deafness, figurative,* Matt. 11:5.

19
3 R. V. at peace with me, and

21
[j] *God, righteousness of,* Gen. 2:2

22
[k] *Judah, kingdom of,* 2 Chr. 11:17.
[l] *Judgments,* vs. 22–25; Ex. 6:6.

did not the LORD, he against whom we have sinned? for they [m,n]would not walk in his ways, [o]neither were they obedient unto his law.

25 Therefore he hath [l]poured upon him the fury of his [p]anger, and the strength of battle: and it hath set him on fire round about, yet he knew not; and it burned him, yet he laid *it* not to heart.[S]

## CHAPTER 43

*God's promises to his chosen people.* 8 *They are witnesses for him of his power to save.* 14 *His purpose to destroy Babylon,* 18 *and to deliver his people.* 22 *He rebukes the people for their sins.*

BUT now thus saith the LORD that [a]created thee, O Jā'cob, and he that formed thee, O Ĭṣ'ra-el, [b]Fear not: for [c]I have [d]redeemed thee, I have called *thee* by thy name; thou *art* mine.[S T]

2 [e]When thou passest through the [f]waters, [g,h,i]I *will be* with thee; and through the rivers, they shall not overflow thee: [e]when thou walkest through the fire, [h,i]thou shalt not be burned; [h,i]neither shall the flame kindle upon thee.[S T]

3 For I *am* the LORD thy God, the [j]Holy One of Ĭṣ'ra-el, thy [k]Saviour: I gave [l]Ē'ġy̆pt *for* thy ransom, [m]Ē-thĭ-ō'pĭ-ȧ and [n,o]Sē'bȧ for thee.[S]

4 Since thou wast precious in my sight, thou hast been honourable, and I have [c]loved thee: therefore will I give men for thee, and people for thy life.[S Q]

5 [b,e]Fear not: for [h,i]I *am* with thee: I will bring thy seed from the east, and gather thee from the west;[S Q]

6 I will say to the north, Give up; and to the south, Keep not back: bring my [p]sons from far, and my daughters from the ends of the earth;[Q]

7 *Even* every one that is [p]called by my name: for I have [q]created him for my [r]glory, I have formed him; yea, I have made him.[S T]

8 ¶ Bring forth the [s]blind people that have eyes, and the [t]deaf that have ears.

9[T] Let all the nations be gathered together, and let the people be assembled: who among them can [u]declare this, and shew us former things? let them bring forth their witnesses, that they may be justified: or let them hear, and say, *It is* truth.

10 [S] Ye *are* my [v]witnesses, saith the LORD, and my servant whom I have [w]chosen; that ye may know[C] and [x]believe me, and understand that I am he: before me there was no God formed, neither shall there be after me.[Q]

11 I, *even* I, *am* the [y]LORD; and beside me *there is* no [k]saviour.[T]

12 I have declared, and have saved, and I have shewed, when *there was* no strange *god* among you: therefore ye *are* my witnesses, saith the LORD, that I *am* God.[S]

13 Yea, [z]before the day *was* I *am* he; and [a]*there is* none that can deliver out of my hand: I will work, and who shall let[C] it?[S Q]

14 ¶ Thus saith the LORD, your [b]redeemer, the [c,d]Holy One of Ĭṣ'ra-el; For your sake [e]I have sent to [f]Băb'y̆-lon, and [1]have brought down all their nobles,[C] and the [g]Chăl-dē'anṣ, whose cry *is* in the ships.[S]

15 I *am* the LORD, your [c,d]Holy One, the [h]creator of Ĭṣ'ra-el, your King.[S]

16 Thus[S] saith the LORD, which maketh a way in the [j]sea, and a path in the mighty waters;

17 [k]Which bringeth forth the chariot and horse, the army and the power; they shall lie down together, they shall not rise: they

**24**
m *Impenitence,* Rom. 2:5.
n *Adversity, obduracy in,* Psa. 10:6.
o *Disobedience to God,* Eph. 5:6.

**25**
p *Anger of God,* 2 Kin. 13:3.

**1**
a *God, creator,* Gen. 2:2.
b *Faith, enjoined,* Mark 11:22.
c *God, love of,* Gen. 2:2.
d *Redemption,* Lev. 25:24.

**2**
e *Adversity, consolation in,* Psa. 10:6.
f *Water, figurative of affliction,* 1 Kin. 17:10.
g *God, preserver,* Gen. 2:2.
h *Promise, to the righteous,* 2 Cor. 1:20.
i *Righteous, promises to,* Psa. 64:10.

**3**
j *God, holiness of,* Gen. 2:2.
k *God, savior,* Gen. 2:2.
l *Egypt,* Gen. 41:8.
m *Ethiopia,* Isa. 18:1.
n Psa. 72:10.
o Or, *Sabeans,* Isa. 45:14.

**6**
p *Spiritual Adoption,* Rom. 8:15.

**7**
q *Man, design of the creation of,* Job 4:17.
r *God, glory of,* Gen. 2:2.

**8**
s *Spiritual Blindness,* 2 Cor. 4:4.
t *Deafness, figurative,* Matt. 11:5.

**9**
u *Prophecies,* Dan. 9:24.

**10**
v *Religious Testimony,* 2 Thess. 1:10.
w *Election of Grace,* Rom. 11:5.
x *Faith,* Mark 11:22.

**11**
y *God, sovereign,* Gen. 2:2.

**13**
z *God, eternity of,* Gen. 2:2.
a *God, power of,* Gen. 2:2.

**14**
b *God, savior,* Gen. 2:2.
c *God, holiness of,* Gen. 2:2.
d *Holiness, attribute of God,* Ex. 39:30.
e *God, providence of,* Gen. 2:2.
f *Babylon, empire of,* Ezra 5:12.
g *Chaldeans,* Dan. 1:4.
1 R. V. I will bring down all of them as fugitives, even the Chaldeans, in the ships of their rejoicing.

**15**
h *God, creator,* Gen. 2:2.
i *God, sovereign,* Gen. 2:2.

**16**
j *Red Sea, divided,* Ex. 10:19.

**17**
k *Egypt, army of, destroyed in the Red Sea,* Gen. 41:8.

are extinct, they are quenched as tow.[G][S]

18 [Q]Remember ye not the former things, neither consider the things of old.

19 Behold, I will do a new thing; now it shall spring forth; shall ye not know it? I will even make a way in the wilderness, *and* rivers in the desert.[Q]

20 The[Q] beast of the field shall honour me, the [2]dragons and the owls: because I [e]give [l]waters in the [m]wilderness, *and* rivers in the desert, to give drink to my people, my chosen.[S]

21 This people have I [h]formed for myself; they shall shew forth my [n]praise.[S][Q]

22 ¶ But [o,p]thou hast [q,r]not called upon me, O Jā′cob; but thou hast been weary of me, O Ĭṣ′ra-el.

23 [o,p]Thou hast not brought me the small cattle[G] of thy [s]burnt offerings; neither hast thou honoured me with thy sacrifices. I have not caused thee to serve with an offering, nor wearied thee with [t]incense.

24 [o,p]Thou hast bought me no [u]sweet cane with [v]money, neither hast thou filled me with the [w]fat of thy sacrifices: but thou hast made me to serve[G] with thy sins, [x]thou hast wearied me with thine iniquities.

25 I, *even* I, *am* he that [y,z]blotteth out thy transgressions for mine own sake, and will not remember thy sins.[T][Q]

26 Put me in [a]remembrance: let us [b]plead together: declare thou, that thou mayest be justified.

27 Thy [c]first father hath [d]sinned, and [3]thy [e]teachers have transgressed against me.

28 Therefore I [4]have [f]profaned the princes of the sanctuary, and [5]have given Jā′cob to the curse, and Ĭṣ′ra-el to reproaches.

**20**
l *Temporal Blessings, from God*, Psa. 103:2.
m *Meribah*, Ex. 17:7.
2 R. V. the jackals and the ostriches:

**21**
n *Praise*, Psa. 150:1.

**22**
o *Backsliders, instances of*, Jer. 3:22.
p *Church, backslidden*, Matt. 16:18.
q *Prayerlessness*, Job 21:15.
r *Ingratitude, of man to God*, Rom. 1:21.

**23**
s *Offerings, burnt*, Lev. 6:17.
t *Frankincense*, 1 Chr. 9:29.

**24**
u *Calamus*, Ezek. 27:19.
v *Money*, Jer. 32:9.
w *Fat, offered in sacrifice*, Lev. 7:24.
x *Sin, repugnant to God*, Rom. 5:12.

**25**
y *Sin, forgiveness of*, Rom. 5:12.
z *God, mercy of*, Gen. 2:2.

**26**
a *Anthropomorphisms*, Gen. 11:5.
b *Reasoning, God reasons with men*, Job 13:6.

**27**
c *Adam, temptation and sin of*, Gen. 2:19.
d *Fall of Man*, Gen. 3:6.
e *Minister, false and corrupt*, Rom. 15:16.
3 R. V. thine interpreters have

**28**
f *Divine Chastisement*, Job 33:19.
4 R. V. will profane
5 R. V. I will make Jacob a curse, and Israel a reviling.

## CHAPTER 44

*Spiritual blessings promised to Israel.* 6 *Jehovah the only true God.* 9 *The folly of idolatry.* 21 *An assurance to Israel of deliverance.*

YET now hear, O Jā′cob my servant; and Ĭṣ′ra-el, whom [a]I have [b]chosen:[S]

2 Thus saith the LORD that [c]made thee, and formed thee from the womb, *which* will help thee; [d]Fear not, O Jā′cob, my servant; and thou, [e]Jĕs′u-rŭn, whom I have [b]chosen.[S]

3 For [f]I will pour [g,h,i]water upon him that is [j]thirsty, and floods upon the [k]dry ground: I will pour my [l]spirit upon thy [m]seed, and my blessing upon thine offspring:[Q]

4 And they shall spring up *as* among the grass, as [n]willows by the water courses.

5 One shall say, I *am* the LORD's; and another shall call *himself* by the name of Jā′cob; and another shall subscribe[G] *with* his hand unto the LORD, and surname *himself* by the name of Ĭṣ′ra-el.

6 Thus saith the LORD the [o]King of Ĭṣ′ra-el, and his [p]redeemer the LORD of hosts; [q]I *am* the first, and [q]I *am* the last; and beside me *there is* no[Q] God.[T][S]

7 And who, as [r]I, shall call, and shall declare it, and set it in order for me, since I appointed the ancient people? and the things that are coming, and shall come, let them shew unto them.[S]

8 [d]Fear ye not, neither be afraid: have not I told thee from that time, and have declared *it*? ye *are* even my [s]witnesses. Is there a God beside me? yea, *there is* no [1]God; I know not *any*.[T]

9 [S][t]They that make a [u]graven[G] [v]image *are* all of them vanity; and their delectable[G] things shall not profit; and they *are* their own witnesses; they see not, nor know; that they may be ashamed.

**1**
a *God, love of*, Gen. 2:2.
b *Election of Grace*, Rom. 11:5.

**2**
c *God, creator*, Gen. 2:2.
d *Faith, enjoined*, Mark 11:22.
e Or, *Jeshurun*, Deut. 32:15.

**3**
f *Righteous, promises to*, Psa. 64:10.
g *Water, figurative of salvation*, 1 Kin. 17:10.
h *Salvation*, Acts 16:17.
i *Spiritual Blessings, from God*, Eph. 1:3.
j *Spiritual Desire*, Psa. 42:1.
k *Drought, figurative*, Gen. 31:40.
l *Holy Spirit, baptism of*, Acts 1:2.
m *Children, of the righteous, blessed of God*, Mark 10:14.

**4**
n *Willow*, Lev. 23:40.

**6**
o *God, sovereign*, Gen. 2:2.
p *God, savior*, Gen. 2:2.
q *God, eternity of*, Gen. 2:2.

**7**
r *God, knowledge of*, Gen. 2:2.

**8**
s *Religious Testimony*, 2 Thess. 1:10.
1 R. V. Rock;

**9**
t *Idolatry, folly of*, vs. 10–20; 1 Sam. 15:23.
u *Carving*, Ex. 35:33.
v *Idol*, 1 Kin. 15:12.

10 [t]Who[Q] hath formed a god, or molten[C] a graven[C] image *that* is profitable for nothing? [S]

11 Behold, all his fellows shall be ashamed: and the workmen, they *are* of men: let them all be gathered together, let them stand up; *yet* they shall fear, *and* they shall be ashamed together.

12 The [w]smith [2]with the tongs both worketh in the coals, and fashioneth it with [x]hammers, and worketh it with the strength of his arms: yea, he is hungry, and his strength faileth: he drinketh no water, and is faint.

13 The [y]carpenter stretcheth out [3]*his* rule; he marketh it out with a [4]line; he fitteth it with planes, and he marketh it out with the compass, and maketh [v]it after the figure of a man, according to the beauty of a man; that it may remain in the house.

14 He heweth him down cedars, and taketh the [5]cypress and the oak, which he strengtheneth for himself among the trees of the forest: he planteth [6]an ash, and the rain doth nourish *it*.

15 Then shall it be for a man to burn: for he will take thereof, and warm himself; yea, he kindleth *it*, and baketh bread; yea, he maketh a [v]god, and worshippeth *it*; he maketh it a graven[C] image, and falleth down thereto.

16 He burneth part thereof in the fire; with part thereof he eateth flesh; he roasteth roast, and is satisfied: yea, he warmeth *himself*, and saith, Aha, I am warm, I have seen the fire:

17 And the residue[C] thereof he maketh a [v]god, *even* his graven[C] image[C]: he [t]falleth down unto it, and worshippeth *it*, and prayeth unto it, and saith, Deliver me; for thou *art* my god.[Q]

18 They have [z]not known nor understood: for he hath shut their eyes, that they cannot see; *and* their hearts, that they cannot understand.

19 And none considereth in his heart, neither *is there* knowledge nor understanding to say, I have burned part of it in the fire; yea, also I have baked [a]bread upon the coals thereof; I have roasted flesh, and eaten *it*: and shall I make the residue thereof an abomination? [b]shall I fall down to the stock of a tree?

20 He feedeth on ashes: a [c]deceived heart hath turned him aside, that he cannot deliver his soul, nor say, *Is there* not a lie in my right hand?

21 ¶ Remember these, O Jā′cob and Ĭs′ra-el; for thou *art* my servant: I have formed thee; thou *art* my servant: O Ĭs′ra-el, [d]thou shalt not be forgotten of me.[S]

22 I have [e]blotted out, as a thick cloud, thy transgressions, and, as a cloud, thy sins: [f]return unto me; for I have [g]redeemed thee.

23 [h]Sing, O ye heavens; for the LORD hath done *it*: shout, ye lower parts of the earth: break forth into singing, ye mountains, O forest, and every tree therein: for the LORD hath redeemed Jă′cob, and glorified himself in Ĭs′ra-el.[S Q]

24 Thus saith the LORD, thy [i]redeemer, and he that [j,k]formed thee from the womb, [l]I *am* the LORD that [j]maketh all *things*; that stretcheth forth the [m]heavens alone; that spreadeth abroad the [7,n]earth by myself;[S T]

25 That frustrateth the tokens of the liars, and maketh [o]diviners mad; that turneth [p]wise *men* backward, and maketh their knowledge foolish;[Q]

26 That confirmeth the word of his servant, and performeth the counsel of his messengers; that saith to [q]Jĕ-ru′sā-lĕm, Thou

12
w *Smith*, Isa. 54:16.
x Jer. 10:4.
2 R. V. maketh an axe, and worketh

13
y *Carpentry*, 2 Kin. 12:11.
3 R. V. a line;
4 R. V. pencil;

14
5 R. V. holm tree
6 R. V. a fir tree,

18
z *Spiritual Blindness*, 2 Cor. 4:4.

19
a *Bread*, Ezek. 4:13.
b *Idolatry, folly of*, 1 Sam. 15:23.

20
c *Delusion*, 2 Thess. 2:11.

21
d *God, faithfulness of*, Gen. 2:2.

22
e *Sin, forgiveness of*, Rom. 5:12.
f *Repentance, enjoined*, Mark 1:4.
g *Redemption, of our souls*, Eph. 1:7.

23
h *Praise, enjoined*, Psa. 150:1.

24
i *God, savior*, Gen. 2:2.
j *God, creator*, Gen. 2:2.
k *Man, created*, Job 4:17.
l *God, sovereign*, Gen. 2:2.
m *Heavens, created*, Psa. 8:3.
n *Earth, created*, Prov. 8:23.
7 R. V. earth; who is with me?

25
o *Sorcery*, Isa. 47:9.
p *Wisdom, worldly*, Prov. 2:2.

26
q *Jerusalem, prophecies of the rebuilding of*, Judg. 19:10.

shalt be inhabited; and to the cities of [r]Jū′dah, Ye shall be built, and I will raise up the decayed places thereof:

27 That saith to the deep, Be dry, and I will dry up thy rivers:[Q S]

28 That saith of [s]Çȳ′rus, *He is* my [t]shepherd, and shall perform all my pleasure: even saying to [q]Jĕ-ru̧′sā-lĕm, Thou shalt be built; and to the [u]temple, Thy foundation shall be laid.[Q]

r *Judah, kingdom of*, 2 Chr. 11:17.

28

s *Cyrus, prophecies concerning*, 2 Chr. 36:22.

t *Shepherd, figurative*, Jer. 31:10.

u *Temple, Second*, 1 Kin. 6:17.

## CHAPTER 45

*God's purpose in calling Cyrus. 9 All opposition thereto in vain. 14 The spiritual conquests of Israel. 17 The security of Israel. 20 The vanity of idols. 22 All nations exhorted to look unto God for salvation.*

[a]THUS saith the LORD to his [b,c]anointed, to [d]Çȳ′rus, whose right hand [e]I have holden,[G] to subdue nations before him; and [e]I will loose the loins of kings, to open [1]before him the two leaved[G] gates; and the [f]gates shall not be shut;

2 [g]I will go before [d]thee, and make the [2]crooked places straight: I will break in pieces the [3]gates of brass,[G] and cut in sunder the bars of iron:[S]

3 And I will give [d]thee the treasures of darkness, and hidden riches of secret places, that thou mayest know that I, the LORD, which [e]call *thee* by thy name, *am* the God of Ĭș′ra-el.[Q]

4 [h]For [i]Jā′cob my servant's sake, and Ĭș′ra-el [4]mine [j]elect, I have even called [d]thee by thy name: I have surnamed thee, though thou hast not known me.[S]

5 [k]I *am* the LORD,[T] and *there is* none else, *there is* no God beside me: I girded [d]thee, though thou hast not known me:

6 That they may know from the rising of the sun, and from the west, that *there is* none beside me. I *am* the LORD, and *there is* none else.[T]

1

a *Government, God in*, Isa. 22:21.

b *Anointing, of kings*, Lev. 8:12.

c *Call, personal*, Phil. 3:14.

d *Cyrus, prophecies concerning*, 2 Chr. 36:22.

e *God, providence of*, Gen. 2:2.

f *Gates*, Deut. 3:5.

1 R. V. the doors before him, and

2

g *God, preserver*, Gen. 2:2.

2 R. V. rugged places plain:

3 R. V. doors

4

h *Intercession, influence of the righteous*, Jer. 27:18.

i *Judah, kingdom of*, 2 Chr. 11:17.

j *Election of Grace*, Rom. 11:5.

4 R. V. my chosen,

5

k *God, sovereign*, Gen. 2:2.

7 [l]I form the [m]light, and create [n]darkness: I make [o,p]peace, and create [q]evil: [k]I the LORD do all these *things*.[S T]

8 Drop down, ye heavens, from above, and let the skies pour down righteousness: let the earth open, and let them bring forth salvation, and let righteousness spring up together; [k]I the LORD have [l]created it.

9 [r]Woe unto him that [s]striveth with his Maker! [5]*Let* the [t]potsherd *strive* with the potsherds of the earth. [u]Shall the clay say to him that fashioneth it, What makest thou? or thy work, He hath no hands?[Q]

10 Woe unto him that saith unto *his* father, What begettest thou? or to the woman, What hast thou brought forth?

11 Thus saith the LORD, the [v]Holy One of Ĭș′ra-el, and his [l]Maker, [w]Ask me of things to come concerning my sons, and concerning the work of my hands command ye me.[S]

12 I have [l]made the [x]earth, and created [y]man upon it: I, *even* my hands, have stretched out the [z]heavens, and all their host have I commanded.[S T]

13 [a]I have raised [b]him up in righteousness, and I will direct all his ways: he shall build my city, and he shall let go my captives, not for price nor reward, saith the LORD of hosts.

14 Thus saith the LORD, The labour of [c]Ē′gȳpt, and [d]merchandise of [e]Ē-thĭ-ō′pĭ-ȧ and of the *Sā-bē′anș, men of stature, shall come over unto thee, and they shall be thine: they shall come after thee; in chains they shall come over, and they shall fall down unto thee, they shall make supplication unto thee, *saying*, Surely God *is* in thee;

7

l *God, creator*, Gen. 2:2.

m *Light, created*, Gen. 1:3.

n *Darkness, God creates*, Gen. 1:2.

o *Peace*, Jer. 29:7.

p *Nation, peace given to, by God*, Isa. 2:4.

q *Adversity, dispensation from God*, Psa. 10:6.

9

r Isa. 29:16; Rom. 9:20, 21.

s *Presumption, in defying God*, Psa. 19:13.

t Job 2:8.

u *Infidelity, arguments against*, 2 Cor. 6:15.

5 R. V. a potsherd among the potsherds of the earth!

11

v *God, holiness of*, Gen. 2:2.

w *God, foreknowledge of*, Gen. 2:2.

12

x *Earth, created*, Prov. 8:23.

y *Man, created*, Job 4:17.

z *Heavens, created*, Psa. 8:3.

13

a *God, providence of*, Gen. 2:2.

b *Cyrus, prophecies concerning*, 2 Chr. 36:22.

14

c *Egypt, prophecies against*, Gen. 41:8.

d *Commerce*, 1 Kin. 10:15.

e *Ethiopia, prophecies concerning*, Isa. 18:1.

---

***SABEANS.** *A people who invaded the land of Uz,* Job 1:15. *Giants among,* Isa. 45:14. *Prophecies concerning,* Isa. 43:3; Joel 3:8. See footnote, SHEBA, 1 Kin. 10:1.

15
*f God, unsearchable,* Gen. 2:2.
*g God, savior,* Gen. 2:2.
16
*h Idolatry, folly of,* 1 Sam. 15:23.
*i Idol,* 1 Kin 15:12.
17
*j Salvation,* Acts 16:17.
18
*k God, creator,* Gen. 2:2.
*l Heavens, created,* Psa. 8:3.
*m Earth, created,* Prov. 8:23.
*n God, sovereign,* Gen. 2:2.
6 R. V. a waste.
19
*o God, righteousness of,* Gen. 2:2.
20
*p Carving,* Ex. 35:33.
21
*q God, justice of,* Gen. 2:2.
22
*r Call, personal,* Phil. 3:14.
*s Promise, or ground of assurance, to sinners,* 2 Cor. 1:20.
23
*t Oath, attributed to God,* Num. 5:19.

and *there is* none else, *there is*
no God.[T Q]
15 Verily thou *art* a [f]God that
hidest thyself, O God of Ĭṣ'ra-el,
the [g]Saviour.[S T Q]
16 [h]They shall be ashamed, and
also confounded, all of them:
they shall go to confusion together *that are* makers of [i]idols.
17 *But* Ĭṣ'ra-el shall be [g]saved
in the LORD with an everlasting [j]salvation: ye shall not be
ashamed nor confounded world
without end.[Q]
18 For thus saith the LORD
that [k]created the [l]heavens; God
himself that formed the [m]earth
and made it; he hath established
it, he created it not [6]in vain,[G] he
formed it to be inhabited: [n]I
*am* the LORD; and *there is* none
else.[S]
19 I have not spoken in secret,
in a dark place of the earth: I
said not unto the seed of Jā'cob,
Seek ye me in vain:[G] I the LORD
speak [o]righteousness, I declare
things that are right.[S]
20 ¶ Assemble yourselves and
come; draw near together, ye
*that are* escaped of the nations:
[h]they have no knowledge that
set up the wood of their [p]graven[G]
[i]image, and pray unto a god *that*
cannot save.
21 Tell ye, and bring *them* near;
yea, let them take counsel together: who hath declared this
from ancient time? *who* hath
told it from that time? *have* not
[n]I the LORD? and *there is* no
God else beside me; a [q]just God
and a [g]Saviour; [n]*there is* none
beside me.[S T Q]
22 [r]Look[T] unto [g]me, and [s]be ye
[j]saved, all the ends of the earth:
for [n]I *am* God, and *there is* none
else.
23 I have [t]sworn by myself, the
word is gone out of my mouth
*in* righteousness, and shall not
return, [u]That unto [n]me [v]every
knee shall bow, every tongue
shall swear.[T Q]
24[T] Surely, shall *one* [w]say, in the
LORD have I [x]righteousness and
[x]strength: *even* to him shall *men*
come; and all that are incensed
against him shall be ashamed.[S]
25 In the LORD shall all the
seed of Ĭṣ'ra-el be [y]justified, and
shall glory.[S T]

## CHAPTER 46

*The prophet shews the folly of idolatry, and exhorts the people of God to trust in him for deliverance.*

[a]BĔL boweth down, Nē'bō
stoopeth, their [b]idols were
upon the beasts, and upon the
cattle: your carriages *were* heavy
loaden;[G] *they are* a burden to the
weary *beast.*[S]
2 They stoop, they bow down
together; they could not deliver
the burden, but themselves are
gone into captivity.
3 ¶ Hearken[S] unto me, O house
of Jā'cob, and all the remnant
of the house of Ĭṣ'ra-el, which
are borne *by* [c]*me* from the belly,[G]
which are carried from the
womb:
4 And *even* to *your* *old age I
*am* he; and *even* to hoar[G] hairs
will [c]I carry *you*: I have made,
and I will bear; even I[S] will carry,
and will deliver *you.*
5 ¶ To whom will ye liken [d]me,
and make *me* equal, and compare me, that we may be like?
6 They lavish gold out of the
bag, and weigh silver in the [e]bal-
ance, *and* hire a [f]goldsmith; and
he maketh it a [g]god: [h]they fall
down, yea, they worship.
7 [h]They bear him upon the
shoulder, they carry him, and
set him in his place, and he

*u* Rom. 14:11.
*v Gentiles, prophecies of the conversion of,* Acts 10:45.
24
*w Religious Testimony,* 2 Thess. 1:10.
*x Spiritual Blessings, from God,* Eph. 1:3.
25
*y Justification,* Rom. 4:25.
1
*a* Jer. 50:2; 51:44.
*b Idolatry,* 1 Sam. 15:23.
3
*c God, providence of,* Gen. 2:2.
5
*d God,* Gen. 2:2.
6
*e Balances,* Prov. 11:1.
*f Goldsmith,* Neh. 3:8.
*g Idol,* 1 Kin. 15:12.
*h Idolatry, folly of,* 1 Sam. 15:23.

* **OLD AGE**, Gen. 47:9; Eccl. 12:1-7. *Wise,* 1 Kin. 12:6-8; 2 Chr. 10:6-8; Job 12:12. *Devout,* Luke 2:37. *Exemplary, enjoined,* Tit. 2:2, 3. *Deference towards,* Lev. 19:32; Job 32:4-9. *Righteous, is glorious,* Prov. 16:31. *Promised to the righteous,* Gen. 15:15; Job 5:26; Psa. 34:12-14; 91:14, 16; Prov. 3:1, 2. *God's care in,* Isa. 46:4. *Psalmist prays not to be forsaken in,* Psa. 71:9, 18. *Infirmities in,* 2 Sam. 19:34-37; Psa. 90:10. *Vigor in,* Deut. 34:7; Psa. 92:12-14. See footnote, LONGEVITY, Psa. 91:16.

standeth; from his place shall
he not remove[G]: yea, *one* shall
cry unto him, yet can he not answer, nor save him out of his
trouble.
8 Remember this, and shew[G]
yourselves men: bring *it* again to
mind, O ye transgressors.
9[S] Re[T]member the former things
of old: for [i]I *am* God, and *there*
*is* none else; *I am* God, and *there*
*is* none like me,
10 [j]Declaring the end from the
beginning, and from ancient
times *the things* that are not
*yet* done, saying, My counsel
shall stand, and I will do all my
pleasure:[T]
11 Calling a ravenous [k,l]bird
from the east, the man that executeth[G] my counsel[G] from a far
country: yea, I have spoken *it*, I
will also bring it to pass; I have
purposed *it*, I will also do it.[S]
12 ¶ Hearken unto me, ye
[m,n]stouthearted, that *are* far
from righteousness:
13 I bring near my [o]righteous-
ness; it shall not be far off, and
my [p,q]salvation shall not tarry[G]:
and I will place salvation in
[r]Zī'ŏn for Is̤'ra-el my glory.[S Q]

## CHAPTER 47

*Babylon to be overthrown, 6 because of her oppression, 7 pride, 10 and self-conceit, 11 notwithstanding her enchantments.*

COME down, and sit in the
dust, O virgin daughter of
[a]Băb'y̆-lon, sit on the ground:
*there is* no throne, O daughter of
the Chăl-dē'ans̤: for thou shalt
no more be called tender and
delicate.[G]
2 Take the [b]millstones, and
grind meal; [1]uncover thy locks,

9
*i God, sovereign,* Gen. 2:2.

10
*j God, foreknowledge of,* Gen. 2:2.

11
*k Birds, figurative,* Eccl. 12:4.
*l Cyrus, prophecies concerning,* 2 Chr. 36:22.

12
*m Impenitence,* Rom. 2:5.
*n Heart, unregenerate,* Psa. 44:21.

13
*o God, righteousness of,* Gen. 2:2.
*p Salvation,* Acts 16:17.
*q God, savior,* Gen. 2:2.
*r Church, prophecies concerning its prosperity,* Matt. 16:18.

1
*a Babylon, empire of, prophetic denunciations against,* vs. 1–15; Ezra 5:12.

2
*b Mill, stones of,* Ex. 11:5.
1 R. V. remove thy veil, strip off the train, uncover the leg,

make bare the leg, uncover the
thigh, pass over the rivers.
3 Thy nakedness shall be uncovered; yea, thy shame shall be
seen: I will take vengeance, and
I will [2]not meet *thee as* a man.
4 ¶ *As for* our [c]redeemer, the
LORD of hosts *is* his name, the
[d,e]Holy One of Is̤'ra-el.[S T]
5 Sit thou silent, and get thee
into darkness, O daughter of
the Chăl-dē'ans̤: for [f]thou shalt
no more be called, The lady of
kingdoms.
6 I was [g]wroth[G] with my people,
I have polluted mine inheritance,
and [h]given them into thine hand:
thou didst [i]shew them no mercy;
upon the ancient hast thou very
heavily[G] laid thy yoke.
7 A[Q]nd thou [j]saidst, I shall be a
lady for ever: *so* that thou didst
not lay these *things* to thy heart,
neither didst remember the latter end of it.
8 Therefore hear now this, *thou*
*that art* [k]given to [l]pleasures, that
dwellest carelessly, that [j]sayest
in thine heart, I *am*, and none
else beside me; I shall not sit *as* a
widow, neither shall I know the
loss of children:[Q]
9 But [j]these two [m]*things* shall
come to thee in a moment in one
day, the loss of children, and
widowhood: [3]they shall come
upon thee in their perfection for
the multitude of thy *sorceries,
*and* for the great abundance of
thine enchantments.[Q]
10 For thou hast [j]trusted in
thy wickedness: thou hast said,
None seeth me. Thy [n]wisdom
and thy knowledge, it hath perverted thee; and thou hast said

3
2 R. V. accept no man.

4
*c God, savior,* Gen. 2:2.
*d God, holiness of,* Gen. 2:2.
*e Holiness, attribute of God,* Ex. 39:30.

5
*f Nation, punishment of,* Isa. 2:4.

6
*g Anger of God,* 2 Kin. 13:3.
*h Divine Chastisement,* Job 33:19.
*i Oppression,* Eccl. 5:8.

7
*j False Confidence,* Psa. 30:6.

8
*k Worldliness,* 1 John 2:15.
*l Worldly Pleasure,* Eccl. 2:1.

9
*m Judgments,* Ex. 6:6.
3 R. V. in their full measure shall they come upon thee, despite of the multitude

10
*n Wisdom, worldly,* Prov. 2:2.

***SORCERY.** *Divination by an alleged assistance of evil spirits,* 1 Sam. 15:23. *Forbidden,* Lev. 19:26, 31; 20:6; Deut. 18:9–14. *Denounced,* Isa. 8:19; Mal. 3:5.
Practiced: *By the Egyptian magicians,* Ex. 7:11, 12, 22; 8:7, 18; Isa. 19:3; *by the Philistines,* 1 Sam. 6:2–5; *by Jezebel,* 2 Kin. 9:22; *by Israel,* Isa. 2:6; *by Manasseh,* 2 Kin. 21:6; 2 Chr. 33:6; *by the Ninevites,* Nah. 3:4, 5; *by the Babylonians,* Isa. 47:9–13; Ezek. 21:21, 22; Dan. 1:20; 2:2, 10, 27; 4:7; 5:7, 15; *by Simon Magus,* Acts 8:9, 11; *by Elymas,* Acts 13:8; *by the damsel at Philippi,* Acts 16:16; *by strolling Jews,* Acts 19:13; *by sons of Sceva,* Acts 19:14, 15; *by false prophets,* Jer. 14:14; 27:9; 29:8, 9; Ezek. 13:6–9; 22:28; Matt. 24:24.
*Divining, by familiar spirits,* Lev. 20:27; 1 Chr. 10:13; 2 Chr. 33:6; Isa. 8:19; 19:3; 29:4; *by entrails,* Ezek. 21:21; *by images,* 2 Kin. 23:24; Ezek. 21:21; *by rods,* Hos. 4:12.
*To cease,* Ezek. 12:23, 24; 13:23; Mic. 5:12.
*Messages of, false,* Ezek. 21:29; Zech. 10:2; 2 Thess. 2:9. *Diviners shall be confounded,* Mic. 3:7. *Belongs to the works of the flesh,* Gal. 5:19, 20. *Wickedness of,* 1 Sam. 15:23. *Vainness of,* Isa. 44:25. *Punishment for,* Ex. 22:18; Lev. 20:27.
*Saul consults the witch of Endor,* 1 Sam. 28:7–25.
*Books of, destroyed,* Acts 19:19.
See footnotes: NECROMANCY, Deut. 18:11; WITCHCRAFT, Ex. 22:18.

in thine heart, I *am*, and none else beside me.

11 [l]Therefore shall [m,o]evil come upon thee; thou shalt not know from whence it riseth: and mischief shall fall upon thee; thou shalt not be able to put it off: and desolation shall come upon thee suddenly, *which* thou shalt not know.

12 Stand now with thine *enchantments, and with the multitude of thy sorceries, wherein thou hast laboured from thy youth; if so be thou shalt be able to profit, if so be thou mayest prevail.

13 Thou art wearied in the multitude of thy counsels. Let now the astrologers, the stargazers, the monthly prognosticators, stand up, and save thee from *these things* that shall come upon thee.

14 Behold, they shall be as [p]stubble; [m,o]the fire shall burn them; they shall not deliver themselves from the power of the flame: *there shall* not *be* a coal to warm at, *nor* fire to sit before it.

15 Thus shall they be unto thee with whom thou hast laboured, *even* thy [q]merchants, from thy youth: they shall wander every one to his quarter; none shall save thee.

## CHAPTER 48

*God rebukes the obstinacy of his people. 9 He saves them for his own sake. 12 His power and providence. 16 His lamentation over their perverseness. 20 The certainty of their deliverance from Babylon.*

HEAR ye this, O house of Jā′cob, which are called by the name of Is̱′ra-el, and are come forth out of the waters of Jū′dah, which [a,b]swear by the name of the LORD, and make mention of the God of Is̱′ra-el, *but* [c]not in truth, nor in righteousness.

2 For [c]they call themselves of the holy city, and stay themselves upon the God of Is̱′ra-el; The LORD of hosts *is* his name.

3 [d]I have declared the former things from the beginning; and they went forth out of my mouth, and I shewed them; I did *them* suddenly, and they came to pass.

4 Because [e]I knew that thou *art* [f,g,h]obstinate, and thy neck *is* an iron sinew, and thy brow [i]brass;

5 [d]I have even from the beginning declared *it* to thee; before it came to pass I shewed *it* thee: lest thou shouldest say, [j]Mine [k]idol hath done them, and my graven image, and my molten image, hath commanded them.

6 Thou hast heard, see all this; and will not ye declare *it*? I have shewed thee new things from this time, even hidden things, and thou [l]didst not know them.

7 They are created now, and not from the beginning; even before the day when thou heardest them not; lest thou shouldest say, Behold, I knew them.

8 Yea, thou heardest not; yea, thou [l]knewest not; yea, from that time *that* thine ear was not opened: for I knew that thou wouldest deal very treacherously, and wast called a transgressor from the womb.

9 ¶ For my name's sake will I [m,n]defer mine [o]anger, and for my praise will I refrain for thee, that I cut thee not off.

10 Behold, I have [p,q]refined thee, but not with silver; I have chosen thee in the [r]furnace of affliction.

11 For mine own sake, *even* for mine own sake, will I do *it*: for how should *my name* be [1]polluted? and [s]I will not give my [t]glory unto another.

12 ¶ Hearken unto me, O Jā′cob and Is̱′ra-el, my called; I *am* he; [u]I *am* the first, [u]I also *am* the last.

11
o *Wicked, punishment of,* Psa. 73:3.

14
p *Stubble,* Isa. 5:24.

15
q *Merchant,* Neh. 3:32.

1
a *Oath,* Num. 5:19.
b *Perjury,* 1 Tim. 1:10.
c *Hypocrisy,* Jas. 3:17.

3
d *God, foreknowledge of,* Gen. 2:2.

4
e *God, knowledge of,* Gen. 2:2.
f *Self-will,* Gen. 49:6.
g *Impenitence,* Rom. 2:5.
h *Obduracy,* Prov. 29:1.
i *Brass, figurative,* Job 28:2.

5
j *Idolatry,* 1 Sam. 15:23.
k *Idol,* 1 Kin. 15:12.

6
l *Spiritual Blindness,* 2 Cor. 4:4.

9
m *God, longsuffering of,* Gen. 2:2.
n *God, mercy of,* Gen. 2:2.
o *Anger of God,* 2 Kin. 13:3.

10
p *Divine Chastisement,* Job 33:19.
q *Afflictions, design of,* Psa. 34:19.
r *Furnace, figurative,* Prov. 17:3.

11
s *God, jealous,* Gen. 2:2.
t *God, glory of,* Gen. 2:2.
1 R. V. profaned?

12
u *God, eternity of,* Gen. 2:2.

13 [v]Mine [w]hand also hath laid the foundation of the [x]earth, and my right hand hath [2]spanned the [y]heavens: *when* I call unto them, they stand up together.[Q]

14 All ye, assemble yourselves, and hear; which among them hath declared these *things*? The LORD hath [z]loved [a]him: he will do his pleasure on [b]Băb′ȳ-lon, and his arm *shall be on* the [c]Chăl-dē′ans̹.

15 I, *even* I, have spoken; yea, I have called [a]him: I have brought him, and he shall make his way prosperous.

16 ¶ Come ye near unto me, hear ye this; I have not spoken in secret from the beginning; from the time that it was, there *am* I: and now the Lord GOD, and his Spirit, hath sent me.[T]

17 Thus saith the LORD, thy [d]Redeemer, the [e]Holy One of Is̹′ra-el; I *am* the LORD thy God which [f,g]teacheth thee to profit, which [h]leadeth thee by the way *that* thou shouldest go.[S T]

18 O that thou hadst hearkened[G] to my commandments! [i]then had thy [j]peace been as a river, and thy [k]righteousness as the waves of the sea:

19 Thy seed also had been as the sand, and the offspring of thy bowels[G] like the [3]gravel thereof; his name should not have been cut off nor destroyed from before me.

20 ¶ Go ye forth of [b]Băb′ȳ-lon, flee ye from the [c]Chăl-dē′ans̹, with a voice of singing declare ye, tell this, utter it *even* to the end of the earth; say ye, The LORD hath redeemed his servant Jā′cob.[Q]

21 And they thirsted not *when* [h]he led them through the deserts: he [l]caused the [m]waters to flow out of the [n]rock for them: he clave[G] the rock also, and the waters gushed out.[S]

**13**
v *God, creator,* Gen. 2:2.
w *God, power of,* Gen. 2:2.
x *Earth, created,* Prov. 8:23.
y *Heavens, created,* Psa. 8:3.
2 R. V. spread out

**14**
z *God, love of,* Gen. 2:2.

a *Cyrus, prophecies concerning,* 2 Chr. 36:22.
b *Babylon, prophecies concerning,* Ezra 5:12.
c *Chaldeans,* Dan. 1:4.

**17**
d *God, savior,* Gen. 2:2.
e *God, holiness of,* Gen. 2:2.
f *God, teacher,* Gen. 2:2.
g *Wisdom, spiritual, from God,* Prov. 2:2.
h *God, guidance of,* Gen. 2:2.

**18**
i *Blessings, contingent upon obedience,* Deut. 11:26.
j *Spiritual Peace, from God,* Gal. 1:3.
k *Righteousness,* Psa. 15:2.

**19**
3 R. V. grains

**21**
l *Miracles,* Luke 23:8.
m *Temporal Blessings, from God,* Psa. 103:2.
n *Meribah,* Ex. 17:7.

22 [o]*There is* no peace, saith the LORD, unto the wicked.

## CHAPTER 49

*The Messiah and the object of his advent. 7 God promises him protection and success. 13 God's unchanging love to Zion. 18 Her glorious enlargement foretold. 24 The enemies of Zion shall be destroyed.*

LISTEN,[T] O isles, unto [a]me; and hearken, ye [b]people, from far; The LORD hath called me from the womb; from the bowels[G] of my mother hath he made mention of my name.[Q]

2 And he hath made my mouth like a sharp sword; in the shadow of his hand hath he hid me, and made me a polished shaft; in his quiver hath he hid me;[T Q]

3[Q] And said unto me, Thou *art* my servant, O Is̹′ra-el, in whom I will be [c]glorified.

4 Then I said, I have laboured in vain, I have spent my strength for nought[G], and in vain: *yet* surely my judgment *is* with the LORD, and my [1]work with my God.[Q]

5 And now, saith the LORD that formed me from the womb *to be* his servant, to bring Jā′cob again to him, [2]Though Is̹′ra-el be not gathered, yet shall I be glorious in the eyes of the LORD, and my God shall be my strength.

6 And he said, It is a light thing that thou shouldest be my servant to raise up the tribes of Jā′cob, and to restore the preserved of Is̹′ra-el: [d,e]I will also give [a]thee [f]for a [g]light to the [b]Gĕn′tīles̹[G], that thou mayest be my salvation unto the end of the earth.[Q T]

7 ¶ Thus [e]saith the LORD, the Redeemer of Is̹′ra-el, *and* his Holy One, to him whom man despiseth, to him whom the nation abhorreth, to a servant of rulers, Kings shall see and arise, princes also shall worship, because of the LORD that is [h]faith-

**22**
o *Wicked, punishment of,* Psa. 73:3.

**1**
a *Jesus, prophecies concerning* (as many learned commentators interpret), vs. 1-12; Matt. 1:21.
b *Gentiles, prophecies of the conversion of,* Acts 10:45.

**3**
c *God, glory of,* v. 26; Gen. 2:2.

**4**
1 R. V. recompence

**5**
2 R. V. and that Israel be gathered unto him: (for I am honourable in the eyes of the Lord, and my God is become my strength:)

**6**
d Isa. 42:6; Luke 2:32; Acts 13:47.
e *Prophecies concerning the Messiah, and their fulfillment,* Gen. 12:3.
f *Jesus, mission of,* Matt. 1:21.
g *Light, figurative,* Matt. 5:14.

**7**
h *God, faithfulness of,* Gen. 2:2.

ful, *and* the [i,j]Holy One of Ĭş′-
ra-el, and he shall choose thee.[T S]
8 Thus saith the LORD, [k]In
an acceptable time have I heard
thee, and in a day of salvation
have I helped thee: and I will
[l]preserve thee, and give thee for
a covenant of the people, to establish the earth, to cause to inherit the desolate heritages;[T Q]
9 [S]That thou mayest say to the
prisoners, Go forth; to them that
*are* in [m]darkness, Shew yourselves. [n]They shall feed in the
ways, and their pastures *shall be*
in all high places.[Q]
10 [n]They shall not hunger nor
thirst; neither shall the heat nor
sun smite them: for [l]he that hath
mercy on them shall lead them,
even by the springs of [o,p]water
shall he guide them.[S Q]
11 And I will make all my
mountains a way, and my highways shall be exalted.
12 Behold, [b]these shall come
from far: and, lo, these from the
north and from the west; and
these from the land of Sī′nim.
13 ¶ [q]Sing, O heavens; and be
[r]joyful, O earth; and break forth
into singing, O mountains: for
[s]the LORD hath [t]comforted his
people, and will have [u]mercy upon his afflicted.[Q]
14 But [v]Zī′ŏn [w,x]said, [3]The
LORD hath forsaken me, and
my Lord hath forgotten me.
15 Can a [y]woman forget her
sucking child, that she should
not have compassion on the son
of her womb? yea, they may forget, yet will [z]I not forget thee.
16 Behold, I have graven[G] [a]thee
upon the palms of *my* hands; thy
walls *are* continually before me.[S]
17 [b]Thy children shall make
haste; thy destroyers and they
that made thee waste shall go
forth of thee.[S]

*i* *God, holiness of,* Gen. 2:2.
*j* *Holiness, attribute of God,* Ex. 39:30.

**8**
*k* 2 Cor. 6:2.
*l* *God, preserver,* Gen. 2:2.

**9**
*m* *Spiritual Blindness,* 2 Cor. 4:4.
*n* *Righteous, promises to,* Psa. 64:10.

**10**
*o* *Water, figurative of salvation,* 1 Kin. 17:10.
*p* *Salvation,* Acts 16:17.

**13**
*q* *Praise,* Psa. 150:1.
*r* *Joy,* Psa. 5:11.
*s* *God, love of,* Gen. 2:2.
*t* *Adversity, consolation in,* Psa. 10:6.
*u* *God, mercy of,* Gen. 2:2.

**14**
*v* *Zion,* 2 Sam. 5:7.
*w* *Doubting,* Rom. 14:23.
*x* *Murmuring,* Num. 14:2.
3 R. V. Jehovah

**15**
*y* *Mother, love of,* 1 Kin. 2:20.
*z* *God, faithfulness of,* Gen. 2:2.

**16**
*a* *Church, God loves,* Matt. 16:18.

**17**
*b* *Adversity, consolation in,* Psa. 10:6.

18 Lift up thine eyes round
about, and behold: all [c]these
gather themselves together, *and*
come to thee. [d]*As* I live, saith
the LORD, thou shalt surely
clothe thee with them all, as with
an ornament, and bind them *on*
*thee,* as a *bride *doeth.*[Q]
19 [e]For [4]thy waste and thy desolate places, and [5]the land of thy
destruction, shall even now be
too narrow by reason of the [c]in-
habitants, and they that swallowed thee up shall be far away.
20 [c,e]The children [6]which thou
shalt have, after thou hast lost
the other, shall say again in thine
ears, The place *is* too strait[G] for
me: give place to me that I may
dwell.
21 [c,e]Then shalt thou say in
thine heart, Who hath begotten
me these, seeing I have lost my
children, and am desolate, a captive, and removing[G] to and fro?
and who hath brought up these?
Behold, I was left alone; these,
where *had* they *been*?
22 [e]Thus saith the Lord GOD,
Behold, I will lift up mine hand
to the [7,c]Gĕn′tīleş,[G] and set up
my [f]standard to the people: and
they shall bring thy sons in *their*
arms, and thy daughters shall be
carried upon *their* shoulders.
23 And kings shall be thy nursing fathers, and their queens thy
nursing mothers: they shall bow[G]
down to thee with *their* face toward the earth, and lick up the
dust of thy feet; and thou shalt
know that I *am* the LORD: for
[g]they shall not be ashamed that
wait for me.[Q]
24 ¶ Shall the prey be taken
from the mighty, or the lawful
captive delivered?[Q]
25 But thus saith the LORD,
Even the captives of the mighty
shall be taken away, and the

**18**
*c* *Gentiles, prophecies of the conversion of,* Acts 10:45.
*d* *Oath, attributed to God,* Num. 5:19.

**19**
*e* *Church, prophecies concerning,* Matt. 16:18.
4 R. V. *inserts* as for
5 R. V. thy land that hath been destroyed, surely now shalt thou be too strait for the inhabitants,

**20**
6 R. V. of thy bereavement shall yet say in

**22**
*f* *Standard, figurative,* Num. 1:52.
7 R. V. nations,

**23**
*g* *Righteous, promises to,* Psa. 64:10.

* **BRIDE.** *Ornaments of,* Isa. 49:18; 61:10; Jer. 2:32; Rev. 21:2. *Presents to,* Gen. 24:53. *Maids of,* Gen. **24:61**; 29:24, 29. **Figurative,** Ezek. 16:8-14; Rev. 19:7, 8; 21:2, 9; 22:17.

prey of the terrible shall be delivered: for I will contend with
him that contendeth with thee,
and I will [h]save thy children.[S]
26 And I will [i]feed them that
oppress thee with their own flesh;
and they shall be drunken with
their own blood, as with sweet
wine: and all flesh shall know
that I the LORD *am* thy [h]Sa-
viour and thy Redeemer, the
mighty One of Jā′cob.[T Q]

## CHAPTER 50

*The sins of Israel the cause of their sufferings, and not God's inability to save.* 4 *God's gifts to the Messiah.* 6 *His patient endurance of reproach.* 10 *An exhortation to trust in God, and not in ourselves.*

THUS saith the LORD, Where
*is* the bill of your [a]mother's
[b]divorcement, whom [c]I have
[d]put away? or which of my creditors *is it* to whom I have sold
you? Behold, for your iniquities[G]
have ye sold yourselves, and for
your transgressions[G] is your
mother put away.
2 Wherefore, when I came, *was*
*there* no man? when I called,
*was there* none to answer? Is
my hand shortened at all, that it
cannot [e]redeem? or have I no
[f]power to deliver? behold, at
my rebuke I dry up the sea, I
make the rivers a wilderness:
their fish stinketh, because *there*
*is* no water, and dieth for thirst.[S]
3 I clothe the heavens with
blackness, and I make sackcloth
their covering.
4 ¶ The Lord GOD hath given
[g]me the tongue of [1]the [h]learned,
that I should know how to [i]speak
a word in season to *him that is*
weary: he wakeneth morning by
morning, he wakeneth mine ear
to hear as [2]the learned.
5 The Lord GOD hath opened
[g]mine ear, and I was not rebellious, neither turned away back.
6 [j,k]I gave my back to the
*smiters[G], and my cheeks to them
that plucked off the hair: I hid
not my face from shame and
[l]spitting.[Q]
7[S]For the Lord GOD will help
me; therefore shall I not be confounded: therefore have I [†]set
my face like a flint, and I know
that I shall not be ashamed.[G]
8 *He is* near that justifieth me;
who will contend with me? let us
stand together: who *is* mine adversary? let him come near to
me.[S Q]
9 Behold, the Lord GOD will
help me; who *is* he *that* shall
condemn me? lo, they all shall
wax[G] old as a garment; the moth
shall eat them up.[S]
10 ¶ Who *is* among you that
[m]feareth the LORD, that [3]obey-
eth the voice of his servant, that
walketh *in* [n,o]darkness, and hath
no [h]light? [p]let him trust in the
name of the LORD, and stay[G]
upon his God.
11 Behold, all ye that kindle
a fire, that [q]compass *yourselves*

**25** h *God, preserver,* Gen. 2:2.

**26** i *Judgments,* Ex. 6:6.

**1** a *Church, backslidden,* Matt. 16:18.
b *Divorce, figurative,* Matt. 19:7.
c *Backsliders, corrective judgments upon,* Jer. 3:22.
d *Divine Chastisement,* Job 33:19.

**2** e *God, savior,* Gen. 2:2.
f *God, power of,* Gen. 2:2.

**4** g *Jesus, prophecies concerning,* Matt. 1:21.
h *Wisdom, spiritual,* Prov. 2:2.
i *Adversity, consolation in,* vs. 7–10; Psa. 10:6.
1 R. V. them that are taught,
2 R. V. they that are taught.

**6** j *Prophecies concerning the Messiah, and their fulfillment,* Gen. 12:3.
k *Jesus, sufferings of, foretold,* Matt. 1:21.
l *Spitting,* Num. 12:14.

**10** m *Fear of God,* Acts 9:31.
n *Darkness, figurative,* Gen. 1:2.
o *Spiritual Blindness,* 2 Cor. 4:4.
p *Faith, enjoined,* Mark 11:22.
3 R. V. obeyeth the voice of his servant? he that walketh in darkness, and hath no light,

**11** q *Delusion,* 2 Thess. 2:11.

* **SMITING AND SCOURGING OF JESUS,** Isa. 50:6; Matt. 20:19; 26:67, 68; 27:26, 30; Mark 10:34; 15:15, 19; Luke 22:63, 64; 23:16; John 18:22; 19:1.

† **DECISION. Injunctions concerning:** *Choosing life,* Deut. 30:19. *Cleaving unto the Lord,* Josh. 23:8; Acts 11:23. *Serving the Lord,* Josh. 24:15; 1 Sam. 12:20; 1 Kin. 18:21; Isa. 50:7; Matt. 6:24; 8:21, 22; Luke 9:59–62; 16:13; 1 Cor. 15:58. *Walking righteously,* Josh. 1:7; 2 Chr. 19:11; Prov. 4:25–27; Matt. 4:17; 2 Thess. 3:13; 1 Tim. 6:11–14; Heb. 12:1; 1 Pet. 1:13; 2 Pet. 1:10. *Abiding in Christ,* John 15: 4, 5, 7, 9; 1 John 2:24, 28.

*Steadfastness, in obedience,* John 8:31; 1 Cor. 15:58; Col. 2:6, 7; 2 Thess. 2:15, 17; 2 Pet. 3:17, 18; 2 John 8; *in grace,* Acts 13:43; 2 Tim. 2:1, 3; *in faith,* Acts 14:22; 1 Cor. 16:13; Phil. 1:27; Col. 1:23; Heb. 3:6–8, 14; 4:14; 10:23, 35; 1 Pet. 5:8, 9; Jude 20, 21; *in Christian liberty,* Gal. 5; *in the Lord,* Phil. 4:1; *in holiness,* 1 Thess. 3:8, 13; *in sound doctrine,* Eph. 4:14; 2 Tim. 1:13, 14; 3:14; Tit. 1:7, 9; Heb. 2:1; 13: 9, 13.

**Instances of:** *Abel,* Heb. 11:4. *Enoch,* Heb. 11:5, 6. *Noah,* Heb. 11:7. *Abraham,* Heb. 11:8, 17–19. *Jacob,* Gen. 28:20–22. *Joseph,* Gen. 39:9. *Moses,* Num. 12:7; Heb. 3:5; 11:24–27. *Israelites,* Ex. 19:7, 8; 24:3, 7; Deut. 4:4; 5:27; 26:17; Josh. 22:34; 24:21–25; 1 Kin. 19:18; 2 Kin. 11:17; 2 Chr. 11:16; 13:10, 11; 15:12, 15; 23:16; 29:10; Ezra 10: 3–44; Neh. 9:38; 10:28–31; Jer. 34:15; 42:5, 6; 50:5; Hos. 11:12. *Levites,* Ex. 32:26. *Caleb,* Num. 14:6–10, 24; Deut. 1:36; Josh. 14:14. *Balaam,* Num. 22:15–18; 24:13. *Phinehas,* Num. 25:7–13. *Joshua,* 24:15. *Gideon,* Judg. 6:25–28. *Ruth,* Ruth 1:16. *Saul,* 1 Sam. 11:4–7. *David,* 1 Sam. 17:32–37; 2 Sam. 22:22–24. *Psalmist,* Psa. 17:3; 26:6, 11; 27:3–8; 40:9, 10; 56:12; 57:7, 8; 71:17; 86:11; 101:2, 3; 108: 1; 116:9, 13, 14, 18; 119:8, 30, 31, 38, 44–46, 57, 94, 106, 115, 125, 145, 146. *A prophet of Judah,* 1 Kin. 13:8–10. *Elijah,* 1 Kin. 18:22. *Jehoshaphat,* 1 Kin. 22:7, 8; 2 Chr. 18:6, 7. *Micaiah,* 1 Kin. 22:13, 14; 2 Chr. 18:12, 13. *Naaman,* 2 Kin. 5:13–17. *Hezekiah,* 2 Kin. 18:6; 2 Chr. 15:17. *Josiah,* 2 Kin. 22:2; 23:3, 25; 2 Chr. 34:31. *Nehemiah,* Neh. 6:11, with chapters 2, 4, 5, 6. *Esther,* Esth. 4:16. *Job,* Job 2:9, 10; *Daniel,* Dan. 1:8. *The three Hebrews,* Dan. 3:16–18; 23:11, 12. *Matthew,* Matt. 9:9. *Joseph,* Mark 15:43. *Nathanael,* John 1:49. *Martha,* John 11:27. *Disciples,* Luke 18:28; John 6:68, 69; Acts 2:42. *Paul,* Acts 9:29; Rom. 1:16; 8:38, 39; Phil. 1:20, 21; 2 Tim. 4:7, 8. *Church, of Ephesus,* Rev. 2:2, 3; *of Sardis,* Rev. 3:4, 8, 10. *Saints,* Rev. 14:4.

See footnote, CHARACTER, Phil. 2:15.

r *Wicked, as devisers of mischief,* Psa. 7:3.
s *Wicked, punishment of,* Psa. 73:3.

1
a *Righteous, described,* Psa. 64:10.
b *Seekers,* Isa. 55:6.

2
c *Abraham, divine call of,* Gen. 17:5.
d *Sarah,* Gen. 17:15.
e *God, providence of,* Gen. 2:2.
f *Call, personal,* Phil. 3:14.
g *Temporal Blessings, from God,* Psa. 103:2.
1 R. V. when he was but one I called him,

3
h *Zion, restoration of,* 2 Sam. 5:7.
i *Church, prophecies concerning its prosperity,* vs. 3–8; Matt. 16:18.
j *Joy,* Psa. 5:11.
k *Praise,* Psa. 150:1.

4
l *Gospel, prophecies relating to,* Mark 13:10.

5
m *Salvation,* Acts 16:17.

6
n *Heavens, destruction of,* Psa. 8:3.
o *Earth, destruction of,* Prov. 8:23.
p *God, faithfulness of,* Gen. 2:2.

about with [r]sparks: walk in the light of your fire, and in the sparks *that* ye have kindled. This shall ye have of mine hand; [s]ye shall lie down in sorrow.[s]

## CHAPTER 51

*Comfort promised to Zion. 4 God's salvation is near. 7 The destruction of Zion's enemies foretold. 9 The people of God pray for his aid as of old. 12 His promise to them. 17 The afflictions of Jerusalem bewailed, 21 and her deliverance promised.*

HEARKEN to me, ye that [a]follow after righteousness, [b]ye that [a]seek the LORD: look unto the rock *whence* ye are hewn, and to the hole of the pit *whence* ye are digged.[s]

2 Look unto [c]Ā'brā-hăm your father, and unto [d]Sā'rah *that* bare you: for [1,e]I [f]called him alone, and blessed him, and [g]increased him.

3 For the LORD shall comfort [h,i]Zī'ŏn: he will comfort all her waste places; and he will make her wilderness like *Ē'dĕn, and her desert like the garden of the LORD; [j]joy and gladness shall be found therein, [k]thanksgiving, and the voice of melody.

4 ¶ Hearken unto me, my [i]people; and give ear unto me, O my nation: for a [l]law shall proceed from me, and I will make my judgment[c] to rest for a light of the people.

5 My[s] righteousness *is* near; my [m]salvation is gone forth, and mine arms shall judge the people; the isles shall wait upon me, and on mine arm shall they trust.

6 Lift up your eyes to the [n]heavens, and look upon the earth beneath: for the heavens shall vanish away like smoke, and the [o]earth shall wax[c] old like a garment, and they that dwell therein shall die in like manner: but [p]my [m]salvation shall be for ever, and [p]my righteousness shall not be abolished.

7 ¶ Hearken unto me, ye that [a,q]know [r]righteousness, the people [a]in whose heart *is* my [s]law; [t]fear ye not the reproach of men, neither be ye afraid of their revilings.

8 For [u]the moth shall eat [v]them up like a garment, and the worm shall eat them like wool: but my [w]righteousness shall be for ever, and my [m]salvation from generation to generation.[s]

9 ¶ [x,y]Awake, awake, put on strength, O arm of the LORD; awake, as in the ancient days, in the generations of old. *Art* thou not it that [2]hath cut [z]Rā'hăb, *and* wounded the dragon?

10 *Art* thou not it [y]which hath dried the [a]sea, the waters of the great deep; that hath made the depths of the sea a way for the ransomed to [b]pass over? [s]

11 Therefore [c,d]the redeemed of the LORD shall return, and come with singing unto Zī'ŏn; and everlasting [e]joy *shall be* upon their head: [c,d]they shall obtain gladness and joy; *and* [c,d]sorrow and mourning shall flee away.

12 I, *even* I, *am* he that [f]comforteth you: [g]who *art* thou, that thou shouldest be afraid of a man *that* [h]shall die, and of the son of man *which* shall be made *as* grass;

13 And forgettest the [i]LORD [j]thy maker, that hath stretched forth the heavens, and laid the foundations of the earth; and hast feared continually every day because of the fury of the oppressor, as if he were ready to destroy? and where *is* the fury of the oppressor?

14 The [k]captive exile [3]hasteneth that he may be loosed, and that he should not die in the pit, nor that his bread should fail.

15 But I *am* the [l]LORD thy

7
q *Wisdom, spiritual,* Prov. 2:2.
r *Righteousness,* Psa. 15:2.
s *Word of God,* Psa. 119:9.
t *Courage, enjoined,* Deut. 31:7.

8
u *Judgments,* Ex. 6:6.
v *Wicked, punishment of,* Psa. 73:3.
w *God, righteousness of,* Gen. 2:2.

9
x *Adversity, prayer in,* Psa. 10:6.
y *God, preserver,* Gen. 2:2.
z Or, *Egypt,* Gen. 41:8.
2 Am. R. V. cut Rahab in pieces, that pierced the monster?

10
a *Red Sea, divided,* Ex. 10:19.
b *Israel, passed through the Red Sea,* Ex. 4:22.

11
c *Promise, to the righteous,* 2 Cor. 1:20.
d *Righteous, promises to,* Psa. 64:10.
e *Joy,* Psa. 5:11.

12
f *Adversity, consolation in,* Psa. 10:6.
g *Cowardice, rebuked,* Lev. 26:36.
h *Death, inevitable,* Num. 23:10.

13
i *God, creator,* Gen. 2:2.
j *Man, created,* Job 4:17.

14
k *Captive,* 1 Sam. 30:3.
3 R. V. shall speedily be loosed; and he shall not die and go down into the pit, neither shall his bread fail.

15
l *God, providence of,* Gen. 2:2.

***EDEN.** *The garden of,* Gen. 2:8–17; 3:23, 24; 4:16; Isa. 51:3; Ezek. 28:13; 31:9, 16, 18; 36:35; Joel 2:3.

God, that divided the [a]sea, whose waves roared: The LORD of hosts *is* his name.

16 And I have [m]put my words in thy mouth, and [n]I have [o]covered thee in the shadow of mine hand, that I may plant[G] the heavens, and lay the foundations of the earth, and [p]say unto Zī′ŏn, Thou *art* my people.[Q]

17 ¶ Awake, awake, stand up, O Jē-ru̧′sā-lĕm, which hast drunk at the hand of the LORD the [q,r]cup of his [s]fury; thou hast drunken the [4]dregs of the cup of trembling, *and* wrung *them* out.[Q]

18 *There is* none to guide her among all the sons *whom* she hath brought forth; neither *is there any* that taketh her by the hand of all the sons *that* she hath brought up.

19 These two *things* are come unto thee; who shall be sorry for thee? [r]desolation, and [r]destruction, and the [r,t]famine, and the [r,u]sword: by whom shall I comfort thee?

20 Thy sons have fainted, they lie at the head of all the streets, as [5]a wild bull in a [†]net: they are full of the fury of the LORD, the [v]rebuke of thy God.

21 ¶ Therefore hear now this, thou afflicted, and [w]drunken, but not with wine:

22 Thus saith thy Lord the LORD, and thy God *that* pleadeth the cause of his people, Behold, I have taken out of thine hand the [q,r]cup of [6]trembling, *even* the dregs of the cup of my [s]fury; thou shalt no more drink it again:

23 But I will put it into the hand of them that afflict thee; which have said to thy soul, Bow down, that we may go over: and thou hast laid thy body as the ground, and as the street, to them that went over.

16

*m Inspiration*, Job 32:8.

*n God, love of*, Gen. 2:2.

*o God, preserver*, Gen. 2:2.

*p Church, God loves*, Matt. 16:18.

17

*q Cup, figurative*, Matt. 20:22.

*r Judgments*, Ex. 6:6.

*s Anger of God*, 2 Kin. 13:3.

4 R. V. bowl of the cup of staggering, and drained it.

19

*t Famine*, 2 Kin. 8:1.

*u War, as a judgment*, Judg. 3:2.

20

*v Divine Chastisement*, Job 33:19.

5 R. V. an antelope

21

*w Drunkenness, figurative*, vs. 21–23; Luke 21:34.

22

6 R. V. staggering, even the bowl of

## CHAPTER 52

*Zion exhorted to awake and prepare for her deliverance from captivity. 7 The herald of this event seen upon the mountains. 9 The waste places of Jerusalem called upon to rejoice. 11 The people commanded to depart out of bondage. 13 The humiliation and exaltation of the Messiah.*

AWAKE, awake; [a]put on thy strength, O Zī′ŏn; put on thy beautiful garments, O [b]Jē-ru̧′sā-lĕm, the holy city: for henceforth there shall no more come into thee the uncircumcised[G] and the unclean.[Q]

2 Shake thyself from the dust; arise, *and* sit down, O Jē-ru̧′sā-lĕm: loose thyself from the bands of thy neck, O captive daughter of Zī′ŏn.

3 For thus saith the LORD, Ye have sold yourselves for nought[G]; and ye shall be redeemed without money.[Q]

4 For thus saith the Lord GOD, My [c]people went down aforetime[G] into [d]Ē′ġy̆pt to sojourn[G] there; and the Ăs-sy̆r′ĭ-an [e]oppressed them without cause.

5 Now therefore, what have I here, saith the LORD, that my people is taken away for nought[G]? [f]they that rule over them [1]make them to howl, saith the LORD; and [g]my name continually every day *is* [h,i]blasphemed[G].[Q]

6 Therefore [j]my people shall know[G] my name: therefore [j]*they shall know* in that day that [k]I *am* he that doth speak: behold, *it is* I.

7 ¶ [l]How [m]beautiful upon the mountains are the feet of him that [n]bringeth [o]good tidings, that publisheth [p]peace; that bringeth good tidings of good, that publisheth salvation; that saith unto Zī′ŏn, Thy [k]God reigneth![S Q]

1

*a Church, prophecies concerning its prosperity*, vs. 1–15; Matt. 16:18.

*b Jerusalem*, Judg. 19:10.

4

*c Israel, in Egypt*, Ex. 4:22.

*d Egypt*, Gen. 41:8.

*e Oppression*, Eccl. 5:8.

5

*f Rulers, wicked*, Ex. 18:21.

*g* Rom. 2:24.

*h Blasphemy*, 2 Sam. 12:14.

*i Profanation, of God's name*, Lev. 22:32.

1 R. V. do howl.

6

*j Adversity, design of*, Psa. 10:6.

*k God, sovereign*, Gen. 2:2.

7

*l* Rom. 10:15.

*m Beauty, spiritual*, Psa. 45:11.

*n Minister, duties of*, Rom. 15:16.

*o Gospel, prophecies concerning*, Mark 13:10.

*p Spiritual Peace*, Gal. 1:3.

† **NET**, Eccl. 9:12; Isa. 19:8; Ezek. 26:5, 14; 47:10. *Of checker work*, 1 Kin. 7:17. *Hidden in a pit*, Psa. 35:7, 8. *Set, for birds*, Prov. 1:17; *for wild animals*, Isa. 51:20. *Fish caught in*, Matt. 4:18–21; 13:47; Luke 5:4; John 21:6–11. See footnote, SNARE, Amos 3:5. **Figurative**, Job 18:8; 19:6; Psa. 9:15; 10:9; 25:15; 31:4; 35:7, 8; 57:6; 66:11; 140:5; 141:10; Prov. 12:12; 29:5; Eccl. 7:26; Hos. 7:12.

**8**

*q* *Watchman,* 2 Sam. 18:24.

*r* *Praise,* Psa. 150:1.

2 R. V. returneth to Zion.

**9**

*s* *Joy,* Psa. 5:11.

*t* *God, savior,* Gen. 2:2.

**10**

*u* *God, holiness of,* Gen. 2:2.

*v* *God, providence of,* Gen. 2:2.

**11**

*w* 2 Cor. 6:17.

*x* *Fellowship, with the wicked forbidden,* 1 Cor. 1:9.

*y* *Holiness, enjoined,* Ex. 39:30.

**12**

*z* *God, guidance of,* Gen. 2:2.

*a* *God, preserver,* Gen. 2:2.

**13**

*b* *Jesus, prophecies concerning,* vs. 13–15; Matt. 1:21.

**14**

*c* *Jesus, sufferings of, foretold,* Matt. 1:21.

*d* *Persecution, of Jesus,* John 15:20.

**15**

*e* Rom. 15:21.

**1**

*a* John 12:38; Rom. 10:16.

*b* *Spiritual Blindness, manifested in unbelief,* 2 Cor. 4:4.

*c* *Minister, discouragements of,* Rom. 15:16.

**2**

*d* *Jesus, prophecies concerning,* vs. 2–12; Matt. 1:21.

*e* *Prophecies concerning the Messiah, and their fulfillment,* Gen. 12:3.

8 Thy [q]watchmen shall [r]lift up the voice; with the voice together shall they sing: for they shall see eye to eye, when the LORD [2]shall bring again Zī'ŏn.

9 Break forth into [s]joy, sing together, ye waste places of Jē-ru̥'-să-lĕm: for the LORD hath comforted his people, he hath [t]redeemed Jē-ru̥'să-lĕm.[Q]

10 The LORD hath made[G] bare his [u]holy arm in the eyes of all the nations; and all the ends of the earth shall see the [v]salvation of our God.[S Q]

11 ¶ [w,x]Depart ye, depart ye, go ye out from thence,[G] touch no unclean *thing*; go ye out of the midst of her; [y]be ye clean, that bear the vessels of the LORD.[S Q]

12 For ye shall not go out with haste, nor go by flight: for the LORD will [z]go before you; and the God of Iș'ra-el *will be* your [a]rereward.[G]

13 ¶ Behold, my [b]servant shall deal prudently, he shall be exalted and extolled, and be very high.[T Q]

14 As many were astonied[G] at thee; [c,d]his visage was so marred more than any man, and his form more than the sons of men:[Q]

15 [b]So shall he sprinkle[G] many nations; the kings shall shut their mouths at him: [e]for *that* which had not been told them shall they see; and *that* which they had not heard shall they consider.[Q]

## CHAPTER 53

*The Messiah despised and rejected. 4 His sufferings in our behalf. 7 His meekness, humiliation, and death. 10 The benefits of his passion.*

[a,b,c]WHO[T] hath believed our report? and to whom is the arm of the LORD revealed?[Q S]

2 For [d,e]he shall grow up before him as a tender plant, and as a root out of a dry ground: he hath no form nor comeliness;[G] and when we shall see him, *there* is no beauty that we should desire him.[Q]

3 [d,e]He is [f]despised and [g]rejected of men; a man of [h]sorrows, and acquainted with grief: and [1]we hid as it were *our* faces from him; he was despised, and we [i]esteemed[G] him not.[Q]

4 ¶ [j]Surely [d,e,h]he hath [k,l]borne our griefs, and [k,l]carried our sorrows: yet we did esteem[G] him [m]stricken,[G] smitten of God, and afflicted.[Q]

5[Q] But [d,e,h]he *was* [l]wounded [n]for our transgressions, *he was* [l]bruised [n]for our iniquities: the chastisement of our [o]peace *was* upon him; and with his stripes[G] we are healed.[S]

6 [p]All we like sheep have [q]gone astray; we have turned every one to his own way; and the LORD hath laid on him the iniquity of us all.[S T Q]

7 He was [f,h]oppressed, and he was afflicted, yet he [r,s]opened not his mouth: [t]he is brought as a lamb to the slaughter, and as a sheep before her shearers is dumb, so he openeth not his mouth.[Q]

8 [2,f]He was taken from prison and from judgment: and who shall declare his generation? for he was [u]cut off out of the land of the living: [n,v]for the transgression of my people was he stricken.[G Q]

9 And [3,d,e]he made his grave with the wicked, and with the rich in his death; [4]because [w]he had done no violence, [x]neither *was any* [y]deceit in his mouth.[Q]

10 Yet it pleased the LORD to bruise him; he hath put *him* to grief: when thou shalt make his soul an [n,u]offering for sin, he shall see *his* seed, he shall prolong *his* days, and the pleasure of the LORD shall prosper in his hand.[T]

11 He shall see of the travail[G] of his soul, *and* shall be satisfied: by

**3**

*f* *Persecution, of Jesus,* vs. 3–10; John 15:20.

*g* *Jesus, rejected,* Matt. 1:21.

*h* *Jesus, sufferings of,* vs. 3–12; Matt. 1:21.

*i* *Unbelievers,* 1 Cor. 6:6.

1 R. V. as one from whom men hide their face he

**4**

*j* Matt. 8:17; 1 Pet. 2:24.

*k* *Jesus, compassion of,* Matt. 1:21.

*l* *Vicarious Sufferings,* Rom. 9:3.

*m* *Divine Chastisement,* Job 33:19.

**5**

*n* *Atonement, by Jesus,* Lev. 17:11.

*o* *Spiritual Peace,* Gal. 1:3.

**6**

*p* 1 Pet. 2:25.

*q* *Depravity, universal,* Job 15:14.

**7**

*r* *Jesus, meekness of,* Matt. 1:21.

*s* *Patience, of Jesus,* Luke 8:15.

*t* Acts 8:32, 33.

**8**

*u* *Jesus, death of,* Matt. 1:21.

*v* *Jesus, design of his death,* Matt. 1:21.

2 Am. R. V. By oppression and judgment he was taken away; and as for his generation, who among them considered that he was cut off out of the land of the living for the transgression of my people to whom the stroke was due?

**9**

*w* 1 Pet. 2:22.

*x* *Jesus, holiness of,* Matt. 1:21.

*y* *Deceit,* Psa. 36:3.

3 R. V. they

4 R. V. although

his knowledge shall my righteous servant [z]justify many; for [a,b]he shall [c,d]bear their iniquities.[S T Q]

12 Therefore will I divide him *a portion* with the great, and he shall divide the spoil with the strong; because [e]he hath poured out his soul unto death: and [f]he was numbered with the transgressors; and [a]he [b,c,d]bare the sin of many, and made intercession for the transgressors.[T Q]

## CHAPTER 54

*God comforts Zion with the promise of great enlargement. 7 His covenant with her firm and immovable. 11 Her future prosperity and glory described. 15 A promise of safety from her enemies.*

[a,b]SING, O [c,d]barren, thou *that* didst not bear; break forth into singing, and cry aloud, thou *that* didst not travail[C] with child: [e]for more *are* the children of the desolate than the children of the married wife, saith the LORD.[Q]

2 Enlarge the place of thy tent, and let them stretch forth the curtains of thine habitations: spare not, lengthen thy cords, and strengthen thy stakes;

3 For [d]thou shalt [1]break forth on the right hand and on the left; and thy seed shall [2]inherit the [e]Gĕn′tīleș,[C] and make the desolate cities to be inhabited.

4 Fear not; for thou shalt not be ashamed: neither be thou confounded[C]; for thou shalt not be put to shame: for thou shalt forget the shame of thy youth, and shalt not remember the reproach of thy widowhood any more.

5 [f]For thy [g]Maker *is* thine [h]husband; the LORD of hosts *is* his name; and thy [i]Redeemer the [j]Holy One of Iș′ra-el; The [k]God of the whole earth shall he be called.[T]

6 For [l]the LORD hath called thee as a [3]woman forsaken and grieved in spirit, and a wife of youth, when [4]thou wast refused, saith thy God.

7 For[T] a small moment have I forsaken thee; but with great [l]mercies will I gather thee.[S]

8 In [5]a little [m]wrath I hid my face from thee for a moment; but [f]with everlasting kindness will I have [l]mercy on thee, saith the LORD thy [i]Redeemer.[S T]

9 For this *is as* the [n]waters of [o]Nō′ah unto me: for [p]*as* I have [q]sworn that the waters of Nō′ah should no more go over the earth; [p]so have I sworn that I would not be wroth[C] with thee, nor rebuke thee.[S]

10 For the mountains shall depart, and the hills be removed; but [f]my kindness shall not depart from thee, [p]neither shall the [r]covenant of my [s]peace be removed, saith the LORD that hath [l]mercy on thee.[S T]

11 ¶[Q]O thou [c]afflicted, tossed with tempest, *and* not comforted, behold, I will lay thy stones with fair colours, and lay thy foundations with [t,u]sapphires.

12 And I will make thy [6]windows of [u,v]agates, and thy gates of [*,u]carbuncles, and all thy borders of pleasant stones.[Q]

13 And [w]all thy children *shall be* [x,y]taught of the LORD; and great *shall be* the [s]peace of thy children.[Q]

14 [z]In righteousness shalt thou be established: thou shalt be far from oppression; for thou shalt not fear: and from terror; for it shall not come near thee.[S]

15 Behold, they shall surely gather together, *but* not by me: whosoever shall gather together against thee shall fall for thy sake.[S]

16 Behold, [a]I have created the [†]smith that bloweth the coals in

**11**
z *Justification,* Rom. 4:25.
a *Jesus, design of his death,* Matt. 1:21.
b *Atonement, by Jesus,* Lev. 17:11.
c *Substitution,* Lev. 1:4.
d *Vicarious Sufferings,* Rom. 9:3.

**12**
e *Jesus, death of,* Matt. 1:21.
f Luke 22:37.

**1**
a *Jesus, kingdom of, prophecies concerning,* vs. 2, 3; Matt. 1:21.
b Gal. 4:27.
c *Church, backslidden,* Matt. 16:18.
d *Church, prophecies concerning its universality,* vs. 1–5; Matt. 16:18.
e *Gentiles, prophecies of the conversion of,* Acts 10:45.

**3**
1 R. V. spread abroad on
2 R. V. possess the nations,

**5**
f *Church, God loves,* Matt. 1:21.
g *God, creator,* Gen. 2:2.
h *Husband, figurative,* Num. 30:6.
i *God, savior,* Gen. 2:2.
j *God, holiness of,* Gen. 2:2.
k *God, sovereign,* Gen. 2:2.

**6**
3 R. V. wife
4 R. V. she is cast off,

**7**
l *God, mercy of,* Gen. 2:2.

**8**
m *Anger of God,* 2 Kin. 13:3.
5 R. V. overflowing

**9**
n *Flood,* Gen. 6:17.
o *Noah,* Gen. 5:29.
p *God, faithfulness of,* Gen. 2:2.
q *Oath, attributed to God,* Num. 5:19.

**10**
r *Covenant, of God with men,* Deut. 29:1.
s *Spiritual Peace,* Gal. 1:3.

**11**
t *Sapphire,* Job 28:6.
u *Precious Stones, figurative,* Ex. 39:10.

**12**
v *Agate,* Ex. 28:19.
6 R. V. pinnacles of rubies,

**13**
w John 6:45.
x *Instruction, in religion,* Prov. 23:23.
y *God, teacher,* Gen. 2:2.

**14**
z *Church, prophecies concerning its prosperity,* Matt. 16:18.

**16**
a *God, providence of,* Gen. 2:2.

* **CARBUNCLE,** possibly emerald. *A precious stone,* Isa. 54:12; Ezek. 28:13. *One of the precious stones set in breastplate,* Ex. 28:17; 39:10.

† **SMITH,** a worker in metals. *Tubal-cain,* Gen. 4:22. *Bezaleel,* Ex. 31:1–9. *The Philistines,* 1 Sam. 13:19. *Jewish, carried captive to Babylon,* 2 Kin. 24:14; Jer. 24:1. *The manufacturers of idols,* Isa. 41:7; 44:12. *Genius of, from God,* Ex. 31:3–5; 35:30–35; Isa. 54:16.

the fire, and that bringeth forth an instrument for his work; and I have created the waster to destroy.[Q]

17 [b]No weapon that is formed against thee shall prosper; and every tongue *that* shall rise against thee in judgment thou shalt condemn. This *is* the heritage of the [c]servants of the LORD, and their [d]righteousness *is* of me, saith the LORD.[S]

## CHAPTER 55

*A gracious invitation to accept God's abundant mercy in the Messiah. 10 God's word shall prosper.*

HO, every one that [a]thirsteth, [b]come ye to the [c,d]waters, and he that hath no money; [e]come ye, buy, and eat; yea, come, buy [f]wine and [g]milk without money and without price.[Q]

2 Wherefore[G] do ye spend money for *that which is* not bread? and your labour for *that which* satisfieth not? hearken [h]diligently unto me, and eat ye *that which is* good, and let your soul [i]delight itself in fatness.

3 Incline your ear, and come unto me: hear, and your soul shall live; and I [j]will make an everlasting [k]covenant with you, *even* [l]the sure[G] mercies[Q] of Dā′vid.[T]

4[T] Behold, I have given [m]him *for* [n]a witness to the [1]people, [n]a leader and commander to the people.[S Q]

5 Behold, [o,p]thou shalt call a [q]nation *that* thou knowest not, and [q]nations *that* knew not thee shall run unto thee because of the LORD thy God, and for the Holy One of Iș′ra-el; for he hath glorified thee.

17
b *Church, prophecies concerning its prosperity,* Matt. 16:18.
c *Righteous, described,* Psa. 64:10.
d *Spiritual Blessings, from God,* Eph. 1:3.

1
a *Spiritual Desire,* Psa. 42:1.
b *Call, to repentance,* Phil. 3:14.
c *Salvation,* vs. 1–3, 6, 7; Acts 16:17.
d *Water, figurative,* 1 Kin. 17:10.
e *Promise, or ground of assurance, to penitents,* vs. 1–3, 7; 2 Cor. 1:20.
f *Wine, figurative,* Prov. 23:31.
g *Milk, figurative,* Job 10:10.

2
h *Diligence,* Rom. 12:8.
i *Spiritual Peace,* Gal. 1:3.

3
j *Prophecies concerning the Messiah, and their fulfillment,* Gen. 12:3.
k *Covenant, of God with men,* Deut. 29:1.
l Acts 13:34.

4
m *Jesus, prophecies concerning,* Matt. 1:21.
n *Church, Christ head of,* Matt. 16:18.
1 R. V. peoples,

5
o *Church, prophecies concerning its prosperity,* Matt. 16:18.
p *Jesus, kingdom of, prophecies concerning,* vs. 10–13; Matt. 1:21.
q *Gentiles, prophecies of the conversion of,* Acts 10:45.

6 ¶ *,[r,s]Seek ye the LORD [t]while he may be found, call ye upon him while he is near:[Q]

7 [s]Let the wicked forsake his way, and the unrighteous man his thoughts: and [r]let him return unto the LORD, and he will have [t]mercy upon him; and to our God, for [u]he will abundantly pardon.[S]

8 ¶[S] For [v,w]my thoughts *are* not your thoughts, neither *are* your ways my ways, saith the LORD.[Q]

9 For *as* the heavens are higher than the earth, so are my ways higher than your ways, and my thoughts than your thoughts.[S]

10 [T x]For as the [y]rain cometh down, and the snow from heaven, and returneth not thither,[C] but watereth the earth, and maketh it bring forth and bud, that it may give seed to the sower, and bread to the eater:[S Q]

11 So shall my [z]word be that goeth forth out of my mouth: it shall not return unto me void,[G] but it shall accomplish that which I please, and it shall prosper *in the thing* whereto I sent it.[S T]

12 For [a]ye shall go out with [b,c]joy, and be led forth with [c,d]peace: the mountains and the hills shall break forth before you into singing, and all the trees of the field shall clap *their* hands.

13 Instead of the [e]thorn shall come up the [c,f]fir tree, and instead of the [g]brier shall come up the [c,h]myrtle tree: and it shall be to the LORD for a name, for an everlasting sign *that* shall not be cut off.

6
r *Commandment, enjoining seeking the Lord,* Deut. 8:2.
s *Repentance, enjoined,* Mark 1:4.
t *God, mercy of,* Gen. 2:2.

7
u *Promise, to penitents,* 2 Cor. 1:20.

8
v *God, incomprehensible,* Gen. 2:2.
w *God, unsearchable,* Gen. 2:2.

10
x *God, providence of,* Gen. 2:2.
y *Temporal Blessings, from God,* Psa. 103:2.

11
z *Word of God,* Psa. 119:9.

12
a *Church, prophecies concerning its prosperity,* Matt. 16:18.
b *Joy,* Psa. 5:11.
c *Righteousness, fruits of,* Psa. 15:2.
d *Spiritual Peace,* Gal. 1:3.

13
e *Thorn, figurative,* Hos. 2:6.
f *Fir Tree, figurative,* 2 Sam. 6:5.
g Isa. 5:6; Ezek. 2:6; 28:24.
h Isa. 41:19; Neh. 8:15.

* **SEEKERS,** Gen. 49:18; 2 Chr. 11:16; 15:12, 13; Psa. 14:2; Acts 17:27. *Must have faith,* Heb. 11:6.
Seeking God: *Enjoined,* 1 Chr. 16:11; 22:19; Psa. 105:4; Isa. 26:8, 9; Hos. 10:12; Joel 2:12, 13; Amos 5:4–6, 8, 14; Zeph. 2:3; Jas. 4:8; Rev. 22:17. *A fruit of adversity,* Psa. 78:34; 83:16; Hos. 5:15.
*By incorrigible sinners, vain,* Amos 8:12; Luke 13:24.
**Promises to,** John 6:37. *Of finding God,* Deut. 4:29; 1 Chr. 28:9; 2 Chr. 15:2; Prov. 8:17, 34, 35; Isa. 45:19, 22; Jer. 29:13. *Of pardon,* Isa. 55:6, 7; Acts 2:21. *Of providential care,* 2 Chr. 26:5; Ezra 8:22; Psa. 34:4; 145:19; Matt. 6:33. *Of spiritual blessings,* Job 8:5, 6; Psa. 9:10; 22:26; 24:3–6; 40:1–4; 63:1–8; 70:4, 5; 119:2; 145:18, 19; Prov. 2:3–5; 28:5; Isa. 45:19, 22; 55:6, 7; Lam. 3:25, 26, 41; Matt. 5:6; 6:33; 7:7–11; Luke 6:21; 11:9–13; Acts 2:21; Rom. 10:12, 13; Heb. 7:25; Rev. 3:20; 21:6.
**Instances of:** *Asa,* 2 Chr. 14:7. *Uzziah,* 2 Chr. 26:5. *Hezekiah,* 2 Chr. 31:21. *Josiah,* 2 Chr. 34:3. *Ezra,* Ezra 7:10. *Psalmist,* Psa. 17:1, 2; 27:4, 8; 33:20; 34:4; 40:1–4; 42:1–4; 63:1–8; 77:1–9; 119:10. *The Magi,* Matt. 2:1, 2. *Cornelius, the centurion,* Acts 10:7, 30–33.
See footnote, PENITENT, Psa. 51:17.

## CHAPTER 56

*God's salvation is near. 2 Blessings promised to all who keep the Sabbath, and observe his covenant. 9 Israel exposed to judgments for the sins of their rulers.*

THUS saith the LORD, [a,b]Keep ye judgment, and do [c]justice: for my [d]salvation *is* near to come, and my [e]righteousness to be revealed.

2 [f,g,h]Blessed *is* the man *that* doeth this, and the son of man *that* layeth hold on it; that keepeth the [i]sabbath from [1]polluting it, and keepeth his hand from doing any evil.

3 ¶ Neither let the [2]son of the stranger, that hath joined himself to the LORD, speak, saying, The LORD [3]hath utterly separated me from his people: neither let the [j]eunuch say, Behold, I *am* a dry tree.

4 For thus saith the LORD unto the [j]eunuchs that keep my [i]sabbaths, and choose *the things* that please me, and [4]take hold of my covenant;

5 Even [g,h]unto [j]them will I give in mine house and within my walls a [5]place and a name better than of sons and of daughters: [g,h]I will give them an everlasting name, that shall not be cut off.

6 Also the [6]sons of the stranger, that join themselves to the LORD, to [k]serve him, and to [l]love the name of the LORD, to be his servants, every one that keepeth the [i]sabbath from [1]polluting it, and [7]taketh hold of my covenant;

7 Even [g]them will I bring to my holy mountain, and make them joyful in my [m,n]house of [o]prayer: their [p]burnt offerings and their sacrifices *shall be* accepted upon mine altar; for [q]mine house shall be called an house of prayer for all [8]people.

8 The Lord GOD which gathereth the outcasts of Is′ra-el saith, Yet will I gather [r]*others* to him, beside those that are gathered unto him.

9 ¶ All ye beasts of the field, come to devour, *yea*, all ye beasts in the forest.

10 His [s]watchmen *are* [t]blind: they are all ignorant, they *are* all dumb [u]dogs, they cannot bark; sleeping, lying down, loving to slumber.

11 Yea, [s]*they are* [v]greedy dogs *which* can never have enough, and they *are* [w]shepherds *that* cannot understand: they [9]all look to their own way, every one for his gain, from his quarter.

12 Come ye, *say* [s]*they*, I will fetch [x]wine, and [y,z]we will [a]fill ourselves with strong drink; and [b,c]to morrow shall be as this day, [10]*and* much more abundant.

## CHAPTER 57

*The blessed death of the righteous. 3 The gross idolatry of the people described. 13 Promises to the humble and contrite. 20 No peace to the wicked.*

THE righteous [a]perisheth, and no man layeth *it* to heart: and merciful men *are* taken away, none considering that the righteous is taken away from the evil *to come*.

2 He shall enter into [b]peace: they shall rest in their beds, *each one* walking *in* his [c]uprightness.

3 ¶ But draw near hither, ye sons of the sorceress, the seed of the adulterer and the whore.

4 Against whom do ye [d]sport yourselves? against whom make ye a wide mouth, *and* draw out the tongue? *are* ye not [e]children of transgression, a [e]seed of [f]falsehood,

5 [g]Enflaming yourselves [1]with idols under every green tree, [g]slaying the [h]children in the valleys under the clifts of the rocks?

6 Among the smooth *stones* of the stream *is* thy portion; they, they *are* thy lot: even to them hast thou poured a drink [i]offer-

---

**1**
a *Commandment, enjoining justice,* Deut. 8:2.
b *Obedience, enjoined,* Heb. 5:8.
c *Justice,* Deut. 33:21.
d *Salvation,* Acts 16:17.
e *God, righteousness of,* Gen. 2:2.

**2**
f *Spiritual Peace,* Gal. 1:3.
g *Righteous, promises to,* Psa. 64:10.
h *Promise, or ground of assurance,* 2 Cor. 1:20.
i *Sabbath, rewards for observance of,* vs. 4–7; Ex. 16:23.
1 R. V. profaning

**3**
j *Eunuch,* Matt. 19:12.
2 R. V. stranger,
3 R. V. will surely separate

**4**
4 R. V. hold fast by

**5**
5 R. V. memorial

**6**
k *Worship,* Gen. 22:5.
l *Love, for God,* 1 John 4:19.
6 R. V. strangers,
7 R. V. holdeth fast by my

**7**
m Matt. 21:13; Mark 11:17; Luke 19:46.
n *Temple,* 1 Kin. 6:17.
o *Prayer,* Acts 6:4.
p *Offerings, burnt,* Lev. 6:17.
q *Church, prophecies concerning its universality,* Matt. 16:18.
8 R. V. peoples.

**8**
r *Gentiles, prophecies of the conversion of,* Acts 10:45.

**10**
s *Minister, false and corrupt,* Rom. 15:16.
t *Spiritual Blindness,* 2 Cor. 4:4.
u *Dog, figurative,* 1 Kin. 21:19.

**11**
v *Covetousness, insatiable,* Isa. 57:17.
w *Shepherd, figurative,* Jer. 31:10.
9 R. V. have all turned to their own way, each one to his gain, from every quarter.

**12**
x *Wine,* Prov. 23:31.
y *Worldly Pleasure,* Eccl. 2:1.
z *Sensuality,* Jude 19.

a *Drunkenness,* Luke 21:34.
b *False Confidence,* Psa. 30:6.
c *Delusion,* 2 Thess. 2:11.
10 R. V. a day great beyond measure.

**1**
a *Death, of the righteous,* Num. 23:10.

**2**
b *Heaven, future home of the righteous,* Luke 18:22.
c *Integrity,* Job 2:3.

**4**
d *Scoffing,* Hab. 1:10.
e *Wicked, described,* Psa. 73:3.
f *Falsehood,* Job 21:34.

**5**
g *Idolatry, wicked practices of,* 1 Sam. 15:23.
h *Human Sacrifices,* Deut. 12:31.
1 R. V. among the oaks,

**6**
i *Offerings, in idolatrous worship,* Lev. 6:17.

2 R. V. be appeased for these things?

**7**

*j Mountain, used for idolatrous worship,* Mic. 7:12.

**8**

3 R. V. memorial:

**9**

*k Perfume,* Prov. 27:9.

*l Hell,* Mark 9:43.

4 R. V. thine ambassadors

**10**

5 R. V. didst find a quickening of thy strength;

6 R. V. faint.

**11**

*m Ingratitude, of man to God,* Rom. 1:21.

*n God, mercy of,* Gen. 2:2.

*o God, longsuffering of,* Gen. 2:2.

**12**

*p Works, insufficient for salvation,* 2 Tim. 1:9.

**13**

*q False Confidence,* Psa. 30:6.

ing, thou hast offered a meat[G]
[i]offering. Should I [2]receive comfort in these?
7 Upon a lofty and high [j]moun-
tain hast thou set thy bed: even
thither[G] wentest thou up to offer
sacrifice.
8 Behind the doors also and the
posts[G] hast thou set up thy [3]re-
membrance: for thou hast discovered[G] *thyself to another* than
me, and art gone up; thou hast
enlarged thy bed, and made thee
*a covenant* with them; [g]thou
lovedst their bed where thou
sawest *it*.
9 And thou wentest to the king
with ointment, and didst increase thy [k]perfumes, and didst
send [4]thy messengers far off, and
didst debase *thyself even* unto
[l]hell.[G]
10 Thou art wearied in the
greatness of thy way; *yet* saidst
thou not, There is no hope: thou
[5]hast found the life of thine hand;
therefore thou wast not [6]grieved.
11 And of whom hast thou been
afraid or feared, that thou hast
[f]lied, and hast [m]not remembered
me, nor laid *it* to thy heart?
[n,o]have not I held[G] my peace even
of old, and thou fearest me not?
12 I will declare thy righteousness, and thy works; for [p]they
shall not profit thee.
13 [q]When thou criest, let thy
companies[G] deliver thee; but the
wind shall carry them all away;

vanity shall take *them*: but he
that [r]putteth his trust in me
[s]shall possess the land, and [s]shall
inherit my holy mountain;
14 And shall say, Cast ye up,
cast ye up, prepare the way, take
up the [t]stumblingblock out of the
way of my [u]people.[S]
15 For thus saith the high and
lofty One that inhabiteth [v]eter-
nity, whose name *is* [w,x]Holy;
[y]I dwell in the high and holy
*place*, with him also *that is* of a
[z,a]contrite and [b]humble spirit, to
revive the spirit of the humble,
and to revive the heart of the
contrite ones.[S T]
16[S] For I will not contend for
ever, [c]neither will I be always
[d]wroth[G]: for the spirit should fail
before me, and the souls *which* I
have made.
17 For the iniquity of his *covetousness was I [d]wroth[G], and
[e]smote[G] him: I hid me, and was
wroth, and he [f,g,h]went on frowardly[G] in the way of his heart.[S]
18 I have seen his ways, and
[c,i,j]will heal him: I will [k]lead
him also, and restore comforts
unto him and to his mourners.[S]
19 I create the fruit of the lips;
[l,m]Peace, peace to *him that is* far
off, and to *him that is* near, saith
the LORD; and [c]I will heal him.[Q]
20 But the wicked *are* [n]like the
troubled sea, when it cannot rest,

**19** *l Spiritual Peace,* Gal. 1:3. *m Spiritual Blessings, from God,* Eph. 1:3.

**20** *n Wicked, described,* Psa. 73:3.

*r Faith,* Mark 11:22.

*s Promise, to the righteous,* 2 Cor. 1:20.

**14**

*t Stumbling, figurative,* Isa. 8:14.

*u Church, God loves,* Matt. 16:18.

**15**

*v God, eternity of,* Gen. 2:2.

*w God, holiness of,* Gen. 2:2.

*x Holiness, attribute of God,* Ex. 39:30.

*y God dwells with the Righteous,* 1 Kin. 6:13.

*z Penitent, promises to,* Psa. 51:17.

*a Repentance, condition of divine favor,* Mark 1:4.

*b Humility, rewards of,* Prov. 22:4.

**16**

*c God, mercy of,* Gen. 2:2.

*d Anger of God,* 2 Kin. 13:3.

**17**

*e Divine Chastisement,* Job 33:19.

*f Adversity, obduracy in,* Psa. 10:6.

*g Obduracy,* Prov. 29:1.

*h Impenitence,* Rom. 2:5.

**18**

*i Backsliders, promises to penitent,* Jer. 3:22.

*j Penitent, promises to,* Psa. 51:17.

*k God, guidance of,* Gen. 2:2.

*** COVETOUSNESS.** *Is idolatry,* Col. 3:5. *Insatiable,* Prov. 21:26; Eccl. 4:8; 5:10, 11; Isa. 56:11. *Root of evil,* 1 Tim. 6:9–11. *Tends to poverty,* Prov. 11:24, 26; 22:16. *Gains of, unstable,* Job 20:15; Prov. 23:4–6; Jer. 17:11. *Debars from sacred offices,* 1 Tim. 3:3; Tit. 1:7, 11; 1 Pet. 5:2. *Debars from kingdom of God,* Matt. 19:23, 24; Luke 18:24, 25; 1 Cor. 6:10; Eph. 5:3, 5. *Denounced,* Isa. 5:8; Jude 11.

*Warnings against,* Deut. 15:9, 10; Prov. 15:27; Hab. 2:5–9; Matt. 6:19–21, 24, 25, 31–33; 13:22; 16:26; Mark 4:19; 7:21–23; Luke 8:14; 12:15–21; John 6:26, 27; 1 Tim. 6:5–8; 2 Tim. 3:2, 5; Heb. 13:5; Jas. 4:2; 1 John 2:15–17. *Commandments against,* Ex. 20:17; Deut. 5:21; Rom. 13:9; 1 Tim. 3:8. *Prayer against,* Psa. 119:36.

*Reproof for,* Neh. 5:7; Isa. 1:23; Jer. 6:13; 22:17; Ezek. 33:31; Hos. 10:1; Mic. 2:2; 3:11; 7:3; Hag. 1:6; Rom. 1:29.

*Punishment for,* Job 31:24, 25, 28; Isa. 57:17; Jer. 8:10; 51:13; Ezek. 22:12, 13; Col. 3:5, 6; 2 Pet. 2:3, 14–17.

**Instances of:** *Eve, in desiring the forbidden fruit,* Gen. 3:6. *Jacob, in defrauding Esau of his father's blessing,* Gen. 27:6–29; *in defrauding Laban of his flocks and herds,* Gen. 30:35–43; *in buying Esau's birthright,* Gen. 25:31. *Laban, in deceiving Jacob in wages,* Gen. 31:7, 15, 41, 42. *Balaam, in loving the wages of unrighteousness,* 2 Pet. 2:15, with Num. 22. *Achan, in taking the treasure,* Josh. 7:21. *Samuel's sons, in taking bribes,* 1 Sam. 8:3. *Saul, in sparing Agag and the booty,* 1 Sam. 15:8, 9. *David, in taking Bath-sheba, the wife of Uriah,* 2 Sam. 11:2–5. *Ahab, in desiring Naboth's vineyard,* 1 Kin. 21:2–16. *Gehazi, in taking a gift from Naaman,* 2 Kin. 5:20–27. *Jews, in exacting usury of their brethren,* Neh. 5:1–11; *in keeping back the portion of the Levites,* Neh. 13:10; *in building fine houses while the house of the Lord laid waste,* Hag. 1:4–9; *in following Jesus for the loaves and fishes,* John 6:26. *The rich young ruler,* Matt. 19:16–22. *The rich fool,* Luke 12:15–21. *Judas, in stealing from the bag,* John 12:6; *in betraying Jesus for thirty pieces of silver,* Matt. 26:15, 16; Mark 14:10, 11; Luke 22:3–6. *The Pharisees,* Luke 16:14. *Ananias and Sapphira, in keeping part of the price of their land,* Acts 5:1–10. *Demetrius, in raising a riot against Paul and Silas,* Acts 19:24–27. *Felix, in hoping for a bribe from Paul,* Acts 24:26. *Demas, in forsaking Paul for love of the world,* 2 Tim. 4:10.

See footnotes: AVARICE, Eccl. 5:10; RICHES, Eccl. 4:8.

whose waters cast up mire and dirt.[Q]

21 *There is* [o]no peace, saith my God, to the wicked.

## CHAPTER 58

*The prophet is commanded to shew the people their sins. 3 Why their fasts have been unprofitable. 8 How God's favor is to be obtained. 13 The reward of keeping the Sabbath.*

[a]CRY aloud, spare[C] not, lift up thy voice like a trumpet, and shew my people their [b]transgression, and the house of Jā'cob their sins.

2 Yet [b,c]they seek me daily, and delight to know my ways, as a nation that did righteousness, and forsook not the ordinance of their God: they ask of me the ordinances of justice; they take delight in approaching to God.

3 [c,d]Wherefore[C] have we [e]fasted, *say they*, and thou seest not? *wherefore* have we afflicted our soul, and thou takest no knowledge? Behold, [b]in the day of your fast ye find pleasure, and exact all your labours.

4 Behold, ye [b,e]fast for [f]strife and debate,[C] and to smite with the fist of wickedness: ye [1]shall not fast as *ye do this* day, to make your voice to be heard on high.

5 [c]Is it such a [b,e]fast that I have chosen? a day for a man to afflict[C] his soul? [c]*is it* to bow down his head as a [g]bulrush, [c]and to spread [h]sackcloth and [i]ashes *under him*? wilt thou call this a fast, and an acceptable day to the LORD?[Q]

6 *Is* not this the fast that I have chosen? [j,k,l]to loose the bands of wickedness, [j,k]to undo the [2]heavy [m]burdens, and [j,k]to let the [n]oppressed go free, and that ye break every yoke?[Q]

7 *Is it* not [k]to [o,p]deal[C] thy bread to the [q]hungry, and that thou [k,r]bring the [q,s]poor that are cast out to thy house? when thou seest the [q]naked, that thou [k]cover him; and that thou hide not thyself from [t]thine own flesh[Q]?

8 ¶ [u,v,w]Then shall thy [x]light break forth as the morning, and thine health[C] shall spring forth speedily: and thy righteousness shall go before thee; the [y]glory of the LORD shall be thy rereward.[C] [Q]

9 Then shalt thou call, and [z]the LORD shall answer; thou shalt cry, and he shall say, Here I *am*. If thou take away from the midst of thee the yoke, the putting forth of the finger, and speaking [3]vanity;

10 And *if* thou [a,b,c]draw out thy soul to the hungry, and satisfy the [d]afflicted[C] soul; [e,f,g]then shall thy [h]light rise in obscurity, and thy darkness *be* as the noon day:

11 And the LORD shall [i]guide thee continually, and [j]satisfy thy soul in drought, and make [4]fat[C] thy bones: and thou shalt be [k]like a [l]watered garden, and [k]like a spring of water, whose waters fail not.[Q]

12 And *they that shall be* of thee shall build the old waste places: thou shalt raise up the foundations of many generations; and thou shalt be called, The repairer of the breach, The restorer of paths to dwell in.

13 ¶ If thou turn away thy foot from the [m]sabbath, *from* doing thy pleasure on my holy day; and call the sabbath a delight, the holy of the LORD, honourable; and shalt honour him, not doing thine own ways, nor finding thine own pleasure, nor speaking *thine own* words:

14 Then shalt thou delight thyself in the LORD; and [n]I will cause thee to ride upon the high places of the earth, and feed thee with the heritage of Jā'cob thy father: for the mouth of the LORD hath spoken *it*.

21
o *Sin, fruits of,* Rom. 5:12.

1
a *Minister, duties of,* Rom. 15:16.
b *Hypocrisy,* vs. 1–5; Jas. 3:17.

2
c *Works, insufficient for salvation,* 2 Tim. 1:9.

3
d *Unbelief,* Heb. 3:12.
e *Fasting,* vs. 4–7; Zech. 8:19.

4
f *Strife,* Prov. 20:3.
1 R. V. fast not this day so as to

5
g *Bulrush,* Ex. 2:3.
h *Sackcloth,* Isa. 15:3.
i *Ashes,* Num. 19:9.

6
j *Rulers, duties of, to rule in righteousness,* Ex. 18:21.
k *Duty of man to man,* Eccl. 12:13.
l *Righteousness, fruits of,* vs. 7–14; Psa. 15:2.
m *Burden, figurative,* Luke 11:46.
n *Oppression, forbidden,* Eccl. 5:8.
2 R. V. bands of the yoke,

7
o *Alms, enjoined,* Matt. 6:2.
p *Liberality, enjoined,* vs. 7–12; 1 Tim. 6:18.
q *Neighbor, kindness to, enjoined,* Luke 10:29.
r *Hospitality, enjoined,* Rom. 12:13.
s *Poor, duty to,* Prov. 21:13.
t *Family, duty to,* 1 Chr. 13:14.

8
u *Blessings, contingent upon obedience,* Deut. 11:26.
v *Righteous, promises to,* Psa. 64:10.
w *Promise to the righteous,* 2 Cor. 1:20.
x *Light, figurative,* Matt. 5:14.
y *God, glory of,* Gen. 2:2.

9
z *Prayer, answer to, promised,* Acts 6:4.
3 R. V. wickedly;

10
a *Adversity, consolation in,* Psa. 10:6.
b *Sympathy,* 1 Pet. 3:8.
c *Righteousness, fruits of,* Psa. 15:2.
d *Afflicted, duty to,* Job 34:28.
e *Poor, liberality to, rewarded,* Prov. 21:13.
f *Liberality, rewards for,* 1 Tim. 6:18.
g *Promise, to the liberal,* 2 Cor. 1:20.
h *Light, figurative,* Matt. 5:14.

11
i *God, guidance of,* Gen. 2:2.
j *Spiritual Blessings, from God,* Eph. 1:3.
k *Righteous, described,* Psa. 64:10.
l *Irrigation,* Eccl. 2:6.
4 R. V. strong

13
m *Sabbath, holy,* Ex. 16:23.

14
n *Temporal Blessings, from God,* Psa. 103:2.

1
*a Hand, figurative,* Ezra 10:19.
*b God, savior,* Gen. 2:2.

2
*c Sin, separates from God,* Rom. 5:12.
*d Wicked, prayers of, not answered,* Psa. 73:3.

3
*e Wicked, described,* vs. 3–8; Psa. 73:3.
*f Falsehood, the wicked practice,* Job 21:34.
*g Speech, evil,* Col. 4:6.

4
*h Justice,* Deut. 33:21.
*i Truth,* John 18:37.
*j Malice,* Eph. 4:31.
1 R. V. sueth in righteousness, and none pleadeth in truth:

5
*k Cockatrice, figurative,* Isa. 11:8.
*l* Job 8:14; Prov. 30:28.
*m Viper, figurative,* Isa. 30:6.

6
*n Sin,* Rom. 5:12.

7
*o* Rom. 3:15–17.
*p Evil Imagination,* Gen. 6:5.

8
*q Peace,* Jer. 29:7.
*r Spiritual Peace,* Gal. 1:3.

9
*s Spiritual Blindness,* 2 Cor. 4:4.

## CHAPTER 59

*The iniquities of Israel have separated them from God. 3 Their sins specified. 9 The calamities thus brought upon them. 16 Salvation is only of God. 20 His covenant with his people.*

BEHOLD, the LORD's [a]hand
is not shortened, that it cannot [b]save; neither his ear heavy,
that it cannot hear:[S]
2 But your [c]iniquities[G] have separated between you and your
God, and your sins have hid *his*
face from you, that [d]he will not
hear.
3 For [e]your hands are defiled
with blood, and your fingers with
iniquity; your lips have spoken
[f,g]lies, your tongue hath muttered
perverseness.
4 [e]None [1]calleth for [h]justice,
nor *any* pleadeth for [i]truth: they
trust in vanity, and speak [f,g]lies;
they [j]conceive mischief, and
bring forth iniquity.
5 [e]They [j]hatch [k]cockatrice[G]'
eggs, and weave the [l]spider's
web: he that eateth of their eggs
dieth, and that which is crushed
breaketh out into a [m]viper.
6 Their webs shall not become
garments, neither shall they cover themselves with their works:
[e]their works *are* works of [n]iniq-
uity, and the act of violence *is*
in their hands.
7 [e,o]Their[Q] feet run to evil, and
they make[G] haste to shed innocent blood: their [p]thoughts *are*
thoughts of iniquity; wasting and
destruction *are* in their paths.
8 [e]The way of [q,r]peace they
know not; and *there is* no judgment[G] in their goings: they have
made them crooked paths: whosoever goeth therein shall not
know [q,r]peace.[Q]
9 ¶ Therefore is judgment[G] far
from us, neither doth justice
overtake us: we wait for light,
but behold [s]obscurity; for brightness, *but* we walk in darkness.
10 We grope for the wall like
the blind, and we grope as if *we*
*had* no eyes: we stumble at noon
day as in the [2]night; *we are* in
desolate places as dead *men*.
11 We roar all like [t]bears, and
mourn sore[G] like [u]doves: we look
for judgment,[G] but *there is* none;
for salvation, *but* it is far off
from us.
12 For [v,w]our transgressions are
multiplied before thee, and our
[x]sins testify against us: for our
transgressions *are* with us; and
*as for* our iniquities, we know[G]
them;
13 [v,x]In transgressing and [3]ly-
ing against the LORD, and [y]de-
parting away from our God,
speaking oppression and revolt,
conceiving and uttering from the
heart words of [f,g]falsehood.
14 [z]And judgment[G] is turned
away backward, and [a]justice
standeth afar off: for [b]truth is
fallen in the street, and equity
cannot enter.
15 Yea, [b]truth faileth; and he
*that* departeth from evil maketh
himself a prey[G]: and the LORD
saw *it*, and it [c]displeased him
that *there was* [d]no judgment.[G]
16 ¶ And he saw that *there was*
no man, and wondered that *there*
*was* no intercessor: therefore his
arm brought salvation unto him;
and his [e]righteousness, it sustained him.[Q]
17 For he put on [e]righteousness
as a [f]breastplate, and an [g]helmet
of salvation upon his head; and
he put on the garments of vengeance *for* clothing, and was clad
with zeal as a cloke.[Q]
18 [h]According to *their* deeds,
accordingly he will repay, [i]fury
to his adversaries, recompence to
his enemies; to the islands he
will repay recompence.[Q]
19 So shall they [j]fear the name
of the LORD from the west, and
his glory from the rising of the
sun. [4]When the enemy shall
come in like a flood, the Spirit of

10
2 R. V. twilight; among them that are lusty we are as

11
*t Bear,* 2 Sam. 17:8.
*u Dove,* Gen. 8:8.

12
*v Prayer, confession in,* vs. 12–15; Acts 6:4.
*w Repentance,* vs. 12–15; Mark 1:4.
*x Sin, confession of,* vs. 12–15; Rom. 5:12.

13
*y Backsliding,* Hos. 11:7.
3 R. V. denying the Lord,

14
*z Rulers, wicked,* v. 15; Ex. 18:21.

*a Justice,* Deut. 33:21.
*b Truth,* John 18:37.

15
*c Anger of God,* 2 Kin. 13:3.
*d Government, corruption in,* Isa. 22:21.

16
*e God, righteousness of,* Gen. 2:2.

17
*f Coat of Mail,* 1 Sam. 17:5.
*g Helmet, figurative,* Jer. 46:4.

18
*h Judgment, according to opportunity and works,* 1 Pet. 1:17.
*i Punishment, according to deeds,* Lev. 26:41.

19
*j Fear of God,* Acts 9:31.
4 Am. R. V. for he shall come as a rushing stream, which the breath of Jehovah driveth.

the LORD shall lift up a standard
against him.[T Q]
20 ¶ And [5, k]the Redeemer shall
come to Zī′ŏn, and [l]unto [m]them
that [n]turn from transgression in
Jā′cob, saith the LORD.[S T Q]
21 As for me, this *is* my [o]cove-
nant with them, saith the LORD;
[p]My spirit that *is* upon thee, and
my [q]words which I have [r]put in
thy mouth, shall not depart out
of thy mouth, nor out of the
mouth of thy seed, nor out of the
mouth of thy seed's seed, saith
the LORD, from henceforth and
for ever.[T Q]

## CHAPTER 60

*The glory of the Lord upon Zion. 3 The Gentiles shall come to her light. 15 Her blessed and glorious state in those times.*

ARISE, shine[Q]; for [a, b]thy light
is come, and the [c]glory of
the LORD is risen upon thee.[S T]
2 For, behold, the darkness
shall cover the earth, and gross[G]
[d]darkness the people: but [a, b]the
LORD shall arise upon thee, and
his [c]glory shall be seen upon thee.[Q S]
3 And [a, b, e]the [1]Gĕn′tīleș[G] shall
come to thy light, and kings to
the brightness of thy rising.[T Q]
4 Lift up thine eyes round
about, and see: [a, b, e]all they gather themselves together, they
come to thee: thy sons shall come
from far, and thy daughters shall
be nursed at *thy* side.
5 [a]Then thou shalt see, and
[2]flow together, and thine heart
shall fear, and be enlarged; because the abundance of the sea
shall be [3]converted unto thee,
the [4]forces of the Gĕn′tīleș[G] shall
come unto thee.[Q]
6 [a, b]The multitude of camels
shall cover thee, the [f]dromeda-
ries of [g]Mĭd′ĭ-an and [h]Ē′phah;
all they from [i]Shē′bȧ shall come:
they shall bring gold and incense; and they shall shew forth
the [j]praises of the LORD.[S Q]
7 [a, b]All the flocks of [k]Kē′där

20
k Rom. 11:26, 27.
l *Penitent, promises to,* Psa. 51:17.
m *Seekers,* Isa. 55:6.
n *Repentance,* Mark 1:4.
5 R. V. a redeemer
21
o *Covenant, of God with men,* Deut. 29:1.
p *Spiritual Blessings, from God,* Eph. 1:3.
q *Word of God, inspiration of,* Psa. 119:9.
r *Inspiration,* Job 32:8.
1
a *Church, prophecies concerning its prosperity,* Matt. 16:18.
b *Jesus, kingdom of, prophecies concerning,* Matt. 1:21.
c *God, glory of,* Gen. 2:2.
2
d *Spiritual Blindness, foretold,* 2 Cor. 4:4.
3
e *Gentiles, prophecies of the conversion of,* Acts 10:45.
1 R. V. nations
5
2 R. V. be lightened,
3 R. V. turned
4 R. V. wealth of the nations
6
f 1 Kin. 4:28; Esth. 8:10.
g *Midianites, prophecies concerning,* Gen. 37:28.
h *Ephah,* Gen. 25:4.
i *Sheba, prophecies concerning,* 1 Kin. 10:1.
j *Praise,* Psa. 150:1.
7
k *Kedar,* Jer. 49:28.

shall be gathered together unto
thee, the rams of [l]Nē-bā′ioth
shall minister unto thee: they
shall come up with acceptance
on mine altar, and I will glorify
the house of my glory.[Q]
8 Who *are* these *that* fly as a
cloud, and as the [m]doves to their
windows?
9 [a, b]Surely the isles shall wait
for me, and the [n]ships of [o]Tär′-
shish first, to bring thy sons
from far, their silver and their
gold with them, unto the name
of the LORD thy God, and to the
Holy One of Iș′ra-el, because he
hath glorified thee.
10[Q] And [5]the sons of [p]strangers[G]
shall build up thy walls, and their
kings shall minister unto thee:
for in my [q]wrath I [r]smote thee,
but in my favour have I had
[s]mercy on thee.[S]
11[S] Therefore [a, b]thy [t]gates shall
be open continually; they shall
not be shut day nor night; that
*men* may bring unto thee the
[4]forces of the Gĕn′tīleș[G], and *that*
their kings *may be* brought.[Q]
12 For the [u]nation and kingdom that will not serve thee shall
perish; yea, *those* nations shall be
utterly wasted.[G]
13 The glory of [v]Lĕb′a-non
shall come unto thee, the [w]fir
tree, the [x]pine tree, and the [x]box
together, to beautify the place of
my sanctuary; and I will make
the place of my feet glorious.
14 [a, b]The sons also of them that
afflicted thee shall come bending
unto thee; and all they that despised thee shall bow themselves
down at the soles of thy feet; and
they shall call thee, The city of
the LORD, The Zī′ŏn of the Holy
One of Iș′ra-el.[Q]
15 [a, b]Whereas thou hast been
forsaken and hated, so that no
man went through *thee*, I will
make thee an eternal excellency,
a joy of many generations.

l Or, *Nebajoth, prophecies concerning,* Gen. 25:13.
8
m *Dove,* Gen. 8:8.
9
n *Ship,* 2 Chr. 8:18.
o *Tarshish,* 2 Chr. 20:36.
10
p *Foreigners,* Deut. 23:20.
q *Anger of God,* 2 Kin. 13:3.
r *Judgments,* Ex. 6:6.
s *God, mercy of,* Gen. 2:2.
5 R. V. And strangers
11
t *Gates, figurative,* Deut. 3:5.
12
u *Nation, judgments denounced against,* Isa. 2:4.
13
v *Lebanon,* Deut. 1:7.
w *Fir Tree,* 2 Sam. 6:5.
x Isa. 41:19.

**16**
*y God, savior,* Gen. 2:2.
*z God, power of,* Gen. 2:2.

**17**
*a Church, prophecies concerning its prosperity,* Matt. 16:18.
*b Jesus, kingdom of, prophecies concerning,* Matt. 1:21.
*c Peace,* Jer. 29:7.
*d Righteousness,* Psa. 15:2.

**18**
*e Salvation,* Acts 16:17.
*f Praise,* Psa. 150:1.

**19**
*g* Rev. 21:23; 22:5.
*h Light, figurative,* Matt. 5:14.

**21**
*i Branch, figurative,* Dan. 4:14.
*j Glorifying God,* Luke 5:25.

**1**
*a* Luke 4:18, 19.
*b Jesus, prophecies concerning,* vs. 1–3; Matt. 1:21.
*c Holy Spirit, Jesus anointed by,* Acts 1:2.
*d Anointing, figurative,* Deut. 28:40.
*e Jesus, mission of,* Matt. 1:21.
*f Gospel, prophecies concerning,* Mark 13:10.
*g Jesus, savior,* Matt. 1:21.
*h Penitent, promises to, of divine favor,* Psa. 51:17.
*i Liberty, spiritual,* Lev. 25:10.
*j Captivity, figurative,* Isa. 5:13.
*k Prisoners, figurative,* Psa. 79:11.

16 [a,b]Thou shalt also suck the milk of the [1]Ġĕn′tīleṣ[C], and shalt suck the breast of kings: and thou shalt know that I the LORD *am* thy [y]Saviour and thy Redeemer, the [z]mighty One of Jā′cob.[S T]

17 [a,b]For brass I will bring gold, and for iron I will bring silver, and for wood brass, and for stones iron: I will also make thy officers [c]peace, and thine exactors[C] [d]righteousness.

18 [a,b]Violence shall no more be heard in thy land, wasting nor destruction within thy borders; but thou shalt call thy walls [e]Salvation, and thy gates [f]Praise.

19[T] [a,b,g]The sun shall be no more thy light by day; neither for brightness shall the moon give light unto thee: but the LORD shall be unto thee an everlasting [h]light, and thy God thy glory.[S Q]

20 [a,b]Thy sun shall no more go down; neither shall thy moon withdraw itself: for the LORD shall be thine everlasting light, and the days of thy mourning shall be ended.[T]

21 [a,b]Thy people also *shall be* all righteous: they shall inherit the land for ever, the [i]branch of my planting, the work of my hands, that I may be [j]glorified.[Q S]

22 A little one shall become a thousand, and a small one a strong nation: I the LORD will hasten it in his time.[S]

## CHAPTER 61

*The office of the Messiah. 4 The glorious results of his coming.*

[a,b]THE[T] [c Q]Spirit of the Lord GOD *is* upon me; because the LORD hath [d]anointed[C] me [e]to preach [f]good tidings unto the meek; he hath sent me [e,g]to bind up the [h]brokenhearted, [e]to proclaim [i]liberty to the [j,k]captives, and the opening of the prison to *them that are* bound;

2 [e]To proclaim [i]the [l]acceptable year of the LORD, and the day of vengeance of our God; [e]to comfort all that mourn;[T Q]

3 [e,m,n]To appoint[C] unto them that mourn in Zī′ŏn, [e]to give unto them [1]beauty for ashes, the oil of [o]joy for mourning, the garment of [p]praise for the spirit of heaviness; that they might be called [q]trees of righteousness, the planting of the LORD, that [r]he might be glorified.[S Q T]

4 ¶ And they shall build the old wastes, they shall raise up the former desolations, and they shall repair the waste cities, the desolations of many generations.

5 And strangers[C] shall stand and feed your flocks, and the sons of the alien *shall be* your plowmen and your vinedressers.

6 But ye shall be named the [s]Priests of the LORD: *men* shall call you the [t]Ministers of our God: ye shall eat the riches of the [2]Ġĕn′tīleṣ[C], and in their glory shall ye [u]boast yourselves.[Q]

7 For your shame *ye shall have* double; and *for* confusion they shall rejoice in their portion: therefore in their land they shall possess the double: everlasting joy shall be unto them.

8 For I the LORD love judgment[C], I [v,w]hate robbery [3]for burnt offering; and I will [4]direct their work in [x]truth, and I will make an everlasting [y]covenant with them.[S T]

9 And [m,n]their seed shall be known among the [2]Ġĕn′tīleṣ[C], and their offspring among the [5]people: all that see them shall acknowledge them, that they *are* the seed *which* the LORD hath blessed.

10 I will greatly [z]rejoice in the LORD, my soul shall be joyful in my God; for he hath [a]clothed

**2**
*l Jubilee, called acceptable year of the Lord,* Lev. 25:10.

**3**
*m Jesus, kingdom of, prophecies concerning,* vs. 3–11; Matt. 1:21.
*n Church, prophecies concerning its prosperity,* vs. 3–11; Matt. 16:18.
*o Joy, under adversity,* Psa. 5:11.
*p Praise,* Psa. 150:1.
*q Righteous, described,* Psa. 64:10.
*r God, glory of, manifested in his church,* Gen. 2:2.
1 R. V. a garland

**6**
*s Priest, figurative,* Lev. 1:5.
*t Righteous, described,* Psa. 64:10.
*u Spiritual Boasting,* Rom. 3:27.
2 R. V. nations,

**8**
*v Hatred, of God, against iniquity,* Prov. 15:17.
*w Sin, repugnant to God,* Rom. 5:12.
*x Truth,* John 18:37.
*y Covenant, of God with men,* Deut. 29:1.
3 R. V. with iniquity;
4 R. V. give them their recompence in

**9**
5 R. V. peoples:

**10**
*z Joy, in the Lord,* Psa. 5:11.
*a Holy, described,* Col. 3:12.

me with the garments of [b]salvation, he hath covered me with
the [c,d]robe of righteousness, as
a +bridegroom decketh *himself*
with [6]ornaments, and as a [e]bride
adorneth *herself* with her jewels.[Q][S]
11 For as the earth bringeth
forth her bud, and as the garden
causeth the things that are sown
in it to spring forth; so [f,g]the
Lord GOD will cause righteousness and praise to spring forth
before all the nations.

## CHAPTER 62

*The prophet's zeal for the prosperity and glory of Zion.* 6 *Her watchmen shall not hold their peace.* 8 *God's promise to Zion.* 10 *An exhortation to prepare the way of the people.*

FOR [a,b]Zī'ŏn's sake [c]will I not
hold[C] my peace, and [d]for Jĕ-
ru'să-lĕm's sake I will not rest,
until the [e]righteousness thereof
go forth as brightness, and the
[f]salvation thereof as a [g]lamp *that*
burneth.
2 And [h,i]the [1]Gĕn'tīles[C] shall see
thy righteousness, and all kings
thy glory: and thou shalt be
called by a new [j]name, which the
mouth of the LORD shall name.[Q][S]
3 [h]Thou shalt also be a [k]crown
of [2]glory in the hand of the
LORD, and a royal diadem in
the hand of thy God.[S]
4 [h]Thou shalt no more be
termed Forsaken; neither shall
thy land any more be termed Desolate: but thou shalt be called
Hĕph'zĭ-bah, and thy land [l]Beū'-
lah: for the [m,n]LORD delighteth
in thee, and thy land shall be
[o]married.
5 For *as* a young man marrieth
a *virgin, *so* shall thy sons [o]marry
thee: and *as* the [p]bridegroom rejoiceth over the bride, *so* shall
thy [m,n]God rejoice over thee.
6 ¶ [b]I have set [q,r]watchmen upon thy walls, O Jĕ-ru'să-lĕm,
*which* [c]shall never hold[C] their
peace day nor night: ye that
[3]make mention of the LORD,
keep not silence,[Q]
7 And [s]give him no rest, till he
establish, and till he make Jĕ-
ru'să-lĕm a praise in the earth.
8 The LORD hath [t]sworn by
his right hand, and by the arm
of his strength, Surely I will no
more give thy corn[C] *to be* meat[C] for
thine enemies; and [4]the sons of
the stranger[C] shall not drink thy
wine, for the which thou hast
laboured:
9 But they that have gathered it shall eat it, and praise
the LORD; and they that have
brought it together shall drink it
in the [u]courts of my [5]holiness.
10 ¶ Go through, go through
the gates; [v]prepare ye the way of
the people; cast up, cast up the
highway; gather out the stones;
lift up a [w]standard for the [6]people.
11 Behold, the LORD hath proclaimed unto the end of the
world, [h]Say ye to the daughter
of Zī'ŏn, Behold, thy salvation
cometh; behold, his reward *is*
with him, and his [7]work before
him.[Q]
12 And they shall call them,
The holy people, The redeemed
of the LORD: and thou shalt be
called, [x]Sought out, A city not
forsaken.

## CHAPTER 63

*The Messiah's triumph over the enemies of Zion.* 7 *A song of thanksgiving to God for his goodness to Israel.* 15 *The prayer of his people in their affliction.*

[a]WHO[Q] *is* this that cometh
from [b]Ē'dom, with [c]dyed
garments from [d]Bŏz'rah? this

b *Salvation*, Acts 16:17.
c *Dress, figurative, of righteousness*, Zech. 3:3.
d *Righteousness, figuratively described as a garment*, Psa. 15:2.
e *Bride, ornaments of*, Isa. 49:18.
6 R. V. a garland,

11
f *Church, prophecies concerning its prosperity*, Matt. 16:18.
g *Spiritual Blessings, from God*, Eph. 1:3.

1
a *Zion*, 2 Sam. 5:7.
b *Church, love for*, Matt. 16:18.
c *Zeal*, 2 Cor. 7:11.
d *Patriotism, instances of*, Psa. 137:1.
e *Righteousness*, Psa. 15:2.
f *Salvation*, Acts 16:17.
g *Lamp*, Ex. 27:20.

2
h *Church, prophecies concerning its prosperity*, vs. 2–12; Matt. 16:18.
i *Gentiles, prophecies of the conversion of*, Acts 10:45.
j *Name*, Prov. 22:1.
1 R. V. nations

3
k *Crown, figurative*, Ex. 29:6.
2 R. V. beauty

4
l *Canaan, called Beulah*, Gen. 37:1.
m *God, love of*, Gen. 2:2.
n *Church, God loves*, Matt. 16:18.
o *Marriage, figurative*, Gen. 34:9.

5
p *Bridegroom*, Isa. 61:10.

6
q *Watchman*, 2 Sam. 18:24.
r *Minister, duties of*, Rom. 15:16.
3 Am. R. V. are Jehovah's remembrancers, take ye no rest,

7
s *Prayer, importunity in*, Acts 6:4.

8
t *Oath, attributed to God*, Num. 5:19.
4 R. V. strangers

9
u *Church, called courts*, 1 Kin. 9:3.
5 R. V. sanctuary.

10
v Isa. 40:3.
w *Standard, figurative*, Num. 1:52.
6 R. V. peoples.

11
7 R. V. recompence

12
x *Church, described*, Matt. 16:18.

1
a *Jesus, prophecies concerning* (as some interpret), Matt. 1:21.
b *Edomites, prophecies concerning*, vs. 1–4; 2 Kin. 8:21.
c *Dyeing*, Ex. 26:14.
d *Bozrah, prophecies concerning*, Gen. 36:33.

+ **BRIDEGROOM**, Psa. 19:5. *Ornaments of*, Isa. 61:10. *Exempt from military duty*, Deut. 24:5. *Companions of*, Judg. 14:11. *Joy with*, Matt. 9:15; Mark 2:19, 20; Luke 5:34, 35. *Parable of*, Matt. 25:1–13. *Song of*, Song 4:1–16.

**Figurative**, Ezek. 16:8–14.

* **VIRGIN**. *Proofs of virginity of*, Deut. 22:13–21. *Dowry of*, Ex. 22:17. *Character of, to be protected*, Deut. 22:17–21. *Betrothal of, a quasi marriage*, Deut. 22:23, 24. *Distinguishing apparel of*, 2 Sam. 13:18. *Priests might marry none but*, Lev. 21:14. *Mourn in the temple*, Lam. 1:4; 2:10. *Virginity of, bewailed*, Judg. 11:37–39. *Parable of the wise and foolish*, Matt. 25:1–13. *Mother of Jesus a*, Isa. 7:14; Matt. 1:23; Luke 1:27. *Advised by Paul not to marry*, 1 Cor. 7:8, 25–35.

**Figurative**: *Of the church*, Isa. 62:5; Jer. 14:17; 31:4, 13; 2 Cor. 11:2.

*that is* glorious in his apparel,
[1]travelling in the greatness of his
strength ? I that speak in righteousness, mighty to save.
2 Wherefore[C] *art thou* [e]red in
thine apparel, and thy garments
like him that treadeth in the
[f]winefat[C] ?
3 [S][a]I have trodden the [f]wine-
press alone; and of the [2]people
*there was* none with me: for I
will tread them in mine anger,
and trample them in my fury;
and their blood shall be sprinkled upon my garments, and I
will stain all my raiment.[Q]
4 For the day of vengeance *is* in
mine heart, and the year of my
redeemed is come.
5 And [a]I looked, and *there was*
none to help; and I wondered
that *there was* none to uphold:
therefore mine own arm brought
salvation unto me; and my fury,
it upheld me.
6 And I will tread down the
[2]people in mine anger, and make
them [g]drunk in my fury, and I
[3]will bring down their strength
to the earth.[S]
7 ¶ [h,i]I [T]will mention the [j]lov-
ing kindnesses of the LORD, *and*
the praises of the LORD, according to all that the LORD hath
bestowed on us, and the great
goodness toward the house of
Iş'ra-el, which he hath bestowed
on them according to his mercies, and according to the multitude of his lovingkindnesses.[S]
8 For he said, Surely [k]they *are*
[l]my people, [k]children *that* will
not [4,m]lie: so he was their [n]Sa-
viour.[T]
9 In all [o]their [p]affliction he was
afflicted, and the [q]angel of his
presence [r]saved them: in his [j]love
and in his [s]pity he [r]redeemed
them; and he bare them, and
carried them all the days of
old.[T Q]
10 But [o]they rebelled, and
vexed his [t]holy Spirit: therefore
he was turned to be their enemy,
*and* he fought against them.[T Q]
11 ¶ Then [u]he remembered the
days of old, [v]Mō'şeş, *and* his
people, *saying*, Where *is* he that
brought them up out of the [w]sea
with the shepherd of his flock ?
where *is* he that put his [t]holy
[5]Spirit within him ?[T Q]
12 That [x,y]led [z]*them* by the
right hand of Mō'şeş with his
glorious arm, [w]dividing the water
before them, to make himself an
everlasting name ?[S]
13 That [x,y]led [z]them through
the deep, as an horse in the wilderness, *that* they should not
stumble ?
14 As [6]a beast goeth down into
the valley, the Spirit of the LORD
caused him to rest: so didst thou
[x,y]lead thy [z]people, to make thyself a glorious name.
15 ¶ [a,b]Look down from
[c]heaven, and behold from the
habitation of thy [d]holiness and
of thy glory: where *is* thy zeal
and thy strength, the [7]sounding
of thy bowels[C] and of thy mercies toward me ? are they restrained ?
16 [e]Doubtless thou *art* [f]our
[g]father, though Ā'brā-hăm be
ignorant of us, and Iş'ra-el acknowledge us not: thou, O
LORD, *art* our father, our [h]re-
deemer; thy name *is* from [i]ever-
lasting.[S T Q]
17 ¶ [a,b]O LORD, why hast thou
made us to err from thy ways,
*and* hardened our heart from thy
fear ? Return for thy servants'
sake, the tribes of thine inheritance.
18 [8,a,b]The people of thy holiness have possessed *it* but a little
while: our adversaries have trodden[C] down thy [j]sanctuary.[Q]
19 [a,b]We are [9]*thine*: thou never
barest rule over them; they were
not called by thy name.

1 R. V. marching

**2**

e *Colors, symbolical*, Ezek. 16:16.

f *Wine Press, figurative*, Isa. 5:2.

**3**

2 R. V. peoples

**6**

g *Drunkenness, figurative*, Luke 21:34.

3 R. V. poured out their lifeblood on the earth.

**7**

h *Thankfulness, to God*, Acts 24:3.

i *Nation, prayer for*, vs. 7–19; Isa. 2:4.

j *God, love of*, Gen. 2:2.

**8**

k *Righteous, described*, Psa. 64:10.

l *Spiritual Adoption*, Rom. 8:15.

m *Integrity*, Job 2:3.

n *God, savior*, Gen. 2:2.

4 R. V. deal falsely:

**9**

o *Israel, in Egypt*, Ex. 4:22.

p *Afflictions, consolation in*, Psa. 34:19.

q *Angel, one of the Holy Trinity*, Ex. 14:19.

r *God, preserver*, Gen. 2:2.

s *Pity, of God*, Job 19:21.

**10**

t *Holy Spirit*, Acts 1:2.

**11**

u *God, longsuffering of*, Gen. 2:2.

v *Moses*, Ex. 2:10.

w *Red Sea, divided*, Ex. 10:19.

5 R. V. spirit in the midst of them?

**12**

x *God, guidance of*, Gen. 2:2.

y *God, providence of*, Gen. 2:2.

z *Israel, led of God*, Ex. 4:22.

**14**

6 R. V. the cattle that go

**15**

a *Nation, in adversity, prayer for*, Isa. 2:4.

b *Adversity, prayer in*, vs. 12–19; Psa. 10:6.

c *Heaven, God's dwelling place*, Luke 18:22.

d *God, holiness of*, Gen. 2:2.

7 R. V. yearning

**16**

e *Faith, exemplified*, Mark 11:22.

f *Spiritual Adoption*, Rom. 8:15.

g *God, fatherhood of*, Gen. 2:2.

h *God, savior*, Gen. 2:2.

i *God, eternity of*, Gen. 2:2.

**18**

j *Temple, Solomon's*, 1 Kin. 6:17.

8 R. V. Thy holy people possessed

**19**

9 R. V. become as they over whom thou never barest rule; as they that were

## CHAPTER 64

*The prayer of God's people for aid; 6 with confession of their unworthiness. 9 The desolation of Zion.*

[a,b] OH that thou wouldest rend[G] the heavens, that thou wouldest come down, that the mountains might flow down at thy presence,

2 As *when* [1]the melting fire burneth, the fire causeth the waters to boil, to make thy name known to thine adversaries, [c]*that* the nations may tremble at thy presence!

3 When thou didst terrible things *which* we looked not for, thou camest down, the mountains flowed down at thy presence.

4 For [2]since the beginning of the world *men* have not heard, nor perceived by the ear, neither hath the eye seen, O [d]God, beside thee, *what* he hath prepared for [e]him that waiteth for him.[Q]

5 [e]Thou meetest him that rejoiceth and worketh righteousness, *those that* remember thee in thy ways: behold, thou [3]art [f]wroth[G]; for [g]we have sinned: in those is continuance, and we shall be saved.

6 [a,b]But [g]we are all [4]as an unclean *thing*, and all [h]our righteousnesses *are* as [5]filthy [i]rags; and we all [j]do fade as a leaf; and our iniquities, like the wind, have taken us away.[S T]

7 [a,b]And *there is* [k]none that calleth upon thy name, that stirreth up himself to take hold of thee: for thou hast hid thy face from us, and hast [l]consumed[G] us, [6]because of our [m]iniquities.

8 But now, O LORD, thou *art* our [n]father; we *are* the [o]clay, and thou our [p]potter; and [q]we all *are* the work of [r]thy hand.[S T Q]

9 [a,b]Be not wroth[G] very sore,[G] O LORD, neither remember iniquity for ever: behold, see, we beseech thee, we *are* all thy people.

10 Thy holy cities are a wilderness, Zī′ŏn is a wilderness, [s]Jė-ru′să-lĕm a desolation.

11 Our holy and our beautiful [t,u]house, where our fathers praised thee, is burned up with fire: and all our pleasant things are laid[G] waste.

12 [a,b,v]Wilt thou refrain[G] thyself for these *things*, O LORD? wilt thou hold thy peace, and afflict[G] us very sore[G]?

## CHAPTER 65

*Call of the Gentiles. 2 Jews to be punished for their rebellious spirit. 8 A remnant shall be saved; 11 but the wicked of the nation shall be cut off. 17 The prosperity of Zion under the new dispensation.*

[a,b] I[Q] AM sought of [c]*them that* asked not *for me*; I am found of *them that* sought me not: I said, Behold me, behold me, unto a nation *that* was not called by my name.[S]

2 [d]I have spread out my hands all the day unto a [e]rebellious people, which walketh in a way *that was* not good, after their own thoughts;[Q]

3 A people that provoketh me to [1,f]anger continually to my face; that [g]sacrificeth in gardens, and burneth [h]incense upon [i]altars of [j]brick;

4 Which remain among the [k]graves, and lodge in the [2]monuments, which eat [l]swine's flesh, and broth of abominable *things is in* their vessels;

5 Which say, Stand by thyself, come not near to me; for *,[m]I

---

**64:1**
a *Nation, in adversity, prayer for,* vs. 1–12; Isa. 2:4.
b *Adversity, prayer in,* vs. 1–12; Psa. 10:6.

**2**
c *Judgments, design of,* Ex. 6:6.
1 R. V. fire kindleth the brushwood, and the fire

**4**
d *God, love of, exemplified,* Gen. 2:2.
e *Righteous, promises to,* Psa. 64:10.
2 R. V. from of old men have not heard, nor perceived by the ear, neither hath the eye seen a God beside thee, which worketh for him that waiteth for him.

**5**
f *Anger of God,* 2 Kin. 13:3.
g *Sin, confession of,* Rom. 5:12.
3 R.V. wast wroth, and we sinned: in them have we been of long time, and shall we be saved?

**6**
h *Self-righteousness,* Luke 18:11.
i *Dress, figurative,* Zech. 3:3.
j *Life, brevity and uncertainty of,* Eccl. 8:15.
4 R. V. become as one that is unclean,
5 R. V. a polluted garment:

**7**
k *Prayerlessness,* Job 21:15.
l *Wicked, punishment of,* Psa. 73:3.
m *Sin, separates from God,* Rom. 5:12.
6 R. V. by means

**8**
n *God, fatherhood of,* Gen. 2:2.
o *Clay, figurative,* Job 33:6.
p *Pottery, figurative,* Jer. 18:3.
q *Man, created,* Job 4:17.
r *God, creator,* Gen. 2:2.

**10**
s *Jerusalem,* Judg. 19:10.

**11**
t *Church, holy,* 1 Kin. 9:3.
u *Temple, Solomon's,* 1 Kin. 6:17.

**12**
v *Prayer, importunity in,* Acts 6:4.

**65:1**
a Rom. 10:20, 21.
b *Church, prophecies concerning its prosperity,* vs. 1–25; Matt. 16:18.
c *Gentiles, prophecies of the conversion of,* Acts 10:45.

**2**
d *God, mercy of,* Gen. 2:2.
e *Backsliders, God's solicitude for,* Jer. 3:22.

**3**
f *Anger of God,* 2 Kin. 13:3.
g *Idolatry,* 1 Sam. 15:23.
h *Incense, offered in idolatrous worship,* Ex. 37:29.
i *Altar, used in idolatrous worship,* Gen. 8:20.
j *Brick,* Gen. 11:3.
1 R. V. my face continually, sacrificing

**4**
k *Burying Places,* Gen. 23:4.
l *Swine,* Lev. 11:7.
2 R. V. secret places;

**5**
m *Self-righteousness,* Luke 18:11.

---

* **BIGOTRY.** *Exhibited, in self-righteousness,* Isa. 65:5; Mark 2:16; Luke 15:2; 18:9–14; *in intolerance,* Luke 9:49, 50; Acts 18:12, 13.

*Rebuke of,* Acts 10:28, 45. *Paul's argument against,* Rom. 3:1–23; 4:1–25.

**Instances of:** *Joshua, through envy, seeking to suppress Eldad and Medad, who were prophesying,* Num. 11:27–29. *Jews, with regard to the Samaritans,* John 4:9, 27; *in rejecting the teachings of Jesus,* Luke 4:28; *in falsely accusing Jesus, of blasphemy,* John 5:18; *and of keeping company with sinners,* Luke 7:39; 15:2; 19:5–7; *and of not conforming to the traditions,* Luke 11:38, 39; *in their treatment of the young man who was born blind, whom Jesus restored to sight,* John 9:28, 29, 34; *with regard to Paul's preaching,* Acts 21:28, 29; 22:22. *John, in forbidding the casting out of devils by one who followed not Jesus,* Mark 9:38–40; Luke 9:49, 50. *James and John, in desiring to call down fire upon the Samaritans who would not receive Jesus,* Luke 9:51–56. *The early Christians,* Acts 10:45; 11:2, 3; *in regard to circumcision,* Acts 15:1–10, 24; Gal. 2:3–5. *Saul, in persecuting the Christians,* Acts 22:3, 4 (with 9:1, 2); 26:9–11; Gal. 1:13, 14; Phil. 3:6.

See footnote, INTOLERANCE, *Religious,* Num. 11:28.

am holier than thou. [n]These *are* a smoke in my nose, a fire that burneth all the day.

6 Behold, *it is* written before me: I will not keep silence, but will recompense, even recompense [o]into their bosom,

7 [p]Your [q]iniquities, and [o]the iniquities of your fathers together, saith the LORD, which have [g]burned [h]incense upon the [r]mountains, and [s]blasphemed me upon the hills: therefore will I measure[G] their former work into their bosom.

8 ¶ Thus saith the LORD, As the new wine is found in the cluster, and *one* saith, Destroy it not; for a blessing *is* in it: so will I do for my servants' sakes, that I may not destroy them all.

9 And I will bring forth a seed out of Jā'cob, and out of Jū'dah an inheritor of my mountains: and mine [t]elect shall inherit it, and my [t]servants shall dwell there.

10 And [u]Shâr'on shall be a fold of flocks, and the valley of [v]Ā'chôr a place for the herds to lie down in, for my people that have sought me.

11 ¶ But ye *are* they that [w]forsake the LORD, that forget my holy mountain, that prepare a table for [3]that troop, and that [4]furnish the drink offering unto that number.

12 [5]Therefore will I number [x]you to the [y,z,a]sword, and ye shall all bow down to the slaughter: because when I called, ye [b,c]did not answer; when I spake, ye did not hear; but did evil before mine eyes, and did choose *that* wherein I delighted not.[S]

13 Therefore thus saith the Lord GOD, Behold, [d,e]my servants shall eat, [f]but ye shall be hungry: behold, [d,e]my servants shall drink, [f]but ye shall be thirsty: behold, [d,e]my servants shall rejoice, [f]but ye shall be ashamed:

14 Behold, [d,e]my servants shall sing for [g]joy of heart, [f]but ye shall cry for sorrow of heart, and shall howl for vexation[G] of spirit.

15 And ye shall leave your name for a curse unto my chosen: for the Lord GOD shall slay thee, and call his servants by another name:[Q]

16 That he who blesseth himself in the earth shall bless himself in the God of [h]truth; and he that sweareth in the earth shall swear by the God of truth; because the former troubles are forgotten, and because they are hid from mine eyes.[S T]

17 ¶ For, behold, [i,j]I create [k,l]new heavens and a [k,m]new earth: and the former shall not be remembered, nor come into mind.[S T Q]

18 But [i,j]be ye glad and rejoice for ever *in that* which I create: for, behold, I create Jĕ-ru̇'să-lĕm a rejoicing, and her people a joy.[T]

19 And [i,j,n]I will rejoice in Jĕ-ru̇'să-lĕm, and joy in my people: and the voice of weeping shall be no more heard in her, nor the voice of crying.[Q]

20 [i,j]There shall be no more thence[G] an infant of days, nor an old man that hath not filled his days: for the child shall die [o]an hundred years old; but the sinner *being* an hundred years old shall be accursed.

21 [i,j]And they shall build houses, and inhabit *them*; and they shall plant vineyards, and eat the fruit of them.

22 [i,j]They shall not build, and another inhabit; they shall not plant, and another eat: for as the days of a tree *are* the days of my people, and [p]mine elect

n *Hypocrisy, abhorred of God,* Jas. 3:17.

6

o *Heredity, results of, judicial,* Ezek. 18:2.

7

p *Children, involved in sins of parents,* Mark 10:14.

q *Sin, consequences of, entailed upon children,* Rom. 5:12.

r *Mountain,* Mic. 7:12.

s *Blasphemy,* 2 Sam. 12:14.

9

t *Righteous, described,* Psa. 64:10.

10

u *Sharon,* 1 Chr. 27:29.

v Josh. 7:24, 26; 15:7; Isa. 65:10; Hos. 2:15.

11

w *Backsliding, of Israel,* Hos. 11:7.

3 R. V. Fortune,

4 R. V. fill up mingled wine unto Destiny;

12

x *Reprobates,* 1 Cor. 9:27.

y *Judgments,* Ex. 6:6.

z *War, as a judgment,* Judg. 3:2.

---

a *Wicked, punishment of,* Psa. 73:3.

b *Impenitence,* Rom. 2:5.

c *Obduracy,* Prov. 29:1.

5 R. V. I will destine you

13

d *God, providence of,* Gen. 2:2.

e *Righteous, promises to,* Psa. 64:10.

f *Wicked, contrasted with the righteous,* Psa. 73:3.

14

g *Joy,* Psa. 5:11.

16

h *God, faithfulness of,* Gen. 2:2.

17

i *Jesus, kingdom of, prophecies concerning* (as some interpret), vs. 17–25; Matt. 1:21.

j *Church, prophecies concerning its prosperity* (as some interpret) vs. 17–25; Matt. 16:18.

k *Millennium* (as some interpret), Rev. 20:2.

l *New Heavens,* Rev. 21:1.

m *Earth, new,* Prov. 8:23.

19

n *God, love of, exemplified,* Gen. 2:2.

20

o *Longevity,* Psa. 91:16.

22

p *Righteous, described,* Psa. 64:10.

shall long enjoy the work of their hands.

23 [i,j]They shall not labour in vain, nor bring forth for trouble; for they *are* the seed of the blessed of the LORD, and their offspring with them.[Q]

24 [i,j]And it shall come to pass, that before they call, [q,r]I will answer; and while they are yet speaking, [q,r]I will hear.

25 [i,j]The [s]wolf and the [t]lamb shall feed together, and the [u]lion shall eat straw like the bullock: and dust *shall be* the [v]serpent's [6]meat.[C] They shall not hurt nor destroy in all my holy mountain, saith the LORD.

## CHAPTER 66

*God delights in the contrite spirit; but rejects hypocrisy.* 5 *Comfort and enlargement promised to Zion.* 10 *An exhortation to rejoice therein.* 15 *The enemies of Zion to be destroyed.* 19 *The message of salvation to be sent to all nations, and the fruits thereof.* 24 *The fearful end of transgressors.*

THUS[Q] saith the LORD, [a]The [b]heaven *is* my [c]throne, and the [d]earth *is* my [e]footstool: where *is* the house that ye build unto me? and where *is* the place of my rest?[S]

2 For all those *things* hath [f]mine hand made, and all those *things* have been, saith the LORD: but to this *man* [g]will I look, *even* to *him that is* [h,i]poor and [i]of a contrite spirit, and [i]trembleth at my word.[Q]

3 [j]He that killeth an ox *is as if* he slew a man; he that sacrificeth a lamb, *as if* he cut off a dog's neck; he that offereth an oblation, *as if he offered* [k]swine's blood; he that burneth [l]incense, *as if* he blessed an idol. Yea, they have chosen their own ways, and their soul delighteth in their abominations.

4 I also will choose[C] their delusions, and will bring their fears upon them; because when I called, [m]none did answer; when I spake, [m]they did not hear: but [m]they did evil before mine eyes, and chose *that* in which I delighted not.

5 ¶ Hear the word of the LORD, ye that tremble at his word; Your brethren that hated you, that [n]cast you out for my name's sake, said, Let the LORD be glorified: [1]but he shall appear to your joy, and they shall be ashamed.[Q]

6 A voice of noise from the city, a voice from the [o]temple, a voice of the LORD that rendereth recompence to his enemies.[Q]

7 Before she travailed,[C] she brought forth; before her pain came, she was delivered of a man child.[Q]

8 Who hath heard such a thing? who hath seen such things? Shall [2]the earth be made to bring forth in one day? *or* shall a nation be born at once? for as soon as [p,q]Zī'ŏn travailed, she brought forth her children.

9 Shall I bring to the birth, and not cause to bring forth? saith the LORD: shall I cause to bring forth, and shut *the womb*? saith thy God.

10 Rejoice ye with Jĕ-ru'să-lĕm, and be glad with her, all ye that [r]love her: rejoice for [s]joy with her, all ye that mourn for her:

11 That ye may suck, and be satisfied with the breasts of her consolations; that ye may milk[C] out, and be delighted with the abundance of her glory.

12 For thus [p,q]saith the LORD, Behold, I will extend peace to her like a river, and the glory of the [3]Gĕn'tīleş[C] like a flowing stream: then shall ye suck, ye shall be borne upon *her* sides, and be dandled[C] upon *her* knees.

13 As one whom his [t]mother comforteth, [u,v]so will I comfort [w]you; and ye shall be comforted in Jĕ-ru'să-lĕm.

24
q *Prayer, answer to, promised,* Acts 6:4.
r *Promise, of answer to prayer,* 2 Cor. 1:20.

25
s *Wolf, figurative,* Jer. 5:6.
t *Lamb, figurative,* Num. 7:15.
u *Lion, figurative,* Mic. 5:8.
v *Serpent, figurative,* Num. 21:6.
6 Am. R. V. food.

1
a Acts 7:49, 50.
b *Heaven, God's dwelling place,* Luke 18:22.
c *Throne, figurative,* 1 Kin. 2:19.
d *Earth,* Prov. 8:23.
e *Footstool, figurative,* 1 Chr. 28:2.

2
f *God, creator,* Gen. 2:2.
g *God, condescension of,* Gen. 2:2.
h *Humility,* Prov. 22:4.
i *Righteous, described,* v. 5; Psa. 64:10.

3
j *Offerings, unavailing when not accompanied by piety,* Lev. 6:17.
k *Swine, used for sacrifice,* Lev. 11:7.
l *Incense, offered in idolatrous worship,* Ex. 37:29.

4
m *Impenitence,* Rom. 2:5.

5
n *Persecution, of the righteous,* John 15:20.
1 R. V. that we may see your joy; but

6
o *Temple, Solomon's,* 1 Kin. 6:17.

8
p *Church, prophecies concerning its prosperity* (as some interpret), vs. 8–23; Matt. 16:18.
q *Jesus, kingdom of, prophecies concerning* (as some interpret), vs. 8–23; Matt. 1:21.
2 R. V. a land be born in

10
r *Church, love for,* Matt. 16:18.
s *Joy,* Psa. 5:11.

12
3 R. V. nations like an overflowing

13
t *Mother, love of,* 1 Kin. 2:20.
u *God, love of, exemplified,* Gen. 2:2.
v *Righteous, promises to,* Psa. 64:10.
w *Church, God loves,* Matt. 16:18.

14 And when ye see *this*, your
heart shall rejoice, and your
bones shall flourish like [4]an
herb: and the hand of the LORD
shall be known toward his servants, and *his* indignation toward
his enemies.[Q]
15 For, behold, the LORD will
come with fire, and with his
[x]chariots like a whirlwind, to
render his [y]anger with fury, and
his rebuke with flames of fire.[Q]
16 For by fire and by his [z]sword
will the LORD plead with all
flesh: and the slain of the LORD
shall be many.
17 [a]They that sanctify themselves, and purify themselves
[5,b]in the gardens behind one *tree*
in the midst, eating [c]swine's
flesh, and the abomination, and
the [d]mouse, [e]shall be consumed
together, saith the LORD.
18 For I [f]*know* their works
and their [g]thoughts: it shall
come, that [h,i]I will gather all
[j]nations and tongues[C]; and they
shall come, and see my [k]glory.[S]
19 [h,i]And I will set a sign
among them, and I will send
those that escape of them unto
the nations, *to* [l]Tär′shish, Pŭl,
and Lŭd, that draw the bow, *to*
Tṵ′bal, and Jā′văn, *to* the isles[C]
afar off, that have not heard
my fame, neither have seen my
[k]glory; and they shall declare
my glory among the [6,j]Ġĕn′tīles̤.[C]
20 And [h,i]they shall bring all
your brethren *for* an offering unto the LORD out of all nations
upon horses, and in chariots, and
in litters, and upon mules, and
upon swift beasts, to my holy
mountain Jė-rṳ′sā-lĕm, saith the
LORD, as the children of Ī̆s̤′ra-el
bring an [m]offering in a clean
vessel into the [n]house of the
LORD.
21 And I will also take of them
for [o]priests *and* for [p]Lē̤′vītes,
saith the LORD.
22 For as the [q]new heavens
and the new [r]earth, which I will
make, shall remain before me,
saith the LORD, so shall your
seed and your name remain.[Q]
23 And [h,i]it shall come to pass,
*that* from one [s]new moon to another, and from one [t]sabbath to
another, shall all flesh come to
[u]worship before me, saith the
LORD.
24 And they shall go forth, and
look upon the carcases of the men
that have transgressed against
me: for [v]their [w]worm shall not
die, neither shall their fire be
quenched; and they shall be an
abhorring[C] unto all flesh.[Q]

**14**
4 R. V. the tender grass:

**15**
*x* *Chariot, figurative,* Josh. 11:4.
*y* *Anger of God,* 2 Kin. 13:3.

**16**
*z* *War, as a judgment,* Judg. 3:2.

**17**
*a* *Reprobates,* 1 Cor. 9:27.
*b* *Idolatry,* 1 Sam. 15:23.
*c* *Swine,* Lev. 11:7.
*d* *Mouse,* Lev. 11:29.
*e* *Wicked, punishment of,* Psa. 73:3.
5 R. V. to go unto the

**18**
*f* *God, knowledge of,* Gen. 2:2.
*g* *Heart, known to God,* Psa. 44:21.
*h* *Jesus, kingdom of, prophecies concerning* (as some interpret), Matt. 1:21.
*i* *Church, prophecy concerning its prosperity* (as some interpret), Matt. 16:18.
*j* *Gentiles, prophecies of the conversion of* (as some interpret), Acts 10:45.
*k* *God, glory of,* Gen. 2:2.

**19**
*l* *Tarshish, prophecies concerning,* 2 Chr. 20:36.

6 R. V. nations.

**20**
*m* *Offerings,* Lev. 6:17.
*n* *Temple, Solomon's,* 1 Kin. 6:17.

**21**
*o* *Priest,* Lev. 1:5.
*p* *Levites,* Deut. 10:8.

**22**
*q* *New Heavens,* Rev. 21:1.
*r* *Earth, new,* Prov. 8:23.

**23**
*s* *New Moon,* Amos 8:5.
*t* *Sabbath,* Ex. 16:23.
*u* *Worship,* Gen. 22:5.

**24**
*v* Mark 9:48.
*w* *Worm, figurative,* Jonah 4:7.

THE

# BOOK OF JEREMIAH

v.1–547 BC
See footnote, *Time*, Rev. 10:6.

1
*a Priest*, Lev. 1:5.
*b Benjamin, tribe of*, Num. 1:37.

2
*c Prophets, inspiration of*, Isa. 3:2.
*d Prophecies, inspired*, Dan. 9:24.
*e Inspiration*, Job 32:8.
*f Josiah*, 1 Kin. 13:2.
*g Amon*, 2 Kin. 21:18.
*h Judah, kingdom of*, 2 Chr. 11:17.

3
*i Jehoiakim*, Jer. 26:1.
*j Zedekiah*, 2 Kin. 25:2.
*k Jerusalem*, Judg. 19:10.
*l Captivity*, Isa. 5:13.
*m Month (August)*, Ex. 12:2.

5
*n God, foreknowledge of*, Gen. 2:2.
*o Sanctification*, 1 Pet. 1:2.
*p Foreordination*, Rom. 8:30.
*q Minister, call of*, Rom. 15:16.

6
*r Doubting, of Jeremiah*, Rom. 14:23.

## CHAPTER 1

*The calling of Jeremiah to the prophetic office. 7 His preparation for the work. 11 Two visions foreshowing speedy judgments upon Jerusalem. 17 God encourages the prophet with the promise of assistance.*

THE words of *Jĕr-e-mī′ah
the son of Hĭl-kī′ah, of the
[a]priests that *were* in †Ăn′a-thŏth
in the land of [b]Bĕn′ja-mĭn:
2 To *,[c]whom the [d]word of the
LORD [e]came in the days of [f]Jō-
sī′ah the son of [g]Ā′mon king of
[h]Jū′dah, in the thirteenth year of
his reign.
3 It came also in the days of
[i]Jĕ-hoi′a-kĭm the son of [f]Jō-sī′ah
king of [h]Jū′dah, unto the end
of the eleventh year of [j]Zĕd-e-
kī′ah the son of Jō-sī′ah king of
Jū′dah, unto the carrying away
of [k]Jĕ-ru′să-lĕm [l]captive in the
fifth [m]month.
4 ¶ Then the [d]word of the
LORD [e]came unto *,[c]me, saying,
5 [n]Before I formed thee in
the belly[C] I knew thee; and before thou camest forth out of the
womb I [o]sanctified thee, *and* I
[p,q]ordained thee a prophet unto
the nations.[S Q]
6 Then [r]said I, Ah, Lord GOD!
behold, [s]I cannot speak: for I
*am* a [t]child.[Q]
7 But the LORD said unto me,
Say not, I *am* a child: for [u]thou
shalt go to all that I shall send
thee, and [v]whatsoever I command thee thou shalt speak.
8 [w]Be not afraid of their faces:
for [x,y]I *am* [z]with thee to [a]deliver
thee, saith the LORD.[Q]
9 Then the LORD [b]put forth his
hand, and touched my mouth.
And the LORD said unto me,
Behold, I have [c]put my words
in thy mouth.
10 See, I have this day [d]set [e]thee
over the nations and over the
kingdoms, to root out, and to
pull down, and to destroy, and
to throw down, to build, and to
plant.[Q]
11 ¶ Moreover the [f]word of the
LORD [c]came unto me, saying,
*Jĕr-e-mī′ah, what [g]seest thou?
And I said, I see a rod of an
[h,i]almond tree.
12 Then said the LORD unto
me, Thou hast well seen: for
[j]I [1]will hasten[G] my word to perform it.
13 And the [f]word of the LORD
[c]came unto me the second time,

*s Excuses*, Luke 14:18.
*t Young Men*, Prov. 1:4.

7
*u Minister, promises to*, Rom. 15:16.
*v Minister, duties of*, Rom. 15:16.

8
*w Courage, enjoined*, Deut. 31:7.
*x Promise, to ministers*, 2 Cor. 1:20.
*y Righteous, promises to*, Psa. 64:10.
*z God dwells with the Righteous*, 1 Kin. 6:13.

*a God, preserver*, Gen. 2:2.

9
*b Anthropomorphisms*, Gen. 11:5.
*c Inspiration*, Job 32:8.

10
*d Minister, call of*, Rom. 15:16.
*e Agency, in executing judgments*, Mark 1:17.

11
*f Word of God, inspired*, Psa. 119:9.
*g Vision*, Acts 9:10.
*h Almond, figurative*, Gen. 43:11.
*i Symbols and Similitudes*, Heb. 9:9.

12
*j God, faithfulness of*, Gen. 2:2.
1 R. V. watch over

---

* **JEREMIAH,** son of Hilkiah. *Prophet and priest*, Jer. 1:1, 5. *Call of*, Jer. 1:4–19. *Time of his prophecies*, Jer. 1: 2, 3; 3:6; 21:1; 24:1; 25:1–3; 26:1; 28:1; 32:1; 34:1; 36:1, 39: 1, 2; 45:1; 49:34. *Letter of, to the captives in Babylon*, Jer. 29. *Sorrow of, under persecution*, Jer. 15:10, 15; 17:15–18. *Conspiracy against*, Jer. 11:21–23; 18:18–23. *Foretells the desolation of Jerusalem*, Jer. 19. *Pashur, the governor of the temple, scourges and confines him in stocks*, Jer. 20:1–3. *Denounces Pashur*, Jer. 20:3–6. *His melancholy and murmuring in consequence of persecution*, Jer. 20:7–18. *Imprisoned*, Jer. 32; 33:1; 37:15–21; 38:6–13; 39:15–18; Lam. 3:53–55. *Nebuchadnezzar directs the release of*, Jer. 39:11–14; 40:1–4. *Has a friend in Ahikam*, Jer. 26:24. *Ebed-melech, the Egyptian, intercedes with the king for him, and secures his release*, Jer. 38:7–13. *Dwells at Mizpah*, Jer. 40:6. *Prayers of*, Jer. 14:7–9; 32:17–25.

*Prophecies of, written by Baruch*, Jer. 36:1–7; 45:1; *destroyed by Jehoiakim*, Jer. 36:8–3; *re-written by Baruch*, Jer. 36:32. *Book of the prophecies of, concerning the utter desolation of Babylon, delivered to Seraiah, with a charge from*, Jer. 51:59–64. *Zedekiah seeks counsel from God by*, Jer. 21:1, 2; 38:14.

His intercession asked: *By Johanan and all the people*, Jer. 42:1–6; *by Zedekiah*, Jer. 37:3. *Johanan carries him into Egypt*, Jer. 43:1–7. *Foretells the conquest of Egypt by Babylon*, Jer. 43:8–12. *Prophecies of, studied by Daniel*, Dan. 9:2. *Celibacy of*, Jer. 16:2. *Purchases a field*, Jer. 32:7–10.

**Lamentations of:** *Over Josiah*, 2 Chr. 35:25. *Over the prosperity of the wicked*, Jer. 12:1–6. *Over the desolations of his people*, Jer. 4:14–18; 8:18–21; 9:1; 10:19–22; 12:7–13. *Over the desolation of Zion and his country, and the destruction of Jerusalem*, see BOOK OF LAMENTATIONS.

† **ANATHOTH.** *A priestly city in Benjamin*, Josh. 21: 18; 1 Chr. 6:60. *Abiathar confined in*, 1 Kin. 2:26. *Jeremiah buys an inheritance in*, Jer. 32:7–12. *Birthplace, of Jeremiah*, Jer. 1:1; *of Abiezer*, 2 Sam. 23:27; *of Jehu*, 1 Chr. 12:3. *Prophecies against*, Jer. 11:21–23. *Inhabitants of, after Babylonian captivity*, Ezra 2:23; Neh. 7:27; 11:32.

saying, What [g]seest thou? And I said, I see a [2,i]seething[C] pot; and the face thereof *is* toward the north.

14 Then the LORD said unto me, Out of the north an [k]evil shall break forth upon all the inhabitants of the land.

15 For, lo, I will call all the families of the kingdoms of the north, saith the LORD; and [k]they shall come, and they shall set every one his throne at the entering of the gates of [l]Jē-rụ′sā-lĕm, and against all the walls thereof round about, and against all the cities of [m]Jū′dah.

16 And I will utter my [k]judgments against them touching[C] all their [n]wickedness, who have [o]forsaken me, and have [p]burned [q]incense unto other gods, and [p]worshipped the works of their own hands.

17 ¶ Thou therefore gird up thy loins, and arise, and speak unto them all that I command thee: [r]be not dismayed at their faces, lest I confound[C] thee before them.[Q]

18 For, behold, [s]I have made thee this day a defenced[C] city, and an iron pillar, and brasen[C] walls against the whole land, against the [t]kings of [m]Jū′dah, against the princes thereof, against the [u]priests thereof, and against the people of the land.

19 And they shall [v]fight against thee; but [s]they shall not prevail against thee; for I *am* [w]with thee, saith the LORD, to [x]deliver thee.

## CHAPTER 2

*God's former kindness to Israel. 4 Their sin in forsaking him. 14 The calamities about to come upon them. 20 The degeneracy and idolatry of Judah. 31 Her forgetfulness of God rebuked.*

MOREOVER the [a]word of the LORD [b]came to me, saying,

2 [c]Go and [d]cry in the ears of [e]Jē-rụ′sā-lĕm, saying, Thus saith the LORD; I remember thee, the kindness of thy youth, the [f]love of thine espousals[C], when [g]thou wentest after me in the [h]wilderness, in a land *that was* not sown.

3 Is̱′ra-el *was* [i]holiness unto the LORD, *and* the [j]firstfruits of his increase: all that devour him shall [1]offend; [k]evil shall come upon them, saith the LORD.[S]

4 ¶ Hear ye the word of the LORD, O house of Jā′cob, and all the families of the house of Is̱′ra-el:

5 Thus saith the LORD, [l]What iniquity have your fathers found in me, that they are [m]gone far from me, and have walked after vanity, and are become vain?[S]

6 [n]Neither said they, Where *is* the LORD that [o]brought [q]us up out of the land of [p]Ē′gy̆pt, that [q]led us through the wilderness, through a land of deserts and of pits, through a land of drought, and of the shadow of death, through a land that no man passed through, and where no man dwelt?[S]

7 And I [o]brought you into a plentiful [r]country, to [s]eat the fruit thereof and the goodness thereof; but when ye entered, ye defiled my land, and made mine heritage an abomination[C].

8 [n]The priests said not, Where *is* the LORD? and [t]they that [u]handle the [v]law [w]knew me not: the [2, x, y]pastors[C] also transgressed against me, and the [z]prophets prophesied by [a]Bā′al, and walked after *things that* do not profit.

9 ¶ Wherefore [b, c]I will yet plead with you, saith the LORD, and with your children's children will I plead.

10 For pass over the isles of [d]Chĭt′tim, and see; and send unto [e]Kē′där, and consider diligently, and see if there be such a thing.

11 Hath a nation changed *their*

13
2 Am. R. V. boiling caldron;

14
k *Divine Chastisement*, Job 33:19.

15
l *Jerusalem*, Judg. 19:10.
m *Judah, kingdom of, prophecies concerning*, 2 Chr. 11:17.

16
n *Sin, repugnant to God*, Rom. 5:12.
o *Backsliding*, Hos. 11:7.
p *Idolatry*, 1 Sam. 15:23.
q *Incense, offered in idolatrous worship*, Ex. 37:29.

17
r *Courage, enjoined*, Deut. 31:7.

18
s *Minister, promises to*, Rom. 15:16.
t *Rulers, wicked*, Ex. 18:21.
u *Priest, corrupt*, Lev. 1:5.

19
v *Persecution, of the righteous*, John 15:20.
w *God dwells with the Righteous*, 1 Kin. 6:13.
x *God, preserver*, Gen. 2:2.

1
a *Prophecies, inspired*, Dan. 9:24.
b *Inspiration*, Job 32:8.

2
c *Minister, call of*, Rom. 15:16.
d *Minister, duties of*, Rom. 15:16.
e *Judah, kingdom of*, 2 Chr. 11:17.
f *Love, for God*, 1 John 4:19.
g *Israel, led of God*, Ex. 4:22.
h *Desert*, Lev. 16:22.

3
i *Holiness*, Ex. 39:30.
j *First Fruits*, Deut. 18:4.
k *Judgments*, Ex. 6:6.
1 R. V. be held guilty;

5
l *God, holiness of*, Gen. 2:2.
m *Backsliding, of Israel*, Hos. 11:7.

6
n *Ingratitude, of man to God*, Rom. 1:21.
o *God, providence of*, Gen. 2:2.
p *Egypt*, Gen. 41:8.
q *God, guidance of*, Gen. 2:2.

7
r *Canaan*, Gen. 37:1.
s *Temporal Blessings, from God*, Psa. 103:2.

8
t *Priest, duties of*, Lev. 1:5.
u *Instruction, in religion*, Prov. 23:23.
v *Law, of Moses*, Deut. 33:2.
w *Spiritual Blindness*, 2 Cor. 4:4.
x *Rulers* (as some interpret), *wicked*, Ex. 18:21.
y *Minister* (as some interpret), *false and corrupt*, Rom. 15:16.
z *Prophets, false*, Isa. 3:2.
a *Baal*, 2 Kin. 17:16.
2 R. V. rulers

9
b *God, longsuffering of*, Gen. 2:2
c *God, mercy of*, Gen. 2:2.

10
d *Chittim*, Dan. 11:30.
e *Kedar*, Jer. 49:28.

11
*f Idolatry, folly of,* 1 Sam. 15:23.
*g Ingratitude, of man to God,* Rom. 1:21.
*h Backsliding, of Israel,* Hos. 11:7.

13
*i Fountain, figurative,* Zech. 13:1.
*j Water, figurative of salvation,* 1 Kin. 17:10.
*k False Confidence,* Psa. 30:6.
*l Cistern, figurative,* Isa. 36:16.

14
3 R. V. become a prey?

15
*m Lion, figurative,* Mic. 5:8.

16
*n Noph,* Isa. 19:13.

17
*o Backsliders, warnings to,* Jer. 3:22.
*p Sin, fruits of,* Rom. 5:12.
*q God, guidance of,* Gen. 2:2.

18
*r Egypt,* Gen. 41:8.
*s* Or, *Nile,* Isa. 11:15.
*t Assyria,* Gen. 25:18.
*u Euphrates,* Gen. 15:18.

gods, [f]which *are* yet no gods? [g]but my people have [h]changed their glory for *that which* doth not profit.[Q]

12 Be astonished, O ye heavens, at [g,h]this, and be horribly afraid, be ye very desolate, saith the LORD.

13 For my people have committed two evils; they have [h]forsaken me the [i]fountain of living [j]waters, *and* [k]hewed them out [l]cisterns, broken cisterns, that can hold no water.[Q]

14 ¶ *Is* Ĭṣ′ra-el a *servant? *is* he a homeborn *slave*? why is he [3]spoiled[G]?

15 The young [m]lions roared upon him, *and* yelled, and they made his land waste: his cities are burned without inhabitant.

16 Also the children of [n]Nŏph and †Tā-hăp′a-nēṣ have broken the crown of thy head.

17 [o,p]Hast thou not procured this unto thyself, in that thou hast [g,h]forsaken the LORD thy God, when he [q]led thee by the way?

18 And now what hast thou to do in the way of [r]Ē′ġȳpt, to drink the waters of [s]Sī′hôr? or what hast thou to do in the way of [t]Ăs-sȳr′ĭ-ȧ, to drink the waters of the [u]river?

19 [o,p,v]Thine own wickedness shall correct thee, and thy [h]backslidings shall reprove thee: know therefore and see that *it is* an evil *thing* and bitter, that thou hast [g,h]forsaken [4]the LORD thy God, and that my fear *is* not in thee, saith the Lord [4]GOD of hosts.

20 For of old time [w]I have broken thy [x]yoke, *and* burst thy bands; and thou saidst, I will not [5]transgress; when upon every high hill and under every green tree thou [6]wanderest, [y]playing the harlot.[S]

21 Yet [w]I had planted thee a noble [z]vine, wholly a right seed: how then art thou turned into the degenerate plant of a strange vine unto me?

22 For [a]though thou wash thee with [7]nitre[G], and take thee much [b]sope, *yet* thine iniquity is marked before me, saith the Lord GOD.

23 How canst thou [c]say, I am not polluted[G], I have not gone after [d]Bā′al-ĭm? see thy way in the valley, know [e]what thou hast done: *thou art* a swift dromedary traversing her ways;

24 A [f]wild ass used to the wilderness, *that* snuffeth up the wind [8]at her pleasure; in her occasion who can turn her away?

19
*v Nation, judgments denounced against,* vs. 35–37; Isa. 2:4.
4 Am. R. V. Jehovah

20
*w God, providence of,* Gen. 2:2.
*x Yoke, figurative,* 1 Sam. 6:7.
*y Idolatry, wicked practices of,* 1 Sam. 15:23.
5 R. V. serve; for
6 R. V. didst bow thyself,

21
*z Grape, figurative,* Lev. 25:5.

22
*a Depravity,* Job 15:14.
*b* Mal. 3:2.
7 R. V. lye,

23
*c Self-righteousness,* Luke 18:11.
*d Baal,* 2 Kin. 17:16.
*e Backsliding, of Israel,* Hos. 11:7.

24
*f Ass, wild,* 2 Chr. 28:15.
8 R. V. in her desire;

* **SERVANT,** a slave. *Laws of Moses concerning,* Ex. 21:1–11, 20, 21, 26, 27, 32; Lev. 19:20–22; 25:6, 10, 44–54; Deut. 15:12–14, 16–18; 24:7.
*Manstealing forbidden,* Deut. 24:7; 1 Tim. 1:10.
*Fugitive, not to be returned to master,* Deut. 23:15, 16; *sought by Shimei,* 1 Kin. 2:39–41; *interceded for by Paul,* Philemon 10–21.
*Homeborn,* Gen. 14:14; 17:13, 27; Ex. 21:4; Eccl. 2:7; Jer. 2:14.
*Bought and sold,* Gen. 17:13, 27; 37:28, 36; 39:17; Lev. 22:11; Deut. 28:68; Esth. 7:4; Ezek. 27:13; Joel 3:6; Rev. 18:13. *Captives of war made,* 2 Kin. 5:2; 2 Chr. 28:8, 10. *Captives of war reduced to servitude were shared with priests and Levites,* Num. 31:28–47. *Owned by priests,* Lev. 22:11. *Thieves punished by being made,* Gen. 43:18; Ex. 22:3. *Defaulting debtors made,* Lev. 25:39; Matt. 18:25. *Children of defaulting debtors sold for,* 2 Kin. 4:1–7. *Voluntary servitude of,* Lev. 25:47; Deut. 15:16, 17; Josh. 9:11–21. *Given as dowry,* Gen. 29:24, 29. *Slaves owned slaves,* 2 Sam. 9:10. *The master might marry, or give in marriage,* Ex. 21:7–10; Deut. 21:10–14; 1 Chr. 2:34, 35.
*Equal status of, with other disciples of Jesus,* 1 Cor. 7:21, 22; 12:13; Gal. 3:28; Eph. 6:8. *Social status of,* Matt. 10:24, 25; Luke 17:7–9; 22:27; John 13:16.
Rights of: *To enjoy religious privileges with the master's household,* Gen. 17:13, 27; Ex. 12:44; Deut. 12:12, 18; 16:11, 14; 29:10, 11; *to have rest on the sabbath,* Ex. 20:10; 23:12; Deut. 5:14.
**Duties of:** *To be obedient,* Matt. 8:9; Eph. 6:5–8; Col. 3:22–25; Tit. 2:9, 10; 1 Pet. 2:18–20. *To honor masters,* Mal. 1:6; 1 Tim. 6:1, 2.
**Kindness to,** Psa. 123:2; Prov. 29:21. *Enjoined,* Lev. 25:43; Eph. 6:9. *Exemplified, by Job,* Job 31:13, 14; *by Boaz,* Ruth 2:4; *by the centurion,* Matt. 8:8–13; Luke 7:2–10. *Redeemed,* Neh. 5:8. *Emancipated,* 2 Chr. 36:23; Ezra 1:1–4; Jer. 34:8–16; Acts 6:9; 1 Cor. 7:21. *Tact in management of,* Eccl. 7:21.
**Cruelty to:** *To Hagar,* Gen. 16:6. *To the Israelites,* Ex. 1:8–22; 5:7–9; Acts 7:19–34. *Sick, abandoned,* 1 Sam. 30:13.
**Good.** INSTANCES OF: *Joseph,* Gen. 39:2–20; 41:9–57. *Of Abraham,* Gen. 24. *Of Jonathan,* 1 Sam. 14:7. *Of Abigail,* 1 Sam. 25:14–17. *Of David,* 2 Sam. 12:18. *Of Naaman,* 2 Kin. 5:2, 3, 13. *In the parable of the pounds and talents,* Matt. 25:14–23; Luke 19:12–19.
**Wicked and Unfaithful.** INSTANCES OF: *Gehazi,* 2 Kin. 5:20–27. *Zimri,* 1 Kin. 16:9, 10; 2 Kin. 9:31. *Ziba,* 2 Sam. 16:1–4, with 19:26, 27. *Of Shimei,* 1 Kin. 2:39. *Of Joash,* 2 Kin. 12:19–21. *Of Amon,* 2 Kin. 21:23. *In the parable of the pounds and talents,* Matt. 25:14–30; Luke 19:12–26.
**Figurative,** Lev. 25:42, 55; Psa. 116:16; Matt. 24:45–51; Luke 12:35–48; 17:7–9; John 8:32–35; Rom. 6:16–22; 7:21–23; Gal. 5:13; 1 Pet. 2:16; 2 Pet. 2:19; Rev. 7:3.
See footnotes: HIRED SERVANT, Lev. 25:40; MASTER, Col. 4:1.

† **TAHAPANES,** called also TAHPANHES and TEHAPHNEHES. *A city in Egypt,* Jer. 2:16; 43:7–9; 44:1; 46:14; Ezek. 30:18.

all they that seek her will not weary themselves; in her month they shall find her.

25 [g]Withhold thy foot from being unshod, and thy throat from thirst: but thou [h]saidst, There is no hope: no; for I have loved [i]strangers, and [j,k]after them will I go.

26 As the [l]thief is ashamed when he is found, so is the house of Is'ra-el ashamed; they, their kings, their princes, and their priests, and their prophets,

27 [m]Saying to a stock, Thou *art* my father; and to a stone, Thou hast brought me forth: for they have [e]turned *their* back unto me, and not *their* face: but [n]in the time of their trouble they will [o]say, Arise, and save us.

28 But [m]where *are* thy [p]gods that thou hast made thee? let them arise, if they can save thee in the time of thy trouble: for *according to* the number of thy cities are thy gods, O Jū'dah.

29 Wherefore will ye plead with me? ye all have transgressed against me, saith the LORD.

30 In vain have I [q,r]smitten your children; they [h,k,s]received no correction: your own sword hath [t]devoured your [u]prophets, like a destroying lion.

31 ¶ O generation, see ye the word of the LORD. Have I been a wilderness unto Is'ra-el? a land of darkness? wherefore say my people, We are [9]lords; we will come no more unto thee?

32 Can a maid forget her ornaments, *or* a bride her [v]attire? yet my [w]people have [e,x]forgotten me days without number.

33 Why trimmest thou thy way to seek love? therefore [10]hast thou also [y]taught the wicked ones thy ways.

34 Also in thy skirts is found the [z]blood of the souls of the [11]poor innocents: I have not found it by secret search, but upon all these.

35 Yet thou [a,b]sayest, Because I am innocent, surely his [c]anger shall turn from me. Behold, I will [12]plead with thee, because thou [a,b]sayest, I have not sinned.

36 Why [d,e]gaddest thou about so much to change thy way? thou also shalt be ashamed of Ē'ġўpt, as thou wast ashamed of Ăs-sўr'ĭ-ȧ.

37 Yea, thou shalt go forth from him, and thine hands upon thine head: for the LORD hath rejected thy confidences, and thou shalt not prosper in them.

## CHAPTER 3

*The greatness of Judah's wickedness. 6 She is worse than Israel was. 12 The people exhorted to repent and turn unto the Lord. 20 Their confession of sin upon their return to him.*

THEY say, If a man [a]put away his wife, and she go from him, and [b]become another man's, shall he return unto her again? shall not that land be greatly polluted? but thou hast [c,d]played the harlot with many lovers; yet [e,f]return again to me, saith the LORD.

2 Lift up thine eyes unto the [1]high places, and see where thou hast not been lien with. In the ways hast thou sat for them, as the Ȧ-rā'bĭ-an in the wilderness; and thou hast polluted the land with thy [d]whoredoms and with thy wickedness.

3 Therefore [g]the [h]showers have been withholden, and there hath been no latter rain; and thou hadst a whore's forehead, thou [i,j]refusedst to be ashamed.

4 [e,f]Wilt thou not from this time cry unto me, My [k]father, thou *art* the [l]guide of my youth?

5 Will he [2]reserve *his* [m]anger for ever? will he keep *it* to the end? Behold, [n]thou hast spoken

25
*g Temptation, admonitions against yielding to,* Luke 11:4.
*h Impenitence,* Rom. 2:5.
*i Evil Company,* Prov. 13:20.
*j Self-will,* Gen. 49:6.
*k Obduracy,* Prov. 29:1.

26
*l Thieves,* Deut. 24:7.

27
*m Idolatry, folly of,* 1 Sam. 15:23.
*n Adversity, benefits of,* Psa. 10:6.
*o Adversity, prayer in,* Psa. 10:6.

28
*p Polytheism,* 1 Cor. 8:5.

30
*q Divine Chastisement,* Job 33:19.
*r Nation, chastisement of,* Isa. 2:4.
*s Afflictions, impenitence in,* Psa. 34:19.
*t Persecution, of the righteous,* John 15:20.
*u Prophets, martyrs,* Isa. 3:2.

31
9 R. V. broken loose;

32
*v Bride, ornaments of,* Isa. 49:18.
*w Godless,* Job 8:13.
*x Ingratitude, of man to God,* Rom. 1:21.

33
*y Influence, evil,* 1 Cor. 7:14.
10 R. V. even the wicked women hast thou taught thy ways.

34
*z Homicide, felonious,* Deut. 5:17.

11 Am. R V. innocent poor: thou didst not find them breaking in: but it is because of all these things:

35
*a Delusion,* 2 Thess. 2:11.
*b Spiritual Blindness,* 2 Cor. 4:4.
*c Anger of God,* 2 Kin. 13:3.
12 R. V. enter into judgement with thee,

36
*d Character, instability of,* Phil. 2:15.
*e Instability,* Jas. 1:8.

1
*a Divorce,* Matt. 19:7.
*b Adultery,* Lev. 20:10.
*c Backsliding, of Israel,* Hos. 11:7.
*d Idolatry, wicked practices of,* 1 Sam. 15:23.
*e God, mercy of,* Gen. 2:2.
*f Repentance, enjoined,* Mark 1:4.

2
1 R. V. bare heights,

3
*g Divine Chastisement,* Job 33:19.
*h Rain,* 2 Sam. 1:21.
*i Obduracy,* Prov. 29:1.
*j Adversity, obduracy in,* Psa. 10:6.

4
*k God, fatherhood of,* Gen. 2:2.
*l God, guidance of,* Gen. 2:2.

5
*m Anger of God,* 2 Kin. 13:3.
*n Wicked, described,* Psa. 73:3.
2 R. V. retain

and done evil things [3]as thou
couldest.
6 ¶ The LORD said also unto
[o]me in the days of [p]Jō-sī'ah the
king, Hast thou seen *that* which
[c]backsliding Īṣ'ra-el hath done?
she is gone up upon every high
[q]mountain and under every
green tree, and there hath [d]play-
ed the harlot.
7 And I said after she had done
all these *things*, [e,f]Turn thou unto me. But she [r]returned not.
And her treacherous sister [s]Jū'-
dah saw *it*.
8 And I saw, when for all the
causes whereby [c]backsliding Īṣ'-
ra-el committed adultery I had
put her away, and given her a
bill of [t]divorce; yet her treacherous sister Jū'dah feared not, but
went and played the harlot also.
9 And it came to pass through
the lightness of her whoredom,[G]
that she defiled the land, and
committed adultery with stones
and with stocks.[G]
10 And yet for all this her
treacherous sister [s]Jū'dah hath
not turned unto me with her
whole [u]heart, but [v]feignedly,[G]
saith the LORD.
11 ¶ And the LORD said unto
[o]me, The [c]backsliding Īṣ'ra-el
hath [4]justified herself more than
treacherous [s]Jū'dah.[T]
12 Go and proclaim these
words toward the north, and
say, [f]Return, thou [c]backsliding
Īṣ'ra-el, saith the LORD; *and* [w]I
will not cause mine [m]anger to
fall upon you: for I *am* [e]merciful,
saith the LORD, *and* I will not
keep *anger* for ever.[S]
13 Only [x]acknowledge thine
iniquity, that thou hast transgressed against the LORD thy
God, and hast scattered thy
ways to the strangers under every
green tree, and ye have [y]not
obeyed my voice, saith the
LORD.

14 Turn, O backsliding children, saith the LORD; for [z]I am
[a]married unto you: and I will
take you one of a city, and two
of a family, and I will bring you
to Zī'ŏn:
15 And I will give you [5]pastors[G]
according to mine heart, which
shall feed you with knowledge
and understanding.
16 And it shall come to pass,
when ye be multiplied and increased in the land, in [b]those
days, saith the LORD, they shall
say no more, The [c]ark of the
covenant of the LORD: neither
shall it come to mind: neither
shall they remember it; neither
shall they visit *it*; neither shall
*that* be done any more.
17 At [b]that time they shall call
[d]Jē-rṳ'sā-lĕm the throne of the
LORD; and all the [e]nations shall
be gathered unto it, to the name
of the LORD, to Jē-rṳ'sā-lĕm:
neither shall they walk any
more after the [6]imagination[G] of
their evil heart.
18 [b]In those days the house of
Jū'dah shall walk with the house
of Īṣ'ra-el, and they shall come
together out of the land of the
north to the land that I have
given for an inheritance unto
your fathers.
19 But I said, How shall I
put thee among the children,
and give thee a pleasant land, a
goodly[G] heritage of the hosts of
nations? and I said, Thou shalt
call me, [f]My [g]father; and shalt
not turn away from [7]me.[T Q]
20 Surely *as* a wife treacherously departeth from her husband, so have ye [h]dealt treacherously with me, O house of Īṣ'-
ra-el, saith the LORD.
21 ¶ A voice was heard upon
the [8]high places, [i]weeping *and*
[j]supplications of the children
of Īṣ'ra-el: for they have perverted their way, *and* they have

3 R. V. and hast had thy way.

6

o *Jeremiah*, Jer. 1:1.

p *Josiah*, 1 Kin. 13:2.

q *Mountain, used for idolatrous worship*, Mic. 7:12.

7

r *Impenitence*, Rom. 2:5.

s *Judah, kingdom of*, 2 Chr. 11:17.

8

t *Divorce, figurative*, Matt. 19:7.

10

u *Heart, known to God*, Psa. 44:21.

v *Hypocrisy*, Jas. 3:17.

11

4 Am. R. V. shown herself more righteous

12

w *Promise, to backsliders*, 2 Cor. 1:20.

13

x *Sin, confession of, enjoined*, Rom. 5:12.

y *Disobedience to God*, Eph. 5:6.

14

z *God, love of, exemplified*, v. 15: Gen. 2:2.

a *Marriage, figurative*, Gen. 34 9.

15

5 R. V. shepherds

16

b *Church, prophecies concerning its prosperity*, Matt. 16.18.

c *Ark, in the tabernacle*, Ex. 25:10.

17

d *Jerusalem*, Judg. 19:10.

e *Gentiles, prophecies of the conversion of*, Acts 10:45.

6 R. V. stubbornness

19

f *Spiritual Adoption*, Rom. 8:15.

g *God, fatherhood of*, Gen. 2:2.

7 R. V. following me.

20

h *Backsliding, of Israel*, Hos. 11:7.

21

i *Repentance, instances of*, Mark 1:4.

j *Nation, in adversity, prayer of*, Isa. 2:4.

8 R. V. bare heights, the

[h,k]forgotten the LORD their
God.
22 [l]Return, ye *,[h]backsliding
children, *and* [m,n]I will heal your
backslidings. Behold,[i,j]we come
unto thee; for thou *art* the LORD
our God.[T]
23 Truly [o]in vain *is* [9]*salvation*[G]
*hoped for* from the hills, [10]*and*
*from* the multitude of mountains: truly in the LORD our
[p]God *is* the [q]salvation[G] of Iṣ'ra-el.
24 [11]For shame hath devoured
the labour of our fathers from
our youth; their flocks and their
herds, their sons and their
daughters.
25 We lie down in our shame,
and our confusion covereth us:
for [i,j,r]we have sinned against
the LORD our God, we and our
fathers, from our youth even unto this day, and have [s]not obeyed
the voice of the LORD our God.

## CHAPTER 4

*God's promise to Israel. 3 He exhorts Judah to repentance in view of coming judgments. 19 The prophet's lamentation over the miseries about to come upon the land.*

IF thou wilt return, O Iṣ'ra-el,
saith the LORD, [a,b]return
unto me: and [c]if thou wilt put
away thine abominations out of
my sight, then shalt thou not
[1]remove.
2 And thou shalt swear, The
LORD liveth, in [d]truth, in judgment,[G] and in [e]righteousness; and
the [f]nations shall bless themselves in him, and in him shall
they glory.[T]
3 ¶ For thus saith the LORD to
the men of [g]Jū'dah and [h]Jē-ru̇'-
sȧ-lĕm, [i]Break up your fallow
ground, and sow not among
thorns.
4 [a,b,j]Circumcise yourselves to
the LORD, and take away the
foreskins of your heart, ye men
of [g]Jū'dah and inhabitants of
[h]Jē-ru̇'sȧ-lĕm: [k]lest my fury
come forth like fire, and burn
that none can quench *it*, because
of the evil of your doings.[S T Q]
5 Declare ye in [g]Jū'dah, and
publish in [h]Jē-ru̇'sȧ-lĕm; and
say, Blow ye the trumpet in the
land: [2]cry, gather together, and
say, Assemble yourselves, and let
us go into the defenced[G] cities.
6 Set up the [l]standard toward
Zī'ŏn: [3]retire, stay[G] not: for [k]I will
bring evil from the north, and a
great destruction.
7 The [m]lion is come up from
his thicket, and the destroyer of
[4]the Gĕn'tīleṣ[G] is on his way;
he is gone forth from his place
to make thy land desolate; *and*
thy cities shall be laid waste
without an inhabitant.
8 For this gird[G] you with [n]sack-
cloth, lament and howl: for the
fierce anger of the LORD is not
turned back from us.[S]
9 And it shall come to pass at
that day, saith the LORD, *that*
the heart of the king shall perish,

k *Ingratitude, of man to God,* Rom. 1:21.

**22**

l *Repentance, enjoined,* Mark 1:4.
m *Nation, penitent, promises to,* Isa. 2:4.
n *Promise, to backsliders,* 2 Cor. 1:20.

**23**

o *False Confidence,* Psa. 30:6.
p *God, savior,* Gen. 2:2.
q *Salvation,* Acts 16:17.
9 R. V. the help that is looked for
10 R. V. the tumult on the mountains:

**24**

11 R. V. But the shameful thing hath

**25**

r *Sin, confession of,* Rom. 5:12.
s *Disobedience to God,* Eph. 5:6.

**1**

a *Repentance, enjoined,* Mark 1:4.
b *Backsliders, called to repentance,* Jer. 3:22.
c *Backsliders, promises to penitent,* Jer. 3:22.
1 R. V. be removed;

**2**

d *God, truth,* Gen. 2:2.
e *God, righteousness of,* Gen. 2:2.
f *Gentiles, prophecies of the conversion of,* Acts 10:45.

**3**

g *Jews, prophecies concerning,* vs. 5-31; Neh. 4:2.
h *Jerusalem,* Judg. 19:10.
i *Agriculture, figurative,* Gen. 3:23.

**4**

j *Circumcision, figurative,* Gen. 17:10.
k *Wicked, punishment of,* Psa. 73:3.

**5**

2 R. V. cry aloud and say,

**6**

l *Standard,* Num. 1:52.
3 R. V. flee for safety,

**7**

m *Lion, figurative,* Mic. 5:8.
4 R. V. nations; he

**8**

n *Sackcloth, symbol of mourning,* Isa. 15:3.

* **BACKSLIDERS.** Described as: *Blind,* 2 Pet. 1:9; Rev. 3:17; *godless,* 2 John 9; *idolaters,* 1 Cor. 10:7; *lukewarm,* Rev. 3:15, 16; *murmurers,* Ex. 17:7; 1 Cor. 10:10; *forsaking God,* Jer. 17:13; *tempting Christ,* 1 Cor. 10:9; *forsaking God's covenant,* Prov. 2:17; Psa. 78:10, 11; *turned aside to evil,* Psa. 125:5; 1 Tim. 5:15; *unfit for God's kingdom,* Luke 9:62.

*God's forbearance with,* Deut. 32:5, 6, 26, 27; Ezra 9:10, 13, 14; Isa. 42:3.

*God's solicitude for,* Deut. 32:28, 29; Psa. 81:13, 14; Isa. 1:4–9, 21, 22; 65:2, 3; Jer. 2:5, 11–13, 17, 31, 32; 18:13–15; 50:6; Hos. 6:4–11; 11:1–4, 7–9; Matt. 23:37.

*Warnings to,* Deut. 4:25–28; 28:58, 59; 31:16–18, 24–29; 1 Kin. 9:6–9; 2 Chr. 7:19–22; Jer. 7:13–34; 11:9–17; Mark 9:50.

*Corrective judgments upon,* Deut. 32:16–25; 1 Kin. 8:33; 2 Chr. 7:19–22; Neh. 9:26–30; Job 34:26, 27; Isa. 50:1; Jer. 8:1–22; Ezek. 22:18–22; Hos. 8:14; 9:1–17.

*Called to repentance,* Isa. 30:9, 15; 31:6; Jer. 3:4–7, 12–14, 21, 22 4:14; 6:16; Hos. 14:1; Mal. 3:7; Rev. 2:4, 5, 20–22; 3:2, 3, 18, 19.

**Promises to Penitent,** Hos. 14:4. *Of finding the Lord,* Deut. 4:29–31; 2 Chr. 15:2–4. *Of spiritual enlightenment,* Isa. 29:24; Jer. 3:14–19; Hos. 6:3. *Of restoration,* Deut. 30:1–10; Prov. 24:16; Isa. 57:18, 19; Hos. 14:4; Zech. 10:6. *Of temporal prosperity,* Lev. 26:40–42; Deut. 30:1–5, 7–10; Job 22:23–30.

**Return of,** Jer. 31:18, 19; 50:4, 5; Hos. 3:5; Jonah 2:4.

**Punishment of:** *By temporal loss,* Deut. 28:15–68; Ezra 8:22; Jer. 13:24, 25; Ezek. 15; Amos 2:4–6. *By being overthrown by enemies,* Num. 14:43; Deut. 4:27, 28; Judg. 2:12–15; 2 Kin. 18:11, 12; 2 Chr. 29:6–8; Psa. 78:40–43, 56–64. *By being forsaken of God,* 2 Chr. 24:20; Isa. 2:6; Jer. 6:30; 12:7; 14:7, 10; 15:1; Hos. 4:6, 10. *By being abandoned to the fruits of their sin,* Prov. 14:14; Ezek. 11:21; 16:43; 23:35.

**Instances of:** *Saul,* 1 Sam. 15:11, 26–28. *Solomon,* 1 Kin. 11:4–40; Neh. 13:26. *Amon,* 2 Kin. 21:22, 23. *Rehoboam,* 2 Chr. 12:1, 2. *Joash,* 2 Chr. 24:24. *Amaziah,* 2 Chr. 25:27. *Jonah,* Jonah 1:3. *Disciples of Jesus,* John 6:66. *Peter,* Matt. 26:69–75. *Corinthian Christians,* 1 Cor 5:1–8. *Galatians,* Gal. 1:6; 3:1; 4:9–11; 5:6, 7. *Hymenæus and Alexander,* 1 Tim. 1:19, 20. *Phygellus and Hermogenes,* 2 Tim. 1:15. *Demas,* 2 Tim. 4:10. *Churches of Asia,* 2 Tim. 1:15; Rev. 2:4; 3:2, 3, 15–18.

See footnote, BACKSLIDING, Hos. 11:7.

and the heart of the princes; and
the priests shall be astonished,
and the prophets shall wonder.
10 Then said I, Ah, Lord GOD!
surely thou hast greatly deceived
this people and Jĕ-ru̥'să-lĕm, saying, Ye shall have peace; whereas the sword reacheth unto the
soul.
11 At that time shall it be said
to this people and to Jĕ-ru̥'să-
lĕm, A [5]dry wind of the high
places in the wilderness toward
the daughter of my people, not
to fan[c], nor to cleanse,
12 *Even* a full wind from those
*places* shall come unto me: now
also will I give sentence[c] against
them.
13 Behold, he shall come up as
clouds, and his [o]chariots *shall be*
as a whirlwind: his [p]horses are
swifter than [q]eagles. [k]Woe unto
us! for we are spoiled[c].
14 O Jĕ-ru̥'să-lĕm, [a,b,r,s]wash
thine [t]heart from wickedness,
that thou mayest be saved. How
long shall thy vain[c] thoughts
lodge within thee?
15 For a voice declareth from
Dăn, and publisheth[c] affliction[c]
from [6]mount Ē'phră-ĭm.
16 Make ye mention to the nations; behold, publish against
Jĕ-ru̥'să-lĕm, *that* watchers come
from a far country, and give out
their voice against the cities of
Jū'dah.
17 As keepers of a field, [k]are
they against her round about;
[k]because she hath been [u]rebel-
lious against me, saith the LORD.
18 [k,v]Thy way and thy doings
have procured these *things* unto thee; this *is* thy wickedness,
because it is bitter, because it
reacheth unto thine heart.
19 ¶ My [w]bowels[c], my bowels[c]! I
am pained at my very heart; my
heart [7]maketh a noise in me; I
cannot hold my peace, because
thou hast heard, O my soul, the
sound of the [x]trumpet, the alarm
of war.
20 [k]Destruction upon destruction is cried; for the whole land
is spoiled[c]: suddenly are my tents
spoiled[c], *and* my curtains in a
moment.
21 How long shall I see the
[l]standard, *and* hear the sound of
the [x]trumpet?
22 For my people *is* [y]foolish,
they have [z]not known me; they
*are* [y]sottish[c] children, and they
[y]have [z]none understanding: they
*are* [y]wise to do evil, but to do
good they have [z]no knowledge.
23 I beheld the earth, and, lo, *it*
*was* without form, and void; and
the heavens, and they *had* no
light.
24 I beheld the mountains, and,
lo, they [a]trembled, and all the
hills moved [8]lightly.
25 I beheld, and, lo, *there was*
no man, and all the birds of the
heavens were fled.
26 I beheld, and, lo, the fruitful
place *was* a wilderness, and all
the cities thereof were broken
down at the presence of the
LORD, *and* [9]by his fierce [b]anger[s].
27 For thus hath the LORD
said, [c]The whole land shall be
desolate; yet [d]will I not make a
full end.
28 For this shall the earth
mourn, and the heavens above
be black: because I have spoken
*it*, I have purposed *it*, and [e]will
not [f]repent, neither will I turn
back from it.
29 The whole city shall flee for
the noise of the [g]horsemen and
[h]bowmen; they shall go into
thickets, and climb up upon the
rocks: [c]every city *shall be* forsaken, and not a man dwell
therein.[Q]
30 And *when* thou *art* spoiled[c],
what wilt thou do? Though
thou clothest thyself with crimson, though thou deckest thee

11
5 R. V. hot wind from the bare heights in

13
o *Chariot*, Josh. 11:4.
p *Horse*, Job 39:19.
q *Eagle*, Lev. 11:13.

14
r *Reproof, faithfulness in*, Prov. 17:10.
s *Spiritual Purification*, Psa 51:2.
t *Heart*, Psa. 44:21.

15
6 R. V. the hills of

17
u *Backsliding, of Israel*, Hos. 11:7.

18
v *Sin, fruits of*, Rom. 5:12.

19
w *Bowels, figurative*, 1 Kin. 3:26.
7 R. V. is disquieted in me;

x *Trumpet*, Josh. 6:4.

22
y *Wicked, described*, Psa. 73:3.
z *Spiritual Blindness*, 2 Cor. 4:4.

24
a *Earthquakes, figurative*, Isa. 29:6.
8 R. V. to and fro.

26
b *Anger of God, destroys*, 2 Kin. 13:3.
9 R. V. before

27
c *Judgments*, Ex. 6:6.
d *God, mercy of*, Gen. 2:2.

28
e *God, immutable*, Gen. 2:2.
f *Repentance, God repenteth not*, Mark 1:4.

29
g *Cavalry*, 1 Sam. 13:5.
h *Archery*, Gen. 21:20.

with ornaments of gold, though
thou [10]rentest thy face with
[i]painting, in vain shalt thou
make thyself fair; *thy* lovers
will despise thee, they will seek
thy life.
31 For I have heard a voice as
of a woman in travail, *and* the
anguish as of her that bringeth
forth her first child, the voice of
the daughter of Zī′ŏn, *that* [11]be-
waileth herself, *that* spreadeth
her hands, *saying*, Woe *is* me
now! for my soul [12]is wearied
because of murderers.

## CHAPTER 5

*God's judgments upon Judah and Israel for their injustice, 3 their perverseness, 7 their adultery, 10 their impiety, 19 their contempt of God, 25 their oppression, 30 and the falsehood of their prophets and priests.*

RUN ye to and fro through the
streets of [a]Jĕ-ru̇′să-lĕm, and
see now, and know, and seek in
the broad places thereof, [b]if ye
can find a man, if there be *any*
that [1]executeth[G] judgment[G], that
seeketh the [c]truth; and I will
[d]pardon [2]it.
2 And though they [e]say, The
LORD liveth; surely they [f,g]swear
falsely.
3 O LORD, [h]*are* not thine eyes
upon the [c]truth? [i]thou hast
stricken[G] them, [j]but they [k]have
not grieved; thou hast consumed[G]
them, *but* they have [l,m]refused to
receive correction: they have
[k]made their faces harder than a
rock; they have refused to return.[S]
4 Therefore I said, Surely
[n]these *are* poor; [n]they are foolish: for [n]they [o]know not the way
of the LORD, *nor* the judgment[G]
of their God.
5 I will get me unto the great
men, and will speak unto them;
for they have known the way of
the LORD, *and* the judgment[G] of
their God: but these have altogether broken the [p]yoke, *and*
burst the bonds.
6 [q]Wherefore a [r]lion out of the
forest shall slay them, *and* a
*wolf of the evenings shall spoil
them[G], a [s]leopard shall watch over
their cities: every one that goeth
out thence shall be torn in pieces:
because their transgressions are
many, *and* their [t]backslidings are
increased.
7 How shall I pardon thee for
this? thy children have [t,u]for-
saken me, and sworn by *them*
*that are* no gods: when I had
[v]fed them to the full, [w]they then
[x]committed [y]adultery, and assembled themselves by troops[G] in
the harlots' houses.
8 [w]They were *as* fed horses in
the morning: every one neighed
after his neighbour's wife.
9 [i]Shall I not [z]visit[G] for these
*things*? saith the LORD: and
shall not my soul be avenged
on such a nation as this?
10 ¶ Go ye up upon her walls,
and [z]destroy; [a]but make not a full
end: take away her battlements;
for they *are* not the LORD's.
11 For the house of Ĭṣ′ra-el and
the house of Jū′dah have [b]dealt
very treacherously against me,
saith the LORD.
12 They have [3]belied the LORD,
and [c,d,e]said, *It is* not he; neither
shall [f]evil come upon us; neither
shall we see [f]sword nor [f]famine:
13 And the prophets shall become wind, and [c,d]the word *is*
not in them: thus shall it be done
unto them.
14 Wherefore [g]thus saith the
LORD God of hosts, Because ye
speak this word, behold, I will
make my words in thy mouth
fire, and this people wood, and it
shall [h]devour them.[Q]
15 Lo, [g,h]I will bring a nation
upon you from far, O house of

**30**
i *Painting, around the eyes,* 2 Kin. 9:30.
10 R. V. enlargest thine eyes with paint,

**31**
11 R. V. gaspeth for breath,
12 R. V. fainteth before the murderers.

**1**
a *Jerusalem,* Judg. 19:10.
b *Intercession, influence of the righteous,* Jer. 27:18.
c *Truth,* John 18:37.
d *Sin, forgiveness of,* Rom. 5:12.
1 R. V. doeth justly,
2 R. V. her.

**2**
e *Hypocrisy,* Jas. 3:17.
f *Oath,* Num. 5:19.
g *Perjury,* 1 Tim. 1:10.

**3**
h *God, knowledge of,* Gen. 2:2.
i *Divine Chastisement,* Job 33:19.
j *Adversity, obduracy in,* Psa. 10:6.
k *Impenitence,* Rom. 2:5.
l *Self-will,* Gen. 49:6.
m *Obduracy,* Prov. 29:1.

**4**
n *Wicked, described,* Psa. 73:3.
o *Spiritual Blindness,* 2 Cor. 4:4.

**5**
p *Yoke, figurative,* 1 Sam. 6:7.

**6**
q *Nation, judgments denounced against,* vs. 6–29; Isa. 2:4.
r *Lion, figurative,* Mic. 5:8.
s *Leopard, figurative,* Song 4:8.
t *Backsliding, of Israel,* Hos. 11:7.

**7**
u *Ingratitude, of man to God,* Rom. 1:21.
v *Riches, a snare,* Eccl. 4:8.
w *Rich, licentious,* Jas. 5:1.
x *Idolatry, wicked practices of,* 1 Sam. 15:23.
y *Adultery,* Lev. 20:10.

**9**
z *Wicked, punishment of,* Psa. 73:3.

**10**
a *God, mercy of,* Gen. 2:2.

**11**
b *Backsliding,* Hos. 11:7.

**12**
c *Infidelity,* 2 Cor. 6:15.
d *Unbelief,* Heb. 3:12.
e *Delusion,* 2 Thess. 2:11.
f *Judgments,* Ex. 6:6.
3 R. V. denied

**14**
g *Nation, judgments denounced against,* Isa. 2:4.
h *Wicked, punishment of,* Psa. 73:3.

* **WOLF.** *Ravenous,* Ezek. 22:27. **Figurative:** Gen. 49:27. *Of divine judgments,* Jer. 5:6. *Of wicked rulers,* Zeph. 3:3. *Of the enemies of the righteous,* Matt. 7:15; 10:16; John 10:12; Acts 20:29. *In ceasing to be ravenous, illustrative of the reconciling power of the gospel,* Isa. 11:6; 65:25.

Ĭṣ′ra-el, saith the LORD: it *is* a
mighty nation, it *is* an ancient
nation, a nation whose language
thou knowest not, neither understandest what they say.
16 Their quiver *is* as an [i]open
sepulchre, they *are* all mighty
men.
17 And [g,h,i]they shall eat[C] up
thine harvest, and thy bread,
*which* thy sons and thy daughters should eat[C]: they shall eat[C] up
thy flocks and thine herds: they
shall eat[C] up thy vines and thy
fig trees: they shall [4]impoverish
thy fenced[C] cities, wherein thou
[j]trustedst, with the sword.
18 Nevertheless in those days,
saith the LORD, [a]I will not make
a full end with you.
19 And it shall come to pass,
when ye shall say, Wherefore[C]
doeth the LORD our God all
these *things* unto us? then shalt
thou answer them, Like as ye
have [b]forsaken me, and [k]served
strange[C] gods in your land, [g,h]so
shall ye serve strangers in a land
*that is* not your's.
20 ¶ Declare this in the house
of Jā′cob, and publish it in Jū′-
dah, saying,
21 Hear now this, O foolish
people, and without understanding; which have eyes, and [l]see not;
which have ears, and hear not:[Q]
22 [m]Fear ye not me? saith the
LORD: will ye not tremble at my
[n]presence, which have placed
the sand *for* the bound of the
†sea by a perpetual decree, that
it cannot pass it: and though the
waves thereof toss themselves, yet
can they not prevail; though they
roar, yet can they not pass over it?
23 But this people hath a revolting and a [o]rebellious [p]heart;
they are [b]revolted and gone.
24 [q]Neither say they in their
heart, Let us now [m]fear the
LORD our God, [r]that giveth
[s,t]rain, both the former and the
latter, in his season: [u]he reserveth unto us the appointed weeks
of the [v]harvest.[Q]
25 ¶ [w,x]Your iniquities have
turned away these *things*, and
[w]your sins have withholden[C] good
*things* from you.
26 For among my people are
found wicked *men*: [y]they [5]lay[C]
wait, as he that setteth snares;
they set a [z]trap, they catch men.
27 As a cage is full of [a]birds, so
*are* their houses full of [b]deceit:
therefore they are become great,
and waxen[C] [c]rich.
28 [c]They are waxen[C] fat, they
shine: yea, they overpass[C] the
deeds of the wicked: they [6]judge
not the cause, the cause of the
[d]fatherless, [7]yet they prosper;
and the right of the [e]needy do
they not judge.
29 [f]Shall I not visit[C] for these
*things*? saith the LORD: [f]shall
not my soul be avenged on such
a nation as this?
30 ¶ A wonderful[C] and horrible
thing is [8]committed in the land;
31 The [g]prophets prophesy[C]
falsely, and the [h]priests bear
rule by their means; and my
people love *to have it* so: and
what will ye do in the end
thereof?

## CHAPTER 6

*Judah about to be invaded.* 4 *The enemy encourage themselves.* 6 *God directs them to besiege Jerusalem,* 9 *and this because of the sins of the people.* 26 *Judah exhorted to mourn.*

[a,b]O YE children of [c]Bĕn′ja-
mĭn, gather yourselves to
flee out of the midst of [d]Jē-ru′-
să-lĕm, and blow the [e]trumpet
in *Tē-kō′ā, and [1]set up a [f]sign

16
i *War, evils of,* Judg. 3:2.

17
j *False Confidence,* Psa. 30:6.
4 Am. R. V. beat down thy fortified

19
k *Idolatry,* 1 Sam. 15:23.

21
l *Spiritual Blindness,* 2 Cor. 4:4.

22
m *Fear of God,* Acts 9:31.
n *God, power of,* Gen. 2:2.

23
o *Obduracy,* Prov. 29:1.
p *Heart,* Psa. 44:21.

24
q *Ingratitude, of man to God,* Rom. 1:21.
r *God, providence of,* Gen. 2:2.
s *Rain, sent by God,* 2 Sam. 1:21.
t *Temporal Blessings, from God,* Psa. 103:2.
u *Agriculture, God to be acknowledged in,* Gen. 3:23.
v *Harvest,* Ex. 34:21.

25
w *Sin, fruits of,* Rom. 5:12.
x *Wicked, punishment of,* Psa. 73:3.

26
y *Wicked, described,* Psa. 73:3.
z Josh. 23:13; Job 18:10.
5 R. V. watch, as fowlers lie in wait;

27
a *Birds,* Eccl. 12:4.
b *Deceit, the wicked practice,* Psa. 36:3.
c *Rich, unscrupulous methods of,* Jas. 5:1.

28
d *Orphan, oppressed,* Lam. 5:3.
e *Poor, oppression of,* Prov. 21:13.
6 R. V. plead
7 R. V. that they should prosper;

29
f *Nation, judgments denounced against,* Isa. 2:4.

30
8 R. V. come to pass in

31
g *Prophets, false,* Isa. 3:2.
h *Priest, corrupt,* Lev. 1:5.

1
a *Judah, kingdom of, prophecies concerning,* vs. 1–30; 2 Chr. 11:17.
b *Reproof, faithfulness in,* Prov. 17:10.
c *Benjamin, tribe of,* Num. 1:37.
d *Jerusalem,* Judg. 19:10.
e *Trumpet,* Josh. 6:4.
f Isa. 30:17.
1 R. V. raise up a signal on

† **SEA.** *Creation of,* Gen. 1:9, 10; Psa. 95:5. *Limits of, established by God,* Gen. 1:9, 10; Job 26:10; 38:8; Psa. 33:7; Jer. 5:22. *Calmed by Jesus,* Matt. 8:24–26; Mark 4:37–39. *Jesus walked on,* Matt. 14:25–31. *Dead to be given up by, at the resurrection,* Rev. 20:13.
SYMBOLICAL: *In Daniel's vision,* Dan. 7:2, 3.

* **TEKOA.** *A city in Judah,* 2 Chr. 11:6. *Home of the woman who interceded for Absalom to be permitted to return to Jerusalem after slaying Amnon,* 2 Sam. 14:2, 4, 9. *Rebuilt and fortified by Rehoboam,* 2 Chr. 11:6. *Desert of,* 2 Chr. 20:20. *People of, work on the new wall of Jerusalem,* Neh. 3:5, 27. *Home of Amos,* Amos 1:1.

of [g]fire in [h]Běth–hăc′çe-rĕm: for
evil appeareth out of the north,
and great destruction.
2 [2]I have likened the daughter
of Zī′ŏn to a comely and delicate
*woman*.
3 The shepherds with their
flocks shall come unto her; they
shall pitch *their* tents against her
round about; they shall feed every one in his place.
4 Prepare ye war against her;
arise, and let us go up at noon.
Woe unto us! for the day goeth
away, for the shadows of the
evening are stretched out.
5 Arise, and let us [i]go by night,
and let us destroy her palaces.
6 ¶ For thus hath the LORD of
hosts [a]said, Hew ye down trees,
and cast a [j]mount against [d]Jĕ-
ru̦′sā-lĕm: this *is* the city to be
visited; she *is* wholly oppression
in the midst of her.
7 As a fountain casteth out her
waters, so she casteth out her
wickedness: violence and spoil is
heard in her; before me continually *is* [3]grief and wounds.
8 [a,b]Be thou instructed, O Jĕ-
ru̦′sā-lĕm, lest my soul [4]depart
from thee; lest I make thee desolate, a land not inhabited.
9 ¶ Thus saith the LORD of
hosts, [k]They shall throughly
glean the remnant of Ĭș′ra-el
as a vine: turn back thine hand
as a grapegatherer into the
baskets.
10 To whom shall I speak, and
give [b]warning, that they may
hear? behold, their ear *is* uncircumcised, and they [l,m]cannot
hearken: behold, the [n]word
of the LORD is unto them a
reproach; they have no delight
in it.
11 Therefore I am full of the
fury of the LORD; I am weary
with holding in: [k]I will pour it
out upon the children [5]abroad,
and upon the assembly of young
men together: for even the husband with the wife shall be
taken, the aged with *him that*
*is* full of days.
12 And [k]their houses shall be
turned unto others, *with their*
fields and wives together: for I
will stretch out my hand upon
the inhabitants of the land, saith
the LORD.
13 For from the least of them
even unto the greatest of them
every one *is* given to [o]covetous-
ness; and from the [p]prophet even
unto the [q]priest every one dealeth falsely.
14 [p,q]They have healed also the
hurt [6]*of the daughter* of my
people slightly, [r]saying, [s]Peace,
peace; when *there is* no peace.
15 Were they ashamed when
they had committed abomination? nay, they were [t]not at
all ashamed, neither could they
[u]blush: therefore [k]they shall fall
among them that fall: at the time
*that* I visit them they shall be
cast down, saith the LORD.
16 Thus [v]saith the LORD,
Stand ye in the ways, and see,
and ask for the old paths, where
*is* the good [w]way, and walk
therein, and [x]ye shall find [y]rest
for your souls. But they[m,z,a]said,
We will not walk *therein*.
17 Also I set [b]watchmen over
you, *saying*, Hearken to the
sound of the [c]trumpet. But they
[a,d]said, We will not hearken.
18 ¶ Therefore hear, ye nations, and know, O congregation, what *is* among them.
19 Hear, O earth: behold, [e]I
will bring evil upon this people,
*even* the [f]fruit of their thoughts,
because they have [g]not hearkened unto my words, nor to my
law, but rejected it.
20 [h]To what purpose cometh
there to me [i]incense from [j]Shē′-
bâ, and the [k]sweet cane from a
far country? your burnt [l]offer-

g *Fire, used as a signal in war*, Ex. 12:8.
h Neh. 3:14.

2

2 R. V. The comely and delicate one, the daughter of Zion, will I cut off.

5

i *Strategy, in war*, Judg. 7:16.

6

j *Fortification*, Ezek. 17:17.

7

3 R. V. sickness

8

4 R. V. be alienated

9

k *Nation, judgments denounced against*, vs. 9–30; Isa. 2:4.

10

l *Spiritual Blindness*, 2 Cor. 4:4.
m *Impenitence*, Rom. 2:5.
n *Word of God*, Psa. 119:9.

11

5 R. V. in the street.

13

o *Covetousness*, Isa. 57:17.
p *Minister, false and corrupt*, Rom. 15:16.
q *Priest, corrupt*, Lev. 1:5.

14

r *False Confidence*, Psa. 30:6.
s *Peace*, Jer. 29:7.
6 R. V. *omits* of the daughter

15

t *Conscience, dead*, Acts 23:1.
u Jer. 8:12; Ezra 9:6.

16

v *Backsliders, called to repentance*, Jer. 3:22.
w *Way, of holiness*, Isa. 35:8.
x *Promise, to backsliders*, 2 Cor. 1:20.
y *Spiritual Peace*, Gal. 1:3.
z *Self-will*, Gen. 49:6.

a *Obduracy*, Prov. 29:1.

17

b *Watchman*, 2 Sam. 18:24.
c *Trumpet*, Josh. 6:4.
d *Self-will*, Gen. 49:6.

19

e *Nation, judgments denounced against*, Isa. 2:4.
f *Sin, fruits of*, Rom. 5:12.
g *Disobedience to God*, Eph. 5:6.

20

h *Hypocrisy, abhorred of God*, Jas. 3:17.
i *Frankincense*, 1 Chr. 9:29.
j *Sheba*, 1 Kin. 10:1.
k *Calamus*, Ezek. 27:19.
l *Offerings, unavailing, when not accompanied by piety*, Lev. 6:17.

ings *are* not acceptable, nor your sacrifices sweet unto me.

21 Therefore thus [e]saith the LORD, Behold, I will lay [m]stumblingblocks before this people, and the fathers and the sons together shall fall upon them; the neighbour and his friend shall perish.

22 Thus saith the LORD, Behold, a people cometh from the north country, and a great nation shall be [7]raised from the [8]sides of the earth.

23 [e]They shall lay hold on bow and spear; they *are* cruel, and have no mercy; their voice roareth like the sea; and they ride upon horses, set in array[G] as men for war [e]against thee, O daughter of Zī'ŏn.

24 We have heard the fame[G] thereof: our hands wax[G] feeble: anguish hath taken hold of us, *and* pain, as of a woman in travail.

25 Go not forth into the field, nor walk by the way; for the [n]sword of the enemy *and* fear *is* on every side.

26 ¶ O daughter of my people, gird *thee* with [o]sackcloth, and wallow thyself in [p]ashes: make thee mourning, *as for* an only son, most bitter lamentation: for [e]the spoiler[G] shall suddenly come upon us.

27 I have set thee *for* a tower *and* a fortress among my people, that thou mayest know and try[G] their way.

28 [q]They *are* all grievous revolters, walking with [r]slanders: *they are* brass and iron; they [9]*are* all corrupters.

29 The bellows [10]are burned, the lead is consumed of the fire; [11]the founder[G] melteth in vain: for the wicked are not plucked away.

30 [12]Reprobate[G] silver shall *men* call them, because [s]the LORD hath [t]rejected [u]them.[S]

21
*m Stumbling, figurative*, Isa. 8:14.

22
7 R. V. stirred up
8 R. V. uttermost parts of

25
*n War, evils of*, Judg. 3:2.

26
*o Sackcloth*, Isa. 15:3.
*p Ashes*, Num. 19:9.

28
*q Wicked, described*, Psa. 73:3.
*r Slander*, Prov. 10:18.
9 R. V. all of them deal corruptly.

29
10 R. V. blow fiercely;
11 R. V. in vain do they go on refining;

30
*s Backsliders, punishment of*, Jer. 3:22.
*t Rejection, by God*, Lam. 5:22.
*u Reprobates*, 1 Cor. 9:27.
12 R. V. Refuse

## CHAPTER 7

*The people of Judah urged to repent. 8 Their trust in lying words rebuked. 12 The impending ruin likened to that of Shiloh. 17 The idolatry of the people, and their punishment. 21 The sacrifices of the disobedient rejected. 29 The abominations of the land, 32 and the judgments about to come upon it.*

THE [a]word that [b]came to [c]Jĕr-e-mī'ah from the LORD, saying,

2 Stand in the gate of the [d]LORD's house, and [e]proclaim there this word, and say, Hear the [f]word of the LORD, all *ye of* [g]Jū'dah, that enter in at these gates to [h]worship the LORD.

3 Thus saith the LORD of hosts, the God of Ĭș'ra-el, [i]Amend your ways and your doings, and [j,k]I will [l]cause you to dwell in this place.

4 [m]Trust ye not in [n]lying words, saying, The temple of the LORD, The temple of the LORD, The temple of the LORD, *are* these.

5 For [j]if ye throughly[G] amend your ways and your doings; [j,o]if ye throughly[G] execute [p]judgment[G] between a man and his [q]neighbour;

6 *If* ye [r]oppress not the [s]stranger[G], the [t]fatherless, and the [u]widow, and [v]shed not innocent blood in this place, neither [w]walk after other gods to your hurt:[G]

7 [j]Then will I cause you to dwell in this place, in the [x]land that I [y]gave to your fathers, for ever and ever.

8 ¶ Behold, [z]ye [a]trust in [b]lying words, that cannot profit.

9 Will ye [c]steal, [d]murder, and commit [e]adultery, and [f,g]swear falsely, and [h]burn [i]incense unto [j]Bā'al, and walk after other gods whom ye know not;

10 And come and stand before me in this house, which is called by my name, and [b]say, We are delivered to do all these abominations?

1
*a Prophecies, inspired*, Dan. 9:24.
*b Prophets, inspiration of*, Isa. 3:2.
*c Jeremiah*, Jer. 1:1.

2
*d Temple, Solomon's*, 1 Kin. 6:17.
*e Preaching*, Matt. 9:35.
*f Word of God*, Psa. 119:9.
*g Judah, kingdom of*, 2 Chr. 11:17.
*h Worship*, Gen 22:5.

3
*i Repentance, enjoined*, Mark 1:4.
*j Blessings, contingent upon obedience*, Deut. 11:26.
*k Promise, to backsliders*, 2 Cor. 1:20.
*l Temporal Blessings, from God*, Psa. 103:2.

4
*m False Confidence*, Psa. 30:6.
*n Hypocrisy*, Jas. 3:17.

5
*o Righteousness, enjoined in official administration*, Psa. 15:2.
*p Justice*, Deut. 33:21.
*q Neighbor*, Luke 10:29.

6
*r Oppression, forbidden*, Eccl. 5:8.
*s Foreigners, justice toward, enjoined*, Deut. 23:20.
*t Orphan, justice to, required*, Lam. 5:3.
*u Widow, oppression of, forbidden*, 2 Sam. 14:5.
*v Homicide, felonious, forbidden*, Deut. 5:17.
*w Idolatry, forbidden*, 1 Sam. 15:23.

7
*x Canaan*, Gen. 37:1.
*y Covenant, of God with men*, Deut. 29:1.

8
*z Reproof, faithfulness in*, Prov. 17:10.
*a False Confidence of the spiritually blind*, Psa. 30:6. *b Hypocrisy*, Jas. 3:17

9 *c Theft*, Mark 7:22. *d Homicide, felonious*, Deut. 5:17. *e Adultery*, Lev. 20:10. *f False Witness*, Matt. 19:18. *g Perjury* 1 Tim. 1:10. *h Idolatry*, 1 Sam. 15:23. *i Incense, offered to idolatrous worship*, Ex. 37:29. *j Baal*, 2 Kin. 17:16.

11 Is this [k,l]house, which is
called by my name, [m]become a
den of [n]robbers in your eyes?
Behold, even I have seen *it*, saith
the LORD.[Q]
12 But go ye now unto my
[o]place which *was* in [p]Shī'lōh,
where I set my name at the first,
and see what [q]I did to it for the
[r]wickedness of my people Ĭṣ'-
ra-el.
13 And now, because ye have
done all these works, saith the
LORD, and [s,t]I [u]spake unto you,
rising up early and speaking, but
ye [v]heard not; and [s,t]I [u]called
you, but ye [w]answered not;
14 Therefore will I do unto *this*
[l]house, [k]which is called by my
name, wherein ye trust, and unto
the place which I gave to you
and to your fathers, as I have
done to [p]Shī'lōh.
15 And [x,y]I will cast you out of
my sight, as I have cast out all
your brethren, *even* the whole
seed of [z]Ē'phrā-ĭm.
16 Therefore [a]pray not thou
for this [b]people, neither lift up
cry nor prayer for them, neither
make [a]intercession to me: for I
will not hear thee.[s]
17 ¶ Seest thou not what they
do in the cities of [c]Jū'dah and in
the streets of [d]Jē-ru̦'sā-lĕm?
18 [e]The [f]children gather wood,
and the fathers kindle the fire,
and the women knead *their*
dough, to [g]make [h]cakes to the
[i,j]queen of heaven, and to pour
out drink [k]offerings unto other
gods, that they may provoke me
to [l]anger.[Q]
19 Do they provoke me to [l]an-
ger? saith the LORD: [m]*do they*
not *provoke* themselves to the
confusion of their own faces?
20 Therefore thus saith the
Lord GOD; Behold, [n,o]mine [l]an-
ger and my fury shall be poured
out upon this place, upon man,
and upon [p]beast, and upon the
trees of the field, and upon the
fruit of the ground; and it shall
burn, and shall not be quenched.[s]
21 ¶ Thus saith the LORD of
hosts, the God of Ĭṣ'ra-el; Put
your burnt [q]offerings unto your
sacrifices, and eat flesh.
22 For I spake not unto your
fathers, nor commanded them in
the day that I [r]brought them out
of the land of [s]Ē'ġy̆pt, concerning burnt offerings or sacrifices:
23[s] But this thing commanded
I them, saying, [t,u,v]Obey my
voice, and I will be your God,
and ye shall be [w]my people: and
[x]walk ye in all the ways that I
have commanded you, that it
may be well unto you.
24 But they [y,z,a,b]hearkened
not, nor inclined their ear, but
walked in the counsels *and* in the
[1]imagination[c] of their evil heart,
and went backward, and not forward.
25 Since the day that your [c]fa-
thers came forth out of the land
of [d]Ē'ġy̆pt unto this day [e]I have
even sent unto you all my servants the [f]prophets, daily rising up
early and sending *them*:[s]
26 Yet they [b,g]hearkened not
unto me, nor inclined their ear,
but [a,h]hardened their neck: they
did worse than their fathers.
27 Therefore thou shalt speak
all these words unto them; but
[i]they will not hearken to thee:
thou shalt also call unto them;
but they will not answer thee.
28 But thou shalt say unto
them, This *is* a nation that
[b]obeyeth not the voice of the
LORD their God, nor receiveth
[2]correction: truth is perished,
and is cut off from their mouth.
29 ¶ [j]Cut off thine hair, *O Jē-
ru̦'sā-lĕm*, and cast *it* away, and
take up a lamentation on [3]high
places; for [k]the LORD hath [l]re-

**11**
k Isa. 56:7; Matt. 21:13; Mark 11:17; Luke 19:46.
l *Temple, Solomon's*, 1 Kin. 6:17.
m *Profanation, of the house of God*, Lev. 22:32.
n *Robbers, dens of*, Hos. 6:9.

**12**
o *Tabernacle*, Ex. 27:9.
p *Shiloh*, Judg. 21:12.
q *Wicked, punishment of*, Psa. 73:3.
r *Backsliding, of Israel*, Hos. 11:7.

**13**
s *God, longsuffering of*, Gen. 2:2.
t *God, mercy of*, Gen. 2:2.
u *Wicked, warned*, Psa. 73:3.
v *Impenitence*, Rom. 2:5.
w *Obduracy*, Prov. 29:1.

**15**
x *Judah, kingdom of, prophecies concerning*, vs. 15–34; 2 Chr. 11:17.
y *Nation, judgments denounced against*, vs. 15–34; Isa. 2:4.
z *Israel, after the revolt*, 1 Kin. 12:1.

**16**
a *Intercession, of man with God, for the obdurate, unavailing*, Jer. 27:18.
b *Reprobates*, 1 Cor. 9:27.

**17**
c *Judah, kingdom of*, 2 Chr. 11:17.
d *Jerusalem*, Judg. 19:10.

**18**
e *Family, idolatrous*, 1 Chr. 13:14.
f *Children*, Mark 10:14.
g *Idolatry, customs of*, 1 Sam. 15:23.
h *Bread, offerings of, by idolaters*, Ezek. 4:13.
i *Moon, worshiped*, Song 6:10.
j *Idolatry, objects of*, 1 Sam. 15:23.
k *Offerings, in idolatrous worship*, Lev. 6:17.
l *Anger of God*, 2 Kin. 13:3.

**19** m *Sin, fruits of*, Rom. 5:12. **20** n *Judah, kingdom of, prophecies concerning*, 2 Chr. 11:17. o *Nation, judgments denounced against*, Isa. 2:4.

p *Animals, suffer under divine judgments*, Jer. 27:5.

**21**
q *Offerings, unavailing when not accompanied by piety*, Lev. 6:17.

**22**
r *God, providence of*, Gen. 2:2.
s *Egypt*, Gen. 41:8.

**23**
t *Obedience, enjoined*, Heb. 5:8.
u *Obedience better than Sacrifice*, 1 Sam. 15:22.
v *Blessings, contingent upon obedience*, Deut. 11:26.
w *Spiritual Adoption*, Rom. 8:15.
x *Walking, figurative*, Gen. 5:22.

**24**
y *Self-will*, Gen. 49:6.
z *Impenitence*, Rom. 2:5.
a *Obduracy*, Prov. 29:1.
b *Disobedience to God*, Eph. 5:6.
1 R. V. stubbornness

**25**
c *Israel*, Ex. 4:22.
d *Egypt*, Gen. 41:8.
e *God, mercy of*, Gen. 2:2.
f *Minister, duties of, to warn*, Rom. 15:16.

**26**
g *Impenitence*, Rom. 2:5.
h *Self-will*, Gen. 49:6.

**27**
i *Minister, message of, rejected*, Rom. 15:16.

**28**
2 R.V. instruction:

**29**
j *Mourning, cutting off the hair in*, Lam. 2:5.
k *Holy Spirit, withdrawn from incorrigible sinners*, Acts 1:2.
l *Rejection, by God*, Lam. 5:22.
3 R. V. the bare heights;

30
m Temple, Solomon's, 1 Kin. 6:17.
n Profanation, of the house of God, Lev. 22:32.

31
o High Places, 1 Kin. 3:2.
p Molech, altar of, 1 Kin. 11:7.
q Or, Topheth, 2 Kin. 23:10.
r Idolatry, wicked practices of, 1 Sam. 15:23.
s Human Sacrifices, Deut. 12:31.

32
t Burying Places, Gen. 23:4.

33
u Nation, judgments denounced against, Isa. 2:4.

34
v Judah, kingdom of, prophecies concerning, 2 Chr. 11:17.
w Jerusalem, prophecies against, Judg. 19:10.
x Marriage, festivities attending, Gen. 34:9.
y War, evils of, Judg. 3:2.

1
a Jerusalem, Judg. 19:10.
b Burying Places, Gen. 23:4.

jected and forsaken the generation of his wrath.
30 For the children of Jū′dah
have done evil in my sight, saith
the LORD: they have set their
abominations in the [m]house
which is called by my name, to
[n]pollute it.
31 And they have built the
[o,p]high places of [q]Tō′phet, which
*is* in the valley of the son of
*Hĭn′nom, to [r]burn their [s]sons
and their daughters in the fire;
which I commanded *them* not,
neither came it into my heart.
32 ¶ Therefore, behold, the
days come, saith the LORD, that
it shall no more be called [q]Tō′phet, nor the valley of the son
of +Hĭn′nom, but the valley of
slaughter: for they shall [t]bury in
Tō′phet, till there be no place.
33 And [u]the carcases[G] of this people shall be meat[G] for the fowls
of the heaven, and for the beasts
of the earth; and none shall fray[G]
*them* away.
34 [u]Then will I cause to cease
from the cities of [v]Jū′dah, and
from the streets of [w]Jē-ru̦′să-lĕm,
the voice of mirth, and the voice
of gladness, the [x]voice of the
bridegroom, and the voice of the
bride: for [y]the land shall be desolate.[Q]

## CHAPTER 8

*The calamities about to come upon the Jews 4 on account of their perverseness. 13 Their approaching alarm and confusion described. 18 The prophet bewails their desperate condition.*

AT that time, saith the LORD,
they shall bring out the
bones of the kings of Jū′dah, and
the bones of his princes, and
the bones of the priests, and the
bones of the prophets, and the
bones of the inhabitants of [a]Jē-ru̦′să-lĕm, out of their [b]graves:
2 And they shall spread them before the [c,d]sun, and the [d,e]moon,
and [d]all the host of heaven, whom
[f]they have loved, and whom they
have served, and after whom they
have walked, and whom they
have sought, and whom they have
worshipped: they shall not be
gathered, nor be buried; they
shall be for dung[G] upon the face
of the earth.[Q]
3 And [g,h]death shall be chosen
rather than life by all the residue[G] of them that remain of this
evil [i]family, which remain in all
the places whither I have driven
them, saith the LORD of hosts.[Q]
4 ¶ Moreover [j]thou shalt say
unto them, Thus saith the LORD;
Shall they fall, and not arise?
shall he turn away, and not return?
5 Why *then* is this people of
[a]Jē-ru̦′să-lĕm [f]slidden back by a
perpetual backsliding? they hold
fast [k]deceit, they [l,m]refuse to return.
6 I hearkened and heard, *but*
they spake not aright: [l,m]no man
repented him of his wickedness,
saying, What have I done? [n]every
one turned to his course, as the
horse rusheth into the battle.
7 Yea, the [o]stork in the heaven
knoweth her appointed times;
and the [p]turtle and the [q]crane and
the [r]swallow observe the time of
their [s]coming; but my people
[t]know not the [1]judgment[G] of the
LORD.
8 How do ye [u]say, We *are* wise,
and the law of the LORD *is* with
us? [2]Lo, certainly in vain[G] made
he *it*; the *pen of the [v]scribes *is*
in vain.
9 The wise *men* are ashamed,
they are dismayed and taken: lo,
they have [l,m]rejected the [w]word
of the LORD; and what wisdom
*is* in them?

2
c Sun, worshiped, Josh. 10:12.
d Idolatry, objects of, 1 Sam. 15:23.
e Moon, worshiped, Song 6:10.
f Backsliding, of Israel, Hos. 11:7.

3
g Death, desired, Num. 23:10.
h Adversity, despondency in, Psa. 10:6.
i Jews, prophecies concerning, Neh. 4:2.

4
j Prophets, inspiration of, Isa. 3:2.

5
k Deceit, Psa. 36:3.
l Impenitence, Rom. 2:5.
m Obduracy, Prov. 29:1.

6
n Wicked, described, Psa. 73:3.

7
o Stork, Lev. 11:19.
p Dove, Gen. 8:8.
q Isa. 38:14.
r Swallow, Psa. 84:3.
s Birds, migrate, Eccl. 12:4.
t Spiritual Blindness, 2 Cor. 4:4.
1 Am. R. V. ordinance of Jehovah.

8
u Self-righteousness, Luke 18:11
v Scribe, 1 Kin. 4:3.
2 R. V. But, behold, the false pen of the scribes hath wrought falsely.

9
w Word of God, Psa. 119:9.

**+ HINNOM.** *A valley W. and S. W. of Jerusalem,* Josh. 15:8; 18:16; Neh. 11:30. *Altar of Molech situated in,* 2 Kin. 23:10; 2 Chr. 28:3; Jer. 7:31; 32:35. *Children offered in sacrifice in,* 2 Chr. 33:6; Jer. 19:2, 4. *Possibly identical with valley of vision,* Isa. 22:1, 5. Tophet a part of, where human sacrifices were burned and other abominations of idolatrous worship were committed. See footnote, TOPHETH, 2 Kin. 23:10.

*** PEN,** Isa. 8:1; 3 John 13. *Made of iron,* Job 19:24. **Figurative,** Psa. 45:1; Jer. 8:8; 17:1.

10 [x]Therefore will I give their wives unto others, *and* their fields to them that shall inherit *them*: for [y]every one from the least even unto the greatest is given to [z]covetousness, from the [a]prophet even unto the [b]priest every one dealeth falsely.

11 For they have healed the hurt of the daughter of my people slightly, [c]saying, [d]Peace, peace; when *there is* no peace.[Q]

12 Were they ashamed when they had committed abomination? nay, they were [e]not at all ashamed, neither could they [f]blush: therefore [g]shall they fall among them that fall: in the time of their visitation[G] they shall be cast down, saith the LORD.

13 [h,i]I will surely consume them, saith the LORD: [i]*there shall be* no [j]grapes on the vine, nor figs on the [k]fig tree, and the leaf shall fade; and *the* [l]*things that* I have given them shall pass away from them.

14 ¶ Why do we sit still? [m]assemble yourselves, and let us enter into the defenced[G] cities, and let us be silent there: for [i]the LORD our God hath put us to silence, and given us water of [n]gall[G] to drink, because [o]we have sinned against the LORD.

15 We looked for peace, but no good *came*; *and* for a time of [3]health, and behold [4]trouble!

16 The snorting of his [p]horses was heard from [q]Dăn: the whole land trembled at the sound of the neighing of his strong ones; for they are come, and have [r]devoured the land, and all that is in it; the city, and those that dwell therein.

17 For, behold, [h]I will send [s]serpents, [5,t]cockatrices,[G] among you, which *will* not *be* [u]charmed, and they shall bite you, saith the LORD.[s]

18 ¶ [6]*When* I would comfort myself against sorrow, [v]my heart *is* faint in me.

19 Behold the voice of the cry of the daughter of my people [7]because of them that [w]dwell in a far country: *Is* not the LORD in Zī′ŏn? *is* not her king in her? Why have they provoked[G] me to [x]anger with their [y]graven[G] images, *and* with strange[G] vanities?

20 [z,a]The [b,c]harvest is past, the [c,d]summer is ended, and [c]we are not saved.

21 [e]For the hurt of the daughter of my people [f]am I hurt; I am black; astonishment[G] hath taken hold on me.

22 [a,g]*Is there* no [h,i]balm[G] in Ḡĭl′e-ăd; *is there* no [j]physician there? why then is not the health of the daughter of my people recovered?

## CHAPTER 9

*The prophet's grief in view of the judgments about to come upon the people for their wickedness. 9 He justifies God in punishing them. 17 He calls to mourning over their calamities; 23 and exhorts the people to trust in God. 25 Both Jews and Gentiles threatened.*

[a,b]OH that my head were waters, and mine eyes a fountain of tears, that [c]I might [d]weep day and night for the slain of the daughter of my people!

2 Oh that I had in the wilderness a lodging place of wayfaring men; [e,f]that I might leave my people, and go from them! for they *be* all [g]adulterers, an assembly of treacherous men.

3 And they bend their tongues *like* their bow *for* [h]lies: [1]but [i]they are [j]not valiant for the [k]truth upon the earth; for they [l]proceed from evil to evil, and they [m]know[G] not me, saith the LORD.

4 Take ye heed every one of his neighbour, and trust ye not in any brother: for every brother [n]will utterly supplant, and every

**10**
x *Divine Chastisement*, Job 33:19.
y *Jews, wickedness of*, Neh. 4:2.
z *Covetousness*, Isa. 57:17.

a *Minister, false and corrupt*, Rom. 15:16.
b *Priest, corrupt*, Lev. 1:5.

**11**
c *False Confidence*, Psa. 30:6.
d *Peace*, Jer. 29:7.

**12**
e *Conscience, dead*, Acts 23:1.
f Jer. 6:15; Ezra 9:6.
g *Wicked, punishment of*, Psa. 73:3.

**13**
h *Nation, judgments denounced against*, Isa. 2:4.
i *Adversity, dispensation from God*, Psa. 10:6.
j *Grape*, Lev. 25:5.
k *Fig Tree*, Luke 13:6.
l *Temporal Blessings, from God*, Psa. 103:2.

**14**
m *Repentance*, Mark 1:4.
n *Gall, figurative*, Job 16:13.
o *Sin, confession of*, Rom. 5:12.

**15**
3 R. V. healing,
4 R. V. dismay!

**16**
p *Horse*, Job 39:19.
q *Dan*, Judg. 18:29.
r *War, evils of*, Judg. 3:2.

**17**
s *Serpent, figurative*, Num. 21:6.
t *Cockatrice, figurative*, Isa. 11:8.
u *Charmers*, Isa. 19:3.
5 Am. R. V. adders,

**18**
6 R. V. Oh that I could comfort myself against sorrow!

v *Doubting*, Rom. 14:23.

**19**
w *Captivity, as a judgment*, Isa. 5:13.
x *Anger of God*, 2 Kin. 13:3.
y *Idolatry*, 1 Sam. 15:23.
7 R. V. from a land that is very far off:

**20**
z *Despondency*, Eccl. 2:20.

a *Adversity, despondency in*, Psa. 10:6.
b *Harvest, figurative*, Ex. 34:21.
c *Opportunity, lost*, Gal. 6:10.
d *Summer, figurative*, Isa. 28:4.

**21**
e *Minister, love of, for the church*, Rom. 15:16.
f *Sympathy*, Jas. 1:27.

**22**
g *Despondency*, Eccl. 2:20.
h *Balm*, Gen. 37:25.
i *Disease, remedies used for*, Ex. 15:26.
j *Physician, figurative*, 2 Chr. 16:12.

**1**
a *Zeal, exemplified*, 2 Cor. 7:11.
b *Patriotism*, Psa. 137:1.
c *Jeremiah*, Jer. 1:1.
d *Weeping*, Ezra 3:13.

**2**
e *Evil Company, shunned by the righteous*, Prov. 13:20.
f *Sin, repugnant to the righteous*, Rom. 5:12.
g *Adultery*, Lev. 20:10.

**3**
h *Falsehood*, Job 21:34.
i *Wicked, described*, Psa. 73:3.
j *Lukewarmness*, Rev. 3:16.
k *Truth*, John 18:37.
l *Sin, progressive*, Rom. 5:12.

m *Spiritual Blindness*, 2 Cor. 4:4. 1 R. V. and they are grown strong in the land, but not for truth: 4 n *Dishonesty*, Ezek. 22:13.

neighbour will walk with [o]slan-
ders.
5 And [i]they will [p]deceive every
one his neighbour, and will [h]not
speak the truth: [i]they have
taught their tongue to speak lies,
*and* weary themselves to commit
iniquity.
6 Thine habitation *is* in the
midst of deceit; through deceit
they [q,r]refuse to know me, saith
the LORD.
7 Therefore thus saith the
LORD of hosts, Behold, [s]I will
melt [t]them, and [u]try[C] them; for
how shall I do for the daughter
of my people?
8 Their tongue *is as* [2]an [v]arrow
shot out; it speaketh deceit: *one*
speaketh peaceably to his neighbour with his mouth, [w]but in
heart [x]he layeth[C] [3]his wait.[C]
9 ¶ Shall I not [y]visit[C] them for
these *things*? saith the LORD:
shall not my soul be avenged on
such a [s,t]nation as this?
10 For the mountains will I
take up a weeping and wailing,
and for the [4]habitations of the
wilderness a lamentation, because they are burned up, so
that none can pass through *them*;
neither can *men* hear the voice of
the cattle; both the fowl of the
heavens and the beast are fled;
they are gone.
11 And [t]I will make [z]Jĕ-ru̇'sâ-
lĕm heaps,[C] [5]*and* a den of dragons; and I will make the cities of
[t]Jū'dah desolate,[C] without an inhabitant.[Q]
12 ¶ Who *is* the wise man, that
may understand this? and *who
is he* to whom the mouth of the
LORD hath spoken, that he may
declare it, for what the land perisheth *and* is burned up like
a wilderness, that none passeth
through?
13 And the LORD saith, Because they have forsaken my
law which I set before them,
and have [a]not obeyed my voice,
neither walked therein;
14 But have walked[C] after
the [6,b]imagination[C] of their own
heart, and [c]after Bā'al-ĭm, which
their fathers [d]taught them:
15 Therefore thus saith the
LORD of hosts, the God of Ĭş'-
ra-el; Behold, [e]I will feed [f]them,
*even* this people, with [g]worm-
wood, and give them water of
[h]gall[C] to drink.[Q]
16 [e]I will [i]scatter [f]them also
among the [7]heathen,[C] whom
neither they nor their fathers
have known: and I will send
a [j]sword after them, till I have
consumed them.
17 ¶ Thus saith the LORD of
hosts, Consider ye, and call for
the mourning women, that they
may come; and send for cunning[C]
*women*, that they may come:
18 And let them make haste,
and take up a wailing for us,
that our eyes may run down with
tears, and our eyelids gush out
with waters.
19 For a voice of wailing is
heard out[C] of [k]Zī'ŏn, How are
we spoiled![C] we are greatly confounded, because we have forsaken the land, because [8]our
dwellings have cast *us* out.
20 Yet hear the word of the
LORD, O ye women, and let
your ear receive the word of his
mouth, and teach your daughters
wailing, and every one her neighbour lamentation.
21 [f]For death is come up into
our windows, *and* is entered into
our palaces, to cut off the children from without,[C] *and* the
young men from the streets.
22 Speak, Thus saith the LORD,
Even the carcases of men shall
fall as dung[C] upon the open field,
and as the handful after the
harvestman, and none shall
gather *them*.
23 ¶ Thus saith the LORD, Let

o *Slander*, Prov. 10:18.

**5**

p *Deceit*, Psa. 36:3.

**6**

q *Obduracy*, Prov. 29:1.

r *Self-will*, Gen. 49:6.

**7**

s *Nation, judgments denounced against*, vs. 7–26; Isa. 2:4.

t *Jews, prophecies concerning* Neh. 4:2.

u *Refining, figurative*, 1 Chr. 28:18.

**8**

v *Arrow, figurative*, 1 Sam. 20:20.

w *Hypocrisy*, Jas. 3:17.

x *Treachery*, 2 Kin. 9:23.

2 R. V. a deadly arrow;

3 R. V. wait for him.

**9**

y *Divine Chastisement*, Job 33:19.

**10**

4 R. V. pastures

**11**

z *Jerusalem, prophecies against*, Judg. 19:10.

5 R. V. a dwelling place of jackals;

**13**

a *Disobedience to God*, Eph. 5:6.

**14**

b *Self-will*, Gen. 49:6.

c *Idolatry*, 1 Sam. 15:23.

d *Influence, evil*, 1 Cor. 7:14.

6 R. V. stubbornness

**15**

e *Divine Chastisement*, Job 33:19.

f *Jews, prophecies concerning*, Neh. 4:2.

g *Wormwood, figurative*, Deut. 29:18.

h *Gall, figurative*, Job 16:13.

**16**

i *Dispersion*, Gen. 11:8.

j *War, as a judgment*, Judg. 3:2.

7 R. V. nations.

**19**

k *Zion*, 2 Sam. 5:7.

8 R. V. they have cast down our dwellings.

not the wise *man* [l,m]glory in his
[n]wisdom, neither let the mighty
*man* glory in his might, let not
[o]the rich *man* glory in his riches:
24 But [p]let him that glorieth
glory in this, that he [q]under-
standeth and knoweth me, that
I *am* the LORD which exercise
[r,s]lovingkindness, [t]judgment,[G]
and [u]righteousness, in the earth:
for in these *things* I delight, saith
the LORD.[S T Q]
25 ¶ Behold, the days come,
saith the LORD, that I will [v]pun-
ish[G] all *them which are* circumcised [9]with the uncircumcised;[Q]
26 Ē′ġy̆pt, and Jū′dah, and
Ē′dom, and the children of Ăm′-
mŏn, and Mō′ab, and all *that*
[10]*are* in the utmost corners, that
dwell in the wilderness: for all
*these* nations *are* uncircumcised,
and all the house of Ĭs̹′ra-el *are*
uncircumcised in the heart.[T Q]

## CHAPTER 10

*The people warned not to learn the way of the heathen.* 17 *The desolations about to come upon the land.* 23 *The prayer of the prophet.*

HEAR ye the word which the
LORD [a]speaketh unto you,
O house of Ĭs̹′ra-el:[S]
2 Thus [b]saith the LORD, Learn
not the way of the [1]heathen,[G] and
be not dismayed at the signs of
heaven; for the heathen are dismayed at them.
3 For [b]the customs of the [2]peo-
ple *are* vain:[G] for *one* cutteth a
tree out of the forest, the work
of the hands of the workman,
with the ax.
4 [b]They deck it with [c]silver and
with [d]gold; they fasten it with
[e]nails and with hammers, that it
move not.
5 [b]They *are* [3]upright as the
palm tree, but speak not: they
must needs be borne, because
they cannot go. [b]Be not afraid of
them; for they cannot do evil,
neither also *is it* in them to do
good.
6 Forasmuch as *there is* none
like unto thee, O LORD; thou
*art* great, and thy name *is* great
in [f]might.
7 Who would not [g]fear thee,
O King of nations? for to thee
doth it appertain: forasmuch as
among all the wise *men* of the
nations, and in all their kingdoms, *there is* none like unto
thee.[S Q]
8 But they are altogether bru-
tish[G] and foolish: [b]the [4]stock *is* a
doctrine of vanities.[S]
9 [c]Silver spread[G] into plates is
[h]brought from [i]Tär′shish, and
[d]gold from [j]Ū′phăz, the work of
the workman, and of the hands
of the [5]founder:[G] [k]blue and [k]pur-
ple *is* their clothing: they *are* all
the work of cunning[G] *men*.
10 But the LORD *is* the true
God, he *is* the [l]living God, and
an [m]everlasting [n]king: at his
[o]wrath the earth shall tremble,
and the nations shall not be able
to abide his indignation.[S Q T]
11 Thus shall ye [p]say unto
them, The gods that have not
made the heavens and the earth,
*even* they shall perish from the
earth, and from under these
heavens.[S]
12 [q,r]He hath [s,t]made the [u]earth
by his [f]power, he hath [s]estab-
lished the world by his [v]wis-
dom, and hath [s]stretched out
the [w]heavens by his discretion.[T S]
13 When [f]he uttereth his voice,
*there is* a multitude of waters in
the heavens, and [x,y]he causeth
the [z]vapours to ascend from the
ends of the earth; he maketh
[a]lightnings with [b]rain, and bringeth forth the wind out of his
[6]treasures.[S]
14 Every man is [7]brutish[G] in *his*
knowledge: every founder[G] is confounded by the graven[G] image:
[c]for his molten[G] image *is* falsehood, and *there is* no breath in
them.[O]

**23**
*l* *Boasting*, Prov. 25:14.
*m* *Pride*, Prov. 16:18.
*n* *Wisdom, worldly*, Prov. 2:2.
*o* *Rich, admonitions to*, Jas. 5:1.

**24**
*p* 1 Cor. 1:31; 2 Cor. 10:17.
*q* *Wisdom, spiritual*, Prov. 2:2.
*r* *God, love of*, Gen. 2:2.
*s* *God, mercy of*, Gen. 2:2.
*t* *God, justice of*, Gen. 2:2.
*u* *God, righteousness of*, Gen. 2:2.

**25**
*v* *Wicked, punishment of*, Psa. 73:3.
9 R. V. in their uncircumcision;

**26**
10 Am. R. V. have the corners of their hair cut off,

**1**
*a* *Word of God, inspired*, Psa. 119:9.

**2**
*b* *Idolatry, folly of*, 1 Sam. 15:23.
1 R. V. nations,

**3**
2 R. V. peoples are vanity:

**4**
*c* *Silver*, 1 Chr. 28:14.
*d* *Gold*, Ezek. 7:19.
*e* *Nail*, Isa. 41:7.

**5**
3 R. V. like a palm tree, of turned work, and speak not:

**6**
*f* *God, power of*, Gen. 2:2.

**7**
*g* *Fear of God*, Acts 9:31.

**8**
4 R. V. instruction of idols, it is but a stock.

**9**
*h* *Commerce*, 1 Kin. 10:15.
*i* *Tarshish*, 2 Chr. 20:36.
*j* Dan. 10:5.
*k* *Colors, symbolical*, Ezek. 16:16.
5 R. V. goldsmith;

**10**
*l* *God, self-existent*, Gen. 2:2.
*m* *God, eternity of*, Gen. 2:2.
*n* *God, sovereign*, Gen. 2:2.
*o* *Anger of God*, 2 Kin. 13:3.

**11**
*p* *Idolatry, prophecies concerning*, 1 Sam. 15:23.

**12**
*q* *Faith, exemplified*, Mark 11:22.
*r* *God, creator*, Gen. 2:2.
*s* *Creation*, Mark 13:19.
*t* *Works of God*, Psa. 40:5.
*u* *Earth, created*, Prov. 8:23.
*v* *God, wisdom of*, Gen. 2:2.
*w* *Heavens, created*, Psa. 8:3.

**13**
*x* *God, providence of*, Gen. 2:2.
*y* *Temporal Blessings, from God*, Psa. 103:2.
*z* *Meteorology*, Matt. 16:2.

*a* *Lightning*, Job 28:26.
*b* *Rain, sent by God*, 2 Sam. 1:21.
6 R. V. treasuries.

**14**
*c* *Idolatry, folly of*, 1 Sam. 15:23.
7 R. V. become brutish and is without knowledge; every goldsmith is put to shame by

15 They *are* vanity, *and* the work of [8]errors: in the time of their visitation[G] [d]they shall perish.

16 The portion of Jā-cob *is* not like them: for he *is* the [e]former of all *things*; and Ĭş′ra-el *is* the [9]rod of his inheritance: The LORD of hosts *is* his name.

17 ¶ Gather up thy wares out of the land, O [10]inhabitant of the fortress.

18 For thus saith the LORD, Behold, [f,g]I will sling out the inhabitants of the land at this once, and will distress them, that they may find *it so*.

19 ¶ [h]Woe is me for my hurt! my wound is grievous[G]: but I said, Truly this *is* a grief, and [i]I must bear it.

20 [h]My tabernacle is spoiled, and all my cords are broken: my children are gone forth of me, and they *are* not: *there is* none to stretch forth my tent any more, and to set up my curtains.

21 For the [11,j,k]pastors[G] are become brutish[G], and [l]have not sought the LORD: therefore they shall not prosper, and all their flocks shall be scattered.

22 [12]Behold, the noise of the bruit[G] is come, and a great commotion out of the north country, [f]to make the cities of Jū′dah [13]desolate, *and* a den of dragons.

23 ¶ O LORD, [m]I know that [n]the way of man *is* [o]not in himself: [n]*it is* not in man that walketh to direct his steps.

24 [p]O LORD, correct me, but with [q,r]judgment[G]; not in thine [s]anger, lest thou bring me to nothing.

25 [t]Pour out thy fury upon the [u]heathen[G] that know thee not, and upon the families that [l]call not on thy name: for they have eaten up Jā′cob, and devoured him, and consumed him, and have made his habitation desolate.[Q]

## CHAPTER 11

*God reminds the people of his covenant. 8 and rebukes their violations of it. 11 Their punishment foretold. 18 A conspiracy against Jeremiah.*

THE word that [a,b]came to [c]Jĕr-e-mī′ah from the LORD, saying,

2 Hear ye the words of this [d]covenant[G], and speak unto the [e]men of Jū′dah, and to the [e]inhabitants of [f]Jĕ-ru̥′să-lĕm;

3 And say thou unto them, Thus saith the LORD God of Ĭş′ra-el; [g]Cursed *be* the man that obeyeth not the [h]words of this covenant,

4 [h]Which I commanded your fathers in the day *that* [i]I brought them forth out of the land of [j]Ē′ġypt, from the iron [k]furnace, saying, [l]Obey my voice, and do [h]them, according to all which I command you: [m,n]so shall [o]ye be my people, and I will be your God:[S T]

5 That I may perform the [p]oath which I have sworn unto your fathers, to give them a [q]land flowing with [r]milk and [s]honey, as *it is* this day. Then answered I, and said, So be it, O LORD.

6 Then the LORD said unto me, Proclaim all these words in the cities of Jū′dah, and in the streets of [f]Jĕ-ru̥′să-lĕm, saying, Hear ye the words of this covenant, and [l]do them.

7 For [t]I earnestly protested unto your fathers in the day *that* I brought them up out of the land of [j]Ē′ġypt, *even* unto this day, rising early and protesting, [l]saying, Obey my voice.

8 Yet they [u]obeyed not, nor inclined their ear, but [v]walked every one in the [1,w,x]imagination[G] of their evil heart: therefore I will bring upon [e]them all the words of this covenant, which I commanded *them* to do; but they did *them* not.

9 And the LORD said unto me,

**15**
d *Idolatry, prophecies concerning,* 1 Sam. 15:23.
8 R. V. delusion:

**16**
e *God, creator,* Gen. 2:2.
9 R. V. tribe

**17**
10 R. V. thou that abidest in the siege.

**18**
f *Nation, judgments denounced against,* Isa. 2:4.
g *Divine Chastisement,* Job 33:19.

**19**
h *Jeremiah, lamentations of,* Jer. 1:1.
i *Afflictions, resignation in,* Psa. 34:19.

**21**
j *Minister* (as some interpret), *false and corrupt,* Rom. 15:16.
k *Rulers* (as some interpret), *wicked,* Ex. 18:21.
l *Prayerlessness,* Job 21:15.
11 R. V. shepherds

**22**
12 Am. R. V. The voice of tidings, behold it cometh,
13 R. V. a desolation, a dwelling place of jackals.

**23**
m *Faith, exemplified,* Mark 11:22.
n *Ignorance,* Acts 3:17.
o *Humility, exemplified,* Prov. 22:4.

**24**
p *Adversity, prayer in,* Psa. 10:6.
q *Justice,* Deut. 32:21.
r *Mercy,* Deut. 5:10.
s *Anger of God,* 2 Kin. 13:3.

**25**
t *Prayer, imprecatory,* Acts 6:4.
u *Heathen,* Lam. 1:10.

**1**
a *Inspiration,* Job 32:8.
b *Prophets, inspiration of,* Isa. 3:2.
c *Jeremiah,* Jer. 1:1.

**2**
d *Covenant, of God with men,* Deut. 29:1.
e *Jews, prophecies concerning,* vs. 2–14; Neh. 4:2.
f *Jerusalem,* Judg. 19:10.

**3**
g *Curse, denounced against the disobedient,* Judg. 5:23.
h *Law of Moses,* Deut. 33:2.

**4**
i *God, providence of,* Gen. 2:2.
j *Egypt,* Gen. 41:8.
k *Furnace, figurative,* Prov. 17:3.
l *Obedience, enjoined,* Heb. 5:8.
m *Contingencies, in divine government,* 1 Kin. 3:14.
n *Blessings, contingent upon obedience,* Deut. 11:26.
o *Spiritual Adoption,* Rom. 8:15.

**5**
p *Oath, attributed to God,* Num. 5:19.
q *Canaan,* Gen. 37:1.
r *Milk, figurative,* Job 10:10.
s *Honey, figurative,* Prov. 25:27.

**7**
t *God, longsuffering of,* Gen. 2:2.

**8**
u *Disobedience to God,* Eph. 5:6.
v *Wicked, described,* Psa. 73:3.
w *Impenitence,* Rom. 2:5.
x *Self-will,* Gen. 49:6.
1 R. V. stubbornness

A [y]conspiracy is found among
the [e]men of Jū′dah, and among
the [e]inhabitants of [f]Jĕ-ru̥′sȧ-lĕm.
10 They are turned back to the
iniquities of their [z]forefathers,
which refused to hear my words;
and they [a]went after other gods
to serve them: the house of Ĭs̱′-
ra-el and the house of Jū′dah
have broken my covenant which
I made with their fathers.
11 Therefore thus saith the
Lord, Behold, I will bring evil
upon them, which they [b]shall not
be able to escape; and though
they shall cry unto me, [c]I will
not hearken unto them.
12 Then shall the cities of Jū′-
dah and inhabitants of Jĕ-ru̥′sȧ-
lĕm go, and [d]cry unto the gods
unto whom they offer [e]incense:
but they shall not save them at
all in the time of their trouble.
13 For *according to* the number
of thy cities were thy [f]gods, O
Jū′dah; and *according to* the
number of the streets of Jĕ-ru̥′-
sȧ-lĕm have ye set up [g]altars to
*that* shameful thing, *even* altars
to [d]burn [e]incense unto [h]Bā′al.
14 Therefore [i]pray not thou for
this people, neither lift up a cry
or prayer for them: for I [c]will
not hear *them* in the time that
they cry unto me for their
trouble.
15 What hath my beloved to do
in mine house, *seeing* she hath
[j]wrought[G] lewdness[G] with many,
and the holy flesh is passed from
thee? when thou doest evil, then
thou rejoicest.[Q]
16 The Lord called thy name,
A green olive tree, fair, *and* of
goodly fruit: with the noise of a
great tumult he hath kindled fire
upon it, and the branches of it
are broken.
17 For the Lord of hosts, that
planted thee, hath pronounced
evil against thee, for the [k]evil
of the house of Ĭs̱′ra-el and of
the house of Jū′dah, which they
have [2]done against themselves to
to provoke me to [l]anger in [d]offer-
ing [e]incense unto [h]Bā′al.
18 ¶ And the Lord hath given
me knowledge *of it,* and I know
*it*: then thou shewedst me their
doings.
19 But I *was* like a lamb *or* an
ox *that* is brought to the slaughter; and I knew not that they had
[m]devised devices[G] against me,
*saying,* Let us destroy the tree
with the fruit thereof, and let us
cut him off from the land of the
living, that his name may be no
more remembered.
20 But, O Lord of hosts, that[G]
[n]judgest [o]righteously, that triest
the reins[G] and the [p]heart[G], [q]let me
see thy vengeance on them: for
unto thee have I revealed my
cause.[S Q]
21 Therefore thus saith the
Lord of the men of [r]Ăn′a-thŏth,
that [s]seek thy life, saying, Prophesy not in the name of the Lord,
that thou die not by our hand:
22 Therefore thus saith the
Lord of hosts, Behold, I will
punish them: the young men shall
die by the [t]sword; their sons and
their daughters shall die by
[u]famine:
23 And there shall be no remnant of them: for I will bring
[v]evil upon the men of [r]Ăn′a-
thŏth, *even* the year of their
visitation.[G]

## CHAPTER 12

*The prophet complains of the prosperity of the wicked. 5 God admonishes him. 7 God's heritage forsaken by him. 14 A promise of return from captivity.*

RIGHTEOUS *art* [a]thou, O
Lord, when I plead with
thee: yet [1]let me talk with thee
of *thy* judgments: [b,c]Where-
fore[G] doth the way of the wicked
[d]prosper? *wherefore*[G] are all they
[2]happy that deal very treacherously?[S]
2 [b,c]Thou hast planted them,

9
*y* *Conspiracy,* 1 Kin. 16:9.

10
*z* *Backsliding, of Israel,* Hos. 11:7.
*a* *Idolatry,* 1 Sam. 15:23.

11
*b* *Punishment, no escape from,* Lev. 26:41.
*c* *Wicked, prayers of, not answered,* v. 14; Psa. 73:3.

12
*d* *Idolatry, customs of,* 1 Sam. 15:23.
*e* *Incense, offered in idolatrous worship,* Ex. 37:29.

13
*f* *Polytheism,* 1 Cor. 8:5.
*g* *Altar, used in idolatrous worship,* Gen. 8:20.
*h* *Baal,* 2 Kin. 17:16.

14
*i* *Intercession, of man with God, for the obdurate, unavailing,* Jer. 27:18.

15
*j* *Idolatry, wicked practices of,* 1 Sam. 15:23.

17
*k* *Backsliding, of Israel,* Hos. 11:7.
*l* *Anger of God,* 2 Kin. 13:3.
2 R. V. wrought for themselves in provoking me

19
*m* *Persecution, of the righteous,* John 15:20.

20
*n* *God, judge,* Gen. 2:2.
*o* *God, justice of,* Gen. 2:2.
*p* *Heart, known to God,* Psa. 44:21.
*q* *Prayer, imprecatory,* Acts 6:4.

21
*r* *Anathoth, prophecies against,* Jer. 1:1.
*s* *Jeremiah, conspiracy against,* Jer. 1:1.

22
*t* *War, as a judgment,* Judg. 3:2.
*u* *Famine, sent as a judgment,* 2 Kin. 8:1.

23
*v* *Wicked, punishment of,* Psa. 73:3.

1
*a* *God, righteousness of,* Gen. 2:2.
*b* *Jeremiah, lamentations of,* Jer. 1:1.
*c* *God, providence of, mysterious,* Gen. 2:2.
*d* *Wicked, prosperity of,* Psa. 73:3.
1 R. V. would I reason the cause with thee:
2 R. V. at ease

yea, they have taken root: they
grow, yea, they bring forth fruit:
[e]thou *art* near in their mouth,
and far from their reins.[G S]
3 But thou, O LORD, know-
est me: thou hast seen me, and
tried[G] mine heart toward thee:
[f]pull them out like sheep for the
slaughter, and prepare them for
the day of slaughter.[Q]
4 [g]How long shall the land
mourn, and the herbs of every
field wither, for the wickedness
of them that dwell therein? [g]the
[h]beasts are consumed, and the
birds; because they [i,j]said, He
shall not see our last end.
5 ¶ If thou hast run with the
footmen,[G] and they have wearied thee, then how canst thou
contend with horses? and [3]*if* in
the land of peace, *wherein* thou
trustedst, *they wearied thee,* then
how wilt thou do in the swelling
of [k]Jôr′dan?
6 For even thy brethren, and
the house of thy father, even
they have [l]dealt treacherously
with thee; [4]yea, they have called
a multitude after thee: believe
them not, though they speak
[m]fair words unto thee.
7 ¶ [n]I have [o]forsaken mine
house, I have left mine heritage;
I have given the dearly beloved
of my soul into the hand of her
enemies.[Q]
8 Mine heritage is unto me as
a [p]lion in the forest; it crieth
out against me: [q]therefore have
I [r]hated it.
9 Mine heritage *is* unto me *as* a
speckled bird, the [s]birds round
about *are* against her; come ye,
assemble all the beasts of the
field, come to devour.
10 Many [5,t,u]pastors[G] have destroyed my vineyard, they have
trodden[G] my portion[G] under foot,
they have made my pleasant portion a desolate wilderness.
11 They have made it desolate,
*and being* desolate it mourneth
unto me; the whole land is made
desolate, because [v]no man layeth
*it* to heart.
12 The spoilers[G] are come upon
all [6]high places through the wilderness: for [w]the sword of the
LORD shall devour from the *one*
end of the land even to the *other*
end of the land: [w]no flesh shall
have peace.
13 They have [x]sown [y]wheat,
but shall reap [z,a]thorns: they
have put themselves to pain, *but*
shall not profit: and they shall be
ashamed of your [7]revenues because of the fierce [b]anger of the
LORD.
14 ¶ Thus saith the LORD
against all mine evil neighbours,
that touch the inheritance which
I have caused my people [c]Iṣ′-
ra-el to inherit; Behold, I will
pluck them out of their land, and
pluck out the house of [d]Jū′dah
from among them.
15 And it shall come to pass,
after that I have plucked them
out I will return, and have [e]com-
passion on them, and will bring
them again, every man to his
heritage, and every man to his
land.[Q]
16 And it shall come to pass,
[f,g]if they will diligently learn the
ways of my people, to [h]swear by
my name, The LORD liveth; as
they taught my people to swear
by [i]Bā′al; then shall they be
built in the midst of my people.
17 But if they [j,k]will not [8]obey,[G]
I will utterly pluck up and destroy that nation, saith the LORD.

## CHAPTER 13

*By the type of a linen girdle, God shews that he will mar the pride of Judah. 12 The whole land to be filled with confusion. 15 The people exhorted to repent and humble themselves. 22 The greatness of their iniquity the cause of God's judgments upon them.*

THUS [a]saith the LORD unto
me, Go and [1,b]get thee a
[c]linen [d,e]girdle,[G] and put it upon

2
e *Hypocrisy,* Jas. 3:17.

3
f *Prayer, imprecatory,* Acts 6:4.

4
g *Judgments,* Ex. 6:6.
h *Animals, suffer under divine judgments,* Jer. 27:5.
i *False Confidence,* Psa. 30:6.
j *Delusion,* 2 Thess. 2:11.

5
k *Jordan,* Gen. 32:10.

6
l *Persecution, of the righteous,* John 15:20.
m *Falsehood,* Job 21:34.
4 R. V. even they have cried aloud after thee:

7
n *Divine Chastisement,* Job 33:19.
o *Wicked, punishment of,* Psa. 73:3.

8
p *Lion,* Mic. 5:8.
q *Sin, repugnant to God,* Rom. 5:12.
r *Hatred, of God, against iniquity,* Prov. 15:17.

9
s *Birds, figurative,* Eccl. 12:4.

10
t *Minister* (as some interpret), *false and corrupt,* Rom. 15:16.
u *Rulers* (as some interpret), *wicked,* Ex. 18:21.
5 R. V. shepherds

11
v *Impenitence,* Rom. 2:5.

12
w *War, evils of,* Judg. 3:2.
6 R. V. the bare heights in the

13
x *Agriculture, figurative,* Gen. 3:23.
y *Wheat, figurative,* Ezra 6:9.
z *Thorn, figurative* Hos. 2:6.

a *Sin, fruits of,* Rom. 5:12.
b *Anger of God,* 2 Kin. 13:3.

14
c *Israel, after the revolt, prophecies concerning the restoration of,* 1 Kin. 12:1.
d *Jews, prophecies concerning restoration of,* Neh. 4:2.

15
e *God, mercy of,* Gen. 2:2.

16
f *Contingencies, in divine government,* 1 Kin. 3:14.
g *Blessings, contingent upon obedience,* Deut. 11:26.
h *Oath,* Num. 5:19.
i *Baal,* 2 Kin. 17:16.

17
j *Self-will,* Gen. 49:6.
k *Impenitence,* Rom. 2:5.
8 R. V. hear,

1
a *Prophets, inspiration of,* Isa. 3:2.
b *Instruction, by object lessons,* vs. 1–11; Prov. 23:23.
c *Linen,* Ezek. 27:16.
d *Girdle, symbolical,* Prov. 31:24.
e *Symbols and Similitudes,* Heb. 9:9.
1 R. V. buy

thy loins, and put it not in water.

2 So I [2]got a [d,e]girdle[c] according to the word of the LORD, and put *it* on my loins.

3 And the word of the LORD [a]came unto me the second time, saying,

4 [b]Take the [d,e]girdle[c] that thou hast [2]got, which *is* upon thy loins, and arise, go to [f]Eū-phrā′-tēs, and hide it there in a hole of the rock.

5 So I went, and hid it by [f]Eū-phrā′tēs, as the LORD commanded me.

6 And it came to pass after many days, that the LORD said unto me, Arise, go to [f]Eū-phrā′-tēs, and take the [d,e]girdle[c] from thence[c], which I commanded thee to hide there.

7 Then I went to [f]Eū-phrā′tēs, and digged, and took the [d,e]girdle[c] from the place where I had hid it: and, behold, the girdle was marred, it was profitable for nothing.

8 Then the word of the LORD [a]came unto me, saying,

9 Thus saith the LORD, [b]After this manner will I mar the [g]pride of [h]Jū′dah, and the great pride of [i]Jē-ru′sā-lĕm.

10 This evil [j]people, which [k,l]refuse to hear my words, which [m]walk in the [3]imagination[c] of their heart, and walk [n]after other gods, to serve them, and to worship them, shall even be as this [d]girdle[c], which is good for nothing.

11 For as the [d]girdle[c] cleaveth[c] to the loins of a man, so have I caused to cleave[c] unto me the whole house of Īs′ra-el and the whole house of Jū′dah, saith the LORD; [o]that they might be unto me for a people, and for a name, and for a praise, and for a glory: but they [k,l]would not hear.

12 ¶ Therefore thou shalt speak unto them this word; Thus saith the LORD God of Īs′ra-el, Every bottle[c] shall be filled with wine: and they shall say unto thee, Do we not certainly know that every bottle shall be filled with wine?

13 Then shalt thou say unto them, Thus saith the LORD, Behold, [h,p]I will fill all the inhabitants of this land, even the kings that sit upon Dā′vid's throne, and the priests, and the prophets, and all the inhabitants of Jē-ru′sā-lĕm, with [q]drunkenness.

14 And [h,p]I will dash them one against another, even the fathers and the sons together, saith the LORD: I will not [r]pity, nor spare, nor have mercy, but destroy them.

15 ¶ [s]Hear ye, and give ear; be not proud: for the LORD hath spoken.

16 Give glory to the LORD your God, before he cause [p,t,u]darkness, and before your feet stumble upon the dark mountains, and, while ye look for light, he turn it into the shadow of death, *and* make *it* gross[c] darkness.

17 But if ye [k,l]will not hear it, [v,w,x,y]my soul shall weep in secret places for *your* pride; and mine eye shall weep sore[c], and run down with tears, because the LORD's flock is carried away captive.

18 Say unto the [z]king and to the [4]queen, [s]Humble yourselves, sit down: for your [5]principalities[c] shall come down, *even* the crown of your glory.

19 The cities of the south shall be shut up, and none shall open *them*: Jū′dah shall be carried away [a]captive all of it, it shall be wholly carried away captive.

20 Lift up your eyes, and behold them that come from the north: where *is* the flock *that* was given thee, thy beautiful flock?

21 What wilt thou say when he

2
2 R. V. bought

4
f *Euphrates*, Gen. 15:18.

9
g *Pride*, Prov. 16:18.
h *Judah, kingdom of, prophecies concerning*, vs. 9–27; 2 Chr. 11:17.
i *Jerusalem*, Judg. 19:10.

10
j *Jews, prophecies concerning*, Neh. 4:2.
k *Self-will*, Gen. 49:6.
l *Impenitence*, Rom. 2:5.
m *Wicked, described*, Psa. 73:3.
n *Idolatry*, 1 Sam. 15:23.
3 R. V. stubbornness

11
o *God, love of*, Gen. 2:2.

13
p *Nation, judgments denounced against*, Isa. 2:4
q *Drunkenness, figurative*, Luke 21:34.

14
r *Pity*, Job 19:21.

15
s *Repentance, exhortations to*, Mark 1:4.

16
t *Darkness, figurative*, Gen. 1:2.
u *Adversity, design of, as a judgment*, Psa. 10:6.

17
v *Minister, faithful*, Rom. 15:16.
w *Love, of man for man* 1 John 4:7.
x *Patriotism*, Psa. 137:1.
y *Zeal*, 2 Cor. 7:11

18
z *Rulers, wicked*, Ex. 18:21.
4 R. V. queen-mother,

19
a *Captivity, of Judah in Babylon*, Isa. 5:13.

shall [6,b]punish thee? for thou
hast taught them *to be* captains,
*and* as chief over thee: shall not
sorrows take thee, as a woman
in travail?
22 ¶ And if thou say in thine
heart, Wherefore[G] come these
things upon me? [b]For the greatness of thine iniquity [c]are thy
skirts discovered,[G] *and* thy heels
[7]made bare.
23 [c,d]Can the [e]Ē-thĭ-ō′pĭ-an
change his skin, or the [f]leopard
his spots? *then* may ye also do
good, that are accustomed to do
evil.[S]
24 Therefore [b]will I scatter
them as the [g]stubble that passeth
away by the wind of the wilderness.
25 [b]This *is* thy lot, the portion
[8]of thy measures from me, saith
the LORD; because thou hast
forgotten me, and [h,i]trusted in
[j]falsehood.[Q]
26 [b]Therefore will I discover[G]
thy skirts upon thy face, that thy
shame may appear.
27 I have seen thine [k]adulteries,
and thy neighings, the lewdness
of thy whoredom,[G] *and* thine
abominations on the hills in the
fields. Woe unto thee, O [l]Jē-
rụ′să-lĕm! wilt thou not be made
clean[G]? when *shall it* once[G] *be*?

## CHAPTER 14

*Dearth upon the land. 7 The prayer of the prophet for its removal. 10 God will not be entreated for the people. 13 Lying prophets no excuse for them. 17 Jeremiah's continued intercession for the people.*

THE word of the LORD that
[a,b]came to Jĕr-e-mī′ah concerning the [c]dearth.[G]
2 Jū′dah [d,e]mourneth, and the
[f]gates thereof languish; they are
black unto the ground; and the
cry of Jē-rụ′să-lĕm is gone up.
3 And their nobles have sent
their little ones to the waters:
they came to the pits,[G] *and* found
[c]no water; they returned with
their vessels empty; they were
ashamed and confounded, and
covered their heads.
4 Because the ground is chapt,[G]
for there was [c]no [g]rain in the
earth, the plowmen were ashamed, they covered their heads.
5 Yea, the [h]hind also calved in
the field, and forsook *it*, because
there was no grass.
6 And the [i]wild asses [1]did stand
in the high places, they snuffed[G]
up the wind like [j]dragons; their
eyes did fail, because *there was*
no grass.
7 ¶ [k]O LORD, though our iniquities testify against us, do thou
*it* for thy name's sake: for our
[l]backslidings are many; [m,n]we
have sinned against thee.
8 [k]O the hope of Ĭs′ra-el, the
[o]saviour thereof in time of
[p]trouble, why shouldest thou be
as a [2]stranger[G] in the land, and as
a wayfaring man *that* turneth
aside to tarry for a night?[T]
9 [k]Why shouldest thou be as a
man astonied,[G] as a mighty man
*that* cannot save? yet [q]thou, O
LORD, *art* in the midst of us, and
we are [r]called by thy name;
leave us not.[S]
10 ¶ Thus saith the LORD unto this people, Thus have they
[s,t]loved to wander, they have
[u]not refrained[G] their feet, therefore the LORD doth not accept
them; he will now remember
their iniquity, and [v]visit[G] their
sins.
11 Then said the LORD unto
me, [w]Pray not for this people for
*their* good.
12 When they [x]fast, [y]I will not
hear their cry; and when they
offer burnt offering and an oblation,[G] [z]I will not accept them:
but [a]I will [b]consume them by the
[c]sword, and by the [d]famine, and
by the [e]pestilence.[Q]
13 ¶ Then said I, Ah, Lord
GOD! behold, the [f]prophets say
unto them, Ye shall not see the

**21**
b *Wicked, punishment of*, Psa. 73:3.
6 Am. R. V. set over thee as head those whom thou hast thyself taught to be friends to thee? shall not

**22**
c *Depravity*, Job 15:14.
7 R. V. suffer violence.

**23**
d *Nature, laws of, uniform in operation*, Jas. 3:12.
e *Ethiopia, inhabitants of, black*, Isa. 18:1.
f *Leopard*, Song 4:8.

**24**
g *Stubble*, Isa. 5:24.

**25**
h *Delusion*, 2 Thess. 2:11.
i *False Confidence*, Psa. 30:6.
j *Falsehood*, Job 21:34.
8 R. V. measured unto thee from me,

**27**
k *Idolatry, wicked practices of*, 1 Sam. 15:23.
l *Jerusalem*, Judg. 19:10.

**1**
a *Inspiration*, Job 32:8.
b *Prophets, inspiration of*, Isa. 3:2.
c *Drought*, Gen. 31:40.

**2**
d *Mourning*, Lam. 2:5.
e *Adversity, despondency in*, Psa. 10:6.
f *Gates, figurative*, Deut. 3:5.

**4**
g *Rain*, 2 Sam. 1:21.

**5**
h *Deer*, Deut. 14:5.

**6**
i *Ass, wild*, 2 Chr. 28:15.
j *Dragon*, Deut. 32:33.
1 R. V. stand on the bare heights, they pant for air like jackals;

**7**
k *Nation, in adversity, prayer for*, Isa. 2:4.
l *Backsliding, of Israel*, Hos. 11:7.
m *Prayer, confession in*, Acts 6:4.
n *Sin, confession of*, Rom. 5:12.

**8**
o *God, preserver*, Gen. 2:2.
p *Adversity, prayer in*, vs. 8, 9, 19-21; Psa. 10:6.
2 R. V. sojourner

**9**
q *Faith, exemplified*, Mark 11:22.
r *Spiritual Adoption*, Rom. 8:15.

**10**
s *Wicked, described*, Psa. 73:3.
t *Sin, love of*, Rom. 5:12.
u *Impenitence*, Rom. 2:5.
v *Wicked, punishment of*, Psa. 73:3.

**11**
w *Intercession, of man with God, for the obdurate, unavailing*, Jer. 27:18.

**12**
x *Fasting*, Zech. 8:19.
y *Wicked, prayers of, not answered*, Psa. 73:3.
z *Offerings, unavailing when not accompanied by piety*, Lev. 6:17.

a *Nation, judgments denounced against*, Isa. 2:4.
b *Wicked, punishment of*, Psa. 73:3.
c *War, as a judgment*, Judg. 3:2.
d *Famine, as a judgment*, 2 Kin. 8:1.
e *Plague, as a judgment*, Ex. 11:1.

**13**
f *Prophets, false*, Isa. 3:2.

sword, neither shall ye have famine; but [g]I will give you assured peace in this place.

14 Then the LORD said unto me, The [i]prophets prophesy lies in my name: I sent them not, neither have I commanded them, neither spake unto them: they prophesy unto you a false vision and [h]divination,[G] and a thing of nought, and the [i]deceit of their heart.[Q]

15 Therefore thus saith the LORD concerning the [i]prophets that prophesy in my name, and I sent them not, yet they say, Sword and famine shall not be in this land; [b]By [c]sword and [d]famine shall those prophets be consumed.

16 And the people to whom they prophesy shall be cast out in the streets of [j]Jĕ-rụ′să-lĕm because of the famine and the sword; and they shall have none to bury them, them, their wives, nor their sons, nor their daughters: for I will pour their wickedness upon them.

17 Therefore thou shalt say this word unto them; [k]Let mine eyes run down with tears night and day, and let them not cease: for the [l]virgin daughter of my people is broken with a great breach,[G] with a very grievous blow.

18 [k]If I go forth into the field, then [m]behold the slain with the [c]sword! and if I enter into the city, then behold them that are sick with [d]famine! yea, both the prophet and the priest go about [3]into a land that they know not.

19 [k,n,o]Hast thou utterly [p]rejected Jū′dah? [q]hath thy soul lothed Zī′ŏn? why hast thou smitten us, and *there is* no healing for us? we looked for peace, and *there is* no good; and for the time of healing, and behold trouble!

20 [o,r]We acknowledge, O LORD, our wickedness, *and* the iniquity of our fathers: for we have sinned against thee.

21 [o]Do not abhor *us*, [s]for thy name's sake, [s]do not disgrace the throne of thy glory: remember, [s]break not thy [t]covenant with us.

22 Are there *any* among the [u]vanities of the [4]Gĕn′tīleṣ[G] that can cause rain? or can the heavens give showers? *art* not thou he, O LORD our God? therefore we will wait upon thee: [v]for thou hast [w]made all [x]these *things*.[S]

## CHAPTER 15

*The rejection and punishment of Israel. 10 God's promise to the prophet. 15 The prayer of Jeremiah. 19 The assurance given him.*

THEN said the LORD unto [a]me, Though [b]Mō′ṣeṣ and [c]Săm′u-el [d]stood before me, *yet*[G] my mind *could* not *be* toward this [e]people: [f]cast *them* out of my sight, and let them go forth.[S]

2 [g]And it shall come to pass, if they say unto thee, Whither[G] shall we go forth? then thou shalt tell[G] them, Thus saith the LORD; [f,h]Such as *are* for [i]death, to death; and such as *are* for the [j]sword, to the sword; and such as *are* for the [k]famine, to the famine; and such as *are* for the [l]captivity, to the captivity.[Q]

3 And [g,h]I will appoint over them four kinds, saith the LORD: the [j]sword to slay, and the dogs to tear, and the fowls of the heaven, and the beasts of the earth, to devour and destroy.[Q]

4 And [g,h]I will cause them to be [1,m]removed into all kingdoms of the earth, [n]because of [o]Mă-năs′seh the son of [p]Hĕz-e-kī′ah king of Jū′dah, for *that* which he did in [q]Jĕ-rụ′să-lĕm.

5 For who shall have pity upon thee, O Jĕ-rụ′să-lĕm? or who shall bemoan thee? or who shall go aside to ask how thou doest?

g *False Confidence*, Psa. 30:6.

14
h *Sorcery*, Isa. 47:9.
i *Deceit*, Psa. 36:3.

16
*Jerusalem*, Judg. 19:10.

17
k *Patriotism*, Psa. 137:1.
l *Virgin, figurative*, Isa. 62:5.

18
m *War, evils of*, Judg. 3:2.
3 R. V. in the land and have no knowledge.

19
n *Adversity, despondency in*, Psa. 10:6.
o *Nation, in adversity, prayer for*, Isa. 2:4.
p *Rejection, by God*, Lam. 5:22.
*Church, love for*, Matt. 16:18.

20
r *Sin, confession of*, Rom. 5:12.

21
s *Prayer, pleas offered in*, Acts 6:4.
t *Covenant, of God with men*, Deut. 29:1.

22
u *Idolatry, folly of*, 1 Sam. 15:23.
v *God, providence of*, Gen. 2:2.
w *God, creator*, Gen. 2:2.
x *Temporal Blessings, from God*, Psa. 103:2.
4 R. V. heathen

1
a *Jeremiah*, Jer. 1:1.
b *Moses*, Ex. 2:10.
c *Samuel*, 1 Sam. 3:1.
d *Intercession, of man with God*, Jer. 27:18.
e *Reprobates*, 1 Cor. 9:27.
f *Wicked, punishment of*, Psa. 73:3.

2
g *Jews, prophecies concerning*, vs. 1–4; Neh. 4:2.
h *Nation, judgments denounced against*, Isa. 2:4.
i *Death, as a judgment*, Num. 23:10.
j *War, as a judgment*, Judg. 3:2.
k *Famine, as a judgment*, 2 Kin. 8:1.
l *Captivity, as a judgment*, Isa. 5:13.

4
m *Dispersion*, Gen. 11:8.
n *Nation, involved in sins of rulers*, Isa. 2:4.
o *Manasseh*, 2 Kin. 21:1.
p *Hezekiah*, 2 Kin. 16:20.
q *Jerusalem*, Judg. 19:10.
1 R. V. tossed to and fro among

6
*r* *Backsliding, of Israel,* Hos. 11:7.
*s* *Repentance, attributed to God,* Mark 1:4.

7
*t* Isa. 30:24; Jer. 51:2; Matt. 3:12.
*u* *Divine Chastisement,* Job 33:19.
*v* *Children, death of, as a judgment upon parents,* Mark 10:14.
*w* *Adversity, obduracy in,* Psa. 10:6.

8
*x* *War, evils of,* Judg. 3:2.
*y* *Widow,* 2 Sam. 14:5.
2 R. V. anguish and terrors to fall upon her suddenly.

9
*z* *Seven, figurative,* Gen. 7:2.

*a* *Sun, figurative,* Josh. 10:12.
*b* *Nation, judgments denounced against,* Isa. 2:4.
*c* *War, as a judgment,* Judg. 3:2.

10
*d* *Murmuring, instances of,* Num. 14:2.
*e* *Adversity, despondency in,* Psa. 10:6.
*f* *Persecution, of the righteous,* John 15:20.

11
*g* *God, providence of,* Gen. 2:2.
*h* *Adversity, consolation in,* Psa. 10:6.
3 R. V. I will strengthen thee for good;
4 R. V. make supplication unto thee in

12
*i* *Iron, figurative,* Prov. 27:17.
5 R. V. Can one break iron, even iron from the north, and brass?

13
*j* *Sin, repugnant to God,* Rom. 5:12.

14
*k* *Anger of God,* 2 Kin. 13:3.

15
*l* *Adversity, prayer in,* Psa. 10:6.
*m* *Prayer, in adversity,* Acts 6:4.
*n* *God, knowledge of,* Gen. 2:2.

6 Thou hast [r]forsaken me, saith
the LORD, thou art gone backward: therefore will I stretch out
my hand against thee, and [f,h]de-
stroy thee; I am weary with [s]re-
penting.
7 And [g]I will fan them with a
[t]fan in the gates of the land; I
will [u]bereave *them* of [v]children, I
will [f,h]destroy my people, *since*
they [w]return not from their ways.
8 [x]Their [y]widows are increased
to me above the sand of the seas:
I have brought upon them
against the mother of the young
men a spoiler at noonday: I have
caused [2]*him* to fall upon it suddenly, and terrors upon the city.
9 She that hath borne [z]seven
languisheth: she hath given up
the ghost[G]; her [a]sun is gone down
while *it was* yet day: she hath
been ashamed and confounded:
and the residue of them will I
[b]deliver to the [c]sword before
their enemies, saith the LORD.
10 ¶ [d,e]Woe is me, my mother,
that thou hast borne me a man of
strife and a man of contention to
the whole earth! I have neither
lent on usury[G], nor men have lent
to me on usury[G]; *yet* every one of
them doth [f]curse me.
11 The LORD said, Verily
[3,g,h]it shall be well with thy
remnant; verily I will cause the
enemy to [4]entreat thee *well* in
the time of evil and in the time
of affliction.
12 [5]Shall [i]iron break the northern iron and the steel[G]?
13 [b]Thy substance and thy
treasures will I give to the spoil
without price, and *that* for all
thy [j]sins, even in all thy borders.
14 And [b]I will make *thee* to pass
with thine enemies into a land
*which* thou knowest not: for a
fire is kindled in mine [k]anger,
*which* shall burn upon you.
15 ¶ [l,m]O LORD, thou [n]know-
est: remember me, and visit[G] me,
and [o]revenge me of my [f]perse-
cutors; take me not away in thy
[p]longsuffering: know that for thy[s]
sake [q,r,s]I have suffered rebuke.
16 Thy [t]words were found, and
[q,r]I did eat them; and thy word
was unto me the joy and rejoicing of mine heart: for I am called
by thy name, O LORD God of
hosts.
17 [u,v]I sat not in the assembly
of [6]the mockers, nor rejoiced; I
sat alone because of thy hand:
for thou hast filled me with indignation.
18 [d,e,w]Why is my pain perpetual, and my wound incurable,
*which* refuseth to be healed?
wilt thou be altogether unto me
as a [7]liar, *and as* waters *that* fail?
19 ¶ Therefore thus saith the
LORD, [x]If thou return, then will
I bring thee again, *and* thou shalt
stand before me: and if thou
take forth the precious[G] from the
vile[G], thou shalt be as my mouth:
let them return unto thee; but
return not thou unto them.
20 And [y,z]I will make thee unto this people a fenced[G] brasen[G]
wall: and they shall fight against
thee, but [y,z]they shall not prevail
against thee: for I *am* [a]with thee
to [b]save thee and to deliver thee,
saith the LORD.[s]
21 And I will [b]deliver thee out
of the hand of the wicked, and I
will redeem thee out of the hand
of the terrible.

## CHAPTER 16

*The utter ruin of the Jews foreshewn. 10 Their sins the cause thereof. 14 A promise of deliverance from captivity. 16 God will doubly recompense their iniquity.*

THE [a]word of the LORD
[b,c]came also unto me,
saying,
2 Thou shalt [d]not take thee a
wife, neither shalt thou have
sons or daughters in this place.
3 For [e]thus saith the LORD
concerning the sons and concerning the daughters that are

*o* *Prayer, imprecatory,* Acts 6:4.
*p* *God, longsuffering of,* Gen. 2:2.
*q* *Zeal,* 2 Cor. 7:11.
*r* *Minister, character of, zealous,* Rom. 15:16.
*s* *Minister, faithful,* Rom. 15:16.

16
*t* *Word of God,* Psa. 119:9.

17
*u* *Evil Company, the righteous shun,* Prov. 13:20.
*v* *Fellowship, with the wicked, avoided,* 1 Cor. 1:9.
6 R. V. them that make merry,

18
*w* *Minister, discouragements of,* Rom. 15:16.
7 R. V. deceitful brook, as

19
*x* *Blessings, contingent upon obedience,* Deut. 11:26.

20
*y* *Adversity, consolation in,* Psa. 10:6.
*z* *Minister, promises to,* Rom. 15:16.

*a* *God dwells with the Righteous,* 1 Kin. 6:13.
*b* *God, preserver,* Gen. 2:2.

1
*a* *Prophecies,* Dan. 9:24.
*b* *Inspiration,* Job 32:8.
*c* *Prophets, inspiration of,* Isa. 3:2.

2
*d* *Jeremiah, celibacy of,* Jer. 1:1.

3
*e* *Jews, prophecies concerning,* vs. 3–21; Neh. 4:2.

born in this place, and concerning their mothers that bare them, and concerning their fathers that begat them in this land;

4 [f,g]They shall [h]die of grievous deaths; they shall not be lamented; neither shall they be [i]buried; *but* they shall be as dung[c] upon the face of the earth: and they shall be consumed by the [j]sword, and by [k]famine; and their carcases shall be meat[c] for the fowls of heaven, and for the beasts of the earth.

5 For thus saith the LORD, Enter not into the house of [l]mourning, neither go to lament nor bemoan them: for [m]I have taken away my peace from this people, saith the LORD, *even* lovingkindness and mercies.

6 [e,f,g]Both the great and the small shall [h]die in this land: they shall not be [i]buried, neither shall *men* [l]lament for them, nor [l,n]cut themselves, nor make themselves [o]bald for them:

7 Neither shall *men* [1]tear *themselves* for them in [l]mourning, to comfort them for the dead; neither shall *men* give them the [p]cup of consolation to drink for their father or for their mother.

8 Thou shalt not also go into the house of [q]feasting, to sit with them to eat and to drink.

9 For thus saith the LORD of hosts, the God of Iş'ra-el; Behold, [e,f]I will cause to cease out of this place in your eyes, and in your days, the voice of mirth, and the voice of gladness, the voice of the bridegroom, and the voice of the bride.[Q]

10 ¶ And it shall come to pass, when thou shalt shew this people all these words, and they shall say unto thee, [r,s,t]Wherefore[c] hath the LORD pronounced all this great evil against us? or [s]what *is* our iniquity? or [s]what *is* our sin that we have committed against the LORD our God?

11 Then shalt thou say unto them, [u]Because your fathers have [v]forsaken me, saith the LORD, and have walked [w]after other gods, and have served them, and have worshipped them, and have forsaken me, and [x]have not kept my law;

12 And [y]ye have done worse than [z]your fathers; for, behold, ye [a]walk every one after the [2,b]imagination[c] of his [c]evil heart, that they may [d]not hearken unto me:

13 Therefore will I [e,f]cast you out of this land [g]into a land that ye know not, *neither* ye nor your fathers; and there shall ye [h]serve other gods day and night; where I will not shew you favour.

14 ¶ Therefore, behold, the days come, saith the LORD, that it shall no more be said, The LORD liveth, that [i]brought up the children of Iş'ra-el out of the land of [j]Ē'ġўpt;

15 But, The LORD liveth, that [i]brought up the children of Iş'ra-el from the land of the north, and from all the lands whither he had [l]driven them: and [k]I will bring them again into their [l]land that I [m]gave unto their fathers.

16 ¶ Behold, I will send for many [n]fishers, saith the LORD, and they shall fish them; and after will I send for many hunters, and they shall [o]hunt them from every mountain, and from every hill, and out of the holes of the rocks.

17 For [p]mine eyes *are* upon all their [q]ways: they are not hid from my face, neither is their iniquity hid from mine eyes.

18 And first I will [r]recompense their iniquity and their sin double; because they have defiled my land, they have filled mine inheritance with the car-

4
f *Nation, judgments denounced against,* Isa. 2:4.
g *Wicked, punishment of,* Psa. 73:3.
h *Death, as a judgment,* Num. 23:10.
i *Burial, lack of, a disgrace,* Acts 8:2.
j *War, as a judgment,* Judg. 3:2.
k *Famine, as a judgment,* 2 Kin. 8:1.

5
l *Mourning,* Lam. 2:5.
m *Adversity, dispensation from God,* Psa. 10:6.

6
n *Cutting, of the flesh for the dead,* Lev. 19:28.
o *Baldness, artificial, in mourning,* Lev. 21:5.

7
p *Cup, figurative,* Matt. 20:22.

8
q *Feasts,* Mark 12:39.

10
r *Spiritual Blindness,* 2 Cor. 4:4.
s *Conscience, dead,* Acts 23:1.
t *God, providence of, misunderstood,* Gen. 2:2.

11
u *Children, involved in sins of parents,* Mark 10:14.
v *Apostasy,* Acts 1:25.
w *Idolatry,* 1 Sam. 15:23.
x *Disobedience to God,* Eph. 5:6.

12
y *Sin, progressive,* Rom. 5:12.
z *Example, bad,* John 13:15.

a *Wicked, described,* Psa. 73:3.
b *Self-will,* Gen. 49:6.
c *Depravity,* Job 15:14.
d *Impenitence,* Rom. 2:5.
2 R. V. stubbornness

13
e *Adversity, dispensation from God,* Psa. 10:6.
f *Dispersion, of the Jews, foretold,* Gen. 11:8.
g *Captivity, as a judgment,* Isa. 5:13.
h *Idolatry,* 1 Sam. 15:23.

14
i *God, providence of,* Gen. 2:2.
j *Egypt,* Gen. 41:8.

15
k *Jews, prophecies concerning restoration of,* Neh. 4:2.
l *Canaan,* Gen. 37:1.
m *Covenant, of God with men,* Deut. 29:1.

16
n *Fishermen, figurative,* Luke 5:2.
o *Hunting, figurative,* Gen. 27:5.

17
p *God, knowledge of,* Gen. 2:2.
q *Sin, known to God,* Rom. 5:12

18
r *Wicked, punishment of,* Psa. 73:3.

19
s *God, preserver,* Gen. 2:2.
t *Faith, exemplified,* Mark 11:22.
u *Adversity, consolation in,* Psa. 10:6.
v *Gentiles, prophecies of the conversion of,* Acts 10:45.
3 R. V. nations

20
w *Idolatry, folly of,* 1 Sam. 15:23.

21
x *Adversity, design of,* Psa. 10:6.
4 R. V. Jehovah.

1
a *Judah, kingdom of, prophecies concerning,* vs. 1–4; 2 Chr. 11:17.
b *Pen, figurative,* Jer. 8:8.
c *Iron, figurative,* Prov. 27:17.
d *Diamond, figurative,* Ex. 39:11.
e *Table, figurative,* Hab. 2:2.
f *Heart,* Psa. 44:21.

2
g *Parents, evil influence of,* 2 Cor. 12:14.
h *Example, bad,* John 13:15.
i *Altar, used in idolatrous worship,* Gen. 8:20.
j *Idolatry,* 1 Sam. 15:23.
k *Groves, worshiped by Israelites,* Judg. 6:28.
1 R. V. Asherim

4
l *Temporal Blessings, from God,* Psa. 103:2.
m *Captivity, as a judgment,* Isa. 5:13.
n *Anger of God,* 2 Kin. 13:3.

5
o *Wicked, punishment of,* Psa. 73:3.
p *Wicked, contrasted with the righteous,* vs. 5–8; Psa. 73:3.
q *False Confidence,* Psa. 30:6.
r *Heart, unregenerate,* Psa. 44:21.
s *Backsliding,* Hos. 11:7.

6
t *Desert,* Lev. 16:22.

cases of their detestable and abominable [h]things.

19 O [s]LORD, [t]my strength, and my fortress, and [u]my refuge in the day of affliction, the [3,v]Gĕn′-tīleṣ[G] shall come unto thee from the ends of the earth, and shall say, Surely our fathers have inherited lies, vanity, and *things* wherein *there is* no profit.[Q]

20 Shall a man make gods unto himself, and [w]they *are* no gods?

21 Therefore, behold, I will this once [x]cause them to know, I will cause them to know mine hand and my might; and they shall know that my name *is* [4]The LORD.

## CHAPTER 17

*The captivity of the Jews for their sins. 5 Their confidence in man rebuked. 12 The prophet prays for protection from his enemies. 19 The Sabbath to be hallowed.*

THE sin of [a]Jū′dah *is* written with a [b]pen of [c]iron, *and* with the point of a [d]diamond: *it is* graven[G] upon the [e]table[G] of their [f]heart, and upon the horns of your altars;

2 Whilst their children [g]remember [h]their [i]altars and their [1,j,k]groves[G] by the green trees upon the high hills.

3 O my mountain in the field, I will give thy substance *and* all thy treasures to the spoil,[G] *and* thy high places for sin, throughout all thy borders.

4 And thou, even thyself, shalt discontinue from thine [l]heritage that I gave thee; and I will cause thee to [m]serve thine enemies in the land which thou knowest not: for ye have kindled a fire in mine [n]anger, *which* shall burn for ever.[S]

5 ¶ Thus saith the LORD; [o]Cursed *be* the [p]man that [q]trusteth in man, and maketh flesh his arm, and whose [r]heart [s]departeth from the LORD.[T]

6 For [o]he shall be like the heath[G] in the [t]desert, and shall not see when good cometh; but shall inhabit the parched places in the wilderness, *in* a salt land and not inhabited.

7 [u,v]Blessed *is* the [w]man that [x,y]trusteth in the LORD, and whose [z]hope the LORD is.

8 For [v]he shall be as a tree planted by the waters, and *that* spreadeth out her roots by the river, and shall not [2]see when heat cometh, but her leaf shall be green; and shall not be careful[G] in the year of drought, neither shall cease from yielding fruit.

9 ¶ The [a]heart *is* [b,c,d]deceitful above all *things*, and desperately [3]wicked: who can know it?[S T]

10 I the LORD [e,f]search the [g]heart,[G] *I* try[G] the reins, even to [h,i]give every man according to his ways, *and* according to the [j]fruits of his doings.[S Q]

11 *As* the [k]partridge [4]sitteth *on eggs*, and hatcheth *them* not; [l]*so* he that [m]getteth [n]riches, and [o]not by right, shall leave them in the midst of his days, and at his end shall be a [p]fool.

12 ¶ [q]A glorious high throne from the beginning *is* the place of our [r]sanctuary.[S]

13 O LORD, the hope of Iṣ′-ra-el, all that forsake thee shall be ashamed, *and* they that [s]depart from me shall be written in the earth, because they have forsaken the LORD, the [t]fountain of living waters.

14 [u,v]Heal me, O LORD, and [q]I shall be healed; save me, and [q]I shall be saved: for thou *art* my praise.

15 Behold, they [w,x]say unto me, [y]Where *is* the word of the LORD? let it come now.

16 As for me, [z,a]I have not hastened[G] from *being* a [5]pastor[G] to follow thee: neither have I desired the woeful day; thou know-

7
u *Spiritual Peace,* Gal. 1:3.
v *Promise, to the righteous,* 2 Cor. 1:20.
w *Righteous, described,* Psa. 64:10.
x *Faith,* Mark 11:22.
y *Anxiety, remedy for,* 1 Pet. 5:7.
z *Hope,* Prov. 13:12.

8
2 R. V. fear

9
a *Heart, unregenerate,* Psa. 44:21.
b *Deceit,* Psa. 36:3.
c *Hypocrisy,* Jas. 3:17.
d *Depravity,* Job 15:14.
3 R. V. sick:

10
e *God, knowledge of,* Gen. 2:2.
f *God, judge,* Gen. 2:2.
g *Heart, known to God,* Psa. 44:21.
h *Judgment, according to opportunity and works* 1 Pet. 1:17.
i *Punishment, according to deeds,* Lev. 26:41.
j *Sin, fruits of,* Rom. 5:12.

11
k 1 Sam. 26:20.
l *Rich, denounced,* Jas. 5:1.
m *Covetousness,* Isa. 57:17.
n *Riches,* Eccl. 4:8.
o *Dishonesty,* Ezek. 22:13.
p *Fool,* Prov. 18:2.
4 Am. R. V. that sitteth on eggs which she hath not laid, so is he

12
q *Faith, exemplified,* Mark 11:22.
r *Temple, Solomon's,* 1 Kin. 6:17.

13
s *Backsliding,* Hos. 11:7.
t *Fountain, figurative,* Zech. 13:1.

14
u *Prayer, in adversity,* Acts 6:4.
v *Adversity, prayer in,* Psa. 10:6.

15
w *Blasphemy, denying the Word of God,* 2 Sam. 12:14.

x *Scoffing,* Hab. 1:10. y *Infidelity,* 2 Cor. 6:15. **16** z *Minister, faithful, instances of,* Rom. 15:16.—a *Zeal,* 2 Cor. 7:11. 5 R. V. shepherd

6 R. V. was before thy face.

**17**

*b Adversity, prayer in,* Psa. 10:6.

7 R. V. refuge

**18**

*c Prayer, imprecatory,* Acts 6:4.

*d Persecution, of the righteous,* John 15:20.

**19**

*e Gates,* Deut. 3:5.

*f Jerusalem, gates of,* Judg. 19:10.

**20**

*g Judah, kingdom of, prophecies concerning,* 2 Chr. 11:17.

**21**

*h Commandment, forbidding Sabbath breaking,* Deut. 8:2.

*i Sabbath, rest on, enjoined,* Ex. 16:23.

**22**

*f* Ex. 20:8–11; Deut. 5:12–14.

**23**

*k Disobedience to God,* Eph. 5:6.

*l Self-will,* Gen. 49:6.

*m Impenitence,* Rom. 2:5.

*n Instruction, in religion,* Prov. 23:23.

**24**

*o Contingencies, in divine government of man,* 1 Kin. 3:14.

**25**

*p Blessings, contingent upon obedience,* Deut. 11:26.

*q Reward, a motive, to obedience,* Matt. 5:12.

est: that which came out of my lips [6]was *right* before thee.

17 [b]Be not a terror unto me: thou *art* my [7]hope in the day of evil.

18 [c]Let them be confounded that [d]persecute me, but let not me be confounded: let them be dismayed, but let not me be dismayed: bring upon them the day of evil, and destroy them with double destruction.

19 ¶ Thus said the LORD unto me; Go and stand in the [e]gate of the children of the people, whereby the kings of Jṳ̄′dah come in, and by the which they go out, and in all the gates of [f]Jē-rṳ′sā-lĕm;

20 And say unto them, Hear ye the [g]word of the LORD, ye kings of Jū′dah, and all Jū′dah, and all the inhabitants of [f]Jē-rṳ′sā-lĕm, that enter in by these [e]gates:

21 [g]Thus saith the LORD; Take heed to yourselves, and [h]bear no burden on the [i]sabbath day, nor bring *it* in by the [e]gates of [f]Jē-rṳ′sā-lĕm;[Q]

22 [h]Neither carry forth a burden out of your houses on the [i]sabbath day, neither do ye any work, but [f]hallow ye the sabbath day, as I commanded your fathers.

23 But they [k,l,m]obeyed not, neither inclined[G] their ear, but made their neck stiff,[G] that they might not hear, nor receive [n]instruction.

24 And it shall come to pass, [o]if ye diligently hearken unto me, saith the LORD, to bring in no burden through the [e]gates of this [f]city on the [i]sabbath day, but [f]hallow the sabbath day, to do no work therein;

25 [p,q]Then shall there enter into the gates of this city kings and princes sitting upon the throne of Dā′vid, riding in chariots and on horses, they, and their princes, the men of Jū′dah, and the inhabitants of Jē-rṳ′sā-lĕm: and this city shall remain for ever.

26 And [p,q]they shall come from the cities of Jū′dah, and from the places about Jē-rṳ′sā-lĕm, and from the land of Bĕn′ja-mĭn, and from the plain, and from the mountains, and from the south, bringing [r]burnt offerings, and sacrifices, and meat[G] offerings, and incense, and bringing sacrifices of [s]praise, unto the [t]house of the LORD.

27 But [o]if ye will not hearken unto me to hallow the sabbath day, and not to bear a burden, even entering in at the gates of Jē-rṳ′sā-lĕm on the sabbath day; [u]then will I kindle a fire in the gates thereof, and it shall devour the palaces of Jē-rṳ′sā-lĕm, and it shall not be quenched.

## CHAPTER 18

*By the type of a potter, God's sovereignty over the nations is shewn. 11 Judgments upon Judah for her idolatry. 18 The prophet's complaint and prayer against his persecutors.*

THE [a]word which [b]came to [c]Jĕr-e-mī′ah from the LORD, saying,

2 Arise, and go down to the *potter's house, and there I will cause thee to hear my words.

3 Then I went down to the *potter's house, and, behold, he [d]wrought[G] a work on the wheels.

4 And the vessel that he made of [e]clay was marred in the hand of the *potter: so he made it again another vessel, as seemed good to the potter to make *it*.

5 Then the [a]word of the LORD [b]came to [c]me, saying,

6 O house of Ĭṣ′ra-el, cannot I do with you as this *potter? saith the LORD. Behold, as the [e]clay *is* in the potter's hand, so

**26**

*r Offerings, burnt* Lev. 6:17.

*s Thankfulness, to God,* Acts 24:3.

*t Church, called House of the Lord,* 1 Kin. 9:3.

**27**

*u Sabbath, punishment for violation of,* Ex. 16:23.

**1**

*a Prophecies,* Dan. 9:24.

*b Inspiration,* Job 32:8.

*c Prophets, inspiration of,* Isa. 3:2.

**3**

*d Art,* 2 Chr. 16:14.

**4**

*e Clay, used by potter,* Job 33:6.

***POTTERY,** Rom. 9:21. *Clay prepared for, by treading,* Isa. 41:25. *Vessels made of,* Jer. 18:3, 4. *Place for manufacture of, outside the wall of Jerusalem, bought as a burying ground for the poor,* Matt. 27:7–10.
**Figurative,** Isa. 64:8. *Of weakness, in the idol in Nebuchadnezzar's vision,* Dan. 2:41.

*are* ye in [f]mine hand, O house of
Iṣ′ra-el.[Q]
7 [g]*At what* instant I shall speak
concerning a nation, and concerning a kingdom, to pluck up,
and to pull down, and to destroy *it*;
8 [h]If that nation, against whom
I have pronounced, [i]turn from
their evil, I will [j]repent of the
evil that I thought to do unto
them.
9 [g]And *at what* instant I shall
speak concerning a nation, and
concerning a kingdom, to [k]build
and to plant *it;*
10 [h]If it do evil in my sight, that
it [l]obey not my voice, then I will
[j]repent of the [m]good, wherewith
I said I would benefit them.
11 Now therefore go to, speak
to the men of Jū′dah, and to
the inhabitants of Jĕ-ru̥′să-lĕm,
[n,o]saying, [b]Thus saith the LORD;
Behold, I frame evil against you,
and devise a device[G] against you:
[p]return ye now every one from
his evil way, and make your ways
and your doings good.
12 And they [q]said, There is no
hope: but [r,s]we will walk after
our own devices[G], and we will
[1]every one do the imagination[G] of
his evil heart.
13 Therefore thus saith the
LORD; Ask ye now among the
[2]heathen[G], who hath heard such
things: the virgin of Iṣ′ra-el hath
done a very horrible thing.
14 [3]Will *a man* leave the [†]snow
of [t]Lĕb′a-non *which cometh* from
the rock of the field? *or* shall the
cold [4]flowing waters that come
from another place be forsaken?
15 Because my people hath
[u]forgotten me, they have burned
[v]incense to [w]vanity[G], and they
have caused them to stumble
in their ways *from* the ancient
paths, to walk in paths, *in* a way
not cast up;
16 [n,o]To make their land desolate, *and* a perpetual hissing;
every one that passeth thereby
shall be astonished[G], and wag his
head.
17 [n,o]I will scatter them as with
an east wind before the enemy;
I will shew them the back, and
not the face, in the day of their
calamity.
18 ¶ Then said they, Come[G],
and let us [x,y]devise devices
against [z,a]Jĕr-e-mī′ah; for the
law shall not perish from the
priest, nor counsel from the wise,
nor the word from the prophet.
Come, and let us smite him with
the tongue, and let us not give
heed to any of his words.
19 [b]Give heed to me, O LORD,
and hearken to the voice of them
that [c]contend with me.
20 Shall [d,e]evil be recompensed
for good? for they have [c]digged
a pit for my soul. Remember
that I stood before thee to [f]speak
good for them, *and* to turn away
thy [g]wrath from them.
21 Therefore [h]deliver up their
children to the [i]famine, and pour
out their *blood* by the force of the
[j]sword; and let their wives be
bereaved of their [k]children, and
*be* widows; and let their men be
put to death; *let* their young men
*be* slain by the sword in battle.
22 [h]Let a cry be heard from
their houses, when thou shalt
bring a troop suddenly upon
them: for they have [c,e]digged a
pit to take me, and hid snares
for my feet.
23 Yet, LORD, thou [l]knowest
all their [c,d]counsel against me
to slay *me*: [h]forgive not their iniquity, neither blot out their sin
from thy sight, but let them be
overthrown before thee; deal

**6**
f *God, sovereign,* Gen. 2:2.

**7**
g *Government, God in,* Isa. 22:21.

**8**
h *Contingencies, in divine government of man,* 1 Kin. 3:14.
i *Repentance, condition of forgiveness,* Mark 1:4.
j *Repentance, attributed to God,* Mark 1:4.

**9**
k *Temporal Blessings, from God,* Psa. 103:2.

**10**
l *Disobedience to God,* Eph. 5:6.
m *Blessings, contingent upon obedience,* Deut. 11:26.

**11**
n *Judah, kingdom of, prophecies concerning,* 2 Chr. 11:17.
o *Nation, judgments denounced against,* Isa. 2:4.
p *Repentance, enjoined,* Mark 1:4.

**12**
q *Self-will,* Gen. 49:6.
r *Obduracy,* Prov. 29:1.
s *Impenitence,* Rom. 2:5.
1 R. V. do every one after the stubbornness of

**13**
2 R. V. nations,

**14**
t *Lebanon,* Deut. 1:7.
3 R. V. Shall the snow of Lebanon fail from
4 R. V. waters that flow down from afar be dried up?

**15**
u *Backsliding,* Hos. 11:7.
v *Incense, offered in idolatrous worship,* Ex. 37:29.
w *Idolatry, folly of,* 1 Sam. 15:23.

**18**
x *Conspiracy, instances of,* 1 Kin. 16:9.
y *Persecution, of the righteous,* John 15:20.
z *Jeremiah, conspiracy against,* Jer. 1:1.
a *Minister, trials and persecutions of,* Rom. 15:16.

**19**
b *Adversity, prayer in,* Psa. 10:6.
c *Persecution, of the righteous,* John 15:20.

**20**
d *Evil for Good,* Psa. 35:12.
e *Ingratitude, of man to man,* Rom. 1:21.
f *Intercession, instances of,* Jer. 27:18.
g *Anger of God,* 2 Kin. 13:3.

**21**
h *Prayer, imprecatory,* Acts 6:4.
i *Famine, as a judgment,* 2 Kin. 8:1.
j *War, as a judgment,* Judg. 3:2.
k *Children, death of, as a judgment,* Mark 10:14.

**23**
l *God, knowledge of,* Gen. 2:2.

† **SNOW.** *In Palestine,* 2 Sam. 23:20. *In Uz,* Job 6:16; 9:30; 37:6. *On Lebanon,* Jer. 18:14. *Illustrative of purity,* Psa. 51:7; Isa. 1:18.

*thus* with them in the time of thine [g]anger.

## CHAPTER 19

*By the type of the breaking of a potter's vessel, is foreshewn the utter desolation of Judah and Jerusalem for their sins.*

THUS saith the LORD, Go and [1,a]get a [b]potter's earthen [c,d]bottle[G], and *take* of the [2]ancients[G] of the people, and of the [2]ancients[G] of the priests;

2 And go forth unto the valley of the son of [e]Hĭn′nom, which *is* by the entry of the [3]east gate, and proclaim there the words that [f]I shall tell thee,

3 And say, Hear ye the word of the LORD, O kings of [g]Jū′dah, and inhabitants of [h]Jē-ru̇′sȧ-lĕm; Thus saith the LORD of hosts, the God of Ĭs̱′ra-el; Behold, [i]I will bring [j]evil upon this place, the which whosoever heareth, his ears shall tingle.

4 Because they have [k]forsaken me, and have estranged[G] this place, and have [l]burned [m]incense in it unto other gods, whom neither they nor their fathers have known, nor the kings of Jū′dah, and have filled this place with the [n]blood of innocents;

5 They have built also the high places of [o]Bā′al, to burn their [p]sons with fire *for* burnt offerings unto Bā′al, which I commanded not, nor spake *it*, neither came *it* into my mind:

6 [h]Therefore, behold, the days come, saith the LORD, that this place shall no more be called [q]Tō′phet, nor The valley of the son of [e]Hĭn′nom, but The valley of slaughter.

7 And [i]I will make void the counsel of [g]Jū′dah and [h]Jē-ru̇′sȧ-lĕm in this place; and I will cause them to fall by the [r]sword before their enemies, and by the hands of them that seek their lives: and their carcases will I give to be meat[G] for the fowls of the heaven, and for the beasts of the earth.

8 And [g,h,i]I will make this city [4]desolate[G], and an hissing[G]; every one that passeth thereby shall be astonished[G] and hiss because of all the plagues thereof.

9 And [g,h,i]I will [s]cause them to [t]eat the flesh of their sons and the flesh of their daughters, and they shall eat every one the flesh of his friend in the [u]siege and straitness[G], wherewith their enemies, and they that seek their lives, shall straiten[G] them.

10 [a]Then shalt thou break the [c,d]bottle in the sight of the men that go with thee,

11 And shalt say unto them, Thus saith the LORD of hosts; [a,i]Even so will I break this people and this city, as *one* breaketh a [b]potter's vessel, that cannot be made whole again: and they shall bury *them* in [q]Tō′phet, till *there be* no place to bury.

12 [g,h,i]Thus will I do unto this place, saith the LORD, and to the inhabitants thereof, and *even* make this city as [q]Tō′phet:

13 And the houses of [h]Jē-ru̇′sȧ-lĕm, and the houses of the kings of Jū′dah, shall be defiled as the place of [q]Tō′phet, because of all the houses upon whose [v]roofs they have [l]burned [m]incense unto all the [w]host of heaven, and have [l]poured out drink offerings unto other gods.[Q]

14 Then came [x]Jĕr-e-mī′ah from [q]Tō′phet, whither the LORD had [f]sent him to prophesy; and he stood in the court of the [y]LORD's house; and said to all the people,

15 Thus saith the LORD of hosts, the God of Ĭs̱′ra-el; Behold, [j]I will bring upon this [h]city and upon all her towns all the evil that I have pronounced against it, because [z]they have

1
*a Instruction, by object lessons,* Prov. 23:23.
*b Pottery,* Jer. 18:3.
*c Bottle,* Gen. 21:14.
*d Symbols and Similitudes,* Heb. 9:9.
1 R. V. buy
2 R. V. elders

2
*e Hinnom,* Jer. 7:31.
*f Prophets, inspiration of,* Isa. 3:2.
3 R. V. gate Harsith,

3
*g Judah, kingdom of, prophecies concerning,* 2 Chr. 11:17.
*h Jerusalem, prophecies against,* 19:10.
*i Nation, judgments denounced against,* Isa. 2:4.
*Adversity, dispensation from God,* Psa. 10:6.

4
*k Backsliding,* Hos. 11:7.
*l Idolatry, customs of,* 1 Sam. 15:23.
*m Incense, offered in idolatrous worship,* Ex. 37:29.
*n Homicide, felonious,* Deut. 5:17.

5
*o Baal,* 2 Kin. 17:16.
*p Human Sacrifices,* Deut. 12:31.

6
*q* Or, *Topheth,* 2 Kin. 23:10.

7
*r War, as a judgment,* Judg. 3:2.

8
4 R. V an astonishment,

9
*s Famine, sent as a judgment,* 2 Kin. 8:1.
*t Cannibalism,* Lam. 2:20.
*u Siege,* Deut. 28:53.

13
*v House, roof of,* Esth. 8:1.
*w Idolatry, objects of,* 1 Sam. 15:23

14
*x Jeremiah,* Jer. 1:1.
*y Temple, Solomon's,* 1 Kin. 6:17.

15
*z Impenitence,* Rom. 2:5.

hardened their necks, that they might not hear my words.

## CHAPTER 20

*The prophet, smitten by Pashur, foretells his fearful doom. 7 The prophet complains of contempt, 10 and of treachery. 14 He curses the day of his birth.*

NOW Păsh′ŭr the son of Ĭm′mēr the priest, who *was* also chief governor in the [a,b]house of the LORD, heard that [c]Jĕr-e-mī′ah prophesied these things.

2 Then [d]Păsh′ŭr [e]smote[G] [c]Jĕr-e-mī′ah the prophet, and put him in the [f]stocks[G] that *were* in the high [g,h]gate of Bĕn′ja-mĭn, which *was* by the [b]house of the LORD.[Q]

3 And it came to pass on the morrow[G], that [d]Păsh′ŭr brought forth [c]Jĕr-e-mī′ah out of the [f]stocks. Then said Jĕr-e-mī′ah unto him, The LORD hath not called thy name Păsh′ŭr, but [1]Mā′gôr–mĭs′sa-bĭb.

4 For thus saith the LORD, Behold, I will make [d]thee a terror to thyself, and to all thy friends: and [i,j]they shall fall by the [k]sword of their enemies, and thine eyes shall behold *it*: and [l]I will give all Jū′dah into the hand of the king of [m]Băb′ȳ-lon, and he shall carry them [n]captive into [o]Băb′ȳ-lon, and shall slay them with the sword.

5 Moreover [i,j,l]I will deliver all the strength of this city, and all the labours thereof, and all the precious things thereof, and all the treasures of the kings of Jū′dah will I give into the hand of their enemies, which shall spoil[G] them, and take them, and carry them to [o]Băb′ȳ-lon.

6 And thou, [d]Păsh′ŭr, and all that dwell in thine house [p]shall go into [n]captivity: and thou shalt come to [o]Băb′ȳ-lon, and there thou shalt die, and shalt be buried there, thou, and all thy friends, to whom thou hast prophesied lies.

7 ¶ [q]O LORD, thou hast deceived me, and I was deceived: thou art stronger than I, and hast prevailed: [r]I am [2,e]in derision daily, every one [s]mocketh me.

8 For since I spake, I cried out, I cried violence and spoil; because [r]the word of the LORD was made a reproach unto me, and a derision, [3]daily.

9 Then I said, I will not make mention of him, nor speak any more in his name. But [t,u]*his word* was in mine [v]heart as a burning [w]fire shut up in my bones, and I was weary with forbearing, and I [4]could not *stay*.[G Q]

10 For I heard the [x]defaming of many, fear on every side. [5]Report, *say they*, and we will report it. All my familiars[G] [y]watched for my halting, *saying*, Peradventure[G] he will be enticed, and we shall prevail against him, and we shall take our [z]revenge on him.

11 But [a,b]the LORD *is* [c]with me as a [d]mighty terrible one: therefore my persecutors shall stumble, and they shall not prevail: they shall be greatly ashamed; [6]for they shall not prosper: *their* everlasting confusion shall never be forgotten.

12 But, O LORD of hosts, that [e]triest[G] the righteous, *and* [f]seest the reins[G] and the [g]heart,[G] [h]let me see thy vengeance on them: for unto thee have I opened my cause.[S]

13 Sing unto the LORD, [i]praise ye the LORD: for he hath delivered the soul[G] of the [j]poor from the hand of evildoers.

14 ¶ [k,l,m]Cursed *be* the [n]day wherein I was born: let not the day wherein my mother bare me be blessed.

15 [k,l,m]Cursed *be* the man who

---

1
a *Church,* 1 Kin. 9:3.
b *Temple, Solomon's,* 1 Kin. 6:17.
c *Jeremiah,* Jer. 1:1.

2
d *Priest, corrupt,* Lev. 1:5.
e *Persecution, of the righteous,* John 15:20.
f *Stocks, in prisons,* Job 13:27.
g *Gates,* Deut. 3:5.
h *Jerusalem, gates of,* Judg. 19:10.

3
1 *That is* Terror, on every side.

4
i *Nation, judgments denounced against,* Isa. 2:4.
j *Judah, kingdom of, prophecies concerning,* 2 Chr. 11:17.
k *War, as a judgment,* Judg. 3:2.
l *Adversity, dispensation from God,* Psa. 10:6.
m *Babylon, empire of,* Ezra 5:12.
n *Captivity, as a judgment,* Isa. 5:13.
o *Babylon, city of,* Ezra 5:12.

6
p *Wicked, punishment of,* Psa. 73:3.

7
q *Adversity, prayer in,* Psa. 10:6.
r *Minister, trials and persecutions of,* Rom. 15:16.
s *Mocking,* 1 Kin. 18:27.
2 R. V. become a laughing-stock all the day,

8
3 R. V. all the day.

9
t *Minister, character of, zealous,* Rom. 15:16.
u *Zeal,* 2 Cor. 7:11.
v *Heart,* Psa. 44:21.
w *Fire, figurative,* Ex. 12:8.
4 R.V. cannot contain.

10
x *Speech, evil,* Col. 4:6.
y *Malice,* Eph. 4:31.
z *Revenge,* Ezek. 25:15.
5 Am. R. V. Denounce, and we will denounce him, say all my familiar friends, they that watch for my fall; peradventure he will be persuaded, and

11
a *Faith, exemplified,* Mark 11:22.
b *Minister, joys of,* Rom. 15:16.
c *God dwells with the Righteous,* 1 Kin. 6:13.
d *God, power of,* Gen. 2:2.
6 R. V. because they have not dealt wisely, even with an everlasting dishonour which shall

12
e *God, judge,* Gen. 2:2.
f *God, knowledge of,* Gen. 2:2.
g *Heart, known to God,* Psa. 44:21.
h *Prayer, imprecatory,* Acts 6:4.

13
i *Praise,* Psa. 150:1.
j *Poor, God's care of,* Prov. 21:13.

14
k *Despondency,* Eccl. 2:20.
l *Adversity, despondency in,* Psa. 10:6.
m *Murmuring, instances of,* Num. 14:2.
n *Birthday, cursed,* Gen. 40:20.

brought tidings to my father,
saying, A man child is born unto
thee; making him very glad.
16 And [h]let that man be as the
[o,p]cities which the LORD [q]over-
threw, and repented not: and let
him hear the cry in the morning,
and the shouting at noontide;
17 Because he slew me not from
the womb; or that my mother
might have been my grave, and
her womb *to be* always great *with*
*me*.
18 [k,l,m]Wherefore[C] came I forth
out of the womb to see labour
and sorrow, that my days should
be consumed with shame?

16
*o Sodom,* Gen. 13:10.
*p Gomorrah,* Gen. 13:10.
*q Wicked, punishment of,* Psa. 73:3.

## CHAPTER 21

*Zedekiah inquires of the prophet the issue of Nebuchadnezzar's war. 3 The prophet foretells the overthrow of the city and the captivity of the people. 8 He counsels them to go over to the Chaldeans; 11 and upbraids the king's house.*

THE word which [a]came unto
[b]Jĕr-e-mī′ah from the LORD,
when king [c]Zĕd-e-kī′ah sēnt unto
him [d]Păsh′ŭr the son of [e]Mĕl-
chī′ah, and *Zĕph-a-nī′ah the
son of [f]Mā-a-sē′iah the priest,
saying,
2 Enquire,[C] I pray thee, of the
LORD for us; for [g]Nĕb-u-chad-
rĕz′zar king of [h]Băb′y̆-lon maketh war against us; if so be that
the LORD will deal with us
according to all his wondrous
works, that he may go up from
us.
3 ¶ Then said [a,b]Jĕr-e-mī′ah
unto them, Thus shall ye say to
[c]Zĕd-e-kī′ah:
4 [i]Thus saith the LORD God
of Īṣ′ra-el; Behold, [j]I will [k]turn
back the weapons of war that
*are* in your hands, wherewith ye
fight against the king of [h]Băb′-
y̆-lon, and *against* the Chăl-dē′-
anṣ, which [l]besiege you without[C]
the walls, and [j]I will assemble
them into the midst of this city.

1
*a Prophets, inspiration of,* Isa. 3:2.
*b Jeremiah,* Jer. 1:1.
*c Zedekiah,* 2 Kin. 25:2.
*d Pashur,* 1 Chr. 9:12.
*e* Neh. 11:12.
*f* Jer. 29:25; 35:4; 37:3.

2
*g* Or, *Nebuchadnezzar,* Dan. 2:1.
*h Babylon, empire of,* Ezra 5:12.

4
*i Judah, kingdom of, prophecies concerning,* 2 Chr. 11:17.
*j Nation, judgments denounced against,* Isa. 2:4.
*k Adversity, dispensation from God,* Psa. 10:6.
*l Siege,* Deut. 28:53.

5 [S]And [j,k]I myself will fight
against you with an outstretched
hand and with a strong arm,
even in [m]anger, and in fury, and
in great wrath.
6 And [i,j,k]I will smite the inhabitants of this [n]city, both man
and [o]beast: they shall die of a
great pestilence.[S]
7 And afterward, saith the
LORD, [i,j]I will [k]deliver [c]Zĕd-e-
kī′ah king of Jū′dah, and his
servants, and the people, and
such as are left in this city from
the pestilence, from the [p]sword,
and from the [q]famine, into the
hand of [g]Nĕb-u-chad-rĕz′zar
king of [h]Băb′y̆-lon, and into the
hand of their enemies, and into
the hand of those that seek their
life: and he shall smite[C] them with
the edge of the sword; he shall not
spare them, neither have [r]pity,
nor have [s]mercy.[Q]
8 ¶ And unto this people thou
shalt say, Thus saith the LORD;
Behold, I set before you the way
of life, and the way of death.[T]
9 He that abideth in this city
shall die by the [p]sword, and by
the [q]famine, and by the [t]pesti-
lence: but he that goeth out, and
falleth to the Chăl-dē′anṣ that
besiege you, he shall live, and
his life shall be unto him for a
prey.[C]
10 For I have set my face
against [n]this city for evil, and
not for good, saith the LORD: it
shall be given into the hand of
the [g]king of [h]Băb′y̆-lon, and he
shall burn it with fire.
11 ¶ And touching the house of
the king of [i]Jū′dah, *say,* Hear ye
the word of the LORD;
12 O house of Dā′vid, thus
saith the LORD; [u,v]Execute judgment in the morning, and deliver *him that is* spoiled[C] out of
the hand of the [w]oppressor, lest

5
*m Anger of God,* 2 Kin. 13:3.

6
*n Jerusalem, prophecies against,* Judg. 19:10.
*o Animals, suffer under divine judgments,* Jer. 27:5.

7
*p War, as a judgment,* Judg. 3:2.
*q Famine, as a judgment,* 2 Kin. 8:1.
*r Pity,* Job 19:21.
*s Mercy,* Deut. 5:10.

9
*t Plague,* Ex. 11:1.

12
*u Rulers, duties of,* Ex. 18:21.
*v Righteousness, enjoined in official administration,* Psa. 15:2.
*w Oppression, forbidden,* Eccl. 5:8.

* **ZEPHANIAH** (*hidden of Jehovah*), a priest in the reign of Zedekiah, king of Judah. *Sent by the king to Jeremiah,* Jer. 21:1, 2; 37:3. *Shows Jeremiah the false prophet's letter,* Jer. 29:25–29. *Taken to Riblah and slain,* 2 Kin. 25:18–21; Jer. 52:24–27.

my fury go out like fire, and burn that none can quench *it*, because of the evil of your doings.

13 Behold, I *am* against thee, O inhabitant of the valley, *and* rock of the plain, saith the LORD; which [x]say, Who shall come down against us? or who shall enter into our habitations?

14 But I will [y]punish you [z,a]according to the fruit of your doings, saith the LORD: and I will kindle a fire in the forest thereof, and it shall devour all things round about it.

## CHAPTER 22

*The king of Judah and his people exhorted to repentance. 10 The judgment upon Shallum, 13 upon Jehoiakim, 20 and upon Coniah.*

THUS saith the LORD; Go down to the house of the king of Jū'dah, and [a]speak there this word,

2 And say, Hear the word of the LORD, O king of Jū'dah, that sittest upon the throne of Dā'vid, thou, and thy servants, and thy people that enter in by these gates:

3 Thus saith the LORD; [b,c,d]Execute ye [e]judgment and righteousness, and deliver the spoiled out of the hand of the oppressor: and [f]do no wrong, do no violence to the [g]stranger, the [h]fatherless, nor the [i]widow, neither [j]shed innocent blood in this place.

4 For [k]if ye do this thing indeed, [l,m]then shall there enter in by the gates of this house kings sitting upon the throne of Dā'vid, riding in chariots and on horses, he, and his servants, and his people.

5 But [k]if ye will not hear these words, I [n]swear by myself, saith the LORD, that [a]this house shall become a desolation.

6 For [a]thus saith the LORD unto the king's house of Jū'dah; Thou *art* [o]Gĭl'e-ăd unto me, *and* the head of [p]Lĕb'a-non: *yet* surely [q]I will make thee a wilderness, *and* cities *which* are not inhabited.

7 And [a,q]I will prepare destroyers against thee, every one with his weapons: and they shall cut down thy choice [r]cedars, and cast *them* into the fire.

8 And many nations shall pass by this [s]city, and they shall say every man to his neighbour, Wherefore hath the LORD done thus unto this great city?

9 Then they shall answer, Because they have [t]forsaken the [u]covenant of the LORD their God, and [v]worshipped other gods, and served them.

10 ¶ [w]Weep ye not for the dead, neither bemoan him: *but* weep sore for [x]him that goeth away: for he shall return no more, nor see his native country.

11 For thus saith the LORD touching [x]Shăl'lum the son of [y]Jō-sī'ah king of Jū'dah, which reigned instead of Jō-sī'ah his father, which went forth out of this place; He shall not return thither any more:

12 But [x]he shall die in [z]the place whither they have led him captive, and shall see this land no more.

13 ¶ [a]Woe unto [b]him that buildeth his house by [c]unrighteousness, and his chambers by wrong; [d]*that* [c]useth his [e,f]neighbour's service without [g,h]wages, and [c]giveth him not for his work;

14 That saith, I will build me a wide [i]house and large chambers, and cutteth him out windows; and *it is* cieled with [j]cedar, and [k]painted with [l]vermilion.

15 Shalt thou reign, because thou [1]closest *thyself* in cedar? did not thy [m]father eat and drink, and [n]do judgment and justice, *and* then [o]*it was* well with him?

16 [m,n]He judged the cause of

13
*x False Confidence*, Psa. 30:6.

14
*y Punishment, according to deeds*, Lev. 26:41.
*z Wicked, punishment of*, Psa. 73:3.

*a Judgment, according to opportunity and works*, 2 Pet. 3:7.

1
*a Judah, kingdom of, prophecies concerning*, vs. 1–30; 2 Chr. 11:17.

3
*b Commandment, enjoining justice*, Deut. 8:2.
*c Righteousness, enjoined in official administration*, Psa. 15:2.
*d Rulers, duties of*, Ex. 18:21.
*e Justice, enjoined*, Deut. 33:21.
*f Injustice, forbidden*, Isa. 26:10.
*g Foreigners, Israelites forbidden to oppress*, Deut. 23:20.
*h Orphan, justice to, required*, Lam. 5:3.
*i Widow, oppression of, forbidden*, 2 Sam. 14:5.
*j Homicide, felonious, forbidden*, Deut. 5:17.

4
*k Contingencies, in divine government*, 1 Kin. 3:14.
*l Blessings, contingent upon obedience*, Deut. 11:26.
*m Reward, a motive, to obedience*, Matt. 5:12.

5
*n Oath, attributed to God*, Num. 5:19.

6
*o Gilead, figurative*, Deut. 3:13.
*p Lebanon, figurative*, Deut. 1:7.
*q Adversity, dispensation from God*, Psa. 10:6.

7
*r Cedar, figurative*, Isa. 9:10.

8
*s Jerusalem, prophecies against*, Judg. 19:10.

9
*t Backsliding, of Israel*, Hos. 11:7.
*u Covenant, of man with God*, Deut. 29:1.
*v Idolatry*, 1 Sam. 15:23.

10
*w Weeping*, Ezra 3:13.
*x Jehoahaz, prophecies concerning*, 2 Kin. 23:30.

11
*y Josiah*, 1 Kin. 13:2.

12
*z Babylon, city of*, Ezra 5:12.

13
*a Rich, denounced*, Jas. 5:1.
*b Jehoiakim*, Jer. 26:1.
*c Dishonesty*, Ezek. 22:13.
*d Employer, required to accord just compensation*, Deut. 24:14.
*e Neighbor, oppression of, denounced*, Luke 10:29.
*f Hired Servant, rights of*, Lev. 25:40.
*g Wages*, Gen. 31:7.
*h Labor, compensation for*, Luke 10:7.

14
*i House, architecture of*, Esth. 8:1.
*j Cedar*, Isa. 9:10.
*k Painting*, 2 Kin. 9:30.
*l* Ezek. 23:14.

15
*m Josiah*, 1 Kin. 13:2.
*n Rulers, righteous*, Ex. 18:21.
*o Obedience, rewarded*, Heb. 5:8.
1 R. V. strivest to excel in cedar?

the [p]poor and needy; then [o]*it*
*was* well *with him*: *was* not this
to [q]know me? saith the LORD.[S]
17 [r]But [b,s]thine eyes and thine
[t]heart *are* not but for thy [u]covet-
ousness, and for to [v]shed innocent blood, and for [w]oppression,
and for violence, to do *it*.
18 Therefore thus saith the
LORD concerning [b]Jĕ-hoi'a-kĭm
the son of [m]Jō-sī'ah king of Jū'-
dah; They shall not lament for
him, *saying*, Ah my brother! or,
Ah sister! they shall not lament
for him, *saying*, Ah lord! or, Ah
his glory!
19 [b]He shall be buried with the
[x]burial of an ass, drawn and
cast forth beyond the gates of
[y]Jĕ-ru'sā-lĕm.
20 ¶ Go up to Lĕb'a-non, and
cry; and lift up thy voice in Bā'-
shăn, and cry from [2]the passages[G]: for all thy lovers are destroyed.
21 I spake unto thee in thy [z]pros-
perity; *but* thou saidst, I [a,b]will
not hear. This *hath been* thy
manner from thy [c]youth, that
thou [d]obeyedst not my voice.
22 The wind shall [3]eat up all
thy pastors[G], and thy lovers shall
go into [e]captivity: surely then
shalt thou be ashamed and confounded for all thy wickedness.
23 O inhabitant of Lĕb'a-non,
that makest thy nest in the cedars, how [4]gracious shalt thou be
when pangs come upon thee, the
pain as of a woman in travail!
24 *As* I live, saith the LORD,
though [f]Cō-nī'ah the son of [g]Jĕ-
hoi'a-kĭm king of Jū'dah were
the signet[G] upon my right hand,
yet would I [h]pluck thee thence[G];
25 And [i]I will give [j]thee into
the hand of them that seek thy
life, and into the hand *of them*
whose face thou fearest, even into the hand of [j]Nĕb-u-chad-rĕz'-
zar king of [k]Băb'y̆-lon, and into
the hand of the [l]Chăl-dē'ans.
26 And [i]I will [h]cast [f]thee out,
and thy mother that bare thee,
into another country, where ye
were not born; and there shall ye
die.
27 But to the land whereunto
they desire to return, thither
shall they not return.
28 *Is* this man [f]Cō-nī'ah a despised broken [5]idol? *is he* a
vessel wherein *is* no pleasure?
wherefore[G] are they cast out, he
and his seed, and are cast into a
land which they know not?
29 O earth, earth, earth, hear
the word of the LORD.
30 Thus saith the LORD, Write
ye this [f]man childless, a man *that*
shall not prosper in his days: for
[i]no man of his seed shall prosper, sitting upon the throne of
Dā'vid, and ruling any more
in Jū'dah.

## CHAPTER 23

*A woe denounced against wicked pastors. 5 Predictions concerning the Messiah. 9 Against false prophets, 33 and mockers of the true prophets.*

WOE[Q] be unto the [1,a]pastors[G]
that destroy and scatter the
sheep of my pasture! saith the
LORD.
2 Therefore thus saith the
LORD God of Iș'ra-el against
the [1,a]pastors that feed my people; Ye have scattered my flock,
and driven them away, and have
not visited them: behold, I will
[b]visit[G] upon you the evil of your
doings, saith the LORD.[Q]
3 And [c]I will gather the remnant of my flock out of all countries whither I have driven them,
and will bring them again to their
folds; and they shall be fruitful
and increase.
4 And I will set up shepherds
over them which shall feed them:
and they shall fear no more, nor
be dismayed, neither shall they
be lacking, saith the LORD.
5 Be[T][Q]hold, the days come, saith
the LORD, that [d]I will raise unto

**16**
p *Poor, righteous treatment of, rewarded*, Prov. 21:13.
q *Wisdom, spiritual*, Prov. 2:2.
**17**
r *Reproof, faithfulness in*, Prov. 17:10.
s *Rulers, wicked*, Ex. 18:21.
t *Heart, unregenerate*, Psa. 44:21.
u *Covetousness*, Isa. 57:17.
v *Homicide, felonious*, Deut. 5:17.
w *Oppression*, Eccl. 5:8.
**19**
x *Burial, lack of, a disgrace*, Acts 8:2.
y *Jerusalem*, Judg. 19:10.
**20**
2 R. V. Abarim;
**21**
z *Prosperity, dangers of*, Eccl. 7:14.

a *Obduracy*, Prov. 29:1.
b *Self-will*, Gen. 49:6.
c *Young Men*, Prov. 1:4.
d *Disobedience to God*, Eph. 5:6.
**22**
e *Captivity, as a judgment*, Isa. 5:13.
3 R. V. feed all thy shepherds,
**23**
4 R. V. greatly to be pitied
**24**
f Or, *Jehoiachin, prophecies concerning*, 2 Kin. 24:6.
g *Jehoiakim*, Jer. 26:1.
h *Wicked, punishment of*, Psa. 73:3.
**25**
i *Adversity, dispensation from God*, Psa. 10:6.
j Or, *Nebuchadnezzar*, Dan. 2:1.
k *Babylon, empire of*, Ezra 5:12.
l *Chaldeans*, Dan. 1:4.

**28**
5 R. V. vessel?
**1**
a *Rulers, wicked*, Ex. 18:21.
1 R. V. shepherds
**2**
b *Wicked, punishment of*, Psa. 73:3.
**3**
c *Jews, prophecies concerning restoration of*, Neh. 4:2.
**5**
d *Jesus, prophecies concerning*, Matt. 1:21.

[e]Dā'vid a [f]righteous [g,h]Branch,
and a [i]King shall reign and
[2]prosper, and shall execute judgment and justice in the earth.
6 [c,d]In his days Jū'dah shall be
saved, and Ĭs'ra-el shall dwell
safely: and this *is* his name
whereby he shall be called,
[h]THE LORD OUR RIGHT-
EOUSNESS.
7 Therefore, behold, the days
come, saith the LORD, that they
shall no more say, The LORD
liveth, which [j]brought up the
children of [k]Ĭs'ra-el out of the
land of [l]Ē'ġy̆pt;
8 But, the LORD liveth, which
[j]brought up and which led the
seed of the house of [k]Ĭs'ra-el out
of the north country, and from
all countries whither I had driven
them; and [c]they shall dwell in
their own land.
9 ¶ Mine heart within me is
broken because of the prophets;
all my bones shake; I am like a
[m]drunken man, and like a man
whom [n]wine hath overcome, because of the LORD, and because
of [3]the words of his holiness.
10 For the land is full of [o,p]adul-
terers; for because of swearing
the land mourneth; the [4]pleasant
places of the wilderness are dried
up, and their course is evil, and
their force *is* not right.
11 For both [q]prophet and
[r]priest are profane; yea, [s]in my
house have I found their wickedness, saith the LORD.
12 Wherefore [t]their way shall
be unto them as slippery *ways* in
the darkness: they shall be driven
on, and fall therein: for I will
bring [b]evil upon them, *even* the
year of their visitation, saith the
LORD.
13 And I have seen folly in
the [q]prophets of [u]Să-mā'rĭ-ȧ;
they prophesied [5]in [v]Bā'al, and
[w]caused my people Ĭs'ra-el to
err.
14 I have seen also in the
[q]prophets of [x]Jĕ-ru'sȧ-lĕm an
horrible thing: they commit
[o]adultery, and walk in lies: they
strengthen also the hands of evildoers, that none doth return
from his wickedness: they are
all of them unto me as [y]Sŏd'om,
and the inhabitants thereof as
[z]Gŏ-mŏr'rah.
15 Therefore thus saith the
LORD of hosts concerning the
[a]prophets; Behold, [b]I will feed
them with [c]wormwood, and
make them drink the water of
[d]gall: for [e]from the [f]prophets of
Jĕ-ru'sȧ-lĕm is profaneness gone
forth into all the land.
16 Thus [g]saith the LORD of
hosts, Hearken not unto the
words of the [a]prophets that
prophesy unto you: they [6]make
you vain: [h]they speak a vision of
their own heart, *and* not out of
the mouth of the LORD.
17 [a,h]They say still unto them
that despise me, The LORD hath
said, Ye shall have peace; and
they say unto every one that
walketh after the [7,i]imagination
of his own heart, No evil shall
come upon you.
18 For who hath stood in the
[8]counsel of the LORD, and hath
perceived and heard his word?
who hath marked his word, and
heard *it*?
19 Behold, a whirlwind of the
LORD is gone forth in fury, even
a grievous whirlwind: [b]it shall
fall grievously upon the head of
the wicked.
20 The [j]anger of the LORD
shall not return, until he have
[b]executed, and till he have performed the thoughts of his heart:
in the latter days ye shall consider it perfectly.
21 I have not sent these
[a,h]prophets, yet they ran: I have
not spoken to them, yet they
prophesied.

e *David,* 1 Sam. 16:13.
f *Jesus, holiness of,* Matt. 1:21.
g *Branch, figurative,* Dan. 4:14.
h *Jesus, names of,* Matt. 1:21.
i *Jesus, king,* Matt. 1:21.
2 R. V. deal wisely,

7
j *God, providence of,* Gen. 2:2.
k *Israel,* Ex. 4:22.
l *Egypt,* Gen. 41:8.

9
m *Drunkenness,* Luke 21:34.
n *Wine, intoxicates,* Prov. 23:31.
3 R. V. his holy words.

10
o *Adultery,* Lev. 20:10.
p *Idolatry, wicked practices of,* 1 Sam. 15:23.
4 R. V. pastures of

11
q *Prophets, false,* Isa. 3:2.
r *Priest, corrupt,* Lev. 1:5.
s *Profanation, of the house of God,* Lev. 22:32.

12
t *Adversity, dispensation from God,* Psa. 10:6.

13
u *Samaria,* Isa. 7:9.
v *Baal,* 2 Kin. 17:16.
w *Influence, evil,* 1 Cor. 7:14.
5 R. V. by

14
x *Jerusalem,* Judg. 19:10.
y *Sodom, wickedness of,* Gen. 13:10.
z *Gomorrah, wickedness of,* Gen. 13:10.

15
a *Prophets, false,* Isa. 3:2.
b *Wicked, punishment of,* Psa. 73:3.
c *Wormwood, figurative,* Deut. 29:18.
d *Gall, figurative,* Job 16:13.
e *Influence, evil,* 1 Cor. 7:14.
f *Example, bad,* John 13:15.

16
g *Inspiration,* Job 32:8.
h *False Teachers,* 2 Pet. 2:1.
6 R. V. teach you vanity:

17
i *Self-will,* Gen. 49:6.
7 R. V. stubbornness

18
8 R. V. council

20
j *Anger of God, destroys,* 2 Kin. 13:3.

22 But if they had stood in my [8]counsel,[G] and had caused my people to hear my words, then they should have turned them from their evil way, and from the evil of their doings.

23 [k]*Am* I a God at hand, saith the LORD, and not a God afar off? [S Q]

24 [k,l]Can any hide himself in secret places that I shall not see him? saith the LORD. Do not I fill [m]heaven and earth? saith the LORD.[S]

25 I have heard what the prophets said, that prophesy [n]lies in my name, saying, I have [o]dreamed, I have dreamed.

26 How long shall *this* be in the heart of the [a]prophets that prophesy [n]lies? yea, *they are* prophets of the [n]deceit of their own heart;

27 Which think to [e]cause my people to [p]forget my name by their [o]dreams which they tell every man to his neighbour, as their fathers have [p]forgotten my name for [q]Bā′al.

28 The [a]prophet that hath a [o]dream, let him tell a dream; and he that hath my word, let him speak my word faithfully. What *is* the [9]chaff to the wheat? saith the LORD.

29 *Is* not my word like as a fire? saith the LORD; and like a hammer *that* breaketh the rock in pieces?

30 Therefore, behold, I *am* against the [a]prophets, saith the LORD, that steal my words every one from his neighbour.

31 Behold, I *am* against the [a]prophets, saith the LORD, that use their tongues, and say, He saith.

32 Behold, I *am* against [a]them that prophesy false [o]dreams, saith the LORD, and do tell them, and [e]cause my people to err by their [n]lies, and by their [10]lightness;[G] yet I sent them not, nor commanded them: therefore they shall not profit this people at all, saith the LORD.

33 ¶ And when this people, or the prophet, or a priest, shall ask thee, saying, What *is* the burden[G] of the LORD? thou shalt then say unto them, What burden[G]? I will even [b]forsake you, saith the LORD.

34 And *as for* the prophet, and the priest, and the people, that shall say, The burden[G] of the LORD, I will even [b]punish[G] that man and his house.

35 Thus shall ye say every one to his neighbour, and every one to his brother, What hath the LORD answered? and, What hath the LORD spoken?

36 And the burden[G] of the LORD shall ye mention no more: for every man's word shall be his burden[G]; for ye have perverted the words of the living God, of the LORD of hosts our God.[T]

37 Thus shalt thou say to the prophet, What hath the LORD answered thee? and, What hath the LORD spoken?

38 But [11]since ye say, The burden of the LORD; therefore thus saith the LORD; Because ye say this word, The burden of the LORD, and I have sent unto you, saying, Ye shall not say, The burden of the LORD;

39 Therefore, behold, I, even I, will utterly [b]forget you, and I will [b]forsake you, and the city that I gave you and your fathers, *and* [b]*cast you* out of my presence:

40 And I will bring an everlasting [b]reproach upon you, and a perpetual shame, which shall not be forgotten.

## CHAPTER 24

*The type of good and bad figs;* 4 *and the meaning thereof.*

THE LORD shewed [a]me, and, behold, two baskets of [b]figs *were* set before the [c]temple of the

**23**
*k God, omnipresent,* Gen. 2:2.

**24**
*l God, knowledge of,* Gen. 2:2.
*m Heaven, God's dwelling place,* Luke 18:22.

**25**
*n Falsehood,* Job 21:34.
*o Dream,* Dan. 1:17.

**27**
*p Backsliding,* Hos. 11:7.
*q Baal,* 2 Kin. 17:16.

**28**
9 R. V. straw

**32**
10 R.V. vain boasting:

**38**
11 R. V. if

**1**
*a Jeremiah,* Jer. 1:1.
*b Fig,* Mark 11:13.
*c Temple, Solomon's,* 1 Kin. 6:17.

d Or, *Nebuchadnezzar*, Dan. 2:1.
e *Babylon, empire of*, Ezra 5:12.
f *Captivity, as a judgment*, Isa. 5:13.
g Or, *Jehoiachin*, 2 Kin. 24:6.
h *Jehoiakim*, Jer. 26:1.
i *Judah, kingdom of*, 2 Chr. 11:17.
j *Carpentry*, 2 Kin. 12:11.
k *Smith*, Isa. 54:16.
l *Jerusalem*, Judg. 19:10.

2

1 R. V. bad

4

m *Jews, prophecies concerning*, vs. 4–10; Neh. 4:2.
n *Prophets, inspiration of*, Isa. 3:2.

5

o *Instruction, by object lessons*, Prov. 23:23.
p *Symbols and Similitudes*, Heb. 9:9.
q *Divine Chastisement, corrective*, Job 33:19.
r *Adversity, design of*, Psa. 10:6.
2 R. V. regard the captives of

6

s *Temporal Blessings, from God*, Psa. 103:2.

7

t *Regeneration*, Tit. 3:5.
u *Wisdom, spiritual, from God*, Prov. 2:2.
v *Repentance, rewards of*, Mark 1:4.
w *Penitent, promises to*, Psa. 51:17.
x *Spiritual Adoption*, Rom. 8:15.

8

y *Zedekiah*, 2 Kin. 25:2.
z *Egypt*, Gen. 41:8.

9

a *Adversity, dispensation from God*, Psa. 10:6.
b *Wicked, punishment of*, Psa. 73:3.
c *Dispersion, of the Jews foretold*, Gen. 11:8.
3 R. V. tossed to and fro among

LORD, after that [d]Nĕb-u-chad-rĕz′zar king of [e]Băb′ȳ-lon had carried away [f]captive [g]Jĕc-o-nī′ah the son of [h]Jĕ-hoi′a-kĭm king of [i]Jū′dah, and the princes of Jū′dah, with the [j]carpenters and [k]smiths, from [l]Jĕ-ru′să-lĕm, and had brought them to Băb′ȳ-lon.

2 One basket *had* very good [b]figs, *even* like the figs *that are* first ripe: and the other basket *had* very [1]naughty[C] figs, which could not be eaten, they were so bad.

3 Then said the LORD unto me, What seest thou, [a]Jĕr-e-mī′ah? And I said, [b]Figs; the good figs, very good; and the evil,[C] very evil, that cannot be eaten, they are so evil.

4 ¶ Again the [m]word of the LORD [n]came unto [a]me, saying,

5 Thus saith the LORD, the God of Ĭs′ra-el; [o]Like these good [b,p]figs, so will I [2]acknowledge [m]them that are carried away [f]captive of Jū′dah, whom I have [q]sent out of this place into the land of the Chăl-dē′ans [r]for *their* good.[S]

6 For I will set mine eyes upon them for good, and I will [s]bring them again to this land: and I will [s]build them, and not pull *them* down; and I will [s]plant them, and not pluck *them* up.

7 And I will [t]give them an heart to [u]know me, that I *am* the LORD: and [v,w]they shall be [x]my people, and I will be their God: for they shall return unto me with their whole heart.[T]

8 ¶ And [o]as the evil figs, which cannot be eaten, they are so evil; surely thus saith the LORD, So will I give [y]Zĕd-e-kī′ah the king of [i]Jū′dah, and his princes, and the residue of [l]Jĕ-ru′să-lĕm, that remain in this land, and them that dwell in the land of [z]Ē′ġy̆pt:

9 And [a,b]I will deliver them to be [3,c]removed into all the kingdoms of the earth for *their* hurt, *to be* a reproach and a proverb, a taunt and a curse, in all places whither I shall drive them.

10 And [b]I will send the [d]sword, the [e]famine, and the pestilence, among them, till they be consumed[C] from off the land that I gave unto them and to their fathers.

## CHAPTER 25

*Judah's disobedience to the warnings of the prophets. 8 Her seventy years' captivity foretold, 12 and after that, the destruction of Babylon. 15 Sundry nations made to drink the wine cup of God's wrath. 34 The howling of the shepherds.*

THE [a]word that [b,c]came to [d]Jĕr-e-mī′ah concerning all the people of Jū′dah in the fourth year of [e]Jĕ-hoi′a-kĭm the son of [f]Jō-sī′ah king of Jū′dah, that *was* the first year of [g]Nĕb-u-chad-rĕz′zar king of [h]Băb′ȳ-lon;

2 The [a]which [d]Jĕr-e-mī′ah the prophet spake unto all the people of Jū′dah, and to all the inhabitants of [i]Jĕ-ru′să-lĕm, saying,

3 From the thirteenth year of [f]Jō-sī′ah the son of [j]Ā′mon king of Jū′dah, even unto this day, that *is* the three and twentieth year, the word of the LORD hath [b]come unto [d]me, and I have [k]spoken unto you, [l]rising early and speaking; but ye have [m]not hearkened.[C]

4 And the LORD hath [k]sent unto you all his servants the [c]prophets, rising early and sending *them*; but ye have [m]not hearkened, nor inclined your ear to hear.

5 They said, [n]Turn ye again now every one from his evil way, and from the evil of your doings, and dwell in the [o,p]land that the LORD hath given unto you and to your fathers for ever and ever:[S]

6 And [q]go not after other gods to serve them, and to worship them, and provoke me not to

10

d *War, as a judgment*, Judg. 3:2.
e *Famine, as a judgment*, 2 Kin. 8:1.

**v.1–525 BC**
See footnote, *Time*, Rev. 10:6.

1

a *Jews, prophecies concerning*, Neh. 4:2.
b *Inspiration*, Job 32:8.
c *Prophets, inspiration of*, Isa. 3:2.
d *Jeremiah*, Jer. 1:1.
e *Jehoiakim*, Jer. 26:1.
f *Josiah*, 1 Kin. 13:2.
g Or, *Nebuchadnezzar*, Dan. 2:1.
h *Babylon, empire of*, Ezra 5:12.

2

i *Jerusalem*, Judg. 19:10.

3

j *Amon*, 2 Kin. 21:18.
k *Wicked, warned*, Psa. 73:3.
l *Zeal, instances of*, 2 Cor. 7:11.
m *Impenitence*, Rom. 2:5.

5

n *Repentance, enjoined*, Mark 1:4.
o *Canaan*, Gen. 37:1.
p *Temporal Blessings, from God*, Psa. 103:2.

6

q *Idolatry, forbidden*, 1 Sam. 15:23.

[r]anger with the works of your hands; and I will do you no hurt.[c]

7 Yet ye have [m]not hearkened[c] unto me, saith the LORD; that ye might [s]provoke me to [r]anger with the works of your hands to your own hurt.

8 ¶ Therefore thus saith the LORD of hosts; Because ye have not heard my words,

9 Behold, [a]I will send and take all the families of the north, saith the LORD, and [g]Nĕb-u-chad-rĕz′zar the king of [h]Băb′ȳ-lon, my servant, and [t]will bring them against this land, and against the inhabitants thereof, and against all these nations round about, and will utterly destroy them, and make them an astonishment,[c] and an hissing,[c] and perpetual desolations.

10 Moreover [t]I will take from them the voice of mirth, and the voice of gladness, the voice of the bridegroom, and the voice of the bride, the sound of the millstones, and the light of the [u]candle.[Q]

11 And [a]this whole land shall be a desolation, *and* an astonishment;[c] and these [t]nations shall [v]serve the [g]king of [h]Băb′ȳ-lon [w]seventy years.

12 ¶ And it shall come to pass, when [w]seventy years are accomplished, *that* I will punish the [g]king of [h]Băb′ȳ-lon, and that [t]nation, saith the LORD, for their iniquity, and the land of the Chăl-dē′anș, and will make it perpetual desolations.

13 And [t]I will bring upon that land all my words which I have pronounced against it, *even* all that is written in this [x]book, which Jĕr-e-mī′ah hath prophesied against all the nations.

14 [t]For many nations and great kings shall serve[c] themselves of them also: and I will [y]recompense them according to their deeds, and according to the works of their own hands.

15 ¶[s]For thus saith the LORD God of Ĭș′ra-el unto me; Take the wine [z]cup of this [a]fury at my hand, and cause all the [b]nations, to whom I send thee, to drink it.[Q]

16[Q]And they shall drink, and [1,c]be moved,[c] and be mad, because of the [d]sword that I will send among them.

17 Then took I the [e]cup at the LORD's hand, and made all the [b]nations to drink, unto whom the LORD had sent me:[s]

18 *To wit,* [f]Jē-ru′sȧ-lĕm, and the cities of [g]Jū′dah, and the kings thereof, and the princes thereof, to make them a desolation, an astonishment,[c] an hissing,[c] and a curse; as *it is* this day;

19 Phā′raōh king of [h]Ē′ġȳpt, and his servants, and his princes, and all his [b]people;

20 [b]And all the mingled[c] people, and all the kings of the land of [i]Ŭz, and all the kings of the land of the [j]Phĭ-lĭs′tĭneș, and [k]Ăsh′ke-lŏn, and [l]Ăz′zah, and [m]Ĕk′rŏn, and the remnant of [n]Ăsh′dŏd,

21 [o]Ē′dom, and [p]Mō′ab, and the [q]children of Ăm′mŏn,

22 And all the kings of [r]Tȳ′rus, and all the kings of [s]Zī′dŏn, and the kings of the isles which *are* beyond the sea,

23 [t]Dē′dan, and [u]Tē′mȧ, and Bŭz, and all [2]*that are* in the utmost corners,

24 And all the kings of [v]Ȧ-rā′-bĭ-ȧ, and all the kings of the mingled people that dwell in the desert,

25 And all the kings of Zĭm′rī, and all the kings of [w]Ē′lăm, and all the kings of the [x]Mēdeș,

26 And all the kings of the north, far and near, one with another, and all the kingdoms of the world, which *are* upon the face of the earth: and the king

r *Anger of God,* 2 Kin. 13:3.

7

s *Sin, repugnant to God,* Rom. 5:12.

9

t *Nation, judgments denounced against,* Isa. 2:4.

10

u *Lamp, figurative of joy,* Ex. 27:20.

11

v *Captivity, of Judah in Babylon,* Isa. 5:13.

w *Seventy, years,* Num. 11:16.

13

x *Book,* Num. 5:23.

14

y *Punishment, according to deeds,* Lev. 26:41.

15

z *Cup, figurative,* Matt. 20:22.

a *Anger of God,* 2 Kin. 13:3.

b *Nation, punishment of,* Isa. 2:4.

16

c *Drunkenness, figurative,* Luke 21:34.

d *War, as a judgment,* Judg. 3:2.

1 R. V. reel to and fro,

17

e *Cup, figurative,* Matt. 20:22.

18

f *Jerusalem, prophecies against,* Judg. 19:10.

g *Judah, kingdom of, prophecies concerning,* 2 Chr. 11:17.

19

h *Egypt, prophecies concerning,* Gen. 41:8.

20

i Job 1:1; Lam. 4:21.

j *Philistines, prophecies concerning,* Gen. 26:14.

k *Ashkelon, prophecies concerning,* Judg. 1:18.

l Or, *Gaza, prophecies concerning,* Gen. 10:19.

m *Ekron, prophecies concerning,* Amos 1:8.

n *Ashdod, prophecies concerning,* 1 Sam. 6:17.

21

o *Edom, prophecies concerning,* Obad. 1.

p *Moabites, prophecies concerning,* Gen. 19:37.

q *Ammonites, prophecies concerning,* Deut. 2:20.

22

r Or, *Tyre, prophecies concerning,* Josh. 19:29.

s *Zidon, prophecies concerning,* Ezek. 28:21.

23

t *Dedan,* Jer. 49:8.

u Job 6:19; Isa. 21:14.

2 Am. R. V. that have the corners of their hair cut off;

24

v *Arabians, prophecies concerning,* 2 Chr. 17:11.

25

w *Elam, prophecies concerning,* Isa. 11:11.

x *Medes, prophecies concerning,* Dan. 5:28.

**27**
*y Nation, judgments denounced against,* Isa. 2:4.
*z Drunkenness, figurative,* Luke 21:34.

*a War, as a judgment,* Judg. 3:2.

**28**
*b Cup, figurative,* Matt. 20:22.
*c Nation, judgments denounced against,* Isa. 2:4.
*d Punishment, no escape from,* Lev. 26:41.

**29**
*e Jerusalem, prophecies against,* Judg. 19:10.

**30**
*f Wine Press, trodden with shouting,* Isa. 5:2.
3 R. V. against his fold;

**31**
*g Wicked, punishment of,* Psa. 73:3.

**32**
4 R. V. uttermost parts

of Shē′shăch shall drink after them.

27 Therefore thou shalt say unto [y]them, Thus saith the LORD of hosts, the God of Ĭş′ra-el; Drink ye, and be [z]drunken, and spue,[G] and fall, and rise no more, because of the [a]sword which I will send among you.[Q]

28 And it shall be, if they refuse to take the [b]cup at thine hand to drink, then shalt thou say unto them, [c]Thus saith the LORD of hosts; [d]Ye shall certainly drink.

29 For, lo, I begin to bring evil on the [e]city which is called by my name, and should ye be utterly unpunished? [c,d]Ye shall not be unpunished: for I will call for a [a]sword upon all the inhabitants of the earth, saith the LORD of hosts.[Q]

30 Therefore prophesy thou against them all these words, and say unto them, The LORD shall roar from on high, and utter his voice from his holy habitation; he shall mightily roar [3]upon his habitation; he shall give a shout, as they that [f]tread[G] *the grapes*, against all the inhabitants of the earth.[Q]

31 A noise shall come *even* to the ends of the earth; for the LORD hath a controversy with the nations, he will plead with all flesh; [g]he will give them *that are* wicked to the [a]sword, saith the LORD.

32 [c]Thus saith the LORD of hosts, Behold, [d]evil shall go forth from nation to nation, and a great whirlwind shall be raised up from the [4]coasts of the earth.

33 And [c,d]the slain of the LORD shall be at that day from *one* end of the earth even unto the *other* end of the earth: they shall not be lamented, neither gathered, nor [h]buried; they shall be dung[G] upon the ground.

34 ¶ Howl, ye shepherds, and cry; and wallow yourselves *in the ashes*, ye principal of the flock: for the days of your slaughter [5]and of your dispersions are accomplished; and ye shall fall like a pleasant vessel.[Q]

35 And the shepherds shall have [d]no way to flee, nor the principal of the flock to escape.

36 A voice of the cry of the shepherds, and an howling of the principal of the flock, *shall be heard*: for the LORD hath spoiled[G] their pasture.

37 [S]And the peaceable [6]habitations are cut down because of the fierce [i]anger of the LORD.

38 He hath forsaken his covert,[G] as the [j]lion: for [c]their land is [7]desolate because of the fierceness of the [8]oppressor, and because of his fierce anger.[S]

## CHAPTER 26

*The prophet exhorts the people to repentance. 8 For this he is seized and arraigned. 12 His defence. 16 He is acquitted.*

IN the beginning of the reign of *Jĕ-hoi′a-kĭm the son of [a]Jō-sī′ah king of [b]Jū′dah [c]came this word from the LORD, saying,

2 Thus saith the LORD; Stand in the court of the LORD's [d]house, and [e,f]speak unto all the cities of [b]Jū′dah, which come to [g]worship in the LORD's house, all the words that I command [h]thee to speak unto them; diminish not a word:

3 If so be they will hearken, and [i]turn every man from his evil way, that I may [j]repent me of the [k]evil, which I purpose to do unto them because of the evil of their doings.[S]

4 And [h]thou shalt say unto them, Thus saith the LORD; If

**33**
*h Burial, lack of, a disgrace,* Acts 8:2.

**34**
5 R. V. are fully come, and I will break you in pieces, and

**37**
*i Anger of God,* 2 Kin. 13:3.
6 R. V. folds are brought to silence because

**38**
*j Lion,* Mic. 5:8.
7 R. V. an astonishment
8 R. V. oppressing sword,

**1**
*a Josiah,* 1 Kin. 13:2.
*b Judah, kingdom of, prophecies concerning,* vs. 1–7; 2 Chr. 11:17
*c Inspiration,* Job 32:8.

**2**
*d Temple, Solomon's,* 1 Kin. 6:17.
*e Minister, duties of,* Rom. 15:16.
*f Wicked, warned,* Psa. 73:3.
*g Worship, public, in the temple,* Gen. 22:5.
*h Jeremiah,* Jer. 1:1.

**3**
*i Repentance, exhortation to,* Mark 1:4.
*j Repentance, attributed to God,* Mark 1:4.
*k Divine Chastisement.* Job 33:19.

* **JEHOIAKIM,** called also ELIAKIM and JECHONIAS; king of Judah. *Ancestor of Jesus,* Matt. 1:11, with 1 Chr. 3:15, 16. *Wicked reign and final overthrow of,* 2 Kin. 23:34–37; 24:1–6; 2 Chr. 36:4–8; Jer. 22:13–19; 26:22, 23; 36; Dan. 1:1, 2. *Dies and is succeeded by his son, Jehoiachin,* 2 Kin. 24:6. *Reigned eleven years,* 2 Kin. 23:36.

ye will [l]not hearken[c] to me, to walk in my law, which I have set before you,

5 To hearken to the words of my servants the prophets, whom I sent unto you, both rising up early, and sending *them,* but ye have [l]not hearkened;

6 Then will I make this house like [m]Shī'lōh, and will make [n]this city a curse to all the nations of the earth.

7 So the priests and the prophets and all the people heard [h]Jĕr-e-mī'ah [o,p]speaking these words in the [d]house of the LORD.

8 ¶ Now it came to pass, when [h]Jĕr-e-mī'ah had made an end of [p]speaking all that the LORD had commanded *him* to speak unto all the people, that the [q]priests and the [r]prophets and all the people [1,s]took him, saying, Thou shalt surely die.

9 Why hast thou prophesied in the name of the LORD, saying, This [d]house shall be like [m]Shī'lōh, and [n]this city shall be desolate without an inhabitant? And all the people were gathered [s]against Jĕr-e-mī'ah in the house of the LORD.

10 ¶ When the princes of Jū'dah heard these things, then they came up from the king's [t]house unto the [d]house of the LORD, and sat down in the entry of the new gate of the LORD's *house.*

11 Then [s]spake the [q]priests and the [r]prophets unto the princes and to all the people, saying, This man *is* worthy to die; for [u]he hath prophesied against this city, as ye have heard with your ears.[c]

12 ¶ Then [v]spake [h,o]Jĕr-e-mī'ah unto all the princes and to all the people, [w]saying, The LORD sent me to prophesy against this house and against this city all the words that ye have heard.

13 [x]Therefore now [p,y,z]amend your ways and your doings, and [a]obey the voice of the LORD your God; and the LORD will [b]repent him of the evil that he hath pronounced against you.

14 [c]As for me, behold, I *am* in your hand: do with me as seemeth good and meet[c] unto you.

15 But know ye for certain, that if ye [d]put me to death, ye shall surely bring innocent blood upon yourselves, and upon this city, and upon the inhabitants thereof: for [c]of a truth the LORD hath sent me unto you to speak all these words in your ears.

16 ¶ Then said the princes and all the people unto the [e]priests and to the [f]prophets; [g]This man *is* not worthy to die: for [c]he hath spoken to us in the name of the LORD our God.

17 [h]Then rose up certain of the elders of the land, and spake to all the assembly of the people, saying,

18 [i]Mī'cah the Mō'ras-thīte prophesied in the days of [j]Hĕz-e-kī'ah king of Jū'dah, and spake to all the people of Jū'dah, saying, [k]Thus saith the LORD of hosts; Zī'ŏn shall be plowed *like* a field, and [l]Jĕ-ru'sā-lĕm shall become heaps, and the mountain of the house as the high places of a forest.

19 Did [j]Hĕz-e-kī'ah king of Jū'dah and all Jū'dah put him at all to death? did he not [m]fear the LORD, and [n]besought[c] the LORD, and the LORD [b]repented him of the evil which he had pronounced against them? Thus [2]might we procure great evil against our souls.

20 And there was also a man that prophesied in the name of the LORD, U-rī'jah the son of Shĕm-a-ī'ah of [o]Kĭr'jath-jē'a-rĭm, who prophesied against this [l]city and against this land ac-

**4**
*l Impenitence,* Rom. 2:5.

**6**
*m Shiloh,* Judg. 21:12.
*n Jerusalem, prophecies against,* Judg. 19:10.

**7**
*o Minister, faithful,* Rom. 15:16.
*p Reproof, faithfulness in,* Prov. 17:10.

**8**
*q Priest, corrupt,* Lev. 1:5.
*r Prophets, false,* Isa. 3:2.
*s Persecution, of the righteous,* John 15:20.
1 R. V. laid hold on

**10**
*t Palace,* 1 Kin. 21:1.

**11**
*u Indictments, instances of,* Matt. 27:37.

**12**
*v Court, accused spoke in his own defense,* Ex. 18:26.
*w Defense,* Acts 19:33.

**13**
*x Zeal, instances of,* 2 Cor. 7:11.
*y Repentance, enjoined,* Mark 1:4.
*z Blessings, contingent upon obedience,* Deut. 11:26.

*a Obedience, enjoined,* Heb. 5:8.
*b Repentance, attributed to God,* Mark 1:4.

**14**
*c Minister, faithful,* Rom. 15:16.

**15**
*d Persecution, of the righteous,* John 15:20.

**16**
*e Priest, corrupt,* Lev. 1:5.
*f Prophets, false,* Isa. 3:2.
*g Minister, defended,* vs. 16–24; Rom. 15:16.

**17**
*h Prudence, instances of,* 2 Chr. 2:12.

**18**
*i Micah,* Mic. 1:1
*j Hezekiah, prophecies concerning,* 2 Kin. 16:20.
*k* Mic. 3:12.
*l Jerusalem, prophecies against,* Judg. 19:10.

**19**
*m Fear of God,* Acts 9:31.
*n Prayer, evils averted by,* Acts 6:4.
2 R. V. should we commit great

**20**
*o Kirjath-jearim,* Josh. 15:9.

cording to all the words of [p]Jĕr-
e-mī'ah:
21 And when Jĕ-hoi'a-kĭm the
king, with all his mighty men,
and all the princes, heard his
words, the king [d]sought to put
him to death: but when U-rī'jah
heard it, he was afraid, and fled,
and went into [q]Ē'ġўpt;
22 And Jĕ-hoi'a-kĭm the king
sent men into [q]Ē'ġўpt, *namely,*
[r]Ĕl'na-thăn the son of [r]Ăch'bôr,
and *certain* men with him into
Ē'ġўpt.
23 And they [s]fetched forth
U-rī'jah out of [q]Ē'ġўpt, and
brought him unto Jĕ-hoi'a-kĭm
the king; [t]who [d]slew him with the
sword, and cast his dead body
into the [u]graves of the common
people.
24 Nevertheless [v]the hand of
[w]Ā-hī'kam the son of [x]Shā'phan
was with [p]Jĕr-e-mī'ah, that they
should not give him into the
hand of the people to put him to
death.

## CHAPTER 27

*The subjugation of the neighboring nations by Nebuchadnezzar prefigured. 12 Zedekiah and his people exhorted to submit to the king of Babylon. 19 The temple to be further spoiled and plundered.*

IN the beginning of the reign
of [a]Jĕ-hoi'a-kĭm the son of
[b]Jō-sī'ah king of Jū'dah [c]came
this [d]word unto [e]Jĕr-e-mī'ah
from the LORD, saying,
2 Thus saith the LORD to me;
[f]Make thee [g]bonds and [1]yokes,
and put them upon thy neck,
3 And send [g]them to the king of
[h]Ē'dom, and to the king of [i]Mō'-
ab, and to the king of the [j]Ăm'-
mon-ītes, and to the king of
[k]Tȳ'rus, and to the king of [l]Zī'-
dŏn, by the hand of the messengers which come to [m]Jē-ru'sā-
lĕm unto [a]Zĕd-e-kī'ah king of
Jū'dah;
4 And command them to say
unto their masters, Thus saith
the LORD of hosts, the God of
Iṣ'ra-el; Thus shall ye say unto
your masters;
5 I have [n]made the [o]earth, the
[p]man and the *beast that *are*
upon the ground, by my great
[q]power and by my outstretched
arm, and [r]have given it unto
whom it seemed meet unto me.
6 And now have I given all
these lands into the hand of
[s,t]Nĕb-u-chad-nĕz'zar the king
of [u]Băb'ȳ-lon, my servant; and
the *beasts of the field have I
given him also to serve him.
7 And [s]all nations shall serve
him, and his son, and his son's
son, until the very time of his
land come: and then many nations and great kings shall serve
themselves of him.
8 And it shall come to pass, *that*
the nation and kingdom which
will not serve the same [s,t]Nĕb-u-
chad-nĕz'zar the king of [u]Băb'ȳ-
lon, and that will not put their
neck under the yoke of the king
of Băb'ȳ-lon, that [v]nation will
I punish, saith the LORD, with

p *Jeremiah,* Jer. 1:1.

21
q *Egypt,* Gen. 41:8.

22
r Jer. 36:12, 25.

23
s *Extradition,* 1 Kin. 18:10.
t *Rulers, wicked,* Ex. 18:21.
u *Burying Places,* Gen. 23:4.

24
v *Friendship,* Prov. 22:24.
w *Ahikam,* 2 Kin. 22:12.
x *Shaphan,* 2 Chr. 34:8.

1
a Or, *Zedekiah,* 2 Kin. 25:2.
b *Josiah,* 1 Kin. 13:2.
c *Prophets, inspiration of,* Isa. 3:2.
d *Prophecies, inspired,* Dan. 9:24.
e *Jeremiah,* Jer. 1:1.
2
f *Instruction, by object lesson,* vs. 2–11; Prov. 23:23.
g *Symbols and Similitudes,* Heb. 9:9.
1 R. V. bars,

3
h *Edomites, prophecies concerning,* 2 Kin. 8:21.
i *Moabites, prophecies concerning,* Gen. 19:37.
j *Ammonites, prophecies concerning,* Deut. 2:20.
k Or, *Tyre, prophecies concerning,* Josh. 19:29.
l *Zidon, prophecies concerning,* Ezek. 28:21.
m *Jerusalem,* Judg. 19:10.

5
n *God, creator,* Gen. 2:2.
o *Earth, created,* Prov. 8:23.
p *Man, created,* Job 4:17.
q *God, power of,* Gen. 2:2.
r *God, sovereign,* Gen. 2:2.

6
s *Nebuchadnezzar, prophecies concerning,* Dan. 2:1.
t *Agency, in executing judgment,* Mark 1:17.
u *Babylon, prophecies concerning,* Ezra 5:12.

8
v *Nation, judgments denounced against,* Isa. 2:4.

* **ANIMALS,** Eccl. 3:21. *Creation of,* Gen. 1:24, 25; 2:19; Jer. 27:5. *Food of,* Gen. 1:30. *Named,* Gen. 2:20. *Ordained as food for man,* Gen. 9:2, 3; Lev. 11:3, 9, 21, 22; Deut. 14:4–6, 9, 11, 20. *God's care of,* Gen. 9:9, 10; Deut. 25:4; Job 38:41; Psa. 36:6; 104:11, 21; 145:15, 16; 147:9; Jonah 4:11; Matt. 6:26; 10:29; Luke 12:6, 24; 1 Cor. 9:9. *Under the curse,* Gen. 3:14; 6:7, 17. *Suffer under divine judgments sent upon man,* Jer. 7:20; 12:4; 21:6; Ezek. 14:13, 17, 19–21; Joel 1:18–20. *Two of every sort preserved in the ark,* Gen. 6:19, 20; 7:2, 9, 14, 15; 8:19. *Seven clean, of every sort, preserved in the ark,* Gen. 7:2, 3. *Suffered the plagues of Egypt,* Ex. 8:17; 9:9, 10, 19; 11:5. *Perish at death,* Eccl. 3:21. *Possessed of devils,* Matt. 8:31, 32; Mark 5:13; Luke 8:33. *Clean and unclean,* Gen. 7:2, 8; 8:20; Lev. 7:21; 11; 20:25; Deut. 14:3–20; Acts 10:11–15; 1 Tim. 4:3–5.

*God's control of,* Psa. 91:13; Luke 10:19. *Instruments of God's will,* Ex. 8; 10:4–15, 19; Num. 21:6; 22:28; Josh. 24:12; Joel 1:4. *Belong to God,* Psa. 50:10–12. *Sent in judgment,* Lev. 26:22; Num. 21:6, 7; Deut. 8:15; Ezek. 5:17; 14:15; Rev. 6:8. *Nature of,* Job 41; Psa. 32:9; Jas. 3:7. *Habits of,* Job 12:7, 8; 37:8; 39; 40:20, 21; Psa. 29:9; 104:20–25; Isa. 13:21, 22; 34:14. *Breeding of,* Gen. 30:35–43; 31:8, 9. *Instincts of,* Deut. 32:11; Job 35:11; 39; 40:15–24; Psa. 104:11–30; Prov. 6:5–8; 30:25–28; Isa. 1:3; Jer. 2:24; 8:7; Lam. 4:3; Matt. 24:28. *Abodes of,* Job 24:5; 37:8; 39:5–10, 27–29; Psa. 104:20, 22, 25; Isa. 34:14, 15; Jer. 2:24; 50:39; Mark 1:13.

**Cruelty to:** *Of Balaam to his ass,* Num. 22:22–33. *Houghing horses,* 2 Sam. 8:4; 1 Chr. 18:4.

**Kindness to,** Deut. 25:4; Prov. 12:10; 1 Tim. 5:18. *In relieving the overburdened,* Ex. 23:5; Deut. 22:4. *In rescuing from pits,* Matt. 12:11; Luke 13:15; 14:5. *In feeding,* Gen. 24:32; 43:24; Judg. 19:21.

INSTANCES OF: *Jacob in erecting booths for his cattle,* Gen. 33:17. *People of Gerar in providing tents for cattle,* 2 Chr. 14:15.

**Laws concerning:** *Sabbath rest for,* Ex. 20:10; Deut. 5:14. *Treatment of vicious,* Ex. 21:28–32, 35, 36. *Penalty for injury of,* Ex. 21:33, 34. *Hybridizing of, forbidden,* Lev. 19:19. *Working of,* Deut. 22:10. *Mother birds and their young,* Deut. 22:6, 7.

*w War, as a judgment*, Judg. 3:2.
*x Famine, as a judgment*, 2 Kin. 8:1.

**9**
*y Prophets, false*, Isa. 3:2.
*z Sorcery*, Isa. 47:9.

*a Dream*, Dan. 1:17.
*b Nebuchadnezzar*, Dan. 2:1.
*c Babylon*, Ezra 5:12.

**10**
*d Falsehood*, Job 21:34.

**11**
*e God, providence of*, Gen. 2:2.

**12**
*f Zedekiah*, 2 Kin. 25:2.

**13**
*g War, as a judgment*, Judg. 3:2.
*h Famine, as a judgment*, 2 Kin. 8:1.

the [w]sword, and with the [x]famine, and with the pestilence, until I have consumed them by his hand.
9 Therefore hearken not ye to
your [y]prophets, nor to your [z]diviners, nor to your [a]dreamers, nor to your enchanters, nor to your sorcerers, which speak unto you, saying, Ye shall not serve the [b]king of [c]Băb′ȳ-lon:
10 For they prophesy a [d]lie un-
to you, to remove you far from your land; and that I should drive you out, and ye should perish.
11 But the nations that bring
their neck under the yoke of the [b]king of [c]Băb′ȳ-lon, and serve him, [e]those will I let remain still in their own land, saith the LORD; and they shall till it, and dwell therein.
12 ¶ I spake also to [f]Zĕd-e-
kī′ah king of Jū′dah according to all these words, saying, Bring your necks under the yoke of the [b]king of [c]Băb′ȳ-lon, and serve him and his people, and live.
13 Why will ye die, thou and
thy people, by the [g]sword, by the [h]famine, and by the pestilence, as the LORD hath spoken against the [i]nation that will not serve the [b]king of Băb′ȳ-lon?
14 Therefore hearken not unto
the words of the [j]prophets that speak unto you, saying, Ye shall not serve the [b]king of [c]Băb′ȳ-lon: for they prophesy a [d]lie unto you.
15 For I have not sent them,
saith the LORD, yet they prophesy a [d]lie in my name; that I might drive you out, and that ye might perish, ye, and the prophets that prophesy unto you.
16 Also I spake to the priests
and to all this people, saying, Thus saith the LORD; Hearken not to the words of your [j]prophets that prophesy unto you, saying, Behold, the vessels of the [k]LORD's house shall now shortly be brought again from [c]Băb′ȳ-lon: for they prophesy a [d]lie unto you.
17 Hearken not unto them;
serve the king of [c]Băb′ȳ-lon, and live: wherefore should this city be laid waste?
18 But if they *be* prophets, and
if the word of the LORD be with them, let them now make †intercession to the LORD of hosts,

*i Nation, judgments denounced against*, Isa. 2:4.

**14**
*j Prophets, false*, Isa. 3:2.

**16**
*k Temple, Solomon's*, 1 Kin. 6:17.

† **INTERCESSION. Of man with God,** Jer. 27:18. *Priestly*, Ex. 28:12, 29, 30, 38; Lev. 10:17. *For spiritual blessing*, Num. 6:23–26; 1 Sam. 12:23; Job 1:5; 42:8–10. *To avert judgment*, Gen. 20:7; Ex. 32:9–14; Num. 14:11–21; 16:45–50; Deut. 9:18–20, 25–29; Isa. 65:8. *For deliverance from enemies*, 1 Sam. 7:5–9; Isa. 37:4. *For healing of disease*, Jas. 5:14–16. See footnote, MEDIATION, Gal. 3:19.

*For the obdurate, unavailing*, Jer. 7:16; 11:14; 14:11.

**Enjoined,** Jer. 29:7; Joel 2:17; Matt. 5:44; Eph. 6:18; 1 Tim. 2:1, 2; 1 John 5:16.

**Intercessional influence of the righteous,** Gen. 18:26–32; 19:22; 26:4, 5, 24; 1 Kin. 11:12, 13, 34; 15:4; 2 Kin. 8:19; Isa. 37:35; Jer. 5:1; Ezek. 14:14, 16, 18, 20; Matt. 24:22; Rom. 11:27, 28.

**Instances of:** *Abraham, for Sodom*, Gen. 18:23–32; *for Abimelech*, Gen. 20:17, 18. *Lot for Zoar*, Gen. 19:21. *Jacob*, Gen. 48:16, 20. *Moses for Israel*, Ex. 17:9–12; 32:31, 32; 34:9; Num. 27:5, 16, 17; Deut. 5:5; 33:6–25. *Joshua*, Josh. 7:6–9. *Deborah and Barak*, Judg. 5:31. *Samuel*, 1 Sam. 12:23. *David*, 2 Sam. 24:17; 1 Chr. 21:17; 29:18, 19. *Solomon*, 1 Kin. 8:31–53; 2 Chr. 6:22–42. *Hezekiah*, 2 Chr. 30:18, 19. *Ezra*, Ezra 9:5–15. *Nehemiah*, Neh. 1:4–9. *Psalmist*, Psa. 51:18; 132:9, 10. *Daniel*, Dan. 9:3–19. *Stephen*, Acts 7:60. *Peter and John*, Acts 8:15. *Paul*, Acts 20:32; 28:8; Rom. 1:9; 10:1; 1 Cor. 1:3 (with Gal. 1:3); 2 Cor. 13:7; Gal. 6:16; Eph. 1:15–19; 3:14–19; Phil. 1:3–5, 9, 10; Col. 1:3, 4, 9; 2:1, 2; 1 Thess. 1:2; 3:10, 12, 13; 5:23; 2 Thess. 1:11; 2:16, 17; 3:5, 16; 2 Tim. 1:3, 16, 18; Philemon 4, 6. *Epaphras*, Col. 4:12. *The churches for Paul*, Acts 14:26; 15:40.

**Solicited:** INSTANCES OF: *By Pharaoh*, Ex. 8:8, 28; 9:28; 10:17; 12:32. *By the Israelites*, Num. 21:7; 1 Sam. 12:19. *By Jeroboam*, 1 Kin. 13:6. *By Hezekiah*, 2 Kin. 19:1–4. *By Zedekiah*, Jer. 37:3. *By Johanan*, Jer. 42:1–6. *By Daniel*, Dan. 2:17, 18. *By Darius*, Ezra 6:10. *By Simon Magus*, Acts 8:24. *By Paul*, Rom. 15:30–32; 2 Cor. 1:11; Eph. 6:19, 20; 1 Thess. 5:25; 2 Thess. 3:1; Heb. 13:18.

**Answered:** INSTANCES OF: *Of Moses, in behalf of Pharaoh, for the abatement, of the plague of frogs*, Ex. 8:12, 15; *of the plague of flies*, Ex. 8:30–32; *of the plague of rain, thunder, and hail*, Ex. 9:27–35; *of the plague of locusts*, Ex. 10:16–20. *Of Moses, for the Israelites, during the battle with the Amalekites*, Ex. 17:11–14; *after the Israelites had made the golden calf*, Ex. 32:11–14, 31–34; Deut. 9:18–29; 10:10; Psa. 106:23; *after the murmuring of the people*, Ex. 33:15–17; *when the fire of the Lord consumed the people*, Num. 11:1, 2; *when the people murmured on account of the report of the spies*, Num. 14:11–20; *when the scourge of the fiery serpents was on Israel*, Num. 21:4–9; *that Miriam's leprosy might be healed*, Num. 12:13; *in behalf of the daughters of Zelophehad*, Num. 27:5–7; *in behalf of Aaron, on account of his sin in making the golden calf*, Deut. 9:20. *Of Samuel, for deliverance of Israel from the oppressions of the Philistines*, 1 Sam. 7:5–14. *The prophet of Judah, for the restoration of Jeroboam's withered hand*, 1 Kin. 13:1–6. *Of Elijah, for the raising from the dead of the son of the hospitable widow*, 1 Kin. 17:20–23. *Of Elisha, for the raising from the dead the son of the Shunammite woman*, 2 Kin. 4:33–36. *Of Isaiah, in behalf of Hezekiah and the people, that they might be delivered from Sennacherib*, 2 Kin. 19:1–7, 20–37.

**Of Man with Jesus**, see footnote, MEDIATION, Gal. 3:19.

**Of man with man:** INSTANCES OF: *Reuben for Joseph*, Gen. 37:21, 22. *Judah for Joseph*, Gen. 37:26, 27. *Judah with Joseph*, Gen. 44:18–34. *Pharaoh's chief baker for Joseph*, Gen. 41:9–13, with 40:14. *Rahab for her people*, Josh. 2:12, 13. *Aaron for Miriam*, Num. 12:12. *Jonathan for David*, 1 Sam. 19:1–7. *Abigail for Nabal*, 1 Sam. 25:23–35.

18
*l Palace,* 1 Kin. 21:1.
*m Jerusalem,* Judg. 19:10.

19
*n Pillar, of Solomon's temple,* Gen. 28:18.
*o Laver,* Ex. 30:18.

20
*p Captivity, as a judgment,* Isa. 5:13.
*q* Or, *Jehoiachin,* 2 Kin. 24:6.
*r Jehoiakim,* Jer. 26:1.

that the vessels which are left in the [k]house of the LORD, and *in* the [l]house of the king of Jū'dah, and at [m]Jė-ru̇'sȧ-lĕm, go not to [c]Băb'ỹ-lon.

19 ¶ For thus saith the LORD of hosts concerning the [n]pillars, and concerning the [o]sea, and concerning the bases, and concerning the residue of the vessels that remain in this city,

20 Which [b]Nĕb-u-chad-nĕz'-zar king of [c]Băb'ỹ-lon took not, when he carried away [p]captive [q]Jĕc-o-nī'ah the son of [r]Jė-hoi'-a-kĭm king of Jū'dah from Jė-ru̇'sȧ-lĕm to Băb'ỹ-lon, and all the nobles of Jū'dah and Jė-ru̇'-sȧ-lĕm; [Q]

21 Yea, thus saith the LORD of hosts, the God of Ĭṣ'ra-el, concerning the vessels that remain *in* the [k]house of the LORD, and *in* the [l]house of the king of Jū'-dah and of Jė-ru̇'sȧ-lĕm;

22 They shall be carried to Băb'ỹ-lon, and there shall they be until the day that I visit them, saith the LORD; then will I bring them up, and restore them to this place.

## CHAPTER 28

*Hananiah falsely prophesies the return of Judah.* 5 *Jeremiah rebukes him.* 10 *Hananiah predicts the deliverance of all nations from Nebuchadnezzar's yoke.* 12 *Jeremiah declares the contrary;* 15 *and foretells the death of the false prophet.*

v.1–514 BC
See footnote, *Time,* Rev. 10:6.

1
*a Zedekiah,* 2 Kin. 25:2.
*b Month (August),* Ex. 12:2.
*c Prophets, false,* Isa. 3:2.
*d Gibeon,* Jer. 41:16.
*e Jeremiah,* Jer. 1:1.
*f Temple, Solomon's,* 1 Kin. 6:17.
*g Church, called house of the Lord,* 1 Kin. 9:3.

AND it came to pass the same year, in the beginning of the reign of [a]Zĕd-e-kī'ah king of Jū'dah, in the fourth year, *and* in the fifth [b]month, *that* [c]Hăn-a-nī'ah the son of Ā'zu̇r the prophet, which *was* of [d]Gĭb'e-on, spake unto [e]me in the [f,g]house of the LORD, in the presence of the priests and of all the people, saying,

2 Thus speaketh the LORD of hosts, the God of Ĭṣ'ra-el, saying, I have broken the [h]yoke of the [i]king of [j]Băb'ỹ-lon.

3 Within two full years will I bring again into this place all the vessels of the [f,g]LORD's house, that [i]Nĕb-u-chad-nĕz'zar king of [j]Băb'ỹ-lon took away from this place, and carried them to Băb'-ỹ-lon:

4 And I will bring again to this place [k]Jĕc-o-nī'ah the son of [l]Jė-hoi'a-kĭm king of Jū'-dah, with all the [m]captives of Jū'dah, that went into [j]Băb'ỹ-lon, saith the LORD: for I will break the [h]yoke of the king of Băb'ỹ-lon.

5 ¶ Then the prophet [e]Jĕr-e-mī'ah said unto the [c]prophet Hăn-a-nī'ah in the presence of the priests, and in the presence of all the people that stood in the house of the LORD,

6 Even the prophet [e]Jĕr-e-mī'-ah said, Amen: the LORD do so: the LORD perform thy words which thou hast prophesied, to bring again the vessels of the [f,g]LORD's house, and all that is carried away [m]captive, from Băb'ỹ-lon into this place.

7 Nevertheless hear thou now this word that I speak in thine ears, and in the ears of all the people;

8 The prophets that have been before me and before thee of old prophesied both against many countries, and against great kingdoms, of war, and of evil, and of pestilence.

9 The prophet which prophesieth of peace, when the word of the prophet shall come to pass, *then* shall the prophet be known, that the LORD hath truly sent him.

10 ¶ Then Hăn-a-nī'ah the

2
*h Yoke, figurative,* 1 Sam. 6:7.
*i Nebuchadnezzar,* Dan. 2:1.
*j Babylon, empire of,* Ezra 5:12.

4
*k* Or, *Jehoiachin,* 2 Kin. 24:6.
*l Jehoiakim,* Jer. 26:1.
*m Captivity, of Judah in Babylon,* Isa. 5:13.

*Joab for Absalom,* 2 Sam. 14:1–24. *Bath-sheba, for Solomon,* 1 Kin. 1:11–22, 28–31; *for Adonijah,* 1 Kin. 2:13–25. *Esther for her people,* Esth. 7:2–6. *Ebed-melech for Jeremiah,* Jer. 38:7–13. *Elisha offers to see the king for the Shunammite,* 2 Kin. 4:13. *The king of Syria for Naaman,* 2 Kin. 5:6–8. *Paul for Onesimus,* Philemon 10–21.
**Of Jesus,** Luke 22:31, 32; 23:33, 34; John 14:16; 17:9, 11 15–17, 20–22; Rom. 8:34; Heb. 7:25; 9:24; 1 John 2:1, 2.

[c]prophet took the [h]yoke from off the prophet [e]Jĕr-e-mī′ah's neck, and brake it.

11 And [c]Hăn-a-nī′ah spake in the presence of all the people, saying, Thus saith the LORD; Even so will I break the [h]yoke of [i]Nĕb-u-chad-nĕz′zar king of [j]Băb′ȳ-lon from the neck of all nations within the space of two full years. And the prophet [e]Jĕr-e-mī′ah went his way.

12 ¶ Then the word of the LORD [n]came unto [e]Jĕr-e-mī′ah *the prophet*, after that Hăn-a-nī′ah the [c]prophet had broken the [h]yoke from off the neck of the prophet Jĕr-e-mī′ah, saying,

13 [n]Go and tell Hăn-a-nī′ah, saying, Thus saith the LORD; Thou hast broken the [h]yokes of wood; but thou shalt make for them [h]yokes of iron.

14 For thus saith the LORD of hosts, the God of Ĭṣ′ra-el; [o]I have put a [h]yoke of iron upon the neck of all these nations, that they may serve [i]Nĕb-u-chad-nĕz′zar king of [j]Băb′ȳ-lon; and they shall serve him: and I have given him the beasts of the field also.

15 ¶ Then said the prophet [e]Jĕr-e-mī′ah unto Hăn-a-nī′ah the [c]prophet, [p]Hear now, Hăn-a-nī′ah; The LORD hath not sent thee; but thou [q]makest this people to [r]trust in a [s]lie.

16 Therefore thus saith the LORD; Behold, I will [t]cast thee from off the face of the earth: this year [t]thou shalt die, because thou hast taught rebellion against the LORD.

17 So Hăn-a-nī′ah the [c]prophet died the same year in the seventh month.

12
*n Prophets, inspiration of,* Isa. 3:2.

14
*o Nation, judgments denounced against,* Isa. 2:4.

15
*p Reproof, faithfulness in,* Prov. 17:10.
*q Influence, evil,* 1 Cor. 7:14.
*r False Confidence,* Psa. 30:6.
*s Falsehood,* Job 21:34.

16
*t Prophets, false, punishment of,* Isa. 3:2.

## CHAPTER 29

*Jeremiah's letter of counsel to the captives in Babylon. 10 Their return after seventy years predicted. 15 The destruction of those who give heed to the false prophets shewn. 20 The fearful end of Ahab and Zedekiah, two false prophets, foretold. 24 Shemaiah's letters against Jeremiah. 30 Jeremiah declares his doom.*

NOW these *are* the words of the [a]letter that [b]Jĕr-e-mī′ah the prophet sent from [c]Jĕ-ru′-sā-lĕm unto the residue of the elders which were carried away [d]captives, and to the [e]priests, and to the prophets, and to all the people whom [f]Nĕb-u-chad-nĕz′zar had carried away captive from Jĕ-ru′sā-lĕm to [g]Băb′ȳ-lon;

2 (After that [h]Jĕc-o-nī′ah the king, and the queen, and the [i]eunuchs, the princes of Jū′dah and Jĕ-ru′sā-lĕm, and the [j]carpenters, and the [k]smiths, were departed from Jĕ-ru′sā-lĕm;)

3 By the hand of Ĕl′a-sah the son of Shā′phan, and Gĕm-a-rī′ah the son of *Hĭl-kī′ah, (whom [l]Zĕd-e-kī′ah king of Jū′dah sent unto [g]Băb′ȳ-lon to [f]Nĕb-u-chad-nĕz′zar king of Băb′ȳ-lon) saying,

4 Thus saith the LORD of hosts, the God of Ĭṣ′ra-el, unto all that are carried away [d]captives, whom [m]I have caused to be carried away from Jĕ-ru′sā-lĕm unto Băb′ȳ-lon;

5 Build ye houses, and dwell *in them*; and plant gardens, and eat the fruit of them;

6 [n]Take ye wives, and beget sons and daughters; and take wives for your sons, and give your daughters to husbands, that they may bear sons and daughters; that ye may be increased there, and not diminished.

7 And [o]seek the †peace of the

1
*a Letters,* Isa. 37:14.
*b Jeremiah,* Jer. 1:1.
*c Jerusalem,* Judg. 19:10.
*d Captivity, of Judah in Babylon,* Isa. 5:13.
*e Priest, taken with the captivity to Babylon,* Lev. 1:5.
*f Nebuchadnezzar,* Dan. 2:1.
*g Babylon, empire of,* Ezra 5:12.

2
*h* Or, *Jehoiachin,* 2 Kin. 24:6.
*i Eunuch,* Matt. 19:12.
*j Carpentry,* 2 Kin. 12:11.
*k Smith,* Isa. 54:16.

3
*l Zedekiah,* 2 Kin. 25:2.

4
*m Adversity, dispensation from God,* Psa. 10:6.

6
*n Marriage,* Gen. 34:9.

7
*o Citizens, duties of,* Luke 15:15.

* **HILKIAH,** the name of a number of men. 1. *The father of Gedaliah,* Jer. 29:3.
2. Priest in the reign of Josiah. *Found the book of the law in the temple,* 2 Kin. 22:4–14; 23:4, 24; 2 Chr. 34:14–22.
3. *A Levite,* 1 Chr. 6:45; 26:11.

† **PEACE,** Psa. 133:1; Prov. 15:17; 17:1, 14; Eccl. 4:6; Isa. 45:7. *Honorable,* Prov. 20:3.
*Enjoined,* Gen. 45:24; Psa. 34:14; Mark 9:50; Rom. 12:18; 14:19; 2 Cor. 13:11; Eph. 4:3, 31, 32; 1 Thess. 5:13; 1 Tim. 2:2; 2 Tim. 2:22; Heb. 12:14; 1 Pet. 3:10, 11.
*Love of, enjoined,* Zech. 8:19.
*Promised,* Lev. 26:6; Job 5:23, 24; Isa. 2:4; 11:6–9, 13; 60:17, 18; Hos. 2:18; see THROUGH CHRIST, below. *The righteous assured of,* Prov. 16:7. *Broken by the gospel,* Matt. 10:21, 22, 34–36; Luke 12:51–53. *Moses' efforts in behalf of, resented,* Ex. 2:13, 14; Acts 7:26–28.

city whither [m]I have caused you
to be carried away [d]captives, and
[p,q]pray unto the LORD [r]for it:
for in the peace thereof shall ye
have peace.
8 ¶ For thus saith the LORD of
hosts, the God of Ĭș′ra-el; Let not
your [s]prophets and your [t]divin-
ers, that *be* in the midst of you,
deceive you, neither hearken to
your [u]dreams which ye cause to
be dreamed.
9 For [s]they prophesy falsely unto you in my name: I have not
sent them, saith the LORD.
10 ¶ For thus saith the LORD,
That after [d,v]seventy years be
accomplished at [g]Băb′y̆-lon [w]I
will visit you, and [x]perform my
good word toward you, [y,z]in causing you to return to this place.
11 For I know the thoughts
that [a]I think toward you, saith
the LORD, thoughts of †peace,
and not of evil, to give you [1]an
expected end.
12 Then shall ye call upon me,
and ye shall go and pray unto
me, and [b]I will hearken unto
you.
13 And [c]ye shall [d]seek me, and
find *me*, when ye shall search for
me with all your heart.
14 And I will be found of you,
saith the LORD: and [e]I will [f]turn
away your [g]captivity, and I will
gather you from all the nations,
and from all the places whither I
have driven you, saith the LORD;
and [h]I will bring you again into
the place whence I caused you to
be carried away captive.
15 ¶ Because ye have said, The
LORD hath raised us up prophets in Băb′y̆-lon;
16 *Know* that thus saith the
LORD of the king that sitteth upon the throne of Dā′vid, and of
all the people that dwelleth in
this city, *and* of your brethren
that are not gone forth with you
into [g]captivity;
17 Thus saith the LORD of
hosts; Behold, [i]I will send upon
them the [j]sword, the [k]famine, and
the pestilence, and will make
them like vile figs, that cannot
be eaten, they are so evil.
18 And I will persecute them
with the [j]sword, with the [k]fam-
ine, and with the pestilence, and
will deliver them to be [2,l]remov-
ed to all the kingdoms of the
earth, to be a curse, and an
astonishment, and an hissing,
and a reproach, among all the
nations whither I have driven
them:
19 Because they have [m]not
hearkened to my words, saith the
LORD, which I sent unto them
by my servants the prophets, rising up early and sending *them;*
but ye would not hear, saith
the LORD.
20 ¶ Hear ye therefore the word
of the LORD, all ye of the [g]cap-
tivity, whom I have sent from
[n]Jė-ru′să-lĕm to [o]Băb′y̆-lon:
21 Thus saith the LORD of
hosts, the God of Ĭș′ra-el, of
Ā′hăb the son of Kŏl-a-ī′ah,
and of Zĕd-e-kī′ah the son of
Mā-a-sē′iah, which prophesy a
[p]lie unto you in my name; Behold, [q]I will deliver them into
the hand of [r]Nĕb-u-chad-rĕz′zar
king of [o]Băb′y̆-lon; and he shall
slay them before your eyes;
22 And of them shall be taken
up a curse by all the [g]captivity of
Jū′dah which *are* in Băb′y̆-lon,
saying, The LORD make thee
like Zĕd-e-kī′ah and like Ā′hăb,
whom the [r]king of [o]Băb′y̆-lon
roasted in the fire;
23 Because they have com-
mitted villany in Ĭș′ra-el, and

p *Prayer, intercessory*, Acts 6:4.
q *Nation, prayer for peace of*, Isa. 2:4.
r *Intercession, of man with God*, Jer. 27:18.

**8**
s *Prophets, false*, Isa. 3:2.
t *Sorcery, by false prophets*, Isa. 47:9.
u *Dream*, Dan. 1:17.

**10**
v *Seventy, years*, Num. 11:16.
w *Adversity, consolation in*, Psa. 10:6.
x *God, faithfulness of*, Gen. 2:2.
y *Prophecies, of the return of the Jews from Babylon*, Dan. 9:24.
z *Temporal Blessings, from God*, Psa. 103:2.

**11**
a *God, goodness of*, Gen. 2:2.
1 R. V. hope in your latter end.

**12**
b *Prayer, answer to, promised*, Acts 6:4.

**13**
c *Seekers*, Isa. 55:6.
d *Spiritual Desire*, Psa. 42:1.

**14**
e *Prophecies, of the return of the Jews from Babylon*, Dan. 9:24.
f *God, providence of*, Gen. 2:2.
g *Captivity, of Judah in Babylon*, Isa. 5:13.
h *Temporal Blessings, from God*, Psa. 103:2.

**17**
i *Wicked, warned*, Psa. 73:3.
j *War, as a judgment*, Judg. 3:2.
k *Famine, as a judgment*, 2 Kin. 8:1.

**18**
l *Dispersion*, Gen. 11:8.
2 R. V. tossed to and fro among

**19**
m *Impenitence*, Rom. 2:5.

**20**
n *Jerusalem*, Judg. 19:10.
o *Babylon, empire of*, Ezra 5:12.

**21**
p *Falsehood*, Job 21:34.
q *Prophets, false, punishment of*, vs. 21–23; Isa. 3:2.
r Or, *Nebuchadnezzar*, Dan. 2:1.

---

Promises to promoters of: *Joy*, Prov. 12:20; *adoption*, Matt. 5:9; *fruit of righteousness*, Jas. 3:17, 18.
Instances of promoters of: *Abraham*, Gen. 13:8, 9; *Abimelech*, Gen. 26:29; *Mordecai*, Esth. 10:3; *psalmist*, Psa. 120:7.
**Through Christ**, Isa. 2:4; 9:6, 7; 11:6, 13; Mic. 4:3, 4; Luke 1:79; John 14:27; Acts 10:36; Rom. 10:15. *To the world*, Isa. 2:4; 11:6–9; Luke 2:14.
See footnote, NATION, *Peace of*, Isa. 2:4.

have committed [s]adultery with
their neighbours' wives, and
have spoken [p]lying words in my
name, which I have not commanded
them; even I [3,t]know,
and *am* a witness, saith the
LORD.
24 ¶ *Thus* shalt [u]thou also
speak to Shĕm-a-ī'ah the Nĕ-hĕl'a-mīte, saying,
25 Thus speaketh the LORD of
hosts, the God of Ĭṣ'ra-el, saying,
Because thou hast sent [v]letters
in thy name unto all the people
that *are* at Jĕ-ru'sā-lĕm, and to
[w]Zĕph-a-nī'ah the son of [x]Mā-a-sē'iah the priest, and to all the
priests, saying,
26 The LORD hath made thee
priest in the stead of Jĕ-hoi'a-dȧ
the priest, that ye should be officers
in the [y]house of the LORD,
for every man *that is* mad, and
maketh himself a prophet, that
thou shouldest put him in [4]prison,
and [z]in the stocks.
27 Now therefore why hast
thou not reproved [a]Jĕr-e-mī'ah
of [b]Ăn'a-thŏth, which maketh
himself a prophet to you?
28 For therefore he sent unto
us *in* [c]Băb'ȳ-lon, saying,
This [d]*captivity is* long: build
ye houses, and dwell *in them*;
and [e]plant gardens, and eat the
fruit of them.
29 And [f]Zĕph-a-nī'ah the priest
read this letter in the ears of
[a]Jĕr-e-mī'ah the prophet.
30 ¶ Then [g]came the [h]word
of the LORD unto [a]Jĕr-e-mī'ah,
saying,
31 Send to all them of the [d]captivity,
saying, Thus saith the
LORD concerning [i]Shĕm-a-ī'ah
the Nĕ-hĕl'a-mīte; Because that
Shĕm-a-ī'ah hath prophesied
unto you, and I sent him not,
and he [j]caused you to [k]trust in
a [l]lie:
32 Therefore thus saith the
LORD; Behold, I will [i]punish
Shĕm-a-ī'ah the Nĕ-hĕl'a-mīte,
and his seed: he shall not have
a man to dwell among this people;
neither shall he behold the
good that I will do for my people,
saith the LORD; because he
hath taught rebellion against the
LORD.

## CHAPTER 30

*The return of Israel predicted. 10 Israel comforted with assurances of quietness and protection. 18 Their former privileges to be restored.*

THE [a]word that came to [b]Jĕr-e-mī'ah from the LORD,
saying,
2 Thus speaketh the LORD God
of Ĭṣ'ra-el, saying, Write thee all
the [c]words that I have spoken
unto thee in a [d]book.
3 For, lo, the days come, saith
the LORD, that [e]I will bring
again the [f]captivity of my people
[g]Ĭṣ'ra-el and [h]Jū'dah, saith the
LORD: and [e]I will cause them to
return to the [i,j]land that I gave
to their fathers, and they shall
possess it.
4 ¶ And these *are* the words
that the LORD spake concerning
[g]Ĭṣ'ra-el and concerning [h]Jū'dah.
5 For thus saith the LORD; We
have heard a voice of trembling,
of fear, and not of peace.
6 Ask ye now, and see whether
a man doth travail with child?
[k]wherefore do I see every man
with his hands on his loins, as a
woman in travail, and all faces
are turned into paleness?
7 Alas! for that day *is* great, so
that none *is* like it: it *is* even
the time of Jā'cob's trouble; but
[g,h,l]he shall be saved out of it.
8 For it shall come to pass in
that day, saith the LORD of hosts,
*that* [m]I will break his [n]yoke from
off thy neck, and will burst thy
bonds, and strangers shall no
more serve themselves of him:
9 But they shall serve the LORD
their God, and [o]Dā'vid their

23
s *Adultery*, Lev. 20:10.
t *Sin, known to God*, Rom. 5:12.
3 R. V. am he that knoweth,

24
u *Jeremiah*, Jer. 1:1.

25
v *Letters*, Isa. 37:14.
w *Zephaniah*, Jer. 21:1.
x Jer. 21:1; 35:4; 37:3.

26
y *Temple, Solomon's*, 1 Kin. 6:17.
z *Prisoners, in stocks*, Psa. 79:11.
4 R. V. the stocks and in shackles.

27
a *Jeremiah*, Jer. 1:1.
b *Anathoth*, Jer. 1:1.

28
c *Babylon*, Ezra 5:12.
d *Captivity, of Judah in Babylon*, Isa. 5:13.
e *Agriculture*, Gen. 3:23.

29
f *Zephaniah*, Jer. 21:1.

30
g *Prophets, inspiration of*, Isa. 3:2.
h *Prophecies, inspired*, Dan. 9:24.

31
i *Prophet, false, punishment of*, Isa. 3:2.
j *Influence, evil*, 1 Cor. 7:14.
k *False Confidence*, Psa. 30:6.
l *Falsehood*, Job 21:34.

1
a *Prophecies, inspired*, Dan. 9:24.
b *Jeremiah*, Jer. 1:1.

2
c *Word of God, inspiration of*, Psa. 119:9.
d *Book*, Num 5:23.

3
e *God, providence of*, Gen. 2:2.
f *Captivity, of Judah in Babylon*, Isa. 5:13.
g *Israel, after the revolt, prophecies concerning restoration of*, 1 Kin. 12:1.
h *Judah, kingdom of, prophecies concerning restoration of*, 2 Chr. 17:11.
i *Canaan*, Gen. 37:1.
j *Temporal Blessings, from God*, Psa. 103:2.

6
k *Adversity, despondency in*, Psa. 10:6.

7
l *Adversity, consolation in*, Psa. 10:6.

8
m *God, preserver*, Gen. 2:2.
n *Yoke, figurative*, 1 Sam. 6:7.

9
o *Jesus, names of*, Matt. 1:21.

p *Jesus, king,* Matt. 1:21.
q *Jesus, prophecies concerning,* Matt. 1:21.

**10**
r *Nation, promises of peace to,* Isa. 2:4.

**11**
s *Dispersion,* Gen. 11:8.
t *God, mercy of,* Gen. 2:2.
u *Divine Chastisement,* Job 33:19.
1 R. V. with judgement, and will in no wise leave thee unpunished.

**12**
v *Disease, figurative,* Ex. 15:26.

**13**
w *Medicine,* Prov. 17:22.
x *Disease, remedies used for,* Ex. 15:26.

**14**
y *Adversity, dispensation from God,* Psa. 10:6.
z *Wicked, punishment of,* Psa. 73:3.

**16**
z *Captivity, as a judgment,* Isa. 5:13.

**17**
b *God, preserver,* Gen. 2:2.

[p]king, [q]whom I will raise up unto them.[Q]

10 Therefore fear thou not, O my servant Jā′cob, saith the LORD; neither be dismayed, O Is̱′ra-el: for, lo, [g,h,l]I will [m]save thee from afar, and thy seed from the land of their [f]captivity; and Jā′cob shall return, and [j,r]shall be in rest, and be quiet, and none shall make *him* afraid

11 For I *am* with thee, saith the LORD, to [m]save thee: though I make a full end of all nations whither I have [s]scattered thee, yet [t]will I not make a full end of thee: but I will [u]correct thee [1]in measure, and will not leave thee altogether unpunished.[S]

12 For thus saith the LORD, Thy [v]bruise *is* incurable, *and* thy wound *is* grievous.

13 *There is* none to plead thy cause, that thou mayest be bound up: thou hast no healing [w,x]medicines.

14 All thy lovers have forgotten thee; they seek thee not; for [y]I have [z]wounded thee with the wound of an enemy, with the chastisement of a cruel one, for the multitude of thine iniquity; *because* thy sins were increased.

15 Why criest thou for thine affliction? thy sorrow *is* incurable for the multitude of thine iniquity: [y,z]*because* thy sins were increased, I have done these things unto thee.

16 Therefore all they that devour thee shall be devoured; and all thine adversaries, every one of them, shall go into [a]captivity; and they that spoil[C] thee shall be a spoil,[C] and all that prey upon thee will I give for a prey.

17[S] For [b]I will restore health unto thee, and I will heal thee of thy wounds, saith the LORD; because they called thee an Outcast, *saying,* This *is* Zī′ŏn, whom no man seeketh after.

18 ¶ Thus saith the LORD; Behold, [c]I will [d]bring again the captivity of Jā′cob's tents, and have [e]mercy on his dwellingplaces; and the [f]city shall be [d]builded upon her own heap,[G] and the palace shall remain after the manner thereof.

19 And out of them shall proceed [g]thanksgiving and the voice of them that make merry: and [c]I will [d]multiply them, and they shall not be few; I will also glorify them, and they shall not be small.[S]

20 [c]Their[T] children also shall be as aforetime,[G] and their congregation shall be established before me, and I will punish all that oppress them.

21 And their nobles shall be of themselves, and their [h]governor shall proceed from the midst of them; and I will cause him to draw near, and he shall approach unto me: for who *is* this that engaged his heart to approach unto me? saith the LORD.

22 And [i]ye shall be [j]my people,[T] and I will be your God.

23 ¶ Behold, the [k]whirlwind of the LORD goeth forth with fury, a continuing whirlwind: [l]it shall fall with pain upon the head of the wicked.

24 The fierce [m]anger of the LORD shall not return, until he have done *it,* and until he have performed the intents of his heart: in the latter days ye shall consider it.

## CHAPTER 31

*The restoration of Israel. 15 Rachel mourning is comforted. 18 To Ephraim repenting mercy is promised. 22 Other gracious promises made to Israel.*

AT the same time, saith the LORD, [a]will I be the God of all the [b,c]families of Is̱′ra-el, and they shall be [d]my people.

2 Thus saith the LORD, The people *which were* left of the

**18**
c *Israel, after the revolt, prophecies concerning restoration of,* 1 Kin. 12:1.
d *Temporal Blessings, from God,* Psa. 103:2.
e *God, mercy of,* Gen. 2:2.
f *Jerusalem, prophecies concerning,* Judg. 19:10.

**19**
g *Thankfulness, to God,* Acts 24:3.

**21**
h *Jesus, prophecies concerning,* Matt. 1:21.

**22**
i *God, love of, exemplified,* Gen. 2:2.
j *Spiritual Adoption,* Rom. 8:15.

**23**
k *Whirlwind, figurative,* Prov. 1:27.
l *Wicked, punishment of,* Psa. 73:3.

**24**
m *Anger of God,* 2 Kin. 13:3.

**1**
a *God, love of,* Gen. 2:2.
b *Israel, after the revolt, prophecies concerning restoration of,* 1 Kin. 12:1.
c *Jews, prophecies concerning restoration of,* Neh. 4:2.
d *Spiritual Adoption,* Rom. 8:15.

2
e *Grace of God,* Rom. 4:16.

4
f *Virgin, figurative,* Isa. 62:5.
g *Music, instruments of,* 2 Chr. 5:13.
h *Dancing, figurative,* Eccl. 3:4.

5
i *Agriculture,* Gen. 3:23.
j *Grape, culture of,* Lev. 25:5.
k *Samaria,* Isa. 7:9.
1 R. V. enjoy the fruit thereof.

6
l *Watchman,* 2 Sam. 18:24.
m *Zion,* 2 Sam. 5:7.
2 R. V. hills of

7
n *Praise,* Psa. 150:1.

8
o *Blindness,* 2 Kin. 6:18.
p *Lameness,* Lev. 21:18.
3 R. V. uttermost parts of

9
q *Repentance,* Mark 1:4.
r *Prayer, penitential,* Acts 6:4.
s *God, guidance of,* Gen. 2:2.
t *God, fatherhood of,* Gen. 2:2.
u *Firstborn, figurative,* Zech. 12:10.

sword found [e]grace in the wilderness; *even* Ĭṣ′ra-el, when I
went to cause him to rest.
3 The LORD hath appeared of
old unto me, *saying,* Yea, I have
[a]loved thee with an everlasting
love: therefore with lovingkindness have I drawn thee.[S] [T]
4 Again I will build thee, and
thou shalt be built, O [f]virgin
of Ĭṣ′ra-el: thou shalt again be
adorned with thy [g]tabrets,[C] and
shalt go forth in the [h]dances of
them that make merry.
5 Thou shalt yet [i]plant [j]vines
upon the mountains of [k]Sā-
mā′rĭ-ȧ: the planters shall plant,
and shall [1]eat *them* as common
things.
6 For [b,c]there shall be a
day, *that* the [l]watchman upon
the [2]mount Ē′phrā-ĭm shall cry,
Arise ye, and let us go up to
[m]Zī′ŏn unto the LORD our God.
7 For thus saith the LORD;
Sing with gladness for Jā′cob,
and shout among the chief of
the nations: publish ye, [n]praise
ye, and say, O LORD, save thy
people, the remnant of Ĭṣ′ra-el.[T]
8 Behold, I will bring [b,c]them
from the north country, and
gather them from the [3]coasts of
the earth, *and* with them the
[o]blind and the [p]lame, the woman
with child and her that travaileth
with child together: a great company shall return thither.[C]
9 [b,c]They[S] shall come with
[q]weeping, and with [r]supplica-
tions will I [s]lead them: I will
cause them to walk by the rivers of waters in a straight way,
wherein they shall not stumble:
for [a]I am a [t]father to Ĭṣ′ra-el,
and Ē′phrā-ĭm *is* [b]my [u]firstborn.[Q] [T]

10 ¶ Hear the word of the
LORD, O ye nations, and declare *it* in the isles afar off, and
say, He that [v]scattered [b,c]Ĭṣ′ra-el
[w]will gather [b,c]him, and [x]keep
him, as a *shepherd *doth* his
flock.[S]
11 For the LORD hath [x]re-
deemed Jā′cob, and ransomed
him from the hand of *him that*
*was* stronger than he.
12 Therefore [b,c]they shall come
and sing in the height of Zī′ŏn,
and shall flow together to the
goodness of the LORD, for
wheat,[C] and for wine, and for
oil, and for the young of the
flock and of the herd: and [y]their
soul shall be as a watered garden; and they shall not sorrow
any more at all.
13 Then shall the virgin [z]re-
joice in the [a]dance, both [b]young
men and old together: for I will
turn their mourning into joy,
and will [c]comfort them, and
make them rejoice from their
sorrow.
14 And I will satiate[C] the soul of
the priests with fatness,[G] and [d]my
people shall be satisfied with my
goodness, saith the LORD.
15 ¶ Thus saith the LORD;
[e,f]A voice was heard in [g]Rā′mah,
[h]lamentation, *and* bitter [i]weep-
ing; Rā′hel weeping for her children refused to be comforted for
her children, because they *were*
not.[Q]
16 Thus saith the LORD; Refrain[G] thy voice from weeping,
and thine eyes from tears: for
[j]thy work shall be rewarded,
saith the LORD; and [k,l]they shall
come again from the land of the
enemy.[Q]

10
v *Adversity, dispensation from God,* Psa. 10:6.
w *Nation, penitent, promises to,* Isa. 2:4.
x *God, preserver,* Gen. 2:2.

12
y *Righteous, described,* Psa. 64:10.

13
z *Joy,* Psa. 5:11.

a *Dancing, figurative,* Eccl. 3:4.
b *Young Men,* Prov. 1:4.
c *Adversity, consolation in,* Psa. 10:6.

14
d *Spiritual Blessings, from God,* Eph. 1:3.

15
e Matt. 2:18.
f *Prophecies, fulfilled,* Dan. 9:24.
g *Ramah, prophecies concerning,* Judg. 19:13.
h *Afflictions, despondency in,* Psa. 34:19.
i *Weeping,* Ezra 3:13.

16
j *Afflictions, consolation in,* Psa. 34:19.
k *Israel, after the revolt, prophecies concerning, of restoration,* 1 Kin. 12:1.
l *Jews, prophecies concerning restoration of,* Neh. 4:2.

* **SHEPHERD.** *One who cares for flocks,* Gen. 31:38–40; Jer. 31:10; Amos 3:12; Luke 2:8. *David the, defends his flock against a lion and a bear,* 1 Sam. 17:34, 35. *Causes the flock to rest,* Psa. 23:2; Song 1:7; Jer. 33:12. *Numbers the flock,* Lev. 27:32; Jer. 33:13. *Knows his flock by name,* John 10:3–5. *Waters the flocks,* Gen. 29:2–10. *Keeps the flocks in folds,* Num. 32:16; 1 Sam. 24:3; 2 Sam. 7:8; John 10:1. *Dogs of,* Job 30:1. *Was an abomination to the Egyptians,* Gen. 46:34. *Angels appear to,* Luke 2:8–20. *Name, given to Cyrus,* Isa. 44:28.
**Instances of:** *Abel,* Gen. 4:2. *Rachel,* Gen. 29:9. *Daughters of Jethro,* Ex. 2:16. *Moses,* Ex. 3:1. *David,* 1 Sam. 16:11; 17:34; 2 Sam. 7:8; Psa. 78:70.
**Figurative,** Gen. 49:24. *Of God's care,* Psa. 23; 78:52; 80:1. *Of prophets, priests, Levites, and civil authorities,* Isa. 56:11; Ezek. 34. *Of Christ,* Zech. 13:7; Matt. 26:31; Mark 14:27; John 10:1–16; Heb. 13:20; 1 Pet. 2:25; 5:4.
See footnote, JESUS, *Shepherd,* Matt. 1:21.

17 And [k,l]there is hope in thine end, saith the LORD, that thy children shall come again to their own border.

18 ¶ I have[T] surely heard [m]Ē′phră-ĭm bemoaning himself *thus;* [n,o]Thou hast [p]chastised me, and I was [q]chastised, as a bullock unaccustomed *to the yoke*: turn thou me,[G] and I shall be turned[G]; for thou *art* the LORD my God.[S]

19 [q]Surely after that I was turned, I [r,s]repented; and after that I was instructed, I smote[G] upon *my* thigh: I was ashamed, yea, even confounded, because I did bear the reproach of my youth.[T]

20 *Is* [m]Ē′phră-ĭm my dear son? *is he* a pleasant child? for [4]since I spake against him, I do earnestly remember him still: therefore my [t]bowels[G] [5]are troubled for him; I will surely have [u]mercy upon him, saith the LORD.

21 Set thee up waymarks[G], make thee [6]high heaps: set thine heart toward the highway, *even* the way *which* thou wentest: turn again, O virgin of Ĭş′ra-el, turn again to these thy cities.

22 ¶ How long wilt thou go about, O thou [v]backsliding daughter? for the LORD hath created a new thing in the earth, A woman shall [7]compass a man.

23 Thus saith the LORD of hosts, the God of Ĭş′ra-el; As yet they shall use this speech in the land of [w]Jū′dah and in the cities thereof, when I shall bring again their [x]captivity; [y]The LORD bless thee, O habitation of justice, *and* mountain of holiness.

24 And there shall dwell in [w]Jū′dah itself, and in all the cities thereof together, husbandmen[G], and *they *that* go forth with flocks.

25 For I have satiated[G] the weary soul, and I have replenished every sorrowful soul.[Q]

26 Upon this I awaked, and beheld; and my sleep was sweet unto me.

27 ¶ Behold, the days come, saith the LORD, that I will sow the house of [l]Ĭş′ra-el and the house of [w]Jū′dah with the seed of man, and with the seed of beast.

28 And it shall come to pass, *that* like as I have watched over them, [z]to pluck up, and to break down, and to throw down, and to destroy, and to afflict; so [a]will I watch over them, to build, and to plant, saith the LORD.[S]

29 [b,c]In those days they shall say no more, [d,e]The fathers have eaten a sour [f]grape, and [g]the children's teeth are set on edge.[T]

30 But [b,c,h]every one shall [i]die [j]for his own [k]iniquity: every man that eateth the sour [f]grape, his teeth shall be set on edge.

31 ¶ [l,m]Behold,[T][Q] the days come, saith the LORD, that I will make a [†,n]new covenant with the house of Ĭş′ra-el, and with the house of Jū′dah:

32 Not according to the [o]covenant that I made with their fathers in the day *that* [a]I took them by the hand to bring them out of the land of [p]Ē′ġȳpt; which my covenant they brake, although I was an [q]husband unto them, saith the LORD:[T]

33 But[Q] [r]this *shall be* the covenant that I will make with the house of Ĭş′ra-el; After those days, saith the LORD, [m,s]I will put my law in their inward parts, and write it in their hearts; and will be their God, and they shall be [t]my people.[T]

34 And [m]they shall teach no more every man his neighbour, and every man his brother, say-

**18**
m *Ephraim, name of, applied to the ten tribes*, Gen. 41:52.
n *Divine Chastisement, penitence under*, Job 33:19.
o *Adversity, prayer in*, Psa. 10:6.
p *Nation, chastisement of*, Isa. 2:4.
q *Adversity, design of*, Psa. 10:6.

**19**
r *Repentance, instances of*, Mark 1:4.
s *Adversity, benefits of*, Psa. 10:6.

**20**
t *Bowels, figurative*, 1 Kin. 3:26.
u *God, mercy of*, Gen. 2:2.
4 R. V. as often as I speak against
5 Am. R. V. yearn for

**21**
6 R. V. guide-posts:

**22**
v *Backsliding, of Israel*, Hos. 11:7.
7 R. V. encompass

**23**
w *Judah, kingdom of, prophecies concerning restoration of*, 2 Chr. 11:17.
x *Captivity, of Judah in Babylon*, Isa. 5:13.
y *Benedictions*, Deut. 21:5.

**28**
z *Adversity, dispensation from God*, Psa. 10:6.

a *God, providence of*, Gen. 2:2.

**29**
b *Innocent, shall not suffer for the guilty*, Deut. 24:16.
c *Children, not punished on account of sins of parents*, Mark 10:14.
d Ezek. 18:2, 3.
e *Proverbs*, 1 Sam. 24:13.
f *Grape, figurative*, Lev. 25:5.
g *Heredity*, Ezek. 18:2.

**30**
h *Punishment, according to deeds*, Lev. 26:41.
i *Sin, punishment of*, Rom. 5:12.
j *Responsibility, personal*, Ezek. 18:20.
k *Sin, consequences of, not entailed on children*, Rom. 5:12.

**31**
l Heb. 8:8-12.
m *Prophecies concerning the Messiah, and their fulfillment*, Gen. 12:3.
n *Gospel, called new covenant*, Mark 13:10.

**32**
o *Covenant, of God with men*, Deut. 29:1.
p *Egypt*, Gen. 41:8.
q *Husband, figurative*, Num. 30:6.

**33**
r Heb. 10:16.
s *Spiritual Blessings, from God*, Eph. 1:3.
t *Spiritual Adoption*, Rom. 8:15.

† **NEW COVENANT.** *The renewal of the Abrahamic covenant, abolishing Mosaic legalism and bringing in the Messianic dispensation of grace*, 2 Cor. 3:6-17. *Prophecy concerning*, Jer. 31:31-34, with Heb. 8:4-13. *In the blood of Jesus*, Matt. 26:28; Mark 14:24; Luke 22:20; 1 Cor. 11:25. *Jesus the mediator of*, Heb. 12:18-24. *Called everlasting*, Heb. 13:20.

**34**
u *Wisdom, spiritual,* Prov. 2:2.
v Heb. 10:17.
w *Sin, forgiveness of,* Rom. 5:12.

**35**
x *God, providence of,* Gen 2:2.
y *God, creator,* Gen. 2:2.
z *Temporal Blessings, from God,* Psa. 103:2.

a *Sun,* Josh. 10:12.
b *Light,* Gen. 1:3.
c *Day,* Gen. 1:5.
d *Astronomy,* Isa. 13:10.
e *Moon,* Song 6:10.
f *Stars,* Judg. 5:20.
g *Night,* Gen. 1:5.
h *Sea,* Jer. 5:22.

**36**
i *God, faithfulness of,* Gen. 2:2.

**37**
j *Heavens, physical,* Psa. 8:3.
k *Geology,* Psa. 104:5.

**38**
l *Jerusalem, prophecies of the rebuilding of,* vs. 38–40; Judg. 19:10.
m *Jerusalem, towers of,* Judg. 19:10.
n *Jerusalem, gates of,* Judg. 19:10.

**39**
8 R. V. out straight onward unto the
9 R. V. turn

**40**
o *Kidron,* 1 Kin. 2:37.

v.1–508 BC
See footnote, *Time,* Rev. 10:6.

**1**
a *Prophecies, inspired,* Dan. 9:24.
b *Jeremiah,* Jer. 1:1.
c *Zedekiah,* 2 Kin. 25:2.

ing, Know[C] the LORD: for they shall all [u]know me, from the least of them unto the greatest of them, saith the LORD: for [v]I will [w]forgive their iniquity, and I will remember their sin no more.[S T Q]

35 ¶ Thus saith the LORD, [x]which [y,z]giveth the [a]sun for a [b]light by [c]day, *and* the [d]ordinances of the [e]moon and of the [f]stars for a light by [g]night, which divideth the [h]sea when the waves thereof roar; The LORD of hosts *is* his name:[S]

36 [i]If[S] those [d]ordinances depart from before me, saith the LORD, *then* the seed of Iş'ra-el also shall cease from being a nation before me for ever.

37 Thus saith the LORD; [i]If [j]heaven above can be measured, and the [k]foundations of the earth searched out beneath, I will also cast off all the seed of Iş'ra-el for all that they have done, saith the LORD.[S]

38 ¶ Behold, the days come, saith the LORD, that [l]the city shall be built to the LORD from the [m]tower of Hă-năn'e-el unto the [n]gate of the corner.

39 And the measuring line shall yet go [8]forth over against it upon the hill Gā'rĕb, and shall [9]compass about to Gō'ăth.

40 And the whole valley of the dead bodies, and of the ashes, and all the fields unto the brook of [o]Kĭd'ron, unto the corner of the [n]horse gate toward the east, *shall be* holy unto the LORD; it shall not be plucked up, nor thrown down any more for ever.

## CHAPTER 32

*Jeremiah's imprisonment. 6 Under the type of buying a field, he is assured of Israel's return. 16 His prayer. 26 The cause of Israel's captivity; 36 and promise of their return.*

THE [a]word that came to [b]Jĕr-e-mī'ah from the LORD in the tenth year of [c]Zĕd-e-kī'ah king of [d]Jū'dah, which *was* the eighteenth year of [e]Nĕb-u-chad-rĕz'zar.

2 For then the [e]king of [f]Băb'ȳ-lon's army [g]besieged [h]Jĕ-ru'-să-lĕm: and [b,i]Jĕr-e-mī'ah the prophet was [j,k]shut up in the [l]court of the [1]prison, which *was* in the king of Jū'dah's house.

3 For [c]Zĕd-e-kī'ah king of [d]Jū'dah had shut him up, saying, Wherefore[C] dost thou [m]prophesy, and say, Thus saith the LORD, Behold, I will give this city into the hand of the king of [f]Băb'ȳ-lon, and he shall take it;

4 And [c]Zĕd-e-kī'ah king of [d]Jū'dah shall not escape out of the hand of the Chăl-dē'anş, but shall surely be [n,o]delivered into the hand of the king of [f]Băb'ȳ-lon, and shall speak with him mouth to mouth, and his eyes shall behold his eyes;

5 And he shall lead [c]Zĕd-e-kī'ah to [f]Băb'ȳ-lon, and there shall he be until I visit him, saith the LORD: though ye fight with the Chăl-dē'anş, ye shall not prosper.

6 ¶ And[Q] [b]Jĕr-e-mī'ah said, The word of the LORD came unto me, saying,

7 Behold, Hă-năm'e-el the son of Shăl'lum thine uncle shall come unto thee, saying, Buy thee my [p,q]field that *is* in [r]Ăn'a-thŏth: for the right of redemption *is* thine to buy *it.*

8 So Hă-năm'e-el mine uncle's son came to me in the [l]court of the [1]prison according to the word of the LORD, and said unto me, Buy my [p,q]field, I pray thee, that *is* in [r]Ăn'a-thŏth, which *is* in the country of [s]Bĕn'ja-mĭn: for the right of [t]inheritance *is* thine, and the redemption *is* thine; buy *it* for thyself. Then I knew that this *was* the word of the LORD.

9 And I bought the [p,q]field of

d *Judah, kingdom of,* 2 Chr. 11:17.
e Or, *Nebuchadnezzar,* Dan. 2:1.

**2**
f *Babylon, empire of,* Ezra 5:12.
g *Siege,* Deut. 28:53.
h *Jerusalem, captured and pillaged,* Judg. 19:10.
i *Prisoners,* Psa. 79:11.
j *Minister, trials and persecutions of,* Rom. 15:16.
k *Persecution, of the righteous,* John 15:20.
l *Prison, court of,* Gen. 39:20.
1 R. V. guard,

**3**
m *Prophecies, fulfilled, of the captivity of the Jews,* Dan. 9:24.

**4**
n *Captivity, as a judgment,* Isa. 5:13.
o *Adversity, dispensation from God,* Psa. 10:6.

**7**
p *Property, in real estate,* Lev. 27:15.
q *Land, sale and redemption of,* vs. 7–16; Ruth 4:3.
r *Anathoth, birthplace of Jeremiah,* Jer. 1:1.

**8**
s *Benjamin, tribe of,* Num. 1:37.
t *Inheritance,* Num. 27:7.

Hă-năm′e-el my uncle's son, that
*was* in [r]Ăn′a-thŏth, and weighed
him the *money, *even* seventeen
[u]shekels[G] of silver.[Q]
10 And I subscribed[G] the [2]evi-
dence, and [v]sealed *it*, and took
[w]witnesses, and weighed *him* the
*money in the [x]balances.
11 So I took the [2]evidence of
the purchase, *both* that which
was [v]sealed *according* to the law
and custom, and that which was
open:
12 And I gave the [2]evidence of
the purchase unto [y]Bā′rṳch the
son of Nē-rī′ah, the son of [z]Mā-
a-sē′iah, in the sight of Hă-năm′-
e-el mine uncle's *son*, and in the
presence of the [a]witnesses that
subscribed[G] the [2]book of the purchase, before all the Jews̱ that
sat in the [b]court of the [1]prison.
13 ¶ And I charged [c]Bā′rṳch
before them, saying,
14 Thus saith the LORD of
hosts, the God of Ĭs̱′ra-el; Take
these evidences, this [2]evidence
of the purchase, both which is
sealed, and this [2]evidence which
is open; and put them in an
earthen vessel, that they may
continue many days.
15 For thus [d]saith the LORD
of hosts, the God of Ĭs̱′ra-el;
[d]Houses and fields and vine-
yards̱ shall be possessed again in
this land.
16 ¶ Now when I had delivered the [2]evidence of the purchase unto [c]Bā′rṳch the son of
Nē-rī′ah, I [e]prayed unto the
LORD, saying,
17 [e]Ah Lord GOD! behold, thou
hast [f]made the [g]heaven and the
[h]earth by thy great [i]power and
stretched[G] out arm, *and* there is
nothing too hard for thee:[S]
18 Thou shewest [j]lovingkind-
ness unto thousands, and [k]rec-
ompensest the [l]iniquity of the
fathers into the bosom of their
children after them: the Great,
the [i]Mighty God, the LORD of
hosts, *is* his name,[S]
19 Great in counsel, and
mighty in work: for [m]thine eyes
*are* open upon all the ways of the
sons of men: to [n,o]give every one
according to his ways, and according to the fruit of his doings:[T S]
20 Which hast set [p]signs and
wonders in the land of [q]Ē′ġy̆pt,
*even* unto this day, and in Ĭs̱′-
ra-el, and among *other* men; and
[p]hast made thee a name, as̱ at
this day;
21 And hast [r]brought forth thy
people Ĭs̱′ra-el out of the land
of [s]Ē′ġy̆pt with signs, and with
wonders, and with a strong hand,
and with a stretched[G] out arm,
and with great terror;
22 And hast [t]given them this
[u]land, which thou didst [v]swear
to their fathers to give them, a
land flowing with [w]milk and
[x]honey;
23 And they came in, and possessed it; but they [y]obeyed not
thy voice, neither walked in thy
law; they have done nothing of
all that thou commandedst them
to do: therefore thou hast caused
all this [z]evil to come upon them:
24 Behold the [a]mounts,[G] they
are come unto the city to take it;
and the city is given into the
hand of the Chăl-dē′ans̱, that
fight against it, because of the
[b]sword, and of the [c]famine, and

**9**
*u Shekel*, Ex. 30:1.

**10**
*v Seal*, 1 Kin. 21:8.
*w Witness, to the transfer of land*, Num. 35:30.
*x Balances*, Prov. 11:1.
2 R. V. deed,

**12**
*y* Jer. 36:4–32; 43: 3–6; 45:1, 2.
*z* Jer. 51:59.
*a Witness, to the transfer of land*, Num. 35:30.
*b Prison, court of*, Gen. 39:20.

**13**
*c* Jer. 36:4–32; 43: 3–6; 45:1, 2.

**15**
*d Adversity, consolation in*, Psa. 10:6.

**16**
*e Adversity, prayer in*, vs. 16–25; Psa. 10:6.

**17**
*f God, creator*, Gen. 2:2.
*g Heavens, created*, Psa. 8:3.
*h Earth, created*, Prov. 8:23.
*i God, power of*, Gen. 2:2.

**18**
*j God, mercy of*, Gen. 2:2.
*k Children, involved in sins of parents*, Mark 10:14.
*l Sin, consequences of, entailed upon children*, Rom. 5:12.

**19**
*m God, knowledge of*, Gen. 2:2.
*n God, judge*, Gen. 2:2.
*o Judgment, according to opportunity and works*, 1 Pet. 1:17.

**20**
*p Miracles, design of*, Luke 23:8.
*q Egypt, plagues in*, Gen. 41:8.

**21**
*r God, providence of*, Gen. 2:2.
*s Egypt, Israelites in bondage in*, Gen. 41:8.

**22**
*t Temporal Blessings, from God*, Psa. 103:2.
*u Canaan, fruitfulness of*, Gen. 37:1.
*v Covenant, of God with men*, Deut. 29:1.
*w Milk, figurative*, Job 10:10.
*x Honey, figurative*, Prov. 25:27.

**23**
*y Disobedience to God*, Eph. 5:6.
*z Adversity, dispensation from God*, Psa. 10:6.

**24**
*a Fortification, field*, Ezek. 17:17.
*b War, as a judgment*, Judg. 3:2.
*c Famine, as a judgment*, 2 Kin. 8:1.

* **MONEY,** Gen. 17:12, 13, 23, 27; 42:25–35, 43:12–23; 44:1–8; 47:14–18; Ex. 12:44; 21:11, 21, 34, 35; 22:7, 17, 25; 30:16; Lev. 22:11; 25:37, 51; 27:15, 18; Num. 3:48–51; 18:16; Deut. 2:6, 28; 14:25, 26; 21:14; 23:19; Judg. 5:19; 16:18; 1 Kin. 21:2, 6, 15; 2 Kin. 5:26; 12:4, 7–16; 22:7, 9; 2 Chr. 24: 5, 11, 14; 34:9, 14, 17; Ezra 3:7; 7:17; Neh. 5:4, 10, 11· Esth. 4:7; Job 31:39; Psa. 15:5; Prov. 7:20; Eccl. 7:12; 10:19; Isa. 43:24; 52:3; 55:1, 2; Jer. 32:9, 10, 25, 44; Lam. 5:4; Mic. 3: 11; Matt. 25:18, 27; 28:12, 15; Mark 14:11; Luke 9:3; 19: 15, 23; 22:5.
*Silver used as*, Gen. 13:2; 20:16; 23:15, 16; 31:15; 37:28; 44:8; Judg. 16:5; 17:1–4; 2 Kin. 15:20; 23:35; Jer. 32:9, 10, 25, 44; Isa. 13:17; 46:6; 60:9; Ezek. 7:19; 28:4; Amos 8:6; Matt. 10: 9; 26:15; Acts 3:6; 7:16; 8:20; 19:19; 20:33; 1 Pet. 1:18.
*Gold used as*, Gen. 13:2; 24:35; 44:8 (with v. 1); 2 Kin. 23:35; 1 Chr. 21:25; Ezra 8:25–30; Isa. 13:17; 46:6; 60:9; Ezek. 7: 19; 28:4; Matt. 2:11; 10:9; Acts 3:6; 20:33; 1 Pet. 1:18.
*Brass used as*, Matt. 10:9; Mark 6:8; 12:41.
*Weighed*, Gen. 23:16; 43:21; Job 28:15; Jer. 32:9, 10; Zech. 11:12. *Image on*, Matt. 22:20, 21. *Conscience*, Judg. 17:2; Matt. 27:3, 5. *Atonement*, Ex. 30:12–16. *Sin*, 2 Kin. 12:16. *Value of, varied corruptly*, Amos 8:5. *Love of, the root of evil*, 1 Tim. 6:10.
See footnotes: GOLD, Ezek. 7:19; SILVER, 1 Chr. 28:14.

25
d *Jeremiah*, Jer. 1:1.

27
e *God, sovereign,* Gen. 2:2.
f *God, power of,* Gen. 2:2.

28
g *Jerusalem, prophecies against,* Judg. 19:10.
h Or, *Nebuchadnezzar, prophecies concerning,* Dan. 2:1.
i *Babylon, empire of,* Ezra 5:12.

29
j *House, roof of,* Esth. 8:1.
k *Idolatry,* 1 Sam. 15:23.
l *Incense, offered in idolatrous worship,* Ex. 37:29.
m *Baal,* 2 Kin. 17:16.
n *Anger of God,* 2 Kin. 13:3.

31
o *Jerusalem, wickedness of,* Judg. 19:10.

32
p *Rulers, wicked,* Ex. 18:21.
q *Priests, corrupt,* Lev. 1:5.
r *Prophets, false,* Isa. 3:2.

33
s *Impenitence,* Rom. 2:5.

of the pestilence: and what thou
hast spoken is come to pass; and,
behold, thou seest *it*.
25 And thou hast said unto
[d]me, O Lord GOD, Buy thee
the field for *money, and take
witnesses; for the city is given
into the hand of the Chăl-dē′ans.
26 ¶ Then came the word of the
LORD unto [d]Jĕr-e-mī′ah, saying,
27 Behold, [e]I *am* the LORD, the
God of all flesh: [f]is there any
thing too hard for me?[S]
28 Therefore thus saith the
LORD; Behold, I will give this
[g]city into the hand of the
Chăl-dē′ans, and into the hand
of [h]Nĕb-u-chad-rĕz′zar king of
[i]Băb′y̆-lon, and he shall take it:
29 And the Chăl-dē′ans, that
fight against this [g]city, shall
come and set fire on this city,
and burn it with the houses, upon whose [j]roofs they have [k]of-
fered [l]incense unto [m]Bā′al, and
[k]poured out drink offerings unto other gods, to provoke me to
[n]anger.
30 For the children of Is′ra-el
and the children of Jū′dah have
only done evil before me from
their youth: for the children of
Is′ra-el have only provoked me
to anger with the work of their
hands, saith the LORD.
31 For this [o]city hath been to
me *as* a provocation of mine [n]an-
ger and of my fury from the day
that they built it even unto this
day; that I should remove it from
before my face,
32 Because of all the evil of the
children of Is′ra-el and of the
children of Jū′dah, which they
have done to provoke me to
[n]anger, they, their [p]kings, their
princes, their [q]priests, and their
[r]prophets, and the men of Jū′-
dah, and the inhabitants of Jē-
ru′să-lĕm.
33 And they have [s]turned unto
me the back, and not the face:
though I [t]taught them, rising up
early and teaching *them*, yet they
have not hearkened to receive
instruction.
34 But they set their [k]abomi-
nations[G] in the [u]house[G], which is
called by my name, to [v]defile it.
35 And they built the [w]high
places of [m]Bā′al, which *are* in
the [x]valley of the son of [y]Hĭn′-
nom, [z]to cause their [a]sons and
their daughters to pass through
*the fire* unto [b]Mō′lech; which I
commanded them not, neither
came it into my mind, that they
should do this abomination, to
cause Jū′dah to sin.
36 ¶ And now therefore thus
saith the LORD, the God of
Is′ra-el, concerning this city,
whereof ye say, It shall be delivered into the hand of the [c]king
of [d]Băb′y̆-lon by the [e]sword, and
by the [f]famine, and by the pestilence;
37 Behold, [g]I will gather them
out of all countries, [h]whither[G] I
have [i]driven them in mine [j]an-
ger, and in my fury, and in great
wrath; and [k]I will bring them
again unto this place, and [k]I will
cause them to dwell safely:[S]
38 And they shall be [l]my people, and [m]I will be their God:[Q]
39 And I will [n]give them one
heart, and one way, that they
may [o]fear me for ever, for the
good of them, and of their [p]chil-
dren after them:
40 And I will make an everlasting [q]covenant with them,
that [r]I will not turn away from
them, to do them good; but I
will put my [o]fear in their [s]hearts,
that they shall not depart from
me.[S T Q]
41 Yea, [m]I will [t]rejoice over
them to [n]do them good, and [m]I
will [u]plant them in this land assuredly with my whole heart and
with my whole soul.
42 For thus [g]saith the LORD;

t *Wicked, warned,* Psa. 73:3.

34
u *Temple, Solomon's,* 1 Kin. 6:17.
v *Profanation,* Lev. 22:32.

35
w *High Places,* 1 Kin. 3:2.
x Or, *Topheth,* 2 Kin. 23:10.
y *Hinnom,* Jer. 7:31.
z *Idolatry, wicked practices of,* 1 Sam. 15:23.

a *Human Sacrifices,* Deut. 12:31.
b *Molech,* 1 Kin. 11:7.

36
c *Nebuchadnezzar,* Dan. 2:1.
d *Babylon, empire of,* Ezra 5:12.
e *War, as a judgment,* Judg. 3:2.
f *Famine, as a judgment,* 2 Kin. 8:1.

37
g *Prophecies, of the return of the Jews from Babylon,* Dan. 9:24.
h *Captivity, as a judgment,* Isa. 5:13.
i *Adversity, dispensation from God,* Psa. 10:6.
j *Anger of God,* 2 Kin. 13:3.
k *Temporal Blessings, from God,* Psa. 103:2.

38
l *Spiritual Adoption,* Rom. 8:15.
m *God, love of, exemplified,* Gen. 2:2.

39
n *Spiritual Blessings, from God,* Eph. 1:3.
o *Fear of God,* Acts 9:31.
p *Children, of the righteous, blessed of God,* Mark 10:14.

40
q *Covenant, of God with men,* Deut. 29:1.
r *God, faithfulness of,* Gen. 2:2.
s *Heart, renewed,* Psa. 44:21.

41
t *Joy, attributed to God,* Psa. 5:11.
u *Temporal Blessings, from God,* Psa. 103:2.

Like as I have brought all this
great [i]evil upon this people, [r]so
will I bring upon them all the
good that I have promised
them.
43 [g]And fields shall be bought
in this land, whereof ye say, *It is*
desolate without man or beast;
it is given into the hand of the
[v]Chăl-dē'anș.
44 [g]Men shall buy fields for
*money, and subscribe[c] [3]evi-
dences, and [w]seal *them,* and take
witnesses in the land of [x]Bĕn'ja-
mĭn, and in the places about
[y]Jē-rṳ'să-lĕm, and in the cities
of [z]Jū'dah, and in the cities of
the mountains, and in the cities
of the valley, and in the cities
of the south: for [g]I will cause
their captivity to return, saith the
LORD.

## CHAPTER 33

*Promises to Israel of return from captivity, 9 and of great prosperity. 15 The Branch of righteousness predicted. 17 Assurances respecting the throne and priesthood of Israel, 20 and perpetuity of descendants.*

MOREOVER the [a]word of
the LORD [b]came unto
[c]Jĕr-e-mī'ah the second time,
while he was yet [d]shut up in the
[e]court of the [1]prison, saying,
2 [a]Thus saith [2]the [f]LORD[c] the
maker thereof, the LORD[c] that
formed it, to establish it; the
LORD *is* his name;
3 [g]Call unto me, and [h,i]I will
answer thee, and shew thee
[3]great and mighty things, which
thou knowest not.[s]
4 For thus saith the LORD, the
God of Ĭș'ra-el, concerning the
houses of this [j]city, and concerning the houses of the kings
of Jū'dah, which are [4]thrown
down by the [k]mounts[c], and by
the sword;
5 They come to fight with the
Chăl-dē'anș, but *it is* to fill them
with the dead bodies of men,
whom I have [l]slain in mine [m]an-
ger and in my fury, and for all
whose [n]wickedness I have hid
my face from this city.[s]
6 B[s]ehold, [o]I will bring it health
and cure, and I will cure them,
and will reveal unto them the
abundance of [p]peace and truth.
7 And [q]I will cause the captivity of Jū'dah and the captivity of
Ĭș'ra-el to return, and will [r]build
them, as at the first.
8 And [s]I will [t]cleanse them
from all their iniquity, whereby
they have sinned against me;
and I will [u]pardon all their
iniquities, whereby they have
sinned, and whereby they have
transgressed against me.[s]
9 And [q]it shall be to me a name
of joy, a praise and an honour
before all the nations of the
earth, which shall hear all the
good that I do unto them: and
they shall fear and tremble for
all the goodness and for all the
prosperity that I procure unto it.[s]
10 ¶ Thus saith the LORD;
Again there shall be heard in
this place, which ye say *shall
be* desolate without man and
without beast, *even* in the cities
of [v]Jū'dah, and in the streets
of [j]Jē-rṳ'să-lĕm, that are desolate, without man, and without
inhabitant, and without beast,
11 [s]The voice of [w]joy, and the
voice of gladness, the voice of
the bridegroom, and the voice of
the bride, the voice of them that
shall say, [x,y]Praise the LORD of
hosts: for the LORD *is* good;
for his [s]mercy *endureth* for ever:
*and* of them that shall bring
the sacrifice[c] of praise into the
[z]house of the LORD. For [q]I
will cause to return the captivity
of the land, as at the first, saith
the LORD.
12 ¶ Thus saith the LORD
of hosts; Again in this place,
which is desolate without man
and without beast, and in all
the cities thereof, shall be an

43

*v Chaldeans*, Dan. 1:4.

44

*w Seal*, 1 Kin. 21:8.
*x Benjamin, tribe of*, Num. 1:37.
*y Jerusalem*, Judg. 19:10.
*z Judah, kingdom of*, 2 Chr. 11:17.
3 R. V. deeds,

1

*a Prophecies, inspired*, Dan. 9:24.
*b Prophets, inspiration of*, Isa. 3:2.
*c Jeremiah, imprisoned by Zedekiah*, Jer. 1:1.
*d Persecution, of the righteous*, John 15:20.
*e Prison, courts of*, Gen. 39:20.
1 R. V. guard,

2

*f God, providence of*, Gen. 2:2.
2 Am. R. V. Jehovah that doeth it, Jehovah that

3

*g Commandment, enjoining prayer*, Deut. 8:2.
*h Promise, of answer to prayer*, 2 Cor. 1:20.
*i Prayer, answer to promised*, Acts 6:4.
3 R. V. great things, and difficult,

4

*j Jerusalem, prophecies concerning*, Judg. 19:10.
*k Fortification, field*, Ezek. 17:17.
4 R. V. broken down to make a defence against the mounts, and against the sword:

5

*l Divine Chastisement*, Job 33:19.
*m Anger of God*, 2 Kin. 13:3.
*n Sin, repugnant to God*, Rom. 5:12.

6

*o God, savior*, Gen. 2:2.
*p Peace*, Jer. 29:7.

7

*q Prophecies, fulfilled, of the return of the Jews from Babylon*, Dan. 9:24.
*r Temporal Blessings, from God*, Psa. 103:2.

8

*s God, mercy of*, Gen. 2:2.
*t Spiritual Purification*, Psa. 51:2.
*u Sin, forgiveness of*, Rom. 5:12.

10

*v Judah, kingdom of, prophecies concerning*, 2 Chr. 11:17.

11

*w Joy*, Psa. 5:11.
*x Praise*, Psa. 150:1.
*y Thankfulness, to God*, Acts 24:3.
*z Temple, Solomon's*, 1 Kin. 6:17.

habitation of [a]shepherds causing
*their* flocks to lie down.
13 In the cities of the mountains, in the cities of the vale,
and in the cities of the south, and
in the land of Bĕn′ja-mĭn, and in
the places about Jĕ-ru̦′sā-lĕm,
and in the cities of Jū′dah, shall
the flocks pass again under the
hands of him that telleth[G] *them*,
saith the LORD.
14 Behold, the days come, saith
the LORD, that [b]I will perform
that good thing which I have
promised unto the house of Ĭs̹′-[S]
ra-el and to the house of Jū′dah.
15 ¶ I[T]n those days, and at that
time, will I cause the [c,d]Branch
of righteousness to grow up unto
[e]Dā′vid; and [f]he shall execute
judgment[G] and righteousness in
the land.[Q]
16 In those days shall [g]Jū′dah
be saved, and [h]Jĕ-ru̦′sā-lĕm shall
dwell safely: and this *is the name*
wherewith she shall be called,
The LORD our righteousness.[T]
17 ¶ For thus saith the LORD;
[e,f]Dā′vid shall never want[G] a man
to sit upon the throne of the
house of Ĭs̹′ra-el;
18 Neither shall the priests the
[i]Lē′vītes want[G] a man before me
to offer [j]burnt offerings, and to
[5]kindle meat[G] offerings, and to do
sacrifice continually.
19 ¶ And the word of the LORD
[k]came unto [l]Jĕr-e-mī′ah, saying,
20[S] T[T]hus saith the LORD; [b]If
ye can break my covenant of
the day, and my covenant of the
night, and [m,n]that there should
not be day and night in their
season;
21 *Then* may also my [o]covenan[G]t
be broken with Dā′vid my servant, [e]that he should not have a
son to reign upon his throne; and
with the [i]Lē′vītes the priests, my
ministers.[S]
22 As the [p]host of heaven cannot be numbered, neither the
sand of the sea measured: [q,r]so
will I multiply the seed of Dā′-
vid my servant, and the Lē′vītes
that minister unto me.[T]
23 ¶ Moreover the word of
the LORD [k]came to [l]Jĕr-e-mī′ah,
saying,
24 Considerest thou not what
this people have spoken, saying, The two families which the
LORD hath chosen, he hath even
cast them off? thus they have
despised my people, that they
should be no more a nation before them.
25[S] Thus saith the LORD; [b]If
my [m,n]covenant [6]*be* not with day
and night, *and if* I have not appointed the ordinances of heaven
and earth;
26 Then will I cast away the
seed of Jā′cob, and Dā′vid my
servant, *so* that I will not take
*any* of his seed *to be* rulers over
the seed of Ā′brā-hăm, Ī′s̹aac,
and Jā′cob: for [s]I will cause
their captivity to return, and
have [t]mercy on them.[S]

## CHAPTER 34

*The prophet foretells the captivity of Zedekiah, 8 and the destruction of Jerusalem on account of the sins of the people.*

THE word which [a]came unto
[b]Jĕr-e-mī′ah from the
LORD, when [c]Nĕb-u-chad-nĕz′-
zar king of [d]Băb′y̆-lon, and all
his [e]army, and all the kingdoms
of the earth of his dominion, and
all the people, fought against
[f]Jĕ-ru̦′sā-lĕm, and against all the
cities thereof, saying,
2 Thus saith the LORD, the
God of Ĭs̹′ra-el; Go and speak to
[g]Zĕd-e-kī′ah king of Jū′dah, and
tell him, Thus saith the LORD;
Behold, [h]I will give this [i]city into
the hand of the [c]king of [d]Băb′y̆-
lon, and [i]he shall burn it with
fire:
3 And [g]thou shalt not escape
out of his hand, but shalt surely
be taken, and delivered into his

12
*a Shepherd,* Jer. 31:10.

14
*b God, faithfulness of,* Gen. 2:2.

15
*c Branch, figurative,* Dan. 4:14.
*d Jesus, names of,* Matt. 1:21.
*e David, type of Christ,* 1 Sam. 16:13.
*f Jesus, prophecies concerning,* Matt. 1:21.

16
*g Judah, kingdom of, prophecies concerning,* 2 Chr. 11:17.
*h Jerusalem,* Judg. 19:10.

18
*i Levites, prophecies concerning,* Deut. 10:8.
*j Offerings, burnt,* Lev. 6:17.
5 R. V. burn oblations,

19
*k Prophets, inspiration of,* Isa. 3:2.
*l Jeremiah,* Jer. 1:1.

20
*m* Gen. 8:22.
*n Nature, laws of, uniform in operation,* Jas. 3:12.

21
*o Covenant,* Deut. 29:1.

22
*p Stars,* Judg. 5:20.
*q Jesus, kingdom of, prophecies concerning,* Matt. 1:21.
*r Church, prophecies concerning its prosperity,* Matt. 16:18.

25
6 R. V. of day and night stand not, if

26
*s Prophecies, fulfilled, of the return of the Jews from Babylon,* Dan. 9:24.
*t God, mercy of,* Gen. 2:2.

1
*a Prophets, inspiration of,* Isa. 3:2
*b Jeremiah,* Jer. 1:1.
*c Nebuchadnezzar,* Dan. 2:1.
*d Babylon, empire of, prophecies of conquest by,* Ezra 5:12.
*e Armies,* Deut. 11:4.
*f Jerusalem, prophecies against,* Judg. 19:10.
**B.C. 590?**

2
*g Zedekiah,* 2 Kin. 25:2.
*h Adversity, dispensation from God,* Psa. 10:6
*i War, evils of,* Judg. 3:2.

hand; and thine eyes shall behold the eyes of the [c]king of [d]Băb'ȳ-lon, and he shall speak with thee mouth to mouth, and thou shalt go to Băb'ȳ-lon.

4 Yet hear the word of the LORD, O [g]Zĕd-e-kī'ah king of Jū'dah; Thus saith the LORD of thee, Thou shalt not die by the sword:

5 *But* thou shalt die in peace: and with the [j,k]burnings of thy fathers, the former kings which were before thee, so shall they [1]burn *odours* for thee; and they will [l]lament thee, *saying*, Ah lord! for I have pronounced the word, saith the LORD.

6 Then [a,b]Jĕr-e-mī'ah the prophet spake all these words unto [g]Zĕd-e-kī'ah king of Jū'dah in Jē-ru'sā-lĕm,

7 When the king of [d]Băb'ȳ-lon's [e]army fought against Jē-ru'sā-lĕm, and against all the cities of Jū'dah that were left, against [m]Lā'chish, and against [n]Ā-zē'-kah: for these defenced[C] [o]cities remained of the cities of Jū'dah.

8 ¶ *This is* the word that [a]came unto [b]Jĕr-e-mī'ah from the LORD, after that the king [g]Zĕd-e-kī'ah had made a [p,q,r]covenant with all the people which *were* at Jē-ru'sā-lĕm, to [s]proclaim [t]liberty unto them;

9 That every man should let his [u]manservant, and every man his maidservant, *being* an [v]Hē'-brew or an Hē'brew-ĕss, go [t]free; that none should serve[C] himself of them, *to wit,* of a [w]Jew his brother.

10 Now when all the princes, and all the people, which had entered into the [p]covenant, heard that every one should let his manservant, and every one his maidservant, go free, that none should serve themselves of them any more, then they obeyed, and let *them* go.

**5**

*j* *Dead, incense burnt for,* 2 Kin. 4:32.

*k* *Burial, rites of,* Acts 8:2.

*l* *Mourning,* Lam. 2:5.

1 R. V. make a burning

**7**

*m* *Lachish,* Josh. 10:5.

*n* *Azekah,* Josh. 10:10.

*o* *Cities, fortified,* Num. 35:8.

**8**

*p* *Covenant, of men with men,* Deut. 29:1.

*q* *Constitution,* vs. 8–11; Dan. 6:12.

*r* *King, constitutional restrictions of,* vs. 8–11; 2 Kin. 3:10.

*s* *Emancipation, proclamation of,* Deut. 15:12.

*t* *Liberty, in sabbatic year,* Lev. 25:10.

**9**

*u* *Servant, emancipated,* vs. 8–22; Jer. 2:14.

*v* *Hebrew,* Gen. 40:15.

*w* *Jews,* Neh. 4:2.

11 But afterward they turned, and [x]caused the servants and the handmaids, whom they had let go free, to return, and [y]brought them into subjection for servants and for handmaids.

12 ¶ Therefore the word of the LORD [a]came to [b]Jĕr-e-mī'ah from the LORD, saying,

13[T] Thus saith the LORD, the God of Ĭs'ra-el; I made a [z]covenant with your fathers in the day that I [a]brought them forth out of the land of [b]Ē'gȳpt, out of the house of bondmen[C], saying,

14 At the end of [c]seven years let ye [d]go every man his brother an [e]Hē'brew, which hath been sold[C] unto thee; and when he hath served thee six years, thou shalt let him go free from thee: but your fathers [f]hearkened not unto me, neither inclined their ear.[T]

15 And ye were now turned, and had done right in my sight, in [g]proclaiming [d]liberty every man to his neighbour; and ye had made a [h]covenant before me in the [i]house which is called by my name:

16 But ye turned and polluted my name, and [j]caused every man his servant, and every man his handmaid, whom he had set at [d]liberty at their pleasure, to return, and [k]brought them into subjection, to be unto you for servants and for handmaids.

17 Therefore thus saith the LORD; Ye have [l]not hearkened unto me, in proclaiming liberty, every one to his brother, and every man to his neighbour: behold, I proclaim a [l,m]liberty for you, saith the LORD, to the [n]sword, to the pestilence, and to the [o]famine; and I will make you to be [2,p]removed into all the kingdoms of the earth.

18 And I will give the men that have [f]transgressed my covenant, which have [l]not performed the

**11**

*x* *Covetousness,* Isa. 57:17.

*y* *Oppression,* Eccl. 5:8.

**13**

*z* *Covenant, of God, with men,* Deut. 29:1.

*a* *God, providence of,* Gen. 2:2.

*b* *Egypt,* Gen. 41:8.

**14**

*c* *Sabbatic Year,* Lev. 25:2.

*d* *Liberty, in sabbatic year,* Lev. 25:10.

*e* *Hebrew,* Gen. 40:15.

*f* *Disobedience to God,* Eph. 5:6.

**15**

*g* *Emancipation, proclamation of,* Deut. 15:12.

*h* *Covenant, of men with men,* Deut. 29:1.

*i* *Temple, Solomon's,* 1 Kin. 6:17.

**16**

*j* *Covetousness,* Isa. 57:17.

*k* *Oppression,* Eccl. 5:8.

**17**

*l* *Wicked, punishment of,* Psa. 73:3.

*m* *Adversity, dispensation from God,* Psa. 10:6.

*n* *War, as a judgment,* Judg. 3:2.

*o* *Famine, as a judgment,* 2 Kin. 8:1.

*p* *Captivity, as a judgment,* Isa. 5:13.

2 R. V. tossed to and fro among

words of the covenant which
they had made before me, when
they cut the calf in twain[c], and
passed between the parts thereof,
19 The princes of Jū'dah, and
the princes of Jē-ru'sā-lĕm, the
eunuchs, and the priests, and
all the people of the land, which
passed between the parts of the
calf;
20 I will even [l,m]give them into
the hand of their enemies, and
into the hand of them that seek
their life: and their dead bodies
shall be for meat[c] unto the fowls
of the heaven, and to the beasts
of the earth.
21 And [q]Zĕd-e-kī'ah king of
Jū'dah and his princes will I
give into the hand of their enemies, and into the hand of them
that seek their life, and into the
hand of the [r]king of [s]Băb'ȳ-lon's
army, which are gone up from
you.
22 Behold, I will command,
saith the LORD, and cause them
to return to this [t]city; and they
shall fight against it, and take it,
and burn it with fire: and I will
make the cities of [u]Jū'dah a desolation[c] without an inhabitant.

21
q *Zedekiah*, 2 Kin. 25:2.
r *Nebuchadnezzar*, Dan. 2:1.
s *Babylon, empire of*, Ezra 5:12.

22
t *Jerusalem, prophecies against*, Judg. 19:10.
u *Judah, kingdom of, prophecies concerning*, 2 Chr. 11:17.

## CHAPTER 35

*The obedience of the Rechabites commended.*
*12 The disobedience of Judah condemned.*
*18 Blessings promised to the Rechabites.*

THE word which [a]came unto
[b]Jĕr-e-mī'ah from the LORD
in the days of [c]Jē-hoi'a-kĭm the
son of [d]Jō-sī'ah king of Jū'dah,
saying,
2 Go unto the house of the
*Rē'chab-ītes, and speak unto
them, and bring them into the
[e,f]house of the LORD, into one of
the chambers, and give them
[g]wine to drink.
3 Then [b]I took Jā-ăz-a-nī'ah
the son of Jĕr-e-mī'ah, the son
of Hăb-a-zĭ-nī'ah, and his breth-

1
a *Prophets, inspiration of*. Isa. 3:2.
b *Jeremiah*, Jer. 1:1.
c *Jehoiakim*, Jer. 26:1.
d *Josiah*, 1 Kin. 13:2.

2
e *Church*, 1 Kin. 9:3.
f *Temple, Solomon's*, 1 Kin. 6:17.
g *Wine*, Prov. 23:31.

ren, and all his sons, and the
whole house of the *Rē'chab-
ītes;
4 And I brought them into the
[e,f]house of the LORD, into the
chamber of the sons of Hā'nan,
the son of Ĭg-da-lī'ah, a man of
God, which *was* by the chamber
of the princes, which *was* above
the chamber of [h]Mā-a-sē'iah the
son of Shăl'lum, the [i]keeper of
the door:
5 And I set before the sons of
the house of the *Rē'chab-ītes
pots full of [g]wine, and cups, and
I said unto them, Drink ye wine.
6 But they [j]said, [k,l]We will
drink no wine: for [m]Jŏn'a-dăb
the son of [m]Rē'chăb our father
commanded us, saying, Ye shall
drink no wine, *neither* ye, nor
your sons for ever:
7 Neither shall ye build house,
nor sow seed, nor plant vineyard, nor have *any*: but all your
days ye shall dwell in tents; that
ye may live many days in the
land where ye *be* strangers[c].
8 Thus have *we obeyed the
voice of [m]Jŏn'a-dăb the son of
[m]Rē'chăb our father in all that
he hath charged us, to [l]drink no
[g]wine all our days, we, our wives,
our sons, nor our daughters;
9 Nor to build houses for us to
dwell in: neither have we vineyard, nor field, nor seed:
10 But we have dwelt in tents,
and have obeyed, and done according to all that [m]Jŏn'a-dăb
our father commanded us.
11 But it came to pass, when
[n]Nĕb-u-chad-rĕz'zar king of
[o]Băb'ȳ-lon came up into the
land, that we said, Come, and let
us go to Jē-ru'sā-lĕm for fear of
the army of the [p]Chăl-dē'anș,
and for fear of the [q]army of the
[r]Sȳr'ĭ-anș: so we dwell **at** Jē-
ru'sā-lĕm.

4
h Jer. 21:1; 29:25; 37:3.
i *Porters, guards of the temple*, 2 Sam. 18:26.

6
j *Temptation, resistance to*, Luke 11:4.
k *Self-denial*, Mark 8:34.
l *Total Abstinence*, Lev. 10:9.
m Or, *Jehonadab*, 2 Kin. 10:15–23.

11
n Or, *Nebuchadnezzar*, Dan. 2:1.
o *Babylon, empire of*, Ezra 5:12.
p *Chaldeans*, Dan. 1:4.
q *Armies*, Deut. 11:4.
r *Syria*, 2 Kin. 6:23.

* **RECHABITES** (*riders, horsemen*). *A family of Kenites descended from Rechab, through Jehonadab*, 2 Kin. 10:15; 1 Chr. 2:55; Jer. 35:6. *Enjoined by Jehonadab to drink no wine*, Jer. 35:6. *Adhere to the injunction of abstinence*, Jer. 35:16. *Perpetuation of the family promised as a reward of obedience*, Jer. 35:19.

12 ¶ Then came the word of the LORD unto [a,b]Jĕr-e-mī′ah, saying,

13 Thus saith the LORD of hosts, the God of Ĭş′ra-el; Go and tell the men of Jū′dah and the inhabitants of Jĕ-ru̥′sā-lĕm, Will ye not receive [s]instruction to hearken[C] to my words? saith the LORD.

14 The words of [m]Jŏn′a-dăb the son of [m]Rē′chăb, that he commanded his sons not to drink wine, are performed; for unto this day they [l]drink none, but obey their father's commandment: notwithstanding I have [s]spoken unto you, rising early and speaking; but ye [t,u]hearkened not unto me.

15 I have [s]sent also unto you all my servants the prophets, rising up early and sending *them*, saying, [v]Return ye now every man from his evil way, and amend your doings, and [w]go not after other gods to serve them, and [x]ye shall dwell in the [y]land which I have given to you and to your fathers: but ye have [t,u]not inclined your ear, nor hearkened unto me.

16 Because the sons of [m]Jŏn′a-dăb the son of [m]Rē′chăb have performed the commandment of their father, which he commanded them; but this people hath [t,u]not hearkened unto me:

17 Therefore thus saith the LORD God of hosts, the God of Ĭş′ra-el; Behold, [z]I will bring upon [a]Jū′dah and upon all the inhabitants of [b]Jĕ-ru̥′sā-lĕm all the evil that I have pronounced against them: because I have spoken unto them, but they have [c,d]not heard; and I have called unto them, but they have not answered.

18 ¶ And [e]Jĕr-e-mī′ah said unto the house of the *Rē′chab-ītes, Thus saith the LORD of hosts, the God of Ĭş′ra-el; Because ye have obeyed the commandment of [f]Jŏn′a-dăb your father, and kept all his precepts, and done according unto all that he hath commanded you:

19 Therefore thus saith the LORD of hosts, the God of Ĭş′ra-el; [f]Jŏn′a-dăb the son of [f]Rē′chăb shall not want[C] a man to stand before me for ever.

## CHAPTER 36

*The prophecies of Jeremiah written out by Baruch, 5 and by him read to the people. 11 The princes require him to read the roll to them. 20 The king burns the roll, and gives orders to apprehend Baruch and Jeremiah. 27 The punishment of the king and of his servants foretold. 32 Baruch writes a new roll.*

AND it came to pass in the fourth year of [a]Jĕ-hoi′a-kĭm the son of [b]Jō-sī′ah king of Jū′dah, *that* this [c]word came unto [d]Jĕr-e-mī′ah from the LORD, saying,

2 Take thee a roll[G] of a [e]book, and write therein all the [c]words that I have spoken unto thee against Ĭş′ra-el, and against Jū′dah, and against all the nations, from the day I spake unto thee, from the days of [b]Jō-sī′ah, even unto this day.

3 [f]It may be that the house of Jū′dah will hear all the evil which I purpose to do unto them; that they may [g]return every man from his evil way; that I may [h]forgive their iniquity and their sin.

4 Then [d]Jĕr-e-mī′ah called [i]Bā′ru̥ch the son of Nē-rī′ah: and Bā′ru̥ch wrote from the mouth of Jĕr-e-mī′ah all the [c]words of the LORD, which he had spoken unto him, upon a roll of a [e]book.

5 And [d]Jĕr-e-mī′ah commanded [i]Bā′ru̥ch, saying, I *am* shut[C] up; I cannot go into the [j]house of the LORD:

6 Therefore go thou, and read in the roll, which thou hast written from my mouth, the [c]words

13
s *Wicked, warned,* Psa. 73:3.

14
t *Disobedience to God,* Eph. 5:6.
u *Impenitence,* Rom. 2:5.

15
v *Repentance, enjoined,* Mark 1:4.
w *Idolatry, forbidden,* 1 Sam. 15:23.
x *Blessings, contingent upon obedience,* Deut. 11:26.
y *Canaan,* Gen. 37:1.

17
z *Adversity, dispensation from God,* Psa. 10:6.

a *Judah, kingdom of, prophecies concerning,* 2 Chr. 11:17.
b *Jerusalem, prophecies against,* Judg. 19:10.
c *Impenitence,* Rom. 2:5.
d *Disobedience to God,* Eph. 5:6.

18
e *Jeremiah,* Jer. 1:1.

f Or, *Jehonadab,* 2 Kin. 10:15–23

v.1–525 BC

1
a *Jehoiakim,* Jer. 26:1.
b *Josiah,* 1 Kin. 13:2.
c *Prophecies, inspired,* Dan. 9:24.
d *Jeremiah,* Jer. 1:1.

2
e *Book,* Num. 5:23.

3
f *God, mercy of,* Gen. 2:2.
g *Repentance,* Mark 1:4.
h *Sin, forgiveness of,* Rom. 5:12.

4
i Jer. 32:12–16; 43:3–6; 45:1, 2.

5
j *Temple, Solomon's,* 1 Kin. 6:17.

of the LORD in the ears of the people in the [i]LORD's house upon the [k]fasting day: and also thou shalt read them in the ears of all Jū'dah that come out of their cities.

6
*k Fasting*, Zech. 8:19.

7 [l]It may be they will present their supplication before the LORD, and will [g]return every one from his evil way: for great *is* the [l]anger and the fury that the LORD hath pronounced against this people.[s]

7
*l Anger of God*, 2 Kin. 13:3.

8 And [i]Bā'ruch the son of Nĕ-rī'ah did according to all that [d]Jĕr-e-mī'ah the prophet commanded him, reading in the [e]book the [c]words of the LORD in the [i]LORD's house.

9 And it came to pass in the fifth year of [a]Jĕ-hoi'a-kĭm the son of [b]Jō-sī'ah king of Jū'dah, in the ninth [m]month, *that* they proclaimed a [k]fast before the LORD to all the people in Jĕ-ru'-să-lĕm, and to all the people that came from the cities of Jū'dah unto Jĕ-ru'să-lĕm.

9
*m Month (December)*, Ex. 12:2.
**v.9–524 BC**

10 Then read [i]Bā-ruch in the [e]book the words of [d]Jĕr-e-mī'ah in the [i]house of the LORD, in the chamber of Ḡĕm-a-rī'ah the son of [n]Shā'phan the [o]scribe, in the higher [p]court, at the entry of the new gate of the LORD's house, in the ears of all the people.

10
*n Shaphan*, 2 Chr. 34:8.
*o Scribe*, 1 Kin. 4:3.
*p Court, of the temple*, Ex. 38:9.

11 ¶ When Mī-chā'iah the son of Ḡĕm-a-rī'ah, the son of [n]Shā'-phan, had heard out of the [e]book all the [c]words of the LORD,

12 Then he went down into the king's house, into the [o]scribe's chamber: and, lo,[c] all the princes sat there, *even* Ĕ-lĭsh'a-mā the scribe, and Dĕl-a-ī'ah the son of Shĕm-a-ī'ah, and [q]Ĕl'na-thăn the son of [q]Ăch'bôr, and Ḡĕm-a-rī'ah the son of [n]Shā'phan, and Zĕd-e-kī'ah the son of Hăn-a-nī'ah, and all the princes.

12
*q* Jer. 26:22.

13 Then Mī-chā'iah declared unto them all the [c]words that he had heard, when [i]Bā'ruch read the [e]book in the ears of the people.

14 Therefore all the princes sent Jĕ-hū'dī the son of Nĕth-a-nī'ah, the son of Shĕl-e-mī'ah, the son of Cu'shī, unto [i]Bā'ruch, saying, Take in thine hand the roll[c] wherein thou hast read in the ears of the people, and come. So Bā'ruch the son of Nĕ-rī'ah took the roll[c] in his hand, and came unto them.

15 And they said unto him, Sit down now, and read it in our ears. So [i]Bā'ruch read *it* in their ears.

16 Now it came to pass, when they had heard all the [c]words, they [1]were afraid both one and other, and said unto [i]Bā'ruch, We will surely tell the king of all these words.

16
1 R. V. turned in fear one toward another,

17 And they asked [i]Bā'ruch, saying, Tell us now, How didst thou write all these words at his mouth?

18 Then [i]Bā'ruch answered them, He pronounced all these words unto me with his mouth, and I wrote *them* with ink in the [e]book.

19 Then said the princes unto [i]Bā'ruch, Go, hide thee, thou and [d]Jĕr-e-mī'ah; and let no man know where ye be.

20 ¶ And they went in to the [a]king into the court, but they laid up the roll in the chamber of Ĕ-lĭsh'a-mā the scribe, and told all the words in the ears of the king.

21 So the [a]king sent Jĕ-hū'dī to fetch the roll:[c] and he took it out of Ĕ-lĭsh'a-mā the scribe's chamber. And Jĕ-hū'dī read it in the ears of the king, and in the ears of all the princes which stood beside the king.

22 Now the [a]king sat in the [r]winterhouse in the ninth

22
*r Winter*, Gen. 8:22.

[m]month: and *there was a fire*
on the [2]hearth burning before
him.
23 And it came to pass, *that*
when Jĕ-hū′dī had read three or
four leaves,[C] [a,s]he cut it with the
penknife, and cast *it* into the fire
that *was* on the [2]hearth, until all
the roll[C] was consumed in the fire
that *was* on the [2]hearth.
24 Yet they were [t]not afraid,
nor rent[C] their garments, *neither*
the king, nor any of his servants
that heard all these words.[Q]
25 Nevertheless Ĕl′na-thăn and
Dĕl-a-ī′ah and Ğĕm-a-rī′ah
had made intercession to the
king that he would not burn
the roll[C]: but he would not hear
them.
26 But the [a,s]king commanded
Jĕ-räh′me-el the [3]son of Hăm′-
me-lĕch, and Sĕr-a-ī′ah the son
of Ăz′rĭ-el, and Shĕl-e-mī′ah the
son of Ăb′de-el, to [u]take [i]Bā′-
ruch the scribe and [d]Jĕr-e-mī′ah
the prophet: but the [v]LORD hid
them.
27 ¶ Then the word of the LORD
came to [d]Jēr-e-mī′ah, after that
the king had burned the roll,[C]
and the words which [i]Bā′ruch
wrote at the mouth of Jĕr-e-mī′-
ah, saying,
28 Take thee again another roll,[C]
and write in it all the former
words that were in the first roll,[C]
which [a,s]Jĕ-hoi′a-kĭm the king of
Jū′dah hath burned.
29 And thou shalt say to [a,s]Jĕ-
hoi′a-kĭm king of Jū′dah, Thus
saith the LORD; Thou hast
burned this roll,[C] saying, Why
hast thou written therein, saying, The king of [w]Băb′ў-lon shall
certainly come and destroy this
land, and shall cause to cease
from thence man and beast?
30 Therefore thus saith the
LORD of Jĕ-hoi′a-kĭm king of
Jū′dah; [x]He shall have none to
sit upon the throne of Dā′vid:
and his dead body shall be cast
out in the day to the heat, and in
the night to the frost.
31 And I will [x]punish him and
his seed and his servants for their
iniquity; and I will bring upon
them, and upon the inhabitants
of Jĕ-ru′să-lĕm, and upon the
men of Jū′dah, all the evil that I
have pronounced against them;
but they [t]hearkened not.
32 ¶ Then took Jĕr-e-mī′ah
another roll,[C] and gave it to Bā′-
ruch the [o]scribe, the son of Nĕ-
rī′ah; who wrote therein from
the mouth of Jēr-e-mī′ah all the
words of the [e]book which Jĕ-
hoi′a-kĭm king of Jū′dah had
burned in the fire: and there
were added besides unto them
many like words.

## CHAPTER 37

*The prophet's warning slighted. 5 The Chaldeans, through fear of the Egyptians, raise the siege of Jerusalem. 6 The prophet foretells their return and victory. 11 He is imprisoned as a deserter. 16 Zedekiah's kindness to him.*

AND king [a]Zĕd-e-kī′ah the son
of [b]Jŏ-sī′ah reigned instead
of [c]Cŏ-nī′ah the son of [d]Jĕ-hoi′-
a-kĭm, whom [e]Nĕb-u-chad-rĕz′-
zar king of [f]Băb′ў-lon made king
in the land of [g]Jū′dah.
2 But [h]neither he, nor his servants, nor the people of the land,
did hearken[C] unto the [i]words of
the LORD, which he spake by
the prophet [j]Jĕr-e-mī′ah.
3 And [a]Zĕd-e-kī′ah the king
sent [k]Jĕ-hū′cal the son of [l]Shĕl-
e-mī′ah and [m]Zĕph-a-nī′ah the
son of [n]Mā-a-sē′iah the priest to
the prophet [j]Jĕr-e-mī′ah, [o]say-
ing, Pray now unto the LORD
our God for us.
4 Now [j]Jĕr-e-mī′ah came in
and went out among the people:
for they had not put him into
prison.
5 Then [p]Phā′raōh's [q]army was
come forth out of Ē′ġўpt: and
when the [r]Chăl-dē′ans that [s]be-

2 R. V. brasier

23
s *Rulers, wicked,* Ex. 18:21.

24
t *Impenitence, instances of,* Rom. 2:5.

26
u *Persecution, of the righteous,* John 15:20.
v *God, preserver,* Gen. 2:2.
3 R. V. king's son.

29
w *Babylon, empire of,* Ezra 5:12.

30
x *Wicked, punishment of,* Ex. 18:21.

v.1–517 BC
See footnote, *Time,* Rev. 10:6.

1
a *Zedekiah,* 2 Kin. 25:2.
b *Josiah,* 1 Kin. 13:2.
c Or, *Jehoiachin,* 2 Kin. 24:6.
d *Jehoiakim,* Jer. 26:1.
e Or, *Nebuchadnezzar,* Dan. 2:1.
f *Babylon, empire of,* Ezra 5:12.
g *Judah, kingdom of,* 2 Chr. 11:17.

2
h *Impenitence, instances of,* Rom. 2:5.
i *Prophecies, inspired,* Dan. 9:24.
j *Jeremiah,* Jer. 1:1.

3
k Or, *Jucal,* Jer. 38:1.
l Jer. 38:1.
m *Zephaniah,* Jer. 21:1.
n Jer. 21:1; 29:25; 35:4.
o *Intercession, solicited,* Jer. 27:18.

5
p *Pharaoh-hophra,* Jer. 44:30.
q *Egyptians, aid the Israelites against the Chaldeans,* Gen. 50:3.
r *Chaldeans,* Dan. 1:4.
s *Siege,* Deut. 28:53.

sieged [t]Jē-ru̧'sā-lĕm heard tidings of them, they departed from Jē-ru̧'sā-lĕm.

6 ¶ Then [i]came the word of the LORD unto the prophet [j]Jĕr-e-mī'ah, saying,

7 Thus saith the LORD, the God of Ĭs̱'ra-el; Thus shall ye say to the king of Jū'dah, that sent you unto me to enquire of me; Behold, [p]Phā'raōh's [q]army, which is come forth to help you, shall return to Ē'ġy̆pt into their own land.

8 And the [r]Chăl-dē'ans̱ shall come again, and fight against this [u]city, and take it, and [v]burn it with fire.

9 [w]Thus saith the LORD; Deceive not yourselves, saying, The Chăl-dē'ans̱ shall surely depart from us: for they shall not depart.

10 For though ye had smitten the whole army of the [r]Chăl-dē'ans̱ that fight against you, and there remained *but* wounded men among them, *yet* should they rise up every man in his tent, and [v]burn this [u]city with fire.

11 ¶ And it came to pass, that when the army of the [r]Chăl-dē'ans̱ was broken up from [t]Jē-ru̧'sā-lĕm for fear of [p]Phā'raōh's army,

12 Then Jĕr-e-mī'ah went forth out of [t]Jē-ru̧'sā-lĕm to go into the land of [x]Bĕn'ja-mĭn, to [1]separate himself thence in the midst of the people.

13 And when he was in the [y]gate of Bĕn'ja-mĭn, a [z]captain of the ward[C] *was* there, whose name *was* Ī-rī'jah, the son of Shĕl-e-mī'ah, the son of Hăn-a-nī'ah; and he took [a]Jĕr-e-mī'ah the prophet, [b]saying, [c]Thou fallest away to the [d]Chăl-dē'ans̱.

14 Then said [a]Jĕr-e-mī'ah, *It is* false; I [c]fall not away to the Chăl-dē'ans̱. But he hearkened not to him: so Ī-rī'jah [e]took Jĕr-e-mī'ah, and brought him to the princes.

15 Wherefore the [f]princes were wroth[C] with [a]Jĕr-e-mī'ah, and [e,g]smote him, and [g]put him in prison in the house of [h]Jŏn'a-than the scribe: for they had made that the prison.[Q]

16 ¶ When [a]Jĕr-e-mī'ah was [2]entered into the [i]dungeon, and into the cabins[G], and Jĕr-e-mī'ah had remained there many days;

17 Then [j]Zĕd-e-kī'ah the king sent, and took him out: and the king asked him secretly in his house, and said, Is there *any* word from the LORD? And [a,k]Jĕr-e-mī'ah said, There is: for, said he, thou shalt be delivered into the hand of the king of Băb'y̆-lon.

18 Moreover Jĕr-e-mī'ah said unto king Zĕd-e-kī'ah, What have I offended against thee, or against thy servants, or against this people, that ye have put me in prison?

19 Where *are* now your [l]prophets which prophesied unto you, saying, The [m]king of [n]Băb'y̆-lon shall not come against you, nor against this land?

20 Therefore hear now, I pray thee, O my lord the king: let my supplication, I pray thee, be accepted before thee; that thou cause me not to return to the house of [h]Jŏn'a-than the scribe, lest I die there.

21 Then [j]Zĕd-e-kī'ah the king commanded that they should commit [a]Jĕr-e-mī'ah into the [o]court of the [3]prison, and that they should give him daily a piece of bread out of the [p]bakers' street, until all the bread in the city were spent. Thus Jĕr-e-mī'ah remained in the court of the [3]prison.

---

t *Jerusalem*, Judg. 19:10.

8
u *Jerusalem, prophecies against*, Judg. 19:10.
v *War, evils of*, Judg. 3:2.

9
w *Minister, faithful, instances of* Rom. 15:16.

12
x *Benjamin, tribe of*, Num. 1:37.
1 R. V. receive his portion there, in

13
y *Jerusalem, gates of*, Judg. 19:10.
z *Captain*, Num. 31:48.

a *Jeremiah*, Jer. 1:1.
b *False Accusation*, 2 Tim. 3:3.
c *Treason*, 2 Kin. 11:14.
d *Chaldeans*, Dan. 1:4.

14
e *Persecution, of the righteous*, John 15:20.

15
f *Rulers, wicked*, Ex. 18:21.
g *Minister, trials and persecutions of*, Rom. 15:16.
h Jer. 38:26.

16
i *Prison, dungeon in*, Gen. 39:20.
2 R. V. come into the dungeon house, and into the cells,

17
j *Zedekiah*, 2 Kin 25:2.
k *Minister, faithful*, Rom. 15:16

19
l *Prophets, false*, Isa. 3:2.
m *Nebuchadnezzar* Dan. 2:1.
n *Babylon, empire of*, Ezra 5:12.

21
o *Prison, court of*, Gen. 39:20.
p *Jerusalem, streets of*, Judg. 19:10.
3 R. V. guard.

## CHAPTER 38

*The prophet is accused, and cast into a dungeon. 7 At the request of Ebed-melech, he is taken out and confined in the court of the prison. 14 The king's conference with the prophet. 24 He is commanded by the king to conceal it from the princes.*

THEN Shĕph-a-tī'ah the son
of Măt'tan, and Ğĕd-a-
lī'ah the son of Păsh'ŭr, and
[a]Jū'cal the son of [b]Shĕl-e-mī'ah,
and [c]Păsh'ŭr the son of [d]Măl-
chī'ah, heard the words that
[e]Jĕr-e-mī'ah had spoken unto
all the people, saying,
2 Thus saith the LORD, He that
remaineth in this [f]city shall die
by the [g]sword, by the [h]famine,
and by the pestilence: but he
that goeth forth to the [i]Chăl-dē'-
ans shall live; for he shall have
his life for a prey[G], and shall live.
3 Thus saith the LORD, This
[f]city shall surely be given into
the hand of the king of Băb'ȳ-
lon's army, which shall take it.
4 Therefore the princes said
unto the king, We beseech thee,
let this [j]man be [k]put to death:
for thus he weakeneth the hands
of the men of war that remain in
this city, and the hands of all the
people, in speaking such words
unto them: for this man seeketh
not the welfare of this people, but
the hurt[G].
5 Then [l,m]Zĕd-e-kī'ah the king
said, Behold, he *is* in your hand:
for the king *is* not *he that* can do
*any* thing against you.
6 Then took they [e,j]Jĕr-e-mī'-
ah, and [k,n,o]cast him into the
dungeon of Măl-chī'ah the [1]son
of Hăm'me-lĕch, that *was* in the
court of the [2,p]prison: and they
let down Jĕr-e-mī'ah with cords.
And in the dungeon *there was* no
water, but mire: so Jĕr-e-mī'ah
sunk in the mire.[Q]
7 ¶ Now when [q]Ē'bed–mē'lech
the [r]Ē-thĭ-ō'pĭ-an, one of the [s]eu-
nuchs which was in the king's
house, heard that they had put
[e]Jĕr-e-mī'ah in the dungeon; the
king then sitting in the [t,u]gate of
Bĕn'ja-mĭn;
8 [q]Ē'bed–mē'lech went forth out
of the king's house, and spake
to the king, saying,
9 [v]My lord the king, these men
have done evil in all that they
have done to [e]Jĕr-e-mī'ah the
prophet, whom they have [n]cast
into the dungeon; and [o]he is like[G]
to die for hunger in the place
where he is: for *there is* no more
bread in the city.
10 Then the king commanded
[q]Ē'bed–mē'lech the [r]Ē-thĭ-ō'pĭ-
an, saying, Take from hence
thirty men with thee, and [w]take
up Jĕr-e-mī'ah the prophet out
of the dungeon, before he die.
11 So [q]Ē'bed–mē'lech took the
men with him, and went into
the house of the king under the
treasury, and took thence old
cast[G] clouts[G] and old rotten rags,
and let them down by cords into
the dungeon to [e]Jĕr-e-mī'ah.
12 [q]Ē'bed–mē'lech the [r]Ē-thĭ-
ō'pĭ-an [w]said unto [e]Jĕr-e-mī'ah,
Put now *these* old cast clouts[G] and
rotten rags under thine armholes[G]
under the cords. And Jĕr-e-mī'-
ah did so.
13 So [w]they drew up [e]Jĕr-e-
mī'ah with cords, and took him
up out of the dungeon: and
Jĕr-e-mī'ah remained in the
court of the [p]prison.
14 ¶ Then [l]Zĕd-e-kī'ah the king
sent, and took [e]Jĕr-e-mī'ah the
prophet unto him into the third
entry that *is* in the [x]house of the
LORD: and the king said unto
Jĕr-e-mī'ah, I will ask thee a
thing; hide nothing from me.
15 Then [e]Jĕr-e-mī'ah said unto
[l]Zĕd-e-kī'ah, If I declare *it* unto
thee, wilt thou not surely put me
to death ? and if I give thee counsel, wilt thou not hearken unto
me ?
16 So [l]Zĕd-e-kī'ah the king
[y,z]sware secretly unto Jĕr-e-

**1**
a Or, *Jehucal*, Jer. 37:3.
b Jer. 37:3.
c *Pashur*, 1 Chr. 9:12.
d 1 Chr. 9:12; Neh. 11:12; Jer. 21:1.
e *Jeremiah*, Jer. 1:1.

**2**
f *Jerusalem, prophecies against*, Judg. 19:10.
g *War, as a judgment*, Judg. 3:2.
h *Famine, as a judgment*, 2 Kin. 8:1.
i *Chaldeans*, Dan. 1:4.

**4**
j *Minister, trials and persecutions of*, Rom. 15:16.
k *Persecution, of the righteous*, John 15:20.

**5**
l *Zedekiah*, 2 Kin. 25:2.
m *Rulers, wicked*, Ex. 18:21.

**6**
n *Prisoners, cruelty to*, Psa. 79:11.
o *Cruelty, instances of*, Psa. 27:12.
p *Prison, court of*, Gen. 39:20.
1 R. V. king's son,
2 R. V. guard:

**7**
q Jer. 39:16–18.
r *Ethiopia*, Isa. 18:1.
s *Eunuch*, Matt. 19:12.
t *Gates, thrones of kings at*, Deut. 3:5.
u *Jerusalem, gates of*, Judg. 19:10.

**9**
v *Intercession, of man with man*, Jer. 27:18.

**10**
w *Prisoners, kindness to*, Psa. 79:11.

**14**
x *Temple, Solomon's*, 1 Kin. 6:17.

**16**
y *Oath*, Num. 5:19.
z *Covenant, of men with men*, Deut. 29:1.

mī′-ah, saying, *As* the LORD liveth, that [a]made us this soul, I will not put thee to death, neither will I give thee into the hand of these men that [b]seek thy life.

17 Then said [c]Jĕr-e-mī′ah unto [d]Zĕd-e-kī′ah, Thus saith the LORD, the God of hosts, the God of Iş′ra-el; If thou wilt assuredly go forth unto the king of Băb′ȳ-lon's princes, then thy soul shall live, and this [e]city shall not be burned with fire; and thou shalt live, and thine house:

18 But if thou wilt not go forth to the king of Băb′ȳ-lon's princes, then shall this [e]city be given into the hand of the [f]Chăl-dē′anş, and they shall [g]burn it with fire, and thou shalt not escape out of their hand.

19 And [d]Zĕd-e-kī′ah the king said unto [c]Jĕr-e-mī′ah, [h]I am [i]afraid of the [j]Jewş that are fallen to the [f]Chăl-dē′anş, lest they deliver me into their hand, and they mock me.

20 But [c]Jĕr-e-mī′ah said, They shall not deliver *thee.* [k]Obey, I beseech thee, the voice of the LORD, which I speak unto thee: [l]so it shall be well unto thee, and thy soul shall live.

21 But if thou refuse to go forth, this *is* the word that the LORD hath shewed me:

22 And, behold, all the women that are left in the king of Jū′dah's house *shall be* brought forth to the king of Băb′ȳ-lon's princes, and those *women* shall say, Thy friends have set thee on, and have prevailed against thee: thy feet are sunk in the mire, *and* they are turned away back.

23 So they shall bring out all thy wives and thy children to the [f]Chăl-dē′anş: and thou shalt not escape out of their hand, but shalt be taken by the hand of the [m]king of Băb′ȳ-lon: and thou shalt cause this [e]city to be [g]burned with fire.

24 ¶ Then said [d]Zĕd-e-kī′ah unto [c]Jĕr-e-mī′ah, Let no man know of these words, and thou shalt not die.

25 But if the princes hear that I have talked with thee, and they come unto thee, and say unto thee, Declare unto us now what thou hast said unto the king, hide it not from us, and we will not put thee to death; also what the king said unto thee:

26 Then thou shalt say unto them, I presented my supplication before the king, that he would not cause me to return to [n]Jŏn′a-than's house, to die there.

27 Then came all the princes unto [c]Jĕr-e-mī′ah, and asked him: and he told them according to all these words that the king had commanded. So they left off speaking with him; for the matter was not perceived.

28 So [c]Jĕr-e-mī′ah abode in the court of the [3,o]prison until the day that [p]Jē-rų′să-lĕm was taken: [4]and he was *there* when Jē-rų′să-lĕm was taken.

## CHAPTER 39

*Jerusalem is taken.* 4 *Zedekiah, attempting to escape, is captured, and his eyes put out.* 8 *The city is burned,* 9 *and the people carried into captivity.* 11 *Nebuchadnezzar's kindness to Jeremiah.* 15 *God's promise to Ebed-melech.*

IN the ninth year of [a]Zĕd-e-kī′ah king of [b]Jū′dah, in the tenth [c]month, came [d]Nĕb-u-chad-rĕz′zar king of [e]Băb′ȳ-lon and all his army against [f]Jē-rų′să-lĕm, and they [g]besieged it.

2 *And* in the eleventh year of [a]Zĕd-e-kī′ah, in the fourth [h]month, the ninth *day* of the month, [1]the [f]city was broken up.

3 And all the princes of the king of [e]Băb′ȳ-lon came in, and sat in the [i]middle [j]gate, *even* Nĕr′gal–shă-rē′zer, Săm′-

---

a *God, creator,* Gen. 2.2.
b *Malice, instances of,* Eph. 4:31.

17
c *Jeremiah,* Jer. 1:1.
d *Zedekiah,* 2 Kin. 25:2.
e *Jerusalem, prophecies concerning,* Judg. 19:10.

18
f *Chaldeans,* Dan. 1:4.
g *War, evils of,* Judg. 3:2.

19
h *King, influenced by popular opinion,* 2 Kin. 3:10.
i *Cowardice,* Lev. 26:36.
j *Public Opinion,* John 12:42.

20
k *Obedience, enjoined,* Heb. 5:8.
l *Blessings, contingent upon obedience,* Deut. 11:26.

23
m *Nebuchadnezzar, prophecies concerning,* Dan. 2:1.

26
n Jer. 37:15, 20.

28
o *Prison, court of,* Gen. 39:20.
p *Jerusalem, captured and pillaged,* Judg. 19:10.
3 R. V. guard
4 R. V. *ends paragraph at* taken *with period. Then follows a new paragraph:* And it came to pass when Jerusalem was taken *ending the chapter with a comma.*

v.1–509 BC
See footnote, *Time,* Rev. 10:6.

1
a *Zedekiah,* 2 Kin. 25:2.
b *Judah, kingdom of,* 2 Chr. 11:17.
c *Month (January),* Ex. 12:2.
d Or, *Nebuchadnezzar,* Dan. 2:1.
e *Babylon,* Ezra 5:12.
f *Jerusalem, captured and pillaged,* Judg. 19:10.
g *Siege,* Deut. 28:53.

2
h *Month (July),* Ex. 12:2.
1 R. V. a breach was made in the city:)

3
i *Jerusalem, gates of,* Judg. 19:10.
j *Gates, thrones of kings at,* Deut. 3:5.

v.3–507 BC
See footnote, *Time*, Rev. 10:6.

4
k *Jerusalem, walls of*, Judg. 19:10.
2 R. V. Arabah.

5
l *Chaldeans*, Dan. 1:4.
m Jer. 52:8; 2 Kin. 25:5.
n *Riblah*, Num. 34:11.
o Or, *Syria*, 2 Kin. 6:23.

6
p *Captive, cruelty to*, 1 Sam. 30:3.
q *Cruelty, instances of*, Psa. 27:12.

8
r *War, evils of*, Judg. 3:2.

9
s *Nebuzar-adan*, 2 Kin. 25:8.
t *Captain*, Num. 31:48.
u *Captivity*, Isa. 5:13.

10
v *Poor, kindness to*, Prov. 21:13.
w *Vineyard*, Isa. 1:8.

11
x *Jeremiah*, Jer. 1:1.

gär–nē′bō, Sär-sē′chim, Răb′–sa-rĭs, Nēr′gal–shā-rē′zer, Răb′–măg, with all the residue of the princes of the king of Băb′y̆-lon.

4 ¶ And it came to pass, *that* when [a]Zĕd-e-kī′ah the king of [b]Jū′dah saw them, and all the men of war then they fled, and went forth out of the city by night, by the way of the king's garden, by the [i]gate betwixt the two [k]walls: and he went out the way of the [2]plain.

5 But the [l]Chăl-dē′ans′ army pursued after them, and overtook [a]Zĕd-e-kī′ah in the [m]plains of Jĕr′ĭ-chō: and when they had taken him, they brought him up to [d]Nĕb-u-chad-nĕz′zar king of [e]Băb′y̆-lon to [n]Rĭb′lah in the land of [o]Hā′math, where he gave judgment upon him.

6 Then the king of [e]Băb′y̆-lon [p,q]slew the sons of [a]Zĕd-e-kī′ah in [n]Rĭb′lah before his eyes: also the king of Băb′y̆-lon slew all the nobles of Jū′dah.

7 Moreover he [p,q]put out [a]Zĕd-e-kī′ah's eyes, and bound him with chains, to carry him to [e]Băb′y̆-lon.

8 And the [l]Chăl-dē′ans [r]burned the king's house, and the houses of the people, with fire, and brake down the walls of Jē-ru′sā-lĕm.

9 ¶ Then [s]Nĕb′u-zär–ā′dan the [t]captain of the guard [u]carried away captive into [e]Băb′y̆-lon the remnant of the people that remained in the [i]city, and those that fell away, that fell to him, with the rest of the people that remained.

10 But [s]Nĕb′u-zär–ā′dan the [t]captain of the guard left of the [v]poor of the people, which had nothing, in the land of Jū′dah, and gave them [w]vineyards and fields at the same time.

11 ¶ Now [d]Nĕb-u-chad-rĕz′zar king of [e]Băb′y̆-lon gave charge concerning [x]Jĕr-e-mī′ah to [s]Nĕb′u-zär–ā′dan the [t]captain of the guard, saying,

12 [y,z]Take him, and look well to him, and do him no harm; but do unto him even as he shall say unto thee.

13 So [s]Nĕb′u-zär–ā′dan the [t]captain of the guard sent, and Nĕb-u-shăs′ban, Răb′–sa-rĭs, and Nēr′gal–shā-rē′zer, Răb′–măg, and all the king of Băb′y̆-lon's princes;

14 Even they sent, and [y,z]took [a]Jĕr-e-mī′ah out of the court of the [3]prison, and committed him unto [b]Gĕd-a-lī′ah the son of [c]Ā-hī′kam the son of [d]Shā′phan, that he should carry him home: so he dwelt among the people.

15 ¶ Now the [e]word of the LORD [f]came unto [a]Jĕr-e-mī′ah, while he was shut up in the court of the [3]prison, saying,

16 Go and speak to [g]Ē′bed-mē′lech the [h]Ē-thĭ-ō′pĭ-an, saying, Thus saith the LORD of hosts, the God of Iş′ra-el; Behold, I will bring my words upon this [i]city for evil, and not for good; and they shall be *accomplished* in that day before thee.

17 But I will [j]deliver thee in that day, saith the LORD: and thou shalt not be given into the hand of the men of whom thou *art* afraid.

18 For I will surely [j]deliver thee, and thou shalt not fall by the sword, but thy life shall be for a prey unto thee: because thou hast put thy [k]trust in me, saith the LORD.

## CHAPTER 40

*Jeremiah, being let go by Nebuzar-adan, goes to Gedaliah. 7 The dispersed Jews repair unto Gedaliah. 13 He believes not the conspiracy of Ishmael.*

THE word that came to [a]Jĕr-e-mī′ah from the LORD, after that [b]Nĕb′u-zär–ā′dan the [c]captain of the guard had [d]let him go from [e]Rā′mah, when he

12
y *Kindness, instances of*, Acts 28:2.
z *Prisoners, kindness to*, Psa. 79:11.

14
a *Jeremiah*, Jer. 1:1.
b *Gedaliah*, 2 Kin. 25:22.
c *Ahikam*, 2 Kin. 22:12.
d *Shaphan*, 2 Chr. 34:8.
3 R. V. guard,

15
e *Prophecies, inspired*, Dan. 9:24.
f *Prophets, inspiration of*, Isa.3:2.

16
g Jer. 38:7–13.
h *Ethiopia*, Isa. 18:1.
i *Jerusalem, prophecies against*, Judg. 19:10.

17
j *God, providence of*, Gen. 2:2.

18
k *Faith, rewards of*, Mark 11:22.

1
a *Jeremiah*, Jer. 1:1.
b *Nebuzar-adan*, 2 Kin. 25:8.
c *Captain*, Num. 31:48.
d *Captive, kindness to*, 1 Sam. 30:3.
e *Ramah*, Judg. 19:13.

f *Chains*, Dan. 5:7.
g *Babylon*, Ezra 5:12.

3
h *Wicked, punishment of*, Psa. 73:3.

5
i *Gedaliah*, 2 Kin. 25:22.
j *Ahikam*, 2 Kin. 22:12.
k *Shaphan*, 2 Chr. 34:8.
l *Government, provincial*, Isa. 22:21.
1 R. V. present,

6
m *Mizpah*, Josh. 18:26.

had taken him being bound in [f]chains among all that were carried away captive of Jê-ru̧'sā-lĕm and Jū'dah, which were carried away captive unto [g]Băb'ȳ-lon.

2 And the [c]captain of the guard took [a]Jĕr-e-mī'ah, and said unto him, The LORD thy God hath pronounced this evil upon this place.

3 Now the LORD hath brought *it*, and done according as he hath said: because [h]ye have sinned against the LORD, and have not obeyed his voice, therefore this thing is come upon you.

4 And now, behold, [b]I [d]loose [a]thee this day from the [f]chains which *were* upon thine hand. If it seem good unto thee to come with me into [g]Băb'ȳ-lon, come; and I will look well unto thee: but if it seem ill unto thee to come with me into Băb'ȳ-lon, forbear: behold, all the land *is* before thee: whither it seemeth good and convenient for thee to go, thither go.

5 Now while he was not yet gone back, [b]*he* [d]*said*, Go back also to [i]Gĕd-a-lī'ah the son of [j]Ā-hī'kam the son of [k]Shā'phan, whom the king of Băb'ȳ-lon hath made [l]governor over the cities of Jū'dah, and dwell with him among the people: or go wheresoever it seemeth convenient unto thee to go. So the [c]captain of the guard gave him victuals and a [1]reward, and let him go.

6 Then went [a]Jĕr-e-mī'ah unto [i]Gĕd-a-lī'ah the son of [j]Ā-hī'kam to [m]Mĭz'pah; and dwelt with him among the people that were left in the land.

7 ¶ Now when all the [c]captains of the forces which *were* in the fields, *even* they and their men, heard that the king of [g]Băb'ȳ-lon had made [i]Gĕd-a-lī'ah the son of [j]Ā-hī'kam [l]governor in the land, and had committed unto him men, and women, and children, and of the [n]poor of the land, of them that were not carried away captive to Băb'ȳ-lon;

8 Then they came to [i]Gĕd-a-lī'ah to [m]Mĭz'pah, even *Ĭsh'-ma-el the son of [o]Nĕth-a-nī'ah, and [p]Jō-hā'nan and Jŏn'a-than the sons of †Kā-rē'ah, and [o]Sĕr-a-ī'ah the son of [o]Tăn'hu-mĕth, and the sons of Ē'phāi the Nĕ-tŏph'a-thīte, and [q]Jĕz-a-nī'ah the son of a Mā-ăch'a-thīte, they and their men.

9 And [i]Gĕd-a-lī'ah the son of [j]Ā-hī'kam the son of [k]Shā'phan [r,s]sware unto them and to their men, saying, Fear not to serve the [t]Chăl-dē'ans: dwell in the land, and serve the king of Băb'ȳ-lon, and it shall be well with you.

10 As for me, behold, I will dwell at [m]Mĭz'pah, to serve the [t]Chăl-dē'ans, which will come unto us: but ye, gather ye [u]wine, and [v]summer fruits, and [w]oil, and put *them* in your vessels, and dwell in your cities that ye have taken.

11 Likewise when all the Jews that *were* in [x]Mō'ab, and among the [y]Ăm'mon-ītes, and in [z]Ē'-dom, and that *were* in all the countries, heard that the king of Băb'ȳ-lon had left a remnant of Jū'dah, and that he had set over them [a]Gĕd-a-lī'ah the son of Ā-hī'kam the son of Shā'phan;

12 Even all the Jews returned out of all places whither they were driven, and came to the land of Jū'dah, to [a]Gĕd-a-lī'ah, unto [b]Mĭz'pah, and gathered wine and summer fruits very much.

13 ¶ Moreover [c]Jō-hā'nan the son of †Kā-rē'ah, and all the

7
n *Poor, kindness to*, Prov. 21:13.

8
o 2 Kin. 25:23.
p *Johanan*, 2 Kin. 25:23.
q Jer. 42:1; or, *Jaazaniah*, 2 Kin. 25:23.

9
r *Oath*, Num. 5:19.
s *Covenant, of men with men*, Deut. 29:1.
t *Chaldeans*, Dan. 1:4.

10
u *Wine*, Prov. 23:31.
v *Summer, fruits of*, Isa. 28:4.
w *Oil*, Deut. 12:17.

11
x *Moab*, Num. 26:3.
y *Ammonites*, Deut. 2:20.
z *Edom*, Obad. 1.

a *Gedaliah*, 2 Kin. 25:22.

12
b *Mizpah*, Josh. 18:26.

13
c *Johanan*, 2 Kin. 25:23.

* **ISHMAEL**, a son of Nethaniah. *Assassinates Gedaliah; defeated by Johanan*, 2 Kin. 25:23–25; Jer. 40:8–16; 41:1–18.

† **KAREAH**, called also CAREAH. *Father of Johanan*, 2 Kin. 25:23; Jer. 40:8, 13; 41:11, 13, 14, 16; 43:2, 4, 5.

[d,e]captains of the forces that *were* in the fields, came to [a]Gĕd-a-lī'ah to [b]Mĭz'pah,

14 And said unto him, Dost thou certainly know that Bā-alis the king of the [f]Ăm'mon-ītes hath sent *Ĭsh'ma-el the son of [g]Nĕth-a-nī'ah to slay thee? But [a]Gĕd-a-lī'ah the son of Ȧ-hī'kam believed them not.

15 Then [c]Jō-hā'nan the son of †Kā-rē'ah spake to [a]Gĕd-a-lī'ah in [b]Mĭz'pah secretly, saying, Let me go, I pray thee, and I will slay *Ĭsh'ma-el the son of [g]Nĕth-a-nī'ah, and no man shall know *it*: wherefore[G] should he slay thee, that all the Jews̤ which are gathered unto thee should be scattered, and the remnant in Jū'dah perish?

16 But [a]Gĕd-a-lī'ah the son of Ȧ-hī'kam said unto [c]Jō-hā'nan the son of †Kā-rē'ah, Thou shalt not do this thing: for thou speakest falsely of *Ĭsh'ma-el.

## CHAPTER 41

*Ishmael treacherously kills Gedaliah and others. 10 He flees with captives to the Ammonites. 11 Johanan recovers the captives, and with them departs toward Egypt.*

NOW it came to pass in the seventh [a]month, *that* [b]Ĭsh'ma-el the son of [c]Nĕth-a-nī'ah the son of [c]Ē-lĭsh'a-mȧ, of the seed royal, and [1]the princes of the king, even ten men with him, came unto [d]Gĕd-a-lī'ah the son of [e]Ȧ-hī'kam to [f]Mĭz'pah; and there they did eat bread together in Mĭz'pah.

2 Then arose [b]Ĭsh'ma-el the son of [c]Nĕth-a-nī'ah, and the ten men that were with him, and [g]smote [d]Gĕd-a-lī'ah the son of [e]Ȧ-hī'kam the son of [h]Shā'phan with the sword, and [g]slew him, whom the king of [i]Băb'ȳ-lon had made [j]governor over the land.

3 [b]Ĭsh'ma-el also [g]slew all the Jews̤ that were with him, *even* with [d]Gĕd-a-lī'ah, at [f]Mĭz'pah, and the [k]Chăl-dē'ans̤ that were found there, *and* the men of war.

4 And it came to pass the second day after [b]he had slain [d]Gĕd-a-lī'ah, and no man knew *it*,

5 That there came certain from [l]Shē'chem, from [m]Shī'lōh, and from [n]Sā-mā'rĭ-ȧ, *even* fourscore men, having their [o]beards shaven, and their clothes [p]rent,[G] and having cut themselves, with offerings and [q]incense in their hand, to bring *them* to the [r]house of the LORD.

6 And [b]Ĭsh'ma-el the son of [c]Nĕth-a-nī'ah went forth from [f]Mĭz'pah to meet them, [s]weeping all along as he went: and it came to pass, as he met them, he said unto them, Come to [d]Gĕd-a-lī'ah the son of [e]Ȧ-hī'kam.

7 And it was *so*, when they came into the midst of the city, that [b]Ĭsh'ma-el the son of [c]Nĕth-a-nī'ah [g]slew them, *and cast them* into the midst of the pit, he, and the men that *were* with him.

8 But ten men were found among them that said unto [b]Ĭsh'ma-el, Slay us not: for we have treasures in the field, of [t]wheat, and of [u]barley, and of [v]oil, and of [w]honey. So he forbare, and slew them not among their brethren.

9 Now the pit[G] wherein [b]Ĭsh'ma-el had cast all the dead bodies of the men, whom he had slain because of [d]Gĕd-a-lī'ah, *was* it which [x]Ā'sȧ the king had made for fear of [y]Bā'a-shȧ king of Ĭs̤'ra-el: *and* Ĭsh'ma-el the son of Nĕth-a-nī'ah filled it with *them that were* slain.

10 Then Ĭsh'ma-el carried away captive all the residue[G] of the people that *were* in Mĭz'pah, *even* the king's daughters, and all the people that remained in Mĭz'pah, whom [z]Nĕb'u-zär–ā'dan the [a]captain of the guard

d *Captain*, Num. 31:48.
e *Armies, how officered*, Deut. 11:4.

14

f *Ammonites, kings of*, Deut. 2:20.
g 2 Kin. 25:23, 25.

v.1–507 BC

1

a *Month (October)*, Ex. 12:2.
b *Ishmael*, Jer. 40:8.
c 2 Kin. 25:25.
d *Gedaliah*, 2 Kin. 25:22.
e *Ahikam*, 2 Kin. 22:12.
f *Mizpah*, Josh. 18:26.
1 R. V. one of the chief officers of the king, and ten

2

g *Homicide, instances of felonious*, Deut. 5:17.
h *Shaphan*, 2 Chr. 34:8.
i *Babylon, empire of*, Ezra 5:12.
j *Government, provincial*, Isa. 22:21.

3

k *Chaldeans*, Dan. 1:4.

5

l *Shechem*, Josh. 20:7.
m *Shiloh*, Judg. 21:12.
n *Samaria*, 1 Kin. 16:24.
o *Beard, cut, as a sign of mourning*, 1 Sam. 21:13.
p *Rending of Garments*, 2 Chr. 34:27.
q *Incense*, Ex. 37:29.
r *Temple, Solomon's*, 1 Kin. 6:17.

6

s *Hypocrisy, instances of*, Jas. 3:17.

8

t *Wheat*, Ezra 6:9.
u *Barley*, Ex. 9:31.
v *Oil*, Deut. 12:17.
w *Honey*, Prov. 25:27.

9

x *Asa*, 1 Kin. 15:8.
y *Baasha*, 1 Kin. 15:16.

10

z *Nebuzar-adan*, 2 Kin. 25:8.

a *Captain*, Num. 31:48.

had committed to [b]Gĕd-a-lī′ah the son of [c]Ă-hī′kam: and [d]Ĭsh′-ma-el the son of [e]Nĕth-a-nī′ah carried them away captive, and departed to go over to the [f]Ăm′-mon-ītes.

11 ¶ But when [g]Jō-hā′nan the son of [h]Kā-rē′ah, and all the [a]captains of the [i]forces that *were* with him, heard of all the evil that [d]Ĭsh′ma-el the son of [e]Nĕth-a-nī′ah had done,

12 Then they took all the men, and went to fight with [d]Ĭsh′ma-el the son of [e]Nĕth-a-nī′ah, and found him by the great waters that *are* in *Gĭb′e-on.

13 Now it came to pass, *that* when all the people which *were* with [d]Ĭsh′ma-el saw [g]Jō-hā′nan the son of [h]Kā-rē′ah, and all the [a]captains of the [i]forces that *were* with him, then they were glad.

14 So all the people that [d]Ĭsh′-ma-el had carried away captive from [j]Mĭz′pah cast about and returned, and went unto [g]Jō-hā′nan the son of [h]Kā-rē′ah.

15 But [d]Ĭsh′ma-el the son of [e]Nĕth-a-nī′ah escaped from [g]Jō-hā′nan with eight men, and went to the [f]Ăm′mon-ītes.

16 Then took [g]Jō-hā′nan the son of [h]Kā-rē′ah, and all the [a]captains of the forces that *were* with him, all the remnant of the people whom he had recovered from [d]Ĭsh′ma-el the son of [e]Nĕth-a-nī′ah, from [j]Mĭz′pah, after *that* he had slain [b]Gĕd-a-lī′ah the son of [c]Ă-hī′kam, *even* mighty men of war, and the women, and the children, and the eunuchs, whom he had brought again from *Gĭb′e-on:

17 And they departed, and dwelt in the habitation of [k]Chĭm′hăm, which is by [l]Bĕth′-lĕ-hĕm, to go to enter into [m]Ē′-gȳpt,

18 Because of the [n]Chăl-dē′ans: for they were afraid of them, because [d]Ĭsh′ma-el the son of [e]Nĕth-a-nī′ah had slain [b]Gĕd-a-lī′ah the son of [c]Ă-hī′kam, whom the king of Băb′ȳ-lon made [o]governor in the land.

## CHAPTER 42

*Johanan desires Jeremiah to inquire of God, and promises obedience to his will.* 7 *The prophet assures him of safety in Judea;* 13 *and warns him against going into Egypt.* 19 *He reproves the hypocrisy of the people.*

THEN all the [a]captains of the [b]forces, and [c]Jō-hā′nan the son of [d]Kā-rē′ah, and [e]Jĕz-a-nī′-ah the son of [f]Hŏsh-a-ī′ah, and all the people from the least even unto the greatest, came near,

2 And said unto [g]Jĕr-e-mī′ah the prophet, Let, we beseech thee, our supplication be accepted before thee, and [h,i]pray for us unto the LORD thy God, *even* for all this remnant; (for we are left *but* a few of many, as thine eyes do behold us:)

3 [j]That the LORD thy God may shew [k]us the way wherein we may walk, and the thing that we may do.

4 Then [g]Jĕr-e-mī′ah the prophet said unto them, I have heard *you*; behold, I will [h]pray unto the LORD your God according to your words; and it shall come to pass, *that* [l]whatsoever thing the LORD shall answer you, I will declare *it* unto you; I will keep nothing back from you.

5 Then they said to [g]Jĕr-e-mī′-ah, [m]The LORD be a true and faithful witness between us, if we do not even according to all [1]things for the which the LORD thy God shall send thee to us.

b *Gedaliah*, 2 Kin. 25:22.
c *Ahikam*, 2 Kin. 22:12.
d *Ishmael*, Jer. 40:8.
e 2 Kin. 25:23, 25.
f *Ammonites*, Deut. 2:20.

11
g *Johanan*, 2 Kin. 25:23.
h *Kareah*, Jer. 40:8.
i *Armies, how officered*, Deut. 11:4.

14
j *Mizpah*, Josh. 18:26.

17
k 2 Sam. 19:37, 38, 40.
l *Bethlehem*, Gen. 48:7.

m *Egypt*, Gen. 41:8.

18
n *Chaldeans*, Dan. 1:4.
o *Government, provincial*, Isa. 22:21.

1
a *Captain*, Num. 31:48.
b *Armies, how officered*, Deut. 11:4.
c *Johanan*, 2 Kin. 25:23.
d *Kareah*, Jer. 40:8.
e Jer. 40:8; or, *Jaazaniah*, 2 Kin. 25:23.
f Jer. 43:2.

2
g *Jeremiah*, Jer. 1:1.
h *Prayer, intercessory*, Acts 6:4.
i *Intercession, solicited*, Jer. 27:18.

3
j *Spiritual Desire*, Psa. 42:1.
k *Seekers*, Isa. 55:6.

4
l *Prophets, inspiration of*, Isa. 3:2.

5
m *Oath, Israelites confirm covenants by*, Num. 5:19.
1 Am. R. V. the word wherewith Jehovah thy God shall

***GIBEON.** *A city of the Hivites*, Josh. 9:3, 17; 2 Sam. 21:2. *The people of, adroitly draw Joshua into a treaty*, Josh. 9; *made slaves by the Israelites, when their sharp practice was discovered*, Josh. 9:27. *The sun stands still over, during Joshua's battle with the five confederated kings*, Josh. 10:12–14. *Allotted to Benjamin*, Josh. 18:25. *Assigned to the Aaronites*, Josh. 21:17. *The tabernacle located at*, 1 Kin. 3:4; 1 Chr. 16:39; 21:29; 2 Chr. 1:2, 3, 13. *Smitten by David*, 1 Chr. 14:16. *Seven sons of Saul slain at, to avenge the inhabitants of*, 2 Sam. 21:1–9. *Solomon worships at, and offers sacrifices*, 1 Kin. 3:4. *God appears to Solomon in dreams at*, 1 Kin. 3:5; 9:2. *Abner slays Asahel at*, 2 Sam. 3:30. *Ishmael, the son of Nethaniah, defeated at, by Johanan*, Jer. 41:11–16. *Pool of*, 2 Sam. 2:13; Jer. 41:12.

6 Whether *it be* good, or whether
er *it be* evil, we will [n]obey the
voice of the LORD our God, [i]to
whom we send thee; [o]that it may
be well with us, when we obey
the voice of the LORD our God.
7 ¶ And it came to pass [p]after
ten days, that [q]the word of the
LORD [l]came unto Jĕr-e-mī'ah.
8 Then called he [c]Jō-hā'nan
the son of [d]Kă-rē'ah, and all the
[a]captains of the [b]forces which
*were* with him, and all the people
ple from the least even to the
greatest,
9 And said unto them, Thus
saith the LORD, the God of Ĭṣ'-
ra-el, unto whom ye sent me to
present your supplication before
him;
10 [o]If ye will still abide in this
land, then will I [r]build you, and
not pull *you* down, and I will
plant you, and not pluck *you* up:
for I [s]repent me of the evil that I
have done unto you.
11 [t]Be not afraid of the [u]king
of [v]Băb'y̆-lon, of whom ye are
afraid; be not afraid of him, saith
the LORD: for I *am* with you to
[w]save you, and to deliver you
from his hand.
12 And I will shew [x]mercies
unto you, that he may have
mercy upon you, and cause you
to return to your own land.
13 But [o]if ye say, We will not
dwell in this land, neither obey
the voice of the LORD your God,
14 Saying, No; but we will go
into the land of [y]Ē'ġy̆pt, where
we shall see no war, nor hear the
sound of the [z]trumpet, nor have
hunger of bread; and there will
we dwell:
15 And now therefore hear the
word of the LORD, ye remnant of
Jū'dah; Thus saith the LORD of
hosts, the God of Ĭṣ'ra-el; If ye
wholly set your faces to enter
into [y]Ē'ġy̆pt, and go to sojourn
there;

6
*n Obedience*, Heb. 5:8.
*o Blessings, contingent upon obedience*, Deut. 11:26.

7
*p Prayer, answer to, delayed*, Acts 6:4.
*q Intercession, of man with God, answered*, Jer. 27:18.

10
*r Temporal Blessings, from God*, Psa. 103:2.
*s Repentance, attributed to God*, Mark 1:4.

11
*t Courage, enjoined*, Deut. 31:7.
*u Nebuchadnezzar*, Dan. 2:1.
*v Babylon*, Ezra 5:12.
*w God, preserver*, Gen. 2:2.

12
*x God, mercy of*, Gen. 2:2.

14
*y Egypt*, Gen. 41:8.
*z Trumpet, used in war*, Josh. 6:4.

16 Then [a]it shall come to pass,
*that* the [b]sword, which ye feared,
shall overtake you there in the
land of [c]Ē'ġy̆pt, and the [d]famine,
whereof ye were afraid, shall follow
low close after you there in Ē'-
ġy̆pt; and there ye shall die.
17 [a]So shall it be with all the
men that set their faces to go into
[c]Ē'ġy̆pt to sojourn there; they
shall die by the [b]sword, by the
[d]famine, and by the [e]pestilence:
and none of them shall remain
or escape from the evil that I
will bring upon them.
18 For thus saith the LORD of
hosts, the God of Ĭṣ'ra-el; As
mine [f]anger and my fury hath
been poured forth upon the inhabitants
habitants of Jē-ru̥'sā-lĕm; [a]so
shall my fury be poured forth
upon you, when ye shall enter
into [c]Ē'ġy̆pt: and ye shall be an
execration, and an astonishment,[G]
and a curse, and a reproach;
and ye shall see this place no
more.[S]
19 ¶ The LORD hath said concerning
cerning you, O ye remnant of
Jū'dah; Go ye not into [c]Ē'ġy̆pt:
know certainly that [g]I have admonished
monished you this day.
20 For ye [2,h]dissembled[G] in your
hearts, when ye sent me unto the
LORD your God, saying, Pray
for us unto the LORD our God;
and according unto all that the
LORD our God shall say, so
declare unto us, and we will
do *it*.
21 And *now* [g]I have this day
declared *it* to you; but ye have
[i]not obeyed the voice of the
LORD your God, nor any *thing*
for the which he hath sent me
unto you.
22 Now therefore know certainly
tainly that [a]ye shall die by the
[b]sword, by the [d]famine, and by
the [e]pestilence, in the place
whither ye desire to go *and* to
sojourn.

16
*a Jews, prophecies concerning*, Neh. 4:2.
*b War, as a judgment*, Judg. 3:2.
*c Egypt*, Gen. 41:8.
*d Famine, as a judgment*, 2 Kin. 8:1.

17
*e Plague, as a judgment*, Ex. 11:1.

18
*f Anger of God*, 2 Kin. 13:3.

19
*g Minister, faithful*, Rom. 15:16.

20
*h Hypocrisy*, Jas. 3:17.
2 R. V. have dealt deceitfully against your own souls; for ye

21
*i Disobedience to God*, Eph. 5:6.

## CHAPTER 43

*Johanan, discrediting Jeremiah's prophecy, carries him and others into Egypt. 8 The prophet foretells by a type the conquest of Egypt by the Babylonians.*

AND it came to pass, *that* when
[a]Jĕr-e-mī′ah had made an
end of speaking unto all the [b]peo-
ple all the words of the LORD
their God, for which the LORD
their God had sent him to them,
*even* all these words,
2 Then spake Ăz-a-rī′ah the
son of [c]Hŏsh-a-ī′ah, and [d]Jō-
hā′nan the son of [e]Kā-rē′ah, and
all the proud men, [f]saying unto Jĕr-e-mī′ah, Thou speakest
falsely: the LORD our God hath
not sent thee to say, Go not into
[g]Ē′ġy̆pt to sojourn there:
3 But [h]Bā′ruch the son of Nē-
rī′ah setteth thee on against us,
for to deliver us into the hand of
the [i]Chăl-dē′anṣ, that they might
put us to death, and carry us
away captives into [i]Băb′y̆-lon.
4 So [d]Jō-hā′nan the son of
[e]Kā-rē′ah, and all the [k]captains
of the forces, and all the people,
[l]obeyed not the voice of the
LORD, to dwell in the land of
Jū′dah.
5 But [d]Jō-hā′nan the son of
[e]Kā-rē′ah, and all the [k]captains
of the forces, took all the remnant of Jū′dah, that were returned from all nations, whither
they had been driven, to dwell in
the land of Jū′dah;
6 *Even* men, and women, and
children, and the king's daughters, and every person that
[m]Nĕb′u-zär-ā′dan the captain of
the guard had left with [n]Ġĕd-a-
lī′ah the son of [o]Ā-hī′kam the
son of [p]Shā′phan, and [a]Jĕr-e-
mī′ah the prophet, and [h]Bā′ruch
the son of Nē-rī′ah.
7 So they came into the land of
[g]Ē′ġy̆pt: for they [l]obeyed not the
voice of the LORD: thus came
they *even* to [q]Täh′pan-hēṣ.
8 ¶ [r]Then came the [s]word of
the LORD unto [a]Jĕr-e-mī′ah in
[q]Täh′pan-hēṣ, saying,
9 [s,t]Take great stones in thine
hand, and [u]hide them in the clay
in the brickkiln, which *is* at the
entry[C] of Phā′raōh's house in
[q]Täh′pan-hēṣ, in the sight of the
men of Jū′dah;
10 And say unto them, [s]Thus
saith the LORD of hosts, the God
of Ĭṣ′ra-el; Behold, I will send
and take [v]Nĕb-u-chad-rĕz′zar
the king of [i]Băb′y̆-lon, my servant, and will set his throne upon
these stones that I have hid; and
he shall spread his royal pavilion
over them.
11 And when he cometh, he
shall smite the land of [r]Ē′ġy̆pt,
*and deliver* such *as are* for death
to death; and such *as are* for
captivity to captivity; and such
*as are* for the sword to the sword.[Q]
12 And I will kindle a fire in the
houses of the gods of [r]Ē′ġy̆pt;
and he shall burn them, and
carry them away captives: and
he shall array himself with the
land of Ē′ġy̆pt, as a shepherd
putteth on his garment; and he
shall go forth from thence in
peace.
13 He shall break also the [1]im-
ages[C] of Bĕth-shē′mesh, that *is*
in the land of Ē′ġy̆pt; and the
houses of the [w]gods of the Ē-ġy̆p′-
tianṣ shall he burn with fire.

## CHAPTER 44

*Jeremiah rebukes the Jews in Egypt for their idolatry, 11 and foretells their destruction. 15 The Jews attempt to justify themselves. 20 The prophet's reply. 29 A sign that God will punish them.*

THE [a]word that came to [b]Jĕr-
e-mī′ah concerning all the
[c]Jews which dwell in the land
of [d]Ē′ġy̆pt, which dwell at [e]Mĭg′-
dol, and at [f]Täh′pan-hēṣ, and
at [g]Nōph, and in the country of
[h]Păth′ros, saying,[T]
2 Thus saith the LORD of hosts,
the God of Ĭṣ′ra-el; Ye have seen
all the [i]evil that I have brought

1
a *Jeremiah*, Jer. 1:1.
b *Jews, prophecies concerning*, Neh. 4:2.

2
c Jer. 42:1.
d *Johanan*, 2 Kin. 25:23.
e *Kareah*, Jer. 40:8.
f *Minister, trials and persecutions of*, Rom. 15:16.
g *Egypt*, Gen. 41:8.

3
h Jer. 32:12–16; 36:4–32; 45:1, 2.
i *Chaldeans*, Dan. 1:4.
*Babylon*, Ezra 5:12.

4
k *Armies, how officered*, Deut. 11:4.
l *Disobedience to God*, Eph. 5:6.

6
m *Nebuzar-adan*, 2 Kin. 25:8.
n *Gedaliah*, 2 Kin. 25:22.
o *Ahikam*, 2 Kin. 22:12.
p *Shaphan*, 2 Chr. 34:8.

7
q Or, *Tahapanes*, Jer. 2:16.

8
r *Egypt, prophecies against*, vs. 8–13; Gen. 41:8.
s *Prophecies, exemplified in pantomime*, Dan. 9:24.

9
t *Instruction, by object lessons*, Prov. 23:23.
u *Pantomime*, Isa. 20:2.

10
v Or, *Nebuchadnezzar, prophecies concerning*, Dan. 2:1.

13
w *Idolatry*, 1 Sam. 15:23.
1 R. V. pillars

B.C. 587?
See footnote, *Time*, Rev. 10:6.

1
a *Prophecies, inspired*, Dan. 9:24.
b *Jeremiah*, Jer. 1:1.
c *Jews, prophecies concerning*, Neh. 4:2.
d *Egypt*, Gen. 41:8.
e Jer. 46:14.
f Or, *Tahapanes*, Jer. 2:16.
g *Noph, prophecy against Jews in*, Isa. 19:13.
h *Pathros, Jewish captives in*, Isa. 11:11.

2
i *Sin, punishment of*, Rom. 5:12.

upon Jē-ru̇'sā-lĕm, and upon all the cities of Jū'dah; and, behold, this day they *are* a desolation,[G] and no man dwelleth therein.

3 Because of their [j]wickedness which they have committed to provoke me to [k]anger, in that they went to [l]burn [m]incense, *and* to serve other gods, whom they knew not, *neither* they, ye, nor your fathers.

4 Howbeit [n]I [o]sent unto you all my servants the [p]prophets, rising early and sending *them*, saying, Oh, do not this [q]abominable thing that I [r]hate.

5 But they [s,t]hearkened not, nor inclined their ear to turn from their wickedness, to burn no incense unto other gods.

6 Wherefore my [k]fury and mine anger was poured forth, and was kindled in the cities of Jū'dah and in the streets of [u]Jē-ru̇'sā-lĕm; and [v]they are wasted *and* desolate, as at this day.[S]

7 Therefore now thus saith the LORD, the God of hosts, the God of Is̩'ra-el; Wherefore[G] commit ye *this* great evil against your souls, [w]to cut off from you man and woman, child and suckling, out of Jū'dah, to leave you none to remain;

8 In that ye provoke me unto [k]wrath with the works of your hands, [l]burning [m]incense unto other gods in the land of [d]Ē'ġy̆pt, whither ye be gone to dwell, that ye might cut yourselves off, and that ye might be a curse and a reproach among all the nations of the earth?

9 Have ye forgotten the [j]wickedness of your fathers, and the wickedness of the [x]kings of Jū'dah, and the wickedness of their [y]wives, and your own wickedness, and the wickedness of your wives, which they have committed in the land of Jū'dah, and in the streets of [u]Jē-ru̇'sā-lĕm?

10 They are [s,t]not humbled *even* unto this day, neither have they feared, nor walked in my [z]law, nor in my statutes, that I set before you and before your fathers.

11 ¶ Therefore thus saith the LORD of hosts, the God of Is̩'ra-el; Behold, [a,b]I will set my face against you for evil, and to cut off all Jū'dah.

12 And I will take the remnant of Jū'dah, that have set their faces to go into the land of [c]Ē'ġy̆pt to sojourn there, and [a,b]they shall all be consumed, *and* fall in the land of Ē'ġy̆pt; they shall *even* be consumed by the [d]sword *and* by the [e]famine: they shall die, from the least even unto the greatest, by the sword and by the famine: and they shall be an execration, *and* an astonishment,[G] and a curse, and a reproach.

13 For I will [a]punish [b]them that dwell in the land of [c]Ē'ġy̆pt, as I have punished Jē-ru̇'sā-lĕm, by the [d]sword, by the [e]famine, and by the [f]pestilence:

14 So that none of the remnant of Jū'dah, which are gone into the land of [c]Ē'ġy̆pt to sojourn there, shall escape or remain, that they should return into the land of Jū'dah, to the which they have a desire to return to dwell there: for none shall return but such as shall escape.

15 ¶ Then all the men which knew that their [g]wives had [h]burned [i]incense unto other gods, and all the women that stood by, a great multitude, even all the people that dwelt in the land of [c]Ē'ġy̆pt, in [j]Păth'ros, answered [k]Jĕr-e-mī'ah, saying,[T]

16 *As for* the word that thou hast spoken unto us in the name of the LORD, we [l,m]will not hearken unto thee.

17 But we [l,m]will certainly do whatsoever thing goeth forth out of our own mouth, to [h]burn [i]in-

3
j *Jews, wickedness of,* Neh. 4:2.
k *Anger of God,* 2 Kin. 13:3.
l *Idolatry, customs of,* 1 Sam. 15:23.
m *Incense, offered in idolatrous worship,* Ex. 37:29.

4
n *God, longsuffering of,* Gen. 2:2.
o *Wicked, warned,* Psa. 73:3.
p *Prophets,* Isa. 3:2.
q *Sin, repugnant to God,* Rom. 5:12.
r *Hatred, of God, against iniquity,* Prov. 15:17.

5
s *Impenitence,* Rom. 2:5.
t *Obduracy,* Prov. 29:1.

6
u *Jerusalem,* Judg. 19:10.
v *Nation, punishment of,* Isa. 2:4.

7
w *Sin, consequences of,* Rom. 5:12.

9
x *Rulers, wicked,* Ex. 18:21.
y *Women, wicked,* Prov. 31:10.

10
z *Law, of Moses,* Deut. 33:2.

11
a *Wicked, punishment of,* Psa. 73:3.
b *Jews, prophecies concerning,* vs. 11–14; Neh. 4:2.

12
c *Egypt,* Gen. 41:8.
d *War, as a judgment,* Judg. 3:2.
e *Famine, as a judgment,* 2 Kin. 8:1.

13
f *Plague, as a judgment,* Ex. 11:1.

15
g *Women, wicked,* Prov. 31:10.
h *Idolatry, customs of,* 1 Sam. 15:23.
i *Incense, offered in idolatrous worship,* Ex. 37:29.
j *Pathros,* Isa. 11:11.
k *Jeremiah,* Jer. 1:1.

16
l *Self-will,* Gen. 49:6.
m *Obduracy,* Prov. 29:1.

17
n *Moon, worshiped,* Song 6:10.
o *Delusion,* 2 Thess. 2:11.

18
p *God, providence of, mysterious and misinterpreted,* Gen. 2:2.

19
1 R. V. husbands?

21
q *Rulers, wicked,* Ex. 18:21.

22
r *Sin, repugnant to God,* Rom. 5:12.
s *Jews, wickedness of,* Neh. 4:2.

23
*Disobedience to God,* Eph. 5:6.

cense unto the [n]queen of heaven,
and to pour out drink offerings
unto her, as we have done, we,
and our fathers, our kings, and
our princes, in the cities of Jū′-
dah, and in the streets of Jē-ru̧′-
sa̐-lĕm: [o]for *then* had we plenty
of victuals,[c] and were well, and
saw no evil.
18 [p]But since we left off to burn
[i]incense to the [n]queen of heaven,
and to pour out drink offerings
unto her, [p]we have wanted[c] all
*things*, and have been consumed
by the [d]sword and by the [e]fam-
ine.
19 [o]And when we burned [i]in-
cense to the [n]queen of heaven,
and poured out drink offerings
unto her, did we make her cakes
to worship her, and pour out
drink offerings unto her, without
our [1]men?
20 ¶ Then [k]Jĕr-e-mī′ah said
unto all the people, to the men,
and to the [g]women, and to all the
people which had given him *that*
answer, saying,
21 The [i]incense that ye burned
in the cities of Jū′dah, and in the
streets of Jē-ru̧′sa̐-lĕm, ye, and
your fathers, your [q]kings, and
your princes, and the people of
the land, did not the LORD remember them, and came it *not*
into his mind?
22 So that [r]the LORD could no
longer bear, because of the [s]evil
of your doings, *and* because of
the abominations which ye have
committed; therefore is your
land a [a]desolation, and an astonishment,[c] and a curse, without an inhabitant, as at this
day.
23 Because ye have [h]burned
[i]incense, and because ye have
sinned against the LORD, and
have [t]not obeyed the voice of the
LORD, nor walked in his law,
nor in his statutes, nor in his
testimonies; therefore this [a]evil
is happened unto you, as at this
day.
24 Moreover [k]Jĕr-e-mī′ah said
unto all the people, and to all
the [g]women, Hear the word of
the LORD, all Jū′dah that *are*
in the land of [c]Ē′ġy̆pt:
25 Thus saith the LORD of
hosts, the God of Ĭs̩′ra-el, saying; Ye and your wives have
both spoken with your mouths,
and fulfilled with your hand,
saying, We will surely perform
our [u]vows that we have vowed,
to [h]burn [i]incense to the [n]queen
of heaven, and to pour out
drink offerings unto her: ye
will surely accomplish your
vows, and surely perform your
vows.
26 Therefore hear ye the word
of the LORD, all Jū′dah that
dwell in the land of [c]Ē′ġy̆pt;
Behold, I have [v,w]sworn by my
great name, saith the LORD,
that my name shall no more be
named in the mouth of any man
of Jū′dah in all the land of
Ē′ġy̆pt, saying, The Lord GOD
liveth.
27 Behold, I will watch over
them for evil, and not for good:
and all the [c]men of Jū′dah that
*are* in the land of [c]Ē′ġy̆pt shall
be [a]consumed by the [d]sword and
by the [e]famine, until there be an
end of them.
28 [b]Yet a small number that
escape the sword shall return out
of the land of [c]Ē′ġy̆pt into the
land of Jū′dah, and all the remnant of Jū′dah, that are gone
into the land of Ē′ġy̆pt to sojourn there, [x]shall know whose
words shall stand, mine, or
their's.
29 ¶ And this *shall be* a sign unto you, saith the LORD, that [b]I
will [a]punish you in this place,
that ye may know that my words
shall surely stand against you
for evil:

25
u *Vows,* Num. 30:2.

26
v *Oath, attributed to God,* Num. 5:19.
w *Covenant, of God with men,* Deut. 29:1.

28
x *Judgments, design of,* Ex. 6:6

30 Thus saith the LORD; Behold, I will give +Phā′raōh-
hŏph′rȧ king of Ē′ġy̆pt into the
hand of his enemies, and into the
hand of them that seek his life;
as I gave [y]Zĕd-e-kī′ah king of
Jū′dah into the hand of [z]Nĕb-u-
chad-rĕz′zar king of Băb′y̆-lon
his enemy, and that sought his
life.

## CHAPTER 45

*The prophet comforts Baruch.*

THE word that [a]Jĕr-e-mī′ah
the prophet spake unto
[b]Bā′ruch the son of Nē-rī′ah,
when he had written these words
in a [c]book at the mouth of Jĕr-e-
mī′ah, in the fourth year of [d]Jė-
hoi′a-kĭm the son of [e]Jō-sī′ah
king of Jū′dah, saying,
2 Thus saith the LORD, the
God of Īs′ra-el, unto thee, O
[b]Bā′ruch;
3 Thou didst say, Woe is me
now! for the LORD hath added
grief to my sorrow; I fainted
in my sighing, and I find no
rest.
4 Thus shalt thou say unto him,
The LORD saith thus; Behold,
*that* which I have built will I
break down, and that which I
have planted I will pluck up,
even this whole land.
5 And [f]seekest thou great things
for thyself? seek *them* not: for,
behold, I will bring [g]evil upon
all flesh, saith the LORD: but
thy life will I give unto thee for
a prey in all places whither thou
goest.

## CHAPTER 46

*Jeremiah prophesies the overthrow of Pharaoh-necho's army at the Euphrates, 13 and the conquest of Egypt by Nebuchadnezzar. 27 He comforts Jacob.*

THE [a]word of the LORD which
[b]came to [c]Jĕr-e-mī′ah the
prophet [1]against the Ġĕn′tīleș;
2 Against [d]Ē′ġy̆pt, against the
army of [e]Phā′raōh-nē′chȯ king
of Ē′ġy̆pt, which was by the river
[f]Eū-phrā′tēș in [g]Cär′che-mĭsh,
which [h]Nĕb-u-chad-rĕz′zar king
of [i]Băb′y̆-lon smote in the fourth
year of [j]Jė-hoi′a-kĭm the son of
[k]Jȯ-sī′ah king of [l]Jū′dah.
3 Order ye the [m]buckler and
[m,n]shield, and draw near to
battle.
4 Harness the [o]horses; and get
up, ye [p]horsemen, and stand
forth with *your* *helmets; furbish the [m,q]spears, *and* put on
the [2]brigandines.
5 Wherefore have I seen them
dismayed *and* turned away back?
and their mighty ones are beaten
down, and are fled apace, and
look not back: *for* fear *was* round
about, saith the LORD.
6 Let not the swift flee away,
nor the mighty man escape; they
shall stumble, and fall toward
the north by the river [f]Eū-phrā′-
tēș.
7 Who *is* this *that* [3]cometh up as
a flood, whose waters are moved
as the rivers?
8 [d]Ē′ġy̆pt riseth up like [4]a flood,
and *his* waters are moved like
the rivers; and he saith, I will
go up, *and* will cover the earth;
I will destroy the city and the inhabitants thereof.
9 Come up, ye horses; and
rage, ye [r]chariots; and let the
mighty men [5]come forth; the
[s]Ē-thĭ-ō′pĭ′anș and the [t]Lĭb′-
y̆-anș, that handle the shield;
and the [6,u]Ly̆d′ĭ-anș, that handle *and* bend the [v]bow.
10 [w]For this *is* the [x]day of the
Lord [7]GOD of hosts, a day of
vengeance, that he may avenge
him of his adversaries: and the
[y]sword shall devour, and it shall
be satiate and made drunk with
their blood: for the Lord [7]GOD
of hosts hath a sacrifice in the

**30**
y *Zedekiah*, 2 Kin. 25:2.
z Or, *Nebuchadnezzar*, Dan. 2:1.

**v.1–525 BC**
See footnote, *Time*, Rev. 10:6.

**1**
a *Jeremiah*, Jer. 1:1.
b Jer. 32:12–16; 36:4–32; 43:3–6.
c *Book, prophecies written in*, Num. 5:23.
d *Jehoiakim*, Jer. 26:1.
e *Josiah*, 1 Kin. 13:2.

**5**
f *Ambition*, Hab. 2:5.
g *Wicked, punishment of*, Psa. 73:3.

**1**
a *Prophecies, inspired*, Dan. 9:24.
b *Prophets, inspiration of*, Isa. 3:2.
c *Jeremiah*, Jer. 1:1.

**2**
d *Egypt, prophecies concerning*, vs. 1–26; Gen. 41:8.

**v.2–525 BC**
e Or, *Pharaoh-nechoh*, 2 Kin. 23:29.
f *Euphrates*, Gen. 15:18.
g Isa. 10:9; 2 Chr. 35:20.
h Or, *Nebuchadnezzar*, Dan. 2:1.
i *Babylon, empire of*, Ezra 5:12.
j *Jehoiakim*, Jer. 26:1.
k *Josiah*, 1 Kin. 13:2.
l *Judah, kingdom of*, 2 Chr. 11:17.

**3**
m *Armor*, 1 Sam. 17:54.
n *Shield*, 1 Kin. 14:27.

**4**
o *Horse*, Job 39:19.
p *Cavalry*, 1 Sam. 13:5.
q *Spear*, 2 Kin. 11:10.
2 R. V. coats of mail.

**7**
3 R. V. riseth up like the Nile, whose waters toss themselves like the rivers?

**8**
4 R. V. the Nile,

**9**
r *Chariot*, Josh. 11:4.
s *Ethiopia, warriors of*, Isa. 18:1.
t Dan. 11:43; Nah. 3:9.
u Or, *Ludim*, Gen. 10:13; 1 Chr. 1:11.
v *Archery*, Gen. 21:10.
5 R. V. go forth: Cush and Put, that
6 R. V. Ludim,

**10**
w *Nation, judgments denounced against*, Isa. 2:4.
x *Day, times of adversity called day of the Lord*, Gen. 1:5.
y *War, evils of*, Judg. 3:2.
7 Am. R. V. Jehovah

+ **PHARAOH-HOPHRA**, Jer. 37:5–7; 44; Ezek. 17:15–17. *Prophecies concerning*, Jer. 44:30; 46:25, 26; Ezek. 29; 30:21–26.

* **HELMET.** *A defensive headgear worn by soldiers*, 1 Sam. 17:5, 38; 2 Chr. 26:14; Jer. 46:4; Ezek. 23:24. **Figurative**, Isa. 59:17; Eph. 6:17; 1 Thess. 5:8.

north country by the river [l]Eū-phrā′tēş.[Q]

11 Go up into [z]Gĭl′e-ăd, and take [a]balm,[C] O virgin, the daughter of [b]Ē′ġy̆pt: in vain shalt thou use many [c,d]medicines; *for* thou shalt not be cured.

12 The nations have heard of thy shame, and thy cry hath filled the land: for the mighty man hath stumbled against the mighty, *and* they are fallen both together.

13 ¶ The [e]word that the LORD spake to [f]Jĕr-e-mī′ah the prophet, how [g]Nĕb-u-chad-rĕz′zar king of [h]Băb′y̆-lon should come *and* smite the land of [b]Ē′ġy̆pt.

14 Declare ye in [b]Ē′ġy̆pt, and publish in [i]Mĭg′dol, and publish in [j]Nŏph and in [k]Täh′pan-hēş: say ye, Stand fast, and prepare thee; for [l]the sword shall devour round about thee.

15 Why are thy valiant *men* swept away? they stood not, because [m]the LORD did drive them.

16 [w]He made many to fall, yea, one fell upon another: and they said, Arise, and let us go again to our own people, and to the land of our nativity, from the oppressing sword.

17 They did cry there, [n]Phā′raōh king of Ē′ġy̆pt *is but* a noise; he hath passed the time appointed.

18 *As* I live, saith the [o]King, whose name *is* the LORD of hosts, Surely as [p]Tā′bôr *is* among the mountains, and as †Cär′mel by the sea, *so* shall he come.

19 O thou daughter dwelling in [b]Ē′ġy̆pt, furnish[C] thyself to go into [q]captivity: for [j]Nŏph shall be waste and desolate without an inhabitant.

20 [b]Ē′ġy̆pt *is like* a very fair heifer, [l]*but* destruction cometh; it cometh out of the north.

21 Also her [r]hired men *are* in the midst of her like fatted bullocks; for they also are turned back, *and* are fled away together: they did not stand, because the day of their calamity was come upon them, *and* the time of their visitation.[C]

22 The voice thereof shall go like a serpent; for [l]they shall march with an army, and come against her with [s]axes, as hewers of wood.

23 [l]They shall cut down her forest, saith the LORD, though it cannot be searched; because they are more than the [t]grasshoppers, and *are* innumerable.

24 The daughter of [b]Ē′ġy̆pt shall be confounded; [l]she shall be delivered into the hand of the people of the north.

25 The LORD of hosts, the God of Ĭş′ra-el, saith; Behold, I will [u]punish the multitude of [v]Nō, and [n]Phā′raōh, and Ē′ġy̆pt, with their gods, and their kings; even Phā′raōh, and *all* them that [w]trust in him:

26 And I will deliver [l]them into the hand of those that seek their lives, and into the hand of [g]Nĕb-u-chad-rĕz′zar king of [h]Băb′y̆-lon, and into the hand of his servants: and afterward it shall be inhabited, as in the days of old, saith the LORD.

27 ¶ But fear not thou, O my servant Jā′cob, and be not dismayed, O Ĭş′ra-el: for, behold, I will [x,y]save thee from afar off, and thy seed from the land of their captivity; and Jā′cob shall return, and be in rest and at ease, and none shall make *him* afraid.

28 Fear thou not, O Jā′cob my

**11**
z *Gilead,* Deut. 3:13.

a *Balm,* Gen. 37:25.
b *Egypt, prophecies concerning,* Gen. 41:8.
c *Medicine,* Prov. 17:22.
d *Disease, remedies used for,* Ex. 15:26.

**13**
e *Prophecies, inspired,* Dan. 9:24.
f *Jeremiah,* Jer. 1:1.
g Or, *Nebuchadnezzar, prophecies concerning,* Dan. 2:1.
h *Babylon, empire of,* Ezra 5:12.

**14**
i Jer. 44:1.
j *Noph, prophecies concerning,* Isa. 19:13.
k Or, *Tahapanes,* Jer. 2:16.
l *Nation, judgments denounced against,* Isa. 2:4.

**15**
m *War, God inflicts defeat in,* Judg. 3:2.

**17**
n *Pharaoh-hophra* (probably), Jer. 44:30.

**18**
o *God, sovereign,* Gen. 2:2.
p *Tabor,* Judg. 8:18.

**19**
q *Captivity, as a judgment,* Isa. 5:13.

**21**
r *Armies, composed of mercenaries,* Deut. 11:4.

**22**
s *Ax,* Deut. 19:5.

**23**
t *Locust,* Nah. 3:17.

**25**
u *Wicked, punishment of,* Psa. 73:3.
v Ezek. 30:14–16; Nah. 3:8.
w *False Confidence,* Psa. 30:6.

**27**
x *God, mercy of,* Gen. 2:2.
y *God, savior,* Gen. 2:2.

† **CARMEL** (*park, garden*). *A fertile and picturesque mountain in Palestine,* Song 7:5; Isa. 33:9; 35:2; Jer. 46:18; 50:19; Amos 1:2. *Caves of,* Amos 9:3; Mic. 7:14. *On the boundary of Asher,* Josh. 19:26 *An idolatrous high place upon; Elijah builds an altar upon, and confounds the worshipers of Baal, putting to death four hundred and fifty of Baal's prophets,* 1 Kin. 18:17–46. *Elisha's abode in,* 2 Kin. 2:25 4:25.

servant, saith the LORD: for I *am* with thee; for I will make a full end of all the nations whither I have driven thee: but [x]I will not make a full end of thee, but [z]correct thee in measure; yet will I not leave thee wholly unpunished.

28
*z* *Divine Chastisement,* Job 33:19.

## CHAPTER 47

*The destruction of the Philistines foretold by Jeremiah.*

THE [a]word of the LORD that came to [b]Jĕr-e-mī′ah the prophet against the [c]Phĭ-lĭs′tĭnes̱, before that [d]Phā′raōh smote [e]Gā′zȧ.

2 Thus saith the LORD; Behold, waters rise up out of the north, and shall be an overflowing flood, and shall overflow the land, and all that is therein; the city, and them that dwell therein: then the men shall cry, and all the inhabitants of the land shall howl.

3 At the noise of the stamping of the hoofs of his strong [1]*horses,* at the rushing of his [f]chariots, *and at* the rumbling of his wheels, the fathers shall not look back to *their* children for feebleness of hands;

4 Because of the day that cometh to spoil all the [c]Phĭ-lĭs′tĭnes̱, *and* to cut off from [g]Tȳ′rus and [h]Zī′dŏn every helper that remaineth: for the LORD will spoil the Phĭ-lĭs′tĭnes̱, the remnant of the country of Căph′tôr.

5 Baldness is come upon [e]Gā′zȧ; [i]Ăsh′ke-lŏn is cut off *with* the remnant of their valley: how long wilt thou cut thyself?

6 O thou [j]sword of the LORD, how long *will it be* ere thou be quiet? put up thyself into thy scabbard, rest, and be still.

7 How can it be quiet, seeing the LORD hath given it a charge against [i]Ăsh′ke-lŏn, and against the sea shore? there hath he appointed it.

1
*a* *Prophecies, inspired,* Dan. 9:24.
*b* *Jeremiah,* Jer. 1:1.
*c* *Philistines, prophecies concerning,* Gen. 26:14.
*d* *Pharaoh-nechoh* (probably), 2 Kin. 23:29.
*e* *Gaza,* Gen. 10:19.

3
*f* *Chariot,* Josh. 11:4.
1 R. V. ones,

4
*g* Or, *Tyre, prophecies concerning,* Josh. 19:29.
*h* *Zidon, prophecies concerning,* Ezek. 28:21.

5
*i* *Ashkelon, prophecies concerning,* Judg. 1:18.

6
*j* *War, as a judgment,* Judg. 3:2.

## CHAPTER 48

*Judgments upon Moab for their pride,* 11 *for their security,* 14 *for their carnal confidence,* 26 *and for their contempt of God and his people.* 47 *The restoration of Moab foretold.*

AGAINST [a]Mō′ab thus saith the LORD of hosts, the God of Īs̱′ra-el; Woe unto [b]Nē′bō! for it is spoiled: [c]Kĭr-ĭ-a-thā′im is confounded *and* taken: Mĭs′găb is confounded and dismayed.

2 [d]*There shall be* no more praise of [a]Mō′ab: in [e]Hĕsh′bŏn they have devised evil against it; come, and let us cut it off from *being* a nation. Also thou [1]shalt be cut down, O Măd′men; the sword shall pursue thee.

3 A voice of crying *shall be* from [f]Hŏr-o-nā′im, spoiling and great destruction.

4 [a]Mō′ab is destroyed; her little ones have caused a cry to be heard.

5 For in the going up of [f]Lu̇′hith continual weeping shall go up; for in the going down of [f]Hŏr-o-nā′im [2]the enemies have heard a cry of destruction.

6 ¶ Flee, save your lives, and be like the heath in the wilderness.

7 For because thou hast [g]trusted in thy works and in thy treasures, [d]thou shalt also be taken: and [h]Chē′mŏsh shall go forth into [i]captivity *with* his priests and his princes together.

8 [d]And the spoiler shall come upon every city, and no city shall escape: the valley also shall perish, and the plain shall be destroyed, as the LORD hath spoken.

9 Give wings unto [a]Mō′ab, that it may flee and get away: for the cities thereof shall be desolate, without any to dwell therein.

10 Cursed *be* he that doeth the work of the LORD [3]deceitfully, and cursed *be* he that keepeth back his [j]sword from blood.

1
*a* *Moabites, prophecies concerning,* vs. 1–47; Gen. 19:37.
*b* *Nebo, prophecies concerning,* Num. 32:3.
*c* Or, *Kirjathaim, prophecies concerning,* Num. 32:37.

2
*d* *Nation, judgments denounced against,* Isa. 2:4.
*e* *Heshbon, prophecies concerning,* Isa. 16:8.
1 R. V. O Madmen, shalt be brought to silence;

3
*f* Isa. 15:5.

5
2 R. V. they have

7
*g* *False Confidence,* Psa. 30:6.
*h* *Chemosh,* Judg. 11:24.
*i* *Captivity, as a judgment,* Isa. 5:13.

10
*j* *War, as a judgment,* Judg. 3:2.
3 R.V. negligently.

11 ¶ [a]Mō′ab hath been at ease from his youth, and he hath settled on his [k]lees,[G] and hath not been emptied from vessel to vessel, neither hath he gone into captivity: therefore his taste remained in him, and his scent is not changed.

12 [d]Therefore, behold, the days come, saith the LORD, that I will send unto him [4]wanderers, that shall cause him to wander, and shall empty his vessels, and break their bottles.[G]

13 And [a]Mō′ab shall be ashamed of [h]Chē′mŏsh, as the house of Ĭṣ′ra-el was ashamed of [l]Bĕth′–el their [g]confidence.

14 ¶ How say ye, We *are* mighty and strong men for the war?

15 [a]Mō′ab is spoiled, and gone up *out of* her cities, and his chosen young men are gone down to the slaughter, saith the [m]King, whose name *is* the LORD of hosts.

16 The calamity of [a,d]Mō′ab *is* near to come, and his affliction hasteth fast.

17 All ye that are about him, bemoan him; and all ye that know his name, say, How is the strong staff broken, *and* the beautiful rod!

18 Thou daughter that dost inhabit [n]Dī′bŏn, come down from *thy* glory, and sit in thirst; for the spoiler[G] of [a]Mō′ab shall come upon thee, *and* he shall destroy thy [o]strong holds.

19 O inhabitant of [p]Är′ō-ēr, stand by the way, and espy;[G] ask him that fleeth, and her that escapeth, *and* say, What is done?

20 [a]Mō′ab is confounded; for it is broken down: howl and cry; tell ye it in Är′nŏn, that Mō′ab is spoiled,

21 And [q]judgment is come upon the plain country; upon Hō′lŏn, and upon [r]Jă-hā′zah, and upon [s]Mĕph′a-ăth,

22 And upon [n]Dī′bŏn, and upon [b]Nē′bō, and upon [t]Bĕth–dĭb-la-thā′im,

23 And upon [c]Kĭr-ĭ-a-thā′im, and upon Bĕth–gā′mul, and upon [u]Bĕth–mē′on,

24 And upon [v]Kē′rī-ŏth, and upon [w]Bŏz′rah, and upon all the cities of the land of Mō′ab, far or near.

25 The horn[G] of Mō′ab is cut off, and his arm is broken, saith the LORD.

26 ¶ Make ye him [x]drunken: for he magnified *himself* against the LORD: [a]Mō′ab also shall wallow in his vomit, and he also shall be in derision.

27 For was not Ĭṣ′ra-el a derision unto thee? was he found among thieves? for [5]since thou spakest of him, thou skippedst for joy.

28 O ye that dwell in [a]Mō′ab, leave the cities, and dwell in the rock, and be like the [y]dove *that* maketh her nest in the sides of the hole's mouth.

29 We have heard the [z]pride of [a]Mō′ab, (he is exceeding proud) his loftiness, and his arrogancy, and his pride, and the haughtiness of his heart.

30 I know his wrath, saith the LORD; [6]but *it shall* not *be* so; his lies shall not so effect *it*.

31 Therefore will I howl for [a]Mō′ab, and I will cry out for all Mō′ab; *mine heart* shall mourn for the men of [b]Kīr–hē′rēṣ.

32 O vine of [c]Sĭb′mah, I will weep for thee with the weeping of [d]Jā′zēr: thy plants are gone over the sea, they reach *even* to the sea of Jā′zēr: the spoiler[G] is fallen upon thy [e]summer fruits and upon thy vintage.

33 [f]And [g]joy and gladness is taken from the plentiful field, and from the land of Mō′ab; and

11
k Psa. 75:8; Isa. 25:6; Zeph. 1:12.

12
4 R. V. them that pour off, and they shall pour him off; and they shall empty his vessels, and break their bottles in pieces.

13
l *Bethel, idolatry at,* Josh. 18:13.

15
m *God, sovereign,* Gen. 2:2.

18
n *Dibon,* Num. 21:30.
o *Fortification,* Ezek. 17:17.

19
p *Aroer,* Deut. 4:48.

21
q *Judgments,* Ex. 6:6.

r Or, *Jahaz,* Judg. 11:20.
s *Mephaath,* Josh. 13:18.

22
t Probably identical with *Almon-diblathaim,* Num. 33:46, 47; or, *Diblath,* Ezek. 6:14.

23
u Or, *Baal-meon,* Num. 32:38.

24
v Amos 2:2.
w *Bozrah, prophecies concerning,* Gen. 36:33.

26
x *Drunkenness, figurative,* Luke 21:34.

27
5 R. V. as often as thou speakest of him, thou waggest the head.

28
y *Dove,* Gen. 8:8.

29
z *Pride,* Prov. 16:18.

30
6 R. V. that it is nought; his boastings have wrought nothing.

31
a *Moabites, prophecies concerning,* Gen. 19:37.
b Or, *Kir-haraseth,* 2 Kin. 3:25.

32
c *Sibmah,* Josh. 13:19.
d *Jazer,* Josh. 13:25.
e *Summer, fruits of,* Isa. 28:4.

33
f *Famine, as a judgment,* 2 Kin. 8:1.
g *Harvest, celebrated with joy,* Ex. 34:21.

I have caused wine to fail from the [h]winepresses: none shall tread with shouting; *their* shouting *shall be* no shouting.

34 From the cry of [i]Hĕsh′bŏn *even* unto [j]Ē-le-ā′leh, *and even* unto Jā′hăz, have they uttered their voice, from [k]Zō′ar *even* unto [l]Hŏr-o-nā′im, *as* an heifer of three years old: for the waters also of [m]Nĭm′rim shall be desolate.

35 Moreover I will cause to cease in [a]Mō′ab, saith the LORD, [n]him that [o]offereth in the [p]high[G] places, and him that burneth [q]incense to his gods.

36 Therefore mine heart shall sound for [a]Mō′ab like pipes[G], and mine heart shall sound like pipes[G] for the men of [b]Kĭr–hē′rēs: because the riches *that* he hath gotten are perished.

37 For every head *shall be* [r]bald, and every [s]beard clipped: upon all the hands *shall be* cuttings, and upon the loins [t]sackcloth.

38 [a]*There shall be* lamentation generally upon all the housetops of Mō′ab, and in the streets thereof: for I have broken Mō′ab like a vessel wherein *is* no pleasure, saith the LORD.

39 [a]They shall howl, *saying,* How is it broken down! how hath Mō′ab turned the back with shame! so shall Mō′ab be a derision and a dismaying to all them about him.

40 For [a]thus saith the LORD; Behold, he shall fly as an [u]eagle, and shall spread his wings over Mō′ab.

41 [v]Kē′rĭ-ŏth is taken, and the strong holds are surprised, and [a]the mighty men's hearts in Mō′ab at that day shall be as the heart of a woman in her pangs.

42 And [a]Mō′ab shall be [w]destroyed from *being* a people, because he hath magnified *himself* against the LORD.

43 [w]Fear, and the pit, and the snare, *shall be* upon thee, O inhabitant of [a]Mō′ab, saith the LORD.

44 [w]He that fleeth from the fear shall fall into the pit; and he that getteth up out of the pit shall be taken in the snare: for I will bring upon it, *even* upon [a]Mō′ab, the year of their visitation[G], saith the LORD.

45 They that fled [7]stood under the shadow of [i]Hĕsh′bŏn because of the force: but a fire shall come forth out of Hĕsh′bŏn, and a flame from the midst of Sī′hŏn, and shall devour the corner of Mō′ab, and the crown of the head of the tumultuous ones.

46 Woe be unto thee, O Mō′ab! the people of [x]Chē′mŏsh perisheth: for thy sons are taken [y]captives, and thy daughters captives.

47 [z]Yet will I bring again the captivity of Mō′ab in the latter days, saith the LORD. Thus far *is* the judgment of Mō′ab.

## CHAPTER 49

*Judgments upon the Ammonites, 7 upon Edom, 23 upon Damascus, 28 upon Kedar, 30 upon Hazor, 34 and upon Elam.*

CONCERNING the [a]Ăm′mon-ītes, thus saith the LORD; Hath Ĭş′ra-el no sons? hath he no heir? why *then* doth [1]their king inherit [b]Găd, and his people dwell in his cities?

2 Therefore, behold, the days come, saith the LORD, that I will cause an alarm of [c]war to be heard in [d]Răb′bah of the [a]Ăm′mon-ītes; and it shall be a desolate heap[G], and her daughters shall be burned with fire: then shall Ĭş′ra-el be heir unto them that were his heirs, saith the LORD.

3 Howl, O [e]Hĕsh′bŏn, for Ā′ī is

---

h *Wine Press, trodden with shouting,* Isa. 5:2.

**34**
i *Heshbon,* Isa. 16:8.
j Num. 32:3, 37; Isa. 15:4; 16:9.
k *Zoar,* Deut. 34:3.
l Isa. 15:5.
m Isa. 15:6.

**35**
n *Priest, idolatrous,* Lev. 1:5.
o *Idolatry, customs of,* 1 Sam. 15:23.
p *High Places,* 1 Kin. 3:2.
q *Incense, offered in idolatrous worship,* Ex. 37:29.

**37**
r *Baldness, as a judgment,* Lev. 21:5.
s *Beard, cut,* 1 Sam. 21:13.
t *Sackcloth,* Isa. 15:3.

**40**
u *Eagle,* Lev. 11:13.

**41**
v Amos 2:2.

**42**
w *Wicked, punishment of,* Psa. 73:3.

**45**
7 R. V. stand without strength under the shadow of Heshbon: for a fire is gone forth

**46**
x *Chemosh,* Judg. 11:24.
y *Captivity, as a judgment,* Isa. 5:13.

**47**
z *God, mercy of,* Gen. 2:2.

**1**
a *Ammonites, prophecies concerning,* vs. 1–6; Deut. 2:20.
b *Gad, tribe of,* Deut. 33:20.
1 R. V. Malcam

**2**
c *War, as a judgment,* Judg. 3:2.
d *Rabbah, prophecies concerning,* Deut. 3:11.

**3**
e *Heshbon, prophecies concerning,* Isa. 16:8.

spoiled: [f]cry, ye daughters of
[d]Răb′bah, gird you with [g]sack-
cloth; lament, and run to and fro
by the [h]hedges; for [1]their king
shall go into [i]captivity, *and* his
priests and his princes together.
4 Wherefore gloriest thou in
the valleys, thy flowing valley,
O backsliding daughter? that
[j]trusted in her treasures, *saying*,
Who shall come unto me?
5 Behold, I will [k]bring a fear
upon thee, saith the Lord [2]GOD
of hosts, from all those that
be about thee; and ye shall be
driven out every man right forth;
and none shall gather up him
that wandereth.
6 And afterward [l]I will bring
again the [i]captivity of the
[a]children of Ăm′mŏn, saith the
LORD.
7 ¶ Concerning [m]Ē′dom, thus
saith the LORD of hosts; *Is* [n]wis-
dom no more in *Tē′man? is
counsel perished from the prudent? is their wisdom vanished?
8 Flee ye, turn back, dwell
deep, O inhabitants of †Dē′dan;
for I will bring the calamity of
[m]Ē′sau upon him, the time *that*
I will visit him.
9 If grapegatherers come to
thee, would they not leave *some*
[o]gleaning grapes? if thieves by
night, they will destroy till they
have enough.
10 But I have made [m]Ē′sau
bare, I have uncovered his secret places, and he shall not be
able to hide himself: his seed
is spoiled, and his brethren, and
his neighbours, and he *is* not.
11 Leave thy [p]fatherless children, [q]I will [r]preserve [s]*them*
alive; and let thy [t]widows [u]trust
in me.
12 For thus saith the LORD;
Behold, they whose judgment
*was* not to drink of the [v]cup have
assuredly drunken; and *art* thou
he *that* shall altogether go unpunished? thou shalt not go
unpunished, but [w, x]thou shalt
surely drink *of it*.
13 For I have [y]sworn by myself, saith the LORD, that [z]Bŏz′-
rah shall become a desolation, a
reproach, a waste, and a curse;
and all the cities thereof shall be
perpetual wastes.
14 I have heard [3]a rumour
from the LORD, and an ambas-
sador is sent unto the [4]heathen,
*saying*, Gather ye together, and
come against her, and rise up to
the battle.
15 For, lo, I will make [a]thee
small among the [4]heathen, *and*
despised among men.
16 Thy terribleness hath [b]de-
ceived thee, *and* the pride of
thine heart, O thou that dwellest
in the clefts of the rock, that
holdest the height of the hill:
though thou shouldest make thy
nest as high as the [c]eagle, I will
[d]bring [a]thee down from thence,
saith the LORD.
17 Also [a]Ē′dom shall be a desolation: every one that goeth by
it shall be astonished, and shall
hiss at all the plagues thereof.
18 As in the overthrow of
[e]Sŏd′om and [f]Gô-mŏr′rah and
the neighbour *cities* thereof, saith
the LORD, no man shall abide
there, neither shall a son of man
dwell in it.
19 Behold, he shall come up
like a [g]lion from the [5]swelling of
Jôr′dan against the habitation of
the strong: but I will suddenly
make him run away from her:
and who *is* a chosen *man*, *that* I
may appoint over her? for who
*is* like me? and who will appoint
[h]me the time? and who *is* that

f *Mourning*, Lam. 2:5.
g *Sackcloth, symbol of mourning*, Isa. 15:3.
h *Hedge, a fence*, Isa. 5:5.
i *Captivity, as a judgment*, Isa. 5:13.

4
j *False Confidence*, Psa. 30:6.

5
k *Adversity, dispensation from God*, Psa. 10:6.
2 Am. R. V. Jehovah

6
l *God, mercy of*, Gen. 2:2.

7
m *Edomites, prophecies concerning*, vs. 7–22; 2 Kin. 8:21.
n *Wisdom, worldly*, Prov. 2:2.

9
o *Gleaning, figurative*, Lev. 23:22.

11
p *Orphan, God the friend of*, Lam. 5:3.
q *Promise, to orphans and widows*, 2 Cor. 1:20.
r *God, preserver*, Gen. 2:2.
s *Children, God's care of*, Mark 10:14.
t *Widow, God the friend of*, 2 Sam. 14:5.
u *Faith, enjoined*, Mark 11:22.

12
v *Cup, figurative*, Matt. 20:22.
w *Wicked, punishment of*, Psa. 73:3.
x *Nation, punishment of*, Isa. 2:4.

13
y *Oath, attributed to God*, Num. 5:19.
z *Bozrah, prophecies concerning*, Gen. 36:33.

14
3 R. V. tidings
4 R. V. nations,

15
a *Edomites, prophecies concerning* 2 Kin. 8:21.

16
b *False Confidence*, Psa. 30:6.
c *Eagle*, Lev. 11:13.
d *Nation, punishment of*, Isa. 2:4.

18
e *Sodom, destroyed*, Gen. 13:10.
f *Gomorrah, destroyed*, Gen. 13:10.

19
5 R. V. pride
g *Lion*, Mic. 5:8.
h *God, sovereign*, Gen. 2:2.

* **TEMAN**, the most important district of Edom, either giving its name to, or taking it from, one of Esau's grandson's. *King of Edom from*, Gen. 36:34. *Eliphaz, Job's friend, from*, Job 2:11. *Prophecies concerning*, Jer. 49:7, 20; Ezek. 25:13; Amos 1:12; Obad. 9; Hab. 3:3.

† **DEDAN.** *Son of Cush*, Gen. 10:7. *A man by the same name is mentioned as son of Keturah*, Gen. 25:3. *Descendants of, dwell in country of the same name, probably bordering on Edom in southern Arabia*, Isa. 21:13; Jer. 25:23; 49:8; Ezek. 25:13; 27:15, 20; 38:13.

shepherd that will stand before me?

20 Therefore hear the counsel of the LORD, that he hath taken against [a]Ē'dom; and his purposes, that he hath purposed against the inhabitants of *Tē'man: Surely the least of the flock shall draw them out: surely he shall [i]make their habitations desolate with them.

21 The earth is moved at the noise of their fall, at the cry the noise thereof was heard in the [j]Red sea.

22 Behold, he shall come up and fly as the [c]eagle, and spread his wings over [k]Bŏz'rah: and at that day shall the heart of the mighty men of [a]Ē'dom be as the heart of a woman in her pangs.

23 ¶ Concerning [l]Dă-măs'cus. [m]Hā'math is confounded, and [n]Är'pad: for they have heard evil tidings: they are [6,o]fainthearted; *there is* sorrow on the sea; it cannot be quiet.

24 [l]Dă-măs'cus is waxed[c] feeble, *and* turneth herself to flee, and fear hath seized on *her*: anguish and sorrows have taken her, as a woman in travail.[c]

25 How is the city of praise not left, the city of my joy!

26 Therefore her [p]young men shall fall in her streets, and all the men of war shall be [7]cut off in that day, saith the LORD of hosts.

27 And I will kindle a fire in the wall of [l]Dă-măs'cus, and it shall consume the palaces of Bĕn–hā'dăd.

28 ¶ Concerning [‡]Kē'där, and concerning the kingdoms of Hā'zôr, which [q]Nĕb-u-chad-rĕz'zar king of [r]Băb'ȳ-lon shall smite, thus saith the LORD; Arise ye, go up to Kē'där, and spoil[c] the men of the east.

29 [s,t]Their tents and their flocks shall they take away: they shall take to themselves their curtains, and all their vessels, and their [u]camels; and they shall cry unto them, Fear *is* on every side.

30 ¶ Flee, get you far off, dwell deep, O ye inhabitants of Hā'zôr, saith the LORD; for [q]Nĕb-u-chad-rĕz'zar king of [r]Băb'ȳ-lon hath taken counsel[c] against you, and hath conceived a purpose against you.

31 Arise, get you up unto [8]the wealthy nation, that dwelleth without care, saith the LORD, which have neither gates nor bars, *which* dwell alone.

32 And their [u]camels shall be a booty, and the multitude of their cattle a [t]spoil: and I will [s]scatter into all winds them *that* [9]*are* in the utmost[c] corners; and I will bring their calamity from all sides thereof, saith the LORD.

33 And Hā'zôr shall be a dwelling [10]for [v]dragons, *and* a desolation for ever: there shall no man abide there, nor *any* son of man dwell in it.

34 ¶ The [w]word of the LORD that came to [x]Jĕr-e-mī'ah the prophet against [y]Ē'lăm in the beginning of the reign of [z]Zĕd-e-kī'ah king of Jū'dah, saying,

35 Thus saith the LORD of hosts; Behold, I will break the bow of [y]Ē'lăm, the chief of their might.

36 And upon [y]Ē'lăm will I bring the four winds from the four quarters of heaven, and will scatter them toward all those winds; and there shall be no nation whither the outcasts of Ē'lăm shall not come.[c]

37 For I will cause [y]Ē'lăm to be dismayed before their enemies, and before them that seek their life: and I will bring [a]evil up-

**20**
*i Adversity, dispensation from God*, Psa. 10:6.

**21**
*j Red Sea*, Ex. 10:19.

**22**
*k Bozrah, prophecies concerning*, Gen. 36:33.

**23**
*l Damascus, prophecies concerning*, vs. 23–27; Isa. 8:4.
*m Hamath, prophecy concerning*, 1 Chr. 18:3.
*n* 2 Kin. 18:34; 19:13; or, *Arphad*, Isa. 36:19; 37:13.
*o Adversity, despondency in*, Psa. 10:6.
6 R. V. melted away:

**26**
*p Young Men*, Prov. 1:4.
7 R. V. brought to silence in

**28**
*q* Or, *Nebuchadnezzar*, Dan. 2:1.
*r Babylon, empire of*, Ezra 5:12.

**29**
*s Nation, judgments denounced against*, Isa. 2:4.
*t Spoils*, 1 Chr. 26:27.
*u Camel*, 1 Sam. 30:17.

**31**
8 R. V. a nation that is at ease,

**32**
9 Am. R. V. have the corners of their hair cut off;

**33**
*v Dragon*, Deut. 32:33.
10 R. V. place of jackals,

**34**
*w Prophecies, inspired*, Dan. 9:24.
*x Jeremiah*, Jer. 1:1.
*y Elam, prophecies concerning*, vs. 34–39; Isa. 11:11.
*z Zedekiah*, 2 Kin. 25:2.

**37**
*a Adversity, dispensation from God*, Psa. 10:6.

‡ **KEDAR** (*dark-skinned*). *A nomadic clan of the Ishmaelites*, Psa. 120:5; Song 1:5; Isa. 21:16, 17; 42:11; 60:7; Jer. 49:28. *Flocks of*, Isa. 60:7; Jer. 49:28, 29. *Princes and commerce of*, Ezek. 27:21.

*b Anger of God,* 2 Kin. 13:3.
*c War, as a judgment,* Judg. 3:2.

39
*d God, mercy of,* Gen. 2:2.

1
*a Prophecies, inspired,* Dan. 9:24.
*b Babylon, city of, prophecies concerning,* vs. 1–46; Ezra 5:12.
*c Jeremiah,* Jer. 1:1.

2
*d Standard, used to call attention to news,* Num. 1:52.
*e* Isa. 46:1; Jer. 51:44.
*f Idol,* 1 Kin. 15:12.
1 R. V. dismayed.

4
*g Repentance, of Israel foretold,* Mark 1:4.
*h Backsliders, return of,* Jer. 3:22.
*i Weeping, penitential,* Ezra 3:13.
*j Seekers,* Isa. 55:6.
*k Spiritual Desire,* Psa. 42:1.

5
*l Zion,* 2 Sam. 5:7.
*m Decision,* Isa. 50:7.
*n Covenant, of man with God,* Deut. 29:1.

6
*o Backsliders, God's solicitude for,* Jer. 3:22.
*p Sheep, figurative,* Deut. 32:14.
*q Rulers, wicked,* Ex. 18:21.
*r Influence, evil,* 1 Cor. 7:14.

on them, *even* my fierce [b]anger,
saith the LORD; and I will send
the [c]sword after them, till I have
consumed them:
38 And I will set my throne
in Ē′lăm, and will destroy from
thence the king and the princes,
saith the LORD.
39 ¶ But it shall come to pass in
the latter days, *that* [d]I will bring
again the captivity of Ē′lăm, saith
the LORD.

## CHAPTER 50

*The destruction of Babylon and the restoration of Israel alternately foretold.*

THE [a]word that the LORD
spake against [b]Băb′ȳ-lon
*and* against the land of the
Chăldē′anș by [c]Jĕr-e-mī′ah the
prophet.
2 Declare ye among the nations, and publish, and set up a
[d]standard[G]; publish, *and* conceal
not: say, [b]Băb′ȳ-lon is taken,
[e]Bĕl is confounded, Mē-rō′dăch
is broken in pieces; her [f]idols
are confounded, her images are
[1]broken in pieces.
3 For [b]out of the north there
cometh up a nation against her,
which shall make her land desolate, and none shall dwell therein: they shall remove, they shall
depart, both man and beast.
4 ¶ In those days, and in that
time, saith the LORD, [g]the children of Ĭș-ra-el [h]shall come, they
and the children of Jū′dah together, going and [i]weeping: they
shall go, and [j,k]seek the LORD
their God.
5 They shall ask the way to
[l]Zī′ŏn with their faces thitherward, *saying,* Come, and [m]let
us join ourselves to the LORD
in a perpetual [n]covenant *that*
shall not be forgotten.
6 [o]My people hath been lost
[p]sheep: their [q]shepherds have
[r]caused them to go astray, they
have turned them away *on* the
mountains: they have gone from
mountain to hill, they have forgotten their restingplace.[Q]
7 All that found them have devoured them: and their adversaries said, We offend not, because they have [s]sinned against
the LORD, the habitation of [t]justice, even the LORD, the hope of
their fathers.[S]
8 Remove out of the midst of
[b]Băb′ȳ-lon, and go forth out of
the land of the Chăl-dē′anș, and
be as the he goats before the
flocks.[Q]
9 ¶ For, lo, [u,v]I will raise and
cause to come up against [b]Băb′-
ȳ-lon [w]an assembly of great nations from the north country:
and [w]they shall [x]set themselves in
array against her; from thence
she shall be taken: their arrows
*shall be* as of a mighty expert
man; none shall return in vain.
10 And [v]Chăl-dē′á shall be a
spoil[G]: all that spoil[G] her shall be
satisfied, saith the LORD.
11 Because ye [2]were glad, because ye rejoiced, O ye destroyers of mine heritage, because ye
are grown fat as the heifer at
grass, and bellow as bulls;
12 [v]Your mother shall be sore[G]
confounded; she that bare you
shall be ashamed: behold, the
hindermost of the nations *shall
be* a wilderness, a dry land, and
a desert.
13 Because of the [y]wrath of the
LORD [u,v]it shall not be inhabited, but it shall be wholly
desolate: every one that goeth by
Băb′ȳ-lon shall be astonished,[G]
and hiss[G] at all her plagues.
14 [v]Put yourselves in array
against Băb′ȳ-lon round about:
all ye that bend the bow, shoot
at her, spare no arrows: for she
hath sinned against the LORD.
15 Shout against her round
about: she hath [3]given her hand:
her foundations are fallen, her
walls are thrown down: for it *is*

7
*s Backsliding, of Israel,* Hos. 11:7.
*t God, justice of,* Gen. 2:2.

9
*u Divine Chastisement,* Job 33:19.
*v Nation, judgments denounced against,* Isa. 2:4.
*w Agency, in executing judgments,* Mark 1:17.
*x War, as a judgment,* Judg. 3:2.

11
2 R. V. are glad, because ye rejoice, O ye that plunder mine heritage, because ye are wanton as an heifer that treadeth out the corn, and neigh as strong horses;

13
*y Anger of God,* 2 Kin. 13:3.

15
3 R. V. submitted herself;

the vengeance of the LORD: take vengeance upon her; as she hath done, do unto her.[Q]

16 [v]Cut off the sower from Băb'ȳ-lon, and him that handleth the [z]sickle in the time of [a]harvest: for fear of the oppressing [b]sword they shall turn every one to his people, and they shall flee every one to his own land.

17 ¶ Ĭş'ra-el *is* a scattered [c]sheep; the [d]lions have driven *him* away: first the king of [e]Ăs-sȳr'ĭ-â hath devoured him; and last this [f]Nĕb-u-chad-rĕz'zar king of Băb'ȳ-lon hath broken his bones.

18 Therefore thus saith the LORD of hosts, the God of Ĭş'ra-el; Behold, I will [g]punish the [f]king of Băb'ȳ-lon and his [h,i]land, as I have punished the king of [e]Ăs-sȳr'ĭ-â.

19 And I will [j]bring [k,l]Ĭş'ra-el again to his [4]habitation, and he shall feed on [m]Cär'mel and [n]Bā'-shăn, and his soul shall be satisfied upon mount Ē'phră-ĭm and Gĭl'e-ăd.

20 In those days, and in that time, saith the LORD, the iniquity of [k,l]Ĭş'ra-el shall be sought for, and *there shall be* none; and the sins of Jū'dah, and they shall not be found: for [o]I will [p]pardon them whom I reserve.

21 ¶ Go up against the land of Mĕr-a-thā'im, *even* against it, and against the inhabitants of [q]Pē'kŏd: [i]waste[G] and utterly destroy after them, saith the LORD, and do according to all that I have commanded thee.

22 [i]A sound of battle *is* in the land, and of great destruction.

23 How is the hammer of the whole earth cut asunder and broken! how is [h]Băb'ȳ-lon become a desolation among the nations!

24 I have laid a snare for thee, and thou art also taken, O [h]Băb'ȳ-lon, and thou wast not aware: thou art found, and also caught, because thou hast striven against the LORD.

25 The LORD hath [b]opened his [r]armoury, and hath brought forth the weapons of his indignation: for [5]this *is* the work of the Lord GOD of hosts in the land of the Chăl-dē'anş.[Q]

26 [i]Come against her from the utmost[G] border, open her storehouses: cast her up as heaps, and destroy her utterly: let nothing of her be left.

27 [i]Slay all her bullocks; let them go down to the slaughter: woe unto them! for their day is come, the time of their visitation.[G]

28 The voice of them that flee and escape out of the land of [h]Băb'ȳ-lon, to declare in Zī'ŏn [i]the vengeance of the LORD our God, the vengeance of his temple.

29 Call together the [s]archers against [h]Băb'ȳ-lon: all ye that bend the bow, camp against it round about; let none thereof escape: [t]recompense her according to her work; according to all that she hath done, do unto her: for she hath been proud against the LORD, against the [u]Holy One of Ĭş'ra-el.[Q]

30 [h,i]Therefore shall her [v]young men fall in the streets, and all her men of war shall be [6]cut off in that day, saith the LORD.

31 Behold, I *am* against thee, *O thou* most proud, saith the LORD [7]GOD of hosts: for thy day is come, the time *that* I will [w]visit[G] thee.

32 [i]And the most proud shall stumble and fall, and none shall raise him up: and I will kindle a fire in his cities, and it shall devour[G] all round about him.

33 ¶ Thus saith the [7]LORD of hosts; The children of Ĭş'ra-el and the children of Jū'dah *were*

**16**

z *Sickle*, Deut. 23:25.

a *Harvest*, Ex. 34:21.

b *War, as a judgment*, Judg. 3:2.

**17**

c *Sheep, figurative*, Deut. 32:14.

d *Lion, figurative*, Mic. 5:8.

e *Assyria*, Gen. 25:18.

f Or, *Nebuchadnezzar*, Dan. 2:1.

**18**

g *Wicked, punishment of*, Psa. 73:3.

h *Babylon, prophecies concerning*, Ezra 5:12.

i *Nation, judgments denounced against*, Isa. 2:4.

**19**

j *Temporal Blessings, from God*, Psa. 103:2.

k *Jews, prophecies concerning*, Neh. 4:2.

l *Israel, after the revolt, prophecies concerning*, 1 Kin. 12:1.

m *Carmel*, Jer. 46:18.

n *Bashan*, Num. 32:33.

4 R. V. pasture,

**20**

o *God, mercy of*, Gen. 2:2.

p *Sin, forgiveness of*, Rom. 5:12.

**21**

q Ezek. 23:23.

**25**

r *Armory, figurative*, Neh. 3:19.

5 Am. R. V. the Lord, Jehovah of hosts, hath a work to do in

**29**

s *Archery, in war*, Gen. 21:20.

t *Punishment, according to deeds*, Lev. 26:41.

u *God, holiness of*, Gen. 2:2.

**30**

v *Young Men*, Prov. 1:4.

6 R. V. brought to silence

**31**

w *Divine Chastisement*, Job 33:19.

7 Am. R. V. Jehovah

33
x *Oppression*, Eccl. 5:8.

34
y *God, savior*, Gen. 2:2.

35
z *War, as a judgment*, Judg. 3:2.

36
8 R. V. boasters,

37
a *Horse*, Job 39:19.
b *Chariot*, Josh. 11:4.

38
c *Drought*, Gen. 31:40.
d *Idolatry*, 1 Sam. 15:23.

39
e *Nation, judgments denounced against*, Isa. 2:4.
f *Animals, abodes of*, Jer. 27:5.
g *Owl*, Lev. 11:16.
9 R. V. wolves

40
h *Sodom, destroyed*, Gen. 13:10.
i *Gomorrah, destroyed*, Gen. 13:10.

41
10 R. V. uttermost parts

42
j *Archery*, Gen. 21:20.
k *War, evils of*, Judg. 3:2.

[x]oppressed together: and all that took them captives held them fast; they refused to let them go.

34 [k,l]Their [y]Redeemer *is* strong; [7]the LORD of hosts *is* his name: [o]he shall throughly[G] plead their cause, that he may give rest to the land, and disquiet the inhabitants of [h]Băb′ȳ-lon.[T Q]

35 ¶ A [z]sword *is* upon the Chăl-dē′anș, saith the LORD, and upon the inhabitants of Băb′ȳ-lon, and upon her princes, and upon her wise *men*.

36 A [z]sword *is* upon the [8]liars; and they shall dote[G]: a sword *is* upon her mighty men; and they shall be dismayed.

37 A [z]sword *is* upon their [a]horses, and upon their [b]chariots, and upon all the mingled[G] people that *are* in the midst of her; and they shall become as women: a sword *is* upon her treasures[G]; and they shall be robbed.

38 A [c]drought *is* upon her waters; and they shall be dried up: for it *is* the land of [d]graven[G] images, and they are mad[G] upon *their* idols.[Q]

39 [e]Therefore the wild beasts of the [f]desert with the [9]wild beasts of the islands shall dwell *there*, and the [g]owls shall dwell therein: and it shall be no more inhabited for ever; neither shall it be dwelt in from generation to generation.[Q]

40 As God overthrew [h]Sŏd′om and [i]Gō-mŏr′rah and the neighbour *cities* thereof, saith the LORD; [e]*so* shall no man abide there, neither shall any son of man dwell therein.

41 Behold, a people shall come from the north, and a great nation, and many kings shall be raised up from the [10]coasts[G] of the earth.

42 They shall hold the [j]bow and the lance: [k]they *are* cruel, and [k]will not shew mercy: their voice shall roar like the sea, and they shall ride upon [a]horses, *every one* put in array, like a man to the battle, against thee, O daughter of [l]Băb′ȳ-lon.

43 The king of Băb′ȳ-lon hath heard the report of them, and [m]his hands waxed[G] feeble: anguish took hold of him, *and* pangs as of a woman in travail.

44 Behold, he shall come up like a [n]lion from the [11]swelling of Jôr′dan unto the habitation of the strong: but [o]I will make them suddenly run away from her: and who *is* a chosen *man*, *that* I may appoint over her? for who *is* like [p]me? and who will appoint me the time? and who *is* that shepherd that will stand before me?

45 Therefore hear ye the counsel[G] of the LORD, that he hath taken against [l]Băb′ȳ-lon; and his purposes, that he hath purposed against the land of the Chăl-dē′anș: Surely [12]the least of the flock shall draw them out: surely he shall make *their* habitation desolate with them.

46 At the noise of the taking of [l]Băb′ȳ-lon the earth is moved, and the cry is heard among the nations.

## CHAPTER 51

*Utter destruction to come upon Babylon for her cruelties to Israel. 59 Her perpetual desolation typified by the book cast into the Euphrates.*

THUS saith the LORD; Behold, I will raise up against [a,b]Băb′ȳ-lon, and against them that dwell in [1]the midst of them that rise up against me, [c]a destroying wind;

2 And will send unto Băb′ȳ-lon [2]fanners[G], that shall [d]fan her, and [c]shall empty her land: for in the day of trouble they shall be against her round about.

3 [3,b]Against *him that* bendeth let the [e]archer bend his bow, and against *him that* lifteth himself

l *Babylon, prophecies concerning*, Ezra 5:12.

43
m *Adversity, despondency in*, Psa. 10:6.

44
n *Lion*, Mic. 5:8.
o *God, power of*, Gen. 2:2.
p *God, sovereign*, Gen. 2:2.
11 R. V. pride

45
12 R. V. they shall drag them away, even the little ones of the flock;

1
a *Babylon, prophecies concerning*, Ezra 5:12.
b *Nation, punishment of*, Isa. 2:4.
c *Judgments, executed by human instrumentality*, Ex. 6:6.
1 R. V. Lebkamai, a destroying wind.

2
d Isa. 30:24; Jer. 15:7; Matt. 3:12.
2 R. V. strangers,

3
e *Archery*, Gen. 21:20.
3 R. V. Let not the archer bend his bow, and let him not lift himself up in his coat of mail:

up in his [l]brigandine[G]: and spare
ye not her young men; destroy ye
utterly all her host.
4 Thus [b]the slain shall fall in
the [a]land of the Chăl-dē′anș, and
*they that are* thrust through in
her streets.
5 For [g,h]Ĭș′ra-el *hath* not *been*
forsaken, nor Jū′dah of his God,
of the LORD of hosts; though
their land was filled with sin
against the [i]Holy One of Ĭș′ra-el.[S]
6 Flee out of the midst of
[a,j]Băb′ȳ-lon, and deliver every
man his [4]soul[G]: be not cut off in
her iniquity; for this *is* the time
of the LORD's vengeance; he will
render unto her a [b]recompence.[Q]
7 Băb′ȳ-lon *hath been* a golden
[k]cup in the LORD's hand, that
made all the earth [l]drunken:
the nations have drunken of her
[m]wine; therefore the nations are
mad.[G][Q]
8 Băb′ȳ-lon is suddenly [b]fallen
and destroyed: howl for her; take
[n,o]balm for her pain, if so be she
may be healed.[Q]
9 We would have healed Băb′ȳ-
lon, but she is not healed: forsake her, and let us go every
one into his own country: for
her [b]judgment reacheth unto
heaven, and is lifted up *even* to
the skies.[Q]
10 The LORD hath brought
forth our righteousness: come,
and let us [p]declare in Zī′ŏn the
work of the LORD our God.[S]
11 Make bright the [e]arrows;
gather the [q]shields: the LORD
hath raised up the spirit of the
kings of the [r]Mēdeș: for his device[G] *is* against [a]Băb′ȳ-lon, to
[b]destroy it; because it *is* the [s]ven-
geance of the LORD, the ven-
geance of his temple.
12 Set up the [t]standard upon
the walls of Băb′ȳ-lon, make the
watch strong, set up the watchmen, prepare the [u,v]ambushes:
for the LORD hath both devised[G] and done that which he
spake against the inhabitants of
Băb′ȳ-lon.
13 O [b]thou that dwellest upon
many waters, abundant in treasures, thine end is come, *and* the
measure of thy [w]covetousness.[Q]
14 The LORD of hosts hath
[x]sworn by himself, *saying*, Surely I will fill thee with men, as
with [5]caterpillers; and they shall
lift up a shout against thee.
15 He hath [y]made the [z]earth by
his [a]power, he hath established
the world by his [b]wisdom, and
hath stretched out the [c]heaven
by his [b]understanding.[S][T]
16 When he uttereth *his* voice,
*there is* a multitude of waters in
the heavens; and [d]he causeth the
[e]vapours to ascend from the ends
of the earth: he maketh [f]light-
nings with [g]rain, and bringeth
forth the [h]wind out of his treasures.[G]
17 Every man is [6]brutish[G] by *his*
knowledge, every founder[G] is confounded by the graven[G] image:
for [i]his molten[G] image *is* falsehood, and *there is* no breath in
them.
18 [i]They *are* vanity, the work
of [7]errors: in the time of their
visitation[G] they shall perish.
19 The portion of Jā′cob *is* not
like them; for he *is* the [j]former of
all things: and *Ĭș′ra-el is* the [8]rod
of his inheritance: the LORD of
hosts *is* his name.
20 [k]Thou *art* my battle [l]ax *and*
weapons of war: for with thee
will I break in pieces the nations,
and with thee will I destroy kingdoms;[S]
21 And with [k]thee will I break
in pieces the [m]horse and his rider;
and with thee will I break in
pieces the [n]chariot and his rider;
22 With [k]thee also will I break
in pieces man and woman; and
with thee will I break in pieces
[o]old and [p]young; and with thee

*l* *Coat of Mail*, 1 Sam. 17:5.

**5**

*g* *God, faithfulness of*, Gen. 2:2.
*h* *God, mercy of*, Gen. 2:2.
*i* *God, holiness of*, Gen. 2:2.

**6**

*j* *Evil Company*, Prov. 13:20.
4 R. V. life;

**7**

*k* *Cup, figurative*, Matt. 20:22.
*l* *Drunkenness, figurative*, Luke 21:34.
*m* *Wine, figurative*, Prov. 23:31.

**8**

*n* *Balm*, Gen. 37:25.
*o* *Medicine*, Prov. 17:22.

**10**

*p* *Religious Testimony*, 2 Thess. 1:10.

**11**

*q* *Shield*, 1 Kin. 14:27.
*r* *Medes, prophecies concerning*, Dan. 5:28.
*s* *Adversity, dispensation from God*, Psa. 10:6.

**12**

*t* *Standard*, Num. 1:52.
*u* *Ambush*, Josh. 8:2.
*v* *Strategy*, Judg. 7:16.

**13**

*w* *Covetousness*, Isa. 57:17.

**14**

*x* *Oath, attributed to God*, Num. 5:19.
5 R. V. the cankerworm,

**15**

*y* *God, creator*, Gen. 2:2.
*z* *Earth, created*, Prov. 8:23.

*a* *God, power of*, Gen. 2:2.
*b* *God, wisdom of*, Gen. 2:2.
*c* *Heavens, created*, Psa. 8:3.

**16**

*d* *God, providence of*, Gen. 2:2.
*e* *Meteorology*, Matt. 16:2.
*f* *Lightning*, Job 28:26.
*g* *Rain*, 2 Sam. 1:21.
*h* *Wind*, Job 37:17.

**17**

*i* *Idolatry, folly of*, 1 Sam. 15:23.
6 R. V. become brutish and is without knowledge: every goldsmith is put to shame by his graven image:

**18**

7 R. V. delusion:

**19**

*j* *God, creator*, Gen. 2:2.
8 R. V. tribe

**20**

*k* *Agency, in executing judgments*, Mark 1:17.
*l* *Ax, figurative*, Deut. 19:5.

**21**

*m* *Horse*, Job 39:19.
*n* *Chariot*, Josh. 11:4.

**22**

*o* *Old Age*, Isa. 46:4.
*p* *Young Men*, Prov. 1:4.

will I break in pieces the young
man and the maid;
23 I will also break in pieces
with [k]thee the shepherd and his
flock; and with thee will I break
in pieces the husbandman and
his yoke of oxen; and with thee
will I break in pieces [9]captains
and rulers.
24 And I will [q]render unto
[r]Băb′ȳ-lon and to all the inhabitants of Chăl-dē′ȧ all their evil
that they have done in Zī′ŏn in
your sight, saith the LORD.
25 Behold, I *am* against thee,
O destroying mountain, saith
the LORD, which destroyest all
the earth: and [s]I will stretch out
mine hand upon thee, and roll
thee down from the rocks, and
will make thee a burnt mountain.
26 And they shall not take of
thee a stone for a corner, nor a
stone for foundations; but [s]thou
shalt be desolate for ever, saith
the LORD.
27 Set ye up a [t]standard in the
land, blow the [u]trumpet among
the nations, prepare the nations against her, call together
against her the kingdoms of
[v]Âr′a-răt, Mĭn′nī, and [w]Ăsh′che-
năz; appoint a captain against
her; cause the horses to come
up as the rough [10]caterpillers.
28 Prepare against her the nations with the kings of the [x]Mē-
deș, the [11]captains thereof, and
all the [12]rulers thereof, and all
the land of his dominion.
29 And the land shall tremble
and sorrow: for every purpose of
the LORD shall be performed
against [r]Băb′ȳ-lon, to [y]make the
land of Băb′ȳ-lon a desolation
without an inhabitant.
30 The mighty men of Băb′ȳ-
lon have forborn to fight, they
have remained in *their* holds:
their might hath failed; they
became as women: [z]they have

23
9 R. V. governors and deputies.

24
*q Wicked, punishment of,* Psa. 73:3.
*r Babylon, prophecies concerning,* Ezra 5:12.

25
*s Nation, judgments denounced against,* Isa. 2:4.

27
*t Standard,* Num. 1:52.
*u Trumpet,* Josh. 6:4.
*v Ararat,* Gen. 8:4.
*w* Or, *Ashkenaz,* Gen. 10:3.
10 R. V. cankerworm.

28
*x Medes, prophecies concerning,* Dan. 5:28.
11 R. V. governors
12 R. V. deputies

29
*y Adversity, dispensation from God,* Psa. 10:6.

30
*z War, evils of,* Judg. 3:2.

burned her dwellingplaces; her
bars are broken.
31 One [a]post shall run to meet
another, and one messenger to
meet another, to shew the king
of [b]Băb′ȳ-lon that his city is
taken [13]at *one* end,
32 And that the passages are
[14]stopped, and the reeds they
have burned with fire, and the
men of war are affrighted.
33 For thus saith the LORD of
hosts, the God of Ĭș′ra-el; The
daughter of [b]Băb′ȳ-lon *is* like
a threshingfloor, [15]*it is* time to
thresh her: yet a little while, and
the time of her harvest shall
come.
34 [c]Nĕb-u-chad-rĕz′zar the king
of Băb′ȳ-lon hath devoured me,
he hath crushed me, he hath
made me an empty vessel, he
hath swallowed me up like a
dragon, he hath filled his belly
with my [16]delicates, he hath cast
me out.
35 The violence done to me and
to my flesh *be* upon [b]Băb′ȳ-lon,
shall the inhabitant of Zī′ŏn say;
and my blood upon the inhabitants of Chăl-dē′ȧ, shall Jē-rṳ′sȧ-
lĕm say.
36 Therefore thus saith the
LORD; Behold, I will plead thy
cause, and take vengeance for
thee; and I will [d]dry up her sea,
and make her springs dry.
37 And [b]Băb′ȳ-lon shall become heaps, a dwellingplace for
[17]dragons, an astonishment, and
an hissing, without an inhabitant.
38 They shall roar together like
[e]lions: they shall [18]yell as lions'
whelps.
39 [d]In their heat I will make
their feasts, and I will make
them [f]drunken, that they may
rejoice, and sleep a perpetual
sleep, and not wake, saith the
LORD.
40 I will bring them down like

31
*a Post,* Job 9:25.
*b Babylon, prophecies concerning,* Ezra 5:12.
13 R. V. on every quarter:

32
14 R. V. surprised,

33
15 R. V. at the time when it is trodden;

34
*c* Or, *Nebuchadnezzar,* Dan. 2:1.
16 Am. R. V. delicacies;

36
*d Nation, judgments denounced against,* Isa. 2:4

37
17 R. V. jackals,

38
*e Lion,* Mic. 5:8.
18 R. V. growl

39
*f Drunkenness, figurative,* Luke 21:34.

lambs to the slaughter, like rams with he goats.

41 How is [g]Shē′shăch taken! and how is the praise of the whole earth surprised! how is Băb′ȳ-lon become [19]an astonishment among the nations!

42 [h]The sea is come up upon Băb′ȳ-lon: she is covered with the multitude of the waves thereof.

43 [h]Her cities are a desolation, a dry land, and a wilderness, a land wherein no man dwelleth, neither doth *any* son of man pass thereby.

44 And [i]I will punish [j]Bĕl in [b]Băb′ȳ-lon, and I will bring forth out of his mouth that which he hath swallowed up: and the nations shall not flow together any more unto him: yea, the [k]wall of Băb′ȳ-lon shall fall.

45 My people, go ye out of the midst of [l]her, and deliver ye every man his soul from the fierce [m]anger of the LORD.

46 And lest your heart faint, and ye fear for the rumour that shall be heard in the land; a rumour shall both come *one* year, and after that in *another* year *shall come* a rumour, and violence in the land, ruler against ruler.

47 Therefore, behold, the days come, that I will do judgment upon the [i]graven images of [b]Băb′ȳ-lon: and her whole land shall be confounded, and all her slain shall fall in the midst of her.

48 Then the heaven and the earth, and all that *is* therein, shall sing for [b]Băb′ȳ-lon: for the spoilers shall come unto her from the north, saith the LORD.

49 As Băb′ȳ-lon *hath caused* the slain of Ĭs′ra-el to fall, so at [b,d]Băb′ȳ-lon shall fall the slain of all the earth.

50 Ye that have escaped the sword, go away, stand not still: remember the LORD afar off, and let [n]Jĕ-ru′să-lĕm come into your mind.

51 We are confounded, because we have heard reproach: shame hath covered our faces: for strangers are come into the sanctuaries of the [o]LORD's house.

52 Wherefore, behold, the days come, saith the LORD, that I will do judgment upon her [i]graven images: and through all her land the wounded shall groan.

53 Though [b]Băb′ȳ-lon should mount up to heaven, and though she should fortify the height of her strength, *yet* [p]from me [d]shall spoilers come unto her, saith the LORD.

54 A sound of a cry *cometh* from Băb′ȳ-lon, and great destruction from the land of the Chăl-dē′ans:

55 Because [h]the LORD hath [p]spoiled Băb′ȳ-lon, and destroyed out of her the great voice; when her waves do roar like great waters, a noise of their voice is uttered:

56 Because [h]the spoiler is come upon her, *even* upon Băb′ȳ-lon, and her mighty men are taken, every one of their bows is broken: for the LORD God of recompences shall surely requite.

57 And I will make [f]drunk her princes, and her wise *men*, her [20]captains, and her [21]rulers, and her mighty men: and they shall sleep a perpetual sleep, and not wake, saith the [q]King, whose name *is* the LORD of hosts.

58 Thus saith the LORD of hosts; The broad [k]walls of [b]Băb′ȳ-lon shall be utterly broken, and her high [r]gates shall be burned with fire; and the people shall labour [22]in vain, and the [23]folk in the fire, and they shall be weary.

59 ¶ The word which [s]Jĕr-e-mī′ah the prophet commanded

41
*g* Jer. 25:26.
19 R. V. a desolation

42
*h Nation, punishment of,* Isa. 2:4.

44
*i Idolatry, prophecies relating to,* 1 Sam. 15:23.
*j* Isa. 46:1; Jer. 50:2.
*k Walls, of Babylon,* 1 Sam. 20:25.

45
*l Evil Company,* Prov. 13:20.
*m Anger of God,* 2 Kin. 13:3.

50
*n Jerusalem,* Judg. 19:10.

51
*o Temple, Solomon's,* 1 Kin. 6:17.

53
*p Adversity, dispensation from God,* Psa. 10:6.

57
*q God, sovereign,* Gen. 2:2.
20 R. V. governors
21 R. V. deputies,

58
*r Babylon, gates of,* Ezra 5:12.
22 R. V. for vanity,
23 R. V. nations for

59
*s Jeremiah,* Jer. 1:1.

Sěr-a-ī′ah the son of Nē-rī′ah,
the son of [t]Mā-a-sē′iah, when
he went with [u]Zěd-e-kī′ah the
king of [v]Jū′dah into Băb′ȳ-lon
in the fourth year of his reign.
And *this* Sěr-a-ī′ah *was* [24]a quiet
prince.
60 So [s]Jěr-e-mī′ah wrote in a
[w]book all the [x]evil that should
come upon [b]Băb′ȳ-lon, *even* all
these [y]words that are written
against Băb′ȳ-lon.
61 And [s]Jěr-e-mī′ah said to
Sěr-a-ī′ah, When thou comest to
Băb′ȳ-lon, and shalt see, and
shalt read all these [y]words;
62 Then shalt thou say, O
LORD, thou hast spoken against
this place, to [p]cut it off, that none
shall remain in it, neither man
nor beast, but that it shall be
desolate for ever.
63 [Q]And it shall be, when thou
hast made an end of reading this
[w]book, *that* [z]thou shalt bind a
stone to it, and [z]cast it into the
midst of [a]Eū-phrā′tēș:
64 And thou shalt say, Thus
shall [b]Băb′ȳ-lon sink, and shall
not rise from the [c]evil that I will
bring upon her: and they shall be
weary. Thus far *are* the words of
[d]Jěr-e-mī′ah.[Q]

## CHAPTER 52

*Zedekiah rebels. 4 Jerusalem is besieged and taken. 8 Zedekiah's sons are killed, his own eyes put out, and he carried captive to Babylon. 12 Nebuzar-adan spoils and burns the temple and city. 24 He carries away the inhabitants of the land as captives. 31 Evil-merodach advances the king, Jehoiachin.*

[a]ZĚD-E-KĪ′AH *was* one and
twenty years old when he
began to reign, and he reigned
eleven years in [b]Jē-ru̥′să-lěm.
And his mother's name *was*
[c]Hă-mū′tal the daughter of [c]Jěr-
e-mī′ah of [c]Lĭb′nah.
2 And [a,d]he did *that which was*
evil in the eyes of the LORD,
[e,f]according to all that [g]Jē-hoi′a-
kĭm had done.
3 For through the [h]anger of the
LORD it came to pass in Jē-ru̥′-
să-lěm and Jū′dah, till he had
[i]cast them out from his presence,
that [a]Zěd-e-kī′ah rebelled against
the [j]king of [k]Băb′ȳ-lon.
4 ¶ And it came to pass in the
ninth year of his reign, in the
tenth [l]month, in the tenth *day* of
the month, *that* [j]Něb-u-chad-
rěz′zar king of [k]Băb′ȳ-lon came,
he and all his army, against [m]Jē-
ru̥′să-lěm, and pitched against it,
and built [n]forts against it round
about.
5 So the [m]city was [o]besieged
unto the eleventh year of king
[a]Zěd-e-kī′ah.
6 And in the fourth [p]month, in
the ninth *day* of the month, the
[q]famine was sore in the city, so
that there was no bread for the
people of the land.
7 Then [1]the [r]city was broken
up, and all the men of war fled,
and went forth out of the city by
night by the way of the [s]gate between the two walls, which *was*
by the king's garden; (now the
[t]Chăl-dē′anș *were* by the city
round about:) and they went by
the way of the [2]plain.
8 But the army of the [t]Chăl-
dē′anș pursued after the king,
and overtook [a]Zěd-e-kī′ah in the
[u]plains of Jěr′ī-chō; and all his
army was scattered from him.
9 Then they took the [a]king, and
carried him up unto the [j]king
of [k]Băb′ȳ-lon to [v]Rĭb′lah in the
land of [w]Hā′math; where he gave
judgment upon him.
10 And the [j]king of [k]Băb′ȳ-lon
[x,y]slew the sons of [a]Zěd-e-kī′ah
before his eyes: he slew also
all the princes of Jū′dah in
[v]Rĭb′lah.
11 Then he [x,y]put out the eyes
of [a]Zěd-e-kī′ah; and the [j]king of
[k]Băb′ȳ-lon bound him in chains,
and carried him to Băb′ȳ-lon,
and put him in [z]prison till the
day of his death.

t Jer. 32:12.
u *Zedekiah*, 2 Kin. 25:2.
v *Judah, kingdom of*, 2 Chr. 11:17.
24 R. V. chief chamberlain.

60
w *Book, prophecies written in*, Num. 5:23.
x *Judgments*, Ex. 6:6.
y *Prophecies, inspired*, Dan. 9:24.

63
z *Instruction, by object lessons*, Prov. 23:23.

a *Euphrates*, Gen. 15:18.

64
b *Babylon, prophecies concerning*, Ezra 5:12.
c *Judgments*, Ex. 6:6.
d *Jeremiah*, Jer. 1:1.

v.1–518 BC
See footnote, *Time*, Rev. 10:6.

1
a *Zedekiah*, 2 Kin. 25:2.
b *Jerusalem*, Judg. 19:10.
c 2 Kin. 23:31; 24:18.

2
d *Rulers, wicked*, Ex. 18:21.
e *Influence, evil*, 1 Cor. 7:14.
f *Example, bad*, John 13:15.
g *Jehoiakim*, Jer. 26:1.

3
h *Anger of God*, 2 Kin. 13:3.
i *Wicked, punishment of*, Psa. 73:3.
j *Nebuchadnezzar*, Dan. 2:1.
k *Babylon, empire of*, Ezra 5:12.

4
l *Month (January)*, Ex. 12:2.
m *Jerusalem, besieged*, Judg. 19:10.
n *Fortification*, Ezek. 17:17.
v.4–509 BC

5
o *Siege*, Deut. 28:53.

6
p *Month (July)*, Ex. 12:2.
q *Famine, instances of*, 2 Kin. 8:1.
v.6–507 BC

7
r *Jerusalem, captured*, Judg. 19:10.
s *Jerusalem, gates of*, Judg. 19:10.
t *Chaldeans*, Dan. 1:4.
1 R. V. a breach was made in the city,
2 R. V. Arabah.

8
u Jer. 39:5; 2 Kin. 25:5.

9
v *Riblah*, Num. 34:11.
w *Hamath*, 1 Chr. 18:3.

10
x *Captive, cruelty to*, 1 Sam. 30:3.
y *Cruelty, instances of*, Psa. 27:12.

11
z *Prison*, Gen. 39:20.

v.12–507 BC
See footnote, *Time*, Rev. 10:6.

12 ¶ Now in the fifth [a]month, in the tenth *day* of the month, which *was* the nineteenth year of [b]Nĕb-u-chad-rĕz′zar king of [c]Băb′ȳ-lon, came [d]Nĕb′u-zär–ā′-dan, [e]captain of the guard, *which* served the king of Băb′ȳ-lon, into [f]Jē-rṳ′sā-lĕm,

13 And [g]burned the [h]house of the LORD, and the [i]king's house; and all the houses of [f]Jē-rṳ′sā-lĕm, and all the houses of the great *men*, burned he with fire:

14 And all the army of the [j]Chăl-dē′anș, that *were* with the [e]captain of the guard, brake down all the [k]walls of Jē-rṳ′sā-lĕm round about.

15 Then [d]Nĕb′u-zär–ā′dan the [e]captain of the guard [l]carried away captive *certain* of the poor of the people, and the residue[G] of the people that remained in the city, and those that fell[G] away, that fell to the king of [c]Băb′ȳ-lon, and the rest of the multitude.

16 But [d]Nĕb′u-zär–ā′dan the [e]captain of the guard left *certain* of the poor of the land for [m]vinedressers and for husbandmen[G].

17 Also the [n]pillars of [o]brass[G] that *were* in the [h]house of the LORD, and the bases, and the [p]brasen[G] sea that *was* in the house of the LORD, the Chăl-dē′anș[G] brake[G], and carried all the brass of them to Băb′ȳ-lon.

18 The [q]caldrons also, and the [r]shovels, and the [s]snuffers, and the [t]bowls, and the [u]spoons, and all the vessels of [o]brass[G] wherewith they ministered, took they away.

19 And the [v]basons, and the [w]firepans[G], and the [t]bowls, and the [q]caldrons, and the [x]candlesticks[G], and the [u]spoons, and the [y]cups; *that* which *was* of [z]gold *in* gold, and *that* which *was* of [a]silver *in* silver, took the [b]captain of the guard away.

20 The [c]two [d]pillars, one [e]sea, and twelve [f]brasen[G] bulls that *were* under the bases, which king [g]Sŏl′o-mon had made [3]in the [h]house of the LORD: the brass[G] of all these vessels was without[G] weight.

21 And *concerning* the [d]pillars, the height of one pillar *was* eighteen [i,j]cubits[G]; and a [4]fillet[G] of twelve cubits[G] did compass[G] it; and the thickness thereof *was* [j,k]four fingers[G]: *it was* hollow.

22 And a [5,l]chapiter[G] of [f]brass[G] *was* upon it; and the height of one [5]chapiter[G] *was* five [i]cubits[G], with network and [m]pomegranates upon the [5]chapiters[G] round about, all *of* brass[G]. The second pillar also and the pomegranates *were* like unto these.

23 And there were ninety and six [m]pomegranates on [6]a side; *and* all the pomegranates upon the network *were* an hundred round about.

24 ¶ And the [b]captain of the guard took [n]Sĕr-a-ī′ah the chief [o]priest, and [p]Zĕph-a-nī′ah the second priest, and the three [q]keepers of the door:

25 He took also out of the city an [7]eunuch, which had the charge of the men of war; and seven men of them that were near the king's person, which were found in the city; and the [8]principal [r]scribe of the host, who mustered the people of the land; and threescore men of the people of the land, that were found in the midst of the city.

26 So [s]Nĕb′u-zär–ā′dan the [b]captain of the guard took them, and brought them to the [t]king of [u]Băb′ȳ-lon to [v]Rĭb′lah.

27 And the [t]king of [u]Băb′ȳ-lon smote[G] them, and [w]put them to death in [v]Rĭb′lah in the land of [x]Hā′math. Thus Jū′dah was [y]carried away captive out of his own land.

28 This *is* the people whom

**12**
a *Month (August)*, Ex. 12:2.
b Or, *Nebuchadnezzar*, Dan. 2:1.
c *Babylon*, Ezra 5:12.
d *Nebuzar-adan*, 2 Kin. 25:8.
e *Captain*, Num. 31:48.
f *Jerusalem*, Judg. 19:10.
**13**
g *War, evils of*, Judg. 3:2.
h *Temple, Solomon's*, 1 Kin. 6:17.
i *Palace*, 1 Kin. 21:1.
**14**
j *Chaldeans*, Dan. 1:4.
k *Jerusalem, walls of*, Judg. 19:10.
**15**
l *Captivity, of Judah in Babylon*, Isa. 5:13.
**16**
m *Vineyard*, Isa. 1:8.
**17**
n *Pillar*, Gen. 28:18.
o *Brass*, Job 28:2.
p *Laver*, Ex. 30:18.
**18**
q *Caldron*, 1 Sam. 2:14.
r *Shovel*, Num. 4:14.
s *Snuffers*, 1 Kin. 7:50.
t *Bowl*, Ex. 25:29.
u *Spoons*, Num. 4:7.
**19**
v *Basin*, 1 Kin. 7:50.
w *Censer*, Lev. 16:12.
x *Candlestick*, Ex. 25:31.
y *Cup*, Gen. 44:2.
z *Gold*, Ezek. 7:19.
a *Silver*, 1 Chr. 28:14.
b *Captain*, Num. 31:48.
**20**
c 1 Kin. 7:21; 2 Chr. 3:17.
d *Pillar*, Gen. 28:18.
e *Laver*, Ex. 30:18.

v.20–507 BC
See footnote, *Time*, Rev. 10:6.

f *Brass*, Job 28:2.
g *Solomon*, 2 Sam. 12:24.
h *Temple, Solomon's*, 1 Kin. 6:17.
3 R. V. for
**21**
i *Cubit*, Ex. 36:9.
j *Measure, linear*, Deut. 25:15.
k *Handbreadth*, 1 Kin. 7:26.
4 R. V. line
**22**
l *Chapiter*, 1 Kin. 7:17.
m *Pomegranate*, Num. 13:23.
5 Am. R. V. capital
**23**
6 R. V. the sides.
**24**
n 2 Kin. 25:18–21; Ezra 7:1.
o *Priest, taken with the captivity to Babylon*, Lev. 1:5.
p *Zephaniah*, Jer. 21:1.
q *Porters*, 2 Sam. 18:26.
**25**
r *Scribe, mustering officer of the army*, 1 Kin. 4:3.
7 R. V. officer that was set over the
8 R. V. scribe of the captain of
**26**
s *Nebuzar-adan*, 2 Kin. 25:8.
t *Nebuchadnezzar*, Dan. 2:1.
u *Babylon*, Ezra 5:12.
v *Riblah*, Num. 34:11.
**27**
w *Captive, of war, put to death*, 1 Sam. 30:3.
x *Hamath*, 1 Chr. 18:3.
y *Jews, captive in Babylon*, Neh. 4:2.

v.28–519 BC
See footnote, *Time*, Rev. 10:6.

29
*z Jerusalem*, Judg. 19:10.
v.29–508 BC

v 30–503 BC

31
*a Jehoiachin*, 2 Kin. 24:6.
*b Month (March)*, Ex. 12:2.

[t]Něb-u-chad-rěz′zar carried away captive: in the seventh year three thousand [y]Jews and three and twenty:

29 In the eighteenth year of [t]Něb-u-chad-rěz′zar he [y]carried away captive from [z]Jē-ru′să-lĕm eight hundred thirty and two persons:

30 In the three and twentieth year of [t]Něb-u-chad-rěz′zar [s]Něb′u-zär–ā′dan the captain of the guard carried away captive of the [y]Jews seven hundred forty and five persons: all the persons *were* four thousand and six hundred.

31 ¶ And it came to pass in the seven and thirtieth year of the captivity of [a]Jē-hoi′a-chĭn king of Jū′dah, in the twelfth [b]month, in the five and twentieth *day* of the month, *that* [c]Ē′vĭl–mĕ-rō′-dach king of [d]Băb′ȳ-lon in the *first* year of his reign [e]lifted[C] up the head of Jē-hoi′a-chĭn king of Jū′dah, and brought him forth out of prison,

32 And [e]spake kindly unto him, and set his throne above the throne of the kings that *were* with him in Băb′ȳ-lon,

33 And [e]changed his prison garments: and [f]he did continually eat bread before him all the days of his life.

34 And [e,f]*for* his [9]diet,[C] there was a continual [9]diet given him of the [c]king of [d]Băb′ȳ-lon, every day a portion until the day of his death, all the days of his life.

v.31–482 BC
See footnote, *Time*, Rev. 10:6.

*c* 2 Kin. 25:27-30.
*d Babylon*, Ezra 5:12.
*e Prisoners, kindness to*, Psa. 79:11.

33
*f Hospitality*, Rom. 12:13.

34
9 R. V. allowance.

THE
# LAMENTATIONS OF JEREMIAH

## CHAPTER 1

*The miserable condition of Jerusalem by reason of her sins. 12 She complains of her afflictions, 18 and confesses God's judgment to be just.*

1
*a Patriotism*, Psa. 137:1.
*b Jerusalem*, Judg. 19:10.

3
*c Captivity, as a judgment*, Isa. 5:13.
*d Jews, captive in Babylon*, Neh. 4:2.

[a]HOW doth the [b]city sit solitary,[C] *that was* full of people! *how* is she become as a widow! she *that was* great among the nations, *and* princess among the provinces, *how* is she become tributary![C]

2 She weepeth sore[C] in the night, and her tears *are* on her cheeks: among all her lovers she hath none to comfort *her*: all her friends have dealt treacherously with her, they are become her enemies.

3 Jū′dah is gone into [c,d]captivity because of affliction, and because of great servitude: she dwelleth among the heathen,[C] she findeth no rest: all her persecutors overtook her between the straits.[C]

4 [e]The ways of [f]Zī′ŏn do mourn, because none come to the [g]solemn [1]feasts: all her gates are desolate: her priests sigh, her virgins are afflicted, and she *is* in bitterness.

5 Her adversaries are the chief, her enemies prosper; for the LORD hath [h,i]afflicted her for the multitude of her transgressions: her children are gone into [c,d]captivity before the enemy.

6 [h,i]And from the daughter of [f]Zī′ŏn all her beauty is departed: her princes are become like harts *that* find no pasture, and they are gone without strength before the pursuer.

7 [b]Jē-ru′să-lĕm [j]remembered in the days of her affliction and of her miseries all her pleasant things that she had in the days of old, when her people fell into the hand of the enemy, and none did help her: the adversaries saw

4
*e Church, love for*, Matt. 16:18.
*f Zion*, 2 Sam. 5:7.
*g Annual Feasts*, Num. 15:3.
1 R. V. assembly;

5
*h Divine Chastisement*, Job 33:19.
*i Nation, punishment of*, Isa. 2:4.

7
*j Adversity, benefits of*, Psa. 10:6.

her, *and* did [k]mock at her [2]sab-
baths.
8 [b]Jē-rṳ′să-lĕm [l]hath grievously sinned; therefore [h]she is
[3]removed: all that honoured her
despise her, because they have
seen her nakedness: yea, she
sigheth, and turneth backward.
9 Her [l]filthiness *is* in her skirts;
she remembereth not her last
end; therefore she came down
wonderfully[c]: she had no comforter. [m]O LORD, behold my
affliction: for the enemy hath
magnified *himself*.
10 The adversary hath spread
out his hand upon all her pleasant things: for she hath seen
*that* the *heathen entered into
her [n]sanctuary, whom thou didst
command *that* they should not
enter into thy congregation.
11 [m]All her people sigh, they
seek bread; they have given their
pleasant things for meat[c] to relieve the soul: see, O LORD, and
consider; for I am become vile.
12 ¶ *Is it* nothing to you, all
ye that pass by? behold, and see
if there be any sorrow like unto
my [o]sorrow, which is done unto
me, wherewith the LORD hath
[h,i]afflicted *me* in the day of his
fierce [p]anger.
13 [h,i]From above hath he sent
[q]fire into my bones, and it pre-
vaileth against them: he hath
spread a net for my feet, he hath
turned me back: he hath made
me desolate *and* faint all the
day.
14 The [r]yoke of my transgressions is bound by his hand: they
are wreathed[c], *and* come up upon
my neck: he hath made my
strength to fall, the Lord hath
delivered me into *their* hands,
*from whom* I am not able to
rise up.
15 [h,i]The Lord hath trodden[G]
under foot all my mighty *men* in
the midst of me: he hath called
an assembly against me to crush
my young men: the Lord hath
trodden[G] the virgin, the daughter
of Jū′dah, *as* in a [s]winepress.[Q]
16 For these *things* I [t]weep;
mine eye, mine eye runneth down
with water, because the comforter that should relieve my
soul is far from me: my children are desolate, because the
enemy prevailed.
17 [e,f]Zī′ŏn spreadeth[G] forth her
hands, *and there is* none to comfort her: the LORD hath commanded concerning Jā′cob, *that*
his adversaries *should be* round
about him: [b]Jē-rṳ′să-lĕm is [4]as
a menstruous[G] woman among
them.
18 ¶ [u]The LORD is [v]righteous;
for I have rebelled against his
commandment: hear, I pray you,
all [5]people, and behold my sorrow: my virgins and my young
men are gone into [c,d]captivity.[S]
19 I called for my lovers, *but*
they deceived me: my priests and
mine elders gave up the ghost[G] in
the city, while they sought their
meat[G] to relieve their souls.
20 [m]Behold, O LORD; for I
*am* in distress: my [w]bowels[G] are
troubled; mine heart is turned
within me; for I have grievously
rebelled: abroad the sword be-
reaveth, at home *there is* as
death.
21 They have heard that I
[o]sigh: *there is* none to comfort
me: all mine enemies have heard

k *Scoffing*, Hab. 1:10.
2 R. V. desolations.

8
l *Jews, wickedness of*, Neh. 4:2.
3 R. V. become as an unclean thing:

9
m *Adversity, prayer in*, Psa. 10:6.

10
n *Temple, Solomon's*, 1 Kin. 6:17.

12
o *Despondency*, Eccl. 2:20.
p *Anger of God*, 2 Kin. 13:3.

13
q *Fire, figurative*, Ex. 12:8.

14
r *Yoke, figurative*, 1 Sam. 6:7.

15
s *Wine Press*, Isa. 5:2.

16
t *Weeping*, Ezra 3:13.

17
4 R. V. among them as an unclean thing.

18
u *Adversity, resignation in, exemplified*, Psa. 10:6.
v *God, justice of*, Gen. 2:2.
5 R. V. ye peoples.

20
w *Bowels, figurative*, 1 Kin. 3:26.

***HEATHEN.** Under this head are grouped all who were not embraced under the Abrahamic covenant. *Cast out of Canaan*, Lev. 18:24, 25; Psa. 44:2; *and their land given to Israel*, Psa. 105:44; 135:10–12; 136:21, 22. *Excluded from the temple*, Lam. 1:10.
Divine revelations given to: *To Abimelech*, Gen. 20:3–7; *to Pharaoh*, Gen. 41:1–32; *to Balaam*, Num. 22:12, 20–35; *to Nebuchadnezzar*, Dan. 2:1, 45; 4:1–18; *to Cyrus*, 2 Chr. 36:23; *to the Magi*, Matt. 2:1, 2, 9–12; *to Cornelius*, Acts 10:1–7.
*Believed in Christ*, Matt. 8:5–13; Luke 7:2–9.
Pious people among, Acts 10:35; *Melchizedek*, Gen. **14:18–20**; *Abimelech*, Gen. 20; *Balaam*, Num. 22; *Jethro*, Ex. 18; *Cyrus*, Ezra 1:1–3; *Eliphaz*, Job 4; *Bildad*, Job 8; *Zophar*, Job 11; *Elihu*, Job 32; *Nebuchadnezzar, after his restoration*, Dan. 4; *the Ninevites, after the preaching of Jonah*, Jonah **3:5–10**; *the Magi, who were first to do homage to Jesus*, Matt. **2:1–12**; *the centurion of Cœsarea*, Acts 10.
*Wicked practices of*, see footnote, **IDOLATRY, 1 Sam. 15:23**.
See footnote, **GENTILES, Acts 10:45.**

of my trouble; they are glad that
thou hast done *it*: thou wilt bring
the day *that* thou hast called, and
they shall be like unto me.
22 [x]Let all their wickedness
come before thee; and do unto
them, as thou hast done unto
me for all my transgressions: for
[o]my sighs *are* many, and my
heart *is* faint.

22
*x Prayer, imprecatory*, Acts 6:4.

## CHAPTER 2

*The chastisement of Zion is from the Lord. 11 The prophet's lamentation. 20 His complaint to God.*

1
*a Church, love for*, Matt. 16:18.
*b Poetry, acrostic*, vs. 1–22; Acts 17:28.
*c Zion*, 2 Sam. 5:7.
*d Anger of God*, 2 Kin. 13:3.
*e Footstool, figurative*, 1 Chr. 28:2.

[a, b]HOW hath the Lord covered
the daughter of [c]Zī'ŏn
with a cloud in his [d]anger, *and*
cast down from heaven unto the
earth the beauty of Iṣ'ra-el, and
remembered not his [e]footstool in
the day of his anger!
2 The Lord hath swallowed up
all the habitations of Jā'cob, and
hath not [f]pitied: he hath thrown
down in his wrath the strong
holds of the daughter of Jū'dah;
he hath brought *them* down to
the ground: he hath polluted the
kingdom and the princes thereof.
3 He hath cut off in *his* fierce
[d]anger all the horn of Iṣ'ra-el: he
hath drawn back his right hand
from before the enemy, and he
burned against Jā'cob like a flaming
fire, *which* devoureth round
about.
4 He hath bent his [g]bow like an
enemy: he stood with his right
hand as an adversary, and slew
all *that were* pleasant to the eye
in the tabernacle of the daughter
of [c]Zī'ŏn: he poured out his fury
like fire.

2
*f Pity*, Job 19:21.

4
*g Bow, figurative*, 2 Sam. 1:18.

5 The Lord was as an enemy:
he hath swallowed up Iṣ'ra-el,
he hath swallowed up all her palaces:
he hath destroyed his strong
holds, and hath increased in the
daughter of Jū'dah *mourning
and lamentation.
6 And he hath violently taken
away his tabernacle, as *if it were*
*of* a garden: he hath destroyed
his places of the assembly: the
LORD hath caused the [h]solemn
[1]feasts and [i]sabbaths to be forgotten
in Zī'ŏn, and hath despised
in the indignation of his
[d]anger the king and the priest.
7 The Lord hath cast off his
altar, he hath abhorred his
[j]sanctuary, he hath given up into
the hand of the enemy the walls
of her palaces; they have made a
noise in the [k]house of the LORD,
as in the day of a solemn feast.
8 The LORD hath purposed to
destroy the wall of the daughter
of [c]Zī'ŏn: he hath stretched out
a line, he hath not withdrawn
his hand from destroying: therefore
he made the rampart and
the wall to lament; they languished
together.
9 [l]Her gates are sunk into the
ground; he hath destroyed and
broken her bars: her king and
her princes *are* among the [2]Gĕn'tīleṣ:
the law *is* no *more*; [m]her
prophets also find no [n]vision
from the LORD.
10 The elders of the daughter
of [c]Zī'ŏn [a]sit upon the ground,
*and* keep silence: they have
cast up [o]dust upon their heads;
they have girded themselves with

6
*h Annual Feasts*, Num. 15:3.
*i Sabbath*, Ex. 16:23.
1 R. V. assembly:

7
*j Sanctuary*, Lev. 4:6.
*k Temple, Solomon's*, 1 Kin. 6:17.

9
*l Jerusalem*, Judg. 19:10.
*m Prophecies, cessation of*, Dan. 9:24.
*n Vision*, Acts 9:10.
2 R. V. nations where the law is not; Yea, her

10
*o Dust, put on the head in mourning*, Eccl. 3:20.

***MOURNING. For the dead:** INDICATED: *By lying on ground*, 2 Sam. 12:16. *By personal appearance neglected*, 2 Sam. 14:2. *By cutting the flesh*, Lev. 19:28; 21:1–5; Deut. 14:1; Jer. 16:6; 41:5. *By lamentations*, Gen. 50:10; Ex. 12:30; 1 Sam. 30:4; Jer. 22:18; Matt. 2:17, 18. *By fasting*, 1 Sam. 31:13; 2 Sam. 1:12; 3:35.

*Revenge inconsistent with*, Gen. 27:41. *Priests prohibited from, except for nearest of kin*, Lev. 21:1–5. *For Nadab and Abihu forbidden*, Lev. 10:6. *Sexes separated in*, Zech. 12:12, 14.

*Of Abraham, for Sarah*, Gen. 23:2. *Of Egyptians, for Jacob seventy days*, Gen. 50:1–3. *Of Israelites, for Aaron thirty days*, Num. 20:29.

*David's lamentations, over the death of Saul and Jonathan*, 2 Sam. 1:17–27; *over the death of Abner*, 2 Sam. 3:33, 34; *over the death of Absalom*, 2 Sam. 18:33.

*Jeremiah and the singing men and singing women lament for Josiah*, 2 Chr. 35:25.

**For calamities and other sorrows:** INDICATED: *By rending the garments*, Gen. 37:29, 34; 44:13; Num. 14:6; Judg. 11:35; 2 Sam. 1:2, 11; 3:31; 13:19, 31; 15:32; 2 Kin. 2:12; 5:8; 6:30; 19:1; 22:11, 19; Ezra 9:3, 5; Job 1:20; 2:12; Isa. 37:1; Jer. 41:5. *By wearing mourning dress*, Gen. 38:14; 2 Sam. 14:2; see footnote, SACKCLOTH, Isa. 15:3. *By cutting or plucking the hair and beard*, Ezra 9:3; Jer. 7:29; see footnote, BALDNESS, Lev. 21:5. *By covering the head and face*, 2 Sam. 15:30; 19:4; Esth. 6:12; Jer. 14:3, 4; *and the upper lip*, Ezek. 24:17, 22; Mic. 3:7 [marg.]. *By laying aside ornaments*, Ex. 33:4, 6. *By walking barefoot*, 2 Sam. 15:30. *By laying the hand on the head*, 2 Sam. 13:19; Jer. 2:37. *By dust on the head*, Josh. 7:6; Ezek. 27:30. *By dressing in black*, Jer. 14:2.

p Sackcloth, symbol of mourning, Isa. 15:3.
q Patriotism, Psa. 137:1.
11
r War, evils of, Judg. 3:2.

[p]sackcloth: [q]the virgins of [l]Jĕ-ru̇'-
sā-lĕm hang down their heads to
the ground.
11 [a,q]Mine eyes do fail with
tears, my bowels are troubled, my
liver is poured upon the earth,
for the destruction of the daughter of my people; because [r]the
children and the sucklings swoon
in the streets of the city.
12 They say to their mothers,
[r]Where *is* corn and wine? [r]when
they swooned as the wounded in
the streets of the city, when their
soul was poured out into their
mothers' bosom.
13 [q]What thing shall I take to
witness for thee? what thing
shall I liken to thee, O daughter
of [l]Jĕ-ru̇'sā-lĕm? [a]what shall I
equal to thee, that I may comfort thee, O virgin daughter of
[c]Zī'ŏn? for thy breach *is* great
like the sea: who can heal
thee?
14 Thy [s]prophets have seen
[3]vain and foolish things for thee:
and they have not discovered
thine iniquity, to [4]turn away thy
captivity; but have seen for thee
false burdens and causes of banishment.
15 All that pass by [t]clap *their*
hands at thee; they hiss and wag
their head at the daughter of
Jĕ-ru̇'sā-lĕm, *saying*, *Is* this the
[l]city that *men* call The perfection of beauty, The joy of the
whole earth?
16 All thine enemies have
opened their mouth against thee:
they hiss and [u]gnash the teeth:
they say, We have swallowed
*her* up: certainly this *is* the day
that we looked for; we have
found, we have seen *it*.
17 The [v]LORD hath done *that*
which he had devised; he hath
fulfilled his word that he had
commanded in the days of old:
he hath thrown down, and hath
not pitied: and he hath caused
*thine* enemy to rejoice over thee.
he hath set up the horn of thine
adversaries.
18 Their heart [w]cried unto the
Lord, O wall of the daughter of
Zī'ŏn, [a]let tears run down like a
river day and night: give thyself
no rest; let not the apple of thine
eye cease.
19 [a,q]Arise, [w]cry out in the night:
in the beginning of the [x]watches
pour out thine heart like water
before the face of the Lord: lift
up thy hands toward him for the
life of thy young children, that
faint for hunger in the top of
every street.
20 [w,y]Behold, O LORD, and
consider to whom thou hast done
this. Shall the women [†]eat their
fruit, [5]*and* children of a span
long? shall the priest and the
prophet be slain in the sanctuary
of the Lord?
21 [r]The young and the old lie
on the ground in the streets: my
virgins and my young men are
fallen by the [z]sword; thou hast
slain *them* in the day of thine anger; thou hast killed, *and* not
pitied.
22 Thou hast called as in a solemn day my terrors round about,
so that in the day of the LORD's
anger none escaped nor remained: those that I have [6]swad-
dled and brought up hath mine
enemy consumed.

14
s Prophets, false, Isa. 3:2.
3 R. V. visions for thee of vanity and foolishness;
4 R. V. bring again thy
15
t Mocking, 1 Kin. 18:27.
16
u Gnashing of Teeth, Job 16:9.
17
v God, immutable, Gen. 2:2.

18
w Nation, in adversity, prayer of, vs. 18–22; Isa. 2:4.
19
x Night, divided into watches, Gen. 1:5.
20
y Prayer, intercessory, Acts 6:4.
5 R. V. the children that are dandled in the hands?
21
z War, as a judgment, Judg. 3:2.
22
6 R. V. dandled

## CHAPTER 3

*The prophet bewails his own calamities. 21 He acknowledges the mercies of God. 37 His humble confession of sin. 55 He prays for deliverance, 64 and for recompense upon his enemies.*

[a,b,c]I AM the man *that* hath
seen [d]affliction by the rod
of his wrath.
2 [b,c]He hath led me, and
brought *me into* [e]darkness, but
not *into* light.
3 [b,c]Surely against me is he

1
a Poetry, acrostic, vs. 1–66; Acts 17:28.
b Despondency, vs. 1–19; Eccl. 2:20.
c Murmuring, against God, vs. 1–19; Num. 14:2.
d Adversity, dispensation from God, Psa. 10:6.
2
e Darkness, figurative, Gen. 1:2.

† CANNIBALISM, Lev. 26:29; Deut. 28:53–57; 2 Kin. 6:28, 29; Jer. 19:9; Lam. 2:20; 4:10; Ezek. 5:10.

turned; he turneth his hand
*against me* all the day.
4 [b,c]My flesh and my skin hath
he made old; he hath broken my
bones.
5 [b,c]He hath builded against
me, and compassed *me* with [f]gall
and travel.
6 [b,c]He hath set me in dark
places, as *they that be* dead of
old.
7 [b,c]He hath hedged me about,
that I cannot get out: he hath
made my [g]chain heavy.
8 [b,c]Also when I cry and shout,
[h]he shutteth out my prayer.
9 [b,c]He hath inclosed my ways
with hewn stone, he hath made
my paths crooked.
10 [b,c]He *was* unto me *as* a [i]bear
lying in wait, *and as* a [j]lion in
secret places.
11 [b,c]He hath turned aside my
ways, and pulled me in pieces:
he hath made me desolate.
12 [b,c]He hath bent his [k]bow,
and set me as a mark for the
[l]arrow.
13 [b,c]He hath caused the [l]ar-
rows of his quiver to enter into
my reins.
14 I was a derision to all my
people; *and* their song all the
day.
15 [b,c]He hath filled me with
bitterness, he hath [1]made me
[m]drunken with [n]wormwood.
16 [b,c]He hath also broken my
teeth with gravel stones, he hath
covered me with ashes.
17 [b,c]And thou hast removed
my soul far off from peace: I forgat prosperity.
18 And I said, [b,c]My strength
and my hope is perished from
the LORD:
19 [2]Remembering mine affliction and my misery, the [n]worm-
wood and the [f]gall.
20 [o]My soul hath *them* still in
remembrance, and [o]is humbled
in me.

21 This I recall to my mind,
therefore have I [p]hope.
22 ¶ [q,r]*It is of* the LORD'S
[s]mercies that we are not consumed, because his compassions
fail not.
23 *They are* new every morning: great *is* thy [t]faithfulness.
24 [u]The LORD *is* my portion,
saith my soul; therefore will I
[p]hope in him.
25 [v,w]The LORD *is* [x]good unto
them that wait for him, to the
soul *that* [y,z]seeketh him.
26 *It is* good that *a man* should
both hope and quietly wait for
the salvation of the LORD.
27 [a]*It is* good for a man that
he [b]bear the [c]yoke in his youth.
28 [3]He sitteth alone and [d]keep-
eth silence, because he hath
[4]borne *it* upon him.
29 [5]He [d]putteth his mouth in
the dust; if so be there may be
hope.
30 [6]He [d]giveth *his* cheek to him
that smiteth him: [7]he is filled
full with reproach.
31 For [e,f,g]the Lord will not
cast off for ever:
32 But though he [h]cause grief,
[f,g]yet will he have compassion
according to the multitude of his
[e]mercies.
33 For [i]he doth not [h]afflict willingly nor grieve the children of
men.
34 To crush under his feet all
the [j]prisoners of the earth,
35 To [k]turn aside the right of a
man before the face of the [l]most
High,
36 To [k]subvert a man in his
cause, the [m]Lord approveth not.
37 ¶ Who *is* he *that* saith, and
it cometh to pass, *when* the [l]Lord
commandeth *it* not?
38 [n,o]Out of the mouth of the
[l]most High proceedeth not evil
and good?

*l God, sovereign,* Gen. 2:2. **36** *m God, righteousness of,* Gen. 2:2. **38** *n God, holiness of,* Gen. 2:2. *o Holiness, attribute of God,* Ex. 39:30.

**5**
*f Gall, figurative of divine judgments,* Job 16:13.

**7**
*g Chains, figurative,* Dan. 5:7.

**8**
*h Doubting,* Rom. 14:23.

**10**
*i Bear,* 2 Sam. 17:8.
*j Lion,* Mic. 5:8.

**12**
*k Bow, figurative,* 2 Sam. 1:18.
*l Arrow, figurative,* 1 Sam. 20:20.

**15**
*m Drunkenness, figurative,* Luke 21:34.
*n Wormwood, figurative,* Deut. 29:18.
1 R. V. sated me

**19**
2 R. V. Remember

**20**
*o Adversity, benefits of,* Psa. 10:6.

**21**
*p Hope,* Prov. 13:12.

**22**
*q Thankfulness, to God,* Acts 24:3.
*r Resignation,* Job 5:17.
*s God, mercy of,* Gen. 2:2.

**23**
*t God, faithfulness of,* Gen. 2:2.

**24**
*u Faith, exemplified,* Mark 11:22.

**25**
*v Promise or Ground of Assurance, to seekers,* 2 Cor. 1:20.
*w Prayer, answer to, promised,* Acts 6:4.
*x God, goodness of,* Gen. 2:2.
*y Seekers,* Isa. 55:6.
*z Spiritual Desire,* Psa. 42:1.

**27**
*a Adversity, benefits of,* Psa. 10:6.
*b Children, punishment of,* Mark 10:14.
*c Yoke, figurative,* 1 Sam. 6:7.

**28**
*d Meekness,* Psa. 45:4.
3 R. V. Let him sit alone and keep
4 R. V. laid it

**29**
5 R. V. Let him put

**30**
6 R. V. Let him give
7 R. V. let him be

**31**
*e God, mercy of,* Gen. 2:2.
*f Afflictions, consolation in,* Psa. 34:19.
*g Promise, to the afflicted,* 2 Cor. 1:20.

**32**
*h Divine Chastisement, administered in love,* Job 33:19.

**33**
*i God, goodness of,* Gen. 2:2.

**34**
*j Prisoners, cruelty to,* Psa. 79:11.

**35**
*k Injustice,* Isa. 26:10.

39 [p]Wherefore[G] doth a living
man [q]complain, a man for the
[r]punishment of his sins?
40 Let us search and [s]try[G]
our ways, and [t]turn again to
the LORD.
41 Let us [u]lift up our heart
with *our* hands unto God in the
[v]heavens.
42 [w, x]We have transgressed and
have rebelled: thou hast not pardoned.
43 Thou hast covered with [y]anger,
and [8, r]persecuted us: thou
hast slain, thou hast not pitied.
44 Thou hast covered thyself
with a cloud, that [z]*our* prayer
should not pass through.
45 [a]Thou hast made us *as*
the offscouring and refuse in the
midst of the [9]people.[Q]
46 All our enemies have opened
their mouths against us.
47 Fear and [10]a snare is come
upon us, [11, a]desolation and destruction.
48 [b, c, d]Mine eye runneth down
with rivers of water for the destruction
of the daughter of my
people.
49 [b, c, d]Mine eye trickleth down,
and ceaseth not, without any intermission,
50 Till the LORD look down,
and behold from [e]heaven.
51 [b, c]Mine eye affecteth mine
heart because of all the daughters
of my city.
52 Mine enemies chased me
sore[G], like a bird, without cause.[Q]
53 They have cut off [f]my life in
the [g]dungeon, and cast a stone
upon me.
54 Waters flowed over mine
head; *then* I said, [d]I am cut
off.
55 ¶ I [h]called upon thy name,
O LORD, out of the low [g]dungeon.
56 Thou [i]hast heard my voice:
[h]hide not thine ear at my breathing,
at my cry.
57 [i]Thou drewest near in the
day *that* I called upon thee: thou
saidst, [j]Fear not.
58 O Lord, [k]thou hast pleaded
the causes of my soul; thou hast
[l]redeemed my life.[T]
59 O LORD, thou hast seen my
wrong: [m]judge thou my cause.
60 Thou hast seen all their vengeance
*and* all their [12]imaginations[G]
against me.
61 Thou hast heard their reproach,
O LORD, *and* all their
[12]imaginations[G] against me;
62 The lips of those that rose
up against me, and their [13]device[G]
against me all the day.
63 Behold their sitting down,
and their rising up; I *am* their
[14]musick.
64 [15]Render unto them a recompence,
O LORD, according to
the work of their hands.
65 [16]Give them sorrow of heart,
thy curse unto them.
66 [17]Persecute and destroy them
in anger from under the heavens
of the LORD.

## CHAPTER 4

*The prophet bewails the changed state of Zion. 13 Her sins the cause of her calamities. 17 Her despair of help. 21 Edom threatened, 22 and Zion comforted.*

[a, b, c]HOW is the [d]gold become
dim! *how* is the most
fine gold changed! the stones of
the sanctuary are poured out in
the top of every street.
2 The [e]precious sons of Zī′ŏn,
comparable to fine gold, how are
they esteemed as earthen pitchers,
the work of the hands of the
potter!
3 Even the [1]sea monsters draw
out the breast, they [f]give suck to
their young ones: the daughter
of my people *is become* cruel, like
the *ostriches in the wilderness.

**39**
p *Resignation, in adversity*, Job 5:17.
q *Murmuring, against God*, Num. 14:2.
r *Wicked, punishment of*, Psa. 73:3.

**40**
s *Self-examination*, 2 Cor. 13:5.
t *Repentance, exhortations to*, Mark 1:4.

**41**
u *Prayer*, Acts 6:4.
v *Heaven, God's dwelling place*, Luke 18:22.

**42**
w *Prayer, confession in*, Acts 6:4.
x *Sin, confession of*, Rom. 5:12.

**43**
y *Anger of God*, 2 Kin. 13:3.
8 R. V. pursued

**44**
z *Wicked, prayers of, not answered*, Psa. 73:3.

**45**
a *Wicked, punishment of*, Psa. 73:3.
9 R. V. peoples.

**47**
10 R. V. the pit are
11 R. V. devastation

**48**
b *Patriotism*, Psa. 137:1.
c *Love, of man for man*, 1 John 4:7.
d *Despondency*, Eccl. 2:20.

**50**
e *Heaven, God's dwelling place*, Luke 18:22.

**53**
f *Prisoners, cruelty to*, Psa. 79:11.
g *Prison, dungeon in*, Gen. 39:20.

**55**
h *Adversity, prayer in*, Psa. 10:6.

**56**
i *Prayer, answered*, Acts 6:4.

**57**
j *Adversity, consolation in*, Psa. 10:6.

**58**
k *God, mercy of*, Gen. 2:2.
l *God, savior*, Gen. 2:2.

**59**
m *God, judge*, Gen. 2:2.

**60**
12 R. V. devices

**62**
13 R. V. imagination

**63**
14 R. V. song.

**64**
15 R. V. Thou wilt render

**65**
16 R. V. Thou wilt give them hardness

**66**
17 R. V. Thou wilt pursue

**1**
a *Poetry, acrostic*, vs. 1–22; Acts 17:28.
b *Jeremiah, lamentations of*, vs. 1–12; Jer. 1:1.
c *War, evils of*, Judg. 3:2.
d *Gold, figurative*, Ezek. 7:19.

**2**
e *Righteous, described*, Psa. 64:10.

**3**
f *Animals, instincts of*, Jer. 27:5.
1 R. V. jackals

*** OSTRICH**, Job 39:13–18; Lam. 4:3; Isa. 13:21 [R. V.]; 34:13; 43:20. *The cry of*, Mic. 1:8. *In the A. V. owl, in the R. V. ostrich in the following scriptures*, Lev. 11:16; Deut. 14:15; Job 30:29; Isa. 43:20; Jer. 50:39; Mic. 1:8.

4 The tongue of the sucking child cleaveth[c] to the roof of his mouth for thirst: [c,g]the young children ask bread, *and* no man breaketh *it* unto them.

5 [c,g]They that did feed delicately are desolate in the streets: [c]they that were brought up in [h]scarlet embrace dunghills.

6 For the [2]punishment of the [i]iniquity of the daughter of my people is greater than [2]the punishment of the sin of [j]Sŏd′om, that was overthrown as in a moment, and no hands stayed on her.

7 Her [3]Năz′a-rītes were [e]purer than snow, they were whiter than milk, they were more ruddy in body than [k]rubies, their polishing *was* of [l]sapphire:

8 [c,g]Their visage is blacker than a coal; they are not known in the streets: their skin cleaveth[c] to their bones; it is withered, it is become like a stick.

9 [c]*They that be* slain with the sword are better than *they that be* slain with [g]hunger: for these pine away, stricken through for *want*[c] *of* the fruits of the field.

10 [c,g,m]The hands of the pitiful women have [4,n]sodden[c] their own children: they were their meat[c] in the destruction of the daughter of my people.

11 The LORD hath accomplished his [o]fury; he hath poured out his fierce anger, and hath kindled a fire in Zī′ŏn, and it hath devoured the foundations thereof.[s]

12 The kings of the earth, and all the inhabitants of the world, would not have believed that the adversary and the enemy should have entered into the gates of Jĕ-ru′să-lĕm.

13 For the [p]sins of her [q]prophets, *and* the iniquities of her [r]priests, that have [s,t]shed the blood of the just in the midst of her,

14 They have wandered *as* blind *men* in the streets, [p]they have [t]polluted themselves with blood, so that men could not touch their garments.

15 They cried unto them, Depart ye; *it is* unclean[c]; depart, depart, touch not: when they fled away and wandered, they said among the [5]heathen[c], They shall no more sojourn *there.*

16 [u]The [o]anger of the LORD hath divided them; he will no more regard them: they respected not the persons of the priests, they favoured not the elders.

17 As for us, our eyes as yet failed for our vain help: in our watching we have [v]watched for a nation *that* could not save *us.*

18 They hunt our steps, that we cannot go in our streets: [w]our end is near, our days are fulfilled; for our end is come.

19 Our [6]persecutors are swifter than the [x]eagles of the heaven: they pursued us upon the mountains, they [y]laid wait for us in the wilderness.

20 The breath of our nostrils, the anointed of the LORD, was taken in their pits, of whom we [v]said, Under his shadow we shall live among the heathen[c].

21 Rejoice and be glad, O daughter of [z]Ē′dom, that dwellest in the land of [a]Ŭz; the [b]cup also shall pass through unto thee: thou shalt be [c]drunken, and shalt make thyself naked.

22 The punishment of thine iniquity is accomplished, O daughter of Zī′ŏn; [d]he will no more carry [e]thee away into captivity: he will visit[c] thine iniquity, O daughter of [f]Ē′dom; he will discover[c] thy sins.

4
g *Famine, described,* 2 Kin. 8:1.

5
h *Colors, symbolical,* Ezek. 16:16.

6
i *Jews, wickedness of,* Neh. 4:2.
j *Sodom, wickedness of,* Gen. 13:10.
2 R. V. *omits* punishment of the

7
k Job 28:18; Prov. 20:15; 31:10.
l *Sapphire,* Job 28:6.
3 R. V nobles

10
m *Prophecies, fulfilled,* Dan. 9:24.
n *Cannibalism,* Lam. 2:20.
4 Am. R. V. boiled

11
o *Anger of God,* 2 Kin. 13:3.

13
p *Jews, wickedness of,* Neh. 4:2.
q *Prophets, false,* Isa. 3:2.
r *Minister, false and corrupt,* Rom. 15:16.
s *Persecution, of the righteous,* John 15:20.
t *Homicide, felonious,* Deut. 5:17.

15
5 R. V. nations

16
u *Wicked, punishment of,* Psa. 73:3.

17
v *False Confidence,* Psa. 30:6.

18
w *Despondency,* Eccl. 2:20.

19
x *Eagle,* Lev. 11:13.
y *Armies, tactics of,* Deut. 11:4.
6 R. V. pursuers

21
z *Edomites, prophecies concerning,* 2 Kin. 8:21.
a Jer. 25:20; Job 1:1.
b *Cup, figurative,* Matt. 20:22.
c *Drunkenness, figurative,* Luke 21:34.

22
d *God, mercy of,* Gen. 2:2.
e *Jews, prophecies concerning,* Neh. 4:2.
f *Edomites, prophecies concerning,* 2 Kin. 8:21.

1
a *Poetry, acrostic,* vs. 1–22; Acts 17:28.
b *Nation, in adversity, prayer for,* vs. 1–22; Isa. 2:4.
c *Adversity, prayer in,* vs. 1–22; Psa. 10:6.
2
d *Assyria, Israelites subject to,* Gen. 25:18.
3
e *Widow,* 2 Sam. 14:5.
4
f *Oppression,* Eccl. 5:8.
5
1 R. V. pursuers are upon our necks: We are weary,
6
g *Alliances,* Josh. 9:15.
h *Hand, clasping of, in token of contract,* Ezra 10:19.
i *Egyptians,* Gen. 50:3.
7
j *Sin, consequences of, entailed upon children,* Rom. 5:12.
k *Children, involved in sins of parents,* Mark 10:14.
l *Punishment, entailed on children,* Lev. 26:41.
10
m *Famine,* 2 Kin. 8:1.
2 R. V. burning heat of famine.
11
n *Rape,* Deut. 22:25.
o *Captive, cruelty to,* 1 Sam. 30:3.
p *Women, treated with cruelty, in war,* Prov. 31:10.

## CHAPTER 5

*Zion's bitter complaint and prayer to God.*

[a,b,c] REMEMBER, O LORD, what is come upon us: consider, and behold our reproach.

2 [b,c]Our inheritance is turned to [d]strangers, our houses to aliens.

3 [b,c]We are +orphans and fatherless, our mothers *are* as [e]widows.

4 [b,c,f]We have drunken our water for money; [f]our wood is sold unto us.

5 [b,c,f]Our [1]necks *are* under persecution: we labour, *and* have no rest.

6 We have [g]given the [h]hand *to* the [i]E-gyp'tians, *and to* the [d]As-syr'i-ans, to be satisfied with bread.

7 Our fathers have [j]sinned, *and are* not; and [k]we have [l]borne their iniquities.

8 Servants have ruled over us: *there is* none that doth deliver *us* out of their hand.

9 We gat our bread with *the peril of* our lives because of the sword of the wilderness.

10 Our skin was black like an oven because of the [2]terrible [m]famine.

11 They [n,o]ravished the [p]women in Zi'on, *and* the maids in the cities of Ju'dah.

12 [o]Princes are hanged up by their hand: the faces of elders were not honoured.

13 [3]They [j]took the [q]young men to [r]grind, and the children [4]fell under the wood.

14 The elders have ceased from the gate, the young men from their musick.

15 The joy of our heart is ceased; our [s]dance is turned into [t]mourning.

16 The crown is fallen *from* our head: woe unto us, that [b,c,u,v]we have sinned!

17 For this our heart is [w]faint; for these *things* our eyes are dim.

18 Because of the mountain of Zi'on, which is desolate, the foxes walk upon it.

19 Thou, O LORD, remainest [x]for ever; [y]thy throne from generation to generation.

20 [z]Wherefore dost thou forget us for ever, *and* forsake us so long time?

21 [b,c]Turn thou us unto thee, O LORD, and we shall be turned; renew our days as of old.

22 But [w,z]thou hast utterly †rejected us; thou art very wroth against us.

13
q *Young Men,* Prov. 1:4.
r *Mill,* Ex. 11:5.
3 R. V. The young men bare the mill,
4 R. V. stumbled
15
s *Dancing,* Eccl. 3:4.
t *Mourning,* Lam. 2:5.
16
u *Prayer, confession in,* Acts 6:4
v *Sin, confession of,* Rom. 5:12.
17
w *Despondency,* Eccl. 2:20.
19
x *God, eternity of,* Gen. 2:2.
y *God, sovereign,* Gen. 2:2.
20
z *Murmuring, against God,* Num. 14:2.

THE

# BOOK OF EZEKIEL

v.1–514 BC
See footnote, *Time,* Rev. 10:6.

1
a *Month (July),* Ex. 12:2.

## CHAPTER 1

*The date of Ezekiel's prophecy at Chebar. 4 His vision of four living creatures, 15 of the four wheels, 26 and of the glory of God.*

NOW it came to pass in the thirtieth year, in the fourth [a]*month,* in the fifth *day* of the month, as I *was* among the [b]captives by the river of *Che'bar, *that* the heavens were opened, and I saw [c]visions of God.

2 In the fifth *day* of the [a]month, which *was* the fifth year of king [d]Je-hoi'a-chin's captivity,

v.2–514 BC
See footnote, *Time,* Rev. 10:6.
b *Jews, captive in Babylon,* Neh. 4:2.
c *Vision,* Acts 9:10.
2
d *Jehoiachin,* 2 Kin. 24:6.

**+ ORPHAN.** *To be visited,* Jas. 1:27. *Beneficent provision for,* Deut. 14:28, 29; 16:10, 11, 14; 24:19–22; 26:12, 13. *Kindness toward,* Job 29:12, 13; 31:16–18, 21. *God the friend of,* Ex. 22:22–24; Deut. 10:18; Psa. 10:14, 17, 18; 68:5; 146:9; Prov. 23:10, 11; Jer. 49:11; Hos. 14:3; Mal. 3:5. *Justice to, required,* Deut. 24:17–22; 27:19; Psa. 82:3; Isa. 1:17, 23; Jer. 7:6, 7; 22:3. *Oppressed,* Job 22:9; 24:3, 9; Isa. 10:1, 2; Jer. 5:28.

**† REJECTION.** *Of God,* 1 Sam. 8:7; 10:19; 2 Kin. 17:15; Luke 7:30. *Of Israel by God,* Num. 14:12, 26–37; 2 Kin. 17:20; Jer. 6:30; 7:29; 14:19; Lam. 5:22. *Of Saul by God,* 1 Sam. 15:23, 26.

**Of Jesus,** see footnote, JESUS, *Rejected,* Matt. 1:21.

*** CHEBAR,** a river of Mesopotamia. *The Jews of the captivity colonize in the valley of,* Ezek. 1:1, 3; 3:15, 23; 10:15, 22; 43:3.

3
*e Prophecies, inspired*, Dan. 9:24.
*f Chaldeans*, Dan. 1:4.

4
*g Whirlwind, figurative*, Prov. 1:27.
*h* Ezek. 8:2.

7
*i Brass*, Job 28:2.

10
*j Lion, similitudes of*, Mic. 5:8.
*k Eagle, similitudes of*, Lev. 11:13.

11
1 R. V. And their faces and their wings were separate above;

3 The [e]word of the LORD came expressly unto †Ē-zē′kĭ-el the priest, the son of Bū′zī, in the land of the [f]Chăl-dē′ans̹ by the river *Chē′bär; and the hand of the LORD was there upon him.

4 ¶ And †I [c]looked, and, behold, a [g]whirlwind came out of the north, a great cloud, and a fire infolding itself, and a brightness *was* about it, and out of the midst thereof as the colour of [h]amber, out of the midst of the fire.

5 Also out of the midst thereof *came* the likeness of four living creatures. And this *was* their appearance; they had the likeness of a man.[Q]

6 And every one had four faces, and every one had four wings.

7 And their feet *were* straight feet; and the sole of their feet *was* like the sole of a calf's foot: and they sparkled like the colour of burnished [i]brass.

8 And *they had* the hands of a man under their wings on their four sides; and they four had their faces and their wings.

9 Their wings *were* joined one to another; they turned not when they went; they went every one straight forward.

10 As for the likeness of their faces, they four had the face of a man, and the face of a [j]lion, on the right side: and they four had the face of an ox on the left side; they four also had the face of an [k]eagle.[Q]

11 [1]Thus *were* their faces: and their wings *were* stretched upward; two *wings* of every one *were* joined one to another, and two covered their bodies.

12 And they went every one straight forward: whither[C] the spirit was to go, they went; *and* they turned not when they went.[T]

13 As for the likeness of the living creatures, their appearance *was* like burning coals of fire, *and* like the appearance of [2]lamps: it went up and down among the living creatures; and the fire was bright, and out of the fire went forth [l]lightning.[Q]

14 And the living creatures ran and returned as the appearance of a flash of lightning.

15 ¶ Now as I beheld the living creatures, behold one [m]wheel upon the earth by the living creatures, [3]with his four faces.

16 The appearance of the [m]wheels and their work *was* like unto the colour of a ‡beryl: and they four had one likeness: and their appearance and their work *was* as it were a wheel in the middle of a wheel.

17 When they went, they went upon their four sides: *and* they turned not when they went.

18 As for their rings, they were so high that they were dreadful; and their rings *were* full of eyes round about them four.[Q]

19 And when the living creatures went, the [m]wheels went by them: and when the living creatures were lifted up from the earth, the wheels were lifted up.

20 Whithersoever[C] the spirit was to go, they went, thither[C] *was their* spirit to go; and the [m]wheels were lifted up over[C] against them: for the spirit of the living creature *was* in the wheels.[T]

21 When those went, *these* went;

13
*l Lightning*, Job 28:26.
2 R. V. torches;

15
*m Wheel, symbolical*, Eccl. 12:6.
3 R. V. for each of the four faces thereof.

† **EZEKIEL** (*God will strengthen*, or *God will prevail*), a priest. *Time of his prophecy*, Ezek. 1:1–3. *Persecution of*, Ezek. 3:25.

Visions of: *Of God's glory*, Ezek. 1; 8:1–4; 10; 11:22–24; *of Jews' abominations*, Ezek. 8:5–18; 22; *and of their punishment*, Ezek. 8:18; 9:5–10; 11:5–12; *of the valley of dry bones*, Ezek. 37:1–14; *of a man with measuring line*, Ezek. chapters 40–48; *of the river*, Ezek. 47:1–5.

Teaches by pantomime: *Feigns dumbness*, Ezek. 3:26; 24:27; 33:22; *symbolizes the siege of Jerusalem by drawings on a tile*, Ezek. 4:1–3; *shaves himself*, Ezek. 5:1–4; *removes his stuff to illustrate the approaching Jewish captivity*, Ezek. 12:3–16; *sighs*, Ezek. 21:6, 7; *uses a boiling pot to symbolize the destruction of Jerusalem*, Ezek. 24:1–14; *omits mourning the death of his wife*, Ezek. 24:16–27. *Prophesies by parable of an eagle*, Ezek. 17:2–10. *Other parables*, Ezek. chapters 15, 16, 19, 23.

*Prophecies of, concerning various nations*, Ezek. chapters 25–32. *His popularity*, Ezek. 33:31, 32.

‡ **BERYL**, or chalcedony. *A precious stone*, Song 5:14; Ezek. 1:16; 10:9. *Set in the breastplate*, Ex. 28:20; 39:13. *John saw, in the foundation of the new Jerusalem*, Rev. 21:20.

and when those stood, *these*
stood; and when those were lifted
up from the earth, the [m]wheels
were lifted up over[C] against them:
for the spirit of the living creature *was* in the wheels.[T]
22 And the likeness of the
firmament upon the heads of the
living creature *was* as the colour
of the terrible [n]crystal, stretched
forth over their heads above.[Q]
23 And under the firmament
*were* their wings straight, the one
toward the other: every one had
two, which covered on this side,
and every one had two, which
covered on that side, their bodies.
24 And when they went, I
heard the noise of their wings,
like the noise of great waters, as
the voice of the Almighty, the
voice of speech, as the noise of
an host: when they stood, they
let[C] down their wings.[Q]
25 And there was a voice [4]from
the firmament that *was* over their
heads, when they stood, *and* had
let down their wings.
26 ¶ [Q]And above the firmament
that *was* over their heads *was*
the likeness of a [o]throne, as the
appearance of a [p,q]sapphire
stone: and upon the likeness of
the throne *was* the likeness as
the appearance of a man above
upon it.
27 And I saw as the colour of
[h]amber, as the appearance of fire
round about within it, from the
appearance of his loins even upward, and from the appearance
of his loins even downward, I
saw as it were the appearance
of fire, and it had brightness
round about.[Q]
28 As the [r]appearance of the
[s]bow that is in the cloud in the
day of [t]rain, so *was* the appearance of the brightness round
about. This *was* the appearance
of the likeness of the [u]glory of
the LORD. And when I saw *it*, I

22
*n* Rev. 4:6; 21:11; 22:1.

25
4 R. V. above

26
*o* *Throne*, 1 Kin. 2:19.
*p* *Sapphire*, Job 28:6.
*q* *Colors, symbolical*, Ezek. 16:16.

28
*r* *Symbols and Similitudes*, Heb. 9:9.
*s* *Rainbow*, Gen. 9:13.
*t* *Rain*, 2 Sam. 1:21.
*u* *God, glory of*, Gen. 2:2.

fell upon my face, and I heard a
voice of one that spake.[Q]

## CHAPTER 2

*Ezekiel's commission. 6 His instructions. 9 The roll of a book spread before him.*

AND he [a]said unto [b]me, Son
of man, stand upon thy
feet, and I will speak unto thee.[Q]
2 And the [a]spirit entered into
[b]me when he spake unto me, and
set me upon my feet, that I heard
him that spake unto me.[T]
3 And he said unto [b]me, Son of
man, I [c]send thee to the children
of Iṣ'ra-el, to [1]a rebellious nation that hath rebelled against
me: they and their fathers have
transgressed against me, *even*
unto this very day.
4 For *they are* impudent children and [d]stiffhearted. I do
[c]send thee unto them; and [a]thou
shalt say unto them, Thus saith
the Lord GOD.
5 And they, whether they will
hear, or whether they will forbear, (for they *are* a rebellious
house,) yet shall know that there
hath been a [a]prophet among
them.
6 ¶ And thou, son of man, [e,f]be
not afraid of them, neither be
afraid of their words, though
[g]briers and [h]thorns *be* with thee,
and thou dost dwell among [i]scor-
pions: [e,f]be not afraid of their
words, nor be dismayed at their
looks, though they *be* a rebellious
house.
7 And [j]thou shalt speak my
words unto them, whether they
will hear, or whether they will
forbear[C]: for they *are* most rebellious.
8 But thou, son of man, hear
what I say unto thee; [k]Be not
thou rebellious like that rebellious house: open thy mouth, and
eat that I give thee.[Q]
9 ¶ [Q]And when I looked, [l]be-
hold, an hand *was* [2]sent unto

1
*a* *Prophets, inspiration of*, Isa. 3:2.
*b* *Ezekiel*, Ezek. 1:3.

3
*c* *Call, personal*, Phil. 3:14.
1 R. V. nations that are rebellious, which have rebelled

4
*d* *Obduracy*, Prov. 29:1.

6
*e* *Commandment, enjoining courage*, Deut. 8:2.
*f* *Courage, exhortations to*, Deut. 31:7.
*g* Ezek. 28:24; Isa. 5:6; 55:13.
*h* *Thorn, figurative*, Hos. 2:6.
*i* *Scorpion, figurative*, Luke 10:19.

7
*j* *Minister, duties of*, Rom. 15:16.

8
*k* *Backsliding, admonitions against*, Hos. 11:7.

9
*l* *Vision*, Acts 9:10.
2 R. V. put forth

me; and, lo, a roll[C] of a [m]book *was* therein;

10 And he spread it before me; and it *was* written within and without: and *there was* written therein lamentations, and mourning, and woe.[Q]

## CHAPTER 3

*The prophet is commanded to eat the roll of the book. 4 God encourages him. 15 The office and duty of the prophet 22 God shuts and opens the prophet's mouth.*

MOREOVER he said unto me, Son of man, eat that thou findest; eat this [a]roll,[C] and go speak unto the house of Is'-ra-el.[Q]

2 So I opened my mouth, and he caused me to eat that [a]roll.[C]

3 And he said unto me, Son of man, cause thy belly to eat, and fill thy bowels[G] with this roll[C] that I give thee. Then did I eat *it*; and it was in my mouth as honey for sweetness.

4 ¶ And he said unto me, Son of man, go, get thee unto the house of Is'ra-el, and [b]speak with my words unto them.

5 For thou *art* not sent to a people of a strange[G] speech and of an hard language, *but* to the house of Is'ra-el;

6 Not to many [1]people of a strange speech and of an hard language, whose words thou canst not understand. Surely, had I sent thee to them, they would have hearkened unto thee.

7 But the house of Is'ra-el will [c]not hearken unto thee; for they will not hearken unto me: for all the house of Is'ra-el *are* [2,d]impudent and hardhearted.

8 Behold, I have made [e]thy face [3]strong against their faces, and thy forehead [3]strong against their foreheads.

9 [e]As an [f]adamant[G] harder than [g]flint have I made thy forehead: [h,i]fear them not, neither be dismayed at their looks, though they *be* a rebellious house.

10 Moreover he said unto me, Son of man, all my words that I shall [j,k]speak unto thee [l]receive in thine heart, and hear with thine ears.

11 And go, get thee to them of the [m]captivity, unto the children of thy people, and [b]speak unto them, and tell them, Thus saith the Lord GOD; whether they will hear, or whether they will forbear.

12 Then the spirit took me up, and I heard behind me a voice of a great rushing, *saying*, Blessed *be* the [n]glory of the LORD from his place.[T]

13 *I heard* also the noise of the wings of the living creatures that touched one another, and the noise of the wheels over[C] against them, and a noise of a great rushing.

14 So the spirit lifted me up, and took me away, and I went in bitterness, in the heat of my spirit; but the hand of the LORD was strong upon me.[T]

15 ¶ Then I came to them of the [m]captivity at Tĕl–ā'bib, that dwelt by the river of [o]Chē'bär, and I sat where they sat, and remained there astonished[C] among them [p]seven days.

16 And it came to pass at the end of [p]seven days, that the [q]word of the LORD [j,k]came unto me, saying,

17 Son of man, I have made [b]thee a [r,s]watchman unto the house of Is'ra-el: therefore hear the word at my mouth, and give them [t]warning from me.[Q]

18 When I say unto the wicked, Thou shalt surely die; and thou givest him not [t]warning, nor speakest to warn the wicked from his wicked way, to save his life; the same wicked *man* shall [u]die in his iniquity; but [v]his blood will I require at thine hand.

*m Book,* Num. 5:23.

1
*a Book,* Num. 5:23.

4
*b Minister, duties of,* Rom. 15:16.

6
1 R. V. peoples

7
*c Obduracy,* Prov. 29:1.
*d Wicked, described,* Psa. 73:3.
2 R. V. of an hard forehead and of a stiff heart.

8
*e Minister, character and qualifications of,* Rom. 15:16.
3 R. V. hard

9
*f* Zech. 7:12.
*g Flint,* Deut. 8:15.
*h Commandment, enjoining courage,* Deut. 8:2.
*i Courage, exhortations to,* Deut. 31:7.

10
*j Inspiration, of prophets,* Job 32:8.
*k Prophets, inspiration of,* Isa. 3:2.
*l Commandment, to ministers,* Deut. 8:2.

11
*m Jews, captive in Babylon,* Neh. 4:2.

12
*n God, glory of,* Gen. 2:2.

15
*o Chebar,* Ezek. 1:1.
*p Seven, days,* Gen. 7:2.

16
*q Prophecies, inspired,* Dan. 9:24.

17
*r Watchman, figurative,* 2 Sam. 18:24.
*s Minister, duties of,* Rom. 15:16.
*t Wicked, warned,* Psa. 73:3.

18
*u Wicked, punishment of,* Psa. 73:3.
*v Ministers, responsibility of.* Rom. 15:16.

19
w *Opportunity, lost,* Gal. 6:10.

20
x *Backsliding,* Hos. 11:7.
y *Stumbling,* Isa. 8:14.

21
z *Sinlessness,* 1 John 5:18.

22
a *Prophets, inspiration of,* Isa. 3:2.
b *Ezekiel,* Ezek. 1:3.

23
c *God, glory of,* Gen. 2:2.
d *Chebar,* Ezek. 1:1.

26
e *Obduracy,* Prov. 29:1.

19 Yet if thou [s,t]warn the
wicked, and he turn not from
his wickedness, nor from his
wicked way, he [w]shall die in his
iniquity; but [v]thou hast delivered
thy soul.
20 Again, When a righteous *man*
doth [x]turn from his righteousness,
and commit iniquity, and
I lay a [y]stumblingblock before
him, he shall die: [v]because thou
hast not given him warning, he
shall die in his sin, and his righteousness
which he hath done
shall not be remembered; but
[v]his blood will I require at thine
hand.
21 Nevertheless if [s]thou warn
the righteous *man,* that the righteous
sin not, and he doth [z]not
sin, he shall surely live, because
he is warned; also [v]thou hast delivered
thy soul.
22 ¶ And [a]the hand of the
LORD was there upon [b]me; and
he said unto me, Arise, go forth
into the plain, and I will there
talk with thee.
23 Then [b]I arose, and went
forth into the plain: and, behold,
the [c]glory of the LORD stood
there, as the glory which I saw
by the river of [d]Chē'bär: and I
fell on my face.
24 Then the spirit[C] entered into
[b]me, and set me upon my feet,
and spake with me, and said
unto me, Go, shut thyself within
thine house.[T]
25 But thou, O son of man, behold,
they shall put bands[C] upon
thee, and shall bind[C] thee with
them, and thou shalt not go out
among them:
26 And I will make thy tongue
cleave[C] to the roof of thy mouth,
that thou shalt be dumb, and
shalt not be to them a reprover:
for they *are* a [e]rebellious house.
27 But when I speak with thee,
I will open thy mouth, and [a]thou
shalt say unto them, Thus saith
the Lord GOD; He that heareth,
let him hear; and he that forbeareth,
let him forbear: for they
*are* a [e]rebellious house.

## CHAPTER 4

*The siege of Jerusalem prefigured, and the punishment to be inflicted on the inhabitants. 9 The severity of the famine typified.*

[a]THOU also, son of man, [b]take
thee a tile,[C] and lay it before
thee, and [c,d] pourtray[C] upon
it the city, *even* [e]Jĕ-ru̇'să-lĕm:
2 [b,c,d]And lay [f]siege against it,
and build a fort against it, and
cast[C] a [g]mount[C] against it; set the
camp also against it, and set
[h]*battering* rams against it round
about.
3 [b]Moreover take thou unto
thee an iron pan, and [c,d]set it
*for* a wall of iron between thee
and the city: and set thy face
against it, and it shall be [f]besieged,
and thou shalt lay siege
against it. This *shall be* a [d]sign
to the house of Ĭṣ'ra-el.
4 [b,c,d]Lie thou also upon thy
left side, and lay the iniquity of
the house of Ĭṣ'ra-el upon it:
*according* to the number of the
days that thou shalt lie upon it
thou shalt bear their iniquity.
5 For I have laid upon thee the
years of their iniquity, according
to the number of the days,
three hundred and ninety days:
so shalt thou bear the iniquity of
the house of Ĭṣ'ra-el.
6 [b,c,d]And when thou hast accomplished
them, [b,c,d]lie again
on thy right side, and thou shalt
bear the iniquity of the house of
Jū'dah [i]forty days: I have appointed
thee each day for a year.
7 Therefore thou shalt set thy
face toward the [f]siege of [e]Jĕ-ru̇'să-lĕm,
and thine arm *shall be*
uncovered, and thou shalt prophesy[C]
against it.
8 [b,c,d]And, behold, I will lay
bands[C] upon thee, and thou shalt
not turn thee from one side to

1
a *Ezekiel,* Ezek. 1:3.
b *Instruction, by object lessons,* Prov. 23:23.
c *Pantomime,* vs. 1–13; Isa. 20:2.
d *Prophecies, exemplified in pantomime,* vs. 1–13: Dan. 9:24.
e *Jerusalem, prophecies against,* vs. 1–17; Judg. 19:10.

2
f *Siege,* Deut. 28:53.
g *Fortification,* Ezek. 17:17.
h Ezek. 21:22.

6
i *Forty, days,* Jonah 3:4.

another, till thou hast ended the days of thy [i]siege.

9 ¶ [b,c,d]Take thou also unto thee [j]wheat, and [k]barley, and [l]beans, and [1,m]lentiles, and millet, and fitches, and put them in one vessel, and make thee *bread thereof, *according* to the number of the days that thou shalt lie upon thy side, three hundred and ninety days shalt thou eat thereof.

10 And thy meat which thou shalt eat *shall be* by weight, twenty [n]shekels a day: from time to time shalt thou eat it.

11 Thou shalt drink also [o]water by [p]measure, the sixth part of an hin: from time to time shalt thou drink.

12 And thou shalt eat it *as* [k]barley *cakes, and thou shalt bake it with dung that cometh out of man, in their sight.

13 And the LORD said, [b,c,d]Even thus shall the children of Ĭṣ'ra-el eat their defiled *bread among the [2]Gĕn'tīleṣ, whither I will drive them.

14 Then said I, Ah Lord GOD! behold, my soul hath not been polluted: for from my youth up even till now have I not eaten of [q]that which dieth of itself, or is torn [3]in pieces; neither came there abominable flesh into my mouth.

15 Then he said unto me, Lo, I have given thee cow's dung for man's dung, and thou shalt prepare thy *bread therewith.

16 Moreover he said unto me, Son of man, behold, [r]I will [s]break the staff of *bread in [e]Jĕ-ru̧'să-lĕm: and they shall eat bread by weight, and with care; and they shall drink [o]water by [p]measure, and with astonishment:

17 That they may [s]want *bread and [o]water, and be astonied one with another, and [4]consume away for their iniquity.

9
*j Wheat*, Ezra 6:9.
*k Barley*, Ex. 9:31.
*l* 2 Sam. 17:28.
*m Lentiles*, Gen. 25:34.
1 R. V. spelt,

10
*n Shekel*, Ex. 30:13.

11
*o Water*, 1 Kin. 17:10.
*p Measure*, Deut. 25:15.

13
2 R. V. nations

14
*q Food, things prohibited as*, Psa. 136:25.
3 R. V. of beasts;

16
*r Adversity, dispensation from God*, Psa. 10:6.
*s Famine, as a judgment*, 2 Kin. 8:1.

## CHAPTER 5

*Under the type of hair, cut with a sword, burnt, and scattered by the wind, are shown the judgments of God upon Jerusalem for her rebellion, 12 by famine, sword, and dispersion.*

AND [a]thou, son of man, [b,c,d]take thee a sharp [1]knife, take thee a barber's razor, and cause *it* to pass upon thine head and upon thy [e]beard: then take thee [f]balances to weigh, and divide the *hair*.

2 [b,c,d]Thou shalt burn with fire a third part in the midst of the city, when the days of the [g]siege are fulfilled: and thou shalt take a third part, *and* smite [2]about it with a knife: and a third part thou shalt scatter in the wind; and I will draw out a sword after them.

3 Thou shalt also take thereof a few in number, and bind them in thy [h]skirts.

4 [b,c,d]Then take of them again, and cast them into the midst of the fire, and burn them in the fire; [i]*for* thereof shall a fire come forth into all the house of Ĭṣ'ra-el.

5 ¶ Thus saith the Lord GOD; [b,d]This *is* [j]Jĕ-ru̧'să-lĕm: I have set it in the midst of the nations and countries *that are* round about her.

6 And she hath [3]changed my

1
*a Ezekiel*, Ezek. 1:3.
*b Instruction, by object lessons*, vs. 1–4; Prov. 23:23.
*c Pantomime*, vs. 1–4; Isa. 20:2.
*d Prophecies, exemplified in pantomime*, vs. 1–4; Dan. 9:24.
*e Beard*, 1 Sam. 21:13.
*f Balances*, Prov. 11:1.
1 R. V. sword, as a barber's

2
*g Siege*, Deut. 28:53.
2 R. V. with the sword round about it;

3
*h Dress, articles of*, Zech. 3:3.

4
*i Wicked, punishment of*, Psa. 73:3.

5
*j Jerusalem, prophecies against*, vs. 5–17; Judg. 19:10.

6
3 R. V. rebelled against my judgements in doing wickedness

* **BREAD.** *Staff of*, Ezek. 4:16; 5:16; 14:13.
**Kinds of:** *Leavened*, Lev. 7:13; 23:17; Hos. 7:4; Amos 4:5; Matt. 13:33. *Unleavened*, Gen. 19:3; Ex. 29:2; Judg. 6:19; 1 Sam. 28:24.
*Made, of wheat flour*, Ex. 29:2; 1 Kin. 4:22; Psa. 81:16; *of manna*, Num. 11:8; *of meal*, 1 Kin. 17:12; *of barley*, Judg. 7:13.
**How prepared:** *Mixed, with oil*, Ex. 29:2, 23; *with honey*, Ex. 16:31; *with leaven, or ferment*, see LEAVENED, in paragraph above. *Kneaded*, Gen. 18:6; Ex. 8:3; 12:34; 1 Sam. 28:24; 2 Sam. 13:8; Jer. 7:18; Hos. 7:4. *Made, into loaves*, 1 Sam. 10:3; 17:17; 25:18; 1 Kin. 14:3; Mark 8:14; *into cakes*, 2 Sam. 6:19; 1 Kin. 17:12, 13; *into wafers*, Ex. 16:31; 29:23. *Baked, in ovens*, Ex. 8:3; Lev. 2:4; 7:9; 11:35; 26:26; Hos. 7:4; *in pans*, Lev. 2:5, 7; 2 Sam. 13:6–9; *on coals*, 1 Kin. 19:6; Isa. 44:19; John 21:9.
*Made by women*, Lev. 26:26; 1 Sam. 8:13; Jer. 7:18. *Traffic in*, Mark 6:37.
**Offerings of**, 1 Sam. 2:36; 2 Kin. 23:9. *By idolaters*, Jer. 7:18; 44:19.
**Figurative**, Lev. 21:6, 8, 17, 21, 22; 22:25; 1 Kin. 22:27; 2 Chr. 18:26; Psa. 127:2; Isa. 30:20; 55:2; Hos. 9:4; 1 Cor. 10:17. *Jesus the bread of life*, John 6:32–35, 48–51.
**Symbolical:** *Of the body of Christ*, Matt. 26:26; Acts 20:7; 1 Cor. 11:23, 24.

k *Jews, wickedness of*, Neh. 4:2.
l *Disobedience to God*, Eph. 5:6.

8
m *Nation, judgments denounced against*, Isa. 2:4.

10
n *Cannibalism*, Lam. 2:20.

11
o *Profanation, of the house of God*, Lev. 22:32.
p *Idolatry, wicked practices of*, 1 Sam. 15:23.
q *Pity, withheld from reprobate sinners*, Job 19:21.

12
r *Plague, as a judgment*, Ex. 11:1.
s *Famine, as a judgment*, 2 Kin. 8:1.
t *War, as a judgment*, Judg. 3:2.

13
u *Anger of God*, 2 Kin. 13:3.

judgments[G] into [k]wickedness more
than the nations, and my statutes
more than the countries that *are*
round about her: for they have
refused my judgments[G] and my
statutes, they have [l]not walked
in them.
7 Therefore thus saith the Lord
GOD; Because ye [4]multiplied
more than the nations that *are*
round about you, *and* have [l]not
walked in my statutes, neither
have kept my judgments[G], neither
have done according to the judgments[G]
of the nations that *are*
round about you;
8 Therefore thus saith the Lord
GOD; Behold, I, even I, *am*
against thee, and will [i]execute
[m]judgments in the midst of thee
in the sight of the nations.
9 And [m]I will do in thee that
which I have not done, and whereunto
I will not do any more the
like, because of all thine abominations.
10 [m]Therefore the fathers shall
[n]eat the sons in the midst of thee,
and the sons shall eat their fathers;
and I will [i]execute judgments
in thee, and the whole
remnant of thee will I scatter
into all the winds.
11 Wherefore, *as* I live, saith
the Lord GOD; Surely, because
thou hast [o]defiled my sanctuary[G]
with all thy [p]detestable things,
and with all thine abominations,
therefore will I also diminish
*thee*; neither shall mine eye spare,
neither will I have any [q]pity.
12 ¶ [m]A third part of thee
shall die with the [r]pestilence, and
with [s]famine shall they be consumed
in the midst of thee: and
a third part shall fall by the
[t]sword round about thee; and I
will scatter a third part into all
the winds, and I will draw out a
sword after them.[Q]
13 Thus shall mine [u]anger be
accomplished, and [m]I will cause
my fury to rest upon them, and
I will be comforted: and [v]they
shall know that I the LORD have
spoken *it* in my zeal, when I have
accomplished my fury in them.
14 [m]Moreover I will make thee
waste, and a reproach among the
nations that *are* round about
thee, in the sight of all that
pass by.
15 So it shall be a reproach and
a taunt, an instruction and an astonishment[G]
unto the nations that
*are* round about thee, when I
shall [i]execute [m]judgments in thee
in [u]anger and in fury and in
furious rebukes. I the LORD
have spoken *it*.
16 When I shall send upon
them the evil [w]arrows of [s]famine,
which shall be for *their* [i]destruction,
*and* which I will send to
destroy you: and I will increase
the famine upon you, and will
break your staff of [x]bread:
17 So will I send upon you
[s]famine and evil [y]beasts, and
they shall bereave thee; and
[r]pestilence and blood shall pass
through thee; and I will bring
the [t]sword upon thee. I the
LORD have spoken *it*.[S Q]

## CHAPTER 6

*Judgments upon Israel for their idolatry.* 8 *A remnant to be left.* 11 *Great calamities thredtened*

AND the [a]word of the LORD
[b]came unto [c]me, saying,
2 Son of man, set[G] thy face toward
the mountains of Is'ra-el,
and prophesy against them,
3 And say, Ye mountains of
Is'ra-el, hear the word of the
Lord GOD; Thus saith the Lord
GOD to the mountains, and to
the hills, to the rivers, and to the
valleys; Behold, [d]I, *even* I, will
bring a [e]sword upon you, and I
will destroy your [f,g]high places.
4 And [d,g]your [h]altars shall
be desolate, and your [1,i]images
shall be broken: and I will cast

v *Judgments, design of*, Ex. 6:6.

16
w *Arrow, figurative*, 1 Sam. 20:20.
x *Bread*, Ezek. 4:13.

17
y *Animals, sent in judgment*, Jer. 27:5.

1
a *Prophecies, inspired*, Dan. 9:24.
b *Prophets, inspiration of*, Isa. 3:2.
c *Ezekiel*, Ezek. 1:3.

3
d *Nation, judgments denounced against*, Isa. 2:4.
e *War, as a judgment*, Judg. 3:2.
f *High Places*, 1 Kin. 3:2.
g *Idolatry, denounced*, 1 Sam. 15:23.

4
h *Altar, used in idolatrous worship*, Gen. 8:20.
i *Sun, worshiped*, Josh. 10:12.
1 R. V. sun-images

down your slain *men* before your idols.

5 [d]And I will lay the dead carcases of the children of Ĭṣ′ra-el before their idols; and I will scatter your bones round about your [h]altars.

6 [d]In all your dwellingplaces the cities shall be laid waste, and the [f,g]high places shall be desolate; that [g]your [h]altars may be laid waste and made desolate, and your idols may be broken and cease, and your [1,i]images may be cut down, and your works may be abolished.

7 [d]And the slain shall fall in the midst of you, and [j]ye shall know that I *am* the LORD.

8 ¶ [k]Yet will I leave a remnant, that ye may have *some* that shall escape the [e]sword among the nations, when ye shall be scattered through the countries.

9 And they that escape of you shall [l]remember me among the nations whither they shall be carried captives, because I am broken with their [m]whorish [n]heart, which hath departed from me, and with their eyes, which go a [m]whoring after their idols: and they shall lothe themselves for the evils which they have committed in all their abominations.

10 And [o]they shall know that I *am* the LORD, *and that* I have not said in vain that I would do this evil unto them.

11 ¶ Thus saith the Lord GOD; [p]Smite with thine hand, and stamp with thy foot, and say, Alas for all the evil [m]abominations of the house of Ĭṣ′ra-el! for they shall fall by the [e]sword, by the [q]famine, and by the [r]pestilence.

12 He that is far off shall die of the [r]pestilence; and he that is near shall fall by the [e]sword; and he that remaineth and is [s]besieged shall die by the [q]famine: thus will I accomplish my fury upon them.

13 [j,o]Then shall ye know that I *am* the LORD, when their slain *men* shall be among their idols round about their [h]altars, upon every high hill, in all the tops of the mountains, and under every green tree, and under every thick oak, the place where they did offer [t]sweet savour to all their idols.

14 [d,u]So will I stretch out my hand upon them, and make the land desolate, yea, more desolate than the wilderness toward Dĭb′lăth, in all their habitations: and [j,o]they shall know that I *am* the LORD.

## CHAPTER 7

*The final desolation of Israel. 16 The mournful condition of them that escape. 20 The sanctuary to be spoiled. 23 Under the type of a chain, is shown their miserable oppression.*

MOREOVER the [a]word of the LORD [b]came unto me, saying,

2 Also, thou son of man, thus saith the Lord GOD unto the land of Ĭṣ′ra-el; An end, the end is come upon the four corners of the land.

3 [c]Now *is* the end *come* upon thee, and I will send mine [d]anger upon thee, and will [e,f]judge thee according to thy ways, and will [g,h]recompense upon thee all thine abominations.

4 And mine eye shall not spare thee, neither will I have [i]pity: but I will [g,h]recompense thy ways upon thee, and thine abominations shall be in the midst of thee: and [j]ye shall know that I *am* the LORD.

5 Thus saith the Lord GOD; An evil, an only evil, behold, is come.

6 An end is come, the end is come: it [1]watcheth for thee; behold, it is come.

7 [2,c]The morning is come unto

---

7
j *Judgments, design of,* Ex. 6:6.

8
k *God, mercy of,* Gen. 2:2.

9
l *Adversity, benefits of,* Psa. 10:6.
m *Idolatry, wicked practices of,* 1 Sam. 15:23.
n *Heart, unregenerate,* Psa. 44:21.

10
o *Adversity, design of,* Psa. 10:6.

11
p *Minister, duties of,* Rom. 15:16.
q *Famine, as a judgment,* 2 Kin. 8:1.
r *Plague, as a judgment,* Ex. 11:1.

12
s *Siege,* Deut. 28:53.

13
t *Incense, offered in idolatrous worship,* Ex. 37:29.

14
u *Adversity, dispensation from God,* Psa. 10:6.

1
a *Prophecies,* Dan 9:24.
b *Prophets, inspiration of,* Isa. 3:2.

3
c *Nation, judgments denounced against,* vs. 3–27; Isa. 2:4.
d *Anger of God,* 2 Kin. 13:3.
e *God, judge,* Gen. 2:2.
f *Judgment, according to opportunity and works,* 1 Pet. 1:17.
g *Punishment, according to deeds,* Lev. 26:41.
h *Wicked, punishment of,* Psa. 73:3.

4
i *Pity, withheld from reprobate sinners,* Job 19:21.
j *Judgments, design of,* Ex. 6:6.

6
1 R. V. awaketh against

7
2 R. V. Thy doom is come unto thee, O inhabitant of the land: the time is come, the day is near: a day of tumult, and not of joyful shouting, upon the mountains.

thee, O thou that dwellest in the
land: the time is come, the day
of trouble *is* near, and not the
sounding[C] again of the mountains.
8 Now will I shortly pour out
my [d]fury upon thee, and accomplish mine anger upon thee:
and I will [e]judge thee [f]according
to thy ways, and will [g,h]recom-
pense thee for all thine abominations.[T]
9 And mine eye shall not spare,
neither will I have [i]pity: I will
[g,h]recompense[C] thee according to
thy ways and thine abominations *that* are in the midst of
thee; and [j]ye shall know that I
*am* the LORD that smiteth.
10 [c]Behold the day, behold, it
is come: [3]the morning is gone
forth; the rod hath blossomed,
pride hath budded.
11 Violence is risen up into
a rod of wickedness: [c]none of
them *shall remain,* nor of their
multitude, nor of [4]any of their's:
neither *shall there be* [5]wailing for
them.
12 [c]The time is come, the day
draweth near: let not the buyer
rejoice, nor the seller mourn: for
wrath *is* upon all the multitude
thereof.
13 For the seller shall not return to that which is sold, although they were yet alive: for
the vision *is* touching the whole
multitude thereof, *which* shall
not return; neither shall any
strengthen himself in the iniquity[C] of his life.
14 They have blown the trumpet, even to make all ready; but
none goeth to the battle: for my
wrath *is* upon all the multitude
thereof.
15 [c]The [k]sword *is* without, and
the [l]pestilence and the [m]famine
within: he that *is* in the field
shall die with the sword; and he
that *is* in the city, famine and
pestilence shall devour him.
16 ¶ But they that escape of
them shall escape, and shall be
on the mountains like [n]doves of
the valleys, all of them mourning, every one for his iniquity.
17 [o]All hands shall be feeble,
and all knees shall be weak *as*
water.
18 They shall also gird *themselves* with [p]sackcloth, and horror shall cover them; and shame
*shall be* upon all faces, and [q]bald-
ness upon all their heads.
19 They shall cast their [r]silver
in the streets, and their *gold
shall be [6]removed: [s,t,u]their silver and their gold shall not be
able to deliver them in the day of
the [d]wrath of the LORD: they
shall not satisfy their souls, neither fill their bowels[C]: because it
is the [v]stumblingblock of their
iniquity.
20 As for the beauty of his
ornament, he set it in majesty:
but [w]they made the images of
their abominations *and* of their
detestable things therein: therefore have I [7]set it far from
them.
21 And I will give it into the
hands of the strangers[C] for a prey,
and to the wicked of the earth

**10**
3 R. V. thy doom

**11**
4 R. V. their wealth:
5 R. V. eminency among them.

**15**
k *War, as a judgment,* Judg. 3:2.
l *Plague, as a judgment,* Ex. 11:1.
m *Famine, as a judgment,* 2 Kin. 8:1.

**16**
n *Dove,* Gen. 8:8.

**17**
o *Adversity, despondency in,* Psa. 10:6.

**18**
p *Sackcloth, symbol of mourning,* Isa. 15:3.
q *Baldness, a judgment,* Lev. 21:5.

**19**
r *Silver* 2 Chr. 28:14.
s *False Confidence, in riches,* Psa. 30:6.
t *Riches, impotent in day of calamity,* Eccl. 4:8.
u *Punishment, no escape from,* Lev. 26:41.
v *Stumbling, figurative,* Isa. 8:14.
6 R. V. as an unclean thing;

**20**
w *Idolatry, denounced,* 1 Sam. 15:23.
7 R. V. made it unto them as an unclean thing.

* **GOLD,** Isa. 13:12. *Exported, from Havilah,* Gen. 2:11, 12; *from Ophir,* 1 Kin. 9:28; 10:11; 1 Chr. 29:4; 2 Chr. 8:18; Job 22:24; *from Tarshish,* 1 Kin. 22:48; *from Parvaim,* 2 Chr. 3:6; *from Sheba,* 1 Kin. 10:10; 2 Chr. 9:9; Psa. 72:15; *from Uphaz,* Jer. 10:9.

*Refined,* Job 28:19; 31:24; Prov. 8:19; 17:3; 27:21; Zech. 13:9; Mal. 3:3. *Wedge of,* Josh. 7:21.

Used in the arts: *Overlaying with,* Ex. 25:11, 13, 24, 28, (with vs. 1–40); 26:27, 29; 30:5; 36:34, 36, 38; 37:2, 4, 11, 15; 1 Kin. 6:20–22, 28, 30, 32, 35.

*Beaten work of,* 2 Chr. 9:15. *Made into wire threads and wrought, into embroidered tapestry,* Ex. 39:3; *into apparel,* Psa. 45:9, 13; *into priests' vestments,* Ex. 39:1–31.

*Modeled, into forms of fruit,* Prov. 25:11; *into ornaments,* Gen. 24:22; Ex. 3:22; 11:2; 28:11; Num. 31:50, 51; Song 1:10, 11; 5:14; Ezek. 16:17.

Articles made of: *Crowns,* Ex. 39:30; Esth. 8:15; Psa. 21:3; Zech. 6:11; *shields,* 1 Kin. 10:16, 17; *bedsteads,* Esth. 1:6. *Vessels and utensils,* 2 Sam. 8:10; 1 Kin. 10:21, 25; 14:26; 1 Chr. 18:10; *for the tabernacle,* Ex. 25:26, 29, 38, 39; 37:16; 38:24; *for the temple,* 1 Chr. 18:11; 22:14, 16; 28:14, 17; 29:2–7. *Altar, candlesticks, lamps, and other articles made of,* Ex. 25:31–38; 37:17–24; 1 Kin. 7:48–51; 2 Kin. 25:15; 2 Chr. 28:15, 16, 18; Jer. 52:19; Ezra 8:27; Dan. 5:3.

*Belongs to God,* Ezek. 16:17.

*Used as money,* Gen. 44:8 (with v. 1); 1 Chr. 21:25; Ezra 8:25–28; Isa. 13:17; 60:9; Ezek. 7:19; 28:4; Matt. 2:11; 10:9; Acts 3:6; 20:33; 1 Pet. 1:18. *Solomon rich in,* 1 Kin. 10:2, 14, 21.

**Figurative,** Eccl. 12:6; Jer. 51:7; Lam. 4:1, 2; 1 Cor. 3:12. **Symbolical.** Dan. 2:32–45; Rev. 21:18, 21.

for a spoil; and they shall pollute it.

22 My face will I turn also from them, and they shall pollute my secret [x]*place*: for the robbers shall enter into it, and defile it.

23 ¶ Make a chain: for the land is full of bloody crimes, and the city is full of violence.

24 Wherefore I will bring the worst of the heathen[C], and they shall possess their houses: I will also make the pomp of the strong to cease; and their holy places shall be defiled.[C]

25 [c]Destruction cometh; and they shall seek peace, and *there shall be* none.

26 Mischief shall come upon mischief, and rumour shall be upon rumour; then shall they seek a vision of the prophet; but the law shall perish from the priest, and counsel from the ancients.[C]

27 [c]The king shall mourn, and the prince shall be clothed with desolation, and the hands of the people of the land shall be troubled: I will [g,h]do unto them after their way, and according to their deserts will I [i]judge them; and [j]they shall know that I *am* the LORD.

## CHAPTER 8

*The prophet in a vision beholds the image of jealousy in the temple; 7 also the elders sacrificing in the chamber of imagery, 13 women weeping for Tammuz, 15 and men worshiping the sun. 17 God's wrath for their idolatry.*

AND it came to pass in the sixth year, in the sixth [a]*month*, in the fifth *day* of the month, *as* [b]I sat in mine house, and the [c]elders of Jū′dah sat before me, that the hand of the Lord GOD [d]fell there upon me.

2 Then I [e]beheld, and lo a likeness as the appearance of fire: from the appearance of his loins even downward, fire; and from his loins even upward, as the appearance of brightness, as the colour of [f]amber.[Q]

3 And he put forth the form of an hand, and took me by a lock of mine head; and the spirit lifted me up between the earth and the heaven, and brought me in the [e]visions of God to [g]Jĕ-rụ′-sā-lĕm, to the door of the [1]inner gate that looketh toward the north; where *was* the seat of the [h]image of [i]jealousy, which provoketh to jealousy.[T]

4 And, behold, the [j]glory of the God of Ĭṣ′ra-el *was* there, according to the [e]vision that I saw in the plain.

5 ¶ Then said he unto me, Son of man, lift up thine eyes now the way toward the north. So I lifted up mine eyes the way toward the north, and behold northward at the gate of the altar this [h]image of [i]jealousy in the entry.

6 He said furthermore unto me, Son of man, seest thou what they do? *even* the great [k]abominations[C] that the house of Ĭṣ′ra-el committeth here, that I should go far off from my [l]sanctuary[C]? but turn thee yet again, *and* thou shalt see greater abominations.[C]

7 ¶ And he brought me to the door of the [m]court; and when I looked, behold a hole in the wall.

8 Then said he unto me, Son of man, dig now in the wall: and when I had digged in the wall, behold a door.

9 And he said unto me, Go in, and behold the wicked [k]abominations that they do here.

10 So I went in and saw; and behold every form of [n,o]creeping things, and abominable beasts, and all the idols of the house of Ĭṣ′ra-el, pourtrayed[C] upon the [p]wall round about.

11 And there stood before them [c]seventy men of the [2]ancients of the house of Ĭṣ′ra-el, and in the

---

22
x *Temple, Solomon's*, 1 Kin. 6:17.

v.1–513 BC
1
a *Month (September)*, Ex. 12:2.
b *Ezekiel*, Ezek. 1:3.
c *Senate*, Num. 11:16.
d *Prophets, inspiration of*, Isa. 3:2.

2
e *Vision*, vs. 1–16; Acts 9:10.

f Ezek. 1:4.

3
g *Jerusalem*, Judg. 19:10.
h *Image, figurative*, 1 Cor. 11:7.
i *Jealousy*, Psa. 78:58.
1 R. V. gate of the inner court

4
j *God, glory of*, Gen. 2:2.

6
k *Idolatry, wicked practices of*, 1 Sam. 15:23.
l *Temple, Solomon's*, 1 Kin. 6:17.

7
m *Court, of the temple*, Ex. 38:9.

10
n *Creeping Things*, Rom. 1:23.
o *Idolatry, objects of*, 1 Sam. 15:23.
p *House, mural paintings of*, Esth. 8:1.

11
2 R. V. elders

midst of them stood Jā-ăz-a-nī'ah the son of Shā'phan, with every man his [q]censer in his hand; and [3]a thick cloud of [r]incense went up.

12 Then said he unto me, Son of man, hast thou seen what the [2]ancients of the house of Ĭș'ra-el [s]do in the dark, every man in the chambers of his imagery[C]? for they [t,u]say, [v,w]The LORD seeth us not; the LORD hath forsaken the earth.

13 ¶ He said also unto me, Turn thee yet again, *and* thou shalt see greater [k]abominations[C] that they do.

14 Then he brought me to the door of the gate of the LORD's [l]house which *was* toward the north; and, behold, there sat [x]women weeping for [o]Tăm'mŭz.

15 ¶ Then said he unto me, Hast thou seen *this,* O son of man? turn thee yet again, *and* thou shalt see greater [k]abominations than these.

16 And he brought me into the [m]inner court of the LORD's house, and, behold, at the door of the [l]temple of the LORD, between the porch and the altar, *were* about five and twenty men, with their backs toward the temple of the LORD, and their faces toward the east; and they worshipped the [o,y]sun toward the east.

17 ¶ Then he said unto me, Hast thou seen *this,* O son of man? Is it a light thing to the house of Jū'dah that they commit the [k]abominations which they commit here? for they have filled the land with violence, and have returned to [z]provoke me to [a]anger: and, lo, they put the branch to their nose.

18 Therefore will I also deal in fury: mine eye shall not spare, neither will I have [b]pity: and though they cry in mine ears with a loud voice, [c]*yet* will I not hear them.

## CHAPTER 9

*A vision typifying the preservation of some of the people,* 5 *and the destruction of the rest.* 8 *God will not be entreated for them.*

HE cried also in mine ears with a loud voice, saying, Cause them that have charge over the city to draw near, even every man *with* his destroying weapon in his hand.

2 And, [a]behold, six men came from the way of the higher gate, which lieth toward the north, and every man a slaughter weapon in his hand; and one man among them *was* clothed with [b]linen, with a writer's inkhorn[C] by his side: and they went in, and stood beside the brasen[G] [c]altar.[Q]

3 And the [d]glory of the God of Ĭș'ra-el was gone up from the [e]cherub, whereupon he was, to the threshold of the house. And he called to the man clothed with [b]linen, which *had* the writer's inkhorn by his side;

4 And[S] the [f]LORD said unto him, Go through the midst of the city, through the midst of [g]Jĕ-ru'să-lĕm, and set a mark upon the foreheads of the men [h]that sigh and that cry for all the [i]abominations[C] that be done in the midst thereof.[Q]

5 And to the others he said in mine hearing, Go ye after him through the city, and [h,j]smite: let not your eye spare, neither have ye [k]pity:

6 [j]Slay[C] utterly[G] old *and* young, both maids, and little children, and women: but [j]come not near any man upon whom *is* the mark; and begin at my [l]sanctuary.[G] Then they began at the ancient[G] men which *were* before the house.[S Q]

7 And he said unto them, Defile the house, and fill the [m]courts

---

[q] *Censer, used in idolatrous rites,* Lev. 16:12.
[r] *Incense, offered in idolatrous worship,* Ex. 37:29.
3 R. V. the odour of the cloud

12
[s] *Sin, in secret,* Rom. 5:12.
[t] *Blasphemy, defying God,* 2 Sam. 12:14.
[u] *Scoffing, of unbelievers,* Hab. 1:10.
[v] *Infidelity, exemplified in impugning God's knowledge,* 2 Cor. 6:15.
[w] *False Confidence, of the infidel,* Psa. 30:6.

14
[x] *Women, wicked,* Prov. 31:10.

16
[y] *Sun, worshiped,* Josh. 10:12.

17
[z] *Sin, repugnant to God,* Rom. 5:12.

[a] *Anger of God,* 2 Kin. 13:3.

18
[b] *Pity, withheld from reprobate sinners,* Job 19:21.

[c] *Wicked, prayers of, not answered,* Psa. 73:3.

2
[a] *Vision,* vs. 1-11; Acts 9:10.
[b] *Linen,* Ezek. 27:16.
[c] *Altar, of burnt offerings,* Gen. 8:20.

3
[d] *Shekinah,* Lev. 16:2.
[e] *Cherubim,* Ex. 37:7.

4
[f] *God, preserver of the righteous,* vs. 4-6; Gen. 2:2.
[g] *Jerusalem,* Judg. 19:10.
[h] *Judgment, according to opportunity and works,* 1 Pet. 1:17.
[i] *Idolatry, wicked practices of,* 1 Sam. 15:23.

5
[j] *Wicked, punishment of,* Psa. 73:3.
[k] *Pity, withheld from reprobate sinners,* Job 19:21.

6
[l] *Temple, Solomon's,* 1 Kin. 6:17.

7
[m] *Court, of the temple,* Ex. 38:9.

with the slain: go ye forth. And they went forth, and [j]slew in the city.

8 ¶ And it came to pass, while they were slaying them, and I was left, that I fell upon my face, and [n]cried, and said, Ah Lord GOD! wilt thou destroy all the residue[C] of Ĭṣ′ra-el in thy pouring out of thy fury upon [g]Jĕ-rṳ′sā̤-lĕm?

9 Then said he unto me, The iniquity of the house of Ĭṣ′ra-el and Jū′dah *is* exceeding great, and the land is full of blood, and the city full of [1]perverseness[C]: for they [o,p]say, [q]The LORD hath forsaken the earth, and [r]the LORD seeth not.

10 And as for me also, mine eye shall not spare, neither will I have [k]pity, *but* I will [j]recompense their way upon their head.

11 And, behold, the man clothed with [b]linen, which *had* the inkhorn by his side, reported the matter, saying, I have done as thou hast commanded me.[Q]

## CHAPTER 10

*The vision of the coals of fire, to be scattered over the city. 8 The vision of the cherubim.*

THEN [a]I looked, and, [b]behold, in the firmament that was above the head of the [c]cherubims there appeared over them as it were a [d,e]sapphire stone, as the appearance of the likeness of a throne.

2 And he spake unto the man clothed with [f]linen, and said, Go in between the wheels, *even* under the [c]cherub, and fill thine hand with coals of fire from between the cherubims, and scatter *them* over the city. And he went in in my sight.

3 Now the [c]cherubims stood on the right side of the [g]house, when the man went in; and the cloud filled the [h]inner court.

4 Then the glory of the LORD went up from the [c]cherub, *and stood* over the threshold of the [g]house; and the house was filled with the cloud, and the [h]court was full of the brightness of the LORD's glory.

5 And the sound of the cherubims' wings was heard *even* to the [h]outer court, as the voice of the [i]Almighty God when he speaketh.

6 And it came to pass, *that* when he had commanded the man clothed with [f]linen, saying, Take fire from between the wheels, from between the [c]cherubims; then he went in, and stood beside the wheels.

7 And *one* cherub stretched forth his hand from between the cherubims unto the fire that *was* between the cherubims, and took *thereof*, and put *it* into the hands of *him that was* clothed with linen: who took *it*, and went out.

8 ¶ And there appeared in the [c]cherubims the form of a man's hand under their wings.

9 And when I [b]looked, behold the four wheels by the cherubims, one wheel by one cherub, and another wheel by another cherub: and the appearance of the wheels *was* as the colour of a [j]beryl stone.

10 And *as for* their appearances, they four had one likeness, as if a wheel had been in the midst of a wheel.

11 When they went, they went upon their four sides; they turned not as they went, but to the place whither the head looked they followed it; they turned not as they went.

12 And their whole body, and their backs, and their hands, and their wings, and the wheels, *were* full of eyes round about, *even* the wheels that they four had.[Q]

8
n *Intercession, exemplified,* Jer. 27:18.

9
o *Blasphemy, defying God,* 2 Sam. 12:14.
p *Scoffing, of unbelievers,* Hab. 1:10.
q *False Confidence, of the infidel,* Psa. 30:6.
r *Infidelity, exemplified in impugning God's knowledge,* 2 Cor. 6:15.
1 R. V. wresting of judgement:

1
a *Ezekiel,* Ezek. 1:3.
b *Vision,* vs. 1–22; Acts 9:10.
c *Cherubim, symbolical,* Ex. 37:7.
d *Sapphire,* Job 28:6.
e *Colors, symbolical,* Ezek. 16:16.

2
f *Linen,* Ezek. 27:16.

3
g *Temple, Solomon's,* 1 Kin. 6:17.
h *Court, of the temple,* Ex. 38:9.

5
i *God, omnipotent,* Gen. 2:2.

9
j *Beryl,* **Ezek. 1:16.**

13 As for the wheels, [1]it was cried unto them in my hearing, O wheel.

14 And every one had four faces: the first face *was* the face of a cherub, and the second face *was* the face of a man, and the third the face of a [k]lion, and the fourth the face of an [l]eagle.[Q]

15 And the [c]cherubims [2]were lifted up. This *is* the living creature that I saw by the river of [m]Chē′bär.

16 And when the [c]cherubims went, the wheels went by them: and when the cherubims lifted up their wings to mount up from the earth, the same wheels also turned not from beside them.

17 When they stood, *these* stood; and when they [2]were lifted up, *these* [2]lifted up themselves *also*: for the spirit of the living creature *was* in them.[T]

18 Then the glory of the LORD departed from off the threshold of the [g]house, and stood over the [c]cherubims.

19 And the [c]cherubims lifted up their wings, and mounted up from the earth in my sight: when they went out, the wheels also *were* beside them, and *every one* stood at the door of the east gate of the LORD's [g]house; and the [n]glory of the God of Iș′ra-el *was* over them above.

20 This *is* the living creature that I saw under the God of Iș′ra-el by the river of [m]Chē′bär; and I knew that they *were* the [c]cherubims.

21 Every one had four faces apiece, and every one four wings; and the likeness of the hands of a man *was* under their wings.

22 And the likeness of their faces *was* the same faces which I saw by the river of [m]Chē′bär, their appearances and themselves: they went every one straight forward.

13
1 R. V. they were called in my hearing, the whirling wheels.

14
*k Lion, similitudes of,* Mic. 5:8.
*l Eagle, similitudes of,* Lev. 11:13.

15
*m Chebar,* Ezek. 1:1.
2 R. V. mounted up

19
*n God, glory of,* Gen. 2:2.

## CHAPTER 11

*The presumption of the princes. 4 Their sin and punishment. 13 God's gracious purpose in the chastisement of his people. 22 The glory of God leaves the city. 24 The end of the vision.*

MOREOVER the spirit lifted [a]me up, and brought me unto the east gate of the LORD's [b]house, which looketh eastward: and behold at the door of the gate five and twenty men; among whom I saw Jā-ăz-a-nī′ah the son of Ā′zụr, and Pĕl-a-tī′ah the son of Bĕ-nā′iah, princes of the people.[T]

2 Then said he unto me, Son of man, these *are* the men that devise[G] [1]mischief, and give wicked counsel in this city:

3 Which [c,d,e]say, [2]*It is* not near; let us build houses: this *city is* the [f]caldron[G], and we *be* the flesh.

4 ¶ Therefore prophesy against them, prophesy, O son of man.

5 And the Spirit of the LORD fell upon [a]me, and said unto me, [g]Speak; Thus saith the LORD; Thus have ye said, O house of Iș′ra-el: for I [h]know the things that come into your [i]mind, *every one of* them.[T]

6 Ye have multiplied your slain in this city, and ye have filled the streets thereof with the slain.

7 Therefore thus saith the Lord GOD; Your slain whom ye have laid in the midst of it, they *are* the flesh, and this *city is* the [f]caldron: but I will bring you forth out of the midst of it.

8 Ye have feared the sword; and [j]I will bring a [k]sword upon you, saith the Lord GOD.

9 And I will bring you out of the midst thereof, and [l]deliver you into the hands of strangers,[G] and will execute judgments among you.

10 [m]Ye[T] shall fall by the [k]sword; I will judge you in the border of Iș′ra-el; and [n]ye shall know that I *am* the LORD.

1
*a Ezekiel,* Ezek. 1:3.
*b Temple, Solomon's,* 1 Kin. 6:17.

2
1 R. V. iniquity,

3
*c Scoffing, of unbelievers,* Hab. 1:10.
*d Infidelity,* 2 Cor. 6:15.
*e Delusion,* 2 Thess. 2:11.
*f Caldron, figurative,* 1 Sam. 2:14.
2 R. V. The time is not near to build houses:

5
*g Prophets, inspiration of,* Isa. 3:2.
*h God, knowledge of,* Gen. 2:2.
*i Heart, known to God,* Psa. 44:21.

8
*j Adversity, dispensation from God,* Psa. 10:6.
*k War, as a judgment,* Judg. 3:2

9
*l Captivity, as a judgment,* Isa. 5:13.

10
*m Wicked, punishment of,* Psa. 73:3.
*n Judgments, design of,* Ex. 6:6.

11 This *city* shall not be your [l]caldron,[G] neither shall ye be the flesh[G] in the midst thereof; *but* I will judge you in the border of Ĭṣ′ra-el:[T]

12 And [n]ye shall know that I *am* the LORD: for ye have [o]not walked in my statutes, neither executed my judgments,[G] but have done after the manners of the [3]heathen[G] that *are* round about you.

13 ¶ And it came to pass, when [a]I [g]prophesied, that Pĕl-a-tī′ah the son of Bē-nā′iah died. Then fell I down upon my face, and cried with a loud voice, and said, [p]Ah Lord GOD! wilt thou make a full end of the remnant of Ĭṣ′ra-el?

14 ¶ Again the [q]word of the LORD [g]came unto [a]me, saying,

15 Son of man, thy brethren, *even* thy brethren, the men of thy kindred, and all the house of Ĭṣ′ra-el wholly, *are* they unto whom the inhabitants of Jē-rụ′-sā-lĕm have said, Get you far from the LORD: unto us is this land given in possession.[S]

16 Therefore say, Thus saith the Lord GOD; Although I have cast them far off among the [3]heathen,[G] and although I have scattered them among the countries, [r,s]yet will I be to them as a [4]little [t]sanctuary[G] in the countries where they shall come.[S]

17 Therefore [q]say, [u]Thus saith the Lord GOD; I will even gather you from the [5]people, and assemble you out of the countries where ye have been scattered, and I will give you the land of Ĭṣ′ra-el.

18 And they shall come thither,[G] and they shall [v]take away all the detestable things thereof and all the abominations[G] thereof from thence.[G]

19[T] And I will [w]give them one [x]heart, and I will [y]put a new spirit within you; and I will take the stony heart out of their flesh, and will give them an heart of flesh:[S Q]

20 That they may [z]walk in my statutes, and [z]keep mine ordinances, and [z]do them: and they shall be [a]my people, and I will be their God.[T]

21 But *as for them* whose heart walketh after the heart of their detestable things and their abominations,[G] I will [b,c]recompense their way upon their own heads, saith the Lord GOD.

22 ¶ [d]Then did the [e]cherubims lift up their wings, and the wheels beside them; and the [f]glory of the God of Ĭṣ′ra-el *was* over them above.

23 And the [f]glory of the LORD went up from the midst of the city, and stood upon the mountain which *is* on the east side of the city.

24 ¶ Afterwards the spirit[G] took me up, and brought me in a [d]vision by the Spirit of God into *,[g]Chăl-dē′ȧ, to them of the [h]captivity. So the vision that I had seen went up from me.[T]

25 Then I spake unto them of the [h]captivity all the things that the LORD had [i]shewed me.

## CHAPTER 12

*The prophet by the type of his removal shows the flight and captivity of Zedekiah. 17 The famine and consternation of the people during the siege typified. 21 Their presumption reproved. 26 The prophecy to be speedily fulfilled.*

THE [a]word of the LORD also [b]came unto [c]me, saying,

2 Son of man, thou dwellest in the midst of a [d,e,f]rebellious house, which have eyes to see, and [g]see not; they have ears to hear, and hear not: for they *are* a rebellious house.[Q]

---

**12**
o *Disobedience to God*, Eph. 5:6.
3 R. V. nations

**13**
p *Prayer, intercessory*, Acts 6:4.

**14**
q *Prophecies, inspired*, Dan. 9:24.

**16**
r *God, mercy of*, Gen. 2:2.
s *Adversity, consolation in*, Psa. 10:6.
t *Sanctuary, figurative*, Lev. 4:6.
4 R. V a sanctuary for a little while

**17**
u *Prophecies, of the return of the Jews from Babylon*, Dan. 9:24.
5 R. V. peoples,

**18**
v *Repentance, of Israel foretold*, Mark 1:4.

**19**
w *Spiritual Blessings, from God*, Eph. 1:3.
x *Heart, renewed*, Psa. 44:21.
y *Regeneration*, Tit. 3:5.

**20**
z *Obedience, rewarded*, Heb. 5:8.
a *Spiritual Adoption*, Rom. 8:15.

**21**
b *Wicked, punishment of*, Psa. 73:3.
c *Idolatry, punishment for*, 1 Sam. 15:23.

**22**
d *Vision*, Acts 9:10.
e *Cherubim, symbolical*, Ex. 37:7.
f *God, glory of*, Gen. 2:2.

**24**
g *Chaldea*, Ezek. 11:24.
h *Jews, captive in Babylon*, Neh. 4:2.

**25**
i *Prophets, inspiration of*, Isa. 3:2.

**1**
a *Prophecies, inspired*, Dan. 9:24.
b *Prophets, inspiration of*, Isa. 3:2.
c *Ezekiel*, Ezek. 1:3.

**2**
d *Jews, wickedness of*, Neh. 4:2.
e *Impenitence*, Rom. 2:5.
f *Obduracy*, Prov. 29:1.
g *Spiritual Blindness*, 2 Cor. 4:4.

---

***CHALDEA**, the southern portion of Babylonia. *Abraham a native of*, Gen. 11:28, 31; 15:7. *Ezekiel prophesies in*, Ezek. 1:3; 11:24. *Army of*, Jer. 52:7, 8, 14, 17. *Prophecies concerning*, Jer. 50:10; 51:35. *Character of its people*, Hab. 1:6. *The name of, sometimes used as an equivalent to Babylon in referring to the Babylonian empire, which embraced in time of the prophets both Chaldea and Babylonia*, Ezek. 16:29; 23:14–16. See footnotes: BABYLON, Ezra 5:12; CHALDEANS, Dan. 1:4.

3 Therefore, thou son of man, [h]prepare thee stuff[G] for removing[G], and [i,j]remove[G] by day in their sight; and thou shalt remove from thy place to another place in their sight: it may be they will [k]consider, though they *be* a rebellious house.

4 [h,i,j]Then shalt thou bring forth thy stuff[G] by day in their sight, as stuff[G] for removing: and thou shalt go forth at even[G] in their sight, as they that go forth into captivity.

5 [h,i,j]Dig thou through the wall in their sight, and carry out thereby.

6 [h,i,j]In their sight shalt thou bear *it* upon *thy* shoulders, *and* carry *it* forth in the [1]twilight: thou shalt cover thy face, that thou see not the ground: for I have set thee *for* a sign unto the house of Ĭş′ra-el.

7 And I did so as I was commanded: [h,i,j]I brought forth my stuff[G] by day, as stuff[G] for [2]captivity[G], and in the even[G] I digged through the wall with mine hand; I brought *it* forth in the twilight, *and* I bare *it* upon *my* shoulder in their sight.

8 And in the morning [b]came the [a]word of the LORD unto [c]me, saying,

9 Son of man, hath not the house of Ĭş′ra-el, the [d,e,f]rebellious house, said unto thee, What doest thou?

10 Say thou unto them, [j]Thus saith the Lord GOD; This burden[G] *concerneth* the [l]prince in Jē-ru̥′sā-lĕm, and all the house of Ĭş′ra-el that *are* among them.

11 [h]Say, I *am* your sign: [i,j]like as I have done, so shall it be done unto them: [m]they shall remove[G] *and* go into [n]captivity.

12 And the [l]prince that *is* among them shall bear upon *his* shoulder in the twilight, and shall go forth: they shall dig through the wall to carry out thereby: he shall cover his face, that he see not the ground with *his* eyes.

13 [o]My net also will I spread upon [l]him, and he shall be taken in my snare: and I will bring him to [p]Băb′ȳ-lon *to* the land of the [q]Chăl-dē′anş; yet shall he not see it, though he shall die there.

14 And I will scatter toward every wind all that *are* about him to help him, and all his bands[G]; and I will draw out the [r]sword after them.

15 And [s]they shall know that I *am* the LORD, when I shall [t]scatter them among the nations, and disperse them in the countries.

16 But I will leave a few men of them from the [r]sword, from the [u]famine, and from the [v]pestilence; that they may declare[G] all their abominations[G] among the [3]heathen[G] whither[G] they come; and [s]they shall know that I *am* the LORD.

17 ¶ Moreover the word of the LORD [b]came to [c]me, saying,

18 Son of man, [i,j]eat thy bread with quaking, and drink thy water with trembling and with carefulness[G];

**19 And say unto the people of the land, [i,j]Thus saith the Lord GOD of the inhabitants of Jē-ru̥′sā-lĕm, *and* of the land of Ĭş′ra-el; [w,x]They shall eat their bread with carefulness[G], and drink their water with astonishment[G], that her land may be desolate from all that is therein, because of the violence of all them that dwell therein.**

**20 And the cities that are inhabited shall be laid waste, and the land shall be desolate; and [s,y]ye shall know that I *am* the LORD.**

21 ¶ And the [z]word of the LORD [a]came unto [b]me, saying,

---

3
h *Instruction, by object lessons,* v. 18; Prov. 23:23.
i *Pantomime,* v. 18; Isa. 20:2.
j *Prophecies, exemplified in pantomime,* v. 18; Dan. 9:24.
k *Repentance,* Mark 1:4.

6
1 R. V. dark;

7
2 R. V. removing,

10
l *Zedekiah,* 2 Kin. 25:2.

11
m *Jews, captive in Babylon,* Neh. 4:2.
n *Captivity, as a judgment,* Isa. 5:13.

13
o *Adversity, dispensation from God,* Psa. 10:6.
p *Babylon, empire of,* Ezra 5:12.
q *Chaldeans,* Dan. 1:4.

14
r *War, as a judgment,* Judg. 3:2.

15
s *Judgments, design of,* Ex. 6:6.
t *Dispersion, foretold,* Gen. 11:8.

16
u *Famine, as a judgment,* 2 Kin. 8:1.
v *Plague, as a judgment,* Ex. 11:1.
3 R. V. nations

19
w *Jews, prophecies concerning,* Neh. 4:2.
x *Wicked, punishment of,* Psa. 7:3.

20
y *Adversity, design of,* Psa. 10:6.

21
z *Prophecies, inspired,* Dan. 9:24

a *Prophets, inspiration of,* Isa. 3:2
b *Ezekiel,* Ezek. 1:3.

22
*c Proverbs*, 1 Sam. 24:13.
*d Infidelity*, 2 Cor. 6:15.
*e Scoffing, of unbelievers*, Hab. 1:10.
*f Vision*, Acts 9:10.

24
*g Sorcery*, Isa. 47:9.

25
*h God, faithfulness of*, Gen. 2:2.
4 R. V. deferred:

1
*a Prophecies, inspired*, Dan. 9:24.
*b Prophets, inspiration of*, Isa. 3:2.
*c Ezekiel*, Ezek. 1:3.

2
*d Prophets, false*, Isa. 3:2.

22 Son of man, what *is* that [c]proverb *that* ye have in the land of Is′ra-el, [d,e]saying, The days are prolonged, and every [f]vision faileth?

23 [a]Tell them therefore, Thus saith the Lord GOD; I will make this [c]proverb to cease, and they shall no more use it as a proverb in Is′ra-el; but say unto them, The days are at hand, and the effect[G] of every [f]vision.

24 For there shall be no more any vain[G] vision nor flattering [g]divination[G] within the house of Is′ra-el.

25 For I *am* the LORD: I will speak, and [h]the word that I shall speak shall come to pass; it shall be no more [4]prolonged: for in your days, O rebellious house, will I say the word, and [h]will perform it, saith the Lord GOD.

26 ¶ Again the word of the LORD [a]came to [b]me, saying,

27 Son of man, behold, *they of* the house of Is′ra-el [d,e]say, The [f]vision that he seeth *is* for many days *to come*, and he prophesieth of the times *that are* far off.

28 Therefore say unto them, Thus saith the Lord GOD; There shall none of my words be prolonged any more, but [h]the word which I have spoken shall be done, saith the Lord GOD.

## CHAPTER 13

*The sin and punishment of false prophets, 17 and of false prophetesses.*

AND the [a]word of the LORD [b]came unto [c]me, saying,

2 Son of man, prophesy against the [d]prophets of Is′ra-el that prophesy, and say thou unto them that prophesy out of their own hearts, Hear ye the word of the LORD;

3 Thus saith the Lord GOD; Woe unto the foolish [d]prophets, that follow their own spirit,[G] and have seen nothing!

4 O Is′ra-el, thy [d]prophets are like the [e]foxes in the deserts.[G]

5 Ye have not gone up into the gaps, neither made up the [1]hedge for the house of Is′ra-el to stand in the battle in the day of the LORD.

6 [d]They have seen vanity and lying [f]divination, saying, The LORD saith: and the LORD hath not sent them: and they have [g]made *others* to [h]hope that [2]they would confirm the word.

7 Have [d]ye not seen a vain vision, and have ye not spoken a lying divination, whereas ye say, The LORD saith *it*; albeit[G] I have not spoken?

8 Therefore thus saith the Lord GOD; [i]Because ye have spoken vanity, and seen lies, therefore, behold, I *am* against you, saith the Lord GOD.

9 And mine hand shall be upon the [d]prophets that see vanity, and that divine[G] lies: they shall not be in the assembly of my people, neither shall they be written in the writing of the house of Is′ra-el, neither shall they enter into the land of Is′ra-el; and ye shall know that I *am* the Lord GOD.

10 Because,[Q] even because they have [g]seduced my people, [h]saying, Peace; and *there was* no peace; and one built up a wall, and, lo, others daubed it with untempered *morter*:

11 Say unto them which daub *it* with untempered *morter*, that it shall fall: there shall be an overflowing shower; and ye, O great hailstones, shall fall; and a stormy wind shall rend[G] *it*.

12 Lo, when the wall is fallen, shall it not be said unto you, Where *is* the daubing wherewith ye have daubed *it*?[Q]

13 Therefore thus saith the Lord GOD; I will even rend[G] *it* with a stormy wind in my fury; and

4
*e Fox, illustrative*, Psa. 63:10.

5
1 R. V. fence

6
*f Sorcery, practiced by false prophets*, Isa. 47:9.
*g Influence, evil*, 1 Cor. 7:14.
*h False Confidence*, Psa. 30:6.
2 R. V. the word should be confirmed.

8
*i Sin, repugnant to God*, Rom. 5:12.

there shall be an overflowing shower in mine [i]anger, and great hailstones in *my* fury to consume *it*.

14 So will I break down the wall that ye have daubed with untempered *morter*, and bring it down to the ground, so that the foundation thereof shall be discovered,[G] and it shall fall, and ye shall be consumed in the midst thereof: and [k]ye shall know that I *am* the LORD.

15 Thus will I accomplish my [i]wrath upon the wall, and upon them that have daubed it with untempered *morter*, and will say unto you, The wall *is* no *more*, neither they that daubed it;[Q]

16 *To wit*, the [d]prophets of Is̱′ra-el which prophesy concerning Jē-rṳ′să-lĕm, and which see visions of peace for her, and *there is* no peace, saith the Lord GOD.

17 ¶ Likewise, thou son of man, set thy face against the [l,m]daughters of thy people, which prophesy out of their own heart; and prophesy thou against them,

18 And say, Thus saith the Lord GOD; Woe to the *women* that [n]sew[G] pillows [3]to all armholes, and make [n]kerchiefs[G] upon the head of every stature to hunt souls! Will ye hunt the souls of my people, and [4]will ye save the souls alive *that come* unto you?

19 And will ye pollute me among my people for handfuls of barley and for pieces of bread, to slay the souls that should not die, and to save the souls alive that should not live, by your lying to my people that hear *your* lies?

20 Wherefore thus saith the Lord GOD; Behold, I *am* against your pillows, wherewith ye there hunt the souls to make *them* fly, and I will tear them from your arms, and will let the souls go, *even* the souls that ye hunt to make *them* fly.

21 Your kerchiefs also will I tear, and deliver my people out of your hand, and they shall be no more in your hand to be hunted; and [k]ye shall know that I *am* the LORD.

22 Because with lies ye have made the heart of the righteous sad, whom I have not made sad; and [h]strengthened the hands of the wicked, that he should not return from his wicked way, [5]by promising him life:

23 Therefore ye shall see no more vanity, nor divine [i]divinations: for [o]I will [p]deliver my people out of your hand: and ye shall know that I *am* the LORD.

## CHAPTER 14

*Idolaters in Israel rebuked,* 6 *and exhorted to repent.* 12 *The certainty of Israel's punishment by famine,* 15 *by noisome beasts,* 17 *by the sword,* 19 *and by pestilence.* 22 *A remnant to be left, and the reason thereof.*

THEN came certain of the [a]elders of Is̱′ra-el unto [b]me, and sat before me.

2 And the [c]word of the LORD [d]came unto [b]me, saying,

3 Son of man, these men have set up their [e]idols in their heart, and put the [f]stumblingblock of their iniquity before their face: [g]should I be enquired of at all by them?

4 Therefore [c,d]speak unto them, and say unto them, Thus saith the Lord GOD; Every man of the house of Is̱′ra-el that setteth up his [e]idols in his heart, and putteth the [f]stumblingblock of his iniquity before his face, and cometh to the prophet; I the LORD will answer him [1]that cometh according to the multitude of his idols;

5 That I may take the house of Is̱′ra-el in their own heart, because [h]they are all estranged from me through their idols.[s]

6 ¶ Therefore [c,d]say unto the

**13**
*i Anger of God,* 2 Kin. 13:3.

**14**
*k Judgments, design of,* Ex. 6:6.

**17**
*l Women, as prophets,* Prov. 31:10.
*m Prophetess,* Judg. 4:4.

**18**
*n Dress,* Zech. 3:3.
3 R. V. upon all elbows, and make kerchiefs for the head of persons of every stature
4 R. V. save souls alive for yourselves?

**22**
5 R. V. and be saved alive:

**23**
*o God, providence of,* Gen. 2:2.
*p God, savior,* Gen. 2:2.

**1**
*a Senate,* Num. 11:16.
*b Ezekiel,* Ezek. 1:3.

**2**
*c Prophecies, inspired,* Dan. 9:24.
*d Prophets, inspiration of,* Isa. 3:2.

**3**
*e Idolatry,* 1 Sam. 15:23.
*f Stumbling, figurative,* Isa. 8:14.
*g Wicked, prayers of, not answered,* Psa. 73:3.

**4**
1 R. V. therein according

**5**
*h Sin, separates from God,* Rom. 5:12.

6
[i] *Repentance, enjoined,* Mark 1:4.
2 R. V. Return ye,

7
3 R. V. inquire for himself of me;

8
[j] *Wicked, punishment of,* Psa. 73:3.
[k] *Judgments, design of,* Ex. 6:6.

9
[l] *Prophets, false,* Isa. 3:2.

10
[m] *Punishment, according to deeds,* Lev. 26:41.

11
[n] *Adversity, benefits of,* Psa. 10:6.
[o] *Spiritual Adoption,* Rom. 8:15.

13
[p] *Nation, judgments denounced against,* Isa. 2:4.
[q] *Famine, as a judgment,* 2 Kin. 8:1.

house of Is̱′ra-el, Thus saith the
Lord GOD; [2,i]Repent, and turn
*yourselves* from your [e]idols; and
turn away your faces from all
your abominations.[s]
7 For every one of the house of
Is̱′ra-el, or of the stranger[C] that
sojourneth in Is̱′ra-el, which separateth himself from me, and
setteth up his [e]idols in his heart,
and putteth the [f]stumblingblock
of his iniquity before his face,
and cometh to a prophet to [3]en-
quire of him concerning me; I
the LORD will answer him by
myself:
8 And I will set my face against
that man, and will make him a
sign and a proverb, and I will
[j]cut him off from the midst of
my people; and [k]ye shall know
that I *am* the LORD.
9 And if the [l]prophet be deceived when he hath spoken a
thing, I the LORD have deceived
that prophet, and I will stretch
out my hand upon him, and will
destroy him from the midst of
my people Is̱′ra-el.
10 And they shall bear [4]the
[m]punishment of their iniquity:
the [5]punishment of the prophet
shall be even as the [5]punish-
ment of him that seeketh *unto*
*him;*
11 [n]That the house of Is̱′ra-el
may go no more astray from
me, neither be polluted[C] any
more with all their transgressions; but that they may be [o]my
people, and I may be their God,
saith the Lord GOD.
12 ¶ The [c]word of the LORD
[d]came again to [b]me, saying,
13 Son of man, when the land
sinneth against me by trespassing
grievously,[C] then will [p]I stretch
out mine hand upon it, and will
break the staff of the bread
thereof, and will send [q]famine
upon it, and will cut off man
and beast from it:
14 [r,s]Though these three men,
[t]Nō′ah, [u]Dăn′iel, and [v]Jōb, were
in it, they should deliver *but* their
own souls by their [w]righteous-
ness, saith the Lord GOD.
15 ¶ If I cause noisome[G] [x]beasts
to pass through the land, and they
spoil[C] it, so that it be desolate,
that no man may pass through
because of the beasts:
16 [r,s]*Though* these [t,u,v]three
men *were* in it, *as* I live, saith
the Lord GOD, they shall deliver
neither sons nor daughters; they
only shall be delivered, but the
land shall be desolate.
17 ¶ Or *if* I bring a [y]sword upon that land, and say, Sword, go
through the land; so that I cut
off man and beast from it:
18 [r,s]Though these [t,u,v]three
men *were* in it, *as* I live, saith
the Lord GOD, they shall deliver
neither sons nor daughters, but
they only shall be delivered themselves.
19 ¶ Or *if* I send a [z]pestilence
into that land, and pour out my
fury upon it in blood, to cut off
from it man and beast:
20 [r,s]Though [t]Nō′ah, [u]Dăn′iel,
and [v]Jōb, *were* in it, *as* I live,
saith the Lord GOD, they shall
deliver neither son nor daughter; they shall *but* deliver their
own souls by their [w]righteous-
ness.
21 For thus saith the Lord
GOD; How much more when I
send my four sore[G] [a]judgments
upon Jē-ru̇′sȧ-lĕm, the [b]sword,
and the [c]famine, and the noisome[G] [d]beast, and the [e]pestilence,
to cut off from it man and
beast?[Q]
22 Yet, behold, [f]therein shall
be left a remnant that shall be
brought forth, *both* sons and
daughters: behold, they shall
come forth unto you, and ye
shall see their way and their
doings: and ye shall be com-

14
[r] *Judgments, no escape from,* Ex. 6:6.
[s] *Intercession, influence of the righteous,* Jer. 27:18.
[t] *Noah, character of,* Gen. 5:29.
[u] *Daniel, devoutness of,* Dan. 1:6.
[v] *Job, righteous,* Job 1:1.
[w] *Works, good,* 2 Tim. 1:9.

15
[x] *Animals, sent in judgment,* Jer. 27:5.

17
[y] *War, as a judgment,* Judg. 3:2.

19
[z] *Plague, as a judgment,* Ex. 11:1.

21
[a] *Nation, judgments denounced against,* Isa. 2:4.
[b] *War, as a judgment,* Judg. 3:2.
[c] *Famine, as a judgment,* 2 Kin. 8:1.
[d] *Animals, sent in judgment,* Jer. 27:5.
[e] *Plague, as a judgment.* Ex. 11:1

22
[f] *God, mercy of,* Gen. 2:2.

23
*g God, justice of,* Gen. 2:2.

1
*a Prophecies, inspired,* Dan. 9:24.
*b Prophets, inspiration of,* Isa. 3:2.
*c Ezekiel,* Ezek. 1:3.

6
*d Wicked, punishment of,* Psa. 73:3.
*e Jews, prophecies concerning,* Neh. 4:2.
*f Jerusalem,* Judg. 19:10.

7
*g Adversity, design of,* Psa. 10:6.

forted concerning the evil that
I have brought upon Jĕ-ru̇′sā-
lĕm, *even* concerning all that
I have brought upon it.
23 And they shall comfort you,
when ye see their ways and their
doings: and ye shall know that
[g]I have not done without cause
all that I have done in it, saith
the Lord GOD.[S]

## CHAPTER 15

*As the vine branch is fit only for fuel, 6 so Jerusalem is fit only for destruction.*

AND the [a]word of the LORD
[b]came unto [c]me, saying,
2 Son of man, What is the vine
tree more than any tree, *or than* a
branch which is among the trees
of the forest?
3[T]Shall wood be taken thereof
to do any work? or will *men* take
a pin of it to hang any vessel
thereon?
4 Behold, it is cast into the fire
for fuel; the fire devoureth both
the ends of it, and the midst of
it is burned. Is it meet[G] for *any*
work?
5 Behold, when it was whole,
it was meet[G] for no work: how
much less shall it be meet[G] yet
for *any* work, when the fire
hath devoured it, and it is
burned?
6 ¶ Therefore thus saith the
Lord GOD; As the vine tree
among the trees of the forest,
which I have given to the fire for
fuel, [d]so will I give the [e]inhabit-
ants of [f]Jĕ-ru̇′sā-lĕm.[T]
7 And [d]I will set my face
against [e]them; they shall go
out from *one* fire, and *another*
fire shall devour them; and
[g]ye shall know that I *am* the
LORD, when I set my face
against them.
8 And [d]I will make the land
desolate, because they have committed a trespass[G], saith the Lord
GOD.

## CHAPTER 16

*Under the similitude of an exposed infant, is shown the state of Jerusalem at first. 6 God's great goodness towards her. 15 Her monstrous idolatry. 35 Her grievous punishment. 44 She is more guilty than Sodom or Samaria. 60 Yet God will remember his covenant with her.*

AGAIN the [a]word of the LORD
[b]came unto [c]me, saying,
2 Son of man, [d]cause [e]Jĕ-ru̇′sā-
lĕm to know her [f]abominations,[G]
3 And[T] say, Thus saith the Lord
GOD unto [e]Jĕ-ru̇′sā-lĕm; Thy
birth and thy nativity[G] *is* of the
land of [g]Cā′năan; thy father *was*
an [h]Ăm′ôr-īte, and thy mother
an [i]Hĭt′tite.
4 [j]And *as for* thy nativity, in the
day thou wast born thy navel
was not cut, [k]neither wast thou
[l]washed in water to [1]supple[G] *thee*;
thou [k]wast not salted at all, nor
[m]swaddled[G] at all.
5 None eye pitied thee, to do
any of these unto thee, to have
compassion upon thee; but thou
wast cast out in the open field, to
the lothing of thy person, in the
day that thou wast born.
6 ¶ And when I passed by thee,
and saw thee [2]polluted[G] in thine
own blood, I said unto thee *when
thou wast* in thy blood, [n]Live;
yea, I said unto thee *when thou
wast* in thy blood, Live[T].
7 [n]I have caused thee to multiply as the bud of the field, and
thou hast increased and waxen[G]
great, and thou art[G] come to excellent ornaments: *thy* breasts
are fashioned, and thine hair is
grown, whereas thou *wast* naked
and bare.
8 Now when [o]I passed by [p]thee,
and looked upon thee, behold,
thy time *was* the time of love;
and I spread my skirt over thee,
and covered thy nakedness: yea,
I sware unto thee, and [q]entered
into a covenant with thee, saith
the Lord GOD, and thou becamest mine.
9 Then [r]washed I thee with

1
*a Prophecies, inspired,* Dan. 9:24.
*b Prophets, inspiration of,* Isa. 3:2.
*c Ezekiel,* Ezek. 1:3.

2
*d Minister, duties of,* Rom. 15:16.
*e Jews, wickedness of,* vs. 1–59; Neh. 4:2.
*f Idolatry, wicked practices of,* 1 Sam. 15:23.

3
*g Canaanites,* Ex. 23:28.
*h Amorites,* Gen. 14:13.
*i Hittites,* Judg. 1:26.

4
*j Children, treatment of, at birth,* Mark 10:14.
*k Sanitation and Hygiene,* Num. 31:23.
*l Ablution,* Judg. 19:21.
*m* Job 38:9; Luke 2:7, 12.
1 R. V. cleanse

6
*n God, mercy of,* Gen. 2:2.
2 R. V. weltering

8
*o Bridegroom, figurative,* Isa. 61:10.
*p Bride, figurative,* Isa. 49:18.
*q Marriage, figurative,* Gen. 34:9.

9
*r Spiritual Purification,* Psa. 51:2.

s *Anointing, figurative,* Deut. 28:40.
t *Oil,* Deut. 12:17.
10
u *Dress,* Zech. 3:3.
v *Embroidery,* Ezek. 26:16.
w *Badger,* Ex. 25:5.
x *Linen,* Ezek. 27:16.
y Rev. 18:12.
3 R. V. sealskin,
11
z *Bracelet,* Gen. 24:22.
a *Chains,* Dan. 5:7.
12
b *Jewel,* Gen. 24:53.
c *Crown,* Ex. 29:6.
4 R.V. a ring upon thy nose,
13
d *Gold,* Ezek. 7:19.
e *Silver,* 1 Chr. 28:14.
f *Dress,* Zech. 3:3.
g *Linen,* Ezek. 27:16.
h Rev. 18:12.
i *Embroidery,* Ezek. 26:16.
j *Honey,* Prov. 25:27.
k *Oil,* Deut. 12:17.
l *Beauty, spiritual,* Psa. 45:11.
14
m *Spiritual Blessings, from God,* Eph. 1:3.
5 R. V. nations
6 R. V. majesty
15
n *False Confidence,* Psa. 30:6.
o *Idolatry, wicked practices of,* 1 Sam. 15:23.
p *Jews, wickedness of,* Neh. 4:2.
16
q *High Places,* 1 Kin. 3:2.

water; yea, I throughly[C] washed away thy blood from thee, and I [s]anointed thee with [t]oil.

10 I [u]clothed thee also with [v]broidered[C] work, and shod thee with [3,w]badgers' skin, and I girded thee about with fine [x]linen, and I covered thee with [y]silk.

11 I decked thee also with ornaments, and I put [z]bracelets upon thy hands, and a [a]chain on thy neck.

12 And I put a [4,b]jewel on thy forehead, and earrings in thine ears, and a beautiful [c]crown upon thine head.

13 Thus wast thou decked with [d]gold and [e]silver; and thy [f]raiment *was of* fine [g]linen, and [h]silk, and [i]broidered[C] work; thou didst eat fine flour, and [j]honey, and [k]oil: and thou wast exceeding [l]beautiful, and thou didst prosper into a kingdom.

14 And thy renown went forth among the [5]heathen[C] for thy [l]beauty: for it *was* perfect through my [6,m]comeliness,[C] which I had put upon thee, saith the Lord GOD.

15 ¶ But thou didst [n]trust in thine own beauty, and [o,p]playedst the harlot because of thy renown, and pouredst out thy fornications on every one that passed by; his it was.

16 [p]And of thy garments thou didst take, and deckedst thy [q]high[C] places with divers[C] *colours, and [o]playedst the harlot thereupon: *the like things* shall not come, neither shall it be *so.*

17 [p]Thou hast also taken thy fair jewels of my [d]gold and of my [e]silver, which I had given thee, and madest to thyself images of men, and didst [o]commit whoredom[C] with them,

18 [p]And tookest thy [i]broidered[C] garments, and coveredst them: and thou hast set mine [k]oil and mine [r]incense before them.

19 My meat[C] also which I gave thee, fine flour, and [k]oil, and [j]honey, *wherewith* I fed thee, [p]thou hast even set it before them for a sweet savour[C]: and *thus* it was, saith the Lord GOD.

20 Moreover [p]thou hast taken thy sons and thy daughters, whom thou hast borne unto me, and [o,s,t]these hast thou sacrificed unto them to be devoured.[C] *Is this* of thy whoredoms[C] a small matter,

21 [p]That thou hast slain my children, and delivered them to [o]cause [s,t]them to pass through *the fire* for them?

22 And in all thine [o,p]abominations and thy whoredoms thou hast not remembered the days of thy youth, when thou wast naked and bare, *and* wast [7]polluted in thy blood.

23 And it came to pass after all thy [p]wickedness, (woe, woe unto thee! saith the Lord GOD;)

24 [p]*That* thou hast also built unto thee an eminent[C] place, and hast made thee an [q]high[C] place in every street.

25 [p]Thou hast built thy [q]high place at every head of the way, and hast made thy beauty to be abhorred,[C] and hast opened thy feet to every one that passed by, and multiplied thy whoredoms.[C]

26 [p]Thou hast also committed fornication with the [u]Ê-ġy̆p'tianș thy neighbours, great of flesh;

18
r *Incense, offered in idolatrous worship,* Ex. 37:29.
20
s *Children, sacrificed,* Mark 10:14.
t *Human Sacrifices, offered,* Deut. 12:31.
22
7 R. V. weltering
26
u *Egyptians,* Gen. 50:3.

***COLORS, FIGURATIVE AND SYMBOLICAL.**
**Black:** *Of affliction,* Job 3:5; Psa. 107:10, 11; 143:3; Isa. 9:19; 24:11. *Of calamity,* Isa. 5:30; 8:22; 50:3; Joel 2:10; 3:14, 15. *Of day of wrath,* Zeph. 1:14, 15. *Of death,* Job 10:20–22. *Of the abode of the lost,* Matt. 25:30; 2 Pet. 2:4; Jude 13; Rev. 16:10.
**Blue:** *Of deity,* Ex. 25:4; 26:1; 28:28, 37; 38:18; 39:1–5, 21, 24, 29, 31; Num. 4:5–12; 15:38–40; 2 Chr. 2:7, 14; 3:14. *Of royalty,* Esth. 8:15; Ezek. 23:6.
**Crimson, Red, Purple and Scarlet:** *Of iniquity,* Isa. 1:18; Rev. 17:3, 4; 18:12, 16. *Of prosperity,* 2 Sam. 1:24; Prov. 31:21; Lam. 4:5. *Of conquest,* Isa. 63:2; Nah. 2:3; Rev. 12:3. *Types and shadows,* Ex. 26:14, 31, 36; 27:16; 28:4–6, 8, 15, 28, 37; 35:6, 7, 23, 25, 35; 36:8, 19, 35, 37; 38:23; 39:8, 29; Lev. 14:4, 6, 49, 51, 52; Num. 4:8, 13; 19:2, 6; Isa. 63:1–3; Heb. 9:19–23.
**White:** *Of holiness,* Lev. 16:4, 32; Psa. 51:7; Isa. 1:18; Dan. 7:9; 11:35; 12:10; Matt. 17:2; Mark 9:3; Matt. 28:3; Rev. 1:14; 2:17; 3:4, 5, 18; 4:4; 6:2, 11; 7:9, 13, 14; 19:8, 11, 14; 20:11.

and hast increased thy whoredoms[G], to [v]provoke me to [w]anger.
27 Behold, therefore I have
[x]stretched out my hand over
thee, and have diminished thine
ordinary *food*, and delivered thee
unto the will of them that hate
thee, the daughters of the [y]Phĭ-
lĭs′tīneș, which are ashamed of
thy lewd[G] way.
28 [p]Thou hast played the
whore[G] also with the [z]Ăs-sy̆r′ĭ-
anș, because thou wast unsati-
able; yea, thou hast played the
harlot with them, and yet couldest not be satisfied.
29 [a]Thou hast moreover multiplied thy fornication in the land
of [b]Cā′năan unto [c]Chăl-dē′ȧ; and
yet thou wast not satisfied herewith.
30 How [d]weak is thine heart,
saith the Lord GOD, seeing thou
doest all these *things*, the work
of an imperious whorish[G] woman;
31 [a]In that thou buildest thine
eminent place in the head of
every way, and makest thine
[e]high place in every street; and
hast not been as an harlot, in
that thou scornest hire;
32 *But as* a wife that committeth adultery, *which* taketh
strangers instead of her husband!
33 They give gifts to all whores[G]:
but [a]thou givest thy gifts to all
thy lovers, and hirest them, that
they may come unto thee on every side for thy whoredom[G].
34 And the contrary is in thee
from *other* women in thy whoredoms[G], whereas none followeth
thee to commit whoredoms[G]: and
in that thou givest a reward, and
no reward is given unto thee,
therefore thou art contrary.
35 ¶ Wherefore, O harlot, hear
the word of the LORD:
36 Thus saith the Lord GOD;
Because thy [a]filthiness was
poured out, and thy nakedness
discovered[G] through thy [f]whore-
doms[G] with thy lovers, and with
all the idols of thy abominations[G],
and by the blood of thy [g,h]chil-
dren, which thou didst give unto
them;
37 [i]Behold, therefore I will
gather all thy lovers, with whom
thou hast taken pleasure, and all
*them* that thou hast loved, with
all *them* that thou hast hated;
I will even gather them round
about against thee, and will discover[G] thy nakedness unto them,
that they may see all thy nakedness.
38 And I will [j]judge thee, as
women that [k]break wedlock and
[g]shed blood are judged; and I
will give [i]thee [l]blood in fury and
jealousy.[T]
39 And [i]I will also give thee
into their hand, and they shall
throw down thine eminent place,
and shall break down thy [e]high
places: they shall strip thee also
of thy clothes, and shall take thy
fair jewels, and leave thee naked
and bare.
40 [i]They shall also bring up a
company against thee, and they
shall [m]stone thee with stones,
and thrust thee through with
their swords.
41 [i]And they shall burn thine
houses with fire, and execute judgments upon thee in the sight of
many women: and I will [n]cause
thee to cease from playing the
harlot, and thou also shalt give
no hire any more.
42 So will I make my [o]fury toward thee to rest, and my [p]jeal-
ousy shall depart from thee, and
I will be quiet, and will be no
more angry.
43 Because thou hast not remembered the days of thy youth,
but hast fretted[G] me in all these
*things*; behold, therefore [i]I also
will recompense thy way upon
*thine* head, saith the Lord GOD:

v *Sin, repugnant to God*, Rom. 5:12.
w *Anger of God*, 2 Kin. 13:3.

27
x *Adversity, dispensation from God*, Psa. 10:6.
y *Philistines*, Gen. 26:14.

28
z *Assyria*, Gen. 25:18.

29
a *Jews, wickedness of*, vs. 29–59; Neh. 4:2.
b *Canaan*, Gen. 37:1.
c *Chaldea*, Ezek. 11:24.
d *Character, instability of*, Phil. 2:15.

31
e *High Places*, 1 Kin. 3:2.

36
f *Idolatry, wicked practices of*, 1 Sam. 15:23.
g *Children, sacrificed*, Mark 10:14.
h *Human Sacrifices*, Deut. 12:31.

37
i *Nation, judgments denounced against*, Isa. 2:4.

38
j *God, judge*, Gen. 2:2.
k *Adultery*, Lev. 20:10.
l *Blood, figurative*, Gen. 9:4.

40
m *Punishment, by stoning*, Lev. 26:41.

41
n *Judgments, design of*, Ex. 6:6.

42
o *Anger of God*, 2 Kin. 13:3.
p *Jealousy, attributed to God*, Psa. 78:58.

and thou shalt not commit this
lewdness above all thine abominations.
44 ¶ Behold, every one that useth
[q]proverbs shall use *this* proverb
against thee, saying, [r]As *is* the
mother, [s]*so is* her daughter.
45 [r,s]Thou *art* thy mother's
daughter, that lotheth her husband and her children; and
thou *art* the sister of thy sisters,
which lothed their husbands and
their children: your mother *was*
an [t]Hĭt'tīte, and your father an
[u]Ăm'ôr-īte.
46 And thine elder sister *is* [v]Să-
mā'rĭ-ȧ, she and her daughters
that dwell at thy left hand: and
thy younger sister, that dwelleth
at thy right hand, *is* [w]Sŏd'om
and her daughters.
47 Yet hast thou not walked
after their ways, nor done after
their abominations: but, as *if*
*that were* a very little *thing*, [x]thou
wast corrupted more than they
in all thy ways.
48 *As* I live, saith the Lord
GOD, [w]Sŏd'om thy sister hath
not done, she nor her daughters,
[x]as thou hast done, thou and thy
daughters.
49 Behold, this was the iniquity of thy sister [w]Sŏd'om, pride,
fulness of bread, and [8]abundance
of [y]idleness was in her and in
her daughters, neither did she
strengthen the hand of the poor
and needy.
50 [T]And they were haughty, and
committed abomination before
me: therefore [z]I took them away
as I saw *good*.
51 Neither hath [a]Să-mā'rĭ-ȧ
committed half of thy sins; but
[b]thou hast multiplied thine abominations[G] more than they, and hast
justified thy sisters in all thine
abominations[G] which thou hast
done.[T]
52 Thou also, which hast judged
thy sisters, bear thine own shame
for thy [b]sins that thou hast committed more abominable[G] than
they: they are more righteous
than thou: yea, be thou confounded also, and bear thy
shame, in that thou hast justified thy sisters.
53 When I shall bring again
their captivity, the captivity of
[c]Sŏd'om and her daughters, and
the captivity of [a]Să-mā'rĭ-ȧ and
her daughters, then *will I bring*
*again* the captivity of thy captives in the midst of them:
54 That thou mayest bear thine
own shame, and mayest be confounded in [b]all that thou hast
done, in that thou art a comfort
unto them.
55 When thy sisters, [c]Sŏd'om
and her daughters, shall return
to their former estate, and [a]Să-
mā'rĭ-ȧ and her daughters shall
return to their former estate, then
thou and thy daughters shall return to your former estate.
56 For thy sister [c]Sŏd'om was
not mentioned by thy mouth in
the day of thy pride,
57 Before thy [b]wickedness was
discovered,[G] as at the time of
*thy* reproach of the daughters of
[d]Sўr'ĭ-ȧ, and all *that are* round
about her, the daughters of the
[e]Phĭ-lĭs'tĭneṣ, [8]which despise thee
round about.
58 Thou hast borne thy [b]lewd-
ness and thine [f]abominations,
saith the LORD.
59 For thus saith the Lord GOD;
I will even [g]deal with thee as thou
hast done, which hast despised
the oath in breaking the [h]cove-
nant.
60 [T]Nevertheless [i]I will remember my [j]covenant with thee in
the days of thy youth, and [k]I will
establish unto thee an everlasting covenant.[S]
61 [S]Then thou shalt remember
thy [b]ways, and be ashamed, when
thou shalt receive thy sisters,

**44**
q *Proverbs,* 1 Sam. 24:13.
r *Parents, evil influence of,* 2 Cor. 12:14.
s *Heredity,* Ezek. 18:2.

**45**
t *Hittites,* Judg. 1:26.
u *Amorites,* Gen. 14:13.

**46**
v *Samaria,* Isa. 7:9.
w *Sodom,* Gen. 13:10.

**47**
x *Jews, wickedness of,* Neh. 4:2.

**49**
y *Idleness,* Eccl. 10:18.
8 R. V. prosperous ease was

**50**
z *God, sovereign,* Gen. 2:2.

**51**
a *Samaria,* Isa. 7:9.
b *Jews, wickedness of,* Neh. 4:2.

**53**
c *Sodom,* Gen. 13:10.

**57**
d *Syria,* 2 Kin. 6:23.
e *Philistines,* Gen. 26:14.
8 Am. R. V. who do despite unto

**58**
f *Idolatry, wicked practices of,* 1 Sam. 15:23.

**59**
g *Judgment, according to opportunity and works,* 1 Pet. 1:17.
h *Covenant, of man with God,* Deut. 29:1.

**60**
i *God, faithfulness of,* Gen. 2:2.
j *Covenant, of God with men,* Deut. 29:1.
k *Jews, prophecies concerning,* Neh. 4:2.

thine [a]elder and thy [c]younger:
and I will give them unto thee
for daughters, but not by thy
covenant.[Q]
62 And [k]I will establish my
[j]covenant with thee; and thou
shalt know that I *am* the LORD:
63 That thou mayest remember, and be confounded, and
never open thy mouth any more
because of thy shame, when I
[9]am [l]pacified toward thee for all
that thou hast done, saith the
Lord GOD.

## CHAPTER 17

*The parable of two eagles and a vine. 11 The explanation of the parable, God's judgment upon Jerusalem for revolting from Babylon. 22 God's promise of prosperity.*

AND the [a]word of the LORD
[b]came unto [c]me, saying,
2 Son of man, put forth a [d]rid-
dle, and speak a [e]parable unto
the [f]house of Is'ra-el;
3 And [e]say, Thus saith the Lord
GOD; A great [g,h]eagle with great
wings, [1]long-winged, full of feathers, which had divers colours,
came unto Leb'a-non, and took
the highest branch of the cedar:
4 [e]He cropped off the [i]top of
his young twigs, and carried it
into a [j]land of traffick; he set it
in a [k]city of [l]merchants.
5 [m]He took also of the [n]seed of
the land, and planted it in a
fruitful field; he placed *it* by
great waters, *and* set it *as* a
willow tree.
6 [m]And [n]it grew, and became a
spreading [o]vine of low stature,
whose branches turned toward
him, and the roots thereof were
under him: so it became a vine,
and brought forth branches, and
shot forth sprigs.
7 [e]There was also another great
[g,p]eagle with great wings and
many feathers: and, behold, this
[m,o]vine did bend her roots toward him, and shot forth her
branches toward him, that he
might water it by the furrows of
her plantation.
8 [m,o]It was planted in a good
[q]soil by great waters, that it
might bring forth branches, and
that it might bear fruit, that it
might be a goodly vine.
9 Say thou, Thus saith the Lord
GOD; Shall it prosper? shall he
not pull up the roots thereof, and
cut off the fruit thereof, that it
wither? [2]it shall wither in all the
leaves of her spring, even without great power or many people to pluck it up by the roots
thereof.
10 Yea, behold, *being* planted,
shall it prosper? shall it not utterly wither, when the [h]east wind
toucheth it? it shall wither in the
furrows where it grew.
11 ¶ Moreover the [a]word of the
LORD [b]came unto [c]me, saying,
12 Say now to the rebellious
house, Know ye not what
[e,m]these *things mean*? tell *them*,
[f]Behold, the [h]king of [k]Bab'y-
lon is come to Je-ru'sa-lem, and
hath taken the [i]king thereof,
and the princes thereof, and led
[r]them with him to Bab'y-lon;
13 And hath taken of the king's
[n]seed, and made a [s]covenant with
him, and hath taken an [t]oath
of him: he hath also taken the
mighty of the land:
14 That the kingdom might be
base, that it might not lift itself
up, *but* that by keeping of his
[s]covenant it might stand.
15 But he [u]rebelled against him
in [v]sending his [w]ambassadors into [x]E'gypt, that they might give
him [y]horses and much people.
Shall he prosper? shall he escape
that doeth such *things*? or shall
he break the covenant, and be
delivered?
16 *As* I live, saith the Lord GOD,
surely in the [k]place *where* the
[h]king *dwelleth* that made [n]him
king, whose [t]oath he despised,

63
l *Sin, forgiveness of*, Rom. 5:12.
9 R. V. have forgiven thee all

1
a *Prophecies, inspired*, Dan. 9:24.
b *Prophets, inspiration of*, Isa. 3:2.
c *Ezekiel*, Ezek. 1:3.
2
d Judg. 14:12-18.
e *Parables, of the two eagles*, vs. 2-24; Ezek. 20:49.
f *Judah, kingdom of, prophecies concerning*, vs. 2-24; 2 Chr. 11:17.
3
g *Eagle, parable of*, Lev. 11:13.
h *Nebuchadnezzar, king of Babylon*, Dan. 2:1.
1 R. V. and long pinions,
4
i *Jehoiachin*, 2 Kin. 24:6.
j *Chaldea*, Ezek. 11:24.
k *Babylon, city of*, Ezra 5:12.
l *Merchant*, Neh. 3:32.
5
m *Parables, of the vine*, vs. 5-10; Ezek. 20:49.
n *Zedekiah*, 2 Kin. 25:2.
6
o *Vine, parables of*, vs. 5-10; Judg. 13:14.
7
p *Pharaoh-hophra*, Jer. 44:30.

8
q *Canaan, land of*, Gen. 37:1.
9
2 R. V. that all its fresh springing leaves may wither; even
12
r *Captive*, 1 Sam. 30:3.
13
s *Covenant, of men with men*, vs. 13-19; Deut. 29:1.
t *Oath*, Num. 5:19.
15
u *Covenant, of men with men, breach of*, Deut. 29:1.
v *Alliances, instances of*, Josh. 9:15.
w *Ambassadors*, Josh. 9:4.
x *Egyptians*, Gen. 50:3.
y *Horse*, Job 39:19.

and whose [s]covenant he brake, *even* with him in the midst of Băb'ȳ-lon he [z]shall die.

17 Neither shall [a]Phā'raōh with *his* mighty army and great company make[C] for [b]him in the war, by casting up mounts[C], and building [+]forts, to cut off many persons:

18 Seeing he despised the oath by [c]breaking the covenant[C], when, lo, he had given his [d]hand, and hath done all these *things*, he shall not escape.

19 Therefore thus saith the Lord GOD; *As* I live, surely mine oath that he hath despised, and my covenant that he hath [c]broken, even it will I [e]recompense upon his own head.

20 And I will spread my net upon [b]him, and he shall be taken in my snare, and I will bring him to [f]Băb'ȳ-lon, and will plead[C] with him there for his trespass that he hath trespassed against me.

21 And all his fugitives with all his bands[C] shall fall by the [g]sword, and they that remain shall be scattered toward all winds: and [h]ye shall know that I the LORD have spoken *it*.

22 ¶ Thus[Q] saith the Lord GOD; [i,j]I will also take of the highest branch of the high cedar, and will set *it*; I will crop off from the top of his young twigs a tender one, and will plant *it* upon an high mountain and eminent[C]:

23 [i,j]In the mountain of the height of Ĭṣ'ra-el will I plant it: and it shall bring forth boughs, and bear fruit, and be a goodly[C] cedar: and under it shall dwell [k]all fowl of every wing; in the shadow of the branches thereof shall they dwell.[Q]

24 [i,j]And all the trees of the field shall know that I the LORD have brought down the high tree, have exalted the low tree, have dried up the green tree, and have made the dry tree to flourish: I the LORD have spoken and have done *it*.

## CHAPTER 18

*God reproves the people for their unjust proverb of the sour grapes. 4 The soul that sins, it shall die. 31 An exhortation to repentance.*

THE[T] word of the LORD [a]came unto [b]me again, saying,

2 What mean ye, that ye use this [c]proverb concerning the land of Ĭṣ'ra-el, [d]saying, The fathers have eaten sour [e]grapes, and *the children's teeth are set on edge?

3 *As* I live, saith the Lord GOD, ye shall not have *occasion* any more to use this [c]proverb in Ĭṣ'ra-el.

4 Behold, all souls are [f]mine; as the soul of the father, so also the soul of the son is mine: [g]the soul that sinneth, [h,i]it shall [j]die.

5 But if a man be [k,l]just, and [m]do that which is lawful and right,

6 *And* hath not [n]eaten upon the mountains, neither hath lifted up his eyes to the idols of the house of Ĭṣ'ra-el, neither hath [o]defiled his neighbour's wife, neither hath come near to a [†]menstruous[C] woman,

7 And hath [m]not oppressed any, *but* hath [m]restored to the debtor his [p]pledge, hath spoiled[C] none by violence, hath [m,q]given his bread to the hungry, and hath [m,q]covered the naked with a garment;

16
z *Wicked, punishment of,* Psa. 73:3.

17
a *Pharaoh-hophra,* Jer. 44:30.
b *Zedekiah,* 2 Kin. 25:2.

18
c *Covenant, of men with men, breach of,* Deut. 29:1.
d *Hand, clasping of, in token of contract,* Ezra 10:19.

19
e *Wicked, punishment of,* Psa. 73:3.

20
f *Babylon,* Ezra 5:12.

21
g *War, as a judgment,* Judg. 3:2.
h *Adversity, design of,* Psa. 10:6.

22
i *Church, prophecies concerning its prosperity* (according to many interpreters), Matt. 16:18.
j *Jesus, kingdom of, prophecies concerning* (according to many interpreters), Matt. 1:21.

23
k *Gentiles, prophecies of the conversion of,* Acts 10:45.

1
a *Prophets, inspiration of,* Isa. 3:2.
b *Ezekiel,* Ezek. 1:3.

2
c *Proverbs,* 1 Sam. 24:13.
d *Infidelity, exemplified in impugning God's righteousness,* vs. 25, 29; 2 Cor. 6:15.
e *Grapes, figurative,* Lev. 25:5.

4
f *God, sovereign,* Gen. 2:2.
g *Judgment, according to opportunity and works,* vs. 5–9, 19–32; 1 Pet. 1:17.
h *Sin, punishment of,* Rom. 5:12.
i *Wicked, punishment of,* Psa. 73:3.
j *Spiritual Death,* 1 John 3:14.

5
k *Righteous, described,* Psa. 64:10.
l *Faithfulness, rewards of,* vs. 5–9, 17; Luke 16:10.
m *Works, good,* vs. 5–9; 2 Tim. 1:9.

6
n *Idolatry, wicked practices of,* 1 Sam. 15:23.
o *Adultery,* Lev. 20:10.

7
p *Pawn, restoration of,* Job 24:3.
q *Liberality,* 1 Tim. 6:18.

+ **FORTIFICATION**, a military defense. *Field, made during military operations,* Deut. 20:19, 20; 2 Kin. 25:1; Jer. 6:6; 32:24; 33:4; Ezek. 4:2; 17:17; 26:8; Dan. 11:15. *Defenses of cities,* 2 Sam. 5:9; 2 Chr. 11:10, 11; 26:9, 15; Neh. 3:8; 4:2; Isa. 22:10; 25:12; 29:3; Jer. 51:53; Nah. 3:14. *Erected in vineyards and herding grounds,* 2 Chr. 26:10; Isa. 5:2; Matt. 21:33; Mark 12:1. *Caves used for,* Judg. 6:2; 1 Sam. 23:29.
**Figurative:** *Of God's care,* 2 Sam. 22:2, 3, 47; Psa. 18:2; 31:3; 71:3; 91:2; 144:2; Prov. 18:10; Nah. 1:7.

* **HEREDITY.** *Like begets like,* Gen. 5:3; Job 14:4; John 3:6, 7.
Results of: *Natural,* Psa. 51:5; John 9:2, 3; Rom. 5:12; Eph. 2:3. *Judicial, ordained consequences of parental conduct,* Ex. 20:5, 6; 34:7; Num. 14:18; Deut. 5:9; Rom. 5:12; 1 Cor. 15:22. *Does not fix moral status,* Jer. 31:29, 30; Ezek. 18:1–32; Matt. 3:9.

† **MENSTRUATION.** *Law relating to,* Lev. 15:19–30; 18:19; 20:18; Ezek. 18:6. *Cessation of, in old age,* Gen. 18:11. *Immunities of women during,* Gen. 31:35. *Of animals,* Jer. 2:24.

8 He *that* hath [m,r]not given
forth upon usury[C], neither hath
taken any increase, *that* hath
withdrawn his hand from iniquity, hath executed [s]true judgment[C] between man and man,
9 Hath [t]walked in my statutes,
and hath kept my judgments,[C]
to [m]deal truly; he *is* [u]just, [v,w]he
shall surely live, saith the Lord
GOD.
10 ¶ If he beget a [x]son *that is*
a [y]robber, a [z]shedder of blood,
and *that* doeth the like to *any*
one of these *things*,
11 And that doeth not any of
those *duties*, but even hath [a]eat-
en upon the mountains, and [b]de-
filed his neighbour's wife,
12 Hath [c]oppressed the poor
and needy, hath spoiled by
violence, hath [d]not restored the
pledge, and hath lifted up his
eyes to the idols, hath [a]commit-
ted abomination,
13 Hath given forth upon
[e]usury[C], and hath taken increase:
[f]shall he then live? [g]he shall not
live: he hath done all these abominations; [‡,g]he shall surely die;
‡his [h]blood[C] shall be upon him.
14 ¶ Now, lo, *if* he beget a [i]son,
that seeth all his father's [j]sins
which he hath done, and considereth, and doeth not such like,
15 *That* hath not [a]eaten upon
the mountains, neither hath lifted up his eyes to the idols of the
house of Is'ra-el, hath not [b]de-
filed his neighbour's wife,
16 Neither hath oppressed any,
hath not [1]withholden the [k]pledge,
neither hath spoiled by violence,
*but* hath [l]given his bread to the
hungry, and hath [l]covered the
naked with a garment,
17 *That* hath taken off his hand
from the poor, *that* hath not received [e]usury[C] nor increase, hath
executed my judgments[C], hath
[m]walked in my statutes; [n]he shall
not die for the iniquity of his
father, [‡,o,p]he shall surely live.
18 *As for* his father, because
he cruelly [c]oppressed, spoiled his
brother by violence, and did *that*
which *is* not good among his
people, lo, even he shall [q]die in
his iniquity.
19 ¶ Yet say ye, Why? doth not
the son bear the iniquity of the
father? When the [n]son hath
done that which is lawful and
right, *and* hath [m]kept all my
statutes, and hath done them,
[‡,o,p]he shall surely live.
20 [‡,r]The[S] soul that sinneth, [g,q]it
shall [r]die. [s]The [n]son shall not
bear the [t]iniquity of the father,
[s]neither shall the father bear the
iniquity of the son: the righteousness of the righteous shall be
upon him, and the wickedness
of the wicked shall be upon
him.[Q]
21 But if the wicked will [u]turn
from all his sins that he hath
committed, and [m]keep all my
statutes, and [m]do that which
is lawful and right, [‡,v,w]he
shall surely live, he shall not
die.
22 [w]All his transgressions that
he hath committed, they shall not
be mentioned unto him: [f]in his
righteousness that he hath done
he shall live.
23 [x]Have I any pleasure at all
that the wicked should die? saith
the Lord GOD: *and* not that he
should return from his ways, and
live?[Q]
24 ¶ But when the righteous
[y]turneth away from his righteousness, and committeth iniquity,
*and* doeth according to all the

**8**
r *Interest, non-exaction of*, Ex. 22:25.
s *Justice*, Deut. 33:21.

**9**
t *Obedience*, Heb. 5:8.
u *Righteousness, imputed on account of obedience*, Psa. 15:2.
v *Promise, to the righteous*, 2 Cor. 1:20.
w *Righteous, promises to*, Psa. 64:10.

**10**
x *Children, wicked*, Mark 10:14.
y *Robbery*, Ezek. 22:29.
z *Homicide, felonious*, Deut. 5:17.

**11**
a *Idolatry, wicked practices of*, 1 Sam. 15:23.
b *Adultery*, Lev. 20:10.

**12**
c *Poor, oppression of*, Prov. 21:13.
d *Pawn, unlawfully retained*, Job 24:3.

**13**
e *Interest*, Ex. 22:25.
f *Judgment, according to opportunity and works*, 2 Pet. 3:7.
g *Wicked, punishment of*, Psa. 73:3.
h *Blood, figurative of guilt*, Gen. 9:4.

**14**
i *Children, good*, Mark 10:14.
j *Example, bad*, John 13:15.

**16**
k *Pawn*, Job 24:3.
l *Liberality*, 1 Tim. 6:18.
1 R. V. taken aught to pledge.

**17**
m *Obedience, rewarded*, Heb. 5:8.
n *Children, not punished on account of sins of parents*, Mark 10:14.
o *Promise, to the righteous*, 2 Cor. 1:20.
p *Righteous, promises to*, Psa. 64:10.

**20**
q *Sin, punishment of*, Rom. 5:12.
r *Spiritual Death*, 1 John 3:14.
s *Innocent, shall not suffer for the guilty*, Deut. 24:16.
t *Sin, consequences of, not entailed upon children*, Rom. 5:12.

**21**
u *Repentance, condition of forgiveness*, Mark 1:4.
v *Penitent, promises to*, vs. 22, 23; Psa. 51:17.
w *Sin, forgiveness of*, Rom. 5:12.

**23**
x *God, mercy of*, Gen. 2:2.

**24**
y *Apostasy, punishment of*, Acts 1:25.

‡ **RESPONSIBILITY.** Attempt to shift: *By Adam*, Gen. 3:12; *by Eve*, Gen. 3:13; *by Sarah*, Gen. 16:5, with v. 2; *by Esau*, Gen. 27:36, with 25:29–34; *by Aaron*, Ex. 32:21–24; *by Saul*, 1 Sam. 15:20, 21; *by Pilate*, Matt. 27:24.
*Assumed by the Jews for the death of Jesus*, Matt. 27:25.
*Personal*, Ezek. 14:14–20; 18:20, 30; Matt. 12:37; John 9:41; 15:22–24; Rom. 14:12; 1 Cor. 3:8, 13–15; Gal. 6:5; 1 Pet. 4:5.
*According to privilege*, Ezek. 33:1–19; Matt. 10:11–15 (with Luke 10:10–15); 11:20–24; 12:41, 42 (with Luke 11:31, 32); 23:31–35 (with Luke 11:49–51); 25:14–30 (with Luke 19:12–27); Luke 13:6–9; 21:1–4; John 3:18, 19; 12:48; 15:22, 24; Acts 17:30, 31; Rom. 12:3, 6–8.
See footnote, JUDGMENT, *According to opportunity and works*, 2 Pet. 3:7.

25
z *Infidelity, exemplified in impugning God's knowledge*, 2 Cor. 6:15.

a *Blasphemy, imputing unrighteousness to God*, 2 Sam. 12:14.
b *Murmuring*, Num. 14:2.
c *God, condescension of, in reasoning with sinners*, Gen. 2:2.
d *God, justice of*, Gen. 2:2.

26
e *Apostasy, punishment of*, Acts 1:25.
f *Judgment, according to opportunity and works*, 1 Pet. 1:17.
g *Wicked, punishment of*, Psa. 73:3.

27
h *Repentance, condition of forgiveness*, Mark 1:4.
i *Sin, forgiveness of*, Rom. 5:12.

29
j *Infidelity, exemplified in impugning God's knowledge*, 2 Cor. 6:15.

30
k *God, judge*, Gen. 2:2.
l *Commandment, enjoining repentance*, Deut. 8:2.
m *Repentance, enjoined*, Mark 1:4.
2 R. V. Return ye,

31
n *Regeneration*, Tit. 3:5.
o *Heart, renewed*, Psa. 44:21.
p *Backsliders, God's solicitude for*, Jer. 3:22.
q *Spiritual Death*, 1 John 3:14.

32
r *God, mercy of*, Gen. 2:2.

abominations that the wicked
*man* doeth, shall he live? All
his righteousness that he hath
done shall not be mentioned:
[f,g]in his trespass that he hath
trespassed, and in his sin that
he hath sinned, in them shall
he die.
25 ¶ Yet ye [z,a,b]say, The way of
the Lord is not equal. [c]Hear
now, O house of Ĭṣ′ra-el; [d]Is
not my way equal? are not your
ways unequal?
26 When a righteous *man* [e]turn-
eth away from his righteousness, and committeth iniquity,
and dieth in them; for his iniquity that he hath done [f,g]shall
he die.
27 Again, when the wicked *man*
[h]turneth away from his wickedness that he hath committed,
and doeth that which is lawful
and right, [f,i]he shall save his soul
alive.
28 Because he considereth, and
[h]turneth away from all his transgressions that he hath committed, [f,i]he shall surely live, he shall
not die.
29 Yet [a,b,j]saith the house of
Ĭṣ′ra-el, The way of the Lord is
not equal. O house of Ĭṣ′ra-el,
are not my ways equal? are not
your ways unequal?
30 Therefore I will [k]judge you,
O house of Ĭṣ′ra-el, every one
[f]according to his ways, saith the
Lord GOD. [2,l,m]Repent, and turn
*yourselves* from all your transgressions; so iniquity shall not
be your ruin.
31 ¶ [l,m]Cast away from you all
your transgressions, whereby ye
have transgressed; and [n]make
you a new [o]heart and a new
spirit: for [p]why will ye [q]die, O
house of Ĭṣ′ra-el?
32 For [r]I have no pleasure in
the death of him that dieth,
saith the Lord GOD: wherefore
[l,m]turn *yourselves*, and live ye.

## CHAPTER 19

*Under the similitude of a lioness and her whelps, the prophet deplores the fall of the royal family. 10 And under the figure of a vine plucked up and wasted, is shewn the desolation of Jerusalem.*

MOREOVER take thou up
a lamentation for the
princes of [a]Ĭṣ′ra-el,
2 And say, What *is* thy mother? A [b]lioness: she lay down
among lions, she nourished her
whelps among young lions.
3 And she brought up [c]one of
her whelps: it became a young
[d]lion, and it learned to catch the
prey; it devoured men.
4 The nations also heard of him;
he was taken in their pit, and they
[e]brought [f]him with [1]chains unto
the land of [g]Ē′gy̆pt.
5 Now when she saw that she
had waited, *and* her hope was
lost, then she took [h]another of
her whelps, *and* made him a
young [d]lion.
6 And he went up and down
among the lions, he became a
young lion, and learned to catch
the prey, *and* devoured men.
7 And he knew their desolate
palaces, and he [i]laid waste their
cities; and the land was desolate, and the fulness thereof, by
the noise of his roaring.
8 Then the nations set against
him on every side from the provinces, and spread their net over
him: he was taken in their pit.
9 And they [e]put [f]him in [2]ward
in chains, and brought him to
the [j]king of [k]Băb′y̆-lon: they
brought him into holds, that his
voice should no more be heard
upon the mountains of Ĭṣ′ra-el.
10 ¶ Thy [l]mother *is* like a
[m]vine in thy blood, planted by
the waters: she was fruitful
and full of branches by reason of many waters.
11 And she had strong rods for
the sceptres of them that bare
rule, and her stature was exalted
among the thick branches, and

1
a *Jews, prophecies concerning*, vs. 1–14; Neh. 4:2.

2
b *Lion, figurative*, Mic. 5:8.

3
c *Jehoahaz*, 2 Kin. 23:30.
d *King*, 2 Kin. 3:10.

4
e *Wicked, punishment of*, Psa. 73:3.
f *Captive*, 1 Sam. 30:3.
g *Egypt*, Gen. 41:8.
1 R. V. hooks

5
h *Jehoiachin*, 2 Kin. 24:6.

7
i *Oppression*, Eccl. 5:8.

9
j *Nebuchadnezzar*, Dan. 2:1.
k *Babylon, empire of*, Ezra 5:12.
2 R. V. a cage with hooks,

10
l *Judah, kingdom of*, 2 Chr. 11:17.
m *Symbols and Similitudes*, vs. 10–14; Heb. 9:9

**12**
*n Nation, punishment of,* Isa. 2:4.

**13**
*o Captivity, of Jews in Babylon,* Isa. 5:13.

**v.1–512 BC**
See footnote, *Time,* Rev. 10:6.

**1**
*a Month (August),* Ex. 12:2.
*b Senate, seeks counsel from prophets,* Num. 11:16.

**2**
*c Prophets, inspiration of,* Isa. 3:2.
*d Prophecies, inspired,* Dan. 9:24.

**3**
*e Wicked, prayers of, not answered,* Psa. 73:3.

**5**
*f Election of Grace,* Rom. 11:5.
*g Egypt,* Gen. 41:8.
*h God, sovereign,* Gen. 2:2.

**6**
*i God, providence of,* Gen. 2:2.

she appeared in her height with
the multitude of her branches.
12 But she was [n]plucked up in
fury, she was cast down to the
ground, and the [j]east wind dried
up her fruit: her strong rods were
broken and withered; the fire
consumed them.
13 And now she *is* [o]planted in
the [k]wilderness, in a dry and
thirsty ground.
14 And fire is gone out of a rod
of her branches, *which* hath devoured her fruit, so that she hath
no strong rod *to be* a sceptre[G] to
rule. This *is* a lamentation, and
shall be for a lamentation.

## CHAPTER 20

*God will not be inquired of by the elders of Israel.* 5 *The history of Israel's rebellions in Egypt,* 10 *in the wilderness,* 27 *and in their own land.* 33 *God shall gather and purify his people.* 45 *The destruction of Jerusalem prefigured.*

AND it came to pass in the
seventh year, in the fifth
[a]*month,* the tenth *day* of the
month, *that* certain of the [b]eld-
ers of Ĭs′ra-el came to enquire[G] of
the LORD, and sat before me.
2 Then [c]came the [d]word of the
LORD unto me, saying,
3 Son of man, speak unto the
[b]elders of Ĭs′ra-el, and say unto
them, Thus saith the Lord GOD;
Are ye come to enquire of me?
*As* I live, saith the Lord GOD, I
[e]will not be enquired of by you.
4 Wilt thou judge them, son of
man, wilt thou judge *them*? cause
them to know the abominations
of their fathers:
5 And say unto them, Thus
saith the Lord GOD; In the day
when I [f]chose Ĭs′ra-el, and lifted
up mine hand unto the seed of
the house of Jā′cob, and made
myself known unto them in the
land of [g]Ē′ġȳpt, when I lifted[G] up
mine hand unto them, saying, [h]I
*am* the LORD your God;
6 In the day *that* I lifted up
mine hand unto them, to [i]bring
them forth of the land of [g]Ē′ġȳpt
into a [j]land that I had espied[G] for
them, flowing with [k]milk and
[l]honey, which *is* the glory of all
lands:
7 Then said I unto them, [m]Cast
ye away every man the abominations of his eyes, and defile not
yourselves with the [n]idols of Ē′-
ġȳpt: [h]I *am* the LORD your God.
8 But they rebelled against me,
and [o,p]would not hearken unto
me: they did not every man cast
away the abominations of their
eyes, neither did they forsake
the [n]idols of Ē′ġȳpt: then I said,
I will [q]pour out my [r]fury upon
them, to accomplish my anger
against them in the midst of the
land of Ē′ġȳpt.
9 But I wrought for my name's
sake, that it should not be
polluted[G] before the [1]heathen[G],
among whom they *were,* in
whose sight I made myself
known unto them, in bringing
them forth out of the land of
[g]Ē′ġȳpt. [s]
10 Wherefore [i]I caused them to
go forth out of the land of [g]Ē′-
ġȳpt, and brought them into the
wilderness.
11 And [s]I gave [t]them my [u]stat-
utes, and shewed[G] them my judgments, which *if* a man [v]do, he
shall even live in them.
12 Moreover also I gave them
my [w]sabbaths, to be a sign between me and them, that they
might know that I *am* the LORD
that [x]sanctify them.
13 But the house of Ĭs′ra-el rebelled against me in the wilderness: they [y]walked not in my
statutes, and they despised my
judgments[G], which *if* a man [v]do,
he shall even live in them; and
my sabbaths they greatly [z]pol-
luted[G]: then I said, I would [a]pour
out my fury upon them in the
wilderness, to consume them.
14 But I wrought for my
name's sake, that it should not

*j Canaan,* Gen. 37:1.
*k Milk, figurative,* Job 10:10.
*l Honey, figurative,* Prov. 25:27.

**7**
*m Idolatry, forbidden,* 1 Sam. 15:23.
*n Egypt, idolatry of,* Gen. 41:8.

**8**
*o Obduracy,* Prov. 29:1.
*p Impenitence,* Rom. 2:5.
*q Wicked, punishment of,* Psa. 73:3.
*r Anger of God,* 2 Kin. 13:3.

**9**
1 R. V. nations.

**11**
*s God, mercy of,* vs. 11–14; Gen. 2:2.
*t Israel, law delivered to,* Ex. 4:22.
*u Law, of Moses,* Deut. 33:2.
*v Works under the Law,* Lev. 18:5.

**12**
*w Sabbath, a sign,* Ex. 16:23.
*x Sanctification, by God,* 1 Pet. 1:2.

**13**
*y Disobedience to God,* Eph. 5:6.
*z Profanation, of the Sabbath,* Lev. 22:32.

*a Wicked, punishment of,* Psa. 73:3.

be polluted[c] before the heathen[c], in whose sight I brought them out.

15 Yet also I lifted[c] up my hand unto them in the wilderness, that I would not bring them into the [b]land which I had given *them*, flowing with [c]milk and [d]honey, which *is* the glory of all lands;

16 Because they [e]despised my judgments[c], and [f]walked not in my statutes, but [g]polluted[c] my sabbaths: for [h]their heart [i]went after their idols.

17 Nevertheless mine eye [j,k]spared them from destroying them, neither did I make an end of them in the wilderness.[s]

18 But I said unto their children in the wilderness, [l]Walk ye not in the statutes of your fathers, neither observe their judgments[c], nor [m]defile yourselves with their idols:

19 [n]I *am* the LORD your God; [o,p]walk in my statutes, and keep my judgments[c], and do them;[s]

20 And hallow my [q]sabbaths; and they shall be a sign between me and you, that ye may know that [n]I *am* the LORD your God.

21 Notwithstanding the children rebelled against me: they [f]walked not in my statutes, neither kept my judgments[c] to do them, which *if* a man do, he shall even live in them; they [g]polluted[c] my sabbaths: then I said, I would [a]pour out my fury upon them, to accomplish my anger against them in the wilderness.

22 Nevertheless [k]I withdrew mine hand, and wrought for my name's sake, that it should not be polluted in the sight of the heathen[c], in whose sight I brought them forth.

23 I lifted[c] up mine hand unto them also in the wilderness, that I would [r,s]scatter them among the heathen[c], and disperse them through the countries;

24 Because they had not executed my judgments[c], but had [f]despised my statutes, and had [g]polluted my sabbaths, and their eyes were after their fathers' idols.

25 Wherefore I gave them also statutes *that were* not good, and judgments[c] whereby they should not live;

26 And I polluted them in their own gifts, in that they [m]caused to pass through *the fire* [t,u]all that openeth[c] the womb, that I might make them desolate, to the end [v]that they might know that I *am* the LORD.

27 ¶ Therefore, son of man, speak unto the house of Iş'ra-el, and say unto them, Thus saith the Lord GOD; Yet in this your fathers have [w]blasphemed me, in that they have committed a trespass against me.

28 *For* when I had brought them into the [b]land, *for* the which I lifted[c] up mine hand to give it to them, then they saw every high hill, and all the thick trees, and they [x]offered there their sacrifices, and there they presented the provocation of their offering: there also they made their [y]sweet savour, and poured out there their drink offerings.

29 Then I said unto them, What *is* the [z]high[c] place whereunto ye go? And the name thereof is called Bā'mah unto this day.

30 Wherefore say unto the house of Iş'ra-el, Thus saith the Lord GOD; Are ye polluted[c] after the [a]manner of your fathers? and commit ye [b]whoredom[c] after their abominations?

31 For when ye offer your gifts, when ye [b]make your [c,d]sons to pass through the fire, ye pollute yourselves with all your idols,

**15**
*b* *Canaan*, Gen. 37:1.
*c* *Milk, figurative*, Job 10:10.
*d* *Honey, figurative*, Prov. 25:27.

**16**
*e* *Wicked, described*, Psa. 73:3.
*f* *Disobedience to God*, Eph. 5:6.
*g* *Profanation, of the Sabbath*, Lev. 22:32.
*h* *Sin, love of*, Rom. 5:12.
*i* *Israel, idolatry of*, Ex. 4:22.

**17**
*j* *God, longsuffering of*, Gen. 2:2.
*k* *God, mercy of*, Gen. 2:2.

**18**
*l* *Example, bad*, John 13:15.
*m* *Idolatry, wicked practices of*, 1 Sam. 15:23.

**19**
*n* *God, sovereign*, Gen. 2:2.
*o* *Commandment, enjoining obedience*, Deut. 8:2.
*p* *Obedience, enjoined*, Heb. 5:8.

**20**
*q* *Sabbath, a sign*, Ex. 16:23.

**23**
*r* *Dispersion, foretold*, Gen. 11:8.
*s* *Captivity, of the Israelites foretold*, Isa. 5:13.

**26**
*t* *Firstborn, of idolaters, sacrificed*, Zech. 12:10.
*u* *Human Sacrifices*, Deut. 12:31.
*v* *Judgments, design of*, Ex. 6:6.

**27**
*w* *Blasphemy, instances of*, 2 Sam. 12:14.

**28**
*x* *Idolatry, customs of*, 1 Sam. 15:23.
*y* *Incense, offered in idolatrous worship*, Ex. 37:29.

**29**
*z* *High Places*, 1 Kin. 3:2.

**30**
*a* *Example, bad*, John 13:15.
*b* *Idolatry, wicked practices of*, 1 Sam. 15:23.

**31**
*c* *Children, sacrificed*, Mark 10:14.
*d* *Human Sacrifices*, Deut. 12:31.

*e Wicked, prayers of, not answered,* Psa. 73:3.

32
*f False Confidence,* Psa. 30:6.
*g Idol, of wood and stone,* 1 Kin. 15:12.

33
*h Nation, judgments denounced against,* Isa. 2:4.

34
2 R. V. peoples.

35
*i God, longsuffering of,* Gen. 2:2.
*j God, mercy of,* Gen. 2.2.

36
*k Egypt,* Gen. 41:8.

37
*l Adversity, dispensation from God,* Psa. 10:6.

38
*m Judgments, design of,* Ex. 6:6.

39
*n Impenitence,* Rom. 2:5.
*o Hypocrisy, abhorred of God,* Jas. 3:17.

even unto this day: and shall I be
enquired of by you, O house of
Ĭş′ra-el? *As* I live, saith the
Lord GOD, [e]I will not be enquired of by you.
32 And that which cometh into
your mind shall not be at all,
that ye say, [f]We will be as the
heathen[G], as the families of the
countries, to serve [g]wood and
stone.
33 *As* I live, saith the Lord GOD,
surely [h]with a mighty hand, and
with a stretched[G] out arm, and
with fury poured out, will I rule
over you:[Q]
34 And [h]I will bring you
out from the [2]people, and will
gather you out of the countries
wherein ye are scattered, with a
mighty hand, and with a stretched[G] out arm, and with fury poured
out.
35 And I will bring you into
the wilderness of the [2]people,
and there will [i,j]I plead[G] with you
face to face.
36 Like [i,j]as I pleaded[G] with
your fathers in the wilderness
of the land of [k]Ē′ġȳpt, so will I
plead[G] with you, saith the Lord
GOD.
37 And I will [l]cause you to pass
under the rod, and I will bring
you into the bond of the covenant[G]:
38 And I will purge out from
among you the rebels, and them
that transgress against me: I will
bring them forth out of the country where they sojourn, and they
shall not enter into the land of
Ĭş′ra-el: and [m]ye shall know that
I *am* the LORD.
39 As for you, O house of Ĭş′-
ra-el, thus saith the Lord GOD;
Go ye, serve ye every one his
idols, and hereafter *also,* if ye
will [n]not hearken unto me: but
[o]pollute[G] ye my holy name no
more with your gifts, and with
your idols.

40 For in mine holy mountain,
in the mountain of the height
of Ĭş′ra-el, saith the Lord GOD,
there shall all the house of Ĭş′-
ra-el, all of them in the land,
serve me: there will I accept
them, and there will I require
your offerings, and the firstfruits
of your oblations[G], with all your
holy things.
41 [3]I will[S] accept you with your
sweet savour, when I bring you
out from the [2]people, and gather
you out of the countries wherein
ye have been scattered; and I
will be sanctified in you before
the [4]heathen.[G Q]
42 And ye shall know that I *am*
the LORD, when I shall bring you
into the [p]land of Ĭş′ra-el, into
the country *for* the which I lifted[G]
up mine hand to give it to your
fathers.[S]
43 And there shall ye [q]remem-
ber your ways, and all your doings, wherein ye have been defiled; and ye shall [r]lothe yourselves in your own sight for all
your evils that ye have committed.[S]
44 And [m]ye shall know that
I *am* the LORD, when I have
wrought with you for my name's
sake, [j]not according to your
wicked ways, nor according to
your corrupt doings, O ye house
of Ĭş′ra-el, saith the Lord GOD.[S]
45 ¶ Moreover the [s]word of the
LORD [t]came unto [u]me, saying,
46 Son of man, set thy face
toward the south, and drop *thy*
[s]*word* toward the south, and
prophesy against the forest of
the south field;
47 And say to the forest of the
south, Hear the word of the
LORD; [s,t]Thus saith the Lord
GOD; Behold, [h]I will kindle a
fire in thee, and it shall devour[G]
every green tree in thee, and
every dry tree: the flaming flame
shall not be quenched, and all

41
3 R. V. As a sweet savour will I accept you, when
4 R. V. nations.

42
*p Canaan,* Gen. 37:1.

43
*q Repentance,* Mark 1:4.
*r Remorse,* Matt. 27:3.

45
*s Prophecies, inspired,* Dan. 9:24.
*t Prophets, inspiration of,* Isa. 3:2.
*u Ezekiel,* Ezek. 1:3.

faces from the south to the north
shall be burned therein.
48 And all flesh shall see that
I the LORD [l]have kindled it: it
shall not be quenched.
49 Then said I, Ah Lord GOD!
they say of me, Doth he not
speak *parables?

## CHAPTER 21

*Ezekiel prophesies against Jerusalem and Israel; and for a sign to them, he sighs with bitterness before them. 8 The sharp and bright sword about to come upon the people. 18 The approach of the king of Babylon described. 25 Sentence against Zedekiah pronounced. 28 The destruction of the Ammonites.*

AND the [a]word of the LORD
[b]came unto [c]me, saying,
2 Son of man, set[G] thy face toward [d]Jĕ-ru̧'sā-lĕm, and drop[G] *thy*
[a]*word* toward the [1]holy places,
and prophesy[G] against the land of
Ĭş'ra-el,
3 And say to the land of Ĭş'ra-
el, Thus saith the LORD; Behold, [e]I *am* against thee, and will
draw forth my [f]sword out of his
sheath, and will cut off from thee
the righteous and the wicked.
4 Seeing then that [e]I will cut
off from thee the righteous and
the wicked, therefore shall my
[f]sword go forth out of his sheath
against all flesh from the south
to the north:
5 [g]That all flesh may know that
I the LORD have drawn forth
my sword out of his sheath: it
shall not return any more.
6 [h]Sigh therefore, thou son of
man, with the breaking of *thy*
loins; and with bitterness sigh
before their eyes.
7 [h]And it shall be, when they
say unto thee, Wherefore[G] [i]sigh-
est thou? that [b]thou shalt answer, For the tidings; because it
cometh: and every heart shall
melt, and all hands shall be
feeble, and every spirit shall faint,
and all knees shall be weak *as*
water: behold, it cometh, and
shall be brought to pass, saith
the Lord GOD.
8 ¶ Again the [a]word of the LORD
[b]came unto [c]me, saying,
9 Son of man, prophesy, and
say, Thus saith the LORD; Say,
A [f]sword, a sword is sharpened,
and also furbished[G]:
10 It is sharpened to make a
sore[G] slaughter; it is furbished[G]
that it may [2]glitter: should we
then make mirth? [3]it contemneth[G]
the rod of my son, *as* every tree.
11 And he hath given it to be
furbished, that it may be handled: this [f]sword is sharpened,
and it is furbished[G], to give it into
the hand of the slayer.
12 Cry and howl, son of man:
for [e]it shall be upon my people,
it *shall be* upon all the princes of
Ĭş'ra-el: [4]terrors by reason of the
sword shall be upon my people:
[h]smite therefore upon *thy* thigh.

1
*a* *Prophecies, inspired*, Dan. 9:24.
*b* *Prophets, inspiration of*, Isa 3:2.
*c* *Ezekiel*, Ezek. 1:3.

2
*d* *Jerusalem*, Judg. 19:10.
1 R. V. sanctuaries,

3
*e* *Nation, judgments denounced against*, Isa. 2:4.
*f* *War, as a judgment*, Judg. 3:2.

5
*g* *Judgments, design of*, Ex. 6:6.

6
*h* *Instruction, by object lessons*, Prov. 23:23.

7
*i* *Adversity, despondency in*, Psa. 10:6.

10
2 R. V. be as lightning:
3 R. V. the rod of my son, it contemneth every tree.

12
4 R. V. they are delivered over to the sword with my people:

*** PARABLES.** *Of the trees*, Judg. 9:8–15. *Of the lamb*, 2 Sam. 12:1–6. *Of the woman of Tekoa*, 2 Sam. 14:5–12. *Of the prisoner of war*, 1 Kin. 20:39–42. *Of the thistle and cedar*, 2 Kin. 14:9. *Of a vine of Egypt*, Psa. 80:8–16. *Of the vineyard*, Isa. 5:1–7; 27:2, 3. *Of the husbandman*, Isa. 28:23–29. *Of the vine*, Ezek. 15; 17:5–10. *Of the two eagles*, Ezek. 17. *Of Aholah and Aholibah*, Ezek. 23. *Of the boiling pot*, Ezek. 24:3–14.

**Of Jesus:** *The wise and foolish builders*, Matt. 7:24–27; Luke 6:47–49.
*Two debtors*, Luke 7:41–47.
*New cloth on the old garment*, Matt. 9:16; Mark 2:21 Luke 5:36.
*New wine in old wine-skins*, Matt. 9:17; Mark 2:22; Luke 5:37–39.
*House divided against itself*, Matt. 12:25–29; Mark 3:23–27; Luke 11:17–22.
*Rich fool*, Luke 12:16–21.
*Servants waiting for their lord*, Luke 12:35–40.
*Barren fig tree*, Luke 13:6–9.
*Sower*, Matt. 13:3–9, 18–23; Mark 4:1–9, 14–20; Luke 8:4–8, 11–15.
*Tares*, Matt. 13:24–30, 36–43.
*Seed growing secretly*, Mark 4:26–29.
*Mustard seed*, Matt. 13:31, 32; Mark 4:30–32; Luke 13:18, 19.
*Leaven*, Matt. 13:33; Luke 13:20, 21.
*Hidden treasure*, Matt. 13:44.
*Pearl of great price*, Matt. 13:45, 46.
*Drag net*, Matt. 13:47–50.
*Unmerciful servant*, Matt. 18:23–35.
*Good Samaritan*, Luke 10:30–37.
*Friend at midnight*, Luke 11:5–8.
*Good shepherd*, John 10:1–16.
*Great supper*, Luke 14:15–24.
*Lost sheep*, Matt. 18:12–14; Luke 15:3–7.
*Lost piece of money*, Luke 15:8–10.
*Prodigal and his brother*, Luke 15:11–32.
*Unjust steward*, Luke 16:1–9.
*Rich man and Lazarus*, Luke 16:19–31.
*Importunate widow*, Luke 18:1–8.
*Pharisee and publican*, Luke 18:9–14.
*Laborers in the vineyard*, Matt. 20:1–16.
*Pounds*, Luke 19:11–27.
*Two sons*, Matt. 21:28–32.
*Wicked husbandmen*, Matt. 21:33–44; Mark 12:1–12 Luke 20:9–18.
*Marriage of the king's son*, Matt. 22:1–14.
*Fig tree leafing*, Matt. 24:32, 33; Mark 13:28, 29.
*Man taking a far journey*, Mark 13:34–37.
*Ten virgins*, Matt. 25:1–13.
*Talents*, Matt. 25:14–30.
*The grain of wheat*, John 12:24.
*Vine*, John 15:1–8.

13 [5]Because *it is* a trial, and what if *the sword* contemn[G] even the rod? it shall be no *more,* saith the Lord GOD.

14 Thou therefore, son of man, prophesy, and [h]smite *thine* hands together, and let the sword be doubled the third time, the sword of the slain: it *is* the sword of the great *men that are* slain, which entereth into their privy[G] chambers.[G]

15 [e]I have set the point of the sword against all their gates, that *their* heart may [6]faint, and *their* ruins be multiplied: ah! *it is* made bright, *it is* wrapped up for the slaughter.

16 [7]Go thee one way or other, *either* on the right hand, *or* on the left, whithersoever[G] thy face *is* set.

17 I will also smite mine hands together, and I will [8]cause my fury to rest: I the LORD have said *it.*

18 ¶ The [a]word of the LORD [b]came unto [c]me again, saying,

19 Also, thou son of man, appoint[G] thee two ways, that the [f]sword of the [i,k]king of [l]Băb′y̆-lon may come: both twain[G] shall come forth out of one land: and choose thou a place, choose *it* at the head of the way to the city.

20 Appoint a way, that the sword may come to [m]Răb′bath of the [n]Ăm′mon-ītes, and to [o]Jū′dah in [d]Jĕ-ru̧′să-lĕm the defenced.[G]

21 For the [f]king of [l]Băb′y̆-lon stood at the parting of the way, at the head of the two ways, to use [p]divination: he [9]made *his* [q]arrows bright, he consulted [10]with images, he looked[G] in the [r]liver.

22 At his right hand was the divination for Jĕ-ru̧′să-lĕm, to [11]appoint captains, to open the mouth in the slaughter, to lift up the voice with shouting, to appoint [s]*battering* rams against the gates, to cast a [t]mount,[G] *and* to build a fort.

23 And it shall be unto them as a [12]false divination[G] in their sight, to them that have sworn oaths: but he will call to remembrance the iniquity, that they may be taken.

24 Therefore thus saith the Lord GOD; Because ye have made your [u]iniquity to be remembered, in that your transgressions are discovered,[G] so that in all your doings your [u]sins do appear; because, *I say,* that ye are come to remembrance, ye shall be taken with the hand.

25 ¶ And thou, [13]profane wicked [v,w]prince of Is̱′ra-el, whose day is come, [14]when iniquity *shall have* an[S] end,

26 Thus saith the Lord GOD; Remove the [15]diadem, and take off the crown: this *shall* not *be* the same: exalt *him that is* low, and abase *him that is* high.[Q]

27 I will overturn, overturn, overturn, it: and it shall be no *more,* until [x]he come whose right it is; and I will give it *him.*[S]

28 ¶ And thou, son of man, prophesy and say, Thus saith the Lord GOD concerning the [n]Ăm′mon-ītes, and concerning their reproach; even say thou, The [f]sword, the sword *is* drawn: for the slaughter *it is* furbished,[G] to [16]consume because of the glittering:

29 Whiles they see vanity unto thee, whiles they [y]divine a lie unto thee, to bring thee upon the necks of *them that are* slain, of the wicked, whose day is come, when their iniquity *shall have* an end.

30 Shall I cause *it* to return into his sheath? I will [z]judge thee in the place where thou wast created, in the land of thy nativity.[G T]

31 And I will pour out mine indignation upon thee, I will blow against thee in the fire of my

**13**

5 R. V. For there is a trial; and what if even the rod that contemneth shall be no more?

**15**

6 R. V. melt, and their stumblings be multiplied: ah! it is made as lightning, it is pointed for slaughter.

**16**

7 R. V. Gather thee together, go to the right; set thyself in array, go to the left;

**17**

8 R. V. satisfy my fury:

**19**

f *Nebuchadnezzar,* Dan. 2:1.

k *Agency, in executing judgments,* Mark 1:17.

l *Babylon,* Ezra 5:12.

**20**

m Or, *Rabbah, prophecies against,* Deut. 3:11.

n *Ammonites, prophecies concerning,* vs. 28–32; Deut. 2:20.

o *Judah, kingdom of,* 2 Chr. 11:17.

**21**

p *Sorcery, practiced by the Babylonians,* Isa. 47:9.

q *Arrow, divination by,* 1 Sam. 20:20.

r *Liver, superstitious rites with,* Lev. 3:4.

9 R. V. shook the arrows to and fro,

10 R. V. the teraphim,

**22**

s Ezek. 4:2.

11 R. V. set battering rams,

t *Fortification,* Ezek. 17:17.

**23**

12 R. V. vain

**24**

u *Sin, known to God,* Rom. 5:12.

**25**

v *Zedekiah,* 2 Kin. 25:2.

w *Rulers, wicked,* Ex. 18:21.

13 R. V. O deadly wounded wicked one, the prince

14 R. V. in the time of the iniquity of the end;

**26**

15 R. V. mitre,

**27**

x *Jesus, prophecies concerning,* Matt. 1:21.

**28**

16 R. V. cause it to devour, that it may be as lightning:

**29**

y *Sorcery,* Isa. 47:9.

**30**

z *God, judge,* Gen. 2:2.

wrath, and deliver thee into the
hand of brutish men[G], *and* skilful
to destroy.
32 Thou shalt be for fuel to the
fire; thy blood shall be in the
midst of the land; thou shalt be
no *more* remembered: for I the
LORD have spoken *it*.

## CHAPTER 22

*The sins of Jerusalem, 13 and the punishment thereof. 23 The general corruption of prophets, priests, princes, and people.*

MOREOVER the [a]word of
the LORD [b]came unto [c]me,
saying,
2 Now, thou son of man, wilt
thou judge[G], wilt thou judge the
bloody[G] city? yea, thou shalt shew
her all her abominations[G].
3 Then [a,b]say thou, Thus saith
the Lord GOD, The [d]city sheddeth blood in the midst of it, that
her time may come, and [e]maketh
idols against herself to defile herself.
4 [d]Thou art become guilty in
thy blood that thou hast shed;
and hast defiled thyself in thine
[e]idols which thou hast made;
and thou hast caused thy days to
draw near, and art come *even*
unto thy years: therefore have I
made [f]thee a reproach unto the
[1]heathen[G], and a mocking to all
countries.
5 *Those that be* near, and *those*
*that be* far from thee, shall mock
thee, *which art* infamous *and*
[2]much vexed[G].
6 Behold, the [g]princes of Is'-
ra-el, every one were in thee to
their power to shed blood.
7 In thee have [h]they set light
by father and mother: in the
midst of thee have they [d]dealt by
[i]oppression with the stranger[G]: in
thee have they [3,d]vexed the [j]fa-
therless and the [k]widow.
8 [d]Thou hast despised mine
holy things, and hast [l]profaned
my [m]sabbaths.
9 In [d]thee are men that carry
tales to [n]shed blood: and in thee
they [o]eat upon the mountains: in
the midst of thee they [o]commit
lewdness.
10 In thee have they [p]discov-
ered[G] their fathers' nakedness: in
thee have they humbled her that
was [4]set apart for pollution[G].
11 And one hath [q]committed
abomination[G] with his neighbour's wife; and another hath
lewdly[G] [p]defiled his daughter in
law; and another in thee hath
[p]humbled his sister, his father's
daughter.
12 In thee have they taken
[5,r]gifts to shed blood; thou hast
[s]taken [t]usury[G] and increase, and
thou hast [s]greedily gained of thy
neighbours by [6,i]extortion, and
hast forgotten me, saith the Lord
GOD.
13 Behold, therefore [u]I have
smitten mine hand [v]at thy *,[d]dis-
honest gain which thou hast
made, and at thy blood which
hath been in the midst of thee.
14 Can thine heart endure, or
can thine hands be strong, in the
days that I shall deal with thee?
[w]I the LORD have spoken *it*, and
will do *it*.
15 And [u,x]I will scatter thee
among the [1]heathen[G], and disperse thee in the countries, and
will [y]consume[G] thy filthiness out
of thee.
16 And thou shalt [7]take thine

1
a *Prophecies, inspired,* Dan. 9:24.
b *Prophets, inspiration of,* Isa. 3:2.
c *Ezekiel,* Ezek. 1:3.

3
d *Jews, wickedness of,* vs. 3–16, 26–31; Neh. 4:2.
e *Idolatry,* 1 Sam. 15:23.

4
f *Nation, punishment of,* Isa. 2:4.
1 R. V. nations,

5
2 R. V. full of tumult.

6
g *Rulers, wicked,* v. 27; Ex. 18:21.

7
h *Children, wicked, disrespectful to parents,* Mark 10:14.
i *Oppression,* Eccl. 5:8.
j *Orphan,* Lam. 5:3.
k *Widow,* 2 Sam. 14:5
3 R. V. wronged

8
l *Profanation, of the Sabbath,* Lev. 22:32.
m *Sabbath, profanation of,* Ex. 16:23.

9
n *Homicide, felonious,* Deut. 5:17.
o *Idolatry, wicked practices of,* 1 Sam. 15:23.

10
p *Incest, defined,* Lev. 18:6.
4 R. V. unclean in her separation.

11
q *Adultery,* Lev. 20:10.

12
r *Bribery, perverts justice,* 1 Sam. 8:3.
s *Covetousness,* Isa. 57:17.
t *Interest, exaction of, rebuked,* Ex. 22:25.
5 R. V. bribes
6 R. V. oppression,

13
u *Nation, judgments denounced against,* Isa. 2:4.
v *Sin, repugnant to God,* Rom. 5:12.

14
w *God, immutable,* Gen. 2:2.

15
x *Captivity, as a judgment,* Isa. 5:13.
y *Judgments, design of,* Ex. 6:6.

16
7 R. V. be profaned in

* **DISHONESTY.** *In not paying debts,* Psa. 37:12; Jas. 5:4. *In collusion with thieves,* Psa. 50:18. *In wicked devices for gain,* Job 24:2–11; Prov. 1:10–14; 20:14; Isa. 32:7; Jer. 22:13; Ezek. 22:29; Hos. 12:7; Amos 3:10; 8:5; Mic. 6:10, 11. *Denounced,* Hos. 4:1, 2; Nah. 3:1. *Forbidden,* Lev. 19:13, 35, 36; Deut. 25:13–16; Psa. 62:10; Prov. 11:1; 20:10, 23; 1 Thess. 4:6. *Penalties for,* Lev. 6:2–7; Prov. 20:17; Zeph. 1:9; Zech. 5:3, 4.
**Instances of:** *Abimelech's servants seize wells of water,* Gen. 21:25; 26:15–22. *Jacob obtains, by unjust advantage, his brother's birthright,* Gen. 25:29–33; *his father's blessing,* Gen. 27:6–29; *Laban's flocks,* Gen. 30:31–43. *Rebekah's guile in Jacob's behalf,* Gen. 27:6–17. *Laban's treatment of Jacob,* Gen. 29:21–30; 31:36–42. *Rachel steals the household gods,* Gen. 31:19. *Simeon and Levi deceive the Shechemites,* Gen. 34:15–31. *Achan appropriates to himself the wedge of gold and the Babylonish garment,* Josh. 7:11–26. *Micah steals eleven hundred pieces of silver,* Judg. 17:2. *Micah's priest steals his images,* Judg. 18:14–21. *Ahab usurps Naboth's vineyard,* 1 Kin. 21:2–16. *The unjust steward defrauds his lord,* Luke 16:1–8. *Judas, in embezzlement of funds,* John 12:6.

inheritance in thyself in the sight of the [1]heathen[C], and thou shalt know that I *am* the LORD.

17 ¶ And the [z]word of the LORD [a]came unto [b]me, saying,

18 Son of man, the house of Is'ra-el is to me [c]become [d]dross: all they *are* [e]brass, and [f]tin, and [g]iron, and †lead, in the midst of the [h]furnace; they are *even* the dross of silver.

19 Therefore thus saith the Lord GOD; Because [c]ye are all become [d]dross, behold, therefore I will gather [i]you into the midst of [j]Jē-ru'sā-lĕm.

20 *As* they gather [k]silver, and [l]brass, and [m]iron, and †lead, and [f]tin, into the midst of the [n]furnace, to blow the fire upon it, to melt *it*; so will I gather [c,o]*you* in mine [p]anger and in my fury, and I will leave *you there*, and melt you.

21 Yea, I will gather [c,o]you, and blow upon you in the fire of my [p]wrath, and ye shall be melted in the midst thereof.

22 As [k]silver is melted in the midst of the [n]furnace, so shall [c,o]ye be melted in the midst thereof; and ye shall know that I the LORD have [q]poured out my fury upon you.

23 ¶ And the [r]word of the LORD [a]came unto [b]me, saying,

24 Son of man, say unto her, Thou *art* the land that is not cleansed, nor rained upon in the day of indignation.

25 *There is* a conspiracy of her prophets in the midst thereof, like a roaring [s]lion ravening the prey; they have devoured souls; they have taken the treasure and precious things; they have made her many widows in the midst thereof.

26 Her [t]priests have violated my law, and have profaned mine holy things: they have put no difference between the [u]holy and [8]profane, neither have they [9]shewed *difference* between the unclean and the clean, and have hid their eyes from my [v]sabbaths, and I am profaned among them.

27 Her [w]princes in the midst thereof *are* like [x]wolves ravening[G] the prey, to shed blood, *and* to destroy souls, [y]to get *dishonest gain.[Q]

28 And her [z]prophets have daubed them with untempered *morter*, seeing vanity, and [a]divining lies unto them, saying, [b]Thus saith the Lord GOD, when the LORD hath not spoken.

29 The people of the land have used oppression, and exercised ‡robbery, and have vexed the [c]poor and needy: yea, they have oppressed the [d]stranger[G] wrongfully.

30 And I sought for a man among them, that should make up the hedge, and [e]stand in the gap before me for the land, that I should not destroy it: but I found none.

31 Therefore have I [f]poured out mine indignation upon them; I have consumed them with the fire of my [g]wrath: [h]their own way have I recompensed upon their heads, saith the Lord GOD.[Q]

## CHAPTER 23

*The harlots Aholah and Aholibah, types of Samaria and Jerusalem. 36 The prophet reproves their idolatries, 45 and shews their ruin.*

THE [a]word of the LORD [b]came again unto [c]me, saying,

2 Son of man, there were [d,e]two women, the daughters of one mother:

3 And they committed [f,g]whoredoms[G] in [h]Ē'gȳpt; they commit-

17
z *Prophecies, inspired*, Dan. 9:24.

a *Prophets, inspiration of*, Isa. 3:2.
b *Ezekiel*, Ezek. 1:3.

18
c *Backsliders, corrective judgments upon*, vs. 18–22; Jer. 3:22.
d *Dross, figurative*, Psa. 119:119.
e *Brass, figurative*, Job 28:2.
f Num. 31:22; Isa. 1:25; Ezek. 27:12.
g *Iron, figurative*, Prov. 27:17.
h *Furnace, figurative*, Prov. 17:3.

19
i *Jews, prophecies concerning*, vs. 19–22; Neh. 4:2.
j *Jerusalem*, Judg. 19:10.

20
k *Silver, refining of*, 1 Chr. 28:14.
l *Brass, smelted*, Job 28:2.
m *Iron*, Prov. 27:17.
n *Furnace*, Prov. 17:3.
o *Nation, judgments denounced against*, Isa. 2:4.
p *Anger of God*, 2 Kin. 13:3.

22
q *Adversity, dispensation from God*, Psa. 10:6.

23
r *Prophecies, inspired*, Dan. 9:24.

25
s *Lion*, Mic. 5:8.

26
t *Priest, corrupt*, Lev. 1:5.
u *Holiness*, Ex. 39:30.
v *Sabbath, profanation of*, Ex. 16:23.
8 R. V. common,
9 R. V. caused men to discern

27
w *Rulers, wicked*, Ex. 18:21.
x *Wolf*, Jer. 5:6.
y *Covetousness*, Isa. 57:17.

28
z *Prophets, false*, Isa. 3:2.

a *Sorcery, practiced by false prophets*, Isa. 47:9.
b *Falsehood*, Job 21:34.

29
c *Poor, oppression of*, Prov. 21:13.
d *Foreigners, oppressed*, Deut. 23:20.

30
e *Intercession, of man with God*, Jer. 27:18.

31
f *Nation, punishment of*, Isa. 2:4.
g *Anger of God*, 2 Kin. 13:3.
h *Judgment, according to opportunity and works*, 1 Pet. 1:17.

1
a *Prophecies, inspired*, Dan. 9:24.
b *Prophets, inspiration of*, Isa. 3:2.
c *Ezekiel*, Ezek. 1:3.

2
d *Israel, after the revolt*, 1 Kin. 12:1.
e *Judah, kingdom of*, 2 Chr. 11:17.

3
f *Whoredom, figurative*, Deut. 31:16.
g *Idolatry, wicked practices of*, 1 Sam. 15:23.
h *Egypt*, Gen. 41:8.

† **LEAD**, a mineral. *Purified by fire*, Num. 31:22; Jer. 6:29; Ezek. 22:18, 20. *Used in making inscriptions in stone*, Job 19:24. *Lead founder*, Jer. 6:29; Ezek. 22:18, 20. *Exported from Tarshish to Tyre*, Ezek. 27:12. *Used for weighing*, Zech. 5:7, 8.

‡ **ROBBERY.** *Forbidden*, Lev. 19:13. *Punishment of, by fine*, Lev. 6:5–7; *by death*, Ezek. 18:10, 13. *Warning against*, Prov. 1:10–14. *Forgiven*, Ezek. 33:15.
**Instances of**, Judg. 9:25; Luke 10:30.
See footnotes: ROBBERS, Hos. 6:9; THEFT, Mark 7:22.

ted whoredoms[G] in their youth: there were their breasts pressed, and there they [1]bruised the teats[G] of their virginity.

4 And the names of them *were* Ā-hō'lah the elder, and Ā-hŏl'ĭ-bah her sister: and they were mine, and they bare sons and daughters. Thus *were* their names; [d]Să-mā'rĭ-ȧ *is* Ā-hō'lah, and [e]Jē-ru'să-lĕm Ā-hŏl'ĭ-bah.

5 And [d]Ā-hō'lah [f]played the harlot when she was mine; and she doted[G] on her lovers, on the [i]Ăs-sy̆r'ĭ-anș *her* neighbours,

6 *Which were* [j]clothed with blue, [2]captains and rulers, all of them desirable young men, [k]horsemen riding upon horses.

7 Thus [d]she committed her [f]whoredoms[G] with them, with all them *that were* the chosen men of [i]Ăs-sy̆r'ĭ-ȧ, and with all on whom she doted[G]: with all their idols she [g]defiled herself.

8 [l]Neither left she her whoredoms [3]*brought* from [h]Ē'ġy̆pt: for in her youth they lay with her, and they [1]bruised the breasts of her virginity, and poured their whoredom[G] upon her.

9 Wherefore I have [m]delivered her into the hand of her lovers, into the hand of the [i,n]Ăs-sy̆r'ĭ-anș, upon whom she doted.

10 These discovered[G] her nakedness: they took her sons and her daughters, and slew her with the sword: and she became [4]famous among women; for [n]they had [o]executed judgment upon her.

11 And when her sister [e]Ā-hŏl'ĭ-bah saw *this*, she was more corrupt in her [5]inordinate love than she, and in her [f,g]whoredoms more than her sister in *her* whoredoms.

12 She doted upon the [i]Ăs-sy̆r'ĭ-anș *her* neighbours, [2]captains and rulers [j]clothed most gorgeously, [k]horsemen riding upon horses, all of them desirable young men.

13 Then I saw that she was defiled, *that* they *took* both one way,

14 And *that* she increased her [f,g]whoredoms: for when she saw men [p]pourtrayed upon the wall, the images of the [q]Chăl-dē'anș pourtrayed with [r]vermilion,

15 Girdled with girdles[G] upon their loins, exceeding in [s]dyed attire upon their heads, all of them princes to look to, after the manner of the [t]Băb-y̆-lō'nĭ-anș of Chăl-dē'ȧ, the land of their nativity:

16 And as soon as [e]she saw them with her eyes, she doted[G] upon them, and sent messengers unto them into Chăl-dē'ȧ.

17 And the [t]Băb-y̆-lō'nĭ-anș came to her into the bed of love, and they defiled[G] her with their [f]whoredom, and she was polluted with them, and her mind was alienated from them.

18 So she discovered[G] her [f]whoredoms[G], and discovered her nakedness: then [u]my mind was alienated from her, like as my mind was alienated from her sister.

19 Yet she multiplied her [f]whoredoms[G], in calling to remembrance the days of her youth, wherein she had played the harlot in the land of [h]Ē'ġy̆pt.

20 For she doted[G] upon their paramours, whose flesh *is as* the flesh of asses, and whose issue *is like* the issue of horses.

21 Thus thou calledst to remembrance the lewdness[G] of thy youth, in [6]bruising thy teats[G] by the [v]Ē-ġy̆p'tianș for the paps[G] of thy youth.

22 ¶ Therefore, O [e]Ā-hŏl'ĭ-bah, thus saith the Lord GOD; Behold, I will [w]raise up thy lovers against thee, from whom thy mind is alienated, and I will

---

1 Am. R. V. handled the bosom of

**5**
i *Assyria*, Gen. 25:18.

**6**
j *Armies, uniforms of*, Deut. 11:4.
k *Cavalry*, 1 Sam. 13:5.
2 R. V. governors

**8**
l *Impenitence*, Rom. 2:5.
3 R. V. since the days of Egypt;

**9**
m *Divine Chastisement*, Job 33:19.
n *Agency, in executing judgments*, Mark 1:17.

**10**
o *Nation, punishment of*, Isa. 2:4.
4 R. V. a byword

**11**
5 R. V. doting than

**14**
p *Painting, of portraits*, 2 Kin. 9:30.
q *Chaldeans*, Dan. 1:4.
r Jer. 22:14.

**15**
s *Dyeing*, Ex. 26:14.
t *Babylon*, Ezra 5:12.

**18**
u *Sin, separates from God*, Rom. 5:12.

**21**
v *Egyptians*, Gen. 50:3.
6 Am. R. V. the handling of thy bosom by

**22**
w *Nation, judgments denounced against*, Isa. 2:4.

bring them against thee on every
side;
23 The [t]Băb-ȳ-lō′nĭ-anș, and all
the [q]Chăl-dē′anș, [x]Pē′kŏd, and
Shō′ȧ, and Kō′ȧ, *and* all the [i]Ăs-
sȳr′ĭ-anș with them: all of them
desirable young men, [2]captains
and rulers, great lords and renowned, all of them riding upon
horses.
24 And [n,w]they shall come
against [e]thee with chariots, wagons, and wheels, and with an assembly of [7]people, *which* shall set
against thee buckler and [y]shield
and [z]helmet round about: and I
will set judgment before them,
and they shall judge thee according to their judgments.
25 And I will set my [a]jealousy
against [b,c]thee, and [d]they shall
deal furiously with thee: they
shall take away thy nose and
thine ears; and thy remnant
shall fall by the [e]sword: they
shall take thy sons and thy
daughters; and thy residue shall
be devoured by the [f]fire.[S]
26 [c,d]They shall also strip thee
out of thy clothes, and take away
thy fair jewels.
27 [g]Thus will I make thy lewdness to cease from thee, and thy
[h]whoredom[G] *brought* from the
land of [i]Ē′ġȳpt: so that thou
shalt not lift up thine eyes unto
them, nor remember Ē′ġȳpt any
more.
28 For thus saith the Lord GOD;
Behold, I will deliver [b,c]thee into
the hand *of* [d]*them* whom thou
hatest, into the hand *of them*
from whom thy mind is alienated:
29 And [d]they shall deal with
[b,c]thee hatefully, and shall take
away all thy labour, and shall
leave thee naked and bare: and
the nakedness of thy [h]whore-
doms[G] shall be discovered,[G] both
thy lewdness and thy whoredoms.[G]

30 [j]I will do these *things* unto
[b,c]thee, because thou hast gone a[G]
whoring after the heathen,[G] *and*
because thou art polluted with
their idols.
31 [b]Thou hast walked in the
[k]way of thy [l]sister; therefore will
I give her [m]cup into thine hand.
32 Thus saith the Lord GOD;
[b,c]Thou shalt drink of thy [l]sis-
ter's [m]cup deep and large: thou
shalt be laughed to scorn and
had in derision; it containeth
much.
33 [b,c]Thou shalt be filled with
[n]drunkenness and sorrow, with
the [m]cup of astonishment[G] and
desolation, with the cup of thy
sister [l]Sȧ-mā′rĭ-ȧ.
34 [b,c]Thou shalt even drink it
and suck *it* out, and thou shalt
[8]break the sherds[G] thereof, and
[9]pluck off thine own breasts: for
I have spoken *it*, saith the Lord
GOD.
35 Therefore thus saith the
Lord GOD; Because thou hast
forgotten me, and cast me behind thy back, therefore [c]bear
thou also thy lewdness and thy
whoredoms.[G]
36 ¶ The LORD said moreover
unto me; Son of man, wilt thou
judge [l]Ȧ-hō′lah and [b]Ȧ-hŏl′ĭ-
bah? yea, declare unto them
their abominations;
37 That [b,l]they have committed
adultery, and blood *is* in their
hands, and with their idols have
they [o]committed adultery, and
have also [o]caused their [p,q]sons,
whom they bare unto me, to pass
for them through *the fire*, to devour *them*.
38 Moreover this they have
done unto me: they have [r]defiled
my [s,t]sanctuary in the same day,
and have [u]profaned my sabbaths.
39 For when they had [o]slain
their [p,q]children to their idols,
then they came the same day in-

23
x Jer. 50:21.

24
y *Shield*, 1 Kin. 14:27.
z *Helmet*, Jer. 46:4.
7 R. V. peoples;

25
a *Jealousy, attributed to God*, Psa. 78:58.
b *Judah, kingdom of*, 2 Chr. 11:17.
c *Nation, judgments denounced against*, Isa. 2:4.
d *Agency, in executing judgments*, Mark 1:17.
e *War, as a judgment*, Judg. 3:2.
f *Fire, torture by*, Ex. 12:8.

27
g *Judgments, design of*, Ex. 6:6.
h *Whoredom, figurative*, Deut. 31:16.
i *Egypt*, Gen. 41:8.

30
j *Divine Chastisement, inflicted for sins*, Job 33:19.

31
k *Example, bad*, John 13:15.
l *Israel, after the revolt*, 1 Kin. 12:1.
m *Cup, figurative*, Matt. 20:22.

33
n *Drunkenness, figurative*, Luke 21:34.

34
8 R. V. gnaw
9 R. V. shall tear thy breasts:

37
o *Idolatry, wicked practices of*, 1 Sam. 15:23.
p *Children, sacrificed*, Mark 10:14.
q *Human Sacrifices, offered by Israelites*, Deut. 12:31.

38
r *Profanation, of the house of God*, Lev. 22:32.
s *Sanctuary*, Lev. 4:6.
t *Church, holy*, 1 Kin. 9:3.
u *Profanation, of the Sabbath*, Lev. 22:32.

to my [s,t]sanctuary to profane it; and, lo, thus have they done in the midst of mine house.

40 And furthermore, that ye have sent for men to come from far, unto whom a messenger *was* sent; and, lo, they came: for whom thou didst wash thyself, paintedst thy eyes, and deckedst thyself with [v]ornaments,

41 And satest upon a stately bed, and a table prepared before it, whereupon thou hast set mine [w]incense and mine [x]oil.

42 And a voice of a multitude being at ease *was* with her: and with the men of the common sort *were* brought [10, y]Să-bē′ans̤ from the wilderness, which put [z]bracelets upon their hands, and beautiful [a]crowns upon their heads.

43 Then said I unto *her that was* old in adulteries, Will they now commit whoredoms[C] with her, and she *with them*?

44 Yet they went in unto her, as they go in unto a woman that playeth the harlot: so went they in unto [b]Ā-hō′lah and unto [c]Ā-hŏl′ī-bah, the lewd[C] women.

45 ¶ And the righteous men, they shall judge them after the manner of adulteresses, and after the manner of women that shed blood; because they *are* adulteresses, and blood *is* in their hands.

46 For thus saith the Lord GOD; I will [d]bring up a [e]company upon them, and will give them to be[11] removed and spoiled.[C]

47 [f]And the [e]company shall stone them with stones, and dispatch them with their swords; they shall slay their sons and their daughters, and burn up their houses with fire.

48 [g]Thus will I cause lewdness to cease out of the land, that all women may be taught not to do after your lewdness.

49 And they shall [h]recompense your lewdness upon you, and ye shall bear the sins of your idols: and ye shall know that I *am* the Lord GOD.

**40**
*v Women, ornaments of,* Prov. 31:10.

**41**
*w Incense, offered in idolatrous worship,* Ex. 37:29.
*x Oil, used in idolatrous worship,* Deut. 12:17.

**42**
*y Drunkard,* Psa. 69:12.
*z Bracelet,* Gen. 24:22.

*a Crown,* Ex. 29:6.
10 R. V. drunkards

**44**
*b Israel, after the revolt,* 1 Kin. 12:1.
*c Judah, kingdom of,* 2 Chr. 11:17.

**46**
*d Adversity, dispensation from God,* Psa. 10:6.
*e Agency, in executing judgments,* Mark 1:17.
11 R. V. tossed to and fro

**47**
*f Nation, judgments denounced against,* Isa. 2:4.

**48**
*g Judgments, design of,* Ex. 6:6.

**49**
*h Punishment, according to deeds,* Lev. 26:41.

## CHAPTER 24

*The commencement of the siege to be noted. 3 The parable of the boiling pot, and its explanation. 15 The prophet is not to mourn for the death of his wife, 19 as a sign that the calamity of the Jews will be beyond all outward sorrow.*

AGAIN in the ninth year, in the tenth [a]month, in the tenth *day* of the month, the [b]word of the LORD [c]came unto [d]me, saying,

2 Son of man, write thee the name of the day, *even* of this same day: the [e]king of [f]Băb′y̆-lon set himself against [g]Jē-ru̇′-să-lĕm this same day.

3 And utter a [h]parable unto the rebellious house, and say unto them, [b]Thus saith the Lord GOD; [i]Set on a pot, set *it* on, and also pour water into it:

4 [i]Gather the pieces thereof into it, *even* every good piece, the thigh, and the shoulder; fill *it* with the choice bones.

5 [i]Take the choice of the flock, and [1]burn also the bones under it, *and* make it boil well, and let them seethe[C] the bones of it therein.

6 ¶ Wherefore [b]thus saith the Lord GOD; [j]Woe to the [k]bloody city, to the pot whose [2]scum *is* therein, and whose [2]scum is not gone out of it! bring it out piece by piece; let no lot fall upon it.

7 For her blood is in the midst of her; she set it upon the top of a rock; she poured it not upon the ground, to cover it with dust;[Q]

8 That it might cause fury to come up to take vengeance; I have set her blood upon the top of a rock, that it should not be covered.

9 Therefore [b]thus saith the Lord GOD; [j]Woe to the [k]bloody city! I will even make the pile for fire great.

10 [j]Heap on wood, [3]kindle the

v.1–510 BC
See footnote, *Time,* Rev. 10:6.

**1**
*a Month (January)*. Ex. 12:2.
*b Prophecies, inspired,* Dan. 9:24.
*c Prophets, inspiration of,* Isa. 3:2.
*d Ezekiel,* Ezek. 1:3.

**2**
*e Nebuchadnezzar* Dan. 2:1.
*f Babylon, empire of,* Ezra 5:12.
*g Jerusalem,* Judg. 19:10.

**3**
*h Parables, boiling pot,* vs. 3–5; Ezek. 20:49.
*i Instruction, by object lessons,* vs. 3–5, 16–27; Prov. 23:23.

**5**
1 R. V. pile

**6**
*j Nation, judgments denounced against,* Isa. 2:4.
*k Jews, wickedness of,* Neh. 4:2.
2 R. V. rust

**10**
3 R. V. make the fire hot, boil well the flesh, and make thick the broth, and let the bones be burned.

fire, consume[G] the flesh, and spice it well, and let the bones be burned.

11 Then set it empty upon the coals thereof, that the brass of it may be hot, and may burn, and *that* the [k]filthiness of it may be molten[G] in it, *that* the [2]scum of it may be consumed[G].

12 [k]She hath wearied *herself* with [4]lies, and her great [2]scum went not forth out of her: her [5]scum *shall be* in the fire.

13 In thy [k]filthiness *is* lewdness[G]: because I have [l]purged thee, and thou wast not purged, thou shalt not be purged from thy filthiness any more, till I have caused my fury to rest upon thee.

14 I the LORD have spoken *it*: it shall come to pass, and [m]I will do *it*; I will not go back, neither will I spare, neither will I repent;[G] [n]according to thy ways, and according to thy doings, shall they judge thee, saith the Lord GOD.

15 ¶ Also the [b]word of the LORD [c]came unto [d]me, saying,

16 Son of man, behold, [i]I take away from thee the [o]desire of thine eyes with a stroke: yet [i,p]neither shalt thou mourn nor weep, neither shall thy tears run down.

17 [6,i,p]Forbear[G] to cry, make no [q]mourning for the dead, bind the [r]tire[G] of thine head upon thee, and put on thy [s]shoes upon thy feet, and cover not *thy* lips, and eat not the bread of men.

18 So [t]I spake unto the people in the morning: and at even[G] my [o]wife died; and I [u]did in the morning as I was commanded.

19 ¶ And the people said unto me, Wilt thou not tell us what these *things are* to us, that thou doest *so*?

20 Then I answered them, The [b]word of the LORD [c]came unto [d]me, saying,

21 Speak unto the house of Ĭş′-ra-el, Thus saith the Lord GOD; Behold, [i]I will profane my sanctuary, the [7]excellency of your strength, the desire of your eyes, and that which your soul pitieth; and [i]your sons and your daughters whom ye have left shall fall by the [v]sword.

22 And [i]ye shall do as I have done: ye shall not cover *your* lips, nor eat the bread of men.

23 And your [r]tires[G] *shall be* upon your heads, and your [s]shoes upon your feet: ye shall not [q]mourn nor weep; but ye shall pine away for your [k]iniquities, and mourn one toward another.

24 [i]Thus [d]Ē-zē′kĭ-el is unto you a sign: according to all that he hath done shall ye do: and when this cometh, [w]ye shall know that I *am* the Lord GOD.

25 Also, thou son of man, *shall it* not *be* in the day when I [x]take from them their strength, the joy of their glory, the desire of their eyes, and that whereupon they set their minds, their sons and their daughters,

26 *That* he that escapeth in that day shall come unto thee, to cause *thee* to hear *it* with *thine* ears?

27 In that day shall thy mouth be opened to him which is escaped, and thou shalt speak, and be no more dumb: and thou shalt be a sign unto them; and [x]they shall know that I *am* the LORD.

## CHAPTER 25

*God's judgments upon the Ammonites for their cruel and insolent conduct towards the Jews; 8 also upon Moab and Seir, 12 upon Edom, 15 and upon the Philistines.*

THE [a]word of the LORD [b]came again unto [c]me, saying,

2 Son of man, set thy face against the [d]Ăm′mon-ītes, and prophesy against them;

3 And say unto the [d]Ăm′mon-ītes, Hear the word of the Lord

---

**12**
4 R. V. toil: yet
5 R. V. rust goeth not forth by fire.

**13**
l *Wicked, punishment of,* Psa. 73:3.

**14**
m *God, immutable,* Gen. 2:2.
n *Judgment, according to opportunity and works,* 1 Pet. 1:17.

**16**
o *Wife,* Prov. 5:18.
p *Bereavement, mourning in, forbidden,* Hos. 9:12.

**17**
q *Mourning, forbidden,* Lam. 2:5.
r *Turban,* Ex. 28:40.
s *Shoe, put off, in mourning,* Josh. 5:15.
6 R. V. Sigh, but not aloud; make

**18**
t *Minister, faithful,* Rom. 15:16.
u *Obedience, exemplified,* Heb. 5:8.

**21**
v *War, as a judgment,* Judg. 3:2.
7 R. V. pride of your power, the desire

**24**
w *Judgments, design of,* Ex. 6:6

**25**
x *Adversity, dispensation from God,* Psa. 10:6.

**1**
a *Prophecies, inspired,* Dan. 9:24.
b *Prophets, inspiration of,* Isa. 3:2.
c *Ezekiel,* Ezek. 1:3.

**2**
d *Ammonites, prophecies concerning,* vs. 2–7; Deut. 2:20.

GOD; [a]Thus saith the Lord
GOD; Because thou saidst, [e]Aha,
against my [f, g]sanctuary, when it
was [h]profaned; and against the
land of Iș'ra-el, when it was desolate; and against the house of
Jū'dah, when they went into
[i]captivity;
4 Behold, therefore [j]I will deliver thee to the men of the east
for a possession, and they shall
set their [1]palaces in thee, and
make their dwellings in thee:
they shall eat thy fruit, and they
shall drink thy milk.
5 And [j]I will make [k]Răb'bah a
stable for [l]camels, and the [d]Ăm'-
mon-ītes a couching[G] place for
flocks: and [m]ye shall know that
I *am* the LORD.
6 For thus saith the Lord GOD;
Because thou hast clapped *thine*
hands, and stamped with the
feet, and rejoiced in heart with
all thy despite[G] against the land of
Iș'ra-el;
7 Behold, therefore [j]I will
stretch out mine hand upon thee,
and will deliver thee for a spoil[G]
to the [2]heathen[G]; and I will cut
thee off from the [3]people, and I
will cause thee to perish out of
the countries: I will destroy thee;
and [m]thou shalt know that I *am*
the LORD.
8 ¶ Thus saith the Lord GOD;
Because that [n]Mō'ab and Sē'ïr
do say, Behold, the house of
Jū'dah *is* like unto all the
heathen[G];
9 Therefore, behold, I will open
the side of [n]Mō'ab from the
cities, from his cities *which are*
on his frontiers, the glory of the
country, [o]Bĕth-jĕsh'ĭ-mŏth, [p]Bā'-
al-mē'on, and [q]Kĭr-ĭ-a-thā'im,
10 Unto the men of the east
[4]with the [d]Ăm'mon-ītes, and will
give them in possession, that the
Ăm'mon-ītes may not be remembered among the nations.
11 And [j]I will execute judgments upon [n]Mō'ab; and [m]they
shall know that I *am* the LORD.
12 ¶ Thus saith the Lord
GOD; Because that [r]Ē'dom hath
dealt against the house of Jū'dah
by taking vengeance, and hath
greatly offended, and *revenged
himself upon them;
13 Therefore thus saith the
Lord GOD; [j]I will also stretch
out mine hand upon [r]Ē'dom,
and will cut off man and beast
from it; and I will make it
desolate from [s]Tē'man; and
they of [t]Dē'dan shall fall by
the [u]sword.
14[s] And [j]I will lay my vengeance upon [r]Ē'dom [v]by the hand
of my people Iș'ra-el: and they
shall do in Ē'dom according to
mine [w]anger and according to
my fury; and they shall know
my vengeance, saith the Lord
GOD.
15 ¶ Thus saith the Lord GOD;
Because the [x]Phĭ-lĭs'tĭneș have
dealt by *revenge, and have
taken vengeance with a despiteful[G] heart, to destroy *it* [5]for the
old hatred;
16 Therefore thus saith the Lord
GOD; Behold, [j]I will stretch out
mine hand upon the [x]Phĭ-lĭs'-
tĭneș, and I will cut off the [y]Chĕr'-
e-thĭmș, and destroy the remnant
of the sea coast.
17 And I will execute great
vengeance upon [x, y]them with
furious rebukes; and [m]they shall
know that I *am* the LORD, when
I shall lay my vengeance upon
them.[s]

**3**
e *Mocking*, 1 Kin. 18:27.
f *Sanctuary*, Lev. 4:6.
g *Church, holy*, 1 Kin. 9:3.
h *Profanation, of the house of God*, Lev. 22:32.
i *Captivity, of Judah in Babylon*, Isa. 5:13.

**4**
j *Nation, judgments denounced against*, Isa. 2·4.
1 R. V. encampments

**5**
k *Rabbah, prophecies against*, Deut. 3:11.
l *Camel*, 1 Sam. 30:17.
m *Judgments, design of*, Ex. 6:6.

**7**
2 R. V. nations;
3 R. V. peoples,

**8**
n *Moabites, prophecies concerning*, Gen. 19:37.

**9**
o *Beth-jeshimoth*, Josh. 12:3.
p *Baal-meon*, Num. 32:38.
q Or, *Kir-jathaim*, Num. 32:37.

**10**
4 R. V. to go against the

**12**
r *Edomites, prophecies concerning*, vs. 12–14; 2 Kin. 8:21.

**13**
s *Teman, prophecies concerning*, Jer. 49:7.
t *Dedan*, Jer. 49:8.
u *War, as a judgment*, Judg. 3:2.

**14**
v *Agency, in executing judgments*, Mark 1:17.
w *Anger of God*, 2 Kin. 13:3.

**15**
x *Philistines, prophecies against*, Gen. 26:14.
5 R. V. with perpetual enmity;

**16**
y Or, *Cherethites*, 1 Sam. 30:14.

* **REVENGE.** *Forbidden*, Lev. 19:18; Prov. 20:22; 24:29; Matt. 5:38–41; Luke 6:27–35; Rom. 12:17, 19; 1 Thess. 5:15; 1 Pet. 3:9. *Rebuked by Jesus*, Luke 9:54, 55. *Proceeds from a spiteful heart*, Ezek. 25:15. *Punishment for*, Ezek. 25:15–17; Amos 1:11, 12.
**Instances of:** *By Simeon and Levi*, Gen. 34:25. *By Joseph*, Gen 42:9–24. *By Samson*, Judg. 15:7, 8; 16:28–30. *By Joab*, 2 Sam. 3:27, 30. *By Absalom*, 2 Sam. 13:23–29. *By Jezebel*, 1 Kin. 19:2. *By Ahab*, 1 Kin. 22:27. *By Haman*, Esth. 3:8–15. *By the Edomites*, Ezek. 25:12. *By the Philistines*, Ezek. 25:15. *By Herodias*, Mark 6:19–24. *By James and John*, Luke 9:54. *By the chief priests*, Acts 5:33. *By the Jews*, Acts 7:54–59.
See footnote, RETALIATION, Deut. 19:19.

## CHAPTER 26

*Tyrus, for exulting against Jerusalem, is threatened with destruction by the hand of Nebuchadnezzar. 15 The mourning and astonishment of the isles at her fall.*

AND it came to pass in the
eleventh year, in the first
*day* of the month, *that* the [a]word
of the LORD [b]came unto [c]me,
saying,
2 Son of man, because that
[d]Tȳ′rus hath [e]said against [f]Jĕ-
ru̇′să-lĕm, Aha, she is broken
*that was* the gates of the [1]peo-
ple: she is turned unto me: I shall
be replenished, *now* she is laid
waste:
3 Therefore thus saith the Lord
GOD; Behold, I *am* against thee,
O [d]Tȳ′rus, and [g]will cause [h]many
nations to come up against thee,
as the sea causeth his waves to
come up.
4 And [h]they shall [g]destroy the
walls of [d]Tȳ′rus, and break down
her towers: I will also scrape her
dust from her, and make her like
the top of a rock.
5 [g]It shall be *a place for* the
spreading of nets in the midst
of the sea: for [i]I have spoken
*it,* saith the Lord GOD: and it
shall become a spoil to the nations.
6 And [g]her daughters which *are*
in the field shall be [j]slain by the
sword; and [k]they shall know that
I *am* the LORD.
7 ¶ For thus saith the Lord
GOD; Behold, [g]I will bring upon [d]Tȳ′rus [h,l]Nĕb-u-chad-rĕz′-
zar king of [m]Băb′ȳ-lon, a king
of kings, from the north, with
[n]horses, and with [o]chariots, and
with [p]horsemen, and companies,
and much people.
8 [h,l]He shall [j]slay with the
sword thy daughters in the field:
and he shall make a fort against
thee, and cast a [q]mount against
thee, and lift up the [r]buckler
against thee.
9 And [h,l]he shall set [s]engines of
war against thy walls, and with
his [t]axes he shall break down thy
towers.
10 [g]By reason of the abundance
of his [n]horses their dust shall
cover thee: thy walls shall shake
at the noise of the [p]horsemen,
and of the [2]wheels, and of the
[o]chariots, when he shall enter
into thy gates, as men enter into
a city wherein is made a breach.
11 [g]With the hoofs of his
[n]horses shall he tread down all
thy streets: he shall [j]slay thy
people by the sword, and [3]thy
strong garrisons shall go down
to the ground.
12 And [g,h]they shall make a
spoil of thy riches, and make a
prey of thy merchandise: and
they shall break down thy walls,
and destroy thy pleasant houses:
and they shall lay thy stones and
thy timber and thy dust in the
midst of the water.
13 And I will [g]cause the noise
of thy [u]songs to cease; and the
sound of thy [v]harps shall be no
more heard.
14 And [g]I will make thee like
the top of a rock: thou shalt be *a*
*place* to spread nets upon; thou
shalt be built no more: for [w]I the
LORD have spoken *it,* saith the
Lord GOD.
15 ¶ Thus saith the Lord GOD
to [d]Tȳ′rus; Shall not the isles
shake at the sound of thy fall,
when the wounded cry, when the
slaughter is made in the midst of
thee?
16 Then all the princes of the
sea shall come down from their
thrones, and lay away their
robes, and put off their *broidered garments: they shall clothe

v.1–508 BC
See footnote, *Time,* Rev. 10:6.

**1**
*a Prophecies, inspired,* Dan. 9:24.
*b Prophets, inspiration of,* Isa. 3:2.
*c Ezekiel,* Ezek. 1:3.

**2**
*d* Or, *Tyre, prophecies relating to,* vs. 1–21; Josh. 19:29.
*e Mocking,* 1 Kin. 18:27.
*f Jerusalem,* Judg. 19:10.
1 R. V. peoples;

**3**
*g Nation, judgments denounced against,* Isa. 2:4.
*h Agency, in executing judgments,* Mark 1:17.

**5**
*i God, immutable,* Gen. 2:2.

**6**
*j War, evils of,* Judg. 3:2.
*k Judgments, design of,* Ex. 6:6.

**7**
*l* Or, *Nebuchadnezzar, prophecies concerning,* vs. 7–12; Dan. 2:1.
*m Babylon, empire of,* Ezra 5:12.
*n Horse,* Job 39:19.
*o Chariot,* Josh. 11:4.
*p Cavalry,* 1 Sam. 13:5.

**8**
*q Fortification,* Ezek. 17:17.
*r Shield,* 1 Kin. 14:27.

**9**
*s* 2 Chr. 26:15.
*t Ax,* Deut. 19:5.

**10**
2 R. V. wagons,

**11**
3 R. V. the pillars of thy strength shall

**13**
*u Music,* 2 Chr. 5:13.
*v Harp,* Dan. 3:10.

**14**
*w God, immutable,* Gen. 2:2.

* **EMBROIDERY.** *In blue and purple and scarlet, on the curtains of the tabernacle,* Ex. 26:1, 36; 27:16; *on the girdle and vestments of the high priest, mingled with gold,* Ex. 28:4–8, 39; 39:3. *On the garments, of Sisera,* Judg. 5:30; *of princes,* Ezek. 26:16; *of women,* Psa. 45:14; Ezek. 16:10, 13, 18. *Bezaleel and Aholiab inspired in,* Ex. 35:30–35; 38:22, 23.
See footnote, TAPESTRY, Prov. 7:16.

themselves with trembling; they shall sit upon the ground, and shall tremble at *every* moment, and be astonished[G] at thee.

17 And they shall take up a lamentation for [d]thee, and say to thee, How art thou destroyed, *that wast* inhabited of [x]seafaring men, the renowned city, which wast strong in the sea, she and her inhabitants, which cause their terror *to be* on all that haunt[G][Q] it!

18 Now shall the isles tremble in the day of thy fall; yea, the isles that *are* in the sea shall be troubled at thy departure.

19 For thus saith the Lord GOD; [g]When I shall make thee a desolate city, like the cities that are not inhabited; when I shall bring up the deep upon thee, and great waters shall cover thee;[Q]

20 [g]When I shall bring thee down with them that descend into the pit, with the people of old time, and shall set thee in the low parts of the earth, in places desolate of old, with them that go down to the pit, that thou be not inhabited; and I shall set glory in the land of the living;

21 [g]I will make thee a terror, and thou *shalt be* no *more*: though thou be sought for, yet shalt thou never be found again, saith the Lord GOD.[Q]

## CHAPTER 27

*The wealth and commerce of Tyre.* **26** *The irreparable ruin thereof.*

THE word of the LORD [a]came again unto [b]me, saying,

2 Now, thou son of man, take up a lamentation for [c]Tȳ′rus;

3 And say unto [c]Tȳ′rus, O thou that art situate[G] at the entry of the sea, *which art* a [d,e]merchant of the [1]people for many isles, Thus saith the Lord GOD; O Tȳ′rus, thou hast said, I *am* of perfect beauty.

4 Thy borders *are* in the midst of the seas, thy builders have perfected thy beauty.

5 They have made all thy *ship* boards of [f]fir trees of [g]Sē′nir: they have taken [h]cedars from [i]Lĕb′a-non to make masts for thee.

6 *Of* the [j]oaks of [k]Bā′shăn have they made thine [l]oars; [2]the company of the Ăsh′ŭr-ītes have made thy benches *of* [m,n]ivory, [e]*brought* out of the isles of [o]Chĭt′-tim.

7 Fine *linen with [n,p]broidered[G] work from Ē′ġy̆pt was [3]that which thou spreadest forth to be thy sail; blue and purple from the isles of Ē-lī′shah was [4]that which covered thee.

8 The inhabitants of [q]Zī′dŏn and [r]Är′văd were thy [s]mariners: thy wise *men*, O [c]Tȳ′rus, *that* were in thee, were thy pilots.

9 The [5]ancients of [t]Gē′bal and the wise *men* thereof were in thee thy calkers: all the [u]ships of the sea with their [s]mariners were in thee to [6]occupy thy merchandise.[Q]

10 They of [v]Pēr′sia and of [w]Lŭd and of [x]Phŭt were in thine army, thy men of war: they hanged[G] the [y]shield and [z]helmet in thee; they set forth thy comeliness.[G]

11 The [a]men of Är′văd with thine army *were* upon thy walls round about, and the Găm′ma-dĭms were in thy towers: they hanged[G] their shields upon thy walls round about; they have made thy beauty perfect.

12 [b]Tär′shish *was* thy [c]merchant by reason of the multitude of all *kind of* [d,e]riches; with [f]silver, [g]iron, [h]tin, and [i]lead, they traded [7]in thy fairs.

13 Jā′văn, [j]Tu̇′bal, and [k]Mē′-shech, they *were* thy [c]merchants: [e]they traded the [l]persons of men

*h* Num. 31:22; Ezek. 22:18, 20. *i* *Lead*, Ezek. 22:18. **7** R. V. for thy wares. **13** *j* *Tubal*, Gen. 10:2. *k* Ezek. 32:26; 38:2, 3. *l* *Servant, bought and sold*, Jer. 2:14.

**17**
*x* *Mariner*, Ezek. 27:27.

**1**
*a* *Prophets, inspiration of*, Isa. 3:2.
*b* *Ezekiel*, Ezek. 1:3.

**2**
*c* Or, *Tyre, prophecies, relating to*, Josh. 19:29.

**3**
*d* *Merchant*, Neh. 3:32.
*e* *Commerce*, 1 Kin. 10:15.
**1** R. V. peoples unto many

**5**
*f* *Fir Tree*, 2 Sam. 6:5.
*g* Or, *Hermon*, Deut. 4:48.
*h* *Cedar*, Isa. 9:10.
*i* *Lebanon, cedars of*, Deut. 1:7.

**6**
*j* *Oak*, Gen. 35:4.
*k* *Bashan*, Num. 32:33.
*l* Isa. 33:21.
*m* *Ivory*, 2 Chr. 9:17.
*n* *Imports*, 1 Kin. 10:11.
*o* *Chittim*, Dan. 11:30.
**2** R. V. they have made thy benches of ivory inlaid in boxwood, from the isles of Kittim.

**7**
*p* *Embroidery*, Ezek. 26:16.
**3** R. V. thy sail, that it might be to thee for an ensign;
**4** R. V. thine awning.

**8**
*q* *Zidon*, Ezek. 28:21.
*r* *Arvadites*, Gen. 10:18.
*s* *Mariner*, Ezek. 27:27.

**9**
*t* Josh. 13:5; 1 Kin. 5:18.
*u* *Ship*, 2 Chr. 8:18.
**5** Am. R. V. old men
**6** Am. R. V. deal in thy merchandise.

**10**
*v* *Persia*, Esth. 1:3.
*w* Or, *Lydia*, Ezek. 30:5.
*x* Or, *Libya*, Acts 2:10.
*y* *Shield*, 1 Kin. 14:27.
*z* *Helmet*, Jer. 46:4.

**11**
*a* *Arvadites*, Gen. 10:18.

**12**
*b* *Tarshish*, 2 Chr. 20:36.
*c* *Merchant*, Neh. 3:32.
*d* *Commerce, articles of*, 1 Kin. 10:15.
*e* *Imports*, vs. 12–25; 1 Kin. 10:11.
*f* *Silver*, 1 Chr. 28:14.
*g* *Iron*, Prov. 27:17.

*m Brass*, Job 28:2.
8 R. V. for thy merchandise.

14
*n* Ezek. 38:6; Gen. 10:3; 1 Chr. 1:6.
*o Horse*, Job 39:19.
*p Mule*, 2 Sam. 18:9.
9 R. V. war-horses

15
*q Dedan*, Jer. 49:8.
*r Ivory*, 2 Chr. 9:17.
10 R. V. mart
11 R. V. in exchange

16
*s Syria*, 2 Kin. 6:23.
*t Emerald*, Rev. 4:3.
*u Embroidery*, Ezek. 26:16.
*v* Job 28:18.
*w Agate*, Ex. 28:19.
12 R. V. traded for thy wares
13 R. V. rubies.

17
*x Canaan, exports of*, Gen. 37:1.
*y Wheat*, Ezra 6:9.
*z* Judg. 11:33.
*a Honey*, Prov. 25:27.
*b Oil*, Deut. 12:17.
*c Balm*, Gen. 37:25.

18
*d Damascus*, Isa. 8:4.
*e Merchant*, Neh. 3:32.
*f Wine*, Prov. 23:31.
*g Wool*, Judg. 6:37.

19
*h Commerce*, 1 Kin. 10:15.
*i Iron*, Prov. 27:17.
14 R. V. traded with yarn for thy wares:

20
*j Dedan*, Jer. 49:8.
15 R. V. cloths for riding.

21
*k Arabia*, 2 Chr. 9:14.
*l Kedar*, Jer. 49:28. *m Sheep*, Deut. 32:14. 16 R. V. were the merchants of thy hand;
22 *n Sheba*, 1 Kin. 10:1.

and vessels of [m]brass [8]in thy
market.[Q]
14 They of the house of [n]Tō-
gär′mah [d]traded [7]in thy fairs
[e]with [o]horses and horsemen and
[9,p]mules.
15 The men of [q]Dē′dan *were*
thy [c]merchants; many isles *were*
the [10]merchandise of thine hand:
[d]they [e]brought thee [11]*for* a present horns of [r]ivory and ebony.
16 [s]Sӯr′ĭ-ȧ *was* thy [c]merchant
by reason of the multitude of the
wares of thy making: [d]they [12]oc-
cupied in thy fairs [e]with [t]eme-
ralds, purple, and [u]broidered[G]
work, and fine *linen, and [v]cor-
al, and [13,w]agate.
17 Jū′dah, and the land of Ĭṣ′-
ra-el, they *were* thy [c]merchants:
they traded [8,x]in thy market
[y]wheat of [z]Mĭn′nith, and Păn′-
năg, and [a]honey, and [b]oil, and
[c]balm.[G][Q]
18 [d]Dă-măs′cus *was* thy [e]mer-
chant in the multitude of the
wares of thy making, for the
multitude of all riches; in the
[f]wine of Hĕl′bon, and white
[g]wool.
19 Dăn also and Jā′văn [14,h]go-
ing to and fro occupied in thy
fairs: bright [i]iron, †cassia, and
‡calamus, were in thy market.
20 [j]Dē′dan *was* thy [e]merchant
in precious [15]clothes for chariots.
21 [k]Ă-rā′bĭ-ȧ, and all the princes
of [l]Kē′där, they [16,h]occupied with
thee in [m]lambs, and rams, and
goats: in these *were they* thy merchants.
22 The [e]merchants of [n]Shē′bȧ
and Rā′a-mah, they *were* thy
merchants: they [12,h]occupied in
thy fairs with chief of all [o]spices,
and with all [p]precious stones, and
[q]gold.[Q]
23 [r]Hā′ran, and [s]Căn′neh, and
[t]Ē′dĕn, the merchants of [n]Shē′-
bȧ, [u]Ăs′shur, *and* Chĭl′măd, *were*
thy merchants.
24 These *were* thy [17,e]merchants
in all sorts *of things*, in blue
clothes, and [v]broidered[G] work,
and in chests of rich apparel,
bound with cords, and made
of [w]cedar, among thy merchandise.
25 The [x]ships of [y]Tär′shish
[18]did sing of thee in thy market:
and thou wast replenished, and
made very glorious in the midst
of the seas.
26 ¶ Thy rowers[G] have brought
thee into great waters: the east
[z,a]wind hath broken thee in the
midst of the seas.
27 [b]Thy riches, and thy [19]fairs,
thy merchandise, thy ‖mariners,
and thy pilots, thy calkers, and
the occupiers of thy merchandise, and all thy men of war, that
*are* in thee, and in all thy company which *is* in the midst of
thee, [c]shall fall into the midst
of the seas in the day of thy
ruin.
28 The[Q] suburbs[G] shall shake at
the sound of the cry of thy pilots.
29 [b]And all that handle the oar,
the ‖mariners, *and* all the pilots
of the sea, shall come down from
their ships, they shall stand upon
the land;[Q]
30[Q] And shall cause their voice
to be heard against thee, and
shall cry bitterly, and shall [d]cast
up dust upon their heads, they

*o Spices*, 1 Kin. 10:2.
*p Precious Stones*, Ex. 39.10.
*q Gold*, Ezek. 7:19.

23
*r Haran*, Gen. 11:31.
*s* Or, *Calneh*, Gen. 10:10; Amos 6:2; or, *Calno*, Isa. 10:9.
*t* 2 Kin. 19:12; Isa. 37:12; Amos 1:5.
*u Assyria*, Gen. 25:18.

24
*v Embroidery*, Ezek. 26:16.
*w Cedar*, Isa. 9:10.
17 R. V. traffickers in choice wares, in wrappings of blue and

25
*x Ship*, 2 Chr. 8:18.
*y Tarshish*, 2 Chr. 20:36.
18 R. V. were thy caravans for thy merchandise:

26
*z Wind*, Job 37:17.
*a Meteorology*, Matt. 16:2.

27
*b Tyre, prophecies relating to*, Josh. 19:29.
*c Wicked, punishment of*, Psa. 73:3.
19 R. V. wares.

30
*d Mourning*, Lam. 2:5.

***LINEN.** *Exported, from Egypt*, Ezek. 27:7; *from Syria*, Ezek. 27:16.
Articles made of: *Curtains of the tabernacle*, Ex. 26:1; 27:9; *curtains of the temple*, 2 Chr. 3:14; *vestments of priests*, Ex. 28:5–8, 15, 39–42; Lev. 6:10; 1 Sam. 2:18; *livery of royal households*, Gen. 41:42; Esth. 8:15; *garments for men*, Gen. 41:42; Ezek. 9:2; Luke 16:19; *and for women*, Isa. 3:23; Ezek. 16:10, 13.
*Mosaic law forbade its being mingled with wool*, Lev. 19:19; Deut. 22:11. *The body of Jesus wrapped in*, Matt. 27:59; Mark 15:46; John 19:40; 20:5.

**Figurative:** *Pure and white, of righteousness*, Rev. 15:6; 19:8, 14.

**† CASSIA.** *An aromatic plant, probably cinnamon*, Psa. 45:8; Ezek. 27:19. *An ingredient of the sacred oil*, Ex. 30:24.

**‡ CALAMUS.** *A sweet cane of Palestine*, Song 4:14; Ezek. 27:19. *An ingredient of the holy ointment*, Ex. 30:23; Isa. 43:24. *Commerce in*, Jer. 6:20; Ezek. 27:19.

‖ **MARINER**, 1 Kin. 9:27, 2 Chr. 8:18; Isa. 42:10; Ezek. 27:27. *Perils of*, Psa. 107:23–30; Jonah 1:5; Acts 27:17–44. *Cowardice of*, Acts 27:30.

shall wallow themselves in the [e]ashes:

31[Q] And [d]they shall make themselves utterly [f]bald for thee, and gird them with [g]sackcloth, and they shall weep for thee with bitterness of heart *and* bitter wailing.

32 And in their [d]wailing they shall take up a lamentation for thee, and lament over thee, *saying*, What *city is* like [b]Tȳ′rus, like [20]the destroyed in the midst of the sea?[Q]

33 When thy wares went forth out of the seas, thou filledst many people; thou didst enrich the kings of the earth with the multitude of thy riches and of thy merchandise.[Q]

34 In the time *when* [b]thou shalt be broken by the seas in the depths of the waters thy merchandise and all thy company in the midst of thee [c]shall fall.

35 All the inhabitants of the isles shall be astonished[G] at thee, and their kings shall be sore[G] afraid, they shall be troubled in *their* [h]countenance.

36 The merchants among the [21]people shall hiss at thee; thou shalt be a terror, and never *shalt be* any more.[Q]

## CHAPTER 28

*God's judgment upon the prince of Tyre for his impious pride. 11 A lamentation over his destruction. 20 Judgments upon Zidon. 24 The restoration of Israel.*

THE [a]word of the LORD came again unto [b]me, saying,

2 Son of man, say unto the [c]prince of [d]Tȳ′rus, Thus saith the Lord GOD; Because thine [e]heart *is* lifted[G] up, and thou hast [f,g]said, [h,i]I *am* a [1]God, I sit *in* the seat of God, in the midst of the seas; yet thou *art* a man, and not God, though thou set thine heart as the heart of God:[Q]

e *Ashes, sitting in,* Num. 19:9.

**31**

f *Baldness, artificial, a sign of mourning,* Lev. 21:5.

g *Sackcloth,* Isa. 15:3.

**32**

20 R. V. her that is brought to silence in

**35**

h *Countenance,* Prov. 15:13.

**36**

21 R. V. peoples

**1**

a *Prophecies, inspired,* Dan. 9:24.

b *Ezekiel,* Ezek. 1:3.

**2**

c *Rulers, wicked,* Ex. 18.21.

d Or, *Tyre, prophecies relating to,* Josh. 19:29.

e *Pride, instances of,* vs. 2–9, 17; Prov. 16:18.

f *Blasphemy, exalting oneself above God,* 2 Sam. 12:14.

g *Boasting,* Prov. 25:14.

h *King, deification of,* 2 Kin. 3:10.

i *Self-exaltation, instances of,* Luke 14:11.

1 R. V. god,

3 Behold, [j]thou *art* wiser than [k]Dăn′iel; there is no secret that they can hide from thee:

4 With thy [l]wisdom and with thine understanding thou hast gotten thee [m]riches, and hast gotten [n]gold and [o]silver into thy treasures[G]:

5 By thy great [l]wisdom *and* by thy [p]traffick[G] hast thou increased thy [q]riches, and thine [e]heart is lifted[G] up because of thy riches:

6 Therefore thus saith the Lord GOD; Because thou hast [h,i]set thine heart as the heart of God;

7 Behold, therefore I will [r,s]bring [t]strangers upon thee, the terrible of the nations: and they shall draw their [u]swords against the beauty of thy wisdom, and they shall defile thy brightness.

8 [r]They shall bring thee down to the pit, and thou shalt [s,v]die the deaths of *them that are* slain in the midst of the seas.

9 Wilt thou yet [f,g]say before him that slayeth thee, [h,i]I *am* God? but thou *shalt be* a man, and no[G] God, in the hand of him that [2]slayeth[G] thee.

10 Thou shalt [s,v]die the deaths of the uncircumcised[G] by the hand of strangers[G]: for I have spoken *it*, saith the Lord GOD.

11 ¶ Moreover the [a]word of the LORD came unto [b]me, saying,

12 Son of man, take up a lamentation upon the [c]king of [d]Tȳ′rus, and say unto him, Thus saith the Lord GOD; Thou sealest up the sum, full of [l]wisdom, and perfect in [w]beauty.

13 Thou hast been in [x]Ē′dĕn the garden of God; every [y]precious stone *was* thy covering, the [z]sardius, *topaz, and the [a]diamond, the [b]beryl, the †onyx, and

**3**

j *Irony, instances of,* vs. 3–5; Mark 12:14.

k *Daniel, wisdom of,* Dan. 1:6.

**4**

l *Wisdom, worldly,* Prov. 2:2.

m *Riches,* Eccl. 4:8.

n *Gold,* Ezek. 7:19.

o *Silver,* 1 Chr. 28:14.

**5**

p *Commerce,* 1 Kin. 10:15.

q *Riches, a snare,* Eccl. 4:8.

**7**

r *Divine Chastisement,* Job 33:19.

s *Wicked, punishment of,* Psa. 73:3.

t *Agency, in executing judgments,* Mark 1:17.

u *War, as a judgment,* Judg. 3:2.

**8**

v *Death, of the wicked, a judgment,* Num. 23:10.

**9**

2 R. V. woundeth

**12**

w *Beauty,* Prov. 6:25.

**13**

x *Eden,* Isa. 51:3.

y *Precious Stones,* Ex. 39:10.

z *Sardius,* Ex. 28:17.

a *Diamond,* Ex. 39:11.

b *Beryl,* Ezek. 1:16.

* **TOPAZ.** *A precious stone,* Ezek. 28:13; Rev. 21:20. *In the breastplate of the high priest,* Ex. 28:17; 39:10. *Of Ethiopia, celebrated,* Job 28:19.

† **ONYX.** *Precious stone,* Job 28:16; Ezek. 28:13. *In the breastplate of the high priest,* Ex. 28:9–12, 20; 39:6, 13. *Contributed by Israelites for the priests' vestments,* Ex. 25:7; 35:9. *Used in the temple,* 1 Chr. 29:2. *Seen in the foundations of the city of the New Jerusalem in John's apocalyptic vision,* Rev. 21:20. *Exported from Havilah,* Gen. 2:12.
See footnote, PRECIOUS STONES, Ex. 39:10.

the [c]jasper, the [d]sapphire, the [e]emerald, and the [f]carbuncle, and [g]gold: the workmanship of thy [h]tabrets[G] and of thy [h]pipes[G] was prepared in thee in the day that thou wast created.[Q]

14 Thou *art* the anointed cherub that covereth; and I have set thee *so*: thou wast upon the holy mountain of God; thou hast walked up and down in the midst of the stones of fire.

15 Thou *wast* perfect in thy ways from the day that thou wast created, till iniquity was found in thee.

16 By the multitude of thy [i]merchandise they have filled the midst of thee with violence, and thou hast sinned: [j]therefore I will [k]cast thee as profane out of the mountain of God: and I will destroy thee, O covering cherub, from the midst of the stones of fire.

17 Thine [l]heart was lifted[G] up because of thy [m]beauty, thou hast corrupted thy [n]wisdom by reason of thy brightness: I will [k]cast thee to the ground, I will lay thee before kings, that they may behold thee.

18 Thou hast defiled thy sanctuaries by the multitude of thine iniquities, by the iniquity of thy traffick[G]; therefore will I bring forth a fire from the midst of thee, it shall [k]devour thee, and I will bring thee to ashes upon the earth in the sight of all them that behold thee.

19 All they that know thee among the [3]people shall be astonished[G] at thee: thou shalt be a terror, and never *shalt* thou *be* any more.

20 ¶ Again the [o]word of the LORD [p]came unto me, saying,

21 Son of man, set thy face against ‡Zī′dŏn, and prophesy against it,

22 And say, Thus saith the Lord GOD; Behold, I *am* against thee, O ‡Zī′dŏn; and I will be glorified in the midst of thee: and [q]they shall know that I *am* the LORD, when I shall have executed judgments in her, and shall be sanctified in her.

23 For I will send into her [r]pestilence, and blood into her streets; and the wounded shall be judged in the midst of her by the [s]sword upon her on every side; and [q]they shall know that I *am* the LORD.

24 ¶ And there shall be no more a pricking brier unto the house of Ĭş′ra-el, nor *any* grieving thorn of all *that are* round about them, that [4]despised them; and [q]they shall know that I *am* the Lord GOD.

25 Thus saith the Lord GOD; When [t]I shall have [u]gathered the [v]house of Ĭş′ra-el from the [3]people among whom they are scattered[G], and shall be sanctified in them in the sight of the [5]heathen[G], then shall they dwell in their [u,w]land that I have given to my servant Jā′cob.

26 And they shall [u]dwell safely therein, and shall build houses, and plant vineyards; yea, they shall dwell with confidence, when I have executed judgments upon all those that [6]despise[G] them round about them; and [q]they shall know that I *am* the LORD their God.

c *Jasper*, Rev. 21:19.
d *Sapphire*, Job 28:6.
e *Emerald*, Rev. 4:3.
f *Carbuncle*, Isa. 54:12.
g *Gold*, Ezek. 7:19.
h *Music, instruments of*, 2 Chr. 5:13.

16
i *Commerce*, 1 Kin. 10:15.
j *Sin, repugnant to God*, Rom. 5:12.
k *Wicked, punishment of*, Psa. 73:3.

17
l *Pride*, Prov. 16:18.
m *Beauty*, Prov. 6:25.
n *Wisdom, worldly*, Prov. 2:2.

19
3 R. V. peoples

20
o *Prophecies, inspired*, Dan. 9:24.
p *Prophets, inspiration of*, Isa. 3:2.

22
q *Judgments, design of*, Ex. 6:6.

23
r *Plague, as a judgment*, Ex. 11:1.
s *War, as a judgment*, Judg. 3:2.

24
4 R. V. did despite unto them;

25
t *God, mercy of*, Gen. 2:2.
u *Temporal Blessings, from God*, Psa. 103:2.
v *Jews, prophecies concerning*, Neh. 4:2.
w *Canaan*, Gen. 37:1.
5 R. V. nations.

26
6 R. V. do them despite round

‡ **ZIDON**, called also SIDON. *A city on the coast of the Mediterranean Sea north of Tyre, and the northern boundary of the Canaanites*, Gen. 10:19. *Designated by Jacob as the border of Zebulun*, Gen. 49:13. *Was on the northern boundary of Asher*, Josh. 19:28; 2 Sam. 24:6. *Belonged to the land of Israel according to promise*, Josh. 13:6. *Idolatry of*, Judg. 10:6; 1 Kin. 11:5. *Inhabitants of, dwelt in security and carelessness*, Judg. 18:7. *Israelites failed to make conquest of*, Judg. 1:31; 3:3. *The inhabitants of, contributed cedar for the first and second temples*, 1 Kin. 5:6; 1 Chr. 22:4; Ezra 3:7. *Solomon marries women of*, 1 Kin. 11:1. *Ahab marries a woman of*, 1 Kin. 16:31. *People of, come to hear Jesus*, Mark 3:8; Luke 6:17. *Inhabitants of, offend Herod*, Acts 12:20–23. *Commerce of*, Isa. 23:2. *Seamen of*, Ezek. 27:8. *Prophecies concerning*, Jer. 25:15–22; 27:3–11; 47:4; Ezek. 28:21–23; 32:30; Joel 3:4–8. *Jesus visits the region of, and heals the daughter of the Syrophenician woman*, Matt. 15:21–28; Mark 7:24–31. *Visited by Paul*, Acts 27:3.

v.1–509 BC
See footnote, *Time*, Rev. 10:6.

1
*a* Esth. 2:16.
*b* *Month* (*January*), Ex. 12:2.
*c* *Prophecies, inspired*, Dan. 9:24.
*d* *Ezekiel*, Ezek. 1:3.

2
*e* *Pharaoh-hophra, prophecies concerning*, vs. 1–21; Jer. 44:30.
*f* *Egypt, prophecies concerning*, Gen. 41:8.

3
*g* *Dragon, symbolical*, Deut. 32:33.
*h* *Boasting*, Prov. 25:14.
*i* *Pride*, Prov. 16:18.
*j* *Nile*, Isa. 11:15.

4
*k* *Nation, judgments denounced against*, Isa. 2:4.

6
*l* *Egyptians*, Gen. 50:3.
*m* *Judgments, design of*, Ex. 6:6.

8
*n* *War, as a judgment*, Judg. 3:2.

## CHAPTER 29

*Pharaoh's destruction foretold. 8 The desolation of Egypt. 13 The restoration thereof after forty years. 17 Egypt to be given to Nebuchadrezzar. 21 A promise to Israel.*

IN the tenth year, in the [a]tenth [b]*month*, in the twelfth *day* of the month, the [c]word of the LORD came unto [d]me, saying,

2 Son of man, set thy face against [e]Phā'raōh king of [f]Ē'ġy̆pt, and prophesy[c] against him, and against all Ē'ġy̆pt:

3 Speak, and say, [c]Thus saith the Lord GOD; Behold, I *am* against thee, [e]Phā'raōh king of [f]Ē'ġy̆pt, the great [g]dragon that lieth in the midst of his rivers, which hath [h,i]said, My [j]river *is* mine own, and I have made *it* for myself.

4 But [k]I will put hooks in thy jaws, and I will cause the fish of thy rivers to stick unto thy scales, and I will bring thee up out of the midst of thy rivers, and all the fish of thy rivers shall stick unto thy scales.

5 And [k]I will leave thee *thrown* into the wilderness, thee and all the fish of thy rivers: thou shalt fall upon the open fields; thou shalt not be brought together, nor gathered: I have given thee for meat[c] to the beasts of the field and to the fowls of the heaven.[Q]

6 And all the [l]inhabitants of [f]Ē'ġy̆pt [m]shall know that I *am* the LORD, because they have been a staff[c] of reed to the house of Ĭs'ra-el.

7 When they took hold of thee by thy hand, thou didst break, and rend[c] all their shoulder: and when they leaned upon thee, thou brakest, and madest all their loins to be at a stand.

8 ¶ Therefore thus saith the Lord GOD; [k]Behold, I will bring a [n]sword upon thee, and cut off man and beast out of thee.

9 [k]And the land of [f]Ē'ġy̆pt shall be desolate and waste; and [m]they shall know that I *am* the LORD: because he hath [h,i]said, The [j]river *is* mine, and I have made *it*.

10 Behold, therefore I *am* against thee, and against thy rivers, and [k]I will make the land of [f]Ē'ġy̆pt utterly waste *and* desolate, from the [o]tower of [p]Sy̆-ē'ne even unto the border of [q]Ē-thĭ-ō'pĭ-ȧ.

11 [f,k]No foot of man shall pass through it, nor foot of beast shall pass through it, neither shall it be inhabited [r]forty years.

12 And I will make the land of [f]Ē'ġy̆pt desolate in the midst of the countries *that are* desolate, and her cities among the cities *that are* laid waste shall be desolate [r]forty years: and [k]I will scatter the [s]Ē-ġy̆p'tians among the nations, and will disperse them through the countries.

13 ¶ Yet thus saith the Lord GOD; At the end of [r]forty years will I gather the [s]Ē-ġy̆p'tians from the [1]people whither[c] they were scattered:

14 And [t]I will bring again the captivity of [f]Ē'ġy̆pt, and will cause [s]them to return *into* the land of [u]Păth'ros, into the land of their habitation; and they shall be there a base[c] kingdom.[T]

15 [f]It shall be the basest of the kingdoms; neither shall it exalt itself any more above the nations: for I will diminish [s]them, that they shall no more rule over the nations.

16 And it shall be no more the [v]confidence of the house of Ĭs'ra-el, which bringeth *their* iniquity to remembrance, when they shall look after them: but [m]they shall know that I *am* the Lord GOD.

17 ¶ And it came to pass in the seven and twentieth year, in the first [w]*month*, in the first *day* of

10
*o* *Tower*, 2 Chr. 26:9.
*p* Ezek. 30:6.
*q* *Ethiopia*, Isa. 18:1.

11
*r* *Forty, years*, Jonah 3:4.

12
*s* *Egyptians, prophecies concerning*, Gen. 50:3.

13
1 R. V. peoples

14
*t* *God, providence of*, Gen. 2:2.
*u* *Pathros*, Isa. 11:11.

16
*v* *False Confidence*, Psa. 30:6.

17
*w* *Month* (*April*), Ex. 12:2.

v.17–492 BC
See footnote, *Time*, Rev. 10:6.

18
x Or, *Nebuchadnezzar, conquests of*, Dan. 2:1.
y *Babylon, empire of*, Ezra 5:12.
z Or, *Tyre*, Josh. 19:29.
a *Baldness, artificial*, Lev. 21:5.

19
b *Government, God in*, Isa. 22:21.
c *God, providence of*, Gen. 2:2.
d *Egypt, prophecies against*, Gen. 41:8.
e Or, *Nebuchadnezzar*, Dan. 2:1.
f *Babylon, empire of*, Ezra 5:12.

20
g *Agency, in executing judgments*, Mark 1:17.

the month, the [c]word of the
LORD came unto me, saying,
18 Son of man, [x]Něb-u-chad-
rĕz′zar king of [y]Băb′ȳ-lon caused
his army to serve a great service against [z]Tȳ′rus: every head
*was* made [a]bald, and every
shoulder *was* peeled[C]: yet had he
no wages, nor his army, for Tȳ′-
rus, for the service that he had
served against it:
19 [S] Therefore thus saith the
Lord GOD; Behold, [b,c]I will give
the land of [d]Ē′ġȳpt unto [e]Něb-
u-chad-rĕz′zar king of [f]Băb′ȳ-
lon; and he shall take her multitude, and take her spoil, and
take her prey; and it shall be the
wages for his army.
20 [c]I have given him the land
of [d]Ē′ġȳpt *for* his labour wherewith he served against it, because [g]they wrought for me,
saith the Lord GOD.[S]
21 In that day will I cause the
horn[C] of the house of Ĭs′ra-el to
bud forth, and I will give thee
the opening of the mouth in the
midst of them; and they shall
know that I *am* the LORD.

## CHAPTER 30

*The desolation of Egypt and her allies. 20 Egypt to be subdued by the king of Babylon.*

1
a *Prophecies, inspired*, Dan. 9:24.
b *Ezekiel*, Ezek. 1:3.

3
c *Day, times of adversity called day of the Lord*, Gen. 1:5.

4
d *War, as a judgment*, Judg. 3:2.
e *Egypt, prophecies against*, Gen. 41:8.
f *Nation, judgments denounced against*, Isa. 2:4.
g *Ethiopia, desolation of*, Isa. 18:1.
1 R. V. anguish shall

5
h *Libya*, Acts 2:10.
i Or, *Lud*, Ezek. 27:10.

THE [a]word of the LORD came
again unto [b]me, saying,
2 Son of man, prophesy and
say, Thus saith the Lord GOD;
Howl ye, Woe[C] worth the day!
3 For the [c]day *is* near, even
the day of the LORD *is* near, a
cloudy day; it shall be the time
of the heathen[C].
4 And the [d]sword shall come
upon [e,f]Ē′ġȳpt, and [1]great pain
shall be in [g]Ē-thĭ-ō′pĭ-ȧ, when
the slain shall fall in Ē′ġȳpt, and
they shall take away her multitude, and her foundations shall
be broken down.
5 [g]Ē-thĭ-ō′pĭ-ȧ, and [h]Lĭb′ȳ-ȧ,
and [i]Lȳd′ĭ-ȧ, and all the mingled
people, and Chŭb, and the men
of the land that is in [j]league,
shall fall with them by the
[d]sword.
6 Thus saith the LORD; They
also that uphold [e]Ē′ġȳpt shall
fall; and the pride of her power
shall come down: from the tower
of [k]Sȳ-ē′ne shall they fall in it by
the [d]sword, saith the Lord GOD.
7 And they shall be desolate in
the midst of the countries *that
are* desolate, and her cities shall
be in the midst of the cities *that
are* wasted.
8 And [l]they shall know that I
*am* the LORD, when I have [m]set
a fire in [e]Ē′ġȳpt, and *when* all
her helpers shall be destroyed.
9 In that day shall [n]messengers
go forth from me in ships to
make the careless[C] [g]Ē-thĭ-ō′pĭ-
ans afraid, and [2]great pain shall
come upon them, as in the day
of Ē′ġȳpt: for, lo[C], it cometh.
10 Thus saith the Lord GOD;
I will also make the multitude
of [e]Ē′ġȳpt to cease [n]by the hand
of [o]Něb-u-chad-rĕz′zar king of
[p]Băb′ȳ-lon.
11 [n,o]He and his people with
him, the terrible of the nations,
shall be brought to destroy the
land: and they shall draw their
[d]swords against [e]Ē′ġȳpt, and fill
the land with the slain.
12 [f]And I will make the rivers
dry, and sell the land into the
hand of the wicked: and I will
make the land waste, and all
that is therein, [n]by the hand of
strangers[C]: I the LORD have
spoken *it*.
13 Thus saith the Lord GOD;
[f]I will also destroy the [q]idols,
and I will cause *their* images to
cease out of [r]Nŏph; and there
shall be no more a prince of the
land of [e]Ē′ġȳpt: and I will put a
fear in the land of Ē′ġȳpt.
14 And I will make [s]Păth′-
ros desolate, and will set fire in

j *Alliances*, Josh. 9:15.

6
k Ezek. 29:10.

8
l *Judgments, design of*, Ex. 6:6.
m *Divine Chastisement*, Job 33:19.

9
n *Agency, in executing judgments*, Mark 1:17.
2 R. V. there shall be anguish upon

10
o Or, *Nebuchadnezzar*, Dan. 2:1.
p *Babylon, empire of*, Ezra 5:12.

13
q *Idolatry, objects of*, 1 Sam. 15:23.
r *Noph, prophecies against*, Isa. 19:13.

14
s *Pathros*, Isa. 11:11.

[t]Zō′an, and will execute judgments in [u]Nō.[T]

15 And I will pour my fury upon Sĭn, the strength of Ē′ġy̆pt; and I will cut[C] off the multitude of [u]Nō.

16 And I will set fire in [e]Ē′ġy̆pt: Sĭn shall have great [3]pain, and [u]Nō shall be rent[G] asunder,[C] and [r]Nŏph *shall have* [4]distresses daily.

17 The young men of Ā′ven and of Pī–be′seth shall fall by the [d]sword: and these *cities* shall go into [v]captivity.

18 At [w]Tĕ-hăph′ne-hēş also the day shall be darkened, when I shall break there the yokes of Ē′ġy̆pt: and the pomp of her strength shall cease in her: as for her, a cloud shall cover her, and her [x]daughters shall go into [v]captivity.

19 [f]Thus will I execute judgments in [e]Ē′ġy̆pt: and [i]they shall know that I *am* the LORD.

20 ¶ And it came to pass in the eleventh year, in the first [y]*month,* in the seventh *day* of the month, *that* the [z]word of the LORD [a]came unto me, saying,

21 Son of man, I have broken the arm of [b]Phā′raōh king of [c]Ē′ġy̆pt; and, lo,[C] it shall not be bound up to [5]be healed, to put a roller[C] to bind it, to make it strong to hold the sword.

22 Therefore thus saith the Lord GOD; Behold, I *am* against [b]Phā′raōh king of [c]Ē′ġy̆pt, and will break his arms, the strong, and that which was broken; and I will cause the sword to fall out of his hand.

23 And I will scatter the [d,e]Ē-ġy̆p′tianş among the nations, and will disperse them through the countries.

24 And I will strengthen the arms of the [f]king of [g]Băb′y̆-lon, and put my [h]sword in his hand: but I will break [b]Phā′raōh's arms, and he shall groan before him with the groanings of a deadly wounded *man.*

25 But I will strengthen the arms of the [f]king of [g]Băb′y̆-lon, and the arms of [b]Phā′raōh shall fall down; and [i]they shall know that I *am* the LORD, when I shall put my [h]sword into the hand of the king of Băb′y̆-lon, and he shall stretch it out upon the land of Ē′ġy̆pt.

26 And I will scatter the [d,e]Ē-ġy̆p′tianş among the nations, and disperse them among the countries; and [i]they shall know that I *am* the LORD.

## CHAPTER 31

*A recital to Pharaoh of the glory of Assyria, 10 and the ruin thereof. 18 Like destruction to come upon Egypt.*

AND it came to pass in the eleventh year, in the third [a]*month,* in the first *day* of the month, *that* the [b]word of the LORD came unto [c]me, saying,

2 Son of man, speak unto [d]Phā′raōh king of [e]Ē′ġy̆pt, and to his multitude; Whom art thou like in thy greatness?

3 Behold, the [f]Ăs-sy̆r′ĭ-an *was* a [g]cedar in Lĕb′a-non with fair branches, and with a shadowing shroud,[C] and of an high stature; and his top was among the thick boughs.

4 The waters made him great, the deep set him up on high with her rivers running round about his plants, and sent out her [1,h]little rivers unto all the trees of the field.

5 Therefore his height was exalted above all the trees of the field, and his boughs were multiplied, and his branches became long because of the multitude of waters, when he shot forth.

6 All the fowls of heaven made their nests in his boughs, and under his branches did all the beasts of the field bring forth their young,

t *Zoan,* Isa. 30:4.
u Jer. 46:25; Nah. 3:8.

**16**
3 R. V. anguish,
4 R. V. adversaries in the daytime.

**17**
v *Captivity, as a judgment,* Isa. 5:13.

**18**
w Or, *Tahapanes,* Jer. 2:16.
x *Women, taken captive,* Prov. 31:10.

**20**
y *Month* (*April*), Ex. 12:2.
z *Prophecies, inspired,* Dan. 9:24.

a *Prophets, inspiration of,* Isa. 3:2.
**v.20–508 BC**

**21**
b *Pharaoh-hophra, prophecies concerning,* Jer. 44:30.
c *Egypt,* Gen. 41:8.
5 R. V. apply healing medicines,

**23**
d *Egyptians, prophecies concerning,* Gen. 50:3.
e *Nation, judgments denounced against,* Isa. 2:4.

**24**
f *Agency, in executing judgments,* Mark 1:17.
g *Babylon,* Ezra 5:12.
h *War, as a judgment,* Judg. 3:2.

**25**
i *Judgments, design of,* Ex. 6:6.

**v.1–508 BC**

**1**
a *Month* (*June*), Ex. 12:2.
b *Prophecies, inspired,* Dan. 9:24.
c *Ezekiel,* Ezek. 1:3.

**2**
d *Pharaoh-hophra,* Jer. 44:30.
e *Egypt, prophecies against,* Gen. 41:8.

**3**
f *Assyria, prophecies concerning,* Gen. 25:18.
g *Cedar, figurative,* Isa. 9:10.

**4**
h *Irrigation,* Eccl. 2:6.
1 R. V. channels

and under his shadow dwelt all
great nations.[Q]
7 Thus was he fair in his
greatness, in the length of his
branches: for his root was by
great waters.
8 The [g]cedars in the garden of
God could not hide him: the fir
trees were not like his boughs,
and the [2]chesnut trees were not
like his branches; nor any tree in
the garden of God was like unto
him in his beauty.[Q]
9 I have made him fair by the
multitude of his branches: so
that all the trees of [i]Ē'dĕn, that
*were* in the garden of God, envied him.
10 ¶ Therefore thus saith the
Lord GOD; Because thou hast
[j]lifted[C] up thyself in height, and
he hath shot up his top among
the thick boughs, and his heart
is lifted[C] up in his height;
11 I have therefore [k,l]delivered
him into the hand of the mighty
one of the [3]heathen[C]; [m]he shall
surely deal with him: I have
driven him out for his wickedness.
12 And [m]strangers, the terrible
of the nations, have cut him off,
and have left him: upon the
mountains and in all the valleys
his branches are fallen, and his
boughs are broken by all the
rivers of the land; and all the
[4]people of the earth are gone
down from his shadow, and have
left him.
13 Upon his ruin shall all the
fowls of the heaven remain, and
all the beasts of the field shall be
upon his branches:
14 [n]To the end that none of
all the trees by the waters exalt
themselves for their height, neither shoot up their top among
the thick boughs, [5]neither their
trees stand up in their height, all
that drink water: for they are
all [l]delivered unto death, to the
nether[C] parts of the earth, in the
midst of the children of men, with
them that go down to the pit.
15 Thus saith the Lord GOD;
In the day when he went down
to [6]the grave[C] I caused a mourning: I covered the deep[C] for him,
and I restrained the floods thereof, and the great waters were
stayed: and I caused Lĕb'a-non
to mourn for him, and all the
trees of the field fainted for him.
16 I made the nations to shake
at the sound of his fall, when I
cast him down to [o]hell[C] with them
that descend into the pit: and
all the trees of [i]Ē'dĕn, the choice
and best of Lĕb'a-non, all that
drink water, shall be comforted
in the nether[C] parts of the earth.
17 They also went down into
[o]hell[C] with him unto *them that be*
slain with the sword; and *they*
*that were* his arm, *that* dwelt under his shadow in the midst of
the [3]heathen[C].
18 ¶ To whom art thou thus
like in glory and in greatness
among the trees of [i]Ē'dĕn? yet
shalt thou be brought down with
the trees of Ē'dĕn unto the nether[C] parts of the earth: [k,l]thou
shalt lie in the midst of the
uncircumcised with *them that*
*be* slain by the sword. This is
[d]Phā'raōh and all his multitude,
saith the Lord GOD.

## CHAPTER 32

*The terrible fall of Egypt. 11 The sword of Babylon shall destroy it. 17 It shall be brought down to the pit, among all the uncircumcised nations.*

AND it came to pass in the
twelfth year, in the twelfth
[a]month, in the first *day* of the
month, *that* the [b]word of the
LORD [c]came unto [d]me, saying,
2 Son of man, take up a lamentation for [e]Phā'raōh king of
[f]Ē'gȳpt, and say unto him, Thou
art like a young lion of the nations, and thou *art* as a [1]whale in

8
2 R. V. plane

9
i *Eden,* Isa. 51:3.

10
j *Self-exaltation,* vs. 10–14; Luke 14:11.

11
k *Divine Chastisement, inflicted for sins,* Job 33:19.
l *Wicked, punishment of,* Psa. 73:3.
m *Agency, in executing judgments,* Mark 1:17.
3 R. V. nations;

12
4 R. V. peoples

14
n *Judgments, design of,* Ex. 6:6.
5 R. V. nor that their mighty ones stand up

15
6 Am. R. V. Sheol

16
o *Hell,* Mark 9:43.

v.1–507 BC
See footnote, *Time* Rev. 10:6.

1
a *Month (March),* Ex. 12:2.
b *Prophecies, inspired,* Dan. 9:24.
c *Inspiration,* Job 32:8.
d *Ezekiel,* Ezek. 1:3.

2
e *Pharaoh-hophra,* Jer. 44:30.
f *Egypt, prophecies against,* vs. 1–32; Gen. 41:8.
1 R. V. dragon

3
g *Nation, judgments denounced against*, vs. 1–32; Isa. 2:4.
h *Agency, in executing judgments*, Mark 1:17.
2 R. V. peoples;

4
3 R. V. settle

10
i *War, as a judgment*, Judg. 3:2.

11
j *Babylon, empire of, prophecies concerning*, Ezra 5:12.

the seas: and thou camest forth with thy rivers, and troubledst the waters with thy feet, and fouledst their rivers.

3 Thus saith the Lord GOD; [g]I will therefore spread out my net over thee with a company of many [2]people; and [h]they shall bring thee up in my net.

4 [f,g]Then will I leave thee upon the land, I will cast thee forth upon the open field, and will cause all the fowls of the heaven to [3]remain upon thee, and I will fill the beasts of the whole earth with thee.[s]

5 [f,g]And I will lay thy flesh upon the mountains, and fill the valleys with thy height.

6 [f,g]I will also water with thy blood the land wherein thou swimmest, *even* to the mountains; and the rivers shall be full of thee.

7 [Q]And [g]when I shall put thee out, I will cover the heaven, and make the stars thereof dark; I will cover the sun with a cloud, and the moon shall not give her light.

8 All the bright lights of heaven will I make dark over thee, and set darkness upon thy land, saith the Lord GOD.[Q]

9 I will also vex[C] the hearts of many [2]people, when I shall bring thy [g]destruction among the nations, into the countries which thou hast not known.

10 Yea, I will make many [2]people amazed[C] at thee, and their kings shall be horribly afraid for thee, when I shall brandish my [i]sword before them; and they shall tremble at *every* moment, every man for his own life, in the day of thy fall.

11 ¶ For thus saith the Lord GOD; The [i]sword of the [h]king of [j]Băb′ȳ-lon shall come upon thee.

12 [g]By the [i]swords of the mighty will I cause thy multitude to fall, the terrible of the nations, all of them: and they shall spoil[C] the [4]pomp of [f]Ē′ġȳpt, and all the multitude thereof shall be destroyed.

13 I will destroy also all the beasts thereof from beside the great waters; neither shall the foot of man trouble them any more, nor the hoofs of beasts trouble them.

14 Then will I make their waters [5]deep, and cause their rivers to run like oil, saith the Lord GOD.

15 When I shall make the land of [f,g]Ē′ġȳpt desolate, and [6]the country shall be destitute of that whereof it was full, when I shall smite all them that dwell therein, [k]then shall they know that I *am* the LORD.

16 This *is* the lamentation wherewith they shall lament her: the daughters of the nations shall lament her: they shall lament for her, *even* for [f]Ē′ġȳpt, and for all her multitude, saith the Lord GOD.

17 ¶ It came to pass also in the twelfth year, in the fifteenth *day* of the month, *that* the [b]word of the LORD [c]came unto [d]me, saying,

18 Son of man, wail for the multitude of [f]Ē′ġȳpt, and cast them down, *even* her, and the daughters of the famous nations, unto the nether[C] parts of the earth, with them that go down into the pit.

19 Whom dost thou pass in beauty? go down, and be thou laid with the uncircumcised.[C]

20 They shall fall in the midst of *them that are* slain by the [i]sword: [g]she is delivered to the sword: draw her and all her multitudes.

21 The strong among the mighty shall speak to him out of the midst of [7]hell[C] with them that

v.17–507 BC
See footnote, *Time*, Rev. 10:6.

12
4 R. V. pride

14
5 R. V. clear,

15
k *Judgments, design of*, Ex. 6:6.
6 R. V. waste, a land destitute

21
7 Am. R. V. Sheol

help him: [g]they are gone down,
they lie uncircumcised, slain by
the sword.
22 Ăs′shụr *is* there and all her
company: his graves *are* about
him: all of them [g]slain, fallen by
the [i]sword:
23 Whose graves are set in the
[8]sides of the pit, and her company is round about her grave:
all of them slain, fallen by the
[i]sword, which caused terror in
the land of the living.
24 There *is* [l]Ē′lăm and all
her multitude round about her
grave, all of them slain, fallen by
the [i]sword, which are gone down
uncircumcised into the nether[C]
parts of the earth, which caused
their terror in the land of the
living; yet have they borne their
shame with them that go down
to the pit.
25 They have set her a bed in
the midst of the slain with all her
multitude: her graves *are* round
about [9]him: all of them uncircumcised, slain by the [i]sword:
though their terror was caused in
the land of the living, yet have
they borne their shame with
them that go down to the pit: he
is put in the midst of *them that be*
slain.
26 There *is* [m]Mē′shech, [n]Tụ′-
bal, and all her multitude: her
graves *are* round about [9]him: all
of them uncircumcised, slain by
the sword, though they caused
their terror in the land of the
living.
27 And they shall not lie with
the mighty *that are* fallen of the
uncircumcised,[C] which are gone
down to [7]hell with their weapons of war: and they have laid
their swords under their heads,
but their iniquities shall be upon
their bones, though *they were* the
terror of the mighty in the land
of the living.
28 Yea, [f, g]thou shalt be broken
in the midst of the uncircumcised, and shalt lie with *them that*
*are* slain with the sword.
29 There *is* [o]Ē′dom, her kings,
and all her princes, which with
their might are laid by *them that*
*were* slain by the [i]sword: they
shall lie with the uncircumcised,
and with them that go down to
the pit.
30 There *be* the princes of the
north, all of them, and all the
[p]Zī-dō′nĭ-anṣ, which are gone
down with the slain; [10]with their
terror they are ashamed of their
might; and they lie uncircumcised[C] with *them that be* slain by
the [i]sword, and bear their shame
with them that go down to the
pit.
31 [e]Phā′raōh shall see them,
and shall be comforted over all
his multitude, *even* Phā′raōh and
all his army slain by the [i]sword,
saith the Lord GOD.
32 For I have caused my terror
in the land of the living: and [e]he
shall be laid in the midst of the
uncircumcised[C] with *them that are*
slain with the [i]sword, *even* Phā′-
raōh and all his [g]multitude, saith
the Lord GOD.

## CHAPTER 33

*The prophet is admonished of his duty as a watchman.* 10 *God hath no pleasure in the death of the wicked.* 21 *The desolation of the land foretold.* 30 *Hypocrites rebuked.*

AGAIN the [a]word of the LORD
came unto [b]me, saying,
2 Son of man, speak to the children of thy people, and say unto
them, When I bring the [c]sword
upon a land, if the people of the
land take a man [1]of their coasts,[C]
and set him for their [d]watch-
man:
3 If when he seeth the [c]sword
come upon the land, he blow the
[e]trumpet, and warn the people;
4 Then whosoever [f]heareth the
sound of the [e]trumpet, and taketh
not warning; if the sword come,

23
8 R. V. uttermost parts of

24
l *Elam, prophecies concerning,* Isa. 11:11.

25
9 R. V. her:

26
m Ezek. 27:13; 38:2, 3.
n *Tubal,* Gen. 10:2.

29
o *Edomites, prophecies concerning,* 2 Kin. 8:21.

30
p *Zidon, prophecies concerning,* Ezek. 28:21.
10 Am. R. V. in the terror which they caused by their might they are put to shame;

1
a *Prophecies, inspired,* Dan. 9:24.
b *Ezekiel,* Ezek. 1:3.

2
c *War, as a judgment,* Judg. 3:2.
d *Watchman,* 2 Sam. 18:24.
1 R.V. from among them,

3
e *Trumpet,* Josh. 6:4.

4
f *Opportunity, measure of responsibility,* Gal. 6:10.

and take him away, [g]his blood shall be upon his own head.

5 He [f]heard the sound of the [e]trumpet, and took not warning; [g]his blood shall be upon him. But he that taketh warning shall deliver[C] his soul.[Q]

6 But if the [d]watchman see the sword come, and [h]blow not the [e]trumpet, and the people be not warned; if the [c]sword come, and take *any* person from among them, he is taken away in his iniquity; but his blood will I require at the watchman's hand.

7 So[S] thou, O son of man, I have set thee a [i,j]watchman unto the house of Ĭș′ra-el; therefore thou shalt hear the word at my mouth, and [k]warn them from me.

8 When I say unto the wicked, O wicked *man*, thou shalt surely [l]die; [j]if thou dost not speak to [k]warn the wicked from his way, that wicked *man* [m]shall die in his iniquity; but [n]his blood will I require at thine hand.[S]

9 Nevertheless, if [j]thou [f,k]warn the wicked of his way to turn from it; [o]if he [o]do not turn from his way, he shall [l,m]die in his iniquity; but [n]thou hast delivered thy soul.[S]

10 Therefore, O thou son of man, speak unto the house of Ĭș′ra-el; Thus ye speak, saying, If our transgressions and our sins *be* upon us, and we [p]pine away in them, how should we then live?[S]

11 Say unto them, *As* I live, saith the Lord GOD, [q]I have no pleasure in the death of the wicked; but that the wicked turn from his way and live: [r,s]turn ye, turn ye from your evil ways; for why will ye [l]die, O house of Ĭș′ra-el?

12 Therefore, thou son of man, say unto the children of thy people, [t]The [u]righteousness of the righteous shall not deliver him in the day of his [v]transgression: as for the wickedness of the wicked, [w,x]he shall not fall thereby in the day that he [y]turneth from his wickedness; neither shall the righteous be able to live for his *righteousness* in the day that he [v]sinneth.

13 When I shall say to the righteous, *that* he shall surely live; [z]if he trust to his [a]own righteousness, and commit iniquity, all his [b]righteousnesses shall not be remembered; but [c,d]for his iniquity that he hath committed, [e]he shall [f]die for it.

14 Again, when I say unto the wicked, Thou shalt surely [f]die; [g]if he [h]turn from his sin, and [i]do that which is lawful and right;

15 [g]*If* the wicked [j,k]restore the [l]pledge, [j,k]give again that he had [m]robbed, [i,k]walk in the statutes of life, without committing iniquity; [n,o,p]he shall surely live, he shall not [f]die.

16 [p]None of his sins that he hath committed shall be mentioned unto him: [k]he hath done that which is lawful and right; [n,o]he shall surely live.

17 ¶ Yet the children of thy people [q,r]say, The way of the Lord is not equal: but as for them, their way is not equal.

18 When the righteous turneth from his righteousness, and committeth iniquity, [c,e]he shall even [f]die thereby.

19 But [g]if the wicked [h]turn from his wickedness, and [i]do that which is lawful and right, [n,o,p]he shall live thereby.

20 Yet ye [q,r]say, The way of the Lord is not equal.[C] O ye house of Ĭș′ra-el, I will [s]judge you every one [c,d]after his ways.[T]

21 ¶ And it came to pass in the twelfth year of our [t,u]captivity, in the tenth [v]*month*, in the fifth *day* of the month, *that* one that had escaped out of [w]Jē-ru̧′sā-lĕm

g *Responsibility, according to privilege*, Ezek. 18:20.

6
h *Watchman, unfaithful*, 2 Sam. 18:24.

7
i *Watchman, figurative*, 2 Sam. 18:24.
j *Minister, duty of*, Rom. 15:16.
k *Wicked, warned*, Psa. 73:3.

8
l *Spiritual Death*, 1 John 3:14.
m *Wicked, punishment of*, Psa. 73:3.
n *Minister, responsibility of*, Rom. 15:16.

9
o *Impenitence*, Rom. 2:5.

10
p *Adversity, despondency in*, Psa. 10:6.

11
q *God, mercy of*, Gen. 2:2.
r *Commandment, enjoining repentance*, Deut. 8:2.
s *Repentance, enjoined*, Mark 1:4.

12
t *Judgment, according to opportunity and works*, 1 Pet. 1:17.
u *Works, insufficient for salvation*, 2 Tim. 1:9.

v.21–507 BC See footnote, *Time*, Rev. 10:6.

v *Apostasy*, Acts 1:25.
w *Penitent, promises to*, Psa. 51:17.
x *Promise, to penitents*, vs. 14–16; 2 Cor. 1:20.
y *Repentance*, Mark 1:4.

13
z *Contingencies in divine Government*, 1 Kin. 3:14.

a *Self-righteousness*, Luke 18:11.
b *Works, insufficient for salvation*, 2 Tim. 1:9.
c *Judgment, according to opportunity and works*, 1 Pet. 1:17.
d *Punishment, according to deeds*, Lev. 26:41.
e *Backsliders, punishment of*, Jer. 3:22.
f *Spiritual Death*, 1 John 3:14.

14
g *Contingencies in divine Government*, 1 Kin. 3:14.
h *Repentance*, Mark 1:4.
i *Obedience*, Heb. 5:8.

15
j *Restitution*, Ex. 22:3.
k *Righteousness, fruits of*, Psa. 15:2.
l *Pawn*, Job 24:3.
m *Robbery*, Ezek. 22:29.
n *Penitent, promises to*, Psa. 51:17.
o *Promise, to penitents*, 2 Cor. 1:20.
p *Sin, forgiveness of*, Rom. 5:12.

17
q *Blasphemy, imputing unrighteousness to God*, 2 Sam. 12:14.
r *Infidelity, exemplified, in impugning God's knowledge*, 2 Cor. 6:15.

20
s *God, judge*, Gen. 2:2.

21
t *Captivity*, Isa. 5:13.
u *Jews, captive in Babylon*, Neh. 4:2.
v *Month (January)*, Ex. 12:2.
w *Jerusalem*, Judg. 19:10.

came unto [x]me, saying, The city
is smitten.

22 Now [y]the hand of the LORD
was upon [x]me in the evening,
afore[c] he that was escaped came;
and had opened my mouth, until
he came to me in the morning;
and my mouth was opened, and
I was no more dumb.

23 Then the [z]word of the LORD
[y]came unto [x]me, saying,

24 Son of man, they that inhabit those wastes of the [a]land
of Ĭṣ'ra-el speak, saying, [b]Ā'brā-
hăm was one, and he inherited
the land: but we *are* many; the
land is given us for inheritance.

25 Wherefore say unto them,
Thus saith the Lord GOD; [c]Ye
eat with the [d]blood, and [e]lift up
your eyes toward your idols, and
[f]shed blood: and shall ye possess
the land?

26 [c]Ye stand upon your sword,
ye work abomination, and ye
[g]defile every one his neighbour's
wife: and shall ye possess the
land?

27 Say thou thus unto them,
Thus saith the Lord GOD; *As* I
live, surely [h]they that *are* in the
wastes[c] shall fall by the [i]sword,
and him that *is* in the open field
will I give to the beasts to be devoured, and they that *be* in the
[j]forts and in the [k]caves shall die
of the [l]pestilence.[Q]

28 For [h]I will [2]lay the land
most desolate, and the pomp
of her strength shall cease; and
the mountains of Ĭṣ'ra-el shall
be desolate, that none shall pass
through.

29 [m]Then shall they know that
I *am* the LORD, when I have laid
the land most desolate because
of all their [c]abominations[c] which
they have committed.

30 ¶ Also, thou son of man, the
children of thy people [3]still are
talking against thee by the walls
and in the doors of the houses,
and speak one to another, every
one to his brother, saying, Come,
I pray you, and hear what is the
word that cometh forth from the
LORD.

31 And they come unto thee as
the people cometh, and they sit
before thee *as* my people, and
they hear thy words, but they
[n]will not do them: for [o]with their
mouth they shew much love,
*but* their heart goeth after their
[4,p]covetousness.

32 And, lo[c], thou *art* unto them
as a very lovely song of [q]one that
hath a pleasant voice, and can
play well on an instrument: for
they hear thy words, but they
[n]do them not.

33 And when this cometh to
pass, (lo, it will come,) then shall
they know that a prophet hath
been among them.

## CHAPTER 34

*Woe denounced against the unfaithful shepherds of Israel. 11 God's care for his flock. 20 A promise of the great Shepherd.*

AND the [a]word of the LORD
came unto [b]me, saying,

2 Son[Q] of man, prophesy against
the [c,d]shepherds of Ĭṣ'ra-el,
prophesy[c], and say unto them,
Thus saith the Lord GOD unto
the shepherds; Woe *be* to the
shepherds of Ĭṣ'ra-el that do
[e,f]feed themselves! should not
the shepherds [g]feed the [h]flocks?

3 [d]Ye [e,f]eat the fat, and ye
clothe you with the [i]wool, ye kill
them that are fed: *but* ye feed not
the flock.[Q]

4 The diseased have [d]ye not
strengthened, neither have ye
healed that which was sick,
neither have ye bound up *that
which was* broken, neither have
ye brought again that which was
driven away, neither have ye
sought that which was lost; but
with force and with [1]cruelty have
ye ruled them.

x *Ezekiel*, Ezek. 1:3.

22
y *Prophets, inspiration of*, Isa. 3:2.

23
z *Prophecies, inspired*, Dan. 9:24.

24
a *Canaan*, Gen. 37:1.
b *Abraham*, Gen. 17:5.

25
c *Jews, wickedness of*, Neh. 4:2.
d *Blood, forbidden as food*, Gen. 9:4.
e *Idolatry*, 2 Sam. 15:23.
f *Homicide, felonious*, Deut. 5:17.

26
g *Adultery*, Lev. 20:10.

27
h *Nation, judgments denounced against*, Isa. 2:4.
i *War, as a judgment*, Judg. 3:2.
j *Fortification*, Ezek. 17:17.
k *Cave*, Judg. 6:2.
l *Plague, as a judgment*, Ex. 11:1.

28
2 R. V. make the land a desolation and an astonishment, and the pride of her power shall cease;

29
m *Judgment, design of*, Ex. 6:6.

30
3 R. V. talk of thee by

31
n *Minister, message of, rejected*, vs. 30–33; Rom. 15:16.
o *Hypocrisy*, Jas. 3:17.
p *Covetousness*, Isa. 57:17.
4 R. V. gain.

32
q *Orator*, Acts 24:1.

1
a *Prophecies, inspired*, Dan. 9:24.
b *Ezekiel*, Ezek. 1:3.

2
c *Shepherd, figurative*, vs. 1–31; Jer. 31:10.
d *Rulers, wicked*, Ex. 18:21.
e *Selfishness*, 2 Tim. 3:2.
f *Covetousness*, Isa. 57:17.
g *Rulers, duties of*, Ex. 18:21.
h *Sheep, figurative*, vs. 1–31; Deut. 32:14.

3
i *Wool*, Judg. 6:37.

4
1 R. V. rigour

5 [Q]And they were scattered, because *there is* no [c]shepherd: and they became meat[G] to all the beasts of the field, when they were scattered.

6 My [h]sheep wandered through all the mountains, and upon every high hill: yea, my flock was scattered upon all the face of the earth, and none did search or seek *after them.*[Q]

7 ¶ Therefore, ye [c,d]shepherds, hear the [a]word of the LORD;

8 *As* I live, saith the Lord GOD, surely because my [h]flock became a prey, and my flock became meat[G] to every beast of the field, because *there was* no [c]shepherd, neither did my shepherds search for my flock, but the [d]shepherds [e,f]fed themselves, and fed not my flock;[Q]

9 Therefore, O ye [c,d]shepherds, hear the [a]word of the LORD;

10 Thus saith the Lord GOD; Behold, I *am* against the [c,d]shepherds; and [j]I will require my flock at their hand, and cause them to cease from feeding the flock; neither shall the shepherds feed themselves any more; for I will [k]deliver my flock from their mouth, that they may not be meat[G] for them.

11 ¶[S]For thus saith the Lord GOD; Behold, I, *even* I, [k]will both search my sheep, and seek them out.[Q]

12 As a [c]shepherd seeketh out his flock in the day that he is among his sheep *that are* scattered; so will [k]I seek out my [h,l]sheep, and will deliver them out of all places where they have been scattered in the cloudy and dark day.

13 And [k]I will bring [l]them out from the [2]people, and gather them from the countries, and will bring them to their own land, and feed them upon the mountains of Is'ra-el by the rivers, and in all the inhabited places of the country.

14 [k]I will feed [l]them in a good pasture, and upon the high mountains of Is'ra-el shall their fold be: there shall they lie in a good fold, and *in* a fat[G] pasture shall they feed upon the mountains of Is'ra-el.

15 [k]I will feed my [h,l]flock, and I will cause them to lie down, saith the Lord GOD.[Q]

16 [k]I will seek that which was lost, and [l]bring again that which was driven away, and will bind up *that which was* broken, and will strengthen that which was sick: but I will [m]destroy the fat[G] and the strong; I will feed them with judgment.[G] [S] [Q]

17 And *as for* you, O my flock, thus saith the Lord GOD; Behold, [n]I judge between cattle[G] and cattle[G], between the rams and the he goats.[S] [Q]

18 *Seemeth it* a small thing unto [d]you to have [e,f]eaten up the good pasture, but ye must tread down with your feet the residue[G] of your pastures? and to have drunk of the [3]deep waters, but ye must foul the residue[G] with your feet?

19 And *as for* my [h]flock, they eat that which [d]ye have trodden[G] with your feet; and they drink that which ye have fouled with your feet.

20 ¶ Therefore thus saith the Lord GOD unto them; Behold, I, *even* I, will [n]judge between the fat cattle[G] and between the lean cattle.

21 Because [d]ye have [o]thrust with side and with shoulder, and pushed all the diseased with your horns, till ye have scattered them abroad;

22 Therefore will [k]I save my flock, and they shall no more be a prey; and I will [n]judge between cattle and cattle.[S]

10
j *Rulers, accountable to God,* Ex. 18:21.
k *God, love of, exemplified,* vs. 10–31; Gen. 2:2.

12
l *Jews, prophecies concerning,* Neh. 4:2.

13
2 R. V. peoples,

16
m *Wicked, punishment of,* Psa. 73:3.

17
n *God, judge,* Gen. 2:2.

18
3 R. V. clear

21
o *Oppression,* Eccl. 5:8.

23 [S][T]And [p]I will set up one [q]shepherd over [r]them, and he shall [s]feed them, *even* my servant [t]Dā′vid; he shall feed them, and he shall be their shepherd.[Q]

24 And [k]I the LORD will be their God, [p]and my servant [t]Dā′vid a prince among them; I the LORD have spoken *it.*[S] [T]

25 And I will make with [r]them a [u]covenant[G] of [v,w]peace, and will cause the evil beasts to cease out of the land: and they shall dwell safely in the wilderness, and sleep in the woods.[T]

26 And [k,r]I will make them and the places round about my hill a blessing; and I will cause the shower to come down in his season; there shall be showers of blessing.[S]

27 And [x]the tree of the field shall yield her fruit, and the earth shall yield her increase, and they shall be safe in their land, and shall know that I *am* the LORD, when I have broken the bands[G] of their yoke, and delivered them out of the hand of those that [o]served[G] themselves of them.

28 And [r]they shall no more be a prey to the heathen[G], neither shall the beast of the land devour them; but they shall dwell safely, and none shall make *them* afraid.[Q]

29 And [k,r]I will raise up [4]for them a plant of renown, and they shall be no more consumed with hunger in the land, neither bear the shame of the heathen[G] any more.[Q]

30 Thus shall they know that I the LORD their God *am* [y,z]with them, and *that* they, *even* the house of Iṣ′ra-el, *are* [a]my people, saith the Lord GOD.

31 And ye my [b]flock, the flock of my pasture, *are* men, *and* [c]I *am* your God, saith the Lord GOD.[S]

**23**
p *Jesus, prophecies concerning,* Matt. 1:21.
q *Jesus, shepherd,* Matt. 1:21.
r *Church, prophecies concerning its prosperity,* vs. 23–31; Matt. 16:18.
s *Gospel, prophecies relating to,* vs. 23–31; Mark 13:10.
t *Jesus, names of,* Matt. 1:21.

**25**
u *Covenant, of God with men,* Deut. 29:1.
v *Peace,* Jer. 29:7.
w *Spiritual Peace,* Gal. 1:3.

**27**
x *Temporal Blessings, from God,* Psa. 103:2.

**29**
4 R. V. unto them a plantation for renown.

**30**
y *God dwells with the Righteous,* 1 Kin. 6:13.
z *Fellowship, with God,* 1 Cor. 1:9.
a *Spiritual Adoption,* Rom. 8:15.

**31**
b *Sheep, figurative,* Deut. 32:14.
c *God, love of, exemplified,* Gen. 2:2.

## CHAPTER 35

*Judgments upon the people of mount Seir for their hatred of Israel.*

MOREOVER the [a]word of the LORD came unto [b]me, saying,

2 Son of man, set thy face against mount [c]Sē′ïr, and prophesy against it,

3 And say unto it, Thus saith the Lord GOD; Behold, O mount [c]Sē′ïr, I *am* against thee, and I will stretch out mine hand against [d]thee, and I will make thee [1]most desolate.

4 [d]I will lay thy cities waste, and thou shalt be desolate, and [e]thou shalt know that I *am* the LORD.

5 Because thou hast had a perpetual [2,f,g]hatred, and hast shed *the blood of* the children of Iṣ′ra-el by the force of the sword in the time of their calamity, in the time [3]*that their* iniquity *had* an end:

6 Therefore, *as* I live, saith the Lord GOD, [d]I will prepare thee unto [h]blood, and blood shall pursue thee: sith[G] thou hast not hated blood, even blood shall pursue thee.

7 Thus will [d]I make mount [c]Sē′ïr [4]most desolate, and cut off from it him that passeth out and him that returneth.

8 And [d]I will fill his mountains with his slain *men*: in thy hills, and in thy valleys, and in all thy rivers, shall they fall that are slain with the [i]sword.

9 [d]I will make thee perpetual desolations, and thy cities shall not [5]return: and [e]ye shall know that I *am* the LORD.

10 Because thou hast said, These two nations and these two countries shall be mine, and we will possess it; whereas[G] the LORD was there:

11 Therefore, *as* I live, saith the Lord GOD, I will even

**1**
a *Prophecies, inspired,* Dan. 9:24.
b *Ezekiel,* Ezek. 1:3.

**2**
c *Edomites, prophecies concerning,* 2 Kin. 8:1.

**3**
d *Nation, judgments denounced against,* Isa. 2:4.
1 R. V. a desolation and an astonishment.

**4**
e *Judgments, design of,* Ex. 6:6.

**5**
f *Hatred,* Prov. 15:17.
g *Malice,* Eph. 4:31.
2 R. V. enmity, and hast given over the children of Israel to the power of
3 R. V. of the iniquity of the end:

**6**
h *Blood, figurative of destruction,* Gen. 9:4.

**7**
4 R. V. an astonishment and a desolation; and I will cut off from it him that passeth through and

**8**
i *War, as a judgment,* Judg. 3:2.

**9**
5 R. V. be inhabited:

[j]do according to thine anger, and according to thine [k]envy which thou hast used out of thy[j,g]hatred against them; and I will make myself known among them, when I have judged thee.

12 And [e]thou shalt know that I *am* the LORD, *and that* I have heard all thy [l]blasphemies which thou hast spoken against the mountains of Is'ra-el, saying, They are laid desolate, they are given us to consume.

13 Thus with your mouth ye have [l]boasted against me, and have multiplied your words against me: I have heard *them*.

14 Thus saith the Lord GOD; When the whole earth rejoiceth, [d]I will make thee desolate.

15 As thou didst rejoice at the inheritance of the house of Is'ra-el, because it was desolate, so will I do unto thee: [c,d]thou shalt be desolate, O mount Sē'ïr, and all [6]Ī-du-mē'ă, *even* all of it: and [e]they shall know that I *am* the LORD.

11
*j Judgment, according to opportunity and works,* 1 Pet. 1:17.
*k Envy,* Prov. 14:30.

12
*l Blasphemy,* 2 Sam. 12:14.

15
6 R. V. Edom.

## CHAPTER 36

*Israel's enemies to be punished. 8 A promise of prosperity to Israel. 16 The people chastised for their sins. 21 Their restoration for the glory of God. 25 Great spiritual blessings promised.*

ALSO, [a]thou son of man, prophesy unto the mountains of [b]Is'ra-el, and say, Ye mountains of Is'ra-el, hear the [c]word of the LORD:

2 Thus saith the Lord GOD; Because the enemy hath said against you, [d]Aha, even the ancient high places are our's in possession:

3 Therefore prophesy and say, Thus saith the Lord GOD; Because they have made *you* desolate, and swallowed you up on every side, that ye might be a possession unto the residue of the [1]heathen, and ye are [d]taken up in the lips of talkers, and [2]*are* an infamy of the people:

1
*a Ezekiel,* Ezek. 1:3.
*b Jews, prophecies concerning,* vs. 1–38; Neh. 4:2.
*c Prophecies, inspired,* Dan. 9:24.

2
*d Scoffing, instances of,* Hab. 1:10.

3
1 R. V. nations,
2 R. V. the evil report of

4 Therefore, ye mountains of Is'ra-el, hear the [b]word of the Lord GOD; Thus saith the Lord GOD to the mountains, and to the hills, to the rivers, and to the valleys, to the desolate wastes, and to the cities that are forsaken, which became a prey and derision to the residue of the [1]heathen that *are* round about;

5 Therefore thus saith the Lord GOD; Surely in the fire of my [e]jealousy have I spoken against the residue of the [1]heathen, and against all [3,f]Ī-du-mē'ă, which have appointed my land into their possession with the joy of all *their* heart, with despiteful minds, to cast it out for a prey.

6 Prophesy therefore concerning the land of [b]Is'ra-el, and say unto the mountains, and to the hills, to the rivers, and to the valleys, Thus saith the Lord GOD; Behold, I have spoken in my [e]jealousy and in my [g]fury, because ye have borne the shame of the heathen:

7 Therefore thus saith the Lord GOD; I have lifted up mine hand, Surely the heathen that *are* about you, they shall bear their shame.

8 ¶ But ye, O mountains of [b]Is'ra-el, ye shall shoot forth your branches, and yield your fruit to my people of Is'ra-el; for they are at hand to come.

9 For, behold, I *am* for you, and [b]I will turn unto you, and ye shall be tilled and sown:

10 And [b]I will multiply men upon you, all the house of Is'ra-el, *even* all of it: and the cities shall be inhabited, and the wastes shall be builded:

11 And [b]I will multiply upon you man and beast; and they shall increase and bring fruit: and I will [4]settle you after your old estates, and will do better *unto you* than at your begin-

5
*e Jealousy, attributed to God,* Psa. 78:58.
*f Edomites, prophecies concerning,* 2 Kin. 8:21.
3 R. V. Edom.

6
*g Anger of God,* 2 Kin. 13:3.

11
4 R. V. cause you to be inhabited after your former estate.

nings: and ye shall know that I *am* the LORD.

12 Yea, I will cause men to walk upon you, *even* my people [b]Iș'ra-el; and they shall possess thee, and thou shalt be their inheritance, and thou shalt no more henceforth bereave them *of* [5]*men.*

13 Thus saith the Lord GOD; Because they say unto you, Thou *land* devourest up men, and hast bereaved thy [6]nations;

14 Therefore thou shalt devour men no more, neither bereave thy [6]nations any more, saith the Lord GOD.

15 [b]Neither will I cause *men* to hear in thee the shame of the heathen any more, neither shalt thou bear the reproach of the [7]people any more, neither shalt thou cause thy [6]nations to fall any more, saith the Lord GOD.

16 ¶ Moreover the [c]word of the LORD came unto [a]me, saying,

17 Son of man, when the house of Iș'ra-el dwelt in their own land, they defiled it by their own way and by their [h]doings: their way was before me as the uncleanness of a [8]removed woman.

18 Wherefore I [i,j]poured my fury upon them for the blood that they had shed upon the land, and for their [k]idols *wherewith* they had polluted it:

19 And I [l]scattered them among the [1]heathen, and they were dispersed through the countries: [m]according to their way and according to their doings I judged them.

20 And when they entered unto the heathen, whither they went, they [n]profaned my [o]holy name, [9]when they said to them, These *are* the people of the LORD, and are gone forth out of his land.

21 ¶ But I had pity for mine [o]holy name, which the [h]house of Iș'ra-el had [n]profaned among the [1]heathen, whither they went.

22 Therefore say unto the house of Iș'ra-el, Thus saith the Lord GOD; I do not *this* for your sakes, O house of Iș'ra-el, but [p]for mine holy name's sake, which ye have [n]profaned among the [1]heathen, whither ye went.

23 And I will sanctify my great name, which was [n]profaned among the [1]heathen, which ye have profaned in the midst of them; and the [1]heathen shall know that I *am* the LORD, saith the Lord GOD, when I shall be sanctified in you before their eyes.

24 For [b]I will take you from among the [1]heathen, and gather you out of all countries, and will bring you into your own land.

25 [q]Then will I [r,s]sprinkle clean [t]water upon you, and ye shall be clean: from all your [h]filthiness, and from all your [k]idols will I [r,s]cleanse you.

26 A [u,v]new heart also will I give you, and a new spirit will I put within you: and I will take away the stony heart out of your flesh, and I will give you an heart of flesh.

27 And I will put my [w]spirit within you, and cause you to [x]walk in my statutes, and ye shall keep my judgments, and do *them.*

28 And ye shall dwell in the [y,z]land that I [a]gave to your fathers; and ye shall be [b]my people, and I will be your God.

29 I will also [c]save [d]you from all your uncleannesses: and I will [e]call for the [f]corn, and will increase it, and lay no famine upon you.

30 And I will [e,f]multiply the fruit of the tree, and the increase of the field, that ye shall receive no more reproach of famine among the [1]heathen.

**12**
5 R. V. children.

**13**
6 R. V. nation;

**15**
7 R. V. peoples

**17**
*h Jews, wickedness of,* Neh. 4:2.
8 R. V. woman in her separation.

**18**
*i Nation, punishment of,* Isa. 2:4.
*j Sin, punishment of,* Rom. 5:12.
*k Idolatry,* 1 Sam. 15:23.

**19**
*l Captivity, as a judgment,* Isa. 5:13.
*m Judgment, according to opportunity and works,* 1 Pet. 1:17.

**20**
*n Profanation, of God's name,* Lev. 22:32.
*o God, holiness of,* Gen. 2:2.
9 R. V. in that men said of them,

**22**
*p Motive, ascribed to God,* Psa. 106:8.

**25**
*q God, mercy of,* Gen. 2:2.
*r Purification, figurative,* Num. 19:19.
*s Spiritual Purification,* Psa. 51:2.
*t Water, figurative,* 1 Kin. 17:10.

**26**
*u Heart, renewed,* Psa. 44:21.
*v Regeneration,* Tit. 3:5.

**27**
*w Holy Spirit,* Acts 1:2.
*x Obedience,* Heb. 5:8.

**28**
*y Canaan,* Gen. 37:1.
*z Temporal Blessings, from God,* vs. 28–38; Psa. 103:2.
*a Covenant, of God with men,* Deut. 29:1.
*b Spiritual Adoption,* Rom. 8:15.

**29**
*c God, savior,* Gen. 2:2.
*d Jews, prophecies concerning,* Neh. 4:2.
*e Prosperity,* Eccl. 7:14.
*f Temporal Blessings, from God,* Psa. 103:2.

31
*g Repentance, of Israel foretold,* Mark 1:4.
*h Remorse,* Matt. 27:3.
*i Jews, wickedness of,* Neh. 4:2.

33
*j Purification, figurative,* Num. 19:19.
*k Spiritual Purification,* Psa. 51:2.

35
*l Eden,* Isa. 51:3.

36
*m God, immutable,* Gen. 2:2.
10 R. V. nations

37
*n Prayer, answer to, promised,* Acts 6:4.

38
*o Annual Feasts,* Num. 15:3.
11 R. V. flock for sacrifice,

1
*a Prophets, inspiration of,* Isa.3:2.
*b Ezekiel.* Ezek. 1:3.

31 Then shall ye [g]remember
your own evil ways, and your
doings that *were* not good, and
shall [h]lothe yourselves in your
own sight for your [i]iniquities and
for your abominations.[T]
32 Not for your sakes do I *this,*
saith the Lord GOD, be it known
unto you: be ashamed and confounded for your own [i]ways, O
house of Iṣ'ra-el.
33 Thus saith the Lord GOD;
In the day that I shall have
[j, k]cleansed you from all your iniquities [d]I will also cause *you* to
dwell in the cities, and the wastes
shall be builded.
34 And [d]the desolate land shall
be tilled, whereas it lay desolate
in the sight of all that passed by.
35 And they shall say, This
land that was desolate is become like the garden of [l]Ē'dĕn;
and the waste and desolate and
ruined cities *are become* fenced,[C]
*and* are inhabited.
36 Then the [10]heathen[C] that are
left round about you shall know
that I the LORD [l]build the ruined
*places, and* plant that that was
desolate: I the LORD have spoken *it,* and [m]I will do *it.*
37 Thus saith the Lord GOD; I
will yet *for* this be [n]enquired of
by the [d]house of Iṣ'ra-el, to do *it*
for them; I will increase them
with men like a flock.
38 As the [11]holy flock, as the
flock of Jē-rụ'să-lĕm in her solemn [o]feasts; [d]so shall the waste
cities be filled with flocks of men:
and they shall know that I *am*
the LORD.[S]

## CHAPTER 37

*The vision of the valley of dry bones.* 11 *Its application.* 15 *The symbol of the two sticks united.* 18 *The explanation thereof,* 20 *and its application to the Messiah's kingdom.*

THE hand of the LORD was
[a]upon [b]me, and carried me
out in the spirit of the LORD, and
set me down in the midst of the
valley which *was* full of *bones,[T]
2 And caused me to pass by
them round about: and, behold,
*there were* very many in the open
valley; and, lo,[C] *they were* very
dry.
3 And he said unto me, Son
of man, can these *bones live?
And I answered, O Lord GOD,
thou knowest.
4 Again he said unto me,
Prophesy upon these *bones, and
say unto them, O ye dry bones,
hear the word of the LORD.
5 Thus[Q] saith the Lord GOD unto
these *bones; Behold, I will cause
[c]breath to enter into you, and
ye shall [d]live:
6 And I will lay sinews upon
you, and will bring up flesh upon
you, and cover you with skin,
and put [c]breath in you, and ye
shall [d]live; and ye shall know
that I *am* the LORD.
7 So I prophesied as I was commanded: and as I prophesied,
there was a noise, and behold
a shaking, and the *bones came
together, bone to his bone.
8 And when I beheld, lo,[C] the
sinews and the flesh came up
upon them, and the skin covered
them above: but *there was* no
breath in them.
9[T] Then said he unto me,
Prophesy[G] unto the wind, prophesy,[G] son of man, and say to the
wind, Thus saith the Lord GOD;
Come from the four winds, O
[e]breath, and breathe upon these
slain, that they may live.[TQ]
10 So I prophesied as he commanded me, and the [c]breath
came into them, and they lived,
and stood up upon their feet, an
exceeding great army.[Q]
11 Then he said unto me, Son
of man, these *bones are the
whole house of Iṣ'ra-el: behold,
they say, [f]Our bones are dried,

5
*c Breath,* Gen. 7:15.
*d Life,* Eccl. 8:15.

9
*e Breath, figurative,* Gen. 7:15.

11
*f Despondency,* Eccl. 2:20.

***BONES.** *Of passover lamb not to be broken,* Ex. 12:46. *Vision of the dry,* Ezek. 37:1–14. *None of Christ's, broken,* Psa. 34:20; John 19:31–37.

and our hope is lost: we are cut off for our parts.

12 Therefore prophesy and say unto them, Thus saith the Lord GOD; Behold, O my [g]people, [h]I will open your graves, and cause you to [i]come up out of your graves, and bring you into the land of Ĭs′ra-el.[Q]

13 And ye shall know that I *am* the LORD, when I have opened your graves, O my people, and [i]brought you up out of your graves,

14 And shall put my spirit[G] in you, and ye shall live, and [g,j]I shall place you in your own [k]land: then shall ye know that I the LORD have spoken *it*, and performed *it*, saith the LORD.[T Q]

15 ¶ The [l]word of the LORD [a]came again unto [b]me, saying,

16 Moreover, thou son of man, [m,n]take thee one stick, and write upon it, For [g]Jū′dah, and for the children of Ĭs′ra-el his companions: then take another stick, and write upon it, For Jō′ṣeph, the stick of [o]Ē′phră-ĭm, and *for* all the house of [p]Ĭs′ra-el his companions:

17 [m,n]And join them one to another into one stick; and they shall become one in thine hand.

18 And when the children of thy people shall speak unto thee, saying, Wilt thou not shew us what thou *meanest* by these?

19 Say unto them, Thus saith the Lord GOD; Behold, I will take the stick of Jō′ṣeph, which *is* in the hand of [o]Ē′phră-ĭm, and the tribes of [p]Ĭs′ra-el his fellows, and will put them with him, *even* with the stick of [g]Jū′dah, and make them one stick, and they shall be one in mine hand.

20 And [m,n]the sticks whereon thou writest shall be in thine hand before their eyes.

21 ¶ And say unto them, Thus saith the Lord GOD; Behold, [j]I will take the children of Ĭs′ra-el from among the [1]heathen, whither[G] they be gone, and will gather them on every side, and bring them into their own land:

22 And I will make [g,p]them one nation in the land upon the mountains of Ĭs′ra-el; and one king shall be king to them all: and they shall be no more two nations, neither shall they be divided into two kingdoms any more at all:

23 [g,p]Neither shall they defile themselves any more with their idols, nor with their detestable[G] things, nor with any of their transgressions: but I will [q]save them out of all their dwellingplaces[G], wherein they have sinned, and will [r,s]cleanse them: [t]so shall they be my people, and I will be their God.[Q]

24 And [u,v]Dā′vid my servant *shall be* [w]king over them; and they all shall have one [x]shepherd: they shall also [y]walk in my judgments[G], and observe my statutes, and [z]do them.[T Q]

25 And they shall dwell in the [a]land that I have [b]given unto Jā′cob my servant, wherein your fathers have dwelt; and they shall dwell therein, *even* they, and their children, and their children's children for ever: and [c]my servant [d]Dā′vid *shall be* their prince for ever.

26 Moreover I will make a [b]covenant of [e]peace with them; it shall be an everlasting covenant with them: and I will place them, and multiply them, and will set my [f]sanctuary in the midst of them for evermore.[T Q]

27 [g]My tabernacle[G] also shall be with them: yea, [h]I will be their God, and they shall be my people.[Q]

28 And the heathen[G] shall know that I the LORD do [i]sanctify Ĭs′-

12
g *Jews, prophecies concerning*, Neh. 4:2.
h *God mercy of*, Gen. 2:2.
i *Resurrection, symbolical of the restoration of Israel*, 1 Cor. 15:12.

14
j *God, providence of*, Gen. 2:2.
k *Canaan*, Gen. 37:1.

15
l *Prophecies, inspired*, Dan. 9:24.

16
m *Pantomime, prophecies illustrated by*, vs. 16–20; Isa. 20:2.
n *Instruction, by object lessons*, Prov. 23:23.
o *Ephraim, name of, applied to the ten tribes*, Gen. 41:52.
p *Israel, prophecies concerning*, 1 Kin. 12:1.

21
1 R. V. nations.

23
q *God, savior*, Gen. 2:2.
r *Sin, forgiveness of*, Rom. 5:12.
s *Spiritual Purification*, Psa. 51:2.
t *God, love of, exemplified*, Gen. 2:2.

24
u *Jesus, names of*, Matt. 1:21.
v *Jesus, prophecies concerning*, Matt. 1:21.
w *Jesus, king*, Matt. 1:21.
x *Jesus, shepherd*, Matt. 1:21.
y *Walking, figurative*, Gen. 5:22.
z *Obedience*, Heb. 5:8.

25
a *Canaan*, Gen. 37:1.
b *Covenant, of God with men*, Deut. 29:1.
c *Jesus, prophecies concerning*, Matt. 1:21.
d *Jesus, names of*, Matt. 1:21.

26
e *Peace*, Jer. 29:7.
f *Sanctuary*, Lev. 4:6.

27
g *God dwells with the Righteous*, 1 Kin. 6:13.
h *God, love of, exemplified*, Gen. 2:2.

28
i *Sanctification*, 1 Pet. 1:2.

ra-el, when my [l]sanctuary shall be in the midst of them for evermore.

## CHAPTER 38

*The army of Gog. 8 His design against Israel. 14 God's judgment against him.*

AND the [a]word of the LORD came unto [b]me, saying,

2 Son of man, set thy face against [c]Gŏg, the land of [d]Mā′-gŏg, the chief prince[G] of [e]Mē′-shech and [f]Tṳ′bal, and prophesy against him,[Q]

3 And say, Thus saith the Lord GOD; Behold, I *am* against thee, O [c]Gŏg, the chief prince[G] of [e]Mē′-shech and [f]Tṳ′bal:

4 And I will turn thee back, and put hooks into thy jaws, and I will bring thee forth, and all thine [g]army, [h]horses and [i]horsemen, all of them clothed [1]with all sorts *of* [j]*armour, even* a great company *with* bucklers and [k]shields, all of them handling [l]swords:

5 [m]Pĕr′s̤ia, [n]Ē-thĭ-ō′pĭ-ȧ, and [o]Lĭb′y̆-ȧ with them; all of them with [k]shield and [p]helmet:

6 Gō′mĕr, and all his bands[G]; the house of [q]Tō-gär′mah [2]of the north quarters, and all his bands: *and* many people with thee.

7 Be thou prepared, and prepare for thyself, thou, and all thy company that are assembled unto thee, and be thou a guard unto them.

8 After many days thou shalt be visited: in the latter years thou shalt come into the land *that is* brought back from the sword, *and is* gathered out of many [3]people, against the mountains of Ĭs̤′ra-el, which have been always waste: but it is brought forth out of the nations, and they shall dwell safely all of them.

9 Thou shalt ascend and come like a storm, thou shalt be like a cloud to cover the land, thou, and all thy bands[G], and many [3]people with thee.

10 Thus saith the Lord GOD; It shall also come to pass, *that* at the same time shall things come into thy mind, and thou shalt [4]think[G] an evil thought:

11 And thou shalt say, I will go up to the land of unwalled villages; I will go to them that are at rest, that dwell safely,[G] all of them dwelling without walls, and having neither bars nor gates,

12 To take a [r]spoil, and to take a prey[G]; to turn thine hand upon the desolate places *that are now* inhabited, and upon the people *that are* gathered out of the nations, which have gotten cattle and goods, that dwell in the midst of the land.

13 [s]Shē′bȧ, and [t]Dē′dan, and the [u]merchants of [v]Tär′shish, with all the young lions thereof, shall say unto thee, Art thou come to take a spoil[G]? hast thou gathered thy company to take a prey[G]? to carry away silver and gold, to take away cattle and goods, to take a great spoil[G]?

14 ¶ Therefore, son of man, prophesy and say unto [c]Gŏg, Thus saith the Lord GOD; In that day when my people of Ĭs̤′ra-el dwelleth safely, shalt thou not know *it*?

15 And thou shalt come from thy place out of the [5]north parts, thou, and many [3]people with thee, all of them [i]riding upon [h]horses, a great company, and a mighty [g]army:

16 And thou shalt come up against my people of Ĭs̤′ra-el, as a cloud to cover the land; it shall be in the latter days, and I will bring thee against my land, [w]that the [6]heathen[G] may know me, when I shall be sanctified[G] in thee, O Gŏg, before their eyes.

17 Thus saith the Lord GOD;

1
a *Prophecies, inspired,* Dan. 9:24.
b *Ezekiel,* Ezek. 1:3.

2
c Ezek. 39; Rev. 20:8.
d *Magog, prophecy concerning,* 1 Chr. 1:5.
e Ezek. 27:13; 32:26; 39:1.
f *Tubal,* Gen. 10:2.

4
g *Armies,* Deut. 11:4.
h *Horse,* Job 39:19.
i *Cavalry,* 1 Sam. 13:5.
j *Armor,* 1 Sam. 17:54.
k *Shield,* 1 Kin. 14:27.
l *Sword,* 1 Chr. 21:5.
1 R. V. in full armour,

5
m *Persia,* Esth. 1:3.
n *Ethiopia,* Isa. 18:1.
o Or, *Phut,* Ezek. 27:10.
p *Helmet,* Jer. 46:4.

6
q Ezek. 27:14; 1 Chr. 1:6.
2 R.V. in the uttermost parts of the north, and all his hordes: even many peoples with thee.

8
3 R. V. peoples,

10
4 R. V. devise an evil device:

12
r *Spoils,* 1 Chr. 26:27.

13
s *Sheba,* 1 Kin. 10:1.
t *Dedan,* Jer. 49:8
u *Merchant,* Neh. 3:32.
v *Tarshish,* 2 Chr. 20:36.

15
5 R. V. uttermost parts of the north,

16
w *Judgments, design of,* Ex. 6:6.
6 R. V. nations

*Art* thou he of whom I have spoken in old time by my servants the [x]prophets of Ĭṣ′ra-el, which prophesied in those days *many* years that I would bring thee against them?

18 And it shall come to pass at the same time when [c]Gŏg shall come against the land of Ĭṣ′ra-el, saith the Lord GOD, *that* my [y]fury shall come up in my face.

19 For in my [z]jealousy *and* in the fire of my wrath have I spoken, Surely in that day there shall be a great shaking in the land of Ĭṣ′ra-el;

20 So that the fishes of the sea, and the fowls of the heaven, and the beasts of the field, and all creeping things that creep upon the earth, and all the men that *are* upon the face of the earth, shall shake at my presence, and the mountains shall be thrown down, and the steep places shall fall, and every wall shall fall to the ground.

21 And [a]I will call for a [b]sword against him throughout all my mountains, saith the Lord GOD: every man's sword shall be against his brother.

22 And [a]I will plead against him with pestilence and with blood; and I will rain upon him, and upon his bands, and upon the many people that *are* with him, an overflowing rain, and great hailstones, fire, and [c]brimstone.

23 Thus will I magnify myself, and sanctify myself; and I will be known in the eyes of many nations, and [d]they shall know that I *am* the LORD.

## CHAPTER 39

*The utter destruction of Gog. 8 The burning of his weapons, 11 and the burial of his slain. 17 The feast of the fowls. 23 The cause of Israel's captivity. 25 God's purpose of mercy towards them.*

THEREFORE, thou son of man, prophesy against [a]Gŏg, and say, Thus saith the Lord GOD; Behold, I *am* against thee, O Gŏg, the chief prince of [b]Mē′shech and [c]Tu̧′bal:

2 And [d]I will turn thee [1]back, and leave but the sixth part of thee, and will cause thee to come up from the north parts, and will bring thee upon the mountains of Ĭṣ′ra-el:

3 And [d]I will smite thy bow out of thy left hand, and will cause thine arrows to fall out of thy right hand.

4 Thou shalt fall upon the mountains of Ĭṣ′ra-el, thou, and all thy [2]bands, and the [3]people that [4]*is* with thee: [d]I will give thee unto the ravenous birds of every sort, and *to* the beasts of the field to be devoured.

5 [d]Thou shalt fall upon the open field: for [e]I have spoken *it*, saith the Lord GOD.

6 And I will send a fire on [f]Mā′gŏg, and among them that dwell [5,g]carelessly in the isles: and [h]they shall know that I *am* the LORD.

7 [h]So will I make my [i]holy name known in the midst of my people Ĭṣ′ra-el; and I will not *let them* [j]pollute my holy name any more: and the [6]heathen shall know that I *am* the LORD, the Holy One in Ĭṣ′ra-el.

8 ¶ Behold, it is come, and it is done, saith the Lord GOD; this *is* the day whereof I have spoken.

9 And they that dwell in the cities of Ĭṣ′ra-el shall go forth, and shall set on fire and burn the weapons, both the [k]shields and the bucklers, the [l]bows and the [m]arrows, and the handstaves, and the [n]spears, and they shall burn them with fire [o]seven years:

10 [d]So that they shall take no wood out of the field, neither cut down *any* out of the forests; for they shall burn the weapons with fire: and they shall spoil those that spoiled them, and rob those

17
x *Prophets, inspiration of,* Isa. 3:2.

18
y *Anger of God,* 2 Kin. 13:3.

19
z *Jealousy, attributed to God,* Psa. 78:58.

21
a *Nation, judgments denounced against,* Isa. 2:4.
b *War, as a judgment,* Judg. 3:2.

22
c *Brimstone, figurative,* Deut. 29:23.

23
d *Judgments, design of,* Ex. 6:6.

1
a Ezek. 38; Rev. 20:8.
b Ezek. 27:13; 32:26; 38:2.
c *Tubal,* Gen. 10:2.

2
d *Nation, judgments denounced against,* Isa. 2:4.
1 R. V. about, and will lead thee on, and will cause thee to come up from the uttermost parts of the north; and

4
2 R. V. hordes,
3 R. V. peoples
4 R. V. are

5
e *God, sovereign,* Gen. 2:2.

6
f *Magog, prophecy concerning,* 1 Chr. 1:5.
g *False Confidence,* Psa. 30:6.
h *Judgments, design of,* Ex. 6:6.
5 R. V. securely

7
i *God, holiness of,* Gen. 2:2.
j *Profanation, of God's name,* Lev. 22:32.
6 R. V. nations

9
k *Shield,* 1 Kin. 14:27.
l *Bow,* 2 Sam. 1:18.
m *Arrow,* 1 Sam. 20:20.
n *Spear,* 2 Kin. 11:10.
o *Seven, years,* Gen. 7:2.

that robbed them, saith the Lord GOD.

11 ¶ And [d]it shall come to pass in that day, *that* I will give unto [a]Gŏg a place [7]there of graves in Ĭṣ′ra-el, the valley of the passengers on the east of the [p]sea: and it shall stop the *noses*[G] of the passengers[G]: and there shall they [q]bury Gŏg and all his multitude: and they shall call *it* The valley of [8]Hā′mon–gŏg.

12 And seven months shall the house of Ĭṣ′ra-el be burying of them, that they may cleanse the land.

13 Yea, all the people of the land shall bury *them*; and it shall be to them a renown the day that I shall be glorified, saith the Lord GOD.

14 And they shall sever[G] out men of continual employment, [9]passing through the land to [q]bury with the passengers[G] those that remain upon the face of the earth, to cleanse it: after the end of seven months shall they search.

15 And the passengers[G] *that* pass through the land, when *any* seeth a man's bone, then shall he set up a sign by it, till the buriers have buried it in the valley of Hā′mon–gŏg.

16 And also the name of [10]the city *shall be* [11]Hā-mō′nah. Thus shall they cleanse the land.

17 ¶ And, thou son of man, thus saith the Lord GOD; Speak unto every feathered fowl, and to every beast of the field, Assemble yourselves, and come; gather yourselves on every side to my [r]sacrifice[G] that I do sacrifice[G] for you, *even* a great sacrifice[G] upon the mountains of Ĭṣ′ra-el, that ye may eat flesh, and drink blood.

18 Ye shall eat the flesh of the mighty, and drink the blood of the princes of the earth, of rams, of lambs, and of goats, of bullocks, all of them fatlings of [s]Bā′shăn.

19 A[Q]nd ye shall eat fat till ye be full, and drink blood till ye be [t]drunken, of my [r]sacrifice which I have sacrificed for you.

20 Thus ye shall be filled at my table with horses and chariots, with mighty men, and with all men of war, saith the Lord GOD.[Q]

21 And I will set my [u]glory among the [6]heathen[G], and all the [6]heathen shall see my judgment that I have executed, and my hand that I have laid upon them.

22 So [h]the house of Ĭṣ′ra-el shall know that I *am* the LORD their God from that day and forward.

23 And the heathen[G] shall know that the house of Ĭṣ′ra-el went into [v]captivity for their iniquity: because they trespassed against me, [w]therefore hid I my face from them, and [x]gave them into the hand of their enemies: so fell they all by the [y]sword.

24 According to their uncleanness and [z]according to their transgressions have I done unto them, and [w]hid my face from them.

25 Therefore thus saith the Lord GOD; Now will I bring again the captivity of Jā′cob, and have [a]mercy upon the whole house of Ĭṣ′ra-el, and will be [b]jealous[G] for my [c]holy name;[S]

26 After that they have borne their shame, and all their trespasses whereby they have trespassed against me, when they dwelt safely in their land, and none made *them* afraid.

27 When I have brought them again from the people, and gathered them out of their enemies' lands, and am sanctified[G] in them in the sight of many nations;

28 Then shall they know that I *am* the LORD their God, which [d]caused them to be led into [e]captivity among the heathen: but [a]I have gathered them unto their

**11**

*p* *Dead Sea*, Gen. 14:3.

*q* *Burial, of Gog*, Acts 8:2.

7 R. V. for burial in Israel, the valley of them that pass through on the east of the sea: and it shall stop them that pass through:

8 *That is* The multitude of Gog.

**14**

9 R. V. that shall pass through the land to bury them that pass through, that remain

**16**

10 R. V. Hamonah shall also be the name of a city.

11 *That is* The multitude.

**17**

*r* *Sacrifices, figurative of divine judgments*, Rom. 12:1.

**18**

*s* *Bashan*, Num. 32:33.

**19**

*t* *Drunkenness, figurative*, Luke 21:34.

**21**

*u* *God, glory of*, Gen. 2:2.

**23**

*v* *Captivity, as a judgment*, Isa. 5:13.

*w* *Sin, repugnant to God*, Rom. 5:12.

*x* *Nation, punishment of*, Isa. 2:4.

*y* *War, as a judgment*, Judg. 3:2.

**24**

*z* *Punishment, according to deeds*, v. 26; Lev. 26:41.

**25**

*a* *God, mercy of*, Gen. 2:2.

*b* *Anthropomorphisms*, Gen. 11:5.

*c* *God, holiness of*, Gen. 2:2.

**28**

*d* *Divine Chastisement*, Job 33:19.

*e* *Captivity, as a judgment*, Isa. 5:13.

own land, and have left none of them any more there.

29 [a]Neither will I hide my face any more from them: for I have poured out my [f]spirit upon the house of Is'ra-el, saith the Lord GOD.[S T]

## CHAPTER 40

*The time and manner of the vision concerning the temple. 6 The description of the east gate, 20 of the north gate, 24 of the south gate, 32 of the east gate, 35 and of the north gate. 39 Eight tables. 44 The chambers. 48 The porch of the house.*

IN the five and twentieth year of our [a]captivity, in the beginning of the year, in the tenth *day* of the month, in the fourteenth year after that the city was smitten, in the selfsame[G] day the hand of the LORD was [b]upon [c]me, and brought me thither[G].

2 In the [d]visions of God brought he me into the land of Is'ra-el, and set me upon a very high mountain, by which *was* as the frame[G] of a city on the south.[Q]

3 And he brought me thither[G], and, behold, *there was* a man, whose appearance *was* like the appearance of brass, with a line of [e]flax in his hand, and a measuring *reed; and he stood in the gate.[Q]

4 And the man said unto me, Son of man, behold with thine eyes, and hear with thine ears, and set thine heart upon all that I shall shew thee; for to the intent that I might shew *them* unto thee *art* thou brought hither[G]: declare all that thou seest to the house of Is'ra-el.

5 And [d]behold a wall on the outside of the [f]house round about, and in the man's hand a measuring *reed[G] of six [g,h]cubits[G] *long* by the cubit and an [h,i]hand breadth: so he measured the breadth of the building, one reed[G]; and the height, one reed[G].[Q]

6 ¶ Then came he unto the [j]gate which looketh toward the east, and went up the stairs thereof, and measured the threshold of the gate, *which was* one *reed[G] broad; and the other threshold [1]*of the gate, which was* one reed[G] broad.

7 And *every* [2]little chamber[G] *was* one *reed[G] long, and one reed[G] broad; and between the [3]little chambers[G] *were* five [g]cubits[G]; and the threshold of the gate by the porch of the gate [4]within *was* one reed[G].

8 He measured also the porch of the gate [4]within, one reed[G].

9 Then measured he the porch of the gate, eight [g]cubits[G]; and the posts thereof, two cubits[G]; and the porch of the gate *was* [4]inward.

10 And the [3]little chambers[G] of the gate eastward *were* three on this side, and three on that side; they three *were* of one measure: and the posts had one measure on this side and on that side.

11 And he measured the breadth of the entry of the [j]gate, ten [g]cubits[G]; *and* the length of the gate, thirteen cubits[G].

12 The space also before the [3]little chambers *was* one [g]cubit[G] *on this side*, and the space *was* one cubit[G] on that side: and the little chambers *were* six cubits[G] on this side, and six cubits[G] on that side.

13 He measured then the gate from the roof of *one* [2]little chamber to the roof of another: the breadth *was* five and twenty cubits[G], door against door.

14 He made also posts of threescore [g]cubits[G], even unto the post of the [k]court round about the gate.

15 And from the face of the

29
*f Holy Spirit,* Acts 1:2.

v.1–494 BC
See footnote, *Time,* Rev. 10:6.

1
*a Jews, captive in Babylon,* Neh. 4:2.
*b Prophets, inspiration of,* Isa. 3:2.
*c Ezekiel,* Ezek. 1:3.

2
*d Vision,* vs. 1–29; Acts 9:10.

3
*e Flax,* Ex. 9:31.

5
*f Temple, Ezekiel's vision of,* 1 Kin. 6:17.
*g Cubit,* Ex. 36:9.
*h Measure, linear,* Deut. 25:15.
*i Handbreadth,* 1 Kin. 7:26.

6
*j Temple, gates of,* 1 Kin. 6:17.
1 R. V. *omits* of the gate, which was

7
2 R. V. lodge was
3 R. V. lodges
4 R. V. toward the house

14
*k Temple, courts of,* 1 Kin. 6:17.

***REED.** *A water plant,* Isa. 19:6, 7; 35:7; Jer. 51:32. *Of six cubits, used as a measuring device,* Ezek. 40:3–8; 41:8; 42:16–19; 45:1; Rev. 11:1; 21:15, 16. *Mockingly given to Jesus as a symbol of royalty, by Roman soldiers,* Matt. 27:29. *Jesus smitten with, while being mocked,* Matt. 27:30; Mark 15:19.
**Figurative:** *Of weakness,* 1 Kin. 14:15; 2 Kin. 18:21; Isa. 36:6; 42:3; Ezek. 29:6; Matt. 11:7; 12:20.

gate of the entrance unto the
face of the porch of the inner
gate *were* fifty cubits.[c]
16 And *there were* [5]narrow
[l]windows to the [3]little chambers, and to their posts within
the gate round about, and likewise to the arches: and windows
*were* round about inward: and
upon *each* post *were* [m]palm trees.
17 Then brought he me into
the outward [k]court, and, lo, *there
were* [n]chambers, and a pavement
made for the court round about:
thirty chambers *were* upon the
pavement.
18 And the pavement by the
side of the gates over against the
length of the gates *was* the lower
pavement.
19 Then he measured the
breadth from the forefront of
the lower [j]gate unto the forefront
of the inner [k]court without, an
hundred [g]cubits eastward and
northward.
20 ¶ And the [j]gate of the
outward court that looked toward the north, he measured the
length thereof, and the breadth
thereof.
21 And the [3]little chambers
thereof *were* three on this side and
three on that side; and the posts
thereof and the arches thereof
were after the measure of the
first gate: the length thereof *was*
fifty [g]cubits,[c] and the breadth five
and twenty cubits.[c]
22 And their [l]windows, and
their arches, and their [m]palm
trees, *were* after the measure of
the [j]gate that looketh toward the
east; and they went up unto it
by seven steps; and the arches
thereof *were* before them.
23 And the [j]gate of the inner
[k]court *was* over[c] against the gate
toward the north, and toward
the east; and he measured from
gate to gate an hundred cubits.
24 ¶ After that he brought me
toward the south, and behold a
[j]gate toward the south: and he
measured the posts thereof and
the arches thereof according to
these measures.
25 And *there were* [l]windows in
it and in the arches thereof round
about, like those windows: the
length *was* fifty [g]cubits,[c] and the
breadth five and twenty cubits.[c]
26 And *there were* seven steps
to go up to it, and the arches
thereof *were* before them: and
it had [m]palm trees, one on this
side, and another on that side,
upon the posts thereof.
27 And *there was* a [j]gate in the
inner [k]court toward the south:
and he measured from gate to
gate toward the south an hundred cubits.[c]
28 And he brought me to the
inner [k]court by the south [j]gate:
and he measured the south gate
according to these meaures;
29 And the [3]little chambers
thereof, and the posts thereof,
and the arches thereof, according
to these measures: and *there were*
[l]windows in it and in the arches
thereof round about: *it was* fifty
[g]cubits long, and five and twenty
cubits broad.
30 And the arches round about
*were* five and twenty cubits[c] long,
and five cubits[c] broad.
31 And the arches thereof *were*
toward the utter[c] [k]court; and
[m]palm trees *were* upon the posts
thereof: and the going up to it
*had* eight steps.
32 ¶ And he brought me into
the inner [k]court toward the east:
and he measured the [j]gate according to these measures.
33 And the [3]little chambers
thereof, and the posts thereof,
and the arches thereof, *were*
according to these measures:
and *there were* [l]windows therein and in the arches thereof
round about: *it was* fifty [g]cubits[c]

**16**
*l Window,* vs. 16–36; Josh. 2:15.
*m Palm Tree,* Song 7:7.
5 R. V. closed

**17**
*n Temple, chambers of,* 1 Kin. 6:17.

long, and five and twenty cubits[G] broad.

34 And the arches thereof *were* toward the outward [k]court; and [m]palm trees *were* upon the posts thereof, on this side, and on that side: and the going up to it *had* eight steps.

35 ¶ And he brought me to the north [j]gate, and measured *it* according to these measures;

36 The [3]little chambers thereof, the posts thereof, and the arches thereof, and the windows to it round about: the length *was* fifty [g]cubits[G], and the breadth five and twenty cubits[G].

37 And the posts thereof *were* toward the utter court; and [m]palm trees *were* upon the posts thereof, on this side, and on that side: and the going up to it *had* eight steps.

38 And the [n]chambers and the entries thereof *were* by the posts of the gates, where they [o]washed the [p]burnt offering.

38
*o Ceremonial Washing,* Ex. 19:10.
*p Offerings, burnt,* Lev. 6:17.

39 ¶ And in the porch of the gate *were* two tables on this side, and two tables on that side, to slay thereon the [p]burnt offering and the [q]sin offering and the [r]trespass offering.

39
*q Offerings, sin,* Lev. 6:17.
*r Offerings, trespass,* Lev. 6:17.

40 And at the side without, as one goeth up to the entry of the north [j]gate, *were* two tables; and on the other side, which *was* at the porch of the gate, *were* two tables.

41 Four tables *were* on this side, and four tables on that side, by the side of the [j]gate; eight tables, whereupon they slew *their sacrifices.*

42 And the four tables *were* of hewn stone for the [p]burnt offering, of a [g]cubit[G] and an half long, and a cubit[G] and an half broad, and one cubit[G] high: whereupon also they laid the instruments wherewith they slew the burnt offering and the sacrifice.

43 And within *were* [s]hooks, an hand[G] broad, fastened round about: and upon the tables *was* the flesh of the offering.

43
*s Hooks,* Ex. 36:36.

44 ¶ And without[G] the inner [j]gate *were* the [n]chambers of the [t,u]singers in the inner court, which *was* at the side of the north gate; and their prospect *was* toward the south: one at the side of the east gate *having* the prospect toward the north.

44
*t Choir,* 1 Chr. 15:16.
*u Music,* 2 Chr. 5:13.

45 And he said unto me, This [n,v]chamber, whose prospect *is* toward the south, *is* for the priests, the [w]keepers of the charge[G] of the [7]house.

45
*v Priest, chambers for, in temple,* Lev. 1:5.
*w Priest, duties of,* Lev. 1:5.

46 And the [n]chamber whose prospect *is* toward the north *is* for the priests, the [w]keepers of the charge of the altar: these *are* the sons of [x]Zā′dŏk among the sons of Lē′vī, which come near to the LORD to minister unto him.

46
*x Zadok,* 2 Sam. 19:11.

47 So he measured the [k]court, an hundred cubits[G] long, and an hundred cubits[G] broad, foursquare; and the [y]altar *that was* before the house.[Q]

47
*y Altar, of burnt offerings,* Gen. 8:20.

48 ¶ And he brought me to the [z]porch of the house, and measured *each* post of the porch, five cubits[G] on this side, and five cubits[G] on that side: and the breadth of the gate *was* three cubits[G] on this side, and three cubits[G] on that side.

48
*z Temple, porch of,* 1 Kin. 6:17.

49 The length of the [z]porch *was* twenty cubits[G], and the breadth eleven cubits[G]; and *he brought me* by the steps whereby they went up to it: and *there were* [a]pillars by the posts, one on this side, and another on that side.

49
*a Temple, pillars of,* 1 Kin. 6:17.

## CHAPTER 41

*The measures, parts, chambers, and ornaments of the temple.*

AFTERWARD he brought [a]me to the [b]temple, and measured the posts, six [c,d]cubits[G] broad on the one side, and six cubits[G] broad on the other side,

1
*a Ezekiel, vision of,* vs. 1–26; Ezek. 1:3.
*b Temple, Ezekiel's vision of,* vs. 1–26; 1 Kin. 6:17.
*c Cubit,* vs. 1–22; Ex. 36:9.
*d Measure, linear,* Deut. 25:15.

*which was* the breadth of the [e]tabernacle.

2 And the breadth of the door *was* ten cubits[G]; and the sides of the door *were* five cubits[G] on the one side, and five cubits[G] on the other side: and he measured the length thereof, forty cubits[G]: and the breadth, twenty cubits[G].

3 Then went he inward, and measured the post of the door, two cubits[G]; and the door, six cubits[G]; and the breadth of the door, seven cubits[G].

4 So he measured the length thereof, twenty cubits[G]; and the breadth, twenty cubits[G], before the [b]temple: and he said unto me, This *is* the [f]most holy *place*.

5 After he measured the wall of the house, six cubits[G]; and the breadth of *every* side chamber, four cubits[G], round about the house on every side.[Q]

6 And the side [g]chambers *were* three, one over another, and thirty in order; and they entered into the wall which *was* of the house for the side chambers round about, that they might have hold, but they had not hold in the wall of the house.

7 And *there was* an enlarging, and a winding about still upward to the side [g]chambers: for the winding about of the house went still upward round about the house: therefore the breadth of the house *was still* upward, and so increased *from* the lowest *chamber* to the highest by the midst.

8 I saw also [1]the height of the house round about: the foundations of the side chambers *were* a full [h]reed[G] of six great cubits.

9 The thickness of the wall, which *was* for the side chamber without[G], *was* five cubits[G]: and *that* which *was* left *was* the place of the side chambers that *were* within.

*e* *Tabernacle*, **Ex. 27:9.**

**4**

*f* *Holy of Holies*, **Ex. 26:33.**

**6**

*g* *Temple, chambers of*, **1 Kin. 6:17.**

**8**

*h* *Reed*, **Ezek. 40:3.**

**1** **R. V. that the house had a raised basement round about:**

10 And between the [g]chambers *was*[G] the wideness of twenty cubits[G] round about the house on every side.

11 And the doors of the side [g]chambers *were* toward *the place that was* left, one door toward the north, and another door toward the south: and the breadth of the place that was left *was* five cubits[G] round about.

12 Now the building that *was* before the separate place at the end toward the west *was* seventy cubits[G] broad; and the wall of the building *was* five cubits[G] thick round about, and the length thereof ninety cubits[G].

13 So he measured the house, an hundred cubits long; and the separate place, and the building, with the walls thereof, an hundred cubits long;

14 Also the breadth of the face of the house, and of the separate place toward the east, an hundred cubits.

15 And he measured the length of the building over[G] against the separate place which *was* behind it, and the galleries thereof on the one side and on the other side, an hundred cubits, with the inner temple, and the [i]porches of the court;

16 The door posts, and the [2]narrow [j]windows, and the galleries round about on their three stories, over[G] against the door, cieled[G] with wood round about, and from the ground up to the windows, and the windows *were* covered;

17 To that above the door, even unto the inner house, and without[G], and by all the wall round about within and without, by measure.

18 And *it was* made with [k]cherubims and [l]palm trees, so that a palm tree *was* between a cherub

**15**

*i* *Temple, porch of*, **1 Kin. 6:17.**

**16**

*j* *Window*, **Josh. 2:15.**

**2** **R. V. closed**

**18**

*k* *Cherubim*, **Ex. 37:7.**

*l* *Palm Tree*, **Song 7:7.**

and a cherub; and *every* cherub
had two faces;
19 So that the face of a man
*was* toward the [l]palm tree on the
one side, and the face of a young
lion toward the palm tree on the
other side: *it was* made through
all the house round about.
20 From the ground unto above
the door *were* [k]cherubims and
[l]palm trees made, and *on* the wall
of the [b]temple.
21 The posts of the [b]temple
*were* squared, *and* the face of the
[m]sanctuary; the appearance *of*
*the one* as the appearance *of the*
*other*.
22 The [n]altar of wood *was*
three cubits high, and the length
thereof two cubits; and the corners thereof, and the length
thereof, and the walls thereof,
*were* of wood: and he said unto
me, This *is* the table that *is* before the LORD.
23 And the [b]temple and the
[m]sanctuary had two [o]doors.
24 And the [o]doors had two
leaves *apiece*, two turning leaves;
two *leaves* for the one door, and
two leaves for the other *door*.
25 And *there were* made on
them, on the [o]doors of the [b]tem-
ple, [k]cherubims and [l]palm trees,
like as *were* made upon the walls;
and *there were* thick planks upon
the face of the [i]porch without.
26 And *there were* [2]narrow [i]win-
dows and [l]palm trees on the one
side and on the other side, on the
sides of the [i]porch, and *upon* the
side chambers of the house, and
thick planks.

21 *m Sanctuary,* Lev. 4:6.

22 *n Altar, of burnt offerings,* Gen. 8:20.

23 *o Door,* Deut. 11:20.

## CHAPTER 42

*The chambers in the court of the temple. 13 Some of them for the priests. 15 The measures of the outward court.*

THEN he brought [a]me forth
into the [1]utter [b]court, the
way toward the north: and he
brought me into the [c]chamber
that *was* over against the separate place, and which *was* before
the building toward the north.
2 Before the length of an
hundred [d]cubits *was* the north
door, and the breadth *was* fifty
cubits.
3 Over against the twenty *cubits*
which *were* for the inner [b]court,
and over against the pavement
which *was* for the [1]utter court,
*was* gallery against gallery in
three *stories*.
4 And before the [c]chambers
*was* a walk of ten cubits breadth
inward, a way of one cubit; and
their doors toward the north.
5 Now the upper [c]chambers *were*
shorter: for the galleries were
higher than these, than the lower,
and than the middlemost of the
building.
6 For they *were* in three *stories*,
but had not pillars as the pillars
of the courts: therefore *the* [2]*build-*
*ing* was straitened more than the
lowest and the middlemost from
the ground.
7 And the wall that *was* without
over against the [c]chambers, toward the [1]utter [b]court on the forepart of the chambers, the length
thereof *was* fifty [d]cubits.
8 For the length of the [c]cham-
bers that *were* in the [1]utter court
*was* fifty cubits: and, lo, before
the temple *were* an hundred cubits.
9 And from under these [c]cham-
bers *was* the entry on the east
side, as one goeth into them from
the [1]utter [b]court.
10 The [c]chambers *were* in the
thickness of the wall of the [b]court
toward the east, over against the
separate place, and over against
the building.
11 And the way before them *was*
like the appearance of the [c]cham-
bers which *were* toward the north,
[3]as long as they, *and* as broad
as they: and all their goings out
*were* both according to their fash-

1 *a Ezekiel, vision of,* vs. 1–20; Ezek. 1:3.
*b Temple, courts of,* 1 Kin. 6:17.
*c Temple, chambers in,* 1 Kin. 6:17.
1 R. V. outer

2 *d Cubit,* Ex. 36:9.

6 2 R. V. uppermost was

11 3 R. V. according to their length so was their breadth:

ions, and according to their doors.

12 And according[C] to the doors of the [c]chambers that *were* toward the south *was* a door in the head of the way, *even* the way directly before the wall toward the east, as one entereth into them.

13 ¶ Then said he unto me, The north [e]chambers *and* the south chambers, which *are* before the separate place, they *be* holy chambers, where the priests that approach unto the LORD shall eat the [e]most holy things: there shall they lay the most holy things, and the [4,f]meat[C] offering, and the [g]sin offering, and the [h]trespass offering; for the place *is* holy.

14 When the priests enter therein, then shall they not go out of the holy *place* into the [1]utter[C] [b]court, but there they shall lay their [i]garments wherein they minister; for they *are* holy; and shall put on other garments, and shall approach to *those things* which *are* for the people.

15 ¶ Now when he had made an end of measuring the inner house, he brought me forth toward the [j]gate whose prospect *is* toward the east, and measured it round about.

16 He measured the east side with the measuring [k]reed, five hundred reeds[C], with the measuring reed round about.

17 He measured the north side, five hundred reeds, with the measuring reed round about.

18 He measured the south side, five hundred reeds, with the measuring reed.

19 He turned about to the west side, *and* measured five hundred reeds with the measuring reed.

20 He measured it by the four sides: it had a wall round about, five hundred *reeds* long, and five hundred broad, to make a separation between [5]the sanctuary and the profane[C] place.

13
*e Priest, emoluments of,* Lev. 1:5.
*f Offerings, meat,* Lev. 6:17.
*g Offerings, sin,* Lev. 6:17.
*h Offerings, trespass,* Lev. 6:17.
4 R. V. meal

14
*i Priest, vestments of,* Lev. 1:5.

15
*j Temple, gates of,* 1 Kin. 6:17.

16
*k Reed,* Ezek. 40:3.

## CHAPTER 43

*The return of God's glory to the temple. 7 His promise to dwell there on condition of his people's repentance and future obedience. 13 The altar of burnt offerings, 18 and the ordinances thereof.*

AFTERWARD he brought [a]me to the [b]gate, *even* the gate that looketh toward the east:

2 And, behold, the [c]glory of the God of Ĭṣ'ra-el came from the way of the east: and his voice *was* like a noise of many waters: and the earth shined with his glory.[Q]

3 And *it was* according to the appearance of the [d]vision which I saw, *even* according to the vision that I saw when I came to destroy the city: and the visions *were* like the vision that I saw by the river [e]Chē'bär; and I fell upon my face.

4 And the [c]glory of the LORD came into the [f]house by the way of the gate whose prospect *is* toward the east.

5 So the spirit [g]took me up, and brought me into the inner [h]court; and, behold, the [c]glory of the LORD filled the house.[T]

6 And I heard [1]*him* speaking unto me out of the house; and the man stood by me.

7 ¶[T] And he said unto me, Son of man, [2]the [f]place of my throne, and the place of the soles of my feet, where [i]I will dwell in the midst of the children of Ĭṣ'ra-el for ever, and my holy name, shall the house of Ĭṣ'ra-el no more defile, *neither* they, nor their kings, by their whoredom[C], nor by the carcases of their kings in their high places.

8 In their setting of their threshold by my thresholds, and their post by my posts, and the wall between me and them, they have even defiled my holy name by their [j]abominations that they have committed: wherefore I

20
5 R. V. that which was holy and that which was common.

1
*a Ezekiel, vision of,* vs. 1–27; Ezek. 1:3.
*b Temple, gates of,* 1 Kin. 6:17.

2
*c God, glory of,* Gen. 2:2.

3
*d Vision, of Ezekiel,* Acts 9:10.
*e Chebar,* Ezek. 1:1.

4
*f Temple, Ezekiel's vision of,* vs. 4–27; 1 Kin. 6:17.

5
*g Prophets, inspiration of,* Isa. 3:2.
*h Temple, courts of,* 1 Kin. 6:17.

6
1 R. V. one

7
*i God dwells with the Righteous,* 1 Kin. 6:13.
2 R. V. this is the place

8
*j Jews, wickedness of,* Neh. 4:2.

k *Wicked, punishment of,* Psa. 73:3.
l *Anger of God,* 2 Kin. 13:3.

10
m *Pattern,* Ex. 25:40.

13
n *Altar, Ezekiel's vision of,* vs. 13–27; Gen. 8:20.
o *Cubit,* Ex. 36:9.
p *Measure, linear,* Deut. 25:15.
q *Handbreadth,* 1 Kin. 7:26.
3 R. V. base of the altar.

15
r *Altar, horns of,* Gen. 8:20.

16
4 R. V. *inserts* hearth

have [k]consumed them in mine
[l]anger.
9 Now let them put away their
[l]whoredom[G], and the carcases[G] of
their kings, far from me, and [i]I
will dwell in the midst of them
for ever.[T]
10 ¶ Thou son of man, shew
the house to the house of Iṣ'-
ra-el, that they may be ashamed
of their [j]iniquities: and let them
measure the [m]pattern.
11 And if they be ashamed of
all that they have [j]done, shew
them the form of the [l]house,
and the fashion thereof, and the
goings out thereof, and the com-
ings in thereof, and all the forms
thereof, and all the ordinances
thereof, and all the forms thereof, and all the laws thereof: and
write *it* in their sight, that they
may keep the whole form thereof, and all the ordinances thereof, and do them.
12 This *is* the law of the [l]house;
Upon the top of the mountain
the whole limit thereof round
about *shall be* most holy. Behold, this *is* the law of the house.
13 ¶ And these *are* the measures of the [n]altar after the [o,p]cu-
bits[G]: The cubit[G] *is* a cubit[G] and
an [p,q]hand breadth; even the
bottom *shall be* a cubit[G], and
the breadth a cubit[G], and the border thereof by the edge thereof
round about *shall be* a [p]span[G]:
and this *shall be* the [3]higher
place of the altar.
14 And from the bottom *upon*
the ground *even* to the lower settle[G] *shall be* two [o,p]cubits[G], and the
breadth one cubit[G]; and from the
lesser settle[G] *even* to the greater
settle[G] *shall be* four cubits[G], and
the breadth *one* cubit[G].
15 So the [n]altar *shall be* four
cubits[G]; and from the altar and
upward *shall be* four [r]horns.
16 And the [n]altar [4]*shall be*
twelve [o,p]*cubits*[G] long, twelve
broad, square in the four squares
thereof.[Q]
17 And the settle *shall be* fourteen *cubits*[G] long and fourteen
broad in the four squares thereof; and the border about it *shall*
*be* half a cubit[G]; and the bottom
thereof *shall be* a cubit[G] about;
and his stairs shall look toward
the east.
18 ¶ And he said unto me, Son
of man, thus saith the Lord GOD;
These *are* the ordinances of the
[s]altar in the day when they shall
make it, to offer [t]burnt offerings
thereon, and to [u]sprinkle [v]blood
thereon.
19 And thou shalt give to the
priests the Lē'vītes that be of the
seed of [w]Zā'dŏk, which approach
unto me, [x]to minister unto me,
saith the Lord GOD, a young
[y]bullock for a [z]sin [a]offering.
20 And thou shalt take of the
[b,c]blood thereof, and put *it* on the
four [d]horns of it, and on the four
corners of the settle[G], and upon
the border round about: thus
shalt thou cleanse and [5]purge it.
21 Thou shalt take the [e]bullock
also of the [f]sin [a]offering, and he
shall burn it in the appointed
place of the house, without[G] the
[g]sanctuary.
22 And on the second day thou
shalt offer a kid of the goats
[h]without [i,j]blemish for a [f]sin
[a]offering; and they shall cleanse
the [k]altar, as they did cleanse *it*
with the [e]bullock.
23 When thou hast made an
end of cleansing [k]*it,* thou shalt
offer a young [e]bullock [h]without
[i,j]blemish, and a ram out of the
flock without blemish.
24 And thou shalt offer them
before the LORD, and the [l]priests
shall cast [m]salt upon them, and
they shall offer them up *for* a
[n]burnt [a]offering unto the LORD.
25 [o]Seven days shalt thou prepare every day a goat *for* a [f]sin

18
s *Altar, how sanctified,* vs. 18–27; Gen. 8:20.
t *Offerings, burnt,* Lev. 6:17.
u *Sprinkling, of blood,* Lev. 14:7.
v *Blood, sacrificial,* Heb. 9:19.

19
w *Zadok,* 2 Sam. 19:11.
x *Priest, duties of,* Lev. 1:5.
y *Bullock,* Ex. 29:3.
z *Offerings, sin,* Lev. 6:17.

a *Jesus, typified in offerings,* Matt. 1:21.

20
b *Blood, sacrificial,* Heb. 9:19.
c *Jesus, atoning blood of, typified,* Matt. 1:21.
d *Altar, horns of,* Gen. 8:20.
5 R. V. make atonement for

21
e *Bullock,* Ex. 29:3.
f *Offerings, sin,* Lev. 6:17.
g *Sanctuary,* Lev. 4:6.

22
h *Holiness, typified,* Ex. 39:30.
i *Blemish,* Lev. 14:10.
j *Sin, typified,* Rom. 5:12.
k *Altar, how sanctified,* Gen. 8:20.

24
l *Priest, duties of,* Lev. 1:5.
m *Salt,* 2 Kin. 2:20.
n *Offerings, burnt,* Lev. 6:17.

25
o *Seven, days,* Gen. 7:2.

[a]offering: they shall also prepare
a young bullock, and a ram out
of the flock, [h]without [i,j]blemish.
26 [o]Seven days shall they [5]purge
the [k]altar and purify it; and they
shall consecrate [6]themselves.
27 And when these days are expired, it shall be, *that* upon the
eighth day, and *so* forward, the
[l]priests shall make your [n]burnt
offerings upon the [k]altar, and
your [q]peace offerings; and I will
accept you, saith the Lord GOD.

## CHAPTER 44

*The east gate assigned only to the prince. 4 The priests reproved for polluting the sanctuary. 9 Idolaters ineligible to the priest's office. 15 The sons of Zadok are appointed thereto. 17 Ordinances for the priests.*

THEN he brought [a]me back
the way of the [1,b]gate of
the outward [c]sanctuary which
looketh toward the east; and it
*was* shut.
2 Then said the LORD unto me;
This [b]gate shall be shut, it shall
not be opened, and no man shall
enter in by it; because the LORD,
the God of Iş'ra-el, hath entered
in by it, therefore it shall be shut.
3 *It is* for the prince; the prince,
he shall sit in it to eat bread
before the LORD; he shall enter
by the way of the porch of *that*
[b]gate, and shall go out by the
way of the same.
4 ¶ Then brought he [a]me the
way of the north [b]gate before
the house: and I looked, and,
behold, the [d]glory of the LORD
filled the [c]house of the LORD:
and I fell upon my face.
5 And the LORD said unto [a]me,
Son of man, mark well, and behold with thine eyes, and hear
with thine ears all that I say
unto thee concerning all the ordinances of the [c]house of the
LORD, and all the laws thereof;
and mark well the entering in of
the house, with every going forth
of the sanctuary.
6 And thou shalt say to the rebellious, *even* to the house of Iş'-
ra-el, Thus saith the Lord GOD;
O ye house of Iş'ra-el, let it suffice you of all your [e]abomina-
tions.
7 In that ye have [f]brought [2]*into my sanctuary* strangers, [g]un-
circumcised in [h]heart, and uncircumcised in flesh, to be in
my [i]sanctuary, to [j]pollute it,
*even* my house, when ye offer
my bread, the fat and the blood,
and they have broken my [k]cove-
nant because of all your abominations.
8 And ye have not kept the
charge of mine holy things: but
ye have set [l]keepers of my charge
in my [i]sanctuary for yourselves.
9 ¶ Thus saith the Lord GOD;
No [3]stranger, [g]uncircumcised in
[h]heart, nor uncircumcised in
flesh, shall enter into my [i]sanc-
tuary, of any stranger that *is*
among the children of Iş'ra-el.
10 And the [m]Lē'vītes that are
gone away far from me, when
Iş'ra-el [n]went astray, which went
astray away from me [o]after their
idols; they shall even bear their
iniquity.
11 Yet [m]they shall be ministers
in my sanctuary, *having* charge
at the gates of the house, and
ministering to the house: they
shall slay the [p]burnt offering and
the sacrifice for the people, and
they shall stand before them to
minister unto them.
12 Because [m]they ministered
unto them before their idols, and
[4,q]caused the house of Iş'ra-el to
[r]fall into iniquity; therefore have
I lifted up mine hand against
them, saith the Lord GOD, and
they shall bear their iniquity.
13 And [m]they shall not come
near unto me, to do the office of
a priest unto me, nor to come
near to any of my holy things, in
the most holy *place*: but they
shall bear their shame, and their

26
5 R. V. it;

27
p *Offerings, peace,* Lev. 6:17.

1
a *Ezekiel, vision of,* vs. 1-31; Ezek. 1:3.
b *Temple, gates of,* 1 Kin. 6:17.
c *Temple, Ezekiel's vision of,* vs. 1-31; 1 Kin. 6:17.
1 R. V. outer gate of the sanctuary,

4
d *God, glory of,* Gen. 2:2.

6
e *Jews, wickedness of,* Neh. 4:2.

7
f *Fellowship, with the wicked,* 1 Cor. 1:9.
g *Wicked, described,* Psa. 73:3.
h *Heart, unregenerate,* Psa. 44:21.
i *Church, holy,* 1 Kin. 9:3.
j *Profanation, of the house of God,* Lev. 22:32.
k *Covenant, of man with God,* Deut. 29:1.
2 R. V. in aliens,

8
l *Minister, false and corrupt,* Rom. 15:16.

9
3 R. V. alien,

10
m *Priest, corrupt,* Lev. 1:5.
n *Backsliding, of Israel,* Hos. 11:7.
o *Idolatry,* vs. 10-12; 1 Sam. 15:23.

11
p *Offerings, burnt,* Lev. 6:17.

12
q *Example, bad,* John 13:15.
r *Stumbling, figurative,* Isa. 8:14.
4 R. V. became a stumblingblock of iniquity unto the house of Israel;

abominations which they have committed.

14 But I will make [m]them keepers of the charge of the house, for all the service thereof, and for all that shall be done therein.

15 ¶ But the priests the Lē′vītes, the sons of [s]Zā′dŏk, that [t]kept the charge of my sanctuary when the children of Ĭş′ra-el [n]went astray from me, they shall come near to me [u]to minister unto me, and they shall stand before me to offer unto me the [v]fat and the [w]blood, saith the Lord GOD:

16 They shall enter into my [i]sanctuary,[G] and they shall come near to my table, [u]to minister unto me, and they shall keep my charge.

17 ¶ And it shall come to pass, *that* when they enter in at the gates of the inner [x]court, they shall be clothed with [y,z]linen garments; and no [a]wool shall come upon them, whiles they minister in the gates of the inner court, and within.

18 They shall have [b]linen [c]bonnets[G] upon their heads, and shall have linen [d]breeches upon their loins; they shall not gird *themselves* with any thing that causeth [e]sweat.

19 And when they go forth into the [5]utter[G] [f]court, *even* into the [5]utter[G] court to the people, they shall put off their [g]garments wherein they ministered, and lay them in the holy [h]chambers, and they shall put on other garments; and they shall not sanctify the people with their garments.

20 Neither shall they *shave their heads, nor suffer their locks to grow long; they shall only poll[G] their heads.

21 Neither shall any priest drink [i]wine, when they enter into the inner [f]court.

22 Neither shall [j]they take for their wives a [k]widow, nor her that is put[G] away: but they shall take maidens of the seed of the house of Ĭş′ra-el, or a widow that had a priest before.

23 And they shall [l,m,n]teach my people *the difference* between the holy and [6]profane,[G] and cause them to discern between the unclean and the clean.

24 And in controversy [o]they shall stand in judgment;[G] *and* they shall [p]judge it according to my judgments:[G] and they shall keep my laws and my statutes in all mine [7,q]assemblies; and they shall hallow my [r]sabbaths.

25 And they shall come at[G] no dead person to [s,t]defile themselves: but for father, or for mother, or for son, or for daughter, for brother, or for sister that hath had no husband, they may defile themselves.

26 And after he is [t]cleansed, they shall reckon unto him seven days.

27 And in the day that he goeth into the [u]sanctuary, unto the inner [f]court, to minister in the sanctuary, he shall [v]offer his [w]sin offering, saith the Lord GOD.

28 And [x]it shall be unto them for an inheritance: [x,y]I *am* their inheritance: and [z]ye shall give them no possession in Ĭş′ra-el: I *am* their possession.

29 [a]They shall eat the [8,b]meat[G] offering, and the [c]sin offering, and the [9,d]trespass offering; and [a]every [10]dedicated thing[G] in Ĭş′ra-el shall be their's.

30 And [a]the first of all the [e]firstfruits of all *things,* and every oblation of all, of every *sort* of your oblations, shall be the

**15**
*s* *Zadok,* 2 Sam. 19:11.
*t* *Faithfulness, instances of,* Luke 16:10.
*u* *Priest, duties of,* Lev. 1:5.
*v* *Fat, offered in sacrifice,* Lev. 7:24.
*w* *Blood, sacrificial,* Heb. 9:19.

**17**
*x* *Temple, courts of,* 1 Kin. 6:17.
*y* *Linen,* Ezek. 27:16.
*z* *Priest, vestments of,* Lev. 1:5.
*a* *Wool,* Judg. 6:37.

**18**
*b* *Linen,* Ezek. 27:16.
*c* *Turban,* Ex. 28:40.
*d* *Breeches,* Ex. 28:42.
*e* *Sweat,* Gen. 3:19.

**19**
*f* *Temple, courts of,* 1 Kin. 6:17.
*g* *Priest, vestments of,* Lev. 1:5.
*h* *Temple, chambers of,* 1 Kin. 6:17.
5 R. V. outer

**21**
*i* *Wine, forbidden to priests while on duty,* Prov. 23:31.

**22**
*j* *Priest, marriage of,* Lev. 1:5.
*k* *Widow,* 2 Sam. 14:5.

**23**
*l* *Instruction, in religion,* Prov. 23:23.
*m* *Priest, duties of,* Lev. 1:5.
*n* *Minister, duties of,* Rom. 15:16.
6 R. V. the common,

**24**
*o* *Judge, priests as,* Judg. 2:18.
*p* *Judge, must judge righteously,* Judg. 2:18.
*q* *Annual Feasts,* Num. 15:3.
*r* *Sabbath, holy,* Ex. 16:23.
7 R. V. appointed feasts;

**25**
*s* *Defilement, of priests,* Lev. 5:2.
*t* *Priest, defilement and purification of,* v. 26; Lev. 1:5.

**27**
*u* *Sanctuary,* Lev. 4:6.
*v* *Priest, atonement for,* Lev. 1:5.
*w* *Offerings, sin,* Lev. 6:17.

**28**
*x* *Priest, emoluments of,* Lev. 1:5.
*y* *Minister, emoluments of,* Rom. 15:16.
*z* *Church, duty of, to ministers,* Matt. 16:18.

**29**
*a* *Priest, emoluments of,* Lev. 1:5.
*b* *Offerings, meat,* Lev. 6:17.
*c* *Offerings, sin,* Lev. 6:17.
*d* *Offerings, trespass,* Lev. 6:17.
8 R. V. meal
9 R. V. guilt
10 R. V. devoted

**30**
*e* *First Fruits,* Deut. 18:4.

*** SHAVING.** *Forbidden, to Nazirites,* Num. 6:5; Judg. 13:5; *to priests,* Ezek. 44:20. *Of the head in mourning,* Job 1:20.

priest's: ye shall also give unto the priest the first of your dough, that he may cause the blessing to rest in thine house.[G]

31 The [f]priests shall not eat of any thing that is dead of itself, or torn, whether it be fowl or beast.

## CHAPTER 45

*The portion of land for the sanctuary; 6 for the city; 7 and for the prince. 9 The ordinances for the princes.*

MOREOVER, when ye shall divide by [a]lot the land for inheritance, [b]ye shall offer an oblation unto the LORD, an holy portion of the land: the length *shall be* the length of five and twenty thousand [c]*reeds*,[G] and the breadth *shall be* ten thousand. This *shall be* holy in all the borders thereof round about.

2 Of this there shall be for the [d]sanctuary five hundred *in length,* with five hundred *in breadth,* square round about; and fifty [e]cubits[G] round about for the suburbs[G] thereof.

3 And of this measure shalt thou measure the length of five and twenty thousand, and the breadth of ten thousand: and in it shall be the [f]sanctuary *and* the most holy *place.*

4 The [g]holy[G] *portion* of the land shall be for the priests the [h]ministers of the sanctuary, which shall come near to minister unto the LORD: and it shall be a place for their houses, and an holy[G] place for the sanctuary.

5 And [i]the five and twenty thousand of length, and the ten thousand of breadth, shall also the Lē′vītes, the ministers of the house, have for themselves, for a possession for twenty chambers.

6 ¶ And ye shall appoint the possession of the [j]city five thousand broad, and five and twenty thousand long, over[G] against the oblation of the holy *portion*: it shall be for the whole house of Ĭṣ′ra-el.

7 ¶ And *a portion shall be* for the prince on the one side and on the other side of the oblation[G] of the holy *portion,* and of the possession of the city, before the oblation[G] of the holy *portion,* and before the possession of the city, from the west side westward, and from the east side eastward: and the length *shall be* over[G] against one of the portions, from the west border unto the east border.

8 In the land shall be his possession in Ĭṣ′ra-el: and my princes shall no more [k]oppress my people; and *the rest of* the land shall they give to the house of Ĭṣ′ra-el according to their tribes.

9 ¶ Thus saith the Lord GOD; Let it suffice you, O [l]princes of Ĭṣ′ra-el: [m,n]remove [o]violence and spoil,[G] and execute judgment and [p]justice, take away your exactions[G] from my people, saith the Lord GOD.

10 [q,r]Ye shall have just [s]balances, and a just [t]ephah,[G] and a just [u,v]bath.[G]

11 [q,r]The [t]ephah and the [u,v]bath shall be of one measure, that the bath may contain the tenth part of an homer,[G] and the ephah the tenth part of an homer[G]: the measure thereof shall be after the homer.[G]

12 And [q]the [w]shekel[G] *shall be* twenty [x]gerahs: twenty shekels,[G] five and twenty shekels,[G] fifteen shekels,[G] shall be your [y]maneh.

13 This *is* the oblation that ye shall offer; the sixth part of an ephah of an homer of [z]wheat, and ye shall give the sixth part of an ephah[G] of an homer of [a]barley:

14 Concerning the ordinance of [b]oil, the [c,d]bath[G] of oil, *ye shall offer* the tenth part of a bath[G] out

**31**
*f* *Priest, holy,* Lev. 1:5.

**1**
*a* *Lot,* Esth. 3:7.
*b* *Commandment, enjoining liberality toward the house of God,* vs. 1–7; Deut. 8:2.
*c* *Reed,* Ezek. 40:3.

**2**
*d* *Temple, in Ezekiel's vision,* 1 Kin. 6:17.
*e* *Cubit,* Ex. 36:9.

**3**
*f* *Sanctuary,* Lev. 4:6.

**4**
*g* *Priest, emoluments of,* Lev. 1:5.
*h* *Minister, called minister of the sanctuary,* Rom. 15:16.

**5**
*i* *Levites, emoluments of,* Deut. 10:8.

**6**
*j* *Jerusalem, measurements of,* Judg. 19:10.

**8**
*k* *Oppression, forbidden,* Eccl. 5:8.

**9**
*l* *Rulers, character and qualifications of,* Ex. 18:21.
*m* *Commandment, enjoining righteousness,* Deut. 8:2.
*n* *Righteousness, enjoined in official administration,* Psa. 15:2.
*o* *Civil Service, corruption in,* Dan. 1:5.
*p* *Justice, enjoined,* Deut. 33:21.

**10**
*q* *Honesty, enjoined,* Rom. 13:13.
*r* *Measure, must be just,* Deut. 25:15.
*s* *Balances, must be just,* Prov. 11:1.
*t* *Measure, dry,* Deut. 25:15.
*u* *Bath,* 1 Kin. 7:26.
*v* *Measure, liquid,* Deut. 25:15.

**12**
*w* *Shekel,* Ex. 30:13.
*x* *Gerah,* Lev. 27:25.
*y* *Weights,* Lev. 19:35.

**13**
*z* *Wheat,* Ezra 6:9.
*a* *Barley,* Ex. 9:31.

**14**
*b* *Oil,* Deut. 12:17.
*c* *Bath,* 1 Kin. 7:26.
*d* *Measure, liquid,* Deut. 25:15.

of the cor, *which is* an homer of ten baths; for ten baths *are* an homer:

15 And one [e,f]lamb out of the flock, out of two hundred, out of the fat pastures of Is'ra-el; for a [1,g]meat offering, and for a [h]burnt offering, and for [i]peace offerings, to make [2,j,k,l]reconciliation for them, saith the Lord GOD.

16 All the people of the land shall give this [m]oblation for the prince in Is'ra-el.

17 And [n]it shall be the prince's part *to give* [h]burnt offerings, and [1,g]meat offerings, and [o]drink offerings, in the feasts, and in the [p]new moons, and in the [q]sabbaths, in all [3,r]solemnities of the house of Is'ra-el: he shall prepare the [s]sin offering, and the [1,g]meat offering, and the [h]burnt offering, and the [i]peace offerings, to make [2,j,k,l]reconciliation for the house of Is'ra-el.

18 Thus saith the Lord GOD; In the first [t]*month,* in the first *day* of the month, thou shalt take a young [u]bullock [v]without [w,x]blemish, and cleanse the sanctuary:

19 And the priest shall take of the [y,z]blood of the [a]sin [b]offering, and put *it* upon the posts of the house, and upon the four corners of the settle of the altar, and upon the posts of the gate of the inner court.

20 And so thou shalt do the seventh *day* of the month for every one that erreth, and for *him that is* [c]simple: so shall ye [4]reconcile the house.

21 In the first [d]*month,* in the fourteenth day of the month, ye shall have the [e]passover, a feast of seven days; [f]unleavened bread shall be eaten.

22 And upon that day shall the [g]prince prepare for himself and for all the people of the land a [h]bullock *for* a [a]sin [b]offering.

23 And [i]seven days of the [e]feast [g]he shall prepare a [j]burnt [b]offering to the LORD, seven [h]bullocks and seven rams [k]without [l,m]blemish daily the seven days; and a kid of the goats daily *for* a [a]sin offering.

24 And he shall prepare a [1,n]meat offering of an [o]ephah for a [h]bullock, and an ephah for a ram, and an [p]hin of [q]oil for an ephah.

25 In the seventh [r]*month,* in the fifteenth day of the month, shall he do the like in the [s]feast of the seven days, according to the [a]sin [b]offering, according to the [j]burnt offering, and according to the [n]meat offering, and according to the [q]oil.

## CHAPTER 46

*Ordinances for the prince in his worship, 9 and for the people. 16 An order for the prince's inheritance. 19 The rear courts designated for boiling and baking.*

THUS saith the Lord GOD; [a]The [b]gate of the inner [c]court that looketh toward the east shall be shut the six working days; but on the [d]sabbath it shall be opened, and in the day of the [e]new moon it shall be opened.

2 And the [f]prince shall enter by the way of the porch of *that* [b]gate without, and shall stand by the post of the gate, and the priests shall [g]prepare his [h]burnt [i]offering and his [j]peace offerings, and he shall worship at the threshold of the gate: then he shall go forth; but the gate shall not be shut until the evening.

3 Likewise [k]the people of the land shall worship at the door of this [b]gate before the LORD in the [d]sabbaths and in the [e]new moons.

4 And the [h]burnt [i]offering that the [f]prince shall offer unto the LORD in the [l]sabbath day *shall be* six [m]lambs [n]without [o,p]blemish, and a ram without blemish.

5 And the [1,q]meat offering *shall*

**15**
*e* *Lamb,* Num. 7:15.
*f* *Jesus, typified in offerings,* Matt. 1:21.
*g* *Offerings, meat,* Lev. 6:17.
*h* *Offerings, burnt,* Lev. 6:17.
*i* *Offerings, peace,* Lev. 6:17.
*j* *Reconciliation, between God and man,* 2 Cor. 5:18.
*k* *Atonement,* Lev. 17:11.
*l* *Jesus, atonement by, typified,* Matt. 1:21.
1 R. V. meal
2 R. V. atonement

**16**
*m* *King, emoluments of,* 2 Kin. 3:10.

**17**
*n* *King, religious duties of,* 2 Kin. 3:10.
*o* *Offerings, drink,* Lev. 6:17.
*p* *New Moon, feast of,* Amos 8:5.
*q* *Sabbath,* Ex. 16:23.
*r* *Annual Feasts,* Num. 15:3.
*s* *Offerings, sin,* Lev. 6:17.
3 R. V. the appointed feasts

**18**
*t* *Month (April),* Ex. 12:2.
*u* *Bullock,* Ex. 29:3.
*v* *Holiness, typified,* Ex. 39:30.
*w* *Blemish,* Lev. 14:10.
*x* *Sin, typified,* Rom. 5:12.

**19**
*y* *Blood, sacrificial,* Heb. 9:19.
*z* *Jesus, atoning blood of, typified,* Matt. 1:21.

*a* *Offerings, sin,* Lev. 6:17.
*b* *Jesus, typified in offerings,* Matt. 1:21.

**20**
*c* *Ignorance, sins of,* Acts 3:17.
4 R. V. make atonement for

**21**
*d* *Month (April),* Ex. 12:2.
*e* *Passover, reinstituted by Ezekiel,* vs. 21–24; Num. 9:5.
*f* *Bread, unleavened,* Ezek. 4:13.

**22**
*g* *King, religious duties of,* 2 Kin. 3:10.
*h* *Bullock,* Ex. 29:3.

**23**
*i* *Seven, days,* Gen. 7:2.
*j* *Offerings, burnt,* Lev. 6:17.
*k* *Holiness, typified,* Ex. 39:30.
*l* *Blemish,* Lev. 14:10.
*m* *Sin, typified,* Rom. 5:12.

**24**
*n* *Offerings, meat,* Lev. 6:17.
*o* *Measure, dry,* Deut. 25:15.
*p* *Measure, liquid,* Deut. 25:15.
*q* *Oil,* Deut. 12:17.

**25**
*r* *Month (October),* Ex. 12:2.
*s* *Tabernacles, feast of,* Deut. 16:13.

**1**
*a* *Vision, of Ezekiel,* vs. 1–24; Acts 9:10.
*b* *Temple, gates of,* 1 Kin. 6:17.
*c* *Temple, courts of,* 1 Kin. 6:17.
*d* *Sabbath, worship on, enjoined,* Ex. 16:23.
*e* *New Moon,* Amos 8:5.

**2**
*f* *King, religious duties of,* 2 Kin. 3:10.
*g* *Priest, duties of,* Lev. 1:5.
*h* *Offerings, burnt,* Lev. 6:17.
*i* *Jesus, typified in offerings,* Matt. 1:21.
*j* *Offerings, peace,* Lev. 6:17.

**3**
*k* *Worship, enjoined,* Gen. 22:5.

**4**
*l* *Sabbath, offerings prescribed for,* Ex. 16:23.
*m* *Lamb,* Num. 7:15.
*n* *Holiness, typified,* Ex. 39:30.
*o* *Blemish,* Lev. 14:10.
*p* *Sin, typified,* Rom. 5:12.

**5**
*q* *Offerings, meat,* Lev. 6:17.
1 R. V. meal

r *Measure, dry,* Deut. 25:15.
s *Measure, liquid,* Deut. 25:15.
t *Oil,* Deut. 12:17.

**6**
u *Bullock,* Ex. 29:3.

**7**
2 R. V. he is able.

**9**
v *Annual Feasts,* Num. 15:3.
w *Worship,* Gen. 22:5.
3 R. V. straight before him.

**12**
x *Offerings, free will,* Lev. 6:17.

*be* an [r]ephah for a ram, and the
[1,q]meat offering for the [m]lambs
as he shall be able to give, and
an [s]hin of [t]oil to an ephah.
6 And in the day of the [e]new
moon *it shall be* a young [u]bul-
lock [n]without [o,p]blemish, and six
[m]lambs, and a ram: they shall be
without blemish.
7 And he shall prepare a
[1,q]meat offering, an [r]ephah for
a [u]bullock, and an ephah for a
ram, and for the [m]lambs according as [2]his hand shall attain unto, and an [s]hin of [t]oil to an
ephah.
8 And when the prince shall enter, he shall go in by the way of
the porch of *that* [b]gate, and he
shall go forth by the way thereof.
9 ¶ But when the people of
the land shall come before the
LORD in the [v]solemn feasts, he
that entereth in by the way of
the north [b]gate to [w]worship shall
go out by the way of the south
gate; and he that entereth by
the way of the south gate shall
go forth by the way of the
north gate: he shall not return
by the way of the gate whereby
he came in, but shall go forth
[3]over against it.
10 And the prince in the midst
of them, when they go in, shall
go in; and when they go forth,
shall go forth.
11 And in the [v]feasts and in the
solemnities the [1,q]meat offering
shall be an [r]ephah to a [u]bullock,
and an ephah to a ram, and to
the [m]lambs as he is able to give,
and an [s]hin of [t]oil to an ephah.
12 Now when the [l]prince shall
prepare a [x]voluntary [h]burnt [i]of-
fering or [j]peace offerings voluntarily unto the LORD, *one* shall
then open him the [b]gate that
looketh toward the east, and he
shall prepare his burnt offering
and his peace offerings, as he did
on the [l]sabbath day: then he
shall go forth; and after his going
forth *one* shall shut the gate.
13 Thou shalt [y]daily prepare
a [h]burnt [i]offering unto the LORD
*of* a [m]lamb of the first year [n]with-
out [o,p]blemish: thou shalt prepare it every morning.
14 And thou shalt prepare a
[1,q]meat offering for it every
morning, the sixth part of an
[r]ephah, and the third part of
an [s]hin of [t]oil, to temper with
the fine flour; a meat offering
continually by a perpetual ordinance unto the LORD.
15 Thus shall they prepare the
[m]lamb, and the [1,q]meat offering,
and the [t]oil, [y]every morning *for*
a continual burnt offering.
16 ¶ Thus saith the Lord GOD;
If [z]the prince give a gift unto
any of his sons, the [a]inherit-
ance thereof shall be his sons'; it
*shall be* their possession by inheritance.
17 But if [b]he give a gift of his
inheritance to one of his servants, then it shall be his to the
[c,d]year of liberty; after it shall
return to the prince: but his [a]in-
heritance shall be his sons' for
them.
18 Moreover [b]the prince shall
not take of the people's [a]inher-
itance [4]by oppression, to thrust
them out of their possession; *but*
he shall give his sons inheritance
out of his own possession: that
my people be not scattered every
man from his possession.
19 ¶ After he brought me
through the entry, which *was* at
the side of the [e]gate, into the holy
[f]chambers of the priests, which
looked toward the north: and,
behold, there *was* a place on the
two sides westward.
20 Then said he unto me, This
*is* the place where the priests
shall boil the [g]trespass offering
and the [h]sin offering, where they
shall bake the [1,i]meat offering;

**13**
y *Offerings, daily,* Lev. 6:17.

**16**
z *King, precepts concerning,* vs. 16–18; 2 Kin. 3:10.

a *Inheritance, of real estate, inalienable,* Num. 27:7.

**17**
b *King, precepts concerning,* 2 Kin. 3:10.
c *Sabbatic Year,* Lev. 25:2.
d *Jubilee, called year of liberty,* Lev. 25:10.

**18**
4 R. V. *omits* by oppression,

**19**
e *Temple, gates of,* 1 Kin. 6:17.
f *Priest, chambers for, in temple,* Lev. 1:5.

**20**
g *Offerings, trespass,* Lev. 6:17.
h *Offerings, sin,* Lev. 6:17.
i *Offerings, meat,* Lev 6:17.

5 R. V. outer
*j Temple, courts of*, 1 Kin. 6:17.

22
*k Cubit*, Ex. 36:9.

24
6 R. V. boiling houses,

1
*a Ezekiel, vision of*, vs. 1–23; Ezek. 1:3.
*b Temple, Ezekiel's vision of*, vs. 1–23; 1 Kin. 6:17.
*c Water, vision of*, vs. 1–5; 1 Kin. 17:10.

2
*d Temple, gates of*, 1 Kin. 6:17.
1 R. V. outer

3
*e Cubit*, Ex. 36:9.

that they bear *them* not out into
the [5]utter[G] [j]court, to sanctify the
people.
21 Then he brought me forth
into the [5]utter[G] [j]court, and caused
me to pass by the four corners of
the court; and, behold, in every
corner of the court *there was* a
court.
22 In the four corners of the
court *there were* courts joined
of forty [k]*cubits*[G] long and thirty
broad: these four corners *were* of
one measure.
23 And *there was* a row *of*
*building* round about in them,
round about them four, and *it*
*was* made with boiling places
under the rows round about.
24 Then said he unto me, These
*are* the [6]places of them that boil,
where the ministers of the house
shall boil the sacrifice of the
people.

## CHAPTER 47

*The vision of the holy waters. 13 The borders of the land. 22 The division of the land by lot.*

AFTERWARD he brought
[a]me again unto the door
of the [b]house; and, behold, [c]waters
issued out from under the
threshold of the house eastward:
for the forefront of the house
*stood toward* the east, and the
waters came down from under
from the right side of the house,
at the south *side* of the altar.[Q]
2 Then brought he [a]me out of
the way of the [d]gate northward,
and led me about the way without[G]
unto the [1]utter[G] gate by the
way that looketh eastward; and,
behold, there ran out [c]waters on
the right side.
3 And when the man that had
the line in his hand went forth
eastward, he measured a thousand
[e]cubits,[G] and he brought me
through the [c]waters; the waters
*were* to the ancles.
4 Again he measured a thousand,
and brought me through
the [c]waters[G]; the waters *were* to
the knees. Again he measured
a thousand, and brought me
through; the waters *were* to the
loins.
5 Afterward he measured a
thousand; *and it was* a [f]river
that I could not pass over: for
the waters were risen, waters to
swim in, a river that could not be
passed over.
6 ¶ And he said unto me, Son of
man, hast thou seen *this*? Then
he brought me, and caused me to
return to the brink of the [f]river.
7 Now when I had returned,
behold, at the bank of the [f]river
*were* very many trees on the one
side and on the other.[Q]
8 Then said he unto me, These
waters issue out toward the east
country, and go down into the
[2]desert,[G] and go into the [g]sea:
*which being* brought forth into
the sea, the waters shall be
healed.
9 And it shall come to pass, *that*
every thing that liveth, which
[3]moveth, whithersoever[G] the [f]rivers
shall come, shall [h]live: and
there shall be a very great multitude
of [i]fish, because[G] these waters
shall come thither: for they shall
be healed; and every thing shall
live whither[G] the river cometh.
10 And it shall come to pass,
*that* the [j]fishers shall stand upon
it from Ĕn–gē′dī even unto Ĕn–
ĕg′la-ĭm; they shall be a *place*
to spread forth [k]nets; their [i]fish
shall be according to their kinds,
as the fish of the [l]great sea, exceeding
many.
11 But the miry[G] places thereof
and the marishes[G] thereof shall
not be healed; they shall be given
to [m]salt.
12 [n,o]And by the [f]river upon
the bank thereof, on this side
and on that side, shall grow all
trees for meat,[G] whose leaf shall

5
*f River, figurative of salvation*, **Psa.** 46:4.

8
*g Dead Sea*, Gen. 14:3.
2 R. V. Arabah:

9
*h Life, spiritual*, Eccl. 8:15.
*i Fish, figurative*, Matt. 17:27.
3 R. V. swarmeth,

10
*j Agency, in salvation of men*, Mark 1:17.
*k Net, figurative*, Isa. 51:20.
*l Mediterranean Sea*, Ex. 23:31.

11
*m Salt, emblematic of barrenness and desolation*, 2 Kin. 2:20.

12
*n Church, prophecies concerning its prosperity* (as some interpret), Matt. 16:18.
*o Jesus, kingdom of, prophecies concerning* (as some interpret), Matt. 1:21.

4 R. V. fail:
5 R. V. every month,
6 R. V. healing.

13
*p* *Canaan, prophecy concerning*, vs. 13–20; Gen. 37:1.
*q* *Israel, tribes of*, Ex. 4:22.

14
*r* *Oath, attributed to God*, Num. 5:19.

15
*s* Ezek. 48:1.
*t* Num. 34:8.

16
*u* *Hamath*, 1 Chr. 18:3.
*v* *Damascus*, Isa. 8:4.

17
*w* Num. 34:9, 10; Ezek. 48:1.

18
*x* *Gilead*, Deut. 3:13.
*y* *Jordan*, Gen. 32:10.

19
*z* Ezek. 48:28.

*a* *Meribah*, Ex. 17:7.
*b* *Kadesh*, Gen. 14:7.
*c* *Egypt, brook of*, Gen. 15:18.
*d* *Mediterranean Sea*, Ex. 23:31.
7 R. V. Meribothkadesh, to the brook of Egypt, unto the great sea.

20
*e* *Hamath*, 1 Chr. 18:3.

not fade, neither shall the fruit thereof [4]be consumed[c]: it shall bring forth new fruit [5]according to his months, because their waters they issued out of the sanctuary: and the fruit thereof shall be for meat[c], and the leaf thereof for [6]medicine.[q]

13 ¶ Thus saith the Lord GOD; This *shall be* the border, whereby ye shall inherit the [p]land according to the twelve [q]tribes of Ĭs̩′ra-el: Jō′s̩eph *shall have two* portions.

14 And ye shall inherit [p]it, one as well as another: *concerning* the which I [r]lifted[c] up mine hand to give it unto your fathers: and this land shall fall unto you for inheritance.

15 And this *shall be* the border of the land toward the north side, from the [l]great sea, the way of [s]Hĕth′lŏn, as men go to [t]Zē′dăd;

16 [u]Hā′math, Bĕ-rō′thah, Sĭb′ra-ĭm, which *is* between the border of [v]Dă-măs′cus and the border of Hā′math; Hā′zar–hăt′tĭ-cŏn, which *is* by the coast of Hau̲′ran.

17 And the border from the [l]sea shall be [w]Hā′zar–ē′nan, the border of [v]Dă-măs′cus, and the north northward, and the border of [u]Hā′math. And *this is* the north side.

18 And the east side ye shall measure from Hau̲′ran, and from [v]Dă-măs′cus, and from [x]Gĭl′e-ăd, and from the [p]land of Ĭs̩′ra-el *by* [y]Jôr′dan, from the border unto the [g]east sea. And *this is* the east side.

19 And the south side southward, from [z]Tā′mar *even* to the [a]waters of [7]strife *in* [b]Kā′desh, the [c]river to the [d]great sea. And *this is* the south side southward.

20 The west side also *shall be* the [d]great sea from the border, till a man come over against [e]Hā′math. This *is* the west side.

21 So shall ye divide this [f]land unto you according to the [g]tribes of Ĭs̩′ra-el.

22 And it shall come to pass, *that* ye shall divide it by [h]lot for an inheritance[c] unto you, and to the [i]strangers[c] that sojourn among you, which shall beget children among you: and they shall be unto you as born in the country among the children of Ĭs̩′ra-el; they shall have inheritance with you among the tribes of Ĭs̩′ra-el.

23 And it shall come to pass, *that* in what tribe the stranger sojourneth, there shall ye give *him* his inheritance, saith the Lord GOD.

## CHAPTER 48

*The portions of the twelve tribes. 8 The portion for the sanctuary; 15 for the city and suburbs: 21 and for the prince. 30 The dimensions and gates of the city.*

NOW these *are* the names of the [a]tribes. From the north end to the coast of the way of [b]Hĕth′lŏn, as one goeth to [c]Hā′math, [d]Hā′zar–ē′nan, the border of [e]Dă-măs′cus northward, to the coast of Hā′math; for these are his sides east *and* west; a *portion for* [f]Dăn.

2 And by the border of [f]Dăn, from the east side unto the west side, a *portion for* [g]Ăsh′ēr.

3 And by the border of [g]Ăsh′ēr, from the east side even unto the west side, a *portion for* [h]Năph′ta-lī.

4 And by the border of [h]Năph′ta-lī, from the east side unto the west side, a *portion for* [i]Mă-năs′seh.

5 And by the border of [i]Mă-năs′seh, from the east side unto the west side, a *portion for* [j]Ē′phră-ĭm.

6 And by the border of [j]Ē′phră-ĭm, from the east side even unto the west side, a *portion for* [k]Reu̲′ben.

7 And by the border of [k]Reu̲′-

21
*f* *Canaan*, Gen. 37:1.
*g* *Israel, tribes of*, Ex. 4:22.

22
*h* *Lot*, Esth. 3:7.
*i* *Foreigners*, Deut. 23:20.

1
*a* *Israel, tribes of*, Ex. 4:22.
*b* Ezek. 47:15.
*c* *Hamath*, 1 Chr. 18:3.
*d* Num. 34:9, 10; Ezek. 47:17.
*e* *Damascus*, Isa. 8:4.
*f* *Dan, tribe of*, Gen. 30 6.

2
*g* *Asher, tribe of*, Num. 1:40.

3
*h* *Naphtali, tribe of*, Num. 1:42.

4
*i* *Manasseh, tribe of*, Gen. 46:20.

5
*j* *Ephraim, tribe of*, Gen. 41:52.

6
*k* *Reubenites*, Josh. 22:1.

7
[l] *Judah, tribe of,* Num. 10:14.

8
[m] *Temple, Ezekiel's vision of,* 1 Kin. 6:17.

10
[n] *Priest, emoluments of,* Lev. 1:5.

11
[o] *Zadok,* 2 Sam. 19:11.
[p] *Faithfulness, instances of,* Luke 16:10.
[q] *Backsliding, of Israel,* Hos. 11:7.
[r] *Priest, corrupt,* Lev. 1:5.

13
[s] *Levites, emoluments of,* Deut. 10:8.

14
[t] *First Fruits,* Deut. 18:4.

15
1 R. V. for common use, for the city.

ben, from the east side unto the
west side, a *portion for* [l]Jū'dah.
8 And by the border of [l]Jū'dah,
from the east side unto the west
side, shall be the offering which
ye shall offer of five and twenty
thousand *reeds*[G] *in* breadth, and
*in* length as one of the *other*
parts, from the east side unto the
west side: and the [m]sanctuary
shall be in the midst of it.
9 The oblation[G] that ye shall offer
unto the LORD *shall be* of five
and twenty thousand in length,
and of ten thousand in breadth.
10 And for them, *even* for the
[n]priests, shall be *this* holy oblation;
toward the north five and
twenty thousand *in length,* and
toward the west ten thousand in
breadth, and toward the east ten
thousand in breadth, and toward
the south five and twenty thousand
in length: and the [m]sanctuary
of the LORD shall be in the
midst thereof.
11 [n]*It shall be* for the priests
that are sanctified of the sons of
[o]Zā'dŏk; which have [p]kept my
charge[G], which went not astray
when the children of Ĭș'ra-el
[q]went astray, as the [r]Lē'vītes
went astray.
12 And *this* oblation[G] of the land
that is offered shall be unto them
a thing most holy by the border
of the Lē'vītes.
13 And over[G] against the border
of the priests the [s]Lē'vītes *shall
have* five and twenty thousand
in length, and ten thousand in
breadth: all the length *shall be*
five and twenty thousand, and
the breadth ten thousand.
14 And they shall not sell of
it, neither exchange, nor alienate
the [t]firstfruits of the land: for *it
is* holy unto the LORD.
15 ¶ And the five thousand,
that are left in the breadth over[G]
against the five and twenty thousand,
shall be [1]a profane[G] *place*
for the [u]city, for dwelling, and
for suburbs[G]: and the city shall be
in the midst thereof.
16[Q] And these *shall be* the measures
thereof; the north side four
thousand and five hundred, and
the south side four thousand and
five hundred, and on the east
side four thousand and five hundred,
and the west side four
thousand and five hundred.
17 And the suburbs[G] of the [u]city
shall be toward the north two
hundred and fifty, and toward
the south two hundred and fifty,
and toward the east two hundred
and fifty, and toward the west
two hundred and fifty.[Q]
18 And the residue in length
over[G] against the oblation of the
holy *portion shall be* ten thousand
eastward, and ten thousand
westward: and it shall be over[G]
against the oblation of the holy
*portion;* and the increase thereof
shall be for food unto them that
[2]serve the city.
19 And they that [2]serve the
city [3]shall serve it out of all the
[a]tribes of Ĭș'ra-el.
20 All the oblation *shall be* five
and twenty thousand by five and
twenty thousand: ye shall offer
the holy oblation foursquare,
with the possession of the [u]city.
21 And the [v,w]residue[G] *shall be*
for the prince, on the one side
and on the other of the holy oblation,
and of the possession of
the [u]city, over[G] against the five
and twenty thousand of the oblation
toward the east border,
and westward over[G] against the
five and twenty thousand toward
the west border, over[G] against the
portions for the prince: and it
shall be the holy oblation; and
the sanctuary of the [m]house *shall
be* in the midst thereof.
22 Moreover [v,w]from the [s]possession
of the Lē'vītes, and from
the possession of the city, *being*

[u] *Jerusalem, prophecies of the rebuilding of,* vs. 15–22; Judg. 19:10.

18
2 R. V. labour in

19
3 R. V. out of all the tribes of Israel, shall till it.

21
[v] *Land, king's part in,* Ruth 4:3.
[w] *King, emoluments of,* 2 Kin. 3:10.

in the midst *of that* which is
the prince's, between the border
of [l]Jū'dah and the border of
[x]Bĕn'ja-mĭn, shall be for the
prince.
23 As for the rest of the tribes,
from the east side unto the west
side, [x]Bĕn'ja-mĭn *shall have* a
*portion*.[C]
24 And by the border of [x]Bĕn'-
ja-mĭn, from the east side unto
the west side, [y]Sĭm'e-on *shall*
*have* a *portion*.
25 And by the border of [y]Sĭm'-
e-on, from the east side unto the
west side, [z]Ĭs'sa-char a *portion*.
26 And by the border of [z]Ĭs'sa-
char, from the east side unto the
west side, [a]Zĕb'u-lŭn a *portion*.
27 And by the border of [a]Zĕb'u-
lŭn, from the east side unto the
west side, [b]Găd a *portion*.
28 And by the border of [b]Găd,
at the south side southward, the
border shall be even from [c]Tā'-
mar *unto* the [d]waters of [4]strife *in*
[e]Kā'desh, *and* to the [f]river toward the [g]great sea.
29 This *is* the land which ye
shall divide by [h]lot unto the
[i]tribes of Ĭs̹'ra-el for inheritance,

22
x *Benjamin, tribe of*, Num. 1:37.

24
y *Simeon, tribe of*, Num. 2:12.

25
z *Issachar, tribe of*, Num. 1:28.

26
a *Zebulun, tribe of*, Gen. 49:13.

27
b *Gad, tribe of*, Deut. 33:20.

28
c Ezek. 47:19.
d *Meribah*, Ex. 17:7.
e *Kadesh*, Gen. 14:7.
f *Egypt, brook of*, Gen. 15:18.
g *Mediterranean Sea*, Ex. 23:31.
4 R. V. Meribath-kadesh, to the brook of Egypt, unto the great sea.

29
h *Lot*, Esth. 3:7.
i *Israel, tribes of*, Ex. 4:22.

and these *are* their portions, saith
the Lord GOD.
30 ¶ And these *are* the goings
out of the city on the north side,
four thousand and five hundred
[5]measures.[C]
31[Q] And the [j]gates of the city
*shall be* after the names of the
[i]tribes of Ĭs̹'ra-el: three gates
northward; one gate of [k]Reu̇'-
ben, one gate of [l]Jū'dah, one
gate of [m]Lē'vī.
32 And at the east side four
thousand and five hundred: and
three [j]gates; and one gate of
[n,o]Jō'se̤ph, one gate of [p]Bĕn'ja-
mĭn, one gate of [q]Dăn.
33 And at the south side four
thousand and five hundred [5]meas-
ures: and three [j]gates; one gate
of [r]Sĭm'e-on, one gate of [s]Ĭs'sa-
char, one gate of [a]Zĕb'u-lŭn.
34 At the west side four thousand and five hundred, *with* their
three gates; one gate of [b]Găd,
one gate of [t]Ăsh'ēr, one gate of
[u]Năph'ta-lī.[Q]
35 *It was* round about eighteen
thousand *measures*:[C] and the
name of the [v]city from *that* day
*shall be*, The LORD *is* there.[Q]

30
5 R. V. reeds by measure:

31
j *Jerusalem, gates of*, Judg. 19:10.
k *Reubenites*, Josh. 22:1.
l *Judah, tribe of*, Num. 10:14.
m *Levites*, Deut. 10:8.

32
n *Ephraim, tribe of*, Gen. 41:52.
o *Manasseh, tribe of*, Gen. 46:20.
p *Benjamin, tribe of*, Num. 1:37.
q *Dan, tribe of*, Gen. 30:6.

33
r *Simeon, tribe of*, Num. 2:12.
s *Issachar, tribe of*, Num. 1:28.

34
t *Asher, tribe of*, Num. 1:40.
u *Naphtali, tribe of*, Num. 1:42.

35
v *Jerusalem*, Judg. 19:10.

---

THE

# BOOK OF DANIEL

v.1–526 BC
See footnote, *Time*, Rev. 10:6.

## CHAPTER 1

*Jehoiakim's captivity. 3 Daniel and three others selected to be taught the learning of the Chaldeans. 8 They refuse to eat the king's meat. 17 Their great attainments in wisdom.*

IN the third year of the reign of
[a]Jĕ-hoi'a-kĭm king of [b]Jū'-
dah came [c]Nĕb-u-chad-nĕz'zar
king of [d]Băb'y̆-lon unto [e]Jē-ru̇'-
sā-lĕm, and [f]besieged it.
2 And the Lord gave [a]Jĕ-hoi'-
a-kĭm king of [b]Jū'dah into his
hand, with part of the vessels of
the [g]house of God: which he
carried into the land of [d]Shī'-

1
a *Jehoiakim*, Jer. 26:1.
b *Judah, kingdom of*, 2 Chr. 11:17.
c *Nebuchadnezzar*, Dan. 2:1.
d *Babylon, empire of*, Ezra 5:12.
e *Jerusalem*, Judg. 19:10.
f *Siege, instances of*, Deut. 28:53.

2
g *Temple, Solomon's*, 1 Kin. 6:17.

när to the house of his god; and
he brought the [h]vessels into the
[i]treasure house of his god.
3 ¶ And the [c]king spake unto
Ăsh'pe-năz the master[C] of his
[j]eunuchs,[C] that he should bring
*certain* of the [k]children of Ĭs̹'-
rael, and of the king's seed, and
of the princes;
4 [1,l]Children[C] in whom *was* no
blemish, but well favoured,[C] and
skilful in all [m]wisdom, and cunning[C] in knowledge, and understanding science, and such as *had*

h *Trophies, placed in temples*, 1 Sam. 21:9.
i *Treasure Houses, heathen temples used for*, Ezra 5:17.

3
j *Eunuch, influential court official*, Matt. 19:12.
k *Jews, captive in Babylon*, Neh. 4:2.

4
l *Young Men*, Prov. 1:4.
m *Wisdom, worldly*, Prov. 2:2.
1 R. V. Youths

n *Instruction, provision for, made by the state,* Prov. 23:23.
o *Government, civil service school provided by,* Isa. 22:21.
p *School, state,* Acts 19:9.
q *Language,* Dan. 3:29.

5
r *Students, in state school,* 2 Kin. 2:3.
s *Wine,* Prov. 23:31.

8
t *Decision, instances of,* Isa. 50:7.
u *Conscience, faithful,* Acts 23:1.
v *Self-denial,* Mark 8:34.
w *Temperance,* vs. 12–16; 2 Pet. 1:6.

9
x *God, providence of,* Gen. 2:2.
y *Temporal Blessings, from God,* Psa. 103:2.
2 Am. R. V. made Daniel to find kindness and compassion

10
z *Government, monarchical,* Isa. 22:21.

ability in them to stand[G] in the
king's palace, and whom they
might [n,o,p]teach the learning
and the [q]tongue of the *Chăl-
dē′ans.
5 And the king appointed
[l,r]them a daily provision of the
king's meat,[G] and of the [s]wine
which he drank: so nourishing
them three years, that at the end
thereof they might †stand[G] before
the king.
6 Now among [k]these were of
the children of Jū′dah, ‡Dăn′iel,
Hăn-a-nī′ah, Mĭsh′a-el, and Ăz-
a-rī′ah:
7 Unto whom the prince of the
[j]eunuchs[G] gave names: for he gave
unto ‡Dăn′iel *the name* of Bĕl-te-
shăz′zar; and to Hăn-a-nī′ah, of
‖Shā′drach; and to Mĭsh′a-el, of
§Mē′shach; and to Ăz-a-rī′ah, of
+Ā-bĕd′–ne-gō.
8 ¶ But ‡Dăn′iel [t]purposed in
his [u]heart that he would [v]not defile himself with the portion of
the king's meat,[G] [w]nor with the
wine which he drank: therefore
he requested of the prince of the
[j]eunuchs that he might not defile
himself.
9 Now God [2]had [x]brought
‡Dăn′iel into [y]favour and tender
love with the prince of the [j]eu-
nuchs.
10 And the prince of the [j]eu-
nuchs[G] said unto ‡Dăn′iel, I fear
my lord the [z]king, who hath
appointed[G] your meat[G] and your
drink: for why should he see
your faces worse[G] liking than the
[3]children[G] which *are* of your sort?
then shall ye make *me* endanger
my head to the king.
11 Then said ‡Dăn′iel to [4]Mĕl′-
zar, whom the prince of the
[a]eunuchs had set over Dăn′iel,
‖Hăn-a-nī′ah, §Mĭsh′a-el, and
+Ăz-a-rī′ah,
12 Prove[G] thy servants, I beseech thee, ten days; and let
them give us pulse[G] to eat, and
water to drink.[Q]
13 Then let our [b]countenances
be looked upon before thee, and
the countenance of the [1,c]chil-
dren[G] that eat of the portion of
the king's meat:[G] and as thou
seest, deal with thy servants.
14 So he consented to them in
this matter, and proved[G] them ten
days.[Q]
15 And at the end of ten days
their [b]countenances appeared
fairer and fatter in flesh than all
the [1,c]children[G] which did eat the
portion of the king's meat.[G]
16 [5]Thus Mĕl′zar took away the
portion of their meat,[G] and the
[d]wine that they should drink; and
gave them pulse.[G]
17 ¶ As for these four [1,c]chil-
dren,[G] God [e]gave them knowledge and skill in all learning and
[f]wisdom: and ‡Dăn′iel had [g]un-
derstanding in all [h]visions and
⊙dreams.
18 Now at the end of the days

11
a *Eunuch,* Matt. 19:12.
4 R. V. the steward,

13
b *Countenance,* Prov. 15:13.
c *Young Men,* Prov. 1:4.

16
d *Wine,* Prov. 23:31.
5 R. V. So the steward took

17
e *God, providence of,* Gen. 2:2.
f *Wisdom, worldly,* Prov. 2:2.
g *Wisdom, spiritual, from God,* Prov. 2:2.
h *Vision,* Acts 9:10.

* **CHALDEANS,** Job 1:17; Isa. 23:13; Jer. 22:25; 24:5; 32:43; 41:3, 18; 43:3; Ezek. 23:14; Dan. 3:8. *Learned and wise men among,* Dan. 1:4; 2:2; 4:7; 5:7.
*Army of,* Jer. 35:11; 50:1. *Besiege and capture Jerusalem,* 2 Kin. 25:1–21; 2 Chr. 36:17–21; Jer. 37:5–11; 39:5, 8; 52:7, 8, 14, 17. *Jeremiah accused of falling away to,* Jer. 37:10–14. *Gedaliah exhorts Jews to serve,* Jer. 40:9, 10.
Prophecies concerning: *Conquest of Jerusalem by,* Jer. 21:4, 9; 25:9–12; 32:24, 28, 29; 37:8–10; 38:2, 18, 19, 23; *captivity of Jews among,* Jer. 32:4, 5; Ezek. 12:13; *judgments upon,* Isa. 43:14; 47:1, 5; 48:14, 20; Jer. 25:12; 33:5; 50:1–10, 35, 45; 51:4, 24, 54.
See footnote, BABYLON, Ezra 5:12.

† **CIVIL SERVICE.** *School for,* Dan. 1:3–20. *Appointment in, on account of merit,* Gen. 39:1–6; 41:38–44; 1 Kin. 11:28; Esth. 6:1–11; Dan. 1:17–21; 6:1–3. *Corruption in,* Neh. 5:15; Dan. 6:4–17; Mark 15:15; Acts 24:26. *Reform in,* Neh. 5:14, 15. *Influence in,* 1 Kin. 1:5–40; 2 Kin. 4:13; Matt. 20:20–23; Mark 10:35.

‡ **DANIEL** (*God is my judge*), a Jewish captive, called also BELTESHAZZAR. *Educated at king's court,* Dan. 1. *Interprets visions,* Dan. chapters 2, 4, 5. *Promotion and executive authority of,* Dan. 2:48, 49; 5:11, 29; 6:2. *Conspiracy against; cast into the lion's den,* Dan. 6.
*Temperance of, in food and drink,* Dan. 1:8–16. *Wisdom of,* Dan. 1:17; Ezek. 28:3. *Devoutness of,* Dan. 2:18; 6; 9; 10; Ezek. 14:14. *Courage and fidelity of,* Dan. 4:27; 5:17–23; 6:10–23. *Worshiped by Nebuchadnezzar,* Dan. 2:46.
*Prophecies of,* Dan. 2:31–45; 4:8, 9, 19–37; chapters 7–12; Matt. 24:15.

‖ **SHADRACH,** called also HANANIAH. *A Hebrew captive in Babylon, of the tribe of Judah,* Dan. 1; 2:17, 49; 3; Heb. 11:34.

§ **MESHACH.** *A name given by the chief eunuch to Mishael, one of the three Hebrew captives,* Dan. 1:7; 2:49; 3:12–30; Heb. 11:34.

+ **ABED-NEGO,** called also AZARIAH. *A Jewish captive in Babylon, of the tribe of Judah,* Dan. 1:6–20; 2:17, 49; 3:12–30; Heb. 11:34.

⊙ **DREAM,** Eccl. 5:3, 7. *Revelations by,* Num. 12:6; Job 33:15–17; Jer. 23:28; Joel 2:28; Acts 2:17.
*Interpreted, by Joseph,* Gen. 40:12, 13, 18, 19; 41:25–32; *by Daniel,* Dan. 2:16–23, 28–30; 4. *Delusive,* Isa. 29:7, 8.

that the king had said he should
bring them in, then the prince of
the [a]eunuchs brought them in
before [i]Něb-u-chad-něz′zar.
19 And the [i]king communed[G] with
them; and among them all was
found none like ‡Dăn′iel, ‖Hăn-
a-nī′ah, §Mĭsh′a-el, and +Ăz-a-
rī′ah: therefore †stood[G] they before the king.
20 And in all matters of [j]wis-
dom *and* understanding, that the
king enquired of them, he found
them ten times better than all
the [j]magicians *and* [5, k]astrologers[G]
that *were* in all his realm.
21 And ‡Dăn′iel continued *even*
unto the first year of king [l]Çȳ′rus.

## CHAPTER 2

*Nebuchadnezzar, forgetting his dream, requires his wise men to show it. 10 They being unable are condemned to die. 14 Daniel obtains some respite. 19 The dream is revealed to him. 20 His thanksgiving. 24 He is brought before the king. 31 The dream. 36 Its interpretation. 46 Daniel's promotion.*

AND in the second year of the
reign of *Něb-u-chad-něz′-
zar Něb-u-chad-něz′zar dreamed
[a]dreams, wherewith his spirit was
troubled, and his [b]sleep[G] brake
from him.
2 Then the *king commanded
to call the [c]magicians, and the
[1]astrologers, and the [d]sorcerers,
and the [e]Chăl-dē′anș, for to shew
the king his [a]dreams. So they
came and stood before the king.
3 And the *king said unto them,
I have dreamed a [a]dream, and
my spirit was troubled to know[G]
the dream.
4 Then spake the [e]Chăl-dē′anș
to the king in [f]Sȳr′ĭ-ăck, [g]O king,
live for ever: tell thy servants the
[a]dream, and we will shew[G] the interpretation.
5 The *king answered and said
to the [e]Chăl-dē′anș, The thing is
gone from me: if ye will not make
known unto me the [a]dream, with
the interpretation thereof, [h]ye
shall be [i]cut in pieces, and your
houses shall be made a dunghill.[G]
6 But if ye shew[G] the [a]dream,
and the interpretation thereof,
ye shall receive of me [j]gifts and
rewards and great honour: therefore shew me the dream, and the
interpretation thereof.
7 They answered again and said,
Let the *king tell his servants
the dream, and we will shew the
interpretation of it.
8 The king answered and said, I
know of certainty that ye would
gain the time, because ye see the
thing is gone from me.
9 But if ye will not make known
unto me the [a]dream, *there is*
*but* one decree for you: for ye
have prepared lying and corrupt
words to speak before me, till the
time be changed: therefore tell
me the dream, and I shall know
that ye can shew me the interpretation thereof.
10 ¶ The [e]Chăl-dē′anș answered
before the king, and said, There
is not a man upon the earth that
can shew[G] the king's matter: therefore *there is* no king, lord, nor
ruler, *that* asked[G] such things at
any [c]magician, or [1, d]astrologer,
or Chăl-dē′an.

18
i *Nebuchadnezzar,* Dan. 2:1.

20
j *Magician,* Ex. 7:11.
k *Sorcery, practiced by Babylonians,* Isa. 47:9.
5 R. V. enchanters

21
l *Cyrus,* 2 Chr. 36:22.

v.1–524 BC
1
a *Dream,* Dan. 1:17.
b *Sleep,* Psa. 127:2.

2
c *Magician,* Ex. 7:11.
d *Sorcery, practiced by Babylonians,* Isa. 47:9.
e *Chaldeans,* Dan. 1:4.
1 R. V. enchanters,

v.4–524 BC
See footnote, *Time,* Rev. 10:6.

4
f *Language,* Dan. 3:29.
g *Salutations,* Luke 1:44.

5
h *Government, monarchical, tyranny in,* vs. 5–13; Isa. 22:21.
i *Punishment, death penalty,* Lev. 26:41.

6
j *Presents, rewards of service,* Gen. 32:13.

*False prophets pretended to receive revelations through,* Deut. 13:1–5; Jer. 23:25–32; 27:9; 29:8; Zech. 10:2.
See footnote, VISION, Acts 9:10.

**Instances of:** *Of Abimelech, concerning Sarah,* Gen. 20:3. *Of Jacob, concerning the ladder,* Gen. 28:12; *concerning the ring-streaked cattle,* Gen. 31:10–13; *concerning his going down into Egypt,* Gen. 46:2. *Of Laban, concerning Jacob,* Gen. 31:24. *Of Joseph, concerning the sheaves,* Gen. 37:5–10. *Of the butler and baker,* Gen. 40:8–23. *Of Pharaoh,* Gen. 41:1–36. *Of the Midianite, concerning the cake of barley,* Judg. 7:13. *Of Solomon, concerning his choice of wisdom,* 1 Kin. 3:3–15. *Of Eliphaz, of a spirit speaking to him,* Job 4:12–21. *Of Nebuchadrezzar,* Dan. 2:1, 31–45; 4:10–27. *Of Daniel, concerning the four beasts,* Dan. 7. *Of Joseph, concerning Mary's innocence,* Matt. 1:20, 21; *concerning the flight into Egypt,* Matt. 2:13; *concerning the return into Palestine,* Matt. 2:19–22. *Of the wise men, not to return to Herod,* Matt. 2:12. *Of Pilate's wife, concerning Jesus,* Matt. 27:19. *Cornelius' vision concerning Peter,* Acts 10:3–6. *Peter's vision of the unclean beasts,* Acts 10:10–16. *Paul's vision, of the man in Macedonia, crying, Come over into Macedonia,* Acts 16:9; *relating to his going to Rome,* Acts 23:11; *concerning the shipwreck, and the safety of all on board,* Acts 27:23, 24.

* **NEBUCHADNEZZAR,** more accurately NEBUCHADREZZAR. *Called* LUCIFER (R. V. day star), Isa. 14:12. *King of Babylon,* Jer. 21:2. *His administration,* Dan. chapters 1–4.
Conquest of: *Of Jerusalem,* 2 Kin. 24:25; 1 Chr. 6:15; 2 Chr. 36:5–21; Ezra 1:7; Jer. 39; *of Egypt,* 2 Kin. 24:7; Jer. 46:2; *of Tyre,* Ezek. 29:18. *An instrument of God's judgments,* Jer. 27:8. *Prophecies concerning,* Jer. 21:7, 10; 22:25; 25:9; 27:6–9; 32:28; 43:10; 46:13; 49:30–33; Ezek. 26:7–12.
See footnote, BABYLON, Ezra 5:12.

v.11–524 BC
See footnote, *Time,* Rev. 10:6.

12
*k Anger,* Psa. 37:8.
*l Babylon,* Ezra 5:12.

13
*m Daniel,* Dan. 1:6.

14
*n Prudence,* 2 Chr. 2:12.
*o Captain,* Num. 31:48.

15
2 R. V. urgent

17
*p Shadrach,* Dan. 1:7.
*q Meshach,* Dan. 1:7.
*r Abed-nego,* Dan. 1:7.

18
*s Intercession, solicited,* Jer. 27:18.
*t God, mercy of,* Gen. 2:2.

19
*u Prayer, answered, instances of,* Acts 6:4.
*v Prophets, inspiration of,* Isa. 3:2.
*w Vision,* Acts 9:10.
*x Worship,* Gen. 22:5.

20
*y Praise, instances of,* Psa. 150:1.
*z God, wisdom of,* Gen. 2:2.

21
*a God, sovereign,* Gen. 2:2.
*b God, providence of,* Gen. 2:2.
*c Government, God in,* Isa. 22:21.
*d King, divinely authorized,* 2 Kin. 3:10.
*e Rulers, appointed by God,* Ex. 18:21.
*f Wisdom, worldly,* Prov. 2:2.
*g Wisdom, spiritual,* Prov. 2:2.

11 And *it is* a rare thing that the king requireth, and there is none other that can shew[C] it before the king, except the gods, whose dwelling is not with flesh.

12 For this cause the *king was [k]angry and very furious, and [h]commanded to destroy all the wise *men* of [l]Băb′ÿ-lon.

13 And [h]the decree went forth that the wise *men* should be slain; and they sought [m]Dăn′iel and his fellows to be slain.

14 ¶ Then [m]Dăn′iel answered with counsel and [n]wisdom to Ā′rĭ-ŏch the [o]captain of the king's guard, which was gone forth to slay the wise *men* of [l]Băb′ÿ-lon:

15 [m]He answered and said to Ā′rĭ-ŏch the king's [o]captain, Why *is* the decree *so* [2]hasty from the king? Then Ā′rĭ-ŏch made the thing known to Dăn′iel.

16 Then [m]Dăn′iel went in, and desired of the king that he would give him time, and that he would shew[C] the king the interpretation.

17 Then [m]Dăn′iel went to his house, and made the thing known to [p]Hăn-a-nī′ah, [q]Mĭsh′a-el, and [r]Ăz-a-rī′ah, his companions:

18 [s]That they would desire [t]mercies of the God of heaven concerning this secret; that [m]Dăn′iel and his fellows should not perish with the rest of the wise *men* of [l]Băb′ÿ-lon.

19 ¶ [u]Then was the secret [v]revealed unto [m]Dăn′iel in a night [w]vision. Then Dăn′iel [x]blessed the God of heaven.[Q]

20 [m]Dăn′iel answered and said, [y]Blessed be the name of God for ever and ever: for [z]wisdom and might are his:[S]

21 And [a]he changeth the times and the †seasons: [a,b,c]he removeth [d,e]kings, and setteth up kings: he giveth [f,g]wisdom unto the wise, and [h]knowledge to them that know understanding:

22 [b]He revealeth the deep and secret things: he [i]knoweth what *is* in the darkness, and the light dwelleth with him.[S]

23 [j]I [k]thank thee, and [l]praise thee, O thou God of my fathers, who hast given me [f,g]wisdom and might, and hast made known unto me now what we desired of thee: for thou hast *now* made known unto us the king's matter.

24 ¶ Therefore [j]Dăn′iel went in unto Ā′rĭ-ŏch, whom the king had ordained[C] to destroy the wise *men* of Băb′ÿ-lon: he went and [m]said thus unto him; Destroy not the [n]wise *men* of Băb′ÿ-lon: bring me in before the king, and I will shew[C] unto the king the [o]interpretation.

25 Then Ā′rĭ-ŏch brought in [j]Dăn′iel before the *king in haste, and said thus unto him, I have found a man of the captives of Jū′dah, that will make known unto the king the [o]interpretation.

26 The *king answered and said to [j]Dăn′iel, whose name *was* Bĕl-te-shăz′zar, Art thou able to make known unto me the [p]dream which I have seen, and the [o]interpretation thereof?

27 [j]Dăn′iel answered in the presence of the king, and said, The secret which the king hath demanded cannot the wise *men*, the [1]astrologers, the [n]magicians, the soothsayers,[C] shew[C] unto the king;

28 But[S] there is a God in heaven that revealeth secrets, and [q]maketh known to the king *Nĕb-u-chad-nĕz′zar what shall be in the latter days. Thy [p]dream, and the visions of thy head upon thy bed, are these;[Q]

29 As for thee, O king, thy

v.21–524 BC
See footnote, *Time,* Rev. 10:6.

*h Knowledge,* Luke 11:52.

22
*i God, knowledge of,* Gen. 2:2.

23
*j Daniel,* Dan. 1:6.
*k Thankfulness, to God,* Acts 24:3.
*l Praise,* Psa. 150:1.

24
*m Intercession, of man with man,* Jer. 27:18.
*n Magician,* Ex. 7:11.
*o Interpreter,* Gen. 40:8.

26
*p Dream, interpreted,* Dan. 1:17.

28
*q God, foreknowledge of,* Gen. 2:2.

† **SEASON.** *A period of time,* Jer. 33:20; Dan. 2:21; Acts 1:7. *A division of the year determined by the earth's position in its orbit,* Gen. 1:14; 8:22; Psa. 104:19; Matt. 21:41; 24:32; Mark 12:2; 1 Thess. 5:1.

v.29–524 BC
See footnote, *Time*, Rev. 10:6.

thoughts came *into thy mind* upon thy bed, what should come to
pass hereafter: and [q]he that revealeth secrets maketh known to
thee what shall come to pass.[S Q]
30 [r]But as for me, [s]this secret is
not revealed to me for *any* wisdom that I have more than any
living, [s]but for *their* sakes that
shall make known the interpretation to the king, and that thou
mightest know[G] the thoughts of
thy heart.
31 ¶ Thou, O king, sawest, and
behold a great image. This great
image, whose brightness *was* excellent, stood before thee; and
the [3]form thereof *was* terrible.[G]
32 This image's head *was* of fine
[t]gold, his breast and his arms of
[u]silver, his belly[G] and his thighs
of [v]brass,
33 His legs of [w]iron, his feet
part of iron and part of [x]clay.
34[Q] Thou sawest[G] till that a
[y,z]stone was cut out without
hands, which smote the image
upon his feet *that were* of [w]iron
and [x]clay, and brake them to
pieces.
35 Then was the [w]iron, the [x]clay,
the [v]brass, the [u]silver, and the
[t]gold, broken to pieces together,
and became like the chaff of the
summer threshing-floors; and the
wind carried them away, that no
place was found for them: and
[z]the [y]stone that smote the image
became a great mountain, and
filled the whole earth.[S Q]
36 ¶ This *is* the [a]dream; and
we will tell the interpretation
thereof before the king.
37 *Thou, O king, *art* a [b]king
of kings: for [c]the God of heaven
[d]hath given [e]thee a kingdom,
power, and strength, and glory.
38 And wheresoever the children of men dwell, the beasts of
the field and the fowls of the
heaven hath he [d]given into thine
hand, and hath made thee [e,f]ruler
over them all. Thou *art* this head
of gold.
39 And after thee shall arise
another kingdom inferior to thee,
and another third kingdom of
[g]brass, which shall bear rule over
all the earth.
40 And the fourth kingdom
shall be strong as [h]iron: forasmuch as iron breaketh in pieces
and subdueth all *things*: and as
iron that breaketh all these, shall
it break in pieces and bruise.
41 And whereas thou sawest
the feet and toes, part of potters' [i]clay, and part of [j]iron, the
kingdom shall be divided; but
there shall be in it of the strength
of the iron, forasmuch as thou
sawest the iron mixed with miry[G]
clay.
42 And *as* the toes of the feet
*were* part of iron, and part of
clay, *so* the kingdom shall be
partly strong, and partly broken.
43 And whereas thou sawest
iron mixed with miry clay, they
shall mingle[G] themselves with the
seed of men: but they shall not
cleave[G] one to another, even as
iron [4]is not mixed with clay.
44[Q] And in the days of these
kings shall the God of heaven
set up a [k]kingdom, which shall
never be destroyed: [5]and the
kingdom shall not be left to other
people, *but* it shall break in pieces
and consume all these kingdoms,[S T]
and it shall stand for ever.
45 Forasmuch as thou sawest
that the [k,l]stone was cut out of
the mountain without hands, and
that it brake in pieces the iron,
the brass, the clay, the silver, and
the gold; the great [m]God hath
made known to the king what
shall come to pass hereafter:
and the dream *is* certain, and
the [a]interpretation thereof sure.[Q S]
46 ¶ Then the king *Nĕb-u-
chad-nĕz'zar fell upon his face,
and [n]worshipped [o]Dăn'iel, and

**30**
r *Humility, instances of*, Prov. 22:4.
s *Miracles, design of*, Luke 23:8.

**31**
3 R. V. aspect

**32**
t *Gold, symbolical*, Ezek. 7:19.
u *Silver, symbolical*, 1 Chr. 28:14.
v *Brass, symbolical*, Job 28:2.

**33**
w *Iron, symbolical*, Prov. 27:17.
x *Clay, symbolical*, Job 33:6.

**34**
y *Stones, symbolical*, Ex. 24:12.
z *Jesus, kingdom of, prophecies concerning* (according to the belief of many learned commentators), Matt. 1:21.

**36**
a *Dream, interpreted*, Dan. 1:17.

**37**
b *Government, imperial*, Isa. 22:21.
c *Government, God in*, Isa. 22:21.
d *God, providence of*, Gen. 2:2.
e *Rulers, appointed by God*, Ex. 18:21.

**38**
f *Man, dominion of*, Job 4:17.

v.38–524 BC
See footnote, *Time*, Rev. 10:6.

**39**
g *Brass, symbolical*, Job 28:2.

**40**
h *Iron*, Prov. 27:17.

**41**
i *Clay, symbolical*, Job 33:6.
j *Iron, symbolical*, Prov. 27:17.

**43**
4 R. V. doth not mingle

**44**
k *Jesus, kingdom of, prophecies concerning* (according to the belief of many learned commentators), Matt. 1:21.
5 R. V. nor shall the sovereignty thereof be left to another people;

**45**
l *Stones, symbolical*, Ex. 24:12.
m *God, foreknowledge of*, Gen. 2:2.

**46**
n *Homage*, Acts 10:25.
o *Daniel*, Dan. 1:6.

v.46–524 BC
See footnote, *Time*, Rev. 10:6.

47
*p* *Miracles, convincing effect of*, Luke 23:8.
*q* *God, sovereign*, Gen. 2:2.

48
*r* *Promotion, instances of*, Psa. 75:6.
*s* *Presents, rewards of service*, Gen. 32:13.
*t* *Minister, an officer in civil government*, 2 Chr. 9:4.
*u* *Government, provincial*, Isa. 22:21.
*v* *Babylon, empire of*, Ezra 5:12.
6 R. V. to be chief governor over

49
*w* *Friendship, instances of*, Prov. 22:24.
*x* *Intercession, of man with man*, Jer. 27:18.
*y* *Shadrach*, Dan. 1:7.
*z* *Meshach*, Dan. 1:7.
*a* *Abed-nego*, Dan. 1:7.

commanded that they should offer an oblation and sweet odours
unto him.
47 The king answered unto
[o]Dăn′iel, and [p]said, Of a truth *it*
*is*, that your God *is* a [q]God of
gods, and a Lord of kings, and a
[m]revealer of secrets, seeing thou
couldest reveal this secret.[Q]
48 Then the king [r]made [o]Dăn′-
iel a great man, and gave him
many great [s]gifts, and made him
[t]ruler over the whole [u]province
of [v]Băb′ȳ-lon, and [6]chief of the
governors over all the wise *men*
of Băb′ȳ-lon.
49 [w]Then [o]Dăn′iel [x]requested
of the king, and he set [y]Shā′-
drach, [z]Mē′shach, and [a]Ă-bĕd′–
ne-gō, over the affairs of the
province of Băb′ȳ-lon: but Dăn′-
iel *sat* in the gate of the king.

## CHAPTER 3

*Nebuchadnezzar dedicates a golden image, 4 and commands all to worship it. 8 Shadrach, Meshach, and Abed-nego are accused of disobedience. 13 Their declaration before the king. 19 They are cast into the fiery furnace. 24 Their miraculous preservation. 26 The king thereupon acknowledges the God of Israel.*

1
*a* *Nebuchadnezzar*, Dan. 2:1.
*b* *Idol, made of gold*, 1 Kin. 15:12.
*c* *Idolatry, objects of*, 1 Sam. 15:23.
*d* *Cubit*, Ex. 36:9.
*e* *Government, provincial*, Isa. 22:21.
*f* *Babylon*, Ezra 5:12.

2
1 R. V. satraps, the deputies, and the governors, the judges,

[a]NĔB-U-CHAD-NĔZ′ZAR
the king made an [b,c]image
of gold, whose height *was* threescore [d]cubits,[C] *and* the breadth
thereof six cubits:[C] he set it up
in the plain of Dṳ′rȧ, in the
[e]province of [f]Băb′ȳ-lon.
2 Then [a]Nĕb-u-chad-nĕz′zar
the king sent to gather together
the [1]princes, the governors, and
the captains, the judges, the
treasurers, the counsellors, the
sheriffs, and all the rulers of
the [e]provinces, to come to the
dedication of the [b,c]image which
Nĕb-u-chad-nĕz′zar the king had
set up.
3 Then the [1]princes, the governors, and captains, the judges,
the treasurers, the counsellors,
the sheriffs, and all the rulers of
the [e]provinces, were gathered
together unto the dedication of
the [b,c]image that [a]Nĕb-u-chad-
nĕz′zar the king had set up; and
they stood before the image that
Nĕb-u-chad-nĕz′zar had set up.
4 Then an herald cried aloud,
To you it is commanded, O people, nations, and languages,[Q]
5 *That* at what time ye hear the
sound of the [g]cornet,[C] [g]flute,[C] [g]harp,[C]
[g]sackbut,[C] [g,h]psaltery,[C] [g]dulcimer,[C]
and all kinds of musick, ye [i]fall
down and [c]worship the golden
[b]image that [a]Nĕb-u-chad-nĕz′zar
the king hath set up:
6 [j,k]And whoso falleth not down
and worshippeth shall the same
hour be cast into the midst of a
burning [l]fiery [m]furnace.[Q]
7 Therefore at that time, when
all the [2]people heard the sound
of the [g]cornet,[C] [g]flute,[C] [g]harp,[C] [g]sack-
but, [g,h]psaltery, and all kinds
of musick, all the [2]people, the
nations, and the languages, fell
down *and* [c]worshipped the golden
[b]image that [a]Nĕb-u-chad-nĕz′-
zar the king had set up.
8 ¶ Wherefore at that time certain [n]Chăl-dē′anṣ came near, and
[o]accused the [p]Jewṣ.
9 They spake and said to the
king [a]Nĕb-u-chad-nĕz′zar, [q]O
king, live for ever.
10 Thou, O king, [k]hast made a
decree, that every man that shall
hear the sound of the [g]cornet,
[g]flute, [g]harp, [g]sackbut, [g,h]psal-
tery, and [g]dulcimer, and all
kinds of musick, shall fall down
and [c]worship the golden image:[Q]
11 And [k]whoso falleth not down
and worshippeth, *that* he should

5
*g* *Music, instruments of*, 2 Chr. 5:13.
*h* *Psaltery*, 1 Chr. 16:5.
*i* *Religious Coercion*, Dan. 6:26.

6
*j* *Rulers, wicked*, Ex. 18:21.
*k* *Government, monarchical, tyranny in*, Isa. 22:21.
*l* *Fire, torture by*, Ex. 12:8.
*m* *Furnace*, Prov. 17:3.

7
2 R. V. peoples

8
*n* *Chaldeans*, Dan. 1:4.
*o* *Persecution, instances of*, vs. 8–23; John 15:20.
*p* *Jews*, Neh. 4:2.

9
*q* *Salutations*, Luke 1:44.

* **HARP**, a stringed instrument of music. *Originated with Jubal*, Gen. 4:21. *Made of almug wood*, 1 Kin. 10:12. *David skilful in playing*, 1 Sam. 16:16, 23. *Used in worship*, 1 Sam. 10:5; 1 Chr. 16:5; 25:1–7; 2 Chr. 5:12, 13; 29:25; Psa. 33:2; 43:4; 49:4; 57:8; 71:22; 81:2; 92:3; 98:5; 108:2; 147:7; 149:3; 150:3. *Used, in national jubilees, after the triumph over the armies of Ammon and Moab*, 2 Chr. 20:28, with verses 20–29; *when the new walls of Jerusalem were dedicated*, Neh. 12:27, 36; *in festivities*, Gen. 31:27; Job 21:11, 12; Isa. 5:12; 23:16; 24:8; 30:32; Ezek. 26:13; Rev. 18:22; *in mourning*, Job 30:31. *Discordant*, 1 Cor. 14:7. *Hung on the willows by the captive Jews*, Psa. 137:2. *Heard in heaven, in John's apocalyptic vision*, Rev. 5:8; 14:2; 15:2. The symbol used in the psalmody to indicate when the harp was to be introduced in the music was Neginoth, see titles of Psa. 4, 6, 54, 55, 61, 67, 76. See footnote, MUSIC, *Instruments of*, 2 Chr. 5:13.

be cast into the midst of a burning [l]fiery [m]furnace.

12 There are certain [p]Jews whom thou hast set over the affairs of the [e]province of [f]Băb′ȳ-lon, [r]Shā′drach, [s]Mē′shach, and [t]Ā-bĕd′–ne-gō; [u]these men, O king, have not regarded[G] thee: they serve not thy gods, nor [c]worship the golden [b]image which thou hast set up.

13 ¶ Then [a]Nĕb-u-chad-nĕz′zar in *his* [v]rage and fury commanded to bring [r]Shā′drach, [s]Mē′shach, and [t]Ā-bĕd′–ne-gō. Then they brought these men before the king.

14 [a]Nĕb-u-chad-nĕz′zar spake and said unto them, *Is it* true, O [r]Shā′drach, [s]Mē′shach, and [t]Ā-bĕd′–ne-gō, do not ye serve my gods, nor [c]worship the golden [b]image which I have set up?

15 [k]Now if ye be ready that at what time ye hear the sound of the [g]cornet, [g]flute, [g]harp, [g]sackbut, [g,h]psaltery, and [g]dulcimer, and all kinds of musick, ye fall down and worship the image which I have made; *well*: [j,k]but if ye worship not, ye shall be cast the same hour into the midst of a burning [l]fiery [m]furnace; and [w]who *is* that God that shall deliver you out of my hands?[Q]

16 [r]Shā′drach, [s]Mē′shach, and [t]Ā-bĕd′–ne-gō, [x]answered and [y,z,a]said to the king, O Nĕb-u-chad-nĕz′zar, we [3]*are* not careful to answer thee in this matter.

17 If it be *so*, [b]our God whom we serve is [c]able to deliver us from the burning fiery furnace, and [b]he will deliver *us* out of thine hand, O king.[S]

18 But if not, [d]be it known unto thee, O king, that [a,e,f,g]we will not serve thy gods, nor worship the golden [h]image which thou hast set up.

19 ¶ Then was [i]Nĕb-u-chad-nĕz′zar full of [j]fury, and the form of his [k]visage[G] was changed against [l]Shā′drach, [m]Mē′shach, and [n]Ā-bĕd′–ne-gō: *therefore* he spake, and [o]commanded that they should heat the [p]furnace one seven times more than it was wont[G] to be heated.

20 And [o]he commanded [4]the most mighty men that *were* in his army to bind [l]Shā′drach, [m]Mē′shach, and [n]Ā-bĕd′–ne-gō, *and* to [q]cast *them* into the burning [r]fiery [p]furnace.

21 Then these men were bound in their [5]coats, their hosen[G], and their hats, and their *other* garments, and were [s]cast into the midst of the burning fiery furnace.

22 Therefore because the king's commandment was urgent, and the [p]furnace exceeding hot, the flame of the fire slew those men that took up [l]Shā′drach, [m]Mē′shach, and [n]Ā-bĕd′–ne-gō.

23[S] And[Q] these three men, [l]Shā′drach, [m]Mē′shach, and [n]Ā-bĕd′–ne-gō, fell down bound into the midst of the burning [r]fiery [p]furnace.

24 Then [i]Nĕb-u-chad-nĕz′zar the king was astonied[G], and rose up in haste, *and* spake, and said unto his counsellors, Did not we cast three men bound into the midst of the fire? They answered and said unto the king, True, O king.

25 He[T] answered and said, Lo, I see four men loose, walking in the midst of the fire, and they [t]have no hurt; and the [6]form of the [u]fourth is like [7]the Son of God.[Q]

26 ¶ Then [i]Nĕb-u-chad-nĕz′zar came near to the mouth of the burning [r]fiery [p]furnace, *and* spake, and said, [l]Shā′drach, [m]Mē′shach, and [n]Ā-bĕd′–ne-gō, ye [v]servants of the most high God, come forth, and come *hither*. Then Shā′drach, Mē′shach, and

**12**
r *Shadrach*, Dan. 1:7.
s *Meshach*, Dan. 1:7.
t *Abed-nego*, Dan. 1:7.
u *Indictments, instances of*, Matt. 27:37.

**13**
v *Anger, instances of*, Psa. 37:8.

**15**
w *False Confidence*, Psa. 30:6.

**16**
x *Zeal, instances of*, 2 Cor. 7:11.
y *Character, stability of*, Phil. 2:15.
z *Courage, instances of*, Deut. 31:7.

a *Faithfulness*, Luke 16:10.
3 R. V. have no need to answer

**17**
b *Faith, exemplified*, Mark 11:22.
c *God, power of*, Gen. 2:2.

**18**
d *Resignation, exemplified*, Job 5:17.
e *Zeal, instances of*, 2 Cor. 7:11.
f *Character, stability of*, Phil. 2:15.
g *Courage, instances of*, Deut. 31:7.
h *Idolatry, objects of*, 1 Sam. 15:23.

**19**
i *Nebuchadnezzar*, Dan. 2:1.
j *Anger*, Psa. 37:8.

k *Countenance*, Prov. 15:13.
l *Shadrach*, Dan. 1:7.
m *Meshach*, Dan. 1:7.
n *Abed-nego*, Dan. 1:7.
o *Rulers, wicked*, Ex. 18:21.
p *Furnace*, Prov. 17:3.

**20**
q *Cruelty*, Psa. 27:12.
r *Fire, torture by*, Ex. 12:8.
4 R. V. certain mighty

**21**
s *Punishment, death penalty*, Lev. 26:41.
5 R. V. hosen, their tunics, and their mantles, and their other

**25**
t *Miracles*, Luke 23:8.
u *Angel, appearances of*, Heb. 1:13.
6 R. V. aspect
7 R. V. a son of the gods.

**26**
v *Righteous, described*, v. 28; Psa. 64:10.

**27**

8 R. V. satraps, the deputies, and the governors, and the king's counsellors,

**28**

*w Miracles, convincing effect of,* Luke 23:8.

*x Praise,* Psa. 150:1.

*y God, preserver,* Gen. 2:2.

*z Faith,* Mark 11:22.

*a Renunciation,* Luke 5:11.

*b Worship,* Gen. 22:5.

**29**

*c Government, monarchical tyranny in,* Isa. 22:21.

*d Shadrach,* Dan. 1:7.

*e Meshach,* Dan. 1:7.

*f Abed-nego,* Dan. 1:7.

*g Miracles, convincing effect of,* Luke 23:8.

**30**

*h Promotion, instances of,* Psa. 75:6.

*i Babylon,* Ezra 5:12.

**1**

*a Nebuchadnezzar,* Dan. 2:1.

*b Government, imperial,* Isa. 22:21.

*c Proclamotion, imperial,* vs. 1–3; 1 Kin. 15:22.

*d Peace,* Jer. 29:7.

**2**

*e Thankfulness, to God,* Acts 24:3.

*f Religious Testimony,* 2 Thess. 1:10.

*g Miracles, convincing effect of,* Luke 23:8.

*h God, sovereign,* Gen. 2:2.

Ȧ-bĕd′–ne-gō, came forth of the midst of the fire.

27 And the [8]princes, governors, and captains, and the king's counsellors, being gathered together, saw these men, upon whose bodies [t]the fire had no power, nor was an hair of their head singed, neither were their coats changed, nor the smell of fire had passed on them.[s]

28 [w]*Then* Nĕb-u-chad-nĕz′zar spake, and said, [x]Blessed *be* the God of [l]Shā′drach, [m]Mē′-shach, and [n]Ȧ-bĕd′–ne-gō, who hath sent his [u]angel, and [y]delivered his servants that [z]trusted in him, and have changed[C] the king's word, and [a]yielded their bodies, that they might not serve nor [b]worship any god, except their own God.[S T]

29 Therefore [c]I make a decree, That every people, nation, and †language, which speak any thing amiss[C] against the God of [d]Shā′drach, [e]Mē′shach, and [f]Ȧ-bĕd′–ne-gō, shall be cut in pieces, and their houses shall be made a dunghill: because [g]there is no other God that can deliver after this sort.

30 ¶ Then the king [h]promoted [d]Shā′drach, [e]Mē′shach, and [f]Ȧ-bĕd′–ne-gō, in the province of [i]Băb′ȳ-lon.

## CHAPTER 4

*Nebuchadnezzar proclaims God's dominion. 4 His dream, which the magicians could not interpret. 8 Its recital to Daniel, 19 and his interpretation thereof. 28 The fulfillment of the dream.*

[a]NĔB-U-CHAD-NĔZ′ZAR the [b]king, [c]unto all people, nations, and languages, that dwell in all the earth; [d]Peace be multiplied unto you.

2 [e]I thought it good to [f]shew the [g]signs and wonders that the [h]high God hath wrought toward me.[Q]

3 [i]How great *are* his signs! and how mighty *are* his wonders! [h]his kingdom *is* an [i]everlasting kingdom, and his dominion *is* from generation to generation.[S]

4 ¶ I [a]Nĕb-u-chad-nĕz′zar was at rest in mine house, and flourishing in my palace:

5 [j]I saw a [k,l]dream which made me afraid, and the thoughts upon my bed and the [m]visions of my head troubled me.

6 Therefore made I a decree to bring in all the wise *men* of [n]Băb′ȳ-lon before me, that they might make known unto me the interpretation of the [k]dream.

7 Then came in the [o]magicians, the [1,p]astrologers,[C] the [q]Chăl-dē′ans, and the soothsayers: and I told the [k]dream before them; but they did not make known unto me the interpretation thereof.

8 But at the last [r]Dăn′iel came in before me, whose name *was* Bĕl-te-shăz′zar, according to the name of my god, and in whom *is* the spirit of the holy [s]gods: and before him I told the dream, *saying,*

9 O [r]Bĕl-te-shăz′zar, master of the magicians, because I know that the spirit of the holy [s]gods *is* in thee, and no secret troubleth thee, tell me the visions of my [k]dream that I have seen, and the interpretation thereof.

10 Thus *were* the [m]visions of mine head in my bed; I saw, and behold a [t]tree in the midst of the earth, and the height thereof *was* great.

11 The [t]tree grew, and was strong, and the height thereof reached unto heaven, and the sight thereof to the end of all the earth:

12 [u]The leaves thereof *were* fair, and the fruit thereof much,

**3**

*i God, eternity of,* Gen. 2:2.

**5**

*j Wicked, warned,* vs. 5–27; Psa. 73:3.

*k Dream,* Dan. 1:17.

*l Heathen, divine revelations given to,* Lam. 1:10.

*m Vision,* Acts 9:10.

**6**

*n Babylon,* Ezra 5:12.

**7**

*o Magician,* Ex. 7:11.

*p Sorcery,* Isa. 47:9.

*q Chaldeans,* Dan. 1:4.

1 R. V. enchanters,

**8**

*r Daniel,* Dan. 1:6.

*s Polytheism,* 1 Cor. 8:5.

**10**

*t Tree, symbolical,* vs. 10–12; Rev. 22:14.

**12**

*u Prosperity,* Eccl. 7:14.

† **LANGUAGE.** *Unity of,* Gen. 11:1, 6. *Confusion of,* Gen. 11:1–9; 10:5, 20, 31. *Dialects of the Jews,* Judg. 12:6; Matt. 26:73. *Many spoken in Jerusalem,* John 19:20; Acts 2:8–11. *Speaking in unknown, in religious assemblies,* 1 Cor. 14:2–28, 39. *Gift of,* Mark 16:17; Acts 2:7, 8; 10:46; 19:6; 1 Cor. 12:10; 14.

and in it *was* meat[G] for all: the beasts of the field had shadow under it, and the fowls of the heaven dwelt in the boughs thereof, and all flesh was fed of it.[Q]

13 I saw in the [m]visions of my head upon my bed, and, behold, a watcher and an holy one came down from heaven;

14 He [l]cried aloud, and said thus, [v]Hew down the tree, and cut off his *branches, shake off his leaves, and scatter his fruit: let the beasts get away from under it, and the fowls from his branches:

15 Nevertheless leave the stump of his roots in the earth, even with a band of iron and brass, in the tender grass of the field; and let it be wet with the †dew of heaven, and *let* his portion *be* with the beasts in the grass of the earth:

16 [v]Let his heart be changed from man's, and let a beast's heart be given unto him; and let [w]seven times pass over him.

17 This matter *is* by the decree of the watchers, and the demand by the word of the holy ones: to the intent [x]that the living may know that [y]the [h]most High ruleth in the kingdom of men, and [z]giveth it to whomsoever he will, and setteth up over it the basest of men.

18 This [a]dream I king [b]Nĕb-u-chad-nĕz′zar have seen. Now thou, O [c]Bĕl-te-shăz′zar, declare the interpretation thereof, forasmuch as all the wise *men* of my kingdom are not able to make known unto me the interpretation: but thou *art* able; for the spirit of the holy gods *is* in thee.

19 ¶ Then [c]Dăn′iel, whose name *was* Bĕl-te-shăz′zar, was astonied[G] for one hour, and his thoughts troubled him. The king spake, and said, Bĕl-te-shăz′zar, let not the dream, or the interpretation thereof, trouble thee. Bĕl-te-shăz′zar answered and said, My lord, the [a]dream *be* to them that [d]hate thee, and the interpretation thereof to thine [e]enemies.

20 The tree that thou sawest, which grew, and was strong, whose height reached unto the heaven, and the sight thereof to all the earth;

21 Whose leaves *were* fair, and the fruit thereof much, and in it *was* meat[G] for all; under which the beasts of the field dwelt, and upon whose branches the fowls of the heaven had their habitation:[Q]

22 It *is* [b]thou, O king, that art grown and become strong: for thy greatness is grown, and reacheth unto heaven, and thy [f]dominion to the end of the earth.

23 And whereas the king saw a watcher and an holy one coming down from heaven, and saying, Hew the tree down, and destroy it; yet leave the stump of the roots thereof in the earth, even with a band of iron and brass, in the tender grass of the field; and let it be wet with the †dew of heaven, and *let* his portion *be* with the beasts of the field, till seven times[C] pass over him;

24 This *is* the [a]interpretation, O king, and this *is* the [g,h]decree of the [i]most High, which is come upon my lord the king:

25 That [g,h]they shall drive [b]thee from men, and thy dwelling shall be with the beasts of the field, and they shall make thee to eat grass as oxen, and they shall wet

14
v *Rulers, divine judgments upon,* Ex. 18:21.

16
w *Seven, years,* Gen. 7:2.

17
x *Afflictions, design of,* Psa. 34:19.
y *Government, God in,* Isa. 22:21.
z *King, divinely authorized,* 2 Kin. 3:10.

18
a *Dream, interpreted,* vs. 18–26; Dan. 1:17.
b *Nebuchadnezzar,* Dan. 2:1.
c *Daniel,* Dan. 1:6.

19
d *Hatred,* Prov. 15:17.
e *Enemy,* Prov. 24:17.

22
f *Government, imperial,* Isa. 22:21.

24
g *Adversity, dispensation from God,* Psa. 10:6.
h *Divine Chastisement,* Job 33:19.
i *God, sovereign,* Gen. 2:2.

***BRANCH. Figurative**, Psa. 80:15; Prov. 11:28; Isa. 4:2; 60:21; Hos. 14:6; John 15:2–8. *Pruning of,* Isa. 18:5; Dan. 4:14; John 15:6; Rom. 11:17, 21. *Fruitless, cut off,* John 15:2, 6. *A title of Christ,* Isa. 11:1; Jer. 23:5; 33:15; Zech. 3:8; 6:12.

**† DEW,** Dan. 4:15, 23, 25, 33; 5:21; Hos. 6:4; 13:3; 14:5. *Forms imperceptibly,* 2 Sam. 17:12; *in the night,* Job 29:19. *Absence of,* 1 Kin. 17:1. *Miraculous profusion, and absence of,* Judg. 6:36–40.
See footnote, METEOROLOGY, Matt. 16:2.
**Figurative,** Deut. 33:28; Psa. 110:3; Isa. 26:19. *Of merciful providence,* Deut. 33:13.

25

*i Seven, years,* Gen. 7:2.
*k Afflictions, design of,* Psa. 34:19.
*l Government, God in,* Isa. 22:21.
*m King, divinely authorized,* 2 Kin. 3:10.

27

*n Wicked, warned,* Psa. 73:3.
*o Reproof, faithfulness in,* Prov. 17:10.
*p Repentance, exhortations to,* Mark 1:4.
*q Sin, repentance for,* Rom. 5:12.
*r Mercy,* Deut. 5:10.
*s Poor, righteous treatment of, rewarded,* Prov. 21:13.

28

*t Prophecies, fulfilled,* Dan. 9:24.

29

*u Palace,* 1 Kin. 21:1.
*v Babylon,* Ezra 5:12.
2 R. V. was walking in the royal palace of Babylon.

30

*w Boasting,* Prov. 25:14.
*x Pride, instances of,* Prov. 16:18.
*y Presumption,* Psa. 19:13.

31

*z Rulers, divine judgment upon,* Ex. 18:21.

32

*a Divine Chastisement,* Job 33:19.
*b Nebuchadnezzar,* Dan. 2:1.
*c Insanity,* Prov. 26:18.
*d Seven, years,* Gen. 7:2.
*e Afflictions, design of,* Psa. 34:19.
*f God, sovereign,* Gen. 2:2.
*g Government, God in,* Gen. 2:2.
*h King, divinely authorized,* 2 Kin. 3:10.

thee with the [†]dew of heaven,
and [i]seven times shall pass over
thee, [k]till thou know that the
[i]most High [l]ruleth in the kingdom of men, and [m]giveth it to
whomsoever he will.
26 And whereas they com-
manded to leave the stump of
the tree roots; thy kingdom shall
be sure[C] unto thee, [k]after that thou
shalt have known that the heavens do rule.
27 Wherefore, O king, let my
counsel be acceptable unto thee,
and [n,o,p]break off thy [q]sins by
righteousness, and thine iniquities by shewing [r]mercy to the
[s]poor; if it may be a lengthening
of thy tranquillity.
28 ¶ [t]All this came upon the
king [b]Nĕb-u-chad-nĕz'zar.
29 At the end of twelve months
[b]he [2]walked in the [u]palace of the
kingdom of [v]Băb'ÿ-lon.
30 The [b]king spake, and
[w,x,y]said, Is not this great [v]Băb'-
ÿ-lon, that I have built for the
house of the kingdom by the
might of my power, and for
the honour of my majesty?[Q]
31 While the word *was* in the
king's mouth, there fell a voice
from heaven, *saying,* O king
Nĕb-u-chad-nĕz'zar, to thee it
is spoken; [z]The kingdom is departed from thee.
32 And [a]they shall drive [b]thee
from men, and [c]thy dwelling
*shall be* with the beasts of the
field: they shall make thee to eat
grass as oxen, and [d]seven times[C]
shall pass over thee, [e]until thou
know that the [f]most High [g]rul-
eth in the kingdom of men,
and [h]giveth it to whomsoever
he will.
33 The same hour was the
thing fulfilled upon [b]Nĕb-u-chad-
nĕz'zar: and [c]he was driven from
men, and did eat grass as oxen,
and his body was wet with the
[†]dew of heaven, till his hairs
were grown like eagles' *feathers,*
and his nails like birds' *claws.*
34[T] And at the end of the days I
[b]Nĕb-u-chad-nĕz'zar lifted up
mine eyes unto heaven, and mine
understanding returned unto me,
and I blessed the [f]most High,
and I [i]praised and honoured
him that liveth [j]for ever, whose
dominion *is* an everlasting dominion, and his kingdom *is* from
generation to generation:[S Q]
35 And all the inhabitants of
the earth *are* reputed as nothing: and [f]he doeth according to
his [k]will in the army of [l]heaven,
and *among* the inhabitants of the
earth: and [m]none can stay[C] his
hand, or say unto him, What
doest thou?[ST]
36 At the same time my reason
returned unto [b]me; and for the
glory of my kingdom, mine honour and brightness returned unto me; and my counsellors and
my lords sought unto me; and I
was established in my kingdom,
and excellent majesty was added
unto me.
37 Now I [b]Nĕb-u-chad-nĕz'zar
[i]praise and extol and honour the
[f]King of heaven, all whose works
*are* [n]truth, and his ways judgment[C]: and those that walk in
[o,p]pride he is [m]able to [q]abase.[Q S T]

## CHAPTER 5

*Belshazzar's feast. 5 The handwriting on the wall. 8 The king's wise men unable to interpret it. 10 Daniel is sent for. 17 He reproves the king, 25 and interprets the writing. 30 The kingdom is transferred to the Medes.*

[a]BĔL-SHĂZ'ZAR the king
[b,c]made a great [d]feast to a
thousand of his lords, and drank
[c]wine before the thousand.
2 [a]Bĕl-shăz'zar, whiles he
tasted the [e]wine, commanded
to bring the [f]golden and [g]silver
vessels which his father [h]Nĕb-
u-chad-nĕz'zar had taken out
of the [i]temple which *was* in
[j]Jĕ-ru'să-lĕm; that the king, and
his princes, his [k,l]wives, and

34

*i Praise,* Psa. 150:1.
*j God, eternity of,* Gen. 2:2.

35

*k Will of God,* Mark 3:35.
*l Heaven, God's dwelling place,* Luke 18:22.
*m God, power of,* Gen. 2:2.

37

*n God, truth,* Gen. 2:2.
*o Pride,* Prov. 16:18.
*p Self-exaltation,* Luke 14:11.
*q Adversity, dispensation from God,* Psa. 10:6.

v.1–460 BC
See footnote, *Time,* Rev. 10:6.

1

*a* Dan. 7:1; 8:1.
*b Worldly Pleasure,* Eccl. 2:1.
*c Wicked, happiness of, brief,* vs. 30, 31; Psa. 73:3.
*d Feasts,* Mark 12:39.
*e Wine,* Prov. 23:31.

2

*f Gold,* Ezek. 7:19.
*g Silver,* 1 Chr. 28:14.
*h Nebuchadnezzar,* Dan. 2:1.
*i Temple, Solomon's,* 1 Kin. 6:17.
*j Jerusalem,* Judg. 19:10.
*k Polygamy,* Deut. 17.17.
*l Women, social status of,* Prov. 31:10.

v.2–460 BC
See footnote, *Time*, Rev. 10:6.

*m Concubinage*, 2 Sam. 21:11.

4

*n Idolatry, objects of*, 1 Sam. 15:23.
*o Brass*, Job 28:2.
*p Iron*, Prov. 27:17.
*q Stones*, Ex. 24:12.

5

*r Wicked, warned*, Psa. 73:3.
*s Miracles*, Luke 23:8.
*t Palace*, 1 Kin. 21:1.

6

*u Countenance*, Prov. 15:13.

7

*v Sorcery*, Isa. 47:9.
*w Chaldeans*, Dan. 1:4.
*x Babylon*, Ezra 5:12.
*y Presents, rewards of service*, Gen. 32:13.
*z Colors, symbolical*, Ezek. 16:16.
1 R. V. enchanters,
2 R. V. purple,

8

*a* Dan. 7:1; 8:1.

9

*b Countenance*, Prov. 15:13.
3 R. V. perplexed.

10

*c Queen*, 1 Kin. 11:19.

his [m]concubines[C], might drink therein.[Q]

3 Then they brought the [f]golden vessels that were taken out of the [i]temple of the house of God which *was* at [j]Jĕ-ru̧′să-lĕm; and the king, and his princes, his [k,l]wives, and his [m]concubines, drank in them.

4 They drank [e]wine, and praised the [n]gods of [f]gold, and of [g]silver, of [o]brass, of [p]iron, of wood, and of [q]stone.[Q]

5 ¶ [c,r]In the same hour [s]came forth fingers of a man's hand, and wrote over against the candlestick[C] upon the plaister of the wall of the king's [t]palace: and the king saw the part of the hand that wrote.

6 Then the king's [u]countenance was changed, and his thoughts troubled him, so that the joints of his loins were loosed, and his knees smote one against another.

7 The king cried aloud to bring in the [1,v]astrologers, the [w]Chăl-dē′ans̡, and the soothsayers. *And* the king spake, and said to the wise *men* of [x]Băb′ y̆-lon, Whosoever shall read this writing, and shew me the interpretation thereof, [y]shall be clothed with [2,z]scarlet[C], and *have* a *chain of gold about his neck, and shall be the third ruler in the kingdom.

8 Then came in all the [a]king's wise *men*: but they could not read the writing, nor make known to the king the interpretation thereof.

9 Then was king [a]Bĕl-shăz′zar greatly troubled, and his [b]countenance[C] was changed in him, and his lords were [3]astonied[C].

10 ¶ *Now* the [c]queen by reason of the words of the king and his lords came into the banquet house: *and* [d,e]the queen spake and said, O king, live for ever: let not thy thoughts trouble thee, nor let thy countenance be changed:

11 There is a [f]man in thy kingdom, in whom *is* the spirit of the holy gods; and in the days of thy [g]father light and understanding and [h,i]wisdom, like the wisdom of the gods, was found in him; whom the king Nĕb-u-chad-nĕz′zar thy father, the king, *I say*, thy father, made master of the [j]magicians, [1,k]astrologers, [l]Chăl-dē′ans̡, *and* soothsayers;

12 Forasmuch as an excellent spirit, and knowledge, and understanding, interpreting of dreams, and shewing[C] of hard sentences, and dissolving of doubts, were found in the same [f]Dăn′iel, whom the king named Bĕl-te-shăz′zar: now [d,e]let Dăn′iel be called, and he will shew the interpretation.

13 Then was [f]Dăn′iel brought in before the [a]king. *And* the king spake and said unto Dăn′iel, *Art* thou that Dăn′iel, which *art* of the children of the [m]captivity of Jū′dah, whom the king my father brought out of Jew′ry̆[C]?

14 [a]I have even heard of [f]thee, that the spirit of the gods *is* in thee, and *that* light and understanding and excellent [h,i]wisdom is found in thee.

15 And now the wise *men*, the [1,k]astrologers[C], have been brought in before me, that they should read this writing, and make known unto me the interpretation thereof: but they could not shew the interpretation of the thing:

16 And I have heard of thee, that thou canst make interpretations, and dissolve[C] doubts: now if thou canst read the writing,

v.10–460 BC
See footnote, *Time*, Rev. 10:6.

*d Women, influential in public affairs*, Prov. 31:10.
*e Statecraft, women in*, Prov. 28:2.

11

*f Daniel*, Dan. 1:6.
*g Nebuchadnezzar*, Dan. 2:1.
*h Wisdom, worldly*, Prov. 2:2.
*i Wisdom, spiritual*, Prov. 2:2.
*j Magician*, Ex. 7:11.
*k Sorcery*, Isa. 47:9.
*l Chaldeans*, Dan. 1:4.

13

*m Captivity*, Isa. 5:13.

* **CHAINS.** *Used as ornaments*, Ezek. 16:11. *Worn by princes*, Gen. 41:42; Dan. 5:7, 29. *Worn, on ankles*, Num. 31:50; *on the breastplate of high priest*, Ex. 28:22; 39:15. *As ornaments on camels*, Judg. 8:26. *A partition of, in the temple*, 1 Kin. 6:21. *Used to confine prisoners*, Psa. 149:8; Jer. 40:4; Acts 12:6, 7; 21:33; 28:20; 2 Tim. 1:16.
See footnote, Fetters, Mark 5:4.
**Figurative**, Psa. 73:6; Prov. 1:9; Lam. 3:7; Ezek. 7:23–27; Jude 6; Rev. 20:1.

and make known to me the interpretation thereof, thou [n]shalt be
clothed with [2,o]scarlet, and *have*
a chain of gold about thy neck,
and shalt be the third ruler in
the kingdom.
17 ¶ Then [l]Dăn′iel answered
and said before the king, [p]Let
thy gifts be to thyself, and give
thy rewards to another; yet I
will read the writing unto the
king, and make known to him
the interpretation.
18 O thou king, the [q]most high
God [r,s]gave [g]Nĕb-u-chad-nĕz′-
zar thy father a [t]kingdom, and
majesty, and glory, and honour:[S]
19 And for the majesty that
[r,s]he gave him, all [4]people, nations, and languages, trembled
and feared before him: [u]whom
he would he slew; and whom he
would he kept alive; and whom
he would he set up; and whom
he would he put down.
20 But when [v]his heart was
lifted up,[C] and his mind [w]hard-
ened in pride, he was [x]deposed
from his kingly throne, and they
took his glory from him:[Q]
21 And he was driven from the
sons of men; and [y]his heart was
made like the beasts, and his
dwelling *was* with the wild asses:
they fed him with grass like
oxen, and his body was wet with
the [z]dew of heaven; [a]till he knew[C]
that the [b]most high God [c]ruled
in the kingdom of men, and *that*
he [d]appointeth over it whomsoever he will.
22 [e]And thou his son, O [f,g]Bĕl-
shăz′zar, hast [h]not humbled thine
heart, though thou knewest all
this;
23 But hast lifted[C] up thyself
against the Lord of [i]heaven; [j]and
they have brought the vessels of
his [k]house before thee, and thou,
and thy lords, thy [l]wives, and thy
[m]concubines, have drunk [n]wine
in them; and thou hast praised
the [o]gods of silver, and gold,
of brass,[C] iron, wood, and stone,
which see not, nor hear, nor
know: and the [p]God in whose
hand thy breath *is*, and whose
*are* all thy ways, hast [q,r]thou
not glorified:[S] [Q]
24 [s]Then was the part of the
hand sent from him; and this
writing was written.
25 ¶ And this *is* the writing
that was written, MĒ′NĒ,
MĒ′NĒ, TĒ′KEL, U-PHÄR′-
SIN.
26 This *is* the interpretation
of the thing: MĒ′NĒ; [t,b,c]God
hath numbered thy kingdom,
and finished it.
27 TĒ′KEL; [t]Thou art weighed in the [u]balances, and art
found wanting.
28 PĒ′RĒS; [t]Thy kingdom is
divided, and given to the †Mēdes
and [v]Pĕr′sians.
29 Then commanded [l]Bĕl-
shăz′zar, and they clothed [w]Dăn′-
iel with [x]scarlet, and *put* a chain
of gold about his neck, and
made a [y]proclamation concerning him, that he should be the
[z]third ruler in the kingdom.
30 ¶ In that night was [l]Bĕl-
shăz′zar the king of the Chăl-
dē′ans slain.
31 And [a]Dā-rī′us the Mē′dĭ-an
took the kingdom, *being* about
threescore and two years old.

## CHAPTER 6

*Daniel is promoted by Darius. 4 His enemies conspire against him, and obtain an impious decree from the king. 10 Daniel is accused of disobedience, and cast into the lions' den. 18 His miraculous preservation. 24 The destruction of his enemies. 25 The king's decree acknowledging the God of Israel.*

1 IT pleased [a,b]Dā-rī′us to set
over the kingdom an hun-
dred and twenty [1]princes, which
should be over the whole [c]king-
dom;

---

v.16–460 BC See footnote, *Time*, Rev. 10:6.

**16**
*n Presents, rewards of service*, Gen. 32:13.
*o Colors, symbolical*, Ezek. 16:16.

**17**
*p Tact*, Prov. 15:1.

**18**
*q God, sovereign*, Gen. 2:2.
*r Government, God in*, Isa. 22:21.
*s God, providence of*, Gen. 2:2.
*t Temporal Blessings, from God*, Psa. 103:2.

**19**
*u Government, monarchical*, Isa. 22:21.
4 R. V. peoples,

**20**
*v Pride, instances of*, Prov. 16:18.
*w Ingratitude, of man to God*, Rom. 1:21.
*x Rulers, divine judgment upon*, Ex. 18:21.

**21**
*y Insanity*, Prov. 26:18.
*z Dew*, Dan. 4:15.
*a Afflictions, design of*, Psa. 34:19.
*b God, sovereign*, Gen. 2:2.
*c Government, God in*, Isa. 22:21.
*d Rulers, appointed by God*, Ex. 18:21.

**22**
*e Reproof, faithfulness in*, Prov. 17:10.
*f* Dan. 7:1; 8:1.
*g Rulers, wicked*, Ex. 18:21.
*h Impenitence, instances of*, Rom. 2:5.

**23**
*i Heaven, God's dwelling place*, Luke 18:22.
*j Worldly Pleasure*, Eccl. 2:1.
*k Temple, Solomon's*, 1 Kin. 6:17.
*l Polygamy*, Deut. 17:17.

v.23–460 BC See footnote, *Time*, Rev. 10:6.

*m Concubinage*, 2 Sam. 21:11.
*n Wine*, Prov. 23:31.
*o Idolatry, objects of*, 1 Sam. 15:23
*p God, preserver*, Gen. 2:2.
*q Godless*, Job 8:13.
*r Ingratitude, of man to God*, Rom. 1:21.

**24**
*s Miracles*, Luke 23:8.

**26**
*t Babylon, prophecies concerning*, Ezra 5:12.

**27**
*u Balances, figurative*, Prov. 11:1.

**28**
*v Persia, prophecies concerning*, Esth. 1:3.

**29**
*w Daniel*, Dan. 1:6.
*x Colors, symbolical*, Ezek. 16:16.
*y Proclamation, imperial*, 1 Kin. 15:22.
*z Promotion*, Psa. 75:6.

**31**
*a* Dan. 6; 9:1.

**1**
*a* Dan. 5:31; 9:1.
*b Government, imperial*, vs. 1–3; Isa. 22:21.
*c Persia*, vs. 1–28; Esth. 1:3.
1 R. V. satraps,

---

† **MEDES**, inhabitants of Media. *Israelites distributed among, when carried to Assyria*, 2 Kin. 17:6; 18:11. *Palace containing archives of the Medo-Persian empire in the Babylonian province of*, Ezra 6:2. *Country of, part of the Medo-Persian empire*, Esth. 1:1–19. *Dominant in the Medo-Persian empire*, Dan. 5:28, 31; 9:1; 11:1.

**2**
d *Daniel*, Dan. 1:6.
e *Minister, an officer in civil government*, 2 Chr. 9:4.

**3**
f *Civil Service, appointment in, on account of merit*, Dan. 1:5.
2 R. V. distinguished

**4**
g *Civil Service, corruption in*, vs. 4–17; Dan. 1:5.
h *Conspiracy, instances of*, vs. 4–17; 1 Kin. 16:9.
i *Persecution, of the righteous*, John 15:20.
j *Malice, instances of*, vs. 4–9; Eph. 4:31.
k *Envy, instances of*, Prov. 14:30.
l *Integrity*, Job 2:3.

**6**
m *King, ceremonial recognition of*, 2 Kin. 3:10.

**7**
n *Flattery*, Prov. 6:24.
o *Lion*, Mic. 5:8.
3 R. V. the deputies and the satraps, the counsellors and the governors, have

**8**
p *King, decrees of*, 2 Kin. 3:10.
q *Babylon, government of, a limited monarchy*, Ezra 5:12.

2 And over these three presidents; of whom [d,e]Dăn′iel *was* first: that the [1]princes might give accounts unto them, and the king should have no damage.

3 Then this [d,e]Dăn′iel was [2,f]preferred above the presidents and princes, because an excellent spirit *was* in him; and the king thought to set him over the whole realm.

4 ¶ Then [g]the presidents and [1]princes [h,i,j,k]sought to find occasion against [d]Dăn′iel concerning the kingdom; but they could find none occasion nor fault; forasmuch as he *was* [l]faithful, neither was there any error or fault found in him.

5 Then said these men, We shall not find any occasion against this [d]Dăn′iel, except we find *it* against him concerning the law of his God.

6 [g,h,i]Then these presidents and [1]princes assembled together to the king, and said thus unto him, [m]King Dā-rī′us, live for ever.

7 [g,h]All the presidents of the kingdom, the [3]governors, and the princes, the counsellors, and the captains, have consulted together to establish a royal statute, and to make a firm decree, that whosoever shall ask a petition of any God or man for thirty days, [n]save[G] of thee, O king, he shall be cast into the den of [o]lions.

8 Now, O king, establish the [p]decree, and sign the writing, [q]that it be not changed, according to the law of the Mēdeș and Pēr′șianș, which altereth not.

9 Wherefore king [a]Dā-rī′us [r]signed the writing and the [p]decree.

10 ¶ Now when [d]Dăn′iel knew that the writing was signed, he went into his house; and his windows being open in his chamber toward [s]Jē-ru̇′sā-lĕm, [t,u,v,w]he [x]kneeled upon his knees [y]three times a day, and [z]prayed, and gave [a]thanks before his God, as he did aforetime.[G]

11 [b]Then these men assembled, and found [c]Dăn′iel [d]praying and making supplication before his God.

12 [b,e]Then they came near, and spake before the king concerning the king's [f]decree; Hast thou not signed a decree, that every man that shall ask *a petition* of any God[G] or man within thirty days, save[G] of thee, O king, shall be cast into the den of [g]lions? The king answered and said, The thing *is* true, according to the *law of the Mēdeș and Pēr′șianș, which altereth not.

13 [b,h]Then answered they and [i]said before the king, That [c]Dăn′iel, which *is* of the children of the [j]captivity of Jū′dah, regardeth not thee, O king, nor the [f]decree that thou hast signed, but [k]maketh his petition three times a day.

14 Then the king, when he heard *these* words, was [l]sore[G] displeased with himself, and set *his* heart on [c]Dăn′iel to deliver him: and he laboured till the going down of the sun to deliver him.

15 [b,e]Then these men assembled unto the king, and said unto the king, Know, O king, that the *law of the Mēdeș and Pēr′-

**9**
r *Seal*, 1 Kin. 21:8.

**10**
s *Jerusalem*, Judg. 19:10.
t *Decision*, Isa. 50:7.
u *Faithfulness*, Luke 16:10.
v *Courage, instances of*, Deut. 31:7.
w *Character, stability of*, Phil. 2:15.
x *Prayer, postures in*, Acts 6:4.
y *Prayerfulness*, 1 Tim. 5:5.
z *Adversity, prayer in*, Psa. 10:6.

a *Thankfulness, to God*, Acts 24:3.

**11**
b *Conspiracy, instances of*, 1 Kin. 16:9.
c *Daniel*, Dan. 1:6.
d *Adversity, prayer in*, Psa. 10:6.

**12**
e *Intolerance*, Num. 11:28.
f *King, decrees of*, 2 Kin. 3:10.
g *Lion*, Mic. 5:8.

**13**
h *Persecution, of the righteous*, John 15:20.
i *Indictments, instances of*, Matt 27:37.
j *Jews, captive in Babylon*, Neh. 4:2.
k *Prayerfulness*, 1 Tim. 5:5.

**14**
l *Conscience, guilty*, Acts 23:1.

* **CONSTITUTION.** It was provided in the law of Moses that in the event of the establishment of a monarchy a copy of the law of Moses should be made, and that the king should be enjoined to study this law all the days of his life and conform his administration thereto, Deut. 17:18–20. This constituted the fundamental law and had its likeness to the constitution of modern governments. When David was crowned king of all Israel he made a league in the nature of a constitution which was a basis of good understanding between himself and the people, 2 Sam. 5:3; 1 Chr. 11:3. When Joash was enthroned a covenant, which must have been in the nature of a limitation of monarchical power, was made between him and the people, 2 Chr. 23:3, 11. In v. 11 this covenant is called a "testimony" and, no doubt, refers to the law of Moses, Deut. 17:18–20, which, it is quite probable, had been preserved sacredly by Jehoiada, the priest. Zedekiah made a covenant with the people proclaiming liberty, Jer. 34:8–11. That the king of the Medes and Persians was restricted by a constitution, which "altereth not," is evident from Dan. 6:12–15.

șianș *is*, That no [l]decree nor
statute which the king establisheth may be changed.
16 Then the king commanded,
and they brought [c]Dăn′iel, and
cast *him* into the den of [g]lions.
*Now* the king spake and [m]said
unto Dăn′iel, Thy God whom
thou servest continually, [m]he will
deliver thee.
17 And a stone was brought,
and laid upon the mouth of the
den; and the king [n]sealed it with
his own signet, and with the signet of his lords; that the purpose
might not be changed concerning [c]Dăn′iel.
18 ¶ Then the king went to his
[o]palace, and [p]passed the night
[q]fasting: neither were instruments of musick brought before
him: and [r]his sleep went from
him.
19 Then the king [p]arose very
early in the morning, and went
in haste unto the den of [g]lions.
20 [S]And when he came to the
den, he cried with a lamentable voice unto [c]Dăn′iel: *and* the
king spake and said to Dăn′iel,
O Dăn′iel, servant of the living
God, is thy God, whom thou
servest continually, able to [s,t]de-
liver thee from the lions?
21 Then said [c]Dăn′iel unto the
king, O king, live for ever.[S Q]
22 My [u]God hath sent his [v]an-
gel, and hath [w]shut the [g]lions'
mouths, that they have not hurt
me: forasmuch as before him
[x]innocency was found in me;
and also before thee, O king,
have I done no hurt.[S T Q]
23 Then was the king exceeding
glad for him, and commanded
that they should take Dăn′iel
up out of the den. So Dăn′iel
was taken up out of the den, and
no manner of hurt was found

16
m *Faith, instances of*, Mark 11:22.

17
n *Seal*, 1 Kin. 21:8.

18
o *Palace*, 1 Kin. 21:1.
p *Anxiety*, 1 Pet. 5:7.
q *Fasting, instances of*, Zech. 8:19.
r *Insomnia, instances of*, Esth. 6:1.

20
s *God, preserver*, Gen. 2:2.
t *Temporal Blessings, from God*, Psa. 103:2.

22
u *God, providence of*, Gen. 2:2.
v *Angel, functions of*, Heb. 1:13.
w *Miracles, convincing effect of*, vs. 20–27; Luke 23:8.
x *Integrity*, Job 2:3.

upon him, because he [m]believed
in his God.
24 ¶ And the king commanded,
and they brought those men
which had accused Dăn′iel, and
they [y,z]cast *them* into the den of
[a]lions, them, their [b]children, and
their wives; and the lions had
the mastery[G] of them, and brake
all their bones in pieces or[G] ever
they came at[C] the bottom of the
den.
25 ¶ Then king [c]Dā-rī′us wrote
unto all [4]people, nations, and
languages, that dwell in all the
earth; Peace be multiplied unto
you.
26 [†]I make a [d]decree, That in
every dominion of my kingdom
men tremble and [e]fear before the
God of [f]Dăn′iel: for he *is* the
living God, and [g]stedfast [h]for
ever, and [i]his kingdom *that*
which shall not be destroyed,
and his dominion *shall be even*
unto the end.[S Q]
27 [j]He delivereth and rescueth,
and he worketh signs and wonders in heaven and in earth, who
hath delivered [f]Dăn′iel from the
power of the [a]lions.
28 So this [f]Dăn′iel prospered in
the reign of [c]Dā-rī′us, and in the
reign of [k]Çȳ′rus the Pēr′șian.

## CHAPTER 7

*Daniel's vision of four beasts*, 9 *and of the Ancient of days*. 15 *The interpretation thereof*.

IN the first year of [a]Bĕl-shăz′-
zar king of [b]Băb′ȳ-lon [c]Dăn′-
iel had a [d]dream and [e]visions of
his head upon his bed: then he
wrote the dream, *and* told the
sum of the matters.
2 [c]Dăn′iel spake and said, I
saw in my vision by night, and,
behold, the four winds of the
heaven strove upon the great sea.[Q]
3 And four great *beasts came

24
y *Wicked, punishment of*, Psa. 73:3.
z *Punishment, death penalty*, Lev. 26:41.
a *Lion*, Mic. 5:8.
b *Children, involved in sins of parents*, Mark 10:14.

25
c Dan. 5:31; 9:1.
4 R. V. peoples.

26
d *Proclamation, imperial*, 1 Kin. 15:22.
e *Fear of God, enjoined*, Acts 9:31.
f *Daniel*, Dan. 1:6.
g *God, immutable*, Gen. 2:2.
h *God, eternity of*, Gen. 2:2.
i *God, sovereign*, Gen. 2:2.

27
j *God, preserver*, Gen. 2:2.

28
k *Cyrus*, 2 Chr. 36:22.

v.1–462 BC
See footnote, *Time*, Rev. 10:6.

1
a Dan. 5:1–30; 8:1.
b *Babylon, prophecies concerning*, vs. 1–28; Ezra 5:12.
c *Daniel*, Dan. 1:6.
d *Dream*, vs. 1–28; Dan. 1:17.
e *Vision, of Daniel*, vs. 1–28; Acts 9:10.

† **RELIGIOUS COERCION**, Ex. 22:20; 2 Chr. 15:12–15; Dan. 3:2–6, 29 (with vs. 1–30); 6:26, 27.
See footnote, INTOLERANCE, Num. 11:28.
* **BEASTS. Figurative:** *Of nations*, Isa. 30:6.

**Symbolical:** Seen in visions: *Of Daniel*, Dan. 7; 8:3–25; *of Peter*, Acts 10:12; *of John*, Rev. 4:6–9; 5:6–14; 6:1–8; 7:11; 11:7; 13; 14:3, 9, 11; 15:2; 16:2, 10–13; 17; 19:4, 19–21; 20:1–4, 10.

v.3—462 BC
See footnote, *Time,* Rev. 10:6.

up from the sea, diverse one from another.

4 The first *was* like a [f]lion, and had [g]eagle's wings: I beheld till the wings thereof were plucked, and it was lifted up from the earth, and made stand upon the feet as a man, and a man's heart was given to it.

5 And behold another *beast, a second, like to a [h]bear, and it raised up itself on one side, and *it had* three ribs in the mouth of it between the teeth of it: and they said thus unto it, Arise, devour much flesh.

6 After this I beheld, and lo another, like a [i]leopard, which had upon the back of it four wings of a fowl; the beast had also four heads; and dominion was given to it.

7 After this I saw in the night visions, and behold a fourth *beast, dreadful and terrible, and strong exceedingly; and it had great iron teeth: it devoured and brake in pieces, and stamped the residue with the feet of it: and it *was* diverse from all the beasts that *were* before it; and it had ten [j]horns.

8 I considered the [j]horns, and, behold, there came up among them another little horn, before whom there were three of the first horns plucked up by the roots: and, behold, in this horn *were* eyes like the eyes of man, and a mouth speaking great things.

9 ¶ I [e]beheld till the thrones were [1]cast down, and the Ancient of days did sit, whose garment *was* [k]white as snow, and the hair of his head like the pure wool: his throne *was like* the fiery flame, *and* his wheels *as* burning fire.

10 A fiery stream issued and came forth from before him: thousand thousands ministered unto him, and ten thousand times ten thousand stood before him: the judgment was set, and the books were opened.

11 I beheld then because of the voice of the great words which the horn spake: I beheld *even* till the *beast was slain, and his body destroyed, and given to the burning flame.

12 As concerning the rest of the beasts, they had their dominion taken away: yet their lives were prolonged for a season and time.

13 I saw in the night visions, and, behold, [l]*one* like the Son of man came with the clouds of heaven, and came to the Ancient of days, and they brought him near before him.

14 And there was given [l]him [m]dominion, and glory, and a [n,o]kingdom, that [p]all [2]people, nations, and languages, should serve him: his dominion *is* an everlasting dominion, which shall not pass away, and his kingdom *that* which shall not be destroyed.

15 ¶ I [c]Dăn'iel was grieved in my spirit in the midst of *my* body, and the [e]visions of my head troubled me.

16 I came near unto one of them that stood by, and asked him the truth of all this. So he told me, and made me know the interpretation of the things.

17 These great *beasts, which are four, *are* four kings, *which* shall arise out of the earth.

18 But the saints of the most High shall take the [n,o]kingdom, and possess the kingdom for ever, even for ever and ever.

19 Then I would know the truth of the fourth *beast, which was diverse from all the others, exceeding dreadful, whose teeth *were of* [q]iron, and his nails *of* [r]brass; *which* devoured, brake in pieces, and stamped the residue with his feet;

20 And of the ten [j]horns that *were* in his head, and *of* the other

4
f *Lion, similitudes of,* Mic. 5:8.
g *Eagle, similitudes of,* Lev. 11:13.

5
h *Bear, similitudes of,* 2 Sam. 17:8.

6
i *Leopard, similitudes of,* Song 4:8.

7
j *Horn, symbolical,* 1 Kin. 1:39.

9
k *Colors, figurative,* Ezek. 16:16.
1 R. V. placed, and one that was ancient of days

v.10—462 BC
See footnote, *Time,* Rev. 10:6.

13
l *Jesus, prophecies concerning* (according to many learned interpreters), Matt. 1:21.

14
m *Jesus, king* (according to many learned interpreters), Matt. 1:21.
n *Jesus, kingdom of, prophecies concerning* (according to many learned interpreters), Matt. 1:21.
o *Church, prophecies concerning its prosperity* (according to many learned interpreters), Matt. 16:18.
p *Gentiles, prophecies of the conversion of* (according to many learned interpreters), Acts 10:45.
2 R. V. the peoples.

19
q *Iron, symbolical,* Prov. 27:17.
r *Brass, symbolical,* Job 28:2.

v.20–462 BC
See footnote, *Time*, Rev. 10:6.

which came up, and before whom three fell; even *of* that horn[G] that had eyes, and a mouth that spake very great things, whose look *was* more stout than his fellows.[Q]

21 I beheld, and the same [i]horn[G] made war with the saints, and prevailed against them;[Q]

22 Until the Ancient of days came, and judgment was given to the saints of the most High; and the time came that the saints possessed the [n,o]kingdom.[Q]

23 Thus he said, The fourth *beast shall be the fourth kingdom upon earth, which shall be diverse from all kingdoms, and shall devour the whole earth, and shall tread it down, and break it in pieces.

24 And the ten [i]horns out of this kingdom *are* ten kings *that* shall arise: and another shall rise after them; and he shall be diverse from the first, and he shall subdue three kings.[Q]

25 And he shall [s]speak *great* words against the [t]most High, and shall wear out the saints of the most High, and think to change times and laws: and they shall be given into his hand until a [u]time and times and the dividing of time.[Q]

26 But the judgment shall sit, and they shall take away his dominion, to consume and to destroy *it* unto the end.

27 And the [3,n,o]kingdom and dominion[G], and the greatness of the kingdom under the whole heaven, shall be given to the people of the saints of the [t]most High, whose kingdom *is* an everlasting kingdom, and all dominions[G] shall serve and [v]obey him.[Q]

28 Hitherto[G] *is* the end of the matter. As for me [c]Dăn′iel, my cogitations[G] much troubled me, and my countenance[G] changed in me: but I kept the matter in my heart.

25
*s* *Blasphemy, reproaching God,* 2 Sam. 12:14.
*t* *God, sovereign,* Gen. 2:2.
*u* *Time,* Rev. 10:6.

27
*v* *Obedience,* Heb. 5:8.
3 R. V. kingdoms

## CHAPTER 8

*Daniel's vision of the ram and he goat. 13 The sanctuary to be trodden down two thousand three hundred days. 15 Gabriel interprets the vision to Daniel.*

IN the third year of the reign of king [a]Běl-shăz′zar a [b]vision appeared unto me, *even unto* me [c]Dăn′iel, after that which appeared unto me at the first.

2 And I saw in a [b]vision; and it came to pass, when I saw, that I *was* at [d]Shṳ′shan *in* the [e]palace, which *is* in the province of [f]Ē′lăm; and I saw in a vision, and I was by the river of Ū′la-ī.

3 Then I lifted up mine eyes, and saw, and, behold, there stood before the river a [g,h]ram which had *two* [i]horns: and the *two* horns *were* high; but one *was* higher than the other, and the higher came up last.

4 I saw the [g,h]ram pushing westward, and northward, and southward; so that no beasts might stand before him, neither *was there any* that could deliver out of his hand; but he did according to his will, and [1,j]became great.

5 And as I was considering, behold, an [h]he goat came from the west on the face of the whole earth, and touched not the ground: and the goat *had* a notable[G] [i]horn between his eyes.

6 And he came to the [g,h]ram that had *two* [i]horns, which I had seen standing before the river, and ran unto him in the fury of his power.

7 And I saw him come close unto the [g,h]ram, and he was moved with choler[G] against him, and smote the ram, and brake his two [i]horns: and there was no power in the ram to stand before him, but he cast him down to the ground, and stamped upon him: and there was none that could deliver the ram out of his hand.

8 Therefore the [h]he goat

v.1–460 BC
See footnote, *Time*, Rev. 10:6.

1
*a* Dan. 5:1-30; 7:1.
*b* *Vision,* vs. 1–27; Acts 9:10.
*c* *Daniel,* Dan. 1:6.

2
*d* *Shushan,* Esth. 1:2.
*e* *Palace,* 1 Kin. 21:1.
*f* *Elam,* Isa. 11:11.

3
*g* *Ram, seen in Daniel's vision,* Ex. 39:34.
*h* *Beasts, symbolical,* Dan. 7:3.
*i* *Horn, symbolical,* vs. 3–9, 20; 1 Kin. 1:39.

4
*j* *Self-exaltation,* Luke 14:11.
1 R. V. magnified himself.

[2,j]waxed[G] very great: and when he was strong, the great [i]horn was broken; and for it came up four notable ones toward the four winds of heaven.

9 And out of one of them came forth a little [i]horn, which waxed[G] exceeding great, toward the south, and toward the east, and toward the [3]pleasant *land.*

10 And it waxed[G] great, *even* to[G] the host of heaven; and it cast[G] down *some* of the host and of the stars to the ground, and stamped upon them.[Q]

11 Yea, [4]he [j]magnified *himself* even to the prince of the host, and [5]by him the [k]daily *sacrifice*[G] was taken away, and the place of his [l]sanctuary was cast down.

12 And [6]an host was given *him* against the [k]daily *sacrifice* by reason of transgression, and it cast down the [m]truth to the ground; and it [7]practised,[G] and prospered.

13 ¶ Then I heard [8]one saint speaking, and another [8]saint said unto that certain *saint* which spake, How long *shall be* the vision *concerning* the [9,k]daily *sacrifice,* and the transgression of desolation, to give both the [l]sanctuary and the host to be trodden[G] under foot?[Q]

14 And he said unto me, Unto two thousand and three hundred [n]days; then shall the [l]sanctuary be cleansed.[G]

15 ¶ And it came to pass, when I, *even* I [c]Dăn′iel, had seen the [b]vision, and sought for the meaning, then, behold, there stood before me as the appearance of a man.

16 And I heard a man's voice between *the banks of* Ū′la-ī, which called, and said, *Gā′-brĭ-el, [o]make this *man* to understand the [b]vision.[Q]

17 So he came near where I stood: and when he came, I was afraid, and fell upon my face: but he said unto me, Understand, O son of man: for [10]at the time of the end *shall be* the vision.

18 Now as he was speaking with me, I was in a deep sleep on my face toward the ground: but he touched me, and set me upright.

19 And he said, Behold, I will [o]make thee know what shall be in the last end of the indignation: for at the time appointed the end *shall be.*

20 The [g,h]ram which thou sawest having *two* horns *are* the kings of [p]Mē′dĭ-ȧ and [q]Pēr′ṣiȧ.

21 And the rough goat *is* the king of [r]Grē′çiȧ: and the great horn that *is* between his eyes *is* the first king.

22 Now that being broken, whereas four stood up for it, four kingdoms shall stand up out of the nation, but not in his power.

23 And in the latter time of their kingdom, when the transgressors are come to the full, a king of fierce [s]countenance, and understanding dark sentences, shall stand up.

24 And his power shall be mighty, but not by his own power: and [t]he shall destroy wonderfully, and shall prosper, and [11]practise,[G] and shall destroy the mighty and the holy people.

25 And through his policy also he shall cause craft[G] to prosper in his hand; and [t]he shall [j]magnify *himself* in his heart, and [12]by peace shall destroy many: he shall also stand up against the Prince of princes; but he shall be broken without hand.

26 And the vision of the evening and the morning which was

---

v.8–460 BC See footnote, *Time,* Rev. 10:6.

**8**
2 R. V. magnified himself exceedingly:

**9**
3 R. V. glorious

**11**
k *Offerings, daily,* Lev. 6:17.
l *Sanctuary,* Lev. 4:6.
4 R. V. it magnified itself,
5 R. V. it took away from him the continual burnt offering, and

**12**
m *Truth,* John 18:37.
6 R. V. the host was given over to it together with the continual burnt offering through transgression;

**13**
8 R. V. a holy one
9 R. V. continual burnt offering, and the transgression that maketh desolate,

**14**
n *Day, prophetic,* Gen. 1:5.

**16**
o *Angel, functions of,* Heb. 1:13.

v.17–460 BC See footnote, *Time,* Rev. 10:6.

**17**
10 R. V. the vision belongeth to the time of the end.

**20**
p *Medes, prophecies concerning,* Dan. 5:28.
q *Persia, prophecies concerning,* Esth. 1:3.

**21**
r *Greece, prophecies concerning,* Zech. 9:13.

**23**
s *Countenance,* Prov. 15:13.

**24**
t *Rulers, wicked,* Ex. 18:21.

**25**
12 R. V. in their security shall he destroy

---

* **GABRIEL,** a messenger of God. *Appeared, to Daniel,* Dan. 8:16–19; 9:21, 22; *to Zacharias,* Luke 1:11–19; *to Mary,* Luke 1:26–38.

v.26–460 BC
See footnote, *Time*, Rev. 10:6.

**27**
*u* Isa. 10:18; Lam. 2:12.

v.1–459 BC
See footnote, *Time*, Rev. 10:6.

**1**
*a* Dan. 5:31; 6.
*b* *Persia, rulers of*, Esth. 1:3.
*c* *Ahasuerus*, Esth. 1:1.
*d* *Medes*, Dan. 5:28.
*e* *Chaldea*, Ezek. 11:24.

**2**
*f* *Daniel*, Dan. 1:6.
*g* *Book, prophecies written in*, Num. 5:23.
*h* *Prophecies, inspired*, Dan. 9:24.
*i* *Jeremiah, prophecies of*, Jer. 1:1.
*j* *Prophets, inspiration of*, vs. 1–22; Isa. 3:2.
*k* *Seventy, years*, Num. 11:16.
*l* *Jerusalem, prophecies against*, Judg. 19:10.

**3**
*m* *Prayer, intercessory*, Acts 6:4.
*n* *Intercession, exemplified*, vs. 3–19; Jer. 27:18.
*o* *Nation, in adversity, prayer for*, Isa. 2:4.
*p* *Fasting, accompanied by prayer*, Zech. 8:19.
*q* *Sackcloth*, Isa. 15:3.
*r* *Ashes*, Num. 19:9.

**4**
*s* *Prayer, confession in*, Acts 6:4.
*t* *God, faithfulness of*, Gen. 2:2.
*u* *God, mercy of*, Gen. 2:2.
*v* *Love, of man for God*, 1 John 4:19.
*w* *Obedience*, Heb. 5:8.

**5**
*x* *Sin, confession of*, vs. 8–11, 15; Rom. 5:12.

**7**
*y* *God, righteousness of*, Gen. 2:2.

told *is* true: wherefore shut[C] thou
up the vision; for it *shall be* for
many days.[Q]
27 And I Dăn′iel [u]fainted, and
was sick *certain* days; afterward
I rose up, and did the king's
business; and I was astonished
at the vision, but none understood *it*.

## CHAPTER 9

*Daniel's confession of sin, 16 and prayer for the restoration of Jerusalem. 20 Gabriel informs him of the seventy weeks.*

IN the first year of [a,b]Dā-rī′us
the son of [c]Ā-hăş-ū-ē′rŭs, of
the seed of the [d]Mēdeş, which
was made king over the [e]realm
of the Chăl-dē′anş;
2 In the first year of his reign I
[f]Dăn′iel understood by [g]books
the number of the years, whereof
the [h]word of the LORD came
to [i]Jĕr-e-mī′ah the [j]prophet, that
he would accomplish [k]seventy
years in the desolations[C] of [l]Jē-
rụ′sā-lĕm.
3 ¶ And I set my face unto the
Lord God, to seek by [m,n,o]prayer
and supplications, with [p]fasting,
and [q]sackcloth, and [r]ashes:
4 And I [m,n,o]prayed unto the
LORD my God, and made my
[s]confession, and said, O Lord, the
great and dreadful[C] God, [t]keep-
ing the covenant and [u]mercy
to them that [v]love him, and to
them that [w]keep his commandments;[S]
5 [s,x]We have sinned, and have
committed iniquity, and have
done wickedly, and have rebelled, even by departing from
thy precepts and from thy judgments:[G]
6 [s,x]Neither have we hearkened
unto thy servants the [j]prophets,
which spake in thy name to our
kings, our princes, and our fathers, and to all the people of the
land.[Q]
7 O Lord, [y]righteousness *belongeth* unto thee, but [s,x]unto us
confusion of faces, as at this day;
to the men of Jū′dah, and to the
inhabitants of Jē-rụ′sā-lĕm, and
unto all Ĭş′ra-el, *that are* near,
and *that are* far off, through all
the countries whither[C] thou hast
[z,a,b]driven [c]them, because of their
trespass that they have trespassed
against thee.[T]
8 [d]O Lord, to us *belongeth* confusion[C] of face, to our kings, to
our princes, and to our fathers,
because [e]we have sinned against
thee.
9 To the Lord our God *be-
long* [f]mercies and [g]forgivenesses,
though we have rebelled against
him;[S]
10 [e,h]Neither have we obeyed
the voice of the LORD our God,
to walk in his [i]laws, which he
set before us by his servants
the [j]prophets.[Q]
11 Yea, all Ĭş′ra-el have [h]trans-
gressed thy [i]law, even by [k]depart-
ing, that they might [h]not obey
thy voice; therefore the [l,m]curse
is poured upon us, and the oath
that *is* written in the law of Mō′-
şeş the servant of God, because
we have sinned against him.
12 And he hath confirmed his
words, which he spake against
us, and against our [n]judges that
judged us, by [l,o]bringing upon
us a great [b]evil: for under the
whole heaven hath not been done
as hath been done upon Jē-rụ′-
sā-lĕm.
13 As [m]*it is* written in the [i]law
of Mō′şeş, all this [b]evil is come
upon us: yet [1,p,q,r]made we not
our prayer before[C] the LORD our
God, that we might turn from
our iniquities, and understand
thy [s]truth.[S T]
14 Therefore hath the LORD
watched upon the [b]evil, and
brought it upon us: for [t]the
LORD our God *is* [u]righteous in
all his works which he doeth:
for [e]we [h]obeyed not his voice.[S]

v.7–459 BC
See footnote, *Time*, Rev. 10:6.

*z* *Captivity, as a judgment*, Isa. 5:13.
*a* *Nation, punishment of*, Isa. 2:4.
*b* *Adversity, dispensation from God*, Psa. 10:6.
*c* *Jews, captive in Babylon*, Neh. 4:2.

**8**
*d* *Nation, in adversity, prayer for*, Isa. 2:4.
*e* *Sin, confession of*, Rom. 5:12.

**9**
*f* *God, mercy of*, Gen. 2:2.
*g* *Sin, forgiveness of*, Rom. 5:12.

**10**
*h* *Disobedience to God*, Eph. 5:6.
*i* *Law, of Moses*, Deut. 33:2.
*j* *Prophets, inspiration of*, Isa. 3:2.

**11**
*k* *Backsliding, of Israel*, Hos. 11:7.
*l* *Wicked, punishment of*, Psa. 73:3.
*m* *Curse, of the Mosaic law*, Judg. 5:23.

**12**
*n* *Judge*, Judg. 2:18.
*o* *Divine Chastisement*, Job 33:19.

**13**
*p* *Adversity, obduracy in*, Psa. 10:6.
*q* *Impenitence*, Rom. 2:5.
*r* *Prayerlessness*, Job 21:15.
*s* *Truth*, John 18:37.
1 R. V. have we not intreated the favour of the Lord

**14**
*t* *Resignation, exemplified*, Job 5:17.
*u* *God, righteousness of*, Gen. 2:2.

v.15–459 BC
See footnote, *Time*, Rev. 10:6.

**15**
v *God, providence of*, Gen. 2:2.
w *Egypt*, Gen. 41:8.

**16**
x *Prayer, pleas offered in*, Acts 6:4.
y *Anger of God*, 2 Kin. 13:3.
z *Jerusalem, called holy mountain*, Judg. 19:10.

a *Children, involved in sins of parents*, Mark 10:14.

**17**
b *Prayer, intercessory*, Acts 6:4.
c *Intercession, exemplified*, Jer. 27:18.
d *Nation, in adversity, prayer for*, Isa. 2:4.
e *Church, called sanctuary*, 1 Kin. 9:3.

**18**
f *Works, are insufficient for salvation*, 2 Tim. 1:9.
g *Prayer, pleas offered in*, Acts 6:4.
h *God, mercy of*, Gen. 2:2.

**19**
i *Sin, forgiveness of*, Rom. 5:12.

15 And now, O Lord our God,
that hast [v]brought thy people
forth out of the land of [w]Ē'ġ̆ypt
with a mighty hand, and hast
gotten thee renown, as at this
day; [e]we have sinned, we have
done wickedly.

16 ¶ O Lord, [x]according to
all thy [u]righteousness, I beseech
thee, [d]let thine [y]anger and thy
fury be turned away from thy city
[z]Jĕ-ru̥'să-lĕm, thy holy mountain:
because for our sins, and [a]for the
iniquities of our fathers, Jĕ-ru̥'-
să-lĕm and thy people *are become*
a reproach to all *that are*
about us.[S T]

17 Now therefore, O our God,
hear the [b,c,d]prayer of thy servant, and his supplications, and
cause thy face to shine[G] upon thy
[e]sanctuary that is desolate[C], for
the Lord's sake.

18 [b,c,d]O my God, incline thine
ear, and hear; open thine eyes,
and behold our desolations[G], and
the city which is called by thy
name: for we do not present
our supplications before thee for
our [f]righteousnesses, but [g]for thy
great [h]mercies.

19 [b,c,d]O Lord, hear; O Lord,
[i]forgive; O Lord, hearken and
do; defer not, [g]for thine own
sake, O my God: [g]for thy city
and thy[T] people are called by thy
name.

20 ¶ And whiles I *was* speaking, and [b,c,d]praying, and [j]con-
fessing my sin and the sin of my
people Ĭs̱'ra-el, and presenting
my supplication before the LORD
my God for the holy mountain
of my God;

21 Yea, whiles I *was* speaking
in [b,c,d]prayer, even the man [k]Gā'-
brĭ-el, whom I had seen in the
[l]vision at the beginning, being
caused to fly swiftly, touched me
about the time of the evening
[m]oblation.[G Q]

22 And [k]he [n,o]informed[C] *me*,
and talked with me, and said, O
[p]Dăn'iel, I am now come forth
to give thee skill and [q]under-
standing.

23 At the beginning of thy
supplications the commandment
came forth, and [k]I am come to
[n]shew *thee*; for thou *art* greatly
beloved: therefore understand
the matter, and consider the
[l]vision.

24 [r,s]Seventy[T] weeks are determined upon thy [t]people and upon thy holy [u]city, [v]to finish the
transgression, and [v]to make an
end of sins, and [v]to make [w]rec-
onciliation for iniquity, and [v]to
bring in everlasting righteousness, and [v]to seal up the vision
and *prophecy[G], and to [x]anoint
the most Holy.[S Q]

25 Know therefore and understand, *that* from the going forth
of the commandment to restore

v.20–459 BC
See footnote, *Time*, Rev. 10:6.

**20**
j *Sin, confession of*, Rom. 5:12.

**21**
k *Gabriel*, Dan. 8:16.
l *Vision*, Acts 9:10.
m *Offerings, daily*, Lev. 6:17.

**22**
n *Angel, functions of*, Heb. 1:13.
o *Prayer, answered*, Acts 6:4.
p *Daniel*, Dan. 1:6.
q *Wisdom, spiritual*, Prov. 2:2.

**24**
r *Seventy, weeks*, Num. 11:16.
s *Jesus, prophecies concerning* (according to many learned interpreters), Matt. 1:21.
t *Jews, prophecies concerning*, Neh. 4:2.
u *Jerusalem, prophecies against*, vs. 24–26; Judg. 19:10.
v *Jesus, mission of* (according to many learned interpreters), Matt. 1:21.
w *Reconciliation, between God and man*, 2 Cor. 5:18.
x *Anointing, figurative*, Deut. 28:40.

* **PROPHECIES.** Concerning Jesus, see footnote, JESUS, PROPHECIES CONCERNING, Matt. 1:21. Concerning church, see footnote, CHURCH, PROPHECIES CONCERNING, Matt. 16:18. Relating to various countries, nations, and cities, see under their respective titles. Respecting individuals, see under their names.

*Inspired*, Isa. 28:22; Luke 1:70; 2 Tim. 3:16; 2 Pet. 1:21. "*The word of the Lord came unto," etc.*: *Elijah*, 1 Kin. 17:8; 21:17, 28; *Isaiah*, Isa. 2:1; 8:5; 13:1; 14:28; 38:4; *Jeremiah*, Jer. 1:4; 7:1; 11:1; 13:8; 16:1; 18:1; 25:1, 2; 26:1; 27:1 29:30; 30:1, 4; 32:1, 6, 26; 33:1, 19, 23; 34:12; 35:12; 36:1; 37:6; 40:1; 43:8; 44:1; 46:1; 49:34; 50:1; *Ezekiel*, Ezek. 3:16; 6:1; 7:1; 11:14; 12:1, 8, 17, 21; 13:1; 14:12; 15:1; 16:1; 17:1, 11; 18:1; 20:45; 21:1, 8, 18; 22:1, 17, 23; 23:1; 24:1, 15, 20; 25:1; 26:1; 27:1; 28:1, 11, 20; 29:1, 17; 30:1, 20; 31:1; 32:1, 17; 33:1, 23; 34:1; 35:1; 36:16; 37:15; 38:1; *Amos*, Amos 7:14, 15; *Jonah*, Jonah 3:1; *Haggai*, Hag. 2:1, 10, 20; *Zechariah*, Zech. 1:7; 4:8; 6:9; 7:1, 4, 8; 8:1, 18.

*Publicly proclaimed*, Jer. 11:6. *Exemplified in pantomime, by Isaiah*, Isa. 20:2, 3; *by Jeremiah*, Jer. 43:9, 10; *by Ezekiel*, Ezek. 4; 5:1–4; Acts 21:11. *Written in books*, Jer. 45:1; 51:60.

*Proof of God's foreknowledge*, Isa. 43:9. *Fulfillment of*, Ezek. 12:22–25, 28; Hab. 2:3; Matt. 5:18; 24:35; Acts 13:27, 29. *Cessation of*, Lam. 2:9; Mic. 3:6.

*Of apostasy*, 1 John 2:18, 19; Jude 17, 18. *Of false teachers*, 2 Pet. 2:1, 3.

**Fulfilled**, Luke 24:27, 44; Acts 3:18; 10:43. *The birth and zeal of Josiah*, 1 Kin. 13:2; 2 Kin. 23:1–20. *Of the prophet of Judah against Jeroboam's altar*, 1 Kin. 13:3–5. *Death of the prophet of Judah*, 1 Kin. 13:21, 22, 24–30. *Extinction, of Jeroboam's house*, 1 Kin. 14:5–17; *of Baasha's house*, 1 Kin. 16:2, 3, 9–13. *Concerning the rebuilding of Jericho*, Josh. 6:26; 1 Kin. 16:34. *Destruction of Ben-hadad's army*, 1 Kin. 20:13–30. *The death of a man who refused to smite a prophet*, 1 Kin. 20:35, 36. *The death of Ahab*, 1 Kin. 20:42; 21:18–24; 22:31–38. *The death of Ahaziah*, 2 Kin. 1:2–17. *Elijah's translation*, 2 Kin. 2:3–11. *Sending of water and victory foretold by Elisha*, 2 Kin. 3:13–26. *The death of the Samaritan lord*, 2 Kin. 7:2, 19, 20. *The end of the famine in Samaria*, 2 Kin. 7:1–18. *Jezebel's tragic death*, 1 Kin. 21:23, with 2 Kin. 9:10, 33–37. *The smiting of Syria by Joash*, 2 Kin. 13:16–25. *Four generations of Jehu to sit upon the throne of Israel*, 2 Kin. 10:30, with 15:12. *Destruction of Sennacherib's army, and his death*, 2 Kin. 19:6, 7, 20–37. *The captivity of Judah*, 2 Kin. 20:17, 18 (with Jer. 25:11, 12; 32:3–5; Dan. 9:2); 24:10–16; 25:11–21. *Return of the Jews from Babylon*, Jer. 29:10, 14; Ezra 1. *Profaning of the temple*, Isa. 56:7; Jer. 7:11; with Matt. 21:13; Mark 11:17; Luke 19:46. *The insanity of Nebuchadnezzar*, Dan. 4:16–37. *Rachel weeping for*

v.25–459 BC
See footnote, *Time,* Rev. 10:6.

**25**
2 R. V. anointed one, the prince, shall be seven weeks: and threescore and two weeks, it shall be built again, with street and moat, even in troublous times.

**26**
*y Temple, Herod's, prophecies concerning its destruction,* 1 Kin. 6:17.
3 R. V. the anointed one be cut off, and shall have nothing:

**27**
*z Judgments,* Ex. 6:6.
4 R. V. make a firm covenant
5 R. V. upon the wing of abominations shall come one that maketh desolate;
6 R. V. wrath be poured out upon the desolator.

and to build [u]Jĕ-ru′să-lĕm unto
the [2,s]Mĕs-sī′ah the Prince *shall*
*be* seven weeks, and threescore
and two weeks: the street shall
be built again, and the wall, even
in troublous times.[T Q]
26 And after threescore and
two weeks shall [3,s]Mĕs-sī′ah be
cut[C]off, but not for himself: and
the people of the prince that
shall come shall destroy the [u]city
and the [y]sanctuary; and the end
thereof *shall be* with a flood, and
unto the end of the war desolations[C] are determined.[S Q]
27 And he shall [4]confirm the
covenant[C] with many for one
week: and in the midst of the
week he shall cause the sacrifice
and the oblation[C] to cease, and
[5]for the overspreading of abominations[C] he shall make *it* desolate[C], even until the consummation, and that determined shall
[6,z]be poured upon the desolate.[Q]

## CHAPTER 10

*Daniel's fasting and humiliation.* 4 *He sees a vision.* 10 *Being troubled he is comforted and strengthened by an angel.*

v.1–455 BC
See footnote, *Time,* Rev. 10:6.

**1**
*a Cyrus,* 2 Chr. 36:22.
*b Persia,* Esth. 1:3.
*c Daniel,* vs. 1–21; Dan. 1:6.
*d Vision,* vs. 1–27; Acts 9:10.
1 R. V. even a great warfare:

**2**
*e Mourning,* Lam. 2:5.

**3**
*f Fasting,* Zech. 8:19.
*g Self-denial,* Mark 8:34.
*h Wine, abstinence from,* Prov. 23:31.

**4**
*i Month (April),* Ex. 12:2.
*j* Gen. 2:14.

IN the third year of [a]Çȳ′rus
king of [b]Pĕr′ṣiȧ a thing was
revealed unto [c]Dăn′iel, whose
name was called Bĕl-te-shăz′zar;
and the thing *was* true, [1]but the
time appointed *was* long: and he
understood the thing, and had
understanding of the [d]vision.
2 In those days I [c]Dăn′iel was
[e]mourning three full weeks.
3 I [f,g]ate no pleasant[C] bread,
neither came flesh nor [h]wine in
my mouth, neither did I anoint
myself at all, till three whole
weeks were fulfilled.
4 And in the four and twentieth
day of the first [i]month, as I was
by the side of the great river,
which *is* [j]Hĭd′de-kĕl;
5 Then [c]I lifted up mine eyes,
and looked, and [d]behold a certain man clothed in [k]linen, whose
loins *were* girded with [2]fine [l]gold
of [m]Ū′phăz:[Q]
6 His body also *was* like the
[n]beryl, and his face as the appearance of [o]lightning, and his
eyes as lamps of fire, and his
arms and his feet like in colour
to polished [p]brass, and the voice
of his words like the voice of a
multitude.[Q]
7 And I [c]Dăn′iel alone saw the
[d]vision: for the men that were
with me saw not the vision; but a
great quaking fell upon them, so
that they fled to hide themselves.
8 Therefore [c]I was left alone,
and saw this great [d]vision, and
there remained no strength in
me: for my comeliness[C] was
turned in me into corruption,
and I retained no strength.
9 Yet heard [c]I the voice of his
words: and when I heard the
voice of his words, then was I in
a deep sleep on my face, and my
face toward the ground.
10 ¶ And, behold, an hand
touched me, which set me upon
my knees and *upon* the palms of
my hands.
11 And he said unto me, O
[c]Dăn′iel, a man greatly beloved,
understand the words that I
speak unto thee, and stand upright: for [q]unto thee am I now
sent. And when he had spoken
this word unto me, I stood trembling.
12 Then said he unto me, Fear
not, [c]Dăn′iel: for from the first
day that thou didst set thine heart
to understand, and to [r]chasten
thyself before thy God, [s]thy words
were heard, and I am come for
thy words.

v.5–455 BC
See footnote, *Time,* Rev. 10:6.

**5**
*k Linen,* Ezek. 27:16.
*l Gold,* Ezek. 7:19.
*m* Jer. 10:9.
2 R. V. pure

**6**
*n Beryl,* Ezek. 1:16.
*o Lightning,* Job 28:26.
*p Brass,* Job 28:2

**11**
*q Angel, functions of,* Heb. 1:13.

**12**
*r Humility,* Prov. 22:4.
*s Prayer, answered,* Acts 6:4.

*her children,* Jer. 31:15, with Matt. 2:16–18. *Invasion of Judah by the Chaldeans,* Hab. 1:6–11, with, 2 Kin. 25; 2 Chr. 36:17–21. *Betrayal of Jesus by Judas,* Psa. 41:9, with John 13:18; 18:1–5. *Judas' destruction,* Psa. 69:25, with Matt. 27: 5· Acts 1:16–20. *Outpouring of the Holy Spirit,* Joel 2:28, 29, with Acts 2:16–21. *Spiritual blindness of the Jews,* Isa. 6:9, 10; 29:13, with Matt. 13:11–15; Mark 7:1–13; Acts 28: 23–27. *Concerning John,* Isa. 40:3, with Matt. 3:3; John 1:23. *Of the destruction of the ship in which Paul sailed,* Acts 27:10, 18–44.

v.13–455 BC
See footnote, *Time*, Rev. 10:6.

13 But the prince of the kingdom of [b]Pĕr′ṣiȧ withstood me one and twenty days: but, lo, *Mī′chaĕl, one of the chief princes, came to help me; and I remained there with the kings of Pĕr′ṣiȧ.[Q]

14 Now I am come [q]to make thee understand what shall befall thy [t]people in the latter days: for yet the [d]vision *is* for *many* days.

15 And when he had spoken such words unto me, I set my face toward the ground, and I became dumb.[G]

16 And, behold, *one* like the similitude of the sons of men touched my lips: then I opened my mouth, and spake, and said unto him that stood before me, O my lord, by the [d]vision my sorrows are turned upon me, and I have retained no strength.[Q]

17 For how can the servant of this my lord talk with this my lord? for as for me, straightway there remained no strength in me, neither is there breath left in me.

18 Then there came again and touched me *one* like the appearance of a man, and he strengthened me,

19 And said, O man greatly beloved, fear not: peace *be* unto thee, be strong, yea, be strong. And when he had spoken unto me, I was strengthened, and said, Let my lord speak; for thou hast strengthened me.[Q]

20 Then said he, Knowest thou wherefore[G] I come unto thee? and now will I return to fight with the prince of [b]Pĕr′ṣiȧ: and when I am gone forth, lo, the prince of [u]Grē′çiȧ shall come.[Q]

21 But I will shew thee that which is noted in the scripture of truth: and *there is* none that holdeth with me in these things, but *Mī′chaĕl your prince.[Q]

14
*t Jews, prophecies concerning*, Neh. 4:2.

20
*u Greece, prophecies concerning*, Zech. 9:13.

v.21–455 BC
See footnote, *Time*, Rev. 10:6.

## CHAPTER 11

*The overthrow of Persia by the king of Grecia.* 5 *Leagues and conflicts between the kings of the south and of the north.* 21 *The rise of a vile person to power.* 30 *His impious conduct.* 40 *His fall.*

ALSO I in the first year of [a]Dȧ-rī′us the [b]Mēde, *even* I, stood to confirm and to strengthen him.

2 And now will I shew thee the truth. Behold, there shall stand up yet three kings in [c]Pĕr′ṣiȧ; and the fourth shall be far richer than *they* all: and by his strength through his riches he shall stir up all against the realm of [d]Grē′çiȧ.

3 And a mighty king shall stand up, that shall rule with great dominion, and do according to his will.

4 And when he shall stand up, his kingdom shall be broken, and shall be divided toward the four winds of heaven; and not to his posterity, nor according to his dominion which he ruled: for his kingdom shall be plucked up, even for others beside those.

5 ¶ And the king of the south shall be strong, and *one* of his princes; and he shall be strong above him, and have dominion; his dominion *shall be* a great dominion.

6 And in the end of years they shall join themselves together; for the king's [e]daughter of the south shall come to the king of the north to make an agreement: but she shall not retain the power of the arm; neither shall he stand, nor his arm: but she shall be given up, and they that brought her, and he that begat her, and he that strengthened her in *these* times.

7 But out of a branch of her roots shall *one* stand up in his [1]estate, which shall come with an

1
*a* Dan. 5:31; 6.
*b Medes*, Dan. 5:28.

2
*c Persia, prophecies concerning*, vs. 1–4; Esth. 1:3.
*d Greece, prophecies concerning*, Zech. 9:13.

6
*e Women, influential in public affairs*, Prov. 31:10.

7
1 R. V. place.

* **MICHAEL**, the Archangel. *His message to Daniel*, Dan. 10:13, 21; 12:1. *Contends with the devil*, Jude 9. *Fights with the dragon*, Rev. 12:7–9.

v.7–455 BC
See footnote, *Time*, Rev. 10:6.

8
*f* *Egypt*, Gen. 41:8.
*g* *Idolatry*, 1 Sam. 15:23.
*h* *Silver*, 1 Chr. 28:14.
*i* *Gold*, Ezek. 7:19.
2 R. V. And also their gods, with their molten images, and with their goodly vessels of silver and of gold, shall he carry captive into Egypt; and he shall refrain some years from the king of the north.

9
3 R. V. And he shall come into the realm of the king of the south, but he shall

10
4 R. V. war,

12
5 R. V. And the multitude shall be lifted up, and his heart shall be exalted:
6 R. V. prevail.

13
7 R. V. he shall come on at the end of the times, even of years,

14
8 R. V. children of the violent among thy people

15
*j* *Fortification*, Ezek. 17:17.
*k* *Cities, fortified* Num. 35:8.

army, and shall enter into the
fortress of the king of the north,
and shall deal against them, and
shall prevail:
8 And [2]shall also carry captives
into [f]Ē′ġy̆pt their [g]gods, with their
princes, *and* with their precious[G]
vessels of [h]silver and of [i]gold; and
he shall continue *more* years than
the king of the north.
9 [3]So the king of the south shall
come into *his* kingdom, and shall
return into his own land.
10 But his sons shall [4]be stirred
up, and shall assemble a multitude of great forces: and *one* shall
certainly come, and overflow, and
pass through: then shall he return, and [4]be stirred up, *even* to
his fortress.
11 And the king of the south
shall be moved with choler,[G] and
shall come forth and fight with
him, *even* with the king of the
north: and he shall set forth a
great multitude; but the multitude shall be given into his hand.
12 *And* [5]when he hath taken
away the multitude, his heart
shall be lifted[G] up; and he shall
cast down *many* ten thousands:
but he shall not [6]be strengthened
*by it.*
13 For the king of the north
shall return, and shall set forth a
multitude greater than the former, and [7]shall certainly come
after certain years with a great
army and with much riches.
14 And in those times there
shall many stand up against the
king of the south: also the [8]rob-
bers of thy people shall exalt
themselves to establish the vision; but they shall fall.
15 So the king of the north shall
come, and cast up a [j]mount,[G] and
take the most [k]fenced[G] cities: and
the arms of the south shall not
withstand, neither his chosen people, neither *shall there be any*
strength to withstand.

16 But he that cometh against
him shall do according to his
own will, and none shall stand
before him: and he shall stand in
the glorious land, [9]which by his
hand shall be consumed.[G]
17 He shall also set his face to
enter with the strength of his
whole kingdom, and upright
ones with him; thus shall he do:
and he shall give him the daughter of women, corrupting her:
but she shall not stand *on his*
*side*, neither be for him.
18 After this shall he turn his
face unto the isles, and shall take
many: but a prince [10]for his own
behalf shall cause the reproach
offered by him to cease; without
his own reproach he shall cause
*it* to turn upon him.
19 Then he shall turn his face
toward the [j]fort of his own land:
but he shall stumble and fall,
and not be found.
20 Then shall stand up in his
[1]estate a [l]raiser of taxes *in* the
glory of the kingdom: but within
few days he shall be destroyed,
neither in anger, nor in battle.
21 And in his [1]estate shall stand
up a vile person, to whom they
shall not give the honour of the
kingdom: but he shall come [11]in
peaceably, and obtain the kingdom by [m]flatteries.
22 And with the arms of a flood
shall they be [12]overflown from
before him, and shall be broken;
yea, also the prince of the covenant.
23 And after the league *made*
with him he shall work deceitfully: for he shall come up, and
shall become strong with a small
people.
24 [13]He shall enter peaceably
even upon the fattest[G] places of
the province; and he shall do
*that* which his fathers have not
done, nor his fathers' fathers; he
shall scatter among them the

v.16–455 BC
See footnote, *Time*, Rev. 10:6.

16
9 R. V. and in his hand shall be destruction.

18
10 R. V. shall cause the reproach offered by him to cease; yea, moreover, he shall cause his reproach to turn upon him.

20
*l* *Tax, collectors of*, Neh. 10:32.

21
*m* *Flattery*, Prov. 6:24.
11 R. V. in time of security,

22
12 R. V. swept away from

24
13 R. V. In time of security shall he come even upon

v.24–455 BC
See footnote, *Time*, Rev. 10:6.

**24**
14 R. V. devise

**26**
*n Treachery*, 2 Kin. 9:23.

**27**
*o Rulers, wicked*, Ex. 18:21.
*p Falsehood*, Job 21:34.

**28**
*q Spoils*, 1 Chr. 26:27.
15 R. V. his pleasure,

**30**
*r Ship*, 2 Chr. 8:18.
16 R. V. regard unto them

**31**
*s Profanation, of the house of God*, Lev. 22:32.
*t Temple, prophecies concerning its destruction*, 1 Kin. 6:17.
*u Offerings, daily*, Lev. 6:17.
17 R. V. continual burnt offering,

prey, and spoil, and riches: *yea*, and he shall [14]forecast his devices[G] against the strong holds, even for a time.

25 And he shall stir up his power and his courage against the king of the south with a great army; and the king of the south shall be stirred up to battle with a very great and mighty army; but he shall not stand: for they shall [14]forecast devices[G] against him.

26 Yea, they that feed of the portion of his meat[G] shall [n]destroy him, and his army shall overflow: and many shall fall down slain.

27 And both these [o]kings' hearts *shall be* to do mischief, and they shall speak [p]lies at one table; but it shall not prosper: for yet the end *shall be* at the time appointed.[S]

28 Then shall he return into his land with great [q]riches; and his heart *shall be* against the holy covenant; and he shall do [15]*exploits*, and return to his own land.

29 At the time appointed he shall return, and come toward the south; but it shall not be as the former, or as the latter.

30 For the [r]ships of *Chĭt′tim shall come against him: therefore he shall be grieved, and return, and have indignation against the holy covenant: so shall he do; he shall even return, and have [16]intelligence with them that forsake the holy covenant.

31 And arms shall stand on his part, and they shall [s]pollute the [t]sanctuary of strength, and shall take away the [17,u]daily *sacrifice*, and they shall place the abomination that maketh desolate.[G][Q]

32 And such as do wickedly against the covenant shall he corrupt by [m]flatteries: but the people that do [v]know their God shall be strong, and do *exploits*.

33 And they that understand among the people shall [w]instruct many: yet they shall fall by the [x]sword, and by flame, by [y]captivity, and by spoil, *many* days.

34 Now when they shall fall, they shall be holpen[G] with a little help: but many shall cleave[G] to them with flatteries.

35 And *some* of them of understanding shall fall, to try[G] them, and to purge, and to make *them* [z]white, *even* to the time of the end: because *it is* yet for a time appointed.

36 [Q]And the king shall do according to his will; and he shall exalt himself, and magnify himself above every god, and shall [a]speak marvellous things against the God of gods, and shall prosper till the indignation[G] be accomplished: for that that is determined shall be done.

37 [T]Neither shall he regard the [18]God[G] of his fathers, nor the desire of women, nor regard any god: for he shall magnify himself above all.[Q]

38 But in his [19]estate shall he honour the [20]God[G] of forces: and a god whom his fathers knew not shall he honour with gold, and silver, and with precious stones, and pleasant[G] things.

39 [21]Thus shall he do in the most strong holds[G] with a strange[G] god, whom he shall acknowledge *and* increase with glory: and he shall cause them to rule over many, and shall divide the land for gain.[G] [T]

40 And at the time of the end shall the king of the south push at him: and the king of the north shall come against him like a whirlwind, with [b]chariots, and

v.32–455 BC
See footnote, *Time*, Rev. 10:6.

**32**
*v Wisdom, spiritual*, Prov. 2:2.

**33**
*w Instruction*, Prov. 23:23.
*x War, as a judgment*, Judg. 3:2.
*y Captivity, as a judgment*, Isa. 5:13.

**35**
*z Colors, figurative*, Ezek. 16:16.

**36**
*a Blasphemy, exalting one's self above God*, 2 Sam. 12:14.

**37**
18 R. V. gods

**38**
19 R. V. place
20 R. V. god of fortresses:

**39**
21 R. V. And he shall deal with the strongest fortresses by the help of a strange god; whosoever acknowledgeth him he will increase with glory:

**40**
*b Chariot*, Josh. 11:4.

***CHITTIM.** *Descendants of Javan, and therefore belonging to the same race as the Greeks, who were also descendants of Javan, along probably with the Latin people*, Gen. 10:4; 1 Chr. 1:7. *Probably inhabited islands of the Mediterranean*, Isa. 23:1, 12; Jer. 2:10. *Their commerce*, Ezek. 27:6. *Prophecies concerning*, Num. 24:24; Dan. 11:30.

with [c]horsemen, and with many [d]ships; and he shall enter into the countries, and shall overflow and pass over.

41 He shall enter also into the glorious land, and many *countries* shall be overthrown: but these shall escape out of his hand, *even* [e]Ē′dom, and [f]Mō′ab, and the chief of the [g]children of Ăm′mŏn.[Q]

42 He shall stretch[G] forth his hand also upon the countries: and the land of [h]Ē′ġȳpt shall not escape.

43 But he shall have power over the treasures of gold and of silver, and over all the precious things of Ē′ġȳpt; and the [i]Lĭb′ȳ-ans and the [j]Ē-thĭ-ō′pĭ-ans *shall be* at his steps.

44 But tidings out of the east and out of the north shall trouble him: therefore he shall go forth with great fury to destroy, and utterly to make[G] away many.

45 And he shall plant the tabernacles of his palace between the seas in the glorious holy mountain; yet he shall [k]come to his end, and none shall help him.

## CHAPTER 12

*The troubles and deliverance of the people of God. 5 The duration of these wonders.*

AND[T] at that time shall [a]Mī′-chaēl stand up, the great prince which standeth for the children of [b]thy [c]people: and there shall be a time of trouble, such as never was since there was a nation *even* to that same time: and at that time [d,e]thy people shall be [f]delivered, every one that shall be found written in the [g]book.[S Q]

2 And many of them that [h]sleep in the dust of the earth shall [i]awake, [e,j]some to [k,l]everlasting life, and some to shame *and* [m,n]everlasting contempt.[T Q]

3 And [e]they that be [o]wise shall shine as the brightness of the [p]firmament; and they that [q]turn many to [r]righteousness as the stars for ever and ever.[Q]

4 But thou, O [c]Dăn′iel, shut up the words, and seal the book, *even* to the time of the end: many shall run to and fro, and [s]knowledge shall be increased.[Q]

5 ¶ Then I [c]Dăn′iel looked, and, behold, there stood other two, the one on this side of the bank of the river, and the other on that side of the bank of the river.

6 And *one* said to the man clothed in [t]linen, which *was* upon the waters of the river, How long *shall it be to* the end of these wonders?

7 And I heard the man clothed in [t]linen, which *was* upon the waters of the river, when he held up his right hand and his left hand unto heaven, and [u]sware by him that liveth for ever that *it shall be* for a [v]time, times, and an half; and when [1]he shall have accomplished to scatter the power of the holy people, all these *things* shall be finished.[Q]

8 And I heard, but I understood not: then said I, O my Lord, what *shall be* the end of these *things*?

9 And he said, Go thy way, [c]Dăn′iel: for the words *are* closed up and [w]sealed[G] till the time of the end.[Q]

10 Many shall be [x]purified, and made [y]white, and [z,a]tried[G]; but the wicked shall do wickedly: and [b]none of the wicked shall understand; but the [c]wise shall understand.

11 And from the time *that* the [2,d]daily *sacrifice* shall be taken away, and the abomination that maketh desolate[G] set up, *there shall be* a thousand two hundred and ninety [e]days.[Q]

v.40–455 BC
See footnote, *Time*, Rev. 10:6.

*c Cavalry*, 1 Sam. 13:5.
*d Ship*, 2 Chr. 8:18.

41
*e Edomites, prophecies concerning*, 2 Kin. 8:1.
*f Moabites, prophecies concerning*, Gen. 19:37.
*g Ammonites, prophecies concerning*, Deut. 2:20.

42
*h Egypt, prophecies concerning*, Gen. 41:8.

43
*i* Jer. 46:9.
*j Ethiopia*, Isa. 18:1.

45
*k Wicked, punishment of*, Psa. 73:3.

1
*a Michael, the archangel*, Dan. 10:13.
*b Daniel*, Dan. 1:6.
*c Jews, prophecies concerning*, Neh. 4:2.
*d Church, prophecies concerning its prosperity*, Matt. 16:18.
*e Righteous, promises to*, vs. 1–3; Psa. 64:10.
*f God, preserver*, Gen. 2:2.
*g Book, figurative, of life*, Psa. 139:16.

2
*h Death, called sleep*, Num. 23:10.
*i Resurrection, prophecies concerning*, vs. 3, 13; 1 Cor. 15:12.
*j* John 5:29.
*k Immortality*, 1 Cor. 15:54.
*l Life, everlasting*, Eccl. 8:15.
*m Punishment, eternal*, Lev. 26:41.
*n Wicked, punishment of*, Psa. 73:3.

v.3–455 BC
See footnote, *Time*, Rev. 10:6.

3
*o Wisdom, spiritual*, Prov. 2:2.
*p Firmament*, Gen. 1:6.
*q Zeal*, 2 Cor. 7:11.
*r Righteousness, winning others to, rewarded*, Psa. 15:2.

4
*s Knowledge*, Luke 11:52.

6
*t Linen*, Ezek. 27:16.

7
*u Oath, a solemn qualification*, Num. 5:19.
*v Time*, Rev. 10:6.
1 R. V. they have made an end of breaking in pieces the power

9
*w Seal, figurative*, 1 Kin. 21:8.

10
*x Spiritual Purification*, Psa. 51:2.
*y Colors, figurative*, Ezek. 16:16.
*z Faith, trial of*, Mark 11:22.

*a Temptation, a test*, Luke 11:4.
*b Spiritual Blindness*, 2 Cor. 4:4.
*c Wisdom, spiritual*, Prov. 2:2.

11
*d Offerings, daily*, Lev. 6:17.
*e Day, a prophetic period*, Gen. 1:5.
2 R. V. continual burnt offering

v.12–455 BC
See footnote, *Time*, Rev. 10:6.

12 Blessed *is* he that waiteth, and cometh to the thousand three hundred and five and thirty [e]days.[Q]

13 But go thou thy way till the end *be*: for thou shalt [f]rest, and stand in thy lot at the end of the days.

v.13–455 BC

13
*f* *Death, of the righteous*, Num. 23:10.

THE

# BOOK OF HOSEA

## CHAPTER 1

*The date of Hosea's prophecy. 2 The prophet, for a sign to the people, takes an adulterous wife. 4 Their children. 10 The restoration and union of Judah and Israel.*

THE [a]word of the LORD that came unto *Hō-ṣē'ȧ, the son of Bē-ē'rī, in the days of [b]Ŭz-zī'-ah, [c]Jō'tham, [d]Ā'hăz, *and* [e]Hĕz-e-kī'ah, kings of [f]Jū'dah, and in the days of [g]Jĕr-o-bō'am the son of [h]Jō'ăsh, king of [i]Ĭṣ'ra-el.

2 The beginning of the [a]word of the LORD by *Hō-ṣē'ȧ. And the LORD said to Hō-ṣē'ȧ, Go, take unto thee a [j]wife of [k,l]whoredoms[G] and children of whoredoms[G]: for the land hath committed great whoredom[G], [m]*departing* from the LORD.

3 So he went and took [j]Gō'mēr the daughter of Dĭb'la-ĭm; which conceived, and bare him a son.

4 And the LORD said unto him, Call his [n]name Jĕz're-el; for yet a little *while*, and [o]I will avenge[G] the blood of [p]Jĕz're-el upon the house of [q]Jē'hū, and will cause to cease the kingdom of the house of [i]Ĭṣ'ra-el.

5 And it shall come to pass at that day, that [o]I will break the [r]bow of [i]Ĭṣ'ra-el in the valley of [p]Jĕz're-el.

6 ¶ And she conceived again, and bare a daughter. And [1]*God* said unto him, Call her [n]name Lō'–rụ-hā'mah[G]: for I will no more have mercy upon the house of [i]Ĭṣ'ra-el; [2]but I will utterly take them away.[Q]

7 But I will have [s]mercy upon the house of [f]Jū'dah, and will [t]save them by the LORD their God, and will not save them by bow, nor by sword, nor by battle, by horses, nor by horsemen.[Q T]

8 ¶ Now when she had weaned Lō'–rụ-hā'mah, she conceived, and bare a son.

9 [3]Then said *God*, Call his [n]name Lō'–ăm'mī[G]: for ye *are* not my people, and I will not be your *God*.

10 Yet the number of the children of Ĭṣ'ra-el shall be as the sand of the sea, which cannot be measured nor numbered; [u]and it shall come to pass, *that* in the place where it was said unto them, Ye *are* not my people, *there* it shall be said unto them, [v]*Ye are* the sons of the living [w]God.[Q]

11 Then shall the children of [f]Jū'dah and the children of [i]Ĭṣ'ra-el be gathered together, and appoint themselves one head, and they shall come up out of the land: for great *shall be* the day of [p]Jĕz're-el.[T]

## CHAPTER 2

*The idolatry of the people. 6 God's judgments against them. 14 His promises of reconciliation.*

SAY ye unto your brethren, Ăm'mī; and to your sisters, Rụ-hā'mah.[Q]

1
*a* *Prophecies, inspired*, Dan. 9:24.
*b* *Uzziah*, 2 Chr. 26:1.
*c* *Jotham*, 2 Kin. 15:5.
*d* *Ahaz*, 2 Kin. 15:38.
*e* *Hezekiah*, 2 Kin. 16:20.
*f* *Judah, prophecies concerning*, 2 Chr. 11:17.
*g* *Jeroboam*, 1 Chr. 5:17.
*h* Or, *Jehoash*, 2 Kin. 13:10.
*i* *Israel, prophecies concerning*, 1 Kin. 12:1.

2
*j* *Women, wicked*, Prov. 31:10.
*k* *Adultery*, Lev. 20:10.
*l* *Idolatry, wicked practices of*, 1 Sam. 15:23.
*m* *Backsliding*, Hos. 11:7.

4
*n* *Name, symbolical*, Prov. 22:1.
*o* *Nation, judgments denounced against*, Isa. 2:4.
*p* *Jezreel, prophecies concerning*, 1 Kin. 18:45.
*q* *Jehu, prophecies concerning*, 2 Chr. 22:8.

5
*r* *Bow, figurative*, 2 Sam. 1:18.

6
1 Am. R. V. Jehovah
2 R. V. that I should in any wise pardon them.

7
*s* *God, mercy of*, Gen. 2:2.
*t* *God, savior*, Gen. 2:2.

9
3 Am. R. V. And Jehovah said.

10
*u* Rom. 9:26.
*v* *Spiritual Adoption*, Rom. 8:15.
*w* *God, fatherhood of*, Gen. 2:2.

*** HOSEA.** *Son of Beeri, prophesies during the reigns of Uzziah, Jotham, Ahaz and Hezekiah, kings of Judah*, Hos. 1:1. *Reproves the abominable, idolatrous practices of the Jews*, Hos. chapters 1, 2. *Denounces the wickedness of priests and people, warns them by the threatened judgments of God, and exhorts to repentance*, Hos. chapters 3–6. *Foretells judgments against Israel*, Hos. chapters 7–10. *Describes the goodness of God to Israel, recounts his mercies, and rebukes their ingratitude; he calls them to repentance, and promises God's blessings*, Hos. chapters 11–14.

2 Plead[G] with your [a,b]mother, plead[G]: for she *is* not my wife, neither *am* I her husband: [c]let her therefore put away her [d]whoredoms[G] out of her sight, and her adulteries from between her breasts;

3 Lest I strip her naked, and set her as in the day that she was born, and make her as a wilderness, and set her like a dry land, and slay her with thirst.

4 And I will not have mercy upon her children; for they *be* the children of [d]whoredoms[G].

5 For their mother hath played the harlot: she that conceived them hath done shamefully: for she said, [e]I will go after my lovers, that give *me* my [f]bread and my [g]water, my [h]wool and my [i]flax, mine [j]oil and my drink.

6 ¶ Therefore, behold, I will hedge up thy way with *thorns, and make a wall, that she shall not find her paths.

7 And she shall follow after her lovers, but she shall not overtake them; and she shall seek them, but shall not find *them*: then shall she say, I will go and return to my first husband; for then *was it* better with me than now.

8 For she did [k]not know that [l]I [m]gave her [n]corn[G], and [o]wine, and [j]oil, and multiplied her [p]silver and [q]gold, [r]*which* they [1]prepared for [s]Bā'al.[S]

9 Therefore will I return, and [t]take away my [n]corn[G] in the time thereof, and my [o]wine in the season thereof, and will recover[G] my [h]wool and my [i]flax *given* to cover her nakedness.

10 And now will I discover[G] her lewdness[G] in the sight of her lovers, and none shall deliver her out of mine hand.

11 [b]I will also cause all her mirth to cease, her [u]feast days, her [v]new moons, and her [w]sabbaths, and all her solemn feasts.

12 And I will [t]destroy her vines and her fig trees, whereof she hath said, These *are* my rewards that my lovers have given me: and I will make them a forest, and the beasts of the field shall eat them.

13 And I will [t]visit[G] upon her the days of [s]Bā'al-ĭm, wherein she burned [x]incense to them, and she decked herself with her earrings and her jewels, and she went after her lovers, and [r]forgat me, saith the LORD.

14 ¶ Therefore, behold, [y]I will allure her, and bring her into the wilderness, and speak comfortably[G] unto her.

15 And [z]I will give her her vineyards from thence[G], and the valley of [a]Ā'chôr for a [b]door of [c]hope: and she shall sing there, as in the days of her youth, and as in the day when she came up out of the land of [d]Ē'ġypt.

16 And it shall be at that day, saith the LORD, *that* thou shalt call me Ī'shī[G]; and shalt call me no more Bā'al-ī.[G]

17 For I will take away the names of Bā'al-ĭm out of her mouth, and they shall no more be remembered by their name.

18 And in that day will I make a covenant[G] for them with the beasts of the field, and with the fowls of heaven, and *with* the creeping things of the ground: and [e,f]I will break the bow and the sword and the battle out of the earth, and will make them to lie down safely.[S T]

19 [S]And [g]I will [h]betroth thee unto [i]me for ever; yea, I will betroth thee unto me in righteous-

**2**
a *Church, backslidden,* vs. 1–23; Matt. 16:18.
b *Israel, prophecies concerning,* vs. 2–23; 1 Kin. 12:1.
c *Repentance, enjoined,* Mark 1:4.
d *Idolatry, wicked practices of,* 1 Sam. 15:23.

**5**
e *Delusion,* 2 Thess. 2:11.
f *Bread,* Ezek. 4:13.
g *Water,* 1 Kin. 17:10.
h *Wool,* Judg. 6:37.
i *Flax,* Ex. 9:31.
j *Oil,* Deut. 12:17.

**8**
k *Spiritual Blindness,* 2 Cor. 4:4.
l *God, providence of,* Gen. 2:2.
m *Temporal Blessings, from God,* Psa. 103:2.
n *Corn,* Psa. 65:13.
o *Wine,* Prov. 23:31.
p *Silver,* 1 Chr. 28:14.
q *Gold,* Ezek. 7:19.
r *Ingratitude, of man to God,* Rom. 1:21.
s *Baal,* 2 Kin. 17:16.
1 R. V. used

**9**
t *Wicked, punishment of,* Psa. 73:3.

**11**
u *Annual Feasts,* Num. 15:3.
v *New Moon, feast of,* Amos 8:5.
w *Sabbath,* Ex. 16:23.

**13**
x *Incense, offered in idolatrous worship,* Ex. 37:29.

**14**
y *God, mercy of,* vs. 14–23; Gen. 2:2.

**15**
z *Israel, prophecies concerning blessing and restoration of,* vs. 14–23; 1 Kin. 12:1.

a Josh. 7:24; 15:7; Isa. 65:10.
b *Door, figurative,* Deut. 11:20.
c *Hope,* Prov. 13:12.
d *Egypt,* Gen. 41:8.

**18**
e *God, preserver,* Gen. 2:2.
f *Nation, promises of peace to,* Isa. 2:4.

**19**
g *God, love of, exemplified,* Gen. 2:2.
h *Betrothal, figurative,* Deut. 20:7.
i *Husband, figurative,* Num. 30:6.

*** THORN.** *The ground cursed with,* Gen. 3:18. *Used for fuel,* Psa. 58:9; 118:12; Eccl. 7:6. *Hedges formed of,* Hos. 2:6; Mic. 7:4. *Crown of, mockingly put on Jesus' head,* Matt. 27:29; Mark 15:17; John 19:2, 5. **Figurative:** *Of afflictions,* Num. 33:55; 2 Cor. 12:7. *Of the adversities of the wicked,* Prov. 22:5. *Of the evils that spring from the heart to choke the truth and prevent it from bearing fruit,* Matt. 13:7, 22.

ness, and in judgment,[G] and in lovingkindness, and in mercies.

20 I will even betroth thee unto me in faithfulness: and thou shalt [j]know the LORD.[S]

21 And it shall come to pass in that day, I will [2]hear, saith the LORD, I will [2]hear the heavens, and they shall [2]hear the earth;

22 And the earth shall [2]hear[G] the corn,[G] and the wine, and the oil; and they shall [2]hear[G] Jĕz′re-el.

23 And I will sow[G] her unto me in the earth; and I will have [k]mercy upon her that had not obtained mercy; and [l]I will say to [m]*them which were* not my people, Thou *art* [n]my people; and they shall say, *Thou art* my God.[Q]

20
*j Wisdom, spiritual,* Prov. 2:2.

21
2 R. V. answer

23
*k God, mercy of,* Gen. 2:2.
l Rom. 9:25.
*m Gentiles, prophecies of the conversion of,* Acts 10:45.
*n Spiritual Adoption,* Rom. 8:15.

## CHAPTER 3

*The desolation and restoration of Israel typified.*

THEN said the LORD unto me, Go yet, love a woman beloved of *her* friend, yet an [a]adulteress, according to the [b]love of the LORD toward the children of Iṣ′ra-el, [1]who [c,d]look to other gods, and love flagons[G] of wine.

2 So I [e]bought [a]her to me for fifteen *pieces* of silver, and *for* an [f]homer[G] of [g]barley, and an half[G] homer[G] of barley:

3 And I said unto her, Thou shalt abide for me many days; thou shalt not play the harlot, and thou shalt not be for *another* man: so *will* I also *be* for thee.

4 For [h]the children of Iṣ′ra-el shall abide many days without a king, and without a prince, and without a sacrifice,[G] and without [2]an image, and without an [i]ephod,[G] and *without* teraphim:

5 Afterward shall the children of Iṣ′ra-el [j]return, and [k,l]seek the LORD their God, and [m]Dā′vid their [n]king; and shall [o]fear the LORD and his [p]goodness in the latter days.[T]

1
*a Women, wicked,* Prov. 31:10.
*b God, love of,* Gen. 2:2.
*c Backsliding, of Israel,* Hos. 11:7.
*d Idolatry,* 1 Sam. 15:23.
1 R. V. though they turn unto other gods, and love cakes of raisins.

2
*e Marriage,* Gen. 34:9.
*f Measure, dry,* Deut. 25:15.
*g Barley,* Ex. 9:31.

4
*h Israel, prophecies concerning,* 1 Kin. 12:1.
*i Ephod,* Ex. 28:6.
2 R. V. pillar,

5
*j Backsliders, return of,* Jer. 3:22.
*k Seekers,* Isa. 55:6.
*l Repentance, of Israel foretold,* Mark 1:4.
*m Jesus, names of,* Matt. 1:21.
*n Jesus, king* (according to many learned interpreters), Matt. 1:21.
*o Fear of God,* Acts 9:31.
*p God, goodness of,* Gen. 2:2.

## CHAPTER 4

*God's controversy with Israel. 6 The sins of the priests. 12 The idolatry of the people. 15 Judah warned by the example of Israel.*

HEAR the word of the LORD, ye [a]children of Iṣ′ra-el: for the LORD hath a controversy with the inhabitants of the land, because *there is* [b]no truth, nor [c]mercy, [d]nor knowledge of God in the land.[Q]

2 [1]By swearing, and [b]lying, and [e]killing, and [f,g]stealing, and committing [h]adultery, they break out, and blood toucheth blood.

3 [i]Therefore shall the land mourn, and every one that dwelleth therein shall languish, with the beasts of the field, and with the fowls of heaven; yea, the fishes of the sea also shall be taken away.

4 Yet let no man strive, nor reprove another: for [a]thy people *are* as they that strive with the [j]priest.

5 [a]Therefore shalt thou fall in the day, and the [k]prophet also shall fall with thee in the night, and I will destroy thy mother.

6 ¶ My people are destroyed for [l]lack of [m]knowledge: because [n]thou hast rejected knowledge, I will also [o]reject thee, that thou shalt be no priest to me: seeing [p]thou hast forgotten the law of thy God, [q]I will also forget thy children.

7 [n,r]As they were increased, [s]so they sinned against me: *therefore* will I change their glory into shame.

8 [n]They eat up the [t]sin of my people, and [u,v]they set their heart on their iniquity.

9 And [w]there shall be, [x,y,z]like people, like priest: and I will punish[G] them [a]for their ways, and reward[G] them their doings.

10 For they shall eat, and not have enough: they shall commit [b]whoredom,[G] and shall not

1
*a Jews, wickedness of,* vs. 1–19; Neh. 4:2.
*b Falsehood, the wicked practice,* Job 21:34.
*c Mercy,* Deut. 5:10.
*d Spiritual Blindness,* 2 Cor. 4:4.

2
*e Homicide, felonious,* Deut. 5:17.
*f Theft,* Mark 7:22.
*g Dishonesty,* Ezek. 22:13.
*h Adultery,* Lev. 20:10.
1 R. V. There is nought but swearing and breaking faith, and killing,

3
*i Nation, judgments denounced against,* Isa. 2:4.

4
*j Priest,* Lev. 1:5.

5
*k Prophets, false,* Isa. 3:2.

6
*l Spiritual Blindness,* 2 Cor. 4:4.
*m Knowledge,* Luke 11:52.
*n Minister, false and corrupt,* vs. 8–13; Rom. 15:16.
*o Wicked, punishment of,* Psa. 73:3.
*p Backsliders, punishment of,* Jer. 3:22.
*q Children, involved in sins of parents,* Mark 10:14.

7
*r Prosperity, evil effects of,* Eccl. 7:14.
*s Ingratitude, of man to God,* Rom. 1:21.

8
*t Offerings, sin,* Lev. 6:17.
*u Wicked, described,* Psa. 73:3.
*v Sin, love of,* Rom. 5:12.

9
*w Church, corruption in,* Matt. 16:18.
*x Proverbs,* 1 Sam. 24:13.
*y Example, bad,* John 13:15.
*z Influence, evil,* 1 Cor. 7:14.

*a Judgment, according to opportunity and works,* 1 Pet. 1:17.

10
*b Idolatry, wicked practices of,* 1 Sam. 15:23.

increase: because they have left
off to take heed to the LORD.
11 [b,c]Whoredom and [d]wine and
new wine [e]take away the heart.
12 ¶ My [f]people [g]ask counsel at
their stocks, and their [h]staff declareth unto them: for the spirit
of [b,c]whoredoms hath caused
*them* to err, and they have gone
a whoring from under their God.
13 [f]They sacrifice upon the tops
of the [i]mountains, and burn [j]in-
cense upon the hills, under [k]oaks
and [l]poplars and [2]elms, because
the shadow thereof *is* good:
therefore your [m]daughters shall
commit whoredom, and your
[3]spouses shall commit adultery.
14 I will not punish your [m]daugh-
ters when they commit whoredom, nor your spouses when they
commit adultery: for [n]themselves
are separated with whores, and
they sacrifice with harlots: therefore the people *that* doth [o,p]not
understand [q,r]shall fall.
15 ¶ Though thou, [s]Ĭs̱'ra-el, play
the harlot, *yet* let not Jū'dah offend; and come not ye unto [t]Gĭl'-
găl, neither go ye up to [u]Bĕth-ā'-
ven, nor [v]swear, The LORD liveth.
16 For Ĭs̱'ra-el [4]slideth back as
a [w]backsliding [x]heifer: now the
LORD will feed them as a lamb
in a large place.
17 [y]Ē'phră-ĭm *is* [g,z,a]joined to
idols: [b,c]let him alone.
18 Their drink is sour: they
have committed [d]whoredom continually: her rulers [5]*with* shame
do love, Give ye.
19 The wind hath bound her up
in her wings, and they shall be
ashamed because of their sacrifices.

## CHAPTER 5

*God's judgments against the priests, the people, and the princes of Israel, for their manifold sins.*

HEAR ye this, O [a]priests; and
hearken, ye house of [b]Ĭs̱'-
ra-el; and give ye ear, O house
of the [c]king; for [d]judgment *is* toward you, because ye have been
a [e]snare on [f]Mĭz'pah, and a net
spread upon [g]Tā'bôr.
2 And the revolters are profound to make slaughter, though
I *have been* a rebuker of them all.
3 I know Ē'phră-ĭm, and [h]Ĭs̱'-
ra-el is [i]not hid from me: for
now, O Ē'phră-ĭm, thou com-
mittest [j]whoredom, *and* Ĭs̱'ra-el
is defiled.
4 [1,k]They will not frame their
doings to turn unto their God:
for the spirit of [j]whoredoms *is* in
the midst of them, and they have
[l]not known the LORD.
5 And the pride of Ĭs̱'ra-el doth
testify to his face: therefore shall
[h]Ĭs̱'ra-el and Ē'phră-ĭm [m]fall in
their iniquity; [n]Jū'dah also shall
[m]fall with them.
6 They shall go with their flocks
and with their herds to seek the
LORD; but [o,p]they shall [q]not find
*him*; [r]he hath withdrawn himself
from them.
7 [h]They have dealt treacherously against the LORD: for they
have begotten strange children:
[m]now shall [2]a month devour them
with their portions.
8 ¶ Blow ye the cornet in [s]Gĭb'-
e-ah, *and* the trumpet in [t]Rā'-
mah: cry aloud *at* [u]Bĕth-ā'ven,
after thee, O Bĕn'ja-mĭn.
9 [v]Ē'phră-ĭm shall be desolate
in the day of rebuke: among
the tribes of Ĭs̱'ra-el [w]have I
made known that which shall
surely be.
10 The [x]princes of [n]Jū'dah
were like them that remove the
[3,y]bound: *therefore* [z]I will pour
out my wrath upon them like
water.
11 Ē'phră-ĭm *is* oppressed *and*
broken in judgment, because he
willingly walked after the commandment.
12 Therefore *will* I *be* unto

11
c *Lasciviousness, demoralizes*, 1 Pet. 4:3.
d *Wine, admonitions against the use of*, Prov. 23:31.
e *Drunkenness, consequences of*, Luke 21:34.

12
f *Jews, wickedness of*, Neh. 4:2.
g *Idolatry, denounced*, vs. 12–19; 1 Sam. 15:23.
h *Sorcery, divining by rods*, Isa. 47:9.

13
i *Mountain, used for idolatrous worship*, Mic. 7:12.
j *Incense, offered in idolatrous worship*, Ex. 37:29.
k *Oak*, Gen. 35:4.
l Gen. 30:37.
m *Women, wicked*, Prov. 31:10.
2 R. V. terebinths,
3 R. V. brides

14
n *Sodomites*, Gen. 19:25.
o *Ignorance, sins of*, Acts 3:17.
p *Spiritual Blindness*, 2 Cor. 4:4.
q *Wicked, punishment of*, Psa. 73:3.
r *Judgments*, Ex. 6:6.

15
s *Israel, after the revolt*, 1 Kin. 12:1.
t *Gilgal, prophecies concerning*, Josh. 4:19.
u *Beth-aven*, Josh. 18:12.
v *Oath*, Num. 5:19.

16
w *Obduracy*, Prov. 29:1.
x *Heifer, intractable*, Num. 19:2.
4 R. V. hath behaved himself stubbornly, like a stubborn heifer:

17
y *Ephraim, name applied to the ten tribes*, Gen. 41:52.
z *Impenitence*, Rom. 2:5.

a *Delusion*, 2 Thess. 2:11.
b *Holy Spirit, withdrawn from incorrigible sinners*, Acts 1:2.
c *Wicked, spirit of God withdrawn from*, Psa. 73:3.

18
d *Idolatry, wicked practices of*, 1 Sam. 15:23. 5 R. V. dearly love shame. 1 *a Minister, false and corrupt*, Rom. 15:16. *b Backsliding, of Israel*, Hos. 11:7.

c *Rulers, wicked*, Ex. 18:21.
d *Judgments*, Ex. 6:6.
e *Influence, evil*, 1 Cor. 7:14.
f *Mizpah*, Gen. 31:49.
g *Tabor*, Judg. 8:18.

3
h *Israel, after the revolt*, 1 Kin. 12:1.
i *Sin, known to God*, Rom. 5:12.
j *Idolatry, wicked practices of*, 1 Sam. 15:23.

4
k *Impenitence*, Rom. 2:5.
l *Spiritual Blindness*, 2 Cor. 4:4.
1 R. V. Their doings will not suffer them to

5
m *Wicked, punishment of*, Psa. 73:3.
n *Judah, kingdom of*, 2 Chr. 11:17.

6
o *Reprobates, rejected of God*, 1 Cor. 9:27.
p *Wicked, prayers of, not answered*, Psa. 73:3.
q *Opportunity, lost*, Gal. 6:10.
r *Holy Spirit, withdrawn from incorrigible sinners*, Acts 1:2.

7
2 R. V. the new moon devour them with their fields.

8
s *Gibeah*, Hos. 9:9.
t *Ramah*, Judg. 19:13.
u *Beth-aven*, Josh. 18:12.

9
v *Ephraim, name applied to the ten tribes*, Gen. 41:52.
w *Israel, prophecies concerning*, 1 Kin. 12:1.

10
x *Rulers, wicked*, Ex. 18:21.
y *Landmarks*, Deut. 19:14.
z *Divine Chastisement*, Job 33:19.
3 R. V. landmark:

Ē′phră-ĭm as a moth, and to the house of Jū′dah as rottenness.[C]

13 When Ē′phră-ĭm saw his [a]sickness, and Jū′dah *saw* his wound, then [b,c]went Ē′phră-ĭm to the [d]Ăs-sȳr′ĭan, and sent to king Jā′reb: yet could he not heal you, nor cure you of your wound.

14 For [e]I *will be* unto [f]Ē′phră-ĭm as a [g]lion, and as a young lion to the house of Jū′dah: I, *even* I, will tear and go away; I will take away, and none shall rescue *him*.

15 [e]I will go *and* return to my place, [h]till they [i]acknowledge their offence, and seek my face: [j]in their affliction they will [k]seek me [4]early.

## CHAPTER 6

*An exhortation to repentance. 4 The instability and wickedness of Israel.*

COME, and [a,b]let us return unto the LORD: for [c,d]he hath torn, and [e]he will heal us; [c,d]he hath smitten, and [e]he will bind us up.

2 After two days will he revive us: in the third day he will raise us up, and we shall live in his sight.[Q]

3 [f]Then shall we [g]know,[C] *if* we follow on to know the LORD: his going forth is prepared as the morning; and [h]he shall come unto us as the [i]rain, as the latter [1]*and* former rain unto the earth.

4 ¶ [j]O Ē′phră-ĭm, what shall I do unto thee? [j]O Jū′dah, what shall I do unto thee? for [k,l]your goodness *is* as a morning cloud, and as the early [m,n]dew it goeth away.

5 Therefore have I [o]hewed[C] *them* by the [p]prophets; I have slain them by the words of my mouth: and thy judgments *are as* the light *that* goeth forth.[Q]

6 For I [q]desired [2,r]mercy, and not [s]sacrifice; and the [t]knowledge[C] of God more than burnt [u]offerings.[Q]

7 But they like [v]men have [w]transgressed the covenant: there have they dealt treacherously against me.

8 Gĭl′e-ăd *is* a city of them that work iniquity, *and is* polluted[C] with blood.

9 And as troops of *robbers wait for a man, *so* the company of [x]priests [y]murder in the way [3]by consent: for they commit lewdness.[C]

10 I have seen an horrible thing in the house of Ĭs′ra-el: there *is* the whoredom[C] of Ē′phră-ĭm, Ĭs′ra-el is defiled.

11 Also, O Jū′dah, he hath set an [z]harvest for thee, when I [4]returned the captivity[C] of my people.

## CHAPTER 7

*Israel rebuked for their sins. 11 Sore chastisement threatened.*

WHEN I would have healed Ĭs′ra-el, then the iniquity of [a]Ē′phră-ĭm was discovered,[C] and the wickedness of [b]Să-mā′rĭ-ă: for they commit [c]falsehood; and the thief cometh in, *and* the troop of [d]robbers spoileth[C] without.

2 And [e]they consider not in their hearts *that* [f]I remember all their wickedness: now [g]their own doings have beset them about; they are before my face.

3 They make the [h]king glad with their wickedness, and the princes with their lies.

4 They *are* all [i]adulterers, [j]as an [k]oven heated by the [l]baker, [1]*who* ceaseth from raising[C] after he hath kneaded the dough, until it be [m]leavened.

5 In the day of our king the princes [2]have made *him* [n]sick

**13**

*a* *Sick, figurative,* Matt. 25:36.
*b* *Alliances,* Josh. 9:15.
*c* *False Confidence,* Psa. 30:6.
*d* *Assyria,* Gen. 25:18.

**14**

*e* *Adversity, dispensation from God,* Psa. 10:6.
*f* *Ephraim, prophecies concerning,* Gen. 41:52.
*g* *Lion, figurative,* Mic. 5:8.

**15**

*h* *Adversity, design of,* Psa. 10:6.
*i* *Repentance,* Mark 1:4.
*j* *Adversity, benefits of,* Psa. 10:6.
*k* *Seekers,* Isa. 55:6.
4 R. V. earnestly.

**1**

*a* *Repentance, exhortation to,* Mark 1:4.
*b* *Church, backslidden,* vs. 1–11; Matt. 16:18.
*c* *Divine Chastisement,* Job 33:19.
*d* *Afflictions, benefits of,* Psa. 34:19.
*e* *Backsliders, promises to penitent,* Jer. 3:22.

**3**

*f* *Faith, exemplified,* Mark 11:22.
*g* *Wisdom, spiritual,* Prov. 2:2.
*h* *Righteous, promises to,* Psa. 64:10.
*i* *Rain,* 2 Sam. 1:21.
1 R. V. rain that watereth

**4**

*j* *Backsliders, God's solicitude for,* Jer. 3:22.
*k* *Character, instability of,* Phil. 2:15.
*l* *Instability,* Jas. 1:8.
*m* *Dew, figurative,* Dan. 4:15.
*n* *Meteorology,* Matt. 16:2.

**5**

*o* *Wicked, warned,* Psa. 73:3.
*p* *Minister, duties of,* Rom. 15:16.

**6**

*q* *Obedience better than Sacrifice,* 1 Sam. 15:22.
*r* *Mercy,* Deut. 5:10.
*s* *Worship, of hypocrites, repugnant to God,* Gen. 22:5.
*t* *Wisdom, spiritual,* Prov. 2:2.
*u* *Offerings, unavailing when not accompanied by piety,* Lev. 6:17.
2 Am. R. V. desire goodness,

**7**

*v* *Adam, temptation and sin of,* Gen. 2:19.
*w* *Fall of Man,* Gen. 3:6.

**9**

*x* *Minister, false and corrupt,* Rom. 15:16.
*y* *Homicide, felonious,* Deut. 5:17.

**11**

*z* *Wicked, punishment of,* Psa. 73:3.
4 R. V. bring again the

**1**

*a* *Ephraim,* Gen. 41:52.
*b* *Samaria,* 1 Kin. 16:24.
*c* *Falsehood,* Job 21:34.
*d* *Robbers,* Hos. 6:9.

**2**

*e* *Godless, described as ignoring God,* Job 8:13.
*f* *Sin, known to God,* Rom. 5:12.
*g* *Judgment, according to opportunity and works,* 2 Pet. 3:7.

**3**

*h* *Rulers, wicked,* Ex. 18:21.

**4**

*i* *Adultery,* Lev. 20:10.
*j* *Lust,* 2 Pet. 1:4.
*k* *Oven,* vs. 6, 7; Ex. 8:3.
*l* *Baker,* 1 Sam. 8:13.
*m* *Leaven,* Lev. 23:17.
1 R.V. he ceaseth to stir the fire, from the kneading of

**5**

*n* *Drunkenness,* Luke 21:34.
2 R. V. made themselves sick with the heat of wine;

*** ROBBERS,** Job 12:6; Prov. 1:11–19. *Dens of,* Jer. 7: 11. *Bands of,* Hos. 6:9; 7:1.
See footnotes: ROBBERY, Ezek. 22:29; THEFT, Mark 7:22.

*o* *Evil Company*, Prov. 13:20.

7
*p* *Prayerlessness*, Job 21:15.

8
*q* *Character, instability of*, Phil. 2:15.
3 R. V. peoples;

10
*r* *Pride*, Prov. 16:18.
*s* *Impenitence*, Rom. 2:5.
*t* *Adversity, obduracy in*, Psa. 10:6.

11
*u* *Spiritual Blindness*, 2 Cor. 4:4.
*v* *False Confidence*, Psa. 30:6.

12
*w* *Net, figurative*, Isa. 51:20.
*x* *Divine Chastisement, inflicted for sins*, Job 33:19.
*y* *Wicked, punishment of*, v. 13; Psa. 73:3.

13
*z* *Ingratitude, of man to God*, Rom. 1:21.

*a* *Blasphemy, speaking lies against God*, 2 Sam. 12:14.

14
*b* *Hypocrisy*, Jas. 3:17.
4 R. V. but they howl

16
*c* *Judgments*, Ex. 6:6.
*d* *Egypt*, Gen. 41:8.
6 R. V. him that is on high;

with bottles of wine; he [o]stretched
out his hand with scorners.
6 For they have made ready
their heart like an [k]oven, whiles
they lie in wait: their baker sleepeth all the night; in the morning
it burneth as a flaming fire.
7 They are all hot as an oven,
and have devoured their judges;
all their kings are fallen: [p]*there*
*is* none among them that calleth
unto me.
8 ¶ [a]Ē'phră-ĭm, he hath mixed
himself among the [3]people; Ē'-
phră-ĭm is [q]a cake not turned.
9 Strangers have devoured his
strength, and he knoweth *it* not:
yea, gray hairs are here and there
upon him, yet he knoweth not.
10 And the [r]pride of Ĭṣ'ra-el
testifieth to his face: and [s,t]they
do not return to the LORD their
God, nor seek him for all this.
11 Ē'phră-ĭm also is like a silly
dove [u]without heart: they [v]call
to Ē'ġy̆pt, they go to Ăs-sy̆r'ĭ-ȧ.
12 When they shall go, I will
spread my [w]net upon them; I will
bring them down as the fowls
of the heaven; I will [x,y]chastise
them, as their congregation hath
heard.
13 [y]Woe unto them! for they
have fled from me: destruction
unto them! because they have
transgressed against me: though
I have redeemed them, [z]yet they
have [a]spoken lies against me.
14 And [b]they have not cried
unto me with their heart, [4]when
they howled upon their beds: they
assemble themselves for corn and
wine, *and* they rebel against me.
15 Though I have [5]bound *and*
strengthened their arms, yet do
they imagine mischief against me.
16 They return, *but* not to [6]the
most High: they are like a deceitful bow: their princes shall [c]fall
by the sword for the rage of their
tongue: this *shall be* their derision in the land of [d]Ē'ġy̆pt.

## CHAPTER 8

*Destruction threatened to Israel and Judah for their impiety and idolatry.*

SET the trumpet to thy mouth.
*He shall come* as an [a]eagle
against the house of the LORD,
[b]because they have transgressed
my covenant, and trespassed
against my law.
2 [c]Ĭṣ'ra-el shall cry unto me,
My God, [d]we know thee.
3 [c]Ĭṣ'ra-el hath cast off *the thing*
*that is* good: the enemy shall pursue him.
4 They have set up [e]kings, but
[f]not by me: they have made
princes, and [f]I knew *it* not: of
their silver and their gold have
they made them [g]idols, that they
may be [b]cut off.
5 ¶ [1,h]Thy [g,i]calf, O [j]Să-mā'-
rĭ-ȧ, hath cast *thee* off; mine [k]an-
ger is kindled against them: how
long *will it be* ere they attain to
innocency?
6 For from Ĭṣ'ra-el *was* it also:
[h]the workman made it; therefore
it *is* not God: but the [g,i]calf of
[j]Să-mā'rĭ-ȧ shall be broken in
pieces.
7 For [l]they have sown the wind,
and [m]they shall reap the whirlwind: [2]it hath no stalk: the bud
shall yield no meal: if so be it
yield, the strangers shall swallow
it up.
8 Ĭṣ'ra-el is swallowed up:
[b,n]now shall they be among the
[3]Gĕn'tīleṣ as a vessel wherein *is*
no pleasure.
9 For they are [o]gone up to [p]Ăs-
sy̆r'ĭ-ȧ, a wild [q]ass alone by himself: Ē'phră-ĭm hath hired [r]lovers.
10 Yea, though they have hired
among the nations, now will I
gather them, and they [4]shall sorrow a little for the burden of the
king of princes.
11 Because Ē'phră-ĭm hath
made many [s]altars to sin, altars
shall be unto him to sin.
12 [5]I have written to him the

1
*a* *Eagle*, Lev. 11:13.
*b* *Sin, punishment of*, Rom. 5:12.

2
*c* *Israel, prophecies concerning*, 1 Kin. 12:1.
*d* *Hypocrisy*, Jas. 3:17.

4
*e* *King*, 2 Kin. 3:10.
*f* *Government, relation of God to*, Isa. 22:21.
*g* *Idol*, 1 Kin. 15:12.

5
*h* *Idolatry, folly of*, 1 Sam. 15:23.
*i* *Calf*, Mic. 6:6.
*j* *Samaria*, 1 Kin. 16:24.
*k* *Anger of God*, 2 Kin. 13:3.
1 R. V. He hath cast off thy calf, O Samaria;

7
*l* *Punishment, according to deeds*, Lev. 26:41.
*m* *Sin, fruits of*, Rom. 5:12.
2 R. V. he hath no standing corn; the blade shall

8
*n* *Backsliders, corrective judgments upon*, Jer. 3:22.
3 R. V. nations

9
*o* *False Confidence*, Psa. 30:6.
*p* *Assyria*, Gen. 25:18.
*q* *Ass, wild*, 2 Chr. 28:15.
*r* *Alliances*, Josh. 9:15.

10
4 Am. R. V. begin to be diminished by reason of the burden of the king of princes.

11
*s* *Altar, used in idolatrous worship*, Gen. 8:20.

12
5 R. V. Though I write for him my law in ten thousand precepts, they are counted

great things of my law, *but* [t]they
were counted as a strange[c] thing.
13 [u]They sacrifice flesh *for* the
sacrifices of mine offerings, and
eat *it*; *but* [v]the LORD accepteth
them not; now will he remember
their iniquity, and [w]visit[c] their
sins: they shall return to [x]Ē'-
ġy̆pt.
14 For Ĭṣ'ra-el hath [y]forgotten
his Maker, and [6]buildeth temples; and Jū'dah hath multiplied
fenced[c] cities: but [z]I will send a
fire upon his cities, and it shall
devour the palaces thereof.

## CHAPTER 9

*The distress and captivity of Israel for their idolatry.*

REJOICE not, O Ĭṣ'ra-el, for
joy, [1]as *other* people: for
thou hast gone a[c] whoring from
thy God, thou hast loved [2]a reward upon every cornfloor.[c]
2 [a]The [b]floor and the [c]wine-
press shall not feed them, and
the new wine shall fail in her.
3 [a]They shall not dwell in the
LORD's [d]land; but Ē'phră-ĭm
[e]shall return to [f]Ē'ġy̆pt, and they
shall eat unclean *things* in [g]Ăs-
sy̆r'ĭ-ȧ.
4 [a]They shall not offer wine *offerings* to the LORD, neither shall
they be pleasing unto him: [h]their
sacrifices *shall be* unto them as
the bread of mourners; all that
eat thereof shall be polluted[c]: for
their bread [3]for their soul shall
not come into the house of the
LORD.
5 What will ye do in the [4]sol-
emn day, and in the day of the
feast of the LORD?
6 For, lo, [a,i]they are gone [5]be-
cause of destruction: [f]Ē'ġy̆pt
shall gather them up, Mĕm'phĭs
shall bury them: the pleasant
*places* for their silver, [j]nettles
shall possess them: [k]thorns *shall
be* in their tabernacles.
7 [i]The days of visitation[c] are
come, the days of recompence
are come; Ĭṣ'ra-el shall know *it*:
the [l]prophet *is* a fool, the [6]spir-
itual man *is* mad, for the multitude of thine iniquity, and the
great hatred.[Q]
8 [7]The watchman of Ē'phră-
ĭm *was* with my God: *but* the
[l]prophet *is* a snare of a fowler in
all his ways, *and* hatred in the
house of his God.
9 They have deeply corrupted
*themselves*, as in the days of
*Ġĭb'e-ah: *therefore* he will [m]re-
member their iniquity, he will
[i,n]visit[c] their sins.
10 [o]I found Ĭṣ'ra-el like grapes
in the wilderness; I saw your fathers as the firstripe in the fig
tree at her first time: *but* they
[p]went to [q]Bā'al-pē'or, and [8]sep-
arated themselves unto *that*
shame; and *their* abominations[c]
were according as [r]they loved.
11 [a]*As for* Ē'phră-ĭm, [i]their
glory shall fly away like a bird,
[9]from the birth, and from the
womb, and from the conception.
12 [a,i,s]Though they bring up
their children, yet will I †bereave
them, *that there shall* not *be* a
man *left*: yea, woe also to them
when [i,u]I depart from them!
13 Ē'phră-ĭm, as I saw [v]Ty̆'rus,
*is* planted in a pleasant place:
but [a,i]Ē'phră-ĭm shall bring forth
his children to the murderer.
14 Give them, O LORD: what
wilt thou give? give them a [w]mis-
carrying womb and dry breasts.

t *Word of God, disbelief in*, Psa. 119:9.

**13**

u *Hypocrisy, punishment for*, Jas. 3:17.

v *Offerings, unavailing when not accompanied by piety*, Lev. 6:17.

w *Judgment, according to opportunity and works*, 1 Pet. 1:17.

x *Egypt*, Gen. 41:8.

**14**

y *Backsliders*, Jer. 3:22.

z *Adversity, dispensation from God*, Psa. 10:6.

6 R. V. builded palaces;

**1**

1 R. V. like the peoples;

2 R. V. hire

**2**

a *Israel, prophecies concerning*, vs. 1–17; 1 Kin. 12:1.

b *Threshing, floors for*, 1 Chr. 21:20.

c *Wine Press*, Isa. 5:2.

**3**

d *Canaan*, Gen. 37:1.

e *Captivity, as a judgment*, Isa. 5:13.

f *Egypt*, Gen. 41:8.

g *Assyria*, Gen. 25:18.

**4**

h *Hypocrisy, abhorred of God*, Jas. 3:17.

3 R. V. shall be for their appetite; it shall not

**5**

4 R. V. day of solemn assembly, and

**6**

i *Wicked, punishment of*, Psa. 73:3.

5 R. V. away from destruction,

j *Nettle, figurative*, Prov. 24:31

k *Thorn, figurative*, Hos. 2:6.

**7**

l *Minister, false and corrupt*, Rom. 15:16.

6 R. V. man that hath the spirit

**8**

7 R. V. Ephraim was a watchman with my God:

**9**

m *Sin, known to God*, Rom. 5:12.

n *Judgment, according to opportunity and works*, 1 Pet. 1:17.

**10**

o *God, love of, exemplified*, Gen. 2:2.

p *Idolatry*, 1 Sam. 15:23.

q *Baal-peor*, Num. 25:3.

r *Sin, love of*, Rom. 5:12.

**11**

9 R. V. there shall be no birth, and none with child, and no conception.

**12**

s *Reprobates, curses denounced against*, 1 Cor. 9:27.

t *Holy Spirit, withdrawn from incorrigible sinners*, Acts 1:2.

u *Sin, separates from God*, Rom. 5:12.

**13**

v Or, *Tyre*, Josh. 19:29.

**14**

w *Abortion, as a judgment*, Ex. 21:22.

***GIBEAH.** *Wickedness of the people of*, Judg. 19:12–30; Hos. 9:9; 10:9. *Destroyed by the Israelites*, Judg. 20. *The city of Saul*, 1 Sam. 10:26; 15:34; 22:6. *The ark of the covenant conveyed to, by the Philistines*, 1 Sam. 7:1; 2 Sam. 6:3. *Deserted*, Isa. 10:29.

**† BEREAVEMENT.** *From God*, Ex. 12:29; Hos. 9:12. *Mourning in, forbidden, to Aaron for Nadab and Abihu*, Lev. 10:6; *to Ezekiel for his wife*, Ezek. 24:16–18.
*Beneficent discipline in*, Eccl. 7:2–4.

**Resignation in:** *Enjoined*, 1 Thess. 4:13–18. *Exemplified, by Job*, Job 1:18–21; *by David*, 2 Sam. 12:22, 23.

**Instances of:** *Abraham, of Sarah*, Gen. 23:2. *Jacob, of Joseph*, Gen. 37:34, 35. *Joseph, of his father*, Gen. 50:1, 4. *The Egyptians, of their firstborn*, Ex. 12:29–33. *Naomi, of her husband*, Ruth 1:3, 5, 20, 21. *David, of his child by Bathsheba*, 2 Sam. 12:15–23; *of Absalom*, 2 Sam. 18:33; 19:4. *Martha and Mary*, John 11:19–21, 33.
See footnote, DEATH, Num. 23:10.

15 All their wickedness *is* in
[x]Gĭl′găl: for there I hated them:
for the wickedness of their doings [u]I will drive them out of
mine house, [y]I will love them no
more: all their princes *are* revolters.
16 [a,i]Ē′phră-ĭm is smitten, their
root is dried up, they shall bear
no fruit: yea, though they bring
forth, yet will I slay *even* the beloved *fruit* of their womb.
17 My God will [u]cast them
away, because [z]they did not
hearken unto him: and they shall
be [a]wanderers among the nations.

## CHAPTER 10

*Judgments upon Israel threatened for their impiety and idolatry.*

IṢ′RA-EL *is* [1]an empty vine,
[a]he bringeth forth fruit unto
himself: according to the multitude of his fruit he hath increased the altars; according to
the goodness of his land [b]they
have made goodly[C] [2]images.
2 [c,d]Their [e]heart is [f]divided;
now shall they be found faulty:
[g]he shall break down their altars, he shall spoil[C] their images.
3 For now they shall say, We
have no king, because we feared
not the LORD; what then should
a king do to us?
4 They have spoken words,
[h]swearing falsely in making a
covenant[C]: thus [i]judgment springeth up as hemlock in the furrows
of the field.
5 The inhabitants of [j]Să-mā′-
rĭ-ȧ shall fear because of the
[k]calves of [l]Bĕth–ā′ven: for the
people thereof shall mourn over
it, and the [m]priests thereof *that*
rejoiced on it, for the glory
thereof, because it is departed
from it.
6 It shall be also carried unto
[n]Ăs-sy̆r′ĭ-ȧ *for* a present to king
Jā′reb: Ē′phră-ĭm shall receive
shame, and Ĭṣ′ra-el shall be
ashamed of his own counsel.[C]
7 *As for* Să-mā′rĭ-ȧ, her king
is cut off as the foam upon the
water.
8 [o]The high places also of Ā′-
ven, the sin of Ĭṣ′ra-el, shall be
destroyed: the thorn and the
*thistle shall come up on their
altars; and [p,q]they shall say to
the mountains, Cover us; and to
the hills, Fall on us.[Q]
9 O Ĭṣ′ra-el, thou hast sinned
from the days of [r]Gĭb′e-ah: there
they stood: [3]the battle in Gĭb′e-
ah against the children of iniquity did not overtake them.
10 *It is* in my desire that I
should [s]chastise them; and the
people shall be gathered against
them, when they [4]shall bind themselves in their two furrows.[S]
11 And Ē-phră-ĭm *is as* an
[t]heifer *that is* taught, *and* loveth
to [u]tread out *the corn*[C]; but I
passed over upon her fair neck:
I will [5]make Ē′phră-ĭm to ride;
Jū′dah shall plow, *and* Jā′cob
shall break his clods.
12 [v]Sow to yourselves in righteousness,[w,x]reap in mercy; break
up your fallow ground: for [y]*it*
*is* time to [z]seek the LORD, till
he come and rain righteousness
upon you.[Q]
13 [a]Ye have plowed wickedness, [a]ye have reaped iniquity;
[a]ye have eaten the fruit of lies:
because thou didst [b]trust in thy
way, in the multitude of thy
mighty men.
14 [c,d]Therefore shall a tumult[C]
arise among thy people, and all
thy fortresses shall be spoiled, as
Shăl′man spoiled Bĕth–är′bel in
the day of battle: [e]the mother
was dashed in pieces upon *her*
children.
15 So shall Bĕth′–el do unto
you because of your great wick-

**15**
x *Gilgal*, Josh. 4:19.
y *Sin, repugnant to God*, Rom. 5:12.

**17**
z *Afflictions, impenitence in*, Psa. 34:19.

a *Jews, dispersion of*, Neh. 4:2.

**1**
a *Unfaithfulness*, Luke 16:11.
b *Idolatry*, 1 Sam. 15:23.
1 R. V. a luxuriant
2 R. V. pillars.

**2**
c *Character, instability of*, Phil. 2:15.
d *Lukewarmness*, Rev. 3:16.
e *Heart, unregenerate*, Psa. 44:21.
f *Indecision*, 1 Kin. 18:21.
g *Idolatry, prophecies relating to*, 1 Sam 15:23.

**4**
h *Perjury*, 1 Tim. 1:10.
i *Judgments*, Ex. 6:6.

**5**
j *Samaria*, Isa. 7:9.
k *Calf, images of*, Mic. 6:6.
l *Beth-aven*, Josh. 18:12.
m *Priest, idolatrous*, Lev. 1:5.

**6**
n *Assyria*, Gen. 25:18.

**8**
o *Idolatry, denounced*, 1 Sam. 15:23.
p Luke 23:30; Rev. 6:16.
q *Terror of the Wicked*, Isa. 2:19.

**9**
r *Gibeah, wickedness of the people of*, Hos. 9:9.
3 R. V. that the battle against the children of iniquity should not overtake them in Gibeah.

**10**
s *Divine Chastisement*, Job 33:19.
4 R. V. are bound to their two transgressions.

**11**
t *Heifer, figurative*, Num. 19:2.
u *Threshing, by treading*, 1 Chr. 21:20.
5 R. V. set a rider on Ephraim;

**12**
v *Sower, figurative*, Matt. 13:3.
w *Righteousness, fruits of*, Psa. 15:2.
x *Reaping, figurative*, 1 Sam. 6:13.
y *Repentance, enjoined*, Mark 1:4.
z *Seekers, seeking God enjoined*, Isa. 55:6.

**13**
a *Sin, fruits of*, Rom. 5:12.
b *False Confidence, in worldly help*, Psa. 30:6.

**14**
c *Wicked, punishment of*, Psa. 73:3.
d *Judgments*, Ex. 6:6.
e *War, evils of*, Judg. 3:2.

* **THISTLE**, Matt. 7:16. *A noxious plant*, Gen. 3:18; Job 31:40; Hos. 10:8. *Parables of*, 2 Kin. 14:9; 2 Chr. 25:18.

edness: in a morning shall the
king of Ĭṣ′ra-el utterly be [c]cut
off.

## CHAPTER 11

*God's goodness to Israel, and their ingratitude.*

WHEN Ĭṣ′ra-el *was* a child,
then I [a]loved him, and
[b]called [c,d]my son out of [e]Ē′ġy̆pt.[Q][S]
2 *As* they called them, so [f,g]they
went from them: they sacrificed
unto [h]Bā′al-ĭm, and burned [i]in-
cense to graven[G] images.
3 [j,k]I taught [l]Ē′phrā-ĭm also
to go, [1]taking them by their
arms; but [m]they [n]knew not that
I healed them.[S]
4 I drew them with [o]cords of a
man, with bands of [a]love: and I
was to them as they that take off
the yoke on their jaws, and [j,k]I
laid meat[G] unto them.
5 ¶ He shall not return into the
land of [e]Ē′ġy̆pt, but the [p]Ăs-sy̆r′-
ĭ-an shall be his king, because
they refused to return.
6 And the [q,r]sword shall abide
on his cities, and shall consume
his [2]branches, and devour *them*,
because of their own counsels.
7 And my people are [s]bent to
*backsliding from me: though
they called them to [3]the most
High, none at all would exalt *him*.
8 [a,t]How shall I give thee up,
Ē′phrā-ĭm? [a,t]*how* shall I deliver thee, Ĭṣ′ra-el? how shall I
make thee as [u]Ăd′mah? *how*
shall I set thee as [u]Ze-bō′im?
mine heart is turned within me,
my [4]repentings are kindled[G] together.
9 [t]I will not execute the fierceness of mine [v]anger, I will not

1
a *God, love of,* Gen. 2:2.
b Matt. 2:15.
c *God, fatherhood of,* Gen. 2:2.
d *Spiritual Adoption,* Rom. 8:15.
e *Egypt,* Gen. 41:8.
2
f *Backsliders,* Jer. 3:22.
g *Impentitence,* Rom. 2:5.
h Or, *Baal,* 2 Kin. 17:16.
i *Incense, offered in idolatrous worship,* Ex. 37:29.
3
j *God, providence of,* Gen. 2.2.
k *Temporal Blessings, from God,* Psa. 103:2.
l *Israel, after the revolt,* 1 Kin. 12:1.
m *Ingratitude, of man to God,* Rom. 1:21.
n *Spiritual Blindness,* 2 Cor. 4:4.
1 R. V. I took them on my arms;
4
o *Rope, figurative,* 1 Kin. 20:31.
5
p *Assyria,* Gen. 25:18.
6
q *Sword, figurative,* 1 Chr. 21:5.
r *War, as a judgment,* Judg. 3:2.
2 R. V. bars,
7
s *Obduracy,* Prov. 29:1.
3 R. V. him that is on high,
8
t *God, mercy of,* Gen. 2:2.
u Gen. 10:19; 14:2, 8; Deut. 29:23.
4 R. V. compassions
9
v *Anger of God, turned away,* 2 Kin. 13:3.

return to destroy Ē′phrā-ĭm: for
I *am* God, and not man; the
[w,x]Holy One in the midst of
thee: and I will not enter into
the city.[S]
10 They shall walk after the
LORD: he shall roar like a lion:
when he shall roar,[5]then the children shall tremble from the west.
11 They shall [6]tremble as a bird
out of Ē′ġy̆pt, and as a dove out
of the land of Ăs-sy̆r′ĭ-á: and I
will [y]place them in their houses,
saith the LORD.
12 Ē′phrā-ĭm compasseth[G] me
about with lies, and the house of
Ĭṣ′ra-el with deceit: but Jū′dah
yet ruleth with God, and is faithful with the [7]saints.

## CHAPTER 12

*Ephraim and Judah reproved for their sins, and exhorted to repentance.*

Ē′PHRĂ-ĬM feedeth on wind,
and followeth after the east
wind: he daily increaseth lies and
desolation[G]; and they do [a]make
a [b]covenant with the [c]Ăs-sy̆r′-
ĭ-anṣ, and [d]oil is carried into
[e]Ē′ġy̆pt.
2 The LORD hath also a controversy[G] with [f]Jū′dah, and will
[g]punish [h]Jā′cob [i]according to his
ways; [i]according to his doings
will he [g]recompense him.
3 ¶ [j]He took his brother by the
heel in the womb, and [1]by his
strength he had power with God:
4 Yea[T], [j]he had power over the
angel, and prevailed: he wept,
and made [k]supplication unto
him: he found him *in* [l]Bĕth′-el,
and there he spake with us;
5 Even the LORD God of hosts;
the LORD *is* his memorial.[T]

w *God, holiness of,* Gen. 2:2.
x *Holiness, attribute of God,* Ex. 39:30.
10
5 R. V. and the children shall come trembling from the west.
11
y *Temporal Blessings, from God,* Psa. 103:2.
6 R. V. come trembling as
12
7 R. V. Holy One.
1
a *False Confidence.* Psa. 30:6.
b *Alliances,* Josh. 9:15.
c *Assyria,* Gen. 25:18.
d *Oil,* Deut. 12:17.
e *Egypt,* Gen. 41:8.
2
f *Judah, kingdom of,* 2 Chr. 11:17.
g *Wicked, punishment of,* Psa. 73:3.
h *Israel, after the revolt, prophecies concerning,* 1 Kin. 12:1.
i *Judgment, according to opportunity and works,* 1 Pet. 1:17.
3
j *Jacob,* Gen. 27:11.
1 R. V. in his manhood he
4
k *Prayer, importunity in,* Acts 6:4.
l *Beth-el,* Josh. 18:13.

* **BACKSLIDING,** Matt. 24:12. *Admonitions against,* Lev. 26:14–39; Deut. 4:9; 29:18 (with vs. 19–28); Josh. 24:27 (with vs. 20–26); 2 Chr. 7:19–22; Psa. 85:8; Ezek. 2:8; Luke 17:32; John 6:66; 1 Cor. 10:11, 12; 2 Cor. 12:20, 21; Gal. 4:9–11; 5:7; 1 Tim. 1:18, 19; 6:20; 2 Tim. 1:8; Heb. 3:12, 13; 4:1, 11; 12:15. *Concealment of, impossible,* Psa. 44:20, 21. *Prayer for help against,* Psa. 80:3–7, 14–19.

SOURCES OF TEMPTATIONS TO: *Desire for evil things,* Psa. 106:13, 14; 1 Cor. 10:1–6. *False teachers,* Isa. 9:16; Gal. 1:6, 7; 3:1. *Love of money,* Mark 4:18, 19; 1 Tim. 6:10. *Love of the world,* 2 Tim. 4:10. *Prosperity,* Deut. 8:11–14; 31:19–21; 32:15. *Tribulation,* Matt. 13:20, 21; Mark 4:16, 17; Luke 8:13.

**Of Israel,** Num. 14:43; Deut. 4:25–31; 32:5, 6, 15; Judg. 2:12; 10:12–14; 2 Chr. 24:20; Neh. 9:26; Psa. 78:10, 40–43, 56–64; 106:13; Isa. 1:4–7, 21, 22; 43:22, 24; 65:2, 3; Jer. 2:5, 11–13, 17, 19, 21, 27, 32; 3:21; 5:19, 23; 8:5; 14:7, 10; 50:6; Ezek. 2:3–8; 5:6; Hos. 1:6, 9; 4:6, 10; 6:4, 7; 11:2, 7. *Warnings against,* Deut. 31:16–30; Amos 2:4. *Punishment for,* Isa. 24:5, 6.

NOTABLE INSTANCES OF THE BACKSLIDING OF ISRAEL: *At Meribah,* Ex. 17:1–7. *When Aaron made the golden calf,* Ex. 32; Deut. 9:16. *After Joshua's death,* Judg. 2:8–23. *During Asa's reign,* 2 Chr. 15:3, 4. *During Jotham's reign,* 2 Chr. 27:2. *During Hezekiah's reign,* 2 Chr. 30:2–12. *In withholding sacrifices,* Isa. 43:22–24.

See footnotes: BACKSLIDERS, Jer. 3:22; APOSTASY, Acts 1:25.

6 Therefore [m,n]turn thou to thy God: keep [o]mercy and judgment[G], and [p,q]wait[G] on thy God continually.

7 ¶ *He is* a [r]merchant, the [s]balances of [t]deceit *are* in his hand: he loveth to [u]oppress.

8 And Ē′phrā-ĭm said, Yet I am become [v]rich, I have found me out substance: *in* all my labours [w,x]they shall find none iniquity in me that *were* sin.[Q]

9 And I *that am* the LORD thy God from the land of [e]Ē′ġy̆pt will yet make thee to dwell in tabernacles, as in the days of the solemn feast.

10 I have also [y,z]spoken by the prophets, and I have multiplied [a]visions, and used [b]similitudes[G], by the ministry of the prophets.

11 *Is* [2]*there* iniquity *in* [c]Gĭl′e-ăd? surely they are vanity: [d]they sacrifice bullocks in [e]Gĭl′găl; yea, their [f]altars *are* as heaps in the furrows of the fields.

12 And [g]Jā′cob fled into the [3]country of Sy̆r′ĭ-ȧ, and Ĭṣ′ra-el [h]served for a wife, and for a wife he kept [i]*sheep*.

13 And by a [j]prophet the LORD [k]brought Ĭṣ′ra-el out of [l]Ē′ġy̆pt, and by a prophet was he preserved.

14 [m]Ē′phrā-ĭm provoked *him* to anger most bitterly: [n,o]therefore shall he leave his blood upon him, and his reproach shall his Lord return unto him.

## CHAPTER 13

*Ephraim's idolatry. 8 God's anger toward. 15 Desolations to follow.*

WHEN Ē′phrā-ĭm spake trembling, he exalted himself in Ĭṣ′ra-el; but when he [a]offended in Bā′al, he died.

2 And [b]now they [c]sin more and more, and have made them molten[G] images of their [d]silver, *and* idols according to their own understanding, all of it the work of the craftsmen: they say of them, Let the men that sacrifice kiss the [e]calves.

3 Therefore [f]they shall be as the morning cloud, and as the early [g]dew that passeth away, as the *chaff *that* is driven with the whirlwind out of the floor, and as the smoke out of the [h]chimney.

4 Yet [i]I *am* the LORD thy God from the land of [j]Ē′ġy̆pt, and [b]thou shalt know no god but me: for *there is* no [k]saviour beside me.[T]

5 I did know thee in the wilderness, in the land of great drought.

6 According to their pasture, so were they filled; [l]they were filled, and their [m]heart was [n]exalted; therefore have they [o]forgotten me.

7 Therefore [f]I will be unto them as a [p]lion: as a [q]leopard by the way will I observe[G] *them*:

8 [f]I will meet them as a [r]bear *that is* bereaved *of her whelps*, and will rend[G] the caul[G] of their heart, and there will I devour them like a [p]lion: the wild beast shall tear them.

9 ¶ [1]O Ĭṣ′ra-el, [s,t]thou hast destroyed thyself; but [u]in me *is* thine help.

10 [2]I will be thy king: where *is any other* that may save thee in all thy cities? and thy judges of whom thou saidst, Give me a king and princes?[S]

11 [v]I gave thee a [w,x]king in mine [y]anger, and took *him* away in my wrath.[S]

12 [z,a]The iniquity of Ē′phrā-ĭm *is* bound up; his sin *is* [3]hid.

13 [b]The sorrows of a travailing woman shall come upon him: he

**6**
*m Commandment, enjoining righteousness*, Deut. 8:2.
*n Repentance, enjoined*, Mark 1:4.
*o Mercy*, Deut. 5:10.
*p Faithfulness*, Luke 16:10.
*q Perseverance, enjoined*, Eph. 6:18.

**7**
*r Merchant*, Neh. 3:32.
*s Balances, false*, Prov. 11:1.
*t Dishonesty*, Ezek. 22:13.
*u Oppression*, Eccl. 5:8.

**8**
*v Riches, a snare*, Eccl. 4:8.
*w Self-righteousness*, Luke 18:11.
*x Delusion, of the self-righteous*, 2 Thess. 2:11.

**10**
*y Prophets, inspiration of*, Isa. 3:2.
*z Wicked, warned*, Psa. 73:3.
*a Vision*, Acts 9:10.
*b Parables*, Ezek. 20:49.

**11**
*c Gilead*, Deut. 3:13.
*d Idolatry*, 1 Sam. 15:23.
*e Gilgal*, Josh. 4:19.
*f Altar, used in idolatrous worship*, Gen. 8:20.
2 R. V. Is Gilead iniquity?

**12**
*g Jacob*, Gen. 27:11.
*h Marriage, wives obtained by purchase*, Gen. 34:9.
*i Sheep*, Deut. 32:14.
3 R. V. field of Aram,

**13**
*j Moses*, Ex. 2:10.
*k God, providence of*, Gen. 2:2.
*l Egypt*, Gen. 41:8.

**14**
*m Ephraim*, Gen. 41:52.
*n Sin, fruits of*, Rom. 5:12.
*o Judgment, according to opportunity and works*, 1 Pet. 1:17.

**1** *a Idolatry*, 1 Sam. 15:23.
**2** *b Idolatry, denounced*, v. 4; 1 Sam. 15:23. *c Sin, progressive*, Rom. 5:12.

*d Silver*, 1 Chr. 28:14.
*e Calf*, Mic. 6:6.

**3**
*f Wicked, punishment of*, Psa. 73:3.
*g Dew*, Dan. 4:15.
*h House, architecture of*, Esth. 8:1.

**4**
*i God, sovereign*, Gen. 2:2.
*j Egypt, Israelites in bondage in*, Gen. 41:8.
*k God, savior*, Gen. 2:2.

**6**
*l Prosperity, dangers of*, Eccl. 7:14.
*m Heart, unregenerate*, Psa. 44:21.
*n Pride*, Prov. 16:18.
*o Ingratitude, of man to God*, Rom. 1:21.

**7**
*p Lion*, Mic. 5:8.
*q Leopard*, Song 4:8.

**8**
*r Bear*, 2 Sam. 17:8.

**9**
*s Sin, fruits of*, Rom. 5:12.
*t Sin, retroactive*, Rom. 5:12.
*u God, preserver*, Gen. 2:2.
1 R. V. It is thy destruction, O Israel, that thou art against me, against thy help.

**10**
2 R. V. Where now is thy king, that he may save thee in all thy cities?

**11**
*v Government, God in*, Isa. 22:21.
*w King, divinely authorized*, 2 Kin. 3:10.
*x Saul*, 1 Sam. 9:2.
*y Anger of God*, 2 Kin. 13:3.

**12**
*z Idolatry, punishment of*, 1 Sam. 15:23.
*a Sin, punishment of*, Rom. 5:12.
3 R. V. laid up in store.

**13**
*b Israel, prophecies concerning*, 1 Kin. 12:1.

***CHAFF.** *Scattering of, illustrative of judgments upon the wicked*, Job 21:18; Psa. 1:4; Isa. 17:13; Dan. 2:35; Hos. 13:3. **Figurative,** Matt. 3:12; Luke 3:17.

is an unwise son; for he should
not stay long in *the place of* the
breaking forth of children.
14 [c]I will ransom them from
the power of the [d]grave; I will
redeem them from death: [e,f]O
death, [4]I will be thy plagues;
O grave, [5]I will be thy destruction: [g]repentance shall be hid
from mine eyes.
15 ¶ Though he be fruitful
among *his* brethren, [h]an [i]east
[j,k]wind shall come, the [6]wind of
the LORD shall come up from
the wilderness, and his spring
shall [l]become dry, and his fountain shall be dried up: he shall
spoil the treasure of all pleasant
vessels.
16 [m,n]Sā-mā′rĭ-ȧ shall [7]become
desolate; [o]for she hath rebelled
against her God: they shall fall
by the sword: [p]their [q]infants
shall be dashed in pieces, and
their [r]women with child shall
be ripped up.

## CHAPTER 14

*Israel is exhorted to repentance. 4 Forgiveness promised.*

O [a]IṢ′RA-EL, [b,c]return unto
the LORD thy God; for [d]thou
hast fallen by thine iniquity.
2 Take with you words, and
[b]turn to the LORD: [e]say unto
him, [f]Take away all iniquity,
and [1]receive *us* graciously: [g,h]so
will we [i]render [2]the calves of our
lips.
3 Ăs′shur shall not save us; we
will not ride upon [j]horses: neither will we [k]say any more to the
work of our hands, *Ye are* our
gods: for in [l]thee the [m]fatherless
findeth mercy.
4 ¶ [l,n,o]I will heal their backsliding, I will [p]love them freely:
for mine [q]anger is turned away
from him.
5 [r]I will be as the [s]dew unto Ĭṣ′-
ra-el: [t]he shall grow as the [u]lily,
and cast forth his roots as [v]Lĕb′-
a-non.
6 [t]His branches shall spread,
and his beauty shall be as the
[w]olive tree, and his smell as
[v]Lĕb′a-non.
7 They that dwell under his
shadow shall return; they shall
revive *as* the [3,x]corn, and grow as
the vine: the scent thereof *shall
be* as the [y]wine of Lĕb′a-non.
8 Ē′phrā-ĭm *shall say*, What
have I to do any more with idols?
I have [4]heard *him*, and observed
him: I *am* like a green fir tree.
From me is thy fruit found.
9 Who *is* wise, and he shall [z]un-
derstand these *things*? [a]prudent,
and he shall know them? for the
[b]ways of the LORD *are* [c,d]right,
and the [e]just shall walk in them:
but the [f]transgressors shall fall
therein.

**14**
c *God, savior*, Gen. 2:2.
d *Grave*, 2 Sam. 3:32.
e 1 Cor. 15:55.
f *Death, apostrophe to*, Num. 23:10.
g *God, immutable*, Gen. 2:2.
4 R. V. where are thy plagues?
5 R. V. where is thy destruction?

**15**
h *Israel, prophecies concerning*, 1 Kin. 12:1.
i *Assyria, prophecies concerning*, Gen. 25:18.
j *Wind, east*, Job 37:17.
k *Meteorology*, Matt. 16:2.
l *Drought, as a judgment*, Gen. 31:40.
6 Am. R. V. breath of Jehovah coming up

**16**
m *Samaria, prophecies concerning*, Isa. 7:9.
n *Wicked, punishment of*, Psa. 73:3.
o *Judgment, according to opportunity and works*, 2 Pet. 3:7.
p *War, evils of*, Judg. 3:2.
q *Cruelty*, Psa. 27:12.
r *Captive, cruelty to*, 1 Sam. 30:3.
7 R. V. bear her guilt;

**1**
a *Backsliding, of Israel*, Hos. 11:7.
b *Repentance, exhortations to*, vs. 1–3; Mark 1:4.
c *God, mercy of*, vs. 1–8; Gen. 2:2.
d *Sin, punishment of*, Rom. 5:12. **2** e *Prayer, enjoined*, Acts 6:4. f *Sin, forgiveness of*, Rom. 5:12. g *Thankfulness, to God*, Acts 24:3. h *Praise*, Psa. 150:1. 1 R. V. accept that which is good:

**2**
i *Sacrifice, figurative*, Rom. 12:1.
2 R. V. as bullocks the offering of

**3**
j *Horse*, Job 39:19.
k *False Confidence*, Psa. 30:6.
l *God, mercy of*, Gen. 2:2.
m *Orphan, God the friend of*, Lam. 5:3.

**4**
n *Promise, to backsliders*, vs. 4–7; 2 Cor. 1:20.
o *Backsliders, promises to penitent*, Jer. 3:22.
p *God, love of*, Gen. 2:2.
q *Anger of God*, 2 Kin. 13:3.

**5**
r *Temporal Blessings, from God*, Psa. 103:2.
s *Dew*, Dan. 4:15.
t *Israel, prophecies concerning*, 1 Kin. 12:1.
u *Lily*, Matt. 6:28.
v *Lebanon*, Deut. 1:7.

**6**
w *Olive*, Deut. 6:11.

**7**
x *Corn*, Psa. 65:13.
y *Wine*, Prov. 23:31.
3 Am. R. V. grain, and blossom as

**8**
4 R. V. answered, and will regard him:

**9**
z *Wisdom, spiritual*, Prov. 2:2.
—a *Prudence*, 2 Chr. 2:12. b *Way, figurative*, Isa. 35:8. c *God, righteousness of*, Gen. 2:2. d *Righteousness*, Psa. 15:2. e *Righteous, described*, Psa. 64:10. f *Wicked, punishment of*, Psa. 73:3.

---

THE

# BOOK OF JOEL

## CHAPTER 1

*The judgments of God upon the land. 8 The prophet exhorts the people to mourn, 14 and to proclaim a fast.*

THE word of the LORD that
[a]came to *Jō′el the son of
Pĕ-thū′el.
2 [b]Hear this, ye old men, and
give ear, all ye inhabitants of the
land. Hath this been in your
days, or even in the days of your
fathers?
3 Tell ye your children of it,

**1**
a *Prophets, inspiration of*, Isa. 33:2.

**2**
b *Nation, punishment of*, vs. 1–20; Isa. 2:4.

* **JOEL** (*Jehovah his God*). *One of the twelve minor prophets, probably lived in the days of Uzziah*, Joel 1:1; Acts 2:16. *Son of Pethuel*, Joel 1:1. *Declares the terribleness of God's judgments*, Joel 1; 2:1–11. *Exhorts to repentance*, Joel 2:12–17. *Denounces judgments against the enemies of God*, Joel 3:1–17. *Foretells blessings for Zion*, Joel 2:18–32; 3:18–21.

and *let* your children *tell* their
children, and their children another generation.
4 [b]That which the [c]palmer-
worm hath left hath the [d]locust
eaten; and that which the locust
hath left hath the [e]cankerworm
eaten; and that which the cankerworm hath left hath the [f]cat-
erpiller eaten.
5 Awake, ye [g]drunkards, and
weep; and howl, all ye [h]drinkers of
[i]wine, because of the [1]new wine;
for it is cut off from your mouth.
6 For a nation is come up upon my land, strong, and without number, whose teeth *are* the
teeth of a [j]lion, and he hath the
cheek teeth of a great lion.
7 [b]He hath laid my [k]vine waste,
and barked my [l]fig tree: he hath
made it clean bare, and cast *it*
away; the branches thereof are
made white.
8 ¶ Lament like a virgin girded
with [m]sackcloth for the husband
of her youth.
9 [b]The [2,n]meat offering and the
[o]drink offering is cut off from the
[p]house of the LORD; the priests,
the LORD's ministers, mourn.
10 [q]The field is wasted, the land
mourneth; for the [r]corn is wasted: the new [i]wine is dried up, the
[s]oil languisheth.
11 Be ye ashamed, O ye husbandmen; howl, O ye vinedressers, for the [t]wheat and for the
[u]barley; because [q]the harvest of
the field is perished.
12 [q]The [k]vine is dried up, and
the [l]fig tree languisheth; the
[v]pomegranate tree, the [w]palm
tree also, and the [x]apple tree,
*even* all the trees of the field, are
withered: because joy is withered
away from the sons of men.
13 ¶ [y,z]Gird yourselves, [3]and
lament, ye priests: howl, ye ministers of the altar: come, lie all
night in [m]sackcloth, ye ministers
of my God: for the [2,n]meat offer-

**4**
*c* Joel 2:25; Amos 4:9.
*d* *Locust, devastation by,* vs. 4–7; Nah. 3:17.
*e* Joel 2:25; Nah. 3:15, 16.
*f* *Caterpillar, as a judgment,* 1 Kin. 8:37.

**5**
*g* *Drunkard,* Psa. 69:12.
*h* *Drunkenness,* Luke 21:34.
*i* *Wine,* Prov. 23:31.
1 R. V. sweet

**6**
*j* *Lion, strength of,* Mic. 5:8.

**7**
*k* *Vineyard, figurative,* Isa. 1:8.
*l* *Fig Tree, figurative,* Luke 13:6.

**8**
*m* *Sackcloth,* Isa. 15:3.

**9**
*n* *Offerings, meat,* Lev. 6:17.
*o* *Offerings, drink,* Lev. 6:17.
*p* *Temple, Solomon's,* 1 Kin. 6:17.
2 R. V. meal

**10**
*q* *Drought, as a judgment,* Gen. 31:40.
*r* *Corn,* Psa. 65:13.
*s* *Oil,* Deut. 12:17.

**11**
*t* *Wheat,* Ezra, 6:9.
*u* *Barley,* Ex. 9:31.

**12**
*v* *Pomegranate,* Num. 13:23.
*w* *Palm Tree,* Song 7:7.
*x* Prov. 25:11; Song 2:3, 5; 7:8; 8:5.

**13**
*y* *Commandment, enjoining penitence,* Deut. 8:2.
3 R. V. *inserts* with sackcloth, and lament,

ing and the [o]drink offering is
withholden from the [p]house of
your God.
14 [z,a]Sanctify ye a fast, [b]call a
solemn assembly, gather the
[4]elders *and* all the inhabitants of
the land *into* the house of the
LORD your God, and cry unto
the LORD,
15 Alas for the [c]day! for the day
of the LORD *is* at hand, and as a
[d]destruction [e]from the Almighty
shall it come.
16 Is not the meat [f]cut off before our eyes, *yea,* joy and gladness from the house of our God?
17 The seed is rotten under
their clods, the garners are laid
desolate, the [g]barns are broken
down; for the corn is withered.
18 How do the [h]beasts groan!
the herds of cattle are perplexed,
because they have no pasture;
yea, the flocks of sheep are made
desolate.
19 O LORD, to thee will I [i]cry:
for [d]the fire hath devoured the
pastures of the wilderness, and
the flame hath burned all the
trees of the field.
20 The [h]beasts of the field [5]cry
also unto thee: for [j]the rivers of
waters are dried up, and the fire
hath devoured the pastures of the
wilderness.

## CHAPTER 2

*Terrible judgments predicted. 12 An exhortation to repent, 15 and to proclaim a fast. 18 Blessings promised thereupon. 28 The outpouring of the Spirit foretold.*

BLOW ye the trumpet in Zī'ŏn,
and sound an alarm in my
holy mountain: let all the inhabitants of the land tremble: for
[a]the [b,c,d]day of the LORD cometh, for *it is* nigh at hand;
2 A day of [e]darkness and of
gloominess, a day of clouds and
of thick darkness, as the morning
spread upon the mountains: a
great [f]people and a strong; there
hath not been ever the like, nei-

*z* *Repentance, enjoined,* Mark 1:4.

**14**
*a* *Fasting, enjoined,* Zech. 8:19.
*b* *Worship, enjoined,* Gen. 22:5.
4 R. V. old men

**15**
*c* *Day, figurative,* Gen. 1:5.
*d* *Nation, punishment of,* Isa. 2:4.
*e* *Adversity, dispensation from God,* Psa. 10:6.

**16**
*f* *Famine, described,* 2 Kin. 8:1.

**17**
*g* *Barn,* Prov. 3:10.

**18**
*h* *Animals, suffer under divine judgments,* Jer. 27:5.

**19**
*i* *Adversity, prayer in,* Psa. 10:6.

**20**
*j* *Drought, as a judgment,* Gen. 31:40.
5 R. V. pant unto

**1**
*a* *Judah, kingdom of, prophecies concerning,* vs. 1–17; 2 Chr. 11:17.
*b* *Day, figurative,* Gen. 1:5.
*c* *Adversity, dispensation from God,* Psa. 10:6.
*d* *Wicked, punishment of,* Psa. 73:3.

**2**
*e* *Darkness, figurative,* Gen. 1:2.
*f* *Locust, symbolical,* vs. 1–11; Nah. 3:17.

3

*g Eden,* Isa. 51:3.

4

*h Cavalry,* 1 Sam. 13:5.

5

*i Chariot,* Josh. 11:4.

7

*j Armies, tactics of,* Deut. 11:4.

9

2 R. V. leap upon the city;

11

*k Agency, in executing judgments,* Mark 1:17.

12

*l Commandment, enjoining penitence,* Deut. 8:2.

*m Repentance, exhortations to,* Mark 1:4.

*n Sincerity,* 1 Cor. 5:8.

ther shall be any more after it, *even* to the years of many generations.[Q]

3 A fire devoureth before them; and behind them a flame burneth: the land *is* as the garden of [g]Ē′dĕn before them, and behind them a desolate wilderness; yea, and nothing shall escape them.[S]

4 The appearance of them *is* as the appearance of horses; and as [h]horsemen, so shall they run.[Q]

5 Like the noise of [i]chariots on the tops of mountains shall they leap, like the noise of a flame of fire that devoureth the stubble, as a strong people set in battle array.[G][Q]

6 Before their face the people shall be much pained: all faces shall gather blackness.

7 They shall run like mighty men; [j]they shall climb the wall like men of war; and they shall march every one on his ways, and they shall not break their ranks:

8 Neither shall one thrust another; they shall walk every one in his path: and [1]*when* they fall upon the sword, they shall not be wounded.[S]

9 They [2]shall run to and fro in the city; they shall run upon the wall, they shall climb up upon the houses; they shall enter in at the windows like a thief.

10 The earth shall quake before them; the heavens shall tremble: the sun and the moon shall be dark, and the stars shall withdraw their shining:[Q]

11 And the LORD shall utter his voice before his army: for his camp *is* very great: for [k]*he is* strong that executeth his word: for the [b,c,d]day of the LORD *is* great and very terrible; and who can abide it?[S T Q]

12 ¶ Therefore also now, saith the LORD, [l,m]Turn ye *even* to me with [n]all your heart, and with [o]fasting, and with [p]weeping, and with mourning:[S T]

13 And rend[G] your heart, and not your garments, and [l,m]turn unto the LORD your God: for he *is* gracious and [q]merciful, [r]slow to anger, and of great kindness, and [s]repenteth him of the evil.[S]

14 Who knoweth *if* he will return and [s]repent, and leave a [t]blessing behind him; *even* a [3]meat[G] offering and a drink offering unto the LORD your God?[S]

15 ¶ Blow the trumpet in Zī′ŏn, [o]sanctify a fast, [u]call a solemn assembly:

16 Gather the people, [v]sanctify the congregation, assemble the [4]elders, gather the children, and those that suck the breasts: let the bridegroom go forth of his chamber, and the bride out of her closet.[G]

17 Let the priests, the ministers of the LORD, [m]weep between the porch and the altar, and [w]let them [x,y]say, Spare thy people, O LORD, and give not thine heritage to reproach, that the [5]heathen[G] should rule over them: wherefore[G] should they say among the [6]people, Where *is* their God?

18 ¶ Then will the LORD be [z]jealous[G] for his land, and [a]pity his people.

19 Yea, the LORD will [b]answer and say unto his people, Behold, [c]I will send you [d,e]corn,[G] and [e,f]wine, and [e,g]oil, and ye shall be satisfied therewith: and I will no more make you a reproach among the heathen[G]:

20 But I will remove far off from you the northern *army*, and will drive him into a land barren and desolate, with his face toward the [h]east sea, and his hinder[G] part toward the [i]utmost[G] sea, and his stink shall come up, and his ill savour[G] shall come up, because he hath done great things.

21 [j,k]Fear not, O land; be glad

*o Fasting, enjoined,* Zech. 8:19.

*p Weeping, penitential,* Ezra 3:13.

13

*q God, mercy of,* Gen. 2:2.

*r God, longsuffering of,* Gen. 2:2.

*s Repentance, attributed to God,* Mark 1:4.

14

*t Temporal Blessings, from God,* Psa. 103:2.

3 R. V. meal

15

*u Worship, enjoined,* Gen. 22:5.

16

*v Purification,* Num. 19:19.

4 R. V. old men,

17

*w Minister, duties of,* Rom. 15:16.

*x Prayer, intercessory,* Acts 6:4.

*y Intercession, of man with God,* Jer. 27:18.

5 R. V. nations

6 R. V. peoples,

18

*z God, jealous,* Gen. 2:2.

*a Pity, of God,* Job 19:21.

19

*b Prayer, answered,* Acts 6:4.

*c God, providence of,* Gen. 2:2.

*d Corn,* Psa. 65:13.

*e Temporal Blessings, from God,* Psa. 103:2.

*f Wine,* Prov. 23:31.

*g Oil,* Deut. 12:17.

20

*h Dead Sea,* Gen. 14:3.

*i Mediterranean Sea,* Ex. 23:31.

21

*j Faith, enjoined,* Mark 11:22.

*k Adversity, consolation in,* Psa. 10:6.

and rejoice: for the LORD will do great things.

22 [i,k]Be not afraid, ye beasts of the field: for [e]the pastures of the wilderness do spring, for the [e]tree beareth her fruit, [e]the fig tree and the vine do yield their strength.

23 [i,k]Be glad then, ye children of Zī′ŏn, and [l]rejoice in the LORD your God: for [c]he hath [e]given you the former [m,n]rain [7]moderately, and he will cause to come down for you the rain, the former rain, and the latter rain in the first *month*.[Q]

24 And [e,o]the [p]floors shall be full of [q]wheat, and [e,o]the fats[C] shall overflow with [f]wine and [g]oil.

25 And [c,o]I will [e]restore to you the years that the [r]locust hath eaten, the [s]cankerworm, and the [t]caterpiller, and the [u]palmerworm,[G] my great army which I sent among you.

26[S] And [o]ye shall eat in plenty, and be satisfied, and [v]praise the name of the LORD your God, that [c]hath dealt wondrously with you: and my people shall never be ashamed.[G]

27 And ye shall know[C] that [w]I *am* in the midst of Iṣ′ra-el, and *that* I *am* the LORD your God, and none else: and [x,y]my people[S] shall never be ashamed.

28 ¶[T Q] And [z]it shall come to pass afterward, *that* [a]I will pour out my [b]spirit upon all flesh; and your sons and your [c]daughters shall [d]prophesy,[G] your old men shall [e]dream dreams, your [f]young men shall see [g]visions:

29 [a]And also upon the servants and upon the handmaids in those days will I pour out my [b]spirit.[T]

30 And I will shew [h]wonders in the heavens and in the earth, blood, and fire, and pillars of smoke.[Q]

31 [h]The [i]sun shall be turned into darkness, and the [j]moon into blood, before the great and the terrible [k]day of the LORD come.[Q]

32 And it shall come to pass, *that* [l]whosoever shall call on the name of the LORD [m,n]shall be delivered: for in mount Zī′ŏn and in [o]Jē-rụ′sā-lĕm [8]shall be deliverance, as the LORD hath said, and [9]in the remnant whom the LORD shall call.[T Q]

## CHAPTER 3

*God's judgments upon the enemies of his people.* 18 *Blessings promised to Zion.*

FOR, behold, in those days, and in that time, [a]when I shall bring again the captivity of Jū′dah and Jē-rụ′sā-lĕm,

2 I will also gather all nations, and will bring them down into the valley of Jē-hŏsh′a-phăt, and will plead[C] with them there for my people and *for* my heritage Iṣ′ra-el, whom they have scattered among the nations, and parted my land.

3 And they have cast [b]lots for my people; and have given a boy for an [c]harlot, and [d]sold a girl for [e]wine, that they might drink.[Q]

4 Yea, and what have ye to do with me, O [f]Tȳre, and [g]Zī′dŏn, and all the [1]coasts of Păl′estīne? will ye render me a recompence? and if ye recompense me, swiftly *and* speedily will I [h,i]return your recompence upon your own head;

5 Because ye have taken my silver and my gold, and have carried into your temples my goodly[G] pleasant[G] things:

6 The children also of Jū′dah and the children of Jē-rụ′sā-lĕm have ye [d]sold unto the [j]Grē′çianṣ, that ye might remove them far from their border.

7 Behold, I will raise[C] them out of the place whither[C] ye have

---

23
l *Joy, enjoined,* Psa. 5:11.
m *Rain,* 2 Sam. 1:21.
n *Meteorology,* Matt. 16:2.
7 R. V. in just measure,

24
o *Prosperity, from God,* Eccl. 7:14.
p *Threshing, floors for,* 1 Chr. 21:20.
q *Wheat,* Ezra 6:9.

25
r *Locust,* Nah. 3:17.
s Joel 1:4; Nah. 3:15, 16.
t *Caterpillar,* 1 Kin. 8:37.
u Joel 1:4; Amos 4:9.

26
v *Thankfulness, enjoined, for providential deliverance,* Acts 24:3.

27
w *God dwells with the Righteous,* 1 Kin. 6:13.
x *Promise, to the righteous,* 2 Cor. 1:20.
y *Righteous, promises to,* Psa. 64:10.

28
z Acts 2:17-21.

a *Prophecies, of the outpouring of the Holy Spirit,* Dan. 9:24.
b *Holy Spirit,* Acts 1:2.
c *Women, as prophets,* Prov. 31:10.
d *Spiritual Gifts,* 1 Cor. 12:4.
e *Dream, revelations by,* Dan. 1:17.
f *Young Men,* Prov. 1:4.
g *Vision, a mode of revelation,* Acts 9:10.

30
h *Celestial Phenomena,* Luke 23:44.

31
i *Sun,* Josh. 10:12.
j *Moon,* Song 6:10.
k *Day, figurative,* Gen. 1:5.

32
l *Penitent, promises to,* Psa. 51:17.
m *Prayer, answer to, promised,* Acts 6:4.
n *Promise, to penitents,* 2 Cor. 1:20.
o *Jerusalem,* Judg. 19:10.
8 R. V. there shall be those that escape,
9 Am. R. V. among the remnant those whom Jehovah doth call.

1
a *Jews, prophecies concerning,* Neh. 4:2.

3
b *Lot,* Esth. 3:7.
c *Harlot,* Prov. 7:10.
d *Servant, bought and sold,* Jer. 2:14.
e *Wine,* Prov. 23:31.

4
f *Tyre,* Josh. 19:29.
g *Zidon,* Ezek. 28:21.
h *Judgment, according to opportunity and works,* 1 Pet. 1:17.
i *Punishment, according to deeds,* Lev. 26:41.
1 R. V. regions of Philistia?

6
j *Greece,* Zech. 9:13.

8
k *Nation, judgments denounced against*, Isa. 2:4.
l *Wicked, punishment of*, Psa. 73:3.
m *Sabeans*, Isa. 45:14.

9
2 R. V. nations;

10
n Isa. 2:4; Mic. 4:3.
o *Sword*, 1 Chr. 21:5.
p *Pruning*, Isa. 18:5.
q *Hooks*, Ex. 36:36.
r *Spear*, 2 Kin. 11:10.

12
s *God, judge*, Gen. 2:2.

13
t *Sickle, figurative*, Deut. 23:25.
u *Harvest, figurative*, Ex. 34:21.
v *Wine Press, figurative*, Isa. 5:2.
3 R. V. tread ye;

14
w *Day, figurative*, Gen. 1:5.

sold them, and will [h,i]return your
recompence upon your own
head:
8 And [k,l]I will sell your sons
and your daughters into the
hand of the children of Jū′dah,
and they shall sell them to the
[m]Să-bē′anș, to a people far off:
for the LORD hath spoken *it*.[Q]
9 ¶ Proclaim ye this among the
[2]Ġĕn′tīleș;[G] Prepare war, wake
up the mighty men, let all the
men of war draw near; let them
come up:
10 Beat your [n]plowshares into
[o]swords, and your [p]pruning-
[q]hooks[G] into [r]spears: let the weak
say, I *am* strong.
11 Assemble yourselves, and
come, all ye heathen,[G] and gather
yourselves together round about:
thither cause thy mighty ones to
come down, O LORD.
12 Let the heathen be wakened,
and come up to the valley of Jĕ-
hŏsh′a-phăt: for there will I sit
to [s]judge all the heathen[G] round
about.[T]
13 [k,l]Put ye in the [t]sickle, for
the [u]harvest is ripe: come, [3]get
you down; for the [v]press is full,
the fats[G] overflow; for their wickedness *is* great.[Q]
14 Multitudes, multitudes in
the valley of decision: for the
[l,w]day of the LORD *is* near in the
valley of decision.[G]

15 The [x]sun and the [y]moon shall
be darkened, and the [z]stars shall
withdraw their shining.[Q]
16[S] The LORD also shall roar
out of Zī′ŏn, and utter his voice
from Jĕ-ru̦′să-lĕm; and the heavens and the earth shall shake: but
[a]the [b]LORD *will be* [4]the [c]hope of
his people, and the strength of
the children of Ĭș′ra-el.[G]
17 So shall ye know that I
*am* the LORD your God dwelling in Zī′ŏn, my holy mountain:
then shall Jĕ-ru̦′să-lĕm be holy,[G]
and there shall no strangers pass
through her any more.[S T]
18 ¶ And [d]it shall come to pass
in that day, *that* the mountains
shall drop down new [e]wine, and
the hills shall flow with [f]milk,
and all the [5]rivers of Jū′dah shall
flow with waters, and a [g]fountain
shall come forth of the house of
the LORD, and shall water the
valley of [h]Shĭt′tim.[Q]
19 [i]Ē′ġy̆pt shall be a desolation, and [j]Ē′dom shall be a desolate wilderness, for the violence
*against* the children of Jū′dah,
because they have shed innocent
blood in their land.
20 But [d]Jū′dah shall dwell for
ever, and Jĕ-ru̦′să-lĕm from generation to generation.
21 For [d,k]I will cleanse[G] their
blood *that* I have not cleansed:[G]
for the LORD dwelleth in Zī′ŏn.[T]

15
x *Sun, darkening of*, Josh. 10:12.
y *Moon, darkening of*, Song 6:10.
z *Stars, darkening of*, Judg. 5:20.

16
a *Righteous, promises to*, Psa. 64:10.
b *God, savior*, Gen. 2:2.
c *Hope*, Prov. 13:12.
4 R. V. a refuge unto his people, and a strong hold to the children of Israel.

18
d *Jews, prophecies concerning*, Neh. 4:2.
e *Wine, figurative*, Prov. 23:31.
f *Milk, figurative*, Job 10:10.
g *Fountain, figurative*, Zech. 13:1.
h *Shittim*, Num. 25:1.
5 R. V. brooks

19
i *Egypt*, Gen. 41:8.
j *Edom*, Obad. 1.

21
k *God, mercy of*, Gen. 2:2.

THE

# BOOK OF AMOS

## CHAPTER 1

*The date of the prophecy of Amos. 2 God's judgment upon Syria, 6 upon the Philistines, 9 upon Tyre, 11 upon Edom, 13 and upon Ammon.*

1
a *Tekoa*, Jer. 6:1.

THE words of *Ā′mos, who
was among the herdmen
of [a]Tĕ-kō′ȧ, which he saw concerning Ĭș′ra-el in the days of
[b]Ŭz-zī′ah king of [c]Jū′dah, and in
the days of [d]Jĕr-o-bō′am the son
of [e]Jō′ăsh king of [f]Ĭș′ra-el, two
years before the [g]earthquake.
2 And he said, The LORD will
roar from Zī′ŏn, and utter his

b *Uzziah*, 2 Chr. 26:1.
c *Judah*, 2 Chr. 11:17.
d *Jeroboam*, 1 Chr. 5:17.
e *Joash*, 2 Kin. 11:2.
f *Israel, after the revolt*, 1 Kin. 12:1.
g *Earthquakes*, Isa. 29:6.

* **AMOS.** *A herdman of Tekoa, and a prophet in the reign of Uzziah*, Amos 1:1. *Denounces divine judgments against heathen nations and against Judah and Israel*, Amos chapters 1–4. *Laments over Israel and exhorts to repentance, reproving pride and luxury*, Amos chapters 5, 6. *His denunciations offend the priest at Beth-el, who reports him to Jeroboam, the king, as a disturber of the peace and a traitor to the king. Amos denounces the priest and foretells his death in captivity.*

voice from Jē-ru̇′să-lĕm; and [h]the [1]habitations of the shepherds shall mourn, and the top of Cär′mel shall wither.

3 ¶ Thus saith the LORD; For three transgressions of [i]Dă-măs′cus, and for four, I will not turn away *the* [h]*punishment* thereof; because they have threshed[C] [j]Gĭl′e-ăd with threshing[C] instruments of iron:

4 But [h]I will send a [k]fire into the house of [l]Hăz′a-el, which shall devour[C] the palaces of [m]Bĕn-hā′dăd.

5 [h]I will break also the bar of [i]Dă-măs′cus, and cut off the inhabitant from the plain of Ā′ven, and him that holdeth the sceptre[C] from the house of Ē′dĕn: and the people of [n]Sȳr′ĭ-ȧ shall go into [o]captivity unto [p]Kĭr, saith the LORD.

6 ¶ Thus saith the LORD; For three transgressions of [q,r]Gā′zȧ, and for four, I will not turn away *the* [h]*punishment* thereof; because they [o]carried away captive [2]the whole captivity, to deliver *them* up to [s]Ē′dom:

7 But [h]I will send a [k]fire on the wall of [q]Gā′zȧ, which shall devour[C] the palaces thereof:

8 And [h]I will cut off the inhabitant from [t]Ăsh′dŏd, and him that holdeth the sceptre from [u]Ăsh′ke-lŏn, and I will turn mine hand against [†]Ĕk′rŏn: and the remnant of the [r]Phĭ-lĭs′tĭneṣ shall perish, saith the Lord GOD.

9 ¶ Thus[Q] saith the LORD; For three transgressions of [v]Tȳ′rus, and for four, I will not turn away *the* [h]*punishment* thereof; because they delivered up the whole captivity to [s]Ē′dom, and remembered not the brotherly covenant[C]:

10 But [h]I will send a [k]fire on the wall of [v]Tȳ′rus, which shall devour the palaces thereof.[Q]

11 ¶ Thus saith the LORD; For three transgressions of [s]Ē′dom, and for four, I will not turn away *the* [h]*punishment* thereof; because he did pursue his brother with the sword, and did cast off all pity, and his anger did tear perpetually[C], and he kept his wrath for ever:

12 But [h]I will send a [k]fire upon [w]Tē′man, which shall devour the palaces of [x]Bŏz′rah.

13 ¶ Thus saith the LORD; For three transgressions of the [y]children of Ăm′mŏn, and for four, I will not turn away *the* [h]*punishment* thereof; because [z]they have [a]ripped up the women with child of [b]Gĭl′e-ăd, that they might enlarge their border:

14 But I will kindle a fire in the wall of [c]Răb′bah, and it shall devour the palaces thereof, with shouting in the day of battle, with a tempest in the day of the whirlwind:

15 And their king shall go into [d]captivity, he and his princes together, saith the LORD.

## CHAPTER 2

*God's judgments upon Moab, 4 upon Judah, 6 and upon Israel. 9 The ingratitude of the people, and their punishment.*

THUS saith the LORD; For three transgressions of [a]Mō′ab, and for four, I will not turn away *the punishment* thereof; because he [b,c]burned the bones of the king of Ē′dom into lime:

2 But [a]I will send a [d]fire upon Mō′ab, and it shall devour[C] the palaces of [e]Kĭr′ĭ-ŏth: and Mō′ab shall die with [f]tumult, with shouting, *and* with the sound of the trumpet:

3 And [a]I will cut off the judge

2
h *Nation, judgments denounced against*, Isa. 2:4.
1 R. V. pastures

3
i *Damascus*, Isa. 8:4.
j *Gilead*, Deut. 3:13.

4
k *Fire, figurative of judgments*, Ex. 12:8.
l *Hazael*, 2 Kin. 9:14.
m 2 Kin. 13:3.

5
n *Syria*, 2 Kin. 6:23.
o *Captivity, as a judgment*, Isa. 5:13.
p *Kir*, 2 Kin. 16:9.

6
q *Gaza*, Gen. 10:19.
r *Philistines*, Gen. 26:14.
s *Edomites*, 2 Kin. 8:21.
2 R. V. people, to

8
t *Ashdod*, 1 Sam. 6:17.
u Or, *Askelon*, Judg. 1:18.

9
v Or, *Tyre*, Josh. 19:29.

12
w *Teman*, Jer. 49:7.
x *Bozrah*, Gen. 36:33.

13
y *Ammonites*, Deut. 2:20.
z *War, evils of*, Judg. 3:2.

a *Captive, cruelty to*, 1 Sam. 30:3.
b *Gilead*, Deut. 3:13.

14
c *Rabbah, prophecies against*, Deut. 3:11.

15
d *Captivity, as a judgment*, Isa. 5:13.

1
a *Moabites, prophecy concerning*, Gen. 19:37.
b *Cremation*, Josh. 7:25.
c *Malice*, Eph. 4:31.

2
d *Fire, figurative of judgments*, Ex. 12:8.
e Or, *Kerioth*, Jer. 48:24, 41.
f *War*, Judg. 3:2.

*the degradation of his wife, and the death of his children by the sword*, Amos chapters 7, 8. *Foretells the desolation of Israel and restoration of Judah*, Amos 9.

† **EKRON** (*eradication, emigration*). *One of the five chief cities of the Philistines*, Josh. 13:3. *Conquered and allotted to Judah*, Josh. 15:11, 45; Judg. 1:18. *Allotted to Dan*, Josh. 19:43. *The ark of God taken to*, 1 Sam. 5:10. *Temple of Baalzebub at*, 2 Kin. 1:2. *Prophecies against*, Jer. 25:20; Amos 1:8; Zeph. 2:4; Zech 9:5.

from the midst thereof, and will
slay all the princes thereof with
him, saith the LORD.
4 ¶ Thus saith the LORD; For
three transgressions of [g]Jū'dah,
and for four, I will not turn away
*the punishment* thereof; because
they have [1,h]despised the law of
the LORD, and have [i]not kept
his commandments, and their
lies caused them to err, [j]after
the which their fathers have
walked:
5 But [g]I will send a fire upon
Jū'dah, and it shall devour the
palaces of Jĕ-ru'să-lĕm.
6 ¶ Thus saith the LORD; For
three transgressions of [k]Ĭs'ra-el,
and for four, I will not turn away
*the punishment* thereof; because
they [l]sold the righteous for [m]sil-
ver, and the [n]poor for a pair of
shoes;
7 That pant after the dust of
the earth on the head of the
[n]poor, and turn aside the way of
the meek: and [o,p]a man and
his father will go in unto the
*same* maid,[C] to [q]profane[C] my holy
name:
8 And [p]they lay *themselves* down
upon clothes laid to [r,s]pledge[C] by
every [t]altar, and [2]they drink the
wine of the condemned *in* the
house of their god.
9 ¶ Yet destroyed I the [u]Ăm'ôr-
īte before them, whose height
*was* like the height of the cedars,
and he *was* strong as the oaks;
yet I destroyed his fruit from
above, and his roots from beneath.
10 Also I [v]brought you up from
the land of [w]Ē'ġўpt, and led you
[x]forty years through the wilderness, to possess the [y]land of the
Ăm'ôr'īte.
11 And I [v,z]raised up of your
sons for prophets, and of your
[a]young men for [b]Năz-a-rītes. *Is*

**4**
*g Judah, prophecies concerning,* 2 Chr. 11:17.
*h Backsliding, of Israel,* Hos. 11:7.
*i Disobedience to God,* Eph. 5:6.
*j Example, bad,* John 13:15.
1 R. V. rejected

**6**
*k Israel, prophecies concerning,* vs. 6–16; 1 Kin. 12:1.
*l Judge, corrupt,* Judg. 2:18.
*m Bribery, punishment for,* 1 Sam. 8:3.
*n Poor, oppression of,* Prov. 21:13.

**7**
*o Lasciviousness,* 1 Pet. 4:3.
*p Idolatry, wicked practices of,* 1 Sam. 15:23.
*q Profanation, of God's name,* Lev. 22:32.

**8**
*r Debt, security for,* 1 Sam. 22:2.
*s Pawn, unlawfully retained,* Job 24:3.
*t Altar, used in idolatrous worship,* Gen. 8:20.
2 R. V. in the house of their God they drink the wine of such as have been fined.

**9**
*u Amorites,* Gen. 14:13.

**10**
*v God, providence of,* Gen. 2:2.
*w Egypt,* Gen. 41:8.
*x Forty, years,* Jonah 3:4.
*y Canaan,* Gen. 37:1.

**11**
*z Minister, call of,* Rom. 15:16.

*a Young Man,* Prov. 1:4.
*b* Or, *Nazirite,* Num. 6:2.

*it* not even thus, O ye children of
Ĭs'ra-el? saith the LORD.
12 But ye [c]gave the Năz'a-rītes
wine to drink; and commanded
the [d]prophets, saying, Prophesy[C]
not.
13 Behold, I [3]am pressed under
you, as a cart is pressed *that is*
full of sheaves.
14 Therefore the flight shall
perish from the swift, and the
strong shall not strengthen his
force, neither shall the mighty
deliver himself:
15 Neither shall he stand that
[e]handleth the bow; and *he that is*
swift of foot shall not deliver
*himself*: neither shall he that
rideth the horse deliver himself.
16 And *he that is* courageous
among the mighty shall flee
away naked in that day, saith
the LORD.

## CHAPTER 3

*The certainty of God's judgments against Israel. 9 The heathen nations called to behold.*

HEAR this word that the
LORD hath spoken against
you, O children of [a]Ĭs'-ra-el,
against the whole family which
I [b]brought up from the land
of [c]Ē'ġўpt, saying,
2 You only have I known of all
the families of the earth: therefore [d]I will [e,f]punish[C] you for all
your [g]iniquities.[S]
3 [h,i]Can two walk together, except they be agreed?
4 Will a [j]lion roar in the forest,
when he hath no prey? will a
young lion cry out of his den, if
he have taken nothing?
5 [k]Can a bird fall in a snare upon the earth, where no gin[C] *is* for
him? shall [1]*one* take up a *snare
from the earth, and have taken
nothing at all?
6 Shall a [l]trumpet be blown in
the city, and the people not be

**12**
*c Temptation, leading into,* Luke 11:4.
*d Prophets, persecutions of,* Isa. 3:2.

**13**
3 R. V. will press you in your place, as a cart presseth that

**15**
*e Archery,* Gen. 21:20.

**1**
*a Israel, prophecies concerning,* 1 Kin. 12:1.
*b God, providence of,* Gen. 2:2.
*c Egypt,* Gen. 41:8.

**2**
*d Divine Chastisement,* Job 33:19.
*e Judgment, according to opportunity and works,* 1 Pet. 1:17.
*f Wicked, punishment of,* Psa. 73:3.
*g Ingratitude, of man to God,* Rom. 1:21.

**3**
*h Fellowship, with God,* 1 Cor. 1:9.
*i Friendship,* Prov. 22:24.

**4**
*j Lion, instincts of,* Mic. 5:8.

**5**
*k Hunting,* Gen. 27:5.
1 R. V. a snare spring up from the ground, and

**6**
*l Trumpet,* Josh. 6:4.

*** SNARE,** Amos 3:5. *For birds,* Prov. 7:23; Eccl. 9:12. **Figurative:** *Of the evils in life of the wicked,* Job 18:5, 9. *Of the devices of the wicked to deceive the righteous,* Psa. 91:3; 119:110; 140:5; 141:9; 142:3; Jer. 18:22.

afraid? shall there be [m]evil in a city, and the LORD hath not done *it*?

7 Surely the Lord GOD will do nothing, but[C] he [n]revealeth his secret unto his servants the prophets.[S Q]

8 The [l]lion hath roared, who will not fear? the Lord GOD hath spoken, who can but prophesy?

9 ¶ Publish in the palaces at [o]Ăsh′dŏd, and in the palaces in the land of [p]Ē′ġy̆pt, and say, Assemble yourselves upon the mountains of [q]Să-mā′rĭ-ȧ, and behold the great tumults in the midst thereof, and the oppressed in the midst thereof.

10 For [r]they [s]know not to do right, saith the LORD, who store up violence and [t,u]robbery in their palaces.

11 Therefore thus saith the Lord GOD; An adversary *there shall be* even round about the land; and he shall bring down thy strength from thee, and thy palaces shall be spoiled.[C]

12 Thus saith the LORD; As the [v]shepherd taketh out of the mouth of the lion two legs, or a piece of an ear; so shall the children of Iș′ra-el be taken out that dwell in [q]Să-mā′rĭ-ȧ in the corner of a [2]bed, and in Dă-măs′-cus *in* a couch.

13 Hear ye, and testify in the house of Jā′cob, saith the Lord GOD, the God of hosts,

14 That [a]in the day that I [w,x]shall visit[C] the transgressions of Iș′ra-el upon him [y]I will also visit the [z]altars of [a]Bĕth′-el: and the horns of the altar shall be cut off, and fall to the ground.

15 And I will smite the [b]winter [c]house with the [d]summer house; and the houses of [e]ivory shall perish, and the great houses shall have an end, saith the LORD.

## CHAPTER 4

*Israel reproved for their oppression, 4 for their idolatry, 6 and for their incorrigibleness.*

HEAR this word, ye [a]kine[C] of [b]Bā′shăn, that *are* in the mountain of [c]Să-mā′rĭ-ȧ, which [d]oppress the [e]poor, which crush the needy, which say to their masters, Bring, and let us drink.

2 The Lord GOD hath [f]sworn by his [g]holiness, that, lo, the days shall come upon you, that [h]he will [i]take you away with hooks, and your posterity with fishhooks.

3 And ye shall go out at the breaches,[C] every [1,a]*cow at that which is* before her; and ye shall cast [2]*them* into the palace, saith the LORD.

4 ¶ [j]Come to [k]Bĕth′-el, and transgress; at [l]Gĭl′găl multiply transgression; and bring your sacrifices every morning, *and* your [m]tithes [3]after three years:

5 [j]And offer a sacrifice[C] of thanksgiving with [n]leaven, and proclaim *and* publish the free [o]offerings: for this liketh[C] you, O ye children of Iș′ra-el, saith the Lord GOD.

6 ¶ And [p]I also have given you [q]cleanness of teeth in all your cities, and [q]want[C] of bread in all your places: [r,s]yet have ye [t,u]not returned unto me, saith the LORD.

7[S] And also I have [v]withholden[C] the [w]rain from you, when *there were* yet three months to the harvest: and I [x]caused it to [y]rain upon one city, and caused it [w]not to rain upon another city: one piece was rained upon, and the piece whereupon it rained not withered.

8 So two *or* three cities wandered unto one city, to drink water; but they were not satisfied: [r,s]yet have ye [t,u]not returned unto me, saith the LORD.

9 [p]I have smitten you with

---

m *Afflictions, from God*, Psa. 34:19.

**7**

n *Prophets, inspiration of*, Isa. 3:2.

**9**

o *Ashdod*, 1 Sam. 6:17.

p *Egypt*, Gen. 41:8.

q *Samaria*, Isa. 7:9.

**10**

r *Rulers, wicked*, Ex. 18:21.

s *Spiritual Blindness*, 2 Cor. 4:4.

t *Robbery*, Ezek. 22:29.

u *Dishonesty, wicked devices for gain*, Ezek. 22:13.

**12**

v *Shepherd*, Jer. 31:10.

2 R. V. couch, and on the silken cushions of a bed.

**14**

w *Judgments*, Ex. 6:6.

x *Wicked, punishment of*, Psa. 73:3.

y *Idolatry, punishment of*, 1 Sam. 15:23.

z *Altar, used in idolatrous worship*, Gen. 8:20.

a *Beth-el, prophecies against*, Josh. 18:13.

**15**

b *Winter*, Gen. 8:22.

c *House*, Esth. 8:1.

d *Summer*, Isa. 28:4.

e *Ivory*, 2 Chr. 9:17.

**1**

a *Women, wicked*, Prov. 31:10.

b *Bashan*, Num. 32:33.

c *Samaria*, Isa. 7:9.

d *Oppression, oppressors punished*, Eccl. 5:8.

e *Poor, oppression of*, Prov. 21:13.

**2**

f *Oath, attributed to God*, Num. 5:19.

g *God, holiness of*, Gen. 2:2.

h *Adversity, dispensation from God*, Psa. 10:6.

i *Wicked, punishment of*, Psa. 73:3.

**3**

1 R. V. one straight before her;

2 R. V. yourselves into Harmon, saith the Lord.

**4**

j *Irony, instances of*, Mark 12:14.

k *Beth-el, idolatry at*, Josh. 18:13.

l *Gilgal, prophecies concerning*, Josh. 4:19.

m *Tithes, customs relating to*, Num. 18:24.

3 R. V. every three days;

**5**

n *Leaven, used in idolatrous worship*, Lev. 23:17.

o *Offerings, in idolatrous worship*, Lev. 6:17.

**6**

p *Adversity, dispensation from God*, Psa. 10:6.

q *Famine*, vs. 6–9; 2 Kin. 8:1.

r *Divine Chastisement, corrective*, Job 33:19.

s *Judgments, design of*, Ex. 6:6.

t *Obduracy*, Prov. 29:1.

u *Adversity, obduracy in*, vs. 7–11; Psa. 10:6.

**7**

v *Drought, sent as a judgment*, Gen. 31:40.

w *Rain, withheld as a judgment*, 2 Sam. 1:21.

x *God, providence of*, vs. 7–12; Gen. 2:2.

y *Temporal Blessings, from God*, Psa. 103:2.

[z]blasting[G] and [a]mildew: when
your gardens and your [b]vine-
yards and your [c]fig trees and
your [d]olive trees increased, the
[e]palmerworm[G] devoured *them*:
[e,f]yet have ye [g]not returned unto
me, saith the LORD.
10 [h]I have sent among you the
[i]pestilence after the manner of
[j]Ē′ġȳpt: your young men have I
slain with the [k]sword, and have
taken away your horses; and I
have made the stink of your
camps to come up unto your nostrils: [e,f]yet have ye [g]not returned
unto me, saith the LORD.
11 [h]I have overthrown *some* of
you, as God overthrew [l]Sŏd′om
and [m]Gō-mŏr′rah, and ye were
as a firebrand plucked out of
the burning: [g]yet have ye not returned unto me, saith the LORD.
12 Therefore thus will I do unto thee, O Iṣ′ra-el: *and* because I
will do this unto thee, [n]prepare
to meet thy God, O Iṣ′ra-el.[S]
13 For, lo, he that [o]formeth
the mountains, and createth the
wind, and [p]declareth unto man
what *is* his thought, that maketh
the morning darkness, and
[q]treadeth upon the high places
of the earth, The LORD, The
God of hosts, *is* his name. [S Q]

## CHAPTER 5

*A lamentation for Israel. 4 An exhortation to repentance. 21 God rejects their hypocritical service.*

HEAR ye this [a]word which I
take up against you, *even* a
lamentation, O house of Iṣ′ra-el.
2 [a]The virgin of Iṣ′ra-el is
fallen; she shall no more rise:
she is forsaken upon her land;
*there is* none to raise her up.
3 For thus saith the Lord GOD;
The city that went out *by* a thousand shall leave an hundred, and
that which went forth *by* an hundred shall leave ten, to the house
of Iṣ′ra-el.
4 ¶ **For thus saith the LORD**
unto the house of Iṣ′ra-el,
[b,c,d]Seek ye me, and [e,f]ye [g]shall
live:
5 But [h]seek not [i]Bĕth′–el, nor
enter into [j]Gĭl′găl, and pass not
to [k]Bē′er–shē′bȧ: for Gĭl′găl shall
surely go into [l]captivity, and
Bĕth′–el shall come to nought.[G]
6 [b,c,d]Seek the LORD, and ye
shall live; lest he break out like
fire in the house of Jō′ṣeph, and
devour *it*, and *there be* none to
quench *it* in Bĕth′–el.
7 [m]Ye who [n]turn judgment[G] to
wormwood, and [1]leave off righteousness in the earth,
8 [b,c,d]*Seek him* that [o,p]maketh
the [2,q,r,s]seven [t]stars and [r]Ō-rī′-
ŏn, and turneth the shadow of
death into the morning, and
maketh the day dark with night:
that calleth for the waters of the
sea, and poureth them out upon
the face of the earth: [3]The LORD
*is* his name:
9 That [4]strengtheneth the
spoiled[G] against the strong, so that
the spoiled shall come against
the fortress.[S]
10 [u]They [v]hate him that rebuketh in the gate, and [u]they
abhor him that speaketh uprightly.[Q]
11 Forasmuch therefore as
[w]your [x]treading *is* upon the
[y]poor, and ye [z]take from him
burdens of wheat: ye have built
houses of hewn stone, but [a]ye
shall not dwell in them; ye have
planted pleasant [b]vineyards, but
[a]ye shall not drink wine of them.
12 For [c]I [d]know your manifold
transgressions and your mighty
sins: they afflict the just, they
take a [e]bribe, and they turn aside
the [f]poor in the gate *from their*
*right*.
13 Therefore the [g]prudent shall
keep silence in that time; for it *is*
an evil time.[Q]

**9**
*z Blasting*, 1 Kin. 8:37.
a Deut. 28:22; Hag. 2:17.
b *Vineyard*, Isa. 1:8.
c *Fig Tree, destroyed as a judgment*, Luke 13:6.
d *Olive*, Deut. 6:11.
e *Divine Chastisement, corrective*, Job 33:19.
f *Judgments, design of*, Ex. 6:6.
g *Obduracy*, Prov. 29:1.

**10**
h *Adversity, dispensation from God*, Psa. 10:6.
i *Plague*, Ex. 11:1.
j *Egypt*, Gen. 41:8.
k *War, as a judgment*, Judg. 3:2.

**11**
l *Sodom, destroyed*, Gen. 13:10.
m *Gomorrah, destroyed*, Gen. 13:10.

**12**
n *Repentance, enjoined*, Mark 1:4.

**13**
o *God, creator*, Gen. 2:2.
p *God, knowledge of*, Gen. 2:2.
q *God, power of*, Gen. 2:2.

**1**
a *Israel, prophecies concerning*, 1 Kin. 12:1.

**4**
b *Seekers*, Isa. 55:6.
c *Commandment, enjoining seeking the Lord*, Deut. 8:2.
d *Repentance, exhortation to*, vs. 4–6; Mark 1:4.
e *Promise, to seekers*, 2 Cor. 1:20.
f *Prayer, answer to, promised*, Acts 6:4.
g *Salvation*, Acts 16:17.

**5**
h *Idolatry, denounced*, 1 Sam. 15:23.
i *Beth-el, prophecies against*, Josh. 18:13.
j *Gilgal, prophecies concerning*, Josh. 4:19.
k *Beer-sheba*, Judg. 20:1.
l *Captivity, as a judgment*, Isa. 5:13.

**7**
m *Rulers, wicked*, Ex. 18:21.
n *Justice, perverted*, Deut. 33:21.
1 R. V. cast down righteousness to the earth;

**8**
o *God, creator*, Gen. 2:2.
p *Works of God*, Psa. 40:5.
q *Seven*, Gen. 7:2.
r Job 9:9; 38:31.
s *Astronomy*, Isa. 13:10.
t *Stars*, Judg. 5:20.
2 R. V. Pleiades
3 Am. R. V. Jehovah is his name;

**9**
4 R. V. that bringeth sudden destruction upon the strong, so that destruction cometh upon the fortress.

**10**
u *Wicked, described*, Psa. 73:3.
v *Reproof, hated*, Prov. 17:10.

**11**
w *Rulers, wicked*, Ex. 18:21.
x *Oppression, oppressors punished*, Eccl. 5:8.
y *Poor, oppression of*, Prov. 21:13.
z *Injustice, its gains unstable*, Isa. 26:10.

a *Wicked, punishment of*, Psa. 73:3.
b *Vineyard*, Isa. 1:8.

**12** c *God, knowledge of*, Gen. 2:2. d *Sin, known to God*, Rom. 5:12. e *Bribery, perverts justice*, 1 Sam. 8:3. f *Poor, oppression of*, Prov. 21:13. **13** g *Prudence, in restraining speech*, 2 Chr. 2:12.

14 [h,i]Seek good, and [j]not evil,
[k]that ye may live: and so the
LORD, the God of hosts, shall be
with you, as ye have spoken.
15 [l]Hate the evil, and love the
good, and [m]establish judgment[G]
in the gate: it may be that the
LORD God of hosts will be [n]gra-
cious unto the remnant of Jō′-
s̩eph.[Q]
16 [o]Therefore the LORD, the
God of hosts, the Lord, saith
thus; [p,q]Wailing *shall be* in all
streets; and they shall say in all
the highways, Alas! alas! and
they shall call the husbandman[G]
to mourning, and such as are
skilful of lamentation to wailing.
17 And in all [b]vineyards *shall*
*be* [p,q]wailing: for I will pass
through thee, saith the LORD.
18 [r]Woe unto you that desire
the [s]day of the LORD! to what
end *is* it for you? the day of
the LORD *is* [t]darkness, and not
light.
19 As if a man did flee from a
[u]lion, and a [o,v]bear met him; or
went into the house, and leaned
his hand on the wall, and a
[o,w]serpent bit him.
20 [o,r]*Shall* not the day of the
LORD *be* darkness, and not light?
even very dark, and no brightness in it?
21 ¶ I [x,y]hate, I despise your
[z]feast days, and I will [5,a]not
smell in your [b]solemn assemblies.
22 Though ye offer me [c]burnt
offerings and your [6,d]meat[G] offerings, I [a]will not accept *them*: neither will I regard the [e]peace offerings of your fat beasts.
23 [a]Take thou away from me
the noise of thy songs; for I will
not hear the melody of thy [f]viols.[G]
24 But [a,g]let judgment[G] run
down as waters, and righteousness as a mighty stream.
25 [h]Have[Q] ye offered unto me
sacrifices and offerings in the
wilderness forty years, O house
of Is̩′ra-el?
26 [h]But ye have borne [7]the tabernacle of your [i]Mō′lŏch and
Chī′un your images, the [j]star of
your god, which ye made to
yourselves.[Q]
27 Therefore will I cause you to
go into [k]captivity beyond [l]Dȧ-
măs′cus, saith the LORD, whose
name *is* The God of hosts.

## CHAPTER 6

*The pride and luxury of Israel. 7 Severe judgments threatened.*

[a,b]WOE to [c]them *that are* at
ease in Zī′ŏn, and [d]trust
in the mountain of Sȧ-mā′rĭ-ȧ,
[1]*which are* named chief of the
nations, to whom the house of
Is̩′ra-el came!
2 Pass ye unto *Căl′neh, and
see; and from thence[G] go ye to
[e]Hā′math the great: then go
down to [f]Găth of the [g]Phĭ-lĭs′-
tīne̩s: *be they* better than these
kingdoms? or their border greater than your border?
3 [b,d]Ye that put far away the
evil day, and cause the seat[G] of
violence to come near;
4 [b,d]That lie upon †beds of
[h]ivory, and stretch themselves
upon their couches, and [i]eat the
lambs out of the flock, and the
calves out of the midst of the
stall;
5 [b]That [2]chant to the sound of
the viol,[G] *and* invent to themselves instruments of [j]musick,
like [k]Dā′vid;
6 [b]That [l]drink [m]wine in bowls,
and [n]anoint themselves with the
chief [o]ointments: but they are
not grieved for the affliction of
Jō′s̩eph.
7 ¶ Therefore now shall they go
[p]captive with the first that go
captive, and the banquet of them

**14**
h *Seekers*, Isa. 55:6.
i *Commandment, enjoining holiness*, v. 15; Deut. 8:2.
j *Sin, repugnant to God*, Rom. 5:12.
k *Blessings, contingent upon obedience*, Deut. 11:26.

**15**
l *Evil, to be abhorred*, 1 Thess. 5:22.
m *Justice, enjoined*, Deut. 33:21.
n *God, mercy of*, Gen. 2:2.

**16**
o *Judgments, no escape from*, vs. 16–20; Ex. 6:6.
p *Weeping*, Ezra 3:13.
q *Adversity, despondency in*, Psa. 10:6.

**18**
r *Wicked, punishment of*, Psa. 73:3.
s *Day, times of adversity called day of the Lord*, Gen. 1:5.
t *Darkness, figurative*, Gen. 1:2.

**19**
u *Lion*, Mic. 5:8.
v *Bear*, 2 Sam. 17:8.
w *Serpent*, Num. 21:6.

**21**
x *Sin, repugnant to God*, Rom. 5:12.
y *Hypocrisy, abhorred of God*, Jas. 3:17.
z *Annual Feasts*, Num. 15:3.

a *Offerings, unavailing, when not accompanied by piety*, Lev. 6:17.
b *Worship, of hypocrites, repugnant to God*, vs. 21–24; Gen. 22:5.
5 R. V. take no delight

**22**
c *Offerings, burnt*, Lev. 6:17.
d *Offerings, meat*, Lev. 6:17.
e *Offerings, peace*, Lev. 6:17.
6 R. V. meal

**23**
f *Music, instruments of*, 2 Chr. 5:13.

**24**
g *Justice, enjoined*, Deut. 33:21.

**25**
h Acts 7:42, 43.

**26**
i Or, *Molech*, 1 Kin. 11:7.
j *Stars, worshiped*, Judg. 5:20.
7 R. V. Siccuth your king and Chiun

**27**
k *Captivity, as a judgment*, Isa. 5:13.
l *Damascus*, Isa. 8:4.

**1**
a *Idolatry, denounced*, 1 Sam. 15:23.
b *Rich, denounced*, vs. 1–6; Jas. 5:1.
c *Backsliders*, Jer. 3:22.
d *False Confidence*, Psa. 30:6.
1 R. V. the notable men of the chief

**2**
e *Hamath*, 1 Chr. 18:3.
f *Gath*, Josh. 11:22.
g *Philistines*, Gen. 26:14.

**4**
h *Ivory*, 2 Chr. 9:17.
i *Gluttony, deadens moral sensibilities*, Prov. 30:22.

**5**
j *Music, instruments of*, 2 Chr. 5:13.
k *David*, 1 Sam. 16:13.
2 R. V. sing idle songs to

**6**
l *Drunkenness*, Luke 21:34.
m *Wine*, Prov. 23:31.
n *Anointing, of the body*, Deut. 28:40.
o *Ointment*, Eccl. 7:1.

**7**
p *Captivity, as a judgment*, Isa. 5:13.

* **CALNEH**, called also CANNEH and CALNO. *A city of Assyria*, Gen. 10:10; Isa. 10:9; Ezek. 27:23; Amos 6:2.
† **BED.** *Made, of iron*, Deut. 3:11; *of ivory*, Amos 6:4; *of gold and silver*, Esth. 1:6. *Used at meals*, Amos 6:4. *Not exempt from execution for debt*, Prov. 22:27. *Perfumed*, Prov. 7:17. **Figurative**, Psa. 139:8.

**8**

*q Oath, attributed to God*, Num. 5:19.

*r Sin, repugnant to God*, Rom. 5:12.

*s Adversity, dispensation from God*, Psa. 10:6.

**10**

*Cremation*, Josh. 7:25.

**12**

*u Gall, figurative of oppression*, Job 16:13.

*v Wormwood, figurative*, Deut. 29:18.

**13**

*w False Confidence*, Psa. 30:6.

*x Self-righteousness*, Luke 18:11.

*y Horn, symbolical*, 1 Kin. 1:39.

**14**

*z Israel, prophecies concerning*, 1 Kin. 12:1.

3 R. V. brook of the Arabah.

**1**

*a Vision*, Acts 9:10.

*b Amos*, Amos 1:1.

*c Divine Chastisement*, Job 33:19.

*d Locusts*, Nah. 3:17.

that stretched themselves shall
be removed.
8 The Lord GOD hath [q]sworn
by himself, saith the LORD the
God of hosts, I [r]abhor the excellency of Jā′cob, and hate his
palaces: therefore will [s]I deliver up the city with all that is
therein.
9 And it shall come to pass, if
there remain ten men in one
house, that they shall die.
10 And a man's uncle shall take
him up, and he that [t]burneth
him, to bring out the bones out
of the house, and shall say unto
him that *is* by the sides of the
house, *Is there* yet *any* with thee?
and he shall say, No. Then
shall he say, Hold thy tongue:
for we may not make mention
of the name of the LORD.
11 For, behold, the LORD commandeth, and he will smite the
great house with breaches, and
the little house with clefts.
12 ¶ Shall horses run upon the
rock? will *one* plow *there* with
oxen? for ye have turned judgment into [u]gall, and the fruit of
righteousness into [v]hemlock:
13 Ye which [w]rejoice in a thing
of nought, which [x]say, Have we
not taken to us [y]horns by our
own strength?
14 But, behold, [z]I will raise up
against you a nation, O house of
Iṣ′ra-el, saith the LORD the God
of hosts; and they shall afflict
you from the entering in of Hē′-
math unto the [3]river of the wilderness.

## CHAPTER 7

*Judgments upon Israel symbolized by grasshoppers, 4 by fire, 7 and by a plumb line. 10 Amaziah complains of Amos to the king. 14 His defence. 16 Amaziah's doom foretold.*

THUS hath the Lord GOD
[a]shewed unto [b]me; and, behold, [c]he formed [d]grasshoppers
in the beginning of the shooting
up of the latter growth; and, lo,
*it was* the latter growth after the
king's [e]mowings.
2 And it came to pass, *that*
when they had made an end of
eating the grass of the land, then
[b]I [f]said, O Lord GOD, forgive,
I beseech thee: [g]by whom shall
Jā′cob arise? for he *is* small.
3 The LORD [h,i]repented for
this: [j]It shall not be, saith the
LORD.
4 ¶ Thus hath the Lord GOD
[a]shewed unto me: and, behold,
[c]the Lord GOD called to contend
by fire, and it devoured the great
deep, and [1]did eat up a part.
5 Then [f]said I, O Lord GOD,
cease, I beseech thee: [g]by whom
shall Jā′cob arise? for he *is*
small.
6 The LORD [h,i]repented for
this: [j]This also shall not be, saith
the Lord GOD.
7 ¶ Thus he [a]shewed me: and,
behold, the Lord stood upon a
wall *made* by a [k]plumbline, with
a plumbline in his hand.
8 And the LORD said unto me,
[b]Ā′mos, what [a]seest thou? And
I said, A [k]plumbline. Then said
the Lord, Behold, I will set a
plumbline in the midst of my
people Iṣ′ra-el: I will not again
pass by [l]them any more:
9 And the high places of Ī′ṣaac
shall be desolate, and the sanctuaries of Iṣ′ra-el shall be laid
waste; and I will rise against the
house of [m]Jĕr-o-bō′am with the
sword.
10 ¶ Then Ăm-a-zī′ah the
priest of Bĕth′-el sent to [m]Jĕr-o-
bō′am king of Iṣ′ra-el, [n,o]saying,
[b]Ā′mos hath conspired against
thee in the midst of the house of
Iṣ′ra-el: the land is not able to
bear all his words.
11 For thus [b]Ā′mos [n,o]saith,
[m]Jĕr-o-bō′am shall die by the
sword, and Iṣ′ra-el shall surely
be led away captive out of [2]their
own land.

*e* Psa. 72:6; 90:6; 129:7.

**2**

*f Adversity, prayer in*, Psa. 10:6.

*g Intercession, instances of*, vs. 2–6; Jer. 27:18.

**3**

*h Repentance, attributed to God*, Mark 1:4.

*i Anthropomorphisms*, Gen. 11:5.

*j God, mercy of*, Gen. 2:2.

**4**

1 R. V. would have eaten up the land.

**7**

*k* Zech. 4:10.

**8**

*l Reprobates*, 1 Cor. 9:27.

**9**

*m Jeroboam, prophecies concerning*, 1 Chr. 5:17

**10**

*n False Accusation*, 2 Tim. 3:3.

*o Minister, trials and persecutions of*, vs. 10–17; Rom. 15:16.

**11**

2 R. V. his land.

12 Also Ăm-a-zī′ah [o]said unto
Ā′mos, O thou seer, go, flee thee
away into the land of Jū′dah,
and there eat bread,[C] and prophesy there:
13 But prophesy not again any
more at [p]Bĕth′-el: for it *is*
the king's [3]chapel, and it *is* the
king's court.
14 ¶ Then answered [b]Ā′mos,
and said to Ăm-a-zī′ah, I *was* no
prophet, neither *was* I a prophet's son; but I *was* an herdman,
and a [4]gatherer of [q]sycomore
fruit:
15 And the LORD [r]took me as I
followed the flock, and the LORD
[s,t,u]said unto me, Go, prophesy
unto my people Ĭs′ra-el.
16 Now therefore hear thou
the word of the LORD: Thou
sayest, Prophesy not against
Ĭs′ra-el, and drop not *thy word*
against the house of Ī′saac.
17 Therefore [t,u]thus saith the
LORD; Thy wife shall be an
[v]harlot in the city, and [w]thy
sons and thy daughters shall
fall by the sword, and thy land
shall be divided by line; and
thou shalt die in a polluted[C]
land: and Ĭs′ra-el shall surely
go into [x]captivity forth[C] of his
land.

13
*p Beth-el*, Josh. 18:13.
3 R. V. sanctuary, and it is a royal house.

14
*q Sycomore*, 2 Chr. 1:15.
4 R. V. dresser of sycomore trees:

15
*r Call, personal*, Phil. 3:14.
*s Minister, charge delivered to*, Rom. 15:16.
*t Prophets, inspiration of*, Isa. 3:2.
*u Prophecies, inspired*, Dan. 9:24.

17
*v Harlot*, Prov. 7:10.
*w War, evils of*, Judg. 3:2.
*x Captivity, as a judgment*, Isa. 5:13.

## CHAPTER 8

*Israel's approaching end typified by a basket of summer fruit. 4 Oppressors of the poor reproved. 11 A famine of the word foretold.*

THUS hath the Lord GOD
[a]shewed unto [b]me: and behold a basket of [c]summer fruit.
2 And he said, [b]Ā′mos, what
[a]seest thou? And I said, A basket of [c]summer fruit. Then [d]said
the LORD unto me, The end is
come upon my people of Ĭs′-
ra-el; I will not again pass by
[e]them any more.
3 And [d]the songs of the temple
shall be howlings in that day,
saith the Lord GOD: [f]*there shall*
*be* many dead bodies in every
place; they shall cast *them* forth
with silence.
4 ¶ Hear this, O ye that [g]swal-
low up the needy, even to make
the [h]poor of the land to fail,
5 Saying, When will the *new
moon be gone, that we may sell
corn[C]? and the [i]sabbath, that we
may set forth wheat, [j]making the
[k]ephah[C] small, and the [l,m]shekel
great, and falsifying the balances
by deceit?
6 That we may [n]buy the [h]poor
for [o]silver, and the needy for a
pair of [p]shoes; *yea*, and [j]sell the
refuse of the wheat?
7 The LORD hath [q]sworn by
the excellency of Jā′cob, Surely
I will never forget any of their
works.[S]
8 [d,r]Shall not the land tremble
for this, and every one mourn
that dwelleth therein? and it
shall rise up wholly [1]as a flood;
and it shall be [2]cast out and
drowned, as *by* the flood of
[s]Ē′ġўpt.
9 And [d]it shall come to pass in
that day, saith the Lord GOD,
that [r]I will cause the [t]sun to [u]go
down at noon, and I will [v]darken
the earth in the clear day:[Q]
10 And [d,r]I will turn your
[w]feasts into mourning, and all
your [x]songs into lamentation;
and I will bring up [y]sackcloth
upon all loins, and [z]baldness upon every head; and I will make
it as the mourning of an only
*son*, and the end thereof as a
bitter day.
11 ¶ Behold, [a]the days come,
saith the Lord GOD, that I will
send a [b,c]famine in the land, not
a famine of bread, nor a [d]thirst
for water, but [e,f]of hearing the
[g]words of the LORD:
12 And they shall wander from
sea to sea, and from the north
even to the east, they shall run to

1
*a Vision*, Acts 9:10.
*b Amos*, Amos 1:1.
*c Summer, fruits of*, Isa. 28:4.

2
*d Israel, prophecies concerning*, 1 Kin. 12:1.
*e Reprobates*, 1 Cor. 9:27.

3
*f War, evils of*, Judg. 3:2.

4
*g Oppression*, vs. 5, 6; Eccl. 5:8.
*h Poor, oppression of*, Prov. 21:13.

5
*i Sabbath, irksome observance of*, Ex. 16:23.
*j Dishonesty, in wicked devices for gain*, Ezek. 22:13.
*k Measure, dry*, Deut. 25:15.
*l Shekel, corrupted*, Ex. 30:13.
*m Balances*, Prov. 11:1.

6
*n Servant, bought and sold*, Jer. 2:14.
*o Silver*, 1 Chr. 28.14
*p Shoe*, Josh. 5:15.

7
*q Oath, attributed to God*, Num. 5:19.

8
*r Judgments*, Ex. 6:6.
*s Egypt*, Gen. 41:8.
1 R. V. like the River;
2 R. V. troubled and sink again, like the River of

9
*t Sun*, Josh. 10:12.
*u Eclipse*, Isa. 13:10.
*v Darkness*, Gen. 1:5.

10
*w Feasts*, Mark 12:39.
*x Music*, 2 Chr. 5:13.
*y Sackcloth*, Isa. 15:3.
*z Baldness, artificial*, Lev. 21:5.

11
*a Israel, prophecies concerning*, 1 Kin. 12:1.
*b Famine, figurative*, 2 Kin. 8:1.
*c Judgments*, Ex. 6:6.
*d Thirst, figurative*, John 4:14.
*e Hunger, figurative of spiritual desire*, Matt. 5:6.
*f Spiritual Desire*, Psa. 42:1.
*g Word of God*, Psa. 119:9.

*** NEW MOON.** *Feast of*, Num. 10:10; 28:11-15; 1 Chr. 23:31; 2 Chr. 31:3. *Traffic at time of, suspended*, Amos 8:5.

12
*h Reprobates,* 1 Cor. 9:27.
14
*i Idol,* 1 Kin. 15:12.
*j Samaria,* 1 Kin. 16:24.
*k Dan, idolatry established at,* Judg. 18:29.
*l Beer-sheba,* Judg. 20:1.
*m Wicked, punishment of,* Psa. 73:3.
3 R. V. As thy God,
4 R. V. As the way

and fro to seek the word of the LORD, and [h]shall not find *it*.

13 In that day shall the fair virgins and young men faint for thirst.

14 They that swear by the [i]sin of [j]Sā-mā′rĭ-ȧ, and say, [3]Thy God, O [k]Dăn, liveth; and, [4]The manner[G] of [l]Bē-er–shē′bȧ liveth; even [h,m]they shall fall, and never rise up again.

## CHAPTER 9

*The certainty of Israel's desolation. 11 The restoring of the tabernacle of David.*

1
*a Vision, of Amos,* Acts 9:10.
*b Prophets, inspiration of.* Isa. 3:2.
*c Wicked, punishment of,* Psa. 73:3.
*d Judgments, no escape from,* Ex. 6:6.
1 Am. R. V. capitals that the thresholds may shake: and break them in pieces on the head of all of them;
2 R V. there shall not one of them flee away, and there shall not one of them escape.
2
*e Hell,* Mark 9:43.
*f God, knowledge of,* Gen. 2:2.
*g Sin, known to God,* Rom. 5:12.
3
*h Carmel,* Jer. 46:18.
4
*i Captivity,* Isa. 5:13.
*j War, as a judgment,* Judg. 3:2.
5
*k God, power of,* Gen. 2:2.
*l Egypt,* Gen. 41:8.
3 R. V. the River;
4 R. V. sink again, like the River of Egypt;
6
*m God, creator,* Gen. 2:2.

I [a]SAW the Lord standing upon the altar: and he [b]said, Smite the [1]lintel[G] of the door, that the posts may shake: and cut them in the head, all of them; and I will [c]slay the last of them with the sword: [2]he that fleeth of them [d]shall not flee away, and he that escapeth of them [d]shall not be delivered.[Q]

2 [S]Though they dig into [e]hell,[G] [d,f,g]thence[G] shall mine hand take them; though they climb up to heaven, [d,f,g]thence[G] will I bring them down:

3 And though they hide themselves in the top of [h]Cär′mel, I will [f,g]search and [c,d]take them out thence[G]; and though they be hid from my sight in the bottom of the sea, [f,g]thence[G] will I command the serpent, and [d]he shall [c]bite them:[S]

4 And though they go into [i]captivity before their enemies, [f,g]thence[G] will I command the [j]sword, and [c,d]it shall slay them: and I will set mine eyes upon them for evil, and not for good.

5 And the [k]Lord GOD of hosts *is* he that toucheth the land, and it shall melt, and all that dwell therein shall mourn: and it shall rise up wholly like [3]a flood; and shall [4]be drowned, as *by* the flood of [l]Ē′ġy̆pt.[S]

6 *It is* [k]he that [m]**buildeth** his [5]stories in the heaven, and hath founded his [6]troop in the earth; he that calleth for the waters of the sea, and [n,o]poureth them out upon the face of the earth: The LORD *is* his name.

7 *Are* ye not as children of the [p]Ē-thĭ-ō′pĭ-anș unto me, O children of Ĭș′ra-el? saith the LORD. Have not I [q]brought up [r]Ĭș′ra-el out of the land of [l]Ē′ġy̆pt? and the [s]Phĭ-lĭs′tĭneș from [t]Căph′tôr, and the [u]Sy̆r′ĭ-anș from [v]Kĭr?

8 Behold, the [w,x]eyes of the Lord GOD *are* upon the sinful kingdom, and [y]I will [z]destroy it from off the face of the earth; saving[G] that [a]I will not utterly destroy the house of Jā′cob, saith the LORD.

9 For, lo, I will command, and [b]I will sift the house of Ĭș′ra-el among all nations, like as *corn*[G] is sifted in a [c]sieve, yet shall not the least grain[G] fall upon the earth.[S Q]

10 All the sinners of my people shall [d]die by the [e]sword, which [f,g]say, The evil shall not overtake nor prevent[G] us.

11 ¶ [b,h]In that[Q] day will I raise up the tabernacle of Dā′vid that is fallen, and close up the breaches thereof; and I will raise up his ruins, and I will build it as in the days of old:

12 That they may possess the remnant of [i]Ē′dom, and of all the [7]heathen[G], which are called by my name[G], saith the LORD that doeth this.[Q]

13 Behold, the days come, saith the LORD, [j,k]that the plowman shall overtake the reaper, and the treader of grapes him that soweth seed; and the mountains shall drop sweet wine, and all the hills shall melt.[S]

14 And [l]I will [j]bring again the captivity of my people of Ĭș′ra-el, and [m]they shall build the waste cities, and inhabit *them*; and they shall plant vineyards,

*n Rain,* 2 Sam. 1:21.
*o Meteorology,* Matt. 16:2.
5 R. V. chambers
6 R. V. vault upon
7
*p Ethiopia,* Isa. 18:1.
*q God, providence of,* Gen. 2:2.
*r Israel,* Ex. 4:22.
*s Philistines,* Gen. 26:14.
*t* Or, *Caphtorim,* Deut. 2:23.
*u Syria,* 2 Kin. 6:23.
*v Kir,* 2 Kin. 16:9.
8
*w Eye, figurative of God's justice,* Matt. 6:22.
*x Government, God in,* Isa. 22:21.
*y Nation, judgments denounced against,* Isa. 2:4.
*z Sin, punishment of,* Rom. 5:12.
*a God, mercy of,* Gen. 2:2.
9
*b Israel, prophecies concerning,* 1 Kin. 12:1.
*c* Isa. 30:28; Luke 22:31.
10
*d Death, of the wicked,* Num. 23:10.
*e War, as a judgment,* Judg. 3:2.
*f False Confidence,* Psa. 30:6.
*g Spiritual Blindness,* 2 Cor. 4:4.
11
*h* Acts 15:16–18.
12
*i Edomites, prophecies concerning,* 2 Kin. 8:21.
7 R. V. nations,
13
*j God, providence of,* Gen. 2:2.
*k Prosperity,* Eccl. 7:14.
14
*l Israel, prophecies concerning restoration of,* 1 Kin. 12:1.
*m Temporal Blessings, from God,* Psa. 103:2.

and drink the wine thereof; they shall also make gardens, and eat the fruit of them.

15 And I will [i,m]plant them upon their land, and they shall no more be pulled up out of their land which I have given them, saith the LORD thy God.

THE

# BOOK OF OBADIAH

*Judgments upon Edom on account of its pride. 10 Edom's violence toward Jacob the cause of its downfall. 15 The judgments of the Lord near at hand. 16 Retribution upon the heathen. 17 Judah's deliverance.*

THE [a]vision of Ō-ba-dī'ah. [b]Thus saith the Lord GOD concerning *,[c]Ē'dom; We have heard [1]a rumour from the LORD, and an [d]ambassador is sent among the [2]heathen, Arise ye, and let us rise up against her in battle.

2 ¶ Behold, I have made [c]thee small among the [2]heathen: thou art greatly despised.

3 The [e,f]pride of thine heart hath deceived thee, thou that dwellest in the clefts of the rock, whose habitation *is* high; that [g,h]saith in his heart, Who shall bring me down to the ground?

4 [c]Though thou [f]exalt *thyself* as the eagle, and though thou set thy nest among the stars, thence will I [i]bring thee down, saith the LORD.

5 If [j]thieves came to thee, if robbers by night, (how art thou cut off!) would they not have stolen till they had enough? if the grapegatherers came to thee, would they not leave *some* grapes?

6 ¶ [c]How are *the things* of Ē'-sau searched out! *how* are his hidden [3]things sought up!

7 All the men of thy [k]confederacy have brought thee *even* to the border: the [l]men that were at peace with thee have [m,n]deceived thee, *and* prevailed against thee; *they that eat* thy bread [m,n]have laid a [4]wound under thee: *there is* none understanding in him.

8 [c,o]Shall I not in that day, saith the LORD, even destroy the [p]wise *men* out of *Ē'dom, and understanding out of the mount of Ē'sau?

9 And thy mighty *men*, O [q]Tē'-man, shall be dismayed, to the end that [c]every one of the mount of Ē'sau may be cut off by slaughter.

10 [c]For *thy* violence against thy brother [r]Jā'cob shame shall cover thee, and thou shalt be cut off for ever.

11 In the day that thou stoodest on the other side, in the day that the strangers carried [5]away captive his forces, and foreigners entered into his gates, and cast lots upon Jē-ru'-sā-lĕm, even thou *wast* as one of them.

12 But [6]thou shouldest not have looked on the day of thy brother in the day that he became a stranger; neither shouldest thou have rejoiced over the children of Jū'dah in the day of their destruction; neither shouldest thou have spoken proudly in the day of distress.

1
a *Vision*, Acts 9:10.
b *Prophets, inspiration of*, Isa. 3:2.
c *Edomites, prophecies concerning*, vs. 1–12; 2 Kin. 8:21.
d *Ambassadors, figurative*, Josh. 9:4.
1 R. V. tidings
2 R. V. nations,

3
e *Pride*, Prov. 16:18.
f *Self-exaltation*, Luke 14:11.
g *Delusion*, 2 Thess. 2:11.
h *False Confidence*, Psa. 30:6.

4
i *Adversity, dispensation from God*, Psa. 10:6.

5
j *Thieves, figurative*, Deut. 24:7.

6
3 R. V. treasures

7
k *Alliances*, Josh. 9:15.
l *Friends, false*, Ex. 33:11.
m *Deception*, Josh. 9:4.
n *Treachery*, 2 Kin. 9:23.
4 R. V. snare

8
o *Nation, judgments denounced against*, Isa. 2:4.
p *Wisdom, worldly*, Prov. 2:2.

9
q *Teman, prophecies concerning*, Jer. 49:7.

10
r *Israel*, Ex. 4:22.

11
5 R. V. away his substance.

12
6 R. V. look not thou on the day of thy brother in the day of his disaster, and rejoice not over the children of Judah in the day of their destruction; neither speak proudly in the day of distress.

* **EDOM** (*red*), called also IDUMEA; the country extending from Elanitic Gulf to the Red Sea. *Occupied by the descendants of Esau*, Gen. 32:3; 36:16, 17, 21; Jer. 40:11. *Noted for its wise men*, Obad. 8. *Sins of*, Obad. 10–14. *Prophecies concerning*, Psa. 60:8, 9; Jer. 25:15, 16, 21; 27:1–11; Dan. 11:41; Obad. 1–21. *Wilderness of*, 2 Kin. 3:8. See footnote, EDOMITES, 2 Kin. 8:21.

13 [7]Thou shouldest not have
entered into the gate of my people in the day of their calamity;
yea, [8]thou shouldest not have
looked on their affliction in the
day of their calamity, [9]nor have
laid *hands* on their substance in
the day of their calamity;
14 [10]Neither shouldest thou
have stood in the crossway, to
cut off those of his that did escape; [11]neither shouldest thou
have delivered up those of his
that did remain in the day of
distress.
15 For the [s]day of the LORD *is*
near upon all the [12]heathen[c]: as
thou hast done, [t]it shall be done
unto thee: thy [13,u]reward shall
return upon thine own head.
16 For as ye have drunk upon
my holy mountain, *so* shall all
the [12]heathen[c] drink continually,
yea, they shall drink, and they
shall swallow down, and they
shall be as though they had not
been.
17 ¶ But upon mount [v]Zī′ŏn
shall be [14]deliverance, and there
shall be holiness; and the [w]house
of Jā′cob shall possess their possessions.
18 And the house of Jā′cob
shall be a fire, and the house of
Jō′ṣeph a flame, and the [c]house
of Ē′sa̤u for stubble, and [x]they
shall kindle in them, and devour them; and there shall not
be *any* remaining of the house
of Ē′sa̤u; for the LORD hath
spoken *it*.
19 And [w]*they of* the south shall
possess the mount of Ē′sa̤u; and
*they of* the plain the Phĭ-lĭs′tĭneṣ:
and they shall possess the fields
of Ē′phră-ĭm, and the fields of
Sā-mā′rĭ-ȧ: and Bĕn′ja-mĭn *shall
possess* Gĭl′e-ăd.
20 And the captivity[c] of this
host of the children of Ĭṣ′ra-el
*shall possess* that of the Cā′-
năan-ītes, *even* unto Zăr′e-phăth;
and the captivity[c] of Jē-ru̇′sā-
lĕm, which *is* in Sĕph′a-răd,
shall possess the cities of the
south.
21 [y,z]And saviours[c] shall come
up on mount Zī′ŏn to judge the
mount of Ē′sa̤u; and the kingdom shall be the LORD's.[Q]

13
7 R. V. Enter not into
8 R. V. look not thou on
9 R. V. neither lay ye hands

14
10 R. V. And stand thou not in
11 R. V. and deliver not up those of his that remain

15
*s Day, times of adversity called day of the Lord,* Gen. 1:5.
*t Judgment, according to opportunity and works,* 1 Pet. 1:17.
*u Sin, retroactive,* Rom. 5:12.
12 R. V. nations:
13 R. V. dealing
**B.C. 585?**

17
*v Zion, restoration of, promised,* 2 Sam. 5:7.
*w Jews, prophecies concerning,* Neh. 4:2.
14 R. V. those that escape, and it shall be holy;

18
*x Agency, in executing judgments* Mark 1:17.

21
*y Jews, prophecies concerning,* Neh 4:2.
*z Edomites, prophecies concerning,* 2 Kin. 8:21.

---

THE

# BOOK OF JONAH

## CHAPTER 1

*Jonah, sent to Nineveh, flees to Tarshish. 4 He is overtaken by a tempest, 11 thrown into the sea, 17 and swallowed by a great fish.*

NOW the [a]word of the LORD
[b]came unto *Jō′nah the son
of [c]Ă-mĭt′ta-ī, saying,
2 [a]Arise, [d]go to †Nĭn′e-veh,
that great[c] city, and [e]cry[c] against
it; for their [f]wickedness is come
up before me.
3 But *Jō′nah rose up [g]to
[h,i]flee unto [j]Tär′shish from the
[k]presence[c] of the LORD, and went
down to [l]Jŏp′pȧ; and he found
a [m]ship going to Tär′shish: [n]so he
paid the fare thereof, and went
down into it, to go with them
unto Tär′shish from the presence[c] of the LORD.

1
*a Minister, call of,* Rom. 15:16.
*b Prophets, inspiration of,* Isa. 3:2.
*c* 2 Kin. 14:25.

2
*d Missions,* Matt. 28:19.
*e Minister, duties of,* Rom. 15:16.
*f Sin, repugnant to God,* Rom. 5:12.

3
*g Minister, unfaithful,* Rom. 15:16.
*h Disobedience to God,* Eph. 5:6.
*i Duty, escape from, sought by Jonah,* Eccl. 12:13.
*j Tarshish,* 2 Chr. 20:36.

*k God, presence of,* Gen. 2:2. *l Joppa,* 2 Chr. 2:16. *m Ship,* 2 Chr. 8:18.
*n Commerce, transportation of passengers,* 1 Kin. 10:15.

* **JONAH,** called also JONAS. *A prophet of Israel,* 2 Kin. 14:25. *Sent by God to warn Nineveh,* Jonah 1:1, 2. *Disobedience and punishment of,* Jonah 1:3–17. *Repentance and deliverance of,* Jonah 2. *Brought Ninevites to repentance,* Jonah 3; Matt. 12:41; Luke 11:32. *Displeased with God's mercy to Nineveh; reproved,* Jonah 4. *His preaching and the repentance of the Ninevites contrasted with the unbelieving Jews,* Matt. 12:39–41; 16:4; Luke 11:29, 30.

† **NINEVEH.** *Capital of the Assyrian empire,* Gen. 10: 11, 12. *Contained a population of children, of upwards of one hundred and twenty thousand, when Jonah preached,* Jonah 4:11. *Extent of,* Jonah 3:4. *Sennacherib in,* 2 Kin. 19:36, 37; Isa. 37:37, 38. *Jonah preaches to,* Jonah 1:1, 2; 3. *Nahum prophesies against,* Nah. chapters 1–3. *Zephaniah foretells the desolation of,* Zeph. 2:13–15. *Ninevites at the judgment,* Matt. 12:41; Luke 11:32.

4
o *Adversity, dispensation from God*, Psa. 10:6.
p *Wind*, Job 37:17.
q *Mediterranean Sea*, Ex. 23:31.

5
r *Mariner, perils of*, Ezek. 27:27.
s *Idolatry*, 1 Sam. 15:23.

6
t *Intercession, solicited*, Jer. 27:18.
u *Adversity, prayer in*, Psa. 10:6.

7
v *Lot*, Esth. 3:7.

9
w *Hebrew*, Gen. 40:15.
x *Fear of God*, Acts 9:31.
y *God, creator*, Gen. 2:2.
z *Sea*, Jer. 5:22.

10
a *Minister, unfaithful*, Rom. 15:16.
b *Duty, escape from, sought by Jonah*, Eccl. 12:13.
c *God, presence of*, Gen. 2:2.

12
d *Conscience, guilty*, Acts 23:1.
e *Self-condemnation*, Job 9:20.

4 ¶ But the LORD [o]sent out a great [p]wind into the [q]sea, and there was a mighty tempest in the sea, so that the ship was like to be broken.

5 Then the [r]mariners were afraid, and [s]cried every man unto his god, and cast forth the wares that *were* in the [m]ship into the sea, to lighten *it* of them. But *,[q]Jō'nah was gone down into the sides of the ship; and he lay, and was fast asleep.

6 So the shipmaster came to him, and said unto him, What meanest thou, O sleeper? arise, [t,u]call upon thy God, if so be that God will think upon us, that we perish not.

7 And they said every one to his fellow, Come, and let us cast [v]lots, that we may know for whose cause this evil *is* upon us. So they cast lots, and the lot fell upon *Jō'nah.

8 Then said they unto him, Tell us, we pray thee, for whose cause this evil *is* upon us; What *is* thine occupation? and whence comest thou? what *is* thy country? and of what people *art* thou?

9 And he said unto them, I *am* an [w]Hē'brew; and I [x]fear the LORD, the God of heaven, which hath [y]made the [z]sea and the dry *land*.

10 Then were the men exceedingly afraid, and said unto him, Why hast thou done this? For the men knew that [a]he [b]fled from the [c]presence of the LORD, because he had told them.

11 Then said they unto him, What shall we do unto thee, that the sea may be calm unto us? for the sea wrought, and was tempestuous.

12 And he said unto them, [d,e]Take me up, and cast me forth into the sea; so shall the sea be calm unto you: for I know that for my sake this great tempest *is* upon you.

13 Nevertheless the men rowed hard to bring *it* to the land; but they could not: for the sea wrought, and was tempestuous against them.

14 Wherefore they [f,g]cried unto the LORD, and said, We beseech thee, O LORD, we beseech thee, let us not perish for this man's life, and lay not upon us innocent blood: for thou, O LORD, hast done as it pleased thee.

15 So they took up *Jō'nah, and cast him forth into the sea: and [h]the sea ceased from her raging.

16 [h]Then the men [i]feared the LORD exceedingly, and [j]offered a sacrifice unto the LORD, and made [k]vows.

17 ¶ Now the LORD had prepared a great [l]fish to swallow up *,[m]Jō'nah. And Jō'nah was in the belly of the fish three days and three nights.

## CHAPTER 2

*Jonah's prayer. 10 His deliverance.*

[a,b]THEN [c]Jō'nah [d,e]prayed unto the LORD his God out of the [f]fish's belly,

2 And said, [a,b,c]I [d]cried by reason of mine [e]affliction unto the LORD, and [g]he heard me; out of the belly of hell cried I, *and* thou heardest my voice.

3 For thou hadst [h]cast me into the deep, in the midst of the seas; and the floods compassed me about: all thy billows and thy waves passed over me.

4 Then I [d,e]said, I am cast out of thy sight; yet I will [b,i]look again toward thy [j]holy temple.

5 The waters compassed me about, *even* to the soul: the [1]depth closed me round about, the weeds were wrapped about my head.

6 [d,e]I went down to the bottoms of the mountains; the earth with

14
f *Prayer, in adversity*, Acts 6:4.
g *Adversity, prayer in*, Psa. 10:6.

15
h *Miracles, convincing effect of*, v. 16; Luke 23:8.

16
i *Fear of God*, Acts 9:31.
j *Thankfulness, to God*, Acts 24:3.
k *Vow*, Num. 30:2.

17
l *Fish, miracles connected with*, Matt. 17:27.
m *Types, of the Savior*, Heb. 10:1.

1
a *Adversity, benefits of*, vs. 1–9; Psa. 10:6.
b *Repentance, instances of*, Mark 1:4.
c *Jonah*, Jonah 1:1.
d *Prayer, in adversity*, Acts 6:4.
e *Adversity, prayer in*, vs. 1–9; Psa. 10:6.
f *Fish, miracles connected with*, vs. 1–10; Matt. 17:27.

2
g *Prayer, answered*, Acts 6:4.

3
h *Adversity, dispensation from God*, Psa. 10:6.

4
i *Backsliders, return of*, Jer. 3:22.
j *Temple, Solomon's*, 1 Kin. 6:17.

5
1 R. V. deep was round about me.

her bars [2]*was* about me for ever:
yet hast [k]thou brought up my
life from [3]corruption,[G] O LORD
my God.
7 When my soul fainted within
me [a]I remembered the LORD:
and my [d]prayer came in unto
thee, into thine [j]holy temple.
8 They that observe lying vanities forsake their own mercy.
9 But [l]I will sacrifice unto thee
with the voice of [m]thanksgiv-
ing; I will pay *that* that I have
[n]vowed. [o]Salvation[G] *is* of the
LORD.[S]
10 ¶ And the LORD spake unto
the [f]fish, and [p,q]it vomited out
[c]Jō′nah upon the dry *land*.[S]

## CHAPTER 3

*Jonah, sent again, preaches to the Ninevites.* 5 *Their repentance.* 10 *God spares them.*

AND the [a]word of the LORD
[b]came unto [c]Jō′nah the
second time, saying,
2 [a]Arise, [d]go unto [e]Nĭn′e-veh,
that great city, and [f]preach[G] unto
it the preaching[G] that I bid thee.
3 [g]So [c,h]Jō′nah arose, and went
unto [e]Nĭn′e-veh, according to the
word of the LORD. Now Nĭn′-
e-veh was an exceeding great city
of three [i]days' journey.
4 And [c]Jō′nah began to enter
into the city a [i]day's journey, and
[h,j]he cried, and said, Yet *forty
days, and [e]Nĭn′e-veh shall be
overthrown.
5 ¶ [k,l,m]So the people of [e]Nĭn′-
e-veh [n]believed God, and [o]pro-
claimed a [p]fast, and put on
[q]sackcloth, from the greatest of
them even to the least of them.[Q]
6 [1]For word came unto the [r]king
of [e]Nĭn′e-veh, and he arose from
his throne, and he laid his robe
from him, and [o]covered *him* with
[q]sackcloth, and sat in [s]ashes.[Q]
7 And he caused *it* to be [t]pro-
claimed and published through
[e]Nĭn′e-veh by the decree of the
king and his nobles, saying, [p]Let
neither man nor beast, herd nor
flock, taste any thing: let them
not feed, nor drink water:
8 But let man and beast be covered with [q]sackcloth, and [u]cry
mightily unto God: yea, let them
[v]turn every one from his evil
way, and from the violence that
*is* in their hands.[Q]
9 Who can tell *if* God will turn
and repent, and turn away from
his fierce [w]anger, that we perish
not?
10 And God saw their works,
that they [o]turned from their evil
way; and God [x]repented of the
evil, that he had said that he
would do unto them; and [y]he
did *it* not.[Q]

## CHAPTER 4

*Jonah's repinings at God's mercy to Nineveh,* 6 *and at the withering of his gourd.* 9 *He is rebuked.*

BUT it displeased [a]Jō′nah exceedingly, and he was very
[b]angry.
2 And he [c]prayed unto the
LORD, and [d]said, I pray thee, O
LORD, *was* not this my saying,
when I was yet in my country?
Therefore I fled before unto
[e]Tär′shish: for I knew that thou
*art* a gracious God, and [f]merci-
ful, [g]slow to anger, and of great
kindness,[S] and repentest thee of
the evil.
3 Therefore now, O LORD,
[h]take, I beseech thee, my life
from me; for [i,j]*it is* better for me
to die than to live.
4 ¶ Then said the LORD, Doest
thou well to be [b]angry?
5 So [a]Jō′nah went out of the

6
k *God, preserver,* Gen. 2:2.
2 R. V. closed upon me for ever:
3 R. V. the pit,
9
l *Thankfulness, exemplified,* Acts 24:3.
m *Praise,* Psa. 150:1.
n *Vows,* Num. 30:2.
o *God, savior,* Gen. 2:2.
10
p *Miracles,* Luke 23:8.
q *Resurrection, typified,* 1 Cor. 15:12.

1
a *Minister, call of,* Rom. 15:16.
b *Prophets, inspiration of,* Isa. 3:2.
c *Jonah,* Jonah 1:1.
2
d *Missions,* vs. 1–8; Matt. 28:19.
e *Nineveh,* Jonah 1:2.
f *Preaching,* Matt. 9:35.
3
g *Obedience, instances of,* Heb. 5:8.
h *Minister, faithful,* Rom. 15:16.
i *Day's Journey,* 1 Kin. 19:4.
4
j *Orator,* Acts 24:1.
5
k *Preaching, effective,* Matt. 9:35.
l *Minister, success attending,* Rom. 15:16.
m *Religious Revivals,* vs. 4–10; Hab. 3:2.
n *Faith, instances of,* Mark 11:22.
o *Repentance, instances of,* Mark 1:4.
p *Fasting,* Zech. 8:19.
q *Sackcloth,* Isa. 15:3.
6
r *Rulers, righteous,* Ex. 18:21.
s *Ashes, repenting in,* Num. 19:9.
1 R. V. And the tidings reached the king

7
t *Proclamation, imperial,* 1 Kin. 15:22.
8
u *Prayer, enjoined,* Acts 6:4.
v *Repentance, enjoined,* Mark 1:4.
9
w *Anger of God,* 2 Kin. 13:3.
10
x *Repentance, attributed to God,* Mark 1:4.
y *God, mercy of,* Gen. 2:2.

1
a *Jonah,* Jonah 1:1.
b *Anger, instances of,* Psa. 37:8.
2
c *Murmuring, against God,* Num. 14:2.
d *Presumption, instances of,* Psa. 19:13.
e *Tarshish,* 2 Chr. 20:36.
f *God, mercy of,* Gen. 2:2.
g *God, longsuffering of.* Gen. 2:2.
3
h *Death, desired,* Num. 23:10.
i *Life, weary of,* Eccl. 8:15.
j *Despondency,* Eccl. 2:20.

*** FORTY.** Remarkable coincidences in the number; believed by some to be mystical.
**Days:** *Of rain, at the time of the flood,* Gen. 7:17. *Of flood, before sending forth the raven,* Gen. 8:6. *For embalming,* Gen. 50:3. *Spies in the land of promise,* Num. 13:25. *Of probation given to the Ninevites,* Jonah 3:4. *Christ's stay after the resurrection,* Acts 1:3. *Symbolical,* Ezek. 4:6.
**Of fasting:** *By Moses,* Ex. 24:18; 34:28; Deut. 9:9, 25; *by Elijah,* 1 Kin. 19:8; *by Jesus,* Matt. 4:2; Mark 1:13; Luke 4:1, 2.
**Years:** *Wanderings of the Israelites in the wilderness,* Ex. 16:35; Num. 14:34. *Peace in Israel,* Judg. 3:11; 5:31; 8:28. *Egypt to be desolated,* Ezek. 29:11.
**Stripes:** *Administered in punishing criminals,* Deut. 25:3; 2 Cor. 11:24.

city, and sat on the east side of
the city, and there made him a
[k]booth, and sat under it in the
shadow, till he might see what
would become of the city.
6 And the LORD God [l,l]pre-
pared a [m,n]gourd, and made *it* to
come up over [a]Jō′nah, that it
might be a shadow over his head,
to deliver him from his grief. So
Jō′nah was exceeding glad of the
gourd.[s]
7 But God prepared a +worm
when the morning rose the next
day, and it smote[c] the [m]gourd
that it withered.[s]
8 And it came to pass, when
the sun did arise, that God prepared a [1]vehement[c] [o]east wind;
and the sun beat upon the head
of [a]Jō′nah, that he fainted, and
[2,h,i]wished in himself to die, and
said, [i]*It is* better for me to die
than to live.
9 And God said to [a]Jō′nah,
Doest thou well to be [b]angry for
the gourd? And he said, I do
well to be angry, *even* unto
death.[Q]
10 Then [p]said the LORD, Thou
hast had[c] pity on the gourd, for
the which thou hast not laboured, neither madest it grow;
which came up in a night, and
perished in a night:
11 [p]And should not **I** spare
[q]Nĭn′e-veh, that great city,
wherein are more than sixscore
thousand persons that cannot
discern between their right hand
and their left hand; and *also*
much [r]cattle?

5
*k Booth, made of boughs,* Lev. 23:42.

6
*l God, providence of,* Gen. 2:2.
*m* 2 Kin. 4:39.
*n Temporal Blessings, from God,* Psa. 103:2.

8
*o Wind, east,* Job 37:17.
1 R. V. sultry

2 R. V. requested for himself that he might

10
*p God, condescension of, in reasoning with Jonah,* Gen. 2:2.

11
*q Nineveh,* Jonah 1:2.
*r Animals, God's care of,* Jer. 27:5.

THE

# BOOK OF MICAH

## CHAPTER 1

*The date of Micah's prophecy. 2 Judgments upon Israel and Judah for idolatry. 10 An exhortation to mourning.*

THE word of the LORD that
[a]came to *Mī′cah the Mō′-
ras-thīte in the days of [b]Jō′-
tham, [c]Ā′hăz, *and* [d]Hĕz-e-kī′ah,
kings of [e]Jū′dah, which he saw
concerning [f,g]Să-mā′rĭ-ȧ and [h]Jē-
ru′să-lĕm.
2 ¶Hear, all ye [1]people; hearken,
O earth, and all that therein is:
and let the Lord GOD be witness against you, the Lord from
his holy temple.
3 For,[s] behold, [i]the LORD cometh forth out of his place, and
will come down, and tread upon
the high places of the earth.
4 And [i]the [j]mountains shall be
molten[c] under him, and the valleys shall be cleft, as wax before
the fire, *and* as the waters *that*
*are* poured down a steep place.[s]
5 [k]For the transgression of Jā′-
cob *is* all this, and for the sins of
the house of Iș′ra-el. What *is*
the transgression of Jā′cob? *is it*
not [f]Să-mā′rĭ-ȧ? and what *are*
the high places of Jū′dah? *are*
*they* not [h]Jē-ru′să-lĕm?
6 Therefore [i]I will make [f,g]Să-
mā′rĭ-ȧ as an heap of the field,
*and* as plantings of a vineyard:
and I will pour down the stones
thereof into the valley, and I will
discover[c] the foundations thereof.
7 And [i]all the [l]graven[c] images[c]
thereof shall be beaten to pieces,
and all the [m]hires[c] thereof shall

1
*a Prophets, inspiration of,* Isa. 3:2.
*b Jotham,* 2 Kin. 15:5.
*c Ahaz,* 2 Kin. 15:38.
*d Hezekiah,* 2 Kin. 16:20.
*e Judah, prophecies concerning,* 2 Chr. 11:17.
*f Samaria,* 1 Kin. 16:24.
*g Israel, prophecies concerning,* 1 Kin. 12:1.
*h Jerusalem, prophecies against,* Judg. 19:10.

2
1 R. V. peoples,

3
*i Nation, judgments denounced against,* Isa. 2:4.

4
*j Mountain,* Mic. 7:12.

5
*k Sin, punishment of,* Rom. 5:12.

6
*l Idolatry, objects of,* 1 Sam. 15:23.
*m Idolatry, wicked practices of,* 1 Sam. 15:23.

+ **WORM**, Ex. 16:20, 24; Deut. 28:39; Jonah 4:7. *Herod, eaten of,* Acts 12:23.
**Figurative**, Job 25:6; Isa. 41:14; 66:24. *Of remorse,* Mark 9:44, 46, 48 (vs. 44, 46 are omitted in R. V.).
* **MICAH**. *One of the minor prophets,* Jer. 26:18, 19; Mic. 1:1. *Denounces, the idolatry of his times,* Mic. 1; *the oppressions of the covetous,* Mic. 2:1-11. *Foretells, the restoration of Israel,* Mic. 2:12, 13; *the injustice of judges and the falsehoods of false prophets,* Mic. 3. *Foretells the coming of the Messiah,* Mic. 4:5. *Denounces oppressions, frauds, and other abominations,* Mic. 6. *Laments the state of Zion, and foretells the triumphs, righteousness, and the mercies of God,* Mic. 7.

be burned with the fire, and all
the idols thereof will I lay desolate: for she gathered *it* of the
hire[G] of an harlot, and they shall
return to the hire[G] of an harlot.
8 Therefore I will [n]wail and
howl, I will go stripped and
naked: I will make a wailing
like the [2,o]dragons, and mourning as the [3,p]owls.
9 For her [k]wound *is* incurable;
for it is come unto Jū'dah; he is
come unto the gate of my people, *even* to [h]Jē-ru̧'să-lĕm.
10 Declare ye *it* not at [q]Găth,
weep ye not at all: [4]in the house of
Ăph'rah roll thyself in the dust.
11 Pass ye away, thou inhabitant of [5]Sā'phĭr, having thy
shame naked: the inhabitant of
[r]Zā'a-năn [6]came not forth in the
mourning of Bĕth–ē'zel; he shall
receive of you his standing.
12 For the inhabitant of Mā'roth
[7]waited carefully[G] for good: [8]but
[s]evil came down from the LORD
unto the gate of Jē-ru̧'să-lĕm.
13 O thou inhabitant of [t]Lā'-
chish, bind the [u]chariot to the
swift beast: she *is* [v,w]the beginning of the sin to the daughter of
Zī'ŏn: for the transgressions of
Ĭs̱'ra-el were found in thee.
14 Therefore shalt thou give
[9]presents to Mŏr'esh-eth–găth:
the houses of [x]Ăch'zĭb *shall be* a
lie[G] to the kings of Ĭs̱'ra-el.
15 Yet will I bring an heir unto
thee, O inhabitant of [y]Mā-rē'-
shah: [10]he shall come unto [z]Ă-
dŭl'lăm the glory of Ĭs̱'ra-el.
16 Make thee bald, and poll[G]
thee for thy delicate children; enlarge thy baldness as the [a]eagle;
for they are gone into [b]captivity
from thee.

## CHAPTER 2

*Woes denounced upon oppressors. 12 The restoration of Israel promised.*

WOE to [a]them that [b]devise
iniquity, and work evil
upon their beds! when the morn-

8
*n* *Mourning*, Lam. 2:5.
*o* *Dragon*, Deut. 32:33.
*p* *Owl*, Lev. 11:17.
2 R. V. jackals,
3 R. V. ostriches.
10
*q* *Gath*, Josh. 11:22.
4 R. V. at Beth-le-Aphrah have I rolled myself in the dust.
11
*r* Probably identical with *Zenan*, Josh. 15:37.
5 R. V. Shaphir, in nakedness and shame:
6 R. V. is not come forth; the wailing of Beth-ezel shall take from you the stay thereof.
12
*s* *Adversity, dispensation from God*, Psa. 10:6.
7 R. V. waiteth anxiously
8 R. V. because evil is come
13
*t* *Lachish, prophecy concerning*, Josh. 10:5.
*u* *Chariot*, Josh. 11:4.
*v* *Influence, evil*, 1 Cor. 7:14.
*w* *Temptation, leading into*, Luke 11:4.
14
*x* Or, *Chezib*, Gen. 38:5.
9 R. V. a parting gift
15
*y* *Mareshah, prophecy concerning*, Josh. 15:44.
*z* *Adullam*, 2 Chr. 11:7.
10 R. V. him that shall possess thee: the glory of Israel shall come even unto Adullam.

16
*a* *Eagle*, Lev. 11:13.
*b* *Captivity, as a judgment*, Isa. 5:13.

1
*a* *Wicked, described*, Psa. 73:3.
*b* *Malice*, Eph. 4:31.

ing is light, they practise it, because it is in the power of their
hand.
2 And [a]they [c]covet fields, and
[d]take *them* by violence; and
houses, and take *them* away: so
they [e]oppress[G] a man and his
house, even a man and his heritage.
3 Therefore thus saith the
LORD; Behold, against this
[f]family do I devise an [g]evil,
from which ye shall not remove your necks; neither shall
ye go haughtily: for this time
*is* evil.
4 In that day shall *one* take up
a parable against you, and lament with a doleful[G] lamentation,
*and* say, We be utterly spoiled[G]:
he hath changed the portion of
my people: how hath he removed
*it* from me! [1]turning away he
hath divided our fields.
5 [f,g]Therefore thou shalt have
none that shall cast a [h]cord by
[i]lot in the congregation of the
LORD.
6 Prophesy[G] ye not, [2]*say they to
them that* prophesy[G]: they shall
not prophesy[G] to them, *that* they
shall not take shame.
7 O *thou that art* named the
house of Jā'cob, is the spirit of
the LORD straitened[G]? *are* these
his doings? do not my words do
good to [j]him that walketh uprightly?
8 Even of late my people is
risen up as an enemy: [3]ye pull off
the robe with the garment from
them that pass by securely[G] as
men averse from war.
9 The women of my people
have ye cast out from their pleasant houses; from their children
have ye taken away my glory for
ever.
10 Arise ye, and depart; for
this *is* not *your* rest: because it
is polluted, it shall destroy *you*,
even with a sore[G] destruction.

2
*c* *Covetousness*, Isa. 57:17.
*d* *Land, monopoly of*, Ruth 4:3.
*e* *Oppression*, Eccl. 5:8.
3
*f* *Nation, judgments denounced against*, Isa. 2:4.
*g* *Wicked, punishment of*, Psa. 73:3.
4
1 R. V. to the rebellious he divideth
5
*h* *Rope*, 1 Kin. 20:31.
*i* *Lot*, Esth. 3:7.
6
2 R. V. thus they prophesy. They shall not prophesy to these: reproaches shall not depart.
7
*j* *Righteous, described*, Psa. 64:10.
8
3 R. V. ye strip the robe from off the garment

11 If a [k]man walking in the [4]spirit and falsehood do [l]lie, *saying,* I will prophesy unto thee of wine and of strong drink; he shall even be the prophet of this people.

12 ¶ [m]I will surely assemble, O Jā′cob, all of thee; I will surely gather the remnant of Ĭṣ′ra-el; I will put them together as the [n]sheep of [o]Bŏz′rah, as the flock in the midst of their fold: they shall make great noise by reason of *the multitude of* men.[S][T]

13 The breaker[C] is come up before them: they have broken[C] up, and have passed through the gate, and are gone out by it: and their king shall pass before them, and the LORD on the head of them.[S]

## CHAPTER 3

*Judgments upon the princes for their cruel exactions, 5 upon the false prophets for their deceptions, 8 and upon Zion for the wickedness of both.*

AND [a]I said, [b]Hear, I pray you, O [c]heads of Jā′cob, and ye princes of the house of [d]Ĭṣ′ra-el; *Is it* not for you to know judgment[C]?

2 [c,e]Who hate the good, and love the evil; who [f]pluck off their skin from off them, and their flesh from off their bones;

3 [c]Who also [f]eat the flesh of my people, and flay their skin from off them; and they break their bones, and chop them in pieces, as for the pot, and as flesh within the caldron.

4 Then shall they [g]cry unto the LORD, but [h]he will not hear them: [i]he will even hide his face from them at that time, as they have behaved themselves ill in their doings.

5 ¶ Thus saith the LORD concerning the [j]prophets that [k,l]make my people err, that bite with their teeth, and cry, Peace; and he that putteth not into their mouths, they even prepare war against him.

6 Therefore night *shall be* unto you, that [j]ye shall not have a vision; and it shall be dark unto you, that ye shall not divine; and the sun shall go down over the prophets, and the day shall be dark over them.

7 Then shall the [j]seers be ashamed, and the diviners confounded: yea, they shall all cover their lips; for [g,h]*there is* no answer of God.

8 But truly [a,m]I am [n]full of power by the spirit[C] of the LORD, and of judgment, and of might, [o]to [b]declare unto Jā′cob his transgression, and to Ĭṣ′ra-el his sin.[T]

9 ¶ Hear this, I pray you, ye [c]heads of the house of Jā′cob, and princes of the house of Ĭṣ′ra-el, [p]that abhor[C] judgment[C], and [p]pervert all equity.[C]

10 [c,q]They build up Zī′ŏn with blood[C], and Jĕ-ru̇-să-lĕm with iniquity.

11 The [r,s]heads thereof judge [t]for [u]reward, and the [v]priests thereof teach [t]for [u]hire, and the [j]prophets thereof divine[C] [t]for [u]money: [w]yet will they lean upon the LORD, and say, *Is* not the LORD among us? none[C] evil can come upon us.

12 Therefore [x]shall Zī′ŏn for your sake be plowed *as* a field, and [y]Jĕ-ru̇-să-lĕm shall become heaps[C], and the mountain of the house as the high places of the forest.

## CHAPTER 4

*The enlargement of Zion in the last days. 3 Her peace, 8 dominion, 11 and victory.*

BUT in the last days [a]it shall come to pass, *that* the [b]mountain of the house of the LORD shall be established in the top of the mountains, and it shall be exalted above the

---

**11**
k *Prophets, false,* Isa. 3:2.
l *Falsehood,* Job 21:34.
4 R. V. wind

**12**
m *God, preserver,* Gen. 2:2.
n *Sheep,* Deut. 32:14.
o *Bozrah,* Gen. 36:33.

**1**
a *Micah,* Mic. 1:1.
b *Reproof, faithfulness in,* Prov. 17:10.
c *Rulers, wicked,* Ex. 18:21.
d *Israel, prophecies concerning,* vs. 1–12; 1 Kin. 12:1.

**2**
e *Wicked, described,* Psa. 73:3.
f *Extortion,* Isa. 16:4.

**4**
g *Prayer, of the wicked not heard,* Acts 6:4.
h *Wicked, prayers of, not answered,* Psa. 73:3.
i *Sin, separates from God,* Rom. 5:12.

**5**
j *Prophets, false,* Isa. 3:2.
k *Influence, evil,* 1 Cor. 7:14.
l *Temptation, leading into,* Luke 11:4.

**8**
m *Zeal, instances of,* 2 Cor. 7:11.
n *Prophets, inspiration of,* Isa. 3:2.
o *Minister, duties of,* Rom. 15:16.

**9**
p *Government, corruption in,* Isa. 22:21.

**10**
q *Oppression,* Eccl. 5:8.

**11**
r *Judge, corrupt,* Judg. 2:18.
s *Court, corrupt,* Ex. 18:26.
t *Covetousness,* Isa. 57:17.
u *Bribery,* 1 Sam. 8:3.
v *Minister, false and corrupt,* Rom. 15:16.
w *False Confidence, of the spiritually blind,* Psa. 30:6.

**12**
x Jer. 26:18.
y *Jerusalem, prophecies against,* Judg. 19:10.

**1**
a *Jesus, kingdom of, prophecies concerning,* vs. 1–7; Matt. 1:21.
b *Church, prophecies concerning its prosperity,* vs. 1–7; Matt. 16:18.

*c Religious Revivals, prophecies concerning,* vs. 1–8; Hab. 3:2.
1 R. V. peoples

2

*d Gentiles, prophecies of the conversion of,* Acts 10:45.
*e Spiritual Desire,* Psa. 42:1.
*f Instruction,* Prov. 23:23.
*g Word of God,* Psa. 119:9.
*h Jerusalem, gospel first preached at,* Judg. 19:10.

3

*i Jesus, judge,* Matt. 1:21.
*j Nation, promises of peace to,* Isa. 2:4.
*k Peace,* Jer. 29:7.
*l War, to cease,* Judg. 3:2.
*m Sword,* 1 Chr. 21:5.
*n* Isa. 2:4; Joel 3:10.
*o Spear,* 2 Kin. 11:10.
*p Pruning,* Isa. 18:5.

4

*q Fig Tree, figurative,* Luke 13:6.
*r God, faithfulness of,* Gen. 2:2.

7

*s God, sovereign,* Gen. 2:2.

8

*t Judah, kingdom of, prophecies concerning,* 2 Chr. 11:17.

hills; and [1,c]people shall flow unto it.

2 [a,b]And many [d]nations shall come, and say, Come, and [c,e]let us go up to the mountain of the LORD, and to the house of the God of Jā′cob; and he will [f]teach us of his ways, and we will walk in his paths: for the law shall go forth of Zī′ŏn, and the [g]word of the LORD from [h]Jĕ-ru̇′să-lĕm.

3 ¶ And [a]he shall [i]judge among many people, and rebuke strong nations afar off; and [j,k,l]they shall beat their [m]swords into [n]plowshares, and their [o]spears into [p]pruninghooks[C]: nation shall not lift up a sword against nation, neither shall they learn war any more.

4 But [a,b]they shall sit every man under his vine and under his [q]fig tree; and *none shall make *them* afraid: for [r]the mouth of the LORD of hosts hath spoken *it.*

5 *For all people will walk every one in the name of his god, and [a,b]we will walk in the name of the LORD our God for ever and ever.

6 ¶[S] In [a]that day, saith the LORD, will I assemble her that halteth[C], and I will gather her that is driven out, and her that I have afflicted;

7 And [a]I will make her that halted[C] a remnant, and her that was cast far off a strong nation: and the [s]LORD shall reign over them in mount Zī′ŏn from henceforth, even for ever.[Q]

8 And thou, [t]O tower of the flock, the strong hold of the daughter of Zī′ŏn, unto thee shall it come, even the first dominion; the kingdom shall come to the daughter of Jĕ-ru̇′să-lĕm.[S]

9 ¶ Now why dost [t]thou cry out aloud? *is there* no king in thee? is thy counsellor perished? for pangs have taken thee as a woman in travail.[Q]

10 Be in pain, and labour to bring forth, O daughter of Zī′ŏn, like a woman in travail: for now shalt [t]thou go forth out of the city, and thou shalt dwell in the field, and thou shalt [u]go *even* to [v]Băb′ȳ-lon; there shalt thou be delivered; there the LORD shall redeem thee from the hand of thine enemies.[Q]

11 ¶ Now also many nations are gathered against thee, that say, Let her be defiled, and let our eye look upon Zī′ŏn.

12 But they [w]know not the [x]thoughts of the LORD, neither understand they his counsel[C]: for he shall gather them as the sheaves into the floor.

13 Arise and thresh, O daughter of Zī′ŏn: for I will make thine [y]horn iron, and I will make thy hoofs brass: and thou shalt beat in pieces many [1]people: and I will consecrate their gain unto the LORD, and their substance unto the [s]LORD of the whole earth.

## CHAPTER 5

*The birthplace of the Messiah. 4 His kingdom, 8 and conquests.*

NOW gather thyself in troops, O daughter of troops: he hath laid siege against us: [a]they shall smite the judge of Ĭs̹′ra-el with a rod upon the cheek.[Q]

2 But [b,c]thou, [d]Bĕth′–lĕ-hĕm Ĕph′ra-tah, *though* thou be little among the thousands of Jū′dah, *yet* out of thee shall [e]he come forth unto me *that is* to be [f]ruler in Ĭs̹′ra-el; whose goings forth *have been* from of old, from everlasting.[S T Q]

3 Therefore will he give them up, until the time *that* she which travaileth[C] hath brought forth: then the remnant of his brethren shall return unto the children of Ĭs̹′ra-el.

10

*u Captivity, as a judgment,* Isa. 5:13.
*v Babylon,* Ezra 5:12.

12

*w Spiritual Blindness,* 2 Cor. 4:4.
*x God, providence of, mysterious,* Gen. 2:2.

13

*y Horn, symbolical,* 1 Kin. 1:39.

1

*a* Matt. 27:30.

2

*b* Matt. 2:6; John 7:42.
*c Prophecies concerning the Messiah, and their fulfillment,* Gen. 12:3
*d Bethlehem,* Gen. 48:7.
*e Jesus, prophecies concerning,* Matt. 1:21.
*f Jesus, king.* Matt. 1:21.

* **TOLERATION.** *Religious.* Mic. 4:4, 5; Mark 9:38–40; Luke 9:49, 50; Acts 28:31; Rom. 14; 1 Cor. 10:27–32.

4 And [e]he shall stand and feed in the strength of the LORD, in the majesty of the name of the LORD his God; and they shall abide: for now shall he be great unto the ends of the earth.

5 And [e]this *man* shall be the [g]peace, when the [h]Ăs-sўr′ĭ-an shall come into our land: and when he shall tread in our palaces, then shall we raise against him [i]seven shepherds, and eight principal men.

6 And they shall [j]waste the land of [h]Ăs-sўr′ĭ-ȧ with the sword, and the land of Nĭm′rŏd in the entrances thereof: thus shall he deliver *us* from the Ăs-sўr′ĭ-an, when he cometh into our land, and when he treadeth within our borders.

7 [k]And the remnant of Jā′cob shall be in the midst of many [1]people as a dew from the LORD, as the showers upon the grass, that tarrieth not for man, nor waiteth for the sons of men.

8 ¶ [k]And the remnant of Jā′cob shall be among the Ġĕn′tīleṣ in the midst of many people as a *lion among the beasts of the forest, as a young lion among the flocks of sheep: who, if he go through, both treadeth down, and teareth in pieces, and none can deliver.

9 [k]Thine hand shall be lifted up upon thine adversaries, and all thine enemies shall be cut off.

10 And it shall come to pass in that day, saith the LORD, that I will cut off thy horses out of the midst of thee, and I will destroy thy chariots:

11 And I will cut off the cities of thy land, and throw down all thy strong holds:

12 And I will cut off [l]witchcrafts out of thine hand; and thou shalt have no *more* soothsayers:

13 [m]Thy graven images also will I cut off, and thy [2]standing images out of the midst of thee; and thou shalt no more worship the work of thine hands.

14 And I will pluck up [3]thy [n]groves out of the midst of thee: so will I destroy thy cities.

15 And [o]I will execute vengeance in [p]anger and fury upon the [4]heathen, such as they have not heard.

## CHAPTER 6

*God's controversy with his people for their ingratitude, 6 ignorance, 10 injustice, 16 and idolatry.*

HEAR ye now what the LORD saith; Arise, contend thou before the mountains, and let the hills hear thy voice.

2 Hear ye, O mountains, the LORD's controversy, and ye strong foundations of the earth: for the LORD hath a controversy with his people, and [a]he will plead with Ĭṣ′ra-el.

3 [b]O my people, what have I done unto thee? and wherein have I wearied thee? testify against me.

4 For [a]I [c]brought thee up out of the land of [d]Ē′ġy̆pt, and [c]redeemed thee out of the house of servants; and I sent before thee [e]Mō′ṣeṣ, [f]Aâr′on, and [g,h]Mĭr′ĭ-am.

5 [a]O my people, remember now what [i]Bā′lăk king of [j]Mō′ab consulted, and what [k]Bā′laam the

5
g *Peace*, Jer. 29:7.
h *Assyria*, Gen. 25:18.
i *Seven*, Gen. 7:2.

6
j *War, evils of*, Judg. 3:2.

7
k *Jews, prophecies concerning*, Neh. 4:2.
1 R. V. peoples

12
l *Sorcery*, Isa. 47:9.

13
m *Idolatry, prophecies concerning*, 1 Sam. 15:23.
2 R. V. pillars out

14
n *Groves, forbidden to be established*, Judg. 6:28.
3 R. V. thine Asherim out

15
o *Nation, judgments denounced against*, Isa. 2:4.
p *Anger of God*, 2 Kin. 13:3.
4 R. V. nations which hearkened not.

2
a *God, love of, exemplified*, Gen. 2:2.

3
b *Ingratitude, of man to God*, Rom. 1:21.

4
c *God, providence of*, Gen. 2:2.
d *Egypt*, Gen. 41:8.
e *Moses*, Ex. 2:10.
f *Aaron*, Ex. 6:20.
g *Miriam*, Ex. 15:20.
h *Women, as prophets*, Prov. 31:10.

5
i *Balak*, Num. 22:4.
j *Moabites*, Gen. 19:37.
k *Balaam, counsel of*, Deut. 23:4.

***LION.** *King of beasts*, Mic. 5:8. *Fierceness of*, Job 4:10; 28:8; Psa. 7:2; Prov. 22:13; Jer. 49:19; 50:44; Hos. 13:8. *The roaring of*, Psa. 22:13; Prov. 20:2; 1 Pet. 5:8. *Strength of*, Prov. 30:30; Isa. 38:13; Joel 1:6. *Instincts of, in taking prey*, Psa. 10:9; 17:12; Lam. 3:10; Amos 3:4; Nah. 2:12. *Lair of, in the jungles*, Jer. 4:7; 25:38. *The bases of the laver in the temple ornamented by mouldings of*, 1 Kin. 7:29, 36. *Twelve statues of, on the stairs leading to Solomon's throne*, 1 Kin. 10:19, 20. *Samson's riddle concerning*, Judg. 14:14, 18. *Proverb concerning*, Eccl. 9:4. *Kept in dens*, Dan. 6:7, 16–24, 27. *Sent as judgment upon the Samaritans*, 2 Kin. 17:25, 26. *Slain, by Samson*, Judg. 14:5–9; *by David*, I Sam. 17:34, 36; *by Benaiah*, 2 Sam. 23:20; *by saints*, Heb. 11:33. *Disobedient prophet slain by*, 1 Kin. 13:24–28. *An unnamed person slain by*, 1 Kin. 20:36. *Used for the torture of criminals*, Dan. 6:16–24.

*A name of Jesus*, Rev. 5:5.

**Similitudes of,** Ezek. 1:10; 10:14; Dan. 7:4; Rev. 4:7; 9:8, 17; 13:2.

**Figurative,** Gen. 49:9; Isa. 65:25; Ezek. 19:2; 2 Tim. 4:17. *Of a ruler's wrath*, Jer. 50:17. *Of enemies*, Psa. 57:4; 58:6. *Of divine judgments*, Isa. 15:9; Jer. 2:15; 4:7; 5:6; Hos. 5:14

son of Bē′or answered him from
[l]Shĭt′tim unto [m]Gĭl′găl; that ye
may know the [n]righteousness of
the LORD.[T]
6 [o]Wherewith[G] shall I [p]come before the LORD, *and* bow myself
before the high God? [q,r]shall I
come before him with [s]burnt offerings, with *calves of a year
old?
7 [q,r]Will the LORD be pleased
with thousands of rams, *or* with
ten thousands of rivers of oil?
shall I give my [t,u]firstborn *for*
my transgression, the fruit[G] of my
body *for* the sin of my soul?
8 He hath shewed thee, O man,
what *is* good; and what doth
the LORD [v]require of thee, but
to [q,w]do justly, and to [w,x]love
[1]mercy, and to [w]walk [y]humbly
with thy God? [S Q]
9 ¶ The LORD's voice crieth
unto the [z]city, and *the man of*
wisdom shall see thy name: [a]hear
ye the rod[G], and [b]who hath appointed it.
10 [c]Are there yet the treasures
of wickedness in the house of the
wicked, and the [d]scant[G] [e]measure
*that is* abominable?
11 Shall I [2]count[G] *them* [f,g]pure
with the wicked [h]balances, and
with the bag of deceitful[i] weights?
12 For the [j]rich men thereof are
full of violence, and the inhabitants thereof have spoken [k]lies,
and their tongue *is* deceitful in
their mouth.
13 Therefore [3]also will I make
*thee* sick in [l]smiting thee, in
[b]making *thee* desolate[G] because
of thy sins.
14 [l]Thou shalt eat, but not be
satisfied; and thy casting down
*shall be* in the midst of thee; and
thou shalt take hold, but shalt
not deliver; and *that* which thou
deliverest will I give up to the
[m]sword.
15 [l]Thou shalt sow, but thou
shalt not reap; thou shalt tread
the [n]olives, but thou shalt not
[o]anoint thee with [p]oil; and [4]sweet
[q]wine, but shalt not drink wine.[Q]
16 For the statutes of [r]Ŏm′rī
are kept, and all the works of the
house of [s]Ā′hăb, and ye walk in
[t]their [u]counsels; that I should
[b,l]make thee a desolation, and
the inhabitants thereof an hissing: therefore ye shall bear the
reproach of my people.

## CHAPTER 7

*The prophet laments the general corruption of his times, 7 and puts his trust in God. 8 He encourages himself against his enemies. 14 His prayer. 16 The ultimate triumph of God's people.*

WOE is me! for I am as when
they have gathered the
summer fruits, as the grape-
[a]gleanings of the vintage: *there is*
no cluster to eat: my soul desired
the firstripe fruit.
2 The [1]good *man* is perished
out of the earth: and *there is*
none upright among men: they
all lie in wait for blood; they
hunt every man his brother with
a net.
3 [2]That they may [b]do evil with
both hands earnestly, the [c]prince
[d]asketh, and the [e,f]judge *asketh*
for a [g]reward; and the great *man*
he uttereth [3]his mischievous desire: so they wrap[G] it up.
4 The best of them *is* as a brier:
the most upright *is sharper* than
a thorn hedge: the [h]day of thy
watchmen *and* thy visitation[G]
cometh; now shall be their perplexity.
5 [i]Trust ye not in a [j]friend, put
ye not *confidence in a guide:
[k]keep the doors of thy mouth
from her that lieth in thy bosom.

l *Shittim, Balaam prophesies in,* Num. 25:1.
m *Gilgal,* Josh. 4:19.
n *God, righteousness of,* Gen. 2:2.

**6**
o *Spiritual Desire,* Psa. 42:1.
p *Worship,* Gen. 22:5.
q *Obedience better than Sacrifice,* vs. 6–8; 1 Sam. 15:22.
r *Offerings, unavailing when not accompanied by piety,* vs. 6–8; Lev. 6:17.
s *Offerings, burnt,* Lev. 6:17.

**7**
t *Firstborn,* Zech. 12:10.
u *Human Sacrifices,* Deut. 12:31.

**8**
v *Righteousness, enjoined,* Psa. 15:2.
w *Christian Graces,* Gal. 5:22.
x *Kindness, enjoined,* Acts 28:2.
y *Humility,* Prov. 22:4.
1 Am. R. V. kindness,

**9**
z *Jerusalem,* Judg. 19:10.

a *Adversity, design of,* Psa. 10:6.
b *Adversity, dispensation from God,* Psa. 10:6.

**10**
c *Reproof, faithfulness in,* Prov. 17:10.
d *Dishonesty, in wicked devices for gain,* Ezek. 22:13.
e *Measure, false, an abomination,* Deut. 25:15.

**11**
f *Purity of Heart,* 2 Tim. 4:12.
g *Holiness,* Ex. 39:30.
h *Balances, false, an abomination,* Prov. 11:1.
i *Weights, must be just,* Lev. 19:35.
2 R. V. be pure

**12**
j *Rich, oppressive,* Jas. 5:1.
k *Falsehood,* Job 21:34.

**13** l *Wicked, punishment of,* Psa. 73:3.
3 R. V. I also have smitten thee with a grievous wound; I have made thee desolate

**14**
m *War, as a judgment,* Judg. 3:2.

**15**
n *Olive,* Deut. 6:11.
o *Anointing, of the body,* Deut. 28:40.
p *Oil,* Deut. 12:17.
q *Wine,* Prov. 23:31.
4 R. V. the vintage,

**16**
r *Omri,* 1 Kin. 16:16.
s *Ahab,* 1 Kin. 16:29.
t *Evil Company,* Prov. 13:20.
u *Influence, evil,* 1 Cor. 7:14.

**1**
a *Gleaning, figurative,* Lev. 23:22.

**2**
1 R. V. godly

**3**
b *Justice, perverted,* Deut. 33:21.
c *Rulers, corrupted by gifts,* Ex. 18:21.
d *Covetousness,* Isa. 57:17.
e *Judge, corrupt,* Judg. 2:18.
f *Court, corrupt,* Ex. 18:26.
g *Bribery, perverts justice,* 1 Sam. 8:3.
2 R. V. Their hands are upon that which is evil to do it diligently;
3 R. V. the mischief of his soul: thus they weave it together.

**4**
h *Wicked, punishment of,* Psa. 73:3.

**5**
i *Hypocrisy, warning against,* Jas. 3:17.
j *Friends, false,* Ex. 33:11.
k *Prudence,* 2 Chr. 2:12.

* **CALF.** *Offered in sacrifice,* Mic. 6:6. *Golden, made by Aaron,* Ex. 32; Deut. 9:16; Neh. 9:18; Psa. 106:19; Acts 7:41. *Images of, set up in Beth-el and Dan,* 1 Kin. 12:28–33; 2 Kin. 10:29; 17:16. *Worshiped by Jehu,* 2 Kin. 10:29. *Prophecies against the golden calves at Beth-el,* 1 Kin. 13:1–5, 32; Jer. 48 13; Hos. 8:5, 6; 10:5, 6, 15; 13:2; Amos 3:14; 4:4; 8:14. *Altars of, destroyed,* 2 Kin. 23:4, 15–20.

* **CONFIDENCE,** Jer. 9:4; 12:6; Mic. 7:5.

6
*l Children, wicked,* Mark 10:14.
*m Daughter-in-law, unfilial,* Lev. 20:12.

7
*n Faith, exemplified,* Mark 11:22.
*o God, savior,* Gen. 2:2.

8
*p Darkness, figurative,* Gen. 1:2.

9
*q Adversity, resignation in,* Psa. 10:6.
*r Sin, confession of,* Rom. 5:12.
*s God, righteousness of,* Gen. 2:2.

12
*t Assyria,* Gen. 25:18.
*u Euphrates,* Gen. 15:18.
4 R. V. the cities of Egypt, and from Egypt even to

6 For †the [l]son dishonoureth the father, the [l]daughter riseth up against her mother, the [m]daughter in law against her mother in law; a man's enemies *are* the men of his own house.[Q]

7 Therefore [n]I will look unto the LORD; I will wait for the [o]God of my salvation: my God will hear me.

8 ¶ Rejoice not against me, O mine enemy: when I fall, [n]I shall arise; when I sit in [p]darkness, [n]the LORD *shall be* a light unto me.

9 [q]I will bear the indignation of the LORD, because [r]I have sinned against him, until he plead my cause, and execute judgment for me: [n]he will bring me forth to the light, *and* I shall behold his [s]righteousness.

10 Then *she that is* mine enemy shall see *it,* and shame shall cover her which said unto me, Where is the LORD thy God? mine eyes shall behold her: now shall she be trodden[C] down as the mire of the streets.

11 ¶ *In* the day that thy walls are to be built, *in* that day shall the decree be far removed.

12 *In* that day *also* he shall come even to thee from [t]Ăs-sȳr'-ĭ-ȧ, and [4]*from* the fortified cities, and from the fortress even to the [u]river, and from sea to sea, and *from* ‡mountain to mountain.

13 Notwithstanding the land shall be desolate[G] because of them that dwell therein, for the [v]fruit of their doings.

14 ¶ [w]Feed thy people with thy rod, the flock of thine heritage, which dwell solitarily[C] *in* the wood[C], in the midst of Cär'mel: let them feed *in* Bā'shăn and Ḡĭl'e-ăd, as in the days of old.

15 According to the days of thy coming out of the land of Ē'ġȳpt will I shew unto him marvellous *things.*

16 The nations shall see and be confounded at all their might: they shall lay *their* hand upon *their* mouth, their ears shall be deaf.

17 They shall lick the dust like a serpent, [5]they shall move out of their holes like worms of the earth: they shall be afraid of the LORD our God, and shall fear because of thee.

18 ¶ Who *is* a God like unto thee, that [x, y]pardoneth iniquity, and passeth by the transgression of the remnant of his heritage? he [z]retaineth not his anger for ever, because he delighteth *in* mercy.[S]

19 He [y]will turn again, he will have compassion upon us; he will subdue our iniquities; and thou wilt [x]cast all their sins into the depths of the sea.

20 [a]Thou wilt perform the truth to [b]Jā'cob, *and* the mercy to [c]Ā-'brā-hăm, which thou hast [d]sworn unto our fathers from the days of old.[S Q]

13
*v Sin, fruits of,* Rom. 5:12.

14
*w Nation, in adversity, prayer for,* Isa. 2:4.

17
5 R. V. like crawling things of the earth they shall come trembling out of their close places: they shall come with fear unto the Lord our God, and shall be afraid because of thee.

18
*x Sin, forgiveness of,* Rom. 5:12.
*y God, mercy of,* Gen. 2:2.
*z God, longsuffering of,* Gen. 2:2.

20
*a Faith, exemplified,* Mark 11:22.
*b Jacob, God confirms the covenant of Abraham to,* Gen. 27:11.
*c Abraham, God's covenant with,* Gen. 17:5.
*d Covenant, of God with men,* Deut. 29:1.

**Betrayed:** *Of Eglon, by Ehud,* Judg. 3:15–23. *Of Sisera, by Jael,* Judg. 4:17–22. *Of Samson, by Delilah,* Judg. 16:17–20. *Of Abner, by Joab,* 2 Sam. 3:27. *Of Amasa, by Joab,* 2 Sam. 20:9, 10. *Of the worshipers of Baal, by Jehu,* 2 Kin. 10:18–28.

See footnote, BETRAYAL, Matt. 26:46.

† **HOSTILITY TO THE RIGHTEOUS,** Micah 7:6; Matt. 10:21, 35, 36; Mark 13:12; Luke 12:53.

‡ **MOUNTAIN.** *Melted,* Deut. 4:11; 5:23; Judg. 5:5; Psa. 97:5; Mic. 1:4. *Overturning and removing of,* Job 9:5; 14:18; 28:9. *Abraham offers Isaac upon Mount Moriah,* Gen. 22:2. *Horeb appointed as a place of worship for the Israelites,* Ex. 3:12. *Used for idolatrous worship,* Deut. 12:2; 1 Kin. 14:23; Jer. 3:6; Hos. 4:13. *Signals from,* Isa. 13:2; 18:3; 30:17. *Removal of, by faith,* Matt. 17:20; 21:21; Mark 11:23. *Jesus, tempted upon,* Matt. 4:8; *preaches from,* Matt. 5:1; *goes up into, for prayer,* Matt. 14:23; Luke 6:12; 9:28; *is transfigured upon,* Matt. 17:1–9; Mark 9:2–9; Luke 9:28–37; *meets his disciples on, after his resurrection,* Matt. 28:16, 17.

## THE

# BOOK OF NAHUM

## CHAPTER 1

*The majesty of God in goodness to his people, and his severity against his enemies.*

THE [a]burden of [b]Nĭn'e-veh. The book of the vision of *Nā'hum the Ĕl'kosh-īte.

2 God *is* [c]jealous,[G] and the LORD revengeth; the LORD revengeth,[G] and *is* [d]furious; the LORD will [e]take [f]vengeance on his adversaries, and he reserveth *wrath* for his enemies.[s]

3 The LORD *is* [g]slow to anger, and great in [h]power, and [e,i,j]will not at all acquit *the wicked*: the LORD *hath* his way in the whirlwind and in the storm, and the clouds *are* the dust of his feet.[s]

4 [h]He[s] rebuketh the sea, and maketh it dry, and drieth up all the rivers: [k]Bā'shăn languisheth, and [l]Cär'mel, and the flower of [m]Lĕb'a-non languisheth.

5 The mountains quake at [h]him, and the hills melt, and the earth is [1]burned at his presence, yea, the world, and all that dwell therein.

6 [h]Who can stand before his [d]indignation? and who can abide in the fierceness of his anger? his fury is poured out like fire, and the rocks are [2]thrown down by him.[s Q]

7 ¶ The LORD *is* [n]good, a [o,p]strong hold[G] in the day of trouble; and [q]he [r]knoweth[G] them that [s]trust in him.[s]

8 But [t]with an overrunning flood he will make an utter end of the place thereof, and [e]darkness shall pursue his enemies.

9 What do ye imagine against the LORD? [t]he will make an utter end: affliction shall not rise up the second time.

10 For [3]while *they be* folden together *as* thorns, and while they are [u]drunken *as* [v]drunkards, [t]they shall be [e]devoured as [w]stubble fully dry.

11 There is *one* come out of thee, that imagineth[G] evil against the LORD, a wicked counsellor.

12 Thus saith the LORD; Though *they be* [4]quiet, and likewise many, yet thus shall they be cut down, when he shall pass through. Though I have afflicted thee, [x]I will afflict thee no more.[s]

13 For now [x]will I break his yoke from off thee, and will burst thy bonds in sunder.

14 And the LORD hath given a commandment concerning thee, *that* no[G] more of thy name be sown: out of the house of thy [y]gods will I cut off the graven[G] image and the molten[G] image: I will make thy grave; for thou art vile.

15 Behold upon the mountains the feet of him that bringeth good tidings, that publisheth [z]peace! O Jū'dah, [a]keep[G] thy solemn [b]feasts, perform thy [c]vows: for the wicked shall no more pass through thee; he is utterly [d]cut off.[Q]

## CHAPTER 2

*The array of God's armies for the destruction of Nineveh.*

[a]HE that dasheth in pieces is come up before thy face: keep the munition,[G] watch the

---

1
*a Prophecies,* Dan. 9:24.
*b Nineveh, Nahum prophesies against,* vs. 1–15; Jonah 1:2.

2
*c God, jealous,* Gen. 2:2.
*d Anger of God,* 2 Kin. 13:3.
*e Wicked, punishment of,* Psa. 73:3.
*f Vengeance, belongs to God,* Psa. 94:1.

3
*g God, longsuffering of,* Gen. 2:2.
*h God, power of,* Gen. 2:2.
*i God, judge,* Gen. 2:2.
*j Punishment, no escape from,* Lev. 26:41.

4
*k Bashan,* Num. 32:33.
*l Carmel,* Jer. 46:18.
*m Lebanon,* Deut. 1:7.

5
1 R. V. upheaved

6
2 R. V. broken asunder

7
*n God, goodness of,* Gen. 2:2.
*o God, preserver,* Gen. 2:2.
*p Adversity, consolation in,* Psa. 10:6.
*q Promise, or ground of assurance, to the righteous,* 2 Cor. 1:20.
*r God, knowledge of,* Gen. 2:2.
*s Faith, rewards of,* Mark 11:22.

8
*t Nation, judgments denounced against,* Isa. 2:4.

10
*u Drunkenness,* Luke 21:34.
*v Drunkard,* Psa. 69:12.
*w Stubble, destruction of, illustrative,* Isa. 5:24.
3 Am. R. V. entangled like thorns and drunken as with their drink they are consumed utterly as dry stubble.

12
*x God, mercy of,* Gen. 2:2.
4 R. V. in full strength, and likewise many, even so shall they be cut down, and he shall pass away.

14
*y Idolatry,* 1 Sam. 15:23.

15
*z Peace,* Jer. 29:7.

*a Worship, enjoined,* Gen. 22:5.
*b Annual Feasts,* Num. 15:3.
*c Vows,* Num. 30:2.
*d Wicked, punishment of,* Psa. 73:3.

1
*a Nineveh, Nahum prophesies against,* vs. 1–13; Jonah 1:2.

---

* **NAHUM,** one of the minor prophets. *Prophesies against the Assyrians: declares the majesty of God and his care for his people,* Nah. 1. *Foretells the destruction of Nineveh,* Nah. chapters 2, 3.

way, make *thy* loins strong, [b]fortify *thy* power mightily.

2 For [1,c]the LORD hath turned away the excellency of Jā′cob, as the excellency of Iṣ′ra-el: for the emptiers have emptied them out, and marred their vine branches.

3 The [d]shield of his mighty [e]men is made red, the valiant men *are* in scarlet: the [f]chariots [2]*shall be* with flaming torches in the day of his preparation, and the fir trees shall be terribly shaken.

4 The [f]chariots shall rage in the streets, they shall justle[G] one against another in the broad ways: they shall seem like torches, they shall run like the [g]lightnings.

5 He shall recount his worthies[G]: they shall stumble in their walk; they shall make haste to the wall thereof, and the [3]defence shall be prepared.

6 The gates of the rivers shall be opened, and the [h]palace shall be dissolved.

7 And Hŭz′zăb[4] shall be led away captive, she shall be brought up, and her maids shall lead *her* as with the voice of doves, tabering[G] upon their breasts.

8 But [a]Nĭn′e-veh *is* of old like a pool of water: yet they shall flee away. Stand, stand, *shall they cry*; but none shall look back.

9 Take ye the [i]spoil[G] of silver, take the spoil[G] of gold: for *there is* none[G] end of the store *and* glory out of all the pleasant[G] furniture.

10 [j]She is empty, and void, and waste: and the heart melteth, and the knees smite together, and much pain *is* in all loins, and the faces of them all gather blackness.

11 Where *is* the dwelling of the [k]lions, and the feedingplace of the young lions, where the lion, *even* the old lion, walked, *and* the lion's whelp, and none made *them* afraid?

12 The [k]lion did tear in pieces enough for his whelps, and strangled for his lionesses, and filled his holes with prey, and his dens with ravin[G].

13 Behold, I *am* against thee, saith the LORD of hosts, and I will burn her chariots in the smoke, and the sword shall devour thy young lions: and I will cut off thy prey from the earth, and the voice of thy messengers shall no more be heard.

## CHAPTER 3

*The utter ruin of Nineveh.*

WOE to the bloody [a]city! it *is* all full of [b,c]lies *and* [d]robbery; the prey departeth not;

2 The noise of a whip, and the noise of the rattling of the wheels, and of the pransing [e]horses, and of the jumping [f]chariots.

3 The [g]horseman lifteth up both the bright [h]sword and the glittering [i]spear: and [j]*there is* a multitude of slain, and a great number of carcases[G]; and *there is* none[G] end of *their* corpses; they stumble upon their corpses:

4 Because of the multitude of the whoredoms[G] of the wellfavoured harlot, the mistress of witchcrafts, that selleth nations through her whoredoms[G], and families through her witchcrafts.

5 Behold, [k]I *am* against thee, saith the LORD of hosts; and I will discover[G] thy skirts upon thy face, and I will shew the nations thy nakedness, and the kingdoms thy shame.

6 And [k]I will cast abominable filth upon thee, and make thee vile, and will set thee as a gazingstock[G].

7 And it shall come to pass, *that* all they that look upon thee shall flee from thee, and say, [a]Nĭn′e-veh is laid waste: who will

b *Fortification*, Ezek. 17:17.

2

c *God, mercy of*, Gen. 2:2.

1 Am. R. V. Jehovah bringeth again the excellency

3

d *Shield*, 1 Kin. 14:27.

e *Soldiers*, Ezra 8:22.

f *Chariot*, Josh. 11:4.

2 R. V flash with steel in the day of his preparation, and the spears are shaken terribly.

4

g *Lightning*, Job 28:26.

5

3 R. V. mantelet is

6

h *Palace*, 1 Kin. 21:1.

7

4 R. V. is uncovered, she is carried away, and her handmaids mourn as with the voice of doves,

9

i *Spoils*, 1 Chr. 26:27.

10

j *War, evils of*, Judg. 3:2.

11

k *Lion, instincts of*, Mic. 5:8.

1

a *Nineveh, Nahum prophesies against*, vs. 1–19; Jonah 1:2.

b *Falsehood, the wicked practice*, Job 21:34.

c *Dishonesty*, Ezek. 22:13.

d *Theft*, Mark 7:22.

2

e *Horse*, Job 39:19.

f *Chariot*, Josh. 11:4.

3

g *Cavalry*, 1 Sam. 13:5.

h *Sword*, 1 Chr. 21:5.

i *Spear*, 2 Kin. 11:10.

j *War, evils of*, Judg. 3:2.

5

k *Nation, judgments denounced against*, Isa. 2:4.

bemoan her? whence shall I seek
comforters for thee?
8 Art thou better than populous
[l]Nō, that was situate among the
rivers, *that had* the waters round
about it, whose rampart *was* the
sea, *and* her wall *was* from the
sea?
9 [m]Ē-thĭ-ō′pĭ-ȧ and [n]Ē′ġy̆pt
*were* her strength, and *it was*
infinite; Pŭt and Lu̥′bĭm were
thy helpers.
10 Yet *was* she carried away, she
went into [o]captivity: [j]her young
children also were [p]dashed in
pieces at the top of all the streets:
and they cast lots for her honourable men, and all her great
men were bound in chains.
11 [k]Thou also shalt be [q]drunk-
en: thou shalt be hid, thou also
shalt seek strength because of the
enemy.
12 [k,r]All thy[1,s]strong holds *shall*
*be like* fig trees with the firstripe
figs: if they be shaken, they shall
even fall into the mouth of the
eater.
13 Behold, [k]thy people in the
midst of thee *are* women: the
gates of thy land shall be set wide
open unto thine enemies: the fire
shall devour thy bars.
14 Draw thee waters for the
[t]siege, fortify thy [s]strong holds:
go into clay, and tread the [u]mor-
ter, make strong the [v]brickkiln.
15 [k]There shall the fire devour
thee; the sword shall cut thee off,
it shall eat thee up like the [w]can-
kerworm: make thyself many as
the cankerworm, make thyself
many as the +locusts.
16 Thou hast multiplied thy
[x,y]merchants above the stars of
heaven: the cankerworm spoileth, and fleeth away.
17 Thy crowned *are* as the +lo-
custs, and thy [2]captains as the
great [z]grasshoppers, which camp
in the hedges in the cold day, *but*
when the sun ariseth they flee
away, and their place is not
known where they *are*.
18 Thy shepherds slumber, O
king of [a]Ăs-sy̆r′ĭ-ȧ: thy [3]nobles
shall dwell *in the dust*: thy people is scattered upon the mountains, and no man gathereth
*them*.
19 *There is* no healing of thy
bruise; thy wound is grievous:
all that hear the bruit of thee
shall clap the hands over thee:
for upon whom hath not thy
wickedness passed continually?

**8**
*l* Jer. 46:25; Ezek. 30:14-16.

**9**
*m* *Ethiopia*, Isa. 18:1.
*n* *Egypt*, Gen. 41:8.

**10**
*o* *Captivity*, Isa. 5:13.
*p* *Cruelty, instances of*, Psa. 27:12.

**11**
*q* *Drunkenness, figurative*, Luke 21:34.

**12**
*r* *False Confidence*, Psa. 30:6.
*s* *Fortification*, Ezek. 17:17.
1 R. V. fortresses

**14**
*t* *Siege*, Deut. 28:53.
*u* *Mortar*, Lev. 14:42.
*v* *Brick*, Gen. 11:3.

**15**
*w* Joel 1:4; 2:25.

**16**
*x* *Merchant*, Neh. 3:32.
*y* *Commerce*, 1 Kin. 10:15.

**17**
*z* Num. 13:33; Eccl. 12:5; Isa. 40:22.
2 R. V. marshals as the swarms of grasshoppers,

**18**
*a* *Assyria*, Gen. 25:18.
3 R. V. worthies are at rest:

---

THE

# BOOK OF HABAKKUK

## CHAPTER 1

*The prophet complains of the violence done in the land. 5 The fearful punishment thereof through the Chaldeans. 12 The prophet's confidence in God.*

THE burden which *Hȧ-băk′-
kuk the [a]prophet did see.
2 [b,c]O LORD, how long shall I
cry, and thou wilt not hear! *even*
cry out unto thee *of* violence, and
thou wilt not save!
3 [b,c]Why dost thou shew me iniquity, and [1]cause *me* to behold
grievance? for [d]spoiling and violence *are* before me: and there
are *that* raise up [e]strife and contention.

**1**
*a* *Prophets, inspiration of*, Isa. 3:2.

**2**
*b* *Minister, discouragements of*, Rom. 15:16.
*c* *Prayer, importunity in*, Acts 6:4.

**3**
*d* *Oppression*, Eccl. 5:8.
*e* *Strife*, Prov. 20:3.
1 R. V. look upon perverseness?

---

**+ LOCUST.** *Authorized as food*, Lev. 11:22. *Used as food*, Matt. 3:4; Mark 1:6. *Plague of*, Ex. 10:1-19; Psa. 78:46; 105:34, 35. *Devastation by*, Deut. 28:38; 1 Kin. 8:37; 2 Chr. 7:13; Isa. 33:4; Joel 1:4-7; Rev. 9:7-10. *Sun obscured by*, Joel 2:2, 10. *Instincts of*, Prov. 30:27.
**In A. V. often inaccurately translated *grasshopper*, as in** Judg. 6:5; 7:12; Job 39:20; Jer. 46:23; Amos 7:1; Nah. 3:17.
**Symbolical**, Joel 2:1-11; Rev. 9:3-11.

*** HABAKKUK.** *A prophet and poet, who prophesied after, probably, the destruction of Nineveh*, Hab. 1:1; 3:1. *His hymn of praise of the majesty of God*, Hab. 3.

4 Therefore [f]the [g]law is slacked,
and [h]judgment[G] doth never go
forth: for the wicked doth compass about the righteous; therefore [h]wrong judgment[G] proceedeth.[S]
5 ¶ [i,j]Behold ye among the
[2]heathen, and regard, and wonder marvellously: for *I* will work
a work in your days, *which* ye
will not believe, though it be
told *you*.[Q]
6 For, lo, [j]I raise up the [k,l]Chăl-
dē′anṣ, *that* bitter and hasty nation, which shall march through
the breadth of the land, to
possess the dwellingplaces *that*
*are* not their's.[Q]
7 They *are* terrible and dreadful:
their judgment and their dignity
shall proceed of themselves.
8 Their [m]horses also are swifter
than the [n]leopards, and are more
fierce than the evening [o]wolves:
and their [p]horsemen shall spread
themselves, and their horsemen
shall come from far; they shall
fly as the [q]eagle *that* hasteth to
eat.
9 They shall come all for violence: their faces[G] [3]shall sup up
*as* the east wind, and they shall
gather [4]the captivity[G] as the sand.
10 [5]And they shall [†]scoff at the
kings, and the princes shall be a
scorn unto them: they shall deride every strong hold; for they
shall heap dust, and take it.
11 Then shall [6]*his* mind change,
and he shall pass over, and [7]of-
fend, *imputing* this his power
unto his god.
12 ¶ [r]*Art* thou not from [s]ever-
lasting, O LORD my God, mine
[t]Holy One? we shall not die. O
LORD, thou hast ordained[8,l] them
for judgment; and, [9]O mighty
God, thou hast established[G] [8,l]them
for [u]correction.[S]
13 [t]*Thou art* of purer [v]eyes than
to behold evil, and [w]canst not
look on iniquity[G]: [x,y]wherefore[G]
lookest thou upon them that
deal treacherously, *and* holdest
thy [10]tongue when the wicked
devoureth *the man that is* more
righteous than he?[S]
14 [y]And makest men as the
fishes of the sea, as the creeping
things, *that have* no ruler over
them?
15 They take up all of them
with the angle[G], they catch them
in their net, and gather them in
their drag[G]: therefore they rejoice
and are glad.
16 Therefore they sacrifice[G] unto
their [z]net, and burn incense unto
their [z]drag[G]; because by them their
portion *is* fat, and their meat[G]
plenteous.
17 [x,y]Shall they therefore empty
their net, and not spare continually to slay the nations?

## CHAPTER 2

*The prophet is directed to wait for the fulfillment of the vision. 5 Woes upon the idolatrous destroyer.*

I WILL stand upon my [a]watch,
and set me upon the tower,
and will watch to see what he will
say unto me, and what I shall answer [1]when I am reproved.
2 And the LORD answered me,
and said, [b]Write the [c]vision, and
make *it* plain upon *tables[G], that
he may run that readeth it.
3[Q] For the [c]vision *is* yet for an
appointed time, [2]but at the end it
shall speak, and not lie: though
it tarry, [d]wait for it; because [e,f]it
will surely come, it will not tarry.

**4**
f *Government, corruption in,* Isa. 22:21.
g *Justice, perverted,* Deut. 33:21.
h *Rulers, wicked,* Ex. 18:21.

**5**
i Acts 13:41.
j *Prophecies, fulfilled,* vs. 6–11; Dan. 9:24.
2 R. V. nations,

**6**
k *Chaldeans,* Dan. 1:4.
l *Agency, in executing judgments,* Mark 1:17.

**8**
m *Horse,* Job 39:19.
n *Leopard,* Song 4:8.
o *Wolf,* Jer. 5:6.
p *Cavalry,* 1 Sam. 13:5.
q *Eagle,* Lev. 11:13.

**9**
3 R. V. are set eagerly as
4 R. V. captives

**10**
5 R. V. Yea, he scoffeth at kings, and princes are a derision unto him: he derideth every strong hold; for he heapeth up dust, and taketh it.

**11**
6 R. V. he sweep by as a wind, and shall
7 R. V. be guilty: even he whose might is his god.

**12**
r *Faith, exemplified,* Mark 11:22.
s *God, eternity of,* Gen. 2:2.
t *God, holiness of,* Gen. 2:2.
8 R. V. him

u *Divine Chastisement, corrective,* Job 33:19.
9 R. V. thou, O Rock, hast

**13**
v *Eye, figurative,* Matt. 6:22.
w *Sin, repugnant to God,* Rom. 5:12.
x *God, longsuffering of,* Gen. 2:2.
y *God, providence of, mysterious,* Gen. 2:2.
10 R. V. peace

**16**
z *Idolatry, objects of,* 1 Sam. 15:23.

**1**
a *Watchfulness,* Matt. 24:42.
1 R. V. concerning my complaint.

**2**
b *Minister, duties of,* Rom. 15:16.
c *Vision,* Acts 9:10.

**3**
d *Faith, enjoined,* Mark 11:22.
e Heb. 10:37.
f *Prophecies, fulfillment of,* Dan. 9:24.
2 R. V. and it hasteth toward the end, and shall not lie:

† **SCOFFING.** *Of unbelievers,* Psa. 42:3, 10; 73:8, 9, 11, 12; Jer. 17:15; Ezek. 8:12; 9:9; 12:22; 2 Pet. 3:3, 4. *Of the wicked at God's requirements,* Job 21:14, 15; Isa. 10:15; 57:4; Ezek. 33:20. *Punishment for,* Isa. 5:18, 19, 24, 25; Heb. 10:29.

**Instances of:** *Ishmael,* Gen. 21:9. *Children at Beth-el,* 2 Kin. 2:23. *Ephraim and Manasseh,* 2 Chr. 30:10. *Priests and people of Judah,* 2 Chr. 36:16. *Sanballat,* Neh. 4:1. *Enemies of Job,* Job 30:1, 9. *Enemies of David,* Psa. 35:15, 16. *Rulers of Israel,* Isa. 28:9, 10, 14. *Ammonites,* Ezek. 25:3. *Tyrians,* Ezek. 26:2. *Heathen,* Ezek. 36:2, 3. *Soldiers,* Matt. 27:28–30; Luke 23:36. *Chief priests,* Matt. 27:41–43. *Pharisees,* Matt. 12:24; Luke 11:15; 16:14. *The soldiers who guarded Jesus,* Luke 22:63, 64. *Herod,* Luke 23:11. *People and rulers,* Luke 23:35. *Some of the multitude,* Acts 2:13. *Jews,* Acts 13:45. *Athenians,* Acts 17:32.

* **TABLE.** *A slab, or tablet, on which inscriptions were made,* Isa. 30:8; Hab. 2:2; Luke 1:63.

**Figurative,** Prov. 3:3; Jer. 17:1; 2 Cor. 3:3.

4 ¶ Behold, his soul *which* is
[g]lifted up is not upright in him:
but †the [h]just shall live [3]by his
[i]faith.[S Q]
5 Yea [4]also, because he transgresseth by [j]wine, *he is* a proud
man, neither keepeth at home,
who enlargeth his desire as[5, k]hell,[C]
and *is* as death, and [l]cannot be
satisfied, but [m]gathereth unto him
all nations, and heapeth unto him
all [6]people:
6 Shall not all these take up a
parable against him, and a taunting proverb against him, and say,
[m]Woe to [n]him that increaseth
*that which is* not his! how long?
and to him that [o]ladeth himself
with [7]thick clay!
7 Shall they not rise up suddenly
that shall bite thee, and awake
that shall vex[C] thee, and thou shalt
be for booties[C] unto them?
8 Because thou hast spoiled
many nations, all the remnant of
the [6]people shall spoil thee; because of men's blood, and *for* the
violence of the land, of the city,
and of all that dwell therein.
9 ¶ [m]Woe to him that [8]coveteth
an evil covetousness to his house,
that ‡he may set his nest on high,
that he may be delivered from the
power of evil!
10 Thou hast consulted[C] shame
to thy house by cutting off many
[6]people, and hast sinned *against*
thy soul.
11 For the stone shall cry out of
the wall, and the beam out of the
timber shall answer it.
12 ¶ Woe to [n]him that buildeth
a town with [p]blood, and stablish-
eth[C] a city by iniquity!
13 Behold, *is it* not of the LORD
of hosts that the [9]people shall
labour in the very fire, and the
people shall weary themselves for
very vanity[C]?
14 For [q, r, s]the earth shall be
filled with the knowledge of the
glory of the LORD, as the waters
cover the sea.
15 ¶ [t]Woe unto him that giveth
his neighbour drink, that [10]put-
test thy bottle[C] to *him*, and makest *him* [u]drunken also, that thou
mayest look on their nakedness!
16 [u]Thou art filled with shame
for glory: drink thou also, and
[11]let thy foreskin[C] be uncovered:
the cup of the LORD's right hand
shall be turned unto thee, and
[12]shameful[C] spewing *shall be* on
thy glory.
17 For the violence [13]of Lĕb′a-
non shall cover thee, and the
spoil of beasts, *which* made them
afraid, because of men's blood,
and for the violence [13]of the
land, [14]of the city, and [14]of all
that dwell therein.
18 ¶ [v]What[Q] profiteth the graven[C]
[w]image that the maker thereof
hath [x]graven[C] it; the molten[C] image, and a teacher of lies, that
the maker of his work trusteth
therein, to make dumb idols[C]?
19 Woe unto him that saith to
the wood, Awake; to the dumb
stone, Arise, it shall teach! Behold, it *is* laid over with gold and
silver, and *there is* no breath at
all in the midst of it.[Q]
20 But the LORD *is* in his holy
temple: [y]let all the earth keep
silence before him.

## CHAPTER 3

*The prayer of Habakkuk. 3 God's majesty and power displayed in the deliverance of his people. 16 The prophet's confidence and joy in God.*

A [a]PRAYER of [b]Hă-băk′kuk
the prophet upon [c]Shĭ-gī′-
o-nŏth.

**4**
*g* *Self-righteousness,* Luke 18:11.
*h* *Righteous, described,* Psa. 64:10.
*i* *Faithfulness,* Luke 16:10.
3 Am. R. V. (*marg.*) *Or,* in his faithfulness.

**5**
*j* *Wine,* Prov. 23:31.
*k* *Hell,* Mark 9:43.
*l* *Drunkard, insatiable appetite of,* Psa. 69:12.
*m* *Covetousness, warnings against,* vs. 5–9; Isa. 57:17.
4 R. V. moreover, wine is a treacherous dealer, a haughty man, and that keepeth not at home;
5 Am. R. V. Sheol,
6 R. V. peoples

**6**
*n* *Rulers, wicked,* vs. 6 13; Ex. 18:21.
*o* *Oppression,* Eccl. 5:8.

**9**
8 R. V. getteth an evil gain for his house,

**12**
*p* *Blood, figurative,* Gen. 9.4.

**13**
9 R. V. peoples labour for the fire, and the nations weary

**14**
*q* Isa. 11:9.
*r* *Jesus, kingdom of, prophecies concerning* (as some interpret), Matt. 1:21.
*s* *Church, prophecies concerning its prosperity* (as some interpret), Matt. 16:18.

**15**
*t* *Drunkenness, woes denounced against,* Luke 21:34.
*u* *Drunkenness, figurative,* Luke 21:34.
10 R. V. that addest thy venom thereto,

**16**
11 R. V. be as one uncircumcised:
12 R. V. foul shame shall be upon thy glory.

**17**
13 R. V. done to
14 R. V. to

**18**
*v* *Idolatry, folly of, illustrated by contrast of idols with the true God,* 1 Sam. 15:23.
*w* *Idol, manufacture of,* 1 Kin. 15:12.
*x* *Carving,* Ex. 35:33.

**20**
*y* *Worship,* Gen. 22:5.

**1**
*a* *Prayer,* Acts 6:4.
*b* *Habakkuk,* Hab. 1:1.
*c* *Music, symbols used in,* 2 Chr. 5:13.

† **THE JUST SHALL LIVE BY FAITH** (R. V. *margin,* in his faithfulness, Hab. 2:4), Rom. 1:17; Gal. 3:11; Heb. 10:38.
‡ **AMBITION,** 1 Tim. 3:1. *Insatiable,* Hab. 2:5, 6. *Parable, illustrating,* 2 Kin. 14:9. *A worldly lust,* Jas. 4:1, 2; 1 John 2:16. *Satan tempts to,* Matt. 4:8–10; Luke 4:5–8. *Moses falsely accused of,* Num. 16:13. *Curse upon,* Isa. 5:8; Hab. 2:9. *Jesus rebukes,* Matt. 16:26; 18:1–3; 20:20–28; Mark 9:33–37; 10:35–45; 12:38, 39; Luke 9:25, 46–48; 11:43; 22:24–30; John 5:44.
**Instances of:** *Lucifer,* Isa. 14:12–15. *Eve,* Gen. 3:5, 6. *Aaron and Miriam,* Num. 12:2–10. *Korah and his co-conspirators,* Num. 16:3–35. *Abimelech,* Judg. 9:1–6. *Absalom,* 2 Sam. 15:1–13; 18:18. *Haman,* Esth. 5:9–13. *Disciples of Jesus,* Matt. 18:1–3; 20:20–24; Mark 9:33–37; 10:35–45; Luke 9:46–48; 22:24–30. *Diotrephes,* 3 John 9, 10.
**Disappointed:** *Ahithophel,* 2 Sam. 17:23. *Adonijah,* 1 Kin. 1:5. *Haman,* Esth. 6:6–9.

2 O LORD, I have [d]heard [1]thy speech, *and* was afraid: [a]O LORD, *,[e]revive thy work in the midst of the years, in the midst of the years make known; [f]in wrath remember mercy.

3 ¶ God came from [g]Tē′man, and the Holy One from mount [h]Pā′ran. [Sē′lah.] His [i]glory covered the heavens, and the earth was full of his praise.

4 And *his* [i]brightness was as the light; he had [2]horns *coming* out of his hand: and there *was* the hiding of his [j]power.

5 Before him went the pestilence, and [3]burning coals went forth at his feet.

6 He stood, and measured the earth: he beheld, and drove asunder the nations; and the everlasting mountains were scattered, the perpetual hills did bow: [4]his ways *are* everlasting.

7 I saw the [k]tents of Cu̧′shan in affliction: *and* the curtains of the land of [l]Mĭd′ĭ-an did tremble.

8 Was the LORD displeased against the rivers? *was* thine [m]anger against the rivers? *was* thy wrath against the sea, that thou didst ride upon thine horses *and* thy chariots of salvation?

9 Thy bow was made quite naked, *according* to the oaths of the tribes, *even thy* word. [Sē′lah.] Thou didst cleave the earth with rivers.

10 The mountains saw thee, *and* they trembled: the overflowing of the water passed by: the deep uttered his voice, *and* lifted up his hands on high.

11 The sun *and* moon stood still in their habitation: at the light of thine arrows they went, *and* at the shining of thy glittering spear.

12 Thou didst march through the land in indignation, thou didst thresh the [5]heathen in anger.

13 Thou wentest forth for the salvation of thy people, *even* for salvation with thine anointed; thou woundedst the head out of the house of the wicked, by discovering the foundation unto the neck. [Sē′lah.

14 Thou didst [6]strike through with his staves the head of his villages: they came out as a whirlwind to scatter me: their rejoicing *was* as to devour the poor secretly.

15 Thou didst walk through the sea with thine horses, *through* the heap of great waters.

16 When I heard, my belly trembled; my lips quivered at the voice: rottenness entered into my bones, and I trembled in [7]myself, that I might rest in the day of trouble: when [8]he cometh up unto the people, he will invade them with his troops.

17 ¶ Although the fig tree shall not blossom, neither *shall* fruit *be* in the vines; the labour of the olive shall fail, and the fields shall yield no meat; the flock shall be cut off from the fold, and *there shall be* no herd in the stalls:

18 Yet [n]I will rejoice in the LORD, I will [o]joy in the God of my salvation.

19 [9,n,p]The LORD God *is* my strength, and he will make my feet like hinds' *feet*, and he will make me to walk upon mine high places. To the chief singer on my [q]stringed instruments.

**2**
*d Prophets, inspiration of*, Isa. 3:2.
*e Spiritual Desire*, Psa. 42:1.
*f Intercession, of man with God*, Jer. 27:18.
1 R. V. the report of thee, and am afraid:

**3**
*g Teman*, Jer. 49:7.
*h Paran*, Gen. 21:21.
*i God, glory of, described*, Gen. 2:2.

**4**
*j God, power of*, Gen. 2:2.
2 R. V. rays

**5**
3 R. V. fiery bolts

**6**
4 R. V. His goings were as of old.

**7**
*k Tent*, Gen. 13:5.
*l Midianites*, Gen. 37:28.

**8**
*m Anger of God*, 2 Kin. 13:3.

**12**
5 R. V. nations

**14**
6 R. V. pierce with his own staves the head of his warriors:

**16**
7 R. V. my place:
8 Am. R. V. When it cometh up against the people that invadeth him in troops.

**18**
*n Faith, exemplified*, Mark 11:22.
*o Joy*, Psa. 5:11.

**19**
*p Spiritual Blessings, from God*, Eph. 1:3.
*q Music*, 2 Chr. 5:13.
9 R. V. Jehovah, the Lord.

* **RELIGIOUS REVIVALS**, Zech. 8:20–23. *Prayer for*, Hab. 3:2. *Prophecies concerning*, Isa. 32:15; Joel 2:28; Mic. 4:1–8.
**Instances of:** *Under, Joshua*, Josh. 5:2–9; *Samuel*, 1 Sam. 7:1–6; *Elijah*, 1 Kin. 18:17–40; *Jehoash and Jehoiada*, 2 Kin. 11:4–20; 12:4–16; 2 Chr. 23; 24:1–14; *Hezekiah*, 2 Kin. 18:1–7; 2 Chr. chapters 29–31; *Josiah*, 2 Kin. 22; 23:1–25; 2 Chr. 34; 35:1–19; *Asa*, 2 Chr. 14:2–5; 15; *Manasseh*, 2 Chr. 33:12–19. *In Nineveh*, Jonah 3:4–10. *Under the preaching of Haggai*, Hag. 1:12–14. *At Pentecost, and in post-pentecostal times*, Acts 2:1–47; 4:4; 5:14; 6:7; 9:35; 11:20, 21; 12:24; 14:1; 19:17–20.

# THE BOOK OF ZEPHANIAH

## CHAPTER 1

*The date of the prophecy. 2 Judgments upon Judah and Jerusalem for their sins.*

THE word of the LORD which [a]came unto *Zĕph-a-nī'ah the son of Cụ'shī, the son of Gĕd-a-lī'ah, the son of Ăm-a-rī'ah, the son of Hĭz-kī'ah, in the days of [b]Jō-sī'ah the son of [c]Ā'-mon, king of Jū'dah.

2 [d]I will utterly[C] consume[C] all *things* from off the land, saith the LORD.

3 [d]I will consume man and beast; I will consume the fowls of the heaven, and the fishes of the sea, and the [e]stumblingblocks[C] with the wicked; and I will [f]cut off man from off the land, saith the LORD.[Q]

4 [d]I will also stretch out mine hand upon [g]Jū'dah, and upon all the inhabitants of [h]Jē-rṳ'sā-lĕm; and I will [f]cut off the remnant of Bā'al from this place, *and* the name of the Chĕm'a-rĭmṣ with the [i]priests;

5 And [d,f]them that worship the [j,k]host of heaven upon the [l]housetops; and [m]them that worship *and* that swear by the LORD, and that swear by Măl'cham;

6 And [d,f]them that are [n]turned back from the LORD; and *those* that have [o]not sought the LORD, nor enquired for him.

7 Hold thy peace at the presence of the Lord GOD: for the [p]day of the LORD *is* at hand: for the LORD hath prepared a [q]sacrifice[C], he hath [1]bid[C] his [†]guests.

8 And it shall come to pass in the day of the LORD's [q]sacrifice, that I will [f]punish[C] the princes, and the king's children, and all such as are clothed with [2]strange[C] [r]apparel.

9 In the same day also will [d]I [f]punish[C] all those that leap[C] on the threshold, which fill their masters' houses with violence and deceit.

10 And [h]it shall come to pass in that day, saith the LORD, *that there shall be* the noise of a cry from the [s]fish gate, and an howling from the second, and a great crashing from the hills.

11 Howl, ye inhabitants of Măk'tesh, for all the [3]merchant people are cut down; all they that bear silver are cut off.

12 ¶ And it shall come to pass at that time, *that* I will search [h]Jē-rṳ'sā-lĕm with [t]candles[C], and [f]punish[C] the men that are settled on their [u]lees[C] that [v,w]say in their heart, The LORD will not do good, neither will he do evil.

13 [d,f,g]Therefore their goods shall become a booty, and their houses a desolation: they shall also build houses, but not inhabit *them*; and they shall plant vineyards, but not drink the wine thereof.

14 The[Q] great [p]day of the LORD *is* near, *it is* near, and hasteth[C]

1
*a Prophets, inspiration of,* Isa. 3:2.
*b Josiah,* 1 Kin. 13:2.
*c Amon,* 2 Kin. 21:18.

2
*d Judgments,* Ex. 6:6.

3
*e Stumbling, figurative,* Isa. 8:14.
*f Wicked, punishment of,* Psa. 73:3.

4
*g Judah, prophecies concerning,* 2 Chr. 11:17.
*h Jerusalem, prophecies against,* Judg. 19:10.
*i Priest, idolatrous,* Lev 1:5.

5
*j Idolatry, objects of,* 1 Sam. 15:23.
*k Stars, worshiped,* Judg. 5:20.
*l House,* Esth. 8:1.
*m Character, instability of,* Phil. 2:15.

6
*n Backsliders,* Jer. 3:22.
*o Prayerlessness,* Job 21:15.

7
*p Day, times of adversity called day of the Lord,* Gen. 1:5.
*q Sacrifice, figurative,* Rom. 12:1.
1 R. V. sanctified

8
*r Dress,* Zech. 3:3.
2 R. V. foreign

10
*s Jerusalem, gates of,* Judg. 19:10.

11
3 R. V. people of Canaan are undone:

12
*t Lamp, figurative,* Ex. 27:20.
*u* Psa. 75:8; Isa. 25:6; Jer. 48:11.
*v False Confidence, of the infidel,* Psa. 30:6.
*w Skepticism,* Psa. 53:1.

* **ZEPHANIAH,** a bold preacher in the reign of Josiah. Foretells great judgments to come from the Lord upon Judah on account of their idolatry and other wickedness; denounces judgments against the Philistines, Moabites, Ethiopians and Assyrians, and exhorts to repentance. He closes his prophecy with a promise of the restoration of the Jews and the flourishing condition of Zion. See BOOK OF ZEPHANIAH.

† **GUEST.** *Salutations to,* Gen. 18:2, 3. *Rules for the conduct of,* Prov. 23:1-3, 6-8; 25:17; Luke 10:5-7; 14:7-11; 1 Cor. 10:27-33. See footnote, HOSPITALITY, Rom. 12:13.

greatly, *even* the voice of the day
of the LORD: the mighty man
shall cry there bitterly.
15 That [p]day *is* a day of wrath,
a day of trouble and distress, a
day of wasteness[C] and desolation,
a day of darkness and gloominess, a day[Q] of clouds and thick
darkness,
16 A day of the [x]trumpet and
alarm against the fenced[C] cities,
and against the high [4]towers.
17 And [d]I will bring [y,z]distress
upon men, that [a]they shall walk
like blind men, because they
have sinned against the LORD:
and their blood shall be poured
out as dust, and their flesh as the
dung.
18 [b,c]Neither their silver nor
their gold shall be able to deliver
them in the day of the LORD's
wrath; but the whole land shall
be devoured by the fire of his
[d]jealousy: for he shall make [5]even
a speedy riddance of all them
that dwell in the land.

## CHAPTER 2

*An exhortation to repentance. 4 Judgments upon the Philistines, 8 upon Moab and Ammon, 12 upon Ethiopia and Assyria.*

[a]GATHER yourselves together,
yea, gather together, O nation [1]not desired;
2 Before the decree bring forth,
*before* the day pass as the chaff,
before the fierce [b]anger of the
LORD come upon you, before the
[c]day of the LORD's anger come
upon you.
3 [d]Seek ye the LORD, all ye meek
of the earth, which have wrought[C]
his judgment[C]; seek [e]righteous-
ness, seek [f]meekness: it may be
ye shall be hid in the day of the
LORD's anger.
4 ¶ For [g]Gā'zȧ shall be forsaken, and [h]Ăsh'ke-lŏn a desolation: they shall drive out [i]Ăsh'-
dŏd at the noon day, and [j]Ĕk'-
rŏn shall be rooted up.
5 [k]Woe unto the [l]inhabitants of
the sea coast, the nation of the
[m]Chĕr'e-thītes! the word of the
LORD *is* against you; O Cā'-
năan, the land of the [n]Phĭ-lĭs'-
tĭneș, I will even destroy thee,
that there shall be no inhabitant.
6 And the sea coast shall be
[2]dwellings *and* cottages for [o]shep-
herds, and folds for flocks.
7 And [p]the coast shall be for the
remnant of the house of Jū'dah;
they shall [3]feed thereupon[C]: in
the houses of Ăsh'ke-lŏn shall
they lie down in the evening: for
[q]the LORD their God shall visit
them, and [4]turn away their captivity.
8 ¶ I have heard the reproach
of [r]Mō'ab, and the revilings of
the [s]children of Ăm'mŏn, whereby they have reproached my people, and magnified *themselves*
against their border.
9 Therefore *as* I live, saith the
LORD of hosts, the God of Ĭș'-
ra-el, Surely [k,l,r]Mō'ab shall be
as [t]Sŏd'om, and the [s]children of
Ăm'mŏn as [u]Gŏ-mŏr'rah, [5]*even*
the breeding[C] of [v]nettles, and
[w]saltpits, and a perpetual desolation: the residue of my people
shall spoil them, and the remnant of my [6]people shall possess
them.
10 [k,l]This shall they have for
their pride, because they have
reproached and magnified *themselves* against the people of the
LORD of hosts.
11 The LORD *will be* terrible
unto them: for [x]he will famish[C]
all the gods of the earth; and
*men* shall worship him, every
one from his place, *even* all the
isles of the [7]heathen[C].
12 ¶ Ye [k,l,y]Ē-thĭ-ō'pĭ-anș also,
ye *shall be* slain by my [z]sword.
13 And he will stretch out his
hand against the north, and destroy [a]Ăs-sy̆r'ĭ-ȧ; and will make
[b]Nĭn-e-veh a desolation, *and* dry
like a wilderness.

16
x *Trumpet,* Josh. 6:4.
4 R. V. battlements.
17
y *Adversity, dispensation from God,* Psa. 10:6.
z *Sin, punishment of,* Rom. 5:12.
a *Wicked, described,* Psa. 73:3.
18
b *Punishment, no escape from,* Lev. 26:41.
c *Riches, impotent in day of calamity,* Eccl. 4:8.
d *Jealousy, attributed to God,* Psa. 78:58.
5 R. V. an end, yea, a terrible end, of all
1
a *Wicked, warned,* Psa. 73:3.
1 R. V. that hath no shame;
2
b *Anger of God,* 2 Kin. 13.3.
c *Day, times of adversity called day of the Lord,* Gen. 1:5.
3
d *Seekers, seeking God, enjoined,* Isa. 55:6.
e *Holiness, enjoined,* Ex. 39:30.
f *Meekness, enjoined,* Psa. 45:4.
4
g *Gaza,* Gen. 10:19.
h Or, *Askelon,* Judg. 1:18.
i *Ashdod,* 1 Sam. 6:17.
j *Ekron,* Amos 1:8.
5
k *Judgments,* Ex. 6:6.
l *Nation, judgments denounced against,* Isa. 2:4.

m *Cherethites,* 1 Sam. 30:14.
n *Philistines,* Gen. 26:14.
6
o *Shepherd,* Jer. 31:10.
2 R. V. pastures, with cottages
7
p *Israel, prophecies concerning,* 1 Kin. 12:1.
q *God, mercy of,* Gen. 2:2.
3 R. V. feed their flocks
4 R. V. bring again
8
r *Moabites,* Gen. 19:37.
s *Ammonites,* vs. 8–11; Deut. 2:20.
9
t *Sodom, destroyed,* Gen. 13:10.
u *Gomorrah, destroyed,* Gen. 13:10.
v *Nettle, figurative,* Prov. 24:31.
w *Salt, emblematic,* 2 Kin. 2:20.
5 R. V. a possession of
6 R. V. nation
11
x *Idolatry, prophecies concerning,* 1 Sam. 15:23.
7 R. V. nations.
12
y *Ethiopia, desolation of,* Isa. 18:1.
z *War, as a judgment,* Judg. 3:2.
13
a *Assyria, prophecies concerning,* Gen. 25:18.
b *Nineveh,* vs. 13–15; Jonah 1:2.

14 And flocks shall lie down in the midst of her, all the beasts of the nations: both the [8]cormorant and the [c]bittern shall lodge in the upper lintels[G] of it; *their* voice shall sing in the windows; desolation *shall be* in the thresholds: for he [9]shall uncover the cedar work.

15 This *is* the rejoicing city that dwelt carelessly, that [d,e]said in her heart, I *am,* and *there is* none beside me: how is she become a desolation, a place for beasts to lie down in! every one that passeth by her shall hiss,[G] *and* wag his hand.

## CHAPTER 3

*Jerusalem rebuked for various sins. 8 An exhortation to wait on God for the restoration of Israel, 14 and to rejoice in their deliverance.*

WOE to her that is [1]filthy and polluted, to the [a]oppressing [b]city!

2 [c]She obeyed not the voice; [d]she received not correction; she trusted not in the LORD; she drew not near to her God.

3 Her [e]princes within her *are* roaring lions; her [f,g]judges *are* evening [h]wolves; they [2]gnaw not the bones till the morrow.

4 Her prophets *are* light *and* treacherous persons: her [i]priests have polluted[G] the sanctuary,[G] they have done violence to the law.

5 The [j]just LORD *is* in the midst thereof; [k]he will not do iniquity: every morning doth he bring his judgment[G] to light, he faileth not; but [l]the [m]unjust knoweth no shame.[S]

6 [n]I have cut off the nations: their [3]towers are desolate; I made their streets waste, that none passeth by: their cities are destroyed, so that there is no man, that there is none[G] inhabitant.

7 I [n]said, Surely thou wilt [o]fear me, thou wilt receive [4]instruction; so their dwelling should not be cut off, howsoever I punished them: but they rose early, *and* corrupted all their doings.

8 ¶ Therefore wait ye upon me, saith the LORD, until the day that I rise up to the prey: for my determination *is* to gather the nations, that I may assemble the kingdoms, to pour upon them mine indignation, *even* all my fierce [p]anger: for all the earth shall be devoured with the fire of my [q]jealousy.[G Q]

9 For [r]then will I [s]turn to the [5]people a pure language, that they may all [t]call upon the name of the LORD, to serve him with one consent.

10 From beyond the rivers of [u]Ē-thĭ-ō′pĭ-ȧ my suppliants, *even* the daughter of my dispersed, shall bring mine offering.

11 In that day shalt thou not be ashamed for all thy doings, wherein thou hast transgressed against me: for then I will take away out of the midst of thee [6]them that rejoice in thy pride, and thou shalt no more be haughty [7]because of my holy mountain.

12 I will also leave in the midst of thee an afflicted and [v]poor people, and they shall [w]trust in the name of the LORD.

13 ¶ [x]The remnant of Ĭş′ra-el shall not do iniquity, nor speak lies; neither shall a [y]deceitful tongue be found in their mouth: for they shall feed and lie down, and none shall make *them* afraid.[S Q]

14 ¶ Sing, O daughter of [z]Zī′-ŏn; shout, O [a]Ĭş′ra-el; be glad and rejoice with all the [b]heart, O daughter of Jĕ-ru̥′să-lĕm.[S]

15 [a,c]The LORD hath taken away thy judgments, he hath cast out thine enemy: the king of Ĭş′ra-el, *even* the LORD, *is* in the midst of thee: thou shalt not see evil any more.[Q]

**14**
c Isa. 14:23; 34:11.
8 Am. R. V. pelican and the porcupine shall lodge in the capitals thereof:
9 R. V. hath laid bare

**15**
d *False Confidence, in self-sufficiency,* Psa. 30:6.
e *Self-exaltation,* Luke 14:11.

**1**
a *Oppression,* Eccl. 5:8.
b *Jerusalem, prophecies against,* Judg. 19:10.
1 R. V. rebellious

**2**
c *Disobedience to God,* Eph. 5:6.
d *Adversity, obduracy in,* v. 7; Psa. 10:6.

**3**
e *Rulers, wicked,* Ex. 18:21.
f *Judge, corrupt,* Judg. 2:18.
g *Court, corrupt,* Ex. 18:26.
h *Wolf, figurative of wicked rulers,* Jer. 5:6.
2 R. V. leave nothing

**4**
i *Minister, false and corrupt,* Rom. 15:16.

**5**
j *God, righteousness of,* Gen. 2:2.
k *God, holiness of,* Gen. 2:2.
l *Wicked, described,* Psa. 73:3.
m *Injustice,* Isa. 26:10.

**6**
n *Judgments, design of,* Ex. 6:6.
3 R. V. battlements

**7**
o *Fear of God,* Acts 9:31.
4 R. V. correction; so her dwelling should not be cut off, according to all that I have appointed concerning her:

**8**
p *Anger of God,* 2 Kin. 13:3.
q *Jealousy, attributed to God,* Psa. 78:58.

**9**
r *Church, prophecies concerning its prosperity,* vs. 9–20; Matt. 16:18.
s *Spiritual Blessings, from God,* Eph. 1:3.
t *Spiritual Desire,* Psa. 42:1.
5 R. V. peoples

**10**
u *Ethiopia,* Isa. 18:1.

**11**
6 R. V. thy proudly exulting ones,
7 R. V. in my

**12**
v *Poor, God's care of,* Prov. 21:13.
w *Faith,* Mark 11:22.

**13**
x *Jews, prophecies concerning,* Neh. 4:2.
y *Deceit,* Psa. 36:3.

**14**
z *Zion, restoration of,* 2 Sam. 5:7.
a *Israel, prophecies concerning restoration of,* vs. 14–20; 1 Kin. 12:1.
b *Heart,* Psa. 44:21.

**15**
c *Grace of God,* Rom. 4:16.

**16**
*d Faith, enjoined,* Mark 11:22.

**17**
*e God, power of,* Gen. 2:2.
*f God, savior,* Gen. 2:2.
*g God, love of, exemplified,* Gen. 2:2.

**18**
*h Afflictions, consolation in,* Psa. 34:19.

16 In that day it shall be [d]said
to Jĕ-ru'să-lĕm, Fear thou not:
*and to* Zī'ŏn, Let not thine hands
be slack.
17 The LORD thy God in the
midst of thee *is* [e]mighty; he will
[f]save, he will rejoice over thee
with joy; he will rest in his [g]love,
he will joy over thee with singing.
18 [h]I will gather *them that are*
sorrowful for the solemn assembly,
*who* are of thee, *to whom* the
reproach of it *was* a burden.
19 Behold, at that time [h]I will
undo all that afflict thee: and I
will save her that halteth[G], and
gather her that was driven out;
and I will get them praise and
[8]fame in every land where they
have been put to shame.
20 At that time [a]will I bring you
*again,* even in the time that I
gather you: for I will make you
a name and a praise among all
[5]people of the earth, when I turn
back your captivity[G] before your
eyes, saith the LORD.[S]

**19**
8 R. V. a name, whose shame hath been in all the earth.

---

THE

# BOOK OF HAGGAI

v 1–441 BC
See footnote, *Time,* Rev. 10:6.

**1**
*a Darius,* Ezra 5:5.
*b Month (September),* Ex. 12:2.
*c Prophets, inspiration of,* Isa. 3:2.
*d Zerubbabel,* Ezra 3:2.
*e Shealtiel,* Ezra 3:2.
*f* Or, *Jeshua,* Ezra 2:2.
*g* Or, *Jozadak,* Neh. 12:26.
*h High Priest,* Lev. 21:10.

**2**
*i Lukewarmness,* Rev. 3:16.
*j Parsimony,* Mal. 3:8.
*k Temple, Solomon's, prophecies of its restoration,* 1 Kin. 6:17.

**3**
*l Reproof, faithfulness in,* Prov. 17:10.

**5**
*m Repentance, enjoined,* Mark 1:4.
*n Self-examination, enjoined,* 2 Cor. 13:5.

**6**
*o Covetousness, reproof for,* Isa. 57:17.

## CHAPTER 1

*The prophet reproves the people for neglecting to build the Lord's house. 7 He exhorts them to build, 12 and promises them God's assistance.*

IN the second year of [a]Dă-rī'us
the king, in the sixth [b]month,
in the first day of the month,
[c]came the word of the LORD by
*Hăg'ga-ī the prophet unto [d]Zĕ-
rŭb'ba-bĕl the son of [e]Shē-ăl'tĭ-
el, governor of Jū'dah, and to
[f]Jŏsh'u-ȧ the son of [g]Jŏs'e-dĕch,
the [h]high priest, saying,
2 [c]Thus speaketh the LORD of
hosts, saying, This people [i,j]say,
The time is not come, the time
that the LORD's [k]house should
be built.
3 Then [c]came the word of the
LORD by *Hăg'ga-ī the prophet,
[l]saying,
4 [l]*Is it* time for you, O ye, to
dwell in your cieled[G] houses, and
this house *lie* waste[G]?
5 Now therefore thus [m,n]saith
the LORD of hosts; Consider your
ways.
6 [o]Ye have sown much, and
bring in little; ye eat, but ye have
not enough; ye drink, but ye are
not filled with drink; ye clothe
you, but there is none warm; and
he that earneth wages earneth
wages *to put it* into a bag with
holes.
7 ¶ Thus [m,n]saith the LORD of
hosts; Consider your ways.
8 Go up to the mountain, and
[p]bring wood, and build the house;
and I will take pleasure in it,
and I will be glorified, saith the
LORD.
9 Ye looked for much, and, lo,
[q,r]*it came* to little; and when ye
brought *it* home, [q,r]I did blow
upon it. Why? saith the LORD
of hosts. Because of mine house
that *is* waste[G], and ye run every
man unto his own house.
10 [q,r]Therefore the heaven over
you is stayed[G] from dew, and
[s,t]the earth is stayed[G] *from* her
fruit.
11 And [t]I called for a [r]drought
upon the land, and upon the
mountains, and upon the corn[G],
and upon the new wine, and upon
the oil, and upon *that* which

v.6–441 BC
See footnote, *Time,* Rev. 10:6.

**8**
*p Liberality, enjoined,* 1 Tim. 6:18.

**9**
*q Parsimony, punishment of,* vs. 9–11; Mal. 3:8.
*r Judgments,* Ex. 6:6.

**10**
*s Famine, sent as a judgment,* v. 11; 2 Kin. 8:1.
*t Adversity, dispensation from God,* Psa. 10:6.

* **HAGGAI**, one of the minor prophets. *Prophesies in the second year of Darius,* Hag. 1:1. *Urges the Jews to rebuild the temple,* Ezra 5:1, 2; 6:14; Hag. 1:1–11. *Encourages the people in the work of rebuilding,* Hag. 2.

v.11–441 BC
See footnote, *Time*, Rev. 10:6.

12
*u* *Preaching, effective*, Matt. 9:35.
*v* *Repentance*, Mark 1:4.
*w* *Obedience*, Heb. 5:8.
*x* *Fear of God*, Acts 9:31.

13
*y* *Righteous, promises to*, Psa. 64:10.

14
*z* *Inspiration*, Job 32:8.

*a* *Liberality, instances of*, 1 Tim. 6:18.

15
*b* *Month (September)*, Ex. 12:2.
*c* *Darius*, Ezra 5:5.

1
*a* *Month (October)*, Ex. 12:2.
*b* *Prophets, inspiration of*, Isa. 3:2.
*c* *Haggai*, Hag. 1:1.

2
*d* *Zerubbabel*, Ezra 3:2.
*e* *Shealtiel*, Ezra 3:2.
*f* *Judah, kingdom of*, 2 Chr. 11:17.
*g* Or, *Jeshua*, Ezra 2:2.
*h* Or, *Jozadak*, Neh. 12:26.
*i* *High Priest*, Lev. 21:10.

3
*j* *Temple, Solomen's*, 1 Kin. 6:17.

the ground bringeth forth, and upon men, and upon cattle, and upon all the labour of the hands.

12 ¶ [u,v]Then [d]Zĕ-rŭb′ba-bĕl the son of [e]Shĕ-ăl′tĭ-el, and [f]Jŏsh′-u-ȧ the son of [g]Jŏs′e-dĕch, the [h]high priest, with all the remnant of the people, [w]obeyed the voice of the LORD their God, and the words of Hăg′ga-ī the prophet, as the LORD their God had sent him, and the people did [x]fear before the LORD.

13 Then spake *Hăg′ga-ī the LORD's[†] messenger in the LORD's [c]message unto the people, [y]saying, I *am* with you, saith the LORD.[S Q]

14 And the LORD [z]stirred up the spirit of Zĕ-rŭb′ba-bĕl the son of Shĕ-ăl′tĭ-el, governor of Jū′dah, and the spirit of Jŏsh′u-ȧ the son of Jŏs′e-dĕch, the high priest, and the spirit of all the remnant of the people; and [a]they came and did work in the house of the LORD of hosts, their God,

15 In the four and twentieth day of the sixth [b]month, in the second year of [c]Dā-rī′us the king.

## CHAPTER 2

*The glory of the latter house to be greater than that of the former. 10 The work hindered by the sins of the people. 20 God's promise to Zerubbabel.*

IN the seventh [a]*month*, in the one and twentieth *day* of the month, [b]came the word of the LORD by the prophet [c]Hăg′-ga-ī, saying,

2 Speak now to [d]Zĕ-rŭb′ba-bĕl the son of [e]Shĕ-ăl′tĭ-el, governor of [f]Jū′dah, and to [g]Jŏsh′u-ȧ the son of [h]Jŏs′e-dĕch, the [i]high priest, and to the residue[G] of the people, saying,

3 Who *is* left among you that saw this [j]house in her first glory? and how do ye see it now? *is it* not in your eyes in comparison of it as nothing?

4 Yet now be strong, O [d]Zĕ-rŭb′ba-bĕl, saith the LORD; and be strong, O [g]Jŏsh′u-ȧ, son of [h]Jŏs′e-dĕch, the [i]high priest; and be strong, all ye people of the land, saith the LORD, and [k]work: for [l]I *am* with you, saith the LORD of hosts:

5 *According to* the word that I [m]covenanted[G] with you when ye came out of [n]Ē′ġy̆pt, [o]so my spirit[G] remaineth among you: fear ye not.[S T]

6 For thus saith the LORD of hosts; [p]Yet once, it *is* a little while, and I will shake the heavens, and the earth, and the sea, and the dry *land*;[Q]

7 And [q,r,s]I will shake all nations, and the [1,t]desire of all nations shall come: and I will fill this house with glory, saith the LORD of hosts.[Q]

8 [u]The silver *is* mine, and the gold *is* mine, saith the LORD of hosts.

9 The glory of this latter house shall be greater than of the former, saith the LORD of hosts: and in this place will I give [v]peace, saith the LORD of hosts.

10 ¶ In the four and twentieth *day* of the ninth [w]*month*, in the second year of [x]Dā-rī′us, [b]came the word of the LORD by [c]Hăg′-ga-ī the prophet, saying,

11 Thus saith the LORD of hosts; Ask now the priests *concerning* the law, saying,

12 [y]If one bear holy flesh[G] in the skirt of his garment, and with his skirt do touch bread, or pottage, or wine, or oil, or any meat,[G] shall it be holy? And the priests answered and said, No.

13 Then said Hăg′ga-ī, If *one that is* unclean by a dead body touch any of these, shall it be unclean? And the priests answered and said, It shall be [z]unclean.

14 Then answered Hăg′ga-ī, and [a]said, [b]So *is* this people, and

v.4–441 BC
See footnote, *Time*, Rev. 10:6.

4
*k* *Zeal, enjoined*, 2 Cor. 7:11.
*l* *Righteous, promises to*, Psa. 64:10.

5
*m* *Covenant, of God with men*, Deut. 29:1.
*n* *Egypt*, Gen. 41:8.
*o* *God, faithfulness of*, Gen. 2:2.

6
*p* Heb. 12:26.

7
*q* *Jesus, kingdom of, prophecies concerning*, vs. 8, 9; Matt. 1:21.
*r* *Church, prophecies concerning its prosperity*, Matt. 16:18.
*s* *Gentiles, prophecies of the conversion of*, Acts 10:45.
*t* *Jesus, prophecies concerning* (as some interpret), Matt. 1:21.
1 R. V. desirable things

8
*u* *God, sovereign*, Gen. 2:2.

9
*v* *Spiritual Peace, from God*, Gal. 1:3.

10
*w* *Month (December)*, Ex. 12:2.
*x* *Darius*, Ezra 5:5.

12
*y* *Minister, character and qualifications of*, Rom. 15:16.

13
*z* *Defilement*, vs. 11–13; Lev. 5:2.

14
*a* *Reproof, faithfulness in*, Prov. 17:10.
*b* *Wicked*, Psa. 73:3.

† **MESSENGER. Figurative,** Hag. 1:13; Mal. 2:7; 3:1; 4:5, 6; Matt. 11:10; Mark 1:2; Luke 7:27.

so *is* this nation before me, saith
the LORD; and so *is* every work
of their hands; and that which
they offer there *is* unclean.
15 And now, I pray you, consider[C] from this day and upward,[C]
from before a stone was laid upon a stone in the [c]temple of the
LORD:
16 [2]Since those *days* were, when
*one* came to an heap of twenty
*measures,* there were *but* ten:
when *one* came to the pressfat[C]
for to draw out fifty *vessels* out
of the press, there were *but*
twenty.
17 I [d]smote you with [e,f]blasting[C]
and with [g]mildew and with [h]hail
in all the labours of your hands;
[i]yet ye *turned* not to me, saith the
LORD.
18 ¶ Consider[C] now from this
day and upward,[C] from the four
and twentieth day of the ninth
*month, even* from the day that
the foundation of the LORD's
[j]temple was laid, consider[C] *it.*
19 Is the seed yet in the [k]barn?
yea, as yet the vine, and the fig
tree, and the pomegranate, and
the olive tree, hath not brought
forth: from this day [l,m,n]will I
bless *you.*[S]
20 ¶ And again the word of the
LORD [o]came unto [p]Hăg′ga-ī in
the four and twentieth *day* of the
month, saying,
21 Speak to [q]Zĕ-rŭb′ba-bĕl, governor of [r]Jū′dah, saying, I will
shake the heavens and the earth;[Q]
22 And [s]I will [t]overthrow the
throne of kingdoms, and I will
destroy the strength of the kingdoms of the [3]heathen;[C] and I
will overthrow the chariots, and
those that ride in them; and the
horses and their riders shall come
down, every one by the sword
of his brother.
23 In that day, saith the LORD
of hosts, will I [u]take thee, O
[q]Zĕ-rŭb′ba-bĕl, my servant, the
son of Shĕ-ăl′tĭ-el, saith the
LORD, and will make thee as a
signet: for I have [v]chosen thee,
saith the LORD of hosts.[S]

v.14—441 BC See footnote, *Time,* Rev. 10:6.

15 c *Temple, Solomon's,* 1 Kin. 6:17.

16 2 R. V. Through all that time, when

17 d *Divine Chastisement, impenitence under,* Job 33:19.
e *Blasting, sent as a judgment,* 1 Kin. 8:37.
f *Judgments, design of,* Ex. 6:6.
g Deut. 28:22; Amos 4:9.
h *Hail,* Job 38:22.
i *Adversity, obduracy in,* Psa. 10:6.

18 j *Temple, Second,* 1 Kin. 6:17.
3 R. V. since the day

19 k *Barn,* Prov. 3:10.

v.19—441 BC See footnote, *Time,* Rev. 10:6.

l *God, providence of,* Gen. 2:2.
m *Temporal Blessings, from God,* Psa. 103:2.
n *Prosperity, from God,* Eccl. 7:14.

20 o *Prophets, inspiration of,* Isa. 3:2.
p *Haggai,* Hag. 1:1.

21 q *Zerubbabel, prophecies relating to,* Ezra 3:2.
r *Judah, kingdom of,* 2 Chr. 11:17.

22 s *Government, God in,* Isa. 22:21.
t *Judgments,* Ex. 6:6.
4 R. V. nations;

23 u *Call, personal,* Phil. 3:14.
v *Foreordination,* Rom. 8:30.

---

THE

# BOOK OF ZECHARIAH

## CHAPTER 1

*An exhortation to repentance. 7 The vision of the horses. 12 At the prayer of the angel mercies are promised to Jerusalem. 18 The vision of the four horns.*

IN the eighth [a]month, in the
second year of [b]Dā-rī′us,
[c]came the [d]word of the LORD
unto *Zĕch-a-rī′ah, the son of
Bĕr-e-chī′ah, the son of [e]Ĭd′dō
the prophet, saying,[Q]
2 The LORD hath been sore[C] displeased with your fathers.
3 Therefore say thou unto
them, Thus saith the LORD of
hosts; [f]Turn ye unto me, saith
the LORD of hosts, and [g,h]I will
turn unto you, saith the LORD of
hosts.[Q]
4 [i]Be ye not as your fathers,
unto whom the former prophets
have cried, saying, Thus saith
the LORD of hosts; [f]Turn ye now
from your evil ways, and *from*
your evil doings: but [j]they did
not hear, nor hearken unto me,
saith the LORD.
5 Your fathers, [k]where *are*
they? and the prophets, [k]do they
live for ever?
6 But my words and my statutes, which I commanded my
servants the prophets, did they

v.1—441 BC See footnote, *Time,* Rev. 10:6.

1 a *Month (November),* Ex. 12:2.
b *Darius,* Ezra 5:5.
c *Prophets, inspiration of,* Isa. 3:2.
d *Prophecies, inspired,* Dan. 9:24.
e Ezra 5:1; 6:14.

3 f *Repentance, enjoined,* Mark 1:4.
g *God, mercy of,* Gen. 2:2.
h *Penitent, promises to,* Psa. 51:17.

4 i *Example, bad, admonitions against,* John 13:15.
j *Impenitence,* Rom. 2:5.

5 k *Death, inevitable,* Num. 23:10.

---

* **ZECHARIAH** (*remembered of Jehovah*), the prophet. *Son of Berechiah,* Zech. 1:1. *Prophesied in the reign of Darius,* Ezra 4:24; 5:1; 6:14; Zech. 1:1, 7; 7:1. *Probably the priest mentioned* in Neh. 12:16.

6
God, judge, Gen. 2:2.
m Judgment, according to opportunity and works, 1 Pet. 1:17.
n Punishment, according to deeds, Lev. 26:41.
1 R. V. overtake your fathers?
7
o Month (February), Ex. 12:2.
v.7–441 BC
8
p Vision, Acts 9:10.
2 R. V. sorrel,
9
q Prophets, inspired by angels, Isa. 3:2.
11
r Isa. 41:19; 55:13.
s Peace, Jer. 29:7.
12
t Prayer, intercessory, Acts 6:4.
u Jerusalem, Judg. 19:10.
v Seventy, Num. 11:16.
13
w Prayer, answered, Acts 6:4.
14
x God, love of, Gen. 2:2.
y Jealousy, attributed to God, Psa. 78:58.
z God, jealous, Gen. 2:2.

not [1]take hold of your fathers? and they returned and said, Like as the LORD of hosts [l]thought to do unto us, [m]according to our ways, and according to our doings, [n]so hath he dealt with us.[Q]

7 ¶ Upon the four and twentieth day of the eleventh [o]month, which *is* the month Sē′băt, in the second year of [b]Dā-rī′us, [c]came the [d]word of the LORD unto *Zĕch-a-rī′ah, the son of Bĕr-e-chī′ah, the son of [e]Ĭd′dō the prophet, saying,

8 I [p]saw[T] by night, and behold a man riding upon a red horse, and he stood among the myrtle trees that *were* in the bottom; and behind him *were there* red horses, [2]speckled,[C] and white.[Q]

9 Then said I, O my lord, what *are* these? And the angel that [q]talked with me said unto me, I will shew thee what these *be*.

10 And the man that stood among the myrtle trees answered and said, These *are they* whom the LORD hath sent to walk to and fro through the earth.

11 And they answered the angel of the LORD that stood among the [r]myrtle trees, and said, We have walked to and fro through the earth, and, behold, all the earth sitteth still, and is at [s]rest.

12 ¶ Then the angel of the LORD answered and [t]said, O LORD of hosts, how long wilt thou not have[C] mercy on [u]Jē-ru̧′sȧ-lĕm and on the cities of Jū′dah, against which thou hast had indignation these [v]threescore and ten years?[Q]

13 And the LORD [w]answered the angel that [q]talked with me *with* good words *and* comfortable[C] words.[G] [S]

14 So the angel that communed[G] with me [q]said unto me, Cry thou, saying, Thus saith the LORD of hosts; [x]I am [y,z]jealous for [u]Jē-ru̧′sȧ-lĕm and for [a]Zī′ŏn with a great jealousy.[S]

15 And I am very sore[C] displeased with the [3]heathen[C] *that are* at ease: for I was but a little displeased, and they helped[C] forward the affliction.

16 Therefore [a,b]thus saith the LORD; I am returned to Jē-ru̧′sȧ-lĕm with [c,d]mercies: my [e]house shall be built in it, saith the LORD of hosts, and a line shall be stretched forth upon Jē-ru̧′sȧ-lĕm.

17 Cry yet, [a,b]saying, Thus saith the LORD of hosts; [c,d]My cities through prosperity shall yet be spread abroad; and the LORD shall yet comfort Zī′ŏn, and shall yet choose Jē-ru̧′sȧ-lĕm.[T]

18 ¶ Then lifted I up mine eyes, and [f]saw, and behold four [g]horns.[C]

19 And I said unto the angel that talked with me, What *be* these? And he answered me, These *are* the [g]horns which have scattered Jū′dah, Ĭs′ra-el, and Jē-ru̧′sȧ-lĕm.

20 And the LORD shewed me four [4]carpenters.

21 Then said I, What come these to do? And he spake, saying, These *are* the [g]horns which have scattered Jū′dah, so that no man did lift up his head: but these are come to fray[G] them, to cast out the horns of the [3]Gĕn′tīles,[C] which lifted up *their* horn over the land of Jū′dah to scatter it.

## CHAPTER 2

*The vision of the angel about to measure Jerusalem. 6 God's people called upon to return from Babylon. 10 The promise of his presence.*

[a]I LIFTED[Q] up mine eyes again, and looked, and [b]behold a [c]man with a measuring line in his hand.

2 Then said I, Whither[C] goest thou? And he said unto me, To measure [d]Jē-ru̧′sȧ-lĕm, to see

a Zion, restoration of, 2 Sam. 5:7.
15
3 R. V. nations
16
b Israel, prophecies concerning, 1 Kin. 12:1.
c God, providence of, Gen. 2:2.
d Temporal Blessings, from God, Psa. 103:2.
e Temple, Second, 1 Kin. 6:17.
18
f Vision, vs. 18–21; Acts 9:10.
g Horn, symbolical, 1 Kin. 1:39.
20
4 R. V. smiths.
1
a Zechariah, Zech. 1:1.
b Vision, Acts 9:10.
c Angel, medium of revelation to prophets, vs. 1–13; Heb. 1:13.
2
d Jerusalem, prophecies concerning, vs. 2–5; Judg. 19:10.

what *is* the breadth thereof, and what *is* the length thereof.[Q]

3 And, behold, the [c]angel that talked with me went forth, and another angel went out to meet him,[T]

4 And said unto him, Run, speak to this young man, saying, [d]Jĕ-rṳ′să-lĕm shall be inhabited *as* towns without walls for the multitude of men and cattle therein:

5 For I, saith the LORD, [d]will be unto her a wall of fire round about, and will be the glory in the midst of her.[S]

6 ¶ Ho, ho, *come forth*, and flee from the land of the north, saith the LORD: for I have spread you abroad as the four winds of the heaven, saith the LORD.[Q]

7 Deliver thyself, O [e]Zī′ŏn, that dwellest *with* the daughter of [f]Băb′ȳ-lon.

8 For thus saith the LORD of hosts; After [1]the glory hath he sent me unto the nations which spoiled[C] you: for he that toucheth you [g]toucheth the apple of his eye.[S]

9 For, behold, I will shake mine hand upon them, and they shall be a spoil[C] to [2]their servants: and [h]ye shall know that the LORD of hosts hath sent [c]me.

10 ¶ Sing[T] and rejoice, O daughter of [i,j]Zī′ŏn: for, lo, I come, and I will [k]dwell in the midst of thee, saith the LORD.[Q]

11 And [i,l]many nations shall be joined to the LORD in that day, and shall be [m]my people: and I will [k]dwell in the midst of thee, and thou shalt know that the LORD of hosts hath sent me unto thee.[T]

12 And the LORD shall inherit [n]Jū′dah his portion in the holy land, and shall choose Jĕ-rṳ′să-lĕm again.

13 Be silent, O all flesh, before the LORD: for he is raised up out of his holy habitation.

## CHAPTER 3

*Under the type of Joshua, the restoration of Zion is prefigured. 8 Messiah the Branch is promised.*

AND he[T Q] [a]shewed me [b]Jŏsh′u-ȧ the [c]high priest standing before the [d]angel of the LORD, and [e]Sā′tan standing at his right hand to resist him.

2 And the LORD said unto [e]Sā′tan, The LORD rebuke thee, O Sā′tan; even the LORD that hath chosen Jĕ-rṳ′să-lĕm rebuke thee: *is* not this a [f]brand plucked out of the fire?[Q]

3 Now [b]Jŏsh′u-ȧ was clothed with filthy *garments, and stood before the angel.[Q]

4 And he answered and spake unto those that stood before him, saying, [g]Take away the filthy *garments from him. And unto him he said, [g]Behold, I have caused thine iniquity to [h,i]pass from thee, and I will clothe thee with [1,j]change of raiment.[S]

5 And I said, Let them set a fair[C] mitre[C] upon his head. So they set a fair[C] mitre[C] upon his head, and clothed him with garments. And the [d]angel of the LORD stood by.

6 And the [d]angel of the LORD protested unto [b]Jŏsh′u-ȧ, saying,

7 Thus saith the LORD of hosts;

**7**

*e* *Zion*, v. 10; 2 Sam. 5:7.

*f* *Babylon, prophecies concerning*, vs. 7–9; Ezra 5:12

**8**

*g* *God, love of*, Gen. 2:2.

1 R. V. *omits* the

**9**

*h* *Judgments, design of*, Ex. 6:6.

2 R. V. those that served them:

**10**

*i* *Church, prophecies concerning its prosperity*, Matt. 16:18.

*j* *Jesus, kingdom of, prophecies concerning*, Matt. 1:21.

*k* *Fellowship, with God*, 1 Cor. 1:9.

**11**

*l* *Gentiles, prophecies of the conversion of*, Acts 10:45.

*m* *Spiritual Adoption*, Rom. 8:15.

**12**

*n* *Jews, prophecies concerning*, Neh. 4:2.

**1**

*a* *Vision*, vs. 1–5; Acts 9:10.

*b* Or, *Jeshua, Zechariah's vision concerning*, Ezra 2:2.

*c* *High Priest*, Lev. 21:10.

*d* *Angel, one of the Holy Trinity* (according to many learned commentators), Ex. 14:19.

*e* *Satan*, Matt. 4:10.

**2**

*f* *Righteous, described*, Psa. 64:10.

**4**

*g* *Instruction, by object lessons*, Prov. 23:23.

*h* *Sin, forgiveness of*, Rom. 5:12.

*i* *Justification*, Rom. 4:25.

*j* *Righteousness, figuratively described as a garment*, Psa. 15:2.

1 R. V. rich apparel.

* **DRESS.** *Of fig leaves*, Gen. 3:7. *Of skins*, Gen. 3:21. *Mixed materials in, forbidden*, Deut. 22:11. *Men forbidden to wear women's, and women forbidden to wear men's*, Deut. 22:5. *Rules with respect to women's*, 1 Tim. 2:9, 10; 1 Pet. 3:3. *Not to be held over night as a pledge for debt*, Ex. 22:26. *Ceremonial purification of*, Lev. 11:32; 13:47–59; 14:55 (with vs. 52, 53); 15:17; Num. 31:20. *Of Israelites waxed not old*, Deut. 8:4; 29:5.

*The folly of excessive changes of raiment*, Job 27:16, 17. *Uniform vestments kept in store, for worshipers of Baal*, 2 Kin. 10:22, 23; *for wedding feasts*, Matt. 22:11. *Presents made of changes of raiment*, Gen. 45:22; 1 Sam. 18:4; 2 Kin. 5:5, 22, 23; Esth. 6:8; Dan. 5:7.

OF THE HEAD: *Bonnets* [R. V. head-tires] *prescribed, by Moses for the priests*, Ex. 28:40; 29:9; 39:28; *by Ezekiel*, Ezek. 44:18. *Turbans* [R. V. head-tires] *worn by women*, Isa. 3:20, 23; Ezek. 24:17, 23.

VARIOUS ARTICLES OF: *Mantle*, 1 Kin. 19:13; 1 Chr. 15:27; Ezra 9:3; Job 1:20. *Robe*, Ex. 28:4; 1 Sam. 18:4; 2 Sam. 13:18; John 19:2, 5. *Shawls* [R. V.], Isa. 3:22. *Embroidered coat*, Ex. 28:4, 39. *Sleeveless shirt, called coat*, Matt. 5:40; Luke 6:29; John 19:23; Acts 9:39. *Cloak*, John 19:2, 5; 2 Tim. 4:13. *Hosen*, Dan. 3:21. *Skirts*, Ezek. 5:3. *Mufflers*, Isa. 3:19. *Sashes* [R. V.], Isa. 3:20.

**Figurative:** *Of righteousness*, Isa. 61:10; Matt. 22:11; Rev. 3:18; 6:11; 7:13, 14; 16:15; 19:8. *Filthy, of unrighteousness*, Isa. 64:6.

**Symbolical:** *Filthy, of iniquity*, Zech. 3:3, 4.

[k]If thou wilt walk in my ways,[G] and [k]if thou wilt keep[G] my charge,[G] [l]then thou shalt also [m]judge my house, and shalt also keep[G] my [n]courts, and I will [o]give thee [2]places to walk among these that stand by.[S]

8 Hear now, O [b]Jŏsh'u-ȧ the [c]high priest, thou, and thy fellows that sit before thee: for they *are* men [3]wondered[G] at: for, behold, [p]I will bring forth my servant the [q,r]BRANCH.[T Q]

9 For behold the [s]stone that I have laid before [b]Jŏsh'u-ȧ; upon one stone *shall be* [t]seven eyes: behold, I will engrave the graving[G] thereof, saith the LORD of hosts, and [u]I will remove the iniquity of that land in one day.

10 [v]In that day, saith the LORD of hosts, shall ye call every man his neighbour under the vine and under the fig tree.

## CHAPTER 4

*The vision of the golden candlestick, 5 and the explanation thereof. 11 The two olive trees are the two anointed ones.*

AND[T] the [a]angel that talked with [b]me came again, and waked me, as a man that is wakened out of his sleep,

2[Q] And said unto me, What [c]seest thou? And I said, I have looked, and behold a [d]candlestick[G] all *of* [e]gold, with a bowl upon the top of it, and his [f]seven lamps thereon, and seven pipes[G] to the seven lamps, which *are* upon the top thereof:

3 And two [g]olive trees by it, one upon the right *side* of the bowl, and the other upon the left *side* thereof.[Q]

4 So I answered and spake to the angel that talked with me, saying, What *are* these, my lord?

5 Then the angel that talked with me answered and said unto me, Knowest thou not what these be? And I said, No, my lord.

6 Then[S] he answered and spake unto me, saying, This *is* the word of the LORD unto [h]Zĕ-rŭb'ba-bĕl, saying, [i]Not by might, nor by power, but by my [j]spirit,[G] saith the LORD of hosts.[T]

7 Who *art* thou, O great mountain? before [h]Zĕ-rŭb'ba-bĕl *thou shalt become* a plain: and he shall bring forth the [k]headstone *thereof with* shoutings, *crying,* Grace, grace unto it.[S T]

8 Moreover the [l]word of the LORD [m]came unto [b]me, saying,

9 The hands of [h]Zĕ-rŭb'ba-bĕl have laid the foundation of this [k]house; his hands shall also finish it; and thou shalt know that the LORD of hosts hath sent me unto you.

10 For who hath despised the day of small things? for they shall rejoice, and shall see the [n]plummet[G] in the hand of [h]Zĕ-rŭb'ba-bĕl *with* those [t]seven; they *are* the eyes of the LORD, which [o]run to and fro through the whole earth.[S Q]

11 ¶ Then answered I, and said unto him, What *are* these two [g]olive trees upon the right *side* of the [d]candlestick[G] and upon the left *side* thereof?[Q]

12 And I answered again, and said unto him, What *be these* two [g,p]olive branches which [1]through the two golden pipes[G] empty the golden [q]*oil* out of themselves?

13 And he answered me and said, Knowest thou not what these *be*? And I said, No, my lord.

14 Then said he, These *are* the two [2]anointed[G] ones, that stand by the Lord of the whole earth.[Q]

## CHAPTER 5

*The vision of the flying roll. 5 The vision of the ephah.*

THEN [a]I turned, and lifted up mine eyes, and looked, and behold a [b]flying roll.[G]

2 And he [c]said unto me, What

**7**

k *Blessings, contingent upon obedience,* Deut. 11:26.

l *Reward, a motive to faithfulness,* Matt. 5:12.

m *High Priest, duties of,* Lev. 21:10.

n *Church, called courts,* 1 Kin. 9:3.

o *God, providence of,* Gen. 2:2.

2 R. V. a place of access among

**8**

p *Jesus, prophecies concerning,* Matt. 1:21.

q *Branch, figurative* Dan. 4:14.

r *Jesus, names of,* Matt. 1:21.

3 Am. R. V. that are a sign:

**9**

s *Stones, figurative,* Ex. 24:12.

t *Seven,* Gen. 7:2.

u *God, mercy of,* Gen. 2:2.

**10**

v *Nation, prophecies of peace to,* Isa. 2:4.

**1**

a *Angel, medium of revelation to prophets,* vs. 1–11; Heb. 1:13.

b *Zechariah,* Zech. 1:1.

**2**

c *Vision, of Zechariah,* Acts 9:10.

d *Candlestick, symbolical,* v. 11; Ex. 25:31.

e *Gold,* Ezek. 7:19.

f *Seven,* Gen. 7:2.

**3**

g *Olive, symbolical,* Deut. 6:11.

**6**

h *Zerubbabel, prophecies relating to,* vs. 6–10; Ezra 3:2.

i *False Confidence, in self-sufficiency,* Psa. 30:6.

j *Holy Spirit, wisdom and strength from,* Acts 1:2.

**7**

k *Temple, Second,* vs. 8–10; 1 Kin. 6:17.

**8**

l *Prophecies, inspired,* Dan. 9:24.

m *Prophets, inspiration of,* Isa. 3:2.

**10**

n Amos 7:7, 8.

o *God, knowledge of,* Gen. 2:2.

**12**

p *Symbols and Similitudes,* Heb. 9:9.

q *Oil, sacred,* Deut. 12:17.

1 R. V. are beside the two golden spouts, that empty the golden oil out of themselves?

**14**

2 R. V. sons of oil,

**1**

a *Zechariah,* Zech. 1:1.

b *Vision,* Acts 9:10.

**2**

c *Instruction, by object lessons,* Prov. 23:23.

seest thou? And I answered, I see a flying roll[C]; the length thereof *is* twenty cubits[C], and the breadth thereof ten cubits[C].

3 Then [c]said he unto me, This *is* the [d]curse that goeth forth over the face of the whole earth: for every one that [e,f]stealeth shall be [1]cut off *as* on this side according to it; and every one that [g,h]sweareth shall be [2]cut off *as* on that side according to it.

4 I will bring [d]it forth, saith the LORD of hosts, and it shall enter into the house of the [e]thief, and into the house of him that [g,h]sweareth[C] falsely by my name: and it shall remain in the midst of his house, and shall consume[C] it with the timber thereof and the stones thereof.

5 ¶ Then the [i]angel that talked with me went forth, and [c]said unto me, Lift up now thine eyes, and see what *is* this that goeth forth.[T]

6 And I said, What *is* it? And he said, This *is* an ephah[C] that goeth forth. He said moreover, This *is* their resemblance through all the earth.

7 And, behold, there was lifted up a talent[C] of lead: and this *is* a [j]woman that sitteth in the midst of the ephah.

8 And he said, This *is* wickedness. And he cast it into the midst of the ephah; and he cast the weight of lead upon the mouth thereof.

9 Then lifted I up mine eyes, and looked, and, behold, there came out two [j]women, and the wind *was* in their wings; for they had wings like the wings of a stork: and they lifted up the ephah between the earth and the heaven.

10 Then said I to the [i]angel that talked with me, Whither[C] do these bear the ephah?[T]

11 And he said unto me, To build it[C] an house in the land of Shī'när: and [3]it shall be established, and set there upon her own base.

3

*d Wicked, punishment of,* Psa. 73:3.

*e Thieves,* Deut. 24:7.

*f Dishonesty,* Ezek. 22:13.

*g False Witness,* Matt. 19:18.

*h Perjury,* 1 Tim. 1:10.

1 R. V. purged out on the one side

2 R. V. purged out on the other side

5

*i Angel, medium of revelation to prophets,* Heb. 1:13.

7

*j Women, symbolical of wickedness,* Prov. 31:10.

11

3 R. V. when it is prepared, she shall be set there in her own place.

## CHAPTER 6

*The vision of the four chariots. 9 The crowning of Joshua the high priest, a type of Messiah the Branch, and of his dominion.*

AND [a]I turned, and lifted up mine eyes, and looked, and, behold, [b]there came four [c]chariots out from between two mountains; and the mountains *were* mountains of [d]brass.

2 In[Q] the first [c]chariot *were* [e]red [f]horses; and in the second chariot black horses;

3 And in the third [c]chariot [e]white [f]horses; and in the fourth chariot grisled[C] and bay horses.[Q]

4 Then I answered and said unto the [g]angel that talked with me, What *are* these, my lord?

5 And the angel answered and said unto me, These *are* the four [1]spirits[C] of the heavens, which go forth from standing before the Lord of all the earth.[Q]

6 The [e,2]black horses which *are* therein go forth into the north country; and the white go forth after them; and the grisled[C] go forth toward the south country.[Q]

7 And the bay went forth, and sought to go that they might walk to and fro through the earth: and he said, Get you hence[C], walk to and fro through the earth. So they walked to and fro through the earth.

8 Then cried he upon me, and spake unto me, saying, Behold, these that go toward the north country have quieted my spirit in the north country.

9 ¶ And the word of the LORD came unto me, saying,

10 Take of *them of* the captivity, *even* of Hĕl'da-ī, of Tō-bī'-jah, and of Jē-dā'iah, which are come from Băb'y̆-lon, and come thou the same day, and go into

1

*a Zechariah,* Zech. 1:1.

*b Vision,* Acts 9:10.

*c Chariot, symbolical,* vs. 1–8; Josh. 11:4.

*d Brass, figurative,* Job 28:2.

2

*e Colors, symbolical,* Ezek. 16:16.

*f Horse, symbolical,* Job 39:19.

4

*g Angel, medium of revelation to prophets,* Heb. 1:13.

5

1 R. V. winds of heaven,

6

2 R. V. chariot wherein are the black horses goeth forth toward the north country; and the white went forth after them; and the grisled went forth toward the south country.

the house of Jō-sī'ah the son of Zěph-a-nī'ah;

11 Then take [h]silver and [i]gold, and make [j]crowns, and set *them* upon the head of [k]Jŏsh'u-ȧ the son of [l]Jŏs'e-děch, the [m]high priest;

12 [Q]And speak unto him, saying, Thus speaketh the LORD of hosts, saying, Behold the man whose name *is* The [n,o,p]BRANCH; and he shall grow up out of his place, and he shall build the [q,r]temple of the LORD:

13 Even he shall build the [q,r]temple of the LORD; and he shall bear the glory, and shall sit and [s]rule upon his throne; and he shall be a [t]priest upon his throne: and the counsel of peace shall be between them both.[T Q]

14 And the crowns shall be to Hē'lem, and to Tō-bī'jah, and to Jē-dā'iah, and to Hěn the son of Zěph-a-nī'ah, for a memorial in the temple of the LORD.

15 And [u]they *that are* far off shall come and [v]build in the temple of the LORD, and ye shall know that the LORD of hosts hath sent me unto you. And *this* shall come to pass, if ye will diligently obey the voice of the LORD your God.

## CHAPTER 7

*The people inquire concerning the keeping of certain fasts. 4 The prophet's answer. 8 Disobedience the cause of their captivity.*

AND it came to pass in the fourth year of king [a]Dā-rī'us, *that* the [b]word of the LORD [c]came unto [d]Zěch-a-rī'ah in the fourth *day* of the ninth [e]month, *even* in Chĭs'leū;

2 [1]When they had sent unto the house of God Shē-rē'zer and Rē'gem-mē'lech, and their men, to [f]pray before the LORD,

3 *And* to speak unto the [g]priests which *were* in the [h]house of the LORD of hosts, and to the [i]prophets, saying, Should I weep in the fifth [j]month, separating myself, as I have done these so many years?

4 ¶ Then came the word of the LORD of hosts unto me, saying,

5 Speak unto all the people of the land, and to the [g,k]priests, saying, When ye fasted and mourned in the [j]fifth and [l]seventh *month*, even those [m]seventy years, [n,o]did ye at all fast unto me, *even* to me?

6 And when ye did eat, and when ye did drink, [o,p]did not ye eat *for yourselves*, and drink *for yourselves*?

7 [q]*Should ye* not *hear* the words which the LORD hath cried by the former prophets, when Jē-ru'sā-lěm was inhabited and in [r]prosperity, and the cities thereof round about her, when *men* inhabited the south and the plain?

8 ¶ And the [b]word of the LORD [c]came unto [d]Zěch-a-rī'ah, saying,

9 Thus [s]speaketh the LORD of hosts, saying, [t,u,v]Execute[G] [w]true judgment, and shew [x]mercy and [y]compassions every man to his brother:

10 And [z]oppress not the [a]widow, nor the [b]fatherless, the [c]stranger,[G] nor the [d]poor; and [e]let none of you imagine evil against his brother in your heart.

11 But [f,g]they refused to hearken, and pulled away the shoulder, and stopped their ears, that they should not hear.

12 Yea, they [h,i]made their hearts *as* an adamant[G] stone, lest they should hear the law, and the [j]words which the LORD of hosts hath [k]sent in his [l]spirit[G] by the former prophets: therefore came a great [m]wrath from the LORD of hosts.

13 Therefore it is come to pass, *that* as he cried, and [h]they would not hear; so they [2,n]cried, and I

**11**
h *Silver*, 1 Chr. 28:14.
i *Gold*, Ezek. 7:19.
j *Crown*, Ex. 29:6.
k Or, *Jeshua*, Ezra 2:2.
l Or, *Jozadak*, Neh. 12:26.
m *High Priest*, Lev. 21:10.

**12**
n *Branch, figurative*, Dan. 4:14.
o *Jesus, names of*, Matt. 1:21.
p *Jesus, prophecies concerning*, Matt. 1:21.
q *Church, prophecies concerning*, Matt. 16:18.
r *Jesus, kingdom of, prophecies concerning*, Matt. 1:21.

**13**
s *Jesus, king*, Matt. 1:21.
t *Jesus, priesthood of*, Matt. 1:21.

**15**
u *Gentiles, prophecies of the conversion of*, Acts 10:45.
v *Church, prophecies concerning its prosperity*, Matt. 16:18.

v.1–439 BC
See footnote, *Time*, Rev. 10:6.

**1**
a *Darius*, Ezra 5:5.
b *Prophecies, inspired*, Dan. 9:24.
c *Prophets, inspiration of*, Isa. 3:2.
d *Zechariah*, Zech. 1:1.
e *Month (December)*, Ex. 12:2.

**2**
f *Prayer*, Acts 6:4.
1 R. V. Now they of Beth-el had sent Sharezer

**3**
g *Priest*, Lev. 1:5.
h *Temple*, 1 Kin. 6:17.
i *Prophets*, Isa. 3:2.
j *Month (August)*, Ex. 12:2.

**5**
k *Minister, false and corrupt*, Rom. 15:16.
l *Month (October)*, Ex. 12:2.
m *Seventy*, Num. 11:16.
n *Fasting, of the disobedient, unacceptable*, Zech. 8:19.
o *Hypocrisy, abhorred of God*, Jas. 3:17.

**6**
p *Selfishness*, 2 Tim. 3:2.

**7**
q *Self-will*, Gen. 49:6.
r *Prosperity, evil effects of, forgetfulness of God*, Eccl. 7:14.

**9**
s *Commandment, enjoining justice*, v. 10; Deut. 8:2.
t *Integrity, enjoined*, Job 2:3.
u *Rulers, duties of*, Ex. 18:21.
v *Duty, of man to man*, Eccl. 12:13.
w *Righteousness, enjoined*, Psa. 15:2.
x *Mercy, enjoined*, Deut. 5:10.
y *Kindness, enjoined*, Acts 28:2.

**10**
z *Oppression, forbidden*, Eccl. 5:8.

a *Widow, oppression of, forbidden*, 2 Sam. 14:5.
b *Orphan, justice to, required*, Lam. 5:3.
c *Foreigners, justice toward, enjoined*, Deut. 23:20.
d *Poor, oppression of*, Prov. 21:13.
e *Malice, forbidden*, Eph. 4:31.

**11**
f *Self-will*, Gen. 49:6.
g *Obduracy*, Prov. 29:1.

**12**
h *Impenitence*, Rom. 2:5.
i *Moral Insensibility*, Luke 8:10.
j *Word of God, inspiration of*, Psa. 119:9.
k *Prophets, inspiration of*, Isa. 3:2.
l *Holy Spirit*, Acts 1:2. m *Anger of God*, 2 Kin. 13:3. **13** n *Wicked, prayers of, not answered*, Psa. 73:3. 2 Am. R. V. shall cry, and I will not hear, said Jehovah of hosts;

**14**
*o* *Captivity, as a judgment,* Isa. 5:13.
*p* *Canaan,* Gen. 37:1.
3 R. V. will scatter them

**1**
*a* *Prophecies, inspired,* Dan. 9:24.
*b* *Zechariah,* Zech. 1:1.

**2**
*c* *Jealousy, attributed to God,* Psa. 78:58.
*d* *Church, God loves,* Matt. 16:18.
*e* *Zion, restoration of, promised,* 2 Sam. 5:7.

**3**
*f* *Grace of God,* Rom. 4:16.
*g* *Jerusalem,* Judg. 19:10.
*h* *Church, called holy mountain,* 1 Kin. 9:3.
*i* *Holiness, of the church,* Ex. 39:30.

**4**
*j* *Nation, prophecies of peace to,* Isa. 2:4.
*k* *Longevity,* Psa. 91:16.

**5**
*l* *Children, amusements of,* Mark 10:14.

**7**
*m* *God, savior,* Gen. 2:2.
*n* *Israel, prophecies concerning,* 1 Kin. 12:1.

**8**
*o* *God, love of, exemplified,* Gen. 2:2.

would not hear, saith the LORD of hosts:

14 But I [3,o]scattered them with a whirlwind among all the nations whom they knew not. Thus the [p]land was desolate after them, that no man passed through nor returned: for they laid the pleasant[C] land desolate.[C]

## CHAPTER 8

*The restoration of Jerusalem.* 9 *The people encouraged in building the Lord's house.* 16 *Sundry duties enjoined.* 18 *Joy and enlargement promised.*

AGAIN the [a]word of the LORD of hosts came *to* [b]*me,* saying,

2 Thus saith the LORD of hosts; I was [c,d]jealous for [e]Zī'ŏn with great jealousy, and I was jealous for her with great fury.

3 Thus saith the LORD; [f]I am returned unto [e]Zī'ŏn, and will dwell in the midst of [g]Jē-ru̧'sā-lĕm: and Jē-ru̧'sā-lĕm shall be called a city of truth; and the mountain of the LORD of hosts the [h,i]holy mountain.[S]

4 Thus [j]saith the LORD of hosts; There shall yet old men and old women dwell in the streets of Jē-ru̧'sā-lĕm, and every man with his staff in his hand for [k]very age.

5 And [j]the streets of the city shall be full of boys and girls [l]playing in the streets thereof.

6 Thus saith the LORD of hosts; If it be marvellous in the eyes of the remnant of this people in these days, should it also be marvellous in mine eyes? saith the LORD of hosts.[Q]

7 Thus saith the LORD of hosts; Behold, [m]I will save [n]my people from the east country, and from the west country;

8 And [m]I will [n]bring them, and they shall dwell in the midst of [g]Jē-ru̧'sā-lĕm: and [o]they shall be my people, and I will be their God, in truth and in righteousness.[T]

9 ¶ Thus saith the LORD of hosts; Let your hands be strong, ye that hear in these days these words by the mouth of the prophets, which *were* in the day *that* the foundation of the [p]house of the LORD of hosts was laid, that the [q]temple might be built.

10 For before these days there was no hire[C] for man, nor any hire[C] for beast; neither *was there any* peace to him that went out or came in because of the [1]affliction: for [r]I set all men every one against his neighbour.

11 But now [s]I *will* not *be* unto the residue[C] of this people as in the former days, saith the LORD of hosts.

12 For [2,n,t,u]the seed *shall be* prosperous; the vine shall give her fruit, and the ground shall give her increase, and the heavens shall give their dew; and [v]I will cause the remnant of this people to possess all these *things.*

13 And it shall come to pass, *that* as ye were a curse among the [3]heathen,[C] O house of Jū'dah, and house of Ĭṣ'ra-el; [n,t]so will I [m,s]save you, and ye shall be a blessing: fear not, *but* let your hands be strong.

14 For thus saith the LORD of hosts; As [w]I thought to punish[C] you, when your fathers provoked me to wrath, saith the LORD of hosts, and I repented not:

15 So again have I thought in these days to do well unto [g]Jē-ru̧'sā-lĕm and to the house of Jū'dah: fear ye not.

16 ¶ These *are* the [x]things that ye shall do; [y,z,a]Speak ye every man the *truth to his [b]neighbour; [c,d,e]execute[C] the [f]judgment of truth and peace in your [g]gates:[Q]

17 And [h]let none of you [i]im-

**9**
*p* *Church, called house of the Lord,* 1 Kin. 9:3.
*q* *Temple, Second,* vs. 9–15; 1 Kin. 6:17.

**10**
*r* *Adversity, dispensation from God,* Psa. 10:6.
1 R. V. adversary:

**11**
*s* *God, mercy of,* Gen. 2:2.

**12**
*t* *Jews, prophecies concerning, of blessings,* Neh. 4:2.
*u* *Temporal Blessings, from God,* Psa. 103:2.
*v* *God, providence of,* Gen. 2:2.
2 R. V. there shall be the seed of peace;

**13**
3 R. V. nations,

**14**
*w* *Judgments, according to opportunity and works,* 1 Pet. 1:17.

**16**
*x* *Commandments,* Deut. 8:2.
*y* Eph. 4:25.
*z* *Commandment, enjoining truthfulness,* vs. 17, 19; Deut. 8:2.
*a* *Speech, wise,* Col. 4:6.
*b* *Neighbor, righteous treatment of,* Luke 10:29.
*c* *Court, civil,* Ex. 18:26.
*d* *Rulers, duties of,* Ex. 18:21.
*e* *Justice, enjoined,* Deut. 33:21.
*f* *Righteousness, enjoined,* Psa. 15:2.
*g* *Gates, place for holding courts of justice,* Deut. 3:5.

**17**
*h* *Malice, forbidden,* Eph. 4:31.
*i* *Evil Imagination,* Gen. 6:5.

* **TRUTHFULNESS.** *Commended,* Prov. 12:17, 19. *Magistrates should be men of,* Ex. 18:21. *Enjoined,* Zech. 8:16; Eph. 4:25; Col. 3:9. *Fearlessness in,* 2 Cor. 12:6; Gal. 4:16. *Of Job,* Job 27:4; 36:4. *Wicked lack,* Jer. 9:5. *Satan devoid of,* John 8:44.

*j Perjury, forbidden*, 1 Tim. 1:10.
*k Sin, repugnant to God*, Rom. 5:12.
*l God, holiness of*, Gen. 2:2.
**18**
*m Prophets, inspiration of*, Isa. 3:2.
*n Inspiration*, Job 32:8.
**19**
*o Month (July)*, Ex. 12:2.
*p Month (August)*, Ex. 12:2.
*q Month (October)*, Ex. 12:2.
*r Month (January)*, Ex. 12:2.
*s Joy*, Psa. 5:11.
*t Annual Feasts*, Num. 15:3.
*u Commandment, enjoining loving truth and peace*, Deut. 8:2.
*v Peace*, Jer. 29:7.
**20**
*w Jesus, kingdom of, prophecies concerning*, vs. 20–23; Matt. 1:21.
*x Church, prophecies concerning its prosperity*, Matt. 16:18.
*y Religious Revivals*, vs. 20–23; Hab. 3:2.
4 R. V. peoples,
**21**
*z Worship*, Gen. 22:5.

*a Seekers*, Isa. 55:6.
5 Am. R. V. intreat the favour of Jehovah,
**22**
*b Gentiles, prophecies of the conversion of*, Acts 10:45.
*c Jerusalem*, Judg. 19:10.
*d Worship*, Gen. 22:5.
**23**
*e God dwells with the Righteous*, 1 Kin. 6:13.

**1**
*a Syria, prophecies concerning*, 2 Kin. 6:23.

agine evil in your hearts against
his [b]neighbour; and [j]love no false
oath: for all these *are* [k]*things*
that [l]I hate, saith the LORD.
18 ¶ And the word of the LORD
of hosts[m, n]came unto me, saying,
19 Thus saith the LORD of hosts;
The †fast of the [o]fourth *month*,
and the fast of the [p]fifth, and the
fast of the [q]seventh, and the fast
of the [r]tenth, shall be to the house
of Jū'dah [s]joy and gladness, and
cheerful [t]feasts; [u]therefore love
the *truth and [v]peace.
20 Thus saith the LORD of hosts;
[w, x]*It shall* yet *come to pass*, that
[y]there shall come [4]people, and
the inhabitants of many cities:
21 And [w, x, y]the inhabitants of
one *city* shall go to another, saying,
Let us go speedily to [5, z]pray
before the LORD, and to [a]seek
the LORD of hosts: I will go also.
22 Yea, [b]many [4]people and
strong nations shall come to
[a]seek the LORD of hosts in [c]Jĕ-rụ'sā-lĕm, and to [5, d]pray before
the LORD.
23 Thus saith the LORD of
hosts; In those days *it shall come
to pass*, that ten men shall take
hold out of all languages of the
nations, even shall take hold of
the skirt of him that is a Jew,
saying, We will go with you: for
we have heard *that* God *is* [e]with
you.

## CHAPTER 9

*Judgments upon the neighboring nations. 9 Zion exhorted to rejoice in the coming of Messiah. 12 God's promises of victory and defense.*

THE burden of the word of the
LORD in the land of Hā'-drach, and [a]Dā-măs'cus *shall be*
the rest thereof: [b]when the eyes
of [c]man, as of all the tribes
of Ĭș'ra-el, *shall be* toward the
LORD.
2 And [d]Hā'math also [1]shall border
thereby; [e]Tȳ'rus, and [f]Zī'-dŏn,
[2]though it be very wise.
3 And [e]Tȳ'rus did [g]build herself
a [h]strong hold, and heaped
up [i]silver as the dust, and fine
[j]gold as the mire of the streets.
4 Behold, the [k]Lord will cast
her out, and he will smite her
power in the sea; and she shall
be devoured with fire.
5 [k, l]Ăsh'ke-lŏn shall see *it*, and
fear; [m]Gā'zȧ also *shall see it*,
and be very sorrowful, and [n]Ĕk'-rŏn;
for her expectation shall be
ashamed; and the king shall perish
from Gā'zȧ, and Ăsh'ke-lŏn
shall not be inhabited.
6 And [k]a [o]bastard shall dwell in
[p]Ăsh'dŏd, and I will cut off the
pride of the [q]Phĭ-lĭs'tĭneș.
7 And I will take away his blood
out of his mouth, and his abominations
from between his teeth:
but he that remaineth, even he,
*shall be* for our God, and he shall
be as a [3]governor in Jū'dah, and
Ĕk'rŏn as a Jĕb'u-sīte.
8 And [r]I will encamp about
mine house [4]because of the army,
because of him that passeth by,
and because of him that returneth:
and no oppressor shall
pass through them any more:
for now have I seen with mine
eyes.
9 ¶ [s]Rejoice greatly, O daughter
of Zī'ŏn; shout, O daughter
of Jĕ-rụ'sā-lĕm: [t, u, v]behold, thy
[w]King cometh unto thee: he *is*

*b Church, prophecies concerning its prosperity*, vs. 2–17; Matt. 16:18.
*c Gentiles, prophecies of the conversion of*, vs. 9–17; Acts 10:45.
**2**
*d Hamath*, 1 Chr. 18:3.
*e* Or, *Tyre*, Josh. 19:29.
*f Zidon*, Ezek. 28:21.
1 R. V. which bordereth thereon: Tyre
2 R. V. because she is
**3**
*g False Confidence*, Psa. 30:6.
*h Cities, fortified*, Num. 35:8.
*i Silver*, 1 Chr. 28:14.
*j Gold*, Ezek. 7:19.
**4**
*k Nation, judgments denounced against*, Isa. 2:4.
**5**
*l* Or, *Askelon*, Judg. 1:18.
*m Gaza*, Gen. 10:19.
*n Ekron*, Amos 1:8.
**6**
*o Bastard, figurative*, Deut. 23:2.
*p Ashdod*, 1 Sam. 6:17.
*q Philistines*, Gen. 26:14.
**7**
3 R. V. chieftain
**8**
*r God, preserver*, Gen. 2:2.
4 R. V. against the army, that none pass through or return:
**9**
*s Joy*, Psa. 5:11.
*t Prophecies concerning the Messiah, and their fulfillment*, Gen. 12:3.
*u Jesus, prophecies concerning*, Matt. 1:21.
*v Triumphal Entry of Jesus into Jerusalem*, Matt. 21:5.
*w Jesus, king*, Matt. 1:21.

† **FASTING.** *Enjoined*, Joel 1:14; 2:12, 13. *Precepts concerning*, Matt. 6:16–18. *Observed, on occasions, of calamities*, 2 Sam. 1:12; Acts 27:33; *of afflictions*, 2 Sam. 12:16; Psa. 35:13; Dan. 6:18; *of approaching danger*, Esth. 4:16; *of ordination of ministers*, Acts 13:3; 14:23.

*Accompanied, by prayer*, Dan. 9:3; *by confession of sin*, 1 Sam. 7:6; Neh. 9:1, 2; *by humiliation*, Deut. 9:18; Neh. 9:1; *by reading the Scriptures*, Jer. 36:6.

*Of the disobedient, unacceptable*, Isa. 58:3–7; Jer. 14:12; Zech. 7:5; Matt. 6:16.

**Prolonged:** *Three weeks, by Daniel*, Dan. 10:2, 3. *Forty days, by Moses*, Ex. 24:18; 34:28; Deut. 9:9, 18; *by Elijah*, 1 Kin. 19:8; *by Jesus*, Matt. 4:2; Mark 1:12, 13; Luke 4:1, 2.

**Instances of:** *The Israelites, in the conflict between the other tribes with the tribe of Benjamin, on account of the wrong suffered by a Levite's concubine*, Judg. 20:26; *when they went to Mizpeh*, 1 Sam. 7:6; *when they went to battle with the Philistines*, 1 Sam. 14:24–30. *The people of Jabesh-gilead, for Saul and his sons*, 1 Sam. 31:13; 1 Chr. 10:12. *Of David, at the death of Saul*, 2 Sam. 1:12; *at the death of Abner*, 2 Sam. 3:35; *during the sickness of the child born to him by Bath-sheba*, 2 Sam. 12:16–22. *Ahab, when Elijah prophesied the destruction of himself and his house*, 1 Kin. 21:27, with vs. 20–29. *Jehoshaphat, at the time of the invasion of the confederated armies of the Canaanites and Syrians*, 2 Chr. 20:3. *Ezra, on account of the idolatrous marriages of the Jews*, Ezra 10:6. *Nehemiah, on account of the desolation of Jerusalem and the*

[x]just, and having [y]salvation[C];
[z]lowly, and riding upon an [a]ass,
and upon a colt the foal of an ass.[Q]
10 And [b]I will cut off the chariot from [c]Ē′phră-ĭm, and the
horse from Jē-ru̇′să-lĕm, and the
battle bow shall be cut off: and
[d]he shall speak peace unto the
[5]heathen[C]: and [e]his dominion
*shall be* from sea *even* to sea, and
from the river *even* to the ends of
the earth.[Q]
11 As for thee also, [f]by the
blood of thy covenant I have
[g]sent forth thy prisoners out of
the pit wherein *is* no water.[S T Q]
12 [h]Turn you to the strong hold,
ye prisoners of [i]hope: even to
day do I declare *that* I will render double unto thee;
13 [6]When I have bent Jū′dah
for me, filled the [j]bow with Ē′-
phră-ĭm, and [7]raised up thy sons,
O [k,l]Zī′ŏn, against thy sons, O
*Greece, and [8]made thee as the
sword of a mighty man.
14[S] And the [m]LORD shall be seen
over them, and his [n]arrow shall
go forth as the [o]lightning: and
the Lord GOD shall blow the
[p]trumpet, and shall go with
[q]whirlwinds of the south.
15 The LORD of hosts shall [r]de-
fend them; and they shall devour, and [9]subdue with [s]sling
stones; and they shall drink, *and*
make a noise as through wine;
and they shall be filled like
bowls, *and* as the corners of the
altar.
16 And the LORD their God
shall [t]save them in that day as
the flock of his people: for *they*
*shall be as* the stones of a crown,
lifted [10]up as an ensign upon his
land.[S]
17 For how great *is* his goodness, and how great *is* his [u]beau-
ty! corn[C] shall make the [v]young
men [11]cheerful, and new wine
the [w]maids.[S Q]

## CHAPTER 10

*God, and not idols, to be sought unto. 5 The Lord will gather and save his people.*

ASK ye of the LORD [a]rain in
the time of the latter rain;
[1]*so* the [b,c]LORD shall make bright
clouds, and give them showers of
[d]rain, to every one grass in the
field.[S]
2 For [e]the [2]idols[C] have spoken
vanity, and the [f]diviners[C] have
seen a lie, and have told false
[g]dreams; they comfort in vain:
therefore they went their way as
a flock, they were troubled, because *there was* no shepherd.[Q]
3 Mine [h]anger [3]was kindled
against the [i,j]shepherds, and I
[4]punished the goats: for the
LORD of hosts hath visited his
flock the house of Jū′dah, and
[5]hath made them as his goodly
horse in the battle.
4 [6]Out of him came forth the
corner, out of him the nail, out of
him the battle bow, out of him
every oppressor together.
5 And [k]they shall be as mighty
*men,* which tread down *their en-*
*emies* in the mire of the streets in
the battle: and they shall fight,
because the [l]LORD *is* with them,
and the [m]riders on horses shall
be confounded.[C]
6 And [k]I will [b]strengthen the
house of Jū′dah, and I will save
the house of Jō′ṣeph, and I will
bring them again to place them;
for I have [n]mercy upon them:
and they shall be as though I had

x *Jesus, justice of,* Matt. 1:21.
y *Jesus, savior,* Matt. 1:21.
z *Jesus, humility of,* Matt. 1:21.

a *Ass, domesticated,* 2 Chr. 28:15.

**10**
b *Nation, promises of peace to,* Isa. 2:4.
c *Ephraim, prophecies concerning,* Gen. 41:52.
d *Gentiles, prophecies of the conversion of,* Acts 10:45.
e *Jesus, kingdom of, prophecies concerning,* Matt. 1:21.
5 R. V. nations:

**11**
f *God, faithfulness of,* Gen. 2:2.
g *God, savior,* Gen. 2:2.

**12**
h *Faith, enjoined,* Mark 11:22.
i *Hope,* Prov. 13:12.

**13**
j *Archery,* Gen. 21:20.
k *Zion,* 2 Sam. 5:7.
l *Jerusalem, called Zion,* Judg. 19:10.
6 R. V. For
7 R. V. I will stir up
8 R. V. will make thee

**14**
m *God, power of,* Gen. 2:2.
n *Arrow, figurative,* 1 Sam. 20:20.
o *Lightning,* Job 28:26.
p *Trumpet, figurative,* Josh. 6:4.
q *Whirlwind,* Prov. 1:27.

**15**
r *God, preserver,* Gen. 2:2.
s *Sling,* 1 Sam. 17:40.
9 R. V. shall tread down the sling stones;

**16**
t *God, savior,* Gen. 2:2.
10 R. V. on high over his land.

**17**
u *Beauty, spiritual,* Psa. 45:11.
v *Young Men,* Prov. 1:4.
w *Women,* Prov. 31:10.
11 R. V. flourish,

**1**
a *Temporal Blessings, prayer for,* Psa. 103:2.
b *God, providence of,* Gen. 2:2.
c *Prayer, answer to, promised,* Acts 6:4.
d *Rain, sent by God,* 2 Sam. 1:21.
1 Am. R. V. even of Jehovah that maketh lightnings; and he shall give

**2**
e *Idolatry, folly of,* 1 Sam. 15:23.
f *Sorcery, message of, false,* Isa. 47:9.
g *Dream,* Dan. 1:17.
2 R. V. teraphim

**3**
h *Anger of God,* 2 Kin. 13:3.
i *Rulers, wicked,* Ex. 18:21.
j *Minister, false and corrupt,* Rom. 15:16.
3 R. V. is
4 R. V. will punish the he-goats:
5 R. V. shall make

**4**
6 R. V. From him shall come forth the corner stone, from him the nail, from him the battle bow, from him every exactor together.

**5**
k *Israel, prophecies concerning,* vs. 5–12; 1 Kin. 12:1.
l *War, God in,* Judg. 3:2.
m *Cavalry,* 1 Sam. 13:5.

**6**
n *God, mercy of,* Gen. 2:2.

*temple,* Neh. 1:4. *The Jews, when Jeremiah prophesied against Judea and Jerusalem,* Jer. 36:9; *in Babylon, with prayer for divine deliverance and guidance,* Ezra 8:21, 23. *Darius, when he put Daniel in the lions' den,* Dan. 6:18. *Daniel, on account of the captivity of the people, with prayer for their deliverance,* Dan. 9:3; *at the time of his vision,* Dan. 10:1–3. *The Ninevites, when Jonah preached to them,* Jonah 3:5–10. *Disciples of John the Baptist,* Matt. 9:14; Mark 2:18. *Anna,* Luke 2:37. *The Pharisees,* Matt. 9:14; Mark 2:18; Luke 18:12. *Paul,* Acts 9:9; 2 Cor. 6:5; 11:27.

* **GREECE.** *Called* JAVAN, Isa. 66:19; Ezek. 27:13. *Prophecies concerning,* Dan. 8:21; 10:20; 11:2.
**Greeks,** Rom. 1:14. *Timothy, son of,* Acts 16:1. *Paul preaches to, in Athens,* Acts 17:16–34; *in Corinth,* Acts 18:1–18; *and writes to the Corinthian Christians,* see 1 Cor. and 2 Cor.
*Poets of,* Acts 17:28. *Philosophy of,* 1 Cor. 1:22, 23. *Schools of,* Acts 19:9. *Prophecy against,* Zech. 9:13. *A term applied to all who were not Jews, equivalent to Gentiles,* John 12:20; Rom. 1:16; 10:12; Gal. 3:28.

**7**
*o Joy, in the Lord,* Psa. 5:11.
*p Wine,* Prov. 23:31.

**8**
*q God, savior,* Gen. 2:2.

**9**
*r Dispersion,* Gen. 11:8.
*s Judgments, design of,* Ex. 6:6.
7 R. V. peoples;

**10**
*t God, providence of,* Gen. 2:2.
*u Egypt,* Gen. 41:8.
*v Assyria,* Gen. 25:18.
*w Gilead,* Deut. 3:13.
*x Lebanon,* Deut. 1:7.

**11**
8 R. V. of affliction,
9 R. V. Nile

**12**
*y Spiritual Blessings, from God,* Eph. 1:3.

**1**
*a Israel, prophecies concerning,* vs. 1–17; 1 Kin. 12.1.

**2**
*b Cedar, figurative,* Isa. 9:10.
*c Bashan,* Num. 32:33.
1 R. V. strong forest is

**3**
*d Adversity, despondency in,* Psa. 10:6.

not cast them off: for I *am* the LORD their God, and will hear them.

7 And [k]*they of* Ē′phră-ĭm shall be like a mighty *man,* and their heart shall [o]rejoice as through [p]wine: yea, their children shall see *it,* and be glad; their heart shall rejoice in the LORD.

8 I will hiss for them, and gather them; for [q]I have redeemed them: and they shall increase as they have increased.

9 And [k]I will [r]sow them among the [7]people: and [s]they shall remember me in far countries; and they shall live with their children, and turn again.

10 [k]I will [t]bring them again also out of the land of [u]Ē′ġȳpt, and gather them out of [v]Ăs-sȳr′-ĭ-ȧ; and I will bring them into the land of [w]Ḡĭl′e-ăd and [x]Lĕb′-a-non; and *place* shall not be found for them.

11 And he shall pass through the sea [8]with affliction, and shall smite the waves in the sea, and all the deeps of the [9]river shall dry up: and the pride of [v]Ăs-sȳr′ĭ-ȧ shall be brought down, and the sceptre of [u]Ē′ġȳpt shall depart away.

12 And I will [y]strengthen them in the LORD; and they shall walk up and down in his name, saith the LORD.

## CHAPTER 11

*The punishment of the Jewish nation. 7 The staves Beauty and Bands. 15 A woe upon the foolish shepherd.*

OPEN thy doors, O [a]Lĕb′a-non, that the fire may devour thy cedars.

2 Howl, fir tree; for the [b]cedar is fallen; because the mighty are spoiled: howl, O ye oaks of [c]Bā′-shăn; for the [1]forest of the vintage is come down.

3 ¶ [d]*There is* a voice of the howling of the shepherds; for their glory is spoiled: a voice of the roaring of young lions; for the pride of Jôr′dan is spoiled.

4 Thus saith the LORD my God; [e]Feed the flock of the slaughter;

5 Whose possessors slay them, and hold themselves not guilty: and [f]they that sell them say, Blessed *be* the LORD; for I am rich: and their own shepherds pity them not.

6 For I will no more [g]pity the inhabitants of the land, saith the LORD: but, lo, I will deliver the men every one into his neighbour's hand, and into the hand of his king: and [h]they shall smite the land, and out of their hand [i]I will not deliver *them.*

7 [2]And I [j]will feed the flock of slaughter, *even* you, O poor of the flock. And I took unto me [k,l]two staves; the one I called Beauty, and the other I called Bands; and I fed the flock.

8 Three shepherds also I cut off in one month; and my soul lothed them, and their soul also abhorred me.

9 Then said I, I will not feed you: that that dieth, let it die; and that that is to be cut off, let it be cut off; and let the rest eat every one the flesh of another.

10 ¶ And I took my staff, *even* Beauty, and [l]cut it asunder, that I might break my covenant which I had made with all the [3]people.

11 And it was broken in that day: and so the poor of the flock that waited upon me knew that it *was* the word of the LORD.

12 And I said unto them, If ye think good, give *me* my [4]price; and if not, forbear. [m,n,o]So they weighed for my price thirty *pieces* of [p,q]silver.

13 And the LORD said unto me, Cast it unto the [r,s]potter: a

**4**
*e Minister, duties of,* Rom. 15:16.

**5**
*f Rulers, wicked,* Ex. 18:21.

**6**
*g Pity, of God, withheld from reprobate sinners,* Job 19:21.
*h Agency, in executing judgments,* Mark 1:17.
*i Judgments, no escape from,* Ex. 6:6.

**7**
*j Poor, God's care of,* Prov. 21:13.
*k Symbols and Similitudes,* Heb. 9:9.
*l Instruction, by object lessons,* vs. 7–14; Prov. 23:23.
2 R. V. So I fed

**10**
3 R. V. peoples.

**12**
*m* Matt. 27:9.
*n Jesus, prophecies concerning,* Matt. 1:21.
*o Prophecies concerning the Messiah, and their fulfillment,* v. 13; Gen. 12:3.
*p Silver,* 1 Chr. 28:14.
*q Money,* Jer. 32:9.
4 R. V. hire;

**13**
*r Pottery,* Jer. 18:3.
*s Art,* 2 Chr. 16:14

goodly[G] price that I was prised[G] at
of them. And I took the thirty
*pieces* of [p]silver, and cast them to
the potter in the house of the
LORD.[Q]

> **14**
> *t* *Judah, kingdom of,* 2 Chr. 11:17.
> *u* *Israel,* 1 Kin. 12:1.

14 Then I [l]cut asunder mine
other staff, *even* Bands[G], that I
might break the *brotherhood
between [t]Jū′dah and [u]Ĭṣ′ra-el.
15 ¶ And the LORD said un-
to me, Take unto thee yet the
instruments of a foolish [f]shep-
herd.

> **16**
> 5 R. V. those that be scattered, nor
> 6 R. V. neither shall he feed that which is sound, but

16 For, lo, I will raise up a
[f]shepherd in the land, *which*
shall not visit those that be cut[G]
off, neither shall seek [5]the young
one, nor heal that that is broken, [6]nor feed that that standeth
still: but he shall eat the flesh of
the fat, and tear their claws in
pieces.

> **17**
> 7 R. V. worthless

17 Woe to the [7]idol[G] [f]shepherd
that leaveth the flock! the sword
*shall be* upon his arm, and upon
his right eye: his arm shall be
clean[G] dried up, and his right eye
shall be utterly darkened.

## CHAPTER 12

*Jerusalem a cup of trembling and a burdensome stone to her adversaries 6 The restoration of Judah. 9 The repentance of Jerusalem.*

> **1**
> *a* *Israel, prophecies concerning,* 1 Kin. 12:1.
> *b* *God, creator,* Gen. 2:2.
> *c* *Heavens, created,* Psa. 8:3.
> *d* *Earth, created,* Prov. 8:23.
> *e* *Man, created,* Job 4:17.

THE [a]burden of the word of
the LORD for Ĭṣ′ra-el, saith
the LORD, [b]which stretcheth
forth the [c]heavens, and layeth
the foundation of the [d]earth, and
formeth the spirit of [e]man within
him.

> **2**
> *f* *Jerusalem, prophecies concerning,* Judg. 19:10.
> 1 R. V. reeling
> 2 R. V. peoples
> 3 R. V. and upon Judah also shall it be in the siege against Jerusalem.

2 Behold, I will make [f]Jē-ru̧′-
sā-lĕm a cup of [1]trembling unto
all the [2]people round about,
[3]when they shall be in the siege
both against Jū′dah *and* against
Jē-ru̧′sā-lĕm.

> **3**
> 4 R. V. sore wounded; and all the nations of the earth shall be

3 And in that day will I make
[f]Jē-ru̧′sā-lĕm a burdensome stone
for all [2]people: all that burden
themselves with it shall be [4]cut
in pieces, though all the people
of the earth be gathered together
against it.[Q]

> **4**
> *g* *Insanity, sent as a judgment,* Prov. 26:18.

4 In that day, saith the LORD,
I will smite every horse with astonishment[G], and his rider with
[g]madness: and I will open mine
eyes upon the house of Jū′dah,
and will smite every horse of the
[2]people with blindness.

> **5**
> 5 R. V. chieftains
> 6 R. V. are my

5 And the [5]governors of Jū′dah
shall say in their heart, The inhabitants of Jē-ru̧′sā-lĕm [6]*shall
be* my strength in the LORD of
hosts their God.

> **6**
> 7 R. V. a pan of

6 In that day will I make the
[5]governors of Jū′dah like [7]an
hearth of fire among the wood,
and like a torch of fire in a sheaf;
and they shall devour all the
[2]people round about, on the
right hand and on the left: and
[f]Jē-ru̧′sā-lĕm shall be inhabited
again in her own place, *even* in
Jē-ru̧′sā-lĕm.

> **7**
> *h* *David,* 1 Sam. 16:13.

7 The LORD also shall save the
tents of Jū′dah first, that the
glory of the house of [h]Dā′vid
and the glory of the inhabitants
of Jē-ru̧′sā-lĕm do not magnify
*themselves* against Jū′dah.

> **8**
> *i* *Spiritual Blessings, from God,* Eph. 1:3.
> *j* *God, preserver,* Gen. 2:2.

8 [i]In that day shall the LORD
[j]defend the inhabitants of [f]Jē-
ru̧′sā-lĕm; and he that is feeble
among them at that day shall be
as Dā′vid; and the house of Dā′-
vid *shall be* as God, as the angel
of the LORD before them.[S T]
9 And it shall come to pass in
that day, *that* I will seek to destroy all the nations that come
against Jē-ru̧′sā-lĕm.

> **10**
> *k* *Holy Spirit, baptism of,* Acts 1:2.
> *l* *Prayerfulness, spirit of, from God,* 1 Tim. 5:5.
> *m* John 19:37.
> *n* *Jesus, prophecies concerning,* Matt. 1:21.
> *o* *Prophecies concerning the Messiah, and their fulfillment,* Gen. 12:3.
> *p* *Repentance, of Israel foretold,* Mark 1:4.

10 And I will pour upon the
house of [h]Dā′vid, and upon the
inhabitants of [f]Jē-ru̧′sā-lĕm, the
[k]spirit of grace and of [l]sup-
plications: and [m,n,o]they shall
look upon me whom they have
pierced, and [p]they shall mourn

---

* **FRATERNITY**, Psa. 133:1-3; Zech. 11:14; Matt. 23:8; Jas. 2:8. *Enjoined, by Moses upon the Israelites,* Deut. 15:7-15; Josh. 1:14, 15; Mal. 2:10; *by Jesus,* Matt. 5:22-24; 18:15-18, 21, 22, 35; John 13:34; 15:12; *by Paul,* Rom. 12:10; 1 Cor. 6:1-8; Gal. 6:1, 2; 1 Thess. 4:9; 2 Thess. 3:14, 15; Heb. 13:1; 1 Pet. 1:22; 2:17; 3:8; 2 Pet. 1:5, 7; 1 John 2:9-11.
*Incompatible, with selfishness,* 1 John 3:17; *with pride of*

for him, as one [q,r]mourneth for *his* only *son*, and [p]shall be in bitterness for him, as one that is in bitterness for *his* *first-born.[S T Q]

11 In that day shall there be a great [q]mourning in [f]Jĕ-ru̥′sā-lĕm, as the mourning of Hā-dad-rĭm′mon in the valley of [s]Mĕ-gĭd′don.[Q]

12 And the land shall [q]mourn, every family apart; the family of the house of [h]Dā′vid apart, and their [t]wives apart; the family of the house of Nā′than apart, and their wives apart;[Q]

13 The family of the house of [u]Lē′vī apart, and their [t]wives apart; the family of Shĭm′e-ī apart, and their wives apart;

14 All the families that remain, every family apart, and their [t]wives apart.

## CHAPTER 13

*A fountain opened for sin. 2 The removal of idolatry and false prophets. 7 The smiting of the Shepherd, and the salvation of a third part of the people.*

IN that day there shall be a *,[a,b,c,d,e]fountain opened to the house of Dā′vid and to the inhabitants of Jĕ-ru̥′sā-lĕm [f]for sin and for [g]uncleanness.[S]

2 And it shall come to pass in that day, saith the LORD of hosts, *that* [h]I will cut off the names of the idols out of the land, and they shall no more be remembered: and also I will cause the [i,j]prophets and the unclean spirit to pass out of the land.

3 And it shall come to pass, *that* when [i]any shall yet prophesy,[C] then his father and his mother that begat him shall say unto him, Thou shalt not live; for thou speakest lies in the name of the LORD: and his father and his mother that begat him shall thrust him through when he prophesieth.[C]

4 And it shall come to pass in that day, *that* the prophets shall be ashamed every one of his vision, when he hath prophesied; neither shall they wear a [1]rough garment to deceive:[Q]

5 But he shall say, I *am* no prophet, I *am* [2]an husbandman;[C] for [3]man taught me to keep cattle from my youth.

6 And *one* shall say unto him, What *are* these wounds [4]in thine hands? Then he shall [k]answer, *Those* with which I was wounded *in* the house of my [l]friends.[Q]

7 ¶ Awake, O [m]sword, against my [n]shepherd, and against the man *that is* my fellow, saith the LORD of hosts: [o,p,q]smite the [r,s]shepherd, and the sheep shall be scattered: and I will turn mine hand upon the little ones.[Q]

8 And it shall come to pass, *that* in all the land, saith the LORD, two parts therein shall be [t]cut off *and* die; but the third shall be left therein.

9 And [u]I will bring the third part through the fire, and will refine them as [v]silver is refined, and will [w]try[C] them as [x]gold is tried:[C] [y]they shall call on my name, and [z]I will hear them: [a]I will say, It *is* my people: and they shall [b,c]say, The LORD *is* my God.[T Q]

q *Mourning*, Lam. 2:5.
r *Bereavement*, Hos. 9:12.

11
s Or, *Megiddo*, Josh. 17:11.

12
t *Wife*, Prov. 5:18.

13
u *Levi*, Gen. 29:34.

1
a *Washing, figurative*, Matt. 27:24.
b *Spiritual Purification, promised*, Psa. 51:2.
c *Types, of the Savior*, Heb. 10:1.
d *Jesus, atonement by*, Matt. 1:21.
e *Atonement, by Jesus, for remission of sins*, Lev. 17:11.
f *Jesus, mission of*, Matt. 1:21.
g *Defilement*, Lev. 5:2.

2
h *Idolatry, prophecies relating to*, 1 Sam. 15:23.
i *Prophets, false, punishment of*, Isa. 3:2.
j *Minister, false and corrupt*, Rom. 15:16.

4
1 R. V. hairy mantle

5
k *Hypocrisy*, Jas. 3:17.
2 R. V. a tiller of the ground;
3 R. V. I have been made a bondman from my youth.

6
l *Friends*, Ex. 33:11.
4 R. V. between thine arms?

7
m *Sword, figurative*, 1 Chr. 21:5.
n *Shepherd, figurative*, Jer. 31:10.
o Matt. 26:31; Mark 14:27.
p *Jesus, prophecies concerning*, Matt. 1:21.
q *Prophecies concerning the Messiah, and their fulfillment*, Gen. 12:3.
r *Jesus, names of*, Matt. 1:21.
s *Jesus, shepherd*, Matt. 1:21.

8
t *Wicked, punishment of*, Psa. 73:3.

9
u *Divine Chastisement*, Job 33:19.
v *Silver*, 1 Chr. 28:14.
w *Temptation, a test*, Luke 11:4.
x *Gold*, Ezek. 7:19.
y *Afflictions, design of*, Psa. 34:19.
z *Prayer, answer to, promised*, Acts 6:4.

a *God, love of*, Gen. 2:2.
b *Faith, exemplified*, Mark 11:22.
c *Religious Testimony*, 2 Thess. 1:10.

---

*title*, Matt. 23:8; *with indifference to another's conscience*, 1 Cor. 8:1–13; 10:28, 29.

**Exemplified:** *By Jonathan and David*, 1 Sam. 18:1; 19: 2–7; 20:17, 41, 42; 23:16–18. *By early Christians*, Acts 2:42–47. *By Paul*, Rom. 9:2, 3; 10:1; 1 Cor. 9:20–22. *By James, Cephas, and John*, Gal 2:9. *By Epaphroditus*, Phil. 2:25, 26. *By the Thessalonian church*, 2 Thess. 1:3.

See footnote, LOVE, *Of man for man*, 1 John 4:7.

*** FIRSTBORN.** *Of man and beast reserved to himself by God*, Ex. 13:2, 12–16; 22:29, 30; 34:19, 20; Lev. 27:26; Num. 3:13; 8:17, 18; 18:15–17; Deut. 15:19–23; Neh.10:36; Luke 2:22–24.

*Redemption of*, Ex. 13:13; 34:20; Lev. 27:27; Num. 3:40–51; 18:15–17. *Levites taken instead of firstborn of the families of Israel*, Num. 3:12, 40–45; 8:16–18.

*Of Egyptians, slain*, Ex. 11:5; 12:12, 29, 30, 33; 13:15; Num. 8:17; 33:4; Psa. 78:51; 105:36; 135:8; 136:10. *Of idolaters, sacrificed*, Ezek. 20:26.

*Jesus, called*, Rom. 8:29; Heb. 1:6; *called firstborn of the dead*, Rev. 1:5.

**Birthright of the:** *A double portion of inheritance*, Deut. 21:15–17. *Royal succession*, 2 Chr. 21:3. *Sold by Esau*, Gen. 25:29–34; 27:36; Rom. 9:12, 13; Heb. 12:16. *Forfeited by Reuben*, Gen. 49:3, 4; 1 Chr. 5:1, 2. *Set aside, that of Manasseh*, Gen. 48:15–20; 1 Chr. 5:1; *of Hosah's son*, 1 Chr. 26:10.

**Figurative,** Ex. 4:22; Psa. 89:27; Jer. 31:9; Heb. 12:23.

*** FOUNTAIN. Figurative:** *Of divine grace*, Psa. 36: 9; Jer. 2:13. *Of the true God*, Zech. 13:1. *Of salvation*, Rev. 7:17.

## CHAPTER 14

*The destroyers of Jerusalem destroyed. 4 The coming of Messiah, and the glory of his kingdom. 12 The plague of Jerusalem's enemies. 16 The remnant of the nations shall turn to the Lord. 20 Holiness unto the Lord.*

BEHOLD, [a]the [b]day of the
LORD cometh, and thy spoil[C]
shall be divided in the midst of
thee.
2 For [a,c]I will gather all nations
against [d]Jē-rṳ'sā-lĕm to battle;
and [e]the city shall be taken, and
the houses rifled,[C] and the [f]wom-
en [g]ravished[C]; and half of the city
shall go forth into [h]captivity, and
the residue[C] of the people shall
not be cut off from the city.
3 ¶ Then shall the LORD go
forth, and fight against those nations, as when he fought in the
day of battle.
4 And his feet shall stand in
that day upon the mount of [i]Ŏl'-
ĭveș, which *is* before [d]Jē-rṳ'sā-
lĕm on the east, and the mount
of Ŏl'ĭveș shall cleave in the
midst thereof toward the east
and toward the west, *and there
shall be* a very great valley; and
half of the mountain shall remove toward the north, and half
of it toward the south.
5 And ye shall flee *to* the valley
of the mountains; for the valley
of the mountains shall reach unto Ā'zăl: yea, ye shall flee, like as
ye fled from before the [j]earth-
quake in the days of [k]Ŭz-zī'ah
king of Jū'dah: and the LORD
my God shall come, *and* all the
[1]saints with thee.[Q]
6 And it shall come to pass in
that [b]day, *that* the light shall not
be clear, *nor* dark:
7 But it shall be one day which
shall be known to the LORD, not
day, nor night: but [l]it shall come
to pass, *that* at evening time it
shall be light.[Q]
8 And [m]it shall be in that day,
*that* living [n,o]waters shall go out
from [d]Jē-rṳ'sā-lĕm; half of them
toward the [2,p]former sea, and
half of them toward the [3,q]hin-
der sea: in summer and in winter
shall it be.[Q]
9 And the LORD shall be [r]king
over [s]all the earth: in that day
shall there be one LORD, and his
name one.[Q]
10 All the land shall be turned
as [4]a plain from [t]Gē'bȧ to *Rĭm'-
mon south of Jē-rṳ'sā-lĕm: and
it shall be lifted up, and inhabited in her place, from Bĕn'ja-
mĭn's [u]gate unto the place of
the first [u]gate, unto the corner
[u]gate, and *from* the [v,w]tower of
Hă-năn'e-el unto the king's winepresses.
11 And *men* shall dwell in it,
and there shall be no more [5]utter
destruction; but [d]Jē-rṳ'sā-lĕm
shall be safely inhabited.[Q]
12 ¶ And this shall be the
[x]plague wherewith the LORD
will smite all the [6]people that
have fought against Jē-rṳ'sā-
lĕm; [y]Their flesh shall consume
away while they stand upon their
feet, and their eyes shall consume away in their holes, and
their tongue shall consume away
in their mouth.
13 And it shall come to pass in
that day, *that* a great tumult[C]
from the LORD shall be among
them; and they shall lay hold
every one on the hand of his
neighbour, and his hand shall
rise up against the hand of his
neighbour.
14 And Jū'dah also shall fight
[7]at Jē-rṳ'sā-lĕm; and the wealth
of all the [8]heathen[C] round about
shall be gathered together, gold,
and silver, and apparel, in great
abundance.
15 And so shall be the [x]plague
of the horse, of the mule, of the

**1**
*a* *Jews, prophecies concerning,* Neh. 4:2.
*b* *Day, figurative,* Gen. 1:5.

**2**
*c* *Adversity, dispensation from God,* Psa. 10:6.
*d* *Jerusalem, prophecies concerning,* Judg. 19:10.
*e* *War, evils of,* Judg. 3:2.
*f* *Captive, cruelty to,* 1 Sam. 30:3.
*g* *Rape,* Deut. 22:25.
*h* *Captivity, as a judgment,* Isa. 5:13.

**4**
*i* *Mount of Olives,* Mark 11:1.

**5**
*j* *Earthquakes,* Isa. 29:6.
*k* *Uzziah,* 2 Chr. 26:1.
1 R. V. holy ones

**7**
*l* *Gospel, prophecies concerning,* Mark 13:10.

**8**
*m* *Jesus, kingdom of, prophecies concerning,* Matt. 1:21.
*n* *Water, figurative of salvation,* 1 Kin. 17:10.
*o* *Salvation,* Acts 16:17.
*p* *Dead Sea,* Gen. 14:3.
*q* *Mediterranean Sea,* Ex. 23:31.
2 R. V. eastern
3 R. V. western

**9**
*r* *Jesus, king,* Matt. 1:21.
*s* *Gentiles, prophecies of the conversion of,* Acts 10:45.

**10**
*t* *Geba,* Josh. 21:17.
*u* *Jerusalem, gates of,* Judg. 19:10.
*v* *Tower,* 2 Chr. 26:9.
*w* *Jerusalem, towers of,* Judg. 19:10.
4 R. V. the Arabah,

**11**
5 R. V. curse;

**12**
*x* *Plague,* Ex. 11:1.
*y* *Judgments,* Ex. 6:6.
6 R. V. peoples

**14**
7 R. V. against
8 R. V. nations

* **RIMMON** (*pomegranate*). *A city S. of Jerusalem,* Zech. 14:10. *Allotted to Judah,* Josh. 15:32; Neh. 11:25, 29; *afterward to Simeon,* Josh. 19:7; 1 Chr. 4:32. *Called* REMMON, Josh. 19:7; *and* EN-RIMMON, Neh. 11:29.

15
[z] *Animals, suffer under divine judgments*, Jer. 27:5.

16
[a] *Gentiles, prophecies of the conversion of*, Acts 10:45.
[b] *Worship*, Gen. 22:5.
[c] *Tabernacles, feast of, penalty for not observing*, Deut. 16:13.

17
[d] *Wicked, punishment of*, vs. 17–19; Psa. 73:3.
[e] *Punishment, according to deeds*, Lev. 26:41.
[f] *Rain, withheld, as a judgment*, 2 Sam. 1:21.

18
[g] *Egypt*, Gen. 41:8.
9 R. V. neither shall it be upon them;

camel, and of the ass, and of [z]all the beasts that shall be in these tents, as this plague.

16 ¶ And it shall come to pass, *that* [a]every one that is left of all the nations which came against Jĕ-rṳ′să-lĕm shall even go up from year to year to [b]worship the King, the LORD of hosts, and to keep the [c]feast of tabernacles.

17 And it shall be, *that* whoso will not come up of *all* the families of the earth unto Jĕ-rṳ′să-lĕm to [b]worship the King, the LORD of hosts, even [d,e]upon them shall be no [f]rain.

18 And if the family of [g]Ē′ġy̆pt go not up, and come not, [9]that *have* no *rain*; there shall be the plague, wherewith the LORD will [d,e]smite the [3]heathen[G] that come not up to keep the [c]feast of tabernacles.

19 This shall be the [d,e]punishment of [g]Ē′ġy̆pt, and the punishment of all nations that come not up to keep the [c]feast of tabernacles.

20 ¶ [h]In that day shall there be upon the [i]bells of the [j]horses, [10,†,k]HOLINESS UNTO THE LORD; and the pots in the LORD's house shall be like the bowls before the altar.

21 Yea, every pot in Jĕ-rṳ′să-lĕm and in Jū′dah shall be [11]holiness unto the LORD of hosts: and all they that sacrifice[G] shall come and take of them, and [12]seethe[G] therein: and in that day there shall be no more the Cā′-năan-īte in the house of the LORD of hosts.

20
[h] *Jesus, kingdom of*, Matt. 1:21.
[i] *Bell*, Ex. 28:33.
[j] *Horse*, Job 39:19.
[k] *Holiness*, Ex. 39:30.
10 R. V. Holy unto the Lord;

21
11 R. V. holy unto
12 Am. R. V. boil

---

THE

# BOOK OF MALACHI

## CHAPTER 1

*Israel's ingratitude. 6 Their polluted offerings, 12 and contempt for God's worship.*

1
[a] *Prophets, inspiration of*, Isa. 3:2.

2
[b] *God, love of, exemplified*, Gen. 2:2.
[c] *Presumption*, Psa. 19:13.
[d] *Unbelief*, Heb. 3:12.
[e] *Esau*, Gen. 25:25.
[f] *Jacob*, Gen. 27:11.
[g] Rom. 9:13.

3
[h] *Adversity, dispensation from God*, Psa. 10:6.
1 R. V. jackals

4
[i] *Edomites, prophecies concerning*, 2 Kin. 8:21.
[j] *False Confidence*, Psa. 30:6.
2 R. V. beaten down, but

THE burden[G] of the word of the LORD to Is̤′ra-el [a]by *Măl′a-chī.

2 [b]I h[Q]ave loved you, saith the LORD. Yet ye [c]say, [d]Wherein[G] hast thou loved us? *Was* not [e]Ē′sa̤u [†]Jā′cob's brother? saith the LORD: yet [g]I loved Jā′cob,[S]

3 And I hated [e]Ē′sa̤u, and [h]laid his mountains and his heritage waste for the [1]dragons of the wilderness.[S Q]

4 Whereas [i]Ē′dom saith, We are [2]impoverished, but [j]we will return and build the desolate places; thus saith the LORD of hosts, They shall build, but [h]I will throw down; and they shall call them, The border of wickedness, and, The people against whom the LORD hath indignation for ever.

5 And your eyes shall see, and ye shall [k]say, The LORD will be magnified from the border of Is̤′ra-el.

6 ¶ A [l]son honoureth *his* father, and a [m]servant his master: if then [n]I *be* a father, where *is* mine honour? and if I *be* a master, where *is* my [o]fear? saith the LORD of hosts unto you, O [p]priests, that despise[G] my name. And ye [q,r]say, Wherein have we despised[G] thy name?[T Q]

5
[k] *Praise*, Psa. 150:1.

6
[l] *Children, good*, Mark 10:14.
[m] *Servant, duties of*, Jer. 2:14.
[n] *God, fatherhood of*, Gen. 2:2.
[o] *Fear of God*, Acts 9:31.
[p] *Minister, false and corrupt*, vs. 7–10; Rom. 15:16.
[q] *Presumption, instances of*, vs. 7, 12; Psa. 19:13.
[r] *Hypocrisy, abhorred of God*, vs. 6–14; Jas. 3:17.

† **LEGENDS.** *"Holiness to the Lord," engraved, on the high priest's mitre*, Ex. 28:36; 39:30; *on bells of horses*, Zech. 14:20. *"This is Jesus, the King of the Jews,"* Matt. 27:39; Mark 15:26; Luke 23:38; John 19:19. *Precepts written on doorposts and gates, and worn on the hand and forehead*, Deut. 6:6–9; 11:18–20.

* **MALACHI** (*messenger*). *Last of minor prophets*, Mal. 1:1. *Reproves Israel for their impiety*, Mal. 1; 2; 3:7–15. *Foretells, the coming of the Messiah*, Mal. 3:1–6; *the judgments on the wicked and the consolations of the righteous*, Mal. 4:1–3; *the coming of the forerunner of the Messiah*, Mal. 4 4–6.

**7**

s *Table, figurative of the altar,* Judg. 1:7.

**8**

t *Offerings, must be without blemish,* Lev. 6:17.

u *Blindness, of animals, disqualified for sacrifice,* 2 Kin. 6:18.

v *Blemish, animals with, forbidden to be used for sacrifice,* Lev. 14:10.

3 R. V. Present it

**9**

w *Wicked, prayer of, not answered,* Psa. 73:3.

**10**

x *Offerings, unavailing when not accompanied by piety,* Lev. 6:17.

4 R. V. Oh that there were one among you that would shut the doors, that ye might not kindle fire on mine altar in vain!

**11**

y *Incense, figurative of praise,* Ex. 37:29.

5 R. V. is

**12**

z *Hypocrisy, abhorred of God,* Jas. 3:17.

---

**13**

a *Blemish,* Lev. 14:10.

b *Offerings, must be without blemish,* Lev. 6:17.

6 R. V. taken by violence,

7 R. V. bring the

**14**

c *Dedication,* Ezra 6:17.

d *God, sovereign,* Gen. 2:2.

8 R. V. blemished

7 [p]Ye offer polluted[G] bread upon mine altar; and ye [q,r]say, Wherein have we polluted[G] thee? In that ye say, The [s]table of the LORD *is* contemptible.[Q]

8 And if ye [t]offer the [u,v]blind for sacrifice,[G] *is it* not evil? and if ye offer the [v]lame and sick, *is it* not evil? [3]offer it now unto thy governor; will he be pleased with thee, or accept thy person? saith the LORD of hosts.

9 And now, I pray you, beseech God that he will be gracious unto us: this hath been by your means[G]: [w]will he regard your persons? saith the LORD of hosts.

10 [4]Who *is there* even among you that would shut the doors *for nought*[G]? neither do ye kindle *fire* on mine altar for nought.[G] [r]I have no pleasure in you, saith the LORD of hosts, [x]neither will I accept an offering at your hand.

11 For from the rising of the sun even unto the going down of the same my name [5]*shall be* great among the Gĕn′tīleș[G]; and in every place [y]incense [5]*shall be* offered unto my name, and a pure offering: for my name [5]*shall be* great among the heathen[G], saith the LORD of hosts.[Q]

12 ¶ But ye have profaned[G] it, in that ye [z]say, The table of the LORD *is* polluted; and the fruit thereof, *even* his meat,[G] *is* contemptible.[Q]

13 Ye [z]said also, Behold, what a weariness *is it*! and ye have snuffed[G] at it, saith the LORD of hosts; and ye brought *that which was* [6]torn, and the [a]lame, and the sick; thus ye [7]brought an [b]offering: should I accept this of your hand? saith the LORD.

14 But cursed *be* the deceiver, which hath in his flock a male, and [c]voweth, and sacrificeth unto the Lord a [8]corrupt thing: for [d]I *am* a great King, saith the LORD of hosts, and my name *is* dreadful[G] among the [9]heathen.[G]

## CHAPTER 2

*The priests reproved for neglecting their covenant; 11 and also the people for their idolatry, 14 adultery, 17 and perverseness.*

AND now, O ye [a]priests, this [b,c]commandment *is* for you.

2 [d]If ye will not hear, and if ye will not lay *it* to heart, to give [e]glory unto my name, saith the LORD of hosts, [f]I will even send a curse upon you, and I will curse your blessings: yea, I have cursed them already, because ye do not lay *it* to heart.

3 Behold, I will [1]corrupt[G] your seed, and spread dung[G] upon your faces, *even* the dung[G] of your solemn feasts; and *one* shall take you away with it.

4 And ye shall know that I have sent this [b,c]commandment unto you, that my [g]covenant might be with [h]Lē′vī, saith the LORD of hosts.

5 My [g]covenant[G] was with [h]him of life and peace; and I gave them to him [2]*for* the fear wherewith he [i]feared me, and was afraid before my name.[T]

6 [j]The law of truth was in his mouth, and iniquity was not found in his lips: he walked with me in peace and [3]equity, and [k,l]did turn many away from iniquity.[T]

7 For[Q] [m,n]the priest's lips should keep [o]knowledge, and [l]they should seek the law at his mouth: for he *is* [p]the messenger of the LORD of hosts.

8 But [q]ye are [r]departed out of the way; ye have [s]caused many to stumble at the [t]law; ye have corrupted the [g]covenant of [h]Lē′vī, saith the LORD of hosts.[Q]

9 Therefore have I also [u]made you contemptible and base before all the people, according as ye have [v]not kept my ways, but have [4]been partial in the law.

9 R. V. Gentiles.

**1**

a *Minister, false and corrupt,* vs. 1–3, 8, 9; Rom. 15:16.

b *Commandment, enjoining righteousness,* Deut. 8:2.

c *Repentance, enjoined,* vs. 1–4; Mark 1:4.

**2**

d *Impenitence, judgments denounced against,* Rom. 2:5.

e *Glorifying God,* Luke 5:25.

f *Judgments, denounced against disobedience,* Ex. 6:6.

**3**

1 R. V. rebuke the seed for your sake, and will spread dung upon your faces, even the dung of your sacrifices; and ye shall be taken away with it.

**4**

g *Covenant, of God with men,* Deut. 29:1.

h *Levites,* Deut. 10:8.

**5**

i *Fear of God,* Acts 9:31.

2 R. V. that he might fear, and he feared me, and stood in awe of my name.

**6**

j *Minister, character and qualifications of,* Rom. 15:16.

k *Influence, good,* 1 Cor. 7:14.

l *Instruction, in religion,* Prov. 23:23.

3 R. V. uprightness,

**7**

m *Priest, duties of,* Lev. 1:5.

n *Minister, duties of,* Rom. 15:16.

o *Knowledge,* Luke 11:52.

p *Messenger, figurative,* Hag. 1:13.

**8**

q *Minister, unfaithful,* Rom. 15:16.

r *Backsliders,* Jer. 3:22.

s *Influence, evil,* 1 Cor. 7:14.

t *Law, of Moses,* Deut. 33:2.

**9**

u *Judgments,* Ex. 6:6.

v *Disobedience to God,* Eph. 5:6.

4 R. V. had respect of persons in the law.

10 Have we not [w]all one father? hath not one God [x]created [y]us? why do we deal treacherously every man against his brother, by profaning the covenant of our fathers?

11 ¶ Jū′dah hath dealt treacherously, and an abomination is committed in Iş′ra-el and in Jĕ-ru̥′să-lĕm; for Jū′dah [z]hath profaned the holiness of the LORD which he loved, and hath [a]married the daughter of a strange god.

12 The LORD will [b]cut off [5]the man that doeth this, the master and the scholar, out of the tabernacles of Jā′cob, and [c]him that [d]offereth an offering unto the LORD of hosts.

13 And this have [c]ye done again, covering the [e]altar of the LORD with tears, with weeping, and with crying out, insomuch that he regardeth not the [d]offering any more, or receiveth *it* with good will at your hand.

14 [f]Yet ye say, Wherefore? Because the LORD hath [g]been witness between thee and the wife of thy youth, against whom thou hast dealt [h]treacherously: yet *is* she thy companion, and the wife of thy covenant.

15 And did not he make one? Yet had he the residue of the spirit. And wherefore one? That he might seek a godly seed. Therefore [i]take heed to your spirit, and let none deal treacherously against the wife of his youth.

16 For the LORD, the God of Iş′ra-el, saith that he [j]hateth [k]putting away: [6]for *one* covereth violence with his garment, saith the LORD of hosts: therefore [i]take heed to your spirit, that ye deal not treacherously.

17 ¶ Ye have wearied the LORD with your words. [l]Yet ye say, Wherein have we wearied *him*? When ye [l,m]say, Every one that doeth evil *is* good in the sight of the LORD, and he delighteth in them; or, [n]Where *is* the God of judgment?

## CHAPTER 3

*The messenger of the covenant coming to his temple. 7 The rebellion, 8 sacrilege, 13 and perverseness of the people. 16 The promise of blessing to them that fear God.*

[a]BEHOLD, [b,c]I will send my [d,e]messenger, and he shall prepare the way before me: and the [f]Lord, whom ye seek, shall suddenly come to his [g]temple, even the messenger of the covenant, whom ye delight in: behold, he shall come, saith the LORD of hosts.

2 But [h]who may abide the day of his coming? and who shall stand when he appeareth? for he *is* like a [i,j]refiner's fire, and like [k]fullers' sope:

3 And [h]he shall sit *as* a [i,j]refiner and purifier of [l]silver: and he shall [m,n]purify the [o]sons of Lē′vī, and purge them as [p]gold and silver, that they may [q]offer unto the LORD an [r]offering in [s]righteousness.

4 Then shall the offering of Jū′dah and Jĕ-ru̥′să-lĕm be pleasant unto the LORD, as in the days of old, and as in former years.

5 And [t]I will come near to you to judgment; and I will be a swift witness against the [u]sorcerers, and against the [v]adulterers, and against [w]false swearers, and against [x]those that [y]oppress the [z,a]hireling in *his* [b]wages, the [c]widow, and the [d]fatherless, and that turn aside the [e]stranger *from his right*, and [f]fear not me, saith the LORD of hosts.

6 For I *am* the LORD, [g]I change not; therefore ye sons of Jā′cob [h]are not consumed.

7 ¶ Even from the days of your fathers ye [1]are gone away from mine ordinances, and have [i]not

*f Fear of God*, Acts 9:31. **6** *g God, immutable*, Gen. 2:2. *h* **God,** *mercy of*, Gen. 2:2. **7** *i Disobedience to God*, Eph. 5:6. **1 R. V.** have turned aside from

**10**
*w Fraternity*, Zech. 11:14.
*x God, creator of man*, Gen. 2:2.
*y Man, created*, Job 4:17.

**11**
*z Idolatry*, 1 Sam. 15:23.

*a Marriage, figurative*, Gen. 34:9.

**12**
*b Wicked, punishment of*, Psa. 73:3.
*c Hypocrisy, abhorred of God*, Jas. 3:17.
*d Offerings, unavailing when not accompanied by piety*, Lev. 6:17.
5 R. V. to the man that doeth this him that waketh and him that answereth, out of the tents of Jacob,

**13**
*e Altar, of burnt offerings*, Gen. 8:20.

**14**
*f Presumption*, Psa. 19:13.
*g Sin, known to God*, Rom. 5:12.
*h Idolatry, wicked practices of*, 1 Sam. 15:23.

**15**
*i Watchfulness, enjoined, over the heart*, Matt. 24:42.

**16**
*j Sin, repugnant to God*, Rom. 5:12.
*k Divorce, unjust, reproved*, vs. 14–16; Matt. 19:7.
6 R. V. and him that covereth his garment with violence,

**17**
*l Godless, described as, impugning God's justice*, Job 8:13.
*m Blasphemy*, 2 Sam. 12:14.

*n Unbelief*, Heb. 3:12.

**1**
*a* Matt. 11:10; Mark 1:2; Luke 7:27.
*b Jesus, prophecies concerning*, Matt. 1:21.
*c Prophecies concerning the Messiah, and their fulfillment*, Gen. 12:3.
*d Messenger, figurative*, Hag. 1:13.
*e John the Baptist*, Luke 1:63.
*f Jesus, divinity of*, Matt. 1:21.
*g Church, called temple*, 1 Kin. 9:3.

**2**
*h Jesus, judge*, Matt. 1:21.
*i Refining*, 1 Chr. 28:18.
*j Art*, 2 Chr. 16:14.
*k* Mark 9:3.

**3**
*l Silver*, 1 Chr. 28:14.
*m Spiritual Purification*, Psa. 51:2.
*n Purity of Heart*, 1 Tim. 4:12.
*o Levites, prophecies concerning*, Deut. 10:8.
*p Gold*, Ezek. 7:19.
*q Worship, preparation for*, Gen. 22:5.
*r Offerings, unavailing, when not accompanied by piety*, Lev. 6:17.
*s Righteousness, required*, Psa. 15:2.

**5**
*t God, judge*, Gen. 2:2.
*u Sorcery*, Isa. 47:9.
*v Adultery*, Lev. 20:10.
*w Perjury*, 1 Tim. 1:10.
*x Employer*, Deut. 24:14.
*y Oppression*, Eccl. 5:8.
*z Employee*, Deut. 24:14.

*a Hired Servant*, Lev. 25:40.
*b Wages*, Gen. 31:7.
*c Widow*, 2 Sam. 14:5.
*d Orphan*, Lam. 5:3.
*e Foreigners*, Deut. 23:20.

j *Backsliders, called to repentance,* Jer. 3:22.
k *Repentance, condition of forgiveness,* Mark 1.4.
l *Presumption,* Psa. 19:13.
m *Spiritual Blindness,* 2 Cor. 4:4.
8
n *Tithes,* Num. 18:24.
o *Offerings,* Lev. 6:17.
9
p *Judgment, according to opportunity and works,* 1 Pet. 1:17.
10
q *Commandment, enjoining liberality in God's service,* Deut. 8:2.
r *Liberality, rewards for,* 1 Tim. 6:18.
s *Blessings, contingent upon obedience,* Deut. 11:26.
t *Promise, to the obedient,* v. 11; 2 Cor. 1:20.
u *God, providence of,* Gen. 2:2.
v *Obedience, rewarded,* Heb. 5:8.
w *Temporal Blessings, from God,* vs. 11, 12; Psa. 103:2.
2 R. V. the whole tithe into
13
x *Blasphemy, defying God,* 2 Sam. 12:14.
14
y *Murmuring,* Num. 14:2.
z *Skepticism,* Psa. 53:1.
15
a *God, providence of, mysterious,* Gen. 2:2.
b *Wicked, prosperity of,* Psa. 73:3.
16
c *Fear of God, bond of fellowship,* Acts 9:31.
d *Communion of Saints,* 1 Cor. 10:16.
e *Fellowship, of the righteous,* 1 Cor. 1:9.
f *God, love of, exemplified,* Gen. 2:2.
g *Book, figurative,* Psa. 139:16.

kept *them.* [j]Return unto me, and
[k]I will return unto you, saith the
LORD of hosts. But ye [l]said,
[m]Wherein[G] shall we return?[Q]
8 ¶ *Will a man rob God? Yet
ye have robbed me. But ye [l]say,
Wherein[G] have we robbed thee?
In [n]tithes[G] and [o]offerings.
9 [p]Ye *are* cursed with a curse:
for ye have robbed me, *even* this
whole nation.
10 [q,r]Bring ye [2]all the [n]tithes[G]
into the storehouse, that there
may be meat[G] in mine house, and
prove[G] me now herewith, saith
the LORD of hosts, [s,t]if I will not
open you the windows of heaven,
and [u,v]pour you out a [w]blessing,
that *there shall* not *be room*
enough *to receive it.*
11 [S]And I will rebuke the de-
vourer for your sakes, and he
shall not destroy[G] the fruits of
your ground; neither shall your
vine cast her fruit before the
time in the field, saith the LORD
of hosts.
12 And all nations[G] shall call you
blessed: for ye shall be a delightsome[G] land, saith the LORD of
hosts.[S]
13 ¶ [x]Your words have been
stout[G] against me, saith the
LORD. Yet ye [l]say, What have
we spoken *so much* against thee?
14 Ye have [y]said, It *is* vain to
serve God: and [z]what profit *is it*
that we have kept his ordinance[G],
and that we have walked mourn-
fully before the LORD of hosts?
15 And now we call the proud
happy; yea, [a]they that work
[b]wickedness are set[G] up; yea,
[a]*they that* tempt[G] God are even
delivered.
16 Then they that [c]feared the
LORD [d,e]spake often one to another: and the LORD [f]hearkened,
and heard *it*, and a [g]book of remembrance was written before
him for them that feared the
LORD, and that [h]thought upon
his name.
17 And [i,j]they shall be mine,
saith the LORD of hosts, in [3]that
day when I make up my jewels;
and I will spare them, as a [k]man
spareth his own [l]son that serveth
him.
18 Then shall ye return, and
[m]discern between the righteous
and the wicked, between him
that serveth God and him that
serveth him not.[S]

## CHAPTER 4

*God's judgment on the wicked, 2 and his blessing on the righteous. 4 The law of Moses to be remembered. 5 The coming of Elijah the prophet.*

FOR, behold, the day cometh,
that shall burn as an oven;
and [a]all the [b]proud, yea, and all
that [c]do wickedly, shall be [d]stub-
ble: and the day that cometh
shall burn them up, saith the
LORD of hosts, that it shall leave
them neither root nor branch.
2 ¶ But [e]unto you that [f]fear my
name shall the [g]Sun of righteousness arise with [h,i]healing in his
wings; and ye shall go forth, and
[1]grow up as calves of the stall.[Q][T]
3 And ye shall tread down the
wicked; for they shall be ashes
under the soles of your feet in the
day that I [2]shall do *this,* saith
the LORD of hosts.[T]
4 ¶ [j]Remember ye the [k]law
of Mō′ṣeṣ my servant, which I
[l]commanded unto him in [m]Hō′-
reb for all Iṣ′ra-el, *with* the statutes and judgments.[G]
5 Behold, [n]I will send you
[o,p,q]Ē-lī′jah the prophet before
the coming of the great and
dreadful[G] [r]day of the LORD:[Q]
6 And he shall [s,t]turn the heart
of the fathers to the children,
and the heart of the children to
their fathers, lest I come and
smite the earth with a curse.

h *Communion, with God,* 2 Cor. 13:14.
17
i *Promise, to the righteous,* 2 Cor. 1:20.
j *Righteous, promises to,* Psa. 64:10.
k *Parents, affection of,* 2 Cor. 12:14.
l *Children, good,* Mark 10:14.
3 Am. R. V. the day that I do make, even mine own possession;
18
m *Wicked, contrasted with the righteous,* Psa. 73:3.
1
a *Wicked, punishment of,* Psa. 73:3.
b *Pride,* Prov. 16:18.
c *Judgment, according to opportunity and works,* 1 Pet. 1:17.
d *Stubble,* Isa. 5:24.
2
e *Righteous, promises to,* Psa. 64:10.
f *Fear of God,* Acts 9:31.
g *Sun, figurative,* Josh. 10:12.
h *Salvation,* Acts 16:17.
i *Spiritual Blessings, from God,* Eph. 1:3.
1 R. V. gambol
3
2 R. V. do make, saith
4
j *Obedience, enjoined,* Heb. 5:8.
k *Law, of Moses,* Deut. 33:2.
l *Revelation,* 2 Cor. 12:1.
m *Horeb,* Ex. 3:1.
5
n *Prophecies concerning the Messiah, and their fulfillment,* Gen. 12:3.
o Matt. 11:14; Mark 9:11; Luke 1:17.
p *John the Baptist, prophecies concerning,* Luke 1:63.
q *Messenger, figurative,* Hag. 1:13.
r *Day, called day of the Lord,* Gen. 1:5.
6
s Luke 1:17.
t *Influence, good,* 1 Cor. 7:14.

* **PARSIMONY.** *Toward the poor,* Jas. 2:16. *Admonition against,* 2 Cor. 9:7; 1 John 3:17. *Of the Jews, toward the temple,* Hag. 1:2, 4, 9; *toward God,* Mal. 3:8, 9. *Of the disciples,* Matt. 26:8, 9; John 12:4, 5. *Punishment of,* Hag. 1:6, 9–11.

# THE

# NEW TESTAMENT

(KING JAMES VERSION, WITH ELABORATE MARGINAL READINGS FROM THE AMERICAN REVISED VERSION)

WITH MARGINAL NOTES AND FOOTNOTES

## THE GOSPEL ACCORDING TO
# MATTHEW

1
a *Genealogy, of Joseph*, 1 Chr. 5:1.
b *Jesus, life of*, vs. 1–17; Matt. 1:21.
c *David, genealogy of*, vs. 1–6; 1 Sam. 16:13.
d *Abraham*, Gen. 17:5.
2
e *Isaac*, Gen. 21:3.
f *Jacob*, Gen. 27:11.
g Or, *Judah*, Gen. 37:26.
3
h Or, *Pharez*, Gen. 38:29.
i Or, *Tamar*, Gen. 38:6.
j Luke 3:33.
k Or, *Ram*, Ruth 4:19.
4
l *Amminadab*, Num. 2:3.
m Or, *Nahshon*, Num. 7:12.
n *Salmon*, Ruth 4:20.
5
o Or, *Boaz*, Ruth 2:1.
p Or, *Rahab*, Josh. 2:1.
q *Obed*, Ruth 4:17.
r *Ruth*, Ruth 1:4.
s *Jesse*, Ruth 4:17.
6
t *King*, 2 Kin. 3:10.
u *Solomon*, 2 Sam. 12:24.
v Or, *Uriah*, 2 Sam. 11:3.
7
w Or, *Rehoboam*, 1 Kin. 11:43.
x Or, *Abijam*, 1 Kin. 15:1.
y *Asa*, 1 Kin. 15:8.
8
z Or, *Jehoshaphat*, 2 Kin. 12:18.

a Or, *Jehoram*, 1 Kin. 22:50.
b Or, *Uzziah*, 2 Chr. 26:1.
9
c Or, *Jotham*, 2 Kin. 15:5.
d Or, *Ahaz*, 2 Kin. 15:38.
e Or, *Hezekiah*, 2 Kin. 16:20.
10
f Or, *Manasseh*, 2 Kin. 21:1.
g *Amon*, 2 Kin. 21:18.
h Or, *Josiah*, 1 Kin. 13:2.
11
i Or, *Jehoiakim*, Jer. 26:1.

## CHAPTER 1

*The genealogy of Jesus Christ. 18 The virgin Mary, while espoused to Joseph, conceives by the Holy Ghost. 19 An angel removes the doubts of Joseph. 21 The name of Jesus. 25 The birth of Jesus.*

THE book of the [a]generation[C]
of [b]Jē′ṣus Chrīst, the son
of [c]Dā′vid, the son of [d]Ā′brā-
hăm.[T][Q]
2 [d]Ā′brā-hăm begat [e]Ī′ṣaac;
and Ī′ṣaac begat [f]Jā′cob; and
Jā′cob begat [g]Jū′das and his
brethren;[Q]
3 And [g]Jū′das begat [h]Phā′rēṣ
and Zā′rȧ of [i]Thā′mar; and
Phā′rēṣ begat [j]Ĕs′rom; and Ĕs′-
rom begat [k]Ā′ram;[Q]
4[Q] And [k]Ā′ram begat [l]Ȧ-mĭn′a-
dăb; and Ȧ-mĭn′a-dăb begat
[m]Nȧ-ăs′son; and Nȧ-ăs′son begat [n]Săl′mŏn;
5 And [n]Săl′mŏn begat [o]Bō′ŏz
of [p]Rā′chăb; and Bō′ŏz begat
[q]Ō′bed of [r]Ruth; and Ō′bed begat [s]Jĕs′se;[Q]
6 And [s]Jĕs′se begat [c]Dā′vid the
[t]king; and Dā′vid the king begat
[u]Sŏl′o-mon of her *that had been
the wife* of [v]U-rī′as;[Q]
7[Q] And [u]Sŏl′o-mon begat [w]Rŏ-
bō′am; and Rŏ-bō′am begat
[x]Ȧ-bī′ȧ; and Ȧ-bī′ȧ begat [y]Ā′sȧ;
8 And [y]Ā′sȧ begat [z]Jŏs′a-phăt;
and Jŏs′a-phăt begat [a]Jō′ram;
and Jō′ram begat [b]Ȯ-zī′as;
9 And [b]Ȯ-zī′as begat [c]Jō′a-
thăm; and Jō′a-thăm begat
[d]Ā′chăz; and Ā′chăz begat
[e]Ĕz-e-kī′as;
10 And [e]Ĕz-e-kī′as begat [f]Mȧ-
năs′sēṣ; and Mȧ-năs′sēṣ begat
[g]Ā′mon; and Ā′mon begat [h]Jŏ-
sī′as;[Q]
11 And [h]Jŏ-sī′as begat [i]Jĕch-o-
nī′as and his brethren, about the
time [j]they were carried away to
[k]Băb′y̆-lon:[Q]
12 And after [j]they were brought
to [k]Băb′y̆-lon, [i]Jĕch-o-nī′as begat [l]Sȧ-lā′thĭ-el; and Sȧ-lā′thĭ-el
begat [m]Zŏ-rŏb′a-bĕl;[Q]
13 And [m]Zŏ-rŏb′a-bĕl begat
Ȧ-bī′ud; and Ȧ-bī′ud begat
[n]Ē-lī′a-kĭm; and Ē-lī′a-kĭm
begat [o]Ā′zôr;
14 And [o]Ā′zôr begat Sā′dŏc;
and Sā′dŏc begat Ā′chim; and
Ā′chim begat Ė-lī′ud;
15 And Ė-lī′ud begat Ē-le-ā′-
zar; and Ē-le-ā′zar begat Măt′-
than; and Măt′than begat Jā′cob;
16 And Jā′cob begat [p]Jō′ṣeph
the husband of [q]Mā′ry̆, of whom
was born *Jē′ṣus, who is called
Chrīst.[T]
17 So all the [r]generations from
[s]Ā′brā-hăm to [t]Dā′vid *are* fourteen generations; and from Dā′-
vid until the [j]carrying away into
[k]Băb′y̆-lon *are* fourteen generations; and from the carrying away into Băb′y̆-lon unto
*Chrīst *are* fourteen generations.
18 ¶ Now[S][T] the birth of[C] *Jē′ṣus
Chrīst was on[C] this wise[C]: When
as his mother [q]Mā′ry̆ was [u,v]es-
poused[C] to [p]Jō′ṣeph, before they
came together, she was found
[w,x]with child of the [y]Holy
Ghost.[C]
19 Then [p]Jō′ṣeph her [z]hus-
band, being a just[C] *man*, and [a]not
willing to make her a publick
example, [b]was minded[C] to put
her away privily.[C]
20 But while [c]he thought on
these things, behold, the [d]angel[C]
of the [e]Lord appeared unto him
in a [f]dream, saying, Jō′ṣeph,
thou son of Dā′vid, fear not to

j *Jews, captive in Babylon*, Neh. 4:2.
k *Babylon*, Ezra 5:12.
12
l Or, *Shealtiel*, Ezra 3:2.
m Or, *Zerubbabel*, Ezra 3:2.
13
n Or, *Shechaniah*, 1 Chr. 3:21.
o Or, *Azrikam*, 1 Chr. 3:23.
16
p *Joseph*, Luke 3:23.
q *Mary*, Luke 1:27.
17
r *Genealogy*, 1 Chr. 5:1.
s *Abraham*, Gen. 17:5.
t *David*, 1 Sam. 16:13.
18
u *Betrothal, a quasi marriage*, Deut. 20:7.
v *Marriage*, Gen. 34:9.
w *Conception, miraculous*, Gen. 21:2.
x *Miracles*, Luke 23:8.
y *Holy Spirit*, Acts 1:2. v.18–5 BC
19
z *Husband, faithful*, v. 20; Num. 30:6.

a *Kindness, instances of*, Acts 28:2.
b *Prudence, instances of*, 2 Chr. 2:12.
20
c *Joseph*, Luke 3:23.
d *Angel, functions of*, Heb. 1.13.
e *God, providence of*, Gen. 2:2.
f *Dream, instances of*, Dan. 1.17.

*g Mary*, Luke 1:27.
*h Conception, miraculous*, Gen. 21:2.
*i Holy Spirit*, Acts 1:2.

21
*j Salvation*, Acts 16:17.

take unto thee [g]Mā'rў thy wife:
for that which is [h]conceived in
her is of the [i]Holy Ghost.
21 And she shall bring forth a
son, and thou shalt call his name
*JĒ'ṢUS: for he shall [j]save his
people from their sins.

22 Now all this was done, that
[k]it might be fulfilled which was
spoken of the Lord by the
[l]prophet, saying,
23 [m]Behold, a [n]virgin shall be
with child, and shall bring forth

22
*k Prophecies concerning the Messiah, and their fulfillment*, Gen. 12:3.
*l Prophets, inspiration of*, Isa. 3:2.

**23** *m* Isa. 7:14. *n Virgin, mother of Jesus*, Isa. 62:5.

***JESUS. Life of:** Facts before the birth of: *The angel Gabriel appears to Mary* [Nazareth], Luke 1:26–38; *Mary visits Elisabeth* [Hebron?], Luke 1:39–56; *Mary's magnificat* [Hebron?], Luke 1:46–55; *an angel appears to Joseph concerning Mary*, Matt. 1:18–25.

*Birth of* [Bethlehem], Matt. 1:18–25; Luke 2:1–7.

*Angels announce the birth of, to the shepherds*, Luke 2:8–14. *Shepherds visit*, Luke 2:15–20. *Magi visit* [Bethlehem], Matt. 2:1–12.

*Circumcision of* [Bethlehem], Luke 2:21. *Is presented in the temple* [Jerusalem], Luke 2:21–38.

*Flight into, and return from, Egypt; dwells at Nazareth*, Matt 2:13–23; Luke 2:39.

*Questions the doctors in the temple* [Jerusalem], Luke 2: 41–52.

*Is baptized by John* [Jordan], Matt. 3:13–17; Mark 1:9–11; Luke 3:21–23.

*Temptation of* [Desert of Judea], Matt. 4:1–11; Mark 1:12, 13; Luke 4:1–13.

*John's testimony concerning*, Matt. 3:11, 12; Mark 1:8; Luke 3:16; John 1:1–34.

*Disciples adhere to*, John 1:35–51.

*Turns water into wine at Cana of Galilee*, John 2:1–12.

*Drives the money changers from the temple* [Jerusalem], John 2:13–16.

*Nicodemus comes to* [Jerusalem], John 3:1–21.

*Baptizes* [Ænon], John 3:22; 4:2.

*Goes to Galilee*, Matt. 4:12; Mark 1:14; Luke 4:14; John 4:1–3.

*Visits Sychar, and teaches the Samaritan woman*, John 4:4–42.

*Teaches in Galilee*, Matt. 4:17; Mark 1:14, 15; Luke 4:14, 15; John 4:43–45.

*Heals a nobleman's son* [Cana of Galilee], John 4:46–54.

*Attends passover* [Jerusalem], John 5:1. *Heals an impotent man at pool of Bethesda, and preaches* [Jerusalem], John 5.

*Is rejected by the people of Nazareth; dwells at Capernaum*, Matt. 4:13–16; Luke 4:16–31.

*Chooses disciples; manifests his omniscience in draught of fishes* [Capernaum], Matt. 4:18–22; Mark 1:16–20; Luke 5:1–11.

*Heals a demoniac* [Capernaum], Mark 1:21–28; Luke 4: 31–37.

*Heals Peter's mother-in-law* [Capernaum], Matt. 8:14–17; Mark 1:29–34; Luke 4:38–41.

*Preaches throughout Galilee*, Matt. 4:23–25; Mark 1:35–39; Luke 4:42–44.

*Heals a leper in Galilee*, Matt. 8:2–4; Mark 1:40–45; Luke 5:12–16.

*Heals a paralytic* [Capernaum], Matt. 9:2–8; Mark 2:1–12; Luke 5:17–26.

*Calls Matthew* [Capernaum], Matt. 9:9; Mark 2:13, 14; Luke 5:27, 28.

*Defines the law of the Sabbath on the occasion of his disciples plucking the ears of corn* [Capernaum], Matt. 12:1–8; Mark 2:23–28; Luke 6:1–5.

*Heals a man having a withered hand* [Capernaum], Matt. 12:9–14; Mark 3:1–6; Luke 6:6–11.

*Withdraws from Capernaum to the Sea of Galilee, where he heals many*, Matt. 12:15–21; Mark 3:7–12.

*Goes up into a mountain, and calls and ordains twelve disciples* [Galilee], Matt. 10:2–4; Mark 3:13–19; Luke 6:12–19.

*Delivers the Sermon on the Mount* [Galilee], Matt. chapters 5–7; Luke 6:20–49.

*Heals the servant of the centurion* [near Capernaum], Matt. 8:5–13; Luke 7:1–10.

*Raises from the dead the son of the widow of Nain*, Luke 7:11–17.

*Receives the message from John the Baptist* [Galilee], Matt. 11:2–19; Luke 7:18–35.

*Upbraids the unbelieving cities about Capernaum*, Matt. 11:20–30.

*Anointed by a sinful woman* [Capernaum], Luke 7:36–50.

*Preaches in the cities of Galilee*, Luke 8:1–3.

*Heals a demoniac, and denounces the scribes and Pharisees* [Galilee], Matt. 12:22–45; Mark 3:19–30; Luke 11:14–54.

*His mother and brethren visit him* [Capernaum], Matt. 12: 46–50; Mark 3:31–35; Luke 8:19–21.

*Parables, of the sower; of the tares; of the mustard seed; of the leaven; of the treasure hidden in the field; of a merchant seeking goodly pearls; of the net* [Sea of Galilee], Matt. 13: 1–53; Mark 4:1–34; Luke 8:4–18.

*Crosses the Sea of Galilee, and stills the tempest*, Matt. 8: 18–27; Mark 4:35–41; Luke 8:22–25.

*Sends demons into the swine* [Gadara], Matt. 8:28–33; Mark 5:1–20; Luke 8:26–39.

*Returns to Capernaum*, Matt. 9:1; Mark 5:21; Luke 8:40.

*Eats with publicans and sinners, and discourses on fasting* [Capernaum], Matt. 9:10–17; Mark 2:15–22; Luke 5:29–39.

*Raises daughter of Jairus, and heals the woman with issue of blood* [Capernaum], Matt. 9:18–26; Mark 5:22–43; Luke 8:41–56.

*Heals two blind men, and casts out a dumb spirit* [Capernaum], Matt. 9:27–34.

*Returns to Nazareth*, Matt. 13:53–58; Mark 6:1–6.

*Teaches in various cities in Galilee*, Matt. 9:35–38.

*Instructs his disciples, and empowers them to heal diseases and cast out unclean spirits*, Matt. 10; Mark 6:6–13; Luke 9:1–6.

*Herod falsely supposes him to be John, whom he had beheaded*, Matt. 14:1, 2, 6–12; Mark 6:14–16, 21–29; Luke 9:7–9.

*The twelve return; he goes to the desert; multitudes follow him; he feeds five thousand* [Sea of Galilee], Matt. 14:13–21; Mark 6:30–44; Luke 9:10–17; John 6:1–14.

*People desire to make him king*, John 6:15.

*Walks on the sea* [Galilee], Matt. 14:22–33; Mark 6:45–52; John 6:15–21.

*Heals many* [Gennesaret], Matt. 13:34, 35; Mark 6:53–56.

*Teaches in the synagogue in Capernaum*, John 6:22–65.

*Disciples forsake him* [Capernaum], John 6:66–71.

*He justifies his disciples in disregarding traditions* [Capernaum], Matt. 15:1–20; Mark 7:1–23.

*Heals the daughter of the Syrophenician woman* [Tyre and Sidon], Matt. 15:21–28; Mark 7:24–30.

*Heals the afflicted* [Decapolis], Matt. 15:29–31; Mark 7: 31–37.

*Feeds four thousand*, Matt. 15:32–39; Mark 8:1–9.

*Refuses to give a sign to the Pharisees* [region of Magdala], Matt. 16:1–4; Mark 8:10–12.

*Cautions his disciples against the leaven of hypocrisy* [Sea of Galilee], Matt. 16:4–12; Mark 8:13–21.

*Heals a blind man* [Bethsaida], Mark 8:22–26.

*Foretells his death and resurrection* [near Cæsarea Philippi], Matt. 16:21–28; Mark 8:31–38; 9:1; Luke 9:21–27.

*Is transfigured*, Matt. 17:1–13; Mark 9:2–13; Luke 9:28–36.

*Heals a demoniac* [Cæsarea Philippi], Matt. 17:14–20; Mark 9:14–29; Luke 9:37–42.

*Foretells his death and resurrection* [Galilee], Matt. 17:22, 23; Mark 9:30–32; Luke 9:43–45.

*Manifests his omniscience in foretelling of the coin in the fish's mouth*, Matt. 17:24–27.

*Reproves the ambition of his disciples* [Capernaum], Matt. 18:1–35; Mark 9:33–50; Luke 9:46–50.

*Reproves the intolerance of his disciples*, Mark 9:38, 39; Luke 9:49, 50.

*Journeys to Jerusalem to attend the feast of tabernacles, passing through Samaria*, Luke 9:51–62; John 7:2–11.

*Teaches in Jerusalem at the feast of tabernacles*, John 7:14–53; 8; 9:39–41; 10:1–21.

*Heals a blind man*, John 9.

*Commissions the seventy* [Samaria], Luke 10:1–16.

*Hears the report of the seventy* [Jerusalem], Luke 10:17–24.

*Answers lawyer's question by parable of the good Samaritan*, Luke 10:25–37.

*Teaches his disciples to pray*, Luke 11:1–13.

*Answers Pharisees*, Luke 11:14–54.

*Discourses to his disciples* [Galilee], Luke 12:1–59.

*Parable of the barren fig tree* [Galilee], Luke 13:6–9.

*Guest of Mary, Martha, and Lazarus, in Bethany*, Luke 10:38–42.

*Teaches in the temple at Jerusalem, at the feast of dedication*, John 10:22–39.

*Goes to Bethabara to escape violence from the rulers* [E. of the Jordan], John 10:40–42; 11:3–16.

*Journeys toward Jerusalem to attend the passover; heals many who are diseased, and teaches the people* [Peræa], Matt. 19:1, 2; Mark 10:1; Luke 13:10–35.

*Dines with a Pharisee* [Peræa], Luke 14:1–24.

*Teaches the multitude* [Peræa], Luke 14:25–35.

*Parables, of the lost sheep; of the lost piece of silver; of prodigal son; of unjust steward* [Peræa], Luke 15:1–32; 16:1–13.

*Reproves hypocrisy of the Pharisees* [Peræa], Luke 16.

*Parable of the rich man and Lazarus* [Peræa], Luke 16: 19–31.

*o* Isa. 7:14.
*p Fellowship, with Christ,* 1 Cor. 1:9.

24
*q Obedience, instances of,* Heb. 5:8.

25
*r Continence, instances of,* Matt. 19:12.

a son, and they shall call his
name [o],*Ĕm-măn′u-el, which
being interpreted is, [p]God with
us. [T] [Q]
24 Then [c]Jō′şeph being raised
from sleep [q]did as the [d]angel of
the Lord had bidden him, and
took unto him his wife:
25 And [r]knew [G] her not till she
had brought forth her firstborn
son: and he called his name
*JĒ′ŞUS. [S]

## CHAPTER 2

*Wise men from the east inquire after Christ. 11 They worship him, and offer presents. 14 The flight into Egypt. 16 Herod slays the children in Bethlehem. 19 After Herod's death Joseph and his family return from Egypt and dwell in Nazareth.*

NOW when [S] [a]Jē′şus was born in
[b]Bĕth′lĕ-hĕm of [c]Jūdæ′ȧ in
the days of Hĕr′od the king, be-

v.1-5 BC
See footnote, *Time,* Rev. 10:6.

1
*a Jesus, life of, birth of,* Matt. 1:21.
*b Bethlehem, birthplace of Jesus,* Gen. 48:7.
*c Judea,* Luke 5:17.

---

*Teaches his disciples concerning offenses* [Peræa], Luke 17:1–10.
*Raises Lazarus from the dead* [Bethany], John 11:1–46.
*Escapes to the city of Ephraim from conspiracy led by Caiaphas* [Judea], John 11:47–54.
*Heals ten lepers,* Luke 17:11–19.
*Teaches the Pharisees concerning the coming of his kingdom* [Peræa], Luke 17:20–37.
*Parables of the unjust judge, and of the Pharisee and publican praying in the temple* [Peræa], Luke 18:1–14.
*Interprets the law concerning marriage and divorce* [Peræa], Matt. 19:3–12; Mark 10:2–12.
*Blesses little children* [Peræa], Matt. 19:13–15; Mark 10:13–16; Luke 18:15–17.
*Receives the rich young ruler* [Peræa], Matt. 19:16–22; Mark 10:17–22; Luke 18:18–24.
*Parable of the vineyard* [Peræa], Matt. 20:1–16.
*Foretells his death and resurrection* [Peræa], Matt. 20:17–19; Mark 10:32–34; Luke 18:31–34.
*Listens to the mother of James and John in behalf of her sons* [Peræa], Matt. 20:20–28; Mark 10:35–45.
*Heals two blind men at Jericho,* Matt. 20:29–34; Mark 10:46–50; Luke 18:35–43.
*Visits Zacchæus,* Luke 19:1–10.
*Parable of the pounds* [Jericho], Luke 19:11–28.
*Goes to Bethany,* John 12:1–9.
*Triumphal entry into Jerusalem,* Matt. 21:1–11; Mark 11:1–11; Luke 19:29–44; John 12:12–19.
*Enters the temple,* Matt. 21:12; Mark 11:11; Luke 19:45.
*Drives the money changers out of the temple,* Matt. 21:12, 13; Mark 11:15; Luke 19:45, 46.
*Heals in the temple,* Matt. 21:14.
*Teaches daily in the temple,* Luke 19:47, 48.
*Causes the barren fig tree to wither,* Matt. 21:17–22; Mark 11:12–14, 20–22.
*Authority of, questioned,* Matt. 21:23–27; Mark 11:27–33; Luke 20:1–8.
*Parables, of the two sons,* Matt. 21:28–31; *of the wicked husbandmen,* Matt. 21:33–46; Mark 12:1–12; Luke 20:9–19; *of the marriage,* Matt. 22:1–14; Luke 14:16–24.
*Tested by the Pharisees and Herodians, and enunciates the duty of the citizen to his government,* Matt. 22:15–22; Mark 12:13–17; Luke 20:20–26.
*Questioned by the Sadducees concerning resurrection of the dead,* Matt. 22:23–33; Mark 12:18–27; Luke 20:27–40. *Questioned by a lawyer,* Matt. 22:34–40; Mark 12:28–34.
*Exposes hypocrisy of the scribes and Pharisees,* Matt. 23; Mark 12:38–40; Luke 20:45–47.
*Laments over Jerusalem,* Matt. 23:37; Luke 19:41–44.
*Extols the widow who casts two mites into the treasury,* Mark 12:41–44; Luke 21:1–4.
*Foretells destruction of the temple, and of Jerusalem,* Matt. 24; Mark 13; Luke 21:5–36.
*Parables of the ten virgins, and of the talents,* Matt. 25:1–30.
*Foretells the scenes of the day of judgment* [Mount of Olives], Matt. 25:31–46.
*Rulers, plot against; bargain with Judas* [Jerusalem], Matt. 26:1–5, 14–16; Mark 14:1, 2, 10, 11; Luke 22:1–6.
*Anointed with box of precious ointment* [Bethany], Matt. 26:6–13; Mark 14:3–9; John 12:1–8.
*Last passover, and institution of the sacrament of the holy eucharist,* Matt. 26:17–30; Mark 14:12–25; Luke 22:7–20.
*Washes disciples' feet,* John 13:1–17.
*Foretells his betrayal by Judas,* Matt. 26:21–25; Mark 14:18–21; Luke 22:21–23; John 13:21–30.
*Teaches his disciples, and comforts them with promise of the gift of the Holy Spirit,* John chapters 14–16.
*Prays for the apostles, and all believers* [Jerusalem], John 17.
*Goes to Gethsemane* [Mount of Olives], Matt. 26:30, 36–46; Mark 14:26, 32–42; Luke 22:39–46; John 18:1.
*Is betrayed and apprehended* [Gethsemane], Matt. 26:47–56; Mark 14:43–54, 66–72; Luke 22:47–54; John 18:2–12.
*Tried before high priest* [Jerusalem], Matt. 26:57–75; Mark 14:53–72; Luke 22:54–71; John 18:13–27.
*Tried, before Pilate,* Matt. 27:1, 2, 11–14; Mark 15:1–5; Luke 23:1–5; John 18:28–38; *before Herod,* Luke 23:6–12.
*Tried again before Pilate, and condemned to death,* Matt. 27:15–26; Mark 15:6–15; Luke 23:13–25; John 18:39, 40; 19:1–16.
*Mocked by the soldiers,* Matt. 27:27–31; Mark 15:16–20.
*Led away to be crucified,* Matt. 27:31–34; Mark 15:20–23; Luke 23:26–32; John 19:16, 17.
*Crucified,* Matt. 27:35–56; Mark 15:24–41; Luke 23:33–49; John 19:18–30.
*Taken from the cross, and buried,* Matt. 27:57–66; Mark 15:42–47; Luke 23:50–56; John 19:31–42.
*Rises from the dead,* Matt. 28:2–15; Mark 16:1–11; Luke 24:1–12; John 20:1–18.

**Appearances of, after his resurrection:** *To Mary Magdalene, and other women,* Matt. 28:1–10; Mark 16:9; Luke 24:1–10; John 20:11–17. *To Peter,* Luke 24:34; 1 Cor. 15:5. *To two disciples who journey to Emmaus,* Mark 16:12, 13; Luke 24:13–31. *In the midst of the disciples, when Thomas is absent* [Jerusalem], John 20:19–23; *when Thomas is present,* Mark 16:14–18; Luke 24:36–49; John 20:26–29; 1 Cor. 15:5. *To certain disciples, Sea of Galilee,* John 21:1–14. *To the eleven disciples, mountain in Galilee,* Matt. 28:16. *To upwards of five hundred* [Galilee], 1 Cor. 15:6. *To James, and also all the apostles* [Jerusalem], Acts 1:3–8; 1 Cor. 15:7. *To Paul,* Acts 9:3–6; 23:11; 26:13–18; 1 Cor. 9:1; 15:8.
*In Stephen's vision,* Acts 7:55, 56. *To John, in a vision, on Patmos,* Rev. 1:10–18.

**Ascension of,** Mark 16:19; Luke 24:50, 51; John 14:2–4; Acts 1:9; 3:21; Eph. 1:20; 4:8–10; 1 Tim. 3:16; Heb. 1:3; 4:14; 9:24. *Foretold,* Psa. 68:18; Luke 24:26, 50; John 6:62; 7:33; 14:2, 3, 12, 28; 16:5, 7, 10, 16, 28; 17:13; 20:17.

**Atonement by,** Rom. 3:24–26; 5:11, 15; 1 Thess. 1:10; Heb. 13:12; 1 John 2:2; 3:5; 4:10; Rev. 5:6, 9; 13:8.
*Made once for all,* Heb. 7:27; 9:24–28; 10:10, 12, 14; 1 Pet. 3:18.
*Vicarious,* Isa. 53:4–12; Matt. 20:28; John 6:51; 11:49–51; Gal. 1:4; 3:13; Eph. 5:2; 1 Thess. 5:9, 10; Heb. 2:9; 1 Pet. 2:24.
*Through his blood,* Luke 22:20; 1 Cor. 1:23; Eph. 2:13–15; Heb. 9:12–15, 25, 26; 12:24; 13:12, 20, 21; 1 John 5:6; Rev. 1:5; 5:9; 7:14; 12:11.
*For reconciliation,* Rom. 5:1–21; 2 Cor. 5:18, 19, 21; Eph. 2:16, 17; Col. 1:20–22; Heb. 2:17.
*For remission of sins,* Zech. 13:1; Matt. 26:28; Luke 24:46, 47; John 1:29; Rom. 4:25; 1 Cor. 15:3; Gal. 1:3, 4; Eph. 1:7; Col. 1:14; Heb. 1:3; 10:1–20; 1 John 1:7; 3:5.

**Atonement by, typified,** Ex. 29:36, 37; 30:10, 15, 16; Lev. 1:4; 5:6, 16, 18; 6:7; 8:34; 9:2, 3, 7; 10:17; 12:7, 8; 14:18–20, 31, 53; 15:14, 15, 29, 30; 16:6, 10, 11, 16–18, 24, 27, 30, 32–34; 17:11; 23:27, 28; 25:9; Num. 8:19, 21; 16:46; 25:13; 28:22, 30; 29:5; 31:50.

**Atoning blood of,** Matt. 26:28; Mark 14:24; Luke 22:20; Eph. 1:7; 2:13; Heb. 9:14; 10:19; 1 John 1:7.

**Atoning blood of, typified,** Ex. 12:7, 13, 22, 23; 24:6, 8; 29:12, 15, 20, 21; 30:10; Lev. 1:5, 10, 11; 3:2, 8, 13; 4:5–7, 17, 18, 25, 30, 34; 5:8, 9; 6:30; 7:2; 8:2, 15, 19, 23, 24, 30; 9:9, 18; 14:6, 14, 15, 25; 16:14, 15, 18, 19, 27; 17:6, 11. Num. 18:17; 19:2–4; Deut. 12:27; 2 Kin. 16:13, 15; 2 Chr. 29:22; 30:16; 35:11; Ezek. 43:20; 45:19, 20; 1 Pet. 1:19.

**Benevolence of:** *Manifested in his companionship with sinners,* Matt. 9:10–12; Mark 2:14–17; Luke 5:30; 15:2; 19:5–10. See COMPASSION OF, and LOVE OF, below.

**Compassion of:** *For those who were in spiritual distress,* Isa. 42:3; Matt. 9:36; 12:20; 18:12, 13; 23:37; Luke 13:34; Mark 1:41; 6:34; Luke 7:13; 15:4–9, 20–24; 19:41, 42; John 11:33–38; 18:8, 9; 2 Cor. 8:9; Heb. 4:15; 5:2. *For those who were in temporal adversity,* Isa. 53:4; Matt. 8:3, 16, 17; 14:14; 15:32; 20:34; Mark 8:2, 3.

**Condescension of,** Luke 22:27; John 13:5, 14; 2 Cor. 8:9; Phil. 2:7, 8; Heb. 2:11.

**Creator,** John 1:3, 10; 1 Cor. 8:6; Col. 1:16, 17; Heb. 1:2, 10; Rev. 3:14.

**Death of,** John 12:32, 33; Acts 5:30; 7:52; Heb. 2:14; 12:2, 24; Rev. 5:12; 13:8. *Foretold, by the psalmist,* **Psa.**

d *Messianic Hope*, vs. 1–12; Gen. 49:10.
e *Seekers, instances of*, Isa. 55:6.
f *Wisdom, of the Magi*, vs. 1–12; Prov. 2:2.
g *Heathen, pious people among*, Lam. 1:10.
h *Jerusalem*, Judg. 19:10.
**2**
i *Jesus, king*, Matt. 1:21.
j *Stars*, Judg. 5:20.
k *Jesus, worship of*, Matt. 1:21.

hold, [d]there came [e,f,g]wise men
from the east to [h]Jĕ-ru̥′sā-lĕm,
2 Saying, [d]Where is he that is
born [i]King of the Jews? for
we have seen his [j]star in the
east, and are come to [k]worship
him.[Q]
3 When Hĕr′od the king had
heard *these things*, he was troubled, and all [h]Jĕ-ru̥′sā-lĕm with
him.
4 And when he had gathered all
the [l]chief [m]priests and [n]scribes
of the people together, he demanded of them where [a]Christ[G]
should be born.
5 And they said unto him,
In [b]Bĕth′lĕ-hĕm of [c]Jū-dæ′ȧ:
for thus it is written by the
[o]prophet.
6 And thou [b,p]Bĕth′lĕ-hĕm, *in*
the land of [c]Jū′dȧ, art not the
least among the princes of Jū′dȧ:
for [q]out of thee shall come a

**4**
l *High Priest*, Lev. 21:10.
m *Priest*, Lev. 1:5.
n *Scribe, member of the council*, 1 Kin. 4:3.
**5**
o *Prophets*, Isa. 3:2.
**6**
p Mic. 5:2; John 7:42.
q *Prophecies concerning the Messiah, and their fulfillment*, Gen. 12:3.

---

22:1 (with Matt. 27:46; Mark 15:34); 22:17 (with Matt. 27:36; Luke 23:35); 22:18 (with Matt. 27:35; Mark 15:24; Luke 23:34; John 19:23, 24); 34:20 (with John 19:36); 69:21 (with Matt. 27:34, 48; Mark 15:36; Luke 23:36; John 19:28–30); *by Isaiah*, Isa. 52:14; 53:7–12; *by Zechariah*, Zech. 12:9, 10 (with Matt. 26:31); *by Jesus, himself*, Matt. 12:40 (with Luke 11:30); 16:4, 21; 17:12, 13, 22, 23; 20:17–19; 21:33–39; 26:2, 12, 18; Mark 8:31; 9:31; 10:32–34; 14:8, 9; Luke 9:22, 44; 12:50; 17:25; 18:31–33; 22:15, 21, 37; John 2:19, 21; 10:11, 15, 17, 18; 12:7, 24, 32–34; 14:19; 18:11.

*Paul's testimony concerning*, Acts 17:3; 26:22, 23; 1 Cor. 1:17, 18, 23, 24; 2:2; 15:3, 4; 2 Cor. 4:10, 11; 13:4; Gal. 3:1; 1 Thess. 2:15; 4:14.

FOR CIRCUMSTANCES OF THE DEATH OF, see LIFE OF, above.

DESIGN OF HIS DEATH: *To make reconciliation*, Rom. 5:6–11; Eph. 2:13–16.

*To redeem*, Isa. 53:4–6, 8, 10–12 (with vs. 1–12); Matt. 20:28; 26:28; Mark 10:45; 14:24; John 6:51; 10:11, 17; 11:49–52; Acts 20:28; 26:23; Rom. 3:24, 25; 8:3, 32; 1 Cor. 5:7; 6:20; 8:11; 15:3; Gal. 1:4; 3:13; 4:4, 5; Eph. 1:6, 7; 5:2, 25–27; Col. 1:14, 20, 22; 2:14, 15; 1 Thess. 1:10; 1 Tim. 2:6; Tit. 2:14; Heb. 2:9, 10, 14, 15, 18; 7:27; 9:12–17, 25, 26, 28; 10:10, 12, 14, 17–20; 1 Pet. 1:18, 19; 2:21, 24; 3:18; 1 John 2:2; 3:16; 4:10; Rev. 1:5, 6; 5:9, 10; 13:8.

*To purge sins*, Zech. 13:1; Luke 24:46, 47; John 1:29; Heb. 1:3; 13:11, 12; 1 John 1:7; Rev. 7:14, 15.

*To secure forgiveness*, Acts 5:30, 31; Rom. 4:25.

*To save*, John 3:14–17; Rom. 6:3–5, 9, 10; 14:9, 15; 2 Cor. 5:14, 15, 19, 21; 8:9; Gal. 2:20; 1 Thess. 5:9, 10.

VICARIOUS DEATH OF, Isa. 53:4–12; Matt. 20:28; John 6:51; 11:49, 51; Gal. 3:13; Eph. 5:2; 1 Thess. 5:9, 10; Heb. 2:9; 1 Pet. 2:24.

VICARIOUS DEATH OF, TYPIFIED, Ex. 29:11, 15, 16, 20, 38–42; Lev. 1:5, 11, 15; 3:2, 8, 13; 4:4, 15, 24, 29; 6:25; 7:2; 8:15, 19; 9:8, 15, 18, 19, 23, 24; 14:13, 19, 25; 2 Chr. 29:22, 24; 30:15; 35:1.

See footnotes: ATONEMENT, Lev. 17:11; REDEMPTION, Eph. 1:7.

VOLUNTARY DEATH OF, Isa. 50:6; 53:12; Luke 9:51; 12:50; 22:15, 42; John 10:17, 18; 18:5, 8, 11; Phil. 2:8; Heb. 7:27; 9:26; 1 John 3:16.

**Divine Sonship of:** Testified to: *By God, at his baptism*, Matt. 3:17; Mark 1:11; Luke 3:22; *at the transfiguration*, Matt. 17:5; Mark 9:7; Luke 9:35; 2 Pet. 1:17; *in his commandment to believe in*, 1 John 3:23.

Testified to: *By himself*, Matt. 11:27 (with Luke 10:22); 26:63, 64; 27:43; Mark 14:61, 62; Luke 22:70; John 3:16–18, 34–36; 6:27, 40, 46, 57; 9:35–37; 11:4; 19:7.

Testified to: *By the disciples*, Matt. 14:33; 1 John 4:14; *by unclean spirits*, Matt. 8:29; Mark 3:11; 5:7 (with Luke 8:28); Luke 4:41; *by Mark*, Mark 1:1; *by John the Baptist*, John 1:34; *by John, the apostle*, John 1:14, 18; 1 John 1:7; 2:22–24; 3:8, 23; 4:9, 10, 14; 5:5, 9, 10, 13, 20; 2 John 3; Rev. 2:18; *by Nathanael*, John 1:49; *by Martha*, John 11:27; *by the centurion*, Matt. 27:54; Mark 15:39; *by Peter*, Acts 3:13; 13:33; *by Paul*, Rom. 1:3, 4, 9; 8:3, 29, 32; 1 Cor. 1:9; 15:24, 27, 28; 2 Cor. 1:3, 19; Gal. 1:16; 4:4; Eph. 1:3; Col. 1:3; 1 Thess. 1:10; *by author of the Epistle to the Hebrews*, Heb. 1:1–3, 5; 4:14; 5:5, 8; 6:6; 7:3; 10:29.

*Declared God to be his Father*, Matt. 15:13; 18:10, 19; 20:23; 26:53, 63, 64; Luke 10:22; 22:29; John 5:19–21, 23, 26, 27, 30, 36, 37; 8:16, 19, 26–29, 38, 49, 54; 10:15, 17, 18, 29, 30, 36–38; 11:41; 12:49, 50; 13:3; 14:7, 9–11, 13, 16, 20, 21, 23, 24, 28, 31; 15:1, 8–10, 15, 23, 24; 16:15, 27, 28, 32; 17:1–26; 20:17, 21.

*Peter's confession of*, Matt. 16:15–17.

*Prophecies concerning*, Psa. 2:7; Luke 1:32, 35.

*Worshipped by the disciples as the Son of God*, Matt. 14:33.

See DIVINITY OF, below; RELATION OF, *To the Father*, below.

**Divinity of:** Indicated by the titles ascribed to him, as: IMMANUEL, Isa. 7:14 (with Matt. 1:23); FIRST AND LAST, Rev. 1:17; 22:13; GOD, Psa. 102:24–27 (with Heb. 1:10–13); John 1:1; 20:28; Rom. 9:5; 1 John 5:20, 21; GOD AND SAVIOUR JESUS CHRIST, 2 Pet. 1:1; GOD OUR SAVIOUR, Tit. 2:13; HOLY ONE, Acts 3:14; KING OF KINGS AND LORD OF LORDS, Rev. 17:14; LORD, Psa. 110:1 (with Matt. 22:42–45); Isa. 40:3 (with Matt. 3:3); Acts 20:28; LORD OF HOSTS, Isa. 8:13, 14 (with 1 Pet. 2:8); MY LORD AND MY GOD, John 20:28; LORD OF ALL, Acts 10:36; Rom. 10:12; MIGHTY GOD, Isa. 9:6; ONLY BEGOTTEN OF THE FATHER, John 1:14, 18; 3:16, 18; 1 John 4:9; SON OF GOD, Matt. 26:63–67; Mark 1:1; 15:39; 1 Cor. 1:9; 2 Cor. 1:19; Gal. 2:20; Eph. 4:13; Heb. 1:2; 2 Pet. 1:17; 1 John 1:2, 3; 3:23; 5:10, 12, 13, 20. See DIVINE SONSHIP OF above.

*Is one with the Father*, John 5:17, 18, 23; 10:30, 33, 38; 12:45; 14:7–10, 11; 17:11, 21, 22.

*Sends the Holy Spirit equally with the Father*, John 14:16.

*Identical with the* ADONAI, *Almighty, of the Old Testament*, John 12:40, 41 (with Isa. 6:8–11); *and the* JEHOVAH *of the Old Testament*, John 19:37, with Zech. 12:10.

TESTIMONY CONCERNING THE: *By the Father*, John 5:32, 34, 37; 6:27; 8:18; Acts 3:33; 1 John 5:9; *at his baptism*, Matt. 3:16, 17; Mark 1:11; Luke 3:22; *at his transfiguration*, Matt. 17:5; Mark 9:7; Luke 9:35; 2 Pet. 1:17.

By Jesus concerning himself, John 5:18, 31, 36; 8:18, 42; 10:33, 36, 38; 12:45; 14:11–13; 16:27, 28; 17:5, 8, 24, 25; 19:7; *to Peter and other disciples*, Matt. 16:16, 17; Mark 8:29, 30; Luke 9:20, 21; *to the Jews*, Matt. 22:43, 44; John 5:23; 10:30, 33, 36, 38; 12:15; *to his disciples*, John 16:27, 28; *to the woman of Samaria*, John 4:25, 26; *to the restored blind man*, John 9:35–37; *to Philip*, John 14:7–11, 20; *to Caiaphas*, Matt. 26:63, 64; Mark 34:61, 62; Luke 22:67–70; *to Pilate*, John 18:36, 37; 1 Tim. 6:13.

*By the angel, to Joseph*, Matt. 1:23; *to Mary*, Luke 1:32, 35.

*By John the Baptist*, John 1:29–34; 5:33.

*By John, the apostle*, John 1:14, 18; 13:3; 1 John 2:22–24.

*By the disciples*, John 16:30.

*By Paul*, Acts 9:20.

*By the author of the Epistle to the Hebrews*, Heb. 11:26.

*By the Scriptures*, John 5:39.

*By Thomas*, John 20:28.

*By demons*, Matt. 8:29; Mark 1:23, 24; 3:11; 5:6, 7; Luke 4:34, 41.

*Is creator of all things*, John 1:3; Col. 1:16, 17.

*Has power to forgive sins*, Matt. 1:21; 9:6; Mark 2:5; Luke 5:20; Col. 3:13.

*Paul's apostleship from*, Gal. 1:1.

*Invoked with the Father and the Holy Spirit in benedictions*, Rom. 1:7; 1 Cor. 1:3; 2 Cor. 1:2; Gal. 1:3; Eph. 1:2; 6:23, 24; 1 Thess. 1:1; 3:11; 2 Thess. 1:1, 2; 2:16, 17; 2 Tim. 1:2.

*All power given to*, Matt. 28:17, 18.

*Eternity ascribed to*, John 1:1, 2; 1 John 1:1. See ETERNITY OF, below.

*Is judge*, 2 Cor. 5:10. See JUDGE, below.

**Eternity of:** *Called everlasting Father*, Isa. 9:6. *Was before creation*, John 1:1, 2, 15; 17:5, 24; Col. 1:17; 2 Tim. 1:9. *Was from the beginning*, 1 John 2:13. *Was from everlasting*, Mic. 5:2. *Continueth forever*, Psa. 102:24–27 (with Heb. 1:10–13); 110:4; Eph. 3:21; Heb. 7:16, 24, 25; Rev. 5:13, 14. *The same yesterday, to-day and forever*, Heb. 13:8.

**Exaltation of,** Psa. 2:8, 9; 68:18; Eph. 4:8. *In glory*, Matt. 26:64; Mark 16:19; Luke 22:69; 24:26; John 7:39; Acts 2:33, 34; 3:20, 21; 7:55, 56; Rom. 8:17, 34; Eph. 1:20–22; 4:10; Col. 3:1; 1 Tim. 3:16; Heb. 1:3; 10:12, 13; 12:2; 1 Pet. 3:22; Rev. 3:21. *As Lord of heaven and earth*, Phil. 2:9–11; Col. 2:15. *To be Savior*, Acts 5:31. *To be priestly mediator*, Heb. 4:10, 14; 6:20; 7:26; 8:1; 9:24.

**Faith in,** see footnote, FAITH IN CHRIST, John 6:69.

**Faithfulness of,** Isa. 11:5; Luke 4:43; John 7:18; 8:29; 9:4; 14:3; 17:8; Heb. 3:2; Rev. 1:5; 3:14. *In mediation*, Heb. 2:17.

**Glorification of,** John 7:39; 12:16; 17:1; Acts 7:55, 56; Heb. 8:1.

r *Jesus, names of,* Matt. 1:21.
1 R. V. be shepherd of

8
s *Deceit,* Psa. 36:3.
t *Hypocrisy, instances of,* Jas. 3:17.

[r]Governor, that shall [1]rule my
people Iṣ′ra-el.[T Q]
7 Then Hĕr′od, when he had
privily[G] called the [e,f,g]wise men,
enquired of them diligently what
time the [j]star appeared.
8 And he sent them to [b]Bĕth′lĕ-
hĕm, and said, Go and search
diligently[G] for the [a]young child;
and when ye have found *him,*
bring me word again, [s,t]that I
may come and worship him also.
9 When [e,g]they had heard the
king, they departed; and, lo, the
[j]star, which they saw in the east,
[u]went before them, till it came
and stood over where the [a]young
child was.[S]

9
u *Guidance,* Psa. 48:14.

**Head of the Church,** Psa. 118:22, 23 (with Matt. 21:42, 43; Mark 12:10); Isa. 28:16 (with Eph. 2:2–22; 1 Pet. 2:6); Luke 20:17, 18 (with 1 Pet. 2:7); John 15:1–8; 1 Cor. 3:11; Eph. 1:22, 23; 4:15; 5:23–32; Col. 1:18; 2:10, 19; 3:11; Rev. 2:2–28; 3:1, 7; 22:16.

**Holiness of:** *Foretold,* Psa. 45:7; Isa. 11:4, 5; Jer. 23:5; Zech. 9:9. *Professed by himself,* John 5:30; 7:18; 8:46; 14:30; Rev. 3:7.

TESTIFIED TO: *By the angel to his mother,* Luke 1:35. *By demons,* Mark 1:24; Luke 4:34. *By the centurion at crucifixion,* Luke 23:47. *By Stephen,* Acts 7:52. *By Peter,* John 6:69; Acts 3:14; 4:27, 30; 1 Pet. 1:19; 2:22. *By John,* 1 John 2:1, 29; 3:5. *By Paul,* Acts 13:35; 2 Cor. 5:21. *By the author of the Epistle to the Hebrews,* Heb. 1:9; 4:15; 7:26–28; 9:14.

**Humanity of,** Psa. 22:22; John 1:14. *Took on himself the nature of man,* Phil. 2:7, 8; Heb. 2:9, 10, 14–18. *Was born of flesh,* Isa. 9:6; Matt. 1:18–25; Luke 2:11–14; 1 John 4:2; 2 John 7.

Called: *Seed of the woman,* Gen. 3:15; Gal. 4:4; *son of man,* Dan. 7:13; Matt. 16:27, 28; 17:22; 20:18, 28; 26:2, 45, 64; Mark 2:28; 8:31; 9:9, 12; 10:33, 45; 14:21, 41, 62; Luke 5:24; 9:22, 44; 17:22, 24; 18:31; 19:10; 21:36; 22:48, 69; 24:7; John 5:27; 12:34; 13:31; Acts 7:56; Rev. 1:13; 14:14; *son of David,* Matt. 20:30, 31; 21:9; 22:42; Mark 12:35; Luke 18:38; *a prophet like unto Moses,* Deut. 18:15–19; Acts 3:22, 23; 7:37.

**Humility of,** 2 Cor. 8:9; Phil. 2:7, 8. *Became a servant,* Luke 22:27; John 13:5, 14. See MEEKNESS OF, below.

**Impeccability of,** see HOLINESS OF, above; TEMPTATION OF, below.

**Incarnation of,** John 16:28; 1 Tim. 3:16. *Foretold,* Gen. 3:15; Deut. 18:15–18; Psa. 2:7 (with Acts 13:33; Heb. 1:5); Isa. 7:14–16; 9:6; 11:1; John 7:42. *Through the generation of the Holy Spirit,* Matt. 1:1, 16–18, 23; Luke 1:26–56. *Made a little lower than the angels,* Heb. 2:9, 14. *Made flesh,* Luke 24:39; John 1:14; 20:27; Rom. 8:3; 1 Cor. 15:47; 2 Cor. 5:16; Gal. 4:4; Phil. 2:7, 8; Heb. 1:3, 6; 2:17, 18 (with vs. 9–17); 10:5; 1 John 1:1–3; 4:2; 2 John 7. *In the lineage of Judah,* Heb. 7:14. *Made of the seed of David,* Matt. 22:45; Rom. 1:3; 9:5; Rev. 22:16. *Was the son of Mary,* Matt. 13:55; Luke 2:1–21.

See HUMANITY OF, above; RELATION OF, *To the Father,* below.

**Intercession of,** see MEDIATION OF, below.

**Judge,** Matt. 3:12 (with Luke 3:17); 25:31–34; Acts 10:42; Rom. 2:16; 1 Cor. 4:4, 5; 2 Cor. 5:10; 2 Tim. 4:1, 8; Rev. 2:23. *Prophecy concerning,* Isa. 2:4 (with Mic. 4:3); 11:3, 4; Mic. 5:1.

*Ordained of God,* John 5:22; Acts 17:31. *Righteous,* 2 Tim. 4:8.

**Justice of,** Zech. 9:9; John 5:30.

**King:** *Prophecies concerning,* Gen. 49:10; 1 Sam. 2:10; 2 Sam. 7:12 (with Acts 2:30); Psa. 2:6; 18:43, 44; 45:3–7; 72:5, 8, 11; 89:3, 4, 19–21, 23, 27, 29, 36, 37; 110:1, 2 (with Matt. 22:42–45); 132:11, 17, 18; Isa. 9:6, 7; 22:22; 32:1; 52:7, 13; Jer. 23:5; 30:9; 33:17; Ezek. 37:24, 25; Dan. 2:35, 44; 7:13, 14; Hos. 3:5; Mic. 5:2, 4; Zech. 6:12, 13; 9:9, 10; Matt. 2:2, 6; 21:5; Luke 1:32, 33. *Appointed by the Father,* Luke 22:29, 30; Acts 2:30, 36 (with 2 Sam. 7:12); Acts 5:31; Eph. 1:20–22; Heb. 2:7, 8.

*Authority of,* Mark 2:28; John 5:27; *universal,* Matt. 11:27 (with Luke 10:22); 28:18; Luke 19:27; John 3:31, 33; 13:3; 17:2; Rom. 9:5; 10:12; 14:9; Col. 2:10; Heb. 1:2–15; 2:7, 8; 1 Pet. 3:22; Rev. 3:7, 14, 21.

*Dominion of, universal,* Acts 10:36; 1 Cor. 15:23–28; Eph. 1:20–22; Phil. 2:9–11; Rev. 1:5–7, 18; 11:15. *Future glory of,* Matt. 19:28; 25:31–34; 26:64; Mark 14:62; Luke 22:69; Heb. 10:12, 13; Rev. 5:13.

KINGSHIP OF: *Avowed by himself,* Matt. 21:5; 27:11; Luke 23:2; John 18:36, 37. *Ascribed, by disciples,* Luke 19:38; John 1:49; 12:13, 15; Acts 17:7; *in superscription on the cross,* John 19:12, 19.

*Symbolical statements concerning,* Rev. 5:5, 12; 6:2, 15–17; 14:14; 17:14; 19:11, 12, 15, 16.

See LORDSHIP OF, below.

**Kingdom of:** *Brings joy and gladness,* Psa. 46:4; Isa. 25:6; 35; 52:9; 55:12. *Brings peace,* Psa. 46:9; Isa. 11:6–9. *Is within us,* Luke 17:21. *Is truth,* John 18:37. *Is not of this world,* John 18:36.

*Keys of,* Matt. 16:19. *Glad tidings of,* Luke 8:1. *Mysteries of,* Luke 8:10. *Is not meat and drink,* Rom. 14:17.

Likened: *To a man who sowed good seed,* Matt. 13:24–30, 38–43; Mark 4:26–29; *to a grain of mustard seed,* Matt. 13:31, 32; Mark 4:30, 31; Luke 13:18, 19; *to leaven,* Matt. 13:33; Luke 13:21; *to a treasure,* Matt. 13:44; *to a pearl,* Matt. 13:45; *to a net,* Matt. 13:47–50; *to a king who called his servants to a reckoning,* Matt. 18:23–35; *to a householder,* Matt. 20:1–16; *to a king who made a marriage feast for his son,* Matt. 22:2–14; Luke 14:16–24; *to ten virgins,* Matt. 25:1–13; *to a man traveling into a far country, who called his servants and delivered to them his goods,* Matt. 25:14–30; Luke 19:12–27.

PROPHECIES CONCERNING THE KINGDOM OF: Its character: *To enlighten,* Jer. 31:34; Heb. 8:11; *to bring peace,* Psa. 46:9; Isa. 65:25; Mic. 4:3–7; *to bring salvation,* Isa. 62:11; *to bring joy,* Isa. 25:6; 35:1–10; 42:1–7, 18–21; Luke 2:10. *Shall be a river of salvation,* Ezek. 47:1–12; Zech. 14:8, 9, 16, 20, 21.

*Its perpetuity,* Isa. 51:6, 8; Luke 1:33; Heb. 1:8; 2 Pet. 1:11.

*Its transforming power,* Isa. 35:1–10; 55:12, 13; 65:17–25.

*Its future glory and greatness,* Isa. 49:22, 23; Hag. 2:7–9; Rev. 21:9–27.

*Its universality,* Gen. 12:3; 22:18; 49:10; Psa. 72:5, 8–11, 16, 17, 19; 89:1–37; 113:3; Isa. 9:6, 7; 40:4–11; 42:1–7; 49:1–26; 52:10; 54:1–3; 59:19–21; Jer. 3:14–19; (according to many learned interpreters, Dan. 2:35, 44; 7:13, 14, 18, 22, 27;) Hab. 2:14; Zech. 9:1, 10; Matt. 8:11; Luke 13:29, 30; Rev. 14:6.

*Its unity,* John 10:16.

*Its growth,* Matt. 13:31–33; Luke 13:21. *Ends of earth shall turn unto Him,* Psa. 66:4; 86:9; Isa. 2:2–4; 45:14; 60:1–9; Jer. 3:17; 16:19–21; 33:16; Ezek. 17:22, 23; Mic. 4:1–4; Zeph. 2:11; Zech. 2:10, 11; 6:15; 8:20–23. *Shall embrace the heathen,* Psa. 2:8; 68:31, 32; 110:4–6; Hos. 2:23; Amos 9:11, 12; Mal. 1:11.

*Its final triumph,* Gen. 3:15; Psa. 2:9; Isa. 11:1–13; Dan. 2:44; 7:9–14, 27; Matt. 16:18; Acts 2:34, 35; 1 Cor. 15:24–28; Eph. 1:10; Phil. 2:10, 11; Heb. 10:13; 12:23, 24, 27, 28; Rev. 5:9, 10, 13, 14; 6:2, 11:15; 12:10; 19:11–21; 20:1–3.

SECULAR NOTIONS CONCERNING: *To restore the kingdom of Israel,* Mark 11:9, 10; John 6:15; Acts 1:6, 7. *Rank of princes in the kingdom of,* Matt. 20:20–23; Mark 10:35–40; Luke 9:46–48.

**Love of,** Psa. 69:9; Rev. 3:9, 19. *Constraining,* 2 Cor. 5:13, 14. *Passeth knowledge,* Eph. 3:17–19.

*For his disciples,* John 10:3, 4, 11, 14–16; 13:1, 23; 14:1–3, 18, 21, 27; 15:9–13, 15; 17:6–26; Rom. 8:35, 37–39; 2 Thess. 2:13. *For children,* Matt. 19:13–15; Mark 10:13, 14, 16; Luke 18:15, 16. *For his mother,* John 19:26, 27. *For the lost,* Isa. 40:11; Matt. 18:12, 13; Mark 8:12; Luke 13:34.

EXEMPLIFIED: *In renunciation,* 2 Cor. 8:9; Phil. 2:6–8. *In compassion,* Isa. 42:3; Matt. 9:36; 14:14; 15:32; Luke 7:13; 22:31, 32; John 11:5, 33–36; Acts 10:38; Heb. 4:15. *In solicitude for others,* Matt. 23:37; Luke 23:28, 34; John 18:8, 9. *In his sacrifice,* Gal. 2:20; Eph. 5:2, 25, 29, 30; 1 John 3:16; Rev. 1:5. *In his vicarious suffering,* Isa. 53:4; Matt. 8:17; Rom. 15:3. *In redemption,* Psa. 72:14; Isa. 63:9.

**Lordship of.** The sovereignty of the Messiah, as conceived by Old Testament writers, seems best described by the word King (see KING, above); but New Testament writers use the word Lord. Jesus said of himself, The son of man is Lord even of the Sabbath, Matt. 12:8; Mark 2:28. The student will find suggestions for profitable reflection in a study of the various forms of expression used by the authors of the epistles in which they attribute Lordship to our Savior, Matt. 12:8; Acts 2:36; Rom. 1:7; 5:1, 11, 21; 6:23; 7:25; 8:39; 10:9; 13:14; 14:14; 15:6, 30; 16:20; 1 Cor. 1:2, 3, 7–10; 5:4; 6:11; 8:6; 9:1; 11:25; 12:3; 15:31, 57; 16:23; 2 Cor. 1:2, 3, 14; 4:5, 14; 8:9; 11:31; 13:14; Gal. 1:3; 6:14, 18; Eph. 1:2, 3, 17; 3:11; 5:20; 6:23, 24; Phil. 1:2, 11; 2:19; 3:20; 4:23; Col. 1:3; 2:6; 3:17, 24; 1 Thess. 1:1, 3, 11, 13; 4:1; 5:10, 24, 28; 2 Thess. 1:1, 2, 7, 12; 2:1, 8, 15, 16; 3:6, 12, 18; 1 Tim. 1:2, 12; 6:3, 14; 2 Tim. 1:2; Philemon 1, 3, 5, 25; Jas. 1:1; 2:1; 1 Pet. 1:3; 3:15; 2 Pet. 1:2, 8, 14, 16; 2:20; 3:18; Jude 4, 18, 21, 25.

**Mediation of,** John 14:6, 14; 16:23, 24, 26; 20:31; Rom.

**10**
*v Joy, instances of,* Psa. 5:11.

**11**
*w Mary,* Luke 1:27.
*x Salutations,* Luke 1:44.

10 When [e,g]they saw the [j]star,
they rejoiced with exceeding
great [v]joy.
11 ¶ And when [g]they were
come into the house, they saw
the young child with [w]Mā'rȳ his
mother, and [x]fell down, and
[k]worshipped him: and when
they had opened their treasures,
they [y]presented unto him gifts;
[z]gold, and [a]frankincense, and
[b]myrrh.[Q]
12 And being [c]warned of [d]God
in a [e]dream that they should not
return to Hĕr'od, they departed
into their own country another
way.
13 ¶ [s]And when they were de-

*y Liberality, instances of, the Magi,* 1 Tim. 6:18.
*z Gold,* Ezek 7:19.
*a Frankincense,* 1 Chr. 9:29.
*b Myrrh,* Ex. 30:23.

**12**
*c God, providence of, overruling,* Gen. 2:2.
*d God, preserver,* Gen. 2:2.
*e Dream,* Dan. 1:17.

1:8; 5:1, 2; 6:23; 1 Cor. 6:11; 15:57; 2 Cor. 1:20; Eph. 3:12; 4:32; 5:20; Col. 3:17; 1 Tim. 2:1, 3, 5; Heb. 9:11–28; 13:15; 1 Pet. 2:5; 1 John 2:1, 2, 12. *As a priest,* Psa. 110:4; Zech. 6:13; Heb. 2:17; 3:1, 2; 4:14, 15; 5:5, 6, 10; 6:19, 20; 7:1, 3, 19, 21, 24–28; 8:1, 2, 6; 9:11; 10:19–21.

*Through his sacrifice,* Eph. 2:13–18; Heb. 10:11, 12; 12:24.

*Exemplified in his intercession,* Isa. 53:12; Luke 13:8, 9; 22:31, 32; 23:33, 34; John 14:16; 17:9, 11, 15–17, 19–22; Rom. 8:34.

See PRIESTHOOD OF, below.

**Meekness of,** Matt. 11:29; Mark 14:60, 61; 15:3–5; 2 Cor. 10:1; Phil. 2:8. *Prophecies concerning,* Psa. 45:4; Isa. 42:1–3; 50:5, 6; 52:1, 14; 53:7; Matt. 12:19, 20; 21:5; Acts 8:32. EXEMPLIFIED: *In not resenting false accusation,* Mark 2:6–11. *In submitting to enemies,* Matt. 26:47–63; 27:12–14; John 8:48–50; Heb. 12:2, 3; 1 Pet. 2:23. *In praying for enemies,* Luke 23:34. *In becoming a servant,* Phil. 2:7.

See HUMILITY OF, above.

**Messiah:** *Messianic Psalms,* Psa. 2; 67:1–7; 68; 69; 72; 96; 98:1–9; 110:1–7.

*Prophecies concerning,* Dan. 9:25, 26; Acts 3:18, 20.

*Simeon's testimony to,* Luke 2:28–32.

*Andrew's belief in,* John 1:41, 45. *Peter's confession of,* Matt. 16:15, 16; Mark 8:29; Luke 9:20; John 6:69.

*His own testimony to his messiahship,* Matt. 11:3–6; 26:63, 64; Luke 24:27; John 4:25, 26, 29, 42; 5:33, 36, 37, 39, 46; 6:27; 8:14, 17, 18, 25, 28, 56; 13:19.

*Called David's son,* Matt. 22:42–45; Mark 12:35–37; Luke 20:41–44.

*Anointed of God,* Psa. 2:2; Acts 4:26, 27.

*Proclaimed, by Apostles,* Acts 9:22; 13:27; 17:2, 3; 26:6, 7, 22, 23; 28:23; Rom. 1:1–3; 1 Cor. 15:3; 1 Pet. 1:10, 11; 2 Pet. 1:16–18; 1 John 5:6–9

See KING, and LORDSHIP, above. See also footnote, MESSIANIC HOPE, Gen. 49:10.

**Miracles of:** *Water made wine,* John 2:1–11.

*Heals the nobleman's son,* John 4:46–54

*Heals demoniac in the synagogue,* Mark 1:23–26; Luke 4:33–36.

*Heals Simon's wife's mother,* Matt. 8:14, 15; Mark 1:29–31; Luke 4:38, 39.

*Heals diseases in Galilee,* Matt. 4:23, 24; Mark 1:34.

*Miracles at Jerusalem,* John 2:23.

*Cleanses the leper,* Matt. 8:1–4; Mark 1:40–45; Luke 5:12–16.

*Heals the paralytic,* Matt. 9:1–8; Mark 2:1–12; Luke 5:17–26.

*Heals the impotent man,* John 5:1–16.

*Restores the withered hand,* Matt. 12:9–13; Mark 3:1–5; Luke 6:6–11.

*Heals multitudes from Judah, Jerusalem, and coasts of Tyre and Sidon,* Luke 6:17–19.

*Heals the centurion's servant,* Matt. 8:5–13; Luke 7:1–10.

*Heals demoniacs,* Matt. 8:16, 17; Luke 4:40, 41.

*Raises the widow's son,* Luke 7:11–16.

*Heals in Galilee,* Luke 7:21, 22.

*Heals a demoniac,* Matt. 12:22–37; Mark 3:19–30; Luke 11:14, 15, 17–23.

*Stills the tempest,* Matt. 8:23–27; Mark 4:35–41; Luke 8:22–25; Matt. 14:32.

*Heals the diseased in the land of Gennesaret,* Matt. 14:34–36.

*Heals the demoniacs in Gadara,* Matt. 8:28–34; Mark 5:1–20; Luke 8:26–39.

*Raises Jairus' daughter,* Matt. 9:18, 19, 23–26; Mark 5:22–24, 35–43; Luke 8:41, 42, 49–56.

*Heals the woman with the issue of blood,* Matt. 9:20–22; Mark 5:25–34; Luke 8:43–48.

*Opens the eyes of two blind men,* Matt. 9:27–31.

*Casts a devil out of and cures the dumb man,* Matt. 9:32, 33.

*Feeds five thousand,* Matt. 14:15–21; Mark 6:35–44; Luke 9:12–17; John 6:5–14.

*Heals sick in Galilee,* Matt. 14:14.

*Walks on the sea,* Matt. 14:22–33; Mark 6:45–52; John 6:14–21.

*Heals the daughter of the Syrophenician woman,* Matt. 15:21–28; Mark 7:24–30.

*Heals lame, blind, dumb, and maimed, near the Sea of Galilee,* Matt. 15:30.

*Feeds four thousand,* Matt. 15:32–39; Mark 8:1–9.

*Cures deaf and dumb,* Mark 7:31–37.

*Cures blind man,* Mark 8:22–36.

*Heals lunatic child,* Matt. 17:14–21; Mark 9:14–29; Luke 9:37–43.

*Cures ten lepers,* Luke 17:11–19.

*Opens the eyes of one born blind,* John 9.

*Raises Lazarus,* John 11:1–54.

*Cures woman with the spirit of infirmity,* Luke 13:10–17.

*Cures dropsy,* Luke 14:1–6.

*Cures two blind men near Jericho,* Matt. 20:29–34; Mark 10:46–52; Luke 18:35–43.

*The fig tree blighted,* Matt. 21:17–22; Mark 11:12–14, 20–24.

*Heals ear of Malchus,* Luke 22:49–51.

*Not particularly described,* Matt. 4:23, 24; 14:14; 15:30; Mark 1:34; Luke 6:17–19; 7:21, 22; John 2:23; 3:2. *Holds the vision of his disciples, that they should not recognize him,* Luke 24:16, 31, 35. *His appearances and disappearances,* Luke 24:13, 31, 36–45; John 20:19, 26. *Opening the understanding of his disciples,* Luke 24:45.

See footnote, MIRACLES, Luke 23:8.

**Mission of,** Isa. 42:7; Matt. 18:12–14; Luke 12:49–53; John 4:25, 34; 18:37.

*To fulfill the law and the prophets,* Mic. 5:2; Matt. 5:17; Rom. 10:4. *To be Lord of all,* Rom. 14:9; 15:8, 9; 2 Cor. 5:15; Eph. 4:10. *To glorify the Father,* John 17:4.

*To preach the gospel,* Isa. 61:1; Matt. 4:23; 9:13; Mark 1:38; Luke 4:18, 19, 43; 5:31, 32; 8:1. *To preach repentance,* Luke 5:30–32; 24:47; Acts 3:26; 5:31. *To bring life,* John 6:51; 10:10; 2 Cor. 5:14, 21. *To give light,* Isa. 9:2; 42:6; Luke 1:78, 79; 2:30–32, 34; John 1:1–9; 9:39; 12:46, 47.

*To condemn sin,* Rom. 8:3, 4. *To die for sinners,* Rom. 5:6–8. *To be propitiation for sin,* Matt. 20:28; Mark 10:45; Luke 24:26, 46; John 6:51; Acts 26:23; Rom. 4:24, 25; 5:6–8; 2 Cor. 5:18; Gal. 1:3, 4; 4:4, 5; Heb. 2:9, 14; 9:26; 1 John 3:5, 8; 4:8, 10. *To purge sins,* Zech. 13:1; Mal. 3:2, 3. *To give remission of sins,* Acts 10:43; Rom. 4:25. *To destroy the works of the devil,* Gen. 3:15; John 3:8.

*To bring salvation,* Matt. 1:21; 15:24; 18:12–14; Luke 19:10; John 3:13–17; Rom. 14:15; 1 Tim. 1:15. *To deliver from fear of death,* Heb. 2:15. *To deliver from temptation,* Heb. 2:18. *To comfort the contrite,* Isa. 61:1–3. *To baptize with the Holy Spirit, and with fire,* Matt. 3:11, 12; Luke 3:16.

*Preaches to spirits in prison,* 1 Pet. 3:19; 4:9; compare Eph. 4:9.

**Names of, and phrases describing:** *Adam,* 1 Cor. 15:45. *Alpha and Omega,* Rev. 21:6; 22:13. *Apostle,* Heb. 3:1. *Author and finisher of our faith,* Heb. 12:2.

*Bishop,* 1 Pet. 2:25. *Blessed and only Potentate,* 1 Tim. 6:15. *Branch,* Jer. 23:5; Zech. 3:8. *Bread of life,* John 6:48. *Bridegroom,* Matt. 9:15. *Bright and morning star,* Rev. 22:16.

*Captain of salvation,* Heb. 2:10. *Chief Shepherd,* 1 Pet. 5:4. *Chief corner stone,* 1 Pet. 2:6; Eph. 2:20. *Chosen of God,* 1 Pet. 2:4. *Christ,* Matt. 1:16. *The Christ,* Matt. 16:20; Mark 14:61. *Christ Jesus,* Rom. 3:24; 8:1; 1 Cor. 1:2; 1 Cor. 1:30. *Christ Jesus our Lord,* Rom. 8:39; 1 Tim. 1:12. *Christ of God,* Luke 9:20. *Christ the Lord,* Luke 2:11. *Christ the power of God,* 1 Cor. 1:24. *Christ the wisdom of God,* 1 Cor. 1:24. *Christ, the Son of God,* Acts 9:20. *Christ, Son of the Blessed,* Mark 14:61. *Counsellor,* Isa. 9:6.

*David,* Jer. 30:9; Ezek. 34:23, 24; 37:24, 25; Hos. 3:5. *Deliverer,* Rom. 11:26. *Door,* John 10:7.

*Emmanuel,* Isa. 7:14; Matt. 1:23. *Everlasting Father,* Isa. 9:6.

*Faithful and True,* Rev. 19:11. *Faithful witness,* Rev. 1:5. *Faithful and true witness,* Rev. 3:14. *Finisher* (R. V. perfecter) *of faith,* Heb. 12:2. *First and last,* Rev. 1:17; 2:8; 22:13. *First begotten* (R. V. firstborn), Heb. 1:6. *First begotten* (R. V. firstborn) *of the dead,* Rev. 1:5. *Forerunner,* Heb. 6:20. *Friend of sinners,* Matt. 11:19.

*God blessed forever,* Rom. 9:5. *God's dear Son,* Col. 1:13. *God with us,* Matt. 1:23. *Governor,* Matt. 2:6. *Good shepherd,* John 10:11. *Great shepherd of the sheep,* Heb. 13:20.

*Head of the church,* Eph. 5:23; Col. 1:18. *Heir of all things,* Heb. 1:2. *High priest,* Heb. 4:14. *Head of the corner,* Matt. 21:42. *Holy One,* Psa. 16:10; Acts 3:14. *Holy One*

**13**

*f* *Angel, functions of*, Heb. 1:13.
*g* *Joseph*, Luke 3:23.
*h* *Jesus, life of*, Matt. 1:21.
*i* *Mary*, Luke 1:27.
*j* *Fugitives, instances of*, Judg. 12:4.
*k* *Egypt*, Gen. 41:8.
*l* *Persecution, of Jesus*, John 15:20.

**14**

*m* *Obedience, instances of*, Heb. 5:8.

**15**

*n* *Prophecies concerning the Messiah, and their fulfillment*, Gen. 12:3.
*o* *Prophets, inspiration of*, Isa. 3:2.
*p* Hos. 11:1.

**16**

*q* *Rulers, wicked, instances of*, Ex. 18:21.

parted, behold, the [f]angel[G] of the
[d]Lord [c]appeareth to [g]Jō′ṣeph in
a [e]dream, saying, Arise, and
take the [h]young child and his
[i]mother, and [j]flee into [k]Ē′-
ġy̆pt, and be thou there until I
bring thee word: for Hĕr′od will
[l]seek the young child to destroy
him.
14 When [g]he arose, he [m]took the
[h]young child and his [i]mother by
night, and departed into [k]Ē′ġy̆pt:
15 And was there until the
death of Hĕr′od: that [n]it might
be fulfilled which was spoken
of the Lord by the [o]prophet,
saying, [p]Out of [k]Ē′ġy̆pt have
I called my son.[Q]
16 ¶ Then [q]Hĕr′od, when he
saw that he was mocked of the
wise men, was exceeding [r]wroth,[G]
and sent forth, and [s,t]slew all the
[2,u]children that were in [v]Bĕth′–
lĕ-hĕm,[G] and in all the [3]coasts
thereof, from two years old and
under, according to the time
which he had diligently enquired
of the wise men.
17 Then was fulfilled [w]that
which was spoken by [x]Jĕr′e-mȳ
the [o]prophet, saying,
18 [y]In [z]Rā′mȧ was there a
voice heard, [a]lamentation, and
weeping, and great mourn-
ing, Rā′chel weeping *for* her
children, and would not be
comforted, [b,c]because they are
not.[Q]

*r* *Anger, instances of*, Psa. 37:8.
*s* *Infanticide*, Ex. 1:16.
*t* *Cruelty, instances of*, Psa. 27:12.
*u* *Children, edict to murder*, Mark 10:14.
*v* *Bethlehem*, Gen. 48:7.
2 R. V. male children
3 R. V. borders

**17**

*w* *Prophecies, fulfilled*, Dan. 9:24.
*x* Or, *Jeremiah*, Jer. 1:1.

**18**

*y* Jer. 31:15.
*z* Or, *Ramah*, Judg. 19:13.

---

*a* *Mourning*, Lam. 2:5.
*b* *Bereavement*, Hos. 9:12.
*c* *Afflictions*, Psa. 34:19.

---

*of God*, Mark 1:24; Luke 4:34. *Image of God*, 2 Cor. 4:4; Heb. 1:3.

*Jesus*, Matt. 1:21; Luke 1:31; 2:21. *Jesus Christ*, Matt. 1:1; John 1:17; 17:3; Acts 2:38; 4:10; 9:34; 10:36; 16:18; Rom. 1:1, 3, 6; 2:16; 5:15, 17; 6:3; 1 Cor. 1:1, 4; 2:2; 2 Cor. 1:19; 4:6; 13:5; Gal. 2:16; Phil. 1:8; 2:11; 1 Tim. 1:15; Heb. 13:8; 1 John 1:7; 2:1. *Jesus Christ our Lord*, Rom. 6:23; 1 Cor. 1:9. *Jesus Christ our Saviour*, Tit. 3:6. *Jesus of Nazareth*, Mark 1:24; Luke 24:19; John 19:19. *Jesus, the Son of God*, Heb. 4:14. *Judge*, Acts 10:42. *Just One*, Acts 3:14; 7:52; 22:14.

*King*, Matt. 21:5. *King of Israel*, John 1:49. *King of kings*, 1 Tim. 6:15; Rev. 17:14; 19:16.

*Lamb*, Rev. 5:6, 8; 6:16; 7:9, 10, 17; 12:11; 13:8, 11; 14:1, 4; 15:3; 17:14; 19:7, 9; 21:9, 14, 22, 23, 27. *Lamb of God*, John 1:29. *Life*, John 14:6; Col. 3:4. *Light of the world*, John 8:12. *Light to the Gentiles*, Isa. 42:6; Luke 2:32; Acts 13:47. *Living bread*, John 6:51. *Living stone*, 1 Pet. 2:4. *Lion of the tribe of Judah*, Rev. 5:5. *Lord of lords*, Rev. 17:14; 19:16. *Lord of all*, Acts 10:36. *Lord our righteousness*, Jer. 23:6. *Lord and Saviour Jesus Christ*, 2 Pet. 1:11; 3:18. *Lord Christ*, Col. 3:24. *Lord Jesus*, Acts 7:59; Col. 3:17; 1 Thess. 4:2. *Lord Jesus Christ*, Acts 11:17; 20:21; Rom. 5:1, 11; 13:14. *Lord Jesus Christ our Saviour*, Tit. 1:4. *Lord of glory*, Jas. 2:1. *Lord over all*, Rom. 10:12.

*Master* (R. V. teacher), Matt. 23:8. *Mediator*, 1 Tim. 2:5. *Messenger of the covenant*, Mal. 3:1. *Messiah*, John 1:41. *Mighty God*, Isa. 9:6. *Morning star*, Rev. 22:16.

*Nazarene*, Matt. 2:23.

*Offspring of David*, Rev. 22:16. *Only begotten of the Father*, John 1:14. *Only begotten Son*, John 1:18.

*Passover*, 1 Cor. 5:7. *Potentate*, 1 Tim. 6:15. *Power of God*, 1 Cor. 1:24. *Precious corner stone*, Isa. 28:16. *Priest*, Heb. 7:17. *Prince*, Acts 5:31. *Prince of life*, Acts 3:15. *Prince of peace*, Isa. 9:6. *Prophet*, Deut. 18:15, 18; Matt. 21:11; Luke 24:19.

*Rabbi*, John 1:49. *Rabboni*, John 20:16. *Ransom*, 1 Tim. 2:6. *Redeemer*, Isa. 59:20. *Rock*, 1 Cor. 10:4. *Rock of offence*, 1 Pet. 2:8. *Root of David*, Rev. 5:5; 22:16. *Root of Jesse*, Isa. 11:10.

*Saviour*, Luke 2:11. *Saviour, Jesus Christ*, 2 Tim. 1:10; Tit. 2:13; 2 Pet. 1:1. *Saviour of the world*, 1 John 4:14. *Shepherd*, Mark 14:27. *Shepherd and bishop of souls*, 1 Pet. 2:25. *Shiloh*, Gen. 49:10. *Son of the Father*, 2 John 3. *Son of God*, see DIVINE SONSHIP OF, above. *Son of Man*, see HUMANITY OF, above. *Son of the Blessed*, Mark 14:61. *Son of the Highest*, Luke 1:32. *Son of David*, Matt. 9:27; 15:22; 22:42; Mark 10:47; Luke 18:38. *Stone of stumbling*, Rom. 9:32, 33; 1 Pet. 2:8.

*Teacher*, John 3:2. *True light*, John 1:9. *True vine*, John 15:1. *Truth*, John 14:6.

*Unspeakable gift*, 2 Cor. 9:15.

*Very Christ*, Acts 9:22.

*Way*, John 14:6. *Witness*, Rev. 1:5. *Wonderful*, Isa. 9:6. *Word*, John 1:1. *Word of God*, Rev. 19:13. *Word of life*, 1 John 1:1.

HIS NAME, 1 Cor. 6:11; Phil. 2:9; Col. 3:17; Rev. 19:16. *Prayer in*, John 14:13; 16:23, 24, 26; Eph. 5:20; Heb. 13:15. *Miracles performed in*, Mark 16:17; Luke 10:17; Acts 3:6; 4:10. *Baptism in*, Matt. 28:19; Acts 2:38. *Preaching in*, Luke 24:47. *Faith in*, Matt. 12:21; John 1:12; 2:23. *Remission of sins in*, Luke 24:47; Acts 10:43; 1 John 2:12. *Life in*, John 20:31. *Salvation in*, Acts 4:12.

**Obedience of:** *Foretold*, Psa. 40:8; Isa. 11:5; 50:5, 6; Heb. 10:7–9.

*To his parents*, Luke 2:51.

*To God*, Luke 2:49; John 4:34; 5:30, 36; 6:38; 8:29, 46, 55; 9:4; 14:31; 15:10; 17:4.

EXEMPLIFIED: *In his baptism*, Matt. 3:15. *In his sufferings*, Matt. 26:39, 42; Mark 14:36; Luke 22:42; Heb. 5:8. *In his death*, John 19:30; Phil. 2:8.

**Omniscience of,** Rev. 2:18, 23; 5:5, 12; Col. 2:3. *Manifested in his knowledge, of the Father*, Matt. 11:27; John 7:29; *of men's hearts*, Matt. 9:4; 12:25; 17:27; 22:18; Mark 2:8; Luke 5:22; 6:8; 9:46–48; 11:17; 22:10–12 (with Mark 14:13–15); John 1:48; 2:24, 25; 4:16–19, 28, 29; 5:42; 6:64; 13:11; 21:17; *of future events*, Matt. 24:25; John 13:1, 3, 10; 16:30, 32; 18:4; 21:6; *of the coin in the fish's mouth*, Matt. 17:27; *of the presence of schools of fishes*, Luke 5:4–7; John 21:6.

**Our example,** John 10:4; Heb. 3:1, 2; 1 John 2:6; Rev. 14:4. *In meekness*, Matt. 11:29; Heb. 12:2–4; 1 Pet. 2:21–24. *In humility*, Luke 22:26, 27; John 13:13–15, 34; 2 Cor. 10:1; Phil. 2:5–8. *In ministering*, Matt. 20:28; Mark 10:43–45; 2 Cor. 8:9 (with context); Gal. 6:2. *In loving others*, John 13:34; Eph. 5:2. *In character*, Rom. 8:29; 15:2, 3, 5, 7; 1 Pet. 1:15, 16; 1 John 3:1–3, 16; 4:17. *In enduring suffering*, 1 Pet. 3:17, 18.

**Parables of:** *The wise and foolish builders*, Matt. 7:24–27; Luke 6:47–49.

*Two debtors*, Luke 7:41–47.

*House divided against itself*, Matt. 12:25–29; Mark 3:23–27; Luke 11:17–22.

*New cloth on the old garment*, Matt. 9:16; Mark 2:21; Luke 5:36.

*New wine in old wine-skins*, Matt. 9:17; Mark 2:22; Luke 5:37–39.

*The rich fool*, Luke 12:16–21.

*The servants waiting for their Lord*, Luke 12:35–40.

*Barren fig tree*, Luke 13:6–9.

*The sower*, Matt. 13:3–9, 18–23; Mark 4:1–9, 14–20; Luke 8:5–8, 11–15.

*The tares*, Matt. 13:24–30, 36–43.

*Seed growing secretly*, Mark 4:26–29.

*Mustard seed*, Matt. 13:31, 32; Mark 4:30–32; Luke 13:18, 19.

*Leaven*, Matt. 13:33; Luke 13:20, 21.

*Hidden treasure*, Matt. 13:44.

*Pearl of great price*, Matt. 13:45, 46.

*Dragnet*, Matt. 13:47–50.

*Unmerciful servant*, Matt. 18:23–35.

*Good Samaritan*, Luke 10:30–37.

*Friend at midnight*, Luke 11:5–8.

*Good shepherd*, John 10:1–16.

*Great supper*, Luke 14:15–24.

*Lost sheep*, Matt. 18:12–14; Luke 15:3–7.

*Lost piece of money*, Luke 15:8–10.

*The prodigal and his brother*, Luke 15:11–32.

*The unjust steward*, Luke 16:1–9.

*Rich man and Lazarus*, Luke 16:19–31.

19
*d Angel, functions of,* Heb. 1:13.
*e God, providence of, instances of,* Gen. 2:2.
*f Dream,* Dan. 1:17.
*g Joseph,* Luke 3:23.
*h Egypt,* Gen. 41:8.
20
*i Guidance,* Psa. 48:14.
*j Jesus, life of, returns from Egypt,* Matt. 1:21.
*k Mary,* Luke 1:27.
21
*l Obedience, instances of,* Heb. 5:8.
22
*m Judea,* Luke 5:17.
*n Galilee,* Mark 6:21.

19 ¶ But when Hĕr′od was
dead, behold, an [d]angel of the
[e]Lord appeareth in a [f]dream to
[g]Jō′ṣeph in [h]Ē′ġȳpt,
20 [i]Saying, Arise, and take the
[j]young child and his [k]mother,
and go into the land of Ĭṣ′ra-el:
for they are dead which sought
the young child's life.[Q]
21 And [g,l]he arose, and took
the young child and his mother,
and came into the land of Ĭṣ′-ra-el.
22 But when he heard that Är-
chĕ-lā′us did reign in [m]Jū-dæ′ȧ
in the room[G] of his father Hĕr′od,
he was afraid to go thither[C]: notwithstanding, being [e]warned of
God in a [f]dream, he turned
aside into the parts of [n]Găl′ĭ-lee:
23 And he came and dwelt in a
city called [o]Năz′a-rĕth: that it
might be fulfilled which was spoken by the [p]prophets, He shall[S Q]
be called a [q]Năz′a-rēne.

## CHAPTER 3

*The preaching of John the Baptist. 7 He reproves the Pharisees and Sadducees. 13 The baptism of Jesus.*

[a]IN those days came [b,c]Jōhn
the Baptist, [d]preaching in
the wilderness of Jū-dæ′ȧ,
2 And saying, [e,f,g]Repent ye:
for the [h]kingdom of heaven is at[C]
hand.[G T]
3 For this is [b]he that was [i]spo-
ken of by the [j]prophet [k]Ē-ṣā′ias,

*g Salvation, conditions of,* Acts 16:17. *h Kingdom of Heaven,* Matt. 13:24. 3 *i Prophecies concerning the Messiah, and their fulfillment,* Gen. 12:3. *j Prophets,* Isa. 3:2. *k* Or, *Isaiah,* Isa. 1:1.

23
*o Nazareth,* John 1:46.
*p Prophets,* Isa. 3:2.
*q Jesus, names of,* Matt. 1:21.

v.1–AD 26
See footnote, *Time,* Rev. 10:6.
1
*a* Mark 1:2-8; Luke 3:2-16.
*b John the Baptist,* Luke 1:63.
*c Minister, faithful, instances of,* Rom. 15:16.
*d Preaching,* Matt. 9:35.
2
*e Commandment, enjoining repentance,* Deut. 8:2.
*f Repentance, enjoined,* Mark 1:4.

*Importunate widow,* Luke 18:1–8.
*Pharisee and publican,* Luke 18:9–14.
*Laborers in the vineyard,* Matt. 20:1–16.
*The pounds,* Luke 19:11–27.
*The two sons,* Matt. 21:28–32.
*Wicked husbandmen,* Matt. 21:33–44; Mark 12:1–11; Luke 20:9–18.
*Marriage of the king's son,* Matt. 22:1–14.
*Fig tree leafing,* Matt. 24:32; Mark 13:28, 29.
*Man taking a far journey,* Mark 13:34–37.
*Ten virgins,* Matt. 25:1–13.
*Talents,* Matt. 25:14–30.
*The grain of wheat,* John 12:24.
*The vine,* John 15:1–6.

**Passion of,** see SUFFERINGS OF, below.

**Peccability of,** see TEMPTATION OF, below.

**Perfections of,** Col. 2:3. *Was the image of God,* 2 Cor. 4:4; Col. 1:15. *All the fullness of the Father dwelt in him,* Col. 1:19; 2:9. *Was righteous,* Isa. 11:5; John 7:18; 2 Cor. 1:19. *Was guileless,* Isa. 53:9. *Was sinless,* Matt. 27:3, 4; Acts 13:28; 2 Cor. 5:21. *Was faithful,* 2 Thess. 3:3; 2 Tim. 2:13; Heb. 3:2. *Was full of grace and truth,* John 1:14, 18; Col. 2:3. *Was just in judgment,* John 5:30.
*Perfected through sufferings,* Heb. 2:10.
*Perfections of, typified,* Lev. 21:17–21.

**Persecutions of,** see footnote, PERSECUTION, John 15:20.

**Popularity of,** Matt. 4:24; 8:1; 13:2; 19:1, 2; 21:8–11 (with Mark 11:8–10; Luke 19:35–38; John 12:12, 13); Mark 1:33; 2:2; 3:7, 20; 5:21; 6:33, 55, 56 (with Matt. 14:13, 35, 36; Luke 9:11; John 6:2); 10:1; 12:37; Luke 4:14, 15, 42; 5:1; 12:1; John 6:15; 12:19.

**Power of,** Psa. 110:3; 1 Cor. 1:24.
*Called* MIGHTY GOD, Isa. 9:6. *Has all power,* Matt. 28:18; John 10:17, 18, 28; 17:2; Phil. 3:20, 21; 2 Thess. 1:9; 1 Tim. 6:16; 2 Pet. 1:16; Rev. 3:7; 5:12.
MANIFESTED: *In creation,* John 1:3, 10; Col. 1:16. *In salvation of men,* Heb. 7:25. *In upholding all things,* Col. 1:17; Heb. 1:3. *In forgiving sins,* Matt. 9:2, 6; Mark 2:5, 10; Luke 5:20, 24; Col. 3:13. *In healing diseases,* Matt. 8:3, 16; 9:6, 7; 12:13; Mark 5:27–34; Luke 5:17; 6:19; Acts 10:38. *In casting out demons,* Matt. 8:16; 12:28, 29; Mark 3:27; Luke 11:20–22. *In stilling the tempest,* Matt. 8:27. *In giving apostles power to heal,* Matt. 10:1; Mark 6:7; Luke 9:11. *In his resurrection,* John 2:19; 10:17, 18,

**Prayers of,** Matt. 11:25, 26; Luke 3:21; 11:1. *In secret,* Matt. 14:23; Mark 1:35; 6:46; Luke 5:16; 6:12; 9:18, 28, 29. *At the grave of Lazarus,* John 11:41, 42. *For Peter,* Luke 22:32. *For believers,* John 17:1–26. *In Gethsemane,* Matt. 26:36–39; Mark 14:32–35; Luke 22:41–44; Heb. 5:7. *On the cross,* Matt. 27:46; Luke 23:34, 46.

**Preëxistence of:** *Was in the beginning,* John 1:1–3; 1 John 2:13, 14; Rev. 3:14. *Came from heaven,* John 3:13; 6:62; Phil. 2:5–7. *Came from the Father,* John 13:3; 16:28. *Was before creation,* John 17:5, 24; 2 Tim. 1:9; 1 John 1:1, 2; 1 Pet. 1:20. *Was maker of all things,* John 1:3; 1 Cor. 8:6; Col. 1:15–17; Heb. 1:1, 2, 8–12; Rev. 4:11. *Was before Abraham,* John 8:56–58. *Was with the Israelites in the wilderness,* 1 Cor. 10:4, 9; Jude 5.

**Priesthood of,** Psa. 110:4; Heb. 2:17; 3:1, 2; 5:4–6; 6:20; 7:11–28; 8:1–6; 9:11–26; 10:12, 21.
TYPIFIED, Ex. 30:1. *In Melchizedek,* Gen. 14:18–20; Psa. 110:4; Heb. 5:6, 10; 7:17, with vs. 1–17. *In Aaronic priesthood,* Ex. 28:1, 12, 29, 30, 38; 40:13; Heb. 4:14, 15; 7.

**Promises of, to his disciples:** *Of everlasting life,* Matt. 19:28; Mark 10:29, 30; Luke 18:29, 30; 23:43; John 5:25–29; 6:54, 57, 58; 12:25, 26. *Of power,* Luke 24:49; John 7:38, 39; Acts 1:4–8. *Of the comforter,* John 14:16, 26; 15:26, 27; 16:7–14. *Of his mediatorship,* John 16:23, 24, 26.

**Prophecies concerning,** Gen. 18:18; 22:18; 26:4; 28:14; Isa. 53:2–12; Matt. 8:17; Gal. 3:8, 16.
Described in prophecy as: *The branch,* Isa. 11:1 (with Rom. 15:12); Jer. 23:5, 6; 33:15; Zech. 3:8; *corner stone,* Psa. 118:22; Isa. 28:16; *ensign to the people,* Isa. 11:10; *fountain for sin,* Zech. 13:1; *king,* Zech. 9:9; *leader and commander,* Isa. 55:4, 5; *light to Gentiles,* Isa. 42:6, 7; 49:6; 52:10, 15; Luke 2:31, 32; *Lord,* Isa. 40:3, 5; 35:2; Jer. 31:34; Mal. 3:1–3; Luke 3:4; *mine elect* (R. V. chosen), Isa. 42:1; *priest,* Psa. 110:4; *prophet,* Deut. 18:15, 18; Acts 3:22–24; *redeemer,* Isa. 59:20; *ruler in Israel,* Mic. 5:2; *savior,* Isa. 62:10, 11; Matt. 1:21; Luke 1:31; *seed of woman,* Gen. 3:15; *shepherd,* Isa. 40:11; Ezek. 34:23; *son of man,* Dan. 7:13, 14.
FUTURE GLORY AND POWER OF, Rev. 19:11, 12, 15. *To have universal dominion,* Psa. 72:5, 8–11, 17, 19; Isa. 2:2–4; 9:6, 7; 60:1–9; (according to many learned interpreters, Dan. 2:35, 44; 7:18, 22, 27;) Mic. 4:1–4. *To be King of kings,* Psa. 72:5, 8–11, 17, 19; Rev. 1:5–7; 11:15; 12:10; 17:14; 19:16; 20:4, 6. *To sit at right hand of God,* Mark 14:62; 1 Pet. 3:22. *To be judge,* Jude 14, 15; Rev. 2:23; 6:16, 17; 14:14–16.

**Prophet,** Deut. 18:15, 18; Matt. 21:11, 46; Luke 7:16; 13:33; 24:19; John 4:19; 6:14; 7:40; 9:17; Acts 3:22, 23; 7:37.

**Received:** *Multitudes attend his ministry,* Matt. 8:1; 13:2; 14:13, 35; 19:1, 2; Mark 1:37, 45; 2:2, 15; 3:7, 20, 21; 4:1; 5:21; 10:1; 11:18; 12:37; Luke 9:11; 12:1; 19:48; 21:38; Mark 11:18; John 6:2; 8:2.
*Many believe on him,* Matt. 4:24; 21:8–11, 15; Mark 2:12; 6:55, 56; 11:8–10; Luke 6:17–19; 7:16, 17; 19:36–38, 47, 48; 23:27; John 2:11, 23; 4:45; 8:30; 10:41, 42; 11:45–48; 12:9, 11–13, 18–21, 42.
*Authority of his teaching confessed,* Mark 1:22; Luke 4:32; John 3:2; 7:46.
*With astonishment and gladness,* Matt. 9:8, 27, 28, 33; 13:54; 15:31; Mark 1:27; 2:12; 5:42; 7:37; Luke 4:36, 37, 42; 5:26; 13:17; 18:43; John 7:31, 40–44; 9:17, 24, 25, 29, 30, 33; 11:37.
Instances of his being received: *By Matthew,* Matt. 9:9; *by Peter and other fishermen,* Mark 1:16–20; Luke 5:3–11; *by Philip,* John 1:43, 45; *by Nathanael,* John 1:45–50; *by Zacchæus,* Luke 19:1–10; *by thief on the cross,* Luke 23:40–42; *by three thousand at Pentecost,* Acts 2:41; 4:4.

**Redeemer,** see SAVIOR, below; see also footnote, REDEMPTION, Eph. 1:7.

**Rejected,** Luke 9:26; 10:16; 11:23; Heb. 6:4, 5, 6; 1 Pet. 2:4, 7, 8; 1 John 2:22, 23; 4:3; 2 John 7.
*By Jews,* Matt. 13:54–58 (with Isa. 6:9, 10); 23:37; Mark 6:3–6; Luke 7:34; 13:34; 19:27, 42; 22:67; John 1:11; 5:38, 40, 43; 7:3–5, 12, 13, 15, 25–27; 8:13, 21, 22, 24, 45–47, 53;

saying, [l]The voice of one crying
in the wilderness, Prepare ye the
way of the [m,n]Lord, make his
[o]paths straight.[Q]
4 And the same [b]Jŏhn had [p]his
[q]raiment of [r]camel's hair, and a
[s]leathern[G] [t]girdle[G] about his loins[G];
and his meat[G] was [u]locusts and
wild [v]honey.[Q]
5 ¶ Then went out to him
[w]Jĕru̇'sȧ-lĕm, and all [x]Jū-dæ'ȧ,
and all the region round about
[y]Jôr'dan,[T]
6 And were [y]baptized of him
in [1]Jôr'dan, confessing their
[z]sins.
7 But when [a]he saw many of
the [b]Phăr'ĭ-seeṣ and [c]Săd'du-
çeeṣ[G] come to his [d]baptism, he
[e]said unto them, [2]O generation[G]
of vipers, who hath warned you
to flee from the [f]wrath to come[T]?
8 [g]Bring forth therefore [h]fruits[G]
[3]meet[G] for [i]repentance:
9 And think not to [j]say within
yourselves, [k]We have [l]Ā'bră-
hăm to *our* father: [m]for I say unto you, that [n]God is able of these
stones to raise up children unto
Ā'bră-hăm.[S]
10 And now also the ax is laid
unto the root of the trees: therefore every tree which [o,p]bringeth

v.3–AD 26
See footnote, *Time*, Rev. 10:6.

*l* Isa. 40:3.
*m* *Jesus, prophecies concerning*, Matt. 1:21.
*n* *Jesus, divinity of*, Matt. 1:21.
*o* *Highways, figurative*, Deut. 2:27.

**4**
*p* *Stoicism*, Acts 17:18.
*q* *Dress*, Zech. 3:3.
*r* *Camel, hair of, made into cloth*, 1 Sam. 30:17.
*s* *Leather*, 2 Kin. 1:8.
*t* *Girdle*, Prov. 31:24.
*u* *Locust*, Nah. 3:17.
*v* *Honey*, Prov. 25:27.

**5**
*w* *Jerusalem*, Judg. 19:10.

v.7–AD 26
See footnote, *Time*, Rev. 10:6.

*b* *Pharisees*, Matt. 15:12.
*c* *Sadducees*, Matt. 22:23.
*d* *Baptism*, Luke 20:4.
*e* *Reproof, faithfulness in, instances of*, vs. 7–12; Prov. 17:10.
*f* *Wicked, punishment of*, Psa. 73:3.
2 R. V. Ye offspring

**8**
*g* *Commandment, enjoining fruits of repentance*, Deut. 8:2.
*h* *Works*, 2 Tim. 1:9.
*i* *Repentance*, Mark 1:4.
3 R. V. worthy of

*x* *Judea*, Luke 5:17. *y* *Baptism*, Luke 20:4. **6** *z* *Sin, confession of*, Rom. 5:12. **1** R. V. the river Jordan, **7**—*a* *John the Baptist*, Luke 1:63.

**9** *j* *Delusion*, 2 Thess. 2:11. *k* *Heredity*, Ezek. 18:2. *l* *Abraham*, Gen. 17:5. *m* *Gentiles, prophecies of the conversion of*, Acts 10:45. *n* *God, power of*, Gen. 2:2.

**10** *o* *Unfruitfulness*, Matt. 7:19. *p* *Unfaithfulness*, Luke 16:11.

9:16, 17, 24; 10:20, 21, 24, 33; 11:46–48; 12:37, 48; Acts 13:46; 18:5, 6; 22:18; 28:24, 25, 27; Rom. 3:3; 9:31, 32; 10: 16, 21; 1 Cor. 1:8. *By Gadarenes*, Matt. 8:34; Mark 5:17; Luke 8:37. *By Greeks*, 1 Cor. 1:23. *By followers*, John 6:36, 60–66.

PROPHECIES CONCERNING HIS REJECTION, Psa. 2:1–3; 118: 22; Isa. 53:1–4; Luke 9:44.

*Foretold by himself*, Matt. 11:16–19 (with Luke 7:31–35); Mark 9:12; Luke 4:23–29; 17:25; John 15:18, 20, 24; *in the parable of the feast*, Luke 14:16–24 (with Matt. 22:2–14); *in the parable of the house built on the sand*, Matt. 7:26, 27; Luke 6:46–49.

PUNISHMENT FOR REJECTION OF, FORETOLD, Matt. 8:12; 10:14, 15, 33; 12:38–45; 21:33–45 (with Mark 12:1–12; Luke 20:9–18); Mark 16:16; 2 Tim. 2:12; Heb. 6:6; 10:29; 2 Pet. 2:1.

**Relation of, to the Father,** Psa. 110:1; Matt. 11:27; 1 Thess. 5:18; Heb. 2:9.

*Called God his father*, Matt. 20:23; 26:39; Mark 13:32; Rev. 2:27.

*In the beginning with God*, John 1:1, 2, 14. *Sent of God*, John 3:34, 35; 4:34; 6:27, 32, 33, 38–40, 44–46; 7:16, 28, 29, 33; 8:16, 19, 28, 29, 38, 40, 42, 49, 54, 55; 9:4; 11:41, 42; 12:44, 49, 50; 17:1–10, 24–26; 1 Cor. 1:30; Heb. 3:2; 1 Pet. 2:4, 23; 1 John 4:9, 10, 14. *Endued with the Holy Spirit*, Isa. 42:1; 61:1; Mic. 5:4; Acts 10:38. *Son of God*, John 5:19–26, 37, 45; Rom. 8:32; 15:6; Heb. 1:2, 3; 5:5–10; 2 Pet. 1:17. *One with the Father*, John 10:18, 25, 30, 32, 33, 36–38; 14:7, 9–14, 20, 24; 15:23–26. *Subject unto the Father*, Psa. 110:1; Mark 10:40; John 20:17; Acts 2:22, 33, 36; 3:13, 26; 4:27; 1 Cor. 15:24, 27, 28. *Image of God*, 2 Cor. 4:4, 6; Phil. 2:6; Col. 1:15, 19. *God raised him from the dead*, Acts 13:37; Rom. 1:4; Eph. 1:17, 20–22; 1 Pet. 1:21.

*Ascended unto the Father*, Luke 24:51; John 16:5, 10, 28; Acts 1:9–11; Rev. 3:12, 21.

See DIVINITY OF, HUMANITY OF, and DIVINE SONSHIP OF, above.

**Resurrection of:** *Prophecies concerning*, Psa. 2:7 (with Acts 13:33); 16:9, 10; Isa. 55:3, with Acts 13:34.

*Foretold by himself*, Matt. 12:40; 16:4, 21; 17:23 (with Luke 9:22; 24:7); 20:19 (with Mark 10:34); 26:32 (with Mark 14:28); 27:52, 53, 63; Mark 8:31; 9:9, 10; Luke 18:33; 24:46; John 2:19, 21, 22, with Mark 14:58.

Certified: *By angels*, Matt. 28:6, 7; Mark 16:6, 7; Luke 24:5–7; *by Mary Magdalene*, Matt. 28:1–8; Mark 16:10; Luke 24:10; John 20:18; *by Cleopas and his fellow disciple*, Mark 16:12, 13; Luke 24:13–35; *by Luke*, Acts 1:3, 22; *by Peter*, Acts 2:24, 31, 32 (with Psa. 16:9, 10); 3:15; 4:10, 33; 5:30–32; 10:40, 41; 1 Pet. 1:3, 21; 3:18, 21; *by Paul*, Acts 13:30–34 (with Psa. 2:7); 17:2, 3, 31; 26:23, 26; Rom. 1:4; 4:24, 25; 5:10; 6:4, 5, 9, 10; 8:11, 34; 1 Cor. 6:14; 15:3, 4, 20–23 (with vs. 5–8, 12–20); 2 Cor. 4:10, 11, 14; 5:15; 13:4; Gal. 1:1; Eph. 1:20; Phil. 3:10; Col. 1:18; 2:12; 1 Thess. 1: 10; 4:14; 2 Tim. 2:8; *by the author of the Epistle to the Hebrews*, Heb. 13:20; *by John*, Rev. 1:5, 18.

*Appears to the eleven apostles after his resurrection*, Mark 16:14; Luke 24:36–51; John 20:19–29.

*For our justification*, Rom. 4:25. *For our salvation*, Rom. 5:10; 10:9.

*An earnest of the general resurrection*, Rom. 6:5; 1 Cor. 6: 14; 15:21–23; 2 Cor. 4:14; 1 Thess. 4:14; 1 Pet. 1:3.

*The theme of apostolic preaching*, Acts 2:24, 31, 32; 3:15; 4:10, 33; 5:30–32; 10:40, 41; 17:2, 3.

See footnote, RESURRECTION, 1 Cor. 15:12.

**Reticence of,** Isa. 53:7; Matt. 26:63; 27:12, 14; Mark 14:61; 15:4, 5; John 19:9; 1 Pet. 2:23.

**Revelations by:** *Concerning his kingdom*, Matt. 8:11, 12 (with Luke 13:28, 29); 10:23, 34; 13:24–50; 16:18, 28 (with Mark 9:1; Luke 9:27); 21:43, 44; 24:14; Mark 16:17, 18; Luke 12:40–53; 13:24–35; 17:20–37; John 4:21, 23; 5:25–29; 6:39, 54; 12:35; 13:19; 14:29; 16:4. *Concerning his rejection by the Jews*, Matt. 21:33–44; Luke 17:25. *Concerning his betrayal*, Matt. 26:21, 23–25. *Concerning his crucifixion*, John 3:14; 8:28; 12:32 (with Luke 24:6, 7). *Concerning judgments upon the Jews*, Matt. 23:37–39. *Concerning the destruction of the temple, and Jerusalem*, Matt. 24; Mark 13; Luke 19:41–44. *Concerning the destruction of Capernaum*, Matt. 11:23; Luke 10:15.

*Concerning persecutions of Christians*, Matt. 23:34–36. *Concerning his being forsaken by his disciples*, John 16:32. *Concerning Lazarus*, John 11:4, 11, 23, 40. *Concerning Peter*, John 21:18–23. *Concerning fame of the woman who anointed his head*, Matt. 26:13; Mark 14:8, 9. *Concerning false christs*, Matt. 24:4, 5, 23–26; Mark 13:5, 6, 21–23; Luke 17:23, 24; 21:8. *Concerning things to come*, Rev. 1:1.

*Concerning his death and resurrection*, Matt. 12:39, 40; 16: 21; 17:12, 22, 23; 20:18, 19; 21:33–39; 26:2, 18, 21, 23, 24, 45, 46; 27:63; Mark 8:31; 9:31; 10:32–34; Luke 9:22–24; 17:25; 18:31–33; 22:15, 37; John 2:19; 10:15, 17; 12:7, 23, 32; 13:18–27; 14:19; 16:20, 32. *Concerning his ascension*, John 7:33, 34; 8:21; 13:33; 16:10, 16.

**Righteousness of,** see HOLINESS OF, above.

**Salvation by,** see footnote, SALVATION, Acts 16:17.

**Savior**, Matt. 1:21; Acts 5:31; 13:23, 38, 39, 47; 15:11; 16:31; 1 Cor. 1:30; 15:57; Eph. 5:23; Phil. 3:20; 1 Tim. 1:1, 15; 2 Tim. 1:9, 10, 12; 2:10; 3:15; Tit. 1:4; Heb. 2:3; 5:9; 2 Pet. 1:11; 2:20; 1 John 3:5; 4:9, 14; 5:11–13.

*Through his death*, Rom. 3:25; 4:25; 5:1, 6, 8–10; Gal. 1: 4; 2:20; Eph. 2:13–18, 20; 5:2, 25, 26; Col. 1:12–14; 1 Thess. 1: 10; 5:9, 10; Tit. 2:13, 14; 1 Pet. 1:18, 19; 3:18; 1 John 4:10.

*Through, his resurrection*, Acts 3:26; Rom. 10:9; 1 Cor. 15: 17; 1 Pet. 3:21; *his intercession*, Heb. 7:22, 25.

*By redemption*, Rom. 3:24. *By reconciliation*, Rom. 5:15, 17–19, 21; 2 Cor. 5:18, 19, 21; Eph. 2:7, 13–18, 20; Heb. 2:17.

*The only*, Acts 4:12; 1 Cor. 3:11.

PROPHECIES CONCERNING HIM AS SAVIOR, Psa. 72:4, 12–14, 17; Isa. 42:6, 7; 49:6, 8, 9; 59:16, 17, 20; 61:1–3; Zech. 9:9; Mal. 4:2; Luke 1:68–77; 4:18, 19.

ILLUSTRATED: *By parables of lost sheep, and lost coin*, Matt. 18:12, 13; Luke 15:1–10.

TESTIFIED TO: *By angels*, Luke 2:11. *By Simeon*, Luke 2:30–32. *By himself*, Luke 5:31, 32 (with Matt. 9:12, 13); 19:10; John 5:33, 34, 40; 6:27, 32, 33, 35, 37, 39, 51, 53–58; 7:37–39; 8:12; 9:5, 39; 10:7, 9–11, 14–16, 27, 28; 11:25, 26; 12:47; 14:6; 17:2, 3, 12. *By John*, John 1:29. *By the people of Sychar*, John 4:42. *By the heavenly host*, Rev. 5:5–14.

See DEATH OF, *Design of*, above.

v.10–AD 26
See footnote, *Time*, Rev. 10:6.

*q Righteousness, fruits of*, Psa. 15:2.
**11**
*r Jesus, perfections of*, Matt. 1:21.
*s Humility, instances of*, Prov. 22:4.
*t Jesus, mission of*, Matt. 1:21.
*u Holy Spirit, baptism of*, Acts 1:2.
*v Fire, figurative*, Ex. 12:8.
**12**
*w Winnowing*, Ruth 3:2.
*x Judgment, the general*, 2 Pet. 3:7.
*y Jesus, judge*, Matt. 1:21.
*z Wheat, figurative*, Ezra 6:9.

*a Righteous, promises to*, Psa. 64:10.
*b Heaven, the future home of the righteous*, Luke 18:22.
*c Punishment, eternal*, Lev. 26:41.
*d Chaff, figurative*, Hos. 13:3.
*e Hell*, Mark 9:43.
4 R. V. cleanse his threshing-floor;
**13**
*f* Mark 1:9–11; Luke 3:21, 22; John 1:32.
*g Galilee*, Mark 6:21.
*h Jordan*, Gen. 32:10.
*i John the Baptist*, Luke 1:63.

not forth [q]good fruit is [l]hewn
down, and cast into the fire.
11 [a]I indeed [d]baptize you with
water unto [i]repentance: but he
that cometh after me is mightier
than I, [r]whose shoes [s]I am not
worthy to bear: [t]he shall baptize
you with the [u]Holy Ghost[G], and
*with* [v]fire:[T]
12 Whose [w]fan[G] *is* in his hand,
and [x,y]he will throughly[G] [4]purge
his floor, and gather his [z,a]wheat
into the [b]garner[G]; but he will
[c]burn up the [d]chaff with unquenchable [e]fire.
13[T] ¶ [f]Then cometh Jē′sus
from [g]Găl′ī-lee to [h]Jôr′dan unto
[i]Jŏhn, to be [d]baptized of him.
14 But [i]Jŏhn [5]forbad him, saying, [j]I have need to be baptized
of thee, and comest thou to me?
15 [f]And Jē′sus answering said
unto him, Suffer[G] *it to be so* now:
for thus it becometh us [k]to fulfil
all righteousness. Then [l]he suffered[G] him.
16 [f]And Jē′sus, when he was
baptized, went up straightway
[6]out of the water: and, lo, the
heavens were opened unto him,
and he [m]saw the [n]Spirit of God
descending [7]like a [o]dove, and
lighting upon him:
17 And lo a voice [8]from heav-
en, saying, This is [p]my beloved
[q,r]Son, in whom I am well
pleased.[T Q]

## CHAPTER 4

*The temptation of Jesus. 13 He dwells in Capernaum, 17 and begins to preach. 18 He calls Peter and Andrew, James and John; 23 and heals the sick.*

THEN[T] was [a]Jē′sus led up of
the [1,b]spirit into the wilderness to be [c]tempted[G] of the *devil.
2 And when he had [d]fasted
[e]forty days and forty nights, he
was afterward an[G] [f,g]hungred[G].[T Q]
3 And when the [c]tempter came
to him, he said, [h]If thou be the
[i]Son of God, command that
these stones be made bread.
4 But he answered and said, It
is written, [j]Man shall not live by
bread alone, but by every word
that proceedeth out of the mouth
of God.[Q T]
5 Then the *devil taketh him
up into the [k]holy city, and setteth
him on a pinnacle[G] of the [l]temple,[Q]
6 And saith unto him, If thou

**14** *j Humility, exemplified*, Prov. 22:4. 5 R. V. would have hindered **15** *k Jesus, obedience of*, Matt. 1:21. *l Obedience, instances of*, Heb. 5:8. **16** 6 R. V. from

v.16–AD 26
See footnote, *Time*, Rev. 10:6.

*m Vision*, Acts 9:10.
*n Holy Spirit, baptism of*, Acts 1:2.
*o Dove*, Gen. 8:8.
7 R. V. as a dove, and coming
**17**
*p God, fatherhood of*, Gen. 2:2.
*q Jesus, divine sonship of*, Matt. 1:21.
*r Jesus, divinity of*, Matt. 1:21.
8 R. V. out of the heavens.

**1**
*a* Mark 1:12, 13; Luke 4:1–13.
*b Holy Spirit, Jesus led by*, Acts 1:2.
*c Temptation, of Jesus*, Luke 11:4.
1 R. V. Spirit
**2**
*d Fasting*, Zech. 8:19.
*e Forty, days*, Jonah 3:4.
*f Hunger, of Jesus*, Neh. 9:15.
*g Appetite, a source of temptation*, Prov. 23:2.
**3**
*h Miracles, design of*, Luke 23:8.
*i Jesus, divine sonship of*, Matt. 1:21.
**4**
*j* Deut. 8:3; Luke 4:4.
**5**
*k Jerusalem*, Judg. 19:10.
*l Temple, Herod's*, 1 Kin. 6:17.

---

**Second coming of,** Matt. 26:64; John 14:28, 29; 21:22; Acts 1:11; 3:20, 21; 1 Cor. 11:26; Phil. 3:20, 21; 1 Thess. 1:10; 2:19; 3:13; 4:15–17; 2 Thess. 2:1–5, 8; 1 Tim. 6:14, 15; Tit. 2:13; 2 Pet. 3:3, 4.

*At an unexpected time*, Matt. 24:3, 27, 30, 31, 37–39, 42–44 (with Mark 13:1–37; Luke 12:40; 17:22–30; 21:5–35); 25:6, 10, 13, 19; Mark 13:32, 35, 36 (with Matt. 24:36); Luke 12:37–40; 1 Thess. 5:2, 3, 23; 2 Pet. 3:8–14; Rev. 16:15; 22:20.

*In heavenly glory*, Matt. 16:27; 25:31; Mark 13:26, 27; 14:62; Luke 9:26 (with Mark 8:38); 21:27.

*To judge the world*, Matt. 16:27; 25:31–46; Luke 19:12, 13, 15; 1 Cor. 1:7, 8; 4:5; 2 Thess. 1:7–10; 2 Tim. 4:1; Rev. 22:12.

*To receive his saints*, John 14:3, 18; 1 Cor. 15:23; Col. 3:4; 2 Thess. 1:10; 2 Tim. 4:8; Heb. 9:28; 1 Pet. 5:4; 1 John 3:2.

*Exhortations in view of*, Jas. 5:7–9; 1 Pet. 1:7, 13; 4:13; 1 John 2:28; Rev. 3:11.

**Shepherd,** Ezek. 34:23; 37:24; Zech. 13:7; Matt. 26:31; John 10:2, 4, 9, 11, 14–16, 27, 28; Heb. 13:20; 1 Pet. 2:25; 5:4.

**Son of Man,** see HUMANITY OF, above.

**Sovereignty of,** see KING, above; LORDSHIP OF, above.

**Sufferings of.** Foretold: *By the psalmist*, Psa. 22:6–8, 11–13, 17–21 (with Matt. 27:35; Mark 15:24; Luke 23:34; John 19:23, 24); 69:7–9, 20; *by prophets*, Isa. 50:6; 52:13, 14; 53:1–12 (with Matt. 26:67; 27:26; Luke 22:37; John 12:38); Mic. 5:1; Zech. 11:12, 13; Luke 24:26, 46; 1 Pet. 1:11; *by himself*, Matt. 16:21; 17:12, 22, 23; 20:17–19 (with Mark 10:32–34; Luke 18:31–33); Mark 8:31; 9:12; Luke 9:22; John 3:14; 13:21.

*In Gethsemane*, Matt. 26:38–45; Mark 14:34–39; Luke 22:42–44; John 18:11.

*In Pilate's judgment hall*, Matt. 27:24–30; Mark 15:15–20; John 19:16–18.

*At his crucifixion*, Matt. 27:31–50; Mark 15:34, 36; Luke 23:33–46; John 19:28.

*Apostolic teaching concerning*, Acts 3:18; 17:3; 2 Cor. 1:5; Phil. 2:8; 3:10; Heb. 2:9; 4:15; 5:7, 8; 12:2, 3; 1 Pet. 1:11; 2:21–23; 3:18; 4:1, 13; Rev. 5:6; 19:13.

**Sympathy of,** see COMPASSION OF, above; LOVE OF, above.

**Teacher,** Matt. 5:1, 2; John 7:46; Acts 1:1.

*From God*, John 3:2.

*Taught, with authority*, Matt. 7:29; 23:8; Mark 1:22; *without respect of persons*, Matt. 22:16; Mark 12:14; Luke 20:21; *by the sea-side*, Mark 4:1; *in cities and villages*, Matt. 11:1; Mark 6:6; Luke 23:5; *in synagogues*, Matt. 4:23; Mark 1:21; Luke 4:15; 6:6; *in the temple*, Matt. 21:23; 26:55; Mark 12:35; Luke 21:37; John 8:2; *in the wilderness*, Mark 6:34.

**Temptation of,** Luke 22:28. *In all points as we are*, Heb. 4:15.

*By the devil*, Matt. 4:1–11; Mark 1:12, 13; Luke 4:1–13.

**Typified:** *In offerings*, Gen. 4:4; 8:20; 22:13; Ex. 12:5–7; 24:5; 29:36, 37; Lev. 1:4, 10–12; 3:6, 12; 4:3–7, 14–18, 20, 23–25, 28–30, 32–34; 5:6–11, 16, 18; 6:6, 7; 7:2; 8:14, 15, 18, 19, 22–24; 9:2, 7–9, 18; 12:6–8; 14:12–14, 25, 30, 31; 15:15, 29, 30; 16:3, 5, 9, 11, 14–16, 21, 22; 19:21, 22; 22:18, 19; 23:12, 18, 19, 27, 28; Num. 6:10, 11, 14, 16, 17; 7; 8:8, 12; 15:24, 25, 27; 28:3, 4, 9, 11, 15, 19, 22, 23, 27, 30; 29:5, 8, 11, 13, 16, 17, 19, 20, 22, 23, 25, 26, 28, 29, 31, 32, 34, 38; 1 Chr. 29:21; 2 Chr. 7:5; 29:21–24; Ezra 6:17, 20; 8:35; Ezek. 43:18–27; 45:15, 18–23.

*In the passover*, Ex. 12:3, 5; Num. 28:16. *In the corner stone*, Psa. 48:21–23; Isa. 28:16; Mark 12:10, 11.

*In David*, Ezek. 34:23, 24; 37:24, 25; Hos. 3:5. *In Solomon*, Psa. 72. *In Hezekiah*, Isa. 32:1.

**Unchangeable,** Heb. 13:8.

**Union of, with the righteous,** see footnote, RIGHTEOUS, *Union of, with Christ*, Psa. 64:10.

**Wisdom of,** Mark 6:2; Luke 2:40, 46, 47, 52; John 7:15.

**Worship of,** 1 Cor. 1:2; 2 Cor. 12:8, 9; Phil. 2:10, 11.

*John's vision of*, Rev. 5:8, 9, 12–14; 7:10.

ENJOINED, John 5:23; Heb. 1:6.

INSTANCES OF: *By the wise men*, Matt. 2:2. *By a certain ruler*, Matt. 9:18. *By the disciples*, Matt. 14:33. *By Canaanitish woman*, Matt. 15:25. *By a leper*, Matt. 8:2. *By women after his resurrection*, Matt. 28:9. *By the eleven*

**6**

*m Presumption, temptation to,* Psa. 19:13.

n Psa. 91:11, 12; Luke 4:10, 11.

*o God, preserver of the righteous,* Gen. 2:2.

*p Angel, functions of,* Heb. 1:13.

**7**

q Deut. 6:16; Luke 4:12.

**8**

*r Mountain,* Mic. 7:12.

**9**

*s Ambition, Satan tempts to,* Hab. 2:5.

**10**

*t Temptation, resistance to,* Luke 11:4.

u Deut. 6:13; 10:20; Luke 4:8.

*v Duty, of man to God,* Eccl. 12:13.

*w Worship,* Gen. 22:5.

**12**

*x John the Baptist,* Luke 1:63.

*y Prison,* Gen. 39:20.

*z Jesus, life of,* Matt. 1:21.

---

*a Galilee,* Mark 6:21.

2 R. V. delivered up,

**13**

*b Nazareth,* John 1:46.

*c Jesus, rejected,* vs. 13–16; Matt. 1:21.

*d Capernaum,* Luke 4:31.

be the [i]Son of God, [m]cast thyself
down: for it is written,[n,o]He shall
give his [p]angels charge concerning
thee: and in *their* hands they shall
bear thee up, lest at any time thou
dash thy foot against a stone.
7 Jē′ṣus said unto him, It is
written again, *,[q]Thou shalt not
tempt the Lord thy God.
8 Again, the *devil taketh
him up into an exceeding high
[r]mountain, and sheweth him all
the kingdoms of the world, and
the glory of them;
9 And saith unto him, [s]All these
things will I give thee, if thou
wilt fall down and worship *me.
10 Then saith Jē′ṣus unto him,
[t]Get thee hence, *Sā′tan: for it
is written, [u,v]Thou shalt [w]wor-
ship the Lord thy God, and him
only shalt thou serve.
11 Then the *devil leaveth him,
and, behold, [p]angels came and
ministered unto him.
12 ¶ Now when Jē′ṣus had
heard that [x]Jŏhn was [2]cast into
[y]prison, [z]he departed into [a]Găl′-
ĭ-lee;
13 And leaving [b]Năz′a-rěth, [c]he
came and dwelt in [d]Că-pēr′na-
ŭm, which is upon the sea coast,
in the borders of [e]Zăb′u-lŏn and
[f]Něph′tha-lĭm:
14 That [g]it might be fulfilled
which was spoken by [h]Ē-ṣā′ias
the prophet, saying,
15 [i]The land of [e]Zăb′u-lŏn, and
the land of [f]Něph′tha-lĭm, *by* the
way of the sea, beyond [j]Jôr′dan,
[a]Găl′ĭ-lee of the Ĝěn′tīleṣ;
16 The [k]people which sat in
[l]darkness [m]saw great [n]light; and
to them which sat in the region and shadow of death light
is sprung up.
17 From that time Jē′ṣus began
to [o]preach, and to say, [p,q]Re-
pent: for the [r]kingdom of heaven
is at hand.
18 ¶ And Jē′ṣus, walking by
the †sea of Găl′ĭ-lee, saw two
brethren, Sī′mon called [s]Pē′tẽr,
and ‡Ăn′drew his brother, casting a [t]net into the sea: for they
were [u]fishers.
19 And [v]he saith unto [w,x]them,
[y,z]Follow me, and [a]I will make
you [b,c]fishers of men.
20 And they straightway

*e* Or, *Zebulun, tribe of,* Gen. 49:13.

*f* Or, *Naphtali, tribe of,* Num. 1:42.

**14**

*g Jesus, prophecies concerning,* Matt. 1:21.

*h* Or, *Isaiah,* Isa. 1:1.

**15**

*i* Isa. 9:1, 2.

*j Jordan,* Gen. 32:10.

**16**

*k Wicked, described,* Psa. 73:3.

*l Darkness, figurative,* Gen. 1:2.

*m Prophecies, fulfilled,* Dan. 9:24.

*n Light, figurative,* Matt. 5:14.

**17**

*o Preaching,* Matt. 9:35.

*p Repentance, burden of preaching of Jesus,* Mark 1:4.

*q Decision, injunctions concerning,* Isa. 50:7.

*r Kingdom of Heaven,* Matt. 13:24.

**18** *s Peter,* Mark 5:37. *t Net,* Isa. 51:20. *u Fishermen,* Luke 5:2.
**19** *v Jesus, chooses disciples,* Matt. 1:21. *w Minister, call of,* Rom. 15:16. *x Apostles, selection of,* Luke 6:13. *y Call, to special religious duty,* Phil. 3:14. *z Commandment, enjoining discipleship,* Deut. 8:2.—*a Promise, to obedient,* 2 Cor. 1:20. *b Fishermen, figurative,* Luke 5:2. *c Agency, in salvation of men,* Mark 1:17.

---

*disciples after his resurrection,* Matt. 28:17; Luke 24:52. *By the multitudes,* Mark 11:9, 10, with Matt. 21:9. *By Simon Peter,* Luke 5:8. *By blind man whom Jesus healed,* John 9:38. *By unclean spirits,* Mark 3:11. *By a man with unclean spirit,* Mark 5:6, 7. *By Stephen,* Acts 7:59, 60. *By Paul,* 1 Tim. 1:12; 2 Pet. 3:18.

**Zeal of:** *For God's house,* Luke 2:49; John 2:17, with Psa. 69:9. *In obedience to God,* John 4:32, 34; 9:4; Rom. 15:3. *In doing good,* Acts 10:38. *In preaching the gospel,* Matt. 4:23; 9:35; Mark 6:6; Luke 4:43 (with Mark 1:38); 8:1. *In giving himself as a sacrifice,* Luke 9:51; 12:50; 13:32, 33; 1 Tim. 6:13.

***SATAN,** Zech. 3:1, 2; Matt. 25:41; Mark 3:22–26 (with Matt. 9:34; Luke 11:15, 18); Luke 10:18; John 16:11; Acts 13:10; Rev. 2:10, 13, 24.

**Called:** APOLLYON, Rev. 9:11. BEELZEBUB, Matt. 12:24; Mark 3:22; Luke 11:15. BELIAL, 2 Cor. 6:15. THE DEVIL, Matt. 4:1; Luke 4:2, 6; Rev. 20:2. SATAN, 1 Chr. 21:1; Job 1:6; Luke 22:31; John 13:27; Acts 5:3; 26:18; Rom. 16:20.

**Character of:** *Sinned from the beginning,* 1 John 3:8. *Subtle,* Gen. 3:1; 2 Cor. 11:3. *Tempter,* Matt. 4:3; 1 Cor. 7:5; 1 Thess. 3:5; 1 Tim. 5:15. *Accuser,* Job 1:6, 7, 9–12; 2:3–7. *Adversary,* Luke 22:31, 53; 1 Pet. 5:8. *Murderer and liar,* John 8:44; Acts 5:3. *Transforms himself into an angel of light,* 2 Cor. 11:14.

**Described as:** *Accuser of our brethren,* Rev. 12:10. *Angel of the bottomless pit,* Rev. 9:11. *Enemy,* Matt. 13:39. *Father of lies,* John 8:44. *Old serpent,* Rev. 12:9; 20:2. *Power of darkness,* Col. 1:13. *Prince, of this world,* John 12:31; 14:30; 16:11; *of devils,* Matt. 12:24; *of the power of the air,* Eph. 2:2. *Ruler of the darkness of this world,* Eph. 6:12. *Spirit that worketh in the children of disobedience,* Eph. 2:2. *The god of this world,* 2 Cor. 4:4. *Wicked one,* Matt. 13:19, 38.

**Instances of temptations by:** *Eve,* Gen. 3:1, 4, 5, 14, 15; 2 Cor. 11:3. *Job,* Job 1:13–22; 2:7–10. *David,* 1 Chr. 21:1. *Jesus,* Matt. 4:1–11; Mark 1:13; Luke 4:1–13; John 14:30. *Judas,* John 13:2, 27.

**Kingdom of:** *Called gates of hell* (R. V. hades), Matt. 16:18. *To be destroyed,* Gen. 3:15; Matt. 13:30; Rom. 16:20; 1 John 3:8.

**Miscellany of facts concerning:** *Sterilizes the heart,* Matt. 13:19, 38, 39; Mark 4:15; Luke 8:12. *Causes, spiritual blindness,* 2 Cor. 4:4; *physical infirmities,* Luke 13:16.

*Devices of,* 2 Cor. 2:11; 12:7; Eph. 6:11, 12, 16; 1 Thess. 2:18; 1 Tim. 3:6, 7.

*Hymeneas and Alexander delivered to,* 1 Tim. 1:20. *Contends with Michael,* Jude 9. *Ministers of, dissemblers,* 2 Cor. 11:15.

*To be resisted,* Eph. 4:27; Jas. 4:7; 1 Pet. 5:8, 9. *Resistance of, effectual,* 1 John 2:13; 5:18. *Gracious deliverance from the power of,* Acts 26:18; Col. 1:13.

*To be cast out of this world,* John 12:31. *To be bound,* Rev. 20:1–3.

**Symbolized:** *By the serpent,* Gen. 3:13; 2 Cor. 11:3. *By the dragon,* Rev. 12:3, 4.

**Synagogue of,** Rev. 2:9; 3:9.

See footnote, DEMONS, Matt. 4:24.

† **SEA OF GALILEE.** *Called* SEA OF CHINNERETH, Num. 34:11; Deut. 3:17; Josh. 13:27; SEA OF CHINNEROTH, Josh. 12:3; LAKE OF GENNESARET, Luke 5:1; SEA OF TIBERIAS, John 21:1. *Jesus calls disciples on the shore of,* Matt. 4:18–22; Luke 5:1–11. *Jesus teaches from a ship on,* Matt. 13:1–3. *Miracles of Jesus on,* Matt. 8:24–32; 14:22–33; 17:27; Mark 4:37–39; Luke 5:1–9; 8:22–24; John 21:1–11.

‡ **ANDREW,** an apostle. *A fisherman,* Matt. 4:18. *Of Bethsaida,* John 1:44. *A disciple of John,* John 1:40. *Finds Peter, his brother, and brings him to Jesus,* John 1:40–42. *Call of,* Matt. 4:18, 19; Mark 1:16, 17. *His name appears in the list of the apostles,* Matt. 10:2; Mark 3:18; Luke 6:14. *Asks the Master privately about the destruction of the temple,* Mark 13:3, 4. *Tells Jesus of the Greeks who sought to see him,* John 12:20–22. *Reports the number of loaves at the feed-*

[d,e,f,g]left *their* [h]nets, and followed him.

21 And going on from thence,[G] [i]he saw other two brethren, [j]James *the son* of [§]Zĕb′e-dee, and [k]Jŏhn his brother, in a ship with Zĕb′e-dee their father, mending their [h]nets; and he called them.

22 And they immediately [d,e,f,g]left the ship and their father, and followed him.

23 ¶ And Jē′sus went about all [l]Găl′ĭ-lee, [m,n]teaching in their [o]synagogues, and [m,p]preaching the [q]gospel of the kingdom, and [m,r]healing all manner of [s]sickness and all manner of disease among the people.[T]

24 And his [t]fame went throughout all [u]Sȳr′ĭ-ȧ: and they brought unto him all [v]sick people that were taken with divers[G] diseases and torments, and those which were possessed with [+]devils,[G] and [3]those which were [w]lunatick,[G] and those that had the [x]palsy; and [s]he healed them.

25 And there followed him great multitudes of people from [l]Găl′ĭ-lee, and *from* [y]Dĕ-căp′o-lĭs, and *from* [z]Jē-ru′sȧ-lĕm, and *from* [a]Jū-dæ′ȧ, and *from* beyond [b]Jôr′dan.

20
*d Obedience, exemplified,* Heb. 5:8.
*e Renunciation, of business for Christ,* Luke 5:11.
*f Faith in Christ, exemplified,* John 6:69.
*g Self-denial, instances of,* Mark 8:34.
*h Net,* Isa. 51:20.
21
*i Jesus, life of,* Matt. 1:21.
*j James,* Luke 5:10.
*k John,* Mark 1:19.
23
*l Galilee,* Mark 6:21.
*m Jesus, mission of,* Matt. 1:21.
*n Jesus, teacher,* Matt. 1:21.
*o Synagogue,* Matt. 12:9.
*p Preaching,* Matt. 9:35.
*q Gospel,* Mark 13:10.
*r Miracles, of Jesus,* Luke 23:8.
*s Disease, healing of, by Jesus,* Ex. 15:26.
24
*t Fame of Jesus,* Luke 5:15.
*u Syria,* 2 Kin. 6:23.
*v Afflictions,* Psa. 34:19.
*w Insanity,* Prov. 26:18.
*x Paralysis,* Mark 2:3.
3 R. V. epileptic, and palsied;
25
*y* Mark 5:20; 7:31.
*z Jerusalem,* Judg. 19:10.
*a Judea,* Luke 5:17.
*b Jordan,* Gen. 32:10.

## CHAPTER 5

*The sermon on the mount: 3 The beatitudes. 13 The disciples of Jesus are the salt of the earth and the light of the world. 17 Jesus came not to destroy the law, but to fulfil it. 21 He compares the teachings of the law of Moses with the Gospel message with reference to killing, 27 to adultery, 31 to divorce, 33 to swearing, 38 to retaliation, 43 and to love of enemies.*

AND seeing the multitudes, [a]he went up into a [b]mountain: and when he was set,[G] his [c]disciples came unto him:

2 And [a]he opened his mouth, and [d]taught them, [e]saying,

3 [f,g]Blessed[S][G] *are* the [h,i,j]poor in spirit: for [k,l]their's is the [m]kingdom of heaven.[T Q]

4 [n]Blessed[G] *are* they that [o,p]mourn: for [l,q,r]they shall be [g]comforted.[Q]

5 [g]Blessed[G] *are* [s]the [j,t]meek: for [l,u]they shall [v]inherit the earth.[Q]

6 Blessed[G] *are* [w]they which do [*,x]hunger and [y]thirst after [z]righteousness: for [a]they [b]shall be filled.

7 [b]Blessed[G] *are* the [c]merciful: for [d,e]they shall obtain mercy.

8 [b]Blessed[G] *are* the [f]pure in [g]heart: for [d,h]they shall see God.[Q]

9 [b]Blessed[G] *are* the [i]peacemakers: for [d,j]they shall be called the [k]children of [l]God.

10 [b]Blessed[G] *are* they which are [m]persecuted for righteousness' sake: for [d,n]their's is the [o]kingdom of heaven.[T]

11 [b,p]Blessed[G] are ye, when *men* shall [1]revile you, and [m]persecute *you*, and shall [q,r,s]say all manner of evil[S] against you falsely, for my sake.

12 [t,u]Rejoice, and be exceeding glad: for great *is* your [†]reward

1
*a Jesus, teacher,* vs. 1–48; Matt. 1:21.
*b Mountain, Jesus preaches from,* Mic. 7:12.

*c Apostles,* Luke 6:13.
2
*d Instruction, in religion,* Prov. 23:23.
*e Preaching,* Matt. 9:35.
3
*f* Luke 6:20.
*g Spiritual Peace,* Gal. 1:3.
*h Righteous, described,* Psa. 64:10.
*i Humility,* Prov. 22:4.
*j Christian Graces,* Gal. 5:22.
*k Promise, to the righteous,* 2 Cor. 1:20.
*l Righteous, promises to,* Psa. 64:10.
*m Kingdom of Heaven,* Matt. 13:24.
4
*n* Luke 6:21.
*o Afflictions, consolation in,* Psa. 34:19.
*p Repentance, rewards of,* Mark 1:4.
*q Penitent, promises to,* Psa. 51:17.
*r Promise, to the penitent,* 2 Cor. 1:20.
5
*s* Psa. 37:11.
*t Meekness, rewards of,* Psa. 45:4.
*u Promise, to the meek,* 2 Cor. 1:20.
*v Inheritance, figurative,* Num. 27:7.
6
*w Seekers, promises to,* Isa. 55:6.
*x Spiritual Desire,* Psa. 42:1.
*y Thirst, figurative,* John 4:14. *z Righteousness,* Psa. 15:2.—*a Promise, to seekers,* 2 Cor. 1:20. *b Spiritual Peace,* Gal. 1:3. **7** *c Mercy, rewards of,* Deut. 5:10. *d Righteous, promises to,* Psa. 64:10. *e Promise, to the merciful,* 2 Cor. 1:20. **8** *f Purity of Heart,* 1 Tim. 4:12. *g Heart, renewed,* Psa. 44:21. *h Promise, to the pure in heart,* 2 Cor. 1:20. **9** *i Peace, promises to promoters of,* Jer. 29:7. *j Promise, to peacemakers,* 2 Cor. 1:20. *k Spiritual Adoption,* Rom. 8:15. *l God, fatherhood of,* Gen. 2:2. **10** *m Persecution, of the righteous,* John 15:20. *n Promise, to the persecuted,* v. 11; 2 Cor. 1:20. *o Kingdom of Heaven,* Matt. 13:24. **11** *p* Luke 6:22. *q False Accusation,* 2 Tim. 3:3. *r Slander,* Prov. 10:18. *s Falsehood,* Job 21:34. 1 R. V. reproach. **12** *t* Luke 6:23. *u Joy, under adversity,* Psa. 5:11.

*ing of the five thousand,* John 6:8, 9. *Meets with the disciples after the Lord's ascension,* Acts 1:13.

§ **ZEBEDEE.** *Father of James and John,* Matt. 4:21; 20:20; 27:56; Mark 1:20; Luke 5:10.

+ **DEMONS.** *Worship of,* Lev. 17:7; Deut. 32:17; Psa. 106:37; 1 Cor. 10:20, 21. *Worship of, forbidden,* Lev. 17:7; Rev. 9:20.

*Cast out by Jesus,* Matt. 4:24; 8:16, 28–32; Mark 1:23–26; 3:11, 12, 22; 16:9; Luke 4:41.

*Power over, given to the disciples,* Matt. 10:1; Mark 6:7; 16:17. *Cast out, by the disciples,* Luke 10:17; *by one who was not associated with the disciples,* Mark 9:38; *by Peter,* Acts 5:16; *by Paul,* Acts 16:16–18; 19:12; *by Philip,* Acts 8:7. *Disciples could not expel,* Mark 9:18, 28, 29. *Sceva's sons could not expel,* Acts 19:13–16. *Parable of the man repossessed of,* Matt. 12:43–45; Luke 11:24–26.

*Jesus falsely accused of being possessed of,* Matt. 12:24; Mark 3:22–30; Luke 11:15; John 7:20; 8:48, 52; 10:20.

*Adversaries of men,* Matt. 12:45.

*Testify to the divinity of Jesus,* Matt. 8:29; Mark 1:23, 24; 3:11; 5:7; Luke 4:34; 8:27, 28.

*Believe and tremble,* Jas. 2:19. *To be judged at the general judgment,* Matt. 8:29; 2 Pet. 2:4; Jude 6.

**Instances of possession by:** *Two men of the Gergesenes,* Matt. 8:28–34; Mark 5:2–20; Luke 8:26–33. *The dumb man,* Matt. 9:32, 33. *The blind and dumb man,* Matt. 12:22; Luke 11:14. *The daughter of the Syrophenician woman,* Matt. 15:22–28; Mark 7:25–30. *The epileptic child,* Matt. 17:14–18; Mark 9:17–27; Luke 9:37–42. *The man in the synagogue,* Mark 1:23–26; Luke 4:33–35. *Mary Magdalene,* Mark 16:9; Luke 8:2, 3. *The herd of swine,* Matt. 8:30–32; Luke 8:32, 33. See footnote, SATAN, Matt. 4:10.

* **HUNGER. Figurative:** *Of spiritual desire,* Psa. 107:9; Prov. 2:3–5; Isa. 55:1, 2; Amos 8:11–13; Matt. 5:6; Luke 1:53; 6:21; John 6:35; 1 Pet. 2:2.

† **REWARD, A MOTIVE,** Isa. 40:10, 11. *In Moses' choice,* Heb. 11:26. *For valor,* 1 Sam. 17:25; Judg. 1:13.

in [v]heaven: for so [m]persecuted
they the [w]prophets which were
before you.[Q]
13 ¶ [x, y]Ye are the [z]salt of the
earth: but if the salt have lost
his [a]savour,[C] wherewith[C] shall it
be salted? it is thenceforth
good for nothing, but to be
[b]cast out, and to be trodden
under foot of men.
14 [c]Ye are the ‡light of the
world. A city that is set on an
hill cannot be hid.
15 [d]Neither do men light a
[e]candle,[C] and put it under a
bushel,[C] but on [2]a candlestick;[C]
and it giveth light unto all that
are in the house.
16 [f]Let your ‡light so shine before men, that they may see your
good [g]works, and [h]glorify your
[i]Father which is in [j]heaven.[T]
17 ¶[T] Think[Q] not that [k]I am
come to destroy the [l]law, or the
prophets: I am not come to destroy, but to fulfil.
18 For verily I say unto you,
[m]Till [n]heaven and [o]earth pass,
one jot[C] or one tittle[C] shall in no
wise[C] pass from the [l]law, till all
be fulfilled.[Q]
19 [p]Whosoever therefore shall
break one of these least commandments, and shall teach men
so, he shall be called the least
in the [q]kingdom of heaven:
but whosoever shall [r]do and
[s]teach *them*, the same shall be
called great in the kingdom of[T]
heaven.
20 For I say unto you, That except your [t]righteousness shall exceed *the righteousness*[C] of the
[u]scribes and [v]Phăr'ĭ-seeș, ye
shall in no case enter into the
[q]kingdom of heaven.[S]
21 ¶ Ye have heard that it was
said by them of old[C] time,
[l, w]Thou shalt not [x]kill; and
whosoever shall kill [y]shall be in
danger of the judgment:[Q]
22 But [z]I say unto you, That
[a]whosoever is [b]angry with his
[c]brother [3]without a cause [d]shall
be in danger of the judgment:
and whosoever shall say to
his brother, [e]Rā'cȧ,[C] [d]shall be
in danger of the council: but
whosoever shall say, Thou fool,
[d]shall be in[C] danger of [f]hell[C] fire.
23 Therefore if thou bring thy
[g]gift to the [h]altar, and there
rememberest that thy [c]brother
hath [4]ought[C] against thee;
24 Leave there thy [g]gift before
the altar, and go thy way; [i]first
be [j]reconciled to thy brother,
and then come and offer thy
gift.
25 Agree with thine adversary
quickly, whiles[C] thou art in the
way with him; ‖, [k]lest [5]at any
time the adversary[C] deliver thee
to the [l]judge, and the judge deliver thee to the officer, and thou
be cast into [m]prison.
26 Verily I say unto thee,
[n]Thou shalt by no means come
out thence, till thou hast paid
the uttermost[C] farthing.[C]
27[T] ¶ Ye have heard that it was
said [6]by them of old time, [o]Thou
shalt not commit [p]adultery:[Q]
28 But [q]I say unto you, [r]That
whosoever looketh on a woman
to [s]lust after her hath committed

v *Heaven, the future home of the righteous,* Luke 18:22.
w *Prophets,* Isa. 3:2.
**13**
x *Righteous, described,* Psa. 64:10.
y *Agency, in the salvation of men,* Mark 1:17.
z *Salt, figurative,* 2 Kin. 2:20.

a *Influence, good,* 1 Cor. 7:14.
b *Backsliders, punishment of,* Jer. 3:22.
**14**
c *Righteous, described,* Psa. 64:10.
**15**
d Mark 4:21; Luke 8:16; 11:33.
e *Lamp,* Ex. 27:20.
2 R. V. the stand;
**16**
f *Commandment, enjoining influence for righteousness,* Deut. 8:2.
g *Works, good,* 2 Tim. 1:9.
h *Glorifying God,* Luke 5:25.
i *God, fatherhood of,* Gen. 2:2.
j *Heaven, God's dwelling place,* Luke 18:22.
**17**
k *Jesus, mission of,* Matt. 1:21.
l *Law, of Moses,* Deut. 33:2.
**18**
m Luke 16:17; 21:32.
n *Heavens, physical, destruction of,* Psa. 8:3.
o *Earth, destruction of,* Prov. 8:23.
**19**
p *False Teachers,* 2 Pet. 2:1.
q *Kingdom of Heaven,* Matt. 13:24.
r *Obedience,* Heb. 5:8.
s *Instruction, in religion,* Prov. 23:23.
**20**
t *Righteousness,* Psa. 15:2.

u *Scribe, hypocrisy of, reproved by Jesus,* 1 Kin. 4:3.
v *Pharisees,* Matt. 15:12.
**21**
w Ex. 20:13.
x *Homicide, felonious,* Deut. 5:17.
y *Punishment, according to deeds,* Lev. 26:41.
**22**
z *Jesus, teacher,* Matt. 1:21.

a *Commandment, forbidding unrighteous anger,* Deut. 8:2.
b *Anger,* Psa. 37:8.
c *Brother,* Prov. 18:24.
d *Punishment, according to deeds,* Lev. 26:41.
e *Speech, evil,* Col. 4:6.
f *Hell,* Mark 9:43.
3 R. V. *omits* without a cause
**23**
g *Offerings,* Lev. 6:17.
h *Altar,* Gen. 8:20.
4 R. V. aught
**24**
i *Commandment, enjoining reconciliation between brethren,* Deut. 8:2.
j *Reconciliation, between man and man,* 2 Cor. 5:18.
**25**
k *Prudence, in avoiding litigation,* 2 Chr. 2:12.
l *Judge,* Judg. 2:18.
m *Prison,* Gen. 39:20.
5 R. V. haply the
**26**
n *Debtor, laws concerning,* Luke 7:41.
**27**
o Ex. 20:14; Deut. 5:18.
p *Adultery, forbidden,* Lev. 20:10.
6 R. V. *omits* by them of old time,
**28**
q *Jesus, teacher,* Matt. 1:21.
r *Chastity, enjoined,* Job 31:1.
s *Lust,* 2 Pet. 1:4.

*To repentance,* Lev. 26:40–45; Isa. 1:16–20; Acts 26:18. *To obedience,* Ex. 20:6; Lev. 25:18, 19; 26:3–13; Deut. 4:40; 6:3, 18; 11:13–16, 18–21, 26–29; Isa. 1:16–20; 3:10; Heb. 12:28. *To faithfulness,* Matt. 24:45–47 (with Luke 12:42–44); 25:14–23 (with Luke 19:12–27); Rev. 2:10; 22:12. *To righteous conduct,* Rom. 2:10; 1 Pet. 3:9–12. *To patience,* Heb. 10:36. *To perseverance,* Matt. 10:22 (with Mark 13:13); 24:13; Rom. 2:6, 7; Gal. 6:9; Rev. 2:17, 25–28; 3:5, 11, 12, 21; 21:7. *To honesty,* Deut. 25:15. *To follow Christ,* Matt. 16:24–27; 20:1–16; 25:34–46; Mark 10:21; Luke 12:8; 2 Pet. 1:10, 11. *To endure persecution,* Luke 6:22, 23; Heb. 10:34. *To endure tribulation,* Rev. 2:7, 10; 7:14–17. *To love enemies,* Luke 6:35. *To deliver the oppressed,* Jer. 22:3, 4. *To honor parents,* Ex. 20:12; Eph. 6:1–3. *To hallow the Sabbath,* Jer. 17:24–26. *To bestow charity,* Deut. 15:9–11; 24:19. *To show kindness to animals,* Deut. 22:7.

‡ **LIGHT. Physical,** see footnote, LIGHT, Gen. 1:3. **Figurative:** *Of the Lord,* Psa. 27:1; Isa. 60:19, 20; Jas. 1:17; 1 John 1:5, 7; 2:8–10. *Of the Lord's word,* Psa. 119:105; Prov. 6:23. *Of personal influence for righteousness,* Matt. 5:14–16; Mark 4:21; Luke 8:16. *Of the righteous,* Luke 16:8; Eph. 5:8, 14; Phil. 2:15; 1 Thess. 5:5. *Of John the Baptist,* John 5:35. *Of spiritual understanding,* Isa. 8:20; Luke 11:33–36; 2 Cor. 4:6. *Of the Gospel,* 2 Cor. 4:4, 6. *Of spiritual wisdom,* Psa. 119:130; Isa. 2:5; 2 Pet. 1:19. *Of righteousness,* Matt. 5:16; Acts 26:18; 1 Pet. 2:9. *Of heavenly glory,* Rev. 21:23. *Of Christ's heavenly glory,* 1 Tim. 6:16. *Of Christ's kingdom,* Isa. 58:8. *Of the Savior,* Isa. 49:6; Mal. 4:2; Matt. 4:16; Luke 2:32; John 1:4, 5, 7–9; 3:19–21; 8:12; 9:5; 12:35, 36, 46; Rev. 21:23.

‖ **LITIGATION.** *To be avoided,* Prov. 17:14; 20:3; 25:8–10; Matt. 5:25, 40; Luke 12:58; 1 Cor. 6:1–8.

[t]adultery with her already in his
[u]heart.[T]
29 [v,w]And if thy right [x]eye
[7,y]offend[G] thee, [z,a]pluck it out,
and cast *it* from thee: for it is
profitable for thee that one of thy
members should perish, and not
*that* thy whole body should be
[b]cast into [c]hell.[G]
30 [d]And if thy right hand [7,e]of-
fend[G] thee, [a,f]cut it off, and cast *it*
from thee: for it is profitable for
thee that one of thy members
should perish, and not *that* thy
whole body should be [b]cast into
[c]hell.
31 ¶ It hath been [g]said, Whosoever shall [h]put away[G] his [i]wife, let
him give her a writing of divorcement:[Q]
32 But [j,k]I say unto you, That
[l,m]whosoever shall [h]put away his
[i]wife, saving[G] for the cause of fornication, causeth her to commit
[n]adultery: and whosoever shall
marry her that is divorced committeth adultery.
33 ¶ Again, ye have heard that
it hath been [g]said by them of old
time, [o]Thou shalt not forswear[G]
thyself, but [p]shalt perform unto
the Lord thine oaths:[Q]
34 But I say unto you, [q]Swear
not at all; neither by [r]heaven;
for it is God's [s]throne:[Q]
35 Nor by the [t]earth; for it is
his [u]footstool: neither by [v]Jĕ-ru̩'-
să-lĕm; for it is the city of the
great [w]King.[Q]
36 [q]Neither shalt thou swear
by thy head, because thou canst
not make one hair white or black.
37 But let your communication
be, Yea, yea; Nay, nay: for
[x]whatsoever is more than these
cometh of evil.
38 ¶ Ye have heard that it hath
been [g]said, [y,z]An eye for an eye,
and a tooth for a tooth:[Q]
39 But [a]I say unto you,
[8,b,c]That ye [d,e]resist not evil: but
whosoever shall smite[G] thee on
thy right cheek, turn to him the
other also.
40 And if any man will sue thee
at the law, and take away thy
coat, [b,e]let him have *thy* cloke[G]
also.
41 And whosoever shall compel
thee to go a mile,[G] [d,e]go with him
twain.[G]
42 [f,g]Give to [h]him that asketh
thee, and from him that would
[i]borrow of [j]thee [k]turn not thou
away.
43 ¶ Ye have heard that it hath
been said, [l,m]Thou shalt [n]love[G]
thy [o]neighbour, and [p]hate thine
[q]enemy.[Q]
44 [r]But [a]I say unto you, [n]Love[G]
your [q]enemies, [9]bless them that
[10,s]curse you, [11]do [t]good to them
that hate you, and [u,v]pray for
them which despitefully[G] use you,
and persecute you;[Q]
45 [w]That [x]ye may be the [y]chil-
dren of your [z]Father which is in
[a]heaven: for [b]he maketh his
[c,d]sun to rise on the [e]evil and on
the [f]good, and sendeth [d,g]rain on
the just[G] and on the unjust.[S T]
46 For [h]if ye love[G] them which
love[G] you, what reward have ye?
do not even the [i]publicans[G] the
same?
47 And if ye [j]salute[G] your brethren only, what do ye more *than*
*others*? do not even the [12]publi-
cans[G] so?
48 [13,k]Be [l]ye therefore [m]perfect,
even [n]as your [o,p,q]Father which
is in [a]heaven is [r]perfect.[S T Q]

t *Adultery, defined,* Lev. 20:10.
u *Heart,* Psa. 44:21.

**29**
v Mark 9:43–48.
w *Holiness,* Ex. 39:30.
x *Eye, figurative, of evil pleasure,* Matt. 6:22.
y *Temptation, to be avoided,* Luke 11:4.
z *Self-denial,* Mark 8:34.
a *Commandment, enjoining holiness,* Deut. 8:2.
b *Wicked, punishment of,* Psa. 73:3.
c *Hell, the future abode of the wicked,* Mark 9:43.
7 R. V. causeth thee to stumble,

**30**
d *Holiness,* Ex. 39:30.
e *Temptation, to be avoided,* Luke 11:4.
f *Self-denial,* Mark 8:34.

**31**
g *Law, of Moses, temporary,* Deut. 33:2.
h *Divorce, Mosaic laws concerning,* Matt. 19:7.
i *Wife,* Prov. 5:18.

**32**
j *Jesus, teacher,* Matt. 1:21.
k Matt. 19:9; Mark 10:11, 12; Luke 16:18.
l *Marriage, indissoluble,* Gen. 34:9.
m *Commandment, enjoining fidelity in marriage,* Deut. 8:2.
n *Adultery,* Lev. 20:10.

**33**
o Lev. 19:12; Num. 30:2.
p *Covenant, binding,* Deut. 29:1.

**34**
q *Commandment, forbidding profane swearing,* Deut. 8:2.
r *Heaven, God's dwelling place,* Luke 18:22.
s *Throne, figurative,* 1 Kin. 2:19.

**35**
t *Earth,* Prov. 8:23. u *Footstool, figurative,* 1 Chr. 28:2. v *Jerusalem, oaths taken in name of,* Judg. 19:10. w *God, sovereign,* Gen. 2:2.
**37** x *Conversation, profane, forbidden,* Psa. 50:23.
**38** y *Retaliation,* Deut. 19:19. z *Malice,* Eph. 4:31.

**39**
a *Jesus, teacher,* Matt. 1:21.
b *Revenge, forbidden,* vs. 30–40; Ezek. 25:15.
c *Forgiveness,* Matt. 18:21.
d *Commandment, forbidding resistance,* Deut. 8:2.
e *Meekness, enjoined,* Psa. 45:4.
8 R. V. Resist not him that is evil:

**42**
f *Kindness, enjoined,* Acts 28:2.
g *Liberality, enjoined,* 1 Tim. 6:18.
h *Poor, liberality to,* Prov. 21:13.
i *Borrowing,* Ex. 22:14.
j *Creditor, laws concerning,* Deut. 15:2.
k *Lending,* Deut. 15:2.

**43**
l Lev. 19:18.
m *Law, of Moses, temporary,* Deut. 33:2.
n *Love, of man for man,* 1 John 4:7.
o *Neighbor,* Luke 10:29.
p *Hatred,* Prov. 15:17.
q *Enemy,* Prov. 24:17.

**44**
r Luke 6:27, 28.
s *Persecution, of the righteous,* John 15:20.
t *Good for Evil,* Luke 6:27.
u *Intercession,* Jer. 27:18.
v *Prayer, for enemies, enjoined,* Acts 6:4.
9 R. V. and pray for
10 R. V. persecute
11 R. V. *omits the remainder of this verse.* **45** w Luke 6:35. x *Promise, to those who love enemies,* 2 Cor. 1:20. y *Spiritual Adoption,* Rom. 8:15. z *God, fatherhood of,* Gen. 2:2.—a *Heaven, God's dwelling place,* Luke 18:22. b *God, goodness of,* Gen 2:2. c *Sun,* Josh. 10:12. d *Temporal Blessings, from God,* Psa. 103:2. e *Wicked,* Psa. 73:3. f *Righteous,* Psa. 64:10. g *Rain,* 2 Sam. 1:21. **46** h Luke 6:32. i *Publicans,* Matt. 11:19. **47** j *Salutations,* Luke 1:44. 12 R. V. Gentiles the same? **48** k *Commandment, enjoining perfection,* Deut. 8:2. l *Righteous, described,* Psa. 64:10. m *Perfection,* Heb. 6:1. n *Example, God our,* John 13:15. o *God, holiness of,* Gen. 2:2. p *God, perfection of,* Gen. 2:2. q *God, fatherhood of,* Gen. 2:2. r *Holiness,* Ex. 39:30. 13 R. V. Ye therefore shall be perfect, as your heavenly Father is perfect.

## CHAPTER 6

*The sermon on the mount continued: Alms-giving, 5 prayer, 16 and fasting. 19 Where our treasure is to be laid up. 24 No man can serve two masters. 25 Anxiety about worldly things forbidden. 33 The kingdom of God to be first sought.*

[a,b]TAKE heed that ye do not
[c] your [1,d,e,f]alms before
men, [g]to be seen of them: otherwise ye have no reward of your
Father which is in heaven.
2 [a,b]Therefore [d]when thou [f]do-
est *thine* *alms, do not sound a
[h]trumpet before thee, as the
[i]hypocrites do in the [j]syna-
gogues and in the streets, [g]that
they may have glory of men.
Verily I say unto you, They
[2]have their reward.
3 [b]But [d]when thou [f]doest
*alms, [k]let not thy left hand
know what thy right hand doeth:
4 That thine *alms may be in
secret: and thy [l]Father which
[m]seeth in secret himself [n]shall
reward [o]thee [3]openly.
5 ¶ And when thou prayest,
thou shalt not be as the [i]hypo-
crites *are*: for they love to [p]pray
standing in the [j]synagogues and
in the corners of the streets, [g]that
they may be seen of men. Verily
I say unto you, They [2]have their
reward.
6 But thou, when thou [q,r]pray-
est, [s]enter into thy closet, and
when thou hast shut thy door,
pray to thy [l]Father which is in
secret; [t]and thy Father which
[m]seeth in secret shall reward
[o]thee [3]openly.
7 But when ye [u]pray, [v]use not
vain repetitions, as the [4,w]hea-
then *do*: for they think that they
shall be heard for their much
speaking.
8 Be not ye therefore like unto
[w]them: for your [l,x]Father knoweth what things ye have need of,
before ye ask him.
9 [y]After this manner therefore
[z]pray ye: Our [a]Father which art in
[b]heaven, Hallowed be thy [c]name.
10 [d]Thy kingdom come. [d]Thy
[e]will be done in earth, as *it is* in
[b]heaven.
11 Give us this day our daily
[f]bread.
12 And [g]forgive us our debts,
as we [5,h]forgive our [i]debtors.
13 And lead us not into [j]temp-
tation, but deliver us from [6]evil:
[7]For [d]thine is the kingdom, and
the [k]power, and the [l]glory, for
ever. Amen.
14 For if ye [h,m]forgive [i]men
their trespasses, your heavenly
[a,n]Father [o]will also [g]forgive
you:
15 But if ye [h,p]forgive not men
their trespasses, neither will your
Father forgive your trespasses.
16 ¶ Moreover when ye [q]fast,
[r]be not, as the [s]hypocrites, of a
sad [t]countenance: for they disfigure their faces, [u]that they may
appear unto men to fast. Verily
I say unto you, They have their
reward.
17 But thou, when thou [q]fast-
est, [v]anoint thine head, and
[w]wash thy face;
18 That thou appear not unto
men to [q]fast, but unto thy [a]Fa-
ther which is in secret: and thy
Father, which [x]seeth in secret,
[y]shall reward [z]thee [8]openly.
19 ¶ [a,b]Lay not up for your-

**1**
a *Commandment, warning against ostentation in giving,* Deut. 8:2.
b *Instruction, in religion,* Prov. 23:23.
c *Watchfulness, enjoined, over motives,* Matt. 24:42.
d *Giving, rules for,* 1 Cor. 16:2.
e *Works, good,* 2 Tim. 1:9.
f *Liberality, without ostentation,* 1 Tim. 6:18.
g *Motive,* Psa. 106:8.
1 R. V. righteousness

**2**
h *Trumpet,* Josh. 6:4.
i *Hypocrisy, warnings against,* Jas. 3:17.
j *Synagogue,* Matt. 12:9.
2 R. V. have received

**3**
k *Commandment, enjoining secrecy in giving alms,* Deut. 8:2.

**4**
l *God, fatherhood of,* Gen. 2:2.
m *God, knowledge of,* Gen. 2:2.
n *Promise, to the liberal,* 2 Cor. 1:20.
o *Righteous, promises to,* Psa. 64:10.
3 R. V. *omits* openly.

**5**
p *Prayer, postures in,* Acts 6:4.

**6**
q *Prayer, private, enjoined,* Acts 6:4.
r *Worship,* Gen. 22:5.
s *Commandment, forbidding ostentation in prayer,* Deut. 8:2.
t *Prayer, answer to, promised,* Acts 6:4.

**7**
u *Prayer, profuse, to be avoided,* Acts 6:4.

v *Commandment, enjoining simplicity in worship,* Deut. 8:2. w *Gentiles, ignorant worship of,* vs. 8, 31, 32; Acts 10:45. 4 R. V. Gentiles

**8**
x *God, foreknowledge of,* Gen. 2:2.

**9**
y Luke 11:2-4.
z *Prayer, Lord's prayer,* Acts 6:4.

a *God, fatherhood of,* Gen. 2:2.
b *Heaven, God's dwelling place,* Luke 18:22.
c *God, name of, to be reverenced,* Gen. 2:2.

**10**
d *God, sovereign,* Gen. 2:2.
e *Will of God, supreme rule of duty,* Mark 3:35.

**11**
f *Temporal Blessings, prayer for,* Psa. 103:2.

**12**
g *Sin, forgiveness of,* Rom. 5:12.
h *Forgiveness, of enemies,* Matt. 18:21.
i *Enemy, forgiveness of,* Prov. 24:17.
5 R. V. also have forgiven

**13**
j *Temptation, prayer against being led into,* Luke 11:4.
k *God, power of,* Gen. 2:2.
l *God, glory of,* Gen. 2:2.
6 R. V. the evil one.
7 R. V. *omits the remainder of this verse.*

**14**
m *Charitableness,* Prov. 10:12.
n *God, mercy of,* Gen. 2:2.
o *Promise, to the forgiving,* 2 Cor. 1:20.

**15**
p *Hatred,* Prov. 15:17.

**16**
q *Fasting, precepts concerning,* Zech. 8:19.

r *Commandment, forbidding ostentation in fasting,* vs. 51, 18; Deut. 8:2. s *Hypocrisy, warnings against,* Jas. 3:17. t *Countenance, sad,* Prov. 15:13. u *Motive,* Psa. 106:8. **17** v *Anointing,* Deut. 28:40. w *Ablution,* Judg. 19:21. **18** x *God, knowledge of,* Gen. 2:2. y *Promise, to the righteous,* 2 Cor. 1:20. z *Righteous, promises to,* Psa. 64:10. 8 R. V. *omits* openly. **19**—a *Commandment, forbidding worldliness,* Deut. 8:2. b *Worldliness, admonitions against,* 1 John 2:15.

* **ALMS.** *Solicited by the unfortunate,* John 9:8; Acts 3:2.

**Giving of:** *To be done, with simplicity,* Matt. 6:1-4; *with liberality,* Deut. 15:11; Rom. 12:8; *with cheerfulness,* 2 Cor. 9:7. *Love of God inspires to,* 1 John 3:17.

*Enjoined,* Lev. 25:35; Deut. 15:7-11; Isa. 58:7; Matt. 5:42; Luke 11:41; 2 Cor. 9:5; Gal. 2:10; 1 Tim. 6:18; Heb. 13:16.

*Rewarded,* Deut. 14:28, 29; 15:10; Matt. 19:21; Luke 12:33; 2 Cor. 9:6.

**Instances of giving:** *Zacchæus,* Luke 19:8. *Dorcas,* Acts 9:36. *Cornelius,* Acts 10:2. *The early Christians,* Acts 2:44, 45; 4:34-37; 6:1-3; 11:29, 30; 24:17; Rom. 15:25-28; 1 Cor. 16:1-4; 2 Cor. 8:1-4; 9:1; Heb. 6:10.

See footnote, LIBERALITY, 1 Tim. 6:18.

c *Treasure,* Luke 12:33.
d *Riches, the heart not to be set upon,* Eccl. 4:8.
e *Moth,* Job 4:19.
f *Theft,* Mark 7:22.
9 R. V. consume,

20

g *Commandment, enjoining laying up treasure in heaven,* Deut. 8:2.
h *Heaven, the future home of the righteous,* Luke 18:22.

22

i *Lamp, figurative,* Ex. 27:20.
j *Conscience,* Acts 23:1.
k *Wisdom, spiritual,* Prov. 2:2.
l *Commandment, implied, enjoining an exact conscience,* vs.22–24; Deut. 8:2.
10 R. V. lamp

23

m *Conscience, corrupt,* Acts 23:1.
n *Wisdom, worldly,* Prov. 2:2.
o *Wicked, described,* Psa. 73:3.
p *Darkness, figurative,* Gen. 1:2.
q *Spiritual Blindness,* 2 Cor. 4:4.

24

r *Decision, injunctions concerning,* Isa. 50:7.
s *Servant,* Jer. 2:14.
t *Obedience,* Heb. 5:8.
u *Master,* Col. 4:1.
v Luke 16:9, 11, 13.

25

w *Jesus, teacher,* Matt. 1:21.
x *Faith, enjoined,* Mark 11:22.
y Luke 12:22–31.
z *Commandment, forbidding anxiety,* Deut. 8:2.

a *Anxiety, forbidden,* 1 Pet. 5:7.
b *Worldliness, admonitions*

selves [c,d]treasures upon earth,
where [e]moth and rust doth [9]cor-
rupt,[G] and where thieves break
through and [f]steal:
20 But [g]lay up for yourselves
[c]treasures in [h]heaven, where neither [e]moth nor rust doth [9]cor-
rupt, and where thieves do not
break through nor [f]steal:
21 For where your [c]treasure
is, there will your heart be
also.
22 The [10,i]light[G] of the body is
the [†,j,k]eye: [l]if therefore thine
eye be single,[G] thy whole body
shall be full of light.
23 But if thine [†,m,n]eye be evil,
[o]thy whole body shall be full of
[p,q]darkness. If therefore the
light that is in thee be darkness, how great *is* that darkness!
24 [r]No [s]man can [t]serve two
[u]masters: for either he will hate
the one, and love the other;
or else he will hold to the
one, and despise the other. [u]Ye
cannot serve God and [v]mam-
mon.[G]
25 Therefore [w]I say unto you,
[11,x,y,z]Take[G] no [‡,a]thought[G] for
your life, [b]what ye shall eat, or
what ye shall drink; nor yet for
your body, what ye shall put
on. Is not the life more than
[12]meat,[G] and the body than raiment[G]?
26 Behold the [c]fowls of the air:
for they sow not, neither do they
reap, nor gather into [d]barns;
yet your heavenly [e,f]Father
[g]feedeth them. [h]Are ye not
[13]much better than they?[S T]
27 Which of you by [14,a]taking[G]
thought can add one [i]cubit unto
his stature?
28 And why [15]take[G] ye [a,j]thought
for [k]raiment? Consider the
[‖]lilies of the field, how they
grow; they toil not, neither do
they spin:
29 And yet [l]I say unto you,
That even [m]Sŏl′o-mon in all his
glory was not arrayed[G] like one of
these.[Q]
30 [S] [n]Wherefore, if [e]God so
clothe the [o]grass of the field,
which to day is, and to morrow
is cast into the [p]oven, [h]*shall he*
not much more *clothe* you, O ye
of little faith?
31 [16]Therefore [j]take[G] no
[a]thought, saying, What shall we
eat? or, What shall we drink?
or, Wherewithal shall we be
[k]clothed?
32 (For after all these things do
the [q]Gĕn′tīleş seek:) [h]for your
heavenly [f]Father [r]knoweth that
ye have need of all these
things.[T]
33 But [s]seek [t]ye first the
[u]kingdom [17]of God, and [v]his
righteousness; and [w,x]all these
things shall be added unto
you.[S Q]
34 [16,y]Take[G] therefore no
[z]thought for the morrow[G]: for the
morrow[G] [18]shall take[G] thought
for the things of itself. Sufficient unto the day *is* the evil
thereof.[Q]

g *Temporal Blessings, from God,* Psa. 103:2.
h *Promise, implied, to the righteous,* 2 Cor. 1:20.
13 R. V. of much more value

27

i *Cubit,* Ex. 36:9.
14 R. V. being anxious

28

j *Commandment, forbidding anxiety,* Deut. 8:2.
k *Dress,* Zech. 3:3.
15 R. V. are ye anxious concerning

29

l *Jesus, teacher,* Matt. 1:21.
m *Solomon,* 2 Sam. 12:24.

30

n *Faith, enjoined,* Mark 11:22.
o *Grass,* Isa. 40:7.
p *Oven,* Ex. 8:3.

31

16 R. V. Be not therefore anxious,

32

q *Gentiles,* Acts 10:45.
r *God, knowledge of,* Gen. 2:2.

33

s *Commandment, enjoining seeking the kingdom of God,* Deut. 8:2.
t *Seekers,* Isa. 55:6.
u *Church, called kingdom of God,* Matt. 16:18.
v *God, righteousness of,* Gen. 2:2.
w *Promise, implied, to the righteous,* 2 Cor. 1:20.
x *Righteous, promises to,* Psa. 64:10.

*against,* 1 John 2:15. 11 R. V. Be not anxious 12 R. V. the food, 26 c *Animals, God's care of,* Jer. 27:5. d *Barn,* Prov. 3:10. e *God, providence of,* Gen. 2:2. f *God, fatherhood of,* Gen. 2:2.

17 R. V. *omits* of God, 34 y *Commandment, forbidding anxiety,* Deut. 8:2. z *Anxiety,* 1 Pet. 5:7. 18 R. V. will be anxious for itself.

† **EYE. Figurative:** *Of God's omniscience,* Psa. 11:4; Prov. 15:3. *Of his justice,* Amos 9:8. *Of his holiness,* Hab. 1:13. *Of his care,* Psa. 33:18; 34:15; 1 Pet. 3:12.

*Of the moral state,* Matt. 7:3–5; 13:15, 16; Mark 7:22. *Of moral perception,* Matt. 6:22, 23; Mark 8:18; Luke 10:23; Acts 26:18.

*Of insatiable desire,* Prov. 27:20; Eccl. 1:8; 2 Pet. 2:14. *Of evil pleasure,* Matt. 5:29; 18:9; Mark 9:47.

*Anthropomorphic uses of,* Deut. 11:12; Psa. 33:18; 34:15; Isa. 1:15; 3:8; Hab. 1:13.

See footnote, ANTHROPOMORPHISMS, Gen. 11:5.

‡ **BORROWING TROUBLE.** *Forbidden,* Matt. 6:25–34; John 14:1; Phil. 4:6; 1 Pet. 5:7.

**Instances of:** *Israelites, at the Red Sea,* Ex. 14:10–12; *about water,* Ex. 15:23–25; 17:2, 3; Num. 20:1–13; *about food,* Ex. 16:2, 3; Num. 11:4–33; *when Moses tarried in the mount,* Ex. 32:1; *when the spies brought their adverse report,* Num. 13:28, 29, 31–33; 14:1–4, with vs. 4–12. *Elijah, under the juniper tree and in the cave,* 1 Kin. 19:4–15. *The disciples, as to how the multitude could be fed,* Matt. 14:15; Mark 6:35–37; *in the tempest, when Jesus was asleep in the ship,* Matt. 8:23–26; Mark 4:36–39; Luke 8:22–24; *when Jesus was crucified,* Luke 24:4–9, 24–31, 36–40. *Mary at the sepulchre,* John 20:11–17. *The people in the shipwreck,* Acts 27:22–25, 30–36.

‖ **LILY.** *The principal chapters of the temple ornamented with carvings of,* 1 Kin. 7:19, 22. *Molded on the rim of the molten laver in the temple,* 1 Kin. 7:26; 2 Chr. 4:5. *Lessons of trust gathered from,* Matt. 6:28–30; Luke 12:27. *Lips of the beloved compared to,* Song 5:13.

**1**
*a* Luke 6:37, 38.
*b* *Commandment, forbidding uncharitable judgment,* Deut. 8:2.
*c* *Charitableness, enjoined,* Prov. 10:12.
**2**
*d* Mark 4:24; Luke 6:38.
1 R. V. *omits* again.
**3**
*e* Luke 6:41, 42.
*f* *Commandment, implied, against self-righteousness,* Deut. 8:2.
*g* *Self-righteousness,* Luke 18:11.
*h* *Eye, figurative,* Matt. 6:22.
*i* Luke 6:41, 42.
**4**
2 R. V. cast
**5**
*j* *Hypocrisy, warnings against,* Jas. 3:17.
**6**
*k* *Prudence,* 2 Chr. 2:12.
*l* *Dog, figurative,* 1 Kin. 21:19.
*m* *Wicked, compared to dogs and swine,* Psa. 73:3.
*n* *Pearl, figurative,* Rev. 17:4.
*o* *Swine, figurative,* Lev. 11:7.
**7**
*p* Luke 11:9–13.
*q* *Spiritual Desire,* Psa. 42:1.
*r* *Commandment, enjoining prayer,* Deut. 8:2.
*s* *Prayer, answer to, promised,* Acts 6:4.
*t* *Righteous, promises to,* Psa. 64:10.
*u* *Seekers,* Isa. 55:6.
*v* *Promise, to seekers,* vs. 8–11; 2 Cor. 1–20.
**9**
*w* *Parents, affection of,* 2 Cor. 12:14.
*x* *Bread,* Ezek. 4:13.

## CHAPTER 7

*The sermon on the mount concluded: Rash judgment reproved. 6 Holy things not to be given to dogs. 7 The duty and efficacy of prayer. 13 The strait gate. 15 False prophets. 24 The house built upon a rock, or upon the sand.*

[*,a] [b,c] JUDGE[G] not, that ye be not
judged.[G]
2 For with what judgment[G] ye
judge,[G] ye shall be judged[G]: and
[d]with what measure ye mete,[G] it
shall be measured to you [1]again.
3 [e,f]And [†]why [g]beholdest thou
the mote[G] that is in thy brother's
[h]eye, but considerest not the
[i]beam[G] that is in thine own
eye?
4 [e]Or how wilt thou say to thy
brother, [†,g]Let me [2]pull out the
mote out of thine [h]eye; and, behold, a [i]beam *is* in thine own
eye?
5 [e,f]Thou [j]hypocrite, first cast
out the [i]beam out of thine own
[h]eye; and then shalt thou see
clearly to cast out the mote out
of thy brother's eye.
6 ¶ [k]Give not that which is holy
unto the [l,m]dogs, neither cast ye
your [n]pearls before [o]swine, lest
they trample them under their
feet, and turn again and rend[G]
you.
7 ¶ [p,q,r]Ask, and [s]it shall be
given [t]you; seek, and [s,u,v]ye
shall find; knock, and [s]it shall
be opened unto you:
8 For [v]every one that [q,s]asketh
receiveth; and he that [u]seeketh
findeth; and to him that knocketh [s,u]it shall be opened.
9 Or what man is there of you,
whom if [w]his son ask[G] [x]bread,
will he give him a stone?
10 Or if he ask a [y]fish, will he
give him a [z]serpent?
11 If [a]ye then, being evil, know
how to give good gifts unto your
children, [b]how much more shall
your [c,d]Father which is in heav-
en give good things to them that
ask him? [S T]
12 [e,f]Therefore[G] all things
[g]whatsoever ye would that men
should do to you, [h]do ye even so
to [i]them: for this is the [j]law and
the prophets.
13 ¶ [k,l]Enter ye in at the [3]strait[G]
[m]gate: for wide *is* the gate, and
broad *is* the [n]way, that leadeth
to [o]destruction, and [p]many there
be which go in thereat:
14 [4]Because strait[G] *is* the [m]gate,
and [5]narrow[G] *is* the [n]way,[G] which
leadeth unto life, and [q]few there
be that find it.
15 ¶ [r,s]Beware of false [t]proph-
ets, which come to you in
[u]sheep's clothing,[G] but inwardly
they are [v]ravening[G] [w]wolves.[Q]
16 [x,y]Ye[S] shall know [t]them by
their fruits.[G] Do men gather
[z]grapes of [a,b]thorns, or [c]figs of
[b,d]thistles?
17 Even so every [e]good tree
bringeth forth [f]good fruit; but a
[b,g,h]corrupt[G] tree bringeth forth
[i]evil fruit.
18 A [e]good tree cannot bring
forth [i]evil fruit, neither *can* a
[b,g,h]corrupt[G] tree bring forth
[f]good fruit. [S]
19 Every tree that [‡]bringeth

**16** *x* Luke 6:43, 44. *y* *Nature, laws of, uniform in operation,* Jas. 3:12. *z* *Grape,* Lev. 25:5.—*a* *Thorn,* Hos. 2:6. *b* *Wicked, described,* Psa. 73:3. *c* *Fig Tree, fruit of,* Luke 13:6. *d* *Thistle,* Hos. 10:8. **17** *e* *Righteous, described,* Psa. 64:10. *f* *Righteousness,* Psa. 15:2. *g* *False Teachers,* 2 Pet. 2:1. *h* *Depravity,* Job 15:14. *i* *Sin,* Rom. 5:12.

**10**
*y* *Fish,* Matt. 17:27.
*z* *Serpent,* Num. 21:6.
**11**
*a* *Parents, affection of,* 2 Cor. 12:14.
*b* *Promise, of answer to prayer,* 2 Cor. 1:20.
*c* *God, fatherhood of,* Gen. 2:2.
*d* *God, goodness of,* Gen. 2:2.
**12**
*e* Luke 6:31.
*f* *Love, of man for man,* 1 John 4:7.
*g* *Golden Rule,* Luke 6:31.
*h* *Duty, of man to man,* Eccl. 12:13.
*i* *Neighbor, duty to,* Luke 10:29.
*j* *Law, of Moses,* Deut. 33:2.
**13**
*k* Luke 13:24.
*l* *Commandment, enjoining repentance,* Deut. 8:2.
*m* *Gates, figurative,* Deut. 3:5.
*n* *Highways, figurative,* Deut. 2:27.
*o* *Spiritual Death,* 1 John 3:14.
*p* *Wicked, punishment of,* Psa. 73:3.
3 R. V. narrow
**14**
*q* *Righteous,* Psa. 64:10.
4 R. V. For narrow is
5 R. V. straitened
**15**
*r* *Commandment, warning against false teachers,* Deut. 8:2.
*s* *Watchfulness,* Matt. 24:42.
*t* *False Teachers, admonitions against,* 2 Pet. 2:1.
*u* *Hypocrisy,* Jas. 3:17.
*v* *Wicked, described,* Psa. 73:3.
*w* *Wolf, figurative,* Jer. 5:6.

* **UNCHARITABLENESS,** Isa. 29:21. *Admonitions against,* Matt. 7:1–5; Luke 6:37–42; 12:57; John 7:24; 8:7; Rom. 2:1; 1 Cor. 4:3–5, 7. *Forbidden,* Jas. 4:11, 12.

**Instances of:** *The Israelites toward Moses, charging him with having made them abhorred by the Egyptians,* Ex. 5:21; *charging him with bringing them out of Egypt to die,* Ex. 14: 11, 12.

*Moses toward the two and a half tribes,* Num. 32:1–33. *The tribes west of the Jordan toward the two and a half tribes,* Josh. 22:11–31. *Eli toward Hannah,* 1 Sam. 1:14–17.

*Eliab toward David, charging him with presumption, when he offered to fight Goliath,* 1 Sam. 17:28. *Princes of Ammon toward David, when he sent commissioners to convey his sympathy to Hanun,* 2 Sam. 10:3; 1 Chr. 19:3. *Bildad toward Job,* Job chapters 18, 25. *Eliphaz toward Job,* Job chapters 15, 22. *Zophar toward Job,* Job chapters 11, 20. *The Jews, charging Paul with teaching contrary to the law and against the temple,* Acts 21:28.

† **INCONSISTENCY,** Matt.7:3–5; 23:3,4; Rom.2:1,21–23.

**Instances of:** *Jehu,* 2 Kin. 10:16–31. *The Jews, in oppressing the poor,* Neh. 5:8, 9; *in accusing Jesus of violating the Sabbath,* John 7:22, 23. *Peter and the other disciples, in requiring of the Gentiles that which they did not practice themselves,* Gal. 2:11–14.

‡ **UNFRUITFULNESS,** Isa. 5:2; Matt. 3:10 (with Luke 3:9); 7:19; 13:3–7 (with Mark 4:3–7, 14–19; Luke 8: 4–14); 21:19, 20 (with Mark 11:13); Luke 3:9; 13:6–9; John 15:2, 4, 6.

See footnote, UNFAITHFULNESS, Luke 16:11.

not forth good fruit is [j]hewn
down, and [j]cast into the fire.
20 Wherefore by their fruits
ye shall know them.
21 ¶ [T] [k]Not every one that
[l]saith unto me, [m]Lord, Lord,
shall enter into the [n]kingdom
of heaven; but he that [o]doeth
the [p]will of my Father which
is in heaven.[S]
22 Many will say to me
in [q]that day, Lord, Lord,
[r]have we not prophesied[G] in
thy name? and in thy name
have cast out devils[G]? and in
thy name done many [6]wonderful [s]works?[T Q]
23 And then will I profess[G] unto
them, I never knew[G] you: [j,t]depart
from me, ye that work
iniquity.[Q]
24 ¶ Therefore [e,u,v]whosoever
[w]heareth these [x]sayings of
mine, and [o,y]doeth them, [z]I will
[a]liken him unto a [b]wise man,
which built his house upon a
[c]rock:
25 And the [d,e]rain descended,
and the floods came, and the
[f]winds blew, and beat upon that
house; and it fell not: for it was
founded upon a [c]rock.
26 And every one that heareth
these [g]sayings of mine,
and [h]doeth them not, shall be
likened unto a [i]foolish man,
which built his house upon the
sand:[T]
27 And the [d,e]rain descended,
and the floods came, and the
[f]winds blew, and beat upon that
house; and it [j]fell: and great was
the fall of it.[Q]
28 ¶ And it came to pass, when
[k]Jē'ṣus had ended these sayings,
the [7]people were astonished at
his doctrine[G]:
29 For [k]he taught them as *one*
having authority, and not as the
[l]scribes.[T]

**19**
*j Wicked, punishment of*, Psa. 73:3.
**21**
*k Delusion, of those who trust in the form of godliness*, 2 Thess. 2:11.
*l Confession of Christ*, Luke 12:8.
*m Wicked, prayer of*, Psa. 73:3.
*n Kingdom of Heaven*, Matt. 13:24.
*o Obedience*, Heb. 5:8.
*p Will of God*, Mark 3:35.
**22**
*q Judgment*, 2 Pet. 3:7.
*r Self-righteousness*, Luke 18:11.
*s Miracles, alleged*, Luke 23:8.
6 R. V. mighty
**23**
*t Sin, separates from God*, Rom. 5:12.
**24**
u Luke 6:47–49.
*v Hearers*, Rom. 2:13.
*w Wisdom, spiritual*, Prov. 2:2.
*x Doctrines of Jesus*, John 7:16.
*y Faith in Christ*, John 6:69.
*z Jesus, parables of*, Matt. 1:21.

*a Parables, of Jesus*, Ezek. 20:49.
*b Wisdom, worldly*, Prov. 2:2.
*c Rock*, Psa. 78:15.
**25**
*d Rain*, 2 Sam. 1:21.
*e Temptation, a test*, Luke 11:4.
*f Wind, figurative of adversity*, Job 37:17.
**26**
*g Doctrines of Jesus*, John 7:16.
*h Jesus, rejected*, Matt. 1:21.
*i Fool*, Prov. 18:2.
**27**
*j Wicked, punishment of*, Psa. 73:3.
**28**
*k Jesus, teacher*, Matt. 1:21.
7 R. V. multitudes
**29**
*l Scribe, instructor in the law*, 1 Kin. 4:3.

## CHAPTER 8

*A leper cleansed.* 5 *The healing of the centurion's servant,* 14 *also of Peter's wife's mother and many others.* 18 *How Jesus must be followed.* 23 *He stills the tempest;* 28 *and heals two men possessed with devils.* 31 *The devils enter into a herd of swine.*

WHEN[T S] he was come down
from the mountain, [a]great
multitudes[G] followed him.
2 [b]And[T], behold, there came a
[c]leper and [d]worshipped him,
saying, [e]Lord, if thou wilt, thou
canst make me clean.
3 And [f,g]Jē'ṣus put forth *his*
hand, and touched him, saying,
I will; be thou clean. And
immediately his [c,h]leprosy was
cleansed.
4 And Jē'ṣus saith unto him,
[i]See thou tell no man; but go thy
way, [j]shew thyself to the priest,
and [k]offer the gift that Mō'ṣeṣ
commanded, for a testimony unto
them.[S Q]
5 ¶ [l]And when Jē'ṣus was entered
into [m]Cā-pēr'na-ŭm, there
[e]came unto him a *centurion,
[n]beseeching him,
6 And [n]saying, Lord, my [o]servant
lieth [1]at home sick of the
[p]palsy[G], grievously[G] tormented.
7 And Jē'ṣus saith unto him, [q]I
will come and heal him.
8 The *centurion answered and
said, Lord, I am [r]not worthy that
thou shouldest come under my
roof: but speak the word only,
and my [o]servant shall be healed.
9 For I am a man under authority,
having [s]soldiers under
me: and I say to this *man*, Go,
and he goeth; and to another,
Come, and he cometh; and to
my servant, Do this, and he doeth
*it*.
10 [S]When Jē'ṣus heard *it*, he
marvelled, and said to them that
followed, Verily, I say unto you,
I have not found so great [e]faith,
no, not in Iṣ'ra-el.

**1**
*a Popularity of Jesus*, John 6:15.
**2**
b Mark 1:40–44; Luke 5:12–14.
*c Leprosy*, Lev. 13:2.
*d Jesus, worship of*, Matt. 1:21.
*e Faith in Christ*, John 6:69.
**3**
*f Jesus, compassion of*, Matt. 1:21.
*g Jesus, miracles of*, Matt. 1:21.
*h Miracles, of Jesus*, Luke 23:8.
**4**
*i Prudence*, 2 Chr. 2:12.
j Lev. 14:2.
*k Commandment, enjoining obedience*, Deut. 8:2.
**5**
l Luke 7:1–10.
*m Capernaum*, Luke 4:31.
*n Mediation*, Gal. 3.19.
**6**
*o Servant, kindness to*, Jer. 2:14.
*p Paralysis*, Mark 2:3.
1 R. V. in the house
**7**
*q Prayer, answered*, Acts 6:4.
**8**
*r Humility, exemplified*, Prov. 22:4.
**9**
*s Armies, Roman*, Deut. 11:4.

***CENTURION.** *A commander of one hundred soldiers*, Mark 15:44, 45; Acts 21:32; 22:25, 26; 23:17, 23; 24:23. *Of Capernaum, comes to Jesus in behalf of his servant*, Matt. 8:5–13; Luke 7:1–10. *In charge of the soldiers who crucified Jesus*, Matt. 27:54; Mark 15:39; Luke 23:47. *Of Cæsarea*, Acts 10:1–33. *Of the cohort of Augustus*, Acts 27:43.

11 And I say unto you, That
[l]many shall come from the east
and west, and shall sit down
with [u]Ā'brā-hăm, and [v]Ī'ṣaac,
and [w]Jā'cob, in the [x, y]kingdom
of heaven.[Q]
12 But the [z]children of the
kingdom shall be [a]cast out into
[b]outer [c]darkness: there shall be
[d, e]weeping and [f]gnashing of
teeth.
13 And [g]Jē'ṣus said unto the
*centurion, Go thy way; and
as thou hast [h]believed, *so* be it
done unto thee. And his [i]serv-
ant was [j, k]healed in the selfsame[G]
hour.
14 ¶ [l]And when Jē'ṣus was
come into [m]Pē'tēr's house, he
saw his [n]wife's mother [2]laid, and
sick of a [o]fever.
15 And he touched her hand,
and the fever [i]left her: and
she arose, and ministered[G] unto
[3]them.
16 ¶ When the even[G] was come,
they brought unto him many
that were [p]possessed with devils[G]: and he [q]cast out the spirits
with *his* word, and [k]healed all
that were [p]sick:
17 That [r]it might be fulfilled[G]
which was spoken by [s]Ē-ṣā'ias
the [t]prophet, saying, [u, v, w]Him-
self took our [p]infirmities, and
bare *our* sicknesses.[S Q T]
18 ¶ Now when Jē'ṣus saw
[x]great multitudes about him, he
gave commandment to depart
unto the other side.
19 And [y]a certain [z]scribe came,
and said unto him, [a]Master,[G] [b]I
will follow thee whithersoever
thou goest.
20 And Jē'ṣus saith unto him,
[c]The [d]foxes have holes, and the
[e]birds of the air *have* nests; but
the Son of man hath not where
to lay *his* head.

21 And another of his disciples
said unto him, Lord, [f, g]suffer[G]
me first to go and [h]bury my
father.[Q]
22 But Jē'ṣus said unto him,
[i, j]Follow me; and let the dead
bury [4]their dead.
23 ¶[S T] And when he was entered
into a [k]ship, his [l]disciples followed him,
24 And, behold[G], there arose a
great [†, m]tempest in the [n]sea, insomuch that the [k]ship was covered with the waves: but he was
asleep.[T]
25 And his [l]disciples came to
*him*, and awoke him, [o]saying,
Lord, save us: [p, q]we perish[G].
26 And he saith unto them,
Why are ye [r]fearful, O ye of [p]lit-
tle [s]faith? Then [t]he arose, and
rebuked the winds and the sea;
and [†, u]there was a great calm.
27 But the [l]men marvelled, saying, What manner of man is
this, that even the winds and
the sea [t, u]obey [v]him!
28 ¶ [w]And when he was come
to the other side into the country
of the [5]Gēr'gē-sēneṣ, there met
him two possessed with [x]devils[G],
coming out of the [y]tombs, exceeding fierce, so that no man
[6]might pass by that way.
29 And, behold, [x]they cried
out, saying, What have we to do
with thee, [7, z]Jē'ṣus, thou Son of
God? art thou come hither to
torment us before the time?[T Q]
30 And there was a good way
off from them an herd of many
[a]swine feeding,
31 So the [b]devils[G] besought[G] him,
saying, If thou cast us out, suffer[G]
us to go away into the herd of
[a]swine.
32 And he said unto them, Go.
And [c]when they were come out,
they went into the herd of
[d]swine: and, behold, the whole
herd of swine ran violently down

**11**
*t Church, prophecies concerning its prosperity,* Matt. 16:18.
*u Abraham,* Gen. 17:5.
*v Isaac,* Gen. 21:3.
*w Jacob,* Gen. 27:11.
*x Kingdom of Heaven,* Matt. 13:24.
*y Jesus, kingdom of,* Matt. 1:21.
*z Wicked, described,* Psa. 73:3
**12**
*a Wicked, punishment of,* Psa. 73:3.

*b Hell, future abode of the wicked,* Mark 9:43.
*c Darkness, figurative,* Gen. 1:2.
*d Weeping, in perdition,* Ezra 3:13.
*e Sorrow, of the lost,* Matt. 13:42.
*f Gnashing of Teeth,* Job 16:9.
**13**
*g Jesus, miracles of,* Matt. 1:21.
*h Faith in Christ,* John 6:69.
*i Servant,* Jer. 2:14.
*j Miracles, of Jesus,* Luke 23:8.
*k Healing, by Jesus,* Acts 4:22.
**14**
*l* Mark 1:29–34; Luke 4:38–41.
*m Peter,* Mark 5:37.
*n Minister, marriage of,* Rom. 15:16.
*o Fever,* Deut. 28:22.
2 R. V. lying
**15**
3 R. V. him.
**16**
*p Afflictions,* Psa. 34:19.
*q Demons, cast out by Jesus,* Matt. 4:24.
**17**
*r Prophecies, concerning the Messiah and their fulfillment,* Gen. 12:3.
*s* Or, *Isaiah,* Isa. 1:1.
*t Prophets,* Isa. 3:2.
*u* Isa. 53:4.
*v Jesus, love of,* Matt. 1:21.
*w Jesus, prophecies concerning,* Matt. 1:21.
**18**
*x Popularity of Jesus,* John 6:15. **19** *y* Luke 9:57–60. *z Scribe,* 1 Kin. 4:3. —*a Master,* John 13:13. *b Zeal, without knowledge,* 2 Cor. 7:11. **20** *c* Luke 9:58. *d Fox,* Psa. 63:10. *e Birds,* Eccl. 12:4.

**21**
*f Procrastination,* Acts 24:25.
*g Excuses,* Luke 14:18.
*h Burial,* Acts 8:2.
**22**
*i Self-denial,* Mark 8:34.
*j Decision, injunctions concerning,* Isa. 50:7.
4 R. V. their own dead.
**23**
*k Ship,* 2 Chr. 8:18.
*l Disciple,* Matt. 9:14.
**24**
*m Meteorology,* Matt. 16:2.
*n Sea of Galilee,* Matt. 4:18.
**25**
*o Adversity, prayer in,* Psa. 10:6.
*p Doubting,* Rom. 14:23.
*q Borrowing Trouble,* Matt. 6:25.
**26**
*r Cowardice, instances of,* Lev. 26:36.
*s Faith, trial of,* Mark 11:22.
*t Jesus, miracles of,* Matt. 1:21.
*u Miracles, of Jesus,* Luke 23:8.
**27**
*v Jesus, power of,* Matt. 1:21.
**28**
*w* Mark 5:1–20; Luke 8:26–39.
*x Demons,* Matt. 4:24.
*y Burying Places, demoniacs dwelt in,* Gen. 23:4.
5 R. V. Gadarenes,
6 R. V. could
**29**
*z Jesus, divine sonship of,* Matt. 1:21.
7 R. V. *omits* Jesus,

**30**
*a Swine,* Lev. 11:7.
**31**
*b Demons,* Matt. 4:24.
**32**
*c Miracles, of Jesus,* Luke 23:8.
*d Animals, possessed of devils,* Jer. 27:5.

† **TEMPEST STILLED,** Matt. 8:23–27; Mark 4:35–41; Luke 8:22–25.

**33**
8 R. V. them that were

**34**
*e Jesus, rejected,* Matt. 1:21.

**1**
*a Capernaum,* Luke 4:31.

**2**
*b Faith in Christ, exemplified,* John 6:69.
*c Paralysis,* Mark 2:3.
*d Jesus, power of, to forgive sins,* Matt. 1:21.
*e Sin, forgiveness of,* Rom. 5:12.
1 R. V. are forgiven.

**3**
*f Scribe,* 1 Kin. 4:3.
*g Blasphemy, false accusations of,* 2 Sam. 12:14.

**4**
*h Jesus, omniscience of,* Matt. 1:21.

**6**
*i Miracles, design of,* Luke 23:8.
*j Healing, by Jesus,* Acts 4:22.

**7**
*k Miracles, of Jesus,* Luke 23:8.

**8**
*l Jesus, received,* Matt. 1:21.
*m Glorifying God,* Luke 5:25.
2 R. V. were afraid,

a steep place into the sea, and
perished in the waters.
33 And they that kept them
fled, and went their ways into
the city, and told every thing,
and what was befallen to [8]the
possessed of the [b]devils.
34 And, behold, the whole city
came out to meet Jē'ṣus: and
when they saw him, they besought [e]*him* that he would depart out of their coasts.

## CHAPTER 9

*Jesus heals one sick of the palsy; 9 calls Matthew; 10 eats with publicans and sinners; 14 and justifies his disciples in not fasting. 18 A ruler entreats him. 20 He heals an issue of blood; 23 raises the ruler's daughter; 27 gives sight to two blind men; 32 heals a dumb man possessed with a devil; 36 and has compassion on the multitude.*

AND he entered into a ship,
and passed over, and came
into his own [a]city.
2 And, behold, they [b]brought
to him a man sick of the [c]palsy,
lying on a bed: and [d]Jē'ṣus seeing their [b]faith said unto the sick
of the palsy; Son, be of good
cheer; thy sins be [1,e]forgiven
thee.
3 And, behold, certain of the
[f]scribes said within themselves,
This *man* [g]blasphemeth.
4 And Jē'ṣus [h]knowing their
thoughts said, Wherefore think
ye evil in your hearts?
5 For whether is easier, to say,
*Thy* sins be forgiven thee; or to
say, Arise, and walk?
6 But [i]that ye may know that
the Son of man hath [j]power on
earth to [e]forgive sins, (then
saith he to the sick of the [c]pal-
sy,) Arise, take up thy bed, and
go unto thine house.
7 And [j,k]he arose, and departed
to his house.
8 [l]But when the multitudes saw
*it,* they [2]marvelled, and [m]glori-
fied God, which had given such
power unto men.
9 ¶ And as Jē'ṣus passed forth
from thence, he saw a man,
named *Măt'thew, sitting at
the [3]receipt of custom: and [n]he
saith unto [o]him, [p,q]Follow me.
And [r,s,t]he arose, and followed
him.
10 ¶ [u]And it came to pass,
as [v]Jē'ṣus sat at meat in the
house, behold, many [w]publicans
and sinners came and sat down
with him and his disciples.
11 And when the [x]Phăr'ĭ-seeṣ
saw *it,* [y,z]they said unto his disciples, Why eateth your [4]Master
with [w]publicans and sinners?
12 But when Jē'ṣus heard *that,*
he said unto them, They that be
[a,b]whole need not a physician,
but they that are sick.
13 But go ye and learn what
*that* meaneth, [c]I will have
[d,e]mercy, and not [f]sacrifice:
for [g]I am not come to call the
[a,b]righteous, but sinners [5]to [h]re-
pentance.
14 ¶ Then came to him the
†disciples of [i]Jŏhn, saying, Why
do we and the [j]Phăr'ĭ-seeṣ [k]fast
oft, but thy disciples fast not?
15 And Jē'ṣus said unto them,
Can the children of the bride-
chamber mourn, as long as the
[l]bridegroom is with them? but
the days will come, when the
bridegroom shall be taken from
them, and then shall they [k]fast.
16 [m,n]No man putteth a piece
of [6]new cloth unto an old garment, for that which is put in to
fill it up taketh from the garment, and the rent is made
worse.
17 [n,o]Neither do men put new
[p]wine into old [7,q]bottles: else the

**9**
*n Jesus, calls Matthew,* Matt. 1:21.
*o Apostles, selection of,* Luke 6:13.
*p Minister, call of,* Rom. 15:16.
*q Call, to special religious duty,* Phil. 3:14.
*r Decision, instances of,* Isa. 50:7.
*s Obedience, instances of,* Heb. 5:8.
*t Renunciation, of business for Christ,* Luke 5:11.
3 R. V. place of toll:

**10**
*u* Mark 2:15–20; Luke 5:29–35.
*v Jesus, benevolence of,* Matt. 1:21.
*w Publicans,* Matt. 11:19.

**11**
*x Pharisees,* Matt. 15:12.
*y Bigotry,* Isa. 65:5.
*z Self-righteousness,* Luke 18:11.
4 Am. R. V. *marg.* teacher

**12**
*a Self-righteousness,* Luke 18: 11.
*b Irony,* Mark 12:14.

**13**
*c* Hos. 6:6.
*d Mercy,* Deut. 5:10.
*e Obedience, better than sacrifice,* 1 Sam. 15:22.
*f Offerings, unavailing without piety,* Lev. 6:17.
*g Jesus, mission of,* Matt. 1:21.
*h Repentance,* Mark 1:4.
5 R. V. *omits* to repentance

**14**
*i John the Baptist,* Luke 1:63.
*j Pharisees,* Matt. 15:12.
*k Fasting,* Zech. 8:19.

**15**
*l Jesus, names of,* Matt. 1:21.

**16**
*m* Mark 2:21; Luke 5:36.

*n Parables, of Jesus,* Ezek. 20:49. 6 R.V. undressed **17** *o* Mark 2:22; Luke 5:37–39. *p Wine,* Prov. 23:31. *q Bottle,* Gen. 21:14. 7 R. V. wine-skins:

* **MATTHEW** (*a gift of Jehovah*), called also LEVI. *A receiver of customs,* Matt. 9:9. *Becomes a disciple of Jesus,* Matt. 9:9, 10; 10:3; Mark 2:14, 15; 3:18; Luke 5:27–29; 6:15; Acts 1:13.

†**DISCIPLES,** a name given to the followers of any teacher. *Of John the Baptist,* Matt. 9:14.
**Of Jesus,** Matt. 10:1; 20:17; Acts 9:26; 14:20; 21:4. *Given power to heal.* Matt. 10:1; Mark 6:6–13, 30; Luke 9:1–6.

8 R. V. skins burst,
9 R. V. skins
10 R. V. fresh wine-skins,

**18**
*r* *Rulers*, Ex. 18:21.
*s* Mark 5:22–43; Luke 8:41–56.
*t* *Jesus, worship of*, Matt. 1:21.
*u* *Faith in Christ, instances of*, John 6:69.

**20**
*v* *Disease*, Ex. 15:26.
*w* *Menstruation*, Ezek. 18:6.

**22**
*x* *Jesus, miracles of*. Matt. 1:21.
*y* *Miracles, of Jesus*, Luke 23:8.

**23**
*z* *Music*, 2 Chr. 5:13.

*a* *Mourning*, Lam. 2:5.
11 R. V. flute-players,

**24**
*b* *Death*, Num. 23:10.
*c* *Sleep, a symbol of death*, Psa. 127:2.

**25**
*d* *Healing, by Jesus*, Acts 4:22.
*e* *Children, miracles in behalf of*, Mark 10:14.
*f* *Miracles, of Jesus*, Luke 23:8.

**26**
*g* *Fame of Jesus*, Luke 5:15.

**27**
*h* *Blindness*, 2 Kin. 6:18.
*i* Mark 10:46.

[8]bottles break, and the wine runneth out, and the [9]bottles perish:[C]
but they put new wine into [10]new
bottles, and both are preserved.
18 ¶ [S]While he spake these
things unto them, behold, there
came a certain [r,s]ruler, and
[t]worshipped him, saying, My
daughter is even now dead: but
[u]come and lay thy hand upon
her, and she shall live.
19 And Jē′sus arose, and followed him, and *so did* his ‖disciples.
20 ¶ And, behold, a woman,
which was [v]diseased with an
‡,[w]issue[C] of blood twelve years,
came behind *him*, and touched
the hem of his garment:[Q]
21 For she said within herself,
[u]If I may but touch his garment,
I shall be whole.[C]
22 But [x]Jē′sus turned him
about, and when he saw her, he
said, Daughter, be of good comfort; thy [u]faith hath made thee
whole.[C] And the woman [x,y]was
made whole[C] from that hour.[S]
23 And when Jē′sus came into
the [r,s]ruler's house, and saw the
[11,z]minstrels[C] and the people
[a]making a noise,
24 He said unto them, Give
place: for the maid is not [b]dead,
but [c]sleepeth. And they laughed
him to scorn.[C]
25 But when the people were
put forth,[C] [d]he went in, and took
her by the hand, and the [e]maid
[f]arose.
26 And the [g]fame hereof went
abroad into all that land.
27 ¶ [S]And when Jē′sus departed
thence, two [h,i]blind men followed him, crying, and saying,
*Thou* [j]son of [k]Dā′vid, have
mercy on us.
28 And when he was come into the house, the [h,i]blind men
[l]came to him: and Jē′sus saith
unto them, Believe ye that I am
able to do this? They said unto
him, [l]Yea, Lord.
29 Then touched [d]he their eyes,
saying, According to your [l]faith
be it unto you.[S]
30 And their eyes were [f]opened;
and Jē′sus [12]straitly[C] [m]charged[C]
them, saying, See *that* no man
know *it*.
31 But they, when they were
departed, [n]spread abroad his
[g]fame[C] in all that country.
32 ¶ As they went out, behold,
they brought to him a [o]dumb
man possessed with a [p]devil.[C]
33 And when the [p]devil[C] was
[f,q]cast out, the [o]dumb [f]spake:
and the multitudes marvelled,
saying, It was never so seen in
Ĭṣ′ra-el.
34 But the [r]Phăr′ĭ-seeṣ [s]said,
He casteth out devils[C] through
the [t]prince of the devils.[C S]
35 ¶ And [u,v]Jē′sus went about
all the cities and villages, [w]teaching in their [x]synagogues, and
‖preaching the [y]gospel of the
kingdom, and [z]healing [13]every
[a]sickness and every [b]disease
among the people.
36 But when he saw the multitudes, [c,d]he was moved with
compassion[C] on them, because
they [14]fainted,[C] and were scattered abroad, as [e]sheep having
no [f]shepherd.[Q]
37 Then saith he unto his †dis-

*j* *Jesus, names of*, Matt. 1:21.
*k* *David, Jesus called son of*, 1 Sam. 16:13.

**28**
*l* *Faith in Christ, exemplified*, John 6:69.

**30**
*m* *Prudence, instances of*, 2 Chr. 2:12.
12 R. V. strictly

**31**
*n* *Zeal, instances of*, 2 Cor. 7:11.

**32**
*o* *Dumb*, Ex. 4:11.
*p* *Demons, possession by*, Matt. 4:24.

**33**
*q* *Demons, cast out by Jesus*, Matt. 4:24.

**34**
*r* *Pharisees*, Matt. 15:12.
*s* *False Accusation*, 2 Tim. 3:3.
*t* *Satan*, Matt. 4:10.

**35**
*u* *Jesus, teacher*, Matt. 1:21.
*v* *Jesus, zeal of*, Matt. 1:21.
*w* *Instruction, in religion*, Prov. 23:23.
*x* *Synagogue, Scriptures read and expounded in*, Matt. 12:9.
*y* *Gospel*, Mark 13:10.
*z* *Healing, by Jesus*, Acts 4:22.

*a* *Afflictions*, Psa. 34:19.
*b* *Disease*, Ex. 15:26.
13 R. V. all manner of disease and all manner of sickness.

**36**
*c* *Jesus, compassion of*, Matt. 1:21.
*d* *Jesus, love of*, Matt. 1:21.
*e* *Sheep, figurative, of lost sinners*, Deut. 32:14.
*f* *Shepherd, figurative*, Jer. 31:10.
14 R. V. were distressed

10. *The seventy, sent forth*, Luke 10:1. *Rulers become*, John 12:42. *Priests become*, Acts 6:7. *First called Christians at Antioch*, Acts 11:26. See footnote, APOSTLES, Luke 6:13.

‡ **HEMORRHAGE.** *A woman suffers twelve years from*, Matt. 9:20–22; Mark 5:25–29; Luke 8:43–48.

See footnote, MENSTRUATION, Ezek. 18:6.

‖ **PREACHING,** the act of exhorting, prophesying, reproving, teaching. *Noah called preacher*, 2 Pet. 2:5; *and Solomon*, Ecc. 1:1. *Sitting while*, Matt. 5:1; Luke 4:20; 5:3.

*Appointed and practiced by Jesus as the method of promulgating the gospel*, Matt. 4:17; 11:1; Mark 16:15, 20; Luke 4:18, 19, 43. *Grave responsibility of*, 2 Cor. 2:14–17.

*Should edify*, 1 Cor. 14:1–25. *Should be skillful*, 2 Tim. 2:15. *Should be, in power*, 1 Thess. 1:5; *with boldness*, Acts 13:46; 2 Cor. 3:12; *not with worldly wisdom*, 1 Cor. 1:17–31; 2:1–8, 12, 13; *not with deceit or flattery*, 1 Thess. 2:3–6.

*Repentance, the subject, of John the Baptist's*, Matt. 3:2; Mark 1:4, 15; Luke 3:3; *of Christ's*, Matt. 4:17; Mark 1:15; *of the apostles'*, Mark 6:12. *The Gospel of the Kingdom of God, the subject of Christ's*, Mark 1:14, 15; 2:2; Luke 8:1. *Christ crucified and risen, the burden of Paul's*, Acts 17:3.

*Jesus preaches to spirits in prison*, 1 Pet. 3:19; 4:9; compare Eph. 4:9.

**Effective:** *By Azariah*, 2 Chr. 15:1–15. *By Jonah*, Jonah 3. *By Haggai*, Hag. 1:7–12. *By Peter*, Acts 2:14–41. *By Philip*, Acts 8:5–12, 27–38. *By Paul*, Acts 9:20–22; 13:16–43.

**Impenitence under:** *Asa*, 2 Chr. 16:7–10. *The Jews*, Acts 13:46.

ciples, The [g]harvest truly *is*
plenteous, but the labourers *are*
few;
38 [h]Pray ye therefore the Lord
of the [g]harvest, that he will send
forth labourers into his harvest.

## CHAPTER 10

*Jesus gives the twelve power to work miracles. 5 He sends them forth to preach, and gives them a charge, 16 Comforts them against persecutions. 40 A blessing promised to those that receive them.*

AND when he had [a]called unto *him* his twelve [b]dis-
ciples, [c]he gave them [1,d]power
*against* [e]unclean spirits, to cast
them out, and to heal all manner
of [f]sickness and all manner of
[g]disease.
2 Now the names of the twelve
[h]apostles are these; The first,
Sī′mon, who is called [i]Pē′tĕr,
and [j]Ăn′drew his brother;
[k]Jāmeș *the son* of [l]Zĕb′e-dee,
and [m]Jŏhn his brother;
3 [n]Phĭl′ĭp, and [o]Bär-thŏl′o-
mew; [p]Thŏm′as, and [q]Măt′thew
the [r]publican; *Jāmeș *the son*
of [s]Ăl-phæ′us, and [2]Lĕb-bæ′us,
whose surname was [t]Thăd-
dæ′us;
4 [u]Sī′mon the Cā′năan-īte, and
[v]Jū′das Ĭs-căr′ĭ-ot, who also
[w]betrayed him.
5 [x]These twelve [y]Jē′șus sent
forth, and [3,z]commanded them,
saying, Go not into the way of
the [a]Gĕn′tīleș, and into *any* city
of the [b]Să-măr′ĭ-tanș enter ye
not:
6 But go rather to the lost
[c]sheep of the [d]house of Ĭș′ra-el.
7 And as [e]ye go, [f]preach, saying, The [g,h]kingdom of heaven
is at hand.
8 [i,j,k]Heal the [l]sick, cleanse the
[m]lepers, raise the [n]dead, cast out
[o]devils: freely ye have received,
freely give.
9 [p]Provide neither [q]gold, nor [r]sil-
ver, nor [s]brass in your †purses.
10 [4]Nor scrip for *your* journey, neither two coats, neither
shoes, nor [5]yet staves: for the
[6,t,u,v]workman is worthy of his
[7,w]meat.
11 And into whatsoever city or
[8]town ye shall enter, [9]enquire
who in it is worthy; and [x]there
abide till ye go thence.
12 And when ye come into an
house, [y]salute it.
13 And if the house be worthy,
let your peace come upon it: but
if it be not worthy, let your peace
return to you.
14 [z]And [a]whosoever shall [b]not
receive you, nor hear your
words, when ye depart out of
that house or city, shake off the
[c]dust of your feet.
15 Verily I say unto you, [d,e]It
shall be more tolerable for the
land of [f]Sŏd′om and [g]Gō-mŏr′-
rhȧ in the day of [h]judgment,
[i]than for that city.
16 ¶ Behold, I send [j]you
forth as [k]sheep in [l]the midst of
[m]wolves: be [n]ye therefore [o]wise
as [p]serpents, and harmless as
[q]doves.
17 But beware of men: for they
will [l]deliver you up to the councils, and they will [r]scourge you
in their [s]synagogues;
18 And ye shall be brought before governors and kings for my

**37**
*g Harvest, figurative,* Ex. 34:21.

**38**
*h Commandment, enjoining prayer for more laborers,* Deut. 8:2.

**1**
*a Minister, call of,* Rom. 15:16.
*b Apostles, miraculous power given to,* Luke 6:13.
*c Jesus, power of,* Matt. 1:21.
*d Charism,* 1 Cor. 12:1.
*e Demons, power over,* Matt. 4:24.
*f Afflictions,* Psa. 34:19.
*g Disease, healing of, by the twelve,* Ex. 15:26.
1 R. V. authority over

**2**
*h Apostles, selection of,* Luke 6:13.
*i Peter,* Mark 5:37.
*j Andrew,* Matt. 4:18.
*k James,* Luke 5:10.
*l Zebedee,* Matt. 4:21.
*m John,* Mark 1:19.

**3**
*n Philip,* Luke 6:14.
*o* Mark 3:18; Luke 6:14.
*p Thomas,* John 11:16.
*q Matthew,* Matt. 9:9.
*r Publicans,* Matt. 11:19.
*s* Mark 3:18.
*t* Mark 3:18.
2 R. V. *omits* Lebbæus, whose surname was

**4**
*u Simon,* Mark 3:18.
*v Judas,* Mark 3:19.
*w Betrayal,* Matt. 26:46.

**5**
*x Apostles, commission of,* Luke 6:13.

*y Jesus, instructs his disciples,* Matt. 1:21. *z Minister, charge delivered to,* Rom. 15:16.—*a Gentiles,* Acts 10:45. *b Samaria,* Isa. 7:9. 3 R. V. charged **6** *c Sheep, figurative of lost sinners,* Deut. 32:14. *d Jews,* Neh. 4:2. **7** *e Ministers, precepts for guidance of,* Rom. 15:16. *f Preaching,* Matt. 9:35. *g Church, called kingdom of heaven,* Matt. 16:18. *h Kingdom of Heaven,* Matt. 13:24.

**8**
*i Charism,* 1 Cor. 12:1.
*j Apostles, miraculous power given to,* Luke 6:13.
*k Healing,* Acts 4:22.
*l Afflicted,* Job 34:28.
*m Leprosy,* Lev. 13:2.
*n Dead,* 2 Kin. 4:32.
*o Demons,* Matt. 4:24.

**9**
*p* Mark 6:8–11; Luke 9:3–5.
*q Gold, used as money,* Ezek. 7:19.
*r Silver, used as money,* 1 Chr. 28:14.
*s Brass, used as money,* Job 28:2.

**10**
*t Employee, rights of, just compensation,* Deut. 24:14.
*u Hired servant, rights of, to receive wages,* Lev. 25:40.
*v Minister, duty, of the church to,* Rom. 15:16.
*w Wages,* Gen. 31:7.
4 R. V. No wallet
5 R. V. staff:
6 R. V. labourer
7 R. V. food.

**11**
8 R. V. village
9 R. V. search out
*x Minister, hospitality to,* Rom. 15:16.

**12**
*y Salutations,* Luke 1:44.

**14**
*z Opportunity, the measure of responsibility,* Gal. 6:10.
*a Unbelievers,* 1 Cor. 6:6.
*b Unbelief,* Heb. 3:12.
*c Dust,* Eccl. 3:20.

**15** *d Responsibility, according to privilege,* Ezek 18:20. *e Judgment, according to opportunity and works,* 2 Pet. 3:7. *f Sodom,* Gen. 13:10. *g* Or, *Gomorrah,* Gen. 13:10. *h Judgment, the general,* 2 Pet. 3:7. *i Opportunity, the measure of responsibility,* Gal. 6:10. **16** *j Ministers, trials and persecutions of,* Rom. 15:16. *k Sheep, figurative.* Deut. 32:14, *l Persecution, of the righteous,* John 15:20. *m Wolf, figurative,* Jer. 5:6. *n Minister, character and qualifications of,* Rom. 15:16. *o Wisdom, worldly,* Prov. 2:2. *p Serpent, subtlety of,* Num. 21:6. *q Dove,* Gen. 8:8. **17** *r Scourging,* Acts 22:24. *s Synagogue,* Matt. 12:9.

*** JAMES,** an apostle. *Son of Alphæus,* Matt. 10:3; Mark 3:18; Luke 6:15; Acts 1:13; 12:17; Gal. 2:9, 12. *The brother, or father, of Judas,* Luke 6:16; Jude 1. *Brother of Joses,* Mark 15:40. *Addresses the council at Jerusalem in favor of liberty for the Gentile converts,* Acts 15:13–21. *Disciples sent by, to Antioch,* Gal. 2:12. *Hears of the success attending Paul's ministry,* Acts 21:18, 19.

† **PURSE,** Prov. 1:14; Matt. 10:9; Mark 6:8; Luke 10:4; 22:35, 36. *Called bag,* Prov. 7:20, John 12:6.

sake, for a testimony against
them and the [t]Gĕn′tīleṣ.
19 But when they [l]delive you
up, [10,u,v]take[G] no thought how or
what ye shall speak: for [w]it shall
be given [x]you in that same hour
what ye shall speak.
20 For it is not ye that speak,
but the [y]Spirit of your [z]Father
which speaketh in you.[T]
21 [a,b]And the brother shall [c]de-
liver up the brother to [d]death,
and the father the child: and the
children shall rise up against
*their* parents, and cause them to
be put to death.[Q]
22 And [e]ye shall be [c,f]hated of
all *men* for my name's sake: [g]but
he that [h,i]endureth to the end
shall be [j]saved.
23 But when they [c]persecute
you in this city, flee ye into another: for verily [k]I say unto you,
Ye shall not have gone over the
cities of Ĭṣ′ra-el, till the [l]Son of
man be come.
24 [m]The [n]disciple is not above
*his* [11]master, nor the [o]servant
above his lord.
25 It is enough for the [n]disciple
that he be as his [11]master, and
the [o]servant as his lord. If they
have [p,q]called the master of the
house [‡]Bē-ĕl′ze-bŭb, how much
more *shall they call* them of his
household?
26 [r]Fear them not therefore:
[s]for there is [t]nothing covered,
that shall not be revealed; and
hid, that shall not be known.
27 What I [u]tell you in darkness,
*that* speak ye in light: and what
ye hear in the ear, *that* [v]preach[G]
ye upon the housetops.
28 And [r,w]fear not them which
[x]kill the body, [y]but are not able
to kill the [z]soul: but rather [a]fear
[b]him which is able to [c,d]destroy[G]
both soul and body in [e]hell.[S]
29 [f,g]Are[S] not two [h]sparrows
sold for a farthing[G]? and one
of [i]them shall not fall on the
ground without your [j,k,l]Father.[T]
30 But [m]the very hairs of [n]your
head are all numbered.[Q]
31 Fear ye not therefore, [o]ye
are of more value than many
[h]sparrows.[S]
32[T] [‖,n,p]Whosoever therefore
shall [q,r]confess me before men,
[m,s]him will I confess also before [t]my Father which is in
[u]heaven.
33 But whosoever shall [v]deny
me before men, [w]him will I also
deny before [t]my Father which
is in [u]heaven.[T]
34 [x]Think not that [y]I am come
to send [z]peace on earth: I came
not to send peace, but a [a,b]sword.
35 For[Q] [c]I am come to set a man
at [b,d]variance[G] against his father,
and the daughter against her
mother, and the [e]daughter in
law against her [§]mother in law.
36 [d]And a man's foes *shall be*
they of his own household.[Q]
37 [f]He that loveth [g]father or
[h]mother more than me is not
worthy of me: and [i]he that loveth [j]son or daughter more than
me is not worthy of me.[Q]
38 And he that taketh not his
[k]cross, and followeth after me,
is not worthy of me.
39 [l]He that [m]findeth his [n]life

**18**
t *Gentiles*, Acts 10:45.

**19**
u Mark 13:11–13; Luke 21:14, 15.
v *Commandment, enjoining fortitude under persecution, and forbidding anxiety*, Deut. 8:2.
w *Promise, to the righteous*, 2 Cor. 1:20.
x *Righteous, promises to*, Psa. 64:10.
10 R. V. be not anxious

**20**
y *Holy Spirit, inspiration of*, Acts 1:2.
z *God, fatherhood of*, Gen. 2:2.

**21**
a *Peace, broken by the gospel*, Jer. 29:7.
b *Hostility to the righteous*, Mic. 7:6.
c *Persecution, of the righteous*, John 15:20.
d *Martyrdom*, Rev. 17:6.

**22**
e Mark 13:13.
f *Hatred*, Prov. 15:17.
g *Blessings, contingent upon obedience*, Deut. 11:26.
h *Faithfulness, rewards of*, Luke 16:10.
i *Perseverance, motives to*, Eph. 6:18.
j *Reward, a motive to perseverance*, Matt. 5:12.

**23**
k *Jesus, prophet*, Matt. 1:21.
l *Jesus, humanity of*, Matt. 1:21.

**24**
m Luke 6:40; John 13:16; 15:20.
n *Disciples*, Matt. 9:14.
o *Servant, social status of*, Jer. 2:14.
11 Am. R. V. *marg.* teacher,

x *Death, not to be feared by the righteous*, Num. 23:10.
y *Immortality, implied*, 1 Cor. 15:54.
z *Man, spirit*, Job 4:17.
a *Fear of God* (as some interpret), Acts 9:31.
b *Satan, to be feared* (as some interpret), Matt. 4:10.
c *Second Death*, Rev. 20:14.
d *Wicked, punishment of*, Psa. 73:3.
e *Hell*, Mark 9:43.

**29**
f *Adversity, consolation in*, Psa. 10:6.
g Luke 12:6, 7.
h *Sparrow*, Psa. 84:3.
i *Birds, divine care of*, Eccl. 12:4.
j *God, fatherhood of*, Gen. 2:2.
k *God, providence of*, Gen. 2:2.
l *God, knowledge of*, Gen. 2:2.

**30**
m *Promise, ground of assurance, to the righteous*, 2 Cor. 1:20.
n *Righteous, promises to*, vs. 29–31; Psa. 64:10.

**31**
o *Man, above other creatures*, Job 4:17.

**32**
p Luke 12:8, 9.
q *Confession of Christ*, Luke 12:8.
r *Religious Testimony*, 2 Thes. 1:10.
s *Reward, a motive, to faithfulness*, Matt. 5:12.
t *Jesus, divine sonship of*, Matt. 1:21.
u *Heaven, God's dwelling place*, Luke 18:22.

**25** p *False Accusation*, 2 Tim. 3:3. q *Blasphemy*, 2 Sam. 12:14.
**26** r *Courage, enjoined*, Deut. 31:7. s Mark 4:22; Luke 8:17. t *Sin, known to God*, Rom. 5:12.
**27** u *Apostles, inspiration of*, Luke 6:13. v *Preaching*, Matt. 9:35.
**28** w *Commandment, enjoining fortitude under persecution*, Deut. 8:2.
**33** v *Jesus, rejected*, Matt. 1:21. w *Wicked*, Psa. 73:3.
**34** x Luke 12:51–53. y *Jesus, mission of*, Matt. 1:21. z *Peace*, Jer. 29:7.—a *Sword, figurative*, 1 Chr. 21:5. b *Strife*, Prov. 20:3.
**35** c *Jesus, mission of*, Matt. 1:21. d *Hostility to the righteous*, Mic. 7:6. e *Daughter-in-law*. Lev. 20:12.
**37** f *Love, of man for Jesus*, 1 John 4:19. g *Father*, Psa. 27:10. h *Mother*, 1 Kin. 2:20. i *Parents*, 2 Cor. 12:14. j *Children*, Mark 10:14. **38** k *Cross, figurative*, John 19:17.
**39** l *Paradox*, 2 Cor. 12:4. m *Worldliness*, 1 John 2:15. n *Life*, Eccl. 8:15.

‡ **BEELZEBUB.** *The prince of devils*, Matt. 9:34; 10:25; 12:24, 27; Mark 3:22; Luke 11:15, 18, 19. *Messengers sent to inquire of, by Ahaziah*, 2 Kin. 1:2.
See footnote, SATAN, Matt. 4:10.

‖ **DISCIPLESHIP OF JESUS. Tests of:** *Confession of, and self-denial*, Matt. 10:32–39; 16:24; 19:21; Luke 12:8, 9. *Renunciation of life and kindred*, Luke 14:26, 27, 33; John 12:25, 26. *Obedience to his commandments*, John 14:15.

§ **MOTHER-IN-LAW,** Matt. 10:35. *Not to be defiled*, Lev. 18:17; 20:14; Deut. 27:23. *Beloved by Ruth*, Ruth 1:14–17; 2:2, 3, 18. *Kindness of*, Ruth 3:1–5. *Peter's, healed by Jesus*, Matt. 8:14, 15; Mark 1:30, 31.

o *Renunciation,* Luke 5:11.
p *Promise, to the righteous,* 2 Cor. 1:20.

**40**
q Mark 9:37; Luke 9:48; 10:16; John 13:20.
r *Love, of man for man,* 1 John 4:7.

**41**
s *Prophets,* Isa. 3:2.

**42**
t Mark 9:41.
u *Kindness,* Acts 28:2.
v *Works,* 2 Tim. 1:9.
w *Disciples,* Matt. 9:14.

**1**
a *Apostles,* Luke 6:13.
b *Jesus, teacher,* Matt. 1:21.
c *Instruction, in religion,* Prov. 23:23.
d *Preaching,* Matt. 9:35.

**2**
e Luke 7:18–35.
f *John the Baptist,* Luke 1:63.
g *Prisoners,* Psa. 79:11.
h *Imprisonment,* Acts 12:4.
i *Disciples,* Matt. 9:14.
1 R. V. by his

**3**
j *Doubting, exemplified,* Rom. 14:23.
k *Jesus, Messiah,* Matt. 1:21.
l *Messianic Hope,* Gen. 49:10.

**4**
m *Miracles, design of,* Luke 23:8.

**5**
n *Blindness, miraculous healing of,* 2 Kin. 6:18.
o *Lameness,* Lev. 21:18.
p *Leprosy,* Lev. 13:2.
q *Poor, God's care of,* Prov. 21:13.
r *Gospel, good tidings,* Mark 13:10.
2 R. V. good tidings

**6**
s *Faith in Christ,* John 6:69.
3 R. V. find none occasion of stumbling

shall lose it: and he that [o]loseth his life for my sake [p]shall find it.

40 [q]He that [r]receiveth you receiveth me, and he that receiveth me receiveth him that sent me.[T]

41 He that receiveth a [s]prophet[G] in the name of a prophet[G] shall receive a prophet[G]'s reward; and he that receiveth a righteous man in the name of a righteous man [p]shall receive a righteous man's reward.[Q]

42 [t]And whosoever shall [u,v]give to drink unto one of these little ones a cup of cold *water* only in the name of a [w]disciple, verily I say unto you, he [p]shall in no wise[G] lose his reward.

## CHAPTER 11

*John the Baptist sends two of his disciples to Jesus.* 7 *Jesus' testimony concerning John.* 16 *The Jews reject both.* 20 *Jesus upbraids Chorazin, Bethsaida, and Capernaum;* 26 *and rejoices that the gospel is revealed unto babes.* 28 *His invitation to the heavy laden.*

AND it came to pass, when Jē'ṣus had made an end of commanding his twelve [a]disciples, [b]he departed thence to [c]teach and to [d]preach in their cities.

2 ¶ [e]Now when [f,g]Jŏhn had heard [h]in the prison the works of Chrīst, he sent [1]two of his [i]disciples,

3 And [j]said unto him, Art thou [k,l]he that should come, or do we look for another?[Q]

4 Jē'ṣus[S] answered and said unto [i]them, Go and shew [f]Jŏhn again those [m]things which ye do hear and see:

5 The [n]blind [m]receive their sight, and the [o]lame walk, the [p]lepers are cleansed, and the *deaf hear, the dead are raised up, and the [q]poor have [2]the [r]gospel [d]preached to them.[Q]

6 And blessed is *he,* whosoever [s]shall [3]not be offended in me.[S]

7 ¶ And as they departed, Jē'ṣus began to say unto the multitudes concerning [f]Jŏhn, What went ye out into the wilderness to see? A [t]reed shaken with the wind?

8 But what went ye out for to see? A man clothed in soft raiment? behold, they that wear soft *clothing* are in kings' houses.

9 But what went ye out for to see? A [u]prophet[G]? yea, I say unto you, and more than a prophet.

10 For this is *he,* of whom [v]it is written, [w]Behold, I send my [x]messenger before thy face, which shall prepare thy way before thee.[Q]

11[T] Verily I say unto you, Among them that are born of women there hath not risen a greater than Jŏhn the Băp'tĭst: notwithstanding [y]he that is [4]least in the [z]kingdom of heaven is greater than he.[S]

12 [a]And from the days of [b]Jŏhn the Băp'tĭst until now the kingdom of heaven suffereth violence[G], and the violent[G] take it by force.[S T]

13 For all the [c]prophets and the [d,e]law [f]prophesied until [b]Jŏhn.

14 And if ye will receive *it,* this is [g]Ē-lī'as, which was for to come.[Q]

15 [h]He that hath ears to hear, let him [i]hear.

16 But whereunto shall I liken this generation? It is like unto [j]children sitting in the [5]markets, and calling unto their fellows,

17 And saying, We have [k]piped unto you, and ye have not [l]danced; we have mourned unto you, and ye have not lamented.

18 For [b,m]Jŏhn came [n]neither eating [o]nor drinking, and [p]they say, He hath a devil[G].

19 The [q,r]Son of man came eating and drinking, [s]and [p]they

**7**
t *Reed, figurative,* Ezek. 40:3.

**9**
u *Prophets,* Isa. 3:2.

**10**
v *Prophecies, concerning the Messiah, and their fulfillment,* Gen. 12:3.
w Mal. 3:1; Mark 1:2.
x *Messenger, figurative,* Hag. 1:13.

**11**
y *Righteous, described,* Psa. 64:10.
z *Kingdom of Heaven,* Matt. 13:24.
4 R. V. but little

**12**
a Luke 16:16.
b *John the Baptist,* Luke 1:63.

**13**
c *Prophets,* Isa. 3:2.
d *Law, of Moses,* Deut. 33:2.
e *Word of God,* Psa. 119:9.
f *Prophecies, concerning the Messiah, and their fulfillment,* Gen. 12:3.

**14**
g Or, *Elijah, antetype of John,* 1 Kin. 17:1.

**15**
h *Commandment, enjoining heed to the truth,* Deut. 8:2.
i *Spiritual Understanding,* Luke 8:8.

**16**
j *Children, amusements of,* Mark 10:14.
5 R. V. marketplaces,

**17**
k *Music,* 2 Chr. 5:13.
l *Dancing,* Eccl. 3:4.

**18**
m *Nazirite, instances of,* Num. 6:2.
n *Abstemiousness, instances of,* Prov. 23:2.
o *Total Abstinence, instances of,* Lev. 10:9.
p *Epicureans, reject John the Baptist,* Acts 17:18.

**19**
q *Jesus, rejected,* Matt. 1:21.
r *Jesus, humanity of,* Matt. 1:21.
s *Unbelief,* Heb. 3:12.

***DEAFNESS.** *Law concerning,* Lev. 19:14. *Inflicted by God,* Ex. 4:11. *Miraculous cure of,* Matt. 11:5; Mark 7:32–35; 9:25. **Figurative:** *Of moral insensibility,* Isa. 6:10; 29:18; 35:5; Ezek. 12:2; Matt. 13:15; Acts 28:26, 27.

[t,u]say, Behold a man [v]glutton-
ous, and a [w]winebibber,[C] a friend
of †publicans[C] and sinners. But
[x]wisdom is justified of her [6]chil-
dren.
20 ¶[C] Then began he to [y]up-
braid the cities wherein most of
his mighty works were done, because they [z]repented not:
21 [a]Woe[Q] unto thee, Chō-rā'zin!
woe unto thee, [b]Bĕth-sā'ĭ-dȧ!
for if the mighty works, which
were done in you, had been done
in [c]Tȳre and [d]Sī'dŏn, they would
have [e]repented long ago in [f]sack-
cloth and [g]ashes.
22 But I say unto you, [h]It shall
be more tolerable for [c]Tȳre and
[d]Sī'dŏn at the day of [i]judgment,
[j]than for you.[Q]
23 [k,l]And thou, [m]Cȧ-pĕr'na-ŭm,
which art exalted unto heaven,
shalt be [n]brought down [7]to
[o]hell:[C] for [h]if the mighty works,
which have been done in thee,
[j]had been done in [p]Sŏd'om, it
would have remained until this
day.[Q]
24 But I say unto you, That [h]it
shall be more tolerable for the
land of [p]Sŏd'om in the day of
[i]judgment, [j]than for thee.
25 ¶[T] At that time [q]Jē'ṣus answered and said, I ‡,[r]thank thee,
O [s]Father, [t]Lord of [u]heaven and
earth, because thou hast hid
these [v]things from the [w]wise and
[8]prudent, and hast revealed
them unto [x,y,z]babes.[S]
26 Even so,[C] [a]Father: for so it
seemed good in thy sight.[S]
27 All things are delivered unto [b]me of my [a]Father: and no
man knoweth the [c]Son, but the
Father; neither knoweth any
man the [d]Father, save[C] the [e]Son,
and *he* to whomsoever the Son
[9]will reveal *him*.[S T]
28 ¶[S] Come unto me, all [f]*ye* that
labour and are [g]heavy laden,[C]
and [h]I will give you [i,j,k]rest.[Q]
29 Take my [l]yoke upon you,
and learn of me; for [m,n,o]I am
[p]meek and [q]lowly in heart: and
ye shall find [i,j]rest unto your
souls.[Q]
30 For my [l]yoke *is* easy, and
my burden is light.[S T]

## CHAPTER 12

*The disciples pluck ears of corn on the Sabbath. 10 A withered hand restored whole. 14 Jesus heals many, and charges them not to make him known. 22 A blind and dumb man possessed with a devil is healed. 31 Blasphemy against the Holy Ghost. 38 The scribes and Pharisees seek a sign. 46 Jesus' true disciples are his nearest relatives.*

[a]AT that time *Jē'ṣus went
on the [b]sabbath day
through the [c]corn;[C] and his [d]dis-
ciples were an [e]hungred,[C] and began to pluck the ears of corn,[C]
and to eat.[Q]
2 But when the [f,g]Phăr'ĭ-seeṣ
saw *it*, they [h]said unto him, Behold, thy [d]disciples do that
which is not lawful to do upon
the sabbath day.[Q]
3 But he said unto them, Have
ye not read [i]what [j]Dā'vid did,
when he was an[C] [e]hungred, and
they that were with him;
4 How he entered into the
[k]house of God, and did eat the
[l]shewbread,[C] which was not lawful for him to eat, neither for
them which were with him, but
only for the [m]priests?[Q]
5 Or have ye not read in the
[n]law, how that on the [b]sabbath
days the [o]priests in the [p]temple

---

*t* *Falsehood, instances of*, Job 21:34.
*u* *False Accusation*, 2 Tim. 3:3.
*v* *Gluttony, Jesus falsely accused of*, Prov. 30:22.
*w* Luke 7:34.
*x* *Wisdom, spiritual*, Prov. 2:2.
6 R. V. works.

**20**
*y* *Jesus, upbraids unbelieving cities*, Matt. 1:21.
*z* *Impenitence*, Rom. 2:5.

**21**
*a* Luke 10:13–15.
*b* *Bethsaida*, John 1:44.
*c* *Tyre*, Josh. 19:29.
*d* Or, *Zidon*, Ezek. 28:21.
*e* *Repentance*, Mark 1:4.
*f* *Sackcloth*, Isa. 15:3.
*g* *Ashes, repenting in*, Num. 19:9.

**22**
*h* *Responsibility, according to privilege*, Ezek. 18:20.
*i* *Judgment, the general*, 2 Pet. 3:7.
*j* *Opportunity, the measure of responsibility*, Gal. 6:10.

**23**
*k* Luke 10:15.
*l* *Judgment, according to opportunity*, 2 Pet. 3:7.
*m* *Capernaum, Christ's prophecy against*, Luke 4:31.
*n* *Wicked, punishment of*, Psa. 73:3.
*o* *Hell*, Mark 9:43.
*p* *Sodom*, Gen. 13:10.
7 R.V. unto Hades:

**25**
*q* *Jesus, prayer of*, Matt. 1:21.
*r* *Thankfulness, Jesus an example of*, Acts 24:3.
*s* *God, fatherhood of*, Gen. 2:2.

*d* *God, incomprehensible*, Gen. 2:2.
*e* *Jesus, omniscience of*, Matt. 1:21.
9 R. V. willeth to

**28**
*f* *Penitent, promises to*, Psa. 51:17.
*g* *Afflictions, consolation in*, Psa. 34:19.
*h* *Promise, to the penitent*, 2 Cor. 1:20.
*i* *Spiritual Peace, from Christ*, Gal. 1:3.
*j* *Rest, spiritual*, Ex. 23:12.
*k* *Salvation*, Acts 16:17.

**29**
*l* *Yoke, figurative*, 1 Sam. 6:7.
*m* *Jesus, our example*, Matt. 1:21.
*n* *Jesus, meekness of*, Matt. 1:21.
*o* *Jesus, humility of*, Matt. 1:21.
*p* *Meekness*, Psa. 45:4.
*q* *Humility*, Prov. 22:4.

**1**
*a* Mark 2:23–28; Luke 6:1–5.
*b* *Sabbath*, Ex. 16:23.
*c* *Corn*, Psa. 65:13.
*d* *Apostles*, Luke 6:13.
*e* *Hunger*, Neh. 9:15.

**2**
*f* *Pharisees*, Matt. 15:12.
*g* *Bigotry*, Isa. 65:5.
*h* *False Accusation, against Jesus*, 2 Tim. 3:3.

**3**
*i* 1 Sam. 21:6.
*j* *David*, 1 Sam. 16:13.

**4**
*k* *Church, called house of God*, 1 Kin. 9:3.
*l* *Shewbread*, Ex. 35:13.
*m* *Priest, emoluments of*, Lev. 1:5.

*t* *God, sovereign*, Gen. 2:2. *u* *Heaven, God's dwelling place*, Luke 18:22. *v* *Mysteries, of redemption*, Mark 4:11. *w* *Wisdom, worldly*, Prov. 2:2. *x* *Babes*, Psa. 8:2. *y* *Minister, character and qualifications of*, Rom. 15:16. *z* *Righteous, described*, Psa. 64:10. 8 R. V. understanding, **26**—*a* *God, fatherhood of*, Gen. 2:2.
**27** *b* *Jesus, king*, Matt. 1:21. *c* *Jesus, divine sonship of*, Matt. 1:21.

**5** *n* *Law, of Moses*, Deut. 33:2. *o* *Priest, duties of*, Lev. 1:5. *p* *Temple, Herod's*, 1 Kin. 6:17.

---

† **PUBLICANS**, Roman tax collectors. *Disreputable*, Matt. 5:46; 9:11; 11:19; 18:17; 21:31; Luke 18:11. *Repent under the preaching of John the Baptist*, Matt. 31:32; Luke 3:12; 7:29. *Hear Jesus gladly*, Luke 15:1, 2. *Matthew, the collector of Capernaum, becomes an apostle*, Matt. 9:9; 10:3; Mark 2:14; Luke 5:27. *Parable concerning*, Luke 18:9–14. *Zacchæus, chief among, receives Jesus into his house*, Luke 19:2–10. *A term of reproach*, Matt. 18:17.

‡ **THANKSGIVING.** *By Jesus*, Matt. 11:25; 15:36; 26:27; Mark 8:6, 7; 14:23; Luke 22:17, 19; John 6:11, 23; 11:41.

* **JESUS DEFINES LAW OF SABBATH,** Matt. 12:1–8; Mark 2:23–28; Luke 6:1–5.

profane the sabbath, and are [1]blameless?

6 But *I say unto you, That in this place is [q]*one* greater than the [p]temple.

7 But if ye had known what *this* meaneth, I will have [r,s]mercy, and not [t]sacrifice, ye would not have condemned the guiltless.

8 For the *Son of man is [2,q]Lord even of the [b]sabbath day.

9 ¶ And when he was departed thence, he went into their †synagogue:

10 And, behold, [u]there was a man which had *his* hand [v]withered. And they asked him, saying, Is it lawful to heal on the sabbath days? that they might accuse him.

11 And *he said unto them, What man shall there be among you, that shall have one [w]sheep, and if it fall into a pit on the [b]sabbath day, will he not lay hold on it, and [x]lift *it* out?

12 How much then is a man [3]better than a [w]sheep? Wherefore it is lawful to do well on the sabbath days.

13 Then saith he to the man, Stretch forth thine hand. And he stretched *it* forth; and it [y]was restored whole, like as the other.

14 ¶ Then the [f]Phăr'ĭ-seeş went out, and [4,z,a]held a council against him, how they might destroy him.

15 [b]But when Jē'şus knew *it*, [c]he [d]withdrew himself from thence: and great multitudes followed him, and he [d,e]healed them all;

16 And [d]charged them that they should not make him known:

17 That [f]it might be fulfilled which was spoken by [g]Ē-şā'ias the [h]prophet, saying,

18 [i]Behold my servant, whom I have chosen; my beloved, in whom my soul is well pleased: I will put my [5,j]spirit upon him, and he shall [k]shew judgment to the [l]Ġĕn'tīleş.

19 [m]He shall not strive, nor cry; neither shall any man hear his voice in the streets.

20 [n]A [o]bruised [p]reed shall [q]he not break, and smoking [r]flax shall he not quench, till he send forth judgment unto victory.

21 And in his [s]name shall the [l]Ġĕn'tīleş [6,t]trust.

22 ¶ [u]Then [v]was brought unto him one possessed with a [w]devil, [x]blind, and [y]dumb: and [z]he [a,b]healed him, insomuch that the blind and dumb both spake and saw.

23 And all the people were amazed, and said, Is not this the [c]son of [d]Dā'vid?

24 But when the [e]Phăr'ĭ-seeş heard *it*, they [f,g]said, [h]This *fellow* doth not cast out [i]devils, but by [j,k]Bē-ĕl'ze-bŭb the prince of the devils.

25 [l]And Jē'şus [m]knew their thoughts, and said unto them, Every kingdom [n]divided against itself is [o]brought to desolation; and every city or house divided against itself [o]shall not stand:

26 And if [k]Sā'tan cast out Sā'tan, he is divided against himself; how shall then his kingdom stand?

27 And if I by [j]Bē-ĕl'ze-bŭb cast out [i]devils, by whom do your children cast *them* out?

---

1 R. V. guiltless?

**6**
q *Jesus, king,* Matt. 1:21.

**7**
r *Mercy,* Deut. 5:10.
s *Offerings, unavailing without piety,* Lev. 6:17.
t *Obedience better than Sacrifice,* 1 Sam. 15:22.

**8**
2 R. V. lord of the sabbath.

**10**
u Mark 3:1–6; Luke 6:6–11.
v *Paralysis,* Mark 2:3.

**11**
w *Sheep,* Deut. 32:14.
x *Animals, kindness to,* Jer. 27:5.

**12**
3 R. V. of more value

**13**
y *Miracles, of Jesus,* Luke 23:8.

**14**
z *Conspiracy, instances of,* 1 Kin. 16:9.

a *Persecution, of Jesus,* John 15:20.
4 R. V. took counsel

**15**
b *Jesus, withdraws from Capernaum, heals many,* Matt. 1:21.
c *Prudence, instances of,* 2 Chr. 2:12.
d *Healing, by Jesus,* Acts 4:22.
e *Disease,* Ex. 15:26.

**17**
f *Prophecies concerning Jesus, and their fulfillment,* Gen. 12:3.
g Or, *Isaiah,* Isa. 1:1.
h *Prophets,* Isa. 3:2.

**18**
i Isa. 42:1–4.
j *Holy Spirit,* Acts 1:2.
k *Jesus, teacher,* Matt. 1:21.
l *Gentiles, prophecies of the conversion of,* Acts 10:45.
5 R. V. Spirit

**19**
m *Jesus, meekness of,* Matt. 1:21.

**20**
n *Promise, to the penitent,* 2 Cor. 1:20.
o *Penitent, promises to,* Psa. 51:17.
p *Reed, figurative,* Ezek. 40:3.
q *Jesus, compassion of,* Matt. 1:21.
r *Flax, figurative,* Ex. 9:31.

**21**
s *Name of Jesus,* John 14:13.
t *Faith in Christ,* John 6:69.
6 R. V. hope.

**22**
u Luke 11:14, 15.
v *Mediation,* Gal. 3:19.
w *Demons,* Matt. 4:24.
x *Blindness, miraculous healing of,* 2 Kin. 6:18.
y *Dumb, miraculously healed,* Ex. 4:11.
z *Jesus, miracles of,* Matt. 1:21.

a *Miracles,* Luke 23:8.
b *Healing, by Jesus,* Acts 4:22.

**23**
c *Jesus, names of,* Matt. 1:21.
d *David, Jesus called son of,* 1 Sam. 16:13.

**24** e *Pharisees,* Matt. 15:12. f *False Accusation,* 2 Tim. 3:3. g *Persecution, of Jesus,* John 15:20. h *Scoffing,* Hab. 1:10. i *Demons,* Matt. 4:24. j *Beelzebub,* Matt. 10:25. k *Satan,* Matt. 4:10. **25** l Mark 3:23–27; Luke 11:17–22. m *Jesus, omniscience of,* Matt. 1:21. n *Strife,* Prov. 20:3. o *Instability,* Jas. 1:8.

---

† **SYNAGOGUE. An assembly,** Acts 13:43 [R. V.]; Jas. 2:2 [R. V.]. *Constitutes a court of justice,* Luke 12:11; Acts 9:2. *Had powers, of criminal courts,* Matt. 10:17; 23:34; Acts 22:19; 26:11; *of ecclesiastical courts,* John 9:22, 34; 12:42; 16:2.

**Place of Assembly.** *Scriptures read and expounded in,* Neh. **8**:1–8; **9**:3, 5; Matt. 4:23; 9:35; 13:54; Mark 1:39; Luke 4:15–33; 13:10; John 18:20; Acts 9:20; 13:5–44; **14**:1; 15:21; 17:2, 10; 18:4, 19, 26.

*In, Jerusalem,* Acts 6:9; *Damascus,* Acts 9:2, 20; *other cities,* Acts 14:1; 17:1, 10; 18:4. *Built by a centurion,* Luke 7:5. *Jesus performed healing in,* Matt. **12:9–13; Luke 13:** 11–14. *Alms given in,* Matt. **6:2.**

**Of Satan,** Rev. 2:9; 3:9.

therefore they shall be your
judges.
28 But if I [p]cast out [i]devils[G]
by the [q]Spirit of God, then the
[r]kingdom of God is come unto
you.[S T]
29 Or else how can one enter
into a strong man's house, and
spoil[G] his goods, except he first
bind the strong man? and then
he will [s]spoil[G] his house.[S Q]
30 [t]He that is not with me is
against me; and he that gathereth not with me scattereth
[7]abroad.
31 Wherefore I say unto you,
[u]All manner of [v]sin and [w]blas-
phemy shall be forgiven unto
men: but the ‡blasphemy *against*
the [x]*Holy* [8]Ghost[G] shall not be
forgiven [9]unto men.[T]
32 And whosoever [w]speaketh a
word against the [y]Son of man,
[u]it shall be forgiven him: but
whosoever ‡speaketh against the
[x]Holy [8]Ghost,[G] it shall not be
forgiven him, neither in this
world,[G] [z]neither in the *world* to
come.[T]
33 [a,b]Either make the [c]tree
good, and his fruit [d]good; or else
make the tree corrupt,[G] and his
fruit [e]corrupt: for the tree is
known by *his* fruit.[S]
34 [10,f]O generation[G] of [g]vipers,
how can ye, being [h]evil, speak
good [i]things? for out of the
abundance of the [c]heart the
mouth speaketh.
35 A good man out of the good
treasure [11]of the [c]heart bringeth
forth good [i]things: and an evil
man out of the evil treasure
bringeth forth evil [i]things.
36 But I say unto you, That
every [j]idle [j]word that men shall
speak, they shall give account
thereof in the day of [k]judg-
ment.
37 For by thy words thou shalt
be [l]justified, and by thy words
thou shalt be [l]condemned.[S T]
38 ¶ [m]Then certain of the
[n]scribes and of the [o]Phăr'ĭ-sees
answered, saying, [12,p]Master, we
would see a [q,r]sign from thee.
39 But he answered and said
unto them, An [g]evil and adulterous generation seeketh after a
[q,r,s]sign; and there shall no sign
be given to it, but the sign of the
[s]prophet [t]Jō'nas:
40 [u,v]For as [t]Jō'nas was three
days and three nights in the
[w]whale's belly; [x]so shall the
Son of man be three days and
three nights in the heart of the
earth.[Q]
41 [y,z]The men of [a]Nĭn'e-veh
shall rise in [b]judgment with this
generation, and shall condemn
it: because they [c,d]repented at
the [e]preaching of [f]Jō'nas; and,
behold, a [g]greater than Jō'nas *is*
here.[Q]
42 [h]The [i]queen of the south
shall rise up in the judgment
with this generation, and shall
condemn it: for she came from
the uttermost[G] parts of the earth
to hear the wisdom of [j]Sŏl'o-
mon; and, behold, a [g]greater
than Sŏl'o-mon *is* here.[Q]
43 When the [k,l]unclean spirit is
gone out of a man, he walketh
through dry places, seeking rest,
and findeth none.
44 Then [l]he saith, I will return
into my house from whence I
came out; and when he is come,
he findeth *it* empty, swept, and
garnished.
45 Then goeth he, and taketh
with himself seven other spirits
more wicked than himself, and
they enter in and dwell there:
and the [m,n]last *state* of that man
is worse than the first. Even so
shall it be also unto this wicked
generation.

**28**
p *Miracles, performed by power of the Holy Spirit,* Luke 23:8.
q *Holy Spirit, power of,* Acts 1:2.
r *Kingdom of Heaven,* Matt. 13:24.

**29**
s *Satan, kingdom of, to be destroyed,* Matt. 4:10.

**30**
t Luke 11:23.
7 R. V. *omits* abroad.

**31**
u *Promise, of forgiveness,* 2 Cor. 1:20.
v *Sin, forgiveness of,* Rom. 5:12.
w *Blasphemy,* 2 Sam. 12:14.
x *Holy Spirit, sin against,* Acts 1:2.
8 R. V. Spirit:
9 R. V. *omits* unto men.

**32**
y *Jesus, humanity of,* Matt. 1:21.
z *Sin, forgiveness of,* Rom. 5:12.

**33**
a *Proverbs,* 1 Sam. 24:13.
b *Holiness, enjoined,* Ex. 39:30.
c *Heart,* Psa. 44:21.
d *Righteousness, figuratively described,* Psa. 15:2.
e *Sin,* Rom. 5:12.

**34**
f *Speech, evil,* Col. 4:6.
g *Wicked, described,* Psa. 73:3.
h *Depravity,* Job 15:14.
i *Speech, wise,* Col. 4:6.
10 R. V. Ye offspring of

**35**
11 R. V. *omits* of the heart

**36**
j *Words, idle,* Luke 4:22.
k *Judgment, the general,* 2 Pet. 3:7.

**37**
l *Judgment, according to opportunity and works,* 2 Pet. 3:7.

**38**
m Luke 11:16-36.
n *Scribe,* 1 Kin. 4:3.
o *Pharisees,* Matt. 15:12.
p *Master,* John 13:13.
q *Sign,* Mark 8:11.
r *Miracles, demanded by unbelievers,* Luke 23:8.
12 Am. R. V. *marg.* teacher,

**39**
s Luke 11:29.
t Or, *Jonah,* Jonah 1:1.

**40**
u *Jesus, resurrection of,* Matt. 1:21.
v *Resurrection, typified,* 1 Cor. 15:12.
w *Fish,* Matt. 17:27.
x *Jesus foretells his Death,* Matt. 17:22.

**41**
y *Jesus, rejected,* Matt. 1:21.
z *Responsibility, according to privilege,* Ezek. 18:20.
a *Nineveh,* Jonah 1:2.
b *Judgment, the general,* 2 Pet. 3:7.
c *Repentance,* Mark 1:4.
d *Conviction of Sin,* John 16:8.
e *Preaching,* Matt. 9:35.
f Or, *Jonah,* Jonah 1:1.
g *Jesus, perfection of,* Matt. 1:21.

**42**
h *Impenitence,* Rom. 2:5.
i *Sheba, queen of,* 1 Kin. 10:1.
j *Solomon, wisdom of,* 2 Sam. 12:24.

**43**
k Luke 11:24-26.
l *Demons,* Matt. 4:24.

**45**
m *Backsliding,* Hos. 11:7.
n *Apostasy,* Acts 1:25.

‡ **UNPARDONABLE SIN,** 2 Kin. 24:4; Matt. 12:31, 32; Luke 12:10; Heb. 6:4-6; 1 John 5:16.
See footnotes: OBDURACY, Prov. 29:1; REPROBATES, 1 Cor. 9:27.
**Instances of:** *Israel,* Num. 14:26-45. *Eli's house,* 1 Sam. 3:14.

46
o Mark 3:31–35; Luke 8:19–21.
p *Mother*, 1 Kin. 2:20.
q *Mary*, Luke 1:27.

49
r *Jesus, love of*, Matt. 1:21.
s *Disciples*, Matt. 9:14.

50
t *Righteous, described*, Psa. 64:10.
u *Obedience*, Heb. 5:8.
v *Duty, of man to God*, Eccl. 12:13.
w *Will of God*, Mark 3:35.
x *God, fatherhood of*, Gen. 2:2.
y *Heaven, God's dwelling place*, Luke 18:22.
z *Brother, expressive of fraternity*, Prov. 18:24.

a *Mother*, 1 Kin. 2:20.

46 ¶ While he yet talked to the
people, behold, [o]*his* [p,q]mother
and his brethren stood without,[C]
desiring to speak with him.
47 Then one said unto him,
Behold, thy mother and thy
brethren stand without,[C] desiring to speak with thee.
48 But he answered and said
unto him that told him, Who is
my mother? and who are my
brethren?
49 And [r]he stretched forth his
hand toward his [s]disciples, and
said, Behold[C] my mother and my
brethren!
50 For [t]whosoever shall [u,v]do
the [w]will of my [x]Father which
is in [y]heaven, the same is my
[z]brother, and sister, and [a]mother.

## CHAPTER 13

*The parable of the sower, 18 and its exposition. 24 The parable of the tares, 31 of the mustard seed, 33 of the leaven, 44 of the hidden treasure, 45 of the pearl, 47 and of the net cast into the sea. 53 Jesus is rejected by his own countrymen.*

1
a *Jesus, parables of*, vs. 3–52; Matt. 1:21.
b *Sea of Galilee*, Matt. 4:18.

2
c *Popularity of Jesus*, John 6:15.
d *Ship*, 2 Chr. 8:18.

3
e *Parables, of Jesus*, Ezek. 20:49.
f *Minister, likened to sower*, Rom. 15:16.
g *Agriculture, figurative*, Gen. 3:23.

4
h *Unfruitfulness*, vs. 4–6; Matt. 7:19.

5
i *Character, instability of*, Phil. 2:15.
j *Instability*, Jas. 1:8.

THE[T] same day went [a]Jē'ṣus
out of the house, and sat
by the [b]sea side.
2 And [c]great multitudes were
gathered together unto him, so
that he went into a [d]ship, and
sat; and the whole multitude
stood on the shore.
3 And [a]he spake many things
unto them in [e]parables,[C] saying,
Behold, a [*,f]sower went forth to
[g]sow;
4 And [h]when he sowed, some
*seeds* fell by the way side, and
the fowls came and devoured
them up:
5 Some fell upon stony places,
where they had not much earth:
and forthwith[C] they sprung up,
because they had [i,j]no deepness
of earth:
6 And when the sun was up,
they were scorched; and because
they had [i,j]no root, they [h]with-
ered away.
7 And some fell among [k]thorns;
and the thorns sprung up, and
[h]choked them:
8 But other fell into good
ground, and brought forth [l]fruit,
some an hundredfold, some six-
tyfold, some thirtyfold.
9 Who hath ears to hear, let
him [m]hear.
10 ¶ [S]And the [n]disciples came,
and said unto him, Why speakest [a]thou unto them in [e]para-
bles[C]?
11 [a]He answered and said unto
them, Because it is given unto
[o]you to [p]know the [q]mysteries[C] of
the [†]kingdom of heaven, but to
them it is not given.
12 For [o,r]whosoever [s]hath, to
him shall be given, and he shall
have more abundance: but whosoever hath not, from him[t,u]shall
be taken away even that he hath.[T]
13 Therefore speak [a]I to them
in [e]parables: because they [v]see-
ing [w,x]see not; and hearing they
hear not, neither do they understand.
14[Q]And in them is [y]fulfilled the
[z]prophecy[C] of [a]Ē-ṣā'ias, which
saith, By hearing [b]ye shall hear,
and [c,d]shall not understand; and
seeing ye shall see, and shall not
perceive:
15 For [e]this people's heart is
[C]waxed[C] gross,[C] and *their* ears are
[f]dull of hearing, and [g]their [h]eyes
they have closed; lest at any time
they should see with *their* eyes,
and hear with *their* ears, and
should understand with *their*
heart, and should be converted,[C]
and I should heal them.[Q]
16 But blessed *are* your eyes,
for they [i,j]see: and your ears, for
they [b]hear.[S]
17 For verily I say unto you,
That many [k]prophets and righteous *men* have [l,m]desired to see
*those things* which ye see, and

7
k *Thorn, figurative*, Hos. 2:6.

8
l *Righteousness*, Psa. 15:2.

9
m *Spiritual Understanding*, Luke 8:8.

10
n *Apostles*, Luke 6:13.

11
o *Righteous, promises to*, Psa. 64:10.
p *Wisdom, spiritual, from God*, Prov. 2:2.
q *Mysteries, of redemption*, Mark 4:11.

12
r *Proverbs*, 1 Sam. 24:13.
s *Prosperity*, Eccl. 7:14.
t *Opportunity, lost*, Gal. 6:10.
u *Wicked, punishment of*, Psa. 73:3.

13
v Ezek. 12:2.
w *Spiritual Blindness*, 2 Cor. 4:4.
x *Unbelief*, Heb. 3:12.

14
y *Moral Insensibility*, Luke 8:10.
z *Prophecies, fulfilled*, Dan. 9:24.

a Cr, *Isaiah*, Isa. 1:1.
b **Isa. 6:9, 10;** Mark 4:12; **Acts 28:25–27.**
c *Spiritual Blindness*, 2 Cor. 4:4.
d *Unbelief*, Heb. 3:12.

15
e *Reprobates*, 1 Cor. 9:27.
f *Deafness, figurative*, Matt. 11:5.
g *Obduracy*, Prov. 29:1.
h *Eye, figurative*, Matt. 6:22.

16
i *Knowledge, of salvation*, Luke 11:52.
j *Wisdom, spiritual*, Prov. 2:2.

17
k *Prophets*, Isa. 3:2.
l *Spiritual Desire*, Psa. 42:1.
m *Messianic Hope*, Gen. 49:10.

*** SOWER.** *Parable of the*, Matt. 13:3–8; Mark 4:3–20; Luke 8:5–8. *Sowing*, Eccl. 11:4; Isa. 28:25. **Figurative**, Job 4:8; Psa. 126:5; Prov. 11:18; Isa. 32:20; Hos. 8:7; 10:12; Gal. 6:7, 8.

have not seen *them*; and to hear
*those* [n]*things* which ye hear, and
have not heard *them*.
18 ¶ [S]Hear[T] ye therefore the
[o]parable of the *sower.
19 When any one heareth the
[p,q,r]word of the kingdom, and
[r]understandeth *it* not, then cometh the [s]wicked *one*, and catcheth away that which was [t]sown
in his heart. This is he which received seed by the way side.
20 [T]But he that received the
[p,q,r]seed into stony places, the
same is he that heareth the
word, and anon[G] with joy receiveth it;
21 Yet [u,v]hath he not root in
himself, but dureth[G] for a while:
for when [w,x]tribulation or [y]per-
secution ariseth because of the
[r]word, [1]by[G] and by [z]he is offended.[T]
22 He also that received
[a,b,c]seed among the [d]thorns is he
that heareth the [a,b,c]word; and
the [e,f,g]care of this world[G], and
the [h]deceitfulness of [g,i]riches,
choke the word, and he becometh [j]unfruitful.
23 But [k]he that received
[a,b,c]seed into the good ground
is he that heareth the [a,b,c]word,
and [l,m]understandeth *it*; which
also beareth [n]fruit, and bringeth forth, some an hundredfold,
some sixty, some thirty.
24 ¶ Another [o]parable put [p]he
forth unto them, saying, The
†,[q]kingdom of heaven is likened
unto a man which [r]sowed [s]good
seed in his field:
25 But while men slept, his
[t,u,v]enemy came and sowed
[w]tares[G] among the [k,x]wheat, and
went his way.
26 But when the blade was
sprung up, and brought forth
fruit, then appeared the [w]tares[G]
also.
27 So the [y]servants of the
householder came and said unto
him, Sir, didst not thou sow good
seed in thy field? from whence[G]
then hath it tares?
28 He said unto them, An [t,u]en-
emy hath done this. The servants
said unto him, Wilt thou then
that we go and gather them up?
29 But he said, Nay; lest while
ye gather up the tares[G], ye root up
also the [z]wheat with them.
30 Let both grow together until
the [a,b]harvest: and in the time of
harvest I will say to the [c]reapers,
[d]Gather ye together first the
[e]tares, and bind them in bundles
to [f]burn them: but gather the
[g]wheat into my [h,i]barn.[S]
31 ¶ Another [j]parable put he
forth unto them, saying, The
†,[k,l]kingdom of heaven is like to
a grain of ‡,[m]mustard seed,
which a man took, and [n]sowed
in his field:
32 Which indeed is the least of
all seeds: but when it is grown,
it is the greatest among herbs,
and becometh a tree, so that the
[o]birds of the air come and lodge
in the branches thereof.[Q]
33 ¶ Another [j]parable spake he
unto them; The †,[k,l]kingdom of
heaven is like unto [p,q]leaven[G],
which a woman took, and hid
in three measures[G] of meal, till
the whole was leavened.[G S T]

n *Gospel*, Mark 13:10.

**18**

o *Parables, of Jesus*, Ezek. 20:49.

**19**

p *Word of God, likened to seed*, Psa. 119:9.
q *Doctrines of Jesus*, vs. 18–23; John 7:16.
r *Truth*, John 18:37.
s *Satan*, Matt. 4:10.
t *Agriculture, figurative*, Gen. 3:23.

**21**

u *Character, instability of*, Phil. 2:15.
v *Instability*, Jas. 1:8.
w *Faith, trial of*, Mark 11:22.
x *Backsliding, temptations to*, Hos. 11:7.
y *Persecution, of the righteous*, John 15:20.
z *Backsliders*, Jer. 3:22.
1 R. V. straightway he stumbleth.

**22**

a *Doctrines of Jesus*, John 7:16.
b *Word of God*, Psa. 119:9.
c *Truth*, John 18:37.
d *Thorn, figurative*, Hos. 2:6.
e *Anxiety*, 1 Pet. 5:7.
f *Worldliness, chokes the word*, 1 John 2:15.
g *Backsliding, temptations to*, Hos. 11:7.
h *Covetousness, warnings against*, Isa. 57:17.
i *Riches, a snare*, Eccl. 4:8.
j *Unfruitfulness*, Matt. 7:19.

**23**

k *Righteous, described*, Psa. 64:10.
l *Wisdom, spiritual*, Prov. 2:2. m *Spiritual Understanding*, Luke 8:8. n *Righteousness*, Psa. 15:2.

**24** o *Parables*, Ezek. 20:49. p *Jesus, parables of*, Matt. 1:21. q *Jesus, kingdom of*, Matt. 1:21. r *Agriculture, figurative*, Gen. 3:23. s *Gospel, likened to good seed*, Mark 13:10.

**25**

t *Enemy, figurative*, Prov. 24:17.
u *Satan*, Matt. 4:10.
v *Malice, the wicked filled with*, Eph. 4:31.
w *Influence, evil*, 1 Cor. 7:14.
x *Wheat, parables of*, Ezra 6:9.

**27**

y *Servant*, Jer. 2:14.

**29**

z *Righteous, compared to wheat*, Psa. 64:10.

**30**

a *Harvest, figurative*, Ex. 34:21.
b *Judgment, the general*, 2 Pet. 3:7.
c *Angel, functions of*, Heb. 1:13.
d *Satan, kingdom of, to be destroyed*, Matt. 4:10.
e *Wicked, punishment of*, Psa. 73:3.
f *Hell*, Mark 9:43.
g *Righteous, promises to*, Psa. 64:10.
h *Barn*, Prov. 3:10.
i *Heaven, future home of the righteous*, Luke 18:22.

**31**

j *Parables*, Ezek. 20:49.
k *Jesus, kingdom of*, Matt. 1:21.
l *Church, prophecies concerning its prosperity*, Matt. 16:18.
m *Gospel, likened to a mustard seed*, Mark 13:10.
n *Agriculture, figurative*, Gen. 3:23.

**32**

o *Birds*, Eccl. 12:4.

**33**

p *Leaven, parables of*, Lev. 23:17.
q *Gospel, likened to leaven*, Mark 13:10.

† **KINGDOM OF HEAVEN**, Matt. 18:3; 19:14; Mark 10:14; Luke 18:16. *Likened, to a man who sowed good seed*. Matt. 13:24–30, 38–43; Mark 4:26–29; *to a grain of mustard seed*, Matt. 13:31, 32; Mark 4:30–32; Luke 13:18, 19; *to leaven*, Matt. 13:33; Luke 13:21; *to a treasure*, Matt. 13:44; *to a pearl*, Matt. 13:45; *to a net*, Matt. 13:47–50; *to a king who called his servants to a reckoning*, Matt. 18:23–35; *to a householder*, Matt. 20:1–16; *to a king who made a marriage feast for his son*, Matt. 22:2–14; Luke 14:16–24; *to ten virgins*, Matt. 25:1–13; *to a man traveling into a far country, who called his servants, and delivered to them his goods*, Matt. 25:14–30; Luke 19:12–27.

*Is not of this world*, John 18:36. *Is not meat and drink*, Rom. 14:17.

*The burden of the preaching, of John the Baptist*, Matt. 3:2; *of Jesus*, Matt. 4:17; Luke 4:43; 9:11; *of the disciples*, Luke 9:2; 10:11. *Mysteries of*, Luke 8:10. *Keys of*, Matt. 16:19. *Glad tidings of*, Luke 8:1. *Rich enter with difficulty*, Matt. 19:23, 24; Mark 10:23–25; Luke 18:24, 25, 29, 30.

See footnotes: CHURCH, Matt. 16:18; JESUS, *Kingdom of*, Matt. 1:21.

‡ **MUSTARD SEED.** *The kingdom of heaven compared to*, Matt. 13:31, 32; Mark 4:31, 32; Luke 13:19. *Faith compared to*, Matt. 17:20.

34 All these things spake [r]Jē′-
ṣus unto the multitude in [j]para-
bles; and without a parable
spake he not unto them:
35 That [s]it might be fulfilled
which was spoken by the [t]proph-
et, saying, [u]I will open my
mouth in [j]parables; I will utter
things which have been kept secret from the foundation of the
world.
36 ¶ Then Jē′ṣus sent the multitude away, and went into the
house: and his [v]disciples came
unto him, saying, Declare unto
us the [j]parable of the tares of
the field.
37 He answered and said unto them, He that soweth the
[w, x, y]good seed is the [z]Son of
man;
38 The field is the world; the
good seed are the [a]children of
the kingdom; but the tares are
the [b]children of the wicked
*one*;
39 The [c]enemy that sowed
them is the [d]devil; the [e]harvest
is the [f]end of the world; and
the reapers are the [g]angels.
40 As therefore the tares are
gathered and burned in the fire;
so shall it be in the [f]end of this
world.
41 The [h]Son of man shall send
forth his [g]angels, and they shall
gather out of [i]his [†]kingdom all
things that [1]offend, and them
which do iniquity;
42 And shall [j]cast them into
a [k, l]furnace of [m]fire: there shall
be ‖wailing and [n]gnashing of
teeth.
43 Then shall the [o, p]righteous
shine forth as the sun in the
[q]kingdom of [r]their [s]Father.
Who hath ears to hear, let
him [t]hear.
44 ¶ Again, [u]the [†]kingdom of
heaven is like unto [v, w]treasure
hid in a field; the which when a
man hath found, he hideth, and
for [x]joy thereof goeth and [y]sell-
eth all that he hath, and buyeth
that field.
45 ¶ Again, [u]the [†]kingdom of
heaven is like unto a [z]merchant
man, seeking goodly [a, b]pearls:
46 Who, when he had found
one [a]pearl of great price, went
and [c]sold all that he had, and
bought it.
47 ¶ Again, [d]the [†]kingdom of
heaven is like unto a net, that
was cast into the sea, and gathered of every kind:
48 Which, when it was full,
they drew to shore, and sat
down, and gathered the good
into vessels, but cast the [e]bad
away.
49 So shall it be at the [f]end of
the world: the [g]angels shall come
forth, and [h]sever the [e]wicked from
among the [i]just,
50 And shall [j]cast [e]them into
the [k, l]furnace of [m]fire: there
shall be ‖wailing and [n]gnashing
of teeth.
51 Jē′ṣus saith unto them,
Have ye [o]understood all these
things? They say unto him,
Yea, [2]Lord.
52 Then said he unto them,
Therefore every [p, q]scribe [3]*which
is* [o]instructed unto the [†]king-
dom of heaven is like unto a man
*that is* an householder, which
bringeth forth out of his [r]treas-
ure *things* new and old.
53 ¶ And it came to pass, *that*
when Jē′ṣus had finished these
[s]parables, [t]he departed thence.
54 [u]And when he was come into his own country, he taught
them in their [v]synagogue, insomuch that they were astonished,
and said, Whence hath this *man*
this [w]wisdom, and *these* mighty
[x]works?

**34**
r *Jesus, parables of,* Matt. 1:21.
**35**
s *Prophecies, concerning Jesus and their fulfillment,* Gen. 12:3.
t *Prophets,* Isa. 3:2.
u Psa. 78:2.
**36**
v *Disciples,* Matt. 9:14.
**37**
w *Truth,* John 18:37.
x *Doctrines of Jesus,* John 7:16.
y *Word of God,* Psa. 119:9
z *Jesus, humanity of,* Matt. 1:21.
**38**
a *Righteous, described,* Psa. 64:10.
b *Wicked, described,* Psa. 73:3.
**39**
c *Enemy, figurative,* Prov. 24:17.
d *Satan,* Matt. 4:10.
e *Harvest, figurative,* Ex. 34:21.
f *Judgment, the general,* 2 Pet. 3:7.
g *Angel, functions of,* Heb. 1:13.
**41**
h *Jesus, humanity of,* Matt. 1:21.
i *Jesus, king,* Matt. 1:21.
1 R. V. cause stumbling,
**42**
j *Wicked, punishment of,* Psa. 73:3.
k *Furnace, figurative,* Prov. 17:3.
l *Hell,* Mark 9:43.
m *Fire, figurative,* Ex. 12:8.
n *Gnashing of Teeth,* Job 16:9.
**43**
o *Righteous, compared to the sun,* Psa. 64:10.
p *Righteous, promises to,* Psa. 64:10.
q *Heaven, the future home of the righteous,* Luke 18:22. r *Spiritual Adoption,* Rom. 8:15. s *God, fatherhood of, taught by Jesus,* Gen. 2:2. t *Spiritual Understanding,* Luke 8:8. **44** u *Parables, of Jesus,* Ezek. 20:49.

v *Treasure,* Luke 12:33.
w *Gospel, likened to a treasure,* Mark 13:10.
x *Joy,* Psa. 5:11.
y *Renunciation,* Luke 5:11.
**45**
z *Merchant,* Neh. 3:32.
a *Pearl,* Rev. 17:4.
b *Gospel, likened to a pearl,* Mark 13:10.
**46**
c *Renunciation,* Luke 5:11.
**47**
d *Parables, of Jesus,* Ezek. 20:49.
**48**
e *Wicked, punishment of,* Psa. 73:3.
**49**
f *Judgment, the general,* 2 Pet. 3:7.
g *Angel, functions of,* Heb. 1:13.
h *Sin, separates from God,* Rom. 5:12.
i *Righteous,* Psa. 64:10.
**50**
j *Wicked, punishment of,* Psa. 73:3.
k *Furnace, figurative,* Prov. 17:3.
l *Hell,* Mark 9:43.
m *Fire, figurative,* Ex. 12:8.
n *Gnashing of Teeth,* Job 16:9.
**51**
o *Spiritual Understanding,* Luke 8:8.
2 R. V. *omits Lord.*
**52**
p *Scribe,* 1 Kin. 4:3.
q *Minister, character and qualifications of,* Rom. 15:16.
r *Treasure, figurative,* Luke 12:33.
3 R. V. who hath been made a disciple to the
**53**
s *Parables, of Jesus,* Ezek. 20:49.
t *Jesus, returns to Nazareth,* Matt. 1:21.
**54**
u Mark 6:1–6.
v *Synagogue,* Matt. 12:9.
w *Wisdom, spiritual,* Prov. 2:2.
x *Miracles,* Luke 23:8.

‖ **SORROW.** *Of the lost,* Matt. 8:12; 13:42, 50; 22:13; 24:51; 25:30; Luke 13:28; 16:23.

**55**
y *Joseph*, Luke 3:23.
z *Carpentry*, 2 Kin. 12:11.

a *Jesus, incarnation of*, Matt. 1:21.
b *Mother*, 1 Kin. 2:20.
c *Mary*, Luke 1:27.
d *Joses*, Matt. 27:56.
e Mark 6:3.
f Or, *Juda*, Mark 6:3.

**57**
g Luke 4:24; John 4:44.
h *Prophets*, Isa. 3:2.
i *Minister, discouragements of*, Rom. 15:16.

**58**
j *Unbelief*, Heb. 3:12.

55 Is not this the [y,z]carpenter's [a]son? is not his [b]mother called [c]Mā'rȳ? and his [§]brethren, [+]Jāmeş, and [d]Jō'sēş, and [e]Sī'mon, and [f]Jū'das?

56 [g]And his sisters, are they not all with us? Whence then hath this *man* all these things?

57 And they were offended in him. But Jē'şus said unto them, A [h,i]prophet is not without honour, save in his own country, and in his own house.

58 And he did not many mighty works there because of their [j]unbelief.

## CHAPTER 14

*Herod's opinion of Jesus. 3 Why John the Baptist was beheaded. 13 Jesus feeds five thousand men with five loaves and two fishes. 22 He walks on the sea. 34 As many as touch the hem of his garment are healed.*

**1**
a *Rulers, wicked, instances of*, Ex. 18:21.
b *Fame of Jesus*, Luke 5:15.

**2**
c *Conscience, guilty*, Acts 23:1.
d *Conviction of Sin, instances of*, John 16:8.
e *John the Baptist*, Luke 1:63.
1 R. V. do these powers work in him.

**3**
f *Malice, instances of*, Eph. 4:31.
g *Persecution, instances of*, John 15:20.
h *Imprisonment*, Acts 12:4.
i *Statecraft, women in*, Prov. 28:2.
j *Women, wicked, instances of*, Prov. 31:10.
k Mark 6:17; Luke 3:19.

AT that time [*,a]Hĕr'od the tetrarch heard of the [b]fame of Jē'şus,

2 [c,d]And said unto his servants, This is [e]Jŏhn the Băp'tĭst; he is risen from the dead; and therefore [1]mighty works do shew forth themselves in him.

3 ¶ For [*,a]Hĕr'od had [f,g]laid hold on [e]Jŏhn, and bound him, and [h]put *him* in prison [i]for [†,j]Hē-rō'dĭ-as' sake, his brother [k]Phĭl'ĭp's wife.

4 For [e]Jŏhn [l]said unto him, It is not lawful for thee to have her.

5 And when [*]he would have put [e]him to death, he [m]feared the multitude, because they counted him as a [n]prophet.

6 But when [*]Hĕr'od's [o]birthday was kept, the daughter of [†,j]Hē-rō'dĭ-as [p]danced before them, and pleased Hĕr'od.

7 Whereupon he promised with an [q]oath to give her whatsoever she would ask.

8 And she, being before [r]instructed of her [†]mother, said, Give me here [e]Jŏhn Băp'tĭst's head in a [s]charger.

9 And the [*]king was sorry: nevertheless for the [q]oath's sake, and them which sat with him at meat, he commanded *it* to be given *her*.

10 And [*]he sent, and [‡,t,u,v]beheaded Jŏhn in the prison.

11 And his head was brought in a [s]charger, and given to the damsel: and she brought *it* to her [†]mother.

12 And [e]his [w]disciples came, and took up the body, and [x]buried it, and went and told Jē'şus.

13 ¶ When [y]Jē'şus heard *of it*, he departed thence by [z]ship into a desert place apart: and when the people had heard *thereof*, they [a]followed [b]him on foot out of the cities.

14 And [c,d]Jē'şus went forth, and saw a great multitude, and was moved with [e]compassion toward them, and he [f,g]healed their sick.

15 ¶ [h]And when it was evening, his disciples came to him, [i]saying, This is a desert place, and the time is now past; send the multitude away, that they may go into the villages, and buy themselves victuals.

16 But Jē'şus said unto them, They need not depart; give ye them to eat.

**4** l *Reproof, faithfulness in*, Prov. 17:10. **5** m *Public Opinion, kings influenced by*, John 12:42. n *Prophets*, Isa. 3:2. **6** o *Birthday*, Gen. 40:20.

p *Dancing*, Eccl. 3:4.

**7**
q *Oath*, Num. 5:19.

**8**
r *Complicity, instances of*, Prov. 29:24.
s *Charger*, Ezra 1:9.

**10**
t *Homicide, felonious*, Deut. 5:17.
u *Punishment, death penalty*, Lev. 26:41.
v *Death, penalty*, Num. 23:10.

**12**
w *Disciples*, Matt. 9:14.
x *Burial*, Acts 8:2.

**13**
y *Jesus, life of*, Matt. 1:21.
z *Ship*, 2 Chr. 8:18.

a *Popularity of Jesus*, John 6:15.
b *Jesus, received*, Matt. 1:21.

**14**
c *Jesus, miracles of*, Matt. 1:21.
d *Jesus, love of*, Matt. 1:21.
e *Jesus, compassion of*, Matt. 1:21.
f *Healing, by Jesus*, Acts 4:22.
g *Miracles*, Luke 23:8.

**15**
h Mark 6:35–44: Luke 9:12–17; John 6:5–13.
i *Borrowing Trouble, instances of*, Matt. 6:25.

---

§ **BROTHERS OF JESUS**, Matt. 12:46; 13:55; Mark 3:31, 32; 6:3; John 7:3, 5; Acts 1:14; 1 Cor. 9:5; Gal. 1:19.

+ **JAMES.** *Brother of Jesus*, Matt. 13:55; Mark 6:3; Gal. 1:19. *Epistle of*, Jas. 1:1.
Whether this James is identical with James the son of Alphæus is one of the most difficult questions in the biographical history of the gospels. For full discussion of the subject the reader is referred to commentaries and biographical works.

* **HEROD.** *Tetrarch of Galilee*, Luke 3:1; 23:7. *Incest of*, Matt. 14:3, 4; Mark 6:17–19. *Beheads John the Baptist*, Matt. 14:3–11; Mark 6:16–28; Luke 9:9. *Mistakes Jesus for John*, Matt. 14:1, 2, 6–12; Mark 6:14–16, 21–29; Luke 9:7–9. *Desires to see Jesus*, Luke 9:7, 9; 23:8. *Tyranny of*, Luke 13:31, 32. *Jesus tried by*, Luke 23:6–12, 15; Acts 4:27.

† **HERODIAS.** *Daughter of Aristobulus*, Matt. 14:3, 6; Mark 6:17, 19, 22; Luke 3:19.

‡ **BEHEADING.** *Of John*, Matt. 14:10; Mark 6:27; Luke 9:9. *Of James*, Acts 12:2. *Of the martyrs*, Rev. 20:4. See footnote, PUNISHMENT, Lev. 26:41.

17 And they say unto him, We have here but five ||loaves, and two [j]fishes.

18 He said, Bring them hither to me.

19 And he commanded the multitude to sit down on the grass, and took the five ||loaves, and the two [j]fishes, and looking up to heaven, [c]he [k,l]blessed[G], and brake, and [g]gave the loaves to *his* [h]disciples, and the disciples to the multitude.

20 And [g]they did all eat, and were filled: and they §took up of the fragments that remained twelve [m]baskets full.[Q]

21 And they that had eaten were about five thousand men, beside women and children.[T]

22 ¶ [n]And[S] straightway[G] Jē'ṣus constrained[G] his [h]disciples to get into a [o]ship, and to go before him unto the other side, while he sent the multitudes away.

23 And when he had sent the multitudes away,[p] he went up into a mountain apart to [q]pray: and when the evening was come, he was there alone.

24[T] But the [o]ship was now in the midst of the [r]sea, tossed with waves: for the wind was contrary.

25 And in the fourth [s]watch[G] of the night +Jē'ṣus went unto them, walking on the [r,t]sea.[T]

26 And when the [h]disciples saw +him walking on the [r,t]sea, they were troubled, saying, It is [2]a spirit; and they cried out for fear.

27 But straightway[G] Jē'ṣus spake unto them, saying, [u]Be of good cheer[G]; it is I; be not afraid.

28 And [v]Pē'tēr answered him and said, Lord, if it be thou, bid[G] me come unto thee on the water.[T]

29[S] And he said, Come. And when [v]Pē'tēr was come down out of the [o]ship, he walked on the water, to go to Jē'ṣus.

30 But when he saw the wind boisterous[G], he was [w]afraid; and beginning to sink, he [x]cried, saying, [y]Lord, save me.

31 And immediately Jē'ṣus stretched forth *his* hand, and caught him, and said unto him, O thou of little [z]faith, wherefore didst thou [x]doubt?[S]

32 And when they were come into the [a]ship, [b]the wind ceased.

33 Then they that were in the [a]ship came and [c]worshipped [d]him, saying, Of a truth [e,f]thou art the [g]Son of God.[S T Q]

34 ¶ [h]And when they were gone over, they came into the land of Gĕn-nĕs'a-rĕt.

35 And when the men of that place had [i]knowledge of him, they sent out into all that country round about, and brought unto him all that were [j]diseased;

36 And besought him that they might only touch the hem of his garment: and as many as touched were [b,j,k]made perfectly whole[G].

## CHAPTER 15

*Jesus reproves the scribes and Pharisees on account of their traditions; 10 teaches that what goes into the mouth defiles not a man; 21 heals the daughter of a woman of Canaan, and many others; 32 and with seven loaves and a few little fishes feeds four thousand men, beside women and children.*

[a]THEN came to [b]Jē'ṣus [c]scribes and [d]Phăr'ĭ-seeṣ, which were of [e]Jė-rụ'sā-lĕm, saying,

2 Why do thy [f]disciples transgress the *,[g,h]tradition of the

17
j *Fish,* Matt. 17:27.

19
k *Prayers, of Jesus,* Luke 5:16.
l *Thanksgiving for Food,* Luke 24:30.

20
m *Basket,* Ex. 29:3.

22
n Mark 6:45–51; John 6:15–21.
o *Ship,* 2 Chr. 8:18.

23
p *Jesus, prayers of,* Matt. 1:21.
q *Prayer, secret,* Acts 6:4.

24
r *Sea of Galilee,* Matt. 4:18.

25
s *Time, division of, into watches,* Rev. 10:6.
t *Water,* 1 Kin. 17:10.

26
2 R. V. an apparition;

27
u *Afflictions, consolation in,* Psa. 34:19.

28
v *Peter,* Mark 5:37.

30
w *Cowardice, instances of,* Lev. 26:36.
x *Doubting, exemplified,* Rom. 14:23.
y *Adversity, prayer in,* Psa. 10:6.

31
z *Faith in Christ,* John 6:69.

32
a *Ship,* 2 Chr. 8:18.
b *Miracles, of Jesus,* Luke 23:8.

33
c *Jesus, worship of,* Matt. 1:21.
d *Jesus, received,* Matt. 1:21.
e *Confession of Christ,* Luke 12:8.
f *Faith in Christ,* John 6:69.
g *Jesus, divinity of,* Matt. 1:21.

34
h Mark 6:53–56.

35
i *Popularity of Jesus,* John 6:15.
j *Disease, healing of,* Ex. 15:26.

36
k *Jesus, miracles of,* Matt. 1:21.

1
a Mark 7:1–23.
b *Jesus, justifies disciples in disregarding traditions,* Matt. 1:21.
c *Scribe,* 1 Kin. 4:3.
d *Pharisees,* Matt. 15:12.
e *Jerusalem,* Judg. 19:10.

2
f *Apostles,* Luke 6:13.
g *Commandments of Men,* Mark 7:7.
h *Purification, traditions concerning,* Num. 19:19.

|| **LOAVES.** *Miracle, of the five,* Matt. 14:15–21; 16:9; Mark 6:37–44; Luke 9:12–17; John 6:5–13; *of the seven,* Matt. 15:34–38; 16:10; Mark 8:1–10.
See footnote, BREAD, Ezek. 4:13.

§ **FRUGALITY,** Prov. 21:17, 20; **23:20, 21.**
*Enjoined by Jesus,* John 6:12.
*Cloak of covetousness,* Mark 14:4, 5.
**Instances of,** Matt. 14:20; 15:37.

+ **JESUS WALKS ON THE SEA,** Matt. 14:25–33; Mark 6:48–52; John 6:19–21.

* **TRADITION.** *The decisions and minor precepts taught by Paul,* 1 Cor. 11:2 [R. V.]; 2 Thess. 2:15; 3:6.
*Commandments of men,* Matt. 12:1–8; 15:2–6; Mark 7:3–9; Luke 6:1–11; Gal. 1:14; Col. 2:8; 1 Pet. 1:18. *Not authoritative,* Matt. 15:2–9.

[i]elders? for they [j]wash not their
[k]hands when they [l]eat bread.
3 But [b]he answered and said
unto them, Why do ye also
[m]transgress the [n]commandment
of God by your *,[g,h]tradition?
4 For God commanded, say-
ing, [o,p,q]Honour thy [r]father and
[r]mother: and, [s]He that [1,t]curseth
father or mother, let him [u]die
the death.
5 But [v]ye say, Whosoever shall
say to *his* father or *his* mother,
[2]*It is* a gift, by whatsoever thou
mightest be profited by me;
6 And honour not his father
or his mother, *he shall be free.*
Thus have [v]ye made the commandment of God of none effect
by your *tradition.
7 *Ye* [w]hypocrites, well did
[x]Ê-sā'ias [y]prophesy of you,
saying,
8 [y,z]This people draweth nigh
unto me with their mouth, and
honoureth me with *their* lips;
[w]but their heart is far from me.
9 But in vain [a,b]they do worship me, teaching *for* doctrines
the [c]commandments of men.
10 ¶ And he called the multitude, and said unto them, Hear,
and understand:
11 Not that which goeth into
the mouth defileth a man; but
that which cometh out of the
mouth, this [d]defileth a man.
12 Then came his [e]disciples,
and said unto him, Knowest
thou that the †Phăr'ĭ-seeş were
offended, after they heard this
saying?
13 But he answered and said,
Every plant, which my heavenly
[f]Father hath not planted, shall
be rooted up.

*i* *Senate*, Num. 11:16.
*j* *Ceremonial Washings*, Ex. 19:10.
*k* *Hand, ceremonial washing of*, Ezra 10:19.
*l* *Eating, ablutions before*, Gen. 18:8.

**3**
*m* *Disobedience to God*, Eph. 5:6.
*n* *Word of God*, Psa. 119:9.

**4**
*o* Ex. 20:12.
*p* *Commandment, enjoining reverence for parents*, Deut. 8:2.
*q* *Children, commandments to*, Mark 10:14.
*r* *Parents, to be reverenced*, 2 Cor. 12:14.
*s* Ex. 21:17.
*t* *Cursing, of parents*, Lev. 24:11.
*u* *Punishment, death penalty*, Lev. 26:41.
1 R. V. speaketh evil of

**5**
*v* *False Teachers*, 2 Pet. 2:1.
2 R.V. That wherewith thou mightest have been profited by me is given to God;

**7**
*w* *Hypocrisy*, Jas. 3:17.
*x* Or, *Isaiah*, Isa. 1:1.
*y* *Prophecies*, Dan 9:24.

**8**
*z* Isa. 29:13.

**9**
*a* *Minister, false and corrupt*, Rom. 15:16.
*b* *False Teachers*, 2 Pet. 2:1.
*c* *Commandments of Men*, Mark 7:7.

**11**
*d* *Defilement*, Lev. 5:2.

**12**
*e* *Apostles*, Luke 6:13.

**13**
*f* *God, fatherhood of*, Gen. 2:2.

14 Let them alone: [g]they be
[h]blind [a,b]leaders of the blind.
[i]And if the blind lead the blind,
both shall fall into the ditch.
15 Then answered [j]Pē'tĕr and
said unto him, Declare unto us
this [k]parable.
16 And Jē'şus said, Are ye also
yet without [l]understanding?
17 [m]Do not ye yet understand,
that whatsoever entereth in at
the mouth goeth into the belly,
and is cast out into the draught?
18 [n]But those things which proceed out of the mouth come forth
from the [o]heart; and they [d]defile
the man.
19 For out of the [o,p]heart proceed [q]evil thoughts, [r]murders,
[s]adulteries, fornications, [t]thefts,
[u,v]false witness, [3,w]blasphemies:
20 These are *the things* which
[d]defile a man: but to eat with
[x]unwashen hands defileth not a
man.
21 ¶ [y]Then Jē'şus went thence,
and departed into the coasts of
[z]Tȳre and [a]Sī'dŏn.
22 And, behold, a [b]woman of
Cā'năan came out of the same
coasts, and [c]cried unto him, saying, [d]Have mercy on me, O
Lord, *thou* [e]son of [f]Dā'vid; [g]my
daughter is grievously vexed
with a [h]devil.
23 But he answered her not a
word. And his [i,j]disciples came
and besought him, saying, Send
her away; for she crieth after
us.
24 But he answered and said,
[k]I am not sent but unto the lost
[l]sheep of the house of Ĭş'ra-el.
25 Then came she and wor-

**23** *i* *Apostles*, Luke 6:13. *j* *Minister, intolerance of*, Rom. 15:16.
**24** *k* *Jesus, mission of*, Matt. 1:21. *l* *Sheep, figurative*, Deut. 32:14.

**14**
*g* *Wicked, compared to the blind*, Psa. 73:3.
*h* *Spiritual Blindness*, 2 Cor. 4:4.
*i* Luke 6:39.

**15**
*j* *Peter*, Mark 5:37.
*k* *Parables, of Jesus*, Ezek. 20:49.

**16**
*l* *Spiritual Understanding*, Luke 8:8.

**17**
*m* Mark 7:15.

**18**
*n* Mark 7:20–23.
*o* *Heart*, Psa. 44:21.

**19**
*p* *Depravity*, Job 15:14.
*q* *Evil Imagination*, Gen. 6:5.
*r* *Homicide, felonious*, Deut. 5:17.
*s* *Adultery*, Lev. 20:10.
*t* *Theft*, Mark 7:22.
*u* *False Witness*, Matt. 19:18.
*v* *Falsehood*, Job 21:34.
*w* *Blasphemy*, 2 Sam. 12:14.
3 R. V. railings:

**20**
*x* *Ceremonial Washings*, Ex. 19:10.

**21**
*y* Mark 7:24–30.
*z* *Tyre*, Josh. 19:29.
*a* Or, *Zidon*, Ezek. 28:21.

**22**
*b* Mark 7:24–30.
*c* *Adversity, prayer in*, Psa. 10:6.
*d* *Faith in Christ*, John 6:69.
*e* *Jesus, names of*, Matt. 1:21.
*f* *David, Jesus called son of*, 1 Sam. 16:13.
*g* *Mediation*, Gal. 3:19.
*h* *Demons*, Matt. 4:24.

† **PHARISEES.** *A sect of the Jews*, Acts 15:5. *Doctrines of*, Matt. 15:9; *concerning the resurrection*, Acts 23:6, 8; *concerning association with publicans and sinners*, Matt. 9:11–13.

Traditions of: *In regard to, fasting*, Matt. 9:14; Luke 18:12; *the washing of hands*, Matt. 15:1, 2; Mark 7:1–15; Luke 11:37, 38; *the duty of children to parents*, Matt. 15:4–9; Mark **7**:10–12; *the Sabbath*, Matt. 12:2–8; Mark 2:23–28; Luke 6:1–11.

*Denounced by Jesus*, Matt. 23:2–36; Luke 11:39–44. *Hypocrisy of, reproved, by John*, Matt. 3:7–10; *by Jesus*, Matt. 6:2–8, 16–18; 15:1–9; 16:1–12; 21:33–46; 23:2–33; Mark **7**:6–15; Luke 11:14–54; 12:1; 15:1–9; 16:14, 15. *Reject John*, Luke 7:30. *Reject Christ*, Matt. 12:38–45; 15:12; John **7**:48. *Come to Jesus with questions*, Matt. 19:3; 22:15–22. *Persecute Jesus*, Matt. 12:14, 24; Mark 3:6; 8:11; Luke 11:16; John 11:47–53.

*Minister to Jesus*, Luke **7**:36; **11**:37; 14:1. *Become disciples of Jesus*, John 3:1; Acts 15:5.

*Paul, a Pharisee*, Acts 23:6; 26:5.

See footnote, SADDUCEES, Matt. 22:23.

**25**
*m Jesus, worship of,* Matt. 1:21.
*n Prayer, importunity in,* Acts 6:4.

**26**
*o Dog,* 1 Kin. 21:19.

**27**
*p Humility, exemplified,* Prov. 22:4.

**28**
*q Faith in Christ,* John 6:69.
*r Jesus, miracles of,* Matt. 1:21.
*s Miracles,* Luke 23:8.

**29**
*t* Mark 7:31–37.
*u Galilee,* Mark 6:21.

**30**
*v Popularity of Jesus,* John 6:15.
*w Lameness,* Lev. 21:18.
*x Blindness,* 2 Kin. 6:18.
*y Dumb,* Ex. 4:11.
*z Healing, by Jesus,* Acts 4:22.

**31**
*a Jesus, received,* Matt. 1:21.
*b Glorifying God,* Luke 5:25.

**32**
*c* Mark 8:1–9.
*d Jesus, compassion of,* Matt. 1:21.
*e Jesus, love of,* Matt. 1:21.
*f Hunger,* Neh. 9:15.

**33**
*g Apostles,* Luke 6:13.
*h Bread,* Ezek. 4:13.

shipped [m]him, [n]saying, Lord,
help me.[Q]
26 But he answered and said,
It is not meet[G] to take the children's
bread, and to cast *it* to
[o]dogs.[G]
27 And she said, [p]Truth, Lord:
yet the [o]dogs[G] eat of the crumbs
which fall from their masters'
table.
28 Then Jē'ṣus answered and
said unto her, O woman, great
*is* thy [q]faith: be it unto thee even
as thou wilt. And her daughter
was [r,s]made[S] whole[G] from that
very hour.
29 ¶ [t]And Jē'ṣus departed from
thence, and came nigh[G] unto the
sea of [u]Găl'ĭ-lee; and went up
into a mountain, and sat down
there.
30 And [v]great multitudes came
unto him, having with them
*those that were* [w]lame, [x]blind,
[y]dumb, maimed[G], and many
others, and cast them down at
Jē'ṣus' feet; and [q]he [s,z]healed
them:
31 Insomuch that the multitude
wondered, when they saw the
[y]dumb [s]to speak, the maimed[G]
[s]to be whole[G], the [w]lame [s]to walk,
and the [x]blind to see: [a]and they
[b]glorified[G] the God of Iṣ'ra-el.[Q]
32 ¶ [c]Then Jē'ṣus called his
disciples *unto him,* and said, I
have [d,e]compassion on the multitude,
because they continue with
me now three days, and have
nothing to eat: and I will not
send them away [f]fasting, lest
they faint in the way.[T]
33 And his [g]disciples say unto
him, Whence should we have so
much [h]bread in the wilderness,
as to fill so great a multitude?
34 And Jē'ṣus saith unto them,
How many [i]loaves have ye?
And they said, Seven, and a few
little [j]fishes.
35 And he commanded the
multitude to sit down on the
ground.
36 And he took the seven
[i]loaves and the [j]fishes, and [k]gave
[l]thanks, and brake *them,* and
[m]gave to his [g]disciples, and the
disciples to the multitude.
37 And [m]they did all eat, and
were filled: and they [n]took up of
the broken meat[G] that was left
seven [o]baskets full.
38 And they that did eat
were four thousand men, beside
women and children.
39 And he sent away the multitude,
and took ship, and came
into the coasts[G] of [4]Măg'da-lă.[T]

## CHAPTER 16

*The Pharisees require a sign. 6 Jesus warns his disciples of the leaven of the Pharisees and Sadducees. 13 What the people think of Jesus. 16 and Peter's confession of him. 21 Jesus foretells his own death and resurrection. 24 Those who will follow him must take up their cross.*

[a]THE [b]Phăr'ĭ-seeṣ also with
the [c]Săd'du-çeeṣ[G] came,
and tempting[G] desired[G] him that
he would shew them a [d]sign[G]
from heaven.
2 He answered and said unto
them, When it is evening, ye say,
**It will be* fair [e]weather: for the
sky is red.
3 And in the morning, *It will
be* foul [e]weather to day: for the
sky is red and lowring[G]. [f,g]O *ye*
hypocrites, ye can discern the
face of the sky; but can ye [h]not
*discern* the signs of the times?
4 [j]A wicked and adulterous
generation seeketh after a
[d,i]sign[G]; and [k]there shall no sign[G]

**34**
*i Loaves,* Matt. 14:17.
*j Fish,* Matt. 17:27.

**36**
*k Jesus, prayers of,* Matt. 1:21.
*l Thanksgiving by Jesus,* Matt. 11:25.
*m Miracles,* Luke 23:8.

**37**
*n Frugality, instances of,* Matt. 14:20.
*o Basket,* Ex. 29:3.

**39**
4 **R. V. Magadan.**

**1**
*a* Mark 8:10–12; Luke 12:54–57.
*b Pharisees, reproved by Jesus,* Matt. 15:12.
*c Sadducees,* Matt. 22:23.
*d Miracles, demanded by unbelievers,* Luke 23:8.

**2**
*e* Job 37:22.

**3**
*f* Luke 12:56.
*g Reproof,* Prov. 17:10.
*h Spiritual Blindness,* 2 Cor. 4:4.
*i Sign, a token,* Mark 8:11.

**4**
*j* Matt. 12:39.
*k Jesus, refuses to give sign to Pharisees,* Matt. 1:21.

* **METEOROLOGY,** Gen. 2:5, 6; 27:39; Job 26:8; Psa. 104:19; 107:25; Eccl. 11:3; Isa. 50:3; Jer. 10:13; 51:16; Amos 9:6; Nah. 1:3; Matt. 24:27; John 3:8; Acts 27:14. *Weather affected by good men's prayers,* 1 Sam. 12:16–18; 1 Kin. 18:41–45; Jas. 5:17, 18.
*In the land of Uz,* Job 27:20, 21; 28:24–27; 29:19; 36:27–33; 37:6–22; 38:8–11, 22, 24–37. *In Palestine,* Psa. 18:10–15; 29:3–10; 48:7; 65:8–12; 133:3; 135:6, 7; 147:7, 8; 148:7, 8; Prov. 25:23; 26:1; 30:4; Eccl. 1:6, 7; Hos. 6:4; 13:15.
*Weather, forecast of,* Matt. 16:2, 3.
*Tempest stilled by Jesus,* Matt. 8:24–27; Luke 8:22–25. *The autumnal storms on the Mediterranean,* Acts 27:9–20, 27.
**Phenomena of:** *The deluge,* Gen. 7:4, 10–12. *Plagues of hail, thunder, and lightning in Egypt,* Ex. 9:22–28, 34; Psa. 78:23, 47, 48. *East wind that divided the Red Sea,* Ex. 14:21. *Dew on Gideon's fleece,* Judg. 6:36–40. *The whirlwind which carried Elijah to heaven,* 2 Kin. 2:1, 11. *Thunder discomfits the Philistine army,* 1 Sam. 7:10. *Wind destroyed Job's children,* Job 1:18, 19.

[l] Or, *Jonah*, Jonah 1:1.

**5**
[m] *Apostles*, Luke 6:13.
[n] Mark 8:14-21.
[o] *Bread*, Ezek. 4:13.

**6**
[p] Luke 12:1.
[q] *Watchfulness, enjoined against false teachers*, Matt. 24:42.
[r] *Leaven, figurative*, Lev. 23:17.
[s] *Hypocrisy, warnings against*, Jas. 3:17.
[t] *Self-righteousness*, Luke 18:11.
[u] *False Teachers*, 2 Pet. 2:1.

**8**
[v] *Faith in Christ*, John 6:69.

**9**
[w] *Spiritual Blindness*, 2 Cor. 4:4.
[x] *Loaves*, Matt. 14:17.
[y] *Miracles, of Jesus*, Luke 23:8.

be given unto it, but the sign[G] of
the prophet [l]Jō'nas. And he left
them, and departed.
5 ¶ And when his [m]disciples
were come to the other side,
[n]they had forgotten to take
[o]bread.
6 Then Jē'ṣus said unto them,
[p,q]Take heed and beware of the
[r,s,t]leaven[G] of the [b,u]Phăr'ĭ-seeṣ
and of the [c,u]Săd'du-çeeṣ[G].
7 And they reasoned among
themselves, saying, *It is* because
we have taken no [o]bread.
8 *Which* when Jē'ṣus perceived,
he said unto them, O [m]ye
of little [v]faith, why reason ye
among yourselves, because ye
have brought no [o]bread?
9 Do ye [w]not yet understand,
neither remember the five
[x,y]loaves of the five thousand,
and how many baskets ye took
up?
10 Neither the seven [x,y]loaves
of the four thousand, and how
many baskets ye took up?
11 How is it that ye do [w]not
understand that I spake *it* not to
you concerning [o]bread, that ye
should beware of the [r,s,t]leaven[G]
of the [b,u]Phăr'ĭ-seeṣ and of the
[c,u]Săd'du-çeeṣ[G]?
12 Then understood they how
that he bade *them* not beware of
the [z]leaven of [o]bread, but of the
[1]doctrine[G] of the [b,u]Phăr'ĭ-seeṣ
and of the [c,u]Săd'du-çeeṣ[G].
13 ¶ [a]When Jē'ṣus came into
the coasts[G] of †Çæs-a-rē'à Phĭlĭp'pī,
he asked his [b]disciples,
saying, [c]Whom do men say that I
the Son of man am?
14 And they said, Some *say that
thou art* [d]Jŏhn the Băp'tĭst:
some, [e]Ē-lī'as; and others, [f]Jĕr-e-mī'as,
or one of the [g]prophets.
15 He saith unto [b]them, But
[2]whom say ye that I am?
16 [S] And [h]Sī'mon Pē'tēr answered
and said, [i,j]Thou art the
[k]Chrīst[G], the [l]Son of the living
God.[T Q]
17 And Jē'ṣus answered and
said unto him, Blessed art thou,
[h]Sī'mon Bär–jō'nȧ: for flesh and
blood hath not revealed [m]*it* unto
thee, but my [n]Father which is in
[o]heaven.[T]
18 And [p]I say also unto thee,
That thou art [h]Pē'tēr, and upon
this [q]rock I will build my
‡church; and the [r]gates of [3,s]hell[G]
shall not prevail[G] against it.[Q]

**12**
[z] *Leaven*, Lev. 23:17.
1 R. V. teaching

**13**
[a] Mark 8:27-30; Luke 9:18-20.
[b] *Apostles*, Luke 6:13.
[c] *Public Opinion*, John 12:42.

**14**
[d] *John the Baptist*, Luke 1:63.
[e] Or, *Elijah*, 1 Kin. 17:1.
[f] Or, *Jeremiah*, Jer. 1:1.
[g] *Prophets*, Isa. 3:2.

**15**
2 R. V. who

**16**
[h] *Peter*, Mark 5:37.
[i] *Faith in Christ, exemplified*, John 6:69.
[j] *Confession of Christ*, Luke 12:8.
[k] *Jesus, Messiah*, Matt. 1:21.
[l] *Jesus, divinity of*, Matt. 1:21.

**17**
[m] *Wisdom, spiritual*, Prov. 2:2.
[n] *God, fatherhood of, taught by Jesus*, Gen. 2:2.
[o] *Heaven, God's dwelling place*, Luke 18:22.

**18** [p] *Jesus, prophet*, Matt. 1:21. [q] *Rock, figurative*, Psa. 78:15. [r] *Gates, figurative*, Deut. 3:5. [s] *Hell*, Mark 9:43. 3 R. V. Hades

† **CÆSAREA PHILIPPI**, a city in the N. of Palestine. *Visited by Jesus*, Matt. 16:13; Mark 8:27; Luke 9:18.

‡ **CHURCH**. The word Church is used here to express the idea of an organized body of believers without regard to the form of institution under which they are associated, whether ancient or modern. No modern term in common use describes the ancient politico-ecclesiastical institution founded by Moses and existing at the time of our Savior. To call the Jewish community a church, combining in itself, as it did, social, political and ecclesiastical functions, may seem, from some points of view, unwarranted, but to all intents and purposes it was a church, and is so classed in this topic. Its priests are classed as ministers and the places of worship are classed as churches. Marginal topics opposite verses containing the church idea employ the word church in order to state the subject in the modern term.

*Called, in the Old Testament*, THE CONGREGATION, Ex. 12:3, 6, 19, 47; 16:1, 2, 9, 10, 22; Lev. 4:13, 15; 10:17; 24:14; ZION, 2 Kin. 19:21, 31; Psa. 9:11; 48:2, 11, 12; 74:2; 132:13; 137:1; Isa. 35:10; 40:9; 49:14; 51:16; 52:1, 2, 7, 8; 60:14; 62:1, 11; Jer. 31:6; 50:5; Lam. 1:4; Joel 2:1, 15; Rom. 9:33; 11:26; 1 Pet. 2:6; DAUGHTER OF ZION, Isa. 62:11; Zech. 9:9; Matt. 21:5; John 12:15.

*Called, in the New Testament*, CHURCH, Matt. 16:18; 18:17; Acts 2:47; 7:38; 20:28; 1 Cor. 11:18; 14:19, 23, 28, 33, 34; 15:9; Gal. 1:13; Eph. 1:22; 1 Tim. 3:15.

**Described as:** *Assembly of the saints*, Psa. 89:7. *Assembly of the upright*, Psa. 111:1. *Body of Christ*, 1 Cor. 12:27; Eph. 4:12. *Branch of God's planting*, Isa. 60:21. *Bride of Christ*, Rev. 21:9. *Christ's body*, Rom. 12:5; 1 Cor. 12:12, 27; Eph. 1:22, 23; 4:12; Col. 1:24. *Church of God*, Acts 20:28. *Church of the living God*, 1 Tim. 3:15. *Church of the firstborn*, Heb. 12:23. *City of the living God*, Heb. 12:22. *Congregation of saints*, Psa. 149:1. *Flock of God*, 1 Pet. 5:2. *Fold*, John 10:16. *General assembly of the firstborn*, Heb. 12:23. *Golden candlestick*, Rev. 1:20. *Heavenly Jerusalem*, Heb. 12:22. *Holy city*, Rev. 21:2. *Holy hill*, Psa. 15:1. *House*, Heb. 3:6. *House of God*, 1 Tim. 3:15; Heb. 10:21. *Household of God*, Eph. 2:19. *Israel of God*, Gal. 6:16. *Joy of the whole earth*, Psa. 48:1, 2, 11-13. *Bride*, Rev. 22:17. *Lamb's wife*, Rev. 19:7-9; 21:9. *Mount Zion*, Heb. 12:22. *Mountain of the Lord's house*, Isa. 2:2. *New Jerusalem*, Rev. 21:2. *Perfection of beauty*, Psa. 50:2. *Pillar and ground of the truth*, 1 Tim. 3:15. *River of gladness*, Psa. 46:4, 5. *Sought out, a city not forsaken*, Isa. 62:12. *Spiritual house*, 1 Pet. 2:5. *Temple of God*, 1 Cor. 3:16, 17. *Temple of the living God*, 2 Cor. 6:16.

*Barren, in the parable of the fruitless fig tree*, Luke 13:6-9; *by the fig tree with nothing but leaves*, Matt. 21:19, 20; Mark 11:13, 14. *Corrupt, in the parables of the vineyard*, Isa. 5:1-7; Matt. 21:33-46; Mark 12:1-12; Luke 20:9-19.

**God loves**, Isa. 27:2, 3; 43:1-7; 49:14-17; Jer. 3:14, 15; 13:11.

**God dwells in**, Psa. 132:14.

**Love for**, Psa. 84:1-12; 102:14.

Manifested: *By prayer for*, Psa. 122:6-9; *by distress at misfortunes of*, Psa. 137:1-6; Isa. 22:4; Jer. 9:1; 14:17; 51:50, 51; Lam. 2:11; 3:48-51; *by joy at prosperity of*, Isa. 66:10, 13, 14; *by zeal for*, Isa. 58:12; 62:1, 6, 7.

**Mission of:** *To be custodians of the oracles of God*, Rom. 3:2; 9:4. *To bring, peace*, Psa. 22:27-31; Isa. 2:3, 4, 5; 11:6-9; 52:1, 2, 7, 8; 61:1-3; 65:25; *spiritual enlightenment*, Isa. 2:3; 29:18, 19; Joel 2:36-32; Hab. 2:14; Acts 2:16-21; *moral transformation*, Isa. 4:2-6; 32:3, 4, 15-17; 35:1, 2, 5-7; 44:3-5; 55:10-13; Zeph. 3:9.

**Prophecies concerning:** *Its universality*, Gen. 12:3; Isa.

19
*t Apostles, authority of,* Luke 6:13.
*u Key, a symbol of authority,* Judg. 3:25.
*v Kingdom of Heaven,* Matt. 13:24.
*w Minister, duties of,* Rom. 15:16.
*x Heaven, figurative,* Luke 18:22.
20
*y Prudence, instances of,* 2 Chr. 2:12.
4 R. V. *omits* Jesus
21
*z Jesus, foretells his death,* Matt. 17:22.

*a Jesus, prophet,* Matt. 1:21.
*b Apostles,* Luke 6:13.
*c Jerusalem,* Judg. 19:10.
*d Persecution, of Jesus,* John 15: 20.
*e Senate,* Num. 11:16.
*f Priest,* Lev. 1:5.
*g Scribe,* 1 Kin. 4:3.
*h Resurrection,* 1 Cor. 15:12.
22
*i Peter,* Mark 5:37.
*j Presumption,* Psa. 19:13.
23
*k Reproof, faithfulness in,* Prov. 17:10.
5 R. V. a stumblingblock
6 R. V. mindest

19 And I will give unto [t]thee
the [u]keys of the [v]kingdom of
heaven: and whatsoever [w]thou
shalt bind on earth shall be
bound in [x]heaven: and whatsoever thou shalt loose on earth
shall be loosed in heaven.[S]
20 Then [y]charged[C] he his [b]dis-
ciples that they should tell no man
that he was [4,k]Jē′şus the Christ.
21 ¶ From that time forth began Jē′şus to [z,a]shew unto his
[b]disciples, how that he must go
unto [c]Jē-ru′sā-lĕm, and [d]suffer
many things of the [e]elders and
chief [f]priests and [g]scribes, and
be killed, and [h]be raised again
the third day.[S]
22 Then [i]Pē′tẽr took him, and
began to [j]rebuke him, saying, Be
it far from thee, Lord: this shall
not be unto thee.
23 But he turned, and [k]said unto [i]Pē′tẽr, Get thee behind me,
Sā′tan: thou art [5]an offence unto
me: for thou [6]savourest[C] not the
things that be of God, but those
that be of men.
24 Then said Jē′şus unto his
disciples, If any [l]*man* will come
after me, [m]let him [n]deny himself, and take up his [o]cross, and
follow me.[T]
25 For whosoever will save his
[p]life shall lose it: and whosoever
will [q]lose his life for my sake
shall [r]find it.
26 [s,t,u,v]For what is a man
profited, if he shall gain the
whole world, and [7,w]lose his own
[p,x]soul[C]? or what shall a man
give in exchange for his [8]soul?
27 For the [y]Son of man shall
[z]come in the glory of his [a]Father
with his [b]angels; and [c]then he
shall [d,e]reward every man according to his works.[T Q]
28 Verily [f]I say unto you,
There be some standing here,
which shall not taste of [g]death,
till they see the [h]Son of man
coming in [i]his kingdom.[T]

## CHAPTER 17

*The transfiguration. 10 Elijah is already come. 14 Jesus heals a lunatic. 22 He foretells his own death and resurrection. 24 The tribute money miraculously provided.*

AND after six days [a]Jē′şus
taketh [b]Pē′tẽr, [c]Jāmeş,
and [d]Jŏhn his brother, and

*o Cross, figurative of duty,* John 19: 17.
25
*p Life,* Eccl. 8:15.
*q Renunciation, of self for Christ,* Luke 5:11.
*r Reward, a motive, to faithfulness,* Matt. 5:12.
26
*s* Mark 8:36, 37; Luke 9:25.
*t Ambition, Christ rebukes,* Hab. 2:5.
*u Worldliness, admonitions against,* 1 John 2:15.
*v Covetousness, warnings against,* Isa. 57:17.
*w Wicked, punishment of,* Psa. 73:3.
*x Immortality,* 1 Cor. 15:54.
7 R. V. forfeit his life?
8 R. V. life?
27
*y Jesus, humanity of,* Matt. 1:21.
*z Jesus, second coming of,* Matt. 1:21.

*a God, fatherhood of,* Gen. 2:2.
*b Angel, functions of,* Heb. 1:13.

**24** *l Righteous, described,* Psa. 64:10. *m Commandment, enjoining self-denial and cross-bearing,* Deut. 8:2. *n Self-denial,* Mark 8:34.

*c Judgment, the general,* 2 Pet. 3:7. *d Reward,* Matt. 5:12. *e Punishment, according to deeds,* Lev. 26:41. **28** *f Jesus, prophet,* Matt. 1:21. *g Death,* Num. 23:10. *h Jesus, humanity of,* Matt. 1:21. *i Jesus, kingdom of,* Matt. 1:21.
**1** *a Jesus, transfigured,* vs. 2–9; Matt. 1:21. *b Peter,* Mark 5:37. *c James,* Luke 5:10. *d John,* Mark 1:19.

2:2; 40:5; 42:3, 4; 45:23; 52:10, 15; 54:1–5; 56:7, 8; 59:19; 60:1, 3–9; 66:12, 19, 23; Jer. 3:17; 4:2; 16:19; 31:7–9, 34; 33:22; Dan. 2:35, 45; 7:13, 14, 18, 22, 27; Amos 9:11, 12; Zeph. 2:11; Zech. 9:1, 10; 14:6–9, 16; Mal. 1:11; Matt. 8:11; John 10:16; Rev. 11:15; 15:4.

*Its prosperity,* **Psa. 72:7–11, 16, 19;** 86:9; 102:15, **16, 18;** 132:15–18; Isa. 4:2–6; 25:6–8; 33:20, 21; 49:6–18; **51: 3–8; 52:1, 2, 7, 8, 10, 15; 54:1–5, 11–14; 55:5, 10–13; 60: 1–9, 19, 20; 61:1–11; 62:2, 3, 12; 65:18, 19, 23–25; 66:12, 19, 23;** Jer. 31:34; Ezek. 17:22–24; 34:26, 29, 30, 31; 47:3–12; Joel 2:26–32; Amos 9:11, 12; Mic. 4:3, 4; 5:2, 4, 7; Hab. 2:14; Zeph. 3:9; Hag. 2:7–9; Zech. 2:10, 11; 6:15; 8: 20–23.

*Its perpetuity,* Isa. 9:7; 33:20; Dan. 7:14, 27; Matt. 16:18.

**Christian:** *Divinely instituted,* Matt. 16:15–18; Eph. 2:20–22; 1 Thess. 1:1; 2 Thess. 1:1; 1 Tim. 3:15. *Founded on the lordship of Jesus,* Matt. 16:18.

*Christ, head of,* Psa. 118:22, 23; Isa. 28:16; Matt. 21:42–43; Mark 12:10; Luke 20:17, 18; John 15:1–8; 1 Cor. 3:11; Eph. 1:22, 23; 2:20–22; 4:15; 5:23–32; Col. 1:18; 2:10, 19; 3:11; 1 Pet. 2:7; Rev. 2:2–28.

*Christ's love for,* John 10:8, 11, 14; Eph. 5:25–32; Rev. 3:9.

*Membership in,* Luke 18:16; Acts 2:41, 47; 4:4; 5:14; 9:35, 42; 11:21; Rom. 12:4, 5; 1 Cor. 12:12–28; Eph. 5:30; Phil. 4:3.

*Rapid growth of,* Acts **2:41, 47;** 4:4; 5:14; 6:7; 9:35; 11:21, **24;** 14:1; 19:17–20.

*Communism in,* Acts 4:32.

*Holiness of,* 2 Cor. 11:2; Eph. 5:27; 2 Pet. 3:14; Rev. 19:8.

*Unity of,* John 10:16; 17:11, 21–23; Rom. 12:4, 5; 1 Cor. **10:17;** 12:5, 12, 13, 26, 27 (with vs. 12–27); Gal. 3:26–28; Eph. **1:10;** 2:14–20; 3:6, 15; 4:4–6, 12, 13, 16, 25; Col. 3:11, 15.

*Union of, with Christ,* John 15:1–7; Rom. 11:17; 2 Cor. 11: **2;** Eph. 5:30, 32; Rev. 19:7; 21:9.

*Diversity of callings in,* 1 Cor. 12:5, 28; Eph. 4:11, 12.

Edified: *By teachers,* Eph. 4:11, 12; *by public worship,* Col. 3:16; Heb. 10:25.

*Pastoral care of,* Acts 20:28.

*Orderly conduct of worship in, enjoined,* 1 Cor. 11:4, 5, 33; 14:26, 33, 40; see also Eccl. 5:1, 2; 1 Tim. 3:15.

**Discipline in the Christian.** Design of: *To save the soul,* Matt. 18:15; 1 Cor. 5:1–13; 2 Thess. 3:14; *to warn others,* 1 Tim. 5:20; *to preserve sound doctrine,* Rom. 16:17; 1 Tim. 1:19, 20; Tit. 1:13; Gal. 5:10.

*Witnesses required in,* Matt. 18:16; 2 Cor. 13:1; 1 Tim. 5:19.

To be exercised: *With kindness,* 2 Cor. 2:6–11; Gal. 6:1; Jude 22, 23; *with forbearance,* Rom. 15:1–3.

*By reproof,* 2 Cor. 7:8; 10:1–11; 13:2, 10; 1 Thess. 5:14; 2 Thess. 3:15; 1 Tim. 5:1, 2; 2 Tim. 4:2; Tit. 2:15.

*For schism,* Rom. 16:17. *For heresy,* 1 Tim. 6:3–5; Tit. 3:10, 11; 2 John 10, 11. *For immorality,* Matt. 18:17, 18; 1 Cor. 5:1–7, 11, 13; 2 Thess. 3:6.

See footnote, DISFELLOWSHIP, Num. 15:31.

**Government of the Christian:** *Authority of apostles in,* Matt. 16:19; John 20:23; Acts 1:15, 23–26; Acts 5:1–11; 1 Cor. 7:17; 11:2, 33, 34; Gal. 2:9. *Authority of apostolic council in,* Acts 15:1–31; 16:4, 5.

*Deacons appointed in,* Acts 6:2–6. *Character of deacons in,* 1 Tim. 3:8–13.

*Bishops or overseers in,* 1 Tim. 3:1–7.

*Elders in,* Acts 14:23; 1 Tim. 5:1, 17, 22; Tit. 1:5. *Duties of elders,* Acts 20:17, 28; Jas. 5:14, 15; 1 Pet. 5:1–3.

*Prophets and teachers in,* Acts 13:1, 3, 5; 1 Tim. 4:14; 2 Tim. 1:6.

*Congregational authority in,* 1 Cor. 16:3, 16; Jude 22, 23.

*Obedience to rulers in, enjoined,* Heb. 13:17, 24.

**Duty of Christian, to Ministers:** *To encourage,* 1 Cor.

bringeth them up into an high
[e]mountain apart,
2 And was *transfigured before
them: and his [f]face did [g]shine as
the [h]sun, and his [i]raiment was
[j]white as the light.
3 And, behold, [k]there appeared
unto them [l]Mō′ṣeṣ and [m]Ē-lī′as
talking with him.
4 Then answered [b]Pē′tēr, and
said unto Jē′ṣus, Lord, [n]it is
good for us to be here: if thou
wilt, let us make here three
tabernacles; one for thee, and
one for [l]Mō′ṣeṣ, and one for
[m]Ē-lī′as.
5 While he yet spake, behold,
a bright [o]cloud overshadowed
them: and behold a voice out of
the cloud, which said, This is my
beloved [p]Son, in whom I am well
pleased; hear ye him.
6 And when the [q]disciples
heard *it*, they fell on their face,
and were sore afraid.
7 And Jē′ṣus came and touched
them, and said, Arise, and be not
afraid.
8 And when they had lifted up
their eyes, they saw no man,
save Jē′ṣus only.
9 ¶ [r]And as they came down
from the [e]mountain, Jē′ṣus
[s]charged them, saying, Tell the
[t]vision to no man, until the Son
of man be [u]risen again from the
dead.
10 And his [q]disciples asked
him, saying, Why then [v]say the
[w]scribes that [x]Ē-lī′as must first
come?
11 And Jē′ṣus answered and
said unto them, [y]Ē-lī′as truly
shall first come, and restore all
things.

*e* *Mountain, Jesus is transfigured upon*, Mic. 7:12.

**2**

*f* *Face, transfigured*, Ex. 34:29.
*g* *Light, miraculous*, Gen. 1:3.
*h* *Sun*, Josh. 10:12.
*i* *Dress*, Zech. 3:3.
*j* *Colors, symbolical*, Ezek. 16:16.

**3**

*k* *Immortality*, 1 Cor. 15:54.
*l* *Moses, on the mount of transfiguration*, Ex. 2:10.
*m* Or, *Elijah, appears to Jesus*, 1 Kin. 17:1.

**4**

*n* *Fellowship, of the righteous*, 1 Cor. 1:9.

**5**

*o* *Pillar of Cloud and Fire*, Ex. 13:21.
*p* *Jesus, divinity of*, Matt. 1:21.

**6**

*q* *Apostles*, Luke 6:13.

**9**

*r* Mark 9:9–13.
*s* *Prudence, instances of*, 2 Chr. 2:12.
*t* *Vision*, Acts 9:10.
*u* *Resurrection*, 1 Cor. 15:12.

**10**

*v* *Prophecies, miscellaneous, fulfilled*, Dan. 9:24.
*w* *Scribe*, 1 Kin. 4:3.
*x* Or, *Elijah*, 1 Kin. 17:1.

**11**

*y* *John the Baptist, mission of*, Luke 1:63.

12 But [z]I say unto you, That
[y]Ē-lī′as is come already, and
they knew him not, but have
done unto him whatsoever they
listed. Likewise shall also the
[a]Son of man [b]suffer of them.
13 Then the disciples understood that he spake unto them
of [c]Jŏhn the Băp′tĭst.
14 ¶ [d]And when they were
come to the multitude, there
came to him a *certain* man,
kneeling down to him, and saying,
15 [e]Lord, have mercy on my
son: for he is [1,f]lunatick, and
sore vexed: for ofttimes he falleth into the fire, and oft into the
water.
16 And I brought him to thy
[g]disciples, and they could not
cure him.
17 Then Jē′ṣus answered and
said, O [h,i]faithless and perverse
[g]generation, how long shall I be
with you? how long shall I suffer
you? bring him hither to me.
18 And [j]Jē′ṣus rebuked the
[k]devil; and he departed out of
him: and †the child was [l]cured
from that very hour.
19 Then came the [g]disciples to
Jē′ṣus apart, and said, Why
could not we cast him out?
20 And Jē′ṣus said unto them,
Because of your [2,h,i]unbelief: for
[m]verily I say unto you, [n]If ye
have [o]faith as a grain of [p]mus-
tard seed, ye shall say unto this
[q]mountain, Remove hence to
yonder place; and [r]it shall remove; and nothing shall be impossible unto you.
21 [3]Howbeit this kind goeth not
out but by [s]prayer and [t]fasting.

**12**

*z* *Jesus, prophet*, Matt. 1:21.

*a* *Jesus, death of*, Matt. 1:21.
*b* *Jesus, sufferings of*, Matt. 1:21.

**13**

*c* *John the Baptist*, Luke 1:63.

**14**

*d* Mark 9:14–29; Luke 9:37–42.

**15**

*e* *Intercession, instances of*, Jer. 27:18.
*f* *Insanity, cured by Jesus*, Prov. 26:18.
**1** R. V. epileptic, and suffers grievously

**16**

*g* *Apostles*, Luke 6:13.

**17**

*h* *Doubting*, Rom. 14:23.
*i* *Unbelief*, Heb. 3:12.

**18**

*j* *Jesus, miracles of*, Matt. 1:21.
*k* *Demons, possession by*, Matt. 4:24.
*l* *Children, miracles in behalf of*, Mark 10:14.

**20**

*m* Matt. 21:21; Mark 11:23; Luke 17:6.
*n* *Promise, to the righteous*, 2 Cor. 1:20.
*o* *Faith, miracles wrought by*, Mark 11:22.
*p* *Mustard Seed*, Matt. 13:31.
*q* *Mountain*, Mic. 7:12.
*r* *Miracles, faith required in those who perform*, Luke 23:8.
2 R. V. little faith:

**21**

*s* *Prayer*, Acts 6:4.
*t* *Fasting*, Zech. 8:19.
3 R. V. *omits this verse.*

---

16:10, 11. *To esteem*, Phil. 2:29; 1 Thess. 5:12, 13; 1 Tim. 5:17. *To provide temporal support of*, 1 Cor. 9:7–23; 2 Cor. 12:13; Gal. 6:6; Phil. 4:10–18; 2 Thess. 3:7–9; 1 Tim. 5:17, 18. *To receive*, Phil. 2:29. *To seek instruction from*, Mal. 2:7. *To imitate the example of*, 1 Cor. 11:1; Phil. 3:17; 2 Thess. 3:7; Heb. 13:7; 1 Pet. 5:3. *To obey*, Heb. 13:17.

**Dissensions in Christian**, 1 Cor. 1:11–13; 3:3, 4; 11:18, 19; 2 Cor. 12:20, 21.

**Persecution of Christian**, Acts 8:1–3; 1 Cor. 15:9; 1 Thess. 2:14, 15. See footnote, PERSECUTION, John 15:20.

**Christian, Backslidden**, Rev. 2:1–5, 12–25; 3:1–4, 14–20. See footnotes: BACKSLIDERS, Jer. 3:22; BACKSLIDING OF ISRAEL, Hos. 11:7.

**Triumphant**, Heb. 12:22, 23; Rev. 3:12; 21:3, 10.

* **TRANSFIGURATION.** *Of Moses*, Ex. 34:29–35. *Of Jesus*, Matt. 17:2–9; Mark 9:2–10; Luke 9:29–36; 2 Pet. 1:16–18. *Of Stephen*, Acts 6:15.

† **DEMONIAC HEALED**, Matt. 17:14–21; Mark 9:14–29; Luke 9:37–43.

22 ¶ And while they abode in
[u]Găl′ĭ-lee, ‡,[v]Jē′ṣus said unto
them, The [w]Son of man shall be
[x]betrayed into the hands of men:
23 And they shall [y]kill him,
and the third day he shall [z]be
raised again. And they were exceeding sorry.
24 ¶ And[T] when they were come
to [a]Că-pēr′na-ŭm, they that received [4,b]tribute[G] *money* came to
[c]Pē′tēr, and said, Doth not your
[5]master [d]pay [4]tribute[G]? [Q]
25 He saith, Yes. And when he
was come into the house, Jē′ṣus
prevented[G] him, saying, What
thinkest thou, [c]Sī′mon? of whom
do the [e]kings of the earth take
custom[G] or [b]tribute[G]? of their own
children, or of strangers[G]?
26 [c]Pē′tēr saith unto him, Of
strangers. Jē′ṣus saith unto him,
Then are the children free.
27 [6]Notwithstanding, lest we
should offend[G] them, go thou to
the [f]sea, and cast an hook, and
take up the ‖fish that first cometh up; and when thou hast
opened his mouth, thou shalt
[g]find a [7]piece[G] of [h]money: that
take, and give unto them for me
and thee.[T]

## CHAPTER 18

*Jesus exhorts his disciples to humility, 7 to avoid offences, 10 and not to despise the little ones. 15 How to deal with an offending brother; 21 and how often to forgive him. 23 The parable of the king who took account of his servants.*

[a]AT the same time came the
[b]disciples unto [c]Jē′ṣus,
saying, [d,e]Who is the greatest in
the [f]kingdom of heaven?
2 And Jē′ṣus called a little
[g]child unto him, and set him in
the midst of them,
3 And said, Verily I say unto
you, [h]Except ye [1]be [i]converted,[G]
and [h]become as little [g]children,
ye shall not enter into the [f]king-
dom of heaven.[S]
4 Whosoever therefore shall
[j]humble himself as this little
[g]child, the same is greatest in
the [f]kingdom of heaven.
5 And [k]whoso shall receive one
such little [g]child in my [l]name receiveth me.
6 [m]But whoso shall [2,n]offend[G]
one of these little ones which
[o]believe [3]in me, it were better
for him that a [p]millstone were
hanged about his neck, and *that*
he were drowned in the depth of
the sea.
7 ¶ [q]Woe unto the world because of [4,n]offences! for it[G] must
needs be that [n]offences[G] come;
but woe to that man by whom
the [5,n]offence[G] cometh!
8 Wherefore [r,s]if thy [t]hand or
thy foot [6]offend[G] thee, [u,v]cut them
off, and cast *them* from thee: it is
better for thee to enter into life
halt or maimed[G], rather than having two hands or two feet to be
cast into [w,x]everlasting[G] [y]fire.
9 And if thine [z]eye [6]offend[G] thee,
[u,v]pluck it out, and cast *it* from
thee: it is better for thee to enter into life with one eye, rather
than having two eyes to be cast
into [w,x]hell[G] [y]fire.
10 ¶ [T][a]Take heed that ye despise not one of these little ones;
for I say unto you, That in
[b]heaven their [c]angels do always
behold the face of [d]my [e]Father
which is in [f]heaven.
11 [7]For the [g]Son of man is come
to [h,i]save that which was [j]lost.[T]
12 How think ye? [k,l]if a man
have an hundred [m]sheep, and

**22**
*u Galilee,* Mark 6:21.
*v Jesus, prophet,* Matt. 1:21.
*w Jesus, humanity of,* Matt. 1:21.
*x Betrayal,* Matt. 26:46.

**23**
*y Jesus death of,* Matt. 1:21.
*z Jesus, resurrection of,* Matt. 1:21.

**24**
*a Capernaum,* Luke 4:31.
*b Tribute,* Ezra 4:13.
*c Peter,* Mark 5:37.
*d Citizens, duties of,* Luke 15:15.
4 R. V. the half-shekel
5 Am. R. V. *marg.* teacher

**25**
*e King, emoluments of,* 2 Kin. 3:10.

**27**
*f Sea of Galilee,* Matt. 4:18.
*g Jesus, omniscience of,* Matt. 1:21.
*h Money,* Jer. 32:9.
6 R. V. But, lest we cause them to stumble,
7 R. V. shekel:

**1**
*a* Mark 9:33-37; Luke 9:46-48.
*b Apostles,* Luke 6:13.
*c Jesus,* Matt. 1:21.
*d Ambition,* Hab. 2:5.
*e Worldliness,* 1 John 2:15.
*f Kingdom of Heaven,* Matt. 13:24.

**2**
*g Children, type of the regenerated,* Mark 10:14.

**3**
*h Salvation, conditions of,* Acts 16:17.
*i Regeneration, necessity of,* Tit. 3:5.
1 R. V. turn,

**4**
*j Humility,* Prov. 22:4.

**5**
*k Minister, duties of,* Rom. 15:16.
*l Name of Jesus,* John 14:13.

**6**
*m* Mark 9:42; Luke 17:2.
*n Temptation, leading into,* Luke 11:4.
*o Faith in Christ,* John 6:69.
*p Millstone,* Judg. 9:53.
2 R. V. cause
3 R. V. on me to stumble, it is profitable for him

**7**
*q* Luke 17:1.
4 R. V. occasions of stumbling!
5 R. V. occasion

**8**
*r* Matt. 5:30; Mark 9:43.
*s Commandment, enjoining renunciation of sources of temptation,* Deut. 8:2.
*t Hand, figurative,* Ezra 10:19.
*u Temptation, to be avoided,* Luke 11:4.
*v Self-denial,* Mark 8:34.
*w Hell, the future abode of the wicked,* Mark 9:43.
*x Punishment, eternal,* Lev. 26:41.
*y Fire, figurative,* Ex. 12:8.
6 R. V. causeth thee to stumble,

**9**
*z Eye, figurative,* Matt. 6:22.

**10**
*a Watchfulness,* Matt. 24:42.
*b Heaven, the future home of the righteous,* Luke 18:22.
*c Angel,* Heb. 1:13.
*d Jesus, divine sonship of,* Matt. 1:21.
*e God, fatherhood of,* Gen. 2:2.

*f Heaven, God's dwelling place,* Luke 18:22. **11** *g Jesus, humanity of,* Matt. 1:21. *h Jesus, mission of,* Matt. 1:21. *i Jesus, Savior,* Matt. 1:21. *j Wicked, described,* Psa. 73:3. 7 R. V. *omits this verse.* **12** *k Parables,* Ezek. 20:49. *l* Luke 15:4-7. *m Sheep, parable of the lost,* Deut. 32:14.

‡ **JESUS FORETELLS HIS DEATH,** Matt. 12:40; 16: 21-28; 17:22, 23; 20:17-19; Mark 8:31-38; 9:30-32; 10:32-34; Luke 9:21-27, 43-45; 18:31-34.

‖ **FISH,** Mark 1:16, 19. *Creation of,* Gen. 1:20-22. *Appointed for food,* Gen. 9:2, 3. *Clean and unclean,* Lev. 11: 9-12; Deut. 14:9, 10. *Taken, with nets,* Eccl. 9:12; Hab. 1:14-17; Matt. 4:18-21; Luke 5:2-6; John 21:6-8; *with hooks,* Isa. 19:8; Amos 4:2; Matt. 17:27; *with spears,* Job 41:7. *Traffic in,* Neh. 13:16. *Broiled,* Luke 24:42; John 21: 9-13. *Great draughts of, through the omniscience of Jesus, in the early period of his ministry,* Luke 5:4-7; *after his resurrection,* John 21:6.
Miracles connected with: *Jonah swallowed by,* Jonah 1:17; 2; Matt. 12:40; *multiplication of the loaves and fishes,* Matt. 14:19; 15:36; Luke 5:6; 9:13-17.
**Figurative,** Jer. 16:16; Ezek. 47:9, 10.

one of them be gone astray, doth he not leave the ninety and nine, and goeth into the mountains, and seeketh that which is gone astray?

13 And if so be that he find it, verily I say unto you, he [n]rejoiceth more of that [m]*sheep,* than of the ninety and nine which went not astray.

14 Even so it is not the [o]will of your [e]Father which is in heaven, that one of these little ones should perish.[T]

15 ¶ Moreover, [p]if thy [q]brother shall [r]trespass against thee, [s,t]go and [u,v]tell him his fault between thee and him [w]alone: if he shall hear thee, thou hast gained thy brother.[Q]

16 But if he will not hear *thee, then* [x]take with thee one or two more, that in the mouth of two or three [y]witnesses every word may be established.[Q]

17 And if he [8]shall neglect to hear them, tell *it* unto the [s,z]church: but if he neglect to hear the church, [a]let him [b]be unto thee as [9]an [c]heathen man and a [d]publican.[G]

18 Verily I say unto you, Whatsoever [e]ye shall bind on earth shall be bound in [f]heaven: and whatsoever ye shall loose on earth shall be loosed in heaven.

19 Again I say unto you, That if [g]two of you shall agree on earth as touching[G] any thing that they shall ask, [h,i,j]it shall be done for them of my [k]Father which is in [l]heaven.[T]

20 For where two or three are gathered together [m]in my name, [h,j,n]there am I in the [o]midst of them.[S T]

21 ¶ Then came [p]Pē′tẽr to him, and said, Lord, how oft[G] shall my [q]brother sin against me, and I *,[r,s]forgive him? till [t]seven times?

22 Jē′ṣus saith unto him, I say not unto thee, Until [t]seven times: but, [u]Until seventy times seven.

23 ¶ [v]Therefore is the [w]kingdom of heaven likened unto a certain [x]king, which would [10]take account of his servants.

24 And when he had begun to reckon, one was brought unto him, which [y]owed him ten thousand [z]talents.[G]

25 But forasmuch as [a]he had not[G] to pay, his lord commanded [b]him to be sold, and his [c]wife, and [d]children, and all that he had, and payment to be made.

26 The servant therefore fell down, and worshipped him, saying, Lord, have [e]patience with me, and I will pay thee all.

27 Then the lord of that servant was moved with [f]compassion, and loosed[G] him, and *forgave him the [g]debt.

28 But the same servant went out, and found one of his fellowservants, which [g]owed him an hundred [h]pence[G]: and [i]he [j]laid hands on him, and took *him* by the throat, saying, Pay me that thou owest.

29 And his fellowservant fell down at his feet, and besought him, saying, Have [e]patience with me, and I will pay thee all.

30 And he would not: but went and [j,k]cast him into prison, till he should pay the [g]debt.

31 So when his fellowservants

**13**
*n Joy,* Psa. 5:11.

**14**
*o God, love of, exemplified,* Gen. 2:2.

**15**
*p* Luke 17:3, 4.
*q Fraternity,* Zech. 11:14.
*r Trespass, of a brother,* Ex. 22:9.
*s Church, rules of discipline in,* vs. 15–18; Matt. 16:18.
*t Commandment, enjoining fraternal reproof,* Deut. 8:2.
*u Duty, of man to man,* Eccl. 12:13.
*v Reproof, enjoined,* Prov. 17:10.
*w Prudence,* 2 Chr. 2:12.

**16**
*x Evidence, laws concerning,* Deut. 17:6.
*y Witness, two necessary to establish a fact,* Num. 35:30.

**17**
*z Court, ecclesiastical,* Ex. 18:26.
*a Fellowship, with the wicked forbidden,* 1 Cor. 1:9.
*b Disfellowship,* Num. 15:31.
*c Gentiles,* Acts 10:45.
*d Publicans,* Matt. 11:19.
8 R. V. refuse
9 R. V. the Gentile and the

**18**
*e Minister,* Rom. 15:16.
*f Heaven, figurative,* Luke 18:22.

**19**
*g Prayer, social,* Acts 6:4.
*h Promise, to the righteous,* 2 Cor. 1:20.
*i Prayer, answer to, promised,* Acts 6:4.
*j Righteous, promises to,* Psa. 64:10. *k God, fatherhood of,* Gen. 2:2. *l Heaven, God's dwelling place,* Luke 18:22. **20** *m Name of Jesus,* John 14:13.

*n Fellowship, with Christ,* 1 Cor. 1:9.
*o Promise, of Christ's presence with believers,* 2 Cor. 1:20.

**21**
*p Peter,* Mark 5:37.
*q Enemy, forgiveness of, enjoined,* Prov. 24:17.
*r Duty, of man to man,* Eccl. 12:13.
*s Charitableness,* Prov. 10:12.
*t Seven,* Gen. 7:2.

**22**
*u Commandment, enjoining forgiveness,* Deut. 8:2.

**23**
*v Parables,* Ezek. 20:49.
*w Kingdom of Heaven,* Matt. 13:24.
*x King,* 2 Kin. 3:10.
10 R. V. make a reckoning with his servants.

**24**
*y Debt,* 1 Sam. 22:2.
*z Talent, parables of,* Ex. 38:25.

**25**
*a Debtor, sold for debt,* Luke 7:41.
*b Servant, defaulting debtors made,* Jer. 2:14.
*Women, sold for debt,* Prov. 31:10.
*d Children, sold for debt,* Mark 10:14.

**26**
*e Christian Graces, patience,* Gal. 5:22.

**27**
*f Pity, instances of,* Job 19:21.
*g Debt,* 1 Sam. 22:2.

**28**
*h Penny,* Matt. 20:2.
*i Creditor, oppressions by,* Deut. 15:2.
*j Debtor, oppressed,* Luke 7:41.

**30**
*k Imprisonment, of debtors,* Acts 12:4.

*** FORGIVENESS.** *Of enemies,* Prov. 24:17; 25:21, 22; Matt. 5:39–41; Rom. 12:20. *Of enemies, a condition of divine forgiveness,* Matt. 6:12, 14, 15; 18:21–35; Mark 11:25; Luke 11:4. *Spirit of, blesses,* Rom. 12:14; 1 Cor. 4:12, 13; 1 Pet. 3:9; *disallows retaliation,* Prov. 24:29; Rom. 12:17, 19; *disallows rejoicing at an enemy's misfortune,* Prov. 24:17. *Enjoined,* Matt. 5:43–48; 18:21–35; Mark 11:25; Luke 6:27–34, 36, 37; 17:3, 4; Eph. 4:32; Col. 3:13; Philemon 10, 18; *in kindness toward an enemy's beast,* Ex. 23:4, 5.

**Instances of:** *Esau, of Jacob,* Gen. 33:4, 11. *Joseph, of his brethren,* Gen. 45:5–15; 50:19–21. *Moses, of Aaron and Miriam,* Num. 12:1–13. *David, of Saul,* 1 Sam. 24:10–12; 26:9; 2 Sam. 1:14–27; *of Shimei,* 2 Sam. 16:9–13; 19:18–23. *Solomon, of Adonijah,* 1 Kin. 1:53. *The prophet of Judah, of Jeroboam,* 1 Kin. 13:3–6. *Jesus, of his enemies,* Luke 23:34. *Stephen, of his murderers,* Acts 7:60. *Paul, of his persecutors,* 1 Cor. 4:12.

**Of sins,** see footnote, SIN, *Forgiveness of,* **Rom. 5:12.**

saw what was done, they were very sorry, and came and told unto their lord all that was done.

32 Then his lord, after that he had called him, said unto him, O thou wicked servant, I forgave thee all that [g]debt, because thou desiredst[C] me:

33 Shouldest not thou also have had [l]compassion on thy fellowservant, even as I had pity on thee?

34 And his lord was [l]wroth[C], and delivered him to the tormentors[C], till he should pay all that was due unto him.

35 So likewise shall my heavenly [m]Father do also unto you, [n]if ye [o]from your hearts forgive not every one his brother their trespasses.

## CHAPTER 19

*Jesus heals the sick. 3 He answers the Pharisees concerning divorce. 10 and his disciples concerning marriage. 13 He blesses little children; 16 answers the rich young man; 23 and declares how hard it is for a rich man to enter the kingdom of God. 27 The reward of those who forsake all and follow him.*

AND [a]it came to pass, *that* when [b]Jē′şus had finished these sayings, he departed from [c]Găl′ĭ-lee, and came into the coasts[C] of [d]Jū-dæ′ȧ beyond [e]Jôr′-dan;

2 And [f]great multitudes [g]followed him; and he [h]healed them there.

3 ¶ [i]The [j]Phăr′ĭ-seeş also came unto him, tempting[C] him, and saying unto him, Is it lawful for a man to *put[C] away his [k]wife for every cause?

4 And he answered and [l]said unto them, Have ye not read, that he which [m]made *them* at the beginning [n]made them [o]male and [p]female,[Q]

5 And said, [q]For this cause shall a [r]man leave father and mother, and shall cleave to his [k]wife: and [s]they twain[C] shall be one flesh?[Q]

6 Wherefore they are no more twain, but [s]one flesh. What therefore God hath joined together, let not man put asunder[C].

7 They say unto him, Why did [t]Mō′şeş then [u]command to give a writing of *divorcement, and to put her away?[Q]

8 He saith unto them, [t]Mō′şeş because of the hardness of your hearts suffered[C] you to *put away your [k]wives: but from the beginning it was not so.[s]

9 And I [l]say unto you, [v]Whosoever shall *put away his wife, except *it be* for fornication, and shall marry another, committeth [w]adultery: and whoso marrieth her which is put away doth commit adultery.

10 ¶ His [x]disciples say unto him, If the case of the man be so with *his* wife, it is [y]not good to marry.

11 But he said unto them, All *men* cannot receive this saying, save[C] *they* to whom it is given.

12 For there are some †eunuchs[C], which were so born from *their* mother's womb: and there are some eunuchs[C], which were made eunuchs[C] of men: and there be eunuchs[C], which have ‡,[z]made themselves †eunuchs[C] for the [a]kingdom of heaven's sake. He that is able to receive *it*, let him receive *it*.

13 ¶ [b]Then were there brought unto him little [c]children, that he should put *his* [d]hands on them,

34
*l* *Anger*, Psa. 37:8.

35
*m* *God, fatherhood of*, Gen. 2:2.
*n* *Malice*, Eph. 4:31.
*o* *Sincerity*, 1 Cor. 5:8.

1
*a* Mark 10:1.
*b* *Jesus, journeys toward Jerusalem*, Matt. 1:21.
*c* *Galilee*, Mark 6:21.
*d* *Judea*, Luke 5:17.
*e* *Jordan*, Gen. 32:10.

2
*f* *Popularity of Jesus*, John 6:15.
*g* *Jesus, received*, Matt. 1:21.
*h* *Healing, by Jesus*, Acts 4:22.

3
*i* Mark 10:2–12.
*j* *Pharisees*, Matt. 15:12.
*k* *Wife*, Prov. 5:18.

4
*l* *Jesus, interprets law of marriage*, Matt. 1:21.
*m* *God, creator*, Gen. 2:2.
*n* Gen. 1:27; Mark 10:6.
*o* *Man, created*, Job 4:17.
*p* *Women, creation of*, Prov. 31:10.

5
*q* Gen. 2:24; Mark 10:7; 1 Cor. 6:16.
*r* *Husband, relation of, to wife*, Num. 30:6.
*s* *Marriage, unity of husband and wife in*, Gen. 34:9.

7
*t* *Moses*, Ex. 2:10.
*u* *Law, of Moses*, Deut. 33:2.

9
*v* Matt. 5:32; Mark 10:11, 12; Luke 16:18.
*w* *Adultery*, Lev. 20:10.

10
*x* *Apostles*, Luke 6:13.
*y* *Celibacy*, 1 Tim. 4:3.

12
*z* *Self-denial*, Mark 8:34.
*a* *Kingdom of Heaven*, Matt. 13:24.

13
*b* Mark 10:13–16; Luke 18:15–17.
*c* *Children, blessed by Jesus*, Mark 10:14.
*d* *Hand*, Ezra 10:19.

* **DIVORCE,** Mark 10:2–12; Luke 16:18. *Mosaic laws concerning*, Ex. 21:7–11; Deut. 21:10–14· 24:1–4. *Authorized for fornication*, Matt. 5:31, 32; 19:3–11. *Unjust, reproved*, Mal. 2:14–16. *From heathen wives, required by Ezra*, Ezra 10:1–16. *Disobedience, a cause for, among the Persians*, Esth. 1:10–22. *Final, after remarriage of either party*, Jer. 3:1. *Paul's injunctions concerning*, 1 Cor. 7:10–17.

**Figurative**, Isa. 50:1; Jer 3:8.

† **EUNUCH,** 2 Kin. 20:18; Matt. 19:11, 12. *Prohibited from certain privileges of the congregation*, Deut. 23:1; Isa. 56:3–5. *Influential court officials*, Jer. 38:7–13; 52:25; Dan. 1:3. *Those who became* (continent, probably), *for the kingdom of heaven's sake*, Matt. 19:12. *Baptism of the Ethiopian*, Acts 8:26–39.

‡ **CONTINENCE.** *Vow of*, Job 31:1. *Enjoined*, Matt. 5; 27, 28; Rom. 13:13; 1 Cor. 7:1–9, 25–29, 36–38; Col. 3:5; 1 Tim. 4:12; 5:1, 2.

**Instances of**: *Joseph*, Gen. 39:7–12. *Uriah*, 2 Sam. 11; 8–13. *Boaz*, Ruth 3:6–13. *Joseph, husband of Mary*, Matt. 1:24, 25. *Eunuchs*, Matt. 19:12. *Paul*, 1 Cor. 7:8; 9:27. *Saints*, Rev. 14:1, 4, 5.

e *Jesus prayers of*, Matt. 1:21.
f *Presumption, instances of*, Psa. 19:13.
g *Children, promises and assurances to*, Mark 10:14.
**14**
**16**
h Mark 10:17–22; Luke 18:18–23.
i *Jesus, names of*, Matt. 1:21.
j *Works*, 2 Tim. 1:9.
k *Salvation, conditions of*, Acts 16:17.
l *Immortality*, 1 Cor. 15:54.
m *Life, everlasting*, Eccl. 8:15.
1 Am. R. V. *marg.* Good Teacher,
**17**
n *God, goodness of*, Gen. 2:2.
o *Commandment, enjoining obedience*, Deut. 8:2.
p *Decalogue*, Ex. 20:3.
2 R. V. askest thou me concerning that which is good?
3 R. V. One there is who is good:
**18**
q Ex. 20:13.
r *Homicide, felonious, forbidden*, Deut. 5:17.
s Ex. 20:14.
t *Adultery, forbidden*, Lev. 20:10.
u Ex. 20:15.
v *Theft, forbidden*, Mark 7:22.
w Ex. 20:16.
x *Falsehood, forbidden*, Job 21:34.
y *Evidence, false, forbidden*, Deut. 17:6.
**19**
z Ex. 20:12.

a *Commandment, enjoining reverence for parents*, Deut. 8:2.
b *Parents, to be reverenced*, 2 Cor. 12:14.

and [e]pray: and the disciples [f]rebuked them.
14 But Jē'sus said, Suffer[C] little
[c]children, and forbid them not,
to come unto me: [g]for of such is
the [a]kingdom of heaven.
15 [c]And he laid *his* hands on
them, and departed thence.[C]
16 ¶ And, behold, [h]one came
and said unto him, [1,i]Good Master, what good thing shall I [j]do,
[k]that I may have [l]eternal [m]life?
17 And he said unto him, Why
[2]callest thou me good? [3]*there is*
none good but one, *that is*,
[n]God: but if thou wilt enter into
[m]life, [o]keep the [p]commandments.[Q T S]
18 He saith unto him, Which?
Jē'sus said, [p,q,r]Thou shalt do
no murder, [s,t]Thou shalt not
commit adultery, [u,v]Thou shalt
not steal, [w,x,y]Thou shalt not
bear ‖false witness,[Q]
19 [p,z,a]Honour thy [b]father and
*thy* [b]mother: and, [c,d]Thou shalt
[e,f,g]love thy [h]neighbour as thyself.[Q]
20 The [i]young man saith unto
him, All these things have I
[4,j]kept from my youth up:
[k]what lack I yet?
21 Jē'sus said unto him, [l]If
thou wilt be [m]perfect, go *and*
[n]sell that thou hast, and [o,p]give
to the [q]poor, and [r]thou shalt
have [s]treasure in [t]heaven: and
come *and* follow me.[S]
22 But when the [i]young man
heard that saying, [u,v]he [w]went
away sorrowful: for he had great
[x]possessions.[Q]

c *Royal Law*, Jas. 2:8. d *Commandment, enjoining love to man*, Deut. 8:2. e *Love, of man for man*, 1 John 4:7. f *Duty, of man to man*, Eccl. 12:13. g *Christian Graces, love*, Gal. 5:22. h *Neighbor, love for, enjoined*, Luke 10:29. **20** i *Young Men*, Prov. 1:4. j *Obedience, instances of*, Heb. 5:8. k *Self-righteousness*, Luke 18:11. 4 R. V. observed: **21** l *Discipleship, tests of*, Matt. 10:32. m *Perfection*, Heb. 6:1. n *Renunciation, of possessions for Christ*, Luke 5:11. o *Liberality*, 1 Tim. 6:18. p *Alms*, Matt. 6:2. q *Poor, duty to*, Prov. 21:13. r *Promise, to the obedient*, 2 Cor. 1:20. s *Treasure*, Luke 12:33. t *Heaven, the future home of the righteous*, Luke 18:22. **22** u *Selfishness*, 2 Tim. 3:2. v *Impenitence, instances of*, Rom. 2:5. w *Counsel, divine, rejected*, Prov. 12:15. x *Riches*, Eccl. 4:8.

23 ¶[T] [y]Then said Jē'sus unto
his [z]disciples, Verily I say unto
you, That a [a,b,c]rich man shall
hardly[C] enter into the [d]kingdom
of heaven.
24 And again I say unto you,
It is easier for a camel to go
through the eye of a [e]needle,
than for a [a,b,c]rich man to enter
into the [d]kingdom of God.
25 When his [f]disciples heard *it*,
they were exceedingly amazed,
saying, Who then can be saved?[T]
26 But Jē'sus beheld *them*, and
said unto them, With men this is
impossible; but with God [g]all
things are possible.[S Q]
27 ¶ [h]Then answered [i]Pē'tēr
and said unto him, Behold, we
have [j]forsaken all, and followed
thee; what shall we have therefore?
28 And Jē'sus said unto [f]them,
Verily I say unto you, That ye
which have followed me, in the
regeneration when the [k,l,m]Son
of man shall sit in the [n]throne of
his glory, [o]ye also shall sit upon twelve thrones, judging the
twelve tribes of Iş'ra-el.[Q]
29 And [p]every one that hath
[j]forsaken houses, or brethren, or
sisters, or father, or mother, or
wife, or children, or lands, for
my name's sake, [q]shall receive
an hundredfold, and shall inherit everlasting [r]life.
30 But many [5]*that are* first
shall be last; and the last *shall
be* first.

## CHAPTER 20

*The parable of the laborers in the vineyard. 17 Jesus again foretells his own death and resurrection. 20 The request of the mother of Zebedee's children. 25 Jesus exhorts to humility. 30 He gives sight to two blind men.*

FOR [a]the [b]kingdom of heaven
is like unto a [c]man *that*
*is* an householder, which went

**23**
y Mark 10:23–27; Luke 18:24–27.
z *Apostles*, Luke 6:13.

a *Rich*, Jas. 5:1.
b *Worldliness*, 1 John 2:15.
c *Covetousness*, Isa. 57:17.
d *Kingdom of Heaven*, Matt. 13:24.
**24**
e Mark 10:25; Luke 18:25.
**25**
f *Apostles*, Luke 6:13.
**26**
g *God, omnipotent*, Gen. 2:2.
**27**
h Mark 10:28–31; Luke 18:28–30.
i *Peter*, Mark 5:37.
j *Self-denial, instances of*, Mark 8:34.
**28**
k *Jesus, humanity of*, Matt. 1:21.
l *Jesus, king*, Matt. 1:21.
m *Jesus, judge*, Matt. 1:21.
n *Throne, figurative*, 1 Kin. 2:19.
o *Jesus, promises of*, Matt. 1:21.
**29**
p *Righteous, promises to*, Psa. 64:10.
q *Promise, to the righteous*, 2 Cor. 1:20.
r *Life, everlasting*, Eccl. 8:15.
**30**
5 R. V. shall be last that are first; and first that are last.
**1**
a *Parables*, vs. 1–10; Ezek. 20:49.
b *Kingdom of Heaven*, Matt. 13:24.
c *Employer*, Deut. 24:14.

‖ **FALSE WITNESS**, Prov. 12:17; 14:5, 8, 25; 25:18. *Forbidden*, Ex. 20:16 (with Deut. 5:20; Matt. 19:18; Luke 18:20); 23:1–3; Lev. 6:1–5; 19:11, 12, 16; Prov. 24:28; Luke 3:14; 1 Tim. 1:9, 10.
*Proceeds from corrupt heart*, Matt. 15:19. *Innocent suffer from*, Psa. 27:12; 35:11. *God hates*, Prov. 6:16–19. *Punishment for*, Deut. 19:16–20; Prov. 19:5, 9; 21:28; Zech. 5:3, 4.
**Instances of:** *Witnesses, against Naboth*, 1 Kin. 21:13; *against Jesus*, Matt. 26:59–61; Mark 14:55–59; *against Stephen*, Acts 6:11, 13; *against Paul*, Acts 16:20, 21; 17:5–7; 24:5; 25:7, 8.

out early in the morning to hire
[d,e,f]labourers into his [g]vineyard.
2 And when [c]he had *agreed
with the [d,e]labourers for a
[†,h]penny a day, he sent them
into his [g]vineyard.
3 And he went out about the
third hour, and saw others standing [i]idle in the marketplace,
4 And said unto them; Go
ye also into the [g]vineyard, and
[h]whatsoever is right [c]I will give
[d,e]you. And they went their way.
5 Again [c]he went out about the
sixth and ninth hour, and did
likewise.
6 And about the eleventh hour
he went out, and found others
standing [i]idle, and saith unto
them, Why stand ye here all the
day idle?
7 They say unto him, Because
no man hath [e]hired us. [c]He saith
unto them, Go [d]ye also into the
[g]vineyard; [1]and whatsoever is
right, [h]*that* shall ye receive.
8 So when even was come, the
[c]lord of the [g]vineyard saith unto
his [j]steward, Call the [d,e]labour-
ers, and give them *their* [h]hire,
beginning from the last unto the
first.
9 And when they came that
*were hired* about the eleventh
hour, they received every man a
[†,h]penny.
10 But when the first came,
they supposed that they should
have received more; and [d,e]they
likewise received every man a
[†,h]penny.
11 And when they had re-
ceived *it*, they [k]murmured
against the [2,c]goodman of the
house,
12 [k]Saying, These last have
wrought *but* one hour, and thou
hast made them equal unto us,
which have borne the burden
and heat of the day.
13 But he answered one of
them, and said, Friend, I do
thee no wrong: didst not thou
*agree with me for a [†,h]penny?
14 Take *that* thine *is*, and go
thy way: I will give unto this
last, even as unto thee.
15 Is it not lawful for me to
do what I will with mine own?
Is thine eye evil, because I
am good?
16 So the last shall be first, and
the first last: [3]for many be
[l]called, but few chosen.
17 ¶ And Jē′sụs going up to
[m]Jĕ-ru̇′să-lĕm took the twelve
[n]disciples apart in the way, and
[o]said unto them,
18 Behold, we go up to [m]Jĕ-ru̇′-
să-lĕm; and [o]the [p]Son of man
shall be [q]betrayed unto the chief
[r]priests and unto the [s]scribes,
and they shall condemn him to
death,
19 [o]And shall deliver him to
the [t]Ġĕn′tīleṣ to mock, and to
[u]scourge, and to [v,w]crucify *him*:
and the third day [x]he shall rise
again.
20 ¶ [y]Then came to him the
[z]mother of [a]Zĕb′e-dee's children with her [b,c]sons, [d]worship-
ping *him*, and [e]desiring a certain
thing of him.
21 And he said unto her, What
wilt thou? She [f]saith unto him,
Grant that these my two [b,c]sons
may sit, the one on thy right
hand, and the other on the left,
in [g]thy kingdom.
22 But Jē′sụs answered and
said, Ye [h]know not what ye ask.

d *Employee*, Deut 24:14.
e *Hired Servant*, vs. 1–15; Lev. 25:40.
f *Labor*, Luke 10:7.
g *Vineyard, parables of*, vs. 1–16; Isa. 1:8.

2
h *Wages*, Gen. 31:7.

3
i *Idleness*, Eccl. 10:18.

7
1 R. V. *omits remainder of verse.*

8
j *Steward*, Gen. 43:19.

11
k *Murmuring*, Num. 14:2.
2 R. V. householder,

16
l *Call, personal*, Phil. 3:14.
3 R. V. *omits remainder of verse.*

17
m *Jerusalem*, Judg. 19:10.
n *Apostles*, Luke 6:13.
o *Jesus foretells his death*, Matt. 17:22.

18
p *Jesus, humanity of*, Matt. 1:21.
q *Betrayal*, Matt. 26:46.
r *Priest*, Lev. 1:5.
s *Scribe*, 1 Kin. 4:3.

19
t *Gentiles*, Acts 10:45.
u *Smiting and Scourging of Jesus*, Isa. 50:6.
v *Crucifixion*, Mark 15:13.
w *Jesus, death of*, Matt. 1:21.
x *Resurrection of Jesus*, Matt. 28:6.

20
y Mark 10:35–41.
z *Salome*, Mark 16:1.

a *Zebedee*, Matt. 4:21.
b *James*, Luke 5:10.
c *John*, Mark 1:19.
d *Jesus, worship of*, Matt. 1:21.
e *Ambition*, Hab. 2:5.

21
f *Statecraft, women in*, Prov. 28:2.
g *Jesus, kingdom of*, Matt. 1:21.

22
h *Spiritual Blindness*, 2 Cor. 4:4.

* **CONTRACTS.** *Binding force of*, Prov. 6:1–5; Matt. 20:1–16; Gal. 3:15.
**Ratified:** *By giving presents*, Gen. 21:25–30. *By consummating in the presence of the public at the gate of the city*, Gen. 23:17, 18; Ruth 4:1–11. *By oaths*, Gen. 26:28, 31; Josh. 9:15, 20. *By joining hands*, Prov. 17:18; 22:26. *By taking off the shoe*, Ruth 4:6–8. *By written instrument*, Jer. 32:10–15. *By boring servant's ear*, Ex. 21:2–6.
**Penalty for breach of**, Lev. 6:1–7.
**Instances of:** *Between Abraham and Abimelech, concerning wells of water*, Gen. 21:25–32; *violated*, Gen. 26:15. *First between Laban and Jacob for Laban's daughter*, Gen. 29:15–20, 27–30; *violated by Laban*, Gen. 29:23–27; *second relating to sharing flocks and herds*, Gen. 30:28–34; *violated in spirit by Jacob*, Gen. 30:37–43. *Between Solomon and Hiram*, 1 Kin 5:8–12; 9:11.

† **PENNY,** *or* DENARIUS, a Roman coin, of different values at different times, but 9 1-2d or 19cts. is a fair estimate of average value (Hastings). Matt. 18:28; 22:19–21; Mark 6:37; 14:5; Luke 7:41; 10:35. A day's wages, Matt. 20:2–14.

Are ye able to drink of the [‡]cup that I shall drink of, [4]and to be [i]baptized with the baptism that I am baptized with? They say unto him, We are able.

23 And he saith unto them, Ye shall drink indeed of my [‡,j]cup, [5]and be baptized with the [i]baptism that I am baptized with: but to sit on my right hand, and on my left, is not mine to give, but *it shall be given to them* for whom it is prepared of [k]my [l]Father.

24 And when the [m]ten heard *it*, they were moved with [n]indignation against the two brethren.

25 [o]But Jē′ṣus called them *unto him*, and said, Ye know that the [p]princes of the [q]Gĕn′tīleṣ exercise dominion over them, and they that are great exercise authority upon them.

26 But it shall not be so among you: but [r]whosoever will be great among you, [s,t,u]let him be your minister;

27 And whosoever will be chief among you, let him be your [v]servant:

28 Even [w,x]as the [y]Son of man came not to be ministered unto, but [z]to minister, and to [a,b,c]give his [d]life a [e,f,g]ransom for many.

29 ¶ And as they departed from [h]Jĕr′ĭ-chō, a great multitude followed him.

30 And, behold, two [i]blind [j]men sitting by the way side, when they heard that Jē′ṣus passed by, cried out, saying, [k]Have mercy on us, O Lord, *thou* [l]son of [m]Dā′vid.

31 And the multitude rebuked them, because they should hold their peace: but they [n]cried the more, saying, Have mercy on us, O Lord, *thou* son of Dā′vid.

32 And Jē′ṣus stood still, and called them, and said, What will ye that I shall do unto you?

33 They say unto him, [k]Lord, that our eyes may be opened.

34 So Jē′ṣus had [o]compassion *on them*, and touched their eyes: and immediately their eyes [p]received sight, and they followed him.

## CHAPTER 21

*Jesus' public entry into Jerusalem. 12 He drives the traders out of the temple; 17 curses a fig tree; 23 and silences those who question his authority. 28 The parable of the two sons; 33 and of the wicked husbandmen.*

AND when they drew nigh unto [a]Jē-ru̧′sā-lĕm, and were come to [b]Bĕth′pha-ġē, unto the mount of [c]Ŏl′īveṣ, then sent Jē′ṣus two [d]disciples,

2 Saying unto them, Go into the village over against you, and straightway ye shall find an [e]ass tied, and a colt with her: loose *them*, and bring *them* unto me.

3 And if any *man* say ought unto you, ye shall say, The Lord hath need of them; and straightway he will send them.

4 All this was done, that [f,g]it might be fulfilled which was spoken by the prophet, saying,

5 [f,g]Tell ye the daughter of [h]Sī′ŏn, Behold, thy [i]King *cometh unto thee, [j]meek, and sitting upon an [e]ass, and a colt the foal of an ass.

6 And the [d]disciples went, and [k]did as Jē′ṣus commanded them,

7 And brought the [e]ass, and the colt, and put on them their clothes, and they set *him* thereon.

8 And [l,m]a very great multitude spread their garments in the

---

i *Baptism, figurative,* Luke 20:4.
4 R. V. *omits* and to be baptized with the baptism that I am baptized with?
**23**
j *Persecution, of Christians, foretold,* John 15:20.
k *Jesus, divine sonship of,* Matt. 1:21.
l *God, fatherhood of, taught by Jesus,* Gen. 2:2.
5 R. V. *omits* and be baptized with the baptism that I am baptized with:
**24**
m *Apostles,* Luke 6:13.
n *Jealousy,* Psa. 78:58.
**25**
o Mark 10:42–45; Luke 22:25–27.
p *Rulers,* Ex. 18:21.
q *Gentiles,* Acts 10:45.
**26**
r *Commandment, enjoining altruistic service,* Deut. 8:2.
s *Humility, enjoined,* Prov. 22:4.
t *Altruism,* Acts 20:35.
u *Minister, character and qualifications of,* Rom. 15:16.
**27**
v *Servant, figurative,* Jer. 2:14.
**28**
w *Example, Christ our, in service,* John 13:15.
x *Jesus, our example,* Matt. 1:21.
y *Jesus, humanity of,* Matt. 1:21.
z *Jesus, mission of,* Matt. 1:21.

a *Atonement, by Jesus,* Lev. 17:11.
b *Jesus, vicarious death of,* Matt. 1:21.
c *Jesus, design of his death,* Matt. 1:21.
d *Life, of Christ, a ransom,* Eccl. 8:15.
e *Ransom, figurative,* Ex. 21:30.
f *Redemption, of our souls,* Eph. 1:7. g *Jesus, savior,* Matt. 1:21. **29** h *Jericho,* Num. 22:1. **30** i *Blindness,* 2 Kin. 6:18. j Mark 10:46–52; Luke 18:35–43. k *Faith in Christ, exemplified,* John 6:69. l *Jesus, names of,* Matt. 1:21. m *David, Jesus called son of,* 1 Sam. 16:13.

**31**
n *Prayer, importunity in,* Acts 6:4.
**34**
o *Jesus, compassion of,* Matt. 1:21.
p *Jesus, miracles of,* Matt. 1:21.

**1**
a *Jerusalem,* Judg. 19:10.
b Mark 11:1; Luke 19:29.
c *Mount of Olives,* Mark 11:1.
d *Apostles,* Luke 6:13.
v.1–AD 30
**2**
e *Ass,* 2 Chr. 28:15.
**4**
f *Prophecies, concerning the Messiah and their fulfillment,* Gen. 12:3.
g *Jesus, kingdom of, prophecies concerning,* Matt. 1:21.
**5**
h Or, *Zion,* 2 Sam. 5:7.
i *Jesus, king,* Matt. 1:21.
j *Jesus, meekness of,* Matt. 1:21.
**6**
k *Obedience,* Heb. 5:8.
**8**
l *Popularity of Jesus,* John 6:15.
m *Jesus, received,* Matt. 1:21.

---

‡ **CUP. Figurative:** *Of judgments,* Psa. 11:6; 75:8; Isa. 51:17, 22; Jer. 25:15–28; Ezek. 23:31–34; Rev. 14:10. *Of sorrow,* Matt. 20:22, 23; 26:39; Mark 14:36; Luke 22:42; John 18:11.
*Of consolation,* Jer. 16:7.
*Of joy,* Psa. 23:5.
*Of salvation,* Psa. 116:13.
*Of the holy communion,* 1 Cor. 10:21; 11:25.
*Of the libations in demon worship,* 1 Cor. 10:21.

* **TRIUMPHAL ENTRY OF JESUS INTO JERUSALEM,** Psa. 118:26; Zech. 9:9; Matt. 21:5, 8–10; Mark 11:7–11; Luke 19:35–38; John 12:12, 13.

way[C]; others cut down branches
from the trees, and strawed[G] *them*
in the way.
9 And the multitudes that went
before, and that followed, cried,
saying, [n]Hō-ṣăn′nȧ to the [o]son of
[p]Dā′vid: Blessed *is* he that cometh in the name of the LORD;
Hō-ṣăn′nȧ in the highest.[Q]
10 ¶ And when he was *come
into [a]Jē-ru̥′sȧ-lĕm, all the city
was moved, saying, Who is this?
11 And the multitude said,
This is Jē′ṣus the [q]prophet of
[r]Năz′a-rĕth of [s]Găl′ĭ-lee.[T]
12 ¶ [t]And Jē′ṣus went into the
[u]temple of God, and [v]cast out all
them that [w]sold and bought in
the temple, and overthrew the
tables of the moneychangers,
and the seats of them that sold
[x]doves,
13 And said unto them, It
is written, My house shall be
called the [y,z]house of prayer;
but ye have [a]made it a den of
[b]thieves.[Q]
14 And the [c]blind and the [d]lame
came to him in the [e]temple; and
he [f,g]healed them.
15 And when the chief [h]priests
and [i]scribes saw the wonderful
[g]things that he did, and the
[j]children crying in the temple,
and saying, [k]Hō-ṣăn′nȧ to the
[l]son of [m]Dā′vid; they were [1]sore[C]
displeased,[Q]
16 And said unto him, Hearest
thou what these say? And Jē′-
ṣus saith unto them, Yea; have
ye never read, [n]Out of the mouth
of [o]babes and sucklings thou
hast perfected [k]praise?[Q]
17[S] And he left them, and went
out of the city into [p]Bĕth′a-nȳ;
and he lodged there.
18 ¶ [q]Now in the morning as
he returned into the city, he
[r]hungered.
19 And when he saw a [s,t]fig
tree in the way, he came to it,
and found [u,v]nothing thereon,
but leaves only, and [w]said unto
it, [x]Let no fruit grow on thee
henceforward for ever. And
[2]presently[C] the fig tree [x,y]with-
ered away.
20 And when the [z]disciples saw
*it*, they marvelled, saying, How
soon is the [s,t]fig tree [x]withered
away!
21 Jē′ṣus answered and said
unto them, [a]Verily I say unto
you, If ye have [b]faith, and [c]doubt
not, [d]ye shall not only [e]do this
*which is done* to the [f]fig tree, but
also if ye shall say unto this
[g]mountain, Be thou removed,
and be thou cast into the sea; it
shall be done.
22 And all things, whatsoever
ye shall ask in [h]prayer, [b]believ-
ing, [i]ye shall receive.[S]
23 ¶ [j]And when he was come
into the [k]temple, the chief
[l]priests and the [m]elders of the
people came unto him as he
was [n]teaching, and said, By
what authority doest thou these
things? and who gave thee this
authority?
24 And Jē′ṣus answered and
said unto them, I also will ask
you one thing, which if ye tell
me, I in like wise will tell you by
what authority I do these things.
25 The [o]baptism of Jŏhn,
whence[C] was it? from [p]heaven,
or of men? And they reasoned
with themselves, saying, If we
shall say, From heaven; he will
say unto us, Why did ye [c,q]not
then believe him?
26 But if we shall say, Of men;
we [r]fear the [s]people; for all hold[C]
[t]Jŏhn as a [u]prophet.[C]
27 And they answered Jē′ṣus,
and said, We cannot tell. And
he said unto them, Neither tell I
you by what authority I do these
things.
28 ¶ But what think ye? [v]A
*certain* man had two sons; and
he came to the first, and said,

v.8–AD 30
See footnote, *Time*, Rev. 10:6.

9
n *Praise*, Psa. 150:1.
o *Jesus, humanity of*, Matt. 1:21.
p *David, Jesus called son of*, 1 Sam. 16:13.
11
q *Jesus, prophet*, Matt. 1:21.
r *Nazareth*, John 1:46.
s *Galilee*, Mark 6:21.
12
t Mark 11:15–17; Luke 19:45, 46; John 2:14, 15.
u *Temple, Herod's*, 1 Kin. 6:17.
v *Zeal*, 2 Cor. 7:11.
w *Sacrilege, instances of*, Lev. 19:8.
x *Dove*, Gen. 8:8.
13
y Isa. 56:7; Jer. 7:11; Mark 11:17; Luke 19:46.
z *Temple, called house of prayer*, 1 Kin. 6:17.

a *Profanation, of the house of God*, Lev. 22:32.
b *Thieves*, Deut. 24:7.
14
c *Blindness*, 2 Kin. 6:18.
d *Lameness*, Lev. 21:18.
e *Temple, Herod's*, 1 Kin. 6:17.
f *Healing, by Jesus*, Acts 4:22.
g *Miracles, of Jesus*, Luke 23:8.
15
h *Priest*, Lev. 1:5.
i *Scribe*, 1 Kin. 4:3.
j *Children*, Mark 10:14.
k *Praise*, Psa. 150:1.
l *Jesus, names of*, Matt. 1:21.
m *David*, 1 Sam. 16:13.
1 R. V. moved with indignation,
16
n *Prophecies, concerning Jesus, and their fulfillment*, Gen. 12:3.
o *Babes*, Psa. 8:2.
17
p *Bethany*, John 11:18.
18
q Mark 11:12–14, 20–24.
r *Hunger*, Neh. 9:15.
19
s *Fig Tree, barren*, Luke 13:6.
t *Ecclesiasticism*, Matt. 23:2.
u *Unfruitfulness*, Matt. 7:19.
v *Unfaithfulness*, Luke 16:11.

v.19–AD 30
See footnote, *Time*, Rev. 10:6.

w *Reproof, instances of*, Prov. 17:10.
x *Wicked, punishment of*, Psa. 73:3.
y *Miracles, of Jesus*, Luke 23:8.
2 R. V. immediately
20
z *Apostles*, Luke 6:13.

21
a Matt. 17:20; Mark 11:23; Luke 17:6.
b *Faith in Christ*, John 6:69.
c *Doubting*, Rom. 14:23.
d *Promise, to the righteous* 2 Cor. 1:20.
e *Miracles, faith required in those who perform*, Luke 23:8.
f *Fig Tree*, Luke 13:6.
g *Mountain*, Mic. 7:12.
22
h *Prayer, answer to, promised*, Acts 6:4.
i *Promise, of answer to prayer*, 2 Cor. 1:20.
23
j Mark 11:27–33; Luke 20:1–8.
k *Temple, Herod's*, 1 Kin. 6:17.
l *Priest*, Lev. 1:5.
m *Senate*, Num. 11:16.
n *Jesus, teacher*, Matt. 1:21.
25
o *Baptism, John's*, Luke 20:4.
p *Heaven, figurative*, Luke 18:22.
q *Unbelief*, Heb. 3:12.
26
r *Cowardice*, Lev. 26:36.
s *Public Opinion*, John 12:42.
t *John the Baptist*, Luke 1:63.
u *Prophets*, Isa. 3:2.
28
v *Parables, of Jesus*, Ezek. 20:49.

v.28–AD 30
See footnote, *Time*, Rev. 10:6.

w *Vineyard, parables of*, Isa. 1:8.

29

x *Repentance*, Mark 1:4.

y *Obedience*, Heb. 5:8.

30

z *Instability*, Jas. 1:8.

31

a *Reproof, faithfulness in*, Prov. 17:10.

b *Publicans*, Matt. 11:19.

c *Harlot*, Prov. 7:10.

d *Kingdom of Heaven*, Matt. 13:24.

32

e *John the Baptist*, Luke 1:63.

f *Unbelief*, Heb. 3:12.

g *Spiritual Blindness*, 2 Cor. 4:4.

h *Impenitence*, Rom. 2:5.

33

i *Parables, of Jesus*, Ezek. 20:49.

j *Vineyard, parables of*, Isa. 1:8.

k *Church, described as corrupt*, vs. 33–46; Matt. 16:18.

l *Ecclesiasticism*, Matt. 23:2.

m *Wine-press*, Isa. 5:2.

n *Tower*, 2 Chr. 26:9.

o *Fortification*, Ezek. 17:17.

p *Renting, of land*, Acts 28:30.

q *Land, leased*, Ruth 4:3.

34

r *Servant*, Jer. 2:14.

s *Prophets*, Isa. 3:2.

35

t *Persecution*, John 15:20.

u *Homicide, felonious*, Deut. 5:17.

37

v *Jesus, son of God*, Matt. 1:21.

38

w *Conspiracy*, 1 Kin. 16:9.

Son, go work to day in my [w]vineyard.

29 He answered and said, I will not: but afterward he [x]repented,[G] and [y]went.

30 And he came to the second, and said likewise. And he answered and said, I *go*, sir: and [z]went not.

31 Whether[G] of them twain[G] did the will of *his* father? They say unto him, The first. Jē′ṣus [a]saith unto them, Verily I say unto you, That the [b]publicans[G] and the [c]harlots go into the [d]kingdom of God before you.

32 For [e]Jŏhn came unto you in the way of righteousness, and ye [f,g]believed him not: but the [b]publicans[G] and the [c]harlots believed him: and ye, when ye had seen *it*, [h]repented[G] not afterward, that ye might believe him.

33 ¶ Hear another [i]parable: †There was a certain householder, which planted a [j,k,l]vineyard, and hedged it round about, and digged[G] a [m]winepress in it, and built a [n,o]tower, and ‡,[p]let[G] [q]it out to ‖husbandmen[G], and went into a far country:[Q]

34 And when the time[G] of the fruit drew near, he sent his [r,s]servants to the ‖husbandmen,[G] that they might receive the fruits of it.

35 †And the ‖husbandmen[G] took his [r,s]servants, and [t]beat one, and [u]killed another, and stoned another.

36 †Again, he sent other [r,s]servants more than the first: and they did unto them likewise.

37 But[T] last of all he sent unto them his [v]son, saying, They will reverence my son.

38 †But when the ‖husbandmen[G] saw the son, they [w]said among themselves, This is the heir; come, let us kill him, and let us seize on his inheritance.

39 †And ‖they caught him, and cast *him* out of the [j,k]vineyard, and [u]slew *him*.[T]

40 When the lord therefore of the [j,k]vineyard cometh, what will he do unto those ‖husbandmen[G]?

41 They say unto him, He will miserably [x,y]destroy those [3,z]wicked men, and will let[G] out *his* vineyard unto other ‖husbandmen, which shall render[G] him the fruits in their [a]seasons.

42 Jē′ṣus saith unto them, Did ye never read in the scriptures, [b]The [c]stone which the builders [d]rejected, the same is become the [e]head of the corner: this is the Lord's doing, and it is marvellous in our eyes?[Q]

43 Therefore [f]say [g]I unto you, The kingdom of God shall be [h]taken from [i,j]you, and given to a nation bringing forth the fruits thereof.[S]

44 And whosoever shall fall on this [c]stone shall be [4]broken: but on whomsoever it shall fall, it will [k]grind him to powder.[Q]

45 And when the chief [l]priests and [m]Phăr′ĭ-seeṣ had heard his parables, they perceived that he spake of [j,n]them.

46 But when they sought to lay hands on him, they [o]feared the [p]multitude, because they took him for a [q]prophet.[T]

## CHAPTER 22

*The parable of the marriage of the king's son. 11 The wedding garment. 15 The question of the Pharisees about paying tribute to Cæsar, 23 and of the Sadducees concerning the resurrection. 34 The two great commandments. 41 Christ the son of David.*

AND Jē′ṣus[S] answered and [a]spake unto them again by [b]parables, and said,

2 [c]The [d]kingdom of heaven is

v.38–AD 30
See footnote, *Time*, Rev. 10:6.

41

x *Punishment*, Lev. 26:41.

y *Wicked, punishment of*, Psa. 73:3.

z Mark 12:9; Luke 20:16.

a *Seasons*, Dan. 2:21.

3 R. V. miserable

42

b *Prophecies, concerning Jesus, and their fulfillment*, Gen. 12:3.

c *Corner Stone, figurative*, Psa. 144:12.

d *Jesus, rejected*, Matt. 1:21.

e *Church, Christ head of*, Matt. 16:18.

43

f *Reproof, faithfulness in*, Prov. 17:10.

g *Jesus, prophet*, Matt. 1:21.

h *Judgments*, Ex. 6:6.

i *Jews, prophecies concerning*, Neh. 4:2.

j *Church, backslidden*, Matt. 16:18.

44

k *Wicked, punishment of*, Psa. 73:3.

4 R. V. broken to pieces:

45

l *Priest*, Lev. 1:5.

m *Pharisees*, Matt. 15:12.

n *Ecclesiasticism*, Matt. 23:2.

46

o *Cowardice*, Lev. 26:36.

p *Public Opinion*, John 12:42.

q *Prophets*, Isa. 3:2.

1

a *Jesus, parables of*, Matt. 1:21.

b *Parables*, Ezek. 20:49.

2

c Compare Luke 14:16–24.

d *Kingdom of Heaven*, Matt. 13:24.

† **CAPITAL AND LABOR.** *Strife between*, Matt. 21:33–41; Mark 12:1–9; Luke 20:9–16. See footnotes: EMPLOYEE, Deut. 24:14; EMPLOYER, Deut. 24:14.

‡ **LEASE.** *Of real estate*, Matt. 21:33–41; Mark 12:1–9; Luke 20:9–16. See footnote, LAND, Ruth. 4:3.

‖ **HUSBANDMAN.** *Parable of, describing the unfaithful Jews, given over to corruption and hypocrisy*, Matt. 21:33–46; Mark 12:1–12; Luke 20:9–19.
**Figurative,** John 15:1; 1 Cor. 3:9.

v.2–AD 30
See footnote, *Time*, Rev. 10:6.

e *Marriage, nuptial feasts*, Gen. 34:9.
1 R. V. marriage feast

**3**
f *Servant*, Jer. 2:14.
g *Prophets*, Isa. 3:2.
h *Call, personal*, Phil. 3:14.
i *Hospitality*, Rom. 12:13.
j *Wicked*, Psa. 73:3.

**4**
k *Feasts*, Mark 12:39.

**5**
l *Worldliness*, 1 John 2:15.

**6**
m *Martyrdom*, Rev. 17:6.
2 R.V. shamefully,

**7**
n *Anger of God*, 2 Kin. 13:3.
o *Judgments*, Ex. 6:6.
p *Wicked, punishment of*, Psa. 73:3.

**9**
3 R. V. unto the partings of the highways,

**11**
q *Judgment, general*, 2 Pet. 3:7.
r *Dress*, Zech. 3:3.
s *Righteousness*, Psa. 15:2.

**12**
t *Self-righteousness*, Luke 18:11.

like unto a certain king, which made a [1,e]marriage for his son,

3 And sent forth his [f,g]servants to [h]call them that were [i]bidden to the [1,e]wedding: and [j]they would not come.

4 Again, he sent forth other [f,g]servants, saying, Tell them which are [h]bidden, Behold, I have prepared my [k]dinner: my oxen and *my* fatlings *are* killed, and all things *are* ready: come unto the [1,e]marriage.

5 But [j]they made light of *it*, and went their ways, [l]one to his farm, [l]another to his merchandise:

6 And the remnant took his [f,g]servants, and entreated *them* [2]spitefully, and [m]slew *them*.

7 But when the king heard *thereof*, he was [n]wroth: and he sent forth his armies, and [o,p]destroyed those murderers, and burned up their city.

8 Then saith he to his [f,g]servants, The wedding is ready, but they which were [h]bidden were not worthy.

9 Go ye therefore [3]into the highways, and as many as ye shall find, [h]bid to the [e]marriage.

10 So those [f,g]servants went out into the highways, and gathered together all as many as they found, both bad and good: and the wedding was furnished with guests.

11 And [q]when the king came in to see the guests, he saw there a man which had not on a wedding [r,s]garment:

12 And he saith unto him, Friend, how [t]camest thou in hither not having a wedding garment? And he was speechless.

13 Then said the king to the servants, Bind him hand and foot, and take him away, and [p]cast *him* into [u]outer [v]darkness; there shall be [w,x]weeping and [y]gnashing of teeth.

14 For many are [h]called, but few *are* [z,a]chosen.

15 ¶ [b]Then went the [c]Phăr'ĭ-seeș, and [d,e]took counsel how they might [4]entangle him in *his* talk.

16 And [c]they sent out unto him their [f]disciples with the [g]Hē-rō'dĭ-anș, [h,i]saying, [5]Master, we know that thou art true, and [j]teachest the way of God in truth, neither carest thou for any *man*: for thou regardest not the person of men.

17 Tell us therefore, What thinkest thou? [k]Is it lawful to give [l]tribute unto Çæ'șar, or not?

18 But Jē'ș̣us [m]perceived their [i]wickedness, and said, Why tempt ye me, *ye* hypocrites?

19 Shew me the [l]tribute money. And they brought unto him a [n]penny.

20 And he saith unto them, Whose *is* this [o]image and superscription?

21 They say unto him, Çæ'șar's. Then saith he unto them, [p]Render therefore unto Çæ'șar the [q]things which are Çæ'șar's; and [r]unto God the things that are God's.

22 When [c]they had heard *these words*, they marvelled, and left him, and went their way.

23 ¶ [s]The same day came to him the *Săd'du-çeeș, which say that there is no [t]resurrection, and asked him,

24 Saying, [5]Master, Mō'ș̣eș [u]said, [v]If a man [w]die, having no children, his [x]brother shall [y]marry his wife, and raise up seed unto his brother.

**24** u *Law, of Moses*, Deut. 33:2. v Deut. 25:5; Mark 12:19; Luke 20:28. w *Death*, Num. 23:10. x *Brother*, Prov. 18:24. y *Marriage, levirate*, Gen. 34:9.

v.13–AD 30
See footnote, *Time*, Rev. 10:6.

**13**
u *Hell*, Mark 9:43.
v *Darkness, figurative*, Gen. 1:2.
w *Weeping, in perdition*, Ezra 3:13.
x *Sorrow, of the lost*, Matt. 13:42.
y *Gnashing of Teeth*, Job 16:9.

**14**
z *Election of Grace*, Rom. 11:5.
a *Foreordination*, Rom. 8:30.

**15**
b Mark 12:13–17; Luke 20:20–25.
c *Pharisees*, Matt. 15:12.
d *Craftiness, instances of*, Psa. 83:3.
e *Persecution, of Jesus*, John 15:20.
4 R. V. ensnare

**16**
f *Disciples*, Matt. 9:14.
g *Herodians*, Mark 3:6.
h *Irony, instances of*, Mark 12:14.
i *Hypocrisy*, Jas. 3:17.
j *Jesus, teacher*, Matt. 1:21.
5 Am. R. V. *marg.* teacher,

**17**
k *Citizens, duties of*, Luke 15:15.
l *Tribute*, Ezra 4:13.

**18**
m *Jesus, omniscience of*, Matt. 1:21.

**19**
n *Penny*, Matt. 20:2.

**20**
o *Money, image on*, Jer. 32:9.

**21**
p *Commandment, enjoining fidelity to God and to government*, Deut. 8:2.
q *King, emoluments of*, 2 Kin. 3:10.
r *Duty, of man to God*, Eccl. 12:13.

**23**
s Mark 12:18–27; Luke 20:27–40.
t *Resurrection*, 1 Cor. 15:12.

* **SADDUCEES**, a sect of the Jews. *Rebuked by John the Baptist*, Matt. 3:7–9; Luke 3:7–9. *Reject the doctrine of the resurrection*, Matt. 22:23–34; Mark 12:18–27; Luke 20:27–40; Acts 23:7, 8. *Jesus warns his disciples against the false doctrines of*, Matt. 16:6–12. *Persecute the apostles*, Acts 4:1–3; 5:17–33.

v.25–AD 30

**29**
z *Spiritual Blindness*, 2 Cor. 4:4.
a *Ignorance*, Acts 3:17.
b *God, power of*, Gen. 2:2.

**30**
c *Resurrection*, 1 Cor. 15:12.
d *Marriage*, Gen. 34:9.
e *Angel*, Heb. 1:13.
f *Heaven, God's dwelling place*, Luke 18:22.

**31**
g *Word of God, inspiration of*, Psa. 119:9.

**32**
h Ex. 3:6.
i *Immortality*, 1 Cor. 15:54.

**33**
j *Doctrines of Jesus*, John 7:16.
6 R. V. teaching.

**34**
k Mark 12:28–34; Luke 10:25–28.
l *Pharisees*, Matt. 15:12.

**36**
m *Law, of Moses*, Deut. 33:2.
n *Decalogue*, Ex. 20:3.

**37**
o Deut. 6:5.
p *Commandment, enjoining love to God*, Deut. 8:2.
q *Love, of man for God*, 1 John 4:19.
r *Duty, of man to God*, Eccl. 12:13.
s *Heart*, Psa. 44:21.

25 Now there were with us seven brethren: and the first, when he had married a wife, [w]deceased, and, having no issue, left his wife unto his brother:

26 Likewise the second also, and the third, unto the seventh.

27 And last of all the woman [w]died also.

28 Therefore in the [t]resurrection whose wife shall she be of the seven? for they all [y]had her.

29 Jē'ṣus answered and said unto them, Ye do err, [z,a]not knowing the scriptures, nor the [b]power of God.

30 For in the [c]resurrection they neither [d]marry, nor are given in marriage, but are as the [e]angels of God in [f]heaven.

31 But as touching the [c]resurrection of the dead, have ye not read that which [g]was spoken unto you by God, saying,

32 [h]I am the God of Ā'brā-hăm, and the God of Ī'ṣaac, and the God of Jā'cob? God is not the God of the dead, but of the [i]living.

33 And when the multitude heard *this*, they were astonished at his [6,j]doctrine.

34 ¶ [k]But when the [l]Phăr'ĭ-seeṣ had heard that he had put the Săd'du-çeeṣ to silence, they were gathered together.

35 Then one of them, *which was* a †lawyer, asked *him a question*, tempting him, and saying,

36 [5]Master, which *is* the great commandment in the [m,n]law?

37 Jē'ṣus said unto him, [n,o,p]Thou shalt [q,r]love the Lord thy God with all thy [s]heart, and with all thy soul, and with all thy mind.

38 [o]This is the first and great commandment.

39 And the second *is* like unto it, [n,t,u]Thou shalt [v,w]love thy [x]neighbour as thyself.

40 On these two commandments hang all the [m]law and the [y]prophets.

41 ¶ While the [z]Phăr'ĭ-seeṣ were gathered together, [a]Jē'ṣus asked them,

42 Saying, What think ye of [b]Christ? whose son is he? They say unto him, *The* [c]*son* of [d]Dā'vid.

43 He saith unto them, How then doth Dā'vid in [7]spirit call him [b]Lord, saying,

44 [e]The LORD said unto my [b]Lord, [f]Sit thou on my right hand, till I make thine enemies thy [g]footstool?

45 If Dā'vid then call him [b]Lord, how is he his [h]son?

46 And no man was able to answer him a word, neither durst any *man* from that day forth ask him any more *questions*.

## CHAPTER 23.

*Jesus directs the people to follow the teaching, but not the example, of the scribes and Pharisees. 13 He denounces woes upon them. 34 The blood of all the prophets to come upon that generation. 37 Jesus' lamentation over Jerusalem.*

THEN [a]spake Jē'ṣus to the multitude, and to his [b]disciples,

2 Saying, *The [c]scribes and the [d]Phăr'ĭ-seeṣ sit in [e]Mō'ṣeṣ' seat:

3 All therefore whatsoever *they bid you observe, *that* observe and do; but do not ye after their [f]works: for [g]they [h]say, and [i]do not.

4 For *they [j]bind heavy [k]burdens and grievous to be borne, and lay *them* on men's shoulders; [i]but they *themselves* will not move them with one of their fingers.

v.39–AD 30
See footnote, *Time*, Rev. 10:6.

**39**
t *Commandment, enjoining love to man*, Deut. 8:2.
u *Royal Law*, Jas. 2:8.
v *Love, of man for man*, 1 John 4:7.
w *Duty, of man to man*, Eccl. 12:13.
x *Neighbor, love for, enjoined*, Luke 10:29.

**40**
y *Prophecies*, Dan. 9:24.

**41**
z *Pharisees*, Matt. 15:12.
a Mark 12:35–37; Luke 20:41–44.

**42**
b *Jesus, Messiah*, Matt. 1:21.
c *Jesus, humanity of*, Matt. 1:21.
d *David, Jesus called son of*, 1 Sam. 16:13.

**43**
7 R. V. the Spirit

**44**
e *Prophecies, concerning the Messiah, and their fulfillment*, Gen. 12:3.
f *Sovereignty of the Messiah*, Psa. 110:1.
g *Footstool, figurative*, 1 Chr. 28:2.

**45**
h *Jesus, incarnation of*, Matt. 1:21.

**1**
a Mark 12:38–40; Luke 20:45, 46.
b *Apostles*, Luke 6:13.

**2**
c *Scribe*, 1 Kin. 4:3.
d *Pharisees*, Matt. 15:12.
e *Law, of Moses*, Deut. 33:2.

**3**
f *Example, bad*, John 13:15.
g *False Teachers*, 2 Pet. 2:1.
h *Hypocrisy*, Jas. 3:17.
i *Inconsistency*, Matt. 7:3.

**4**
j *Oppression*, Eccl. 5:8.
k *Burden, figurative*, Luke 11:46.

† **LAWYER**, one versed in the Mosaic law. *Tests Jesus with questions*, Matt. 22:35; Luke 10:25–37. *Jesus' denunciations against*, Luke 11:45–52. *Zenas, a*, Tit. 3:13. See footnote, LITIGATION, Matt. 5:25.

* **ECCLESIASTICISM**, the authority and power of the church, as exercised by constituted authorities. *Traditional rules of Jewish*, Matt. 15:1–20; Mark 7:2–23. *Arrogance of*, Matt. 12:2–7; 23:4. *The Jewish, rebuked by Jesus*, Matt. 23:2–4, 8–10, 13–35. *Corrupt, illustrated by the parable of the wicked husbandman*, Matt. 21:28–44; Mark 12:1–12; Luke 20:9–16. *Overthrow of, symbolized in the withering of the fruitless fig tree*, Matt. 21:19, 20.

v.5–AD 3
See footnote, *Time*, Rev. 10:6.

**5**
*l* Matt. 6:1.
**6**
*m* *Pride*, Prov. 16:18.
*n* *Feasts*, Mark 12:39.
*o* *Synagogue*, Matt. 12:9.
**7**
*p* *Salutations*, Luke 1:44.
**8**
*q* *Church, Christ the head of*, Matt. 16:18.
*r* *Jesus, teacher*, Matt. 1:21.
*s* *Man, equality of*, Job 4:17.
*t* *Fellowship, of the righteous*, 1 Cor. 1:9.
*u* *Fraternity*, Zech. 11:14.
*v* *Unity, of the righteous*, Psa. 133:1.
1 R. V. teacher,
2 R. V. *omits* even Christ;
**9**
*w* *Father*, Psa. 27:10.
*x* *God, fatherhood of*, Gen. 2:2.
*y* *Heaven, God's dwelling place*, Luke 18:22.
**10**
*z* *Master, Jesus called*, John 13:13.

**11**
*a* *Altruism*, Acts 20:35.
**12**
*b* *Humility*, Prov. 22:4.
*c* *Promise, to the humble*, 2 Cor. 1:20.
**13**
*d* *Reproof, faithfulness in*, Prov. 17:10.
*e* *Scribe*, 1 Kin. 4:3.
*f* *Pharisees*, Matt. 15:12.
*g* *Hypocrisy*, Jas. 3:17.
*h* *Kingdom of Heaven*, Matt. 13:24.
**14**
*i* *Punishment, according to deeds*, Lev. 26:41.
*j* *Wicked, punishment of*, Psa. 73:3.
3 R. V. *omits this verse.*
**15**
*k* *Hell*, Mark 9:43.

5 But all their works they do
[l]for to be seen of men: they
make broad their †phylacteries,[C]
and enlarge the borders of their
garments,[Q]
6 And [m]love the uppermost
rooms[C] at [n]feasts, and the chief
seats in the [o]synagogues,
7 And [l,p]greetings in the markets, and to be called of men,
‡Răb′bī,[C] Răb′bī.[C]
8 But be not ye called ‡Răb′bī:
for one is [q]your [1,r]Master, [2]*even*
Chrīst; and all [s,t]ye are [u,v]breth-
ren.
9 And call no *man* your [w]fa-
ther upon the earth: for one
is your [x]Father, which is in
[y]heaven.[T]
10 Neither be ye called masters[C]: for one is your [z]Master,[C]
*even* Chrīst.[T]
11 But he that is greatest
among you [a]shall be your servant.
12 And whosoever shall exalt
himself shall be abased[C]; and he
that shall [b]humble himself [c]shall
be exalted.[Q]
13 ¶ But [d]woe unto *you,
[e]scribes and [f]Phăr′ĭ-seeş, [g]hypo-
crites! for ye shut up the [h]king-
dom of heaven against men: for
ye neither go in *yourselves*,
neither suffer[C] ye them that are
entering to go in.
14 [3,d]Woe unto *you, [e]scribes
and [f]Phăr′ĭ-seeş, hypocrites! for
ye devour[C] widows' houses, and
[g]for a pretence make long prayer: [i]therefore [j]ye shall receive
the greater damnation[C].
15 [d]Woe unto *you, [e]scribes
and [f]Phăr′ĭ-seeş, [g]hypocrites! for
ye compass[C] sea and land to make
one proselyte[C], and when he is
made, ye make him twofold
more the child of [k]hell[C] than yourselves.

16 [d]Woe unto *you, [l]*ye* [m]blind
guides, which say, Whosoever
shall [n]swear by the [o]temple, it
is nothing; but whosoever shall
swear by the [p]gold of the temple,
he is a debtor!
17 [d]*Ye* [q]fools and [m]blind: for
whether is greater, the [p]gold, or
the [o]temple that [r]sanctifieth[C] the
gold?
18 And, Whosoever shall [n]swear
by the [s]altar, it is nothing; but
whosoever sweareth by the gift
that is upon it, he is [4]guilty.
19 [d]*Ye* [q]fools and [m]blind: for
whether *is* greater, the gift, or
[t]the [s]altar that [r]sanctifieth the
gift?[Q]
20 Whoso therefore shall [n]swear
by the [s]altar, sweareth by it, and
by all things thereon.
21 And whoso shall [n]swear by
the [o]temple, sweareth by it, and
by him that dwelleth therein.[Q]
22 And he that shall [n]swear by
[u]heaven, sweareth by the [v]throne
of God, and by him that sitteth
thereon.[Q]
23 [d]Woe unto you, scribes and
Phăr′ĭ-seeş, hypocrites! for ye
pay [w]tithe of [x]mint and anise and
[y]cummin, and have omitted the
[z]weightier *matters* of the law,
[a,b]judgment[C], [a,c]mercy, and [d]faith:
these ought ye to have done, and
not to leave the other undone.[Q]
24 [e,f]*Ye* [g]blind guides, which
strain [5]at a gnat, and swallow a
camel.
25 [e]Woe unto you, [h]scribes and
[i]Phăr′ĭ-seeş, hypocrites! for ye
make clean the outside of the
cup and of the platter,[C] [j]but
within they are full [6]of [k]extor-
tion and excess.
26 [e]*Thou* [g]blind [i]Phăr′ĭ-see,
[l]cleanse first that *which is* within
the cup and platter, that the outside of them may be clean also.

v.16–AD 30
See footnote, *Time*, Rev. 10:6.

**16**
*l* *False Teachers*, 2 Pet. 2:1.
*m* *Spiritual Blindness*, 2 Cor. 4:4.
*n* *Oath*, Num. 5:19.
*o* *Temple*, 1 Kin. 6:17.
*p* *Gold*, Ezek. 7:19.
**17**
*q* *Fool*, Prov. 18:2.
*r* *Sanctification*, 1 Pet. 1:2.
**18**
*s* *Altar, of burnt offerings*, Gen. 8:20.
4 R. V. a debtor.
**19**
*t* Ex. 29:37.

**22**
*u* *Heaven, figurative*, Luke 18:22.
*v* *Throne, figurative*, 1 Kin. 2:19.
**23**
*w* *Tithes*, Num. 18:24.
*x* Luke 11:42.
*y* Isa. 28:25, 27.
*z* *Duty, of man to God*, Eccl. 12:13.

*a* *Duty, of man to man*, Eccl. 12:13.
*b* *Righteousness, required*, Psa. 15:2.
*Mercy, enjoined*, Deut. 5:10.
*d* *Faith*, Mark 11:22.
**24**
*e* *Reproof, faithfulness in*, Prov. 17:10.
*f* *False Teachers*, 2 Pet. 2:1.
*g* *Spiritual Blindness*, 2 Cor. 4:4.
5 R. V. out the gnat,
**25**
*h* *Scribe*, 1 Kin. 4:3.
*i* *Pharisees*, Matt. 15:12.
*j* *Hypocrisy*, Jas. 3:17.
*k* *Extortion*, Isa. 16:4.
6 R. V. from
**26**
*l* *Spiritual Purification, enjoined*, Psa. 51:2.

† **PHYLACTERY.** *A small box containing slips of parchment on which were written portions of the law*, Ex. 13:9, 16; Deut. 6:4–9; 11:18. *Worn ostentatiously by the Jews*, Matt. 23:5.
‡ **RABBI.** *The title, of a teacher*, Matt. 23:7, 8; John 3:2; *ostentatiously used by the Pharisees*, Matt. 23:7; *used in addressing John*, John 3:26; *used in addressing Jesus*, John 1:38, 49; 3:2; 6:25 [R. V., Matt. 26:25, 49; Mark 9:5; 11:21; 14:45; John 4:31; 9:2; 11:8]. *Jesus called Rabboni*, [R. V. Mark 10:51]; John 20:16. *Forbidden by Jesus as a title to his disciples*, Matt. 23:8.

v.27–AD 30
See footnote, *Time*, Rev. 10:6.

27
*m* *Wicked, described*, Psa. 73:3.

30
*n* *Self-righteousness*, Luke 18:11.

31
*o* *Self-condemnation*, Job 9:20.
*p* *Example, bad*, John, 13:15.

33
*q* *Viper, figurative*, Isa. 30:6.
*r* *Punishment, no escape from*, Lev. 26:41.
*s* *Sin, no escape from consequences of*, Rom. 5:12.
*t* *Judgments*, Ex. 6:6.
*u* *Wicked, punishment of*, Psa. 73:3.
*v* *Hell*, Mark 9:43.
7 R. V. judgment

34
*w* Luke 11:49–51.
*x* *Jesus, prophet*, Matt. 1:21.
*y* *Opportunity, the measure of responsibility*, Gal. 6:10.
*z* *Prophets, persecutions of*, Isa. 3:2.

*a* *Minister, trials and persecutions of*, Rom. 15:16.
*b* *Martyrdom*, Rev. 17:6.
*c* *Crucifixion*, Mark 15:13.
*d* *Scourging*, Acts 22:24.
*e* *Synagogue*, Matt. 12:9.
*f* *Persecution, of the righteous*, John 15:20.

35
*g* *Responsibility*, Ezek. 18:20.
*h* *Abel*, Gen. 4:2.
*i* Luke 11:51.
*j* Or, *Berechiah*, Zech. 1:1, 7.
*k* *Altar, in the temple*, Gen. 8:20.
8 R. V. sanctuary

36
*l* *Jesus, prophet*, Matt. 1:21.

37
*m* Luke 13:34, 35; 19:41–44.
*n* *Jerusalem*, Judg. 19:10.
*o* *Backsliders, God's solicitude for*, Jer. 3:22.
*p* *Prophets, persecution of*, Isa. 3:2.
*q* *Opportunity, lost*, Gal. 6:10.

27 [e]Woe unto *you, [h]scribes and
[i]Phăr′ĭ-seeș, [j]hypocrites! for [m]ye
are like unto whited sepulchres,
which indeed appear beautiful
outward, but are within full of
dead *men's* bones, and of all
uncleanness.
28 [e]Even so ye also outwardly
appear righteous unto men, but
[m]within ye are full of [j]hypocrisy
and iniquity.
29 [e]Woe unto you, [h]scribes and
[i]Phăr′ĭ-seeș, [j]hypocrites! because
ye build the tombs of the prophets, and garnish the sepulchres
of the righteous,
30 And [n]say, If we had been
in the days of our fathers, we
would not have been partakers
with them in the blood of the
prophets.
31 Wherefore [o]ye be witnesses
unto yourselves, that ye are the
children of [p]them which killed
the prophets.
32 Fill ye up then the measure
of your fathers.
33 [m]*Ye* serpents, *ye* generation
of [q]vipers, [r,s]how can ye escape
the [7,t,u]damnation of [v]hell?
34 Wherefore, behold, [w,x,y]I
send unto you [z,a]prophets, and
wise men, and scribes: and
[a]*some* of them ye shall [b]kill
and [c]crucify; and *some* of them
shall ye [d]scourge in your [e]syna-
gogues, and [f]persecute *them* from
city to city:
35 That [g]upon *you may come
all the righteous blood shed upon the earth, from the blood of
righteous [h]Ā′bĕl unto the blood
of [i]Zăch-a-rī′as son of [j]Băr-a-
chī′as, whom ye [b,f]slew between
the [8]temple and the [k]altar.
36 Verily [l]I say unto you, All
these things shall come upon
this generation.
37 [m]O [n]Jē-ru̧′sā-lĕm, Jē-ru̧′-
sā-lĕm, [o]*thou* that [b,f]killest the
[p]prophets, and stonest them
which are sent unto thee, [q]how
often would [r]I have gathered
thy children together, even as a
hen gathereth her chickens under *her* wings, and ye [s]would not!
38 Behold, your house is left
unto you desolate.
39 For [l]I say unto you, Ye shall
not see me henceforth, till ye
shall say, [t]Blessed *is* he that
cometh in the name of the Lord.

## CHAPTER 24

*Jesus foretells the destruction of the temple, 3 and the calamities which shall precede it. 29 The signs of his coming. 34 The day and hour thereof unknown. 42 The duty of all to watch.*

[a]AND Jē′ş̦us went out, and
departed from the [b]tem-
ple: and his [c]disciples came to
*him* for to shew him the buildings of the temple.
2 And Jē′ş̦us said unto them,
See ye not all these things? verily [d]I say unto you, There shall
not be left here one stone upon
another, that shall not be thrown
down.
3 ¶ And as he sat upon the
mount of [e]Ŏl′ĭveș, the [c]disciples
came unto him privately, saying,
Tell us, when shall these things
be? and what *shall be* the [f]sign
of [g]thy coming, and of the end
of the [h]world?
4 And Jē′ş̦us answered and
said unto them, [i]Take heed that
no man [1,j,k]deceive you.
5 For [l,m]many shall come in my
name, saying, I am Chrīst; and
shall [2,j,k]deceive many.
6 And ye shall hear of [n]wars
and rumours of wars: see that
ye be not troubled: for all *these*
*things* must come to pass, but
the end is not yet.
7 For nation shall rise against
nation, and kingdom against
kingdom: and there shall be
[o]famines, [3]and pestilences, and
[p]earthquakes, in divers places.
8 All these *are* the beginning
of [4,q]sorrows.
9 [r]Then shall they [s]deliver you

v.37–AD 30
See footnote, *Time*, Rev. 10:6.

*r* *Jesus, love of*, Matt. 1:21.
*s* *Impentience*, Rom. 2:5.

39
*t* Psa. 118:26; Matt. 21:9; Mark 11:9; Luke 13:35; 19:38; John 12:13.

1
*a* Mark 13; Luke 21:5–36.
*b* *Temple, Herod's* 1 Kin. 6:17.
*c* *Apostles*, Luke 6:13.

2
*d* *Jesus, prophet*, Matt. 1:21.

3
*e* *Mount of Olives*, Mark 11:1.
*f* *Sign, a token*, Mark 8:11.
*g* *Jesus, second coming of*, Matt. 1:21.
*h* *Earth, destruction of*, Prov. 8:23.

4
*i* *Watchfulness, enjoined*, Matt. 24:42.
*j* *Temptation, leading into*, Luke 11:4.
*k* *Apostasy*, Acts 1:25.
1 R. V. lead you astray.

5
*l* *False Teachers*, 2 Pet. 2:1.
*m* *Antichrist*, 2 John 7.
2 R. V. lead many astray.

6
*n* *War*, Judg. 3:2.

7
*o* *Famine*, 2 Kin. 8:1.
*p* *Earthquakes, as judgments*, Isa. 29:6.
3 R. V. *omits* and pestilences

8
*q* *Afflictions*, Psa. 34:19.
4 R. V. travail.

9
*r* *Malice*, Eph. 4:31.
*s* *Persecution, of the righteous*, John 15:20.

v.9–AD 30
See footnote, *Time*, Rev. 10:6.

*t* *Martyrdom*, Rev. 17:6.
*u* *Hatred*, Prov. 15:17.

**10**
*v* *Apostasy*, Acts 1:25.
*w* *Betrayal*, Matt. 26:46.
5 R. V. stumble,

**12**
*x* *Backsliding, temptation to*, Hos. 11:7.

**13**
*y* *Blessings, contingent upon obedience*, Deut. 11:26.
*z* *Faithfulness*, Luke 16:10.

*a* *Perseverance*, Eph. 6:18.
*b* *Christian Graces, perseverance*, Gal. 5:22.
*c* *Righteous, rewarded*, Psa. 64:10.
*d* *Promise, to the righteous*, 2 Cor. 1:20.
*e* *Reward, a motive to perseverance*, Matt. 5:12.
*f* *Salvation*, Acts 16:17.

**14**
*g* *Jesus, prophet*, Matt. 1:21.
*h* *Gospel, prophecies relating to*, Mark 13:10.
*i* *Preaching*, Matt. 9:35.
*j* *Missions*, Matt. 28:19.

**15**
*k* Dan. 9:27; 11:31; 12:11.
*l* *Jerusalem, destruction of, foretold by Jesus*, Judg 19:10.
*m* *Daniel, prophecies of*, Dan. 1:6.
*n* *Prophets*, Isa. 3:2.

**16**
*o* *Judea*, Luke 5:17.

**17**
*p* *House, roof of*, Esth. 8:1.

**18**
*q* *Dress*, Zech. 3:3.
6 R. V. cloke.

**20**
*r* *Winter*, Gen. 8:22.
*s* *Sabbath*, Ex. 16:23.

**21**
*t* *Faith, trial of*, Mark 11:22.
*u* *Adversity*, Psa. 10:6.

up to be afflicted, and shall [t]kill you: and ye shall be [u]hated of all nations for my name's sake.

10 And then shall many [5]be [v]offended, and shall [w]betray one another, and shall [u]hate one another.[Q]

11 And many [l,m]false prophets shall rise, and shall [2,i]deceive many.

12 And because iniquity[G] shall abound, the love of many shall [x]wax[C] cold.

13 [y]But he that shall [z,a,b]endure unto the end, [c,d]the same [e]shall be [f]saved.

14 And [g]this [h]gospel of the kingdom shall be [i]preached in [j]all the world for a witness unto all nations; and then shall the end come.

15 [k,l]When ye therefore shall see the abomination of desolation, spoken of by [m]Dăn′iel the [n]prophet, stand in the holy place, (whoso readeth, let him understand:)[Q]

16 Then let them which be in [o]Jū-dæ′ȧ flee into the mountains:

17 Let him which is on the [p]housetop not come down to take any thing out of his house:

18 Neither let him which is in the field return back to take his [6,q]clothes.

19 And woe unto them that are with child, and to them that give suck in those days!

20 But pray ye that your flight be not in the [r]winter, neither on the [s]sabbath day:

21 For then shall be great [t,u]tribulation, such as was not since the beginning of the world to this time, no, nor ever shall be.[Q]

22 And except those days should be shortened, there should no flesh be saved: but for the [v,w]elect's[G] [x]sake those days shall be shortened.[S]

23 [y]Then if any man shall say unto you, Lo, here *is* [z]Christ, or, There; believe *it* not.

24 For there shall arise [z]false Christs, and [a]false prophets, and shall shew great [b,c]signs and wonders; insomuch that, if *it were* possible, they shall [7,d]deceive the very [e]elect.[Q]

25 Behold, [f,g]I have told you before.

26 Wherefore if [a]they shall say unto you, Behold, he is in the desert; go not forth: behold, *he is* in the secret chambers[G]; believe *it* not.

27 For as the [h,i]lightning cometh out of the east, and shineth even unto the west; so shall also the [j]coming of the Son of man be.

28 [k]For wheresoever the carcase is, there will the [l]eagles be gathered together.

29 ¶ Immediately after the [m]tribulation[G] of those days shall the [n]sun [o]be [p,q]darkened, and the [r]moon [o]shall [p]not give her light, and the [s]stars shall [o]fall from [t]heaven, and [o]the powers of the heavens shall be shaken:[Q]

30 And then shall appear the [u]sign of the [v]Son of man in heaven: and then shall all the tribes of the earth [w]mourn, and they shall see the [v]Son of man coming in the clouds of heaven with power and great glory.[Q]

31 And he shall send his [x]angels with a great sound of a [y]trumpet, and [z]they shall gather together his [e]elect from the four winds, from one end of heaven to the other.[S Q]

32 ¶ [a]Now learn a [b]parable of the [c]fig tree; When his branch is yet tender, and putteth forth leaves, ye know that [d]summer *is* nigh[G]:

v.22–AD 30
See footnote, *Time*, Rev. 10:6.

**22**
*v* *Righteous, promises to*, Psa. 64:10.
*w* *Foreordination*, Rom. 8:30.
*x* *Intercession, influence of the righteous*, Jer. 27:18.

**23**
*y* Mark 13:21–27; Luke 21:24–28.
*z* *Antichrist*, 2 John 7.

**24**
*a* *False Teachers*, 2 Pet. 2:1.
*b* *Miracles, performed by false christs*, Luke 23:8.
*c* *Sorcery*, Isa. 47:9.
*d* *Deception*, Josh. 9:4.
*e* *Foreordination*, v. 31; Rom. 8:30.
7 R. V. lead astray

**25**
*f* *Jesus, omniscience of*, Matt. 1:21.
*g* *Jesus, prophet*, Matt. 1:21.

**27**
*h* *Lightning*, Job 28:26.
*i* *Meteorology*, Matt. 16:2.
*j* *Jesus, second coming of*, Matt. 1:21.

**28**
*k* *Parables*, Ezek. 20:49.
*l* *Eagle*, Lev. 11:13.

**29**
*m* *Adversity*, Psa. 10:6.
*n* *Sun*, Josh. 10:12.
*o* *Celestial Phenomena*, Luke 23:44.
*p* *Eclipse*, Isa. 13:10.
*q* *Darkness, figurative*, Gen. 1:2.
*r* *Moon, darkening of*, Song 6:10.
*s* *Stars, falling of*, Judg. 5:20.
*t* *Heavens, physical*, Psa. 8:3.

**30**
*u* *Sign*, Mark 8:11.
*v* *Jesus, humanity of*, Matt. 1:21.
*w* *Despondency*, Eccl. 2:20.

**31**
*x* *Angel, functions of*, Heb. 1:13.
*y* *Trumpet*, Josh. 6:4.

*z* *Righteous, promises to*, Psa. 64:10. **32**—*a* Mark 13:28–31; Luke 21:29–33. *b* *Parables*, Ezek. 20:49. *c* *Fig Tree*, Luke 13:6. *d* *Summer*, Isa. 28:4.

v.33–AD 30
See footnote, *Time*, Rev. 10:6.

**33**
*e* *Sign*, Mark 8:11.
*f* *Celestial Phenomena*, Luke 23:44.

**34**
*g* *Jesus, prophet*, Matt. 1:21.

**35**
*h* *Heavens, physical, destruction of*, Psa. 8:3.
*i* *Earth, destruction of*, Prov. 8:23.
*j* *Doctrines of Jesus*, John 7:16.
*k* *Prophecies, fulfillment of*, Dan. 9:24.

**36**
*l* Mark 13:32–37; Luke 21:34–36.
*m* *Judgment, the general*, 2 Pet. 3:7.
*n* *Angel*, Heb. 1:13.
*o* *God, foreknowledge of*, Gen. 2:2.
*p* *God, fatherhood of*, Gen. 2:2.

**37**
*q* Or, *Noah*, Gen. 5:29.
*r* *Antediluvians, destruction of*, Gen. 6:1.
*s* *Jesus, second coming of*, Matt. 1:21.

**38**
*t* *Worldliness, instances of*, 1 John 2:15.
*u* *Spiritual Blindness*, 2 Cor. 4:4.
*v* *Marriage*, Gen. 34:9.
*w* *Ark*, Gen. 6:14.

**39**
*x* *Flood*, Gen. 6:17.
*y* *Judgments*, Ex. 6:6.

**41**
*z* *Women, duties of*, Prov. 31:10.

*a* *Labor*, Luke 10:7.
*b* *Mill*, Ex. 11:5.

**42**

33 So likewise ye, when ye
shall see all these [e,f]things,
know that it is near, *even* at
the doors.
34 Verily [g]I say unto you, This
generation shall not pass, till all
these things be fulfilled.
35 [h]Heaven and [i]earth shall
pass away, but my [j,k]words
shall not pass away.
36 ¶ [l]But of that [m]day and hour
knoweth no *man*, no, not the
[n]angels of heaven, but [o,p]my
Father only.
37 But as the days of [q,r]Nō'e
*were*, so shall also the [s]coming
of the Son of man be.
38 For as in the days that
were before the flood they were
[t,u]eating and drinking, [v]marrying and giving in marriage, until the day that [q]Nō'e entered
into the [w]ark,
39 And knew not until the
[x,y]flood came, and took them
all away; so shall also the [s]coming of the Son of man be.
40 Then shall two be in the
field; the one shall be taken, and
the other left.
41 Two [z]*women shall be* [a]grinding at the [b]mill; the one shall be
taken, and the other left.
42 ¶ [*,c,d]Watch therefore: for
ye know not what hour your
[e]Lord doth come.
43 [f]But know this, that if the
[8]goodman of the house had
known in what [g]watch the
[h,i]thief would come, he would
have *watched, and would not
have suffered his house to be
broken up.

44 Therefore be ye also [j]ready:
for in such an hour as ye
think not the [k]Son of man
[e]cometh.
45 [l]Who then is a [m,n]faithful
and [o]wise [p,q]servant, whom his
[r]lord hath made ruler over his
household, to give them [9]meat
in due season?
46 [s,t]Blessed *is* that [p,q]servant,
whom his [r]lord when he cometh
shall find so doing.
47 Verily I say unto you, That
he shall [s,t]make him ruler over
all his goods.
48 But and if that evil [p]servant
shall [u,v]say in his [w]heart, My
[x]lord delayeth his coming;
49 And shall begin to [y]smite
*his* fellowservants, and to eat
and drink with the [z]drunken;
50 The lord of that [p]servant
shall come in a day when he
looketh not for *him*, and in an
hour that he is not aware of,
51 And shall [a,b,c]cut him asunder, and appoint *him* his portion
with the [d]hypocrites: there shall
be [e,f]weeping and [g]gnashing of
teeth.

## CHAPTER 25

*The parable of the ten virgins, 14 and of the talents. 31 The last judgment described.*

[a,b,c]THEN shall the [d]kingdom
of heaven be likened unto ten [e]virgins, which took their
[f]lamps, and went forth to meet
the [g]bridegroom.
2 And five of [h]them were [i,j]wise,
and [k]five *were* [l]foolish.
3 [k]They that *were* [l]foolish took

v.44–AD 30
See footnote, *Time*, Rev. 10:6.

**44**
*j* *Preparedness*, Luke 12:40.
*k* *Jesus, humanity of*, Matt. 1:21.

**45**
*l* Luke 12:42–48.
*m* *Faithfulness, exhortations to*, Luke 16:10.
*n* *Righteous, described*, Psa. 64:10.
*o* *Wisdom, worldly*, Prov. 2:2.
*p* *Servant, figurative*, Jer. 2:14.
*q* *Minister, character and qualifications of*, Rom. 15:16.
*r* *Master*, Col. 4:1.
9 R. V. food

**46**
*s* *Reward, a motive, to faithfulness*, Matt. 5:12.
*t* *Righteous, promises to*, Psa. 64:10.

**48**
*u* *Procrastination*, Acts 24:25.
*v* *Delusion*, 2 Thess. 2:11.
*w* *Heart*, Psa. 44:21.
*x* *God, longsuffering of, abused*, Gen. 2:2.

**49**
*y* *Oppression*, Eccl. 5:8.
*z* *Drunkenness*, Luke 21:34.

**51**
*a* *Probation, ended*, Rom. 5:4.
*b* *Opportunity, lost*, Gal. 6:10.
*c* *Wicked, punishment of*, Psa. 73:3.
*d* *Hypocrisy*, Jas. 3:17.
*e* *Weeping, in perdition*, Ezra 3:13.
*f* *Sorrow, of the lost*, Matt. 13:42.
*g* *Gnashing of Teeth*, Job 16:9.

*c* *Commandment, enjoining watchfulness*, vs. 42–51; Deut. 8:2. *d* *Temptation, admonitions against yielding to*, Luke 11:4. *e* *Jesus, second coming of*, Matt. 1:21. **43** *f* Luke 12:39, 40. *g* *Time*, Rev. 10:6. *h* *Thieves*, Deut. 24:7. *i* *Temptation*, Luke 11:4. 8 R. V. master

**1** *a* *Parables*, Ezek. 20:49. *b* *Judgment, the general*, 2 Pet. 3:7. *c* *Opportunity, the measure of responsibility*, vs. 1–16; Gal. 6:10. *d* *Kingdom of Heaven*, Matt. 13:24. *e* *Virgin, parable of*, Isa. 62:5. *f* *Lamp*, Ex. 27:20. *g* *Bridegroom*, Isa. 61:10. **2** *h* *Women, good, illustrated*, Prov. 31:10. *i* *Wisdom, worldly*, Prov. 2:2. *j* *Wisdom, spiritual*, Prov. 2:2. *k* *Women, wicked, illustrated*, Prov. 31:10. *l* *Spiritual Blindness*, 2 Cor. 4:4.

* **WATCHFULNESS,** Psa. 102:7. *Over the tongue*, Psa. 39:1; 141:3.
**With prayer,** Neh. 4:9; Matt. 26:41; Mark 13:33; Eph. 6:18; Col. 4:2; 1 Pet. 4:7.
**Enjoined,** Deut. 4:15; Josh. 23:11; Matt. 18:10; 24:42–51; 25:13; Mark 4:24; 13:32–37; Luke 11:35; 12:35–40; 17:3; 21:34–36; Rom. 11:20; 1 Cor. 10:12; 11:28; 16:13; Gal. 6:1; Eph. 5:15; Col. 2:8; 1 Thess. 5:4, 6, 21; 1 Pet. 5:8; Heb. 2:1; Rev. 16:15.
*Upon young men*, Psa. 119:9; Prov. 4:23–27. *Upon married men*, Mal. 2:15 *Upon ministers*, Acts 20:28–31; 1 Cor. 3:10; Col. 4:2, 17; 1 Tim. 4:16.
*Over motives*, Matt. 6:1–5. *Over conscience*, Luke 11:35. *Over the heart*, Prov. 4:23.
*Against apostasy*, 2 John 8. *Against backsliding*, Deut. 4:9, 23; Heb. 3:12; 12:15; Rev. 3:2, 3, 11. *Against covetousness*, Luke 12:15. *Against idolatry*, Ex. 23:13; Deut. 4:23; 11:16; 12:13. *Against evil associations*, Ex. 34:12; Phil. 3:2; 2 Pet. 3:17. *Against false teachers*, Matt. 7:15; Mark 13:22, 23; Acts 20:28–31; 1 John 4:1.

their [l]lamps, and [m]took no [n,o]oil
with them:
4 But the [h]wise [p]took [n,o]oil in
their vessels with their [l]lamps.
5 While the [g]bridegroom tarried, they all [q]slumbered and
[r]slept.
6 And at [b]midnight there was a
cry made, Behold, the [q,s]bride-
groom cometh; go ye out to
meet him.
7 Then all those [e]virgins [t]arose,
and trimmed their [l]lamps.
8 And the [k,l]foolish said unto
the [h,i,j]wise, [u]Give us of your
[n,o]oil; [v]for our [l]lamps are [1]gone
out.
9 But the [h,i]wise answered,
saying, *Not so*; lest there be not
enough for us and you: but go
ye rather to them that [w]sell, and
buy for yourselves.
10 And while they went to
[w]buy, the [g,s]bridegroom came;
and they that were [p]ready went
in with him to the [2,x]marriage:
and [y,z]the [a]door was shut.
11 [b]Afterward came also the
other [c,d]virgins, [e]saying, Lord,
Lord, open to us.
12 But he answered and said,
Verily I say unto [f]you, I know
you not.
13 [g,h,i]Watch therefore, for ye
know neither the day nor the
hour [3]wherein the [j,k]Son of man
cometh.
14 ¶ [l,m,n]For *the* [o]*kingdom of*
*heaven is* as [p]a man travelling
into [4]a far country, *who* called
his own [q,r]servants, and delivered unto them his goods.
15 And unto one he gave five
[s]talents, to another two, and to
another one; to every man according to his several ability;
and straightway took his journey.

16 Then he that had received
the five [s]talents went and [t]traded
with the same, and made *them*
other five talents.
17 And likewise he that *had*
*received* two, he also [t]gained
other two.
18 But he that had received one
went and digged in the earth,
and hid his lord's [u]money.
19 After a long time the [k]lord
of those [q,r]servants cometh, and
reckoneth with them.
20 And so he that had received
five [s]talents came and brought
other five talents, saying, Lord,
thou deliveredst unto me five
talents: behold, I have [t,v,w]gain-
ed beside them five talents more.
21 His lord [x]said unto him,
Well done, *thou* good and [v]faith-
ful [q,r]servant: thou hast been
[y]faithful over a few things, [z]I
will make thee ruler over many
things: enter thou into the [a]joy
of thy [b]lord.
22 He also that had received
two [c]talents came and said,
Lord, thou deliveredst unto me
two talents: behold, I have
[d,e]gained two other talents beside them.
23 His lord [f]said unto him,
Well done, good and [g]faithful
servant; thou hast been [h]faithful
over a few things, [i]I will make
thee ruler over many things:
enter thou into the [a]joy of thy
[b]lord.
24 Then [j]he which had received
the one [c]talent came and said,
Lord, I knew thee that thou art
an hard man, reaping where thou
hast not sown, and gathering
where thou [5]hast not strawed:
25 And [j,k]I was afraid, and
went and [l]hid thy talent in the
earth: lo, *there* thou hast *that is*
thine.
26 His lord answered and said
unto him, *Thou* wicked and
[m]slothful [j]servant, thou knewest

v.3–AD 30
See footnote, *Time*, Rev. 10:6.

3
m *Procrastination*, Acts 24:25.
n *Oil, illuminating*, Deut. 12:17.
o *Oil, figurative*, Deut. 12:17.

4
p *Preparedness*, Luke 12:40.

5
q *Sleep*, Psa. 127:2.
r *Death, called sleep*, Num. 23:10.

6
s *Jesus, second coming of*, Matt. 1:21.

7
t *Resurrection*, 1 Cor. 15:12.

8
u *Preparedness, lack of*, Luke 12:40.
v *Unfaithfulness*, Luke 16:11.
1 R. V. going

9
w *Commerce*, 1 Kin. 10:15.

10
x *Marriage, figurative*, Gen. 34:9.
y *Probation, ended*, Rom. 5:4.
z *Opportunity, lost*, Gal. 6:10.

a *Door, figurative*, Deut. 11:20.
2 R. V. marriage feast:

11
b *Delusion*, 2 Thess. 2:11.
c *Virgin, parable of*, Isa. 62:5.
d *Women, wicked, illustrated*, Prov. 31:10.
e *Wicked, prayer of*, Psa. 73:3.

12
f *Reprobates*, 1 Cor. 9:27.

13
g *Watchfulness, enjoined*, Matt. 24:42.
h *Commandment, enjoining watchfulness*, Deut. 8:2.
i *Temptation, admonitions against yielding to*, Luke 11:4.

j *Jesus, humanity of*, Matt. 1:21. k *Jesus, second coming of*, Matt. 1:21. 3 R. V. *omits the remainder of this verse.* **14** l *Parables*, Ezek. 20:49. m *Faithfulness, required.* vs. 14–23; Luke 16:10. n *Probation*, Rom. 5:4. o *Kingdom of Heaven*, Matt. 13:24. p Compare Luke 19:12–26. q *Servant*, Jer. 2:14. r *Steward*, Gen. 43:19. 4 R. V. another **15** s *Talent*, Ex. 38:25.

v.16–AD 30
See footnote, *Time*, Rev. 10:6.

16
t *Works*, 2 Tim. 1:9.

18
u *Money*, Jer. 32:9.

20
v *Faithfulness, exemplified*, Luke 16:10.
w *Diligence, exemplified*, Rom. 12:8.

21
x *Judgment, according to opportunity and works*, 1 Pet. 1:17.
y *Christian Graces, faithfulness*, Gal. 5:22.
z *Righteous, promises to*, Psa. 64:10.

a *Joy*, Psa. 5:11.
b *Jesus, king*, Matt. 1:21.

22
c *Talent*, Ex. 38:25.
d *Diligence, exemplified*, Rom. 12:8.
e *Works*, 2 Tim. 1:9.

23
f *Judgment, according to opportunity and works*, 1 Pet. 1:17.
g *Faithfulness, exemplified*, Luke 16:10.
h *Christian Graces, faithfulness*, Gal. 5:22.
i *Righteous, promises to*, Psa. 64:10.

24
j *Servant, wicked and unfaithful*, Jer. 2:14.
5 R. V. didst not scatter:

25
k *Self-condemnation*, Job 9:20.
l *Unfaithfulness*, Luke 16:11.

26
m *Laziness*, Prov. 19:15.

that I [n]reap where I sowed not,
and gather where I have not
strawed:
27 Thou oughtest therefore to
have put my [o]money to the [6]ex-
changers, and *then* at [p]my coming I should have received mine
own with [7,q]usury.
28 [r]Take therefore the [c]talent
from him, and give *it* unto him
which hath ten talents.
29 [s]For unto every one that
[t]hath shall be given, and he shall
have [t]abundance: but from [t]him
that hath not shall be taken
away even that which he hath.
30 And [u]cast ye the [v]unprofit-
able servant into [w,x]outer [y]dark-
ness: there shall be [z,a]weeping
and [b]gnashing of teeth.
31 ¶ When the [c,d]Son of man
shall come in his glory, and all
the holy [e]angels with him, then
shall [f,g]he sit upon the [h]throne
of his glory:
32 And [i]before him shall be
gathered all nations: and he
shall [j]separate them one from
another, as a [k]shepherd divideth
*his* [l]sheep from the [m]goats:
33 And he shall set the [l]sheep
on his right hand, but the [m]goats
on the left.
34 Then shall the [n]King say
unto them on his right hand,
[o,p,q]Come, ye blessed of my
Father, inherit the [r,s]kingdom
prepared for you from the foundation of the world:
35 For [t]I was an [u]hungred, and
[v,w,x,y]ye [z,a,b]gave me meat: I
was thirsty, and [c,d]ye [a,b,e]gave
me drink: I was a [f]stranger,
and ye [c,d,g]took me in:
36 Naked, and [c,d]ye [b,e,h]clothed
me: I was *sick, and ye [i]visited
me: [j]I was in prison, and ye
[b,e]came unto me.
37 [k]Then shall the righteous
answer him, saying, Lord, when
saw we thee an hungred, and fed
*thee*? or thirsty, and gave *thee*
drink?
38 [k]When saw we thee a stranger, and took *thee* in? or naked,
and clothed *thee*?
39 Or when saw we thee *sick,
or in prison, and came unto thee?
40 And the [l,m]King shall answer and say unto them, Verily
I say unto you, Inasmuch as ye
have done [b]*it* unto one of the
least of these my [n]brethren, ye
have done *it* unto me.
41 Then shall [l,m]he say also
unto [o]them on the left hand,
[p]Depart from me, ye cursed,
into [q]everlasting [r]fire, prepared
for the [s]devil and his [t]angels:
42 For I was an hungred, and
[u]ye gave me no meat: I was
thirsty, and [u]ye gave me no
drink:
43 I was a [f]stranger, and [u]ye
took me not in: naked, and [u]ye
[h]clothed me not: *sick, and [j]in
prison, and [u]ye [i]visited me not.
44 Then shall they also answer
him, saying, Lord, when saw
we thee an hungred, or athirst,
or a [f]stranger, or naked, or
*sick, or [j]in prison, and did not
minister unto thee?
45 Then shall he answer them,
saying, Verily I say unto you,
Inasmuch as [u]ye did *it* not to
one of the least of these, ye did
*it* not to me.
46 And [o]these shall go away
into [8]everlasting [v]punishment:
but [w]the righteous into [x,y]life
eternal.

v.26–AD 30
See footnote, *Time*, Rev. 10:6.

n *Reaping, figurative*, 1 Sam. 6:13.

**27**
o *Money*, Jer. 32:9.
p *Jesus, second coming of*, Matt. 1:21.
q *Interest*, Ex. 22:25.
6 R. V. bankers
7 R. V. interest.

**28**
r *Probation, ended*, Rom. 5:4.

**29**
s *Proverbs*, 1 Sam. 24:13.
t *Prosperity*, Eccl. 7:14.

**30**
u *Punishment, according to deeds*, Lev. 26:41.
v *Wicked, punishment of*, Psa. 73:3.
w *Second Death*, Rev. 20:14.
x *Hell*, Mark 9:43.
y *Darkness, figurative*, Gen. 1:2.
z *Weeping, in perdition*, Ezra 3:13.
a *Sorrow, of the lost*, Matt. 13:42.
b *Gnashing of Teeth*, Job 16:9.

**31**
c *Jesus, humanity of*, Matt. 1:21.
d *Jesus, second coming of*, Matt. 1:21.
e *Angel, holy*, Heb. 1:13.
f *Jesus, judge*, vs. 31–34; Matt. 1:21
g *Jesus, king*, vs. 31–34; Matt. 1:21.
h *Throne, figurative*, 1 Kin. 2:19.

**32**
i *Judgment, the general*, 2 Pet. 3:7.
j *Sin, separates from God*, Rom. 5:12.
k *Shepherd*, Jer. 31:10.

l *Righteous, compared to sheep*, Psa. 64:10. m *Wicked, compared to goats*, Psa. 73:3. **34** n *Jesus, King*, Matt. 1:21. o *Reward, a motive, to faithfulness*, Matt. 5:12. p *Righteous, promises to*, Psa. 64:10. q *Promise, implied, to the righteous*, 2 Cor. 1:20. r *Heaven, the future home of the righteous*, Luke 18:22. s *Inheritance, figurative*, Num. 27:7. **35** t *Poor, duty to*, Prov. 21:13. u *Afflicted, duty to*, Job 34:28. v *Kindness, enjoined*, vs. 35–40; Acts 28:2. w *Duty, of man to man*, Eccl. 12:13. x *Altruism*, Acts 20:35. y *Love, of man for man*, 1 John 4:7. z *Faithfulness*, Luke 16:10. —a *Liberality*, 1 Tim. 6:18. b *Works, good*, 2 Tim. 1:9. c *Love, of man for man*, 1 John 4:7. d *Duty, of man to man*, Eccl. 12:13. e *Altruism*, Acts 20:35.

v.35–AD 30
See footnote, *Time*, Rev. 10:6.

f *Foreigners*, Deut. 23:20.
g *Hospitality*, Rom. 12:13.

**36**
h *Poor, duty to*, Prov. 21:13.
i *Afflicted, duty to*, Job 34:28.
j *Prisoners*, Psa. 79:11.

**37**
k *Humility, exemplified*, Prov. 22:4.

**40**
l *God, sovereign*, Gen. 2:2.
m *God, judge*, Gen. 2:2.
n *Brother*, Prov. 18:24.

**41**
o *Wicked, punishment of*, Psa. 73:3.
p *Sin, separates from God*, Rom. 5:12.
q *Hell*, Mark 9:43.
r *Fire, figurative*, Ex. 12:8.
s *Satan*, Matt. 4:10.
t *Demons, punishment of*, Matt. 4:24.

**42**
u *Unfaithfulness*, Luke 16:11.

**46**
v *Punishment, eternal*, Lev. 26:41.
w *Promise, to the righteous*, 2 Cor. 1:20.
x *Life, everlasting*, Eccl. 8:15.
y *Immortality*, 1 Cor. 15:54.
8 R. V. eternal

*** SICK, THE.** *Visiting*, Psa. 41:6. *Visiting, a duty*, Matt. 25:36, 43; Jas. 1:27. **Figurative**, Isa. 1:5, 6; Hos. 5:13. See footnotes; AFFLICTED, Job 34:28; AFFLICTIONS, Psa. 34:19; DISEASE, Ex. 15:26.

## CHAPTER 26

*The rulers conspire against Jesus.* 6 *At Bethany a woman anoints his head.* 14 *Judas conspires against him.* 17 *Jesus keeps the passover;* 26 *institutes the Lord's supper;* 36 *prays in the garden;* 47 *and is betrayed with a kiss.* 57 *He is brought before the high priest and condemned.* 69 *Peter denies him.*

AND it came to pass, when Jē'ṣus had finished all these sayings, [a]he said unto his [b]disciples,

2 Ye know that [c]after two days is *the* [d]*feast of* the [e]passover, and the [f]Son of man is [g]betrayed to be [h]crucified.[Q]

3 ¶ Then assembled together the chief [i]priests, [1]and the scribes, and the elders of the people, unto the [2]palace of the high [j]priest, who was called *Cā'ia-phăs,

4 And [k,l]consulted that they might take Jē'ṣus by [m]subtilty,[C] and kill *him.*

5 But they said, Not on the [d]feast *day,* lest there be an uproar among the people.

6 ¶[n]Now when Jē'ṣus was in [o]Bĕth'a-nȳ, in the house of [p]Sī'-mon the [q]leper,

7 [r]There came unto him a [s]woman having an [t]alabaster[C] [u]box of very precious [v]ointment,[C] and [w]poured it on [x]his head, as he sat *at meat.*[C]

8 But when his [b]disciples saw *it,* they had indignation,[y]saying, To what purpose *is* this waste?

9 For this [v]ointment might have been sold for much, and given to the [z]poor.

10 When Jē'ṣus understood *it,* he said unto them, Why trouble ye the woman? for she hath wrought a good work upon me.

11 For ye have the [z]poor always with you; but me ye have not always.[Q]

12 [a,b]For in that she hath poured this [c]ointment on my body, she did *it* [3]for my [d]burial.

13 Verily [e]I say unto you, Wheresoever this [f]gospel shall be [g]preached in the whole world, *there* shall also this, that this woman hath done, be told for a memorial of her.

14 ¶ [h]Then one of the [i]twelve, called [j]Jū'das Ĭs-căr'ĭ-ot, [k,l,m]went unto the chief priests,

15 [k,l,m]And said *unto them,* [n]What will ye give me, and I will deliver him unto you? And they [4,o]covenanted[C] with him for thirty pieces[G] of [p]silver.[Q]

16 And from that time [j]he [k]sought opportunity to betray him.

17 ¶ [q]Now the first *day* of the [r]*feast of* unleavened bread the [i]disciples came to Jē'ṣus, saying unto him, Where wilt thou that we prepare for thee to eat the [s]passover?[Q]

18 And he said, Go into the city to such a man, and say unto him, The [5,t]Master saith, My time is at hand; I will keep the [s]passover at thy house with my [i]disciples.

19 And the [u,v]disciples did as Jē'ṣus had appointed them; and they made ready the [s]passover.

20 ¶ [w]Now when the even[C] was come, he sat down with the [i]twelve.

21 And as they did eat, he said, Verily [e]I say unto you, that [j]one of you shall betray me.[S]

22 And they were exceeding sorrowful, and [x]began every one of them to say unto him, Lord, is it I?

23 And he answered and said, He that dippeth *his* hand with me in the dish, the same shall betray me.[Q]

24 The Son of man goeth as it is written of him: but [y]woe unto that man by whom the Son of man is betrayed! it had been

---

v.1–AD 30 See footnote, *Time,* Rev. 10:6.

**1**
a *Jesus, prophet,* Matt. 1:21.
b *Apostles,* Luke 6:13.

**2**
c Mark 14:1, 2; Luke 22:1, 2.
d *Annual Feasts,* Num. 15:3.
e *Passover,* Num. 9:5.
f *Jesus, humanity of,* Matt 1:21.
g *Betrayal,* Matt. 26:46.
h *Jesus, death of,* Matt. 1:21.

**3**
i *Priest,* Lev. 1:5.
j *High Priest,* Lev. 21:10.
1 R. V. *omits* and the scribes
2 R. V. court

**4**
k *Conspiracy, instances of,* 1 Kin. 16:9.
l *Persecution, of Jesus,* John 15:20.
m *Craftiness,* Psa. 83:3.

**6**
n Mark 14:3–9; John 12:1–8; see also Luke 7:36–39.
o *Bethany,* John 11:18.
p Mark 14:3.
q *Leprosy,* Lev. 13:2.

**7**
r *Love, for Jesus, instances of,* 1 John 4:19.
s *Mary, anoints Jesus,* John 11:2.
t Mark 14:3; Luke 7:37.
u *Cruse,* 1 Sam. 26:11.
v *Ointment,* Eccl. 7:1.
w *Anointing, symbolical,* Deut. 28:40.
x *Jesus, anointed,* Matt. 1:21.

**8**
y *Parsimony, of the disciples,* Mal. 3:8.

**9**
z *Poor,* Prov. 21:13.

**12**
a *Anointing, the dead,* Deut. 28. 40.
b *Dead, anointing of,* 2 Kin. 4:32.
c *Ointment,* Eccl. 7:1.
d *Burial,* Acts 8:2.
3 R. V. to prepare me for burial.

v.13–AD 30 See footnote, *Time,* Rev. 10:6.

**13**
e *Jesus, prophet,* Matt. 1:21.
f *Gospel,* Mark 13:10.
g *Preaching,* Matt. 9:35.

**14**
h Mark 14:10, 11; Luke 22:3–6.
i *Apostles,* Luke 6:13.
j *Judas,* Mark 3:19.
k *Infidelity, of friends,* 2 Cor. 6:15.
l *Apostasy, instances of,* Acts 1:25.
m *Conspiracy,* 1 Kin. 16:9.

**15**
n *Covetousness, instances of,* Isa. 57:17.
o *Bribery, instances of,* 1 Sam. 8:3.
p *Silver, used for money,* 1 Chr. 28:14.
4 R. V. weighed unto him thirty

**17**
q Mark 14:12–16; Luke 22:7–13.
r *Annual Feasts,* Num. 15:3.
s *Passover, observed by Jesus,* vs. 17–20; Num. 9:5.

**18**
t *Master,* John 13:13.
5 Am. R. V. *marg.* teacher

**19**
u *John,* Mark 1:19.
v *Peter,* Mark 5:37.

**20**
w Mark 14:17–26; Luke 22:14–38.

**22**
x *Self-examination,* 2 Cor. 13:5.

**24**
y *Wicked, punishment of,* Psa. 73:3.

---

* **CAIAPHAS.** *High priest,* Luke 3:2. *Son-in-law of Annas,* John 18:13. *Prophesies concerning Jesus,* John 11:49–51; 18:14. *Jesus tried before,* Matt. 26:2, 3, 57, 63–65; Mark 14:53–65; 15:1; Luke 22:54, 66–71; John 18:24, 28. *Peter and other disciples accused before; Peter's defense, and Peter and John's bold statement of rights,* Acts 4:1–22.

v.24–AD 30
See footnote, *Time*, Rev. 10:6.

**25**
z *Hypocrisy, instances of*, Jas. 3:17.
6 R. V. Is it I, Rabbi?

**26**
a *Passover, Lord's supper ordained at*, Num. 9:5.
b *Eucharist*, Mark 14:22.
c *Bread, symbolical*, 1 Cor. 11:23.
d *Symbols and Similitudes*, Heb. 9:9.
e *Jesus, prayers of*, Matt. 1:21.
f *Apostles*, Luke 6:13.

**27**
g *Cup*, Gen. 44:2.
h *Wine, sacramental use of*, Prov. 23:31.
i *Thankfulness, to God*, Acts 24:3.

**28**
j *Blood, of Christ*, Heb. 9:19.
k *New Covenant*, Jer. 31:31.
l *Atonement, made by Jesus*, Lev. 17:11.
m *Jesus, design of his death*, Matt. 1:21.
n *Sin, forgiveness of*, Rom. 5:12.
7 R. V. covenant,

**29**
o *Fellowship, with Christ*, 1 Cor. 1:9.
p *God, fatherhood of*, Gen. 2:2.
q *Heaven, the future home of the righteous*, Luke 18:22.

**30**
r *Praise*, Psa. 150:1.
s *Song*, Psa. 77:6.
t *Mount of Olives*, Mark 11:1.

**31**
u Mark 14:27–31.
v *Temptation*, Luke 11:4.
w *Backsliding, temptations to*, Hos. 11:7.
x *Prophecies, concerning the Messiah, and their fulfillment*, Gen. 12:3.
y Zech. 13:7.
z *Shepherd, figurative*, Jer. 31:10.

good for that man if he had not
been born.[S Q]
25 Then [j]Jū′das, which betrayed him, answered and said,
[6,t,z]Master, is it I? He said unto
him, Thou hast said.
26 ¶ [a,b]And as they were eating,
Jē′ṣus took [c,d]bread, and [e]bless-
ed *it*, and brake *it*, and gave *it*
to the [f]disciples, and said, Take,
eat; this is my body.
27 And he took the [d,g,h]cup,
and [i]gave thanks, and gave *it* to
them, saying, Drink ye all of it;
28 For [h]this is my [j]blood of the
[7,k]new testament, which is [l]shed
for many [m]for the [n]remission of
sins.[S T Q]
29 But I say unto you, I will
not drink henceforth of this
[h]fruit of the vine, until that day
when I drink it new [o]with you
in my [p]Father's [q]kingdom.
30 ¶ And when they had [r]sung
an [s]hymn, they went out into the
mount of [t]Ŏl′ĭveṣ.[Q]
31 [u]Then saith Jē′ṣus unto
them, All ye shall be [v,w]offended
because of me this night: for
[x]it is written, I will [y]smite the
[z,a]shepherd, and the [b]sheep of the
flock shall be scattered abroad.[Q]
32 [c]But after I am [d]risen again,
I will go before you into [e]Găl′ilee.
33 [f]Pē′tĕr answered and said
unto him, Though all *men* shall
be [g]offended because of thee, *yet*
[h]will I never be offended.
34 Jē′ṣus said unto him, [i]Verily
[c]I say unto thee, That this night,
before the cock crow, thou shalt
deny me thrice.[S]
35 [f]Pē′tĕr said unto him,
Though I should die with thee,
yet [h]will I not deny thee. Likewise also said all the disciples.

—a *Jesus, shepherd*, Matt. 1:21. b *Sheep, figurative*, Deut. 32:14. **32** c *Jesus, prophet*, Matt. 1:21. d *Jesus, resurrection of*, Matt. 1:21. e *Galilee*, Mark 6:21. **33** f *Peter*, Mark 5:37. g *Backsliding*, Hos. 11:7. h *False Confidence*, Psa. 30:6. **34** i Mark 14:30, 68, 72; Luke 22:34, 60, 61; John 13:38; 18:27.

36 ¶ [j]Then cometh Jē′ṣus with
them unto a place called [k]Gĕth-
sĕm′a-nē, and saith unto the disciples, Sit ye here, while I go and
[l,m]pray yonder.
37 And he took with him [f]Pē′-
tĕr and the two [n,o]sons of [p]Zĕb′-
e-dee, and began to be sorrowful
and very heavy.[T]
38 Then saith he unto them,
[q]My soul is exceeding sorrowful,
even unto death: tarry ye here,
and [r]watch with me.[Q]
39 And he went a little farther, and fell on his face, and
[l,m,s]prayed, saying, O [t]my Father, [u]if it be possible, let this
[v]cup pass from me: [w]nevertheless
[x]not as I will, but [y]as thou [z]*wilt*.[T]
40 And he cometh unto the
[a]disciples, and findeth them
[b]asleep, and saith unto [c]Pē′tĕr,
What, could ye not [d]watch with
me one hour?
41 [d]Watch and [e]pray, that ye
enter not into [f]temptation: the
[g]spirit indeed *is* willing, but [h]the
flesh *is* weak.
42 He went away again the second time, and [i,j]prayed, saying,
O [k]my Father, [l]if this [m]cup may
not pass away from me, except
I drink it, [n,o]thy [p]will be done.[T]
43 And he came and found
them [b]asleep again: for their
eyes were heavy.
44 And he left them, and went
away again, and [i,j]prayed the third
time, saying the same words.
45 Then cometh he to his
[a]disciples, and saith unto them,
Sleep on now, and take *your*
rest: behold, the hour is at hand,
and the Son of man is †betrayed
into the hands of sinners.
46 Rise, let us be going: [q]behold,
[r]he is at hand that doth †betray me.

v.36–AD 30

**36**
j Mark 14:32–40; Luke 22:39–46; John 18:1.
k *Gethsemane, Jesus betrayed in*, Mark 14:32.
l *Prayers of Jesus*, Luke 5:16.
m *Prayer, secret*, Acts 6:4.

**37**
n *James*, Luke 5:10.
o *John*, Mark 1:19.
p *Zebedee*, Matt. 4:21.

**38**
q *Jesus, sufferings of*, Matt. 1:21.
r *Watchfulness*, Matt. 24:42.

**39**
s *Adversity, prayer in*, Psa. 10:6.
t *Jesus, relation of, to the Father*, Matt. 1:21.
u *Contingencies, in divine government of man*, 1 Kin. 3:14.
v *Cup, figurative*, Matt. 20:22.
w *Jesus, death of, voluntary*, Matt. 1:21.
x *Resignation, exemplified*, Job 5:17.
y *Obedience, instances of*, Heb. 5:8.
z *Will of God, the supreme rule of duty*, Mark 3:35.

**40**
a *Apostles*, Luke 6:13.
b *Sleep*, Psa. 127:2.
c *Peter*, Mark 5:37.
d *Watchfulness*, Matt. 24:42.

**41**
e *Prayer, enjoined*, Acts 6:4.
f *Temptation, admonitions against yielding to*, Luke 11:4.
g *Man, spirit*, Job 4:17.
h *Indecision*, 1 Kin. 18:21.

**42**
i *Prayers of Jesus*, Luke 5:16.
j *Adversity, prayer in*, Psa. 10:6.
k *Jesus, relation of, to the Father*, Matt. 1:21.
l *Contingencies, in divine government of man*, 1 Kin. 3:14.
m *Cup, figurative*, Matt. 20:22.

n *Resignation, exemplified*, Job 5:17. o *Obedience, instances of*, Heb. 5:8. p *Will of God, the supreme rule of duty*, Mark 3:35. **46** q *Jesus, omniscience of*, Matt. 1:21. r *Judas*, Mark 3:19.

† **BETRAYAL.** Of cities: *Of Jericho by Rahab*, Josh. 2:1–21; *of Luz*, Judg. 1:24, 25.
*Of David, by Doeg*, 1 Sam. 22:9, 10, with 21:1–10. *Of the righteous, foretold*, Matt. 24:10; Mark 13:12; Luke 21:16.
**Of Jesus**, Matt. 10:4; 26:14–16, 45–50; Mark 14:10, 11; Luke 22:3–6, 21, 47, 48; John 13:21; 18:2, 5. *Foretold by himself*, Matt. 17:22; 20:18; 26:2, 21, 23–25; Mark 14:18–21, 41, 42; Luke 22:21; John 13:18, 21.

v.47–AD 30
See footnote, *Time,*
Rev. 10:6.

**47**
s Mark 14:43–50; Luke 22:47–53; John 18:3–11.
t *Sword,* 1 Chr. 21:5.
u *Priest,* Lev. 1:5.
v *Senate,* Num. 11:16.
**48**
w *Friends, false,* Ex. 33:11.
x *Kiss, of Judas,* Ruth 1:14.
**49**
y *Treachery,* 2 Kin. 9:23.
z *Salutations,* Luke 1:44.

a *Master,* John 13:13.
b *Kiss, of Judas,* Ruth 1:14.
c *Hypocrisy,* Jas. 3:17.
8 R. V. Rabbi;
**50**
d *Jesus, meekness of,* Matt. 1:21.
e *Persecution, of Jesus,* John 15: 20.
f *Prisoners,* Psa. 79:11.
9 R. V. do that for which thou art come.
**51**
g *Peter,* Mark 5:37.
h *Sword,* 1 Chr. 21:5.
i *Rashness, instances of,* 2 Sam. 6:7.
j Mark 14:47; Luke 22:50, 51; John 18:10.
k *High Priest,* Lev. 21:10.
**52**
l *Homicide, punishment of,* Deut. 5:17.
**53**
m *Jesus, divine sonship of,* Matt. 1:21.
n *God, fatherhood of,* Gen. 2:2.
o *Angel, minister to the righteous,* Heb. 1:13.
**54**
p *Prophecies, concerning Jesus, and their fulfillment,* Gen. 12:3.
**55**
q *Thieves,* Deut. 24:7.
r *Jesus, teacher,* Matt. 1:21.
s *Temple, Herod's,* 1 Kin. 6:17.
**56**
t *Prophets,* Isa. 3:2.

47 ¶ [s]And while he yet spake,
lo, [r]Jū'das, one of the [a]twelve,
came, and with him a great multitude with [t]swords and staves,
from the chief [u]priests and [v]el-
ders of the people.
48 Now [r,w]he that [†]betrayed
him gave them a sign, saying,
Whomsoever I shall [x]kiss, that
same is he: hold him fast.
49 And forthwith he [y]came to
Jē'ṣus, and said, [z]Hail, [8,a]mas-
ter; and [b,c]kissed him.
50 And [d]Jē'ṣus said unto
him, Friend, [9]wherefore art thou
come? Then came they, and
[e]laid hands on Jē'ṣus, and [‡]took
[f]him.
51 And, behold, [g]one of them
which were with Jē'ṣus stretched
out *his* hand, and drew his
[h]sword, and [i]struck a [j]servant of
the [k]high priest's, and smote off
his ear.
52 Then said [d]Jē'ṣus unto him,
Put up again thy [h]sword into
his place: for [l]all they that take
the sword shall perish with the
sword.
53 Thinkest thou that I cannot
now pray to [m]my [n]Father, and
he shall presently give me more
than twelve legions of [o]angels?
54 But how then shall the
[p]scriptures be fulfilled, that thus
it must be?
55 In that same hour said [d]Jē'-
ṣus to the multitudes, Are ye
come out as against a [q]thief with
[h]swords and staves for to take
me? I sat daily with you [r]teach-
ing in the [s]temple, and ye laid no
hold on me.
56 But all this was done, that
the [p]scriptures of the [t]prophets
might be fulfilled. [u]Then all the
[v,w]disciples [x]forsook him, and
fled.

57 ¶ [y]And they that had [‡,e]laid
hold on Jē'ṣus led *him* away to
*Cā'ia-phăs the [k,z]high priest,
where the [a]scribes and the [b]eld-
ers were assembled.
58 But [c]Pē'tēr followed him
afar off unto the [10,d]high priest's
palace, and went in, and sat with
the [11]servants, to see the end.
59 [e]Now the chief [f]priests, and
[b,f]elders, and all the [f]council,
[g]sought [h,i,j]false witness against
Jē'ṣus, to put him to death;
60 [12]But found none: yea,
though many [h]false witnesses
came, *yet* found they none. At
the last came two false witnesses,
61 And said, [k]This *fellow* said,
I am able to destroy the [l]temple
of God, and to build it in three
days.
62 And the [*,d]high priest arose,
and said unto him, [m]Answerest
thou nothing? what *is it which*
these witness against thee?
63 But Jē'ṣus [m,n]held his peace.
And the high priest answered
and said unto him, I adjure thee
[o]by the living God, that thou tell
us whether thou be the [p]Christ,
the [q]Son of God.
64 Jē'ṣus saith unto him, Thou
hast said: nevertheless I say unto you, Hereafter shall ye see the
[r]Son of man [s,t]sitting on the right
hand of power, and [u]coming in
the clouds of heaven.
65 Then the [*,d]high priest
[v]rent his clothes, [w]saying, He
hath spoken [x]blasphemy; what
further need have we of witnesses? behold, now ye have
heard his blasphemy.
66 What think ye? They answered and said, He is guilty of
death.
67 [y]Then did they [g,z]spit in his
face, and buffeted him; and oth-

v.57 AD 30
See footnote, *Time,*
Rev. 10:6.

**57**
y *Trial of Jesus,* vs. 57–68; Mark 14:53.
z *Judge, priests as,* Judg. 2:18.

a *Scribe,* 1 Kin. 4:3.
b *Senate,* Num. 11:16.
**58**
c *Peter,* Mark 5:37.
d *High Priest,* Lev. 21:10.
10 R. V. court of the high priest,
11 R. V. officers,
**59**
e *Court, corrupt,* Ex. 18:26.
f *Rulers, wicked, instances of,* Ex. 18:21.
g *Persecution, of Jesus,* John 15: 20.
h *False Witness,* Matt. 19:18.
i *False Accusation,* 2 Tim. 3:3.
j *Perjury,* 1 Tim. 1:10.
**60**
12 R. V. And they found it not, though many false witnesses came. But afterward came two,
**61**
k *Indictments, instances of,* Matt. 27:37.
l *Temple, figurative,* 1 Kin. 6·17.
**62**
m *Pleading,* Deut. 17:8.
**63**
n *Reticence of Jesus,* Mark 14:61.
o *Oath,* Num. 5:19.
p *Jesus, Messiah,* Matt. 1:21.
q *Jesus, divinity of,* Matt. 1:21.
**64**
r *Jesus, humanity of,* Matt. 1:21.
s *Jesus, exaltation of,* Matt. 1:21.
t *Jesus, king,* Matt. 1:21.
u *Jesus, second coming of,* Matt. 1:21.
**65**
v *Rending of Garments,* 2 Chr. 34:27.
w *Falsehood, instances of,* Job 21:34.

u *Adversity, forsaken by friends in,* Psa. 10:6. v *Apostles,* Luke 6:13. w *Friends, false,* Ex. 33:11. x *Cowardice, instances of,* Lev. 26:36.

x *Blasphemy, false accusations of,* 2 Sam. 12:14. **67** y *Prophecies, concerning the Messiah, and their fulfillment,* Gen. 12:3. z *Spitting,* Num. 12:14.

‡ **ARREST.** *Of Jesus,* Matt. 26:50, 57; Mark 14:46; Luke 22:54; John 18:12. *Of the apostles,* Acts 5:17, 18; 6:12. *Of Paul and Silas,* Acts 16:19. *Of Paul,* Acts 21:30. *Paul authorized to arrest Christians,* Acts 9:2.

v.67–AD 30
See footnote, *Time*, Rev. 10:6.

*a Smiting of Jesus*, Isa. 50:6.

**68**

*b Mocking*, 1 Kin. 18:27.

**69**

c Mark 14:66–72; Luke 22:55–62; John 18:15–18, 25–27.
*d Peter*, Mark 5:37.
*e Galilee*, Mark 6:21.
13 R. V. court:

**70**

*f Falsehood, instances of*, Job 21:34.
*g Cowardice, instances of*, Lev. 26:36.
*h Temptation, instances of yielding to*, Luke 11:4.

**71**

*i Nazareth*, John 1:46.
14 R. V. man

**72**

*j Perjury, instances of*, 1 Tim. 1:10.

**74**

k Mark 14:30, 68, 72; Luke 22:34, 60, 61; John 13:38.

**75**

*l Conscience, guilty, instances of*, Acts 23:1.
*m Jesus, prophet*, Matt. 1:21.
*n Weeping, by Peter*, Ezra 3:13.
*o Repentance, instances of*, Mark 1:4.
*p Remorse, instances of*, Matt. 27:3.

**1**

*a Priest*, Lev. 1:5.
*b Senate*, Num. 11:16.
*c Conspiracy, instances of*, 1 Kin. 16:9.

**2**

*d Prisoners*, Psa. 79:11.

ers [a]smote *him* with the palms
of their hands,
68 Saying, [b]Prophesy unto us,
thou Chrīst, Who is he that
smote thee?
69 ¶ [c]Now [d]Pē′tēr sat without in
the [13]palace: and a damsel came
unto him, saying, Thou also wast
with Jē′ṣus of [e]Găl′ĭ-lee.
70 But he [f,g,h]denied before
*them* all, saying, I know not
what thou sayest.
71 And when [d]he was gone out
into the porch, another *maid* saw
him, and said unto them that
were there, This [14]*fellow* was
also with Jē′ṣus of [i]Năz′a-rĕth.
72 And again he [f,g,h]denied
with an [j]oath, I do not know the
man.
73 And after a while came unto
*him* they that stood by, and said
to [d]Pē′tēr, Surely thou also art
*one* of them; for thy speech bewrayeth thee.
74 Then began [d]he to curse and
to [j]swear, *saying*, [f,g]I know not
the man. And immediately the
[k]cock crew.
75 And [d]Pē′tēr [l]remembered
the word of [m]Jē′ṣus, which said
unto him, Before the [k]cock crow,
thou shalt deny me thrice. And
he went out, and [n,o,p]wept bitterly.

## CHAPTER 27

*Jesus delivered to Pilate.* 3 *Judas hangs himself.* 19 *The message of Pilate's wife.* 24 *Pilate washes his hands, releases Barabbas, and delivers Jesus to be crucified.* 29 *Jesus is crowned with thorns,* 34 *crucified,* 40 *reviled,* 50 *dies, and is buried.* 62 *The sepulchre made sure.*

WHEN the morning was
come, all the chief [a]priests
and [b]elders of the people [c]took
counsel against Jē′ṣus to put
him to death:
2 And when they had bound
[d]him, they led *him* away, and
delivered him to *,[1],[e]Pŏn′tĭ-ŭs
Pī′late the [f]governor.
3 ¶ Then [g,h]Jū′das, which had
[i]betrayed him, when he saw
that he was condemned, †,[j,k,l]re-
pented himself, and brought
again the [m]thirty pieces of [n]silver
to the chief [a]priests and [b]elders,
4 †Saying, [j,l,o]I have sinned in
that I have [i]betrayed the [p]inno-
cent [q]blood. And they said,
What *is that* to us? see thou *to
that.*
5 And [g]he cast down the pieces
of [n]silver in the [2,r]temple, and
departed, and went and [s,t]hanged
himself.
6 And the chief [a]priests took
the [n]silver pieces, and said, It is
not lawful for to put them into
the [u]treasury, because it is the
price of blood.
7 And they took counsel, and
bought with them the [v]potter's
field, to bury [w]strangers in.
8 Wherefore that field was
called, The [x]field of blood, unto
this day.
9 Then was [t]fulfilled that which
was spoken by [y]Jĕr′e-mȳ the
[z]prophet, saying, [a]And they took
the thirty pieces of [b]silver, the
price of him that was valued,
whom they of the children of Ĭṣ′-
ra-el did value;
10 And gave them for the [c]pot-
ter's field, as the Lord appointed
me.
11 ¶ [d]And Jē′ṣus stood before
the *governor: and the governor
asked him, saying, [e]Art thou the
[f]King of the Jews? And Jē′ṣus
said unto him, [g]Thou sayest.
12 And when he was accused of
the chief [h]priests and [i]elders, [j]he
[k]answered nothing.

v.2–AD 30
See footnote, *Time*, Rev. 10:6.

*e Court, civil*, Ex. 18:26.
*f Government, provincial*, Isa. 22:21.
1 R. V. *omits* Pontius,

**3**

*g Judas*, Mark 3:19.
*h Minister, false and corrupt*, Rom. 15:16.
*i Betrayal, of Jesus*, Matt. 26:46.
*j Repentance*, Mark 1:4.
*k Conscience, guilty*, Acts 23:1.
*l Conviction of Sin, instances of*, John 16:8.
*m Conscience Money*, Judg. 17:2.
*n Silver*, 1 Chr. 28:14.

**4**

*o Sin, confession of*, Rom. 5:12.
*p Jesus, perfections of*, Matt. 1:21.
*q Blood, of Christ*, Heb. 9:19.

**5**

*r Temple, Herod's*, 1 Kin. 6:17.
*s Suicide, instances of*, 1 Kin. 16:18.
*t Prophecies, fulfilled*, Dan. 9:24.
2 R. V. sanctuary,

**6**

*u Treasure Houses*, Ezra 5:17.

**7**

*v Pottery*, Jer. 18:3.
*w Foreigners*, Deut. 23:20.

**8**

x Acts 1:19.

**9**

y Or, *Jeremiah*, Jer. 1:1.
*z Prophets*, Isa. 3:2.

a Zech. 11:12, 13.
*b Silver*, 1 Chr. 28:14.

**10**

*c Pottery*, Jer. 18:3.

**11**

*d Trial of Jesus*, Mark 14:53.
*e Treason, Jesus falsely accused of*, 2 Kin. 11:14.
*f Jesus, king*, Matt. 1:21. *g Defense*, Acts 19:33. **12** *h Priest*, Lev. 1:5. *i Senate*, Num. 11:16. *j Jesus, meekness of*, Matt. 1:21. *k Reticence of Jesus*, Mark 14:61.

* **PILATE.** *Roman governor of Judea*, Matt. 27:2; Luke 3:1.
*Causes slaughter of Galileans*, Luke 13:1.
*Tries Jesus and orders his crucifixion*, Matt. 27; Mark 15; Luke 23; John 18:28–40; 19; Acts 3:13; 4:27; 13:28; 1 Tim. 6:13.
*Allows Joseph of Arimathea to take Jesus's body*, Matt. 27:57, 58; Mark 15:43–45; Luke 23:52; John 19:38.

† **REMORSE.** Ezek. 7:16–18, 25, 26; 33:10; 1 John 3:20. *Of the lascivious*, Prov. 5:7–13. *Of the lost*, Luke 13:28.
**Instances of:** *David*, Psa. 31:10; 51. *Peter*, Matt. 26:75. *Judas*, Matt. 27:3–5. *The Jews*, Acts 2:37.

13 Then said *Pī'late unto him, Hearest thou not how many things they witness against thee?

14 And [j]he answered him to [k]never a word; insomuch that the governor marvelled greatly.[Q]

15 ¶ Now at *that* [l]feast the governor was wont[G] to release unto the people a [‡,m]prisoner, whom they would.

16 And they had then a notable[G] [‡,m]prisoner, called [‖]Bȧ-răb'bas.

17 [d]Therefore when they were gathered together, *Pī'late said unto them, Whom will ye that I release unto you? [‖]Bȧ-răb'bas, or Jē'ṣus which is called Christ?

18 For he knew that for [n,o]envy[G] they had delivered him.

19 ¶ [d]When [*,p]he was set down on the [q]judgment seat, his [r,s]wife sent unto him, saying, Have thou nothing to do with that [t]just[G] man: for I have suffered many things this day in a [u]dream because of him.

20 But the chief [h]priests and [i]elders persuaded the multitude that they should ask [‖]Bȧ-răb'bas, and destroy Jē'ṣus.

21 The governor answered and said unto them, Whether of the [‡]twain[G] will ye that I release unto you? They said, [‖]Bȧ-răb'bas.

22 *Pilate saith unto them, What shall I do then with Jē'ṣus which is called Christ? *They* all say unto him, Let him be crucified.

23 And the governor said, Why, what evil hath he done? But they cried out the more, saying, Let him be crucified.

24 [v,w]When [*,x]Pī'late saw that he could prevail[G] nothing, but *that* rather a tumult was made, he took water, and [§,y]washed *his* [z]hands before the multitude, saying, [a]I am innocent of the blood of this just[G] person: [b]see ye *to it.*[Q]

25 Then answered all the people, and said, [c,d,e]His blood *be* on us, and on our children.[Q]

26 Then released he [‖]Bȧ-răb'bas unto them: and when he had [f]scourged[G] [g]Jē'ṣus, he delivered *him* to be crucified.

27 ¶ [h]Then the [i]soldiers of the *governor took Jē'ṣus into the [3]common[G] hall, and gathered unto him the whole band of *soldiers*.

28 And they stripped him, and put on him a [j]scarlet [k]robe.

29 ¶ And when they had platted[G] a [l]crown of thorns, they [m,n]put *it* upon his head, and a [o]reed in his right hand: and they [n]bowed the knee before him, and [p,q]mocked him, saying, [n]Hail, King of the Jews!

30 And they [r]spit upon him, and took the [o]reed, and [f]smote him on the head.[Q]

31 [s]And after that they had [p]mocked him, they took the [k]robe off from him, and put his own raiment on him, and led him away to crucify *him*.

32 And as they came out, they found a man of Çȳ-rē'nē, [t]Sī'mon by name: him they compelled to bear his [u]cross.

33 [v]And when they were come unto a place called [w]Gŏl'gȯ-thȧ, that is to say, a place of a skull,

34 [x]They gave him [4,y]vinegar to drink mingled with [z]gall: and when he had tasted *thereof*, he would not drink.[Q]

35 And they [a]crucified [b]him,

v.13–AD 30
See footnote, *Time*, Rev. 10:6.

**15**
*l* *Passover*, Num. 9:5.
*m* *Prisoners, released at feasts*, Psa. 79:11.

**18**
*n* *Envy, instances of*, Prov. 14:30.
*o* *Malice, instances of*, Eph. 4:31.

**19**
*p* *Judge*, Judg. 2:18.
*q* *Judgment-seat*, Acts 25:10.
*r* *Women, good, instances of*, Prov. 31:10.
*s* *Statecraft, women in*, Prov. 28:2.
*t* *Jesus, perfections of*, Matt. 1:21.
*u* *Dream*, Dan. 1:17.

**24**
*v* *Government, corruption in*, Isa. 22:21.
*w* *Public Opinion, corrupt yielding to*, John 12:42.
*x* *Judge, corrupt, instances of*, Judg. 2:18.
*y* *Ablution, of the hands*, Judg. 19:21.

v.24–AD 30
See footnote, *Time*, Rev. 10:6.

*z* *Hand, washing of, a symbol of innocency*, Ezra 10:19.

*a* *Hypocrisy, instances of*, Jas. 3:17.
*b* *Responsibility, attempt to shift*, Ezek. 18:20.

**25**
*c* *Curse, assumed for others*, Judg. 5:23.
*d* *Punishment, assumed for others*, Lev. 26:41.
*e* *Responsibility*, Ezek. 18:20.

**26**
*f* *Smiting and Scourging of Jesus*, Isa. 50:6.
*g* *Prisoners, scourged*, Psa. 79:11.

**27**
*h* Mark 15:16–19; John 19:2, 3.
*i* *Soldiers*, Ezra 8:22.
3 Am. R. V. Prætorium,

**28**
*j* *Colors, symbolical*, Ezek. 16:16.
*k* *Dress*, Zech. 3:3.

**29**
*l* *Crown, of thorns*, Ex. 29:6.
*m* *Cruelty, instances of*, vs. 28–34; Psa. 27:12.
*n* *Irony, instances of*, Mark 12:14.
*o* *Reed*, Ezek. 40:3.
*p* *Mocking*, 1 Kin. 18:27.
*q* *Scoffing*, Hab. 1:10.

**30**
*r* *Spitting*, Num. 12:14.

**31**
*s* Mark 15:20, 21; Luke 23:26–32; John 19:16, 17.

**32**
*t* Mark 15:21; Luke 23:26.
*u* *Cross, borne by Simon*, John 19:17.

**33**
*v* Mark 15:22–37; Luke 23:33–46; John 19:18–30.
*w* Mark 15:22; John 19:17.

**34** *x* *Death, scenes of*, Num. 23:10. *y* *Wine*, Prov. 23:31. *z* *Gall*, Job 16:13. 4 R. V. wine **35**—*a* *Crucifixion, of Jesus*, Mark 15:13. *b* *Jesus, sufferings of*, Matt. 1:21.

‡ **CRIMINALS.** *Confined, in prisons*, Gen. 39:20–23; Ezra 7:26; Acts 16:25; *in dungeons*, Gen. 40:15; 41:14; Ex. 12:29; Isa. 24:22; Jer. 37:16; 38:10; Lam. 3:53, 55.
*Released at feasts*, Matt. 27:15, 21; Mark 15:6.
*Sentence upon, to be executed speedily*, Ezra 7:26.
See footnote, PRISONERS, Psa. 79:11.

‖ **BARABBAS.** *A prisoner released by Pilate*, Matt. 27:16–26; Mark 15:7–15; Luke 23:18–25; John 18:40; Acts 3:14.

§ **WASHING.** *Of hands, a token of innocency*, Deut. 21:6; Psa. 26:6; 73:13; Matt. 27:24. *Of the disciples' feet by the Savior, as an example of willing service*, John 13:5–15.
See footnotes: ABLUTION, Judg. 19:21; CEREMONIAL WASHINGS, Ex. 19:10; PURIFICATION, Num. 19:19; SPIRITUAL PURIFICATION, Psa. 51:2.
**Figurative:** *Of regeneration*, Psa. 51:7; Prov. 30:12; Isa. 1:16; 4:4; Zech. 13:1; 1 Cor. 6:11; Eph. 5:26; Tit. 3:5.

v.35–AD 30 See footnote, *Time*, Rev. 10:6.

c *Lot*, Esth. 3:7.
d Psa. 22:18; Mark 15:24; Luke 23:34; John 19:24.
5 R. V. *omits remainder of verse.*

**37**
e *Inscription, on the cross*, Mark 15:26.
f *Legends*, Zech. 14:20.
g *Irony, instances of*, Mark 12:14.

**38**
h *Thieves*, Deut. 24:7.
i Luke 23:32, 39.
6 R. V. robbers,

**39**
j *Mocking*, 1 Kin. 18:27.
k *Scoffing, instances of*, Hab. 1:10.

**40**
l *Temple, figurative*, 1 Kin. 6:17.
m *Jesus, divine sonship of*, Matt. 1:21.
n *Cross*, John 19:17.

**41**
o *Priest*, Lev. 1:5.
p *Scribe*, 1 Kin. 4:3.
q *Senate*, Num. 11:16.

**42**
r *Unbelief, instances of*, Heb. 3:12.
7 R. V. He is the King of Israel; let

**44**
8 R. V. upon him the same reproach.

**45**
s *Darkness, at the crucifixion*, Gen. 1:2.
t *Celestial Phenomena*, Luke 23:44.

**46**
u *Prayers of Jesus*, Luke 5:16.

and parted his garments, casting [c]lots: [5]that it might be fulfilled which was spoken by the
prophet, [d]They parted my garments among them, and up-
on my vesture did they cast
lots.[Q]
36 And sitting down they
watched him there;
37 And set up over his head
his [+]accusation written, [e,f]THIS
IS JĒ′ṢUS [g]THE KING OF
THE JEWṢ.
38 Then were there two
[6,h,i]thieves [a]crucified with him,
one on the right hand, and another on the left.[Q]
39 ¶ And they that passed by
[j,k]reviled[G] him, wagging their
heads,[Q]
40 And [j,k]saying, Thou that
destroyest the [l]temple, and buildest *it* in three days, save thyself.
If thou be the [m]Son of God, come
down from the [n]cross.
41 Likewise also the chief
[o]priests [j,k]mocking *him*, with
the [p]scribes and [q]elders, said,
42 [j,k]He saved others; [r]himself
he cannot save. [7,j,k]If he be the
King of Ị̄ṣ′ra-el, let him now
come down from the [n]cross, and
we will believe him.
43 [j,k]He trusted in God; [r]let
him deliver him now, if he will
have him: for he said, I am the
[m]Son of God.[Q]
44 The [h,i]thieves also, which
were [a]crucified with him, [j,k]cast
[8]the same in his teeth.
45 ¶ Now from the sixth hour
there was [s,t]darkness over all
the land unto the ninth hour.[Q]
46 And about the ninth hour
Jē′ṣus [u]cried with a loud voice,
saying, [v]Ē′lī, Ē′lī, lā′mȧ sȧ-
băch′tha-nī? that is to say, [w]My
God, my God, why hast thou
forsaken me?[T Q]
47 Some of them that stood
there, when they heard *that*, said,
This *man* calleth for [x]Ė-lī′as.
48 And straightway one of them
ran, and took a [y]spunge, and
filled *it* with [z]vinegar, and put *it*
on a reed, and gave him to drink.[Q]
49 The rest said, Let be, let us
see whether Ė-lī′as will come to
save him.
50 ¶ [a]Jē′ṣus, when he had cried
again with a loud voice, [b]yielded
up [9]the ghost.[G]
51 And, behold, [c]the [d]veil of
the [e]temple was rent[G] in twain[G]
from the top to the bottom; and
the earth did [f]quake[G], and the
rocks rent[G];[Q]
52[Q] And the [g]graves were
opened; and many bodies of
the saints which slept [h]arose,
53 And came out of the [g]graves
after his [i]resurrection[G], and went
into the [j]holy city, and appeared
unto many.[Q]
54 Now when the [k,l]centurion,
and they that were with him,
watching Jē′ṣus, saw the [f]earth-
quake, and those things that
were done, they feared greatly,
saying, Truly this was the [m]Son
of God.[T]
55 [n,o]And many [p]women were
there beholding afar off, which
followed Jē′ṣus from [q]Găl′ĭ-lee,
ministering unto him:
56 Among which was [©]Mā′rȳ
Măg-da-lē′nē, and [r]Mā′rȳ the
mother of [s]Jāmeṣ and [▲]Jō′sēṣ,
and the [t]mother of [u]Zĕb′e-dee's
[v,w]children.

v.46–AD 30
v Psa. 22:1; Mark 15:34.
w *Despondency*, Eccl. 2:20.

**47**
x Or, *Elijah*, 1 Kin. 17:1.

**48**
y Mark 15:36; John 19:29.
z *Wine*, Prov. 23:31.

**50**
a *Jesus, death of*, Matt. 1:21.
b *Death*, Num. 23:10.
9 R. V. his spirit.

**51**
c Mark 15:38–41; Luke 23:45, 47–49.
d *Vail, of temple*, 2 Chr. 3:14.
e *Temple, Herod's*, 1 Kin. 6:17.
f *Earthquakes, instances of*, Isa. 29:6.

**52**
g *Grave*, 2 Sam. 3:32.
h *Resurrection*, 1 Cor. 15:12.

**53**
i *Resurrection of Jesus*, Matt. 28:6.
j *Jerusalem*, Judg. 19:10.

**54**
k *Centurion*, Matt. 8:5.
l *Armies, Roman*, Deut. 11:4.
m *Jesus, divine sonship of*, Matt. 1:21.

**55**
n *Friendship, instances of*, Prov. 22:24.
o *Love, for Jesus, instances of*, 1 John 4:19.
p *Women, last at the cross*, Prov. 31:10.
q *Galilee*, Mark 6:21.

**56**
r *Mary*, Mark 15:40.
s *James*, Matt. 10:3.
t *Salome*, Mark 16:1.
u *Zebedee*, Matt. 4:21.
v *James*, Luke 5:10.
w *John*, Mark 1:19.

---

**+ INDICTMENTS. Instances of:** *Naboth, for blasphemy*, 1 Kin. 21:13, with vs. 1–16. *Jeremiah, for treasonable prophecy, but of which he was acquitted*, Jer. 26:1–24; *a second indictment*, Jer. 37:13–15. *Three Hebrew captives, for contumacy*, Dan. 3:12, with vs. 1–28; *Daniel, for contumacy*, Dan. 6:13, with vs. 1–24. *Jesus, under two charges, first, for blasphemy*, Matt. 26:61, 63–65; Mark 14:58, 61–64; Luke 22:67–71; John 19:7; *second, for treason*, Matt. 27:11, 37; Mark 15:2, 26; Luke 23:2, 3, 38; John 18:30, 33; 19:12, 19–22.

*Stephen, for blasphemy*, Acts 6:11, 13. *Paul*, Acts 17:7; 18:13; 24:5; 25:18, 19, 26, 27. *Paul and Silas*, Acts 16:20, 21.

*Quashed*, Acts 18:14–16.

**© MARY MAGDALENE.** *Possessed of devils; delivered by Jesus*, Mark 16:9; Luke 8:2, 3. *Present, at the crucifixion*, Matt. 27:56; Mark 15:40; John 19:25; *at the sepulchre*, Matt. 27:61; 28:1–7; Mark 15:47; 16:1–7; Luke 23:55, 56; 24:1–7; John 20:1, 11–13. *Recognizes Jesus after his resurrection*, Matt. 28:8–10; Mark 16:9; John 20:14–18.

**▲ JOSES.** *A brother of Jesus*, Matt. 13:55; 27:56; Mark 6:3; 15:40, 47.

57 ¶ [x]When[Q] the even[G] was come,
there came a [y]rich man of [z]Ăr-ĭ-
mă-thæ'ȧ, named [a]Jō'ṣeph, who
also himself was Jē'ṣus' disciple:
58 [a]He went to Pī'late, and
begged the body of Jē'ṣus. Then
Pī'late commanded the body to
be delivered.[Q]
59 And when [a]Jō'ṣeph had
taken the [b]body, he wrapped it
in a clean linen cloth,
60 And laid it in his own new
[c]tomb, which he had hewn out
in the rock: and he rolled a great
[d]stone to the door of the [c]sepul-
chre, and departed.
61 And there was ⊙Mā'rȳ Măg-
da-lē'nē, and the other [e]Mā'rȳ,
sitting over[G] against the [c]sepul-
chre.
62 ¶ Now the [f]next day, that
followed the day of the [g]prep-
aration, the chief [h]priests and
[i]Phăr'ĭ-seeṣ came together unto
Pī'late,
63 Saying, Sir, we remember
that that deceiver [j]said, while he
was yet alive, After three days
[k]I will rise again.
64 Command therefore that the
[c]sepulchre be made sure until
the third day, lest his [l]disciples
come [10]by night, and steal him
away, and say unto the people,
He is risen from the dead: so
the last error shall be worse than
the first.
65 Pī'late said unto them, Ye
have a [m]watch[G]: go your way,
make [c]*it* as sure as ye can.
66 So they went, and made
the [c]sepulchre sure, [n]sealing the
stone, and setting a [m]watch[G].

## CHAPTER 28

*The resurrection of Jesus. 9 He appears to the women. 11 The soldiers bribed. 16 Jesus meets his disciples on a mountain in Galilee. 18 The great commission.*

[a]IN[T] the end of the [b]sabbath,
as it began to dawn toward
the first *day* of the week, [c,d]came
[e]Mā'rȳ Măg-da-lē'nē and the
other [f]Mā'rȳ to see the [g]sepul-
chre.
2 And, behold, there was a
great [h]earthquake: for the [i]angel
of the Lord descended from
heaven, and came and rolled
back the stone [1]from the door,
and sat upon it.[T]
3 His [2]countenance was like
[j]lightning, and his raiment[G]
[k]white as [l]snow:
4 And for [m]fear of him the keepers did shake, and became as
dead *men*.
5 And the [i]angel answered and
said unto the women, [n]Fear not
ye: for I know that ye seek Jē'-
ṣus, which was [o]crucified.
6 He is not here: for he is
*risen, as he said. Come, see
the place where the Lord lay.[T]
7 And go quickly, and tell his
[p]disciples that he is *risen from
the dead; and, behold, he goeth
before you into [q]Găl'ĭ-lee; there
shall ye see him: lo, I have told
you.
8 And they departed quickly
from the [g]sepulchre[G] with fear
and great [r]joy; and did run to
bring his [p]disciples word.
9 ¶ And [3]as they went to tell his
[p]disciples, behold, [s]Jē'ṣus met
them, saying, [t]All[G] hail. And
they came and [u]held him by the
feet, and [v]worshipped him.
10 Then said Jē'ṣus unto them,
Be not afraid: go tell my brethren that they go into [q]Găl'ĭ-lee,
and there shall they see me.
11 ¶ Now when they were going, behold, some of the [w]watch[G]
came into the city, and shewed
unto the chief [x]priests all the
things that were done.
12 And when [x]they were assembled with the [y]elders, and
had taken counsel, they [z]gave
large [a]money unto the [b]soldiers,

---

v.57–AD 30
See footnote, *Time,* Rev. 10:6.

**57**
x Mark 15:42–47; Luke 23:50–56; John 19:38–42.
y *Rich, instances of,* Jas. 5:1.
z *Arimathea,* John 19:38.

a *Joseph,* John 19:38.

**59**
b *Dead, prepared for burial,* 2 Kin. 4:32.

**60**
c *Burying Places,* Gen. 23:4.
d *Stones,* Ex. 24:12.

**61**
e *Mary,* Mark 15:40.

**62**
f *Sabbath, preparation for,* Ex. 16:23.
g Mark 15:42; Luke 23:54; John 19:14, 31, 42.
h *Priest,* Lev. 1:5.
i *Pharisees,* Matt. 15:12.

**63**
j *Jesus, prophet,* Matt. 1:21.
k *Jesus, resurrection of,* Matt. 1:21.

**64**
l *Disciples,* Matt. 9:14.
10 **R. V. *omits* by night,**

**65**
m *Soldiers,* Ezra 8:22.

**66**
n *Seal, on sepulchre of Jesus,* 1 Kin. 21:8.

**1**
a Mark 16:1–8; Luke 24:1–10; John 20:1.
b *Sabbath,* Ex. 16:23.
c *Friendship, instances of,* Prov. 22:24.
d *Love, for Jesus, instances of,* 1 John 4:19.

v.1–AD 30
See footnote, *Time,* Rev. 10:6.

e *Mary Magdalene,* Matt. 27:56.
f *Mary,* Mark 15:40.
g *Burying Places,* Gen. 23:4.

**2**
h *Earthquakes, instances of,* Isa. 29:6.
i *Angel, functions of,* Heb. 1:13.
1 R. V. *omits* from the door,

**3**
j *Lightning,* Job 28:26.
k *Colors,* Ezek. 16:16.
l *Snow,* Jer. 18:14.
2 R. V. appearance was as

**4**
m *Fear of God, guilty,* Acts 9:31.

**5**
n *Afflictions, consolation in,* Psa. 34:19.
o *Crucifixion, of Jesus,* Mark 15:13.

**7**
p *Apostles,* Luke 6:13.
q *Galilee,* Mark 6:21.

**8**
r *Joy,* Psa. 5:11.

**9**
s *Jesus, appearances of,* Matt. 1:21.
t *Salutations,* Luke 1:44.
u *Love, for Jesus,* 1 John 4:19.
v *Jesus, worship of,* Matt. 1:21.
3 R. V. *omits* as they went to tell his disciples,

**11**
w *Soldiers,* Ezra 8:22.
x *Priest,* Lev. 1:5.

**12**
y *Senate,* Num. 11:16.
z *Bribery, instances of,* 1 Sam. 8:3.

a *Money,* Jer. 32:9.
b *Witness, corrupted by money,* Num. 35:30.

---

* **RESURRECTION OF JESUS,** Matt. 27:53; 28:2–15; Mark 16:1–11; Luke 24:1–12; John 20:1–18. *Foretold by himself,* Matt. 16:21; 17:9, 23; 20:19; 26:61; 27:63; Mark 8:31; 9:9, 10, 31; 10:34; Luke 9:22; 18:33; 24:7, 46; John 2:19–21; 10:17, 18.

v.13—AD 30
See footnote, *Time*, Rev. 10:6.

**13**
*c Falsehood*, Job 21:34.
*d Disciples*, Matt. 9:14.
*e Sleep*, Psa. 127:2.

**14**
*f Government, provincial*, Isa. 22:21.
4 R. V. rid you of care.

**15**
*g Bribery, instances of*, 1 Sam. 8:3.
*h Watchman, unfaithful*, 2 Sam. 18:24.

**16**
*i* John 21:1, 2.
*j Apostles*, Luke 6:13.
*k Galilee*, Mark 6:21.

13 Saying, [c]Say ye, His [d]dis-
ciples came by night, and stole
him *away* while we [e]slept.
14 And if this come to the [f]gov-
ernor's ears, we will persuade
him, [4]and secure[G] you.
15 [g]So [h]they took the [a]money,
and did as they were taught: and
this saying is commonly reported
among the Jews until this day.
16 ¶ [i]Then the eleven [j]disciples
went away into [k]Găl'ĭ-lee, into a
[l]mountain where Jē'ṣus had appointed them.
17 And when they saw [m]him,
they [n]worshipped him: but some
[o]doubted.

*l Mountain*, Mic. 7:12. **17** *m Jesus, appearances of*, Matt. 1:21. *n Jesus, worship of*, Matt. 1:21. *o Unbelief*, Heb. 3:12.

18 And [m]Jē'ṣus came and spake
unto them, saying, All [5]power[G] is
given unto [p]me in heaven and in
earth.[T] [Q]
19[T] [†, q, r]Go [s]ye therefore, and
[6, t]teach[G] all nations, [u]baptizing
them in the name of the [v]Father,
and of the [v, w]Son, and of the
[v, x]Holy Ghost[G]:
20 [i]Teaching them to [y]ob-
serve all things whatsoever I
have commanded you: and, lo,
[z, a]I am with you alway, *even*
unto the end of the world[G].
Amen.[S T Q]

v.18—AD 30
See footnote, *Time*, Rev. 10:6.

**18**
*p Jesus, king*, Matt. 1:21.
5 R. V. authority

**19**
*q* Mark 16:15; Luke 24:47.
*r Commandment, enjoining evangelism*, Deut. 8:2.
*s Apostles, commission of*, Luke 6:13.
*t Instruction*, Prov. 23:23.

*u Baptism, Christian*, Luke 20:4. *v Holy Trinity*, Luke 3:22. *w Jesus, divinity of*, Matt. 1:21. *x Holy Spirit*, Acts 1:2. 6 R. V. make disciples of
**20** *y Obedience, enjoined*, Heb. 5:8. 2 *a Promise, to the righteous*, 2 Cor. 1:20. *a Righteous, promises to*, Psa. 64:10.

---

THE GOSPEL ACCORDING TO

# MARK

v.1—AD 26
See footnote, *Time*, Rev. 10:6.

**1**
*a Gospel*, Mark 13:10.
*b Jesus, Messiah*, Matt. 1:21.
*c Jesus, divine sonship of*, Matt. 1:21.

**2**
*d Word of God*, Psa. 119:9.
*e Prophecies, concerning the Messiah, and their fulfillment*, Gen. 12:3.
*f* Mal. 3:1; Matt. 11:10.
*g Messenger, figurative*, Hag. 1:13.
*h John the Baptist*, Luke 1:63.
1 R. V. Isaiah the prophet,

## CHAPTER 1

*The preaching of John the Baptist. 9 Jesus is baptized. 12 His temptation. 14 He preaches in Galilee, 16 and calls Peter and Andrew, James and John. 23 A man with an unclean spirit healed; 29 also Peter's wife's mother, 32 and many others. 40 A leper cleansed.*

THE beginning of the [a]gospel
of [b]Jē'ṣus Chrīst, the [c]Son
of God;[T]
2 As it is [d]written in [1]the [e]pro-
phets, [f]Behold, I send my [g]mes-
senger before thy face, [h]which
shall prepare thy way before thee.[Q T]
3 [i]The voice of [h]one crying in
the wilderness, Prepare ye the
way of the Lord, make his paths
straight.[Q]
4 [h]Jŏhn did [j]baptize in the [k]wil-
derness, and [l]preach the baptism

**3** *i* Isa. 40:3; Matt. 3:3; Luke 3:4–6. **4** *j Baptism, John's*, Luke 20:4. *k Beth-arabah*, Josh. 15:6. *l Preaching*, Matt. 9:35.

of *repentance [2]for the [m, n]remis-
sion of sins.
5 And there went out unto [o]him
all the land of [p]Jū-dæ'ȧ, and
they of [q]Jĕ-ru̥'sȧ-lĕm, and were
all [j]baptized of him in the river of
[r]Jôr'dan, *confessing their [s]sins.
6 And [t]Jŏhn was [u]clothed with
[v]camel's hair, and with a girdle[G]
of a [w]skin about his loins[G]; and
he did eat [x, y]locusts and wild
[z]honey;[Q]
7 And [a]preached, [b]saying,
There cometh [c]one mightier
than I after me, the latchet[G] of
whose [d]shoes I am [e]not worthy
to stoop down and unloose[G].

v.4—AD 26
See footnote, *Time*, Rev. 10:6.

*m Sin, forgiveness of*, Rom. 5:12.
2 R. V. unto
*n Salvation, conditions of*, Acts 16:17.

**5**
*o John, his influence upon the public mind*, Luke 1:63.
*p Judea*, Luke 5:17.
*q Jerusalem*, Judg. 19:10.
*r Jordan, John baptizes in*, Gen. 32:10.
*s Sin, confession of* Rom. 5:12.

**6**
*t Stoicism*, Acts 17:18.
*u Dress*, Zech. 3:3.

*v Camel*, 1 Sam. 30:17. *w Leather*, 2 Kin. 1:8. *x Locust, used as food*, Nah. 3:17. *y Food, articles of*, Psa. 136:25. *z Honey*, Prov. 25:27.—**7** *a Preaching*, Matt. 9:35. *b John, testifies to the messiahship of Jesus*, Luke 1:63. *c Jesus, Messiah*, Matt. 1:21. *d Shoe*, Josh. 5:15. *e Humility, instances of*, Prov. 22:4.

---

† **MISSIONS.** *Religious propagandism*, 2 Kin. 17:27, 28; 1 Chr. 16:23, 24. *Enjoined*, Psa. 96:3, 10; Matt. 28:19; Mark 16:15; Luke 24:47, 48. *Prophecy concerning*, Matt. 24:14; Mark 13:10. *Peter's vision concerning*, Acts 10:9–20.
*Ordained by Jesus*, Matt. 24:14; 28:19; Mark 16:15, 16; Luke 24:47–49. *Saul and Barnabas ordained for*, Acts 13:2–4, 47. *Paul appointed to*, Acts 26:14–18; 1 Cor. 16:9.
*Symbolized by the flying angel*, Rev. 14:6, 7.
*The first to do homage to the Messiah were heathen*, Matt. 2:11.
*Missionary hymn*, Psa. 96.
See footnotes: GENTILES, *Prophecies concerning the conversion of*, Acts 10:45; JESUS, *Kingdom of, prophecies concerning*, Matt. 1:21.

* **REPENTANCE**, Psa. 34:14, 18; Isa. 22:12.
*Exhortations to*, Prov. 1:22, 23; Jer. 6:16–18; 7:3; 26:3; Hos. 6:1; 14:1–2; Amos 5:4–6.
*Enjoined*, Deut. 32:29; 2 Chr. 30:7–9; Job 36:10; Isa. 22:12; 31:6; 44:22; 55:6, 7; Jer. 3:4, 12–14, 19, 22; 18:11; 25:5, 6; 26:13; 35:15; Ezek. 12:1–5; 14:6; 18:30–32; 33:10–12, 14–16, 19; Dan. 4:27; Hos. 10:12; 14:1, 2; Joel 1:14; 2:12, 13, 15–17; Amos 4:12; Jonah 3:8, 9; Hag. 1:7; Zech. 1:3; Matt. 4:17; Mark 1:4, 15; 6:12; Luke 3:3; Acts 2:38; 3:19; 8:22; 17:30; Rev. 2:5, 16; 3:2, 3, 19.
*Gift, of God*, 2 Tim. 2:25; *of Christ*, Acts 5:31. *Goodness of God, leads to*, Rom. 2:4. *Tribulation leads to*, Deut. 4:30; 30:1–3; 1 Kin. 8:33–50; 2 Chr. 6:36–39; Job 34:31, 32.

v.8–AD 26
See footnote, *Time*, Rev. 10:6.

**8**

*f Baptism, John's*, Luke 20:4.

*g Holy Spirit, baptism of*, Acts 1:2.

3 Am. R. V. I baptized you in water; but he shall baptize you in the Holy Spirit.

**9**

*h* Matt. 3:13–16; Luke 3:21, 22.

*i Jesus, baptized by John*, Matt. 1:21.

*j Nazareth*, John 1:46.

*k Galilee*, Mark 6:21.

*l Jordan, John baptizes Jesus in*, Gen. 32:10.

**10**

*m Vision*, Acts 9:10.

*n Holy Spirit*, Acts 1:2.

*o Dove*, Gen. 8:8.

**11**

*p Jesus, divine sonship of*, Matt. 1:21.

*q God, fatherhood of*, Gen. 2:2.

8 [3]I indeed have [f]baptized you
with water: but [e]he shall baptize
you with the [g]Holy Ghost.[G T]
9 ¶ [h]And it came to pass in those
days, that [i]Jē'ṣus came from
[j]Năz'a-rĕth of [k]Găl'ĭ-lee, and was
[f]baptized of Jŏhn in [l]Jôr'dan.
10 And straightway coming up
out of the water, he [m]saw the heavens opened, and the [n]Spirit like
a [o]dove descending upon him:[T]
11 And there came a voice from
heaven, *saying*, [p]Thou art [q]my
beloved Son, in whom I am well
pleased.[Q T]
12 ¶ And [r]immediately the
[4,n]spirit driveth him into the
wilderness.[T]
13 And he was there in the wilderness [r]forty days, [s]tempted[G] of
[t]Sā'tan; and was with the wild
[u]beasts; and the [v]angels ministered[G] unto[S] him.
14 ¶ [w]Now after that Jŏhn was
[x]put in prison, Jē'ṣus came into
[k]Găl'ĭ-lee, [y]preaching the [z,a]gos-
pel of the [b]kingdom of God,[T]
15 And saying, The [c]time is
fulfilled,[G] and the [b]kingdom of
God is at hand: [d]repent ye, and
[e]believe the [a,f]gospel.[S T]
16 ¶ [g]Now as [h]he walked by
the [i]sea of Găl'ĭ-lee, he saw [j]Sī'-
mon and [k]Ăn'drew his brother
casting a [l]net into the sea: for
they were [m]fishers.
17 And [h]Jē'ṣus said unto
[n,o]them, [p,q]Come ye after me,
and I will make you to become
[†,r]fishers of men.
18 And straightway[G] [s]they [t,u,v]for-
sook their[G] [l]nets, and followed him.
19 And when he had gone a little farther thence, he saw [w]Jāmeṣ
the *son* of [x]Zĕb'e-dee, and [‡]Jŏhn

**12** *r* Matt. 4:1–11; Luke 4:1–13. **4** R. V. Spirit **13** *s Forty, days*, Jonah 3:4. *t Satan*, Matt. 4:10. *u Animals, abodes of*, Jer. 27:5. *v Angel, functions of*, Heb. 1:13. **14** *w* Isa. 9:1, 2; Matt. 4:12–17.

v.14–AD 26
See footnote, *Time*, Rev. 10:6.

*x Persecution, of the righteous*, John 15:20.

*y Preaching, repentance the subject of Christ's*, Matt. 9:35.

*z Gospel*, Mark 13:10.

*a Word of God*, Psa. 119:9.

*b Kingdom of Heaven*, Matt. 13:24.

**15**

*c Time, fulness of*, Rev. 10:6.

*d Commandment, enjoining repentance*, Deut. 8:2.

*e Faith, enjoined*, Mark 11:22.

*f Gospel*, Mark 13:10.

**16**

*g* Matt. 4:18–22.

*h Jesus, history of*, Matt. 1:21.

*i Sea of Galilee*, Matt. 4:18.

*j Peter*, Mark 5:37. *k Andrew*, Matt. 4:18. *l Net*, Isa. 51:20. *m Fishermen*, Luke 5:2. **17** *n Apostles, selection of*, Luke 6:13. *o Minister, call of*, Rom. 15:16. *p Call, to special religious duty*, Phil. 3:14. *q Commandment, enjoining discipleship*, Deut. 8:2. *r Fisherman, figurative*, Luke 5:2. **18** *s Faith in Christ, exemplified*, John 6:69. *t Obedience, exemplified*, Heb. 5:8. *u Self-denial, instances of*, Mark 8:34. *v Renunciation, of business for Christ*, vs. 18–20; Luke 5:11. **19** *w James*, Luke 5:10. *x Zebedee*, Matt. 4:21.

---

*Condition, of forgiveness*, Lev. 26:40–42; Deut. 4:29–31; 30:1–3, 8; 1 Kin. 8:33–50; 2 Chr. 6:36–39; 7:14; Neh. 1:9; Job 11:13–15; 22:23; Psa. 34:18; Prov. 28:13; Isa. 55:7; Jer. 3:4, 12–14, 19; 7:5–7; 18:7, 8; 36:3; Ezek. 18:21–23, 27, 28, 30, 31; Amos 5:6; Mal. 3:7; Matt. 5:4; Luke 13:1–5; 1 John 1:9; *of divine favor*, Lev. 26:40–42; 2 Chr. 7:14; Isa. 57:15.

*To be preached to all nations*, Luke 24:47.

*Joy in heaven over*, Luke 15:1–10. *Of Israel foretold*, Jer. 50:4, 5; Ezek. 11:18–20; Hos. 3:5; Zech. 12:10. *Universal, foretold*, Psa. 22:27; Rom. 14:11. *Rewards of*, Prov. 1:23; Isa. 59:20; Jer. 7:3, 5, 7; 24:7; Ezek. 18:21–23, 27, 28.

*The burden of the preaching, of John the Baptist*, Matt. 3:2, 7, 8; Mark 1:4, 15; Luke 3:3; *of Jesus*, Matt. 4:17; Mark 1:15; Luke 5:32; *of Peter*, Acts 2:38, 40; 3:19; 8:22; *of Paul*, Acts 17:30; 20:21; 26:20; *of the apostles*, Mark 6:12.

*Unavailing, to Israel*, Num. 14:39–45; *to Esau*, Heb. 12:16, 17.

**Attributed to God,** Gen. 6:6, 7; Ex. 32:14; Deut. 32:36; Judg. 2:18; 1 Sam. 15:11, 35; 2 Sam. 24:16; 1 Chr. 21:15; Psa. 106:45; 135:14; Jer. 15:6; 18:8, 10; 26:3; 42:10; Joel 2:13; Amos 7:3, 6; Jonah 3:9, 10. *God repenteth not*, Num. 23:19; 1 Sam. 15:29; Psa. 110:4; Rom. 11:29.

**Exemplified:** *By Job*, Job 7:20, 21; 9:20; 13:23; 40:4; 42:6. *By David*, Psa. 32:5; 38:3, 4, 18; 40:12; 41:4; 51:1–4, 7–17. *By the Israelites*, Jer. 3:21, 22, 25; 14:7–9, 20; 31:18, 19; Lam. 3:40, 41. *By Daniel for the Jews*, Dan. 9:5–7; 10:12. *By the prodigal*, Luke 15:17–20.

**Instances of:** *Joseph's brethren, for their ill treatment of Joseph*, Gen. 42:21; 50:17, 18. *Pharaoh, for his hardness of heart*, Ex. 9:27; 10:16, 17. *Balaam, for his spiritual blindness*, Num. 22:34, with vs. 24–35. *Israelites, for worshiping the golden calf*, Ex. 33:3, 4; *for their murmuring on account of lack of bread and water, when the plague of fiery serpents came upon them*, Num. 21:4–7; *when rebuked by an angel for not expelling the Canaanites*, Judg. 2:1–5; *for their idolatry, when afflicted by the Philistines*, Judg. 10:6–16; 1 Sam. 7:3–6; *for asking for a king*, 1 Sam. 12:16–20; *in the time of Asa, under the preaching of Azariah*, 2 Chr. 15:1–15; *under the preaching of Oded*, 2 Chr. 28:9–15; *under the influence of Hezekiah*, 2 Chr. 30:11. *Achan, for his theft*, Josh. 7:20. *Job*, Job 42:6; *David, at the rebuke of Nathan, the prophet, for his sins of adultery and murder*, 2 Sam. 12:11, 13 (with vs. 7–14); Psa. 32:5; 38:3, 4, 18; 40:12; 41:4; 51:1–4, 7–17; *for numbering Israel*, 2 Sam. 24:10, 17. *Psalmist*, Psa. 106:6; 119:59, 176; 130:1–3. *Rehoboam, when his kingdom was invaded, and Jerusalem besieged*, 2 Chr. 12:1–12; Isa. 6:5. *Hezekiah, for his pride*, Isa. 38:15; *at the time of his sickness*, 2 Chr. 32:26; *when reproved by the prophet Micah*, Jer. 26:18, 19. *Ahab, when reproved by Elijah for his idolatry*, 1 Kin. 21:27, with vs. 17:29. *Jehoahaz*, 2 Kin. 13:4. *Josiah, when he heard the law which had been discovered in the temple, by Hilkiah*, 2 Kin. 22:11–20. *Manasseh, when he was carried captive to Babylon by the king of Assyria*, 2 Chr. 33:12, 13. *The Jews of the captivity, at the dedication of the temple*, Ezra 6:21; 9:4, 6, 10, 13, 14; *for their idolatrous marriages*, Ezra 10; *for their oppressive usury*, Neh. 5:1–13; *after hearing the law expounded by Ezra*, Neh. 9:1–3; *under the preaching of Haggai*, Hag. 1. *Jonah, after his punishment*, Jonah 2:2–9. *The Ninevites, under the preaching of Jonah*, Jonah 3:5–9, 10. *The Jews, under the preaching of John the Baptist*, Matt. 3:6. *The woman who anointed Jesus with oil*, Luke 7:37–48. *The disobedient son*, Matt. 21:29. *The prodigal son*, Luke 15:17–21. *The publican*, Luke 18:13. *Peter, of his denial of Jesus*, Matt. 26:75; Mark 14:72; Luke 22:62. *The Ephesians, under the preaching of Paul*, Acts 19:18.

See footnotes: CONVICTION OF SIN, John 16:8; REMORSE, Matt. 27:4.

† **AGENCY.** *In salvation of men*, Ezek. 47:10; Matt. 4:19; 5:13–16; Luke 1:17; 5:10; 10:17, 21; 1 Cor. 1:26–29; 1 Thess. 2:4; 1 Tim. 1:11, 12; Jas 5:20. *In executing judgments*, 1 Sam. 15:1–19; 2 Sam. 7:14; 2 Kin. 9:6, 7; 19:25, 26; 2 Chr. 22:7; Isa. 10:5, 6; 13:5; 41:15; Jer. 27:8; 51:20–23; Ezek. 23:24.

‡ **JOHN,** the Apostle. *A fisherman; son of Zebedee*, Matt. 4:21. *Call of*, Mark 1:19, 20. *Intimately associated with Jesus*, John 13:23–26; 21:20. *Is present when Jesus performs the following miracles: Healing of Peter's mother-in-law*, Mark 1:30, 31; *raising of the daughter of Jairus*, Mark 5:37; Luke 8:51; *the two draughts of fishes*, Luke 5:10; John 21:1–7. *Is present with Jesus, at the transfiguration*, Matt. 17:1; Mark 9:2; Luke 9:28; *in the garden*, Matt. 26:37; Mark 14:33; Luke 22:39.

*Intolerance of*, Mark 9:38; Luke 9:49, 50, 54–56. *Civil ambitions of*, Matt. 20:20–24; Mark 10:35–41. *With Peter prepares the passover*, Matt. 26:18, 19; Mark 14:13–16; Luke 22:8–13. *Present, at the trial of Jesus before the high priest*, John 18:15, 16; *at the crucifixion*, John 19:26, 27; *at the sepulchre*, John 20:2–8; *when Jesus manifested himself at the Sea of Galilee*, John 21. *Is intrusted with the care of Mary, the mother of Jesus*, John 19:26. *Dwells in Jerusalem*, Acts 1:13. *With Peter in the temple*, Acts 3:1–11. *Imprisoned*

his brother, who also were in the
[5]ship mending their [l]nets.
20 And straightway he [o,p]called
[m,n]them: and [s,t]they [u,v]left their
father [x]Zĕb′e-dee in the ship
with the [y]hired servants, and
went after him.
21 [z]And they went into [a]Că-
pēr′na-ŭm; and straightway on
the [b]sabbath day he entered into
the [c]synagogue, and [d,e]taught.
22 And [f]they were astonished
at his [6,g]doctrine: for he taught
them as one that had authority,
and not as the [h]scribes.
23 And there was in their [c]syn-
agogue a man [i]with an [j]unclean
spirit; and he cried out,
24 Saying, [7]Let *us* alone; what
have we to do with thee, thou
[k]Jē′ṣus of [l]Năz′a-rĕth? art thou
come to destroy us? I know thee
who thou art, the [m,n]Holy One
of God.
25 And Jē′ṣus rebuked him, saying, Hold thy peace, and come
out of him.
26 And when the [j]unclean spirit
had torn him, and cried with a
loud voice, he [o]came out of
him.
27 And they were all amazed,
insomuch that they questioned
among themselves, saying, What
thing is this? what new [g]doctrine
*is* this? for with authority commandeth he even the [j]unclean
spirits, and they do obey him.
28 And immediately his [p]fame
spread abroad throughout all the
region [8]round about [q]Găl′ĭ-lee.
29 ¶ And forthwith, when they
were come out of the [c]synagogue,
they entered into the house of
[r]Sī′mon and [s]Ăn′drew, with
[t]Jāmeṣ and ‡Jŏhn.
30 [u]But [r,v]Sī′mon's [w]wife's
[x]mother lay sick of a [y]fever,
and anon they tell him of her.
31 And he came and took her
by the hand, and lifted her up;
and immediately the [y]fever [o,z]left
her, and she ministered unto
them.
32 ¶ And at even, when the sun
did set, they [a]brought unto him
all that were [b,c]diseased, and
them that were possessed with
[d]devils.
33 And [e]all the city was gathered together at the door.
34 And he [f]healed many that
were [c]sick of divers [b]diseases,
and [f]cast out many [d]devils; and
[g]suffered not the devils to speak,
because they knew him.
35 ¶ And in the morning,
[h]rising up a great while before
day, he went out, and departed
into a [9]solitary place, and there
[i]prayed.
36 And [j]Sī′mon and they that
were with him followed after him.
37 And when they had found
him, they said unto him, [e]All
*men* seek for thee.
38 And [k]he said unto them, Let
us go into the next towns, that
I may [l]preach there also: for
[m]therefore came I forth.
39 And he [l]preached in their
[n]synagogues throughout all
[o]Găl′ĭ-lee, and [f]cast out [d]devils.
40 ¶ [p]And there came a [q]leper
to him, beseeching him, and
[r]kneeling down to him, and saying unto him, If thou wilt, [s]thou
canst make me clean.
41 And Jē′ṣus, moved with
[t]compassion, put forth *his* hand,
and touched him, and saith unto
him, I will; be thou clean.
42 And as soon as he had spoken, immediately the [b]leprosy
[f]departed from him, and he was
cleansed.
43 And he straitly [g]charged
him, and forthwith sent him
away;
44 And [o]saith unto him, See

5 R. V. boat

**20**

y *Hired Servant*, Lev. 25:40.

**21**

z Luke 4:31–37.

a *Capernaum*, Luke 4:31.
b *Sabbath*, Ex. 16:23.
c *Synagogue, place of assembly*, Matt. 12:9.
d *Jesus, teacher*, Matt. 1:21.
e *Instruction, in religion*, Prov. 23:23.

**22**

f *Jesus, received*, Matt. 1:21.
g *Doctrines of Jesus*, John 7:16.
h *Scribe*, 1 Kin. 4:3.
6 R. V. teaching:

**23**

i *Afflictions*, Psa. 34:19.
j *Demons, possession by*, Matt. 4:24.

**24**

k *Jesus, names of*, Matt. 1:21.
l *Nazareth*, John 1:46.
m *Jesus, holiness of*, Matt. 1:21.
n *Jesus, divinity of*, Matt. 1:21.
7 R. V. *omits* Let us *alone;*

**26**

o *Miracles, of Jesus*, Luke 23:8.

**28**

p *Fame of Jesus*, Luke 5:15.
q *Galilee*, Mark 6:21.
8 R. V. of Galilee round about.

**29**

r Or, *Peter*, Mark 5:37.
s *Andrew*, Matt. 4:18.
t *James*, Luke 5:10.

**30**

u Matt. 8:14–17; Luke 4:38–41.
v *Minister, marriage of*, Rom. 15:16.
w *Wife*, Prov. 5:18.
x *Mother-in-law*, Matt. 10:35.
y *Fever*, Deut. 28:22.

**31**

z *Disease, healing of, by Jesus*, Ex. 15:26.

**32**

a *Mediation*, Gal. 3:19.
b *Disease, healing of, by Jesus*, Ex. 15:26.
c *Afflictions*, Psa. 34:19.
d *Demons*, Matt. 4:24.

**33**

e *Popularity of Jesus*, John 6:15.

**34**

f *Miracles, of Jesus*, Luke 23:8.
g *Prudence, instances of*, 2 Chr. 2:12.

**35**

h *Diligence, Jesus an example of*, Rom. 12:8.
i *Prayers of Jesus*, Luke 5:16.
9 R. V. desert

**36**

j *Peter*, Mark 5:37.

**38**

k *Jesus, zeal of*, Matt. 1:21.
l *Preaching*, Matt. 9:35.
m *Jesus, mission of*, Matt. 1:21.

**39**

n *Synagogue*, Matt. 12:9.
o *Galilee*, Mark 6:21.

**40**

p Matt. 8:2–4; Luke 5:12–14.
q *Leprosy, healed by Jesus*, Lev. 13:2.
r *Humility*, Prov. 22:4.
s *Faith in Christ, instances of*, John 6:69.

**41**

t *Jesus, compassion of*, Matt. 1:21.

*by the rulers of the Jews*, Acts 4:1–21. *Sent by the church with a commission to Samaria*, Acts 8:14–17. *A pillar of the church*, Gal. 2:9. *Writes biography of Jesus*, John 19:35; 21:24, 25. *Writes to the churches*, see the EPISTLES OF JOHN. *Writes his apocalyptic vision from Patmos*, Rev. 1:9. *Prophecy concerning*, Rev. 10:11.

**44**
*u Priest,* Lev. 1:5.
*v Purification,* Num. 19:19.
*w Law, of Moses,* Deut. 33:2.
*x* Lev. 14:2–32.

**45**
*y Fame of Jesus,* Luke 5:15.
*z Zeal, instances of,* 2 Cor. 7:11.

*a Popularity of Jesus,* John 6:15.

**1**
*a Jesus, history of,* vs. 1–22; Matt. 1:21.
*b Capernaum,* Luke 4:31.

**2**
*c Popularity of Jesus,* John 6:15.
*d Jesus, received,* Matt. 1:21.
*e Preaching, the gospel,* Matt. 9:35.

**3**
*f Mediation,* Gal. 3:19.

**4**
*g House, roof of,* Esth. 8:1.

**5**
*h Jesus, power of,* Matt. 1:21.
*i Faith in Christ, exemplified,* John 6:69.
*j Healing, by Jesus,* Acts 4:22.
*k Sin, forgiveness of,* Rom. 5:12.
1 R. V. are forgiven.

**6**
*l Scribe,* 1 Kin. 4:3.

**7**
*m Unbelief, instances of,* Heb. 3:12.
*n Blasphemy, Jesus falsely accused of,* 2 Sam. 12:14.

**8**
*o Jesus, omniscience of,* Matt. 1:21.

thou say nothing to any man: but go thy way, shew thyself to the [u]priest, and offer for thy [v]cleansing those things which [w]Mō′ṣeṣ [x]commanded, for a testimony unto them.

45 But he went out, [y]and [z]began to publish *it* much, and to blaze abroad the matter, insomuch that Jē′ṣus could no more openly enter into the city, but was without in desert places: and [a]they came to him from every quarter.

## CHAPTER 2

*Jesus heals one sick of the palsy; 14 calls Levi; 15 eats with publicans and sinners; 18 and justifies his disciples in not fasting. 23 The disciples pluck ears of corn on the Sabbath.*

AND again [a]he entered into [b]Că-pĕr′na-ŭm after *some* days; and it was noised that he was in the house.

2 And straightway [c]many were gathered together, insomuch that there was no room to receive *them,* no, not so much as about the door: and [d]he [e]preached the word unto them.

3 And they come unto him, [f]bringing one sick of the *palsy, which was borne of four.

4 And when they could not come nigh unto him for the press, they uncovered the [g]roof where he was: and when they had broken *it* up, they let down the bed wherein the sick of the *palsy lay.

5 When [h]Jē′ṣus saw their [i]faith, he said unto the sick of the *palsy, Son, [j]thy sins [1]be [k]forgiven thee.

6 But there were certain of the [l]scribes sitting there, and reasoning in their hearts,

7 [m]Why doth this *man* thus speak [n]blasphemies? [m]who can forgive sins but God only?

8 And immediately when [o]Jē′ṣus perceived in his spirit that they so reasoned within themselves, he said unto them, Why reason ye these things in your hearts?

9 Whether is it easier to say to the sick of the *palsy, *Thy* sins be forgiven thee; or to say, Arise, and take up thy bed, and walk?

10 But [p]that ye may know that the [h,q]Son of man hath power on earth to forgive sins, (he saith to the sick of the *palsy,)

11 I say unto thee, Arise, and take up thy bed, and go thy way into thine house.

12 And immediately he [i,r]arose, took up the bed, and went forth before them all; insomuch that they were all amazed, and glorified God, saying, We never saw it on this fashion.

13 ¶ And [a]he went forth again by the [s]sea side; and all the multitude resorted unto him, and he [t,u]taught them.

14 And as he passed by, he saw [v,w]Lē′vī the *son* of Ăl-phæ′us sitting at the receipt of [2,x]custom, and said unto him, [y,z,a]Follow me. And he [b]arose and followed him.

15 [c]And it came to pass, that, as Jē′ṣus [d]sat at meat in his house, many [e]publicans and sinners sat also together with Jē′ṣus and his [f]disciples: [g]for there were many, and they followed him.

16 And when the [h]scribes [3]and [i]Phăr′ĭ-seeṣ saw him eat with [e]publicans and sinners, they said unto his [f]disciples, [j,k]How is it that he eateth and drinketh with publicans and sinners?

17 When Jē′ṣus heard *it,* he saith unto them, They that are whole have no need of the [l]physician, but they that are [m]sick: [n]I came not to call the [k,o]right-

**10**
*p Miracles, design of,* Luke 23:8.
*q Jesus, humanity of,* Matt. 1:21.

**12**
*r Miracles, of Jesus,* Luke 23:8.

**13**
*s Sea of Galilee,* Matt. 4:18.
*t Jesus, teacher,* Matt. 1:21.
*u Instruction, in religion,* Prov. 23:23.

**14**
*v* Or, *Matthew,* Matt. 9:9.
*w Publicans,* Matt. 11:19.
*x Tax,* Neh. 10:32.
*y Apostles, selection of,* Luke 6:13.
*z Minister, call of,* Rom. 15:16.

*a Call, to special religious duty,* Phil. 3:14.
*b Obedience, instances of,* Heb. 5:8.
2 R. V. toll,

**15**
*c* Matt. 9:10–13; Luke 5:29–32.
*d Hospitality,* Rom. 12:13.
*e Publicans,* Matt. 11:19.
*f Disciples,* Matt. 9:14.
*g Popularity of Jesus,* John 6:15.

**16**
*h Scribe,* 1 Kin. 4:3.
*i Pharisees,* Matt. 15:12.
*j Bigotry, instances of,* Isa. 65:5.
*k Self-righteousness,* Luke 18:11.
3 R. V. of the

**17**
*l Physician, proverbs about,* 2 Chr. 16:12.
*m Sick,* Matt. 25:36.
*n Jesus, mission of,* Matt. 1:21.
*o Irony, instances of,* Mark 12:14.

* **PARALYSIS.** *Cured, by Jesus,* Matt. 4:24; 8:6, 13; 9:2, 6; Mark 2:3–12; Luke 5:18–25; *by Philip,* Acts 8:7; *by Peter,* Acts 9:33, 34.

eous, but [p]sinners [4]to [q]repent-
ance.
18 ¶ And the [r]disciples of [r]Jŏhn
and of the [i]Phăr′ĭ-seeş used to
[s]fast: and they come and say unto him, Why do the disciples of
Jŏhn and of the Phăr′ĭ-seeş fast,
but thy disciples fast not?
19 And Jē′şus said unto them,
Can the children of the bride-
chamber fast, while the [t]bride-
groom is with them? as long as
they have the bridegroom with
them, they cannot fast.
20 [u]But the days will come,
when the [t]bridegroom shall be
taken away from them, and then
shall they fast in those days.
21 [v]No man also seweth a piece
of [5]new[G] cloth on an old [w]gar-
ment: else the new piece that
filled it up taketh away from the
old, and the rent[G] is made worse.
22 [x]And no man putteth new[G]
[y]wine into old [6,z]bottles[G]: else the
new wine doth burst the bottles[G],
and the wine is spilled, and the
bottles[G] will be marred[G]: but new
wine must be put into new bottles[G].
23 ¶ [a]And it came to pass, that
he went through the [b]corn[G] fields
on the [c]sabbath day; and his
[d]disciples began, as they went,
to pluck the ears of corn.[Q]
24 And the [e]Phăr′ĭ-seeş said unto him, Behold, why do they on
the [c]sabbath day that which is
not lawful?
25 And [f]he said unto them,
Have ye never read what [g]Dā′vid
did, when he had need, and was
an[G] [h]hungred, he, and they that
were with him?
26 How he went into the [i]house
of God in the days of [j]Ā-bī′a-
thär the [k]high priest, and did eat
the [l]shewbread[G], which is not
lawful to eat but for the priests,
and gave also to them which
were with him?[Q]
27 And [f]he said unto them, The
[c]sabbath was made for man, and
not man for the sabbath:[Q]
28 Therefore the [m,n]Son of man
is [7,o]Lord also of the sabbath.

## CHAPTER 3

*Jesus heals a withered hand. 7 Great multitudes follow him, of whom he heals many. 13 He chooses the twelve apostles. 22 Blasphemy against the Holy Ghost. 31 His true disciples are his nearest relatives.*

[a]AND[S] he entered again into
the [b]synagogue; and there
was a man there which had a
withered hand.
2 And [c]they watched him,
whether he would heal him
on the [d]sabbath day; that they
might accuse him.
3 And he saith unto the man
which had the withered hand,
Stand forth.
4 And he saith unto them, Is it
lawful to do good on the [d]sab-
bath days, or to do evil? to save
life, or to kill? But they held
their peace.
5 And when he had looked
round about on them with [e]an-
ger, being grieved for the [f,g]hard-
ness of their hearts, [h]he saith
unto the man, Stretch forth
thine hand. [h]And he stretched *it*
out: and his hand was [i]restored
whole[G] as the other.[S]
6 And the [j]Phăr′ĭ-seeş went
forth, and straightway[G] [k]took
counsel[G] with the *Hē-rō′dĭ-anş[G]
against him, [l]how they might
destroy him.
7 ¶ [m]But Jē′şus [n]withdrew himself with his [o]disciples to the
[p]sea: and [q]a great multitude
from [r]Găl′ĭ-lee followed [s]him,
and from [t]Jū-dæ′ă,
8 And from [u]Jē-ru′să-lĕm, and
from [v]Ī-du-mæ′ă, and *from* beyond [w]Jôr′dan; and they about
[x]Tȳre and [y]Sī′dŏn, a great multitude, when they had heard

p *Wicked,* Psa. 73:3.
q *Repentance,* Mark 1:4.
4 R. V. *omits* to repentance.

18
r *John the Baptist,* Luke 1:63.
s *Fasting, habitual,* Zech. 8:19.

19
t *Bridegroom,* Isa. 61:10.

20
u *Jesus, prophet,* Matt. 1:21.

21
v Matt. 9:16; Luke 5:36.
w *Dress,* Zech. 3:3.
5 R. V. undressed

22
x Matt. 9:17; Luke 5:37–39.
y *Wine,* Prov. 23:31.
z *Bottle,* Gen. 21:14.
6 R. V. wine-skins: else the wine will burst the skins, and the wine perisheth, and the skins: but they put new wine into fresh wine-skins.

23
a Matt. 12:1–8; Luke 6:1–5.
b *Corn,* Psa. 65:13.
c *Sabbath,* Ex. 16:23.
d *Disciples,* Matt. 9:14.

24
e *Pharisees,* Matt. 15:12.

25
f *Jesus, life of, defines law of Sabbath,* Matt. 1:21.
g *David,* 1 Sam. 16:13.
h *Hunger,* Neh. 9:15.

26
i *Tabernacle,* Ex. 27:9.
j Or, *Abimelech,* Judg. 8:13.
k *High Priest,* Lev. 21:10.
l *Shewbread,* Ex. 35:13.

28
m *Jesus, humanity of,* Matt. 1:21.
n *Jesus, names of,* Matt. 1:21.
o *Jesus, king,* Matt. 1:21.
7 R. V. lord

1
a *Capernaum,* Luke 4:31.
b *Synagogue,* Mark 12:9.

2
c *Malice,* Eph. 4:31.
d *Sabbath,* Ex. 16:23.

5
e *Anger,* Psa. 37:8.
f *Spiritual Blindness,* 2 Cor. 4:4.
g *Impenitence, instances of,* Rom. 2:5.
h Matt. 12:9–14; Luke 6:6–11.
i *Jesus, miracles of,* Matt. 1:21.

6
j *Pharisees, persecute Jesus,* Matt. 15:12.
k *Conspiracy, instances of,* 1 Kin. 16:9.
l *Persecution, of Jesus,* John 15:20.

7
m Matt. 12:15.
n *Prudence, instances of,* 2 Chr. 2:12.
o *Disciples,* Matt. 9:14.
p *Sea of Galilee,* Matt. 4:18.
q *Popularity of Jesus,* John 6:15.
r *Galilee,* Mark 6:21.
s *Jesus, received,* Matt. 1:21.
t *Judea,* Luke 5:17.

8
u *Jerusalem,* Judg. 19:10.
v Or, *Edom,* Obad. 1.
w *Jordan,* Gen. 32:10.
x *Tyre,* Josh. 19:29.
y Or, *Zidon,* Ezek. 28:21.

* **HERODIANS,** a political faction among the Jews. *Seek to entangle Jesus,* Matt. 22:16; Mark 12:13. *Conspire to slay Jesus,* Matt. 12:14; Mark 3:6.

what great things he did, came
unto him.
9 And he spake to his [o]disciples,
that a [1]small [z]ship should wait
on him because of the multitude,
lest they should throng him.
10 For he had [a]healed many;
insomuch that they [b]pressed
upon him for to touch him, as
many as had [c]plagues.
11 And [d]unclean spirits, when
they saw him, fell down before
him, and cried, saying, Thou art
the [e]Son of God.
12 And he straitly [f]charged
them that they should not make
him known.
13 ¶ And he goeth up into a
mountain, and [g]calleth *unto him*
whom he would: and they came
unto him.
14 And he [h]ordained [i]twelve,
that they should be with him,
and that he might send them
forth to [j]preach,
15 And to [k]have [2]power to
[l,m]heal [c]sicknesses, and to cast
out [n]devils:
16 [o]And Sī′mon he surnamed
[p]Pē′tēr;
17 And [q]Jāmeș the *son* of [r]Zĕb′-
e-dee, and [s]Jŏhn the brother of
Jāmeș; and he surnamed them
Bō-a-nēr′ġēș, which is, The sons
of [t]thunder:
18 And [u]Ăn′drew, and [v]Phĭl′-
ĭp, and [w]Bär-thŏl′o-mew, and
[x]Măt′thew, and [y]Thŏm′as, and
[z]Jāmeș the *son* of [a]Ăl-phæ′us,
and [b]Thăd-dæ′us, and [†]Sī′mon
the [3]Că′năan-īte,
19 And [‡]Jū′das Ĭs-căr′ĭ-ot,
which also [c]betrayed him: and
they went into an house.
20 ¶ And [d,e]the multitude cometh together again, so that
they could not so much as eat
bread.
21 And when his friends heard
*of it*, they went out to lay hold on
him: for they said, He is [f]beside
himself.
22 ¶ And the [g]scribes which
came down from [h]Jė-ru̇′să-lĕm
[i,j,k,l]said, He hath [m]Bė-ĕl′ze-
bŭb, and by the prince of the
[n]devils casteth he out devils.
23 [o]And he called them *unto*
*him*, and [p]said unto them in
[q]parables, How can [r]Sā′tan cast
out Sā′tan?
24 And if a kingdom be [s]di-
vided against itself, that kingdom cannot stand.
25 And if a house be [s]divided
against itself, that house cannot
stand.
26 And if [r]Sā′tan rise up against
himself, and be divided, he cannot stand, but hath an end.
27 No man can enter into a
strong man's house, and spoil
his goods, except he will first
bind the strong man; and then
he will spoil his house.
28 Verily I say unto you, All
sins shall be [t]forgiven unto the
sons of men, and blasphemies
wherewith soever they shall
blaspheme:
29 But [u]he that shall [v,w]blas-
pheme against the [x]Holy Ghost
hath never forgiveness, but is [4]in
danger of eternal [y]damnation:
30 Because they [i,j,k,l]said, He
hath an [n]unclean spirit.
31 ¶ [z]There came then his
[a]brethren and his [b]mother, and,

**9** *z Ship*, 2 Chr. 8:18. 1 R. V. little boat

**10** *a Healing, by Jesus*, Acts 4:22. *b Faith in Christ, exemplified*, John 6:69. *c Disease, healing of*, Ex. 15:26.

**11** *d Demons, testify to the divinity of Jesus*, Matt. 4:24. *e Jesus, divine sonship of*, Matt. 1:21.

**12** *f Prudence, instances of*, 2 Chr. 2:12.

**13** *g Call, personal*, Phil. 3:14.

**14** *h Ordination, of apostles*, Ex. 29:1. *i Apostles, commission of*, Luke 6:13. *Preaching*, Matt. 9:35.

**15** *k Apostles, miraculous power given to*, Luke 6:13. *l Healing*, Acts 4:22. *m Miracles, power to work, given the disciples*, Luke 23:8. *n Demons*, Matt. 4:24. 2 R. V. authority to cast out devils:

**16** *o Apostles, names of*, Luke 6:13. *p Peter*, Mark 5:37.

**17** *q James, son of Zebedee*, Luke 5:10. *r Zebedee*, Mark 4:21. *s John*, Mark 1:19. *t Thunder, sons of Zebedee called sons of*, 1 Sam. 7:10.

**18** *u Andrew*, Matt. 4:18. *v Philip*, Luke 6:14. *w* Matt. 10:3; Luke 6:14; Acts 1:13. *x Matthew*, Matt. 9:9. *y Thomas*, John 11:16. *z James, son of Alpheus*, Matt. 10:3.—*a* Matt. 10:3. *b* Matt. 10:3. 3 R. V. Cananæan,

**19** *c Betrayal, of Jesus*, Matt. 26:46.

**20** *d Jesus, received*, Matt. 1:21. *e Popularity of Jesus*, John 6:15.

**21** *f Insanity, Jesus accused of*, Prov. 26:18.

**22** *g Scribe*, 1 Kin. 4:3. *h Jerusalem*, Judg. 19:10. *i False Accusation, instances of*, 2 Tim. 3:3. *j Infidelity, exemplified*, 2 Cor. 6:15. *k Scoffing*, Hab. 1:10. *l Persecution, of Jesus*, John 15:20. *m Beelzebub, the prince of devils*, Matt. 10:25. *n Demons*, Matt. 4:24.

**23** *o* Matt. 12:25–29; Luke 11:17–26. *p Instruction*, Prov. 23:23. *q Parables, of Jesus*, Ezek. 20:49. *r Satan*, Matt. 4:10.

**24** *s Strife*, Prov. 20:3.

**28** *t Sin, forgiveness of*, Rom. 5:12.

**29** *u Reprobates*, 1 Cor. 9:27. *v Blasphemy, against the Holy Spirit*, 2 Sam. 12:14. *w Sin, unpardonable*, Rom. 5:12. *x Holy Spirit, sin against*, Acts 1:2. *y Punishment, eternal*, Lev. 26:41.

**31** *z* Matt. 12:46–50; Luke 8:19–21. *a Brothers of Jesus*, Matt. 13:55. *b Mary*, Luke 1:27.

† **SIMON,** one of the twelve apostles. *Called*, THE CANAANITE, Matt. 10:4; Mark 3:18; ZELOTES, Luke 6:15; Acts 1:13.

‡ **JUDAS**, surnamed Iscariot. *Chosen as an apostle*, Matt. 10:4; Mark 3:19; Luke 6:16; Acts 1:17. *Treasurer of the disciples*, John 12:6; 13:29. *His covetousness exemplified, by his protest against the breaking of the box of ointment*, John 12:4–6; *by his bargain to betray Jesus for a sum of money*, Matt. 26:14–16; Mark 14:10, 11; Luke 22:3–6; John 13:2. *Jesus accuses him of infidelity*, Matt. 26:21–25; Mark 14:18–21; Luke 22:21–23; John 13:10, 11, 18–30. *His apostasy*, John 17:12. *Betrays the Lord*, Matt. 26:47–50; Mark 14:43–45; Luke 22:47–49; John 18:2–5; Acts 1:16. *Returns the money to the rulers of the Jews*, Matt. 27:3–10. *Hangs himself*, Matt. 27:5; Acts 1:18.

*Prophecies concerning*, Matt. 26:21–25; Mark 14:18–21; Luke 22:21–23; John 13:18–26; 17:12; Acts 1:16, 20 (with Psa. 41:9; Zech. 11:12, 13).

standing without,[c] sent unto him,
calling him.
32 And the multitude sat about
him, and they said unto him,
Behold, thy [b]mother and thy
[a]brethren without seek for
thee.
33 And he answered them, saying, Who is my mother, or my
brethren?
34 And he looked round about
on them which sat about him,
and [c]said, Behold my mother
and my brethren![G]
35 For [d]whosoever shall [e]do
the ‖will of God, the same is
my brother, and my sister, and
mother.

## CHAPTER 4

*The parable of the sower, 14 and its exposition. 21 A candle not to be put under a bushel. 26 The parable of the seed growing, 30 and of the mustard seed. 35 Jesus stills a storm on the sea.*

AND[T] he began again to
[a,b]teach by the [c]sea side:
and [d]there was gathered unto
him a great multitude, so that he
entered into a ship, and sat in
the sea; and the whole multitude
was by the sea on the land.
2 And he [a,b]taught them many
things by [e]parables, and said
unto them in his [1]doctrine,[G]
3 Hearken;[G] Behold, there went
out a [f,g]sower to [h]sow:
4 And it came to pass, as he
[h]sowed, some fell by the way
side, [i]and the fowls of the air
came and devoured it up.
5 And some fell on stony
ground, where it had not much
earth; and immediately it sprang
up, because it had [j,k]no depth of
earth:
6 But when the sun was up, it
was scorched; and because it had
[j,k]no root, it [i]withered away.
7 And some fell among [l]thorns,
and the thorns grew up, and
choked it, and it [i]yielded no
fruit.[G]
8 And other fell on good
ground, and did [m]yield fruit that
sprang up and increased; and
[m]brought forth, some thirty, and
some sixty, and some an hundred.
9 And he said unto them, [n]He
that hath ears to hear, let him
[o]hear.
10 ¶ And when he was alone,
they that were about him with
the [p]twelve asked of him the
parable.
11 And he said unto them, Unto [p,q]you it is given to [r]know
the *mystery[G] of the [s]kingdom of
God: but unto them that are
without,[G] all *these* things are done
in parables:[s]
12 That seeing they may see,
and [u,v]not perceive; and hearing they may hear, and not [u,v]un-
derstand; lest at any time
they should [2]be converted,[G] and
*their* sins should be [w]forgiven
them.[Q]
13 And he said unto [x]them,
Know[G] ye not this parable? and
how then will ye know all parables?
14 ¶ The sower soweth the
[y,z,a]word.
15 And these are they by the
way side, where the [a,b,c]word is
sown; but when they have heard,
[d,e]Sā'tan cometh immediately,
and taketh away the word that
was sown in their hearts.
16 And these are they likewise
which are sown on stony ground;
who, when they have heard the
[a,b,c]word, immediately receive it
with gladness;
17 And have no root in themselves, and so endure [f,g]but for
a time: afterward, when [h]afflic-
tion or [h,i]persecution ariseth for

**34**
c *Jesus, love of,* Matt. 1:21.

**35**
d *Righteous, promises to,* Psa. 64:10.
e *Obedience, rewarded,* Heb. 5:8.

**1**
a *Jesus, teacher,* Matt. 1:21.
b *Instruction, in religion,* Prov. 23:23.
c *Sea of Galilee,* Matt. 4:18.
d *Jesus, received,* Matt. 1:21.

**2**
e *Parables,* Ezek. 20:49.
1 R. V. teaching,

**3**
f *Sower, parable of the,* vs. 3–20; Matt. 13:3.
g *Minister, likened to sower,* Rom. 15:16.
h *Agriculture, figurative,* Gen. 3:23.

**4**
i *Unfruitfulness,* Matt. 7:19.

**5**
j *Character, instability of,* Phil. 2:15.
k *Instability,* Jas. 1:8.

**7**
l *Thorn, figurative,* Hos. 2:6.

**8**
m *Righteousness,* Psa. 15:2.

**9**
n *Commandment, enjoining heed to the truth,* Deut. 8:2.
o *Spiritual Understanding,* Luke 8:8.

**10**
p *Apostles,* Luke 6:13.

**11**
q *Righteous, promises to,* Psa. 64:10.
r *Wisdom, spiritual,* Prov. 2:2.
s *Kingdom of Heaven.* Matt. 13:24.

**12**
t Isa. 6:9, 10; Matt. 13:14, 15; Acts 28:25–27.
u *Moral Insensibility,* Luke 8:10.
v *Spiritual Blindness,* 2 Cor. 4:4.
w *Sin, forgiveness of,* Rom. 5:12.
2 R. V. turn again,

**13**
x *Apostles, fail to comprehend the nature of Jesus' kingdom,* Luke 6:13.

**14**
y *Word of God,* Psa. 119:9.
z *Truth,* John 18:37.

a *Doctrines of Jesus,* vs. 14–20; John 7:16.

**15**
b *Word of God,* Psa. 119:9.
c *Truth,* John 18:37.
d *Satan,* Matt. 4:10.
e *Temptation, sources of,* Luke 11:4.

**17**
f *Character, instability of,* Phil. 2:15.
g *Instability,* Jas. 1:8.
h *Backsliding, temptations to,* Hos. 11:7.
i *Persecution, of the righteous,* John 15:20.

‖ **WILL OF GOD.** *The supreme rule of duty,* Matt. 6:10; 12:50 (with Mark 3:35); 26:39, 42; Mark 14:36; Luke 22:42; John 4:34; 5:30; 6:38–40; Rom. 12:2; Eph. 5:17. *Plans of the righteous subject to,* Acts 18:21; Rom. 1:10; 15:32; 1 Cor. 4:19; 16:7; Heb. 6:3; Jas. 4:15.

* **MYSTERIES,** Deut. 29:29. *Of redemption,* Matt. 11:25; 13:11, 35; Mark 4:11; Luke 8:10; Rom. 16:25, 26; 1 Cor. 2:7–10; 2 Cor. 3:12–18; Eph. 1:9, 10; 3:3–5, 9, 18, 19; 6:19; Col. 1:25–27; 2:2; 4:3, 4; 1 Tim. 3:9, 16; 1 Pet. 1:10–12; Rev. 10:7. *Of regeneration,* John 3:8–12.

the [b,c]word's sake, immediately
[j]they [3]are offended.
18 And these are they which
are sown among [k]thorns; such
as hear the [a,b,c]word,
19 And the [h,l,m]cares of this
world,[G] and [n]the deceitfulness
of [h,o]riches, and the [p]lusts of
other things entering in, choke
the word, and it becometh [q]un-
fruitful.
20 And [r]these are they which
are sown on good ground; such
as hear the [a,b,c]word, and [s]re-
ceive *it*, and bring forth [t]fruit,
some thirtyfold, some sixty, and
some an hundred.
21 ¶ And he [u]said unto them,
Is a [v,w,x]candle[G] brought to be
put under a bushel, or under
a bed? and not to be set on a
candlestick[G]?
22 [y]For there is nothing [z]hid,
which shall not be manifested;
neither was any thing kept
secret, but that it should come
[4]abroad.
23 If any man have ears to
hear, let him [a]hear.
24 And he said unto them,
Take heed what ye hear: [b,c]with
what measure ye mete,[G] it shall
be measured to you: and [5,d]un-
to you that hear shall more be
given.
25 For [c,d]he that [e]hath, to him
shall be given: and he that hath
not, from him shall be taken even
that which he hath.
26 ¶ [S][T]And he [f]said, So is
the [g,h]kingdom of God, as if a
man should cast seed into the
ground;
27 And should sleep, and rise
night and day, and the seed
should spring and grow up, he
knoweth not how.
28 For [i]the earth bringeth forth
fruit of herself; first the blade,
then the ear, after that the full
[j]corn[G] in the ear.
29 But when the fruit is
brought forth, immediately he
putteth in the [k]sickle, because
the harvest is come.[Q]
30 ¶ And he [f]said, Whereunto
shall we liken the [g,h]kingdom of
God? or with what [6]comparison
shall we compare it?[T]
31 [g,h]*It is* like a grain of [l]mus-
tard seed, which, when it is sown
in the earth, is less than all the
seeds that be in the earth:
32 But when it is sown, it groweth up, and becometh greater
than all herbs, and shooteth out
great branches; so that the fowls
of the air may lodge under the
shadow of it.[S][Q]
33 And with many such [f]par-
ables [m]spake he the word unto
them, as they were able to hear *it*.
34 But without a [f]parable
[m]spake he not unto them: and
when they were alone, he expounded all things to his [n]dis-
ciples.
35 ¶ [S]And the same day, when
the even[G] was come, he saith unto
them, Let us pass over unto the
other side.
36 And when they had sent
away the multitude, they took
him even as he was in the
[7,o]ship. And there were also
with him other little [8]ships.
37 [p]And there arose a great
storm of [q]wind, and the waves
beat into the ship, so that it was
now full.
38 And he was in the hinder
part of the ship, [r]asleep on a pillow: and they awake him, and
say unto him, Master,[G] [s,t]carest
thou not that we perish?
39 [T]And he arose, and rebuked[G]
the wind, and said unto the sea,
Peace, be still. And the [q]wind
[u,v]ceased, and there was a great
calm.
40 And he said unto them,
[w]Why are ye so [s,t]fearful? [9]how
is it that ye have no [x]faith?
41 And they feared exceedingly,

j *Backsliders*, Jer. 3:22.
3 R. V. stumble.

**18**
k *Thorn, figurative*, Hos. 2:6.

**19**
l *Anxiety*, 1 Pet. 5:7.
m *Worldliness*, 1 John 2:15.
n *Covetousness, warnings against*, Isa. 57:17.
o *Riches, a snare*, Eccl. 4:8.
p *Lust, chokes the word*, 2 Pet. 1:4.
q *Unfruitfulness*, Matt. 7:19.

**20**
r *Righteous, described*, Psa. 64:10.
s *Obedience, exemplified*, Heb. 5:8.
t *Righteousness*, Psa. 15:2.

**21**
u Matt. 5:15; Luke 8:16; 11:33.
v *Lamp*, Ex. 27:20.
w *Influence, good*, 1 Cor. 7:14.
x *Religious Testimony*, 2 Thess. 1:10.

**22**
y Matt. 10:26; Luke 8:17; 12:2.
z *Sin, known to God*, Rom. 5:12.
4 R. V. to light.

**23**
a *Spiritual Understanding*, Luke 8:8.

**24**
b Matt. 7:2; Luke 6:38.
c *Proverbs*, 1 Sam. 24:13.
d *Righteous, promises to*, Psa. 64:10.
5 R. V. more shall be given unto you.

**25**
e *Righteousness*, Psa. 15:2.

**26**
f *Parables, of Jesus*, Ezek. 20:49.
g *Jesus, kingdom of*, Matt. 1:21.
h *Church, prophecies concerning its prosperity*, Matt. 16:18.

**28**
i *Nature*, Jas. 3:12.
j *Corn*, Psa. 65:13.

**29**
k *Sickle*, Deut. 23:25.

**30**
6 R. V. parable shall we set it forth.

**31**
l *Mustard Seed*, Matt. 13:31.

**33**
m *Jesus, teacher*, Matt. 1:21.

**34**
n *Apostles*, Luke 6:13.

**36**
o *Ship*, 2 Chr. 8:18
7 R. V. boat.
8 R. V. boats

**37**
p *Sea of Galilee*, Matt. 4:18.
q *Wind*, Job 37:17

**38**
r *Sleep*, Psa. 127:2
s *Doubting*, Rom. 14:23.
t *Borrowing Trouble*, Matt. 6:25.

**39**
u *Jesus, miracles of*, Matt. 1:21.
v *Tempest, stilled*, Matt. 8:26.

**40**
w *Unbelievers*, 1 Cor. 6:6.
x *Faith, trial of*, vs. 38–40; Mark 11:22.
9 R. V. have ye not yet faith?

and said one to another, What manner of man is this, that even the wind and the sea obey him?

## CHAPTER 5

*Jesus casts out the legion of devils, 11 which enter into a herd of swine. 22 Jairus entreats him. 25 He heals the woman of an issue of blood; 35 and raises the daughter of Jairus.*

AND [a]they came over unto the other side of the [b]sea, into the country of the [1]Găd′a-rēneș.

2 And when he was come out of the [2,c]ship, immediately there met him out of the [d]tombs a man with an [e]unclean spirit,

3 Who had *his* dwelling among the [d]tombs; and no man could bind him, no, not with [f]chains:

4 Because that he had been often bound with *fetters and [f]chains, and the chains had been plucked asunder by him, and the fetters broken in pieces: [3]neither could any *man* tame him.

5 And always, [g]night and [h]day, he was in the mountains, and in the [d]tombs, crying, and cutting himself with stones.

6 But when he saw Jē′șus afar off, he ran and [i]worshipped him,

7 And cried with a loud voice, and [j]said, What have I to do with thee, Jē′șus, *thou* [k]Son of the most high God? I adjure thee by God, that thou torment me not.

8 For he said unto him, Come out of the man, *thou* unclean spirit.

9 And he asked [e]him, What *is* thy name? And he answered, saying, My name *is* Legion: for we are many.

10 And [e]he besought him much that he would not send them away out of the country.

11 Now there was there nigh unto the mountains a great herd of [l]swine feeding.

12 And all the [e]devils besought him, saying, Send us into the

1
a Matt. 8:28–34; Luke 8:26–39.
b *Sea of Galilee*, Matt. 4:18.
1 R. V. Gerasenes.
2
c *Ship*, 2 Chr. 8:18.
d *Burying Places*, Gen. 23:4.
e *Demons*, Matt. 4:24.
2 R. V. boat,
3
f *Chains*, Dan. 5:7.
4
3 R. V. and no man had strength to tame him.
5
g *Night*, Gen. 1:5.
h *Day*, Gen. 1:5.
6
i *Jesus, worship of*, Matt. 1:21.
7
j *Demons, testify to the divinity of Jesus*, Matt. 4:24.
k *Jesus, divine sonship of*, Matt. 1:21.
11
l *Swine*, Lev. 11:7.

[l]swine, that we may enter into them.

13 And forthwith [m]Jē′șus gave them leave. And the unclean spirits went out, and entered into the swine: and the herd ran violently down a steep place into the [b]sea, (they were about two thousand;) and were choked in the sea.

14 And they that fed the [l]swine fled, and told *it* in the city, and in the country. And they went out to see what it was that was done.

15 And they come to Jē′șus, and see him that was possessed with the [e]devil, and had the legion, sitting, and clothed, and in his right mind: and they were afraid.

16 And they that saw *it* told them how it befell to him that was possessed with the devil, and *also* concerning the [l]swine.

17 And they began to pray [n]him to depart out of their coasts.

18 And when he was come into the [c]ship, he that had been possessed with the devil [o]prayed him that he might be with him.

19 Howbeit Jē′șus suffered him not, but saith unto him, [p]Go home to thy friends, and [q]tell them how great things the Lord hath done for thee, and hath had [r]compassion on thee.

20 And he departed, and [s,t]began to publish in [u]Dē-căp′o-lĭs how great things Jē′șus had done for him: and all *men* did marvel.

21 ¶ And when Jē′șus was passed over again by [2]ship unto the other side, [v]much people gathered unto him: and he was nigh unto the [b]sea.

22 And, behold, there [w]cometh one of the rulers of the [x]synagogue, [y,z]Jā-ī′rus by name; and

13
m *Jesus, miracles of*, Matt. 1:21.
17
n *Jesus, rejected*, Matt. 1:21.
18
o *Love, of man for Jesus*, 1 John 4:19.
19
p *Commandment, enjoining witnessing for Christ*, Deut. 8:2.
q *Religious Testimony*, 2 Thess. 1:10.
r *Jesus, compassion of*, Matt. 1:21.
20
s *Zeal, exemplified*, 2 Cor. 7:11.
t *Thankfulness, to God*, Acts 24:3.
u Matt. 4:25; Mark 7:31.
21
v *Popularity of Jesus*, John 6:15.
22
w *Faith in Christ, exemplified*, John 6:69.
x *Synagogue*, Matt. 12:9.
y Matt. 9:18–26; Luke 8:41–56.
z *Parents, affection of, exemplified*, 2 Cor. 12:14.

***FETTERS.** *Used for securing prisoners*, 2 Chr. 33:11; 36:6; Mark 5:4. *Made of brass*, Judg. 16:21; 2 Kin. 25:7.

when he saw him, he [a,b]fell at his feet,

23 And [c]besought him greatly, saying, [d]My little [e]daughter lieth [f]at the point of [g]death: *I pray thee,* [h]come and lay thy [i]hands on her, that she may be healed; and she shall live.

24 And [j]*Jē′s̱us* went with him; and much people followed him, and thronged him.

25 ¶ And a certain woman, which had an [1,k]issue of blood twelve years,

26 And had [l]suffered many things of many [m]physicians, and had spent all that she had, and was nothing bettered, but rather grew worse,

27 When she had heard of Jē′s̱us, [h]came in the press behind, and touched his garment.

28 For she said, [h]If I may touch but his clothes, I shall be whole.

29 And straightway the fountain of her blood [n]was dried up; and she felt in *her* body that she was [o]healed of that [k]plague.

30 And [p]Jē′s̱us, immediately knowing in himself that [4]virtue had gone out of him, turned him about in the press, and said, Who touched my clothes?

31 And his [q]disciples said unto him, Thou seest the multitude thronging thee, and sayest thou, Who touched me?

32 And he looked round about to see her that had done this thing.

33 But the woman fearing and trembling, knowing what was done in her, [r]came and fell down before him, and told him all the truth.

34 And [j]he said unto her, Daughter, thy [h]faith hath made thee whole; go in [s]peace, and be [o]whole of thy [k]plague.

35 ¶ While he yet spake, there came from the ruler of the [t]synagogue's *house certain* which said, Thy [e]daughter is [g]dead: why troublest thou the [u]Master any further?

36 As soon as Jē′s̱us heard the word that was spoken, he saith unto the ruler of the [t]synagogue, [v,w]Be not afraid, only [x]believe.

37 And he suffered no man to follow him, save [†]Pē′tẽr, and [y]Jāmes̱, and [z]Jŏhn the brother of Jāmes̱.

38 And he cometh to the house of the ruler of the synagogue, and seeth the tumult, and them that [a]wept and wailed greatly.

39 And when he was come in, he saith unto them, Why make ye

a *Humility,* Prov. 22:4.
b *Salutations,* Luke 1:44.

23
c *Mediation,* Gal. 3:19.
d *Parents, affection of, exemplified,* 2 Cor. 12:14.
e *Children,* Mark 10:14.
f *Disease,* Ex. 15:26.
g *Death,* Num. 23:10.
h *Faith in Christ, exemplified,* John 6:69.
i *Hand, imposition of,* Ezra 10:19.

24
j *Jesus, compassion of,* Matt. 1:21.

25
k *Hemorrhage,* Matt. 9:20.

26
l *Afflictions,* Psa. 34:19.
m *Physician,* 2 Chr. 16:12.

29
n *Miracles, of Jesus,* Luke 23:8.
o *Healing,* Acts 4:22.

30
p *Jesus, omniscience of,* Matt. 1:21.
4 R. V. the power proceeding from him had gone forth,

31
q *Apostles,* Luke 6:13.

33
r *Thankfulness,* Acts 24:3.

34
s *Spiritual Peace,* Gal. 1:3.

35
t *Synagogue,* Matt. 12:9.
u *Jesus, names of,* Matt. 1:21.

36
v *Commandment, forbidding fear and enjoining faith,* Deut. 8:2.
w *Afflictions, consolation in,* Psa. 34:19.
x *Faith, enjoined,* Mark 11:22.

37
y *James,* Luke 5:10.
z *John,* Mark 1:19.

38
a *Mourning,* Lam. 2:5.

† **PETER** *(a rock). Called also* SIMON BAR-JONA *and* CEPHAS, Matt. 16:16–19; Mark 3:16; John 1:42; *and* SIMEON (R. V. Symeon), Acts 15:14. *A fisherman,* Matt. 4:18; Luke 5:1–7; John 21:3. *Call of,* Matt. 4:18–20; Mark 1:16–18; Luke 5:1–11. *An apostle,* Matt. 10:2; 16:18, 19; Mark 3:16; Luke 6:14; Acts 1:13.

*His wife's mother healed,* Matt. 8:14, 15; Mark 1:29, 30; Luke 4:38, 39. *Confesses Jesus as Christ,* Matt. 16:16–19; Mark 8:29; Luke 9:20; John 6:68, 69. *His presumption in rebuking Jesus,* Matt. 16:22, 23; Mark 8:32, 33; *when the throng was pressing Jesus and the woman of infirmity touched him,* Luke 8:45; *when Jesus foretold his persecution and death,* Matt. 16:21–23; Mark 8:31–33; *in refusing to let Jesus wash his feet,* John 13:6–11.

*Present at the healing of Jairus' daughter,* Mark 5:37; Luke 8:51; *at the transfiguration,* Matt. 17:1–4; Mark 9:2–6; Luke 9:28–33; 2 Pet. 1:16–18; *in Gethsemane,* Matt. 26:36–46; Mark 14:33–42; Luke 22:40–46.

*Seeks the interpretation, of the parable of the steward,* Luke 12:41; *of the law of forgiveness,* Matt. 18:21; *of the law of defilement,* Matt. 15:15; *of the prophecy of Jesus concerning his second coming,* Mark 13:3, 4.

*Walks upon the water of the Sea of Galilee,* Matt. 14:28–31. *Sent with John to prepare the Passover,* Matt. 26:18, 19; Mark 14:13–16; Luke 22:8–13. *Calls attention to the withered fig tree,* Mark 11:21.

*His perfidy foretold by Jesus; and his profession of fidelity,* Matt. 26:33–35; Mark 14:29–31; Luke 22:31–34; John 13:36–38. *Cuts off the ear of Malchus,* Matt. 26:51; Mark 14:47; Luke 22:50. *Follows Jesus to the high priest's palace,* Matt. 26:58; Mark 14:54; Luke 22:54; John 18:15. *His denial of Jesus, and his repentance,* Matt. 26:69–75; Mark 14:66–72; Luke 22:55–62; John 18:17, 18, 25–27. *Visits the sepulchre,* Luke 24:12; John 20:2–6. *Jesus sends message to, after the resurrection,* Mark 16:7. *Jesus appears to,* Luke 24:34; 1 Cor. 15:4, 5. *Present at the Sea of Tiberias when Jesus appeared to his disciples; is commissioned to feed the flock of Christ,* John 21:1–23.

*Abides in Jerusalem,* Acts 1:13. *Recommends filling vacancy in the apostleship caused by the death of Judas,* Acts 1:15–22. *Preaches at Pentecost,* Acts 2:14–40. *Heals the impotent man in the portico of the temple,* Acts 3.

*Accused by the council; his defense,* Acts 4:1–23. *Foretells the death of Ananias and Sapphira,* Acts 5:1–11. *Heals the sick,* Acts 5:15. *Imprisoned and scourged; his defense before the council,* Acts 5:17–42.

*Goes to Samaria,* Acts 8:14. *Prays for the baptism of the Holy Spirit,* Acts 8:15–18. *Rebukes Simon, the sorcerer,* Acts 8:18–24. *Returns to Jerusalem,* Acts 8:25. *Receives Paul,* Gal. 1:18; 2:9. *Visits Lydda; heals Æneas,* Acts 9:32–34. *Visits Joppa; dwells with Simon, the tanner; raises Dorcas from the dead,* Acts 9:36–43. *Has a vision of a sheet containing clean and unclean animals,* Acts 10:9–16. *Receives the servant of the centurion; goes to Cæsarea; preaches and baptizes the centurion and his household,* Acts 10. *Advocates, the preaching of the gospel to the Gentiles,* Acts 11:1–18; 15:7–11. *Imprisoned, and delivered by an angel,* Acts 12:3–19. *Writes two epistles,* 1 Pet. 1:1; 2 Pet. 1:1.

**39**

*b Death, called sleep,* Num. 23:10.

*c Sleep, a symbol of death,* Psa. 127:2.

**40**

*d Scoffing,* Hab. 1:10.

*e Father,* Psa. 27:10.

*f Mother,* 1 Kin. 2:20.

**42**

*g Children, miracles in behalf of,* Mark 10:14.

*h Dead,* 2 Kin. 4:32.

*i Miracles, of Jesus,* Luke 23:8.

**43**

*j Prudence, instances of,* 2 Chr. 2:12.

*k Food,* Psa. 136:25.

**1**

*a* Matt. 13:53–58; Luke 4:16–30.

*b Nazareth,* John 1:46.

*c Apostles,* Luke 6:13.

**2**

*d Sabbath, religious instruction on,* Ex. 16:23.

*e Jesus, teacher,* Matt. 1:21.

*f Instruction, in religion,* Prov. 23:23.

*g Synagogue,* Matt. 12:9.

*h Jesus, wisdom of,* Matt. 1:21.

*i Miracles, of Jesus,* Luke 23:8.

**3**

*j Carpentry,* 2 Kin. 12:11.

*k Jesus, humanity of,* Matt. 1:21.

*l Mary,* Luke 1:27.

*m Brothers of Jesus,* Matt. 13:55.

*n James,* Matt. 13:55.

*o Joses,* Matt. 27:56.

*p* Or, *Judas,* Matt. 13:55.

*q* Matt. 13:55.

*r* Matt. 13:56.

*s Unbelief,* Heb. 3:12.

*t Jesus, rejected,* Matt. 1:21.

**4**

*u Proverbs,* 1 Sam. 24:13.

*v Prophets,* Isa. 3:2.

this ado, and [a]weep? the damsel is not [b]dead, but [c]sleepeth.

40 And they [d]laughed him to scorn. But when he had put them all out, he taketh the [e]father and the [f]mother of the damsel, and them that were with him, and entereth in where the damsel was lying.

41 And he took the damsel by the hand, and said unto her, Tăl′ĭ-thȧ cū′mī; which is, being interpreted, Damsel, I say unto thee, arise.

42 And straightway the [g,h]damsel [i]arose, and walked; for she was *of the age* of twelve years. And they were astonished with a great astonishment.

43 And he [j]charged them straitly that no man should know it; and commanded that [k]something should be given her to eat.

## CHAPTER 6

*Jesus is contemned of his own countrymen. 7 He gives the twelve power over unclean spirits, and sends them forth to preach. 14 Herod's opinion of Jesus. 17 Why John the Baptist was beheaded. 30 The twelve return. 34 With five loaves and two fishes Jesus feeds five thousand men. 47 He walks on the sea. 53 All that touch him are healed.*

[a] AND he went out from thence, and came into his [b]own country; and his [c]disciples follow him.

2 And when the [d]sabbath day was come, he began to [e,f]teach in the [g]synagogue: and many hearing *him* were astonished, saying, From whence hath this *man* these things? and what [h]wisdom *is* this which is given unto him, that even such mighty [i]works are wrought by his hands?

3 Is not this the [j]carpenter, the [k]son of [l]Mā′rȳ, the [m]brother of [n]Jāmes, and [o]Jō′sēs, and of [p]Jū′dȧ, and [q]Sī′mon? and are not his [r]sisters here with us? And they were [s]offended at [t]him.

4 But Jē′sus said unto them, [u]A [v]prophet is not without honour, but in his own country, and among his own kin, and in his own house.

5 And he could there do no mighty [w]work, save that he laid his [x]hands upon a few sick folk, and [y]healed *them.*

6 And he marvelled because of their [s]unbelief. And [z]he went round about the villages, [a,b]teaching.

7 ¶ And he called *unto him* the [c]twelve, and began to send them forth by two and two; and gave [c]them [1]power over [d]unclean spirits;

8 [e]And commanded [f]them that they should [g]take nothing for *their* journey, save a staff only; [2]no scrip, no bread, no [h]money in *their* purse:

9 But *be* shod with sandals; and not put on two coats.

10 And he said unto them, [i]In what place soever [j]ye enter into an house, there abide till ye depart from that place.

11 [k]And whosoever [l]shall not [j]receive you, nor hear you, when ye depart thence, shake off the dust under your feet for a testimony against them. [3]Verily I say unto you, It shall be more tolerable for [m]Sŏd′om and [n]Gō-mŏr′rhȧ in the day of [o]judgment, than for that city.

12 And they went out, and [p]preached that men should [q]repent.

13 And they [c]cast out many [d]devils, and [r]anointed with oil many that were sick, and [s]healed *them.*

14 ¶ And king [t]Hĕr′od heard [4]*of him;* (for his name was spread abroad:) and he [u]said, That [v]Jŏhn the Băp′tĭst was [w]risen from the dead, and therefore [x]mighty works do shew forth themselves in him.

*x Miracles,* Luke 23:8. 4 R. V. thereof: for his name had become known: and he said, John the Baptist is risen from the dead, and therefore do these powers work in him.

**5**

*w Miracles,* Luke 23:8.

*x Hand, imposition of,* Ezra 10:19.

*y Healing, by Jesus,* Acts 4:22.

**6**

*z Jesus, zeal of,* Matt. 1:21.

*a Jesus, teacher,* Matt. 1:21.

*b Instruction, in religion,* Prov. 23:23.

**7**

*c Apostles, miraculous power given to,* Luke 6:13.

*d Demons, power over, given the disciples,* Matt. 4:24.

1 R. V. authority

**8**

*e* Matt. 10:9–15; Luke 9:3–5.

*f Minister, charge delivered to,* Rom. 15:16.

*g Minister, emoluments of,* Rom. 15:16.

*h Money,* Jer. 32:9.

2 R. V. no bread, no wallet,

**10**

*i Church, duty of, to minister,* Matt. 16:18.

*j Ministers, hospitality to,* Rom. 15:16.

**11**

*k Responsibility,* Ezek. 18:20.

*l Opportunity, lost,* Gal. 6:10.

*m Sodom,* Gen. 13:10.

*n* Or, *Gomorrah,* Gen. 13:10.

*o Judgment, the general,* 2 Pet. 3:7.

3 R. V. *omits the rest of this verse.*

**12**

*p Preaching,* Matt. 9:35.

*q Repentance, enjoined,* Mark 1:4.

**13**

*r Anointing,* Deut 28:40.

*s Healing,* Acts 4:22.

**14**

*t Herod,* Matt. 14:1.

*u Conscience, guilty,* Acts 23:1.

*v John the Baptist,* Luke 1:63.

*w Resurrection,* 1 Cor. 15:12.

**15**
y Or, *Elijah*, 1 Kin. 17:1.
z *Prophets*, Isa. 3:2.

**16**
a *Herod*, Matt. 14:1.
b *Conscience, guilty*, Acts 23:1.
c *John the Baptist*, Luke 1:63.
d *Martyrdom*, Rev. 17:6.

**17**
e *Prisoners*, Psa. 79:11.
f *Prison*, Gen. 39:20.
g *Statecraft, women in*, Prov. 28:2.
h *Herodias*, Matt. 14:3.
i *Women, wicked*, Prov. 31:10.
j Matt. 14:3; Luke 3:19.
k *Marriage, incestuous forbidden*, Gen. 34:9.

**18**
l *Minister, faithful*, Rom. 15:16.
m *Reproof, faithfulness in*, Prov. 17:10.

**19**
n *Malice, instances of*, Eph. 4:31.
o *Revenge, exemplified*, Ezek. 25:15.

**20**
p *John the Baptist, character of*, Luke 1:63.
q *Holiness*, Ex. 39:30.
5 R. V. was much perplexed; and

**21**
r *Feasts*, Mark 12:39.

**22**
s *Dancing*, Eccl. 3:4.
t *Rashness*, 2 Sam. 6:7.

**23**
u *Oath*, Num. 5:19.

15 Others said, That it is [y]Ē-lī′as. And others said, That it is a [z]prophet[G], or as one of the prophets.

16 But when [a]Hĕr′od heard *thereof*, he [b]said, It is [c]Jŏhn, whom I [d]beheaded: he is risen from the dead.

17 For [a]Hĕr′od himself had sent forth and laid hold upon [c]Jŏhn, and bound [e]him in [f]prison [g]for [h,i]Hē-rō′dĭ-as′ sake, his brother [j]Phĭl′ĭp's wife: for he had [k]married her.

18 For [c,l]Jŏhn had [k,m]said unto [a]Hĕr′od, It is not lawful for thee to have thy brother's wife.[Q]

19 Therefore [h,i]Hē-rō′dĭ-as had a quarrel against him, and [n,o]would have killed him; but she could not:

20 For [a]Hĕr′od feared [c]Jŏhn, knowing that he was a [p]just[G] man and an [p,q]holy, and observed[G] him; and when he heard him, he [5]did many things, and heard him gladly.

21 And when a convenient day was come, that [a]Hĕr′od on his birthday made a [r]supper to his lords, high captains, and chief *estates*[G] of *Găl′ĭ-lee;

22 And when the daughter of the said [h]Hē-rō′dĭ-as came in, and [s]danced, and pleased [a]Hĕr′-od and them that sat with him, the king [t]said unto the damsel[G], Ask of me whatsoever thou wilt, and I will give *it* thee.

23 And he [i,u]sware unto her, Whatsoever thou shalt ask of me, I will give *it* thee, unto the half of my kingdom.[Q]

24 And she went forth, and said unto her [h,i]mother, What shall I ask? And she [n,o]said, The head of [c]Jŏhn the Băp′tĭst.

25 [v]And she came in straightway with haste unto the [a]king, and asked, saying, I will[G] that thou give me by[G] and by[G] in a charger[G] the head of [c]Jŏhn the Băp′tĭst.

26 And the [a]king was exceeding sorry; *yet* for his [u]oath's sake, and [w]for their sakes which sat with him, he would not reject her.

27 And immediately the king sent an executioner, and [x]commanded his head to be brought: and he went and [y,z,a]beheaded [b]him in the [c]prison,

28 And brought his head in a charger[G], and gave it to the damsel[G]: and the damsel gave it to her [d,e]mother.

29 And when his [f]disciples heard *of it*, they came and took up his corpse, and [g]laid it in a tomb.

30 ¶ And the [h]apostles gathered themselves together unto Jē′sus, and told him all things, both what they had done, and what they had taught.

31 And he said unto [i]them, Come ye yourselves apart[G] into a desert[G] place, and [j]rest a while: for there were many coming and going, and they had no leisure so much as to eat.

32 And [k]they departed into a desert place by [6,l]ship privately.

33 And the people saw them departing, and many knew him, and [m]ran afoot thither out of all cities, and outwent[G] them, and came together unto him.

34 And Jē′sus, when he came out, saw much people, and was moved with [n,o]compassion toward them, because they were as sheep not having a [p]shepherd:

**25**
v *Complicity, instances of*, Prov. 29:24.

**26**
w *Public Opinion*, John 12:42.

**27**
x *Government, monarchical, tyranny in*, Isa. 22:21.
y *Beheading, of John*, Matt. 14:10.
z *Martyrdom, instances of*, Rev. 17:6.

a *Persecution, of the righteous*, John 15:20.
b *Prisoners*, Psa. 79:11.
c *Prison*, Gen. 39:20.

**28**
d *Herodias*, Matt. 14:3.
e *Women, wicked*, Prov. 31:10.

**29**
f *Disciples*, Matt. 9:14.
g *Burial*, Acts 8:2.

**30**
h *Apostles*, Luke 6:13.

**31**
i *Minister, recreations for*, Rom. 15:16.
j *Rest, recommended by Jesus*, Ex. 23:12.

**32**
k Matt. 14:13–21; Luke 9:10–17; John 6:1–13.
l *Ship*, 2 Chr. 8:18.
6 R. V. boat

**33**
m *Popularity of Jesus*, John 6:15.

**34**
n *Jesus, compassion of*, Matt. 1:21.
o *Pity, of Jesus*, Job 19:21.
p *Shepherd*, Jer. 31:10.

* **GALILEE**, the northern district of Palestine. *Kedesh, a city of refuge in*, Josh. 20:7; 21:32; *and later a city for priests*, 1 Chr. 6:76. *Cities in, given to Hiram*, 1 Kin. 9:11, 12. *Taken by king of Assyria*, 2 Kin. 15:29. *Prophecy concerning*, Isa. 9:1; Matt. 4:15, 16. *Called* GALILEE OF THE NATIONS, Isa. 9:1. *Herod, tetrarch of*, Mark 6:21; Luke 3:1; 23:6, 7. *Jesus resides in*, Matt. 17:22; 19:1; John 7:1, 9. *Teaching and miracles of Jesus in*, Matt. 4:23, 25; 15:29–31; Mark 1:14, 28, 39; 3:7; Luke 4:14, 44; 5:17; 23:5; John 1:43; 4:3, 43–45; Acts 10:37. *People of, receive Jesus*, John 4:45, 53. *Disciples were chiefly from*, Acts 1:11; 2:7. *Women from, ministered to Jesus*, Matt. 27:55, 56; Mark 15:41; Luke 23:49, 55. *Jesus appeared to his disciples in, after his resurrection*, Matt. 26:32; 28:7, 10, 16, 17; Mark 14:28; 16:7; John 21.
*Routes from, to Judea*, Judg. 21:19; John 4:3–5. *Dialect of*, Mark 14:70. *Churches in*, Acts 9:31.

and he began to [q,r]teach them many things.[Q]

35 And when the day was now far spent, his [h]disciples came unto him, and [s]said, This is a desert place, and now the time *is* far passed:

36 Send them away, that they may go into the country round about, and into the villages, and buy themselves [t]bread: for they have nothing to eat.

37 [n]He answered and said unto [h]them, Give ye them to eat. And they say unto him, Shall we go and buy two hundred [u]pennyworth of bread, and give them to eat?

38 He saith unto them, How many [v]loaves have ye? go and see. And when they knew, they say, Five, and two [w]fishes.

39 And he commanded them to make all sit down by companies upon the green grass.

40 And they sat down in ranks, by hundreds, and by fifties.

41 [x]And when he had taken the five [v]loaves and the two [w]fishes, he looked up to heaven, and [y,z]blessed, and brake the loaves, and gave *them* to his [a]disciples to set before them; and the two fishes divided he among them all.

42 [b]And they did all eat, and were filled.

43 [b]And they [c]took up twelve [d]baskets full of the fragments, and of the fishes.

44 [b]And they that did eat of the loaves were about five thousand men.

45 ¶ [e]And straightway he constrained his [a]disciples to get into the [6,f]ship, and to go to the other side before unto [g]Bĕth-sā'ĭ-dȧ, while he sent away the people.

46 And when he had sent them away, he departed into a mountain to [h,i]pray.

47 And when even was come, the [j]ship was in the midst of the [j]sea, and he alone on the land.

48 And he saw [a]them [7]toiling in rowing; for the [k]wind was contrary unto them: and about the fourth [l]watch of the night he cometh unto them, [m]walking upon the [j]sea, and would have passed by them.

49 But when they saw [m]him walking upon the sea, they supposed it [8]had been a spirit, and cried out:

50 For [a]they all saw him, and were troubled. And immediately he talked with them, and saith unto them, Be of good cheer: it is I; be not afraid.

51 And he went up unto [a]them into the [6]ship; and the wind [b]ceased: and they were sore amazed in themselves [9]beyond measure, and wondered.

52 For they [10]considered not *the miracle* of the [n]loaves: for [o]their [p]heart was hardened.

53 [q]And when they had passed over, they came into the land of Gĕn-nĕs'a-rĕt, and [11]drew to the shore.

54 And when they were come out of the [6]ship, straightway they knew him,

55 [r]And ran through that whole region round about, and [s,t]began to carry about in beds those that were sick, where they heard he was.

56 [r]And whithersoever he entered, into villages, or cities, or country, they [s,t]laid the sick in the [12]streets, and besought him that they might touch if it were but the border of his garment: and as many as touched him were made [u]whole.

## CHAPTER 7

*The Pharisees find fault with the disciples for eating with unwashen hands. 6 Jesus teaches concerning defilement, 24 heals the daughter of a Syrophenician woman; 31 and also one that was deaf and had an impediment in his speech.*

[a]THEN came together unto him the [b]Phăr'ĭ-seeş, and certain of the [c]scribes, which came from [d]Jē-ru̇'sā-lĕm.

---

*q Jesus, teacher,* Matt. 1:21.
*r Instruction, in religion,* Prov. 23:23.

35
*s Borrowing Trouble, instances of,* Matt. 6:25.

36
*t Bread, traffic in,* Ezek. 4:13.

37
*u Penny,* Matt. 20:2.

38
*v Loaves,* Matt. 14:17.
*w Fish,* Matt. 17:27.

41
*x Miracles, of Jesus,* Luke 23:8.
*y Prayers of Jesus,* Luke 5:16.
*z Thanksgiving for Food,* Luke 24:30.

*a Apostles,* Luke 6:13.

42
*b Miracles, of Jesus,* Luke 23:8.

43
*c Frugality,* Matt. 14:20.
*d Basket,* Ex. 29:3.

45
*e* Matt. 14:22–33; John 6:15–21.
*f Ship,* 2 Chr. 8:18.
*g Bethsaida,* John 1:44.

46
*h Prayers of Jesus,* Luke 5:16.
*i Prayer, private,* Acts 6:4.

47
*j Sea of Galilee,* Matt. 4:18.

48
*k Wind,* Job 37:17.
*l Time,* Rev. 10:6.
*m Jesus walks on the Sea,* Matt. 14:25.
7 R. V. distressed

49
8 R. V. was an apparition,

51
9 R. V. *omits the rest of this verse.*

52
*n Loaves,* Matt. 14:17.
*o Spiritual Blindness,* 2 Cor. 4:4.
*p Heart,* Psa. 44:21.
10 R.V. understood not concerning the loaves, but

53
*q* Matt. 14:34–36.
11 R. V. moored

55
*r Popularity of Jesus,* John 6:15.
*s Faith in Christ, exemplified,* John 6:69.
*t Mediation,* Gal. 3:19.

56
*u Miracles, of Jesus,* Luke 23:8.
12 R. V. market-places,

1
*a* Matt. 15:1–28.
*b Pharisees,* Matt. 15:12.
*c Scribe,* 1 Kin. 4:3.
*d Jerusalem,* Judg. 19:10.

2 And when they saw some of his [e]disciples eat bread with [f]defiled, that is to say, with unwashen, [g]hands, they found fault.

3 [h]For the [b]Phăr′ĭ-seeṣ, and all the Jewṣ, except they [i,j]wash *their* [g]hands oft, [k]eat not, holding the [l]tradition of the elders.

4 [h]And *when they come* from the market, except they [i,j]wash, they [k]eat not. And many other things there be, which they have [l]received to hold, *as* the [i]washing of cups, and pots, [m]brasen vessels, [1]and of tables.

5 Then the [b]Phăr′ĭ-seeṣ and [c]scribes asked him, Why walk not thy [e]disciples according to the [l]tradition of the elders, but eat bread with [2,f]unwashen [g]hands?

6 He answered and [n]said unto them, Well hath [o]Ē-ṣā′ias [p]prophesied of you hypocrites, as it is written, [q,r]This people honoureth me with *their* lips, but their heart is far from me.

7 Howbeit in vain do they worship me, teaching *for* doctrines the [*,l]commandments of [s]men.

8 For laying aside the [t,u]commandment of God, ye hold the [l]tradition of men, [3]*as* the [i]washing of pots and cups: and many other such like things ye do.

9 And he [n]said unto them, Full well ye reject the [t,u]commandment of God, that ye may keep your own [l]tradition.

10 For Mō′ṣeṣ [v]said, [w]Honour thy [x]father and thy [y]mother; and, [4,z,a]Whoso [b]curseth father or mother, let him [c]die the death:

11 But [d,e]ye say, [f]If a man shall say to his father or mother, [5]*It is* Côr′băn, that is to say, a gift, by whatsoever thou mightest be profited by me; *he shall be free*.

12 And [d,e]ye suffer him no more to do ought for his father or his mother;

13 Making the [g,h]word of God of none effect through your [i]tradition, which ye have delivered: and many such like things do ye.

14 ¶ And when he had called all the people *unto him*, he [j]said unto them, Hearken unto me every one *of you*, and understand:

15 [k]There is nothing from without a man, that entering into him can defile him: but the things which come out of him, those are they that defile the man.

16 [6,l]If any man have ears to hear, let him [m]hear.

17 And when he was entered into the house from the people, his [n]disciples asked him concerning the [o]parable.

18 And he saith unto them, Are ye so [p]without understanding also? Do ye not perceive, that whatsoever thing from without entereth into the man, *it* cannot defile him;

19 Because it entereth not into his [q]heart, but into [7]the belly, and goeth out into the draught, purging all meats?

20 And he [j]said, That which cometh out of the man, that defileth the man.

21 For from within, [r]out of the [q]heart of men, [s]proceed [t]evil thoughts, [u]adulteries, fornications, [v]murders,

22 [†,s]Thefts, [w]covetousness, wickedness, [x]deceit, [y]lascivious-

**2**
*e Disciples*, Matt. 9:14.
*f Defilement*, Lev. 5:2.
*g Hand*, Ezra 10:19.
**3**
*h Ecclesiasticism*, Matt. 23:2.
*i Ceremonial Washings*, Ex. 19:10.
*j Purification*, Num. 19:19.
*k Eating*, Gen. 18:8.
*l Tradition*, Matt. 15:2.
**4**
*m Brass*, Job 28:2.
1 R. V. *omits* and of tables.
**5**
2 R. V. defiled hands?
**6**
*n Reproof, faithfulness in*, Prov. 17:10.
*o* Or, *Isaiah*, Isa. 1:1.
*p Prophecies*, Dan. 9:24.
*q* Isa. 29:13.
*r Hypocrisy, described*, Jas. 3:17.
**7**
*s False Teachers*, 2 Pet. 2:1.
**8**
*t Commandments*, Deut. 8:2.
*u Word of God*, Psa. 119:9.
3 R. V. *omits the rest of the verse.*
**10**
*v Law, of Moses*, Deut. 33:2.
*w* Ex. 20:12.
*x Father, to be honored*, Psa. 27:10.
*y Mother, reverence for, enjoined*, 1 Kin. 2:20.
*z* Ex. 21:17; Matt. 15:4.
*a Children, wicked*, Mark 10:14.
*b Cursing*, Lev. 24:11.
*c Punishment, death penalty*, Lev. 26:41.
4 R. V. He that speaketh evil of
**11**
*d Pharisees*, Matt. 15:12.
*e Scribe*, 1 Kin. 4:3.
*f Vows*, Num. 30:2.

5 R. V. That wherewith thou mightest have been profited by me is Corban, that is to say, Given to God;
**13**
*g Word of God*, Psa. 119:9.
*h Commandments*, Deut. 8:2.
*i Tradition*, Matt. 15:2.
**14**
*j Instruction, in religion*, Prov. 23:23.
**15**
*k* Matt. 15:17–20.
**16**
*l Commandment, enjoining heed to the truth*, Deut. 8:2.
*m Spiritual Understanding*, Luke 8:8.
6 R. V. *omits* this verse.
**17**
*n Apostles*, Luke 6:13.
*o Parables*, Ezek. 20:49.
**18**
*p Spiritual Blindness*, 2 Cor. 4:4
**19**
*q Heart*, Psa. 44:21.
7 R. V. his belly, and goeth out into the draught? This he said, making all meats clean.
**21**
*r Depravity*, Job 15:14.
*s Sin, fruits of*, Rom. 5:12.
*t Evil Imagination*, Gen. 6:5.
*u Adultery*, Lev. 20:10.
*v Homicide, felonious*, Deut. 5:17.
**22**
*w Covetousness*, Isa. 57:17.
*x Deceit*, Psa. 36:3.
*y Lasciviousness*, 1 Pet. 4:3.

* **COMMANDMENTS OF MEN**, commonly called traditions, being interpretations of the law rendered by the elders, or legislative senate, which, like decisions of courts in present times, had more weight and authority than the law itself. Isa. 29:13; Gal. 1:14; Col. 2:8; 1 Tim. 4:1–3. *Rejected by Jesus*, Matt. 15:2–6; Mark 7:3–9.

† **THEFT**, Matt. 15:19; Mark 7:21, 22; Rev. 9:21. *Forbidden*, Ex. 20:15; Lev. 19:11, 13; Deut. 5:19; 23:24, 25; Psa. 62:10; Matt. 19:18; Luke 18:20; Rom. 13:9; Eph. 4:28; Tit. 2:10; 1 Pet. 4:15. *Restitution for things stolen required of the penitent*, Ezra 33:15. *Penalty for*, Ex. 21:16; 22:1–4, 10, 12; Lev. 6:2–5; Prov. 6:30, 31; Zech. 5:3; Matt. 27:38, 44.
See footnotes: DISHONESTY, Ezek. 22:13; THIEVES, Deut. 24:7.

**Instances of:** *Rachel, of the household gods*, Gen. 31: 19, 34, 35. *Achan*, Josh. 7:11. *Micah*, Judg. 17:2. *The spies of Laish*, Judg. 18:14–27. *Israelites*, Ezek. 22:29; Hos. 4:1, 2. *Judas*, John 12:6.

ness, an evil [z]eye, [8,a]blasphemy,
[b]pride, foolishness:
23 [c]All these evil things come
from within, and defile the man.
24 ¶ [d]And from thence [e]he
arose, and went into the borders
of [f]Tȳre and [g]Sī′dŏn, and entered into an house, and would
have no man know *it*: but he
could not be hid.
25 For a *certain* [h]woman, whose
young daughter had an [i]unclean
spirit, heard of him, and [j,k]came
and [l]fell at his feet:
26 The woman was a [m]Greek,
a [n]Sȳ-rō-phē-nĭ′çian by nation;
and [h]she [k]besought him that he
would cast forth the [i]devil out of
her daughter.
27 But Jē′ṣus said unto her, Let
the children first be filled: for it
is not meet to take the children's
bread, and to cast *it* unto the
dogs.
28 And [h]she answered and said
unto him, [j]Yes, Lord: [l]yet the
dogs under the table eat of the
children's crumbs.
29 And [e]he said unto her, For
this saying go thy way; the [i]devil
is [o]gone out of thy [p]daughter.
30 And when she was come to
her house, she found the [i]devil
[o]gone out, and her [p]daughter
laid upon the bed.
31 ¶ [q]And again, departing
from the coasts of [f]Tȳre and
[g]Sī′dŏn, [r]he came unto the [s]sea
of Găl′ĭ-lee, through the midst
of the coasts of [t]Dē-căp′o-lĭs.
32 And they [j,k]bring unto him
one that was [u]deaf, and had an
impediment in his speech; and
they beseech him to put his
[v]hand upon him.
33 And [r]he took him aside from
the multitude, and put his fingers into his ears, and he [w]spit,
and touched his tongue;
34 And looking up to heaven,
[r]he sighed, and saith unto him,
Ĕph′pha-thȧ, that is, Be opened.

z *Eye, figurative,* Matt. 6:22.

a *Blasphemy,* 2 Sam. 12:14.
b *Pride,* Prov. 16:18.
8 R. V. railing.

**23**
c *Sin, fruits of,* Rom. 5:12.

**24**
d Matt. 15:21–28.
e *Jesus, life of, heals daughter of Syrophenician,* vs. 24–30; Matt. 1:21.
f *Tyre,* 1 Kin. 5:1.
g Or, *Zidon*. Ezek. 28:21.

**25**
h *Parents, affection of, exemplified,* 2 Cor. 12:14.
i *Demons,* Matt. 4:24.
j *Faith in Christ, exemplified,* John 6:69.
k *Mediation,* Gal. 3:19.
l *Humility,* Prov. 22:4.

**26**
m *Greece,* Zech. 9:13.
n *Syria,* 2 Kin. 6:23.

**29**
o *Miracles, of Jesus,* Luke 23:8.
p *Children, healing of,* Mark 10:14.

**31**
q Matt. 15:29–37.
r *Jesus, life of, heals an infirm man,* vs. 31–37; Matt. 1:21.
s *Sea of Galilee,* Matt. 4:18.
t Mark 5:20; Matt. 4:25.

**32**
u *Deafness,* Matt. 11:5.
v *Hand, imposition of,* Ezra 10:19.

**33**
w *Spitting,* Num. 12:14.

35 And straightway his ears
were [o]opened, and the string of
his tongue was [o]loosed, and he
spake plain.
36 And he [x]charged them that
they should tell no man: but the
more he charged them, [y]so much
the more a great deal they published *it*;
37 And were beyond measure
astonished, saying, He hath done
all things well: [z]he maketh both
the [a]deaf to hear, and the [b]dumb
to speak.

## CHAPTER 8

*Jesus feeds four thousand.* **10** *The Pharisees require a sign.* **14** *Jesus warns his disciples of the leaven of the Pharisees and of Herod.* **22** *He heals a blind man.* **27** *What the people think of Jesus,* **29** *and Peter's confession of him.* **31** *Jesus foretells his own death and resurrection.* **34** *Those who will follow him must take up their cross.*

[a]IN those days the multitude
being very great, and hav-
ing nothing to eat, [b]Jē′ṣus called
his [c]disciples *unto him*, and saith
unto them,
2 I have [d]compassion on the
multitude, because they have
now been with me three days,
and have nothing to eat:
3 And if I send them away [e]fast-
ing to their own houses, they will
faint by the way: for divers of
them came from far.
4 And his [c]disciples answered
him, From whence can a man
satisfy these *men* with bread here
in the wilderness?
5 And he asked them, How
many [f]loaves have ye? And they
said, Seven.
6 And he commanded the people to sit down on the ground:
[g]and he took the seven [f]loaves,
and [h,i]gave [j]thanks, and brake,
and gave to his [c]disciples to set
before *them*; and they did set
*them* before the people.
7 And they had a few small
[k]fishes: and he [i]blessed, and commanded to set them also before
*them*.

**36**
x *Prudence, instances of,* 2 Chr. 2:12.
y *Zeal, instances of,* 2 Cor. 7:11.

**37**
z *Miracles, of Jesus,* Luke 23:8.

a *Deafness,* Matt. 11:5.
b *Dumb,* Ex. 4:11.

**1**
a Matt. 15:32–39.
b *Jesus, life of, feeds four thousand,* vs. 1–9; Matt. 1:21.
c *Apostles,* Luke 6:13.

**2**
d *Jesus, compassion of,* Matt. 1:21.

**3**
e *Hunger,* Neh. 9:15.

**5**
f *Loaves,* Matt. 14:17.

**6**
g *Miracles, of Jesus,* Luke 23:8.
h *Food, thanksgiving before taking,* Psa. 136:25.
i *Thanksgiving, by Jesus,* Matt. 11:25.
j *Thankfulness, to God,* Acts 24:3.

**7**
k *Fish,* Matt. 17:27.

8 [g]So they did eat, and were filled: and they [l]took up of the broken *meat* that was left seven [m]baskets.

9 [g]And they that had eaten were about four thousand: and he sent them away.[S]

10 ¶ And straightway[G] he entered into a [1,n]ship with his [c]disciples, and came into the parts of Dăl-ma-nū′thȧ.

11 [o]And the [p]Phăr′ĭ-seeş came forth, and began to question with him, seeking of him a *sign from heaven, [q]tempting[G] him.

12 And he sighed deeply in his spirit, and [r]saith, Why doth this generation seek after a *sign? verily I say unto you, There shall no sign be given unto this generation.

13 And he left them, and entering into the [1,n]ship again departed to the other side.

14 ¶ [s]Now *the* [c]*disciples* had forgotten to take [t]bread, neither had they in the [1,n]ship with them more than one loaf.

15 And he charged them, saying, [u]Take heed, [v]beware of the [w,x]leaven[G] of the [p]Phăr′ĭ-seeş, and *of* the leaven[G] of [y]Hĕr′od.

16 And [z]they reasoned among themselves, saying, *It is* because we have no bread.

17 And when Jē′şus [a]knew *it*, he saith unto them, Why reason ye, because ye have no bread? [b]perceive ye not yet, neither understand? have ye your heart yet hardened?

18 Having [c]eyes, [b]see ye not? and having [d]ears, [b]hear ye not? and do ye not remember?[Q]

19 [e]When I brake the five loaves among five thousand, how many baskets full of fragments took ye up? They say unto him, Twelve.

20 And [e]when the seven among four thousand, how many baskets full of fragments took ye up? And they said, Seven.

21 And he said unto them, How is it that ye [b]do not understand?

22 ¶ [S]And [f]he cometh to [g]Bĕth-sā′ĭ-dȧ; and they [h]bring a [i]blind man unto him, and besought[G] him to touch him.

23 And [f]he took the blind man by the hand, and led him out of the town; and when he had [j]spit on his eyes, and put his hands upon him, he asked him if he saw ought[G].

24 And he looked up, and said, I see men as trees, walking.

25 After that [f]he put *his* hands again upon his eyes, and made him look up: and he was [e]restored, and saw every man clearly.

26 And he sent him away to his house, [k]saying, Neither go into the town, nor tell *it* to any in the town.[S]

27 ¶ [l]And Jē′şus went out, and his [m]disciples, into the towns of [n]Çæs-a-rē′ȧ Phĭ-lĭp′pī: and by the way he asked his disciples, saying unto them, Whom do men say that I am?

28 And they answered, [o]Jŏhn the Băp′tĭst: but some *say*, [p]Ē-lī′as; and others, One of the [q]prophets.

29 And he saith unto them, But whom say ye that I am? And [r]Pē′tĕr answereth and saith unto him, [s]Thou art the [t]Chrīst.[T]

30 And he [k]charged[G] them that they should tell no man of him.

31 ¶ And [u,v]he began to teach them, that the [w]Son of man must [x]suffer many things, and be rejected of the [y]elders, and *of* the chief [z]priests, and [a]scribes, and be [b]killed, and after three days [c]rise again.

32 And he spake that saying

8
*l Frugality*, Matt. 14:20.
*m Basket*, Ex. 29:3.

10
*n Ship*, 2 Chr. 8:18.
1 R. V. boat

11
*o* Matt. 16:1–4; Luke 12:54–57.
*p Pharisees*, Matt. 15:12.
*q Temptation*, Luke 11:4.

12
*r Reproof, faithfulness in*, Prov. 17:10.

14
*s* Matt. 16:5–12; Luke 12:1.
*t Bread*, Ezek. 4:13.

15
*u Watchfulness*, Matt. 24:42.
*v Hypocrisy, warnings against*, Jas. 3:17.
*w Leaven, figurative*, Lev. 23:17.
*x Self-righteousness*, Luke 18:11.
*y Herod*, Matt. 14:1.

16
*z Spiritual Blindness*, 2 Cor. 4:4.

17
*a Jesus, omniscience of*, Matt. 1:21.
*b Spiritual Blindness*, 2 Cor. 4:4.

18
*c Eye, figurative*, Matt. 6:22.
*d Ear, figurative*, Lev. 8:23.

19
*e Miracles, of Jesus*, Luke 23:8.

22
*f Jesus, life of, heals a blind man*, vs. 22–26; Matt. 1:21.
*g Bethsaida*, John 1:44.
*h Mediation*, Gal. 3:19.
*i Blindness*, 2 Kin. 6:18.

23
*j Spitting*, Num. 12:14.

26
*k Prudence*, 2 Chr. 2:12.

27
*l* Matt. 16:13–20; Luke 9:18–20.
*m Apostles*, Luke 6:13.
*n Cæsarea Philippi*, Matt 16:13.

28
*o John the Baptist*, Luke 1:63.
*p* Or, *Elijah*, 1 Kin. 17:1.
*q Prophets*, Isa. 3:2.

29
*r Peter*, Mark 5:37.
*s Faith in Christ*, John 6:69.
*t Jesus, Messiah*, Matt. 1:21.

31
*u Jesus foretells his Death*, Matt. 17:22.
*v Jesus, prophet*, Matt. 1:21.
*w Jesus, humanity of*, Matt. 1:21.
*x Jesus, sufferings of*, Matt. 1:21.
*y Senate*, Num. 11:16.
*z Priest*, Lev. 1:5.
*a Scribe*, 1 Kin. 4:3.
*b Jesus, death of*, Matt. 1:21.
*c Jesus, resurrection of*, Matt. 1:21.

***SIGN.** *A miracle to confirm faith*, Matt. 12:38; 16:4; Mark 8:11, 12; John 2:11; 3:2; 4:48.
*Asked for by, and given to, Abraham*, Gen. 15:8–17; *Moses*, Ex. 4:1–9; *Gideon*, Judg. 6:17, 36–40; *Hezekiah*, 2 Kin. 20:8–11; *Zacharias*, Luke 1:18–22. *Given to Jeroboam*, 1 Kin. 13:3–5.
*A token of coming events*, Matt. 16:3, 4; 24:3; Luke 12:54–56. See footnote, MIRACLES, Luke 23:8.

**32**
d *Peter, presumption of,* Mark 5:37.
e *Presumption, instances of,* Psa. 19:13.
**33**
f *Apostles,* Luke 6:13.
g *Reproof, faithfulness in,* Prov. 17:10.
2 R. V. mindest not
**34**
h *Righteous, described,* Psa. 64:10.
i *Commandment, enjoining self-denial and cross-bearing,* Deut. 8:2.
j *Cross, figurative,* John 19:17.
**35**
k *Paradox,* 2 Cor. 12:4.
l *Worldliness,* 1 John 2:15.
m *Persecution, of the righteous,* John 15:20.
n *Promise, to the righteous,* 2 Cor. 1:20.
**36**
o Matt. 16:26; Luke 9:25.
p *Wicked, punishment of,* Psa. 73:3.
q *Life,* Eccl. 8:15.
3 R. V. forfeit his life?
**37**
4 R. V. life?
**38**
r *Wicked, described,* Psa. 73:3.
s *Jesus, rejected,* Matt. 1:21.
t *Jesus, humanity of,* Matt. 1:21.
u *Judgment, the general,* 2 Pet. 3:7.
v *Jesus, second coming of,* Matt. 1:21.
w *God, fatherhood of,* Gen. 2:2.
x *Angel,* Heb. 1:13.
**1**
a *Jesus, prophet,* Matt. 1:21.

openly. And [d]Pē'tēr took him, and [e]began to rebuke him.

33 But when he had turned about and looked on his [f]disciples, he [g]rebuked [d]Pē'tēr, saying, Get thee behind me, Sā'tan: for thou [2]savourest not the things that be of God, but the things that be of men.

34 ¶ And when he had called the people *unto him* with his [f]disciples also, he said unto them, [h]Whosoever will come after me, [i]let him †deny himself, and take up his [j]cross, and follow me.

35 For [k]whosoever will [l]save his life shall lose it; [k]but whosoever shall [m]lose his life for my sake and the gospel's, the [n]same shall save it.

36 [o]For what shall it profit a man, if he shall gain the whole world, and [3,p]lose his own [q]soul?

37 Or what shall a man give in exchange for his [4,q]soul?

38 [r]Whosoever therefore shall be [s]ashamed of me and of my words in this adulterous and sinful generation; of him also shall the [t]Son of man be ashamed, [u]when [v]he cometh in the glory of his [w]Father with the holy [x]angels.

## CHAPTER 9

*The transfiguration. 14 Jesus casts out a dumb spirit; 30 and foretells his own death and resurrection. 33 He exhorts his disciples to humility. 38 They are not to reject those who are not against them; 42 but to avoid giving cause for stumbling.*

AND he said unto them, Verily [a]I say unto you, That there be some of them that stand here, which shall not taste of [b]death, till they have seen the [c]kingdom of God come with power.

2 ¶ And after six days Jē'ṣus taketh *with him* [d]Pē'tēr, and [e]Jāmeṣ, and [f]Jŏhn, and leadeth them up into an high mountain apart by themselves: and he was [g]transfigured before them.

3 And his raiment became [1]shining, exceeding [h]white as snow; so as no [i]fuller on earth can white them.

4 And there [j]appeared unto them [k]Ē-lī'as with [l]Mō'ṣeṣ: and they were talking with Jē'ṣus.

5 And [d]Pē'tēr answered and said to Jē'ṣus, [2,m]Master, it is good for us to be here: and let us make three tabernacles; one for thee, and one for [l]Mō'ṣeṣ, and one for [k]Ē-lī'as.

6 For he wist not what to say; for they were sore afraid.

7 And there was a cloud that overshadowed them: and a voice came out of the cloud, saying, This is [n]my beloved [o]Son: hear him.

8 And suddenly, when they had looked round about, they saw no man any more, save Jē'ṣus only with themselves.

9 [p]And as they came down from the mountain, he [q]charged them that they should tell no man what things they had seen, till the [r]Son of man were [s,t]risen from the dead.

10 And they kept that saying with themselves, questioning one with another what the [s,t]rising from the dead should mean.

b *Death,* Num. 23:10.
c *Kingdom of Heaven,* Matt. 13:24.
**2**
d *Peter,* Mark 5:37.
e *James,* Luke 5:10.
f *John,* Mark 1:19.
g *Transfiguration, of Jesus,* Matt. 17:2.
**3**
h *Colors, symbolical,* Ezek. 16:16.
i Mal. 3:2.
1 R. V. glistering,
**4**
j *Immortality, implied in the appearance of Moses and Elijah,* 1 Cor. 15:54.
k Or, *Elijah,* 1 Kin. 17:1.
l *Moses,* Ex. 2:10.
**5**
m *Jesus, names of,* Matt. 1:21.
2 R. V. Rabbi,
**7**
n *God, fatherhood of,* Gen. 2:2.
o *Jesus, divine sonship of,* Matt. 1:21.
**9**
p Matt. 17:9–13.
q *Prudence,* 2 Chr. 2:12.
r *Jesus, humanity of,* Matt. 1:21.
s *Resurrection of Jesus,* Matt. 28:6.
t *Jesus, resurrection of,* Matt. 1:21.

† **SELF-DENIAL,** Luke 21:2–4; 1 Cor. 6:12; 9:12, 15, 18, 19, 23, 25–27; 10:23, 24; 2 Cor. 6:3; Phil. 2:4–8; 3:7–9; 2 Tim. 2:4; Tit. 2:12; Heb. 13:13; Rev. 12:11. *In respect to, appetite,* Prov. 23:2; Dan. 10:3; *sinful pleasures,* Matt. 5:29, 30; 18:8, 9; Mark 9:43; *deeds of the flesh,* Rom. 6:6; 8:12, 13, 35, 36; 13:14; 1 Cor. 9:27; Gal. 5:16, 17, 24; Col. 3:5; Tit. 2:12; 1 Pet. 2:11, 12, 14–16.

*Required of Christ's disciples,* Matt. 8:19–22 (with Luke 9:57, 58); 10:37–39; 16:24, 25; Mark 8:34, 35; Luke 9:23, 24 (with Matt. 19:12, 21); 5:11; 12:33; 14:26, 27, 33; 18:27–29 (with Mark 10:29), 30; John 12:25 (with Matt. 16:25; Mark 8:35); 1 Pet. 4:1; 3 John 7.

*For a brother's sake,* Rom. 14:1–22; 15:1–5; 1 Cor. 8:10–13. See footnote, CROSS, John 19:17.

**Instances of:** *Abraham, when he accorded to Lot his preference for the grazing lands of Canaan,* Gen. 13:9 (with 17:8); *in offering Isaac,* Gen. 22:12. *Moses, in choosing rather to suffer affliction with the people of God than to enjoy the pleasures of sin,* Heb. 11:25; *in taking no compensation from the Israelites for his services,* Num. 16:15. *The widow of Zarephath, in sharing with Elijah the last of her sustenance,* 1 Kin. 17:12–15. *Daniel, in his abstemiousness,* Dan. 1:8; *in refusing rewards from Belshazzar,* Dan. 5:16, 17. *Esther, in risking her life for the deliverance of her people,* Esth. 4:16. *The Rechabites, in refusing to drink wine or strong drink, or even to plant vineyards,* Jer. 35:6, 7.

*Peter and other apostles, in abandoning their vocations to follow Jesus,* Matt. 4:20; 9:9; Mark 1:16–20; 2:14; Luke 5:11, 27, 28; *in forsaking all and following Jesus,* Matt. 19:27; Mark 10:28; Luke 5:28. *The widow, who cast her all into the treasury,* Luke 21:4. *The early Christians, in having everything in common,* Acts 2:44, 45; 4:34. *Joses, in selling his possessions, and giving all that he received to the apostles,* Acts 4:36, 37. *Paul, in not counting even his life dear to himself,* Acts 20:24; Phil. 3:7, 8; *in laboring for his own support while he also taught,* Acts 20:34, 35; 1 Cor. 4:12; 10:33.

**11**
*u Scribe*, 1 Kin. 4:3.

**12**
*v Prophecies, concerning the Messiah, and their fulfillment*, Gen. 12:3.

**13**
*w John the Baptist*, Luke 1:63.

**14**
*x* Matt. 17:14–18; Luke 9:37–42.
*y Apostles*, Luke 6:13.

**15**
*z Salutations*, Luke 1:44.

**16**
3 R. V. them?

**17**
*a Parents, affection of, exemplified*, 2 Cor. 12:14.
*b Dumb*, Ex. 4:11.
*c Demons*, Matt. 4:24.

**18**
*d Apostles*, Luke 6:13.
4 R. V. it
5 R. V. it dasheth him down:

**22**
*e Mediation*, Gal. 3:19.

11 ¶ And they asked him, saying, Why say the [u]scribes that [k]Ē-lī′as must first come?

12 And he answered and told them, [k]Ē-lī′as verily cometh first, and restoreth all things; and how [v]it is written of the [r]Son of man, that he must suffer many things, and be set at nought.

13 But I say unto you, That [w]Ē-lī′as is indeed come, and they have done unto him whatsoever they listed, as it is written of him.

14 ¶ [x]And when he came to *his* [y]disciples, he saw a great multitude about them, and the [u]scribes questioning with them.

15 And straightway all the people, when they beheld him, were greatly amazed, and running to *him* [z]saluted him.

16 And he asked [3]the scribes, What question ye with them?

17 And one of the multitude answered and said, Master, [a]I have brought unto thee my son, which hath a [b]dumb [c]spirit;

18 And wheresoever [4]he taketh him, [5]he teareth him: and he foameth, and gnasheth with his teeth, and pineth away: and I spake to thy [d]disciples that they should cast [4]him out; and they could not.

19 He answereth him, and saith, O faithless generation, how long shall I be with you? how long shall I suffer you? bring him unto me.

20 And they brought him unto him: and when he saw him, straightway the [c]spirit tare him; and he fell on the ground, and wallowed foaming.

21 And he asked his father, How long is it ago since this came unto him? And he said, Of a child.

22 And ofttimes it hath cast him into the fire, and into the waters, to destroy him: but [e]if thou canst do any thing, have compassion on us, and help us.

23 Jē′ṣus said unto him, If thou canst [6]believe, all things *are* possible to him that [f]believeth.

24 And straightway the [a]father of the child cried out, and said [7]with tears, Lord, I [f]believe; [g]help thou mine [h]unbelief.

25 When Jē′ṣus saw that the people came running together, he rebuked the [c]foul spirit, saying unto him, *Thou* [b]dumb and [i]deaf spirit, I charge thee, come out of him, and enter no more into him.

26 And *the spirit* cried, and rent him sore, and [j,k]came out of him: and he was as one dead; insomuch that many said, He is dead.

27 But Jē′ṣus took him by the hand, and lifted him up; and [j,k]he arose.

28 And when he was come into the house, his [d]disciples asked him privately, Why could not we cast him out?

29 And he said unto them, This kind can come forth by nothing, but by [l]prayer [8]and fasting.

30 ¶ And they departed thence, and passed through [m]Găl′ĭ-lee; and he would not that any man should know *it*.

31 For he taught his disciples, and [n,o]said unto them, The [p]Son of man is delivered into the hands of men, and they shall [q]kill him; and after that he is killed, he shall [r]rise the third day.

32 But [s]they understood not that saying, and were afraid to ask him.

33 ¶ [t]And he came to [u]Că-pēr′na-ŭm: and being in the house [v]he asked them, What [9]was it that ye disputed among yourselves by the way?

34 But they held their peace: for by the way they had [w]dis-

**23**
*f Faith in Christ*, John 6:69.
6 R. V. *omits* believe,

**24**
*g Faith, prayer for*, Mark 11:22.
*h Unbelief*, Heb. 3:12.
7 R. V. *omits* with tears, Lord,

**25**
*i Deafness*, Matt. 11:5.

**26**
*j Miracles, of Jesus*, Luke 23:8.
*k Demoniac Healed*, Matt. 17:18.

**29**
*l Prayer*, Acts 6:4.
8 R. V. *omits* and fasting.

**30**
*m Galilee*, Mark 6:21.

**31**
*n Jesus, prophet*, Matt. 1:21.
*o Jesus foretells his Death*, Matt. 17:22.
*p Jesus, humanity of*, Matt. 1:21.
*q Jesus, death of*, Matt. 1:21.
*r Resurrection of Jesus*, Matt. 28:6.

**32**
*s Spiritual Blindness*, 2 Cor. 4:4.

**33**
*t* Matt. 18:1–4; Luke 9:46–48.
*u Capernaum*, Luke 4:31.
*v Jesus, omniscience of*, Matt. 1:21.
9 R. V. were ye reasoning in the way?

**34**
*w Strife, instances of*, Prov. 20:3.

x *Ambition*, Hab. 2:5.
y *Worldliness*, 1 John 2:15.

**35**
z *Jesus, life of, reproves ambition of the disciples*, vs. 35–37; Matt. 1:21.

a *Apostles*, Luke 6:13.
b *Commandment, enjoining altruistic service*, Deut. 8:2.
c *Humility*, Prov. 22:4.
d *Altruism*, Acts 20:35.
10 R. V. minister

**36**
e *Children*, Mark 10:14.
11 R. V. little child,

**37**
f Matt. 18:5; Luke 9:48.
g *Fellowship, with Christ*, 1 Cor. 1:9.
h *Fellowship, with God*, 1 Cor. 1:9.
12 R. V. little children

**38**
i Luke 9:49, 50.
j *John, intolerance of*, Mark 1:19.
k *Demons*, Matt. 4:24.
l *Intolerance*, Num. 11:28.
m *Bigotry, instances of*, Isa. 65:5.
13 R. V. *omits* and he followeth not us:

**39**
n *Toleration*, Mic. 4:4.
o *Commandment, forbidding intolerance*, Deut. 8:2.
p *Miracles*, Luke 23:8. 14 R. V. mighty work **41** q Matt. 10:41, 42. r *Liberality*, 1 Tim. 6:18. s *Love, of man for man*, 1 John 4:7. t *Works*, 2 Tim. 1:9. u *Love, of man for Jesus*, 1 John 4:19. v *Promise, to the righteous*, 2 Cor. 1:20. 15 R. V. *omits* in my name, **42** w Matt. 18:6; Luke 17:2. x *Temptation, leading into*, Luke 11:4. y *Faith in Christ*, John 6:69. 16 R. V. cause one 17 R. V. on me to stumble,

puted among themselves, [x,y]who *should be* the greatest.

35 And [z]he sat down, and called the [a]twelve, and saith unto them, If any man desire to be first, [b]*the same* shall be [c]last of all, and [10,d]servant of all.

36 And he took a [11,e]child, and set him in the midst of them: and when he had taken him in his arms, he said unto them,

37 [f]Whosoever shall receive one of such [12,e]children in my name, [g]receiveth me: and whosoever shall [g]receive me, receiveth not me, [h]but him that sent me.[T]

38 ¶ [i]And [j]Jŏhn answered him, saying, Master,[G] we saw one casting out [k]devils in thy name, [13]and he followeth not us: and [l,m]we forbad him, because he followeth not us.[S]

39 But Jē'ṣus [n]said, [o]Forbid him not: for there is no man which shall do a [14,p]miracle in my name, that can lightly[G] speak evil of me.[S]

40 For he that is not against us is on our part.

41 [q]For whosoever shall [r,s,t]give you a cup of water to drink [15]in my name, [u]because ye belong to Christ, verily I say unto you, [v]he shall not lose his reward.

42 [w]And whosoever shall [16,x]offend[G] one of *these* little ones that [y]believe [17]in me, it is better for him that a [z]millstone were hanged[G] about his neck, and he were cast into the sea.

43 [a]And if thy [b]hand [18,c]offend[G] thee, [d,e]cut it off: it is better for[G] thee to enter into life maimed, than having two hands [f]to go into *hell,[G] into the [g,h]fire that never shall be quenched:[S]

44 [19]Where their [i]worm dieth not, and the [g]fire is not quenched.

45 And if thy foot [18,c]offend[G] thee, [d,e]cut it off: it is better for thee to enter halt[G] into life, than having two feet to be cast into [20]*hell,[G] into the [g,h]fire that never shall be quenched:

46 [19]Where their [i]worm dieth not, and the [g]fire is not quenched.

47 [j]And if thine [k]eye [18,c]offend[G] thee, [d,e]pluck it out: it is better for thee to enter into the [l]kingdom of God with one eye, than having two eyes to be cast into *,[h]hell[G] [g]fire:

48 Where their [i]worm dieth not, and the [g,h]fire is not quenched.[Q]

49 For every one shall be [m]salted with [g]fire, [21]and every sacrifice shall be salted with salt.

50 Salt *is* good: but if the salt have lost his saltness, wherewith will ye season it? Have [m,n]salt in yourselves, and have [o]peace one with another.

z *Millstone*, Judg. 9:53.

**43**
a Matt. 5:30; 18:8.
b *Hand, figurative*, Ezra 10:19.
c *Temptation, leading into*, Luke 11:4.
d *Commandment, enjoining renunciation of sources of temptation*, vs. 45–48; Deut. 8:2.
e *Self-denial*, Mark 8:34.
f *Wicked, punishment of*, Psa. 73:3.
g *Fire, figurative*, Ex. 12:8.
h *Punishment, eternal*, Lev. 26:41.
18 R. V. cause thee to stumble,

**44**
i *Worm, figurative*, Jonah 4:7.
19 R. V. *omits this verse.*

**45**
20 R. V. hell. *Rest of verse is omitted.*

**47**
j Matt. 5:29; 18:9.
k *Eye, figurative*, Matt. 6:22.
l *Kingdom of Heaven*, Matt. 13:24.

**49**
m *Salt, figurative*, 2 Kin. 2:20.
21 R. V. *omits the rest of this verse.*

**50**
n *Influence, good*, 1 Cor. 7:14.
o *Peace, enjoined*, Jer. 29:7.

* **HELL.** *Used in the King James version of the O. T. to translate the Hebrew word* SHEOL, *signifying the unseen state*, see 2 Sam. 22:6; Job 11:8; 26:6; Psa. 9:17; 16:10; 18:5; 55:15; 86:13; 116:3; 139:8; Prov. 5:5; 7:27; 9:18; 15:11, 24; 23:14; 27:20; Isa. 5:14; 14:9, 11, 15; 28:15, 18; 57:9; Ezek. 31:16, 17; 32:21, 27; Amos 9:2; Jonah 2:2; Hab. 2:5.

*Figurative of divine judgments*, Deut. 32:22; Ezek. 31: 15–17.

This word is used also in the King James version of the N. T. as the translation of the Greek word HADES, signifying the unseen world, Matt. 11:23; 16:18; Luke 10:15; 16:23; Acts 2:27, 31; Rev. 1:18; 6:8; 20:13, 14; and of the Greek word GEHENNA, signifying the place of torment, Matt. 5:22, 29, 30; 10:28; 18:9; 23:15, 33; Mark 9:43, 45, 47; Luke 12:15; Jas. 3:6. It is also used as the translation of the Greek word TARTARUS, signifying the infernal region, 2 Pet. 2:4. In the King James version for the Hebrew word SHEOL are used the English words GRAVE, in Gen. 37:35; 42:38; 44:29, 31; 1 Sam. 2:6; 1 Kin. 2:6, 9; Job 7:9; 14:13; 17:13; 21:13; 24:19; Psa. 6:5; 30:3; 31:17; 49:14, 15; 88:3; 89:48; 141:7; Prov. 1:12; 30:16; Eccl. 9:10; Song 8:6; Isa. 14:11; 38:10, 18; Hos. 13:14; and PIT, in Num. 16:30, 33; Job 17:16.

The English revisers use the Hebrew word SHEOL in all places where HELL, GRAVE, and PIT were used in the King James version, except in Deut. 32:22; Psa. 55:15; 86:13; and except in the prophetical books. The American revisers invariably use SHEOL in the American text, where SHEOL occurs in the Hebrew.

**The future state, or abode, of the wicked,** Psa. 9:17; Prov. 5:5; 9:18; 15:24; 23:14; Isa. 30:33; 33:14; Matt. 5:22, 29, 30; 7:13, 14; 8:11, 12; 10:28; 13:30, 38–42, 49, 50; 18:8, 9, 34, 35; 22:13; 25:30, 41, 46; Mark 9:43–48 (with Matt. 5:29, 30); Luke 3:17 (with Matt. 3:12); 16:23–28; Acts 1:25; 2 Thess. 1:9; 2 Pet. 2:4; Jude 6, 23; Rev. 9:1, 2; 11:7; 14:10, 11; 19:20; 20:10, 15; 21:8, with 2:11.

See footnote, WICKED, *Punishment of*, Psa. 73:3.

## CHAPTER 10

*Jesus answers the Pharisees concerning divorce. 13 He blesses little children; 17 answers the rich young man; 23 and shews how hard it is for a rich man to enter the kingdom of God. 28 The reward of those who forsake all and follow him. 32 He again foretells his own death and resurrection. 35 The request of James and John. 42 Jesus exhorts to humility. 46 He heals blind Bartimæus at Jericho.*

[a]AND he arose from thence,
and cometh into the coasts[G]
of [b]Jū-dæ′à by the farther side
of [c]Jŏr′dan: and [d]the people resort unto [e]him again; and, as
he was wont[G], he [f]taught them
again.
2 ¶ [g]And the [h]Phăr′ĭ-seeş came
to him, and asked him, Is it lawful for a man to [i]put away *his*
[j]wife? tempting[G] him.
3 And he answered and said
unto them, What did Mō′şeş
[k]command you?
4 And they said, Mō′şeş suffered[G] to write a bill of [i]divorce-
ment, and to put *her* away.[Q]
5 And Jē′şus answered and said
unto them, For the [l]hardness of
your heart he wrote you this
precept.
6 But from the beginning of
the creation [m]God [n]made them
[o]male and [p]female.[T][Q]
7 [q]For[Q] this cause shall a [r]man
leave his father and mother, and
cleave to his [j]wife;
8 And [s]they twain[G] shall be [t]one
flesh: so then they are no more
twain, but one flesh.[S][Q]
9 [u]What therefore God hath
joined together, let not man put
asunder.
10 And in the house his [v]dis-
ciples asked him again of the
same *matter*.
11 And he saith unto them,
[w]Whosoever shall put away his
[j]wife, and [t]marry another, committeth [x]adultery against her.
12 And if a [j]woman shall put
away her [r]husband, and be
[t]married to another, she committeth [x]adultery.
13 ¶ And [y]they brought young
children to him, that he should
touch them: and *his* [v]disciples [z]re-
buked[G] those that brought *them*.
14[S] But when Jē′şus saw *it*, he
was [1]much displeased, and said
unto them, Suffer[G] the little *chil-

**1**
*a* Matt. 19:1, 2.
*b* *Judea*, Luke 5:17.
*c* *Jordan*, Gen. 32:10.
*d* *Popularity of Jesus*, John 6:15.
*e* *Jesus, received*, Matt. 1:21.
*f* *Jesus, teacher*, Matt. 1:21.

**2**
*g* Matt. 19:3–12.
*h* *Pharisees*, Matt. 15:12.
*i* *Divorce*, Matt. 19:7.
*j* *Wife*, Prov. 5:18.

**3**
*k* *Law, of Moses*, Deut. 33:2.

**5**
*l* *Obduracy*, Prov. 29:1.

**6**
*m* Gen. 1:27; 5:2; Matt. 19:4.
*n* *God, creator*, Gen. 2:2.
*o* *Man, created*, Job 4:17.
*p* *Women, creation of*, Prov. 31:10.

**7**
*q* Gen. 2:24.
*r* *Husband*, Num. 30:6.

**8**
*s* Matt. 19:5; 1 Cor. 6:16; Eph. 5:31.
*t* *Marriage*, Gen. 34:9.

**9**
*u* *Commandment, enjoining indissolubility of marriage*, Deut. 8:2.

**10**
*v* *Apostles*, Luke 6:13.

**11**
*w* Matt. 5:32; 19:9; Luke 16:18.
*x* *Adultery*, Lev. 20:10.

**13**
*y* Matt. 19:13–15; Luke 18:15–17.
*z* *Presumption*, Psa. 19:13.

**14**
1 R.V. moved with indignation,

* **CHILDREN.** *A blessing*, Gen. 5:29; Psa. 127:3–5; Prov. 17:6.
*The gift of God*, Gen. 4:1, 25; 17:16, 20; 22:17; 28:3; 29:32–35; 30:2, 6, 17–24; 33:5; 48:9, 16; Ruth 4:13; Job 1:21; Psa. 107:38, 41; 113:9; 127:3.
*Promised to the righteous*, Deut. 7:12, 14; Job 5:25; Psa. 128:2–4, 6.
Given in answer to prayer: *To Abraham*, Gen. 15:2–5; 21:1, 2; *to Isaac*, Gen. 25:21; *to Leah*, Gen. 30:17–21; *to Rachel*, Gen. 30:22–24; *to Hannah*, 1 Sam. 1:9–20; *to Zacharias*, Luke 1:13.
*Treatment of, at birth*, Ezek. 16:4–6; Luke 2:7, 12. *Circumcision of*, see footnote, CIRCUMCISION, Gen. 17:10.
*Weaning of*, Gen. 21:8; 1 Sam. 1:22; 1 Kin. 11:20; Psa. 131:2; Isa. 28:9. *Nurses for*, Ex. 2:7–9; Ruth 4:16; 2 Sam. 4:4; 2 Kin. 11:2.
*Amusements of*, Job 21:11; Zech. 8:5; Matt. 11:16, 17; Luke 7:31, 32.
*Tutors and governors for*, 2 Kin. 10:1; Acts 22:3; Gal. 3:24; 4:1, 2.
Dedicated to God in infancy: *Samson*, Judg. 13:5, 7; *Samuel*, 1 Sam. 1:24–28.
*God's care of*, Ex. 22:22–24; Deut. 10:18; 14:29; Psa. 10:14, 17, 18; 27:10; 68:5; 146:9; Jer. 49:11; Hos. 14:3; Mal. 3:5.
Early piety of: *Samuel*, 1 Sam. 2:18; 3; *Jeremiah*, Jer. 1:5–7; *John the Baptist*, Luke 1:15, 80.
*Attend divine worship*, Ex. 34:23; Josh. 8:35; 2 Chr. 20:13; Ezra 8:21; Neh. 8:2, 3; 12:43; Matt. 21:15. *Entitled to enjoy religious privileges*, Deut. 12:12, 18.
*Share benefits of covenant privileges guaranteed to parents*, Gen. 6:18; 12:7; 13:15; 17:7, 8; 21:13; 26:3–5, 24; Lev. 26:44, 45; Isa. 65:23; 1 Cor. 7:14. *Bound by covenants of parents*, Gen. 17:9–14. *Involved in sins of parents*, Ex. 20:5; 34:7; Lev. 20:5; 26:39–42; Num. 14:18, 33; 1 Kin. 16:12; 21:29; Psa. 37:28; Isa. 14:20, 21; 65:6, 7; Jer. 32:18; Dan. 6:24. *Not punished on account of sins of parents*, 2 Kin. 14:6; Jer. 31:29, 30; Ezek. 18:1–30.
Death of, as a judgment upon parents: *Firstborn of Egypt*, Ex. 12:29; Num. 8:17; Psa. 78:5; *sons of Eli*, 1 Sam. 3:13, 14; *sons of Saul*, 1 Sam. 28:18, 19; *David's child by Uriah's wife*, 2 Sam. 12:14–19.
*Bastard, excluded from the privileges of the congregation*, Deut. 23:2; Heb. 12:8.
*Difference made between male and female in Mosaic law*, Lev. 12.
*Status of minor*, Gal. 4:1, 2.
Partiality of parents among: *Rebekah for Jacob*, Gen. 27:6–17; *Jacob for Joseph*, Gen. 37:3, 4. *Partiality among, forbidden*, Deut. 21:15–17.
*Counsel of parents to*, 1 Kin. 2:1–4; 1 Chr. 22:6–12; 28:9, 10, 20.
*Intercessional sacrifices in behalf of*, Job 1:5.
*Sacrificed*, 2 Kin. 17:31; Ezek. 16:20, 21. *Caused to pass through fire*, 2 Kin. 16:3; 17:17; Jer. 32:35; Ezek. 16:21.
*Taken for debt*, 2 Kin. 4:1; Neh. 5:5; Job 24:9; Matt. 18:25.
Sold in marriage: *Law concerning*, Ex. 21:7–11; *instance of, Leah and Rachel*, Gen. 29:15–30.
Edict to murder: *Of Pharaoh*, Ex. 1:22; *of Jehu*, 2 Kin. 10:1–8; *of Herod*, Matt. 2:16–18.
*Blessed by Jesus*, Matt. 19:13–15; Mark 10:13–16; Luke 18:15, 16, 17.
*Type of the regenerated*, Matt. 18:2–5, 10; 19:14, 15; Mark 9:37; 10:13–16; Luke 9:48; 18:15, 17.
**Commandments to:** *To honor and obey parents*, Ex. 20:12; Lev. 19:3; Deut. 5:16; Prov. 1:8, 9; 6:20–23; 23:22; Matt. 15:4; 19:19; Mark 10:19; Luke 18:20; Eph. 6:1–3; Col. 3:20; 1 Tim. 3:4.
*To seek wisdom*, Prov. 4:1–11, 20–22; 5:1, 2; 8:32, 33; 27:11. *To praise the Lord*, Psa. 148:12, 13. *To remember their Creator*, Prov. 23:26; Eccl. 12:1.
**Good:** *Obey parents*, Prov. 13:1. *A joy to parents*, Prov. 10:1; 15:20; 23:24; 29:3. *Keep the law*, Prov. 28:7. *Extol the Savior*, Matt. 21:15, 16, with Psa. 8:2. *Are filial*, Mal. 1:6.
INSTANCES OF FILIAL: *Shem and Japheth*, Gen. 9:23. *Isaac*, Gen. 22:6–12. *Jacob*, Gen. 28:7. *Judah*, Gen. 44:18–34. *Joseph*, Gen. 45:9–11; 46:29; 47:12, 29, 30. *Moses*, Ex. 15:2. *Daughter of Jephthah*, Judg. 11:36–39. *Saul*, 1 Sam. 9:5. *David*, 1 Sam. 22:3, 4. *Solomon*, 1 Kin. 2:19, 20.
INSTANCES OF GOOD: *The captive maid*, 2 Kin. 5:2–4. *Jewish children*, 2 Chr. 20:13; Neh. 8:3; 12:43. *Josiah*, 2 Chr. 34:1–3. *Daniel and the three Hebrews*, Dan. 1:8–20. *The*

dren to come unto me, and forbid them not: for [a]of such is the
[b,c]kingdom of God.
15 Verily I say unto you, Whosoever shall not receive the [b]king-
dom of God [d]as a little *child, he
shall not enter therein.
16 And he took *them up in his
arms, put *his* [e]hands upon them,
and blessed them.
17 ¶ And when he was gone
forth into the way, there came
[f]one running, and [g]kneeled to
him, and asked him, Good Master, what shall I [h]do that I may
inherit eternal [i]life?
18 And Jē'ṣus said unto him,
Why callest thou me good? *there is*
none good but one, *that is*, [j,k]God.
19 Thou knowest the [l]com-
mandments, [m]Do not commit
[n]adultery, [o]Do not [p]kill, [q]Do not
[r]steal, [s]Do not bear [t]false witness, [u]Defraud not, [v]Honour thy
[w]father and [x]mother.
20 And he answered and said
unto him, Master, [y]all these have
I [z]observed from my youth.
21 Then Jē'ṣus beholding him
[a]loved him, and said unto him,
One thing thou lackest: go thy
way, [b,c]sell whatsoever thou hast,
and [d]give to the [e]poor, and
[f,g]thou [h]shalt have treasure in
heaven: and [i,j]come, [2]take up
the [k]cross, and follow me.
22 And [l]he was sad at that saying, and went away grieved: for
he had great [m,n]possessions.
23 ¶ [o]And Jē'ṣus looked round
about, and saith unto his [p]dis-
ciples, How hardly shall they
that have [m]riches enter into the
[q]kingdom of God!
24 And the disciples were astonished at his words. But Jē'ṣus
answereth again, and [r]saith unto
them, Children, how hard is it
for them that [s]trust in [m,n]riches
to enter into the [q]kingdom of
God!
25 It is easier for a [t]camel to
go through the eye of a [u]needle,
than for a rich man to enter into
the [q]kingdom of God.
26 And they were astonished
out of measure, saying among
themselves, Who then can be
[v]saved?
27 And Jē'ṣus looking upon
them saith, With men *it is*
impossible, but not with God:
for with [w]God all things are
possible.
28 ¶ [x]Then [y]Pē'tēr began to say
unto him, Lo, we have [z,a]left
all, and have followed thee.
29 And [b]Jē'ṣus answered and
said, Verily I say unto you, There
is no man that hath [a,c]left house,
or brethren, or sisters, or father,
or mother, [3]or wife, or children,
or lands, for my sake, and the
[d]gospel's,
30 But [e]he shall receive an
[f]hundredfold now in this time,
houses, and brethren, and sisters, and mothers, and children,

*a Promise, to children,* 2 Cor. 1:20.
*b Kingdom of Heaven,* Matt. 13:24.
*c Church, membership in,* Matt. 16:18.
**15**
*d Righteous, described,* Psa. 64:10.
**16**
*e Hand, imposition of,* Ezra 10:19.
**17**
*f* Matt. 19:16–22; Luke 18:18–23.
*g Salutations,* Luke 1:44.
*h Works,* 2 Tim. 1:9.
*i Life, everlasting,* Eccl. 8:15.
**18**
*j God, goodness of,* Gen. 2:2.
*k God, holiness of,* Gen. 2:2.
**19**
*l Decalogue,* Ex. 20:3.
*m* Ex. 20:14.
*n Adultery, forbidden,* Lev. 20:10.
*o* Ex. 20:13.
*p Homicide, forbidden,* Deut. 5:17.
*q* Ex. 20:15.
*r Theft, forbidden,* Mark 7:22.
*s* Ex. 20:16.
*t False Witness, forbidden,* Matt. 19:18.
*u Honesty, enjoined,* Rom. 13:13.
*v* Ex. 20:12.
*w Father, to be honored,* Psa. 27:10.
*x Mother, reverence for, enjoined,* 1 Kin. 2:20.

**20** *y Self-righteousness,* Luke 18:11. *z Obedience,* Heb. 5:8. —**21** *a Jesus, love of,* Matt. 1:21. *b Commandment, enjoining self-denial,* Deut. 8:2. *c Renunciation, of possessions for Christ,* Luke 5:11. *d Liberality, enjoined,* 1 Tim. 6:18. *e Poor,* Prov. 21:13. *f Promise, to the righteous of treasure in heaven,* 2 Cor. 1:20. *g Righteous, promises to,* Psa. 64:10. *h Reward, a motive, to faithfulness,* Matt. 5:12. *i Call, personal,* Phil. 3:14. *j Discipleship of Jesus,* Matt. 10:32. *k Cross, figurative,* John 19:17. 2 R. V. *omits* take up the cross, and

**22**
*l Worldliness,* 1 John 2:15.
*m Riches, a snare,* Eccl. 4:8.
*n Temptation, sources of,* Luke 11:4.
**23**
*o* Matt. 19:23–26; Luke 18:24–27.
*p Apostles,* Luke 6:13.
*q Kingdom of Heaven,* Matt. 13:24.
**24**
*r Instruction, in religion,* Prov. 23:23.
*s False Confidence, in riches,* Psa. 30:6.
**25**
*t Camel,* 1 Sam. 30:17.
*u* Matt. 19:24; Luke 18:25.
**26**
*v Salvation,* Acts 16:17.
**27**
*w God, power of,* Gen. 2:2.
**28**
*x* Matt. 19:27–30; Luke 18:28–30.
*y Peter,* Mark 5:37.
*z Self-denial, instances of,* Mark 8:34.

*a Renunciation,* Luke 5:11.
**29**
*b Jesus, promises of,* Matt. 1:21.
*c Self-denial, instances of,* Mark 8:34.
*d Gospel,* Mark 13:10.
3 R. V. *omits* or wife,
**30**
*e Promise, to the righteous,* 2 Cor. 1:20.
*f Reward,* Matt. 5:12.

---

Rechabites, Jer. 35:18, 19. *Jesus,* Luke 2.51, 52; *Timothy,* 2 Tim. 1:5. *John,* Luke 1:15.

**Instruction of:** *In the law,* Deut. 6:6–9; 11:19, 20; 31:12, 13; Josh. 8:35; Psa. 78:1–8. *In the scriptures,* Acts 22:3; Eph. 6:4; 2 Tim. 3:15. *In the fear of the Lord,* Psa. 34:11. *In righteousness,* Prov. 1:1–4; 22:6; Isa. 28:9, 10; 38:19.

*By rehearsing to them God's providences,* Ex. 10:2; 12:26, 27; 13:8–10, 14–16; Deut. 4:9, 10.

**Miracles in behalf of:** *Raised from the dead, by Elijah,* 1 Kin. 17:17–23; *by Elisha,* 2 Kin. 4:17–36; *by Jesus,* Matt. 9:18, 24–26; Mark 5:35–42; Luke 7:13–15; 8:49–56.

*Healing of,* Matt. 15:28; 17:18; Mark 7:29, 30; 9:17–27; Luke 8:41–56; 9:38–42; John 4:46–54.

**Of the righteous, blessed of God:** *In escaping judgments,* Gen. 6:18; 7:1; 19:12, 15, 16; Lev. 26:44, 45. *In temporal prosperity,* Gen. 12:7; 13:15; 17:7, 8; 21:13; 26:3, 4, 24; Deut. 4:37; 10:15; 12:28; 1 Kin. 15:4; Psa. 37:26; 102:28; 112:2. *In divine mercy,* Psa. 103:17, 18; Prov. 20:7; Jer. 32:39; Acts 2:39; 1 Cor. 7:14.

**Prayer in behalf of:** *For healing,* 2 Sam. 12:16. *For divine favor,* Gen. 17:18. *For spiritual wisdom,* 1 Chr. 22:12; 29:19.

**Promises and assurances to,** Acts 2:39. *Of long life to the obedient,* Ex. 20:12; Deut. 5:16; Prov. 3:1–10; Eph. 6:2, 3. *Of divine instruction,* Isa. 54:13.

**Wicked.** *Disrespectful, to parents,* Deut. 27:16; Prov. 15:20; 30:11; Ezek. 22:7; Mic. 7:6; Job 19:18; 2 Kin. 2:23; *to the aged,* Isa. 3:5. *Disobedient to parents,* Deut. 21:18–20; Prov. 13:1; 15:5; 30:17; Rom. 1:30; 2 Tim. 3:2. *Defraud parents,* Prov. 28:7, 24. *Disgrace parents,* Prov. 10:1; 17:2, 21, 25; 19:13, 26. *Betray parents,* Mark 13:12.

PUNISHMENT OF, Ex. 21:15, 17; Lev. 20:9; Deut. 21:21; 27:16; Prov. 20:20; 22:15; Matt. 15:4; Mark 7:10. *Enjoined,* Prov. 19:18; 23:13; 29:17. *By reproof,* Prov. 29:15. *By the rod,* Prov. 13:24; 22:15; 23:13, 14; 29:15.

and lands, with [g]persecutions;
and in the world to come [h]eter-
nal [i]life.
31 [j]But many *that are* first shall
be last; and the last first.
32 ¶ And they were in the way
going up to [k]Jĕ-ru̥′să-lĕm; and
Jē′ṣus went before them: and
they were amazed; and as they
followed, they were afraid. And
[l]he took again the [m]twelve, and
began to tell them what things
should happen unto him,
33 [l,n]*Saying,* Behold, we go
up to [k]Jĕ-ru̥′să-lĕm; and the
[o]Son of man shall be [p]delivered
unto the chief [q]priests, and unto the [r]scribes; and they shall
condemn him to death, and
shall deliver him to the Ġĕn′-
tīleṣ:
34 And they shall [s]mock him,
and shall [t]scourge him, and shall
spit upon him, and shall [u]kill
him: and the third day [v]he shall
rise again.
35 ¶ [w]And [x]Jāmeṣ and [y]Jōhn,
the sons of [z]Zĕb′e-dee, come
unto him, saying, Master, [a]we
would that thou shouldest do for
us whatsoever we shall desire.
36 And he said unto them,
What would ye that I should do
for you?
37 They said unto him, [a]Grant
unto us that we may sit, one on
thy right hand, and the other on
thy left hand, in [b]thy glory.
38 But Jē′ṣus said unto them,
Ye know not what ye ask: can
ye drink of the [c]cup that [d]I
drink of? and be [e]baptized with
the baptism that I am baptized
with?
39 And they said unto him,
We can. And Jē′ṣus said unto
them, Ye shall indeed drink of
the [c]cup that [d]I drink of; and
with the [e]baptism that I am
baptized withal shall ye be
baptized:
40 But to sit on my right hand
and on my left hand is not [f]mine
to give; but *it shall be given to*
*them* for whom it is prepared.
41 And when the [g]ten heard
*it*, they began to be much [h]dis-
pleased with [i]Jāmeṣ and [j]Jŏhn.
42 [k]But Jē′ṣus called them *to*
*him*, and saith unto them, Ye
know that they which are accounted to rule over the [l]Ġĕn′-
tīleṣ exercise lordship over them;
and their great ones exercise
authority upon them.
43 But so shall it not be among
you: but whosoever [a]will be great
among you, [m,n]shall be your
[o]minister:
44 And whosoever [4]of you [a]will
be the chiefest, [m,n]shall be [o]serv-
ant of all.
45 [p]For even the [q]Son of man
came not to be ministered unto,
but [r]to minister, and to give his
[s]life a [t,u]ransom for many.
46 ¶ [v]And they came to [w]Jĕr′-
ĭ-chō: and as [x]he went out of
Jĕr′ĭ-chō with his [y]disciples
and a great number of people,
[z]blind Bär-ti-mæ′us, the son of
Tī-mæ′us, sat by the highway
side [a]begging.
47 And when he heard that it
was [b]Jē′ṣus of [c]Năz′a-rĕth, he
began to cry out, and say, Jē′-
ṣus, *thou* [b]son of [d]Dā′vid, [e]have
[f]mercy on me.
48 And many charged him
that he should hold his peace:
but he [g]cried the more a great
deal, *Thou* [b]son of [d]Dā′vid, [e]have
[f]mercy on me.
49 And [h]Jē′ṣus stood still, and
commanded him to be called.
And they call the [i]blind man,
saying unto him, [j]Be of good
comfort, rise; he calleth thee.
50 And [e]he, casting away his
garment, rose, and came to Jē′-
ṣus.
51 And Jē′ṣus answered and
said unto him, What wilt thou
that I should do unto thee?

g *Persecution, of the righteous,* John 15:20.
h *Immortality,* 1 Cor. 15:54.
i *Life, everlasting,* Eccl. 8:15.

31
j Luke 13:30.

32
k *Jerusalem,* Judg. 19:10.
l *Jesus, revelations by,* vs. 32–34; Matt. 1:21.
m *Apostles,* Luke 6:13.

33
n *Jesus foretells his Death,* Matt. 17:22.
o *Jesus, humanity of,* Matt. 1:21.
p *Persecution, of Jesus,* John 15:20.
q *Priest,* Lev. 1:5.
r *Scribe,* 1 Kin. 4:3.

34
s *Mocking,* 1 Kin. 18:27.
t *Smiting and Scourging, of Jesus,* Isa. 50:6.
u *Jesus, death of,* Matt. 1:21.
v *Jesus, resurrection of,* Matt. 1:21.

35
w Matt. 20:20–28.
x *James, civil ambitions of,* Luke 5:10.
y *John, civil ambitions of,* Mark 1:19.
z *Zebedee,* Matt. 4:21.

---

a *Ambition,* Hab. 2:5.

37
b *Jesus, kingdom of,* Matt. 1:21.

38
c *Cup, figurative,* Matt. 20:22.
d *Jesus, sufferings of,* Matt. 1:21.
e *Baptism, figurative,* Luke 20:4.

40
f *Jesus, relation of, to the Father,* Matt. 1:21.

41
g *Apostles,* Luke 6:13.
h *Jealousy,* Psa. 78:58.
i *James,* Luke 5:10.
j *John,* Mark 1:19.

42
k Matt. 20:25–28; Luke 22:25–27.
l *Gentiles,* Acts 10:45.

43
m *Commandment, enjoining altruistic service,* Deut. 8:2.
n *Humility, enjoined,* Prov. 22:4.
o *Altruism,* Acts 20:35.

44
4 R. V. would be first among you,

45
p *Example, Christ our,* John 13:15.
q *Jesus, humanity of,* Matt. 1:21.
r *Jesus, mission of,* Matt. 1:21.
s *Life,* Eccl. 8:15.
t *Jesus, design of his death,* Matt. 1:21.
u *Redemption of our Souls,* Eph. 1:7.

46
v Matt. 20:29–34; Luke 18:35–43.
w *Jericho,* Num. 22:1.
x *Jesus, life of, heals blind men at Jericho,* Matt. 1:21.
y *Apostles,* Luke 6:13.
z *Blindness,* 2 Kin. 6:18.

---

a *Beggars,* Luke 16:20.

47
b *Jesus, names of,* Matt. 1:21.
c *Nazareth,* John 1:46.
d *David,* 1 Sam. 16:13.
e *Faith in Christ,* John 6:69.
f *Mercy,* Deut. 5:10.

48
g *Prayer, importunity in,* Acts 6:4.

49
h *Jesus, compassion of,* Matt. 1:21.
i *Blindness,* 2 Kin. 6:18.
j *Afflictions, consolation in,* Psa. 34:19.

The [i]blind man said unto him, [5,e]Lord, that I might receive my sight.

52 And Jē′şus said unto him, Go thy way; thy [e]faith hath made thee whole.[G] And immediately he [k]received his sight, and [l]followed Jē′şus in the way.[S]

## CHAPTER 11

*Jesus' public entry into Jerusalem. 12 He curses the fig tree; 15 drives the traders out of the temple; 20 and exhorts to faith and forgiveness. 27 He silences those who question his authority.*

AND [a]when they came nigh[G] to [b]Jē-rṳ′sā-lĕm, unto [c]Bĕth′-pha-ġē and [d]Bĕth′a-nȳ, at the mount of *Ŏl′ĭveş, he sendeth forth two of his [e]disciples,

2 And saith unto them, Go your way into the village over[G] against you: and as soon as ye be entered into it, ye shall find a colt tied, whereon never man sat; loose him, and bring *him*.

3 And if any man say unto you, Why do ye this? say ye that the Lord hath need of him; and straightway[G] he will send him hither.

4 And [e]they went their way, and found the colt tied by the door without[G] in [1]a place where two ways met; and they loose him.

5 And certain of them that stood there said unto them, What do ye, loosing the colt?

6 And they said unto them even as Jē′şus had commanded: and they let them go.

7 [f]And they brought the colt to Jē′şus, and cast their garments on him; and he sat upon him.

8 [f]And [g]many spread their garments in the way[G]: and others cut down branches off the trees, and strawed[G] *them* in the way.

51
5 R. V. Rabboni,

52
k *Miracles, of Jesus*, Luke 23:8.
l *Love, for Jesus*, 1 John 4:19.

1
a Matt. 21:1–9; Luke 19:29–38.
b *Jerusalem*, Judg. 19:10.
c Matt. 21:1; Luke 19:29.
d *Bethany*, John 11:18.
e *Apostles*, Luke 6:13.
v.1–AD 30

4
1 R. V. the open street;

7
f *Triumphal Entry of Jesus into Jerusalem*, Matt. 21:5.

8
g *Popularity of Jesus*, John 6:15.

9 [f,g][Q]And they that went before, and they that followed, cried, saying, [h,i]Hō-şăn′nȧ; [j]Blessed *is* he that cometh in the name of the Lord:

10 [h,i,j]Blessed [2]*be* the [k]kingdom of our father [l]Dā′vid, that cometh in the name of the Lord: Hō-şăn′nȧ in the highest.[Q]

11 And Jē′şus entered into [b]Jē-rṳ′sā-lĕm, and into the [m]temple: and when he had looked round about upon all things, and now the eventide[G] was come, he went out unto [d]Bĕth′a-nȳ with the [e]twelve.

12 ¶ [n][S]And on the morrow[G], when they were come from [d]Bĕth′a-nȳ, he was [o]hungry:

13 And seeing a †fig tree afar off having leaves, he came, if haply[G] he might find any thing thereon: and when he came to it, he found [p]nothing but leaves; for the time of figs was not *yet*.

14 And Jē′şus answered and said unto †it, No man eat fruit of thee hereafter for ever. And his [e]disciples heard *it*.[S]

15 ¶ [q]And they come to [b]Jē-rṳ′sā-lĕm: and Jē′şus went into the [m]temple, and began to cast out them that sold and bought in the temple, and overthrew[G] the tables of the moneychangers, and the seats of them that sold [r]doves;

16 And would not suffer[G] that any man should carry *any* vessel through the [m]temple.

17 And he [s]taught, [t]saying unto them, Is it not written, My [u]house shall be called [3]of all nations the [v]house of [w]prayer? but ye have [x]made it a den of [y]thieves.[Q]

18 And the [z]scribes and chief

v.9–AD 30
See footnote, *Time*, Rev. 10:6.

9
h *Joy, instances of*, Psa. 5:11.
i *Praise*, Psa. 150:1.
j *Love, for Jesus*, 1 John 4:19.

10
k *Jesus, kingdom of*, Matt. 1:21.
l *David*, 1 Sam. 16:13.
2 R. V. is the kingdom that cometh, the kingdom of our father David:

11
m *Temple, Herod's*, 1 Kin. 6:17.

12
n Matt. 21:18–22.
o *Hunger*, Neh. 9:15.

13
p *Unfruitfulness*, Matt. 7:19.

15
q Matt. 21:12, 13; Luke 19:45, 46; John 2:14, 15.
r *Dove*, Gen. 8:8.

17
s *Jesus, teacher*, Matt. 1:21.
t *Reproof, faithfulness in*, Prov. 17:10.
u *Church*, 1 Kin. 9:3.
v Isa. 56:7; Matt. 21:13; Luke 19:46.
w *Prayer, in the temple*, Acts 6:4.
x *Profanation, of the house of God*, Lev. 22:32.
y *Thieves*, Deut. 24:7.
3 R. V. a house of prayer for all the nations?

18
z *Scribe*, 1 Kin. 4:3.

***MOUNT OF OLIVES,** east of Jerusalem. *Called* MOUNT OF CORRUPTION, 2 Kin. 23:13. *The highway, to the E. of Jerusalem, passed over*, 2 Sam. 15:30. *Solomon built idolatrous shrines on*, 1 Kin. 11:7; 2 Kin. 23:13. *Jesus' triumphant entry into Jerusalem by way of*, Matt. 21:1; Mark 11:1; Luke 19:29, 37; John 12:12–15. *Jesus repairs to*, Matt. 24:3; 26:30; Mark 13:3; 14:26; Luke 21:37; 22:39; John 8:1. *Jesus makes his ascension from*, Acts 1:12.

† **FIG.** *Common, to Palestine*, Num. 13:23; Deut. 8:8; *to Egypt*, Psa. 105:33. *Employed as a remedy*, 2 Kin. 20:7; Isa. 38:21. *Traffic in*, Neh. 13:15. *Cakes of, dried and preserved*, 1 Sam. 30:12; 1 Chr. 12:40; *sent by Abigail to David, to placate David after Nabal's refusal to contribute to the support of David's army*, 1 Sam. 25:18. *Jeremiah's vision of good and bad*, Jer. 24:1–10.
See footnote, FIG TREE, Luke 13:6.

v.18–AD 30
See footnote, *Time*, Rev. 10:6.

*a Priest*, Lev. 1:5.
*b Persecution, of Jesus*, John 15:20.
*c Public Opinion*, John 12:42.
*d Doctrines of Jesus*, John 7:16.

**20**
*e Miracles, of Jesus*, Luke 23:8.

**21**
*f Peter*, Mark 5:37.
*g Jesus, names of*, Matt. 1:21.
**4** R. V. Rabbi,

**22**
*h Commandment, enjoining faith*, Deut. 8:2.

[a]priests heard *it*, and [b]sought
how they might destroy him:
for they feared him, because all
the [c]people was astonished at
his [d]doctrine.[G]
19 And when even[c] was come,
he went out of the city.
20 ¶ [s]And in the morning, as
they passed by, they saw the †fig
tree [e]dried up from the roots.
21 And [f]Pē′tēr calling to remembrance saith unto him,
[4,g]Master, behold, the †fig tree
which thou cursedst is withered away.
22 And Jē′ṣus answering saith
unto them, [h]Have ‡faith in
God.
23 For [i]verily I say unto you,
That whosoever shall say unto
this [j]mountain, Be thou removed, and be thou cast into
the sea; and shall not [k]doubt in
his heart, but shall ‡believe that
those things which he saith shall
come to pass; [l,m]he shall have
whatsoever he saith.
24 Therefore I say unto you,
What things soever ye desire,
when ye [n]pray, ‡believe that ye
[5]receive *them*, and [o]ye shall have
*them*.[s]
25 [T]And when ye stand praying,
[p,q,r]forgive, if ye have ought[G]

v.23–AD 30
See footnote, *Time*, Rev. 10:6.

**23**
*i* Matt. 17:20; 21:21; Luke 17:6.
*j Mountain*, Mic. 7:12.
*k Doubting*, Rom. 14:23.
*l Righteous, promises to*, Psa. 64:10.
*m Promise, to the righteous*, 2 Cor. 1:20.

**24**
*n Prayer, answer to, promised*, Acts 6:4.
*o Promise, to the righteous, of answer to prayer*, 2 Cor. 1:20.

5 R. V. have received **25** *p Commandment, enjoining forgiveness*, Deut. 8:2. *q Forgiveness, of enemies, enjoined*, Matt. 18:21. *r Duty, of man to man*, Eccl. 12:13.

‡ **FAITH,** Psa. 118:8, 9; Hab. 2:4 (with Rom. 1:17; Gal. 3:11; Heb. 10:38); Luke 17:6; 18:8; 1 Tim. 4:12; Heb. 11:1–3, 6. *The gift of God*, Rom. 12:3. *Weak*, Matt. 6:25–34; 14:31; Luke 9:40; 17:5. *Prayer for increase of*, Mark 9:24; Luke 17:5.

*Secures salvation*, Col. 2:12; 2 Thess. 2:13; Heb. 4:1–11; 6:1, 12, 18.

*Inspired, by God's goodness*, Psa. 36:7, 9; *by the Holy Spirit*, 1 Cor. 12:8, 9.

*Miracles wrought by*, Matt. 17:18–20; 21:21, 22; Mark 9:23; 11:23, 24.

Strengthened by miracles: *Of Abraham*, Gen. 15:8–18; *of Gideon*, Judg. 6:17, 36–40; *of Hezekiah*, 2 Kin. 20:8–11; *of Zacharias*, Luke 1:18–20, 64.

*In affliction, exemplified by Job*, Job 13:15, 16; 14:15; 16:19; 19:25–27.

In adversity: *Exemplified, by Hagar*, Gen. 16:13; *by Moses*, Num. 14:8, 9; *by Asa*, 2 Chr. 14:11; *by Jehoshaphat*, 2 Chr. 20:12; *by Hezekiah*, 2 Chr. 32:7, 8; *by Nehemiah*, Neh. 1:10; 2:20; *by the psalmist*, Psa. 3:3, 5, 6; 4:3, 8; 6:8, 9; 7:1, 10; 9:3, 4; 11:1; 13:5; 17:6; 20:5–7; 31:1, 3–6, 14, 15; 32:7; 33:20–22; 35:10; 38:9, 15; 42:5, 6, 8; 43:5; 44:5, 8; 46:1–3, 5, 7; 54:4; 55:16, 17, 23; 56:3, 4, 8, 9; 57:1–3; 59:9, 17; 60:9, 10, 12; 61:2, 4, 6, 7; 62:1, 5, 6, 7; 63:6, 7; 69:19, 35, 36; 70:5; 71:1, 3, 5–7, 14, 16, 20, 21; 73:23, 24, 26, 28; 86:2, 7; 89:18, 26; 91:1, 2, 9, 10; 92:10, 15; 94:14, 15, 17, 18, 22; 102:13; 108:10–13; 118:6, 7, 10, 14, 17; 119:42, 57, 74, 81, 114, 166; 121:2; 138:7, 8; 140:6, 7, 12; 142:3, 5; 143:8, 9; *by Jeremiah*, Lam. 3:24; *by Daniel*, Dan. 3:16, 17; *by Jonah*, Jonah 2:2; *by Micah*, Mic. 7:7–9, 20; *by Paul*, Acts 27:25; 2 Cor. 1:10; 4:8, 9, 13, 16–18; Phil. 1:19–21; 1 Tim. 4:10; 2 Tim. 1:12, 13; 4:7, 8, 18; *by the author of Epistle to the Hebrews*, Heb. 10:34.

**Enjoined,** Psa. 4:5; 115:9, 11; Eccl. 11:1; Isa. 26:4; Matt. 6:25–34; Mark 1:15; 11:22; Luke 12:32; 1 Tim. 6:11, 12, 17; Jas. 1:6. *In time of public danger*, Ex. 14:13; Num. 21:34; Deut. 1:21, 29, 30; 3:2, 22; 7:17–21; 20:1; 31:8, 23; Josh. 10:25; Judg. 6:14–16; 2 Kin. 19:6, 7; 2 Chr. 20:15, 17, 20; 32:7, 8; Neh. 4:14; Isa. 37:6; Jer. 42:11. *In time of adversity*, Psa. 37:3, 5, 7; 55:22; 62:8; Isa. 43:1, 2, 5, 10; 44:2, 8.

*Upon public leaders*, Josh. 1:9 (with vs. 5–9); 2 Chr. 15:7. *Upon the young*, Prov. 3:5, 6, 24–26. *Upon the discouraged*, Isa. 35:3, 4; 41:10, 13, 14; 50:10. *Upon widows*, Jer. 49:11.

**Exemplified:** *By Asa*, 2 Chr. 14:11. *By Jehoshaphat*. 2 Chr. 20:12. *By Hezekiah*, 2 Chr. 32:8. *By Job*, Job 1:21, 22; 2:10; 5:8, 9; 19:25–27. *By the psalmists, in the great hymns prepared for public worship and private meditation, setting forth supreme confidence in God*, Psa. 4:3, 8; 11:1; 13:5, 6; 16:1, 2, 5, 8–11; 18:1–3, 30–50; 20:5–8; 23; 25:1–15; 27:1–14; 31:1–5, 22–24; 40:1–11; 46:1–11; 56:10–13; 57:1–11; 60:6–12; 61:1–8; 62:5–12; 63:1–8; and the following psalms in their entirety, 91, 95, 105–108, 115–118, 121, 123–126, 130, 135, 136, 138, 139, 140, 145–150. *By Isaiah*, Isa. 8:10, 17; 12:2; 17:13, 14; 25:9; 26:1, 8; 33:1, 22; 50:7–9; 63:16; 64:8. *By Jeremiah*, Jer. 14:9, 22; 16:19; 17:17; 20:11.

**Instances of:** *Abel*, Heb. 11:4. *Noah, in building the ark*, Gen. 6:14–22; Heb. 11:7. *Abraham, in forsaking the land of his nativity at the command of God*, Gen. 12:1–4; Heb. 11:8; *in believing the promise of many descendants*, Gen. 12:7; 15:4–6; Rom. 4:18–21; Heb. 11:11, 12; *in the offering up of Isaac*, Gen. 22:1–10; Heb 11:17–19. *Jacob, in blessing Joseph's sons*, Gen. 48:8–21; Heb. 11:21. *Joseph, concerning God's providence in his being sold into Egypt, and the final deliverance of Israel*, Gen. 50:20, 24; Heb. 11:22. *Jochebed, in caring for Moses*, Ex. 2:2, 3; Heb. 11:23. *Pharaoh's servants, who obeyed the Lord*, Ex. 9:20. *Moses, in espousing the cause of his people*, Heb. 11:24–28; *at the death of Korah*, Num. 16:28, 29.

*Israelites*, Psa. 22:4, 5; *when Aaron declared the mission of himself and Moses*, Ex. 4:31; *in the battle with the Canaanites*, 1 Chr. 5:20; *and other conquests*, 2 Chr. 13:8–18. *Caleb, in advising to take the land of promise*, Num. 13:30; 14:6–9; *when he asked for Hebron*, Josh. 14:12. *Rahab, in hospitality to the spies*, Josh. 2:9, 11; Heb. 11:31. *The spies, sent to reconnoiter Jericho*, Josh. 2:24. *Conquest of Jericho*, Josh. 6; Heb. 11:30. *Manoah's wife*, Judg. 13:23. *Hannah*, 1 Sam. 1. *Jonathan, in smiting the Philistines*, 1 Sam. 14:6.

*David, in smiting Goliath*, 1 Sam. 17:37, 45–47; *in choosing to fall into the hands of the Almighty in his punishment for numbering Israel*, 2 Sam. 24:14; *in believing God's promise, that his kingdom would be a perpetual kingdom*, Acts 2:30.

*Job*, Job 1:21, 22; 2:10. *Eliphaz, in the overruling providence of God, that afflictions are for the good of the righteous*, Job 5:6–27. *Mordecai, in deliverance of the Jews*, Esth. 4:14.

*Elijah, in his controversy with the priests of Baal*, 1 Kin. 18:32–38. *Widow of Zarephath in feeding Elijah*, 1 Kin. 17:13–15. *Amaziah, in dismissing the Ephraimites in obedience to the command of God, and going alone to battle against the Edomites*, 2 Chr. 25:7–10. *Hezekiah*, 2 Kin. 18:5; 19.

*Daniel, in the lion's den*, Dan. 6. *The three Hebrews, who refused to worship Nebuchadnezzar's idol*, Dan. 3:13–27. *Nebuchadnezzar*, Dan. 6:16.

*Ninevites, in obeying Jonah*, Jonah 3:5. *Ezra, in making the journey from Babylon to Jerusalem without a military escort*, Ezra 8:22. *Habakkuk*, Hab. 3:17–19.

*Mary*, Luke 1:38. *Joseph, in obeying the vision about Mary and to flee into Egypt*, Matt. 1:18–24; 2:13, 14. *Simeon, when he saw Jesus in the temple*, Luke 2:25–35. *The ancient worthies*, Heb. 11:32–34. *Paul*, Rom. 8:18, 28, 38, 39; 1 Cor. 9:26; 2 Cor. 5:7; Gal. 5:5.

**Trial of**, Deut. 8:2. *Is precious*, 1 Pet. 1:7. *By tribulations*, Matt. 24:21–25; 2 Thess. 1:3–5. *By deferred hope*, Heb. 6:13–15. *By temptations*, Jas. 1:3, 12; see footnote, TEMPTATION, Luke 11:4.

INSTANCES OF TRIAL OF: *Noah*, Gen. 6:14–22; Heb. 11:7. *Abraham, when commanded to leave his native land and go he knew not whither*, Gen. 12:1–4; Heb. 11:8; *when commanded to offer Isaac*, Gen. 22:1–19; Heb. 11:17–19. *Moses, when sent to Pharaoh*, Ex. 3:11, 12; 4:10–17; Heb. 11:25–29; *at the Red Sea, by the murmurings of the people*, Ex. 14:15; Heb. 11:9. *Joshua and the children of Israel, in the method of taking Jericho*, Josh. 6; Heb. 11:30. *Gideon, when commanded to deliver Israel*, Judg. 6:36–40; 7; Heb. 11:32. *Job, by affliction and adversity*, Job 1; 2. *Ezra, in leaving Babylon without a military escort*, Ezra 8:22. *Daniel, when forbidden by decree to pray to Jehovah*, Dan. 6:4–23; Heb. 11:32, 33. *The three Hebrews, when commanded to worship Nebuchadnezzar's image*, Dan. 3:8–30; Heb. 11:32–34.

*The Syrophenician woman*, Matt. 15:21–28; Mark 7:24–30. *The two blind men who appealed to Jesus for sight*, Matt. 9:28.

The disciples: *By the question of Jesus, as to who he was,*

v.25–AD 30
See footnote, *Time*, Rev. 10:6.

*s Enemy*, Prov. 24:17.
*t God, fatherhood of*, Gen. 2:2.
*u Heaven, God's dwelling place*, Luke 18:22.
*v Sin, forgiveness of*, Rom. 5:12.

**26**
6 R. V. *omits this verse.*

**27**
*w* Matt. 21:23–27; Luke 20:1–8.
*x Jerusalem*, Judg. 19:10.
*y Temple, Herod's*, 1 Kin. 6:17.
*z Priest*, Lev. 1:5.

*a Scribe*, 1 Kin. 4:3.

**28**
*b Presumption*, Psa. 19:13.

**30**
*c Baptism, John's*, Luke 20:4.

**32**
*d Cowardice*, Lev. 26:36.
*e Public Opinion*, John 12:42.
*f John the Baptist*, Luke 1:63.
*g Prophets*, Isa. 3:2.

**33**
*h Falsehood*, Job 21:34.

**1**
*a Parables, of Jesus*, Ezek. 20:49.
*b Capital and Labor*, Matt. 21:33.
*c Vineyard, parable of*, Isa. 1:8.

against [s]any: that your [t]Father
also which is in [u]heaven may
[v]forgive you your trespasses.
26 [6]But if ye do not [q,r]forgive,
neither will your [t]Father which
is in [u]heaven forgive your trespasses.[T]
27 ¶ [w]And they come again to
[x]Jĕ-ru̦′să-lĕm: and as he was
walking in the [y]temple, there
come to him the chief [z]priests,
and the [a]scribes, and the elders,
28 And [b]say unto him, By
what authority doest thou these
things? and who gave thee this
authority to do these things?
29 And Jē′ṣus answered and
said unto them, I will also ask of
you one question,[G] and answer
me, and I will tell you by what
authority I do these things.
30 The [c]baptism of Jŏhn, was
*it* from heaven, or of men? answer me.
31 And they reasoned with
themselves, saying, If we shall
say, From heaven; he will say,
Why then did ye not believe
him?
32 But if we shall say, Of men;
they [d]feared the [e]people: for all
*men* counted [f]Jŏhn, that he was
a [g]prophet indeed.
33 And they answered and
[h]said unto Jē′ṣus, We cannot
tell. And Jē′ṣus answering saith
unto them, Neither do I tell you
by what authority I do these
things.

## CHAPTER 12

*The parable of the wicked husbandmen. 13 The question of the Pharisees about paying tribute to Cæsar, 18 and of the Sadducees concerning the resurrection. 28 The two great commandments. 35 Christ the son of David. 38 The evil example of the scribes to be avoided. 41 The widow's two mites.*

AND he began to speak unto
them by [a]parables. [b]A *cer-*
*tain* man planted a [c]vineyard, and
set an [d]hedge about *it*, and digged[G]
*a place for* the [e]winefat,[G] and
built a [f,g]tower, and [h]let[G] [i]it out
to [j,k]husbandmen,[G] and went into
a far country.[Q]
2 And at the [l]season he sent
to the [j]husbandmen[G] a [m]servant,
that he might receive from the
husbandmen[G] of the [n]fruit of the
[c]vineyard.
3 [o]And they caught *him*, and
beat him, and sent *him* away
empty.
4 And again he sent unto them
another [m]servant; and [1,o,p]at him
they cast stones, and wounded
*him* in the head, and sent *him*
away shamefully handled.
5 And again he sent [m]another;
[o]and him they [q]killed, and many
others; beating some, and killing
some.
6 Having yet therefore one
[r]son, his wellbeloved, he sent
him also last unto them, saying,
They will reverence[G] my son.[Q]
7 But those [j]husbandmen[G] [o]said
among themselves, This is the
heir; come, [p]let us kill him, and
the inheritance shall be our's.
8 And [o]they took him, and
[q]killed [s]*him*, and cast *him* out of
the [c]vineyard.[S]
9 What shall therefore the lord[G]
of the [c]vineyard do? he will come
and [t]destroy the [j,u]husbandmen,[G]
and will give the vineyard unto
others.
10[Q] And have ye not read this
[v]scripture; The [w,x]stone which
the builders rejected is become
the [y]head of the corner:
11 [v]This was the Lord's doing,
and it is marvellous in our eyes[Q]?
12 And they [z,a]sought to lay
hold on him, but [b]feared the
[c]people: for they knew that he
had spoken the [d]parable against

v 1–AD 30
See footnote, *Time*, Rev. 10:6.

*d Hedge*, Isa. 5:5.
*e Wine-press*, Isa. 5:2.
*f Tower*, 2 Chr. 26:9.
*g Fortification*, Ezek. 17:17.
*h Lease*, Matt. 21:33.
*i Land, leased*, Ruth 4:3.
*j Husbandman*, Matt. 21:33.
*k Ecclesiasticism*, Matt. 23:2.

**2**
*l Seasons*, Dan. 2:21.
*m Prophets, martyrs*, vs. 2–5; Isa. 3:2.
*n Grape*, Lev. 25:5.

**3**
*o Unfaithfulness*, vs. 4–8; Luke 16:11.

**4**
*p Malice*, Eph. 4:31.
1 R. V. *omits* and at him they cast stones,

**5**
*q Homicide, felonious*, Deut. 5:17.

**6**
*r Jesus, divine sonship of*, Matt. 1:21.

**8**
*s Jesus, rejected*, Matt. 1:21.

**9**
*t Wicked, punishment of*, Psa. 73:3.
*u* Matt. 21:41; Luke 20:16.

**10**
*v Prophecies*, Dan. 9:24.
*w Corner Stone, figurative*, Psa. 144:12.
*x Jesus, typified in the corner stone*, Matt. 1:21.
*y Jesus, head of the church*, Matt. 1:21.

**12**
*z Persecution, of Jesus*, John 15:20.

*a Malice, instances of*, Eph. 4:31.
*b Cowardice*, Lev. 26:36.
*c Public Opinion*, John 12:42.
*d Parables, of Jesus*, Ezek. 20:49.

Matt. 16:15–20; Luke 9:20, 21; *by their inability to cast out the evil spirit from the epileptic*, Matt. 17:14–21; Mark 9:14–29; Luke 9:37–42; *in the tempest at sea*, Matt. 8:23–27; Mark 4:36–41; Luke 8:22–26. *Of Philip, when questioned by Jesus as to how the multitude would be fed*, John 6:5, 6. *Of Peter, when asked whether he loved Jesus*, John 21:15–17.

**Rewards of:** *Protection*, 2 Sam. 22:31; Psa. 5:11; 9:9, 10; 18:30; 33:18–20; Prov. 29:25; 30:5; Jer. 39:18; Nah. 1:7; Heb. 13:5, 6. *Prosperity*, Prov. 28:25; Isa. 57:13; Jer. 17:7, 8. *Spiritual peace*, Psa. 2:12; 32:10; 40:4; 84:5, 12; Isa. 26:3; Rom. 15:13. *Eternal life*, 2 Tim. 1:1, 8.
See footnote, FAITH IN CHRIST, John 6:69.

v.12–AD 30
See footnote, *Time*, Rev. 10:6.

**13**
e Matt. 22:15–22; Luke 20:20–26.
f *Pharisees*, Matt. 15:12.
g *Herodians*, Mark 3:6.
h *Craftiness, instances of*, Psa. 83:3.

**14**
i *Hypocrisy, instances of*, Jas. 3:17.
j *Jesus, teacher*, Matt. 1:21.
k *Temptation, leading into*, Luke 11:4.
l *Tribute*, Ezra 4:13.
m *Rulers*, Ex. 18:21.
n *Government, duty of citizens to*, Isa. 22:21.

**15**
o *Penny*, Matt. 20:2.

**17**
p *Commandment, enjoining obedience to civil government*, Deut. 8:2.

**18**
q Matt. 22:23–33; Luke 20:27–40.
r *Sadducees*, Matt. 22:23.
s *Resurrection*, 1 Cor. 15:12.

**19**
t *Law, of Moses*, Deut. 33:2.
u *Brother*, Prov. 18:24.
v *Wife*, Prov. 5:18.
w *Marriage, levirate*, Gen. 34:9.

them: and they left him, and
went their way.
13 ¶ And [e]they send unto him
certain of the [f]Phăr'ĭ-seeş and of
the [g]Hē-rō'dĭ-anş, [h]to catch him
in *his* words.
14 And when [f,g]they were come,
they [i]say unto him, Master, *we
know that thou art true, and
carest for no man: for thou regardest not the person of men,
but [j]teachest the way of God in
truth: [k]Is it lawful to give [l]trib-
ute to [m,n]Çæ'şar, or not?[T]
15 Shall we give, or shall we
not give? But he, knowing
their [i]hypocrisy, said unto them,
Why [k]tempt ye me? bring me a
[o]penny, that I may see *it*.
16 And they brought [o]*it*. And
he saith unto them, Whose *is*
this image and superscription?
And they said unto him, Çæ'-
şar's.
17 And Jē'şus answering said
unto them, [p]Render to [m,n]Çæ'-
şar the things that are Çæ'şar's,
and to God the things that are
God's. And they marvelled at
him.
18 ¶ Then come unto [q]him the
[r]Săd'du-çeeş, which say there is
no [s]resurrection; and they asked
him, saying,
19 Master, Mō'şeş [t]wrote unto
us, If a man's [u]brother die, and
leave *his* [v]wife *behind him*, and
leave no children, that his
brother should [w]take his wife,
and raise up seed unto his
brother.[Q]
20 Now there were seven [u]breth-
ren: and the first took a [v]wife,
and dying left no seed.
21 And the second [w]took her,
and died, neither left he any
seed: and the third likewise.
22 And the seven [w]had her,
and left no seed: last of all the
woman died also.
23 In the [s]resurrection therefore, when they shall rise, whose
[v]wife shall she be of them? for
the seven had her to [w]wife.
24 And Jēşus answering said
unto them, Do ye not therefore
err, because ye [x,y]know not the
[z]scriptures, neither the [a]power
of God?
25 For when they shall [b]rise
from the dead, they neither
[c]marry, nor are given in marriage; but are as the [d]angels
which are in [e]heaven.
26 And as touching the dead,
that they [b]rise: have ye not read
in the [f]book of Mō'şeş, how in
the [g]bush God spake unto him,
saying, I *am* the God of [h]Ā'bră-
hăm, and the God of [i]Ī'şaac, and
the God of [j]Jā'cob?[Q]
27 He is not the God of the
dead, but the God of the [k]living:
ye therefore do greatly err.
28 ¶ [l]And one of the scribes
came, and having heard them
reasoning together, and perceiving that he had answered them
well, asked him, Which is the
first [m]commandment of all?
29 [Q]And Jē'şus answered him,
The first [2]of all the [m]command-
ments *is*, Hear, O Ĭş'ra-el; The
Lord our [n,o]God is one Lord:[T]
30 And [p,q]thou shalt [r,s]love the
Lord thy God with all thy heart,
and with all thy soul, and with
all thy mind, and with all thy
strength: [3]this *is* the first commandment.[Q]
31 And the second *is* like,
*namely* this, [t,u]Thou shalt
[v,w]love thy [x]neighbour as thyself. There is none other commandment greater than these.[Q]
32 [Q]And the scribe said unto

v.22–AD 30
See footnote, *Time*, Rev. 10:6.

**24**
x *Ignorance, of the Scriptures*, Acts 3:17.
y *Spiritual Blindness*, 2 Cor. 4:4.
z *Word of God*, Psa. 119:9.
a *God, power of*, Gen. 2:2.

**25**
b *Resurrection, taught by Jesus*, 1 Cor. 15:12.
c *Marriage, none in the resurrection state*, Gen. 34:9.
d *Angel*, Heb. 1:13.
e *Heaven, future home of the righteous*, Luke 18:22.

**26**
f *Law, of Moses*, Deut. 33:2.
g *Burning Bush*, Ex. 3:2.
h *Abraham*, Gen. 17:5.
i *Isaac*, Gen. 21:3.
j *Jacob*, Gen. 27:11.

**27**
k *Immortality*, 1 Cor. 15:54.

**28**
l Matt. 22:34–40; Luke 10:25–28.
m *Commandments*, Deut. 8:2.

**29**
n *God, sovereign*, Gen. 2:2.
o *God, unity of*, Gen. 2:2.
2 R. V. *omits* of all the commandments

**30**
p Deut. 6:5.
q *Commandment, enjoining love to God*, Deut. 8:2.
r *Love, of man for God*, 1 John 4:19.
s *Duty, of man to God*, Eccl. 12:13.
3 R. V. *omits* this is the first commandment.

**31**
t *Commandment, enjoining love to man*, Deut. 8:2.
u *Royal Law*, Jas. 2:8.
v *Love, of man for man*, 1 John 4:7.
w *Duty, of man to man*, Eccl. 12:13.
x *Neighbor, love for, enjoined*, Luke 10:29.

* **IRONY. Instances of:** *Michal to David*, 2 Sam. 6:20. *Elijah to the priests of Baal*, 1 Kin. 18:27. *Job to his accusers*, Job 12:2. *Ezekiel to the prince of Tyre*, Ezek. 28:3–5. *Micaiah*, 1 Kin. 22:15; 2 Chr. 18:14. *Amos to the Samaritans*, Amos 4:4. *Jesus to Pharisees*, Mark 2:17; Luke 5:31, 32. *Pharisees and Herodians to Jesus*, Matt. 22:16. *Roman soldiers to Jesus*, Matt. 27:29; Mark 15:17–19; Luke 23:11; John 19:2, 3. *Pilate, calling Jesus king*, Mark 15:19; John 19:15. *Superscription of Pilate on the cross over Jesus*, Matt. 27:37; Mark 15:26; Luke 23:38; John 19:19. *Paul to the Corinthians*, 2 Cor. 11:19. *Agrippa to Paul*, Acts 26:28.
See footnotes: SARCASM, Judg. 10:4; SATIRE, 1 Sam. 2:3.

v.32–AD 30
See footnote, *Time*, Rev. 10:6.

**33**
*y Offerings, unavailing when not accompanied by piety*, Lev. 6:17.
4 R. V. *omits* and with all the soul,

**34**
*z Speech, wise*, Col. 4:6.

*a Kingdom of Heaven*, Matt. 13:24.

**35**
*b Jesus, teacher*, Matt. 1:21.
*c Instruction, in religion*, Prov. 23:23.
*d Temple, Herod's*, 1 Kin. 6:17.
*e Scribe*, 1 Kin. 4:3.
*f Jesus, Messiah*, Matt. 1:21.
*g Jesus, humanity of*, Matt. 1:21.
*h David*, 1 Sam. 16:13.

**36**
*i Prophets, inspiration of*, Isa. 3:2.
*j Holy Spirit, inspiration of*, Acts 1:2.
*k Sovereignty of the Messiah*, Psa. 110:1.
*l Prophecies, concerning the Messiah, and their fulfillment*, Gen. 12:3.
*m Jesus, pre-existence of*, Matt. 1:21.
*n Footstool, figurative*, 1 Chr. 28:2.
5 R. V. Spirit,

**37**
*o Jesus, received*, Matt. 1:21.
*p Popularity of Jesus*, John 6:15.

**38**
*q* Matt. 23; Luke 20:45–47.
*r Doctrines of Jesus*, John 7:16.
*s Commandment, admonishing against hypocrisy*, Deut. 8:2.
*t Pride, admonitions against*, Prov. 16:18.

him, Well, Master, thou hast said the truth: for there is one [n,o]God; and there is none other but he:

33 And to [r,s]love him with all the heart, and with all the understanding, [4]and with all the soul, and with all the strength, and [u]to [v,w]love *his* [x]neighbour as himself, is more than all whole burnt [y]offerings and sacrifices.

34 And when Jē′ṣus saw that he [z]answered discreetly, he said unto him, Thou art not far from the [a]kingdom of God. And no man after that durst ask him *any question*.

35 ¶ And Jē′ṣus answered and said, while he [b,c]taught in the [d]temple, How say the [e]scribes that [f]Chrīst is the [g]son of [h]Dā′vid?

36 For Dā′vid himself [i]said by the [j]Holy [5]Ghost, [k,l]The LORD said to my [m]Lord, Sit thou on my right hand, till I make thine enemies thy [n]footstool.

37 [h]Dā′vid therefore himself calleth him Lord; and whence is he *then* his son? And the common people [o]heard him [p]gladly.

38 ¶ And [q]he said unto them in his [r]doctrine, [s,t,u]Beware of the [e]scribes, which love to [v]go in long clothing, and *love* [w]salutations in the marketplaces,

39 And [v]the chief seats in the [x]synagogues, and [v]the [6]uppermost rooms at †feasts:

40 Which [y]devour [z]widows' houses, and for a [a]pretence make long [b]prayers: these shall receive greater [7,c]damnation.

*u Ambition, Christ rebukes*, Hab. 2:5. *v Self-exaltation*, Luke 14:11. *w Salutations*, Luke 1:44. **39** *x Synagogue*, Matt. 12:9. 6 R. V. chief places **40** *y Oppression*, Eccl. 5:8. *z Wisdom*, 2 Sam. 14:5.—*a Hypocrisy*, Jas. 3:17. *b Prayer, of scribes*, Acts 6:4. *c Punishment*, Lev. 26:41. 7 R. V. condemnation.

41 ¶ [d]And Jē′ṣus sat over against the treasury, and beheld how the people cast [e]money into the treasury: and many that were [f]rich cast in [g]much.

42 And there came a certain [h]poor [i,j]widow, and she threw in two [k]mites, which make a farthing.

43 And [l]he called *unto him* his [m]disciples, and saith unto them, Verily I say unto you, That this [h]poor [i]widow hath [g]cast more in, than all they which have cast into the treasury:

44 For all *they* did cast in of their [8,n]abundance; but she of her want did [g]cast in [o]all that she had, *even* [o]all her living.

## CHAPTER 13

*Jesus foretells the destruction of the temple, 3 and the calamities that shall precede it. 24 The signs of his coming. 32 The day and the hour thereof unknown. 33 The duty of all to watch.*

AND [a]as he went out of the [b]temple, one of his [c]disciples saith unto him, Master, see what manner of [d]stones and what buildings *are here*!

2 And Jē′ṣus answering [e]said unto him, Seest thou these great buildings? there shall not be left one [d]stone upon another, that shall not be thrown down.

3 And as he sat upon the mount of [f]Ōl′īveṣ over against the [b]temple, [g]Pē′tẽr and [h]Jāmeṣ and [i]Jŏhn and [j]Ăn′drew asked him privately,

4 Tell us, when shall these things be? and what *shall be* the [k]sign when all these things shall be fulfilled?

5 And Jē′ṣus answering them began to say, [l,m]Take heed lest any *man* [1,n]deceive you:

v.41–AD 30
See footnote, *Time*, Rev. 10:6.

**41**
*d* Luke 21:1–4.
*e Money*, Jer. 32:9.
*f Rich*, Jas. 5:1.
*g Liberality*, 1 Tim. 6:18.

**42**
*h Poor*, Prov. 21:13.
*i Widow*, 2 Sam. 14:5.
*j Women, good*, Prov. 31:10.
*k* Luke 21:2.

**43**
*l Jesus, teacher*, Matt. 1:21.
*m Apostles*, Luke 6:13.

**44**
*n Riches*, Eccl. 4:8.
*o Self-denial*, Mark 8:34.
8 R. V. superfluity;

**1**
*a* Matt. 24; Luke 21:5–36.
*b Temple, Herod's*, 1 Kin. 6:17.
*c Apostles*, Luke 6:13.
*d Stones*, Ex. 24:12.

**2**
*e Jesus, revelations by*, Matt. 1:21.

**3**
*f Mount of Olives*, Mark 11:1.
*g Peter*, Mark 5:37.
*h James*, Luke 5:10.
*i John*, Mark 1:19.
*j Andrew*, Matt. 4:18.

**4**
*k Sign*, Mark 8:11.

**5**
*l Commandment, enjoining watchfulness against false christs*, Deut. 8:2.
*m Watchfulness, enjoined*, Matt. 24:42.
*n Apostasy, admonitions against*, Acts 1:25.
1 R. V. lead you astray.

† **FEASTS.** *Men alone present at*, Esth. 1:8; Mark 6:21; Luke 14:24; *women alone at*, Esth. 1:9. *Men and women attend*, Ex. 32:6 (with vs. 2, 3); Dan. 5:1–3. *Riddles propounded at*, Judg. 14:12. *Marriage feasts provided by the bridegroom*, Judg. 14:10, 17. *Guests arranged, according to age*, Gen. 43:33; *according to rank*, 1 Sam. 9:22; Luke 14:8–10.
*Guests at, reclined on couches at table*, Amos 6:4, 7; John 13:25. *Wine served at*, Esth. 5:6; 7:7.
*Covenants ratified by*, Gen. 26:28–30.
*Music at*, Isa. 5:12; Amos 6:5; Luke 15:25. *Dancing at*, Matt. 14:6; Luke 15:25.
*Given by kings*, Esth. 1:3–8; Dan. 5:1–4. *Drunkenness at*, 1 Sam. 25:36; Esth. 1:10; Dan. 5:1–4.
*Parable of*, Matt. 22:1–14; Luke 14:16–24.
CELEBRATIONS BY: *Of birthdays*, Gen. 40:20; Mark 6:21. *Of weaning of children*, Gen. 21:8. *Of coronations*, 1 Kin. 1:25; 1 Chr. 12:38–40. *Of national deliverances*, Esth. 8:17; 9:17–19.
**Figurative**, Rev. 19:9, 17.

v.6–AD 30
See footnote, *Time*, Rev. 10:6.

**6**
*o False Teachers*, 2 Pet. 2:1.
*p Antichrist*, 2 John 7.
2 R. V. lead many astray.

**7**
*q War*, Judg. 3:2.
*r Adversity, consolation in*, Psa. 10:6.

**8**
*s Earthquakes*, Isa. 29:6.
*t Famine*, 2 Kin. 8:1.
3 R. V. *omits* and troubles:

**9**
*u* Matt. 10:17–22.
*v Commandment, enjoining fortitude under persecution*, vs. 11–13; Deut. 8:2.
*w Persecution, of Christians foretold*, John 15:20.
*x Synagogue*, Matt. 12:9.
*y Beating*, Ex. 5:14.

**10**
*z Missions*, Matt. 28:19.

**11**
*a* Matt. 10:19.
*b Persecution of Christians, foretold*, John 15:20.
*c Commandment, enjoining fortitude under persecution*, Deut. 8:2.
*d Anxiety*, 1 Pet. 5:7. *e Promise, or ground of assurance*, 2 Cor. 1:20. *f Righteous, promises to*, Psa. 64:10. 4 R. V. be not anxious 5 R. V. *omits* neither do ye premeditate: *g Inspiration*, Job 32:8. *h Holy Spirit, inspiration of*, Acts 1:2. **12** *i Hostility to the righteous*, Mic. 7:6.

6 For [o,p]many shall come in my
name, saying, I am *Christ*; and
shall [2]deceive many.
7 And when ye shall hear of
[q]wars and rumours of wars, [r]be
ye not troubled: for *such things*
must needs be; but the end *shall*
not *be* yet.[Q]
8 For nation shall [q]rise against
nation, and kingdom against
kingdom: and there shall be
[s]earthquakes in divers[G] places,
and there shall be [t]famines [3]and
troubles: these *are* the beginnings of sorrows.[G Q]
9 ¶ But [u,v]take heed to yourselves: for they shall [w]deliver you
up to councils[G]; and in the [x]syna-
gogues ye shall be [y]beaten: and
ye shall be brought before rulers
and kings for my sake, for a testimony against them.
10 And the *gospel must first
be [z]published[G] among all nations.
11 But [a]when they shall lead
*you*, and [b]deliver you up, [4,c]take
no [d]thought beforehand what ye
shall speak, [5]neither do ye premeditate: but [e,f]whatsoever shall
be [g]given you in that hour, that
speak ye: for it is not ye that
speak, but the [h]Holy Ghost[G].[T]
12 Now [i]the brother shall [b]be-
tray the brother to death, and
the father the son; and [j]children
shall rise up against *their* parents, and shall cause them to be
[k]put to death.[Q]
13 And ye shall be [l]hated of all
*men* for my name's sake: [m]but
he that shall [n,o]endure unto the
end, [e,f]the same [p]shall be [q]saved.[S]
14 ¶ But [r,s]when ye shall see
the abomination of desolation,
[6]spoken of by [t]Dăn'iel the [u]pro-
phet, standing where [7]it ought
not, (let him that readeth understand,) then let them that
be in [v]Jū-dæ'ȧ flee to the mountains:[Q]
15 And let him that is on the
[w]housetop not go down into the
house, neither enter *therein*, to
take any thing out of his house:
16 And let him that is in the
field not turn back again for to
take up his garment.[S]
17 But woe to them that are
with child, and to them that give
suck in those days!
18 And pray ye that your flight
be not in the winter.
19 For *in* those days shall be
[x]affliction[G], such as was not from
the beginning of the †creation
which God [y]created unto this
time, neither shall be.[T Q]
20 And except that the [z]Lord
had shortened those days, no

v.12–AD 30
See footnote, *Time*, Rev. 10:6.

*j Children, wicked*, Mark 10:14.
*k Martyrdom*, Rev. 17:6.

**13**
*l Hatred*, Prov. 15:17.
*m Blessings, contingent upon obedience*, Deut. 11:26.
*n Perseverance, motives to*, Eph. 6:18.
*o Faithfulness, rewards of*, Luke 16:10.
*p Reward, a motive, to faithfulness*, Matt. 5:12.
*q Salvation*, Acts 16:17.

**14**
*r* Dan. 9:27; 11:31; 12:11; Matt. 24:15.
*s Jerusalem, destruction of, foretold*, vs. 14–23; Judg. 19:10.
*t Daniel*, Dan. 1:6.
*u Prophets*, Isa. 3:2.
*v Judea*, Luke 5:17.
6 R. V. *omits* spoken of by Daniel the prophet,
7 R. V. he

**15**
*w House, roof of*, Esth. 8:1.

**19**
*x Adversity*, Psa. 10:6.
*y God, creator*, Gen 2:2.

**20**
*z God, preserver*, Gen. 2:2.

***GOSPEL**, Matt. 13:17; Mark 1:14, 15; Luke 2:10, 11; 4:18, 19, 43, 44; Acts 10:36; 12:24; 19:20; Gal. 3:8; Col. 1:5, 23, 26–28; Rev. 14:6, 7. *From God*, John 17:7, 8, 14. *Called* THE NEW COVENANT, Jer. 31:31–34; Heb. 7:22; 8:6–13; 9:8–15; 10:9; 12:22–24.

Described as: *Gospel of the kingdom*, Matt. 4:23; 24:14; *gospel of God*, Rom. 1:1; 15:16; 1 Thess. 2:8; 1 Pet. 4:17; *gospel of Christ*, Mark 1:1; 1 Cor. 9:12, 18; Gal. 1:7; Phil. 1:27; 1 Thess. 3:2; *the dispensation of the grace of God*, Eph. 3:2; *gospel of the grace of God*, Acts 20:24; *gospel of your salvation*, Eph. 1:13; *gospel of peace*, Eph. 6:15; *good tidings*, Isa. 40:9; 41:27; 52:7; 61:1; [R. V.] Matt. 11:5; Luke 7:22; Acts 13:32, 33; 1 Pet. 1:25; *the kingdom of God*, Luke 16:16; *law of liberty*, Jas. 1:25; *word of God*, 1 Thess. 2:13; 1 Pet. 1:23; *word of the Lord*, 1 Pet. 1:25; *word of Christ*, Col. 3:16; *word of this salvation*, Acts 13:26; *word of reconciliation*, 2 Cor. 5:19; *word of truth*, Eph. 1:13; *word of faith*, Rom. 10:8; *words of this life*, Acts 5:20; *words of life*, Phil. 2:16; *doctrine according to godliness*, 1 Tim. 6:3; *everlasting gospel* (Am. R. V. eternal good tidings), Rev. 14:6; *the faith*, Jude 3.

*Likened to, a mustard seed*, Matt. 13:31, 32; Mark 4:30–33; Luke 13:18, 19; *good seed*, Matt. 13:24–30, 36–43; *leaven*, Matt. 13:33; *a pearl of great price*, Matt. 13:45, 46; Luke 13:20, 21; *a hidden treasure*, Matt. 13:44; *a householder*, Matt. 20:1–16; *a feast*, Luke 14:16–24.

*Contrasted with the law*, John 1:16, 17.

*Dissemination of*, Acts 14:3; 16:17; 20:24. *Dissemination of, enjoined*, Matt. 24:14; 28:18–20; Mark 13:10; Mark 16:15; Acts 5:20; Rom. 10:15–18; 16:25, 26; 1 Cor. 1:18, 21, 24, 25; 9:16–18; Eph. 3:8–11.

*Life and immortality brought to light in*, 2 Tim. 1:10. *Salvation through*, Rom. 1:16, 17; 1 Cor. 15:1, 2; Eph. 1:13, 14; Jas. 1:21; 1 Pet. 1:23. *Preached to the dead*, 1 Pet. 3:19; 4:6.

*Prophecies concerning*, Isa. 2:3–5; 4:2–6; 9:2, 6, 7; 25:7–9; 29:18, 24; 32:3, 4; 35:5–10; 40:9; 41:27; 42:6, 7; 49:13; 51:4–6; 52:7; 55:1–5; 60:1–22; 61:1–3; Jer. 31:31–34; Ezek. 34:23–31; 47:1–12; Joel 2:28–32; Mic. 4:1–7; Matt. 24:14, Luke 1:67–79; 2:12–14, 34.

See footnotes: JESUS, *Kingdom of, prophecies concerning*, Matt. 1:21; CHURCH, *Prophecies concerning its prosperity*, Matt. 16:18.

† **CREATION**, Psa. 148:3–5; Prov. 16:4; Isa. 45:7; 66:2; Jer. 51:19; Amos 4:13; Mark 13:19; Acts 7:50; Rom. 1:20; 1 Cor. 11:12; Heb. 2:10; 3:4; Rev. 4:11.

*Of the earth*, Gen. 1:1, 2, 9, 10; 2:1–4; Ex. 20:11; 1 Sam. 2:8; 2 Kin. 19:15; Neh. 9:6; Job 38:4, 7–10; Psa. 24:1, 2; 89:11; 90:2; 95:5; 102:25; 104:2, 3, 5, 6, 24, 30; 119:90; 121:2; 124:8; 136:5–9; 146:5, 6; Prov. 3:19; 8:26–29; Isa. 37:16; 40:28; 42:5; 44:24; 45:12, 18; 48:13; 51:13, 16; Jer. 10:12; 27:5; 32:17; 51:15; Jonah 1:9; Acts 4:24; 14:15; 17:24, 25; Rev. 10:6; 14:7.

*Of the heavens*, Gen. 1:1, 6–8; 2:1–4; Ex. 20:11; 2 Kin. 19:15; 1 Chr. 16:26; Neh. 9:6; Job 9:8, 9; 37:16, 18; Psa. 8:3; 19:1, 4; 96:5; 102:25; 104:2, 3, 5, 6, 24, 30; 121:2; 124:8; 136:5; 146:5, 6; Prov. 3:19; 8:26–28; Isa. 37:16; 42:5; 44:

v.20–AD 30
See footnote, *Time,* Rev. 10:6.

*a* *Intercession, influence of the righteous,* Jer. 27:18.
*b* *Foreordination,* Rom. 8:30.

**21**
*c* Matt. 24:23–31; Luke 21:24–28.
*d* *False Teachers,* 2 Pet. 2:1.
*e* *Antichrist,* 2 John 7.
*f* *Commandment, enjoining watchfulness against false christs,* Deut. 8:2.

**22**
*g* *Prophets, false,* Isa. 3:2.
*h* *Sign,* Mark 8:11.
*i* *Temptation, leading into,* Luke 11:4.

**23**
*j* *Watchfulness, enjoined,* Matt. 24:42.
*k* *Jesus, prophet,* Matt. 1:21.

**24**
*l* *Adversity,* Psa. 10:6.
*m* *Astronomy,* Isa. 13:10.
*n* *Sun, darkening of,* Josh. 10:12.
*o* *Eclipse,* Isa. 13:10.
*p* *Moon, darkening of,* Song 6:10.

**25**
*q* *Stars, falling of,* Judg. 5:20.

**26**
*r* *Jesus, humanity of,* Matt. 1:21.
*s* *Jesus, second coming of,* Matt. 1:21.
*t* *Jesus, power of,* Matt. 1:21.

**27**
*u* *Judgment, the general,* 2 Pet. 3:7.
*v* *Angel, functions of,* Heb. 1:13.
*w* *Righteous, promises to,* Psa. 64:10.
*x* *Earth,* Prov. 8:23.

flesh should be saved: but [a]for
the [b]elect's sake, whom he hath
chosen, he hath shortened the
days.[S]
21 [c]And then if any [d]man shall
say to you, Lo, [e]here *is* Christ; or,
Lo, *he is* there; [f]believe *him* not:
22 For [e]false Christs and false
[g]prophets shall rise, and shall
shew [h]signs and wonders, to [i]seduce,[G] if *it were* possible, even the
[b]elect.[G] [S Q]
23 But [f,j]take ye heed: behold,
[k]I have foretold you all things.
24 ¶ But in those days, after
that [l]tribulation, [m]the [n]sun shall
be [o]darkened, and the [p]moon
shall [o]not give her light,[Q]
25 And the [q]stars of heaven
shall fall, and the powers that
are in heaven shall be shaken.[Q]
26 And then shall they see the
[r]Son of man [s]coming in the
clouds with great [t]power and
glory.[Q]
27 And [u]then shall he send his
[v]angels, and [w]shall gather together his [b]elect from the four
winds, from the uttermost part
of the [x]earth to the uttermost
part of heaven.[Q]
28 [y]Now learn a [z]parable[G] of the
[a]fig tree; When her branch is yet
tender, and putteth forth leaves,
ye know that [b]summer is near:
29 So ye in like manner, when
ye shall see these [c]things come to
pass, know that [8,d]it is nigh,[G] *even*
at the doors.
30 Verily[G] [e]I say unto you, that
this generation shall not pass,
till all these things be done.
31 [f]Heaven and [g]earth shall
pass away: but my [h,i]words shall
not pass away.[Q]
32 ¶ [j]But of that [k]day and *that*
hour knoweth no man, no, not
the angels which are in heaven,
neither the [l]Son, [m]but the [n]Father.[S T]
33 [o,p]Take ye heed, [q]watch and
[r]pray: for ye know not when the
time is.
34 [9,s]*For the Son of man is* as a
man taking a far journey, who
left his house, and gave authority to his servants, and to every
man his work, and commanded
the porter to watch.
35 [o,q]Watch ye therefore: for ye
know not when the [d]master of
the house cometh, at even,[G] or at
midnight, or at the cockcrowing,[G]
or in the morning:
36 Lest coming suddenly he
find you sleeping.
37 And what I say unto you I
say unto all, [o,q]Watch.

## CHAPTER 14

*The rulers conspire against Jesus.* 3 *At Bethany a woman anoints his head.* 10 *Judas conspires against him.* 12 *Jesus keeps the passover;* 22 *institutes the Lord's supper;* 32 *prays in the garden;* 43 *and is betrayed with a kiss.* 53 *He is brought before the high priest and condemned.* 66 *Peter denies him.*

[a]AFTER two days was *the*
*feast of* the [b]passover, and
of unleavened bread: and the
chief [c]priests and the [d]scribes
[e]sought how they might take him
by [f]craft,[G] and put *him* to death.
2 But they said, Not on the
[b]feast *day,* [g]lest there be an
uproar of the people.
3 ¶ [h]And being in [i]Bĕth'a-ny̆ in
the [j]house of [k]Sī'mon the [l]leper,
as he sat at meat,[G] there came a
[m,n]woman having an [o]alabaster

v.31–AD 30
See footnote, *Time,* Rev. 10:6.

*g* *Earth, destruction of,* Prov. 8:23.
*h* *Word of God,* Psa. 119:9.
*i* *Doctrines of Jesus,* John 7:16.

**32**
*j* Matt. 24:36–51; Luke 21:34–36.
*k* *Judgment, the general,* 2 Pet. 3:7.
*l* *Jesus, relation of, to the Father,* Matt. 1:21.
*m* *God, foreknowledge of,* Gen. 2:2.
*n* *God, fatherhood of,* Gen. 2:2.

**33**
*o* *Commandment, enjoining watchfulness,* vs. 34–37; Deut. 8:2.
*p* *Preparedness,* Luke 12:40.
*q* *Watchfulness, enjoined,* Matt. 24:42.
*r* *Prayer, enjoined,* Acts 6:4.

**34**
*s* *Parables, of Jesus,* Ezek. 20:49.
9 R. V. It is as when a man, sojourning in another country,

**1**
*a* Matt. 26:1–5; Luke 22:1, 2.
*b* *Passover,* Num. 9:5.
*c* *Priest,* Lev. 1:5.
*d* *Scribe,* 1 Kin. 4:3.
*e* *Persecution, of Jesus,* John 15:20.
*f* *Craftiness,* Psa. 83:3.

**2**
*g* *Public Opinion,* John 12:42.

**3**
*h* Matt. 26:6–13; John 12:1–8; see also Luke 7:36–39.
*i* *Bethany,* John 11:18.

**28** *y* Matt. 24:32–35; Luke 21:29–33. *z* *Parables, of Jesus,* Ezek. 20:49.—*a* *Fig Tree,* Luke 13:6. *b* *Summer,* Isa. 28:4. **29** *c* *Sign,* Mark 8:11. *d* *Jesus, second coming of,* Matt. 1:21. 8 R. V. he **30** *e* *Jesus, prophet,* Matt. 1:21. **31** *f* *Heavens, physical, destruction of,* Psa. 8:3.

*j* *Hospitality,* Rom. 12:13. *k* Matt. 26:6. *l* *Leprosy,* Lev. 13:2. *m* *Women, good, instances of,* Prov. 31:10. *n* *Mary,* John 11:2. *o* Matt. 26:7; Luke 7:37.

24; 45:18; Jer. 32:17; Amos 5:8; Acts 4:24; 14:15; Rev. 10:6; 14:7.
*Of the sun, moon and stars,* Gen. 1:14–19; Psa. 136:7–9.
*Of the seas,* Gen. 1:9, 10; Ex. 20:11; Neh. 9:6; Psa. 95:5; 146:5, 6; Prov. 8:26–29; Jonah 1:9; Acts 4:24; 14:15; Rev. 10:6; 14:7.
*Of vegetation,* Gen. 1:11, 12.
*Of animals,* Gen. 1:20–25; Job 12:7–9; Jer. 27:5.
*Of man,* Gen. 1:26–28; 2:7; 5:1, 2; 9:6; Ex. 4:11; Deut. 4:32; 32:6, 15, 18; Job 10:3, 8, 9, 11, 12; 31:15; 33:4; 34:19; Psa. 94:9; 95:6; 100:3; 119:73; 149:2; Prov. 20:12; 22:2; Eccl. 7:29; 12:1; Isa. 17:7; 42:5; 43:1, 7, 15; 44:2, 24; 45:12; 51:13; 64:8; Jer. 27:5; Zech. 12:1; Mal. 2:10; Mark 10:6; Acts 17:24–29.
*By God's word,* Psa. 33:6, 7, 9; 2 Cor. 4:6; Heb. 11:3; 2 Pet. 3:5. *By God's will,* Rev. 4:11.
*By Christ,* John 1:3, 10; Rom. 11:36; 1 Cor. 8:6; Eph. 3:9; Col. 1:16, 17; Heb. 1:1, 2, 10; Rev. 3:14.

v.3–AD 30
See footnote, *Time*, Rev. 10:6.

*p Cruse*, 1 Sam. 26:11.
*q Ointment*, Eccl. 7:1.
*r Spikenard*, Song 4:13.
*s Love, for Jesus*, 1 John 4:19.
*t Anointing*, Deut. 28:40.
1 R. V. costly;

**4**
*u Frugality, cloak of covetousness*, Matt. 14:20.

**5**
*v Penny*, Matt. 20:2.
*w Poor*, Prov. 21:13.

**7**
*x Kindness*, Acts 28:2.

**9**
*y Gospel*, Mark 13:10.
*z Preaching*, Matt. 9:35.

*a Missions*, Matt. 28:19.
*b Mary*, John 11:2.

**10**
*c Judas*, Mark 3:19.
*d Apostles*, Luke 6:13.
*e Apostasy, instances of*, Acts 1:25.
*f Priest*, Lev. 1:5.
*g Infidelity, of friends*, 2 Cor. 6:15.
*h Betrayal, of Jesus*, Matt. 26:46.

**11**
*i Church, corruption in*, Matt. 16:18.
*j Bribery*, 1 Sam. 8:3.
*k Money*, Jer. 32:9.

**12**
*l* Matt. 26:17–19; Luke 22:7–13.
*m Passover*, Num. 9:5.

**13**
*n Peter*, Mark 5:37.
*o John*, Mark 1:19.
*p Jesus, omniscience of*, Matt. 1:21.

[p]box of [q]ointment of [r]spikenard
very [1]precious; and [s]she brake
the box, and [t]poured *it* on his
head.
4 And there were some that had
indignation within themselves,
and said, [u]Why was this waste
of the [q]ointment made?
5 For [u]it might have been sold
for more than three hundred
[v]pence, and have been given to
the [w]poor. And they murmured
against her.
6 And Jē′ṣus said, Let [m,n]her
alone; why trouble ye her? she
hath wrought a good work on
me.
7 For ye have the [w]poor with
you always, and whensoever ye
will ye may [x]do them good: but
me ye have not always.
8 [n]She hath done what she
could: she is come aforehand to
[t]anoint my body to the burying.
9 Verily I say unto you, Wheresoever this [y]gospel shall be
[z]preached [a]throughout the whole
world, *this* also that [b]she hath
done shall be spoken of for a
memorial of her.
10 ¶ And [c]Jū′das Ĭs-căr′ĭ-ot,
one of the [d]twelve, [e]went unto
the chief [f]priests, [g]to [h]betray
him unto them.
11 And [i]when [j]they heard *it*,
they were glad, and promised
to [j]give him [k]money. And he
sought how he might conven-
iently [h]betray him.
12 ¶ [l]And the first day of unleavened bread, when they killed
the [m]passover, his [d]disciples said
unto him, Where wilt thou that
we go and prepare that thou
mayest eat the passover?
13 And he sendeth forth [n,o]two
of his [d]disciples, and saith unto
them, Go ye into the city, and
[p]there shall meet you a man
bearing a pitcher of water: follow him.
14 And wheresoever he shall go
in, say ye to the goodman of the
house, The Master saith, Where
is the [q]guestchamber, where I
shall eat the [m]passover with my
[d]disciples?
15 And he will shew you a large
upper room furnished *and* prepared: there make ready for us.
16 And his disciples went forth,
and came into the city, and
found as he had said unto them:
and they made ready the passover.
17 And in the evening he cometh with the [d]twelve.
18 And as they sat and did eat,
Jē′ṣus said, Verily I say unto
you, [c]One of you which eateth
with me shall [h]betray me.
19 And they began to be sorrowful, and to say unto him one
by one, [r]*Is* it I? and another
*said, Is* it I?
20 And he answered and said
unto them, *It is* one of the
[d]twelve, that dippeth with me in
the dish.
21 The [s]Son of man indeed goeth, as [t]it is written of him: but
woe to that man by whom the
Son of man is [h]betrayed! good
were it for that man if he had
never been born.
22 ¶ *And as they did eat, Jē′-
ṣus took [u,v]bread, and [w]blessed,
and brake *it*, and gave to them,
and said, Take, eat: this is my
body.
23 And he took the [x,y]cup, and
when he had given [w]thanks, he
gave *it* to them: and they all
drank of it.
24 And he said unto them,
[y]This is my [z,a]blood of the
[2,b]new testament, which is [c]shed
for many.

v.13–AD 30
See footnote, *Time*, Rev. 10:6.

**14**
*q House, architecture of*, Esth. 8:1.

**19**
*r Self-examination*, 2 Cor. 13:5.

**21**
*s Jesus, humanity of*, Matt. 1:21.
*t Prophecies, concerning the Messiah, and their fulfillment*, Gen. 12:3.

**22**
*u Bread, symbolical*, 1 Cor. 11:23.
*v Symbols and Similitudes*, Heb. 9:9.
*w Thanksgiving, for food*, Luke 24:30.

**23**
*x Cup*, Gen. 44:2.
*y Wine, symbolical*, Prov. 23:31.

**24**
*z Blood, of Christ*, Heb. 9:19.

*a Jesus, atoning blood of*, Matt. 1:21.
*b New Covenant*, Jer. 31:31.
*c Jesus, design of his death*, Matt. 1:21.
2 R. V. covenant,

* **EUCHARIST.** *Instituted*, Matt. 26:17–29; Mark 14:22–25; Luke 22:19, 20; John 13:1–4. *Celebrated by the disciples*, Acts 2:42, 46; 20:7; 1 Cor. 11:26. *Bread and cup of, are symbols of the body and blood of our Lord*, Matt. 26:26–28; 1 Cor. 10:16, 17, 21, 22; 11:23–25. *Self-examination before taking, enjoined*, 1 Cor. 11:27–32. *Profanation of, forbidden*, 1 Cor. 11:20–22, 33, 34.

v.25–AD 30
See footnote, *Time*, Rev. 10:6.

**25**
*d Wine*, Prov. 23:31.

**26**
*e Music*, 2 Chr. 5:13.
*f Praise*, Psa. 150:1.
*g Song*, Psa. 77:6.
*h Mount of Olives*, Mark 11:1.

**27**
*i* Matt. 26:31–35.
*j Prophecies, concerning the Messiah, and their fulfillment*, Gen. 12:3.
*k Shepherd, figurative*, Jer. 31:10.
*l Jesus, names of*, Matt. 1:21.
*m Sheep, figurative*, Deut. 32:14.
3 R. V. *omits* because of me this night:

**28**
*n Jesus, resurrection of*, Matt. 1:21.
*o Galilee*, Mark 6:21.

**29**
*p Peter*, Mark 5:37.
*q False Confidence*, Psa. 30:6.
*r Zeal, exemplified*, 2 Cor. 7:11.

**30**
*s Jesus, prophet*, Matt. 1:21.
*t* Matt. 26:34, 74, 75; Luke 22:34, 60, 61; John 13: 38; 18:27.

**32**
*u Apostles*, Luke 6:13.
*v Prayers of Jesus*, Luke 5:16.

**33**
*w James*, Luke 5:10.
*x John*, Mark 1:19.
*y Despondency*, Eccl. 2:20.
4 R. V. sore troubled.

**34**
*z Jesus, sufferings of*, Matt. 1:21.

*a Watchfulness, enjoined*, Matt. 24: 42.

**35**
*b Prayer, postures in*, Acts 6:4.

25 Verily I say unto you, I will drink no more of the [d]fruit of the vine, until that day that I drink it new in the kingdom of God.

26 ¶ And when they had [e,f]sung an [g]hymn, they went out into the mount of [h]Ŏl′ĭveṣ.

27 [i]And Jē′ṣus saith unto them, All ye shall be offended [3]because of me this night: for it is [j]written, I will smite the [k,l]shepherd, and the [m]sheep shall be scattered.[Q]

28 But after that [n]I am risen, I will go before you into [o]Găl′ĭ-lee.

29 But [p]Pē′tẽr said unto him, Although all shall be offended, [q,r]yet *will* not I.

30 And [s]Jē′ṣus saith unto him, Verily I say unto thee, That this day, *even* in this night, before the [t]cock crow twice, thou shalt deny me thrice.

31 But he spake the more vehemently, [q,r]If I should die with thee, I will not deny thee in any wise.[C] Likewise also said they all.

32 ¶ And they came to a place which was named †Gĕth-sĕm′a-nē: and he saith to his [u]disciples, Sit ye here, while I shall [v]pray.

33 And he taketh with him [p]Pē′tẽr and [w]Jāmeṣ and [x]Jŏhn, and began to be sore[C] amazed, and to be [4]very [y]heavy[C];

34 And saith unto them, [y,z]My soul is exceeding sorrowful unto death: tarry ye here, and [a]watch.[Q]

35 And he went forward a little, and [b]fell on the ground, and [c,d]prayed that, if it were possible, the hour might pass from him.

36 And he [c]said, Ăb′bȧ, [e]Father, all things *are* possible unto [f]thee; take away this [g]cup from me: nevertheless [h,i,j]not what I will, but [k]what thou [l]wilt.[C][T]

37 And he cometh, and findeth [m]them [n]sleeping, and saith unto [o]Pē′tẽr, Sī′mon, sleepest thou? couldest not thou watch one hour?

38 [p]Watch ye and [q]pray, lest ye enter into [r]temptation. The [s]spirit truly *is* ready, but the flesh *is* weak.

39 And [t]again he went away, and [c,d]prayed, and spake the same words.

40 And when he returned, he found [m]them [n]asleep again, (for their eyes were heavy,) neither wist[C] they what to answer him.

41 And he cometh the third time, and saith unto them, [n]Sleep on now, and take *your* rest: it is enough, the hour is come; behold, the [u]Son of man is [v]betrayed into the hands of [w]sinners.

42 Rise up, let us go; lo, [x]he that [v]betrayeth me is at hand.

43 ¶ And immediately, while he yet spake, cometh [x]Jū′das, one of the [m]twelve, and with him a great multitude with [y]swords and staves[C], from the chief [z]priests and the [a]scribes and the [b]elders.

44 And he that [c]betrayed him had given them a [d]token[C], [e]saying, Whomsoever I shall [f]kiss, that same is he; take him, and lead *him* away safely.

45 And as soon as he was come, he goeth straightway to him, and [g]saith, [5,h]Master, master; and [f]kissed him.

46 And they [i]laid their hands on him, and [j]took him.

47 And [k]one of them that stood by drew a [l]sword, and smote a [m,n]servant of the [o]high priest, and cut off his ear.

48 And Jē′ṣus answered and said unto them, Are ye come out, as against a [p]thief, with [l]swords and *with* staves[C] to take me?

v.37–AD 30
See footnote, *Time*, Rev. 10:6.

**37**
*m Apostles*, Luke 6:13.
*n Sleep*, Psa. 127:2.
*o Peter*, Mark 5:37.

**38**
*p Commandment, enjoining watchfulness*, Deut. 8:2.
*q Prayer, enjoined*, Acts 6:4.
*r Temptation, admonitions against yielding to*, Luke 11:4.
*s Man, spirit*, Job 4:17.

**39**
*t Prayer, importunity in*, Acts 6:4.

**41**
*u Jesus, humanity of*, Matt. 1:21.
*v Betrayal, of Jesus*, Matt. 26:46.
*w Wicked*, Psa. 73:3.

**42**
*x Judas*, Mark 3:19.

**43**
*y Sword*, 1 Chr. 21:5.
*z Priest*, Lev. 1:5.

*a Scribe*, 1 Kin. 4:3.
*b Senate*, Num. 11:16.

**44**
*c Betrayal, of Jesus*, Matt. 26:46.
*d Sign*, Mark 8:11.
*e Treachery*, 2 Kin. 9:23.
*f Kiss*, Ruth 1:14.

**45**
*g Friends, false*, Ex. 33:11.
*h Hypocrisy*, Jas. 3:17.
5 R. V. Rabbi;

**46**
*i Arrest, of Jesus*, Matt. 26:57.
*j Prisoners*, Psa. 79:11.

**47**
*k Peter*, Mark 5:37.
*l Sword*, 1 Chr. 21:5.
*m Servant*, Jer. 2:14.
*n* Matt. 26:57; Luke 22:50.
*o High Priest*, Lev. 21:10.

**48**
*p Thieves*, Deut. 24:7.

*c Prayers of Jesus*, Luke 5:16. *d Adversity, prayer in*, Psa. 10:6. **36** *e God, fatherhood of*, Gen. 2:2. *f God, power of*, Gen. 2:2. *g Cup, figurative*, Matt. 20:22. *h Adversity, resignation in*, Psa. 10:6. *i Jesus, death of, voluntary*, Matt. 1:21. *j Renunciation*, Luke 5:11. *k Jesus, obedience of*, Matt. 1:21. *l Will of God, the supreme rule of duty*, Mark 3:35.

† **GETHSEMANE**, a garden near Jerusalem. *Jesus betrayed in*, Matt. 26:36–50; Mark 14:32–46; Luke 22:39–49; John 18:1–12.

v.49–AD 30
See footnote, *Time,* Rev. 10:6.

**49**
*q Temple, Herod's,* 1 Kin. 6:17.
*r Jesus, teacher,* Matt. 1:21.
*s Instruction, in religion,* Prov. 23:23.
*t Prophecies, concerning the Messiah, and their fulfillment,* Gen. 12:3.
*u Word of God,* Psa. 119:9.

**50**
*v Apostles, forsake Jesus,* Luke 6:13.
*w Cowardice,* Lev. 26:36.

**53**
*x High Priest,* Lev. 21:10.
*y Caiaphas,* Matt. 26:3.
*z Priest,* Lev. 1:5.
*a Senate,* Num. 11:16.
*b Scribe,* 1 Kin. 4:3.

**54**
*c Peter,* Mark 5:37.
*d Palace,* 1 Kin. 21:1.
*e High Priest,* Lev. 21:10.
*f Caiaphas,* Matt. 26:3.
6 R. V. court
7 R. V. officers,

**55**
*g Priest,* Lev. 1:5.
*h Court, corrupt,* Ex. 18:26.
*i Malice,* Eph. 4:31.
*j Persecution, of Jesus,* John 15:20.

**56**
*k Perjury, instances of,* 1 Tim. 1:10.
*l False Witness,* Matt. 19:18.

**60**
*m Defense,* Acts 19:33.

**61**
*n Jesus, meekness of,* Matt. 1:21.

49 I was daily with you in
the [q]temple [r,s]teaching, and ye
took me not: but the [t,u]scrip-
tures must be fulfilled.
50 And [v]they all [w]forsook him,
and fled.[Q]
51 And there followed him a
certain young man, having a
linen cloth cast about *his* naked
*body*; and the young men laid
hold on him:
52 And he left the linen cloth,
and fled from them naked.
53 ¶ ‡And they led Jē′ṣus away
to the [x,y]high priest: and with
him were assembled all the chief
[z]priests and the [a]elders and the
[b]scribes.
54 And [c]Pē′tēr followed him
afar off, even into the [6,d]palace
of the [e,f]high priest: and he sat
with the [7]servants, and warmed
himself at the fire.
55 ‡And the chief [g]priests and
all the [h]council[G] [i,j]sought[G] for
witness against Jē′ṣus to put
him to death; and found
none.
56 ‡For many [k]bare [l]false[G] witness against him, but their witness agreed not together.
57 ‡And there arose certain[G],
and [k]bare [l]false[G] witness against
him, saying,
58 We heard him say, I will destroy this temple that is made
with hands, and within three
days I will build another made
without hands.
59 But neither so did their witness[G] agree together.
60 ‡ And[Q] the [e,f]high priest stood
up in the midst, and asked Jē′-
ṣus, saying, [m]Answerest thou
nothing? what *is it which* these
witness against thee?
61 ‡But[T] [n]he ‖held his peace, and
[m]answered nothing. Again the
[e,f]high priest asked him, and said
unto him, Art thou the [o]Chrīst,
the [p]Son of the Blessed?[Q]
62 And Jē′ṣus said, I am: and
[q]ye shall see the Son of man [r]sit-
ting on the right hand of power,
and [s]coming in the clouds of
heaven.[T Q]
63 Then the [e,f]high priest [t]rent[G]
his clothes, and saith, What need
we any further witnesses?[Q]
64 ‡,[u]Ye have heard the [v]blas-
phemy[G]: what think ye? And
[w]they all condemned him to be
[8]guilty[G] of death.[Q]
65 [x]And some began to [y]spit
on him, and to cover his face,
and to buffet[G] him, and to [z]say
unto him, Prophesy[G]: and the
[9]servants did strike him with
the palms of their hands.
66 ¶ [a]And as [b]Pē′tēr was beneath in the [c]palace, there cometh one of the maids of the [d]high
priest:
67 And when she saw [b]Pē′tēr
warming himself, she looked upon him, and said, And thou also
wast with [e]Jē′ṣus of Năz′a-rĕth.
68 [f]But he [g]denied, saying, I
know not, neither understand I
what thou sayest. And he went
out into the porch; and the [h]cock
crew[G].
69 And a maid saw him again,
and began to say to them that
stood by, This is *one* of them.
70 [f]And he [g]denied it again.
And a little after, they that
stood by said again to [b]Pē′tēr,
Surely thou art *one* of them: for
thou art a [i]Găl′ĭ-læ′an, [10]and thy
[j]speech agreeth *thereto*.
71 But he began to curse and to
[k,l]swear[G], *saying*, I know not this
man of whom ye speak.
72 And the second time the
[h]cock crew[G]. And [b]Pē′tēr [m]called

10 R. V. *omits the rest of this verse.*
**71** *k Oath,* Num. 5:19. *l Perjury, instances of,* 1 Tim. 1:10.
**72** *m Conscience, guilty,* Acts 23:1.

v.61–AD 30
See footnote, *Time,* Rev. 10:6.
*o Jesus, Messiah,* Matt. 1:21.
*p Jesus, names of,* Matt. 1:21.

**62**
*q Jesus, revelations by,* Matt. 1:21.
*r Jesus, king,* Matt. 1:21.
*s Jesus, second coming of,* Matt. 1:21.

**63**
*t Rending of Garments,* 2 Chr. 34:27.

**64**
*u False Accusation,* 2 Tim. 3:3.
*v Blasphemy, false indictments for,* 2 Sam. 12:14.
*w Court, corrupt,* Ex. 18:26.
8 R. V. worthy

**65**
*x Persecution, of Jesus,* John 15:20.
*y Spitting,* Num. 12:14.
*z Mocking,* 1 Kin. 18:27.
9 R. V. officers

**66**
*a* Matt. 26:69–75; Luke 22:55–62; John 18:15–18, 25–27.
*b Peter,* Mark 5:37.
*c Palace,* 1 Kin. 21:1.
*d High Priest,* Lev. 21:10.

**67**
*e Jesus, names of,* Matt. 1:21.

**68**
*f Temptation, yielding to,* Luke 11:4.
*g Falsehood, instances of,* Job 21:34.
*h* Matt. 26:34, 74, 75; Luke 22:34, 60, 61; John 13:38; 18:27.

**70**
*i Galilee, dialect of,* Mark 6:21.
*j Language,* Dan. 3:29.

‡ **TRIAL OF JESUS. Jewish:** *First examined by Annas,* John 18:13, 19–24; *then by Caiaphas and the council,* Matt. 26:57–68; Mark 14:53–65; Luke 22:54, 66–71; John 18:24, 28.
**Roman:** *By Pilate,* Matt. 27:2, 11–26; Mark 15:1–15; Luke 23:1–7; John 18:28–40; 19:1–16. *By Herod,* Luke 23:7–12. *Remanded to Pilate,* Luke 23:13–24.
‖ **RETICENCE OF JESUS,** Isa. 53:7; Matt. **26:63; 27:**12, 14; Mark 14:61; 15:4, 5; John 19:9; 1 Pet. 2:23.
See PRUDENCE, *Of Jesus,* 2 Chr. 2:12.

v.72–AD 30
See footnote, *Time*, Rev. 10:6.

n *Jesus, prophet*, Matt. 1:21.
o *Weeping*, Ezra 3:13.
p *Repentance*, Mark 1:4.

to mind the [n]word that Jē′ṣus said unto him, Before the cock crow twice, thou shalt deny me thrice. And when he thought thereon, he [o,p]wept.[T]

## CHAPTER 15

*Jesus is delivered over to Pilate;* 15 *who releases Barabbas and delivers Jesus to be crucified.* 17 *The crown of thorns.* 22 *The crucifixion.* 29 *The priests and others mock.* 37 *Jesus dies.* 42 *His burial.*

AND straightway in the morning the chief [a]priests held a consultation with the [b]elders and [c]scribes and the whole council,[G] and [d]bound [e]Jē′ṣus, and carried *him* away, and [f]delivered *him* to [g]Pī′late.

2 [f]And [g]Pī′late asked him, Art thou the [h]King of the Jewṣ? And he answering said unto him, [i]Thou[G] sayest *it*.

3 [f]And the chief [a]priests [j]accused him of many things: [1]but [k]he [l]answered nothing.

4[Q] [f]And [g,m]Pī′late asked him again, saying, Answerest thou nothing? behold how many things they witness against thee.

5 [f]But [k]Jē′ṣus yet [l]answered nothing; so that [g]Pī′late marvelled.[Q]

6 ¶ Now at *that* [n]feast he [2]released unto them one [o]prisoner, whomsoever they desired.

7 And there was *one* named [p]Bă-răb′bas, *which lay* bound with [q]them that had made insurrection with him, who had committed [r]murder in the insurrection.

8 And the multitude [s]crying aloud began to desire[G] *him to do* as he had ever done unto them.

9 But [g]Pī′late answered them, saying, Will ye that I release unto you the [t]King of the Jewṣ?

10 For he knew that the chief [u,v]priests had delivered him for [w,x]envy.

11 But the chief [u]priests [y]moved[G] the people, that he should rather release [p]Bă-răb′bas unto them.

12 And [g]Pī′late answered and said again unto them, What will ye then that I shall do *unto him* whom ye call the [t]King of the Jewṣ?

13 And [z]they [w,x]cried out again, *Crucify him.

14 Then [a]Pī′late said unto them, Why, what evil hath he done? And they cried out the more exceedingly, *Crucify him.

15 And *so* [a,b,c]Pī′late, [d]willing to content[G] the [e]people, released [f]Bă-răb′bas unto them, and delivered Jē′ṣus, when he had [g,h]scourged[G] [i]*him*, to be *crucified.

16 ¶ [j]And the [k]soldiers led him away into the hall, called †Præ-tō′rĭ-um; and they call together the whole band.

17 And they clothed him with [l]purple,[G] and platted a [m]crown of [n]thorns, and put it about his *head*,

18 And began to [o]salute him, Hail,[G] [p]King of the Jewṣ!

19 And they [g]smote[G] him on the head with a [q]reed,[G] and did spit upon him, and [o,p]bowing *their* knees worshipped him.

20 [r]And when they had [o]mocked him, they took off the [l]purple from him, and put his own clothes on him, and led him out to *crucify him.

21 And they compel one [s]Sī′mon a Çy̆-rē′nĭ-an, who passed by, coming out of the country, the father of Ăl-ĕx-ăn′dẽr and [t]Ru̧′fus, to bear his [u]cross.

22 [v]And they bring him unto the place [w]Gŏl′gō-thȧ, which is, being interpreted, The place of a skull.

23 And they gave him to drink

1
a *Priests, conspire to destroy Jesus*, Lev. 1:5.
b *Senate*, Num. 11:16.
c *Scribe*, 1 Kin. 4:3.
d *Persecution, of Jesus*, John 15:20.
e *Prisoners*, Psa. 79:11.
f *Trial of Jesus*, vs. 1–15; Mark 14:53.
g *Pilate*, Matt. 27:2.
2
h *Indictments, instances of*, Matt. 27:37.
i *Pleading*, Deut. 17:8.
3
j *False Accusation*, 2 Tim. 3:3.
k *Jesus, meekness of*, Matt. 1:21.
l *Reticence of Jesus*, Mark 14:61.
1 R. V. *omits* but he answered nothing.
4
m *Court, civil*, Ex. 18:26.
6
n *Passover, prisoners released at*, Num. 9:5.
o *Prisoners, released at feasts*, Psa. 79:11.
2 R. V. used to release unto
7
p *Barabbas*, Matt. 27:16.
q *Citizens, wicked and treasonable*, Luke 15:15.
r *Homicide, felonious*, Deut. 5:17.
8
s *Intercession, of man with man*, Jer. 27:18.
9
t *Jesus, king*, Matt. 1:21.
10
u *Priest*, Lev. 1:5.
v *Court, corrupt*, Ex. 18:26.
w *Envy, instances of*, Prov. 14:30.
x *Malice, instances of*, Eph. 4:31.

v.11–AD 30
See footnote, *Time*, Rev. 10:6.

11
y *Complicity, instances of*, Prov. 29:24.
13
z Matt. 27:22, 23; Luke 23:21; John 19:6.
14
a *Pilate*, Matt. 27:2.
15
b *Civil Service, corruption in*, Dan. 1:5.
c *Rulers, wicked*, Ex. 18:21.
d *Demagogism, instances of*, 2 Sam. 15:2.
e *Public Opinion, corrupt yielding to*, John 12:42.
f *Barabbas*, Matt. 27:16.
g *Smiting and Scourging of Jesus*, Isa. 50:6.
h *Jesus, sufferings of*, Matt. 1:21.
i *Prisoners, scourged*, Psa. 79:11.
16
j Matt. 27:27–30; John 19:2, 3.
k *Soldiers*, Ezra 8:22.
17
l *Colors, symbolical*, Ezek. 16:16.
m *Crown, of thorns*, Ex. 29:6.
n *Thorns*, Hos. 2:6.
18
o *Mocking, instances of*, 1 Kin. 18:27.
p *Irony*, Mark 12:14.
19
q *Reed*, Ezek. 40:3.
20
r Matt. 27:31, 32; Luke 23:26–32; John 19:16, 17.
21
s Matt. 27:32; Luke 23:26.
t Rom. 16:13.
u *Cross*, John 19:17.
22
v Matt. 27:33–50; Luke 23:33–46; John 19:18–30.
w Matt. 27:33; John 19:17.

* **CRUCIFIXION.** *A reproach*, Gal. 3:13; 5:11. *Of Jesus*, Matt. 27:35–54; Mark 15:24–39; Luke 23:33–49; John 19:17–30. *Of Jesus, the theme of Paul's preaching*, 1 Cor. 1:23; 2:2; Gal. 3:1. *Of two malefactors*, Matt. 27:38.
*Of disciples, foretold*, Matt. 23:34.

See footnotes: CROSS, John 19:17; PUNISHMENT, Lev. 26:41.
**Figurative**, Rom. 6:6; 2 Cor. 4:10; Gal. 2:20; 5:24; 6:14, 17.

† **PRETORIUM.** *Called also Common Hall, Judgment Hall, and Palace*, Matt. 27:27; Mark 15:16; John 18:28, 33; 19:9; Acts 23:35; Phil. 1:13.

v.23–AD 30
See footnote, *Time*, Rev. 10:6.

**23**
x *Vinegar*, Num. 6:3.
y *Myrrh*, Ex. 30:23.

**24**
z Psa. 22:18; Matt. 27:35; Luke 23:34; John 19:23, 24.

a *Prophecies, concerning the Messiah, and their fulfillment*, Gen. 12:3.
b *Lot*, Esth. 3:7.

**25**
c *Time*, Rev. 10:6.

**26**
d *Indictments*, Matt. 27:37.
e *Irony, instances of*, Mark 12:14.

**27**
f *Thieves*, Deut. 24:7.

**28**
g Isa. 53:12.
3 R. V. *omits this verse.*

**29**
h *Mocking*, 1 Kin. 18:27.
i *Presumption*, Psa. 19:13.
j *Sarcasm*, Judg. 10:14.

**30**
k *Cross*, John 19:17.

**31**
l *Priest*, Lev. 1:5.
m *Scribe*, 1 Kin. 4:3.

**33**
n *Sun, darkening of*, Josh. 10:12.
o *Darkness, at the crucifixion*, Gen. 1:2.

**34**
p *Afflictions, despondency in*, Psa. 34:19.
q *Despondency*, Eccl. 2:20.
r *Jesus, sufferings of*, Matt. 1:21.
s *Prayer, in adversity*, Acts 6:4.
t *Prayers of Jesus*, Luke 5:16.
u Psa. 22:1; Matt. 27:46.
v *Prophecies, concerning the Messiah, and their fulfillment*, Gen. 12:3.

**35**
w Or, *Elijah*, 1 Kin. 17:1.

[x]wine mingled with [y]myrrh: but he received *it* not.[Q]

24 [z,a]And when they had *crucified him, they parted his garments, casting [b]lots upon them, what every man should take.[Q]

25 And it was the [c]third hour, and they *crucified him.

26 And the ‡superscription[G] of his [d]accusation was written over, [e]THE KING OF THE JEWS.

27 And with him they *crucify two [f]thieves; the one on his right hand, and the other on his left.

28 [3]And the [a]scripture was fulfilled, which saith, [g]And he was numbered with the transgressors.[Q]

29 ¶ And they that passed by [h,i]railed[G] on him, wagging their heads, and [j]saying, Ah, thou that destroyest the temple, and buildest *it* in three days,[Q]

30 [h,j]Save thyself, and come down from the [k]cross.

31 Likewise also the chief [l]priests [h]mocking said among themselves with the [m]scribes, He saved others; himself he cannot save.

32 [e,j]Let Christ the King of Is'ra-el descend now from the [k]cross, that we may see and believe. And they that were *crucified with him reviled[G] him.

33 ¶ And when the [c]sixth hour was come, [n]there was [o]darkness over the whole land until the ninth hour.[Q]

34 And at the [c]ninth hour Jē'sus [p,q,r]cried with a loud voice, [s]saying, [t,u,v]Ē-lō'ī, Ē-lō'ī, lā'ma sā-băch'tha-nī? which is, being interpreted, My God, my God why hast thou forsaken me?[T Q]

35 And some of them that stood by, when they heard *it*, said, Behold, he calleth [w]Ē-lī'as.

36 And one ran and filled a [x]spunge full of [y]vinegar, and put *it* on a [z]reed, and gave him to drink, saying, Let alone; let us see whether [w]Ē-lī'as will come to take him down.[Q]

37 And [a]Jē'sus cried with a loud voice, and [b]gave up the ghost.[G]

38 And the [c,d]veil[G] of the [e]temple was rent[G] in twain[G] from the top to the bottom.

39 ¶ [f]And when the [g]centurion, which stood over[G] against him, saw that he so cried out, and [b]gave up the ghost[G], he said, Truly this man was the [h]Son of God.[T]

40 There were also [i]women looking on afar off: among whom was [j]Mā'rȳ Măg-da-lē'nē, and ‖Mā'rȳ the mother of [k]Jāmes the less and of [l]Jō'sēs, and [m]Sā-lō'mē;

41 (Who also, when he was in [n]Găl'ĭ-lee, followed him, and ministered unto him;) and many other women which came up with him unto [o]Jē-ru'sā-lĕm.

42 ¶ And now when the even[G] was come, because it was the [p]preparation, that is, the day before the [q]sabbath,

43 [r]Jō'seph of [s]Ăr-ĭ-mă-thæ'ă, an honourable [t]counsellor, which also [u]waited for the [v]kingdom of God, came, and [w]went in [x]boldly unto [y]Pī'late, and craved[G] the body of Jē'sus.

44 And [y]Pī'late marvelled if he were already dead: and calling *unto him* the [g]centurion, he asked him whether he had been any while dead.

45 And when [y]he knew *it* of the [g]centurion, he gave the body to [r]Jō'seph.

46 And [r]he bought fine [z]linen, and took him down, and wrap-

v.36–AD 30
See footnote, *Time*, Rev. 10:6.

**36**
x Matt. 27:48; John 19:29.
y *Vinegar*, Num. 6:3.
z *Reed*, Ezek. 40:3.

**37**
a *Jesus, death of*, Matt. 1:21.
b *Death, called giving up the ghost*, Num. 23:10.

**38**
c *Vail, of the temple, rent*, 2 Chr. 3:14.
d *Symbols and Similitudes*, Heb. 9:9.
e *Temple, Herod's*, 1 Kin. 6:17.

**39**
f Matt. 27:54; Luke 23:47.
g *Centurion*, Matt. 8:5.
h *Jesus, divine sonship of*, Matt. 1:21.

**40**
i *Women, last at the cross*, Prov. 31:10.
j *Mary Magdalene*, Matt. 27:56.
k *James*, Matt. 10:3.
l *Joses*, Matt. 27:56.
m *Salome*, Mark 16:1.

**41**
n *Galilee*, Mark 6:21.
o *Jerusalem*, Judg. 19:10.

**42**
p Matt. 27:62; Luke 23:54; John 19:14, 31, 42.
q *Sabbath, preparation for*, Ex. 16:23.

**43**
r *Joseph*, John 19:38.
s *Arimathea*, John 19:38.
t *Counselor*, Prov. 11:14.
u *Messianic Hope*, Gen. 49:10.
v *Kingdom of Heaven*, Matt. 13:24.
w *Decision, instances of*, Isa. 50:7.
x *Courage*, Deut. 31:7.
y *Pilate*, Matt. 27:2.

**46**
z *Linen*, Ezek. 27:16.

‡ **INSCRIPTIONS.** *On the miter of the high priest*, Ex. 28:36. *On the holy crown*, Ex. 39:30. *On the bells of horses*, Zech. 14:20.
*Over Jesus at the crucifixion*, Matt. 27:37; Mark 15:26; Luke 23:38; John 19:19.

‖ **MARY.** *Wife of Cleophas*, John 19:25. *Mother of James and Joses*, Matt. 27:56; Mark 15:40. *Assists in preparing the body of Jesus for burial*, Matt. 28:1; Mark 16:1. *At the sepulchre*, Matt. 27:61; Mark 15:47. *A witness to the resurrection*, Luke 24:10.

v.46–AD 30
See footnote, *Time*,
Rev. 10:6.

*a* Matt. 27:59–66; Luke 23:53–56; John 19:38–42.
*b* *Burying Places*, Gen. 23:4.

**47**
*c* *Mary Magdalene*, Matt. 27:56.
*d* *Women, first at the sepulchre*, Prov. 31:10.
*e* *Joses*, Matt. 27:56.

**1**
*a* Matt. 28:1–8; Luke 24:1–10; John 20:1.
*b* *Sabbath*, Ex. 16:23.
*c* *Mary Magdalene*, Matt. 27:56.
*d* *Women, first at the sepulchre*, Prov. 31:10.
*e* *Mary*, Mark 15:40.
*f* Matt. 27:56; Luke 24:10.
*g* *Spices*, 1 Kin. 10:2.
*h* *Anointing, of the dead*, Deut. 28:40.

**5**
*i* *Angel, appearances of*, Heb. 1:13.
*j* *Colors*, Ezek. 16:16.
1 R. V. amazed:

**6**
*k* *Afflictions, consolation in*, Psa. 34:19.
*l* *Crucifixion*, Mark 15:13.
*m* *Resurrection of Jesus*, Matt. 28:6.

**7**
*n* *Apostles*, Luke 6:13.
*o* *Peter*, Mark 5:37.
*p* *Galilee*, Mark 6:21.

ped him in the linen, and [a]laid
him in a [b]sepulchre[G] which was
hewn out of a rock, and rolled
a stone unto the door of the
sepulchre.[G]
47 And [c,d]Mā′rȳ Măg-da-lē′nē
and ‖Mā′rȳ *the mother* of [e]Jō′sēṣ
beheld where he was laid.

## CHAPTER 16

*Jesus' resurrection. 9 He appears to Mary Magdalene, to two disciples, and to the eleven, 15 whom he sends forth into all the world to preach the gospel to every creature. 19 His ascension.*

[a]AND when the [b]sabbath
was past, [c,d]Mā′rȳ Măg-
da-lē′nē, and [e]Mā′rȳ the *mother* of [f]Jāmeṣ, and *Sā-lō′mē,
had bought sweet [g]spices, that
they might come and [h]anoint
him.
2 And[T] very early in the morning
the first *day* of the week, [d]they
came unto the sepulchre at the
rising of the sun.
3 And they said among themselves, Who shall roll us away
the stone from the door of the
sepulchre?
4 And when they looked, they
saw that the stone was rolled
away: for it was very great.
5 And entering into the sepulchre, they saw a [i]young man sitting on the right side, clothed in
a long [j]white garment; and they
were [1]affrighted.[C]
6 And he saith unto them, [k]Be
not [1]affrighted[G]: Ye seek Jē′ṣus
of Năz′a-rĕth, which was [l]cruci-
fied: he is [m]risen; he is not here:
behold the place where they laid
him.[T]
7 But go your way, tell his
[n]disciples and [o]Pē′tĕr that he
goeth before you into [p]Găl′ĭ-lee:
there shall ye see him, as he said
unto you.
8 And they went out quickly,
and fled from the sepulchre;
for they trembled and were
amazed: neither said they any
thing to any *man*; for they
were afraid.
9 ¶ Now when *Jē′ṣus* was
[m]risen early the †first *day* of
the week, he ‡appeared first
to [c,q]Mā′rȳ Măg-da-lē′nē, out
of whom he had cast seven
[r]devils.[G T]
10 *And* [c]she went and told them
that had been with him, as they
mourned and wept.
11 And they, when they had
heard that he was [m]alive, and
had been seen of her, [s,t]believed
not.
12 ¶ [u]After that he ‡appeared in
another form unto two of them,
as they walked, and went into
the country.
13 And they went and told *it*
unto the residue[G]: [s,t]neither believed they them.
14 ¶ Afterward he ‡,[2]appeared
unto the [n]eleven as they sat at
meat,[G] and upbraided them with
their [t,v]unbelief and hardness of
heart, because they believed not
them which had seen him after
he was [m]risen.
15 [w]And he said unto [x]them,
[y]Go ye into all the world, and
[z]preach the [a]gospel to every
creature.
16 He that [b]believeth and is
[c]baptized [d]shall be [e]saved; but
he that [f,g]believeth not shall be
[3,h]damned.[G S T]
17 And these signs shall follow
[i]them that [b]believe; In my [j]name

v.7 AD 30
See footnote, *Time*
Rev. 10:6.

**9**
*q* *Women, first to whom the risen Lord appeared*, Prov. 31:10.
*r* *Demons, possession by*, Matt. 4:24.

**11**
*s* *Doubting*, Rom. 14:23.
*t* *Unbelief*, Heb. 3:12.

**12**
*u* Luke 24:13–35.

**14**
*v* *Spiritual Blindness*, 2 Cor. 4:4.
2 R. V. was manifested

**15**
*w* Matt. 28:19; Luke 24:47.
*x* *Apostles, commission of*, Luke 6:13.
*y* *Missions*, Matt. 28:19.
*z* *Preaching*, Matt. 9:35.

*a* *Gospel*, Mark 13:10.

**16**
*b* *Faith in Christ*, John 6:69.
*c* *Baptism, Christian*, Luke 20:4.
*d* *Promise, to believers*, 2 Cor. 1:20.
*e* *Salvation*, Acts 16:17.
*f* *Unbelief*, Heb. 3:12.
*g* *Jesus, rejected*, Matt. 1:21.
*h* *Wicked, punishment of*, Psa. 73:3.
3 R. V. condemned.

**17**
*i* *Apostles, miraculous power given to*, Luke 6:13.
*j* *Name of Jesus*, John 14:13.

* **SALOME** (*peaceful*). *Mother of James and John*, Matt. 27:56, with Mark 15:40; 16:1. *Asks Jesus to promote her sons*, Matt. 20:20, 21. *Present, at the cross*, Mark 15:40; *at the sepulchre*, Mark 16:1, 2.

† **CHRISTIAN SABBATH**, Matt. 28:1, 5, 6, 7; Mark 16:9; John 20:19, 26 (with vs. 1, 11–16); Acts 20:7; 1 Cor. 16:2; Rev. 1:10.

‡ **APPEARANCES OF JESUS AFTER HIS RESURRECTION**, Acts 10:40–42; 13:31.

*To Mary Magdalene*, Matt. 28:1–10; Mark 16:9; John 20:11–17. *To Peter*, Luke 24:34; 1 Cor. 15:5.

*To the two disciples who journey to Emmaus*, Mark 16:12, 13; Luke 24:13–35.

*To the disciples, when Thomas was absent* [Jerusalem], John 20:19–23; *when Thomas was present* [Jerusalem], Mark 16:14–18; Luke 24:36–49; John 20:26–29. *To certain disciples, at the Sea of Galilee*, John 21:1–14. *To the eleven disciples in a mountain of Galilee*, Matt. 28:16. *To upwards of five hundred brethren*, 1 Cor. 15:6, 7.

*To James and to all the apostles* [Jerusalem], Acts 1:3–8; 1 Cor. 15:7.

*To Paul*, Acts 9:3–6; 23:11; 26:15; 1 Cor. 9:1; 15:8,

v.17–AD 30 See footnote, *Time*, Rev. 10:6.

*k Miracles, power to work, given the disciples*, Luke 23:8.
*l Demons*, Matt. 4:24.
*m Tongues, the miraculous gift of the early Christians*, 1 Cor. 12: 10.

shall they [k]cast out [l]devils[G];
they shall speak with new
[m]tongues;[S]
18 [i]They shall take up [n]ser-
pents; and if they drink any
deadly thing, it shall not hurt
them; they shall lay [o]hands on
the [p]sick, and they shall [q]re-
cover.

19 ¶ So then [4]after the Lord had
spoken unto them, he was [r]re-
ceived up into [s]heaven, and sat
on the right hand of God.[T Q]
20 And [i]they went forth, and
[t,u]preached [v]every where, the
Lord working with *them*, and
confirming the [w,x]word with
[k]signs following. Amen.

v.19–AD 30 See footnote, *Time*, Rev. 10:6.

**19**
*r Ascension, of Jesus*, 2 Kin. 2:1.
*s Heaven, God's dwelling place*, Luke 18:22
4 R. V. the Lord Jesus, after he had spoken unto them, was

**20**
*t Preaching*, Matt. 9:35.

**18** *n Serpent*, Num. 21:6. *o Hand, imposition of*, Ezra 10:19. *p Disease, miraculous healing of*, Ex. 15:26. *q Healing*, Acts 4:22. *u Zeal, exemplified*, 2 Cor. 7:11. *v Missions*, Matt. 28:19. *w Gospel*, Mark 13:10. *x Doctrines of Jesus*, John 7:16.

---

THE GOSPEL ACCORDING TO

# LUKE

## CHAPTER 1

*Luke's preface. 5 Zacharias and Elisabeth. 6 The angel Gabriel foretells to Zacharias the birth and office of John; 26 and also to Mary the birth and character of Jesus. 39 Mary visits Elisabeth. 42 The song of Elisabeth, 46 and of Mary. 57 The birth and circumcision of John. 67 The song of Zacharias.*

FORASMUCH as many have
taken in hand to [1]set forth
in order a declaration of those
things which are most surely believed among us,
2 Even as they delivered them
unto [a]us, which from the beginning were eyewitnesses, and
[b]ministers of the word;
3 [c]It seemed good to [d]me also,
having [2]had perfect[G] understanding of all things from the very
first, to write unto thee in order,
most excellent [e]Thē-ŏph′ĭ-lŭs,
4 That thou mightest know the
certainty of those things, wherein
thou hast been instructed.

5 ¶ There was in the days of
Hĕr′od, the [f]king of [g]Jū-dæ′ă, a
certain [h]priest named [i]Zăch-a-
rī′as, of the course of [j]Ā-bī′ă:
and his wife *was* of the daughters of [k]Aăr′on, and her name
*was* Ē-lĭș′a-bĕth.[Q]
6 And [i,l]they were both righteous before God, [m,n]walking in
all the [o]commandments and ordinances of the Lord [p]blameless.
7 And they had no child, because that Ē-lĭș′a-bĕth was [q]bar-
ren, and they both were *now*
[r]well[G] stricken[G] in years.
8 And it came to pass, that
while [i]he executed[G] the [h]priest's
office before God in the order
of his course,
9 [T]According to the custom of
the priest's office, his lot was [s]to
burn [t]incense when he went into
the [u]temple of the Lord.[Q]
10 And the whole multitude of
the people were [v]praying without[G] at the time of [t]incense.[T]
11 And there [w]appeared unto
[i]him an [x,y]angel of the Lord
standing on the right side of the
[z]altar of incense.
12 And when [a]Zăch-a-rī′as saw
[b]*him*, he was troubled, and fear
fell upon him.
13 But the [c]angel said unto
him, Fear not, [a]Zăch-a-rī′as: for
thy [d]prayer is heard; and thy
wife Ē-lĭș′a-bĕth shall bear thee
a [e]son, and thou shalt call his
name Jŏhn.
14 And thou shalt have [f]joy
and gladness; and many shall
rejoice at his birth.
15 For he shall be great in
the sight of the Lord, and [g]shall
drink neither [h]wine nor strong
drink; and [i]he shall be [j,k]filled
with the [l]Holy Ghost[G], even from
his mother's womb.[Q]

**1**
1 R. V. draw up a narrative concerning those matters which have been fulfilled among us,

**2**
*a Apostles*, Luke 6:13.
*b Minister*, Rom. 15:16.

**3**
*c Friendship, instances of*, Prov. 22:24.
*d Luke*, Col. 4:14.
e Acts 1:1.
2 R. V. traced the course of all things accurately from the first,

**5**
*f Rulers*, Ex. 18:21.
*g Judea*, Luke 5:17.
*h Priest*, Lev. 1:5.
i Luke 3:2.
j Or, *Abijah*, 1 Chr. 24:10.
*k Aaron*, Ex. 6:20.

**6**
*l Women, good*, Prov. 31:10.
*m Righteous, described*, Psa. 64:10.
*n Faithfulness*, Luke 16:10.
*o Law, of Moses*, Deut. 33:2.
*p Perfection* Heb. 6:1.

**7**
*q Barrenness*, Deut. 7:14.
*r Old Age*, Isa. 46:4.

**9**
*s Priest, duties of*, Lev. 1:5.
*t Incense*, Ex. 37:29.
*u Temple, Herod's*, 1 Kin. 6:17.

**10**
*v Prayer*, Acts 6:4.

**11**
*w Vision*, Acts 9:10.
*x Angel*, Heb. 1:13.
*y Gabriel*, vs. 19, 26; Dan. 8:16.
*z Altar, of incense*, Ex. 30:1.

**12**
a Luke 3:2.
*b Vision*, Acts 9:10.

**13**
*c Gabriel*, vs. 19, 26; Dan. 8:16.
*d Prayer, answered*, Acts 6:4.
*e Children, in answer to prayer*, Mark 10:14.

**14**
*f Joy*, Psa. 5:11.

**15**
*g Total Abstinence*, Lev. 10:9.
*h Wine*, Prov. 23:31.
*i Children, early piety of*, Mark 10:14.
*j Prophets, inspiration of*, Isa. 3:2.
*k Inspiration*, Job 32:8.
*l Holy Spirit, inspiration of*, Acts 1:2.

17
m Mal. 4:6.
n *Spiritual Power,* Luke 24:49.
o Or, *Elijah, antetype of John the Baptist,* 1 Kin. 17:1.
p *Wisdom, spiritual,* Prov. 2:2.
18
q *Doubting,* Rom. 14:23.
r *Faith, strengthened by miracles,* vs. 18–20, 22; Mark 11:22.
s *Sign,* Mark 8:11.
t *Old Age,* Isa. 46:4.
19
u *Angel, functions of,* Heb. 1:13.
20
v *Dumb,* Ex. 4:11.
w *Unbelief,* Heb. 3:12.
21
x *Temple, Herod's,* 1 Kin. 6:17.
22
y *Vision,* Acts 9:10.
3 R. V. continued making signs unto
v.24–6 BC
24
z *Conception,* Gen. 21:2.
25
a *Barrenness,* Deut. 7:14.
26
b *Angel, appearances of,* Heb. 1:13.
c *Gabriel, appeared to Mary,* Dan. 8:16.

16 And many of the children of Ĭş′ra-el shall he turn to the Lord their God.

17 [m]And he shall go before him in the spirit and [n]power of [o]Ē-lī′as, to turn the hearts of the fathers to the children, and the disobedient to the [p]wisdom of the just; to make ready a people prepared for the Lord.[Q]

18 And [a]Zăch-a-rī′as said unto the [c]angel, [q,r,s]Whereby shall I know this ? for I am an [t]old man, and my wife [t]well[G] stricken in years.[Q]

19 And the angel answering said unto him, I am [c]Gā′brĭ-el, that stand in the presence of God; and am [u]sent to speak unto thee, and to shew thee these glad tidings.[Q]

20 And, behold, thou shalt be [s,v]dumb, and not able to speak, until the day that these things shall be performed, because thou [w]believest not my words, which shall be fulfilled in their season.

21 And the people waited for [a]Zăch-a-rī′as, and marvelled that he tarried so long in the [x]temple.

22 And when he came out, he [v]could not speak unto them: and they perceived that he had seen a [y]vision in the [x]temple: for he [3]beckoned unto them, and remained speechless.

23 And it came to pass, that, as soon as the days of his ministration were accomplished, he departed to his own house.[Q]

24 And after those days his wife Ē-lĭş′a-bĕth [z]conceived, and hid herself five months, saying,

25 Thus hath the Lord dealt with me in the days wherein he looked on *me*, to take away my [a]reproach among men.[Q]

26 ¶ And in the sixth month the [b]angel [c]Gā′brĭ-el was sent from God unto a city of [d]Găl′ĭ-lee, named [e]Năz′a-rĕth,[S]

27 To a [f]virgin [g,h]espoused[G] to a man whose name was [i]Jō′şeph, of the house of [j]Dā′vid; and the virgin's name *was* *Mā′rȳ.

28 And[S] the [b,c]angel came in unto *her, and said, Hail, *thou that art* highly favoured, the Lord *is* with thee: [4]blessed art thou among women.

29 And when *she saw *him*, she was troubled at his saying, and cast[G] in her mind what manner of salutation[G] this should be.

30 And the [b,c]angel said unto her, Fear not, *Mā′rȳ: for [k]thou hast found [l]favour with God.[S]

31[T] And, behold, thou shalt [m]conceive in thy womb, and bring forth a son, and shalt call his name [n]JĒ′ŞUS.[T Q G]

32 [o]He[T] shall be great, and shall be called the [n,p]Son of the Highest: and the Lord God shall give unto [q]him the [r]throne of his father [j]Dā′vid:[Q]

33 And [q]he shall reign over the house of Jā′cob for ever; and of his [s]kingdom there shall be no end.[T Q]

34 Then said *Mā′rȳ unto the [b,c]angel, How shall this be, seeing I know not a man ?

35 And the [b,c]angel answered and said unto her, The [t,u]Holy Ghost[G] shall come upon thee, and the power of the [u]Highest shall overshadow thee: therefore also that [v]holy thing which shall be born of thee shall be called the [p,u]Son of God.[T Q]

36 And, behold, thy cousin[G] Ē-lĭş′a-bĕth, she hath also [m]conceived a son in her [w]old age: and this is the sixth month with her, who was called [a]barren.

37 For [5]with [x]God nothing shall be impossible.[Q]

v.26–5 BC See footnote, *Time,* Rev. 10:6.
d *Galilee,* Mark 6:21.
e *Nazareth,* John 1:46.
27
f *Virgin,* Isa. 62:5.
g *Betrothal, a quasi marriage,* Deut. 20:7.
h *Marriage,* Gen. 34:9.
i *Joseph,* Luke 3:23.
j *David,* 1 Sam. 16:13.
28
4 R. V. *omits the rest of this verse.*
30
k *Women, good,* Prov. 31:10.
l *Grace of God,* Rom. 4:16.
31
m *Conception,* Gen. 21:2.
n *Jesus, names of,* Matt. 1:21.
32
o *Prophecies, concerning Jesus, and their fulfillment,* Gen. 12:3.
p *Jesus, divine sonship of,* Matt. 1:21.
q *Jesus, king,* Matt. 1:21.
r *Throne,* 1 Kin. 2:19.
33
s *Jesus, kingdom of, prophecies concerning,* Matt. 1:21.
35
t *Holy Spirit,* Acts 1:2.
u *Holy Trinity,* Luke 3:22.
v *Jesus, holiness of,* Matt. 1:21.
36
w *Old Age,* Isa. 46:4.
37
x *God, power of,* Gen. 2:2.
5 R. V. no word from God shall be void of power.

* **MARY.** *The mother of Jesus,* Matt. 1:16; 13:55; Luke 1:26–38; 2:5–19; 6:3. *Visits her cousin Elisabeth,* Luke 1:39–56. *Attends the feast at Jerusalem with Joseph, her husband, and Jesus, her son; starts on the return; misses Jesus, seeks and finds him in the temple,* Luke 2:41–51. *Is present with Jesus at a marriage in Cana of Galilee,* John 2:1–10. *Seeks Jesus when he is teaching,* Matt. 12:46, 47; Mark 3:31; Luke 8:19. *Present at the cross,* John 19:25–27. *Is committed to the care of John,* John 19:27. *With the disciples in Jerusalem,* Acts 1:14. *Prophecies concerning,* Isa. 7:14; Luke 2:35.

v.38–5 BC
See footnote, *Time*, Rev. 10:6.

38
*y* *Faith, instances of*, Mark 11:22.

39
*z* Or, *Judea*, Luke 5:17.

40
*a* Luke 3:2.

41
*b* *Prophetess, Elisabeth*, Judg. 4:4.
*c* *Holy Spirit, inspiration of*, Acts 1:2.

42
*d* *Women, as poets*, Prov. 31:10.
*e* *Poetry, sacred lyrics*, vs. 42–55; Acts 17:28.

43
*f* *Humility, instances of*, Prov. 22:4.

45
*g* *Faith*, Mark 11:22.
*h* *God, faithfulness of*, Gen. 2:2.
6 R. V. fulfilment

46
*i* *Praise*, Psa. 150:1.

47
*j* *Joy, instances of*, Psa. 5:11.
*k* *God, savior*, Gen. 2:2.

48
*l* *God, providence of*, Gen. 2:2.

49
*m* *God, power of*, Gen. 2:2.
*n* *God, holiness of*, Gen. 2:2.

50
*o* *God, mercy of*, Gen. 2:2.
*p* *Fear of God*, Acts 9:31.

38 And *Mā′rȳ said, Behold the handmaid of the Lord; [y]be it unto me according to thy word. And the angel departed from her.

39 ¶ And *Mā′rȳ arose in those days, and went into the hill country with haste, into a city of [z]Jū′dȧ;

40 And entered into the house of [a]Zăch-a-rī′as, and saluted Ē-lĭs′a-bĕth.

41 And it came to pass, that, when Ē-lĭs′a-bĕth heard the [†]salutation of *Mā′rȳ, the babe leaped in her womb; and [b]Ē-lĭs′a-bĕth was [c]filled with the Holy Ghost:

42 And [b,d]she spake out with a loud voice, and said, [e]Blessed *art* thou among women, and blessed *is* the fruit of thy womb.

43 [e,f]And whence *is* this to me, that the mother of my Lord should come to me?

44 [e]For, lo, as soon as the voice of thy [†]salutation sounded in mine ears, the babe leaped in my womb for joy.

45 [e]And blessed *is* she that [g]believed: for there shall be a [6,h]performance of those things which were told her from the Lord.

46 ¶ And *[d]Mā′rȳ said, [e]My soul doth [i]magnify the Lord,

47 [e]And my spirit hath [j]rejoiced in God my [k]Saviour.

48 [e]For he hath [l]regarded the [f]low estate of his handmaiden: for, behold, from henceforth all generations shall call me blessed.

49 For he that is [m]mighty hath done to me great things; and [n]holy *is* his name.

50 And his [o]mercy *is* on them that [p]fear him from generation to generation.

51 He hath shewed [m]strength with his [q,r]arm; he hath scattered the [s,t]proud in the imagination of their hearts.

52 He hath put down the mighty from *their* seats, and [u]exalted them of low degree.

53 He hath filled the [v,w]hungry with good things; and the [t]rich [x]he hath sent empty away.

54 He hath [k]holpen his servant Ĭș′ra-el, in [h]remembrance of *his* [o]mercy;

55 As he [y,z]spake to our fathers, to Ā′brā-hăm, and to his seed for ever.

56 And *Mā′rȳ abode with her about three months, and returned to her own house.

57 ¶ Now Ē-lĭs′a-bĕth's full time came that she should be delivered; and she brought forth a son.

58 And her neighbours and her [7]cousins heard how the Lord had shewed great [a]mercy upon her; and they rejoiced with her.

59 And it came to pass, that on the eighth day they came to [b]circumcise the child; and they called him [c]Zăch-a-rī′as, after the name of his father.

60 And his mother answered and said, Not *so*; but he shall be called [‡]Jŏhn.

61 And they said unto her, There is none of thy kindred that is called by this name.

62 And they made signs to his [c]father, how he would have him called.

63 And he asked for a writing [8]table, and wrote, saying, His name is [‡]Jŏhn. And they marvelled all.

64 And his mouth was opened immediately, and his tongue

v.51–5 BC
See footnote, *Time*, Rev. 10:6.

51
*q* *Arm, figurative*, Psa. 89:13.
*r* *Anthropomorphisms*, Gen. 11:5.
*s* *Pride*, Prov. 16:18.
*t* *Ambition*, Hab. 2:5.

52
*u* *Humility, rewards of*, Prov. 22:4.

53
*v* *Hunger, figurative*, Matt. 5:6.
*w* *Spiritual Desire*, Psa. 42:1.
*x* *God, sovereign*, Gen. 2:2.

55
*y* *Prophecies, concerning Jesus, and their fulfillment*, Gen. 12:3.
*z* *Covenant, of God with men*, Deut. 29:1.

58
*a* *God, mercy of*, Gen. 2:2.
7 R. V. kinsfolk

59
*b* *Circumcision*, Gen. 17:10.
*c* Luke 3:2.

63
8 R. V. tablet.

† **SALUTATIONS.** *By kissing*, 2 Sam. 20:9; Matt. 26:49. *By bowing*, Gen. 18:2; 19:1, 2; 23:7; 27:29; 33:3; 37:10; 41:43; 42:6; 43:26, 28; 49:8; 2 Sam. 18:28; 1 Kin. 1:16. *By prostrating*, 1 Sam. 25:23; Esth. 8:3; Matt. 2:11; Mark 5:22.
Addresses in: *My lords*, Gen. 19:2; *God be gracious unto thee*, Gen. 43:29; *Blessed be thou of the Lord*, 1 Sam. 15:13; *Peace*, 1 Sam. 25:6; *Art thou in health, my brother*, 2 Sam. 20:9; *Hail, Master*, Matt. 26:49; *All hail*, Matt. 28:9; *Peace to this house*, Luke 10:5; *Peace unto you*, John 20:21, 26; *from a master to his servants, The Lord be with you*, Ruth 2:4; *servants to their masters, The Lord bless thee*, Ruth 2:4.
By letter, 1 Cor. 16:21; 2 Cor. 13:13; Col. 4:18; Phil. 4:21 (with Matt. 10:12, 13); 2 Thess. 3:17; 1 Pet. 1:2; 2 Pet. 1:2; 2 John 13; 3 John 14.
See footnote, MANNERS, Gen. 18:2.

‡ **JOHN THE BAPTIST.** *Prophecies concerning*, Isa. 40:

*loosed,* and he spake, and
[d]praised God.
65 And fear came on all that
dwelt round about them: and
all these sayings were noised[G]
abroad throughout all the hill
country of [e]Jū-dæ'ȧ.
66 And all they that heard *them*
laid *them* up in their hearts, saying, What manner of child shall
this be! And the hand of the
Lord was with him.
67 ¶ And his father [c,f]Zăch-a-
rī'as was [g]filled with the Holy
Ghost[G], and prophesied[G], saying,
68 [d,h]Blessed[S T] *be* the Lord God
of Ĭṣ'ra-el; for he hath visited
and [i,j]redeemed his people,[Q]
69 [k,l]And hath raised up an
[m]horn of [n]salvation[G] for us in the
house of his servant [o]Dā'vid;[Q]
70 As he [f,k]spake by the mouth
of his holy prophets, which have
been since the world began:
71 That we should be saved
from our enemies, and from the
hand of all that hate us;[Q]
72 [Q]To perform the [a]mercy
*promised* to our fathers, and to
remember his holy [p]covenant;[T]
73 The [q]oath which he sware to
our father [r]Ā'brā-hăm,[S Q]
74 That he would grant unto
us, that we being delivered out
of the hand of our enemies might
serve him without fear,[Q]
75 In [s]holiness and [t]righteous-
ness before him, all the days of
our life.[T]
76 [k]And [‡]thou, child, shalt be
called the prophet of the Highest: for thou shalt go before the
face of the Lord to prepare his
ways;[Q]
77 To[T] give [u,v]knowledge of [w]sal-
vation unto his people by the [x]re-
mission of their sins,
78 Through[Q] the tender [y]mercy
of our God; whereby the [m]day-
spring[G] from on high hath visited
us,[T]
79 [z]To give light to [a]them that
sit in [b,c]darkness and *in* the
shadow of [d]death, to [e]guide our
feet into the way of [f]peace.[S Q]
80 And the [‡,g]child grew, and
waxed[G] strong in spirit, and was
in the deserts till the day of his
shewing unto Ĭṣ'ra-el.

## CHAPTER 2

*The enrollment.* 6 *The birth of Jesus at Bethlehem.* 8 *An angel announces it to the shepherds.* 13 *The song of the heavenly host.* 21 *The circumcision and purification.* 25 *The song of Simeon.* 36 *Anna the prophetess.* 39 *Jesus at Nazareth.* 42 *At twelve years of age he questions the doctors in the temple.*

AND it came to pass in those
days, that there went out
a decree from [a,b]Çæ'ṣar Au-
gŭs'tus, that all the world should
be [1,c]taxed.
2 (*And* this [2,c]taxing was first
made when Çȳ-rē'nĭ-ŭs was [d]gov-
ernor of [e]Sȳr'ĭ-ȧ.)
3 And all went to [3]be [c]taxed,
every one into his own city.
4 And [f]Jō'ṣeph also went up
from [g]Găl'ĭ-lee, out of the city
of [h]Năz'a-rĕth, into [i]Jū-dæ'ȧ,
unto the city of Dā'vid, which
is called [j]Bĕth'lĕ-hĕm; (because
he was of the house[G] and lineage[G]
of [k]Dā'vid:)
5 To [4]be taxed with [l]Mā'rȳ his
[m]espoused[G] wife, being great with
child.

v.64–5 BC See footnote, *Time,* Rev. 10:6.

**64** *d Praise,* Psa. 150:1.

**65** *e Judea,* Luke 5:17.

**67** *f Prophets, inspiration of,* Isa. 3:2. *g Holy Spirit, inspiration of,* Acts 1:2.

**68** *h Poetry, sacred lyrics,* Acts 17:28. *i Redemption of our Souls,* Eph. 1:7. *j God, savior,* Gen. 2:2.

**69** *k Prophecies, concerning Jesus, and their fulfillment,* Gen. 12:3. *l Messianic Hope,* Gen. 49:10. *m Jesus, names of,* Matt. 1:21. *n Salvation,* Acts 16:17. *o David,* 1 Sam. 16:13.

**72** *p Covenant, of God with men,* Deut. 29:1.

**73** *q Oath, attributed to God,* Num. 5:19. *r Abraham, God's covenant with,* Gen. 17:5.

**75** *s Holiness,* Ex. 39:30. *t Righteousness,* Psa. 15:2.

v.77–5 BC See footnote, *Time,* Rev. 10:6.

**77** *u Knowledge, of salvation,* Luke 11:52. *v Wisdom, spiritual,* Prov. 2:2. *w Salvation,* Acts 16:17. *x Sin, forgiveness of,* Rom. 5:12.

**78** *y God, mercy of,* Gen. 2:2.

**79** *z Jesus, mission of,* Matt. 1:21.

*a Wicked, described,* Psa. 73:3. *b Darkness, figurative,* Gen. 1:2. *c Spiritual Blindness,* 2 Cor. 4:4. *d Spiritual Death,* 1 John 3:14. *e Guidance,* Psa. 48:14. *f Spiritual Peace,* Gal. 1:3.

**80** *g Children, good,* Mark 10:14.

v.1–5 BC

**1** *a Government, imperial,* Isa. 22:21. *b Cæsar,* Acts 25:8. *c Census,* 2 Sam. 24:1. 1 R. V. enrolled.

**2** *d Government, provincial,* Isa. 22:21. *e Syria,* 2 Kin. 6:23. 2 R. V. enrolment

**3** 3 R. V. enrol themselves

**4** *f Joseph,* Luke 3:23. *g Galilee,* Mark 6:21. *h Nazareth,* John 1:46. *i Judea,* Luke 5:17. *j Bethlehem,* Gen. 48:7. *k David,* 1 Sam. 16:13.

**5** *l Mary,* Luke 1:27. *m Betrothal,* Deut. 20:7. 4 R. V. To enrol himself with

3-5 (with Matt. 3:3; 11:10; Mark 1:2, 3; Luke 3:4-6; John 1:23); Mal. 3:1; 4:5, 6; Luke 1:11-17. *Extraordinary conception and birth of,* Luke 1:11-20, 57-66. *Dwells in the desert,* Matt. 3:1; Mark 1:4; Luke 1:80; 3:2, 3. *Mission of,* Matt. 17:11; Mark 1:2-8; Luke 1:15-17, 76-79; 3:4-6; John 1:7, 8, 15, 22-28, 31-34; 5:32-35; Acts 13:24, 25; 19:4. *Ministry of,* Matt. 3:1-3; Mark 1:4; Luke 3:2, 3; John 1:6-8. *His influence upon the public mind,* Matt. 3:5, 6; 14:5; 21:32; Mark 1:5; 11:32; Luke 3:7, 15; 20:6. *Rejected by chief priests and elders,* Matt. 21:23-32. *Testifies to the messiahship of Jesus,* Matt. 3:11, 12; Mark 1:7, 8; Luke 3:16, 17; John 1:15, 26-36; 3:26-30; 5:32, 33; 10:41; Acts 13:25. *Teaches his disciples, to pray,* Luke 11:1; *to fast,* Luke 5:33; 20:4. *Baptizes Jesus,* Matt. 3:13-16; Mark 1:9-11; Luke 3:21, 22; John 1:31 32. *The testimony of Jesus concerning,* John 5:32-35; Matt. 11:9, 11; 17:12, 13; 21:32; Mark 9:13. *His ministry not attested by miracles,* John 10:41. *Reproves Herod on account of his adultery; Herod imprisons him, and beheads him,* Matt. 4:12; 14:1-12; Mark 6:17-29; 9:13; Luke 3:18-20. *Sends two disciples to Jesus,* Matt. 11:2-6; Luke 7:18-23. *Herod supposes Jesus to be,* Matt. 14:1, 2; 16:14; Mark 6:14, 16; Luke 9:19. *Character of,* Mark 6:20; John 5:35. *Jesus discourses upon,* Matt. 11:7-19; Luke 7:24-33. *Affected probably by the doctrines of the Stoics,* Matt. 11:18; Mark 1:6; Luke 1:80. *A Nazirite,* Matt. 11:18; Luke 1:15; 7:33.

6 And so it was, that, while [f,l]they were [j]there, the days were accomplished that she should be delivered.

7 And she [n]brought forth her firstborn son, and [o]wrapped him in [p]swaddling[G] clothes, and laid him in a manger; because there was no room for them in the inn.

8 ¶ And there were in the same country [q]shepherds abiding in the field, keeping watch over their flock by night.

9 And, lo, the [r]angel of the Lord came upon them, and the [s]glory of the Lord shone round about them: and they were sore[G] afraid.[S]

10 And the [r]angel said unto them, Fear not: for, [t]behold, I bring you [u]good tidings of great [v]joy, which shall be to all people.

11 For unto you is [n,w]born this day in the [j]city of Dā'vid a [x]Saviour, which is [y]Christ the Lord.[T]

12 And this *shall be* a sign unto you; Ye shall find the babe wrapped in [p]swaddling clothes, lying in a manger.

13 And suddenly there was with the [r]angel a multitude of the heavenly host [z]praising God, and saying,

14 [a]Glory to God in the highest, and on earth [b,c]peace, [5]good will toward men.[T]

15 And it came to pass, as the [d]angels were gone away from them into heaven, the [e]shepherds said one to another, Let us now go even unto [f]Bĕth'lĕ-hĕm, and see this thing which is come to pass, which the Lord hath made known unto us.

16 And they [g]came with haste, and found [h]Mā'rȳ, and [i]Jō'ṣeph, and the babe lying in a manger.

17 And when they had seen *it*, they [j,k]made known abroad the saying which was told them concerning this child.

18 And all they that heard *it* wondered at those things which were told them by the [e]shepherds.

19 But [h]Mā'rȳ kept all these things, and pondered *them* in her heart.

20 And the [e]shepherds returned, [a,l]glorifying and praising God for all the things that they had heard and seen, as it was told unto them.

21[T] ¶ [m]And when eight days were accomplished for the [n]circumcising of the child, his name was called [o]JĒ'ṢUS,[G] which was so named of the [d]angel before he was conceived in the womb.[Q]

22 And when the days of [p]her [q]purification according to the [r]law of Mō'ṣeṣ were accomplished, they brought [s]him to [t]Jĕ-ru̇'sȧ-lĕm, to present *him* to the Lord;[Q]

23 (As it is written in the [r]law of the Lord, [u]Every [v]male that openeth the womb shall be called holy to the Lord;)[Q]

24 And to offer a [w]sacrifice according to that which is said in the [r]law of the Lord, [x]A pair of [y]turtledoves, or two young [z]pigeons.[Q]

25 And, behold, there was a man in [a]Jĕ-ru̇'sȧ-lĕm, whose name *was* Sĭm'e-on; and the same man *was* just[G] and devout, [b,c]waiting for the consolation of Ĭṣ'ra-el: and the [d]Holy [6]Ghost[G] was [e,f]upon him.[T Q]

26 And it was [g]revealed unto him by the [d]Holy [6]Ghost,[G] [h]that he should not see [i]death, before he had seen the Lord's Christ.

27 And he came by the [d]Spirit into the [j]temple: and when the [k]parents brought in the child Jē'ṣus, to [l]do for him after the custom of the [m]law,[T]

28 Then took he him up in his arms, and [n,o]blessed God, and said,

v.6–5 BC
See footnote, *Time*, Rev. 10:6.

**7**
n *Jesus, birth of*, Matt. 1:21.
o *Children, treatment of, at birth*, Mark 10:14.
p Job 38:9; Ezek. 16:4.

**8**
q *Shepherd*, Jer. 31:10.

**9**
r *Angel, appearances of*, Heb. 1:13.
s *God, glory of*, Gen. 2:2.

**10**
t *Jesus, kingdom of, prophecies concerning*, Matt. 1:21.
u *Gospel*, Mark 13:10.
v *Joy*, Psa. 5:11.

**11**
w *Jesus, humanity of*, Matt. 1:21.
x *Jesus, savior*, Matt. 1:21.
y *Jesus, king*, Matt. 1:21.

**13**
z *Praise*, Psa. 150:1.

**14**
a *Glorifying God*, Luke 5:25.
b *Peace*, Jer. 29:7.
c *Spiritual Peace*, Gal. 1:3.
5 R. V. among men in whom he is well pleased.

**15**
d *Angel*, Heb. 1:13.
e *Shepherd*, Jer. 31:10.
f *Bethlehem*, Gen. 48:7.

**16**
g *Faith, instances of*, Mark 11:22.
h *Mary*, Luke 1:27.
i *Joseph*, Luke 3:23.

**17**
j *Religious Testimony*, 2 Thess. 1:10.
k *Zeal, instances of*, 2 Cor. 7:11.

v.18–5 BC
See footnote, *Time*, Rev. 10:6.

**20**
l *Joy, instances of*, Psa. 5:11.

**21**
m *Family, religion in*, 1 Chr. 13:14.
n *Circumcision*, Gen. 17:10.
o *Jesus*, Matt. 1:21.

**22**
p *Women, purification of*, Prov. 31:10.
q *Purification*, Num. 19:19.
r *Law, of Moses*, Deut. 33:2.
s *Jesus, life of*, Matt. 1:21.
t *Jerusalem*, Judg. 19:10.

**23**
u Ex. 13:2, 12.
v *Firstborn*, Zech. 12:10.

**24**
w *Offerings*, Lev. 6:17.
x Lev. 12:8.
y *Dove*, Gen. 8:8.
z *Pigeon*, Gen. 15:9.

**25**
a *Jerusalem*, Judg. 19:10.
b *Faith, exemplified*, Mark 11:22.
c *Messianic Hope*, Gen. 49:10.
d *Holy Spirit, inspiration of*, Acts 1:2.
e *Inspiration*, Job 32:8.
f *Prophets, inspiration of*, Isa. 3:2.
6 R. V. Spirit

**26**
g *Revelation*, 2 Cor. 12:1.
h *Jesus, prophecies concerning*, Matt. 1:21.
i *Death*, Num. 23:10.

**27**
j *Temple, Herod's*, 1 Kin. 6:17.
k *Parents*, 2 Cor. 12:14.
l *Firstborn, redemption of*, Zech. 12:10.
m *Law, of Moses*, Deut. 33:2.

**28**
n *Thankfulness, to God, exemplified*, Acts 24:3.
o *Joy, instances of*, Psa. 5:11.

29 Lord, now [p]lettest thou thy servant depart in [q]peace, according to thy word:

30 For[Q] [r]mine eyes have seen thy [s]salvation,

31 Which thou hast prepared before the face of all people;[Q]

32 [t,u]A [v]light [w]to lighten[G] the [x]Ġĕn'tīleş, and the glory of thy people Ĭş'ra-el.[T] [Q]

33 And [7,y]Jō'şeph and his [z]mother marvelled at those things which were spoken of him.

34 And Sĭm'e-on [a]blessed them, and said unto [b]Mā'rȳ his mother, Behold, [c]this *child* is set for the fall and rising again of many in Ĭş'ra-el; and for a sign which shall be spoken against;[Q]

35 (Yea, a sword shall pierce through [b]thy own soul also,) that the thoughts of many hearts may be revealed.[T]

36 And there was one Ăn'nȧ, a [d,e]prophetess, the daughter of Phā-nū'el, of the tribe of Ā'sēr: she was of a [f,g]great age, and had lived with an husband seven years from her virginity;

37 And she *was* a [h]widow of about [f,g]fourscore and four years, [i]which [j]departed not from the [k]temple, [8]but served *God* with [l]fastings and [m]prayers night and day.

38 And [d]she coming in that instant [n]gave thanks likewise unto the Lord, and [o,p]spake of him to all them that [q]looked for [r]redemption in [s]Jē-ru̥'sā-lĕm.[Q]

39 And when [b,t]they had performed all things according to the [u]law of the Lord, they returned into [v]Găl'ĭ-lee, to their own city [w]Năz'a-rĕth.

40 And the child grew, and waxed[G] strong [9]in spirit, filled with [x]wisdom: and the [y]grace of God was upon him.[T]

41 ¶ Now his parents went to [s]Jē-ru̥'sā-lĕm every year at the [z]feast of the [a]passover.[Q]

42 And when [b]he was twelve years old, they went up to [c]Jē-ru̥'sā-lĕm after the custom of the [a]feast.

43 And when they had fulfilled the days, as they returned, the child [b]Jē'şus tarried behind in [c]Jē-ru̥'sā-lĕm; and [10,d]Jō'şeph and his [e]mother knew not of *it.*

44 But they, supposing [b]him to have been in the company,[G] went a day's journey; and they sought him among *their* kinsfolk[G] and acquaintance.

45 And when they found [b]him not, they turned back again to [c]Jē-ru̥'sā-lĕm, seeking him.

46[T] And it came to pass, that after three days they found [b]him in the [f]temple, sitting in the midst of the *doctors,[G] both hearing them, and asking them questions.

47 And all that heard [b]him were astonished at his [g]understanding and answers.[T]

48 And when they saw [b]him, they were amazed: and his [e]mother said unto him, Son, why hast thou thus dealt with us? behold, [h]thy father and I have sought thee sorrowing.[Q]

49 And [b]he said unto them, How is it that ye sought me? wist[G] ye not that [i]I must be [11]about my [j]Father's [12]business?[T]

50 And they understood not the saying which he spake unto them.

51 And he went down with them, and came to [k]Năz'a-rĕth, and was [l]subject unto them: but his [e]mother kept all these sayings in her heart.

**29**
*p Death, desired,* Num. 23:10.
*q Spiritual Peace,* Gal. 1:3.

**30**
*r Messianic Hope,* Gen. 49:10.
*s Salvation,* Acts 16:17.

**32**
*t Prophecies, concerning the Messiah, and their fulfillment,* Gen. 12:3.
*u Jesus, prophecies concerning,* Matt. 1:21.
*v Light, figurative,* Matt. 5:14.
*w Jesus, mission of,* Matt. 1:21.
*x Gentiles,* Acts 10:45.

**33**
*y Joseph,* Luke 3:23.
*z Mary,* Luke 1:27.
7 R. V. his father

**34**
*a Benedictions, instances of,* Deut. 21:5.
*b Mary,* Luke 1:27.
*c Jesus, prophecies concerning,* Matt. 1:21.

**36**
*d Prophetess,* Judg. 4:4.
*e Women, as prophets,* Prov. 31:10.
*f Old Age,* Isa. 46:4.
*g Longevity,* Psa. 91:16.

**37**
*h Widow,* 2 Sam. 14:5.
*i Women, good,* Prov. 31:10.
*j Zeal, instances of,* 2 Cor. 7:11.
*k Temple, Herod's,* 1 Kin. 6:17.
*l Fasting,* Zech. 8:19.
*m Prayerfulness, exemplified,* 1 Tim. 5:5.

8 R. V. worshipping with **38** *n Thankfulness, to God,* Acts 24:3. *o Religious Testimony,* 2 Thess. 1:10. *p Witnessing for Christ,* Luke 24:48. *q Messianic Hope,* Gen. 49:10. *r Redemption of our Souls,* Eph. 1:7. *s Jerusalem,* Judg. 19:10.
**39** *t Joseph,* Luke 3:23. *u Law, of Moses,* Deut. 33:2. *v Galilee,* Mark 6:21. *w Nazareth,* John 1:46.

**40**
*x Jesus, wisdom of,* Matt. 1:21.
*y Grace of God,* Rom. 4:16.
9 R. V. *omits* in spirit,

**41**
*z Annual Feasts,* Num. 15:3.
*a Passover,* Num. 9:5.

**42**
*b Jesus,* vs. 43–49; Matt. 1:21.
*c Jerusalem,* Judg. 19:10.

**43**
*d Joseph,* Luke 3:23.
*e Mary,* Luke 1:27.
10 R. V. his parents knew it not;

**46**
*f Temple, Herod's,* 1 Kin. 6:17.

**47**
*g Jesus, wisdom of,* Matt. 1:21.

**48**
*h Parents, affection of, exemplified,* 2 Cor. 12:14.

**49**
*i Jesus, zeal of,* Matt. 1:21.
*j God, fatherhood of,* Gen. 2:2.
11 R. V. in
12 R. V. house?

**51**
*k Nazareth,* John 1:46.
*l Jesus, obedience of,* Matt. 1:21.

* **DOCTOR.** *A teacher, or master,* Matt. 8:19; Luke 2:46; 5:17; Acts 5:34; 1 Tim. 1:7.

52 And Jē'ṣus increased in [g]wisdom and stature, and in [m]favour with God and [13]man.[T][Q]

## CHAPTER 3

*The preaching of John the Baptist. 15 His testimony concerning Christ. 19 Herod imprisons John. 21 Jesus is baptized. 23 His genealogy.*

[a]NOW in the fifteenth year of the reign of [b]Tī-bē'-rĭ-ŭs Çæ'ṣar, Pŏn'tĭ-ŭs [c]Pī'late being [d]governor of [e,f]Jū-dæ'ȧ, and [g]Hĕr'od being tetrarch[G] of [f,h]Găl'ĭ-lee, and his brother [i]Phĭl'ĭp tetrarch of [f]Ī-tụ-ræ'ȧ and of the region of [f]Trăch-o-nī'tis, and Lȳ-sā'nĭ-as the tetrarch[G] of [f]Ăb-ĭ-lē'nē,

2 [j]Ăn'nas and [k]Cā'ia-phăs being the [l]high priests, the [m]word of God [n]came unto [o]Jŏhn the son of [p]Zăch-a-rī'as in the wilderness.

3 And [o]he came into all the country about [q]Jôr'dan, [r]preaching the [s]baptism of [t]repentance [1]for the [u]remission of sins;

4[Q] As it is written in the book of the words of [v]Ê-ṣā'ias the prophet, [w]saying, [x]The voice of [o]one crying in the wilderness, Prepare ye the way of the [y]Lord, make his paths straight.

5 [w,x]Every valley shall be filled, and every mountain and hill shall be brought low; and the crooked shall be made straight, and the rough ways *shall be* made smooth;

6 [w,x]And all flesh shall see the [z,a]salvation of God.[Q]

7 Then [b]said [c]he to the multitude that came forth to be [d]baptized of him, [2]O generation[G] of [e]vipers, who hath warned you to flee from the [f]wrath to come?[T]

8 [g]Bring forth therefore [h]fruits worthy of [i]repentance, and begin not to[G] [j]say within yourselves, We have [k]Ā'brā-hăm to *our* father: for I say unto you, That God is [l]able of these stones to raise up children unto Ā'brā-hăm.

9 And now also the axe is laid unto the root of the trees: every tree therefore which [m]bringeth not forth good fruit is [f]hewn down, and [f]cast into the fire.

10 And the [n]people asked him, saying, What shall we do then?

11 He answereth and saith unto them, He that hath two coats, [o,p]let him impart to [q]him that hath none; and he that hath [3]meat[G], let him do likewise.

12 Then came also [n,r]publicans[G] to be [d]baptized, and said unto him, Master[G], what shall we do?

13 And he said unto [s]them, [t,u,v,w]Exact no more than that which is appointed you.

14 And the [n,x]soldiers likewise demanded of him, saying, And what shall we do? And he said unto them, [y]Do violence to no man, [z,a]neither [b]accuse *any* falsely; and [c]be content with your [d]wages.

15 ¶ And as the people were in [e]expectation, and all men mused[G] in their hearts of [f]Jŏhn, whether he were the Chrĭst, or not;

16 [f]Jŏhn answered, saying unto *them* all, I indeed [g]baptize you with water; but [h]one mightier than I cometh, the latchet[G] of [i]whose [j]shoes [k]I am not worthy to unloose[G]: [l]he shall baptize you with the [m]Holy Ghost[G] and with [n]fire:[T]

17 Whose [o]fan[G] *is* in his hand, and [p]he will throughly[G] purge his [4]floor, and will gather the [q,r]wheat into his [s]garner[G]; but the [t]chaff he will [u]burn with [v,w]fire unquenchable.

---

52
*m Grace of God,* Rom. 4:16.
13 R. V. men.

v.1–AD 26

1
*a Roman Empire,* John 11:48.
*b Cæsar,* Acts 25:8.
*c Pilate,* Matt. 27:2.
*d Government, provincial,* Isa. 22:21.
*e Judea,* Luke 5:17.
*f Canaan, Roman provinces of,* Gen. 37:1.
*g Herod,* Matt. 14:1.
*h Galilee,* Mark 6:21.
*i* Matt. 14:3.

2
*j* John 18:13, 19–24; Acts 4:6.
*k Caiaphas,* Matt. 26:3.
*l High Priest,* Lev. 21:10.
*m Inspiration,* Job 32:8.
*n Prophets, inspiration of,* Isa. 3:2.
*o John the Baptist,* Luke 1:63.
*p* Luke 1:5–80.

3
*q Jordan,* Gen. 32:10.
*r Preaching, repentance,* Matt. 9:35.
*s Baptism, John's,* Luke 20:4.
*t Repentance, enjoined,* Mark 1:4.
*u Sin, forgiveness of,* Rom. 5:12.
1 R. V. unto

4
*v* Or, *Isaiah,* Isa. 1:1.
*w Prophecies, concerning the Messiah, and their fulfillment,* Gen. 12:3.
*x* Isa. 40:3–5.
*y Jesus, prophecies concerning,* Matt. 1:21.

6
*z Salvation,* Acts 16:17.

*a Gospel,* Mark 13:10.

7
*b Reproof, faithfulness in,* Prov. 17:10.
*c Minister, faithful,* Rom. 15:16.

v.8–AD 26
See footnote, *Time,* Rev. 10:6.

*k Abraham,* Gen. 17:5.
*l God, power of,* Gen. 2:2.

9
*m Unfruitfulness,* Matt. 7:19.

10
*n Seekers,* Isa. 55:6.

11
*o Commandment, enjoining fruits of righteousness,* Deut. 8:2.
*p Liberality, enjoined,* 1 Tim. 6:18.
*q Poor, duty to,* Prov. 21:13.
3 R. V. food,

12
*r Publicans,* Matt. 11:19.

13
*s Tax, collectors of,* Neh. 10:32.
*t Commandment, enjoining honesty in office,* Deut. 8:2.
*u Honesty, enjoined,* Rom. 13:13.
*v Integrity, enjoined,* Job 2:3.
*w Extortion, forbidden,* Isa. 16:4.

14
*x Soldiers,* Ezra 8:22.
*y Commandment, enjoining justice, and contentment,* Deut. 8:2.
*z False Witness, forbidden,* Matt. 19:18.

*a Injustice, forbidden,* Isa. 26:10.
*b False Accusation,* 2 Tim. 3:3.
*c Contentment, enjoined,* 1 Tim. 6:6.
*d Wages,* Gen. 31:7.

15
*e Messianic Hope,* Gen. 49:10.
*f John the Baptist,* Luke 1:63.

16
*g Baptism, John's,* Luke 20:4.
*h Jesus, prophecies concerning,* Matt. 1:21.
*i Jesus, perfections of,* Matt. 1:21.
*j Shoe,* Josh. 5:15.

---

*d Baptism, John's,* Luke 20:4. *e Viper, figurative,* Isa. 30:6. *f Wicked, punishment of,* Psa. 73:3. 2 R. V. Ye offspring of **8** *g Commandment, enjoining repentance,* Deut. 8:2. *h Salvation, conditions of,* Acts 16:17. *i Repentance,* Mark 1:4. *j False Confidence,* Psa. 30:6.

*k Humility, instances of,* Prov. 22:4. *l Promise, to the righteous,* 2 Cor. 1:20. *m Holy Spirit, baptism of,* Acts 1:2. *n Fire, figurative,* Ex. 12:8. **17** *o Winnowing, figurative,* Ruth. 3:2. *p Jesus, judge,* Matt. 1:21. *q Wheat, figurative,* Ezra 6:9. *r Righteous, promises to,* Psa. 64:10. *s Heaven, future home of the righteous,* Luke 18:22. *t Chaff, figurative,* Hos. 13:3. *u Wicked, punishment of,* Psa. 73:3. *v Fire, everlasting,* Ex. 12:8. *w Punishment, eternal,* Lev. 26:41. 4 R. V. threshing-floor.

v.18–AD 26
See footnote, *Time*, Rev. 10:6.

18
x *Preaching*, Matt. 9:35.

19
y *Herod*, Matt. 14:1.
z *Reproof, faithfulness in*, Prov. 17:10.

a *Herodias*, Matt. 14:3.
b *Women, wicked*, Prov. 31:10.
c Matt. 14:3; Mark 6:17.

20
d *Prisoners*, Psa. 79:11.

21
e *Baptism, John's*, Luke 20:4.
f Matt. 3:13–16; Mark 1:9, 11.
g *Prayers of Jesus*, Luke 5:16.

22
h *Holy Spirit, baptism of*, Acts 1:2.
i *Jesus, divine sonship of*, Matt. 1:21.
5 R. V. form, as a

23
j *Jesus, incarnation of*, Matt. 1:21.
k *Genealogy, of the ancestors of Joseph*, vs. 23–38; 1 Chr. 5:1.
6 R. V. when he began to teach, was about

27
l Or, *Zerubbabel*, Ezra 3:2.

18 And many other things in
his exhortation [x]preached he unto the people.
19 ¶ But [y]Hĕr'od the tetrarch,
being [z]reproved[C] by him for
[a,b]Hê-rō'dĭ-as his brother [c]Phĭl'-
ĭp's wife, and for all the evils
which Hĕr'od had done,
20 Added yet this above all,
that he [d]shut up Jŏhn in prison.
21 ¶ Now[T] when all the people
were [e]baptized, [f]it came to pass,
that Jē'ṣus also being baptized,
and [g]praying, the heaven was
opened,
22 And the *,[h]Holy Ghost[C] descended in a bodily [5]shape like a
dove upon him, and a voice came
from heaven, which said, [i]Thou
art *my beloved *Son; in thee I
am well pleased.[T Q]
23 ¶ And Jē'ṣus himself [6]began
to be about thirty years of age,
being (as was supposed) the [j]son
of †Jō'ṣeph, [k]which was *the son*
of Hē'lī,
24 [k]Which was *the son* of Măt'-
that, which was *the son* of Lē'vī,
which was *the son* of Mĕl'chī,
which was *the son* of Jăn'nȧ,
which was *the son* of Jō'ṣeph,
25 [k]Which was *the son* of Măt-
ta-thī'as, which was *the son* of
Ā'mos, which was *the son* of
Nā'um, which was *the son* of
Ĕs'lī, which was *the son* of
Năg'ge,
26 [k]Which was *the son* of Mā'-
ath, which was *the son* of Măt-
ta-thī'as, which was *the son* of
Sĕm'e-ī, which was *the son* of
Jō'ṣeph, which was *the son* of
Jū'dȧ,
27 [k]Which was *the son* of Jō-
ăn'nȧ, which was *the son* of
Rhē'sȧ, which was *the son* of
[l]Zō-rŏb'a-bĕl, which was *the son*
of [m]Sȧ-lā'thĭ-el, which was *the*
*son* of Nē'rī,[Q]
28 [k]Which was *the son* of Mĕl'-
chī, which was *the son* of Ăd'dī,
which was *the son* of Cō'sam,
which was *the son* of Ĕl-mō'-
dam, which was *the son* of Ēr,
29 [k]Which was *the son* of Jō'se,
which was *the son* of Ē-li-ē'zēr,
which was *the son* of Jō'rim,
which was *the son* of Măt'that,
which was *the son* of Lē'vī,
30 [k]Which was *the son* of Sĭm'-
e-on, which was *the son* of Jū'dȧ,
which was *the son* of Jō'ṣeph,
which was *the son* of Jō'nan,
which was *the son* of Ē-lī'a-kĭm,
31[Q] [k]Which was *the son* of Mē'-
le-ȧ, which was *the son* of Mē'-
nan, which was *the son* of Măt'-
ta-thȧ, which was *the son* of
Nā'than, which was *the son* of
[n]Dā'vid,
32 [k]Which was *the son* of [o]Jĕs'-
se, which was *the son* of [p]Ō'bed,
which was *the son* of [q]Bō'ŏz,
which was *the son* of [r]Săl'mŏn,
which was *the son* of [s]Nȧ-ăs'son,
33 [k]Which was *the son* of
[t]Ā-mĭn'a-dăb, which was *the son*
of Ā'ram, which was *the son* of
[u]Ĕs'rom, which was *the son* of
[v]Phā'rēṣ, which was *the son* of
[w]Jū'dȧ,[Q]
34 [k]Which[Q] was *the son* of [x]Jā'-
cob, which was *the son* of [y]Ī'-
ṣaac, which was *the son* of [z]Ā'-
brȧ-hăm, which was *the son* of
Thā'rȧ, which was *the son* of
Nā'chôr,
35 Which was *the son* of [a]Sā'-
ruch, which was *the son* of [b]Rā'-
gau, which was *the son* of [c]Phā'-
lec, which was *the son* of [d]Hē'-
bēr, which was *the son* of [e]Sā'lȧ,
36 Which was *the son* of Cȧ-ī'-
nan, which was *the son* of [f]Ăr-

v.27–AD 26
See footnote, *Time*, Rev. 10:6.

m Or, *Shealtiel*, Ezra 3:2.

31
n *David*, 1 Sam. 16:13.

32
o *Jesse*, Ruth 4:17.
p *Obed*, Ruth 4:17.
q Or, *Boaz*, Ruth 2:1.
r *Salmon*, Ruth 4:20.
s Or, *Nahshon*, Num. 7:12.

33
t Or, *Amminadab*, Num. 2:3.
u Matt. 1:3.
v Or, *Pharez*, Gen. 38:29.
w Or, *Judah*, Gen. 37:26.

34
x *Jacob*, Gen. 27:11.
y *Isaac*, Gen. 21:3.
z *Abraham*, Gen. 17:5.

35
a Or, *Serug*, Gen. 11:20.
b Or, *Reu*, Gen. 11:18.
c Or, *Peleg*, Gen. 10:25.
d Or, *Eber*, Gen. 10:21.
e Or, *Salah*, Gen. 10:24.

36
f *Arphaxad*, Gen. 10:22.

* **THE HOLY TRINITY**, Matt. 28:19; Luke 3:22 (with Matt. 3:16); John 1:32, 33; 14:16, 17, 26; 16:7, 13–15; Acts 1:2, 4, 5; 2:33; 10:38; Rom. 8:9, 11; 1 Cor. 12:3; 2 Cor. 1:21, 22; 13:14; Gal. 4:4, 6; 2 Thess. 2:13, 14, 16; Tit. 3:4–6; Heb. 9:14; 1 Pet. 1:2.
See footnotes: God, Gen. 2:2; Jesus, *Divinity of*, Matt. 1:21; Holy Spirit, Acts 1:2.

† **JOSEPH.** *Husband of Mary*, Matt. 1:18–25; 13:55; Luke 1:27. *His genealogy*, Matt. 1:1–16; Luke 3:23–38. *An angel appears and testifies to the innocency of his betrothed*, Matt. 1:19–24. *Dwells at Nazareth*, Luke 2:4. *Belongs to the city of Bethlehem*, Luke 2:4. *Goes to Bethlehem to be enrolled*, Luke 2:1–4. *Jesus born to*, Matt. 1:25; Luke 2:7. *Presents Jesus in the temple*, Luke 2:22–39. *Returns to Nazareth*, Luke 2:39. *Warned in a dream to escape to Egypt*, Matt. 2:13–15. *Warned in a dream to return to Nazareth*, Matt. 2:19–23. *Attends the annual feast at Jerusalem with his family*, Luke 2:42–51.

phăx′ad, which was *the son* of [g]Sĕm, which was *the son* of [h]Nō′e, which was *the son* of [i]Lā′mech,

37 Which was *the son* of [j]Mă-thu̥′sa-lȧ, which was *the son* of [k]Ē′nŏch, which was *the son* of [l]Jā′red, which was *the son* of [m]Mȧ-lē′le-el, which was *the son* of [n]Că-ī′nan,

38 Which was *the son* of [o]Ē′nos, which was *the son* of [p]Sĕth, which was *the son* of [q]Ăd′ăm, which was *the son* of God.

## CHAPTER 4

*The temptation of Jesus. 14 He returns to Galilee; 16 and is rejected at Nazareth. 33 A man with an unclean spirit is healed; 38 also Peter's wife's mother, 40 and many others. 43 Jesus preaches in Galilee.*

AND [a]Jē′şus being full of the [b]Holy [1]Ghost returned from [c]Jŏr′dan, and was led by the Spirit into the wilderness,

2 Being [d]forty days [e,f]tempted of the [g]devil. And in those days he [h]did eat nothing: and when they were ended, he afterward [i]hungered.

3 And the [g]devil [e,f]said unto him, If thou be the [j]Son of God, command this stone [k]that it be made bread.

4 And Jē′şus [l]answered him, saying, It is written, That [m]man shall not live by bread alone, [2]but by every word of God.

5 And the [g]devil, taking him up [3]into an high mountain, [f,n]shewed unto him all the kingdoms of the world in a moment of time.

6 And the [g]devil [e,f]said unto him, [n,o]All this power will I give thee, and the glory of them: for that is delivered unto me; and to whomsoever I will I give it.

7 If thou therefore wilt [p]worship me, [n]all shall be thine.

8 And Jē′şus answered and said unto him, [4,l]Get thee behind me, [g]Sā′tan: for it is written, [q]Thou shalt [r]worship the Lord thy God, and [s]him only shalt thou serve.

9 And [g]he brought him to [t]Jē-ru̥′sȧ-lĕm, and set him on a pinnacle of the [u]temple, and [e,f]said unto him, If thou be the [j]Son of God, [v]cast thyself down from hence:

10 For it is written, [w]He shall give his [x]angels charge over thee, to keep thee:

11 [w]And in *their* hands they shall bear thee up, lest at any time thou dash thy foot against a stone.

12 And Jē′şus [l]answering said unto him, It is said, [y]Thou shalt not tempt the Lord thy God.

13 And when the [g]devil had ended all the [e,f]temptation, he departed from him for a season.

14 ¶ And [z]Jē′şus returned in the [a]power of the Spirit into [b]Găl′ĭ-lee: [c]and there went out a [d]fame of him through all the region round about.

15 And he [e,f]taught in their [g]synagogues, being glorified of all.

16 ¶ [h]And he came to [i]Năz′a-rĕth, where he had been brought up: and, as his custom was, he went into the [g]synagogue on the [j]sabbath day, and stood up for to [k]read.

17 And there was delivered unto him the [l]book of the [m]prophet [n]Ē-şā′ias. And when he had opened the book, he found the place where it was written,

18 [o]The [p]Spirit of the Lord *is* upon me, because he hath [q]anointed me [r]to [s]preach the [t]gospel to the [u]poor; he hath sent me [r]to [5]heal the [v]brokenhearted, [r]to preach deliverance to the [w]captives, and recovering of sight to the [x]blind, [r]to set at [y]liberty them that are bruised,

19 [r]To [s]preach the acceptable year of the Lord.

20 And he closed the book, and he gave *it* again to the minister, and sat down. And the eyes of

v.36–AD 26 See footnote, *Time*, Rev. 10:6.

g Or, *Shem*, Gen. 6:10.
h Or, *Noah*, Gen. 5:29.
i *Lamech*, Gen. 5:25.

**37**
j Gen. 5:21–27.
k *Enoch*, Gen. 5:18.
l *Jared*, Gen. 5:15.
m Or, *Mahalaleel*, Gen. 5:12.
n *Cainan*, Gen. 5:9.

**38**
o Or, *Enosh*, 1 Chr. 1:1.
p *Seth*, Gen. 4:25.
q *Adam*, Gen. 2:19.

**1**
a Matt. 4:1–11; Mark 1:12, 13.
b *Holy Spirit, Jesus anointed and led by*, Acts 1:2.
c *Jordan*, Gen. 32:10.
1 R. V. Spirit

**2**
d *Forty, days*, Jonah 3:4.
e *Temptation*, Luke 11:4.
f *Jesus, temptation of*, Matt. 1:21.
g *Satan*, Matt. 10:4.
h *Fasting*, Zech. 8:19.
i *Hunger*, Neh. 9:15.

**3**
j *Jesus, divine sonship of*, Matt. 1:21.
k *Miracles, design of*, Luke 23:8.

**4**
l *Temptation, resistance to*, Luke 11:4.
m Deut. 8:3; Matt. 4:4.
2 R. V. *omits the rest of this verse.*

**5**
n *Ambition, Satan tempts to*, Hab. 2:5.
3 R. V. *omits* into an high mountain,

**6**
o *Falsehood*, Job 21:34.

**7**
p *Demons, worship of*, Matt. 4:24.

**8**
q Deut. 6:13; Matt. 4:10.
r *Worship*, Gen. 22:5.
s *God, sovereign*, Gen. 2:2.
4 R. V. *omits* Get thee behind me, Satan: for

**9**
t *Jerusalem*, Judg. 19:10.
u *Temple, Herod's*, 1 Kin. 6:17.
v *Presumption, temptation to* Psa. 19:13.

**10**
w Psa. 91:11, **12**; Matt. 4:6.
x *Angel, functions of*, Heb. 1:13.

**12**
y Deut. 6:16; Matt. 4:7.

**14**
z Matt. 4:12; Mark 1:14.

a *Holy Spirit, power of*, Acts 1:2.
b *Galilee*, Mark 6:21.
c *Jesus, received*, Matt. 1:21.
d *Fame of Jesus*, Luke 5:15.

**A.D. 30**

**15**
e *Instruction, in religion*, Prov. 23:23.
f *Jesus, teacher*, Matt. 1:21.
g *Synagogue*, Matt. 12:9.

**16**
h Matt. 13:54–58; Mark 6:1–6.
i *Nazareth*, John 1:46.
j *Sabbath, religious instruction on*, Ex. 16:23.
k *Worship, the word of God read in public assemblies*, Gen. 22:5.

**17**
l *Word of God, expounded by Jesus*, v. 21; Psa. 119:9.
m *Prophets*, Isa. 3:2.
n Or, *Isaiah*, Isa. 1:1.

**18**
o Isa. 61:1, 2.
p *Holy Spirit*, Acts 1:2
q *Anointing, figurative*, Deut. 28:40.
r *Jesus, mission of*, Matt. 1:21.
s *Preaching*, Matt. 9:35.
t *Gospel*, Mark 13:10.
u *Poor, God's care of*, Prov. 21:13.
v *Penitent, promises to*, Psa. 51:17.
w *Prisoners, figurative*, Psa. 79:11.
x *Spiritual Blindness*, 2 Cor. 4:4.
y *Liberty, spiritual*, Lev. 25:10.
5 R. V. proclaim release to the captives, And

all them that were in the synagogue were fastened on him.
21 And he began to say unto
them, This day is this [z,a]scrip-
ture fulfilled in your ears.[T]
22 And all bare him witness,
and wondered at the gracious
*words which proceeded out of
his mouth. And they said, Is not
this Jō′ṣeph's [b]son?[Q]
23 And he said unto them, [c]Ye
will surely say unto me this
[d]proverb, [e]Physician, heal thyself: whatsoever we have heard
done in Că-pĕr′na-ŭm, do also
here in thy country.[T]
24 And he said, Verily I say
unto you, [f]No [g,h]prophet is accepted in his own country.
25 But I tell you of a truth,
many [i]widows were in Ĭṣ′ra-el
in the days of [j]Ē-lī′as, when the
heaven was shut up three years
and six months, when great [k]fam-
ine was throughout all the land;[Q]
26 But unto none of them was
[j]Ē-lī′as sent, save[G] unto [l]Să-rĕp′-
tȧ, *a city* of Sī′dŏn, unto a woman *that was* a [i]widow.[Q]
27 And many [m]lepers were in
Ĭṣ′ra-el in the time of [n]Ĕl-ĭ-sē′-
us the [g]prophet; and none of
them was cleansed, saving[G] [o]Nā′-
a-man the [p]Sўr′ĭ-an.[Q]
28 And all they in the [q]syna-
gogue, when they heard these
things, [r,s]were filled with [t]wrath,[G]
29 And rose up, and [u,v,w]thrust
him out of the city, and led him
unto the brow[G] of the hill whereon their city was built, that they
might cast him down headlong.
30 But he passing through the
midst of them went his way,
31 [x]And came down to †Că-
pĕr′na-ŭm, a city of [y]Găl′ĭ-lee,
and [z,a]taught them on the [b]sab-
bath days.
32 And they were astonished at
his [6,a,c]doctrine:[G] for his word
was with [7,d]power.
33[†] ¶ [e]And[S] in the [f]synagogue
there was a man, which had a
spirit of an unclean devil,[G] and
cried out with a loud voice,
34 Saying, Let *us* alone; what
have we to do with thee, *thou*
Jē′ṣus of [g]Năz′a-rĕth? art thou
come to destroy us? I know thee
who thou art; the [h]Holy One of
God.
35 And Jē′ṣus rebuked him,
saying, Hold thy peace, and
come out of him. And when the
devil[G] had thrown him in the
midst, he [i]came out of him, and
hurt him not.[S]
36 And they were all amazed,
and spake among themselves,
saying, What a word *is* this! for
with authority and power he
commandeth the unclean[G] spirits,
and they come out.[Q]
37 And the [j]fame of him went
out into every place of the country round about.
38 ¶ [k]And he arose out of
the [f]synagogue, and entered into
[l]Sī′mon's house. And Sī′mon's
[m]wife's [n]mother was taken with
a great [o]fever; and they [p]be-
sought[G] him for her.
39 And he stood over her, and
rebuked the [o,q]fever; and it [i,r]left
her: and immediately she arose
and ministered unto them.[S]
40 ¶ Now when the sun was setting, all they that had any sick

**21**
z *Prophecies, concerning Jesus, and their fulfillment*, Gen. 12:3.
a *Word of God*, Psa. 119:9.

**22**
b *Jesus, incarnation of*, Matt. 1:21.

**23**
c *Scorners*, Prov. 19:25.
d *Proverbs*, 1 Sam. 24:13.
e *Physician*, 2 Chr. 16:12.

**24**
f Matt. 13:57; John 4:44.
g *Prophets*, Isa. 3:2.
h *Minister, discouragements of*, 2 Chr. 9:4.

**25**
i *Widow*, 2 Sam. 14:5.
j Or, *Elijah*, 1 Kin. 17:1.
k *Famine*, 2 Kin. 8:1.

**26**
l Or, *Zarephath*, 1 Kin. 17:8–24.

**27**
m *Leprosy*, Lev. 13:2.
n Or, *Elisha*, 1 Kin. 19:16.
o 2 Kin. 5:1–23.
p *Syria*, 2 Kin. 6:23.

**28**
q *Synagogue*, Matt. 12:9.
r *Bigotry, instances of*, Isa. 65:5.
s *Reproof, despised*, Prov. 17:10.
t *Anger, instances of*, Psa. 37:8.

**29**
u *Persecution, of Jesus*, John 15:20.
v *Intolerance*, Num. 11:28.
w *Jesus, rejected*, Matt. 1:21.

**31**
x Mark 1:21–28.
y *Galilee*, Mark 6:21.
z *Instruction, in religion*, Prov. 23:23.
a *Jesus, teacher*, Matt. 1:21.
b *Sabbath*, Ex. 16:23.

**32**
c *Doctrines of Jesus*, John 7:16.
d *Spiritual Power*, Luke 24:49.
6 R. V. teaching;
7 R. V. authority.

**33**
e Mark 1:23–28.
f *Synagogue*, Matt. 12:9.

**34**
g *Nazareth*, John 1:46.
h *Jesus, holiness of*, Matt. 1:21.

**35**
i *Miracles, of Jesus*, Luke 23:8.

**37**
j *Fame of Jesus*, Luke 5:15.

**38**
k Matt. 8:14–17; Mark 1:29–34.
l *Peter*, Mark 5:37.
m *Minister, marriage of*, Rom. 15:16.
n *Mother-in-law*, Matt. 10:35.
o *Fever*, Deut. 28:22.
p *Mediation*, Gal. 3:19.

**39**
q *Disease, healing of, by Jesus*, Ex. 15:26.
r *Healing, by Jesus*, Acts 4:22.

* **WORDS.** *Should be acceptable to God*, Psa. 19:14. *Fitly spoken, are like apples of gold in setting of silver*, Prov. 25:11. *Spoken in season*, Prov. 15:23; Isa. 50:4.
*Of the teacher, should be plain*, 1 Cor. 14:9, 19. *Of the perfect man, wise*, Jas. 3:2.
*In a multitude of, is sin*, Prov. 10:19. *Fool known by the multitude of*, Eccl. 5:3. *Of a fool will swallow him up*, Eccl. 10:12–14.
*Idle, account must be given for, in the day of judgment*, Matt. 12:36, 37. *Vain, not to be regarded*, Ex. 5:9; Job 8:2. *Unprofitable, to be avoided*, Eph. 5:6; 2 Tim. 2:14. *Folly of hasty*, Prov. 29:20. *Seditious, beguile*, Rom. 16:18. *Without knowledge, darken counsel*, Job 38:2.
Of the wise: *As goads, and as nails well fastened*, Eccl. 12:11; *gracious*, Eccl. 10:12.
*Of the hypocrite, deceitful*, Psa. 55:21. *Of the talebearer, dainty morsels to a corrupt heart*, Prov. 18:8.
**Of Jesus:** *Gracious*, Luke 4:22. *Spirit and life*, John 6:63. *Eternal life*, John 6:68. *Shall judge*, John 12:47, 48. See footnote, DOCTRINES OF JESUS, John 7:16.
See footnote, SPEECH, Col. 4:6.

† **CAPERNAUM**, a city on the shore of the Sea of Galilee. *Jesus chose, as the place of his abode*, Matt. 4:13; Luke 4:31. *Miracles of Jesus performed at*, Matt. 9:1–26; 17:24–27; Mark 1:21–45; 2; 3:1–6; Luke 7:1–10; John 4:46–53; 6:17–25, 59. *Jesus' prophecy against*, Matt. 11:23; Luke 10:15.

with divers[G] [q]diseases [p]brought
them unto him; and he laid his
[s]hands on every one of them, and
[i,r]healed them.
41 And [t]devils[G] also [t]came out
of many, crying out, and [u]say-
ing, Thou art [8]Chrīst the Son
of God. And he rebuking *them*
suffered[G] them not to speak:
for they[T] knew that he was
Chrīst.
42 And when it was day, he
departed and went into a desert place: and [v]the people sought
him, and came unto him, and
stayed[G] him, that he should not
depart from them.
43 And he said unto them, I
must [w]preach the [x]kingdom of
God to other cities also: for
[y]therefore am I sent.
44 And he [w]preached in the
synagogues of [z]Găl'ĭ-lee.

## CHAPTER 5

*Jesus teaches the people. 4 The miraculous draught of fishes. 10 The calling of Peter, James, and John. 12 Jesus cleanses a leper; 16 prays in the wilderness; 18 heals one sick of the palsy; 27 and calls Levi, 29 who makes a feast, at which Jesus eats with publicans and sinners. 33 He justifies his disciples in not fasting. 36 New cloth not put on old garments, nor new wine in old wine-skins.*

AND it[s] came to pass, that, as
[a]the people pressed upon
[b]him [c]to [d]hear the [e,f]word of God,
he stood by the [g]lake of Gĕn-
nĕs'a-rĕt,
2 And saw two [1,h]ships standing by the [g]lake: but the *fishermen were gone out of them, and
were washing *their* [i]nets.
3 And he entered into one of
the [1,h]ships, which was [j]Sī'mon's,
and prayed[G] him that he would
thrust out a little from the land.
And [k]he sat down, and [d,l]taught
the people out of the ship.
4[T] Now when he had left speaking, he [m]said unto [j]Sī'mon,
Launch out into the deep, and
let down your [i]nets for a draught[G].
5 And [j]Sī'mon answering said
unto him, Master, we have toiled
all the night, and have taken
nothing: nevertheless [n]at thy
word I will [o]let down the [i]net.
6 And when they had this done,
they inclosed a great multitude
of [p]fishes: and their net brake.
7 And they beckoned unto
*their* partners, which were in
the other [h]ship, that they should
come and help them. And they
came, and filled both the [1]ships,
so that they began to sink.
8 When [j]Sī'mon Pē'tĕr saw *it*,
he [q]fell down at Jē'şus' knees,
saying, Depart from me; for [r,s]I
am a sinful man, O Lord.
9 For he was astonished, and
all that were with him, at the
draught[G] of the [p]fishes which
they had taken:
10 And so *was* also †Jāmeş,
and [t]Jŏhn, the sons of [u]Zĕb'e-
dee, which were partners with
Sī'mon. And Jē'şus said unto
[j]Sī'mon, Fear not; [v]from henceforth *,[w]thou shalt catch men.
11 And when they had brought
their ships to land, they ‡forsook
all, and [x]followed him.[T]
12 ¶ And it came to pass, when
he was in a certain city, [y]behold a
man full of [z]leprosy: who seeing
Jē'şus fell on *his* face, and besought[G] him, [a]saying, Lord, if thou
wilt, thou canst make me clean.

**40**
s *Hand, imposition of, in healing,* Ezra 10:19.

**41**
t *Demons, cast out by Jesus,* Matt. 4:24.
u *Jesus, divinity of, testified to by demons,* Matt. 1:21.
8 R. V. *omits* Christ

**42**
v *Popularity of Jesus,* John 6:15.

**43**
w *Preaching,* Matt. 9:35.
x *Kingdom of Heaven,* Matt. 13:24.
y *Jesus, mission of,* Matt. 1:21.

**44**
z *Galilee,* Mark 6:21.

**1**
a *Popularity of Jesus,* John 6:15.
b *Jesus, received,* vs. 17, 19, 26; Matt. 1:21.
c *Hunger figurative,* Matt. 5:6.
d *Instruction, in religion,* Prov. 23:23.
e *Word of God,* Psa. 119:9.
f *Doctrines of Jesus,* John 7:16.
g Or, *Sea of Galilee,* Matt. 4:18.

**2**
h *Ship,* 2 Chr. 8:18.
i *Net,* Isa. 51:20.
1 R. V. boats

**3**
j Or, *Peter,* Mark 5:37.
k *Jesus, teacher,* Matt. 1:21.
l *Preaching,* Matt. 9:35.

**4**
m *Jesus, omniscience of,* Matt. 1:21.

**5**
n *Faith in Christ, exemplified,* John 6:69.
o *Obedience,* Heb. 5:8.

**6**
p *Fish,* Matt. 17:27.

**8**
q *Humility, instances of,* Prov 22:4.
r *Miracles, convincing effect of,* Luke 23:8.
s *Conviction of Sin, instances of,* John 16:8.

**10**
t *John,* Mark 1:19.
u *Zebedee,* Matt. 4:21.
v *Call, to special religious duty,* Phil. 3:14.
w *Agency, in salvation of men,* Mark 1:17.

**11**
x *Discipleship, of Jesus,* Matt. 10:32.

**12**
y Matt. 8:2-4; Mark 1:40-44.
z *Leprosy,* Lev. 13:2.
a *Faith in Christ, instances of,* John 6:69.

*** FISHERMEN.** *Certain apostles,* Matt. 4:18-21; Mark 1:16, 17, 19; Luke 5:1-10; John 21:2, 3.
**Figurative,** Jer. 16:16; Matt. 4:19; Mark 1:17; Luke 5:10.

**† JAMES,** an apostle. *Son of Zebedee and Salome,* Matt. 4:21; 27:56. *A fisherman,* Luke 5:10. *Called to be an apostle,* Matt. 4:21, 22; 10:2; Mark 1:19, 20; Luke 6:14; Acts 1:13. *Surnamed* BOANERGES, Mark 3:17.
An intimate companion of Jesus and present with him: *At the great draught of fishes,* Luke 5:10; *at the healing of Peter's mother-in-law,* Mark 1:29; *at the raising of the daughter of Jairus,* Mark 5:37; Luke 8:51; *at the transfiguration of Jesus,* Matt. 17:1; Mark 9:2; Luke 9:28; *in Gethsemane,* Matt. 26:37; Mark 14:33. *Asks Jesus concerning his second coming,* Mark 13:3.
*Bigotry of,* Luke 9:54. *Civil ambitions of,* Matt. 20:20-23; Mark 10:35-41. *Present at the sea of Galilee when Jesus revealed himself to the disciples after his resurrection,* John 21:2. *Martyred,* Acts 12:2.

**‡ RENUNCIATION,** Phil. 3:7, 8. *Of self for others, exemplified, by Moses,* Ex. 32:32; *by Jesus,* Phil. 2:7; *by Paul,* Rom. 9:3; 2 Cor. 13:7.
*Of self for Christ,* Matt. 16:25; Luke 14:26-33; 17:33; John 12:25. *Of business for Christ,* Matt. 4:20; 9:9; Mark 1:18-20; 2:14; Luke 5:27, 28. *Of possessions for Christ,* Matt. 19:21-29; Mark 10:21-30; Luke 18:22-30. *Of one's all for Christ, illustrated by parables of the man who found the treasure and the merchant who bought the pearl of great price,* Matt. 13:44-46.
*Of the will, to the Father, exemplified by Jesus,* Mark 14:36; Luke 22:42; John 5:30; 6:38.

13 And he put forth *his* hand,
and touched him, saying, I will:
be thou clean. And immediately
the [b]leprosy[c,d] departed from him.
14 And he [e]charged him to
tell no man: but go, and [f]shew
thyself to the priest, and [g]offer
for thy cleansing, according as
[h]Mō'ṣeṣ [i]commanded, for a testimony unto them.[Q]
15 But so much the more went
there a ‖fame[G] abroad of him: and
great multitudes came together
[j]to hear, and to be [c]healed by
him of their [b]infirmities.
16 And he withdrew himself into the wilderness, and §prayed.
17 ¶ And it came to pass on a
certain day, as he was [k,l]teach-
ing, that there were [m]Phăr'ĭ-
seeṣ and [n]doctors[G] of the [i]law
sitting by, which were come out
of every town of [o]Găl'ĭ-lee, and
+Jū-dæ'ȧ, and [p]Jĕ-ru'sȧ-lĕm: and
the [q]power of the Lord was *present* to [c]heal them.
18 ¶ And, behold, men
[r,s,t]brought in a bed a man which
was taken with a [u]palsy[G]: and
they sought *means* to bring him
in, and to lay *him* before him.[T]
19 And when they could not find
by what *way* they might bring
him in because of the multitude,
[v]they went upon the [w]housetop,
and [r,s,t]let him down through
the tiling with *his* couch into the
midst before Jē'ṣus.
20 And[T] when he saw their [r]faith,
[x]he said unto him, Man, thy sins
are [y]forgiven thee.
21 And the [z]scribes and the
[a]Phăr'ĭ-seeṣ began to [b]reason,
saying, Who is this which speaketh [c]blasphemies? Who can forgive sins, but God alone?[T Q]
22 But when Jē'ṣus [d]perceived
their thoughts, he answering said
unto them, What [b]reason ye in
your hearts?
23 Whether is easier, to say,
Thy sins be forgiven thee; or to
say, Rise up and walk?
24 But that ye may know that
the [e]Son of man hath [f]power[G] upon earth to forgive sins, (he said
unto the sick of the palsy,) I say
unto thee, Arise, and take up thy
couch, and go into thine house.
25 And immediately he [g,h]rose
up before them, and took up that
whereon he lay, and departed to
his own house, ⊙,[i]glorifying God.
26 And they were all amazed,
and [j]they ⊙glorified God, and
were filled with fear, saying, We
have seen strange things to day.[S]
27 ¶ And after these things he
went forth, and saw a [k]publican[G],
named [l]Lē'vī, sitting at the [2]re-
ceipt[G] of [m]custom[G]: and he said
unto [n]him, [o]Follow me.
28 And he ‡left all, rose up, and
followed him
29 And [l]Lē'vī [p]made [q]him a
great [r]feast in his own house:
and there was a great company
of [k,s]publicans[G] and of others that
sat down with them.
30 But their [t]scribes and [a]Phăr'-
ĭ-seeṣ [u]murmured[G] against his [v]dis-
ciples, saying, [w,x]Why do ye eat
and drink with [k]publicans[G] and
sinners?
31 And Jē'ṣus answering said
unto them, They that are
[x,y]whole[G] need not a [z]physician;
but they that are sick.
32 [a]I came not to call the
[b,c]righteous, but [d]sinners to [e]re-
pentance.
33 ¶ And they said unto him,

**13**
*b* *Disease, healing of, by Jesus,* Ex. 15:26.
*c* *Healing, by Jesus,* Acts 4:22.
*d* *Miracles, of Jesus,* Luke 23:8.

**14**
*e* *Prudence, instances of,* 2 Chr. 2:12.
*f* *Leprosy, law concerning,* Lev. 13:2.
*g* *Offerings,* Lev. 6:17.
*h* *Moses,* Ex. 2:10.
*i* *Law, of Moses,* Deut. 33:2.

**15**
*j* *Hunger, figurative,* Matt. 5:6.

**17**
*k* *Jesus, teacher,* Matt. 1:21.
*l* *Instruction, in religion,* Prov. 23:23.
*m* *Pharisees,* Matt. 15:12.
*n* *Doctor,* Luke 2:46.
*o* *Galilee,* Mark 6:21.
*p* *Jerusalem,* Judg. 19:10.
*q* *God, power of,* Gen. 2:2.

**18**
*r* *Faith in Christ, instances of,* John 6:69.
*s* *Mediation,* Gal. 3:19.
*t* *Kindness,* Acts 28:2.
*u* *Paralysis,* Mark 2:3.

**19**
*v* *Perseverance,* Eph. 6:18.
*w* *House, roof of,* Esth. 8:1.

**20**
*x* *Jesus, power of, to forgive sins,* Matt. 1:21.
*y* *Sin, forgiveness of,* Rom. 5:12.

**21**
*z* *Scribe,* 1 Kin. 4:3.

---

*a* *Pharisees,* Matt. 15:12.
*b* *Reasoning, of the Pharisees,* Job 13:6.
*c* *Blasphemy,* 2 Sam. 12:14.

**22**
*d* *Jesus, omniscience of,* Matt. 1:21.

**24**
*e* *Jesus, humanity of,* Matt. 1:21.
*f* *Jesus, divinity of,* Matt. 1:21.

**25**
*g* *Healing, by Jesus,* Acts 4:22.
*h* *Miracles, of Jesus,* Luke 23:8.
*i* *Thankfulness, to God,* Acts 24:3.

**26**
*j* *Miracles, convincing effect of,* Luke 23:8.

**27**
*k* *Publicans,* Matt. 11:19.
*l* Or, *Matthew,* Matt. 9:9.
*m* *Tax, collectors of,* Neh. 10:32.
*n* *Minister, call of,* Rom. 15:16.
*o* *Call, personal,* Phil. 3:14.
2 R. V. place of toll

**29**
*p* *Hospitality,* Rom. 12:13.
*q* Matt. 9:10–13; Mark 2:15–17.
*r* *Feasts,* Mark 12:39.
*s* *Guest,* Zeph. 1:7.

**30**
*t* *Scribe,* 1 Kin. 4:3.
*u* *Uncharitableness,* Matt. 7:1.
*v* *Apostles,* Luke 6:13.
*w* *Bigotry,* Isa. 65:5.
*x* *Self-righteousness,* Luke 18:11.

**31**
*y* *Irony,* Mark 12:14.
*z* *Physician, proverbs about,* 2 Chr. 16:12.

---

**32**
*a* *Jesus, mission of,* Matt. 1:21.
*b* *Self-righteousness,* Luke 18:11.
*c* *Irony,* Mark 12:14.
*d* *Wicked,* Psa. 73:3.
*e* *Repentance,* Mark 1:4.

---

‖ **FAME OF JESUS,** Matt. 4:24, 25; 9:31; 14:1; Mark 1:28; Luke 4:14, 37; 5:15.

§ **PRAYERS OF JESUS,** Matt. 11:25, 26; Luke 3:21; 11:1; John 12:27, 28. *In secret,* Matt. 14:23; Mark 1:35; 6:46; Luke 5:16; 6:12; 9:18, 28, 29. *Thanksgiving before eating,* Matt. 14:19; 15:36; 26:26, 27; Mark 6:41; 8:6; 1 Cor. 11:24. *In blessing children,* Matt. 19:13, 15; Mark 10:16. *At the grave of Lazarus,* John 11:41, 42. *For Peter,* Luke 22:32. *For believers,* John 17:1–26. *In Gethsemane,* Matt. 26:36–44; Mark 14:32–35; Luke 22:41–44; Heb. 5:7. *On the cross,* Matt. 27:46; Luke 23:34, 46.

+ **JUDEA,** the southern division of Palestine. *It extended from the Jordan and Dead Sea on the E. to the Mediterranean, and from Shiloh on the N. to the wilderness on the S.,* Matt. 4:25; Luke 5:17; John 4:47, 54. In Luke 1:5 the term applies to all Palestine. In Matt. 19:1, Mark 10:1, and Luke 23:5 it included the inhabited territory E. of Jordan.

⊙ **GLORIFYING GOD,** Luke 2:14, 20; 7:16; 13:13; 18:43.

33
*f Disciples*, Matt. 9:14.
*g John the Baptist*, Luke 1:63.
*h Fasting*, Zech. 8:19.
*i Prayer*, Acts 6:4.
*j Pharisees*, Matt. 15:12.

34
*k Bridegroom*, Isa. 61:10.

36
*l Parables, of Jesus*, Ezek. 20:49.
*m* Matt. 9:16, 17; Mark 2:21, 22.
*n Wisdom, worldly*, Prov. 2:2.
3 R. V. rendeth a piece from a new garment and putteth it upon an old garment; else he will rend the new, and also the piece from the new will not agree with the old.

37
*o Wine*, v. 38; Prov. 23:31.
*p Bottle*, Gen. 21:14.
4 R. V. wine-skins;
5 R. V. skins,
6 R. V. skins will

38
7 R. V. fresh wine-skins.
8 R. V. *omits* and both are preserved.

39
9 R. V. good.

1
*a* Matt. 12:1; Mark 2:23.
*b Sabbath*, Ex. 16:23.
*c Corn*, Psa. 65:13.
*d Disciples*, Matt. 9:14.

2
*e Pharisees*, Matt. 15:12.

3
*f Jesus defines Law of Sabbath*, Matt. 12:1.

Why do the [f]disciples of [g]Jŏhn
[h]fast often, and make [i]prayers,
and likewise *the disciples* of the
[j]Phăr′ĭ-seeș; but thine eat and
drink?
34 And he said unto them, Can
ye make the children[G] of the bride-
chamber [h]fast, while the [k]bride-
groom is with them?
35 But the days will come, when
the [k]bridegroom shall be taken
away from them, and then shall
they [h]fast in those days.
36 ¶ And he spake also a [l]par-
able unto them; [m,n]No man [3]put-
teth a piece of a new garment
upon an old; if otherwise[G], then
both the new maketh a rent[G], and
the piece that was *taken* out of
the new agreeth not with the old.
37 And [m,n]no man putteth new
[o]wine into old [4,p]bottles[G]; else the
new wine will burst the [5]bottles[G],
and be spilled, and the [6]bottles[G]
shall perish.
38 But [n]new [o]wine must be put
into [7]new [p]bottles[G]; [8]and both are
preserved.
39 No man also having drunk old
[o]*wine* straightway[G] desireth new:
for he saith, The old is [9]better.

## CHAPTER 6

*The disciples pluck ears of corn on the Sabbath. 6 Jesus heals a withered hand. 12 He chooses the twelve apostles; 17 and heals the multitudes. 20 The beatitudes. 27 Love towards enemies. 37 Rash judgment reproved. 47 The house built upon a rock, or upon the sand.*

AND it came to pass [a]on
the second [b]sabbath after
the first, that he went through the
[c]corn fields[G]; and his [d]disciples
plucked the ears of corn[G], and did
eat, rubbing *them* in *their* hands.[Q]
2 And certain of the [e]Phăr′ĭ-
seeș said unto them, Why do ye
that which is not lawful to do
on the sabbath days?
3 And [f]Jē′șus answering them
said, Have ye not read so much
as this, what [g]Dā′vid did, when
himself was an[G] [h]hungred, and
they which were with him;
4 How [g]he went into the [i]house
of God, and did take and eat
the [j]shewbread[G], and gave also to
them that were with him; which
it is not lawful to eat but for the
[k]priests alone?[Q]
5 And [l]he said unto them, That
the [l]Son of man is Lord also of
the [b]sabbath.[G]
6 ¶ [S]And it came to pass also
on another [b]sabbath, that he entered into the [m]synagogue and
[n,o]taught: and [p]there was a man
whose right hand was withered.
7 And the [q]scribes and [e]Phăr′-
ĭ-seeș watched him, whether he
would heal on the sabbath day;
that they might find an accusation against him.
8 But he [r]knew their thoughts,
and said to the man which had
the withered hand, Rise up, and
stand forth in the midst. And he
arose and stood forth.[T Q]
9 Then said Jē′șus unto them, I
will ask you one thing; Is it lawful on the sabbath days to do
good, or to do [1]evil? to save life,
or to destroy *it*?
10 And looking round about
upon them all, he said unto the
man, Stretch forth thy hand.
And he did so: and his hand [s]was
restored whole[G] as the other.
11 And they were filled with
[t]madness[G]; and communed[G] one
with another what they might
[u]do to Jē′șus.[S]
12 ¶ And it came to pass in
those days, that he went out into
a [v]mountain to [w,x]pray, and continued all night in prayer to God.
13 And when it was day, he
called *unto him* his [y]disciples:
and of them he [z]chose twelve,
whom also he named *apostles;

*g David*, 1 Sam. 16:13.
*h Hunger*, Neh. 9:15.

4
*i Tabernacle*, Ex. 27:9.
*j Shewbread*, Ex. 35:13.
*k Priest*, Lev. 1:5.

5
*l Jesus, king*, Matt. 1:21.

6
*m Synagogue*, Matt. 12:9.
*n Jesus, teacher*, Matt. 1:21.
*o Instruction, in religion*, Prov. 23:23.
*p* Matt. 12:10–13; Mark 3:1–5.

7
*q Scribe*, 1 Kin. 4:3.

8
*r Jesus, omniscience of*, Matt. 1:21.

9
1 R. V. harm

10
*s Miracles, of Jesus*, Luke 23:8.

11
*t Malice*, Eph. 4:31.
*u Persecution, of Jesus*, John 15:20.

12
*v Mountain*, Mic. 7:12.
*w Prayers of Jesus*, Luke 5:16.
*x Prayer, private*, Acts 6:4.

13
*y Disciples*, Matt. 9:14.
*z Call, to special religious duty*, Phil. 3:14.

*Enjoined*, 1 Chr. 16:28, 29; Psa. 22:23; Isa. 42:12; 1 Cor. 6:20; 10:31.
* **APOSTLES**, the twelve disciples, whom Jesus selected to be intimately associated with himself.

*Names of*, Matt. 10:2; Mark 3:16–19; Luke 6:13–16; Acts 1:13, 26. *Selection of*, Matt. 4:18–22; 9:9; 10:2–4; Mark 1:16–20; 3:13–19; Luke 5:1–11; 6:13–16; John 1:43. *Unlearned*, Matt. 11:25; Acts 4:13.

14 Sī'mon, (whom he also
named [a]Pē'tẽr,) and [b]Ăn'drew
his brother, [c]Jāmeș and [d]Jŏhn,
†Phĭl'ĭp and [e]Bär-thŏl'o-mew,
15 [f]Măt'thew and [g]Thŏm'as,
[h]Jāmeș the *son* of Ăl-phæ'us,
and [i]Sī'mon called [2]Zē-lō'tēș,[G]
16 And [j]Jū'das *the* [3]*brother* of
Jāmeș, and [k]Jū'das Ĭs-căr'ĭ-ot,
which also was the [l]traitor.
17 And he came down with
*them, and stood in the plain,
and the company of his [m]dis-
ciples, and a great multitude
of people out of all [n]Jū-dæ'ȧ
and [o]Jē-ru̧'sȧ-lĕm, and from the
sea coast of [p]Tȳre and [q]Sī'dŏn,
which came to [r]hear him, and to
be [s,t]healed of their [u]diseases;[G]
18 And they that were vexed
with [v]unclean spirits: and they
were [s,u]healed.
19 And the whole multitude
sought to touch him: for there
went [4,w]virtue[G] out of him, and
[s,u]healed *them* all.
20 ¶ [S]And he lifted up his
eyes on his [m]disciples, and
said, [x,y]Blessed *be ye* [z,a]poor:
for [b,c]your's is the [d]kingdom of
God.[T]
21 [e]Blessed *are* [f]*ye* that [g,h]hun-
ger now: for [i]ye shall be filled.
[e]Blessed *are ye* that weep now:
for ye shall laugh.[Q]
22 [e,j,k]Blessed are ye, when men
shall [l]hate you, and when they
shall [m,n]separate you *from their*
*company*, and shall reproach *you*,
and cast out your name as evil,
for the Son of man's sake.
23 Rejoice ye in that day, and
leap for [o]joy: for, behold, [j,k]your
[p]reward *is* great in heaven: for
in the like manner did their fathers unto the [q]prophets.[Q]
24 But woe unto you that are
[r]rich! for ye have received your
consolation.
25 Woe unto you that are full!
for ye shall hunger. Woe unto
[s]you that laugh now! for ye shall
mourn and weep.
26 Woe unto you, when all men
shall [t]speak well of you! for so
did their fathers to the false
[u]prophets.
27 ¶ But I say unto you which
hear, [v,w,x]Love your [y]enemies,
do ‡good[Q] to them which [l]hate
you,[Q]
28 [y]Bless them that [z,a]curse
you, and [b]pray for them which
despitefully use you.
29 And unto him that [c]smiteth
thee on the *one* cheek [d,e]offer
also the other; and him that
taketh away thy cloke [d,e]forbid
not *to take thy* coat also.
30 [f,g,h]Give to every man that
asketh of thee; and of him that
taketh away thy goods ask *them*
not again.
31 And [i]as ye would that men
should do to you, [j]do ye also to
them likewise.
32 For if ye [k]love them which

**14**
a *Peter*, Mark 5:37.
b *Andrew*, Matt. 4:18.
c *James*, Luke 5:10.
d *John*, Luke 1:63.
e *Bartholomew*, Acts 1:13.

**15**
f *Matthew*, Matt. 9:9.
g *Thomas*, John 11:16.
h *James*, Matt. 10:3.
i *Simon*, Mark 3:18.
2 R. V. the Zealot,

**16**
j Acts 1:13; Jude 1.
k *Judas*, Mark 3:19.
l *Treason*, 2 Kin. 11:14.
3 R. V. son

**17**
m *Disciples*, Matt. 9:14.
n *Judea*, Luke 5:17.
o *Jerusalem*, Judg. 19:10.
p *Tyre*, Josh. 19:29.
q Or, *Zidon*, Ezek. 28:21.
r *Jesus, received*, Matt. 1:21.
s *Healing, by Jesus*, Acts 4:22.
t *Miracles, of Jesus*, Luke 23:8.
u *Disease, healing of*, Ex. 15:26.

**18**
v *Demons*, Matt. 4:24.

**19**
w *Jesus, power of*, Matt. 1:21.
4 R. V. power

**20**
x Matt. 5:3-12.
y *Spiritual Peace*, Gal. 1:3. z *Poor, figurative*, Prov. 21:13. —a *Humility*, Prov. 22:4. b *Promise, to the humble*, 2 Cor. 1:20. c *Righteous, promises to*, Psa. 64:10. d *Kingdom of Heaven*, Matt. 13:24. **21** e *Spiritual Peace*, Gal. 1:3. f *Seekers*, Isa. 55:6. g *Hunger, figurative*, Matt. 5:6. h *Spiritual Desire*, Psa. 42:1. i *Promise, to those who have spiritual desire*, 2 Cor. 1:20.
**22** j *Promise, to the persecuted*, 2 Cor. 1:20. k *Adversity, consolation in*, Psa. 10:6. l *Hatred*, Prov. 15:17.

m *Persecution, of the righteous*, John 15:20.
n *Intolerance*, Num. 11:28.

**23**
o *Joy*, Psa. 5:11.
p *Reward, a motive, to faithfulness*, Matt. 5:12.
q *Prophets*, Isa. 3:2.

**24**
r *Rich*, Jas. 5:1.

**25**
s *Wicked, happiness of*, Psa. 73:3.

**26**
t *Flattery*, Prov. 6:24.
u *Prophets, false*, Isa. 3:2.

**27**
v *Commandment, enjoining love for enemies*, Deut. 8:2.
w *Love, of man for man*, 1 John 4:7.
x *Forgiveness, enjoined*, Matt. 18:21.
y *Enemy, kindness to, enjoined*, Prov. 24:17.

**28**
z *Cursing*, Lev. 24:11.

a *Malice*, Eph. 4:31.
b *Prayer, for enemies, enjoined*, Acts 6:4.

**29**
c *Persecution, of the righteous*, John 15:20.
d *Commandment, enjoining meekness*, Deut. 8:2.
e *Meekness, enjoined*, Psa. 45:4.

**30**
f *Commandment, enjoining liberality*, vs. 35, 38; Deut. 8:2.
g *Kindness, enjoined*, Acts 28:2.
h *Poor, liberality toward*, Prov. 21:13.

**31** i *Golden Rule*, Matt. 7:12. j *Commandment, enjoining the golden rule in conduct*, Deut. 8:2.
**32** k *Love, of man for man*. 1 John 4:7.

---

*Commission of*, Matt. 10; 28:19, 20; Mark 3:14, 15; 6:7–11; 16:15; Luke 9:1–5; 22:28–30; John 20:23; 21:15–19; Acts 1:1–8; 10:42. *Miraculous power given to*, Matt. 10:1; Mark 3:15; 6:7; 16:17; Luke 9:1, 2; 10:9, 17; Acts 2:4, 43; 5:12–16. *Authority of*, Matt. 16:19; 18:18; 19:28.

*Inspiration of*, Matt. 16:17–19; Luke 24:45; Acts 1:2; 13:9. *Duties of*, see COMMISSION OF, above, and Luke 24:46–48; John 15:27; Acts 1:8, 21, 22; 2:32; 3:15; 4:33; 5:32; 10:39–41; 13:31.

*Moral state of, before Pentecost*, Matt. 16:22, 23; 17:19, 20; 18:3; Mark 8:32, 33; Luke 9:54, 55. *Forsake Jesus*, Mark 14.50.

*Fail to comprehend the nature and mission of Jesus, and the nature of the kingdom he came to establish*, Matt. 8:25–27; 15:23; 16:8–12, 21, 22; 19:25; Mark 4:13; 6:51, 52; 8:17, 18; 9:9, 10, 31, 32; 10:13, 14; Luke 24:19, 21; John 4:32–34; 10:6; 12:16; 13:6–8; 14:5–9; Acts 1:6.

**Paul**, 1 Cor. 1:1; 2 Cor. 1:1; Gal. 1:1; Eph. 1:1; Col. 1:1; 1 Tim. 1:1; 2 Tim. 1:1; Tit. 1:1. See footnote, PAUL, Acts 13:9.

† **PHILIP.** *One of the twelve apostles*, Matt. 10:3; Mark 3:18; Luke 6:14; Acts 1:13. *Call of*, John 1:43. *Brings Nathanael to Jesus*, John 1:45–50. *Assists in caring for the multitude whom Jesus miraculously feeds*, John 6:5–7. *Brings certain Greeks to Jesus, who desire to see him*, John 12:20–22. *Asks Jesus to show the Father*, John 14:8–13.

‡ **GOOD FOR EVIL**, Prov. 25:21 (with Rom. 12:20); Matt. 5:44–48; Luke 6:27–36.

INSTANCES OF: *Abraham, to Abimelech*, Gen. 20:14–18. *Joseph, to his brethren*, Gen. 45:3–15. *David, to Saul*, 1 Sam. 24:17; 26. *Prophet, to Jeroboam*, 1 Kin. 13:6, with v. 4. *Elisha, to the Syrians*, 2 Kin. 6:22, 23. *David, to his enemies*, Psa. 35:12–14. *Jesus, to his crucifiers*, Luke 23:34. *Stephen*, Acts 7:60.

See footnote, EVIL FOR GOOD, Psa. 35:12.

love you, what thank have ye?
for sinners also love those that
love them.
33 And if ye do good to them
which do good to you, what
thank have ye? for sinners also
do even the same.
34 And if [l]ye [m]lend *to them* of
whom ye hope to receive, what
thank have ye? for sinners also
lend to sinners, to receive as
much again.
35 But [k,n,o]love ye your
enemies, and [5,q]do good, and
[l,m]lend, [6]hoping for nothing
again; and your [p]reward shall
be great, and ye shall be [q]the
children of the Highest: for he
is [r,s]kind unto the [t]unthankful
and *to* the evil.[S Q]
36 [u,v]Be ye therefore merciful,
[w]as your [x]Father also is [y]merciful.[T]
37 [z,a,b]Judge not, and ye shall
not be judged: [b]condemn not, and
ye shall not be condemned: [c]forgive,
and ye shall be forgiven:
38 [d]Give, and it shall be given
unto you; good measure, pressed
down and shaken together, and
running over, shall men give into
your bosom. For [e]with the same
measure that ye mete[G] withal[G] it
shall be measured to you again.
39 And he spake a [f]parable unto
them, [g]Can the [h]blind lead the
blind? shall they not both fall
into [7]the ditch?
40 [i]The disciple is not above
his master[C]: but every one [8]that
is [j]perfect[C] shall be as his master.
41 And [k]why beholdest thou
the mote[G] that is in thy brother's
eye, but perceivest not the beam[G]
that is in thine own eye?
42 [k]Either how canst thou say
to thy brother, Brother, let me
pull out the mote that is in thine
eye, when thou thyself beholdest
not the beam[G] that is in thine own
eye? Thou [l]hypocrite, cast out
first the beam[G] out of thine own
eye, and then shalt thou see
clearly to pull out the mote[C] that
is in thy brother's eye.
43 [m]For [n]a [o]good tree bringeth
not forth corrupt[C] fruit; neither
doth a [p,q]corrupt[C] tree bring forth
good fruit.
44 For [r]every tree is known
by his own fruit. For of thorns
men do not gather [s]figs, nor of
a [t]bramble bush gather they
[u]grapes.
45 A [o]good man out of the good
treasure of his heart [v]bringeth
forth [w]that which is good; and
an evil man out of the evil treasure
of his heart [x]bringeth forth
that which is evil: for of the
abundance of the heart his
mouth speaketh.
46 ¶ And [y]why call ye me,
Lord, Lord, and do not the
things which I [z]say?[Q]
47 [a]Whosoever cometh to me,
and [b,c]heareth my [d]sayings, and
[c,e,f]doeth them, I will shew you
to whom he is like:
48 [g]He is like a man which built
an house, and digged[C] deep, and
laid the foundation on a rock:
and when the [h,i]flood arose, the
stream beat vehemently[G] upon
that house, and could not shake
it: [9]for it was founded upon a
rock.
49 But he that [b]heareth, and
[j]doeth not, is like a man that
without a foundation built an
house upon the earth; against
which the [i]stream did beat vehemently,
and immediately it
fell; and the [k]ruin of that house
was great.

## CHAPTER 7

*Jesus heals the centurion's servant; 9 declares greatness of the centurion's faith; 11 and raises a widow's son at Nain. 19 John the Baptist sends two of his disciples to Jesus. 24 His testimony concerning John. 31 The Jews reject both. 36 A woman anoints the feet of Jesus.*

[a]NOW[S] when [b]he had ended all
his [c]sayings in the audience[C]
of the people, he entered
into [d]Că-pĕr′na-ŭm.

34
*l Creditor, laws concerning*, Deut. 15:2.
*m Lending*, Deut. 15:2.

35
*n Commandment, enjoining love for enemies*, Deut. 8:2.
*o Forgiveness, enjoined*, Matt. 18:21.
*p Reward, a motive*, Matt. 5:12.
*q Spiritual Adoption*, Rom. 8:15.
*r God, goodness of*, Gen. 2:2.
*s Kindness, of God*, Acts 28:2.
*t Ingratitude, of man to God*, Rom. 1:21.
5 R. V. do them good,
6 R. V. never despairing;

36
*u Commandment, enjoining mercy*, Deut. 8:2.
*v Mercy, enjoined*, Deut. 5:10.
*w Example, God our*, John 13:15.
*x God, fatherhood of*, Gen. 2:2.
*y God, mercy of*, Gen. 2:2.

37
z Matt. 7:1, 2.
*a Commandment, enjoining charitableness and forgiveness*, Deut. 8:2.
*b Charitableness, enjoined*, Prov. 10:12.
*c Forgiveness, enjoined*, Matt. 18:21.

38
*d Liberality, enjoined*, 1 Tim. 6:18.
e Matt. 7:2; Mark 4:24.

39
*f Parables, of Jesus*, Ezek. 20:49.
g Matt. 15:14.
*h Spiritual Blindness*, 2 Cor. 4:4.
7 R. V. a pit?

40
i Matt. 10:24, 25; John 13:16; 15:20.
*j Perfection*, Heb. 6:1.
8 R. V. when he is perfected

41
k Matt. 7:3-5.

42
*l Hypocrisy*, Jas. 3:17.

43
m Matt. 7:17-20.
*n Nature, laws of, uniform in operation*, Jas. 3:12.
*o Righteous, described*, Psa. 64:10.
*p Wicked, compared to corrupt trees*, Psa. 73:3.
*q Sin, fruits of*, Rom. 5:12.

44
*r Proverbs*, 1 Sam. 24:13.
*s Fig*, Mark 11:13.
t Judg. 9:14, 15.
*u Grape*, Lev. 25:5.

45
*v Speech, wise*, Col. 4:6.
*w Righteousness, fruits of*, Psa. 15:2.
*x Speech, evil*, Col. 4:6.

46
*y Hypocrisy, rebuked by Jesus*, Jas. 3:17.
*z Jesus, teacher*, Matt. 1:21.

47
a Matt. 7:24-27.
*b Hearers*, Rom. 2:13.
*c Faith in Christ*, John 6:69.
*d Doctrines of Jesus*, John 7:16.
*e Obedience*, Heb. 5:8.
*f Faithfulness*, Luke 16:10.

48
*g Righteous, described*, Psa. 64:10.
*h Adversity*, Psa. 10:6.
*i Temptation*, Luke 11:4.
9 R. V. because it had been well builded.

49
*j Unfaithfulness*, Luke 16:11.
*k Wicked, punishment of*, Psa. 73:3.

1
a Matt. 8:5-13.
*b Jesus, teacher*, Matt. 1:21.
*c Doctrines of Jesus*, John 7:16.
*d Capernaum*, Luke 4:31.

**2**
e *Centurion*, Matt. 8:5.
f *Armies, Roman*, Deut. 11:4.
g *Master, good*, Col. 4:1.
h *Servant, kindness to*, Jer. 2:14.
i *Love, of man for man*, 1 John 4:7.
**3**
j *Kindness, instances of*, Acts 28:2.
k *Faith in Christ*, John 6:69.
**4**
l *Mediation*, Gal. 3:19.
1 R. V. earnestly,
**5**
m *Liberality, instances of*, 1 Tim. 6:18.
n *Synagogue*, Matt. 12:9.
**6**
o *Humility, exemplified*, Prov. 22:4.
**10**
p *Miracles, of Jesus*, Luke 23:8.
**11**
q *Disciples*, Matt. 9:14.
**12**
r *Dead* 2 Kin. 4:32

2 [T]And a certain [e,f,g]centurion's[G]
[h]servant, who [i]was dear unto
him, was sick, and ready to die.
3 And when he heard of Jē'ṣus,
[j,k]he sent unto him the elders of
the Jewṣ, beseeching[G] him that he
would come and heal his [h]serv-
ant.
4 And when they came to
Jē'ṣus, they [l]besought him [1]in-
stantly, saying, That [e]he was
worthy for whom he should do
this:
5 For [e]he loveth our nation, and
he [m]hath built us a [n]synagogue.
6 Then Jē'ṣus went with them.
And when he was now not far
from the house, the [e]centurion
sent friends to him, saying unto
him, Lord, trouble not thyself:
for [o]I am not worthy that thou
shouldest enter under my roof:
7 Wherefore [o]neither thought
I myself worthy to come unto
thee: but [k]say in a word, and
my [h]servant shall be healed.
8 For I also am a man set under
authority, having under me soldiers, and I say unto one, Go,
and he goeth; and to another,
Come, and he cometh; and to
my servant, Do this, and he doeth *it*.
9 When Jē'ṣus heard these
things, he marvelled at him, and
turned him about, and said unto
the people that followed him, I
say unto you, I have not found
so great [k]faith, no, not in Ĭṣ'-
ra-el.
10 And they that were sent, returning to the house, found the
servant [p]whole[G] that had been
sick.[S]
11 ¶ And it came to pass the
day after, that he went into a
city called Nā'in; and many of
his [q]disciples went with him, and
much people.[T]
12 Now when he came nigh[G]
to the gate of the city, behold,
there was a [r]dead man carried
out, the only son of his mother,
and she was a [s]widow: and much
people of the city was with her.[Q]
13 And when the Lord saw her,
he had [t]compassion on her, and
[u]said unto her, Weep not.
14 And he came and touched
the [v]bier: and they that bare
*him* stood still. And he said,
Young man, I say unto thee,
Arise.
15 And he that was [r]dead [p]sat
up, and began to speak. And he
delivered him to his mother.[Q]
16 And there came a fear on
all: and they [w,x]glorified God,
saying, That a great [y]prophet is
risen up among us; and, That
God hath visited his people.[T]
17 And this [z]rumour[G] of him
went forth throughout all [a]Jū-
dæ'ȧ, and throughout all the region round about.
18 ¶ [b]And the [c]disciples of
[d]Jŏhn shewed him of all these
things.
19 And [d]Jŏhn calling *unto him*
two of his [c]disciples sent *them*
to [2]Jē'ṣus, saying, Art thou [e,f]he
that should come? or look we
for another?[Q]
20 When the men were come
unto him, they said, [d]Jŏhn Băp'-
tĭst hath sent us unto thee, saying, Art thou [e,f]he that should
come? or [f]look we for another?
21 And in that same hour he
[g]cured many of *their* infirmities[G]
and plagues[G], and of evil spirits;
and unto many *that were* blind
he [g]gave sight.[S]
22 Then Jē'ṣus answering said
unto them, Go your way, and
tell [d]Jŏhn what [h]things ye have
seen and heard; how that the
[i]blind see, the [j]lame walk, the
[k]lepers are cleansed, the [l]deaf
hear, the [m]dead are raised, to the
poor the [n]gospel is [o]preached.[Q]
23 And blessed is *he*, whosoever
shall [3]not be offended[G] in me.
24 ¶ And when the messengers

s *Widow*, 2 Sam. 14:5.
**13**
t *Jesus, compassion of*, Matt. 1:21.
u *Afflictions, consolation in*, Psa. 34:19.
**14**
v 2 Sam. 3:31.
**16**
w *Glorifying God*, Luke 5:25.
x *Jesus, received*, Matt. 1:21.
y *Jesus, prophet*, Matt. 1:21.
**17**
z *Fame of Jesus*, Luke 5:15.
a *Judea*, Luke 5:17.
**18**
b Matt. 11:2-19.
c *Disciples*, Matt. 9:14.
d *John the Baptist*, Luke 1:63.
**19**
e *Jesus, Messiah*, Matt. 1:21.
f *Messianic Hope*, Gen. 49:10.
2 R. V. the Lord.
**21**
g *Miracles, of Jesus*, Luke 23:8.
**22**
h *Miracles, design of*, vs. 22, 23; Luke 23:8.
i *Blindness*, 2 Kin. 6:18.
j *Lameness*, Lev. 21:18.
k *Leprosy*, Lev. 13:2.
l *Deafness*, Matt. 11:5.
m *Dead*, 2 Kin. 4:32.
n *Gospel*, Mark 13:10.
o *Preaching*, Matt. 9:35.
**23**
3 R. V. find none occasion of stumbling in me.

of [d]Jŏhn were departed, he began to speak unto the people concerning Jŏhn, What went ye out into the wilderness for to see? A reed shaken with the wind?

25 But what went ye out for to see? A man clothed in soft raiment? Behold, they which are gorgeously apparelled, and live delicately, are in kings' courts.

26 But what went ye out for to see? A [p]prophet[C]? Yea, I say unto you, and much more than a prophet.

27 This is *he*, of whom it is written, [q,r]Behold, I send my [s]messenger before thy face, which shall prepare thy way before thee.[Q]

28 For I say unto you, Among those that are born of women there is not a greater [4,p]prophet[C] than [d]Jŏhn the Băp'tĭst: but he that is [5]least in the kingdom of God is greater than he.

29 And all the people that heard *him*, and the [t]publicans[C], justified[C] God, being baptized with the [u]baptism of Jŏhn.

30 But the Phăr'ĭ-sees̹ and lawyers rejected the counsel of God against themselves, [v]being not baptized of him.[T]

31 ¶ And the Lord said, [w]Whereunto then shall I liken the men of this generation? and to what are they like?

32 They are like unto [x]children sitting in the marketplace, and calling one to another, and saying, We have piped unto you, and ye have not danced; we have [6]mourned to you, and ye have not wept.

33 For [y]Jŏhn the Băp'tĭst came [z,a]neither eating bread [b]nor drinking wine; and ye [c]say, He hath a devil.[C]

34 The [d]Son of man is come eating and drinking; and ye [c,e,f,g]say, Behold a [h]gluttonous man, and a [i]winebibber[C], a friend of [j]publicans[C] and sinners!

35 But [k]wisdom is justified[C] of all her children.

36[T] ¶ And one of the [l]Phăr'ĭ-sees̹ [m]desired[C] him that he would eat with him. And he went into the Phăr'ĭ-see's house, and sat down to meat.[C]

37 And, behold, a woman in the city, which was a sinner, when she knew that *Jē'sus* sat at meat[C] in the [l]Phăr'ĭ-see's house, brought an [n]alabaster [o]box of [p]ointment,

38 And [q]stood at his feet behind *him* [r]weeping, and began to [7]wash his [s]feet with tears, and did wipe *them* with the hairs of her head, and [t]kissed his feet, and [u]anointed[C] *them* with the [p]ointment.[C]

39 Now when the [l]Phăr'ĭ-see which had [m]bidden[C] him saw *it*, he [v,w]spake within himself, saying, This man, if he were a prophet[C], would have known who and what manner of woman *this is* that toucheth him: for she is a sinner.

40 And Jē'sus answering said unto him, Sī'mon, I have somewhat to say unto thee. And he saith, Master, say on.

41 [x]There was a certain [8,y]creditor which had two *debtors: the one owed five hundred [z]pence[C], and the other fifty.

42 And when they had nothing to pay, [y]he frankly[C] forgave them both. Tell me therefore, which of them will [a]love him most?

43 Sī'mon answered and said, I suppose that *he*, to whom he forgave most. And he said unto him, Thou hast rightly judged.

44 And he turned to the woman, and said unto Sī'mon, Seest thou this woman? I entered into

**26**
p *Prophets*, Isa. 3:2.

**27**
q Mal. 3:1.
r *Prophecies, concerning the Messiah, and their fulfillment*, Gen. 12:3.
s *Messenger, figurative*, Hag. 1:13.

**28**
4 R. V. *omits* prophet
5 R. V. but little in

**29**
t *Publicans*, Matt. 11:19.
u *Baptism, John's*, Luke 20:4.

**30**
v *Pharisees, reject John*, Matt. 15:12.

**31**
w Matt. 11:16–19.

**32**
x *Children, amusements of*, Mark 10:14.
6 R. V. wailed,

**33**
y *John the Baptist*, Luke 1:63.
z *Nazrite, instances of*, Num. 6:2.
a *Stoicism*, Acts 17:18.
b *Total Abstinence*, Lev. 10:9.
c *False Accusation*, 2 Tim. 3:3.

**34**
d *Jesus, humanity of*, Matt. 1:21.
e *Jesus, rejected*, Matt. 1:21.
f *Unbelief*, Heb. 3:12.
g *Persecution, of Jesus*, John 15:20.
h *Gluttony, Jesus falsely accused of*, Prov. 30:22.
i Matt. 11:19.
j *Publicans*, Matt. 11:19.

**35**
k *Wisdom*, Prov. 2:2.

**36**
l *Pharisees, minister to Jesus*, Matt. 15:12.
m *Hospitality*, Rom. 12:13.

**37**
n Matt. 26:7; Mark 14:3.
o *Cruse*, 1 Sam. 26:11.
p *Ointment*, Eccl. 7:1.

**38**
q *Love, for Jesus*, 1 John 4:19.
r *Weeping*, Ezra 3:13.
s *Feet*, 2 Sam. 4:4.
t *Kiss*, Ruth 1:14.
u *Anointing, of Jesus*, Deut. 28:40.
7 R. V. wet

**39**
v *Bigotry*, Isa. 65:5.
w *Self-righteousness*, Luke 18:11.

**41**
x *Parables, of Jesus*, Ezek. 20:49.
y *Creditor, merciful*, Deut. 15:2.
z *Penny*, Matt. 20:2.
8 R. V. lender

**42**
a *Thankfulness*, Acts 24:3.

*** DEBTOR.** *Laws concerning*, Lev. 25:35–38; Deut. 24:10–13; Neh. 10:31; Matt. 5:25, 26, 40; 18:25. *Sold for debt*, 2 Kin. 4:1–7; Neh. 5:3–5; Matt. 18:25. *Imprisoned for debt*, Matt. 18:30. *Oppressed*, 2 Kin. 4:1–7; Neh. 5:3–5; Job 20:18, 19; Matt. 18:28–30. *Mercy toward, enjoined*, Matt. 18:23–27. *Wicked*, Luke 20:9–16.

thine house, thou gavest me [b]no
water for my feet: but [c]she hath
[9]washed my feet with tears, and
wiped *them* with the hairs of her
head.
45 Thou gavest me no [d]kiss:
but [c]this woman since the time I
came in hath not ceased to kiss
my feet.
46 My head with [e]oil thou didst
not [f]anoint: but [c]this woman
hath [g]anointed my [b]feet with
[h]ointment.
47 Wherefore I [i]say unto thee,
Her sins, which are many, are
[j]forgiven; for she [c]loved much:
but to whom little is forgiven,
*the same* loveth little.
48 And he [i]said unto her, Thy
sins are [j]forgiven.
49 And they that sat at meat
with him began to say within
themselves, Who is this that for-
giveth sins also?
50 And he said to the woman,
Thy [k]faith hath saved thee; go
in [l]peace.

## CHAPTER 8

*Women minister unto Jesus of their substance. 4 The parable of the sower, 11 and its exposition. 16 A candle not to be put under a bushel. 19 Jesus' true disciples are his nearest relatives. 22 He stills a tempest; 26 and casts out the legion of devils, 33 which enter into a herd of swine. 41 Jairus entreats him. 43 He heals an issue of blood; 49 and raises the daughter of Jairus.*

AND it came to pass afterward,
that [a]he went throughout
every city and village, [b,c]preach-
ing and shewing the [d]glad tidings of the [e]kingdom of God:
and the [f]twelve *were* with him,
2 And certain [g]women, which
had been [h]healed of [i]evil spirits
and [j]infirmities, [k]Mā′rȳ called
Măg-da-lē′nē, out of whom went
seven devils,
3 And [l]Jō-ăn′nȧ the wife of
Chū′zȧ Hĕr′od's steward, and
Sụ-săn′nȧ, and many others,
which [m,n]ministered unto him
of their substance.
4 ¶ And when much people
were gathered together, and
were come to him out of every
city, he [o,p]spake by a [q]parable:
5 A [r,s]sower went out to [t]sow his
[u,v]seed: and as he sowed, some
fell by the way side; and it was
trodden down, and the fowls of
the air devoured it.
6 And some fell upon a rock;
and as soon as it was sprung up,
it [w,x]withered away, because it
lacked moisture.
7 And some fell among thorns;
and the thorns sprang up with it,
and [y]choked it.
8 And other fell on good ground,
and sprang up, and bare [z]fruit an
hundredfold. And when he had
said these things, he cried, He
that hath ears to hear, let him
*hear.
9 ¶ And his [a]disciples asked
him, saying, What might this
[b]parable be?
10 And he said, Unto you it is
given to know the [c]mysteries of
the [d]kingdom of God: but to
others in parables; that seeing
they might †,[e]not see, and hearing they might not understand.
11 Now the [b]parable is this:
The seed is the [f,g,h]word of
God.
12 Those by the way side are
[i]they that hear; then cometh the
[j]devil, and [k]taketh away the
[h]word out of their hearts, lest
they should believe and be
saved.
13 They on the rock *are they*,
which, when they [i]hear, receive the [f,g,h]word with joy; and
[l]these have [m]no root, [n]which for

**44**
b *Ablution, of the feet,* Judg. 19:21.
c *Love, for Jesus,* 1 John 4:19.
9 R. V. wetted
**45**
d *Kiss,* Ruth 1:14.
**46**
e *Oil,* Deut. 12:17.
f *Anointing, of guests,* Deut. 28:40.
g *Anointing, of Jesus,* Deut. 28:40.
h *Ointment,* Eccl. 7:1.
**47**
i *Jesus, power of, to forgive sins,* Matt. 1:21.
j *Sin, forgiveness of,* Rom. 5:12.
**50**
k *Faith in Christ,* John 6:69.
l *Spiritual Peace,* Gal. 1:3.
**1**
a *Jesus, zeal of,* Matt. 1:21.
b *Preaching,* Matt. 9:35.
c *Jesus, mission of,* Matt. 1:21.
d *Gospel,* Mark 13:10.
e *Kingdom of Heaven,* Matt. 13:24.
f *Apostles,* Luke 6:13.
**2**
g *Women, good,* Prov. 31:10.
h *Healing, by Jesus,* Acts 4:22.
i *Demons, possession by,* Matt. 4:24.
j *Disease, healing of,* Ex. 15:26.
k *Mary Magdalene,* Matt. 27:56.
**3**
l Luke 24:10.

m *Love, for Jesus,* 1 John 4:19.
n *Liberality,* 1 Tim. 6:18.
**4**
o *Jesus, teacher,* Matt. 1:21.
p *Instruction, in religion,* Prov. 23:23.
q *Parables, of Jesus,* Ezek. 20:49.
**5**
r *Sower, parable of,* Matt. 13:3.
s *Minister,* Rom. 15:16.
t *Agriculture, figurative,* Gen. 3:23.
u *Doctrines of Jesus,* John 7:16.
v *Truth,* John 18:37.
**6**
w *Character, instability of,* Phil. 2:15.
x *Instability,* Jas. 1:8.
**7**
y *Unfruitfulness,* Matt. 7:19.
**8**
z *Righteousness,* Psa. 15:2.
**9**
a *Disciples,* Matt. 9:14.
b *Parables, of Jesus,* Ezek. 20:49.
**10**
c *Mysteries, of redemption,* Mark 4:11.
d *Kingdom of Heaven,* Matt. 13:24.
e *Spiritual Blindness,* 2 Cor. 4:4.
**11**
f *Word of God,* Psa. 119:9.
g *Doctrines of Jesus,* vs. 11–15; John 7:16.
h *Truth,* John 18:37.
**12**
i *Hearers,* Rom. 2:13.
j *Satan,* Matt. 4:10.
k *Faith, trial of,* Mark 11:22.
**13**
l *Character, instability of,* Phil. 2:15.
m *Instability,* Jas. 1:8.
n *Backsliders,* Jer. 3:22.

* **SPIRITUAL UNDERSTANDING,** Matt. 13:23; Luke 10:21, 22; John 7:17.

*Of apostles,* Matt. 13:16, 17; Luke 8:10; 10:23, 24. *Of Peter,* Matt. 16:16, 17. *Of Mary,* Luke 10:39, 42.

*Lacking, in disciples,* Matt. 15:15, 16; Luke 24:25; *in Jews,* Matt. 13:11–16; John 6:26, 41, 52; 9:28, 29, 39–41; 12:37–40; Acts 28:24–27; *in Simon Magus,* Acts 8:18–23.

**Enjoined:** *Concerning, the import of prophecy,* Matt. 11:13–15; *the import of parables,* Matt. 13:9, 43; Luke 8:8; *the character of the disciples of Jesus,* Luke 14:33–35; *the Holy Spirit's message to the churches,* Rev. 2:7.
See footnote, WISDOM, *Spiritual,* Prov. 2:2.

† **MORAL INSENSIBILITY,** Isa. 6:10; Matt. 13:14, 15; Mark 4:12; Luke 8:10; John 12:40; Acts 28:26, 27; Rom. 11:8.

a while believe, and in time of [k,o]temptation[G] [p]fall away.

14 And that which fell among thorns are they, which, when they have heard, go forth, and are choked [q]with [r,s]cares and [s,t]riches and [s,u,v]pleasures of *this* life, and [w]bring no fruit to perfection.[G]

15 But that on the good ground are they, which in an honest and good [x]heart, having heard the word, [y]keep *it*, and bring forth [z]fruit with ‡patience.

16 ¶ [a]No man, when he hath lighted a [1]candle[G], covereth it with a vessel, or putteth *it* under a bed; but [b,c]setteth [d]*it* on a [2]candlestick[G], that they which enter in may see the light.

17 [e]For [f]nothing is secret, that shall not be made manifest; neither *any thing* hid, that shall not be known and come abroad.[G]

18 [g]Take heed therefore how ye hear: for [h,i]whosoever [j]hath, to him shall be given; and whosoever hath not, from [k]him shall be taken even that which he [3]seemeth to have.

19 ¶ [l]Then came to him *his* [m]mother and his [n]brethren, and could not come at him for the press.[G]

20 And it was told him *by certain* which said, Thy mother and thy brethren stand without[G], desiring to see thee.

21 And he answered and said unto them, [o]My mother and my brethren are these which hear the [p,q]word of God, and [r]do it.

22 ¶ [s]Now[S] it came to pass on a certain day, that he went into a [t]ship with his [u]disciples: and he said unto them, Let us go over unto the other side of the [v]lake. And they launched forth.

23 But as they sailed he fell [w]asleep: and there came down a [x,y]storm of wind on the lake; and they were filled *with water*, and were in jeopardy.[G]

24 And they came to him, and awoke him, [z]saying, [a]Master, master, [b]we perish[G]. Then he arose, and rebuked[G] the [c]wind and the raging of the water: and they [d,e]ceased, and there was a [c]calm.[T]

25 And he said unto them, Where is your [f]faith? And they being afraid wondered[G], saying one to another, What manner of man is this! for he commandeth even the winds[Q] and water, and they obey him.

26 ¶ [g]And they arrived at the country of the [4]Găd′a-rēneṣ, which is over[G] against [h]Găl′ĭ-lee.

27 And when he went forth to land, there met him out of the city a[G] certain man, which had [i]devils[G] long time, and ware[G] no clothes, neither abode[G] in *any* house, but in the [j]tombs.

28 When he saw Jē′ṣus, he cried out, and fell down before him, and with a loud voice said, What have I to do with thee, Jē′ṣus, [k]*thou* Son of God most high? I beseech thee, torment me not.[S T]

29 (For he had commanded the [i]unclean spirit to come out of the man. For oftentimes[G] it had caught him: and he was kept bound with chains and in fetters[G]; and he brake the bands[G], and was driven of the devil[G] into the wilderness.)

30 And Jē′ṣus asked him, saying, What is thy name? And

*o Temptation,* Luke 11:4.
*p Backsliding,* Hos. 11:7.

**14**

*q Covetousness, warning against,* Isa. 57:17.
*r Anxiety,* 1 Pet. 5:7.
*s Temptation, sources of,* Luke 11:4.
*t Riches,* Eccl. 4:8.
*u Worldly Pleasure,* Eccl. 2:1.
*v Sin, pleasures of,* Rom. 5:12.
*w Unfruitfulness,* Matt. 7:19.

**15**

*x Heart, renewed,* Psa. 44:21.
*y Obedience,* Heb. 5:8.
*z Righteousness, fruits of,* Psa. 15:2.

**16**

*a* Matt. 5:15; Mark 4:21; Luke 11:33.
*b Religious Testimony,* 2 Thess. 1:10.
*c Zeal,* 2 Cor. 7:11.
*d Influence, good,* 1 Cor. 7:14.
1 R. V. lamp.
2 R. V. stand,

**17**

*e* Matt. 10:26; Mark 4:22; Luke 12:2.
*f Sin, known to God,* Rom. 5:12.

**18**

*g Watchfulness, enjoined,* Matt. 24:42.
*h Proverbs,* 1 Sam. 24:13.
*i Righteous, promises to,* Psa. 64:10.
*j Righteousness,* Psa. 15:2.
*k Wicked, punishment of,* Psa. 73:3.
3 R. V. thinketh he hath.

**19**

*l* Matt. 12:46–50; Mark 3:31–35.
*m Mary,* Luke 1:27.
*n Brothers of Jesus,* Matt. 13:55.

**21** *o Fellowship, with Christ,* 1 Cor. 1:9. *p Word of God,* Psa. 119:9; *q Doctrines of Jesus,* John 7:16. *r Obedience,* Heb. 5:8. **22** *s* Matt. 8:23; Mark 4:35. *t Ship,* 2 Chr. 8:18. *u Disciples,* Matt. 9:14.

*v Sea of Galilee,* Matt. 4:18.

**23**

*w Sleep, of Jesus,* Psa. 127:2.
*x Meteorology,* Matt. 16:2.
*y Adversity,* Psa. 10:6.

**24**

*z Doubting,* Rom. 14:23.
*a Master,* John 13:13.
*b Borrowing Trouble,* Matt. 6:25.
*c Meteorology,* Matt. 16:2.
*d Tempest Stilled,* Matt. 8:26.
*e Miracles, of Jesus,* Luke 23:8.

**25**

*f Faith in Christ,* John 6:69.

**26**

*g* Matt. 8:28–34; Mark 5:1–20.
*h Galilee,* Mark 6:21.
4 R. V. Gerasenes,

**27**

*i Demons,* Matt. 4:24.
*j Burying Places,* Gen. 23:4.

**28**

*k Jesus, divinity of,* Matt. 1:21.

‡ **PATIENCE,** Rev. 1:9. *Commended,* Eccl. 7:8, 9. *Enjoined,* Psa. 37:7–9; Eph. 4:2; Col. 3:12, 13; 1 Thess. 5:14; 1 Tim. 6:11; 2 Tim. 2:24, 25; Tit. 2:2; Heb. 12:1; Jas. 5:7, 8; 2 Pet. 1:5, 6. *A fruit of tribulation,* Rom. 5:3, 4. *A grace of the righteous,* Luke 8:15; 21:19; Rom. 2:7; 8:25; 12:12; 15:4, 5; 1 Cor. 13:4, 5; 2 Cor. 6:4–6; 12:12; 1 Thess. 1:3; Heb. 6:12; 10:36; Jas. 1:3, 4, 19; **1 Pet. 2:19–23; Rev. 14:12.** ***Strife appeased by,*** **Prov. 15:18.**

See footnotes: LONGSUFFERING, 2 Cor. 6:6; MEEKNESS, Psa. 45:4.

**Instances of:** *Isaac toward the people of Gerar,* Gen. 26:15–22. *Moses,* Ex. 16:7, 8. *Job,* Job 1:21; Jas. 5:11. *David,* Psa. 40:1. *Jesus,* 1 Pet. 2:21–23; Rev. 1:9. *Paul,* 2 Tim. 3:10. *Prophets* Jas. 5:10. *The Thessalonians,* 2 Thess. 1:4. *The church, at Ephesus,* Rev. 2:2, 3; *at Thyatira,* Rev. 2:19. *John,* Rev. 1:9.

he said, Legion: because many
devils were entered into him.
31 And they besought him that
he would not command them to
go out into the deep.
32 And there was there an herd
of many [l]swine feeding on the
mountain: and they besought
him that he would suffer them
to enter into them. And he suffered them.
33 [e]Then went the [i]devils out of
the man, and entered into the
[l,m]swine: and the herd ran violently down a steep place into
the lake, and were choked.
34 When they that fed *them*
saw what was done, they fled,
and went and told *it* in the city
and in the country.
35 Then they went out to see
what was done; and came to
Jē'ṣus, and found the man, out
of whom the [i]devils were departed, sitting at the feet of Jē'-
ṣus, clothed, and in his right
mind: and they were afraid.
36 They also which saw *it* told
them by what means he that was
possessed of the devils was
healed.
37 ¶ Then the whole multitude
of the country of the [4]Găd'a-
rēneṣ round about [n]besought
him to depart from them; for
they were taken with great fear:
and he went up into [5]the ship,
and returned back again.
38 Now the man out of whom
the [i]devils were departed [o]be-
sought him that he might be
with him: but Jē'ṣus sent him
away, saying,
39 Return to thine own house,
and shew how great things God
hath done unto thee. And he
went his way, and [p,q]published
throughout the whole city how
great things Jē'ṣus had done unto him.
40 And it came to pass, that,
when [r]Jē'ṣus was returned, the

32
*l Swine*, Lev. 11:7.

33
*m Animals, possessed of devils*, Jer. 27:5.

37
*n Jesus, rejected*, Matt. 1:21.
5 R. V. a boat,

38
*o Love, for Jesus*, 1 John 4:19.

39
*p Religious Testimony*, 2 Thess. 1:10.
*q Thankfulness, to God, instances of*, Acts 24:3.

40
*r* Matt. 9:1; Mark 5:21.

people *gladly* [s]received him: for
they were all waiting for him.
41 ¶ [t]And, behold, there came
a man named Jā-ī'rus, and he
was a ruler of the [u]synagogue:
and he fell down at Jē'ṣus' feet,
and [v]besought him that he would
come into his house:
42 For he had one only [w]daugh-
ter, about twelve years of age,
and she lay a dying. But as he
went the people thronged him.
43 ¶ And a woman having an
[x]issue of blood twelve years,
which had spent all her living
upon [y]physicians, neither could
be healed of any,
44 Came behind *him*, and
[z]touched the border of his garment: and immediately her [a]is-
sue of blood [b]stanched.
45 And Jē'ṣus said, Who
touched me? When all denied,
[c]Pē'tēr and they that were with
him [d]said, Master, the multitude
throng thee and press *thee*, [6]and
sayest thou, Who touched me?
46 And Jē'ṣus said, Somebody
hath touched me: for I perceive
that [7]virtue is gone out of me.
47 And when the woman saw
that she was not hid, she came
trembling, and falling down before him, she declared unto him
before all the people for what
cause she had touched him, and
how she was [b]healed immediately.
48 And he [e]said unto her,
Daughter, [8]be of good comfort:
thy [f]faith hath made thee whole;
go in [g]peace.
49 ¶ While he yet spake, there
cometh one from the ruler of
the [h]synagogue's *house*, saying
to him, Thy daughter is [i]dead;
trouble not the Master.
50 But when Jē'ṣus heard *it*, he
answered him, saying, Fear not:
[j]believe only, and she shall be
made whole.
51 And when he came into the

*s Jesus, received*, Matt. 1:21.

41
*t* Matt. 9:18-26; Mark 5:22-43.
*u Synagogue*, Matt. 12:9.
*v Mediation*, Gal. 3:19.

42
*w Children*, Mark 10:14.

43
*x Hemorrhage*, Matt. 9:20.
*y Physician*, 2 Chr. 16:12.

44
*z Faith in Christ, exemplified*, John 6:69.

*a Hemorrhage*, Matt. 9:20.
*b Miracles, of Jesus*, Luke 23:8.

45
*c Peter*, Mark 5:37.
*d Presumption, instances of*, Psa. 19:13.
6 R. V. *omits the rest of the verse.*

46
7 R. V. power

48
*e Afflictions, consolation in*, Psa. 34:19.
*f Faith in Christ*, John 6:69.
*g Spiritual Peace*, Gal. 1:3.
8 R. V. *omits* be of good comfort:

49
*h Synagogue*, Matt. 12:9.
*i Dead*, 2 Kin. 4:32.

50
*j Faith in Christ, enjoined*, John 6:69.

51
*k James*, Luke 5:10.
*l John*, Mark 1:19.
52
*m Mourning*, Lam. 2:5.
*n Sleep, a symbol of death*, Psa. 127:2.
53
*o Scorners*, Prov. 19:25.
54
9 R. V. But he, taking her by the hand, called, saying, Maiden, arise.
55
10 R. V. that something be given her to eat.
56
*p Prudence*, 2 Chr. 2:12.

house, he suffered no man to go
in, save [c]Pē′tēr, and [k]Jāmeş, and
[l]Jŏhn, and the father and the
mother of the maiden.
52 And all [m]wept, and bewailed
her: but he [e]said, Weep not; she
is not [i]dead, but [n]sleepeth.
53 And [o]they laughed him to
scorn, knowing that she was
dead.
54 [9]And he put them all out,
and took her by the hand, and
called, saying, Maid, arise.
55 And her spirit [b]came again,
and she arose straightway: and
he commanded [10]to give her
meat.
56 And her parents were astonished: but he [p]charged them that
they should tell no man what
was done.

## CHAPTER 9

*Jesus gives the twelve power to work miracles, and sends them forth to preach.* 3 *His charge to them.* 7 *Herod desires to see Jesus.* 10 *The twelve return.* 12 *With five loaves and two fishes Jesus feeds five thousand men.* 18 *What the people think of Jesus;* 20 *and Peter's confession of him.* 22 *Jesus foretells his own death and resurrection.* 23 *Those who follow him must take up their cross.* 28 *The transfiguration.* 37 *Jesus casts out an unclean spirit;* 43 *and again foretells his own death.* 46 *He exhorts his disciples to humility;* 49 *and not to reject those who are not against them.* 51 *James and John are rebuked.* 57 *How Jesus must be followed.*

THEN he called his twelve disciples together, and [a]gave
[b]them power and authority over
all [c]devils, and to [d]cure [e]diseases.
2 And he sent [b,f]them to
[g]preach the [h]kingdom of God,
and to [d]heal the [e]sick.
3 And he said unto [f]them,
[i]Take nothing for *your* journey,
neither [1]staves, nor scrip, neither
bread, neither [j]money; neither
have two coats apiece.
4 And [k]whatsoever house [l]ye
enter into, there abide, and
thence depart.
5 And [m,n,o]whosoever will not
receive you, when ye go out of
that city, shake off the very dust
from your feet for a testimony
against them.

1
*a Jesus, power of*, Matt. 1:21.
*b Apostles, miraculous power given to*, Luke 6:13.
*c Demons*, Matt. 4:24.
*d Healing, by the apostles*, Acts 4:22.
*e Disease, healing of*, Ex. 15:26.
2
*f Minister, charge delivered to*, Rom. 15:16.
*g Preaching*, Matt. 9:35.
*h Kingdom of Heaven*, Matt. 13:24.
3
*i* Matt. 10:9–15; Mark 6:8–11.
*j Money*, Jer. 32:9.
1 R. V. staff, nor wallet,
4
*k Church, duty of, to ministers*, Matt. 16:18.
*l Minister, hospitality to*, Rom. 15:16.
5
*m Opportunity*, Gal. 6:10.
*n Responsibility, according to privilege*, Ezek. 18:20.
*o Judgment, according to opportunity and works*, 2 Pet. 3:7.

6 And [b]they departed, and went
through the towns, [g]preaching
the [p]gospel, and [d]healing every
where.
7 ¶ Now [q]Hĕr′od the tetrarch
heard of all that was done by
him: and he was [r]perplexed, because that it was said of some,
that [s]Jŏhn was [t]risen from the
dead;
8 And of some, that [u]Ē-lī′as
had appeared; and of others,
that one of the old [v]prophets
was risen again.
9 And [q]Hĕr′od said, [s]Jŏhn have
I [w,x]beheaded: but who is this,
of whom I hear such things?
And he desired to see him.
10 ¶ And the [y]apostles, when
they were returned, told him all
that they had done. And he took
them, and went aside privately
into a desert place belonging to
the city called [z]Bĕth-sā′ĭ-dȧ.
11 And the people, when they
knew *it*, [a,b]followed him: and he
received them, and [c,d]spake unto
them of the [e]kingdom of God,
and [f]healed them that had need
of healing.
12 ¶ And [g]when the day began
to wear away, then came the
twelve, and said unto him, Send
the multitude away, that they
may go into the towns and country round about, and lodge, and
get victuals: for we are here in a
desert place.
13 But he said unto them, Give
ye them to eat. And they said,
We have no more but five [h]loaves
and two [i]fishes; except we
should go and buy [2]meat for all
this people.
14 For they were about five
thousand men. And he said to
his disciples, Make them sit down
by fifties in a company.
15 And they did so, and made
them all sit down.
16 Then he took the five [h]loaves
and the two [i]fishes, and looking

6
*p Gospel*, Mark 13:10.
7
*q Herod*, Matt. 14:1.
*r Conscience, guilty, instances of*, Acts 23:1.
*s John the Baptist*, Luke 1:63.
*t Resurrection*, 1 Cor. 15:12.
A.D. 32
8
*u* Or, *Elijah*, 1 Kin. 17:1.
*v Prophets*, Isa. 3:2.
9
*w Beheading, of John*, Matt. 14:10.
*x Persecution, of the righteous*, John. 15:20.
10
*y Apostles*, Luke 6:13.
*z Bethsaida*, John 1:44.

11
*a Popularity of Jesus*, John 6:15.
*b Jesus, received*, Matt. 1:21.
*c Jesus, teacher*, Matt. 1:21.
*d Preaching*, Matt. 9:35.
*e Kingdom of Heaven*, Matt. 13:24.
*f Healing*, Acts 4:22.
12
*g* Matt. 14:15–21; Mark 6:35–44; John 6:5–13.
13
*h Loaves*, Matt. 14:17.
*i Fish*, Matt. 17:27.
2 R. V. food

up to heaven, he [j,k]blessed them, and brake, and gave to the disciples to set before the multitude.

17 And [l]they did eat, and were all filled: and there was taken up of fragments that remained to them twelve [m]baskets.[Q]

18 ¶ [n]And it came to pass, as he was alone [o]praying, his disciples were with him: and he asked them, saying, Whom say the people that I am?

19 They answering said, [p]Jŏhn the Băp′tĭst; but some *say*, [q]Ē-lī′as; and others *say*, that one of the old [r]prophets is [s]risen again.

20 He said unto them, But whom say ye that I am? [t]Pē′tĕr answering [u]said, The [v]Chrīst of God.[T]

21 And he straitly[G] [w]charged[G] them, and commanded *them* to tell no man that thing;

22 [x]Saying, The [y]Son of man must [z]suffer[G] many things, and be rejected of the elders and chief priests and scribes, and be [a]slain, and be [b]raised the third day.

23 ¶ And he said to *them* all, If any *man* will come after me, [c]let him [d,e]deny himself, and [e]take up his [f]cross daily, and follow me.

24 For whosoever will save his [g]life [h]shall lose it: but whosoever will [i,j]lose his life for my sake, [k]the same shall [l]save it.

25 [m,n]For what is a man advantaged, if he gain the whole world, and lose [3]himself, or be cast away?

26 For whosoever shall be ashamed of me and of my words, of him shall the Son of man be ashamed, [c]when he shall [p]come in his own glory, and *in his* [q]Father's, and of the holy [r]angels.[T]

27 But [s]I tell you of a truth, there be some standing here, which shall not taste of death, till they see the kingdom of God.

28 ¶ And it came to pass about an eight days after these sayings, he took [t]Pē′tĕr and [u]Jŏhn and [v]Jāmes, and went up into a [w]mountain to [x]pray.

29 And as he [x]prayed, the fashion[G] of his [y]countenance was [z]altered, and his raiment[G] *was* [a]white *and* glistering.[G]

30 [S]And, behold, [b]there talked with him two men, which were [c]Mō′ṣeṣ and [d]Ē-lī′as:

31 Who appeared in glory, and spake of his decease[G] which he should accomplish at [e]Jĕ-ru′sā-lĕm.[S]

32 But [f]Pē′tĕr and they that were with him were heavy with sleep: and when they were awake, they [g]saw his glory, and the [c,d]two men that stood with him.

33 And it came to pass, as they departed from him, [f]Pē′tĕr said unto Jē′ṣus, Master, it is good for us to be here: and let us make three tabernacles[G]; one for thee, and one for [c]Mō′ṣeṣ, and one for [d]Ē-lī′as: not knowing what he said.

34 While he thus spake, there came a [h]cloud, and overshadowed them: and they feared as they entered into the cloud.[T]

35 And there came a voice out of the [h]cloud, saying, This is [i]my [4]beloved [j]Son: hear him.[T] [Q]

36 And when the voice was past, Jē′ṣus was found alone. And they kept *it* close[G], and told no man in those days any of those things which they had seen.

37 ¶ [k]And it came to pass, that on the next day, when they were come down from the [5]hill, much people met him.

38 And, behold, a man of the company cried out, [l]saying,

**16**
*j* *Prayer, thanksgiving for food,* Acts 6:4.
*k* *Thanksgiving, by Jesus,* Matt. 11:29.

**17**
*l* *Miracles, of Jesus,* Luke 23:8.
*m* *Basket,* Ex. 29:3.

**18**
*n* Matt. 16:13–20; Mark 8:27–30.
*o* *Prayers of Jesus,* Luke 5:16.

**19**
*p* *John the Baptist,* Luke 1:63.
*q* Or, *Elijah,* 1 Kin. 17:1.
*r* *Prophets,* Isa. 3:2.
*s* *Resurrection,* 1 Cor. 15:12.

**20**
*t* *Peter, confesses Jesus as Christ,* Mark 5:37.
*u* *Faith in Christ,* John 6:69.
*v* *Jesus, Messiah,* Matt. 1:21.

**21**
*w* *Prudence, instances of,* 2 Chr. 2:12.

**22**
*x* *Jesus foretells his Death,* Matt. 17:22.
*y* *Jesus, humanity of,* Matt. 1:21.
*z* *Jesus, sufferings of,* Matt. 1:21.

*a* *Jesus, death of,* Matt. 1:21.
*b* *Resurrection of Jesus,* Matt. 28:6.

**23**
*c* *Commandment, enjoining self-denial,* Deut. 8:2.
*d* *Self-denial,* Mark 8:34.
*e* *Righteous, described,* Psa. 64:10.
*f* *Cross, figurative of duty,* John 19:17.

**24**
*g* *Life,* Eccl. 8:15.
*h* *Wicked, punishment of,* Psa. 73:3.
*i* *Martyrdom, spirit of, required by Jesus,* Rev. 17:6.
*j* *Renunciation,* Luke 5:11.
*k* *Promise, to the righteous, of eternal life,* 2 Cor. 1:20.

*l* *Immortality,* 1 Cor. 15:54. **25** *m* Matt. 16:26; Mark 8:36, 37. *n* *Ambition, Jesus rebukes,* Hab. 2:5. 3 R. V. or forfeit his own self? **26** *o* *Judgment, the general,* 2 Pet. 3:7. *p* *Jesus, second coming of,* Matt. 1:21. *q* *God, fatherhood of,* Gen. 2:2. *r* *Angel,* Heb. 1:13.

**27**
*s* *Jesus, prophet,* Matt. 1:21.

**28**
*t* *Peter,* Mark 5:37.
*u* *John,* Mark 1:19.
*v* *James,* Luke 5:10.
*w* *Mountain,* Mic. 7:12.
*x* *Prayers of Jesus,* Luke 5:16.

**29**
*y* *Countenance, transfigured,* Prov. 15:13.
*z* *Transfiguration, of Jesus,* Matt. 17:2.

*a* *Colors, symbolical,* Ezek. 16:16.

**30**
*b* *Immortality, implied in the appearance of Moses and Elijah,* 1 Cor. 15:54.
*c* *Moses,* Ex. 2:10.
*d* Or, *Elijah,* 1 Kin. 17:1.

**31**
*e* *Jerusalem,* Judg. 19:10.

**32**
*f* *Peter,* Mark 5:37.
*g* *Vision,* Acts 9:10.

**34**
*h* *Pillar of Cloud and Fire,* Ex. 13:21.

**35**
*i* *God, fatherhood of,* Gen. 2:2.
*j* *Jesus, divine sonship of,* Matt. 1:21.
4 R. V. Son, my chosen:

**37**
*k* Matt. 17:14–19; Mark 9:14–29.
5 R. V. mountain

**38**
*l* *Parents, affection of, exemplified,* 2 Cor. 12:14.

*m Mediation*, Gal. 3:19.

**39**

*n Demons, possession by*, Matt. 4:24.

**40**

*o Apostles*, Luke 6:13.

*p Faith, weak*, Mark 11:22.

**41**

*q Doubting*, Rom. 14:23.

**42**

*r Healing, by Jesus*, Acts 4:22.

*s Miracles, of Jesus*, Luke 23:8.

*t Demoniac Healed*, Matt. 17:18.

**43**

6 R. V. astonished at the majesty of God. But while all were marvelling at all the things which he did,

**44**

*u Jesus foretells his Death*, Matt. 17:22.

**46**

*v* Matt. 18:1–6; Mark 9:33–37.

*w Minister, false and corrupt*, Rom. 15:16.

*x Pride*, Prov. 16:18.

*y Ambition*, Hab. 2:5.

*z Worldliness*, 1 John 2:15.

**47**

*a Jesus, omniscience of*, Matt. 1:21.

*b Children, type of the regenerated*, Mark 10:14.

**48**

*c Minister, character and qualifications of*, Rom. 15:16.

*d Fellowship, with Christ*, 1 Cor. 1:9.

*e Fellowship, with God*, 1 Cor. 1:9.

*f Humility*, Prov. 22:4.

*g Righteous, promises to*, Psa. 64:10.

**49**

*h* Mark 9:38, 39.

*i John*, Mark 1:19.

Master, I [m]beseech thee, look
upon my son: for he is mine only
child.
39 And, lo, a [n]spirit taketh him,
and he suddenly crieth out; and
it teareth him that he foameth
again, and bruising him hardly
departeth from him.
40 And I besought thy [o]disciples to cast him out; and [p]they
could not.
41 And Jē'ṣus answering said,
O [p,q]faithless and perverse generation, how long shall I be with
you, and suffer you? Bring thy
son hither.
42 And as he was yet a coming,
the [n]devil threw him down, and
tare *him*. And Jē'ṣus rebuked
the unclean spirit, and [r,s]healed
the [t]child, and delivered him
again to his father.
43 ¶ And they were all [6]amazed
at the mighty power of God.
But while they wondered every
one at all things which Jē'ṣus
did, he said unto his [o]disciples,
44 Let these sayings sink down
into your ears: for [u]the Son of
man shall be delivered into the
hands of men.
45 But they understood not
this saying, and it was hid from
them, that they perceived it not:
and they feared to ask him of
that saying.
46 ¶ [v]Then there arose a reasoning among [o,w]them, [x,y,z]which of
them should be greatest.
47 And Jē'ṣus, [a]perceiving the
thought of their heart, took a
[b]child, and set him by him,
48 And said unto them, [c]Whosoever shall receive this [b]child
in my name [d]receiveth me: and
whosoever shall receive me [e]receiveth him that sent me: for he
that is [f]least among you all, [g]the
same shall be great.
49 [h]And [i]Jŏhn answered and
said, Master, we saw one casting
out [j]devils in thy name; and we
[k,l]forbad him, because he followeth not with us.
50 And Jē'ṣus said unto him,
[m,n]Forbid *him* not: for he that is
not against [7]us is for us.
51 ¶ [o]And it came to pass,
when the time was come that he
should be received up, [p,q]he stedfastly set his face to go to [r]Jē-ru'sā-lĕm,
52 And sent messengers before
his face: and they went, and entered into a village of the [s]Sā-măr'ĭ-tanṣ, to make ready for
him.
53 And they *did not receive
[t]him, because his face was as
though he would go to [r]Jē-ru'-sā-lĕm.
54 And when his [u]disciples
[v]Jāmeṣ and [i]Jŏhn saw *this*, they
[w,x,y]said, Lord, [z]wilt thou that
we command fire to come down
from heaven, and consume them,
[8]even as Ē-lī'as did?
55 But he turned, and [a]rebuked
them, [9]and said, Ye know not
what manner of spirit ye are of.
56 [10]For the Son of man is not
come to destroy men's lives, but
[b]to [c]save *them*. And they went to
another village.
57 ¶ [d]And it came to pass, that,
as they went in the way, a certain *man* [e]said unto him, Lord, I
will follow thee whithersoever
thou goest.
58 And Jē'ṣus said unto him,
[f]Foxes have holes, and [g]birds of
the air *have* nests; but the Son of
man hath not where to lay *his*
head.
59 And he said unto another,
[h,i]Follow me. But he [j,k]said,
Lord, [l]suffer me first to go and
bury my father.

*j Demons*, Matt. 4:24.

*k Intolerance, exemplified*, Num. 11:28.

*l Bigotry, instances of*, Isa. 65:5.

**50**

*m Toleration*, Mic. 4:4.

*n Catholicity, inculcated*, Eph. 2:14.

7 R. V. you is for you.

**51**

*o* John 7:2–11.

*p Jesus, death of, voluntary*, Matt. 1:21.

*q Jesus, zeal of*, Matt. 1:21.

*r Jerusalem*, Judg. 19:10.

**52**

*s Samaria*, Isa. 7:9.

**53**

*t Jesus, rejected*, Matt. 1:21.

**54**

*u Apostles*, Luke 6:13.

*v James*, Luke 5:10.

*w Presumption*, Psa. 19:13.

*x Rashness*, 2 Sam. 6:7.

*y Zeal, without knowledge*, 2 Cor. 7:11.

*z Revenge*, Ezek. 25.15.

8 R. V. *omits* even as Elias did?

**55**

*a Retaliation, malicious, forbidden*, Deut. 19:19.

9 R. V. *omits the rest of this verse*.

**56**

*b Jesus, mission of*, Matt. 1:21.

*c Jesus, savior*, Matt. 1:21.

10 R. V. *omits all of this verse except* And they went to another village.

**57**

*d* Matt. 8:19–22.

*e Zeal, without knowledge*, 2 Cor. 7:11.

**58**

*f Fox*, Psa. 63:10.

*g Birds*, Eccl. 12:14.

**59**

*h Decision, injunctions concerning*, Isa. 50:7.

*i Call, personal*, Phil. 3:14. *j* Matt. 8:21, 22. *k Excuses, for release from duty*, Luke 14:18. *l Procrastination*, Acts 24:25.

* **INHOSPITABLENESS. Instances of:** Toward the Israelites: *Edom*, Num. 20:18–21; *Sihon*, Num. 21:22, 23; *Ammonites and Moabites*, Deut. 23:3–6. *Men of Gibeah, toward a Levite*, Judg. 19:15. *Nabal, toward David*, 1 Sam. 25:10–17. *Samaritans, toward Jesus*, Luke 9:53. See footnote, HOSPITALITY, Rom. 12:13.

**60**
*m Preaching,* Matt. 9:35.
*n Kingdom of Heaven,* Matt. 13:24.

**62**
*o Backsliders, described,* Jer. 3:22.

**1**
*a Seventy,* v. 17; Num. 11:16.
*b Disciples, the seventy sent forth,* Matt. 9:14.
*c Minister, call of,* Rom. 15:16.

**2**
*d Harvest, figurative,* Ex. 34:21.
*e Prayer, enjoined,* Acts 6:4.
*f Minister, charge delivered to,* Rom. 15:16.

**3**
*g Righteous, described,* Psa. 64:10.
*h Wicked, described,* Psa. 73:3.

**4**
*i* 2 Kin. 4:29.

**5**
*j Salutations,* Luke 1:44.

**6**
1 R. V. a
2 R. V. him:

**7**
*k Church, duty of, to ministers,* Matt. 16:18.
*l Minister, hospitality to,* Rom. 15:16.
*m Guest, rules for conduct of,* Zeph. 1:7.
*n Employee, rights of,* Deut. 24:14.
*o Servant,* Jer. 2:14.
*p Wages,* Gen. 31:7.

60 Jē'sus said unto him, Let
the dead bury their dead: but go
thou and [m]preach the [n]kingdom
of God.
61 And another also said, Lord,
I will follow thee; but let me
first go bid them farewell, which
are at home at my house.
62 And Jē'sus said unto him,
No man, having put his hand to
the plough, and [o]looking back,
is fit for the [n]kingdom of God.

## CHAPTER 10

*Jesus sends forth the seventy.* 2 *His charge to them.* 17 *The seventy return.* 21 *Jesus rejoices in spirit.* 23 *The disciples' privilege.* 25 *A lawyer questions Jesus.* 30 *The parable of the good Samaritan.* 38 *Martha and Mary.*

AFTER these things the Lord
appointed other [a,b,c]seventy
also, and sent them two and two
before his face into every city
and place, whither he himself
would come.
2 Therefore said he unto them,
The [d]harvest truly *is* great, but
the labourers *are* few: [e,f]pray ye
therefore the Lord of the harvest,
that he would send forth
labourers into his harvest.
3 [f]Go your ways: behold, I
send you forth as [g]lambs among
[h]wolves.
4 [i]Carry neither purse, nor
scrip, nor shoes: and [j]salute no
man by the way.
5 And into whatsoever house ye
enter, first say, [j]Peace *be* to this
house.
6 And if [1]the son of peace be
there, your peace shall rest upon
[2]it: if not, it shall turn to you
again.
7 And [k,l]in the same house remain,
[m]eating and drinking such
things as they give: for the *[n,o]labourer
is worthy of his [p]hire. Go
not from house to house.
8 And into whatsoever city ye
enter, and [k]they [l]receive you,
[m]eat such things as are set before
you:
9 And heal the [q]sick that are
therein, and [r]say unto them,
[s]The [t]kingdom of God is come
nigh unto you.
10 But [u]into whatsoever city ye
enter, and they [v]receive you not,
go your ways out into the streets
of the same, and say,
11 Even the very dust of your
city, which cleaveth on us, we do
wipe off against you: notwithstanding
be ye sure of this, that
[s]the [t]kingdom of God is come
nigh unto you.
12 But I say unto you, that
[u,w]it shall be more tolerable in
[x]that day for [y]Sŏd'om, than for
that city.
13 [z,a]Woe unto thee, [b]Chō-rā'-zin!
woe unto thee, [c]Bĕth-sā'ĭ-dȧ!
for if the mighty works had been
done in [d]Tȳre and [e]Sī'dŏn, which
have been done in you, they had
a great while ago [f]repented, sitting
in [g]sackcloth and [h]ashes.
14 But [i]it shall be more tolerable
for [d]Tȳre and [e]Sī'dŏn at the
[j]judgment, [k]than for you.
15 [l]And thou, [m]Că-pēr'na-ŭm,
which art exalted to heaven,
shalt be [n]thrust down [3]to [o]hell.
16 [p]He that heareth you heareth
me; and he that despiseth
you [q,r]despiseth me; and he that
despiseth me despiseth him that
sent me.
17 ¶ And the seventy returned
again with [s]joy, [t]saying, Lord,
even the [u]devils are [v]subject unto
us through thy name.
18 And he said unto them, I
beheld [w]Sā'tan as [x]lightning fall
from heaven.

**9**
*q Disease, healing of, by the seventy,* Ex. 15:26.
*r Preaching,* Matt. 9:35.
*s Opportunity,* Gal. 6:10.
*t Kingdom of Heaven,* Matt. 13:24.

**10**
*u Responsibility, according to privilege,* Ezek. 18:20.
*v Opportunity, lost,* Gal. 6:10.

**12**
*w Judgment, according to opportunity and works,* 2 Pet. 3:7.
*x Judgment, the general,* 2 Pet. 3:7.
*y Sodom,* Gen. 13:10.

**13**
*z* Matt. 11:21-23.
*a Impenitence,* Rom. 2:5.
*b* Matt. 11:21.
*c Bethsaida,* John 1:44.
*d Tyre,* Josh. 19:29.
*e* Or, *Zidon,* Ezek. 28:21.
*f Repentance,* Mark 1:4.
*g Sackcloth,* Isa. 15:3.
*h Ashes,* Num. 19:9.

**14**
*i Responsibility, according to privilege,* Ezek. 18:20.
*j Judgment, the general,* 2 Pet. 3:7.
*k Opportunity,* Gal. 6:10.

**15**
*l* Matt. 11:23.
*m Capernaum, prophecy against* Luke 4:31.
*n Wicked, punishment of,* Psa. 73:3.
*o Hell,* Mark 9:43.
3 R. V. unto Hades.

**16**
*p* Matt. 10:40; John 13:20.

*q Jesus, rejected,* Matt. 1:21. *r Unbelief,* Heb. 3:12.
**17** *s Joy, instances of,* Psa. 5:11. *t Boasting, instances of,* Prov. 25:14. *u Demons,* Matt. 4:24. *v Miracles, of the disciples,* Luke 23:8.
**18** *w Satan,* Matt. 4:10. *x Lightning,* Job 28:26.

* **LABOR.** *Sleep of the laborer sweet,* Eccl. 5:12. *Enjoined,* Gen. 3:19; Ex. 20:9-11; 23:12; 34:21; Luke 13:14; Acts 20:35; Eph. 4:28; 1 Thess. 4:11; 2 Thess. 3:10-12.
*Compensation for,* Lev. 19:13; Deut. 25:4; 1 Cor. 9:9; 1 Tim. 5:18; Jer 22:13; Mal. 3:5; Matt. 20:1-15; Luke 10:7; Jas. 5:4; *of servants must not be oppressive,* Deut. 24:14, 15.
*Paul, an example in,* 2 Thess. 3:8-13.
See footnotes: CAPITAL AND LABOR, Matt. 21:33. EMPLOYEE, Deut. 24:14; MASTER, Col. 4:1.

19 Behold, [y,z]I give unto you [4]power to tread on [a]serpents and [†]scorpions, and over all the power of the enemy: and nothing shall by any means hurt you.

20 Notwithstanding in this rejoice not, that the spirits are subject unto you; but rather rejoice, because [b]your names are [c]written in [d]heaven.

21 ¶ [e]In that hour Jē'ṣus rejoiced in [5]spirit, and said, I thank thee, O [f]Father, [g]Lord of heaven and earth, that thou hast hid these things from the [h]wise and prudent, and hast revealed them unto [i,j]babes: even so, Father; for so it seemed good in thy sight.

22 All things are delivered to [k]me of my [l]Father: and no man knoweth who the [l]Son is, but the Father; and who the Father is, but the [m]Son, and *he* to whom the Son will reveal *him*.

23 ¶ And he turned him unto *his* [n]disciples, and said privately, Blessed *are* the [o]eyes which [p]see the [q]things that ye see:

24 [r]For I tell you, that many prophets and kings have [s]desired to see those things which ye see, and have not seen *them*; and to hear those things which ye hear, and have not heard *them*.

25 ¶ [t]And, behold, a certain [u]lawyer stood up, and tempted him, saying, Master, what shall I do to inherit eternal [v]life?

26 He said unto him, What is written in the [w]law? how readest thou?

27 And he answering said, [x,y]Thou shalt [z,a]love the Lord thy God with all thy heart, and with all thy soul, and with all thy strength, and with all thy mind; and [b,c,d,e,f]thy [‡]neighbour as thyself.

28 And he said unto him, Thou hast answered right: this [g]do, and [h]thou shalt live.

29 But [i]he, willing to justify himself, said unto Jē'ṣus, And who is my [‡]neighbour?

30 And Jē'ṣus answering [j]said, A certain *man* went down from [k]Jē-rụ'sā-lĕm to [l]Jĕr'ĭ-chō, and fell among [m]thieves, which [n]stripped [o]him of his raiment, and wounded *him*, and departed, leaving *him* half dead.

31 And by chance there came down a certain [p]priest that way: [q]and when he saw [o]him, he passed by on the other side.

32 And likewise a [r]Lē'vīte, when he was at the place, [q]came and looked *on* [o]*him*, and passed by on the other side.

33 But a certain [s]Sā-măr'ĭ-tan, as he journeyed, came where he was: and when he saw [o]him, he had [t]compassion *on him*,

34 And [t]went to *him*, and bound up his [u]wounds, [v]pouring in [w]oil and wine, and set him on his own beast, and brought him to an inn, and took care of him.

35 And on the morrow when he departed, he took out two [x]pence, and [y]gave *them* to the host, and [o,t]said unto him, Take care of him; and whatsoever thou spendest more, when I come again, I will repay thee.

36 Which now of these three, thinkest thou, was [‡]neighbour unto [o]him that fell among the [m]thieves?

**19**

*y Jesus, power of,* Matt. 1:21.
*z Minister, promises to,* Rom. 15:16.

*a Serpent,* Num. 21:6.
4 R. V. authority

**20**

*b Righteous, promises to,* Psa. 64:10.
*c Book, figurative,* 139:16.
*d Heaven, the future home of the righteous,* Luke 18:22.

**21**

*e* Matt. 11:25–27.
*f God, fatherhood of,* Gen. 2:2.
*g God, sovereign,* Gen. 2:2.
*h Wisdom, worldly,* Prov. 2:2.
*i Babes,* Psa. 8:2.
*j Humility,* Prov. 22:4.
5 R. V. the Holy Spirit.

**22**

*k Jesus, king,* Matt. 1:21.
*l Jesus, divinity of,* Matt. 1:21.
*m Jesus, omniscience of,* Matt. 1:21.

**23**

*n Disciples,* Matt. 9:14.
*o Eye, figurative,* Matt. 6:22.
*p Wisdom, spiritual,* Prov. 2:2.
*q Gospel,* Mark 13:10.

**24**

*r Messianic Hope,* Gen. 49:10.
*s Spiritual Desire,* Psa. 42:1.

**25**

*t* Matt. 22:34–40; Mark 12:28–34
*u Lawyer,* Matt. 22:35.
*v Life, everlasting,* Eccl. 8:15.

**26**

*w Law, of Moses,* Deut. 33:2.

**27** *x Commandment, enjoining love to God,* Deut. 8:2. *y* Deut. 6:5. *z Love, for God,* 1 John 4:19.—*a Duty, of man to God,* Eccl. 12:13.

*b Commandment, enjoining love for man,* Deut. 8:2.
*c Royal Law,* Jas. 2:8.
*d Love, of man for man,* 1 John 4:7.
*e Duty, of man to man,* Eccl. 12:13.
*f Altruism,* Acts 20:35.

**28**

*g Works under the Law,* Lev. 18:5.
*h Righteous, promises to,* Psa. 64:10.

**29**

*i Lawyer,* Matt. 22:35.

**30**

*j Parables, of Jesus,* Ezek. 20:49.
*k Jerusalem,* Judg. 19:10.
*l Jericho,* Num. 22:1.
*m Thieves,* Deut. 24:7.
*n Robbery,* Ezek. 22:29.
*o Afflicted, help for,* vs. 30–37; Job 34:28.

**31**

*p Priest, corrupt,* Lev. 1:5.
*q Hypocrisy, instances of,* Jas. 3:17.

**32**

*r Levites,* Deut. 10:8.

**33**

*s Samaria,* Isa. 7:9.
*t Poor, kindness to,* Prov. 21:13.

**34**

*u* Isa. 1:6.
*v Anointing, the sick,* Deut. 28:40.
*w Medicine,* Prov. 17:22.

**35**

*x Penny,* Matt. 20:2.
*y Liberality, instances of,* 1 Tim. 6:18.

**† SCORPION.** *A venomous reptile common in the wilderness through which the children of Israel journeyed,* Deut. 8:15. *Power over, given to the seventy,* Luke 10:19. *Unfit for food,* Luke 11:12. *Sting of, in the tail,* Rev. 9:10.

**Figurative:** *Of enemies,* Ezek. 2:6. *Of cruelty,* 1 Kin. 12:11, 14; 2 Chr. 10:11, 14.

**‡ NEIGHBOR.** *Duty to, defined in Golden Rule,* Matt. 7:12. *Love worketh no ill to,* Rom. 13:10. *Love for, enjoined,* Lev. 19:18; Matt. 19:19; 22:39; Mark 12:31–33; Luke 10:25–37; Rom. 13:9, 10; Gal. 5:14; Jas. 2:8, 9. *Kindness to, enjoined,* Ex. 23:4, 5; Deut. 22:1–4; Isa. 58:6, 7; Gal. 6:10. *Charitableness toward, enjoined,* Rom. 15:2. *Benevolence toward, enjoined,* Prov. 3:28, 29. *Righteous treatment of, enjoined,* Zech. 8:16, 17. *Honesty toward, enjoined,* Lev. 19:13. *Kindness to, rewarded,* Isa. 58:8–14; Matt. 25:34–46. *Righteous treatment of, rewarded,* Psa. 15:1–3. *False witness against, forbidden,* Ex. 20:16; Lev. 19:16. *Hatred of, forbidden,* Lev. 19:17. *Oppression of, denounced,* Jer. 22:13. *Penalty for violation of the rights of,* Lev. 6:2–5.

37
*z* *Mercy*, Deut. 5:10.

*a* *Duty, of man to man*, Eccl. 12:13.

38
*b* *Bethany*, John 11:18.
*c* *Friendship, instances of*, Prov. 22:24.
*d* *Hospitality, instances of*, Rom. 12:13.

39
*e* *Mary*, John 11:2.
*f* *Humility*, Prov. 22:4.
*g* *Love, for Jesus*, 1 John 4:19.
*h* *Feet*, 2 Sam. 4:4.
*i* *Faith in Christ, exemplified*, John 6:69.
6 R. V. the Lord's

40
*j* *Anxiety*, 1 Pet. 5:7.

41
7 R. V. But the Lord answered
8 R. V. anxious

42
*k* *Women, good*, Prov. 31:10.
*l* *Spiritual Desire, exemplified*, Psa. 42:1.

37 And he said, He that shewed
[z]mercy on him. Then said Jē'-
ṣus unto him, Go, and [a]do thou
likewise.
38 ¶ Now it came to pass, as
they went, that he entered into
a certain [b]village: and a certain
woman named ‖Mär'thȧ [c,d]re-
ceived him into her house.
39 And she had a sister called
[e]Mā'rȳ, which also [f,g]sat at [6]Jē'-
ṣus' [h]feet, and [i]heard his word.
40 But ‖Mär'thȧ was [j]cum-
bered about much serving, and
came to him, and said, Lord,
dost thou not care that my sister
hath left me to serve alone? bid
her therefore that she help me.
41 [7]And Jē'ṣus answered and
said unto her, ‖Mär'thȧ, Mär'-
thȧ, thou art [8]careful and [j]trou-
bled about many things:
42 But one thing is needful: and
[e,k]Mā'rȳ [l]hath chosen that good
part, which shall not be taken
away from her.

## CHAPTER 11

*Jesus teaches his disciples to pray. 5 The efficacy of prayer. 14 He heals a dumb man possessed with a devil; 17 and reproves those who ascribe his power to Beelzebub. 29 The sign of Jonas. 33 A candle is not to be put under a bushel. 37 Jesus dines with one of the Pharisees, and denounces woes upon them. 49 The blood of all the prophets to come upon this generation.*

A.D. 33

1
*a* *Prayers of Jesus*, Luke 5:16.

AND it came to pass, that, as
he was [a]praying in a certain place, when he ceased, one
of his [b]disciples said unto him,
Lord, teach us to pray, as [c]Jŏhn
also taught his disciples.
2 And [1]he said unto them,
[d]When ye [e]pray, say, Our [f]Fa-
ther which art in [g]heaven, Hallowed be thy [h]name. [i]Thy [j]king-
dom come. [i]Thy [k]will be done,
as in heaven, so in earth.
3 Give us day by day our daily
[l]bread.
4 And [m]forgive us our sins; for
we also [n]forgive every one that is
indebted to us. And [2]lead us not
into *temptation; [3]but deliver us
from evil.
5 And he [o]said unto them,
Which of you shall have a friend,
and shall go unto him at midnight, and say unto him, Friend,
lend me three loaves;
6 For a friend of mine in his
journey is come to me, and I
have nothing to set before him?
7 And he from within shall answer and say, Trouble me not:
the door is now shut, and my
children are with me in bed; I
cannot rise and give thee.
8 I say unto you, Though he
will not rise and give him, because he is his friend, yet because of his importunity he will
rise and give him as many as he
needeth.
9 And I say unto you, [p,q]Ask,
and [r,s]it shall be given you;

*b* *Disciples*, Matt. 9:14.
*c* *John the Baptist*, Luke 1:63.

2
*d* Matt. 6:9–13
*e* *Prayer, the Lord's prayer*, Acts 6:4.
*f* *God, fatherhood of*, Gen. 2:2.
*g* *Heaven, God's dwelling place*, Luke 18:22.
*h* *God, name of, to be reverenced*, Gen. 2:2.
*i* *God, sovereign*, Gen. 2:2.
*j* *Kingdom of Heaven*, Matt. 13:24.
*k* *Will of God, the supreme rule of duty*, Mark 3:35.
1 R. V. And he said unto them, When ye pray, say, Father, Hallowed be thy name. Thy kingdom come.

3
*l* *Temporal Blessings, from God*, Psa. 103:2.

4
*m* *Sin, forgiveness of*, Rom. 5:12.
*n* *Forgiveness*, Matt. 18:21.
2 R. V. bring us
3 R. V. *omits the rest of this verse.*

5
*o* *Parables, of Jesus*, Ezek. 20:49.

9
*p* Matt. 7:7–11.
*q* *Prayer, answer to, promised*, Acts 6:4.
*r* *Promise, to the righteous, of answer to prayer*, 2 Cor. 1:20.
*s* *Righteous, promises to*, Psa. 64:10.

‖ **MARTHA.** *Sister of Mary and Lazarus*, John 11:1. *Ministers to Jesus*, Luke 10:38–42; John 12:2. *Beloved by Jesus*, John 11:5.

* **TEMPTATION,** Prov. 12:26; Rom. 8:35–39. *Called snares of death*, Prov. 13:14; 14:27.

*Way of escape from*, 1 Cor. 10:13. *Christ succors in*, Heb. 2:18; 4:15; Rev. 3:10. *The Lord delivers from*, 2 Pet. 2:9. *To be avoided*, Matt. 18:8, 9 (with 5:29, 30); Mark 9:43–48.

**Benefits of,** Jas. 1:2–4, 12; 1 Pet. 1:6, 7.

**Design of:** *A test*, Psa. 119:101, 110; Zech. 13:9; 1 Pet. 1:6, 7; 4:12. *A test, of fidelity*, Deut. 13:1–3; 2 Chr. 32:31; Job 1:8–22; 2:3–10; *of obedience*, Gen. 22:1–14; Deut. 8:2, 5; Heb. 11:17.

**Leading into:** *To be avoided*, Matt. 18:6, 7; Mark 9:42; Luke 17:1; Rom. 14:13, 15, 21; 1 Cor. 7:5; 8:9–13; 10:28–32. *Prayer against being led into*, Matt. 6:13; 26:41; Mark 14:38; Luke 22:40, 46.

INSTANCES OF LEADING OTHERS INTO: *Abraham, of Pharaoh*, Gen. 12:18, 19; *of Abimelech*, Gen. 20:9. *Rebekah, of Jacob*, Gen. 27:6–14. *Balak, of Balaam*, Num. 22:5–7, 16, 17; 23:11–13, 25–27. *Eli's sons, of Israel*, 1 Sam. 2:24, 25. *Gideon, of Israel*, Judg. 8:27. *The old prophet of Bethel, of the prophet of Judah*, 1 Kin. 13:15–19. *Jeroboam, of Israel*, 1 Kin. 15:30, 34.

**Resistance to:** *Enjoined*, Deut. 7:25, 26; Prov. 1:10–19; 4:14, 15; 5:3, 8; Matt. 26:41; Mark 14:37, 38; Rom. 12:21; Eph. 6:11, 13–17; Jas. 4:7; 1 Pet. 5:8, 9.

*Rewards to those who resist*, Isa. 33:15, 16; Jas. 1:12.

INSTANCES OF THOSE WHO RESISTED: *Joseph*, Gen. 39:7–12. *Balaam*, Num. 22:7–18, 38; 23:7–12, 18–24. *David*, 1 Sam. 26:5–25. *Rechabites*, Jer. 35:5–9. *Nehemiah*, Neh. 4:9. *Job*, Job 31:1, 5–17, 19–34, 38–40. *Jesus*, Matt. 4:1–11; 26:38–42; Luke 4:1–13; Heb. 4:15; 12:3, 4.

**Sources of:** *Cherished pleasures*, Matt. 5:29, 30; 18:7–9; Mark 9:43–48. *Evil company*, Ex. 34:12–16; Prov. 2:10–16. *Harlots and carnal desires*, Prov. 5:1–20; 6:24–29; 7:1–27; 9:15–18; Eccl. 7:26. *Carnal desires*, Rom. 7:5; Gal. 5:17; Jas. 1:13–15; 2 Pet. 2:18; 1 John 2:16, 17. *False teachers*, Matt. 18:6, 7; Luke 17:1; 1 John 2:26; 4:1–3; Rev. 2:20. *Persecutions*, John 16:1, 2. *Prosperity*, Deut. 8:10–17; Luke 12:16–21. *Riches*, Matt. 19:16–24; Mark 10:17–30; 1 Tim. 6:9, 10. *Cares, riches and pleasures*, Matt. 13:22; Luke 8:13, 14; 21:34–38.

*Satan*, Gen. 3:1–5; 1 Chr. 21:1; Mark 4:15, 17; Luke 22:3, 31, 32; 2 Cor. 2:11; 11:3, 14, 15; 12:7; Eph. 4:27; 6:11, 13–17; 1 Thess. 3:5; 1 Tim. 5:15; Jas. 4:7; 1 Pet. 5:8, 9; Rev. 12:10, 11, 17.

*Wicked men*, Prov. 16:29; 28:10; Hos. 7:5; Amos 2:12; Matt. 5:19; 2 Tim. 3:13.

**Warnings against yielding to,** Ex. 34:12–16; Deut. 8:11–20; Prov. 2:10–16; 5:1–21; 6:27, 28; 7:1–27; 9:15–18;

[t]seek, and [q]ye shall find; knock, and [r,s]it shall be opened unto you.

10 [r,s]For every one that [q]asketh receiveth; and [t]he that seeketh findeth; and to him that knocketh it shall be opened.

11 If a son shall ask bread of any of you that is a [u]father, will he give him a stone? or if *he ask* a fish, will he for a fish give him a serpent?

12 Or if he shall ask an egg, will he offer him a [v]scorpion?

13 If [w]ye then, being evil, know how to give good gifts unto your children: [q]how much more shall *your* heavenly [x]Father give the [y]Holy Spirit to them that ask him?[T]

14 ¶ [z]And[S] he was [a]casting out a [b]devil,[G] and it was dumb. And it came to pass, when the devil was gone out, the dumb spake; and the people wondered.[G]

15 But [c]some of them [d,e,f]said, He casteth out devils[G] through [g,h]Bē-ĕl′ze-bŭb the chief of the devils.[G][S]

16 [i]And others, tempting[G] *him*, sought of him a sign from heaven.

17 But he, [j]knowing their thoughts, said unto them, Every kingdom [k]divided against itself is brought to desolation;[G] and a house *divided* against a house falleth.[Q]

18 If [h]Sā′tan also be divided against himself, how shall his kingdom stand? because ye [d]say that I cast out devils[G] through [g]Bē-ĕl′ze-bŭb.[S]

19 And if I by [g]Bē-ĕl′ze-bŭb cast out devils,[G] by whom do your sons cast *them* out? therefore shall they be your judges.

20 But if I with the finger of [l]God [a]cast out [b]devils,[G] no doubt the [m]kingdom of God is come upon you.[T][Q]

21 When [4]a strong man armed keepeth his palace, his goods are in peace:

22 But when a stronger than he shall come upon him, and overcome him, he taketh from him all his armour wherein he trusted, and divideth his spoils.[G]

23 [n]He that is not with me is against me: and he that gathereth not with me scattereth.

24 When the [b,o]unclean[G] spirit is gone out of a man, he walketh through dry places, seeking rest; and finding none, he saith, I will return unto my house whence I came out.

25 And when he cometh, he findeth *it* swept and garnished.[G]

26 Then goeth he, and taketh *to him* seven other spirits more wicked than himself; and they enter in, and dwell there: and the [p]last *state* of that [q]man is worse than the first.

27 ¶ And it came to pass, as he spake these things, a certain woman of the company lifted up her voice, and said unto him, Blessed *is* the womb that bare thee, and the paps[G] which thou hast sucked.

28 But he said, Yea rather, [r,s]blessed *are* they that hear the [t,u]word of God, and [v,w]keep it.

29 ¶ And when the people were gathered thick together, he began to say, This is an evil generation: they seek a [x]sign; and there shall no sign be given it, but the sign of [y]Jō′nas the prophet.

30 For as [y]Jō′nas was a [x]sign unto

t *Seekers*, Isa. 55:6.

**11**
u *Father*, Psa. 27:10.

**12**
v *Scorpion*, Luke 10:19.

**13**
w *Parents*, 2 Cor. 12:14.
x *God, fatherhood of*, Gen. 2:2.
y *Holy Spirit*, Acts 1:2.

**14**
z Matt. 12:22–24.
a *Miracles, of Jesus*, Luke 23:8.
b *Demons, possession by*, Matt. 4:24.

**15**
c Matt. 12:24–30; Mark 3:22–27.
d *False Accusation*, 2 Tim. 3:3.
e *Scoffing*, Hab. 1:10.
f *Persecution, of Jesus*, John 15:20.
g *Beelzebub*, Matt. 10:25.
h *Satan*, Matt. 4:10.

**16**
i Matt. 12:38.

**17**
j *Jesus, omniscience of*, Matt. 1:21.
k *Strife*, Prov. 20:3.

**20**
l *God, power of*, Gen. 2:2.
m *Kingdom of Heaven*, Matt. 13:24.

**21**
4 R. V. the strong man fully armed guardeth his own court,

**23**
n Matt. 12:30.

**24**
o Matt. 12:43–45.

**26**
p *Apostasy*, Acts 1:25.
q *Backsliders*, Jer. 3:22.

**28**
r *Righteous, promises to*, Psa. 64:10.
s *Blessings, contingent upon obedience*, Deut. 11:26.
t *Word of God*, Psa. 119:9.
u *Doctrines of Jesus*, John 7:16.
v *Obedience*, Heb. 5:8.
w *Doer of the Word*, Jas. 1:22.

**29**
x *Sign*, Mark 8:11.
y Or, *Jonah*, Jonah 1:1.

Eccl 7:26; Jer. 2:25; Matt. 26:31, 41; Mark 14:37, 38; Luke 21:34–36; 1 Cor. 16:13; Eph. 6:11, 13–17; Heb. 12:3, 4; 1 Pet. 4:7; 5:8, 9; 2 Pet. 3:17; Rev. 3:2, 3.

**Yielding to:** INSTANCES OF: *Adam and Eve*, Gen. 3:1–19. *Sarah, to lie*, Gen. 18:13–15. *Isaac, to lie*, Gen. 26:7. *Jacob, to defraud Esau*, Gen. 27:6–14, 18–29. *Balaam*, Num. 22:15–22; 2 Pet. 2:15. *Achan*, Josh. 7:21. *David, to commit adultery*, 2 Sam. 11:2–5; *to number Israel*, 1 Chr. 21. *Solomon, to become an idolater through the influences of his wives*, 1 Kin. 11:4; Neh. 13:26. *The prophet of Judah*, 1 Kin. 13:11–19. *Hezekiah*, 2 Kin. 20:12–20; Isa. 39:1–7. *Peter*, Matt. 26:69–74; Mark 14:67–71; Luke 22:55–60.

**Of Jesus**, Luke 22:28. *In all points as we are*, Heb. 4:15. *By the devil*, Matt. 4:1–11; Mark 1:12, 13; Luke 4:1–13.

**30**

z *Nineveh*, Jonah 1:2.

a *Responsibility, according to privilege*, Ezek. 18:20.

b *Jesus, humanity of*, Matt. 1:21.

**31**

c *Judgment, according to opportunity and works*, 2 Pet. 3:7.

d *Sheba*, 1 Kin. 10:1.

e *Judgment, the general*, 2 Pet. 3:7.

f *Wisdom, worldly*, Prov. 2:2.

g *Solomon*, 2 Sam. 12:24.

h *Jesus, perfections of*, Matt. 1:21.

**32**

i Or, *Nineveh*, Jonah 1:2.

j *Repentance*, Mark 1:4.

k *Conviction of Sin, instances of*, John 16:8.

l *Preaching*, Matt. 9:35.

m Or, *Jonah*, Jonah 1:1.

**33**

n Matt. 5:15; Mark 4:21; Luke 8:16.

o *Parables, of Jesus*, Ezek. 20:49.

p *Influence, good*, 1 Cor. 7:14.

q *Lamp*, Ex. 27:20.

**34**

r Matt. 6:22, 23.

s *Light, figurative*, Matt. 5:14.

t *Conscience, faithful*, Acts 23:1.

u *Wisdom, spiritual*, Prov. 2:2.

v *Conscience, corrupt*, Acts 23:1.

w *Spiritual Blindness*, 2 Cor. 4:4.

5 R. V. lamp

**35**

x *Watchfulness, over conscience, enjoined*, Matt. 24:42.

y *Self-examination*, 2 Cor. 13:5.

**36**

z *Spiritual Understanding*, Luke 8:8.

**37**

a *Pharisees*, Matt. 15:12.

b *Hospitality, instances of*, Rom. 12:13. **38** c *Self-righteousness*, Luke 18:11. d *Ceremonial Washings*, Ex. 19:10. e *Purification*, Num. 19:19. **39** f *Reproof, faithfulness in*, Prov. 17:10. g *Satire*, 1 Sam. 2:3. h *Hypocrisy, rebuked by Jesus*, Jas. 3:17.

the [z]Nĭn'e-vītes, [a]so shall also the
[b]Son of man be to this generation.
31 [c]The [d]queen of the south
shall rise up in the [e]judgment
with the men of this generation,
and condemn them: for she
came from the utmost parts of
the earth to hear the [f]wisdom
of [g]Sŏl'o-mon; and, behold, [h]a
greater than Sŏl'o-mon *is* here.
32 The men of [i]Nĭn'e-ve shall
rise up in the [e]judgment with
this generation, and shall condemn
it: for they [j,k]repented at
the [l]preaching of [m]Jō'nas; and,
behold, [h]a greater than Jō'nas
*is* here.
33 [n,o]No man, when he hath
lighted a [p,q]candle, putteth *it* in
a secret place, neither under
a bushel, but on a candlestick,
that they which come in may see
the light.
34 [r]The [5,s]light of the body is
the eye: therefore when thine
[t]eye is single, thy whole body
also is [t]full of [u]light; but when
*thine* [v]*eye* is evil, thy body also *is*
full of [w]darkness.
35 [x,y]Take heed therefore that
the light which is in thee be not
darkness.
36 If thy whole body therefore
*be* full of [z]light, having no part
dark, the whole shall be full of
light, as when the bright shining
of a candle doth give thee light.
37 ¶ And as he spake, a certain
[a]Phăr'ĭ-see [b]besought him
to dine with him: and he went
in, and sat down to meat.
38 And when the [a]Phăr'ĭ-see
saw *it*, he [c]marvelled that he had
not first [d,e]washed before dinner.
39 And the Lord [f]said unto
him, [g]Now do ye [a]Phăr'ĭ-sees
[h]make clean the outside of the
cup and the platter; but your [i]inward
part is full of [6,j]ravening
and wickedness.
40 *Ye* [k]fools, did not he that
[l]made that which is without
make that which is within also?
41 [7]But rather [m,n]give alms of
such things as ye have; and, behold,
all things are clean unto
you.
42 [f]But woe unto you, [o]Phăr'ĭ-sees!
for ye [o]tithe [p]mint and rue
and all manner of herbs, and
pass over judgment and the [q]love
of God: these ought ye to have
done, and not to leave the other
undone.
43 [f]Woe unto you, [a]Phăr'ĭ-sees!
[r,s]for ye love the [8]uppermost
seats in the [t]synagogues, and
[u]greetings in the markets.
44 [f]Woe unto you, [9,v]scribes
and [a]Phăr'ĭ-sees, [h]hypocrites! for
ye are as [w]graves which appear
not, and the men that walk over
*them* are not aware *of them*.
45 Then answered one of the
[x]lawyers, and said unto him,
Master, thus saying thou reproachest
us also.
46 And he said, Woe unto you
also, *ye* [x]lawyers! for [y]ye lade
men with †burdens grievous to
be borne, and ye yourselves
touch not the burdens with one
of your fingers.
47 Woe unto you! for [z]ye build
the sepulchres of the [a]prophets,
and your fathers [b,c]killed them.
48 Truly ye bear witness that ye
allow the deeds of your fathers:
for they indeed [b,c]killed them,
and ye build their sepulchres.
49 Therefore also said the wisdom
of God, [d,e]I will send them
prophets and apostles, and *some*
of them they shall [b]slay and [c]persecute:
50 [e]That the blood of all the
prophets, which was [b]shed from

i *Heart, unregenerate*, Psa. 44:21.

j *Extortion*, Isa. 16:4.

6 R. V. extortion

**40**

k *Fool*, Prov. 18:2.

l *God, creator*, Gen. 2:2.

**41**

m *Liberality, enjoined*, 1 Tim. 6:18.

n *Poor, duty to*, Prov. 21:13.

7 R. V. Howbeit give for alms those things which are within;

**42**

o *Tithes*, Num. 18:24.

p Matt. 23:23.

q *Love, for God*, 1 John 4:19.

**43**

r *Ambition, Jesus rebukes*, Hab. 2:5.

s *Pride, rebuked*, Prov. 16:18.

t *Synagogue*, Matt. 12:9.

u *Salutations*, Luke 1:44.

8 R. V. chief

**44**

v *Scribe*, 1 Kin. 4:3.

w *Burying Places*, Gen. 23:4.

9 R. V. *omits* scribes and Pharisees, hypocrites!

**45**

x *Lawyer*, Matt. 22:35.

**46**

y *Minister, false and corrupt*, Rom. 15:16.

**47**

z *Satire*, 1 Sam. 2:3.

a *Prophets*, Isa. 3:2.

b *Martyrdom, of prophets*, Rev. 17:6.

c *Persecution, of the righteous*, John 15:20.

**49**

d Matt. 23:34–46.

e *Judgment, according to opportunity and works* 2 Pet. 3:7.

† **BURDEN. Figurative,** Psa. 55:22; Matt. 11:30; Gal. 6:2, 5. *Of oppression*, Isa. 58:6; Matt. 23:4; Luke 11:46. *Of the prophetic message*, Isa. 13:1, 15:1; 17:1; 19:1.

the foundation of the world, may
be required of this generation;
51 From the blood of [f]Ā'bĕl
unto the blood of [g]Zăch-a-rī'as,
which perished between the [h]al-
tar and the [10,i]temple: verily I say
unto you, [e]It shall be required of
this generation.[Q]
52 [j]Woe unto you, [k]lawyers! for
[l]ye have taken away the key of
‡knowledge: ye [m]entered not in
yourselves, and them that were
entering in ye [n]hindered.
53 And as he said these things
unto them, the [o]scribes and the
[p]Phăr'ĭ-seeș began to urge *him*
vehemently, and to provoke him
to speak of many things:
54 [q]Laying wait for him, and
seeking to catch something out
of his mouth, [11]that they might
accuse him.

## CHAPTER 12

*Jesus warns his disciples of the leaven of the Pharisees. 4 They must not fear man. 10 Blasphemy against the Holy Ghost. 13 The people warned against covetousness. 16 The parable of the rich man who would build greater barns. 22 Anxiety about worldly things forbidden. 31 The kingdom of God to be first sought. 35 The duty of watchfulness. 49 The coming of Jesus an occasion of division. 54 The signs of the times to be regarded.*

IN the mean time, when [a]there
were gathered together an
innumerable multitude of people, insomuch that they trode
one upon another, he began to
say unto his [b]disciples first of
all, [c,d,e]Beware ye of the [f,g]leaven
of the [h]Phăr'ĭ-seeș, which is hypocrisy.
2 For [i]there is [j]nothing covered, that shall not be revealed;
neither hid, that shall not be
known.
3 Therefore whatsoever ye
have spoken in darkness shall
be heard in the light; and that
which ye have spoken in the ear
in closets[G] shall be proclaimed
upon the [k]housetops.
4 And I say unto you my
friends, [l,m]Be not afraid of them
that kill the body, and after that
have no more that they can do.
5 But I will forewarn you whom
ye shall fear: [n]Fear [o]him, which
after he hath killed hath power
to [p]cast into [q]hell[G]; yea, I say unto
you, Fear him.
6 [r,s]Are[S] not five [t]sparrows sold
for two farthings[G], and not one of
them is forgotten before [u]God?
7 But [r]even the very hairs of
your head are all numbered.
[s]Fear not therefore: [v]ye are of
more value than many sparrows.[S]
8 Also[T] I say unto you, [w,x,y]Who-
soever shall *,[z]confess me before
men, [a,b]him shall the Son of man
also confess before the angels of
God:
9 But he that [c]denieth me before men shall be [d]denied before
the angels of God.
10 And whosoever shall speak a
word against the Son of man,
[e,f]it shall be forgiven him: but
unto him that [g]blasphemeth
against the [h]Holy Ghost[G] [i]it shall
not be forgiven.[T]
11 And when they [j]bring you
unto the [k]synagogues, and [1]*unto*
[l]magistrates, and powers, [m]take[G]
ye no [n]thought how or what
thing ye shall answer, or what
ye shall say:

**51**
*f Abel*, Gen. 4:2.
*g* Matt. 23:35.
*h Altar*, Gen. 8:20.
*i Temple, Solomon's*, 1 Kin. 6:17.
10 R. V. sanctuary:

**52**
*j Reproof, faithfulness in*, Prov. 17:10.
*k Lawyer*, Matt. 22:35.
*l Minister, false and corrupt*, Rom. 15:16.
*m Spiritual Blindness*, 2 Cor. 4:4.
*n Stumbling, figurative*, Isa. 8:14.

**53**
*o Scribe*, 1 Kin. 4:3.
*p Pharisees*, Matt. 15:12.

**54**
*q Malice, instances of*, Eph. 4:31.
11 R. V. *omits the rest of this verse.*

**1**
*a Popularity of Jesus*, John 6:15.
*b Disciples*, Matt. 9:14.
*c* Matt. 16:5–12; Mark 8:14–21.
*d Commandment, admonishing against hypocrisy*, Deut. 8:2.
*e Hypocrisy, warnings against*, Jas. 3:17.
*f Leaven, figurative*, Lev. 23:17.
*g Influence, evil*, 1 Cor. 7:14.
*h Pharisees, hypocrisy of*, Matt. 15:12.

**2**
*i* Matt. 10:26–33; Mark 4:22; Luke 8:17.
*j Sin, known to God*, Rom. 5:12.

**3**
*k House, roof of*, Esth. 8:1.

**4**
*l Commandment, enjoining fortitude under persecution*, Deut. 8:2.
*m Courage, exhortations to*, Deut. 31:7.

**5**
*n Fear of God* (as some interpret), Acts 9:31.
*o Satan* (as some interpret), Matt. 4:10.
*p Wicked, punishment of*, Psa. 73:3.
*q Hell*, Mark 9:43.

**6**
*r* Matt. 10:29–31.
*s Afflictions, consolation in*, Psa. 34:19.
*t Birds, divine care of*, Eccl. 12:4.
*u God, providence of*, Gen. 2:2.

**7**
*v Righteous, promises to*, Psa. 64:10.

**8**
*w* Matt. 10:32, 33.
*x Decision, exhortation to*, Isa. 50:7.
*y Discipleship of Jesus, tests of*, Matt. 10:32.
*z Religious Testimony*, 2 Thess. 1:10.
*a Reward, a motive, to faithfulness*, Matt. 5:12.
*b Promise, to the righteous*, 2 Cor. 1:20.

**9**
*c Jesus, rejected*, Matt. 1:21.
*d Wicked, punishment of*, Psa. 73:3.

**10** *e Sin, forgiveness of*, Rom. 5:12. *f Penitent, promises to*, Psa. 51:17. *g Blasphemy, against the Holy Spirit*, 2 Sam. 12:14. *h Holy Spirit, sin against*, Acts 1:2. *i Sin, unpardonable*, Rom. 5:12. **11** *j Persecution, of the righteous*, John 15:20. *k Synagogue*, Matt. 12:9. *l Magistrate*, Ezra 7:25. *m Commandment, forbidding anxiety*, Deut. 8:2. *n Anxiety*, 1 Pet. 5:7. 1 R. V. the rulers, and the authorities, be not anxious how or what ye shall answer, or what ye shall say:

‡ **KNOWLEDGE.** *Is power*, Prov. 24:5. *A divine gift*, 1 Cor. 12:8. *Is pleasant*, Prov. 2:10. *Is of more value than gold*, Prov. 8:10. *Shall be increased*, Dan. 12:4.
*The earth shall be full of*, Isa. 11:9. *Fear of the Lord is the beginning of*, Prov. 1:7. *The priest's lips should keep*, Mal. 2:7. *Righteous should increase in*, 2 Pet. 1:6.
*Desire for*, 1 Kin. 3:9; Psa. 119:66; Prov. 2; 12:1; 15:14; 18:15. *Key of*, Luke 11:52. *Rejected*, Hos. 4:6.
See footnote, WISDOM, Prov. 2:2.
**Of God**, see footnote, GOD, *Knowledge of*, Gen. 2:2.
**Of Jesus**, see footnote, JESUS, *Knowledge of*, Matt. 1:21.

* **CONFESSION OF CHRIST.** *In baptism*, Acts 19:4, 5; Gal 3:27. *Unto salvation*, Rom. 10:9–11 (with Matt. 10:32; Luke 12:8).
*Inspired by the Holy Spirit*, 1 Cor. 12:3; 1 John 4:2, 3. *Fellowship with the Father through*, 1 John 2:23; 4:15.
*Timid believers deterred from*, John 12:42, 43. *Those refusing to make, rejected*, Matt. 10:33; Mark 8:38; Luke 12:9; 2 Tim. 2:12.
*Enjoined*, 2 Tim. 1:8.
*Exemplified*, Matt. 3:11; 14:33; 16:16; John 6:69; 9:22–38; 11:27; Acts 8:35–37 (v. 37 is omitted in R. V.); 9:20; 18:5; Rom. 1:16.
*Hypocritical*, Matt. 7:21–23; Luke 13:26; 1 John 1:6; 2:4.

12 For [o,p]the [q]Holy Ghost[G]
shall [r]teach you in the same hour
[s]what ye ought to say.[T]
13 ¶ And one of the company
said unto him, Master, speak to
my brother, that he divide the
inheritance with me.
14 And he said unto him, Man,
who made me a judge or a di-
vider over you?[Q]
15 And he said unto them,
[t]Take heed, and [u,v]beware of
covetousness: for a man's life
consisteth not in the [w]abun-
dance of the things which he
possesseth.
16 And he spake a [x]parable
unto them, saying, The ground
of a certain [y]rich man brought
forth plentifully:
17 And he [z]thought within himself, saying, What shall I do, because I have no room where to
bestow[G] my fruits[G]?
18 And he said, This will I
do: [z]I will pull down my [a]barns,
and build greater; and there will
I bestow[G] all my fruits[G] and my
goods.
19 And I will [b]say to my soul,
Soul, [c]thou hast much [d]goods
laid up for many years; [e]take
thine ease, [f]eat, [f]drink, *and* [g]be
merry.
20 But God said unto him,
*Thou* fool, [h]this night thy soul
shall be [i]required of thee: then
whose shall those things be,
which thou hast provided?
21 So *is* he that layeth up treasure [j]for himself, and is not [k]rich
toward God.
22 ¶ And he said unto his [l]dis-
ciples, Therefore I say unto you,
[2,m,n,o]Take[G] no [p]thought for your
life, what ye shall eat; neither
for the body, what ye shall put
on.
23 The life is more than meat[G],
and the body *is more* than raiment[G].
24[S] Consider the [q]ravens: for
they neither sow nor reap; which
neither have storehouse nor barn;
and God [r,s]feedeth them: how
much more are ye better than
the fowls?[Q]
25 And which of you [3]with taking[G] [p]thought can add to his stature one [t]cubit?
26 If ye then be not able to do
that thing which is least, why
[4]take[G] ye [p]thought for the rest?
27 Consider the [u]lilies how they
grow: they toil not, they spin
not; and yet I say unto you, that
[v]Sŏl'o-mon in all his glory was
not arrayed[G] like one of these.[Q]
28 If then God so [r]clothe the
[w]grass, which is to day in the
field, and to morrow is cast into
the [x]oven; how much more *will
he* [r,s]*clothe* you, O ye of [y]little
faith?[S]
29 And seek not ye what ye
shall eat, or what ye shall drink,
neither be ye of doubtful mind.
30 For all these things do the
nations of the world seek after:
and your [z]Father [a]knoweth that
ye have need of these things.[T]
31 But rather [b]seek ye the
[c]kingdom of God; and [d]all these
things shall be added unto you.
32 [e]Fear not, little [f]flock; for
[g]it is your Father's good pleasure to give you the [c]kingdom.[S T]
33 [h,i]Sell that ye have, and
[j,k,l]give [m]alms; provide yourselves bags which wax[G] not old,
[n]a †treasure in the heavens that
faileth not, where no thief ap-
proacheth, neither moth cor-
rupteth.
34 For where your treasure is,
there will your heart be also.
35 [o,p]Let your loins be girded
about, and *your* lights[G] burning;[Q]

**12**
o *Promise, to the righteous, of divine guidance,* 2 Cor. 1:20.
p *Righteous, promises to,* Psa. 64:10.
q *Holy Spirit, inspiration of,* Acts 1:2.
r *Inspiration, of the disciples,* Job 32:8.
s *Wisdom, spiritual,* Prov. 2:2.

**15**
t *Watchfulness, enjoined,* Matt. 24:42.
u *Commandment, warning against covetousness,* Deut. 8:2.
v *Covetousness, warnings against,* Isa. 57:17.
w *Riches,* Eccl. 4:8.

**16**
x *Parables, of Jesus,* Ezek. 20:49.
y *Rich,* Jas. 5:1.

**17**
z *Worldliness, instances of,* 1 John 2:15.

**18**
a *Barn,* Prov. 3:10.

**19**
b *Presumption,* Psa. 19:13.
c *False Confidence,* Psa. 30:6.
d *Riches, delusive,* Eccl. 4:8.
e *Sensuality,* Jude 19.
f *Appetite,* Prov. 23:2.
g *Wicked, happiness of,* Psa. 73:3.

**20**
h *Life, brevity and uncertainty of,* Eccl. 8:15.
i *Death, of the wicked,* Num. 23:10.

**21**
j *Selfishness,* 2 Tim. 3:2.
k *Righteousness,* Psa. 15:2.

**22**
l *Disciples,* Matt. 9:14.
m Matt. 6:25-33.
n *Commandment forbidding anxiety,* vs. 22-32; Deut. 8:2.
o *Faith, enjoined,* Mark 11:22.
p *Anxiety,* 1 Pet. 5:7.
2 R. V. Be not anxious

**24**
q *Raven,* Job 38:41.
r *God, providence of,* Gen. 2:2.
s *Temporal Blessings, from God,* Psa. 103:2.

**25**
t *Cubit,* Ex. 36:9.
3 R. V. by being anxious

**26**
4 R. V. are ye anxious concerning

**27**
u *Lily,* Matt. 6:28.
v *Solomon,* 2 Sam. 12:24.

**28**
w *Grass,* Isa. 40:7.
x *Oven,* Ex. 8:3.
y *Doubting,* Rom. 14:23.

**30**
z *God, fatherhood of,* Gen. 2:2.

a *God, knowledge of,* Gen. 2:2.

**31**
b *Commandment, enjoining seeking the kingdom of God,* Deut. 8:2.
c *Kingdom of Heaven,* Matt. 13:24.
d *Righteous, promises to,* Psa. 64:10.

**32**
e *Faith, enjoined,* Mark 11:22.
f *Sheep, figurative,* Deut. 32:14.
g *Promise, to the righteous,* 2 Cor. 1:20.

**33**
h *Self-denial,* Mark 8:34.
i *Worldliness, admonitions against,* 1 John 2:15.
j *Commandment, enjoining liberality,* Deut. 8:2.
k *Liberality,* 1 Tim. 6:18.
l *Poor, duty to,* Prov. 21:13.
m *Alms,* Matt. 6:2.
n *Reward, a motive, to obedience,* Matt. 5:12.

**35**
o *Commandment, enjoining watchfulness,* vs. 35-40; Deut. 8:2.
p *Faithfulness, exhortations to,* Luke 16:10.

† **TREASURE,** a thing of highly estimated value. *Money,* Gen. 42:25, 27, 28, 35; 43:23, with vs. 18, 21, 22. *Precious stones,* 1 Chr. 29:8. *Jesus forbids the hoarding of,* Matt. 6:19-21; 19:21; Luke 12:33.
**Figurative:** *Of spiritual understanding,* Matt. 13:52; Col. 2:3. *Of the object of the affections,* Matt. 6:19-21; Luke 12:34. *Of knowledge,* 2 Cor. 4:6, 7; Col. 2:3.
*Parable of,* Matt. 13:44.

36 [q]And ye yourselves like unto
men that [‡]wait for their lord,
when he will return from the
wedding; that when he cometh
and knocketh, they may open
unto him immediately.
37 Blessed *are* those [r,s,t]serv-
ants, whom the lord when he
[u]cometh shall find [v]watching:
verily I say unto you, that he
shall gird himself, and [w]make
them to sit down to meat, and
will come forth and serve them.
38 And if he shall come in the
second [x]watch, or come in the
third watch, and find *them* so,
blessed are those servants.
39 [y]And this know, that if the
[5]goodman of the house had
known what hour the thief
would come, he would have
watched, and not have suffered
his house to be broken through.
40 Be ye therefore [‡]ready also:
for the Son of man [u]cometh at an
hour when ye think not.
41 ¶ Then [z]Pē′tēr said unto
him, Lord, speakest thou this
[a]parable unto [b]us, or even to
[c]all?
42 And the Lord said, [d,e]Who
then is that [f]faithful and wise
[c,g]steward, whom *his* lord [h,i]shall
make ruler over his household, to
give *them their* portion of meat
in due season?
43 Blessed *is* that [c,j]servant,
whom his lord when he cometh
shall find so doing.
44 Of a truth I say unto you,
that [h,i]he will make [c,j]him ruler
over all that he hath.
45 But and if that [c,k]servant
[l]say in his heart, My lord delayeth his coming; and shall begin
to [m]beat the menservants and
maidens, and to [n]eat and drink,
and to be [o]drunken;
46 The lord of that servant will
come in a day when he looketh
not for *him*, and at an hour
when he is not aware, and will
[p]cut him in sunder, and will appoint him his portion with the
[q]unbelievers.
47 And that servant, which
[r,s]knew his lord's will, and [‡,t]pre-
pared not *himself*, neither did
according to his will, shall be
[u]beaten with many *stripes*.
48 But he that [v,w]knew not, and
did commit things worthy of
stripes, shall be [s,u]beaten with
few *stripes*. For [r]unto whomsoever much is given, [x]of him shall
be much required: and to whom
men have committed much, of
him they will ask the more.
49 ¶ [y]I am come to send [z]fire
on the earth; and what will I, if
it be already kindled?
50 But [a]I have a [b,c]baptism to
be baptized with; and how am
I straitened till it be accomplished!
51 [d]Suppose ye that I am come
to give [e]peace on earth? I tell
you, Nay; but rather [f]division:
52 For from henceforth there
shall be five in one house divided, three against two, and
two against three.
53 [g]The father shall be divided
against the son, and the son
against the father; the mother
against the daughter, and the
daughter against the mother;
the mother in law against her
daughter in law, and the daughter in law against her mother in
law.
54 ¶ [h]And he said also to the
people, When ye see a [i,j]cloud
rise out of the west, straightway ye say, There cometh a
[j,k]shower; and so it is.
55 And when *ye see* the south
[j,l]wind blow, ye say, There will
be heat; and it cometh to pass.
56 *Ye* [m]hypocrites, ye can dis-

**36**
q *Parables, of Jesus*, Ezek. 20:49.
**37**
r *Servant, figurative*, Jer. 2:14.
s *Minister, faithful*, Rom. 15:16.
t *Disciples*, Matt. 9:14.
u *Jesus, second coming of*, Matt. 1:21.
v *Watchfulness*, Matt. 24:42.
w *Obedience, rewarded*, Heb. 5:8.
**38**
x *Night, divided into watches*, Gen. 1:5.
**39**
y Matt. 24:43–45.
5 R. V. master
**41**
z *Peter*, Mark 5:37.
a *Parables, of Jesus*, Ezek. 20:49.
b *Apostles*, Luke 6:13.
c *Disciples*, Matt. 9:14.
**42**
d Matt. 24:45–51.
e *Minister, character and qualifications of*, Rom. 15:16.
f *Faithfulness, exhortation to*, Luke 16:10.
g *Steward, figurative*, Gen. 43:19.
h *Promise, to the faithful*, 2 Cor. 1:20.
i *Reward, a motive, to faithfulness*, Matt. 5:12.
**43**
j *Minister, faithful*, Rom 15:16.
**45**
k *Minister, false and corrupt*, Rom. 15:16.
l *Procrastination*, Acts 24:25.
m *Cruelty*, Psa. 27:12.
n *Sensuality*, Jude 19.
o *Drunkenness*, Luke 21:34.

**46**
p *Wicked, punishment of*, Psa. 73:3.
q *Unbelievers*, 1 Cor. 6:6.
**47**
r *Opportunity, the measure of responsibility*, Gal. 6:10.
s *Judgment, according to opportunity and works*, 1 Pet. 1:17.
t *Sin, defined*, Rom. 5:12.
u *Punishment, according to deeds*, Lev. 26:41.
**48**
v *Ignorance, sins of*, Acts 3:17.
w *Spiritual Blindness*, 2 Cor. 4:4.
x *Responsibility, according to privilege*, Ezek. 18:20.
**49**
y *Jesus, mission of*, Matt. 1:21.
z *Fire, figurative*, Ex. 12:8.
**50**
a *Jesus, zeal of*, Matt. 1:21.
b *Jesus, death of, voluntary*, Matt. 1:21.
c *Baptism, figurative*, Luke 20:4.
**51**
d Matt. 10:34, 35.
e *Peace*, Jer. 29:7.
f *Strife*, Prov. 20:3.
**53**
g *Hostility to the Righteous*, Mic. 7:6.
**54**
h Matt. 16:1–4; Mark 8:10–12.
i *Sign*, Mark 8:11.
j *Meteorology*, Matt. 16:2.
k *Rain*, 2 Sam. 1:21.
**55**
l *Wind*, Job 37:17
**56**
m *Hypocrisy*, Jas. 3:17.

‡ **PREPAREDNESS**, Matt. 24:44; 25:1–13; Mark 13:32–37; Luke 12:35–48; 19:41–44.
See footnote, FAITHFULNESS, Luke 16:10.

cern the face of the sky and of
the earth; but how is it that ye
do not discern this time?
57 Yea, and why even of yourselves [n]judge ye not what is right?
58 ¶ When thou goest with
thine adversary to the [o]magis-
trate, *as thou art* in the way,
‖give diligence [p]that thou mayest be delivered from him; lest
[q]he hale thee to the judge, and
the judge deliver thee to the officer, and the officer cast thee into
[r]prison.
59 I tell thee, thou shalt not
depart thence, till thou hast
paid the very last mite.

## CHAPTER 13

*The slaughter of certain Galileans. 6 The parable of the barren fig tree. 10 Jesus heals an infirm woman. 18 The kingdom of God is like a grain of mustard seed; 20 and like leaven. 23 The strait gate. 41 Jesus' message to Herod. 34 His lamentation over Jerusalem.*

THERE were present at that
season some that told him
of the [a]Găl-ĭ-læ'anṣ, whose blood
[b]Pī'late had mingled with their
sacrifices.
2 And Jē'ṣus answering said
unto them, Suppose ye that these
[a]Găl-ĭ-læ'anṣ were sinners above
all the Găl-ĭ-læ'anṣ, because they
suffered such things?
3 I tell you, Nay: but, [c,d]except
ye [e]repent, ye shall all likewise
[f]perish.
4 Or those eighteen, upon
whom the tower in [g]Sĭ-lō'am
fell, and slew them, think ye that
they were [1]sinners above all men
that dwelt in [h]Jĕ-ru̧'sā-lĕm?
5 I tell you, Nay: but, [c,d]except
ye [e]repent, ye shall all likewise
[f]perish.
6 ¶ He spake also this [i]parable;
A certain *man* had a *fig tree
planted in his [j]vineyard; [k]and he
came and sought [l]fruit [m]thereon,
and found [n,o]none.
7 Then said he unto the dresser
of his [j]vineyard, Behold, these
[p,q]three years I come seeking
[l]fruit on this *fig tree, and find
none: [f,r,s,t]cut it down; why
cumbereth it the ground?
8 And [u]he answering [v]said unto
him, Lord, [p,q]let it alone this
year also, till I shall dig about
it, and dung *it*:
9 And if it bear [l]fruit, *well*: and
if not, *then* after [q]that thou shalt
[f,r,s,t]cut it down.
10 ¶ And he was [w,x]teaching in
one of the [y]synagogues on the
[z]sabbath.
11 And, behold, there was a
woman which had a spirit of [a]in-
firmity eighteen years, and was
bowed together, and could in no
wise lift up *herself*.
12 And when Jē'ṣus saw her, [b]he
called *her to him*, and said unto
her, Woman, thou art loosed
from thine [a]infirmity.
13 And he laid *his* hands on her:
and immediately she was [c,d]made
straight, and [e,f]glorified God.
14 And the ruler of the [g]syna-
gogue answered with indignation, because that Jē'ṣus had
[d]healed on the [h]sabbath day, and
said unto the people, [i]There are
six days in which men ought to
[j]work: in them therefore come
and be healed, and not on the
sabbath day.
15 The Lord then answered
him, and [k]said, [2]*Thou* [l]hypo-
crite, doth not each one of you
on the sabbath [m]loose his ox or
*his* ass from the stall, and lead
*him* away to watering?
16 And ought not this woman,
being a daughter of [n]Ā'brā-hăm,
whom [o]Sā'tan hath [p]bound, lo,
these eighteen years, be loosed
from this bond on the [h]sabbath
day?

**57**
n *Uncharitableness,* Matt. 7:1.

**58**
o *Magistrate,* Ezra 7:25.
p *Litigation, to be avoided,* Matt. 5:25.
q *Creditor, oppressions by,* Deut. 15:2.
r *Prison,* Gen. 39:20.

**1**
a *Galilee,* Mark 6:21.
b *Pilate,* Matt. 27:2.

**3**
c *Commandment, enjoining repentance,* Deut. 8:2.
d *Reproof, faithfulness in,* Prov. 17:10.
e *Repentance, enjoined,* Mark 1:4.
f *Wicked, punishment of,* Psa. 73:3.

**4**
g *Siloam, tower of,* John 9:11.
h *Jerusalem,* Judg. 19:10.
1 R. V. offenders

**6**
i *Parables, of Jesus,* Ezek. 20:49.
j *Vineyard, parables of,* Isa. 1:8.
k *Responsibility, according to privilege,* Ezek. 18:20.
l *Righteousness, fruits of,* Psa. 15:2.
m *Church, backslidden,* Matt. 16:18.
n *Unfruitfulness,* Matt. 7:19.
o *Unfaithfulness,* Luke 16:11.

**7**
p *God, longsuffering of,* Gen. 2:2.
q *Probation,* Rom. 5:4.
r *Holy Spirit, withdrawn from incorrigible sinners,* Acts 1:2.
s *Opportunity, lost,* Gal. 6:10.
t *Judgment, according to opportunity and works,* 1 Pet. 1:17.

**8**
u *Jesus, mediation of,* Matt. 1:21.
v *Intercession, exemplified,* Jer. 27:18.

**10**
w *Jesus, teacher,* Matt. 1:21.
x *Instruction, in religion,* Prov. 23:23.
y *Synagogue,* Matt. 12:9.
z *Sabbath, religious instruction on,* Ex. 16:23.

**11**
a *Afflictions,* Psa. 34:19.

**12**
b *Jesus, compassion of,* Matt. 1:21.

**13**
c *Miracles, of Jesus,* Luke 23:8.
d *Healing, by Jesus,* Acts 4:22.
e *Glorifying God,* Luke 5:25.
f *Thankfulness, to God,* Acts 24:3.

**14**
g *Synagogue,* Matt. 12:9.
h *Sabbath,* Ex. 16:23.
i Ex. 20:8, 9.
j *Labor,* Luke 10:7.

**15**
k *Reproof, faithfulness in,* Prov. 17:10.
l *Hypocrisy,* Jas. 3:17.
m *Animals, kindness to,* Jer. 27:5.
2 R. V. Ye hypocrites,

**16**
n *Abraham,* Gen. 17:5.
o *Satan,* Matt. 4:10.
p *Afflictions, from Satan,* Psa. 34:19.

‖ **COMPROMISE.** *Before litigation, enjoined,* Prov. 25:8–10; Luke 12:58, 59; Matt. 5:25, 26.

* **FIG TREE,** Jas. 3:12. *Leaves of, used for clothing,* Gen. 3:7. *Common, to Palestine,* Num. 13:23; Deut. 8:8; *to Egypt,* Psa. 105:33. *Destroyed as a judgment,* Amos 4:9. *Barren, cursed by Jesus,* Matt. 21:19, 20; Mark 11:12–14, 20, 21. **Parables of,** Judg. 9:10, 11; Luke 13:6–9; 21:29–31. **Figurative,** 1 Kin. 4:25; 2 Kin. 18:31 (with Isa. 36:16); Mic. 4:4. See footnote, FIG, Mark 11:13.

17 And when he had said these things, all his adversaries were ashamed: and [q]all the people rejoiced for all the glorious things that were done by him.[s]

18 ¶ Then [r]said he, Unto what is the [s]kingdom of God like? and whereunto shall I resemble[G] it?

19 [s,t]It is like a grain of [u]mustard seed, which a man took, and cast into his garden; and it grew, and waxed[G] a great tree; and the fowls of the air lodged in the branches of it.[Q]

20 ¶ And again he [r]said, Whereunto shall I liken the kingdom of God?

21 [s,t]It is like [v]leaven, which a woman took and hid in three measures[G] of meal, till the whole was leavened.

22 And he went through the cities and villages, [w,x]teaching, and journeying toward [y]Jĕ-rụ′să-lĕm.

23 ¶ Then[T] said one unto him, Lord, are there few that be saved? And he said unto them,

24 [z,a]Strive[G] to enter in at the strait[G] gate: for many, I say unto you, will seek to enter in, and shall not be able.

25 When once the master[G] of the house is risen up, and hath [b]shut to the [c]door, and ye begin to stand without,[G] and to knock at the door, [d]saying, Lord, Lord, open unto us; and he shall answer and say unto you, I know [e]you not whence ye are:

26 Then shall ye begin to [f]say, We have eaten and drunk in thy presence, and thou hast taught in our streets.

27 But he shall say, I tell you, I know you not whence ye are; [g,h]depart from me, all *ye* [e]workers of iniquity.[Q]

28 There shall be [i]weeping and [j]gnashing of teeth, when ye shall see [k]Ā′bră-hăm, and [l]Ī′şaac, and [m]Jā′cob, and all the prophets, in the [n]kingdom of God, and you *yourselves* [g,h]thrust out.[s]

29 And [o,p]they shall come from the east, and *from* the west, and from the north, and *from* the south, and shall sit down in the kingdom of God.[Q]

30 And, behold, there are last which shall be first, and there are first which shall be last.[T]

31 ¶ The same day there came certain of the [q]Phăr′ĭ-seeş, [r]saying unto him, Get thee out, and depart hence: for [s]Hĕr′od will[G] [t]kill thee.

32 And he said unto them, Go ye, and tell that [s,u]fox, Behold, [v]I [w]cast out [x]devils,[G] and I do [y]cures to day and to morrow, and the third *day* I shall be perfected.[G]

33 Nevertheless I must walk to day, and to morrow, and the *day* following: for it cannot be that a [z]prophet perish[G] out of [a]Jĕ-rụ′să-lĕm.[T]

34 [b]O [a]Jĕ-rụ′să-lĕm, Jĕ-rụ′să-lĕm, which [c]killest the [d]prophets, and [e]stonest them that are sent unto thee; how often would [f]I have gathered thy children together, as a hen *doth gather* her brood under *her* wings, and [g,h]ye would not![s]

35 Behold, [i]your house is left unto you desolate[G]: and verily I say unto you, Ye shall not see me, until *the time* come when ye shall say, [j]Blessed *is* he that cometh in the name of the Lord.[Q]

## CHAPTER 14

*Jesus on the Sabbath heals one who had dropsy. 7 The chief rooms not to be chosen. 12 Kindness to the poor enjoined. 15 The parable of the great supper, from which the guests excuse themselves. 25 Jesus' disciples must count the cost of becoming his followers.*

AND[s] it came to pass, as he went into the house of one of the chief [a]Phăr′ĭ-seeş to eat bread on the [b]sabbath day, that they watched him.

2 And, behold, there was a cer-

17
q *Jesus, received,* Matt. 1:21.
18
r *Parables, of Jesus,* Ezek. 20:49.
s *Kingdom of Heaven,* Matt. 13:24.
19
t *Jesus, kingdom of, prophecies concerning,* Matt. 1:21.
u *Mustard Seed* Matt. 13:31.
21
v *Leaven,* Lev. 23:17.
22
w *Jesus, teacher,* Matt. 1:21.
x *Instruction, in religion,* Prov. 23:23.
y *Jerusalem,* Judg. 19:10.
24
z Matt. 7:13.
a *Commandment, enjoining righteousness,* Deut. 8:2.
25
b *Opportunity, lost,* Gal. 6:10.
c *Door, figurative,* Deut. 11:20.
d *Delusion,* 2 Thess. 2:11.
e *Reprobates,* 1 Cor. 9:27.
26
f *Hypocrisy* Jas. 3:17.
27
g *Sin, separates from God,* Rom. 5:12.
h *Wicked, punishment of,* Psa. 73:3.
28
i *Sorrow, of the lost,* Matt. 13:42.
j *Gnashing of Teeth,* Job 16:9.
k *Abraham,* Gen. 17:5.
l *Isaac,* Gen. 21:3.
m *Jacob,* Gen. 27:11.

n *Kingdom of Heaven,* Matt. 13:24.
29
o *Jesus, kingdom of, prophecies concerning,* Matt. 1:21.
p *Gentiles, prophecies of the conversion of,* Acts 10:45.
31
q *Pharisees,* Matt. 15:12.
r *Jesus, rejected,* Matt. 1:21.
s *Herod,* Matt. 14:1.
t *Persecution, of Jesus,* John 15:20.
32
u *Fox, figurative,* Psa. 63:10.
v *Jesus, zeal of,* Matt. 1:21.
w *Miracles, of Jesus,* Luke 23:8.
x *Demons,* Matt. 4:24.
y *Healing, by Jesus,* Acts 4:22.
33
z *Jesus, prophet,* Matt. 1:21.

a *Jerusalem,* Judg. 19:10.
34
b Matt. 23:37–39.
c *Martyrdom, of prophets,* Rev. 17:6.
d *Prophets,* Isa. 3:2.
e *Persecution, of the righteous,* John 15:20.
f *Jesus, compassion of,* Matt. 1:21.
g *Impenitence,* Rom. 2:5.
h *Jesus, rejected,* Matt. 1:21.
35
i *Jerusalem, destruction of, foretold,* Judg. 19:10.
j Psa. 118:26; Matt. 21:9; 23:39; Mark 11:9; Luke 19:38; John 12:13.

1
a *Pharisees,* Matt. 15:12.
b *Sabbath,* Ex. 16:23.

3
*c* *Lawyer,* Matt. 22:35.

4
*d* *Healing, by Jesus,* Acts 4:22.
*e* *Miracles, of Jesus,* Luke 23:8.

5
*f* *Animals, kindness to,* Jer. 27:5.

7
*g* *Parables, of Jesus,* Ezek. 20:49.
*h* *Presumption,* Psa. 19:13.
1 R. V. seats;

8
*i* *Guest, rules for conduct of,* Zeph. 1:7.
*j* *Hospitality,* Rom. 12:13.
*k* *Feasts,* Mark 12:39.
*l* *Manners,* Gen. 18:2.
*m* *Pride, rebuked,* Prov. 16:18.
2 R. V. marriage feast,
3 R. V. chief seat;

9
4 R. V. place,

10
*n* *Humility, enjoined,* Prov. 22:4.

11
*o* *Humility, rewards of,* Prov. 22:4.

12
*p* *Hospitality, unselfish,* Rom. 12:13.
*q* *Friends,* Ex. 33:11.

tain man before him which had the dropsy.

3 And Jē´ṣus answering spake unto the [c]lawyers and [a]Phăr´ĭ-seeṣ, saying, Is it lawful to heal on the [b]sabbath day?

4 And they held their peace. And he took *him,* and [d,e]healed him, and let him go;

5 And answered them, saying, Which of you shall have an [f]ass or an ox fallen into a pit, and will not straightway pull him out on the sabbath day?

6 And they could not answer him again to these things.

7 ¶ And he put forth a [g]parable to those which were bidden, when he marked how they [*,h]chose out the chief [1]rooms; saying unto them,

8 When [i]thou art [j]bidden of any *man* to a [2,k]wedding, [l,m]sit not down in the [3]highest room; lest a more honourable man than thou be bidden of him;

9 And he that bade thee and him come and say to thee, Give this man place; and thou begin with shame to take the lowest [4]room.

10 But [i]when thou art [j]bidden, go and [l,n]sit down in the lowest room; that when he that bade thee cometh, he may say unto thee, Friend, go up higher: then shalt thou have worship in the presence of them that sit at meat with thee.

11 For whosoever *exalteth himself shall be abased; and he that [o]humbleth himself shall be exalted.

12 ¶ Then said he also to him that bade him, When thou makest a [k]dinner or a supper, [p]call not thy [q]friends, nor thy brethren, neither thy kinsmen, nor *thy* rich neighbours; lest they also bid thee again, and a recompence be made thee.

13 But when thou makest a [k]feast, call the [r]poor, the maimed, the lame, the blind:

14 And [s]thou [t]shalt be blessed; for they cannot recompense thee: for thou shalt be recompensed at the [u]resurrection of the just.

15 ¶ And when one of them that sat at meat with him heard these things, he said unto him, Blessed *is* he that shall eat bread in the [v]kingdom of God.

16 [w]Then [g]said he unto him, A certain man made a great [x]supper, and [y]bade many:

17 And sent his servant at supper time to say to them that were bidden, Come; for all things are now ready.

18 And they all with one *consent* began to make †excuse. The first [z]said unto him, I have bought a piece of ground, and I must needs go and see it: [z]I pray thee have me excused.

19 And another [†,z]said, I have bought five yoke of oxen, and I go to prove them: [z]I pray thee have me excused.

20 And another [†,z]said, I have married a wife, and [z]therefore I cannot come.

21 So that servant came, and shewed his lord these things. Then the master of the house being angry said to his servant, Go out quickly into the streets and lanes of the city, and [y]bring in hither the poor, and the maimed, and the halt, and the blind.

22 And the servant said, Lord, it is done as thou hast commanded and yet there is room.

13
*r* *Poor, duty to,* Prov. 21:13.

14
*s* *Righteous, promises to,* Psa. 64:10.
*t* *Reward, a motive, to obedience,* Matt. 5:12.
*u* *Resurrection,* 1 Cor. 15:12.

15
*v* *Kingdom of Heaven,* Matt. 13:24.

16
*w* See Matt. 22:1–14.
*x* *Feasts,* Mark 12:39.
*y* *Call, personal,* Phil. 3:14.

18
*z* *Worldliness, leads to the rejection of the gospel,* 1 John 2:15.

* **SELF-EXALTATION,** Mark 12:38, 39; Luke 14:7–11; 2 Cor. 10:5, 17; Gal. 6:3; 2 Thess. 2:4. See footnotes: PRIDE, Prov. 16:18; SELF-RIGHTEOUSNESS, Luke 18:11.
**Instances of:** *Pharaoh,* Ex. 9:17. *Korah, Dathan, and Abiram,* Num. 16:1–11. *Sennacherib,* 2 Chr. 32:9–19. *Prince of Tyre, making himself God,* Ezek. 28:2, 9, 10. *Nebuchadnezzar,* Dan. 4:30; 5:20. *Belshazzar,* Dan. 5:22, 23. *Simon the sorcerer,* Acts 8:9–11. *Herod, when deified by the people,* Acts 12:20–23.

† **EXCUSES.** *For disobedience,* Gen. 3:12, 13; Ex. 32:22–24; Deut. 30:11–14.
For release from duty: *By Moses, when commissioned to deliver Israel,* Ex. 3:11; 4:1, 10–14; *by Gideon.* Judg. 6:12–17; *by Jesus' disciples,* Matt. 8:21; Luke 9:59–62.
When called to be a prophet: *Elisha,* 1 Kin. 19:19–21; *Isaiah,* Isa. 6:5–8; *Jeremiah,* Jer. 1:5–10.
*For rejecting salvation,* Luke 14:18–20; John 15:22; Acts 24:25; Rom. 1:20, 21; 3:19.

23 And the lord said unto the servant, Go out into the highways and hedges, and compel *them* to come in, that my house may be filled.

24 For I say unto you, That none of those [a]men which [b]were bidden shall taste of my [c]supper.

25 ¶ And [d]there went great multitudes with him: and he turned, and said unto them,

26 [e,f]If any [g]*man* [h]come to me, and [i,j]hate not his father, and mother, and wife, and children, and brethren, and sisters, yea, and his own [k]life also, he cannot be my disciple.

27 And [e]whosoever doth not bear his [l]cross, and come after me, cannot be my disciple.

28 For which of you, intending to build a [m]tower, [n]sitteth not down first, and counteth the cost, whether he have *sufficient* to finish *it*?

29 [n]Lest haply, after he hath laid the foundation, and is not able to finish *it*, all that behold *it* begin to mock him,

30 Saying, This man began to build, and was not able to finish.

31 Or what king, going to make [o]war against another king, [n]sitteth not down first, and consulteth whether he be able with ten thousand to meet him that cometh against him with twenty thousand?

32 Or else, while the other is yet a great way off, he [p]sendeth an [q]ambassage, and desireth conditions of peace.

33 So likewise, [e]whosoever he be of you that [i]forsaketh not all that he hath, he cannot be my disciple.

34 ¶ [r]Salt *is* good: but [s]if the salt have [t]lost his savour, wherewith shall it be seasoned?

35 It is neither fit for the land, nor yet for the dunghill; *but* men cast it out. He that hath ears to hear, let him [u]hear.

## CHAPTER 15

*The parable of the lost sheep; 8 of the piece of silver; 11 of the prodigal son.*

THEN [a]drew near unto him all the [b]publicans and sinners for to hear him.

2 And the [c]Phăr'ĭ-seeş and [d]scribes [e,f]murmured, saying, This man [g]receiveth sinners, and eateth with them.

3 ¶ And he spake this [h]parable unto them, saying,

4 [i,j]What man of you, having an hundred sheep, if he lose one of them, doth not leave the ninety and nine in the wilderness, and go after that which is lost, until he find it?

5 And when he hath found *it*, [j]he layeth *it* on his shoulders, rejoicing.

6 And when he cometh home, he calleth together *his* friends and neighbours, saying unto them, Rejoice with me; for I have found my sheep which was lost.

7 I say unto you, that likewise [k]joy shall be in [l]heaven over one [m]sinner that [n]repenteth, more than over ninety and nine [f,o]just persons, which need no repentance.

8 ¶ [h]Either what woman having ten pieces of silver, if she lose one piece, doth not light a candle, and sweep the house, and seek diligently till she find *it*?

9 And when she hath found *it*, she calleth *her* friends and *her* neighbours together, saying, Rejoice with me; for I have found the piece which I had lost.

10 Likewise, I say unto you, there is [k]joy in the presence of the [p]angels of God over one [m]sinner that [n]repenteth.

11 ¶ And he [h]said, A certain man had two [q]sons:

12 And the younger of [q]them

---

**24**
a *Reprobates,* 1 Cor. 9:27.
b *Opportunity, lost,* Gal. 6:10.
c *Feasts,* Mark 12:39.

**25**
d *Popularity of Jesus,* John 6:15.

**26**
e *Discipleship of Jesus, tests of,* Matt. 10:32.
f *Salvation, condition of,* Acts 16:17.
g *Seekers,* Isa. 55:6.
h *Love, for Jesus,* 1 John 4:19.
i *Self-denial,* Mark 8:34.
j *Renunciation, of self for Christ,* Luke 5:11.
k *Life,* Eccl. 8:15.

**27**
l *Cross, figurative,* John 19:17.

**28**
m *Tower, parable of,* 2 Chr. 26:9.
n *Prudence,* 2 Chr. 2:12.

**31**
o *War,* Judg. 3:2.

**32**
p *Diplomacy,* 2 Kin. 16:7.
q *Ambassadors,* Josh. 9:4.

**34**
r *Salt,* 2 Kin. 2:20.
s *Proverbs,* 1 Sam. 24:13.
t *Apostasy,* Acts 1:25.

**35**
u *Spiritual Understanding,* Luke 8:8.

**1**
a *Spiritual Desire,* Psa. 42:1.
b *Publicans,* Matt. 11:19.

**2**
c *Pharisees,* Matt. 15:12.
d *Scribe,* 1 Kin. 4:3.
e *Bigotry, instances of,* Isa. 65:5.
f *Self-righteousness,* Luke 18:11.
g *Jesus, benevolence of,* Matt. 1:21.

**3**
h *Parables, of Jesus,* Ezek. 20:49.

**4**
i Matt. 18:12, 13.
j *Jesus, compassion of,* Matt. 1:21.

**7**
k *Joy, in heaven,* Psa. 5:11.
l *Heaven, future home of the righteous,* Luke 18:22.
m *Penitent, promises to,* Psa. 51:17.
n *Repentance,* Mark 1:4.
o *Irony,* Mark 12:14.

**10**
p *Angel,* Heb. 1 13.

**11**
q *Young Men,* Prov. 1:4.

said to *his* father, Father, give
me the portion[G] of goods that
[r]falleth *to me*. And he divided
unto them *his* living.
13 And not many days after
the younger [q]son gathered all
together, and took his journey
into a far country, and there
wasted his substance with riotous[G] living.[Q]
14 And when he had spent all,
there arose a mighty [s]famine in
that land; and he began to be in
want.[G]
15 And he went and joined
[t,u]himself to a *citizen of that
country; and he sent him into
his fields to feed [v]swine.
16 And he would [w]fain[G] have
filled his belly with the husks
that the [v]swine did eat: and no
man gave unto him.
17 And when [x,y]he came to himself, he said, How many [t]hired
servants of my father's [z]have
bread enough and to spare, and
I perish[G] with [a]hunger!
18 [b,c]I will arise and go to my
father, and will say unto him,
[d]Father, [e]I have sinned against[Q]
heaven, and before thee,
19 And [f]am no more worthy to
be called thy son: make me as
one of thy [g]hired servants.
20 And he arose, and [b]came to
his father. But when he was yet
a great way off, his father saw
him, and [h]had [i,j]compassion,
and ran, and fell on his neck,
and [k]kissed him.
21 And the son said unto him,
Father, [b,e]I have sinned against
heaven, and in thy sight, and
[f]am no more worthy to be called
thy son.[T]
22 But the father said to his
servants, Bring forth the best
robe, and put *it* on him; and put
a ring on his hand, and shoes on
*his* feet:
23 And bring hither the fatted[G]
calf, and kill *it*; and let us [l]eat,
and be merry:
24 For this my son was dead,
and is [j]alive again; he was lost,
and [j]is found. And they began
to [m]be merry.
25 Now his elder son was in the
field: and as he came and drew
nigh[G] to the house, he heard
musick and [n]dancing.
26 And he called one of the
servants, and asked what these
things meant.
27 And he said unto him, Thy
brother is come; and thy father
hath killed the fatted calf, because he hath received him safe
and sound.
28 And he was [o]angry, and
would not go in: therefore [p]came
his father out, and intreated him.
29 And he answering [q]said to
*his* father, Lo, [r]these many years
do I serve[G] thee, neither transgressed I at any time thy commandment: and [s]yet thou never
gavest me a kid, that I might
make merry with my friends:
30 [q,s]But as soon as this thy son
was come, which hath devoured[G]
thy living[G] with harlots, thou hast
killed for him the fatted calf.
31 And he said unto him, Son,

**12**
r *Inheritance,* Num. 27:7.

**14**
s *Famine,* 2 Kin. 8:1.

**15**
t *Hired Servant,* Lev. 25:40.
u *Employee,* Deut. 24:14.
v *Swine,* Lev. 11:7.

**16**
w *Hunger,* Neh. 9:15.

**17**
x *Adversity, benefits of,* Psa. 10:6.
y *Conviction of Sin,* John 16:8.
z *Employee, kindness to,* Deut. 24:14.

a *Hunger,* Neh. 9:15.

**18**
b *Repentance,* Mark 1:4.
c *Conviction of Sin,* John 16:8.
d *God, fatherhood of,* Gen. 2:2.
e *Sin, confession of,* Rom. 5:12.

**19**
f *Humility,* Prov. 22:4.
g *Hired Servant,* Lev. 25:40.

**20**
h *Parents, affection of, exemplified,* 2 Cor. 12:14.
i *God, love of,* Gen. 2:2.
j *Sin, forgiveness of,* Rom. 5:12.
k *Kiss,* Ruth 1:14.

**23**
l *Feasts,* Mark 12:39.

**24**
m *Joy,* Psa. 5:11.

**25**
n *Dancing,* Eccl. 3:4.

**28**
o *Anger,* Psa. 37:8.
p *God, longsuffering of,* Gen. 2:2.

**29**
q *Murmuring,* Num. 14:2.
r *Self-righteousness,* Luke 18:11.
s *Jealousy,* Psa. 78:58.

*** CITIZENS. Duties of:** *To honor rulers,* Ex. 22:28; Num. 27:20; Job 34:18; Prov. 16:14, 15; 24:21; 25:6, 7, 15; Eccl. 10:4, 20; Acts 23:5; 1 Pet. 2:17. *To pray for rulers,* Ezra 6:10; 1 Tim. 2:1, 2. *To promote peace,* Jer. 29:7. *To obey the law,* Ezra 7:26; 10:8; Eccl. 8:2–4; Acts 19:35–41; Rom. 13:1–7; Tit. 3:1; 1 Pet. 2:13–16.

*To pay taxes,* Matt. 17:24–27; 22:17–21; Mark 12:14–17; Luke 20:22–25; Rom. 13:5–7.

**Rights of:** *Public vindication when falsely accused,* Acts 16:37. *Protection from mob violence,* Acts 19:36–41. *Fair trial in courts,* Acts 22:25–29; 24:18, 19; 25:16, with vs. 5, 10, 11.

**Loyal.** INSTANCES OF: *Israelites,* Josh. 1:16–18; 2 Sam. 3:36, 37; 15:23, 30; 18:3; 21:17. *David,* 1 Sam 24:6–11; 26:6–16; 2 Sam. 1:14. *Hushai,* 2 Sam. 17:15, 16. *David's soldiers,* 2 Sam. 18:12, 13; 23:15, 16. *Joab,* 2 Sam. 19:5, 6. *Barzillai,* 2 Sam. 19:32. *Jehoiada,* 2 Kin. 11:4–12. *Isaiah,* Isa. 22:4. *Jeremiah,* the Book of Lamentations. *Mordecai,* Esth. 2:21–23.

**Wicked and treasonable,** Prov. 17:11; 19:10, 12; 2 Tim. 3:1–4; 2 Pet. 2:10; Jude 8.

INSTANCES OF WICKED: *Miriam and Aaron,* Num. 12:1–11. *Korah, Dathan and Abiram,* Num. 16:1–35; 26:9. *Shechemites,* Judg. 9:1–6, 23, 25, 46–49. *Ephraimites,* Judg. 12:1–4. *Israelites,* 1 Sam. 10:27; 1 Kin. 12:16–19. *Absalom,* 2 Sam. 15:10–13. *Ahithophel,* 2 Sam. 15:12; 17:1–4. *Sheba* 2 Sam. 20:1, 2. *Adonijah,* 1 Kin. 1:5–7. *Jeroboam,* 1 Kin. 11:26; 12:20; 2 Chr. 13:5–9. *Baasha,* 1 Kin. 15:27. *Zimri,* 1 Kin. 16:9, 10. *Jozachar and Jozabad,* 2 Kin. 12:20, 21; 14:5. *Shallum,* 2 Kin. 15:10. *Menahem,* 2 Kin. 15:14. *Pekah,* 2 Kin. 15:25. *Hoshea,* 2 Kin. 15:30. *Sons of Sennacherib,* 2 Kin. 19:37; 2 Chr. 32:21. *Ishmael,* Jer. 40:14–16; 41. *Bigthan and Teresh,* Esth. 2:21. *Jews,* Ezek. 17:12–20. *Barabbas,* Mark 15:7. *Theudas and four hundred seditious persons,* Acts 5:36. *Judas,* Acts 5:37.

**Figurative,** Eph. 2:19; Phil. 3:20 [R. V.].

thou art ever with me, and all that I have is thine.

32 It was meet that we should make merry, and be glad: for this thy brother was dead, and is alive again; and was lost, and is found.

## CHAPTER 16

*The parable of the unjust steward. 13 Jesus reproves the covetous Pharisees. 19 The parable of the rich man and Lazarus.*

AND he [a]said also unto his [b]disciples, There was a certain rich man, which had a [c]steward; and the same was accused unto him that he had [d,e]wasted his goods.

2 And he called him, and [f]said unto him, How is it that I hear this of thee? give an account of thy [g]stewardship; for thou mayest be no longer steward.

3 Then the [c]steward said within himself, What shall I do? for my lord taketh away from me the stewardship: I cannot dig; to beg I am ashamed.

4 I am resolved what to do, that, when I am put out of the stewardship, they may receive me into their houses.

5 So he called every one of his lord's debtors *unto him*, and said unto the first, How much owest thou unto my lord?

6 And he said, An hundred [h]measures of [i]oil. And he said unto him, Take thy bill, and sit down quickly, and write fifty.

7 Then said he to another, And how much owest thou? And he said, An hundred [j]measures of [k]wheat. And he said unto him, Take thy bill, and write fourscore.

8 And the lord commended the unjust steward, because he had done wisely: for the children of this world are in their generation [l]wiser than the [m]children of [n,o]light.

9 And I say unto you, Make to yourselves friends of the [p,q]mammon of unrighteousness; that, when ye fail, they may receive you into everlasting habitations.

10 He that is [*,r]faithful in that which is least is faithful also in much: and he that is [s]unjust in the least is unjust also in much.

11 If therefore ye have [†]not been faithful in the unrighteous [p,q]mammon, who will commit to your trust the true *riches*?

12 And if ye have [†]not been faithful in that which is another man's, who shall give you that which is your own?

13 [u]No servant can [v]serve two masters: for either he will hate the one, and love the other; or else he will hold to the one, and despise the other. Ye cannot serve God and [p,w]mammon.

14 ¶ And the [x]Phăr'ĭ-seeş also, who were [y]covetous, heard all these things: and they [z]derided him.

15 And he said unto them, Ye are they which [a,b]justify yourselves before men; but God [c]knoweth your [d]hearts: for that which is highly esteemed among men is [e]abomination in the sight of God.

16 [f]The [g]law and the [h]prophets *were* until [i]Jŏhn: since that time the [j,k]kingdom of God is [l]preached, and every man presseth into it.

17 And [m]it is easier for heaven

**1**
a *Parables, of Jesus*, Ezek. 20:49.
b *Disciples*, Matt. 9:14.
c *Steward*, Gen. 43:19.
d *Dishonesty*, Ezek. 22:13.
e *Worldliness*, 1 John 2:15.

**2**
f *Reproof, faithfulness in*, Prov. 17:10.
g *Probation*, Rom. 5:4.

**6**
h *Measure, liquid*, Deut. 25:15.
i *Oil*, Deut. 12:17.

**7**
j *Measure, dry*, Deut. 25:15.
k *Wheat*, Ezra 6:9.

**8**
l *Wisdom, worldly*, Prov. 2:2.
m *Righteous, described*, Psa. 64:10.
n *Light, figurative*, Matt. 5:14.
o *Wisdom, spiritual*, Prov. 2:2.

**9**
p Matt. 6:24.
q *Riches*, Eccl. 4:8.

**10**
r *Christian Graces, faithfulness*, Gal. 5:22.
s *Injustice*, Isa. 26:10.

**11**
t *Opportunity, the measure of responsibility*, Gal. 6:10.

**13**
u *Servant*, Jer. 2:14.
v *Hypocrisy*, Jas. 3:17.
w *Worldliness*, 1 John 2:15.

**14**
x *Pharisees*, Matt. 15:12.
y *Covetousness*, Isa. 57:17.
z *Scoffing, instances of*, Hab. 1:10.

**15**
a *Self-righteousness*, Luke 18:11.
b *Hypocrisy*, Jas. 3:17.
c *God, knowledge of*, Gen. 2:2.
d *Heart, known to God*, Psa. 44:21.
e *Sin, repugnant to God*, Rom. 5:12.

**16**
f Matt. 11:12.
g *Law, of Moses, temporary*, Deut. 33:2.
h *Prophecies*, Dan. 9:24.
i *John the Baptist*, Luke 1:63.
j *Kingdom of Heaven*, Matt. 13:24.
k *Gospel*, Mark 13:10.
l *Preaching*, Matt. 9:35.

**17**
m Matt. 5:18; Luke 21:32, 33.

* **FAITHFULNESS**, Psa. 12:1; Prov. 20:6. *Required*, Matt. 24:45–51 (with Luke 12:36–48); 25:14–30 (with Luke 19:12–27). *A fruit of the Spirit*, Gal. 5:22.

**Rewards of**, Psa. 31:23; Prov. 28:20; Matt. 10:22; 13:12; 25:29; Mark 13:13; Heb. 10:34; Rev. 2:10.

INSTANCES AND EXEMPLIFICATIONS OF: *Abraham*, Gal. 3:9. *Abraham's servant*, Gen. 24:33. *Moses*, Num. 12:7; Heb. 3:5. *David*, 2 Sam. 22:22–25. *Elijah*, 1 Kin. 19:10, 14. *Josiah*, 2 Kin. 22:2. *Abijah*, 2 Chr. 13:10–12. *Jehoshaphat*, 2 Chr 20:1–30. *Workmen in temple repairs*, 2 Kin. 12:15; 2 Chr. 34:12. *Hanani and Hananiah*, Neh. 7:1, 2. *Nehemiah's treasurer*, Neh. 13:13. *Job*, Job 1:21, 22; 2:9, 10. *The three Hebrew captives*, Dan. 3:16–18. *Daniel*, Dan. 6:10. *Jesus*, John 4:34; Heb. 3:2. *Paul*, 1 Tim. 1:12; 2 Tim. 4:7.

See footnote, REWARD, A MOTIVE, *To faithfulness*, Matt. 5:12.

† **UNFAITHFULNESS.** *Unfaithful in little, unfaithful in much*, Luke 16:10. *Brings, spiritual bankruptcy*, Matt. 13:12; 25:29; *destruction*, John 15:2. *Denounced in parables, of the vineyard*, Isa. 5:1–7; Matt. 21:33–43; Mark 12:1–9; *of the slothful servant*, Matt. 25:24–30; Luke 19:20–27. *Illustrated by the unfruitful branch*, John 15:2, 4, 6.

and earth to pass, than one tittle[C]
of the [g]law to fail.
18 Whosoever [n]putteth away
his [o]wife, and [p]marrieth another,
committeth [q]adultery: and whosoever marrieth her that is put
away from *her* husband committeth adultery.
19 ¶ [r]There was a certain
[s]rich man, which was [t,u]clothed
in purple and fine [v]linen, and
fared[C] sumptuously[C] every day:
20 And there was a certain
[‡]beggar named Lăz′a-rŭs, which
was laid at his gate, full of sores,
21 And desiring to be fed with
the crumbs which fell from the
[s]rich man's table: moreover the
[w]dogs came and licked his sores.
22 And it came to pass, that
the [‡,x]beggar [y]died, and was carried by the [z]angels[C] [a]into [b]Ā′bră-
hăm's bosom: the rich man also
[c]died, and was [d]buried;
23 And in [1,e]hell[C] he lift up his
eyes, being in [f,g]torments, and
seeth [b]Ā′bră-hăm afar off, and
Lăz′a-rŭs in his bosom.
24 And he cried and said, Father [b]Ā′bră-hăm, have mercy on
me, and send Lăz′a-rŭs, that he
may dip the tip of his finger in
water, and cool my tongue; for I
am [f,g]tormented in this flame.
25 But [b]Ā′bră-hăm said, Son,
remember that thou in thy
lifetime [h]receivedst thy good
things, and likewise Lăz′a-rŭs
evil things: but now he is comforted, and thou art tormented.
26 And beside all this, between
us and you there is a great gulf
fixed: so that they which would
pass from hence[C] to you cannot;
neither can they pass to us, that
*would come* from thence[C].
27 Then he said, I pray thee
therefore, father, that thou wouldest send him to my father's house:
28 For I have five brethren;
that he may testify unto them,
lest they also come into this
place of torment.
29 [b]Ā′bră-hăm saith unto him,
They have [i]Mō′ṣeṣ and the
[i]prophets; let them hear them.
30 And he said, Nay[C], father
Ā′bră-hăm: but if one went unto
them from the dead, they will
[j]repent.
31 And he said unto him, If
they [k,l]hear not [i]Mō′ṣeṣ and the
[i]prophets, [m]neither will they be
persuaded, though one [n]rose
from the dead.

## CHAPTER 17

*Jesus exhorts to avoid offences.* 3 *How to deal with an offending brother.* 5 *The necessity and power of faith.* 7 *All are unprofitable servants.* 11 *Ten lepers healed.* 20 *The kingdom of God.* 22 *The coming of the Son of man.*

THEN said he unto the disciples, [a]It is impossible
but that [1,b,c]offences will come:
but woe *unto him*, through whom
they come!
2 [d]It were better for him that a
[e]millstone were hanged about his
neck, and he cast into the sea,
than that he should [2,b,c]offend[C]
one of these little ones.
3 ¶ [f,g]Take heed to yourselves:
[h]If thy brother [i]trespass against
thee, [j]rebuke[C] him; and if he [k]re-
pent, [l,m,n]forgive him.
4 And if he [i]trespass[C] against
thee [o]seven times in a day, and
seven times in a day turn again
to thee, [p]saying, I [k]repent; thou
shalt [l,m,n]forgive him.
5 ¶ And the [q]apostles [r]said unto
the Lord, Increase our faith.[S T]
6 And the Lord said, [s]If ye had
[t]faith as a grain of mustard seed,
ye might say unto this sycamine
tree, Be thou plucked up by the
root, and be thou planted in the
sea; and it should obey you.
7 But which of you, having a
[u]servant plowing or feeding cattle, will say unto him by and by,

**18**
*n* *Divorce,* Matt. 19:7.
*o* *Wife,* Prov. 5:18.
*p* *Marriage,* Gen. 34:9.
*q* *Adultery,* Lev. 20:10.

**19**
*r* *Parables, of Jesus,* Ezek. 20:49.
*s* *Rich,* Jas. 5:1.
*t* *Wicked, prosperity of,* Psa. 73:3.
*u* *Worldliness, instances of,* 1 John 2:15.
*v* *Linen,* Ezek. 27:16.

**21**
*w* *Dog,* 1 Kin. 21:19.

**22**
*x* *Poor, God's care of,* Prov. 21:13.
*y* *Death, of the righteous,* Num. 23:10.
*z* *Angel, functions of,* Heb. 1:13.
*a* *Heaven, future home of the righteous,* Luke 18:22.
*b* *Abraham,* Gen. 17:5.
*c* *Death, of the wicked,* Num. 23:10.
*d* *Burial,* Acts 8:2.

**23**
*e* *Hell,* Mark 9:43.
*f* *Sorrow, of the lost,* Matt. 13:42.
*g* *Wicked, punishment of,* Psa. 73:3.
1 R. V. Hades

**25**
*h* *Wicked, prosperity of,* Psa. 73:3.

**29**
*i* *Word of God,* Psa. 119:9.

**30**
*j* *Repentance,* Mark 1.4.

**31**
*k* *Impenitence,* Rom. 2:5.
*l* *Unbelief,* Heb. 3:12.
*m* *Obduracy,* Prov. 29:1.
*n* *Resurrection,* 1 Cor. 15:12.

**1**
*a* Matt. 18:6, 7; Mark 9:42.
*b* *Temptation, leading into,* Luke 11:4.
*c* *Unbelief,* Heb. 3:12.
1 R. V. occasions of stumbling should come:

**2**
*d* *Wicked, punishment of,* Psa. 73:3.
*e* *Millstone,* Judg. 9:53.
2 R. V. cause one of these little ones to stumble.

**3**
*f* *Commandment, enjoining watchfulness and forgiveness,* Deut. 8:2.
*g* *Watchfulness, enjoined,* Matt. 24:42.
*h* Matt. 18:15–35.
*i* *Trespass,* Ex. 22:9.
*j* *Reproof, enjoined,* Prov. 17:10.
*k* *Repentance,* Mark 1:4.
*l* *Forgiveness,* Matt. 18:21.
*m* *Duty, of man to man,* Eccl. 12:13.
*n* *Charitableness, enjoined,* Prov. 10:12.

**4**
*o* *Seven,* Gen. 7:2.
*p* *Sin, confession of,* Rom. 5:12.

**5**
*q* *Apostles,* Luke 6:13.
*r* *Faith, prayer for increase of,* Mark 11:22.

**6**
*s* Matt. 17:20; 21:21; Mark 11:23.
*t* *Faith, enjoined,* Mark 11:22.

**7**
*u* *Servant,* Jer. 2:14.

‡ **BEGGARS,** 1 Sam. 2:8; Psa. 37:25; Prov. 20:4; Luke 16:3.
**Instances of:** *Bartimæus,* Mark 10:46. *Lazarus,* Luke 16:20–22. *The blind man,* John 9:8. *The lame man,* Acts 3:2–6.
See footnote, POOR, Prov. 21:13.

when he is come from the field,
Go and sit down to meat?
8 And will not rather say unto
him, Make ready wherewith I
may sup, and gird thyself, and
serve me, till I have eaten and
drunken; and afterward thou
shalt eat and drink?
9 Doth he thank that servant
because he did the things that
were commanded him? I trow
not.
10 [v]So likewise ye, when ye
shall have done all those things
which are commanded you, say,
We are unprofitable servants:
we have done that which was our
[w]duty to do.
11 ¶ And it came to pass, as
he went to [x]Jĕ-rṳ'să-lĕm, that he
passed through the midst of [y]Să-
mā'rĭ-ȧ and [z]Găl'ĭ-lee.
12 And as he entered into a certain village, there met him ten
men that were [a]lepers, which
stood [b]afar off:
13 And they lifted up *their*
voices, and [c]said, Jē'ṣus, Master, have mercy on us.
14 And when he saw *them*, he
said unto them, Go [d]shew yourselves unto the [e]priests. And it
came to pass, that, as they went,
they were [f,g]cleansed.
15 And one of them, when he
saw that he was [f]healed, turned
back, and with a [h]loud voice
[i,j]glorified God,
16 And fell down on *his* face at
his feet, giving him [k]thanks: and
he was a [l]Să-măr'ĭ-tan.
17 And Jē'ṣus answering said,
Were there not ten cleansed? but
[m]where *are* the nine?
18 There are not found that
returned to give [i]glory to God,
save this [n]stranger.
19 And he said unto him,
Arise, go thy way: thy [c]faith
hath made thee whole.
20 ¶ And when he was de-
manded of the [o]Phăr'ĭ-seeṣ,
when the [p]kingdom of God
should come, he answered them
and said, The kingdom of God
cometh not with observation:
21 Neither shall they say, Lo
here! or, Lo there! for, behold,
the kingdom of God is within
you.
22 ¶ And he [q]said unto the [r]dis-
ciples, The days will come, when
ye shall desire to see one of the
days of the Son of man, and ye
shall not see *it*.
23 And [s]they shall say to you,
See here; or, See there: go not
after *them*, nor follow *them*.
24 For as the [t]lightning, that
lighteneth out of the one *part*
under heaven, shineth unto the
other *part* under heaven; [q]so
shall also the Son of man be
[u]in his day.
25 [q]But first must he [v]suffer
many things, and be [w]rejected of
this generation.
26 And as it was in the days of
[x]Nō'e, so shall it be also in the
days of the Son of man.
27 [y,z]They did eat, they drank,
they [a]married wives, they were
given in marriage, until the day
that [b]Nō'e entered into the [c]ark,
and the [d]flood came, and [e,f]de-
stroyed them all.
28 Likewise also as it was in
the days of [g]Lŏt; [h,i]they did eat,
they drank, they bought, they
sold, they planted, they builded;
29 But the same day that [g]Lŏt
went out of [j]Sŏd'om it rained
fire and brimstone from heaven,
and [e]destroyed *them* all.
30 Even thus shall it be in the
day when the Son of man is [k]re-
vealed.
31 [l]In that day, he which shall
be upon the housetop, and his
stuff in the house, let him not
come down to take it away: and
he that is in the field, let him
likewise not return back.
32 [m,n]Remember [g]Lŏt's [o]wife.

10
*v Humility, enjoined*, Prov. 22:4.
*w Duty, of man to God*, Eccl. 12:13.

11
*x Jerusalem*, Judg. 19:10.
*y Samaria*, Isa. 7:9.
*z Galilee*, Mark 6:21.

12
*a Leprosy*, Lev. 13:2.
*b Sanitation and Hygiene, isolation*, Num. 31:23.

13
*c Faith in Christ*, John 6:69.

14
*d Leprosy, law concerning*, Lev. 13:2.
*e Priest*, Lev. 1:5.
*f Healing, by Jesus*, Acts 4:22.
*g Miracles, of Jesus*, Luke 23:8.

15
*h Shouting*, 2 Chr. 15:14.
*i Glorifying God*, Luke 5:25.
*j Praise*, Psa. 150:1.

16
*k Thankfulness, to God*, Acts 24:3.
*l Samaria*, Isa. 7:9.

17
*m Ingratitude, of man to God*, Rom. 1:21.

18
*n Foreigners*, Deut. 23:20.

20
*o Pharisees*, Matt. 15:12.

*p Kingdom of Heaven*, Matt. 13:24.

22
*q Jesus, prophet*, Matt. 1:21.
*r Disciples*, Matt. 9:14.

23
*s False Teachers*, 2 Pet. 2:1.

24
*t Lightning*, Job 28:26.
*u Jesus, second coming of*, Matt. 1:21.

25
*v Jesus, death of*, Matt. 1:21.
*w Jesus, rejected*, Matt. 1:21.

26
*x* Or, *Noah*, Gen. 5:29.

27
*y Worldliness, instances of*, 1 John 2:15.
*z False Confidence*, Psa. 30:6.
*a Marriage*, Gen. 34:9.
*b* Or, *Noah*, Gen. 5:29.
*c Ark*, Gen. 6:14.
*d Flood*, Gen. 6:17.
*e Wicked, punishment of*, Psa. 73:3.
*f Antediluvians, destruction of*, Gen. 6:1.

28
*g Lot*, Gen. 11:27.
*h Worldliness, instances of*, 1 John 2:15.
*i False Confidence*, Psa. 30:6.

29
*j Sodom*, Gen. 13:10.

30
*k Jesus, second coming of*, Matt. 1:21.

31
*l Jerusalem, destruction of, foretold*, Judg. 19:10.

32
*m Backsliding, admonitions against*, Hos. 11:7.
*n Instability, instances of*, Jas. 1:8.
*o Women, wicked*, Prov. 31:10.

33 [p]Whosoever shall seek to save his life shall [e]lose it; and whosoever shall [q]lose his life shall preserve it.

34 I tell you, in that night there shall be two *men* in one bed; the one shall be taken, and the other shall be left.

35 [r]Two *women* shall be grinding together; the one shall be taken, and the other left.

36 Two *men* shall be in the field; the one shall be taken, and the other left.

37 And they answered and said unto him, Where, Lord? And he said unto them, [s]Wheresoever the body *is*, thither will the eagles be gathered together.

## CHAPTER 18

*The parables of the importunate widow;* 9 *and of the Pharisee and publican.* 15 *Jesus receives little children.* 18 *The rich ruler answered.* 34 *It is hard for a rich man to enter the kingdom of God.* 28 *The reward of those who forsake all and follow Jesus.* 31 *Jesus foretells his own death and resurrection.* 35 *He heals a blind man at Jericho.*

AND he spake a [a]parable unto them *to this end,* that men ought always to [b,c]pray, and not to [d,e]faint;

2 Saying, There was in a city a [f]judge, which feared not God, neither regarded man:

3 And there was a [g]widow in that city; and she came unto him, saying, Avenge me of mine adversary.

4 And he would not for a while: but afterward he said within himself, Though I fear not God, nor regard man;

5 Yet [h]because this [g]widow troubleth me, I will avenge her, lest by her continual coming she weary me.

6 And the Lord said, Hear what the unjust [f]judge saith.

7 And [i,j]shall not God [k]avenge his own [l]elect, which cry day and night unto him, though [m]he bear long with them?

8 I tell you that he will avenge them speedily. Nevertheless when the Son of man [n]cometh, [o]shall he find [p]faith on the earth?

9 ¶ And he spake this [a]parable unto certain which [q]trusted in themselves that they were righteous, and [r]despised others:

10 Two men went up into the [s]temple to [t]pray; the one a [u]Phăr′ĭ-see, and the other a [v]publican.

11 The [u]Phăr′ĭ-see [w,x]stood and prayed thus with himself, God, I thank thee, that *,[y,z]I am not as other men *are,* [a]extortioners, [b]unjust, [c]adulterers, or even as this [d]publican.

12 *I [e,f]fast twice in the week, I [e]give [g]tithes of all that I possess.

13 And the [d]publican, standing afar off, [h]would not lift up so much as *his* eyes unto heaven, but smote upon his breast, [i,j,k]saying, God be [l]merciful to me a sinner.

14 I tell you, [m]this man went down to his house [n,o]justified *rather* than the other: [e]for every one that [p,q]exalteth himself shall be abased; and he that [r]humbleth himself shall be exalted.

15 ¶ And they brought unto him also infants, that he would touch them: but when *his* [s]disciples saw *it,* [t]they [u]rebuked them.

16 But Jē′ṣus called them *unto*

**33** *p Paradox,* 2 Cor. 12:4. *q Renunciation, of self for Christ,* Luke 5:11.

**35** *r* Matt. 24:41.

**36** 3 R. V. *omits this verse.*

**37** *s* Matt. 24:28.

**1** *a Parables, of Jesus,* Ezek. 20:49. *b Prayer, enjoined,* Acts 6:4. *c Adversity, prayer in,* Psa. 10:6. *d Despondency,* Eccl. 2:20. *e Adversity, despondency in,* Psa. 10:6.

**2** *f Judge,* Judg. 2:18.

**3** *g Widow,* 2 Sam. 14:5.

**5** *h Selfishness,* 2 Tim. 3:2.

**7** *i Prayer, answer to, promised,* Acts 6:4. *j Righteous, promises to,* Psa. 64:10. *k Vengeance,* Psa. 94:1. *l Election of Grace,* Rom. 11:5. *m God, longsuffering of,* Gen. 2:2.

**8** *n Jesus, second coming of,* Matt. 1:21. *o Unbelief,* Heb. 3:12. *p Faith in Christ,* John 6:69.

**9** *q False Confidence,* Psa. 30:6. *r Bigotry,* Isa. 65:5.

**10** *s Temple, Herod's,* 1 Kin. 6:17. *t Worship, public,* Gen. 22:5. *u Pharisees,* Matt. 15:12. *v Publicans,* Matt. 11:19.

**11** *w Prayer, postures in,* Acts 6:4. *x* Matt. 6:1. *y Presumption,* Psa. 19:13. *z Delusion,* 2 Thess. 2:11.

*a Extortion,* Isa. 16:4. *b Injustice,* Isa. 26:10. *c Adultery,* Lev. 20:10. *d Publicans,* Matt. 11:19.

**12** *e Works, insufficiency of, for salvation,* v. 14; 2 Tim. 1:9. *f Fasting,* Zech. 8:19. *g Tithes,* Num. 18:24.

**13** *h Humility, exemplified,* Prov. 22:4. *i Prayer, penitential,* Acts 6:4. *j Sin, confession of,* Rom. 5:12. *k Repentance, instances of,* Mark 1:4. *l God, mercy of,* Gen. 2:2. **14** *m Penitent, promises to,* Psa. 51:17. *n Justification,* Rom. 4:25. *o Sin, forgiveness of,* Rom. 5:12. *p Self-exaltation,* Luke 14:11. *q Pride,* Prov. 16:18. *r Humility, rewards of,* Prov. 22:4. **15** *s Disciples,* Matt. 9:14. *t Minister, intolerance of,* Rom. 15:16. *u Presumption, instances of,* Psa. 19:13.

* **SELF-RIGHTEOUSNESS,** Prov. 30:12, 13; Jer. 2:13, 22, 23, 34, 35; 8:8; Hab. 2:4; Gal. 6:3; Rev. 3:17, 18. *Assertive,* Prov. 20:6; Matt. 7:22, 23. *Delusive,* Prov. 12:15; 16:2; 21:2; 28:26; Isa. 28:20; 50:11; 64:6; Hos. 12:8; Matt. 7:22, 23; 22:12, 13.

*Admonitions against,* Deut. 9:4–6; 2 Cor. 10:17, 18. *Denounced,* Isa. 5:21; 65:5; Jer. 17:5; Matt. 16:6; 22:12, 13; 23:29–31; Mark 8:15.

*Job accused of,* Job 11:4; 32:1, 2; 33:8, 9; 35:2, 7, 8.

See footnotes: HYPOCRISY, Jas. 3:17; SELF-EXALTATION, Luke 14:11.

**Instances of:** *Saul,* 1 Sam. 15:13–21. *The rich young ruler,* Matt. 19:16–22; Mark 10:17–22; Luke 18:18–23. *Lawyer,* Luke 10:25–29. *Pharisees,* Matt. 9:11–13; Mark 2:16, 17; Luke 7:39; 15:2; 16:14, 15; 18:9–14; John 9:28–41. *Israel,* Rom. 10:3. *Church of Laodicea,* Rev. 3:17.

*him,* and [v,w]said, Suffer little
children to come unto me, and
forbid them not: for of such is
the [x,y]kingdom of God.
17 Verily I say unto you, Whosoever shall not receive the [x]king-
dom of God [z]as a little child shall
in no wise enter therein.
18 ¶ [a]And a certain [b]ruler asked
him, saying, Good Master, what
shall I do to inherit [c]eternal
[d]life?
19 And Jē′ṣus said unto him,
Why callest thou me good? none
*is* good, save one, *that is,* [e]God.
20 Thou knowest the com-
mandments, [f]Do not commit
[g]adultery, [h]Do not [i]kill, [j]Do
not [k]steal, [l]Do not bear [m]false
witness, [n,o,p]Honour thy [q]father
and thy [r]mother.
21 And he said, *All these have
I [s]kept from my youth up.
22 Now when Jē′ṣus heard
these things, he said unto him,
Yet lackest thou one thing:
[t,u,v]sell all that thou hast, and
[w]distribute unto the poor, and
[x]thou shalt have treasure in
†heaven: and come, follow me.
23 And when he heard this, he
was very sorrowful: for [y]he was
very rich.
24 And [1]when Jē′ṣus saw that
he was very sorrowful, he said,
How hardly shall [y]they that have
[z]riches enter into the [a]kingdom
of God!
25 For [b]it is easier for a camel
to go through a needle's eye,
than for a [c]rich man to enter
into the [a]kingdom of God.
26 And they that heard *it* said,
Who then can be saved?
27 And he said, [d]The things
which are impossible with men
are possible with God.
28 ¶ [e]Then [f]Pē′tĕr said, Lo, we
have [g,h,i]left all, and followed
thee.
29 And he said unto them, Verily I say unto you, There is no
man that hath [h,i]left house, or
parents, or brethren, or wife, or
children, for the [a]kingdom of
God's sake,
30 [j,k]Who shall not receive
manifold more in this present
time, and in the world to come
[l,m]life everlasting.
31 ¶ Then he took *unto him* the
[n]twelve, and said unto them,
Behold, we go up to [o]Jĕ-ru̥′să-
lĕm, and all [p]things that are
written by the [q]prophets concerning the Son of man shall be
accomplished.
32 For he shall be delivered
unto the Ġĕn′tīleṣ, and shall
be [r]mocked, and [r]spitefully entreated, and [r]spitted on:
33 And they shall [s]scourge *him,*
and [t]put him to death: and the
third day he shall [u]rise again.
34 And they [v]understood none
of these things: and this saying was hid from them, neither
knew they the things which were
spoken.
35 ¶ [w]And it came to pass, that
as he was come nigh unto [x]Jĕr′ĭ-
chō, a certain [y]blind man sat by
the way side [z]begging:
36 And hearing the multitude
pass by, he asked what it meant.
37 And they told him, that [a]Jē′-
ṣus of [b]Năz′a-rĕth passeth by.

16
v *Commandment, enjoining discipling of children,* Deut. 8:2.
w *Jesus, love of,* Matt. 1:21.
x *Kingdom of Heaven,* Matt. 13:24.
y *Church, membership in,* Matt. 16:18.

17
z *Children, type of the regenerated,* Mark 10:14.

18
a Matt. 19:16–22; Mark 10:17–22.
b *Young Men,* Prov. 1:4.
c *Immortality,* 1 Cor. 15:54.
d *Life, everlasting,* Eccl. 8:15.

19
e *God, goodness of,* Gen. 2:2.

20
f Ex. 20:14.
g *Adultery,* Lev. 20:10.
h Ex. 20:13.
i *Homicide,* Deut. 5:17.
j Ex. 20:15.
k *Theft,* Mark 7:22.
l Ex. 20:16.
m *False Witness,* Matt. 19:18.
n Ex. 20:12.
o *Commandment, enjoining reverence for parents,* Deut. 8:2.
p *Children, commandments to,* Mark 10:14.
q *Father, to be revered,* Psa. 27:10.
r *Mother, reverence for, enjoined,* 1 Kin. 2:20.

21
s *Obedience, instances of,* Heb. 5:8.

22
t *Commandment, enjoining self-denial,* Deut. 8:2.
u *Discipleship of Jesus, tests of,* Matt. 10:32.
v *Renunciation, of possessions,* Luke 5:11. w *Poor, liberality to, rewarded,* Prov. 21:13. x *Promise, to the righteous, of treasure in heaven,* 2 Cor. 1:20. **23** y *Rich,* Jas. 5:1. **24** z *Riches, a snare,* Eccl. 4:8.—a *Kingdom of Heaven,* Matt. 13:24. 1 R. V. Jesus seeing him said, How **25** b Matt. 19:24; Mark 10:25. c *Rich,* Jas. 5:1.

27
d *God, power of,* Gen. 2:2.

28
e Matt. 19:27–30; Mark 10:28–31.
f *Peter,* Mark 5:37.
g *Decision, instances of,* Isa. 50:7.
h *Renunciation,* Luke 5:11.
i *Self-denial,* Mark 8:34.

30
j *Promise, to the righteous,* 2 Cor. 1:20.
k *Righteous, promises to,* Psa. 64:10.
l *Life, everlasting,* Eccl. 8:15.
m *Immortality,* 1 Cor. 15:54.

31
n *Apostles,* Luke 6:13.
o *Jerusalem,* Judg. 19:10.
p *Prophecies concerning the Messiah, and their fulfillment,* Gen. 12:3.
q *Prophets,* Isa. 3:2.

32
r *Jesus, sufferings of,* Matt. 1:21.
s *Smiting and Scourging of Jesus,* Isa. 50:6.
t *Jesus foretells his Death,* Matt. 17:22.
u *Resurrection of Jesus,* Matt. 28:6.

34
v *Spiritual Blindness,* 2 Cor. 4:4.

35
w Mark 10:46–52.
x *Jericho,* Num. 22:1.
y *Blindness,* 2 Kin. 6:18.
z *Beggars,* Luke 16:20.

37
a *Jesus, names of,* Matt. 1:21.
b *Nazareth,* John 1:46.

† **HEAVEN. God's dwelling place,** Deut. 26:15; 1 Kin. 8:30, 39, 43, 49; 1 Chr. 21:26; 2 Chr. 6:21, 27, 30, 33, 35, 39; 7:14; 30:27; Neh. 9:27; Job 22:12, 14; Psa. 2:4; 11:4; 20:6; 33:13; 102:19; 103:19; 113:5, 6; 123:1; Eccl. 5:2; Isa. 57:15; 63:15; 66:1; Lam. 3:41; Matt. 5:34; 6:9; 10:32, 33; 12:50; 16:17; 18:10, 14; Mark 11:25; Acts 7:49, 55, 56; Heb. 8:7.

Figurative: *Of the divine government,* Matt. 16:19; 18:18; 23:22. *Of God,* Matt. 21:25.

**The future home of the righteous,** Matt. 5:12; 13:30, 43; Luke 16:22; John 12:26; 13:36; 17:24; Phil. 3:20; Col. 1:5, 12; 1 Thess. 4:17; Rev. 2:7; 3:21; 14:13.

Called: *A city,* Heb. 11:10, 16; *a garner,* Matt. 3:12; *a house,* John 14:2, 3; 2 Cor. 5:1; *a kingdom,* Matt. 25:34; Luke 12:32; 22:29, 30; *kingdom of Christ and of God,* Eph. 5:5; *a heavenly country,* Heb. 11:16; *paradise,* Luke 23:43; 2 Cor. 12:2, 4.

*Everlasting,* 2 Cor. 5:1; Heb. 10:34; 13:14; 1 Pet. 1:4; 2 Pet. 1:11. *Allegorical representations of,* Rev. 4:1–11; 5:1–14; 7:9–17; 14:1–3; 15:1–8; 21; 22:1–5. *No marriage in,* Matt. 22:30; Luke 20:34–36. *Names of the righteous written in,* Luke 10:20; Heb. 12:22–24. *Treasure in,* Matt. 6:20; 19:21; Luke 12:33. *Joy in,* Psa. 16:11; Luke 15:6, 7, 10. *Righteousness dwells in,* 2 Pet. 3:13. *No sorrow in,* Rev. 7:16, 17; 21:4.

38
c *Prayer, importunity in,* Acts 6:4.
d *David,* 1 Sam. 16:13.
e *Faith in Christ, exemplified,* John 6:69.

40
f *Jesus, love of,* Matt. 1:21.

43
g *Miracles, of Jesus,* Luke 23:8.
h *Glorifying God,* Luke 5:25.
i *Thankfulness, to God,* Acts 24:3.
j *Jesus, received,* Matt. 1:21.
k *Praise,* Psa. 150:1.

1
a *Jericho,* Num. 22:1.

2
b *Publicans,* Matt. 11:19.
c *Rich, instances of,* Jas. 5:1.

4
d *Sycomore,* 2 Chr. 1:15.

6
e *Hospitality, instances of,* Rom. 12:13.

38 And he [c]cried, saying, Jē′-
ṣus, *thou* [a]son of [d]Dā′vid, [e]have
mercy on me.
39 And they which went before rebuked him, that he should
hold his peace: but he [c]cried so
much the more, *Thou* [a]son of
[d]Dā′vid, [e]have mercy on me.
40 And [f]Jē′ṣus stood, and commanded him to be brought unto
him: and when he was come
near, he asked him,
41 [f]Saying, What wilt thou that
I shall do unto thee? And he
said, [e]Lord, that I may receive
my sight.
42 And Jē′ṣus said unto him,
Receive thy sight: thy [e]faith
hath saved thee.
43 And immediately he [g]re-
ceived his sight, and followed
him, [h,i]glorifying God: and [j]all
the people, when they saw *it*,
gave [k]praise unto God.

## CHAPTER 19

*Zacchæus the publican. 11 The parable of the ten pounds. 28 Jesus' public entry into Jerusalem. 41 He weeps over the city; 45 drives the traders out of the temple; 47 and teaches daily in it.*

AND *Jē′ṣus* entered and
passed through [a]Jĕr′ĭ-chō.
2 And, behold, *there was* a
man named Zăc-chæ′us, which
was the chief among the [b]pub-
licans, and he was [c]rich.
3 And he sought to see Jē′ṣus
who he was; and could not for
the press, because he was little
of stature.
4 And he ran before, and
climbed up into a [d]sycomore
tree to see him: for he was to
pass that *way*.
5 And when Jē′ṣus came to the
place, he looked up, and saw
him, and said unto him, Zăc-
chæ′us, make haste, and come
down; for to day I must abide
at thy house.
6 And he made haste, and
came down, and [e]received him
joyfully.
7 And when they saw *it*, they
all murmured, [f]saying, That he
was gone to be guest with a
man that is a sinner.
8 And Zăc-chæ′us stood, and
said unto the Lord; Behold,
Lord, the half of my goods I
[g,h]give to the [i]poor; and if I
have [1]taken any thing from any
man by [j]false accusation, I [k,l]re-
store *him* fourfold.
9 And Jē′ṣus said unto him,
This day is [m]salvation come to
this house, forsomuch as he also
is a son of [n]Ā′brā-hăm.
10 [o]For the Son of man is
come [p]to seek and [p]to [q]save
that which was [r]lost.
11 ¶ And as they heard these
things, he added and spake a
[s]parable, because he was nigh
to [t]Jē-ru̦′să-lĕm, and because
they thought that the [u]king-
dom of God should immediately
appear.
12 He said therefore, [s,v]A certain nobleman went into a far
country to receive for himself a kingdom, and to [w]re-
turn.
13 And he called his ten servants, and [x]delivered them ten
pounds, and said unto them,
[2,y]Occupy till I come.
14 But his citizens hated him,
and sent [3]a message after him,
saying, We will not have this
*man* to reign over us.
15 And it came to pass, that
when he was [w,z]returned, having
received the kingdom, then he
commanded these servants to
be called unto him, to whom
he had given the money, that
he might know how much
every man had gained by trading.
16 Then came the first, saying,
Lord, [a]thy pound hath gained
ten pounds.
17 And he [b]said unto him,
Well, thou good [c]servant: [d]be-

7
f *Bigotry, instances of,* Isa. 65:5.

8
g *Liberality, instances of,* 1 Tim. 6:18.
h *Alms,* Matt. 6:2.
i *Poor, kindness to,* Prov. 21:13.
j *False Accusation,* 2 Tim. 3:3.
k *Restitution,* Ex. 22:3.
l *Integrity, instances of,* Job 2:3.
1 R. V. wrongfully exacted aught of any man, I restore

9
m *Salvation,* Acts 16:17.
n *Abraham,* Gen. 17:5.

10
o *Penitent, promises to,* Psa. 51:17.
p *Jesus, mission of,* Matt. 1:21.
q *Jesus, savior,* Matt. 1:21.
r *Wicked, described,* Psa. 73:3.

11
s *Parables, of Jesus,* Ezek. 20:49.
t *Jerusalem,* Judg. 19:10.
u *Kingdom of Heaven,* Matt. 13:24.

12
v Matt. 25:14-30.
w *Jesus, second coming of,* Matt. 1:21.

13
x *Opportunity, the measure of responsibility,* Gal. 6:10.
y *Probation,* Rom. 5:4.
2 R. V. Trade ye herewith

14
3 R. V. an ambassage

15
z *Judgment, the general,* 2 Pet. 3:7.

16
a *Opportunity, the measure of responsibility,* Gal. 6:10.

17
b *Judgment, according to opportunity and works,* 1 Pet. 1:17.
c *Servant, good,* Jer. 2:14.
d *Responsibility, according to privilege,* Ezek. 18:20.

*e Faithfulness,* Luke 16:10.
*f Righteous, described,* Psa. 64:10.
*g Reward, a motive, to faithfulness,* Matt. 5:12.
*h Righteous, promises to,* Psa. 64:10.

20
*i Servant, wicked and unfaithful,* Jer. 2:14.
*j Unfaithfulness,* Luke 16:11.
*k Idleness,* Eccl. 10:18.

21
*l Self-condemnation,* Job 9:20.

22
*m God, judge,* Gen. 2:2.

23
4 R. V. interest?

26
*n Proverbs,* 1 Sam. 24:13.
*o Promise, to the righteous,* 2 Cor. 1:20.
*p Righteousness,* Psa. 15:2.
*q Prosperity,* Eccl. 7:14.
*r Wicked, punishment of,* Psa. 73:3.

27
*s Jesus, rejected,* Matt. 1:21.
*t Jesus, king,* Matt. 1:21.

28
*u Jerusalem,* Judg. 19:10.

29
*v* Matt. 21:1; Mark 11:1.
*w Bethany,* John 11:18.
*x Mount of Olives,* Mark 11:1.
*y Apostles,* Luke 6:13.

cause thou hast been [e,f]faithful
in a very little, [g,h]have thou authority over ten cities.
18 And the second came, saying, Lord, [a]thy pound hath
gained five pounds.
19 And he [b]said likewise to him,
[g,h]Be thou also over five cities.
20 And [i]another came, saying,
Lord, behold, *here is* thy pound,
which I have [j]kept [k]laid up in a
napkin:
21 For [l]I feared thee, because
thou art an austere man: thou
takest up that thou layedst not
down, and reapest that thou
didst not sow.
22 And he saith unto him,
Out of thine own mouth will
I [b,m]judge thee, *thou* wicked
[i]servant. Thou knewest that I
was an austere man, taking up
that I laid not down, and reaping that I did not sow:
23 Wherefore then gavest not
thou my money into the bank,
that at my coming I might have
required mine own with [4]usury?
24 And he said unto them that
stood by, Take from him the
pound, and give *it* to him that
hath ten pounds.
25 (And they said unto him,
Lord, he hath ten pounds.)
26 For I say unto you, That
[n,o]unto every one which [p,q]hath
shall be given; and from him
that hath not, even that he hath
[r]shall be taken away from him.
27 But those mine enemies,
which [s]would not that I should
[t]reign over them, bring hither,
and [r]slay *them* before me.
28 And when he had thus spoken, he went before, ascending
up to [u]Jė-ru̥′sȧ-lĕm.
29 ¶ And it came to pass,
when he was come nigh to
[v]Bĕth′pha-ġē and [w]Bĕth′a-nȳ,
at the mount called *the mount*
of [x]Ŏl′ĭveș, he sent two of his
[y]disciples,

30 Saying, Go ye into the village over against *you*; in the
which at your entering ye shall
find a colt tied, whereon yet
never man sat: loose him, and
bring *him hither*.
31 And if any man ask you,
Why do ye loose *him*? thus shall
ye say unto him, Because the
Lord hath need of him.
32 And they that were sent
went their way, and found even
as he had said unto them.
33 And as they were loosing the
colt, the owners thereof said unto them, Why loose ye the colt?
34 And they said, The Lord
hath need of him.
35 And they brought him to
Jē′șus: and [z]they cast their garments upon the colt, and they set
Jē′șus thereon.
36 And as he went, [z]they spread
their clothes in the way.
37 And when he was [a]come
nigh, even now at the descent
of the [b]mount of Ŏl′ĭveș, [c]the
whole multitude of the [d]disci-
ples began to rejoice and [e]praise
God with a loud voice for all the
mighty works that they had seen;
38 [c]Saying, [e,f]Blessed *be* the
King that cometh in the name
of the Lord: peace in heaven,
and glory in the highest.
39 And some of the [g]Phăr′ĭ-
seeș from among the multitude
said unto him, Master, rebuke
thy [d]disciples.
40 And he answered and said
unto them, I tell you that, if
these should hold their peace,
the stones would immediately
cry out.
41 ¶ And when he was come
near, he beheld the [h]city, and
[i,j]wept over it,
42 Saying, If [k]thou hadst
known, even thou, at least in
this thy day, the things *which*
*belong* unto thy [l]peace! but now
they are [m]hid from thine eyes.

v.30–AD 30
See footnote, *Time,* Rev. 10:6.

35
*z Popularity of Jesus,* vs. 35–38; John 6:15.

37
*a Triumphal Entry of Jesus into Jerusalem,* vs. 35–38; Matt. 21:5.
*b Mount of Olives,* Mark 11:1.
*c Popularity of Jesus,* vs. 35–38; John 6:15.
*d Disciples,* Matt. 9:14.
*e Praise,* Psa. 150:1.

38
*f* Psa. 118:26; Matt. 21:9; 23:39; Mark 11:9; John 12:13.

39
*g Pharisees,* Matt. 15:12.

41
*h Jerusalem, destruction of, foretold,* vs. 42–44; Judg. 19:10.
*i Weeping,* Ezra 3:13.
*j Jesus, compassion of,* Matt. 1:21.

42
*k Unbelievers,* 1 Cor. 6:6.
*l Peace,* Jer. 29:7.
*m Spiritual Blindness,* 2 Cor. 4:4.

v.43–AD 30
See footnote, *Time*, Rev. 10:6.

**43**
*n* *Jesus, prophet*, Matt. 1:21.

**44**
*o* *Judgments*, Ex. 6:6.

**45**
*p* Matt. 21:12–14; Mark 11:15–18.
*q* *Temple, Herod's*, 1 Kin. 6:17.
5 R. V. *omits the rest of this verse.*

**46**
*r* *Prophecies, fulfilled*, Dan. 9:24.
*s* Isa. 56:7; Matt. 21:13; Mark 11:17.
*t* *Profanation, of the house of God*, Lev. 22:32.
*u* *Sacrilege, instances of*, Lev. 19:8.
*v* *Thieves*, Deut. 24:7.

**47**
*w* *Jesus, teacher*, Matt. 1:21.
*x* *Instruction, in religion*, Prov. 23:23.
*y* *Malice*, Eph. 4:31.
*z* *Persecution, of Jesus*, John 15:20.

**48**
*a* *Popularity of Jesus*, John 6:15.
*b* *Jesus, received*, Matt. 1:21.
*c* *Spiritual Desire*, Psa. 42:1.

**1**
*a* Matt. 21:23–27; Mark 11:27–33.
*b* *Jesus, teacher*, Matt. 1:21.
*c* *Instruction, in religion*, Prov. 23:23.
*d* *Temple, Herod's*, 1 Kin. 6:17.
*e* *Preaching*, Matt. 9:35.
*f* *Gospel*, Mark 13:10.
*g* *Priest*, Lev. 1:5.
*h* *Scribe*, 1 Kin. 4:3.

**3**
*i* *Tact*, Prov. 15:1.

43 [h,n]For the days shall come
upon thee, that thine enemies
shall cast a trench about thee,
and compass thee round, and
keep thee in on every side,
44 And [n]shall [o]lay [h]thee even
with the ground, and thy children within thee; and they shall
not leave in thee one stone upon
another; because thou [m]knewest
not the time of thy visitation.
45 [p]And he went into the [q]temple, and began to cast out them
that sold [5]therein, and them that
bought;
46 Saying unto them, It is
[r]written, My house is the [s]house
of prayer: but ye have [t,u]made it
a den of [v]thieves.
47 And he [w,x]taught daily
in the [q]temple. But the chief
priests and the scribes and the
chief of the people [y,z]sought to
destroy him,
48 And could not find what
they might do: for [a,b]all the
people were very attentive [c]to
hear him.

## CHAPTER 20

*Jesus silences those who question his authority. 9 The parable of the wicked husbandmen. 19 The question of the priests about paying tribute to Cæsar, 27 and of the Sadducees concerning the resurrection. 39 Christ the Son of David. 45 He warns the disciples to beware of the scribes.*

[a]AND it came to pass, *that* on
one of those days, as he
[b,c]taught the people in the [d]temple, and [e]preached the [f]gospel,
the chief [g]priests and the [h]scribes
came upon *him* with the elders,
2 And spake unto him, saying,
Tell us, by what authority doest
thou these things? or who is he
that gave thee this authority?
3 And he answered and [i]said
unto them, I will also ask you
one thing; and answer me:
4 [i]The *baptism of [j]Jŏhn, was
it from heaven, or of men?
5 And they [k]reasoned with themselves, saying, If we shall say,
From heaven; he will say, Why
then believed ye him not?
6 But and if we say, Of men;
[l]all the people will stone us: for
they be persuaded that [j]Jŏhn
was a [m]prophet.
7 And they answered, that they
could not tell whence *it was.*
8 And Jē'sus said unto them,
Neither tell I you by what authority I do these things.
9 Then began he to speak to the
people this [n]parable; [o]A certain
man planted a [p]vineyard, and
[q]let [r]it forth to [s,t]husbandmen,
and went into a far country for a
long time.
10 And at the [u]season he sent a
[v]servant to the [s,t]husbandmen,
that they should give him of the
[w]fruit of the [p]vineyard: but [x]the
husbandmen [y]beat [v]him, and
sent *him* away empty.
11 And again [z]he sent another
[v]servant: and they beat him also,
and entreated *him* shamefully,
and sent *him* away empty.
12 And again he sent a [v]third:
and [x]they [y]wounded him also,
and cast *him* out.
13 Then said the lord of the
[a]vineyard, What shall I do? I
will send my beloved [b]son: it
may be they will reverence *him*
[1]when they see him.
14 But when the [c,d]husbandmen saw him, they reasoned
among themselves, saying, This
is the heir: come, let us kill him,
that the inheritance may be
ours.
15 So they [e]cast him out of
the [a]vineyard, and [f,g]killed *him.*

v.4–AD 30
See footnote, *Time*, Rev. 10:6.

**4**
*j* *John the Baptist*, Luke 1:63.

**5**
*k* *Reasoning*, Job 13:6.

**6**
*l* *Public Opinion*, John 12:42.
*m* *Prophets*, Isa. 3:2.

**9**
*n* *Parables, of Jesus*, Ezek. 20:49.
*o* *Capital and Labor, strife between*, Matt. 21:35.
*p* *Vineyard, parable of*, Isa. 1:8.
*q* *Lease*, Matt. 21:33.
*r* *Land*, Ruth 4:3.
*s* *Husbandman, parable of*, Matt. 21:33.
*t* *Ecclesiasticism*, Matt. 23:2.

**10**
*u* *Seasons*, Dan. 2:21.
*v* *Prophets, persecutions of*, Isa. 3:2.
*w* *Grape*, Lev. 25:5.
*x* *Unfaithfulness*, Luke 16:11.
*y* *Persecution, of the righteous*, John 15:20.

**11**
*z* *God, longsuffering of*, Gen. 2:2.

**13**
*a* *Vineyard, parable of*, Isa. 1:8.
*b* *Jesus, divinity of*, Matt. 1:21.
1 R. V. *omits* when they see him.

**14**
*c* *Husbandman, parable of*, Matt. 21:33.
*d* *Ecclesiasticism*, Matt. 23:2.

**15**
*e* *Jesus, rejected*, Matt. 1:21.
*f* *Jesus, death of*, Matt. 1:21.
*g* *Homicide*, Deut. 5:17.

***BAPTISM.** *Of John the Baptist*, Matt. 3:5–8, 11 (with Mark 1:8; Luke 3:7, 8, 16; John 10:40); 21:25 (with Mark 11:30; Luke 20:4); Mark 1:4, 5; Luke 3:3, 7, 12, 16, 21; 7:29, 30; John 1:25, 26, 28, 31, 33; 3:23; Acts 1:5, 22; 10:37; 11:16; 13:24; 18:25; 19:3, 4.
*Of Jesus*, Matt. 3:13–16; Mark 1:9–10; Luke 3:21.
**Christian.** *Into the discipleship of Jesus*, Matt. 28:19; Mark 16:16; John 3:22, 26; 4:1, 2; Acts 2:38, 41; 8:12, 13, 16, 36–38; 9:18; 10:46–48; 16:14, 15, 33; 18:8; 19:4, 5; 22:16; Rom. 6:3, 4; 1 Cor. 1:13–17; Gal. 3:27; Eph. 4:5; Col. 2:12; 1 Pet. 3:21.
*To be administered in the name of the Father, and of the Son, and of the Holy Spirit*, Matt. 28:19. *For the dead*, 1 Cor. 15:29. *Of Holy Spirit*, see footnote, HOLY SPIRIT, Acts 1:2.
**Figurative**, Matt. 20:22, 23; Mark 10:38, 39; Luke 12:50. *Unto Moses*, 1 Cor. 10:1, 2.

v.15–AD 30
See footnote, *Time*, Rev. 10:6.

16
*h Wicked, punishment of*, Psa. 73:3.
*i Jews, prophecies concerning*, Neh. 4:2.
*j* Mark 12:9.

17
*k Reproof, faithfulness in*, Prov. 17:10.
*l Prophecies concerning the Messiah, and their fulfillment*, Dan. 9:24.
*m Corner Stone, figurative*, Psa. 144:12.
*n Church, Christ, the head of*, Matt. 16:18.
*o Jesus, head of the church*, Matt. 1:21.

18
2 R. V. broken to pieces;

19
*p Priest*, Lev. 1:5.
*q Scribe*, 1 Kin. 4:3.
*r Malice*, Eph. 4:31.
*s Public Opinion*, John 12:42.
*t Parables, of Jesus*, Ezek. 20:49.

20
*u* Matt. 22:15–22; Mark 12:13–17.
*v Spies*, Josh. 6:23.
*w Hypocrisy*, Jas. 3:17.
*x Deception, instances of*, Josh. 9:4.

21
*y Flattery*, Prov. 6:24.
*z Jesus, teacher*, Matt. 1:21.

22
*a Citizens, duties of*, Luke 15:15.
*b Tax*, Neh. 10:32.
*c Government, duty of citizens to*, Isa. 22:21.

23
*d Craftiness, instances of*, Psa. 83:3.
3 R. V. *omits* Why tempt ye me?

24
*e Penny*, Matt. 20:2.

25
*f Commandment, enjoining obedience to civil government*, Deut. 8:2.

What therefore shall the lord of
the vineyard do unto them?
16 He shall come and [h]destroy
these [c,i,j]husbandmen[C], and shall
give the [a]vineyard to others.
And when they heard *it*, they
said, God forbid.
17 And he beheld them, and
[k]said, What is [l]this then that
is written, The [m]stone which
the builders rejected, the same
is become the [n,o]head of the
corner?[Q]
18 Whosoever shall fall upon
that stone shall be [2]broken; but
on whomsoever it shall fall, it
will [h]grind him to powder.[T][Q]
19 And the chief [p]priests and
the [q]scribes the same hour [r]sought[C]
to lay hands on him; and they
feared the [s]people: for they perceived that he had spoken this
[t]parable against them.
20 ¶ [u]And they watched *him*,
and sent forth [v]spies, which
should [w,x]feign[C] themselves just[C]
men, that they might take hold
of his words, that so they might
deliver him unto the power and
authority of the governor.
21 And they asked him, [y]say-
ing, Master, we know that thou
sayest and [z]teachest rightly, neither acceptest thou the person *of*
*any*, but teachest the way of God
truly:
22 Is it lawful for [a]us to give
[b]tribute[C] unto [c]Çæ′şar, or no?
23 But he perceived their
[d]craftiness, and said unto them,
[3]Why tempt[C] ye me?
24 Shew me a [e]penny[C]. Whose
image and superscription[C] hath
it? They answered and said,
Çæ′şar's.
25 And he said unto them,
[f]Render[C] therefore unto [c]Çæ′şar
the things which be Çæ′şar's,
and unto God the things which
be God's.
26 And they could not take hold
of his words before the people:
and they marvelled at his answer, and held their peace.
27 ¶ [g]Then came to *him* certain
of the [h]Săd′du-çeeş[C], which deny
that there is any [i]resurrection:
and they asked him,
28 Saying, Master, Mō′şeş
[j]wrote unto us, If any man's
[k]brother [l]die, having a [m]wife,
and he die without children,
that his brother should [n]take
his wife, and raise up seed
unto his brother.[Q]
29 There were therefore seven
brethren[C]: and the first took a
wife, and died without children.
30 And the second [n]took her to
wife, and he died childless.
31 And the third [n]took her; and
in like manner the seven also:
and they left no children, and
died.
32 Last of all the woman died
also.
33 Therefore in the [i]resurrec-
tion[C] whose wife of them is she?
for seven had her to wife.
34 And Jē′şus answering said
unto them, The children of this
world[C] [o]marry, and are given in
marriage:
35 But they which shall be accounted [p]worthy to obtain [q]that
world[C], and the [i]resurrection[C] from
the [r]dead, neither [o]marry, nor
are given in marriage:
36 [s,t]Neither can they [l]die any
more: for they are equal unto the
[u]angels; and are the [v]children of
God, being the children of the
resurrection.
37 Now that the [r]dead are
[i]raised, even [w]Mō′şeş shewed [4]at
the [x]bush, when he calleth the
Lord the God of [y]Ā′bră-hăm,
and the God of [z]Ī′şaac, and the
God of [a]Jā′cob.[Q]
38 For he is not [5]a God of the
dead, but of the [b]living: for all
live unto him.
39 Then certain of the [c]scribes

v.26–AD 30
See footnote, *Time*, Rev. 10:6.

27
*g* Matt. 22:23–33; Mark 12:18–27.
*h Sadducees*, Matt. 22:23.
*i Resurrection*, 1 Cor. 15:12.

28
*j Law, of Moses*, Deut. 33:2.
*k Brother*, Prov. 18:24.
*l Death*, Num. 23:10.
*m Wife*, Prov. 5:18.
*n Marriage, levirate*, Gen. 34:9.

34
*o Marriage*, Gen. 34:9.

35
*p Righteous, described*, Psa. 64:10.
*q Heaven, future home of the righteous*, Luke 18:22.
*r Dead*, 2 Kin. 4:32.

36
*s Immortality*, 1 Cor. 15:54.
*t Life, everlasting*, Eccl. 8:15.
*u Angel*, Heb. 1:13.
*v Spiritual Adoption*, Rom. 8:15.

37
*w Moses*, Ex. 2:10.
*x Burning Bush*, Ex. 3:2–5.
*y Abraham*, Gen. 17:5.
*z Isaac*, Gen. 21:3.
*a Jacob*, Gen. 27:11.
4 R. V. in the place concerning the Bush,

38
*b Immortality*, 1 Cor. 15:54.
5 R. V. the

39
*c Scribe*, 1 Kin. 4:3.

answering said, Master, thou hast well said.

40 And after that they durst[G] not ask him any *question at all.*

41 ¶ And he said unto them, [d]How say they that Christ is [e]Dā′vid's [f]son?

42 [Q]And [e]Dā′vid himself saith in the [g]book of Psälms, The LORD said unto my Lord, [h]Sit thou on my right hand,

43 Till I make thine enemies thy [i]footstool.[Q]

44 [e]Dā′vid therefore calleth him Lord, how is he then his [f]son?

45 ¶ Then in the audience[G] of all the people he said unto his [j]disciples,

46 [k,l,m]Beware of the [c]scribes, which desire [n]to walk in long robes, and love [o]greetings in the markets, and the [6,n]highest seats in the [p]synagogues, and the [n]chief [7]rooms at [q]feasts;

47 Which [r]devour [s]widows' houses, and [l]for a shew make long [t]prayers: [u]the same [v]shall receive [w]greater [8]damnation.[G]

## CHAPTER 21

*A widow's two mites. 5 Jesus foretells the destruction of the temple, 7 and the calamities which shall precede it. 25 The signs of his coming, 34 and the duty of watchfulness and prayer. 37 Jesus abides by night in the mount of Olives.*

[a]AND he looked up, and saw the [b]rich men [c]casting their gifts into the treasury.

2 And he saw also a certain [d]poor [e,f]widow [c]casting in thither two [g]mites.[G]

3 And he said, [h,i]Of a truth I say unto you, that this poor widow hath [c]cast in more than they all:

4 For [h,i]all these have of their [1]abundance cast in unto the offerings of God: but she of her [j]penury[G] hath [c,k]cast in all the living that she had.

5 ¶ And as some spake of the [l]temple, how it was adorned with goodly[G] stones and gifts, he said,

6 [m]*As for* these things which ye behold, the days will come, in the which there shall not be left one stone upon another, that shall not be thrown down.

7 And they asked him, saying, Master, but when shall these things be? and what [n]sign[G] *will there be* when these things shall come to pass?

8 And he said, [o]Take heed that ye be not [2,p]deceived: [q]for [r,s]many shall come in my name, saying, I am [3]*Christ*; and the time draweth near: go ye not therefore after them.[Q]

9 But [t]when ye shall hear of [u]wars and commotions, be not terrified: for these things must first come to pass; but the end *is* not by[G] and by.[Q]

10 Then said he unto them, [v]Nation shall [u]rise against nation, and kingdom against kingdom:[Q]

11 And great [w]earthquakes shall be in divers[G] places, and [x]famines, and [y]pestilences; and fearful sights and great [n]signs shall there be from heaven.

12 But before all these, [z]they shall lay their hands on you, and [a]persecute *you,* delivering *you* up to the [b]synagogues, and into [c]prisons, being brought before kings and rulers for my name's sake.

13 And it shall turn to you for a testimony.

14 [d,e]Settle *it* therefore in your hearts, not to meditate before what ye shall answer:

15 For [f,g]I will [h]give you a mouth and [i]wisdom, which all your adversaries shall not be able to gainsay[G] nor resist.

16 And ye shall be [a]betrayed both by parents, and brethren, and kinsfolks, and friends; and

v.39–AD 30 See footnote, *Time,* Rev. 10:6.

**41**
d Matt. 22:41–46; Mark 12:35–37.
e *David,* 1 Sam. 16:13.
f *Jesus, incarnation, of,* Matt. 1:21.

**42**
g *Prophecies concerning the Messiah, and their fulfillment,* Gen. 12:3.
h *Sovereignty of the Messiah,* Psa. 110:1.

**43**
i *Footstool, figurative,* 1 Chr. 28:2.

**45**
j *Disciples,* Matt. 9:14.

**46**
k *Commandment, admonishing against hypocrisy,* Deut. 8:2.
l Matt. 23; Mark 12:38–40.
m *Pride, rebuked,* Prov. 16:18.
n *Self-exaltation,* Luke 14:11.
o *Salutations,* Luke 1:44.
p *Synagogue,* Matt. 12:9.
q *Feasts,* Mark 12:39.
6 R. V. chief
7 R. V. places

**47**
r *Oppression,* Eccl. 5:8.
s *Widow,* 2 Sam. 14:5.
t *Prayer,* Acts 6:4.
u *Wicked, punishment of,* Psa. 73:3.
v *Judgment, according to opportunity and works,* 1 Pet. 1:17.
w *Punishment, according to deeds,* Lev. 26:41.
8 R. V. condemnation.

**1**
a Mark 12:41–44.
b *Rich,* Jas. 5:1.
c *Liberality, instances of,* 1 Tim. 6:18.

**2**
d *Poor,* Prov. 21:13.
e *Widow,* 2 Sam. 14:5.
f *Women, good,* Prov. 31:10.
g Mark 12:42. **3** h *Responsibility, according to privilege,* Ezek. 18:20. i *Judgment, according to opportunity and works,* 1 Pet. 1:17.
**4** j *Poverty,* Prov. 30:8. k *Self-denial, instances of,* Mark 8:34.
1 R. V. superfluity

v.5–AD 30 See footnote, *Time,* Rev. 10:6.

**5**
l *Temple, Herod's,* 1 Kin. 6:17.

**6**
m Matt. 24; Mark 13.

**7**
n *Sign,* Mark 8:11.

**8**
o *Watchfulness,* Matt. 24:42.
p *Apostasy,* Acts 1:25.
q Matt. 24:24; Mark 13:22.
r *Minister, false and corrupt,* Rom. 15:16.
s *Antichrist,* 2 John 7.
2 R. V. led astray:
3 R. V. he;

**9**
t *Adversity, consolation in,* Psa. 10:6.
u *War,* Judg. 3:2.

**10**
v Matt. 24:7; Mark 13:8.

**11**
w *Earthquakes,* Isa. 29:6.
x *Famine,* 2 Kin. 8:1.
y *Plague,* Ex. 11:1.

**12**
z Matt. 24:9; Mark 13:9.
a *Persecution, of Christians foretold,* John 15:20.
b *Synagogue,* Matt. 12:9.
c *Prison,* Gen. 39:20.

**14**
d Matt. 10:19.
e *Commandment, enjoining fortitude under persecution,* Deut. 8:2.

**15**
f *Righteous, promises to,* Psa. 64:10.
g *Promise, to the righteous,* 2 Cor. 1:20.
h *Inspiration, of disciples,* Job 32:8.
i *Wisdom, spiritual, from God,* Prov. 2:2.

some of you shall they cause to be [j]put to death.

17 And ye shall be [a,k]hated of all *men* for my name's sake.

18 [f,g,l,m]But there shall not an hair of your head perish.[G S Q]

19 In your [n,o]patience [4]possess ye your souls.

20 And when ye shall see [p]Jĕ-rṳ′să-lĕm [q]compassed with armies, then know that the desolation thereof is nigh.[C]

21 Then let them which are in [r]Jū-dæ′ȧ flee to the mountains; and let them which are in the midst of it depart out; and let not them that are in the countries enter thereinto.

22 For these be the days of [s]vengeance, that all [t]things which are written may be fulfilled.[S Q]

23 [u]But woe unto them that are with child, and to them that give suck, in those days! for there shall be great [v]distress in the land, and wrath upon this people.

24 And they shall fall by the edge of the sword, and shall be led away [w]captive into all nations: and [p]Jĕ-rṳ′să-lĕm shall be trodden down of the [x]Ġĕn′tīleș, until the times of the Ġĕn′tīleș be fulfilled.[Q]

25 ¶ And [y]there shall be [z]signs in the [a]sun, and in the [b]moon, and in the [c]stars; and upon the earth [d]distress of nations, with perplexity; the sea and the waves roaring;[Q]

26 Men's hearts [d]failing them for fear, and for looking after those things which are coming on the [e]earth: for the powers of [f]heaven shall be shaken.[Q]

27 [g]And then shall they see the Son of man [h]coming in a cloud with power and great glory.[Q]

28 And when these things begin to come to pass, then look up, and lift up your heads; for your redemption draweth nigh.[C]

29 And he spake to them a [i]parable; [j]Behold the [k]fig tree, and all the trees;

30 When they now shoot forth, ye see and know of your own selves that [l]summer is now nigh[C] at hand.

31 So likewise ye, when ye see these things come to pass, know ye that the [m]kingdom of God is nigh at hand.

32 [n]Verily I say unto you, This generation shall not pass away, till all be fulfilled.

33 [f]Heaven and [e]earth shall pass away: but my words shall not pass away.

34 ¶ [o]And [p,q,r]take heed to yourselves, [s]lest at any time your hearts be overcharged[C] with [t]surfeiting,[C] and *drunkenness, and [u]cares of this life, and *so* that day come upon you unawares.

35 For as a snare shall it come on all them that dwell on[S Q] the face of the whole earth.

36 [q,r,v]Watch ye therefore, and [w]pray always, that ye may [5]be accounted worthy to escape all these things that shall come to pass, and to stand before the Son of man.

37 And in the day time he was [x,y]teaching in the [z]temple; and at night he went out, and abode[C] in the mount that is called *the mount* of [a]Ŏl′ĭveș.

38 And [b,c]all the people came

v.16–AD 30 See footnote, *Time*, Rev. 10:6.

16

*j Martyrdom, followers of Jesus exposed to*, Rev. 17:6.

17

*k Hatred*, Prov. 15:17.

18

*l God, preserver*, Gen. 2:2.

*m Adversity, consolation in*, Psa. 10:6.

19

*n Patience*, Luke 8:15.

*o Resignation*, Job 5:17.

4 R. V. ye shall win your souls.

20

*p Jerusalem, destruction of, foretold by Jesus*, Judg. 19:10.

*q Siege*, Deut. 28:53.

21

*r Judea*, Luke 5:17.

22

*s Judgments*, Ex. 6:6.

*t Prophecies*, Dan. 9:24.

23

*u* Matt. 24:19–21; Mark 13:17–19.

*v Adversity*, Psa. 10:6.

24

*w Captive*, 1 Sam. 30:3.

*x Gentiles, prophecies of the conversion of*, Acts 10:45.

25

*y* Matt. 24:29; Mark 13:24, 25.

*z Astronomy, sidereal phenomena*, Isa. 13:10.

*a Sun*, Josh. 10:12.

*b Moon*, Song 6:10.

*c Stars*, Judg. 5:20.

*d Adversity, despondency in*, Psa. 10:6.

26

*e Earth, destruction of*, Prov. 8:23.

*f Heavens, physical, destruction of*, Psa. 8:3.

v.27–AD 30 See footnote, *Time*, Rev. 10:6.

27

*g* Matt. 24:30; Mark 13:26.

*h Jesus, second coming of*, Matt. 1:21.

29

*i Parables, of Jesus*, Ezek. 20:49.

*j* Matt. 24:32–35; Mark 13:28–31.

*k Fig Tree, parable of*, Luke 13:6.

30

*l Summer*, Isa. 28:4.

31

*m Kingdom of Heaven*, Matt. 13:24.

32

*n* Matt. 5:18; Luke 16:17.

34

*o* Matt. 24:36–51; Mark 13:32–37.

*p Commandment, warning against sinful indulgence*, Deut. 8:2.

*q Watchfulness, enjoined*, Matt. 24:42.

*r Temptation, resistance to*, Luke 11:4.

*s Worldliness, admonitions against*, 1 John 2:15.

*t Gluttony, warnings against*, Prov. 30:22.

*u Anxiety*, 1 Pet. 5:7.

36

*v Commandment, enjoining watchfulness*, Deut. 8:2.

*w Prayer, enjoined*, Acts 6:4.

5 R. V. prevail to escape

37

*x Instruction, in religion*, Prov. 23:23.

*y Jesus, teacher*, Matt. 1:21.

*z Temple, Herod's*, 1 Kin. 6:17.

*a Mount of Olives*, Mark 11:1.

38

*b Popularity of Jesus*, John 6:15.

*c Jesus, received*, Matt. 1:21.

* **DRUNKENNESS**, Isa. 28:7, 8; 56:12; Hos. 7:5; Joel 1:5; 3:3; Amos 2:8, 12; Matt. 24:49; Luke 12:45.

*Mockery in*, Psa. 69:12. *Consequences of*, Prov. 21:17; 23:21, 29, 30, 32–35; Isa. 19:14; 24:9–11; 28:7; Hos. 4:11.

*Forbidden*, 1 Sam. 1:14; Prov. 23:20, 31, 32; 31:4–7; Luke 21:34; Rom. 13:13; 1 Cor. 11:21–30; Eph. 5:18; 1 Thess. 5:7, 8; 1 Pet. 4:3.

*Woes denounced against*, Isa. 5:11, 12, 22; 28:1, 3, 7, 8; Amos 6:1, 6; Nah. 1:10; Hab. 2:15, 16.

*Death penalty for*, Deut. 21:20, 21; Jer. 25:27. *Excludes from kingdom of God*, 1 Cor. 6:9, 10; Gal. 5:19–21.

Falsely accused of: *Hannah*, 1 Sam. 1:12–16; *Jesus*, Matt. 11:19; *the Apostles*, Acts 2:13–15.

**Figurative**, Isa. 51:17; 63:6; Jer. 51:7–9; Ezek. 23:31–34; Hab. 2:15, 16.

**Instances of**: *Noah*, Gen. 9:21. *Lot*, Gen. 19:33, 35. *Nabal*, 1 Sam. 25:36. *Uriah*, 2 Sam. 11:13. *Amnon*, 2 Sam. 13:28. *Elah*, 1 Kin. 16:9. *Ben-hadad and his thirty-two confederate kings*, 1 Kin. 20:16. *Ahasuerus*, Esth. 1:10, 11. *Belshazzar*, Dan. 5:1–6. *Degenerate Christians*, 1 Cor. 11:21.

See footnotes: TOTAL ABSTINENCE, Lev. 10:9; DRUNKARD, Psa. 69:12; WINE, Prov. 23:31.

v.38–AD 30
See footnote, *Time*, Rev. 10:6.

d *Spiritual Desire*, Psa. 42:1.

early in the morning to him in the temple, for [d]to hear him.

## CHAPTER 22

*The rulers conspire against Jesus, and arrange with Judas for his betrayal. 7 Jesus keeps the passover; 19 institutes the Lord's supper; 24 exhorts his disciples to humility; 31 and foretells Peter's denial of him. 39 He prays in the garden; 47 is betrayed with a kiss; 54 and is brought into the high priest's house, where Peter denies him. 63 He is mocked; 66 and condemned before the council.*

[a]NOW the feast of unleavened bread drew nigh,[G] which is called the [b]Passover.[G]

2 And the chief [c]priests and [d]scribes [e,f]sought[G] how they might kill him; for they feared the [g]people.

3 ¶ [h]Then [i,j]entered [k,l]Sā′tan into [m]Jū′das surnamed Ĭs-căr′ĭ-ot, being of the number of the [n]twelve.

4 And he [i]went his way, and [j,o]communed[G] with the chief [c]priests and [p]captains, how he might [q]betray him unto them.

5 [r]And they were glad, and covenanted[G] to [s]give [t]him [u]money.

6 And he promised, and [i,j]sought opportunity to [q]betray him unto them in the absence of the multitude.

7 ¶ [v]Then came the day of unleavened bread, when[Q] the [b]passover must be killed.

8 And he sent [w]Pē′tēr and [x]Jŏhn, saying, Go and prepare us the [b]passover,[G] that we may eat.[Q]

9 And they said unto him, Where wilt thou that we prepare?

10 [T]And [y]he said unto them, Behold, when ye are entered into the city, there shall a man meet you, bearing a pitcher of water; follow him into the house where he entereth in.

11 And ye shall say unto the goodman[G] of the house, The Master saith unto thee, Where is the guestchamber, where I shall eat the [b]passover with my disciples?

12 And he shall shew you a large upper room furnished: there make ready.[T]

13 And [w,x]they went, and found as he had said unto them: and they made ready the [b]passover.

14 [z]And when the hour was come, he sat down, and the twelve [a]apostles with him.

15 And he said unto them, With desire I have desired to eat this [b]passover with you before [c]I suffer:

16 For I say unto you, I will not any more eat thereof, until it be fulfilled in the kingdom of God.

17 And [d]he took the [e,f,g]cup, and [h]gave [i]thanks, and said, Take this, and divide *it* among yourselves:

18 For I say unto you, I will not drink of the fruit of the vine, until the kingdom of God shall come.

19 ¶ [d]And he took bread, and [h]gave [i]thanks, and brake *it*, and gave unto them, saying, This is my body which is given [j]for you: this do in [k]remembrance of me.

20 Likewise also the [e,f,l]cup after supper, saying, This cup *is* the [m]new [1]testament in my[Q] [n]blood, which is [o]shed [j]for you.

21 ¶ But, [p]behold, the hand of [q]him that [r]betrayeth me *is* with me on the table.[Q]

22 And truly the Son of man goeth, [s]as it was determined: but woe unto that man by whom he is [r]betrayed!

23 And they began to [t]enquire among themselves, which of them it was that should do this thing.

24 ¶ And there was also a [u]strife among them, [v]which of them should be accounted the greatest.

25 And he said unto them, [w]The kings of the Ġĕn′tīleș exercise lordship over them; and they that exercise authority

**1**
a Matt. 26:1–5; Mark 14:1, 2.
b *Passover*, Num. 9:5.

**2**
c *Priest*, Lev. 1:5.
d *Scribe*, 1 Kin. 4:3.
e *Malice*, Eph. 4:31.
f *Persecution, of Jesus*, John 15:20.
g *Public Opinion*, John 12:42.

**3**
h Matt. 26:14–16; Mark 14:10, 11.
i *Apostasy, instances of*, Acts 1:25.
j *Infidelity, of friends*, 2 Cor. 6:15.
k *Satan*, Matt. 4:10.
l *Temptation, sources of, Satan*, Luke 11:4.
m *Judas*, Mark 3:19.
n *Apostles*, Luke 6:13.

**4**
o *Conspiracy*, 1 Kin. 16:9.
p *Soldiers*, Ezra 8:22.
q *Betrayal, of Jesus*, Matt. 26:46.

**5**
r *Prophecies of the Messiah, and their fulfillment*, Gen. 12:3.
s *Bribery, instances of*, 1 Sam. 8:3.
t *Covetousness*, Isa. 57:17.
u *Money, silver used as*, Jer. 32:9.

**7**
v Matt. 26:17–19; Mark 14:12–16.

**8**
w *Peter*, Mark 5:37.
x *John*, Mark 1:19.

**10**
y *Jesus, omniscience of*, Matt. 1:21.

v.12–AD 30
See footnote, *Time*, Rev. 10:6.

**14**
z Matt. 26:20–30; Mark 14:17–26.
a *Apostles*, Luke 6:13.

**15**
b *Passover*, Num. 9:5.
c *Jesus, death of*, Matt. 1:21.

**17**
d *Eucharist, instituted*, Mark 14:22.
e *Cup*, Gen. 44:2.
f *Symbols and Similitudes*, Heb. 9:9.
g *Wine, sacramental use of*, Prov. 23:31.
h *Thankfulness*, Acts 24:3.
i *Thanksgiving, by Jesus*, Matt. 11:25.

**19**
j *Jesus, design of his death*, Matt. 1:21.
k *Memorial, Lord's supper*, Num. 16:40.

**20**
l *Wine, symbolical*, Prov. 23:31.
m *New Covenant*, Jer. 31:31.
n *Blood, of Jesus, atoning*, Heb. 9:19.
o *Atonement, by Jesus*, Lev. 17:11.
1 R. V. covenant

**21**
p *Jesus, prophet*, Matt. 1:21.
q *Judas, prophecies concerning*, Mark 3:19.
r *Betrayal, of Jesus*, Matt. 26:46.

**22**
s *Foreordination, of the death of Jesus*, Rom. 8:30.

**23**
t *Self-examination*, 2 Cor. 13:5.

**24**
u *Strife, instances of*, Prov. 20:3.
v *Ambition*, Hab. 2:5.

**25**
w Matt. 20:25–28; Mark 10:42–45.

upon them are called bene-
factors.
26 But ye *shall* not *be* so: but he
that is greatest among you, [x]let
him be as the younger; and he
that is chief, [y]as he that doth
[z]serve.
27 For whether *is* greater, he
that sitteth at meat[G], or [a]he that
serveth? *is* not he that sitteth at
meat[G]? but [b]I am among you [c]as
[d]he that serveth.
28 [e]Ye are they which have continued with me in my [f]tempta-
tions[G].
29 [T]And [g,h]I appoint unto you a
[i]kingdom, as my [j]Father hath
appointed unto [k]me;
30 [g,h]That ye may eat and
drink at my table in my kingdom, and sit on thrones judging
the twelve tribes of Ĭṣ′ra-el.[T]
31 ¶ And the Lord said, [l]Sī′-
mon, Sī′mon, behold, [m]Sā′tan
hath desired *to have* you, that[Q]
he may [n,o]sift *you* as wheat:
32 But [p]I have [q,r]prayed for
thee, that thy [s]faith [t]fail not:
and when thou [2]art converted[G],
[u]strengthen thy brethren.
33 And he [v,w]said unto him,
Lord, I am ready to go with
thee, both into [x]prison, and to
[y]death.
34 [z]And he said, [a]I tell thee,
[b]Pē′tēr, the cock shall not crow
this day, before that thou shalt
thrice deny that thou knowest
me.
35 ¶ And he said unto them,
When I sent you without [c]purse,
and [c]scrip[G], and [c]shoes, lacked
ye any thing? And they said,
Nothing.
36 Then said he unto them,
But now, he that hath a purse,
let him take *it*, and likewise [3]*his*
scrip[G]: and he that hath no sword,
let him sell his garment, and buy
one.
37 For I say unto you, that [d]this
that is written must yet be accomplished in me, [e]And he was
reckoned among the transgressors: for the things concerning
me have an end.[Q]
38 And they said, Lord, behold,
here *are* two swords. And he
said unto them, It is enough.
39 ¶ [f]And he came out, and
went, as he was wont[G], to the
mount of [g]Ŏl′ĭveṣ; and his [h]dis-
ciples also followed him.
40 And when he was at the
[i]place, he said unto them, [j,k]Pray
that ye enter not into [l]tempta-
tion.
41 And he was withdrawn from
them about a stone's cast, and
[m]kneeled down, and [n]prayed,
42 [o]Saying, Father, if thou be
willing, remove this [p]cup from
me: nevertheless [q,r,s,t]not my
will, but [u]thine, be done.[T]
43 And there appeared an
[v]angel unto him from heaven,
[w]strengthening him.
44 And being in an [x]agony he
[n,y]prayed more earnestly: and
his [z]sweat was as it were great
drops of blood falling down to
the ground.
45 And when he rose up from
prayer, and was come to his [a]dis-
ciples, he found them [b]sleeping
for sorrow,
46 And said unto them, Why
sleep ye? rise and [c]pray, lest ye
enter into [d]temptation.
47 ¶ [e]And while he yet spake,
behold a multitude, and he that
was called [f]Jū′das, one of the
[a]twelve, went before them, and
[g]drew near unto Jē′ṣus to [h]kiss
him.
48 But Jē′ṣus said unto him,
[f]Jū′das, [i]betrayest thou the Son
of man with a [h]kiss?
49 [S]When they which were about
him saw what would follow, they

v.25–AD 30
See footnote, *Time*, Rev. 10:6.

**26**
x *Humility, enjoined*, Prov. 22:4.
y *Commandment, enjoining altruistic service*, Deut. 8:2.
z *Altruism*, Acts 20:35.

**27**
a *Servant, social status of*, Jer. 2:14.
b *Jesus, an example*, Matt. 1:21.
c *Jesus, humility of*, Matt. 1:21.
d *Minister, character and qualifications of*, Rom. 15:16.

**28**
e *Apostles*, Luke 6:13.
f *Jesus, temptation of*, Matt. 1:21.

**29**
g *Promise, to the righteous*, 2 Cor. 1:20.
h *Righteous, promises to*, Psa. 64:10.
i *Heaven, future home of the righteous*, Luke 18:22.
j *God, fatherhood of*, Gen. 2:2.
k *Jesus, kingdom of*, Matt. 1:21.

**31**
l *Peter*, Mark 5:37.
m *Satan*, Matt. 4:10.
n Isa. 30:28; Amos 9:9.
o *Temptation, a test*, Luke 11:4.

**32**
p *Jesus, love of*, Matt. 1:21.
q *Prayers of Jesus*, Luke 5:16.
r *Jesus, mediation of*, Matt. 1:21.
s *Faith in Christ*, John 6:69.
t *Perseverance*, Eph. 6:18.
u *Minister, duties of*, Rom. 15:16.
2 R.V. hast turned again, stablish thy brethren.

**33**
v *Zeal*, 2 Cor. 7:11.
w *False Confidence*, Psa. 30:6.
x *Prison*, Gen. 39:20.
y *Death*, Num. 23:10.

**34**
z Matt. 26:34, 74, 75; Mark 14:30, 68, 72; John 13:38; 18:27.—a *Jesus, prophet*, Matt. 1:21. b *Peter*, Mark 5:37. **35** c *Minister, emoluments of*, Rom. 15:16. **36** 3 R. V. a wallet:

v.37–AD 30
See footnote, *Time*, Rev. 10:6.

**37**
d *Prophecies concerning the Messiah, and their fulfillment*, Gen. 12:3.
e Isa. 53:12.

**39**
f Matt. 26:36–46; Mark 14:32–42; John 18:1.
g *Mount of Olives*, Mark 11:1.
h *Apostles*, Luke 6:13.

**40**
i *Gethsemane*, Mark 14:32.
j *Prayer, enjoined*, Acts 6:4.
k *Commandment, enjoining prayerfulness*, Deut. 8:2.
l *Temptation*, Luke 11:4.

**41**
m *Prayer, postures in*, Acts 6:4.
n *Prayers of Jesus*, Luke 5:16.

**42**
o *Afflictions, prayer in*, Psa. 34:19.
p *Cup, figurative*, Matt. 20:22.
q *Resignation, exemplified*, Job 5:17.
r *Renunciation, of the will to the Father*, Luke 5:11.
s *Prayer, submission in*, Acts 6:4.
t *Jesus, obedience of*, Matt. 1:21.
u *Will of God*, Mark 3:35.

**43**
v *Angel, functions of*, Heb. 1:13.
w *Afflictions, consolation in*, Psa. 34:19.

**44**
x *Jesus, sufferings of*, Matt. 1:21.
y *Prayer, importunity in*, Acts 6:4.
z *Sweat, of blood*, Gen. 3:19.

**45**
a *Apostles*, Luke 6:13.
b *Sleep*, Psa. 127:2.

**46**
c *Prayer, enjoined*, Acts 6:4.
d *Temptation*, Luke 11:4.

**47**
e Matt. 26:47–56; Mark 14:43–50; John 18:3–11. f *Judas*, Mark 3:19. g *Treachery*, 2 Kin. 9:23. h *Kiss, of Judas*, Ruth 1:14. **48** i *Betrayal, of Jesus*, Matt. 26:46.

v.49–AD 30
See footnote, *Time*, Rev. 10:6.

**49**
*i* *Sword*, 1 Chr. 21:5.
**50**
*k* *Peter*, Mark 5:37.
*l* Matt. 26:51; Mark 14:47; John 18:10.
*m* *High Priest*, Lev. 21:10.
**51**
*n* *Miracles, of Jesus*, Luke 23:8.
**52**
*o* *Priest*, Lev. 1:5.
*p* *Temple, Herod's*, 1 Kin. 6:17.
*q* *Senate*, Num. 11:16.
**53**
*r* *Darkness, figurative*, Gen. 1:2.
**54**
*s* *Arrest, of Jesus*, Matt. 26:50.
*t* *Prisoners*, Psa. 79:11.
*u* *Trial of Jesus*, Mark 14:53.
*v* *Cowardice, instances of*, Lev. 26:36.
**55**
*w* Matt. 26:69–75; Mark 14:66–72; John 18:15–18, 25–27.
4 R. V. court,
**57**
*x* *Temptation, yielding to*, Luke 11:4.
*y* *Falsehood, instances of*, Job 21:34.
**59**
*z* *Galilee*, Mark 6:21.

**60**
*a* *Peter*, Mark 5:37.
*b* *Falsehood, instances of*, Job 21:34.
*c* Matt. 26:34, 74, 75; Mark 14:30, 68, 72; John 13:38; 18:27.
**61**
*d* *Jesus, compassion of*, Matt. 1:21.
*e* *Conscience, guilty*, Acts 23:1.

said unto him, Lord, shall we
smite with the [i]sword?
50 ¶ And [k]one of them smote
the [l]servant of the [m]high priest,
and cut off his right ear.
51 And Jē′ṣus answered and
said, Suffer ye thus far. And he
touched his ear, and [n]healed
him.
52 Then Jē′ṣus said unto the
chief [o]priests, and captains of
the [p]temple, and the [q]elders,
which were come to him, Be ye
come out, as against a thief, with
[i]swords and staves?
53 When I was daily with you
in the [p]temple, ye stretched forth
no hands against me: but this is
your hour, and the power of
[r]darkness.
54 ¶ Then [s]took they [t]him, and
led *him*, and [u]brought him into
the high priest's house. And
[k]Pē′tēr [v]followed afar off.
55 And when they had kindled
a fire in the midst of the [4]hall,
and were set down together,
[k,w]Pē′tēr sat down among them.
56 But a certain maid beheld
him as he sat by the fire, and
earnestly looked upon him, and
said, This man was also with
him.
57 And [x]he [y]denied him, saying, Woman, I know him not.
58 And after a little while another saw him, and said, Thou
art also of them. And [k]Pē′tēr
[y]said, Man, I am not.
59 And about the space of one
hour after another confidently
affirmed, saying, Of a truth this
*fellow* also was with him: for he
is a [z]Găl-ĭ-læ′an.
60 And [a]Pē′tēr [b]said, Man,
I know not what thou sayest.
[c]And immediately, while he yet
spake, the cock crew.
61 And the [d]Lord turned, and
looked upon [a]Pē′tēr. And Pē′tēr
[e]remembered the word of the
Lord, how he had said unto him,
[c]Before the cock crow, thou shalt
deny me thrice.
62 And [a]Pē′tēr went out, and
[f,g,h]wept bitterly.
63 ¶ And the men that held Jē′-
ṣus [i,j]mocked him, and [k,l]smote
*him.*
64 And when they had blind-
folded him, [5]they [k,l]struck him
on the face, and asked him, [i]say-
ing, Prophesy, who is it that
smote thee?
65 And many other things
[6,m]blasphemously [n]spake they
against [7]him.
66 ¶ And as soon as it was day,
the [o]elders of the people and the
chief [p]priests and the [q]scribes
came together, and [r]led him into
their council, saying,
67 [r]Art thou [s]the [t]Chrīst? tell
us. And he said unto them, If I
tell you, [u]ye will [v,w]not believe:
68 And if I also ask *you*, ye will
not answer [8]me, nor let *me* go.
69 Hereafter shall the Son of
man [x,y]sit on the right hand of
the power of God.
70 [r]Then said they all, Art thou
then the [z]Son of God? And he
said unto them, [a]Ye say that I am.
71 And they said, What need
we any further witness? for we
ourselves have heard of his own
mouth.

## CHAPTER 23

*Jesus is delivered over to Pilate, who sends him to Herod. 8 Herod mocks him. 13 Pilate, yielding, releases Barabbas and delivers Jesus to be crucified. 27 The daughters of Jerusalem bewail him. 33 The crucifixion. 34 The rulers deride him. 39 The penitent thief. 46 Jesus dies. 50 His burial.*

AND the whole multitude of
them arose, and [a]led [b]him
unto [c]Pī′late.
2 And [a]they began to [d]accuse
him, [e,f]saying, We found this *fellow* [g]perverting the nation, and
forbidding to give [h]tribute to
Çæ′ṣar, saying that he himself
is Chrīst a [i]King.

*f* *Slander, instances of*, Prov. 10:18. *g* *Treason, Jesus falsely accused of*, 2 Kin. 11:14. *h* *Tribute*, Ezra 4:13. *i* *Jesus, king*, Matt. 1:21.

v.61–AD 30
See footnote, *Time*, Rev. 10:6.

**62**
*f* *Weeping*, Ezra 3:13.
*g* *Remorse*, Matt. 27:3.
*h* *Repentance*, Mark 1:4.
**63**
*i* *Mocking*, 1 Kin. 18:27.
*j* *Persecution, of Jesus*, John 15:20.
*k* *Cruelty, instances of*, Psa. 27:12.
*l* *Smiting of Jesus*, Isa. 50:6.
**64**
5 R. V. *omits* they struck him on the face,
**65**
*m* *Blasphemy*, 2 Sam. 12:14.
*n* *False Accusation*, 2 Tim. 3:3.
6 R. V. *omits* blasphemously
7 R. V. him, reviling him.
**66**
*o* *Senate*, Num. 11:16.
*p* *Priest*, Lev. 1:5.
*q* *Scribe*, 1 Kin. 4:3.
*r* *Trial of Jesus*, Mark 14:53.
**67**
*s* *Indictments, instances of*, Matt. 27:37.
*t* *Jesus, Messiah*, Matt. 1:21.
*u* *Unbelievers*, 1 Cor. 6:6.
*v* *Unbelief, instances of*, Heb. 3:12.
*w* *Jesus, rejected*, Matt. 1:21.
**68**
8 R. V. *omits the rest of this verse.*
**69**
*x* *Jesus, exaltation of*, Matt. 1:21.
*y* *Jesus, king*, Matt. 1:21.
**70**
*z* *Jesus, divine sonship of*, Matt. 1:21.

*a* *Pleading*, Deut. 17:8.
**1**
*a* *Trial of Jesus*, Mark 14:53.
*b* *Prisoners*, Psa. 79:11.
*c* *Pilate*, Matt. 27:2.
**2**
*d* *False Accusation, instances of*, 2 Tim. 3:3.
*e* *Indictments*, Matt. 27:37.

v.3–AD 30
See footnote, *Time*, Rev. 10:6.

3
*f Pleading*, Deut. 17:8.

5
*k Jesus, teacher*, Matt. 1:21.
*l Judea*, Luke 5:17.
*m Galilee*, Mark 6:21.

3 [a]And [c]Pī′late asked him,
saying, Art thou [e]the King of
the Jewṣ? And he answered
him and said, [f]Thou sayest *it*.
4 [a]Then said [c]Pī′late to the
chief priests and *to* the people,
I find no fault in this man.
5 [a]And they were the more
fierce, [d,f]saying, He stirreth up
the people, [k]teaching throughout all [l]Jew′rȳ, beginning from
[m]Găl′ĭ-lee to this place.
6 When [c]Pī′late heard of [m]Găl′-
ĭ-lee, he asked whether the man
were a Găl-ĭ-læ′an.
7 And as soon as he knew that
he belonged unto [n]Hĕr′od's jurisdiction, he sent [a]him to Hĕr′od,
who himself also was at [o]Jē-ru̇′-
sȧ-lĕm at that time.
8 ¶ And [a]when [n]Hĕr′od saw
Jē′ṣus, he was exceeding glad:
for he was [p]desirous to see him
of a long *season*, because he had
heard many things of him; and
he hoped to have seen some
*miracle done by him.
9 [a]Then he questioned with
him in many words; but he
[q]answered him nothing.

v.7–AD 30
See footnote, *Time*, Rev. 10:6.

7
*n Herod*, Matt. 14:1.
*o Jerusalem*, Judg. 19:10.

8
*p Curiosity, instances of*, Prov. 27:20.

9
*q Reticence of Jesus*, Mark 14:61.

---

***MIRACLES.** Called: *Marvelous things*, Psa. 78:12; *marvelous works*, Isa. 29:14; *signs and wonders*, Jer. 32:21; John 4:48; 2 Cor. 12:12.

*Performed, through the power of God*, John 3:2; Acts 14:3; 15:12; 19:11; *and of the Holy Spirit*, Matt. 12:28; Rom. 15:19; 1 Cor. 12:9, 10, 28, 30; *in the name of Christ*, Mark 9:38, 39; 16:17; Luke 9:49, 50; Acts 3:16; 4:30. *Faith required in those who perform*, Matt. 17:20; 21:21; John 14:12; Acts 3:16. *Faith required in those for whom they were performed*, Matt. 9:28; Mark 9:22–24; Acts 14:9. *Power to work, given the disciples*, Mark 3:14, 15; 16:17, 18, 20. *Demanded by unbelievers*, Ex. 7:9, 10; Matt. 12:38, 39; 16:1; Luke 11:16, 29; 23:8; John 2:18; 6:30; Cor. 1:22.

**Design of**: *To reveal God*, Ex. 7:5, 17; 8:8–10, 22; 9:4–16, 29; 10:1, 2; 14:4, 18; Deut. 4:33–39; Josh. 4:23, 24; 1 Kin. 18:24, 37–39; Jer. 32:20. *To produce faith in God*, Ex. 14:31; Num. 14:11; Josh. 3:7–17; 2 Chr. 7:1–3; Psa. 106:9–12. *To produce the fear of God*, 1 Sam. 12:17, 18; Dan. 6:20–27; Jonah 1:14–16. *To constrain to obedience*, Ex. 16:4–6; 19:4, 5; Deut. 11:1–8; 29:1–9; Judg. 2:7; Psa. 78:10–32. *To glorify God*, Luke 5:26; John 11:4; Acts 4:21, 22. *To attest the messiahship of Jesus*, Matt. 11:2–5 (with Luke 7:19–22); Mark 2:9–12 (with Luke 5:24–26); Luke 18:42, 43; John 2:11; 4:48; 5:36; 11:4, 40–42; 14:11; 15:24. *To glorify Jesus*, Acts 3:1–13. *To attest God's servants*, Ex. 4:2–9; 19:9; Num. 16:28–35; 1 Sam. 12:17, 18; Zech. 2:9; Acts 2:22; Heb. 2:4. *To preserve the righteous*, Dan. 3:28, 29; 6:20–27. *To change wicked purposes*, Ex. 3:19, 20; 9:16, 17; 10:16, 17; 11:1–10; 12:29–33; 14:24, 25.

**Convincing effect of:** *On children of Israel*, Ex. 4:28–31; 14:31; Num. 17:1–13. *On Pharaoh's servants*, Ex. 10:7. *On Pharaoh*, Ex. 10:16, 17; 12:31, 32. *On Egyptians*, Ex. 12:33; 1 Sam. 6:6. *On the Canaanites*, Josh. 2:9–11; 5:1. *On Gideon*, Judg. 6:17–22, 36–40; 7:1. *On people who witnessed Elijah's*, 1 Kin. 18:24, 37–39. *On Naaman*, 2 Kin. 5:14, 15. *On Nebuchadnezzar*, Dan. 2:47; 3:28, 29; 4:2, 3. *On Darius*, Dan. 6:20–27. *On Simon Peter*, Luke 5:4–11. *On disciples of Jesus*, John 2:11, 22, 23; 20:30, 31. *On the nobleman whose child Jesus healed*, John 4:48–53. *On people who witnessed Christ's*, John 7:31; 11:43–45; 12:10, 11. *On people who witnessed Philip's*, Acts 8:6. *On people who witnessed Peter's*, Acts 9:32–42. *On Sergius Paulus, the deputy*, Acts 13:8–12. *On Gentiles*, Rom. 15:18, 19.

*Resisted by the obdurate*, Neh. 9:17; Psa. 78:10–32; John 9:24–28; 15:24, 25.

**Alleged:** *Performed, by magicians*, Ex. 7:10–12, 22; 8:7; *by impostors*, Matt. 7:22. *Performed through the powers of evil*, 2 Thess. 2:9; Rev. 16:14. *Wrought, in support of false religions*, Deut. 13:1, 2; *by false christs*, Matt. 24:24; *by false prophets*, Matt. 24:24; Rev. 19:20. *Of false prophets not to be regarded*, Deut. 13:1–3. *Deceive the ungodly*, Rev. 13:14; 19:20. *A mark of apostasy*, 2 Thess. 2:3, 9; Rev. 13:13.

**Catalogue of:** *Fire on Abraham's sacrifice*, Gen. 15:17. *Conception of Isaac*, Gen. 21:2. *Blinding of the Sodomites*, Gen. 19:11. *Destruction of Sodom*, Gen. 19:24. *Flaming bush*, Ex. 3:2. *Transformation of Moses' rod into a serpent*, Ex. 4:3, 4, 30; 7:10, 12. *Moses' leprosy*, Ex. 4:6, 7, 30. *Plagues in Egypt*, see footnote, PLAGUES, Ex. 11:1. *Pillar of cloud and fire*, Ex. 13:21, 22; 14:19, 20. *Passage of the Red Sea*, Ex. 14:21, 23. *Destruction of Pharaoh and his army*, Ex. 14:23–30. *Sweetening the waters of Marah*, Ex. 15:25. *Manna*, Ex. 16:4–31; *double portion of, on sixth day*, Ex. 16:5, 29; *preservation of manna over Sabbath*, Ex. 16:24. *Quails*, Ex. 16:13. *Defeat of Amalek*, Ex. 17:9–13. *Water from the rock*, Ex. 17:5, 7. *Miriam's leprosy*, Num. 12:10–15. *Judgment by fire*, Num. 11:1–3. *Destruction of Korah*, Num. 16:31–35; Deut. 11:6, 7. *Plague*, Num. 16:46–50. *Aaron's rod buds*, Num. 17:1–9. *Waters from the rock in Kadesh*, Num. 20:8–11. *Scourge of serpents*, Num. 21:6–9. *Destruction of Nadab and Abihu*, Lev. 10:1, 2. *Jordan divided*, Josh. 3:14–17; 4:16–18. *Fall of Jericho*, Josh. 6:20; Heb. 11:30. *Sun and moon stand still*, Josh. 10:12–14. *Dew on Gideon's fleece*, Judg. 6:37–40. *Destruction of the people of Beth-shemesh*, 1 Sam. 6:19, 20. *Plague in Israel*, 1 Chr. 21:14–26. *Fire on the sacrifices, of Aaron*, Lev. 9:24; *of Gideon*, Judg. 6:21; *of Solomon*, 2 Chr. 7:1; *of Elijah*, 1 Kin. 18:38. *Jeroboam's hand withered*, 1 Kin. 13:3–6. *Rending of the altar*, 1 Kin. 13:5, with vs. 1, 3. *Elijah is fed, by ravens*, 1 Kin. 17:6; *by an angel*, 1 Kin. 19:1–8. *Elijah, increases the widow's meal and oil*, 1 Kin. 17:9–16; Luke 4:26; *raises the widow's son*, 1 Kin. 17:17–24. *Rain in answer to Elijah's prayer*, 1 Kin. 18:41–45. *Elijah, brings fire on Ahaziah's army*, 2 Kin. 1:10–12; *divides Jordan*, 2 Kin. 2:8. *Elijah's translation*, 2 Kin. 2:11.

*Elisha divides Jordan*, 2 Kin. 2:14; *sweetens the waters of Jericho*, 2 Kin. 2:19–22; *increases a widow's oil*, 2 Kin. 4:1–7; *raises the Shunammite's child*, 2 Kin. 4:18–37; *renders harmless the poisoned pottage*, 2 Kin. 4:38–41; *feeds one hundred men*, 2 Kin. 4:42–44; *cures Naaman*, 2 Kin. 5:1–19; *smites Gehazi with leprosy*, 2 Kin. 5:26, 27; *causes the ax to float*, 2 Kin. 6:6; *reveals the counsel of the king of Syria*, 2 Kin. 6:12; *causes the eyes of his servant to be opened*, 2 Kin. 6:17; *smites with blindness the army of the king of Syria*, 2 Kin. 6:18. *The dead man restored to life on touching Elisha's bones*, 2 Kin. 13:21.

*Destruction of Sennacherib's army*, 2 Kin. 19:35; Isa. 37:36. *A return of the shadow on the sundial*, 2 Kin. 20:9–11. *Deliverance, of Shadrach, Meshach, and Abed-nego*, Dan. 3:20–27; *of Daniel*, Dan. 6:22. *Preservation of Jonah in the fish's belly*, Jonah 1:17; 2:10.

*The incarnation of Jesus*, Matt. 1:18–25; Luke 1:26–38; 2:1–7. *The appearance of the star of Bethlehem*, Matt. 2:1–9.

**Of Jesus**, IN CHRONOLOGICAL ORDER: *Water made wine*, John 2:1–11.

*Heals the nobleman's son*, John 4:46–54.

*Heals the demoniac*, Mark 1:23–26; Luke 4:33–35.

*Heals Peter's mother-in-law*, Matt. 8:14–17; Mark 1:29–31; Luke 4:38, 39.

*Cleanses the leper*, Matt. 8:1–4; Mark 1:40–45; Luke 5:12–15.

*Heals the paralytic*, Matt. 9:1–8; Mark 2:1–12; Luke 5:17–26.

*Heals the impotent man*, John 5:1–16.

*Restores the withered hand*, Matt. 12:9–13; Mark 3:1–5; Luke 6:6–11.

*Heals the centurion's servant*, Matt. 8:5–13; Luke 7:1–10.

*Raises the widow's son to life*, Luke 7:11–16.

*Heals a demoniac*, Matt. 12:22, 23; Luke 11:14.

*Stills the tempest*, Matt. 8:23–27; 14:32; Mark 4:35–41; Luke 8:22–25.

*Casts devils out of two men of Gadara*, Matt. 8:28–34; Mark 5:1–20; Luke 8:26–39.

*Raises from the dead the daughter of Jairus*, Matt. 9:18, 19, 23–26; Mark 5:22–24, 35–43; Luke 8:41, 42, 49–56.

*Cures the woman with the issue of blood*, Matt. 9:20–22; Mark 5:25–34; Luke 8:43–48.

*Restores the sight of two blind men*, Matt. 9:27–31.

*Heals a demoniac*, Matt. 9:32, 33.

*Feeds five thousand men*, Matt. 14:15–21; Mark 6:35–44; Luke 9:12–17; John 6:5–14.

*Walks on the sea*, Matt. 14:22–33; Mark 6:45–52; John 6:16–21.

*Heals the daughter of the Syrophenician woman*, Matt. 15:21–28; Mark 7:24–30.

v.10–AD 30
See footnote, *Time*, Rev. 10:6.

10
*r Priest*, Lev. 1:5.
*s Scribe*, 1 Kin. 4:3.
*t Malice*, Eph. 4:31.

11
*u Soldiers*, Ezra 8:22.
*v Persecution, of Jesus*, John 15:20.
*w Mocking*, 1 Kin. 18:27.
*x Sarcasm, instances of*, Judg. 10:14.

12
*y Reconciliation*, 2 Cor. 5:18.
*z Friends*, Ex. 33:11.

13
*a Pilate*, Matt. 27:2.
*b Priest*, Lev. 1:5.

14
*c Trial of Jesus*, Mark 14:53.

15
*d Herod*, Matt. 14:1.
1 R.V. he sent him back unto us;

16
*e Scourging of Jesus*, Isa. 50:6.

17
*f Passover*, Num. 9:5.
2 R. V. *omits this verse.*

18
*g Persecution, of Jesus*, John 15:20.
*h Barabbas*, Matt. 27:16.

19
*i Citizens, wicked and treasonable*, Luke 15:15.
*j Homicide, felonious*, Deut. 5:17.
*k Prison*, Gen. 39:20.

21
*l Crucifixion*, Mark 15:13.

10 And the chief [r]priests and [s]scribes stood and [t]vehemently accused him.
11 [a]And [n]Hĕr′od with his [u]men of war [t,v]set him at nought, and [w]mocked *him*, and [x]arrayed him in a gorgeous robe, and sent him again to Pī′late.
12 ¶ And the same day Pī′late and [n]Hĕr′od were [y]made [z]friends together: for before they were at enmity between themselves.
13 ¶ And [a]Pī′late, when he had called together the chief [b]priests and the rulers and the people,
14 Said unto them, Ye have brought this man unto me, as one that perverteth the people: and, behold, I, having examined [c]*him* before you, have found no fault in this man touching those things whereof ye accuse him:
15 [c]No, nor yet [d]Hĕr′od: for [1]I sent you to him; and, lo, nothing worthy of death is done unto him.
16 I will therefore [e]chastise him, and release *him.*
17 [2](For of necessity he must release one unto them at the [f]feast.)
18 And they cried out all at once, saying, [g]Away with this *man*, and release unto us [h]Bȧ-răb′bas:
19 ([i]Who for a certain sedition made in the city, and for [j]murder, was cast into [k]prison.)
20 [a]Pī′late therefore, willing to release Jē′ṣus, spake again to them.
21 But they cried, saying, [g,l]Crucify *him*, crucify him.
22 And he said unto them the third time, Why, what evil hath he done? I have found no cause of death in him: I will therefore [e]chastise him, and let *him* go.
23 And they were instant with loud voices, [g]requiring that he might be [l]crucified. And [3,m]the voices of them and of the chief [b]priests prevailed.
24 [c]And [a,n]Pī′late gave sentence that it should be [o]as they required.
25 And he released unto them [i]him that for sedition and [j]murder was cast into [k]prison, whom [o]they had desired; but he delivered Jē′ṣus to their [g]will.
26 ¶ [p]And as they led him away, they laid hold upon one [q]Sī′mon, a Çȳ-rē′nĭ-an, coming out of the country, and on him they laid the [r]cross, that he might bear *it* after Jē′ṣus.
27 And [s]there [t]followed him a great company of people, and of [u]women, which also [v,w]bewailed and lamented him.
28 But [x]Jē′ṣus turning unto them said, Daughters of [y]Jē-ru′-sȧ-lĕm, weep not for me, but weep for yourselves, and for your children.
29 [y]For, behold, the days are coming, in the which they shall say, Blessed *are* the barren, and the wombs that never bare, and the paps which never gave suck.
30 [y,z,a]Then shall they begin to say to the mountains, Fall on us; and to the hills, Cover us.
31 For if they do these things in a green tree, what shall be done in the dry?

v.22–AD 30
See footnote, *Time*, Rev. 10:6.

23
*m Public Opinion*, John 12:42.
3 R. V. their voices prevailed.

24
*n Statecraft, corruption in*, Prov. 28:2.
*o Demagogism*, 2 Sam. 15:2.

26
*p* Matt. 27:31, 32; Mark 15:20, 21; John 19:16, 17.
*q* Matt. 27:32; Mark 15:21.
*r Cross*, John 19:17.

27
*s Jesus, received*, Matt. 1:21.
*t Love, for Jesus*, 1 John 4:19.
*u Women*, Prov. 31:10.
*v Mourning*, Lam. 2:5.
*w Death, scenes of*, Num. 23:10.

28
*x Jesus, love of*, Matt. 1:21.
*y Jerusalem*, vs. 29–31; Judg. 19:10.

30
*z Punishment, no escape from*, Lev. 26:41.
*a Terror of the Wicked*, Isa. 2:19.

*Feeds four thousand men*, Matt. 15:32–39; Mark 8:1–9.
*Restores one deaf and dumb*, Mark 7:31–37.
*Restores the sight of a blind man*, Mark 8:22–26.
*Heals lunatic child*, Matt. 17:14–20; Mark 9:14–29; Luke 9:37–43.
*Heals ten lepers*, Luke 17:11–19.
*Opens the eyes of a man born blind*, John 9.
*Raises Lazarus from the dead*, John 11:1–46.
*Heals the woman with an infirmity*, Luke 13:10–17.
*Cures a man afflicted with dropsy*, Luke 14:1–6.
*Restores the sight of two blind men near Jericho*, Matt. 20:29–34; Mark 10:46–52; Luke 18:35–43.
*Fig tree withered*, Matt. 21:17–22; Mark 11:12–14, 20–24.
*Heals the ear of Malchus*, Luke 22:49–51.
**Of the disciples of Jesus:** *By the seventy*, Luke 10:17–20. *By other disciples*, Mark 9:38, 39; John 14:12. *By the apostles*, Acts 3:6, 7, 12, 13, 16; 4:10, 30; 9:34, 35; 16:18. *Peter, heals the sick*, Acts 5:15, 16; *heals Æneas*, Acts 9:33, 34; *raises Dorcas to life*, Acts 9:40; *causes the death of Ananias and Sapphira*, Acts 5:5, 10. *Peter and other apostles delivered from prison*, Acts 5:19–23; 12:6–11; 16:26. *Philip carried away by the Spirit*, Acts 8:39. *Paul, strikes Elymas with blindness*, Acts 13:11; *heals a cripple*, Acts 14:10; *casts out evil spirits, and heals sick*, Acts 16:18; 19:11, 12; 20:9–12; 28:5, 8, 9; *raises Eutychus to life*, Acts 20:9–12; *shakes a viper off his hand*, Acts 28:5. *Paul cured of blindness*, Acts 9:3–6, 17, 18.

v.32–AD 30
See footnote, *Time*, Rev. 10:6.

**32**
*b* Matt. 27:38–44.
*c* *Punishment*, Lev. 26:41.
**33**
*d* Matt. 27:33–50; Mark 15:22–37; John 19:17, 30.
*e* Matt. 27:33; Mark 15:22; John 19:17.
*f* *Crucifixion*, Mark 15:13.
4 R. V. The skull,
**34**
*g* *Good for Evil*, Luke 6:27.
*h* *Forgiveness, instances of*, Matt. 18:21.
*i* *Jesus, meekness of*, Matt. 1:21.
*j* *Meekness, of Jesus*, Psa. 45:4.
*k* *Prayer, intercessory*, Acts 6:4.
*l* *Prayers of Jesus*, Luke 5:16.
*m* *Spiritual Blindness*, 2 Cor. 4:4.
*n* *Ignorance, sins of*, Acts 3:17.
*o* Psa. 22:18; Matt. 27:35; Mark 15:24; John 19:24.
*p* *Prophecies concerning the Messiah, and their fulfillment*, Gen. 12:3.
*q* *Lot*, Esth. 3:7.
**35**
*r* *Scoffing, instances of*. Hab. 1:10.
*s* *Jesus, names of*, Matt. 1:21.
**36**
*t* *Soldiers*, Ezra 8:22.
*u* *Mocking*, 1 Kin. 18:27.
*v* *Vinegar*, Num. 6:3.
**38**
*w* *Inscriptions*, Mark 15:26.
*x* *Language*, Dan. 3:29.
*y* *Irony, instances of*, Mark 12:14.
5 R. V. *omits* in letters of Greek, and Latin, and Hebrew,
**39**
*z* Matt. 27:38–44.

---

**40**
*a* *Fear of God*, Acts 9:31.
**42**
*b* *Faith in Christ, exemplified*, John 6:69.
*c* *Jesus, kingdom of*, Matt. 1:21.
6 R. V. said, Jesus, remember me

32 ¶ [b]And there were also two
other, malefactors, led with him
to be [c]put to death.
33 [d]And when they were come
to the place, which is called
[4,e]Căl′va-rў, there they [f]crucified
him, [b]and the malefactors, one
on the right hand, and the other
on the left.
34 [g]Then [h,i,j]said Jē′ṣus, [k,l]Father, forgive them; for they
[m,n]know not what they do. And
[o,p]they parted his raiment, and
cast [q]lots.
35 And the people stood beholding. And the rulers also
with them [r]derided *him*, saying,
He saved others; let him save
himself, if he be [s]Chrīst, the
chosen of God.
36 And the [t]soldiers also [u]mocked him, coming to him, and offering him [v]vinegar,
37 And [r,u]saying, If thou be
the king of the Jewṣ, save thyself.
38 And a [w]superscription also
was written over him [5]in letters of [x]Greek, and [x]Lăt′in,
and [x]Hē′brew, [y]THIS IS THE
KING OF THE JEWṢ.
39 ¶ And one of the [z]malefactors which were hanged [r]railed
on him, [u]saying, If thou be
[s]Chrīst, save thyself and us.
40 But the other answering rebuked him, saying, Dost
not thou [a]fear God, seeing
thou art in the same condemnation?
41 And we indeed justly; for we
receive the due reward of our
deeds: but this man hath done
nothing amiss.
42 And he [6,b]said unto Jē′ṣus,
Lord, remember me when thou
comest into [c]thy kingdom.
43 And Jē′ṣus said unto him,
Verily I say unto thee, [d]To
day shalt thou be with me in
[e,f]paradise.
44 ¶ And it was about the sixth
hour, and there was a [†,g,h]darkness over all the earth until the
ninth hour.
45 [i]And the [j]sun was [g]darkened, and the [k,l]veil of the [m]temple was rent in the midst.
46 And [n]when Jē′ṣus had cried
with a loud voice, he [o,p]said,
[q]Father, [r]into thy hands I commend my spirit: and having said
thus, he [s,t]gave up the ghost.
47 ¶ Now when the [u,v]centurion saw what was done, he
[w]glorified God, saying, Certainly
this was a righteous man.
48 And all the people that
came together to that sight, beholding the things which were
done, smote their breasts, and
returned.
49 And all his acquaintance,
and the [x]women that followed
him from [y]Găl′ĭ-lee, stood afar
off, beholding these things.
50 ¶ [z]And, behold, *there was* a
man named [a]Jō′ṣeph, a [7,b]counsellor; *and he was* a good man,
and a just:
51 (The same had not consented to the counsel and deed
of them;) *he was* of [c]Ăr-ĭ-mă-thæ′ā, a city of the [d]Jewṣ: who
also himself [e]waited for the
[f]kingdom of God.
52 This *man* went unto [g]Pī′lăte,
and begged the body of Jē′ṣus.
53 And he took it down, and
wrapped it in linen, and laid it in
a [h]sepulchre that was hewn in
stone, wherein never man before
was laid.
54 And that day was the

**51** *c* *Arimathea*, John 19:38. *d* *Jews*, Neh. 4:2. *e* *Messianic Hope*, Gen. 49:10. *f* *Kingdom of Heaven*, Matt. 13:24. **52** *g* *Pilate*, Matt. 27:2. **53** *h* *Burying Places*, Gen. 23:4.

v.43–AD 30
See footnote, *Time*, Rev. 10:6.

**43**
*d* *Death, of the righteous, a transition*, Num. 23:10.
*e* 2 Cor. 12:4; Rev. 2:7.
*f* *Heaven, future home of the righteous*, Luke 18:22.
**44**
*g* *Darkness*, Gen. 1:2.
*h* *Astronomy, sidereal phenomena*, Isa. 13:10.
**45**
*i* Matt. 27:51–56; Mark 15:38–41.
*j* *Sun, darkening of*, Josh. 10:12.
*k* *Vail*, 2 Chr. 3:14.
*l* *Symbols and Similitudes*, Heb. 9:9.
*m* *Temple, Herod's*, 1 Kin. 6:17.
**46**
*n* *Prophecies concerning the Messiah, and their fulfillment*, Gen. 12:3.
*o* *Prayers of Jesus*, Luke 5:16.
*p* *Afflictions, prayer in*, Psa. 34:19.
*q* *God, fatherhood of*, Gen. 2:2.
*r* Psa. 31:5.
*s* *Death*, Num. 23:10.
*t* *Jesus, death of*, Matt. 1:21.
**47**
*u* *Centurion*, Matt. 8:5.
*v* *Armies, Roman*, Deut. 11:4.
*w* *Glorifying God*, Luke 5:25.
**49**
*x* *Women*, Prov. 31:10.
*y* *Galilee*, Mark 6:21.
**50**
*z* Matt. 27:57–66; Mark 15:42–47; John 19:38–42.

---

*a* *Joseph*, John 19:38.
*b* *Counselor*, Prov. 11:14.
7 R. V. councillor.

---

† **CELESTIAL PHENOMENA.** *Fire from heaven, on the cities of the plain*, Gen. 19:24, 25; *on the two captains and their fifties*, 2 Kin. 1:10–14; *on the flocks and servants of Job*, Job 1:16. *Hail, on the Egyptians*, Ex. 9:22–34.
*Darkness, on the Egyptians*, Ex. 10:22, 23; *at the crucifixion of Jesus*, Matt. 27:45; Luke 23:44, 45. *Pillar of cloud and fire*, Ex. 13:21, 22; 14:19, 24; 40:38; Num. 9:15–23; Psa. 78:14. *Thunder and lightning on Mt. Sinai*, Ex. 19:16, 18; 20:18. *Sun stood still*, Josh. 10:12, 13.
*Prophecy of darkening of sun, moon, and stars*, **Joel 2:30, 31;** Matt. 24:29; Luke 21:25; Acts 2:19, 20.
See footnote, ASTRONOMY, Isa. 13:10.

v.54–AD 30
See footnote, *Time*, Rev. 10:6.

54
*i* Matt. 27:62; Mark 15:42; John 19:14, 31, 42.
*j* *Sabbath, preparation for*, Ex. 16:23.

55
*k* *Women*, Prov. 31:10.
*l* *Galilee*, Mark 6:21.

56
*m* *Anointing, of the dead*, Deut. 28:40.
*n* *Spices*, 1 Kin. 10:2.
*o* *Ointment*, Eccl. 7:1.
*p* *Sabbath, observance of*, Ex. 16:23.
*q* Ex. 20:8.

1
*a* Matt. 28:1–8; Mark 16:1–8; John 20:1.
*b* *Christian Sabbath*, Mark 16:9.
*c* *Rising, early*, Gen. 19:2.
*d* *Women, first at the sepulchre*, Prov. 31:10.
*e* *Love, for Jesus, instances of*, 1 John 4:19.
*f* *Spices*, 1 Kin. 10:2.
1 R. V. *omits the rest of this verse.*

6
*g* *Resurrection of Jesus*, Matt. 28:6.
*h* *Jesus, revelations by*, Matt. 1:21.
*i* *Galilee*, Mark 6:21.

9
*j* *Apostles*, Luke 6:13.

10
*k* *Mary Magdalene*, Matt. 27:56.
*l* Luke 8:3.
*m* *Mary*, Mark 15:40.

[i]preparation, and the [j]sabbath drew on.

55 ¶ And the [k]women also, which came with him from [l]Găl′ĭ-lee, followed after, and beheld the [h]sepulchre, and how his body was laid.

56 And they returned, and [m]prepared [n]spices and [o]ointments; and rested the [p]sabbath day according to the [q]commandment.[Q]

## CHAPTER 24

*The resurrection of Jesus. 9 The report of the women. 12 Peter runs to the sepulchre. 13 Jesus appears to two disciples on their way to Emmaus; 36 and to the eleven. 50 His ascension.*

[a]NOW[T] upon the [b]first *day* of the week, very [c]early in the morning, [d]they [e]came unto the sepulchre, bringing the [f]spices which they had prepared, [1]and certain *others* with them.

2 And they found the stone rolled away from the sepulchre.

3 And they entered in, and found not the body of the Lord Jē′ṣus.[T]

4 And it came to pass, as they were much perplexed thereabout, behold, two men stood by them in shining garments:

5 And as they were afraid, and bowed down *their* faces to the earth, they said unto them, Why seek ye the living among the dead?[Q]

6 He is not here, but is [g]risen: remember how he [h]spake unto you when he was yet in [i]Găl′ĭ-lee,

7 [h]Saying, The Son of man must be delivered into the hands of sinful men, and be crucified, and the third day rise again.

8 And they remembered his words,

9 And returned from the sepulchre, and told all these things unto the [j]eleven, and to all the rest.

10 It was [k]Mā′rȳ Măg-da-lē′nē, and [l]Jō-ăn′nȧ, and [m]Mā′rȳ *the mother* of [n]Jāmeṣ, and other *women that were* with them, which told these things unto the [j]apostles.

11 And their words seemed to them as idle tales, and [o]they [p,q]believed them not.

12 Then arose [r]Pē′tēr, and ran unto the sepulchre; and stooping down, he beheld the linen clothes laid by themselves, and departed, wondering in himself at that which was come to pass.

13 ¶[T] [s]And, behold, two of [j]them went that same day to a village called Ĕm-mā′us, which was from [t]Jē-ru′sȧ-lĕm *about* threescore [u,v]furlongs.[G]

14 And they [w]talked together of all these things which had happened.

15 And it came to pass, that, while they communed *together* and reasoned, Jē′ṣus himself [x]drew near, and went with them.

16 But their eyes were [y]holden[G] that they should not know him.

17 And he said unto them, What manner of communications[G] *are* these that ye have one to another, as ye walk, and are sad?

18 And the one of them, whose name was Clē′o-păs, answering said unto him, Art thou only a stranger in [t]Jē-ru′sȧ-lĕm, and hast not known the things which are come to pass there in these days?

19 And he said unto them, What things? And they said unto him, Concerning Jē′ṣus of [z]Năz′a-rĕth, which was a [a]prophet mighty in deed and word before God and all the people:

20 And how the chief [b]priests and our rulers [c]delivered him to be condemned to death, and have [d]crucified him.

21 But we [e]trusted that it had

v.10–AD 30
See footnote, *Time*, Rev. 10:6.
*n* Mark 16:1.

11
*o* *Unbelievers*, 1 Cor. 6:6.
*p* *Unbelief, instances of*, Heb. 3:12.
*q* *Jesus, rejected*, Matt. 1:21.

12
*r* *Peter*, Mark 5:37.

13
*s* Mark 16:12, 13.
*t* *Jerusalem*, Judg. 19:10.
*u* John 11:18; Rev. 21:16.
*v* *Measure, linear*, Deut. 25:15.

14
*w* *Fellowship, of the righteous*, 1 Cor. 1:9.

15
*x* *Appearances of Jesus after his Resurrection*, vs. 15–31; Mark 16:9.

16
*y* *Miracles, of Jesus*, Luke 23:8.

19
*z* *Nazareth*, John 1:46.
*a* *Jesus, prophet*, Matt. 1:21.

20
*b* *Priest*, Lev. 1:5.
*c* *Persecution, of Jesus*, John 15:20.
*d* *Crucifixion*, Mark 15:13.

21
*e* *Messianic Hope*, Gen. 49:10.

v.21–AD 30
See footnote, *Time*, Rev. 10:6.

22
f *Women, first at the sepulchre*, Prov. 31:10.

23
g *Vision*, Acts 9:10.
h *Angel, appearances of*, Heb. 1:13.

25
i *Doubting*, Rom. 14:23.
j *Prophecies concerning the Messiah, and their fulfillment*, Gen. 12:3.
k *Prophets*, Isa. 3:2.

26
l *Jesus, mission of*, Matt. 1:21.
m *Jesus, Messiah*, Matt. 1:21.
n *Jesus, sufferings of*, Matt. 1:21.
o *Jesus, exaltation of*, Matt. 1:21.

27
p *Law, of Moses*, Deut. 33:2.
q *Instruction, in religion*, Prov. 23:23.
r *Word of God, expounded*, Psa. 119:9.
s *Jesus, prophecies concerning*, Matt. 1:21.

29
t *Hospitality*, Rom. 12:13.

31
u *Miracles, of Jesus*, Luke 23:8.

32
v *Fellowship, with Christ*, 1 Cor. 1:9.

been he which should have
redeemed Iṣ'ra-el: and beside
all this, to day is the third day
since these things were done.
22 Yea, and certain [f]women
also of our company made us
astonished, which were early at
the sepulchre;
23 And when they found not
his body, they came, saying, that
they had also seen a [g]vision of
[h]angels, which said that he was
alive.
24 And certain of them which
were with us went to the sepulchre, and found *it* even so as the
[f]women had said: but him they
saw not.
25 Then he said unto them, O
fools, and [i]slow of heart to believe [j]all that the [k]prophets have
spoken:
26 [l]Ought not [m]Christ to have
[n]suffered these things, and to
[o]enter into his glory?
27 And beginning at [p]Mō'ṣeṣ
and all the prophets, he [q]ex-
pounded[G] unto them in all the
[r]scriptures the [j]things concerning [s]himself.[T] [Q]
28 And they drew nigh[G] unto
the village, whither[G] they went:
and he made[G] as though he
would have gone further.
29 But they constrained him,
saying, [t]Abide with us: for it is
toward evening, and the day is
far spent. And he went in to
tarry with them.
30 And it came to pass, as he
sat at meat[G] with them, he took
bread, and *blessed *it*, and
brake, and gave to them.
31 And their eyes were [u]opened,
and they knew him; and he vanished out of their sight.
32 And they said one to another, Did not our heart burn
within us, while he [v]talked
with us by the way[G], and
while he [q]opened to us the
[r]scriptures?
33 And they rose up the same
hour, and returned to [w]Jē-ru'sā-
lĕm, and found the [x]eleven gathered together, and them that
were with them,
34 Saying, The Lord is [y]risen
indeed, and hath [z]appeared to
Sī'mon.
35 And they told what things
*were done* in the way, and how he
was known of them in breaking
of bread.
36 ¶ And as they thus spake,
Jē'ṣus himself [z]stood in the
midst of them, and saith unto
them, [a]Peace *be* unto you.[T]
37 But they were terrified and
affrighted[G], and supposed that
they had seen a spirit.
38 And he said unto them, Why
are ye troubled? and why do
thoughts arise in your hearts?
39 Behold[G] my hands and my
feet, that it is [b]I myself: handle
me, and see; for a spirit[G] hath
not flesh and bones, as ye see
me have.
40 And when he had thus
spoken, he shewed them *his*
hands and *his* feet.
41 And while they yet [c]believed
not for [d]joy, and wondered, he
said unto them, Have ye here
[2]any meat[G]?
42 And they gave him a piece
of a broiled [e]fish, [3]and of an
[f]honeycomb.
43 And he took *it*, and did [b]eat
before them.
44 And he said unto them,
These *are* the words which I
spake unto you, while I was yet
with you, that all [g]things must
be fulfilled, which were written
in the [h]law of Mō'ṣeṣ, and *in*
the prophets, and *in* the psalms,
concerning me.[T]
45 Then opened he their [i]un-

v.32–AD 30
See footnote, *Time*, Rev. 10:6.

33
w *Jerusalem*, Judg. 19:10.
x *Apostles*, Luke 6:13.

34
y *Resurrection of Jesus*, Matt. 28:6.
z *Appearances of Jesus after his Resurrection*, Mark 16:9.

36
a *Salutations*, Luke 1:44.

39
b *Jesus, humanity of*, Matt. 1:21.

41
c *Unbelief, instances of*, Heb. 3:12.
d *Joy, instances of*, Psa. 5:11.
2 R. V. anything to eat?

42
e *Fish*, Matt. 17:27.
f *Honey*, Prov. 25:27.
3 R. V. *omits* and of an honeycomb.

44
g *Prophecies concerning the Messiah, and their fulfillment*, Gen. 12:3.
h *Law, of Moses*, Deut. 33:2.

45
i *Spiritual Understanding*, Luke 8:8.

* **THANKSGIVING FOR FOOD**, 1 Sam. 9:13; Matt. 14:19 (with Mark 6:41; Luke 9:16; John 6:11, 23); Mark 8:6, 7 (with Matt. 15:36); Luke 24:30; Acts 27:35; Rom. 14:6; 1 Cor. 10:30, 31; 1 Tim. 4:3–5.

v.45–AD 30
See footnote, *Time,* Rev. 10:6.

*j Word of God,* Psa 119:9.

46

*k Jesus, sufferings of,* Matt. 1:21.
*l Atonement, by Jesus,* Lev. 17:11.
*m Resurrection of Jesus,* Matt. 28:6.

47

*n* Matt. 28:19; Mark 16:15.
*o Repentance,* Mark 1:4.
*p Sin, forgiveness of,* Rom. 5:12.
*q Preaching,* Matt. 9:35.
*r Name of Jesus,* John 14:13.

derstanding, that they might
understand the [j]scriptures,
46 And said unto them, Thus it
is written, and thus it behoved
Christ to [k,l]suffer, and to [m]rise
from the dead the third day:
47 [n]And that [o]repentance and
[p]remission of sins should be
[q]preached in his [r]name among
[s]all nations, beginning at [t]Jĕ-ru̇'sȧ-lĕm.
48 And [u]ye are [†,v]witnesses of
these things.
49 ¶ And, behold, [w,x,y]I send
the promise of my [z]Father upon
you: but tarry ye in the city of
[a]Jĕ-ru̇'sȧ-lĕm, until ye be [b,c]en-
dued with [‡]power from on
high.
50 ¶ And he led them out
as far as to [d]Bĕth'a-ny̆, and
he lifted up his [e]hands, and
[f]blessed them.
51 And it came to pass, while
he blessed them, he was parted
from them, and [g]carried up into
heaven.
52 And they [h]worshipped him,
and returned to [a]Jĕ-ru̇'sȧ-lĕm
with great [i]joy:
53 And were continually in the
[j]temple, [4,k,l]praising and blessing God. Amen.

*s Missions,* Matt. 28:19. *t Jerusalem,* Judg. 19:10. **48** *u Minister, duties of,* Rom. 15:16. *v Religious Testimony,* 2 Thess. 1:10. **49** *w Jesus, promises of,* Matt. 1:21. *x Promise, of the Holy Spirit,* 2 Cor. 1:20. *y Minister, promises to,* Rom. 15:16. *z God, fatherhood of,* Gen. 2:2.

*i Joy,* Psa. 5:11. **53** *j Temple, Herod's,* 1 Kin. 6:17. *k Praise,* Psa. 150:1. *l Worship, public,* Gen. 22:5. 4 R. V. *omits* praising and

v.49–AD 30
See footnote, *Time,* Rev. 10:6.

*a Jerusalem,* Judg. 19:10.
*b Minister, character and qualifications of,* Rom. 15:16.
*c Holy Spirit, baptism of,* Acts 1:2.

50

*d Bethany,* John 11:18.
*e Hand,* Ezra 10:19.
*f Benedictions,* Deut. 21:5.

51

*g Ascension, of Jesus,* 2 Kin. 2:1.

52

*h Jesus, worship of,* Matt. 1:21.

THE GOSPEL ACCORDING TO

# JOHN

## CHAPTER 1

*The divinity, humanity, and office of Jesus Christ. 15 The testimony of John the Baptist. 39 The calling of Andrew, Peter, and others.*

1

*a Jesus, pre-existence of,* Matt. 1:21.
*b Jesus, eternity of,* Matt. 1:21.
*c* 1 John 1:1; Rev 19:13.
*d Jesus, names of,* Matt. 1:21.
*e Jesus, divinity of,* Matt. 1:21.

3

*f Creation, by Christ,* Mark 13:19.
*g Jesus, creator,* Matt. 1:21.

4

*h Life, spiritual,* Eccl. 8:15.
*i Light, figurative,* Matt. 5:14.
*j Wisdom spiritual,* Prov. 2:2.

5

*k Darkness, figurative,* Gen. 1:2.
*l Spiritual Blindness,* 2 Cor. 4:4.
1 R.V. apprehended

6

*m John the Baptist,* Luke 1:63.
v.6–AD 26

[a,b]IN the beginning was the
[c,d]Word, and the Word
was with God, and the [e]Word
was God.
2 [a,b]The same was in the beginning with God.
3 All things were [f]made by
[g]him; and without him was not
any thing made that was made.
4 In him was [h]life; and the life
was the [i,j]light of men.
5 And the [i]light shineth in
[k,l]darkness; and the darkness
[1]comprehended it not.
6 ¶ There was a man sent from
God, whose name *was* [m]Jŏhn.
7 The same came for a witness,
to bear witness of the [d]Light,
that all *men* through him might
[n]believe.
8 [m]He was not that [d]Light,
but *was sent* to bear witness of
that Light.
9 *That* was the true [d]Light,
which [o]lighteth every man that
cometh into the world.
10 He was in the world, and
the world was [f]made by [g]him,
and the world [l,p]knew him not.
11 He came unto his own, and
his own [p,q]received him not.
12 But as many as [r]received
him, to them gave he [2]power to
become the [s]sons of God, *even* to
them that [r]believe on his [t]name:
13 Which were [u]born, not of
blood, nor of the will of the flesh,
nor of the will of man, but of
God.
14 And the [v,w]Word was [x]made

v.7–AD 26
See footnote, *Time,* Rev. 10:6.

7

*n Faith in Christ,* John 6:69.

9

*o Jesus, mission of,* Matt. 1:21.

10

*p Unbelief,* Heb. 3:12.

11

*q Jesus, rejected,* Matt. 1:21.

12

*r Faith in Christ, salvation by,* John 6:69.
*s Spiritual Adoption,* Rom. 8:15.
*t Name of Jesus,* John 14:13.
2 R. V. the right

13

*u Regeneration,* Tit. 3:5.

14

*v* 1 John 1:1; Rev. 19:13.
*w Jesus, names of,* Matt. 1:21.
*x Jesus, incarnation of,* Matt. 1:21.

† **WITNESSING FOR CHRIST,** Luke 2:17, 38; 24:48; Acts 1:8; 10:39; 22:15; 23:11; 26:22. *Of John the Baptist,* John 1:15; 3:26. *Of the apostles,* John 15:27; 19:35; Acts 10:39–43; 1 John 1:1–5; *to his resurrection,* Acts 1:22; 2:32; 3:15; 4:33; 5:32; 1 Cor. 15:3–8.

‡ **SPIRITUAL POWER.** *From God,* Isa. 40:29–31; Luke 24:49; 1 Cor. 1:24–28; Phil. 2:13; 2 Tim. 1:7. *From the Holy Spirit,* John 7:38, 39; Acts 1:8; 2:2–4. *On believers,* Acts 6:8, 10; 1 Cor. 4:19, 20; Heb. 6:5. *In preaching,* Acts 4:33; 6:10; 1 Thess. 1:5. *Through prayer,* Gen. 32:28; Luke 24:49; Acts 1:14, with 2:1–4. See footnote, HOLY SPIRIT, Acts 1:2.

v.14–AD 26 See footnote, *Time*, Rev. 10:6.

*y Fellowship, with Christ*, 1 Cor. 1:9.
*z Transfiguration, of Jesus*, Matt. 17:2.

*a Jesus, divine sonship of*, Matt. 1:21.
*b God, fatherhood of*, Gen. 2:2.
*c Jesus, perfections of*, Matt. 1:21.
*d Truth*, John 18:37.

**15**
*e John the Baptist*, Luke 1:63.
*f Witnessing for Christ*, Luke 24:48.

**16**
*g Spiritual Blessings, from Christ*, Eph. 1:3.

**17**
*h Law, temporary*, Deut. 33:2.
*i Moses*, Ex. 2:10.
*j Salvation*, Acts 16:17.

**18**
*k God, invisible*, Gen. 2:2.
*l Jesus, relation of, to the Father*, Matt. 1:21.

**19**
*m Jews*, Neh. 4:2.
*n Priest*, Lev. 1:5.
*o Levites*, Deut. 10:8.
*p Jerusalem*, Judg. 19:10.

**21**
*q* Or, *Elijah, antetype of John the Baptist*, 1 Kin. 17:1.

**23**
*r* Isa. 40:3; Matt. 3:3; Luke 3:4.
*s Prophets*, Isa. 3:2.
*t* Or, *Isaiah*, Isa. 1:1.

**24**
*u Pharisees*, Matt. 15:12.

**25**
*v Baptism, of John the Baptist*, Luke 20:4.

flesh, and [y]dwelt among us, (and we beheld his [z]glory, the glory as of the [a]only begotten of the [b]Father,) [c]full of grace and [d]truth.[Q]

15 ¶ [e]Jŏhn [f]bare witness of him, and cried, saying, This was he of whom I spake, He that cometh after me is preferred[G] before me: for he was before me.[T][S]

16 And of his [g]fulness have all we received, and grace for grace.

17 For the [h]law was given by [i]Mō′ṣeṣ, *but* [j]grace and [d]truth came by Jē′ṣus Chrīst.[T][Q]

18 [k]No man hath seen God at any time; the only begotten [a]Son, which is [l]in the bosom of the [b]Father, he hath declared[G] *him.*[T][Q]

19 ¶ And this is the record[G] of [e]Jŏhn, when the [m]Jewṣ sent [n]priests and [o]Lē′vītes from [p]Jē-rụ′sā-lĕm to ask him, Who art thou?

20 And [e]he confessed, and denied not; but confessed, I am not the Chrīst.

21 And they asked [e]him, What then? Art thou [q]Ē-lī′as? And he saith, I am not. Art thou that prophet? And he answered, No.[Q]

22 Then said they unto him, Who art thou? that we may give an answer to them that sent us. What sayest thou of thyself?

23 He said, [e]I *am* [r]the voice of one crying in the wilderness, Make straight the way of the Lord, as said the [s]prophet [t]Ē-ṣā′ias.[Q]

24 And they which were sent were of the [u]Phăr′ĭ-seeṣ.

25 And they asked him, and said unto him, Why [v]baptizest thou then, if thou be not that Chrīst, nor [q]Ē-lī′as, neither that prophet?

26 [e]Jŏhn answered them, saying, I baptize with water: but there standeth [w]one among you, whom ye know not;

27 [w]He it is, who coming after me is preferred before me, [x]whose shoe's latchet I am [y]not worthy to unloose.[G]

28 These things were done in [3,z]Bĕth-ăb′a-rȧ beyond [a]Jôr′dan, where [b]Jŏhn was [c]baptizing.

29 ¶ The next day [b]Jŏhn seeth Jē′ṣus coming unto him, and saith, Behold the *,[d,e,f]Lamb of God, which [g,h]taketh away the sin of the world.[Q]

30 This is he of whom I said, After me cometh a man which is preferred before me: for he was before me.[T]

31 And I knew him not: but that he should be made manifest to Ĭṣ′ra-el, therefore am [b]I come [c]baptizing with water.

32[T] And [b]Jŏhn bare record,[G] saying, I [i]saw the Spirit descending from heaven like a [j]dove, and it abode upon him.

33 And I knew him not: but he that sent me to [k]baptize with water, the same said unto me, Upon whom thou shalt see the Spirit descending, and remaining on him, the same is he which baptizeth with the [l]Holy [4]Ghost.[G]

34 And [b]I saw, and bare record[G] that this is the [m]Son of God.[T]

35 ¶ Again the next day after [b]Jŏhn stood, and two of his [n]disciples;

36 And looking upon Jē′ṣus as he walked, he saith, Behold the *,[d,e,f]Lamb of God![Q]

37 And the two [n]disciples heard him speak, and they followed Jē′ṣus.

38 Then Jē′ṣus turned, and saw them following, and saith unto them, What seek ye? They said unto him, [o]Răb′bī,[G] (which is to say, being interpreted, Master,) where dwellest thou?

v.26–AD 26 See footnote, *Time*, Rev. 10:6.

**26**
*w Jesus, prophecies concerning*, Matt. 1:21.

**27**
*x Jesus, perfections of*, Matt. 1:21.
*y Humility*, Prov. 22:4.

**28**
*z* John 10:39–42.

*a Jordan*, Gen. 32:10.
*b John the Baptist*, Luke 1:63.
*c Baptism, of John the Baptist*, Luke 20:4.
3 R. V. Bethany

**29**
*d Jesus, names of*, Matt. 1:21.
*e Symbols and Similitudes*, Heb. 9:9.
*f Types, of the Savior*, Heb. 10:1.
*g Jesus, design of his death*, Matt. 1:21.
*h Atonement, by Jesus*, Lev. 17:11.

**32**
*i Vision*, Acts 9:10.
*j Dove*, Gen. 8:8.

**33**
*k Baptism, of John the Baptist*, Luke 20:4.
*l Holy Spirit, baptism of*, Acts 1:2.
4 R. V. Spirit.

**34**
*m Jesus, divine sonship of*, Matt. 1:21.

**35**
*n Disciples*, Matt. 9:14.

**38**
*o Rabbi*, Matt. 23:7.

***LAMB.** *An appellation of Jesus*, John 1:29; Rev. 6:16; 7:9, 10, 14, 17; 12:11; 13:8; 14:1, 4; 15:3; 17:14; 19:7; 21:9, 14, 22, 23, 27; 22:1, 3.

v.39–AD 26
See footnote, *Time*, Rev. 10:6.

**40**
*p Andrew*, Matt. 4:18.
*q Peter*, Mark 5:37.

**41**
*r Zeal, instances of*, 2 Cor. 7:11.
*s Faith in Christ, exemplified*, John 6:69.
*t Jesus, Messiah*, Matt. 1:21.

**42**
*u* John 21:15–17.
5 R. V. Peter.

**43**
*v Galilee*, Mark 6:21.
*w Philip*, Luke 6:14.
*x Minister, call of*, Rom. 15:16.
*y Call, personal*, Phil. 3:14.

**45**
*z* John 21:2.

*a Faith in Christ, exemplified*, John 6:69.
*b Jesus, prophecies concerning*, Matt. 1:21.
*c Moses*, Ex. 2:10.
*d Law, of Moses*, Deut. 33:2.
*e Prophecies concerning the Messiah, and their fulfillment*, Gen. 12:3.
*f Joseph*, Luke 3:23.

**46**
*g* John 21:2.
*h Proverbs*, 1 Sam. 24:13.
*i Philip*, Luke 6:14.

**47**
*j Holy, described*, Col. 3:12.

39 He saith unto them, Come and see. They came and saw where he dwelt, and abode with him that day: for it was about the tenth[G] hour.

40 One of the two which heard [b]Jŏhn *speak*, and followed him, was [p]Ăn′drew, Sī′mon [q]Pē′tẽr's brother.

41 [p]He first [r]findeth his own brother [q]Sī′mon, and saith unto him, [s]We have found the [t]Mĕs-sī′as, which is, being interpreted, the [d]Chrīst.[G T Q]

42 And [p]he [r]brought him to Jē′ṣus. And when Jē′ṣus beheld him, he said, Thou art [q]Sī′mon the son of [u]Jō′nȧ: thou shalt be called Çē′phas, which is by interpretation, [5]A stone.

43 ¶ The[T] day following Jē′ṣus would go forth into [v]Găl′ĭ-lee, and findeth [w]Phĭl′ĭp, and saith unto [x]him, [y]Follow me.

44 Now [w]Phĭl′ĭp was of †Běth-sā′ĭ-dȧ, the city of [p]Ăn′drew and [q]Pē′tẽr.

45 [w]Phĭl′ĭp findeth [z]Nā-thăn′a-el, and [a]saith unto him, We have found him, of [b]whom [c]Mō′ṣeṣ in the [d]law, and the [e]prophets, did write, Jē′ṣus of ‡Năz′a-rĕth, the son of [f]Jō′ṣeph.[T Q]

46 And [g]Nā-thăn′a-el said unto him, [h]Can there any good thing come out of ‡Năz′a-rĕth? [i]Phĭl′ĭp saith unto him, Come and see.

47 Jē′ṣus saw [g]Nā-thăn′a-el coming to him, and saith of him, Behold an Īṣ′ra-el-īte indeed, [j]in whom is ‖no guile[G]!

48 [g]Nā-thăn′a-el saith unto him, Whence[G] knowest thou me? Jē′ṣus answered and said unto him, Before that [i]Phĭl′ĭp called thee, when thou wast under the [k]fig tree, I [l]saw thee.

49 [g]Nā-thăn′a-el answered and [a]saith unto him, [m]Răb′bī,[G] [n]thou art the [o]Son of God; thou art the [p]King of Īṣ′ra-el.[T Q]

50 Jē′ṣus answered and said unto him, Because I said unto thee, I [l]saw thee under the [k]fig tree, believest thou? thou shalt see greater things than these.

51 And he [q]saith unto him, Verily, verily, I say unto you, Hereafter ye shall see heaven open, and the [r]angels of God ascending and descending upon the [s]Son of man.[T Q]

## CHAPTER 2

*Jesus at Cana turns water into wine. 13 He goes up to Jerusalem, and drives the traders out of the temple. 18 He foretells his own death and resurrection. 23 Many believe on him.*

AND[S T] the third day there was a [a]marriage in *Cā′nȧ of [b]Găl′ĭ-lee; and the [c,d]mother of Jē′ṣus was there:

2 And both Jē′ṣus was called, and his [e]disciples, to the [a]marriage.

3 And when they wanted[G] [f]wine, the [c,d]mother of Jē′ṣus saith unto him, They have no wine.

4 Jē′ṣus saith unto her, Woman, what have I to do with thee? mine hour is not yet come.

5 His [c,d]mother saith unto the servants, Whatsoever he saith unto you, do *it*.[Q]

6 And there were set there six waterpots of stone, after the manner of the [g]purifying of the Jewṣ, containing two or three [h]firkins[G] apiece.

7 Jē′ṣus saith unto them, Fill the waterpots with [i]water. And they filled them up to the brim.

v.48–AD 26
See footnote, *Time*, Rev. 10:6.

**48**
*k Fig Tree*, Luke 13:6.
*l Jesus, omniscience of*, Matt. 1:21.

**49**
*m Rabbi*, Matt. 23:7.
*n Jesus, received*, Matt. 1:21.
*o Jesus, divine sonship of*, Matt. 1:21.
*p Jesus, king*, Matt. 1:21.

**51**
*q Jesus, prophet*, Matt. 1:21.
*r Angel*, Heb. 1:13.
*s Jesus, humanity of*, Matt. 1:21.

**1**
*a Marriage*, Gen. 34:9.
*b Galilee*, Mark 6:21.
*c Mother*, 1 Kin. 2:20.
*d Mary*, Luke 1:27.

**2**
*e Disciples*, Matt. 9:14.

**3**
*f Wine*, Prov. 23:31.

**6**
*g Purification*, Num. 19:19.
*h Measure, liquid*, Deut. 25:15.

**7**
*i Water*, 1 Kin. 17:10.

† **BETHSAIDA** (*house*, or *place of fishing*), a city of Galilee. *The city of Philip, Andrew, and Peter*, John 1:44; 12:21. *Jesus, visits*, Mark 6:45; *cures a blind man in*, Mark 8:22; *prophesies against*, Matt. 11:21, 22; Luke 10:13, 14.
Desert of, E. of the sea of Galilee. *Jesus feeds five thousand people in*, Matt. 14:13; Mark 6:32; Luke 9:10.

‡ **NAZARETH**, a village in Galilee. *Joseph and Mary dwell at*, Matt. 2:23; Luke 1:26, 27, 56; 2:4, 39, 51. *Jesus from*, Matt. 21:11; Mark 1:24; 10:47; Luke 4:34; 18:37; 24:19. *People of, reject Jesus*, Luke 4:16–30. *Its name opprobrious*, John 1:46.

‖ **GUILELESSNESS.** *Enjoined*, Psa. 34:13 (with 1 Pet. 3:10); 1 Pet. 2:1. *Of Jesus*, 1 Pet. 2:22. *Of Nathanael*, John 1:47. *A grace of the righteous*, Psa. 32:2.

* **CANA** (*reedy*, *a nest* or *cave*). *Marriage at; and Jesus' first miracle, the changing of water into wine, at*, John 2:1–11. *Nobleman's son healed at*, John 4:46, 47. *Nathanael's home at*, John 21:2.

8 And he saith unto them,
Draw out now, and bear unto
the governor of the [j]feast. And
they bare *it*.
9 When the ruler of the [j]feast
had tasted the [i]water that was
[k]made [l]wine, and knew not
whence it was: (but the servants
which drew the water knew;) the
governor of the feast called the
bridegroom,
10 And saith unto him, Every
man at the beginning doth set
forth good [l]wine; and when
men have [1]well drunk, then
that which is worse: *but* thou
hast kept the good [l]wine until
now.
11 This beginning of [2,k]mir-
acles did Jē'ṣus in *Cā'nȧ of
[b]Găl'ĭ-lee, and [m]manifested forth
his glory; and his [e]disciples
[n,o]believed on him.
12 ¶ After this he went down
to [p]Că-pēr'na-ŭm, he, and his
[c,d]mother, and his [q]brethren, and
his [e]disciples: and they continued there not many days.
13 ¶ And the [r]Jews' [s]passover
was at hand, and Jē'ṣus went up
to [t]Jē-ru̥'sā-lĕm,
14 [u]And found in the [v]tem-
ple those that [w,x]sold oxen and
sheep and doves, and the changers of money sitting:
15 [u]And when he had made a
scourge of small cords, he drove
them all out of the [v]temple, and
the sheep, and the oxen; and
poured out the changers' money,
and overthrew the [y]tables;
16 And said unto them that
sold doves, Take these things
hence; [w,x]make not my [z]Fa-
ther's house an house of merchandise.
17 And his [a]disciples remembered that it was written, The
[b,c]zeal of thine house [3]hath eaten
me up.
18 ¶ Then answered the [d]Jews
and said unto him, What [e]sign

8
j *Feasts*, Mark 12:39.

9
k *Miracles, of Jesus*, Luke 23:8.
l *Wine, made by Jesus*, Prov. 23:31.

10
1 R. V. drunk freely,

11
m *Miracles, design of*, Luke 23:8.
n *Faith in Christ*, John 6:69.
o *Jesus, received*, Matt. 1:21.
2 R. V. his signs

12
p *Capernaum*, Luke 4:31.
q *Brothers of Jesus*, Matt. 13:55.

13
r *Jews*, Neh. 4:2.
s *Passover*, Num. 9:5.
t *Jerusalem*, Judg. 19:10.

14
u Matt. 21:12, 13; Mark 11:15–17; Luke 19:45, 46.
v *Temple, Herod's*, 1 Kin. 6:17.
w *Sacrilege*, Lev. 19:8.
x *Profanation, of God's house*, Lev. 22:32.

15
y *Table*, Judg. 1:7.

16
z *God, fatherhood of*, Gen. 2:2.

17
a *Disciples*, Matt. 9:14.
b *Zeal*, 2 Cor. 7:11.
c *Jesus, zeal of*, Matt. 1:21.
3 R. V. shall eat me up.

18
d *Jews*, Neh. 4:2.
e *Miracles, demanded by unbelievers*, Luke 23:8.

shewest thou unto us, seeing that
thou doest these things?
19 Jē'ṣus answered and said
unto them, [f]Destroy this [g]tem-
ple, and in three days [h]I will
[i]raise it up.
20 Then said the [d]Jews, Forty
and six years was this [j]temple in
building, and wilt thou rear it up
in three days?
21 But he spake of the [g]temple
of his body.
22 When therefore he was [i]risen
from the dead, his [a]disciples remembered that he had said this
unto them; and they believed
the [k]scripture, and the word
which Jē'ṣus had said.
23 ¶ Now when he was in [l]Jē-
ru̥'sā-lĕm at the [m]passover, in
the feast *day*, many believed in
his [n]name, [4]when they saw the
[o]miracles which he did.
24 But Jē'ṣus [p]did not commit
himself unto them, because he
[q]knew all *men*,
25 And needed not that any
should testify of man: for he
[q]knew what was in man.

## CHAPTER 3

*Nicodemus comes to Jesus. 3 Jesus teaches the necessity of regeneration, 14 his mission and the love of the Father. 23 John baptizes, 27 and testifies that Jesus is the Messiah.*

THERE was a man of the
[a]Phăr'ĭ-seeṣ, named [b]Nĭc-
o-dē'mus, a ruler of the [c]Jewṣ:
2 The same came to Jē'ṣus [d]by
night, and said unto him, Răb'-
bī, [e]we know that thou art a
[f]teacher come from God: for no
man can do these [1,g]miracles that
thou doest, except God be with
him.
3 Jē'ṣus answered and said unto him, Verily, verily, I say unto
thee, [h]Except a man be [i,j,k]born
[2]again, he cannot see the [l]king-
dom of God.
4 [b,m]Nĭc-o-dē'mus saith unto
him, [n]How can a man be born
when he is old? can he enter the

A.D. 30
See footnote, *Time*, Rev. 10:6.

19
f *Jesus, death of*, Matt. 1:21.
g *Temple, figurative*, 1 Kin. 6:17.
h *Jesus, power of*, Matt. 1:21.
i *Resurrection of Jesus*, Matt. 28:6.

20
j *Temple, Herod's*, 1 Kin. 6:17.

22
k *Word of God*, Psa. 119:9.

23
l *Jerusalem*, Judg. 19:10.
m *Passover*, Num. 9:5.
n *Name of Jesus*, John 14:13.
o *Miracles, of Jesus*, Luke 23:8.
4 R. V. beholding his signs

24
p *Prudence*, 2 Chr. 2:12.
q *Jesus, omniscience of*, Matt. 1:21.

v.23–AD 27

1
a *Pharisees*, Matt. 15:12.
b John 7:50–53.
c *Jews*, Neh. 4:2.

2
d *Cowardice*, Lev. 26:36.
e *Public Opinion*, John 12:42.
f *Jesus, teacher*, Matt. 1:21.
g *Miracles, of Jesus*, Luke 23:8.
1 R. V. signs

3
h *Salvation, conditions of*, Acts 16:17.
i *Regeneration*, Tit. 3:5.
j *Heart, renewed*, Psa. 44:21.
k *Life, spiritual*, Eccl. 8:15.
l *Kingdom of Heaven*, Matt. 13:24.
2 R. V. anew,

4
m *Unbelievers*, 1 Cor. 6:6.
n *Spiritual Blindness*, 2 Cor. 4:4.

second time into his mother's
womb, and be born?
5 Jē'ṣus answered, Verily, verily, I say unto thee, [h]Except a
man be [i,j,k]born of water and *of*
the [o]Spirit, he cannot enter into
the [l]kingdom of God.
6 [p]That which is born of the
flesh is flesh; and that which is
born of the Spirit is spirit.
7 Marvel not that I said unto thee, Ye must be [i,j,k]born
[2]again.
8 [q]The [r]wind bloweth where
it listeth, and thou hearest the
sound thereof, but canst not tell
whence it cometh, and whither
it goeth: [s]so is every one that is
born of the [o]Spirit.
9 [b]Nĭc-o-dē'mus answered and
said unto him, [n]How can these
things be?
10 Jē'ṣus answered and said
unto him, Art thou [3]a master of
Ĭṣ'ra-el, and [n]knowest not these
things?
11 Verily, verily, I say unto
thee, We speak that we do know,
and testify that we have seen;
and ye [t]receive not our witness.
12 If I have told you earthly
things, and ye [u]believe not, how
shall ye believe, if I tell you *of*
heavenly things?
13 And no man hath ascended
up to heaven, but [v]he that came
down from heaven, *even* the
[w]Son of man which is in heaven.
14 And [x]as [y]Mō'ṣeṣ lifted up
the [z,a,b]serpent in the wilderness,
[c]even so must the Son of man
[d]be lifted up:
15 [e]That [f]whosoever [g]believeth
[4]in him should not [h]perish, but
have [i]eternal [j]life.
16 For God so [k]loved the
[l]world, that he gave his only
begotten [m]Son, that whosoever
[g]believeth in him should not
[h]perish, but have everlasting
[i,j]life.
17 For [k]God sent not his [m]Son
into the world to [5]condemn
the world; but [n]that the world
through him might be [o]saved.
18 He that [g]believeth on him
is not [6]condemned: but he that
[p,q]believeth not [7]is condemned
already, because he hath not believed in the [r]name of the only
begotten [m]Son of God.
19 And this is the [8,s]condemna-
tion, that [t,u]light is come into the
world, and men [v,w]loved [x,y]dark-
ness rather than light, because
their deeds were evil.
20 For every one that [p]doeth
[z]evil [w]hateth the [u]light, neither
cometh to the light, lest his deeds
should be reproved.
21 But he that [a,b]doeth [c]truth
cometh to the light, that his
[d]deeds may be made manifest,
that they are wrought in God.
22 ¶ After these things came
Jē'ṣus and his [e]disciples into the
land of [f]Jū-dæ'ȧ; and there he
tarried with them, and [g]baptized.
23 And [h]Jŏhn also was [i]bap-
tizing in Æ'nŏn near to Sā'lĭm,
because there was much water
there: and they came, and were
baptized.
24 For [h]Jŏhn was not yet cast
into [j]prison.
25 ¶ Then there arose a question between *some* of Jŏhn's
[c]disciples and the [k]Jewṣ about
[l]purifying.
26 [m]And they came unto [h]Jŏhn,
and said unto him, [n]Răb'bī, he
that was with thee beyond [o]Jôr'-
dan, to whom thou barest witness, behold, the same [g]baptiz-
eth, and all *men* come to him.
27 [h]Jŏhn answered and said, A
[p]man can receive nothing, except
[q,r]it be given him from heaven.
28 Ye yourselves bear me witness, that I said, I am not the
Christ, but that I am sent before
him.

**5**
o *Holy Spirit*, Acts 1:2.

**6**
p *Heredity*, Ezek. 18:2.

**8**
q *Meteorology*, Matt. 16:2.
r *Wind*, Job 37:17.
s *Mysteries*, Mark 4:11.

**10**
3 R. V. the teacher

**11**
t *Jesus, rejected*, Matt. 1:21.

**12**
u *Unbelief*, Heb. 3:12.

**13**
v *Jesus, pre-existence of*, Matt. 1:21.
w *Jesus, humanity of*, Matt. 1:21.

**14**
x Num. 21:9.
y *Moses*, Ex. 2:10.
z *Brazen Serpent*, 2 Kin. 18:4.

a *Symbols and Similitudes*, Heb. 9:9.
b *Types of the Savior*, Heb. 10:1.
c *Jesus, prophet*, Matt. 1:21.
d *Jesus, death of*, Matt. 1:21.

**15**
e *Jesus, design of his death*, Matt. 1:21.
f *Righteous, promises to*, Psa. 64:10.
g *Faith in Christ*, John 6:69.
h *Wicked, punishment of*, Psa. 73:3.
i *Immortality*, 1 Cor. 15:54.
j *Life, everlasting*, Eccl. 8:15.
4 R. V. may in him have eternal life.

**16**
k *God, love of*, Gen. 2:2.
l *Wicked, God's love for*, Psa. 73:3.
m *Jesus, divine sonship of*, Matt. 1:21.

**17**
n *Jesus, mission of*, Matt. 1:21.
o *Jesus, savior*, Matt. 1:21.
5 R. V. judge

**18**
p *Wicked, described*, Psa. 73:3.
q *Unbelief*, Heb. 3:12.
r *Name of Jesus*, John 14:13.
6 R. V. judged:
7 R. V. hath been judged

**19**
s *Judgment, according to opportunity and works*, 1 Pet. 1:17.
t *Responsibility, according to privilege*, Ezek. 18:20.
u *Light, figurative*, Matt. 5:14.
v *Sin, love of*, Rom. 5:12.
w *Depravity*, Job 15:14.
x *Darkness, figurative*, Gen. 1:2.
y *Spiritual Blindness*, 2 Cor. 4:4.
8 R. V. judgment,

**20**
z *Sin*, Rom. 5:12.

**21**
a *Righteous, described*, Psa. 64:10.
b *Righteousness, fruits of*, Psa. 15:2.
c *Truth*, John 18:37.
d *Works*, 2 Tim. 1:9.

**22**
e *Disciples*, Matt. 9:14.
f *Judea*, Luke 5:17.
g *Baptism, Christian*. Luke 20:4.

**23**
h *John the Baptist*, Luke 1:63.
i *Baptism, of John the Baptist*, Luke 20:4.

**24**
j *Prison*, Gen. 39:20.

**25**
k *Jews*, Neh. 4:2.
l *Purification*, Num. 19:[illegible]

**26**
m *Jealousy, instances of*, Psa. 78:58.
n *Rabbi*, Matt. 23:7.
o *Jordan*, Gen. 32:10.

**27** p *Minister, character and qualifications of*, Rom. 15:16. q *Spiritual Blessings, from God*, Eph. 1:3. r *Spiritual Gifts*, 1 Cor. 12:4.

29 [s]He that hath the bride is
the bridegroom: but the friend
of the bridegroom, which standeth and heareth him, rejoiceth
greatly because of the bridegroom's voice: this my [t]joy
therefore is fulfilled.
30 He must increase, but I *must*
decrease.
31 [u]He that cometh from above
is [v]above all: he that is of the
earth is earthly, and speaketh of
the earth: he that cometh from
heaven is above all.[T] [Q]
32 And what he hath [w]seen and
heard, that he testifieth[G]; and [x]no
man receiveth his testimony[G].
33[T] He that hath [y]received his
testimony[G] hath set[G] to his seal
that God is [z]true.
34 For [a]he whom God hath
sent speaketh the words of God:
for [9]God giveth not the Spirit by
measure *unto him*.[T]
35 The [b]Father [c]loveth the [d]Son,
and [e]hath given all things into
his hand.
36 He that [f]believeth on the
[d]Son hath [g]everlasting [h]life: and
he that [10]believeth not the Son
shall not see life; but [i]the wrath
of God abideth[G] on him.[S] [T]

## CHAPTER 4

*Jesus converses with a woman of Samaria. 27 His disciples marvel. 31 The fields white for the harvest. 39 Many of the Samaritans believe on him. 43 He departs into Galilee; 46 and heals a nobleman's son sick at Capernaum.*

WHEN therefore the Lord
knew how the [a]Phăr'ĭ-
seeṣ had heard that Jē'ṣus made
and [b]baptized more [c]disciples
than [d]Jŏhn,[T]
2 (Though Jē'ṣus himself [b]bap-
tized not, but his [c]disciples,)
3 [e]He left [f]Jū-dæ'ȧ, and departed again into [g]Găl'ĭ-lee.
4 And he must needs go
through [h]Să-mā'rĭ-ȧ.
5 Then cometh [e]he to a city
of [h]Să-mā'rĭ-ȧ, which is called

29
s *Marriage, figurative*, Gen. 34:9.
t *Joy*, Psa. 5:11.
31
u *Jesus, divinity of*, Matt. 1:21.
v *Jesus, king*, Matt. 1:21.
32
w *Jesus, omniscience of*, Matt. 1:21.
x *Jesus, rejected*, Matt. 1:21.
33
y *Faith*, Mark 11:22.
z *God, truth*, Gen. 2:2.

34
a *Jesus, relation of, to the Father*, Matt. 1:21.
9 R. V. he giveth not the Spirit by measure.
35
b *God, fatherhood of*, Gen. 2:2.
c *God, love of*, Gen. 2:2.
d *Jesus, divine sonship of*, Matt. 1:21.
e *Jesus, king*, Matt. 1:21.
36
f *Faith in Christ*, John 6:69.
g *Immortality*, 1 Cor. 15:54.
h *Life, everlasting*, Eccl. 8:15.
i *Wicked, punishment of*, Psa. 73:3.
10 R. V. obeyeth

1
a *Pharisees*, Matt. 15:12.
b *Baptism, Christian*, Luke 20:4.
c *Disciples*, Matt. 9:14.
d *John the Baptist*, Luke 1:63.
3
e *Jesus, life of, goes to Galilee*, Matt. 1:21.
f *Judea*, Luke 5:17.
g *Galilee*, Mark 6:21.
4
h *Samaria*, Isa. 7:9.

[i]Sȳ'-chär, near to the [j]parcel[G]
of ground that [k]Jā'cob gave to
his son [l]Jō'ṣeph.[Q]
6 Now [k]Jā'cob's [m]well was
there. Jē'ṣus therefore, being
[n]wearied with *his* journey, sat
thus on the well: *and* it was
about the sixth[G] hour.
7 There cometh a woman of
[h]Să-mā'rĭ-ȧ to draw water: Jē'-
ṣus saith unto her, Give me to
drink.
8 (For his [c]disciples were gone
away unto the city to buy
[1]meat[G].)
9 Then saith the woman of
[h]Să-mā'rĭ-ȧ unto him, How is
it that thou, being a [o]Jew, askest drink of me, which am a
woman of Să-mā'rĭ-ȧ? for the
Jewṣ [p]have no dealings with
the Să-măr'ĭ-tanṣ.[Q]
10 Jē'ṣus answered and said
unto her, [q,r]If thou knewest the
[s]gift of God, and who it is that
saith to thee, Give me to drink;
thou wouldest have asked of
him, and [t]he would have given
thee living [u]water.
11 The woman saith unto him,
Sir, thou hast nothing to draw
with, and the well is deep: from
whence then hast thou that living [u]water?
12 Art thou greater than our
father [k]Jā'cob, which gave us
the [m]well, and drank thereof
himself, and his children, and
his cattle?
13 Jē'ṣus answered and said
unto her, Whosoever drinketh of
this water shall thirst again:
14 But [v]whosoever drinketh of
the [u]water that I shall give him
shall never *,[w]thirst; but [x]the
water that [s]I shall give him shall
be[G] in him a well of water springing up into [y]everlasting [z]life.[T]
15 The woman saith unto him,
Sir, give me this [u]water, that I

5
i Or, *Shechem*, Josh. 20:7.
j Gen. 33:19; Josh. 24:32.
k *Jacob*, Gen. 27:11.
l *Joseph*, Gen. 33:2.
6
m *Wells*, Gen. 21:19.
n *Jesus, humanity of*, Matt. 1:21.
8
1 R. V. food.
9
o *Jews*, Neh. 4:2.
p *Bigotry*, Isa. 65:5.
10
q *Spiritual Blindness*, 2 Cor. 4:4.
r *Ignorance*, Acts 3:17.
s *Jesus, savior*, Matt. 1:21.
t *Jesus, mission of*, Matt. 1:21.
u *Water, figurative*, 1 Kin. 17:10.
14
v *Righteous, promises to*, Psa. 64:10.
w *Spiritual Desire*, Psa. 42:1.
x *Promise, to the righteous, of eternal life*, 2 Cor. 1:20.
y *Immortality*, 1 Cor. 15:54.
z *Life, everlasting*, Eccl. 8:15.

*** THIRST.** *Figurative of the ardent desire of the devout mind*, Psa. 42:1–4; 63:1; 143:6; Isa. 55:1; Amos 8:11–13; Matt. 5:6; John 4:14, 15; 6:35; 7:37; Rev. 21:6; 22:17. See footnote, SPIRITUAL DESIRE, Psa. 42:1.

17
a *Jesus, omniscience of*, Matt. 1:21.
18
b *Adultery, instances of*, Lev. 20:10.
19
c *Jesus, prophet*, Matt. 1:21.
20
d *Worship*, Gen. 22:5.
e *Gerizim*, Deut. 11:29.
f *Jerusalem*, Judg. 19:10.
21
g *God, fatherhood of*, Gen. 2:2.
22
h *Salvation*, Acts 16:17.
i *Jews*, Neh. 4:2.
23
j *Duty, of man to God*, Eccl. 12:13.
k *Man, spirit*, Job 4:17.
l *Truth*, John 18:37.
24
m *God, spirit*, Gen. 2:2.
25
n *Messianic Hope*, Gen. 49:10.
o *Jesus, Messiah*, Matt. 1:21.
p *Jesus, mission of*, Matt. 1:21.
27
q *Disciples*, Matt. 9:14.
2 R. V. a
28
r *Zeal, instances of*, 2 Cor. 7:11.

thirst not, neither come hither to draw.

16[T] Jē'ṣus saith unto her, Go, call thy husband, and come hither.[C]

17 The woman answered and said, I have no husband. Jē'ṣus [a]said unto her, Thou hast well said, I have no husband:

18 [a]For thou hast had [b]five husbands; and he whom thou now hast is not thy husband: in that saidst thou truly.

19 The woman saith unto him, Sir, I perceive that thou art a [c]prophet.[T]

20 Our fathers [d]worshipped in this [e]mountain; and ye say, that in [f]Jė-ru̥'să-lĕm is the place where men ought to worship.[Q]

21 Jē'ṣus [c]saith unto her, Woman, believe me, the hour cometh, when ye shall neither in this [e]mountain, nor yet at [f]Jė-ru̥'să-lĕm, [d]worship the [g]Father.

22 Ye [d]worship ye know not what: we know what we worship: for [h]salvation[C] is of the [i]Jewṣ.[Q T]

23 But the hour cometh, and now is, when the true worshippers shall [d,j]worship the [g]Father in [k]spirit and in [l]truth: for the Father seeketh such to worship him.[T]

24 [m]God *is* a Spirit: and they that [d]worship him must worship *him* in [k]spirit and in [l]truth.[S T]

25 The[T] woman saith unto him, [n]I know that [o]Mĕs-sī'as cometh, which is called Chrīst: when he is come, [p]he will tell us all things.

26 Jē'ṣus saith unto her, I that speak unto thee am [o]*he*.[T]

27 ¶ And upon this came his [q]disciples, and marvelled that he talked with [2]the woman: yet no man said, What seekest thou? or, Why talkest thou with her?

28[T] The woman then left her waterpot, and went her way into the city, and [r]saith to the men,

29 [s,t]Come, see a man, which told me all things that ever I did: is not this the Chrīst?[T]

30 Then they went out of the city, and came unto him.

31 ¶ In the mean while his [q]disciples prayed[C] him, saying, [u]Master, eat.

32 But he [v]said unto them, I have meat[C] to eat that ye know not of.[T]

33 Therefore said the [q]disciples one to another, Hath any man brought him *ought*[C] to eat?

34 Jē'ṣus saith unto them, [v,w]My meat[C] is to [x,y]do the [z]will of [a]him that sent me, and to finish his work.[T]

35 Say not ye, [b]There are yet four months, and *then* cometh harvest? behold, I say unto you, Lift up your eyes, and look on the fields; for they are white already to [c]harvest.

36 And [d]he that reapeth receiveth wages, and gathereth fruit unto [e]life eternal: that both he that soweth and he that reapeth may rejoice together.

37 And herein is that saying true, One[Q] soweth, and another reapeth.

38 I sent [f]you to reap that whereon ye bestowed[C] no labour: other men laboured, and ye are entered into their labours.

39 ¶ And many of the Să-măr'-ĭ-tanṣ of that city [g]believed on him for the saying of the woman, which [h]testified, He told me all that ever I did.

40 So when the Să-măr'ĭ-tanṣ were come[C] unto him, they [i]besought[C] him that he would tarry with them: and he abode there two days.

41 And many more [g]believed because of his own word;

42 And said unto the woman, Now we [g]believe, not because of thy [h]saying: for we have heard *him* ourselves, and know that

29
s *Faith in Christ, exemplified*, John 6:69.
t *Religious Testimony*, 2 Thess. 1:10.
31
u *Rabbi*, Matt. 23:7.
32
v *Jesus, zeal of*, Matt. 1:21.
34
w *Faithfulness, instances of*, Luke 16:10.
x *Jesus, obedience of*, Matt. 1:21.
y *Diligence*, Rom. 12:8.
z *Will of God, the supreme rule of duty*, Mark 3:35.
a *Jesus, relation of, to the Father*, Matt. 1:21.
35
b Matt. 9:37; Luke 10:2.
c *Harvest, figurative*, Ex. 34:21.
36
d *Minister, promises to, and joys of*, Rom. 15:16.
e *Life, everlasting*, Eccl. 8:15.
38
f *Minister, duties of, to save men*, vs. 35-38; Rom. 15:16.
39
g *Faith in Christ*, John 6:69.
h *Religious Testimony*, 2 Thess. 1:10.
40
i *Jesus, received*, Matt. 1:21.

this is indeed [2]the Christ, the [j]Saviour of the world.[T]

43 ¶ [T]Now after two days he departed thence, and went into [k]Găl′ĭ-lee.

44 For Jē′ṣus himself testified, that [l]a [m,n]prophet hath no honour in his own country.

45 Then when he was come into [k]Găl′ĭ-lee, the Găl-ĭ-læ′anṣ [i]received him, having seen all the things that he did at [o]Jē-ru̇′sā-lĕm at the [p]feast: for they also went unto the feast.[T]

46 [S]So [T]Jē′ṣus came again into [q]Cā′nȧ of [k]Găl′ĭ-lee, where he made the water wine. And there was a certain nobleman, whose son was sick at [r]Cȧ-pēr′na-ŭm.

47 When he heard that Jē′ṣus was come out of [s]Jū-dæ′ȧ into [k]Găl′ĭ-lee, [t]he [u]went unto him, and [v]besought[G] him that he would come down, and heal his son: for he was at the point of death.

48 Then said Jē′ṣus unto him, Except ye see [w]signs and wonders, [x]ye will not believe.[Q]

49 The nobleman [t,u]saith unto him, Sir, [v]come down ere[G] my child die.

50 Jē′ṣus saith unto him, Go thy way; thy [y]son [w]liveth. And the man [u]believed the word that Jē′ṣus had spoken unto him, and he went his way.

51 And as he was now going down, his servants met him, and told *him*, saying, Thy son liveth.

52 Then enquired he of them the hour when he began to amend. And they said unto him, Yesterday at the seventh hour the fever left him.

53 So the father knew that *it was* at the same hour, in the which Jē′ṣus said unto him, Thy son liveth: and himself [u]believed, and his whole house.

54 This *is* again the second [3,w]miracle *that* Jē′ṣus did, when he was come out of [s]Jū-dæ′ȧ into [k]Găl′ĭ-lee.[S T]

## CHAPTER 5

*The pool of Bethesda. 5 An impotent man healed on the Sabbath. 10 The Jews find fault. 17 Jesus answers them, declaring himself to be the Son of God; 32 and proving it by the testimony of John, 36 by his works, 37 and by the witness of the Father in the Scriptures.*

AFTER[S] this there was a [a]feast of the [b]Jewṣ; and Jē′ṣus went up to [c]Jē-ru̇′sā-lĕm.

2 [T]Now there is at [c]Jē-ru̇′sā-lĕm by the [d]sheep [1]*market* a [e]pool, which is called in the [f]Hē′brew [g]tongue Bē-thĕṣ′dȧ, having five porches.

3 In these lay a great multitude of [h]impotent[G] folk, of [i]blind, halt[G], withered, [2]waiting for the moving of the water.

4 [3]For an [j]angel went down at a certain season into the [e]pool, and troubled the water: whosoever then first after the troubling of the water stepped in was made whole[G] of whatsoever [h]disease he had.

5 And a certain man was there, which had an *infirmity thirty and eight years.

6 When Jē′ṣus saw him lie, and knew that he had been now a long time *in that case*, he [k]saith unto him, Wilt thou be made whole[G]?

7 The [4]impotent man answered him, Sir, I have no man, when the water is troubled, to put me into the [e]pool: but while I am coming, another steppeth down before me.

8 Jē′ṣus saith unto him, Rise, take up thy bed, and walk.

9 And immediately the man was made [l,m]whole[G], and took up his bed, and walked: and on the same day was the [n]sabbath.[T]

10 ¶ The [b]Jewṣ therefore said unto him that was cured, It is

**42**
j *Jesus, savior,* Matt. 1:21.
2 R. V. *omits* the Christ.
**43**
k *Galilee,* Mark 6:21.
**44**
l Matt. 13:57; Luke 4:24.
m *Prophets,* Isa. 3:2.
n *Minister, discouragements of,* Rom. 15:16.
**45**
o *Jerusalem,* Judg. 19:10.
p *Annual Feasts,* Num. 15:3.
**46**
q *Cana* John 2:1.
r *Capernaum, miracles at,* Luke 4:31.
**47**
s *Judea,* Luke 5:17.
t *Parents, affection of, exemplified,* 2 Cor. 12:14.
u *Faith in Christ, exemplified,* John 6:69.
v *Mediation,* Gal. 3:19.
**48**
w *Miracles, of Jesus,* Luke 23:8.
x *Unbelievers,* 1 Cor. 6:6.
**50**
y *Children, miracles in behalf of,* Mark 10:4.

**A.D. 30**
See footnote, ***Time,*** Rev. 10:6.
**54**
3 R. V. sign
v.1–AD 28
**1**
a *Annual Feasts,* Num. 15:3.
b *Jews,* Neh. 4:2.
c *Jerusalem,* Judg. 19:10.
**2**
d *Jerusalem, gates of,* Judg. 19:10.
e *Pool,* 2 Sam. 2:13.
f *Hebrew,* Gen. 40:15.
g *Language,* Dan. 3:29.
1 R. V. gate
**3**
h *Disease,* Ex. 15:26.
i *Blind,* Deut. 27:18.
2 R. V. *omits remainder of verse.*
**4**
j *Angel, functions of,* Heb. 1:13.
3 R. V. *omits this verse.*
**6**
k *Jesus, compassion of,* Matt. 1:21.
**7**
4 R. V. sick
**9**
l *Miracles, of Jesus,* Luke 23:8.
m *Healing, by Jesus,* Acts 4:22.
n *Sabbath, Jesus performs miracles on,* Ex. 16:23.

* **INFIRMITY, PHYSICAL.** Eccl. 12:3. *Of Isaac,* Gen. 27:1. *Of Jacob,* Gen. 48:10. ***Of Eli,*** **1 Sam. 3:2.** ***Of Barzillai,*** 2 Sam. 19:35. Exemption from: *Moses,* Deut. 34:7; *Caleb,* Josh. 14:11.

13
5 Am. R. V. knew

14
o *Temple, Herod's,* 1 Kin. 6:17.
p *Wicked, punishment of,* Psa. 73:3.

15
q *Religious Testimony,* 2 Thess. 1:10.

16
r *Persecution, of Jesus,* John 15:20.
s *Malice,* Eph. 4:31.
6 R. V. *omits* and sought to slay him,

17
t *God, fatherhood of,* Gen. 2:2.
u *Jesus, mission of,* Matt. 1:21.

18
v *Bigotry, instances of,* Isa. 65:5.
w *Jesus, divine sonship of,* Matt. 1:21.
x *Jesus, relation of, to the Father,* Matt. 1:21.

20
y *God, love of,* Gen. 2:2.

21
z *Life, spiritual,* Eccl. 8:15.

a *Jesus, power of,* Matt. 1:21.

22
b *God, fatherhood of,* Gen. 2:2.

the [n]sabbath day: it is not lawful
for thee to carry *thy* bed.
11 He answered them, He that
made me [l,m]whole, the same said
unto me, Take up thy bed, and
walk.
12 Then asked they him, What
man is that which said unto thee,
Take up thy bed, and walk?
13 And he that was healed [5]wist
not who it was: for Jē'ṣus had
conveyed himself away, a multitude being in *that* place.
14 Afterward Jē'ṣus findeth
him in the [o]temple, and said unto him, Behold, thou art made
whole: sin no more, lest a worse
[p]thing come unto thee.
15 The man departed, and [q]told
the [b]Jewṣ that it was Jē'ṣus,
which had made him [l,m]whole.
16 And therefore did the [b]Jewṣ
[r]persecute Jē'ṣus, [6]and [s]sought
to slay him, because he had done
these things on the [n]sabbath day.
17 ¶ But Jē'ṣus answered them,
My [t]Father worketh hitherto,
and [u]I work.
18 Therefore the [v]Jewṣ [s]sought
the more to kill him, because he
not only had broken the [n]sabbath, but said also that God was
[w,x]his [t]Father, making himself
[x]equal with God.
19 ¶ Then answered Jē'ṣus and
said unto them, Verily, verily, I
say unto you, The [w,x]Son can
do nothing of himself, but what
he seeth the [t]Father do: for
what things soever he doeth,
these also doeth the Son likewise.
20 For the [t]Father [y]loveth the
[w,x]Son, and sheweth him all
things that himself doeth: and
he will shew him greater works
than these, that ye may marvel.
21 For as the [t]Father raiseth up
the dead, and [z]quickeneth *them;*
even so the [a]Son quickeneth
whom he will.
22 For the [b]Father judgeth no
man, but hath committed all
judgment unto the [c,d]Son:
23 That all *men* should honour
the [c]Son, even as they honour
the [b]Father. He that honoureth
not the [c]Son honoureth not the
[b]Father which hath sent him.
24 Verily, verily, I say unto you,
He that heareth my [e,f]word, and
[g,h]believeth on him that sent me,
[i]hath [j]everlasting life, and [7,k]shall
not come into condemnation;
but is [l]passed from [m]death unto
life.
25 Verily, verily, I say unto you,
The hour is coming, and now is,
when the dead shall hear the
voice of the [n]Son of God: and
[i]they that hear shall live.
26 For as the [b]Father hath life
in himself; so hath he given to
the [o]Son to have life in himself;
27 And hath given him [p]authority to execute judgment also, because he is the [q]Son of
man.
28 Marvel not at this: for the
hour is coming, in the which [r]all
that are in the [s]graves shall hear
his voice,
29 [t]And shall [r]come forth; [u]they
that have [v]done good, unto the
resurrection of [j]life; and they
that have done evil, unto the
resurrection of [8,w,x]damnation.
30 [y]I can of mine own self do
nothing: as I hear, I judge: and
[z]my judgment is [a]just; because
[b]I seek [c]not mine own will, but
the [d]will of [9]the [e]Father which
hath sent me.
31 If I bear witness of myself,
my witness is not true.
32 There is [f]another that beareth witness of [g]me; and I know
that the witness which he witnesseth of me is true.
33 Ye sent unto [h]John, and he
bare witness unto the [i]truth.

c *Jesus, divinity of,* Matt. 1:21.
d *Jesus, judge,* Matt. 1:21.

24
e *Doctrines of Jesus,* John 7:16.
f *Gospel,* Mark 13:10.
g *Faith in Christ,* John 6:69.
h *Salvation, conditions of,* Acts 16:17.
i *Promise to the righteous, of eternal life,* 2 Cor. 1:20
j *Life, everlasting,* Eccl. 8:15.
k *Justification,* Rom. 4:25.
l *Regeneration,* Tit. 3:5.
m *Spiritual Death,* 1 John 3:14.
7 R. V. cometh not into judgment,

25
n *Jesus, divine sonship of,* Matt. 1:21.

26
o *Jesus, savior,* Matt. 1:21.

27
p *Jesus, king,* Matt. 1:21.
q *Jesus, humanity of,* Matt. 1:21.

28
r *Resurrection, of all the dead,* 1 Cor. 15:12.
s *Burying Places,* Gen. 23:4.

29
t Dan. 12:2.
u *Righteous, described,* Psa. 64:10.
v *Works, good,* 2 Tim. 1:9.
w *Punishment, eternal,* Lev. 26:41.
x *Wicked, punishment of,* Psa. 73:3.
8 R. V. judgment.

30
y *Jesus, relation of, to the Father,* Matt. 1:21.
z *Jesus, justice of,* Matt. 1:21.

a *Jesus, perfections of,* Matt. 1:21.
b *Jesus, obedience of,* Matt. 1:21.
c *Renunciation, of the will to the Father,* Luke 5:11.

d *Will of God, the supreme rule of duty,* Mark 3:35. e *God, fatherhood of,* Gen. 2:2. 9 R. V. him that sent me.
32 f *God,* Gen. 2:2. g *Jesus, divinity of,* Matt. 1:21.
33 h *John the Baptist, mission of,* Luke 1:63. i *Truth,* John 18:37.

34 But I receive not testimony[G] from man: but these [j,k]things I say, [l]that ye might be [m]saved.

35 [h]He was [10]a burning and a shining [n]light: and ye were willing [o,p]for a season[G] to [q]rejoice in his light.

36 But I have greater witness than *that* of [h]John: for the works which the [e]Father [r]hath given me to finish, the same works that I do, [s]bear witness of me, that the Father [r]hath sent me.

37 And the [e]Father himself, which hath sent me, hath borne witness of [g]me. Ye have neither heard his voice at any time, [t]nor seen his shape.

38 And ye [u]have not his [v]word abiding[G] in you: for whom he hath sent, [w]him ye [u,x]believe not.[T]

39 [11,y]Search the scriptures; for in them ye think ye have [z]eternal life: and they are they which testify of me.

40 And [a]ye will not come to me, that ye might have [b]life.[T]

41 I receive not honour from men.

42 [c]But I [d]know you, that [e]ye have not the [f]love of God in you.[T]

43 I am come [g]in my Father's name, and ye [h]receive me not: if another shall come in his own name, him ye will receive.[T]

44 How can ye believe, which [i,j]receive honour one of another, and seek not the honour that *cometh* from[T] God only?

45 Do not think that I will accuse you to the [k]Father: there is *one* that accuseth you, *even* [l]Mō'ṣeṣ, [12]in whom ye [m]trust.[Q]

46 [n]For [o]had ye believed[G] [l,p,q]Mō'ṣeṣ, ye would have [r]believed[G] me: for he wrote of me.[T Q]

47 But if ye [o]believe not his [p,q]writings, how shall ye believe my [s]words?

34
*j* *Doctrines of Jesus*, John 7:16.
*k* *Gospel*, Mark 13:10.
*l* *Jesus, mission of*, Matt. 1:21.
*m* *Salvation*, Acts 16:17.

35
*n* *Light, figurative*, Matt. 5:14.
*o* *Character, instability of*, Phil. 2:15.
*p* *Instability*, Jas. 1:8.
*q* *Joy*, Psa. 5:11.
10 R. V. the lamp that burneth and shineth:

36
*r* *Jesus, relation of, to the Father*, Matt. 1:21.
*s* *Miracles, design of*, Luke 23:8.

37
*t* *God, invisible*, Gen. 2:2.

38
*u* *Spiritual Blindness*, 2 Cor. 4:4.
*v* *Word of God*, Psa. 119:9.
*w* *Jesus, rejected*, Matt. 1:21.
*x* *Unbelief*, Heb. 3:12.

39
*y* *Word of God, searching of*, Psa. 119:9.
*z* *Life, everlasting*, Eccl. 8:15.
11 R. V. Ye search

40
*a* *Salvation, offered and rejected*, Acts 16:17.
*b* *Life, spiritual*, Eccl. 8:15.

42
*c* *Reproof, faithfulness in*, Prov. 17:10.
*d* *Sin, known to God*, Rom. 5:12.
*e* *Wicked, described*, Psa. 73:3.
*f* *Love, for God*, 1 John 4:19.

43
*g* *Jesus, relation of, to the Father*, Matt. 1:21.
*h* *Jesus, rejected*, Matt. 1:21.

44
*i* *Ambition*, Hab. 2:5.
*j* *Worldliness*, 1 John 2:15.

45
*k* *God, fatherhood of*, Gen. 2:2.
*l* *Moses*, Ex. 2:10. *m* *False Confidence, of the self-righteous*, Psa. 30:6. 12 R. V. on whom ye have set your hope. **46** *n* Deut. 18:15. *o* *Unbelief*, Heb. 3:12. *p* *Law, of Moses, prophecies in, of the Messiah*, Deut. 33:2. *q* *Word of God, disbelief in*, Psa. 119:9. *r* *Faith in Christ*, John 6:69. **47** *s* *Doctrines of Jesus*, John 7:16.

## CHAPTER 6

*Jesus passes over the Sea of Galilee; 5 and feeds five thousand men with five loaves and two fishes. 15 He walks on the sea. 22 The people follow him to Capernaum. 26 He reproves their carnal motives; 30 and declares himself to be the bread of life. 66 Many of his disciples walk no more with him. 68 Peter confesses him.*

AFTER these things Jē'ṣus went over the [a]sea of Găl'ĭ-lee, which is *the sea* of Tī-bē'rĭ-as.

2 And [b]a great multitude followed him, because they [1]saw his [c,d]miracles[G] which he did on them that were diseased.

3 And Jē'ṣus went up into a mountain, and there he sat with his [e]disciples.

4 And the [f]passover, a feast of the Jewṣ, was nigh.[G]

5 [S] [g]When Jē'ṣus then lifted up *his* eyes, and saw a great company come unto him, he saith unto [h]Phĭl'ĭp, Whence shall we buy bread, that these may eat?

6 And this he said to [i]prove[G] him: for he himself knew what he would do.

7 [h]Phĭl'ĭp answered him, Two hundred pennyworth[G] of bread is not sufficient for them, that every one of them may take a little.

8 One of his disciples, [j]Ăn'drew, Sī'mon [k]Pē'tēr's brother, saith unto him,

9 There is a lad here, which hath five [l]barley [m]loaves, and two small [n]fishes: but what are they among so many?

10 And Jē'ṣus said, Make the men sit down. Now there was much grass in the place. So the men sat down, in number about five thousand.

11 And Jē'ṣus took the [m]loaves; and when he had [o]given [p]thanks, he distributed [2]to the [e]disciples, and the disciples to them that were set down; and likewise of the [n]fishes as much as they would.[G]

12 When they were filled, he [q]said unto his [e]disciples, Gather

A.D. 32
See footnote, *Time*, Rev. 10:6.

1
*a* *Sea of Galilee*, Matt. 4:18.

2
*b* *Jesus, received*, Matt. 1:21.
*c* *Miracles, of Jesus*, Luke 23:8.
*d* *Healing, by Jesus*, Acts 4:22.
1 R. V. beheld the signs

3
*e* *Disciples*, Matt. 9:14.

4
*f* *Passover*, Num. 9:5.
v.4–AD 29

5
*g* Matt. 14:15–21; Mark 6:34–44; Luke 9:12–17.
*h* *Philip*, Luke 6:14.

6
*i* *Faith, trial of*, Mark 11:22.

8
*j* *Andrew*, Matt. 4:18.
*k* *Peter*, Mark 5:37.

9
*l* *Barley*, Ex. 9:31.
*m* *Loaves*, Matt. 14:17.
*n* *Fish*, Matt. 17:27.

11
*o* *Prayers of Jesus*, Luke 5:16.
*p* *Thanksgiving for Food*, Luke 24:30.
2 R. V. *omits* to the disciples, and the disciples

12
*q* *Frugality, enjoined by Jesus*, Matt. 14:20.

up the fragments that remain, that nothing be lost.

13 Therefore they gathered *them* together, and filled twelve [r]baskets with the fragments of the five barley loaves, which remained over and above unto them that had eaten.

14 ¶ Then those men, when they had seen the [3,c]miracle that Jē′ṣus did, said, This is of a truth that [s]prophet that should come into the world.[T] [Q]

15 When Jē′ṣus therefore perceived that *they would come and take him by force, to make him a king, he departed again into a mountain himself alone.

16 ¶ And when even[G] was *now* come, his [e]disciples went down unto the [a]sea,

17 And entered into a [4]ship, and went over the sea toward [t]Cā-pēr′na-ŭm. And it was now dark, and Jē′ṣus was not come to them.

18 And the sea arose by reason of a great wind that blew.

19 So when they had rowed about five and twenty or thirty [u]furlongs,[G] they see [v]Jē′ṣus walking on the sea, and drawing nigh unto the ship: and they were afraid.

20 But he saith unto them, It is I; be not afraid.

21 Then they willingly received him into the ship: and immediately the ship was at the land whither they went.[S]

22 ¶ The day following, when the people which stood on the other side of the sea saw that there was none other boat there, save[G] [5]that one [6]whereinto his [e]disciples were entered, and that Jē′ṣus went not with his disciples into the boat, but *that* his disciples were gone away alone;

23 (Howbeit[G] there came other boats from Tī-bē′rĭ-as nigh unto the place where they did eat bread, after that the Lord had [o]given [p]thanks:)

24 When the people therefore saw that Jē′ṣus was not there, neither his [e]disciples, they also took shipping, and came to [t]Cā-pēr′na-ŭm, seeking for Jē′ṣus.

25 And when they had found him on the other side of the sea, they said unto him, [w]Răb′bī, when camest thou hither?

26 Jē′ṣus answered them and said, Verily, verily, I say unto you, [x]Ye seek me, [y]not because ye saw [3]the [z]miracles, but because ye did eat of the loaves, and were filled.

27 [a]Labour not for the meat[G] which perisheth, but for that [b,c]meat which endureth unto [d]everlasting life, [e]which the Son of man shall give unto you: for [f]him hath God the [g]Father [h]sealed.

28 Then said they unto him, What shall we do, that we might work the works of God?

29 Jē′ṣus answered and said unto them, [i]This is the work of God, that ye [j]believe on him whom he hath sent.[S] [T]

30 They [k]said therefore unto him, What sign shewest thou then, that we may see, and believe thee? what dost thou work?

31 Our fathers did eat [l,m,n]manna in the desert; as it is written, [o]He gave them [p]bread from heaven to eat.[Q]

32 Then[T] Jē′ṣus said unto them, Verily,[G] verily, I say unto you, [q]Mō′ṣeṣ gave you not that bread from heaven; but my [g]Father giveth you the true [c,r]bread from heaven.

33 For the [c,r]bread of God is he which cometh down from

13
r *Basket*, Ex. 29:3.

14
s *Jesus, prophet*, Matt. 1:21.
3 R. V. sign

17
t *Capernaum*, Luke 4:31.
4 R. V. boat,

19
u Luke 24:13; Rev. 21:16.
v *Jesus walks on the Sea*, Matt. 14:25.

22
5 R. V. *omits* that
6 R. V. *omits* whereinto his disciples were entered,

25
w *Rabbi*, Matt. 23:7.

26
x *Covetousness, instances of*, Isa. 57:17.
y *Hypocrisy, rebuked by Jesus*, Jas. 3:17.
z *Miracles, of Jesus*, Luke 23:8.

27
a *Commandment, enjoining zeal for righteousness*, Deut. 8:2.
b *Life, spiritual*, Eccl. 8:15.
c *Spiritual Gifts*, 1 Cor. 12:4.
d *Life, everlasting*, Eccl. 8:15.
e *Promise, to the righteous, of eternal life*, 2 Cor. 1:20.
f *Jesus, relation of, to the Father*, Matt. 1:21.
g *God, fatherhood of*, Gen. 2:2.
h *Seal, figurative*, 1 Kin. 21:8.

29
i *Commandment, enjoining faith*, Deut. 8:2.
j *Faith in Christ*, John 6:69.

30
k *Miracles, demanded by unbelievers*, Luke 23:8.

31
l *Manna*, Ex. 16:31.
m *Symbols and Similitudes*, Heb. 9:9.
n *Types of the Savior*, Heb. 10:1.
o *God, providence of*, Gen. 2:2.
p *Temporal Blessings, from God*, Psa. 103:2.

32
q *Moses*, Ex. 12:10.
r *Bread, figurative*, Ezek. 4:13.

* **POPULARITY OF JESUS**, Matt. 4:24; 8:1; 13:2; 19:1, 2; 21:8, 9 (with Mark 11:8–10; Luke 19:35–38; John 12: 12, 13); Mark 1:33; 2:2; 3:7, 20; 5:21; 6:33, 55, 56 (with Matt. 14:13, 35; Luke 9:11; John 6:2); 10:1; 12:37; Luke 4:14, 15, 42; 5:1; 12:1; John 6:15; 12:19.

heaven, and [s]giveth life unto the world.[T]

34 Then [t]said they unto him, Lord, evermore give us this [c,r]bread.

35[S] And Jē′ṣus said unto them, I[G] am the [r,u]bread of life: he that cometh to me shall never [v]hunger; and he that [i]believeth on me shall never [w]thirst.[T]

36 But I said unto you, That [x]ye also have seen me, and [y]believe not.

37[T] All that the [z]Father [a]giveth me shall come to me; and [b,c,d]him that cometh to me I will in no wise cast out.

38 For [e]I came down from heaven, [f]not to do mine own will, but [g]the [h]will of him that sent me.

39 And this is the [i]Father's [h]will which hath sent me, that of all which he hath [a]given me I should lose nothing, but [j]should [k,l]raise it up again at the last day.

40 And this is the will of him that sent me, that every one which seeth the [m]Son, and [n]believeth on him, [d]may have [l]everlasting [o]life: and [d]I will [k]raise him up at the last day.[S T]

41 The Jewṣ then [p]murmured[G] at him, because he said, I am the [q]bread which came down from heaven.

42 And they said, Is not this Jē′ṣus, the son of Jō′ṣeph, whose father and mother we know? how is it then that he [r]saith, I came down from heaven?[T]

43 Jē′ṣus therefore answered and said unto them, Murmur[G] not among yourselves.

44 No[T] man can come to me, except the Father which hath sent me draw him: and [s]I will [k]raise him up at the last day.[S]

45 It is written in the [t]prophets, [u]And they shall be all [v]taught of [w]God. Every man therefore that hath heard, and hath [x]learned of the Father, cometh unto me.[S Q]

46 [y]Not that any man hath seen the Father, save [z]he which is [7]of God, [a]he hath seen the Father.[T]

47 Ve[T]rily, verily, I say unto you, He that [b]believeth on me hath [c]everlasting [d]life.[S]

48 I[G] am that [e]bread of [f]life.[T]

49 Your fathers did eat [g]manna in the wilderness, and are dead.

50 This is the [e,f]bread which cometh down from heaven, that a man may eat thereof, and not [h]die.

51 [i]I[G] am the living [e]bread which came down from heaven: if any man eat of this bread, he shall [c,d]live for ever: and the bread that I[G] will [j,k]give is my flesh, which I[G] will [j,k]give for the [l]life of the world.[S]

52 The Jewṣ therefore strove[G] among themselves, [m]saying, How can this man give us *his* flesh to eat?

53 Then[T] Jē′ṣus said unto them, Verily, verily, I say unto you, Except ye eat the flesh of the Son of man, and drink his [n]blood, ye have no [f]life in you.

54 Whoso eateth my flesh, and drinketh my [n]blood, [o]hath [c]eternal [d]life; and [p]I will [q]raise him up at the last day.[T]

55 For my flesh is meat[G] indeed, and my [n]blood is drink indeed.

56 He that eateth my flesh, and drinketh my [n]blood, [r]dwelleth in me, and I in him.

57 As the living [s]Father hath [t]sent me, and I live by the Father: so he that eateth me, even he shall [t,u]live by me.[T]

58 This is that [e]bread which came down from heaven: not as your fathers did eat [g]manna, and are dead: he that eateth of this bread shall [d]live for ever.

59 These things said he in the [v]synagogue, as he [w,x]taught in [y]Că-pēr′na-ŭm.

**33**
s *Jesus, mission of,* Matt. 1:21.
**34**
t *Spiritual Desire,* Psa. 42:1.
**35**
u *Salvation,* Acts 16:17.
v *Hunger, figurative,* Matt. 5:6.
w *Thirst, figurative,* John 4:14.
**36**
x *Unbelievers,* 1 Cor. 6:6.
y *Jesus, rejected,* Matt. 1:21
**37**
z *God, fatherhood of,* Gen. 2:2.

a *Foreordination,* Rom. 8:30.
b *Penitent, promises to,* Psa. 51:17.
c *Seekers, promises to,* Isa. 55:6.
d *Promise, to seekers,* 2 Cor. 1:20.
**38**
e *Jesus, mission of,* Matt. 1:21.
f *Renunciation, of the will to the Father,* Luke 5:11.
g *Jesus, obedience of,* Matt. 1:21.
h *Will of God, the supreme rule of duty,* Mark 3:35.
**39**
i *God, love of,* Gen. 2:2.
j *Righteous, promises to,* Psa. 64:10.
k *Resurrection,* 1 Cor. 15:12.
l *Immortality,* 1 Cor. 15:54.
**40**
m *Jesus, divinity of,* Matt. 1:21.
n *Faith in Christ,* John 6:69.
o *Life, everlasting,* Eccl. 8:15.
**41**
p *Murmuring, instances of,* Num. 14:2.
q *Bread, figurative,* Ezek. 4:13.
**42**
r *Jesus, pre-existence of,* Matt. 1:21.
**44**
s *Promise, to the righteous, of resurrection,* 2 Cor. 1:20.
**45**
t *Prophecies concerning the Messiah, and their fulfillment,* Gen. 12:3.
u Isa. 54:13.
v *Instruction, in religion,* Prov. 23:23.
w *God, teacher,* Gen. 2:2.

x *Wisdom, spiritual, from God,* Prov. 2:2.
**46**
y *God, incomprehensible,* Gen. 2:2.
z *Jesus, relation of, to the Father,* Matt. 1:21.

a *Jesus, omniscience of,* Matt. 1:21.
7 R. V. from
**47**
b *Faith in Christ,* John 6:69.
c *Immortality,* 1 Cor. 15:54.
d *Life, everlasting,* Eccl. 8:15.
**48**
e *Bread, figurative,* Ezek. 4:13
f *Life, spiritual,* Eccl. 8:15.
**49**
g *Manna,* Ex. 16:31.
**50**
h *Spiritual Death,* 1 John 3:14.
**51**
i *Jesus, mission of,* Matt. 1:21.
j *Jesus, vicarious death of,* Matt. 1:21.
k *Atonement, by Jesus,* Lev. 17:11.
l *Redemption,* Eph. 1:7.
**52**
m *Spiritual Blindness,* 2 Cor. 4:4.
**53**
n *Blood, of Jesus,* Heb. 9:19.
**54**
o *Jesus, promises of,* Matt. 1:21.
p *Promise, to the righteous, of resurrection,* 2 Cor. 1:20.
q *Resurrection,* 1 Cor. 15:12.
**56**
r *Fellowship, with Christ,* 1 Cor. 1:9.
**57**
s *God, fatherhood of,* Gen. 2:2.
t *Jesus, relation of, to the Father,* Matt. 1:21.
u *Regeneration,* Tit. 3:5.
**59**
v *Synagogue,* Matt. 12:9.
w *Jesus, teacher,* Matt. 1:21.
x *Instruction, in religion,* Prov. 23:23.
y *Capernaum,* Luke 4:31.

**60**
*z* *Disciples*, Matt. 9:14.

**61**
8 R. V. cause you to stumble?

**62**
*a* *Jesus, ascension of*, Matt. 1:21.
*b* *Jesus, pre-existence of*, Matt. 1:21.
*c* *Jesus, eternity of*, Matt. 1:21.

**63**
*d* *Life, spiritual*, Eccl. 8:15.
*e* *Doctrines of Jesus*, John 7:16.

**64**
*f* *Unbelief*, Heb. 3:12.
*g* *Jesus, omniscience of*, Matt. 1:21.
*i* *Sin, known to God*, Rom. 5:12.

**66**
*i* *Disciples*, Matt. 9:14.
*j* *Instability, instances of*, Jas. 1:8.
*k* *Apostasy, instances of*, Acts 1:25.

**67**
*l* *Apostles*, Luke 6:13.

**68**
*m* *Peter*, Mark 5:37.
*n* *Life, everlasting*, Eccl. 8:15.

60 Many therefore of his [z]disciples, when they had heard *this*, said, This is an hard saying; who can hear it?

61 When Jē'ṣus knew in himself that his [z]disciples murmured[G] at it, he said unto them, Doth this [8]offend[C] you?

62 *What* and if ye shall see the Son of man [a]ascend up where [b,c]he was before?[S T Q]

63 It is the spirit that [d]quickeneth[C]; the flesh profiteth nothing: the [e]words that I speak unto you, *they* are spirit, and *they* are life.[T]

64[S] But[T] there are some of you that [f]believe not. For Jē'ṣus [g,h]knew from the beginning who they were that believed not, and who should betray him.[T]

65 And he said, Therefore said I unto you, that no man can come unto me, except it were given unto him of my Father.[S T]

66 ¶ From that *time* many of his [i]disciples [j]went back, and [k]walked no more with him.

67 Then said Jē'ṣus unto the [l]twelve, Will[C] ye also go away?

68[T] Then Sī'mon [m]Pē'tēr answered him, Lord, to whom shall we go? thou hast the [e]words of eternal [n]life.

69 And we [†]believe and are sure that [o]thou art [9]that [p]Chrīst, the [q]Son of the living God.[T]

70 Jē'ṣus answered them, Have not I chosen you [l]twelve, and one of you is a devil?

71 He spake of [10,r]Jū'das Ĭs-căr'ĭ-ot *the son* of [s]Sī'mon: for he it was that should [t]betray him, being one of the [l]twelve.

## CHAPTER 7

*Jesus in Galilee reproves his own brethren; 10 goes up to the feast of tabernacles; 14 and teaches in the temple. 40 What the people think of Jesus. 45 The officers sent to take him return without him. 50 Nicodemus takes his part.*

AFTER these things Jē'ṣus walked in [a]Găl'ĭ-lee: for he would not walk in [b]Jew'rȳ[G], because the [c]Jewṣ [d,e]sought[G] to kill him.

2 ¶ [f]Now the Jewṣ' feast of [g,h]tabernacles was at hand.[Q]

3 [i]His [j]brethren therefore [k]said unto him, Depart hence, and go into [b]Jū-dæ'ȧ, that thy [l]disciples also may see the [m]works that thou doest.

4 For *there is* no man *that* doeth any thing in secret, and he himself seeketh to be known openly. If thou do these [m]things, shew thyself to the world.

5 For [n]neither did his brethren believe in him.

6 Then Jē'ṣus said unto them,

**69**
*o* *Confession of Christ*, Luke 12:8.
*p* *Jesus, Messiah*, Matt. 1:21.
*q* *Jesus, divine sonship of*, Matt. 1:21.
9 R. V. the Holy One of God.

**71**
*r* *Judas*, Mark 3:19.
*s* John 13:2, 26.
*t* *Betrayal, of Jesus*, Matt. 26:46.
10 R. V. Judas, the son of Simon Iscariot,

**1**
*a* *Galilee*, Mark 6:21.
*b* *Judea*, Luke 5:17.
*c* *Jews*, Neh. 4:2.
*d* *Malice*, Eph. 4:31.
*e* *Persecution, of Jesus*, John 15:20.

**2**
*f* Luke 9:51–62.
*g* *Tabernacles, feast of*, Deut. 16:13.
*h* *Annual Feasts*, Num. 15:3.

**3**
*i* *Jesus, rejected*, Matt. 1:21.
*j* *Brothers of Jesus*, Matt. 13:55.
*k* *Presumption, instances of*, Psa. 19:13.
*l* *Disciples*, Matt. 9:14.
*m* *Miracles, of Jesus*, Luke 23:8.

**5**
*n* *Unbelief, instances of*, Heb. 3:12.

---

† **FAITH IN CHRIST**, Psa. 2:12. *Enjoined*, Matt. 17:7; John 6:20; 20:27, 29; 1 John 3:23. *Prayer for increase of*, Mark 9:24. *Salvation by*, Mark 16:16; Luke 7:50; John 1:12; 3:14–18, 36; 5:24; 6:40, 47; 7:38; 12:36, 46; 20:31; Acts 10: 43; 13:48; 15:9, 11; 16:31; 20:21; 26:18; Rom. 1:16, 17; 3: 22–28; 4:1–25; 5:1, 2; 9:31–33; 10:4–10; 11:20; 1 Cor. 1:21; 2:5; Gal. 2:16; 3:1–29; 5:5, 6; Eph. 1:12–14; 2:8; 3:12, 17; 1 Tim. 1:16; 2 Tim. 1:13; 3:15; 1 Pet. 1:9; 2:6, 7; 2 Pet. 1:1.

*The Christian triumphs by*, 2 Cor. 1:24; Eph. 6:16; Phil. 3:9; Col. 1:23; Heb. 10:22, 38, 39; 13:7; 1 Pet. 1:5, 7–9, 21; 1 John 5:4, 5, 10, 14.

*Fruitful of good works*, John 14:12; Jas. 2:1–26.

**Exemplified by:** *Abraham*, John 8:56. *The wise men of the East*, Matt. 2:1, 2, 11. *The disciples*, Matt. 4:18–22; Mark 1:16–20; Luke 5:4–11; John 1:35–49; 6:68, 69; 16:27, 30, 33. *The disciples, through the miracle at Cana of Galilee*, John 2:11. *Philip*, John 1:45, 46. *Nathanael*, John 1:49. *Jews at Jerusalem*, John 2:23; 8:30; 11:45; 12:11. *The Samaritans, who believed through the preaching of Jesus*, John 4: 39–42.

*The nobleman, for the healing of his son*, John 4:46, 47, 50. *The leper*, Matt. 8:2; Mark 1:40; Luke 5:12, 13. *Those who brought the paralytic to Jesus*, Matt. 9:1, 2; Mark 2:1–5; Luke 5:18–20. *The centurion, for the healing of his servant*, Matt. 8:5–10, 13; Luke 7:3–9. *The woman who was a sinner*, Luke 7:38, 44–48, 50. *The sick of Gennesaret*, Matt. 14:36; Mark 3:10; 6:54–56. *The disciples, in the storm*, Matt. 14:33.

*The woman with the issue of blood*, Matt. 9:21, 22; Mark 5: 28; Luke 8:44, 48. *Jairus, for the healing of his daughter*, Matt. 9:18, 23–25; Mark 5:22, 23; Luke 8:41, 42. *Two blind men*, Matt. 9:27–30. *The people who saw the feeding of the five thousand*, John 6:14. *The Syrophenician woman*, Matt. 15:22–28; Mark 7:25–30. *Those who brought the deaf and dumb man to Jesus*, Mark 7:32. *The people of Decapolis*, Matt. 15:30. *The father of the demoniac child*, Matt. 17:14, 15; Mark 9:24; Luke 9:38, 42.

*The blind man whom Jesus healed on the Sabbath*, John 9: 13–38. *Mary, the sister of Martha*, Luke 10:38–42; John 11:32. *The people in Bethany beyond the Jordan*, John 10: 41, 42. *The Samaritan leper*, Luke 17:11–19. *Blind Bartimæus, and a fellow blind man*, Matt. 20:30–34; Mark 10:46–52; Luke 18:35–42. *Zacchæus*, Luke 19:1–6.

*The thief, on the cross*, Luke 23:42. *John, the disciple, after the resurrection*, John 20:8. *Thomas, after the resurrection*, John 20:28.

*By three thousand, at Pentecost*, Acts 2:41. *By five thousand*, Acts 4:4 *By multitudes*, Acts 5:14. *By the Ethiopian eunuch*, Acts 8:36, 38. *By the cripple at Lystra*, Acts 14:8–10. *By Stephen*, Acts 6:8, 55–56. *By Paul*, 2 Cor. 12:9, 10; Gal. 2:20; Phil. 4:13; 2 Tim. 1:12; 4:18.

*Samaritans, through the preaching of Philip*, Acts 8:9–12. *People, of Lydda and Saron*, Acts 9:35; *of Joppa*, Acts 9:42; *of Antioch*, Acts 11:21–24. *Barnabas*, Acts 11:24. *Eunice, Lois, and Timothy*, Acts 16:1; 2 Tim. 1:5. *Lydia*, Acts 16: 14. *Philippian jailer*, Acts 16:31–34. *Crispus*, Acts 18:8. *The Corinthians*, Acts 18:8; 1 Cor. 15:11. *Jews at Rome*, Acts 28:24. *Ephesians*, Eph. 1:13, 15. *Colossians*, Col. 1: 2, 4. *Thessalonians*, 1 Thess. 1:6; 3:6–8; 2 Thess. 1:3, 4. *Philemon*, Philemon 5. *Church at Thyatira*, Rev. 2:19.

My time is not yet come: but
your time is alway ready.
7 The world cannot [o]hate you;
but me it hateth, because I [p]tes-
tify of it, that the works thereof
are evil.
8 Go ye up unto this [g,h]feast: I
go not up yet unto this feast; for
my time is not yet full come.
9 When he had said these words
unto them, he abode[G] *still* in
[a]Găl′ĭ-lee.
10 ¶ But when his [j]brethren
were gone up, then went he also
up unto the [g]feast, [q]not openly,
but as it were in secret.
11 Then the Jewṣ sought him
at the [g]feast, and said, Where
is he?
12 And there was much murmuring[G] among the people concerning him: for some said, [r]He
is a good man: others said, Nay;
but [i]he deceiveth the people.
13 Howbeit no man spake
openly of him for fear of the
[c]Jewṣ.
14 ¶ Now about the midst of
the [g]feast Jē′ṣus went up into the
[s]temple, and [t,u]taught.
15 And the [c]Jewṣ marvelled,
saying, How knoweth this man
letters, having never learned?
16[T] Jē′ṣus answered them, and
said, My *,[1]doctrine is not mine,
but [w]his that sent me.
17 If any man [2,x]will[G] do his
[y]will, he shall [z]know of the
*,[1]doctrine, whether it be of
God, or *whether* I speak of myself.[T]
18 He that [a]speaketh of himself
seeketh his own glory: but he
that [b]seeketh his glory that [c]sent
him, the same is [d]true, and [d]no
unrighteousness is in him.[T]
19 [e]Did not Mō′ṣeṣ give you the
[f]law, and *yet* [g]none of you keepeth the law? Why [h]go ye about
to kill me?
20 The people answered and
[i]said, Thou hast a [j]devil:[G] who
[h]goeth[G] about to kill thee?
21 Jē′ṣus answered and said
unto them, I have done one
work, and ye all marvel.
22 [f]Mō′ṣeṣ therefore gave unto you [k]circumcision; (not because it is of Mō′ṣeṣ, but of the
fathers;) and ye on the [l]sabbath
day circumcise a man.[Q]
23 If a man on the [l]sabbath day
receive [k]circumcision, that the
[f]law of Mō′ṣeṣ should not be
broken; [m]are ye [n]angry at me,
because I have made a man every whit[G] [o]whole on the sabbath
day?
24 [p,q]Judge not according to
the appearance, but [q,r]judge
[s]righteous judgment.[Q]
25 Then said some of them
of [t]Jē-ru′sā-lĕm, Is not this he,
whom they [h,u]seek to kill?
26 But, lo, he speaketh [3]boldly,
and they say nothing unto him.
Do the rulers know indeed that
this is the very[G] Chrīst?
27 Howbeit[G] we know this man
whence he is: but when Chrīst
cometh, no man knoweth whence
he is.
28[T] Then cried Jē′ṣus in the
[v]temple as he [w]taught, saying,
Ye both know me, and ye know
whence I am: and I am not come
of myself, but [x]he that sent me is
true, whom ye [y]know not.
29 But [z]I know him: for I am
from him, and he hath sent me.[T]
30 Then they [a]sought[G] to take
him: but no man laid hands on
him, because his hour was not
yet come.

7
o *Hatred*, Prov. 15:17.
p *Reproof, hated*, Prov. 17:10.

10
q *Prudence, instances of*, 2 Chr. 2:12.

12
r *Jesus, received*, Matt. 1:21.

14
s *Temple, Herod's*, 1 Kin. 6:17.
t *Instruction, in religion*, Prov. 23:23.
u *Jesus, teacher*, Matt. 1:21.

15
v *Jesus, wisdom of*, Matt. 1:21.

16
w *Jesus, relation of, to the Father*, Matt. 1:21.
1 R. V. teaching

17
x *Decision*, Isa. 50:7.
y *Will of God, the supreme rule of duty*, Mark 3:35.
z *Wisdom, spiritual*, Prov. 2:2.
2 R. V. willeth to

18
a *Self-exaltation*, Luke 14:11.
b *Jesus, obedience of*, Matt. 1:21.
c *Jesus, relation of, to the Father*, Matt. 1:21.
d *Jesus, perfections of*, Matt. 1:21.

19
e *Reproof, faithfulness in*, Prov. 17:10.
f *Law, of Moses*, Deut. 33:2.
g *Disobedience to God*, Eph. 5:6.
h *Persecution, of Jesus*, John 15:20.

20
i *Falsehood*, Job 21:34.
j *Demons*, Matt. 4:24.

22
k *Circumcision*, Gen. 17:10.
l *Sabbath*, Ex. 16:23.

23
m *Inconsistency, instances of*, Matt. 7:3.
n *Anger*, Psa. 37:8.
o *Miracles, of Jesus*, Luke 23:8.

24
p *Uncharitableness*, Matt. 7:1.
q *Commandment, enjoining charitableness*, Deut. 8:2.
r *Charitableness, enjoined*, Prov. 10:12.
s *Justice*, Deut. 33:21.

25
t *Jerusalem*, Judg. 19:10.
u *Malice*, Eph. 4:31.

26
3 R. V. openly,

28
v *Temple, Herod's*, 1 Kin. 6:17.
w *Instruction, in religion*, Prov. 23:23.
x *God, holiness of*, Gen. 2:2.
y *Spiritual Blindness*, 2 Cor. 4:4.

29
z *Jesus, omniscience of*, Matt. 1:21.

30
a *Persecution, of Jesus*, John 15:20.

* **DOCTRINES OF JESUS**, Matt. 13:18–23; 22:33; Mark 4:16–20; Luke 8:11–15; John 5:24; 8:43; 15:20; 17:20; Acts 17:11; 2 Cor. 1:18; Gal. 6:6; Col. 1:5; 3:16; Tit. 1:9; Jas. 1:21; 1 Pet. 2:2; 2 John 9:10. *Called, word of God*, Luke 5:1; Acts 6:2; 13:7; 1 Thess. 2:13; 2 Tim. 2:9; Tit. 2:5; Heb. 6:5; 13:7; 1 John 2:14; *sound doctrine*, Tit. 2:1.
*From the Father*, John 7:16; 14:24. *Everlasting*, Matt. 24:35; 1 Pet. 1:23. *Sanctifying*, John 15:3; Eph. 5:26. *The standard of the final judgment*, John 12:48.
*Spoken with boldness*, Acts 4:31; Phil. 1:14. *Faithfully declared*, 2 Cor. 2:17; 4:2; Phil. 2:16. *Confirmed by miracles*, Mark 16:20. *Joyously received*, 1 Thess. 1:6.
*Obedience to, enjoined*, Jas. 1:22–24. *Perseverance in, a proof of discipleship*, John 8:31. *Obedience to, rewarded*, Luke 8:21; 11:28; John 14:23; 15:7; Jas. 1:25.
*Success of*, Acts 6:7; 8:14; 12:24; 13:44; 19:20.
*Rejected*, John 8:37; 12:47; Acts 13:46; Heb. 4:2; 1 Pet. 2:8.
See footnotes: GOSPEL, Mark 13:10; WORD OF GOD, Psa. 119:9.

31 And [b]many of the people [c,d]believed on him, and said, When Christ cometh, will he do more [4]miracles[G] than these which this *man* hath done?

32 ¶ The [e]Phăr'ĭ-seeș heard that the people murmured[T G] such things concerning him; and the Phăr'ĭ-seeș and the chief [f]priests sent officers to take him.

33 Then [g]said Jē'șus unto them, Yet a little while am I with you, and *then* [h]I go unto him that sent me.

34 [i]Ye shall seek me, and [j]shall not find *me*: and where I[G] am, [j]*thither* ye cannot come.

35 Then [k]said the Jewș among themselves, Whither will he go, that we shall not find him? will he go unto the [l]dispersed among the [5]Ġĕn'tīleș,[G] and teach the [5]Ġĕn'tīleș[G]?

36 [k]What *manner of* saying is this that he said, Ye shall seek me, and shall not find *me:* and where I am, *thither*[G] ye cannot come?

37 ¶ In the last day, that great *day* of the [m]feast, Jē'șus stood and cried, saying, If any man [n]thirst, let him come unto [o]me,[G] and drink.[Q]

38 [p,q]He that [r]believeth on me, as the scripture hath said, out of his [s]belly[G] shall flow [t]rivers of living [u]water.[S Q]

39 (But this spake he of the [v]Spirit, which they that believe on him should receive: for the [6]Holy Ghost[G] was not yet *given;* because that Jē'șus was not yet [w]glorified.)[T Q]

40 Many of the people therefore, when they heard this saying, said, Of a truth this is the [x]Prophet.[T Q]

41 Others said, This is the [y]Christ. But some [z]said, Shall Christ come out of [a]Găl'ĭ-lee?

42 Hath not the [b,c]scripture said, That [d]Christ cometh of the seed of [e]Dā'vid, and out of the town of [f]Bĕth'lĕ-hĕm, where Dā'vid was?[Q]

43 So there was a division among the people because of him.

44 And some of them would have taken him; but no man laid hands on him.

45 ¶ Then came the officers to the chief [g]priests and [h]Phăr'ĭ-seeș; and they said unto them, Why have ye not brought him?

46 The officers answered, Never man [i]spake like this man.[Q]

47 Then answered them the [h]Phăr'ĭ-seeș, Are ye also deceived?

48 Have any of the rulers or of the [h]Phăr'ĭ-seeș believed on him?

49 But this people who [j]knoweth not the [k]law are cursed.

50 [l]Nĭc-o-dē'mus saith unto them, (he that came to [7]Jē'șus by night, being one of them,)

51 Doth our [k]law judge *any* man, before it [†]hear him, and know what he doeth?[Q]

52 They answered and said unto him, Art thou also of [a]Găl'ĭlee? Search, and look: for out of Găl'ĭ-lee ariseth no prophet.

53 And every man went unto his own house.

## CHAPTER 8

*A woman taken in adultery. 12 Jesus, the light of the world. 14 He justifies himself. 31 The unbelieving Jews not Abraham's true seed. 59 Jesus hides himself from them.*

JĒ'ȘUS went unto the mount of [a]Ŏl'īveș.

2 And early in the morning he came again into the [b]temple, and [c]all the people came unto him; and he sat down, and [d,e]taught them.

3 And the [f]scribes and [g]Phăr'ĭ-

**31**
b *Miracles, convincing effect of,* Luke 23:8.
c *Faith in Christ,* John 6:69.
d *Jesus, received,* Matt. 1:21.
4 R. V. signs

**32**
e *Pharisees,* Matt. 15:12.
f *Priest,* Lev. 1:5.

**33**
g *Jesus, prophet,* Matt. 1:21.
h *Jesus, ascension of,* Matt. 1:21.

**34**
i *Seekers,* Isa. 55:6.
j *Sin, separates from God,* Rom. 5:12.

**35**
k *Spiritual Blindness,* 2 Cor. 4:4.
l *Dispersion, of the Jews,* Gen. 11:8.
5 R. V. Greeks,

**37**
m *Tabernacles, feast of,* Deut. 16:13.
n *Thirst, figurative,* John 4:14.
o *Jesus, savior,* Matt. 1:21.

**38**
p *Prophecies concerning the Messiah, and their fulfillment,* Gen. 12:3.
q *Righteous, described,* Psa. 64:10.
r *Faith in Christ, salvation by,* John 6:69.
s *Belly,* Prov. 20:27.
t *Influence, good,* 1 Cor. 7:14.
u *Water, figurative,* 1 Kin. 17:10.

**39**
v *Holy Spirit,* Acts 1:2.
w *Jesus, exaltation of,* Matt. 1:21.
6 R. V. Spirit was

**40**
x Deut. 18:15.

**41**
y *Jesus, Messiah,* Matt. 1:21.
z *Doubting,* Rom. 14:23.

a *Galilee,* Mark 6:21.

**42**
b *Word of God,* Psa. 119:9.
c *Prophecies concerning the Messiah, and their fulfillment,* Gen. 12:3.
d Psa. 89:3, 4; Mic. 5:2.
e *David,* 1 Sam. 16:13.
f *Bethlehem,* Gen. 48:7.

**45**
g *Priest,* Lev. 1:5.
h *Pharisees,* Matt. 15:12.

**46**
i *Jesus, teacher,* Matt. 1:21.

**49**
j *Ignorance,* Acts 3:17.
k *Law, of Moses,* Deut. 33:2.

**50**
l John 3:1-10.
7 R. V. him before,

**1**
a *Mount of Olives,* Mark 11:1.

**2**
b *Temple, Herod's,* 1 Kin. 6:17.
c *Jesus, received,* Matt. 1:21.
d *Jesus, teacher,* Matt. 1:21.
e *Instruction, in religion,* Prov 23:23.

**3**
f *Scribe,* 1 Kin. 4:3.
g *Pharisees,* Matt. 15:12.

† **TRIAL.** *Before court,* Lev. 24:10-14. *Right of,* John 7:51; Acts 16:37-39; 22:25-30.

h *Women, wicked,* Prov. 31:10.
i *Adultery,* Lev. 20:10.

5
j *Law, of Moses,* Deut. 33:2.
k *Adultery, penalties for,* Lev. 20:10.
l *Stoning,* 1 Sam. 30:6.
m *Punishment, mode of,* Lev. 26:41.

6
n *Hypocrisy, instances of,* Jas. 3:17.
1 R. V. *omits the rest of this verse.*

7
o *Reproof, faithfulness in,* Prov. 17:10.
p *Sin,* Rom. 5:12.

9
q *Conviction of Sin,* John 16:8.
r *Conscience, guilty,* Acts 23:1.
2 R. V. *omits* being convicted by their own conscience,

10
3 R. V. And Jesus lifted up himself, and said unto her, Woman, where are they? did no man condemn thee?

11
s *Adultery, forgiveness of,* Lev. 20:10.
t *Sin, forgiveness of,* Rom. 5:12.

12
u *Jesus, mission of,* Matt. 1:21.
v *Light, figurative,* Matt. 5:14.
w *Righteous, promises to,* Psa. 64:10.
x *Promise, to the righteous, of spiritual enlightenment,* 2 Cor. 1:20.
y *Darkness, figurative,* Gen. 1:2.
z *Spiritual Blindness,* 2 Cor. 4:4.

a *Wisdom, spiritual, from God,* Prov. 2:2.

13
b *Jesus, rejected,* Matt. 1:21.
c *Pharisees,* Matt. 15:12.

seeş brought unto him a [h]woman taken in [i]adultery; and when they had set her in the midst,

4 They say unto him, Master, this [h]woman was taken in [i]adultery, in the very act.

5 Now Mō′şeş in the [j]law commanded us, that [k]such should be [l,m]stoned[G]: but what sayest thou[Q T]?

6 This they [n]said, tempting[G] him, that they might have to accuse him. But Jē′şus stooped down, and with *his* finger wrote on the ground, [1]*as though he heard them not.*

7 So [n]when they continued asking him, he lifted up himself, and [o]said unto them, He that is without [p]sin among you, let him first cast a stone at her. [Q]

8 And again he stooped down, and wrote on the ground.

9 And they which heard *it,* [2]being [q]convicted by *their own* [r]conscience, went out one by one, beginning at the eldest, *even* unto the last: and Jē′şus was left alone, and the [h]woman standing in the midst.

10 [3]When Jē′şus had lifted up himself, and saw none but the woman, he said unto her, Woman, where are those thine accusers? hath no man condemned[G] thee?[S]

11 She said, No man, Lord. And Jē′şus said unto her, [s,t]Neither do I condemn thee: go, and sin no more.

12 ¶ Then spake Jē′şus again unto them, saying, [u]I[C] am the [v]light of the world: [w,x]he that followeth me shall not walk in [y,z]darkness, but shall have the [a]light of life.[T] [Q]

13 [b]The [c]Phăr′ĭ-seeş therefore said unto him, Thou bearest record of thyself; thy record[G] is not true.[T]

14 Jē′şus answered and said unto them, Though I bear record[G] of myself, *yet* my record[G] is true: for I know whence I came, and whither I go; but [d]ye cannot tell whence I come, and whither I go.[Q]

15[T] [d]Ye judge after[C] the flesh; I judge no man.

16 And yet if I judge, my judgment is true: for I am not alone, but [e]I and the [f]Father that [g]sent me.

17 It is also written in your [h]law, that the [i]testimony of two men is true.[Q]

18 I[C] am one that bear witness of myself, and the [f]Father that [g]sent me beareth witness of [e]me.

19 Then said they unto him, Where is thy [f]Father? Jē′şus answered, Ye [d]neither know me, nor my Father: if ye had known me, ye should have known my Father also.[T]

20 These words spake Jē′şus in the treasury, as he [j,k]taught in the [l]temple: and no man laid hands on him; for his hour was not yet come.

21 Then said Jē′şus again unto them, I go my way, and [m]ye shall seek me, and shall [n]die in your sins: whither I go, [o]ye cannot come.

22 [d]Then said the [p]Jewş[G], Will he [q]kill himself? because he saith, Whither I go, [o]ye cannot come.

23 And he said unto them, Ye are from beneath; I am from above: ye are of this world; I am not of this world.[S]

24 I said therefore unto you, that ye shall [n]die in your sins: for if [r]ye [s]believe not that I am *he,* ye shall [n]die in your sins.

25 Then said they unto him, Who art thou? And Jē′şus saith unto them, Even *the same* that I said unto you from the beginning.

26[T] I have many things to [t]say and to judge of you: but he that sent me is [u]true; and I speak to the world those [t]things which I have heard of him.[S]

14
d *Spiritual Blindness,* 2 Cor. 4:4.

16
e *Jesus, divinity of,* Matt. 1:21.
f *God, fatherhood of,* Gen. 2:2.
g *Jesus, relation of, to the Father,* Matt. 1:21.

17
h *Law, of Moses,* Deut. 33:2.
i *Witness,* Num. 35:30.

20
j *Jesus, teacher,* Matt. 1:21.
k *Instruction, in religion,* Prov. 23:23.
l *Temple, Herod's,* 1 Kin. 6:17.

21
m *Seekers,* Isa. 55:6.
n *Wicked, punishment of,* Psa. 73:3.
o *Sin, separates from God,* Rom. 5:12.

22
p *Jews,* Neh. 4:2.
q *Suicide,* 1 Kin. 16:18.

24
r *Unbelievers,* 1 Cor. 6:6.
s *Unbelief,* Heb. 3:12.

26
t *Doctrines of Jesus,* John 7:16.
u *God, truth,* Gen. 2:2.

27 They [d]understood not that
he spake to them of the [f]Father.
28 Then said Jē'ṣus unto them,
When ye have [v]lifted up the Son
of man, then shall ye know that
I[G] am *he*, and *that* I[G] do nothing of
myself; but as my [f]Father hath
taught me, I[G] [t]speak these things.
29 And he that [g]sent me is with
me: [4]the [f]Father hath not left
me alone; for I [w,x]do always
those things that please him.[T]
30 As he spake these words,
[y]many [z]believed on him.
31[S] Then said Jē'ṣus to those
Jewṣ which [z]believed on him, If
[a]ye [b]continue in my [c]word, *then*
are ye my [d]disciples indeed;
32 And [e]ye shall [f]know the
[g]truth, and [e]the truth shall make
you [h]free.[S T]
33 They [i]answered him, We be
[j]Ā'brā-hăm's seed, and [k]were
never in bondage to any man:
how sayest thou, Ye shall be
made free?[Q]
34 Jē'ṣus answered them, Verily, verily, I say unto you, Whosoever committeth [l]sin is the
[5,m,n]servant of sin.[S]
35 And the [5]servant abideth
not in the house for ever: *but* the
[o,p]Son abideth ever.[Q]
36 If the [o]Son therefore shall
make you [h]free, [e]ye shall be free
indeed.
37 I know that ye are [j]Ā'brā-
hăm's seed; but ye [q,r]seek to kill
me, because my [c]word hath [6]no
place in you.
38 I speak that which I have
seen with my [s]Father: and ye [7]do
that which ye have seen with
[t]your father.[I]
39 They answered and said unto him, [j]Ā'brā-hăm is our father.
Jē'ṣus saith unto them, If ye
were Ā'brā-hăm's children, ye
would do the works of Ā'brā-
hăm.
40 But now ye [q,r]seek to kill
me, a man that hath [u]told you
the truth, which [v]I have heard of
God: this did not Ā'brā-hăm.
41 Ye[T] do the deeds of [t]your father. Then said they to him, We
be not born of fornication; we
have one [s]Father, *even* God.[Q]
42 Jē'ṣus said unto them, If
God were your Father, ye would
[w]love me: for [o,v]I proceeded
forth and came from God; neither came I of myself, but he
sent me.[T]
43 Why do ye [x]not understand
my [y]speech? *even* because ye
[x]cannot hear my [y]word.
44 [z]Ye are of *your* father the
[a]devil, and the [b,c]lusts[G] of your
father ye will do. He was a
murderer from the beginning,
and abode[G] not in the [d]truth, because there is no truth in him.
When he speaketh a [e]lie, he
speaketh of his own: for he is a
liar, and the father of it.[S Q]
45 And because I tell *you* the
[d]truth, [f]ye [g]believe me not.
46 [h]Which of you convinceth[G]
me of sin? And if I say the
[d]truth, why do ye not believe
me?
47 [i]He that is of God heareth
God's [j]words: ye therefore hear
*them* not, because ye are [k]not of
God.
48 Then answered the [l]Jewṣ,
and said unto him, [m]Say we not
well that thou art a Să-măr'ĭ-tan,
and hast a [n]devil?[G]
49 Jē'ṣus [o]answered, I have not
a [n]devil;[G] but I honour my [p]Fa-
ther, and ye do dishonour me.[T]
50 And I [o]seek not mine own
glory: there is one that seeketh
and [q]judgeth.[S]
51 Verily, verily, I say unto you,
[r]If a man keep my saying, [s]he
shall never see [t]death.
52 Then [m]said the [l]Jewṣ unto
him, Now we know that thou
hast a [n]devil.[G] [u]Ā'brā-hăm is
dead, and the [v]prophets; and
thou sayest, If a man keep my

**28**
v *Crucifixion,* Mark 15:13.

**29**
w *Jesus, obedience of,* Matt. 1:21.
x *Faithfulness,* Luke 16:10.
4 R. V. he hath

**30**
y *Jesus, received,* Matt. 1:21.
z *Faith in Christ,* John 6:69.

**31**
a *Righteous, described,* Psa. 64:10.
b *Perseverance, a proof of discipleship,* Eph. 6:18.
c *Doctrines of Jesus,* John 7:16.
d *Disciples,* Matt. 9:14.

**32**
e *Promise, to the righteous,* 2 Cor. 1:20.
f *Wisdom, spiritual,* Prov. 2:2.
g *Truth,* John 18:37.
h *Liberty, spiritual,* Lev. 25:10.

**33**
i *Self-righteousness, instances of,* Luke 18:11.
j *Abraham,* Gen. 17:5.
k *Delusion,* 2 Thess. 2:11.

**34**
l *Sin,* Rom. 5:12.
m *Servant, figurative,* Jer. 2:14.
n *Wicked, described,* Psa. 73:3.
5 R. V. bond-servant

**35**
o *Jesus, divinity of,* Matt. 1:21.
p *Jesus, eternity of,* Matt. 1:21.

**37**
q *Malice,* Eph. 4:31.
r *Persecution, of Jesus,* John 15:20.
6 R. V. not free course

**38**
s *God, fatherhood of,* Gen. 2:2.
t *Satan,* Matt. 4:10.
7 R. V. also do the things which ye heard from your father.

**40**
u *Jesus, teacher,* Matt. 1:21.
v *Jesus, relation of, to the Father,* Matt. 1:21.

**42**
w *Love, for Jesus,* 1 John 4:19.

**43**
x *Spiritual Blindness,* 2 Cor. 4:4.
y *Doctrines of Jesus,* John 7:16.

**44**
z *Wicked, described,* Psa. 73:3.
a *Satan,* Matt. 4:10.
b *Lust,* 2 Pet. 1:4.
c *Malice,* Eph. 4:31.
d *Truth,* John 18:37.
e *Falsehood,* Job 21:34.

**45**
f *Unbelievers,* 1 Cor. 6:6.
g *Unbelief,* Heb. 3:12.

**46**
h *Jesus, holiness of,* Matt. 1:21.

**47**
i *Righteous, described,* Psa. 64:10.
j *Truth, of the gospel,* John 18:37
k *Wicked, described,* Psa. 73:3.

**48**
l *Jews,* Neh. 4:2.
m *False Accusation,* 2 Tim. 3:3.
n *Demons,* Matt. 4:24.

**49**
o *Jesus, meekness of,* Matt. 1:21.
p *God, fatherhood of,* Gen. 2:2.

**50**
q *God, judge,* Gen. 2:2.

**51**
r *Obedience, rewarded,* Heb. 5:8.
s *Promise, to the righteous, of eternal life,* 2 Cor. 1:20.
t *Spiritual Death,* 1 John 3:14.

**52**
u *Abraham,* Gen. 17:5.
v *Prophets,* Isa. 3:2.

saying, he shall never taste of death.

53 Art thou greater than our father [u]Ā′bră-hăm, which is dead? and the [v]prophets are dead: whom makest thou thyself?

54[T] Jē′şus answered, If I honour myself, my honour is nothing: it is my [p]Father that [w]honoureth [x]me; of whom ye say, that he is your God:

55 Yet ye have [y]not known him; but I know him: and if I should say, I know him not, I shall be a liar like unto you: but I know him, and [z]keep his saying.

56 Your father Ā′bră-hăm [a]rejoiced [b]to see my day: and he saw *it*, and was glad.[T]

57 Then said the Jewş unto him, Thou art not yet fifty years old, and hast thou seen Ā′bră-hăm?

58 Jē′şus said unto them, Verily, verily, I[G] say unto you, [c,d]Before Ā′bră-hăm was, I[G] am.[S T]

59 Then [e,f]took they up stones to cast at him: but Jē′şus hid himself, and went out of the [g]temple, [8]going through the midst of them, and so passed by.

## CHAPTER 9

*A man born blind is healed.* 13 *The Pharisees are offended, and cast him out.* 35 *Jesus receives him.* 39 *Those whom Jesus came to enlighten.*

AND as[T] *Jē′şus* passed by, he saw a man which was [a]blind from *his* birth.

2 And his [b]disciples asked him, saying, [c]Master, who did sin, this man, or his parents, that he [d]was born [a]blind?[Q]

3 Jē′şus answered, Neither hath this man sinned, nor his parents: [e]but that the works of God should be made manifest in him.

4 [1,f]I must [g]work the works of him that [h]sent me, while it is day: the [i]night cometh, when no man can work.[T]

5 As long as I am in the world, [j]I am the [k,l]light of the world.[T Q]

6 When he had thus spoken, he spat on the ground, and made [m]clay of the spittle, and he anointed[G] the eyes of the [a]blind man with the clay,

7 And said unto him, Go, wash in the [n]pool of *Sī-lō′am, (which is by interpretation, Sent.) He went his way therefore, and washed, and came [o]seeing.[S Q T]

8 ¶ The neighbours therefore, and they which before had seen him that he was [2]blind, said, Is not this he that sat and [p]begged?

9 Some said, This is he: others *said*, He is like him: *but* he said, I am *he*.

10 Therefore said they unto him, How were thine eyes opened?

11 He answered and said, A man that is called Jē′şus made [m]clay, and anointed[G] mine eyes, and said unto me, Go to the [n]pool of *Sī-lō′am, and wash: and I went and washed, and I [o]received sight.

12 Then said they unto him, Where is he? He said, I know not.

13 ¶ They brought to the [q]Phăr′ĭ-seeş him that aforetime[G] was [a]blind.

14 And it was the [r]sabbath day when Jē′şus made the [m]clay, and [o]opened his eyes.

15 Then again the [q]Phăr′ĭ-seeş also asked him how he had received his sight. He said unto them, He put [m]clay upon mine eyes, and I washed, and [o]do see.

16 Therefore [s]said some of the [q]Phăr′ĭ-seeş, This man is not of God, because he keepeth not the

**54**
*w* *Jesus, relation of, to the Father,* Matt. 1:21.
*x* *Jesus, divine sonship of,* Matt. 1:21.

**55**
*y* *Spiritual Blindness,* 2 Cor. 4:4.
*z* *Jesus, obedience of,* Matt. 1:21.

**56**
*a* *Faith in Christ, exemplified,* John 6:69.
*b* *Messianic Hope,* Gen. 49:10.

**58**
*c* *Jesus, pre-existence of,* Matt. 1:21.
*d* *Jesus, eternity of,* Matt. 1:21.

**59**
*e* *Persecution, of Jesus,* John 15:20.
*f* *Malice,* Eph. 4:31.
*g* *Temple, Herod's,* 1 Kin 6:17.
8 R. V. *Omits the rest of this verse.*

**1**
*a* *Blindness,* 2 Kin. 6:18.

**2**
*b* *Disciples,* Matt. 9:14.
*c* *Rabbi,* Matt. 23:7.
*d* *Heredity, results of,* Ezek. 18:2.

**3**
*e* *Afflictions, design of,* Psa. 34:19.

**4**
*f* *Zeal,* 2 Cor. 7:11.
*g* *Obedience, exemplified,* Heb. 5:8.
1 R. V. We

*h* *Jesus, relation of, to the Father,* Matt. 1:21.
*i* *Death, preparation for,* Num. 23:10.

**5**
*j* *Jesus, mission of,* Matt. 1:21.
*k* *Light, figurative,* Matt. 5:14.
*l* *Wisdom, spiritual,* Prov. 2:2.

**6**
*m* *Clay,* Job 33:6.

**7**
*n* *Pool,* 2 Sam. 2:13.
*o* *Miracles, of Jesus,* Luke 23:8.

**8**
*p* *Beggars,* Luke 16:20.
2 R. V. a beggar.

**13**
*q* *Pharisees,* Matt. 15:12.

**14**
*r* *Sabbath,* Ex. 16:23.

**16**
*s* *Jesus, rejected,* Matt. 1:21.

* **SILOAM,** called also SHILOAH and SILOAH. *A pool in Jerusalem,* Neh. 3:15; Isa. 8:6. *Jesus directs the blind man, whom he healed, to wash in,* John 9:1-11. *Tower of, in the wall of Jerusalem, falls and kills eighteen people,* Luke 13:4.

3 R. V. signs?

**17**

t *Religious Testimony*, 2 Thess. 1:10.

u *Faith in Christ*, John 6:69.

**18**

v *Blindness*, 2 Kin. 6:18.

**22**

w *Cowardice, instances of*, Lev. 26:36.

x *Public Opinion*, John 12:42.

y *Confession of Christ*, Luke 12:8.

z *Church, rules of discipline in*, Matt. 16:18.

a *Disfellowship*, Num. 15:31.

b *Persecution, of the righteous*, John 15:20.

c *Synagogue*, Matt. 12:9.

**24**

d *Blindness*, 2 Kin. 6:18.

e *Hypocrisy, instances of*, Jas. 3:17.

[r]sabbath day. Others said, How can a man that is a sinner do such [3,o]miracles? And there was a division among them.

17 [q]They say unto the blind man again, What sayest thou of him, that he hath opened thine eyes? He [t,u]said, He is a prophet.[T]

18 But the Jewṣ did not believe concerning him, that he had been [v]blind, and received his sight, until they called the parents of him that had received his sight.

19 And they asked them, saying, Is this your son, who ye say was born [v]blind? how then doth he now see[G]?

20 His parents answered them and said, We know that this is our son, and that he was born blind:

21 But by what means he now seeth, we know not; or who hath opened his eyes, we know not: he is of age; ask him: he shall speak for himself.

22 These *words* spake his parents, because they [w]feared the [x]Jewṣ: for the Jewṣ had agreed already, that if any man did [y]confess that he was Christ, he should be [z,a,b]put out of the [c]synagogue.

23 Therefore said his parents, He is of age; ask him.

24 Then again called they the man that was [d]blind, and [e]said unto him, Give God the praise: we know that this man is a sinner.[Q]

25 He answered and said, Whether he be a sinner *or no*, I know not: one thing I know, that, whereas I was [d]blind, now I see.

26 Then said they to him again, What did he to thee? how opened he thine eyes?

27 He answered them, I have told you already, and ye did not hear: wherefore would ye hear *it* again? will ye also be his disciples?

28 Then they reviled[G] him, and said, Thou art his [f]disciple; but [g,h]we are [i]Mō′ṣeṣ' disciples.

29 We know that God [j]spake unto Mō′ṣeṣ: *as for* this [4]*fellow*, we [k]know not from whence he is.

30 The man answered and said unto them, Why herein is a marvellous thing, that ye [k]know not from whence he is, and *yet* he hath opened mine eyes.

31 Now we know that God [l]heareth not sinners: but if any [m]man be a worshipper of God, and [n]doeth his will, him [o]he heareth.[T Q]

32 Since the world[G] began was it not heard that any man opened the eyes of one that was born [d]blind.

33 If this man were not of God, he could do nothing.

34 They answered and said unto him, Thou wast altogether born in sins, and [g]dost thou teach us? And they [a,b]cast him out.[Q]

35 ¶ Jē′ṣus[T] heard that they had cast him out; and when he had found him, he said unto him, Dost thou believe on the [p]Son of God?

36 He[S] answered and said, Who is he, Lord, that I might believe on him?

37 And Jē′ṣus said unto him, Thou hast both seen him, and it is he that talketh with thee.[T]

38 And he said, Lord, I [q]believe. And he [r]worshipped him.[S]

39 ¶ And Jē′ṣus said, [s]For judgment I am come into this world, that they which [k]see not might see; and that they which [t]see might be made blind.[T]

40 And *some* of the [u]Phăr′ĭ-seeṣ which were with him heard these words, and said unto him, Are we blind also?

**28**

f *Disciples*, Matt. 9:14.

g *Self-righteousness, instances of*, Luke 18:11.

h *Bigotry, instances of*, Isa. 65:5.

i *Moses*, Ex. 2:10.

**29**

j *Prophets, inspiration of*, Isa. 3:2.

k *Spiritual Blindness*, 2 Cor. 4:4.

4 R. V. man,

**31**

l *Wicked, prayer of, not answered*, Psa. 73:3.

m *Righteous, promises to*, Psa. 64:10.

n *Obedience*, Heb. 5:8.

o *Prayer, answer to, promised*, Acts 6:4.

**35**

p *Jesus, divine sonship of*, Matt. 1:21.

**38**

q *Faith in Christ, exemplified*, John 6:69.

r *Jesus, worship of*, Matt. 1:21.

**39**

s *Jesus, mission of*, Matt. 1:21.

t *Self-righteousness*, Luke 18:11.

**40**

u *Pharisees*, Matt. 15:12.

41 Jē'ṣus said unto them, If ye were [v]blind, ye should have no sin: but now ye say, [t]We see; [w, x]therefore your [y]sin remaineth.

## CHAPTER 10

*Jesus is the door, and the good shepherd. 19 A division among the Jews concerning him. 22 His works prove him to be the Son of God. 39 He escapes from the Jews, and goes again beyond Jordan; 41 where many believe on him.*

VERILY,[G] verily, I [a]say unto you, [b]He that entereth not by the door into the sheepfold, but climbeth up some other way, the same is a [c]thief and a robber.

2 But [d]he that entereth in by the door is the [e]shepherd of the [f, g]sheep.

3[S] To him the porter openeth; and the [f]sheep hear [d, e, h]his voice: and he calleth his own sheep by name, and [i]leadeth them out.

4 And when he putteth forth his own [f]sheep, [j]he [i]goeth before them, and the sheep follow him: for they [k]know his voice.

5 And a stranger will they not follow, but will flee from him: for they know not the voice of strangers.

6 This [a]parable[G] spake Jē'ṣus unto them: but they [l]understood not what things they were which he spake unto them.[S]

7 Then said Jē'ṣus unto them again, Verily,[G] verily, I[G] say unto you, [m]I[G] am the [n]door of the [f]sheep.[T]

8 [o]All that ever came before [h]me are [c]thieves and robbers: but the [f]sheep did not hear them.[Q]

9 [m]I[G] am the [n]door: by [h]me if any man enter in, [p]he shall be [q]saved, and shall go in and out, and find pasture.[Q]

10 The [c]thief cometh not, but for to steal, and to kill, and to destroy: [r]I am come that they might have [s]life, and that they might have *it* [1]more abundantly.[T]

11 I[G] am the good [h]shepherd: the good shepherd [2, t]giveth his life [u]for the [f]sheep.[T S Q]

12 But he that is an [v, w]hireling,[G] and not the [e]shepherd, whose own the [f]sheep are not, seeth the [x]wolf coming, and leaveth the sheep, and fleeth: and the wolf catcheth them, and scattereth the sheep.

13 The [v, w]hireling fleeth, because he is an hireling, and careth not for the sheep.

14[S] [h]I[G T] am the good shepherd, and know[G] my [f]*sheep*, and am [k]known[G] of mine.

15 As the [y]Father knoweth[G] me, even so know[G] [z]I the Father: and [a]I [b]lay down my life [c]for the sheep.[T]

16 And [d]other sheep I have, which are not of this fold: [e]them also I must bring, and they shall hear my voice; and [f]there shall be one fold, *and* one [g]shepherd.[Q]

17 Therefore[T] doth my [h]Father [i]love [j]me, because [a]I [b]lay down my life, that I might [k, l]take it again.[T]

18 No man taketh it from me, but [a]I [b]lay it down of myself. I have [m]power to lay it down, and I have power to take it again. This commandment have I received of my [h]Father.[S T]

19 ¶ There was a [n]division therefore again among the [o]Jewṣ for these sayings.

20 [p]And many of them [q, r]said, He hath a [s]devil,[G] and is [t]mad;[G] why hear ye him?

21 [u]Others said, These are not the words of him that hath a [s]devil. Can a devil[G] open the eyes of the blind?

22 ¶ And it was at [v]Jē-ru'sā-lĕm the [w]feast of the [x]dedication, and it was winter.

23 And Jē'ṣus walked in the [y]temple in [z]Sŏl'o-mon's porch.

---

**41**
v *Ignorance,* Acts 3:17.
w *Judgment, according to opportunity and works,* 1 Pet. 1:17.
x *Responsibility, personal,* Ezek. 18:20.
y *Sin,* Rom. 5:12.

**1**
a *Parables, of Jesus,* Ezek. 20:49.
b *Minister, false and corrupt,* Rom. 15:16.
c *Thieves,* Deut. 24:7.

**2**
d *Minister, character and qualifications of,* Rom. 15:16.
e *Shepherd, figurative,* Jer. 31:10.
f *Sheep, figurative,* Deut. 32:14.
g *Righteous,* Psa. 64:10.

**3**
h *Jesus, shepherd,* Matt. 1:21.
i *Guidance,* Psa. 48:14.

**4**
j *Jesus, our example,* Matt. 1:21.
k *Wisdom, spiritual,* Prov. 2:2.

**6**
l *Spiritual Blindness,* 2 Cor. 4:4.

**7**
m *Jesus, savior,* Matt. 1:21.
n *Door, figurative,* Deut. 11:20.

**8**
o *False Teachers,* 2 Pet. 2:1.

**9**
p *Penitent, promises to,* Psa. 51:17.
q *Salvation,* Acts 16:17.

**10**
r *Jesus, mission of,* Matt. 1:21.
s *Life, spiritual,* Eccl. 8:15.
1 R. V. *omits* more

**11**
t *Jesus, vicarious death of,* Matt. 1:21.
u *Jesus, design of his death,* Matt. 1:21.
2 R. V. layeth down

**12**
v *Hired Servant, unfaithful,* Lev. 25:40.
w *Minister, false and corrupt,* Rom. 15:16.
x *Wolf,* Jer. 5:6.

**15**
y *God, fatherhood of,* Gen. 2:2.
z *Jesus, relation of, to the Father,* Matt. 1:21.

a *Jesus, death of, voluntary,* Matt. 1:21.
b *Jesus, vicarious death of,* Matt. 1:21.
c *Jesus, design of his death,* Matt. 1:21.

**16**
d *Gentiles, prophecies of the conversion of,* Acts 10:45.
e *Church, prophecies concerning its prosperity,* Matt. 16:18.
f *Church, unity of,* Matt. 16:18.
g *Jesus, shepherd,* Matt. 1:21.

**17**
h *God, fatherhood of,* Gen. 2:2.
i *God, love of,* Gen. 2:2.
j *Jesus, relation of, to the Father,* Matt. 1:21.
k *Jesus, resurrection of,* Matt. 1:21.
l *Ressurection,* 1 Cor. 15:12.

**18**
m *Jesus, power of,* Matt. 1:21.

**19**
n *Strife, instances of,* Prov. 20:3.
o *Jews,* Neh. 4:2.

**20**
p *Jesus, rejected,* Matt. 1:21.
q *False Accusation,* 2 Tim. 3:3.
r *Persecution, of Jesus,* John 15:20.

s *Demons,* Matt. 4:24. t *Insanity, Jesus falsely accused of,* Prov. 26:18. **21** u *Jesus, received,* Matt. 1:21. **22** v *Jerusalem,* Judg. 19:10. w *Annual Feasts,* Num. 15:3. x *Dedication, feast of,* Ezra 6:17.
**23** y *Temple, Herod's,* 1 Kin. 6:17. z Acts 3:11; 5:12.

24 Then[S] came the [a]Jews round about him, and said unto him, How long dost thou make[C] us to doubt? If thou be the Christ, tell us plainly.

25 Jē'ṣus answered them, I told you, and ye [b]believed not: the [c]works that I do in my [d]Father's name, they bear witness of me.[T]

26 But ye [b]believe not, because [e]ye are not of my sheep, [3]as I said unto you.[T]

27[T] [f]My sheep hear my voice, and I know[C] them, and they follow me:

28 And [g]I [h]give unto them [i]eternal [j]life; and [h]they shall never perish, neither shall any *man* pluck them out of my hand.[T]

29 My [d]Father, which gave *them* me, is [k]greater than all; and no *man* is able to pluck *them* out of my Father's hand.[S]

30 [l]I and *my* [d]Father are one.[T]

31 ¶ Then[T] the [a]Jews [m]took up stones again to stone him.

32 Jē'ṣus answered them, Many good [c]works have I shewed you from my [d]Father; for which of those works do ye stone me?

33 The [a]Jews answered him, saying, For a good work we stone thee not; but for [n]blasphemy; and because that thou, being a man, [l]makest thyself God.[Q]

34 Jē'ṣus answered them, Is it not written in your [o,p]law, [q]I said, Ye are gods?[Q]

35 If he called them gods, unto whom the [p]word of God came, and the scripture cannot be broken;

36 [n]Say ye of him, whom the [d]Father hath sanctified, and sent into the world, Thou blasphemest; because I said, I am the [l]Son of God?

37 If I do not the works of my [d]Father, believe me not.

**24**
*a Jews*, Neh. 4:2.

**25**
*b Unbelief*, Heb. 3:12.
*c Miracles, of Jesus*, Luke 23:8.
*d God, fatherhood of*, Gen. 2:2.

**26**
*e Reprobates*, 1 Cor. 9:27.
3 R. V. *omits* as I said unto you.

**27**
*f Jesus, shepherd*, Matt. 1:21.

**28**
*g Jesus, power of*, Matt. 1:21.
*h Righteous, promises to*, Psa. 64:10.
*i Immortality*, 1 Cor. 15:54.
*j Life, everlasting*, Eccl. 8:15.

**29**
*k God, sovereign*, Gen. 2:2.

**30**
*l Jesus, divinity of*, Matt. 1:21.

**31**
*m Persecution, of Jesus*, John 15:20.

**33**
*n Blasphemy, false accusations of*, 2 Sam. 12:14.

**34**
*o Law, of Moses*, Deut. 33:2.
*p Word of God*, Psa. 119:9.
*q* Psa. 82:6.

38 But if I do, though ye believe not me, believe the [c]works: that ye may know, and [4]believe, that the Father *is* in [r]me, and I in [r]him.[T]

39 ¶ Therefore they [m]sought again to take him: but he [s]escaped out of their hand,

40 And went away again beyond [t]Jôr'dan into the [u]place where [v]Jŏhn at first [w]baptized; and there he abode.[C]

41 And [x,y]many resorted unto him, and said, [v]Jŏhn did no [5]miracle: but all things that Jŏhn spake of this man were true.

42 And many [y,z]believed on him there.

## CHAPTER 11

*The raising of Lazarus from the dead.* 45 *Many Jews believe.* 47 *The chief priests and Pharisees conspire against Jesus.* 49 *The counsel of Caiaphas.* 54 *Jesus retires to the city of Ephraim.* 55 *At the passover many inquire after him.*

NOW[T] a certain *man* was [a]sick, *named* *Lăz'a-rŭs, of Bĕth'-a-nȳ, the town of †Mā'rȳ and her sister [b]Mär'thȧ.

2 (It was *that* †Mā'rȳ which [c]anointed the Lord with ointment,[C] and wiped his feet with her hair, whose brother *Lăz'a-rŭs was [a]sick.)

3 Therefore his sisters sent unto him, saying, Lord, behold, he whom thou [d]lovest is sick.

4 When Jē'ṣus heard *that*, he said, This [e]sickness is not unto death, but [f]for the [g]glory of God, [f]that the [h]Son of God might be glorified[C] thereby.[T]

5 Now Jē'ṣus [d,i]loved [b,j]Mär'thȧ, and her [†,j]sister, and *Lăz'a-rŭs.

6 When he had heard therefore that *he was [a]sick, he abode[C] two days still in the same place where he was.

7 Then after that saith he to *his*

**38**
*r Jesus, relation of, to the Father*, Matt. 1:21.
4 R. V. understand

**39**
*s Prudence, of Jesus*, 2 Chr. 2:12.

**40**
*t Jordan*, Gen. 32:10.
*u* John 1:28.
*v John the Baptist*, Luke 1:63.
*w Baptism, of John the Baptist*, Luke 20:4.

**41**
*x Popularity of Jesus*, John 6:15.
*y Jesus, received*, Matt. 1:21.
5 R. V. sign:

**42**
*z Faith in Christ*, John 6:69.

**1**
*a Afflictions*, Psa. 34:19.
*b Martha*, Luke 10:38.

**2**
*c Anointing, of Jesus*, Deut. 28:40.

**3**
*d Jesus, love of*, Matt. 1:21.

**4**
*e Afflictions, design of*, Psa. 34:19.
*f Miracles, design of*, Luke 23:8.
*g God, glory of*, Gen. 2:2.
*h Jesus, divine sonship of*, Matt. 1:21.

**5**
*i Friendship*, Prov. 22:24.
*j Women, good*, Prov. 31:10.

* **LAZARUS**, brother of Mary and Martha. *Sickness and death of*, John 11:1-14. *Jesus raises, from the dead*, John 11:38-44; 12:17, 18 *Supped with Jesus*, John 12:1, 2, 9. *Plotted against by the chief priests*, John 12:10, 11.

† **MARY**, sister of Lazarus. *Sits at Jesus' feet for instruction*, Luke 10:38-42. *Beloved of Jesus*, John 11:1, 5. *Jesus calls for*, John 11:29. *Anoints Jesus*, Matt. 26:7-13; Mark 14:3-9; John 11:2; 12:3.

[k]disciples, Let us go into [l]Jū-
dæ′ȧ again.
8 *His* [k]disciples say unto
him, [m]Master, the [n]Jews̱ of late
[o]sought[G] to stone thee; and goest
thou thither again?
9 Jē′ṣus answered, Are there
not twelve hours in the [p]day? If
any man walk in the [q]day, he
stumbleth not, because he seeth
the [r]light of this world.
10 But if a man walk in the
[s]night, he stumbleth, because
there is [t]no light in him.
11 These things said he: and
after that he saith unto them,
Our [u]friend *Lăz′a-rŭs [v,w]sleep-
eth; but I go, that I may awake
him out of sleep.
12 Then said his [k]disciples,
Lord, if he [x]sleep, he [1]shall do
well.
13 Howbeit Jē′ṣus spake of his
[w]death: but they thought that
he had spoken of taking of rest
in sleep.
14 Then said Jē′ṣus unto them
plainly, *Lăz′a-rŭs is [y]dead.
15 And I am glad for your
sakes that I was not there, [z]to
the intent ye may believe; nevertheless let us go unto him.
16 Then [a]said ‡Thŏm′as, which
is called Dĭd′y̆-mŭs, unto his
fellowdisciples, [b,c]Let us also go,
that we may die with him.
17 Then when Jē′ṣus came, he
found that he had *lain* in the
grave four days already.
18 Now ‖Bĕth′a-ny̆ was nigh[G]
unto [d]Jē-ru′sȧ-lĕm, about fifteen
[e]furlongs[G] off:
19 And many of the [f]Jews̱
[c,g]came to [h]Mär′thȧ and †Mā′ry̆,
to [i]comfort them [j]concerning
their brother.
20 Then [h]Mär′thȧ, as soon as
she heard that Jē′ṣus was coming, went and met him: but
†Mā′ry̆ sat *still* in the house.
21 Then said [h]Mär′thȧ unto
Jē′ṣus, Lord, [k]if thou hadst been
here, my brother had not died.
22 But I [k]know, that even now,
whatsoever thou wilt ask of God,
God will give *it* thee.
23 Jē′ṣus [l,m]saith unto her, Thy
brother shall rise again.
24 [h]Mär′thȧ saith unto him,
I know that he shall rise again
in the [n]resurrection at the last
day.[Q]
25 [S] Jē′ṣus said unto her, I[G]
am the resurrection, and the
[o]life: [p]he that [q,r]believeth in
[s]me, though he [2]were [t]dead, yet
[u]shall he [v]live:[T]
26 And [p]whosoever liveth and
[q,r]believeth in me [u]shall never
[w]die. Believest thou this?[S]
27 She saith unto him, Yea,
Lord: [x]I [k]believe that thou art
the [y]Christ, the [z]Son of God,
which should come into the
world.[S]
28 And when she had so said,
she went her way, and called
†Mā′ry̆ her sister secretly, saying, The Master is come, and
calleth for thee.
29 As soon as she heard *that*,
she arose quickly, and came unto
him.
30 Now Jē′ṣus was not yet
come into the town, but was in
that place where [a]Mär′thȧ met
him.
31 The [b]Jews̱ then which were
with her in the house, and
[c,d]comforted her, when they saw
†Mā′ry̆, that she rose up hastily
and went out, followed her, saying, She goeth unto the [e,f]grave
to [g,h]weep there.

**7**
k *Apostles*, Luke 6:13.
l *Judea*, Luke 5:17.

**8**
m *Rabbi*, Matt. 23:7.
n *Jews*, Neh. 4:2.
o *Persecution, of Jesus*, John 15:20.

**9**
p *Day, figurative*, Gen. 1:5.
q *Wisdom, spiritual*, Prov. 2:2.
r *Light, figurative*, Matt. 5:14.

**10**
s *Darkness, figurative*, Gen. 1:2.
t *Spiritual Blindness*, 2 Cor. 4:4.

**11**
u *Friends*, Ex. 33:11.
v *Sleep, a symbol of death*, Psa. 127:2.
w *Death*, Num. 23:10.

**12**
x *Sleep*, Psa. 127:2.
1 R. V. will recover.

**14**
y *Dead*, 2 Kin. 4:32.

**15**
z *Miracles, design of*, Luke 23:8.

**16**
a *Courage, instances of*, Deut. 31:7.
b *Love, for Jesus*, 1 John 4:19.
c *Friendship, instances of*, Prov. 22:24.

**18**
d *Jerusalem*, Judg. 19:10.
e Luke 24:13.

**19**
f *Jews*, Neh. 4:2.
g *Kindness, instances of*, Acts 28:2.
h *Martha*, Luke 10:38.
i *Sympathy*, 1 Pet. 3:8.
j *Bereavement*, Hos. 9:12.

**21**
k *Faith in Christ, exemplified*, John 6:69.

**23**
l *Condolence, instances of*, 2 Sam. 10:2.
m *Afflictions, consolation in*, Psa. 34:19.

**24**
n *Resurrection*, 1 Cor. 15:12.

**25**
o *Life, spiritual*, Eccl. 8:15.
p *Righteous, promises to*, Psa. 64:10.
q *Faith in Christ*, John 6:69.
r *Salvation, conditions of*, Acts 16:17.
s *Jesus, savior*, Matt. 1:21.
t *Dead*, 2 Kin. 4:32.
u *Promise, to believers*, 2 Cor. 1:20.
v *Immortality*, 1 Cor. 15:54.
2 R. V. die.

**26**
w *Spiritual Death*, 1 John 3:14.

**27**
x *Confession of Christ, exemplified*, Luke 12:8.
y *Jesus, Messiah*, Matt. 1:21.
z *Jesus, divinity of*, Matt. 1:21.

**30**
a *Martha*, Luke 10:38.

**31**
b *Jews*, Neh. 4:2.
c *Kindness*, Acts 28:2.
d *Sympathy*, 1 Pet. 3:8.
e *Grave*, 2 Sam. 3:32.
f *Burying Places*, Gen. 23:4.
g *Weeping*, Ezra 3:13.
h *Mourning*, Lam. 2:5.

‡ **THOMAS** (*twin*), called DIDYMUS. *One of the twelve apostles*, Matt. 10:3; Mark 3:18; Luke 6:15. *Present at the raising of Lazarus*, John 11:16. *Asks Jesus the way to the Father's house*, John 14:5. *Absent when Jesus first appeared to the disciples after the resurrection*, John 20:24. *Skepticism of*, John 20:25. *Sees Jesus after the resurrection and believes*, John 20:26–29; 21:1, 2. *Dwells with the other apostles in Jerusalem*, Acts 1:13, 14. *Loyalty of, to Jesus*, John 11:16; 20:28.

‖ **BETHANY.** *A village on the eastern slope of the Mount of Olives, on the highway from Jerusalem to Jericho*, John 11:18. *Mary, Martha, and Lazarus dwell in*, Luke 10:38–41. *Lazarus dies, and is raised to life at*, John 11. *Jesus attends a feast in*, Matt. 26:6–13; John 12:1–9. *The colt, on which Jesus made his triumphal entry into Jerusalem, obtained in*, Mark 11:1–11. *Jesus sojourns in*, Matt. 21:17; Mark 11:11, 12, 19.

32 Then when †Mā′rȳ was come where Jē′ṣus was, and saw him, she fell down at his feet, [i]saying unto him, Lord, if thou hadst been here, my brother had not died.

33 When Jē′ṣus therefore saw her [g,h]weeping, and the [b]Jewṣ also [d]weeping [j]which came with her, [k]he groaned in the spirit, and was troubled,

34 And said, Where have ye laid him? They said unto him, Lord, come and see.

35 Jē′ṣus [d,g]wept.[T]

36 Then said the Jewṣ, Behold how he [f,l]loved[C] him!

37 And some of them said, Could not this man, which [m]opened the eyes of the [n]blind, have caused that even this man should not have died?

38 Jē′ṣus therefore again groaning in himself cometh to the [e,f]grave. It was a [o]cave, and a stone lay upon it.

39 Jē′ṣus said, Take ye away the stone. [a]Mär′thȧ, the sister of him that was dead, saith unto him, Lord, by this time he stinketh: for he hath been *dead* four days.

40 Jē′ṣus saith unto her, Said I not unto thee, that, if thou wouldest believe, thou shouldest see the glory of God?[S]

41[T] Then they took away the stone [3]*from the place* where the dead was laid. And Jē′ṣus lifted up *his* eyes, and [p]said, [q]Father, I [r]thank thee that thou hast heard me.

42 And [p]I knew that thou hearest me always: but because of the people which stand by I said *it*, that they may believe that thou hast sent me.[T]

43[S] And when he thus had spoken, he cried with a loud voice, *Lăz′a-rŭs, come forth.

32
*i* *Faith in Christ, exemplified*, John 6:69.

33
*j* *Friendship, instances of*, Prov. 22:24.
*k* *Jesus, compassion of*, Matt. 1:21.

36
*l* *Jesus, love of*, Matt. 1:21.

37
*m* *Miracles, of Jesus*, Luke 23:8.
*n* *Blindness*, 2 Kin. 6:18.

38
*o* *Cave*, Judg. 6:2.

41
*p* *Prayers of Jesus*, Luke 5:16.
*q* *God, fatherhood of*, Gen. 2:2.
*r* *Thankfulness, Jesus set an example of*, Acts 24:3.
3 R. V. *omits* from the place where the dead was laid.

44 And he that was [s]dead [m]came forth, bound hand and foot with graveclothes: and his face was bound about with a napkin.[C] Jē′ṣus saith unto them, Loose[C] him, and let him go.[S]

45 Then many of the [b]Jewṣ which came to †Mā′rȳ, and had seen the things which Jē′ṣus did, [t]believed on him.

46 But [u]some of them went their ways to the [v]Phăr′ĭ-seeṣ, and told them what things Jē′ṣus had done.

47 ¶ [w]Then gathered the chief [x]priests and the [v]Phăr′ĭ-seeṣ a council, and said, What do we? for this man doeth many [4,t]miracles.

48 [w]If we let him thus alone, all *men* will believe on him: and the §Rō′manṣ shall come and take away both our place and nation.

49 And one of them, *named* [y]Cā′ia-phăs, being the [z]high priest that same year, said unto them, Ye know nothing at all,

50 Nor[S] consider that it is expedient for us, that one man should [a]die for the people, and that the whole nation perish not.

51[T] And this spake [b]he not of himself: but being high priest that year, he [c]prophesied that [d]Jē′ṣus should [a,e]die [f,g]for that nation;

52 And not for that nation only, but that also he should gather together in [h]one the [i,j]children of God that were scattered abroad.[C][T]

53 Then from that day forth they [k,l,m]took counsel together for to put him to [n]death.[S]

54 Jē′ṣus therefore [o]walked no more openly among the [p]Jewṣ; but [o]went thence unto a country near to the wilderness, into a city called [q]Ē′phrā-ĭm, and there continued with his [r]disciples.

55 ¶ And the [p]Jewṣ' [s]passover

44
*s* *Dead*, 2 Kin. 4:32.

45
*t* *Miracles, convincing effect of*, Luke 23:8.

46
*u* *Jesus, rejected*, Matt. 1:21.
*v* *Pharisees*, Matt. 15:12.

47
*w* *Envy, instances of*, Prov. 14:30.
*x* *Priest*, Lev. 1:5.
4 R. V. signs.

49
*y* *Caiaphas*, Matt. 26:3.
*z* *High Priest*, Lev. 21:10.

50
*a* *Suffering, vicarious*, Col. 1:24.

51
*b* *Caiaphas*, Matt. 26:3.
*c* *Inspiration*, Job 32:8.
*d* *Jesus, mission of*, Matt. 1:21.
*e* *Jesus, vicarious death of*, Matt. 1:21.
*f* *Atonement, by Jesus*, Lev. 17:11.
*g* *Jesus, design of his death*, Matt. 1:21.

52
*h* *Church, unity of*, Matt. 16:18.
*i* *Spiritual Adoption, of the righteous*, Rom. 8:15.
*j* *Gentiles, prophecies concerning*, Acts 10:45.

53
*k* *Conspiracy*, 1 Kin. 16:9.
*l* *Malice*, Eph. 4:31.
*m* *Persecution, of Jesus*, John 15:20.
*n* *Jesus, death of*, Matt. 1:21.

54
*o* *Prudence, instances of*, 2 Chr. 2:12.
*p* *Jews*, Neh. 4:2.
*q* 2 Chr. 13:19.
*r* *Apostles*, Luke 6:13.

55
*s* *Passover*, Num. 9:5.

§ **ROMAN EMPIRE.** *Ruled, by Augustus Cæsar*, Luke 2:1; *by Tiberius Cæsar*, Luke 3:1; *by Claudius Cæsar*, Acts 18:2; *by Nero*, Phil. 4:22. *Citizenship in, by nativity*, Acts 22:28; *by purchase*, Acts 22:28. *Rights of citizens of*, Acts 16:37; 22:25–29; *to trial*, Acts 25:16; *to appeal*, Acts 25:10, 21.

A.D. 33
See footnote, *Time*, Rev. 10:6.

t *Jerusalem*, Judg. 19:10.
u *Purification*, Num. 19:19.

56
v *Temple, Herod's*, 1 Kin. 6:17.

57
w *Priest*, Lev. 1:5.
x *Pharisees*, Matt. 15:12.

v.1–AD 30

1
a Compare Matt. 26:6–13; Mark 14:3–9; and Luke 7:36–39.
b *Passover*, Num. 9:5.
c *Bethany*, John 11:18.
d *Lazarus*, John 11:1.
1 R. V. *omits* which had been dead,

2
e *Hospitality, instances of*, Rom. 12:13.
f *Martha*, Luke 10:38.

3
g *Love, for Jesus, instances of*, 1 John 4:19.
h *Mary*, John 11:2.
i *Ointment*, Eccl. 7:1.
j *Spikenard*, Song 4:13.
k *Anointing, of Jesus*, Deut. 28:40.

4
l *Presumption*, Psa. 19:13.
m *Apostles*, Luke 6:13.
n *Judas*, Mark 3:19.
o *Minister, false and corrupt*, Rom. 15:16.
p John 6:71.
q *Betrayal, of Jesus*, Matt. 26:46.

5
r *Hypocrisy, instances of*, Jas. 3:17.
s *Parsimony*, Mal. 3:8.
t *Poor*, Prov. 21:13.

6
u *Dishonesty, instances of*, Ezek. 22:13.
v *Covetousness, instances of*, Isa. 57:17.
w *Thieves*, Deut. 24:7.
2 R. V. took away

7
x *Jesus, prophet*, Matt. 1:21.
y *Jesus, death of*, Matt. 1:21.
z *Burial*, Acts 8:2.

was nigh[G] at hand: and many went out of the country up to [t]Jĕ-ru'sȧ-lĕm before the passover, to [u]purify themselves.[Q]

56 Then sought[G] they for Jē'ṣus, and spake among themselves, as they stood in the [v]temple, What think ye, that he will not come to the [s]feast?

57 Now both the chief [w]priests and the [x]Phăr'ĭ-seeṣ had given a commandment, that, if any man knew where he were, he should shew *it*, [l,m]that they might take him.[T]

## CHAPTER 12

*The supper at Bethany.* 3 *Mary anoints the feet of Jesus.* 10 *The chief priests consult to put Lazarus to death.* 12 *Jesus' public entry into Jerusalem.* 20 *Certain Greeks desire to see him.* 23 *He foretells his own death and resurrection.* 37 *The Jews are blinded.* 42 *Many rulers believe, but do not confess him.* 44 *The danger of rejecting him.*

[a]THEN Jē'ṣus six days before the [b]passover came to [c]Bĕth'a-nȳ, where [d]Lăz'a-rŭs was [1]which had been dead, whom he raised from the dead.

2 There [e]they made him a supper; and [f]Mär'thȧ served: but [d]Lăz'a-rŭs was one of them that sat at the table with him.

3 [g]Then took [h]Mā'rȳ a pound[G] of [i]ointment of [j]spikenard, very costly, and [k]anointed the feet of Jē'ṣus, and wiped his feet with her hair: and the house was filled with the odour of the ointment.

4 Then [l]saith one of his [m]disciples, [n,o]Jū'das Ĭs-căr'ĭ-ot, [p]Sī'mon's *son*, which should [q]betray him,

5 [r,s]Why was not this [t]ointment[G] sold for three hundred pence[G], and given to the [t]poor?

6 This he [l]said, not that he cared for the [t]poor; but because he [u]was a [v,w]thief, and had the bag, and [2]bare what was put therein.

7 Then [x]said Jē'ṣus, Let her alone: against the day of my [y,z]burying hath she kept this.

8 For the [t]poor always ye have with you[Q]; but me ye have not always.

9 ¶ Much people of the [a]Jewṣ therefore knew that he was there: and they came not for Jē'ṣus' sake only, but [b]that they might see [c]Lăz'a-rŭs also, whom he had [d]raised from the dead.

10 But the chief [e]priests [f,g]consulted that they might put [c]Lăz'a-rŭs also to death;

11 Because that by reason of him many of the [a]Jewṣ went away, and [h,i,j]believed on Jē'ṣus.

12 ¶ On the next day much people that were come to the [k,l]feast, when they heard that Jē'ṣus was coming to [m]Jĕ-ru'sȧ-lĕm,

13 [i,n,o]Took branches of [p]palm trees, and went forth to meet him, and cried, Hō-ṣan'nȧ[G]: [q]Blessed *is* the [r]King of Ĭṣ'ra-el that cometh in the name of the Lord.[Q]

14 And Jē'ṣus, when he had found a young [s]ass, sat thereon; as it is written,

15 [t]Fear not, daughter of [u]Sī'ŏn: behold, thy [r]King cometh, sitting on an [s]ass's colt.[Q]

16 These things understood not his [v]disciples at the first: but when Jē'ṣus was [w]glorified, then remembered they that these [q]things were written of him, and *that* they had done these things unto him.

17 The people therefore that was with him when he called [x]Lăz'a-rŭs out of his [y]grave, and raised him from the [z]dead, bare record[G].

18 For this cause the people also met him, for that they heard that he had done this [3,a]miracle.

19 The [b]Phăr'ĭ-seeṣ therefore said among themselves, Perceive ye how ye prevail[G] nothing? behold, [c]the world[G] is gone after him.

20 ¶ [d]And there were certain

v.8–AD 30
See footnote, *Time*, Rev. 10:6.

9
a *Jews*, Neh. 4:2.
b *Curiosity*, Prov. 27:20.
c *Lazarus*, John 11:1.
d *Miracles, of Jesus*, Luke 23:8.

10
e *Priest*, Lev. 1:5.
f *Malice*, Eph. 4:31.
g *Persecution, instances of*, John 15:20.

11
h *Faith in Christ*, John 6:69.
i *Jesus, received*, Matt. 1:21.
j *Miracles, convincing effect of*, Luke 23:8.

12
k *Passover*, Num. 9:5.
l *Annual Feasts*, Num. 15:3.
m *Jerusalem*, Judg. 19:10.

13
n *Triumphal Entry of Jesus into Jerusalem*, Matt. 21:5.
o *Popularity of Jesus*, John 6:15.
p *Palm Tree*, Song 7:7.
q *Prophecies concerning the Messiah, and their fulfillment*, Gen. 12:3.
r *Jesus, king*, Matt. 1:21.

14
s *Ass, domesticated*, 2 Chr. 28:15.

15
t Zech. 9:9.
u Or, *Zion*, 2 Sam. 5:7.

16
v *Apostles*, Luke 6:13.
w *Jesus, death of*, Matt. 1:21.

17
x *Lazarus, resurrection of*, John 11:1.
y *Grave*, 2 Sam. 3:32.
z *Dead*, 2 Kin. 4:32.

18
a *Miracles, of Jesus*, Luke 23:8.
3 R. V. sign.

19
b *Pharisees*, Matt. 15:12.
c *Popularity of Jesus*, John 6:15.

20
d *Jerusalem, annual feasts at*, Judg. 19:10.

v.20–AD 30
See footnote, *Time,* Rev. 10:6.

*e Greece,* Zech. 9:13.
*f Worship,* Gen. 22:5.
*g Passover,* Num. 9:5.
*h Annual Feasts,* Num. 15:3.

21
*i Philip,* Luke 6:14.
*j Bethsaida,* John 1:44.
*k Galilee,* Mark 6:21.
*l Spiritual Desire,* Psa. 42:1.

22
*m Andrew,* Matt. 4:18.

23
*n Jesus, death of,* Matt. 1:21.

24
*o Parables, of Jesus,* Ezek. 20:49.
*p Wheat,* Ezra. 6:9.
*q Suffering, vicarious,* Col. 1:24.
4 R. V. grain

25
*r Paradox,* 2 Cor. 12:4.
*s Worldliness,* 1 John 2:15.
*t Discipleship of Jesus, tests of,* Matt. 10:32.
*u Righteous, promises to,* Psa. 64:10.
*v Renunciation, of self for Christ,* Luke 5:11.
*w Martyrdom, spirit of, required by Jesus,* Rev. 17:6.
*x Life, everlasting,* Eccl. 8:15.

26
*y Heaven, future home of the righteous,* Luke 18:22
*z Obedience, rewarded,* Heb. 5:8.

*a Promise, to the righteous,* 2 Cor. 1:20.
*b God, fatherhood of,* Gen. 2:2.

27
*c Jesus, sufferings of,* Matt. 1:21.
*d Prayers of Jesus,* Luke 5:16.
*e Jesus, mission of,* Matt. 1:21.

[e]Greeks among them that came
up to [f]worship at the [g,h]feast:
21 The same came therefore to
[i]Phĭl′ĭp, which was of [j]Bĕth-sā′-
ĭ-dȧ of [k]Găl′ĭ-lee, and desired[G]
him, saying, Sir, we [l]would[G] see
Jē′ṣus.
22 [i]Phĭl′ĭp cometh and telleth
[m]Ăn′drew: and again Ăn′drew
and Phĭl′ĭp tell Jē′ṣus.
23 ¶ And Jē′ṣus answered them,
saying, The hour is come, that
the Son of man should be [n]glori-
fied.[G]
24 Verily, verily, I [o]say unto
you, Except a [4]corn[G] of [p]wheat
fall into the ground and [q]die, it
abideth alone: but if it die, it
bringeth forth much fruit.
25 [r,s]He that [t]loveth his life
shall lose it; and [u]he that [v,w]hateth
his life in this world shall keep it
unto [x]life eternal.
26[T] [t]If any man serve me, let
him follow me; and [y]where I am,
there shall also my servant be: if
any man [z]serve me, [u,a]him will
*my* [b]Father honour.
27 Now is my soul [c]troubled;
and what shall I [d]say? Father,
save me from this hour: but [e]for
this cause came I unto this hour.[Q]
28 [b,d]Father, [f]glorify thy name.
Then came there a voice from
heaven, *saying,* I have both glorified *it,* and will glorify *it* again.
29 The people therefore, that
stood by, and heard *it,* said that
it thundered: others said, An
[g]angel spake to him.
30 Jē′ṣus answered and said,
This voice came not because of
me, but for your sakes.[T]
31[T] Now is the judgment of this
world: [h]now shall the [i]prince of
this world be [j]cast out.[S]
32 And I, if I be [k,l]lifted[G] up
from the earth, will [m,n]draw [o]all
*men* unto me.
33 This he said, signifying
[k]what death[G] he should [l]die.
34 The people answered him,
[p]We have heard out of the [q]law
that [r]Chrĭst [s]abideth[G] for ever:
and how sayest thou, The [t]Son
of man must be [k,l]lifted[G] up? who
is this Son of man?[T Q]
35 Then[T] Jē′ṣus said unto them,
Yet a little while is the [u,v,w]light
with you. Walk [x]while ye have
the light, lest [y,z,a]darkness come
upon you: for he that walketh in
darkness knoweth not whither
he goeth.
36 While ye have [b]light, [c,d,e]be-
lieve in the light, that ye may be
the [f]children of light. These
things spake Jē′ṣus, and departed, and [g]did hide himself from
them.[S T]
37 ¶ But though he had done
so many [5,h]miracles[G] before them,
yet [i]they [j,k,l]believed not on him:
38 That the [m]saying of [n]Ē-ṣā′-
ias the [o]prophet might be fulfilled, which he spake, Lord,
[j,l,p]who hath believed our report? and to whom hath the arm
of the Lord been revealed?[Q]
39[S] Therefore they could [j,l]not
believe, because that [n]Ē-ṣā′ias
said again,
40 He hath [l]blinded their eyes,
and hardened their [q]heart; [r]that
they should not see with *their*
eyes, nor understand with *their*
heart, and be converted,[G] and I
should heal them.[S Q]
41 These things said [n]Ē-ṣā′ias,
[s]when he saw his glory, and
spake of him.[S T]
42 ¶ Nevertheless among
the chief rulers also many [d]be-
lieved on him; but [*,t]because
of the [u]Phăr′ĭ-seeṣ they [v]did not

v.32–AD 30
See footnote, *Time,* Rev. 10:6.

*m Jesus, mission of,* Matt. 1:21.
*n Salvation,* Acts 16:17.
*o Gentiles, prophecies of the conversion of,* Acts 10:45.

34
*p Messianic Hope,* Gen. 49:10.
*q Law, of Moses,* Deut. 33:2.
*r Jesus, Messiah,* Matt. 1:21.
*s Jesus, eternity of,* Matt. 1:21.
*t Jesus, humanity of,* Matt. 1:21.

35
*u Light, figurative,* Matt. 5:14.
*v* John 1:4–9.
*w Jesus, teacher,* Matt. 1:21.
*x Opportunity,* Gal. 6:10.
*y Darkness, figurative,* Gen. 1:2.
*z Spiritual Blindness,* 2 Cor. 4:4.

*a Opportunity, lost,* Gal. 6:10.

36
*b Light, figurative,* Matt. 5:14.
*c Commandment, enjoining faith,* Deut. 8:2.
*d Faith in Christ,* John 6:69.
*e Salvation, conditions of,* Acts 16:17.
*f Righteous, described,* Psa. 64:10.
*g Prudence, instances of,* 2 Chr. 2:12.

37
*h Miracles, of Jesus,* Luke 23:8.
*i Unbelievers,* 1 Cor. 6:6.
*j Unbelief,* Heb. 3:12.
*k Jesus, rejected,* Matt. 1:21.
*l Spiritual Blindness,* 2 Cor. 4:4.
5 R. V. signs

38
*m Prophecies concerning the Messiah, and their fulfillment,* Gen. 12:3.
*n* Or, *Isaiah,* Isa. 1:1.
*o Prophets,* Isa. 3:2.
*p* Isa. 53:1.

40
*q Heart,* Psa. 44:21.
*r Moral Insensibility,* Luke 8:10.

**28** *f God, glory of,* Gen. 2:2. **29** *g Angel,* Heb. 1:13.
**31** *h Jesus, prophet,* Matt 1:21. *i Satan, described as prince of this world,* Matt. 4:10. *j Satan, kingdom of, to be destroyed,* Matt. 4:10.
**32** *k Crucifixion,* Mark 15:13. *l Jesus, death of,* Matt. 1:21.

**41** *s Jesus, pre-existence of,* Matt. 1:21. **42** *t Cowardice, instances of,* Lev. 26:36. *u Pharisees,* Matt. 15:12. *v Indecision, instances of,* 1 Kin. 18:21.

* **PUBLIC OPINION.** Kings influenced by: *Saul,* 1 Sam. 14:45; 15:24; *David,* 2 Chr. 20:21; *Hezekiah,* 2 Chr. 30:2; *Zedekiah,* Jer. 38:19, 24–27; *Herod,* Matt. 14:5; Acts 12:2, 3; *Pilate,* John 19:6–13.

v.42–AD 30

w *Confession of Christ, timid believers deterred from,* Luke 12:8.
x *Disfellowship,* Num. 15:31.
y *Persecution, of the righteous,* John 15:20.
z *Synagogue,* Matt. 12:9.

43
a *Worldliness, leads to the rejection of Christ,* 1 John 2:15.

44
b *Faith in Christ,* John 6:69.
c *Jesus, relation of, to the Father,* Matt. 1:21.

45
d *Jesus, divinity of,* Matt. 1:21.

46
e *Jesus, mission of,* Matt. 1:21.
*Light, figurative,* Matt. 5:14.
g *Salvation, conditions of,* Acts 16:17.
h *Wisdom, spiritual, from God,* Prov. 2:2.
i *Darkness, figurative,* Gen. 1:2.
j *Spiritual Blindness,* 2 Cor. 4:4.

47
k *Doctrines of Jesus,* John 7:16.
l *Jesus, savior,* Matt. 1:21.
6 R. V. sayings, and keep them not,

48
m *God, judge* Gen. 2:2.
n *Judgment, according to opportunity and works,* 2 Pet. 3:7.
o *Responsibility, according to privilege,* Ezek. 18:20.

49
p *God, fatherhood of,* Gen. 2:2.
q *Jesus, teacher,* Matt. 1:21.

50
r *Life, everlasting,* Eccl. 8:15.
s *Obedience, instances of,* Heb. 5:8.

1
a *Passover,* Num. 9:5.
b *Jesus, omniscience of,* Matt. 1:21.
c *God, fatherhood of,* Gen. 2:2.
d *Jesus, love of,* Matt. 1:21.

[w]confess *him*, lest they should be
[x,y]put out of the [z]synagogue:
43 For they [a]loved the praise of
men more than the praise of God.
44 ¶ [S]Jē'ṣus cried and said, He
that [b]believeth on me, believeth
not on me, but on [c]him that sent
me.
45 And he that seeth [d]me seeth
[c]him that sent me.[T]
46 [e]I am come a [f]light into the
world, that whosoever[C] [b,g]believ-
eth on me should [h]not abide[C] in
[i,j]darkness.[S T]
47 And if any man hear my
[6,k]words, and believe not, I
judge him not: for [e,l]I came not
to judge the world, but to save
the world.
48 He that rejecteth me, and
receiveth not my [k]words, hath
[m]one that judgeth him: [n,o]the
word that I have spoken, the
same shall judge him in the last
day.
49 For[T] I have not spoken of myself; but the [p]Father which [c]sent
me, he gave me a command-
ment, what I should [q]say, and
what I should speak.
50 And I know that his commandment is [r]life everlasting[C]:
whatsoever I speak therefore,
even as the Father said unto me,
[s]so I speak.[T]

## CHAPTER 13

*Jesus washes his disciples' feet; 12 and exhorts them to humility and brotherly love. 18 He foretells that one of them would betray him. 31 The Son of man glorified. 34 The new commandment to love one another. 36 Peter forewarned of his denial.*

NOW[T] before the feast of the
[a]passover, when Jē'ṣus [b]knew
that his hour was come that he
should depart out of this world
unto the [c]Father, having [d]loved
his own which were in the world,
he loved them unto the end.[T]
2 And [1]supper being ended,
the [e]devil having now put into the [f]heart of [g]Jū'das Ĭs-căr'-
ĭ-ot, [h]Sī'mon's *son*, to [i]betray
him;
3 Jē'ṣus [b]knowing that the [c]Fa-
ther had [j]given all things into his
hands, and that [k]he was [l]come
from God, and [l]went to God;[T]
4 He riseth from supper, and
laid aside his garments; [m]and
took a towel, and girded himself.
5 [n,o]After that he poureth water
into a bason, and began to wash
the [p]disciples' [q]feet, and to wipe
*them* with the towel wherewith
he was girded.
6 Then cometh he to Sī'mon
[r]Pē'tēr: and Pē'tēr saith unto
him, Lord, dost thou wash my
feet?
7 Jē'ṣus answered and said unto him, What I do thou [s]knowest
not now; but thou shalt know
hereafter.[S]
8 [r]Pē'tēr [t]saith unto him, Thou
shalt never wash my feet. Jē'ṣus
answered him, If I wash thee
not, thou hast no part with
me.
9 Sī'mon [r]Pē'tēr saith unto him,
Lord, not my feet only, but also
*my* hands and *my* head.
10 [T]Jē'ṣus saith to him, He that
is washed needeth not save[G] to
wash *his* feet, but is clean every
[G]whit: and ye are clean, but not
all.[S]
11 For he [b,u]knew who should
[v]betray him; therefore said he,
Ye are not all clean.[T]
12 [m]So after he had washed
their feet, and had taken his garments, and was set down again,
he said unto them, Know ye what
I have done to you?

v.2–AD 30
See footnote, *Time,* Rev. 10:6.

2
e *Satan,* Matt. 4:10.
f *Heart,* Psa. 44:21.
g *Judas,* Mark 3:19.
h John 6:71.
i *Infidelity, of friends,* 2 Cor. 6:15.
1 R. V. during supper, the devil

3
j *Jesus, king,* Matt. 1:21.
k *Jesus, divinity of,* Matt. 1:21.
l *Jesus, relation of, to the Father,* Matt. 1:21.

4
m *Altruism, Jesus sets an example of,* Acts 20:35.

5
n *Jesus, humility of,* Matt. 1:21.
o *Jesus, condescension of,* Matt. 1:21.
p *Apostles,* Luke 6:13.
q *Feet, washing of,* 2 Sam. 4:4.

6
r *Peter,* Mark 5:37.

7
s *Ignorance,* Acts 3:17.

8
t *Presumption, instances of,* Psa. 19:13.

11
u *Sin, known to God,* Rom. 5:12.
v *Betrayal, of Jesus,* Matt. 26:46.

*Jesus inquires about,* Matt. 16:13; Mark 8:27; Luke 9:18. *Feared, by Nicodemus,* John 3:2; *by Joseph of Arimathea,* John 19:38; *by the parents of the man who was born blind,* John 9:21, 22; *by rulers, who believed in Jesus but feared the Pharisees,* John 12:42, 43; *by Herod,* Matt. 14:5; *by chief priests,* Matt. 21:26; Mark 11:18, 32; Luke 20:6; 12:12; *by those who feared to further persecute the disciples,* Acts 4:21; 5:26.
**Concessions to:** *By Paul, in circumcising Timothy,* Acts 16:3. *By James and the Christian elders, who required Paul to observe certain rites,* Acts 21:18–26. *By disciples, who urged circumcision,* Gal. 6:12. *By Peter and Barnabas with others,* Gal. 2:11–14.
**Corrupt yielding to:** *By Herod, in the case, of John the Baptist,* Mark 6:26; *of Peter,* Acts 12:3. *By Peter, concerning Jesus,* Matt. 26:69–75; Mark 14:66–72; Luke 22:54–62. *By Pilate,* Matt. 27:23–27; Mark 15:15; Luke 23:13–25; John 18:38, 39; 19:4–16. *By Felix and Festus, concerning Paul,* Acts 24:27; 25:9.

13 Ye call me *Master and
[w, x]Lord: and ye say well; for
*so* I am.
14 If I then, *your* Lord and
Master, have washed your feet;
[y, z]ye also [a]ought to wash one
another's feet.
15 For [b]I have given you an
[†]example, that ye should do as
I have done to you.[T]
16 Verily, verily, I say unto you,
[c]The [d]servant is not greater than
his lord; neither [e]he that is sent
greater than he that sent him.
17 If ye know these things,
[2, f]happy are ye if ye do them.
18 ¶ I speak not of you all: I
know whom I have chosen: but
that the [g]scripture may be fulfilled, [h, i]He that eateth bread
with me hath [j]lifted up his heel
against me.[Q]
19 Now [k]I tell you before it
come, that, when it is come to
pass, ye may believe that I am [l]*he*.[Q]
20 Verily, verily, I say unto you,
[m]He that receiveth [n]whomsoever
I send [o]receiveth me; and he
that receiveth me receiveth him
that [p]sent me.[S T]
21 When Jē'şus had thus said,
he was [q]troubled in spirit, and
testified, and said, Verily, verily,
I say unto you, that [i]one of you
shall [r]betray me.
22 Then the [s]disciples looked
one on another, doubting of
whom he spake.
23 Now there was [3]leaning on
Jē'şus' bosom [t]one of his [s]disci-
ples, whom Jē'şus [u]loved.
24 Sī'mon [v]Pē'tēr therefore
beckoned to him, that he should
ask who it should be of whom he
spake.
25 [t]He then [4]lying on Jē'şus'
breast saith unto him, Lord, who
is it?
26 Jē'şus answered, He it is, to
whom I shall give a sop, when I
have dipped *it*. And when he
had dipped the sop,[C] he gave *it*
to [w]Jū'das Ĭs-căr'ĭ-ot, *the son* of
[x]Sī'mon.
27 And after the sop [y]Sā'tan
entered into him. Then said
Jē'şus unto [w]him, That thou
doest, do quickly.
28 Now no man at the table
knew for what intent he spake
this unto him.
29 For some *of them* thought,
because [w]Jū'das had the bag,
that Jē'şus had said unto him,
Buy *those things* that we have
need of against the [z]feast; or,
that he should give something to
the [a]poor.
30 He then having received the
sop[G] went immediately out: and
it was night.
31 ¶[T] Therefore, when he was
gone out, Jē'şus said, Now is the
Son of man glorified,[C] and God is
glorified in him.
32 [5]If God be glorified[C] in him,
God shall also [b]glorify him in
himself, [b]and shall straightway
glorify him.[T]
33 Little children, yet a little
while I am with you. Ye shall
seek me: and as I said unto the
Jews, Whither I go, ye cannot
come; so now I say to you.
34 A new commandment I give
unto you, [c]That ye [d, e, f]love one
another; [†, g]as I have loved you,
that ye also love one another.

v.13–AD 30
See footnote, *Time*, Rev. 10:6.

**13**
*w Church, Christ, head of*, Matt. 16:18.
*x Jesus, king*, Matt. 1:21.

**14**
*y Minister, character and qualifications of*, Rom. 15:16.
*z Commandment, enjoining altruistic service*, Deut. 8:2.

*a Humility, enjoined*, Prov. 22:4.

**15**
*b Jesus, our example*, Matt. 1:21.

**16**
*c* Matt. 10:24, 25; Luke 6:40; John 15:20.
*d Servant*, Jer. 2:14.
*e Minister*, Rom. 15:16.

**17**
*f Obedience, rewarded*, Heb. 5:8.
2 R. V. blessed

**18**
*g Prophecies concerning the Messiah, and their fulfillment*, Gen. 12:3.
*h* Psa. 41:9.
*i Judas, prophecies concerning*, Mark 3:19.
*j Infidelity, of friends*, 2 Cor. 6:15.

**19**
*k Jesus, prophet*, Matt. 1:21.
*l Jesus, Messiah*, Matt. 1:21.

**20**
*m* Matt. 10:40; Luke 10:16.
*n Minister*, Rom. 15:16.
*o Faith in Christ*, John 6:69.
*p Jesus, relation of, to the Father*, Matt. 1:21.

**21**
*q Jesus, sufferings of*, Matt. 1:21.
*r Betrayal, of Jesus*, Matt. 26:46.

**22** *s Apostles*, Luke 6:13. **23** *t John*, Mark 1:19. *u Jesus, love of*, Matt. 1:21. 3 R.V. at the table reclining in **24** *v Peter*, Mark 5:37.

v.24–AD 30
See footnote, *Time*, Rev. 10:6.

**25**
4 R. V. leaning back, as he was on

**26**
*w Judas*, Mark 3:19.
*x* John 6:71.

**27**
*y Satan*, Matt. 4:10.

**29**
*z Passover*, Num. 9:5.

*a Poor*, Prov. 21:13.

**32**
*b Jesus, exaltation of*, Matt. 1:21.
5 R. V. *omits* If God be glorified in him,

**34**
*c Commandment, enjoining love*, Deut. 8:2.
*d Love, of man for man*, 1 John 4:7.
*e Duty, of man to man*, Eccl. 12:13.
*f Christian Graces, love*, Gal. 5:22.
*g Jesus, our example*, Matt. 1:21.

* **MASTER.** *Jesus called*, Matt. 8:19; 10:25; 23:8; 26:18, 25, 49; Mark 14:45; Luke 8:24; John 13:13, 14. *Prohibited as an appellation of the disciples*, Matt. 23:8.

† **EXAMPLE. Bad:** *Debauching*, Prov. 22:24, 25; Jer. 17:1, 2; Ezek. 20:18; Hos. 4:9; 5:5. *To be shunned*, Lev. 18:2, 3; 20:23; Deut. 18:9; 2 Chr. 30:7; Isa. 8:11; Hos. 4:15; Zech. 1:4; Matt. 23:1–3; 1 Cor. 10:6; Eph. 4:17; 3 John 11.

**Good:** *Enjoined*, 1 Tim. 4:12; Tit. 2:7, 8; 1 Pet. 5:3. *Inspiring*, Neh. 5:8–19; 1 Thess. 1:6–8; 1 Pet. 2:11–21. *To be imitated*, Heb. 13:7; Jas. 5:10, 11.

**God, our:** *In holiness*, Lev. 11:44; 19:2. *In perfection*, Matt. 5:48. *In mercy*, Luke 6:36.

**Christ, our:** *In service*, Matt. 20:28; Mark 10:43–45; Luke 22:27; John 13:13–17; Phil. 2:5–8. *In meekness*, 2 Cor. 10:1; 1 Pet. 2:20–25. *In self-renunciation*, Rom. 15:2–7; 2 Cor. 8:9; Eph. 5:1, 2; 1 John 3:16. *In enduring persecution*, 1 Pet. 3:17, 18; 4:1. *In forgiving*, Col. 3:13. *In obedience*, 1 John 2:6. *In steadfastness*, Heb. 12:2, 3. *In perseverance*, Rev. 3:21. See footnote, JESUS, *Our example*, Matt. 1:21.

**Paul, our,** 1 Cor. 4:16; 11:1; Phil. 3:17; 4:9; 1 Tim. 1:16; 2 Tim. 1:13. *In self-control*, 1 Cor. 7:7, 8. *In self-maintenance*, 2 Thess. 3:7–10. *In beneficence*, Acts 20:35. See footnote, INFLUENCE, 1 Cor. 7:14.

v.35–AD 30
See footnote, *Time*, Rev. 10:6.

**35**
*h* *Righteousness, fruits of*, Psa. 15:2.
*i* *Disciples*, Matt. 9:14.
*j* *Righteous, described*, Psa. 64:10.
**36**
*k* *Peter*, Mark 5:37.
*l* *Heaven, future home of the righteous*, Luke 18:22.
*m* *Righteous, promises to*, Psa. 64:10.
**37**
*n* *Love, for Jesus*, 1 John 4:19.
*o* *False Confidence*, Psa. 30:6.
**38**
*p* Matt. 26:34, 74, 75; Mark 14:30, 68, 72; Luke 22:34, 60, 61; John 18:27.
*q* *Jesus, prophet*, Matt. 1:21.

**1**
*a* *Commandment, forbidding anxiety*, Deut. 8:2.
*b* *Afflictions, consolation in*, Psa. 34:19.
*c* *Borrowing Trouble*, Matt. 6:25.
*d* *Anxiety*, 1 Pet. 5:7.
*e* *Commandment, enjoining faith*, Deut. 8:2.
*f* *Faith in Christ, enjoined*, John 6:69.
1 R. V. *omits* ye
**2**
*g* *God, fatherhood of*, Gen. 2:2.
*h* *House, figurative*, Esth. 8:1.
*i* *Heaven, future home of the righteous*, Luke 18:22.
*j* *Promise, to the righteous*, 2 Cor. 1:20.
*k* *Righteous, promises to*, Psa. 64:10.
*l* *Jesus, ascension of*, Matt. 1:21.
2 R. V. for I go
**3**
*m* *Jesus, second coming of*, Matt. 1:21.
**5**
*n* *Thomas*, John 11:16.
**6**
*o* *Way, figurative*, Isa. 35:8.
*p* *Truth*, John 18:37.
*q* *Life, spiritual*, Eccl. 8:15. *r* *God, access to, through Christ*, Gen. 2:2. *s* *Jesus, mediation of*, Matt. 1:21. *t* *Jesus, savior*, Matt. 1:21. **7** *u* *Jesus, divinity of*, Matt. 1:21. *v* *Jesus, relation of, to the Father*, Matt. 1:21.

35 [h]By this shall all *men* know
that ye are my [i]disciples, if ye
have [d,f,j]love one to another.
36 ¶ Sī'mon [k]Pē'tẽr said unto
him, Lord, whither goest thou?
Jē'ṣus answered him, [l]Whither
I go, thou canst not follow me
now; but [m]thou shalt follow me
afterwards.
37 [k]Pē'tẽr said unto him, Lord,
why cannot I follow thee now?
I [n,o]will lay down my life for thy
sake.
38 Jē'ṣus answered him, Wilt
thou lay down thy life for my
sake? [p]Verily, verily, [q]I say unto thee, The cock shall not crow,
till thou hast denied me thrice.

## CHAPTER 14

*Jesus discourses with his disciples, and comforts them. 6 He is the way, the truth, and the life. 15 He promises to send the Holy Spirit, the Comforter; 27 and leaves his peace with them.*

[a,b]LET[T] not your heart be
[c,d]troubled: [1]ye believe
in God, [e,f]believe also in me.[S]
2 In my [g]Father's [h,i]house are
many mansions[G]: if *it were* not *so*,
I would have told you. [2,j,k]I [l]go
to prepare a place for you.[S]
3 And if I[G] [l]go and prepare a
place for you, I[G] will [m]come again,
and receive you unto myself;
that [i]where I[G] am, *there* ye may
be also.[S T]
4 And whither I go ye know,
and the way ye know.
5 ¶ [n]Thŏm'as saith unto him,
Lord, we know not whither thou
goest; and how can we know the
way?
6 Jē'ṣus[T] saith unto him, I[G] am
the [o]way, the [p]truth, and the
[q]life: no man [r]cometh unto the
Father, but [s]by [t]me.[S]
7 If ye had known [u,v]me, ye
should have known my [g]Father
also: and from henceforth ye
know him, and have seen him.
8 ¶ [w]Phĭl'ĭp [x]saith unto him,
Lord, shew us the [g]Father, and
it sufficeth[G] us.
9 Jē'ṣus saith unto him, Have I
been so long time with you, and
yet hast thou not known me,
[w]Phĭl'ĭp? he that hath seen [u]me
hath seen the Father; and how
sayest thou *then*, Shew us the
Father?
10 Believest thou not that [v]I am
in the Father, and [v]the Father in
me? the words that [y]I speak unto you I speak not of myself: but
the Father that dwelleth in me,
he doeth the works.
11 [z]Be[S]lieve me that [v]I *am* in the
Father, and [v]the Father in me:
or else believe me for the very
[a]works' sake.[Q]
12 Verily, verily, I say unto you,
He that [b]believeth on me, the
[a]works that I do shall he do also;
and greater *works* than these
shall he do; because I go unto
my Father.[S]
13 And whatsoever ye shall
[c]ask [d]in my *name, [e,f]that will
I do, that the Father may be
[g]glorified[G] in the Son.
14 If ye shall [c]ask any thing in
my name, [e,f]I will do *it*.[T]
15 ¶ If ye [h,i]love me, [3,j,k]keep
my commandments.
16[S T] And [d,l]I will pray the [l,m]Fa-
ther, and [n]he shall give you another [l,o]Comforter[G], that he may
[p]abide[G] with you for ever;
17 *Even* the [o]Spirit of truth;
whom the world cannot receive,
because [q]it [r]seeth him not, neither knoweth[G] him: but ye know[G]
him; for he [p]dwelleth with you,
and [n]shall be in you.[S T]
18 [f,s]I will not leave you comfortless[G]: [l]I will come to you.

v.7–AD 30
See footnote, *Time*, Rev. 10:6.
**8**
*w* *Philip*, Luke 6:14.
*x* *Doubting, exemplified*, Rom. 14:23.
**10**
*y* *Jesus, prophet*, Matt. 1:21.
**11**
*z* *Commandment, enjoining faith*, Deut. 8:2.
*a* *Miracles, of Jesus*, Luke 23:8.
**12**
*b* *Faith in Christ*, John 6:69.
**13**
*c* *Prayer, answer to, promised*, Acts 6:4.
*d* *Jesus, mediation of*, Matt. 1:21.
*e* *Promise, to the righteous*, 2 Cor. 1:20.
*f* *Righteous, promises to*, Psa. 64:10.
*g* *God, glory of*, Gen. 2:2.
**15**
*h* *Love, for Jesus*, 1 John 4:19.
*i* *Duty, of man to God*, Eccl. 12:13.
*j* *Discipleship of Jesus, tests of*, Matt. 10:32.
*k* *Obedience, a proof of love*, Heb. 5:8.
3 R. V. ye will keep
**16**
*l* *Holy Trinity*, Luke 3:22.
*m* *God, fatherhood of*, Gen. 2:2.
*n* *Promise, of the Holy Spirit*, 2 Cor. 1:20.
*o* *Holy Spirit*, Acts 1:2.
*p* *Fellowship, of the Holy Spirit*, 1 Cor. 1:9.
**17**
*q* *Unbelievers*, 1 Cor. 6:6.
*r* *Spiritual Blindness*, 2 Cor. 4:4.
**18**
*s* *Adversity, consolation in*, Psa. 10:6.

***NAME OF JESUS**, 1 Cor. 6:11; Phil. 2:9; Col. 3:17; Rev. 2:13. *Prayer in*, John 14:13; 16:23, 24, 26; Eph. 5:20; Col. 3:17. *Miracles performed in*, Acts 3:6; 4:10; 19:13. *Baptism in*, Matt. 28:19; Acts 2:38. *Faith in*, Matt. 12:21; John 1:12; 2:23. *Remission of sins in*, Luke 24:47 Acts 10:43; 1 Cor. 6:11; 1 John 2:12. *Life in*, John 20:31. *Salvation in*, Acts 4:12. *Persecutions on account of*, Acts 5:41.

19 Yet a little while, and the
world seeth me no more; but ye
see me: because I [t]live, ye shall
[u,v]live also.[S]
20[T] At that day ye shall know
that [w]I *am* in my Father, and
[x,y]ye in me, and [x,y]I in you.
21 He that hath my commandments, and [z]keepeth[G] them, he it
is that [a]loveth me: and he that
loveth me shall be [b]loved of my
[c]Father, and [d]I will [e]love him,
and will manifest[G] myself to him.[T] [S]
22 [f]Jū'das saith unto him, not
Ĭs-căr'ĭ-ot, Lord, how is it that
thou wilt manifest thyself unto
us, and not unto the world?
23[T] Jē'ṣus answered and said
unto him, [g]If a man [a]love me,
[h]he will [i]keep my [j,k]words: and
my Father will [b]love him, and we
will come unto him, and make[G]
our [l,m]abode with him.[S]
24 He that loveth me not [n]keep-
eth not my [j,k]sayings: and the
word which ye hear is not mine,
but the Father's which [o]sent me.[T]
25 These [j]things have [k]I spoken unto you, being *yet* present
with you.
26 But the Comforter,[G] *which
is* the [p]Holy Ghost,[G] [q]whom the
Father will send in my name, he
shall teach you all things, and
bring all things to your remembrance, whatsoever I have said
unto you.[T]
27 [r,s,t]Peace I leave with you,
my peace I give unto you: not as
the world giveth, give I unto you.
[u]Let not your heart be [v,w]trou-
bled, neither let it be afraid.
28[T] Ye have heard how I said
unto you, I go away, and [x]come
*again* unto you. If ye loved me,
ye would rejoice, because I said,
I go unto the Father: for [o]my
Father is greater than I.
29 And now [y]I have told you
before it come to pass, that, when
it is come to pass, ye might [z]be-
lieve.
30 Hereafter I will not talk
much with you: for the [a]prince
of this world cometh, and [b]hath
nothing in me.
31 But that the world may
know that I love the [c]Father;
and as the Father gave me
commandment, even [d]so I do.
Arise, let us go hence.[T]

## CHAPTER 15

*Jesus' discourse continued: He is the true vine. 9 The mutual love of Christ and his members. 18 He comforts them in view of persecution. 26 The office of the Holy Spirit, and of the apostles.*

I[G] AM the true[T] [a,b]vine, and my
[c]Father is the [d]husbandman.[G]
2 Every [e]branch [f]in me that
[g,h,i]beareth not fruit he [j,k]taketh
away: and every [e,l]*branch* that
beareth [m,n]fruit, he [o,p,q]purgeth[G]
it, that it may bring forth more
fruit.[T]
3 Now ye are clean through the
[r]word which I have [s]spoken unto
you.
4 [f,t,u]Abide[G] in me, and I in
you. As the [e]branch cannot
bear [m,n]fruit of itself, [v]except it
abide[G] in the [a,b]vine; no more
can ye, except [f]ye abide[G] in me.
5[T] I[G] am the [a,b]vine, ye *are*
the [e]branches: He that [f]abideth
in me, and I[G] in him, the same
bringeth forth much [m,n]fruit: for
without me ye can do nothing.[S]
6 If a man [f]abide not in me, he
is [j,k]cast forth as a branch, and
is withered; and men gather
them, and [j,k]cast *them* into the
fire, and they are burned.
7 If ye [f]abide[G] in me, and my
[r]words abide[G] in you, [w]ye shall
[x]ask what ye will, and it shall
be done unto you.
8 Herein is my [y]Father [z]glori-
fied,[G] that ye bear much [a,b]fruit;
so shall ye be my [c]disciples.

v.19–AD 30
See footnote, *Time*, Rev. 10:6.

**19**
t *Jesus, eternity of*, Matt. 1:21.
u *Immortality*, 1 Cor. 15:54.
v *Life, everlasting*, Eccl. 8:15.

**20**
w *Jesus, relation of, to the Father*, Matt. 1:21.
x *Fellowship, with Christ*, 1 Cor. 1:9.
y *Righteous, union of, with Christ*, Psa. 64:10.

**21**
z *Obedience, a proof of love*, Heb. 5:8.
a *Love, for Jesus*, 1 John 4:19.
b *God, love of*, Gen. 2:2.
c *God, fatherhood of*, Gen. 2:2.
d *Promise, to the righteous*, 2 Cor. 1:20.
e *Jesus, love of*, Matt. 1:21.

**22**
f Luke 6:16; Acts 1:13.

**23**
g *Contingencies in Divine Government*, 1 Kin. 3:14.
h *Righteous, described*, Psa. 64:10.
i *Obedience, a proof of love*, Heb. 5:8.
j *Doctrines of Jesus*, John 7:16.
k *Jesus, teacher*, Matt. 1:21.
l *Fellowship, with Christ*, 1 Cor. 1:9.
m *Fellowship, with God*, 1 Cor. 1:9.

**24**
n *Wicked, described*, Psa. 73:3.
o *Jesus, relation of, to the Father*, Matt. 1:21.

**26**
p *Holy Spirit*, Acts 1:2.
q *Promise, to the righteous, of the Holy Spirit*, 2 Cor. 1:20.

**27**
r *Spiritual Peace*, Gal. 1:3.
s *Promise, to the righteous*, 2 Cor. 1:20.
t *Christian Graces, peace*, Gal. 5:22.

v.29–AD 30
See footnote, *Time*, Rev. 10:6.

z *Faith in Christ*, John 6:69.

**30**
a *Satan*, Matt. 4:10.
b *Jesus, holiness of*, Matt. 1:21.

**31**
c *God, fatherhood of*, Gen. 2:2.
d *Jesus, obedience of*, Matt. 1:21.

**1**
a *Vine, symbolical*, Judg. 13:14.
b *Jesus, names of*, Matt. 1:21.
c *God, fatherhood of*, Gen. 2:2.
d *Husbandman*, Matt. 21:33.

**2**
e *Branch, figurative*, Dan. 4:14.
f *Righteous, union of, with Christ*, Psa. 64:10.
g *Unfruitfulness*, Matt. 7:19.
h *Unfaithfulness*, Luke 16:11.
i *Backsliding*, Hos. 11:7.
j *Sin, separates from God*, Rom. 5:12.
k *Wicked, punishment of*, Psa. 73:3.
l *Righteous, described*, Psa. 64:10.
m *Works, good*, 2 Tim. 1:9.
n *Righteousness, fruits of*, Psa. 15:2.
o *Pruning*, Isa. 18:5.
p *Divine Chastisement*, Job 33:19.
q *Afflictions, design of*, Psa. 34:19.

**3**
r *Doctrines of Jesus*, John 7:16.
s *Jesus, teacher*, Matt. 1:21.

**4**
t *Commandment, enjoining abiding in Christ*, Deut. 8:2.
u *Decision, injunctions concerning*, Isa. 50:7.
v *Perseverance, a condition of fruitfulness*, Eph. 6:18.

**7**
w *Promise, to the righteous, of answer to prayer*, 2 Cor. 1:20.

u *Commandment, forbidding anxiety*, Deut. 8:2. v *Borrowing Trouble*, Matt. 6:25. w *Anxiety*, 1 Pet. 5:7. **28** x *Jesus, second coming of*, Matt. 1:21. **29** y *Jesus, prophet*, Matt. 1:21.

x *Prayer, answer to, promised*, Acts 6:4. **8** y *God, fatherhood of*, Gen. 2:2. z *Glorifying God*, Luke 5:25.—a *Works, good*, 2 Tim. 1:9. b *Righteousness, fruits of*, Psa. 15:2. c *Disciples*, Matt. 9:14.

v.9–AD 30
See footnote, *Time*, Rev. 10:6.

**9**

*d* *God, fatherhood of*, Gen. 2:2.
*e* *God, love of*, Gen. 2:2.
*f* *Jesus, relation of, to the Father*, Matt. 1:21.
*g* *Jesus, love of*, Matt. 1:21.
*h* *Perseverance*, Eph. 6:18.
*i* *Love, for Jesus*, 1 John 4:19.

**10**

*j* *Obedience, rewarded*, Heb. 5:8.
*k* *Righteous, union of, with Christ*, Psa. 64:10.
*l* *Jesus, obedience of*, Matt. 1:21.

**11**

*m* *Instruction, in religion*, Prov. 23:23.
*n* *Jesus, teacher*, Matt. 1:21.
*o* *Righteous, promises to*, Psa. 64:10.
*p* *Joy*, Psa. 5:11.

**12**

*q* *Doctrines of Jesus*, John 7:16.
*r* *Commandment, enjoining love*, Duet. 8:2.
*s* *Love, of man for man*, 1 John 4:7.
*t* *Christian Graces, love*, Gal. 5:22.

**13**

*u* *Jesus, death of*, Matt. 1:21.
*v* *Vicarious Sufferings*, Rom. 9:3.
*w* *Substitution*, Lev. 1:4.
*x* *Friends*, Ex. 33:11.

**14**

*y* *Obedience*, Heb. 5:8.
*z* *Duty, of man to God*, Eccl. 12:13.

**16**

*a* *Call, to special religious duty*, Phil. 3:14.

9 As the [d]Father hath [e]loved [f]me, so have I [g]loved you: [h]continue ye in my [g,i]love.

10 If ye [j]keep my commandments, ye shall [k]abide[G] in my love; even as I have [l]kept my [d]Father's commandments, and [f]abide[G] in his [e]love.[T]

11 These things have I [m,n]spoken unto you, [o]that my [p]joy might remain in you, and *that* your joy might be full.

12 This is my [q]commandment, [r]That ye [b,s,t]love one another, as I have [g]loved you.

13 Greater [g]love hath no man than this, that a man [u,v]lay down his life [w]for his [x]friends.

14 Ye are my [x]friends, if ye [y,z]do whatsoever I command you.

15 Henceforth I call you not servants; for the servant knoweth not what his lord doeth: but I have called you [x]friends; for all things that I have heard of my Father I have [m,n]made known unto you.[T]

16 Ye have not chosen me, but I have [a]chosen you, and ordained[G] you, that ye should go and bring forth fruit, and *that* your fruit should remain: that whatsoever ye shall [b]ask of the [c]Father [d]in my [e]name, he may give it you.[S] [T]

17 These things [f]I command you, that ye [g]love one another.

18 ¶ If the world [h]hate you, ye know that [i]it hated me before *it hated* you.

*b* *Prayer, answer to, promised*, Acts 6:4. *c* *God, fatherhood of*, Gen. 2:2. *d* *Jesus, mediation of*, Matt. 1:21. *e* *Name of Jesus*, John 14:13. **17** *f* *Commandment, enjoining love*, Deut. 8:2. *g* *Love, of man for man, enjoined*, 1 John 4:7. **18** *h* *Hatred, toward the righteous*, Prov. 15:17. *i* *Adversity, consolation in*, Psa. 10:6.

19 If ye were [j]of the world, the world would love his own: but because ye are [k]not of the world, but I have [a]chosen you out of the world, therefore the world [h]hateth you.[S]

20 Remember the word that I said unto you, [l]The servant is not greater than his lord. If they have *persecuted me, they will also persecute you; if they have kept my saying, they will keep your's also.

21 But [m]all these *things will they do unto you for my [e]name's sake, because they [n]know not him that sent me.[T]

22 [o,p]If I had not come and spoken unto them, they had not had [q]sin: but [o,p]now they have no cloke[G] for their sin.

23 [r]He that [h]hateth me hateth my Father also.

24[T] [o,p]If I had not done among them the [s]works which none other man did, they had not had [q]sin: but now have they both seen and [h]hated both me and my Father.

25 But *this cometh to pass*, that the [t]word might be fulfilled that is written in their law, [u]They hated [v]me without a cause.[T Q]

26 But when the [w,x]Comforter[G] is come, [y]whom [x]I will send unto you from the [x,z]Father, *even* the Spirit of truth, which proceedeth from the Father, he shall testify of me:[T]

27 And [a]ye also shall bear [b,c]witness, because ye have been with me from the beginning.

v.19–AD 30
See footnote, *Time*, Rev. 10:6.

**19**

*j* *Worldliness*, 1 John 2:15.
*k* *Righteous, described*, Psa. 64:10.

**20**

*l* Matt. 10:24, 25; Luke 6:40; John 13:16.

**21**

*m* *Jesus, prophet*, Matt. 1:21.
*n* *Spiritual Blindness*, 2 Cor. 4:4.

**22**

*o* *Responsibility, according to privilege*, Ezek. 18:20.
*p* *Judgment, according to opportunity and works*, 1 Pet. 1:17.
*q* *Sin*, Rom. 5:12.

**23**

*r* *Godless, described*, Job 8:13.

**24**

*s* *Miracles, design of*, Luke 23:8.

**25**

*t* *Prophecies concerning the Messiah, and their fulfillment*, Gen. 12:3.
*u* Psa. 35:19; 69:4.
*v* *Jesus, holiness of*, Matt. 1:21.

**26**

*w* *Holy Spirit*, Acts 1:2.
*x* *Holy Trinity*, Luke 3:22.
*y* *Jesus, promises of*, Matt. 1:21.
*z* *God, fatherhood of*, Gen. 2:2.

**27**

*a* *Minister, duties of*, Rom. 15:16.
*b* *Religious Testimony*, 2 Thess. 1:10.
*c* *Witnessing for Christ*, Luke 24:48.

* **PERSECUTION.** **Of Jesus,** Acts 4:27; Heb. 12:2, 3.
*Foretold*, Isa. 50:6; 52:14; 53:2–10; Matt. 2:13; John 15:24, 25.
*Typified in the persecutions of Israel's kings*, Psa. 2:1–5; 22:1, 2, 6–8, 11–21; 69:1–21, with Rom. 15:3.
*Meekly endured*, Isa. 50:6.
*By the Jews*, Matt. 12:14; 26:3, 4; Mark 15:14; Luke 6:11; 22:2–5, 52, 53; 23:23; John 5:16; 7:1, 7, 19; 11:57; 15:18, 20, 21; 19:6, 15; 18:22, 23; Acts 2:23; *in making false imputation*, Matt. 12:24; Mark 3:22; Luke 11:15; John 10:20; *in bringing false accusation*, Matt. 11:19; Luke 7:34; John 18:29, 30; *in acts of violence*, Luke 4:28, 29; 22:63–65 (with Matt. 26:67; Mark 14:65); *in seeking false testimony*, Matt. 26:59; *in seeking his death*, Matt. 26:14–16 (with Mark 14:1, 48); Mark 3:6, 21; 11:18; Luke 19:47; John 7:20, 30, 32; 8:37, 40, 48, 52, 59; 10:31; *in crucifying him*, Acts 3:13–15; 7:52; 13:27–29; 1 Cor. 2:8.
*By Herod*, Luke 13:31; 23:11.
*By the Roman soldiers*, Matt. 27:25–30; Mark 15:15–20; John 19:2, 3.
**Of the righteous,** Gen. 49:23; Psa. 11:2; 37:32; 38:20; Isa. 26:20; 59:15; Jer. 15:10; Lam. 1:3; Rom. 8:35; 2 Cor. 12:10; Gal. 4:29; 6:17.
*By mocking*, Psa. 42:3, 10; 69:9–12; 119:51; Jer. 20:7, 8.
*By violence*, Psa. 94:5; Jer. 2:30; 50:7; Acts 5:29, 40–42; 7:52; Gal. 6:12, 17; 1 Thess. 2:2, 14, 15; Jas. 2:6.
*By ecclesiastical censure*, John 9:22, 34; 12:42; 2 Tim. 4:16, 17.
*Divine permission of, mysterious*, Hab. 1:13.
*Extension of church by*, Acts 8:1, 4; 11:19–21; Phil. **1:12**.

v.1–AD 30
See footnote, *Time*, Rev. 10:6.

**1**

1 R. V. made to stumble.

**2**

*a* *Jesus, prophet*, Matt. 1:21.
*b* *Temptation, sources of*, Luke 11:4.
*c* *Church, rules of discipline in*, Matt. 16:18.
*d* *Disfellowship*, Num. 15:31.
*e* *Persecution, of Christians foretold*, John 15:20.
*f* *Disciples*, Matt. 9:14.
*g* *Synagogue*, Matt. 12:9.
*h* *Zeal, without knowledge*, 2 Cor. 7:11.
*i* *Ignorance, sins of*, Acts 3:17.
*j* *Spiritual Blindness*, 2 Cor. 4:4.
*k* *Delusion*, 2 Thess. 2:11.

**3**

*l* *God, fatherhood of*, Gen. 2:2.

**5**

*m* *Jesus, ascension of*, Matt. 1:21.
*n* *Jesus, relation of, to the Father*, Matt. 1:21.

## CHAPTER 16

*Jesus' discourse concluded: He renews the promise of the Comforter; 17 removes the perplexity of his disciples; 23 and assures them that prayer in his name is acceptable. 33 Peace in Jesus, but in the world tribulation.*

THESE things have I spoken unto you, that ye should not be [1]offended.[G]

2 [a,b,c]They shall [d,e]put [f]you out of the [g]synagogues: yea, the time cometh, that [h]whosoever [i]killeth you will [j,k]think that he doeth God service.

3 And these [a,e]things will they do unto you, because they have [j]not known the [l]Father, nor me.[T]

4 But these things have [a]I told you, that when the time shall come, ye may remember that I told you of them. And these things I said not unto you at the beginning, because I was with you.

5 But now [m]I go my way to him that [n]sent me; and none of you asketh me, Whither[G] goest thou[T]?

6 But because I have said these things unto [f]you, sorrow hath filled your heart.

7[T] Nevertheless I tell you the truth; It is expedient for you that I go away: for if I go not away, the [o]Comforter[G] will not come unto you; but if I depart, [p]I will send him unto you.

8[Q] And when [o]he is come, he will *,[2]reprove[G] the world of [q]sin, and of [r]righteousness,[G] and of judgment:[G,T]

9 Of sin, because they [s]believe not on me;

10 Of [r]righteousness, because [m]I go to my [l]Father, and ye see me no more;

11 Of judgment, because the [t]prince of this world is judged.[T S Q]

12 I have yet many things to [u]say unto you, but ye cannot bear them now.

13 Howbeit[G] when he, the [o]Spirit of [v]truth, is come, [p]he will [w]guide you into all [3,v]truth: for he shall not speak of himself; but whatsoever he shall hear, *that* shall he speak: and [p]he will shew you things to come.[S]

14 He shall glorify me: for he shall receive of mine, and [p]shall shew *it* unto you.

15 All things that the [l]Father hath are [n]mine: therefore said I, that he shall take of mine, and shall shew *it* unto you.

16 A little while, and ye shall not see me: and again, a little

v.7–AD 30
See footnote, *Time*, Rev. 10:6.

**7**

*o* *Holy Spirit*, Acts 1:2.
*p* *Promise, of the Holy Spirit*, 2 Cor. 1:20.

**8**

*q* *Sin*, Rom. 5:12.
*r* *Righteousness*, Psa. 15:2.
2 R. V. convict

**9**

*s* *Unbelief*, Heb. 3:12.

**11**

*t* *Satan*, Matt. 4:10.

**12**

*u* *Jesus, teacher*, Matt. 1:21.

**13**

*v* *Truth*, John 18:37.
*w* *Guidance*, Psa. 48:14.
3 R. V. the truth:

14, 18. *Impotent to separate from the love of Christ*, Rom. 8:17, 35–39.

*Exhortations to courage under*, Isa 51:12, 16; Heb. 12:3, 4; 13:13; 1 Pet. 3:14, 16, 17; 4:12–14, 16, 19.

*Courageously endured*, Jer. 26:11–14; 1 Cor. 4:9–13; 2 Cor. 4:8–12; 6:4, 5, 8–10; 11:23–27; 12:10; 2 Thess. 1:4; 2 Tim. 1:8, 12; 2:9, 10, 12; Heb. 11:25–27, 33–38; Jas. 5:6, 10.

*Rejoicing under*, Rom. 5:3; Col. 1:24; 1 Thess. 1:6; Heb. 10:32–34. *Perseverance under*, Psa. 44:15–18, 22.

*Prayer for deliverance from*, Psa. 70:1–5; 83:1; 142:6. *Deliverance from*, Psa. 124; 129:1, 2. *John's vision concerning*, Rev. 2:3, 10, 13; 6:9–11; 7:13–17; 12:10, 11; 17:6; 20:4.

*Of Christians, foretold*, Matt. 20:22; 23:34, 35; 24:8–10; Mark 13:9, 11–13; Luke 21:12–19; John 15:18–21; 16:1, 2; 2 Tim. 3:12.

*Promises to those who endure*, Matt. 5:10–12; 10:16–18, 21–23, 28–31; Luke 6:22, 23.

INSTANCES OF: *Abel*, Gen. 4:8; Matt. 23:35; 1 John 3:12. *Lot*, Gen. 19:9. *Moses*, Ex. 17:4. *The psalmist*, Psa. 31:13; 56:5; 59:1, 2. *Prophets martyred by Jezebel*, 1 Kin. 18:4. *Gideon*, Judg. 6:28–32. *Elijah*, 1 Kin. 18:10; 19; 2 Kin. 1:9; 2:23 *Micaiah*, 1 Kin. 22:24, 26; 2 Chr. 18:23, 26. *Elisha*, 2 Kin. 6:31. *Hanani*, 2 Chr. 16:10. *Zachariah*, 2 Chr. 24:21. *The prophets*, 2 Chr. 36:16; Matt. 21:35, 36; 1 Thess. 2:15. *Job*, Job 30:1–10. *Jeremiah*, Jer. 11:19; 15:10, 15; 17:15–18; 18:18–23; 26; 32:2; 33:1; 36:26; 37; 38:1–6. *Urijah*, Jer. 26:23.

*The three Hebrews of the captivity, in the fiery furnace*, Dan. 3:8–23. *Daniel*, Dan. 6. *The Jews*, Ezra 4; Neh. 4. *John the Baptist*, Matt. 14:3–12. *James*, Acts 12:2. *The disciples*, John 9:22, 34; 20:19. *Lazarus*, John 12:10. *The apostles*, Acts 4:3–18; 5:18–42; 12:1–19; Rev. 1:9. *Stephen*, Acts 6:9–15; 7. *The church*, Acts 8:1; 9:1–14; Gal. 1:13. *Paul*, Acts 9:16, 23–25, 29; 16:19–25; 21:2–33; 22:22–24; 23:10, 12–15; 1 Cor. 4:9, 11–13; 2 Cor. 1:8–10; 4:8–12; 6:4, 5, 8–10; 11:23–27, 32, 33; Col. 1:24; 1 Thess. 2:2, 14, 15; 2 Tim. 1:8, 12; 2:9, 10; 3:11, 12; 4:16, 17. *Timothy*, Heb. 13:23. *John*, Rev. 1:9. *Antipas*, Rev. 2:13.

* **CONVICTION OF SIN.** *Produced, by dreams*, Job 33:14–17; *by visions*, Acts 9:3–9; *by adversity*, Job 33:18–30; Lam. 1:20: Luke 15:17–21; *by the gospel*, Acts 2:37; 1 Cor. 14:24, 25; *by conscience*, John 8:9; Rom. 2:15; *by the Holy Spirit*, John 16:7–11.

**Instances of:** *Adam and Eve, after their disobedience*, Gen. 3:8–10. *Joseph's brethren, on account of their cruelty to Joseph*, Gen. 42:21, 22; 44:16; 45:3; 50:15–21.

Pharaoh: *After, the plague of hail*, Ex. 9:27, 28; *the plague of locusts*, Ex. 10:16, 17; *the death of the firstborn*, Ex. 12:31.

The Israelites: *After, being rebuked and punished for worshiping the golden calf*, Ex. 33:4; *the death of the ten spies, and their being sentenced to wander forty years*, Num. 14:39, 40; *their murmuring against God and being bitten by fiery serpents*, Num. 21:7.

*Saul, after sparing Agag and the best of the spoils*, 1 Sam. 15:24. *David, after the pestilence sent on account of his numbering the people*, 1 Chr. 21:8, 30; *after his sin with Bathsheba*, 2 Sam. 12–13; Psa. 51:1–17. *Widow of Zarephath, when her son died*, 1 Kin. 17:18. *Isaiah, after his vision of God's throne*, Isa. 6:5. *Belshazzar, when he saw the writing on the wall*, Dan. 5:6. *Ninevites, at the preaching of Jonah*, Jonah 3; Matt. 12:41; Luke 11:32. *Jonah, in the whale's belly*, Jonah 2. *Herod, when he heard of the fame of Jesus*, Matt. 14:2; Mark 6:14; Luke 9:7. *Jews, when Jesus commanded the guiltless man to cast the first stone at the woman taken in adultery*, John 8:9. *Simon Peter, after the large draught of fishes*, Luke 5:8. *Judas, after his betrayal of Jesus*, Matt. 27:3–5. *Saul of Tarsus, when he saw Jesus on the way to Damascus*, Acts 9:4–18. *Felix, under the preaching of Paul*, Acts 24:25. *Philippian jailer, after the earthquake*, Acts 16:29, 30.

while, and ye shall see me, [3]be-
cause I [m]go to the [l]Father.
17 Then said *some* of his [l]dis-
ciples among themselves, What
is this that he saith unto us, A
little while, and ye shall not see
me: and again, a little while, and
ye shall see me: and, Because I
go to the [l]Father?
18 They said therefore, What
is this that he saith, A little
while? we cannot tell what he
saith.
19 Now Jē'ṣus [x]knew that they
were desirous to ask him, and
said unto them, Do ye enquire
among yourselves of that I said,
A little while, and ye shall not
see me: and again, a little while,
and ye shall see me?
20 Verily, verily, I say unto you,
That ye shall weep and lament,
but the world shall rejoice: and
ye shall be sorrowful, but [y]your
sorrow shall be turned into joy.
21 A woman when she is in
travail[G] hath sorrow, because her
hour is come: but as soon as she
is delivered of the child, she
remembereth no more the anguish, for joy that a man is born
into the world.[Q]
22 And ye now therefore have
sorrow: but I will see you again,
and [y]your heart shall rejoice, and
your[Q] joy no man taketh from
you.
23 And in that day ye shall ask
me nothing. Verily, verily, I say
unto you, [4]Whatsoever ye shall
[z]ask the [a]Father [b]in my [c]name,
[d,e]he will [f]give *it* you.
24 Hitherto[G] have ye asked nothing [b]in my [c]name: [g]ask, and [d,e]ye
shall receive, that your [h,i]joy may
be full.
25 These things have I spoken
unto you in [5]proverbs: but the
time cometh, when I shall no
more speak unto you in [5]prov-
erbs, but I shall shew you plainly
of the [a]Father.

26 At that day ye shall ask in
my [c]name: and I say not unto
you, that I will pray the Father
for you:
27 For the [a]Father himself [j]lov-
eth you, because ye have [k]loved
me, and have [l]believed that [m,n]I
came out from God.[S]
28 [m,n]I came forth from the
Father, and am [o]come into the
world: again, I leave the world,
and [p]go to the Father.
29 ¶ His [q]disciples said unto
him, Lo,[G] now speakest thou
plainly, and speakest no [6]prov-
erb.[G]
30 [T]Now are we sure that thou
[r]knowest all things, and needest
not that any man should ask thee:
by this we [l]believe that [m,n]thou
camest forth from God.[T]
31 Jē'ṣus answered them, Do
ye now believe?
32 [s]Behold, the hour cometh,
yea, is now come, that ye shall be
scattered, every man to his own,
and shall leave me alone: and
yet I am not alone, because the
[a]Father is [m]with me.[T Q]
33 These things I have spoken
unto you, [t]that in me ye might
have [u]peace. In the world[G] ye
shall have [v]tribulation: but be of
good cheer; [t]I have overcome
the world.[S]

## CHAPTER 17

*Jesus prays to his Father to glorify him, 6 to preserve his apostles, 20 to glorify them, and all other believers with him in heaven.*

THESE[T] words spake Jē'ṣus,
and lifted up his eyes to
heaven, and [a]said, [b]Father, the
hour is come; glorify[G] thy [c]Son,
that thy Son also may [d]glorify[G]
thee:[S]
2 As thou hast given him
[1,e]power over all flesh, that [f]he
should [g]give [h,i]eternal [j]life to
as many as thou hast [k]given
him.[S T]
3 And this is [j]life eternal, that
they might [l]know[G] thee the only

v.16–AD 30
See footnote, *Time*, Rev. 10:6.

**16**
3 R. V. *omits* because I go to the Father.

**19**
*x Jesus, omniscience of*, Matt. 1:21.

**20**
*y Afflictions, consolation in*, Psa. 34:19.

**23**
*z Prayer, answer to, promised*, Acts 6:4.

*a God, fatherhood of*, Gen. 2:2.
*b Jesus, mediation of*, Matt. 1:21.
*c Name of Jesus*, John 14:13.
*d Promise, to the righteous, of answer to prayer*, 2 Cor. 1:20.
*e Righteous, promises to*, Psa. 64:10.
*f God, providence of*, Gen. 2:2.
4 R. V. If ye shall ask anything of the Father, he will give it you in my name.

**24**
*g Prayer, answer to promised*, Acts 6:4.
*h Joy*, Psa. 5:11.
*i Christian Graces, joyfulness*, Gal. 5:22.

**25**
5 Am. R. V. dark sayings:

v.26–AD 30
See footnote, *Time* Rev. 10:6.

**27**
*j God, love of*, Gen. 2:2.
*k Love, for Jesus*, 1 John 4:19.
*l Faith in Christ*, John 6:69.
*m Jesus, relation of, to the Father*, Matt. 1:21.
*n Jesus, pre-existence of*, Matt. 1:21.

**28**
*o Jesus, incarnation of*, Matt. 1:21.
*p Jesus, ascension of*, Matt. 1:21.

**29**
*q Disciples*, Matt. 9:14.
6 Am. R. V. dark saying.

**30**
*r Jesus, omniscience of*, Matt. 1:21.

**32**
*s Jesus, prophet*, Matt. 1:21.

**33**
*t Jesus, mission of*, Matt. 1:21.
*u Spiritual Peace*, Gal. 1:3.
*v Adversity, consolation in*, Psa. 10:6.

**1**
*a Prayers of Jesus*, vs. 1–26; Luke 5:16.
*b God, fatherhood of*, Gen. 2:2.
*c Jesus, divine sonship of*, Matt. 1:21.
*d God, glory of*, Gen. 2:2.

**2**
*e Jesus, power of*, Matt. 1:21.
*f Jesus, savior*, Matt. 1:21.
*g Jesus, mission of*, Matt. 1:21.
*h Righteous, promises to*, Psa. 64:10.
*i Immortality*, 1 Cor. 15:54.
*j Life, everlasting*, Eccl. 8:15.
*k Election of Grace*, Rom. 11:5.
1 R. V. authority

**3**
*l Wisdom, spiritual*, Prov. 2:2.

v.3–AD 30
See footnote, *Time*, Rev. 10:6.

m *God*, Gen. 2:2.
n *Jesus, Messiah*, Matt. 1:21.
o *Jesus, relation of, to the Father*, Matt. 1:21.

**4**
p *Glorifying God*, Luke 5:25.
q *Obedience, instances of*, Heb. 5:8.
r *Jesus, obedience of*, Matt. 1:21.
s *Salvation, plan of*, Acts 16:17.

**5**
t *Jesus, eternity of*, Matt. 1:21.
u *Jesus, pre-existence of*, Matt. 1:21.

**6**
v *Disciples*, Matt. 9:14.

**8**
w *Gospel*, Mark 13:10.
x *Doctrines of Jesus*, John 7:16.
y *Faith*, Mark 11:22.
z *Jesus, divinity of*, Matt. 1:21.

a *Faith in Christ*, John 6:69.

**9**
b *Prayer, intercessory*, Acts 6:4.
c *Prayers of Jesus*, Luke 5:16.
d *Jesus, mediation of*, Matt. 1:21.
e *Grace of God*, Rom. 4:16.
f *Election of Grace*, Rom. 11:5.

**10**
g *Jesus, relation of, to the Father*, Matt. 1:21.

**11**
h *Disciples*, Matt. 9:14.
i *God, holiness of*, Gen. 2:2.
j *God, savior*, Gen. 2:2.
k *Spiritual Blessings, from God*, Eph. 1:3.
l *Church, unity of*, Matt. 16:18.
m *Fellowship, of the righteous*, 1 Cor. 1:9.
n *Unity, of the righteous*, Psa. 133:1.
o *Jesus, divinity of*, Matt. 1:21.

**12**
p *Jesus, love of*, Matt. 1:21.
q *Reprobates*, 1 Cor. 9:27.

true [m]God, and Jē'şus [n]Christ, [o]whom thou hast sent.[S T]

4 I have [p]glorified thee on the earth: I have [q,r]finished the [g,s]work which thou gavest me to do.[T]

5 [a]And now, O Father, glorify thou me with thine own self with the glory which [t,u]I had with thee before the world[G] was.[S T]

6 I have manifested thy name unto the [v]men which thou [k]gavest me out of the world: thine they were, and thou gavest them me; and they have [q]kept thy word.[S T]

7 Now they have [l]known that all things whatsoever thou hast given me are of thee.

8 For [q]I have given unto [v]them the [w,x]words which thou gavest me; and they have [y]received *them*, and have known[G] surely that [o,z]I came out from thee, and they have [a]believed that thou didst send me.[T]

9 I [b,c]pray [d]for them: I pray not for the world[G], but for them which [e]thou hast [f]given me; for they are thine.[S T]

10 And [g]all mine are thine, and thine are mine; and I am glorified[G] in them.[S T]

11 [S]And now I am no more in the world[G], but [h]these are in the world, and I [b,c]come to thee. [i]Holy Father, [j,k]keep through thine own name [h]those whom thou hast [f]given me, that they may be [l,m,n]one, [o]as we *are*.[T]

12 While I was with them [2]in the world,[G] [p]I kept them in thy name: those that thou gavest me I have kept, and none of them is [q]lost, but the [r]son of perdition; that the [s]scripture might be fulfilled.[Q]

13 And now come I to thee; and these things I speak in the world, that they might have my [t]joy fulfilled in themselves.

14 I have given [h]them thy [u,v,w]word; and the world[G] hath [x]hated them, because they are [y]not of the world,[G] even [z]as I am not of the world.[G]

15 [a]I [b,c]pray not that thou shouldest take them out of the world,[G] but that thou shouldest keep them from the [3]evil.[S]

16 [d,e]They are [f]not of the world,[G] even as I am not of the world.[G]

17 [b,c,g]Sanctify[G T] [d]them through thy [h]truth: thy [i]word is truth.[S]

18 As thou hast [j]sent me into the world,[G] even so have I also sent [d]them into the world.[G]

19 And for their sakes I [k,l]sanctify myself, that they also might be [g]sanctified through the [h]truth.[S]

20 Neither [b,c]pray [a]I for [d]these alone, but for [d]them also which shall [m]believe on me [n]through their [o]word;[S T]

21 That they all may be [p]one; as thou, Father, *art* [j]in me, and [j]I in thee, that [q]they also may be [r,s]one in us: that the world[G] may [m]believe that thou hast [j]sent me.[T]

22 And the glory[G] which thou gavest me I have given them; that they may be [p]one, even as we are one:

23 [r]I in [q]them, and thou [j]in me, that they may be [4]made [t]perfect[G] in one; and that the world[G] may know that thou hast [j]sent me, and hast [u]loved them, as thou hast loved me.[S T]

24 [S][b,c,v]Father, I[G] will that they also, whom thou hast [w]given me, be with me [x]where I[G] am; that they may behold my glory, which thou hast given me: for thou [u]lovedst me [y,z]before the foundation of the world.[G T Q]

25 O [a]righteous Father, the world[G] hath [b]not known thee: but I have known thee, and these have known that thou hast [c]sent me.[T]

v.14–AD 30
See footnote, *Time*, Rev. 10:6.

**14**
u *Truth*, John 18:37.
v *Gospel*, Mark 13:10.
w *Doctrines of Jesus*, John 7:16.
x *Hatred*, Prov. 15:17.
y *Righteous, described*, Psa. 64:10.
z *Jesus, our example*, Matt. 1:21.

**15**
a *Jesus, mediation of*, Matt. 1:21.
b *Prayer, intercessory*, Acts 6:4.
c *Prayers of Jesus*, Luke 5:16.
3 R. V. evil one.

**16**
d *Disciples*, Matt. 9:14.
e *Minister, character and qualifications of*, Rom. 15:16.
f *Righteous, described*, Psa. 64:10.

**17**
g *Sanctification*, 1 Pet. 1:2.
h *Truth*, John 18:37.
i *Word of God*, Psa. 119:9.

**18**
j *Jesus, relation of, to the Father*, Matt. 1:21.

**19**
k *Jesus, holiness of*, Matt. 1:21.
l *Jesus, perfections of*, Matt. 1:21.

**20**
m *Faith in Christ*, John 6:69.
n *Agency, in salvation of men*, Mark 1:17.
o *Preaching*, Matt. 9:35.

**21**
p *Church, unity of*, Matt. 16:18.
q *Righteous, union of, with Christ*, Psa. 64:10.
r *Fellowship, with Christ*, 1 Cor. 1:9.
s *Fellowship, with God*, 1 Cor. 1:9.

**23**
t *Perfection*, Heb. 6:1.
u *God, love of*, Gen. 2:2.
4 R. V. perfected into one;

**24**
v *God, fatherhood of*, Gen. 2:2.
w *Election of Grace*, Rom. 11:5.
x *Heaven, future home of the righteous*, Luke 18:22.

r *Judas*, Mark 3:19. s Psa. 109:8; Acts 1:20. 2 R. V. I kept them in thy name which thou hast given me: and I guarded them, and not one of them perished, but **13** t *Joy*, Psa. 5:11.

y *Jesus, pre-existence of*, Matt. 1:21. z *Jesus, eternity of*, Matt. 1:21. **25**—a *God, righteousness of*, Gen. 2:2. b *Spiritual Blindness*, 2 Cor. 4:4. c *Jesus, relation of, to the Father*, Matt. 1:21.

26 And I have [d]declared[C] unto them thy name, and will declare *it*: that the [e]love wherewith thou hast loved me may be in them, and [f,g]I in them.[S T]

## CHAPTER 18

*Judas betrays Jesus. 10 Peter smites the high priest's servant. 12 Jesus is bound and led away, first to Annas. 15 Peter's first denial 19 Jesus before Caiaphas. 25 Peter's second denial. 28 Jesus is delivered over to Pilate, 38 who seeks to release him, but the Jews demand Barabbas.*

[a]WHEN Jē'ṣus had spoken these words, he went forth with his [b]disciples over the [c]brook [d]Çē'dron, where was a [e]garden, into the which he entered, and his disciples.

2 And [f]Jū'das also, which [g,h]betrayed him, knew the place: for Jē'ṣus ofttimes resorted[C] thither[C] with his [b]disciples.

3 [f,i]Jū'das then, having received a band *of* [1]*men* and officers from the chief [j]priests and [k]Phăr'ĭ-seeṣ, cometh thither[C] with lanterns and torches and weapons.

4 Jē'ṣus therefore, [l]knowing all things that should come upon him, went forth, and said unto them, Whom seek ye?

5 They answered him, Jē'ṣus of [m]Năz'a-rĕth. Jē'ṣus saith unto them, I[C] am *he*. And [f]Jū'das also, which [g,h]betrayed him, stood with them.

6 As soon then as he had said unto them, I[C] am *he*, they went backward, and fell to the ground.

7 Then asked he them again, Whom seek ye? And they said, Jē'ṣus of [m]Năz'a-rĕth.

8 Jē'ṣus answered, I[C] have told you that I[C] am *he*: if therefore ye seek me, [n]let these go their way:

9 That the saying might be fulfilled, which he spake, Of them which thou gavest me have I lost none.

10 [o]Then Sī'mon [p]Pē'tēr having a [q]sword drew it, and [r]smote the high priest's servant, and cut off his right ear. The servant's name was [s]Măl'chus.

11 Then said Jē'ṣus unto [p]Pē'tēr, Put up thy [q]sword into the sheath: the [t,u]cup which my Father hath given me, [v]shall I not drink it?

12 Then the band[C] and the [2]captain and officers of the [w]Jewṣ [3,x]took [y]Jē'ṣus, and bound him,

13 And led him away [z]to [a,b]Ăn'nas first; for he was father in law to [c]Cā'ia-phăs, which was the [d]high priest that same year.

14 Now [c]Cā'ia-phăs was he, which gave counsel to the [e]Jewṣ, that it was expedient that one man should die for the people.[T]

15 ¶ And Sī'mon [f]Pē'tēr followed Jē'ṣus, and *so did* [g]another disciple: that disciple was known unto the [d]high priest, and went in with Jē'ṣus into the [4]palace of the high priest.

16 But [f]Pē'tēr stood at the door without.[C] Then went out that [g]other disciple, which was known unto the [d]high priest, and spake unto [h]her that kept the door, and brought in Pē'tēr.

17 Then saith the [h]damsel[C] that kept the door unto [f]Pē'tēr, Art not thou also *one* of this man's [i]disciples? He [j,k]saith, I am not.

18 And the servants and officers stood there, who had made a fire of coals; for it was cold: and they warmed themselves: and [f]Pē'tēr stood with them, and warmed himself.

19 ¶ [l]The high priest then asked Jē'ṣus of his [i]disciples, and of his [5,m]doctrine.[C]

20 [l]Jē'ṣus answered him, I [m]spake openly to the world; I ever [n,o]taught in the [p]synagogue, and in the [q]temple, whither the [e]Jews always resort[C]; and in secret have I said nothing.

21 [l]Why askest thou me? ask them which heard me, what I

v.26–AD 30
See footnote, *Time*, Rev. 10:6.

**26**
d *Jesus, teacher*, Matt. 1:21.
e *God, love of*, Gen. 2:2.
f *Fellowship, with Christ*, 1 Cor. 1:9.
g *Righteous, union of, with Christ*, Psa. 64:10.

**1**
a Matt. 26:36–46; Mark 14:32–42; Luke 22:39–46.
b *Apostles*, Luke 6:13.
c *Brook*, Deut. 8:7.
d Or, *Kidron*, 1 Kin. 2:37.
e *Gethsemane*, Mark 14:32.

**2**
f *Judas*, Mark 3:19.
g *Betrayal, of Jesus*, Matt. 26:46.
h *Infidelity, of friends*, 2 Cor. 6:15.

**3**
i Matt. 26:47–56; Mark 14:43–50; Luke 22:47–53.
j *Priest*, Lev. 1:5.
k *Pharisees*, Matt. 15:12.
1 R. V. soldiers,

**4**
l *Jesus, omniscience of*, Matt. 1:21.

**5**
m *Nazareth*, John 1:46.

**8**
n *Jesus, compassion of*, Matt. 1:21.

**10**
o *Love, for Jesus*, 1 John 4:19.
p *Peter*, Mark 5:37.
q *Sword*, 1 Chr. 21:5.
r *Rashness*, 2 Sam. 6:7.

v.10–AD 30
See footnote, *Time*, Rev. 10:6.

s Matt. 26:51; Mark 14:47; Luke 22:50, 51.

**11**
t *Cup, figurative*, Matt. 20:22.
u *Jesus, sufferings of*, Matt. 1:21.
v *Resignation, exemplified*, Job 5:17.

**12**
w *Jews*, Neh. 4:2.
x *Arrest, of Jesus*, Matt. 26:57.
y *Prisoners*, Psa. 79:11.
2 R. V. chief captain,
3 R. V. seized

**13**
z *Trial of Jesus*, Mark 14:53.

a Luke 3:2; Acts 4:6.
b *Court, ecclesiastical*, Ex. 18:26.
c *Caiaphas*, Matt. 26:3.
d *High Priest*, Lev. 21:10.

**14**
e *Jews*, Neh. 4:2.

**15**
f *Peter*, Mark 5:37.
g *John*, Mark 1:19.
4 R. V. court

**16**
h *Women*, Prov. 31:10.

**17**
i *Disciples*, Matt. 9:14.
j *Falsehood*, Job 21:34.
k *Cowardice, instances of*, Lev. 26:36.

**19**
l *Trial of Jesus*, Mark 14:53.
m *Doctrines of Jesus*, John 7:16.
5 R. V. teaching.

**20**
n *Instruction, in religion*, Prov. 23:23.
o *Jesus, teacher*, Matt. 1:21.
p *Synagogue*, Matt. 12:9.
q *Temple, Herod's*, 1 Kin. 6:17.

v.21–AD 30
See footnote, *Time*, Rev. 10:6.

**22**
*r* *Malice, of Christ's enemies,* Eph. 4:31.
*s* *Smiting and Scourging of Jesus,* Isa. 50:6.
*t* *Persecution, of Jesus,* John 15:20.

**23**
*u* *Jesus, meekness of,* Matt. 1:21.

**24**
*v* Luke 3:2; Acts 4:6.
*w* *Caiaphas,* Matt. 26:3.
*x* *High Priest,* Lev. 21:10.

**26**
*y* *Gethsemane,* Mark 14:32.

**27**
*z* Matt. 26:34, 74, 75; Mark 14:30, 68, 72; Luke 22:34, 60, 61; John 13:38.

**28**
*a* *Trial of Jesus,* Mark 14:53.
*b* *Pretorium,* Mark 15:16.
*c* *Hypocrisy, instances of,* Jas. 3:17.
*d* *Defilement,* Lev. 5:2.
*e* *Passover,* Num. 9:5.

**29**
*f* *Pilate,* Matt. 27:2.
*g* *Persecution, of Jesus,* John 15:20

**30**
*h* *False Accusation,* 2 Tim. 3:3.
*i* *Indictments, instances of,* Matt. 27:37.

have said unto them: behold,
they know what I said.
22 And when he had thus
spoken, [r]one of the officers
which stood by [s,t]struck Jē'ṣus
with the palm of his hand,
saying, Answerest thou the high
priest so? [Q]
23 [u]Jē'ṣus answered him, If I
have spoken evil, bear witness of
the evil: but if well, why smitest
thou me?
24 Now [v]Ăn'nas had sent him
bound unto [w]Cā'ia-phăs the
[x]high priest.
25 ¶ And Sī'mon [f]Pē'tēr stood
and warmed himself. They said
therefore unto him, Art not thou
also *one* of his [i]disciples? He
[j,k]denied *it*, and said, I am not.
26 One of the servants of the
high priest, being *his* kinsman[C]
whose ear [f]Pē'tēr cut off, saith,
Did not I see thee in the [y]garden
with him?
27 [f]Pē'tēr then [j,k]denied again:
and immediately the [z]cock crew.[C]
28 ¶ [a]Then led they Jē'ṣus from
Cā'ia-phăs unto the [b]hall of
judgment: and it was early; and
they themselves went not into
the judgment hall, [c]lest they
should be [d]defiled; but that they
might eat the [e]passover.
29 [a,f]Pī'late then went out unto
them, and said, What [g]accusa-
tion bring ye against this man?
30 They answered and said unto him, [h]If he were not a [i]male-
factor,[C] we would not have delivered him up unto thee.

31 [a]Then said [f]Pī'late unto
them, Take ye him, and judge
him according to your law. The
Jewṣ therefore said unto him, It
is not lawful for us to put any
man to death:
32 That the [j]saying of Jē'-
ṣus might be fulfilled, which he
spake, signifying [k]what death he
should die.
33 [a]Then [f]Pī'late entered into
the [b]judgment hall again, and
called Jē'ṣus, and said unto
him, Art thou the [i,l]King of
the Jewṣ?
34 Jē'ṣus answered him, Sayest
thou this thing of thyself, or did
others tell it thee of me?
35 [f]Pī'late answered, Am I a
Jew? Thine own nation and the
chief priests have delivered thee
unto me: what hast thou done?[Q]
36 [T] [a]Jē'ṣus [m]answered, My
[n]kingdom is not of this world: if
my kingdom were of this world,
then would my servants fight,
that I should not be delivered to
the Jewṣ: but now is my kingdom not from hence.[S]
37 [f]Pī'late therefore said unto
him, Art thou a [l]king then? Jē'-
ṣus [m]answered, Thou sayest that
I am a king. [o]To this end was I
born, and for this cause came I
into the world, that I should bear
witness unto the *truth. Every
one that is of the truth heareth
my voice.[S Q T]
38 [f]Pī'late saith unto him,
What is *truth? And when he
had said this, he went out again

v.31–AD 30
See footnote, *Time*, Rev. 10:6.

**32**
*j* *Prophecies, fulfilled,* Dan. 9:24.
*k* *Crucifixion,* Mark 15:13.

**33**
*l* *Jesus, king,* Matt. 1:21.

**36**
*m* *Pleading,* Deut. 17:8.
*n* *Jesus, kingdom of,* Matt. 1:21.

**37**
*o* *Jesus, mission of,* Matt. 1:21.

* **TRUTH,** Psa. 85:10, 11. *Precious,* Prov. 23:23. *Preserves,* Psa. 46:11; 61:7; 91:4; Prov. 20:28. *Purifies,* Prov. 16:6; 1 Pet. 1:22. *Sanctifies,* **John 17:17, 19; 2** Thess. 2:13. *Brings freedom,* John 8:32.

*Reacheth unto the clouds,* Psa. 108:4. *Endureth forever,* Psa. 100:5; 117:2. *Ways of the Lord in,* Psa. 25:10.

*The foundation, of which Christ is the corner stone,* Eph. 2:20.

*Came by Jesus Christ,* John 1:17; 8:45; 14:6; 18:37, 38; Eph. 2:20. *Revealed to the righteous,* Psa. 57:3; 86:11.

*Word of God called word of,* **John 17:17; Eph. 1:13;** Col. 1:5; 2 Tim. 2:15; Jas. 1:18.

*Acceptance of, necessary to salvation,* 2 Thess. **2:12, 13;** 1 Tim. 2:4; 2 Tim. 2:25; 3:7; Heb. 10:26.

*Rejection of, brings condemnation,* 2 Thess. 2:10–12; Tit. 1:14.

*Ministers must preach,* 2 Cor. 4:2; 2 Tim. 2:15.

*To be taught by parents to children,* Isa. 38:19. *Church is pillar of,* 1 Tim. 3:15.

*The wicked, destitute of,* **Dan. 9:13; 1 Tim. 6:5;** *resist,* **2 Tim. 3:8; 4:4.**

**Of the gospel,** 2 Tim. 4:3, 4; Tit. 1:1, 14; 2:1; Jas. 1:18, 21, 23, 25; 2:12; 5:19; 1 Pet. 1:22–25; 2:2, 8; 3:1; 5:12; 2 Pet. 1:12. See footnotes: DOCTRINES OF JESUS, John 7:16; GOD, *Truth*, Gen. 2:2.

**Attribute of God,** Ex. 34:6; Deut. 32:4; Psa. 31:5; 40:10, 11; 71:22; 86:15; 89:14; 115:1; 117:2; 138:2; 146:6; Isa. 25:1; 65:16; Jer. 4:2. *Exhibited, in his government,* Psa. 119:151; *in his judgments,* Psa. 96:13; Rom. 2:2; *in his word,* John 17:17; *in his works,* Psa. 111:7, 8; Dan. 4:37.

**Attribute of Christ,** John 1:14; 14:6.

**Attribute of the Holy Spirit,** John 14:17; 16:13; 1 John 5:7.

**Grace of the Righteous,** Psa. 51:6; Prov. 3:3; John 3:21; 3 John 3.

*Righteous, should be girded with,* Eph. 6:14; *should know,* 1 Tim. 4:3; 1 John 2:21; 3:19; 4:6; *should walk in,* 2 John 4; 3 John 4; *should obey,* Rom. 2:8; *should love,* Zech. 8:19; 2 Thess. 2:10; *should rejoice in,* **1** Cor. **13:6;** *should meditate upon,* **Phil. 4:8.**

v.38–AD 30
See footnote, *Time*, Rev. 10:6.

**38**
*p Jews*, Neh. 4:2.
6 R. V. crime

**39**
*q Prisoners, kindness to*, Psa. 79:11.
*r Irony*, Mark 12:14.

**40**
*s Public Opinion*, John 12:42.
*t Barabbas*, Matt. 27:16.
*u Robbers*, Hos. 6:9.

**1**
*a Trial of Jesus*, vs. 1–16; Mark 14:53.
*b Pilate*, Matt. 27:2.
*c Prisoners, Jesus*, Psa. 79:11.
*d Punishment, by scourging*, Lev. 26:41.
*e Scourging of Jesus*, Isa. 50:6.

**2**
*f* Matt. 27:27–31; Mark 15:16–20.
*g Soldiers*, Ezra 8:22.
*h Crown*, Ex. 29:6.
*i Thorn*, Hos. 2:6.
*j Sarcasm, instances of*, Judg. 10:14.
*k Irony, instances of*, Mark 12:14.
*l Colors, symbolical*, Ezek. 16:16.

**3**
*m Smiting of Jesus*, Isa. 50:6.
*n Cruelty, instances of*, Psa. 27:12
1 R. V. they came unto him, and said,

**4**
2 R. V. crime

**6**
*o Priest*, Lev. 1:5.
*p Public Opinion*, John 12:42.
*q* Matt. 27:22, 23; Luke 23:21.
*r Crucifixion*, Mark 15:13.
*s King, influenced by popular opinion*, 2 Kin. 3:10.
*t Character, instability of*, Phil. 2:15.

**7**
*u Blasphemy, false accusation of*, 2 Sam. 12:14.

unto the [p]Jews, and saith unto them, I find in him no [6]fault *at all*.

39 But ye have a custom, that I should release unto you [q]one at the [e]passover: will ye therefore that I release unto you the [r]King of the Jews?

40 Then [s]cried they all again, saying, Not this man, but [t]Bă-răb′bas. Now Bă-răb′bas was a [u]robber.

## CHAPTER 19

*Jesus is scourged, and crowned with thorns. 4 Pilate seeks again to release him; 8 again the third time; 13 but yields and delivers him to be crucified. 17 The crucifixion. 23 The soldiers cast lots for his garments. 25 He commends his mother to John. 28 He dies. 38 His burial.*

[a]THEN [b]Pī′late therefore took [c]Jē′ṣus, and [d,e]scourged *him*.[C]

2 [f]And the [g]soldiers platted[C] a [h]crown of [i]thorns, and put [j]*it* on his head, and they [k]put on him a [l]purple robe,

3 And [1,j,k]said, Hail, King of the Jews! and they [m,n]smote[C] him with their hands.[Q]

4 [b]Pī′late therefore went forth again, and saith unto them, Behold, I bring him forth to you, that ye may know that I find no [2]fault in him.

5 Then came Jē′ṣus forth, wearing the [h]crown of [i]thorns, and the [l]purple robe. And [b]*Pī′late* saith unto them, Behold the man!

6 When the chief [o]priests therefore and officers saw him, they [p]cried out, saying, [q,r]Crucify *him*, crucify *him*. [s]Pī′late saith unto them, [t]Take ye him, and crucify *him*: for I find no fault in him.

7 The Jews answered him, We have a law, and by our law he ought to die, because [u]he made himself the Son of God.[Q]

8 ¶ When Pī′late therefore heard that [p]saying, he was the more afraid;

9 And went again into the [v]judgment hall, and [a]saith unto Jē′ṣus, Whence art thou? But [w]Jē′ṣus [x]gave him no answer.

10 [a]Then saith [y]Pī′late unto him, Speakest thou not unto me? knowest thou not that I have power[C] to crucify thee, and have power to release thee?

11 Jē′ṣus answered, Thou couldest have no power *at all* against me, except it were given thee from [z]above: therefore [a]he that delivered me unto thee hath the greater sin.[S T]

12 And from thenceforth [b]Pī′late sought to release him: but the Jews cried out, saying, [c]If thou let this man go, thou art not [d]Çæ′ṣar's friend: [c]whosoever maketh himself a [e]king speaketh against Çæ′ṣar.

13 ¶ When [b]Pī′late therefore heard that saying, he brought Jē′ṣus forth, and sat down in the judgment seat in a place that is called the Pavement, but in the Hē′brew, Găb′ba-thȧ.

14 And it was the [f]preparation of the [g]passover, and about the sixth hour: and he saith unto the Jews, [h]Behold your King!

15 But they [i]cried out, Away with *him*, away with *him*, [j]crucify him. [b]Pī′late saith unto them, Shall I crucify [h]your King? The chief [k]priests [l]answered, We have no king but [d]Çæ′ṣar.

16 [m,n]Then [o]delivered [p,q]he him therefore unto them to be crucified. And they took Jē′ṣus, and led *him* away.

17 [r]And he bearing his *cross went forth into a place called *the place* of a skull, which is called in the Hē′brew [s]Gŏl′gŏ-thȧ:

v.8–AD 30
See footnote, *Time*, Rev. 10:6.

**9**
*v Pretorium*, Mark 15:16.
*w Jesus, meekness of*, Matt. 1:21.
*x Reticence of Jesus*, Mark 14:61.

**10**
*y Government, monarchical, tyranny in*, Isa. 22:21.

**11**
*z God, sovereign*, Gen. 2:2.
*a Caiaphas*, Matt. 26:3.

**12**
*b Pilate*, Matt. 27:2.
*c Treason*, 2 Kin 11:14.
*d Cæsar*, Acts 25:8.
*e Jesus, king*, Matt. 1:21.

**14**
*f* Matt. 27:62; Mark 15:42; Luke 23:54.
*g Passover*, Num. 9:5.
*h Sarcasm*, Judg. 10:14.

**15**
*i Persecution, of Jesus*, John 15:20.
*j Crucifixion*, Mark 15:13.
*k Priest*, Lev. 1:5.
*l Hypocrisy, instances of*, Jas. 3:17.

**16**
*m* Matt. 27:31, 32; Mark 15:20, 21; Luke 23:26–32.
*n Demagogism*, 2 Sam. 15:2.
*o Character, instability of*, Phil. 2:15.
*p Rulers, wicked, instances of*, Ex. 18:21.
*q Government, corruption in*, Isa. 22:21.

**17**
*r* Matt. 27:33–50; Mark 15:22–37; Luke 23:33–46.
*s* Matt. 27:33; Mark 15:22.

*** CROSS.** *Jesus and two malefactors crucified on*, Matt. 27:32; Mark 15:21; Luke 23:26; Eph. 2:16; Phil. 2:8; Col. 1:20; 2:14; Heb. 12:2. *Borne, by Simon*, Matt. 27:32; Mark 15:21; Luke 23:26; *by Jesus*, John 19:17. *Death on, a disgrace*, Gal. 3:13. **Figurative:** *Of duty*, Matt. 10:38; 16:24; Mark 8:34; Luke 9:23; 14:27. *Of Christ's vicarious death*, 1 Cor. 1:17, 18; Gal. 5:11; 6:14; Phil. 3:18.
See footnotes: CRUCIFIXION, Mark 15:13; SELF-DENIAL, Mark 8:34.

18 Where they [i]crucified him,
and two other with him, on
either side one, and Jē'ṣus in the
midst.
19 ¶ And [b]Pī'late wrote a title,
and put *it* on the *cross. And
the [t]writing was, JĒ'ṢUS OF
NĂZ'A-RĔTH THE KING
OF THE JEWṢ.
20 This title then read many of
the Jewṣ: for the place where
Jē'ṣus was [i]crucified was nigh[G]
to the [u]city: and it was written
in [v]Hē'brew, *and* [v]Greek, *and*
[v]Lăt'in.
21 Then said the chief [k]priests
of the Jewṣ to Pī'late, Write not,
The King of the Jewṣ; but
that he said, I am King of the
Jewṣ.
22 Pī'late [w]answered, What I
have written I have written.
23 ¶ Then the [x]soldiers, when
they had crucified Jē'ṣus, took
his garments, and made four
parts, to every soldier a part; and
also *his* coat: now the coat was
without seam, woven from the
top throughout.
24 [x]They said therefore among
themselves, Let us not rend[G] it,
but cast [y]lots for it, whose it
shall be: that the [z,a]scripture
might be fulfilled, which saith,
[b]They parted my raiment among
them, and for my vesture they
did cast lots. These things therefore the soldiers did.[Q]
25 ¶ Now there stood by the
*cross of Jē'ṣus his [c,d]mother,
and his mother's sister, [e]Mā'rȳ
the *wife* of Clē'o-phăs, and
[f]Mā'rȳ Măg-da-lē'nē.
26 When Jē'ṣus therefore saw
his [c,d]mother, and the [g]disciple
standing by, whom he [h]loved, he
saith unto his mother, Woman,
behold thy son!
27 Then saith he to the [g]disci-
ple, Behold thy [c]mother! And
from that hour that disciple [i]took
[d]her unto his own *home.*
28 ¶[Q]After this, Jē'ṣus knowing that all [j]things were now accomplished, that the [k]scripture
might be fulfilled, saith, I thirst.
29 Now there was set a vessel
full of [l]vinegar: and they filled a
[m]spunge with vinegar, and put *it*
upon [n]hyssop, and put *it* to his
mouth.[Q]
30 When Jē'ṣus therefore had
received the [l]vinegar, he said,
[o]It is finished: and he bowed his
head, and [p]gave up [3]the ghost.[G T Q]
31 ¶ The Jewṣ therefore, be-
cause it was the [q]preparation,
[r]that the bodies should not remain upon the cross on the [s]sab-
bath day, (for that sabbath day
was an high day,) besought[G]
[t]Pī'late that their legs might be
broken, and *that* they might be
taken away.[Q]
32 Then came the [u]soldiers,
and brake the legs of the first,
and of the other which was crucified with him.
33 But when they came to Jē'-
ṣus, and saw that he was dead
already, they brake not his legs:
34 But one of the [u]soldiers
with a [v]spear pierced his side,
and forthwith[G] came there out
[w]blood and water.
35 And [y]he that saw *it* [x]bare
[y]record,[G] and his record[G] is true:
and he knoweth that he [x,y]saith
true, that ye might believe.
36 For these things were done,
that the [k]scripture should be
fulfilled, [z]A [a]bone of him shall
not be broken.[Q]
37 And again another [b]scrip-
ture saith, [c]They shall look on
him whom they pierced.[T Q]
38 ¶ And after this †Jō'ṣeph of
‡Ăr-ĭ-mă-thæ'ă, being a [d]disci-
ple of Jē'ṣus, but secretly for
[e]fear of the [f]Jewṣ, besought[G] [g]Pī'-

v.18–AD 30
See footnote, *Time,* Rev. 10:6.

19
t *Inscriptions,* Mark 15:26.

20
u *Jerusalem,* Judg. 19:10.
v *Language,* Dan. 3:29.

22
w *Character, stability of,* Phil. 2:15.

23
x *Soldiers,* Ezra 8:22.

24
y *Lot,* Esth. 3:7.
z *Prophecies concerning the Messiah, and their fulfillment,* Gen. 12:3.

a *Word of God,* Psa. 119:9.
b Psa. 22:18; Matt. 27:35; Mark 15:24; Luke 23:34.

25
c *Mother,* 1 Kin. 2:20.
d *Mary,* Luke 1:27.
e *Mary,* Mark 15:40.
f *Mary Magdalene,* Matt. 27:56.

26
g *John,* Mark 1:19.
h *Jesus, love of,* Matt. 1:21.

v.27–AD 30
See footnote, *Time,* Rev. 10:6.

27
i *Kindness, instances of,* Acts 28:2.

28
j *Salvation, plan of,* Acts 16:17.
k *Prophecies concerning the Messiah, and their fulfillment,* Gen. 12:3.

29
l *Vinegar,* Num. 6:3.
m Matt. 27:48; Mark 15:36.
n *Hyssop,* Ex. 12:22.

30
o *Jesus, mission of,* Matt. 1:21.
p *Jesus, death of,* Matt. 1:21.
3 R. V. his spirit.

31
q Matt. 27:62; Mark 15:42; Luke 23:54.
r Deut. 21:23.
s *Sabbath,* Ex. 16:23.
t *Pilate,* Matt. 27:2.

32
u *Soldiers,* Ezra 8:22.

34
v *Spear,* 2 Kin. 11:10.
w *Blood, of Jesus,* Heb. 9:19.

35
x *Religious Testimony,* 2 Thess. 1:10.
y *Witnessing for Christ,* Luke 24:48.

36
z Ex. 12:46; Num. 9:12.

a *Bones,* Ezek. 37:1.

37
b *Prophecies concerning the Messiah, and their fulfillment,* Gen. 12:3.
c Zech. 12:10.

38
d *Disciples,* Matt. 9:14.
e *Cowardice, instances of,* Lev. 26:36.
f *Public Opinion,* John 12:42.
g *Pilate,* Matt. 27:2.

† **JOSEPH,** of Arimathea. *Begs the body of Jesus for burial in his own tomb,* Matt. 27:57–60; Mark 15:42–47; Luke 23:50–56; John 19:38–42.

‡ **ARIMATHEA,** a city five miles N. of Jerusalem. *The city of Joseph, who secured the body of Jesus,* Matt. 27:57; Mark 15:43; Luke 23:51; John 19:38.

v.38–AD 30
See footnote, *Time*, Rev. 10:6.

39
*h Love, for Jesus*, 1 John 4:19.
*i* John 3:1-10.
*j Myrrh*, Ex. 30:23.
*k Aloes*, Psa. 45:8.

40
*l Spices*, Josh. 6:23.
*m Burial, with spices*, Acts 8:2.

41
*n Burying Places*, Gen. 23:4.

42
*o* Matt. 27:57-66; Mark 15:45-47; Luke 23:50-56.
*p* Matt. 27:62; Mark 15:42; Luke 23:54.

1
*a* Matt. 28:1-8; Mark 16:1-8; Luke 24:1-10.
*b Christian Sabbath*, Mark 16:9.
*c Love, for Jesus, instances of*, 1 John 4:19.
*d Mary Magdalene*, Matt. 27:56.
*e Women, first at the sepulchre*, Prov. 31:10.

2
*f Peter*, Mark 5:37.
*g John*, Mark 1:19.
*h Jesus, love of*, Matt. 1:21.

5
*i Linen*, Ezek. 27:16.

late that he might take away the body of Jē′ṣus: and Pī′late gave *him* leave. He came therefore, and took the body of Jē′ṣus.

39 And [h]there came also [i]Nĭc-o-dē′mus, which at the first came to Jē′ṣus by night, and brought a mixture of [j]myrrh and [k]aloes, about an hundred pound[C] *weight*.

40 Then took they the body of Jē′ṣus, and wound[C] it in linen clothes with the [l]spices, as the manner[C] of the Jewṣ is to [m]bury.

41 Now in the place where he was crucified there was a [n]garden; and in the garden a new sepulchre[C], wherein was never man yet laid.

42 There [o]laid they Jē′ṣus therefore because of the Jewṣ' [p]preparation *day*; for the [n]sepulchre was nigh[C] at[C] hand.

## CHAPTER 20

*Mary Magdalene comes to the sepulchre and finds it empty.* 3 *Peter and John run thither.* 11 *Jesus appears to Mary Magdalene;* 19 *and also at evening to the disciples.* 24 *The unbelief of Thomas.* 26 *After eight days Jesus again appears to the disciples, and Thomas believes.* 30 *The object for which John wrote his gospel.*

[a]THE [b]first *day* of the week [c]cometh [d,e]Mā′rȳ Măg-da-lē′nē early, when it was yet dark, unto the sepulchre[C], and seeth the stone taken away from the sepulchre[G T].

2 Then she runneth, and cometh to Sī′mon [f]Pē′tĕr, and to the [g]other disciple, whom Jē′ṣus [h]loved[C], and saith unto them, They have taken away the Lord out of the sepulchre, and we know not where they have laid him.

3 [f]Pē′tĕr therefore went forth, and that [g]other disciple, and came to the sepulchre.

4 So they ran both together: and the [g]other disciple did outrun [f]Pē′tĕr, and came first to the sepulchre[C].

5 And he stooping down, *and looking in*, saw the [i]linen clothes lying; yet went he not in.

6 Then cometh Sī′mon [f]Pē′tĕr following him, and went into the sepulchre, and seeth the [i]linen clothes lie,

7 And the napkin[C], that was about his head, not lying with the linen clothes, but wrapped together in a place by itself.

8 Then went in also that [g]other disciple, which came first to the sepulchre[C], and he saw, and [j]believed.

9 For as yet they [k]knew not the scripture, that he must [l]rise again from the dead.[Q]

10 Then the [m]disciples went away again unto their own home.

11 ¶ But [d]Mā′rȳ stood without[C] at the sepulchre[C] [c,n,o]weeping: and as she wept, she stooped down, *and looked* into the sepulchre[C],

12 And seeth two [p]angels in white sitting, the one at the head, and the other at the feet, where the body of Jē′ṣus had lain.

13 And they say unto her, Woman, why weepest thou? She saith unto them, [q]Because they have taken away my Lord, and I know not where they have laid him.

14 And when [d]she had thus said, [r]she turned herself back, and [s]saw Jē′ṣus standing, and knew not that it was Jē′ṣus.

15 Jē′ṣus saith unto her, Woman, why weepest thou? whom seekest thou? She, supposing him to be the gardener, saith unto him, Sir, if thou have borne[C] him hence, tell me where thou hast laid him, and I will take him away.

16 Jē′ṣus saith unto her, [d]Mā′rȳ. She turned herself, and saith unto him, [t,u]Răb-bō′nī; which is to say, Master[C].

17 Jē′ṣus saith unto her, Touch me not; for I am not yet ascended to [v]my [w]Father: but go to my brethren, and say unto them, I

v.6–AD 30
See footnote, *Time*, Rev. 10:6.

8
*j Faith in Christ*, John 6:69.

9
*k Ignorance, of the scriptures*, Acts 3:17.
*l Resurrection of Jesus*, Matt. 28:6.

10
*m Apostles*, Luke 6:13.

11
*n Weeping*, Ezra 3:13.
*o Friendship, instances of*, Prov. 22:24.

12
*p Angel, appearances of*, Heb. 1:13.

13
*q Borrowing Trouble, instances of*, Matt. 6:25.

14
*r Women, first to whom our risen Lord appeared*, Prov. 31:10.
*s Appearances of Jesus after his Resurrection*, Mark 16:9.

16
*t Rabbi*, Matt. 23:7.
*u Jesus, names of*, Matt. 1:21.

17
*v Jesus, relation of, to the Father*, Matt. 1:21.
*w God, fatherhood of*, Gen. 2:2.

v.17–AD 30
See footnote, *Time*, Rev. 10:6.

*x Jesus, ascension of*, Matt. 1:21.

19
*v Christian Sabbath*, Mark 16:9.
*z Peace*, Jer. 29:7.

*a Salutations*, Luke 1:44.

20
*b Apostles*, Luke 6:13.

21
*c Peace*, Jer. 29:7.
*d God, fatherhood of*, Gen. 2:2.
*e Jesus, relation of, to the Father*, Matt. 1:21.
*f Apostles, commission of*, Luke 6:13.

22
*g Holy Spirit, baptism of*, Acts 1:2.

23
*h Church, government of*, Matt. 16:18.
*i Court, ecclesiastical*, Ex. 18:26.
*j Sin, forgiveness of*, Rom. 5:12.

24
*k Thomas*, John 11:16.

25
*l Unbelievers*, 1 Cor. 6:6.

26
*m Appearances of Jesus after his Resurrection*, Mark 16:9.

[x]ascend unto my Father, and
your Father; and *to* my God, and
your God.[T]
18 [d]Mā′rȳ Măg-da-lē′nē came
and told the [m]disciples that she
had seen the Lord, and *that* he
had spoken these things unto
her.
19 ¶ Then the same day at
evening, being the [v]first *day* of
the week, when the doors were
shut where the [m]disciples were
assembled for fear of the Jews,
[s]came Jē′şus and stood in the
midst, and saith unto them,
[z,a]Peace *be* unto you.[T]
20 And when he had so said, he
shewed unto them *his* hands and
his side. Then were the [b]disci-
ples glad, when they saw the
Lord.
21[T] Then said Jē′şus to them
again, [a,c]Peace *be* unto you: as
*my* [d]Father hath [e]sent me, even
so [f]send I you.
22 And when he had said this,
he breathed on *them*, and saith
unto them, Receive ye the [g]Holy
Ghost:[G T]
23 [h,i]Whose soever sins ye
[j]remit, they are remitted unto
them; *and* whose soever *sins* ye
retain, they are retained.
24 ¶ But [k]Thŏm′as, one of the
[b]twelve, called Dĭd′ȳ-mŭs, was
not with them when Jē′şus came.
25 The other [b]disciples therefore said unto him, We have seen
the Lord. But he [l]said unto
them, Except I shall see in his
hands the print of the nails, and
put my finger into the print of
the nails, and thrust my hand
into his side, I will not believe.
26 ¶ And after eight days
again his [b]disciples were within,[G]
and [k]Thŏm′as with them: *then*
[m]came Jē′şus, the doors being
shut, and stood in the midst,
and said, [a,c]Peace *be* unto you.[T]
27 Then saith he to [k]Thŏm′as,
Reach hither thy finger, and behold my hands; and reach hither
thy hand, and thrust *it* into my
side: and [n,o]be not faithless, but
believing.[S]
28[T] And [k]Thŏm′as answered
and [p,q]said unto him, [r]My Lord
and my God.
29 Jē′şus saith unto him,
[k]Thŏm′as, because thou hast
seen me, thou hast believed:
blessed *are* they that have not
seen, and *yet* have believed.[S T]
30 ¶ And many other [s]signs[G]
truly did Jē′şus in the presence
of his [b]disciples, which are not
written in this book:
31 But these are written, that ye
might [t]believe that Jē′şus is the
[u]Chrīst, the [r]Son of God; and
that [v]believing ye might have
[w]life [x]through his [y]name.[S T]

## CHAPTER 21

*Jesus appears to the disciples at the sea of Tiberias. 6 The great draught of fishes. 15 He tries Peter's love; 18 signifies by what death he should die; 20 and rebukes his curiosity concerning John. 24 The conclusion.*

[a]AFTER these things Jē′şus
[b]shewed himself again to
the [c]disciples at the [d]sea of Tī-
bē′rĭ-as; and on this wise[G] shewed
he *himself*.
2 There were together Sī′mon
[e]Pē′tēr, and [f]Thŏm′as called
Dĭd′ȳ-mŭs, and [g]Nȧ-thăn′a-el
of [h]Cā′nȧ in [i]Găl′ĭ-lee, and the
[j,k]*sons* of Zĕb′e-dee, and two
other of his disciples.
3 Sī′mon [e]Pē′tēr saith unto
them, I go a fishing. They say
unto him, We also go with thee.
They went forth, and entered
into [1]a ship immediately; and
that night they caught nothing.
4 But when the morning was
now come, Jē′şus [b]stood on the
shore: but the disciples knew not
that it was Jē′şus.
5 Then Jē′şus saith unto them,
Children, have ye [2]any meat[G]?
They answered him, No.
6 And he said unto them, Cast
the [l]net on the right side of the

v.27–AD 30
See footnote, *Time*, Rev. 10:6.

27
*n Faith in Christ, enjoined*, John 6:69.
*o Commandment, enjoining faith*, Deut. 8:2.

28
*p Confession of Christ*, Luke 12:8.
*q Faith in Christ, exemplified*, John 6:69.
*r Jesus, divinity of*, Matt. 1:21.

30
*s Miracles, of Jesus*, Luke 23:8.

31
*t Faith in Christ*, John 6:69.
*u Jesus, Messiah*, Matt. 1:21.
*v Salvation, conditions of*, Acts 16:17.
*w Life, spiritual*, Eccl. 8:15.
*x Jesus, mediation of*, Matt. 1:21.
*y Name of Jesus*, John 14:13.

1
*a* Matt. 28:16.
*b Appearances of Jesus after his Resurrection*, Mark 16:9.
*c Apostles*, Luke 6:13.
*d* Or, *Sea of Galilee*. Matt. 4:18.

2
*e Peter*, Mark 5:37.
*f Thomas*, John 11:16.
*g* John 1:45–49.
*h Cana*, John 2:1.
*i Galilee*, Mark 6:21.
*j James*, Luke 5:10.
*k John*, Mark 1:19.

3
1 **R. V. the boat;**

5
2 **R. V. aught to eat?**

6
*l Net*, **Isa. 51:20.**

v.6–AD 30
See footnote, *Time*, Rev. 10:6.

3 R. V. boat,
*m* *Jesus, omniscience of*, Matt. 1:21.
*n* *Fish*, Matt. 17:27.

**7**
*o* *Jesus, love of*, Matt. 1:21.
*p* *Love, for Jesus*, 1 John 4:19.
4 R. V. his coat about him

**9**
*q* *Bread*, Ezek. 4:13.

**14**
*r* *Resurrection of Jesus*. Matt. 28:6.

**15**
*s* *Discipleship of Jesus, tests of*, vs. 15–19; Matt. 10:32.
*t* John 1:42.
*u* *Apostles, commission of*, Luke 6:13.
*v* *Minister, duties of*, Rom. 15:16.
*w* *Lamb, a type of young believers*, Num. 7:15.

[3]ship,[G] and [m]ye shall find. They cast therefore, and now they were not able to draw it for the multitude of [n]fishes.[S]

7 Therefore that [k]disciple whom Jē′ṣus [o]loved saith unto [e]Pē′tĕr, It is the Lord. Now when Sī′mon Pē′tĕr heard that it was the Lord, he girt[G] [4]*his* fisher's coat *unto him*, (for he was naked,) and did [p]cast himself into the sea.

8 And the other disciples came in a little [3]ship;[G] (for they were not far from land, but as it were two hundred cubits,) dragging the [l]net with [n]fishes.

9 As soon then as they were come to land, they saw a fire of coals there, and [n]fish laid thereon, and [q]bread.

10 Jē′ṣus saith unto them, Bring of the [n]fish which ye have now caught.

11 Sī′mon [e]Pē′tĕr went up, and drew the [l]net to land full of great fishes, an hundred and fifty and three: and for[G] all there were so many, yet was not the net broken.

12 Jē′ṣus saith unto them, Come *and* dine. And none of the [c]disciples durst[G] ask him, Who art thou? knowing that it was the Lord.

13 Jē′ṣus then cometh, and taketh [q]bread, and giveth them, and [n]fish likewise.

14 This is now the third time that Jē′ṣus [b]shewed himself to his [c]disciples, after that he was [r]risen from the dead.

15 ¶[T]So when they had dined, Jē′ṣus [s]saith to Sī′mon [e]Pē′tĕr, Sī′mon, *son* of [t]Jō′nas, lovest[G] thou me more than these? He saith unto him, Yea, Lord; thou knowest that I [p]love[G] thee. He saith unto him, [u,v]Feed my [w]lambs.

16 He [s]saith to him again the second time, [e]Sī′mon, *son* of [t]Jō′nas, lovest[G] thou me? He saith unto him, Yea, Lord; thou knowest that I [p]love[G] thee. He saith unto him, [5,u,v]Feed my [x]sheep.

17 He [s]saith unto him the third time, [e]Sī′mon, *son* of [t]Jō′nas, lovest[G] thou me? Pē′tĕr was grieved because he said unto him the third time, Lovest[G] thou me? And he said unto him, Lord, thou [y]knowest all things; thou knowest that I [p]love[G] thee. Jē′ṣus saith unto him, [u,v]Feed my [x]sheep.[S T]

18 Verily,[G] verily, I say unto thee, When thou wast young, thou girdedst[G] thyself, and walkedst whither thou wouldest: but when thou shalt be old, [z]thou shalt stretch forth thy hands, and another shall gird thee, and carry *thee* whither thou wouldest not.

19 This spake he, signifying by what [a]death he should [b,c]glorify[G] God. And when he had spoken this, he saith unto him, Follow me.

20 Then [d]Pē′tĕr, turning about, seeth the [e]disciple whom Jē′ṣus [f]loved following; which also leaned on his breast at supper, and said, Lord, which is he that betrayeth thee?

21 [d]Pē′tĕr seeing him saith to Jē′ṣus, Lord, and what *shall* this man *do*?

22 Jē′ṣus saith unto him, If I will that he tarry[G] till I [g]come, what *is that* to thee? follow thou me.

23 Then went this saying abroad among the brethren, that [e]that disciple should not die: yet Jē′ṣus said not unto him, He shall not die; but, If I will[G] that he tarry[G] till I come, what *is that* to thee?

24 [e]This is the disciple which [h,i]testifieth of these things, and wrote these things: and we know that his testimony is true.

25 And there are also many

v.16–AD 30
See footnote, *Time*, Rev. 10:6.

**16**
*x* *Sheep, figurative*, Deut. 32:14.
5 R. V. Tend

**17**
*y* *Jesus, omniscience of*, Matt. 1:21.

**18**
*z* *Jesus, prophet*, Matt. 1:21.

**19**
*a* *Death*, Num. 23:10.
*b* *Glorifying God*, Luke 5:25.
*c* *Afflictions, design of*, Psa. 34:19.

**20**
*d* *Peter*, Mark 5:37.
*e* *John*, Mark 1:19.
*f* *Jesus, love of*, Matt. 1:21.

**22**
*g* *Jesus, second coming of*, Matt. 1:21.

**24**
*h* *Religious Testimony*, 2 Thess. 1:10.
*i* *Witnessing for Christ*, Luke 24:48.

v.25–AD 30
See footnote, *Time*, Rev. 10:6.

other things which Jē′ṣus did,
the which, if they should be written every one, I suppose that
even the world itself could not
contain the books that should be
written. Amen.

v.25–AD 30
See footnote, *Time*, Rev. 10:6.

THE

# ACTS OF THE APOSTLES

v.1–AD 30

1

*a* *Luke*, Col. 4:14.
*b* *Witnessing for Christ*, Luke 24:48.
*c* Luke 1:3.
*d* *Jesus, teacher*, Matt. 1:21.
*e* *Instruction, in religion*, Prov. 23:23.

2

*f* *Ascension, of Jesus*, 2 Kin. 2:1.
*g* *Apostles*, Luke 6:13.
*h* *Call, personal*, Phil. 3:14.

3

*i* 1 Cor. 15:7.
*j* *Resurrection of Jesus*, Matt. 28:6.
*k* *Appearances of Jesus after his Resurrection*, Mark 16:9.
*l* *Forty, days*, Jonah 3:4.
*m* *Kingdom of Heaven*, Matt. 13:24.
1 R. V. *omits* infallible

## CHAPTER 1

*Jesus is seen of his apostles forty days after his resurrection. 4 His charge to them. 9 His ascension. 10 Two angels foretell his second coming. 12 The disciples return from mount Olivet, and give themselves to prayer. 15 Matthias is chosen an apostle in the place of Judas.*

THE former treatise have [a]I
[b]made, O [c]Thē-ŏph′ĭ-lŭs, of
all that Jē′ṣus began both to do
and [d,e]teach,
2 Until the day in which he was
[f]taken up, after that he through
the *Holy Ghost had given commandments unto the [g]apostles
whom he had [h]chosen:
3 [i,j]To whom also he [k]shewed
himself alive after his passion by
many [1]infallible proofs, being
seen of them [l]forty days, and
speaking of the things pertaining
to the [m]kingdom of God:
4 And, [k]being assembled together with *them*, commanded
them that they should not depart from [n]Jĕ-rụ′să-lĕm, but wait
for the [o]promise of the [p]Father,
which, *saith he*, ye have heard
of me.
5 For [q]Jŏhn truly [r]baptized with
water; but [s]ye shall be baptized
with the *Holy Ghost not many
days hence.
6 When they therefore were
come together, they asked of
him, [t]saying, Lord, wilt thou at
this time restore again the kingdom to Ĭṣ′ra-el?
7 And he said unto them, It is
not for you to know the times or
the [u]seasons, which the [p,v]Father
hath put in his own [2]power.
8 But [g]ye shall receive [w,x]power

v.4–AD 30
See footnote, *Time*, Rev. 10:6.

4

*n* *Jerusalem*, Judg. 19:10.
*o* *Jesus, promises of*, Matt. 1:21.
*p* *God, fatherhood of*, Gen. 2:2.

5

*q* *John the Baptist*, Luke 1:63.
*r* *Baptism, John's*, Luke 20:4.
*s* *Promise, of the Holy Spirit*, 2 Cor. 1:20.

6

*t* *Spiritual Blindness*, 2 Cor. 4:4.

7

*u* *Seasons*, Dan. 2:21.
*v* *God, sovereign*, Gen. 2:2.
2 R. V. authority.

8

*w* *Minister, character and qualifications of*, Rom. 15:16.
*x* *Spiritual Power*, Luke 24:49.

* **HOLY SPIRIT**, Gen. 1:2; Psa. 51:11; Matt. 1:18, 20; Gal. 3:2, 3, 14; 6:8; Col. 1:8; Heb. 6:4. *Convinces of sin*, Gen. 6:3; John 16:8–11. *Comforts*, John 14:16, 17, 26; 15:26; 16: 7–14; Acts 9:31. *Guides*, John 16:13; Acts 13:2–4; 15:8, 28; 16:6, 7; Rom. 8:4, 14; Gal. 5:16, 18, 25. *Helps our infirmities*, Rom. 8:26. *Regenerates*, John 3:5, 6; 2 Cor. 3:3, 18; Tit. 3:5, 6. *Sanctifies*, Rom. 15:16; 1 Cor. 6:11; 2 Thess. 2: 13; 1 Pet. 1:2. *Dwells in believers*, Rom. 8:11.

*Invites to salvation*, Rev. 22:17.

*Communion with*, 2 Cor. 13:14; Phil. 2:1. *Given to every man*, 1 Cor. 12:7. *Given, in answer to prayer*, Luke 11:13; Acts 8:15; *through imposition of hands*, Acts 8:17–19; 19:6.

*Access to the Father by*, Eph. 2:18, 22. *Prayer in*, Eph. 6: 18; Jude 20. *Wisdom and strength from*, Neh. 9:20; Zech. 4:6; Eph. 3:16. *Liberty from*, 2 Cor. 3:17. *Love of God given by*, Rom. 5:5.

*Ministers commissioned by*, Acts 20:28. *Christian baptism in the name of, with the name of Father and Son*, Matt. 28:19. *Gospel preached in power of*, 1 Cor. 2:4, 10; 1 Thess. 1:5; 1 Pet. 1:12. *Word of God, sword of*, Eph. 6:17. *Water, a symbol of*, John 7:38, 39.

*Demons cast out by*, Matt. 12:28. *Power to bestow, not purchasable*, Acts 8:18–20.

Poured upon: *Israel*, Isa. 32:15; Ezek. 39:29; *the Gentiles*, Acts 10:19, 20, 44–47; 11:15, 16; *all flesh*, Joel 2:28, 29; Acts 2:17.

*Christians, are temples of*, 1 Cor. 3:16; 6:19; *are filled with*, Acts 2:4, 33; 4:8, 31; 6:5; 8:17; 11:24; 13:9, 52; Eph. 5:18; 2 Tim. 1:14; *have fellowship with*, Rom. 8:9, 11; 1 Cor. 3:16; 6:19; 2 Cor. 13:14; Phil. 2:1; *receive earnest of*, 2 Cor. 1:22; 5:5; Eph. 1:13, 14; *are sealed with*, 2 Cor. 1:22; Eph. 1:13; 4: 30; *have righteousness, peace, and joy in*, Rom. 14:17; 15:13; 1 Thess. 1:6; *are unified by*, 1 Cor. 12:13.

*Immaculate conception of Mary by*, Matt. 1:20; Luke 1:35.

*Jesus anointed and led by*, Isa. 61:1; Matt. 3:16; 4:1; Mark 1:10; Luke 3:22; 4:18; John 1:32, 33; Acts 10:38; Heb. 9:14.

*Testifies that Jesus is Lord*, John 15:26; 16:14; 1 Cor. 12:3.

**Baptism of**, Matt. 3:11; Mark 1:8; Luke 3:16; John 1:33 (with Acts 11:16); 20:22 (with Acts 1:5); Acts 19:2–6; 1 John 2:20, 27.

**Fruits of**, Rom. 8:23; Gal. 5:22, 23.

**Gifts of**: *Foretold*, Isa. 44:3; Joel 2:28, 29. *Of different kinds*, 1 Cor. 2:4–6, 8–10, 28. *Bestowed for the confirmation of the gospel*, Rom. 15:19; Heb. 2:4.

**Inspiration of**, Matt. 10:20; Mark 13:11; Luke 12:12; 1 Cor. 2:4, 10–14; 1 Tim. 4:1.

INSTANCES OF INSPIRATION OF: *Joseph*, Gen. 41:38. *Bezaleel*, Ex. 31:3; 35:31. *The seventy elders*, Num. 11:17. *Balaam*, Num. 24:2.

The Judges: *Othniel*, Judg. 3:10; *Gideon*, Judg. 6:34; *Jephthah*, Judg. 11:29.

*King Saul*, 1 Sam. 11:6. *King David*, 1 Chr. 28:11, 12.

*The prophets*, 2 Pet. 1:21. *Azariah*, 2 Chr. 15:1. *Zechariah*, 2 Chr. 24:20. *Zacharias*, Luke 1:67. *Elizabeth*, Luke 1:41. *Simeon*, Luke 2:25, 26. *John the Baptist*, Luke 1:15.

*The disciples*, Acts 6:3; 7:55; 8:29; 9:17; 10:45.

**Intercession of**, Rom. 8:26, 27.

**Power of**: *Promised*, Luke 24:49; Acts 1:8; 2:38. *On Christ*, Matt. 12:28; Luke 4:14. *On ministers*, Acts 2:4; Rom. 15:19. *On the righteous*, Rom. 15:13; Eph. 3:16.

**Revelations from**, Mark 12:36; Luke 2:26, 27; John 16: 13; 1 Cor. 2:10, 11; Eph. 3:5; 1 Tim. 4:1; Heb. 3:7; 2 Pet. 1:21; Rev. 2:7, 11, 29; 14:13.

**Sin against**, Acts 8:18–22; 1 John 5:16. *By grieving*, Isa. 63:10, 11, 14; Eph. 4:30. *By resisting*, Acts 5:9; 7:51; Eph. 4:30; 1 Thess. 5:19; Heb. 10:29. *By blaspheming*, Matt. 12: 31, 32; Mark 3:29; Luke 12:10. *By lying to*, Acts 5:3.

**Withdrawn from incorrigible sinners**, Gen. 6:3; Deut. 32:30; Jer. 7:29; Hos. 4:17, 18; 9:12; Rom. 1:24, 26, 28.

INSTANCES OF WITHDRAWAL FROM INCORRIGIBLE SINNERS: *Antediluvians*, Gen. 6:3–7. *Israelites*, Deut. 1:42; 28:15–68; 31:17, 18. *Saul*, 1 Sam. 16:14; 18:12; 28:15, 16; 2 Sam. 7:15.

**Witness of**, Acts 5:32; Rom. 8:15, 16; 9:1; 2 Cor. 1:22; 5:5; Gal. 4:6; Eph. 1:13, 14; Heb. 10:15; 1 John 3:24; 4:13; 5: 6–8.

v.8–AD 30
See footnote, *Time*, Rev. 10:6.

y *Minister, duties of*, Rom. 15:16.
z *Witnessing for Christ*, Luke 24:48.
a *Jerusalem*, Judg. 19:10.
b *Judea*, Luke 5:17.
c *Samaria*, Isa. 7:9.
d *Missions*, Matt. 28:19.
9
e *Ascension, of Jesus*, 2 Kin. 2:1.
10
f *Angel, appearances of*, Heb. 1:13.
11
g *Apostles*, Luke 6:13.
h *Galilee*, Mark 6:21.
i *Jesus, second coming of*, Matt. 1:21.
12
j *Mount of Olives*, Mark 11:1.
k *Day's Journey*, 1 Kin. 19:4.
13
l *Peter*, Mark 5:37.
m *James*, Luke 5:10.
n *John*, Mark 1:19.
o *Andrew*, Matt. 4:18.
p *Philip*, Luke 6:14.
q *Thomas*, John 11:16.
r Matt. 10:3; Mark 3:18; Luke 6:14.
s *Matthew*, Matt. 9:9.
t *James*, Matt. 10:3.
u *Simon*, Mark 3:18.
v Luke 6:16; Jude 1.
3 R. V. son
14
w *Fellowship, of the righteous*, 1 Cor. 1:9.
x *Prayer, social*, Acts 6:4.
y *Women*, Prov. 31:10.
z *Mary*, Luke 1:27.
a *Brothers of Jesus*, Matt. 13:55.
15
b *Peter*, Mark 5:37.
c *Disciples*, Matt. 9:14.
16
d *Word of God, inspiration of*, Psa. 119:9.

after that the *Holy Ghost[G] is come upon you: and [y]ye shall be [z]witnesses unto me both in [a]Jē-ru'sā-lĕm, and in all [b]Jū-dæ'ā, and in [c]Sā-mā'rĭ-ā, and [d]unto the uttermost part of the earth.[T]

9 And when he had spoken these things, while they beheld, he was [e]taken up; and a cloud received him out of their sight.[Q]

10 And while they looked stedfastly toward heaven as he went up, behold, two [f]men stood by them in white apparel;

11 Which also said, [g]Ye men of [h]Găl'ĭ-lee, why stand ye gazing up into heaven? this same Jē'ṣus, which is [e]taken up from you into heaven, shall so [i]come in like manner as ye have seen him go into heaven.

12 ¶[T]Then returned they unto [a]Jē-ru'sā-lĕm from the mount called [j]Ŏl'ĭ-vĕt, which is from Jē-ru'sā-lĕm a sabbath[G] [k]day's journey.

13 And when they were come in, they went up into an upper room, where abode both [l]Pē'tēr, and [m]Jāmeṣ, and [n]Jŏhn, and [o]Ăn'drew, [p]Phĭl'ĭp, and [q]Thŏm'as, [r]Bär-thŏl'o-mew, and [s]Măt'thew, [t]Jāmeṣ *the son* of Ăl-phæ'us, and [u]Sī'mon Zē-lō'tēṣ,[G] and [v]Jū'das *the* [3]*brother* of Jāmeṣ.

14 These all continued [w]with one accord in [x]prayer and supplication, with the [y]women, and [z]Mā'rȳ the mother of Jē'ṣus, and with his [a]brethren.[T]

15 ¶ And in those days [b]Pē'tēr stood up in the midst of the [c]disciples, and said, (the number of names together were about an hundred and twenty,)

16 Men *and* brethren, this [d]scripture must needs have been [e]fulfilled, which the *Holy Ghost[G] by the mouth of [f]Dā'vid spake before concerning [g]Jū'das, which was [h,i]guide to them that took Jē'ṣus.[T Q]

17 For he was numbered with [j]us, and had obtained part of this ministry.

18 Now [k]this man purchased a [l]field with the reward of iniquity; and [m]falling headlong, he burst asunder in the midst, and all his bowels gushed out.

19 And it was known unto all the dwellers at [n]Jē-ru'sā-lĕm; insomuch as that field is called in their proper[G] tongue, [o]Ā-çĕl'da-mā, that is to say, The field of blood.

20 For it is written in the book of Psālms, [c,p]Let his habitation be desolate, and let no man dwell therein: and his [4]bishoprick let another take.[Q]

21 Wherefore of these men which have [q]companied with[G] us all the time that the Lord Jē'ṣus went in and out among us,

22 Beginning from the [r]baptism of [s]Jŏhn, unto that same day that he was [t]taken up from [j]us, must one be ordained[G] to be a [u]witness with us of his [v]resurrection.

23 And they appointed two, Jō'ṣeph called Bär'sa-băs, who was surnamed Jŭs'tus, and Măt-thī'as.

24 And they [w]prayed, and said, Thou, Lord, which [x]knowest the [y]hearts of all *men*, [z]shew whether[G] of these two thou hast [a,b]chosen,[S]

25 That [c]he may take part of this ministry and apostleship, from which [d]Jū'das by transgression [†]fell, that he might go to his own [e]place.

v.16–AD 30
See footnote, *Time*, Rev. 10:6.

e *Prophecies, fulfilled*, Dan. 9:24.
f *David*, 1 Sam. 16:13.
g *Judas*, Mark 3:19.
h *Treason*, 2 Kin. 11:14.
i *Betrayal, of Jesus*, Matt. 26:46.
17
j *Apostles*, Luke 6:13.
18
k *Minister, false and corrupt*, Rom. 15:16.
l *Burying Places*, Gen. 23:4.
m *Suicide, instances of*, 1 Kin. 16:18.
19
n *Jerusalem*, Judg. 19:10.
o Matt. 27:8.
20
p Psa. 69:25; 109:8.
4 R. V. office
21
q *Fellowship, of the righteous*, 1 Cor. 1:9.
22
r *Baptism, John's*, Luke 20:4.
s *John the Baptist*, Luke 1:63.
t *Ascension, of Jesus*, 2 Kin. 2:1.
u *Witnessing for Christ*, Luke 24:48.
v *Resurrection of Jesus*, Matt. 28:6.
24
w *Guidance, prayer for*, Psa. 48:14.
x *God, knowledge of*, Gen. 2:2.
y *Heart, known to God*, Psa. 44:21.
z *God, guidance of*, Gen. 2:2.
a *Minister, call of*, Rom. 15:16.
b *Call, personal*, Phil. 3:14.
25
c *Minister, duties of*, Rom. 15:16.
d *Judas*, Mark 3:19.
e *Hell*, Mark 9:43.

† **APOSTASY.** *Described*, Deut. 32:15; Matt. 12:45; Luke 11:24–26; 1 Tim. 4:1–3; 2 Tim. 3:6–9; 4:3, 4; 2 Pet. 2:15–22; Jude 8. *Foretold*, 2 Thess. 2:3; 1 Tim. 4:1–3; 2 Tim. 3:1–5; 2 Peter 2:1.
*Admonitions against*, Matt. 24:4, 5; Mark 13:5, 6; Heb. 3:12; 2 Pet. 3:17; 2 John 8; Jude 4–6.
*Caused by persecution*, Matt. 13:21 (with Mark 4:17); 24:9–12. *No remedy for*, Heb. 6:4–8; 10:26–29. *Punishment of*, 1 Chr. 28:9; Isa. 1:28; Jer. 17:5, 6; Ezek. 18:24, 26; 33:12, 13, 18; Zeph. 1:4–6; John 15:6; 2 Thess. 2:11, 12; Heb. 10:38, 39; Jude 6.
**Instances of:** *Israelites*, Ex. 32; Num. 14; Acts 7:39–43. *Saul*, 1 Sam. 18:12. *Amaziah*, 2 Chr. 25:14, 27. *Disciples*, John 6:66. *Judas*, Matt. 26:14–16; 27:3–5; Mark 14:10, 11; Luke 22:3–6, 47, 48; Acts 1:16–18. *Hymenæus and Alexander*, 1 Tim. 1:19, 20. *Phygellus and Hermogenes*, 2 Tim. 1:15.

v.26–AD 30
See footnote, *Time*, Rev. 10:6.

**26**
*f* *Lot*, Esth. 3:7.
*g* *Apostles*, Luke 6:13.

**1**
*a* *Annual Feasts*, Num. 15:3.
*b* *Apostles*, Luke 6:13.
*c* *Fellowship, of the righteous*, 1 Cor. 1:9.

**3**
*d* *Vision*, Acts 9:10.
*e* *Fire*, Ex. 12:8.
1 R. V. tongues parting asunder,

**4**
*f* *Inspiration*, Job 32:8.
*g* *Holy Spirit, power of*, Acts 1:2.
*h* *Charism*, 1 Cor. 12:1.
*i* *Miracles*, Luke 23:8.
*j* *Tongues, miraculous gift of*, 1 Cor. 12:10.

**5**
*k* *Jerusalem*, Judg. 19:10.
*l* *Jews*, Neh. 4:2.

**6**
*m* *Preaching*, Matt. 9:35.
*n* *Language*, Dan. 3:29.

**7**
*o* *Galilee*, Mark 6:21.

**9**
*p* *Medes*, Dan. 5:28.
*q* *Elam*, Isa. 11:11.
*r* *Mesopotamia*, Gen. 24:10.
*s* *Judea*, Luke 5:17.

26 And they gave forth their [f]lots; and the lot fell upon Măt-thī′as; and he was numbered with the eleven [g]apostles.[S] [Q]

## CHAPTER 2

*The outpouring of the Spirit on the day of Pentecost, and the gift of tongues. 14 Peter's discourse. 37 Three thousand repent and are baptized. 44 The disciples have all things common. 47 Converts are daily added to the church.*

AND[T] when the day of *,[a]Pĕn′te-cŏst was fully come, [b]they were all with [c]one accord in one place.[Q]

2 And suddenly there came a sound from heaven as of a rushing mighty wind, and it filled all the house where they were sitting.

3 And there appeared unto them [1,d]cloven[G] tongues like as of [e]fire, and it sat upon each of them.

4 And [b]they were all [f]filled with the [g]Holy Ghost[G], and began to [h]speak [i]with other [j]tongues,[G] as the Spirit [f]gave them utterance.[T]

5 And there were dwelling at [k]Jĕ-ru′să-lĕm [l]Jews, devout men, out of every nation under heaven.

6 Now when this was noised abroad, the multitude came together, and were confounded[G], because that every man heard them [m]speak in his own [i,n]language.

7 And they were all amazed and marvelled, saying one to another, Behold, are not all these which speak [o]Găl-ĭ-læ′ans?

8 And how hear we every man in our own [j]tongue[G], wherein we were born?

9 Pär′thĭ-ans, and [p]Mēdes, and [q]Ē′lam-ītes, and the dwellers in [r]Mĕs-o-pŏ-tā′mĭ-ȧ, and in [s]Jū-dæ′ȧ, and [t]Căp-pa-dō′çĭ-ȧ, in [u]Pŏn-tus, and †Ā′șiȧ,

10 [v]Phrȳġ′ĭ-ȧ, and [w]Păm-phȳl′-ĭ-ȧ, in [x]Ē′ġȳpt, and in the parts of ‡Lĭb′ȳ-ȧ about ‖Çy-rē′nē, and [2]strangers[G] of [y]Rōme, [l]Jews and proselytes[G],

11 [z]Crētes and [a]Ā-rā′bĭ-ans, we do hear them [b,c]speak in our [d]tongues[G] the wonderful [e]works of God.

12 And they were all amazed, and were [f]in doubt, saying one to another, What meaneth this?

13 [f]Others [g]mocking said, These men are [h]full of new [i]wine.

14 ¶ But [j]Pē′tēr, standing up with the [k]eleven, lifted up his voice, and [l]said unto them, Ye men of [m]Jū-dæ′ȧ, and all *ye* that dwell at [n]Jē-ru′să-lĕm, be this known unto you, and hearken[G] to my words:

15 For these are not [h]drunken, as ye suppose, seeing it is *but* the [o]third[G] hour of the day.

16[T] But this is [p]that which was spoken by the [q]prophet [r]Jō′el;

17 [s]And[Q] it shall come to pass in the last days, saith God, I will [t]pour out of my [u]Spirit upon all flesh: and your sons and your daughters shall prophesy[G], and your [v]young men shall see [w]visions, and your [x]old men shall dream [y]dreams:

18 [s]And on my servants and on my handmaidens I will [t]pour out in those days of my [u]Spirit; and they shall prophesy:

19 And [s]I will shew [z]wonders in [a]heaven above, and [b]signs in the

v.9–AD 30
See footnote, *Time*, Rev. 10:6.

*t* 1 Pet. 1:1.
*u* Acts 18:2; 1 Pet. 1:1.

**10**
*v* Acts 16:6; 18:23.
*w* *Pamphylia*, Acts 14:24.
*x* *Egypt*, Gen. 41:8.
*y* *Rome*, Acts 19:21.
2 R. V. sojourners from

**11**
*z* *Crete*, Acts 27:7.
*a* *Arabians*, 2 Chr. 17:11.
*b* *Witnessing for Christ*, Luke 24:48.
*c* *Preaching*, Matt. 9:35.
*d* *Language*, Dan. 3:29.
*e* *Redemption of our Souls*, Eph. 1:7.

**12**
*f* *Spiritual Blindness*, 2 Cor. 4:4.

**13**
*g* *Scoffing*, Hab. 1:10.
*h* *Drunkenness*, Luke 21:34.
*i* *Wine*, Prov. 23:31.

**14**
*j* *Peter*, Mark 5:37.
*k* *Apostles*, Luke 6:13.
*l* *Zeal*, 2 Cor. 7:11.
*m* *Judea*, Luke 5:17.
*n* *Jerusalem*, Judg. 19:10.

**15**
*o* *Time*, Rev. 10:6.

**16**
*p* *Prophecies, fulfilled*, Dan. 9:24.
*q* *Prophets*, Isa. 3:2.
*r* *Joel*, Joel 1:1.

**17**
*s* Joel 2:28–32.
*t* *Inspiration*, Job 32:8.
*u* *Holy Spirit*, Acts 1:2.
*v* *Young Men*, Prov. 1:4.
*w* *Vision*, Acts 9:10. *x* *Old Age*, Isa. 46:4. *y* *Dream*, Dan. 1:17.

**19** *z* *Celestial Phenomena*, Luke 23:44.—*a* *Heavens, physical*, Psa. 8:3. *b* *Sign*, Mark 8:11.

See footnotes: BACKSLIDING, *Of Israel*, Hos. 11:7; BACKSLIDERS, Jer. 3:22; REPROBATES, 1 Cor. 9:27.

* **PENTECOST,** an annual feast, held on the fiftieth day after offering the first barley sheaf at the beginning of harvest, which occurred during the feast of the Passover. *Called, feast of weeks*, Ex. 34:22; Deut. 16:10; *feast of harvest*, Ex. 23:16; *day of first fruits*, Num. 28:26; *day of Pentecost*, Acts 2:1; 20:16; 1 Cor. 16:8.

*Institution of*, Ex. 23:16; 34:22; Lev. 23:15–21; Num. 28:26–31; Deut. 16:9–12, 16.

*Holy Spirit given to apostles on*, Acts 2.

See footnotes: FEASTS, Mark 12:39; ANNUAL FEASTS, Num. 15:3.

† **ASIA,** signifying, usually, Asia Minor and the regions of Asia contiguous to Palestine, and not the remote parts of the continent reaching to India and China. *Jews of the dispersion from, in Jerusalem*, Acts 2:9; 21:27; 24:18. *Paul and Silas forbidden by the Holy Spirit to preach in*, Acts 16:6. *Gospel preached in, by Paul*, Acts 19; 20:4. *Paul leaves*, Acts 20:16. *Churches of*, 1 Cor. 16:19; Rev. 1:4, 11.

‡ **LIBYA.** *Region W. of Egypt*, Acts 2:10. *Called also* PHUT, Ezek. 27:10; 30:5; 38:5. *Inhabitants of, called* LUBIM, 2 Chr. 12:3; 16:8; Nah. 3:9.

‖ **CYRENE.** *A city of Libya*, Acts 2:10; 13:1. *Simon, the father of Alexander and Rufus, belonged to*, Matt. 27:32; Mark 15:21; Luke 23:26; Acts 13:1.

v.19–AD 30
See footnote, *Time*, Rev. 10:6.

*c Earth*, Prov. 8:23.

**20**

*d* Joel 2:31, 32.
*e Celestial Phenomena*, Luke 23:44.
*f Sun*, Josh. 10:12.
*g Eclipse*, Isa. 13:10.
*h Moon*, Song 6:10.

**21**

*i Seekers*, Isa. 55:6.
*j God, savior*, Gen. 2:2.

**22**

*k Reproof, faithfulness in*, Prov. 17:10.
*l Nazareth*, John 1:46.
*m Jesus, humanity of*, Matt. 1:21.
*n Jesus, relation of, to the Father*, Matt. 1:21.
*o Miracles, design of*, Luke 23:8.
3 R. V. mighty works

**23**

*p Foreordination*, Rom. 8:30.
*q God, foreknowledge of*, Gen. 2:2.
*r Crucifixion*, Mark 15:13.
4 R. V. by the hand of lawless men did crucify and slay:

**24**

*s God, power of*, Gen. 2:2.
*t Resurrection, of Jesus*, 1 Cor. 15:12.
*u Death*, Num. 23:10.

**25**

*v David*, 1 Sam. 16:13.
*w Prophecies concerning the Messiah, and their fulfillment*, Gen. 12:3.
*x* Psa. 16:8–11.
*y Faith, exemplified*, vs. 26–28; Mark 11:22.

**26**

*z Joy*, Psa. 5:11.

*a Resurrection*, 1 Cor. 15:12.
*b Hope*, Prov. 13:12.

**27**

*c* Psa. 16:10, 11.
*d Resurrection, of Jesus*, 1 Cor. 15:12.
*e Hell*, Mark 9:43.
*f Jesus, holiness of*, Matt. 1:21.

[c]earth beneath; blood, and fire, and vapour of smoke:

20 [d,e]The [f]sun shall be [g]turned into darkness, and the [h]moon into blood, before that great and notable[G] day of the Lord come:

21 [d]And it shall come to pass, *that* [i]whosoever shall call on the name of the [j]Lord shall be saved.[T Q]

22 [k]Ye men of Ĭṣ′ra-el, hear these words; Jē′ṣus of [l]Năz′a-rĕth, a [m]man [n]approved[G] of God among you by [3,o]miracles and wonders and signs, which God did [n]by him in the midst of you, as ye yourselves also know:[T]

23 [k]Him, being delivered by the [p]determinate[G] counsel and [q]foreknowledge[G] of God, ye [4]have taken, and by wicked hands have [r]crucified and slain:[S]

24 Whom [s]God hath raised [t]up, having loosed the pains of [u]death: because it was not possible that he should be holden[G] of[G] it.[Q]

25 For[Q] [v]Dā′vid [w]speaketh concerning him, [x]I foresaw the Lord always before my face, for he is on my right hand, that [y]I should not be moved:

26 [x]Therefore did my heart [z]rejoice, and my tongue was glad; moreover also [y,a]my flesh shall rest in [b]hope:

27 Because [c,d]thou wilt not leave[G] my soul in [5,e]hell,[G] neither wilt thou suffer[G] thine [f]Holy One to see [g]corruption.[G]

28 [c]Thou hast [h]made known to me the ways of life; thou shalt make me full of [i]joy with thy countenance.[G S Q]

29[T] Men *and* brethren, let me freely speak unto you of the patriarch [j]Dā′vid, that he is both dead and buried, and his [k]sepulchre[G] is with us unto this day.[Q]

30 Therefore being a [l]prophet,[G] and knowing that God had [m]sworn with an [n]oath to him, [o]that [p]of the fruit of his loins, [6]according to the flesh, he would raise up [q]Christ to sit on his [r]throne;[Q]

31 [l]He seeing this before spake of the [d]resurrection[G] of Christ, that his soul was not left in [5,e]hell,[G] neither his flesh did see [g]corruption.[Q]

32 This Jē′ṣus hath [s]God [d]raised up, whereof [t]we all are [u]witnesses.

33 Therefore [v]being by the right hand of God [w]exalted, and having received of the [x,y]Father the promise of the [y,z]Holy Ghost,[G] [y]he hath shed forth this, which ye now see and hear.

34[Q T] For [a]Dā′vid is not ascended into the heavens: but he saith himself, [b]The LORD said unto my [c]Lord, [d]Sit thou on my right hand,

35 Until I make thy foes thy [e]footstool.[T Q]

36 Therefore let all the house of Ĭṣ′ra-el know assuredly, that God hath made that same Jē′ṣus, whom ye have [f]crucified, both [g]Lord and [h]Christ.[T]

37 ¶ Now[T] when they heard *this*, they were [i,j]pricked[G] in their heart, and said unto [k]Pē′tĕr and to the rest of the [l]apostles, Men *and* brethren, what shall [m]we do?

38 Then [k]Pē′tĕr said unto them, [n,o,p]Repent, and be [q]baptized every one of you in the [r]name of Jē′ṣus Christ [7]for the [s]remission of sins, and [t]ye shall receive the gift of the [u]Holy Ghost.[G]

39 For the [t]promise is unto you, and to your [v]children, and to all that are afar off, *even* as many as the Lord our God shall [w]call.[G T Q]

v.30–AD 30
See footnote, *Time*, Rev. 10:6.

**30**

*l Prophets, inspiration of*, Isa. 3:2.
*m Covenant, of God with men*, Deut. 29:1.
*n Oath*, Num. 5:19.
*o Prophecies concerning the Messiah, and their fulfillment*, Gen. 12:3.
*p Jesus, incarnation of*, Matt. 1:21.
*q Jesus, king*, Matt. 1:21.
*r Throne, figurative*, 1 Kin. 2:19.
6 R. V. he would set one upon his throne;

**32**

*s God, power of*, Gen. 2:2.
*t Apostles*, Luke 6:13.
*u Witnessing for Christ*, Luke 24:48.

**33**

*v Jesus, relation of, to the Father*, Matt. 1:21.
*w Jesus, exaltation of*, Matt. 1:21.
*x God, fatherhood of*, Gen. 2:2.
*y Holy Trinity*, Luke 3:22.
*z Holy Spirit*, Acts 1:2.

**34**

*a David*, 1 Sam. 16:13.
*b* Psa. 110:1.
*c Jesus, divinity of*, Matt. 1:21.
*d Sovereignty of the Messiah*, Psa. 110:1.

**35**

*e Footstool, figurative*, 1 Chr. 28:2.

**36**

*f Crucifixion*, Mark 15:13.
*g Jesus, worship of*, Matt. 1:21.
*h Jesus, Messiah*, Matt. 1:21.

**37**

*i Conscience, guilty*, Acts 23:1.
*j Conviction of Sin*, John 16:8.
*k Peter*, Mark 5:37.
*l Apostles*, Luke 6:13.
*m Seekers*, Isa. 55:6.

**38**

*n Commandment, enjoining repentance*, Deut. 8:2.

*g Corruption*, Job 17:14. 5 R. V. Hades. **28** *h God, guidance of*, Gen. 2:2. *i Joy*, Psa. 5:11. **29** *j David*, 1 Sam. 16:13. *k Burying Places*, Gen. 23:4.

*o Repentance, the burden of the preaching of Peter*, Mark 1:4. *p Salvation, conditions of*, Acts 16:17. *q Baptism, Christian*, Luke 20:4. *r Name of Jesus*, John 14:13. *s Sin, forgiveness of*, Rom. 5:12. *t Promise, of the Holy Spirit*, 2 Cor. 1:20. *u Holy Spirit*, Acts 1:2. 7 R. V. unto **39** *v Children, of the righteous*, Mark 10:14. *w Call, personal*, Phil. 3:14.

v.40–AD 30
See footnote, *Time*, Rev. 10:6.

**40**

x *Preaching*, Matt. 9:35.
y *Commandment, enjoining righteousness*, Deut. 8:2.
z *Fellowship, with the wicked, forbidden*, 1 Cor. 1:9.
8 R. V. crooked

**41**

a *Faith in Christ*, John 6:69.
b *Jesus, received*, Matt. 1:21.
c *Baptism, Christian*, Luke 20:4.
d *Church, Christian, growth of*, Matt. 16:18.
e *Church, membership in*, Matt. 16:18.

**42**

f *Faithfulness*, Luke 16:10.
g *Apostles*, Luke 6:13.
h *Instruction, in religion*, Prov. 23:23.
i *Fellowship*, 1 Cor. 1:9.
j *Eucharist*, Mark 14:22.
k *Prayer*, Acts 6:4.
9 R. V. teaching

**43**

l *Miracles, of the disciples*, Luke 23:8.

**45**

m *Self-denial, instances of*, Mark 8:34.
n *Liberality, instances of*, 1 Tim. 6:18.
o *Love, of man for man*, 1 John 4:7.

**46**

p *Temple, Herod's*, 1 Kin. 6:17.
q *Joy, instances of*, Psa. 5:11.
r *Thankfulness, to God*, Acts 24:3.
s *Heart, renewed*, Psa. 44:21.
10 R. V. day by day, continuing stedfastly with one accord in the temple, and breaking bread at home, they did take their food with

**47**

t *Praise*, Psa. 150:1.
u *Righteous, described*, Psa. 64:10.

40 And with many other words did he [x]testify and exhort, saying, [y,z]Save yourselves from this [8]untoward[G] generation.[Q]

41 ¶ Then they that gladly [a,b]received his word were [c]baptized: and the same day there were [d]added *unto* [e]*them* about three thousand souls.

42 And they [f]continued stedfastly in the [g]apostles' [9,h]doctrine and [i]fellowship, and in [j]breaking of bread, and in [k]prayers.

43 And fear came upon every soul: and many [l]wonders and signs[G] were done by the [g]apostles.

44 And all that [a]believed were together, and [§]had all things common;

45 And [m]sold their possessions and goods, and [n,o]parted them to all *men*, as every man had need.

46 And [10]they, continuing daily with one accord in the [p]temple, and [j]breaking bread from house to house, did eat their meat[G] with [q,r]gladness and singleness of [s]heart,

47 [t]Praising God, and having favour with all the people. And the Lord [d,e]added to [11]the church daily [u]such as should be saved.[G S T]

## CHAPTER 3

*Peter and John go up to the temple. 2 A lame man healed. 12 Peter's discourse in Solomon's porch. 19 He exhorts to repentance and faith in Christ.*

NOW [a]Pē′tēr and [b]Jŏhn went up together into the [c]temple at the hour of [d]prayer, *being* the ninth *hour*.

2[S] And a certain man [e]lame from his mother's womb [f]was carried, whom they laid daily at the [1]gate of the [c]temple which is called Beautiful, to [g]ask [h]alms of them that entered into the temple;

3 [g]Who seeing [a]Pē′tēr and [b]Jŏhn about to go into the [c]temple asked an [h]alms.[G]

4 And [a]Pē′tēr, fastening his eyes upon him with [b]Jŏhn, said, Look on us.

5 And he gave heed unto them, expecting to receive something of them.

6 Then [a]Pē′ter said, [i]Silver and [j]gold have I none; but such as I have give I thee: In the [k]name of Jē′şus Chrīst of [l]Năz′a-rĕth rise up and walk.

7 And he took him by the right hand, and lifted *him* up: and immediately his feet and ancle bones [m,n]received strength.

8 And [o]he leaping up stood, and walked, and entered with them into the [c]temple, walking, and leaping, and [p,q,r]praising God.

9 And all the people saw him walking and [p]praising God:

10 And they knew that it was [o]he which sat for [h]alms at the Beautiful gate of the [c]temple: and they were filled with wonder and amazement at that which had happened unto him.

11 ¶ And as the [e]lame man which was [n]healed held [a]Pē′tēr and [b]Jŏhn, all the people ran together unto them in the [s]porch that is called Sŏl′o-mon's, greatly wondering.

12 And when [t]Pē′tēr saw *it*, he [u,v]answered unto the people, Ye men of Ĭş′ra-el, why marvel ye at this? or why look ye so earnestly on us, [w]as though by our own power or holiness we had made this man to walk?

13 The God of Ā′bră-hăm, and of Ī′şaac, and of Jā′cob, the God of our fathers, hath glorified his [2,x]Son Jē′şus; [y]whom ye [z]delivered up, and [a]denied him in the presence of [b]Pī′late, when he was determined to let *him* go.[S Q]

**6**

i *Silver*, 1 Chr. 28:14.
j *Gold*, Ezek. 7:19.
k *Name of Jesus*, John 14:13.
l *Nazareth*, John 1:46.

**7**

m *Miracles, of the disciples*, Luke 23:8.
n *Healing, by the apostles*, Acts 4:22.

**8**

o *Joy, instances of* Psa. 5:11.
p *Praise*, Psa. 150:1.
q *Shouting*, 2 Chr. 15:14.
r *Thankfulness, to God*, Acts 24:3.

**11**

s Acts 5:12; John 10:23.

**12**

t *Orator*, Acts 24:1.
u *Courage, instances of*, Deut. 31:7.
v *Zeal, instances of*, 2 Cor. 7:11.
w *Humility*, Prov. 22:4.

**13**

x *Jesus, relation of, to the Father*, Matt. 1:21.
y *Reproof, faithfulness in*, Prov. 17:10.
z *Persecution, of Jesus*, John 15:20.
a *Jesus, rejected*, Matt. 1:21.
b *Pilate*, Matt. 27:2.
2 R. V. Servant Jesus;

11 Am. R. V. them day by day those that were saved.
1 a *Peter*, Mark 5:37. b *John*, Mark 1:19. c *Temple, Herod's*, 1 Kin. 6:17. d *Prayer*, Acts 6:4.
2 e *Lameness*, Lev. 21:18. f *Kindness*, Acts 28:2. g *Beggars*, Luke 16:20. h *Alms*, Matt. 6:2. 1 R. V. door

§ **COMMUNISM.** *Christians in apostolic church in Jerusalem had all property in common*, Acts 2:44, 45; 4:32, 34–37; 5:1–10.

14 But ye [a]denied the [3,c,d]Holy
One and the [c]Just, and desired a
[e,f]murderer to be granted unto
you;[Q]
15 And killed the [c]Prince of life,
whom [g]God hath [h]raised from
the dead; whereof [i]we are [j]wit-
nesses.[T]
16 And his [k]name through
[l]faith in his name hath [m]made
this man strong, whom ye see
and know: yea, the faith which
is by him hath given him this
perfect soundness in the presence of you all.[S]
17 And now, brethren, I wot[G]
that through *,[n]ignorance ye did
*it*, as *did* also your rulers.
18 But those [o,p]things, which
[q]God before had [r]shewed by the
mouth of all his prophets, that
[s]Chrīst should [t]suffer, he hath so
fulfilled.[S]
19 [u,v]Repent[G] ye therefore, and
[4]be converted[G], that your sins
may be [w]blotted out, when the
[x]times of refreshing shall come
from the presence of the Lord;[S]
20 And he shall [y]send Jē′-
ṣus [s]Chrīst, which before was
preached unto you:
21 [z]Whom the heaven must receive until the times of restitution[G] of all things, which God
hath [a]spoken by the mouth of
all his holy prophets since the
world[G] began.
22 [T]For [b]Mō′ṣeṣ truly [c,d]said
unto the fathers, [e]A [f]prophet
shall the Lord your God raise
up unto you [g]of[G] your brethren,
like unto me; him shall ye hear
in all things whatsoever he shall
say unto you.[Q]
23 And it shall come to pass,
*that* every soul, which will not
hear that [f]prophet, shall be [h]de-
stroyed from among the people.[Q]
24 Yea, and all the [a]prophets
from [i]Săm′u-el and those that
follow after, as many as have
spoken, have likewise foretold of
these days.
25 Ye are the children of the
prophets, and of the [j]covenant[G]
which God made with our
fathers, saying unto Ā′brā-
hăm, And in thy [g]seed shall
all the [k]kindreds[G] of the earth be
blessed.[Q]
26 Unto you first God, having
raised up his [2,l]Son Jē′ṣus, sent
[m]him [n]to bless you, in [o]turning
away every one of you from his
iniquities.[S T]

## CHAPTER 4

*Peter and John imprisoned. 4 Five thousand believe. 5 Peter and John brought before the council. 8 Peter's defence. 13 The rulers command them not to teach in the name of Jesus. 23 They return to their own company, who lift up their voice in prayer. 31 They are all filled with the Holy Spirit. 34 Barnabas and others sell their possessions.*

AND as [a,b]they [c]spake unto
the people, the [d]priests,
and the captain of the [e]temple,
and the [f]Săd′du-çeeṣ[G] came upon
them,
2 Being [g]grieved that [a,b]they
[c,h]taught the people, and
[i]preached through Jē′ṣus the
[j]resurrection[G] from the dead.
3 And [g]they laid hands on
them, and [k]put *them* in [l]hold unto the next day: for it was now
eventide.[G]
4 Howbeit [m,n]many of them
which heard the word [o,p]be-
lieved; and the number of the
men was about five thousand.
5 ¶ And it came to pass on the

**14**
c *Jesus, names of,* Matt. 1:21.
d *Jesus, holiness of,* Matt. 1:21.
e *Barabbas,* Matt. 27:16.
f *Homicide, felonious,* Deut. 5:17.
3 R. V. Holy and Righteous One,

**15**
g *God, power of,* Gen. 2:2.
h *Resurrection, of Jesus,* 1 Cor. 15:12.
i *Apostles,* Luke 6:13.
j *Witnessing for Christ,* Luke 24:48.

**16**
k *Name of Jesus,* John 14:13.
l *Faith in Christ,* John 6:69.
m *Miracles,* Luke 23:8.

**17**
n *Spiritual Blindness,* 2 Cor. 4:4.

**18**
o *Prophecies, fulfilled,* Dan. 9:24.
p *Salvation, plan of,* Acts 16:17.
q *God, foreknowledge of,* Gen. 2:2.
r *Prophets, inspiration of,* Isa. 3:2.
s *Jesus, Messiah,* Matt. 1:21.
t *Jesus, sufferings of,* Matt. 1:21.

**19**
u *Repentance, enjoined,* Mark 1:4.
v *Commandment, enjoining repentance,* Deut. 8:2.
w *Sin, forgiveness of,* Rom. 5:12.
x *Spiritual Blessings, from God,* Eph. 1:3.
4 R. V. turn again,

**20**
y *Jesus, second coming of,* Matt. 1:21.

**21**
z *Jesus, exaltation of,* Matt. 1:21.

---

a *Prophets, inspiration of,* Isa. 3:2.

**22**
b *Moses,* Ex. 2:10.
c *Prophecies concerning the Messiah, and their fulfillment,* Gen. 12:3. d *Jesus, prophecies concerning,* Matt. 1:21. e Deut. 18:15, 18, 19; Acts 7:37. f *Jesus, prophet,* Matt. 1:21. g *Jesus, incarnation of,* Matt. 1:21.

**23**
h *Wicked, punishment of,* Psa. 73:3.

**24**
i *Samuel,* 1 Sam. 3:1.

**25**
j *Covenant, of God with men,* Deut. 29:1.
k *Nations blessed in Abraham,* Gen. 18:18.

**26**
l *Jesus, relation of, to the Father,* Matt. 1:21.
m *Jesus, savior,* Matt. 1:21.
n *Jesus, mission of,* Matt. 1:21.
o *Regeneration,* Tit. 3:5.

**1**
a *Peter,* Mark 5:37.
b *John,* Mark 1:19.
c *Zeal,* 2 Cor. 7:11.
d *Priest,* Lev. 1:5.
e *Temple, Herod's,* 1 Kin. 6:17.
f *Sadducees,* Matt. 22:23.

**2**
g *Intolerance,* Num. 11:28.
h *Instruction, in religion,* Prov. 23:23.
i *Preaching,* Matt. 9:35.
j *Resurrection,* 1 Cor. 15:12.

**3**
k *Persecution, instances of,* John 15:20.
l *Prison,* Gen. 39:20.

**4**
m *Church, growth of,* Matt. 16:18.
n *Religious Revivals,* Hab. 3:2.
o *Faith in Christ,* John 6:69.
p *Jesus, received,* Matt. 1:21.

---

* **IGNORANCE,** Job 8:9; 28:12, 13, 20, 21; Prov. 8:5; 19:2; Eccl. 7:23, 24; Jer. 10:23; Hos. 4:14; John 13:7.
*Concerning God,* 1 Sam. 3:7; Job 11:7, 8, 12; 36:26, 29; 37:5, 15, 16, 19, 23; Psa. 139:6; Prov. 30:3, 4; Acts 17:23, 30; *his works,* Eccl. 3:11; 8:17; 11:5; *his wisdom,* 1 Cor. 2:7–10.
*Concerning the future,* Prov. 27:1; Eccl. 8:6, 7; Acts 1:7; 1 Cor. 13:9, 12. *Concerning the Holy Spirit,* Acts 19:2. *Concerning the Scriptures,* Matt. 22:29; Mark 12:24; John 20:9; 1 Tim. 1:7.
*Concerning snares of the wicked,* Prov. 7:6–23; 9:14–18; 22:3; 27:12.
*Remedy for,* Jas. 1:5, 6.
**Sins of:** *Sacrifices for,* Lev. 4:1–35; 5:4–19; Num. 15:22–29; Ezek. 45:20. *Forgiven,* 1 Tim. 1:12, 13; Heb. 5:2. *Forgiven on account of reparation,* Gen. 20:1–7.
**Evil consequences of,** Isa. 5:13; Hos. 4:6. *Alienates from God,* Eph. 4:18, 19. *Darkens understanding,* Luke 23:34; John 16:2, 3; Acts 3:17; 1 Cor. 2:8.
**Punishment of,** Ezek. 3:18; 33:6, 8; Luke 12:48. *By fines,* Lev. 22:14.
INSTANCES OF PUNISHMENT OF SINS OF: *Pharaoh,* Gen. 12:11–17. *Abimelech,* Gen. 20:1–18.

morrow, that their rulers, and [q]elders, and [r]scribes,

6 And *Ăn′nas the [s]high priest, and [t]Cā′ia-phăs, and Jŏhn, and Ăl-ĕx-ăn′dẽr, and as many as were of the kindred of the high priest, were gathered together at [u]Jē-ru′să-lĕm.

7 And when [v]they had set them in the midst, they asked, By what [w]power, or by what name, have ye done this?

8 Then [x,y]Pē′tẽr, [z]filled with the [a]Holy Ghost, [b]said unto them, Ye [c]rulers of the people, and [d]elders of Ĭs′ra-el,

9 [b,e]If we this day be examined of the good deed done to the impotent man, by what means he is [f]made whole;

10 [b,e]Be it known unto you all, and to all the people of Ĭs′ra-el, that by the [g]name of Jē′sus Christ of [h]Năz′a-rĕth, [i]whom ye [j]crucified, whom [k]God [l]raised from the dead, *even* by him doth this man stand here before you whole.

11 [m]This is the [n]stone which was [o,p]set at nought of you builders, which is become the [q,r]head of the corner.

12 Neither is there [s,t]salvation in any other: for there is none other name under heaven given among men, whereby we must be saved.

13 ¶ Now when they saw the [u]boldness of [v]Pē′tẽr and [w]Jŏhn, and perceived that they were unlearned and ignorant men, they marvelled; and they took knowledge of them, that [x]they had been with Jē′sus.

14 And beholding the man which was †healed standing with them, they could say nothing against it.

15 But when they had commanded them to go aside out of the council, [y]they conferred among themselves,

16 [y]Saying, What shall we do to these men? for that indeed a notable [f]miracle hath been done by them *is* manifest to all them that dwell in [z]Jē-ru′să-lĕm; and we cannot deny *it*.

17 [y]But that it spread no further among the people, let us straitly [a]threaten them, that they speak henceforth to no man in this [b]name.

18 And they called them, and [a,c]commanded them not to [d]speak at all nor [e,f]teach in the [b]name of Jē′sus.

19 But [g]Pē′tẽr and [h]Jŏhn [i,j,k]answered and said unto them, Whether it be right in the sight of God to hearken unto you more than [l]unto God, judge ye.

20 For [l,m]we cannot but [d]speak the things which we have seen and heard.

21 So when they had further [a]threatened them, they let them go, finding nothing how they might punish them, because of the [n]people: for all *men* [o]glorified God for [p]that which was done.

22 For the man was above forty years old, on whom this [p]miracle of †healing was shewed.

**5**
*q* *Senate*, Num. 11:16.
*r* *Scribe*, 1 Kin. 4:3.

**6**
*s* *High Priest*, Lev. 21:10.
*t* *Caiaphas*, Matt. 26:3.
*u* *Jerusalem*, Judg. 19:10.

**7**
*v* *Court*, Ex. 18:26.
*w* *Apostles, commission of*, Luke 6:13.

**8**
*x* *Orator*, Acts 24:1.
*y* *Minister, faithful*, Rom. 15:16.
*z* *Minister, character and qualifications of*, Rom. 15:16.

*a* *Holy Spirit*, Acts 1:2.
*b* *Defense*, Acts 19:33.
*c* *Court*, Ex. 18:26.
*d* *Senate*, Num. 11:16.

**9**
*e* *Courage, instances of*, vs. 9–12; Deut. 31:7.
*f* *Miracles*, Luke 23:8.

**10**
*g* *Name of Jesus*, John 14:13.
*h* *Nazareth*, John 1:46.
*i* *Reproof, faithfulness in*, Prov. 17:10.
*j* *Crucifixion*, Mark 15:13.
*k* *God, power of*, Gen. 2:2.
*l* *Resurrection, of Jesus*, 1 Cor. 15:12.

**11**
*m* *Prophecies concerning the Messiah, and their fulfillment*, Gen. 12:3.
*n* *Corner Stone, figurative*, Psa. 144:12. *o* *Unbelief*, Heb. 3:12. *p* *Jesus, rejected*, Matt. 1:21. *q* *Jesus, head of the church*, Matt. 1:21. *r* *Church, Christ the head of*, Matt. 16:18. **12** *s* *Salvation*, Acts 16:17. *t* *Jesus, savior*, Matt. 1:21. **13** *u* *Boldness of the Righteous*, Phil. 1:20. *v* *Peter*, Mark 5:37. *w* *John*, Mark 1:19.

*x* *Wisdom, spiritual*, Prov. 2:2.

**15**
*y* *Court, corrupt*, Ex. 18:26.

**16**
*z* *Jerusalem*, Judg. 19:10.

**17**
*a* *Persecution, of the righteous*, John 15:20.
*b* *Name of Jesus*, John 14:13.

**18**
*c* *Intolerance*, Num. 24:28.
*d* *Preaching*, Matt. 9:35.
*e* *Instruction, in religion*, Prov. 23:23.
*f* *Minister, duties of*, Rom. 15:16.

**19**
*g* *Peter*, Mark 5:37.
*h* *John*, Mark 1:19.
*i* *Conscience, faithful*, Acts 23:1.
*j* *Character, firmness of*, Phil. 2:15.
*k* *Courage, instances of*, Deut. 31:7.
*l* *Duty, of man to God*, Eccl. 12:13.

**20**
*m* *Zeal*, 2 Cor. 7:11.

**21**
*n* *Public Opinion*, John 12:42.
*o* *Glorifying God*, Luke 5:25.
*p* *Miracles, convincing effect of*, Luke 23:8.

* **ANNAS.** *Associate high priest with Caiaphas*, Luke 3:2. *Jesus taken before*, John 18:13, 19, 24. *Sits with others in judgment on the disciples*, Acts 4:6.

† **HEALING.** *The Lord the healer*, Gen. 20:17; Ex. 15:26; Psa 6:2; 30:2; 103:3; Acts 4:30.

*In answer to prayer*, Jas. 5:14–16; *of Miriam*, Num. 12:10–15; *of Jeroboam*, 1 Kin. 13:1–6; *of Hezekiah*, 2 Kin. 20:1–7.

*By Elisha, of Naaman*, 2 Kin. 5:1–14.

**By Jesus:** *The nobleman's son*, John 4:46–53. *The impotent man*, John 5:2–9. *A leper*, Matt. 8:2–4; Mark 1:40–17; Luke 5:12–13. *Peter's mother-in-law*, Matt. 8:14, 15. *Man with palsy*, Matt. 9:2–8; Mark 2:1–12; Luke 5:17–26. *The man with the withered hand*, Matt. 12:9–13; Mark 3:1–5; Luke 6:6–10. *The centurion's servant*, Matt. 8:5–13; Luke 2:1–10. *Demoniacs*, Matt. 8:28–34 (with Mark 5:1–20; Luke 8:26–36); 12:22; 17:14–18; Mark 9:14–27; Luke 9:38–42; 11:14. *Blind and dumb*, Matt. 9:27–33; 12:22; 20:30–34; Mark 8:22–25; 10:46–52; Luke 18:35–43. *Woman with issue of blood*, Matt. 9:20–22; Mark 5:25–34; Luke 8:43–48. *Many sick*, Matt. 8:16; 9:35; 14:14, 35, 36; 15:30, 31; 19:2; Mark 6:5, 53–56; Luke 4:40; Luke 9:11. *Daughter of the Syrophenician woman*, Matt. 15:22–28; Mark 7:25–30. *Woman with an infirmity*, Luke 13:10–13. *Ten lepers*, Luke 17:12–14. See footnote, MIRACLES, *Of Jesus*, Luke 23:8.

*Power of, given, to the apostles*, Matt. 10:1, 8; Mark 3:13–15; 6:7, 13; Luke 9:1, 2, 6; *to the seventy*, Luke 10:9, 17; *to all believers*, Mark 16:18. *Special gifts of*, 1 Cor. 12:9, 28, 30.

**By the apostles:** *The lame man, in Jerusalem*, Acts 3:2

23 ¶ And being let go, [g,h]they went to their own company, and reported all that the chief priests and elders had said unto them.

24 [T]And when they heard that, they lifted up their voice to God with one accord, and [q]said, [r]Lord, thou *art* God, which hast [s]made [t]heaven, and [u]earth, and the [Q][v]sea, and all that in them is:[Q]

25 Who [w]by the [1]mouth of thy servant [x]Dā'vid hast said, [y]Why did the [2,z]heathen[G] rage, and the people imagine vain things?

26 [y,a]The kings of the earth stood up, and the [b]rulers were gathered together against the [c]Lord, and [d]against his [3,e]Chrīst.[Q]

27 [S]For of a truth [d]against thy [f]holy [4,g]child Jē'şus, whom thou hast [h]anointed, both [i]Hĕr'od, and Pŏn'tĭ-ŭs [j]Pī'late, with the Ġĕn'tīleş,[G] and the people of Ĭş'ra-el, were gathered together,[T][Q]

28 For to do whatsoever thy hand and thy counsel [k]determined before to be done.[S]

29 [l,m]And now, Lord, behold their threatenings: and grant unto thy [n]servants, that with all [o]boldness they may [p,q]speak thy [r]word,

30 [T][m]By stretching forth thine hand to [†]heal; and that [s]signs and wonders may be done by the [t]name of thy [f]holy [4,g]child Jē'şus.[S][Q]

31 And when they had [l]prayed, the place was shaken where they were assembled together; and [u]they were all [o]filled with the [v]Holy Ghost,[G] and they [p,q]spake the [r]word of God with boldness.[T]

32 ¶ And the multitude of them that [w]believed were of [x,y]one heart and of one soul: [z,a,b]neither said any *of them* that ought[G] of the things which he possessed was his own; but [c]they had all things common.

33 And with great [d]power gave the [e]apostles [f,g]witness of the [h]resurrection[G] of the Lord Jē'şus: and great grace was upon them all.[S]

34 Neither was there any among them that lacked: for as many as were possessors of [i]lands or houses [a]sold them, and [j]brought the prices of the things that were sold,

35 And [a,b,j]laid *them* down at the [e]apostles' feet: and [c]distribution was made unto every man according as he had need.

36 And Jō'sēş, who by the [e]apostles was surnamed [‡]Bär'na-băs, (which is, being interpreted, [5]The son of consolation,[G]) a [k]Lē'vīte, *and* of the country of [l]Çy̆'prus,

37 Having [i]land, [a]sold *it*, and [j]brought the [m]money, and laid *it* at the [e]apostles' feet.

## CHAPTER 5

*The death of Ananias and Sapphira.* 12 *Signs and wonders wrought by the apostles.* 17 *They are imprisoned;* 19 *but are delivered by an angel, and teach in the temple.* 29 *Their defense before the council.* 33 *Gamaliel's advice.* 40 *The apostles are beaten and dismissed.* 41 *They rejoice that they are counted worthy to suffer shame for Christ.*

BUT a certain man named Ăn-a-nī'as, with Săp-phī'rȧ his [a]wife, sold a [b,c]possession,

2 And [d,e]kept back *part* of the price, his [a,f]wife also [g]being privy[G] *to it*, and [h]brought a certain part, and [i]laid *it* at the [j]apostles' feet.

3 But[T] [k]Pē'tēr [l]said, Ăn-a-nī'as,

**24**
q *Prayer, in adversity,* Acts 6:4.
r *Praise,* Psa. 150:1.
s *God, creator,* Gen. 2:2.
t *Heavens, created,* Psa. 8:3.
u *Earth, created,* Prov. 8:23.
v *Sea,* Jer. 5:22.

**25**
w *Prophets, inspiration of,* Isa. 3:2.
x *David,* 1 Sam. 16:13.
y Psa. 2:1, 2.
z *Gentiles,* Acts 10:45.
1 R. V. Holy Ghost, by the mouth of our father David thy servant, didst say,
2 R. V. Gentiles

**26**
a *Prophecies concerning the Messiah, and their fulfillment,* Gen. 12:3.
b *Rulers, wicked,* Ex. 18:21.
c *Jesus, lordship of,* Matt. 1:21.
d *Persecution, of Jesus, foretold,* John 15:20.
e *Jesus, Messiah,* Matt. 1:21.
3 R. V. Anointed:

**27**
f *Jesus, holiness of,* Matt. 1:21.
g *Jesus, relation of, to the Father,* Matt. 1:21.
h *Anointing, figurative,* Deut. 28:40.
i *Herod,* Matt. 14:1.
j *Pilate,* Matt. 27:2.
4 R. V. Servant

**28**
k *Foreordination,* Rom. 8:30.

**29**
l *Prayer, in adversity,* Acts 6:4.
m *Adversity, prayer in,* Psa. 10:6.
n *Minister, prayer for,* Rom. 15:16.
o *Minister, character and qualifications of,* Rom. 15:16. p *Instruction, in religion,* Prov. 23:23. q *Preaching,* Matt. 9:35. r *Doctrines of Jesus,* John 7:16. **30** s *Miracles,* Luke 23:8. t *Name of Jesus,* John 14:13. **31** u *Prayer, answered,* Acts 6:4. v *Holy Spirit,* Acts 1:2.

**32**
w *Faith in Christ,* John 6:69.
x *Church, unity of,* Matt. 16:18.
y *Unity, of the righteous,* Psa. 133:1.
z *Love, of man for man,* 1 John 4:7.
a *Self-denial,* Mark 8:34.
b *Liberality, instances of,* 1 Tim. 6:18.
c *Communism,* Acts 2:44.

**33**
d *Spiritual Power,* Luke 24:49.
e *Apostles,* Luke 6:13.
f *Witnessing for Christ,* Luke 24:48.
g *Religious Testimony,* 2 Thess. 1:10.
h *Resurrection, of Jesus,* 1 Cor. 15:12.

**34**
i *Land,* Ruth 4:3.
j *Unselfishness,* 1 Cor. 10:24.

**36**
k *Levites,* Deut. 10:8.
l *Cyprus,* Acts 21:3.
5 R. V. Son of exhortation),

**37**
m *Money,* Jer 32:9.

**1**
a *Wife,* Prov. 5:18.
b *Land, bought and sold,* Ruth 4:3.
c *Property,* Lev. 27:15.

**2**
d *Covetousness,* Isa. 57:17.
e *Deception,* Josh. 9:4.
f *Women, wicked,* Prov. 31:10.
g *Complicity,* Prov. 29:24.
h *Hypocrisy,* Jas. 3:17.
i *Communism,* Acts 2:44.
j *Apostles,* Luke 6:13.

**3**
k *Peter,* Mark 5:37.
l *Reproof, faithfulness in,* Prov. 17:10.

10; *in Lystra,* Acts 14:8–10. *Sick, in Jerusalem,* Acts 5:15, 16; *in the island of Melita,* Acts 28:8, 9. *Æneas,* Acts 9:34.

**Figurative,** Psa. 41:4; 147:3.

‡ **BARNABAS** (*son of prophecy*). *Called also* JOSES (R. V. Joseph). Acts 4:36; *and* JUPITER, Acts 14:12–18. *A prophet,* Acts 13:1. *An apostle,* Acts 14:14. *A Levite who gave his possessions to be owned in common with other disciples,* Acts 4:36, 37. *Presents Paul to the apostles in Jerusalem,* Acts 9:25–27. *Accompanies Paul from Antioch to Jerusalem,* Acts 11:30. *Returns with Paul to Antioch,* Acts 12:25. *Goes with Paul, to Seleucia,* Acts 13:4; *to Iconium,* Acts 13:51; 14:1–7. *Goes to Derbe,* Acts 14:20. *Is sent as a commissioner to Jerusalem,* Acts 15; Gal. 2:1–9. *Disaffected toward Paul,* Acts 15:36–39. *Is reconciled to Paul,* 1 Cor. 9:6. *Piety of* Acts 11:24. *Devotion of, to Jesus,* Acts 15:26.

m *Satan*, Matt. 4:10.
n *Heart*, Psa. 44:21.
o *Falsehood*, Job 21:34.
p *Holy Spirit, sin against*, Acts 1:2.

5
q *Death, of the wicked*, Num. 23:10.
r *Wicked, punishment of*, Psa. 73:3.
s *Miracles*, Luke 23:8.

6
t *Burial*, Acts 8:2.

12
u John 10:23; Acts 3:11.
v *Temple, Herod's*, 1 Kin. 6:17.

why hath [m]Sā′tan filled thine [n]heart to [o]lie to the [p]Holy Ghost,[G] and to [d,e]keep back *part* of the price of the [b,c]land?

4 [l]Whiles it remained, was it not thine own? and after it was sold, was it not in thine own power? why hast thou conceived this thing in thine heart? thou hast not [o]lied unto men, but unto God.[T]

5 And Ăn-a-nī′as hearing these words fell down, and [q,r,s]gave up the ghost:[G] and great fear came on all them that heard these things.

6 And the young men arose, wound[G] him up, and carried *him* out, and [t]buried *him*.

7 And it was about the space of three hours after, when his [a,f]wife, not knowing what was done, came in.

8 And [k]Pē′tẽr answered unto her, Tell me whether ye sold the land for so much? And she said, [o]Yea, for so much.

9 Then [k]Pē′tẽr [l]said unto her, How is it that ye have agreed together to tempt[G] the [p]Spirit of the Lord? behold, the feet of them which have [t]buried thy husband *are* at the door, and shall carry thee out.[T]

10 Then fell she down straightway[G] at his feet, and [q,r,s]yielded up the ghost:[G] and the young men came in, and found her dead, and, carrying *her* forth, [t]buried *her* by her husband.[S]

11 And great fear came upon all the church, and upon as many as heard these things.

12 ¶ And by the hands of the [j]apostles were many [s]signs and wonders wrought[G] among the people; (and they were all with one accord in [u,v]Sŏl′o-mon's porch.

13 And of the rest durst[G] no man join himself to them: but the people magnified them.

14 And [w,x]believers were the more [y]added to the Lord, multitudes both of men and women.)

15 Insomuch[S] that [w]they brought forth the sick into the streets, and laid *them* on beds and couches, that at the least the shadow of [k]Pē′tẽr passing by might overshadow some of them.

16 There came also a multitude *out* of the cities round about unto [z]Jē-ru̦′sȧ-lĕm, bringing sick folks,[S] and them which were vexed[G] with [a]unclean spirits: and they were [b,c]healed every one.[S]

17 ¶ [d]Then the [e]high priest rose up, and all they that were with him, (which is the sect of the [f]Săd′du-çeeș,[G]) and were filled with [1,g]indignation,[G]

18 And [d]laid their hands on the [h]apostles, and [i]put [j]them in the common [k]prison.

19 But the [l]angel of the Lord by night [m]opened the prison doors, and brought them forth, and said,[S]

20[S] Go, [n]stand and [o]speak in the [p]temple to the people all the [q,r]words of this life.

21 And when they heard *that*, [h,s]they [t,u]entered into the [p]temple early in the morning, and [o]taught. But the [v]high priest came, and they that were with him, and called the [w]council[G] together, and all the [x]senate of the children of Ĭș′ra-el, and sent to the prison to have them brought.

22 But when the officers came, and found them not in the [k]prison, they returned, and told,

23 Saying, The prison truly found we shut with all safety, and the keepers standing without[G] before the doors: but when we had opened, we found no man within.[S]

24 Now when the [v]high priest and the captain of the [p]temple and the chief priests heard these

14
w *Faith in Christ, exemplified*, John 6:69.
x *Religious Revivals*, Hab. 3:2.
y *Church, increase of*, Matt. 16:18.

16
z *Jerusalem*, Judg. 19:10.

a *Demons*, Matt. 4:24.
b *Healing*, Acts 4:22.
c *Miracles, of the disciples*, Luke 23:8.

17
d *Intolerance, religious*, Num. 11:28.
e *High Priest*, Lev. 21:10.
f *Sadducees*, Matt. 22:23.
g *Jealousy*, Psa. 78:58.
1 R. V. jealousy,

18
h *Apostles*, Luke 6:13.
i *Arrest*, Matt. 26:50.
j *Minister, instances of persecution of*, Rom. 15:16.
k *Prison*, Gen. 39:20.

19
l *Angel, functions of*, Heb. 1:13.
m *Miracles*, Luke 23:8.

20
n *Minister, duties of*, Rom. 15:16.
o *Instruction, in religion*, Prov. 23:23.
p *Temple, Herod's*, 1 Kin. 6:17.
q *Gospel*, Mark 13:10.
r *Doctrines of Jesus*, John 7:16.

21
s *Minister, faithful*, Rom. 15:16.
t *Zeal*, 2 Cor. 7:11.
u *Courage, instances of*, Deut. 31:7.
v *High Priest*, Lev 21:10.
w *Court*, Ex. 18:26.
x *Senate*, Num. 11:16.

things, they doubted of them whereunto this would grow.

25 Then came one and told them, saying, Behold, the [h,j]men whom ye put in [k]prison are standing in the [p]temple, and [o]teaching the people.

26 Then went the captain with the officers, and brought them without violence[G]: for they feared the [y]people, lest they should have been stoned.

27 And when they had brought them, they set *them* before the [w]council: and the [v]high priest asked them,

28 Saying, [z]Did we not straitly[G] command you that ye should not teach in this [a]name? and, behold, ye have filled [b]Jē-ru̦'sā-lĕm with your [2,c]doctrine, and intend to bring this man's blood upon us.

29 Then [d]Pē'tēr and the *other* apostles answered and [e,f,g]said, We ought to obey [h,i]God rather than men.[S]

30 The[S] God[T] of our fathers [j]raised up Jē'şus, [k]whom ye [l]slew and hanged on a tree.[Q]

31 Him hath God [m]exalted with his right hand *to be* a [n,o]Prince and a [n,p]Saviour, for [q]to give [r]repentance to Is̩'ra-el, and [q,s]forgiveness of [t]sins.[S] [T]

32 And [u,v]we are his [w]witnesses of these things; and *so is* also the [x]Holy Ghost[G], whom God hath given to them that [h,i]obey him.[T]

33 ¶ When they heard *that*, they were cut *to the heart*, and [3,y,z]took counsel to slay them.

34 Then stood there up one in the [a]council, a [b]Phăr'ĭ-see, named [c]Gā-mā'lĭ-el, a [d]doctor[G] of the law, had in reputation among all the people, and commanded to put the [e]apostles forth a little space[G];

35 And [f]said unto them, Ye men of Is̩'ra-el, take heed to yourselves what ye intend to do as touching these men.

36 For before these days rose up [g]Theū'das, [h]boasting himself to be somebody; to whom a number of men, about four hundred, joined themselves: who was [i]slain; and all, as many as obeyed him, were scattered, and brought to nought[G].

37 After this man rose up Jū'das of [j]Găl'ĭ-lee in the days of the taxing, and drew away much people after him: he also perished; and all, *even* as many as obeyed him, were dispersed.

38 And now I [f]say unto you, Refrain from these men, and let them alone: for if this counsel[G] or this work be of men, it will come to nought[G]:[S]

39 But if it be of [k]God, ye cannot overthrow it; lest haply[G] ye be found even to fight against God.

40 And to him they agreed: and when they had called the [e]apostles, and [l,m]beaten *them*, they commanded that [n]they should not speak in the [o]name of Jē'şus, and let them go.

41 And they departed from the presence of the [a]council, [p,q]rejoicing that they were counted worthy to [r]suffer [m,s]shame for [4]his [o]name.

42 And daily in the [t]temple, and [5,u]in every house, they [v]ceased not to [w]teach and [x]preach Jē'şus [6,y]Chrīst.

## CHAPTER 6

*For the care of the poor, seven deacons are chosen. 7 The number of disciples greatly multiplied. 8 Stephen works miracles; 11 is falsely accused of blasphemy; 12 and brought before the council.*

AND in those days, when the number of the [a]disciples was multiplied, there arose a murmuring of the [1]Grē'çianş[G] against the [b]Hē'brewş, because their [c]widows were neglected in the daily ministration[G].

2 Then the [d]twelve called the

26
y *Public Opinion*, John 12:42.

28
z *Intolerance*, Num. 11:28.

a *Name of Jesus*, John 14:13.
b *Jerusalem*, Judg. 19:10.
c *Doctrines of Jesus*, John 7:16.
2 R. V. teaching,

29
d *Peter*, Mark 5:37.
e *Defense*, Acts 19:33.
f *Conscience, faithful*, Acts 23:1.
g *Courage*, Deut. 31:7.
h *Obedience*, Heb. 5:8.
i *Duty, of man to God*, Eccl. 12:13.

30
j *Resurrection, of Jesus*, 1 Cor. 15:12.
k *Reproof, faithfulness in*, Prov. 17:10.
l *Jesus, death of*, Matt. 1:21.

31
m *Jesus, exaltation of*, Matt. 1:21.
n *Jesus, names of*, Matt. 1:21.
o *Jesus, king*, Matt. 1:21.
p *Jesus, savior*, Matt. 1:21.
q *Jesus, mission of*, Matt. 1:21.
r *Repentance*, Mark 1:4.
s *Jesus, power of, to forgive sins*, Matt. 1:21.
t *Sin, forgiveness of*, Rom. 5:12.

32
u *Apostles*, Luke 6:13.
v *Minister, called witness*, Rom. 15:16.
w *Witnessing for Christ*, Luke 24:48.
x *Holy Spirit*, Acts 1:2.

33
y *Revenge*, Ex. 25:15.
z *Malice*, Eph. 4:31.
3 R. V. were minded

34
a *Court*, Ex. 18:26.
b *Pharisees*, Matt. 15:12.
c Acts 22:3.
d *Doctor*, Luke 2:46.
e *Apostles*, Luke 6:13.

35
f *Tact*, Prov. 15:1.

36
g *Citizens, wicked and treasonable*, Luke 15:15.
h *Presumption, instances of*, Psa. 19:13.
i *Punishment, death penalty*, Lev. 26:41.

37
j *Galilee*, Mark 6:21.

39
k *God, providence of, overruling*, Gen. 2:2.

40
l *Beating*, Ex. 5:14.
m *Persecution, of the righteous*, John 15:20.
n *Intolerance*, Num. 11:28.
o *Name of Jesus*, John 14:13.

41
p *Joy, under adversity*, Psa. 5:11.
q *Resignation, exemplified*, Job 5:17.
r *Suffering for Christ*, Phil. 1:29.
s *Adversity, resignation in, exemplified*, Psa. 10:6.
4 R. V. the Name.

42
t *Temple, Herod's*, 1 Kin. 6:17.
u *Worship, in private homes*, Gen. 22:5.
v *Diligence*, Rom. 12:8.
w *Instruction, in religion*, Prov. 23:23.
x *Preaching*, Matt. 9:35.
y *Jesus, Messiah*, Matt. 1:21.
5 R. V. at home,
6 R. V. as the Christ.

1
a *Disciples*, Matt. 9:14.
b *Hebrew*, Gen. 40:15.
c *Widow*, 2 Sam. 14:5.
1 R. V. Grecian Jews

2
d *Apostles*, Luke 6:13.

[e]multitude of the [a]disciples *unto*
*them*, and said, [f]It is not reason[G]
that we should leave the [g,h,i]word
of God, and serve [j]tables.
3 Wherefore, [e]brethren, look ye
out among you [k]seven men of
honest [l]report, full of the [2,m]Holy
Ghost[G] and [n]wisdom, whom we
may appoint [o]over this business.
4 But we will [p,q]give ourselves continually to [*,r]prayer,
and to the [g,h]ministry of the
[i]word.
5 And the saying pleased the
whole multitude: and they chose

*e Church, government of,* Matt. 16:18.
*f Minister, duties of,* Rom. 15:16.
*g Instruction, in religion,* Prov. 23:23.
*h Preaching,* Matt. 9:35. *i Doctrines of Jesus,* John 7:16. *j Table, figurative,* Judg. 1:7. **3** *k Seven,* Gen. 7:2. *l Name,* Prov. 22:1. *m Holy Spirit,* Acts 1:2. 2 R. V. Spirit

*n Wisdom, spiritual,* Prov. 2:2.
*o Deacon,* 1 Tim. 3:8.
**4**
*p Diligence,* Rom. 12:8.
*q Zeal,* 2 Cor. 7:11.
*r Prayerfulness, exemplified by the apostles,* 1 Tim. 5:5.

---

*** PRAYER,** Psa. 17:1, 6; 22:1, 2, 19; 28:1, 2; 35:22; 55:1, 2, 16, 17; 57:2; 61:1, 2; 70:5; 102:1, 2, 130:1, 2; 141:1, 2; 142:1, 2.

*Daily, in the morning,* Psa. 5:3; 88:13. *Morning and evening,* Psa. 92:2. *Thrice daily,* Dan. 6:10. *In the night,* Psa. 119:55, 62.' *All night,* Luke 6:12. *Without ceasing,* 1 Thess. 5:17.

*Private, enjoined,* Matt. 6:6.

*Lord's Prayer,* Matt. 6:9–13; Luke 11:2–4.

*Weeping in,* Ezra 10:1. *In loud voice, satirized by Elijah,* 1 Kin. 18:27. *Of scribes, long,* Mark 12:40; Luke 20:47. *Hypocritical, forbidden,* Matt. 6:5. *Should be discreet,* Eccl. 5:2. *Vain repetitions of, to be avoided,* Matt. 6:7. *Test of, proposed by Elijah,* 1 Kin. 18:24–39.

*Power of,* Mark 9:28, 29; Jas. 5:16–18. *Accompanied by works,* Neh. 4:9. *Kept in divine remembrance,* Rev. 5:8; 8:3, 4.

*Of the righteous, acceptable,* Prov. 15:8, 29. *Spirit of, from God,* Zech. 12:10. *Divine help in,* Rom. 8:26.

*Public, should edify,* 1 Cor. 14:14, 15. *Perseverance in,* Rom. 12:12; Eph. 6:18; see IMPORTUNITY IN, below. *Evils averted by,* Jer. 26:19.

*Disbelief in,* Job 21:15.

**Penitential:** *Of David,* Psa. 51:1–17. *Of the publican,* Luke 18:13. See CONFESSION IN, below, and footnote, SIN, *Confession of,* Rom. 5:12.

**Submission in:** *Exemplified, by Job,* Job 1:20, 21; *by Jesus,* Matt. 26:39; Mark 14:36; Luke 22:42.

**Postures in:** *Bowing,* Gen. 24:26, 48, 52; Ex. 4:31; 34:8, 9; 2 Chr. 29:29. *Kneeling,* 1 Kin. 8:54; 2 Chr. 6:13; Ezra 9:5; Psa. 95:6; Dan. 6:10; Luke 22:41; Acts 20:36; 21:5. *Spreading forth the hands,* 1 Kin. 8:22; 2 Chr. 6:12, 13; Ezra 9:5; Isa. 1:15; Lam. 3:41; 1 Tim. 2:8. *Standing,* Luke 18:11, 13.

**Family:** *By Abraham,* Gen. 12:7, 8; 13:4, 18. *By Jacob,* Gen. 35:3, 7.

**Social,** Matt. 18:19; Acts 1:13, 14; 16:16, 25; 20:36; 21:5. *Held in private houses,* Acts 1:13, 14; 12:12.

**Enjoined,** 1 Chr. 16:11, 35; Psa. 105:3, 4; Isa. 55:6; Lam. 3:41; Luke 18:1; Eph. 1:18; Phil. 4:6; Col. 4:2; 1 Thess. 5:17, 18; 1 Tim. 2:8; Heb. 4:16.

**Exemplified:** *By Eliezer,* Gen. 24:12. *By Jacob,* Gen. 32:9–12. *By Gideon,* Judg. 6:22, 36, 39. *By Hannah,* 1 Sam. 1:10, 13. *By David,* 2 Sam. 7:18–29. *By Solomon, at the dedication of the temple,* 1 Kin. 8:23–53; 2 Chr. 6:14–42. *By Hezekiah,* 2 Kin. 20:2. *By Isaiah,* 2 Kin. 20:11. *By Manasseh,* 2 Chr. 33:18, 19. *By Ezra,* Ezra 9:5–15. *By Nehemiah,* Neh. 2:4. *By Jeremiah,* Jer. 32:16–25. *By Daniel,* Dan. 9:3–19. *By Jonah,* Jonah 2:1–9. *By Habakkuk,* Hab. 1:2. *By Anna,* Luke 2:37. *By Jesus,* Matt. 14:23; 26:36, 39; Mark 1:35; 6:46; Luke 5:16; 6:12; 9:18, 28, 29. *By Paul,* Acts 9:11. *By Peter,* Acts 9:40; 10:9. *By Cornelius,* Acts 10:30.

**In adversity:** *By Jacob,* Gen. 43:14. *By Moses,* Ex. 32:32. *By the Israelites,* Num. 20:16; Deut. 26:7; Judg. 3:9. *By David,* 2 Sam. 22:7. *By Hezekiah,* 2 Kin. 19:16, 19. *By Jehoshaphat,* 2 Chr. 20:4–13. *By Manasseh,* 2 Chr. 33:12, 13. *By the psalmist,* Psa. 5:1–12; 7:1, 2, 6, 7; 13:1–4; 22:1–21; 25:2, 16–19, 22; 27:11, 12; 28:1; 31:1–4, 9, 14–18; 35:1–28; 38:1–22; 43:1–5; 44:4, 23–26; 54:1–3; 55:1–17; 56:1–13; 57:1, 2; 59:1–17; 64:1, 2; 69:1–36; 70:1–5; 71:1–24; 74:1–23; 79:1–13; 94:1–23; 102; 108:6, 12; 109:1, 2, 21, 26–28; 120:2; 140:1–13; 142:1, 2, 5–7; 143:1–12. *By Jeremiah,* Jer. 15:15. *By Jonah,* Jonah 2:1–9. *By Stephen,* Acts 7:59, 60. *By Paul and Silas,* Acts 16:25.

**Intercessory,** Gen. 20:7; Jer. 27:18; 29:7; Matt. 5:44; Eph. 6:18, 19; 1 Tim. 2:1; Heb. 13:20, 21; Jas. 5:14–16. *Priestly,* Ex. 28:12, 29, 30, 38; Lev. 10:17. *For spiritual blessing,* Num. 6:23–26; 1 Sam. 12:23; Job 1:5; 42:8–10. *To avert judgments,* Gen. 20:7; Ex. 32:9–14; Num. 14:11–21; 16:45–50; Deut. 9:18–20, 25–29; Isa. 65:8. *For deliverance from enemies,* 1 Sam. 7:5–9; Isa. 37:4. *For healing disease,* Jas. 5:14–16.

*For the obdurate, unavailing,* Jer. 7:16; 11:14; 14:11.

*Of Moses for Israel,* Ex. 32:11–14, 31, 32; 34:9; Num. 14:19; 21:7; Deut. 9:18, 20, 25–29. *Of Joshua for Israel,* Josh. 7:6, 7. *Of Boaz for Ruth,* Ruth 2:12. *Of Eli for Hannah,* 1 Sam. 1:17. *Of Samuel for Israel,* 1 Sam. 7:9; 12:23. *Of David, for Israel,* 2 Sam. 24:17; 1 Chr. 29:18; *for Solomon,* 1 Chr. 29:19. *Of Solomon,* 1 Kin. 8:31–53; 2 Chr. 6:22–42. *Of Hezekiah for transgressors,* 2 Chr. 30:18, 19. *Of Job for his three friends,* Job 42:8–10. *Of the psalmist for the righteous,* Psa. 7:9; 28:9; 36:10; 80:14, 15. *Of Daniel for Israel,* Dan. 9:3–19. *Of Jesus for his murderers,* Luke 23:34. *Of Stephen for his murderers,* Acts 7:60. *Of Peter and John for Samaritan believers,* Acts 8:15. *Of the recipients of bounty for Corinthian donors,* 2 Cor. 9:14.

*Of Paul, for unbelieving Jews,* Rom. 10:1; *for Roman Christians,* Rom. 1:9; *for Ephesian Christians,* Eph. 1:15–19; 3:14–19; *for Philippian Christians,* Phil. 1:3–5, 9; *for Colossian Christians,* Col. 1:3, 9; *for Thessalonian Christians,* 1 Thess. 1:2; 3:10, 12, 13; 5:23; 2 Thess. 1:11, 12; 2:16, 17; 3:5, 16; *for Onesiphorus,* 2 Tim. 1:16, 18; *for Philemon,* Philemon 4. *Of Philemon for Paul,* Philemon 22.

See footnote, MEDIATION, Gal. 3:19.

SOLICITED, Num. 21:7; Rom. 15:30–32; 2 Cor. 1:11; Eph. 6:19; Col. 4:3; 1 Thess. 5:25; 2 Thess. 3:1; Heb. 13:18. See footnote, INTERCESSION, *Solicited,* Jer. 27:18.

**Importunity in,** Psa. 86:3, 6; 88:1, 2, 9, 13; 102; 119:145–147; Hos. 12:4; Luke 11:5–8; 18:1–7.

INSTANCES OF IMPORTUNITY IN: *Abraham,* Gen. 18:23–32. *Jacob,* Gen. 32:24–30. *Moses,* Ex. 32:32; 33:12–16; 34:9; Deut. 9:18, 25. *Gideon,* Judg. 6:36–40. *Samson,* Judg. 16:28. *Hannah,* 1 Sam. 1:10, 11. *Elijah,* 1 Kin. 18:24–44; Jas. 5:17, 18. *Hezekiah,* 2 Kin. 19:15–19; Isa. 38:2, 3. *Asa,* 2 Chr. 14:11. *Ezra,* Ezra 9:5. *Nehemiah,* Neh. 1:4–11; 9:32. *Isaiah,* Isa. 64:12. *Daniel,* Dan. 9:3, 17–19. *Mariners,* Jonah 1:14. *Habakkuk,* Hab. 1:2. *Jesus,* Matt. 26:39, 42; Mark 14:36, 39; Luke 22:42–44; Heb. 5:7. *Paul,* 2 Cor. 12:8.

**Confession in,** Lev. 26:40; Ezra 10:1; Luke 15:21; 18:13. *Enjoined,* Lev. 5:5; Num. 5:6, 7; Jer. 3:13, 25. *A condition of forgiveness,* 1 Kin. 8:47, 49, 50; Prov. 28:13; 1 John 1:9.

INSTANCES OF, Judg. 10:10, 15; 1 Sam. 12:10; Neh. 9:2, 3, 33–35; Psa. 31:10; 32:5; 38:4, 18; 40:11, 12; 41:4; 51:2–5; 69:5; 106:6; 119:176; 130:3. *Moses for Israel,* Ex. 32:31, 32; 34:9. *Ezra for Judah,* Ezra 9:6–15. *Nehemiah for Judah,* Neh. 1:4–11. *Isaiah for Judah,* Isa. 14:20, 21; 59:12–15; 64:5–7. *Jeremiah for Judah,* Jer. 14:7, 20; Lam. 1:18, 20; 3:42. *Daniel for Judah,* Dan. 9:5–15.

**Pleas in,** Ex. 33:13; Num. 14:13–19; 16:22; Deut. 3:24, 25; 9:26–29; Josh. 7:7–9; 2 Sam. 7:25–29; 2 Kin. 19:15–19; Psa. 9:19, 20; 74:10, 11, 18, 20–23; 83:1, 2, 18; Isa. 37:15–20; Joel 2:17.

*God's mercy,* Psa. 69:13, 16; 109:21, 26, 27; 115:1; 119:124. *God's providences,* Psa. 4:1; 27:9. *God's promises,* Gen. 32:9–12; Ex. 32:13; 1 Kin. 8:25, 26, 59, 60; Neh. 1:8, 9; Psa. 89:49–51; 119:43, 49, 116; Jer. 14:21. *Personal consecration,* Psa. 119:94. *Personal righteousness,* Psa. 86:1, 2, 4, 5, 17; 119:38, 145, 173–176; Jer. 18:20.

**Tokens of answer to, asked for:** *By Abraham's servant,* Gen. 24:14, 42–44. *By Gideon,* Judg. 6:36–40.

**Rebuked:** *Of Moses, at the Red Sea,* Ex. 14:15; *when he prayed to see Canaan,* Deut. 3:23–27. *Of Joshua,* Josh. 7:10.

**Imprecatory,** Num. 16:15; Josh. 8:33, 34; Judg. 16:28; Neh. 4:4, 5; 5:13; Job 27:7; Psa. 5:10; 9:20; 10:2, 15; 28:4; 31:17, 18; 35:4, 8, 26; 40:14, 15; 54:5; 55:9, 15; 56:7; 58:7; 59:5, 11, 15; 68:1, 2; 69:23, 24, 27, 28; 70:2, 3; 71:13; 79:10, 12; 83:13–17; 94:2; 109:7, 9–20, 28, 29; 119:78, 84; 129:5; 140:9, 10; 143:12; 144:6; Jer. 11:20; 12:3; 15:15; 17:18; 18:21–23; 20:12; Lam. 1:22; Gal. 1:8, 9.

**Answer to:** PROMISED, 2 Chr. 7:14; Job 22:27; 33:26; Psa. 10:17; 145:18, 19; Prov. 10:24; 15:8, 29; 16:1; Isa. 58:9; 65:24; Jer. 33:3; Matt. 7:7–11; 18:19, 20; 21:22; Mark 11:24; Luke 11:9–13; 18:1–8; John 14:13, 14; 15:7, 16; 16:23, 24, 26; Rom. 10:12, 13; Heb. 4:16; Jas. 4:8; 5:16; 1 John 3:22; 5:14. *To those in adversity,* Ex. 6:5, 6 (with Acts 7:34); Psa. 32:6; 34:15, 17; 37:4, 5; 50:15; 55:16, 17; 65:2, 5; 69:32, 33; 86:7; 91:15; 102:17–20; Isa. 19:20; 30:19; Joel 2:18, 19, 32; Zech. 10:1, 6; 13:9. *To the meek,* Mark 11:25. *To the penitent,* Deut. 4:30, 31; 2 Chr. 7:13–15.

DELAYED, Psa. 22:1, 2; Jer. 42:2–7; Luke 18:7.

WITHHELD: *Of Balaam,* Deut. 23:5; Josh. 24:10. *Of Job,* Job 30:20. *Of the Israelites, when attacked by the Amorites,*

5
*s Faith in Christ,* John 6:69.
*t Philip,* Acts 8:5.
6
*u Deacon, ordained,* 1 Tim. 3:8.
*v Ordination, of ministers,* Ex. 29:1.
*w Hand, imposition of,* Ezra 10:19.
7
*x Religious Revivals,* Hab. 3:2.
*y Church, growth of,* Matt. 16:18.
*z Disciples,* Matt. 9:14.
*a Jerusalem,* Judg. 19:10.
*b Priest,* Lev. 1:5.
*c Disciples, priests become,* Matt. 9:14.
*d Faith in Christ,* John 6:69.
8
*e Righteous, described,* Psa. 64:10.
*f Minister, character and qualifications of,* Rom. 15:16.
*g Spiritual Power,* Luke 24:49.
*h Miracles,* Luke 23:8.
3 R. V. grace

†Stē′phen, a man full of [s]faith
and of the [m]Holy [2]Ghost,[G] and
[t]Phĭl′ĭp, and Prŏch′o-rŭs, and Nī-
cā′nor, and Tī′mon, and Pär′me-
năs, and Nĭc′o-lăs a proselyte[G] of
Ăn′tĭ-ŏch:
6 [u]Whom they set before the
[d]apostles: and when they had
prayed, they [v]laid *their* [w]hands
on them.
7 And the [i]word of God increased; and [x, y]the number of
the [z]disciples multiplied in [a]Jē-
ru̦′sā-lĕm greatly; and a great
company of the [b]priests were
[c]obedient to the [d]faith.
8 ¶ And †Stē′phen, [e,f]full of
[3]faith and [g]power, did great
wonders and [h]miracles among
the people.
9 Then there arose certain of
the [i]synagogue, which is called
*the synagogue* of the [j]Lĭb′ĕr-
tīneș, and [k]Çȳ-rē′nĭ-anș, and
[l]Ăl-ĕx-ăn′drĭ-anș, and of them of
[m]Çĭ-lĭ′çiȧ and of [n]Ā′șiȧ, disputing with †Stē′phen.

10 And they were not able to
resist the [o]wisdom and the spirit
by which †he spake.
11 Then they suborned[G] [p]men,
which [q, r, s]said, We have heard
him speak [t]blasphemous words
against [u]Mō′șeș, and *against*
God.
12 And they stirred up the people, and the [v]elders, and the
[w]scribes, and [x]came upon *him*,
and [y]caught him, and brought
*him* to the [z]council,[G]
13 And set up [a]false witnesses,
which said, This man ceaseth not to speak [b]blasphemous[G]
words against [c]this holy place,
and the [d]law:[Q]
14 For we have heard him say,
that this Jē′șus of [e]Năz′a-rĕth
shall destroy this place, and shall
change the [f]customs which Mō′-
șeș delivered us.
15 And all that sat in the [g]coun-
cil, looking stedfastly on him,
saw his face [h]as it had been the
face of an [i]angel.

10
*o Wisdom, spiritual,* Prov. 2:2.
11
*p Witness,* Num. 35:30.
*q Falsehood,* Job 21:34.
*r False Accusation,* 2 Tim. 3:3.
*s Perjury,* 1 Tim. 1:10.
*t Blasphemy, false accusations of,* 2 Sam. 12:14.
*u Law, of Moses,* Deut. 33:2.
12
*v Senate,* Num. 11:16.
*w Scribe,* 1 Kin. 4:3.
*x Persecution, of the righteous,* John 15:20.
*y Arrest,* Matt. 26:50.
*z Court,* Ex. 18:26.
13
*a False Witness,* Matt. 19:18.
*b Blasphemy, false accusations of,* 2 Sam. 12:14.
*c Temple, Herod's,* 1 Kin. 6:17.
*d Law, of Moses,* Deut. 33:2.

**9** *i Synagogue,* Matt. 12:9. *j Servant, emancipated,* Jer. 2:14. *k Cyrene,* Acts 2:10. *l Alexandria,* Acts 27:6. *m Cilicia,* Gal. 1:21. *n Asia,* Acts 2:9.

**14** *e Nazareth,* John 1:46. *f Law, temporary,* Deut. 33:2. **15** *g Court,* Ex. 18:26. *h Transfiguration,* Matt. 17:2. *i Angel,* Heb. 1:13.

Deut. 1:45. *The prayer of Jesus, Let this cup pass,* Matt. 26: 39, 42, 44, with vs. 45–75 and chapter 27.

Exceeds Petition: *Solomon asked wisdom; the answer included wisdom, riches, honor, and long life,* 1 Kin. 3:7–14; 2 Chr. 1:7–12.

Different from the Request: *Moses asked to see God's face; God revealed his goodness,* Ex. 33:18–20. *Moses asked to be permitted to cross the Jordan; the answer was permission to view the land of promise,* Deut. 3:23–27. *The Israelites lusted for the fleshpots of Egypt; the answer gave them flesh, but also leanness of soul,* Psa. 106:14, 15. *Martha and Mary asked Jesus to come and heal their brother Lazarus; Jesus delayed, but raised Lazarus from the dead,* John 11:1–44. *Paul asked that the thorn in the flesh be removed; the answer was a promise of grace to endure it,* 2 Cor. 12:8, 9.

**Answered,** Job 34:28; Psa. 3:4; 6:8, 9; 18:6; 22:4, 5, 24; 28:6; 30:2; 31:22; 34:4–6; 40:1; 66:19, 20; 81:7; 99:6–8; 106: 44; 107:6, 13; 116:1–8; 118:5, 21; 119:26; 120:1; 138:3; Lam. 3:57, 58; Acts 4:31.

Instances of Answered: *Cain,* Gen. 4:13–15. *Abraham, for a son,* Gen. 15; 21:2; *entreating for Sodom,* Gen. 18: 23–33; *for Ishmael,* Gen. 17:20; *for Abimelech,* Gen. 20:17. *Abraham's servant, for guidance,* Gen. 24:12–52. *Isaac, for children,* Gen. 25:21. *Rebecca, concerning her pains in pregnancy,* Gen. 25:22, 23. *Jacob, for deliverance from Esau,* Gen. 32:9–32; 33:1–17; Hos. 12:4. *Moses, for help, at the Red Sea,* Ex. 14:15, 16; *at the waters of Marah,* Ex. 15:25; *at Horeb,* Ex. 17:4–6; *in the battle with the Amalekites,* Ex. 17:8–14; *concerning the murmuring of the Israelites for flesh,* Num. 11: 11–35; *in behalf of Miriam's restoration from leprosy,* Num. 12: 13–15. *Moses, Aaron, and Samuel,* Psa. 99:6.

Israelites: *For deliverance, from bondage,* Ex. 2:23–25; 3: 7–10; Acts 7:34; *from Pharaoh's army,* Ex. 14:10–30; *from the king of Mesopotamia,* Judg. 3:9; *from Eglon,* Judg. 3:15; *from Sisera,* Judg. 4:2, 3, 15, 16; 1 Sam. 12:9–11; *from Ammon,* Judg. 10:6–18; 11:1–33; *for God's favor under the reproofs of Azariah,* 2 Chr. 15:1–15; *from the Canaanites,* Neh. 9:27.

*Gideon, asking the token of dew,* Judg. 6:36–40. *Manoah, asking about Samson,* Judg. 13:8, 9. *Samson, asking for strength,* Judg. 16:28–30. *Hannah, asking for a child,* 1 Sam. 1:10–17, 19, 20. *David, asking whether Keilah would be delivered into his hands,* 1 Sam. 23:10–12; *and Ziklag,* 1 Sam. 30:8; *whether he should go into Judah after Saul's death,* 2 Sam. 2:1; *whether he should go against the Philistines,* 2 Sam. 5:19–25. *David, in adversity,* Psa. 118:5; 138:3. *Solomon, asking for wisdom,* 1 Kin. 3:9–13; 9:2, 3. *Elijah, raising the widow's son,* 1 Kin. 17:22; *asking for fire on his sacrifice,* 1 Kin. 18:36–38; *asking for rain,* 1 Kin. 17:1; 18:1, 42–45; Jas. 5:17, 18. *Elisha, leading the Syrian army,* 2 Kin. 6:17–20. *Jabez, asking for prosperity,* 1 Chr. 4:10. *Abijah, for victory over Jeroboam,* 2 Chr. 13:14–18. *Asa, for victory over Zerah,* 2 Chr. 14: 11–15. *The people of Judah,* 2 Chr. 15:15. *Jehoshaphat, for victory, over the Syrians,* 2 Chr. 18:31; *over the Ammonites and Moabites,* 2 Chr. 20:6–27. *Jehoahaz, for victory over Hazael,* 2 Kin. 13:4. *Priests and Levites, when blessing the people,* 2 Chr. 30:27. *Hezekiah and Isaiah, for deliverance from Sennacherib,* 2 Kin. 19:14–20; 2 Chr. 32:20–23; *to save Hezekiah's life,* 2 Kin. 20:1–7, 11; 2 Chr. 32:24. *Manasseh, for deliverance from the king of Babylon,* 2 Chr. 33:13, 19. *Reubenites, for deliverance from the Hagarites,* 1 Chr. 5:20. *The Jews returning from the captivity,* Ezra 8:21, 23. *Ezekiel, to have the baking of his bread of affliction changed,* Ezek. 4:12–15. *Daniel, for the interpretation of Nebuchadnezzar's dream,* Dan. 2:19–23; *interceding for the people,* Dan. 9:20–23; *in a vision,* Dan. 10:12. *Jonah, for deliverance,* Jonah 2:1, 2, 7. *Zacharias, for a son,* Luke 1:13. *Peter, asking that Tabitha be restored,* Acts 9:40. *Cornelius,* Acts 10:31. *The disciples, for Peter,* Acts 12:5–17.

**Of the wicked not heard,** Deut. 1:45; 2 Sam. 22:42; Job 35:12, 13; Psa. 18:41; 66:18; Prov. 1:24–28; 15:8, 29; 21:13, 27; 28:9; Isa. 1:15; 45:19; 59:2; Jer. 11:11; 14:12; 15:1; 18:17; Lam. 3:8, 44; Ezek. 8:18; 20:3, 31; Hos. 5:6; Mic. 3:4; Zech. 7:12, 13; Mal. 2:11–13; John 9:31; Jas. 1:6, 7; 4:3.

**Of Jesus.** See footnote, Prayers of Jesus, Luke 5:16.

**In behalf of Nations.** See footnote, Nations, *Prayer for,* Isa. 2:4.

† **STEPHEN,** a Christian martyr. *One of the seven deacons appointed to oversee the daily ministration,* Acts 6:3, 5, 6. *Faith and power of,* Acts 6:5, 8–10. *False charges against,* Acts 6: 11–15. *Defense of,* Acts 7. *Stoned,* Acts 7:54–60; 8:1; 22: 20. *Burial of,* Acts 8:2. *Gentle and forgiving spirit of,* Acts 7:59, 60.

## CHAPTER 7

*Stephen's defense. 51 He accuses the Jews of slaying the prophets and the Just One; 54 at which they are enraged. 55 His vision of the Son of man. 57 He is stoned to death.*

THEN said the [a]high priest,
Are these things so?
2 And [b]he [c]said, Men, brethren,
and fathers, hearken; The God
of glory appeared unto our father [d]Ā'brā-hăm, when he was
in [e]Měs-o-pō-tā'mĭ-â, before he
dwelt in [f]Chăr'ran,
3 And said unto [d]him, [g]Get
thee out of thy country, and
from thy kindred, and come into
the [h]land which I shall shew
thee.
4 Then [i]came [d]he out of the
land of the [j]Chăl-dæ'anș, and
dwelt in [f]Chăr'ran: and from
thence, when his [k]father was
dead, he removed him into [h]this
land, wherein ye now dwell.
5 And he gave him none inheritance in it, no, not *so much as* to
set his foot on: yet he [l]promised
that he would give [m]it to him for a
possession, and to his [n]seed after
him, when *as yet* he had no child.
6 And God spake on this wise,
[o]That his [n,p]seed should sojourn
in a strange [q]land; and that they
should [r]bring them into bondage, and entreat *them* evil four
hundred years.
7 And [o]the nation to whom they
shall be in [r]bondage will I [s]judge,
said God: and after that shall
they come forth, and serve me in
this place.
8 And he gave him the covenant of [t]circumcision: and so
[d]*Ā'brā-hăm* begat [u]Ī'șaac, and
circumcised him the eighth day;
and Ī'șaac *begat* [v]Jā'cob; and
Jā'cob *begat* the twelve patriarchs.
9 And the patriarchs, moved
with [w,x]envy, sold [y]Jō'șeph into
[q]Ē'ġȳpt: but [z,a]God was with
him,
10 And [b]delivered him out
of all his afflictions, and gave
him favour and [c]wisdom in
the sight of [d]Phā'raōh [e]king
of [f]Ē'ġȳpt; and he made him
governor over Ē'ġȳpt and all
his house.
11 Now there came a [g]dearth
over all the land of [f]Ē'ġȳpt and
[h]Chā'năan, and great affliction:
and our fathers found no sustenance.
12 But when [i]Jā'cob heard that
there was [j]corn in Ē'ġȳpt, he sent
out our fathers first.
13 And at the second *time* [k]Jō'-
șeph was made known to his
brethren; and Jō'șeph's kindred
was made known unto [d]Phā'-
raōh.
14 Then sent [k]Jō'șeph, and
called his father [i]Jā'cob to *him*,
and all his kindred, [l]threescore
and fifteen souls.
15 So [i]Jā'cob went down into
[f]Ē'ġȳpt, and [m]died, he, and our
fathers,
16 And were carried over into
[n]Sȳ'chem, and laid in the [o,p]sep-
ulchre that [q]Ā'brā-hăm bought
for a sum of [r]money of the sons
of [s]Ĕm'môr *the father* of Sȳ'-
chem.
17 But when the time of the
[t]promise drew nigh, which God
had sworn to [q]Ā'brā-hăm, the
people grew and multiplied in
[f]Ē'ġȳpt,
18 [u]Till another king arose,
which knew not [k]Jō'șeph.
19 The same [v]dealt subtilly
with our kindred, and evil entreated our fathers, so that they
[w]cast out their [1]young children,
to the end they might not
live.
20 In which time [x]Mō'șeș was
born, and was exceeding fair,
and nourished up in his father's
house three months:
21 And when he was cast out,
[y]Phā'raōh's daughter took him

1
a *High Priest*, Lev. 21:10.
2
b *Stephen*, Acts 6:9.
c *Defense*, Acts 19:33.
d *Abraham*, Gen. 17:5.
e *Mesopotamia*, Gen. 24:10.
f Or, *Haran*, Gen. 11:31.
3
g Gen. 12:1.
h *Canaan*, Gen. 37:1.
4
i *Obedience, exemplified*, Heb. 5:8.
j *Chaldea*, Ezek. 11:24.
k *Terah*, Gen. 11:24.
5
l *Covenant, of God with men*, Deut. 29:1.
m *Canaan, promised to Abraham, and his seed*, Gen. 37:1.
n *Israel, prophecies concerning*, Ex. 4:22.
6
o Gen. 15:13, 14.
p *Israel, in Egypt*, Ex. 4:22.
q *Egypt*, Gen. 41:8.
r *Oppression*, Eccl. 5:8.
7
s *God, judge*, Gen. 2:2.
8
t *Circumcision*, Gen. 17:10.
u *Isaac*, Gen. 21:3.
v *Jacob*, Gen. 27:11.
9
w *Envy*, Prov. 14:30.
x *Jealousy*, Psa. 78:58.
y *Joseph*, Gen. 33:2.
z *God dwells with the Righteous*, 1 Kin. 6:13.
a *Righteous, God is with*, Psa. 64:10.

10
b *God, providence of*, Gen. 2:2.
c *Wisdom, worldly*, Prov. 2:2.
d *Pharaoh*, Gen. 37:36.
e *Rulers*, Ex. 18:21.
f *Egypt*, Gen. 41:8.
11
g *Famine* (R.V.), 2 Kin. 8:1.
h Or, *Canaan, famine in*, Gen. 37:1.
12
i *Jacob*, Gen. 27:11.
j *Corn*, Psa. 65:13.
13
k *Joseph*, Gen. 33:2.
14
l *Israel, number of, who went into Egypt*, Ex. 4:22.
15
m *Death*, Num. 23:10.
16
n Or, *Shechem*, Josh. 20:7.
o *Burying Places*, Gen. 23:4.
p *Machpelah*, Gen. 23:9.
q *Abraham*, Gen. 17:5.
r *Money*, Jer. 32:9.
s Or, *Hamor*, Gen. 34:18.
17
t *Covenant, of God with men*, Deut. 29:1.
18
u Ex. 1:8.
19
v *Oppression*, Eccl. 5:8.
w *Infanticide*, Ex. 1:16.
1 R. V. babes.
20
x *Moses*, Ex. 2:10.
21
y *Pharaoh*, Ex. 1:11.

z *Adoption, of children*, Gen. 48:5.

22

a *Moses*, Ex. 2:10.
b *Wisdom, worldly*, Prov. 2:2.
c *Egypt*, Gen. 41:8.

23

2 R. V. well-nigh

24

d *Love, of man for man*, 1 John 4:7.
e *Rashness, instances of*, 2 Sam. 6:7.
f *Homicide, felonious*, Deut. 5:17.

25

g *God, providence of*, Gen. 2:2.

26

h *Strife*, Prov. 20:3.
i *Peace*, Jer. 29:7.
j *Fraternity*, Zech. 11:14.

29

3 R. V. became a sojourner in the land of Midian,

30

k Or, *Sinai*, Ex. 16:1.
l *Angel*, Heb. 1:13.
m *Burning Bush*, Ex. 3:2.

32

n Ex. 3:6.

33

o Ex. 3:5.
p *Reverence, for sacred places*, Lev. 19:30.
q *Shoe*, Josh. 5:15.

up, and [z]nourished him for her own son.

22 And [a]Mō′ṣeṣ was learned in all the [b]wisdom of the [c]Ė-ġy̆p′-tianṣ, and was mighty in words and in deeds.

23 And when he was [2]full forty years old, it came into his heart to visit his brethren the children of Ĭṣ′ra-el.

24 And seeing one *of them* suffer wrong, [d]he [d]defended *him*, and avenged him that was oppressed, and [e,f]smote the Ė-ġy̆p′tian:

25 For he supposed his brethren would have understood how that [g]God by his hand would deliver them: but they understood not.

26 And the next day he shewed himself unto them as they [h]strove, and would have set them at [i]one again, saying, Sirs, ye are [j]brethren; why do ye wrong one to another?

27 But he that did his neighbour wrong thrust him away, saying, Who made thee a ruler and a judge over us?

28 Wilt thou kill me, as thou diddest the Ė-ġy̆p′tian yesterday?

29 Then fled [a]Mō′ṣeṣ at this saying, and [3]was a stranger in the land of Mā′dĭ-an, where he begat two sons.

30 And when forty years were expired, there appeared to him in the wilderness of mount [k]Sī′-nȧ an [l]angel of the Lord in a flame of fire in a [m]bush.

31 When [a]Mō′ṣeṣ saw *it*, he wondered at the sight: and as he drew near to behold *it*, the voice of the Lord came unto him,

32 *Saying*, [n]I *am* the God of thy fathers, the God of Ā′brȧ-hăm, and the God of Ī′ṣaac, and the God of Jā′cob. Then Mō′ṣeṣ trembled, and durst not behold.

33 Then said the Lord to him, [o,p]Put off thy [q]shoes from thy feet: for the place where thou standest is holy ground.

34 [r]I have seen, I have seen the [s]affliction of my people which is in [c]Ē′ġy̆pt, and [t]I have heard their groaning, and am come down [g]to deliver them. And now [u]come, I will send thee into Ē′ġy̆pt.

35 This Mō′ṣeṣ whom they refused, saying, Who made thee a ruler and a judge? the same did [g]God send *to be* a ruler and a deliverer by the hand of the [l]angel which appeared to him in the [m]bush.

36 He brought them out, after that he had shewed [v,w]wonders and signs in the land of Ē′ġy̆pt, and in the [x]Red sea, and in the wilderness forty years.

37 This is that Mō′ṣeṣ, which said unto the children of Ĭṣ′ra-el, [y]A [z]prophet shall [4]the Lord your God raise up unto you of your brethren, like unto [a]me; [5]him shall ye hear.

38 This is he, that was in the [b]church in the wilderness with the [c]angel which spake to him in the mount [d]Sī′nȧ, and *with* our [e]fathers: who received the [6]lively [f,g]oracles to give unto us:

39 To whom our fathers would [h]not obey, but thrust *him* from them, and in their hearts turned back again into [i]Ē′ġy̆pt,

40 Saying unto [j]Aâr′on, [k]Make us gods to go before us: for *as for* this Mō′ṣeṣ, which brought us out of the land of Ē′ġy̆pt, we [7]wot not what is become of him.

41 And they made a [l]calf in those days, and [m]offered sacrifice unto the idol, and rejoiced in the works of their own hands.

42 Then God turned, and gave [n]them up to worship the [o]host of heaven; as it is written in the book of the prophets, [p]O ye house of Ĭṣ′ra-el, have ye offered to me slain beasts and sacrifices

34

r *God, knowledge of*, Gen. 2:2.
s *Adversity, prayer in*, Psa. 10:6.
t *Prayer, answered, instances of*, Acts 6:4.
u *Call, personal*, Phil. 3:14.

36

v *Plague, as a judgment*, Ex. 11:1.
w *Miracles*, Luke 23:8.
x *Red Sea*, Ex. 10:19.

37

y Deut. 18:15; Acts 3:22.
z *Jesus, prophet*, Matt. 1:21.

a *Moses, type of Christ*, Ex. 2:10.
4 R. V. God raise
5 R. V. *omits* him shall ye hear.

38

b *Church*, Matt. 16:18.
c *Angel*, Heb. 1:13.
d Or, *Sinai*, Ex. 16:1.
e *Jews, entrusted with oracles*, Neh. 4:2.
f *Oracle*, 1 Kin. 6:5.
g *Law, of Moses*, Deut. 33:2.
6 R. V. living

39

h *Disobedience to God*, Eph. 5:6.
i *Egypt*, Gen. 41:8.

40

j *Aaron*, Ex. 6:20.
k Ex. 32:1, 23.
7 Am. R. V. know

41

l *Calf, golden*, Mic. 6:6.
m *Idolatry*, 1 Sam. 15:23.

42

n *Reprobates, instances of*, 1 Cor. 9:27.
o *Idolatry, objects of*, 1 Sam. 15:23.
p Amos 5:25–27.

**43**
*q* Or, *Molech*, 1 Kin. 11:7.
*r* *Babylon*, Ezra 5:12.

**44**
*s* *Tabernacle*, Ex. 27:9.
*t* *Moses*, Ex. 2:10.
*u* *Pattern*, Ex. 25:40.

**45**
*v* Or, *Joshua*, Josh. 1:1.
*w* *Canaanites*, Ex. 23:28.
*x* *God, providence of*, Gen. 2:2.
*y* *David*, 1 Sam. 16:13.

**46**
*z* *Grace of God*, Rom. 4:16.

*a* *Zeal*, 2 Cor. 7:11.
*b* *Temple*, 1 Kin. 6:17.
8 R. V. habitation

**47**
*c* *Solomon*, 2 Sam. 12:24.

**48**
*d* *God, sovereign*, Gen. 2:2.
*e* *God, omnipresent*, Gen. 2:2.
*f* *Prophets*, Isa. 3:2.

**49**
*g* *Heaven, God's dwelling place*, Luke 18:22.
*h* Isa. 66:1, 2.
*i* *Throne, figurative*, 1 Kin. 2:19.
*j* *Footstool, figurative*, 1 Chr. 28:2.

**50**
*k* *God, creator*, Gen. 2:2.

**51**
*l* *Reproof, faithfulness in*, Prov. 17:10.
*m* *Self-will*, Gen. 49:6.
*n* *Wicked, described*, Psa. 73:3.
*o* *Holy Spirit*, Acts 1:2.

**52**
*p* *Persecution, of the righteous*, John 15:20.
*q* *Jesus, names of*, Matt. 1:21.
*r* *Jesus, holiness of*, Matt. 1:21.
*s* *Betrayal, of Jesus*, Matt. 26:46.
9 R. V. Righteous One;

*by the space of* forty years in the wilderness?

43 Yea, ye took up the tabernacle of [q]Mō′lŏch, and the star of your god Rĕm′phan, figures which ye made to worship them: and I will carry you away beyond [r]Băb′ȳ-lon.

44 Our fathers had the [s]tabernacle of witness in the wilderness, as he had appointed, speaking unto [t]Mō′ṣeṣ, that he should make it according to the [u]fashion that he had seen.

45 Which also our fathers that came after brought in with [v]Jē′ṣus into the possession of the [w]Ġĕn′tīleṣ, whom [x]God drave out before the face of our fathers, unto the days of [y]Dā′vid;

46 Who found [z]favour before God, and [a]desired to find a [8, b]tabernacle for the God of Jā′cob.

47 But [c]Sŏl′o-mon built him an [b]house.

48 Howbeit the [d]most High [e]dwelleth not in temples made with hands; as saith the [f]prophet,

49 [g, h]Heaven *is* [d]my [i]throne, and earth *is* my [j]footstool: what house will ye build me? saith the Lord: or what *is* the place of my rest?

50 [h]Hath not my hand [k]made all these things?

51 ¶ [l]Ye [m, n]stiffnecked and [n]uncircumcised in heart and ears, ye do always resist the [o]Holy Ghost: as your fathers *did*, so *do* ye.

52 Which of the [f]prophets have not your fathers [p]persecuted? and they have slain them which shewed before of the coming of the [9, q, r]Just One; of whom ye have been now the [s]betrayers and murderers:

53 [t]Who have received the [u]law [10]by the disposition of [v]angels, and have [w]not kept *it*.

54 ¶ When they heard these things, they were cut to the heart, and they [x]gnashed on [y]him with *their* teeth.

55 But [y]he, being [z]full of the [a]Holy Ghost, looked up stedfastly into heaven, and [b]saw the [c]glory of God, and [d]Jē′ṣus standing on the right hand of God,

56 And said, Behold, I see the heavens opened, and the [d]Son of man standing on the right hand of God.

57 Then they cried out with a loud voice, and stopped their ears, and [e, f]ran upon him with one accord,

58 And [e, f]cast *him* out of the city, and [g, h, i]stoned *him*: and the [j]witnesses laid down their clothes at a [k]young man's feet, whose name was [l]Saul.

59 And they [g]stoned [m]Stē′phen, [n, o]calling upon [11]*God*, and [p]saying, [q]Lord Jē′ṣus, receive [r]my spirit.

60 And [m]he kneeled down, and [s, t]cried with a loud voice, Lord, [u, v, w, x]lay not this sin to [y]their charge. And when he had said this, he fell [z]asleep.

## CHAPTER 8

*The disciples are scattered abroad and preach the Word. 5 Philip preaches at Samaria. 9 Simon the sorcerer is baptized. 14 Peter and John are sent to Samaria; in answer to whose prayer, and with the laying on of their hands, the Holy Spirit is given. 18 Simon offers them money for the like power. 20 Peter rebukes him. 26 Philip is sent to teach and to baptize the Ethiopian eunuch.*

AND [a]Saul was [b]consenting unto [c]his death. And at that time there was a great [d, e]persecution against the [f]church which was at [g]Jē-ru′să-lĕm; and they were all scattered abroad throughout the regions of [h]Jū-dæ′ȧ and [i]Sȧ-mā′rĭ-ȧ, except the [j]apostles.

2 And devout men carried [c]Stē′-

**54**
*x* *Anger, instances of*, Psa. 37:8.
*y* *Stephen*, Acts 6:9.

**55**
*z* *Inspiration*, Job 32:8.

*a* *Holy Spirit*, Acts 1:2.
*b* *Vision*, Acts 9:10.
*c* *God, glory of*, Gen. 2:2.
*d* *Jesus, exaltation of*, Matt. 1:21.

**57**
*e* *Intolerance*, Num. 11:28.
*f* *Persecution, of the righteous*, John 15:20.

**58**
*g* *Stoning*, 1 Sam. 30:6.
*h* *Punishment, death penalty*, Lev. 26:41.
*i* *Martyrdom*, Rev. 17:6.
*j* *Witness*, Num. 35:30.
*k* *Complicity*, Prov. 29:24.
*l* Or, *Paul*, Acts 13:9.

**59**
*m* *Stephen*, Acts 6:9.
*n* *Adversity, prayer in*, Psa. 10:6.
*o* *Death, scenes of*, Num. 23:10.
*p* *Resignation*, Job 5:17.
*q* *Jesus, worship of*, Matt. 1:21.
*r* *Man, spirit*, Job 4:7.
11 R. V. the Lord,

**60**
*s* *Prayer, intercessory*, Acts 6:4.
*t* *Intercession*, Jer. 27:18.
*u* *Forgiveness*, Matt. 18:21.

**A.D. 34**
*v* *Good for Evil*, Luke 6:27.
*w* *Love, of man for man*, 1 John 4:7.
*x* *Meekness*, Psa. 45:4.
*y* *Enemy, instances of forgiveness of*, Prov. 24:17.
*z* *Death, called sleep*, Num. 23:10.

**53** *t* *Prophets, inspired by angels*, Isa. 3:2. *u* *Law, of Moses*, Deut. 33:2. *v* *Angel, functions of*, Heb. 1:13. *w* *Disobedience to God*, Eph. 5:6. 10 R. V. as it was ordained by angels,

**1** *a* Or, *Paul*, Acts 13:9. *b* *Complicity, instances of*, Prov. 29:24. *c* *Stephen*, Acts 6:9. *d* *Persecution, of the righteous*, John 15:20. *e* *Intolerance*, Num. 11:28. *f* *Church, persecution of*, Matt. 16:18. *g* *Jerusalem*, Judg. 19:10. *h* *Judea*, Luke 5:17. *i* *Samaria*, Isa. 7:9. *j* *Apostles*, Luke 6:13.

phen *to his *burial,* and made
great lamentation over him.
3 As for [a]Saul, he [1,d,e]made
havock of the [f]church, entering
into every house, and haling men
and women committed *them* to
[k]prison.
4 Therefore they that were
scattered abroad [l]went every
where [m]preaching the [n]word.
5 ¶ Then †Phĭl′ĭp went down
to the city of [i]Să-mā′rĭ-ȧ, and
[m]preached [o]Chrīst unto them.
6 And the people with one accord gave heed unto those things
which †Phĭl′ĭp [m]spake, hearing
and seeing the [p]miracles which
he did.
7 For [q]unclean spirits, crying
with loud voice, [p]came out of
many that were possessed *with*
*them*: and many taken with [r]pal-
sies, and that were [s]lame, were
[t]healed.
8 And there was great [u]joy in
that city.
9 But there was a certain man,
called Sī′mon, which beforetime in the same city used [v]sor-
cery, and [2,w]bewitched the people of [i]Să-mā′rĭ-ȧ, [x]giving out
that himself was some great
one:
10 To whom they all gave heed,
from the least to the greatest,
saying, This man is the great
power of God.
11 And to him they had regard, because that of long time
he had [2,w]bewitched them with
[v]sorceries.
12 But when they [y]believed
†Phĭl′ĭp [m]preaching [3]the things
concerning the [z]kingdom of God,
and the [a]name of Jē′sus Chrīst,
they were [b]baptized, both men
and women.
13 Then Sī′mon himself [c]be-
lieved also: and when he was
[b]baptized, he continued with
†Phĭl′ĭp, and [4]wondered, beholding the [d]miracles and signs which
were done.
14 ¶ Now when the [e]apostles
which were at [f]Jē-ru′să-lĕm
heard that [g]Să-mā′rĭ-ȧ had received the [h]word of God, they sent
unto them [i]Pē′tēr and [j]Jŏhn:
15 Who, when they were come
down, [k]prayed for them, that they
might receive the [l]Holy Ghost:
16 (For as yet he was fallen
upon none of them: only they
were [b]baptized [5]in the [a]name of
the Lord Jē′sus.)
17 Then laid they *their* [m]hands
on them, and they received the
[l]Holy Ghost.
18 And when Sī′mon saw that
through laying on of the apostles' [m]hands the [l]Holy Ghost was
given, he offered them [n]money,
19 Saying, [o]Give me also this
power, that on whomsoever I lay
hands, he may receive the [l]Holy
Ghost.
20 But [p,q]Pē′tēr [r]said unto him,
Thy [n]money perish with thee,
because thou hast thought that
the [l]gift of God may be purchased with money.
21 [r]Thou hast neither part
nor lot in this matter: for thy
[s,t,u]heart is not right in the sight
of God.
22 [v]Repent therefore of this
thy wickedness, and [w]pray God,
if perhaps the thought of thine
heart may be [x]forgiven thee.
23 For I perceive that thou art

3
k *Prison,* Gen. 39:20.
1 R. V. laid waste the
4
l *Zeal,* 2 Cor. 7:11.
m *Preaching,* Matt. 9:35.
n *Doctrines of Jesus,* John 7:16.
5
o *Jesus, Messiah,* Matt. 1:21.
6
p *Miracles,* Luke 23:8.
7
q *Demons,* Matt. 4:24.
r *Paralysis,* Mark 2:3.
s *Lameness,* Lev. 21:18.
t *Healing,* Acts 4:22.
8
u *Joy,* Psa. 5:11.
9
v *Sorcery,* Isa. 47:9.
w *Deception,* Josh. 9:4.
x *Self-exaltation,* Luke 14:11.
2 R. V. amazed
12
y *Faith in Christ,* John 6:69.
z *Kingdom of Heaven,* Matt. 13:24.

a *Name of Jesus,* John 14:13.
3 R. V. good tidings

b *Baptism, Christian,* Luke 20:4.
13
c *Faith in Christ,* John 6:69.
d *Miracles,* Luke 23:8.
4 R. V. he was amazed.
14
e *Apostles,* Luke 6:13.
f *Jerusalem,* Judg. 19:10.
g *Samaria,* Isa. 7:9.
h *Doctrines of Jesus,* John 7:16.
i *Peter,* Mark 5:37.
j *John,* Mark 1:19.
15
k *Prayer, intercessory,* Acts 6:4.
l *Holy Spirit,* Acts 1:2.
16
5 R. V. into
17
m *Hand, imposition of,* Ezra 10:19.
18
n *Money,* Jer. 32:9.
19
o *Covetousness,* Isa. 57:17.
20
p *Peter,* Mark 5:37.
q *Minister, incorruptible,* Rom. 15:16.
r *Reproof, faithfulness in,* Prov. 17:10.
21
s *Heart,* Psa. 44:21.
t *Sin, known to God,* Rom. 5:12.
u *Wicked, described,* Psa. 73:3.
22
v *Repentance, enjoined,* Mark 1:4.
w *Prayer, enjoined,* Acts 6:4.
x *Sin, forgiveness of,* Rom. 5:12.

* **BURIAL.** *Rites of,* Jer. 34:5. *Soon after death,* Deut. 21:23; Josh. 8:29; John 19:38–42; Acts 5:9, 10. *With spices,* 2 Chr. 16:14; Mark 16:1; Luke 23:56. *Bier used at,* 2 Sam. 3:31; Luke 7:14.

Attended by relatives and friends: *Of Jacob,* Gen. 50:5–9; *of Abner,* 2 Sam. 3:31–39; *of child of Jeroboam,* 1 Kin. 14:13; *of the son of the widow of Nain,* Luke 7:12, 13; *of Stephen,* Acts 8:2.

*Lack of, a disgrace,* 2 Kin. 9:10; Prov. 30:17; Jer. 16:4; 22:19; Ezek. 39:15.

Directions given about, before death: *By Jacob,* Gen. 49:29, 30; *by Joseph,* Gen. 50:25.

*Of Gog* [multitude], *requiring seven months,* Ezek. 39:11–13.

**Figurative,** Rom. 6:4; Col. 2:12.

See footnote, BURYING PLACES, Gen. 23:4.

† **PHILIP.** *One of the seven deacons,* Acts 6:5. *Successfully preaches in Samaria,* Acts 8:4–14. *Expounds the Scriptures to the Ethiopian eunuch whom he baptizes,* Acts 8:27–38. *Caught away by the Spirit to Azotus; preaches in the cities, and goes to Cæsarea,* Acts 8:39, 40. *Abides at Cæsarea, and entertains Paul,* Acts 21:8. *Has four daughters, prophetesses,* Acts 21:9, 10.

[u]in the [y,z]gall of bitterness, and
*in* the bond of iniquity.
24 Then answered Sī'mon, and
said, [a]Pray ye to the Lord for me,
that none of these things which
ye have spoken come upon me.
25 And they, when they had
[b]testified and [c]preached the
[d]word of the Lord, returned to
[e]Jē-ru'sā-lĕm, and preached the
[d,f]gospel in many villages of the
[g]Să-măr'ĭ-tans.
26 ¶ And the [h]angel of the
Lord spake unto †Phĭl'ĭp, saying, Arise, and go toward the
south unto the way that goeth
down from [e]Jē-ru'sā-lĕm unto
[i]Gā'zȧ, which is desert.
27 And he arose and went:
and, behold, a man of [j]Ē-thĭ-
ō'pĭ-ȧ, an [k]eunuch of great authority under [l]Căn'dā-çē [m]queen
of the Ē-thĭ-ō'pĭ-ans, who had
the charge of all her treasure,
and had come to [e]Jē-ru'sā-lĕm
for to [n]worship,
28 Was returning, and sitting in
his [o]chariot read [p]Ē-ṣā'ias the
[q]prophet.
29 Then the Spirit [r]said unto
†Phĭl'ĭp, [s]Go near, and join thyself to this [o]chariot.
30 And †Phĭl'ĭp ran thither to
*him*, and heard him read the
[q]prophet [p]Ē-ṣā'ias, and said,
Understandest thou what thou
readest?
31 And he said, How can I, except some man should [t]guide
me? And he [u]desired †Phĭl'ĭp
that he would come up and sit
with him.
32 The place of the scripture
which he read was this, [v]He was
led as a sheep to the slaughter;
and like a [w]lamb dumb before
his shearer, [x]so opened he not
his mouth:
33 [v]In his humiliation his judgment was taken away: and who
shall declare his generation? for
his life is taken from the earth.
34 And the [k]eunuch answered
†Phĭl'ĭp, and said, I pray thee,
of whom speaketh the [p]prophet
this? of himself, or of some other
[6]man?
35 Then †Phĭl'ĭp opened his
mouth, and began at the same
scripture, and [i,y]preached unto
him Jē'ṣus.
36 And as they went on *their*
way, they came unto a certain
water: and the [k]eunuch said, See,
*here is* water; what doth hinder
me to be [z]baptized?
37 [7]And Phĭl'ĭp said, [a]If thou
believest with all thine heart,
thou mayest. And he answered
and said, I [b,c]believe that Jē'ṣus
Christ is the [d]Son of God.
38 And he commanded the
[e]chariot to stand still: and they
went down both into the water,
both †Phĭl'ĭp and the [f]eunuch;
and he [g]baptized him.
39 And when they were come
up out of the water, the [h]Spirit of
the Lord caught away †Phĭl'ĭp,
that the [f]eunuch saw him no
more: and he went on his way
[i]rejoicing.
40 But †Phĭl'ĭp was found at
[j]Ȧ-zō'tus: and passing through
he [k]preached [8]in all the cities,
till he came to [l]Çæs-a-rē'ȧ.

## CHAPTER 9

*Saul's conversion near Damascus.* 10 *Ananias baptizes him.* 20 *He preaches Christ boldly.* 23 *After many days the Jews lay wait to kill him.* 25 *He escapes and comes to Jerusalem;* 29 *where the Grecians go about to slay him;* 30 *but he is taken by the brethren and sent to Tarsus.* 32 *Peter heals Eneas of the palsy;* 36 *and restores Tabitha to life.*

AND [a]Saul, yet [b,c,d]breath-
ing out threatenings and
slaughter against the [e]disciples
of the Lord, went unto the [f]high
priest,
2 [g]And [h]desired of him letters
to [i]Dā-măs'cus to the [j]syna-
gogues, that if he found any of
[1]this [k,l]way, whether they were
men or women, he might [m]bring
them bound unto [n]Jē-ru'sā-lĕm.

23
y *Gall, figurative,* Job 16:13.
z *Depravity,* Job 15:14.

24
a *Intercession, solicited,* Jer. 27:18.

25
b *Religious Testimony,* 2 Thess. 1:10.
c *Preaching,* Matt. 9:35.
d *Doctrines of Jesus,* John 7:16.
e *Jerusalem,* Judg. 19:10.
f *Gospel,* Mark 13:10.
g *Samaria,* Isa. 7:9.

26
h *Angel, appearances of,* Heb. 1:13.
i *Gaza,* Gen. 10:19.

27
j *Ethiopia,* Isa. 18:1.
k *Eunuch,* Matt. 19:12.
l *Women, as rulers,* Prov. 31:10.
m *Queen,* 1 Kin. 11:19.
n *Worship,* Gen. 22:5.

28
o *Chariot,* Josh. 11:4.
p Or, *Isaiah,* Isa. 1:1.
q *Prophets,* Isa. 3:2.

29
r *Holy Spirit, inspiration of,* Acts 1:2.
s *Guidance,* Psa. 48:14.

31
t *Instruction, in religion,* Prov. 23:23.
u *Spiritual Desire,* Psa. 42:1.

32
v Isa. 53:7, 8.
w *Lamb, symbol of Christ,* Num. 7:15.
x *Jesus, meekness of,* Matt. 1:21.

34
6 R. V. *omits* man

35
y *Preaching,* Matt. 9:35.

36
z *Baptism, Christian,* Luke 20:4.

37
a *Salvation, conditions of,* Acts 16:17.
b *Faith in Christ,* John 6:69.
c *Jesus, received,* Matt. 1:21.
d *Jesus, divinity of,* Matt. 1:21.
7 R. V. *omits this verse.*

38
e *Chariot,* Josh. 11:4.
f *Eunuch,* Matt. 19:12.
g *Baptism, Christian,* Luke 20:4.

39
h *Holy Spirit,* Acts 1:2.
i *Joy,* Psa. 5:11.

40
j Or, *Ashdod,* 1 Sam. 6:17.
k *Preaching,* Matt. 9:35.
l *Cæsarea,* Acts 21:8.
8 R. V. the gospel to all

1
a Or, *Paul,* Acts 13:9.
b *Malice,* Eph. 4:31.
c *Bigotry, instances of,* Isa. 65:5.
d *Persecution, of the righteous,* John 15:20.
e *Disciples,* Matt. 9:14.
f *High Priest,* Lev. 21:10.

2
g *Extradition,* 1 Kin. 18:10.
h *Intolerance, religious,* Num. 11:28.
i *Damascus,* Isa. 8:4.
j *Synagogue,* Matt. 12:9.
k *Way, figurative,* Isa. 35:8.
l *Doctrines of Jesus,* John 7:16.
m *Arrest,* Matt. 26:50.
n *Jerusalem,* Judg. 19:10.
1 R. V. the Way.

3
o *Light, miraculous,* Gen. 1:3.
p *Miracles,* Luke 23:8.

4
q *Appearances of Jesus after his Resurrection,* Mark 16:9.
r *Persecution, of Jesus,* John 15:20.

5
2 R. V. *omits the rest of the verse.*

6
3 R. V. *omits* And he trembling and astonished said, Lord, what wilt thou have me to do? And the Lord said unto him,

8
s *Blindness,* 2 Kin. 6:18.
4 R. V. nothing;

9
t *Fasting, instances of,* Zech. 8:19.

10
u Acts 22:12–16.

3 And as he journeyed, he came
near [i]Dă-măs′cus: and suddenly
there shined round about him a
[o,p]light from heaven:
4 [q]And he fell to the earth,
and heard a voice saying unto
him, [a]Saul, Saul, why [r]persecutest
thou me?
5 And he said, Who art thou,
Lord? And the Lord said, I am
Jē′sus whom thou [r]persecutest:
[2]*it is* hard for thee to kick
against the pricks.
6 [3]And he trembling and astonished
said, Lord, what wilt thou
have me to do? And the Lord
*said* unto him, Arise, and go into
the city, and it shall be told thee
what thou must do.
7 And the men which journeyed
with him stood speechless, hearing
a voice, but seeing no man.
8 And [a]Saul arose from the
earth; and when his eyes were
opened, he saw [4,s]no man: but
they led him by the hand, and
brought *him* into [i]Dă-măs′cus.
9 And he was three days [s]without
sight, and [t]neither did eat
nor drink.
10 ¶ And there was a certain
[e]disciple at [i]Dă-măs′cus, named
[u]Ăn-a-nī′as; and to him said the
Lord in a *vision, Ăn-a-nī′as.
And he said, Behold, I *am here,*
Lord.
11 And the Lord *said* unto him,
Arise, and go into the street
which is called Straight, and enquire
in the house of Jū′das for
*one* called Saul, of †Tär′sus: for,
behold, he [v]prayeth,
12 And hath seen [5]in a *vision
a man named [u]Ăn-a-nī′as coming
in, and putting *his* hand on
him, that he might receive his
sight.
13 Then [u]Ăn-a-nī′as [w,x,y]answered,
Lord, I have heard by
many of this man, how much
evil he hath done to thy saints
at Jē-ru′să-lĕm:
14 And here he hath authority
from the chief priests to [z]bind all
that call on thy name.
15 But the Lord said unto him,
Go thy way: for he is a [a]chosen
vessel unto me, to bear my
[b]name before the [c]Ġĕn′tīles, and
kings, and the children of Īs′-
ra-el:
16 For I will shew him how
[6]great things [d]he must [e]suffer for
my [b]name's sake.
17 And Ăn-a-nī′as went his
way, and entered into the house;
and putting his hands on him
said, Brother Saul, the Lord,
*even* Jē′sus, that [f]appeared unto
thee in the way as thou camest,
hath sent me, that thou mightest
receive thy sight, and be filled
with the [g]Holy Ghost.
18 And immediately there fell
from his eyes as it had been
scales: and he [h]received sight
forthwith, and arose, and was
[i]baptized.
19 And [7]when he had received
meat, he was strengthened.

11
v *Prayer,* Acts 6:4.

12
5 R. V. *omits* in a vision

13
w *Doubting,* Rom. 14:23.
x *Excuses,* Luke 14:18.
y *Duty, escape from, sought by Ananias,* Eccl. 12:13.

14
z *Intolerance,* Num. 11:28.

15
a *Election of Grace,* Rom. 11:5.
b *Name of Jesus,* John 14:13.
c *Gentiles, prophecies of the conversion of,* Acts 10:45.

16
d *Paul, persecutions of,* Acts 13:9.
e *Suffering for Christ,* Phil. 1:29.
6 R. V. many

17
f *Appearances of Jesus after his Resurrection,* Mark 16:9.
g *Holy Spirit,* Acts 1:2.

18
h *Miracles,* Luke 23:8.
i *Baptism, Christian,* Luke 20:4.

19
7 R. V. he took food and was

***VISION.** *A mode of revelation,* Num. 12:6; 1 Sam. 3:1; 2 Chr. 26:5; Psa. 89:19; Prov. 29:18; Jer. 23:16; Dan. 1:17; Hos. 12:10; Joel 2:28; Obad. 1; Hab. 2:2; Acts 2:17.

*Of Abraham, concerning his descendants,* Gen. 15:1–17. *Of Jacob, of the ladder,* Gen. 28:2–15; *at Beer-sheba,* Gen. 46:2. *Of Moses, of the burning bush,* Ex. 3:2–5; *of the glory of God,* Ex. 24:9–11; 33:18–23. *Of Joshua, of the captain of the Lord's host,* Josh. 5:13–15.

*Of the Israelites, of the manifestation of the glory of God,* Ex. 24:10, 17; Heb. 12:18–21.

*Of David, of the angel of the Lord by the threshing floor of Ornan,* 1 Chr. 21:15–20. *Of Elisha, at the translation of Elijah,* 2 Kin. 2:11,12. *Of Elisha's servant, of the chariots of the Lord,* 2 Kin. 6:17. *Of Micaiah, of the defeat of the Israelites; of the Lord on his throne; and of a lying spirit,* 1 Kin. 22:17–23; 2 Chr. 18:16–22. *Of Job, of a spirit,* Job 4:12–16.

*Of Isaiah, of the Lord and his glory in the temple,* Isa. 6; *of the valley of vision,* Isa. 22.

*Of Jeremiah, of an almond rod,* Jer. 1:11, 12; *of the boiling pot,* Jer. 1:13–19.

*Of Ezekiel, of the glory of God,* Ezek. 1:1–28; 23; *of the roll,* Ezek. 2:9, 10; *of the man of fire,* Ezek. 8; 9; *of the coals of fire,* Ezek. 10:1–7; *of the dry bones,* Ezek. 37:1–14; *of the city and temple,* Ezek. chapters 40–48; *of the waters,* Ezek. 47:1–12.

*Of Daniel, of the beasts,* Dan. 7; *of the Ancient of days,* Dan. 7: 9–27; *of the ram and the he-goat,* Dan. 8; *of the angel,* Dan. 10.

*Of Amos, of grasshoppers,* Amos 7:1, 2; *of fire,* Amos 7:4; *of a plumb line,* Amos 7:7, 8; *of summer fruit,* Amos 8:1–3.

*Of Zechariah, of horses,* Zech. 1:8–11; *of the golden candlestick,* Zech. 4; *of the flying roll,* Zech. 5:1–4.

*Of Zacharias, in the temple,* Luke 1:13–22. *Of John the Baptist, at the baptism of Jesus,* Matt. 3:16, 17; Mark 1:10, 11; Luke 3:21, 22; John 1:32–34.

*Of Paul, of Christ, on the way to Damascus,* Acts 9:3–6; 1 Cor. 9:1; *of Ananias,* Acts 9:12; *of a man of Macedonia,* Acts 16:9; *of paradise,* 2 Cor. 12:1–4. *Of Cornelius, the centurion, of an angel,* Acts 10:3–7. *Of Peter, of the sheet let down from heaven,* Acts 10:9–18.

† **TARSUS,** capital of Cilicia, in Asia Minor. *Paul's birthplace,* Acts 9:11; 21:39; 22:3. *Paul sent to, from Jerusalem to avoid assassination,* Acts 9:30. *Paul brought from, to Antioch by Barnabas,* Acts 11:25, 26.

Then was [j]Saul certain days
with the [k]disciples which were
at [l]Dă-măs′cus.[S]
20 [T] And [m]straightway[G] [8,j]he
[n]preached [o]Chrīst in the [p]syna-
gogues, that he is the [q]Son of
God.
21 But all that heard *him* were
amazed, and said; Is not this he
that destroyed them which called
on this [b]name in [r]Jĕ-ru′să-lĕm,
and came hither for that intent,
that he might bring them bound
unto the chief priests?
22 But [j]Saul increased the more
in strength, and confounded the
[s]Jews which dwelt at [l]Dă-măs′-
cus, proving that this is very[G]
[o]Chrīst.[T]
23 ¶ And after that many days
were fulfilled, the Jews [d,t]took
counsel to kill him:
24 But their [9,t]laying await
was known of [j]Saul. And [t]they
watched the gates day and night
to kill him.
25 Then the disciples took him
by night, and let *him* down by
the wall in a [u]basket.
26 And when [j]Saul was come to
[r]Jĕ-ru′să-lĕm, he assayed[G] to join
himself to the [k]disciples: but
they were all afraid of him, and
believed not that he was a disciple.
27 But [v]Bär′na-băs took him,
and brought *him* to the [w]apos-
tles, and declared unto them
how he had seen the Lord in the
way, and that he had spoken to
him, and how he had [n]preached
[x]boldly at [l]Dă-măs′cus in the
[y]name of Jē′sus.
28 And he was with them coming in and going out at [r]Jĕ-ru′-
să-lĕm.
29 And he [n,z]spake [x]boldly in
the [y]name of the Lord Jē′sus,
and disputed against the [10,a]Grē′-
cians[G]: but they went about to
[b]slay him.
30 *Which* when the brethren
knew, they brought [b]him down
to [c]Çæs-a-rē′ȧ, and sent him
forth to [†]Tär′sus.
31 Then had the [11]churches
rest throughout all [d]Jū-dæ′ȧ and
[e]Găl′ĭ-lee and [f]Să-mā′rĭ-ȧ, and
were edified[G]; and walking in the
[‡]fear of the Lord, and in the
comfort of the [g]Holy Ghost[G],
were [h]multiplied.
32 ¶ And it came to pass, as
[i]Pē′tēr passed throughout all
*quarters*, he came down also
to the saints[G] which dwelt at
[j]Lўd′dȧ.
33 And there he found a certain man named Æ′ne-ăs, which
had kept his bed eight years, and
was sick of the [k]palsy.
34[S] And [i]Pē′tēr said unto him,
Æ′ne-ăs, [l]Jē′sus Chrīst maketh
thee whole[G]: arise, and make thy
bed. And [m]he [n]arose immediately.
35 And [o]all that dwelt at [j]Lўd′-
dȧ and [p]Sā′ron saw him, and
[n,q,r]turned to the Lord.[S]
36 ¶ Now there was at [s]Jŏp′pȧ

**19**
*j* Or, *Paul*, Acts 13:9.
*k* *Disciples*, Matt. 9:14.
*l* *Damascus*, Isa. 8:4.
**20**
*m* *Zeal*, 2 Cor. 7:11.
*n* *Preaching*, Matt. 9:35.
*o* *Jesus, Messiah*, Matt. 1:21.
*p* *Synagogue*, Matt. 12:9.
*q* *Jesus, divinity of*, Matt. 1:21.
8 R. V. in the synagogues he proclaimed Jesus,
**21**
*r* *Jerusalem*, Judg. 19:10.
**22**
*s* *Jews*, Neh. 4:2.
**23**
*t* *Malice*, Eph. 4:31.
**A.D. 37**
**24**
9 R. V. plot became known to
**25**
*u* *Basket*, Ex. 29:3.
**27**
*v* *Barnabas*, Acts 4:36.
*w* *Apostles*, Luke 6:13.

*x* *Courage*, Deut. 31:7.
*y* *Name of Jesus*, John 14:13.
**29**
*z* *Witnessing for Christ*, Luke 24:48.
*a* *Greece*, Zech. 9:13.
*b* *Paul, persecutions of*, Acts 13:9.
10 R. V. Grecian Jews;
**30**
*c* *Cæsarea*, Acts 21:8.
**31**
*d* *Judea*, Luke 5:17.
*e* *Galilee*, Mark 6:21.
*f* *Samaria*, Isa. 7:9.
*g* *Holy Spirit*, Acts 1:2.
*h* *Church, Christian, rapid growth of*, Matt. 16:18.
11 R. V. church
**32**
*i* *Peter*, Mark 5:37.
*j* Or, *Lod*, 1 Chr. 8:12.
**A.D. 38**
**33**
*k* *Paralysis*, Mark 2:3.
**34**
*l* *Name of Jesus, miracles performed in*, John 14:13.
*m* *Healing, by the apostles*, Acts 4:22.
*n* *Miracles, convincing effect of*, v. 35; Luke 23:8.
**35**
*o* *Church, Christian, membership in*, Matt. 16:18.
*p* Or, *Sharon*, 1 Chr. 27:29.
*q* *Religious Revivals*, Hab. 3:2.
*r* *Faith in Christ, exemplified*, John 6:69.
**36**
*s* *Joppa*, 2 Chr. 2:16.

‡ **FEAR OF GOD**, Ex. 18:21; Deut. 4:10; 6:2; 10:12; 14:23; 17:13; 1 Kin. 8:40; Ezra 10:3; Job 28:28; Psa. 34:11; 52:6; 89:7; Prov. 2:5, 6; 15:16; Eccl. 3:14; 2 Cor. 5:11; Rev. 19:5.

Described: *As clean*, Psa. 19:9; *as hating evil*, Prov. 8:13; *as prolonging life*, Prov. 10:27; *as a fountain of life*, Prov. 14:27; *as wisdom*, Job 28:28; Prov. 15:33; *as the beginning of wisdom*, Psa. 111:10; Prov. 1:7; 9:10; 15:33.

*Deters from sin*, Ex. 20:18–20; Prov. 16:6; Jer. 32:39, 40. *Averts temporal calamity*, Deut. 28:49, 58; 2 Kin. 17:36, 39; Prov. 19:23.

*Secures divine blessing*, Deut. 5:29; Psa. 25:12, 13; 31:19; 33:18; 34:7, 9; 85:9; 103:11, 13, 17; 111:5; 112:1; 115:11, 13; 128:1–4; 145:19; Prov. 22:4; Eccl. 7:18; 8:12; Mal. 4:2; Luke 1:50; Acts 10:35.

*Is a bond of fellowship among the righteous*, Mal. 3:16.

*Universality of, foretold*, Psa. 6:11; 9; 102:15.

**A motive**: *To obedience*, Deut. 31:12; 2 Pet. 3:11. *To filial obedience*, Deut. 21:21. *To truthfulness*, Deut. 19:20.

**Enjoined**, Lev. 19:14, 32; 25:19, 36, 43; Deut. 6:13; 10:20; 13:4; Josh. 24:14; 1 Sam. 12:24; 2 Kin. 17:36; 1 Chr. 16:30; 2 Chr. 19:7, 9; Neh. 5:9; Psa. 2:11; 4:4; 22:23; 34:9; 96:4; Prov. 3:7; 23:17; 24:21; Eccl. 5:7; 12:13; Isa. 8:13; 29:23; Rom. 11:20; Col. 3:22; 1 Pet. 2:17; Rev. 14:7.

**Motives to**: *God's majesty*, Jer. 10:7; *power*, Josh. 4:24; Psa. 99:1; Jer. 5:22; Matt. 10:28; Luke 12:5; *power and justice*, Job 37:23, 24; *wrath*, Psa. 90:11; *judgments*, Isa. 1:20; *providence*, 1 Sam. 12:2–4; *forgiveness*, Psa. 130:4.

**Instances of those who feared God**: *Noah, in preparing the ark*, Heb. 11:7. *Abraham, tested in the offering of his son Isaac*, Gen. 22:12. *Jacob, in the vision of the ladder, and the covenant of God*, Gen. 28:16, 17. *Joseph*, Gen. 42:18. *The midwives of Egypt, in refusing to take the lives of the Hebrew children*, Ex. 1:17, 21. *Job*, Job 1:8; 2:3. *David*, Psa. 5:7. *Cornelius, who feared God with all his house*, Acts 10:2.

**Guilty**, Job 15:20–25; 18:11; Prov. 1:24–27; 10:24; Isa. 2:19–21; 33:14; Mic. 7:17; Rom. 8:15; 2 Tim. 1:7; Jas. 2:19; Rev. 6:16.

INSTANCES OF GUILTY FEAR: *Adam and Eve*, **Gen. 3:8–13.** *Judas*, Matt. 27:3–5. *Devils*, Jas. 2:19.

a certain [t]disciple named Tăb′ĭ-thȧ, which by interpretation is called Dôr′cas: this [u]woman was full of [v]good [w]works and [v,x,y]almsdeeds[G] which she did.

37 And it came to pass in those days, that she was sick, and died: [z]whom when they had [a]washed, they laid *her* in an [b]upper chamber.

38 And forasmuch as [c]Lўd′dȧ was nigh[G] to [d]Jŏp′pȧ, and the [e]disciples had heard that [f]Pē′tēr was there, they sent unto him two men, [12]desiring *him* that he would not delay to come to them.

39 Then [f]Pē′tēr arose and went with them. When he was come, they brought him into the [b]upper chamber: and all the widows stood by him weeping, and shewing the [g,h]coats and garments which Dôr′cas made, while she was with them.

40 But [f]Pē′tēr put them all forth, and kneeled down, and [i]prayed; and turning *him* to the body said, Tăb′ĭ-thȧ, arise. And she [j]opened her eyes: and when she saw Pē′tēr, she sat up.[S]

41 And he gave her *his* hand, and lifted her up, and when he had called the saints[G] and widows, presented her [j]alive.

42 And it was known throughout all [d]Jŏp′pȧ; and many [j,k]believed in the Lord.

43 And it came to pass, that he [l]tarried many days in [d]Jŏp′pȧ with one [m]Sī′mon a [n]tanner[G].

## CHAPTER 10

*The vision of Cornelius.* **7** *He sends for Peter.* **9** *Peter's vision.* **19** *He goes to Cornelius,* **24** *who receives him gladly.* **34** *Peter preaches Christ.* **44** *The Holy Ghost falls on all that heard the word;* **47** *and they are baptized.*

THERE was a certain man in [a]Çæs-a-rē′ȧ called Côr-nē′lĭ-ŭs, a [b,c]centurion[G] of the [c]band called the Ĭ-tăl′ian *band*,

2 A devout *man*, and one that [d]feared God with all his [e]house[G], which [f,g]gave much [h]alms[G] to the [i]people, and [j]prayed to God alway.

3 He saw in a [k]vision [1]evidently[G] about the ninth[G] hour of the day an [l]angel of God coming in to him, and saying unto him, Côr-nē′lĭ-ŭs.

4 And when he looked on him, he was afraid, and said, What is it, Lord? And he [m]said unto him, Thy prayers and thine [f,g,h]alms are come up for a memorial before God.

5 And now send men to [n]Jŏp′pȧ, and [2]call for *one* Sī′mon, whose surname is [o]Pē′tēr:

6 He [p]lodgeth with one [q]Sī′mon a [r]tanner, whose house is by the sea side: [3]he shall tell thee what thou oughtest to do.

7 And when the [l]angel which spake unto Côr-nē′lĭ-ŭs was departed, he called two of his household [s]servants, and a devout soldier of them that waited[G] on him continually;

8 And when he had declared all *these* things unto them, he sent them to [n]Jŏp′pȧ.

9 ¶ On the morrow[G], as they went on their journey, and drew nigh[G] unto the city, [o]Pē′tēr went up upon the [t]housetop to [u]pray about the sixth[G] hour:

10 And he became very [v]hungry, and would have eaten: but while they made ready, he fell into a [w]trance,

11 And [x]saw heaven opened, and a certain vessel descending unto him, as it had been a great sheet [4]knit at the four corners, and let down to the earth:

12 [y]Wherein were all manner of fourfooted [z]beasts [5]of the earth, and wild beasts, and creeping things, and fowls of the air.

13 And there came a voice to him, Rise, [a]Pē′tēr; kill, and eat.

14 But Pē′tēr said, Not so, Lord; for I have never eaten any thing that is common[G] or unclean.[GQ]

t *Disciples,* Matt. 9:14.
u *Women, good,* Prov. 31:10.
v *Righteousness, fruits of,* Psa. 15:2.
w *Works, good,* 2 Tim. 1:9.
x *Alms, instances of giving,* Matt. 6:2.
y *Poor, kindness to,* Prov. 21:13.

37
z *Dead, prepared for burial,* 2 Kin. 4:32.

a *Ablution, of the dead,* Judg. 19:21.
b *House, architecture of,* Esth. 8:1.

38
c Or, *Lod,* 1 Chr. 8:12.
d *Joppa,* 2 Chr. 2:16.
e *Disciples,* Matt. 9:14.
f *Peter,* Mark 5:37.
12 R. V. intreating

39
g *Dress,* Zech. 3:3.
h *Works, good,* 2 Tim. 1:9.

40
i *Prayer, answered,* Acts 6:4.
j *Miracles, convincing effect of,* vs. 41, 42; Luke 23:8.

42
k *Faith in Christ,* John 6:69.

43
l *Minister, hospitality to,* Rom. 15:16.
m Acts 10:6, 17, 32.
n *Art,* 2 Chr. 16:14.

A.D. 41
See footnote, *Time,* Rev. 10:6.

1
a *Cæsarea,* Acts 21:8.
b *Centurion,* Matt. 8:5.
c *Armies, Roman army,* Deut. 11:4.

2
d *Fear of God,* Acts 9:31.
e *Family, religion in the,* 1 Chr. 13:14.
f *Liberality,* 1 Tim. 6:18.
g *Works, good,* 2 Tim. 1:9.
h *Alms,* Matt. 6:2.

i *Poor, kindness to,* Prov. 21:13.
j *Prayerfulness,* 1 Tim. 5:5.

3
k *Vision,* Acts 9:10.
l *Angel, functions of,* Heb. 1:13.
1 R. V. openly, as it were,

4
m *Heathen, divine revelations given to,* Lam. 1:10.

5
n *Joppa,* 2 Chr. 2:16.
o *Peter,* Mark 5:37.
2 R. V. fetch one

6
p *Hospitality,* Rom. 12:13.
q Acts 9:43.
r *Art,* 2 Chr. 16:14.
3 R. V. *omits* he shall tell thee what thou oughtest to do.

7
s *Servant,* Jer. 2:14.

9
t *House, roof of,* Esth. 8:1.
u *Prayer,* Acts 6:4.

10
v *Hunger,* Neh. 9:15.
w Acts 11:5; 22:17.

11
x *Vision, of Peter,* Acts 9:10.
4 R. V. let down by four corners upon the earth:

12
y *Food, Peter's vision concerning,* Psa. 136:25.
z *Animals, clean and unclean,* Jer. 27:5.

5 R. V. and creeping things of the earth and fowls of the heaven.

13
a *Peter,* Mark 5:37.

15 And the voice *spake* unto him again the second time, What God hath cleansed, *that* call not thou common.

16 This was done thrice: and the vessel was received up again into heaven.

17 Now while [a]Pē′tēr [6]doubted in himself what this [b]vision which he had seen should mean, behold, the men which were sent from Côr-nē′lĭ-ŭs had made enquiry for [c]Sī′mon's house, and stood before the gate,

18 And called, and asked whether Sī′mon, which was surnamed [a]Pē′tēr, were lodged there.

19 While Pē′tēr thought on the [b]vision, the [d]Spirit said unto him, Behold, three men seek thee.

20 [e]Arise therefore, and get thee down, and go with them, doubting nothing: for I have sent them.

21 Then [a]Pē′tēr went down to the men [7]which were sent unto him from Côr-nē′lĭ-ŭs; and said, Behold, I am he whom ye seek: what *is* the cause wherefore ye are come?

22 And they said, Côr-nē′lĭ-ŭs the centurion, a just man, and one that [f]feareth God, and of good report among all the nation of the Jews, was warned from God by an holy [g]angel to send for thee into his house, and to hear words of thee.

23 Then called he them in, and [h]lodged *them*. And on the morrow [a]Pē′tēr went away with them, and certain brethren from [i]Jŏp′pȧ accompanied him.

24 And the morrow after they entered into [j]Çæs-a-rē′ȧ. And Côr-nē′lĭ-ŭs waited for them, and had called together his kinsmen and near friends.

25 And as [a]Pē′tēr was coming in, Côr-nē′lĭ-ŭs met him, and fell down at his feet, and *worshipped *him*.

26 [k]But Pē′tēr took him up, saying, Stand up; I myself also am a man.

27 And as he talked with him, he went in, and found many that were come together.

28 And he said unto them, Ye know how that it is an unlawful thing for a man that is a Jew to keep company, or come unto one of another nation; but [l]God hath shewed me that I should not call any [m]man common or unclean.

29 Therefore came I *unto you* without gainsaying, as soon as I was sent for: I ask therefore for what intent ye have sent for me?

30 And Côr-nē′lĭ-ŭs said, Four days ago [8]I was [n]fasting until this hour; and at the ninth hour I [o]prayed in my house, and, behold, a [g]man stood before me in bright clothing,

31 And [p]said, Côr-nē′lĭ-ŭs, thy [q]prayer is heard, and thine [r,s,t]alms are had in remembrance in the sight of God.

32 Send therefore to [i]Jŏp′pȧ, and call hither Sī′mon, whose surname is [a]Pē′tēr; he is lodged in the house of *one* [c]Sī′mon a tanner by the sea side: [9]who, when he cometh, shall speak unto thee.

33 Immediately therefore I sent to thee; and thou hast well done that thou art come. Now therefore are we all here present before God, to hear all things that are commanded thee of [10]God.

34 ¶ Then [u]Pē′tēr opened *his* mouth, and said, Of a truth I perceive that [v]God is [w]no [x]respecter of persons:

35 But [w]in every [y]nation he that [z]feareth him, and worketh righteousness, is [11]accepted with him.

17
*b* *Vision*, Acts 9:10.
*c* Acts 9:43.
6 R. V. was much perplexed in

19
*d* *Holy Spirit*, Acts 1:2.

20
*e* *Guidance*, Psa. 48:14.

21
7 R. V. *omits* which were sent unto him from Cornelius;

22
*f* *Fear of God*, Acts 9:31.
*g* *Angel*, Heb. 1:13.

23
*h* *Hospitality*, Rom. 12:13.
*i* *Joppa*, 2 Chr. 2:16.

24
*j* *Cæsarea*, Acts 21:8.

26
*k* *Worship, to be rendered to God only*, Gen. 22:5.

28
*l* *Bigotry, God's rebuke of*, Isa. 65.5.
*m* *Man, equality of*, Job 4:17.

30
*n* *Fasting*, Zech. 8:19.
*o* *Prayer*, Acts 6:4.
8 R. V. until this hour, I was keeping the ninth hour of prayer in my house;

31
*p* *Heathen, divine revelations given to*, Lam. 1:10.
*q* *Prayer, answered*, Acts 6:4.
*r* *Alms*, Matt. 6:2.
*s* *Liberality*, 1 Tim. 6:18.
*t* *Works, good*, 2 Tim. 1:9.

32
9 R. V. *omits* who, when he cometh, shall speak unto thee.

33
10 R. V. the Lord.

34
*u* *Orator*, Acts 24:1.
*v* *God, impartial*, Gen. 2:2.
*w* *Catholicity, inculcated*, Eph. 2:14.
*x* *Respect of Persons*, Prov. 24:23.

35
*y* *Heathen, pious people among*, Lam. 1:10.
*z* *Fear of God*, Acts 9:31.
11 R. V. acceptable to

* **HOMAGE.** *Rendered, to Joseph*, Gen. 41:43; *to kings*, 1 Kin. 1:16, 23, 31; *to princes*, Esth. 3:2, 5; *to Mordecai*, Esth. 6:11; *to Daniel*, Dan. 2:46. *Refused, by Peter*, Acts 10:25, 26; *by Paul and Barnabas*, Acts 14:11–18; *by the angel seen by John in his vision*, Rev 19:10; 22:8, 9.

**36**
*a Gospel*, Mark 13:10.
*b Spiritual Peace*, Gal. 1:3.
*c Jesus, king*, Matt. 1:21.
*d Jesus, names of*, Matt. 1:21.
12 R. V. good tidings of peace
**37**
*e Judea*, Luke 5:17.
*f Galilee*, Mark 6:21.
*g Baptism, John's*, Luke 20:4.
**38**
*h Anointing, figurative*, Deut. 28:40.
*i Jesus, relation of, to the Father*, Matt. 1:21.
*j Holy Spirit, baptism of*, Acts 1:2.
*k Jesus, power of*, Matt. 1:21.
*l Jesus, zeal of*, Matt. 1:21.
*m Jesus, benevolence of*, Matt. 1:21.
*n Works, good*, 2 Tim. 1:9.
*o Altruism*, Acts 20:35.
*p Healing, by Jesus*, Acts 4:22.
*q Afflictions, from Satan*, Psa. 34:19.
*r Satan*, Matt. 4:10.
**39**
*s Apostles*, Luke 6:13.
*t Witnessing for Christ*, Luke 24:48.
*u Jerusalem*, Judg. 19:10.
*v Jews, reject Christ*, Neh. 4:2.
*w Crucifixion, of Jesus*, Mark 15:13.
**40**
*x Resurrection, of Jesus*, 1 Cor. 15:12.
*y Appearances of Jesus after his Resurrection*, Mark 16:9.
**42**
*z Apostles, commission of*, Luke 6:13.

*a Minister, duties of*, Rom. 15:16.
*b Preaching*, Matt. 9:35.
*c Religious Testimony*, 2 Thess. 1:10.
*d Jesus, judge*, Matt. 1:21.

36[T] The [a]word which *God* sent
unto the children of Iṣ'ra-el,
preaching [12,b]peace by Jē'ṣus
Chrīst: (he is [c,d]Lord of all:)[Q]
37 That [a]word, *I say*, ye know,
which was published throughout all [e]Jū-dæ'ȧ, and began from
[f]Găl'ĭ-lee, after the [g]baptism
which Jŏhn preached;
38 How God [h,i]anointed [d]Jē'-
ṣus of Năz'a-rĕth with the [j]Holy
Ghost[G] and with [k]power: who
[l]went about [m,n,o]doing good, and
[p]healing all that were [q]oppressed
of the [r]devil; for God was [i]with
him.[T Q]
39 And [s]we are [t]witnesses of all
things which he did both in the
land of the Jewṣ, and in [u]Jē-
ru'sā-lĕm; whom [v]they slew and
[w]hanged on a tree:[Q]
40 Him God [x]raised up the
third day, and [y]shewed him
openly;
41 Not to all the people, but
[y]unto witnesses chosen before of
God, *even* to us, who did eat and
drink with him after he rose
from the dead.
42 And he [z]commanded us [a]to
[b]preach unto the people, and [a]to
[c]testify that it is he which was
ordained of God *to be* the [d]Judge
of quick[G] and dead.[T Q]
43 To him give all the prophets witness, that [e]through his
[f]name whosoever [g]believeth in
him shall receive [h,i]remission of
sins.[S T Q]
44 ¶ While [j]Pē'tēr yet spake
these words, [k]the [l]Holy Ghost[G]
[l]fell on all them which heard
the word.
45 And they of the [m]circum-
cision which [g]believed were [n]as-
tonished, as many as came with
[j]Pē'tēr, because that on the
†Gĕn'tīleṣ also was poured out
the [k]gift of the [l]Holy Ghost.[G Q]
46 For they heard them speak
with [o]tongues,[G] and [p]magnify[G]
God. Then [n]answered [j]Pē'tēr,
47 [n]Can any man forbid water,
that these should not be [q]bap-
tized, which [r]have received the
[l]Holy Ghost[G] as well as we?
48 And he commanded them to
be baptized [q]in the name of [13]the
Lord. Then prayed[G] they him to
tarry[G] certain days.

## CHAPTER 11

*Peter accused of consorting with the Gentiles. 4 His defense. 19 The gospel is preached to the Gentiles in Antioch. 22 Barnabas is sent from Jerusalem to Antioch, 25 and seeks for Saul. 26 The disciples are called Christians first in Antioch. 27 A great dearth foretold. 29 The disciples send relief to the brethren in Judea.*

AND the [a]apostles and brethren that were in [b]Jū-dæ'ȧ
heard that the [c]Ġĕn'tīleṣ had also
received the [d]word of God.
2 And when [e]Pē'tēr was come
up to [f]Jē-ru'sā-lĕm, they that
were of the [g]circumcision [h]con-
tended with him,
3 [h]Saying, Thou wentest in to
men uncircumcised, and didst
eat with them.
4 But [i]Pē'tēr rehearsed[G] *the matter* from the beginning, and expounded[G] *it* by order unto them,
saying,
5 [e]I was in the city of [j]Jŏp'pȧ
[k]praying: and in a [l]trance I saw
a [m]vision, A certain vessel descend, as it had been a great
sheet, let down from heaven by
four corners; and it came even
to me:
6 Upon the which when I had
fastened mine eyes, I considered, and saw fourfooted beasts
of the earth, and wild beasts,
and creeping things, and fowls
of the air.
7 And I heard a voice saying unto me, Arise, [e]Pē'tēr; slay and eat.

**46**
*o Tongues, miraculous gift of*, 1 Cor. 12:10.
*p Praise*, Psa. 150:1.
**47**
*q Baptism, Christian*, Luke 20:4.
*r Righteous, described*, Psa. 64:10.
**48**
13 R. V. Jesus Christ.

**1**
*a Apostles*, Luke 6:13.
*b Judea*, Luke 5:17.
*c Gentiles, conversion of*, vs. 1–18; Acts 10:45.
*d Gospel*, Matt. 13:10.
**2**
*e Peter*, Mark 5:37.
*f Jerusalem*, Judg. 19:10.
*g Circumcision, figurative*, Gen. 17:10.
*h Bigotry, instances of*, Isa. 65:5.
**4**
*i Orator*, Acts 24:1.
**5**
*j Joppa*, 2 Chr. 2:16.
*k Prayer*, Acts 6:4.
*l* Acts 10:11; 22:17.
*m Vision*, Acts 9:10.

**43** *e Jesus, mission of*, Matt. 1:21. *f Name of Jesus*, John 14:13. *g Faith in Christ*, John 6:69. *h Salvation*, Acts 16:17. *i Sin, forgiveness of*, Rom. 5:12. **44** *j Peter*, Mark 5:37. *k Charism*, 1 Cor. 12:1. *l Holy Spirit*, Acts 1:2. **45** *m Circumcision, figurative*, Gen. 17:10 *n Bigotry, rebuke of*. vs. 46, 47; Isa. 65:5.

† **GENTILES.** *Ways of, condemned*, Jer. 10:2, 3; Eph. 4:17–19. *God's forbearance toward*, Acts 14:16. *Ignorant worship of*, Matt. 6:7, 8, 31, 32; Acts 17:4, 16, 17, 22–27; 1 Cor. 10:20; 12:2. *Wicked practices of*, Rom. 1:18–32; Gal. 2:15; Eph. 5:12; 1 Thess. 4:5; 1 Pet. 4:3, 4. *Moral responsibility of*, Rom. 2:14, 15. *Prophecies of the conversion of*,

8 But I said, Not so, Lord:
for nothing common[C] or unclean
hath at any time entered into my
mouth.
9 But the voice answered me
again from heaven, What God
hath cleansed, *that* call not thou
common.[C]
10 And this was done three
times: and all were drawn up
again into heaven.
11 And, behold, immediately
there were three men already
come unto the house where I
was, sent from [n]Çæs-a-rē′ȧ unto
me.
12 And the spirit [o]bade me go
with them, [1]nothing doubting.
Moreover these six brethren accompanied me, and we entered
into the man's house:
13 And he shewed us how he
had seen an [p]angel in his house,
which stood and said unto him,
Send men to [f]Jŏp′pȧ, and [2]call
for Sī′mon, whose surname is
[e]Pē′tĕr;
14 Who shall tell thee words,
whereby thou and all thy house
shall be saved.
15 And as I began to speak, the
[q]Holy Ghost[G] fell on them, as on
us at the beginning.
16 Then remembered I the
word of the Lord, how that he
said, Jŏhn indeed [r]baptized with
water; but ye shall be baptized[G]
with the [q]Holy Ghost.
17 Forasmuch then as God
[s]gave them the like[C] [q,t,u]gift as
*he did* unto us, who [v]believed on
the [w]Lord Jē′ṣus Christ; what
was I, that I could withstand
God?[S]
18 When they heard these
things, they held their peace, and
[x]glorified[G] God, saying, Then
hath God also to the [y]Gĕn′tīleṣ
granted [t,u]repentance unto [z]life.[T S]
19 ¶ Now they which were scattered abroad upon the [a]persecu-
tion that arose about [b]Stē′phen
travelled as far as [c]Phē-nī′çē,
and [d]Çȳ′prus, and *Ăn′tĭ-ŏch,
[e,f]preaching the [g]word to none
but unto the [h]Jewṣ only.
20 And some of them were
men of [d]Çȳ′prus and [i]Çȳ-rē′nē,
which, when they were come
to *Ăn′tĭ-ŏch, spake unto the
[j]Grē′çianṣ,[G] [e]preaching the [k]Lord
Jē′ṣus.
21 And the [l]hand of the Lord
was with them: and [m,n]a great
number [o]believed, and turned
unto the Lord.[S]
22 ¶ Then tidings[G] of these
things came unto the ears of the
church which was in [p]Jē-ru̇′sȧ-
lĕm: and [q]they sent forth [r]Bär′-
na-băs, [3]that he should go as far
as *Ăn′tĭ-ŏch.
23 Who, when he came, and
had seen the [s]grace of God, was
[t]glad, and [u]exhorted[G] them all,
that with [v]purpose of heart they
would cleave[C] unto the Lord.
24 For he was a good man, and
[w]full of the [x]Holy Ghost[G] and of
[y]faith: and [n]much people was
added unto the Lord.
25 Then departed [r]Bär′na-băs
to [z]Tär′sus, for to seek [a]Saul:
26 And when he had found
him, he brought him unto *Ăn′-
tĭ-ŏch. And it came to pass, that
a whole year they assembled
themselves with the [b]church, and
[c]taught much people. And the

**11**
n *Cæsarea,* Acts 21:8.

**12**
o *Guidance,* Psa. 48:14.
1 R. V. making no distinction.

**13**
p *Angel,* Heb. 1:13.
2 R. V. fetch

**15**
q *Holy Spirit, baptism of,* Acts 1:2.

**16**
r *Baptism, John's,* Luke 20:4.

**17**
s *Catholicity, inculcated,* Eph. 2:14.
t *Salvation,* Acts 16:17.
u *Spiritual Gifts,* 1 Cor. 12:4.
v *Faith in Christ,* John 6:69.
w *Jesus, lordship of,* Matt. 1:21.

**18**
x *Glorifying God,* Luke 5:25.
y *Gentiles, conversion of,* Acts 10:45.
z *Life, spiritual,* Eccl. 8:15.

**19**
a *Persecution,* John 15:20.
b *Stephen,* Acts 6:9.
c Acts 15:3.
d *Cyprus,* Acts 21:3.
e *Preaching,* Matt. 9:35.
f *Zeal,* 2 Cor. 7:11.
g *Doctrines of Jesus,* John 7:16.
h *Jews,* Neh. 4:2.

**20**
i *Cyrene,* Acts 2:10.
j *Greeks,* Zech. 9:13.
k *Jesus, lordship of,* Matt. 1:21.

**A.D. 42**

**21**
l *Hand, figurative,* Ezra 10:19.
m *Religious Revivals,* Hab. 3:2.
n *Church, Christian, rapid growth of,* Matt. 16:18.
o *Faith in Christ,* John 6:69.

**22**
p *Jerusalem,* Judg. 19:10.
q *Church, government of,* Matt. 16:18.
r *Barnabas,* Acts 4:36.
3 R. V. *omits* that he should go

**A.D. 43**

**23**
s *Grace of God,* Rom. 4:16.
t *Joy, instances of,* Psa. 5:11.
u *Perseverance, exhortation to,* Eph. 6:18.
v *Decision, injunctions concerning,* Isa. 50:7.

**24** w *Righteous, described,* Psa. 64:10. x *Holy Spirit,* Acts 1:2.
y *Faith,* Mark 11:22.
**25** z *Tarsus,* Acts 9:11.—a Or, *Paul,* Acts 13:9.
**26** b *Church,* Matt. 16:18. c *Instruction, in religion,* Prov. 23:23.

Gen. 12:3; 22:18; 49:10; Psa. 2:8; 22:27–31; 46:10; 65:2, 5; 66:4; 68:31, 32; 86:9; 102:15, 18–22; Isa. 2:2–4; 9:2, 6, 7; 11:6–10; 18:7; 35:1, 2, 5–7; 40:5; 42:1–12; 45:6, 8, 22–24; 49:1, 5, 6, 18–23; 54:1–3; 55:5; 56:3, 6–8; 60:1–14; 65:1; 66:12, 19, 23; Jer. 3:17; 4:2; 16:19–21; Dan. 2:35, 44, 45; 7:13, 14; Hos. 2:23; Joel 2:28–32; Amos 9:11, 12; Mic. 4:3, 4; Hag. 2:7; Zech. 2:10, 11; 6:15; 8:20–23; 9:1, 10; 14:8, 9, 16; Matt. 3:9; 8:11; 12:17–21; 19:30; Mark 10:31; Luke 13:29, 30; 21:24; John 10:16; Acts 9:15.
*Conversion of,* Acts 10:45; 11:1–18; 13:2, 46–48; 14:27; 15:7–31; 18:4–6; 26:16–18; 28:28; Rom. 1:5–7; 9:22–30; 10:19, 20; 11:11–13, 17–21; 15:9–12; Gal. 1:15, 16; 2:2; 3:14; Eph. 3:1–8; Col. 3:11; 1 Thess. 2:16; 1 Tim. 3:16; Rev. 11:15; 15:4.

* **ANTIOCH,** a city of Syria. *Disciples called Christians first in,* Acts 11:19–30. *Church in,* Acts 13:1; 14:26, 27. *Paul and Barnabas sent as missionaries by church in,* Acts 13:2, 3; 14:26. *Barnabas and Paul make second visit to,* Acts 14:26–28. *Paul returns to,* Acts 18:22. *Dissension in church of,* Acts 15:22, with vs. 1–35. *Paul and Peter's controversy at,* Gal. 2:11–15.

[d]disciples were called †Chrĭs'-
tians first in Ăn'tĭ-ŏch.
27 ¶ And in these days came
[e]prophets from [f]Jĕ-ru'să-lĕm unto Ăn'tĭ-ŏch.
28 And there stood up one of
[e]them named [g]Ăg'a-bŭs, and
signified [h]by the [i]spirit that there
should be great [4,j]dearth throughout all the world: which came
to pass in the days of Clau'dĭ-ŭs
[5]Çæ'şar.
29 Then the [d]disciples, every
man according to his ability,
[k,l]determined to send relief unto
the [m,n]brethren which dwelt in
[o]Jū-dæ'ȧ:
30 Which also they did, and
sent it to the [p]elders by the hands
of [q]Bär'na-băs and [a]Saul.

## CHAPTER 12

*Herod kills James and imprisons Peter. 6 An angel delivers him from prison. 20 Herod's miserable death. 24 The word of God increases.*

NOW about that time Hĕr'od
the [a]king stretched forth
*his* hands to [b]vex certain of the
[c]church.
2 And [a,d]he [b,e]killed [f,g]Jāmeş
the brother of [h]Jŏhn with the
[i]sword.
3 And [j]because he saw it
pleased the [k,l]Jewş, he proceeded further to [b,m]take
[g,n]Pē'tēr also. (Then were the
[o]days of unleavened bread.)
4 And when he had apprehended him, he *,[b,g]put [m,n]*him* in
[p]prison, and delivered *him* to four
quaternions of [q]soldiers to keep
him; intending after [1,o]Ēas'tēr to
bring him forth to the people.
5 [n]Pē'tēr therefore was [m]kept
*in [p]prison: but [r,s,t]prayer was
made [2]without ceasing of the
[u]church unto God for him.
6 And when Hĕr'od would have
brought him forth, the same
night [n]Pē'tēr was sleeping [m]be-
tween two [q]soldiers, bound with
two [v]chains: and the keepers before the door kept the [p]prison.
7 And, behold, the [w]angel of
the Lord came upon *him*, and
a light shined in the [3]prison: and
he smote [n]Pē'tēr on the side,
and [4]raised him up, saying, Arise
up quickly. And his chains [x]fell
off from *his* hands.
8 And the [w]angel said unto him,
Gird thyself, and bind on thy
sandals. And so he did. And he
saith unto him, Cast thy garment about thee, and follow me.
9 And he went out, and followed him; and [5]wist not that it
was true which was done by the
[w]angel; but thought he saw a
[y]vision.
10 When they were past the
first and the second ward, they
came unto the [z]iron [a]gate that
leadeth unto the city; which
[b]opened to them of his own accord: and they went out, and
passed on through one street;
and forthwith the angel departed
from him.
11 And when [c]Pē'tēr was come
to himself, he said, Now I know
of a surety, that the [d]Lord hath
sent his angel, and hath [e]deliv-
ered me out of the hand of
Hĕr'od, and *from* all the expectation of the people of the Jewş.
12 And when he had considered *the thing*, he came to the
[f]house of [g,h]Mā'rÿ the mother
of Jŏhn, whose surname was
†Märk; where many were gathered together [i,j]praying.

d *Disciples*, Matt. 9:14.
27
e *Prophets*, Isa. 3:2.
f *Jerusalem*, Judg. 19:10.
28
g Acts 21:10.
h *Inspiration*, Job 32:8.
i *Holy Spirit*, Acts 1:2.
j *Famine*, 2 Kin. 8:1.
4 R. V. Famine over all
5 R. V. *omits* Cæsar.
29
k *Liberality*, 1 Tim. 6:18.
l *Righteousness, fruits of, liberality*, Psa. 15:2.
m *Fraternity*, Zech. 11:14.
n *Poor, kindness to*, Prov. 21:13.
o *Judea*, Luke 5:17.
30
p *Elders*, Acts 14:23.
q *Barnabas*, Acts 4:36.
1
a *Rulers, wicked*, Ex. 18:21.
b *Persecution*, John 15:20.
c *Church, persecution of*, Matt. 16:18.
2
d *Government, monarchical, tyranny in*, Isa. 22:21.
e *Martyrdom*, Rev. 17:6.
f *James*, Luke 5:10.
g *Minister, persecutions of*, Rom. 15:16.
h *John*, Mark 1:19.
i *Sword*, 1 Chr. 21:5.
3
j *Demagogism*, 2 Sam. 15:2.
k *Jews*, Neh. 4:2.
l *Public Opinion*, John 12:42.
m *Prisoners, Peter*, Psa. 79:11. n *Peter*, Mark 5:37. o *Passover*, Num. 9:5. 4 p *Prison*, Gen. 39:20. q *Soldiers*, Ezra 8:22. 1 R. V. the Passover
5 r *Prayer, intercessory*, Acts 6:4. s *Minister, prayer for*, Rom. 15:16. t *Adversity, prayer in*, Psa. 10:6.

u *Church*, Matt. 16:18.
2 R. V. earnestly
6
v *Chains*, Dan. 5:7.
7
w *Angel, functions of*, Heb. 1:13.
x *Miracles*, Luke 23:8
3 R. V. cell:
4 R. V. awoke him,
9
y *Vision*, Acts 9:10.
5 Am. R. V. knew
10
z *Iron*, Prov. 27:17.
a *Gates*, Deut. 3:5.
b *Miracles*, Luke 23:8.
11
c *Peter*, Mark 5:37.
d *God, providence of*, Gen. 2:2.
e *God, preserver*, Gen. 2:2.
12
f *House, used for worship*, Esth. 8:1.
g Col. 4:10.
h *Women, religious privileges of*, Prov. 31:10.
i *Prayer, social*, Acts 6:4.
j *Worship, in private houses*, Gen. 22:5.

† **CHRISTIAN.** *Believers called*, Acts 26:28; 1 Pet. 4:16. *Disciples called, first at Antioch*, Acts 11:26.

* **IMPRISONMENT.** *Of Joseph*, Gen. 39:20. *Of Jeremiah*, Jer. 38:6. *Of John the Baptist*, Matt. 11:2; 14:3. *Of Apostles*, Acts 5:18. *Of Paul and Silas*, Acts 16:24. *Of Peter*, Acts 12:4.
*Of debtors*, Matt 5:25, 26; 18:30.

See footnotes: PRISON, Gen. 39:20; PRISONERS, Psa. 79:11.

† **MARK.** *A cousin, or nephew, of Barnabas*, Col. 4:10. *A disciple of Jesus*, Acts 12:12, 25; 13:5, 13. *Paul and Barnabas contend concerning*, Acts 15:36–39. *A convert of Peter*, 1 Pet. 5:13. *Fellow-worker with Paul at Rome*, Col. 4:10, 11; 2 Tim. 4:11; Philemon 24. *Tradition identifies, as the young man who fled naked when Jesus was apprehended*, Mark 14:51.

14
[k] *Joy, instances of,* Psa. 5:11.

15
6 R. V. confidently

17
[l] Acts 15:13.
[m] *Prudence, instances of,* 2 Chr. 2:12.

18
[n] *Soldiers,* Ezra 8:22.

19
[o] *Watchman,* 2 Sam. 18:24.
[p] *Punishment, death penalty,* Lev. 26:41.
[q] *Judea,* Luke 5:17.
[r] *Cæsarea,* Acts 21:8.

20
[s] *Tyre,* Josh. 19:29.
[t] *Sidon,* Ezek. 28:21.
[u] *Diplomacy, instances of,* 2 Kin. 16:7.
[v] *Statecraft, influence in,* Prov. 28:2.
[w] *Chamberlain,* 2 Kin. 23:11.
7 R. V. they asked for peace,

21
[x] *Throne,* 1 Kin. 2:19.
[y] *Orator,* Acts 24:1.

22
[z] *Flattery, instances of,* Prov. 6:24.

13 And as [c]Pē′tēr knocked at the door of the gate, a damsel came to hearken, named Rhō′dȧ.

14 And when she knew [c]Pē′tēr's voice, she opened not the gate for [k]gladness, but ran in, and told how Pē′tēr stood before the gate.

15 And they said unto her, Thou art mad. But she [6]constantly affirmed that it was even so. Then said they, It is his angel.

16 But [c]Pē′ter continued knocking: and when they had opened *the door,* and saw him, they were astonished.

17 But he, beckoning unto them with the hand to hold their peace, declared unto them how the [d]Lord had [e]brought him out of the prison. And he said, Go shew these things unto [l]Jāmeṣ, and to the brethren. And he [m]departed, and went into another place.

18 Now as soon as it was day, there was no small stir among the [n]soldiers, what was become of [c]Pē′tēr.

19 And when Hĕr′od had sought for him, and found him not, he examined the [o]keepers, and commanded that *they* should be [p]put to death. And he went down from [q]Jū-dæ′ȧ to [r]Çæs-a-rē′ȧ, and *there* abode.

20 ¶ And Hĕr′od was highly displeased with them of [s]Tȳre and [t]Sī′dŏn: but they came with one accord to him, and, [u,v]having made Blăs′tus the king's [w]chamberlain their friend, [7]desired peace; because their country was nourished by the king's *country.*

21 And upon a set day Hĕr′od, arrayed in royal apparel, sat upon his [x]throne, and made an [y]oration unto them.

22 And the people gave a shout, [z]*saying, It is* the voice of a god, and not of a man.

23 And immediately the [a]angel of the Lord [b]smote him, because he [c]gave not God the [d]glory: and he was eaten of [e]worms, and gave up the ghost.

24 ¶ But [f]the [g,h]word of God grew and multiplied.

25 And [i]Bär′na-băs and [j]Sạul returned from [k]Jē-rụ′sȧ-lĕm, when they had fulfilled *their* ministry, and took with them John, whose surname was †Märk.

## CHAPTER 13

*Paul and Barnabas sent forth to the Gentiles. 4 Of Sergius Paulus and Elymas the sorcerer in Cyprus. 14 Paul preaches Jesus at Antioch in Pisidia. 42 Many believe. 45 The Jews opposing and blaspheming, Paul and Barnabas turn to the Gentiles. 50 They are driven away, and go to Iconium.*

NOW there were in the church that was at [a]Ăn′tĭ-ŏch certain [b]prophets and [c,d]teachers; as [e]Bär′na-băs, and Sĭm′e-on that was called Nī′gẽr, and Lụ′çius of [f]Çȳ′rē′nē, and Măn′a-ĕn, [1]which had been brought up with [g]Hĕr′od the tetrarch, and Sạul.

2 As they ministered to the Lord, and [h]fasted, the [i]Holy Ghost said, [j]Separate me [e]Bär′na-băs and Sạul for the work whereunto I have [k]called them.

3 And when they had [h]fasted and [l]prayed, and [m,n]laid *their* [o]hands on them, they [p]sent *them* away.

4 ¶ So they, being [p]sent forth by the [i]Holy Ghost, departed unto Sē-leū′çĭ-ȧ; and from thence they sailed to [q]Çȳ′prus.

5 And when they were at Săl′a-mĭs, they [r]preached the [s]word of God in the [t]synagogues of the Jewṣ: and they had also [u]Jŏhn [2]to *their* minister.

6 And when they had gone through the isle unto Pā′phos, they found a certain [v]sorcerer, a false prophet, a Jew, whose name *was* Bär-jē′ṣus:

[t] *Synagogue,* Matt. 12:9. [u] Or, *Mark,* Acts 12:12. 2 R. V. as their attendant.
6 [v] *Sorcery,* Isa. 47:9.

23
[a] *Angel,* Heb. 1:13.
[b] *Judgments,* Ex. 6:6.
[c] *Ingratitude, of man to God,* Rom. 1:21.
[d] *Glorifying God,* Luke 5:25.
[e] *Worm,* Jonah 4:7.

24
[f] *Church, Christian,* Matt. 16:18.
[g] *Doctrines of Jesus,* John 7:16.
[h] *Gospel,* Mark 13:10.

25
[i] *Barnabas,* Acts 4:36.
[j] Or, *Paul,* Acts 13:9.
[k] *Jerusalem,* Judg. 19:10.

1
[a] *Antioch,* Acts 11:19.
[b] *Prophets,* Isa. 3:2.
[c] *Teachers,* 1 Chr. 25:8.
[d] *Instruction, in religion,* Prov. 23:23.
[e] *Barnabas,* Acts 4:36.
[f] *Cyrene,* Acts 2:10.
[g] *Herod,* Matt. 14:1.
1 R. V. the foster-brother of

2
[h] *Fasting,* Zech. 8:19.
[i] *Holy Spirit,* Acts 1:2.
[j] *Minister, call of,* Rom. 15:16.
[k] *Call, personal,* Phil. 3:14.

3
[l] *Prayer,* Acts 6:4.
[m] *Ordination, of ministers,* Ex. 29:1.
[n] *Minister, ordination of,* Rom. 15:16.
[o] *Hand, imposition of,* Ezra 10:19.
[p] *Missions,* Matt. 28:19.

4
[q] *Cyprus,* Acts 21:3.

5
[r] *Preaching,* Matt. 9:35.
[s] *Doctrines of Jesus,* John 7:16.

7
*w Deputy*, 1 Kin. 22:47.
*x Prudence*, 2 Chr. 2:12.
*y Spiritual Desire*, Psa. 42:1.
3 R. V. proconsul

7 Which was with the [3,w]dep-
uty[c] of the country, Sẽr'ġĭ-ŭs
Pau̥'lus, a [x]prudent man; who
called for [e]Bär'na-băs and Sau̥l,
and [y]desired to hear the [s]word of
God.
8 But Ĕl'y̆-măs the [v]sorcerer
(for so is his name by interpretation) withstood them, seeking to
turn away the [3,w]deputy from the
faith.
9 Then Sau̥l, (who also *is called*
*Pau̥l,) [z]filled with the [a]Holy
Ghost,[c] set his eyes on him,

9
*z Apostles, inspiration of*, Luke 6:13.
*a Holy Spirit*, Acts 1:2.

* **PAUL.** *Called also* SAUL, Acts 8:1; 9:1; 13:9. *Of the tribe of Benjamin*, Rom. 11:1; Phil. 3:5. *Personal appearance of*, 2 Cor. 10:1, 10.

*Born in Tarsus*, Acts 9:11; 21:39; 22:3. *Educated in the school of Gamaliel*, Acts 22:3; 26:4. *A zealous Pharisee*, Acts 22:3; 23:6; 26:5; 2 Cor. 11:22; Gal. 1:14; Phil. 3:5, 6. *A Roman*, Acts 16:37; 22:25–28. *Persecutes the Christians*, Acts 8:3; 9:1, 13, 14; 22:4, 19; Gal. 1:13; 1 Tim. 1:13. *Present at, and gives consent to, the stoning of Stephen*, Acts 7:58; 8:1; 22:20. *Sent to Damascus with letters for the arrest and return to Jerusalem of Christians*, Acts 9:1, 2.

*His vision and conversion*, Acts 9:3–22; 22:4–19; 26:9–15; 1 Cor. 9:1; 15:8; Gal. 1:16; 1 Tim. 1:12, 13. *Is baptized*, Acts 9:18; 22:16. *Called to be an apostle*, Acts 22:14–21; 26:16–18; Rom. 1:1; 1 Cor. 1:1; 9:1, 2; 15:9; Gal. 1:1, 15, 16; Eph. 1:1; Col. 1:1; 1 Tim. 1:1; 2:7; 2 Tim. 1:1, 11; Tit. 1:1, 3.

*Preaches in Damascus*, Acts 9:20, 22. *Is persecuted by the Jews*, Acts 9:23, 24. *Goes, to Arabia*, Gal. 1:17; *to Jerusalem*, Acts 9:25, 26; Gal. 1:18, 19. *Received by the disciples in Jerusalem*, Acts 9:26–29. *Goes to Cæsarea*, Acts 9:30; 18:22.

*Sent to the Gentiles*, Acts 13:2, 3, 47, 48; 22:17–21; 26:17; Rom. 11:13; 15:16; Gal. 1:15, 16. *Has Barnabas as his companion*, Acts 11:25, 26. *Teaches at Antioch one year*, Acts 11:26. *Conveys the contributions of the Christians in Antioch to the Christians in Jerusalem*, Acts 11:27–30. *Returns with John to Antioch*, Acts 12:25.

*Visits, Seleucia*, Acts 13:4; *Cyprus*, Acts 13:4. *Preaches, at Salamis*, Acts 13:5; *at Paphos*, Acts 13:6. *Sergius Paulus, deputy of the country, is a convert of*, Acts 13:7–12. *Contends with Elymas the sorcerer*, Acts 13:6–12. *Visits Perga in Pamphylia*, Acts 13:13. *John, a companion of, departs for Jerusalem*, Acts 13:13. *Visits Antioch in Pisidia, and preaches in the synagogue*, Acts 13:14–41. *His message received gladly by the Gentiles*, Acts 13:42, 49. *Persecuted and expelled*, Acts 13:50, 51.

*Visits Iconium, and preaches to the Jews and Greeks; is persecuted; escapes to Lystra; goes to Derbe*, Acts 14:1–6. *Heals an impotent man*, Acts 14:8–10. *The people attempt to worship him and Barnabas*, Acts 14:11–18. *Is persecuted by certain Jews from Antioch and Iconium, and is stoned*, Acts 14:19; 2 Cor. 11:25; 2 Tim. 3:11. *Escapes to Derbe, where he preaches the gospel, and returns to Lystra, and to Iconium, and to Antioch; confirms the souls of the disciples, exhorts them to continue in the faith, and ordains elders*, Acts 14:19–23.

*Revisits Pisidia, Pamphylia, Perga, Attalia, and Antioch in Syria, where he abode*, Acts 14:24–28. *Contends with the Judaizing Christians against circumcision*, Acts 15:1, 2. *Refers the question as to circumcision to the apostles and elders at Jerusalem*, Acts 15:2, 4. *He declares to the apostles at Jerusalem the miracles and wonders God had wrought among the Gentiles*, Acts 15:12. *Returns, with letters to the Gentiles, to Antioch, accompanied by Barnabas, Judas, and Silas*, Acts 15:22, 25.

*Makes his second tour of the churches*, Acts 15:36. *Chooses Silas as his companion; and passes through Syria and Cilicia, confirming the churches*, Acts 15:36–41. *Visits Lystra; circumcises Timothy*, Acts 16:1–5. *Goes through Phrygia and Galatia; is forbidden by the Holy Spirit to preach in Asia; visits Mysia; essays to go to Bithynia, but is restrained by the Spirit; goes to Troas, where he has a vision of a man saying, Come over into Macedonia, and help us; immediately proceeds to Macedonia*, Acts 16:6–10; 2 Cor. 2:12, 13; *and tribulations in*, 2 Cor. 7:5. *Visits Samothracia and Neapolis; comes to Philippi, the chief city of Macedonia; visits a place of prayer at the river side; preaches the word; the merchant, Lydia, of Thyatira, is converted and baptized*, Acts 16:11–15. *Causes the evil spirit to come out of a damsel who practices divination*, Acts 16:16–18. *Persecuted, beaten, and cast into prison with Silas; sings songs of praise in the prison; an earthquake shakes the prison; he preaches to the alarmed jailer, who believes, and is baptized with his household*, Acts 16:19–34. *Is released by the civil authorities on the ground of his being a Roman citizen*, Acts 16:35–39. *Is received at the house of Lydia*, Acts 16:15, 40.

*Visits Amphipolis, and Apollonia, and Thessalonica; preaches in the synagogue*, Acts 17:1–4. *Is persecuted*, Acts 17:5–9; 2 Thess. 1:1–4. *Escapes to Berea by night; preaches in the synagogue; many honorable women, and men, not a few, believe*, Acts 17:10–12. *Persecuted by the Jews who come from Thessalonica; is conducted by the brethren to Athens*, Acts 17:13–15. *Disputes on Mars' Hill with Grecians*, Acts 17:16–34.

*Visits Corinth; dwells with Aquila and Priscilla, who were tentmakers; joins in their handicraft; reasons in the synagogue every Sabbath; is rejected of the Jews, turns to the Gentiles; makes his abode with Justus; continues there one year and six months teaching the word of God*, Acts 18:1–11. *Persecuted by Jews; drawn before the deputy; takes his leave after many days, and sails unto Syria, accompanied by Aquila and Priscilla*, Acts 18:12–18.

*Visits Ephesus, where he leaves Aquila and Priscilla; enters into a synagogue, where he reasons with the Jews; starts on his return journey to Jerusalem; visits Cæsarea; goes over the country of Galatia and Phrygia, in order, strengthening the disciples*, Acts 18:18–23. *Returns to Ephesus; baptizes in the name of the Lord Jesus, and lays his hands upon John's disciples, who are baptized with the Holy Ghost; preaches in the synagogue; remains in Ephesus for the space of two years; heals the sick*, Acts 19:1–12. *Tribulations of, at Ephesus*, 1 Cor. 15:32. *Reproves the exorcists; casts an evil spirit out of a man, and many believe, bringing their books of sorcery to be burned*, Acts 19:13–20; 1 Cor. 16:8, 9. *Purposes visiting Jerusalem, and then Rome*, Acts 19:21; 20:22; 23:11; Rom. 15:24, 25. *Sends Timothy and Erastus into Macedonia, but remains himself in Asia for a season*, Acts 19:21, 22. *The spread of the gospel through his preaching interferes with the makers of idols; he is persecuted, and a great uproar of the city is created; the town clerk appeases the people, dismisses the accusation against Paul, and disperses the people*, Acts 19:23–41; 2 Tim. 4:14.

*Proceeds to Macedonia after confirming the churches in those parts; comes into Greece and abides three months; returns through Macedonia*, Acts 20:1–6. *Visits Troas; preaches until break of day; restores to life the young man who fell from the window*, Acts 20:6–12. *Visits Assos, and sails by Mitylene, Chios, Samos, and Miletus, hastening to Jerusalem, to be there at Pentecost*, Acts 20:13–16. *Sends for the elders of the church of Ephesus; rehearses to them how he had preached in Asia, and his trials and afflictions for preaching repentance toward God; declares he was going bound in spirit to Jerusalem; exhorts them to take heed to themselves and the flock over whom the Holy Ghost had made them overseers; kneels down and prays, and takes his departure*, Acts 20:17–38.

*Visits Coos, Rhodes, Patara; takes ship for Tyre; tarries at Tyre seven days; is brought on his way by the disciples to the outskirts of the city; kneels down and prays; takes ship; comes to Ptolemais; salutes the brethren, and abides one day*, Acts 21:1–7.

*Departs for Cæsarea; enters the house of Philip, the Evangelist; is admonished by Agabus not to go to Jerusalem; proceeds nevertheless to Jerusalem*, Acts 21:8–15. *Is received by the brethren gladly; talks of the things that had been wrought among the Gentiles by his ministry; enters the temple; the people are stirred against him by Jews from Asia; an uproar is created; he is thrust out of the temple; the chief captain of the garrison interposes and arrests him*, Acts 21:17–33. *Bound with chains*, Acts 21:33; 22:29; 28:20; Eph. 6:20; 2 Tim. 1:16. *His defense*, Acts 21:33–40; 22:1–21. *Is confined in the castle*, Acts 22:24–30. *Is brought before the council; his defense*, Acts 22:30; 23:1–5. *Is returned to the castle*, Acts 23:10. *Is cheered by a vision, promising him that he shall bear witness in Rome*, Acts 23:11.

*Jews conspire against his life*, Acts 23:12–15; 25:2, 3. *Are thwarted by his nephew*, Acts 23:16–22. *Is escorted to Cæsarea by a military guard*, Acts 23:23–33. *Is confined in Herod's judgment hall* [R. V. Prætorium] *in Cæsarea*, Acts 23:35. *His trial before Felix*, Acts 24:1–23. *Remains in custody for two years*, Acts 24:27. *His trial before Festus*, Acts 25:1–12. *Appeals to Cæsar*, Acts 25:10–12. *His examination before Agrippa*, Acts 25:13–27; 26. *Accused of insanity*, Acts 26:24; 2 Cor. 5:13.

*Is taken to Rome in custody of Julius, a centurion, and a guard of soldiers; takes shipping, accompanied by other prisoners, and sails by way of the coasts of Asia; stops at Sidon and at Myra*, Acts 27:1–5. *Transferred to a ship of Alexandria; sails by way of Cnidus, Crete, Salamis, and the Fair Havens*, Acts 27:6–8. *Predicts misfortune to the ship; his counsel not heeded, and the voyage resumed*, Acts 27:9–13. *The ship encounters a tempest; Paul encourages and comforts the officers and crew; the soldiers advise putting the prisoners to death; the centurion interferes, and all on board, consisting of two hundred and seventy-six souls, are saved*, Acts 27:14–44. *The ship is*

**10**
*b Reproof, faithfulness in*, Prov. 17:10.
*c Wicked, described*, Psa. 73:3.
*d Satan*, Matt. 4:10.
4 R. V. guile
5 R. V. villany,

**11**
*e Blindness, as a judgment*, 2 Kin. 6:18.
*f Miracles, convincing effect of*, v. 12; Luke 23:8.

**12**
*g Deputy*, 1 Kin. 22:47.
*h Faith in Christ*, John 6:69.
*i Doctrines of Jesus*, John 7:16.
6 R. V. teaching

**13**
*j* Acts 14:25.
*k Pamphylia*, Acts 14:24.
*l* Or, *Mark*, Acts 12:12.
*m Jerusalem*, Judg. 19:10.

**14**
*n* Acts 14:24.
*o Synagogue*, Matt. 12:9.
*p Sabbath*, Ex. 16:23.

**15**
*q Word of God, to be read publicly*, Psa. 119:9.
7 R. V. *omits* Ye men and

**16**
*r Orator*, Acts 24:1.
*s Zeal*, 2 Cor. 7:11.
*t Preaching*, Matt. 9:35.
*u Catholicity, instances of*, Eph. 2:14.
*v Fear of God*, Acts 9:31.

**17**
*w God, providence of*, Gen. 2:2.

10 And [b]said, O [c]full of all [4]subtilty and all [5]mischief, *thou* [c]child of the [d]devil, [c]*thou* enemy of all righteousness, wilt thou not cease to pervert the right ways of the Lord?

11 And now, behold, the hand of the Lord *is* upon thee, and thou shalt be [e]blind, not seeing the sun for a season. And immediately there [f]fell on him a mist and a darkness; and he went about seeking some to lead him by the hand.

12 Then the [3,g]deputy, when he saw what was done, [i,h]believed, being astonished at the [6,i]doctrine of the Lord.

13 ¶ Now when *Pa̤ul and his company loosed from Pā′phos, they came to [j]Pĕr′gȧ in [k]Păm-phy̆l′ĭ-ȧ: and [l]Jŏhn departing from them returned to [m]Jē-rṳ′-sȧ-lĕm.

14 ¶ But when they departed from [j]Pĕr′gȧ, they came to †Ăn′-tĭ-ŏch in [n]Pĭ-sĭd′ĭ-ȧ, and went into the [o]synagogue on the [p]sabbath day, and sat down.

15 And after the reading of the [q]law and the prophets the rulers of the [o]synagogue sent unto them, saying, [7]*Ye* men *and* brethren, if ye have any word of exhortation for the people, say on.

16 Then *,[r,s]Pa̤ul stood up, and beckoning with *his* hand [t]said, Men of Ĭs̤′ra-el, [u]and ye that [v]fear God, give audience.

17 The [w]God of this people of Ĭs̤′ra-el chose our [x]fathers, and exalted the people when they dwelt as strangers in the land of [y]Ē′ġy̆pt, and with an high [z]arm brought he them out of it.

18 And about the time of [a]forty years suffered he their manners in the wilderness.

19 And when he had [b]destroyed seven nations in the land of [c]Chā′-năan, he [8]divided their land to them by [d]lot.

20 And after [9]that he gave *unto* [e]*them* [f]judges about the space of four hundred and fifty years, until [g]Săm′u-el the prophet.

21 And afterward [e]they desired a [h]king: and [i]God gave unto them [j,k]Sa̤ul the son of [l]Çĭs, a man of the tribe of [m]Bĕn′ja-mĭn, by the space of forty years.

22 And when [i]he had removed [j]him, he raised up unto them [k,n]Dā′vid to be their king; to whom also he gave testimony, and said, I have found Dā′vid the *son* of Jĕs′se, [o]a man after mine own heart, which [p]shall fulfil all my will.

23 [q]Of this man's seed hath [r]God according to *his* [s]promise raised unto Ĭs̤′ra-el a [t]Saviour, Jē′s̤us:

24 When [u]Jŏhn had first [v]preached before his coming the [w]baptism of [x]repentance to all the people of Ĭs̤′ra-el.

25 And as [u]Jŏhn fulfilled his course, he said, Whom think ye

*x Israel*, Ex. 4:22.
*y Egypt*, Gen. 41:8.
*z Arm, figurative*, Psa. 89:13.

**18**
*a Forty, years*, Jonah 3:4.

**19**
*b Judgments*, Ex. 6:6.
*c* Or, *Canaan*, Gen. 37:1.
*d Lot*, Esth. 3:7.
8 R. V. gave them their land for an inheritance, for about four hundred and fifty years:

**20**
*e Israel, under the judges*, Ex. 4:22.
*f Judge, of Israel*, Judg. 2:16.
*g Samuel*, 1 Sam. 3:1.
9 R. V. these things he gave them judges until Samuel the prophet.

**21**
*h King*, 2 Kin. 3:10.
*i Government, God in*, Isa. 22:21.
*j Saul*, 1 Sam. 9:2.
*k Rulers, appointed by God*, Ex. 18:21.
*l* Or, *Kish*, 1 Sam. 9:1.
*m Benjamin, tribe of*, Num. 1:37.

**22**
*n David*, 1 Sam. 16:13.
*o Righteous, described*, Psa. 64:10.
*p Obedience*, Heb. 5:8.

**23**
*q Jesus, incarnation of*, Matt. 1:21.
*r God, faithfulness of*, Gen. 2:2.
*s Covenant, of God with men*, Deut. 29:1.
*t Jesus, savior*, Matt. 1:21. **24** *u John the Baptist*, Luke 1:63. *v Preaching*, Matt. 9:35. *w Baptism, John's*, Luke 20:4. *x Repentance*, Mark 1:4.

---

*wrecked, and all on board take refuge on the island of Melita*, Acts 27:14–44; 28:1. *Kind treatment by the inhabitants of the island*, Acts 28:1, 2. *Is bitten by a viper and miraculously preserved*, Acts 28:3–6. *Heals the ruler's father and others*, Acts 28:7–10. *Is delayed in Melita three months; proceeds on the voyage; delayed at Syracuse; sails by Rhegium and Puteoli; meets brethren who accompany him to Rome from Appii forum; arrives at Rome; is delivered to the captain of the guard; is permitted to dwell by himself in custody of a soldier*, Acts 28: 11–16. *Forsaken by friends in his first defense*, 2 Tim. 4:16. *Calls the chief Jews together; states his situation; is kindly received; expounds the gospel; testifies to the kingdom of heaven*, Acts 28:17–29.

*Dwells two years in his own hired house, preaching and teaching*, Acts 28:30, 31. *Luke a companion of*, 2 Tim. 4:11.

*Caught up to the third heaven*, 2 Cor. 12:1–4. *Has a thorn in the flesh*, 2 Cor. 12:7–9; Gal. 4:13, 14.

**Persecutions of,** Acts 9:16, 23–25, 29; 14:19; 16:19–24; 20:22, 23; 21:13, 27, 28–33; 22:22–24; 23:10, 12–15; 1 Cor. 4:9, 11–13; 2 Cor. 1:8–10; 4:8, 9; 6:4, 5, 8–10; 11:23–27, 32, 33; 12:10; Gal. 5:11; 6:17; Phil. 1:30; Col. 1:24; 1 Thess. 2:2; 2 Tim. 1:12; 2:9, 10; 3:11, 12; 4:16, 17.

**Character of,** 2 Cor. 10:1, 10; 11:6; Gal. 4:13. *Cheerful in adversity*, Acts 16:25; Rom. 8:35–37; 2 Cor. 4:8–10; 12:10; 2 Tim. 2:10; 3:11, 12; 4:16, 17. *Courageous*, Acts 9:29; 20:22–24; 21:13; Eph. 6:20; 1 Thess. 2:2. *Purposeful, even in the face of the admonitions of the Holy Spirit not to go to Jerusalem*, Acts 20:22, 23; 21:4, 10–14. *Indomitable*, Rom. 8:35–37; 1 Cor. 4:9–13; 2 Cor. 4:8–12; 6:4–10; 11:23–33; 12:10; 1 Thess. 2:2; 2 Tim. 1:12; 3:11; 4:17. *Joyous in sufferings*, Phil. 2: 17; Col. 1:24; 2 Tim. 2:9. *Meek*, 1 Cor. 4:12, 13; 2 Tim. 4:16. *Self forgetful*, 1 Cor. 4:9, 11–13. *Self-supporting*, Acts 18:3; 20:33–35; 2 Cor. 11:7, 9; 1 Thess. 2:9; 2 Thess. 3:8. *Tactful*, 1 Cor. 9:19–22; 10:33; Philemon 7–14. *Zealous*, Rom. 9:3; 2 Cor. 5:11–14; 6:4–10; 11:22–33; 12:10, 14, 15; Phil. 3:6–16; Col. 1:29. *Ready for death*, 2 Tim. 4:6–8.

† **ANTIOCH.** *A city of Pisidia*, Acts 13:14. *People of, persecute Paul*, Acts 13:14–52; 14:19–22; 2 Tim. 3:11.

**25**
*y Humility,* Prov. 22:4.

**26**
*z Brother, expressive of fraternity,* Prov. 18:24.

*a Abraham,* Gen. 17:5.
*b Catholicity, instances of,* Eph. 2:14.
*c Fear of God,* Acts 9:31.
*d Gospel,* Mark 13:10.
*e Salvation,* Acts 16:17.
10 R. V. *Omits* Men and

**27**
*f Jerusalem,* Judg. 19:10.
*g Spiritual Blindness,* 2 Cor. 4:4.
*h Word of God,* Psa. 119:9.
*i Jesus, prophecies concerning,* Matt. 1:21.
*j Sabbath,* Ex. 16:23.
*k Prophecies, fulfillment of,* Dan. 9:24.
*l Persecution, of Jesus,* John 15:20.
11 R. V. *omits* day

**28**
*m Innocency,* Psa. 26:6.
*n Malice,* Eph. 4:31.
*o Pilate,* Matt. 27:2.

**29**
*p Crucifixion,* Mark 15:13.
*q* Matt. 27:57–60; Mark 15:42–46; Luke 23:50–53; John 19:38–42.

**30**
*r God, power of,* Gen. 2:2.
*s Resurrection, of Jesus,* 1 Cor. 15:12.

**31**
*t Appearances of Jesus after his Resurrection,* Mark 16:9.
*u Apostles,* Luke 6:13.
*v Galilee,* Mark 6:21.
*w Witnessing for Christ,* Luke 24:48.
*x Religious Testimony,* 2 Thess. 1:10.

that I am? I am not *he.* But,
behold, there cometh one after
me, whose shoes of *his* feet [y]I
am not worthy to loose.
26 [10]Men *and* [z]brethren, children of the stock of [a]Ā′brā-
hăm, and [b]whosoever among
you [c]feareth God, to you is the
[d]word of this [e]salvation sent.[Q]
27 For they that dwell at [f]Jĕ-
ru̦′să-lĕm, and their rulers, because they [g]knew him not, nor
yet the [h,i]voices of the prophets
which are read every [j]sabbath
[11]day, they have fulfilled [k]*them* in
[l]condemning *him.*
28 And though they found [m]no
cause of death *in him,* yet [n]de-
sired they [o]Pī′late that he should
be slain.
29 And when they had [p]fulfilled
all that was [k]written of him, they
took *him* down from the tree,
and [q]laid *him* in a sepulchre.[S]
30 But [r]God [s]raised him from
the dead:[T]
31 And he was [t]seen many days
of [u]them which came up with
him from [v]Găl′ĭ-lee to [f]Jĕ-ru̦′să-
lĕm, who are his [w,x]witnesses
unto the people.
32 [S]And we declare unto you
[y]glad tidings, how that the
[z]promise which was made unto
the fathers,
33 God hath [a]fulfilled the same
unto us their children, in that he
hath [b]raised up Jē′ṣus again; as
[c]it is also written in the second
psalm, [d]Thou art my [e]Son, this
day have I [f]begotten thee.[S T Q]
34 And as concerning that [g]he
[b]raised him up from the dead,
*now* no more to return to [h]cor-
ruption, he said on this wise,[G] I
will give you [i]the [12]sure mercies
of [j]Dā′vid.[T Q]

35 Wherefore he saith also in
another *psalm,* [k]Thou shalt not
suffer[G] thine [l]Holy One to see
corruption.[Q]
36 For Dā′vid, after he had
[13]served his own generation by
the will of God, fell on [m]sleep,[G]
and was laid unto his fathers,
and saw [h]corruption:[G Q]
37 But[S] he, whom [g]God [b]raised
again, saw no [h]corruption.[G]
38 ¶ [T]Be it known unto you
therefore, men *and* brethren, that
[n]through this man is preached
unto you the [o]forgiveness of sins:
39 And by him all that [p]believe
are [q]justified from all things,
from which ye [r]could not be justified by the [s]law of Mō′ṣeṣ.[S T]
40 Beware therefore, lest that
come upon you, which is spoken
of in the prophets;
41 [t]Behold, ye [u]despisers, and
wonder, and perish: for I work a
work in your days, a work which
[v]ye [w]shall in no wise[G] believe,
though a man declare it unto
you.[Q]
42 ¶ And [x]when the Jewṣ were
gone out of the [y]synagogue,[G] the
Ġĕn′tīleṣ [z]besought that these
[a,b]words might be [c]preached to
them the next [d]sabbath.
43 Now when the congregation
was broken up, [e]many of the
Jewṣ and religious proselytes[G] followed *Pa̦ul and [f]Bär′na-băs:
who, speaking to them, [g]per-
suaded them to [h]continue in the
grace of God.
44 ¶ And the next [d]sabbath day
[e]came almost the whole city together to hear the [a,b]word of
God.
45 But when the Jewṣ saw the
[e]multitudes, they were filled with
[i,j]envy, and [k,l]spake against
those [b]things which were spoken
by *Pa̦ul, contradicting and
[m]blaspheming.
46 Then *Pa̦ul and [f]Bär′na-băs
waxed[G] [n]bold, and [o]said, It was

**35**
*k* Psa. 16:10.
*l Jesus, holiness of,* Matt. 1:21.

**36**
*m Death, called sleep,* Num. 23:10.
13 R. V. in his own generation served the counsel of God,

**38**
*n Jesus, mission of,* Matt. 1:21.
*o Sin, forgiveness of,* Rom. 5:12.

**39**
*p Faith in Christ,* John 6:69.
*q Justification, through Christ,* Rom. 4:25.
*r Works, insufficient for salvation,* 2 Tim. 1:9.
*s Law, temporary,* Deut. 33:2.

**41**
*t* Hab. 1:5.
*u Reprobates,* 1 Cor. 9:27.
*v Unbelievers,* 1 Cor. 6:6.
*w Spiritual Blindness,* 2 Cor. 4:4.

**42**
*x Minister, success attending,* vs. 42–44; Rom. 15:16.
*y Synagogue,* Matt. 12:9.
*z Spiritual Desire,* Psa. 42:1.

*a Gospel,* Mark 13:10.
*b Doctrines of Jesus,* John 7:16.
*c Preaching,* Matt. 9:35.
*d Sabbath,* Ex. 16:23.

**43**
*e Minister, success attending,* Rom. 15:16.
*f Barnabas,* Acts 4:36.
*g Perseverance, exhortation to,* Eph. 6:18.
*h Character, stability of,* Phil. 2:15.

**45**
*i Envy,* Prov. 14:30.
*j Jealousy,* Psa. 78:58.
*k Jesus, rejected,* Matt. 1:21.
*l Bigotry,* Isa. 65:5.
*m Blasphemy,* 2 Sam. 12:14.

**46**
*n Boldness of the Righteous,* Phil. 1:20.
*o Preaching,* Matt. 9:35.

**32** *y Gospel,* Mark 13:10. *z Covenant, of God with men,* Deut. 29:1. **33**—*a God, faithfulness of,* Gen. 2:2. *b Resurrection, of Jesus,* 1 Cor. 15:12. *c Prophecies of the Messiah, and their fulfillment,* Gen. 12:3. *d* Psa. 2:7. *e Jesus, divine sonship of,* Matt. 1:21. *f Jesus, incarnation of,* Matt. 1:21.
**34** *g God, power of,* Gen. 2:2. *h Corruption,* Job 17:14. *i* Isa. 55:3. *j David,* 1 Sam. 16:13. 12 R. V. holy and sure blessings

necessary that the [p]word of God should first have been spoken to you: but seeing [q]ye [r,s]put [t]it from you, and judge yourselves unworthy of everlasting [u]life, lo, we [v]turn to the [w]Ġĕn'tīleṣ.

47 For so hath the Lord commanded us, *saying,* [x,y]I have set thee to be a light of the [w]Ġĕn'tīleṣ,[C] that thou shouldest be for [z,a]salvation unto the ends of the earth.[T Q]

48 And when the [b]Ġĕn'tīleṣ heard this, they were [c]glad, and [d]glorified[C] the word of the Lord: and as many as were [e]ordained[C] to [f]eternal [g]life [h]believed.[S T]

49 And the [i,j]word of the Lord was [k]published throughout all the region.

50 But the Jewṣ stirred up the devout and honourable women, and the chief men of the city, and raised [l]persecution against *Pa̤ul and [m]Bär'na-băs, and expelled them out of their coasts.[C]

51 But they shook off the dust of their feet against them, and came unto ‡Ī-cō'nĭ-ŭm.

52 And the [n]disciples were filled with [c]joy, and with the [o]Holy Ghost.[C]

## CHAPTER 14

*At Iconium Paul and Barnabas are persecuted, 6 and flee to Lystra, 8 where Paul heals a cripple. 11 The people hold them to be gods. 19 Paul is stoned. 21 He and Barnabas pass through various provinces, confirming the churches. 26 Returning to Antioch, they rehearse what God had done.*

AND it came to pass in [a]Ī-cō'nĭ-ŭm, that [b,c]they went both together into the [d]synagogue of the Jewṣ, and [e]sȯ spake, that [f,g]a great multitude both of the [h]Jewṣ and also of the [i]Greeks [j]believed.

2 But the [1]unbelieving [h]Jewṣ [k]stirred up the [l]Ġĕn'tīleṣ, and made their minds evil[C] affected against the brethren.

3 Long time therefore abode they speaking [m]boldly in the Lord, which gave testimony unto the [n]word of his grace, and granted [o]signs and wonders to be done by their hands.

4 But the multitude[C] of the city was divided: and part held[C] with the [h]Jewṣ, and part with the [p]apostles.

5 And when there was an [k]assault made both of the [l]Ġĕn'tīleṣ, and also of the [h]Jewṣ with their rulers, to use [p,q]*them* despitefully,[C] and to stone them,

6 They were ware[C] of *it,* and [r]fled unto *Lȳs'trȧ and †Dēr'bē, cities of [s]Lȳc-a-ō'nĭ-ȧ, and unto the region that lieth round about:

7 And there they [t]preached the [n]gospel.

8[T] ¶ And there sat a certain man at *Lȳs'trȧ, [u]impotent[C] in his feet, being a cripple from his mother's womb, who never had walked:

9 The same heard [b]Pa̤ul speak: who stedfastly beholding him, and perceiving that he had [j]faith to be healed,

10 Said with a loud voice, Stand upright on thy feet. And [v]he [w]leaped and walked.[S]

11 And when the people saw what [b]Pa̤ul had done, they lifted up their voices, saying in the [x]speech of [s]Lȳc-a-ō'nĭ-ȧ, The gods are come down to us in the likeness of men.

12 And they called [c]Bär'na-băs, [y]Jū'pĭ-tēr; and [b]Pa̤ul, Mēr-cū'rĭ-ŭs, because he was the chief speaker.

13 Then the [z]priest of [y]Jū'pĭ-tēr, [2]which was before their city, brought oxen and garlands unto

*p* *Truth, of the gospel,* John 18:37.
*q* *Reprobates,* 1 Cor. 9:27.
*r* *Jesus, rejected,* Matt. 1:21.
*s* *Unbelief,* Heb. 3:12.
*t* *Word, of God, rejected,* Psa. 119:9.
*u* *Life, everlasting,* Eccl. 8:15.
*v* *Missions,* Matt. 28:19.
*w* *Gentiles,* Acts 10:45.

**47**
*x* *Prophecies of the Messiah, and their fulfillment,* Gen. 12:3.
*y* Isa. 49:6.
*z* *Jesus, savior,* Matt. 1:21.
*a* *Salvation,* Acts 16:17.

**48**
*b* *Gentiles,* Acts 10:45.
*c* *Joy,* Psa. 5:11.
*d* *Glorifying God,* Luke 5:25.
*e* *Foreordination,* Rom. 8:30.
*f* *Immortality,* 1 Cor. 15:54.
*g* *Life, everlasting,* Eccl. 8:15.
*h* *Faith in Christ,* John 6:69.

**49**
*i* *Doctrines of Jesus,* John 7:16.
*j* *Gospel,* Mark 13:10.
*k* *Preaching,* Matt. 9:35.

**50**
*l* *Persecution, of the righteous,* John 15:20.
*m* *Barnabas,* Acts 4:36.

**52**
*n* *Disciples,* Matt. 9:14.
*o* *Holy Spirit,* Acts 1:2.

**1**
*a* *Iconium,* Acts 13:51.
*b* *Paul,* Acts 13:9.
*c* *Barnabas,* Acts 4:36.
*d* *Synagogue,* Matt. 12:9.
*e* *Zeal,* 2 Cor. 7:11.
*f* *Religious Revivals,* Hab. 3:2. *g* *Church, Christian, rapid growth of,* Matt. 16:18. *h* *Jews,* Neh. 4:2. *i* *Greece,* Zech. 9:13. *j* *Faith in Christ,* John 6:69. **2** 1 R. V. Jews that were disobedient

*k* *Persecution, of the righteous,* John 15:20.
*l* *Gentiles,* Acts 10:45.

**3**
*m* *Boldness of the Righteous,* Phil. 1:20.
*n* *Gospel,* Mark 13:10.
*o* *Miracles, of the disciples,* Luke 23:8.

**A.D. 46**

**4**
*p* *Apostles,* Luke 6:13.

**5**
*q* *Minister, persecutions of,* Rom. 15:16.

**6**
*r* *Prudence, instances of,* 2 Chr. 2:12.
*s* v. 11.

**7**
*t* *Preaching,* Matt. 9:35.

**8**
*u* *Lameness,* Lev. 21:18.

**10**
*v* *Healing, by the apostles,* Acts 4:22.
*w* *Miracles, of the disciples,* Luke 23:8.

**11**
*x* *Language,* Dan. 3:29.

**12**
*y* Acts 19:35.

**13**
*z* *Idolatry,* 1 Sam. 15:23.
2 R. V. whose temple was

‡ **ICONIUM,** a city of Asia Minor. *Paul preaches in,* Acts 13:51; 14:1–5, 21, 22; 16:2; *and is persecuted by the people of,* Acts 14:1–6, 19; 2 Tim. 3:11.

* **LYSTRA.** *One of two cities of Lycaonia, to which Paul and Barnabas fled from persecutions in Iconium,* Acts 14:6–23; 2 Tim. 3:11. *Elders ordained for church in, by Paul and Barnabas,* Acts 14:23. *Timothy a resident of,* Acts 16:1–4.

† **DERBE,** a city of Lycaonia. *Paul flees to,* Acts 14:6, 20. *Visited by Paul and Silas,* Acts 16:1 *Gaius resided in,* Acts 20:4.

a *Gates, place for religious services,* Deut. 3:5.
b *Homage,* Acts 10:25.

**14**

c *Apostles,* Luke 6:13.
d *Barnabas,* Acts 4:36.
e *Paul,* Acts 13:9.
f *Zeal,* vs. 14–18; 2 Cor. 7:11.
g *Rending of Garments,* 2 Chr. 34:27.

**15**

h *Integrity, instances of,* Job 2:3.
i *Idolatry, folly of,* 1 Sam. 15:23.
j *Worship, to be rendered to God only,* Gen. 22:5.
k *God, personality of,* Gen. 2:2.
l *God, creator,* Gen. 2:2.
m *Heavens, physical,* Psa. 8:3.
n *Earth,* Prov. 8:23.
o *Sea,* Jer. 5:22.
3 R. V. bring you good tidings, that

**16**

p *God, longsuffering of,* Gen. 2:2.

**17**

q *Natural Religion,* Psa. 19:1.
r *God, providence of,* Gen. 2:2.
s *Rain,* 2 Sam. 1:21.
t *Temporal Blessings, from God,* Psa. 103:2.
u *Food, from God,* Psa. 136:25.

**19**

v *Jews,* Neh. 4:2.
w *Antioch,* Acts 13:14.
x *Iconium,* Acts 13:51.
y *Persecution, of the righteous,* John 15:20.
z *Stoning, instances of,* 1 Sam. 30:6.

a *Paul,* Acts 13:9.

**20**

b *Disciples,* Matt. 9:14.
c *Barnabas,* Acts 4:36.

**21**

d *Preaching,* Matt. 9:35.

the [a]gates, and would have [b]done
sacrifice with the people.
14 *Which* when the [c]apostles,
[d]Bär'na-băs and [e]Paul, heard *of,*
[f]they [g]rent their clothes, and ran
in among the people, crying out,
15 And [h]saying, Sirs, why do ye
these things? We also are men
of like passions with you, and
[3]preach unto you that ye should
turn from these [i]vanities [j]unto
the living [k]God, which [l]made
[m]heaven, and [n]earth, and the
[o]sea, and all things that are
therein:
16 Who in times past [p]suffered
all nations to walk in their own
ways.
17 [q]Nevertheless he left not
himself without witness, in that
he did good, and [r]gave us [s,t]rain
from heaven, and fruitful seasons, filling our hearts with [u]food
and gladness.
18 And with these sayings
scarce restrained they the people, that they had not [b]done sacrifice unto them.
19 ¶ And there came thither
*certain* [v]Jews from [w]Ăn'tĭ-ŏch
and [x]Ī-cō'nĭ-ŭm, who persuaded
the people, and, having [y,z]stoned
[a]Paul, drew *him* out of the city,
supposing he had been dead.
20 Howbeit, as the [b]disciples
stood round about him, he rose
up, and came into the city: and
the next day he departed with
[c]Bär'na-băs to †Dĕr'bē.
21 And when they had [d]preached
the [e]gospel to that city, and had
[4]taught many, they returned again
to *Lўs'trȧ, and *to* [f]Ī-cō'nĭ-ŭm,
and [g]Ăn'tĭ-ŏch,
22 Confirming the souls of the
[b]disciples, *and* [h]exhorting them

e *Gospel,* Mark 13:10. f *Iconium,* Acts 13:51. g *Antioch,* Acts 13:14. 4 R. V. made many disciples,
**22** h *Perseverance, exhortation to,* Eph. 6:18.

to [i]continue in the [j]faith, and
that we must through much
[k,l]tribulation enter into the
[m]kingdom of God.
23 And when [n]they had [5]or-
dained them ‡elders in every
church, and had [o,p]prayed with
[q]fasting, they commended them
to the Lord, on whom they [r]be-
lieved.
24 And after [a,c]they had passed
throughout [s]Pĭ-sĭd'ĭ-ȧ, they came
to ‖Păm-phўl'ĭ-ȧ.
25 And when [a,c]they had
preached the word in [s]Pĕr'gȧ,
they went down into Ăt-tā'lĭ-ȧ:
26 And thence sailed to [t]Ăn'tĭ-
ŏch, from whence they had been
[6,u]recommended to the [v]grace
of God for the work which they
fulfilled.
27 And when [a,c]they were
come, and had gathered the
church together, they rehearsed
all that God had done with
them, and how he had opened
the door of faith unto the [w]Gĕn'-
tīles.
28 And there [a,c]they abode long
time with the [b]disciples.

## CHAPTER 15

*Dissension at Antioch about circumcision. 2 Paul and Barnabas sent to Jerusalem. 6 In assembly of the apostles and elders, after much disputing, Peter and James give their advice. 22 The decision of the assembly is sent by letters to the Gentile churches. 36 Paul and Barnabas separate from one another.*

AND certain men which
came down from [a]Jū-
dæ'ȧ taught the brethren, *and*
[b]*said,* Except ye be [c]circumcised
after the [1]manner of [d]Mō'ṣeṣ, ye
cannot be saved.
2 When therefore [e]Paul and
[f]Bär'na-băs had no small [g]dis-
sension and [2]disputation with
them, they determined that Paul
and Bär'na-băs, and certain other

i *Decision, injunctions concerning,* Isa. 50:7.
j *Doctrines of Jesus,* John 7:16.
k *Faith, trial of,* Mark 11:22.
l *Temptation, a test,* Luke 11:4.
m *Kingdom of Heaven,* Matt. 13:24.

**23**

n *Church, government of,* Matt. 16:18.
o *Prayer,* Acts 6:4.
p *Minister, prayer for,* Rom. 15:16.
q *Fasting,* Zech. 8:19.
r *Faith in Christ,* John 6:69.
5 R. V. appointed for them

**24**

s Acts 13:14.

**26**

t *Antioch,* Acts 11:19.
u *Intercession,* Jer. 27:18.
v *Grace of God,* Rom. 4:16.
6 R. V. committed

**27**

w *Gentiles, conversion of,* Acts 10:45.

**1**

a *Judea,* Luke 5:17.
b *Bigotry, instances of,* Isa. 65:5.
c *Circumcision,* Gen. 17:10.
d *Law, of Moses,* Deut. 33:2.
1 R. V. custom

**2**

e *Paul,* Acts 13:9.
f *Barnabas,* Acts 4:36.
g *Strife,* Prov. 20:3.
2 R. V. questioning

‡ **ELDERS.** *Ordained,* Acts 14:23; Tit. 1:5–9. *Disbursed alms,* Acts 11:29, 30. *Overseers of the Church,* Acts 15:2–29; 16:4, 5; 20:17, 28–32; 21:18; 1 Tim. 5:17–19; 1 Pet. 5:1–5. *Performed ecclesiastical rites,* 1 Tim. 4:14, Jas. 5:14, 15. *In the Mosaic politico-ecclesiasticism,* see SENATE, Num. 11:16.

APOCALYPTIC VISION OF, Rev. 4:4, 10; 5:5, 6, 8, 11, 14; 7:11, 13; 11:16; 14:3; 19:4.

‖ **PAMPHYLIA,** a province in Asia Minor. *Bordered on the Mediterranean Sea,* Acts 27:5. *Men of, in Jerusalem,* Acts 2:10. *Paul goes to,* Acts 13:13, 14; 14:24. *John, surnamed Mark, in,* Acts 13:13; 15:38.

of them, should go up to [h]Jē-
rṳ'sā-lĕm unto the [i]apostles and
[j]elders about this question.
3 And being brought on their
way by the [k]church, they passed
through [l]Phē-nī'çē and [m]Sā-mā'-
rĭ-ȧ, declaring the conversion of
the [n]Ġĕn'tīle̤ṣ: and they caused
great [o]joy unto all the brethren.
4 And when they were come to
[h]Jē-rṳ'sā-lĕm, they were received of the [k]church, and *of* the
[i]apostles and [j]elders, and they
declared all things that God had
done with them.
5 ¶ But there rose up certain
of the sect of the [p]Phăr'ĭ-see̤ṣ
which believed, saying, That it
was needful to [c]circumcise them,
and to command *them* to keep
the [d]law of Mō'ṣe̤ṣ.
6 And the [i]apostles and [j]elders
came together for to consider of
this matter.
7 And when there had been
much [2]disputing, [q]Pē'tĕr rose
up, and said unto them, [3]Men
*and* brethren, ye know how that
a good while ago God [r]made
choice among us, that the [n]Ġĕn'-
tīle̤ṣ [r]by my mouth should hear
the word of the [s]gospel, and [t]be-
lieve.
8 And God, which [u]knoweth
the [v]hearts, bare them witness,
giving [n]them the [w]Holy Ghost,
even as *he did* unto us;
9 And [x]put no difference between us and them, [4, y]purifying
their hearts by [t]faith.
10 Now therefore why tempt ye
God, to put a [z, a]yoke upon the
neck of the [b]disciples, which neither our fathers nor we were able
to bear?
11 But we [c]believe that through
the grace of the [d]Lord Jē'ṣus
[5]Christ we shall be [e, f]saved, even
as they.
12 ¶ Then all the multitude
kept silence, and gave audience

*h Jerusalem,* Judg. 19:10.
*i Apostles,* Luke 6:13.
*j Elders,* Acts 14:23.

3
*k Church,* Matt. 16:18.
*l* Acts 11:19; 21:2–4.
*m Samaria,* Isa. 7:9.
*n Gentiles, conversion of,* Acts 10:45.
*o Joy,* Psa. 5:11.

5
*p Pharisees,* Matt. 15:12.

7
*q Peter,* Mark 5:37.
*r Call, personal,* Phil. 3:14.
*s Gospel,* Mark 13:10.
*t Faith in Christ,* John 6:69.
3 R. V. *omits* Men and

8
*u God, knowledge of,* Gen. 2:2.
*v Heart, known to God,* Psa. 44:21.
*w Holy Spirit,* Acts 1:2.

9
*x Respect of Persons,* Prov. 24:23.
*y Regeneration,* Tit. 3:5.
4 R. V. cleansing

10
*z Yoke, figurative,* 1 Sam. 6:7.

*a Circumcision,* Gen. 17:10.
*b Disciples,* Matt. 9:14.

11
*c Faith in Christ, salvation by,* John 6:69.
*d Jesus, lordship of,* Matt. 1:21.
*e Jesus, savior,* Matt. 1:21.
*f Salvation,* Acts 16:17.
5 R. V. *omits* Christ

to [g]Bär'na-băs and [h]Pa̤ul, declaring what [i]miracles and wonders God had wrought among
the [j]Ġĕn'tīle̤ṣ by [k]them.
13 ¶ And after they had held
their peace, [l]Jāme̤ṣ answered,
saying, [3]Men *and* brethren,
hearken unto me:
14 [m]Sĭm'e-on hath declared
how God at the first did visit the
[j]Ġĕn'tīle̤ṣ, to take out of them a
people for his name.
15 And to this agree the [n]words
of the prophets; as it is written,
16 [o]After this I will return, and
will build again the tabernacle of
[p]Dā'vid, which is fallen down;
and I will build again the ruins
thereof, and I will set it up:
17 That the residue of men
might [q, r]seek after the Lord, and
all the [j]Ġĕn'tīle̤ṣ, [s]upon whom
my name is called, saith the Lord,
who doeth all these things.
18 [6, t]Known unto God are all
his works from the beginning of
the world.
19 Wherefore [u]my [7]sentence is,
that we trouble not them, which
from among the [j]Ġĕn'tīle̤ṣ are
turned to God:
20 But that we write unto them,
that they [v, w]abstain from pollutions of idols, and *from* [x]fornica-
tion, and *from* [y]things strangled,
and *from* [z]blood.
21 For [a]Mō'ṣe̤ṣ of old time hath
in every city them that preach
him, being read in the [b]syna-
gogues every [c]sabbath day.
22 ¶ Then pleased it the [d]apos-
tles and [e]elders, with the whole
[f]church, to send chosen men of
their own company to [g]Ăn'tĭ-
ŏch with [h]Pa̤ul and [i]Bär'na-băs;
*namely,* Jū'das surnamed Bär'-
sa-băs, and *Sī'las, chief men
among the brethren:
23 And they wrote [8]*letters* by

*e Elders,* Acts 14:23. *f Church, government of,* Matt. 16:18. *g Antioch,* Acts 11:19. *h Paul,* Acts 13:9. *i Barnabas,* Acts 4:36.
**23** 8 R. V. thus by them, The apostles and the elder brethren

12
*g Barnabas,* Acts 4:36.
*h Paul,* Acts 13:9.
*i Miracles, of the disciples,* Luke 23:8.
*j Gentiles, conversion of,* Acts 10:45.
*k Agency, in salvation of men,* Mark 1:17.

13
*l* Acts 12:17.

14
*m* Or, *Peter,* Mark 5:37.

15
*n Prophecies concerning the Messiah, and their fulfillment,* Gen. 12:3.

16
*o* Amos 9:11, 12.
*p David,* 1 Sam. 16:13.

17
*q Seekers,* Isa. 55:6.
*r Spiritual Desire,* Psa. 42:1.
*s Spiritual Adoption, of the Gentiles,* Rom. 8:15.

18
*t God, foreknowledge of,* Gen. 2:2.
6 R. V. Saith the Lord, who maketh these things known from the beginning of the world.

19
*u Catholicity, inculcated,* Eph. 2:14.
7 R. V. judgement

20
*v Chastity, enjoined,* Job 31:1.
*w Idolatry, forbidden,* 1 Sam. 15:23.
*x Adultery, forbidden,* Lev. 20:10.
*y* Acts 21:25.
*z Blood, forbidden as food,* Gen. 9:4.

21
*a Law, of Moses, publicly taught,* Deut. 33:2.
*b Synagogue,* Matt. 12:9.
*c Sabbath, religious observance of,* Ex. 16:23.

22
*d Apostles,* Luke 6:13.

* **SILAS,** called also SILVANUS. *Sent from Jerusalem to Paul in Antioch,* Acts 15:22–34. *Becomes Paul's companion,* Acts 15:40, 41; 2 Cor. 1:19; 1 Thess. 1:1; 2 Thess. 1:1. *Imprisoned with Paul in Philippi,* Acts 16:19–40. *Driven, with*

j Gentiles, conversion of, Acts 10:45.
k Syria, 2 Kin. 6:23.
l Cilicia, Gal. 1:21.

**24**
m Heresy, Tit. 3:10.
9 R. V. subverting your souls; to whom we gave no commandment;

**25**
n Love, of man for man, 1 John 4:7.

**26**
o Righteous, described, Psa. 64:10.
p Zeal, 2 Cor. 7:11.
q Name of Jesus, John 14:13.
r Jesus, lordship of, Matt. 1:21.

**27**
s Minister, sent forth two and two, Rom. 15:16.

**28**
t Holy Spirit, Acts 1:2.
u Church, decrees of, Matt. 16:18.

**29**
v Blood, forbidden as food, Gen. 9:4.
w Acts 21:25.
x Adultery, forbidden, Lev. 20:10.
10 R. V. things sacrificed

**31**
y Joy, Psa. 5:11.

**32**
z Prophets, Isa. 3:2.

---

a Minister, duties of, Rom. 15:16.

**33**
11 R. V. those that had sent them forth.

them after this manner; The [d]apostles and [e]elders and brethren *send* greeting unto the brethren which are of the [j]Gĕn'tīleş in [g]Ăn'tĭ-ŏch and [k]Sỹr'ĭ-ȧ and [l]Çĭ-lĭ'çiȧ:

24 Forasmuch as we have heard, that certain which went out from us have troubled you with [m]words, [9]subverting your souls, saying, *Ye must* be circumcised, and keep the law: to whom we gave no *such* commandment:

25 It seemed good unto us, being assembled with one accord, to send chosen men unto you with our [n]beloved [i]Bär'na-băs and [h]Pa̤ul,

26 [o]Men that have [p]hazarded their lives for the [q]name of our [r]Lord Jē'şus Chrīst.

27 We have sent therefore [s]Jū'das and *Sī'las, who shall also tell *you* the same things by mouth.

28 For it seemed good to the [t]Holy Ghost, and to us, to lay upon you no greater burden than these necessary [u]things;

29 [u]That ye abstain from [10]meats offered to idols, and from [v]blood, and from [w]things strangled, and from [x]fornication: from which if ye keep yourselves, ye shall do well. Fare ye well.

30 So when they were dismissed, they came to [g]Ăn'tĭ-ŏch: and when they had gathered the multitude together, they delivered the epistle:

31 *Which* when they had read, they [y]rejoiced for the consolation.

32 And Jū'das and *Sī'las, being [z]prophets also themselves, [a]exhorted the brethren with many words, and confirmed *them.*

33 And after they had tarried *there* a space, they were let go in peace from the brethren unto [11]the apostles.

34 [12]Notwithstanding it pleased *Sī'las to abide there still.

35 [b]Pa̤ul also and [c]Bär'na-băs continued in [d]Ăn'tĭ-ŏch, [e]teaching and [f]preaching the [g,h]word of the Lord, with many others also.

36 ¶ And some days after [b]Pa̤ul said unto [c]Bär'na-băs, Let us go again and visit our brethren in every city where we have preached the word of the Lord, *and see* how they do.

37 And [c]Bär'na-băs determined to take with them Jŏhn, whose surname was [i]Märk.

38 But [b]Pa̤ul thought not good to take him with them, who [j]departed from them from [k]Păm-phỹl'ĭ-ȧ, and went not with them to the work.

39 And the [l]contention was so sharp between them, that they departed asunder one from the other: and so [c]Bär'na-băs took [i]Märk, and sailed unto [m]Çỹ'prus;

40 And [b]Pa̤ul chose *Sī'las, and departed, being [n]recommended by the brethren unto the [o]grace of [13]God.

41 And he went through [p]Sỹr'ĭ-ȧ and [q]Çĭ-lĭ'çiȧ, confirming the [r]churches.

## CHAPTER 16

*Paul circumcises Timothy. 6 Being forbidden by the Spirit to preach in Asia and Bithynia, he comes to Troas. 9 By a vision he is led to pass into Macedonia. 14 Lydia converted. 16 A spirit of divination cast out. 19 Paul and Silas scourged and imprisoned. 25 The prison doors miraculously opened. 31 The jailer converted. 35 Paul and Silas set at liberty.*

THEN came [a]he to [b]Dĕr'bē and [c]Lỹs'trȧ: and, behold, a certain [d]disciple was there, named [1,e]Tĭ-mō'the-ŭs, the son of a certain [f]woman, which was a Jew'ess, and [g]believed; but his father *was* a [h]Greek:

2 Which was well reported of

**34**
12 R. V. omits this verse.

**35**
b Paul, Acts 13:9.
c Barnabas, Acts 4:36.
d Antioch, Acts 11:19.
**A.D. 53**
e Instruction, in religion, Prov. 23:23.
f Preaching, Matt. 9:35.
g Word of God, Psa. 119:9.
h Doctrines of Jesus, John 7:16.

**37**
i Mark, Acts 12:12.

**38**
j Instability, instances of, Jas. 1:8.
k Pamphylia, Acts 14:24.

**39**
l Strife, Prov. 20:3.
m Cyprus, Acts 21:3.

**40**
n Intercession, instances of, Jer. 27:18.
o Grace of God, Rom. 14:16.
13 R. V. the Lord.

**41**
p Syria, Paul preaches in, 2 Kin. 6:23.
q Cilicia, Gal. 1:21.
r Church, Matt. 16:18.

**1**
a Paul, Acts 13:9.
b Derbe, Acts 14:6.
c Lystra, Acts 14:6.
d Disciples, Matt. 9:14.
e Or, Timothy, 1 Cor. 4:17.
f 2 Tim. 1:5.
g Faith in Christ, John 6:69.
h Greeks, Zech. 9:13.
1 Am. R. V. Timothy, the son of a Jewess who believed; but his father was a Greek.

---

*Paul, from Thessalonica,* Acts 17:4-10. *Left by Paul at Berea,* Acts 17:14. *Rejoins Paul at Corinth,* Acts 18:1, 5. *Carries Peter's epistle to the disciples of the Dispersion in Asia Minor,* 1 Pet. 5:12.

by the [i]brethren that were at
[c]Lȳs′trȧ and [j]Ī-cō′nĭ-ŭm.
3 Him would [a]Paul have to go
forth [k]with him; and took and
[l,m]circumcised him [n,o]because of
the [p,q]Jews which were in those
quarters: for they knew all that
his father was a [h]Greek.
4 And as they went through the
cities, they delivered them the
[r]decrees for to keep, that were
ordained of the [s]apostles and
[t]elders which were at [u]Jē-ru′sȧ-
lĕm.
5 And so were the churches [2]es-
tablished in the [v]faith, and [w]in-
creased in number daily.
6 Now when they had gone
throughout [x]Phrȳg′ĭ-ȧ and the
region of *Gȧ-lā′tiȧ, and were
forbidden of the [y]Holy Ghost to
[z]preach the word in [a]Ā′ṣiȧ,
7 After they were come to
Mȳs′iȧ, they assayed to go into
[b]Bī-thȳn′ĭ-ȧ: but the Spirit [3]suf-
fered them not.
8 And they passing by Mȳs′iȧ
came down to [c]Trō′as.
9 ¶ And a [d]vision appeared to
[e]Paul in the night; There stood
a man of †Măç-e-dō′nĭ-ȧ, and
prayed him, saying, Come over
into Măç-e-dō′nĭ-ȧ, and help us.
10 And after he had seen the
[d]vision, immediately [e,f]we [g]en-
deavoured to go into Măç-e-
dō′-nĭ-ȧ, assuredly gathering
that [4]the Lord had called us
for to [h]preach the [i]gospel unto
them.
11 Therefore loosing from
[c]Trō′as, we came with a straight
course to Săm-o-thrā′çiȧ, and
the next *day* to Nē-ăp′o-lĭs;
12 And from thence to [j]Phĭ-
lĭp′pī, which is [5]the chief city of
that part of †Măç-e-dō′nĭ-ȧ, *and*
a colony: and we were in that
city abiding certain days.
13 And on the [k]sabbath we
went [6]out of the city by a river
side, where [l]prayer was wont to
be made; and we sat down, and
spake unto the women which resorted *thither*.
14 ¶ And a certain [m]woman
named Lȳd′ĭ-ȧ, a seller of purple, of the city of [n]Thȳ-a-tī′rȧ,
which [o]worshipped God, heard
*us*: [p]whose [q]heart the Lord
opened, that she attended unto
the things which were spoken of
[e]Paul.
15 And when she was [r]bap-
tized, and her [s]household, she
besought *us*, saying, If ye have
judged me to be faithful to the
Lord, [t,u]come into my house,
and abide *there*. And she constrained us.
16 ¶ And it came to pass, as we
went to [7]prayer, a certain damsel possessed with a spirit of divination met us, which brought
her masters much gain by soothsaying:
17 The same followed [e]Paul
and us, and cried, saying, These
men are the servants of the most
high God, which [v]shew unto us
the [w]way of ‡salvation.
18 And this did she many days.

**2**
*i* *Fraternity, of Christian believers*, Zech. 11:14.
*j* *Iconium*, Acts 13:51.
**3**
*k* *Minister, sent forth two and two*, Rom. 15:16.
*l* *Circumcision*, Gen. 17:10.
*m* *Expediency, of Paul*, 1 Cor. 6:12.
*n* *Tact*, Prov. 15:1.
*o* *Prudence*, 2 Chr. 2:12.
*p* *Jews*, Neh. 4:2.
*q* *Public Opinion*, John 12:42.
**4**
*r* *Church, decrees of*, Matt. 16:18.
*s* *Apostles*, Luke 6:13.
*t* *Elders*, Acts 14:23.
*u* *Jerusalem*, Judg. 19:10.
**5**
*v* *Faith, the doctrines of Jesus*, 1 Cor. 16:13.
*w* *Church, Christian, rapid growth of*, Matt. 16:18.
2 R. V. strengthened
**6**
*x* Acts 2:10; 18:23.
*y* *Holy Spirit*, Acts 1:2.
*z* *Preaching*, Matt. 9:35.

*a* *Asia*, Acts 2:9.
**7**
*b* 1 Pet. 1:1.
3 R. V. Spirit of Jesus suffered them not;
**8**
*c* Acts 20:5, 6; 2 Cor. 2:12; 2 Tim. 4:13.
**9**
*d* *Vision*, Acts 9:10.
*e* *Paul*, Acts 13:9.
**10**
*f* *Luke*, Col. 4:14.
*g* *Zeal*, 2 Cor. 7:11.
*h* *Preaching*, Matt. 9:35.
*i* *Gospel*, Mark 13:10.
4 R. V. God

**12**
*j* *Philippi*, Acts 20:6.
5 R. V. a city of Macedonia, the first of the district, a Roman colony:
**13**
*k* *Sabbath, religious instruction on*, Ex. 16:23.
*l* *Prayer*, Acts 6:4.
6 R. V. forth without the gate by a river side, where we supposed there was a place of prayer;
**14**
*m* *Women, good*, Prov. 31:10.
*n* Rev. 1:11; 2:18, 24.
*o* *Worship*, Gen. 22:5.
*p* *Conviction of Sin, from God*, John 16:8.
*q* *Heart*, Psa. 44:21.
**15**
*r* *Baptism, Christian*, Luke 20:4.
*s* *Family, good*, 1 Chr. 13:14.
*t* *Hospitality*, Rom. 12:13.
*u* *Minister, hospitality to*, Rom. 15:16.
**16**
7 R. V. the place of prayer,
**17**
*v* *Minister, duties of*, Rom. 15:16.
*w* *Gospel*, Mark 13:10.

***GALATIA**, a province of Asia Minor. *Its churches visited by Paul*, Acts 16:6; 18:23. *Collection taken in, for Christians at Jerusalem*, 1 Cor. 16:1. *Peter's epistle to*, 1 Pet. 1:1. *Churches in*, Gal. 1:1, 2.
See Paul's Epistle to Galatians.

†**MACEDONIA**, a country in southeastern Europe. *Paul, has a vision concerning*, Acts 16:9; *preaches in, at Philippi*, Acts 16:12; *revisits*, Acts 20:1–6; 2 Cor. 2:13; 7:5. *Churches in, send contributions to the poor in Jerusalem*, Rom. 15:26; 2 Cor. 8:1–5. *Timothy visits*, Acts 19:22. *Paul's tribulations in*, 2 Cor. 7:5. *Titus joins Paul in*, 2 Cor. 7:6. *Aristarchus from*, Acts 27:2.

‡**SALVATION.** *Call to*, Isa. 55:1–3, 6, 7; Luke 3:6.
Signifying: *Gracious providences*, Deut. 32:15; Psa. 68:19, 20; 91:16; 95:1; 116:13; 149:4; Isa. 12:2, 3; *personal deliverance from enemies*, 2 Sam. 22:36; Psa. 3:8; 18:2; 37:39; *national deliverance from enemies*, Ex. 15:2; 1 Chr. 16:35; Psa. 98:2, 3; 106:8; Isa. 46:12, 13; Jer. 3:23; *a divine standard of righteousness*, Isa. 56:1; *the saving power of divine truth*, Isa. 45:17; *the light and glory of Zion*, Isa. 62:1; *the promised Messiah*, John 4:22; *personal righteousness*, 2 Chr. 6:41; Psa. 132:16, *eternal life*, 1 Thess. 5:8, 9; 1 Pet. 1:5, 9.

**Through Christ**, Isa. 61:10; Matt. 1:21; Luke 19:10; 24:46, 47; John 3:14–17; 11:51, 52; Acts 4:12; 13:26, 38, 39, 47; 16:30, 31; Rom. 5:15–21; 7:24, 25; 9:30–33; 1 Cor. 6:11; Eph. 1:9, 10, 13; 2 Tim. 1:9, 10; 2:10; Tit. 3:5–7; Heb. 2:3, 10; 5:9; 7:25; 1 John 4:9, 10; 5:11; Jude 3. *By the atonement*, 1 Cor. 1:18, 21, 24, 25; Gal. 1:4; 3:8, 13, 14, 21, 26–28; Col. 1:20–23, 26, 27; 1 Tim. 2:6; Rev. 5:9. *By his resurrection*, Rom. 5:10. *By the gospel*, Rom. 1:16; Jas. 1:21. *By the grace of God*, Eph. 2:8, 9; Tit. 2:11; 2 Pet. 3:15.

*Foretold by, prophets*, Luke 2:31, 32; 1 Pet. 1:10; *by angels*, Luke 2:9–14. *Preached by apostles*, Acts 16:17. *Wisdom in, derived from the Scriptures*, 2 Tim. 3:15. *Praise for, ascribed unto God and the Lamb*, Rev. 7:9, 10.

*For the Gentiles*, Acts 11:17, 18; 15:7–9, 11; 28:28; Rom.

But [e]Pa̤ul, being grieved, turned
and said to the [x]spirit, I command thee in the name of Jē′sus
Christ to come out of her. And
he [y]came out the same hour.[s]
19 ¶ And when her masters saw
that the [z]hope of their gains was
gone, they [a,b]caught [c]Pa̤ul and
[d]Sī′las, and drew[G] *them* into the
marketplace unto the rulers,
20 And brought [c,d]them to
the [e]magistrates, [f,g]saying, These
men, being Jews, do exceedingly
trouble our city,[Q]
21 And [f,g]teach [h]customs, which
are not lawful for us to receive,
neither to observe, being Rō′-
mans.
22 And the multitude rose up
together against them: and the
[e]magistrates rent[C] off their clothes,
and commanded to [8,i]beat *them*.
23 And when they had [j]laid
many stripes upon [k]them, they
cast *them* into prison, charging
the jailor to keep them safely:
24 Who, having received such a
charge, [l]thrust [c,d]them into the
inner [m]prison, and made their
[n]feet fast[C] in the [o]stocks.
25 ¶ And at midnight [c,p]Pa̤ul
and [d,p]Sī′las [q,r]prayed, and
[s,t,u]sang [v]praises unto God: and
the prisoners heard them.
26 And suddenly there was a
great [w]earthquake, so that the
foundations of the [m]prison were
shaken: and immediately all the
doors were opened, and every
one's bands were loosed.[S]
27 And the keeper of the [m]pris-
on awaking out of his sleep, and
seeing the prison doors open, he
drew out his sword, and would
have [x]killed himself, supposing
that the prisoners had [9]been
fled.
28 But [c]Pa̤ul cried with a loud
voice, saying, Do thyself no
harm: for we are all here.
29 Then he called for a light,
and sprang in, and [10]came trembling, and fell down before [c]Pa̤ul
and [d]Sī′las,
30 And brought them out, and
[y,z]said, Sirs, what must I do to
be saved?
31 And they said, [a,b]Believe
on the [c,d]Lord Jē′sus [11]Christ,
and thou shalt be saved, and
thy [e]house.[S T]
32 And they [f,g]spake unto him
the [h]word of the Lord, and to all
that were in his house.
33 And he took them the same
hour of the night, and [i]washed
*their* [j]stripes; and was [k]baptized,
he and all his, straightway.[G]
34 And when he had brought
[l]them into his house, he set
meat[C] before them, and rejoiced,
[m]believing in God with all his
[e]house.
35 And when it was day, the
[n]magistrates sent the serjeants,
saying, Let those men go.
36 And the keeper of the prison
told this saying to [o]Pa̤ul, The
[n]magistrates have sent to let you
go: now therefore depart, and go
in peace.
37 But [o]Pa̤ul said unto them,
They have [j,p]beaten us openly
[q]uncondemned, being [r]Rō′mans,
and have cast *us* into prison; and
now do they thrust us out priv-

**18**
x *Demons*, Matt. 4:24.
y *Miracles, of the disciples*, Luke 23:8.

**19**
z *Covetousness, instances of*, Isa. 57:17.

a *Malice*, Eph. 4:31.
b *Arrest*, Matt. 26:50.
c *Paul*, Acts 13:9.
d *Silas*, Acts 15:22.

**20**
e *Magistrate*, Ezra 7:25.
f *False Accusation*, 2 Tim. 3:3.
g *Indictments* Matt. 27:37.

**21**
h *Heresy*, Tit. 3:10.

**22**
i *Beating*, Ex. 5:14.
8 R. V. beat them with rods.

**23**
j *Scourging*, Acts 22:24.
k *Prisoners, scourged*, Psa. 79:11.

**24**
l *Imprisonment*, Acts 12:4.
m *Prison*, Gen. 39:20.
n *Feet*, 2 Sam. 4:4.
o *Stocks, in prisons*, Job 13:27.

**25**
p *Prisoners, joyful*, Psa. 79:11.
q *Prayer*, Acts 6:4.
r *Worship, in the night*, Gen. 22:5.
s *Resignation, exemplified*, Job 5:17.
t *Adversity, resignation in*, Psa. 10:6.
u *Joy, instances of*, Psa. 5:11.
v *Praise*, Psa. 150:1.

**26**
w *Earthquakes*, Isa. 29:6.

**27**
x *Suicide*, 1 Kin. 16:18.
9 R. V. escaped.

**29**
10 R. V. trembling for fear, fell

**30**
y *Conviction of Sin*, John 16:8.
z *Spiritual Desire*, Psa. 42:1.

**31**
a *Faith in Christ, salvation by*, John 6:69.
b See footnote *Salvation*, on preceding page.
c *Jesus, lordship of*, Matt. 1:21.
d *Jesus, savior*, Matt. 1:21.
e *Family, religion in*, 1 Chr. 13:14.
11 R. V. *omits* Christ,

**32**
f *Preaching*, Matt. 9:35.
g *Instruction, in religion*, Prov. 23:23.
h *Doctrines of Jesus*, John 7:16.

**33**
i *Prisoners, kindness to*, Psa. 79:11.
j *Prisoners, scourged*, Psa. 79:11.
k *Baptism, Christian*, Luke 20:4.

**34**
l *Minister, hospitality to*, Rom. 15:16.
m *Faith, instances of*, Mark 11:22.

**35**
n *Magistrate*, Ezra 7:25.

**36**
o *Paul*, Acts 13:9.

**37**
p *Beating*, Ex. 5:14.
q *Trial, right of*, John 7:51.
r *Roman Empire, rights of citizens of*, John 11:48.

11:11; 15:9, 16; Gal. 3:8; Eph. 3:6, 9. *For all men*, 1 Tim. 2:3, 4; 4:10; 2 Pet. 3:9; Rev. 14:6; 22:17.
*From sin*, Matt. 1:21; Mark 2:17; Luke 5:31, 32. *From spiritual hunger and thirst*, John 4:14; 6:35; 7:37, 38.
*Not by works*, Rom. 3:28; 4:1–25; 9:30–33; 11:6; Gal. 2:16; Eph. 2:8, 9; Tit. 3:5–7.
*Offered and rejected*, Matt. 22:3–13; 23:37; Luke 14:16–24; John 5:40.
**Conditions of:** *Repentanse*, Matt. 3:2; Mark 1:4; Luke 3:8; Acts 2:38; 3:19; 2 Cor. 7:10. *Faith in Christ*, Mark 16:15, 16; John 3:14–18; 5:24; 6:47; 11:25, 26; 12:36; 20:31; Acts 2:21; 16:30, 31; 20:21; Rom. 1:16, 17; 3:21–30; 4:1–25; 5:1, 2; 10:4, 8–13; Gal. 2:16; 3:8; Eph. 2:8; Phil. 3:9; 2 Thess. 2:13; 1 Tim. 1:15, 16; 1 Pet. 1:9. *Supreme love to Christ*, Luke 14:25–27. *Renunciation of the world*, Matt. 19:16–21; Luke 14:33; 18:18–26.
**Plan of,** John 17:4; Heb. 6:17–20. *Foreordained*, Eph. 1:4–6; 3:11. *Described as a mystery*, Matt. 13:11; Mark 4:11; Luke 8:10; Rom. 16:25, 26; 1 Cor. 2:7–9; Eph. 3:9, 10; 6:19; Col. 1:26, 27; 1 Tim. 3:16.
Includes: *The incarnation of Christ*, Gal. 4:4, 5; *the atonement by Christ*, John 18:11; 19:28–30; Acts 3:18; 17:3; Rom. 16:25, 26; 1 Cor. 1:21–25; 2:7–9; Eph. 1:7–11; 3:1–8; 6:19; Col. 1:26, 27; Heb. 2:9–18; 10:10; *initial grace*, John 6:37, 44, 45, 65; *the election of grace*, 2 Thess. 2:13, 14; 2 Tim. 1:9, 10.
Sets forth: *Reconciliation to God through Christ*, 2 Cor. 5:18, 19; Col. 1:9, 20–23; *righteousness by faith in the atonement of Christ, as opposed to righteousness by works*, Rom. 10:3–9; 16:25, 26; Eph. 2:6–10.
**Final:** *Conditioned on perseverance*, Matt. 24:13.
See footnote, Jesus, *Savior*, Matt. 1:21.

40
*s* *Prison*, Gen. 39:20.
*t* *Fellowship, of the righteous*, 1 Cor. 1:9.
*u* *Fraternity*, Zech. 11:14.
*v* *Minister, duties of*, Rom. 15:16.

1
*a* *Thessalonica*, Phil. 4:16.
*b* *Synagogue*, Matt. 12:9.
*c* *Jews*, Neh. 4:2.

2
*d* *Paul*, Acts 13:9.
*e* *Zeal, exemplified*, 2 Cor. 7:11.
*f* *Sabbath, religious instruction on*, Ex. 16:23.
*g* *Reasoning*, Job 13:6.
*h* *Instruction, in religion*, Prov. 23:23.
*i* *Word of God*, Psa. 119:9.

3
*j* *Salvation, plan of*, Acts 16:17.
*k* *Jesus, Messiah*, Matt. 1:21.
*l* *Jesus, sufferings of*, Matt. 1:21.
*m* *Jesus, death of*, Matt. 1:21.
*n* *Resurrection, of Jesus*, 1 Cor. 15:12.
*o* *Preaching*, Matt. 9:35.

4
*p* *Faith in Christ*, John 6:69.
*q* *Fellowship, of the righteous*, 1 Cor. 1:9.
*r* *Silas*, Acts 15:22.
*s* *Gentiles, conversion of*, Acts 10:45.
*t* *Greeks*, Zech. 9:13.
*u* *Women*, Prov. 31:10.
1 R. V. were persuaded,

5
*v* *Unbelievers*, 1 Cor. 6:6.
*w* *Intolerance, exemplified*, Num. 11:28.
*x* *Malice*, Eph. 4:31.
*y* *Envy*, Prov. 14:30.
*z* *Jealousy*, Psa. 78:58.

*a* *Persecution, of the righteous*, John 15:20.
*b* *Minister, persecutions of*, Rom. 15:16.
2 R. V. being moved with jealousy, took

ily[G]? nay verily; but let them come themselves and fetch[G] us out.

38 And the serjeants told these words unto the [n]magistrates: and they feared, when they heard that they were Rō'mans̩.

39 And they came and besought them, and brought *them* out, and desired *them* to depart out of the city.

40 And they went out of the [s]prison, and [t]entered into *the house of* Lȳd'ĭ-ȧ: and when they had [t]seen the [u]brethren, [v]they comforted them, and departed.

## CHAPTER 17

*Paul preaches at Thessalonica with success; 5 but is persecuted by the Jews. 10 He is sent to Berea, and preaches there. 13 Being persecuted there also, he comes to Athens. 16 He disputes publicly. 22 His discourse on Mars' hill. 32 Some mock and others believe.*

NOW when they had passed through Ăm-phĭp'o-lĭs and Ăp-ŏl-lō'nĭ-ȧ, they came to [a]Thĕs-sa-lō-nī'cȧ, where was a [b]synagogue of the [c]Jews̩:

2 And [d]Pa̤ul, [e]as his manner was, went in unto them, and three [f]sabbath days [g,h]reasoned with them out of the [i]scriptures,

3 Opening[G] and alleging,[G] [j]that [k]Chrīst must needs have [l,m]suffered, and [n]risen again from the dead; and that this Jē'ṣus, whom I [o]preach unto you, is [k]Chrīst.

4 And some of them [1,p]believed, and [q]consorted[G] with [d]Pa̤ul and [r]Sī'las; and of the devout [s,t]Greeks a great multitude, and of the chief [u]women not a few.

5 ¶ But the [v]Jews̩ [2]which believed not, [w,x]moved with [y,z]envy, took unto them certain lewd[G] fellows of the baser[G] sort,[G] and gathered a *company, and set all the city on an uproar, and [a,b]assaulted the house of Jā'son, and sought to bring them out to the people.

6 And when they found them not, they [a]drew[G] Jā'son and certain brethren unto the rulers of the city, crying, These that have turned the world upside down are come hither also;

7 Whom Jā'son hath received: and [c,d]these all [e]do contrary to the decrees of Çæ'ṣar, saying that there is another [f]king, *one* Jē'ṣus.

8 And they troubled the people and the rulers of the city, when they heard these things.

9 And when they had taken security of Jā'son, and of the other, they let them go.

10 ¶ And the brethren immediately [g]sent away [h]Pa̤ul and [i]Sī'las by night unto [j]Bĕ-rē'ȧ: who coming *thither* went into the [k]synagogue of the Jews̩.

11 These were more noble than those in [l]Thĕs-sa-lō-nī'cȧ, in that they received the [m]word with all readiness of mind, and [n]searched the [o]scriptures daily, whether those things were so.

12 Therefore many of them [p]believed; also of honourable [q]women which were [r]Greeks, and of men, not a few.

13 But when the [s]Jews̩ of [l]Thĕs-sa-lō-nī'cȧ had knowledge that the [o]word of God was [t]preached of [h]Pa̤ul at [j]Bĕ-rē'ȧ, they came thither also, and [u,v,w]stirred up the people.

14 And then immediately the brethren [g,x]sent away [h]Pa̤ul to go as it were to the sea: but [i]Sī'las and [y]Tĭ-mō'the-ŭs abode there still.

15 And they that conducted [h]Pa̤ul brought him unto [z]Ăth'ĕns̩: and receiving a commandment unto [i]Sī'las and [x]Tĭ-mō'the-ŭs for to come to him with all speed, they departed.

16 ¶ Now while [a]Pa̤ul waited for them at [b]Ăth'ĕns̩, his spirit was [3]stirred in him, when he

7
*c* *False Accusation*, 2 Tim. 3:3.
*d* *Indictments*, Matt. 27:37.
*e* *Treason, Paul falsely accused of*, 2 Kin. 11:14.
*f* *Jesus, king*, Matt. 1:21.

10
*g* *Prudence*, 2 Chr. 2:12.
*h* *Paul*, Acts 13:9.
*i* *Silas*, Acts 15:22.
*j* Acts 20:4.
*k* *Synagogue*, Matt. 12:9.

11
*l* *Thessalonica*, Phil. 4:16.
*m* *Doctrines of Jesus*, John 7:16.
*n* *Spiritual Desire*, Psa. 42:1.
*o* *Word of God*, Psa. 119:9.

12
*p* *Faith in Christ*, John 6:69.
*q* *Women*, Prov. 31:10.
*r* *Greeks*, Zech. 9:13.

13
*s* *Jews*, Neh. 4:2.
*t* *Preaching*, Matt. 9:35.
*u* *Malice*, Eph. 4:31.
*v* *Intolerance*, Num. 11:28.
*w* *Persecution, of the righteous*, John 15:20.

14
*x* *Tact*, Prov. 15:1.
*y* Or, *Timothy*, 1 Cor. 4:17.

15
*z* Acts 18:1; 1 Thess. 3:1.

16
*a* *Paul*, Acts 13:9.
*b* Acts 18:1; 1 Thess. 3:1.
3 R. V. provoked within him, as he beheld the city full of idols.

***MOB.** *At, Thessalonica*, Acts 17:5; *Jerusalem*, Acts 21:28, 30; *Ephesus*, Acts 19:29–40.

c *Idolatry*, 1 Sam. 15:23.
d *Sin, repugnant to the righteous*, Rom. 5:12.

**17**
e *Reasoning*, Job 13:6.
f *Instruction, in religion*, Prov. 23:23.
g *Synagogue*, Matt. 12:9.
h *Zeal*, 2 Cor. 7:11.

**18**
i *Philosophy, Greek schools of*, Col. 2:8.
j *Scoffing*, Hab. 1:10.
k *Minister, duties of*, Rom. 15:16.
l *Resurrection*, 1 Cor. 15:12.

**21**
m *Idleness*, Eccl. 10:18.

**22**
n *Orator*, Acts 24:1.
4 R. V. the Areopagus,
5 Am. R. V. very religious.

**23**
o *Altar, used in idolatrous worship*, Gen. 8:20.
p *Inscriptions*, Mark 15:26.
q *Ignorance, concerning God*, Acts 3:17.
r *Spiritual Blindness*, 2 Cor. 4:4.
6 R. V. observed the objects of your worship,

**24**
s *God, creator*, Gen. 2:2.
t *God, sovereign*, Gen. 2:2.

saw the city wholly given to
[c,d]idolatry.
17 Therefore [e,f]disputed he in
the [g]synagogue with the Jews,
and with the devout persons,
and in the market [h]daily with
them that met with him.
18 Then certain [i]philosophers
of the †Ĕp-ĭ-cū-rē'ans, and of
the ‡Stō'ĭcks, encountered him.
And some [j]said, What will this
babbler say? other some, He
seemeth to be a setter forth
of strange gods: because he
[k]preached unto them Jē'sus,
and the [l]resurrection.
19 And they took him, and
brought him unto Ăr-e-ŏp'a-
gŭs, saying, May we know what
this new doctrine, whereof thou
speakest, *is*?
20 For thou bringest certain
strange things to our ears: we
would know therefore what these
things mean.
21 (For all the Â-thē'nĭ-ans
and strangers which were there
[m]spent their time in nothing else,
but either to tell, or to hear some
new thing.)
22 ¶ Then [a,n]Paul stood in the
midst of [4]Märs' hill, and said,
*Ye* men of [b]Ăth'ĕns, I perceive
that in all things ye are [5]too
superstitious.
23 For as I passed by, and [6]be-
held your devotions, I found
an [o]altar with this [p]inscription,
TO THE UNKNOWN GOD.
Whom therefore ye [q,r]ignorantly
worship, him declare I unto you.
24 God that [s]made the world
and all things therein, seeing
that he is [t]Lord of heaven and
earth, dwelleth not in temples
made with hands;
25 Neither is [7]worshipped with
men's hands, [u]as though he
needed any thing, seeing he [s]giv-
eth to all [v]life, and [w]breath, and
all things;
26 And hath [s]made of one
blood all nations of ‖,[x]men for
to dwell on all the face of the
earth, and [y]hath determined [8]the
times before appointed, and the
bounds of their habitation;
27 That they should [z]seek [9]the
Lord, if haply they might feel
after him, and find him, though
[a]he be not far from every one of
us:
28 For in [a,b]him we live, and
move, and have our being; as
certain also of your own §,[c]poets
have said, For we are also his
offspring.
29 Forasmuch then as we are
the offspring of God, we ought
not to think that the [d]Godhead
is like unto gold, or silver, or
stone, graven by art and man's
device.
30 And the times of this [e,f]ig-
norance God [10,g,h]winked at; but
now [i,j]commandeth all men every
where to repent:
31 Because he hath appointed a
[k]day, in the which he will judge
the world in [l]righteousness by
*that* [m]man whom he hath ordained; *whereof* he hath given
assurance unto all *men*, in that
he hath [n]raised him from the
dead.
32 ¶ And when they heard of
the [n]resurrection of the dead,
some [o]mocked: and others said,

**25**
u *God, self-existent*, Gen. 2:2.
v *Life, from God*, Eccl. 8:15.
w *Breath, of life*, Gen. 7:15.
7 R. V. he served by

**26**
x *Man, equality of*, Job 4:17.
y *Foreordination*, Rom. 8:30.
8 R. V. their appointed seasons,

**27**
z *Seekers*, Isa. 55:6.
a *God, immanence of*, Gen. 2:2.
9 R. V. God,

**28**
b *God, preserver*, Gen. 2:2.
c *Greece, poets of*, Zech. 9:13.

**29**
d *God, spirit*, Gen. 2:2.

**30**
e *Ignorance*, Acts 3:17.
f *Spiritual Blindness*, 2 Cor. 4:4.
g *God, longsuffering of*, Gen. 2:2.
h *God, mercy of*, Gen. 2:2.
i *Commandment, enjoining repentance*, Deut. 8:2.
j *Repentance, enjoined*, Mark 1:4
10 R. V. overlooked;

**31**
k *Judgment, the general*, 2 Pet. 3:7.
l *God, justice of*, Gen. 2:2.
m *Jesus, judge*, Matt. 1:21.
n *Resurrection, of Jesus*, 1 Cor. 15:12.

**32**
o *Scoffing*, Hab 1:10.

† **EPICUREANS**, Isa. 22:13; Luke 12:19. *Doctrines propagated by, familiar to the author of Ecclesiastes*, Eccl. 2:1–10; *and to Paul*, 1 Cor. 15:32. *Dispute with Paul*, Acts 17:18.

‡ **STOICISM**, a Grecian philosophy, inculcating doctrines of severe morality, self-denials, and inconvenient services. Scripture analogies to: *John the Baptist, wears camel's hair, and subsists on locusts and wild honey*, Matt. 3:4; Mark 1:6; *comes neither eating nor drinking*, Matt. 11:18; Luke 7:33. *Jesus requires, self-denials and crosses*, Matt. 10:38, 39; 16:24; Mark 8:34, 35; Luke 9:23–26; 14:27; *the subordination of natural affection*, Matt. 10:37; Luke 14:26. *Paul teaches, that the law of the mind is at war with the law of the members*, Rom. 7:23 (with vs. 14–24); 8:3–10; *that the body must be kept under*, Rom. 8:3–13, 18–23; 1 Cor. 9:27; *and advises celibacy*, 1 Cor. 7:1–9, 25, 26, 32, 33, 39, 40.
*School of, at Athens*, Acts 17:18.

‖ **RACE**, human. *Unity of*, Gen. 3:20; Mal. 2:10; Acts 17:26.

§ **POETRY**, Acts 17:28.
**Acrostic**, Psa. 25; 34; 37; 111; 112; 119; 145; Prov. 31:10–31; Lam. chapters 1–5.
**Didactic**: *Moses' song*, Deut. 32. *The Book of Job, the Proverbs, Ecclesiastes, Lamentations of Jeremiah, the didactic psalms.* See footnote, PSALMS, *Didactic*, Psa. 1.

We will hear thee again of this
*matter*.
33 So [p]Paul departed from
among them.
34 Howbeit certain men clave
unto him, and [q]believed: among
the which *was* Dī-o-nȳs'ĭ-ŭs the
Ăr-e-ŏp'a-gīte, and a [r]woman
named Dăm'a-rĭs, and others
with them.

## CHAPTER 18

*At Corinth Paul labors with his hands, and preaches. 6 The Jews oppose him. 9 The Lord encourages him in a vision. 12 He is brought before Gallio, but dismissed. 18 He comes to Ephesus on his way to Syria; 23 and afterward visits Galatia and Phrygia. 24 Apollos preaches at Ephesus and in Achaia.*

AFTER these things [a]Paul departed from [b]Ăth'ĕns, and
came to *Cŏr'inth;
2 And found a certain [c]Jew
named †Ăq'uĭ-lȧ, born in [d]Pŏn'-
tus, lately come from [e]Ĭt'a-lȳ,
with his wife †Prĭs-çĭl'lȧ; (because that [f]Clau'dĭ-ŭs had [g]com-
manded all [c]Jews to depart from
[h]Rōme:) and came unto them.
3 And because [a]he was of
the same [1]craft, he [i]abode with
†them, and [j]wrought: for by their
occupation they were [k,l]tent-
makers.
4 And he [m,n]reasoned in the
[o]synagogue [p]every [q]sabbath, and
persuaded the [c]Jews and the
[r]Greeks.
5 And when [s]Sī'las and [t]Tĭ-mō'-
the-ŭs were come from [u]Măç-e-
dō'nĭ-ȧ, Paul was [2,p,v]pressed in
the spirit, and [w,x]testified to the
Jews *that* Jē'sus *was* [y]Christ.
6 And when they [z]opposed
themselves, and blasphemed,
he shook *his* raiment, and said
unto them, Your blood *be* upon
your own heads; [a]I *am* clean:
from henceforth I will go unto
the [b]Ġĕn'tīles.
7 And he departed thence, and
[c]entered into a certain *man's*
house, named Jŭs'tus, [d]*one* that
[e]worshipped God, whose house
joined hard to the [f]synagogue.
8 And [g]Crĭs'pus, the chief ruler
of the [f]synagogue, [h]believed on
the Lord with all his [i]house; and
many of the Cŏ-rĭnth'ĭ-ans hearing [h]believed, and were [j]bap-
tized.
9 Then spake the Lord to [k]Paul
in the night by a [l]vision, [m]Be not
afraid, but [n]speak, and hold not
thy peace:
10 For [o,p]I am with thee, and
[q]no man shall set on thee to hurt
thee: for I have much people in
this city.
11 And he continued *there* a
year and six months, [r]teaching
the [s]word of God among them.
12 ¶ And when Găl'lĭ-ō was
the [3,t]deputy of ‡Ȧ-chā'iȧ, the
[u]Jews [v,w,x]made insurrection
with one accord against [k,y]Paul,
and brought him to the [z]judg-
ment seat,
13 [a]Saying, This [4]*fellow* persuadeth men [b]to worship God
contrary to the [c]law.
14 And when [d]Paul was now
about to open *his* mouth, Găl'-
lĭ-ō said unto the Jews, If it were
a matter of wrong or wicked
[5]lewdness, O *ye* Jews, reason
would that I should bear with
you:
15 But if it be a question of
words and names, and *of* your

33
*p Paul*, Acts 13:9.
34
*q Faith in Christ*, John 6:69.
*r Women*, Prov. 31:10.
1
*a Paul*, Acts 13:9.
*b* Acts 17:15, 22; 1 Thess. 3:1.
2
*c Jews*, Neh. 4:2.
*d* Acts 2:9; 1 Pet. 1:1.
*e* Acts 27:1; Heb. 13:24.
*f* Acts 11:28.
*g Banishment*, Ezra 7:26.
*h Rome, Jews excluded from*, Acts 19:21.
3
*i Minister, hospitality to*, Rom. 15:16.
*j Industry*, 1 Kin. 11:28.
*k Tent*, Gen. 13:5.
*l Art, of the tentmaker*, 2 Chr. 16:14.
1 R. V. trade,
4
*m Reasoning*, Job 13:6.
*n Instruction, in religion*, Prov. 23:23.
*o Synagogue*, Matt. 12:9.
*p Zeal*, 2 Cor. 7:11.
*q Sabbath, religious observance of*, Ex. 16:23.
*r Gentiles, conversion of*, Acts 10:45.
5
*s Silas*, Acts 15:22.
*t* Or, *Timothy*, 1 Cor. 4:17.
*u Macedonia*, Acts 16:12.
*v Minister, character and qualifications of*, Rom. 15:16.
*w Religious Testimony*, 2 Thess. 1:10.
*x Confession of Christ*, Luke 12:8.
*y Jesus, Messiah*, Matt. 1:21.
2 R.V. constrained by the word,
6
*z Jesus, rejected*, Matt. 1:21.

*a Minister, responsibility of*, Rom. 15:16.
*b Gentiles*, Acts 10:45.
7
*c Minister, hospitality to*, Rom. 15:16.
*d Righteous, described*, Psa. 64:10.
*e Worship*, Gen. 22:5.
*f Synagogue*, Matt. 12:9.
8
*g* 1 Cor. 1:14.
*h Faith in Christ*, John 6:69.
*i Family, religion in*, 1 Chr. 13:14.
*j Baptism, Christian*, Luke 20:4.
9
*k Paul*, Acts 13:9.
*l Vision*, Acts 9:10.
*m Courage, enjoined*, Deut. 31:7.
*n Minister, duties of*, Rom. 15:16.
10
*o Minister, promises to*, Rom. 15:16.
*p Righteous, promises to*, Psa. 64:10.
*q God, preserver*, Gen. 2:2.
11
*r Instruction, in religion*, Prov. 23:23.
*s Doctrines of Jesus*, John 7:16.
12
*t Deputy*, 1 Kin. 22:47.
*u Jews*, Neh. 4:2.
*v Conspiracy*, 1 Kin. 16:9.
*w Bigotry*, Isa. 65:5.
*x Intolerance*, Num. 11:28.
*y Minister, persecutions of*, Rom. 15:16.
*z Judgment Seat*, Acts 25:10.
3 R. V. proconsul

**13**—*a Indictments, instances of*, Matt. 27:37. *b Heresy*, Tit. 3:10. *c Law, of Moses*, Deut. 33:2. 4 R. V. man **14** *d Paul*, Acts 13:9. 5 R. V. villany,

**Elegy:** *On the death, of Saul*, 2 Sam. 1:19–27; *of Abner*, 2 Sam. 3:33, 34.
**Epic:** *Moses' song*, Ex. 15:1–19. *Miriam's song*, Ex. 15:21. *Deborah's song*, Judg. 5.
**Sacred Lyrics:** *Songs, of Moses and Miriam*, Ex. 15; *of Hannah*, 1 Sam. 2:1–10; *of Mary*, Luke 1:46–55; *of Zacharias*, Luke 1:68–79. *The Psalms*, which see.
* **CORINTH**, a city in Achaia. *Visited, by Paul*, Acts 18; 2 Cor. 12:14; 13:1, with 1 Cor. 16:5–7; and 2 Cor. 1:16; *by Apollos*, Acts 19:1; *by Titus*, 2 Cor. 8:16, 17; 12:18. *Erastus, a Christian of*, Rom. 16:23; 2 Tim. 4:20.
**Church of:** *Schism in*, 1 Cor. 1:12; 3:4. *Immoralities in*, 1 Cor. 5; 11. *Writes to Paul*, 1 Cor. 7:1. *Alienation of, from Paul*, 2 Cor. 10. *Abuse of ordinances in*, 1 Cor. 11:20–22; 14. *Heresies in*, 1 Cor. 15:12; 2 Cor. 11. *Lawsuits in*, 1 Cor. 6. *Liberty of*, 2 Cor. 9. *Paul's letters to*, 1 Cor. 1:2; 16:21–24; 2 Cor. 1:1, 13.
† **AQUILA AND PRISCILLA.** *Christians at Corinth*, Acts 18:1–3, 18, 19, 26. *Friends of Paul*, Rom. 16:3, 4. *Send salutations to Corinthians*, 1 Cor. 16:19. *Paul sends salutations to*, 2 Tim. 4:19.
‡ **ACHAIA**, a region of Greece. *Paul visits*, Acts 18; 19:21; 1 Cor. 16:15; 2 Cor. 1:1. *Benevolence of the Christians in*, Rom. 15:26; 2 Cor. 9:2; 11:10.

[c]law, look ye *to it*; for I will be no judge of such *matters*.

16 And he drave them from the [e]judgment seat.

17 Then all the [f]Greeks took Sŏs′the-nēs̱, the chief ruler of the [g]synagogue, and beat *him* before the [e]judgment seat. And Găl′lĭ-ō cared for none of those things.

18 ¶ And [d]Pa̤ul *after this* tarried[C] *there* yet a good while, and then took his leave of the brethren, and sailed thence into [h]Sy̆r′-ĭ-ȧ, and with him †Prĭs-çĭl′lȧ and †Ăq′uĭ-lȧ; having shorn *his* head in [i]Çĕn′chre-ȧ: for he had a [j]vow.[Q]

19 And he came to ‖Ĕph′e-sŭs, and left †them there: but he himself entered into the [g]synagogue, and [k,l]reasoned with the [m]Jews̱.

20 When they desired *him* to tarry longer time with them, he consented not;

21 But [6]bade them farewell, saying, I must by all means keep this [n]feast that cometh in Jė-ru̇′-sȧ-lĕm: but I will return again unto you, if God [o]will. And he sailed from ‖Ĕph′e-sŭs.

22 And when [d]he had landed at [p]Çæs-a-rē′ȧ, and gone up, and saluted[G] the [q]church, he went down to [r]Ăn′tĭ-ŏch.

23 And after he had spent some time *there*, he departed, and went over *all* the country of [s]Gȧ-lā′tiȧ and [t]Phry̆ġ′ĭ-ȧ in order, [u]strengthening all the [v]disciples.

24 ¶ And a certain Jew named [w]*Ȧ-pŏl′los, born at [x]Ăl-ĕx̱-ăn′-drĭ-ȧ, [7]an eloquent man, *and* mighty in the [y]scriptures, came to ‖Ĕph′e-sŭs.

25 [w]This man was instructed in the [z,a]way of the Lord; and being fervent[G] in the spirit, [b]he spake and [c]taught [8]diligently the things of the Lord, knowing only the [d]baptism of Jŏhn.

26 And he began to speak [e]boldly in the [f]synagogue: whom when †Ăq′uĭ-lȧ and †,[g]Prĭs-çĭl′lȧ had heard, they took him unto *them*, and [c]expounded[G] unto him the [h,i]way of God more [9]perfectly.[C]

27 And when he was disposed to pass into ‡Ȧ-chā′iȧ, the brethren [10]wrote, exhorting the [j]disciples to receive him: who, when he was come, helped them much which had [k]believed through grace:[S]

28 For he [11]mightily convinced[G] the Jews̱, *and that* publickly, shewing by the [l,m]scriptures that Jē′s̱us was [n]Chrīst.[T]

## CHAPTER 19

*At Ephesus Paul baptizes certain disciples of John. 9 Being opposed by the Jews in the synagogue, he disputes daily in the school of Tyrannus. 13 Certain Jewish exorcists are overcome. 19 Many of those who used curious arts burn their books. 21 Paul's purposed journey. 23 Demetrius, the silversmith, excites a tumult against him; 35 which is appeased by the town clerk.*

AND it came to pass, that, while *Ȧ-pŏl′los was at [a]Cŏr′inth, [b]Pa̤ul having passed through the upper coasts[G] came to [c]Ĕph′e-sŭs: and finding certain [d]disciples,

2 He said unto them, [1]Have ye received the [e]Holy Ghost[G] since ye [f]believed? And they said unto him, [2,g]We have not so much as heard whether there be any Holy Ghost.[C]

3 And he said unto them, [3]Unto[G] what then were ye baptized? And they said, [3]Unto[G] Jŏhn's [h]baptism.

4 Then said [b]Pa̤ul, [i]Jŏhn verily [h]baptized with the baptism of [j]repentance, saying unto the

**16**
e *Judgment Seat,* Acts 25:10.

**17**
f *Greeks,* Zech. 9:13.
g *Synagogue,* Matt. 12:9.

**18**
h *Syria,* 2 Kin. 6:23. Rom. 16:1.
j *Vows,* Num. 30:2.

**19**
k *Reasoning,* Job 13:6.
l *Instruction, in religion,* Prov. 23:23.
m *Jews,* Neh. 4:2.

**21**
n *Annual Feasts,* Num. 15:3.
o *Will of God, the supreme rule of duty,* Mark 3:35.
6 R. V. taking his leave of them, and saying, I will return again unto you, if God will, he set sail from Ephesus.

**22**
p *Cæsarea,* Acts 21:8.
q *Church,* Matt. 16:18.
r *Antioch,* Acts 11:19.

**A.D. 56**

**23**
s *Galatia,* Acts 16:6.
t Acts 2:10; 16:6.
u *Minister, duties of,* Rom. 15:16.
v *Disciples,* Matt. 9:14.

**24**
w *Apollos,* Acts 19:1.
x *Alexandria,* Acts 27:6.
y *Word of God,* Psa. 119:9.
7 R. V. a learned

**25**
z *Way,* Isa. 35:8.

a *Doctrines of Jesus,* John 7:16.
b *Zeal, exemplified,* 2 Cor. 7:11.
c *Instruction, in religion,* Prov. 23:23.
d *Baptism, John's,* Luke 20:4.
8 R. V. carefully the things concerning Jesus,

**26**
e *Boldness of the Righteous,* Phil. 1:20.
f *Synagogue,* Matt. 12:9.
g *Women, good,* Prov. 31:10.
h *Gospel,* Mark 13:10.
i *Doctrines of Jesus,* John 7:16.
9 R. V. carefully.

**27**
j *Disciples,* Matt. 9:14.
k *Faith in Christ,* John 6:69.
10 R. V. encouraged him, and wrote to the

**28**
l *Prophecies,* Dan. 9:24.
m *Word of God,* Psa. 119:9.
n *Jesus, Messiah,* Matt. 1:21.
11 R. V. powerfully confuted

**1**
a *Corinth,* Acts 18:1.
b *Paul,* Acts 13:9.
c *Ephesus,* Acts 18:19.
d *Disciples,* Matt. 9:14.

**2**
e *Holy Spirit, baptism of,* Acts 1:2.
f *Faith in Christ,* John 6:69.
g *Ignorance, concerning the Holy Spirit,* Acts 3:17.
1 R. V. Did ye receive the Holy Ghost when ye believed?
2 R. V. Nay, we did not so much as hear whether the Holy Ghost was given.

**3**
h *Baptism, John's,* Luke 20:4.
3 R. V. Into

**4**
i *John the Baptist,* Luke 1:63.
j *Repentance,* Mark 1:4.

‖ **EPHESUS.** *Paul visits and preaches in,* Acts 18:19–21; 19; 20:16–38. *Apollos visits and preaches in,* Acts 18:24–28. *Sceva's sons attempt to expel a demon in,* Acts 19:13–16. *Temple of Diana in,* Acts 19:24, 27, 28, 35. *Timothy directed by Paul to remain at,* 1 Tim. 1:3. *Paul sends Tychicus to,* 2 Tim. 4:12. *Onesiphorus lives at,* 2 Tim. 1:18. *Church at,* Rev. 1:11. *Apocalyptic message to,* Rev. 2:1–7. See Paul's Epistle to the Ephesians.

* **APOLLOS.** *An eloquent Christian convert, preaches. in Ephesus,* Acts 18:24–28; *in Corinth,* Acts 19:1; 1 Cor. 1:12; 3:4–7. *Refuses to return to Corinth,* 1 Cor. 16:12. *Paul writes Titus about,* Tit. 3:13.

people, that they should [l]believe
on him which should come after
him, that is, on [4]Christ Jē′ṣus.
5 When they heard *this*, they
were [k,l]baptized [5]in the [m]name
of the [n]Lord Jē′ṣus.
6 And when [b]Pa̤ul had laid *his*
[o]hands upon them, the [e]Holy
Ghost[C] came on them; and they
[p,q,r]spake with [s]tongues,[C] and
prophesied.[C]
7 And all the men were about
twelve.
8 And he went into the [t]synagogue,
and [u]spake [v]boldly for the
space[C] of three months, [6,w,x]disputing[C]
and persuading the things
concerning the [y]kingdom of
God.
9 But when [7]divers[C] were [z,a]hardened,
and believed not, but
spake evil of that [b,c]way before
the multitude, he departed from
them, and separated the [d]disciples,
[6]disputing daily in the
[†,e]school of one Ty̆-răn′nus.
10 And this continued by the
space[C] of two years; so that all
they which dwelt in [f]Ā′ṣiȧ heard
the [g]word of the [h]Lord [8]Jē′ṣus,
both Jewṣ and Greeks.
11[S] And God wrought special
[i]miracles by the hands of [j]Pa̤ul:
12 So that from his body were
brought unto the sick handkerchiefs
or aprons, and the [k]diseases
[i,l]departed from them, and
the [m]evil spirits [i,l]went out of
them.[S]
13 ¶ Then certain of the [9]vagabond[C]
Jewṣ, [n]exorcists,[C] [o]took
upon them to call over them
which had [m]evil spirits the [p]name
of the [h]Lord Jē′ṣus, saying, We
adjure you by Jē′ṣus whom
Pa̤ul preacheth.
14 And there were seven sons of
*one* Sçē′vȧ, a Jew, *and* chief of
the [q]priests, which did so.
15 And the [m]evil spirit answered
and said, Jē′ṣus I know,
and Pa̤ul I know; but who
are ye?[S]
16 And the man in whom the
[m]evil spirit was leaped on them,
and overcame them, and prevailed
against them, so that they
fled out of that house naked and
wounded.
17 And this was known to all
the Jewṣ and Greeks also dwelling
at [r]Ĕph′e-sŭs; and fear fell
on them all, and [s,t]the [p]name of
the Lord Jē′ṣus was magnified.
18 And [s,t]many that [u]believed
came, and [v,w]confessed, and
shewed their deeds.
19 Many of them also which
used curious[C] arts brought their
[x]books together, and [y,z]burned
them before all *men*: and they
counted the price of them, and
found *it* fifty thousand *pieces*[C] of
[a]silver.
20 [b]So mightily grew the [c]word
of [10]God and prevailed.
21 ¶ After these things were
ended, [d]Pa̤ul purposed in the
spirit, when he had passed
through [e]Măç-e-dō′nĭ-ȧ and [f]A-chā′iȧ,
to go to [g]Jē-ru̥′sȧ-lĕm,
saying, After I have been there
I must also see [‡]Rōme.
22 So he sent into [e]Măç-e-dō′nĭ-ȧ
[h]two of them that ministered
unto him, [i]Tī-mō′the-ŭs and
[j]Ē-răs′tus; but he himself stayed
in [k]Ā′ṣiȧ for a season.[C]

4 R. V. on Jesus.

**5**
*k Baptism, Christian*, Luke 20:4.
*l Confession of Christ*, Luke 12:8.
*m Name of Jesus*, John 14:13.
*n Jesus, lordship of*, Matt. 1:21.
5 R. V. into

**6**
*o Hand, imposition of*, Ezra 10:19.
*p Spiritual Gifts*, 1 Cor. 12:4.
*q Charism*, 1 Cor. 12:1.
*r Miracles*, Luke 23:8.
*s Tongues, the miraculous gift of*, 1 Cor. 12:10.

**8**
*t Synagogue*, Matt. 12:9.
*u Zeal*, 2 Cor. 7:11.
*v Boldness of the Righteous*, Phil. 1:20.
*w Reasoning*, Job 13:6.
*x Instruction, in religion*, Prov. 23:23.
*y Kingdom of Heaven*, Matt. 13:24.
6 R. V. reasoning

**9**
*z Obduracy*, Prov. 29:1.
*a Unbelief, instances of*, Heb. 3:12.
*b Way*, Isa. 35:8.
*c Gospel*, Mark 13:10.
*d Disciples*, Matt. 9:14.
*e Greece, schools of*, Zech. 9:13.
7 R. V. some were hardened and disobedient, speaking evil of the Way

**10**
*f Asia*, Acts 2:9.
*g Doctrines of Jesus*, John 7:16. *h Jesus, lordship of*, Matt. 1:21. 8 R. V. *omits* Jesus.
**11** *i Miracles, of the disciples*, Luke 23:8. *j Paul*, Acts 13:9.
**12** *k Disease, healing of*, Ex. 15:26. *l Healing*, Acts 4:22. *m Demons*, Matt. 4:24.
**13** *n Sorcery*, Isa. 47:9. *o Presumption, instances of*, Psa. 19:13.
9 R. V. strolling

*p Name of Jesus*, John 14:13.

**14**
*q Priest*, Lev. 1:5.

**17**
*r Ephesus*, Acts 18:19.
*s Religious Revivals*, Hab. 3:2.
*t Church, Christian, rapid growth of*, Matt. 16:18.

**18**
*u Faith in Christ*, John 6:69.
*v Sin, confession of*, Rom. 5:12.
*w Repentance, instances of*, Mark 1:4.

**19**
*x Book, on magic*, Num. 5:23.
*y Sorcery, books on, destroyed*, Isa. 47:9.
*z Righteousness, fruits of*, Psa. 15:2.
*a Money*, Jer. 32:9.

**20**
*b Church, Christian, rapid growth of*, Matt. 16:18.
*c Doctrines of Jesus*, John 7:16.
10 R. V. the Lord and

**21**
*d Paul*, Acts 13:9.
*e Macedonia*, Acts 16:12.
*f Achaia*, Acts 18:2.
*g Jerusalem*, Judg. 19:10.

**A.D. 59**

**22**
*h Minister, sent forth two and two*, Rom. 15:16.
*i* Or, *Timothy*, 1 Cor. 4:17.
*j* 2 Tim. 4:20.
*k Asia*, Acts 2:9.

† **SCHOOL.** *Of the prophets, at Naioth*, 1 Sam. 19:20; *at Beth-el*, 2 Kin. 2:3; *at Jericho*, 2 Kin. 2:5, 15; *at Gilgal*, 2 Kin. 4:38. *Crowded attendance at*, 2 Kin. 6:1.
*In the home*, Deut. 4:9, 10; 6:7, 9; 11:19, 20; Psa. 78:5–8. *State*, 2 Chr. 17:7–9; Dan. 1:3–21.
*Of Gamaliel*, Acts 5:34; 22:3. *Of Tyrannus*, Acts 19:9.
*Schoolmaster* [tutor, R. V.], Gal. 3:24, 25.
See footnote, INSTRUCTION, Prov. 23:23.

‡ **ROME,** the capital of the Roman empire. *Jews excluded from, by Claudius*, Acts 18:2. *Visited by Onesiphorus*, 2 Tim. 1:16, 17. *Paul, in vision, is told he must preach in*, Acts 23:11; *desires to preach in*, Rom. 1:15; *appeals to Cæsar in*, Acts 25.10–12; *comes to*, Acts 28:14; *justifies himself before the chief Jews in, and preaches the gospel to them*, Acts 28:17–21; *dwells two years a prisoner in, preaching the kingdom of God to all who come to him*, Acts 28:16, 30, 31. *Abominations in*, Rom. 1:18–32. *Christians in*, Rom. 16:5–16; Phil. 1:12–18; 4:22; 2 Tim. 4:21. *Paul's letter to the Christians in*, Rom. 1:7.

**23**
*l* *Way,* Isa. 35:8.
*m* *Doctrines of Jesus,* John 7:16.
11 R. V. the Way.
**24**
*n* *Silver, workers in,* 1 Chr. 28:14.
*o* *Idol, manufacture of,* 1 Kin. 15:12.
12 R. V. little business
**26**
*p* *Ephesus,* Acts 18:19.
**27**
*q* *Temple, idolatrous,* 1 Kin. 6:17.
**29**
*r* Acts 20:4; 27:2; Col. 4:10; Philemon 24.
*s* *Mob,* Acts 17:5.
**30**
*t* *Disciples,* Matt. 9:14.
*u* *Prudence,* 2 Chr. 2:12.
*v* *Friendship,* Prov. 22:24.
**31**
13 R. V. chief officers

23 ¶ And the same time there
arose no small stir about [11]that
[l,m]way.
24 For a certain *man* named
Dē-mē′trĭ-ŭs, a [n]silversmith,
which [o]made silver shrines for
Dī-ăn′ȧ, brought no [12]small gain
unto the craftsmen;
25 Whom he called together
with the workmen of like occupation,
and said, Sirs, ye know
that by this craft we have our
wealth.
26 Moreover ye see and hear,
that not alone at [p]Ĕph′e-sŭs, but
almost throughout all [k]Ā′ṣiȧ,
this [d]Pa̤ul [b]hath persuaded and
turned away much people, saying
that they be no gods, which
are made with hands:
27 So that not only this our craft
is in danger to be set at nought;
but also that the [q]temple of the
great goddess Dī-ăn′ȧ should be
despised, and her magnificence
should be destroyed, whom all
[k]Ā′ṣiȧ and the world worshippeth.
28 And when they heard *these
sayings,* they were full of wrath,
and cried out, saying, Great *is*
Dī-ăn′ȧ of the Ė-phē′ṣiaṉṣ.
29 And the whole city was filled
with confusion: and having
caught Gā′ius and [r]Ăr-ĭs-tär′-chus,
men of [e]Măç-e-dō′nĭ-ȧ,
Pa̤ul's companions in travel,
[s]they rushed with one accord
into the theatre.
30 And when [d]Pa̤ul would
have entered in unto the people,
the [t]disciples [u,v]suffered him
not.
31 And certain of the [13]chief of
[k]Ā′ṣiȧ, which were his friends,
sent unto him, [u,v]desiring *him*
that he would not adventure himself
into the theatre.
32 [s]Some therefore cried one
thing, and some another: for the
assembly was confused; and the
more part knew not wherefore
they were come together.
33 And they drew Ăl-ĕx̣-ăn′-dēr
out of the multitude, the
Jews̤ putting him forward. And
Ăl-ĕx̣-ăn′dēr beckoned with the
hand, and would have made his
‖defence unto the people.
34 [s]But when they knew that he
was a Jew, all with one voice
about the space of two hours
cried out, Great *is* Dī-ăn′ȧ of
the Ė-phē′ṣiaṉṣ.
35 And when the [w]townclerk
had appeased the [s]people, [x]he
said, [y]*Ye* men of [p]Ĕph′e-sŭs,
what man is there that knoweth
not how that the city of the
Ė-phē′ṣiaṉṣ is a [14]worshipper of
the great goddess Dī-ăn′ȧ, and
of the *image* which fell down
from [z]Jū′pĭ-tēr?
36 Seeing then that these things
cannot be spoken against, [a]ye
ought to be quiet, and to do
nothing rashly.
37 For ye have brought hither
these [b]men, which are neither
robbers of [15]churches, nor yet
blasphemers of your goddess.
38 Wherefore if Dē-mē′trĭ-ŭs,
and the craftsmen which are
with him, have a matter against
any man, the [16]law is open, and
there are [c]deputies: let them implead
one another.
39 But if ye enquire any thing
concerning other matters, [b]it shall
be determined in a lawful assembly.
40 For [b]we are in danger to
be [17]called in question for this
day's uproar, there being no cause
whereby we may give an account
of this concourse.
41 And when he had thus spoken,
he dismissed the assembly.

**35**
*w* *Cities, town clerk of,* Num. 35:8.
*x* *Orator,* vs. 35-46; Acts 24:1.
*y* *Tact,* vs. 35-41; Prov. 15:1.
*z* Acts 14:12, 13.
14 R. V. temple-keeper
**36**
*a* *Citizens, duties of, to obey the law,* Luke 15:15.
**37**
*b* *Citizens, rights of, protection from mob violence,* vs. 36-41; Luke 15:15.
15 R. V. temples
**38**
*c* *Deputy,* 1 Kin. 22:47.
16 R. V. the courts are open, and there are proconsuls:
**40**
17 R. V. accused concerning this day's riot, there being no cause for it: and as touching it we shall not be able to give account of this concourse.

‖ **DEFENSE,** an argument made before a court by the accused. *Of Jeremiah,* Jer. 26:12-16. *Of Peter before the council, when called to explain concerning the healing of the lame man,* Acts 4:8-12; 5:29-32. *Of Stephen before the council,* Acts 7:1-53. *Of Paul before the mob,* Acts 22:1-21; *the council,* 23:1-6; *the governor,* 24:10-21; *Agrippa,* 26:1-23. *Right to make,* John 7:51. *Jesus declined to make,* Matt. 27:11-14; Mark 15:2-5.

## CHAPTER 20

*Paul goes from Ephesus through Macedonia into Greece. 4 He returns through Macedonia to Troas. 7 He celebrates the Lord's supper; 9 and restores Eutychus. 13 His journey to Miletus. 17 He sends for the elders of the church at Ephesus. 18 His farewell charge to them, 36 and prayer.*

AND after the uproar was ceased, [a]Paul called unto *him* the [b]disciples, and [1]embraced *them,* and departed for to go into [c]Măç-e-dō′nĭ-ȧ.

2 And when he had gone over those parts, and had given them much [d]exhortation[G], he came into [e]Greeçe,

3 And *there* abode[G] three months. And when [2]the Jews [f]laid wait for him, as he was about to sail into [g]Sỹr′ĭ-ȧ, he purposed to return through [c]Măç-e-dō′nĭ-ȧ.

4 And there accompanied him into [h]Ā′ṣiȧ Sŏp′a-tēr of [i]Bē-rē′ȧ; and of the [j]Thĕs-sa-lō′nĭ-anṣ, [k]Ăr-ĭs-tär′chus and Sĕ-cŭn′dus; and Gā′ius of [l]Dẽr′bē, and [m]Tĭ-mō′the-ŭs; and of Ā′ṣiȧ, *Tỹch′-ĭ-cŭs and †Trŏph′ĭ-mŭs.

5 These going before tarried[G] for [a,n]us at [o]Trō′as.

6 And [a,n]we sailed away from ‡Phĭ-lĭp′pī after the days of [p]unleavened bread, and came unto them to [o]Trō′as in five days; where we abode seven days.

7 ¶ And upon the [q]first *day* of the week, when the [b]disciples came together [r,s]to break [t]bread, [a]Paul [u]preached unto them, ready to depart on the morrow[G]; and [v]continued his speech until midnight.[T]

8 And there were many lights in the [w]upper chamber, where they were gathered together.

9 And[S] there sat in a [x]window a certain young man named Eū′tỹ-chŭs, being fallen into a deep [y]sleep: and as [a]Paul was long [u]preaching, he sunk down with sleep, and fell down from the third [3]loft[G], and was taken up [z]dead.

10 And [a]Paul went down, and fell on him, and embracing *him* said, Trouble not yourselves; for his life is in him.[Q]

11 When he therefore was come up again, and had [b]broken [c]bread, and eaten, and talked a long while, even till break of day, so he departed.[S]

12 And they brought the [4]young man alive, and were not a little comforted.

13 ¶ And we went before to [d]ship, and sailed unto Ăs′sŏs, there intending to take in [a]Paul: for so had he appointed, minding[G] himself to go [5]afoot.

14 And when he met with us at Ăs′sŏs, we took him in, and came to Mĭt-ỹ-lē′nē.

15 And we sailed thence, and came the next *day* over[G] against Chī′os; and the next *day* we arrived at Sā′mos, [6]and tarried at Trō-ġỹl′lĭ-ŭm; and the next *day* we came to [e]Mī-lē′tus.

16 For [a]Paul had determined to sail by [f]Ĕph′e-sŭs, because he would not spend the time in [g]Ā′ṣiȧ: for he hasted[G], if it were possible for him, to be at [h]Jĕ-ru′sȧ-lĕm the day of [i]Pĕn′te-cŏst.

17 ¶ And from [e]Mī-lē′tus he sent to [f]Ĕph′e-sŭs, and called the [j]elders[G] of the church.

18 And when [j]they were come to him, he said unto them, Ye know, from the first day that I came into [g]Ā′ṣiȧ, after what

1
a *Paul,* Acts 13:9.
b *Disciples,* Matt. 9:14.
c *Macedonia,* Acts 16:12.
1 R. V. having sent for the disciples and exhorted them, took leave of them,

2
d *Instruction, in religion,* Prov. 23:23.
e *Greece,* Zech. 9:13.

3
f *Minister, persecutions of,* Rom. 15:16.
g *Syria,* 2 Kin. 6:23.
2 R. V. a plot was laid against him by the Jews, as

4
h *Asia,* Acts 2:9.
i Acts 17:10, 13.
j *Thessalonica,* Phil. 4:16.
k Acts 19:29; 27:2; Col. 4:10; Philemon 24.
l *Derbe,* Acts 14:6.
m Or, *Timothy,* 1 Cor. 4:17.

5
n *Luke* (probably), Col. 4:14.
o Acts 16:8; 2 Cor. 2:12; 2 Tim. 4:13.

6
p *Annual Feasts, passover,* Num. 15:3.

7
q *Christian Sabbath,* Mark 16:9.
r *Eucharist,* Mark 14:22.
s *Worship,* Gen. 22:5.
t *Bread, symbolical,* Ezek. 4:13.
u *Preaching,* Matt. 9:35.
v *Zeal,* 2 Cor. 7:11.

8
w *House, architecture of,* Esth. 8:1.

9
x *Window,* Josh. 2:15.
y *Sleep,* Psa. 127:2.
z *Dead,* 2 Kin. 4:32.
3 R. V. story,

10
a *Paul,* Acts 13:9.

11
b *Eucharist,* Mark 14:22.
c *Bread, symbolical,* Ezek. 4:13.

12
4 R. V. lad

13
d *Ship,* 2 Chr. 8:18.
5 R. V. by land.

15
e 2 Tim. 4:20.
6 R. V. *omits* and tarried at Trogyllium;

16
f *Ephesus,* Acts 18:19.
g *Asia,* Acts 2:9.
h *Jerusalem,* Judg. 19:10.
i *Pentecost,* Acts 2:1.

17
j *Elders,* Acts 14:23.

* **TYCHICUS** (*faithful*), a companion of Paul. *Accompanies Paul from Greece to Asia,* Acts 20:4. *With Paul in Nicopolis,* Tit. 3:12. *With Paul in Rome,* Eph. 6:21, 22; Col. 4:7, 8. *Paul's amanuensis in writing to the Ephesians and Colossians,* see the postscripts to EPHESIANS and COLOSSIANS. *Sent to Ephesus,* Eph. 6:21, 22; 2 Tim. 4:12. *Sent to Colosse,* Col. 4:7, 8.

† **TROPHIMUS,** an Ephesian, companion of Paul. *Accompanies Paul from Greece to Asia,* Acts 20:4. *With Paul in Jerusalem; made the occasion of an attack on Paul,* Acts 21:27–30. *Left ill at Miletus,* 2 Tim. 4:20.

‡ **PHILIPPI,** a city of Macedonia. *Paul preaches in,* Acts 16:12–40; 20:1–6; 1 Thess. 2:1, 2. *Paul and Silas are imprisoned in,* Acts 16:12–40. *Contributes to the maintenance of Paul,* Phil. 4:10–18. *Paul sends Epaphroditus to,* Phil. 2:25. *Paul writes a letter to the Christians of,* Phil. 1:1.

**18**
*k Minister, faithful,* Rom. 15:16.
*l Zeal, of Paul,* 2 Cor. 7:11.
**19**
*m Humility,* Prov. 22:4.
*n Minister, trials and persecutions of,* Rom. 15:16.
*o Jews,* Neh. 4:2.
7 R. V. with trials which
8 R. V. plots of the Jews:
**20**
*p Instruction, in religion,* Prov. 23:23.
9 R. V. that I shrank not from declaring unto you anything that was profitable, and teaching you publicly,
**21**
*q Greeks,* Zech. 9:13.
*Repentance, the burden of Paul's preaching,* Mark 1:4.
*s Faith in Christ,* John 6:69.
*t Jesus, lordship of,* Matt. 1:21.
**22**
*u Paul, purposes to go to Jerusalem,* Acts 13:9.
*v Courage,* Deut. 31:7.
*w Rashness,* 2 Sam. 6:7.
**23**
*x Holy Spirit,* Acts 1:2.
**24**
*y Renunciation,* Luke 5:11.
*z Gospel,* Mark 13:10.

*a Grace of God,* Rom. 4:16.
10 R. V. I hold not my life of any account, as dear unto myself, so that I may accomplish my course, and the ministry,
**25**
*b Preaching,* Matt. 9:35.
*c Kingdom of Heaven,* Matt. 13:24.
11 R. V. *omits* of God,
**26**
*d Minister, responsibility of,* Rom. 15:16.

manner [k,l]I have been with you
at all seasons,[G]
19 [k,l]Serving the Lord with all
[m]humility of [n]mind, and with
many tears, and [7]temptations,[G]
which befell me by the [8]lying[G] in
wait of the [o]Jews:
20 *And* [k,l]how [9]I kept back
nothing that was profitable *unto*
*you,* but have shewed you, and
have [p]taught you publickly, and
from house to house,
21 [T] [p]Testifying both to the
[o]Jews, and also to the [q]Greeks,
[r]repentance toward God, and
[s]faith toward our [t]Lord Jē′sus
Chrīst.[S]
22 And now, behold, [l,u]I [v,w]go
bound in the spirit unto [h]Jĕ-ru′-
sā-lĕm, not knowing the things
that shall befall me there:
23 Save[G] that the [x]Holy Ghost[G]
witnesseth in every city, saying
that bonds and afflictions abide[G]
me.[T]
24 But [10,w]none of these things
move me, [y]neither count I my
life dear[G] unto myself, [l]so that I
might finish my course with joy,
and the ministry, which I have
received of the [t]Lord Jē′sus, to
testify[G] the [z]gospel of the [a]grace
of God.
25 And now, behold, I know
that ye all, among whom I have
gone [b]preaching the [c]kingdom
[11]of God, shall see my face no
more.
26 Wherefore I take you to record[G] this day, that [d,e]I *am* pure
from the blood of all *men.*
27 For [e]I have not shunned[G]
[d,f]to declare unto you all the
counsel of God.[T]
28 [g,h]Take heed therefore unto

*e Minister, faithful, instances of,* Rom. 15:16. **27** *f Minister, duties of,* Rom. 15:16. **28** *g Watchfulness, enjoined,* Matt. 24:42. *h Commandment, to ministers,* Deut. 8:2.

yourselves, and to all the [i,j]flock,[G]
[12]over the which the [k]Holy Ghost[G]
hath made you [13,l]overseers,[G] [j]to
feed the [j]church of God, which
he hath [m,n,o]purchased with his
own [p]blood.[S T Q]
29 For I know this, that after my departing shall grievous
[q,r]wolves enter in among you, not
sparing the flock.
30 Also of your own selves
shall men arise, speaking perverse things, to [s]draw away disciples after them.
31 Therefore watch, and remember, that by the space[G] of
three years [e,t]I [u]ceased not to
warn every one night and day
with tears.
32 And now, [14]brethren, I [v]com-
mend you to God, and to the
word of his grace, [w]which is able
to build you up, and to give you
an [x,y]inheritance among all them
which are [z,a]sanctified.[Q]
33 [b,c,d]I have coveted no man's
[e]silver, or [f]gold, or apparel.[Q]
34 Yea, ye yourselves know,
that [g,h]these hands have [i]minis-
tered unto my necessities, and
‖[j,k]to them that were [l]with me.
35 [15,g,h]I have shewed you all
things, how that so [i]labouring
[m]ye ought [k,n]to ‖support the
[o]weak, and to remember the
words of the Lord Jē′sus, how
he said, It is more blessed to
give than to receive.
36 ¶ And when he had thus
spoken, he [p]kneeled down, and
[q]prayed with them all.
37 And they all wept sore,[G] and

*e Silver,* 1 Chr. 28:14. *f Gold,* Ezek. 7:19. **34** *g Minister, faithful,* Rom. 15:16. *h Example, Paul our,* John 13:15. *i Industry,* 1 Kin. 11:28. *j Kindness,* Acts 28:2. *k Liberality,* 1 Tim. 6:18. *l Fellowship, of the righteous,* 1 Cor. 1:9. **35** *m Commandment, enjoining liberality,* Deut. 8:2. *n Church, duties of,* Matt. 16:18. *o Poor, duty to,* Prov. 21:13. 15 R. V. In all things I gave you an example, **36** *p Prayer, postures in,* Acts 6:4. *q Prayer, social,* Acts 6:4.

*i Sheep, figurative of the righteous,* Deut. 32:14.
*j Church, pastoral care of,* Matt. 16:18.
*k Holy Spirit,* Acts 1:2.
*l Bishop,* 1 Tim. 3:1.
*m Redemption of our Souls,* Eph. 1:7.
*n Atonement, by Jesus,* Lev. 17:11.
*o Jesus, design of his death,* Matt. 1:21.
*p Blood, of Christ, redeeming,* Heb. 9:19.
12 R. V. in
13 R. V. bishops
**29**
*q Wolf, figurative,* Jer. 5:6.
*r False Teachers,* 2 Pet. 2:1.
**30**
*s Apostasy,* Acts 1:25.
**31**
*t Love, of man for man,* 1 John 4:7.
*u Zeal,* 2 Cor. 7:11.
**32**
*v Intercession, instances of,* Jer. 27:18.
*w Promise, or ground of assurance, to the righteous,* 2 Cor. 1:20.
*x Inheritance, figurative,* Num. 27:7.
*y Immortality,* 1 Cor. 15:54.
*z Sanctification,* 1 Pet. 1:2.

*a Righteous, described,* Psa. 64:10.
14 R. V. *omits* brethren,
**33**
*b Paul,* Acts 13:9.
*c Minister, emoluments of,* Rom. 15:16.
*d Integrity,* Job 2:3.

‖ **ALTRUISM. Jesus inculcates:** BY PRECEPT: *He who would be greatest must be servant of all,* Matt. 20:26, 27; Mark 9:35; 10:43, 44; Luke 22:26, 27; John 13:4–17. *Giving better than receiving,* Acts 20:35.

BY EXAMPLE, John 13:4–17. *Came to serve,* Matt. 20:28; Phil. 2:7. *Went about doing good,* Acts 10:38. *Pleased not himself,* Rom. 15:3. *Became poor to make others rich,* 2 Cor. 8:9.

**Paul inculcates:** BY PRECEPT: *To help the weak,* Acts 20:35; Rom. 15:1, 2. *To promote the welfare of others,* 1 Cor. 10:24, 33; Gal. 6:1, 2, 10; Phil. 2:4–9.

BY EXAMPLE: *Became servant of all,* 1 Cor. 9:19–22; 2 Cor. 4:5. *Made many rich,* 2 Cor. 6:10.

**Motives inspiring to:** *Love of neighbor,* Luke 10:25–37. *To save men,* 1 Cor. 9:22. *For Jesus' sake,* 2 Cor. 4:5. *Example of Jesus,* 2 Cor. 8:9; Phil. 2:3–8.

**37**
*r Minister, beloved,* Rom. 15:16.
*s Kiss, of affection,* Ruth 1:9.

**1**
*a Paul,* Acts 13:9.
*b Luke* (probably), Col. 4:14.

**2**
*c Ship,* 2 Chr. 8:18.
*d* Acts 15:3.

**3**
*e Syria,* 2 Kin. 6:23.
*f Tyre,* Josh. 19:29.

**4**
*g Disciples,* Matt. 9:14.
*h Prophets, inspiration of,* Isa. 3:2.
*i Holy Spirit,* Acts 1:2.
*j Jerusalem,* Judg. 19:10.

**5**
*k Self-will,* Gen. 49:6.
*l Rashness, instances of,* 2 Sam. 6:7.
*m Disobedience to God,* Eph. 5:6.
*n Minister, beloved,* Rom. 15:16.
*o Prayer, postures in,* Acts 6:4.
*p Prayer, social,* Acts 6:4.

fell on [b,r]Păul's neck, and [s]kissed him,

38 [r]Sorrowing most of all for the words which he spake, that they should see his face no more. And they accompanied him unto the ship.

## CHAPTER 21

*Paul, sailing to Syria, lands first at Tyre;* 5 *and afterward at Cæsarea,* 8 *where he abides with Philip the evangelist.* 10 *He will not be dissuaded from going to Jerusalem.* 15 *He journeys thither, and is gladly received by the brethren.* 20 *Their advice to him.* 27 *He is seized in the temple by the Jews;* 31 *but is rescued by the chief captain,* 37 *and permitted to speak to the people.*

AND it came to pass, that after [a,b]we were gotten from them, and had launched, we came with a straight course unto Cō'ŏs, and the *day* following unto Rhōdeș, and from thence unto Păt'a-rȧ:

2 And finding a [c]ship sailing over unto [d]Phĕ-nī'çiȧ, we went aboard, and set forth.

3 Now when we had discovered *Çȳ'prus, we left it on the left hand, and sailed into [e]Sȳr'ĭ-ȧ, and landed at [f]Tȳre: for there the [c]ship was to unlade her burden.

4 And finding [g]disciples, we tarried there seven days: who said to [a]Păul [h]through the [i]Spirit, that he should not go up to [j]Jĕ-ru'să-lĕm.

5 And when we had accomplished those days, [a,b]we [k,l,m]departed and went our way; and they all brought [n]us on our way, with wives and children, till *we were* out of the city: and we [o]kneeled down on the shore, and [p]prayed.

6 And when [a,b]we had taken our leave one of another, we took [c]ship; and they returned home again.

7 And when [a,b]we had finished [1]*our* course from [f]Tȳre, we came to Ptŏl-e-mā'is, and saluted the brethren, and abode with them one day.

8 And the next *day* we [2]that were of Păul's company departed, and came unto †Çæs-a-rē'ȧ: and [q]we entered into the house of [r]Phĭl'ĭp the [s]evangelist, which was *one* of the seven; and abode with him.

9 And the same man had four [t,u]daughters, virgins, which did prophesy.

10 And as we tarried *there* many days, there came down from [v]Jū-dæ'ȧ a certain prophet, named [w]Ăg'a-bŭs.

11 And when [w]he was come unto us, he took Păul's [x]girdle, and [y]bound his own hands and feet, and said, [h]Thus saith the [i]Holy Ghost, [z]So shall the Jewș at [a]Jĕ-ru'să-lĕm [b]bind the man that owneth this girdle, and [b]shall deliver *him* into the hands of the [c]Ġĕn'tīleș.

12 And when we heard these things, both we, and they of that place, [d]besought him not to go up to [a]Jĕ-ru'să-lĕm.

13 Then [e]Păul answered, What mean ye to [f]weep and to break mine heart? for [g,h,i,j]I am ready not to be bound only, [k]but also to die at [a]Jĕ-ru'să-lĕm for the name of the Lord Jē'șus.

14 And when he [g]would not be persuaded, we ceased, saying, The [l]will of the Lord be done.

15 And after those days [e,m]we took up our [3]carriages, and went up to [a]Jĕ-ru'să-lĕm.

16 There went with us also *certain* of the [n]disciples of †Çæs-a-rē'ȧ, and brought with them one Mnā'son of *Çȳ'prus, an [4]old

**7**
1 R. V. the voyage from

**8**
*q Minister, hospitality to,* Rom. 15:16.
*r Philip,* Acts 8:5.
*s* Eph. 4:11; 2 Tim. 4:5.
2 R. V. *omits* that were of Paul's company

**9**
*t Women, as prophets,* Prov. 31:10.
*u Prophetess,* Judg. 4:4.

**10**
*v Judea,* Luke 5:17.
*w* Acts 11:28.

**11**
*x Girdle,* Prov. 31:24.
*y Pantomime,* Isa. 20:2.
*z Prophecies,* Dan. 9:24.
*a Jerusalem,* Judg. 19:10.
*b Persecution, of the righteous,* John 15:20.
*c Gentiles,* Acts 10:45.

**12**
*d Love, of man for man,* 1 John 4:7.

**13**
*e Paul,* Acts 13:9.
*f Weeping,* Ezra. 3:13.
*g Character, stability of,* Phil. 2:15.
*h Love, for Jesus,* 1 John 4:19.
*i Zeal, exemplified,* 2 Cor. 7:11.
*j Resignation,* Job 5:17.
*k Renunciation,* Luke 5:11.

**14**
*l Will of God,* Mark 3:35.

**15**
*m Luke* (probably), Col. 4:14.
3 R. V. baggage.

**16**
*n Disciples,* Matt. 9:14.
4 R. V. early

*** CYPRUS.** *An island in the Mediterranean,* Acts 21:3; 13:4, 6; 27:4. *Barnabas born in,* Acts 4:36. *Persecuted Jews preached the gospel in,* Acts 11:19, 20. *Visited, by Barnabas and Paul, under the guidance of the Holy Spirit,* Acts 13:4–12; *by Barnabas and Mark,* Acts 15:39. *Mnason, a disciple of,* Acts 21:16.

† **CÆSAREA,** a seaport in Palestine. *Home, of Philip,* Acts 8:40; 21:8; *of Cornelius, the centurion,* Acts 10:1, 24. *Provincial capital, of Herod,* Acts 12:19–23; *of Felix,* Acts 23:23, 24. *Paul conveyed to, by the disciples to save him from his enemies,* Acts 9:30; *by Roman soldiers to be tried by Felix,* Acts 23:23–35.

disciple, with whom we should
[o]lodge.
17 And when we were come to
[a]Jė-rṳ′să-lĕm, the brethren received us gladly.
18 And the *day* following [e]Pạul
went in with us unto [p]Jāmeṣ;
and all the [q]elders were present.
19 And when he had saluted[G]
them, he declared particularly[G]
what things God had wrought
among the [r]Ġĕn′tīleṣ by his
ministry.
20 And when they heard *it*, they
[s]glorified [5]the Lord, and [t]said
unto him, Thou seest, [u]brother,
how many thousands of Jewṣ
there are which [v]believe; and they
are all [w]zealous of[G] the [x]law:
21 And they are informed of
thee, that thou teachest all the
Jewṣ which are among the Ġĕn′-
tīleṣ [x]to forsake Mō′ṣeṣ, saying
that they ought not to [y]circum-
cise *their* children, neither to walk
after the customs.
22 What is it therefore? [6]the
multitude must needs come together: for they will hear that
thou art come.
23[Q] [t]Do therefore this that we
say to thee: We have four men
which have a [z]vow on them;
24 [t,a]Them take, and [b]purify
thyself with them, and be at
charges with them, that they
may shave *their* heads: and all
may know that those things,
whereof they were informed concerning thee, are nothing; but
*that* thou thyself also walkest
orderly, and keepest the law.[Q]
25 As touching the [c]Ġĕn′tīleṣ
which [d]believe, we [7]have written
*and* concluded[G] that they observe
no such thing, save only that
they keep themselves from *things*
offered to idols, and from [e]blood,
and from [f]strangled, and from
[g]fornication.
26 [a,h]Then [i]Pạul took the men,
and the next day [b]purifying himself with them entered into the
[j]temple, to signify the accomplishment of the days of purification, until that an offering
should be offered for every one
of them.[Q]
27 And when the seven days
were almost ended, the Jewṣ
which were of [k]Ā′ṣiȧ, when they
saw him in the temple, [l]stirred
up all the [m]people, and laid hands
on him,
28 [m]Crying out, Men of Ĭṣ′rael,
help: [n,o]This is the man, that
teacheth all *men* every where
against the people, and the [p]law,
and this place: and further
brought [q]Greeks also into the
temple, and hath polluted[G] this
[r]holy place.[Q]
29 (For they had seen before
with him in the city Trŏph′ĭ-mŭs
an Ē-phē′ṣian, whom they supposed that Pạul had brought
into the [j]temple.)
30 And all the city was moved,
and the [m]people ran together:
and they [s]took [t]Pạul, and drew[G]
him out of the temple: and forthwith[G] the doors were shut.
31 And as they went about to
kill him, tidings came unto the
[t]chief captain of the band, that
[m]all [u]Jė-rṳ′să-lĕm was in an
uproar.
32 [t]Who immediately took [v]sol-
diers and [w]centurions, and ran
down unto them: and when they
saw the [t]chief captain and the
soldiers, they left[G] [x]beating of
Pạul.
33 Then the [t]chief captain came
near, and took him, and commanded *him* to be bound with
two [y]chains; and demanded who
he was, and what he had done.
34 And some cried one thing,
some another, among the [m]mul-
titude: and when he could not
know the certainty[G] for the tumult[G], he commanded him to be
carried into the castle.

*o Hospitality,* Rom. 12:13.

18
*p* Acts 12:17; 15:13.
*q Elders,* Acts 14:23.

19
*r Gentiles, conversion of,* Acts 10:45.

20
*s Glorifying God,* Luke 5:25.
*t Diplomacy, ecclesiastical,* vs. 20–24; 2 Kin. 16:7.
*u Brother,* Prov. 18:24.
*v Faith in Christ,* John 6:69.
*w Bigotry,* Isa. 65:5.
*x Law, of Moses, temporary,* Deut. 33:2.
5 R. V. God;

21
*y Circumcision,* Gen. 17:10.

22
6 R. V. *omits* the multitude must needs come together: for

23
*z Vows,* Num. 30:2.

24
*a Public Opinion, concession to,* vs. 19–26; John 12:42.
*b Purification,* Num. 19:19.

25
*c Gentiles, conversion of,* Acts 10:45.
*d Faith in Christ,* John 6:69.
*e Blood, forbidden as food,* Gen. 9:4.
*f* Acts 15:20, 29.
*g Adultery, forbidden,* Lev. 20:10.
7 R. V. wrote, giving judgement that they should keep

26
*h Expediency,* 1 Cor. 6:12.
*i Paul,* Acts 13:9.

*j Temple, Herod's,* 1 Kin. 6:17.

27
*k Asia,* Acts 2:9.
*l Minister, trials and persecutions of,* Rom. 15:16.
*m Mob,* Acts 17:5.

28
*n False Accusation,* 2 Tim. 3:3.
*o Intolerance,* Num. 11:28.
*p Law, of Moses,* Deut. 33:2.
*q Greeks,* Zech. 9:13.
*r Church, called Holy Place,* 1 Kin. 9:3.

30
*s Arrest,* Matt. 26:50.

31
*t* Acts 22:24–30; 23:10–35.
*u Jerusalem,* Judg. 19:10.

32
*v Soldiers,* Ezra 8:22.
*w Centurion,* Matt. 8:5.
*x Persecution, of the righteous,* John 15:20.

33
*y Chains,* Dan. 5:7.

35 And when he came upon the stairs, so it was, that he was borne[c] of the soldiers for the violence of the [m]people.

36 For the [m]multitude of the people followed after, crying, Away with him.

37 And as [i]Pa̤ul was to be led into the castle, he said unto the [i]chief captain, May I speak unto thee? Who said, [8]Canst thou speak [z]Greek?

38 Art not thou that Ē-ġ̆y̆p′-tian, which before these days [9]madest an uproar, and leddest out into the wilderness four thousand men [10]that were murderers?

39 But [a]Pa̤ul said, I am a man *which am* a Jew of [b]Tär′sus, *a city* in [c]Çĭ-lĭ′çiȧ, a citizen of no mean city: and, I beseech thee, suffer[c] me to speak unto the people.

40 And when he had given him licence, [a]Pa̤ul stood on the stairs, and beckoned with the hand unto the people. And when there was made a great silence, he [d]spake unto *them* in the [e]Hē′brew [f]tongue, saying,

## CHAPTER 22

*Paul declares to the people the manner of his conversion. 22 They cry out against him. 24 The chief captain commands to scourge him. 25 He declares himself a Roman, and is spared. 30 He is brought before the council.*

[1]MEN, brethren, and fathers, hear ye my [a]defence *which* [b]*I make* now unto you.

2 (And when they heard that he [c]spake in the [d]Hē′brew [e]tongue to them, they kept the more silence: and he saith,)

3 [c]I am [2]verily a man *which am* a Jew, born in [f]Tär′sus, *a city* in [g]Çĭ-lĭ′çiȧ, yet brought up in this city [h]at the feet of [i]Gȧ-mā′lĭ-el, *and* [j,k]taught according to the [3]perfect manner of the [l]law of the fathers, and was [m]zealous toward God, as ye all are this day.

4 And I [n,o]persecuted this [p,q]way unto the death, [r]binding and delivering into prisons both men and women.

5 As also the [s]high priest doth bear me witness, and all the estate[c] of the elders: from whom also I received [t]letters unto the brethren, and went to [u]Dȧ-măs′cus, to bring [r]them which were there bound unto [v]Jē-rṳ′sȧ-lĕm, for to be punished.

6 And it came to pass, that, as I made my journey, and was come nigh[c] unto [u]Dȧ-măs′cus about noon, suddenly there shone from heaven a great light round about me.

7 And I fell unto the ground, and heard a [w]voice saying unto me, Sa̤ul, Sa̤ul, why [x]persecutest thou me?

8 And I answered, Who art thou, Lord? And he said unto me, I am Jē′ṣus of Năz′a-rĕth, whom thou [x]persecutest.

9 And they that were with me saw indeed the light, [4]and were afraid; but they heard not the voice of him that spake to me.

10 And I said, What shall I do, Lord? And the Lord said unto me, Arise, and go into [u]Dȧ-măs′cus; and there it shall be told thee of all things which are appointed for thee to do.

11 And when I could [y]not see for the glory[c] of that light, being led by the hand of them that were with me, I came into [u]Dȧ-măs′cus.[s]

12 And one [z]Ăn-a-nī′as, a devout man according to the law, having a good report of all the Jews̱ which dwelt *there*,

13 Came unto me, and stood, and said unto me, Brother Sa̤ul, receive thy sight. And the same hour I [a]looked up upon him.

14 And he said, The God of our fathers hath [b]chosen thee, that thou shouldest know his will,

**37**
*Language*, Dan. 3:29.
8 R. V. Dost thou know

**38**
9 R. V. stirred up to sedition and led out
10 R. V. of the Assassins?

**39**
a *Paul*, Acts 13:9.
b *Tarsus*, Acts 9:11.
c *Cilicia*, Gal. 1:21.

**40**
d *Defense*, Acts 19:33.
e *Hebrew*, Gen. 40:15.
f *Language*, Dan. 3:29.

**1**
a *Defense*, Acts 19:33.
b *Orator*, Acts 24:1.
1 R. V. *omits* Men,

**2**
c *Tact*, Prov. 15:1.
d *Hebrew*, Gen. 40:15.
e *Language*, Dan. 3:29.

**3**
f *Tarsus*, Acts 9:11.
g *Cilicia*, Gal. 1:21.
h *School*, Acts 19:9.
i Acts 5:34.
j *Instruction, of children*, Prov. 23:23.
k *Children, instruction of*, Mark 10:14.
l *Law, of Moses*, Deut. 33:2.
m *Zeal, of Paul*, 2 Cor. 7:11.
2 R. V. *omits* verily a man which am
3 R. V. strict

**4**
n *Bigotry, instances of*, Isa. 65:5.
o *Intolerance*, Num. 11:28.
p *Way, figurative*, Isa. 35:8.
q *Doctrines of Jesus*, John 7:16.
r *Persecution, of the righteous*, John 15:20.

**5**
s *High Priest*, Lev. 21:10.
t *Extradition*, 1 Kin. 18:10.
u *Damascus*, Isa. 8:4.
v *Jerusalem*, Judg 19:10.

**7**
w *Appearances of Jesus after his Resurrection*, Mark 16:9.
x *Persecution, of Jesus*, John 15:20.

**9**
4 R. V. *omits* and were afraid;

**11**
y *Blindness*, 2 Kin. 6:18.

**12**
z Acts 9:10–18.

**13**
a *Miracles*, Luke 23:8.

**14**
b *Call, personal*, Phil. 3:14.

and see [5]that [c]Just One, and shouldest hear the voice of his mouth.

15 For thou shalt be his [d,e]witness unto all men of what thou hast seen and heard.

16 And now why tarriest thou? arise, and be [f]baptized, and [g]wash away thy sins, calling on [6]the name of the Lord.

17 And it came to pass, that, when I was come again to [h]Jĕ-ru'să-lĕm, even while I [i]prayed in the [j]temple, I was in a [k]trance;

18 And [l]saw him saying unto me, [m]Make haste, and get thee quickly out of [h]Jĕ-ru'să-lĕm: for they [n,o]will not receive thy [d,p]testimony concerning me.

19 And I said, Lord, they know that I [q]imprisoned and [q]beat in every [r]synagogue them that [s]believed on thee:

20 And when the blood of [7]thy [t]martyr [u]Stē'phen was shed, I also was standing by, and [v]consenting unto his death, and kept the raiment of them that slew him.

21 And he said unto me, [w]Depart: for I will send thee far hence unto the [x]Gĕn'tīleș.

22 ¶ And they gave him audience unto this word, and *then* lifted up their voices, and said, [y,z,a]Away with such a *fellow* from the earth: for it is not fit that he should live.

23 And as they cried out, and cast off *their* clothes, and threw dust into the air,

24 The [b,c]chief captain commanded [d]him to be brought into the castle, and bade that he should be examined by *·[e]scourging; [f]that he might know wherefore they cried so against him.

25 And as they bound him with thongs, [g]Paul said unto the [b,h]centurion that stood by, Is it lawful for you to scourge a man that is a [i]Rō'man, and [j]uncondemned?

26 When the [h]centurion heard *that*, he went and told the [c]chief captain, saying, [8]Take heed what thou doest: for this man is a [i]Rō'man.

27 Then the [c]chief captain came, and said unto him, Tell me, art thou a Rō'man? He said, Yea.

28 And the [c]chief captain answered, With a great sum †obtained I this [9,k]freedom. And [g]Paul said, But [l]I was *free* born.

29 Then straightway they departed from him which should have examined him: and the [c]chief captain also was afraid, after he knew that he was a Rō'man, and because he had bound him.

30 On the morrow, because he would have known the certainty wherefore he was accused of the Jews, he loosed him from *his* bands, and commanded the chief [m]priests and all their [n]council to appear, and brought Paul down, and set him before them.

## CHAPTER 23

*Paul's defense before the council.* **7** *Dissension between the Pharisees and Sadducees, his accusers.* **11** *The Lord encourages him.* **12** *The Jews conspire against him.* **16** *The chief captain informed thereof. He sends Paul to Cæsarea, to Felix the governor.*

AND [a]Paul, earnestly beholding the [b]council, [c]said, [1]Men *and* brethren, I have lived [d]in all

c *Jesus, names of,* Matt. 1:21.
5 R. V. the Righteous One,

**15**
d *Witnessing for Christ,* Luke 24:48.
e *Minister, duties of,* Rom. 15:16.

**16**
f *Baptism, Christian,* Luke 20:4.
g *Spiritual Purification,* Psa. 51:2.
6 R. V. his name.

**17**
h *Jerusalem,* Judg. 19:10.
i *Prayer,* Acts 6:4.
j *Temple, Herod's,* 1 Kin. 6:17.
k Acts 10:10; 11:5.

**18**
l *Vision,* Acts 9:10.
m *Guidance,* Psa. 48:14.
n *Unbelief,* Heb. 3:12.
o *Jesus, rejected,* Matt. 1:21.
p *Religious Testimony,* 2 Thess. 1:10.

**19**
q *Persecution, of the righteous,* John 15:20.
r *Synagogue,* Matt. 12:9.
s *Faith in Christ,* John 6:69.

**20**
t *Martyrdom,* Rev. 17:6.
u *Stephen,* Acts 6:5.
v *Complicity,* Prov. 29:24.
7 R. V. Stephen thy witness

**21**
w *Minister, call of,* Rom. 15:16.
x *Gentiles,* Acts 10:45.

**22**
y *Bigotry,* Isa. 65:5.
z *Intolerance,* Num. 11:28.

---

a *Malice,* Eph. 4:31.

**24**
b *Armies, Roman army,* Deut. 11:4.
c Acts 21:31-40; 23:10-35.
d *Prisoners,* Psa. 79:11.
e *Punishment, for minor offenses,* Lev. 26:41.

f *Self-crimination,* Josh. 7:20.

**25**
g *Paul,* Acts 13:9.
h *Centurion,* Matt. 8:5.
i *Citizens, rights of,* Luke 15:15.
j *Trial, right of,* John 7:51.

**26**
8 R. V. What art thou about to do?

**28**
k *Liberty, political,* Lev. 25:10.
l *Roman Empire, citizenship in, by nativity,* John 11:48.
9 R. V. citizenship. And Paul said, But I am a Roman born,

**30**
m *Priest,* Lev. 1:5.
n *Court,* Ex. 18:26.

**1**
a *Paul,* Acts 13:9.
b *Court,* Ex. 18:26.
c *Defense,* Acts 19:33.
d *Integrity,* Job 2:3.
1 R. V. *omits* Men and

---

* **SCOURGING,** corporal punishment by stripes. *Prescribed in the Mosaic law, for fornication,* Lev. 19:20; *for slander,* Deut. 22:18; *for other offenses,* Deut. 25:2. *Forty stripes the maximum limit,* Deut. 25:3. *Fatal,* Job 9:23. *Of servants avenged,* Ex. 21:20. *Foretold by Jesus, as a persecution of his followers,* Matt. 10:17; *as a persecution of himself,* Matt. 20:19; Mark 10:34; Luke 18:33.

*Of children,* see footnote, CHILDREN, *Correction of,* Mark 10:14.

**Instances of:** *Of Jesus,* Matt. 27:26; Mark 15:15; John 19:1. *Of Paul and Silas,* Acts 16:23. *Of Paul,* Acts 21:32; 22:24; 2 Cor. 11:24, 25.

**Figurative:** *Of the oppressions of rulers,* 1 Kin. 12:11; 2 Chr. 10:11, 14. *Of the evil tongue,* Job 5:21.

† **NATURALIZATION.** *Giving rights of citizenship to aliens,* Acts 22:28.

**Figurative,** Eph. 2:12, 13, 19.

good *conscience before God until this day.

2 And [e]the [f,g]high priest [h]Ăn-a-nī'as commanded them that stood by him to smite[c] him on the mouth.

3 Then [i,j]said [a]Paul unto him, God shall smite thee, *thou* [k]whited[c] wall: for sittest thou to judge me after the law, and commandest me to be smitten contrary to the law?[Q]

4 And they that stood by said, Revilest[c] thou God's high priest?

5 Then said [a]Paul, I [2]wist[c] not, brethren, that he was the [f]high priest: for it is written, [l]Thou shalt not [m]speak evil of the [n]ruler of thy people.[Q]

6 But when [a]Paul perceived that the one part were [o]Săd'du-çeeș[c], and the other [p]Phăr'ĭ-seeș, he [q]cried out in the council, [1]Men *and* brethren, I am a Phăr'ĭ-see, the son of a Phăr'ĭ-see: of the [r]hope and [s]resurrection of the dead I am called in question.

7 And when he had so said, there arose a [t]dissension between the [p]Phăr'ĭ-seeș and the [o]Săd'du-çeeș[c]: and the multitude was divided.

8 For the [o]Săd'du-çeeș[c] say that there is no [s]resurrection, neither angel, nor spirit: but the [p]Phăr'ĭ-seeș confess both.

9 And there arose a great cry: and the [u]scribes *that were* of the [p]Phăr'ĭ-seeș' part arose, and [t]strove[c], saying, We find no evil in this man: [3]but if a spirit or an [v]angel hath spoken to him, let us not fight against God.

10 And when there arose a great [t]dissension, the [w]chief captain, fearing lest [a]Paul should have been pulled in pieces of them, commanded the [x]soldiers to go down, and to take him by force from among them, and to bring *him* into the castle.

11 And the night following the Lord [y,z]stood by him, and [a]said, Be of good cheer[c], [b]Paul: for as thou hast [c]testified of me in [d]Jĕ-ru'să-lĕm, so must thou bear [c]witness also at [e]Rōme.

12 And when it was day, [4]certain of the Jews [f,g]banded together, and bound themselves under a [h]curse, saying that they would neither eat nor drink till they had killed [b]Paul.

13 And they were more than forty which had made this [f]conspiracy.

14 And they came to the chief priests and elders, and said, We have [f,g]bound ourselves under a great [h]curse, that we will eat nothing until we have slain [b]Paul.

15 Now therefore ye with the council signify to the chief captain that he bring him down unto you to morrow, as though ye would [5]enquire something more perfectly[c] concerning him: and we, or[c] ever he come near, are ready to kill him.

16 And when Paul's sister's son heard of their lying[c] in wait, he

**2**
e *Intolerance, exemplified,* Num. 11:28.
f *High Priest, duties of, judicial,* Lev. 21:10.
g *Rulers, wicked, instances of,* Ex. 18:21.
h Acts 24:1.

**3**
i *Reproof, faithfulness in,* Prov. 17:10.
j *Court, contempt of,* Ex. 18:26.
k *Hypocrisy, described,* Jas. 3:17.

**5**
l Ex. 22:28.
m *Speech, evil,* Col. 4:6.
n *Rulers, must not be reviled,* Ex. 18:21.
2 Am. R. V. knew

**6**
o *Sadducees,* Matt. 22:23.
p *Pharisees,* Matt. 15:12.
q *Tact,* Prov. 15:1.
r *Hope,* Prov. 13:12.
s *Resurrection,* 1 Cor. 15:12.

**7**
t *Strife,* Prov. 20:3.

**9**
u *Scribe,* 1 Kin. 4:3.
3 R. V. and what if a spirit hath spoken to him, or an angel? *Omits* let us not fight against God.

v *Angel,* Heb. 1:13.

**10**
w Acts 21:31–40; 22:24–30.
x *Soldiers,* Ezra 8:22.

**11**
y *Vision,* Acts 9:10.
z *Appearances of Jesus after his Resurrection,* Mark 16:9

a *Adversity, consolation in,* Psa. 10:6.
b *Paul,* Acts 13:9.
c *Witnessing for Christ,* Luke 24:48.
d *Jerusalem,* Judg. 19:10.
e *Rome,* Acts 19:21.

**12**
f *Conspiracy, instances of,* 1 Kin. 16:9.
g *Malice, instances of,* Eph. 4:31.
h *Oath,* Num. 5:19.
4 R. V. *omits* certain of

**15**
5 R. V. judge of his case more exactly:

* **CONSCIENCE**, Psa. 51:3; Matt. 6:22; Luke 11:33–36; Rom. 2:14, 15; 7:15–23; 2 Cor. 5:11. *Approving,* Job 27:6; Prov. 21:2 (with 1 Cor. 4:4 [R. V.]); Acts 23:1; 24:16; Rom. 9:1; 1 Cor. 4:4; 2 Cor. 1:12; 1 Tim. 1:5, 19; 3:9; 2 Tim. 1:3; Heb. 13:18; 1 Pet. 2:19; 3:16, 21; 1 John 3:20, 21.

*Purged,* Heb. 9:14; 10:22.

*Of another, to be respected,* Rom. 14:2–20; 1 Cor. 8:7, 9–13; 10:27–32; 2 Cor. 4:2.

*Corrupt,* Matt. 6:23; Luke 11:34. *Seared,* 1 Tim. 4:2. *Dead,* Prov. 16:25; 30:20; Jer. 6:15; Amos 6:1, 3–6; Rom. 1:21–25; Eph. 4:17–19.

**Faithful:** INSTANCES OF: *Pharaoh, when he took Abraham's wife into his harem,* Gen. 12:18, 19. *Abimelech, when he took Isaac's wife into his harem,* Gen. 26:9–11. *Jacob, in his care of Laban's property,* Gen. 31:39. *Joseph, when Potiphar's wife tried to corrupt him,* Gen. 39:7–12. *Nehemiah, in the matter of taxes,* Neh. 5:15. *Daniel, in refusing to eat of the king's meat and wine,* Dan. 1:8. *Peter, in declaring the whole counsel of God,* Acts 4:19, 20; 5:29.

See footnotes: HONESTY, Rom. 13:13; INTEGRITY, Job 2:3.

**Guilty,** Job 15:21, 24; Psa. 51:1–14; 73:21; Prov. 28:1; Matt. 14:2 (with Mark 6:14, 16); 27:3–5; John 8:9; Acts 2:37; Tit. 1:15; Heb. 10:26, 27.

INSTANCES OF GUILTY: *Adam and Eve, after they sinned,* Gen. 3:7, 8. *Jacob, after he defrauded Esau,* Gen. 33:1–12. *Joseph's brethren,* Gen. 42:21. *Pharaoh, after the plagues,* Ex. 9:27. *Micah, after stealing,* Judg. 17:2. *David, for his indignity to Saul,* 1 Sam. 24:5; *for his adultery, and murder of Uriah,* Psa. 32; 38; 40:11, 12; 51; *for numbering Israel,* 2 Sam. 24:10; 1 Chr. 21:1–8. *The old prophet of Beth-el,* 1 Kin. 13:29–32, with v. 18. *The lepers of Samaria,* 2 Kin. 7:8–10. *Jonah,* Jonah 1:12. *Herod, for beheading John the Baptist,* Matt. 14:2; Luke 9:7. *Peter, after denying the Lord,* Matt. 26:75; Mark 14:72; Luke 22:62. *Judas, after betraying the Lord,* Matt. 27:3–5. *The accusers of the woman taken in adultery, when challenged to cast the first stone if innocent,* John 8:9.

went and entered into the castle,
and [i]told Paul.
17 Then [b]Paul called one of the
[j]centurions unto *him*, and said,
Bring this young man unto the
chief captain: for he hath a certain thing to tell him.
18 So he took him, and brought
*him* to the chief captain, and said,
Paul the prisoner called me unto
*him*, and prayed[G] me to bring this
young man unto thee, who hath
something to say unto thee.
19 Then the chief captain took
him by the hand, and went *with*
*him* aside privately, and asked
*him*, What is that thou hast to
tell me?
20 And he said, The Jews
have agreed to desire thee that
thou wouldest bring down Paul
to morrow into the council, as
though [6]they would enquire somewhat of him more perfectly[G].
21 But do not thou yield unto
them: for there [g]lie in wait for
him of them more than forty
men, which have [f]bound themselves [7]with an [h]oath, that they
will neither eat nor drink till
they have killed him: and now
are they ready, looking for a
promise from thee.
22 So the chief captain *then*
let the young man depart, and
[k]charged *him*, *See thou* tell no
man that thou hast shewed these
things to me.
23 And he called unto *him*
two [j]centurions, saying, Make
ready two hundred [l]soldiers to
go to [m]Çæs-a-rē′ă, and horsemen threescore and ten, and
spearmen two hundred, at the
third[G] hour of the night;
24 And provide *them* beasts,
that they may set Paul on, and
[n]bring *him* safe unto [o]Fē′lĭx the
[p]governor.
25 And he wrote a [q]letter after
this manner:
26 [r]Clau′dĭ-ŭs Lȳ′sĭ-as unto the

16
*i* *Love, of man for man*, 1 John 4:7.
17
*j* *Centurion*, Matt. 8:5.
20
6 R. V. thou wouldest inquire somewhat more exactly concerning him.
21
7 R. V. under a curse.
22
*k* *Prudence*, 2 Chr. 2:12.
23
*l* *Soldiers*, Ezra 8:22.
*m* *Cæsarea*, Acts 21:8.
24
*n* *Change of Venue*, Acts 26:32.
*o* *Felix*, Acts 25:14.
*p* *Government, provincial*, Isa. 22:21.
25
*q* *Letters*, Isa. 37:14.
26
*r* Acts 21:31-40; 22:24-30.

most excellent governor [o]Fē′lĭx
*sendeth* greeting.
27 This man was taken of the
Jews, and [8]should have been
killed of them: then came I with
an army, and rescued him, having understood that he was a
[s,t]Rō′man.
28 And when I would have
known the cause wherefore they
accused him, I brought him forth
into their council:
29 Whom I perceived to be accused of questions of their law,
but to have nothing laid to his
charge worthy of death or of
bonds.
30 And when it was told me
how that [9]the Jews [f]laid wait for
the man, I sent straightway[G] to
thee, and gave commandment to
his accusers also to say before
thee what *they had* against him.
Farewell.
31 Then the [l]soldiers, as it was
commanded them, took Paul,
and brought *him* by night to
Ăn-tĭp′a-trĭs.
32 On the morrow[G] they left the
[u]horsemen to go with him, and
returned to the castle:
33 Who, when they came to
[m]Çæs-a-rē′ă, and delivered the
[q]epistle[G] to the [p]governor, presented Paul also before him.
34 And when the [v]governor had
read *the letter*, he asked of what
province he was. And when he
understood that *he was* of [w]Çĭ-
lĭ′çiă;
35 I will hear thee, said he, when
thine accusers are also come. And
he commanded him to be kept in
Hĕr′od's [x]judgment hall.

## CHAPTER 24

*Paul, accused by Tertullus, 10 answers for himself. 24 He preaches Christ before Felix and Drusilla. 25 Felix trembles. 27 He is succeeded by Festus, and leaves Paul bound.*

AND after five days [a]Ă-na-
nī′as the [b]high priest descended with the elders, and *with*

27
*s* *Roman Empire, rights of citizens of*, John 11:48.
*t* *Citizens, rights of, fair trial in courts*, Luke 15:15.
8 R. V. was about to be slain of them, when I came upon them with the soldiers,
30
9 R. V. there would be a plot against the man, I sent him to thee forthwith, charging his accusers also to speak against him before thee Omits Farewell.
32
*u* *Cavalry*, 1 Sam. 13:5.
34
*v* *Judge, rulers as*, Judg. 2:18.
*w* *Cilicia*, Gal. 1:21.
35
*x* *Prætorium*, Mark 15:16.
1
*a* Acts 23:2-5.
*b* *High Priest*, Lev 21:10.

c *Minister, persecutions of,* Rom. 15:16.
d *Government, provincial,* Isa. 22:21.
e *Felix,* Acts 25:14.
f *Paul,* Acts 13:9.

2

g *Flattery,* Prov. 6:24.
1 R. V. much peace, and that by thy providence evils are corrected for this nation,

5

h *False Accusation,* 2 Tim. 3:3.
i *False Witness,* Matt. 19:18.
j *Indictments,* Matt. 27:37.
k *Heresy,* Tit. 3:10.
2 R. V. insurrections

6

3 R. V. *omits* and would have judged according to our law.

7

l Acts 21:31-40; 22:24-30; 23:10-35.
4 R. V. *omits this verse.*

8

5 R. V. From whom thou wilt be able, by examining him thyself, to take knowledge

a certain *orator *named* Tĕr-
tŭl′lus, who [c]informed the [d,e]gov-
ernor against [f]Pa̤ul.
2 And when he was called forth,
Tĕr-tŭl′lus began to accuse *him,*
saying, [g]Seeing that by [e]thee we
enjoy [1]great quietness, and that
very worthy deeds are done unto
this nation by thy providence,[C]
3 [g]We accept *it* always, and in
all places, most noble [e]Fē′lĭx,
with all †thankfulness.
4 Notwithstanding, that I be not
further tedious unto thee, I pray[C]
thee that thou wouldest hear us
of thy clemency a few words.
5 For [h,i,j]we have found this
man *a* pestilent *fellow,* and a
mover of [2]sedition among all the
Jews̱ throughout the world, and
a ringleader of the [k]sect of the
Năz′a-rēnes̱:
6 [h,i,j]Who also hath gone
about to profane the temple:
whom we took, [3]and would have
judged according to our law.
7 [4]But the [l]chief captain Lȳ′sĭ-
as came *upon us,* and with great
violence took *him* away out of
our hands,
8 [5]Commanding his accusers
to come unto thee: by examining of whom thyself mayest take
knowledge of all these things,
whereof we accuse him.
9 And the Jews̱ also assented,
saying that these things were so.
10 ¶ Then [f]Pa̤ul, after that the
[d]governor had beckoned unto
him to speak, [g,m]answered, Forasmuch as I know that thou hast
been of many years a judge unto
this nation, I do the more cheerfully [6,n]answer for myself:
11 Because that thou mayest
understand, that there are yet
but twelve days since I went up
to [o]Jē-rṳ′să-lĕm for to [p,q]wor-
ship.
12 [n]And they neither found me
in the [r]temple disputing with any
man, neither raising up the people, neither in the [s]synagogues,
nor in the city:
13 [n]Neither can they prove the
things whereof they now accuse
me.
14 But this [t]I confess unto thee,
that after the [u,v]way which they
call [7,k]heresy,[C] so worship I the
God of my fathers, [w]believing all
things which are written in the
[x,y]law and in the [z]prophets:
15 And have [a]hope toward God,
which they themselves [8]also allow, that there shall be a [b]resur-

10

m *Tact,* Prov. 15:1.
n *Defense,* vs. 10-21; Acts 19:33.
6 R. V. make my defence:

11

o *Jerusalem,* Judg. 19:10.
p *Worship,* Gen. 22:5.
q *Annual Feasts,* Num. 15:3.

12

r *Temple, Herod's,* 1 Kin. 6:17.
s *Synagogue,* Matt. 12:9.

14

t *Courage, instances of,* Deut. 31:7.
u *Way,* Isa. 35:8.
v *Doctrines of Jesus,* John 7:16.
w *Faith,* Mark 11:22.
x *Law, of Moses,* Deut. 33:2.
y *Word of God,* Psa. 119:9.
z *Prophecies,* Dan. 9:24.
7 R. V. a sect, so serve I

15

a *Hope,* Prov. 13:12.
b *Resurrection,* 1 Cor. 15:12.
8 R. V. look for,

***ORATOR. Instances of:** *Judah,* Gen. 44:18-44. *Aaron,* Ex. 4:14-16. *Moses,* Deut. chapters 1 to 4:40. *Jonah,* Jonah 3:4-10. *Peter,* Acts 2:14-40; 3:12-26; 4:8-12; 10:34-48; 11:4-17. *Stephen,* Acts 7:2-60. *Paul and Barnabas,* Acts 14:14-17. *Paul,* Acts 13:16-41; 17:22-31; 22:1-21; 24:10-21; 26:1-29; 27:21-25. *James,* Acts 15:13-21. *Apollos,* Acts 18:24-28. *Herod,* Acts 12:21. *Tertullus,* Acts 24:1. *The townclerk,* Acts 19:35-41.

**† THANKFULNESS. To God,** Psa. 30:4; 50:14; 75:1; 92:1; 97:12; 106:1; 118:1; 2 Cor. 9:11; Eph. 5:4, 19, 20; Phil. 4:6; Col. 1:12; 2:7; 3:15-17; 4:2; 1 Thess. 5:18; 1 Tim. 2:1; Heb. 13:15. *Of the heavenly host,* Rev. 7:11, 12; 11:16, 17.

*Should be offered, through Christ,* Rom. 1:8; Col. 3:17; Heb. 13:15; *in the name of Christ,* Eph. 5:20. *Should be offered in private worship,* Dan. 6:10; *in public worship,* 1 Chr. 23:30; 25:3; Neh. 11:17; Psa. 35:18.

*Jesus set an example of,* Matt. 11:25; 15:36; 26:27; Mark 8:6, 7; 14:23; Luke 22:17, 19; John 6:11, 23; 11:41.

*Ministers appointed to offer in public,* 1 Chr. 16:4, 7; 2 Chr. 31:2.

*Before taking food,* Matt. 14:19; Mark 8:7; Luke 24:30; John 6:11; Acts 27:35.

*For his goodness and mercy,* Psa. 68:19; 79:13; 89:1; 100:4; 106:1; 107:1; 116:12-14, 17; 136:1-3; Isa. 63:7. *For the gift of Christ,* 2 Cor. 9:15. *For deliverance from adversity,* Psa. 31:7, 21; 35:9, 10; 44:7, 8; 54:6, 7; 66:8, 9, 12-16, 20; 98:1. *For providential deliverance,* Ex. 12:14, 17, 42; 13:3, 8-10, 14-16; Judg. 5:11; Psa. 105:1-45; 107:1, 2, 15, 22, 42, 43; 136:1-26; Joel 2:26. *For deliverance from the power of sin,* Rom. 7:23-25. *For promised victory over death and the grave,* 1 Cor. 15:57. *For temporal blessings,* Rom. 14:6, 7; 1 Tim. 4:3-5.

*Cultivated, by the Feast of Tabernacles,* Deut. 16:9-15; *by thank offerings,* Ex. 34:26; Lev. 19:24; 23:14; Deut. 12:18; 26:10; Prov. 3:9, 10; *by songs,* 1 Chr. 16:7-36; Psa. 95:2; 100.

*Enjoined,* Eph. 1:16; 5:20; 1 Thess. 5:18; 1 Tim. 2:1.

INSTANCES OF: *Noah,* Gen. 8:20. *Melchizedek,* Gen. 14:20. *Lot,* Gen. 19:19. *Abraham,* Gen. 12:7. *Abraham's servant,* Gen. 24:27. *Leah,* Gen. 29:32-35. *Jacob,* Gen. 32:10; 35:3, 7; 48:11, 15, 16. *Joseph,* Gen. 41:51, 52. *Moses,* Ex. 15:1-18. *Miriam,* Ex. 15:20-22. *Jethro,* Ex. 18:10. *Israel,* Ex. 4:31; 15:1-21; Num. 21:17; 31:49-54; 1 Chr. 29:22. *Deborah,* Judg. 5. *Hannah,* 1 Sam. 1:27, 28; 2:1-10. *Samuel,* 1 Sam. 7:12. *David,* 2 Sam. 6:21; 1 Chr. 29:13. *Solomon,* 1 Kin. 8:15, 56; 2 Chr. 6:4. *Jehoshaphat's army,* 2 Chr. 20:27, 28. *Ezra,* Ezra 7:27. *The Levites,* 2 Chr. 5:12, 13; Neh. 9:4-38. *The Jews,* Neh. 12:31, 40, 43. *Daniel,* Dan. 2:23. *Nebuchadnezzar,* Dan. 4:2, 34. *The mariners,* Jonah 1:16. *Jonah,* Jonah 2:9. *The shepherds,* Luke 2:20. *Simeon,* Luke 2:28. *Anna,* Luke 2:38.

Those whom Jesus healed: *The man with palsy,* Luke 5:25; *the demoniac,* Luke 8:39; *the woman bent with infirmity,* Luke 13:13; *one of the ten lepers,* Luke 17:15, 16; *blind Bartimæus,* Luke 18:43.

*The lame man healed by Peter,* Acts 3:8.

*Paul,* Acts 27:35; 28:15; Rom. 1:8; 6:17; 1 Cor. 1:4; 2 Cor. 2:14; Phil. 1:3-5; Col. 1:3-6; 2 Thess. 1:3; 1 Tim. 1:12.

See footnote, PRAISE, Psa. 150:1.

**Of Man to Man.** *The Israelites, to Joshua,* Josh. 19:49, 50. *The spies, to Rahab,* Josh. 6:22-25. *Saul, to the Kenites,* 1 Sam. 15:6. *David, to the men of Jabesh-gilead,* 2 Sam. 2:5-7; *to Hanun,* 2 Sam. 10:2; *to Barzillai,* 1 Kin. 2:7. *Paul, to Onesiphorus,* 2 Tim. 1:16-18. *The people of Melita, to Paul,* Acts 28:10.

9 R. V. *omits* of the dead,

**16**

*c Conscience, approving,* Acts 23:1.

*d Obedience,* Heb. 5:8.

*e Sinlessness,* 1 John 5:18.

*f Holiness,* Ex. 39:30.

*g Honesty,* Rom. 13:13.

*h Integrity,* Job 2:3.

**17**

*i Liberality,* 1 Tim. 6:18.

*j Alms,* Matt. 6:2.

**18**

*k Asia,* Acts 2:9.

*l Temple, Herod's,* 1 Kin. 6:17.

10 R. V. Amidst which they found me purified in the temple, with no crowd, nor yet with tumult: but there were certain Jews from Asia—

**19**

*m Citizens, rights of, fair trial in courts,* Luke 15:15.

11 R. V. aught

**22**

*n Felix,* Acts 25:14.

*o Way,* Isa. 35:8.

*p* Acts 21:31–40; 22:24–30; 23: 10–35.

12 R. V. But Felix, having more exact knowledge concerning the Way, deferred

**23**

*q Centurion,* Matt. 8:5.

*r Prisoners, kindness to,* Psa. 79:11.

*s Kindness,* Acts 28:2.

*t Friends,* Ex. 33:11.

**24**

*u Women, social status of,* Prov. 31:10.

*v Faith in Christ,* John 6:69.

13 R. V. Christ Jesus.

**25**

*w Reasoning,* Job 13:6.

*x Righteousness,* Psa. 15:2.

*y Temperance,* 2 Pet. 1:6.

rection [9]of the dead, both of the just and unjust.

16 And herein do I exercise myself, to have always a [c]conscience [d,e,f]void of offence toward God, and [g,h]*toward* men.

17 Now after many years I came [i]to bring [j]alms to my nation, and offerings.

18 [10]Whereupon certain Jews from [k]Ā′ṣiȧ found me purified in the [l]temple, neither with multitude, nor with tumult.

19 [m]Who ought to have been here before thee, and object, if they had [11]ought against me.

20 Or else let these same *here* say, if they have found any evil doing in me, while I stood before the council,

21 Except it be for this one voice, that I cried standing among them, Touching the [b]resurrection of the dead I am called in question by you this day.

22 ¶ [12]And when [n]Fē′lĭx heard these things, having more perfect knowledge of *that* [o]way, he deferred them, and said, When [p]Lȳ′sĭ-as the chief captain shall come down, I will know the uttermost of your matter.

23 And he commanded a [q]centurion to keep [r]Pa̤ul, and [s]to let *him* have liberty, and that he should forbid none of his [t]acquaintance to minister or come unto him.

24 And after certain days, when [n]Fē′lĭx came with his [u]wife Drṳ-sĭl′lȧ, which was a Jew′ess, he sent for Pa̤ul, and heard him concerning the [v]faith in [13]Christ.

25 And as he [w]reasoned of [x]righteousness, [y]temperance, and [z]judgment to come, [a]Fē′lĭx [14,b]trembled, and answered, [‡,c,d]Go thy way for this time; when I have a convenient season, I will call for thee.

26 [e,f]He hoped also that [g]money should have been given him of Pa̤ul, [15]that he might loose him: wherefore he sent for him the oftener, and communed with him.

27 But [16]after two years [h]Pôr′çĭ-ŭs Fĕs′tus came into [a]Fē′lĭx′ room: and Fē′lĭx, [i]willing to shew the [j]Jews a pleasure, left [k,l]Pa̤ul bound.

## CHAPTER 25

*The Jews inform Festus, in Jerusalem, against Paul. 6 At Cæsarea he hears the apostle and his accusers. 10 Paul appeals unto Cæsar. 13 Festus declares the matter to king Agrippa. 23 Paul is brought forth before Festus and Agrippa.*

NOW when [a]Fĕs′tus was come into the province, after three days he ascended from [b]Çæs-a-rē′ȧ to [c]Jē-rṳ′sā-lĕm.

2 Then the [1]high [d]priest and the chief of the Jews [e]informed [a]him against [f]Pa̤ul, and besought him,

3 And desired favour against him, that he would send for him to [c]Jē-rṳ′sā-lĕm, [g]laying wait in the way to kill him.

4 But [a]Fĕs′tus answered, that [f]Pa̤ul should be kept at [b]Çæs-a-rē′ȧ, and that he himself would depart shortly *thither*.

5 [h]Let them therefore, said he, which [2]among you are able, go down with *me*, and accuse this man, if there be any wickedness in him.

6 And when [a]he had tarried among them [3]more than ten days, he went down unto [b]Çæs-a-rē′ȧ; and the next day sitting on the judgment seat commanded Pa̤ul to be brought.

7 And when he was come, the Jews which came down from [c]Jē-rṳ′sā-lĕm stood round about, and [e,g]laid many and grievous complaints against [f]Pa̤ul, which they could not prove.

8 While [f,i]he [j]answered for him-

**26**

*e Judge, corrupt,* Judg. 2:18.

*f Court, corrupt,* Ex. 18:26.

*g Bribery,* 1 Sam. 8:3.

15 R. V. *omits* that he might loose him:

**27**

*h* Acts 25; 26:24, 25.

**A.D. 62**

*i Demagogism,* 2 Sam. 15:2.

*j Public Opinion, corrupt yielding to,* John 12:42.

*k Paul,* Acts 13:9.

*l Prisoners,* Psa. 79:11.

16 R. V. when two years were fulfilled, Felix was succeeded by Porcius Festus; and desiring to gain favour with the Jews, Felix left Paul in bonds.

**1**

*a* Acts 24:27; 26: 24, 25.

*b Cæsarea,* Acts 21:8.

*c Jerusalem,* Judg. 19:10.

**2**

*d Priest,* Lev. 1:5.

*e False Accusation,* 2 Tim. 3:3.

*f Paul,* Acts 13:9.

1 R.V. chief priests and the principal men of the Jews

**3**

*g Malice,* Eph. 4:31.

**5**

*h Citizens, rights of, fair trial in courts,* Luke 15:15.

2 R. V. are of power among you, go down with me, and if there is anything amiss in the man, let them accuse him.

**6**

3 R. V. not more than eight or ten

**8**

*i Prisoners, permitted to make defense,* Psa. 79:11.

*j Defense,* Acts 19:33.

*z Judgment, the general,* 2 Pet. 3:7.—*a Felix,* Acts 25:14. *b Conviction of Sin,* John 16:8. *c Indecision,* 1 Kin. 18:21. *d Excuses for rejecting salvation,* Luke 14:18. 14 R. V. was terrified,

‡ **PROCRASTINATION,** Ezek. 11:2, 3; Matt. 25:2–13. *Rebuked,* Matt. 8:21, 22; Luke 9:59, 61. *Admonition against,* 1 Thess. 5:2, 3. *Forbidden,* Ex. 22:29. See footnote, EXCUSES, Luke 14:18. **Instances of:** *Elisha,* 1 Kin. 19:20, 21. *Felix,* Acts 24:25.

self, Neither against the law of the Jewṣ, neither against the temple, nor yet against *Çæ'ṣar, have I offended any thing at all.

9 But [a,k]Fēs'tus, [4,l]willing to do the [m]Jewṣ a pleasure,[c] answered [l]Pạul, and said, [n]Wilt thou go up to [c]Jē-rụ'sā-lĕm, and there be judged of these things before me?

10 Then said Pạul, I stand at *Çæ'ṣar's [†,o]judgment seat, where I ought to be judged: to the Jewṣ [p]have I done no wrong, as thou very well knowest.

11 For if I [5]be an offender, or have committed any thing worthy of death, I refuse not to die: but if there be none of these things whereof these accuse me, no man may deliver me unto them. [n,h,q]I appeal unto *Çæ'ṣar.

12 Then [a]Fēs'tus, when he had conferred with the council,[c] answered, Hast [h,q]thou [n]appealed unto *Çæ'ṣar? unto Çæ'ṣar shalt thou go.

13 ¶ And after certain days king Ȧ-grĭp'pȧ and [r]Bĕr-nī'çē came unto [b]Çæs-a-rē'ȧ to salute[c] [a]Fēs'tus.

14 And when they had been there many days, [a]Fēs'tus declared [l]Pạul's cause unto the king, saying, There is a certain man left in bonds by [‡]Fē'lĭx:

15 About whom, when I was at [c]Jē-rụ'sā-lĕm, the chief priests and the elders of the Jewṣ informed *me*, desiring *to have* judgment against him.

16 To whom I answered, It is not the manner of the [s]Rō'manṣ to deliver any [h]man [6]to die, before that he which is accused have the accusers face to face, and have [7]licence to [t,u]answer for himself concerning the crime laid against him.

17 Therefore, when they were come hither, without any delay on the morrow[c] I sat on the [†]judgment seat, and commanded the man to be brought forth.

18 Against whom when the accusers stood up, they brought none [v]accusation of such things as I supposed:

19 But had certain questions against him of their own [8]superstition, and of one Jē'ṣus, which was [w]dead, whom Pạul [x]affirmed to be [y]alive.

20 And [9]because I doubted of such manner of questions, I asked *him* whether he would go to [c]Jē-rụ'sā-lĕm, and there be judged of these matters.

21 But when [l]Pạul had [n,z]appealed to be reserved unto the hearing of *[,10]Ạu-gŭs'tus, I commanded him to be kept till I might send him to *Çæ'ṣar.

22 Then Ȧ-grĭp'pȧ said unto [a]Fēs'tus, I would also hear the man myself. To morrow, said he, thou shalt hear him.

23 And on the morrow, when Ȧ-grĭp'pȧ was come, and [b]Bĕr-nī'çē, with great pomp, and was entered into the place of hearing, with the chief captains, and principal men of the city, at [a]Fēs'tus' commandment [c]Pạul was brought forth.

24 And [a]Fēs'tus said, King Ȧ-grĭp'pȧ, and all men which are here present with us, ye see this man, about whom all the multitude of the Jewṣ have dealt with me, both at Jē-rụ'sā-lĕm, and *also* here, [d]crying that he ought not to live any longer.

25 But when I found that he had committed nothing worthy of death, and that he himself hath [e]appealed to *[,10]Ạu-gŭs'tus, I have determined to send him.

9
*k Court, corrupt,* Ex. 18:26.
*l Demagogism,* 2 Sam. 15:2.
*m Public Opinion,* John 12:42.
*n Change of Venue,* Acts 26:32.
4 R. V. desiring to gain favour with the Jews, answered Paul, and said,

10
*o Court,* Ex. 18:26.
*p Conscience, approving,* Acts 23:1.
*q Rashness,* 2 Sam. 6:7.

11
5 Am. R. V. am a wrong-doer, and have

13
*r* Acts 26:30.

16
*s Roman Empire, rights of citizens of,* John 11:48.
*t Defense,* Acts 19:33.
*u Pleading,* Deut. 17:8.
6 R. V. *omits* to die,
7 R. V. opportunity

18
*v Indictments,* Matt. 27:37.

19
*w Jesus, death of,* Matt. 1:21.
*x Religious Testimony,* 2 Thess. 1:10.
*y Jesus, resurrection of,* Matt. 1:21.
8 R. V. religion,

20
9 R. V. I, being perplexed how to inquire concerning these things, asked

21
*z Appeal,* Acts 28:19.
10 R. V. the emperor,

22
*a* Acts 24:27; 26:24, 25.

23
*b* Acts 26:30.
*c Paul,* Acts 13:9.

24
*d Persecution, of the righteous,* John 15:20.

26
*e Appeal,* Acts 28:19.

*** CÆSAR.** *Augustus decrees that a census of the Jews shall be taken,* Luke 2:1. *Tiberius exacts tribute from the Jews,* Mark 12:14–17; Luke 3:1; 20:22; John 19:12, 15. *Claudius,* Acts 11:28; 18:2. *Nero reigned at the time of Paul's persecutions,* Acts 25:8–12, 21, 25; 26:32; 28:19.

**† JUDGMENT SEAT,** Matt. 27:19; Acts 18:12; 25:10. *Of Christ* (R. V. God), Rom. 14:10.

**‡ FELIX,** governor of Judea. *Paul tried before,* Acts 23:24–35; 24. *Trembles under Paul's preaching,* Acts 24:25. *Leaves Paul in bonds,* Acts 24:26, 27; 25:14.

26 Of whom [a]I have no certain
thing to write unto my lord.
Wherefore I have brought him
forth before you, and specially
before thee, O king Ȧ-grĭp′pȧ,
that, after examination had, I
might have somewhat to write.
27 For it seemeth to me unreasonable to send a prisoner, and
not withal to signify the [11]crimes
*laid* against him.

## CHAPTER 26

*Paul before Agrippa declares his life, 12 and the manner of his conversion. 24 Festus declares him to be mad. 25 Paul's reply. 28 Agrippa almost persuaded to be a Christian. 30 Paul pronounced innocent.*

THEN Ȧ-grĭp′pȧ said unto
[a]Paul, [b]Thou art permitted to [c]speak for thyself. Then
[d]Paul stretched forth the hand,
and answered for himself:
2 [e,f]I think myself happy, king
Ȧ-grĭp′pȧ, [1]because I shall answer for myself this day before
thee touching all the things
whereof I am [g]accused of the
Jews:
3 Especially *because* [e,f]*I know*
thee to be expert in all customs
and questions which are among
the Jews: wherefore I beseech
thee to hear me patiently.
4 My manner of life from my
youth, which was at the first
among mine own nation at [h]Jē-
ru′sȧ-lĕm, know all the Jews;
5 Which knew me from the beginning, if they would testify,
that after the [2]most straitest sect
of our religion I lived a [i]Phăr′ĭ-
see.
6 And now [a]I stand and am
judged for the [j,k]hope of the
[l]promise made of God unto our
fathers:
7 Unto which [l]*promise* our
[m]twelve tribes, [3]instantly [n]serv-
ing *God* day and night, [j,k]hope
to come. For which hope's sake,
king Ȧ-grĭp′pȧ, I am accused of
the Jews.
8 Why should it be thought a
thing incredible with you, that
[o]God should [p]raise the dead?
9 [a]I verily [q]thought with myself, that I ought to do many
things contrary to the name of
Jē′sus of Năz′a-rĕth.
10 Which thing I also did in
[h]Jē-ru′sȧ-lĕm: and [r]many of the
saints did I [s]shut up in [t]prison,
having received authority from
the chief priests; and when they
were [u]put to death, I gave my
voice against *them*.
11 And I [s]punished them oft
in [4]every [v]synagogue, and compelled *them* to [w]blaspheme;
and [q,r]being exceedingly [x,y]mad
against them, I [s]persecuted *them*
even unto strange cities.
12 Whereupon as I went to [z]Dȧ-
măs′cus with authority and commission from the chief [a]priests,
13 At midday, O king, [b,c]I [d]saw
in the way a [e]light from heaven,
above the brightness of the sun,
shining round about me and them
which journeyed with me.
14 And when we were all fallen
to the earth, I heard a [f]voice
speaking unto me, and saying
in the [g]Hē′brew [h]tongue, Saul,
Saul, why [i]persecutest thou me?
*it is* hard for thee to kick against
the [5]pricks.
15 And I said, Who art thou,
Lord? And he said, I am Jē′sus
whom thou [i]persecutest.
16 But rise, and stand upon thy
feet: for I have [l]appeared unto
thee for this purpose, [j]to make
thee a minister and a [k]witness
both of these things which thou
hast seen, and of those things
in the which I will appear unto
thee;
17 Delivering thee from the
people, and *from* the Ġĕn′tīles,
unto whom now I [l,m]send [b,j]thee,
18 [k]To open their [n]eyes, *and*
[k]to turn *them* from [o,p]darkness
to [q,r]light, and *from* the power of
[s]Sā′tan unto God, that they may

**27**
11 R. V. charges against

**1**
*a* *Paul*, Acts 13:9.
*b* *Prisoners, permitted to make defense*, Psa. 79:11.
*c* *Defense*, vs. 1–23; Acts 19:33.
*d* *Orator*, Acts 24:1.

**2**
*e* *Flattery, instances of*, Prov. 6:24.
*f* *Tact*, Prov. 15:1.
*g* *Indictments*, Matt. 27:37.
1 R. V. that I am to make my defence before thee

**4**
*h* *Jerusalem*, Judg. 19:10.

**5**
*i* *Pharisees*, Matt. 15:12.
2 R. V. *omits* most

**6**
*j* *Hope*, Prov. 13:12.
*k* *Messianic Hope*, Gen. 49:10.
*l* *Covenant, of God with men*, Deut. 29:1.

**7**
*m* *Israel*, Ex. 4:22.
*n* *Obedience*, Heb. 5:8.
3 R. V. earnestly

**8**
*o* *God, omnipotent*, Gen. 2:2.
*p* *Resurrection*, 1 Cor. 15:12.

**9**
*q* *Bigotry*, Isa. 65:5.

**10**
*r* *Intolerance*, Num. 11:28.
*s* *Persecution, of the righteous*, John 15:20.
*t* *Prison*, Gen. 39:20.
*u* *Martyrdom*, Rev. 17:6.

**11**
*v* *Synagogue*, Matt. 12:9.
*w* *Blasphemy*, 2 Sam. 12:14.
*x* *Malice*, Eph. 4:31.
*y* *Hatred*, Prov. 15:17.
4 R. V. all the synagogues, I strove to make them blaspheme;

**12**
*z* *Damascus*, Isa. 8:4.

*a* *Priest*, Lev. 1:5.

**13**
*b* *Paul*, Acts 13:9.
*c* *Religious Testimony*, vs. 13–23; 2 Thess. 1:10.
*d* *Vision*, Acts 9:10.
*e* *Light, miraculous*, Gen. 1:3.

**14**
*f* *Appearances of Jesus after his Resurrection*, Mark 16:9.
*g* *Hebrew*, Gen. 40:15.
*h* *Language*, Dan. 3:29.
*i* *Persecution, of Jesus*, John 15:20.
5 R. V. goad.

**16**
*j* *Minister, call of*, Rom. 15:16.
*k* *Minister, duties of*, Rom. 15:16.

**17**
*l* *Call, personal*, Phil. 3:14.
*m* *Missions*, Matt. 28:19.

**18**
*n* *Eye, figurative*, Matt. 6:22.
*o* *Darkness, figurative*, Gen. 1:2.
*p* *Spiritual Blindness*, 2 Cor. 4:4.
*q* *Light, figurative*, Matt. 5:14.
*r* *Wisdom, spiritual*, Prov. 2:2.
*s* *Satan*, Matt. 4:10.

t *Sin, forgiveness of,* Rom. 5:12.
u *Inheritance, figurative,* Num. 27:7.
v *Sanctification,* 1 Pet. 1:2.
w *Faith in Christ,* John 6:69.
6 R. V. *omit* that is

**19**

x *Strenuousness, of Paul,* Eccl. 9:10.
y *Obedience,* Heb. 5:8.

**20**

z *Damascus,* Isa. 8:4.
a *Jerusalem,* Judg. 19:10.
b *Judea,* Luke 5:17.
c *Gentiles, conversion of,* Acts 10:45.
d *Repentance, the burden of the preaching of Paul,* Mark 1:4.

**21**

e *Intolerance,* Num. 11:28.
f *Temple, Herod's,* 1 Kin. 6:17.
7 R. V. seized me in the temple, and assayed to kill me.

**22**

g *Grace of God,* Rom. 4:16.
h *Witnessing for Christ,* Luke 24:48.
i *Religious Testimony,* 2 Thess. 1:10.
j *Prophecies concerning the Messiah, and their fulfillment,* Gen. 12:3.
k *Law, of Moses,* Deut. 33:2.

**23**

l *Jesus, Messiah,* Matt. 1:21.
m *Jesus, mission of,* Matt. 1:21.
n *Jesus, sufferings of,* Matt. 1:21.
o *Jesus, death of,* Matt. 1:21.
p *Resurrection, of Jesus,* 1 Cor. 15:12.
q *Light, figurative,* Matt. 5:14.

**24**

r *Defense,* Acts 19:33.
s Acts 24:27; 25.
t *Paul, accused of insanity,* Acts 13:9.
u *Insanity,* Prov. 26:18.

**25**

v *Truth,* John 18:37.
8 R. V. excellent

receive [t]forgiveness of sins, and [u]inheritance among them which are [v]sanctified by [w]faith [6]that is in me.

19 Whereupon, O king Ȧ-grĭp'-pȧ, [x]I was [y]not disobedient unto the heavenly [d]vision:

20 But shewed first unto them of [z]Dȧ-măs'cus, and at [a]Jē-ru'-sȧ-lĕm, and throughout all the coasts of [b]Jū-dæ'ȧ, and *then* to the [c]Ġĕn'tīleṣ, that they should [d]repent and turn to God, and do works meet for repentance.

21 For these causes the Jewṣ [7,e]caught me in the [f]temple, and [e]went about to kill *me.*

22 Having therefore obtained [g]help of God, I continue unto this day, [h,i]witnessing both to small and great, saying none other things than those which the [j]prophets and [k]Mō'ṣeṣ did say should come:

23 That [l,m]Chrīst should [n,o]suffer, *and* that he should be the first that should [p]rise from the dead, and should shew [q]light unto the people, and to the [c]Ġĕn'-tīleṣ.

24 ¶ And as he thus [r]spake for himself, [s]Fĕs'tus said with a loud voice, [t]Paul, thou art [u]beside thyself; much learning doth make thee mad.

25 But he said, I am not mad, most [8]noble [s]Fĕs'tus; but speak forth the words of [v]truth and soberness.

26 For the king knoweth of these things, before whom also I speak freely: for I am persuaded that none of these things are hidden from him; for this thing was not done in a corner.

27 King Ȧ-grĭp'pȧ, believest thou the [j]prophets? I know that thou believest.

28 Then Ȧ-grĭp'pȧ said unto Paul, [9,w]Almost thou persuadest me to be a [x]Chrĭs'tian.

29 And Paul said, [y,z]I would to God, that [10]not only thou, but also all that hear me this day, were both almost, and altogether such as I am, except these bonds.

30 And when he had thus spoken, the [a]king rose up, and the [a,b]governor, and [c,d]Bĕr-nī'çē, and they that sat with them:

31 And when they were gone aside, they talked between themselves, saying, This man doeth nothing worthy of death or of bonds.

32 Then said Ȧ-grĭp'pȧ unto [e]Fĕs'tus, This man might have been set at liberty, if he had not [*,f]appealed unto Çæ'ṣar.

## CHAPTER 27

*Paul, sailing toward Rome, 9 foretells the danger of the voyage; 11 but is not believed. 14 They are driven up and down by a tempest; 27 and, after fourteen days, draw near to land. 39 They suffer shipwreck, 43 but all escape safe to land.*

AND when it was determined that [a,b]we should sail into [c]Ĭt'a-lȳ, they delivered Paul and certain other [d]prisoners unto *one* named Jū'lĭ-ŭs a [e]centurion of [f]Au-gŭs'tus' band.

2 And entering into a [g]ship of Ăd-ra-mȳt'tĭ-ŭm, we launched, meaning to sail by the coasts of [h]Ā'ṣiȧ; *one* [i]Ăr-ĭs-tär'chus, a [j]Măç-e-dō'nĭ-an of [k]Thĕs-sa-lō-nī'cȧ, being with us.

3 And the next *day* we touched at [l]Sī'dŏn. And Jū'lĭ-ŭs [1,m]courteously entreated [a]Paul, and gave *him* liberty to go unto his [n]friends to refresh himself.

4 And [2]when we had launched from thence, we sailed under [o]Çȳ'prus, because the winds were contrary.

5 And when we had sailed over the sea of [p]Çĭ-lĭ'çiȧ and [q]Păm-

**28**

w *Sarcasm, instances of,* Judg. 10:14.
x *Christian,* Acts 11:26.
9 R. V. With but little persuasion thou wouldest fain make me a Christian.

**29**

y *Love, of man for man,* 1 John 4:7.
z *Zeal,* 2 Cor. 7:11.
10 R. V. whether with little or with much, not thou only, but also all that hear me this day, might become such as I am, except these bonds.

**30**

a *Rulers,* Ex. 18:21.
b *Government, provincial,* Isa. 22:21.
c Acts 25:13, 23.
d *Women, social status of,* Prov. 31:10.

**32**

e Acts 24:27; 25.
f *Appeal,* Acts 28:19.

**1**

a *Paul,* Acts 13:9.
b *Luke* (probably), Col. 4:14.
c Acts 18:2; Heb. 13:24.
d *Prisoners,* Psa. 79:11.
e *Centurion,* Matt 8:5.
f *Cæsar,* Acts 25:8.

**2**

g *Ship,* 2 Chr. 8:18.
h *Asia,* Acts 2:9.
i Acts 19:29; 20:4; Col. 4:10; Philemon 24.
j *Macedonia,* Acts 16:12.
k *Thessalonica,* Phil. 4:16.

**3**

l Or, *Zidon,* Ezek. 28:21.
m *Kindness, instances of,* Acts 28:2.
n *Friends,* Ex. 33:11.
1 R. V. treated Paul kindly,

4 o *Cyprus,* Acts 21:3. 2 R. V. putting to sea from thence, we sailed under the lee of Cyprus. 5 p *Cilicia,* Gal. 1:21. q *Pamphylia,* Acts 14:24.

*** CHANGE OF VENUE.** *Granted Paul,* Acts 23:17-35; 25:12, 21; 26:32; 28:19. *Declined by Paul,* Acts 25:9, 11.

phy̆l′ĭ-ȧ, we came to My̆′rȧ, *a city* of Ly̆′çiȧ.

6 And there the [e]centurion found a [g]ship of *Ăl-ĕx-ăn′drĭ-ȧ sailing into [c]Ĭt′a-ly̆; and he put us therein.

7 And when we had sailed slowly many days, and scarce were come over against Cnī′dus, the wind not suffering us, we sailed under †Crēte, over against Săl-mō′nē;

8 And, [3]hardly passing it, came unto a place which is called The fair havens; nigh whereunto was the city *of* Lȧ-sē′ȧ.

9 ¶ Now when much time was spent, and when sailing was now dangerous, because the [r, s]fast was now already past, Paul admonished *them*, [Q]

10 And said unto them, Sirs, I perceive that [t]this voyage will be with hurt and much damage, not only of the lading and [g]ship, but also of our lives.

11 Nevertheless the centurion believed the master and the owner of the ship, more than those things which were spoken by Paul.

12 And because the haven was not commodious to [u]winter in, the more part advised to depart thence also, if by any means they might attain to [4]Phē-nī′çē, *and there* to winter; *which is* an haven of †Crēte, [5]and lieth toward the south west and north west.

13 And when the [v]south wind blew softly, supposing that they had obtained *their* purpose, loosing *thence*, they sailed close by †Crēte.

14 But [t]not long after there arose against it a [v]tempestuous wind, called [6]Eū-rŏc′ly̆-dŏn.

15 And when the [g]ship was caught, and could not bear up into the [v]wind, we let *her* drive.

16 And [7]running under a certain island which is called Clau′dȧ, we had much work to come by the boat:

17 Which when they had taken up, they used helps, undergirding the ship; and, [t]fearing lest they should [8]fall into the quicksands, strake sail, and so were driven.

18 And we [t]being exceedingly tossed with a [v]tempest, the next *day* they [9]lightened the ship;

19 And the third *day* we cast out with our own hands the tackling of the [g]ship.

20 And [t]when neither sun nor stars in many days appeared, and no small tempest lay on *us*, [w, x]all hope that we should be saved was then taken away.

21 ¶ But after long abstinence Paul stood forth in the midst of them, and [y]said, Sirs, ye should have hearkened unto me, and not have loosed from †Crēte, and to have gained this harm and loss.

22 And now I exhort you to be of good cheer: for there shall be no loss of *any man's* life among you, but of the ship.

23 For [z]there stood by me this night the [a]angel of God, [b]whose I am, [b]and whom I [c]serve,

24 Saying, Fear not, Paul; thou must be brought before Çæ′şar: and, lo, [d]God hath given thee all them that sail with thee.

25 Wherefore, sirs, be of good cheer: for I [e]believe God, that it shall be even as it was told me.

26 Howbeit we must be cast upon a certain island.

27 But when the fourteenth night was come, as we were driven [10]up and down in Ā′drĭ-ȧ, about midnight the [f]shipmen deemed that they drew near to some country;

**8**
3 R. V. with difficulty coasting along it we came

**9**
*r Fasting*, Zech. 8:19.
*s Day of Atonement (October)*, Lev. 23:27.

**10**
*t Prophecies, fulfilled*, vs. 18–44; Dan. 9:24.

**12**
*u Winter*, Gen. 8:22.
4 R. V. Phœnix,
5 R. V. looking north-east and south-east.

**13**
*v Meteorology*, Matt. 16:2.

**14**
6 R. V. Euraquilo:

**16**
7 R. V. running under the lee of a small island called Cauda, we were able, with difficulty, to secure the boat:

**17**
8 R. V. be cast upon the Syrtis, they lowered the gear, and so were driven.

**18**
9 R. V. began to throw the freight overboard;

**20**
*w Despondency, instances of*, Eccl. 2:20.
*x Borrowing Trouble*, Matt. 6:25.

**21**
*y Orator*, Acts 24:1.

**23**
*z Vision*, Acts 9:10.

*a Angel, functions of*, v. 24; Heb. 1:13.
*b Decision*, Isa. 50:7.
*c Obedience*, Heb. 5:8.

**24**
*d God, preserver*, Gen. 2:2.

**25**
*e Faith, instances of*, Mark 11:22.

**27**
*f Mariner*, Ezek. 27:27.
10 R. V. to and fro in the sea of Adria, about midnight the sailors surmised that they were drawing near

* **ALEXANDRIA.** *A city of Egypt*, Acts 6:9. *Ships of*, Acts 27:6; 28:11. *Apollos, the learned Christian orator, was born in*, Acts 18:24.

† **CRETE**, an island in the Mediterranean Sea. *Visited, by Paul*, Acts 27:7, 12, 13, 21; *by Titus*, Tit. 1:5. *Character of the inhabitants of*, Acts 2:11; Tit. 1:12.

28 And sounded, and found *it* twenty [g]fathoms: and when they had gone a little further, they sounded again, and found *it* fifteen fathoms.

29 Then fearing lest we should have fallen upon rocks, they cast four [h]anchors out of the stern, and wished for the day.

30 And as the [i]shipmen were about to flee out of the ship, when they had let down the boat into the sea, under colour as though they would have cast [h]anchors out of the foreship,

31 Paul said to the [i]centurion and to the [j]soldiers, Except these abide in the ship, ye cannot be saved.

32 Then the soldiers cut off the ropes of the boat, and let her fall off.

33 And while the day was coming on, Paul besought *them* all to take [k]meat, saying, This day is the fourteenth day that ye have tarried and continued [l]fasting, having taken nothing.

34 Wherefore I pray you to take *some* [11]meat: for this is for your [12]health: for [m]there shall not an hair fall from the head of any of you.

35 And when he had thus spoken, he took bread, and [n]gave thanks to God in presence of them all: and when he had broken *it*, he began to eat.

36 Then were they all of good cheer, and they also took *some* [11,k]meat.

37 And we were in all in the ship two hundred threescore and sixteen souls.

38 And when they had eaten enough, they lightened the ship, and cast out the wheat into the sea.

39 And when it was day, they knew not the land: but they discovered a certain [13]creek with a shore, into the which they were minded, if it were possible, to thrust in the ship.

40 And [14]when they had taken up the [h]anchors, they committed *themselves* unto the sea, and loosed the [o]rudder bands, and hoised up the mainsail to the wind, and made toward shore.

41 [p]And falling into a place where two seas met, they ran the [q]ship aground; and the forepart stuck fast, and remained unmoveable, but the hinder part was broken with the violence of the waves.

42 And the [j]soldiers' counsel was to kill the [r]prisoners, lest any of them should swim out, and escape.

43 But the [i]centurion, willing to save Paul, kept them from *their* purpose; and commanded that they which could swim should cast *themselves* first *into the sea*, and get to land:

44 And the rest, some on boards, and some on [15]*broken pieces* of the ship. And so it came to pass, that they escaped all safe to land.

## CHAPTER 28

*Paul is kindly entertained by the barbarous people of Melita. 3 A viper fastens on his hand without harm. 8 He heals many who had diseases. 11 His journey to Rome. 17 He declares to the Jews the cause of his coming, and persuades them concerning Jesus. 24 Some believe. 30 Paul preaches two whole years in his own hired house at Rome.*

AND when [1,a,b]they were escaped, then [1]they knew that the island was called Mĕl'ĭ-tȧ.

2 And the [c]barbarous people shewed us no little *,[d]kindness: for they kindled a [e]fire, and [f]received us every one, because of

28
g *Measure, linear,* Deut. 25:15.

29
h Heb. 6:19.

31
i *Centurion,* Matt. 8:5.
j *Soldiers,* Ezra 8:22.

33
k *Food,* Psa. 136:25.
l *Fasting,* Zech. 8:19.

34
m *Adversity, consolation in,* Psa. 10:6.
11 R. V. food:
12 R. V. safety

35
n *Thanksgiving for Food,* Luke 24:30.

39
13 R. V. bay with a beach.

40
o Jas. 3:4.
14 R. V. casting off the anchors, they left them in the sea, at the same time loosing the bands of the rudders; and hoisting up the foresail to the wind, they made for the beach.

41
p *Prophecies, fulfilled,* Dan. 9:24.
q *Ship, wrecked,* 2 Chr. 8:18.

42
r *Prisoners,* Psa. 79:11.

44
15 R. V. other things from the ship.

1
a *Paul,* Acts 13:9.
b *Luke* (probably), Col. 4:14.
1 R. V. we

2
c *Barbarian,* Rom. 1:14.
d *Christian Graces, kindness,* Gal. 5:22.
e *Fire,* Ex. 12:8.
f *Hospitality,* Rom. 12:13.

* **KINDNESS.** *Enjoined,* Zech. 7:9, 10; Matt. 5:42; Luke 6:30, 34, 35; Acts 20:35; Rom. 12:15; 15:1, 2; Gal. 6:1, 2, 10; Eph. 4:32; Col. 3:12; 1 Pet. 3:8, 9; 1 John 3:17, 18. *Enjoined, to enemies,* Ex. 23:4, 5; Luke 6:34, 35; *to strangers,* Lev. 19:34; *to a brother,* Deut. 22:1.
*Inspired by love,* 1 Cor. 13:4-7. *Commends ministers,* 2 Cor. 6:6. *Rewards of,* Prov. 14:21; Matt. 5:7; 25:34, 35.
*Of God,* Luke 6:35. *Of good women,* Prov. 31:26; 1 Tim. 5:9, 10. *Of good men,* Psa. 112:5; Heb. 5:2.
*Of Jesus,* see footnote, JESUS, *Compassion of,* Matt. 1:21.
**Instances of:** *Sons of Heth to Abraham,* Gen. 23:6, 11.

the present [g]rain, and because of
the cold.
3 And when [a]Pa̤ul had gathered
a bundle of sticks, and laid *them*
on the [e]fire, there came a [h]viper[C]
out of the heat, and fastened on
his hand.
4 And when the [c]barbarians[C]
saw the *venomous* beast hang
on his hand, they said among
themselves, No doubt this man
is a murderer, whom, though he
hath escaped the sea, yet [2]ven-
geance suffereth[C] not to live.
5 And he shook off the beast
into the [e]fire, and [i]felt no harm.[S]
6 Howbeit they looked when he
should have swollen, or fallen
down dead suddenly: but after
they had looked[C] a great while,
and saw [i]no harm come to him,
they changed their minds, and
said that he was a god.
7 ¶ In the same quarters were
possessions of the chief man of
the island, whose name was
Pŭb′lĭ-ŭs; who received us, and
[f]lodged[C] us three days courte-
ously.
8 [S]And it came to pass, that the
father of Pŭb′lĭ-ŭs lay sick of a
[j,k]fever and [3]of a bloody flux[C]:
to whom Pa̤ul entered in, and
[l]prayed, and laid his [m]hands
on him, and [i,n]healed him.
9 So when this was done,
others also which had [k]diseases
in the island, came, and were
[i,n]healed:[S]
10 Who also honoured us with
many honours; and when we departed, they [o]laded[C] *us* with such
things as were necessary.
11 ¶ And after three months we
departed in a [p]ship of [q]Ăl-ĕx-
ăn′drĭ-ȧ, which had [r]wintered in
the isle, whose sign was [4]Căs′tŏr
and Pŏl′lux.
12 And landing at Sy̆r′a-cūse,
we tarried[C] *there* three days.
13 And from thence we [5]fetched[C]
a compass, and came to Rhē′gĭ-
ŭm: and after one day the [s]south
wind blew, and we came the next
day to Pū-tē′o-lī:
14 Where we found [t]brethren,
and were [f]desired to tarry with
them [u]seven days: and so we
went toward [v]Rōme.
15 And from thence, when the
[t]brethren heard of us, they [w]came
to meet us as far as [6]Ăp′pĭ-ī
fō′rum, and The three taverns[C]: whom when Pa̤ul saw, he
[x]thanked God, and took [y]cour-
age.
16 And when we came to
[v]Rōme, [7]the [z]centurion delivered
the prisoners to the captain of
the guard: but [a,b]Pa̤ul was suffered[C] to dwell by himself with a
[c]soldier that kept him.
17 And it came to pass, that
after three days [a]Pa̤ul called the
chief of the Jews̤ together: and
when they were come together,
he said unto them, [8]Men *and*
brethren, though I have committed nothing against the people, or customs of our fathers,
yet was I delivered prisoner from
[d]Jē-ru̇′să-lĕm into the hands of
the Rō′mans̤.
18 Who, when they had examined me, would have let *me* go,
because there was no cause of
death in me.
19 But when the Jews̤ spake
against *it*, I was constrained to
[†,e]appeal unto Çæ′s̤ar; not that

g *Rain*, 2 Sam. 1:21.

3

h *Viper*, Isa. 30:6.

4

2 R. V. Justice

5

i *Miracles*, Luke 23:8.

8

j *Fever*, Deut. 28:22.

k *Disease, healing of, by Paul*, Ex. 15:26.

l *Intercession, of man with God*, Jer. 27:18.

m *Hand, imposition of*, Ezra 10:19.

n *Healing, by the apostles*, Acts 4:22.

3 R. V. dysentery:

10

o *Liberality*, 1 Tim. 6:18.

11

p *Ship*, 2 Chr. 8:18.

q *Alexandria*, Acts 27:6.

r *Winter*, Gen. 8:22.

4 R. V. The Twin Brothers.

13

s *Meteorology*, Matt. 16:2.

5 R. V. made a circuit,

14

t *Fraternity*, Zech. 11:14.

u *Seven, days*, Gen. 7:2.

v *Rome*, Acts 19:21.

15

w *Love, of man for man*, 1 John 4:7.

x *Thankfulness, to God*, Acts 24:3.

y *Courage*, Deut. 31:7.

6 R. V. The Market of Appius, and The Three Taverns:

16

z *Centurion*, Matt. 8:5.

a *Paul*, Acts 13:9.

b *Prisoners, kindness to*, Psa. 79:11.

c *Soldiers*, Ezra 8:22.

7 R. V. *omits* the centurion delivered the prisoners to the captain of the guard: but

17

d *Jerusalem*, Judg. 19:10.

8 R. V. I, brethren, though

19

e *Change of Venue*, Acts 26:32.

*Keeper of the prison to Joseph*, Gen. 39:21–23. *Pharaoh to Jacob*, Gen. 45:16–20; 47:5, 6. *Pharaoh's daughter to Moses*, Ex. 2:6–10. *Moses to Jethro's daughters*, Ex. 2:17, 19. *Jethro to Moses*, Ex. 2:20. *Rahab to the spies*, Josh. 2:4–16. *Boaz to Ruth*, Ruth 2:8–16; 3:15. *David to Nabal*, 1 Sam. 25:15, 16. *Abigail to David*, 1 Sam. 25:14–35. *David to Mephibosheth*, 2 Sam. 9:1–13. *Joab to Absalom*, 2 Sam. 14:1–24. *Obadiah, to the prophets of the Lord*, 1 Kin. 18:4. *Ahab to Ben-hadad*, 1 Kin. 20:32–34. *The Shunammite woman to Elisha*, 2 Kin. 4:8–10. *Elisha to the Shunammite woman*, 2 Kin. 4:13–17, 28–37; 8:1. *Evil-merodach to Jehoiachin*, 2 Kin. 25:28–30. *Jehoshabeath to Joash*, 2 Chr. 22:11. *Nehemiah and the nobles to the people*, Neh. 5:8–19. *Mordecai to Esther*, Esth. 2:7. *Ebed-melech to Jeremiah*, Jer. 38:7–13. *Nebuchadrezzar to Jeremiah*, Jer. 39:11, 12.

*Joseph to Mary*, Matt. 1:19, 24. *Centurion to his servant*, Luke 7:2–6. *Jews to Mary and Martha*, John 11:19, 33. *John to Mary*, John 19:27. *Felix to Paul*, Acts 24:23. *Julius to Paul*, Acts 27:3, 43. *Barbarians to Paul*, Acts 28:2, 7. *Onesiphorus to Paul*, 2 Tim. 1:16–18.

† **APPEAL.** *Paul makes, to Cæsar*, Acts 25:10, 11, 21–27; 26:32; 28:19.

I had [9]ought to accuse my nation of.

20 For this cause therefore [10]have I called for you, to see *you*, and to speak with *you*: because that for the [f,g]hope of Iș′ra-el I am bound with this [h]chain.

21 And they said unto him, We neither received letters out of [i]Jū-dæ′ȧ concerning thee, neither any of the brethren that came shewed or spake any harm of thee.

22 But we desire to hear of thee what thou thinkest: for as concerning this sect, we know that every where it is [j]spoken against.

23 And when they had appointed [a]him a day, there came many to him into *his* lodging; to whom [k]he [l]expounded and [m]testified the [n]kingdom of God, persuading them concerning [o]Jē′șus, both out of the [p,q]law of Mō′ṣeș, and *out of* the [r]prophets, from morning till evening.

24 And some [s]believed the things which were spoken, and [t]some [u,v]believed not.

25 And when they agreed not among themselves, they departed, after that Pa̤ul had spoken one word, [w]Well [x]spake the [y]Holy Ghost by [z]Ē-șā′ias the [a]prophet unto our fathers,

26 Saying, Go unto this people, and say, Hearing ye shall hear, and shall [b]not understand; and seeing ye shall see, and [c]not perceive:

27 For [b]the [d]heart of this people is waxed gross, and their ears are [e]dull of hearing, and their eyes have they [c]closed; lest they should see with *their* eyes, and hear with *their* ears, and understand with *their* heart, and should [11]be converted, and I should heal them.

28 Be it known therefore unto you, that the [f]salvation of God is sent unto the [g]Ġĕn′tīleș, and *that* they will hear it.

29 [12]And when he had said these words, the Jewș departed, and had great reasoning among themselves.

30 ¶ And [h]Pa̤ul dwelt two whole years in his own ‡hired house, and received all that came in unto him,

31 [i]Preaching the [j]kingdom of God, and [k]teaching those things which concern the [l]Lord Jē′șus [m]Christ, with all confidence, [n,o]no man forbidding him.

9 R. V. aught

**20**

*f* *Hope*, Prov. 13:12.

*g* *Messianic Hope*, Gen. 49:10.

*h* *Chains*, Dan. 5:7.

10 R. V. did I intreat you to see and to speak with me: for because of the hope

**21**

*i* *Judea*, Luke 5:17.

**22**

*j* *Persecution, of the righteous*, John 15:20.

**23**

*k* *Zeal, exemplified by Paul*, 2 Cor. 7:11.

*l* *Instruction, in religion*, Prov. 23:23.

*m* *Religious Testimony*, 2 Thess. 1:10.

*n* *Kingdom of Heaven*, Matt. 13:24.

*o* *Jesus, Messiah*, Matt. 1:21.

*p* *Law, of Moses*, Deut. 33:2.

*q* *Word of God*, Psa. 119:9.

*r* *Prophecies concerning the Messiah, and their fulfillment*, Gen. 12:3.

**24**

*s* *Faith in Christ*, John 6:69.

*t* *Unbelievers*, 1 Cor. 6:6.

*u* *Unbelief*, Heb. 3:12.

*v* *Jesus, rejected*, Matt. 1:21.

**25**

*w* *Prophecies, fulfilled*, Dan. 9:24.

*x* Isa. 6:9, 10; Matt. 13:14, 15; Mark 4:12.

*y* *Holy Spirit*, Acts 1:2.

*z* Or, *Isaiah*, Isa. 1:1.

*a* *Prophets, inspiration of*, Isa. 3:2.

**26**

*b* *Moral Insensibility*, Luke 8:10.

*c* *Spiritual Blindness*, 2 Cor. 4:4.

**27**

*d* *Heart*, Psa. 44:21.

*e* *Deafness, figurative*, Matt. 11:5.

11 R. V. turn again.

**28**

*f* *Salvation*, Acts 16:17.

*g* *Gentiles, conversion of*, Acts 10:45.

**29**

12 R. V. *omits this verse.*

**30**

*h* *Paul*, Acts 13:9.

**31**

*i* *Preaching*, Matt. 9:35.

*j* *Kingdom of Heaven*, Matt. 13:24.

*k* *Instruction, in religion*, Prov. 23:23.

*l* *Jesus, lordship of*, Matt. 1:21.

*m* *Jesus, Messiah*, Matt. 1:21.

*n* *Toleration*, Mic. 4:4.

*o* *Liberty, religious*, Lev. 25:10.

## THE EPISTLE OF PAUL TO THE

# ROMANS

## CHAPTER 1

*Paul's call to the apostleship, and salutation to the saints in Rome. 8 His prayer for them, 11 and desire to see them. 16 The gospel the power of God unto salvation. 18 The Gentiles are under condemnation. 21 Their wickedness.*

[a]PA̤UL, a servant of Jē′șus [b]Christ, [c]called *to be* an apostle, separated unto the [d]gospel of God,

2 ([e]Which he had [f]promised afore by his [g]prophets in the [h]holy scriptures,)

3 [e]Concerning [i]his [j,k]Son [1]Jē′șus Christ our Lord, which was made [l]of the seed of [m]Dā′vid according to the flesh;

4 And declared *to be* the [j,k]Son of [i]God with power, according

**1**

*a* *Paul*, Acts 13:9.

*b* *Jesus, Messiah*, Matt. 1:21.

*c* *Call, personal*, Phil. 3:14.

*d* *Gospel*, Mark 13:10.

**2**

*e* *Jesus, prophecies concerning*, Matt. 1:21.

*f* *Covenant, of God with men*, Deut. 29:1.

*g* *Prophets, inspiration of*, Isa. 3:2.

*h* *Word of God*, Psa. 119:9.

**3**

*i* *God, fatherhood of*, Gen. 2:2.

*j* *Jesus, divine sonship of*, Matt. 1:21.

*k* *Jesus, relation of, to the Father*, Matt. 1:21.

*l* *Jesus, incarnation of*, Matt. 1:21.

*m* *David*, 1 Sam. 16:13.

1 R. V. *omits* Jesus Christ our Lord,

‡ **RENTING.** *Of land*, Matt. 21:33–41; Luke 20:9–16. *Of houses*, Acts 28:30.

to the spirit of holiness, by the
[2,n]resurrection from the dead:[T]
5 By whom we have received
grace and apostleship, for [o]obe-
dience to the [p]faith among all
[q]nations, for his [3,r]name:
6 [S T]Among whom are ye also the
[c]called[G] [4]of Jē′ṣus Chrīst:
7 To all that be in [s]Rōme, [t,u]be-
loved of God, called *to be* saints[S]:
[v,w]Grace to you and [x]peace from
God our [i]Father, and the [y]Lord
Jē′ṣus Chrīst.[S T Q]
8 First, I [z]thank my God
[a]through Jē′ṣus [b]Chrīst for you
all, that your [c]faith is spoken of
throughout the whole world.
9 For God is my witness, whom
I serve with my [d]spirit in the
[e]gospel of his [f]Son, that [g]without
ceasing I make mention of you
always in my [h]prayers;[T]
10 [5,i]Making request, if by any
means now at length I might have
a prosperous journey by the [j]will
of God to come unto you.[S]
11 For I [k]long to see you, that I
may [l,m]impart unto you some
spiritual gift, to the end ye may
be established;
12 That is, that I [6]may be
comforted [n]together with you by
the mutual [c]faith both of you
and me.
13 Now I would not have you
ignorant, brethren, that [k]often-
times I purposed to come unto
you, ([7]but was let[G] hitherto[G],) that
I might have some fruit among
you also, even as among other
Gĕn′tīleṣ.[G]
14 [k]I am debtor[G] both to the
Greeks[G], and to the *Bär-bā′-
rĭ-anṣ[G]; both to the wise, and to
the unwise.
15 So, as much as in me is, [k]I
am ready to [m,o]preach the [e]gos-
pel to you that are at [p]Rōme also.
16 [S]For [q]I am not ashamed of
the [e]gospel [8]of Chrīst: for it is
the [r]power of God unto [s]salvation[G]
to everyone that [c]believeth; to the
Jew first, and also to the Greek.[G Q]
17 For therein is the [t]righteous-
ness of God revealed from faith
to faith: as it is written, [u]The
just shall live by [c]faith.[S T Q]
18 For [v]the [w]wrath of God is
revealed from [x]heaven against
all ungodliness and unrighteousness of men, [y]who hold[G] the truth
in unrighteousness;[S T]
19 [T]Because [z,a]that which may
be known of God is manifest in
them; for God hath shewed *it*
unto them.
20 [a,b]For the [c]invisible things
of him from the [d]creation of the
world are clearly seen, being [9]un-
derstood by the things that are
made, *even* his [e]eternal [f]power
and Godhead; so that they are
without [g]excuse:[S T Q]
21 Because that, [h]when they
knew God, [i]they [j]glorified[G] *him*
not as God, †neither were
[k]thankful; but became [i]vain in
their [10,l]imaginations[G], and their
foolish [i,m]heart was [n]darkened.[T]
22 [o]Professing themselves to be
[p]wise, they became [q,r]fools,[Q]

**4**
n *Resurrection, of Jesus,* 1 Cor. 15:12.
2 R. V. resurrection of the dead; even Jesus Christ our Lord,

**5**
o *Obedience,* Heb. 5:8.
p *Faith in Christ,* John 6:69.
q *Gentiles, conversion of,* Acts 10:45.
r *Name of Jesus,* John 14:13.
3 R. V. name's sake:

**6**
4 R. V. to be Jesus Christ's:

**7**
s *Rome,* Acts 19:21.
t *God, love of,* Gen. 2:2.
u *Righteous, described,* Psa. 64:10.
v *Grace of God,* Rom. 4:16.
w *Benedictions,* Deut. 21:5.
x *Spiritual Peace,* Gal. 1:3.
y *Jesus, lordship of,* Matt. 1:21.

**8**
z *Thankfulness, to God,* Acts 24:3.
a *Jesus, mediation of,* Matt. 1:21.
b *Jesus, Messiah,* Matt. 1:21.
c *Faith in Christ,* John 6:69.

**9**
d *Man, spirit,* Job 4:17.
e *Gospel,* Mark 13:10.
f *Jesus, divine sonship of,* Matt. 1:21.
g *Prayerfulness,* 1 Tim. 5:5.
h *Prayer, intercessory,* Acts 6:4. **10** i *Temporal Blessings, prayer for,* Psa. 103:2. j *Will of God, supreme rule of duty,* Mark 3:35.
5 R. V. Always in my prayers making request, if by any means now at length I may be prospered by the will
**11** k *Love, of man for man,* 1 John 4:7. l *Instruction, in religion,* Prov. 23:23. m *Minister, duties of,* Rom. 15:16.
**12** n *Fellowship, of the righteous,* 1 Cor. 1:9. 6 R. V. with you may be comforted in you, each of us by the other's faith, both yours and mine.
**13** 7 R. V. (and was hindered hitherto),

**15**
o *Preaching,* Matt. 9:35.
p *Rome,* Acts 19:21.

**16**
q *Confession of Christ,* Luke 12:8.
r *God, power of,* Gen. 2:2.
s *Salvation, plan of,* Acts 16:17.
8 R. V. omits of Christ:

**17**
t *God, righteousness of,* Gen. 2:2.
u *The Just shall live by Faith,* Hab. 2:4.

**18**
v *Wicked, punishment of,* Psa. 73:3.
w *Anger of God,* 2 Kin. 13:3.
x *Heaven, God's dwelling place,* Luke 18:22.
y *Infidelity,* 2 Cor. 6:15.

**19**
z *Wisdom, spiritual,* Prov. 2:2.
a *Natural Religion,* Psa. 19:1.

**20**
b *Infidelity, argument against,* 2 Cor. 6:15.
c *God, invisible,* Gen. 2:2.
d *God, creator,* Gen. 2:2.
e *God, eternity of,* Gen. 2:2.
f *God, power of,* Gen. 2:2.
g *Excuses,* Luke 14:18.
9 R. V. perceived through the things that are made, even his everlasting power and divinity; that they may be without excuse:

**21**
h *Sin, against knowledge,* Rom. 5:12.
i *Wicked, described,* Psa. 73:3.
j *Glorifying God,* Luke 5:25. k *Thankfulness, to God,* Acts 24:3. l *Evil Imagination,* Gen. 6:5. m *Heart, unregenerate,* Psa. 44:21. n *Conscience, dead,* Acts 23:1. 10 R V. reasonings,
**22** o *Conceit,* Prov. 26:5. p *Wisdom, worldly,* Prov. 2:2. q *Fool,* Prov. 18:2. r *Spiritual Blindness,* 2 Cor. 4:4.

* **BARBARIAN.** *A foreigner,* Acts 28:2–4; Rom. 1:14; 1 Cor. 14:11; Col. 3:11.
See footnote, FOREIGNERS, Deut. 23:20.

† **INGRATITUDE. To God,** Rom. 1:21; 2 Tim. 3:2. *Prosperity tempts to,* Deut. 6:10–12; 8:12–14; 32:6, 13, 15, 18; 2 Chr. 26:15, 16; Jer. 5:7–9, 24; Hos. 13:6. *Punishment for,* Deut. 28:47, 48; 1 Kin. 16:1–3; 2 Chr. 32:25; Psa. 78:16, 17, 27–32, 42–68; Dan. 5:18, 20, 21.

INSTANCES OF: *Levites,* Num. 16:9, 10. *Israel,* Deut. **31**:16; Judg. 2:10–12; 8:34, 35; 10:11, 13, 14; 1 Sam. 8:7, 8; **10**:19; Neh. 9:25, 26, 35; Psa. 106:7, 21; Isa. 1:2; Jer. 2:6, 7, 17, 31; Hos. 11:1, 3. *David,* 2 Sam. 12:7–9. *Baasha,* 1 Kin. 16:1, 2.

**To Jesus:** *The nine lepers,* Luke 17:12–18.

**Of Man to Man,** Prov. 17:13; 2 Tim. 3:2.

INSTANCES OF: *Pharaoh's butler to Joseph,* Gen. 40:23. *Israelites to Moses,* Ex. 16:3; 17:2–4; Num. 16:12–14; *to Gideon,* Judg. 8:35. *Shechemites,* Judg. 9:17, 18. *Men of Keilah to David,* 1 Sam. 23:5–12. *Saul to David,* 1 Sam. 24. *Nabal,* 1 Sam. 25:21. *David's companions to David,* Psa. 35:11–16; 38:20; 41:9; 109:4, 5. *Citizens,* Eccl. 9:14–16. *Joash,* 2 Chr. 24:22. *Jeremiah's enemies,* Jer. 18:20.

23 And changed the [s]glory of
the [t]uncorruptible God [u]into an
[v]image made like to corruptible
[v]man, and to [v]birds, and [v]four-
footed beasts, and [‡,v]creeping
things.
24 Wherefore God also [w]gave
[x]them up to [y]uncleanness through
the [z]lusts of their own hearts, to
[a]dishonour their own bodies between themselves:
25 Who [11]changed the [b]truth of
God into a lie, and [c]worshipped
and served the creature [12]more
than the [d]Creator, [e]who is blessed
for ever. Amen.
26 For this cause God gave them
up unto [f]vile [13]affections: for even
their [g]women did change the natural use into [a]that which is against
nature:
27 And likewise also the men,
leaving the natural use of the
woman, burned in their [a,h]lust
one toward another; men with
men working that which is unseemly, and [i]receiving in themselves that recompence of their
error which was meet.
28 And even as [j]they [14,k]did not
like to retain God in *their* knowledge, God gave them over to
a [l]reprobate mind, to do those
things which are not [15]convenient;
29 [k]Being filled with all unrighteousness, [16]fornication, wickedness, [m]covetousness, [n]malicious-
ness; full of [o]envy, [p]murder,
[17,q]debate, [r]deceit, [n]malignity;
[s]whisperers,
30 [k,t]Backbiters, [18]haters of
God, despiteful, proud, [u]boasters,
inventors of evil things, [v]disobe-
dient to parents,
31 [k,w]Without understanding,
covenantbreakers, without [x]nat-
ural affection, [19]implacable, unmerciful:
32 [k]Who knowing the judgment of God, that they which
commit such things are worthy
of [y]death, [z]not only do the same,
but [20,z]have pleasure in them
that do them.

## CHAPTER 2

*He that sins cannot excuse himself, 3 nor escape the judgment of God, 6 who will render to every man according to his deeds. 12 The Gentiles will be judged by the law written in their hearts. 17 The greater privileges of the Jews will increase their guilt, if they keep not the law.*

THEREFORE thou art in-
excusable, O man, who-
soever thou art that [a]judgest:
for wherein thou judgest another, thou [b]condemnest thyself;
for thou that judgest [c,d]doest the
same things.
2 But we are sure that the judgment of God is [e]according to
[f]truth against them which commit such things.
3 And [g,h]thinkest thou this, O
man, that [a]judgest them which
do such things, and [c,d]doest the
same, that thou shalt escape the
judgment of God?
4 Or despisest thou the riches
of his [i]goodness and forbearance
and [j]longsuffering; [k]not knowing
that the goodness of God leadeth
thee to [l]repentance?
5 But after thy [m]hardness and
*impenitent [n]heart treasurest up
unto thyself [o,p]wrath against the
[q]day of wrath and revelation of

**23**
s *God, glory of,* Gen. 2:2.
t *God, holiness of,* Gen. 2:2.
u *Idolatry, folly of,* 1 Sam. 15:23.
v *Idolatry, objects of,* 1 Sam. 15:23.

**24**
w *Holy Spirit, withdrawn from incorrigible sinners,* Acts 1:2.
x *Reprobates,* 1 Cor. 9:27.
y *Idolatry, wicked practices of,* 1 Sam. 15:23.
z *Lust,* 2 Pet. 1:4.

a *Sodomy,* Lev. 18.22.

**25**
b *Truth,* John 18:37.
c *Idolatry, folly of,* 1 Sam. 15:23.
d *God, creator,* Gen. 2:2.
e *Praise,* Psa. 150:1.
11 R. V. exchanged
12 R. V. rather than

**26**
f *Lasciviousness,* 1 Pet. 4:3.
g *Women, wicked,* Prov. 31:10.
13 R. V. passions:

**27**
h *Lust,* 2 Pet. 1:4.
i *Sin, fruits of,* Rom. 5:12.

**28**
j *Godless,* Job 8:13.
k *Wicked, described,* Psa. 73:3.
l *Reprobates,* 1 Cor. 9:27.
14 R. V. refused to have God
15 R. V. fitting;

**29**
m *Covetousness,* Isa. 57:17.
n *Malice,* Eph 4:31.
o *Envy,* Prov. 14:30.
p *Homicide, felonious,* Deut. 5:17. q *Strife,* Prov. 20:3. r *Deceit,* Psa. 36:3. s *Slander,* Prov. 10:18. 16 R. V. *omits* fornication, 17 R. V. strife,
**30** t *Backbiting,* Prov. 25:23. 18 R. V. hateful to God, insolent, haughty, boastful,

u *Boasting,* Prov. 25:14.
v *Children, wicked,* Mark 10:14.

**31**
w *Spiritual Blindness,* 2 Cor. 4:4.
x *Affections, natural,* 2 Cor. 7:15.
19 R. V. *omits* implacable,

**32**
y *Second Death,* Rev. 20:14.
z *Obduracy,* Prov. 29:1.
20 R. V. also consent with them that practise them.

**1**
a *Uncharitableness.* Matt. 7:1.
b *Self-condemnation,* Job 9:20.
c *Inconsistency,* Matt. 7:3.
d *Hypocrisy,* Jas. 3:17.

**2**
e *God, justice of,* Gen. 2:2.
f *Truth,* John 18:37.

**3**
g *False Confidence,* Psa. 30:6.
h *Punishment, no escape from,* Lev. 26:41.

**4**
i *God, goodness of,* Gen. 2:2.
j *God, longsuffering of,* Gen. 2:2.
k *Spiritual Blindness,* 2 Cor. 4:4.
l *Repentance,* Mark 1:4.

**5**
m *Obduracy,* Prov. 29:1.
n *Heart, unregenerate,* Psa. 44:21.
o *Anger of God,* 2 Kin. 13:3.
p *Wicked, punishment of,* Psa. 73:3.
q *Judgment, the general,* 2 Pet. 3:7.

‡ **CREEPING THINGS.** *A general term for animals,* Gen. 1:26; Lev. 11:20–23, 29–31, 42; Psa. 104:20, 25; Rom. 1:23. *Unclean,* Lev. 5:2; 11:20, 29–44; Deut. 14:19. *Clean,* Lev. 11:21, 22. *Uses of, in idolatrous worship,* Ezek. 8:10.

* **IMPENITENCE,** Eccl. 8:11; Isa. 26:10; 48:4, 8; 57:11; Jer. 2:25; 3:7–10; 5:21–24; 6:10, 16, 17; 7:13, 14, 24; 8:5–7; 11:8; 16:12; 17:23; 18:12; 22:21; 25:4; 35:14–17; 44:10, 16, 17; Ezek. 2:4, 5; 3:19; 20:8; 33:9; Hos. 4:17; 5:4; 11:2, 7; Zech. 7:11–13; Matt. 11:21; 12:41, 42; 13:15; 23:37, 38; Luke 10:13; 16:31; Acts 7:51; Rev. 9:20, 21. *Admonitions against,* Psa. 95:8; 2 Cor. 12:21; Heb. 3:8; Rev. 2:5, 16, 21, 22; 3:3. *Leads to destruction,* Matt. 24:38, 39, 48–51; Luke 13:3, 5; Rev. 16:9, 21. *Judgments, denounced against,* Lev. 23:29; 26:21–43; Deut. 29:19–21; 1 Sam. 15:23; Psa. 7:11–13; 68:21; 81:11, 12; 107:11, 12; Prov. 1:24–31; 19:16; 28:13, 14; 29:1; Ezek. 33:4, 5; Rom. 2:4, 5; *denounced against Israel's,* Isa. 65:12, 15; 66:4; 12:11; 14:10; 15:6, 7; Jer. 19:15; 26:4–6; Dan. 9:13; Mal. 2:2.

See footnotes: OBDURACY, Prov. 29:1; REPROBATES, 1 Cor. 9:27.

**Instances of:** *Pharaoh,* Ex. 9:30, 34. *Israelites,* Num. 14:22, 23; 2 Kin. 17:14; 2 Chr. 24:19; 36:15, 17; Neh. 9:16, 17, 29, 30; Jer. 29:19; 36:31; Zech. 1:4. *Eli's sons,* 1 Sam. 2:25. *Amaziah,* 2 Chr. 25:16. *Manasseh,* 2 Chr. 33:10. *Amon,* 2 Chr. 33:23. *Jehoiakim and his servants,* Jer. 36:22–24. *Zedekiah,* 2 Chr. 36:12, 13; Jer. 37:2. *Belshazzar,* Dan. 5:22, 23. *Jews,* Matt. 27:4, 25; Mark 3:5.

*r* *God, righteousness of*, Gen. 2:2.

**6**
*s* *God, impartial*, Gen. 2:2.
*t* *Judgment, according to opportunity and works*, 2 Pet. 3:7.

**7**
*u* *Righteous, promises to*, Psa. 64:10.
*v* *Patience, a grace of the righteous*, Luke 8:15.
*w* *Perseverance, motives to*, Eph. 6:18.
*x* *Immortality*, 1 Cor. 15:54.
*y* *Reward, a motive, to perseverance*, Matt. 5:12.
*z* *Life, everlasting*, Eccl. 8:15.
1 R. V. incorruption,

**8**
*a* *Wicked, contrasted with the righteous*, vs. 8–10; Psa. 73:3.
*b* *Strife*, Prov. 20:3.
*c* *Truth*, John 18:37.
*d* *Wicked, punishment of*, Psa. 73:3.
2 R. V. factious,

**9**
*e* *Evil*, 1 Thess. 5:22.
3 R. V. Greek;

**10**
*f* *Reward, a motive, to faithfulness*, Matt. 5:12.
*g* *Spiritual Peace*, Gal. 1:3.

**11**
*h* *God, justice of*, Gen. 2:2.
*i* *Respect of Persons*, Prov. 24:23.

**12**
*j* *Law, of Moses*, Deut. 33:2.
*k* *Responsibility, according to privilege*, Ezek. 18:20.

**13**
*l* *Doer of the Word*, Jas. 1:22.
*m* *Works*, 2 Tim. 1:9. *n* *Justification*, Rom. 4:25.
**14** *o* *Heathen, pious people among*, Lam. 1:10. **15** *p* *Heart*, Psa. 44:21. *q* *Conscience*, Acts 23:1.
**16** *r* *Judgment, the general*, 2 Pet. 3:7. *s* *God, judge*, Gen. 2:2. *t* *Sin, secret*, Rom. 5:12. *u* *Jesus, Messiah*, Matt. 1:21.

the [e,r]righteous judgment of
God;
6 [e,r,s]Who will [t]render to every
man according to his deeds:
7 To [u]them who by [v]patient
[w]continuance in well doing seek
for glory and honour and [1]im-
mortality, [x,y]eternal [z]life:
8 But unto [a]them that are
[2,b]contentious, and do not obey
the [c]truth, but obey unrighteousness, [d]indignation and wrath,
9 [d]Tribulation and anguish, upon every soul of man that doeth
[e]evil, of the Jew first, and also of
the [3]Ġĕn'tīle;
10 [a]But [f]glory, [f]honour, and
[f,g]peace, to every man that worketh good, to the Jew first, and
also to the [3]Ġĕn'tīle:
11 For there is [h]no [i]respect of
persons with God.
12 For as many as have sinned
without [j]law [k]shall also [d]perish
without law: and as many as
have sinned in the law [k]shall be
judged by the law;
13 (For not the †hearers of the
law *are* just before God, but the
[l,m]doers of the law shall be [n]jus-
tified.
14 For when the [o]Ġĕn'tīleṣ,
which have not the [j]law, do by
nature the things contained in the
law, these, having not the law, are
a law unto themselves:
15 Which shew the work of the
[j]law written in their [p]hearts, their
[q]conscience also bearing witness,
and *their* thoughts the mean while
accusing or else excusing one another;)
16 In the [r]day when God shall
[s]judge the [t]secrets of men by
Jē'ṣus [u]Chrīst according to my
gospel.
17 Behold, thou art called a
Jew, and [v]restest in the [j]law, and
makest thy boast of God,
18 And knowest *his* will, and
approvest the things that are
more excellent, being [w]instructed
out of the [j]law;
19 And art [x]confident that [y]thou
thyself art a guide of the [z]blind,
a [a]light of them which are in
[b]darkness,
20 [4]An [c]instructor of the foolish, a teacher of [d]babes, which
hast the form of knowledge and
of the truth in the [e]law.
21 [c]Thou therefore which teachest another, [f]teachest thou not
thyself? thou that preachest a
man should not [g]steal, [f]dost thou
steal?
22 [c]Thou that sayest a man
should not commit [h]adultery,
[f]dost thou commit adultery?
thou that abhorrest [i]idols, dost
thou [5]commit sacrilege?
23 [c]Thou that makest thy boast
of the [e]law, through breaking the
law [f]dishonourest thou God?
24 For the [j]name of God is
[k,l]blasphemed among the [m]Ġĕn'-
tīleṣ through [n]you, as it is written.
25 For [o]circumcision verily
profiteth, if thou keep the [e]law:
but if thou be a [6]breaker of the
law, thy circumcision is made
uncircumcision.
26 Therefore if the uncircumcision keep the [7]righteousness of
the law, shall not his uncircumcision be counted for circumcision?
27 And [p]shall not uncircumcision which is by nature, if it
fulfil the law, judge thee, who by
the letter and circumcision dost
transgress the law?
28 For he is not a Jew, which is
one [f]outwardly; neither *is that*
[o]circumcision, which is outward
in the flesh:
29 But he *is* a Jew, which is one

**17**
*v* *Self-righteousness*, Luke 18:11.

**18**
*w* *Instruction, in religion*, Prov. 23:23.

**19**
*x* *False Confidence*, Psa. 30:6.
*y* *False Teachers*, 2 Pet. 2:1.
*z* *Spiritual Blindness*, 2 Cor. 4:4.
*a* *Light, figurative*, Matt. 5:14.
*b* *Darkness, figurative*, Gen. 1:2.

**20**
*c* *False Teachers*, 2 Pet. 2:1.
*d* *Babes, figurative*, Psa. 8:2.
*e* *Law, of Moses*, Deut. 33:2.
4 R. V. A corrector of

**21**
*f* *Hypocrisy*, Jas. 3:17.
*g* *Theft*, Mark 7:22.

**22**
*h* *Adultery*, Lev. 20:10.
*i* *Idol*, 1 Kin. 15:12.
5 R. V. rob temples?

**24**
*j* *God, name of, not to be profaned*, Gen. 2:2.
*k* *Blasphemy*, 2 Sam. 12:14.
*l* *Profanation, of God's name*, Lev. 22:32.
*m* *Gentiles*, Acts 10:45.
*n* *Influence, evil*, 1 Cor. 7:14.

**25**
*o* *Circumcision*, Gen. 17:10.
6 R. V. transgressor

**26**
7 R. V. ordinances

**27**
*p* *Responsibility, according to privilege*, Ezek. 18:20.

† **HEARERS.** *Heedless*, Ezek. 33:30–32; Matt. 7:26, 27 (with Luke 6:49); 13:14, 15, 19–22; Luke 8:11–14; Rom. 2:13; Jas. 1:22–24. *Obedient*, Matt. 7:24, 25; 13:23; Luke 6:47, 48; 8:15; Jas. 1:25.

inwardly; and [q,r]circumcision *is*
*that* of the [s]heart, in the [t]spirit,
*and* not in the letter; whose
praise *is* not of men, but of God.

## CHAPTER 3

*Objections answered. 9 All men are under sin. 20 No flesh justified by the law. 28 A man is justified by faith without the deeds of the law. 31 The law is not made void through faith.*

WHAT advantage then hath
the Jew? or what profit *is*
*there* of [a]circumcision?
2 Much every way: chiefly, because that unto [b,c]them were
committed the [d,e]oracles of God.
3 For what if some [1]did [f]not believe? shall their unbelief make
the [g]faith of God without effect?
4 God forbid: yea, let [h]God be
[i]true, but every man a [j]liar; as it
is written, [k]That thou mightest
be justified in thy sayings, and
mightest [2]overcome when thou
art [l]judged.
5 But if our unrighteousness
commend the [h]righteousness of
God, what shall we say? *Is*
God unrighteous who [3]taketh
vengeance? (I speak as a man)
6 God forbid: for then how
shall God [l]judge the world?
7 For if the [m]truth of God hath
more abounded through my lie
unto his [n]glory; why yet am I
also judged as a sinner?
8 And not *rather*, (as we be
[o,p]slanderously reported, and as
some affirm that we say,) Let us
do evil, that good may come?
whose [4]damnation is just.
9 What then? are we [5]better
*than they*? No, in no wise: for
we have before proved both Jews
and Gĕn′tīleş, that they are [q]all
under [r]sin;
10 As it is written, [q,s]There is
none righteous, no, not one:
11 [t]There is none that understandeth, [t]there is none that
[u]seeketh after God.
12 They are all gone out of the
way, they are together become
unprofitable; [q]there is none that
doeth good, no, not one.
13 [t,v]Their throat *is* an open
sepulchre; with their [w]tongues
they have used [x]deceit; [y]the [z]poi-
son of [a]asps *is* under their lips:
14 [b]Whose mouth *is* full of cursing and bitterness:
15 [c]Their feet *are* swift to shed
blood:
16 Destruction and misery *are*
in their ways:
17 And the way of peace have
they not known:
18 [d,e]There is no [f]fear of God
before their eyes.
19 Now we know that what
things soever the [g]law saith, it
saith to them who are under the
law: that every [h]mouth may be
stopped, and all the world may
[6]become guilty before God.
20 Therefore by the [i]deeds of
the [g]law there shall no flesh be
[j]justified in his sight: for by the
law *is* the knowledge of sin.
21 But now the [k]righteousness
of God without the law is manifested, being witnessed by the
[g,l]law and the [l]prophets;
22 Even the [k]righteousness of
God *which is* by [m]faith of Jē′-
şus Chrīst unto all and upon all
them that believe: for there is
no [7]difference:
23 For *all have sinned, and
[8]come short of the glory of God;
24 Being [n]justified freely by his
[o]grace through the [p,q,r]redemp-
tion that is in [s,t]Chrīst Jē′şus:
25 Whom God hath set forth
*to be* a †,[q,s]propitiation through
[m]faith in his [u]blood, to declare
his righteousness [9]for the [n,v]re-

**29**
q *Circumcision, figurative*, Gen. 17:10.
r *Holiness*, Ex. 39:30.
s *Heart, renewed*, Psa. 44:21.
t *Man, spirit*, Job 4:17.

**1**
a *Circumcision*, Gen. 17:10.

**2**
b *Jews, entrusted with oracles of God*, Neh. 4:2.
c *Church, mission of*, Matt. 16:18.
d *Oracle*, 1 Kin. 6:5.
e *Law, of Moses*, Deut. 33:2.

**3**
f *Unbelief*, Heb. 3:12.
g *God, faithfulness of*, Gen. 2:2.
1 R. V. were without faith? shall their want of faith make of none effect the faithfulness of God?

**4**
h *God, righteousness of*, Gen. 2:2.
i *God, truth of*, Gen. 2:2.
j *Falsehood*, Job 21:34.
k Psa. 51:4.
l *God, judge*, Gen. 2:2.
2 R. V. prevail when thou comest into judgement.

**5**
3 R. V. visiteth with wrath? (I speak after the manner of men.)

**7**
m *Truth*, John 18:37.
n *God, glory of*, Gen. 2:2.

**8**
o *Slander*, Prov. 10:18.
p *False Accusation*, 2 Tim. 3:3.
4 R. V. condemnation

**9**
q *Depravity, universal*, Job 15:14.
r *Sin, dominion of*, Rom. 5:12.

u *Seekers*, Isa. 55:6.

**13**
v Psa. 5:9.
w *Speech, evil*, Col. 4:6.
x *Deceit*, Psa. 36:[illegible]
y Psa. 140:3.
z *Venom*, Deut. 32:33.
a *Asp*, Job 20:14.

**14**
b Psa. 10:7.

**15**
c Prov. 1:16; Isa. 59:7, 8.

**18**
d Psa. 36:1.
e *Wicked, described*, Psa. 73:3.
f *Fear of God*, Acts 9:31.

**19**
g *Law, of Moses*, Deut. 33:2.
h *Excuses, for rejecting salvation*, Luke 14:18.
6 R. V. be brought under the judgement of God:

**20**
i *Works, insufficient for salvation*, 2 Tim. 1:9.
j *Justification, not by the law*, Rom. 4:25.

**21**
k *God, righteousness of*, Gen. 2:2.
l *Word of God*, Psa. 119:9.

**22**
m *Faith in Christ, salvation by*, John 6:69.
7 R. V. distinction;

**23**
8 R. V. fall

**24**
n *Justification, by faith*, Rom. 4:25.
o *Grace of God*, Rom. 4:16.
p *Redemption of our Souls*, Eph. 1:7.
q *Atonement, by Jesus*, Lev. 17:11.
r *Jesus, design of his death*, Matt. 1:21.
s *Jesus, atonement by*, Matt. 1:21.

5 R. V. in worse case than they? No, in no wise: for we before laid to the charge both of Jews and Greeks. **10** s Psa. 14:1–3; 53:1–3. **11** t *Wicked, described*, Psa. 73:3.

t *Jesus, savior*, Matt. 1:21. **25** u *Blood, of Christ, atoning*, Heb. 9:19. v *Sin, forgiveness of*, Rom. 5:12. 9 R. V. because of the passing over of the sins done aforetime, in the forbearance of God;

* **SINFULNESS.** *Universal*, 1 Kin. 8:46; 2 Chr. 6:36; Psa. 14:3; Eccl. 7:20; Rom. 3:23; 11:32; 1 John 1:8, 10. See footnote, DEPRAVITY, Job 15:14.

† **PROPITIATION**, Rom. 3:25; 5:1, 10, 11; Col. 1:20–22; 1 John 2:2; 4:10. See footnote, ATONEMENT, Lev. 17:11.

mission[G] of sins that are past,
through the [w]forbearance of
God;[T]
26 To declare, *I say*, at this
time his righteousness: that he
might be [x]just,[G] and the [n]justifier
of him which [m]believeth in Jē′-
ṣus.
27 Where [10]*is* [‡, y]boasting then?
It is excluded. By what law? of
works? Nay: but by the law of
[z]faith.
28 Therefore we conclude that
a man is [a]justified[G] by [b]faith without[G] the deeds of the [c]law.[T]
29 *Is he* the [d]God of the [e]Jewṣ
only? *is* [d]*he* not also of the
[f]Ġĕn′tīleṣ? Yes, of the Ġĕn′-
tīleṣ also:
30 Seeing *it is* [d]one God, which
shall [a]justify the [g]circumcision
by [b]faith, and [f]uncircumcision
through faith.[S T Q]
31 Do we then make void[G]
the [c]law through [b]faith? God
forbid: [11]yea,[G] we establish the
law.[T]

## CHAPTER 4

*Abraham's faith was counted unto him for righteousness, 10 before he was circumcised. 13 The promise to him was through the righteousness of faith. 18 The strength of his faith. 23 His example recorded for our sake.*

WHAT shall we say then that
[a]Ā′bră-hăm our [1]father,
as pertaining to the flesh, hath
found?
2[T] For if [a]Ā′bră-hăm were [b]jus-
tified[G] by [c]works, he hath *whereof*
to glory; but not before God.
3 For what saith the [d]scrip-
ture? [a]Ā′bră-hăm [e]believed God,
and it was [2]counted unto him for
[f]righteousness.[T Q]
4 [g]Now[S] to [h, i]him that worketh
is the [f]reward not reckoned of
grace, but of debt.
5[T] But to him that worketh not,
but [e]believeth on him that [b, k]jus-
tifieth the ungodly, his [e]faith is
[2]counted for [f]righteousness.
6 Even as Dā′vid also [3]de-
scribeth the [l]blessedness[G] of the
man, unto whom God imputeth
[f]righteousness without[G] works,
7 *Saying*,[Q] [l, m]Blessed *are* they
whose iniquities are [k]forgiven,
and whose sins are covered.
8 [l, m]Blessed *is* the man to
whom the Lord [k]will not [4]im-
pute[G] sin.[S T Q]
9 *Cometh* this blessedness[G] then
upon the [n]circumcision *only*, or
upon the [o]uncircumcision also?
for we say that [e]faith was reckoned to [a]Ā′bră-hăm for [f]right-
eousness.[Q]
10 How was it then reckoned?
when he was in [p]circumcision, or
in uncircumcision? Not in circumcision, but in uncircumcision.
11 And he received the sign
of [p]circumcision, a [p]seal of the
righteousness of the [e]faith which
*he had yet* being uncircumcised:
that he might be the father of all
them that [e]believe, though they
be not circumcised; that [f]right-
eousness might be [5]imputed unto them also:[T Q]
12 And the father of [p]circum-
cision to them who are not of the
circumcision only, but who also
walk in the steps of that [e]faith of
our father [a]Ā′bră-hăm, which *he
had* being *yet* uncircumcised.
13 For the [q]promise, that he
should be the heir of the world,
*was* not to [a]Ā′bră-hăm, or to
his seed, through the [r]law, but
through the [f]righteousness of
[e]faith.[T Q]
14 For if they which are of the
[r]law *be* heirs, [s]faith is made void,[G]
and the [q]promise made of none
effect:
15 Because the [r]law worketh
wrath: for [t]where no law is, *there
is* no transgression.[T]
16 Therefore *it is* of [s]faith, that

*w God, longsuffering of*, Gen. 2:2.

**26**
*x God, justice of*, Gen. 2:2.

**27**
*y Self-righteousness*, Luke 18:11.
*z Faith*, Mark 11:22.
10 R. V. then is the glorying? It is excluded. By what manner of law?

**28**
*a Justification, by faith*, Rom. 4:25.
*b Faith*, Mark 11:22.
*c Law, of Moses*, Deut. 33:2.

**29**
*d God, unity of*, v. 30; Gen. 2:2.
*e Jews*, Neh. 4:2.
*f Gentiles*, Acts 10:45.

**30**
*g Jews*, Neh. 4:2.

**31**
11 R. V. nay,

**1**
*a Abraham*, Gen. 17:5.
1 R. V. forefather according to the flesh,

**2**
*b Justification*, see footnote on opposite page.
*c Works, insufficient, for salvation*, 2 Tim. 1:9.

**3**
*d Word of God*, Psa. 119:9.
*e Faith, reckoned for righteousness*, Gen. 15:6.
*f Righteousness, imputed on account of faith*, Psa. 15:2.
2 R. V. reckoned

**4**
*g Employer, to accord just compensation*, Deut. 24:14.
*h Hired Servant, rights of*, Lev. 25:40.
*i Employee, rights of*, Deut. 24:14.
*j Wages*, Gen. 31:7.

**5**
*k Sin, forgiveness of*, Rom. 5:12.

**6**
*l Spiritual Peace*, Gal. 1:3.
3 R. V. pronounceth blessing upon the man, unto whom God reckoneth righteousness apart from works,

**7**
*m* Psa. 32:1, 2.

**8**
4 R. V. reckon

**9**
*n Jews*, Neh. 4:2.
*o Gentiles*, Acts 10:45.

**10**
*p Circumcision, a seal of righteousness*, Gen. 17:10.

**11**
5 R. V. reckoned

**13**
*q Covenant, of God with men*, Deut. 29:1.
*r Law, of Moses*, Deut. 33:2.

**14**
*s Faith in Christ*, John 6:69.

**15**
*t Sin, defined*, Rom. 5:12.

‡ **SPIRITUAL BOASTING**, Rom. 11:18–21. *Incompatible, with faith*, Rom. 3:27; Eph. 2:8–10; *with humility*, 1 Cor. 1:29 (with vs. 17–31); 4:6, 7; 2 Cor. 10:12–16. *In the Lord, approved*, Jer. 9:24; 2 Cor. 10:17, 18; Gal. 6:14.

*it might be* by [+]grace; to the
end the [q]promise might be sure
to all the seed; not to that only
which is of the [r]law, but to
that also which is of the [s]faith
of [a]Ā'brā-hăm; who is the father
of us all,[T]
17 (As it is written, I have made
thee a father of many [u]nations,)
before him whom he [v]believed,
*even* God, who [w]quickeneth[G] the
dead, and calleth those things
which be not as though they
were.[T Q]
18 Who against [x]hope [v]be-
lieved in hope, that he might
become the father of many
[u]nations, according to [q]that
which was spoken, So shall thy
[u]seed be.[Q]
19 And being not weak in
[v]faith, he considered not his own
body now dead, when he was
about an hundred years old, neither yet the [y]deadness of Sā'-
rah's womb:[Q]
20[S] He[T] staggered[G] not at the
promise of God through [y]unbe-
lief; but was strong in [v]faith,
[a]giving glory to God;
21 And being fully persuaded
that, what he had [b]promised, he
was [c]able also to perform.[T]
22[T] A[Q]nd therefore [d]it was [5]im-
pute[G]d to him for [e]righteousness.
23 Now it was not written for
his sake alone, that [e]it was [5]im-
puted to him;
24 But for us also, to whom [e]it
shall be [5]imputed, if we [f]believe
on [c]him that [g]raised up Jē'sus
our Lord from the dead;[S T Q T]
25 [h]Who was [i,j,k]delivered [l]for
our offences, and was [g,h]raised
again for our [†]justification.[S Q]

17
*u Descendants of Abraham*, Gen. 22:17.
*v Faith*, Mark 11:22.
*w Life, from God*, Eccl. 8:15.

18
*x Hope*, Prov. 13:12.

19
*y Barrenness*, Deut. 7:14.

20
*z Unbelief*, Heb. 3:12.

*a Glorifying God*, Luke 5:25.

21
*b Covenant, of God with men*, Deut. 29:1.
*c God, power of*, Gen. 2:2.

22
*d Faith, reckoned for righteousness*, Gen. 15:6.
*e Righteousness, imputed on account of faith*, Psa. 15:2.

24
*f Faith*, Mark 11:22.
*g Resurrection, of Jesus*, 1 Cor. 15:12.

25
*h Jesus, mission of*, Matt. 1:21.
*i Jesus, sufferings of*, Matt. 1:21.
*j Crucifixion, of Jesus*, Mark 15:13.
*k Atonement, by Jesus*, Lev. 17:11.
*l Jesus, design of His death*, Matt. 1:21.

## CHAPTER 5

*The fruits of justification by faith: Peace with God, 2 joy, 3 glorying in tribulation, 5 and assurance of hope. 12 As sin and death came by Adam, 17 so righteousness and life came by Jesus Christ. 20 Where sin abounded, grace did much more abound.*

THEREFORE b[T]eing [a]justifi[G]ed
by [b]faith,[1] we have [c,d,e]peace
with God [f]through our [g]Lord Jē'-
sus [h]Christ:[S]
2 By whom also we have [i]access
by [b]faith into this [a,d]grace wherein we stand, and [2,j,k]rejoice in
[l]hope of the [m]glory of God.[S T]
3 A[S]nd not only *so*, but [3]we glory
in tribulations also: knowing that
[n]tribulation worketh [o,p]patience;
4 And [o]patience, [*,4]experience;
and experience, [l]hope:[S]
5 And [l]hope maketh not
ashamed; because the [q]love of
God is shed abroad in our
[r]hearts by the [s]Holy[G] Ghost[G]
which is given unto us.[S T Q]

1
*a Justification*, vs. 1–21; Rom. 4:25.
*b Faith in Christ*, John 6:69.
*c Spiritual Peace*, Gal. 1:3.
*d Reconciliation*, 2 Cor. 5:18.
*e Justification, fruits of*, Rom. 4:25.
*f Atonement, by Jesus*, Lev. 17:11.
*g Jesus, lordship of*, Matt. 1:21.
*h Jesus, savior*, Matt. 1:21.
1 R. V. let us have

2
*i Access to God*, Eph. 3:12.
*j Joy*, Psa. 5:11.
*k Righteous, happiness of*, Psa. 64:10.
*l Hope*, Prov. 13:12.
*m God, glory of*, Gen. 2:2.
2 R. V. let us rejoice

3 *n Adversity, benefits of*, Psa. 10:6. *o Patience*, Luke 8:15. *p Christian Graces*, Gal. 5:22. 3 R. V. let us also rejoice in our tribulations: 4 4 R. V. probation;
5 *q God, love of*, Gen. 2:2. *r Heart*, Psa. 44:21. *s Holy Spirit*, Acts 1:2.

+ **GRACE OF GOD.** *Unmerited favor*, Deut. 7:7, 8; 2 Chr. 30:9; Eph. 1:6; Tit. 2:11; Heb. 4:16. *No warrant for sinful indulgence*, Rom. 6:1, 15.
*Divine help*, Psa. 84:11; 1 Cor. 10:13; 2 Cor. 1:12; 12:9; 1 Pet. 1:5.
Manifested: *In drawing men to Christ*, John 6:44, 45; *in redemption*, Eph. 1:5–9, 11, 12; *in justification*, Gen. 15:6; Rom. 3:22–24; 4:4, 5, 16; 5:2, 6–8, 15–21; Tit. 3:7; *in passing over transgressions*, Num. 23:20, 21; Neh. 9:17; Rom. 3:25; *in salvation*, Rom. 11:5, 6; Eph. 2:8, 9; 2 Tim. 1:9; *in calling to service*, Gal. 1:15, 16; *in spiritual growth*, Eph. 3:16; *in spiritual gifts*, 1 Cor. 1:4–8; Eph. 4:7, 11.
Manifested: *In character and conduct*, 2 Cor. 1:12; Phil. 2:13; *in the character and conduct of the righteous*, 1 Cor. 15:10; 2 Cor. 1:12; Phil. 2:13; *in sustaining the righteous*, 1 Chr. 17:8; 2 Cor. 12:9; 1 Pet. 1:5; Jude 24; *in sustaining in temptation*, 1 Cor. 10:13; Rev. 3:10.
*Intercessory prayer for*, John 17:11, 12, 15; 1 Thess. 1:1; 5:28; 2 Pet. 1:2.
*With respect to Jacob and Esau*, Rom. 9:10–16.
*Exhortation against rejecting*, 2 Cor. 6:1, 2.
**Manifestations of:** *To Enoch*, Gen. 5:24. *To Noah*, Gen. 6:8, 17, 18. *To Abraham*, Gen. 12:2; 21:22. *To Ishmael*, Gen. 21:20. *To Isaac*, Gen. 26:24. *To Jacob*, Gen. 46:3, 4; 48:16. *To Joseph*, Gen. 39:2, 3, 23. *To Moses*, Ex. 3:12; 33:12–17. *To Israel*, Deut. 4:7. *To Naphtali*, Deut. 33:23. *To Joshua*, Josh. 1:5, 9. *To Job*, Job 10:12. *To David*, 1 Sam. 25:26, 34; 2 Sam. 7:8–16. *To Jeremiah*, Jer. 15:20. *To the righteous*, Psa. 5:12; Acts 4:33.

† **JUSTIFICATION,** the act of divine grace which restores the sinner to the relation toward God that he would have sustained if he had not sinned; pardon of sin. The word is used also to denote the state of the sinner after he is restored to divine favor.
*Not imputing guilt to the sinner*, Psa. 32:2; Isa. 53:11; Zech. 3:4; John 5:24; Rom. 8:1.
*From God*, Isa. 45:24, 25; 50:8; 54:17; 61:10; Rom. 3:25; 8:30, 33; 2 Cor. 5:19, 21; Tit. 3:7.
*Not by the law*, Rom. 3:20; Gal. 2:16; 3:11; 5:4–6. *By faith*, Gen. 15:6; Rom. 3:20–22, 24–26, 28, 30; 4:2–25; 5:1; 9:30–32; 10:4, 6, 8–11; Gal. 2:14–21; 3:6, 8, 9, 21, 22, 24; Phil. 3:8, 9; Heb. 11:4, 7; Jas. 2:20–23, 26. *Through Christ*, Isa. 53:11; Jer. 23:6; Acts 13:39; Rom. 3:20–25; 5:9, 11, 16–18, 21; 1 Cor. 1:30; 6:11; Col. 2:13, 14.
**Fruits of:** *Peace*, Rom. 5:1. *Holiness*, Rom. 6:22.
See footnotes: SIN, *Forgiveness of*, Rom. 5:12; REGENERATION, Titus 3:5.

* **PROBATION** [R. V.], Rom. 5:4. *Adam on*, Gen. 2:15–17; 3:3. *Amorites on*, Gen. 15:16. *Solomon on*, 1 Kin. 3:14; 9:4–9, with 11:9–12. *Taught in parables of, the talents and pounds*, Matt. 25:14–30; Luke 19:12–27; *the fig tree*, Luke 13:6–9; *embezzling steward*, Luke 16:1–12.
*Ended*, Jer. 8:20; Matt. 24:50; 25:10, 28. See footnote, REPROBATE, 1 Cor. 9:27.

6 For when we were yet without strength, in due time Chrīst
[t,u]died [v,w]for the [x]ungodly.[s]
7 For scarcely for a righteous
man will one die: yet peradventure[C] [y]for a good man some
would even dare to die.
8 But God commendeth his
[z,a]love toward us, in that, while
we were yet sinners, Chrīst [b]died
[c]for us.[s]
9[s] Much more then, being now
[d]justified by his [e,f]blood, we
[g]shall be saved from [5,h]wrath
through him.
10 For if, when we were enemies, we were [d,i]reconciled to
God by the [b,f]death of his [j]Son,
much more, being reconciled, we
shall be saved by his [k]life.[s]
11 And not only so, but we
also [l]joy[C] in God through our
Lord Jē'sus Chrīst, by whom we
have now received the [6,f]atone-
ment.[G,S]
12 [T] Wherefore, as [m]by one [n]man
[†]sin entered into the world, and

6
*t Jesus, mission of*, Matt. 1:21.
*u Jesus, death of*, Matt. 1:21.
*v Jesus, design of his death*, Matt. 1:21.
*w Vicarious Sufferings*, Rom. 9:3.
*x Wicked, described*, Psa. 73.3.
7
*y Love, of man for man*, 1 John 4:7.
8
*z God, love of*, Gen. 2:2.
—*a God, condescension of*, Gen. 2:2. *b Jesus, vicarious death of*, Matt. 1:21. *c Jesus, mission of*, Matt. 1:21. **9** *d Justification, through Christ*, Rom. 4:25. *e Blood, of Christ*, Heb. 9:19. *f Atonement, by Jesus*, Lev. 17:11.

*g Righteous, promises to*, Psa. 64:10.
*h Anger of God*, 2 Kin. 13:3.
5 R. V. the wrath of God
**10**
*i Reconciliation*, 2 Cor. 5:18.
*j Jesus, divine sonship of*, Matt. 1:21.
*k Resurrection, of Jesus*, 1 Cor. 15:12.
**11** *l Joy*, Psa. 5:1 . 6 R. V. reconciliation. **12** *m Fall of Man*, Gen. 3:6. *n Adam*, Gen. 2:19.

† **SIN.** *Of Adam*, Hos. 6:7; Rom. 5:12, 15–19, with Gen. 3:6.

† **SIN.** *The inherited tendencies to evil*, Matt. 7:17, 18; 12:33–35; Mark 7:20–23; Luke 6:45; Rom. 6:6; 7:17, 20, 23, 25; 8:3, 5–7; Gal. 5:16, 17; Eph. 2:3; Jas. 1:14; 4:17. *Is besetting*, Heb. 2:1. *Fruits of*, Gal. 5:19–21; 1 Pet. 4:3.

† **SIN,** transgression of the law: *Defined*, **Prov. 24:9; Hos. 6:8; Matt. 5:28; 1 Cor. 8:12; Jas. 2:10, 11; 4:17; 1 John 3:4; 5:17.**

*Defiles*, Psa. 51:2, 7; Isa. 1:18; Heb. 12:15; **1 John 1:7.** *Enslaves*, John 8:34; Rom. 6:16; 2 Pet. 2:19.

*Progressive*, Isa. 30:1; Jer. 9:3; 16:11, 12; Hos. 13:2; 2 Tim. 3:13; Jas. 1:14, 15. *Retroactive*, Psa. 7:15, 16; 9:15, 16; 10:2; 94:23; Prov. 1:31; 5:22, 23; 8:36; 11:5, 6, 27, 29; Isa. 3:9, 11; Jer. 2:19; 4:18; 7:19. *A root of bitterness*, Deut. 29:18; Heb. 12:15.

*From the heart*, Isa. 44:20; Jer. 7:24; 17:9; Ezek. 20:16; Matt. 5:28; 7:17, 18; 12:33–35; 15:8, 11, 16–19; Luke 6:45. *Of the tongue*, Eccl. 5:6. *In thought*, Prov. 24:9. *In secret*, Psa. 19:12; 90:8; Eccl. 12:14; Ezek. 8:12; John 3:20; Rom. 2:16; Eph. 5:12. *Against conscience*, Rom. 14:23. *Against knowledge*, Luke 12:47, 48; John 9:41; 15:22; Rom. 1:21, 32; 2:17–23; Heb. 10:26; Jas. 4:17; 2 Pet. 2:21, 22.

INCITEMENTS TO: *The devil*, Matt. 13:24, 25, 38, 39; John 8:44; Eph. 2:2; 1 John 3:8, 10. *The fallen nature*, Gal. 5:16, 17; Eph. 2:3; Jas. 1:14, 15; 4:1–3.

*Degrees in*, Luke 7:41–47; 12:47, 48.

*Separates from God*, Deut. 31:17, 18; Josh. 7:12; 2 Chr. 24:20; Psa. 78:59–60; Isa. 59:1, 2; 64:7; Ezek. 23:18; Amos 3:2, 3; Mic. 3:4; Matt. 7:23; 25:41; Luke 13:27; Heb. 12:14.

*Works spiritual death*, Rom. 5:12, 21; 6:21, 23; 7:13; Eph. 2:1; Jas. 1:15.

*Pleasures of*, Job 20:12–16; Luke 8:14; Heb. 11:25. *Sinfulness of*, Rom. 7:13. *Dominion of*, Rom. 3:9. *Fools mock at*, Prov. 14:9. *Attempts to cover, vain*, Gen. 3:10; Job 31:33; Isa. 29:15.

*Not imputed, where there is no law*, Rom. 4:15; 5:13; *to the redeemed*, 2 Cor. 5:19; *to the righteous*, Psa. 32:2; Rom. 4:6–8.

*Known to God*, Gen. 3:11; 4:10; Ex. 16:8, 9, 12; Num. 12:2; 14:26, 27; Deut. 1:34; 31:21; 32:34; Josh. 7:10–15; Job 11:11; 14:16, 17; 34:21, 22, 25; Psa. 44:20, 21; 69:5; 90:8; 94:11; Eccl. 5:8; Isa. 29:15; Jer. 2:22; 16:17; 29:23; Ezek. 21:24; Hos. 5:3; 7:2; Amos 5:12; 9:1–4, 8; Mal. 2:14; Matt. 10:26.

*Known to Christ*, Rev. 2:23.

*Repugnant to God*, Gen. 6:6, 7; Lev. 18:24–30; Num. 22:32; Deut. 25:16; 32:19; 2 Sam. 11:27; 1 Kin. 14:22; Psa. 5:4–6; 10:3; 11:5; 78:59; 95:10; 106:40; Prov. 3:32; 6:16–19; 11:20; 15:8, 9, 26; 21:27; Isa. 43:24; Jer. 25:7; 44:4, 21, 22; Hab. 1:13; Zech. 8:17; Luke 16:15.

*Repugnant to Christ*, Rev. 2:6, 15.

*Repugnant to the righteous*, Gen. 39:7–9; Deut. 7:26; Job 1:1; 21:16; 22:18; Psa. 26:5, 9; 84:10; 101:3, 4, 7; 119:104, 113, 128, 163; 139:19–22; Prov. 8:13; 29:27; Jer. 9:2; Rom. 7:15, 19, 23, 24; 2 Pet. 2:7, 8; Jude 23; Rev. 2:2.

*By righteous, dishonors God*, 2 Sam. 12:14.

*Against the Holy Spirit, unpardonable*, Matt. 12:31; Mark 3:29; Luke 12:10.

*Consequences of, entailed upon children*, Ex. 20:5; 34:7; Lev. 26:39, 40; Num. 14:33; Deut. 5:9; Prov. 14:11; Isa. 14:20–22; Jer. 32:18; Lam. 5:7; Rom. 5:12–21. *Guilt of, and punishment for, not entailed upon children*, Deut. 24:16; 2 Kin. 14:6; 2 Chr. 25:4; Jer. 31:29, 30; Ezek. 18:2–4, 20.

**Love of,** Job 15:16; 20:12, 13; Prov. 2:14; 4:16, 17; 10:**23**; 26:11; Jer. 14:10; **Ezek. 20:16; Hos. 4:8; 9:10; Mic. 7:3; John 3:19, 20; 2 Pet. 2:22.**

**Fruits of,** Deut. 29:18; Job 4:8; Prov. 22:8; Hos. 8:7; **10:13;** Mark 7:21–23; Rom. 6:23; 7:5; Gal. 5:19–21; **6:7, 8; Jas. 1:15.** *Moral insensibility*, Prov. 30:20.

**Consequences of:** *Debauched countenance*, Isa. 3:9. *Guilty fear*, Gen. 3:7–10; Prov. 10:24; 28:1. *Depraved conscience*, Prov. 30:20. *Privations*, Jer. 5:25. *Trouble*, Isa. 57:20, 21; Jer. 4:18.

**No escape from consequences of,** Gen. 3:8–19; Isa. 28:18–22; Amos 9:2–4; Matt. 23:33; Heb. 2:3.

**Conviction of:** *Produced, by dreams*, Job 33:14–17; *by visions*, Acts 9:3–9; *by afflictions*, Job 33:18–30; Lam. 1:20; Luke 15:17–21; *by adversity*, Psa. 107:4–6, 10–14, 17–20, 23–30; *by the gospel*, Acts 2:37; *by religious testimony*, 1 Cor. 14:24, 25; *by the conscience*, John 8:9; Rom. 2:15; *by the Holy Spirit*, John 16:7–11.

**Repentance for:** *Enjoined*, 2 Chr. 30:7–9; Job 36:10; Psa. 34:14; Prov. 1:22, 23; Isa. 22:12; 31:6; 44:22; 55:6, 7; Jer. 3:4, 12–14, 19; 6:8, 16; 18:11; 25:5; 26:13; 35:15; Ezek. 14:6; 18:30–32; 33:10–12; Dan. 4:27; Hos. 6:1; 10:12; 14:1, 2; Joel 1:14; 2:12, 13, 15–18; Amos 4:12; Jonah 3:8, 9; Zech. 1:3; Matt. 4:17; Mark 1:15; 6:12; Acts 2:38, 40; 3:19; 8:22; 17:30; 20:21; Jas. 4:8–10; Rev. 2:5, 16; 3:2, 3, 19.

*Gift, of God*, 2 Tim. 2:25; *of Christ*, Acts 5:31. *Tribulation leads to*, Deut. 4:30; 1 Kin. 8:33–50; 2 Chr. 6:36–39; Psa. 107:4–6, 10–14, 17–20, 23–30. *Goodness of God leads to*, Rom. 2:4.

*A condition of pardon*, Lev. 26:40–42; Deut. 4:29–31; 30:1–3; 2 Chr. 7:14; Neh. 1:9; Prov. 28:13; Jer. 7:5–7; 36:3; Ezek. 18:21–23, 27, 28, 30, 31; Mal. 3:7; 1 John 1:9.

**Confession of,** 1 Kin. 8:47; Prov. 28:13. *Signified by placing hands on head of offering*, Lev. 3:2, 13; 4:4, 15, 24, 29, 33; 16:21; Num. 8:12. *Illustrated in parables, of prodigal son*, Luke 15:17–21; *of Pharisee and publican*, Luke 18:13.

*To God, enjoined*, Lev. 5:5–10; 16:21. *To saints, enjoined*, Jas. 5:16.

*To God, exemplified, by Israel*. Num. 14:40; Judg. 10:10; 1 Sam. 7:6; *by Saul*, 1 Sam. 15:2, 4; *by David*, 2 Sam. 12:13; 24:10, 17; 1 Chr. 21:17; *by the psalmist*, Psa. 32:5; 38:3, 4, 18; 40:11, 12; 41:4; 51:2–5; 69:5; 73:21, 22; 119:59, 60, 176; *by the Jews*, Ezra 9:4–7, 10–15; Neh. 9:2, 3, 5–38; *by Job*, Job 42:5, 6; *by Isaiah*, Isa. 6:5.

**Forgiveness of,** Acts 26:18; Eph. 1:7. *Promised*, Ex. 34:6, 7; Lev. 4:20, 26, 31, 35, 40–42; 5:4–13; Deut. 4; Isa. 1:18; 43:25, 26; 44:21, 22; Jer. 31:34; 33:8; Ezek. 18:21, 22; 33:14–16; Matt. 12:31; Mark 3:28, Heb. 8:12; 10:17; Jas. 5:15; 1 John 1:7, 9. *Blessedness of*, Psa. 32:1, 2; Rom. 4:7, 8.

INSTANCES OF: *Israelites*, Num. 14:20; Psa. 85:2, 3; 99:8; 103:12. *David*, 2 Sam. 12:13; Psa. 32:5. *Isaiah*, Isa. 6:7. *Man with palsy*, Matt. 9:2, 6; Mark 2:5; Luke 5:20, 24. *The prostitute*, Luke 7:48; John 8:11. *Believers*, Col. 2:13.

CONDITIONS OF: *Repentance*, Luke 3:3; 13:3, 5; Acts 2:38; 3:19. *Faith*, Acts 10:36, 43; 13:38, 39; 26:16–18. *Confession of sins*, 1 John 1:7, 9.

*Through shedding of blood*, Heb. 9:22. *Spirit of*, Matt. 6:12, 14, 15; 18:35; Mark 11:25.

*The mission of Christ, to secure*, Matt. 1:21; 26:28; Luke 24:47; 1 John 2:1, 2, 12; Rev. 1:5.

*Prayer for*, Psa. 19:12; 25:7, 11; 51:9; 79:9. *Intercessory prayer for*, 1 Kin. 8:22–50.

*Apostolic*, John 20:23.

**Punishment of,** Gen. 2:17; 3:16–19; 4:10–14; 6:5–7; 19:13; Ex. 32:33, 34; 34:7; Lev. 19:8; 26:14–21; Num. 15:30, 31; 32:23; Deut. 28:15–68; 1 Kin. 13:33, 34; 1 Chr. 21:7–27; Psa. 95:10, 11; Prov. 1:24–32; Jer. 44:2–6; Ezek. 18:4; Matt. 25:41, 46; Rom. 6:23. See footnote, WICKED, *Punishment of*, Psa. 73:3.

**Typified. [The design of the Mosaic ordinances was to**

o *Spiritual Death*, 1 John 3:14.
p *Death, universal to mankind*, Num. 23:10.
q *Wicked, punishment of*, Psa. 73:3.
r *Heredity*, Ezek. 18:2.

13
s *Law, of Moses*, Deut. 33:2.

14
t *Adam, type of Christ*, Gen. 2:19.
u *Moses*, Ex. 2:10.
v *Types, of the Savior, Adam*, Heb. 10:1.

15
w *Grace of God*, Rom. 4:16.
x *Atonement, by Jesus*, Lev. 17:11.
y *Jesus, humanity of*, Matt. 1:21.

16
z *Justification, through Christ*, Rom. 4:25.

17
a *Adam*, Gen. 2:19.
b *Fall of Man*, Gen. 3:6.
c *Spiritual Death*, 1 John 3:14.
d *Grace of God*, Rom. 4:16.
e *Justification, through Christ*, Rom. 4:25.
f *Life, spiritual*, Eccl. 8:15.
g *Atonement, by Jesus*, Lev. 17:11.

18
h *Salvation*, Acts 16:17.
7 R. V. So then as through one trespass the judgement came unto all men to condemnation; even so through one act of righteousness the free gift

20
i *Law, of Moses*, Deut. 33:2.

[o]death by sin; and so [p,q]death
[r]passed upon all men, for that
all have sinned:[S][Q]
13 (For until the [s]law †sin was
in the world: but sin is not imputed[G] when there is no law.
14 Nevertheless [p]death reigned
from [t]Ă′dăm to [u]Mō′ṣeṣ, even
over them that had not sinned
after the similitude[G] of Ă′dăm's
†,[m]transgression, who is the [v]fig-
ure of him that was to come.[T]
15[S] But[T] not as the †offence, so
also *is* the free gift. For if
through the †,[m]offence of one
many be dead, much more the
[w]grace of God, and the [x]gift by
grace, *which is* by one [y]man,
Jē′-ṣus Christ, hath abounded
unto many.
16 And not as *it was* by [n]one
that †sinned, *so is* the gift: for
the judgment *was* by one to condemnation, but the free [x]gift *is*
of many offences unto [z]justifica-
tion.[T]
17 F[T]or if by one [a]man's †,[b]of-
fence [c]death reigned by one;
much more they which receive
abundance of [d]grace and of the
gift of [e]righteousness shall reign
in [f]life [g]by one Jē′ṣus Christ.)
18 [7]Therefore as by the [b]offence
of one *judgment came* upon all
men to condemnation; even so
[g]by the righteousness of one *the
free* [h]*gift came* upon all men unto
[e]justification of [f]life.
19 For as by one man's †dis-
obedience many were made sinners, so by the obedience of one
shall many be made righteous.[T][S][Q]
20[T] Moreover the [i]law entered,
that the offence might abound.
But where †sin abounded, [d]grace
did much more abound:
21 That as †sin hath reigned unto [c]death, even so might [d]grace
reign through righteousness unto eternal [j]life [g,k]by Jē′ṣus Christ
our [l]Lord.[S][T]

## CHAPTER 6

*We may not live in sin, 2 for we are dead unto it. 12 Believers exhorted to holiness. 23 The wages of sin is death.*

WHAT shall we say then?
Shall we continue in [a]sin,
that [b]grace may abound?
2 God forbid. How shall we,
that are [c,d]dead to sin, live any
longer [e]therein?
3 Know ye not, that so many
of us as were [f]baptized into
Jē′ṣus Christ were baptized into
his [g]death?
4 Therefore we are [h]buried with
him by [f]baptism into [g]death: that
like[C] as Christ was [i]raised up from
the dead by the glory of the [j]Fa-
ther, even so we also should walk
in [k,l]newness of [m]life.
5 For[S] if we have [1]been planted
together in the likeness of his
[n]death, we shall be also [2]*in the
likeness* of *his* [i]resurrection:
6 Knowing this, that our [e,o]old
man is [p]crucified with *him*, that
the body of [e]sin might be [3]de-
stroyed, that henceforth we
should [q]not serve sin.
7 For he that [4]is [c]dead is [q]freed
from sin.
8 Now if we [5]be [c]dead with
Christ, we believe that we shall
also [r]live with him:[S]
9 Knowing that Christ being

3 R. V. done away, that so we should no longer be in bondage to sin; **7** 4 R. V. hath died is justified from sin. **8** r *Immortality*, 1 Cor. 15:54. 5 R. V. died

21
j *Life, everlasting*, Eccl. 8:15.
k *Jesus, atonement by*, Matt. 1:21.
l *Jesus, lordship of*, Matt. 1:21.

1
a *Sin, transgression of the law*, Rom. 5:12.
b *Grace of God*, Rom. 4:16.

2
c *Death, constructive, of the race, in the vicarious death of Jesus*, vs. 2–11; Num. 23:10.
d *Righteous, described*, Psa. 64:10.
e *Sin, the inherited tendencies to evil*, Rom. 5:12.

3
f *Baptism, Christian*, Luke 20:4.
g *Death, figurative, of the benefits of Christ's death*, Num. 23:10.

4
h *Burial, figurative*, Acts 8:2.
i *Resurrection, of Jesus*, 1 Cor. 15:12.
j *God, fatherhood of*, Gen. 2:2.
k *Resurrection, figurative*, 1 Cor. 15:12.
l *Regeneration*, Tit. 3:5.
m *Life, spiritual*, Eccl. 8:15.

5
n *Jesus, death of*, Matt. 1:21.
1 R. V. become united with him by the likeness
2 R. V. by

6
o *Depravity*, Job 15:14.
p *Crucifixion, figurative*, Mark 15:13.
q *Liberty, spiritual*, Lev. 25:10.

impress the Israelites, and through them the consciences of all people for all time, with the sinfulness of sin. In order to produce this effect the Mosaic law contained numerous types of sin, the design of which was to teach that sin is repugnant to God, and that it separates from God and from the righteous. Hence, we find many object lessons about uncleanness and defilement, blemishes, separation from the congregation, atonements and atoning sacrifices, washings and purifications; all of which were designed to typify the sinfulness of sin and the necessity, in order to please a holy Jehovah, that sin must be purged, and the heart purified.]

*By blemishes that disqualified animals for sacrifices*, Ex. 12:5; Lev. 1:10; 3:1, 6; 4:3, 23; 5:15; 6:6; 9:2, 3; 22:19–22; Num. 28:3, 9, 11, 19, 31; 29:2, 8, 13, 17, 20, 23, 26, 29, 32, 36. *By blemishes of priests, disqualifying them from performing sacred offices*, Lev. 21:17–23. *By unclean animals*, Lev. 11:1–47; 20:25; Deut. 14:3–20.

*Its effect, in separating the wicked from God and from the righteous, by excluding the defiled and unclean from the congregation*, Lev. 7:20, 25, 27; 13:5, 26, 33; 15:19; 17:9, 10, 15; 18:29; 19:8; 20:3–6; Num. 5:2, 3; 19:20; Deut. 23:10, 11.

**Pollution of:** *Typified, by the defilement caused by touching any unclean thing*, Lev. 5:2, 3; 11:24–28, 31; 22:5; *by eating any unclean thing*, Lev. 11:41–47; *by touching a dead body*, Lev. 21:1; Num. 5:2; 9:6, 10; 19:11, 13, 16; 31:19; *by leprosy*, Lev. 13:3, 8, 11, 20, 25, 27, 30, 36, 44–46, 51, 55; 14:44; Num. 5:2, 3; *by sexual impurities*, Lev. 15:1–33; 22:4; Deut. 23:10, 11.

11
[s] *Holiness,* Ex. 39:30.
[t] *Life, spiritual,* Eccl. 8:15.
[u] *Jesus, lordship of,* Matt. 1:21.

12
[v] *Temptation,* Luke 11:4.

13
[w] *Consecration, personal,* Lev. 7:37.

14
[x] *Law,* Deut. 33:2.
[y] *Gospel,* Mark 13:10.

16
[z] *Servant, figurative,* Jer. 2:14.

[a] *Sin, the inherited tendencies to evil,* Rom. 5:12.
[b] *Spiritual Death,* 1 John 3:14.
[c] *Wicked, punishment of,* Psa. 73:3.
[d] *Righteousness,* Psa. 15:2.

17
[e] *Thankfulness, to God,* Acts 24:3.
[f] *Obedience,* Heb. 5:8.
[g] *Heart,* Psa. 44:21.
[h] *Doctrines of Jesus,* John 7:16.
6 R. V. teaching whereunto ye were delivered;

18
[i] *Liberty, spiritual,* Lev. 25:10.
[j] *Righteous, described,* Psa. 64:10.
[k] *Righteousness,* Psa. 15:2.

19
[l] *Sanctification,* 1 Pet. 1:2.
7 R. V. sanctification.

[i]raised from the [n]dead dieth no more; death hath no more dominion over him.

10 For in that he [n]died, he died unto [a]sin once[G]: but in that he liveth, he liveth unto God.

11 Likewise reckon ye also yourselves to be [c,s]dead indeed unto [e]sin, but [t]alive unto God through Jē′ṣus Chrīst our [u]Lord.[T]

12[T] Let not [e]sin therefore reign in your mortal body, that ye should obey it in the [v]lusts[G] thereof.

13 Neither yield ye your members *as* instruments[G] of unrighteousness unto [a]sin: but [w]yield yourselves unto God, as those that are [m]alive from the [c]dead, and your members *as* instruments[G] of righteousness unto God.

14 For [e]sin shall not have dominion[G] over you: for ye are not under the [x]law, but under [y]grace.[S T]

15 What then? shall we sin, because we are not under the [x]law, but under [y]grace? God forbid.

16 Know ye not, that to whom ye yield yourselves servants[G] to obey, his [z]servants[G] ye are to whom ye obey; whether of [a]sin unto [b,c]death, or of obedience unto [d]righteousness?

17[S] But God be [e]thanked, that ye were the servants[G] of [a]sin, but ye have [f]obeyed from the [g]heart that form of [6,h]doctrine which was delivered you.

18 Being then made [i,j]free from [a]sin, ye became the servants[G] of [k]righteousness.

19 I speak after the manner of men because of the infirmity of your flesh: for as ye have yielded your members servants[G] to uncleanness and to iniquity unto iniquity; even so now yield your members servants to [k]righteousness unto [7,l]holiness.[G S T]

20 For when ye were the servants[G] of [a]sin, ye were free from righteousness.[S]

21 What fruit had ye then in those things whereof ye are now ashamed? for the end of those things *is* [b,m]death.[Q]

22 But[T] now being made [i]free from [a]sin, and become servants[G] to God, [n]ye have your fruit unto [7,l,o]holiness, and the end [p]everlasting [q]life.[S]

23 For the [r]wages of [s]sin *is* [m]death; but the [t]gift of God *is* [p]eternal [q]life [u,v]through Jē′ṣus Chrīst our [w]Lord.[T]

## CHAPTER 7

*Believers are dead to the law by the body of Christ. 7 Conviction of sin is by the law. 12 The law is holy. 14 The conflict between the law in the members and the law of the mind. 24 Deliverance through Jesus Christ.*

KNOW ye not, brethren, (for I speak to them that know the [a]law,) how that the law hath dominion[G] over a man as long as he liveth?

2 For [b]the [c]woman which hath an [d]husband is bound by the [a]law to *her* husband so long as he liveth; but if the husband be dead, [e]she is loosed from the law of *her* husband.

3 So then if, while *her* [d]husband liveth, she be married to another man, she shall be called an [f]adulteress: but if her husband be dead, [e]she is free from that [a]law; so that she is no adulteress, though she be [g]married to another man.

4 Wherefore, my brethren, ye also are become [h]dead to the law by the body of Chrīst; that ye should be [i]married to another, *even* to him who is [j]raised from the dead, that we should bring forth [k]fruit unto God.[S]

5 For when we were in the [l]flesh[G], the [1]motions[G] of sins, which were by the law, did [m]work in our members to bring forth fruit unto [n]death.

6 But now we [2]are delivered

21
[m] *Second Death,* Rev. 20:14.

22
[n] *Righteous, promises to,* Psa. 64:10.
[o] *Justification, fruits of,* Rom. 4:25.
[p] *Immortality,* 1 Cor. 15:54.
[q] *Life, everlasting,* Eccl. 8:15.

23
[r] *Wages, figurative,* Gen. 31:7.
[s] *Sin, punishment of,* Rom. 5:12.
[t] *Spiritual Gifts,* 1 Cor. 12:4.
[u] *Atonement, by Jesus,* Lev. 17:11.
[v] *Jesus, vicarious death of,* Matt. 1:21.
[w] *Jesus, lordship of,* Matt. 1:21.

1
[a] *Law,* Deut. 33:2.

2
[b] *Marriage,* Gen. 34:9.
[c] *Wife,* Prov. 5:18.
[d] *Husband,* Num. 30:6.
[e] *Widow,* 2 Sam. 14:5.

3
[f] *Adultery, defined,* Lev. 20:10.
[g] *Marriage, of widows,* Gen. 34:9.

4
[h] *Death, constructive, of the race in the vicarious death of Jesus,* Num. 23:10.
[i] *Fellowship, with Christ,* 1 Cor. 1:9.
[j] *Resurrection, of Jesus,* 1 Cor. 15:12.
[k] *Righteousness, fruits of,* Psa. 15:2.

5
[l] *Sin, the inherited tendencies to evil,* Rom. 5:12.
[m] *Temptation, sources of,* Luke 11:4.
[n] *Spiritual Death,* 1 John 3:14.
1 R. V. sinful passions, which were through the law, wrought in

6
2 R. V. have been discharged from the law, having died to that wherein we were holden, so that we serve

from the [a]law, that being dead
wherein we were held; that we
should [o]serve in [p]newness of
spirit, and not *in* the oldness
of the letter.[T]
7 What shall we say then? *Is*
the law sin? God forbid. Nay, I
had not known [q]sin, but by the
[a]law: for I had not known [3]lust,
except the law had said, [r]Thou
shalt not [s]covet.[T] [Q]
8 But [l]sin, taking occasion by
the commandment, wrought[G] in
me all manner of [3]concupis-
cence.[G] For without[G] the [a]law
[q]sin *was* dead.
9 For I was alive without[G] the
law once: but when the [a]com-
mandment came, [q]sin revived,
and I [n]died.
10 And the commandment,
which *was ordained* to [t]life, I
found *to be* unto [n]death.[Q]
11 For [l]sin, taking occasion
by the commandment, [4]deceived
me, and by it [n]slew *me*.[Q]
12[T] Wherefore the [a]law *is* holy,
and the commandment holy, and
just, and good.
13 Was then that which is good
made [n]death unto me? God forbid. But [q]sin, that it might appear [u]sin, working death in me
by that which is good; that [q]sin
by the commandment might become exceeding [u]sinful.[T]
14 For[T] we know that the [a]law is
spiritual: but I am [v]carnal,[G] [w]sold
under sin.[Q]
15 For [v]that which I do I [5]al-
low[G] not: for what I [x]would,[G] that
do I not; but what I [y]hate, that
do I.
16 If then I do that which I
[x]would not, I consent unto[G] the
[z]law that *it is* good.
17 Now then it is no more I
that do it, but [a]sin that [b]dwelleth
in me.
18 For [c]I know that in me (that
is, in my flesh,) [b]dwelleth no good
thing: for to [d]will is present with

o *Obedience*, Heb. 5:8.
p *Regeneration*, Tit. 3:5.

**7**
q *Sin, transgression of the law*, Rom. 5:12.
r Ex. 20:17; Deut. 5:21.
s *Covetousness*, Isa. 57:17.
3 R. V. coveting.

**10**
t *Life, spiritual*, Eccl. 8:15.

**11**
4 R. V. beguiled

**13**
u *Sin, sinfulness of*, Rom. 5:12.

**14**
v *Carnal Mind, in conflict with the inward man*, vs. 14–22; 1 Cor. 3:3.
w *Wicked, described*, Psa. 73:3.

**15**
x *Conscience*, Acts 23:1.
y *Sin, repugnant to the righteous*, Rom. 5:12.
5 R. V. know

**16**
z *Law*, Deut. 33:2.

**17**
a *Sin, the inherited tendencies to evil*, Rom. 5:12.
b *Depravity*, Job 15:14.

**18**
c *Humility, exemplified*, Prov. 22:4.
d *Conscience*, Acts 23:1.

me; but *how* to perform[Q] that
which is good I find not.
19 For the good that I [d]would
I do not: but the [e]evil which I
[f]would not, that I do.[G]
20 Now if I do that I would not,
it is no more I that do it, but [a]sin
that [b]dwelleth in me.
21 I find then a law, that, when
I [d]would do good, [a]evil is present
[6]with me.
22 For I delight in the [g]law of
God after the [h]inward man:
23 But I see [7]another law in my
members, warring against the
law of my [h]mind, and bringing
me into [i]captivity to the law of
[a]sin which is in my members.
24 O wretched man that I am!
who shall deliver me from the
[a]body of this [j]death?
25 I [k]thank God [l,m]through
Jē'şus [n]Christ our Lord. So then
[8]with the [h]mind I myself serve
the law of God; but with the
flesh the law of [a]sin.[T]

## CHAPTER 8

*The security of believers: They are free from condemnation. 5 They are not in the flesh, but in the Spirit. 12 They are children of God. 18 The glory to be revealed in them. 26 The Spirit helps their infirmities. 28 All things work together for their good. 32 God gave his Son to save them. 35 Nothing can separate them from his love.*

THERE[T] *is* therefore now
[a,b]no condemnation to [c]them
which are [d]in Christ Jē'şus,[1] who
walk not after the flesh,[G] but after
the Spirit.[S]
2 For the law of the [e]Spirit of
[f]life in [g]Christ Jē'şus [h]hath made
me [a,i]free from the law of [j]sin and
[k,l]death.
3 For what the [m,n]law could not
do, in that it was weak through
the flesh, God sending his own
[o]Son [p]in the likeness of sinful
flesh, and [2,q]for sin, condemned
[j]sin in the flesh:[S]
4 That the [3]righteousness of
the law might be fulfilled in us,

p *Jesus, incarnation of*, Matt. 1:21. q *Jesus, mission of*, Matt. 1:21. 2 R. V. as an offering for sin. **4** 3 R. V. (*marg.*) requirement

**19**
e *Sin, transgression of the law*, Rom. 5:12.
f *Sin, repugnant to the righteous*, Rom. 5:12.

**21**
6 R. V. *omits* with me.

**22**
g *Law*, Deut. 33:2.
h *Man, a spirit*, Job 4:17.

**23**
i *Captivity, figurative*, Isa. 5:13.
7 R. V. a different

**24**
j *Spiritual Death*, 1 John 3:14.

**25**
k *Thankfulness, to God*, Acts 24:3.
l *Faith in Christ, exemplified*, John 6:69.
m *Atonement, by Jesus*, Lev. 17:11.
n *Jesus, Messiah*, Matt. 1:21.
8 Am. R. V. I of myself with the mind, indeed, serve

**1**
a *Sin, forgiveness of*, Rom. 5:12.
b *Justification*, Rom. 4:25.
c *Righteous, described*, Psa. 64:10.
d *Fellowship, with Christ*, 1 Cor. 1:9.
1 R. V. *omits* who walk not after the flesh, but after the spirit.

**2**
e *Holy Spirit*, Acts 1:2.
f *Life, spiritual*, Eccl. 8:15.
g *Jesus, savior*, Matt. 1:21.
h *Regeneration*, Tit. 3:5.
i *Liberty, spiritual*, Lev. 25:10.
j *Sin, transgression of the law*, Rom. 5:12.
k *Spiritual Death*, 1 John 3:14.
l *Wicked, punishment of*, Psa. 73:3.

**3**
m *Law*, Deut. 33:2.
n *Works, insufficient for salvation*, 2 Tim. 1:9.
o *Jesus, divine sonship of*, Matt. 1:21.

[r]who walk not after the [s]flesh,[G] but after the [4,t]Spirit.[T]

5[T] For [u,v]they that are after the [s]flesh do mind the things of the flesh; but [r]they that are after the [4,t]Spirit the things of the [4]Spirit.

6 For [5]to be [u,w]carnally[G] minded *is* [x]death; but to be spiritually minded *is* [y]life and [z]peace.

7[S] Because the [6,a,b]carnal[G] mind *is* enmity against God: for it is not subject to the [c]law of God, neither indeed can be.

8 So then [d]they that are in the [a,b]flesh[G] cannot please God.[S T]

9 But [e]ye are not in the [a]flesh, but in the [4]Spirit, if so be that the [f,g]Spirit of [g]God [h]dwell in you. Now if any man have not the Spirit of [g,i]Christ, he is none of his.[T]

10 And [j]if [i]Christ *be* in you, the body *is* [k]dead because of sin; but the [4]Spirit *is* [l]life because of righteousness.[T]

11 But if the [f,g]Spirit of [g,m]him that [n]raised up [g]Jē′sus from the dead [h]dwell in you, he that raised up [7,i]Christ from the dead shall also [o]quicken[G] your mortal bodies by his Spirit that dwelleth in you.[T]

12 Therefore, brethren, we are debtors, not to the [a]flesh, to live after the flesh.

13 For if ye live after the [a]flesh, ye [8]shall [p]die: but if ye through the [4]Spirit do mortify[G] the [q]deeds of the body, ye shall [r]live.[S]

14 For as many as are led by the [f]Spirit of God, [s]they are the sons of God.[T]

15 For[S T] ye have not received the spirit of bondage again to [t]fear; but [u]ye have received the [4]Spirit of *adoption, whereby we cry, Ăb′bå, [v]Father.

16 The [f]Spirit [9]itself [w,x]beareth witness with our spirit, that we *are the children of God:[S T]

17[T] And if *children, then [y]heirs; heirs of God, and [z]joint-heirs with Christ; [a,b]if so be that we [c]suffer with *him*, that we may be also [d]glorified together.[S]

18 For [e]I reckon[G] that the [f]sufferings of this present time *are* not worthy *to be compared* with the glory which shall be revealed [10]in us.[S]

19 For the earnest expectation of the [11]creature[G] waiteth for the manifestation of the sons of God.[T]

20[T] For the [12]creature was made subject to vanity, not willingly, but by reason of him who hath subjected *the same* in hope,[Q]

21 Because the [12]creature itself also shall be delivered from the bondage of [g]corruption[G] into the [13]glorious [h]liberty of the *children of God.

22 For we know that the whole creation groaneth and travaileth[G] in pain together until now.

23 And not only *they*, but ourselves also, which have the [i]firstfruits of the Spirit, even we ourselves groan within ourselves, waiting for the adoption,[G] *to wit*, the redemption of our body.[T]

24 For we [14]are saved by [j]hope: but hope that is seen is not hope: for what a man seeth, why doth he yet hope for?

25 But if we hope for that we see not, *then* do we with [k]patience wait for *it*.

26[T] Likewise the [l]Spirit also helpeth our infirmities:[G] for we [m]know not what we should [n]pray for as we ought: but the Spirit

r *Righteous, described*, Psa. 64:10.
s *Sin, the inherited tendencies to evil*, Rom. 5:12.
t *Holy Spirit* (as some interpret), Acts 1:2.
4 R. V. spirit.

**5**
u *Wicked, described*, Psa. 73:3.
v *Wicked, contrasted with the righteous*, Psa. 73:3.

**6**
w *Carnal Mind*, 1 Cor. 3:3.
x *Spiritual Death*, 1 John 3:14.
y *Life, spiritual*, Eccl. 8:15.
z *Spiritual Peace*, Gal. 1:3.
5 R. V. the mind of the flesh is death; but the mind of the spirit is life and peace:

**7**
a *Carnal Mind*, 1 Cor. 3:3.
b *Heart, unregenerate*, Psa. 44:21.
c *Law*, Deut. 33:2.
6 R. V. mind of the flesh is

**8**
d *Wicked, described*, Psa. 73:3.

**9**
e *Righteous, described*, Psa. 64:10.
f *Holy Spirit*, Acts 1:2.
g *Holy Trinity*, Luke 3:22.
h *Fellowship, with the Holy Spirit*, 1 Cor. 1:9.
i *Jesus, Messiah*, Matt. 1:21.

**10**
j *Regeneration*, Tit. 3:5.
k *Death, figurative*, Num. 23:10.
l *Life, spiritual*, Eccl. 8:15.

**11**
m *God, power of*, Gen. 2:2.
n *Jesus, resurrection of*, Matt. 1:21.
o *Resurrection*, 1 Cor. 15:12.

7 R. V. Christ Jesus **13** p *Spiritual Death*, 1 John 3:14. q *Sin, the inherited tendencies to evil*, Rom. 5:12. r *Life, spiritual*, Eccl. 8:15. 8 R. V. must die;
**14** s *Righteous, promises to*, Psa. 64:10. **15** t *Fear of God, guilty*, Acts 9:31.

u *Liberty*, Lev. 25:10.
v *God, fatherhood of*, Gen. 2:2.

**16**
w *Holy Spirit, witness of*, Acts 1:2.
x *Assurance, of acceptance*, Heb. 10:22.
9 R. V. himself

**17**
y *Heir, figurative of spiritual adoption*, Gen. 15:3.
z *Inheritance, figurative*, Num. 27:7.

a *Adversity, consolation in*, Psa. 10:6.
b *Afflictions, consolation in*, Psa. 34:19.
c *Suffering for Christ*, Phil. 1:29.
d *Jesus, exaltation of*, Matt. 1:21.

**18**
e *Faith, exemplified*, Mark 11:22.
f *Persecution, of the righteous*, John 15:20.
10 R. V. to usward.

**19**
11 R. V. creation waiteth for the revealing of the sons of God.

**20**
12 R. V. creation

**21**
g *Corruption, figurative*, Job 17:14.
h *Liberty, spiritual*, Lev. 25:10.
13 R. V. liberty of the glory of the children of God.

**23**
i *First Fruits, figurative*, Deut. 18:4.

**24**
j *Hope*, Prov. 13:12.
14 R. V. were

**25**
k *Patience, a grace of the righteous*, Luke 8:15

**26**
l *Holy Spirit*, Acts 1:2.
m *Ignorance*, Acts 3:17.
n *Prayer, divine help in*, Acts 6:4.

* **SPIRITUAL ADOPTION.** *Of Israel*, Ex. 4:22, 23; Num. 6:27; Deut. 14:1; 26:18; 27:9; 28:10; 32:5, 6; 2 Chr. 7:14; Jer. 3:19; 31:9, 20; Isa. 63:8, 16; Hos. 1:9, 10; 11:1; Rom. 9:4. *Of Solomon*, 2 Sam. 7:14; 1 Chr. 22:10; 28:6.
*Of the righteous*, Prov. 14:26; Isa. 43:1-6; 63:8, 16; Matt. 5:9, 45; 12:50; 13:43; Luke 6:35; John 11:52; Rom. 9:8; 2 Cor. 6:17, 18; Eph. 2:19; Phil. 2:15; Heb. 12:6, 7, 9; 1 John 3:1, 2, 10; Rev. 21:7.
*Of the Gentiles, through the gospel*, Eph. 3:6. *By faith in Christ*, John 1:12, 13; Gal. 3:26, 29; Eph. 1:5; Heb. 2:10, 11, 13. *Testified to by the Holy Spirit*, Rom. 8:14-17, 19, 21, 29; Gal. 4:5-7.

15 R. V. himself

**27**
o *Heart, known to God,* Psa. 44:21.
p *God, knowledge of,* Gen. 2:2.
q *Righteous,* Psa. 64:10.

**28**
r *God, providence of,* Gen. 2:2.
s *Promise, or Ground of Assurance, to the righteous,* 2 Cor. 1:20.
t *Adversity, consolation in,* Psa. 10:6.
u *Love, for God,* 1 John 4:19.
v *Call, personal,* Phil. 3:14.
w *Election of Grace,* Rom. 11:5.

**29**
x *God, foreknowledge of,* Gen. 2:2.
y *Image, figurative,* 1 Cor. 11:7.
z *Jesus, divine sonship of,* Matt. 1:21.

a *Firstborn, birthright of,* Zech. 12:10.
16 R. V. foreordained

**30**
b *Call, personal,* Phil. 3:14.
c *Election of Grace,* Rom. 11:5.
d *Justification, from God,* Rom. 4:25.

**31**
e *Faith,* Mark 11:22.
f *God, preserver,* Gen. 2:2.

**32**
g *God, love of,* Gen. 2:2.
h *Jesus, divine sonship of,* Matt. 1:21.
i *Jesus, design of his death,* Matt. 1:21.
j *Promise, to the righteous,* 2 Cor. 1:20.

[15]itself maketh intercession for
us with groanings which cannot
be uttered.
27 And he that searcheth the
[o]hearts [p]knoweth what *is* the
mind of the [l]Spirit, because he
maketh intercession for the
[q]saints according to *the will of*
God.
28 And [e,r]we know that [s,t]all
things work together for good to
them that [u]love God, to them
who are the [v,w]called according
to *his* purpose.
29 For whom he did [x]fore-
know, he also [16]did †predes-
tinate *to be* conformed to the
[y]image of his [z]Son, that he might
be the [a]firstborn among many
brethren.
30 Moreover whom he [16]did
†predestinate, them he also
[b]called: and whom he [b,c]called,
them he also [d]justified: and
whom he justified, them he also
glorified.
31 What shall we then say to
these things? [e,f]If God *be* for
us, who *can be* against us?
32 [g]He that spared not [h]his own
Son, but delivered him up [i]for us
all, how [j]shall he not with him
also freely give us all things?
33 Who shall lay any thing to
the charge of God's [†,c]elect? *It
is* God that [d]justifieth.
34 Who *is* he that condemneth?
*It is* [17,k]Christ that [i]died, yea
rather, that is [l]risen again, who
is even [m]at the right hand of
God, who also [n]maketh intercession for us.

35 [o,p,q,r]Who shall [s]separate us
from the [t]love of [k]Christ? *shall*
[u]tribulation, or distress, or [v]per-
secution, or [w]famine, or nakedness, or peril, or sword?
36 As it is written, [p,x,y]For thy
sake [z]we are killed all the day
long; we are accounted as [a]sheep
for the slaughter.
37 Nay, in all these [b]things
we are more than conquerors
[c]through him that [d]loved us.
38 For [e]I am [f]persuaded, that
[b]neither [g]death, nor life, nor
[h]angels, nor principalities, nor
powers, nor things present, nor
things to come,
39 [b]Nor height, nor depth, nor
any other creature, shall be able
to [i]separate us from the [j]love of
God, which is in [k]Christ Jē'şus
our [l]Lord.

## CHAPTER 9

*Paul's sorrow for the Jews. 6 All are not Israel who are of Israel. 3 The children of the promise are counted for the seed of Abraham. 18 God has mercy upon whom he will. 25 The calling of the Gentiles and the rejection of the Jews were foretold. 32 The reason why the Jews were rejected.*

I [a]SAY the truth in Christ, I
lie not, my [b]conscience also
bearing me witness in the [c]Holy
Ghost,
2 That I have great heaviness and continual sorrow in
my heart.
3 For [d,e]I could wish that
myself were [*,1,f]accursed from
Christ for my brethren, my kinsmen according to the flesh:
4 Who are [g]Is'ra-el-ītes; to
[h]whom *pertaineth* the [i]adoption,

**35**
o *Faith in Christ, exemplified,* John 6:69.
p *Love, for Jesus* (as some interpret), 1 John 4:19.
q *Temptation,* Luke 11:4.
r *Perseverance,* Eph. 6:18.
s *Apostasy,* Acts 1:25.
t *Jesus, love of* (as some interpret), Matt. 1:21.
u *Adversity,* Psa. 10:6.
v *Persecution,* John 15:20.
w *Famine,* 2 Kin. 8:1.

**36**
x Psa. 44:22.
y *Zeal,* 2 Cor. 7:11.
z *Martyrdom, spirit of,* Rev. 17:6.

a *Sheep, figurative,* Deut. 32:14.

**37**
b *Temptation,* Luke 11:4.
c *Jesus, savior,* Matt. 1:21.
d *Jesus, love of,* Matt. 1:21.

**38**
e *Faith, exemplified,* Matt. 11:22.
f *Assurance, of grace,* v. 39; Heb. 10:22.
g *Death,* Num. 23:10.
h *Angel,* Heb. 1:13.

**39**
i *Apostasy,* Acts 1:25.
j *God, love of,* Gen. 2:2.
k *Jesus, Messiah,* Matt. 1:21.
l *Jesus, lordship of,* Matt. 1:21.

**1**
a *Integrity,* Job 2:3.

**34** k *Jesus, Messiah,* Matt. 1:21. l *Resurrection, of Jesus,* 1 Cor. 15:12. m *Jesus, exaltation of,* Matt. 1:21. n *Jesus, mediation of,* Matt. 1:21. 17 R. V. Christ Jesus

b *Conscience, approving,* Acts 23:1. c *Holy Spirit,* Acts 1:2. **3** d *Love, of man for man,* 1 John 4:7. e *Renunciation, of self,* Luke 5:11. f *Penalty, vicariously assumed,* 1 Sam. 25:24. 1 R. V. anathema **4** g *Jews, entrusted with the oracles of God,* Neh. 4:2. h *Church, mission of,* Matt. 16:18. i *Spiritual Adoption,* Rom. 8:15.

† **FOREORDINATION.** *According to purpose of grace,* Ex. 33:19; Isa. 44:1, 2, 7; Mal. 1:2, 3; Acts 13:48; Rom. 8:28–30, 33; 9:11–29; 11:5, 7, 8; 1 Cor. 1:26–29; Eph. 1:4, 5, 9–11; 3:11; 2 Thess. 2:13; 2 Tim. 1:9; Tit. 1:1, 2; 1 Pet. 1:2. *Of posterity to Abraham,* Gen. 21:12; Neh. 9:7, 8. *Of Joseph's mission in Egypt,* Gen. 45:5–7; Psa. 105:17–22. *Of Israel as a nation,* Gen. 21:12; Deut. 4:37; 7:7, 8; 10:15; 32:8. *Of Ishmael as a nation,* Gen. 21:12, 13; 25:12–18. *Of famine in Egypt,* Gen. 41:30–32. *Of David as king,* 2 Chr. 6:6. *Of Jehu's dynasty,* 2 Kin. 10:30; 15:12. *Of the rending of Solomon's kingdom,* 1 Kin. 11:11, 12, 31–39; 12:15. *Of the destruction, of the Canaanites,* Josh. 11:20; *of Benhadad,* 1 Kin. 20:42; *of Ahaziah,* 2 Chr. 22:7; *of Amaziah and the idolatrous Jews,* 2 Chr. 25:20. *Of agent to execute divine judgments,* 2 Kin. 19:25; 2 Chr. 22:7; Hab. 1:12. *Of Jeremiah as prophet,* Jer. 1:4, 5. *Of the death of Jesus,* Mark 14:21; Luke 22:22; 24:26, 27; Acts 2:23; 3:18; 4:28; Rev. 13:8. *Of Paul to the ministry,* Acts 9:15; Gal. 1:15, 16; 1 Tim. 2:7. *Of the times and bounds of nations,* Acts 17:26. *Of the standard of righteousness,* Eph. 2:10. *Of the kingdom prepared for the righteous,* Matt. 25:34. *Of the wicked, to day of evil,* Prov. 16:4; *to condemnation,* Jude 4. *Of the day of judgment,* Acts 17:31.

* **VICARIOUS SUFFERINGS,** John 15:13; Rom. 9:3; 1 Pet. 2:21–24; 1 John 3:16.
See footnotes: JESUS, *Sufferings of,* Matt. 1:21; PENALTY, *Vicariously assumed,* 1 Sam. 25:24.

and the glory, and the [i]covenants, and the giving of the [k]law, and the service *of God*, and the promises;[T Q]

5 Whose *are* the fathers,[C] and of whom [l]as concerning the flesh Christ *came*, [m]who is over all, [n]God blessed for ever. Amen.[T Q]

6 Not as though the [o]word of God hath taken none effect. For they *are* not all Ĭṣ′ra-el, which are of Ĭṣ′ra-el:[Q]

7 Neither, because they are the seed of [p]Ā′bră-hăm, *are they* all children: but, [q,r]In [s]Ī′ṣaac shall thy seed be called.[T Q]

8 That is, They which are the [t]children of the flesh, these *are* not the [u,v]children of God: but the [u]children of the [w]promise are [2]counted for the seed.

9 For this *is* the word of [w]promise, [x]At this time will I come, and [y]Sā′rah shall have a son.[Q]

10 And not only *this*; but when [z]Rē-bĕc′cȧ also had conceived by one, *even* by our father Ī′ṣaac;[S Q]

11[T] (For *the children* being not yet born, neither having done any good or evil, that the [a]purpose of God according to [b]election might stand, not of works, but of him that calleth;)[S]

12 It was said unto her, [c]The [d]elder shall serve the younger.[S Q]

13 As it is written, [e,f]Jā′cob have I [g,h]loved, but [i]Ē′ṣau have I [h]hated.[S T Q]

14 What shall we say then? [j,k]*Is there* unrighteousness with God? God forbid.[S Q]

15 For he saith to [l]Mō′ṣeṣ, [m]I will have [n]mercy on whom I will have mercy, and I will have compassion on whom I will have compassion.[S Q]

16 So then *it is* not of him that [o]willeth,[C] nor of him that [o]runneth, but of [p]God that sheweth [n]mercy.[S T]

17 For the [q]scripture saith unto [r]Phā′raōh, [s]Even for this same [a]purpose have I raised thee up, that I might shew my [t]power in thee, and [u]that my name might be declared throughout all the earth.[S Q]

18 Therefore hath he [n]mercy on whom he will *have mercy*, and whom he will he hardeneth.[S Q]

19 Thou wilt say then unto me, Why doth he yet find fault? For who hath resisted [v]his [w]will?[S]

20 Nay but, O [x]man, who art thou that [y,z]repliest against God? [a,b]Shall the thing formed say to him that formed *it*, Why hast thou made me thus?[S T Q]

21 Hath not the [c]potter [3]power over the [d,e]clay, of the same lump to make one vessel unto honour, and another unto dishonour?[S Q]

22 *What* if God, willing to shew *his* [f]wrath, and to make his [g]power known, endured with much [h]longsuffering the [i]vessels of wrath [j]fitted to [k]destruction:[Q T S]

23 And that he might make known the [l,m]riches of his glory on the [n]vessels of mercy, which he had afore[C] [j]prepared unto glory,[S]

24 Even us, whom he hath [o]called, not [C]of the [p]Jews only, but also [C]of the [q]Ġĕn′tīleṣ?[S]

25 As he saith also in Ō′ṣee, [r]I will call them [s]my people, which were not my people; and her beloved, which was not beloved.[Q]

26 [t]And it shall come to pass, *that* in the place where it was said unto them, Ye *are* not my people; there shall they be called [4]the [n,s]children of the living God.[Q]

27 [Q] [u]Ē-ṣā′ias also crieth concerning Ĭṣ′ra-el, [v]Though the number of the children of Ĭṣ′ra-el be as the sand of the sea, [5]a remnant shall be saved:[S]

i *Covenant, of God with men,* Deut. 29:1.
k *Law, of Moses,* Deut. 33:2.

**5**
l *Jesus, incarnation of,* Matt. 1:21.
m *Jesus, king,* Matt. 1:21.
n *Jesus, divinity of,* Matt. 1:21.

**6**
o *Word of God,* Psa. 119:9.

**7**
p *Abraham,* Gen. 17:5.
q Gen. 21:12.
r *Foreordination,* Rom. 8:30.
s *Isaac, prophecies concerning,* Gen. 21:3.

**8**
t *Wicked, described,* Psa. 73:3.
u *Righteous, described,* Psa. 64:10.
v *Spiritual Adoption,* Rom. 8:15.
w *Covenant, of God with men,* Deut. 29:1.
2 R. V. reckoned for a seed.

**9**
x Gen. 18:10, 14.
y *Sarah,* Gen. 17:15.

**10**
z *Rebekah,* Gen. 24:15.

**11**
a *Foreordination, according to purpose of grace,* Rom. 8:30.
b *Election of Grace,* Rom. 11:5.

**12**
c Gen. 25:23.
d *Firstborn, birthright of,* v. 13; Zech. 12:10.

**13**
e Mal. 1:2, 3.
f *Jacob,* Gen. 27:11.
g *God, love of,* Gen. 2:2.
h *Anthropomorphisms,* Gen. 11:5.
i *Esau,* Gen. 25:25.

**14**
j *God, justice of,* Gen. 2:2.
k *God, righteousness of,* Gen. 2:2. **15** l *Moses,* Ex. 2:10. m Ex. 33:19. n *God, mercy of,* Gen. 2:2.
**16** o *Works, insufficient for salvation,* 2 Tim. 1:9.

p *Grace of God,* Rom. 4:16.

**17**
q *Word of God,* Psa. 119:9.
r *Pharaoh,* Ex. 3:10.
s Ex. 9:16.
t *God, power of,* Gen. 2:2.
u *Judgments, design of,* Ex. 6:6.

**19**
v *God, sovereign,* Gen. 2:2.
w *Will of God,* Mark 3:35.

**20**
x *Man, insignificance of,* Job 4:17.
y *Murmuring, against God,* Num. 14:2.
z *Presumption,* Psa. 19:13.
a Isa. 29:16; 45:9.
b *Infidelity, arguments against,* 2 Cor. 6:15.

**21**
c *Pottery,* Jer. 18:3.
d *Clay,* Job 33:6.
e *Man, insignificance of,* Job 4:17.
3 R. V. a right over

**22**
f *Anger of God,* 2 Kin. 13:3.
g *God, power of,* Gen. 2:2.
h *God, longsuffering of,* Gen. 2:2.
i *Wicked, described,* Psa. 73:3.
j *Foreordination,* Rom. 8:30.
k *Wicked, punishment of,* Psa. 73:3.

**23**
l *Grace of God,* Rom. 4:16.
m *Spiritual Blessings, from God,* Eph. 1:3.
n *Righteous, described,* Psa. 64:10.

**24**
o *Call, personal,* Phil. 3:14.
p *Jews,* Neh. 4:2.
q *Gentiles,* Acts 10:45.

**25**
r Hos. 2:23.
s *Spiritual Adoption,* Rom. 8:15.

**26**
t Hos. 1:10.
4 R. V. sons

**27**
u Or, *Isaiah,* Isa. 1:1.
v Isa. 10:22, 23.
5 R. V. it is the remnant that shall be saved:

28 For [6,w]he will finish the work, and cut *it* short in righteousness: because a short work will the Lord make upon the earth.[S Q]

29 And as [u]Ē-ṣā′ias said before, [x]Except the Lord of Săb′a-ōth[G] had left us a seed, we had been as [y]Sŏd′o-mȧ, and been made like unto [z]Gŏ-mŏr′rhȧ.[Q]

30 What shall we say then? That the [a]Ġĕn′tīleṣ, which followed not after righteousness, have attained to [b,c]righteousness, even the [b,c]righteousness which is of [d]faith.[S]

31 But Ĭṣ′ra-el, [7]which followed after the [e]law of righteousness, hath not attained to the law of [b,c]righteousness.[S]

32 Wherefore[G]? Because *they sought it* not by [d]faith, but as it were [8]by the [f]works of the [e]law. For they [g,h,i]stumbled at that stumblingstone;[S Q]

33 As it is [j]written, [k]Behold, I lay in [l]Sī′ŏn a [g]stumblingstone and rock of offence: and whosoever [d]believeth on him [m]shall not be [9]ashamed.[S Q]

## CHAPTER 10

*Paul's desire for the salvation of Israel. 2 The difference between the righteousness of the law and that of faith. 11 All, both Jew and Gentile, who believe shall be saved. 19 Israel not ignorant of these things.*

BRETHREN, [a]my heart's desire and [b]prayer to God [1]for Ĭṣ′ra-el is, that they might be [c]saved.

2 For I bear them record[G] that they have a [d]zeal of God, but not according to knowledge.

3 [T]For they being [e]ignorant of God's [f,g]righteousness, and going[G] about to establish their own [h]righteousness, have not submitted themselves unto the [i]righteousness of God.

4 For[S] Chrīst *is* the [j]end of the [k]law [2]for [l]righteousness to every one that [m]believeth.[T]

5 For Mō′ṣeṣ [3]describeth the righteousness which is of the [n]law, That the man which [o]doeth those things shall live by them.[Q]

6 But[T Q] the [l]righteousness which is of [m]faith speaketh on this wise, Say not in thine heart, [p]Who shall ascend into heaven? (that is, to bring Chrīst down [4]*from above*:)

7 Or, [p]Who shall descend into the [5]deep? (that is, to bring up Chrīst again from the dead.)[S]

8 [S]But what saith it? [p]The [q]word is nigh[G] thee, *even* in thy mouth, and in thy heart: that is, the word of [m]faith, which we preach;[T]

9 That if thou shalt [r,s]confess with thy mouth [6]the [t]Lord [u]Jē′ṣus, and shalt [m]believe in thine heart that God hath [v]raised him from the dead, thou [w]shalt be [x]saved.[Q]

10 For with the [y]heart man [m]believeth unto [l]righteousness; and with the mouth [s]confession is made unto [x]salvation.

11 For the [z]scripture saith, Whosoever [a]believeth on [b]him shall not be [7]ashamed.[T Q]

12 For there is [c]no [8]difference between the Jew and the Greek: for the same [d]Lord over all is [e]rich unto [f]all that [g]call upon him.

13 For [h]whosoever shall [g]call upon the name of the Lord shall be [i]saved.[S Q T]

14 How then shall they call on him in whom they have not believed? and how shall they believe in him of whom they have not heard? and how shall they hear without a [j]preacher?

15 And how shall they preach, except they be [k]sent? as it is

**28**
*w* *God, sovereign,* Gen. 2:2.
6 R. V. the Lord will execute his word upon the earth, finishing it and cutting it short.
**29**
*x* Isa. 1:9.
*y* *Sodom, destroyed,* Gen. 13:10.
*z* *Gomorrah, destroyed,* Gen. 13:10.

**30**
*a* *Gentiles, conversion of,* Acts 10:45.
*b* *Justification, by faith,* Rom. 4:25.
*c* *Salvation,* Acts 16:17.
*d* *Faith in Christ,* John 6:69.
**31**
*e* *Law, of Moses,* Deut. 33:2.
7 R. V. following after a law of righteousness, did not arrive at that law.
**32**
*f* *Works, insufficient for salvation,* 2 Tim. 1:9.
*g* *Stumbling, figurative,* Isa. 8:14.
*h* *Unbelief,* Heb. 3:12.
*i* *Jesus, rejected,* Matt. 1:21.
8 R. V. by works. They stumbled at the stone of stumbling;
**33**
*j* *Prophecies concerning the Messiah, and their fulfillment,* Gen. 12:3.
*k* Isa. 8:14; 28:16.
*l* Or, *Zion,* 2 Sam. 5:7.
*m* *Righteous, promises to,* Psa. 64:10.
9 R. V. put to shame.

**1**
*a* *Love, of man for man,* 1 John. 4:7.
*b* *Prayer, intercessory,* Acts 6:4.
*c* *Salvation,* Acts 16:17.
1 R. V. is for them,
**2**
*d* *Zeal, without knowledge,* 2 Cor. 7:11.

*k* *Law, of Moses, temporary,* Deut. 33:2.
*l* *Justification, by faith,* Rom. 4:25.
*m* *Faith in Christ,* John 6:69.
2 R. V. unto
**5**
*n* *Law, of Moses,* Deut. 33:2.
*o* *Works under the Law,* Lev. 18:5.
3 R. V. writeth that the man that doeth the righteousness which is of the law shall live thereby.
**6**
*p* Deut. 30:12–14.
4 R. V. *omits* from above:
**7**
5 R. V. abyss?
**8**
*q* *Gospel,* Mark 13:10.
**9**
*r* *Religious Testimony,* 2 Thess. 1:10.
*s* *Confession of Christ,* Luke 12:8.
*t* *Jesus, lordship of,* Matt. 1:21.
*u* *Jesus, savior,* Matt. 1:21.
*v* *Resurrection, of Jesus,* 1 Cor. 15:12.
*w* *Penitent, promises to,* Psa. 51:17.
*x* *Salvation,* Acts 16:17.
6 R. V. Jesus as Lord,
**10**
*y* *Heart, renewed,* Psa. 44:21.
**11**
*z* *Word of God,* Psa. 119:9.

*a* *Faith in Christ,* John 6:69.
*b* *Jesus, savior,* Matt. 1:21.
7 R. V. put to shame.
**12**
*c* *Respect of Persons,* Prov. 24:23.
*d* *God, sovereign,* Gen. 2:2.
*e* *God, mercy of,* Gen. 2:2.
*f* *Seekers,* Isa. 55:6.
*g* *Prayer, answer to, promised,* Acts 6:4.
8 R. V. distinction between Jew and Greek: for the same Lord is Lord of all, and is rich

**3** *e* *Spiritual Blindness,* 2 Cor. 4:4. *f* *God, righteousness of,* Gen. 2:2. *g* *Salvation, plan of,* Acts 16:17. *h* *Self-righteousness,* Luke 18:11. *i* *Atonement, by Jesus,* Lev. 17:11.
**4** *j* *Jesus, mission of,* Matt. 1:21.
**13** *h* Joel 2:32; Acts 2:21. *i* *Salvation,* Acts 16:17. **14** *j* *Instruction, in religion,* Prov. 23:23. **15** *k* *Minister, call of,* Rom. 15:16.

written, [l]How beautiful are the
[m]feet of them that [9]preach the
[n]gospel of [o]peace, and bring
glad tidings of good things![Q]
16 But [p]they [10]have not all
obeyed the [n]gospel. For [q]Ē-ṣā'-
ias saith, [r]Lord, [s]who hath believed our [t]report?[Q]
17 So then [u]faith *cometh* by
hearing, and hearing by the
[v]word of [11]God.[T]
18 But I say, Have they not
heard? Yes verily, [v,w]their
sound went into all the earth,
and their words unto the ends
of the world.[Q]
19 But I say, Did not Ĭṣ'ra-el
know? First [x]Mō'ṣeṣ saith, [y]I
will provoke you to [z]jealousy
[12]by [a]*them that are* no people,
*and* by a foolish nation I will
anger you.[Q]
20[Q] But [b]Ē-ṣā'ias is very bold,
and saith, [c]I was found of [a]them
that sought me not; I was made
manifest unto them that asked
not after me.[S]
21 But to Ĭṣ'ra-el he saith, [d]All
day long I have stretched forth
my hands unto a [e]disobedient
and [f]gainsaying[G] people.[Q]

## CHAPTER 11

*God has not cast off all Israel. 5 There is a remnant according to the election of grace, and the rest are blinded. 11 Through their fall salvation is come unto the Gentiles. 12 If the fall of them be the riches of the world, how much more their fullness. 24 They will be restored. 33 God's judgments are unsearchable.*

[a]I SAY[Q] then, Hath God cast
away his people? God for-
bid. For I also am an Ĭṣ'ra-el-
īte, of the seed of [b]Ā'brā-hăm, *of*
the tribe of [c]Bĕn'ja-mĭn.
2 God hath not cast away his
people which he [d]foreknew.
[1]Wot[G] ye not what the [e]scripture
saith of [f]Ē-lī'as? how he [2]mak-
eth intercession to God against
Ĭṣ'ra-el, saying,[S] [Q]
3 [g]Lord, they have [h,i]killed thy
[j]prophets, and digged[G] down
thine altars; and I am left alone,
and they seek my life.[Q]
4 But[S] what saith the answer of
God unto him? [k]I have [l]re-
served to myself seven thousand
men, who have [m]not bowed the
knee to [3]*the image of* Bā'al.[Q]
5 Even so then at this present time also there is a remnant[G]
according to the *,[l]election of
[n]grace.[T]
6 And if by [n]grace, then *is it* no
more of [o]works: otherwise grace
is no more grace. [4]But if *it be*
of works, then is it no more
grace: otherwise work is no more
work.[S]
7[S] What then? [p]Ĭṣ'ra-el hath
not obtained[G] that which he seeketh for; but the *election hath
obtained[G] it, and the [q]rest were
[5,r,s]blinded
8 (According as it is written,
God hath given them the spirit
of [6,s]slumber, eyes that they
should [r]not see, and ears that
they should [t]not hear;) unto this
day.[S] [Q]
9[Q] And [u]Dā'vid saith, [v,w]Let
their table be made a snare,
and a trap, and a stumblingblock, and a recompence unto
them:
10 Let their eyes be [r,s]dark-
ened, that they may not see, and
bow down their back alway.[Q]
11 I say then, Have they stumbled that they should fall? God
forbid: but *rather* through their
fall [x]salvation *is come* unto the
[y]Ġĕn'tīleṣ, for to provoke them
to [z]jealousy.[Q]
12 Now if the fall of them *be*
the riches of the world, and [7]the
diminishing of them the riches
of the [y]Ġĕn'tīleṣ; how much more
their fulness?
13 For [a]I speak to you Ġĕn'tīleṣ,
inasmuch as I am the [b,c]apostle

l Isa. 52:7.
m *Feet*, 2 Sam. 4:4.
n *Gospel*, Mark 13:10.
o *Spiritual Peace*, Gal. 1:3.
9 R. V. bring glad tidings of good things!

**16**
p *Jesus, rejected*, Matt. 1:21.
q Or, *Isaiah*, Isa. 1:1.
r Isa. 53:1.
s *Unbelief*, Heb. 3:12.
t *Prophecies concerning the Messiah, and their fulfillment*, Gen. 12:3.
10 R. V. they did not all hearken to the glad tidings.

**17**
u *Faith in Christ*, John 6:69.
v *Doctrines of Jesus*, John 7:16.
11 R. V. Christ.

**18**
w Psa. 19:4.

**19**
x *Law, of Moses*, Deut. 33:2.
y Deut. 32:21.
z *Jealousy*, Psa. 78:58.

a *Gentiles, conversion of*, Acts 10:45.
12 R. V. with that which is no nation, With a nation void of understanding will I anger you.

**20**
b Or, *Isaiah*, Isa. 1:1.
c Isa. 65:1, 2.

**21**
d *God, longsuffering of*, Gen. 2:2.
e *Disobedience to God*, Eph. 5:6.
f *Unbelievers*, 1 Cor. 6:6.

**1**
a *Paul*, Acts 13:9.
b *Abraham*, Gen. 17:5.
c *Benjamin, tribe of*, Num. 1:37.

**2**
d *God, foreknowledge of*, Gen. 2:2.
e *Word of God*, Psa. 119:9.
f Or, *Elijah*, 1 Kin. 17:1.
1 Am. R. V. know
2 R. V. pleadeth with God

**3**
g 1 Kin. 19:10, 14.
h *Persecution, of the righteous*, John 15:20.
i *Martyrdom*, Rev. 17:6.

j *Prophets*, Isa. 3:2.

**4**
k 1 Kin. 19:18.
l *Foreordination*, Rom. 8:30.
m *Faithfulness*, Luke 16:10.
3 R. V. *omits* the image of

**5**
n *Grace of God*, Rom. 4:16.

**6**
o *Works, insufficient for salvation*, 2 Tim. 1:9.
4 R. V. *omits the rest of this verse.*

**7**
p *Jews*, Neh. 4:2.
q *Reprobates*, 1 Cor. 9:27.
r *Spiritual Blindness*, 2 Cor. 4:4.
s *Moral Insensibility*, Luke 8:10.
5 R. V. hardened:

**8**
t *Deafness, figurative*, Matt. 11:5.
6 R. V. stupor,

**9**
u *David*, 1 Sam. 16:13.
v Psa. 69:22, 23.
w *Prayer, imprecatory*, Acts 6:4.

**11**
x *Salvation*, Acts 16:17.
y *Gentiles, conversion of*, Acts 10:45.
z *Jealousy*, Psa. 78:58.

**12**
7 R. V. their loss the riches

**13**
a *Paul*, Acts 13:9.
b *Apostles, commission of*, Luke 6:13.
c *Minister, call of*, Rom. 15:16.

* **ELECTION OF GRACE**, **Matt. 22:14; John 15:16; 17:6; Rom. 11:5; Eph. 1:4; 2:10; 1 Pet. 2:9.** See footnote, FOREORDINATION, Rom. 8:30.

d *Zeal*, 2 Cor. 7:11.
8 R. V. glorify my ministry:

**14**
9 R. V. jealousy

**15**
e *Reconciliation, between God and man*, 2 Cor. 5:18.

**16**
f *First Fruits, figurative*, Deut. 18:4.
g *Holiness*, Ex. 39:30.
h *Branch, figurative*, Dan. 4:14.

**17**
i *Jews, reject Jesus*, Neh. 4:2.
j *Gentiles, conversion of*, Acts 10:45.
k *Olive, figurative*, Deut. 6:11.
l *Church*, Matt. 16:18.
10 R. V. were broken off, and thou, being a wild olive, wast grafted in among them, and didst become partaker with them of the root of the fatness of the olive tree;

**18**
m *Spiritual Boasting*, Rom. 3:27.
n *Humility, enjoined*, Prov. 22:4.

**19**
11 R. V. grafted

**20**
o *Unbelief*, Heb. 3:12.
p *Faith in Christ*, John 6:69.
q *Fear of God*, Acts 9:31.

**21**
12 R. V. neither will he spare thee.

**22**
r *God, goodness of*, Gen. 2:2.
s *God, judge*, Gen. 2:2.
t *Perseverance*, Eph. 6:18.
u *Wicked, punishment of*, Psa. 73:3.
13 R. V. God's goodness,

**23**
v *Repentance*, Mark 1:4.
14 R. V. graft

of the Ġĕn′tīleș, [d]I [8]magnify mine office:

14 If by any means I may provoke to †,[9]emulation *them which are* my flesh, and might save some of them.

15 For if the casting away of them *be* the [e]reconciling of the world, what *shall* the receiving *of them be*, but life from the dead?

16 For if the [f]firstfruit *be* [g]holy, the lump *is* also *holy*: and if the root *be* holy, so *are* the [h]branches.

17 And if some of the [h,i]branches [10]be broken off, and [j]thou, being a wild [k]olive tree, wert graffed in among them, and with them partakest of the root and fatness of the [l]olive tree;

18 [m,n]Boast not against the [h,i]branches. But if [j]thou boast, thou bearest not the root, but the root thee.

19 [j]Thou wilt [m]say then, The [h,i]branches were broken off, that I might be [11]graffed in.

20 Well; because of [o]unbelief [i]they were broken off, and [j]thou standest by [p]faith. Be not [m]highminded, but [q]fear:

21 For if God spared not the natural [h,i]branches, [12]*take heed* lest he also spare not [j]thee.

22 Behold therefore the [r]goodness and [s]severity of God: on [i]them which fell, severity; but toward thee, [13]goodness, if [j]thou [t]continue in *his* goodness: otherwise thou also shalt be [u]cut off.

23 And [i]they also, if they [v]abide not still in unbelief, shall be [11]graffed in: for God is able to [14]graff them in again.

24 For if [j]thou wert cut out of the [k]olive tree which is wild by nature, and wert [11]graffed contrary to nature into a good [l]olive tree: how much more shall these, which be the natural [h,i]*branches*, be [11]graffed into their own olive tree?

25 For I would not, brethren, that ye should be [w]ignorant of this mystery, lest ye should be wise in your own [x]conceits; that [15]blindness in part is happened to [i]Ĭș′ra-el, until the fulness of the [j]Ġĕn′tīleș be come in.

26 And so all [i]Ĭș′ra-el shall be saved: as it is written, [y,z]There shall come out of [a]Sī′ŏn the [b]Deliverer, and shall [c]turn away ungodliness from Jā′cob:

27 For this *is* my [d]covenant unto [e]them, when I shall [f]take away their sins.

28 As concerning the [g]gospel, [e]*they are* enemies for [h]your sakes: but as touching the *election, *they are* [i]beloved [j]for the fathers' sakes.

29 For the [k]gifts and [l]calling of [m]God *are* [16]without repentance.

30 For as [h]ye in times past [17]have [n]not believed God, yet have now obtained [o]mercy through [e]their unbelief:

31 Even so have these also now [18,n]not believed, that through [h]your mercy [e]they also may obtain [o]mercy.

32 For God hath [19]concluded them [p]all in [n]unbelief, that he might have [o]mercy upon all.

33 O the depth of the riches both of the [q]wisdom and [r]knowledge of God! how [s]unsearchable *are* his judgments, and his ways past finding out!

34 For who hath known the mind of the [t]Lord? or who hath been his counsellor?

35 Or who hath first given to him, and it shall be recompensed unto him again?

36 For [u]of him, and [v]through

19 R. V. shut up all unto disobedience,
**33** q *God, wisdom of*, Gen. 2:2. r *God, knowledge of*, Gen. 2:2. s *God, unsearchable*, Gen. 2:2.
**34** t *God, sovereign*, Gen. 2:2. **36** u *God, creator*, Gen. 2:2. v *God, providence of*, Gen. 2:2.

**25**
w *Spiritual Blindness*, 2 Cor. 4:4.
x *Conceit, warnings against*, Prov. 26:5.
15 R. V. a hardening in part hath befallen Israel,

**26**
y Isa. 59:20, 21.
z *Prophecies concerning the Messiah, and their fulfillment*, Gen. 12:3.

a Or, *Zion*, 2 Sam. 5:7.
b *Jesus, names of*, Matt. 1:21.
c *Jesus, mission of*, Matt. 1:21.

**27**
d *Covenant, of God with men*, Deut. 29:1.
e *Jews*, Neh. 4:2.
f *Sin, forgiveness of*, Rom. 5:12.

**28**
g *Gospel*, Mark 13:10.
h *Gentiles, conversion of*, Acts 10:45.
i *God, love of*, Gen. 2:2.
j *Intercession, intercessional influence of the righteous*, Jer. 27:18.

**29**
k *Spiritual Gifts*, 1 Cor. 12:4.
l *Call, personal*, Phil. 3:14.
m *God, immutable*, Gen. 2:2.
16 Am. R. V. (*marg.*) not repented of.

**30**
n *Disobedience to God*, Eph. 5:6.
o *God, mercy of*, Gen. 2:2.
17 R. V. were disobedient to God, but now have obtained mercy by their disobedience,

**31**
18 R. V. been disobedient, that by the mercy shewn to you they also may now obtain mercy.

**32**
p *Sinfulness*, Rom. 3:23.

† **EMULATION**, Rom. 11:11, 14; 2 Cor. 8:1–8; 9:1–5; Heb. 10:24. Illustrated: *In Esau's marriage*, Gen. 28:6–9; *in Jacob's household*, Gen. 30:1–24.

w *God, glory of*, Gen. 2:2.
x *Praise*, Psa. 150:1.

**1**
a *Love, of man for man*, 1 John 4:7.
b *Consecration, personal*, Lev. 7:37.
c *Body, to be consecrated to God*, 1 Cor. 6:19.
d *Holiness, exhortations to*, Ex. 39:30.

**2**
e *Commandment, forbidding worldliness*, Deut. 8:2.
f *Worldliness, admonitions against*, 1 John 2:15.
g *Regeneration*, Tit. 3:5.
h *Will of God*, Mark 3:35.
1 R. V. fashioned according to

**3**
i *Grace of God*, Rom. 4:16.
j *Pride, admonition against*, Prov. 16:18.
k *Humility, enjoined*, Prov. 22:4.
l *Self-exaltation*, Luke 14:11.
m *Sober-mindedness*, Tit. 2:6.
n *Responsibility, according to privilege*, Ezek. 18:20.
o *Faith, gift of God*, Mark 11:22.

**5**
p *Righteous, union of, with Christ*, Psa. 64:10.
q *Unity, of the righteous*, Psa. 133:1.

him, and [t]to him, *are* all things:
to whom *be* [w,x]glory for ever.
Amen.[S]

## CHAPTER 12

*Believers are exhorted to devote themselves to the service of God, 3 to be humble, 6 and to use diligently their various gifts. 9 Sundry other duties enjoined.*

I [a]BESEECH you therefore,
brethren, by the mercies of
God, that ye [b]present your [c]bod-
ies a living *sacrifice,[C] [d]holy, acceptable unto God, *which is* your
reasonable service.
2 And [e]be not [1,f]conformed to
this world:[C] but be ye [g]trans-
formed by the renewing of your
mind, that ye may prove what *is*
that good, and acceptable, and
perfect, [h]will of God.[T]
3 For I say, through the [i]grace
given unto me, to every man that
is among you, [j,k]not to think *of*
*himself* [l]more highly than he
ought to think; but to think
[m]soberly, [n]according as God
hath dealt to every man the
measure of [o]faith.
4 For as we have many members in one body, and all members have not the same office:
5 So [p]we, *being* many, are [q,r]one
[s]body [t]in Christ, and [2]every one
members one of another.
6 Having then [u]gifts differing
according to the [i]grace that is
given to us, whether prophecy,[C]
[v]*let us prophesy*[C] [n]according to
the proportion of [3,o]faith;
7 [v]Or ministry, *let us* [4,w]*wait*
on *our* ministering: or [x]he that
teacheth, [5]on teaching;
8 [v]Or he that exhorteth,[C] on
exhortation: he that [y]giveth, [z]*let*
*him do it* with [6,a]simplicity;[C] [b]he
that ruleth, with †diligence; he
that sheweth [c]mercy, with cheerfulness.
9 [d]*Let* [e,f]love be [g]without [7]dis-
simulation.[C] [d,h]Abhor that which is
[i]evil; [j]cleave[C] to that which is good.[S Q]
10 [k]*Be* [l]kindly [m]affectioned[C] one
to another with [n]brotherly [e,f]love;
[k,l]in honour preferring one another;
11 [†,8,o,p]Not [q]slothful in business; [f,r,s]fervent in spirit; serving the Lord;
12 [t]Rejoicing in [u]hope; [f,t,v,w]pa-
tient in [x]tribulation; [f,t]continu-
ing [9]instant[C] in [y,z]prayer;
13 [a,b]Distributing to the necessity of saints; [a]given to ‡hospi-
tality.
14 [c,d,e,f]Bless[C] [g]them which persecute you: bless, and [h]curse not.

v *Commandment, enjoining zeal*, Deut. 8:2.
3 R. V. our faith;

**7**
w *Minister, duties of*, Rom. 15:16.
x *Teachers*, 1 Chr. 25:8.
4 R. V. give ourselves to our ministry;
5 R. V. to his teaching;

**8**
y *Poor, liberality to*, Prov. 21:13.
z *Alms*, Matt. 6:2.
a *Liberality*, 1 Tim. 6:18.
b *Rulers*, Ex. 18:21.
c *Mercy*, Deut. 5:10.
6 R. V. liberality;

**9**
d *Commandment, enjoining love, and the abhorrence of evil*, Deut. 8:2.
e *Love, of man for man*, 1 John 4:7.
f *Christian Graces*, Gal. 5:22.
g *Sincerity*, 1 Cor. 5:8.
h Amos 5:15.
i *Evil, to be abhorred*, 1 Thess. 5:22.
j *Perseverance*, Eph. 6:18.
7 R. V. hypocrisy.

**10**
k *Commandment, enjoining love and helpfulness*, Deut. 8:2. l *Duty, of man to man*, Eccl. 12:13. m *Affections, benevolent*, 2 Cor. 7:15. n *Fraternity, enjoined*, Zech. 11:14. **11** o *Strenuousness, enjoined*, Eccl. 9:10. p *Industry, enjoined*, 1 Kin. 11:28. q *Laziness*, Prov. 19:15. r *Zeal*, 2 Cor. 7:11. s *Commandment, enjoining spiritual diligence*, Deut. 8:2. 8 R. V. In diligence not slothful; **12** t *Commandment, enjoining joyfulness, patience, and steadfastness*, Deut. 8:2. u *Hope*, Prov. 13:12. v *Patience, a grace of the righteous*, Luke 8:15. w *Resignation*, Job 5:17. x *Adversity, resignation in*, Psa. 10:6. y *Prayerfulness, enjoined*, 1 Tim. 5:5. z *Prayer, perseverance in*, Acts 6:4. 9 R. V. stedfastly **13**—a *Commandment, enjoining liberality, and hospitality*, Deut. 8:2. b *Liberality, enjoined*, 1 Tim. 6:18. **14** c *Commandment, enjoining forgiveness*, Deut. 8:2. d *Meekness, enjoined*, Psa. 45:4. e *Forgiveness, of enemies*, Matt. 18:21. f *Good for Evil*, Luke 6:27. g *Enemy, kindness to*, Prov. 24:17. h *Cursing*, Lev. 24:11.

r *Church, unity of*, Matt. 16:18. s *Church, membership in*, Matt. 16:18. t *Fellowship, with Christ*, 1 Cor. 1:9. 2 R. V. severally members **6** u *Spiritual Gifts*, 1 Cor. 12:4.

*** SACRIFICE. Figurative:** *Of divine judgments*, Isa. 34:6; Ezek. 39:17; Zeph. 1:7, 8. *Of self*, Rom. 12:1; Phil. 2:17. *Of self-denial*, Phil. 3:7, 8. *Of praise*, Psa. 116:17; Jer. 33:11; Hos. 14:2; Heb. 13:15.

See footnote, OFFERINGS, Lev. 6:17.

**† DILIGENCE.** Required: *In business*, Prov. 27:23; Eccl. 9:10; Rom. 12:11; *in keeping the heart*, Deut. 4:9; Prov. 4:23; Heb. 12:15; *in keeping the commandments of the Lord*, Ex. 15:26; Deut. 6:17; 11:13; Josh. 22:5; Psa. 119:4; Luke 13:24; Heb. 4:11; *in doing the work of the Lord*, John 9:4; 1 Cor. 7:29–31; 15:58; *in the religious instruction of children*, Deut. 6:7; 11:19; *in adding Christian virtues*, 2 Pet. 1:5; *in making our calling and election sure*, 2 Pet. 1:10; 3:14.

*Of ministers*, Acts 6:4; 2 Tim. 4:2; Rom. 12:8.

**Rewarded:** *By prosperity*, Deut. 11:14; Prov. 10:4; 13:4. *By preferment*, Prov. 12:24; 22:29. *By eternal inheritance*, Heb. 6:10–12; 11:6.

**Exemplified:** *By Hezekiah*, 2 Chr. 31:21. *By Nehemiah and his helpers*, Neh. 4:6. *By the faithful servants in the parables of the talents and pounds*, Matt. 25:20–23; Luke 19:16–18. *By the Apostles*, Acts 5:42. *By Paul*, Phil. 3:13, 14; 1 Thess. 2:9.

**‡ HOSPITALITY.** *Unselfish*, Luke 14:12–14. *Deceitful*, Prov. 23:6–8. *Parable of*, Matt. 22:2–10. *Enjoined*, Isa. 58:6, 7; Matt. 25:34–39; Rom. 12:13; 1 Tim. 3:2; 5:10; Tit. 1:7, 8; Heb. 13:2; 1 Pet. 4:9–11; 3 John 5–8. *To strangers, enjoined*, Lev. 19:10, 33, 34; Deut. 10:18, 19; 26:12, 13.

**Instances of:** *Pharaoh to Abraham*, Gen. 12:16. *Melchizedek to Abraham*, Gen. 14:18. *Abraham to angels*, Gen. 18:1–8. *Lot to an angel*, Gen. 19:1–11. *Abimelech to Abraham*, Gen. 20:14, 15. *Laban, to Abraham's servant*, Gen. 24:31–33; *to Jacob*, Gen. 29:13, 14. *Isaac to Abimelech*, Gen. 26:30. *Joseph to his brethren*, Gen. 43:31–34. *Pharaoh to Jacob*, Gen. 45:16–20; 47:7–12. *Jethro to Moses*, Ex. 2:20. *Rahab to the spies*, Josh. 2:1–16. *Man of Gibeah to the Levite*, Judg. 19:16–21. *Pharaoh to Hadad*, 1 Kin. 11:17, 22. *Jeroboam to the prophet of Judah*, 1 Kin. 13:7. *The widow of Zarephath to Elijah*, 1 Kin. 17:10–24. *The Shunammite to Elisha*, 2 Kin. 4:8. *Elisha to the Syrian spies*, 2 Kin. 6:22. *Job to strangers*, Job 31:32. *David to Mephibosheth*, 2 Sam. 9:7–13. *King of Babylon to Jehoiachin*, 2 Kin. 25:29, 30. *Nehemiah to rulers and Jews*, Neh. 5:17–19.

*Martha to Jesus*, Luke 10:38; John 12:1, 2. *Pharisees to Jesus*, Luke 11:37, 38. *Zaccheus to Jesus*, Luke 19:1–10. *Disciples to Jesus*, Luke 24:29. *The tanner to Peter*, Acts 10:6, 23. *Lydia to Paul and Silas*, Acts 16:15. *Barbarians, to Paul*, Acts 28:2. *Publius to Paul*, Acts 28:7. *Phebe to Paul*,

15 [i,j,k,l]Rejoice with them that
do rejoice, and [i,j,k,l]weep with
them that weep.
16 *Be* of the same mind one
toward another. [10,m]Mind not
high things, but condescend to
men of low estate. [n,o]Be not
wise in your own conceits.
17 [p,q]Recompense to no man
evil for evil. [11,r]Provide things
honest in the sight of all men.
18 If it be possible, as much as
lieth in you, [12,s]live [t,u]peaceably
with all men.
19 Dearly beloved, [q,v]avenge
not yourselves, but *rather* give
place unto wrath: for it is written, [w,x]Vengeance *is* mine; I will
repay, saith the Lord.
20 Therefore [y]if thine enemy
[z]hunger, [a,b]feed him; if he thirst,
[a,b]give him drink: for in so doing
thou shalt heap coals of fire on
his head.
21 [c,d]Be not overcome of evil,
but overcome evil with [e]good.

## CHAPTER 13

*Subjection, and many other duties, we owe to magistrates. 8 Love is the fulfilling of the law. 11 Gluttony, drunkenness, and other works of darkness are to be put away.*

[a]LET every soul [b]be subject
unto the [c]higher powers.
For [d]there is no power but of
God: [d]the [e]powers that be are
ordained of God.
2 [f]Whosoever therefore resisteth the [c,e]power, resisteth the
[d]ordinance of God: and they
that resist shall receive to themselves [1]damnation.
3 For [g]rulers are not a terror to
good works, but to the evil. Wilt
thou then not be afraid of the
power? do that which is good,
and thou shalt have praise of the
same:
4 For [e]he is the minister of God
to thee for good. But if [f]thou
do that which is evil, be afraid;
for [g]he beareth not the sword
in vain: for he is the minister
of God, a [h]revenger to *execute*
wrath upon [f]him that doeth evil.
5 Wherefore *ye* must needs [b]be
subject, not only for wrath, but
also for [i]conscience sake.
6 For for this cause pay [b]ye
[j]tribute also: for [e]they are [2]God's
ministers, attending continually
upon this very thing.
7 [b,k]Render therefore to all
their dues: [j]tribute to whom tribute *is due*; custom to whom custom; fear to whom fear; honour
to whom honour.
8 [l]Owe no man any thing, but
to [m,n,o]love one another: for he
that loveth [3]another hath fulfilled the [p]law.
9 For this, [q]Thou shalt not
commit [r]adultery, [s]Thou shalt
not [t]kill, [u]Thou shalt not [v]steal,
[4,w]Thou shalt not bear [x]false
witness, [y]Thou shalt not [z]covet;
and if *there be* any other commandment, it is briefly comprehended in this saying, namely,
[a]Thou shalt [b,c]love thy [d]neigh-
bour as thyself.
10 [b]Love worketh no ill to his
[d]neighbour: therefore love *is* the
fulfilling of the [e]law.
11 And that, knowing the time,
that now *it is* high time to [f]awake
out of sleep: for now *is* our [g]sal-
vation nearer than when we
[h]believed.
12 The [i]night is far spent, the day
is at hand: let us therefore [j]cast
off the works of [k]darkness, and let
us [j,l]put on the [m]armour of [n]light.
13 [o]Let us walk *honestly,

**15**
*i* *Duty, of man to man,* Eccl. 12:13.
*j* *Kindness, enjoined,* Acts 28:2.
*k* *Sympathy, enjoined,* 1 Pet. 3:8.
*l* *Commandment, enjoining sympathy,* Deut. 8:2.

**16**
*m* *Commandment, enjoining humility,* Deut. 8:2.
*n* *Conceit, warnings against,* Prov. 26:5.
*o* *False Confidence, warning against,* Psa. 30:6.
10 R. V. Set not your mind on high things, but condescend to things that are lowly.

**17**
*p* *Retaliation, malicious, forbidden,* Deut. 19:19.
*q* *Revenge, forbidden,* Ezek. 25:15.
*r* *Commandment, enjoining discreet conduct,* Deut. 8:2.
11 R. V. Take thought for things honourable in

**18**
*s* *Commandment, enjoining peaceableness,* Deut. 8:2.
*t* *Peace, enjoined,* Jer. 29:7.
*u* *Strife, exhortations against,* Prov. 20:3.
12 R. V. be at peace with all men.

**19**
*v* *Malice, forbidden,* Eph. 4:31.
*w* Deut. 32:35.
*x* *Vengeance,* Psa. 94:1.

**20**
*y* Prov. 22:21, 22.
*z* *Hunger,* Neh. 9:15.

*a* *Commandment, enjoining kindness to enemies,* Deut. 8:2. *b* *Forgiveness, of enemies,* Matt. 18:21. **21** *c* *Commandment, enjoining steadfastness,* Deut. 8:2. *d* *Temptation, resistance to, enjoined,* Luke 11:4. *e* *Good for Evil,* Luke 6:27. **1** *a* *Commandment, enjoining obedience to civil government,* Deut. 8:2. *b* *Citizens, duties of,* Luke 15:15. *c* *Government, duty of citizens to,* Isa. 22:21. *d* *Government, God in,* Isa. 22:21. *e* *Rulers, ordained of God,* Ex. 18:21. **2** *f* *Citizens, wicked,* Luke 15:15. 1 R. V. judgement. **3** *g* *Rulers, a terror to evil doers,* Ex. 18:21.

**4**
*h* *Avenger of Blood, figurative,* Deut. 19:6.

**5**
*i* *Conscience,* Acts 23:1.

**6**
*j* *Tribute,* Ezra 4:13.
2 R. V. Ministers of God's service.

**7**
*k* *Commandment, enjoining righteousness,* Deut. 8:2.

**8**
*l* *Debt, forbidden,* 1 Sam. 22:2.
*m* *Commandment, enjoining love for man,* Deut. 8:2.
*n* *Love, of man for man,* 1 John 4:7.
*o* *Duty, of man to man,* Eccl. 12:13.
*p* *Law,* Deut. 33:2.
3 R. V. his neighbor

**9**
*q* Ex. 20:14.
*r* *Adultery,* Lev. 20:10.
*s* Ex. 20:13.
*t* *Homicide,* Deut. 5:17.
*u* Ex. 20:15.
*v* *Theft,* Mark 7:22.
*w* Ex. 20:16.
*x* *False Witness,* Matt. 19:18.
*y* Ex. 20:17.
*z* *Covetousness,* Isa. 57:17.

*a* *Royal Law,* Jas. 2:8.
*b* *Love, of man for man,* 1 John 4:7.
*c* *Duty, of man to man,* Eccl. 12:13.
*d* *Neighbor, love for,* Luke 10:29.
4 R. V. *omits* Thou shalt not bear false witness,

**10**
*e* *Law,* Deut. 33:2.

**11**
*f* *Watchfulness,* Matt. 24:42.
*g* *Salvation,* Acts 16:17.
*h* *Faith in Christ,* John 6:69.

**12**
*i* *Night, figurative,* Gen. 1:5.
*j* *Commandment, enjoining spiritual diligence,* Deut. 8:2.
*k* *Darkness, figurative,* Gen. 1:2.
*l* *Holiness, exhortations to,* Ex. 39:30.
*m* *Armor, figurative* 1 Sam. 17:54. *n* *Light, figurative,* Matt. 5:14. **13** *o* *Commandment, forbidding various vices,* Deut. 8:2.

Rom. 16:2. *Onesiphorus to Paul,* 2 Tim. 1:16. *Gaius,* 3 John 5–8.
**Rewarded:** INSTANCES OF: *Rahab's,* Josh. 6:17, 22–25. *Widow of Zarephath's,* 1 Kin. 17:10–24.

* **HONESTY,** Psa. 7:3, 4; Prov. 11:1; 12:22; 16:11; 20:10; Isa. 33:15, 16; Job 27:6; Acts 24:16; 2 Cor. 7:2; 8:21; Heb. 13:18.
**Enjoined,** Lev. 19:35, 36; Deut. 16:20; 25:13–16; **Prov.**

as in the day; [p]not in [5]rioting
and [q]drunkenness, [r]not in [s]cham-
bering and wantonness, not in
[t]strife and [6,u]envying.
14 But [v,w]put ye on the [x]Lord
Jē'ṣus Chrīst, and [y]make not
[z]provision for the flesh, to *fulfil*
the lusts *thereof*.

## CHAPTER 14

*Men may not despise nor condemn one another for things indifferent; 13 but must take heed that they give no offence in them.*

HIM that is [a]weak in the faith
[b,c]receive ye, [d]*but* not [1]to
doubtful disputations.
2 [2]For one believeth that he
may eat all things: another, who
is weak, eateth herbs.
3 [a,e,f]Let not him that eateth
despise him that eateth not; and
[a,e,f]let not him which eateth not
judge him that eateth: for God
hath received him.
4 Who art thou that judgest
[3]another man's servant? to his
own master he standeth or falleth. Yea, he shall be holden up:
for God is able to make him
stand.
5 One man esteemeth one day
above another: another esteemeth every day *alike*. Let every
man be fully persuaded in his
own mind.
6 He that regardeth the day,
regardeth *it* unto the Lord; and
[4]he that regardeth not the day,
to the Lord he doth not regard
*it*. He that eateth, eateth to the
Lord, for he giveth God [g]thanks;
and he that eateth not, to the
Lord he eateth not, and giveth
God thanks.
7 For [h]none of us liveth to himself, and no man [i]dieth to himself.
8 For whether we live, we live
unto the Lord; and whether we
[i]die, we die unto the Lord:
whether we live therefore, or die,
we are the Lord's.
9 For to this end Chrīst [5]both
died, and [j]rose, and revived,
[k]that he might be [l]Lord both of
the [m]dead and living.
10 But [f]why dost thou judge
thy brother? or why dost thou
set at nought thy brother? for
we shall all stand before the
[n,o]judgment seat of [6,p]Chrīst.
11 For it is [q]written, [r]*As* I live,
saith the Lord, [s]every knee shall
[t]bow to [u]me, and every tongue
shall [v]confess to God.
12 [o]So then every one of us shall
[w]give account of himself to [p]God.
13 [x,y]Let us not therefore judge
one another any more: but judge
this rather, that no man put a
[z,a]stumblingblock or an occasion
to fall in *his* brother's way.
14 I know, and am persuaded
by the [b]Lord Jē'ṣus, that *there is*
nothing unclean of itself: but to
him that esteemeth any thing
to be unclean, to him *it is* unclean.
15 But if thy brother be grieved
with *thy* meat, [7]now walkest thou
[c]not [d]charitably. [a,e]Destroy not
him with thy meat, [f]for whom
Chrīst [g,h]died.
16 [i]Let not then your good be
evil spoken of:
17 For the [j]kingdom of God is
not [8]meat and drink; but [k]right-
eousness, and [l]peace, and [m]joy
in the [n]Holy Ghost.
18 For [o]he that in these things
serveth Chrīst [p]*is* acceptable to
God, and approved of men.
19 [q]Let us therefore [d,r]follow
after the things which make for

*p Temperance, enjoined*, 2 Pet. 1:6.
*q Drunkenness, forbidden*, Luke 21:34.
*r Continence, enjoined*, Matt. 19:12.
*s Lasciviousness, forbidden*, 1 Pet. 4:3.
*t Strife, exhortations against*, Prov. 20:3.
*u Jealousy, forbidden*, Psa. 78:58.
5 R. V. revelling
6 R. V. jealousy.

**14**
*v Commandment, enjoining imitation of Christ*, Deut. 8:2.
*w Jesus, our example*, Matt. 1:21.
*x Jesus, lordship of*, Matt. 1:21.
*y Self-denial*, Mark 8:34.
*z Worldliness*, 1 John 2:15.

**1**
*a Weak, duty of strong to*, 1 Cor. 8:9.
*b Duty, of man to man*, Eccl. 12:13.
*c Fellowship, of the righteous*, 1 Cor. 1:9.
*d Conscience, another's, to be respected*, vs. 1–23; Acts 23:1.
1 Am. R. V. (*marg.*) for decisions of doubts.

**2**
2 R. V. One man hath faith to eat all things: but he that is weak eateth herbs.

**3**
*e Church, Christian, discipline in*, Matt. 16:18.
*f Charitableness, enjoined*, Prov. 10:12.

**4**
3 R. V. the servant of another? to his own lord he standeth or falleth. Yea, he shall be made to stand; for the Lord hath power to make him stand.

**6**
*g Thanksgiving for Food*, Luke 24:30.
4 R. V. *omits* and he that regardeth not the day, to the Lord he doth not regard it. **7** *h Unselfishness*, 1 Cor. 10:24. *i Death, of the righteous*, Num. 23:10.

**9**
*j Resurrection, of Jesus*, 1 Cor. 15:12.
*k Jesus, design of his death*, Matt. 1:21.
*l Jesus, lordship of*, Matt. 1:21.
*m Dead*, 2 Kin. 4:32.
5 R V. died, and lived again, that he

**10**
*n Judgment Seat*, Acts 25:10.
*o Judgment, the general*, 2 Pet. 3:7.
*p God, judge*, Gen. 2:2.
6 R. V. God.

**11**
*q Word of God*, Psa. 119:9.
*r* Isa. 45:23.
*s Repentance, universal, foretold*, Mark 1:4.
*t Worship, to become universal*, Gen. 22:5.
*u God, sovereign*, Gen. 2:2.
*v Sin, confession of*, Rom. 5:12.

**12**
*w Responsibility, personal*, Ezek. 18:20.

**13**
*x Commandment, enjoining charitableness*, Deut. 8:2.
*y Charitableness, enjoined*, Prov. 10:12.
*z Stumbling, figurative*, Isa. 8:14.
*a Temptation, leading into, to be avoided*, Luke 11:4.

**14**
*b Jesus, lordship of*, Matt. 1:21.

**15**
*c Selfishness*, 2 Tim. 3:2.
*d Love, of man for man*, 1 John 4:7.
*e Expediency*, 1 Cor. 6:12.
*f Jesus, design of his death*, Matt. 1:21. *g Jesus, death of*, Matt. 1:21. *h Atonement, by Jesus*, Lev. 17:11. 7 R. V. thou walkest no longer in love. **16** *i Evil, appearance of, to be avoided*, 1 Thess. 5:22. **17** *j Kingdom of Heaven*, Matt. 13:24. *k Righteousness*, Psa. 15:2. *l Spiritual Peace*, Gal. 1:3. *m Joy*, Psa. 5:11. *n Holy Spirit*, Acts 1:2. 8 R. V. eating and drinking, **18** *o Righteous, promises to*, Psa. 64:10. *p Promise, or Ground of Assurance*, 2 Cor. 1:20.
**19** *q Commandment, enjoining charitableness*, Deut. 8:2. *r Meekness, enjoined*, Psa. 45:4.

4:25; Ezek. 45:10; Mark 10:19; Luke 3:12, 13; Rom. 13:13; Col. 3:22; 1 Thess. 4:11, 12; 1 Tim. 2:2.
**Instances of:** *Samuel, who in his judicial duties was incorruptible*, 1 Sam. 12:3–5. *The overseers of the temple repairs, with whom no reckoning was kept*, 2 Kin. 12:15; 22:4–7. *Treasurers of the temple*, Neh. 13:13.

*s* *Peace, enjoined,* Jer. 29:7.
*t* *Wisdom, spiritual,* Prov. 2:2.
**20**
9 R. V. clean;
**21**
*u* *Appetite, restrained for a brother's sake,* Prov. 23:2.
*v* *Food,* Psa. 136:25.
*w* *Wine, admonitions against the use of,* Prov. 23:31.
10 R. V. *omits* or is offended, or is made weak.
**22**
*x* *Faith,* Mark 11:22.
11 R. V. judgeth not himself in that which he approveth.
**23**
*y* *Conscience,* Acts 23:1.
*z* *Sin, against conscience,* Rom. 5:12.
12 R. V. condemned

**1**
*a* *Righteous, described,* Psa. 64:10.
*b* *Commandment, enjoining Christian tolerance toward the weak,* Deut. 8:2.
*c* *Charitableness, enjoined,* Prov. 10:12.
*d* *Kindness, enjoined,* Acts 28:2.
*e* *Love, of man for man,* 1 John 4:7.
*f* *Fellowship, of the righteous,* 1 Cor. 1:9.
*g* *Altruism,* Acts 20:35.
*h* *Weak, duty of strong to,* 1 Cor. 8:9.
*i* *Commandment, enjoining self-denial,* Deut. 8:2.
*j* *Unselfishness,* 1 Cor. 10:24.
*k* *Self-denial,* Mark 8:34.

[s]peace, and things wherewith one
may [t]edify[G] another.
20 For meat[G] destroy not the
work of God. All things indeed
*are* [9]pure; but *it is* evil for that
man who eateth with offence.
21 *It is* good neither to [u]eat
[v]flesh[G], nor to [u]drink [w]wine, nor
*any thing* whereby thy brother
[a]stumbleth, [10]or is offended, or
is made weak.
22 Hast thou [x]faith? have *it* to
thyself before God. Happy *is* he
that *,[11]condemneth not himself
in that thing which he alloweth.
23 And he that †,[y]doubteth is
[12]damned[G] if he eat, because *he
eateth* not of faith: for whatsoever
*is* not of faith is [z]sin.[T]

## CHAPTER 15

*The strong must bear with the weak: we may not please ourselves, for so did not Christ. 7 We must receive one another, as Christ received us, both Jews and Gentiles. 15 Paul excuses his manner of writing, 28 and promises to see them, 30 and requests their prayers.*

WE then that are [a]strong
[b,c]ought to [d,e,f,g]bear the
infirmities[G] of the [h]weak, and
[i,j,k]not to [l]please ourselves.
2 [i]Let every one of us please *his*
[m]neighbour for [1]*his* good to [n]edification[G].
3 For even Christ [o]pleased not
himself; but, as it is [p]written,
[q]The reproaches of them that
reproached thee fell on me.[Q]
4 For whatsoever things were
written aforetime[G] were written
for our [n]learning, that we through
[r]patience and [s]comfort of the
[p]scriptures might have [t]hope.
5[T] Now [u]the [v]God of patience
and [2,s]consolation[G] grant you to
be [w]likeminded one toward another
according to [x]Christ Jē'ṣus:
6 That ye may with [w]one mind
*and* one mouth [y]glorify[G] God,
even the [z]Father of our [a]Lord
Jē'ṣus Christ.[T]
7 Wherefore [b,c]receive ye one
another, [d]as Christ also received
us to the glory of God.
8 [3]Now I say that Jē'ṣus Christ
was a minister of the [e]circumcision[G]
for the [f]truth of God, to confirm
the [g]promises *made* unto the
fathers:[S T Q]
9 And that the [h]Gĕn'tīleṣ[G] might
[i]glorify[G] God for *his* [j,k]mercy; as
it is written, [4,l]For this cause I
will confess to thee among the
Gĕn'tīleṣ[G], and sing unto thy
name.[Q]
10 And again he saith, [m,n]Rejoice,
ye Gĕn'tīleṣ[G], with his people.[Q]
11 And again, [o,p]Praise the
Lord, all ye Gĕn'tīleṣ[G]; and [5]laud[G]
him, all ye people.[Q]
12 And again, [q]Ē-ṣā'ias saith,
[r,s]There shall be a [t]root of Jĕs'se,
and he that shall rise to reign
over the Gĕn'tīleṣ[G]; in him shall
the [h]Gĕn'tīleṣ[G] [6,u]trust.[T Q]
13 [v]Now the God of [u]hope fill
you with all [n,w]joy and [w,x]peace
in [y]believing, that ye may
abound in hope, through the
power of the [z]Holy[G] Ghost.[G T]
14 And [a]I myself also am persuaded
of you, my brethren, that
ye also are [b]full of goodness,
[b]filled with all [c]knowledge, [b]able
also to admonish[G] one another.

*w* *Unity, of the righteous,* Psa. 133:1.
*x* *Jesus, Messiah,* Matt. 1:21.
2 R. V. comfort
**6**
*y* *Glorifying God,* Luke 5:25.
*z* *God, fatherhood of,* Gen. 2:2.

*a* *Jesus, lordship of,* Matt. 1:21.
**7**
*b* *Fraternity,* Zech. 11:14.
*c* *Fellowship, of the righteous,* 1 Cor. 1:9.
*d* *Jesus, our example,* Matt. 1:21.
**8**
*e* *Circumcision, figurative,* Gen. 17:10.
*f* *God, faithfulness of,* Gen. 2:2.
*g* *Covenant, of God with men,* Deut. 29:1.
3 R. V. For I say that Christ hath been made a minister
**9**
*h* *Gentiles, conversion of,* Acts 10:45.
*i* *Glorifying God,* Luke 5:25.
*j* *God, mercy of,* Gen. 2:2.
*k* *Salvation,* Acts 16:17.
*l* 2 Sam. 22:50.
4 R. V. Therefore will I give praise unto thee among the Gentiles,
**10**
*m* Deut. 32:43.
*n* *Joy,* Psa. 5:11.
**11**
*o* Psa. 117:1.
*p* *Praise,* Psa. 150:1.
5 R. V. let all the peoples praise him.
**12**
*q* Or, *Isaiah,* Isa. 1:1.
*r* Isa. 11:10.
*s* *Prophecies concerning the Messiah, and their fulfillment,* Gen. 12:3.

*l* *Selfishness,* 2 Tim. 3:2. **2** *m* *Neighbor, charitableness toward, enjoined,* Luke 10:29. *n* *Wisdom, spiritual,* Prov. 2:2. 1 R. V. that which is good unto edifying. **3** *o* *Example, Christ our, in self-renunciation,* John 13:15. *p* *Word of God,* Psa. 119:9. *q* Psa. 69:9. **4** *r* *Patience, a grace of the righteous,* Luke 8:15. *s* *Afflictions, consolation in,* Psa. 34:19. *t* *Hope,* Prov. 13:12. **5** *u* *Benedictions, apostolic,* Deut. 21:5. *v* *God, long-suffering of,* Gen. 2:2.

*t* *Jesus, prophecies concerning,* Matt. 1:21. *u* *Hope,* Prov. 13:12. 6 R. V. hope. **13** *v* *Prayer, intercessory,* Acts 6:4. *w* *Spiritual Blessings, from God,* Eph. 1:3. *x* *Spiritual Peace,* Gal. 1:3. *y* *Faith in Christ,* John 6:69. *z* *Holy Spirit,* Acts 1:2. **14**—*a* *Paul,* Acts 13:9. *b* *Righteous, described,* Psa. 64:10. *c* *Wisdom, spiritual,* Prov. 2:2.

* **CONSISTENCY.** Neh. 5:9; Matt. 6:24; Luke 16:13; Rom. 14:22; 1 Cor. 10:21.

† **DOUBTING.** *In prayer,* Matt. 21:21; Jas. 1:6–8.
**Instances of:** *Abram,* Gen. 15:8. *Sarah,* Gen. 18:12–14. *Moses,* Ex. 3:11; 4:1, 10; 5:22, 23; 6:12; Num. 11:21, 22. *Israelites,* Ex. 14:10–12, 15; 1 Sam. 17:11, 24. *Gideon,* Judg. 6:13, 15. *Samuel,* 1 Sam. 16:1, 2. *Job,* Job 3; 4:3–6; 9:16–23; 30:20, 21. *Psalmist,* Psa. 22:2; 31:22; 42:5, 6; 49:5; 73:13–17; 77:3, 7–9. *Obadiah,* 1 Kin. 18:7–14. *Elijah,* 1 Kin. 19:13–18. *Jeremiah,* Jer. 1:6; 15:18; 32:24, 25; Lam. 3:8, 17, 18; 5:20, with chapters 1–5.
*Christ's disciples,* Matt. 8:23–27; 14:29–31; 17:14–21; 28:17; Mark 4:38, 40; 9:14–29; 16:10, 11; Luke 8:25; 9:40, 41; John 14:8–11; 20:24–27. *John the Baptist,* Matt. 11:2, 3. *Ananias,* Acts 9:13, 14. *Peter, walking on the sea,* Matt. 14:30. *Thomas,* John 20:25.

**15**
*d* *Zeal, exemplified,* 2 Cor. 7:11.
*e* *Apostles, commission of,* Luke 6:13.
7 R. V. measure,

15 Nevertheless, brethren, [a,d]I
have written the more boldly unto you in some [7]sort, as putting
you in mind, because of the
[e]grace that is given to me of God,[S]
16 That [a]I should be the *minister of Jē'ṣus [f]Christ to the
[g]Ġĕn'tīleṣ, ministering the [h]gos-
pel of God, that the offering up
of the Ġĕn'tīleṣ might be acceptable, being [i]sanctified by the
[j]Holy Ghost.[C T]

**16**
*f* *Jesus, Messiah,* Matt. 1:21.
*g* *Gentiles, conversion of,* Acts 10:45.
*h* *Gospel,* Mark 13:10.
*i* *Sanctification,* 1 Pet. 1:2.
*j* *Holy Spirit,* Acts 1:2.

*** MINISTER.** *Likened to sowers,* Psa. 126:6; Matt. 13: 3–8; Mark 4:3–8; Luke 8:5–8.

*Teachers of schools,* 1 Sam. 19:20; 2 Kin. 2:3, 5, 15; 4:38; 2 Chr. 15:3; 17:7–9; Acts 13:1.

*Hired,* Judg. 17:10; 18:4. *In politics,* 2 Sam. 15:24–27. *In war,* 2 Chr. 13:12, 14.

Influential in public affairs, 1 Sam. 12:6–10; *designate kings,* 1 Sam. 9:15, 16; 10:1; 16:1–13; *recommend civil and military appointments,* 2 Kin. 4:13.

Expostulate with rulers: *Samuel with Saul,* 1 Sam. 13: 11–14; 15:10–31; *Nathan with David,* 2 Sam. 12:1–14; *Elijah with Ahab,* 1 Kin. 18:17, 18.

*Recreation for,* Mark 6:31, 32. *Take leave of congregations,* Acts 20:17–38. *Personal bearing of,* Tit. 2:7, 8. *Preach without ecclesiastical authority,* Gal. 1:15–24; 2:1–9. *Work of, will be tried,* 1 Cor. 3:12–15. *Responsibility of,* Ezek. 3:17–21; 33:8; Matt. 10:14–40; Acts 18:6; 20:26, 27; 1 Cor. 1:23; 2 Cor. 2:15–17; 5:11, 18, 19; 1 Tim. 6:20. *Speaking evil of, forbidden,* Jude 8–10. *Clothed with authority,* 1 Thess. 5:12; Tit. 1:13, 14; 2:15; 3:1, 2, 8, 9; Heb. 13:6, 7, 17 (see Epistles to Timothy and Titus in full). *Clothed with salvation,* 2 Chr. 6:41. *Exhorted to grow in grace,* 1 Tim. 6:11; 2 Tim. 2:22.

*Marriage of,* Lev. 21:7–15; Matt. 8:14; Mark 1:30; 1 Cor. 9:5; 1 Tim. 3:2, 12; Tit. 1:5–7.

Incorruptible: *Balaam,* Num. 22:18, 37, 38; 23:8, 12; 24: 12–14, with 2 Pet. 2:15, 16; *Micaiah,* 1 Kin. 22:13, 14; *Peter,* Acts 8:18–23.

*Love of, for the church, exemplified by Paul,* Phil. 1:7; 1 Thess. 1:2–4; 2:8, 11. *Kindness to, Ebed-melech to Jeremiah,* Jer. 38:7–13. *Fear of,* 1 Sam 16:4. *Example to the flock,* Phil. 3:17; 2 Thess. 3:9; 1 Tim. 4:12; Tit. 2:1, 7, 8; 1 Pet. 5:3. *Intolerance of,* Matt. 15:23. *Message of, rejected,* Jer. 7:27; Ezek. 33:30–33. *God's care of,* 1 Kin. 17:1–16; 19:1–8; Matt. 10:29–31; Luke 12:6, 7. *Their calling, glorious,* 2 Cor. 3:7–11. *Discouragements of,* Isa. 30:10, 11; 53:1; Ezek. 3:8, 9, 14; Hab. 1:2, 3; Matt. 13:57; Mark 6:3, 4; Luke 4:24; John 4:44. *Defended,* Jer. 26:16–24; Acts 23:9. *Beloved,* Acts 20: 37, 38; 21:5, 6.

Sent forth two and two: *Disciples,* Mark 6:7; *Paul and Barnabas,* Acts 13:2, 3; *Judas and Silas,* Acts 15:27; *Barnabas and Mark,* Acts 15:37, 39; *Paul and Silas,* Acts 15:40; *Paul and Timothy,* Acts 16:1–4; *Paul and Titus,* 2 Cor. 8: 19, 23; *Timothy and Erastus,* Acts 19:22; *Titus and a companion,* 2 Cor. 12:18.

**Described as:** *Ambassadors for Christ,* 2 Cor. 5:20; Eph. 6:20. *Angels of the church,* Rev. 1:20; 2:1, 8, 12, 18; 3:1, 7, 14. *Apostles,* Luke 6:13; Rev. 18:20. *Apostles of Jesus Christ,* Tit. 1:1. *Men of God,* Deut. 33:1; 1 Tim. 6:11. *Messengers of the church,* 2 Cor. 8:23. *Messengers of the Lord of Hosts,* Mal. 2:7.

*Ministers, of God,* Isa. 61:6; 2 Cor. 6:4; *of the Lord,* Joel 2: 17; *of Christ,* Rom. 15:16; 1 Cor. 4:1; *of the sanctuary,* Ezek. 45:4; *of the Gospel,* Eph. 3:7; Col. 1:23; *of the Word,* Luke 1:2; *of the New Testament,* 2 Cor. 3:6; *of the church,* Col. 1:24, 25; *of righteousness,* 2 Cor. 11:15. *Overseers,* Acts 20:28. *Pastors,* Jer. 3:15; John 21:16, 17; Eph. 4:11. *Preachers,* Rom. 10:14; 1 Tim. 2:7. *Preachers of righteousness,* 2 Pet. 2:5.

*Servants, of God,* Tit. 1:1; Jas. 1:1; *of the Lord,* 2 Tim. 2:24; *of Jesus Christ,* Phil. 1:1; Jude 1. *Shepherds,* Jer. 23:4. *Soldiers of Christ,* 2 Tim. 2:3, 4. *Stars,* Rev. 1:20; 2:1. *Stewards, of God,* Tit. 1:7; *of the mysteries of God,* 1 Cor. 4:1. *Teachers,* Isa. 30:20; Eph. 4:11. *Watchmen,* Isa. 62:6; Ezek. 33:7.

**Call of,** Matt. 9:38; Rom. 10:14, 15; Eph. 4:11, 12; Heb. 5:4. *Aaron and his sons,* Ex. 28:1; 1 Chr. 23:13; Heb. 5:4. *Levites,* Num. 3:5–13; 16:5, 9. *Elisha,* 1 Kin. 19:16, 19. *Isaiah,* Isa. 6:8–10. *Jeremiah,* Jer. 1:5. *Jonah,* Jonah 1:1, 2; 3:1, 2. *The twelve apostles,* Matt. 4:18–22 (with Mark 1: 17–20); 9:9 (with Mark 2:14; Luke 5:27); 10:1–5; John 1:43. *The seventy disciples,* Luke 10:1, 2. *Paul,* Acts 13:2, 3; 20: 24; 22:12–15; 26:14–18; Rom. 1:1; 1 Cor. 1:1, 27, 28 (with 2 Cor. 1:1; Col. 1:1); 9:16–19; 2 Cor. 5:18–20; Gal. 1:15, 16; Eph. 3:7, 8; Col. 1:25–29; 1 Tim. 1:12–14; 2:7; 2 Tim. 1:11; Tit. 1:3. *Barnabas,* Acts 13:2, 3. *Archippus,* Col. 4:17. See footnote, CALL, *Personal,* Phil. 3:14.

**Character and qualifications of:** *Blameless,* 1 Tim. 3: 2–4, 7–13; Tit. 1:5–9. *Compassionate,* Heb. 5:2. *Consistent,* Rom. 2:21–23. *Courageous,* Jer. 1:7, 8, 17–19; Acts 20: 22, 24; 2 Tim. 1:7. *Diligent,* 2 Chr. 29:11; 1 Cor. 15:10. *Eager to serve,* Isa. 6:8. *Endued with power,* Luke 24:49; Acts 1:8; 4:8, 31; Gal. 2:8. *Gentle,* 2 Tim. 2:24, 25. *Holy,* Lev. 21:6; Isa. 6:7; 52:11; Mal. 2:6; John 17:17; 1 Cor. 9:27; 2 Tim. 2:21; Tit. 1:5–9. *Humble,* Matt. 20:25–28; 23:8, 10, 11; Luke 22:27; John 13:13–17; 15:20; 2 Cor. 4:5. *Meek,* 1 Cor. 4:12, 13; 2 Cor. 10:1. *Patient,* Jas. 5:10. *Persevering,* Matt. 10:22–24; 2 Cor. 4:1, 8–10. *Sincere,* 2 Cor. 4:1, 2. *Tactful,* 1 Cor. 9:18–23; 10:23, 28–33; 2 Cor. 6:3; 12:16. *Willing to suffer hardship,* 2 Tim. 2:3; 4:5. *Wise,* Mal. 2:7; Matt. 10: 16; Luke 6:39; 2 Cor. 4:6; 2 Tim. 2:7; 3:14, 16, 17.

*Not contentious,* 2 Tim. 2:14, 23, 24; Tit. 3:9. *Not of the world,* John 15:19; 17:16. *Not entangled with the world,* 2 Tim. 2:4, 5.

*Zealous,* Jer. 20:9; Ezek. 34:1–31; 2 Tim. 1:6–8; 4:2. See footnote, ZEAL, 2 Cor. 7:11.

Instances of zealous: *Titus,* 2 Cor. 8:16, 17; *Epaphroditus,* Phil. 2:25–30; *Epaphras,* Col. 4:12, 13; *John, in his vision,* Rev. 5:4, 5.

*Faithful,* 1 Sam. 2:35; Matt. 24:45; Luke 12:42–44; Acts 20:22, 24; 1 Cor. 2:2; 2 Cor. 6:4–7.

Instances of faithful: *Moses,* Deut. 4:26; 30:19; Heb. 3:2, 5; *Micaiah,* 2 Chr. 18:12, 13; *Azariah,* 2 Chr. 26:16–20; *Balaam,* Num. 22:18, 38; 23:8, 12; 24:12–14; *Nathan,* 2 Sam. 12:1–14; *Isaiah,* Isa. 22:4, 5; 39:3–7; *Jeremiah,* Jer. 17:16; 26:1–15; 28; 37:9, 10, 16–18; *John the Baptist,* Matt. 3:2–12; Mark 6:18; Luke 3:7–19; *the apostles,* Acts 4:19, 20, 31; 5: 21, 29–32; *Peter,* Acts 2:14–40; 3:12–26; 4:8–12; 8:18–23; *Paul,* Acts 15:25, 26; 17:16, 17; 19:8; 20:26, 27; *Tychicus,* Col. 4:7.

**Ordination of:** *Priests,* Ex. 29:1–9, 19–35; 40:12–16; Lev. 8:6–35; Heb. 7:21. *Matthias,* Acts 1:26. *Paul and Barnabas,* Acts 13:3. *Timothy,* 1 Tim. 4:14.

**Duties of,** Eph. 4:11, 12. *To preach,* Matt. 10:7; Rom. 1:14, 15. *To preach the unsearchable riches of Christ,* Eph. 3:8–12. *To admonish,* Isa. 58:1; 62:6, 7. *To exhort,* 2 Cor. 5:20; 1 Tim. 4:13; 6:17, 18; 2 Pet. 1:12–16. *To warn,* Jer. 7:25; Ezek. 33:1–9. *To reprove,* Ezek. 6:11; 34:2–31; Jonah 1:2; 2 Cor. 7:8; see footnote, REPROOF, Prov. 17:10. *To teach,* Lev. 10:11; 2 Kin. 17:27, 28; 2 Chr. 15:3; Ezra 7:10; Jer. 26:2; Ezek. 44:23; Matt. 10:7, 27; 28:19, 20; Acts 5:20; 6:4; 16:4; 18:9, 10; 26:16–18; Rom. 1:15; 12:6, 7; 2 Cor. 10: 8; Eph. 3:8–10; 4:11, 12; 1 Tim. 2:7; 4:13–16; 2 Tim. 2:2, 14, 15, 24, 25; 4:1, 2, 5. *To teach the lordship of Jesus,* 2 Cor. 4:5. *To serve,* Matt. 20:25–28; Mark 10:43–45; 2 Cor. 4:5. *To make converts to Christ,* Matt. 28:19, 20. *To win souls,* Prov. 11:30; John 4:35–38; 2 Cor. 5:18, 20. *To witness for Christ,* Luke 24:48; John 15:27; Acts 1:22; 10:42; 22:15. *To do the work of an evangelist,* 2 Tim. 4:5. *To give himself continually to prayer,* Acts 6:4. *To lament over the worldliness and sins of the church,* Joel 1:13–15; 2:17. *To speak boldly,* Eph. 6:20. *To minister to all without respect of persons or races,* Rom. 1:14, 15. *To exercise authority in the church,* Matt. 16:19; 18:18; 1 Cor. 4:19–21; 2 Cor. 7:8, 9, 12, 15; 13: 2, 3, 10; 2 Thess. 3:4; 1 Tim. 1:3, 4, 11, 18; 5:19–22; 1 Pet. 5:1–3. *To feed the flock,* Jer. 3:15; 23:4, 22, 28; John 21:15–17; Acts 20:28; 1 Cor. 14:1–33; 1 Pet. 5:2–4. *To strengthen the discouraged,* Luke 22:32. *To comfort the people,* Isa. 40:1, 2, 9, 11; 1 Thess. 3:2.

For further study of *Duties of,* see CHARGES DELIVERED TO, below.

**Charges delivered to,** Num. 18:1–7; Deut. 31:7, 8, 14–23; Josh. 1:1–9; Jer. 1:17–19; Ezek. 3:4; Matt. 10:5–42; Luke 10:1–16; 1 Tim. 1:18–20; 2:1–15; 3:1–16; 4:1–16; 5:1–22; 6:1–21; 2 Tim. 1:6–13; 2:1–26; 3:1–17; 4:1–8.

**Precepts for guidance of,** Jer. 1:7, 8, 17–19; Ezek. 2:6–8; Matt. 7:6; 10:7, 8, 11–13, 16, 25–28; Luke 10:1–11; Col. 4:17; 1 Tim. 1:3, 4, 11, 18, 19; 4:6, 7, 12–16; 5:1–3, 7–11, 19–22; 6:3, 4, 10–14, 17–21; 2 Tim. 1:6–8; 2:2–7, 14–16, 23–25; 4:1, 2, 5; 1 Pet. 5:1–4; 2 Pet. 1:12–16.

**Promises to,** Jer. 1:7–10, 17–19; 15:20, 21; Dan. 12:3; Matt. 10:28–31; 28:20; Luke 10:19; 12:11, 12; 24:49; Acts 1: 4, 5, 8; 18:9, 10; 1 Cor. 3:8; 9:9, 10; 1 Pet. 5:4.

**Joys of,** John 4:36–38; 2 Cor. 2:14; 7:6, 7; Phil. 2:16; 1 Thess. 2:13, 19, 20; 3:8, 9; 2 John 4; 3 John 4.

**Success attending:** *Jonah,* Jonah 1:5, 6, 9, 14, 16; 3: 4–10. *Apostles,* Acts 2:1–4, 41. *Philip,* Acts 8:6, 8, 12, 36, 38. *Peter,* Acts 9:32–35; 10:44–48. *Paul,* Acts 13:42–44; 14:1, 8–10, 27; 17:34; 28:24; 1 Cor. 4:15; 9:2; 15:11; 2 Cor. 3: 2, 3; 12:12; Phil. 2:16; 1 Thess. 1:5. *Apollos,* Acts 18:24–28. See footnote, RELIGIOUS REVIVALS, Hab. 3:2.

**Trials and Persecutions of:** *Foretold,* Matt. 10:16–27; (with John 13:16); 23:34.

INSTANCES OF TRIALS AND PERSECUTIONS OF: *Elijah,* 1 Kin. 17:2–7; 18:7–10; 19:1–10. *Micaiah,* 1 Kin. 22:24–

17 I have therefore [s]whereof I
may glory[C] through Jē′ṣus [j]Chrīst
in those things which pertain to
God.
18 For [a,d]I will not dare to
speak of any [9]of those [k]things
which [j]Chrīst hath not wrought
by me, [k]to make the [g]Ġĕn′-
tīleṣ obedient, by word and
deed,
19 Through mighty [k]signs and
wonders, by the power of the
[10,j]Spirit of God; so that from
[l]Jĕ-ru̧′să-lĕm, and round about
unto [m]Ĭl-lyr′ĭ-cŭm, [a,d]I have
fully [n]preached the [h]gospel of
[j]Chrīst. [T]
20 Yea, [11]so have I strived to
[n]preach the [h]gospel, not where
[j]Chrīst was named, lest I should
build upon another man's foundation:
21 But as it is [o]written, [p,q]To
whom he was not spoken of,[g] they
shall see: and they that have not
heard shall understand.[Q]
22 For which cause also I have
been much hindered from coming to you.
23 But now having no more
place in these parts, and [r]having
a great desire these many years
to come unto you;
24 Whensoever I take my journey into Spāin, I will come to
you: for I trust to see you in my
journey, and to be brought on
my way thitherward by you, if
first I be somewhat filled with
your [s]*company*.
25 But now I go unto [l]Jĕ-ru̧′-
să-lĕm to minister[C] unto the
saints.
26 For it hath pleased them of
[t]Măç-e-dō′nĭ-ȧ and [u]Ȧ-chā′iȧ to
[v]make a certain [w]contribution
for the [x]poor saints which are at
[l]Jĕ-ru̧′să-lĕm.
27 It hath pleased them verily; and their debtors they are.
For if the [g]Ġĕn′tīleṣ have been
made partakers of their spiritual
things, [y]their duty is also [z]to
minister unto them in carnal[C]
things.
28 When therefore I have performed this, and have sealed to
them this fruit, I will come by
you into Spāin.
29 And I am sure that, when I

**17**
8 R. V. my glorying in Christ Jesus in things pertaining to God.

**18**
*k Miracles, design of*, Luke 23:8.
9 R. V. things save those which Christ wrought through me, for the obedience of the Gentiles, by word and deed,

**19**
*l Jerusalem*, Judg. 19:10.
*m* Or, *Dalmatia*, 2 Tim. 4:10.
*n Preaching*, Matt. 9:35.
10 R. V. Holy Ghost;

**20**
11 R. V. making it my aim so to preach the gospel, not where Christ was already named, that I might not build

**21**
*o Word of God*, Psa. 119:9.
*p* Isa. 52:15.
*q Prophecies*, Dan. 9:24.

**23**
*r Love, of man for man*, 1 John 4:7.

**24**
*s Fellowship, of the righteous*, 1 Cor. 1:9.

**26**
*t Macedonia*, Acts 16:12.
*u Achaia*, Acts 18:12.
*v Liberality*, 1 Tim. 6:18.
*w Alms*, Matt. 6:2.
*x Poor, kindness to*, Prov. 21:13.

**27**
*y Thankfulness, enjoined*, Acts 24:3.
*z Reciprocity*, 1 Cor. 9:11.

---

27; 2 Chr. 18:23–26. *Hanani*, 2 Chr. 16:10. *Zechariah*, 2 Chr. 24:20–22, 25; Matt. 23:35; Luke 11:51. *Jeremiah*, Jer. 11:19–21; 15:10, 15; 17:15–18; 18:18–23; 20:1–3, 7–18; 32:2, 3; 33:1; 37:15–21; 38:6–13; 39:15; 43:1–7; Lam. 3:53–55. *Ezekiel*, Ezek. 3:24, 25. *Amos*, Amos 7:10–17. *The apostles*, Acts 5:17–42. *Peter*, Acts 12:3–19. *Paul*, Acts 9:23–25, 29, 30; 14:4–6, 11–20; 16:16–24; 17:5–10, 13, 14; 18:12, 13; 20:3; 21:27–40; 22:22–30; 23:10–35; 24:26, 27; 27:9–44; 1 Cor. 4:9–13; 2 Cor. 6:4–10; 7:5; 11:23–33; 12:7–10; Eph. 3:1, 13; 2 Tim. 1:8, 16; 2:9; 4:16, 17; see footnote, PAUL, *Persecutions of*, Acts 13:9.

**Duty of the church to:** *To esteem*, 1 Thess. 5:13. *To pray for*, 2 Chr. 6:41; Psa. 132:9; Matt. 9:37, 38; Acts 4:29; 12:5; Rom. 15:30–32; 2 Cor. 1:11; Eph. 6:18–20; Phil. 1:19; Col. 4:2–4; 1 Thess. 5:25; 2 Thess. 3:1, 2; Philemon 22; Heb. 13:18, 19. *To imitate the example of*, 1 Cor. 11:1; Phil. 3:17; 2 Thess. 3:7; Heb. 13:7. *To submit to the authority of*, 1 Cor. 11:2; 16:16; 1 Thess. 5:12, 13; 2 Thess. 3:4; Heb. 13:7, 17.

*To provide for the support, of priest and Levite*, Num. 18:20, 21; Deut. 10:9; 14:27; 18:1–4; Josh. 13:14; 18:7; Jer. 31:14; Ezek. 44:28; *of the twelve apostles*, Matt. 10:9, 10; Mark 6:8; Luke 22:35; *of the seventy disciples*, Luke 10:7, 8; *of Christian preachers*, 1 Cor. 9:3, 4, 7–14; Gal. 6:6; Phil. 4:10–18; 1 Tim. 5:18.

*Right of support, waived by Paul*, Acts 20:33–35; 1 Cor. 9:15–18; 2 Cor. 11:7–10; 12:13–18; 1 Thess. 2:5, 6, 9; 2 Thess. 3:7–9.

**Hospitality to:** INSTANCES OF, Matt. 10:11–14; Luke 10:5–11. *To Elijah, by the woman of Zarephath*, 1 Kin. 17:10–16. *To Elisha, by the Shunammite woman*, 2 Kin. 4:8–10. *To Paul, by Lydia*, Acts 16:14, 15, 40; *by the Philippian jailer*, Acts 16:33 34; *by Aquila and Priscilla*, Acts 18:3; *by Justus*, Acts 18:7; *by Philip the evangelist*, Acts 21:8–10; *by the barbarians*, Acts 28:1–10.

**False and corrupt**, 1 Kin. 12:31; Neh. 13:29; Jer. 2:8; 6:13, 14; 8:10, 11; 12:10; Lam. 2:14; Ezek. 22:25, 28; 44:8, 10; Hos. 9:7, 8; Zeph. 3:4; Mal. 1:6–10; 2 Tim. 4:3. *Mercenary*, 1 Sam. 8:3; Isa. 56:11; Mic. 3:11. *Presumptuous*, Deut. 18:20–22; John 5:43. *Insincere*, Phil. 1:15, 16. *Brutish*, Jer. 10:21. *Adulterous*, 1 Sam. 2:22; Jer. 23:14; Hos. 6:9. *Murderous*, Hos. 6:9.

*Pervert the truth*, 2 Cor. 2:17; 11:3, 4, 13–15; Gal. 1:6–8; 1 Tim. 4:1–3, 7. *Cause the people to err*, Isa. 3:12; Jer. 50:6. *Addicted to strong drink*, Isa. 28:7; 56:12. *Indifferent to good and evil*, Isa. 56:10; Ezek. 22:26.

*Desired by the wicked*, Isa. 30:10, 11; Jer. 5:13, 14, 30, 31; Amos 2:11, 12; Mic. 2:11.

*Denunciations against*, Isa. 5:20; Jer. 23:11–40; Lam. 4:13, 14; Ezek. 13:1–23; 34:1–10, 16–22; Matt. 23:4–7, 13–36; 2 Pet. 2:1–22.

*Warnings against*, Deut. 13:1–4; Isa. 8:19, 20; Jer. 14:13–16; 27:9–18; Matt. 5:19; 7:15–23; 15:9, 13, 14 (with Luke 6:39); 23:3, 4, 13; 24:4, 5, 11, 24, 26, 48–51; Mark 13:21, 22; Luke 21:8; John 10:1, 5, 8, 10, 12, 13; Acts 20:29, 30; Eph. 4:14; Phil. 3:2; Col. 2:4, 8, 18, 19; 1 Tim. 1:3–7; 6:3–5; 2 Tim. 2:17 18; Tit. 1:10–14; 1 John 2:18, 19, 22, 23, 26; 4:1–3, 5; 2 John 7, 10, 11; Rev. 2:12, 14, 15, 18, 20–23.

*Judgments upon*, Isa. 29:10, 11; Hos. 5:1; Gal. 5:10.

*Punishment of*, Deut. 13:1, 5; 18:20; Isa. 43:27, 28; Jer. 14:15; 23:1, 2, 11, 15, 21; 27:9–18; Lam. 4:13, 14; Ezek. 14:9, 10; Hos. 4:5, 6, 8–13; Mic. 3:5–7; Zech. 10:3; 13:2–5; Mal. 2:1–3, 8, 9; Luke 12:45, 46; 2 Pet. 2:3; Jude 4, 11.

INSTANCES OF FALSE AND CORRUPT: *Nadab and Abihu*, Lev. 10:1, 2. *Korah, Dathan, and Abiram*, Num. 16:1–40. *Eli's sons*, 1 Sam. 2:12–17, 22, 25, 29, 34; 3:13; 4:11. *Samuel's sons*, 1 Sam. 8:1–3. *The old prophet of Beth-el*, 1 Kin. 13:11–32. *Jonathan*, Judg. 17:7–13; 18. *Noadiah*, Neh. 6:14. *Priests under, Jehoash*, 2 Kin. 12:7; 2 Chr. 24:5, 6; *Hezekiah*, 2 Chr. 30:3, 5. *Priests and Levites*, Ezra 2:61, 62; 9:1, 2; 10:18–24; Neh. 13:4–9, 28, 29; Zech. 7:5, 6. *Hananiah*, Jer. 28. *Jonah*, Jonah 1:1–6. *Scribes and Pharisees*, Matt. 23:15, 16; *Caiaphas*, Matt. 26:2, 3, 57, 63–65; John 11:49–51; 18:14. *Judas*, Matt. 26:14–16, 21–25, 47–50; 27:3–5; John 12:4–6; Acts 1:18. *Judaizing Christians*, Gal. 3:1, 2; 4:17; 6:12, 13. *Hymenæus*, 1 Tim. 1:20; 2 Tim. 2:17, 18. *Alexander*, 1 Tim. 1:20. *Philetus*, 2 Tim. 2:17, 18.

come unto you, I shall come in
the fulness of the blessing[G] [12]of
the [a]gospel of Christ.
30 Now I beseech you, brethren, for the Lord Jē'ṣus Christ's
sake, and for the love of the
Spirit, that ye [b]strive together
with me in *your* [c]prayers to God
for me;[T]
31 That I may be delivered
from [d]them that [13]do not believe
in [e]Jū-dæ'ȧ; and that my service
which I *have* for [f]Jē-ru̥'sȧ-lĕm
may be accepted[G] of the saints;
32 That I may come unto you
with [g]joy by the [h]will of God,
and [14]may [i]with you be refreshed.
33 Now [j]the God of [k]peace *be*
with you all. Amen.

## CHAPTER 16

*The apostle commends Phebe, and desires the brethren to greet many; 17 he beseeches them to mark those who cause divisions and offences, 21 and after sundry salutations ends with praise and thanks to God.*

I COMMEND unto you Phē'-
bē our sister, which is a
servant of the [a]church which is
at [b]Çĕn'chre-ȧ:
2 That ye [c]receive her in the
Lord, as becometh[G] saints,[G] and
that ye assist her in whatsoever
[1]business she hath need of you:
for [d]she hath been a succourer[G] of
many, and of myself also.
3 [2,e]Greet [f]Pris-çĭl'lȧ and [f]Ăq'-
uĭ lȧ my helpers in Christ Jē'ṣus:
4 Who [g,h,i]have for my life laid
down their own necks: unto
whom not only I give [j]thanks,
but also all the churches of the
[k]Ġĕn'tīleṣ.
5 Likewise [2,e]*greet* the church
that is in their [l]house. Salute[G] my
[m]wellbeloved Ē-pæn'e-tŭs, who
is the [n]first fruits of [o]Ā-chā'iȧ
unto Christ.
6 [2,e]Greet [d]Mā'rȳ, who bestowed much labour on [3]us.
7 [e]Salute[G] Ăn-drō-nī'cus and
Jū'niȧ, my kinsmen, and my fel-
lowprisoners, who are of note
among the [p]apostles, who also
[4]were in Christ before me.
8 [2,e]Greet Ăm'plĭ-as my [m]be-
loved in the Lord.
9 [e]Salute[G] Ûr'băne, our helper
in Christ, and Stā'chȳs my [m]be-
loved.
10 [e]Salute[G] Ā-pĕl'lēṣ approved
in Christ. Salute them which are
of Ăr-ĭs-to-bū'lus' *household*.[G]
11 [e]Salute[G] Hē-rō'dĭ-ŏn my kinsman.[G] Greet them that be of the
*household* of Năr-çĭs'sus, which
are in the Lord.
12 [e]Salute[G] Trȳ-phē'nȧ and Trȳ-
phō'sȧ, who labour in the Lord.
Salute the [m]beloved Pĕr'sis,
which laboured much in the
Lord.
13 [e]Salute[G] Ru̥'fus chosen in the
Lord, and his mother and mine.
14 [e]Salute[G] Ā-syn'crĭ-tŭs, Phlē'-
gon, Hĕr'mas, Păt'ro-băs, Hĕr'-
mēṣ, and the brethren which are
with them.
15 Salute[G] Phĭ-lŏl'o-gŭs, and
[d]Jū'liȧ, Nē're-ŭs, and his [d]sister,
and Ō-lȳm'pas, and all the saints
which are with them.
16 Salute[G] one another with an
holy [q]kiss. The churches of
Christ salute you.
17 Now I beseech you, brethren, [r]mark [s]them which [5]cause
[t,u]divisions and offences contrary to the [v]doctrine which ye
have learned; and [w,x,y]avoid
them.
18 For they that are such serve
not our [z]Lord [6]Jē'ṣus Christ, but
their own belly[G]; and by [7,a,b]good
words and fair speeches [c]deceive
the hearts of the simple.[G]
19 For your [d,e]obedience is come
abroad unto all *men*. I am glad
therefore on your behalf: but yet
I would have you [f,g]wise unto
that which is good, and [f]simple[G]
concerning evil.
20 And the God of [h]peace
shall bruise[G] [i]Sā'tan under your
feet shortly. [j]The grace of our

**29**
a *Gospel*, Mark 13:10.

**30**
b *Prayer, importunity in*, Acts 6:4.
c *Intercession, solicited*, Jer. 27:18.

**31**
d *Unbelievers*, 1 Cor. 6:6.
e *Judea*, Luke 5:17.
f *Jerusalem*, Judg. 19:10.
13 R. V. are disobedient in Judæa,

**32**
g *Joy*, Psa. 5:11.
h *Will of God, supreme rule of duty*, Mark 3:35.
i *Fellowship, of the righteous*, 1 Cor. 1:9.
14 R. V. together with you find rest.

**33**
i *Benedictions, apostolic*, Deut. 21:5.
k *Spiritual Peace*, Gal. 1:3.

**1**
a *Church, Christian*, Matt. 16:18.
b Acts 18:18.

**2**
c *Hospitality*, Rom. 12:13.
d *Women, good*, Prov. 31:10.
1 R. V. matter

**3**
e *Salutations*, Luke 1:44.
f *Aquila and Priscilla*, Acts 18:2.
2 R. V. Salute

**4**
g *Unselfishness*, 1 Cor. 10:24.
h Rom. 5:7.
i *Friendship*, Prov. 22:24.
j *Thankfulness, of man to man*, Acts 24:3.
k *Gentiles*, Acts 10:45.

**5**
l *House, used for worship*, Esth. 8:1.
m *Love, of man for man*, 1 John 4:7.
n *First Fruits, figurative*, Deut. 18:4.
o *Achaia*, Acts 18:12.

**6**
3 R. V. you.

**7**
p *Apostles*, Luke 6:13.
4 R. V. have been

**16**
q *Kiss, holy*, Ruth 1:9.

**17**
r *Church, discipline in*, Matt. 16:18.
s *False Teachers*, 2 Pet. 2:1.
t *Strife*, Prov. 20:3.
u *Church, dissensions in*, Matt. 16:18.
v *Doctrines of Jesus*, John 7:16.
w *Disfellowship*, Num. 15:31.
x *Evil Company, forbidden*, Prov. 13:20.
y *Fellowship, with the wicked, forbidden*, 1 Cor. 1:9.
5 R. V. are causing the divisions and occasions of stumbling, contrary

**18**
z *Jesus, lordship of*, Matt. 1:21.

a *Flattery*, Prov. 6:24.
b *Hypocrisy*, Jas. 3:17.
c *Deceit*, Psa. 36:3.
6 R. V. *omits* Jesus
7 R. V. their smooth and fair speech they beguile the hearts of the innocent.

**19**
d *Obedience*, Heb. 5:8.
e *Holiness*, Ex. 39:30.
f *Righteous, described*, Psa. 64:10.
g *Wisdom, spiritual*, Prov. 2:2.

**20**
h *Spiritual Peace*, Ga.. 1:3.
i *Satan*, Matt. 4:10.
j *Benedictions, apostolic*, Deut. 21:5.

[k]Lord Jē′ṣus Chrīst *be* with you.
[8]Amen.[T S Q]
21 [l]Tĭ-mō′the-ŭs my workfel-
low, and Lu̧′çius, and [m]Jā′son,
and Sō-sĭp′a-tēr, my kinsmen,
salute[G] you.
22 I Tēr′tius, who wrote *this*
epistle,[G] salute[G] you in the Lord.
23 [n]Gā′ius mine [o]host, and of
the whole church, saluteth[G] you.
Ē-răs′tus the [9,p]chamberlain[G] of
the [q]city saluteth you, and Quär′-
tus a [r]brother.
24 [10,j]The grace of our Lord
Jē′ṣus Chrīst *be* with you all.
Amen.
25 Now to him that is of power
to stablish[G] you according to my
gospel, and the [s]preaching of
Jē′ṣus Chrīst, according to the
revelation of the [t,u]mystery, which
[11]was kept secret since the world
began,
26 But now is made manifest,
and by the [v]scriptures of the
prophets, according to the commandment of the [w]everlasting
God, made known to all nations
for the [x]obedience of [y]faith:[S]
27 To [z]God only wise, *be* [a]glory
[b]through Jē′ṣus Chrīst for ever.
Amen.[S]

Written to the Romans from Corinthus, *and sent* by Phebe servant of the church at Cenchrea.

*k Jesus, lordship of,* Matt. 1:21.
8 R. V. *omits* Amen.
**21**
*l* Or, *Timothy,* 1 Cor. 4:17.
*m* Acts 17:5–7, 9.
**23**
*n* 1 Cor. 1:14.
*o Hospitality,* Rom. 12:13.
*p Chamberlain,* 2 Kin. 23:11.
*q Corinth,* Acts 18:1.
*r Brother,* Prov. 18:24.
9 R. V. treasurer
**24**
10 R. V. *omits this verse.*

**25**
*s Doctrines of Jesus,* John 7:16.
*t Mysteries, of redemption,* Mark 4:11.
*u Salvation, plan of,* Acts 16:17.
11 R. V. hath been kept in silence through times eternal.
**26**
*v Word of God,* Psa. 119:9.
*w God, eternity of,* Gen. 2:2.
*x Obedience,* Heb. 5:8.
*y Faith in Christ,* John 6:69.

**27** *z God, wisdom of,* Gen. 2:2.—*a Praise,* Psa. 150:1. *b Jesus, mediation of,* Matt. 1:21.

THE FIRST EPISTLE OF PAUL TO THE

# CORINTHIANS

## CHAPTER 1

*The apostle's salutation and thanksgiving. 10 He reproves their contentions. 18 The preaching of the cross the power of God. 26 No flesh may glory before him.*

[a]PAUL,[T] [b,c]called[G] *to be* an [d]apos-
tle of Jē′ṣus Chrīst through
the [e]will of God, and Sŏs′the-nēṣ
*our* brother,
2 Unto the [f]church of God
which is at [g]Cŏr′inth, to [h]them
that are [i]sanctified[G] in Chrīst Jē′-
ṣus, [b]called *to be* saints,[G] with all
that in every place [j]call upon the
name of Jē′ṣus Chrīst our [k]Lord,
both their's and our's:[S]
3 [l,m]Grace *be* unto you, and
[n]peace, from God our [o]Father,
and *from* the [k]Lord Jē′ṣus Chrīst.[T]
4 I [p]thank my God always [q]on
your behalf, for the [r]grace of
God which is given you by
Jē′ṣus Chrīst;
5 That in every thing ye are
[s]enriched by him, in all utterance, and *in* all [t]knowledge;
6 Even as the [u]testimony of
Chrīst was confirmed[G] in you:
7 So that ye come behind in no
[s]gift; waiting for the [1,v]coming
of our Lord Jē′ṣus Chrīst:
8 Who [w]shall also confirm you
unto the end, *that ye* [2]*may be*
blameless in the [v,x]day of our
Lord Jē′ṣus Chrīst.[S]
9 God *is* [y]faithful,[G] [3]by whom
ye were called unto the *fellow-

**1**
*a Paul,* Acts 13:9.
*b Call, personal,* Phil. 3:14.
*c Minister, call of,* Rom. 15:16.
*d Apostles,* Luke 6:13.
*e Will of God,* Mark 3:35.
**2**
*f Church, Christian,* Matt. 16:18.
*g Corinth,* Acts 18:1.
*h Righteous, described,* Psa. 64:10.
*i Sanctification,* 1 Pet. 1:2.
*j Jesus, worship of,* Matt. 1:21.

**4**
*p Thankfulness, to God,* Acts 24:3.
*q Love, of man for man,* 1 John 4:7.
*r Grace of God,* Rom. 4:16.
**5**
*s Spiritual Gifts,* 1 Cor. 12:4.
*t Wisdom, spiritual,* Prov. 2:2.
**6**
*u Preaching,* Matt. 9:35.
**7**
*v Jesus, second coming of* (as some interpret), Matt. 1:21.
1 R. V. revelation

*k Jesus, lordship of,* Matt. 1:21. **3** *l Benedictions, apostolic,* Deut. 21:5. *m Prayer, intercessory,* Acts 6:4. *n Spiritual Peace,* Gal. 1:3. *o God, fatherhood of,* Gen. 2:2.

**8** *w Righteous, promises to,* Psa. 64:10. *x Judgment, general* (as some interpret), 2 Pet. 3:7. 2 R. V. be unreproveable **9** *y God, faithfulness of,* Gen. 2:2. 3 R. V. through whom

* **FELLOWSHIP. With God,** Ex. 33:11, 14–17; Lev. 26:12; Amos 3:3; 2 Cor. 13:11; 1 John 1:3, 5–7. *Signified, in men walking with God,* Gen. 5:22, 24; 6:9; *in God dwelling with men,* Ex. 29:45; Psa. 101:6; Isa. 57:15; Zech. 2:10; John 14:23; 2 Cor. 6:16; 1 John 3:24; 4:13; Rev. 21:3, 4.

**With Christ,** Matt. 18:20; Luke 24:32; 1 Cor. 1:9; 10:16; 1 John 1:3; Rev. 3:20. *Signified, in Christ dwelling with men,* John 6:56; 14:23; Eph. 3:17; Col. 1:27; 1 John 3:24; *in our union with Christ,* John 15:1–8; Rom. 8:1, 10, 17; 12:5; 1 Cor. 12:12, 27; 2 Cor. 13:5; Eph. 5:30; Col. 3:3; 1 Thess. 5:9, 10; Heb. 2:11; 1 John 5:12, 20.

**With the Holy Spirit,** John 14:16, 17; Rom. 8:9; 1 Cor. 3:16; 2 Cor. 13:14; Gal. 4:6; Phil. 2:1.

**Of the righteous,** Psa. 55:14; Mal. 3:16; Rom. 1:12; 1 Cor. 12:13; Col. 2:2; 1 John 1:3, 7. *In unity of purpose,* Psa. 133:1–3; Amos 3:3; John 17:11, 21–23; Acts 1:14; 2:1, 42, 44–47; 17:4; 1 Pet. 3:8, 9. *In worship,* 1 Cor. 10:16, 17; Eph. 5:19; Col. 3:16. *In ministry,* 1 Thess. 4:18; 5:11, 14. *In brotherhood,* 1 Sam. 23:16; Matt. 23:8. *Exemplified,* Luke 24:13–15; Gal. 2:9.

**With the wicked,** Prov. 12:11. *Impoverishing,* Prov. 28:19. *Debauching,* Psa. 50:18; Prov. 29:24; 1 Cor. 15:33; 2 Pet.

ship of his [z]Son Jē′ṣus Christ our
[a]Lord.[S T Q]
10 Now [b]I beseech you, brethren, by the [c]name of our [a]Lord
Jē′ṣus Christ, that ye all speak
the same thing, and *that* there be
[d, e]no [f]divisions among you; but
*that* ye be [4]perfectly *joined together in the same mind and in
the same judgment.
11 For it hath been declared[G]
unto me of you, my brethren, by
them *which are of the house* of
Chlō′ē, that there are [f, g]conten-
tions among you.
12 Now this [b]I say, that every
one of [h]you saith, I am of Pa̤ul;
and I of [i]A-pŏl′los; and I of
[j]Çē′phas; and I of Christ.
13 [k]Is Christ divided? was
Pa̤ul [l]crucified for you? or were
ye [m]baptized in the name of
Pa̤ul?
14 I thank God that I [m]bap-
tized none of you, but [n]Cris′pus
and [o]Gā′ius;
15 Lest any should say that
I had [m]baptized in mine own
name.
16 And I [m]baptized also the
[p]household of [q]Stĕph′a-năs: besides, I know not whether I baptized any other.
17 For Christ sent me not to
baptize, but to [r, s]preach the
[t, u]gospel: not with [v, w]wisdom of
words, lest the [x, y, z]cross of
Christ should be [5]made of none
effect.
18 For the [6]preaching of the
[u, x]cross is to [a]them that [b]perish
foolishness; but unto us which
are [c, d]saved it is the [e]power of
God.[T]

19 For it is written, [f]I will
destroy the [g]wisdom of the
wise, and [7]will bring to nothing the understanding of the
prudent.[Q]
20 Where *is* the [g]wise? where *is*
the [h]scribe? where *is* the [i]dis-
puter of this world[G]? hath not
God made foolish the [g]wisdom
of this world?[Q]
21 For after that in the [j]wisdom
of God the world [8]by [g]wisdom
[b]knew not God, it pleased God
by the foolishness of [k]preaching
to [l]save them that [m]believe.[T]
22 For the [n]Jews require a
[o]sign, and the [p]Greeks seek after
[g]wisdom:
23 But [q]we preach Christ
[r, s]crucified, unto the [t]Jews a
[u]stumblingblock[G], and unto [9]the
[t]Greeks[G] foolishness;
24 But unto them which are
[v]called, both Jews and Greeks,
Christ the [e]power of God, and
the [j]wisdom of God.[S]
25 Because the foolishness of
God is wiser than men; and the
weakness of God is stronger than
men.[S]
26[S] For ye see your [v]calling,
brethren, how that not many
[g]wise men after the flesh, not
many mighty, not many noble,
*are called*:[T]
27 But God hath [w]chosen the
foolish things of the world [10, x]to
confound[G] the wise; and God
hath chosen the weak things of
the world [x]to confound[G] the
things which[G] are mighty;
28 And base[G] things of the world,
and things which are despised,
hath God [w]chosen, *yea*, and
things which are not, to bring to
nought[G] things that are:[S]

z *Jesus, divine sonship of*, Matt. 1:21.

a *Jesus, lordship of*, Matt. 1:21.

**10**

b *Paul*, Acts 13:9.
c *Name of Jesus*, John 14:13.
d *Church, unity of*, Matt. 16:18.
e *Unity, of the righteous*, Psa. 133:1.
f *Church, dissensions in*, Matt. 16:18.
4 R. V. perfected together

**11**

g *Strife*, Prov. 20:3.

**12**

h *Corinth, church of*, Acts 18:1.
i *Apollos*, Acts 19:1.
j Or, *Peter*, Mark 5:37.

**13**

k *Reproof, faithfulness in*, Prov. 17:10.
l *Crucifixion*, Mark 15:13.
m *Baptism, Christian*, Luke 20:4.

**14**

n Acts 18:8.
o Rom. 16:23.

**16**

p *Family, religion in*, 1 Chr. 13:14.
q 1 Cor. 16:15, 17.

**17**

r *Preaching*, Matt. 9:35.
s *Minister, duties of*, Rom. 15:16.
t *Gospel*, Mark 13:10.
u *Doctrines of Jesus*, John 7:16.
v *Reasoning*, Job 13:6.
w *Philosophy*, Col. 2:8.
x *Cross, figurative*, John 19:17.
y *Jesus, death of*, Matt. 1:21.
z *Atonement, by Jesus*, Lev. 17:11.
5 R. V. made void.

**18**

a *Unbelievers*, 1 Cor. 6:6.
b *Spiritual Blindness*, 2 Cor. 4:4.
c *Righteous, described*, Psa. 64:10. d *Salvation*, Acts 16:17. e *God, power of*, Gen. 2:2. 6 R. V. word of the cross is to them that are perishing foolishness; but unto us which are being saved

**19**

f Isa. 29:14.
g *Wisdom, worldly*, Prov. 2:2.
7 R. V. the prudence of the prudent will I reject.

**20**

h *Scribe*, 1 Kin. 4:3.
i *Reasoning*, Job 13:6.

**21**

j *God, wisdom of*, Gen. 2:2.
k *Doctrines of Jesus*, John 7:16.
l *Salvation, plan of*, Acts 16:17.
m *Faith in Christ, salvation by*, John 6:69.
8 R. V. through its wisdom knew not God, it was God's good pleasure through the foolishness of the preaching

**22**

n *Jews*, Neh. 4:2.
o *Miracles, demanded by unbelievers*, Luke 23:8.
p *Greeks*, Zech. 9:13.

**23**

q *Minister, faithful*, Rom. 15:16.
r *Crucifixion*, Mark 15:13.
s *Jesus, death of*, Matt. 1:21.
t *Unbelievers*, 1 Cor. 6:6.
u *Stumbling, figurative*, Isa. 8:14.
9 R. V. Gentiles

**24**

v *Call, personal*, Phil. 3:14.

**27**

w *Foreordination*, Rom. 8:30.
x *Agency, in salvation of men*, Mark 1:17.
10 R. V. that he might put to shame them that are wise; and God chose the weak things of the world, that he might put to shame the things that are strong;

---

2:18, 19. *Abhorred by the righteous*, Gen. 49:6; Psa. 6:8; 26: 4, 5.

*Forbidden*, Ex. 23:32, 33; 34:12–16; Num. 16:26; Deut. 7: 2–4; 12:30; 13:6–11; Josh. 23:6, 7; Ezra 9:12; 10:11; Psa. 1: 1; Prov. 1:10–15; 4:14, 15; 9:6; Isa. 52:11; Matt. 18:17; Rom. 16:17; 1 Cor. 5:9–11; 2 Cor. 6:14–17; Eph. 5:11; 2 Thess. 3:6, 14, 15; 2 Tim. 3:2–7; 2 Pet. 3:17; 2 John 9–11; Rev. 18:1–4.

*Punishment on account of*, Num. 25:1–8; 33:55, 56; Deut. 31:16, 17; Josh. 23:12, 13; Judg. 3:5–8; Psa. 106:34, 35, 41, 42.

INSTANCES OF: *Solomon*, 1 Kin. 11:1–8. *Rehoboam*, 1 Kin. 12:8, 9. *Jehoshaphat*, 2 Chr. 18:3; 19:2; 20:35–37. *Jehoram*, 2 Chr. 21:6. *Ahaziah*, 2 Chr. 22:3–5. *Israelites*, Num. 25:1–8; Ezra 9:1, 2; Ezek. 44:7. *Judas Iscariot*, Matt. 26:14–16.

AVOIDED: *Man of God*, 1 Kin. 13:7–10. *Children of the captivity*, Ezra. 6:21. *Nehemiah*, Neh. 6:2–4; 10:29–31. *David*, Psa. 101:4–7; 119:115. *Jeremiah*, Jer. 15:17. *Joseph of Arimathea*, Luke 23:51. *Church of Ephesus*, Rev. 2:6.

29 That no flesh should [y]glory [11]in his presence.

30 But of him are ye in [z]Christ Jē′ṣus, who of God is made unto us [a]wisdom, and [b]righteousness, and [c]sanctification, and [d]redemption:

31 That, according as it is written, He that glorieth, [e]let him glory in the Lord.

## CHAPTER 2

*The manner in which the apostle had preached the gospel to them. 6 The wisdom of God is revealed in the gospel, 14 but the natural man receives it not.*

AND [a]I, brethren, when I came to you, came [b]not with excellency of speech or of [c,d,e]wisdom, [f]declaring unto you the [1]testimony of God.

2 For [a,g]I determined [h,i]not to know any thing among you, save Jē′ṣus [j]Christ, and him [k,l]crucified.

3 And [b]I was with you in weakness, and in fear, and in much trembling.

4 And my speech and my [f]preaching [2]*was* not with enticing words of man's [c,d,e]wisdom, but in demonstration of the [m]Spirit and of power:

5 That your [n]faith should not stand in the [c,d,e]wisdom of men, but in the [o]power of God.

6 Howbeit we speak [p]wisdom among them that are perfect: yet not the [c]wisdom of this world, nor of the [3]princes of this world, that come to nought:

7 But we speak the wisdom of [q]God in a [l,r,s]mystery, *even* the hidden *wisdom,* which God [4,t]ordained before the world unto our glory:

8 Which [u]none of the princes of this world [5]knew: for had they known *it,* they would not have [v,w,x]crucified the [y]Lord of glory.

9 But as it is written, [6,z]Eye hath not seen, nor ear heard, neither have entered into the heart of man, the [a]things which [b]God [c]hath prepared for [d]them that [e]love him.

10 But God hath revealed *them* unto us by his [f]Spirit: for the Spirit searcheth all things, yea, the [g]deep things of God.

11 For what man knoweth the things of a man, save the [h]spirit of man which is in him? even so the things of [g]God knoweth no man, but the [f]Spirit of God.

12 Now [i]we have received, not the spirit of the world, but the [j]spirit which is of God; that we might know the [k]things that are freely given to us of God.

13 Which things also we speak, not in the words which man's [l]wisdom teacheth, but which the [7,f]Holy Ghost teacheth; comparing spiritual things with spiritual.

14 But the natural man [m]receiveth not the things of the [f]Spirit of God: for they are foolishness unto [n]him: [o]neither can he know *them,* because they are spiritually [8]discerned.

15 But he that is spiritual judgeth all things, yet he himself is judged of no man.

16 [p]For who hath known the mind of the [q]Lord, that he may instruct him? But we have the mind of Christ.

## CHAPTER 3

*The apostle speaks unto them as unto babes and as carnal. 5 He and Apollos, ministers by whom they believed. 11 Christ the only foundation. 16 Believers are the temple of God. 19 The wisdom of the world is foolishness with God.*

AND [a]I, brethren, could not speak unto you as unto spiritual, but as unto carnal, *even* as unto [b]babes in Christ.

2 I have fed you with [c]milk, and not with meat: for hitherto ye were not able *to bear it,* neither yet now are ye able.

**29**
y *Spiritual Boasting,* Rom. 3:27.
11 R. V. before God.

**30**
z *Jesus, savior,* Matt. 1:21.
a *Wisdom, spiritual,* Prov. 2:2.
b *Justification, through Christ,* Rom. 4:25.
c *Sanctification,* 1 Pet. 1:2.
d *Redemption of our Souls,* Eph. 1:7.

**31**
e *Spiritual Boasting,* Rom. 3:27.

**1**
a *Paul,* Acts 13:9.
b *Humility,* Prov. 22:4.
c *Wisdom, worldly,* Prov. 2:2.
d *Philosophy,* Col. 2:8.
e *Reasoning,* Job 13:6.
f *Preaching,* Matt. 9:35.
1 R. V. mystery

**2**
g *Zeal,* 2 Cor. 7:11.
h *Renunciation,* Luke 5:11.
i *Minister, character and qualifications of,* Rom. 15:16.
j *Jesus, Messiah,* Matt. 1:21.
k *Jesus, death of,* Matt. 1:21.
l *Atonement, by Jesus,* Lev. 17:11.

**4**
m *Holy Spirit,* Acts 1:2.
2 R. V. were not in persuasive words

**5**
n *Faith in Christ,* John 6:69.
o *God, power of,* Gen. 2:2.

**6**
p *Wisdom, spiritual,* Prov. 2:2.
3 R. V. rulers

**7**
q *God, wisdom of,* Gen. 2:2.
r *Mysteries, of redemption,* Mark 4:11.
s *Salvation, plan of,* Acts 16:17.
t *Foreordination,* Rom. 8:30.
4 R. V. foreordained before the worlds

**8** u *Spiritual Blindness,* 2 Cor. 4:4. v *Crucifixion,* Mark 15:13. w *Ignorance, sins of,* Acts 3:17. x *Zeal, without knowledge,* 2 Cor. 7:11. y *Jesus, lordship of,* Matt. 1:21. 5 R. V. knoweth:

**9**
z Isa. 64:4.
a *Spiritual Blessings, from God,* Eph. 1:3.
b *God, love of,* Gen. 2:2.
c *God, providence of,* Gen. 2:2.
d *Righteous, promises to,* Psa. 64:10.
e *Love, for God,* 1 John 4:19.
6 R. V. Things which eye saw not, and ear heard not, And which entered not into the heart of man, Whatsoever things God prepared for them that love him.

**10**
f *Holy Spirit,* Acts 1:2.
g *God, unsearchable,* Gen. 2:2.

**11**
h *Man, a spirit,* Job 4:17.

**12**
i *Righteous, described,* Psa. 64:10.
j *Wisdom, spiritual,* Prov. 2:2.
k *Mysteries, of redemption,* Mark 4:11.

**13**
l *Wisdom, worldly,* Prov. 2:2.
7 R. V. Spirit

**14**
m *Unbelief,* Heb. 3:12.
n *Unbelievers,* 1 Cor. 6:6.
o *Spiritual Blindness,* 2 Cor. 4:4.
8 R. V. judged.

**16**
p Isa. 40:13.
q *God, incomprehensible,* Gen. 2:2.

**1**
a *Paul,* Acts 13:9.
b *Babes, figurative,* Psa. 8:2.

**2**
c *Milk, figurative,* Job 10:10.

3 For ye are yet [*,d]carnal[G]: for
whereas *there is* among you
[1,d,e,f]envying, and [d,g]strife, and
[d,h,i]divisions, are ye not carnal,[G]
and walk as men?
4 For while one saith, I am
of [a]Paul; and another, I *am* of
[j]Ă-pŏl'los; are [k]ye not [2]carnal[G]?
5 [3]Who then is [a]Paul, and who
*is* [j]Ă-pŏl'los, but [l]ministers by
[m]whom ye [n]believed, even as the
Lord [o]gave to every man?
6[S] I have [p]planted, [j]Ă-pŏl'los
[p,q]watered; but [r]God gave the
[s]increase.
7 So then neither is he that
planteth any thing, neither he
that watereth; but [r]God that giveth the [s]increase.[S]
8 Now he that [p]planteth and
he that [q]watereth are one: and
every [t]man [u]shall receive his
own [v]reward according to his
own labour.
9 For we are [4,m]labourers together with God: ye are God's
[w]husbandry,[G] *ye are* God's building.
10 According to the [x]grace of
God which is given unto me, as a
wise [†]masterbuilder, I have laid
the foundation, and another
buildeth thereon. But let every
man [y]take heed how he buildeth
thereupon.
11 [z]For other foundation can
no man lay than that is laid,
which is [a]Jē'ṣus Christ.[Q]
12 Now if any [b]man build upon
this foundation [c]gold, [d]silver,
precious stones, wood, [e]hay,
stubble;
13 Every [b]man's work shall be
made manifest: for the [f,g]day
shall declare it, because it shall
be revealed by fire; and the fire
shall [5]try[G] every man's work of
what sort it is.
14 If any [b]man's work abide
which he hath built thereupon,
he shall receive a [h]reward.
15 If any man's work shall be
burned, he shall suffer loss: but
he himself shall be saved; yet so
as by[G] fire.
16 Know ye not that ye are the
[i,j]temple of God, and *that* the
[k]Spirit of God [l]dwelleth in you[T S]?
17 If any man [6]defile[G] the [i]tem-
ple of God, him shall God [m]de-
stroy; for the temple of God is
[n]holy, which [i]*temple* ye are.
18 Let no man [o]deceive[G] himself.
If any man [7]among you [p]seemeth
to be [q]wise in this world,[G] [r,s]let
him become a fool, that he may
[8]be [t]wise.
19 For the [q]wisdom of this
world is foolishness with God.
For it is written, [u]He taketh the
wise in their own craftiness.[Q]
20 And again, [v]The Lord
[w]knoweth the [9,x]thoughts of the
[q]wise, that they are vain.[G S Q]
21[S] Therefore [y]let no man glory
in men. For [z]all things are
your's;
22 Whether [a]Paul, or [b]Ă-pŏl'-
los, or [c]Çē'phas, or the world, or
[d]life, or [e]death, or things present,
or things to come; all are your's;
23 And ye are Christ's; and
[f]Christ *is* God's.[S T]

## CHAPTER 4

*Paul and his fellow-laborers, the ministers of Christ. 7 Vain boasting reproved. 9 The apostles a spectacle to the world, angels, and men. 14 As his beloved sons the apostle warns the Corinthians. 16 His example to be imitated. 20 Kingdom of God not in word, but in power.*

LET a man so account[G] of
us, as of the [a]ministers[G] of
Christ, and [b]stewards of the
mysteries[G] of God.

**3**
*d Sin, fruits of,* Rom. 5:12.
*e Envy,* Prov. 14:30.
*f Jealousy,* Psa. 78:58.
*g Strife,* Prov. 20:3.
*h Dissension, in churches,* 1 Cor. 1:10–13; 11:18, 19.
*i Church, dissensions in,* Matt. 16:18.
1 R. V. jealousy and strife, are ye not carnal, and walk after the manner of men?

**4**
*j Apollos,* Acts 19:1.
*k Corinth, church of,* Acts 18:1.
2 R. V. men?

**5**
*l Minister,* Rom. 15:16.
*m Agency, in salvation of men,* Mark 1:17.
*n Faith in Christ,* John 9:69.
*o Spiritual Gifts,* 1 Cor. 12:4.
3 R. V. What then is Apollos? and what is Paul? Ministers through whom ye believed; and each as the Lord gave to him.

**6**
*p Works,* 2 Tim. 1:9.
*q Irrigation, figurative,* Eccl. 2:6.
*r God, power of,* Gen. 2:2.
*s Spiritual Blessings, from God,* Eph. 1:3.

**8**
*t Minister, promises to,* Rom. 15:16.
*u Judgment, according to opportunity and works,* 1 Pet. 1:17.
*v Reward, a motive, to faithfulness,* Matt. 5:12.

**9**
*w Husbandman, figurative,* Matt. 21:33.
4 R. V. God's fellow-workers:

**10** *x Grace of God,* Rom. 4:16. *y Watchfulness, enjoined,* Matt. 24:42.
**11** *z Jesus, savior,* Matt. 1:21.—*a Jesus, head of church,* Matt. 1:21.
**12** *b Minister, work of, will be tried,* Rom. 15:16. *c Gold, figurative,* Ezek. 7:19. *d Silver, figurative,* 1 Chr. 28:14. *e* Prov. 27:25.
**13** *f Judgment, the general* (as some interpret), 2 Pet. 3:7. *g Jesus, second coming of* (as some interpret), Matt. 1:21.

5 R. V. prove each man's

**14**
*h Reward, a motive, to faithfulness,* Matt. 5:12.

**16**
*i Temple, figurative,* 1 Kin. 6:17.
*j Righteous, described,* Psa. 64:10.
*k Holy Spirit, Christians are temples of,* Acts 1:2.
*l Fellowship, with the Holy Spirit,* 1 Cor. 1:9.

**17**
*m Wicked, punishment of,* Psa. 73:3.
*n Holiness,* Ex. 39:30.

**18**
*o Delusion,* 2 Thess. 2:11.
*p Conceit, warnings against,* Prov. 26:5.
*q Wisdom, worldly,* Prov. 2:2.
*r Paradox,* 2 Cor. 12:4.
*s Humility, enjoined,* Prov. 22:4.
*t Wisdom, spiritual,* Prov. 2:2.
7 R. V. thinketh that he is wise among you in this world,
8 R. V. become

**19**
*u* Job 5:13.

**20**
*v* Psa. 94:11.
*w God, knowledge of,* Gen. 2:2.
*x Heart, known to God,* Psa. 44:21.
9 R. V. reasonings

**21**
*y False Confidence, warnings against,* Psa. 30:6.
*z Righteous, promises to,* vs. 21, 22; Psa. 64:10.

**22**
*a Paul,* Acts 13:9.
*b Apollos,* Acts 19:1.
*c* Or, *Peter,* Mark 5:37.
*d Life,* Eccl. 8:15.
*e Death, of the righteous,* Num. 23:10.

**23**
*f Jesus, relation of, to the Father,* Matt. 1:21.

**1** *a Minister, duties of,* Rom. 15:16. *b Steward, figurative,* Gen. 43:19.

* **CARNAL MIND.** *Is in conflict, with the inward man,* Rom. 7:14–22; *with the Holy Spirit,* Gal. 5:17. *Is at enmity with God,* Rom. 8:6–8; Jas. 4:4. *In children of wrath,* Eph. 2:3. *To be crucified,* Rom. 8:13; Gal. 5:24. *Excludes from kingdom of God,* Gal. 5:19–21.

† **MASTER WORKMAN,** Prov. 8:30 (R. V.); 1 Cor. 3:10. **Instances of:** *Tubal-cain,* Gen. 4:22. *Of the tabernacle, Bezaleel,* Ex. 31:2–11; 35:30–35; *Aholiab,* Ex. 31:6–11; 35:34, 35. *Of the temple, Hiram,* 1 Kin. 7:13–50; 2 Chr. 2:13, 14; 4:11–18.

2 Moreover it is required in
[a,b]stewards, that a man be found
[c,d]faithful.
3 But with [e]me it is a very small
thing that I should be [f]judged of
you, or of man's judgment: yea,
I judge not mine own self.
4 For [e,g]I know nothing [1]by[C]
myself; yet am I not hereby justified: but he that [h]judgeth me is
the Lord.[S] [Q]
5 Therefore [i]judge nothing before the [j]time, until the [k]Lord
[l]come, who both will bring to light
the hidden things of [m]darkness,
and will make manifest the counsels[C] of the hearts: and [n]then shall
every man have praise of God.
6 And these things, brethren, [e]I
have in a figure transferred to
myself and *to* [o]Ȧ-pŏl′los for your
sakes; that ye might learn in us
not to [2]think *of men* above that
which is written, that [p]no one
of you be [q,r]puffed[C] up for [s]one
against another.
7 For who maketh thee to differ
[3]*from another*? and [t]what hast
thou that thou didst not receive?
now if thou didst receive *it*, why
dost thou [r]glory, as if thou hadst
not received *it*?[S]
8 [4,u,v]Now ye are full, now ye
are rich, ye have reigned as kings
without us: and I would[C] to God
ye did reign, that we also might
reign with you.
9 For I think that God hath set
forth us the [w,x]apostles last, [5]as it
were [y]appointed to death: for we
are made a [z]spectacle unto the
world, and to [a]angels, and to men.
10 [b]We *are* [c]fools for Chrīst's
sake, but [d]ye *are* wise in Chrīst;
[b]we *are* [c]weak, but [d]ye *are* strong;
[d]ye [6]*are* honourable, but [b]we *are*
[c]despised.[C]
11 Even unto this present hour
we both [e,f]hunger, and [f]thirst,
and are [f]naked, and are [f]buf-
feted,[C] and [f]have no certain[C]
dwellingplace;
12 [g]And [7,h]labour, working with
our own hands: being [i]reviled,
we [j,k]bless; being [i]persecuted, we
[8,j]suffer[C] it: [Q]
13 Being [l]defamed, we intreat:[C]
we are made as the filth of the
world, *and are* the offscouring of
all things unto this day.[Q]
14 I write not these things to
shame you, but [9]as my [m]beloved
sons I warn *you*.
15 For though ye have ten thousand [n]instructors in Chrīst, yet
*have ye* not many fathers: for in
Chrīst Jē′ṣus [o]I have begotten
you through the [p]gospel.
16 Wherefore I beseech you, be
ye [10]followers of [q]me.
17 For this cause have I sent
unto you *Tĭ-mō′the-ŭs, who is
my [m,r]beloved son, and [s]faithful
in the Lord, who shall [q]bring
you into remembrance of my
ways which be in Chrīst, as I
[n]teach every where in every
church.[S]
18 Now some are puffed[C] up, as
though I [11]would not come to you.
19 But I will come to you
shortly, if the [t]Lord [u]will, and
will know, not the [12]speech of
them which are puffed up, but
the [v,w]power.

**2**
c *Faithfulness*, Luke 16:10.
d *Christian Graces*, Gal. 5:22.

**3**
e *Paul*, Acts 13:9.
f *Uncharitableness*, Matt. 7:1.

**4**
g *Conscience, approving*, Acts 23:1.
h *Jesus, judge*, Matt. 1:21.
1 R. V. against myself;

**5**
i *Charitableness, enjoined*, Prov. 10:12.
j *Judgment, the general* (as some interpret), 2 Pet. 3:7.
k *Jesus, lordship of*, Matt. 1:21.
l *Jesus, second coming of* (as some interpret), Matt. 1:21.
m *Darkness, figurative*, Gen. 1:2.
n *Judgment, according to opportunity and works*, 2 Pet. 3:7.

**6**
o *Apollos*, Acts 19:1.
p *Humility, enjoined*, Prov. 22:4.
q *Pride*, Prov. 16:18.
r *Spiritual Boasting*, Rom. 3:27.
s *Strife*, Prov. 20:3.
2 R. V. go beyond the things which are written;

**7**
t *Spiritual Blessings, from God*, Eph. 1:3.

**8**
u *Irony*, Mark 12:14.
v *Reproof, faithful, ness in*, Prov. 17:10.
4 R. V. Already are ye filled, already ye are become rich, ye have reigned without us: yea and I would that ye did reign,
**9** w *Apostles*, Luke 6:13. x *Minister, trials and persecutions of*, Rom. 15:16. y *Persecutions, of the righteous*, John 15:20. z *Games, figurative*, 1 Cor. 9:24.—a *Angel*, Heb. 1:13. 5 R. V. of all, as men doomed to death:

**10**
b *Humility*, Prov. 22:4.
c *Minister, character and qualifications of*, Rom. 15:16.
d *Irony*, Mark 12:14.
6 R. V. have glory, but we have dishonour.

**11**
e *Hunger*, Neh. 9:15.
f *Suffering for Christ*, Phil. 1:29.

**12**
g *Self-denial*, Mark 8:34.
h *Industry*, 1 Kin. 11:28.
i *Persecution, of the righteous*, John 15:20.
j *Meekness*, Psa. 45:4.
k *Forgiveness, of enemies*, Matt. 18:21.
7 R. V. toil,
8 R. V. endure;

**13**
l *Slander*, Prov. 10:18.

**14**
m *Love, of man for man*, 1 John 4:7.
9 R. V. to admonish you as my beloved children.

**15**
n *Instruction, in religion*, Prov. 23:23.
o *Agency, in salvation of men*, Mark 1:17.
p *Gospel*, Mark 13:10.

**16**
q *Example, Paul our*, John 13:15.
10 R. V. imitators

**17**
r *Friendship*, Prov. 22:24.
s *Faithfulness*, Luke 16:10.

**18** 11 R. V. were not coming to you. **19** t *God, providence of*, Gen. 2:2. u *Will of God*, Mark 3:35. v *Spiritual Power*, Luke 24:49. w *Righteousness, fruits of*, Psa. 15:2. 12 R. V. word

*** TIMOTHY** (*honoring God*), called also TIMOTHEUS. *Parentage of*, Acts 16:1. *Reputation and Christian faith of*, Acts 16:2; 1 Cor. 4:17; 16:10; 2 Tim. 1:5; 3:15. *Circumcised; becomes Paul's companion*, Acts 16:3; 1 Thess. 3:2. *Left by Paul at Berea*, Acts 17:14. *Rejoins Paul at Corinth*, Acts 17:15; 18:5. *Sent into Macedonia*, Acts 19:22. *Rejoined by Paul; accompanies Paul to Asia*, Acts 20:1–4. *Sends salutation to the Romans*, Rom. 16:21. *Sent to the Corinthians*, 1 Cor. 4:17; 16:10, 11; see postcript to 1 Corinthians. *Preaches to the Corinthians*, 2 Cor. 1:19. *Sent to the Philippians*, Phil. 2:19, 23. *Sent to the Thessalonians*, 1 Thess. 3:2, 6. *Left by Paul in Ephesus*, 1 Tim. 1:3. *Confined with Paul in Rome*, Phil. 2:19–23; Philemon 1; Heb. 13:23; with the postscripts to Philippians and Philemon. *Ordained bishop of the Ephesians*, see postscript to 2 Timothy. *Joins Paul in the Epistle, to the Philippians*, Phil. 1:1; *to the Colossians*, Col. 1:1, 2; *to the Thessalonians*, 1 Thess. 1:1; 2 Thess. 1:1: *to Philemon*, Philemon 1. *Acts as Paul's amanuensis in writing the first letter to the Corinthians*, see postscript to 1 Corinthians. *Writes the letter to the Hebrews*, see postscript to Hebrews. *Zeal of*, Phil. 2:19–22; 1 Tim. 6:12. *Power of*, 1 Tim. 4:14; 2 Tim. 1:6. *Paul's love for*, 1 Cor. 4:17; Phil. 2:22; 1 Tim. 1:2, 18; 2 Tim. 1:2–4. *Paul writes to*, 1 Tim. 1:1, 2; 2 Tim. 1:1, 2.

20 For the [x]kingdom of God *is* not in word, but in [v]power.

21 What will ye? shall I come unto you with a rod, or in love, and *in* the spirit of [j]meekness?

## CHAPTER 5

*The immoralities in the Corinthian Church. 5 The discipline of erring members. 9 Admonitions against evil company.*

IT is reported commonly *that there is* [a]fornication among [b]you, and such fornication as is not so much as named among the [c]Gĕn′tīleṣ, that [d]one should [e]have his father's wife.

2 And ye are [f]puffed up, and have not rather mourned, that [d]he that hath done this [a,e]deed might be [g,h]taken away from among you.

3 For I verily, as absent in body, but present in spirit, have judged already, as though I were present, *concerning* [d]him that hath so done this [a,e]deed,

4 In the [i]name of our Lord Jē′ṣus [1]Chrīst, when ye are gathered together, and my spirit, with the power of our Lord Jē′ṣus [1]Chrīst,

5 [j,k]To deliver such an one unto [l]Sā′tan for the destruction of the flesh, that the spirit may be [m]saved in the [n]day of the [o]Lord Jē′ṣus.

6 Your [p]glorying *is* not good. Know ye not that a little [q,r,s]leaven leaveneth the whole lump?

7 [t,u,v]Purge out therefore the old [q]leaven, that ye may be a new lump, as ye are unleavened. For even Chrīst our [w,x]passover is [y]sacrificed [z]for us:

8 Therefore let us keep the feast, not with [a]old [b]leaven, neither with the leaven of [c]malice and wickedness; but with the unleavened *bread* of *sincerity and truth.

9 I wrote unto you in [2]an epistle [d,e]not to [f]company with [g]fornicators:

10 [d,e]Yet not altogether with the [f,g]fornicators of this world, or with the [h]covetous, or [i]extortioners, or with [j]idolaters; for then must ye needs go out of the world.

11 But now I have [d]written unto you [e,f,k]not to keep company, if any man that is called a brother be a [g]fornicator, or [h]covetous, or an [j]idolater, or a [3,l]railer, or a [m]drunkard, or an [i]extortioner; with such an one no not to eat.

12 For what have I to do to judge them also that are without? do not ye judge them that are within?

13 But them that are without God [n]judgeth. Therefore [o]put away from among yourselves that wicked person.

## CHAPTER 6

*The apostle reproves them for going to law with each other before unbelievers, 8 and for defrauding one another. 12 All things are not expedient. 15 Their bodies are the members of Christ, 19 and temples of the Holy Ghost.*

DARE any of you, having a matter against [1]another, [a]go to law before the unjust, and not before the saints?

2 Do ye not know that the saints shall [b]judge the world? and if the world shall be judged by you, are ye unworthy to judge the smallest matters?

3 Know ye not that we shall judge [c]angels? how much more things that pertain to this life?

4 If then ye have [2]judgments of things pertaining to this life, set

---

**20**
x *Kingdom of Heaven,* Matt. 13:24.

**1**
a *Adultery,* Lev. 20:10.
b *Corinth, church of,* Acts 18:1.
c *Gentiles,* Acts 10:45.
d *Backsliders,* vs. 1–8; Jer. 3:22.
e *Incest,* Lev. 18:6.

**2**
f *Pride,* Prov. 16:18.
g *Church, discipline in,* Matt. 16:18.
h *Disfellowship,* Num. 15:31.

**4**
i *Name of Jesus,* John 14:13.
1 R. V. *omits* Christ,

**5**
j *Judgments, design of,* Ex. 6:6.
k *Wicked, punishment of,* Psa. 73:3.
l *Satan,* Matt. 4:10.
m *Salvation,* Acts 16:17.
n *Judgment, the general,* 2 Pet. 3:7.
o *Jesus, lordship of,* Matt. 1:21.

**6**
p *Spiritual Boasting,* Rom. 3:27.
q *Leaven, type of sin,* Lev. 23:17.
r *Influence, evil,* 1 Cor. 7:14.
s *Evil Company,* Prov. 13:20.

**7**
t *Commandment, enjoining holiness,* Deut. 8:2.
u *Holiness, enjoined,* Ex. 39:30.
v *Spiritual Purification,* Psa. 51:2.
w *Passover, lamb of, a type of Christ,* Num. 9:5.
x *Types, of the Savior,* Heb. 10:1.
y *Atonement, by Jesus,* Lev. 17:11.
z *Jesus, design of his death,* Matt. 1:21.

**8**
a *Hypocrisy,* Jas. 3:17.
b *Leaven, type of sin,* Lev. 23:17.
c *Malice, forbidden,* Eph. 4:31.

**9**
d *Commandment, forbidding fellowship with the wicked,* Deut. 8:2.
e *Fellowship, with wicked forbidden,* 1 Cor. 1:9.
f *Evil Company,* Prov. 13:20.
g *Adultery,* Lev. 20:10.
2 R. V. my

**10**
h *Covetousness,* Isa. 57:17.
i *Extortion,* Isa. 16:4.
j *Idolatry,* 1 Sam. 15:23.

**11**
k *Disfellowship,* Num. 15:31.
l *Railing, forbidden,* Jude 9.
m *Drunkard, fellowship with, forbidden,* Psa. 69:12.
3 R. V. reviler,

**13**
n *God, judge,* Gen. 2:2.
o *Church, discipline in,* Matt. 16:18.

**1**
a *Litigation,* Matt. 5:25.
1 R. V. his neighbour, go to law before the unrighteous,

**2**
b *Judgment, the general,* 2 Pet. 3:7.

**3**
c *Angel, to be judged by men,* Heb. 1:3.

**4**
2 R. V. to judge things pertaining to this life, do ye set them to judge who are of no account in the church?

---

* **SINCERITY.** *In preaching,* Phil. 1:16, 17. *In forgiving others,* Matt. 18:35. *In love to Christ,* Eph. 6:24. *In service to God,* Josh. 24:14. *In fraternal love,* Rom. 12:9; 2 Cor. 8:8, 24; 1 Pet. 1:22; 1 John 3:18.
*Of ministers,* 2 Cor. 1:12; 2:17; 1 Thess. 2:3–5. *Of Jesus,* 1 Pet. 2:22. *A grace of the righteous,* Psa. 32:2. *The wicked devoid of,* Psa. 55:21. *Enjoined,* Matt. 18:35; 1 Cor. 5:8; Phil. 1:10; 1 Pet. 2:1. *Enjoined upon servants,* Eph. 6:5–7; Col. 3:22.
**Exemplified:** *By the two and one-half tribes,* Josh. 22:21–30, 33. *By men of Zebulun,* 1 Chr. 12:33. *By David* 1 Sam. 24:4–7; 25:31–33, 39–42; 26:6–22. *By Hezekiah,* Isa 38:3. *By Nathanael,* John 1:47. *By Paul,* 2 Cor. 1:12. *By Timothy,* 2 Tim. 1:5. *By Lois and Eunice,* 2 Tim. 1:5.

5
d *Reproof, faithfulness in,* Prov. 17:10.
e *Arbitration,* 1 Kin. 3:16.
3 R. V. say this to move you to shame. Is it so, that there cannot be found among you one wise man, who shall be able to decide between his brethren,

7
f *Retaliation, malicious, forbidden,* v. 8; Deut. 19:19.
g *Meekness, enjoined,* Psa. 45:4.
4 R. V. Nay, already it is altogether a defect in you, that ye have lawsuits one with another.

8
h *Honesty, required,* Rom. 13:13.
i *Fraternity,* Zech. 11:14.

9
j *Wicked, punishment of,* Psa. 73:3.
k *Sin, fruits of,* Rom. 5:12.
l *Kingdom of Heaven,* Matt. 13:24.
m *Lasciviousness,* 1 Pet. 4:3.
n *Idolatry,* 1 Sam. 15:23.
o *Adultery,* Lev. 20:10.
p *Sodomy,* Lev. 18:22.
6 R. V. men,

10
q *Thieves,* Deut. 24:7.

them to judge who are least esteemed in the church.
5 I [3,d]speak to your shame. Is
it so, that there is not a wise man
among you? no, not one that
shall be able to [e]judge between
his brethren?
6 But brother [a]goeth to law
with brother, and that before
the *unbelievers.
7 [4]Now therefore there is utterly a fault among you, because ye [a]go to law one with another. [f,g]Why do ye not rather
take wrong? [f,g]why do ye not
rather *suffer yourselves to* be defrauded?
8 [h]Nay, [5]ye do wrong, and defraud, and that *your* [i]brethren.
9 Know ye not that the unrighteous [j,k]shall not inherit the
[l]kingdom of God? Be not deceived: neither [m]fornicators, nor
[n]idolaters, nor [o]adulterers, nor
effeminate, nor [p]abusers of themselves with [6]mankind,
10 Nor [q]thieves, nor [r]covet-
ous, nor [s]drunkards, nor [t]revil-
ers, nor [u]extortioners, shall inherit the [l]kingdom of God.
11 And such were some of you:
but ye are [v,w,x]washed, but ye
are [x,y,z]sanctified, but ye are
[a]justified [b]in the [c]name of the
[7,d,e]Lord Jē'sus, and by the
[e,f]Spirit of our [e]God.

r *Covetousness, debars from the kingdom of God,* Isa. 57:17. s *Drunkard, excluded from kingdom of God,* Psa. 69:12. t *Speech, evil,* Col. 4:6. u *Extortion, excludes from kingdom of God,* Isa. 16:4.
11 v *Washing, figurative,* Matt. 27:24. w *Spiritual Purification, by the Holy Spirit,* Psa. 51:2. x *Righteous, described,* Psa. 64:10. y *Sanctification,* 1 Pet. 1:2. z *Holiness,* Ex. 39:30.—a *Justification, through Christ,* Rom. 4:25. b *Jesus, mediation of,* Matt. 1:21. c *Name of Jesus,* John 14:13. d *Jesus, lordship of,* Matt. 1:21. e *Holy Trinity,* Luke 3:22. f *Holy Spirit, sanctifies,* Acts 1:2.
7 R. V. Lord Jesus Christ, and in the Spirit of our God.

12 All things are lawful unto me, but all things are not
[†,g]expedient: all things are lawful for me, but [h]I will not
be brought under the power of
any.
13 Meats for the belly, and
the belly for meats: but God
shall [8]destroy both it and them.
Now [i]the [‡]body *is* not for
[j]fornication, but [k]for the
Lord; and the Lord [k]for the
body.
14 And God hath both [l]raised
up the [d]Lord, and will also [m]raise
up us by his own [n]power.
15 Know ye not that your [‡]bod-
ies [k]are the members of Christ?
shall I then take [k]the members
of Christ, and [i]make *them* the
members of an [j]harlot? God
forbid.
16 [9]What? know ye not that
he which is [o]joined to an harlot
is one body? for [p]two, saith he,
shall be one flesh.
17 But he that is [k]joined unto
the Lord is one spirit.
18 Flee [j]fornication. Every sin
that a man doeth is without the
[‡]body; but he that committeth
fornication [q]sinneth against his
own body.
19 [9]What? know ye not that
your [‡]body is [10]the [r]temple of
the [s]Holy Ghost *which is* in
you, which ye have of God, and
ye are not your own?
20 For ye are [t,u]bought with a
price: [v]therefore [w]glorify God in
your [‡]body, [11]and in your spirit,
which are God's.

12
g *Prudence,* 2 Chr. 2:12.
h *Self-denial,* Mark 8:34.

13
i *Chastity, enjoined,* Job 31:1.
j *Adultery,* Lev. 20:10.
k *Righteous, union of, with Christ,* Psa. 64:10.
8 R. V. bring to nought both

14
l *Jesus, resurrection of,* Matt. 1:21.
m *Resurrection,* 1 Cor. 15:12.
n *God, power of,* Gen. 2:2.

16
o *Marriage, unity of husband and wife in,* Gen. 34:9.
p Gen. 2:24; Matt. 19:5; Mark 10:8; Eph. 5:31.
9 R. V. *omits* What?

18
q *Sin, retroactive,* Rom. 5:12.

19
r *Temple, figurative,* 1 Kin. 6:17.
s *Holy Spirit,* Acts 1:2.
10 R. V. a temple

20
t *Redemption of our Souls,* Eph. 1:7.
u *Jesus, design of his death,* Matt. 1:21.
v *Holiness, motives to,* Ex. 39:30.
w *Glorifying God, enjoined,* Luke 5:25.
11 R. V. *omits* and in your spirit, which are God's.

* **UNBELIEVERS.** *Are spiritually blind,* John 14:17; 1 Cor. 2:14; 2 Pet. 3:4–7. *Are impure,* Tit. 1:15. *Make God a liar,* 1 John 5:10. *Will not be convinced,* Luke 16:31; 22:67; John 4:48; 12:37–40. *God's forbearance toward,* Rom. 10:16, 21. *Shall be destroyed,* Jer. 5:12–14; Matt. 10:14, 15; Luke 12:46; John 8:24; 12:48; Acts 13:41; 1 Cor. 1:18; 2 Thess. 2:11, 12; Jude 5–7; Rev. 21:8.

**Instances of:** *Eve,* Gen. 3:4–6. *Moses,* Num. 11:22, 23. *Moses and Aaron,* Num. 20:12. *Israelites,* Deut. 9:23; 2 Kin. 17:14; Psa. 78:8–67; 95:8–11; 106:7, 24. *Naaman,* 2 Kin. 5:12. *Zacharias,* Luke 1:20. *Chief priests and scribes,* Mark 15:31, 32; Luke 22:67. *The Jews,* Matt. 21:32; Mark 2:6–11; 8:11, 12; 15:29, 30; Luke 13:34; 19:41, 42; John 8:45–47, 52, 53; 12:37, 39, 40. *Disciples,* Matt. 17:20; Mark 4:38, 40; Luke 24:11, 21, 25, 26, 36–45; John 6:36, 60–66. *People of Nazareth,* Mark 6:2–6. *Brethren of Jesus,* John 7:5. *Thomas,* John 20:25.

† **EXPEDIENCY.** *To avoid offending a weak brother,* Rom. 14:1, 2, 14–22; 1 Cor. 6:12; 8:8–13; 9:22, 23; 10:23–29, 32, 33. *To save men,* 1 Cor. 9:19–23. *Rule governing,* 1 Cor. 10:30, 31.

*Of Paul, in circumcising Timothy,* Acts 16:3; *in purifying himself in the temple,* Acts 21:23–27.

See footnote, PRUDENCE, 2 Chr. 2:12.

‡ **BODY.** *Called, house,* 2 Cor. 5:1; *house of clay,* Job 4:19; *golden bowl,* Eccl. 12:6; *earthen vessel,* 2 Cor. 4:7; *tabernacle,* 2 Pet. 1:13; *temple of God,* 1 Cor. 3:16, 17; 6:19; *member of Christ,* 1 Cor. 6:15.

*Corruptible,* Job 17:14; 1 Cor. 15:53, 54.

*To be consecrated to God,* Rom. 12:1.

*To be kept unto holiness,* 1 Cor. 6:13–20. *Resurrection of,* 1 Cor. 15:19–54; Phil. 3:21; see footnote, RESURRECTION, 1 Cor. 15:12.

**Spiritual,** 1 Cor. 15:42–44; 2 Cor. 5:1–4.

1
*a Corinth, church of,* Acts 18:1.
*b Letters,* Isa. 37:14.
*c Continence,* Matt. 19:12.
*d Chastity,* Job 31:1.
1 R. V. *omits* unto me:

2
*e Adultery, forbidden,* Lev. 20:10.
*f Marriage, enjoined,* Gen. 34:9.
*g Wife,* Prov. 5:18.
*h Husband,* Num. 30:6.
2 R. V. But, because of fornications,

3
3 R. V. her due:

4
4 R. V. over

5
*i Fasting,* Zech. 8:19.
*j Prayer,* Acts 6:4.
*k Satan,* Matt. 4:10.
*l Temptation,* Luke 11:4.
5 R. V. *omits* fasting

7
*m Example, Paul, our,* John 13:15.
*n Celibacy,* 1 Tim. 4:3.
6 R. V. own gift from God,

8
*o Widow,* 2 Sam. 14:5.
*p Marriage, discouraged among the Corinthians,* Gen. 34:9.

9
7 R. V. have not continency,

## CHAPTER 7

*The apostle treats of marriage and its duties. 10 The believing partner is not to forsake the unbelieving. 17 Every man must be content with the lot to which God has called him.*

NOW concerning the things
whereof [a]ye [b]wrote [1]unto
me: *It is* good for a man [c,d]not
to touch[G] a woman.
2 [2]Nevertheless, *to avoid* [e]for-
nication, [f]let every man have his
own [g]wife, and let every woman
have her own [h]husband.
3 Let the [h]husband render unto
the [g]wife [3]due[G] benevolence: and
likewise also the wife unto the
husband.
4 The [g]wife hath not power[G] [4,G]of
her own body, but the [h]husband:
and likewise also the husband
hath not power[G] [4,G]of his own body,
but the wife.
5 Defraud[G] ye not one the other,
except *it be* with consent for a
time, that ye may give yourselves
to [5,i]fasting and [j]prayer; and
come together again, that [k]Sā'-
tan [l]tempt you not for your in-
continency.
6 But I speak this by permission, *and* not of commandment.
7 For [c,d]I would that all men
were even [m,n]as I myself. But
every man hath his [6]proper[G] gift
of God, one after this manner,
and another after that.
8 I say therefore to the unmarried and [o]widows, [p]It is good for
them if they abide[G] even [m,n]as I.
9 But if they [7]cannot contain,[G]
let them marry: for it is better to
marry than to burn.[G]
10 And unto the married I
command, *yet* not I, [q]but the
Lord, [r]Let not the [g]wife [s]depart
from *her* [h]husband:
11 But and if [g]she [s]depart, let
her remain unmarried, or be reconciled to *her* [h]husband: and let
not the husband [8,s]put[G] away *his*
wife.
12 But to the rest speak I, not
the Lord: If any [t]brother hath a
[g]wife that [u]believeth not, and she
be pleased to dwell with him, let
him not [9,s]put[G] her away.
13 And the woman which hath
an [h]husband that [u]believeth not,
and if he be pleased to dwell with
her, let her not leave him.
14 For the [u]unbelieving [h]hus-
band is *sanctified by the [g]wife,
and the unbelieving wife is sanctified by the [10]husband: else were
your children unclean;[G] but now
are [v]they holy.
15 But if the [u]unbelieving depart, let him [s]depart. A brother
or a sister is not under bondage in such *cases*: but God hath
called us [11]to [w]peace.
16 For what knowest thou, O
[g]wife, whether thou shalt *save
*thy* [h]husband? or how knowest
thou, O man, whether thou shalt
save *thy* wife?
17 But as God hath distributed
to every man, as the Lord hath
[x]called every one, [y]so let him
walk. And so ordain[G] I in all
[z]churches.
18 [x]Is any man called being [a]cir-
cumcised? let him not become
uncircumcised. Is any called in
uncircumcision? let him not be
circumcised.

10
*q Word of God, inspiration of,* Psa. 119:9.
*r Commandment, enjoining fidelity in wedlock,* Deut. 8:2.
*s Divorce, injunctions concerning,* Matt. 19:7.

11
8 R. V. leave

12
*t Brother,* Prov. 18:24.
*u Unbelievers,* 1 Cor. 6:6.
9 R. V. leave her.

14
*v Children, of the righteous, blessed of God,* Mark 10:14.

15
*w Peace,* Jer. 29:7.
11 R. V. in peace.

17
*x Call, personal,* Phil. 3:14.
*y Obedience, enjoined,* Heb. 5:8.
*z Church, government of,* Matt. 16:18.

18
*a Circumcision,* Gen. 17:10.

* **INFLUENCE.** *Solicited, Bath-sheba for Adonijah,* 1 Kin. 2:13–18.
*Proffered, Elisha for Shunammite woman,* 2 Kin. 4:12, 13.
Intercessional in behalf of friends: *Of Jonathan for David,* 1 Sam. 19:1–6; 20:4–9; *of nobles of Judah in behalf of Tobiah,* Neh. 6:17–19; *of mother of Zebedee's children for sons,* Matt. 20:20–24; *of Blastus for Tyre and Sidon,* Acts 12:20.
**Good,** Matt. 5:13–16; Mark 4:21, 22; Luke 8:16; 11:33–36; John 7:38; 1 Cor. 7:14, 16; Phil. 2:15; 1 Thess. 1:7, 8; 1 Tim. 6:1; Heb. 11:4; 1 Pet. 2:11, 12; 3:1, 2, 15, 16.
INSTANCES OF: *David over his successors,* 1 Kin. 3:3; 2 Kin. 18:3; 22:2; 2 Chr. 29:2; 34:2. *Asa over Jehoshaphat,* 1 Kin. 22:42, 43. *Joash over Amaziah,* 2 Kin. 14:3. *Amaziah over Azariah,* 2 Kin. 15:1–3. *Uzziah over Jotham,* 2 Kin. 15:34. *Josiah, in religious zeal,* 2 Kin. 22; 23:1–25; 2 Chr. 34; 35. *Hezekiah, for religious reform,* 2 Chr. 29; 30; 31. *Ezra, against marriage with idolaters,* Ezra 10:1, 9. *Nehemiah, during the rebuilding of the walls of Jerusalem,* Neh. 4:7–23; 5.
**Evil,** Prov. 29:12; Matt. 13:24, 25. *Of wicked parents over children,* Jer. 17:1, 2. *Of wicked priest and people,* Hos. 4:9. *Warnings against,* Prov. 22:24, 25; Luke 12:1; 1 Cor. 5:6–8; Gal. 5:7–9; 2 Tim. 2:14, 17, 18; Heb. 12:15.
INSTANCES OF: *Eve over Adam,* Gen. 3:6. *Solomon's wives,* 1 Kin. 11:3, 4. *The young men over Rehoboam,* 1 Kin. 12:8–14; 2 Chr. 10:8–14. *Rehoboam over Abijam,* 1 Kin. 15:3. *Jezebel over Ahab,* 1 Kin. 21:4–16, 25. *Ahab over Ahaziah,* 1 Kin. 22:52, 53; 2 Kin. 8:25–27. *Ahab over Jehoram,* 2 Kin. 8:16, 18; 2 Chr. 21:5, 6; 22:3–5. *Jeroboam over Israel,* 2 Kin. 17:21, 22. *Manasseh over Judah,* 2 Kin. 21:9; 2 Chr. 33:9. *Manasseh over Amon,* 2 Kin. 21:20, 21. *Jehoiakim over Jehoiachin,* 2 Kin. 24:9.
See footnote, EXAMPLE, John 13:15.

19 [a]Circumcision is nothing, and uncircumcision is nothing, but the keeping[G] of the commandments of God.

20 [b]Let every man abide in the same calling wherein he was [c]called.[S]

21 Art thou [c]called *being* a [12]servant? [b]care not for it: but if [d]thou [13]mayest be made free, use *it* rather.

22 For he that is [c]called in the Lord, *being* a [12,e]servant, is [f]the Lord's [g]freeman: likewise also he that is called, *being* free, is [f]Christ's [12,h]servant.

23 Ye are [i]bought with a [j]price; [14]be not ye the servants of men.

24 Brethren, let every man, wherein[G] he is [c]called, [b]therein abide with God.

25 Now concerning [k]virgins I have no commandment of the Lord: yet I give my judgment, as one that hath obtained mercy of the [l]Lord to be [15,m]faithful.

26 I [16]suppose therefore that this is good for the present distress, *I say*, that *it is* good for a man so to be.

27 Art thou bound unto a [n]wife? [b]seek not to be loosed. Art thou loosed from a wife? [b]seek not a wife.

28 But and if thou marry, thou hast not sinned; and if a [k]virgin marry, she hath not sinned. Nevertheless such shall have [17]trouble in the flesh: but I spare you.

29 But this I say, brethren, [o]the time *is* [18]short: [p]it remaineth, [q]that both they that have wives be as though they had none;

30 And they that [r]weep, as though they wept not; and they that [s]rejoice, as though they rejoiced not; and they that [q]buy, as though they possessed not;

31 And they that [q]use this world, as not [19]abusing *it*: for the fashion[G] of this world passeth away.

32 But I would have you[20]without [t]carefulness.[G] He that is [u]unmarried careth for the things that belong to the Lord, how he may please the Lord:

33 But he that is married [q]careth for the things that are of the world, how [v]he may please *his* [n]wife.

34 There is difference *also* between a [n]wife and a [k]virgin. The unmarried woman careth for the things of the Lord, that she may be [w]holy both in body and in [x]spirit: but she that is married [21,q]careth for the things of the world, how she may please *her* [v]husband.

35 And this I speak for your own profit; not that I may cast a snare upon you, but for that which is [22]comely,[C] and that ye may attend upon the Lord without distraction.

36 But if any [y]man think that he behaveth himself [23]uncomely[G] toward his [k]virgin, if she pass the flower of *her* age, and need so require, let him do what he will, he sinneth not: let them [z]marry.

37 Nevertheless [y]he that standeth stedfast in his heart, having no necessity, but hath power over his own will, and hath [24]so decreed in his heart that he will keep his [k]virgin, doeth well.

38 So then [y]he that giveth [25,k]*her* in [z]marriage doeth well; but he that giveth *her* not in marriage doeth better.

39 [a]The [b]wife is bound by the law as long as her [c]husband liveth; but if her husband be dead, [d]she is at liberty to be married to whom she will; only in the Lord.

40 But she is happier if she so abide, after my judgment: and I think also that [e]I have the [f]Spirit of God.

**20**
b *Contentment, enjoined*, 1 Tim. 6:6.
c *Call, to special religious duty*, Phil. 3:14.

**21**
d *Servant, emancipation of*, Jer. 2:14.
12 R. V. bondservant?
13 R. V. canst become free.

**22**
e *Servant, equal status of, with other disciples of Jesus*, Jer. 2:14.
f *Righteous, described*, Psa. 64:10.
g *Liberty, spiritual*, Lev. 25:10.
h *Servant, figurative*, Jer. 2:14.

**23**
i *Redemption of our Souls*, Eph. 1:7.
j *Jesus, design of his death*, Matt. 1:21.
14 R. V. become not bondservants

**25**
k *Virgin*, Isa. 62:5.
l *Jesus, lordship of*, Matt. 1:21.
m *Faithfulness*, Luke 16:10.
15 Am. R. V. trustworthy.

**26**
16 R. V. think therefore that this is good by reason of the present distress, namely, that it is good for a man to be as he is.

**27**
n *Wife*, Prov. 5:18.

**28**
17 R. V. tribulation

**29**
o *Zeal*, 2 Cor. 7:11.
p *Diligence*, vs. 29–31; Rom. 12:8.
q *Worldliness, admonitions against*, 1 John 2:15.
18 R. V. shortened, that henceforth both those that

**30**
r *Weeping*, Ezra 3:13.
s *Joy*, Psa. 5:11.

**31**
19 Am. R. V. using it to the full:

**32**
t *Anxiety*, 1 Pet. 5:7.
u *Celibacy*, 1 Tim. 4:3.
20 R. V. to be free from cares.

**33**
v *Husband*, Num. 30:6.

**34**
w *Holiness*, Ex. 39:30.
x *Man, a spirit*, Job 4:17.
21 R. V. is careful for

**35**
22 R. V. seemly,

**36**
y *Parents*, 2 Cor. 12:14.
z *Marriage*, Gen. 34:9.
23 R. V. unseemly toward his virgin daughter, if she be past the flower of her age, and if need so requireth,

**37**
24 R. V. determined this in his own heart, to keep his own virgin daughter, shall do well.

**38**
25 R. V. his own virgin daughter in marriage

**39**
a *Marriage, indissoluble*, Gen. 34:9.
b *Wife*, Prov. 5:18.
c *Husband*, Num. 30:6.
d *Widows, marriage of*, 2 Sam. 14:5.

**40**
e *Prophets, inspiration of*, Isa. 3:2.
f *Holy Spirit*, Acts 1:2.

**1**
*a* *Idolatry,* 1 Sam. 15:23.
*b* *Offerings, offered in idolatrous worship,* Lev. 6:17.
*c* *Wisdom, worldly,* Prov. 2:2.
*d* *Pride,* Prov. 16:18.
*e* *Love, of man for man,* 1 John 4:7.
1 R. V. love

**2**
*f* *False Confidence,* Psa. 30:6.

**3**
*g* *Love, for God,* 1 John 4:19.
*h* *Righteous, promises to,* Psa. 64:10.
*i* *God, knowledge of,* Gen. 2:2.

**4**
*j* *Food,* Psa. 136:25.
*k* *Idolatry,* 1 Sam. 15:23.
*l* *Idol,* 1 Kin. 15:12.
*m* *God, unity of,* Gen. 2:2.

**6**
*n* *God, fatherhood of,* Gen. 2:2.
*o* *Jesus, lordship of,* Matt. 1:21.
*p* *Jesus, divinity of,* Matt. 1:21.
*q* *Jesus, creator,* Matt. 1:21.

**7**
*r* *Conscience, another's, to be respected,* Acts 23:1.
2 R. V. but some, being used until now to the idol, eat as of a thing sacrificed to an idol;

**9**
*s* *Watchfulness, enjoined,* Matt. 24:42.
*t* *Evil, appearance of, to be avoided,* 1 Thess. 5:22.
*u* *Stumbling, figurative,* Isa. 8:14.
*v* *Temptation, leading into, to be avoided,* Luke 11:4.

**10**
*w* *Temple, idolatrous,* 1 Kin. 6:17.

## CHAPTER 8

*Concerning meat offered to idols. 9 Their Christian liberty must not become a stumblingblock to them that are weak.*

NOW as touching[G] things
[a,b]offered unto idols, we
know that we all have knowledge. [c]Knowledge [d]puffeth[G] up,
but [1,e]charity[G] edifieth.[G]
2 And if any man [f]think that he
knoweth[G] any thing, he knoweth[G]
nothing yet as he ought to know.
3 But if any man [g]love God,
[h]the same is [i]known[G] of him.[S]
4 As concerning therefore the
eating of those [j]things that are
[b,k]offered in sacrifice[G] unto [l]idols,
we know that an idol *is* nothing
in the world, and that *there is*
none other [m]God but one.[T Q]
5 For though there be that are
called gods, whether in heaven
or in earth, (as there be *gods
many, and lords many,)
6 But to us *there is but* [m]one
God, the [n]Father, of whom *are*
all things, and we in him; and
one [o,p]Lord Jē'ṣus Chrīst, [q]by
whom *are* all things, and we by
him.[S T Q]
7 Howbeit *there is* not in every
man that knowledge: [2]for some
with conscience[G] of the [l]idol unto
this hour eat *it* as a thing [b]offered
unto an idol; and their [r]con-
science being weak is defiled.
8 But meat[G] commendeth us not
to God: for neither, if we eat, are
we the better; neither, if we eat
not, are we the worse.
9 But [s,t]take heed lest by any
means this liberty of your's become a [u,v]stumblingblock to them
that are †weak.
10 For [i]if any man see thee
which hast knowledge sit at
meat[G] in the idol's [w]temple, shall
not the [r]conscience of him which
is †weak be emboldened to eat
those things which are [k]offered
to idols;
11 And through thy knowledge
shall the weak [x]brother perish,
[y]for whom Chrīst died?
12 But when ye [z]sin so against
the [x]brethren, and wound their
weak [a]conscience, ye sin against
Chrīst.
13 Wherefore, [b]if meat[G] make
my [c]brother to [3]offend, [d,e,f]I will
[g]eat no flesh[G] while the world
standeth, lest I make my brother
to offend.

## CHAPTER 9

*Paul asserts his apostleship, 7 and that they who preach the gospel ought to live by it; 15 yet that he himself had not been chargeable to them, 19 and had made himself the servant of all. 24 He strives for an incorruptible crown.*

AM [a]I not an [b]apostle? am I
not free? have I not [c,d]seen
Jē'ṣus [1]Chrīst our [e]Lord? are
not ye [f]my work in the Lord?
2 If [a]I be not an [b]apostle unto
others, yet [2]doubtless I am to
you: for [g]the seal[G] of mine apostleship are ye in the Lord.
3 [3]Mine answer to them that do
examine[G] me is this,
4 [h]Have we [4]not power[G] to eat
and to drink?
5 [h]Have [i]we [5]not power[G] to
[j]lead about a sister, a [k]wife, as
well as other [b]apostles, and *as*
the [l]brethren of the [e]Lord, and
[m]Çē'phas?
6 Or [a]I only and [n]Bär'na-băs,
have [6]not we power[G] to forbear[G]
working?
7 [7,o,p,q]Who goeth a warfare[G]
any time at his own charges[G]?
who planteth a vineyard, and
eateth not of the fruit thereof?

**11**
*x* *Fraternity,* Zech. 11:14.
*y* *Jesus, design of his death,* Matt. 1:21.

**12**
*z* *Sin, defined,* Rom. 5:12.
*a* *Conscience, another's, to be respected,* Acts 23:1.

**13**
*b* *Love, of man for man,* 1 John 4:7.
*c* *Fraternity,* Zech. 11:14.
*d* *Expediency,* 1 Cor. 6:12.
*e* *Evil, appearance of, to be avoided,* 1 Thess. 5:22.
*f* *Self-denial,* Mark 8:34.
*g* *Appetite, restrained for a brother's sake,* Prov. 23:2.
3 R. V. stumble, I will eat no flesh for evermore, that I make not my brother to stumble.

**1**
*a* *Paul,* Acts 13:9.
*b* *Apostles,* Luke 6:13.
*c* *Vision,* Acts 9:10.
*d* *Appearances of Jesus after his Resurrection,* Mark 16:9.
*e* *Jesus, lordship of,* Matt. 1:21.
*f* *Agency, in salvation of men,* Mark 1:17.
1 R. V. *omits* Christ

**2**
*g* *Minister, success attending,* Rom. 15:16.
2 R. V. at least I am

**3**
3 R. V. My defence to

**4**
*h* *Self-denial,* Mark 8:34.
4 R. V. no right

**5**
*i* *Celibacy, not obligatory,* 1 Tim. 4:3. *j* *Minister, marriage of,* Rom. 15:16. *k* *Wife,* Prov. 5:18. *l* *Brothers of Jesus,* Matt. 13:55. *m* Or, *Peter,* Mark 5:37. 5 R. V. no right to lead about a wife that is a believer, even as the rest of the apostles. **6** *n* *Barnabas,* Acts 4:36. 6 R. V. we not a right to **7** *o* *Soldiers,* Ezra 8:22. *p* *Minister, emoluments of,* Rom. 15:16. *q* *Church, duty of, to ministers,* Matt. 16:18. 7 R. V. What soldier ever serveth at his own charges?

* **POLYTHEISM**, the belief that there are many gods, Josh. 24:2, 23; Judg. 3:7; 10:16; 17:5; Jer. 2:28; 11:13; 1 Cor. 8:5.
See footnote, IDOLATRY, 1 Sam. 15:23.

† **WEAK.** *Duty of strong to,* Job 4:3, 4; Isa. 35:3–7; Matt. 25:35, 40; Rom. 14:1–23; 15:1–3; 1 Cor. 8:7–13; 9:22; 2 Cor. 11:29; Gal. 6:1, 2; Jas. 5:19, 20.
See footnote, KINDNESS, Acts 28:2.

or who feedeth a flock, and eateth not of the [r]milk of the flock?
8 [s]Say I these things as a man?
or saith not the [s]law the same
also?
9 For it is written in the [s]law
of Mō′ṣeṣ, [p,t,u]Thou shalt not
muzzle the mouth of the ox that
treadeth out the corn.[C] Doth God
[v]take care for [w]oxen?[Q]
10 Or saith he *it* altogether for
our sakes? For our sakes, no
doubt, *this* is written: that [p,u]he
that ploweth should plow in
[x]hope; and that he that thresh-
eth [9]in hope should be partaker
of his hope.
11 *If we have sown unto you
spiritual things, *is it* a great
thing if we shall [*,p,u]reap your
carnal[C] things?
12 If others be partakers of *this*
[10]power[C] over you, *are* not we
rather? Nevertheless we have
not used this [11]power[C]; but [y,z]suf-
fer[C] all things, lest we should hinder the [a]gospel of Chrīst.
13 Do ye not know that [b,c]they
which minister about holy things
live *of the* [d]*things* of the temple?
and [b,c]they which wait at the [e]al-
tar are partakers with the altar?[Q]
14 Even so hath the Lord ordained that [c]they which [f]preach
the [a]gospel should [c,g]live of the
gospel.
15 But [h]I have used none of
[c]these things: neither have I written these things, that it should
be so done unto me: for [i]*it were*
better for me to die, than that
any man should make my glorying void.[C]
16 For though I [f,j]preach the
[a]gospel, I have nothing to glory
of: for [k]necessity is laid upon
me; yea, [l]woe is unto me, if I
preach not the gospel![Q]
17 For if I do this thing [m]will-
ingly, I have a [n]reward: but if
[12]against my will, a [k,o]dispensa-
tion[C] *of the gospel* is committed
unto me.
18 What is my [n]reward then?
*Verily* that, when I [f]preach the
[a]gospel, I may make the gospel
[13]of Chrīst [h]without charge, that
I abuse not my [c]power[C] in the
gospel.
19 For though I be free from
all *men*, [l]yet have I [14,p,q]made
myself [m,r]servant unto all, that I
might gain the more.
20 And unto the Jewṣ I [l,p,s]be-
came as a Jew, that I might gain
the Jewṣ; to them that are under
the law, [15,l,p,s]as under the law,
that I might gain them that are
under the law;
21 To them that are without
law, [l,p,s]as without law, (being
not without law to God, but under the law to Chrīst,) that I
might gain them that are without law.[T]
22 To the [t]weak [l,p,s]became I
as weak, that I might gain the
weak: [l,p,s]I am made all things
to all *men*, that I might by all
means save some.
23 And [16,l]this I do for the
[a]gospel's sake, that I might be
partaker thereof with *you*.
24 Know ye not that [u]they
which run in a [†]race run all, but
one receiveth the [v]prize? [w]So
[x]run, that ye may [17]obtain.
25 And every man that striv-
eth [18,†]for the mastery[C] is [y]tem-
perate in all things. Now they
*do it* to obtain a corruptible
[z,a]crown; but we [a]an incorruptible.
26 I therefore so [†]run, [b]not as
uncertainly; so fight I, [b]not as
one that beateth the air:
27 But I [19,c]keep under my
body, and bring *it* into [d]subjec-

r *Milk*, Job 10:10.

**8**

s *Law, of Moses*, Deut. 33:2.

8 R. V. Do I speak these things after the manner of men?

**9**

t Deut. 25:4.

u *Labor, compensation for*, Luke 10:7.

v *God, providence of*, Gen. 2:2.

w *Animals, God's care of*, Jer. 27:5.

**10**

x *Hope*, Prov. 13:12.

9 R. V. to thresh in hope of partaking.

**12**

y *Zeal*, 2 Cor. 7:11.

z *Self-denial*, Mark 8:34.

a *Gospel*, Mark 13:10.

10 R. V. right over you, do not we yet more?

11 R. V. right;

**13**

b *Priest, emoluments of*, Lev. 1:5.

c *Minister, emoluments of*, Rom. 15:16.

d *Offerings, holy*, Lev. 6:17.

e *Altar, of burnt offerings*, Gen. 8:20.

**14**

f *Preaching*, Matt. 9:35.

g *Church, duty of, to ministers*, Matt. 16:18.

**15**

h *Self-denial*, Mark 8:34.

i *Renunciation*, Luke 5:11.

**16**

j *Minister, duties of*, Rom. 15:16.

k *Minister, call of*, Rom. 15:16.

l *Zeal*, 2 Cor. 7:11.

**17**

m *Minister, character and qualifications of*, Rom. 15:16.

n *Reward, a motive, to faithfulness*, Matt. 5:12.

o *Minister, responsibility of*, Rom. 15:16.

12 R. V. not of mine own will, I have a stewardship intrusted to me.

**18**

13 R. V. without charge, so as not to use to the full my right in the gospel.

**19**

p *Tact*, Prov. 15:1.

q *Unselfishness*, 1 Cor. 10:24.

r *Altruism*, Acts 20:35.

14 R. V. brought myself under bondage to all,

**20**

s *Minister, tactful*, Rom. 15:16.

15 R. V. not being myself under the law, that I might

**22**

t *Weak, duty of strong to*, 1 Cor. 8:9.

**23**

16 R. V. I do all things for the gospel's sake, that I may be a joint partaker thereof.

**24**

u *Righteous, compared to runners in a race*, Psa. 64:10.

v Phil. 3:14.

w *Faithfulness*, Luke 16:10.

x *Strenuousness, enjoined*, Eccl. 9:10.

17 R. V. attain.

**25**

y *Temperance*, 2 Pet. 1:6.

z *Crown, figurative*, Ex. 29:6.

a *Reward, a motive, to faithfulness*, Matt. 5:12.

18 R. V. in the games is

**26**

b *Faith*, Mark 11:22.

**27**

c *Continence*, Matt. 19:12.

d *Captivity, figurative*, Isa. 5:13.

19 R. V. buffet my body, and bring it into bondage:

* **RECIPROCITY**, Rom. 15:27; 1 Cor. 9:11; Gal. 6:6. *Treaty of*, 1 Kin. 5:1–12, with 9:11–14.

† **GAMES.** *Foot races*, 1 Cor. 9:24, 26; Gal. 2:2; Phil. 2:16; Heb. 12:1. *Gladiatorial*, 1 Cor. 4:9; 9:26; 2 Tim. 4:7, 8. **Figurative:** *Of the Christian life*, 1 Cor. 9:24, 26; Gal. 5:7; Phil. 2:16; 3:13, 14; Heb. 12:1. *Of a successful ministry*, Gal. 2:2; Phil. 2:16. *Of spiritual conflict*, 1 Cor. 4:9; 9:26; 15:32; 2 Tim. 4:7, 8.

*e Wicked, punishment of,* Psa. 73:3.

20 R. V. rejected.

tion: lest that by any means,
when I have preached to others,
I myself should be [20]a [‡,e]castaway.

## CHAPTER 10

*Certain miracles in the Old Testament used as types of our sacraments. 5 The punishment of the rebellious Jews a warning to us to avoid the like sins. 15 especially in partaking of the Lord's supper. 24 In things indifferent we must have regard to our brethren and the glory of God.*

1
*a Israel,* Ex. 4:22.
*b Pillar of Cloud and Fire, symbol of the Lord's presence,* Ex. 13:21.
*c Red Sea, divided,* Ex. 10:19.

2
*d Baptism, unto Moses,* Luke 20:4.
*e Moses,* Ex. 2:10.

3
*f Manna, figurative,* Ex. 16:31.
*g Types, of the Savior,* Heb. 10:1.

4
*h Meribah,* Ex. 17:7.
*i Symbols and Similitudes,* Heb. 9:9.
*j Rock, figurative,* Psa. 78:15.
*k Jesus, names of,* Matt. 1:21.
1 R. V. rock

5
*l Wicked, punishment of,* Psa. 73:3.
*m Unbelieving Israelites destroyed,* Num. 14:11.

6
*n Lust, warnings against,* 2 Pet. 1:4.
*o Worldliness, admonitions against,* 1 John 2:15.
*p Example, bad,* John 13:15.

7
*q Commandment, forbidding idolatry,* Deut. 8:2.
*r* Ex. 32:6.

MOREOVER, brethren, I
would not that ye should
be ignorant, how that all our [a]fathers were under the [b]cloud, and
all passed through the [c]sea;
2 And were all [d]baptized unto
[e]Mō′ṣeṣ in the [b]cloud and in the
[c]sea;
3 And did all eat the same
[f,g]spiritual meat;
4 And did all drink the same
spiritual [h]drink: for they drank
of that spiritual [1,i,j]Rock that
followed them: and that [1,k]Rock
was Chrīst.
5 But with many of [l]them God
was not well pleased: for they
were [m]overthrown in the wilderness.
6 Now these things were our examples, to the intent we should
not [n,o]lust after evil things, [p]as
they also lusted.
7 [q]Neither be ye idolaters, as
*were* some of them; as it is
written, [r]The people sat down
to eat and drink, and rose up
to [s]play.
8 [t]Neither let us commit [u]fornication, as some of them committed, and [l,v]fell in one day
three and twenty thousand.
9 Neither let us [w]tempt [2,x]Chrīst,
as some of them also tempted,
[y]and were [l,v]destroyed of [z]serpents.
10 [a]Neither [b]murmur ye, as
some of them also murmured,
and were [c]destroyed of the destroyer.
11 Now all these things happened unto them [3]for ensamples: and [d]they are [e]written for
our [f]admonition, upon whom the
ends of the [4]world are come.
12 Wherefore let him that
[g]thinketh he standeth [h,i,j]take
heed lest he fall.
13 [k]There hath no temptation
taken you but such as [5]is common to man: but God *is* [l]faithful, [m,n]who will not suffer you to
be tempted above that ye are
able; but [n,o]will with the [p]temptation also [q]make a way to escape, that ye may be able to
bear *it.*
14 Wherefore, my dearly [r]beloved, [s]flee from [t]idolatry.
15 I speak as to [u]wise men;
judge ye what I say.
16 The [v]cup of blessing which
we bless, is it not [6]the *communion of the [w]blood of Chrīst?
The [v]bread which we break, is it
not [6]the communion of the body
of Chrīst?
17 For we *being* many are one
[x]bread, *and* [y]one body: for we
are all partakers of [7]that one
bread.
18 Behold Īṣ′ra-el after the
flesh: [8]are not [z]they which eat

*y* Num. 21:6.
*z Serpent,* Num. 21:6.

10
*a Commandment, forbidding murmuring,* Deut. 8:2.
*b Murmuring, against God, forbidden,* Num. 14:2.
*c Wicked, punishment of,* Psa. 73:3.

11
*d Backsliding, admonitions against,* Hos. 11:7.
*e Word of God,* Psa. 119:9.
*f Instruction, in religion,* Prov. 23:23.
3 R. V. by way of example; and they were written
4 R. V. ages are come.

12
*g False Confidence,* Psa. 30:6.
*h Commandment, enjoining watchfulness,* Deut. 8:2.
*i Watchfulness, enjoined,* Matt. 24:42.
*j Sin, warnings against,* Rom. 5:12.

13
*k Afflictions, consolation in,* Psa. 34:19.
*l God, faithfulness of,* Gen. 2:2.
*m God, preserver,* Gen. 2:2.
*n Righteous, promises to,* Psa. 64:10.
*o Promise, of deliverance from temptation,* 2 Cor. 1:20.
*p Temptation, way of escape from,* Luke 11:4.

*s Idolatry, wicked practices of,* 1 Sam. 15:23. **8** *t Commandment, forbidding adultery,* Deut. 8:2. *u Adultery, forbidden,* Lev. 20:10. *v Judgments,* Ex. 6:6. **9** *w Presumption, warnings against,* Psa. 19:13. *x Jesus, lordship of,* Matt. 1:21. 2 R. V. the Lord

*q Grace of God,* Rom. 4:16. 5 R. V. man can bear: **14** *r Love, of man for man,* 1 John 4:7. *s Commandment, forbidding idolatry,* Deut. 8:2. *t Idolatry,* 1 Sam. 15:23.
**15** *u Wisdom, spiritual,* Prov. 2:2.
**16** *v Eucharist, bread and cup of, symbols,* Mark 14:22. *w Blood, of Christ, symbolized in the Eucharist,* Heb. 9:19. 6 R. V. a
**17** *x Bread, figurative,* Ezek. 4:13. *y Church, unity of,* Matt. 16:18. 7 R. V. the
**18** *z Priest, emoluments of,* Lev. 1:5. 8 R. V. have not they which eat the sacrifices communion with the altar?

‡ **REPROBATES,** Jer. 6:30; 2 Tim. 3:8; Jude 4–13. *Called, men of corrupt minds,* 2 Tim. 3:8; *vessels of wrath,* Rom. 9:22.
*Moral insensibility of,* Isa. 22:12–14; 28:13; 29:9–12; Matt. 13:14, 15; 15:14; Rom. 11:7, 8. *Rejected of God,* Prov. 1:24–28; Jer. 6:30; 7:16; 15:1; Hos. 5:6; Matt. 15:14; 25:8–13; Luke 13:24–28; 14:24; John 10:26; 2 Thess. 2:10, 11; Heb. 3:10–12, 17–19; 6:4–8; 10:26–31. *Admonitions against reprobacy,* Heb. 12:15–17. *Curses denounced against,* Deut. 28:15–68; 31:17, 18; Isa. 65:12; Hos. 9:12; Mark 3:29; Heb. 10:26–31.
INSTANCES OF: *Antediluvians,* Gen. 6:5–7. *Sodomites,* Gen. 13:13; 19:13; Jude 7. *Israel,* Num. 14:26–45; Deut. 1:42; Jude 5. *Eli's house,* 1 Sam. 3:14. *Saul,* 1 Sam. 15:23; 16:14; 18:12; 28:15. *Judas,* John 17:12. *Angels,* Jude 6.
See footnote, OBDURACY, Prov. 29:1.

* **COMMUNION OF SAINTS,** Psa. 133:1–3; Amos 3:3; 1 John 1:3, 7.
*Enjoined,* 1 Thess. 4:18; 5:11, 14; 10:24, 25; Jas. 5:16.
**Exemplified,** Psa. 55:14; Mal. 3:16; Luke 24:32 (with v 17); Acts 2:42.
See footnote, FELLOWSHIP, 1 Cor. 1:9.

of the [a]sacrifices partakers of
the [b]altar? [Q]
19 What say I then? that the
[c]idol is any thing, or that which
is offered in sacrifice to idols is
any thing?
20 But *I say*, that the things
which the [d]Gĕn′tīleṣ sacrifice,
they sacrifice to [e]devils,[G] and not
to God: and I would not that
ye should have [9,f]fellowship with
devils.[G Q]
21 [f,g]Ye cannot drink the [h]cup
of the Lord, and the [h]cup of devils:[G] ye cannot be partakers of the
Lord's [i,j]table, and of the table
of devils.[G Q]
22 Do we provoke[G] the Lord to
[k]jealousy? are we stronger than
he? [Q]
23 All things are lawful [10]for
me, but [l]all things are not [m]ex-
pedient: all things are lawful
[10]for me, but all things edify not.
24 [n]Let no man seek his own,
but [11,†,o,p]every man another's
*wealth*.
25 [q]Whatsoever is sold in the
shambles,[G] *that* eat, [m,r]asking no
question for [s]conscience sake:
26 For [t]the [u]earth *is* the [v]Lord's,
and the fulness thereof.[Q]
27 If any of [w]them that believe
not bid [x]you *to a feast*, and ye be
disposed to go; [m,r,y]whatsoever
is set before you, eat, asking no
question for [s]conscience sake.
28 But if any man say unto
you, This is offered in sacrifice
[12]unto [z]idols, [a,b,c]eat not [d]for
[e]his sake that shewed it, and for
conscience sake: [13]for the [f]earth
*is* the [g]Lord's, and the fulness
thereof.
29 [e]Conscience, I say, not thine
own, but of the other: for why
is my liberty judged of another
*man's* conscience?
30 For if I by grace be a partaker, why am I evil spoken of
for that for which I give [h]thanks?
31 Whether therefore ye eat, or
drink, or whatsoever ye do, [i,j]do
all to the glory of God.
32 [k,l,m]Give [14]none offence,
neither to the Jewṣ, nor to the
Gĕn′tīleṣ,[G] nor to the [n]church of
God:
33 Even [o]as [p,q]I please all
*men* in all *things*, [†,r]not seeking
mine own profit, but the *profit*
of many, that they may be saved.

## CHAPTER 11

*The apostle reproves the practice of men praying with their heads covered, and of women with theirs uncovered. 17 He rebukes them for their divisions, 20 and for profaning the Lord's supper. 23 His account of its institution.*

BE [a]ye [1]followers of me, even
[b]as [c]I also *am* of Chrīst.
2 Now I praise you, brethren,
that ye remember me in all
things, and [2]keep the [d]ordi-
nances, as I delivered *them* to
you.
3 But I would have you know,
that the [e,f]head of every man is
[g]Chrīst; and [h]the head of the
[i]woman *is* the [j]man; and [k]the
head of Chrīst *is* God.[T Q]
4 [l,m]Every man [n]praying or
prophesying, having *his* head
covered, dishonoureth his head.
5 But [l,m]every [o]woman that
[n]prayeth or prophesieth[G] with *her*
head uncovered dishonoureth her
head: for that is even all one as if
she were shaven.

a *Offerings*, Lev. 6:17.
b *Altar, of burnt offerings*, Gen. 8:20.

**19**
c *Idol*, 1 Kin. 15:12.

**20**
d *Gentiles, ignorant worship of*, Acts 10:45.
e *Demons, worship of*, Matt. 4:24.
f *Fellowship, with the wicked*, 1 Cor. 1:9.
9 R. V. communion

**21**
g *Consistency*, Rom. 14:22.
h *Cup, figurative*, Matt. 20:22.
i *Eucharist*, Mark 14:22.
j *Table, figurative*, Judg. 1:7.

**22**
k *Jealousy, attributed to God*, Psa. 78:58.

**23**
l *Self-denial*, Mark 8:34.
m *Expediency*, 1 Cor. 6:12.
10 R. V. *omits* for me,

**24**
n *Commandment, enjoining helpfulness, forbidding selfishness*, Deut. 8:2.
o *Altruism*, Acts 20:35.
p *Christian Graces, unselfishness*, Gal. 5:22.
11 R. V. each his neighbour's good.

**25**
q *Food*, Psa. 136:25.
r *Minister, tactful*, Rom. 15:16.
s *Conscience*, Acts 23:1.

**26**
t Psa. 24:1.
u *Earth, the Lord's*, Prov. 8:23.
v *God, sovereign*, Gen. 2:2.

**27** w *Unbelievers*, 1 Cor. 6:6. x *Guest, rules for the conduct of*, Zeph. 1:7. y *Manners, rules for guests*, Gen. 18:2.

**28** z *Idol*, 1 Kin. 15:12.—a *Evil, appearance of, to be avoided*, 1 Thess. 5:22. b *Temptation, leading into*, vs 28–32; Luke 11:4. c *Commandment, enjoining regard for the consciences of others*, Deut. 8:2. d *Charitableness, enjoined*, Prov. 10:12. e *Conscience, another's, to be respected*, Acts 23:1. f *Earth, the Lord's*, Prov. 8:23. 12 R. V. *omits* unto idols, 13 R. V. *omits the rest of this verse*.

g *God, sovereign*, Gen. 2:2.

**30**
h *Thanksgiving for Food*, Luke 24:30.

**31**
i *Holiness, exhortations to*, Ex. 39:30.
j *Glorifying God, enjoined*, Luke 5:25.

**32**
k *Expediency*, 1 Cor. 6:12.
l *Tact*, Prov. 15:1.
m *Commandment, forbidding giving cause for stumbling*, Deut. 8:2.
n *Church*, Matt. 16:18.
14 R. V no occasion of stumbling, either to Jews, or to Greeks, or to

**33**
o *Example, Paul, our*, John 13:15.
p *Minister, faithful*, Rom. 15:16.
q *Zeal*, 2 Cor. 7:11.
r *Self-denial*, Mark 8:34.

**1**
a *Corinth, church of*, Acts 18:1.
b *Example, Paul, our*, John 13:15.
c *Minister, faithful*, Rom. 15:16.
1 R. V. imitators

**2**
d *Tradition*, Matt. 15:2.
2 R. V. hold fast the traditions, even as

**3**
e *Church, Christ head of*, Matt. 16:18.
f *Jesus, head of church*, Matt. 1:21.
g *Jesus, Messiah*, Matt. 1:21.
h *Family, government of*, 1 Chr. 13:14.
i *Wife, relation of, to husband*, Prov. 5:18.
j *Husband, relation of, to wife*, Num. 30:6.
k *Jesus, relation of, to the Father*, Matt. 1:21.

**4** l *Worship, proprieties in*, Gen. 22:5. m *Church, orderly conduct of worship in, enjoined*, Matt. 16:18. n *Prayer*, Acts 6:4.

**5** o *Women, religious privileges of*, Prov. 31:10.

† **UNSELFISHNESS.** *Royal law of*, Jas. 2:8. *Enjoined*, Rom. 12:10; 15:1, 2; 1 Cor. 10:24; Gal. 6:2; Phil. 2:3, 4. *Love inspires*, 1 Cor. 13:4, 5.
*Jesus an example of*, Rom. 15:3.
**Instances of:** *Abraham*, Gen. 13:9; 14:23, 24. *King of Sodom*, Gen. 14:21. *Judah*, Gen. 44:33, 34. *Moses*, Num. 11:29; 14:12–19. *Gideon*, Judg. 8:22, 23. *Saul*, 1 Sam. 11:12, 13. *Jonathan*, 1 Sam. 23:17, 18. *David*, 1 Sam. 24:17; 2 Sam. 15:19, 20; 23:16, 17; 1 Chr. 21:17; Psa. 69:6. *Joab*, 2 Sam. 12:28. *Araunah*, 2 Sam. 24:22–24. *Nehemiah*, Neh. 5:14–18. *Daniel*, Dan. 5:17. *Joseph*, Matt. 1:19. *The disciples*, Acts 4:34, 35. *Priscilla and Aquila*, Rom. 16:3, 4. *Paul*, 1 Cor. 9:19–23; 10:33; 2 Cor. 11:9–12; Phil. 1:18; 4:17; 2 Thess. 3:8. *Onesiphorus*, 2 Tim. 1:16–18.

6 For if the woman be not [3]cov-
ered, let her also be shorn: but if
it be a shame for a woman to be
shorn or shaven, let her be [3]cov-
ered.
7 For a man indeed ought not
to [4]cover *his* head, forasmuch as
[p,q]he is the *image and glory of
God: but the woman is the glory
of the man.[Q]
8 For [r]the man is not of the
woman; but the woman of the
man.[Q]
9 Neither was the man created
for the woman; but the woman
for the man.[Q]
10 For this cause ought the
woman to have [5]power[G] on *her*
head because of the [s]angels.
11 Nevertheless [t]neither is the
man without the woman, neither
the woman without the man, in
the Lord.
12 For as the woman *is* of the
man, even so *is* the man also by
the woman; but all things of
[u]God.
13 Judge [6]in yourselves: [l,m]is
it comely[G] that a woman [n]pray
unto God uncovered?
14 Doth not even nature itself
teach you, that, if a man have
long hair, it is a shame unto
him?
15 But if a woman have long
hair, it is a glory to her: for *her*
hair is given her for a covering.
16 But if any man seem to be
[v]contentious, we have no such
custom, neither the [w]churches
of God.
17 [7]Now in this that I declare
*unto you* I praise *you* not, that
ye [x]come together not for the
better, but for the worse.
18 For first of all, when ye come
together in the [y]church, I hear
that there be [v]divisions among
you; and I partly believe it.
19 For there must be also [8]her-
esies[G] among you, that they which
are [z]approved may be made manifest among you.[S] [Q]
20 When [9]ye come together
therefore into one place, [a,b]*this*
is not to eat the [c]Lord's supper.
21 For in eating every one taketh before *other* his own supper:
and one is [d]hungry, and another
is [e]drunken.
22 What? [b,f]have [g]ye not
houses to eat and to drink in?
or despise ye the church of God,
and [10]shame them that have not?
What shall I say to you? shall I
praise you in this? I praise *you*
not.
23 For I have [h]received of the
Lord that which also I delivered
unto you, That the [i]Lord Jē'ṣus
the *same* night in which he was
[j]betrayed [k]took [l]bread:
24 And when he had given
[m,n]thanks, he brake [l]*it*, and said,
[11,k]Take, eat: this is my body,
which is broken for you: this do
in [o]remembrance of me.
25 After the same manner also
[12]*he* [k]*took* the cup, when he had
supped,[G] saying, This [p,q]cup is
the [r]new testament[G] in my [s]blood:
this do ye, as oft as ye drink *it*, in
[o]remembrance of me.[Q]
26 For as often as ye [k]eat this
[l]bread, and [k]drink this [p,q]cup,
ye [13]do [t]shew[G] the Lord's [u]death
till he [v]come.
27 Wherefore whosoever shall
[k]eat this [l]bread, and [k]drink *this*
[p]cup of the Lord, [w]unworthily,[G]
shall be guilty of the body and
blood of the [i]Lord.
28 But let a man [14,x]examine[G]
himself, and so let him [k]eat of
[15]*that* [l]bread, and [k]drink of
[15]*that* [p,q]cup.
29 [w]For he that eateth and

**26** t *Religious Testimony,* 2 Thess. 1:10. u *Jesus, death of,* Matt. 1:21. v *Jesus, second coming of,* Matt. 1:21. 13 R. V. proclaim the Lord's death till he come.
**27** w *Sacrilege,* Lev. 19:8.
**28** x *Self-examination,* 2 Cor. 13:5. 14 R. V. prove 15 R. V. the

**7**
p *Man, created in the image of God,* Job 4:17.
q Gen. 1:26.

**8**
r *Marriage, unity of husband and wife in,* Gen. 34:9.

**10**
s *Angel,* Heb. 1:13.
5 R. V. a sign of authority on

**11**
t *Marriage, based on law of nature,* Gen. 34:9.

**12**
u *God, creator,* Gen. 2:2.

**13**
6 R. V. ye in yourselves: is it seemly that a woman pray unto God unveiled?

**16**
v *Strife,* Prov. 20:3.
w *Church,* Matt. 16:18.

**17**
7 R. V. But in giving you this charge, I praise
x *Worship, proprieties in,* Gen. 22:5.

**18**
y *Church, dissensions in,* Matt. 16:18.

**19**
8 Am. R. V. factions
z *Temptation, a test,* Luke 11:4.

**20**
a *Worship, proprieties in,* Gen. 22:5.
b *Church, orderly conduct of worship in, enjoined,* Matt. 16:18.
c *Eucharist, profanation of,* Mark 14:22.
9 R. V. therefore ye assemble yourselves together, it is not possible to eat

**21**
d *Hunger,* Neh. 9:15.
e *Drunkenness,* Luke 21:34.

**22**
f *Reproof, faithfulness in,* Prov. 17:10.
g *Corinth, church of,* Acts 18:1.
10 R. V. put them to shame that have not?

**23**
h *Inspiration,* Job 32:8.
i *Jesus, lordship of,* Matt. 1:21.
j *Betrayal, of Jesus,* Matt. 26:46.
k *Eucharist,* Mark 14:22.
l *Bread, symbolical,* Ezek. 4:13.

**24**
m *Thanksgiving for Food,* Luke 24:30.
n *Prayers of Jesus,* Luke 5:16.
o *Memorial, Lord's Supper,* Num. 16:40.
11 R. V. This is my body, which is for you:

**25**
p *Cup, figurative,* Matt. 20:22.
q *Wine, symbolical of the blood of Jesus,* Prov. 23:31.
r *New Covenant,* Jer. 31:31.
s *Blood, of Christ,* Heb. 9:19.
12 R. V. the cup, after supper, saying, This cup is the new covenant in my blood:

***IMAGE.** *Seen in Nebuchadnezzar's vision,* Dan. 2. **Figurative:** *Man created in image of God,* Gen. 1:26, 27; 5:1; 9:6; 1 Cor. 11:7; Jas. 3:9. *Regeneration into image of God,* Psa. 17:15; Rom. 8:29; 2 Cor. 3:18; Col. 3:10; 1 John 3:1-3. *Christ, of God,* Col. 1:15; Heb. 1:3. *Of jealousy,* Ezek. 8:3, 5. See footnotes: IDOL, 1 Kin. 15:12; IDOLATRY, 1 Sam. 15:23.

**29**
16 R. V. eateth and drinketh judgement unto himself, if he discern not the body.

**30**
*y Judgments,* Ex. 6:6.
*z Death, as a judgment,* Num. 23:10.

**31**
17 R. V. discerned ourselves,

**32**
*a Afflictions, benefits of,* Psa. 34:19.
*b Afflictions, design of,* Psa. 34:19.
*c Divine Chastisement,* Job 33:19.

**33**
*d Fraternity,* Zech. 11:14.
*e Church, orderly conduct of worship in, enjoined,* Matt. 16:18.

**34**
*f Apostles, authority of,* Luke 6:13.
18 R. V. judgement.

**2**
*a Gentiles,* Acts 10:45.
*b Idolatry,* 1 Sam. 15:23.

**3**
*c Holy Spirit,* Acts 1:2.
*d Holy Trinity,* Luke 3:22.
*e Blasphemy,* 2 Sam. 12:14.
*f Religious Testimony,* 2 Thess. 1:10.
*g Confession of Christ,* Luke 12:8.
*h Jesus, lordship of,* Matt. 1:21.
*i Jesus, divinity of,* Matt. 1:21.
1 R. V. saith, Jesus is anathema;

**5**
*j Jesus, head of church,* Matt. 1:21.
2 R. V. diversities of ministrations,

**6**
*k God, power of,* Gen. 2:2.
3 R. V. workings,

**7**
*l Inspiration,* Job 32:8.

drinketh [16]unworthily, eateth and
drinketh damnation[G] to himself,
[w]not discerning the Lord's
body.
30 For this cause many *are*
[y]weak and [y]sickly among you,
and many [y,z]sleep.
31 For if we[17]would [x]judge[G] ourselves, we should not be judged.
32 But when we are [a,b]judged,
we are [c]chastened of the Lord,
that we should not be condemned
with the world.
33 Wherefore, my [d]brethren,
[e]when ye come together to eat,
tarry[G] one for another.
34 And [e]if any man hunger, let
him eat at home; that ye come
not together unto [18]condemna-
tion.[G] And [f]the rest will I set in
order when I come.

## CHAPTER 12

*Concerning spiritual gifts. 4 Diversities of gifts, but the same Spirit. 12 As in the natural body there are many members, and all have not the same office, 27 so in the church there are different gifts and offices.*

NOW concerning *, †spiritual
*gifts,* brethren, I would not
have you ignorant.
2 Ye know that ye were [a]Gĕn′-
tīleș,[G] carried away unto these
dumb [b]idols, even as ye were led.[Q]
3 [T]Wherefore I give you to understand, that no man speaking
by the [c,d]Spirit of [d]God [1,e]calleth
[d]Jē′șus accursed[G]: and *that* no
man can [f,g]say that Jē′șus is
the [h,i]Lord, but by the [d]Holy[G]
Ghost.[S]
4 Now there are diversities of
*, †gifts, but the same [c]Spirit.
5 And there are [2]differences of
administrations,[G] but the same
[j]Lord.
6 And there are diversities of
[3]operations, but it is the same
God which [k]worketh all in[T] all.[S]
7 But the [l]manifestation of the
[c]Spirit is given to every man to
profit withal.
8 For to one is *,†given by the
[c]Spirit the word of [m]wisdom; to
another the word of [n]knowledge
by the same Spirit;
9 [f,†]To another [o]faith by the
same [c]Spirit; to another the gifts
of [p]healing by the same Spirit;
10 *, †To another the working
of [q]miracles; to another [r]proph-
ecy; to another discerning of
spirits; to another *divers* kinds
of ‡,[s]tongues; to another the [t]in-
terpretation of tongues:
11 But all these worketh that
one and the selfsame[G] [c]Spirit, dividing to every man severally[G] as
he will.[T]
12 [u,v]For as the [w]body is one,
and hath many members, and
all the members of that one body,
being many, are one body: so
also *is* Christ.
13 For by one [x]Spirit are [y]we
all [z]baptized into [u,v]one [w]body,
whether *we be* Jewș or [4]Gĕn′-
tīleș,[G] whether *we be* [a]bond or
free; and have been all made to
drink [5]into one Spirit.
14 For the [b]body is not one
member,[G] but many.
15 If the [c]foot shall say, Because I am not the [d]hand, I am
not of the [b]body; is it therefore
not of the body?
16 And if the [e]ear shall say,
Because I am not the [f]eye, I am
not of the [b]body; is it therefore
not of the body?
17 If the whole [b]body *were* an
[f]eye, where *were* the hearing?
If the whole *were* hearing, where
*were* the smelling?
18 But now hath [g]God set the
members every one of them in
the [b]body, as it hath pleased
him.

**8**
*m Wisdom, spiritual,* Prov. 2:2.
*n Knowledge,* Luke 11:52.

**9**
*o Faith, inspired,* Mark 11:22.
*p Healing,* Acts 4:22.

**10**
*q Miracles,* Luke 23:8.
*r Prophecies,* Dan. 9:24.
*s Language,* Dan. 3:29.
*t Interpreter,* Gen. 40:8.

**12**
*u Church, unity of,* Matt. 16:18.
*v Unity, of the righteous,* Psa. 133:1.
*w Body,* 1 Cor. 6:19.

**13**
*x Holy Spirit, baptism of,* Acts 1:2.
*y Church, membership in,* Matt. 16:18.
*z Baptism, Christian,* Luke 20:4.
*a Servant,* Jer. 2:14.
4 R. V. Greeks,
5 R. V. of

**14**
*b Body,* 1 Cor. 6:19.

**15**
*c Feet,* 2 Sam. 4:4.
*d Hand,* Ezra 10:19.

**16**
*e Ear,* Lev. 8:23.
*f Eye,* Matt. 6:22.

**18**
*g God, creator,* Gen. 2:2.

***CHARISM.** *An inspired gift, bestowed on the apostles and early Christians,* Matt. 10:1, 8; Mark 16:17, 18; Luke 10:1, 9, 17, 19; Acts 2:4; 10:44–46; 19:6; 1 Cor. 12.

**† SPIRITUAL GIFTS,** Rom. 11:29; 12:6–8; 1 Cor. 12:4–11; 1 Pet. 4:10, 11.

See footnotes: CHARISM, above; HOLY SPIRIT, Acts 1:2; TONGUES, below.

**‡ TONGUES.** *The miraculous gift to the early Christians,* Mark 16:17; Acts 2:1–18; 10:46, 19:6; 1 Cor. 12:10, 28, 30; 13:8; 14:2–19, 21–28, 39.

19 And if they were all one member, where *were* the [b]body?

20 But now *are they* many members, yet but one [b]body.

21 And the [f]eye cannot say unto the [d]hand, I have no need of thee: nor again the head to the [e]feet, I have no need of you.

22 Nay, much more those members of the [b]body, which seem to be more feeble, are necessary:

23 And those [6]*members* of the [b]body, which we think to be less honourable, upon these we bestow more abundant honour; and our uncomely *parts* have more abundant comeliness.

24 For our comely *parts* have no need: but [g]God hath tempered the body together, having given more abundant honour to that *part* which lacked:

25 That there should be no schism in the [h]body; but *that* the members should have the same [i,j]care one for another.

26 And whether one member [k]suffer, all the members [l]suffer with it; or one member be honoured, all the members [l]rejoice with it.

27 Now [m]ye are the body [n]of Christ, and [7]members in particular.

28 And God hath set some in the [o]church, first [p]apostles, [8]secondarily [q]prophets, thirdly [r,s]teachers, after that [t]miracles, then [*,†]gifts of [u]healings, helps, [v]governments, diversities of [‡]tongues.

29 *Are* all [p]apostles? *are* all [q]prophets? *are* all [r]teachers? *are* all workers of [t]miracles?

30 Have all the [*,†]gifts of [u]healing? do all speak with [‡]tongues? do all [w]interpret?

31 But [9]covet earnestly the best [†]gifts: and yet shew I unto you a [i,j]more excellent way.

23
6 R. V. parts

25
*h* *Church, unity of,* Matt. 16:18.
*i* *Altruism,* Acts 20:35.
*j* *Love, of man for man,* 1 John 4:7.

26
*k* *Afflictions,* Psa. 34:19.
*l* *Sympathy,* Jas. 1:27.

27
*m* *Righteous, union of, with Christ,* Psa. 64:10.
*n* *Fellowship, with Christ,* 1 Cor. 1:9.
7 R. V. severally members thereof.

28
*o* *Church, diversity of calling in,* Matt. 16:18.
*p* *Apostles,* Luke 6:13.
*q* *Prophets,* Isa. 3:2.
*r* *Teachers,* 1 Chr. 25:8.
*s* *Instruction, provision for,* Prov. 23:23.
*t* *Miracles,* Luke 23:8.
*u* *Healing,* Acts 4:22.
*v* *Church, government of,* Matt. 16:18.
8 R. V. secondly

30
*w* *Interpreter,* Gen. 40:8.

31
9 R. V desire earnestly the greater gifts.

## CHAPTER 13

*All gifts, however excellent, are worth nothing without love. 4 The praises thereof. 13 It is greater than hope and faith.*

THOUGH I [a,b]speak with the tongues of men and of angels, and have not [1,c,d,e]charity, I am become *as* [f]sounding [g]brass, or a [f]tinkling [h]cymbal.

2 And though I have *the gift of* prophecy, and understand all mysteries, and all [i]knowledge; and though I have all [j]faith, so that I could remove mountains, and have not [1,c]charity, I am nothing.

3 And though I [e,k]bestow all my goods to feed *the* [l]*poor*, and though I [m]give my body to be [n,o]burned, and have not [1,c]charity, it profiteth me nothing.

4 [1,c]Charity [d,e,p,q]suffereth long, *and* is [d,e,r,s]kind; [1]charity [t]envieth not; [1]charity [u]vaunteth not itself, is [v]not puffed up,

5 [w]Doth not behave itself unseemly, [x,y]seeketh not her own, is not [2]easily [z]provoked, [y]thinketh no evil;

6 [a]Rejoiceth not in [3]iniquity, but rejoiceth in the [b]truth;

7 [c,d,e]Beareth all things, believeth all things, [f]hopeth all things, [c,d,e]endureth all things.

8 [1,e,g]Charity never faileth: but whether *there be* prophecies, they shall [4]fail; whether *there be* [h]tongues, they shall cease; whether *there be* [i]knowledge, it shall [4]vanish away.

9 For we know in part, and we prophesy in part.

10 But when that which is perfect is come, then that which is in part shall be done away.

11 When I was a [j]child, I spake as a child, I [5]understood as a child, I thought as a child: but when I became a man, I put away childish things.

1
*a* *Religious Testimony,* 2 Thess. 1:10.
*b* *Works, insufficient for salvation,* 2 Tim. 1:9.
*c* *Love,* 1 John 4:7.
*d* *Christian Graces,* Gal. 5:22.
*e* *Righteousness, fruits of,* Psa. 15:2.
*f* *Hypocrisy, described,* Jas. 3:17.
*g* *Brass,* Job 28:2.
*h* *Cymbal,* 1 Chr. 13:8.
1 R. V. love,

2
*i* *Knowledge,* Luke 11:52.
*j* *Faith,* Mark 11:22.

3
*k* *Liberality,* 1 Tim. 6:18.
*l* *Poor,* Prov. 21:13.
*m* *Zeal,* 2 Cor. 7:11.
*n* *Persecution, of the righteous,* John 15:20.
*o* *Martyrdom,* Rev. 17:6.

4
*p* *Longsuffering,* 2 Cor. 6:6.
*q* *Patience, a grace of the righteous,* Luke 8:15.
*r* *Kindness, inspired by love,* Acts 28:2.
*s* *Meekness, described,* Psa. 45:4.
*t* *Envy,* Prov. 14:30.
*u* *Pride,* Prov. 16:18.
*v* *Humility,* Prov. 22:4.

5
*w* *Prudence,* 2 Chr. 2:12.
*x* *Unselfishness,* 1 Cor. 10:24.
*y* *Christian Graces, charitableness,* Gal. 5:22.
*z* *Anger,* Psa. 37:8.
2 R. V. provoked, taketh not account of evil;

6
*a* *Righteousness,* Psa. 15:2.
*b* *Truth,* John 18:37.
3 R. V. unrighteousness, but rejoiceth with the truth;

**7** *c* *Patience,* Luke 8:15. *d* *Meekness,* Psa. 45:4. *e* *Christian Graces, love,* Gal. 5:22. *f* *Hope,* Prov. 13:12. **8** *g* *Love,* 1 John 4:7. *h* *Tongues,* 1 Cor. 12:10. *i* *Knowledge,* Luke 11:52. 4 R. V. be done away
**11** *j* *Children,* Mark 10:14. 5 R. V. felt

12

*k Mirror, figurative*, Job 37:18.

*l Wisdom, spiritual*, Prov. 2:2.

6 R. V. in a mirror,

7 R. V. have been known.

13

*m Faith*, Mark 11:22.

1

*a Love*, 1 John 4:7.

*b Spiritual Gifts*, 1 Cor. 12:4.

*c Preaching, should edify*, Matt. 9:35.

1 R. V. love; yet desire earnestly spiritual

2

*d Language*, Dan. 3:29.

3

*e Afflictions, consolation in*, Psa. 34:19.

3 R. V. comfort, and consolation.

4

*f Church*, Matt. 16:18.

5

*g Interpreter*, Gen. 40:8.

6

4 R. V. teaching?

7

*h Music, instruments of*, 2 Chr. 5:13.

*i Harp*, Dan. 3:10.

5 R. V. a voice,

8

*j Trumpet, in war*, Josh. 6:4.

12 For now we see [6]through a [k]glass,[C] darkly; but then face to face: now I know in part; but then shall I [l]know even as also I [7]am known.

13 And now abideth [m]faith, [e,f]hope, [1,e,g]charity,[C] these three; but the greatest of these *is* [1]charity.[C]

## CHAPTER 14

*The gift of prophecy preferred to speaking with tongues. 12 The end of both is the edification of the church. 26 Directions how to use these gifts. 34 Women forbidden to speak in the church.*

FOLLOW after [1,a]charity,[C] and desire [b]spiritual *gifts*, but rather that ye may [c]prophesy.[C]

2 For he that speaketh in [2]an *unknown* [d]tongue speaketh not unto men, but unto God: for no man understandeth *him*; howbeit in the spirit he speaketh mysteries.

3 But he that [c]prophesieth[C] [e]speaketh unto men *to* edification,[C] and [3]exhortation, and comfort.

4 He that speaketh in [2]an *unknown* [d]tongue edifieth[C] himself; but he that [c]prophesieth[C] edifieth the [f]church.

5 I would that ye all spake with [d]tongues, but rather that ye [c]prophesied: for greater *is* he that prophesieth than he that speaketh with tongues, except he [g]interpret, that the [f]church may receive edifying.[GQ]

6 Now, brethren, if I come unto you speaking with [d]tongues, what shall I profit you, except I shall speak to you either by revelation, or by knowledge, or by prophesying, or by [4]doctrine[G]?

7 And even things without life giving [5]sound, whether [h]pipe[C] or [h,i]harp, except they give a distinction in the sounds, how shall it be known what is piped or harped?

8 For if the [j]trumpet give an uncertain[C] [5]sound, who shall prepare himself [6]to the battle?

9 So likewise ye, except ye utter by the tongue [7,k]words easy to be understood, how shall it be known what is spoken? for ye shall speak into the air.

10 There are, it may be, so many kinds of voices in the world, and none of them *is* without signification.[C]

11 Therefore if I know not the meaning of the voice, I shall be unto him that speaketh a [l]barbarian, and he that speaketh *shall be* a barbarian[C] unto me.

12 Even so ye, forasmuch as ye are [m]zealous of [b]spiritual *gifts*, seek that ye may excel to the edifying of the [f]church.

13 Wherefore let him that speaketh in [2]an *unknown* [d]tongue [n]pray that he may [g]interpret.

14 For if I [n]pray in [2]an *unknown* [d]tongue, my [o]spirit[C] prayeth, but my understanding is unfruitful.

15 What is it then? [p]I will [n]pray with the [o]spirit, and I will pray with the understanding also: I will [q,r]sing with the spirit, and I will sing with the understanding also.

16 Else when thou shalt bless with the [o]spirit, how shall he that occupieth the room[C] of the unlearned say Amen at thy giving of [s]thanks, seeing he understandeth not what thou sayest?

17 For thou verily givest [s]thanks well, but the other is not edified.[C]

18 I [s]thank my God, I speak with [d]tongues more than ye all:

19 Yet in the [f]church I had rather speak five words with my understanding, that [8]*by my voice* I might [t]teach others also, than ten thousand words in [2]an *unknown* tongue.

20 Brethren, [u]be not [v]children in [9]understanding: howbeit in

6 R. V. for war?

9

*k Words*, Luke 4:22.

7 R. V. speech

11

*l Barbarian*, Rom. 1:14.

12

*m Zeal*, 2 Cor. 7:11.

13

*n Prayer*, Acts 6:4.

14

*o Man, a spirit*, Job 4:17.

15

*p Worship, in spirit and in truth*, Gen. 22:5.

*q Music*, 2 Chr. 5:13.

*r Praise*, Psa. 150:1.

16

*s Thankfulness, to God*, Acts 24:3.

19

*t Instruction, in religion*, Prov. 23:23.

8 R. V. I might instruct others also,

20

*u Commandment, enjoining manly gravity*, Deut. 8:2.

*v Children*, Mark 10:14.

9 R. V. mind:

[w]malice be ye [10]children, but [u]in [9]understanding be men.

21 In the [x]law it is written, [y]With *men of* other tongues and [11]other lips will I speak unto this people; and yet for all that [z]will they not hear me, saith the Lord.[Q]

22 Wherefore [a]tongues are for a sign, not to them that [b]believe, but to them that [c]believe not: but [d]prophesying[G] [12]*serveth* not for them that believe not, but for them which believe.

23 If therefore the whole [e]church be [f]come together into one place, and all speak with [a]tongues, and there come in *those that are* unlearned, or [c]unbelievers, will they not say that ye are mad[G]?

24 But if all [d]prophesy, and there come in one that [c]believeth not, or *one* unlearned, he is [13]convinced[G] of all, he is judged of all:

25 And thus are the secrets of his heart made manifest; and so [g]falling down on *his* face he will [f]worship God, [14]and report that God is in you of a truth.[Q]

26 How is it then, brethren? when ye come together, every one of you hath a psalm, hath a [4]doctrine, hath a [a]tongue, hath a revelation, hath an interpretation. [h,i]Let all things be done unto edifying.

27 [h,i]If any man speak in [2]an *unknown* [a]tongue, *let it be* by two, or at the most *by* three, and *that* [15]by course[G]; and let one [j]interpret.

28 But if there be no [j]interpreter, [h,i]let him keep silence in the church; and let him speak to himself, and to God.

29 [h,i]Let the prophets[G] speak two or three, and let the [16]other judge.

30 [17,h,i]If *any thing* be revealed to another that sitteth by, let the first hold his peace.

31 For ye may all prophesy[G] one by one, that all may learn, and all may be comforted.[G]

32 And the spirits of the prophets are subject to the prophets.

33 For God is not [18]*the author* of confusion[G], but of [k]peace, as in all churches of the saints.

34 [l]Let your women keep silence in the churches: for it is not permitted unto them to speak; but [19]*they are commanded* to be under [m]obedience, as also saith the law.[Q]

35 And if they will learn any thing, let [n]them ask their [o]husbands at home: for it is a shame for [l]women to speak in the church.

36 What? came the word of God out from you? or came it unto you only?

37 If any man think himself to be a prophet, or spiritual, let him acknowledge that the things that [p]I write unto you are the [q]commandments of the Lord.

38 But if any man be ignorant, let him be ignorant.

39 Wherefore, brethren, [20]covet[G] to prophesy, and forbid not to speak with [a]tongues.

40 [h,i]Let all things be done decently[G] and in order.

## CHAPTER 15

*The certainty of the resurrection proved by the resurrection of Christ. 35 The manner of the resurrection. 51 Those then living on the earth shall be changed, and the dead raised incorruptible. 54 Death swallowed up in victory.*

MOREOVER,[T] brethren, [a]I declare unto you the [b]gospel which I [c,d]preached unto you, which also ye have [e]received, and wherein ye stand;

2 By which also ye are [1,f]saved, if ye keep[G] in memory what I [c,d]preached unto you, unless ye have [e]believed in vain.[G T]

3 For [a]I [c,d]delivered unto you first of all that which I also received, how that Christ [g,h]died

w *Malice, forbidden*, Eph. 4:31.
10 R. V. babes,

21
x *Word of God*, Psa. 119:9.
y Isa. 28:11, 12.
z *Obduracy*, Prov. 29:1.
11 R. V. by the lips of strangers will

22
a *Language*, Dan. 3:29.
b *Faith in Christ*, John 6:69.
c *Unbelief*, Heb. 3:12.
d *Preaching*, Matt. 9:35.
12 R. V. is for a sign, not to the unbelieving, but

23
e *Church*, Matt. 16:18.
f *Worship*, Gen. 22:5.

24
13 R. V. he is reproved by all,

25
g *Conviction of Sin*, John 16:8.
14 R. V. declaring that God is among you indeed.

26
h *Commandment, enjoining orderly conduct of divine worship*, vs. 27-33; Deut. 8:2.
i *Church, orderly conduct of worship in*, Matt. 16:18.

27
j *Interpreter*, Gen. 40:8.

29
16 R. V. others discern.

30
17 R. V. But if a revelation be made to another sitting by, let the first keep silence.

33
k *Peace*, Jer. 29:7.
18 R. V. a God of confusion,

34
l *Women, Paul's precepts concerning*, Prov. 31:10.
m *Family, government of*, 1 Chr. 13:14.
19 R. V. let them be in subjection, as also saith the law.

35
n *Wife*, Prov. 5:18.
o *Husband*, Num. 30:6.

37
p *Apostles, inspiration of*, Luke 6:13.
q *Word of God, is inspired*, Psa. 119:9.

39
20 R. V. desire earnestly to prophesy,

1
a *Paul*, Acts 13:9.
b *Gospel*, Mark 13:10.
c *Preaching*, Matt. 9:35.
d *Witnessing for Christ*, Luke 24:48.
e *Faith in Christ*, John 6:69.

2
f *Salvation*, Acts 16:17.
1 R. V. saved: I make known, I say, in what words I preached it unto you, if ye hold it fast, except ye believed in vain.

3
g *Jesus, death of*, Matt. 1:21.
h *Atonement, by Jesus*, Lev. 17:11.

*i* *Jesus, design of his death*, Matt. 1:21.
*j* *Word of God*, Psa. 119:9.
4
*k* *Jesus, resurrection of*, Matt. 1:21.
5
*l* *Appearances of Jesus after his Resurrection*, Mark 16:9.
*m* Or, *Peter*, Mark 5:37.
*n* *Apostles*, Luke 6:13.
6
*o* *Death, called sleep*, Num. 23:10.
7
*p* *James, an apostle*, Luke 6:13.
8
*q* *Vision, of Paul*, Acts 9:10.
9
*r* *Humility*, Prov. 22:4.
*s* *Sin, confession of*, Rom. 5:12.
*t* *Persecution, of the righteous*, John 15:20.
*u* *Church, persecution of*, Matt. 16:18.
10
*v* *Religious Testimony*, 2 Thess. 1:10.
*w* *Grace of God*, Rom. 4:16.
*x* *Spiritual Blessings, from God*, Eph. 1:3.
*y* *Minister, character and qualifications of*, Rom. 15:16.
*z* *Zeal*, 2 Cor. 7:11.

11
*a* *Preaching*, Matt. 9:35.
*b* *Minister, success attending*, Rom. 15:16.
*c* *Faith in Christ*, John 6:69.
12
*d* *Corinth, church of*, Acts 18:1.
13
*e* *Jesus, resurrection of*, Matt. 1:21.

[i]for our sins according to the
[j]scriptures; [S T Q]
4 And that he was buried, and
that he *,[k]rose again the third
day according to the [j]scriptures: [Q]
5 And that he was [l]seen of
[m]Çē′phas, then of the [n]twelve:
6 After that, he was [l]seen of
above five hundred brethren at
once; of whom the greater part
remain unto this present, but
some are fallen [o]asleep. [G]
7 After that, he was [l]seen of
[p]Jāmeș; then of all the [n]apostles.
8 And last of all he was [l,q]seen
of [a]me also, as of one born out of
due time.
9 For I am the least of the
[n]apostles, that am [r]not meet [G] to
be called an apostle, because [s]I
[t]persecuted the [u]church of God.
10 [r,v]But by the [w,x]grace of
God I am what I am: and his
[y]grace which *was bestowed* upon
me was not in vain; but [z]I laboured more abundantly than
they all: yet not I, but the [y]grace
of God which was with me.
11 Therefore whether *it were* I
or they, so we [a]preach, and so
[b]ye [c]believed.
12 Now if Chrīst be preached
that he rose from the dead, how
say some among [d]you that there
is no *resurrection of the dead?
13 But if there be no *resurrection of the dead, then is Chrīst
not [e]risen:
14 And if Chrīst be not risen,
then *is* our [a]preaching vain, and
your [c]faith *is* also vain.
15 Yea, and we are found false
witnesses of God; because we
have [j]testified of God that he
*,[e]raised up Chrīst: whom he
raised not up, if so be that the
dead rise not.
16 For if the [g]dead *rise not,
then is not Chrīst [e]raised:
17 And if Chrīst be not *,[e]raised,
your [c]faith *is* vain; ye are yet in
your sins.
18 Then they also which are
fallen [h]asleep [G] in Chrīst are perished.
19 If in this life only we have
[i]hope in Chrīst, we are of all men
most [2]miserable.
20 But now is Chrīst *risen
from the dead, *and* become the
[j]firstfruits of them that [3,h]slept. [G]
21 For since by [k]man *came*
[l,m,n]death, by [o]man *came* also
the *,[e]resurrection of the dead. [Q T]
22 For as in [p]Ăd′ăm all die,
even so in Chrīst shall [q]all be
made *alive. [T]
23 But every man in his own
order: Chrīst the [j]firstfruits; afterward they that are [r]Chrīst's
at his [s]coming.
24 [t]Then *cometh* the end, when
[u]he shall have delivered up the
[v]kingdom to God, even the [w]Father; when [x]he shall have put
down [y]all rule and all authority
and power. [S T Q]
25 [t]For [z]he must reign, till he
hath put all [4]enemies under his
feet. [T Q]
26 The last enemy *that* shall be
destroyed *is* [a]death.

*y* *Satan, kingdom of, to be destroyed*, Matt. 4:10. 25 *z* *Jesus, king*, Matt. 1:21. 4 R. V. his enemies
26—*a* *Death, to be destroyed*, Num. 23:10.

15
*Religious Testimony*, 2 Thess. 1:10.
16
*g* *Dead*, 2 Kin. 4:32.
18
*h* *Death, called sleep*, Num. 23:10.
19
*i* *Hope, of resurrection*, Prov. 13:12.
2 R. V. pitiable.
20
*j* *First Fruits, figurative*, Deut. 18:4.
3 R. V. are asleep.
21
*k* *Man, mortal*, Job 4:17.
*l* *Fall of Man*, Gen. 3:6.
*m* *Death*, Num. 23:10.
*n* *Wicked, punishment of*, Psa. 73:3.
*o* *Jesus, humanity of*, Matt. 1:21.
22
*p* *Adam*, Gen. 2:19.
*q* *Jesus, mission of*, Matt. 1:21.
23
*r* *Jesus, Messiah*, Matt. 1:21.
*s* *Jesus, second coming of*, Matt. 1:21.
24
*t* *Millennium*, vs. 24–28; Rev. 20:4.
*u* *Jesus, relation of, to the Father*, Matt. 1:21.
*v* *Jesus, kingdom of, prophecies concerning*, vs. 24–28; Matt. 1:21.
*w* *God, fatherhood of*, Gen. 2:2.
*x* *Jesus, power of*, Matt. 1:21.

* **RESURRECTION,** Matt. 22:23–32 (with Mark 12:18–27; Luke 20:27–37); Matt. 25:6–7; Luke 14:14; 20:35, 36; Heb. 6:2; 11:35. *First, of the dead in Christ*, 1 Thess. 4:16. Rev. 20:4–6; *at Christ's second coming*, 1 Thess. 4:14, 16.

*Of all the dead*, John 5:28, 29; Acts 24:15; 1 Cor. 15:20, 21; Rev. 20:13.

*Prophecies concerning*, Isa. 26:19; Dan. 12:2, 3, 13; Hos. 13:14.

*Job's views concerning*, Job 19:25–27.

Taught: *By Jesus*, Matt. 22:30–32 (with Mark 12:25–27; Luke 20:37, 38); John 5:21, 25, 28, 29; 6:39, 40, 44, 54; 11:23–25; *by the apostles*, Acts 4:1, 2; 17:18, 31, 32; 23:6, 8; 24:14, 15; 26:6–8; Rom. 8:10, 11, 19, 21–23; 1 Cor. 6:14; 15:12–57; 2 Cor. 4:14; 5:1–5; Phil. 3:11, 21; Rev. 20:5, 6.

*Believed in by the Pharisees*, Acts 23:6, 8; 24:14, 15; 26:6–8.

*Denied by the Sadducees*, Matt. 22:23–28; Acts 23:6, 8.

*Of saints after Christ's resurrection*, Matt. 27:52, 53.

*Error concerning*, 2 Tim. 2:18.

**Figurative:** *Of regeneration*, Rom. 6:4; Eph. 2:1, 5, 6; Col. 2:12; 3:1.

**Typified:** *Isaac*, Gen. 22:13, with Heb. 11:19. *Jonah*, Jonah 2:10, with Matt. 12:40.

**Symbolical**, Rev. 11:11. *Of the restoration of Israel*, Ezek. 37:1–14.

**Of Jesus:** *Denied by the Jews*, Matt. 28:12–15. *Raised by the power of God*, Acts 2:24, 32; 3:15, 26; 4:10; 5:30; 10:40; 15:20, 30, 33, 34, 37; 17:31; Rom. 4:24; 8:11; 10:9; 1 Cor. 6:14; 15:15; 2 Cor. 4:14; Gal. 1:4; Eph. 1:20; Col. 2:12; 1 Tim. 1:10; 1 Pet. 1:21. *For our justification*, Rom. 4:25; 1 Pet. 3:21. *Earnest of general resurrection*, 1 Cor. 15:12–15; 1 Pet. 1:3.

*The theme of apostolic preaching*, Acts 2:24, 31, 32; 3:15; 4:10, 33; 5:30–32; 10:40, 41; 17:2, 3, 18.

See footnote, JESUS, *Resurrection of*, Matt. 1:21.

27
b Psa. 8:6.
c *Jesus, king,* Matt. 1:21.
5 R. V. in subjection under his feet.
6 R. V. in subjection, it is

28
d *Millennium,* Rev. 20:4.
e *Jesus, divinity of,* Matt. 1:21.
f *God, sovereign,* Gen. 2:2.

29
g *Baptism, for the dead,* Luke 20:4.

30
h *Paul, persecutions of,* Acts 13:9.

31
7 R. V. that glorying in you, brethren, which I have

32
i *Games, figurative,* 1 Cor. 9:24.
j *Animals, figurative,* Jer. 27:5.
k *Ephesus,* Acts 18:19.
l *Dead,* 2 Kin. 4:32.
m Isa. 22:13.
n *Worldliness,* 1 John 2:15.
o *Epicureans,* Acts 17:18.
p *Sensuality,* Jude 19.

33
q *Proverbs,* 1 Sam. 24:13.
r *Fellowship, with the wicked,* 1 Cor. 1:9.
s *Evil Company,* Prov. 13:20.

34
t *Holiness, enjoined,* Ex. 39:30.
u *Spiritual Blindness, manifested in ignorance of God,* 2 Cor. 4:4.
v *Reproof, faithfulness in,* Prov. 17:10.

36
w *Seed, sowing of,* Lev. 19:19.
11 R. V. foolish one,

37
x *Nature, laws of, uniform in operation,* Jas. 3:12.
y *Wheat,* Ezra 6:9.

38
z *God, creator,* Gen. 2:2.

27 [b]For he hath put all things
[5]under [c]his feet. But when he
saith all things are put [6]under
*him, it is* manifest that he is ex-
cepted, which did put all things
under him.[Q]
28 [d]And when all things shall
be subdued unto him, then shall
the [e]Son also himself be subject
unto him that put all things under him, that [f]God may be all in
all.[T]
29 Else what shall they do
which are [g]baptized for the
dead, if the dead *rise not at
all? why are they then baptized
for the dead?
30 And why stand we in [h]jeop-
ardy[G] every hour?
31 I protest by [7]your rejoicing
which I have in Chrīst Jē'ṣus our
Lord, I die daily.
32 If after the manner[G] of men
I have [i]fought with [j]beasts at
[k]Ĕph'e-sŭs, what advantageth[G] it
me, if the [l]dead rise not? [m,n]let
[o]us [p]eat and drink; for to morrow we die.[Q]
33 Be not deceived: [q]evil[8,r,s]com-
munications[G] corrupt good manners.
34 Awake to [9]righteousness,
and [t]sin not; for some [u]have not
the knowledge of God: [v]I speak
*this* to [10]your shame.
35 But some *man* will say, How
are the dead *raised up? and
with what body do they come?
36 *Thou* [11]fool, [w]that which thou
sowest is not quickened,[G] except
it die:
37 And [w]that which thou sowest, thou sowest not that body
that shall be, but [x]bare grain,
it may chance of [y]wheat, or of
some other *grain*:
38 But [z]God giveth it a body as
it hath pleased him, and to every
seed his own body.[Q]
39 All flesh *is* not the same
flesh: but *there is* one *kind of*
[x]flesh of men, another [z]flesh of
beasts, another of fishes, *and*
[x]another of birds.
40 *There are* also [a]celestial[G] bodies, and bodies terrestrial: but
the glory of the celestial[G] *is* one,
and the *glory* of the terrestrial[G] *is*
another.
41 *There is* one glory[G] of the
[b]sun, and another glory[G] of the
[c]moon, and another glory[G] of the
[a]stars: for *one* star differeth from
*another* star in glory.[G]
42 So also *is* the *resurrection
of the dead. It is sown in corruption; [d]it is [e]raised in incorruption:
43 It is sown in dishonour; [d]it
is [e]raised in glory[G]: it is sown in
weakness; [d]it is [e]raised in power:[S]
44 It is sown a natural body;
it is [e]raised a [d]spiritual body.
[12]There is a natural body, and
there is a [d]spiritual body.
45 And so it is written, [f]The
first man [g]Ăd'ăm was made a
living soul; the last [h,i]Ăd'ăm
[13]*was made* a [j]quickening[G] [Q] spirit.[T]
46 Howbeit that *was* not first
which is spiritual, but that which
is natural; and afterward that
which is spiritual.
47 The first [k]man *is* of the earth,
earthy: the second [l]man *is* [14]the
Lord from heaven.[T] [Q]
48 As *is* the earthy, such *are*
they also that are earthy: and as
*is* the heavenly, such *are* they
also that are heavenly.
49 And as we have borne the
[m]image of the earthy, [n]we shall
also bear the image of the heavenly.[Q]
50 Now this I say, brethren,
that flesh and blood cannot
inherit the [o]kingdom of God;
neither doth corruption inherit
incorruption.
51 [T]Behold, I shew[G] you a mystery[G]; We shall not all [p,q]sleep,
but we shall all be changed,
52 In a moment, in the twin-
kling of an eye, at the last trump[G]:

40
a *Stars,* Judg. 5:20.

41
b *Sun,* Josh. 10:12.
c *Moon,* Song 6:10.

42
d *Body, spiritual,* 1 Cor. 6:19.
e *Body, resurrection of,* 1 Cor. 6:19.

44
12 R. V. If there is a natural body, there is also a spiritual body.

45
f Gen. 2:7.
g *Adam, creation of,* Gen. 2:19.
h *Jesus, names of,* Matt. 1:21.
i *Jesus, savior,* Matt. 1:21.
j *Jesus, mission of,* Matt. 1:21.
13 R. V. became a life-giving spirit.

47
k *Man, mortal,* Job 4:17.
l *Jesus, humanity of,* Matt. 1:21.
14 R. V. of heaven. *Omits* the Lord

49
m *Image, figurative,* 1 Cor. 11:7.
n *Righteous, promises to,* Psa. 64:10.

50
o *Heaven, future home of the righteous,* Luke 18:22.

51
p *Sleep, a symbol of death,* Psa. 127:2.
q *Death, exemption from,* Num. 23:10.

52
r *Translation, of the saints, at the last day,* Heb. 11:5.

53
s *Body, corruptible,* 1 Cor. 6:19.
t *Life, everlasting,* Eccl. 8:15.

54
u *Death,* Num. 23:10.
v Isa. 25:8.
w *Prophecies concerning the Messiah, and their fulfillment,* Gen. 12:3.

55
x Hos. 13:14.
15 R. V. death,

56
y *Sin,* Rom. 5:12.
16 R. V. power

57
z *Thankfulness, to God,* Acts 24:3.

a *Praise,* Psa. 150:1.
b *Jesus, mission of,* Matt. 1:21.
c *Salvation,* Acts 16:17.
d *Jesus, lordship of,* Matt. 1:21.

58
e *Commandments, enjoining steadfastness,* Deut. 8:2.
f *Faithfulness,* Luke 16:10.
g *Character, stability of,* Phil. 2:15.
h *Christian Graces,* Gal. 5:22.
i *Perseverance, exhortation to,* Eph. 6:18.
j *Diligence, required,* Rom. 12:8.
k *Zeal,* 2 Cor. 7:11.
l *Righteous, promises to,* Psa. 64:10.

for the trumpet shall sound,
and the [e]dead shall be raised
incorruptible, and we shall be
[r]changed.
53 For this [s]corruptible[G] must
put on incorruption, and this
mortal *must* put on [†,t]immortality.
54 So when this [s]corruptible
shall have put on incorruption,
and this mortal shall have put
on [†]immortality, then shall be
brought to pass the saying that
is written, [u,v,w]Death is swallowed up in victory.[Q]
55 [x]O [u]death, where *is* thy
sting? O [15]grave,[G] where *is* thy
victory?[T Q]
56 The sting of [u]death *is* [y]sin;
and the [16]strength of sin *is* the
law.[T]
57 But [z,a]thanks *be* to God,
which [b]giveth us the [c]victory
through our [d]Lord Jē′ṣus Chrĭst.
58 Therefore, my beloved
brethren, [e,f]be ye [‡,g,h]stedfast,
[h,i]unmoveable, always [h,j,k]abounding in the work of the
Lord, forasmuch as ye know
that [l]your labour is not in vain
in the Lord.[Q]

## CHAPTER 16

*The apostle exhorts them to relieve the wants of the brethren at Jerusalem; 10 commends Timothy; 13 and after friendly admonitions, 19 concludes his epistle with divers salutations.*

NOW[T] concerning the [a]collection for the [b]saints, as [c,d]I
have given order to the churches
of [e]Gă-lā′tiȧ, even so [f]do ye.
2 *Upon the [g]first *day* of the
week let every one of you lay
by him in store, as [1]*God* hath
[h]prospered him, that there be
no gatherings when I come.[S T]
3 And when I come, whomsoever [i]ye shall approve by *your*
[j]letters, them will [c,d]I send to
[2]bring your liberality[G] unto [k]Jĕ-ru′sȧ-lĕm.
4 And if it be meet[G] that I go
also, they shall go with me.
5 Now I will come unto you,
when I shall pass through [l]Măç-e-dō′nĭ-ȧ: for I do pass through
Măç-e-dō′nĭ-ȧ.
6 And it may be that I will
abide, yea, and winter with you,
that ye may bring me on my
journey whithersoever I go.
7 For I [3]will not see you now
by the way; but I trust[G] to tarry[G]
a while with you, if the Lord
[m]permit.
8 But [c]I will tarry[G] at [n]Ĕph′e-sŭs until [o]Pĕn′te-cŏst.[Q]
9 For a great [p,q]door and effectual is opened unto me, and
*there are* many adversaries.
10 Now if [r]Tĭ-mō′the-ŭs come,
[s]see that he may be with you
without fear: for [t]he worketh
the work of the Lord, as [t]I
also *do*.
11 [s]Let no man therefore despise[G] [r]him: but [4]conduct him
forth in peace, that he may come
unto me: for I look for him
with the brethren.
12 As touching *our* brother
[u]Ȧ-pŏl′los, I greatly desired him
to come unto you with the brethren: but his will was not at all to
come at this time; but he will

2
h *Prosperity,* Eccl. 7:14.
1 R. V. he may prosper, that no collections be made when I come.

3
i *Church, government of,* Matt. 16:18.
j *Letters, of commendation,* Isa. 37:14.
k *Jerusalem,* Judg. 19:10.
2 R. V. to carry your bounty unto Jerusalem:

5
l *Macedonia,* Acts 16:12.

7
m *Will of God, supreme rule of duty,* Mark 3:35.
3 R. V. do not wish to see you now

8
n *Ephesus,* Acts 18:19.
o *Pentecost,* Acts 2:1.

9
p *Door, figurative,* Deut. 11:20.
q *Opportunity,* Gal. 6:10.

10
r Or, *Timothy,* 1 Cor. 4:17.
s *Church, duty of, to ministers,* Matt. 16:18.
t *Minister, faithful,* Rom. 15:16.

11
4 R. V. set him forward on his journey in peace,

12
u *Apollos,* Acts 19:1.

1 a *Alms,* Matt. 6:2. b *Poor,* Prov. 21:13. c *Paul,* Acts 13:9. d *Apostles, authority of,* Luke 6:13. e *Galatia,* Acts 16:6. f *Liberality, enjoined,* 1 Tim. 6:18. 2 g *Christian Sabbath,* Mark 16:9.

† **IMMORTALITY,** Job 14:13–15; Prov. 14:32; Matt. 19:16; 25:46; Mark 10:30; Luke 10:25–28; John 3:14–16, 36; 5:39; 6:47, 50–54, 58; 10:28; 11:26; 14:19; 17:2, 3; Rom. 2:7; 6:22, 23; 2 Cor. 5:1; Gal. 6:8; Col. 1:5; 1 Tim. 4:8; 6:12, 19; 2 Tim. 1:9, 10; Tit. 1:2; 3:7; Heb. 10:34; 11:10, 13–16; 13:14; 1 John 2:17, 25; 5:13; Jude 21.

*Moses at the bush assured of,* Ex. 3:6 (with Matt. 22:32; Mark 12:26, 27; Luke 20:36–38; Acts 7:32). *Hope of, sustained Abraham,* Heb. 11:10; *comforted David,* 2 Sam. 12:23.

Implied: *In the translation, of Enoch,* Gen. 5:24; Heb. 11:5; *of Elijah,* 2 Kin. 2:11; *in redemption from Sheol,* Psa. 16:10, 11; *in the spirit returning to God,* Eccl. 3:21; 12:7; *in the soul surviving the death of the body,* Matt. 10:28; *in the appearance of Moses and Elijah at the transfiguration of Jesus,* Matt. 17:2–9; Mark 9:2–10; Luke 9:29–36; *in the abolition of death,* Isa. 25:8; *in the Savior's promise to his disciples,* John 14:2, 3; *in the resurrection,* Isa. 26:19; Dan. 12:2, 3; John 6:40; 1 Thess. 4:13–18; 5:10; see footnote, RESURRECTION, 1 Cor. 15:12; *in eternal inheritance,* Acts 20:32; 26:18; Heb. 9:15; 1 Pet. 1:3–5; *in the everlasting punishment of the wicked,* 2 Thess. 1:7–9; *in the judgment,* see footnote, JUDGMENT, 2 Pet. 3:7.

‡ **STEADFASTNESS,** Psa. 57:7; 108:1; 112:7; Rom. 14:4; 1 Thess. 3:8; Col. 1:23; Jas. 1:25.

*Enjoined,* 1 Cor. 7:20; 15:58; 16:13; Gal. 6:1; Eph. 6:11, 13, 14; Phil. 1:27; 4:1; 1 Thess. 5:21; 2 Thess. 2:15; 3:13; Heb. 10:23; 13:9; Jas. 1:25; 1 Pet. 5:9.

**Rewards of,** Matt. 10:22; 24:13; Mark 13:13; Rev. 2:7, 10, 11, 17, 25–28; 3:5, 11, 12, 21; 21:17.

* **GIVING.** Rules for: *Without ostentation,* Matt. 6:1–4; *regularly,* 1 Cor. 16:2; *liberally,* 2 Cor. 9:6–15; *cheerfully,* 2 Cor. 8:11, 12; 9:7. See footnote, LIBERALITY, 1 Tim. 6:18.

come when he shall have [5]con-
venient time.
13 [v,w]Watch ye, [x,y]stand [z]fast
in the [†]faith, [a]quit you like men,
be strong. [Q]
14 [b,c]Let all your things[G] be
done [6]with [d]charity.[G]
15 I beseech[G] you, brethren,
(ye know the house of [e]Stĕph'-
a-năs, that it is the firstfruits of
[f]Ȧ-chā'-iȧ, and *that* they have
[7,g]addicted[G] themselves to the
[h]ministry of the saints,)
16 That ye [i]submit yourselves
unto such, and to every one that
helpeth with *us*, and laboureth.
17 I am glad of the coming
of [e]Stĕph'a-năs and Fôr-tū-nā'-
tus and Ȧ-chā'i-cŭs: for that
which was lacking on your part
they have supplied.
18 For they have refreshed my
spirit and your's: therefore acknowledge ye them that are such.
19 The churches of [j]Ā'ṣiȧ
[k]salute[G] you. [l]Ăq'uĭ-lȧ and [l]Prĭs-
çĭl'lȧ salute[G] you much in the
Lord, with the [m]church that is
in their [n]house.
20 All the brethren [k]greet you.
Greet ye one another with an
holy [o]kiss.
21 The [k]salutation of *me* [p]Pạul
with mine own hand.
22 If any man [q]love[G] not the
[r]Lord [7]Jē'ṣus Chrīst, let him be
Ȧ-năth'e-mȧ[G] Mär'an–ā'thȧ.[G]
23 [s]The grace of our Lord
Jē'ṣus Chrīst *be* with you.
24 My [g]love *be* with you all in
Chrīst Jē'ṣus. Amen.

[8]The first *epistle* to the Corinthians was written from Philippi by Stephanas, and Fortunatus, and Achaicus, and Timotheus.

5 R. V. opportunity.
**13**
v *Commandment, enjoining watchfulness,* Deut. 8:2.
w *Watchfulness, enjoined,* Matt. 24:42.
x *Temptation, resistance to,* Luke 11:4.
y *Perseverance, exhortation to,* Eph. 6:18.
z *Character, stability of,* Phil. 2:15.
a *Courage, enjoined upon Christians,* Deut. 31:7.
**14**
b *Commandment, enjoining love for man,* Deut. 8:2.
c *Charitableness, enjoined,* Prov. 10:12.
d *Love,* 1 John 4:7.
6 R. V. in love.
**15**
e 1 Cor. 1:16.
f *Achaia,* Acts 18:12.
g *Love, of man for man,* 1 John 4:7. h *Altruism,* Acts 20:35.
7 R. V. set themselves to minister unto the saints).
**16** i *Church, discipline in,* Matt. 16:18.

**19**
j *Asia, churches of,* Acts 2:9.
k *Salutations,* Luke 1:44.
l *Aquila and Priscilla,* Acts 18:2.
m *Fellowship, of the righteous,* 1 Cor. 1:9.
n *Worship, in private homes,* Gen. 22:5.
**20**
o *Kiss,* Ruth 1:9.
**21**
p *Paul,* Acts 13:9.
**22**
q *Love, for Jesus,* 1 John 4:19.
r *Jesus, lordship of,* Matt. 1:21.
7 R. V. *omits* Jesus Christ,
**23**
s *Benedictions, apostolic,* Deut. 21:5.
**24**
8 R. V. *omits postscript.*

THE SECOND EPISTLE OF PAUL TO THE

# CORINTHIANS

## CHAPTER 1

*The apostle's salutation. 3 The consolation God had given him in his tribulation enabled him to comfort others. 8 His trouble in Asia. 12 The ground of his rejoicing. 15 His reasons for not visiting them.*

[a]PAUL, an [b]apostle of Jē'ṣus
Chrīst [c]by the [d]will of God,
and [e]Tĭm'o-thȳ *our* brother, unto
the [f]church of God which is at
[g]Cŏr'inth, with all the saints
which are in all [h]Ȧ-chā'iȧ:[T]
2 [i,j]Grace *be* to you and [k]peace
from God our [l]Father, and *from*
the [m]Lord [n]Jē'ṣus Chrīst.
3 [o,p]Blessed *be* God, even the
Father of our [m]Lord [n]Jē'ṣus
Chrīst, the Father of [q]mercies,
and the God of all comfort;
4 Who [r]comforteth[G] us in all
our [1]tribulation,[G] that we may
be able to [s,t]comfort them which
are in any [1]trouble, by the comfort wherewith we ourselves [r]are
comforted of God.[T]
5 For as the [u]sufferings of
Chrīst abound in [v,w]us, so our
[r]consolation[G] also aboundeth by
Chrīst.[Q]
6 And whether we be afflicted,
*it is* [t]for your consolation and
[2]salvation, which is effectual[G] in
the [x]enduring of the same sufferings which we also [v,w]suffer: or
whether we be comforted, *it is* for
your consolation and salvation.[G]
7 And our hope of you *is* stedfast, knowing, that as ye are
partakers of the sufferings, [y]so
*shall ye be* also of the consolation.

**1**
a *Paul,* Acts 13:9.
b *Apostles,* Luke 6:13.
c *Minister, call of,* Rom. 15:16.
d *Will of God,* Mark 3:35.
e *Timothy,* 1 Cor. 4:17.
f *Church,* Matt. 16:18.
g *Corinth,* Acts 18:1.
h *Achaia,* Acts 18:12.
**2**
i *Grace of God,* Rom. 4:16.
j *Benedictions, apostolic,* Deut. 21:5.
k *Spiritual Peace,* Gal. 1:3.
l *God, fatherhood of,* Gen. 2:2.
m *Jesus, lordship of,* Matt. 1:21.
n *Jesus, divinity of,* Matt. 1:21. **3** o *Thankfulness, to God,* Acts 24:3. p *Praise,* Psa. 150:1. q *God, mercy of,* Gen. 2:2.
**4** r *Adversity, consolation in,* Psa. 34:19.

s *Sympathy,* Jas. 1:27.
t *Love, of man for man,* 1 John 4:7.
1 R. V. affliction,
**5**
u *Jesus, sufferings of,* Matt. 1:21.
v *Minister, trials and persecutions of,* Rom. 15:16.
w *Persecution, of the righteous,* John 15:20.
**6**
x *Patience,* Luke 8:15.
2 R. V. salvation; or whether we be comforted, it is for your comfort, which worketh in the patient enduring of the same sufferings which we also suffer:
**7**
y *Righteous, promises to,* Psa. 64:10.

† **FAITH,** the doctrines of Jesus. *The belief held, in common, by apostles and early Christians,* Acts 6:7; 16:5; 1 Cor. 16:13; Gal. 1:23; 3:23, 25; 6:10; Phil. 1:27; 1 Tim. 3:9; 4:1; 5:8; 6:10, 21; 2 Tim. 3:8; 4:7; Tit. 1:1, 4, 13; 3:15; Jude 3; Rev. 2:13.

8
z *Afflictions*, Psa. 34:19.
a *Asia*, Acts 2:9.
9
b *Self-righteousness*, Luke 18:11.
c *Faith*, Mark 11:22.
d *God, power of*, Gen. 2:2.
e *Resurrection*, 1 Cor. 15:12.
3 R. V. answer
10
f *God, providence of*, Gen. 2:2.
4 R. V. and will deliver: on whom we have set our hope that he will also still deliver us;
11
g *Minister, duty of church to*, Rom. 15:16.
h *Intercession, solicited*, Jer. 27:18.
i *Thankfulness, to God*, Acts 24:3.
12
j *Conscience, approving*, Acts 23:1.
k *Sincerity*, 1 Cor. 5:8.
l *Wisdom, worldly*, Prov. 2:2.
m *Grace of God*, Rom. 4:16.
5 R. V. holiness and sincerity of God,
6 R. V. behaved ourselves in
13
n *Paul*, Acts 13:9.

8 For we would not, brethren, have you ignorant of our
[1,v,w,z]trouble which came to us
in [a]Ā′ṣiȧ, that we were pressed[G]
out of measure, above strength,
insomuch that we despaired even
of life:
9 But we had the [3]sentence
of death in ourselves, that we
should not [b]trust in ourselves,
but [c]in [d]God which [e]raiseth the
dead:
10 Who [f]delivered us from so
great a death, and [4]doth deliver:
in whom we [c]trust that he will
yet deliver *us*;
11 Ye also [g]helping together by
[h]prayer for us, that for the gift
*bestowed*[G] upon us by the means
of many persons [i]thanks may be
given by many on our behalf.
12 For our rejoicing is this, the
testimony of our [j]conscience,
that in [5]simplicity[G] and godly
[k]sincerity, not with fleshly [l]wis-
dom, but by the [m]grace of God,
we [6]have had our conversation[G]
in the world, and more abundantly to you-ward.
13 For we write none other
things unto you, than what ye
read or acknowledge[G]; and [n]I
trust ye shall acknowledge[G] even
to the end;
14 As also ye have acknowledged us in part, that we are
your rejoicing, even as ye also
*are* our's in the day of the [o]Lord
Jē′ṣus.
15 And in this confidence [n]I
was minded[G] to come unto you
before, that ye might have a second benefit;
16 And to pass by you into
[p]Măç-e-dō′nĭ-ȧ, and to come
again out of Măç-e-dō′nĭ-ȧ unto
you, and of you to be brought on
my way toward [q]Jū-dæ′ȧ.
17 When I therefore was thus
minded, did [n]I [7]use lightness[G]?
or the things that I purpose, do I
purpose according to the flesh,
that with me there should be yea
yea, and nay nay?
18 But *as* God *is* [8,r]true, our
[s]word toward you was not yea
and nay.
19 For the [t]Son of God, Jē′-
ṣus Chrīst, who was [u]preached
among you by us, *even* by [n]me
and [v]Sĭl-vā′nus and [w]Tĭ-mō′the-
ŭs, was not yea and nay, but in
him [9]was yea.
20 For [10]all the [*,x]promises of

14
o *Jesus, lordship of*, Matt. 1:21.
16
p *Macedonia*, Acts 16:12.
q *Judea*, Luke 5:17.
17
7 Am. R. V. show fickleness?
18
r *God, faithfulness of*, Gen. 2:2.
s *Doctrines of Jesus*, John 7:16.
8 R. V. faithful.
19
t *Jesus, divine sonship of*, Matt. 1:21.
u *Preaching*, Matt. 9:35.
v Or, *Silas*, Acts, 15:22.
w Or, *Timothy*, 1 Cor. 4:17.
9 R. V. is yea.
20
x *Prophecies concerning the Messiah, and their fulfillment*, Gen. 12:3.
10 R. V. how many soever be the promises of God, in him is the yea: wherefore also through him is the Amen, unto the glory of God through us.

*** PROMISES, OR GROUND OF ASSURANCE**, Heb. 6:12; Jas. 2:5; 2 Pet. 1:4; 3:13. *Against the recurrence of universal flood*, Gen. 9:11.
*Of answer to prayer*, 2 Chr. 7:14; Job 22:27; Psa. 2:8; 145:19; Isa. 58:9; 65:24; Jer. 29:12; 33:3; Matt. 6:6; 7:7, 8, 11; 17:20; 18:19; 21:22; Mark 11:24; Luke 11:13; John 14:13, 14; 15:7, 16; 16:23, 24; Jas. 1:5; 5:15, 16; 1 John 5:14, 15.
*Of blessings upon worshipers*, Ex. 20:24; Isa. 40:31.
*Of comfort in sorrow*, Psa. 46:1; 50:15; 55:22; 146:8; 147:3; Isa. 43:2; Luke 6:21; 2 Cor. 1:3, 4; 7:6.
*Of spiritual enlightenment*, Isa. 29:18, 24; 35:5, 6; 42:16; Matt. 10:19; Luke 21:14, 15; John 7:17; 8:12, 32; Heb. 8:10.
*Of God's presence*, Ex. 3:12; Deut. 31:8; 1 Sam. 10:7.
*Of Christ's presence with believers*, Matt. 18:20; 28:20.
*Of forgiveness*, Psa. 130:4; Isa. 1:18; 43:25; 55:7; Jer. 31:34; 33:8; Matt. 6:14; 12:31, 32; Mark 3:28; Luke 12:10; Acts 10:43; 13:38, 39; Jas. 5:15, 16; 1 John 1:9.
*Of healing*, Jas. 5:15.
*Of the Holy Spirit*, Joel 2:28; Luke 11:13; 24:49; John 7:38, 39; 14:16, 17, 26; 15:26; 16:7; Acts 2:38.
*Of spiritual adoption*, Lev. 26:12; 2 Cor. 6:17, 18; Heb. 8:10.
*Of victory of the Messiah over Satan*, Gen. 3:15.
*To believers*, Jer. 17:7, 8; Mark 16:16–18; John 3:15, 16; 5:24; 6:35, 40, 47; 7:38; 11:25; 14:12–14; Rom. 9:33; 10:9, 11.
*To backsliders*, Lev. 26:40–42; Deut. 30:1–3; 2 Chr. 30:9; Jer. 3:12–15; Hos. 14:4; Mal. 3:7.
*To children*, Ex. 20:12; Deut. 5:16; Matt. 19:14; Mark 10:14; Luke 18:15, 16; Eph. 6:3.
*To the burdened*, Matt. 11:28, 29.
*To the afflicted*, Job 33:24–28; 36:15; Psa. 9:9; 12:5; 18:27; 41:3; Lam. 3:31.
*To orphans and widows*, Deut. 10:18; Psa. 68:5; 146:9; Prov. 15:25; Jer. 49:11.
*To seekers*, Deut. 4:29; 1 Chr. 28:9; 2 Chr. 15:2; Ezra 8:22; Psa. 34:10; 145:18; Jer. 29:13; Matt. 5:6; 6:33; Luke 6:21; John 6:37; Rom. 10:13; Heb. 11:6.
*To the faithful*, Matt. 25:21, 23; Luke 12:42–44; 19:16–19; Rom. 2:7, 10; Rev. 2:10.
*To the forgiving, of divine forgiveness*, Matt. 6:14; Mark 11:25; Luke 6:37.
*To the humble*, Isa. 57:15; Matt. 5:3; 18:4; 23:12; Luke 6:20; 14:11; 18:14; Jas. 4:6; 1 Pet. 5:5, 6.
*To the liberal*, Psa. 41:1–3; 112:9; Prov. 3:9, 10; 11:25; 22:9; 28:27; Eccl. 11:1; Isa. 58:10, 11; Matt. 6:4; Luke 6:38; 2 Cor. 9:6, 8.
*To the meek*, Psa. 10:17; 22:26; 25:9; 37:11; 147:6; 149:4; Prov. 29:23; Isa. 29:19; Matt. 5:5.
*To the merciful*, 2 Sam. 22:26; Psa. 18:25; 41:1–3; Matt. 5:7.
*To ministers*, Psa. 126:5, 6; Jer. 1:8; 20:11; Dan. 12:3; Matt. 28:20; John 4:36, 37; 1 Pet. 5:4.
*To the obedient*, Ex. 15:26; 19:5, 6; 20:6 (with Deut. 5:11); 23:22, 25, 26; Deut. 4:40; 6:2, 3; 12:28; 28:1–6; 30:2–10; 1 Kin. 3:14; Neh. 1:5; Psa. 1:1, 3; 25:10; 103:17, 18; 119:1, 2; Prov. 1:33; Isa. 1:19; Jer. 7:23; Ezek. 18:19; Mal. 3:10, 11; Matt. 5:19; 12:50; Mark 3:35; Luke 8:21; 11:28; John 8:51; 12:26; 14:21, 23; 15:10; 1 John 2:5, 17; 3:24.
*To those who fear the Lord*, Psa. 34:7; 103:11–13, 17; 112:1; 115:13; 128:1–6; 145:19; Prov. 10:27; 19:23; Eccl. 7:18; 8:12.
*To those who have spiritual desire*, Isa. 55:1; Matt. 5:6; Luke 6:21.
*To those who endure to the end*, Matt. 10:22; 24:13; Mark 13:13; Rev. 2:7, 11, 17, 26–28; 3:5, 12, 21; 21:7.
*To those who love their enemies*, Matt. 5:44, 45.
*To those who rebuke the wicked*, Prov. 24:25.
*To those who confess Christ*, Matt. 10:32; Rom. 10:9; 1 John 2:23; 4:15.
*To peacemakers, of sonship*, Matt. 5:9.
*To penitents*, Lev. 26:40–42; Deut. 4:29–31; 2 Chr. 7:14; 30:9; Psa. 34:18; 147:3; Isa. 1:18; 55:7; Matt. 5:4.
*To the poor*, Ex. 22:27; Job 36:15; Psa. 12:5; 35:10; 69:33; 72:2, 4, 12–14; 109:31; 132:15; Prov. 22:22, 23; Isa. 41:17.
*To the pure in heart*, Matt. 5:8.

*y Jesus, mission of,* Matt. 1:21.
*z God, glory of,* Gen. 2:2.

**21**
*a Spiritual Blessings,* Eph. 1:3.
*b Unity, of the righteous,* Psa. 133:1.
*c Righteous, union of, with Christ,* Psa. 64:10.
*d Anointing, figurative,* Deut. 28:40.

**22**
*e Seal, figurative,* 1 Kin. 21:8.
*f Holy Spirit, witness of,* Acts 1:2.

**23**
*g Oath,* Num. 5:19.
*h Corinth,* Acts 18:1.
11 R. V. witness

**24**
*i Faith in Christ,* John 6:69.
*j Minister, duties of,* Rom. 15:16.
*k Joy,* Psa. 5:11.
12 R. V. lordship

**1**
1 R. V. with sorrow.

God [y]in him *are* yea,[G] and in him Amen, unto the [z]glory of God by us.[S T]

21 Now he which [a]stablisheth[G] us [b,c]with you in Christ, and hath [d]anointed us, *is* God;

22 Who hath also [e]sealed us, and given the [†]earnest[G] of the [f]Spirit in our hearts.

23 Moreover [g]I call God for a [11]record[G] upon my soul, that to spare you I came not as yet unto [h]Cŏr'inth.

24 Not for that we have [12]dominion[G] over your [i]faith, but are [j]helpers of your [k]joy: for by faith ye stand.

## CHAPTER 2

*Having shewn why he came not to them,* 6 *the apostle directs them to receive again the excommunicated person.* 12 *His disappointment in not finding Titus at Troas.* 14 *His thanksgiving to God for his success in preaching the gospel.*

BUT I determined this with myself, that I would not come again to you [1]in heaviness.[G]

2 For if I make you sorry, who is he then that maketh me glad, but the same which is made sorry by me?

3 And I wrote this same unto you, lest, when I came, I should have sorrow from them of whom I ought to rejoice; having confidence in you all, that my [a]joy is *the joy* of you all.

4 For out of much [b]affliction[G] and anguish of heart I wrote unto you with many tears; not that ye should be grieved, but that ye might know the [c]love which I have more abundantly unto you.

5 But if any have caused [2]grief, he hath not grieved me, but in part: that I may not overcharge[G] you all.

6 [d]Sufficient to such a man *is* this punishment,[G] which *was inflicted* [3]of many.

7 So that contrariwise[G] [e]ye *ought* rather to [f]forgive *him,* and comfort *him,* lest perhaps such a one should be swallowed[G] up with overmuch sorrow.

8 Wherefore I beseech you that ye would confirm[G] *your* [c]love toward him.

9 For to this end also did I write, that I might know the proof of you, whether ye be [g]obedient in all things.

10[S] To whom [d]ye [f]forgive any thing,[G] I *forgive* also: for if I forgave any thing, to whom

**3**
*a Joy,* Psa. 5:11.

**4**
*b Afflictions,* Psa. 34:19.
*c Love, of man for man,* 1 John 4:7.

**5**
2 R. V. sorrow, he hath caused sorrow, not to me, but in part (that I press not too heavily) to you all.

**6**
*d Church, discipline in,* Matt. 16:18.
3 R. V. by the many;

**7**
*e Charitableness, enjoined,* Prov. 10:12.
*f Forgiveness,* Matt. 18:21.

**9**
*g Obedience,* Heb. 5:8.

**PROMISES**—Continued

*To persecuted saints,* Matt. 5:10, 11; Luke 6:22, 23; 21:12–18; 1 Pet. 4:14.

*To the wise of heart,* Prov. 2:10–21.

**To the righteous,** Job 17:9; 36:11; Psa. 1:1–3; 34:7, 22; 37:4, 5; 55:22; 119:1, 105; 138:8; 145:20; 146:8; Prov. 25:22; Isa. 58:8; Jer. 17:7; Matt. 6:30, 33; 10:22, 42; 24:13; Luke 6:35; 18:6–8; Rom. 5:9; 8:30, 31; 1 Cor. 2:9; 3:21, 22; Gal. 6:9; Phil. 4:7; 2 Thess. 3:3; Rev. 2:17, 26, 28; 3:5; 14:13.

*Of answer to prayer,* Prov. 15:29; Mark 11:23, 24; John 14:13, 14; Acts 10:4; 1 Pet. 3:12; 1 John 3:22.

*Of blessings upon their children,* Psa. 103:17; 112:2, 3; Isa. 59:21.

*Of comfort,* Isa. 25:8; 66:13, 14; Matt. 5:4; John 14:16–18; Rev. 21:4.

*Of deliverance, from temptation,* 1 Cor. 10:13; Jas. 4:7; 2 Pet. 2:9; *from trouble,* Job 5:19–24; Psa. 33:18, 19; 34:15, 17; 50:15; 97:10, 11; Prov. 3:25, 26; Isa. 41:10–13; 43:2.

*Of divine help,* Psa. 55:22; Isa. 41:10, 11, 13; 2 Cor. 12:9; Phil. 4:19; Heb. 13:5, 6.

*Of divine guidance,* Psa. 25:12; 32:8; 37:23, 24; 48:14; 73:24; Prov. 3:5, 6.

*Of divine mercy,* Psa. 32:10; 103:17, 18; Mal. 3:17.

*Of divine presence,* Gen. 26:3, 24; 28:15; 31:3; Ex. 33:14; Deut. 31:6, 8; Josh. 1:5; 1 Kin. 6:13; Hag. 1:13; 2:4, 5; Matt. 18:20; 28:20; John 14:17, 23; 2 Cor. 6:16; 13:11; Phil. 4:9; Heb. 13:5; Jas. 4:8; Rev. 21:3.

*Of divine likeness,* 1 John 3:2.

*Of guidance in the church,* Isa. 4:5, 6.

*Of peace,* Isa. 26:3; John 16:33; Rom. 2:10.

*Of refuge in adversity,* Psa. 33:18, 19; 62:8; 91:1, 3–7, 9–12; Prov. 14:26; Nah. 1:7.

*Of strength in adversity,* Psa. 29:11.

*Of security,* Psa. 32:6, 7; 84:11; 121:3–8; Isa. 33:16.

*Of providential care,* Gen. 15:1; Ex. 23:22; Lev. 26:5, 6, 10; Deut. 33:27; 1 Sam. 2:9; 2 Chr. 16:9; Ezra 8:22; Job 5:15; Psa. 34:9, 10; 37:23–26; 121:2–8; 125:1–3; 145:19, 20; Prov. 1:33; 2:7; 3:6; 10:3; 16:7; Isa. 49:9–11; 65:13, 14; Ezek. 34:11–17, 22–31; Luke 12:7; 21:18; 1 Pet. 5:7.

*Of overruling providence,* Rom. 8:28; 2 Cor. 4:17.

*Of temporal blessings,* Lev. 25:18, 19; 26:5; Deut. 28:1–13; Psa. 37:9; 128:1–6; Prov. 2:21; 3:1–4, 7–10; Matt. 6:26–33; Mark 10:30; Luke 18:29, 30.

*Of spiritual enlightenment,* Isa. 2:3; John 8:12.

*Of seeing God,* Matt. 5:8.

*Of inconceivable spiritual blessings,* Isa. 64:4; 1 Cor. 2:9.

*Of the rest of faith,* Heb. 4:9.

*Of wisdom,* Jas. 1:5.

*Of ministry of angels,* Heb. 1:14.

*Of dwelling with Christ,* John 14:2, 3; 17:24; Col. 3:4; 1 Thess. 4:17; 5:10.

*Of everlasting remembrance,* Psa. 112:6.

*Of having names written in heaven,* Luke 10:20.

*Of resurrection,* John 5:29; 1 Cor. 15:48–57; 2 Cor. 4:14; 1 Thess. 4:16.

*Of heavenly rest,* Heb. 4:9.

*Of future glory,* Matt. 13:43; Rom. 8:18; Col. 3:4; 2 Tim. 2:10; 1 Pet. 1:5; 5:4; Rev. 7:14–17.

*Of treasure in heaven,* Matt. 10:21; Luke 18:22.

*Of inheritance,* Matt. 25:34; Acts 20:32; 26:18; Col. 1:12; 3:24; Tit. 3:7; Heb. 9:15; Jas. 2:5; 1 Pet. 1:4.

*Of heavenly reward,* Matt. 5:12; 13:43; 2 Tim. 4:8; Heb. 11:16; Jas. 1:12; 2 Pet. 1:11; Rev. 2:7, 10; 22:5, 12, 14.

*Of eternal life,* Dan. 12:2, 3; Matt. 19:29; 25:46; Mark 10:29, 30; Luke 18:29, 30; John 3:15, 16, 36; 4:14; 5:24, 29; 6:40; 10:28; 12:25; 17:2; Rom. 2:7; 6:22, 23; Gal. 6:8; 1 Thess. 4:15–17; 1 Tim. 1:16; 4:8; Tit. 1:2; 1 John 2:25; 5:13; Rev. 22:5.

*To reign forever,* Rev. 22:5; compare Matt. 25:21, 23; Luke 19:17, 18.

† **EARNEST.** *A pledge or token,* Psa. 86:17; 2 Cor. 1:22; 5:5; Eph. 1:14. See footnote, TOKEN, Psa. 86:17.

11
*h Satan*, Matt. 4:10.
*i Temptation, sources of*, Luke 4:11.
12
*j* Acts 16:8, 11; 20:5, 6; 2 Tim. 4:13.
*k Gospel*, Mark 13:10.
*l Doctrines of Jesus*, John 7:16.
*m Opportunity, providential*, Gal. 6:10.
*n God, providence of*, Gen. 2:2.
4 R. V. for the gospel of Christ, and when a door
13
*o Titus*, Tit. 1:4.
*p Brother*, Prov. 18:24.
*q Macedonia*, Acts 16:12.
14
*r Thankfulness, to God*, Acts 24:3.
15
*s Agency, in salvation of men*, Mark 1:17.
*t Salvation*, Acts 16:17.
*u Wicked, punishment of*, Psa. 73:3.
5 R. V. are perishing;
16
*v Spiritual Death*, 1 John 3:14.
*w Life, spiritual*, Eccl. 8:15.
6 R. V. a savour from death
17
*x Minister, faithful*, Rom. 15:16.
*y False Teachers*, 2 Pet. 2:1.
*z Doctrines of Jesus*, John 7:16.
*a Sincerity*, 1 Cor. 5:8.

I forgave *it*, for your sakes
*forgave I it* in the person of
Christ;
11 Lest [h,i]Sā′tan should get an
advantage of us: for we are not
ignorant of his devices.
12 Furthermore, when I came
to [j]Trō′ăs [4]to *preach* Christ's
[k,l]gospel, and a [m]door was opened
unto me of the [n]Lord,
13 [c]I had no rest in my spirit,
because I found not [o]Tī′tus my
[p]brother: but taking my leave of
them, I went from thence into
[q]Măç-e-dō′nĭ-ȧ.
14 Now [r]thanks *be* unto God,
which always causeth us to triumph
in Christ, and maketh
manifest the savour of his knowledge
by us in every place.
15 For [s]we are unto God a
sweet savour of Christ, in them
that are [t]saved, and in them that
[5,u]perish:
16 To the one [6]*we are* the savour
of [v]death unto death; and
to the other the savour of [w]life
unto life. And who *is* sufficient
for these things?
17 For [x]we are not as [y]many,
which corrupt the [z]word of God:
but as of [a]sincerity, but as of
God, in the sight of God speak
we in Christ.

## CHAPTER 3

*They are his epistle of commendation. 6 The ministration of the Spirit shewn to be more glorious than the ministration of condemnation. 14 The veil on Israel's heart. 17 Where the Spirit of the Lord is, there is liberty.*

1
*a Letters, of commendation*, Isa. 37:14.
1 R. V. as do some, epistles of commendation to you or from you?
2
*b Minister, success attending*, Rom. 15:16.
*c Love, of man for man*, 1 John 4:7.

DO we begin again to commend
ourselves? or need we, [1]as
some *others*, [a]epistles of commendation
to you, or *letters* of
commendation from you?
2 [b]Ye are our epistle [c]written in
our hearts, known and read of
all men:
3 *Forasmuch as ye are* manifestly
declared to be the epistle
of Christ ministered by us, written
not with ink, but with the
[d]Spirit of the living God; not
in tables of stone, but in [2]fleshy
tables of the heart.
4 And such trust have we
through Christ to God-ward:
5 [e]Not that we are sufficient of
ourselves to think any thing as
of ourselves; but [e]our [f]sufficiency
*is* of God;
6 Who also hath made us [3]able
ministers of the [g,h]new testament;
not of the letter, but of the
spirit: for the letter killeth, but
the spirit giveth [i]life.
7 But if the [j]ministration of
death, written *and* engraven in
stones, [4]was glorious, so that the
children of Iș′ra-el could not
stedfastly behold the face of
[k]Mō′ṣeṣ for the glory of his
[l]countenance; which *glory* was
[5]to be done away:
8 How shall not the [h]ministration
of the spirit be rather
glorious?
9 For if the [j]ministration of condemnation
*be* glory, much more
doth the [h]ministration of righteousness
exceed in glory.
10 For even [j]that which was
made glorious had no glory in
this respect, by reason of the
[h]glory that excelleth.
11 For if [j]that which [6]is done
away *was* glorious, much more
[h]that which remaineth *is* [7]glorious.
12 Seeing then that we have
such [m]hope, we use great [8]plainness
of speech:
13 And not as [k]Mō′ṣeṣ, *which*
put a [n]vail over his face, that
the children of Iș′ra-el could not
stedfastly look to the end of that
which [9]is abolished:
14 But their minds were
[10,o]blinded: for until this day remaineth
the same [o]vail untaken
away in the reading of the [p]old
[11]testament; which *vail* is done
away in [q]Christ.
15 But even unto this day,

3
*d Holy Spirit, regenerates*, Acts 1:2.
2 R. V. tables that are hearts of flesh.
5
*e Minister, character and qualifications of*, Rom. 15:16.
*f Spiritual Blessings, from God*, Eph. 1:3.
6
*g New Covenant*, Jer. 31:31.
*h Gospel*, Mark 13:10.
*i Life, spiritual*, Eccl. 8:15.
3 R. V. sufficient as ministers of a new covenant;
7
*j Law, temporary*, Deut. 33:2.
*k Moses, face of, transfigured*, Ex. 2:10.
*l Countenance, transfigured*, Prov. 15:13.
4 R. V. came with glory,
5 R. V. passing away:
11
6 R. V. passeth away was with glory,
7 R. V. in glory.
12
*m Hope*, Prov. 13:12.
8 R. V. boldness
13
*n Veil*, Gen. 24:65.
9 R. V. was passing away:
14
*o Spiritual Blindness*, 2 Cor. 4:4.
*p Law, of Moses*, Deut. 33:2.
*q Jesus, mission of*, Matt. 1:21.
10 R. V. hardened:
11 R. V. covenant

when [p]Mō′şeş is read, the [o]vail
is upon their heart.[S]
16 Nevertheless when [r]it shall
turn to the [s]Lord, the [o]vail shall
be taken away.[Q]
17 Now[S T] the Lord is [12]that [t]Spir-
it: and where the Spirit of the
Lord *is,* there *is* [u]liberty.
18 But we all, with [13]open face
beholding as in a [v]glass[G] the
[w]glory of the Lord, are changed
into the same [x]image from glory
to glory, *even* as by the Spirit of
the Lord.[S T Q]

## CHAPTER 4

*The apostle's sincerity and diligence in preaching the gospel. 7 How his troubles and persecutions did redound to the praise of God's power, 12 to the benefit of the church, 16 and to the apostle's own eternal glory.*

THEREFORE seeing we have
this ministry, as we have received mercy, [a]we [b]faint not;
2 But have [c,d]renounced the hidden things of [1]dishonesty,[G] [c,d]not
walking in [e]craftiness, [c]nor handling the [f]word of God [e]deceit-
fully; but by [c]manifestation of
the [g]truth commending ourselves
to every man's [h]conscience in the
sight of God.
3 But if our [g]gospel be [2]hid,[G] it
is [2]hid[G] to them that [3]are [i,j]lost:
4 In whom the [k]god of this
world[G] hath *blinded the minds
of [l]them which [m]believe not, lest
the [n]light of the [4]glorious[G] gospel
of Christ, who is the [o,p,q]image
of God, should shine unto them.[T]
5 For [r]we [s]preach not ourselves,
but Christ Jē′şus [5]the [t]Lord;
and [u]ourselves your [v,w]servants
for Jē′şus' sake.
6 For God, [x]who commanded
the [y]light to shine out of [z]dark-
ness, hath shined[G] in our [a]hearts,
[b]to *give* the [c]light of the [d]knowl-
edge of the [e]glory of God in the
face of Jē′şus Christ.[Q]
7 But we have this [f]treasure
in [g]earthen vessels, that the [6]ex-
cellency of the [h]power may be of
God, and [i]not of us.
8 *We are* [7,j]troubled on every
side, [k,l,m]yet not [8]distressed; *we
are* perplexed, [k,l,m]but not in despair;
9 [9,j]Persecuted, [k,l,m]but not forsaken; [j]cast down, [k,l,m]but not
destroyed;
10 Always [n]bearing about in
the body the [o]dying of [10]the Lord
Jē′şus, that the life also of Jē′şus
might be made manifest in our
body.
11 For we which live are alway
[n]delivered unto death for Jē′şus'
sake, [p]that the life also of Jē′şus
might be made manifest in our
mortal flesh.
12 So then death worketh in us,
but life in you.
13 We[T] having the same spirit of
[q]faith, according as it is written,
[r]I believed, and therefore have I
[s]spoken; we also [q]believe, and
therefore [s]speak;[Q]

**16**
r *Jews,* Neh. 4:2.
s *Jesus, lordship of,* Matt. 1:21.
**17**
t *Holy Spirit,* Acts 1:2.
u *Liberty, under the gospel,* Lev. 25:10.
12 R. V. the
**18**
v *Mirror, figurative,* Job 37:18.
w *God, glory of,* Gen. 2:2.
x *Image, figurative,* 1 Cor. 11:7.
13 R. V. unveiled face reflecting as a mirror the glory of the Lord, are transformed into the same image from glory to glory, even as from the Lord the Spirit.

**1**
a *Zeal, exemplified,* 2 Cor. 7:11.
b *Courage,* Deut. 31:7.
**2**
c *Minister, character and qualifications of,* Rom. 15:16.
d *Righteous, described,* Psa. 64:10.
e *Hypocrisy,* Jas. 3:17.
f *Word of God,* Psa. 119:9.
g *Truth,* John 18:37.
h *Conscience, another's, to be respected,* Acts 23:1.
1 R. V. shame,
**3**
i *Moral insensibility,* Luke 8:10.
j *Wicked, described,* Psa. 73:3.
2 R. V. veiled,
3 Am. R. V. perish:

**5**
r *Minister, humble,* Rom. 15:16.
s *Preaching,* Matt. 9:35.
t *Jesus, lordship of,* Matt. 1:21.
u *Love, of man for man,* 1 John 4:7.
v *Servant, figurative,* Jer. 2:14.
w *Altruism,* Acts 20:35.
5 R. V. as Lord,
**6**
x *God, creator,* Gen. 2:2.
y *Light,* Gen. 1:3.
z *Darkness,* Gen. 1:2.

a *Heart, renewed,* Psa. 44:21.
b *Jesus, mission of,* Matt. 1:21.
c *Light, figurative,* Matt. 5:14.
d *Wisdom, spiritual,* Prov. 2:2.
e *God, glory of,* Gen. 2:2.
**7**
f *Treasure, figurative,* Luke 12:33.
g *Body,* 1 Cor. 6:19.
h *God, power of,* Gen. 2:2.
i *Humility,* Prov. 22:4.
6 R. V. greatness of the power
**8**
j *Persecution, of the righteous,* John 15:20.
k *Paul, character of,* Acts 13:9.
l *Faith, exemplified,* Mark 11:22.
m *Adversity, resignation in,* Psa. 10:6.
7 R. V. pressed
8 R. V. straitened;
**9**
9 R. V. Pursued, yet not forsaken; smitten down,

**4** k *Satan,* Matt. 4:10. l *Unbelievers,* 1 Cor. 6:6. m *Jesus, rejected,* Matt. 1:21. n *Light, figurative of the gospel,* Matt. 5:14. o *Image, figurative,* 1 Cor. 11:7. p *Jesus, relation of, to the Father,* Matt. 1:21. q *Jesus, perfections of,* Matt. 1:21. 4 R. V. gospel of the glory of Christ,

**10** n *Suffering for Christ,* Phil. 1:29. o *Jesus, death of,* Matt. 1:21. 10 R. V. *omits* the Lord **11** p *Afflictions, design of,* Psa. 34:19.
**13** q *Faith in Christ,* John 6:69. r Psa. 116:10. s *Religious Testimony,* 2 Thess. 1:10.

* **SPIRITUAL BLINDNESS,** Deut. 29:4; Job 5:14; Isa. 29:10–12; 56:10; 59:10; Jer. 2:8; 5:21; 9:3; Ezek. 12:2; Rom. 11:8. *Foretold,* Isa. 60:2; Rom. 2:4; 11:10.

**Manifested:** IN IGNORANCE: *Of God,* Ex. 5:2; Isa. 1:3; Jer. 4:22; Hos. 4:1, 6; John 7:28; 15:21; 16:2, 3; 17:25; Acts 17:23; 1 Cor. 1:18, 20, 21; 2:8, 14, 15; 15:34; Gal. 4:8; Eph. 4:17–19; 1 Thess. 4:4, 5; 1 John 4:8; 3 John 11.

*Of Christ,* Matt. 16:3, 9; Luke 23:34; John 1:5, 10; 4:10, 22 (with vs. 11, 15); 8:15, 19, 27, 33, 42, 43, 52, 54, 55, 57; 9:29, 30, 39 (with vs. 30–38); Acts 3:17 (with v. 14); Rom. 11:7, 8, 25 (with context); 1 Pet. 1:14; 1 John 3:1, 6.

*Of the Holy Spirit,* John 14:17; Acts 19:2.

*Of the Scriptures,* Matt. 22:29; Mark 12:24; Acts 13:27; 2 Cor. 3:14, 15; Heb. 5:11, 12; 2 Pet. 3:16.

*Of moral truth,* Deut. 32:28, 29; Prov. 4:19; 28:5; Isa. 5:13; Dan. 12:10; Matt. 15:14, 16; 16:3, 9; 23:19, 24, 26 (with vs. 16–24); Mark 7:18; Luke 6:39; 12:48, 57; 2 Tim. 3:7; Jude 10.

*Of the way of salvation,* Luke 19:42; John 3:4; 6:52, 60; 2 Pet. 1:9; 1 John 1:6, 8; 2:4, 9, 11; Rev. 3:17.

*Of God's ways,* Psa. 95:10; Jer. 5:4; 8:7–9; Mic. 4:12.

IN UNBELIEF, Psa. 14:1, 4; Isa. 53:1; Mark 16:14; John 12:35, 38; Acts 28:25, 27; 2 Cor. 4:3, 4, 6; 2 Thess. 2:11, 12.

IN INSENSIBILITY, Deut. 29:4; Judg. 16:20; Prov. 7:7–23; 17:16; Isa. 6:9, 10; 42:18–20; 44:18–20; 48:8; Jer. 16:10; Hos. 7:11; Matt. 6:23; 13:13–15; Mark 4:11, 12; 6:52; 8:18; Luke 8:10; John 12:40; Acts 28:25, 26, 27.

IN PRESUMPTION, Psa. 10:5, 6; 94:7, 8; Isa. 28:10–13, 15; 40:21, 27, 28; Jer. 8:8, 9; Amos 9:10.

IN PERVERSITY, Job 21:14, 15; Prov. 1:7, 22, 29, 30; 13:18; 19:2, 3; Isa. 5:20; 26:10, 11; Jer. 9:3, 6; Ezek. 12:2, 3; Hos. 5:4; Matt. 21:32; Mark 3:5; Luke 11:52; John 3:19; Rom. 1:19–23, 28–31.

IN HYPOCRISY, Tit. 1:15, 16.

**Consequences of,** Prov. 10:21; 14:12, Isa. 27:11; Hos. 4:6, 14; 2 Thess. 1:8.

**Remedy for,** Isa. 9:2; 25:7; 35:5; 42:6, 7; Luke 4:18; John 8:12; Acts 26:18; 2 Cor. 4:6; Eph. 5:8; Col. 1:13; 1 Pet. 2:9.

14 Knowing that he which
[t]raised up the [u]Lord Jē´ṣus
[v]shall [w]raise up us also [11]by Jē´-
ṣus, and shall present *us* with
you.[T]
15 For all things *are* for your
sakes, [x]that the [12]abundant grace
might through the [y]thanksgiving
of many redound[G] to the [e]glory of
God.[S]
16 For which cause we faint not;
but though our outward [z]man
[13]perish, yet the inward *man* is
renewed day by day.
17 For our light [a]affliction,
which is but for a moment, [b]work-
eth for us a far more exceeding
*and* eternal weight of glory;
18 While we look not at the
things which are seen, but at the
things which are not seen: for
the things which are seen *are*
temporal; but the things which
are not seen *are* eternal.

## CHAPTER 5

*The apostle's assurance of eternal life, 2 and desire to be absent from the body, and to be present with the Lord. 9 He labors to be accepted of him. 12 The love of Christ constrains him to act. 18 The ministry of reconciliation.*

FOR [a]we [b]know that if our
earthly [c,d]house of *this* tabernacle were [e]dissolved, [f]we have
a [g]building of God, an house
not made with hands, [h,i]eternal
in the [j]heavens.[Q]
2 For in this we groan, earnestly [k]desiring to be clothed upon
with our [g]house[G] which is from
[j]heaven:
3 If so be that being [o]clothed
we shall not be found naked.[G]
4 For [l]we that are in *this* [d]tab-
ernacle do groan, being burdened: not for that we would
be unclothed, but [g]clothed upon,
that [1]mortality might be swallowed up of [h,i]life.
5[T] Now [m]he that hath wrought[G]
us for the selfsame[G] [h,n]thing *is*
God, who also hath given unto
us the [o,p]earnest[G] of the [q]Spirit.[S]
6 Therefore *we are* always [2,r]con-
fident, knowing that, [s]whilst [l]we
are at home in the body, we are
absent from the Lord:[T]
7 (For we walk by [r]faith, not by
sight:)
8 We are [2,r]confident, *I say*, and
[s]willing rather to be [l]absent from
the body, and [s]to be [3]present with
the Lord.
9 Wherefore [4,l]we labour, that,
whether present or absent, we
may be [s]accepted of him.[G]
10 For we must all appear
before the [t]judgment seat of
[u]Christ; that every one may [v]re-
ceive the things *done* in *his* body,
[w]according to that he hath done,
whether *it be* good or bad.[T Q]
11 Knowing therefore the [5,x]ter-
ror of the Lord, [y]we persuade
men; but we are made manifest unto God; and I trust also
are made manifest in your [z]con-
sciences.
12 For we commend not ourselves again unto you, but give
you occasion to glory[G] on our behalf, that ye may have somewhat
to *answer* them which glory[G] [a]in
appearance, and not in heart.
13 For whether we be [b]be-
side ourselves, *it is* to God: or
whether we [6]be sober,[G] *it is* [c,d]for
your cause.
14[S T] For the [e]love of Christ constraineth us; because we thus
judge, that if one [f,g]died [h]for all,
[7]then were all dead:
15 And *that* he [f,g]died [h]for
all, that they which live [i]should
not henceforth [j]live unto themselves, but unto him which died
for them, and [k]rose again.[S T]
16 Wherefore henceforth know
we no man after[G] the flesh: yea,
though we have known Christ
after[G] the [l]flesh, yet now henceforth know we *him* no more.
17 Therefore[S] if any man *be* [m]in

**14**
*t Jesus, resurrection of,* Matt. 1:21.
*u Jesus, lordship of,* Matt. 1:21.
*v Righteous, promises to,* Psa. 64:10.
*w Resurrection,* 1 Cor. 15:12.
11 R. V. with

**15**
*x Adversity, benefits of,* Psa. 10:6.
*y Thankfulness, to God,* Acts 24:3.
12 R. V. grace, being multiplied through the many, may cause the thanksgiving to abound unto the glory of God.

**16**
*z Man, mortal,* Job 4:17.
13 R. V. is decaying,

**17**
*a Afflictions, benefits of,* Psa. 34:19.
*b Faith,* Mark 11:22.

**1**
*a Religious Testimony,* 2 Thess. 1:10.
*b Faith, exemplified,* Mark 11:22.
*c House, figurative,* Esth. 8:1.
*d Body,* 1 Cor. 6:19.
*e Death, of the righteous, anticipated with confidence,* Num. 23:10.
*f Promise, or Ground of Assurance,* 2 Cor. 1:20.
*g Body, spiritual,* 1 Cor. 6:19.
*h Immortality,* 1 Cor. 15:54.
*i Life, everlasting,* Eccl. 8:15.
*j Heaven, future home of the righteous,* Luke 18:22.

**2**
*k Spiritual Desire,* Psa. 42:1.

**4**
*l Man, a spirit,* Job 4:17.
1 R. V. what is mortal may be

**5**
*m God, creator,* Gen. 2:2.
*n Man, design of his creation,* Job 4:17.
*o Earnest,* 2 Cor. 1:22.
*p Spiritual Blessings,* Eph. 1:3.
*q Holy Spirit,* Acts 1:2.

**6**
*r Faith, exemplified,* Mark 11:22.
*s Love, for Jesus,* 1 John 4:19.
2 R. V. of good courage,

**8**
3 R. V. at home

**9**
4 R. V. also we make it our aim, whether at home or absent, to be well-pleasing unto him.

**10**
*t Judgment, general,* 2 Pet. 3:7.
*u Jesus, judge,* Matt. 1:21.
*v Judgment, according to opportunity and works,* 2 Pet. 3:7.
*w Responsibility, personal,* Ezek. 18:20.

**11**
*x Fear of God,* Acts 9:31.
*y Minister, faithful,* Rom. 15:16.
*z Conscience, another's, to be respected,* Acts 23:1.
5 R. V. fear of

**12**
*a Hypocrisy,* Jas. 3:17.

**13**
*b Insanity, Paul accused of,* Prov. 26:18.
*c Love, of man for man,* 1 John 4:7.
*d Unselfishness,* 1 Cor. 10:24.
6 R. V. are of sober mind,

**14**
*e Jesus, love of,* Matt. 1:21.
*f Jesus, mission of,* Matt. 1:21.
*g Atonement, by Jesus,* Lev. 17:11.
*h Jesus, vicarious death of,* Matt. 1:21.
7 R. V. therefore all died;

**15** *i Righteous, described,* Psa. 64:10. *j Selfishness,* 2 Tim. 3:2. *k Resurrection, of Jesus,* 1 Cor. 15:12. **16** *l Jesus, incarnation of,* Matt. 1:21. **17** *m Righteous, union of, with Christ,* Psa. 64:10.

n Gal. 6:15.
o *Regeneration*, Tit. 3:5.

**18**

p *God, mercy of*, Gen. 2:2.
q *Minister, duties of, to save men*, Rom. 15:16.
8 R. V. through Christ,

**19**

r *Sin, forgiveness of*, Rom. 5:12.
s *Justification*, Rom. 4:25.
t *Gospel*, Mark 13:10.

**20**

u *Agency, in salvation of men*, Mark 1:17.
v *Ambassadors, figurative*, Josh. 9:4.
9 R. V. were intreating by us: we beseech you on behalf of Christ,

**21**

w *Jesus, holiness of*, Matt. 1:21.
x *Jesus, perfections of*, Matt. 1:21.

Christ, *he is* a [n,o]new creature:
old things are passed away;
behold, all things are become
new.[Q]
18 And all things *are* of God,
who hath [+,p]reconciled us to
himself [8,t,q]by Jē'ṣus Christ, and
hath given to us the [q]ministry of
reconciliation;
19 To[C] wit, that God was in
Christ, [+,p]reconciling the world
unto himself, [r,s]not imputing[C]
their trespasses unto them; and
hath committed unto us the
[t]word of reconciliation.[S]
20 Now then [u]we are [q,v]ambassadors for Christ, as though God
[9]did beseech *you* by us: we pray[C]
*you* in Christ's stead, be ye [+]reconciled to God.[Q]
21 For he hath made him [†]*to
be* sin for us, who knew [w,x]no
sin; that we might be made the
righteousness of God in him.[S]

## CHAPTER 6

*Paul beseeches them not to receive the grace of God in vain. 3 His faithful and self-denying labors in the ministry. 11 His strong affection for them, 13 and desire that they should live as becomes the gospel. 14 Separation from unbelievers.*

**1**

a 1 Cor. 3:9.
b *Grace of God*, Rom. 4:16.

**2**

c Isa. 49:8.
d *Salvation*, Acts 16:17.
e *God, mercy of*, Gen. 2:2.

**3**

f *Minister, character and qualifications of*, Rom. 15:16.
g *Zeal, exemplified*, 2 Cor. 7:11.
h *Minister, duties of*, vs. 3–10; Rom. 15:16.
1 R. V. occasion of stumbling in anything, that our ministration be not blamed;

**4**

i *Patience*, Luke 8:15.
j *Resignation, exemplified*, Job 5:17.

WE then, *as* [a]workers together
*with him*, beseech *you* also
that ye receive not the [b]grace of
God in vain.[C]
2 (For he saith, [c]I have heard
thee in a time accepted, and in
the day of [d]salvation have I [e]succoured[C] thee: behold, now *is* the
accepted time; behold, now *is*
the day of salvation.)[Q]
3 [f,g,h]Giving no [1]offence in any
thing, that the ministry be not
blamed:
4 [f,g]But in all *things* [2]approving[C] ourselves as the [h]ministers
of God, in much [i,j]patience, in
[k,l]afflictions, in [l]necessities, in
[l]distresses,
5 [l]In [m]stripes,[C] in [n]imprisonments, in tumults, in labours, in
watchings,[C] in [o]fastings;
6 [f]By [p]pureness, by [q]knowledge,
by *longsuffering,[C] by [r]kindness,
by the [s]Holy[C] Ghost,[C] by [t]love unfeigned,[C]
7 [f]By the [u]word of [v]truth, by
the [w]power of God, by the [x]armour of [y]righteousness on the
right hand and on the left,
8 By honour and dishonour, by
[z]evil report and good report: [a]as
deceivers, and [a]*yet* true;
9 [a,b]As unknown, and [a]*yet* well
known; as dying, and, behold,
we live; as chastened, and not
killed;
10 [a,b]As sorrowful, [a]yet alway
[c]rejoicing; [a]as poor, yet [d]making
many rich; [a]as having nothing,
and [a]*yet* possessing all things.
11 O *ye* [e]Cŏ-rinth'ĭ-anṣ, [f]our
mouth is open unto you, [g]our
heart is enlarged.[Q]
12 Ye are not straitened in us,
but ye are straitened in your
own [3]bowels.[C]
13 Now for a recompence[C] in the
same, (I speak as unto *my* children,)[C] be ye also enlarged.
14 [h]Be ye not unequally [i]yoked[C]
together with [j]unbelievers: for
what [k]fellowship hath righteousness with unrighteousness? and
what communion hath [l]light
with [m]darkness?
15 And what concord hath
Christ with [n]Bē'lĭ-al[C]? or what
part hath he that [o]believeth with
an [†,4]infidel[C]?

k *Afflictions*, Psa. 34:19.
l *Minister, trials and persecutions of*, Rom. 15:16.
2 R. V. commending

**5**

m *Scourging*, Acts 22:24.
n *Imprisonment*, Acts 12:4.
o *Fasting*, Zech. 8:19.

**6**

p *Purity, of heart*, 1 Tim. 4:12.
q *Wisdom, spiritual*, Prov. 2:2.
r *Kindness*, Acts 28:2.
s *Holy Spirit*, Acts 1:2.
t *Love*, 1 John 4:7.

**7**

u *Gospel*, Mark 13:10.
v *Truth*, John 18:37.
w *God, power of*, Gen. 2:2.
x *Armor, figurative*, 1 Sam. 17:54.
y *Righteousness*, Psa. 15:2.

**8**

z *Slander*, Prov. 10:18.
a *Paradox*, 2 Cor. 12:4.

**9**

b *Minister, character and qualifications of*, Rom. 15:16.

**10**

c *Joy, under adversity*, Psa. 5:11.
d *Altruism*, Acts 20:35.

**11**

e *Corinth, church of*, Acts 18:1.
f *Zeal, exemplified*, 2 Cor. 7:11.
g *Love, of man for man*, 1 John 4:7.

**12**

3 R. V. affections.

**14** h *Church, discipline in*, Matt. 16:18. i *Marriage* (as some interpret), Gen. 34:9. j *Unbelievers*, 1 Cor. 6:6. k *Fellowship, with the wicked, forbidden*, 1 Cor. 1:9. l *Light, figurative*, Matt. 5:14. m *Darkness, figurative*, Gen. 1:2. **15** n *Satan*, Matt. 4:10. o *Faith in Christ*, John 6:69. 4 R. V. unbeliever?

**+ RECONCILIATION. Between God and Man:** *Through Christ*, Rom. 5:1, 10; 11:15; 2 Cor. 5:18–21; Eph. 2:15–17; Col. 1:20–22; Heb. 2:17.

**Between man and man**, Matt. 5:23–26. *Between Esau and Jacob*, Gen. 33:4, 11. *Between Saul and David*, 1 Sam. 19:7. *Between Pilate and Herod*, Luke 23:12.

***LONGSUFFERING**, 1 Tim. 1:16. *A Christian grace*, 1 Cor. 13:4, 7; 2 Cor. 6:4–6; Gal. 5:22; Col. 1:11; 2 Tim. 3:10; 4:2. *Enjoined*, Eph. 4:2; Col. 3:12, 13.

See footnotes: CHARITABLENESS, Prov. 10:12; GOD, *Longsuffering of*, Gen. 2:2; PATIENCE, Luke 8:15.

**† INFIDELITY. Disbelief in God**, Num. 15:30, 31; 2 Chr. 32:14–19; Isa. 29:16.

*Prosperity tempts to*, Deut. 32:15. *Arguments against*, Job 12:7–25; Psa. 94:8, 9; Isa. 10:15; 29:16; 45:9, 10; Rom. 1:20; 9:20, 21.

Exemplified: *In mocking God*, Psa. 14:1, 6; Isa. 57:4–11; Dan. 3:15; Acts 17:18; 2 Pet. 3:3, 4; Jude 18, 19. *In mocking*

16 And what agreement hath
[5]the [p,q,r]temple of God with
idols? for [6]ye are the temple of
the living God; as God hath
said, [s,t,u]I will [v]dwell in them,
and walk in *them*; and I will
be their God, and they shall be
my people.[T Q]
17 Wherefore [w]come out from
among them, and [x]be ye separate, saith the Lord, and touch
[7]not the unclean[C] *thing*; and [y]I
will receive you,[S Q]
18 And will be a [z]Father unto
you, and ye shall be [a]my sons
and daughters, saith the Lord
Almighty.[S T Q]

## CHAPTER 7

*The apostle exhorts them to purity of life, and to bear him like affection as he does to them. 4 He declares what comfort he received in his afflictions from the coming of Titus, 7 and from the report he gave of the godly sorrow his former epistle had wrought in them. 13 Their kindness to Titus.*

HAVING therefore these
promises, dearly [a]beloved,
[b,c]let us [d]cleanse ourselves from
all [1]filthiness of the flesh and
spirit, [c]perfecting holiness in the
[e]fear of God.[S T]
2 [2]Receive us; [f,g]we have
wronged no man, we have corrupted[C] no man, we have defrauded no man.
3 I speak not *this* to condemn
*you*: for I have said before, that
ye are in our hearts to die and
live with *you*.
4 Great *is* my [h]boldness of
speech toward you, great *is* my
glorying[C] [3]of you: [i]I am filled
with comfort, [i]I am exceeding
joyful in all our [j]tribulation.
5 For, when we were come into
[k]Măç-e-dō′nĭ-ȧ, our flesh had
[l]no rest, but we were [l]troubled
on every side; without *were*
[l]fightings, within *were* [l]fears.
6 Nevertheless God, that [m]com-
forteth [4,n]those that are cast
down, comforted us by the [o]com-
ing of [p]Tī′tus;[Q]
7 And not by his coming only,
but by the consolation wherewith he was comforted in you,
when he told us your earnest
desire, your [q,r]mourning, your
[5]fervent mind toward me; so that
I rejoiced the more.
8 For [s]though I made you sorry
with [6]a letter, I do not [7]repent,[C]
though I did [7]repent[C]: for I perceive that the same epistle hath
made you sorry, though *it were*
but for a season.
9[S] Now I rejoice, not that ye
were made sorry, but that ye
sorrowed to [t]repentance[C]: for ye
were made sorry after[C] a godly
manner, that ye might [8]receive
damage by us in nothing.
10 For godly sorrow worketh
[t]repentance[C] to [u]salvation [9]not to
be repented[C] of: but the sorrow of
the world worketh [v,w]death.[S T]
11 For behold this selfsame[C]
thing, that ye [t]sorrowed after a
godly sort,[C] what carefulness[C] it
wrought in you, yea, *what* clearing of yourselves, yea, *what* indignation, yea, *what* fear, yea,
*what* vehement desire, yea, *what*
*zeal, yea, *what* [10]revenge! In all

**16**
p *Temple, figurative*, 1 Kin. 6:17.
q *Church*, Matt. 16:18.
r *Righteous, described*, Psa. 64:10.
s Lev. 26:12.
t *God, love of, exemplified*, Gen. 2:2.
u *God dwells with the Righteous*, 1 Kin. 6:13.
v *Fellowship, with God*, 1 Cor. 1:9.
5 R. V. a
6 R. V. we are a temple

**17**
w Isa. 52:11.
x *Holiness, enjoined*, Ex. 39:30.
y *Righteous, promises to*, Psa. 64:10.
7 R. V. no unclean thing;

**18**
z *God, fatherhood of*, Gen. 2:2.

a *Spiritual Adoption*, Rom. 8:15.

**1**
a *Love, of man for man*, 1 John 4:7.
b *Commandment, enjoining purity*, Deut. 8:2.
c *Holiness, enjoined*, Ex. 39:30.
d *Spiritual Purification*, Psa. 51:2.
e *Fear of God*, Acts 9:31.
1 R. V. defilement

**2**
f *Honesty*, Rom. 13:13.
g *Integrity*, Job 2:3.
2 R. V. Open your hearts to us: we wronged no man, we corrupted no man, we took advantage of no man. **4** *h Minister, character and qualifications of*, Rom. 15:16. *i Resignation, exemplified*, Job 5:17. 3 R. V. on your behalf:

j *Afflictions, resignation in*, Psa. 34:19.

**5**
k *Macedonia*, Acts 16:12.
l *Minister, trials and persecutions of*, Rom. 15:16.

**6**
m *Afflictions, consolation in*, Psa. 34:19.
n *Humility*, Prov. 22:4.
o *Temporal Blessings*, Psa. 103:2.
p *Titus*, Tit. 1:4.
4 R. V. the lowly,

**7**
q *Love, of man for man*, 1 John 4:7.
r *Sympathy*, Jas. 1:27.
5 R. V. zeal for me;

**8**
s *Church, discipline in*, Matt. 16:18.
6 R.V. my epistle,
7 R. V. regret it,

**9**
t *Repentance*, Mark 1:4.
8 R. V. suffer loss by us

**10**
u *Salvation*, Acts 16:17.
v *Spiritual Death*, 1 John 3:14.
w *Wicked, punishment of*, Psa. 73:3.
9 R. V. a repentance which bringeth no regret:

**11**
10 R. V. avenging!

*God's servants*, 2 Kin. 2:23; 2 Chr. 30:6, 10; 36:16; Jer. 17:15; Ezek. 20:49. *In rejecting God*, Job 21:14, 15; Psa. 14:1; 53:1. *In rejecting Christ*, Matt. 12:24; 27:39–44; Mark 3:22; Luke 11:15; 19:14, 27. *In doubting God's help*, Psa. 3:2. *In impugning, God's holiness*, Job 35:3; Psa. 10:11, 13; Ezek. 18:2, 29; Mal. 1:7; 3:14; *God's knowledge*, Job 22:13, 14, 17; Psa. 59:7; 64:5; 73:11; Isa. 29:15; Ezek. 8:12; *God's mercy*, Psa. 42:3; *God's righteousness*, Ezek. 18:2, 29.

Punishment for, Num. 15:30, 31; Deut. 29:19–21; Isa. 5:18, 19, 24, 25; 28:9, 10, 14, 15, 17–22; 47:10, 11; Jer. 5:12, 14; Ezek. 9:9, 10; 33:20; Luke 19:14, 27; Heb. 10:28, 29; 2 Pet. 2:1.

**Of friends**, Psa. 41:9; Matt. 26:14–16, 47–50; Mark 14:10, 11, 43–46; Luke 22:3–6, 47, 48; John 13:18; 18:2–5.

***ZEAL.** *Without love, unprofitable*, 1 Cor. 13:3. *Without knowledge*, Num. 11:27, 28; Judg. 11:30, 31, 34, 35; Eccl. 7:16; Matt. 8:19, 20; Luke 9:57, 58; John 16:2; Acts 21:20; Rom. 10:2, 3; Gal. 1:13, 14.

*Required*, Isa. 62:6, 7; Matt. 5:13–16; 1 Cor. 15:58; Tit. 2:14; 3:1.

*Enjoined*, Psa. 96:2; Eccl. 9:10; Hag. 2:4; Rom. 12:11; 1 Cor. 7:29–35; Gal. 6:9; Eph. 5:15, 16; 6:10–20; Phil. 1:27, 28; Col. 4:5; 2 Thess. 3:13; Heb. 12:1, 2; 13:13–15; 1 Pet. 2:2; 2 Pet. 1:10, 11; 3:14; Jude 3, 22, 23; Rev. 3:19.

*Rewards of*, Dan. 12:3; Matt. 25:21, 23; Luke 19:17–19; Jas. 5:20.

**Exemplified in the following instances:** *Moses*, Ex. 2:12; 32:19, 20, 31, 32; Num. 10:29; 11:29; Deut. 9:18, 19. *Phinehas*, Num. 25:7–13; Psa. 106:30. *Joshua*, Num. 11:27–29; Josh. 7:6; 24:14–16. *Gideon*, Judg. 6:11–32. *Jephthah*, Judg. 11:30, 31, 34–39. *Samuel*, 1 Sam. 12:23; 15:11, 35; 16:1. *David*, 1 Sam. 17:26; 2 Sam. 6; 7:2; 8:11, 12; 24:24; 1 Chr. 29:17; Psa. 40:8–10; 42:1, 2; 51:13; 69:7–9; 71:17, 18. *Solomon*, 1 Kin. 8:31–53; 2 Chr. 6:22–42. *Elijah*, 1 Kin. 19:10. *Obadiah*, 1 Kin. 18:3, 4. *Micaiah*, 1 Kin. 22:14. *Jehu*,

*things* ye have approved yourselves to be [11,x]clear in this matter.
12 Wherefore, though I wrote
unto you, *I did it* not for his
cause that had done the wrong,
nor for his cause that suffered
wrong, but that [12]our care for
you in the sight of God might
appear unto you.
13 Therefore we were comforted
in your comfort: yea, and exceedingly the more joyed we for the
joy of [p]Tī'tus, because [y]his spirit
was refreshed by you all.
14 For if I have boasted any
thing to him of you, I am not
ashamed; but as we spake all
things to you in truth, even so
our boasting, which *I made* before [p]Tī'tus, is found a truth.
15 And his inward [†,z]affection
is more abundant toward you,
whilst he remembereth the obedience of you all, how with fear
and trembling ye received him.
16 I rejoice [13]therefore that I
have confidence in you in all
*things*.

## CHAPTER 8

*He stirs them up to a liberal contribution for the poor saints at Jerusalem; 9 cites the grace of our Lord Jesus Christ; 16 and commends to them Titus and others, who were coming to them in reference to this business.*

MOREOVER, [a]brethren, [b,c]we
[1]do you to wit of the [d]grace
of God bestowed on the [e]churches
of [f]Măç-e-dō'nĭ-ȧ;
2 How that in [2]a great trial
of [g]affliction the abundance of
their [h]joy and their deep [i]pov-
erty [j]abounded unto the riches
of their [k]liberality.
3 For [3]to *their* power, I bear
record, yea, and [j]beyond *their*
power *they* [4,k]*were* willing of
themselves;
4 [l]Praying us with much in-
treaty [5]that we would receive the
[k]gift, and *take upon us* the fellowship of the ministering to the
saints.
5 And *this they did*, not as we
hoped, but first [m,n]gave their own
selves to the Lord, and [o]unto us
by the [p]will of God.
6 Insomuch that we [6]desired
[q]Tī'tus, that as he had begun,
so he would also finish in you
the same [k]grace also.
7 Therefore, as ye abound in
every *thing, in* [r]faith, and utterance, and [s]knowledge, and *in*
all [7,j]diligence, and *in* your [o]love
to us, [t]*see* that ye abound in this
grace also.
8 I speak not by command-
ment, but [8]by occasion of the [u]for-
wardness of others, and to prove
the [v]sincerity of your [n]love.
9 For ye know the [w]grace of
our [x]Lord Jē'ṣus Chrīst, that,
though he was rich, yet [y]for your
sakes [z]he became poor, that ye
through his poverty might be
rich.
10 And herein I give *my* [9]ad-

x *Purity*, 1 Tim. 4:12.
11 R. V. pure

**12**
12 R. V. your earnest care for us might be made manifest unto you in the sight of God.

**13**
y *Fellowship, of the righteous*, 1 Cor. 1:9.

**15**
z *Love, of man for man*, 1 John 4:7.

**16**
13 R. V. that in everything I am of good courage concerning you.

**1**
a *Corinth, church of*, Acts 18:1.
b *Tact*, vs. 1–8; Prov. 15:1.
c *Emulation*, vs. 1–9; Rom. 11:14.
d *Grace of God*, Rom. 4:16.
e *Church, Christian*, Matt. 16:18.
f *Macedonia*, Acts 16:12.
1 R. V. make known to you the grace of God which hath been given in the

**2**
g *Afflictions*, Psa. 34:19.
2 R. V. much proof of

h *Joy, under adversity*, Psa. 5:11.
i *Poverty*, Prov. 30:8.
j *Zeal, exemplified*, 2 Cor. 7:11.
k *Liberality*, 1 Tim. 6:18.

**3**
3 R. V. according to
4 R. V. gave of their own accord,

**4**
l *Poor, kindness to*, Prov. 21:13.
5 R. V. in regard of this grace and the fellowship in the

**5**
m *Consecration, personal*, Lev. 7:37.
n *Love, for God*, 1 John 4:19.
o *Love, of man for man*, 1 John 4:7.
p *Will of God*, Mark 3:35.

**6**
q *Titus*, Tit. 1:4.
6 R. V. exhorted

**7**
r *Faith in Christ*, John 6:69.
s *Wisdom, spiritual*, Prov. 2:2.
t *Liberality, enjoined*, 1 Tim. 6:18.
7 R. V. earnestness,

**8**
u *Altruism*, Acts 20:35.
v *Sincerity*, 1 Cor. 5:8.
8 R. V. as proving through the earnestness of others the sincerity also of your love.

**9** w *Jesus, love of*, Matt. 1:21. x *Jesus, lordship of*, Matt. 1:21. y *Jesus, compassion of*, Matt. 1:21. z *Example, Christ our*, John 13:15. **10** 9 R. V. judgement:

2 Kin. 9; 10. *Jehoiada*, 2 Kin. 11:4–17; 2 Chr. 23:1–17. *Asa*, 1 Kin. 15:11–15; 2 Chr. 14:1–5, 15. *Israelites*, 2 Chr. 15:15; Ezek. 9:4. *Jehoshaphat*, 2 Chr. 17:3–10; 19. *Isaiah*, Isa. 6:8; 62:1. *Hezekiah*, 2 Chr. 30:31; Isa. 37:1. *Josiah*, 2 Kin. 22; 23; 2 Chr. 34:3–7, 29–33. *Priests*, Ezek. 44:15. *Ezra*, Ezra 7:10; 9; 10; Neh. 8:1–6, 13, 18. *Nehemiah*, Neh. 4; 5; 13:7–9, 15–28. *Psalmist*, Psa. 119:53, 126, 136, 139, 158. *Jeremiah*, Jer. 9:1–3; 13:17; 18:20; 20:9; 25:3, 4; 26:12–15. *Three Hebrews*, Dan. 3:17, 18. *Habakkuk*, Hab. 1:2–4.

*Jesus*, Matt. 23:37; Luke 19:41; John 4:34, 35; 9:4. *Anna*, Luke 2:38. *Andrew and Philip*, John 1:41–46. *Apostles*, Mark 16:20; Acts 4:31, 33; 5:21, 25, 29–32, 41, 42; 8:4, 25, 30, 35, 40; 11:19, 20, 24, 26. *Two blind men proclaiming the miracle of healing, contrary to the injunction of Jesus*, Matt. 9:30, 31. *The restored leper*, Mark 1:44, 45. *Man healed of demons*, Mark 5:19, 20. *Peter*, Matt. 16:22; Mark 14:29–31; Luke 22:33; Acts 2:14–40; 3:12–26; 4:2, 8–12, 18–20; 5:29–32; 2 Pet. 1:12–15. *Samaritan woman*, John 4:28–30, 39.

Paul: *For the evangelization of the Jews*, Rom. 9:1–3; 10:1; 11:14; *in his ministry*, Acts 9:20–29; 14:1–28; 15:25, 26; 17:16, 17, 22–31; 19:8–10; 20:18–24, 26, 27, 31, 33, 34; 21:13; 24:14–25; 26:1–29; 28:23, 30, 31; Rom. 1:1, 14, 15; 15:15–32; 1 Cor. 4:1–21; 9:12–27; 2 Cor. 1:12, 17–19; 5:9, 11, 13, 14, 20; 6:3–11; 11:16–33; 12:10–21; Gal. 1:15, 16; 2:2; 4:19; Eph. 6:20; Phil. 1:18, 20, 24, 25, 27; 2:16, 17; 3:4–16; Col. 1:28, 29; 2:1, 5; 1 Thess. 1:5, 6; 2:2–6, 8–11; 2 Thess. 3:7–9; 2 Tim. 1:3, 7, 11–13; *in his piety*, 1 Cor. 4:12; 10:33; 15:31; 2 Cor. 4:8–18; 11:22–33; 12:10; Phil. 3:4–16; 4:11, 12, 17; 2 Tim. 3:10, 11; *in providing self-support*, Acts 20:33, 34; 1 Cor. 4:12; 2 Cor. 11:7–12; 2 Thess. 3:7–9; *in suffering for Christ*, Acts 21:13; 2 Cor. 6:4, 5, 8–10; 11:22–33; 12:10, 14, 15, 21; 2 Tim. 2:9, 10; 3:10, 11.

*Paul and Barnabas*, Acts 14:14, 15. *Timothy*, Phil. 2:22. *Phebe*, Rom. 16:1, 2. *Epaphroditus*, Phil. 2:26, 30. *Corinthians*, 1 Cor. 14:12; 2 Cor. 7:11; 9:2. *Thessalonians*, 1 Thess. 1:2–8. *Ephesians*, Rev. 2:2, 3, 6. *Christian Jews*, Heb. 10:34. *John*, Acts 4:8–12, 13, 18–20; 3 John 4; Rev. 5:4.

† **AFFECTIONS.** *Set upon the Lord's house*, 1 Chr. 29:3; Psa. 69:9. *Should be set upon heavenly things*, Col. 3:1, 2. *Benevolent, toward one another, enjoined*, Rom. 12:10. *Natural*, Rom. 1:31; 2 Tim. 3:3. *Vile*, Rom. 1:26; Gal. 5:24; Col. 3:5.

*a Liberality, enjoined,* vs. 10–14; 1 Tim. 6:18.

10 R. V. who were the first to make a beginning a year ago, not only to do, but also to will.

**11**

*b Giving, rules for,* 1 Cor. 16:2.

**14**

*c Reciprocity,* 1 Cor. 9:11.

**15**

*d* Ex. 16:18.

**16**

*e Thankfulness, to God,* Acts 24:3.

*f Zeal, exemplified,* 2 Cor. 7:11.

*g Titus,* Tit. 1:4.

*h Minister, zealous,* Rom. 15:16.

*i Corinth, church of,* Acts 18:1.

**17**

11 R. V. very earnest,

**18**

*j Church, Christian,* Matt. 16:18.

**19**

*k Church, government of,* Matt. 16:18.

*l Minister, call of,* Rom. 15:16.

*m Liberality,* 1 Tim. 6:18.

12 R. V. in the matter of this grace, which is ministered by us to the glory of the Lord, and to shew our readiness:

**20**

*n Prudence,* 2 Chr. 2:12.

13 R. V. the matter of this bounty

**21**

*o Honesty,* Rom. 13:13.

14 R. V. For we take thought for things honourable, not only

vice: for [a]this is expedient[G] for
you, [10]who have begun before,
not only to do, but also to be
forward[G] a year ago.
11 Now therefore [a]perform the
[b]doing *of it*; that as *there was* a
readiness to will, so *there may be*
a performance[G] also out of that
which ye have.
12 For [b]if there be first a willing
mind, *it is* accepted according to
that a man hath, *and* not according to that he hath not.[Q]
13 For *I mean* not that other
men be eased, and ye burdened:
14 But by an equality, *that* now
at this time [c]your abundance
*may be a supply* for their want,
that [c]their abundance also may
be *a supply* for your want[G]: that
there may be equality:
15 As it is written, [d]He that *had*
*gathered* much had nothing over;
and he that *had gathered* little
had no lack.[Q]
16 But [e]thanks *be* to God, which
put the same [f]earnest care into
the heart of [g,h]Tī'tus for [i]you.
17 For indeed he accepted the
exhortation[G]; but being [11,f,h]more
forward[G], of his own accord he
went unto [i]you.
18 And we have sent with him
the [h]brother, whose [j]praise *is*
in the gospel throughout all the
[j]churches;
19 And not *that* only, but
who was also [k,l]chosen of the
churches to travel with us [12]with
this [m]grace, which is administered[G]
by us to the glory of the same
Lord, and *declaration of* your
ready mind:
20 [n]Avoiding this, that no man
should blame us in [13]this [m]abun-
dance which is administered[G] by
us:
21 [14]Providing[G] for [o]honest
things, not only in the sight of
the Lord, but also in the sight
of men.[Q]
22 And we have sent with them
our [h]brother, whom we have
oftentimes proved [15]diligent in
many things, but now much
more [16]diligent, upon the great
confidence which *I have* in you.
23 Whether *any do enquire* of
[g]Tī'tus, *he is* my partner and fel-
lowhelper concerning you: or our
brethren *be enquired of*, *they are*
the messengers of the churches,
*and* the glory of Christ.
24 [p]Wherefore shew ye to them,
and before the churches, the proof
of your [q]love, and of our boasting on your behalf.

## CHAPTER 9

*The apostle shews why, though he knew their forwardness, he yet sent Titus and his brethren beforehand; 6 and exhorts them to give bountifully. 15 God's unspeakable gift.*

FOR as touching[G] the [a]minis-
tering[G] to the [b]saints, [c]it is
superfluous for me to write to
[d]you:
2 For I know [1]the forwardness[G]
of your mind, for which I boast
of you to them of [e]Măç-e-dō'nĭ-ȧ,
that [f]Ā-chā'iȧ was ready a year
ago; and [g]your [h,i]zeal hath provoked[G] very many.
3 Yet have I sent the brethren,
lest our boasting of [d]you should
be in vain in this behalf; that, as
I said, ye may be ready:
4 Lest haply[G] if they of [e]Măç-e-
dō'nĭ-ȧ come with me, and find
you unprepared, we (that we say
not, ye) should be [2]ashamed in
this same confident boasting.
5 Therefore I thought it necessary to [3]exhort[G] the brethren, that
they would go before unto you,
and make up beforehand your
[a,f]bounty, whereof ye had notice
before, that the same might be
ready, as *a matter of* bounty,
and not as *of* covetousness.
6 But this *I say*, [k]He which
[l]soweth sparingly shall [l]reap also sparingly; and [k]he which soweth [a]bountifully shall reap also
bountifully.[Q]

**22**

15 R. V. earnest

16 R. V. earnest, by reason of the great confidence which he hath in you.

**24**

*p Tact, of Paul,* Prov. 15:1.

*q Love, of man for man,* 1 John 4:7.

**1**

*a Liberality,* 1 Tim. 6:18.

*b Poor, liberality to,* Prov. 21:13.

*c Tact, of Paul,* vs. 1–5; Prov. 15:1.

*d Corinth, church of,* Acts 18:1.

**2**

*e Macedonia,* Acts 16:12.

*f Achaia,* Acts 18:12.

*g Emulation,* Rom. 11:14.

*h Zeal,* 2 Cor. 7:11.

*i Influence, good,* 1 Cor. 7:14.

1 R. V. your readiness, of which I glory on your behalf to them of Macedonia, that Achaia hath been prepared for a year past; and your zeal hath stirred up very many of them.

**4**

2 R. V. put to shame in this confidence.

**5**

*f Alms,* Matt. 6:2.

3 Am. R. V. intreat the brethren, that they would go before unto you, and make up beforehand your before-promised bounty, that the same might be ready, as a matter of bounty, and not of extortion.

**6**

*k Giving, rules for,* 1 Cor. 16:2.

*l Agriculture,* Gen. 3:23.

7 [a, k][S]Every man according as he purposeth in his heart, *so let him give*; [k]not [m]grudgingly, or of necessity: for [n]God loveth a cheerful giver.[Q]

8 And [o]God *is* [p]able to make all [q]grace abound toward you; that ye, always having all sufficiency[G] in all *things*, may abound to every good [r]work:

9 (As it is written, [s]He hath [a]dispersed abroad; he hath [a]given to the poor: his righteousness remaineth for ever.[Q]

10 Now [t]he that ministereth[G] [u]seed to the sower [4]both minister[G] [u]bread for *your* food, and [q]multiply your seed sown, and increase the [v,w]fruits of your righteousness;)[S Q]

11 Being [q]enriched in every thing to all [5,w]bountifulness, which causeth through us [x]thanksgiving to God.

12 For the administration[G] of this service not only [y]supplieth the want[G] of the saints, but is abundant also by many [x]thanksgivings unto God;

13 [6]Whiles[G] by the experiment[G] of this ministration[G] they [z]glorify God for your professed subjection unto the gospel of Christ, and for *your* [w]liberal distribution unto them, and unto all *men*;

14 And by their [a]prayer for you, which [b]long after you [7]for the exceeding [c]grace of God in you.

15 [d]Thanks *be* unto God for his unspeakable gift.

## CHAPTER 10

*Against those who disparaged his bodily presence and speech, he asserts his spiritual might and authority; 12 and reproves them for stretching themselves beyond their measure, and for boasting themselves of other men's labors.*

NOW I [a]Paul myself beseech you by the [b,c]meekness and *gentleness of Christ, who in presence *am* [1,d,e]base[G] among you, but being absent am [2,f]bold toward you:

2 But I beseech *you*, that I may not be bold when I am present with that confidence, wherewith I think to be bold against some, which think of us as if we walked according to the [g]flesh:

3 For though we walk in the [g]flesh, we do not war after the flesh:

4 (For the [h,i]weapons of our warfare *are* not [3,g]carnal,[G] but mighty through God to the pulling down of strong holds;)[T]

5 [j]Casting down [k]imaginations, and every [l]high thing that [m]exalteth itself against the [n]knowledge of God, and bringing into [o]captivity every thought to the obedience of [p]Christ;

6 And having in a readiness to [4]revenge all disobedience, when your obedience is fulfilled.

7 Do ye look on things after the outward appearance? If any man [q]trust to himself that he is Christ's, let him of himself think this again, that, as he *is* Christ's, even so *are* we Christ's.

8 For though I should [5]boast somewhat more of our [r]authority, which the Lord hath given us for edification,[G] and not for your destruction, I should not be ashamed:

9 That I may not seem as if I would terrify you by letters.

10 For *his* letters, say they, *are* weighty and powerful; but [s]*his* bodily presence *is* weak, and *his* speech [6]contemptible.

11 Let such an one think this, that, such as we are in word by letters when we are absent, such *will we be* also in deed when we are present.

12 For we [7]dare not make ourselves of the number, or com-

**7**
*m Parsimony, admonition against*, Mal. 3:8.
*n God, love of*, Gen. 2:2.
**8**
*o Promise, or Ground of Assurance*, 2 Cor. 1:20.
*p God, power of*, Gen. 2:2.
*q Prosperity, from God*, Eccl. 7:14.
*r Works*, 2 Tim. 1:9.
**9**
*s* Psa. 112:9.
**10**
*t God, providence of*, Gen. 2:2.
*u Temporal Blessings, from God*, Psa. 103:2.
*v Righteousness, fruits of*, Psa. 15:2.
*w Liberality*, 1 Tim. 6:18.
4 R. V. and bread for food, shall supply and multiply your seed for sowing, and increase
**11**
*x Thankfulness, to God*, Acts 24:3.
5 R. V. liberality,
**12**
*y Poor, liberality to*, Prov. 21:13.
**13**
*z Glorifying God*, Luke 5:25.
6 R. V. Seeing that through the proving of you by this ministration they glorify God for the obedience of your confession unto the gospel of Christ, and for the liberality of your contribution unto them and unto all;
**14**
*a Prayer, intercessory*, Acts 6:4.
*b Love, of man for man*, 1 John 4:7.
*c Spiritual Blessings, from God*, Eph. 1:3.
7 R. V. by reason of the
**15**
*d Thankfulness, to God*, Acts 24:3.
**1**
*a Paul*, Acts 13:9.
*b Jesus, meekness of*, Matt. 1:21.
*c Example, Christ our*, John 13:15.
*d Humility*, Prov. 22:4.
*e Christian Graces, humility*, Gal. 5:22.
*f Minister, character and qualifications of*, Rom. 15:16.
1 R. V. lowly
2 R. V. of good courage
**2**
*g Carnal Mind*, 1 Cor. 3:3.
**4**
*h Armor, figurative*, 1 Sam. 17:54.
*i Gospel*, Mark 13:10.
3 R. V. of the flesh, but mighty before God to the casting down of strong holds);
**5**
*j Wisdom, worldly*, Prov. 2:2.
*k Evil Imagination*, Gen. 6:5.
*l Pride*, Prov. 16:18.
*m Self-exaltation*, Luke 14:11.
*n Wisdom, spiritual*, Prov. 2:2.
*o Captivity, figurative*, Isa. 5:13.
*p Jesus, lordship of*, Matt. 1:21.
**6**
4 R. V. avenge
**7**
*q Self-righteousness*, Luke 18:11.
**8**
*r Minister, duties of*, Rom. 15:16.
5 R. V. glory somewhat abundantly concerning our authority (which the Lord gave for building you up, and not for casting you down), I shall not
**10**
*s Paul, personal appearance of*, Acts 13:9.
6 R. V. of no account.
**12**
7 R. V. are not bold to number or compare

* **GENTLENESS.** *Of Christ*, Matt. 11:29; 2 Cor. 10:1. *Of God*, 2 Sam. 22:36; Psa. 18:35; Isa. 40:11. *Of Paul*, 1 Thess. 2:7. *A fruit of the Spirit*, Gal. 5:22. *Required, in ministers*, 2 Tim. 2:24–26; *in all Christians*, Tit. 3:1, 2. See footnote, CHRISTIAN GRACES, Gal. 5:22.

pare ourselves with some that [q,t]commend themselves: but they measuring themselves by themselves, and comparing themselves among themselves, are not wise.

13 But we will not [8,t]boast of things without[c] *our* measure, but according to the measure of the rule which God hath distributed to us, a measure to reach even unto you.

14 For we stretch not ourselves beyond *our measure,* as though we reached not unto you: for [u]we are come as far as to you also in [9]*preaching* the [i]gospel of Christ:

15 Not [10,t]boasting of things without *our* measure, *that is,* of other men's labours; but having hope, when your faith is increased, that we shall be enlarged by you according to our rule abundantly,

16 [11,v]To [w]preach the [i]gospel in the *regions* beyond you, *and* not to [t]boast[c] in another man's line of things made ready to our hand.

17 But he that [t]glorieth,[c] let him glory in the Lord.[Q]

18 For not he that [q,t]commendeth himself is approved, but whom the Lord commendeth.

## CHAPTER 11

*The apostle's jealousy over them. He is not behind the chiefest of the apostles. 7 His preaching the gospel freely to them. 13 The false apostles. 16 He asks to be indulged in boasting himself a little; 21 and shews that, in respect to birth, he was not inferior to those deceitful workers, 23 and, as to sufferings and labors for Christ, far superior.*

WOULD to God [a]ye could bear with [b]me [1]a little in *my* folly: and indeed bear with me.

2 For I am [c]jealous over you with godly jealousy: for I have [d]espoused[c] [e,f]you to one husband, [g]that I may present *you as* a chaste [h]virgin to Christ.

3 But I fear, lest by any means, as [i]the [j,k,l]serpent beguiled [m,n]Eve through his [o]subtilty,[c] so your minds should be corrupted from the [p]simplicity[c] [2]that is in Christ.[Q]

4 For if [q]he that cometh [r]preacheth [s]another Jē′ṣus, whom we have not preached, or *if* ye receive another spirit, which ye have not received, or another gospel, which ye have not accepted, ye might well bear[c] with *him.*

5 For [b]I suppose [t]I was not a whit[c] behind the very chiefest apostles.

6 But though *I be* rude[c] in speech, yet not in [u]knowledge; [3]but we have been throughly[c] made manifest among you in all things.

7 Have I committed an offence in abasing[c] myself that ye might be exalted,[c] because I have [r]preached to you the [v]gospel of God [4]freely[c]?

8 I robbed other churches, [w]taking wages *of them,* to do you service.

9 And when I was present with you, and wanted,[c] I was chargeable[c] to no man: for [w]that which was lacking to me the brethren which came from [x]Măç-e-dō′-nĭ-ȧ supplied: and in all *things* I have kept myself from being burdensome unto you, and *so* will I keep *myself.*

10 As the truth of Christ is in me, no man shall stop me of this boasting in the regions of [y]Ā-chā′iȧ.[T]

11 Wherefore? because I [z]love you not? God [a]knoweth.

12 But what I do, that I will do, that I may cut off occasion from them which desire occasion; that wherein they glory, they may be found even as we.

13 For such *are* [b]false apostles, [c]deceitful workers, [5,d]transforming themselves into the apostles of Christ.

14 And no marvel; for [e]Sā′tan

t *Spiritual Boasting,* Rom. 3:27.

**13**

8 R. V. glory beyond our measure, but according to the measure of the province which

**14**

u *Zeal, exemplified,* 2 Cor. 7:11.

9 R. V. *omits* preaching

**15**

10 R. V. glorying beyond our measure, that is, in other men's labours; but having hope that, as your faith groweth, we shall be magnified in you according to our province unto further abundance,

**16**

v *Missions,* Matt. 28:19.

w *Preaching,* Matt. 9:35.

11 R. V. So as to preach the gospel even unto the parts beyond you, and not to glory in another's province in regard of things ready to our hand.

**1**

a *Corinth, church of,* Acts 18:1.

b *Paul,* Acts 13:9.

1 R. V. in a little foolishness:

**2**

c *Love, of man for man,* 1 John 4:7.

d *Marriage, figurative,* Gen. 34:9.

e *Church, union of, with Christ,* Matt. 16:18.

f *Righteous, union of, with Christ,* Psa. 64:10.

g *Holiness, enjoined upon the church,* Ex. 39:30.

h *Virgin, figurative,* Isa. 62:5.

**3**

i Gen. 3:4; 1 Tim. 2:14.

j *Serpent,* Num. 21:6.

k *Satan,* Matt. 4:10.

l *Temptation, sources of,* Luke 11:4.

m *Women, fall of,* Prov. 31:10.

n *Fall of Man,* Gen. 3:6.

o *Craftiness,* Psa. 83:3.

p *Truth,* John 18:37.

2 R. V. and the purity that is toward Christ.

**4**

q *False Teachers,* 2 Pet. 2:1.

r *Preaching,* Matt. 9:35.

s *Heresy,* Tit. 3:10.

**5**

t *Sarcasm,* Judg. 10:14.

**6**

u *Wisdom, spiritual,* Prov. 2:2.

3 R. V. nay, in everything we have made it manifest among all men to you-ward.

**7**

v *Gospel,* Mark 13:10.

4 R. V. for nought?

**8**

w *Minister, emoluments of,* Rom. 15:16.

**9**

x *Macedonia,* Acts 16:12.

**10**

y *Achaia,* Acts 18:12.

**11**

z *Love, of man for man,* 1 John 4:7.

a *God, knowledge of,* Gen. 2:2.

**13**

b *False Teachers,* 2 Pet. 2:1.

c *Deceit, the wicked practice,* Psa. 36:3.

d *Hypocrisy,* Jas. 3:17.

5 R. V. fashioning

**14**

e *Satan,* Matt. 4:10.

6 R. V. fashioneth himself into
**15**
*f Minister, false and corrupt,* Rom. 15:16.
*g Judgment, according to opportunity and works,* 1 Pet. 1:17.
*h Wicked, punishment of,* Psa. 73:3.
7 R. V. fashion themselves as
**16**
8 R. V. foolish; but if ye do, yet as foolish receive me, that I also may glory a little.
**19**
*i Sarcasm,* Judg. 10:14.
*j Irony,* Mark 12:14.
9 R. V. bear with the foolish gladly, being wise yourselves.
**20**
10 R. V. bear with a man, if he bringeth you into bondage, if he devoureth you, if he taketh you captive,
**21**
11 R. V. by way of disparagement,
**22**
*k Hebrew,* Gen. 40:15.
*l Zeal,* 2 Cor. 7:11.
*m Abraham,* Gen. 17:5.
**23**
*n Minister, faithful,* Rom. 15:16.
*o Strenuousness,* Eccl. 9:10.
*p Paul, persecutions of,* Acts 13:9.
*q Scourging,* Acts 22:24.
*r Minister, trials and persecutions of,* Rom. 15:16.
12 R. V. one beside himself
**24**
*s Jews, persecuted Paul,* Neh. 4:2.
*t Forty, stripes,* Jonah 3:4.
**25**
*u Stoning,* 1 Sam. 30:6.
*v Ship, wrecked,* 2 Chr. 8:18.

[6]himself is transformed into an
angel of light.[S]
15 Therefore *it is* no great thing
if [e]his [f]ministers also [7]be [d]trans-
formed as the ministers of righteousness; whose [g,h]end shall be
according to their works.
16 I say again, Let no man
think me a [8]fool; if otherwise,
yet as a fool receive me, that I
may boast myself a little.
17 That which I speak, I speak
*it* not after the Lord, but as it
were foolishly, in this confidence
of boasting.
18 Seeing that many glory[G] after
the flesh, I will glory[G] also.
19 For [i]ye [9]suffer[G] fools gladly,
seeing [i]ye *yourselves* are wise.
20 For ye [10]suffer,[G] if a man
bring you into bondage, if a man
devour *you*, if a man take[G] *of you*,
if a man exalt himself, if a man
smite you on the face.
21 I speak [11]as concerning reproach,[G] as though we had been
weak. Howbeit whereinsoever
any is bold, (I speak foolishly,)
I am bold also.
22 Are they [k]Hē'brews? [l]so
*am* I. Are they Is'ra-el-ītes?
[l]so *am* I. Are they the seed of
[m]Ā'brā-hăm? [l]so *am* I.
23 Are they ministers of Chrīst?
(I speak as [12]a fool) [l,n]I *am*
more; in [o]labours more abundant, in [p,q,r]stripes[G] above measure, in [p,r]prisons more frequent,
in [p,r]deaths oft.
24 Of the [s]Jews five times received I [t]forty [q]*stripes*[G] save one.
25 Thrice was I [q]beaten with
rods, once was I [u]stoned, thrice I
suffered [v]shipwreck, a night and
a day I have been in the deep;
26 [l,r]*In* journeyings often, *in*
perils of waters, *in* perils of
[w]robbers, *in* perils by *mine own*
countrymen, *in* perils by the
[13]heathen,[G] *in* perils in the city, *in*
perils in the wilderness, *in* perils
in the sea, *in* perils among false
[x]brethren;
27 [l]In [14]weariness and painful-
ness, in watchings[G] often, in [y]hun-
ger and thirst, in [z]fastings often,
in cold and nakedness.
28 Beside those things that are
without, that which cometh upon me daily, [15,a]the care of all
the churches.
29 Who is [b]weak, and [c,d]I am
not weak? who is [16]offended,
and I [c,d]burn[G] not?
30 If I must needs glory, [e]I will
glory of the things which concern mine infirmities.
31 The God and [f,g]Father of
our [h]Lord Jē'sus [17]Chrīst, which
is blessed for evermore, knoweth
that [i]I lie not.[T]
32 In [j]Dā-măs'cus the [k]gov-
ernor under Ăr'e-tăs the king
kept the city of the Dăm'as-çēnes
with a garrison, [l,m]desirous to
apprehend me:
33 And [n]through a window in a
basket was I let down by the
[o]wall, and escaped his hands.

## CHAPTER 12

*Though he might glory in his wonderful revelations, 9 yet he rather chooses to glory in his infirmities. 11 They had forced him to his vain boasting. 14 He promises to come to them again; but yet in the affection of a father, 20 although he fears he shall find many offenders.*

[1]IT is not expedient for [a]me
doubtless to glory. I will
come to [b]visions and *revelations of the Lord.

**26**
*w Robbers,* Hos. 6:9.
*x Friends, false,* Ex. 33:11.
13 R. V. Gentiles,
**27**
*y Hunger,* Neh. 9:15.
*z Fasting,* Zech. 8:19.
14 R. V. labour and travail,
**28**
*a Minister, duties of,* Rom. 15:16.
15 R. V. anxiety for all
**29**
*b Weak, duty of strong to,* 1 Cor. 8:9.
*c Sympathy,* Jas. 1:27.
*d Love, of man for man,* 1 John 4:7.
16 R. V. made to stumble,
**30**
*e Humility,* Prov. 22:4.
**31**
*f God, fatherhood of,* Gen. 2:2.
*g Jesus, divine sonship of,* Matt. 1:21.
*h Jesus, lordship of,* Matt. 1:21.
*i Integrity,* Job 2:3.
17 R. V. he who is blessed
**32**
*j Damascus,* Isa. 8:4.
*k Government, municipal,* Isa. 22:21.
*l Minister, trials and persecutions of,* Rom. 15:16.
*m Righteous, persecutions of,* Psa. 64:10.
**33**
*n Paul, escapes from Damascus,* Acts 13:9.
*o Damascus, walled,* Isa. 8:4.
**1**
*a Paul,* Acts 13:9.
*b Vision,* Acts 9:10.
1 R. V. I must needs glory, though it is not expedient;

* **REVELATION.** *Of the name of Deity,* Ex. 3:14; 34:6, 7. *Of the commandments,* Ex. 20:1–17; 34:27, 28; Deut. 5:7–21. *Of statutes,* Ex. chapters 21–23; Lev. 19:1–37; 20:1–27; Deut. chapters 22–25.

*Concerning, offerings for the tabernacle,* Ex. 25:1–9; *furniture of the tabernacle,* Ex. 25:10–40; *curtains, coverings and boards of the tabernacle,* Ex. 26:1–37; *pattern of the altar,* Ex. 27:1–8; *court of the tabernacle,* Ex. 27:9–19; *priesthood and holy vestments,* Ex. 28:1–43; Lev. 21:1–23; *consecration of priests,* Ex. 29:1–35; Lev. 8:1–33; *sanctifying the altar,* Ex. 29:36–44.

*Concerning, atonement money,* Ex. 30:11–16; *offerings,* Lev. chapters 1–6; 7:1–34; 22:17–30; Num. 15:1–28; 28; 29; *sins of ignorance,* Lev. 4:1–35; *clean and unclean animals,* Lev. 11; Deut. 14:3–20.

*Concerning, purification,* Lev. 12:1–8; *treatment of diseases,* Lev. 13:1–46; *purification of garments,* Lev. 13:47–59; *purification of lepers,* Lev. 14:1–32; *purification of leprous houses,* Lev. 14:33–57; *defilement,* Lev. 15:1–33; *ceremonies on the day of atonement,* Lev. 16:1–34; 23:26–32; *marriage,* Deut. 24:1–5; *feasts,* Lev. 23:1–8, 33–44; 28; 29; Deut. 16:1–17; *first fruits,* Lev. 23:9–25; Deut. 26:1–11.

2 I knew a man in Christ above fourteen years ago, ([c]whether in the body, I cannot tell; or whether out of the body, I cannot tell: God knoweth;) such an one caught up to the third [d]heaven.

3 And I knew such a man, ([c]whether in the body, or out of the body, I cannot tell: God knoweth;)

4 How that he was caught up into [e]paradise, and heard †unspeakable [f]words, which it is not lawful for a man to utter.

5 Of such an one will I glory: yet [g]of myself I will not glory, but in mine infirmities.

6 For though I would desire to glory, I shall not be [2]a fool; for I will say the [h]truth: but *now* I forbear, [g]lest any man should think of me above that which he seeth me *to be*, or *that* he heareth of me.

7 And [3,g]lest [a]I should be [i]exalted above measure through the abundance of the *revelations, [j]there was given to me a [k,l]thorn in the flesh, the [m]messenger of [n,o]Sā'tan to buffet me, lest I should be exalted above measure.

8 For [p]this thing I [q]besought the Lord thrice, that it might depart from me.

9 And he [r]said unto me, [s]My [t,u]grace is sufficient for thee: for my [v]strength is made perfect in weakness. [w,x]Most gladly therefore will I rather glory in my infirmities, that the [y]power of Christ may rest upon me.

10 Therefore [z,a]I take [b]pleasure in [c]infirmities, in reproaches, in necessities, in [d]persecutions, in distresses [e]for Christ's sake: for †when I am weak, then am I strong.

11 I am become [4]a fool in glorying; ye have compelled me: for I ought to have been commended of you: for †in nothing am I behind the [f]very chiefest apostles, though I be nothing.

12 [g]Truly the signs of an apostle were wrought among you in all [h]patience, in [i]signs, and wonders, and mighty deeds.

13 For what is it wherein [j]ye were inferior to other churches, except *it be* that [k]I myself was [l]not burdensome to you? forgive me this wrong.

14 Behold, the third time [a]I am ready to come to you; and [k]I [m,n]will not be burdensome to you: for I [o]seek not your's, but you: for the children ought not to lay up for the ‡parents, but the parents for the children.

**2**
c *Man, a spirit,* Job. 4:17.
d *Heaven, future home of the righteous,* Luke 18:22.
**4**
e Luke 23:43; Rev. 2:7.
f *Words,* Luke 4:22.
**5**
g *Humility, exemplified,* Prov. 22:4.
**6**
h *Truth,* John 18:37.
2 R. V. foolish;
**7**
i *Self-exaltation,* Luke 14:11.
j *Afflictions, design of,* Psa. 34:19.
k *Thorn, figurative,* Hos. 2:6.
l *Afflictions, from Satan,* Psa. 34:19.
m *Messenger, figurative,* Hag. 1:13.
n *Satan,* Matt. 4:10.
o *Temptation, sources of,* Luke 11:4.
3 R. V. by reason of the exceeding greatness of the revelations—wherefore, that I should not be exalted overmuch,
**8**
p *Afflictions, prayer in,* Psa. 34:19.
q *Prayer, importunity in,* Acts 6:4.
**9**
r *Prayer, answer to, different from the request,* Acts 6:4.
s *Afflictions, consolation in,* Psa. 34:19.
t *Grace of God,* Rom. 4:16.
u *God, mercy of, in comforting the afflicted,* Gen. 2:2.
v *God, power of,* Gen. 2:2.
w *Afflictions, resignation in,* Psa. 34:19.
x *Faith in Christ,* John 6:69.
y *Spiritual Power,* Luke 24:49.
**10**
z *Meekness, exemplified,* Psa. 45:4.
a *Zeal, exemplified,* 2 Cor. 7:11.
b *Afflictions, resignation in,* Psa. 34:19.
c *Suffering for Christ,* Phil. 1:29.
d *Persecution, of the righteous,* John 15:20.
e *Love, for Jesus,* 1 John 4:19.
**11**
f *Sarcasm,* Judg. 10:14.
4 R. V. foolish:
**12**
g *Minister, character and qualifications of,* Rom. 15:16.
h *Patience, a grace of the righteous,* Luke 8:15.
i *Miracles,* Luke 23:8.
**13**
j *Church, duty of, to ministers,* Matt. 16:18.
k *Paul, self-supporting,* Acts 13:9. l *Minister, emoluments of,* Rom. 15:16.
**14** m *Unselfishness,* 1 Cor. 10:24. n *Love, of man for man,* 1 John 4:7. o *Minister, duties of,* Rom. 15:16.

*Concerning, sabbatic year and year of jubilee,* Lev. 25:1–55; Deut. 15:1–18; *penalties for disobedience,* Lev. 26:1–45; *vows,* Lev. 27:1–29; *tithes,* Lev. 27:30–33; Deut. 14:22–29; 26:12.

*Concerning, camp and order of march of the Israelites,* Num. 2:1–34; *the Levites,* Num. 3:5–50; 4; *the Nazirite,* Num. 6:1–21; *priestly benedictions,* Num. 6:22–27.

*Concerning, emoluments of priests,* Num. 18:8–32; *water of separation,* Num. 19:1–22; *Moses' successor,* Num. 27:18–21; *property rights of women,* Num. 27:7, 8; *boundaries of Canaan,* Num. 34; *cities of refuge and Levitical cities,* Num. 35:1–34; *worldwide mission of the Gospel,* Eph. 3:3–6.

**By Jesus,** see footnote, JESUS, *Revelations by,* Matt. 1:21.

See footnotes: INSPIRATION, Job 32:8; PROPHETS, *Inspiration of,* Isa. 3:2; WORD OF GOD, *Is inspired,* Psa. 119:9.

† **PARADOX,** Prov. 13:7; Matt. 10:39; 16:25 (with Mark 8:35; Luke 17:33; John 12:25); 1 Cor. 3:18; 2 Cor. 6:4, 8–10; 12:4, 10, 11; Eph. 3:17–19; Phil. 3:18, 19.

‡ **PARENTS.** *To be reverenced,* Ex. 20:12; Lev. 19:3; Deut. 5:16; Matt. 15:4; 19:19; Mark 7:10; 19:19; Luke 18:20. *To be obeyed,* Prov. 1:8; 6:20; 23:22; Eph. 6:1; Col. 3:20. *Covenant benefits of, entailed upon children,* Gen. 6:18; Ex. 20:6; Psa. 103:17. *Curses upon, entailed upon children,* Ex. 20:5; Lev. 20:5; Isa. 14:20; Jer. 9:14; Lam. 5:7. *Involved in children's wickedness,* 1 Sam. 2:31–36; 4:10–18.

*Fathers, to rule household,* Gen. 18:19; Prov. 3:12; 13:24; 1 Tim. 3:4, 5, 12; Tit. 1:6; Heb. 12:7; *to govern with kindness,* Eph. 6:4; Col. 3:21. *Mother, beloved,* Prov. 31:28.

*Cursing of, to be punished,* Ex. 21:17; Lev. 20:9.

**Partiality of:** *Isaac, for Esau,* Gen. 25:28. *Rebekah, for Jacob,* Gen. 25:28; 27:6–17. *Jacob, for Joseph,* Gen. 33:2; 37:3; 48:22; *for Benjamin,* Gen. 42:4. See footnote, PARTIALITY, 1 Tim. 5:21.

**Prayers of, in behalf of children:** *Of David,* 2 Sam. 7:25–29 (with 1 Chr. 17:16–27); 2 Sam. 12:16; 1 Chr. 22:11, 12; 29:19.

**Paternal blessings:** *Of Noah,* Gen. 9:24–27. *Of Abraham,* Gen. 17:18. *Of Isaac,* Gen. 27:4, 10–40; 28:3, 4. *Of Laban,* Gen. 31:55. *Of Jacob,* Gen. 48:15–20; 49:1–28; Heb. 11:20.

**Paternal imprecations,** Gen. 9:24, 25; 49:3–7.

**Evil influence of,** 1 Kin. 15:26; 22:52, 53; 2 Kin. 8:27; 21:20; 2 Chr. 21:6; 22:3.

**Good influence of,** 1 Kin. 22:43; 2 Kin. 15:3, 34.

**Indulgent:** *Eli,* 1 Sam. 2:27–36; 3:13, 14. *David,* 1 Kin. 1:6.

**Love of,** Psa. 103:13; Prov. 3:12; Isa. 49:15; 66:13; Matt. 7:9; 10:37; Luke 11:11–13. *Exemplified by, Hagar,* Gen. 21:15, 16; *Rebekah's mother,* Gen. 24:55; *Isaac and Rebekah,* Gen. 25:28; *Isaac,* Gen. 27:26, 27; *Laban,* Gen. 31:26–28; *Jacob,* Gen. 37:3, 4; 42:4, 38; 43:13, 14; 45:26–28; 48:10, 11; *Moses' mother,* Ex. 2:1–3, 9, 10; *Naomi,* Ruth 1:8, 9; *Han-*

**15**
*p Ingratitude, of man to man,* Rom. 1:21.
5 R. V. your souls. If I love you more abundantly, am I loved the less?
**16**
*q Minister, tactful,* Rom. 15:16.
**17**
*r Minister, faithful,* Rom. 15:16.
6 R. V. take advantage
**18**
*s Titus,* Tit. 1:4.
7 R. V. take any advantage
**19**
*t Responsibility, personal,* Ezek. 18:20.
8 R. V. Ye think all this time that we are excusing ourselves unto you. In the sight of God speak we in Christ. But all things, beloved, are for your edifying.
**20**
*u Reproof, faithfulness in,* Prov. 17:10.
*v Church, dissensions in,* Matt. 16:18.
*w Envy,* Prov. 14:30.
*x Anger,* Psa. 37:8.
*y Strife,* Prov. 20:3.
*z Backbiting,* Prov. 25:23.

*a Slander,* Prov. 10:18.
**21**
*b Backsliding, admonitions against,* Hos. 11:7.
*c Impenitence,* Rom. 2:5.
*d Adultery,* Lev. 20:10.
*e Lasciviousness,* 1 Pet. 4:3.

**1**
*a Paul,* Acts 13:9.
*b Minister, duties of,* vs. 1–10; Rom. 15:16.
*c Corinth, church of,* Acts 18:1.
*d* Deut. 19:15.
*e Church, discipline in,* Matt. 16:18.
*f Witness,* Num. 35:30.

15 And [g,n]I will very gladly
spend and be spent for [5]you;
though the more abundantly I
[n]love you, [p]the less I be loved.
16 But be it so, [k,m]I did not
burden you: nevertheless, being
[q]crafty, I caught you with guile.
17 [r]Did I [6]make a gain of you
by any of them whom I sent unto you?
18 I desired [C] [s]Tī′tus, and with
*him* I sent a brother. [r]Did Tī′tus
[7]make a gain of you? walked we
not in the same spirit? *walked
we* not in the same steps?
19 [8]Again, think ye that we excuse ourselves unto you? [g,r,t]we
speak before God in Christ: but
*we do* all things, dearly [n]beloved,
for your edifying.[C]
20 For [u]I fear, lest, when I
come, I shall not find you such as
I would, and *that* I shall be found
unto you such as ye would not:
lest *there be* [v]debates, [w]envyings,
[x]wraths, [y]strifes, [z,a]backbitings,[C]
whisperings, swellings,[C] tumults:[C]
21 *And* lest, when I come again,
my God will humble me among
you, and *that* I shall bewail[C] many
which have [b]sinned already, and
have [c]not repented of the uncleanness and [d]fornication and
[e]lasciviousness which they have
committed.

## CHAPTER 13

*The apostle threatens obstinate offenders. 5 Exhorts to self-examination, 7 and to a reformation of life. 11 Concludes his epistle with a general exhortation, a salutation, and benediction.*

THIS *is* the third *time* [a,b]I
am coming to [c]you. [d,e]In
the mouth of two or three [f]witnesses shall every word be established.[Q]
2 I told you before, and foretell
you, as if I were present, the second time; and being absent now
I write to them which heretofore
have sinned, and to all other,
that, if I come again, [b,g]I will not
spare:
3 Since ye seek a proof of Christ
speaking in me, which to you-ward[C] is not weak, but is mighty
in you.
4 For though he was [h,i]crucified through weakness, yet he
[j]liveth by the [k]power of God.
For we also are weak in him, but
we shall live with him by the
power of God toward you.
5 *,[l]Examine[C] yourselves, whether ye be in the [m]faith; prove your
own selves. Know ye not your
own selves, how that Jē′sus
[n]Christ is in [o]you, except ye be
[p]reprobates?[C][S]
6 But I trust that ye shall know
that we are not [p]reprobates.[C]
7 Now [q]I [r]pray to God that ye
[s]do no evil; [t,u]not that we should
appear approved, but [v]that ye
should do that which is [1]honest,[C]
though we be as reprobates.[C]
8 For we can do nothing against
the [w]truth, but for the truth.
9 For [u]we are glad, when we
are weak, and ye are strong: and
this also we wish, *even* your
[2,x]perfection.[C]
10 Therefore [b]I write these
things being absent, lest being
present I should use sharpness,
according to the [3]power which
the Lord hath given me to edification, and not to destruction.
11 Finally, brethren, farewell.
[y]Be [4,x]perfect,[C] be of good comfort, be of [z]one mind, [a]live in
[b]peace; and [c]the God of [d]love
and [e]peace shall be [f]with you.[S]

**2**
*g Reproof, faithfulness in,* Prov. 17:10.
**4**
*h Crucifixion, of Jesus,* Mark 15:13.
*i Jesus, death of,* Matt. 1:21.
*j Jesus, resurrection of,* Matt. 1:21.
*k God, power of,* Gen. 2:2.
**5**
*l Commandment, enjoining self-examination,* Deut. 8:2.
*m Faith, the doctrines of Jesus,* 1 Cor. 16:13.
*n Jesus, Messiah,* Matt. 1:21.
*o Righteous, union of, with Christ,* Psa. 64:10.
*p Reprobates,* 1 Cor. 9:27.
**7**
*q Zeal,* 2 Cor. 7:11.
*r Prayer, intercessory,* Acts 6:4.
*s Holiness,* Ex. 39:30.
*t Renunciation, of self, by Paul,* Luke 5:11.
*u Unselfishness,* 1 Cor. 10:24.
*v Love, of man for man,* 1 John 4:7.
1 R. V. honourable,
**8**
*w Truth,* John 18:37.
**9**
*x Perfection,* Heb. 6:1.
2 R. V. perfecting.
**10**
3 R. V. authority which the Lord gave me for building up, and not for casting down.
**11**
*y Commandment, enjoining Christian graces,* Deut. 8:2.
*z Unity, of the righteous,* Psa. 133:1.

*a Meekness, enjoined,* Psa. 45:4.
*b Peace, enjoined,* Jer. 29:7.
*c Righteous, promises to,* Psa. 64:10. *d God, love of,* Gen. 2:2.
*e Spiritual Peace,* Gal. 1:3. *f Fellowship, with God,* 1 Cor. 1:9.
4 R. V. perfected; be comforted;

*nah,* 1 Sam. 2:19; *David,* 2 Sam. 12:18–23; 13:38, 39; 14:1, 33; 18:5, 12, 13, 33; 19:1–6; *Rizpah,* 2 Sam. 21:8–11; *the mother of the infant brought to Solomon by the harlots,* 1 Kin. 3:22–28; *Job,* Job 1:5; *Mary,* Luke 2:48; John 19:25; *Jairus,* Mark 5:23; *the Syrophenician mother,* Mark 7:25–28; *father of demoniac,* Mark 9:17–24; *nobleman,* John 4:46–49.

*God's love, likened to love of,* Psa. 103:13; Prov. 3:12.

**Duties of:** *To provide for children,* 2 Cor. 12:14; 1 Tim. 5:8. *To instruct children in righteousness,* Ex. 10:2; 12:27; 13:8, 14; Deut. 4:9, 10; 6:7, 20–25; 11:18–21; 32:46; Psa. 78:5, 6; Prov. 22:6; Isa. 38:19; Joel 1:3; Eph. 6:4; 1 Thess. 2:11.

**Beloved:** *By Joseph,* Gen. 46:29. *By Rahab,* Josh. 2:12, 13. *By Jesus,* John 19:27. *By Ruth,* Ruth 1:16, 17. *By Elisha,* 1 Kin. 19:20.

* **SELF-EXAMINATION.** *Enjoined,* Psa. 4:4; Hag. 1:7; 1 Cor. 11:28, 31; 2 Cor. 13:5; Gal. 6:4. *Conversion as*

12 [g]Greet one another with an
holy [h]kiss.
13 All the saints [g]salute[G] you.
14 [i]The grace of the [j,k]Lord
Jē'sus Christ, and the [l]love of
[k]God, and the †communion[G] of
the [k,m]Holy[G] Ghost,[G] *be* with you
all. Amen.[S T]

[5]The second *epistle* to the Corinthians was written from Philippi, *a city* of Macedonia, by Titus and Lucus.

**12**
*g Salutations,* Luke 1:44.
*h Kiss, holy,* Ruth 1:9. **14** *i Benedictions, apostolic,* Deut. 21:5. *j Jesus, lordship of,* Matt. 1:21. *k Holy Trinity,* Luke 3:22.
*l God, love of,* Gen. 2:2.
*m Holy Spirit,* Acts 1:2.
5 R. V. *omits postscript.*

---

THE EPISTLE OF PAUL TO THE

# GALATIANS

## CHAPTER 1

*The apostle's salutation. 6 He marvels that they are so soon turned to another gospel, 8 and accurses those that preach any other gospel than he did. 11 He learned the gospel not of men, but of God. 13 What he was before his conversion, 15 and what he did immediately after it.*

[a]PAUL, an apostle, (not of
men, neither by man, but
[b,c]by Jē'sus Christ, and God the
[d]Father, who [e]raised him from
the dead;)[T]
2 And all the [f]brethren which
are with me, unto the [g]churches
of [h]Gā-lā'tia:
3 [i,j,k]Grace[S T] *be* to you and*peace
from God the [d]Father, and *from*
our [l]Lord Jē'sus Christ,
4 Who [m,n]gave [o]himself [p,q]for
our sins, that he might [n,r]deliver
us from this present evil world,[G]
according to the [s]will of God and
our [d]Father:[S T]
5 To whom *be* [t]glory for ever
and ever. Amen.
6 I marvel that ye are [u,v]so soon
[w]removed from him that called
you into the grace of Christ unto
another gospel:
7 Which is not [1]another; but
there be [x]some that trouble you,
and would [y]pervert[G] the [z]gospel
of Christ.
8 But though we, or an [a]angel
from heaven, [b]preach any other
gospel unto you than [c]that which
we have preached unto you, [d]let
him be [2,e]accursed.
9 As we said before, so say [f]I
now again, If any [g]*man* preach
any other gospel unto you than
[c]that ye have received, [d]let him
be [2,e]accursed.[S]
10 [h]For do [f]I now [i]persuade[G]
men, or God? or do I seek to
[j]please men? for if I yet pleased
men, I should not be the servant
of Christ.
11 But [f]I certify[G] you, brethren,
that the [c]gospel which was
[b]preached of me is not after[G] man.
12 For [f,k]I neither received it of
man, neither was I [l]taught *it,* but
[3]by the revelation of Jē'sus Christ.
13 For ye have heard of my
[4]conversation[G] in time past in the
Jews' †religion, how that beyond
measure [f]I [m,n,o,p]persecuted the
church of God, and [5]wasted[G] it:

**1**
*a Paul,* Acts 13:9.
*b Apostles, commission of,* Luke 6:13.
*c Call, personal,* Phil. 3:14.
*d God, fatherhood of,* Gen. 2:2.
*e Resurrection, of Jesus,* 1 Cor. 15:12.
**2**
*f Fraternity,* Zech. 11:14.
*g Church, Christian,* Matt. 16:18.
*h Galatia,* Acts 16:6.
**3**
*i Prayer, intercessory,* Acts 6:4.
*j Benedictions, apostolic,* Deut. 21:5.
*k Grace of God,* Rom. 4:16.
*l Jesus, lordship of,* Matt. 1:21.
**4**
*m Atonement, by Jesus,* Lev. 17:11.
*n Jesus, mission of,* Matt. 1:21.
*o Jesus, savior,* Matt. 1:21.
*p Jesus, atonement by,* Matt. 1:21.
*q Jesus, design of his death,* Matt. 1:21.
*r Redemption of our Souls,* Eph. 1:7.
*s Will of God,* Mark 3:35.
**5**
*t Praise,* Psa. 150:1. **6** *u Character, instability of,* Phil. 2:15. *v Instability,* Jas. 1:8. *w Backsliding,* Hos. 11:7. **7** 1 R. V. another gospel

**7**
*x False Teachers,* 2 Pet. 2:1.
*y Heresy,* Tit. 3:10.
*z Gospel,* Mark 13:10.
**8**
*a Angel,* Heb. 1:13
*b Preaching,* Matt 9:35.
*c Doctrines of Jesus,* John 7:16.
*d Prayer, imprecatory,* Acts 6:4.
*e Accursed,* Deut. 21:23.
2 R. V. anathema.
**9**
*f Paul,* Acts 13:9.
*g Minister, false and corrupt,* Rom. 15:16.
**10**
*h Zeal, exemplified,* 2 Cor. 7:11.
*i Minister, duties of,* Rom. 15:16.
*j Flattery,* Prov. 6:24.
**12**
*k Apostles, commission of,* Luke 6:13.
*l Instruction, in religion,* Prov. 23:23.
3 R. V. it came to me through revelation of Jesus Christ.
**13**
*m Persecution,* John 15:20.
*n Bigotry,* Isa. 65:5.
*o Ignorance, sins of,* Acts 3:17.
*p Zeal, without knowledge,* 2 Cor. 7:11. 4 R. V. manner of life in time 5 R. V. made havock of it:

---

*result of,* Psa. 119:59; Lam. 3:40. *Exemplified by the disciples,* Matt. 26:22; Mark 14:19.

† **COMMUNION. With God,** John 14:23; 2 Cor. 6:16; 1 John 1:3.
**With Christ,** John 14:23; 1 John 1:3; Rev. 3:20.
**With the Holy Spirit,** John 14:16–18; 2 Cor. 13:14; Gal. 4:6.
**Instances of:** *Enoch,* Gen. 5:22, 24. *Noah,* Gen. 6:9. *Abraham,* Gen. 18:1–33. *Hagar,* Gen. 16:8–12. *Moses,* Ex. 3; 4:1–17; 33:9, 11; 34:29–35; Num. 12:8. *Joshua,* Josh. 7:10–15. *Gideon,* Judg. 6:11–24.

* **SPIRITUAL PEACE,** Isa. 27:5; 54:1, 10, 13; 55:2, 12; 57:19; Ezek. 34:25; Luke 2:14, 29; Rom. 5:1; 1 Cor. 14:33. *Christ's Kingdom, a kingdom of,* Isa. 9:6; 11:6–9, 13; Mic. 5:5; Luke 1:79; Acts 10:36.
*From God,* Job 34:29; Psa. 29:11; 72:3, 7; 85:8; Jer. 33:6; Hag. 2:9; Rom. 15:13, 33; 16:20; 1 Cor. 1:3; 2 Cor. 1:2; Gal. 1:3; Phil. 4:7, 9; 1 Thess. 1:1; 5:23; 2 Thess. 3:16; 1 Tim. 1:2; 2 Tim. 1:2; Tit. 1:4; Philemon 3; Heb. 13:20; Rev. 1:4.
*From Christ,* Matt. 11:29; John 14:27; 16:33; 20:19; Eph. 2:14–17; Col. 3:15 (R. V.); Rev. 1:4, 5.
*A fruit of the Holy Spirit,* Rom. 14:17; Gal. 5:22 *of righteousness,* Rom. 2:10. *Assured to the righteous,* Psa. 37:4, 11, 37; 125:1, 5; Prov. 3:17, 24; Isa. 26:3, 12; 32:2, 17, 18; Rom. 8:6.
*Through the reconciliation of Christ,* Isa. 53:5; Col. 1:20. *Through acquaintance with God,* Job 22:21, 26. *Through loving God's law,* Psa. 119:165. *Through obedience,* Isa. 48:18; Jer. 6:16.
*None, to the wicked,* Isa. 57:20, 21.

† **NATIONAL RELIGION.** *Supported by taxes,* Ex. 30:11–16; 38:26. *Ministers of, supported by the state,* 1 Kin. 18:19; 2 Chr. 11:13–15. *Subverted by Jeroboam,* 1 Kin. 12:26–33; 2 Chr. 11:13–15. *Idolatrous, established by Jeroboam,* 1 Kin. 12:26–33.

14 And [6]profited in the Jews' [†]religion above many my equals in mine own nation, being more exceedingly [p,q]zealous of the [r]traditions of my fathers.

15 But when it pleased God, who separated me from my mother's womb, and [s,t]called *me* by his [u]grace,

16 To reveal his [v]Son in me, that I might [b]preach him among the [7,w]heathen; immediately I conferred not with flesh and blood:

17 Neither went I up to [x]Jē-ru'sā-lĕm to them which were apostles before me; but I went into [y]Ā-rā'bĭ-ȧ, and returned again unto [z]Dā-măs'cus.

18 Then after three years [a]I went up to [b]Jē-ru'sā-lĕm to see [c]Pē'tĕr, and abode with him fifteen days.

19 But other of the [d]apostles saw I none, save [e]Jāmes the Lord's [f]brother.

20 Now the things which I write unto you, behold, [g]before God, I lie not.

21 Afterwards I came into the regions of [h]Sўr'ĭ-ȧ and [‡]Çĭ-lĭ'çiȧ;

22 And was unknown by face unto the [i]churches of [j]Jū-dæ'ȧ which were in Christ:

23 But they had heard only, That he which [k]persecuted us in times past now [l]preacheth the [m]faith [8]which once he destroyed.

24 And they [n]glorified God in me.

## CHAPTER 2

*The apostle shews when and for what purpose he went up again to Jerusalem; 3 that Titus was not compelled to be circumcised; 11 and that he withstood Peter at Antioch for his dissimulation, 14 because, through fear of the Jews, he acted as if justification came by works of law. 20 His life by the faith of the Son of God.*

THEN fourteen years after [a]I went up again to [b]Jē-ru'sā-lĕm with [c]Bär'na-băs, and took [d]Tī'tus with *me* also.

2 And I went up by [e,f]revelation, and communicated unto them that [g]gospel which I [h]preach among the [i]Gĕn'tīles, but privately to them which were of reputation, lest by any means I should [j]run, or had run, in vain.

3 But neither [d]Tī'tus, who was with me, being a [k]Greek, was compelled to be [l]circumcised:

4 And that because of [m,n]false brethren [1]unawares brought in, who came in privily to [o]spy out our [p]liberty which we have in Christ Jē'sus, that they might bring us into bondage:

5 To whom we gave place by subjection, no, not for an hour; that the truth of the [g]gospel might continue with you.

6 But of these who seemed to be somewhat, (whatsoever they were, it maketh no matter to me: [q]God accepteth no man's person:) [2]for they who seemed *to be somewhat* in conference added nothing to me:

7 But contrariwise, when they saw that the gospel of the uncircumcision was [f]committed unto me, as *the gospel* of the circumcision *was* [t]unto [r]Pē'tĕr;

8 (For he that wrought [3]effectually in [r]Pē'tĕr to the apostleship of the [s]circumcision, the same was mighty in me toward the [t]Gĕn'tīles:)

9 And when [u]Jāmes, [r]Çē'phas, and [v]Jŏhn, who seemed to be pillars, perceived the grace that was given unto me, [w]they gave to me and Bär'na-băs the right hands of [x]fellowship; that we *should* [y]*go* unto the [4,t]heathen, and they unto the [s]circumcision.

10 Only [w]*they would* that we should [z]remember the [a]poor; the same which [b]I also was [5]forward to do.

11 But when [c]Pē'tĕr was come

**14** q *Paul, character of*, Acts 13:9. r *Tradition*, Matt. 15:2. 6 R. V. I advanced in the Jews' religion beyond many of mine own age among my countrymen,

**15** s *Minister, call of*, Rom. 15:16. t *Foreordination*, Rom. 8:30. u *Grace of God*, Rom. 4:16.

**16** v *Jesus, divine sonship of*, Matt. 1:21. w *Gentiles, conversion of*, Acts 10:45. 7 R. V. Gentiles;

**17** x *Jerusalem*, Judg. 19:10. y *Arabia*, 2 Chr. 9:14. z *Damascus*, Isa. 8:4.

**18** a *Paul*, Acts 13:9. b *Jerusalem*, Judg. 19:10. c *Peter*, Mark 5:37.

**19** d *Apostles*, Luke 6:13. e *James*, Matt. 13:55. f *Brothers of Jesus*, Matt. 13:55.

**20** g *Oath*, Num. 5:19.

**21** h *Syria*, 2 Kin. 6:23.

**22** i *Church, Christian*, Matt. 16:18. j *Judea*, Luke 5:17.

**23** k *Persecution, of Christians*, John 15:20. l *Preaching*, Matt. 9:35. m *Faith, the doctrines of Jesus*, 1 Cor. 16:13. 8 R. V. of which he once made havock;

**24** n *Glorifying God*, Luke 5:25.

**1** a *Paul*, Acts 13:9. b *Jerusalem*, Judg. 19:10. c *Barnabas*, Acts 4:36. d *Titus*, Tit. 1:4.

**2** e *Inspiration*, Job 32:8. f *Call, personal*, Phil. 3:14. g *Doctrines of Jesus*, John 7:16. h *Preaching*, Matt. 9:35. i *Gentiles, conversion of*, Acts 10:45. j *Foot Race, figurative*, Psa. 19:5.

**3** k *Greek*, Zech. 9:13. l *Circumcision, abrogated*, Gen. 17:10.

**4** m *False Teachers*, 2 Pet. 2:1. n *Heresy, teachers of*, Tit. 3:10. o *Spies*, Josh. 6:23. p *Liberty, spiritual*, Lev. 25:10. 1 R. V. privily brought in,

**6** q *God, impartial*, Gen. 2:2. 2 R. V. they, I say, who were of repute imparted nothing to me:

**7** r *Peter*, Mark 5:37.

**8** s *Jews*, Neh. 4:2. t *Gentiles*, Acts 10:45. 3 R. V. *omits* effectually

**9** u *James*, Matt. 10:3. v *John*, Mark 1:19. w *Church, government of*, Matt. 16:18. x *Fellowship, of the righteous*, 1 Cor. 1:9. y *Missions*, Matt. 28:19. 4 R. V. Gentiles,

**10** z *Liberality*, 1 Tim. 6:18. a *Poor*, Prov. 21:13. b *Paul*, Acts 13:9. 5 R. V. zealous

**11** c *Peter*, Mark 5:37.

‡ **CILICIA.** *Maritime province of Asia Minor*, Acts 27:5. *Jews dwell in*, Acts 6:9. *Churches of*, Acts 15:23, 41; Gal. 1:21

to [d]Ăn'tĭ-ŏch, [b]I withstood him to the face, because he [6]was to be blamed.

12 For before that certain came from [e]Jāmeș, [c]he [f]did eat with the [g]Ġĕn'tīleș: but when they were come, he [f]withdrew and separated himself, [h]fearing [i,j]them which were of the circumcision.

13 And the other [i]Jewș [k,l]dissembled likewise with him; insomuch that [m]Bär'na-băs also was [n]carried away with their dissimulation.

14 But when I saw that they walked not uprightly according to the truth of the [o]gospel, I [p,q]said unto [c]Pē'tēr before *them* all, If thou, being a [i]Jew, livest after the manner of [g]Ġĕn'tīleș, and not as do the Jewș, why compellest thou the Ġĕn'tīleș to live as do the Jewș?

15 We *who are* [i]Jewș by nature, and not sinners of the [g]Ġĕn'tīleș,

16 Knowing that a man is not [r]justified by the [s]works of the [t]law, but [u]by the [v]faith of Jē'șus [w]Chrīst, even we have believed in Jē'șus Chrīst, that we might be justified by the faith of Chrīst, and not by the works of the law: for by the works of the law shall no flesh be justified.

17 But if, while we seek to be [u]justified by Chrīst, we ourselves also are found sinners, *is* therefore Chrīst the minister of sin? God forbid.

18 For if I build again the things which I destroyed, I make myself a transgressor.

19 For I through the [c]law am dead to the law, that I might [x,y]live unto God.

20 [z]I am [a]crucified with Chrīst: nevertheless I [b]live; yet not I, but Chrīst liveth in [c]me: and the life which I now live in the flesh I live by the [d]faith of the [e]Son of God, who [f]loved me, and [g,h]gave himself for me.

21 I do not frustrate the [i]grace of God: for if [j]righteousness *come* by the [k]law, then Chrīst is dead in vain.

## CHAPTER 3

*The apostle reproves them for being drawn away from the simplicity of the gospel; 6 and shews that those who believe are justified, 9 and blessed with faithful Abraham. 24 The law was our schoolmaster. 28 Unity of believers in Christ.*

O FOOLISH Gă-lā'tianș, who hath [a,b]bewitched you, [1]that ye should not obey the [c]truth, before whose eyes Jē'șus Chrīst hath been evidently [d]set forth, [e]crucified among you?

2 This only would I learn of you, Received ye the [f]Spirit by the [g]works of the [h]law, or by the hearing of [i]faith?

3 Are ye so foolish? having begun in the [f]Spirit, are ye now made perfect by the flesh?

4 Have ye suffered so many things in vain? if *it be* yet in vain.

5 He therefore that [2]ministereth to you the [f]Spirit, and worketh [j]miracles among you, *doeth he it* by the works of the [h]law, or by the hearing of [i]faith?

6 Even as [k]Ā'bră-hăm [l]believed God, and it was accounted to him for [m,n]righteousness.

7 Know ye therefore that they which are of [i]faith, the same are the [o]children of [k]Ā'bră-hăm.

8 And the [p]scripture, foreseeing that God would [n]justify the [3,q]heathen through [i,r]faith, preached [4]before the [s]gospel unto [k]Ā'bră-hăm, *saying,* In thee shall all [t]nations be blessed.

9 So then they which be of [i]faith are blessed with [u]faithful [k]Ā'bră-hăm.

10 For as many as are of the [g]works of the [h]law are under the [v]curse: for it is written, [v,w]Cursed *is* every one that [x]continueth

d *Antioch,* Acts 11:19.
6 R. V. stood condemned.

**12**
e *James,* Matt. 10:3
f *Inconsistency,* Matt. 7:3.
g *Gentiles,* Acts 10:45.
h *Cowardice.* Lev. 26:36.
i *Jews,* Neh. 4:2.
j *Public Opinion,* John 12:42.

**13**
k *Dissembling,* Josh. 7:11.
l *Hypocrisy,* Jas. 3:17.
m *Barnabas,* Acts 4:36.
n *Influence, evil,* 1 Cor. 7:14.

**14**
o *Doctrines of Jesus,* John 7:16.
p *Courage,* Deut. 31:7.
q *Reproof, faithfulness in,* Prov. 17:10.

**16**
r *Justification, not by the law,* Rom. 4:25.
s *Works, insufficient for salvation,* 2 Tim. 1:9.
t *Law, of Moses,* Deut. 33:2.
u *Justification, by faith,* Rom. 4:25.
v *Faith in Christ,* John 6:69.
w *Jesus, Messiah,* Matt. 1:21.

**19**
x *Life, spiritual,* Eccl. 8:15.
y *Regeneration,* Tit. 3:5.

**20**
z *Religious Testimony,* 2 Thess. 1:10.

a *Crucifixion, figurative,* Mark 15:13.
b *Life, spiritual,* Eccl. 8:15.
c *Righteous, union of, with Christ,* Psa. 64:10.
d *Faith in Christ,* John 6:69.
e *Jesus, divine sonship of,* Matt. 1:21.
f *Jesus, love of,* Matt. 1:21.
g *Jesus, design of his death,* Matt. 1:21.
h *Redemption of our Souls,* Eph. 1:7.

**21**
i *Grace of God,* Rom. 4:16.
j *Justification, not by the law,* Rom. 4:25.
k *Law, of Moses,* Deut. 33:2.

**1**
a *Backsliding, temptation to,* Hos. 11:7.
b *Spiritual Blindness,* 2 Cor. 4:4.
c *Truth, of the gospel,* John 18:37.
d *Instruction, in religion,* Prov. 23:23.
e *Jesus, death of,* Matt. 1:21.
1 R. V. *omits* that ye should not obey the truth,

**2**
f *Holy Spirit,* Acts 1:2.
g *Works, insufficient for salvation,* 2 Tim. 1:9.
h *Law, of Moses,* Deut. 33:2.
i *Faith in Christ,* John 6:69.

**5**
j *Miracles,* Luke 23:8.
2 R. V. supplieth

**6**
k *Abraham,* Gen. 17:5.
l *Faith, reckoned for righteousness,* Gen. 15:6.
m *Righteousness, imputed on account of faith,* Psa. 15:2.
n *Justification,* Rom. 4:25.

**7**
o *Unity, of the righteous,* Psa. 133:1.

**8**
p *Word of God,* Psa. 119:9.
q *Gentiles, prophecies concerning the conversion of,* Acts 10:45.
r *Salvation, conditions of,* Acts 16:17.
s *Gospel,* Mark 13:10.
t *Nations to be blessed in Abraham,* Gen. 18:18.
3 R. V. Gentiles
4 R. V. the gospel beforehand unto

**9**
u *Faithfulness,* Luke 16:10.

**10**
v *Curse,* Judg. 5:23.
w Deut. 27:26.
x *Disobedience,* Eph. 5:6.

not in all things which are written
in the book of the law to do them.
11 But that no man is [n]justified
by the law in the sight of God, *it*
*is* evident: for, The [5,y]just shall
live by [z]faith.
12 And the law is not of [z]faith:
but, The man that [a]doeth them
shall live in them.
13 [b]Chrīst hath [c]redeemed us
from the curse of the law, [d,e]be-
ing made a curse [f,g]for us: for it
is written, [h]Cursed *is* every one
that [i]hangeth on a tree:
14 That the [j]blessing of [k]Ā′brā-
hăm might come on the [l]Gĕn′-
tīleș [m]through Jē′șus Chrīst; that
we might receive the promise of
the [n]Spirit through [o]faith.
15 Brethren, I speak after the
manner of men; Though *it be*
but a man's [p]covenant, yet *if it*
*be* confirmed, no man disannul-
leth, or addeth thereto.
16 Now to [k]Ā′brā-hăm and his
seed were the [q,r]promises made.
He saith not, And to seeds, as of
many; but as of one, And to thy
[s]seed, which is Chrīst.
17 And this I say, *that* the [q]cov-
enant, that was confirmed before
of God [6]in Chrīst, the [t]law,
which was [u]four hundred and
thirty years after, cannot disannul, that it should make the
promise of none effect.
18 For if the [v]inheritance *be* of
the law, *it is* no more of [w]prom-
ise: but God gave *it* to [k]Ā′brā-
hăm by [w]promise.
19 [7]Wherefore then *serveth* the
[x]law? It was added because
of [y]transgressions, till the [s]seed
should come to whom the promise was made; *and it was* ordained by [z]angels in the hand of
a *,[a]mediator.
20 Now a *mediator is not
*a mediator* of one, but God is
[b]one.
21 *Is* the [c]law then against the
[d]promises of God? God forbid:
for if there had been a law given
which could have given life, verily [e]righteousness should have
been by the [f]law.
22 [8]But the scripture hath concluded all under [g]sin, that the
[h]promise by [i]faith of Jē′șus
Chrīst might be given to them
that believe.
23 But before [i,k]faith came, we
were kept [9]under the [f]law, shut
up unto the [i,k]faith which should
afterwards be revealed.
24 Wherefore the [l]law was our
[10,l]schoolmaster *to bring us* unto
Chrīst, that we might be [h]justi-
fied by [i]faith.
25 But after that [i,k]faith is
come, we are no longer under a
[10,f,l]schoolmaster.
26 For [m]ye are all the [n,o]chil-
dren of God by [i]faith in Chrīst
Jē′șus.
27 For as many of you as have
been [p]baptized into Chrīst have
put on Chrīst.
28 [q]There is [r]neither [s]Jew nor
[t]Greek, there is neither bond nor
free, there is neither male nor
female: for ye are all [m,o]one in
Chrīst Jē′șus.
29 And if ye *be* Chrīst's, then
are ye [u]Ā′brā-hăm's seed, and
[v]heirs according to the [d]promise.

**11**
y *Just shall live by Faith*, Hab. 2:4.
z *Faith*, Mark 11:22.
5 R. V. righteous

**12**
a *Works under the Law*, Lev. 18:5.

**13**
b *Jesus, savior*, Matt. 1:21.
c *Redemption of our Souls*, Eph. 1:7.
d *Jesus, vicarious death of*, Matt. 1:21.
e *Penalty, vicariously assumed*, 1 Sam. 25:24.
f *Substitution*, Lev. 1:4.
g *Jesus, design of his death*, Matt. 1:21.
h Deut. 21:23.
i *Crucifixion, a reproach*, Mark 15:13.

**14**
j *Justification, by faith*, Rom. 4:25.
k *Abraham*, Gen. 17:5.
l *Gentiles, conversion of*, Acts 10:45.
m *Jesus, atonement by*, Matt. 1:21.
n *Holy Spirit*, Acts 1:2.
o *Faith in Christ*, John 6:69.

**15**
p *Covenant, binding*, Deut. 29:1.

**16**
q *Covenant, of God with men*, Deut. 29:1.
r *Nations to be blessed in Abraham*, Gen. 18:18.
s *Prophecies concerning the Messiah, and their fulfillment*, Gen. 12:3.

**17**
t *Law, of Moses*, Deut. 33:2.
u Ex. 12:40, 41.
6 R. V. *omits* in Christ,

**18** v *Inheritance*, Num. 27:7. w *Grace of God*, Rom. 4:16.
**19** x *Law, of Moses, temporary*, Deut. 33:2. 7 R. V. What then is the law?

y *Sin, transgression of the law*, Rom. 5:12.
z *Angel, functions of*, Heb. 1:13.
a *Moses*, Ex. 2:10.

**20**
b *God, unity of*, Gen. 2:2.

**21**
c *Law, of Moses*, Deut. 33:2.
d *Covenant, of God with men*, Deut. 29:1.
e *Righteousness*, Psa. 15:2.
f *Works under the Law*, Lev. 18:5.

**22**
g *Sin, transgression of the law*, Rom. 5:12.
h *Justification, by faith*, Rom. 4:25.
i *Faith in Christ*, John 6:69.
8 R. V. Howbeit the scripture hath shut up all things under sin,

**23**
j *Faith, the doctrines of Jesus*, 1 Cor. 16:13.
k *Gospel*, Mark 13:10.
9 R. V. in ward under

**24**
l *School*, Acts 19:9.
10 R. V. tutor

**26**
m *Church, unity of*, Matt. 16:18.
n *Spiritual Adoption*, Rom. 8:15.
o *Unity, of the righteous*, Psa. 133:1.

**27**
p *Baptism, Christian*, Luke 20:4.

**28**
q *Catholicity, taught*, Eph. 2:14.
r *Man, equality of, under the gospel*, Job 4:17.
s *Jews*, Neh. 4:2.
t *Gentile*, Acts 10:45.

**29**
u *Abraham*, Gen. 17:5.
v *Heir, figurative*, Gen. 15:3.

* **MEDIATION. Between men and God**, Ex. 18:19; Job 9:33; Gal. 3:19. *Solicited by Israel*, Ex. 20:19, 20; Deut. 5:27.
INSTANCES OF: *By Moses*, Ex. 32:11–13; 34:9; Num. 14:13–19; 27:5; Deut. 5:5; 9:18–20, 25–29. *By Aaron*, Num. 16:47, 48. *By Joshua*, Josh. 7:6–9. *By Samuel*, 1 Sam. 8:10, 21. *By David*, 2 Sam. 24:17.
**Between men and Jesus:** *In behalf of the afflicted*, Matt. 12:22; 15:30; Mark 1:32. *The four friends for the paralytic*, Mark 2:3; Luke 5:18–20. *Jairus*, Matt. 9:18; Mark 5:23; Luke 8:41. *The nobleman for his son*, John 4:47, 49. *The father of the epileptic for his son*, Matt. 17:15; Mark 9:17, 18. *The Syrophenician woman for her daughter*, Matt. 15:22; Mark 7:24–26. *The disciples for Peter's wife's mother*, Mark 1:30; Luke 4:38, 39.
**Between men and men:** *Reuben for Joseph*, Gen. 37:21, 22. *Judah for Joseph*, Gen. 37:26, 27. *Pharaoh's chief baker for Joseph*, Gen. 41:9–13, with 40:14. *Jonathan for David*, 1 Sam. 19:1–7. *Abigail for Nabal*, 1 Sam. 25:23–35. *Joab for Absalom*, 2 Sam. 14:1–24. *Bath-sheba, for Solomon*, 1 Kin. 1:15–31; *for Adonijah*, 1 Kin. 2:13–25. *Ebed-melech for Jeremiah*, Jer. 38:7–13 *Elisha offers to see the king for the Shunammite*, 2 Kin. 4:13. *The king of Syria for Naaman*, 2 Kin. 5:6–8. *Paul for Onesimus*, Philemon 10–21.
See footnote, INTERCESSION, Jer. 27:18.

## CHAPTER 4

*We were under the law till Christ came, as the heir is under his guardian till he is of age. 5 But Christ freed us from the law: 7 therefore we are no longer servants to it. 14 He remembers their good will to him; 22 and shews that we are Abraham's seed according to the promise.*

NOW I say, *That* the [a]heir, as
long as he is a [b]child, differeth nothing from a [1,c]servant,
though he be lord of all;
2 But is under [2,d]tutors and
governors until the time appointed of the father.
3 Even so we, when we were
children, were in bondage under
the [3]elements of the world:
4 But when the fulness of the
time was come, God sent forth
[e]his [f]Son, [4,g]made of a woman,
made under the [h]law,
5 [i]To [j]redeem them that were
under the [h,k]law, that we might
receive the [l]adoption of sons.
6 And because ye are [l]sons, [m]God
hath sent forth the [m,n]Spirit of his
[f,m]Son [o]into [5]your hearts, crying,
Ăb′bă, [p]Father.
7 Wherefore thou art [q]no more
a [6]servant, but a [l]son; and if
a son, then an [r]heir of God
[7]through Chrīst.
8 Howbeit then, when ye [s]knew
not God, ye [8,t]did service unto
them which by nature are no
gods.
9 But now, after that ye have
[u]known God, or rather are
[v,w]known of God, how [x,y,z]turn
ye again to the [a]weak and beggarly [3]elements, whereunto ye
desire again to be in bondage?
10 Ye observe days, and
months, and times, and years.
11 I am afraid of you, lest I
have bestowed upon you labour
in vain.
12 [b]Brethren, I beseech you, be
[c]as I *am*; for I *am* as ye *are*: ye
[9]have not injured me at all.
13 Ye know [10]how through infirmity of the flesh I [d]preached
the [e]gospel unto you at the first.
14 And [11]my [f]temptation which
was in my flesh ye despised not,
nor rejected; but [g]received me as
an angel of God, *even* as Chrīst
Jē′ṣus.
15 Where [12]is then the blessedness ye spake of? for I bear you
record, that, if *it had been* possible, [g]ye would have plucked out
your own eyes, and have given
them to me.
16 Am I therefore become your
enemy, because I [h]tell you the
[i]truth?
17 [j]They [k]zealously [13]affect you,
*but* not well; yea, they would ex-
clude you, that ye might affect
them.
18 But *it is* good to be [l]zealously
[14]affected always in *a* good *thing*,
and not only when I am present
with you.
19 My little children, of whom
I travail in birth again until
Chrīst be formed in you,
20 I desire to be present with
you now, and to change my
voice; for I [15]stand in doubt of
you.
21 Tell me, ye that desire to be
under the law, do ye not hear the
law?
22 For it is written, that [m]Ā-
brā-hăm had two [n,o]sons, the
[p]one by a [q,r]bondmaid, the other
by a [s]freewoman.
23 But [n]he *who was* of the
[q,r]bondwoman was born after
the flesh; but [o]he of the [s]free-
woman *was* by promise.
24 Which things [16]are an *allegory: for [q,s]these are the two
covenants; the [t]one from the
mount [u]Sī′nāi, which gendereth
to bondage, which is [q]Ā′găr.

**1**
a *Heir,* Gen. 15:3.
b *Children, minors,* Mark 10:14.
c *Servant,* Jer. 2:14.
1 R. V. bondservant,

**2**
d 2 Kin. 10:1; Acts 22:3.
2 R. V. guardians and stewards until

**3**
3 R. V. rudiments

**4**
e *God, fatherhood of,* Gen. 2:2.
f *Jesus, divine sonship of,* Matt. 1:21.
g *Jesus, incarnation of,* Matt. 1:2.
h *Law, of Moses,* Deut. 33:2.
4 R. V. born of a woman, born under the law,

**5**
i *Jesus, mission of,* Matt. 1:21.
j *Redemption of our Souls,* Eph. 1:7.
k *Works under the Law,* Lev. 18:5.
l *Spiritual Adoption,* Rom. 8:15.

**6**
m *Holy Trinity,* Luke 3:22.
n *Holy Spirit, witness of,* Acts 1:2.
o *Communion, with the Holy Spirit,* 2 Cor. 13:14.
p *God, fatherhood of,* Gen. 2:2.
5 R. V. our hearts,

**7**
q *Liberty, spiritual,* Lev. 25:10.
r *Heir, figurative,* Gen. 15:3.
6 R. V. bondservant,
7 R. V. *omits* through Christ.

**8**
s *Spiritual Blindness,* 2 Cor. 4:4.
t *Idolatry,* 1 Sam. 15:23.
8 R. V. were in bondage to

**9** u *Wisdom, spiritual,* Prov. 2:2. v *God, knowledge of,* Gen. 2:2. w *Righteous, described,* Psa. 64:10. x *Backsliding,* Hos. 11:7. y *Character, instability of,* Phil. 2:15. z *Instability,* Jas. 1:8. —a *Works under the Law,* Lev. 18:5. **12** b *Love, of man for man,* 1 John 4:7.

c *Example, Paul our,* John 13:15.
9 R. V. Ye did me no wrong:

**13**
d *Preaching,* Matt. 9:35.
e *Gospel,* Mark 13:10.
10 R. V. that because of an infirmity

**14**
f *Temptation,* Luke 11:4.
g *Love, of man for man,* 1 John 4:7.
11 R. V. that which was a temptation to you in my flesh

**16**
h *Reproof,* Prov. 17:10.
i *Truth, of the gospel,* John 18:37.

**17**
j *False Teachers,* 2 Pet. 2:1.
k *Zeal, without knowledge,* 2 Cor. 7:11.
13 R. V. seek you in no good way; nay, they desire to shut you out, that ye may seek them.

**18**
l *Zeal,* 2 Cor. 7:11.
14 R. V. sought in a good matter at all times,

**20**
15 R. V. am perplexed about

**22**
m *Abraham,* Gen. 17:5.
n *Ishmael,* Gen. 16:11.
o *Isaac,* Gen. 21:3.
p *Bastard,* Deut. 23:2.
q *Hagar,* Gen. 16:1.
r *Concubinage,* 2 Sam. 21:11.
s *Sarah,* Gen. 17:15.

**24**
t *Law, of Moses,* Deut. 33:2.
u *Sinai,* Ex. 16:1.
16 R. V. contain an allegory: for these women are two covenants; one from mount Sinai, bearing children unto bondage, which is Hagar.

* **ALLEGORY.** *Of the trees seeking a king,* Judg. 9:8–15. *Messiah's kingdom represented under, of the wolf and the lamb dwelling together,* Isa. 11:6–8. *Wilderness to blossom as the rose,* Isa. 35:1, 2. *The two covenants,* Gal. 4:24.

25 For this [q]Ā′gär is mount
[u]Sī′nāi in Ā-rā′bĭ-ȧ, and answereth[G] to Jē-ru′sȧ-lĕm which now
is, and is in bondage with her
children.
26 But [v]Jē-ru′sȧ-lĕm which is
above is free, which is [17]the
mother of us all.
27 For it is written, [w,x]Rejoice,
*thou* barren that bearest not;
break forth and cry, thou that
travailest not; for the desolate
hath many more children than
she which hath an husband.[Q]
28 Now we, brethren, as [o]Ī′-
ṣaac was, are the children of
promise.
29 But as then [n,p]he that was
born after the flesh [y]persecuted
[o]him *that was born* after the
Spirit, even so *it is* now.[Q]
30 Nevertheless what saith the
scripture? [z]Cast out the [a]bond-
woman and her [b]son: for the son
of the bondwoman shall not be
[c]heir with the [d]son of the [e]free-
woman.[Q]
31 So then, brethren, we are not
children of the bondwoman, but
of the [18,f]free.[T]

## CHAPTER 5

*The apostle urges them to stand fast in their liberty, 3 and not to observe circumcision: 13 but by love to serve one another. 19 He reckons up the works of the flesh, 22 and the fruits of the Spirit, 25 and exhorts to walk in the Spirit.*

[a,b]STAND [c,d]fast therefore in
the [e]liberty wherewith
[f]Chrīst hath made us free, and
be not entangled again with the
[g]yoke of bondage.
2 Behold, I [h]Paul say unto
you, that if ye be [i,j]circum-
cised, Chrīst shall profit you
nothing.
3 For I testify again to every
man that is circumcised, that he
is a debtor[G] to do the whole [k]law.
4[S] [1]Chrīst[G] is become of no effect unto you, whosoever of you
are [l]justified by the [k]law; ye are
[m]fallen from grace.
5 For we through the [n]Spirit
wait for the [o]hope of [p]righteous-
ness by [q]faith.
6 For in Jē′ṣus Chrīst neither [i,j]circumcision availeth any
thing, nor uncircumcision; but
[q]faith [2]which worketh by [r]love.[S]
7 Ye did [s]run well; [t]who did
[u,v]hinder you that ye should
[w]not obey the [x]truth?
8 This persuasion *cometh* not of
him that [y]calleth you.
9 A little [z,a,b]leaven leaveneth[G]
the whole lump.
10 I have confidence in you
through the Lord, that ye will be
none otherwise minded: but [c,d]he
that troubleth you shall bear his
judgment, whosoever he be.
11 And I, brethren, if I yet
[e]preach [f]circumcision, why do I
yet suffer [g]persecution? then [3]is
the [h]offence[G] of the [i,j]cross ceased.
12 I would [4]they were even
[k]cut[G] off which trouble you.
13 For, brethren, ye have been
called unto [5,l]liberty; only *use*
not [5]liberty for an occasion to
the flesh, but by [m]love [n]serve one
another.
14 For all the [o]law is fulfilled in
one word, *even* in this; [p,q]Thou
shalt [r]love thy [s]neighbour as thyself.[Q]
15 But if ye [t]bite and devour
one another, take heed that ye be
not consumed[G] one of another.
16[T] *This* I say then, [u]Walk in
the [v]Spirit, and ye shall [w]not fulfil the [x]lust of the flesh.
17 For the [y]flesh [z]lusteth
against the Spirit, and the Spirit
against the flesh: and these are
contrary the one to the other: so
that ye cannot do the things that
ye would.

4 Am. R. V. that they who unsettle you would even go beyond circumcision. **13** *l Liberty, spiritual,* Lev. 25:10. *m Love, of man for man,* 1 John 4:7. *n Altruism,* Acts 20:35. 5 R. V. freedom **14** *o Law, of Moses,* Deut. 33:2. *p Commandment, enjoining love to man,* Deut. 8:2. *q Royal Law,* Jas. 2:8. *r Duty, of man to man,* Eccl. 12:13. *s Neighbor, love for, enjoined,* Luke 10:29. **15** *t Strife,* Prov. 20:3. **16** *u Commandment, enjoining spirituality,* Deut. 2:8. *v Holy Spirit,* Acts 1:2. *w Self-denial,* Mark 8:34. *x Carnal Mind,* 1 Cor. 3:3. **17** *y Depravity,* Job 15:14. *z Temptation, sources of, carnal desires,* Luke 11:4.

**26**
*v Kingdom of Heaven,* Matt. 13:24.
17 R. V. our mother.

**27**
*w* Isa. 54:1.
*x Church, prophecies concerning its prosperity,* Matt. 16:18.

**29**
*y Persecution, of the righteous,* John 15:20.

**30**
*z* Gen. 21:10.

*a Hagar,* Gen. 16:1.
*b Ishmael,* Gen. 16:11.
*c Heir,* Gen. 15:3.
*d Isaac,* Gen. 21:3.
*e Sarah,* Gen. 17:15.

**31**
*f Liberty, spiritual,* Lev. 25:10.
18 R. V. freewoman.

**1**
*a Commandment, enjoining steadfastness,* Deut. 8:2.
*b Perseverance, exhortation to,* Eph. 6:18.
*c Character, stability of,* Phil. 2:15.
*d Steadfastness, enjoined,* 1 Cor. 15:58.
*e Liberty, spiritual,* Lev. 25:10.
*f Jesus, Messiah,* Matt. 1:21.
*g Works under the Law,* Lev. 18:5.

**2**
*h Paul,* Acts 13:9.
*i Circumcision, abrogated,* Gen. 17:10.
*j Works, insufficient for salvation,* 2 Tim. 1:9.

**3**
*k Law, of Moses,* Deut. 33:2.

**4**
*l Justification, not by the law,* Rom. 4:25.
*m Backsliders,* Jer. 3:22.
1 R. V. Ye are severed from Christ, ye who would be justified

**5**
*n Holy Spirit,* Acts 1:2.
*o Hope,* Prov. 13:12.
*p Righteousness,* Psa. 15:2.
*q Faith in Christ,* John 6:69.

**6**
*r Love, for Jesus,* 1 John 4:19.
2 R. V. working through love.

**7**
*s Foot Race, figurative,* Psa. 19:5.
*t Minister, false and corrupt,* Rom. 15:16.
*u Temptation, leading into,* Luke 11:4.
*v Influence, evil,* 1 Cor. 7:14.
*w Backsliding,* Hos. 11:7.
*x Truth, of the gospel,* John 18:37.

**8**
*y Call, personal,* Phil. 3:14.

**9**
*z Leaven, figurative,* Lev. 23:17.

*a Evil Company,* Prov. 13:20.
*b Influence, evil,* 1 Cor. 7:14.

**10**
*c False Teachers,* 2 Pet. 2:1.
*d Church, discipline in,* Matt. 16:18.

**11**
*e Preaching,* Matt. 9:35.
*f Works under the Law,* Lev. 18:5.
*g Paul, persecutions of,* Acts 13:9.
*h Crucifixion, a reproach,* Mark 15:13.
*i Cross, figurative,* John 19:17.
*j Atonement, by Jesus,* Lev. 17:11.
3 R. V. hath the stumblingblock of the cross been done away.

**12**
*k Disfellowship,* Num. 15:31.

**18**
a *Righteous, described*, Psa. 64:10.

**19**
b *Sin, fruits of*, Rom. 5:12.
c *Carnal Mind*, 1 Cor. 3:3.
d *Adultery*, Lev. 20:10.
e *Lasciviousness*, 1 Pet. 4:3.
6 R. V. *omits* Adultery,

**20**
f *Idolatry*, 1 Sam. 15:23.
g *Sorcery*, Isa. 47:9.
h *Hatred*, Prov. 15:17.
i *Jealousy*, Psa. 78:58.
j *Anger*, Psa. 37:8.
k *Strife*, Prov. 20:3.
l *Heresy*, Tit. 3:10.
7 R. V. sorcery, enmities, strife, jealousies, wraths, factions, divisions, heresies.

**21**
m *Envy*, Prov. 14:30.
n *Drunkenness*, Luke 21:34.
o *Wicked, punishment of*, Psa. 73:3.
p *Heaven, future home of the righteous*, Luke 18:22.
8 R. V. *omits* murders,

18 But if ye be [a]led of the Spirit, ye are not under the law.
19 Now the [b]works of the [c]flesh
are manifest, which are *these*;
[6]Adultery, [d]fornication, uncleanness, [e]lasciviousness,
20 [f]Idolatry, [7,g]witchcraft, [h]ha-
tred, variance, [i]emulations,
[j]wrath, [k]strife, seditions, [l]her-
esies,
21 [m]Envyings, [8]murders, [n]drunk-
enness, revellings, and such like:
of the which I tell you before, as
I have also told *you* in time past,
that they which do such things
[o]shall not inherit the [p]kingdom
of God.
22 But the *,[q]fruit of the [r]Spirit
is [s]love, [t]joy, [u]peace, [v]longsuf-
fering, [9,w]gentleness, goodness,
[10,x]faith,
23 [y]Meekness, [z]temperance:
against such there is no law.
24 And they that are [11]Christ's
have [a,b]crucified the flesh with
the [c]affections and lusts.
25 If we [b,d]live in the [e]Spirit, let
us also walk in the Spirit.
26 Let us [b]not be desirous of
vain glory, provoking one another, [f]envying one another.

## CHAPTER 6

*They are exhorted to deal mildly with an offending brother, 2 and to bear one another's burdens; 6 to be liberal to their teachers, 9 and not to be weary in well doing. 12 He shews what they intend that preach circumcision; 14 and glories in nothing, save in the cross of Christ.*

BRETHREN, [a]if a man be
overtaken in [1]a fault, ye
which are [b]spiritual, [c,d,e]restore
such an [f]one in the spirit of
[b,g]meekness; [h]considering thyself, lest thou also be [i]tempted.
2 [e,j,k,l]Bear ye one another's
[m]burdens, and so fulfil the [n]law
of Christ.
3 For if a man [o,p,q]think
himself to be something, when
he is nothing, he deceiveth himself.
4 But let every man [r]prove his
own [s]work, and then shall he
have rejoicing in himself alone,
and not [2]in another.
5 For every man shall [t]bear his
own [u]burden.
6 [v,w,x]Let him that is [y]taught
in the [n]word [x]communicate unto
him that teacheth in [z]all good
things.
7 Be not [a]deceived; God is
not mocked: for [b,c]whatsoever a

**1**
a *Church, discipline in*, Matt. 16:18.
b *Christian Graces*, Gal. 5:22.
c *Commandment, enjoining helpfulness*, Deut. 8:2.
d *Charitableness, enjoined*, Prov. 10:12.
e *Duty, of man to man*, Eccl. 12:13.
f *Weak, duty of the strong to*, 1 Cor. 8:9.
g *Meekness*, Psa. 45:4.
h *Watchfulness*, Matt. 24:42.
i *Temptation*, Luke 11:4.
1 R. V. any trespass,

**2**
j *Kindness, enjoined*, Acts 28:2.
k *Fellowship, of the righteous*, 1 Cor. 1:9.
l *Altruism, Paul inculcates*, Acts 20:35.
m *Burden, figurative*, Luke 11:46.
n *Doctrines of Jesus*, John 7:16.

**3**
o *Conceit*, Prov. 26:5.
p *Self-righteousness*, Luke 18:11.

**22** q *Righteousness, fruits of*, Psa. 15:2. r *Holy Spirit*, Acts 1:2. s *Love, of man for man*, 1 John 4:7. t *Joy*, Psa. 5:11. u *Spiritual Peace*, Gal. 1:3. v *Longsuffering*, 2 Cor. 6:6. w *Gentleness*, 2 Cor. 10:1. x *Faithfulness*, Luke 16:10. 9 R. V. kindness, 10 R. V. faithfulness,
**23** y *Meekness*, Psa. 45:4. z *Temperance*, 2 Pet. 1:6.
**24** a *Crucifixion, figurative*, Mark 15:13. b *Righteous, described*, Psa. 64:10. c *Affections, vile*, 2 Cor. 7:15. 11 R. V. of Christ Jesus have crucified the flesh with the passions and the lusts thereof,
**25** d *Life, spiritual*, Eccl. 8:15. e *Holy Spirit*, Acts 1:2.
**26** f *Envy, forbidden*, Prov. 14:30.

q *Delusion*, 2 Thess. 2:11. **4** r *Self-examination*, 2 Cor. 13:5. s *Works*, 2 Tim. 1:9. 2 R. V. of his neighbour. **5** t *Judgment, according to opportunity and works*, 1 Pet. 1:17. u *Responsibility, personal*, Ezek. 18:20.
**6** v *Commandment, enjoining the temporal support of ministers*, Deut. 8:2. w *Church, duty of, to ministers*, Matt. 16:18. x *Reciprocity*, 1 Cor. 9:11. y *Instruction, in religion*, Prov. 23:23. z *Minister, emoluments of*, Rom. 15:16.
**7**—a *Delusion*, 2 Thess. 2:11. b *Proverbs*, 1 Sam. 24:13. c *Nature, laws of, uniform in operation*, Jas. 3:12.

* **CHRISTIAN GRACES.** *Benevolence*, Matt. 19:19; John 15:12; Rom. 12:10; Gal. 5:22.
*Charitableness*, 1 Cor. 13:5–7; Gal. 6:1; Col. 3:13. See footnote, CHARITABLENESS, Prov. 10:12.
*Chastity*, Prov. 6:25; Matt. 5:28; Eph. 5:3; Col. 3:5. See footnote, CHASTITY, Job 31:1.
*Contentment*, Luke 3:14; 1 Cor. 7:20–24; 1 Tim. 6:8; Heb. 13:5. See footnote, CONTENTMENT, 1 Tim. 6:6.
*Faith, in the sense of trust*, Isa. 26:3; Rom. 4:20.
*Faithfulness*, Matt. 18:26; 25:21, 23; Luke 16:10; 1 Cor. 4:2.
*Fortitude*, 2 Pet. 1:5.
*Generosity*, see footnote, GENEROSITY, Gen. 20:14.
*Gentleness*, Jas. 3:17; 2 Tim. 2:24; Tit. 3:2.
*Godliness*, Mic. 6:8; 1 Tim. 2:2, 3; 4:8; 6:6.
*Holiness*, Isa. 52:1, 11; Matt. 5:8; Phil. 2:15; Tit. 1:15; 1 Pet. 1:15. See footnote, HOLINESS, Ex. 39:30.
*Hope*, Rom. 5:3–5; 12:12; 1 Cor. 13:13. See footnote, HOPE, Prov. 13:12.
*Humility*, Matt. 18:2–4; 1 Cor. 13:4; Eph. 4:2; Col. 3:12, 13. See footnote, HUMILITY, Prov. 22:4.
*Joyfulness*, John 16:24; 17:13; Gal. 5:22; Phil. 4:4; 1 Thess. 5:16. See footnote, JOY, Psa. 5:11.
*Kindness*, 1 Cor. 13:4; Gal. 6:2, 10; Eph. 4:32; 2 Pet. 1:5, 7. See footnote, KINDNESS, Acts 28:2.
*Longsuffering*, Gal. 5:22; Col. 3:12, 13; 2 Tim. 3:10; 1 Cor. 13:4, 7. See footnote, LONGSUFFERING, 2 Cor. 6:6.
*Love*, John 13:35; Rom. 12:10; 1 Cor. 13:1–9, 13. See footnote, LOVE, 1 John 4:7.
*Meekness*, Prov. 15:1, 13; 16:32; Matt. 5:5; 1 Cor. 13:4; Phil. 2:14, 15; 2 Tim. 2:24, 25; 1 Pet. 3:4. See footnote, MEEKNESS, Psa. 45:4.
*Mercy*, Psa. 85:10; Matt. 5:7; Col. 3:12. See footnote, MERCY, Deut. 5:10.
*Patience*, Rom. 5:3; 1 Cor. 13:4; 2 Cor. 6:4; 1 Thess. 5:14; 2 Tim. 2:24. See footnote, PATIENCE, Luke 8:15.
*Peace*, John 14:27; 16:33; Rom. 8:6; Gal. 5:22. See footnotes: PEACE, Jer. 29:7; SPIRITUAL PEACE, Gal. 1:3.
*Perseverance*, Matt. 24:13; 1 Cor. 15:58. See footnote, PERSEVERANCE, Eph. 6:18.
*Purity*, Psa. 51:7; Matt. 5:8; 1 Tim. 5:22; 1 John 3:3. See footnote, PURITY, 1 Tim. 4:12.
*Steadfastness*, 1 Cor. 15:58; 2 Thess. 2:15. See footnote, STEADFASTNESS, 1 Cor. 15:58.
*Temperance*, Dan. 1:8; 1 Cor. 9:25; 1 Tim. 3:3; 2 Pet. 1:5, 6. See footnote, TEMPERANCE, 2 Pet. 1:6.
*Tolerance*, Luke 9:49, 50; Rom. 14:1. See footnote, TOLERATION, Mic. 4:4.
*Unselfishness*, Rom. 12:10; 1 Cor. 10:24; 13:5; Phil. 2:3, 4. See footnote, UNSELFISHNESS, 1 Cor. 10:24.
*Zeal*, Eccl. 9:10; Dan. 12:3; John 4:34; 9:4; Rom. 12:11; 1 Cor. 7:29–31; Phil. 3:7–14; Heb. 12:1; Jude 22, 23 See footnote, ZEAL, 2 Cor. 7:11.

 Goodness Gal. 5:22, Ro. 15:14, Eph. 5:9, 2 Thess. 1:11

[d]man [e]soweth, [f,g]that shall he
also [e]reap.
8 For he that soweth to his
[h]flesh [i]shall of the flesh reap
[g,j]corruption[G]; but he that soweth
to the [k]Spirit [l,m]shall of the Spirit reap [n,o]life everlasting.[T]
9 And [p]let us [q]not be weary in
well doing: for in due season
[l,m]we shall [r]reap, if we [s]faint[G] not.
10 As we have therefore +op-
portunity, [t]let us [u]do good unto
all *men*, especially unto them
who are of the [v]household of
[w]faith.
11 [3]Ye see how large a letter I
have written unto you with mine
own hand.
12 [x]As many as [y]desire to make
a fair shew in the flesh, [z]they constrain you to be [a]circumcised;
only[4,b]lest they should suffer[c]per-
secution for the [d]cross of Chrīst.
13 For neither they themselves
who are [a]circumcised keep[G] the
[e]law; but desire to have you circumcised, that they may glory[G] in
your flesh.
14 But [5,f]God forbid that I
should [g]glory, [h]save[G] in the [d]cross
of our [i]Lord Jē'ṣus Chrīst, by
whom [j]the world is [k]crucified
unto me, and I unto the world.[S]
15 For [6]in Chrīst Jē'ṣus [l]nei-
ther circumcision availeth any
thing, nor uncircumcision, but a
[j,m]new creature.[S]
16 And as many as walk according to this rule, [n,o]peace *be*
on them, and [p,q]mercy, and upon the [r]Is'ra-el of God.[Q]
17 From henceforth let no man
trouble me: for I bear[7]in my body
the marks[G] of the Lord Jē'ṣus.
18 Brethren, [n]the [q]grace of our
[i]Lord Jē'ṣus Chrīst *be* with your
[s]spirit. Amen.

[8]Unto the Galatians written from Rome.

*d Sower,* Matt. 13:3. *e Agriculture,* Gen. 3:23. *f Righteousness, fruits of,* Psa. 15:2. *g Sin, fruits of,* Rom. 5:12. **8** *h Carnal Mind,* 1 Cor. 3:3. *i Wicked, punishment of,* Psa. 73:3. *j Corruption, figurative,* Job 17:14. *k Holy Spirit,* Acts 1:2. *l Righteous, promises to,* Psa. 64:10. *m Promise, to the righteous,* 2 Cor. 1:20. *n Life, everlasting,* Eccl. 8:15. *o Immortality,* 1 Cor. 15:54. **9** *p Contentment,* 1 Tim. 6:6. *q Zeal,* 2 Cor. 7:11. *r Reward, a motive, to perseverance,* Matt. 5:12. *s Perseverance, motives to,* Eph. 6:18. **10** *t Kindness, enjoined,* Acts 28:2. *u Altruism, Paul inculcates,* Acts 20:35. *v Fraternity,* Zech. 11:14. *w Faith, doctrines of Jesus,* 1 Cor. 16:13. **11** 3 Am. R. V. See with how large letters I write **12** *x Public Opinion, concessions to,* John 12:42. *y Hypocrisy,* Jas. 3:17. *z False Teachers,* 2 Pet. 2:1.—*a Circumcision,* Gen. 17:10. *b Cowardice,* Lev. 26:36. *c Persecution, of the righteous,* John 15:20.

*d Cross, figurative,* John 19:17. 4 R. V. that they may not be persecuted for **13** *e Law, of Moses,* Deut. 33:2. **14** *f Humility,* Prov. 22:4. *g Spiritual Boasting,* Rom. 3:27. *h Love, for Jesus,* 1 John 4:19. *i Jesus, lordship of,* Matt. 1:21. *j Righteous, described,* Psa. 64:10. *k Crucifixion, figurative,* Mark 15:13. 5 R. V. far be it from me to glory, **15** *l Works, insufficient for salvation,* 2 Tim. 1:9. *m Regeneration,* Tit. 3:5. 6 R. V. neither is circumcision anything, **16** *n Benedictions, apostolic,* Deut. 21:5. *o Spiritual Peace,* Gal. 1:3. *p God, mercy of,* Gen. 2:2. *q Grace of God,* Rom. 4:16. *r Church, called Israel of God,* Matt. 16:18. **17** 7 R. V. branded on my body the marks of Jesus. **18** *s Man, a spirit,* Job 4:17. 8 R. V. *omits postscript.*

THE EPISTLE OF PAUL TO THE

# EPHESIANS

## CHAPTER 1

*The apostle's salutation and thanksgiving. 4 He treats of our election and adoption by grace. 13 They trusted in Christ, and were sealed by the Holy Spirit of promise. 15 Wherefore he prays that they may come to a full knowledge of the salvation wrought in Christ, 20 whom God had exalted to his own right hand.*

[a]PAUL,[T] an apostle of Jē'ṣus
[b]Chrīst [c]by the [d]will of
God, to the saints which are at
[e]Ĕph'e-sŭs, and to the [f]faithful[G]
[g]in Chrīst Jē'ṣus:
2 [h,i]Grace *be* to you, and [j]peace,
from God our [k]Father, and *from*
the [l]Lord Jē'ṣus Chrīst.[T]
3 [m]Blessed *be* the God and [k]Father
of our [l]Lord Jē'ṣus Chrīst, who
hath [n]blessed us with all *spirit-

**1** *a Paul,* Acts 13:9. *b Jesus, Messiah,* Matt. 1:21. *c Call, personal,* Phil. 3:14. *d Will of God,* Mark 3:35. *e Ephesus,* Acts 18:19. *f Righteous, described,* Psa. 64:10. *g Righteous, union of, with Christ,* Psa. 64:10. **2** *h Grace of God,* Rom. 4:16. *i Benedictions, apostolic,* Deut. 21:5. *j Spiritual Peace,* Gal. 1:3. *k God, fatherhood of,* Gen. 2:2. *l Jesus, lordship of,* Matt. 1:21. **3** *m Praise,* Psa. 150:1. *n God, love of,* Gen. 2:2.

**+ OPPORTUNITY.** *Providential,* 1 Cor. 16:9; 2 Cor. 2:12. *Neglected,* Luke 12:47. *Spurned,* Prov. 1:24, 25; Matt. 23:34–38; Luke 14:16–24. *Lost,* Num. 14:40–43; Prov. 1:28; Jer. 8:20; Hos. 5:6; Matt. 24:50, 51; 25:1–10, 24–28 (with Luke 19:20–24); Luke 13:25–28.

*Terrible consequences, of neglecting,* Ezek. 3:19; Matt. 25:3–13, 24–30, 41–46; *of spurning,* Prov. 1:24–32; Matt. 10:14, 15; 11:20–24.

*The measure of responsibility,* Prov. 1:24–30; Ezek. 3:19; 33:1–17; Matt. 10:14, 15; 11:20–24; 23:34–48; 25 (with Luke 19:20–24); Luke 12:47; 14:16–24.

See footnote, JUDGMENT, ACCORDING TO OPPORTUNITY AND WORKS, 1 Pet. 1:17.

*** SPIRITUAL BLESSINGS. From God,** Deut. 33:25, 27; Psa. 18:28, 32, 35, 36; 29:11; 37:6, 17, 24, 39; 63:8; 66:8, 9; 68:19, 28, 35; 84:5, 11; Isa. 40:11, 29, 31; 41:10, 13, 14, 17, 18; Jer. 31:14; Hab. 3:19; Zech. 10:12; 12:8; John 1:16; Acts 3:19; 1 Cor. 2:9; Phil. 4:13; Jas. 1:17; Jude 24.

*Guidance,* Ex. 33:16; Psa. 23:2, 3; 119:102; Isa. 40:11, 58:11.

*Sanctification,* Ex. 31:13; Lev. 21:8; Isa. 1:25; 4:3, 4; 6:6, 7; 1 John 1:9; Jude 1.

*The perfecting of salvation,* 2 Cor. 1:21; Phil. 1:6; 2:13, 4:19; Col. 1:11, 12; 1 Thess. 5:24; Heb. 13:20, 21; 1 Pet. 1:5, 2 Pet. 1:2–4.

*The earnest of the Spirit,* 2 Cor. 1:22; 5:5.

ual blessings in heavenly *places* in Christ:

4 According as he hath [o,p]chosen us in him before the foundation of the world, that we should be [f,q]holy and [f]without [1]blame before him in love:

5 Having [2,p]predestinated us unto the [r]adoption of children by Jē′ṣus Christ to himself, according to the [h]good pleasure of his [d]will,

6 To the [m]praise of the [s]glory of his [t]grace, [3]wherein he hath made us accepted in the beloved.

7 [u]In whom we have [†,v,w]redemption through his [x,y]blood, the [w,z]forgiveness of sins, according to the riches of his grace;

8 [4]Wherein he hath abounded toward us in all [a]wisdom and prudence;

9 Having made known unto us the [b]mystery of his [c]will, according to his good pleasure which he hath [d]purposed in himself:

10 [5,e]That in the dispensation of the fulness of times he might gather together in [f]one all things in Christ, both which are in heaven, and which are on earth; *even* in him:

11 In whom also we [6]have obtained an [g]inheritance, being [d]predestinated according to the purpose of him who worketh all things after the counsel of his own [c]will:

12 [7]That we should be to the praise of his glory, who first [h]trusted in Christ.

13 In whom ye also *trusted,* after that ye heard the [i]word of truth, the [j]gospel of your [k]salvation: in whom also, after that ye [h]believed, ye were [l,m]sealed with that [n]holy Spirit of promise,

14 Which is the [o]earnest of our [g]inheritance until the [†]redemption of [8]the purchased possession, unto the praise of his [p]glory.

15 [9]Wherefore I also, after I heard of your [h]faith in the Lord Jē′ṣus, and [q]love unto all the saints,

16 [r]Cease not to give [s]thanks for you, making mention of you in my [t]prayers;

17 That the God of our [u]Lord Jē′ṣus Christ, the [v]Father of glory, may give unto you the *spirit of [w]wisdom and revelation in the knowledge of him:

18 The eyes of your [10]understanding being enlightened; that ye may know what is the [x]hope of his calling, and what the riches of the glory of his [y]inheritance in the saints,

19 And what *is* the exceeding greatness of his [z]power to us-ward who [a]believe, according to the working of his mighty power,

20 Which he wrought in Christ, when he [b]raised him from the dead, and set *him* [c,d]at his own right hand in the heavenly *places,*

21 [c,d]Far above all [11]principality, and power, and might, and dominion, and every name that is named, not only in this world, but also in that which is to come:

22 [e]And hath put all *things* under his feet, and gave him *to be* the [f]head over all *things* to the [g]church,

23 Which is his body, the fulness of him that filleth all in all.

**4**
*o Election of Grace,* Rom. 11:5.
*p Foreordination,* Rom. 8:30.
*q Holiness,* Ex. 39:30.
1 R. V. blemish

**5**
*r Spiritual Adoption,* Rom. 8:15.
2 R. V. foreordained us

**6**
*s God, glory of,* Gen. 2:2.
*t God, mercy of,* Gen. 2:2.
3 R. V. which he freely bestowed on us in the Beloved:

**7**
*u Salvation, plan of,* Acts 16:17.
*v Atonement, by Jesus,* Lev. 17:11.
*w Jesus, design of his death,* Matt. 1:21.
*x Blood, of Christ,* Heb. 9:19.
*y Jesus, atoning blood of,* Matt. 1:21.
*z Sin, forgiveness of,* Rom. 5:12.

**8**
*a God, wisdom of,* Gen. 2:2.
4 R. V. Which he made to abound

**9**
*b Mysteries, of redemption,* Mark 4:11.
*c Will of God,* Mark 3:35.
*d Foreordination,* Rom. 8:30.

**10**
*e Jesus, kingdom of, prophecies concerning,* Matt. 1:21.
*f Church, unity of,* Matt. 16:18.
5 R. V. Unto a dispensation of the fulness of the times, to sum up all things in Christ, the things in the heavens, and the things upon the earth; in him, I say,

**11** *g Inheritance, figurative,* Num. 27:7. 6 R. V. were made a heritage, having been foreordained according
**12** *h Faith in Christ,* John 6:69. 7 R. V. To the end that we should be unto the praise of his glory, we who had before hoped in Christ: **13** *i Doctrines of Jesus,* John 7:16. *j Gospel,* Mark 13:10. *k Salvation,* Acts 16:17.

*l Seal, figurative,* 1 Kin. 21:8.
*m Righteous, described,* Psa. 64:10.
*n Holy Spirit,* Acts 1:2.

**14**
*o Earnest,* 2 Cor. 1:22.
*p God, glory of,* Gen. 2:2.
8 R. V. God's own possession,

**15**
*q Love, of man for man,* 1 John 4:7.
9 R. V. For this cause I also, having heard of the faith in the Lord Jesus which is among you, and which ye shew toward all the saints,

**16**
*r Prayerfulness, exemplified,* 1 Tim. 5:5.
*s Thankfulness, to God,* Acts 24:3.
*t Prayer, intercessory,* Acts 6:4.

**17**
*u Jesus, lordship of,* Matt. 1:21.
*v God, fatherhood of,* Gen. 2:2.
*w Wisdom, spiritual,* Prov. 2:2.

**18**
*x Hope,* Prov. 13:12.
*y Inheritance, figurative,* Num. 27:7.
10 R. V. heart

**19**
*z God, power of,* Gen. 2:2.
*a Faith in Christ,* John 6:69.

**20**
*b Resurrection, of Jesus,* 1 Cor. 15:12.
*c Jesus, exaltation of,* Matt. 1:21.
*d Sovereignty of the Messiah,* Psa. 110:1.

**21** 11 R. V. rule, and authority, and power, and dominion,
**22** *e* Psa. 8:6. *f Jesus, head of the church,* Matt. 1:21. *g Church, Christ head of,* Matt. 16:18.

*Peace,* Isa. 26:12; 57:19; Mal. 4:2; Phil. 4:7.
**From Christ,** John 1:16; Rom. 1:7; 16:20; 1 Cor. 1:3; 16:23; 2 Cor. 1:2; 13:14; Gal. 1:3; 6:16, 18; Eph. 1:2; 6:23, 24; Phil. 1:2; 4:23; 1 Thess. 5:28; 2 Thess. 1:2; 3:16, 18; 1 Tim. 1:2; 2 Tim. 1:2; Philemon 3, 25; 2 Pet. 1:1; 2 John 1:3.
See footnotes: TEMPORAL BLESSINGS, *From God,* Psa. 103:2; BLESSINGS, *Contingent upon obedience,* Deut. 11:27.

† **REDEMPTION OF OUR SOULS,** Matt. 20:28; Mark 10:45; Luke 2:38; Acts 20:28; Rom. 3:24-26; 1 Cor. 1:30; 6:20; 7:23; Gal. 1:4; 2:20; 4:4, 5; Eph. 1:7; 5:2; Col. 1:14, 20-22; 1 Tim. 2:6; Tit. 2:14; Heb. 9:12, 15; 1 Pet. 1:18, 19; Rev. 5:9, 10.
See footnotes: ATONEMENT, Lev. 17:11; RANSOM, Ex. 21:30.

## CHAPTER 2

*Their former state. 4 God's great mercy in their deliverance. 10 They are created in Christ Jesus unto good works. 11 Wherefore he reminds them of their former alienation, 13 and exhorts them, being now made nigh by the blood of Christ, 19 to live not as aliens, but as fellow citizens with the saints.*

AND you [1]*hath he* [a,b,c,d]*quickened*, who were [e,f]dead in trespasses and [g]sins;

2 Wherein in time past ye walked according to the course of this world, according to the [h]prince of the power of the air, the spirit that now worketh in the [f]children of disobedience:

3 Among whom also we all [2]had our conversation in times past in the [i]lusts of our flesh, fulfilling the desires of the flesh and of the [j]mind; and were by [k]nature the [f]children of wrath, even as others.

4 But God, who is rich in [l]mercy, for his great [m]love wherewith he loved us,

5 Even when we were [e,f]dead [3]in [g]sins, hath [b,c,d]quickened us together with Chrīst, (by [n]grace [4]ye are [o]saved;)

6 And hath raised *us* up together, and made *us* sit [p]together in heavenly *places* [q]in Chrīst Jē′ṣus:

7 [r]That in the ages to come he might shew the exceeding riches of his [l]grace in *his* [s]kindness toward us through Chrīst Jē′ṣus.

8 For by [n]grace [4]are ye [o]saved through [t]faith; and that not of yourselves: *it is* the [u]gift of God:

9 Not of [v]works, [5]lest any man should [w]boast.

10 For we are [d]his workmanship, created in Chrīst Jē′ṣus unto good [x]works, which God [6]hath before [y,z]ordained that we should walk in them.

1
- a *Resurrection, figurative*, 1 Cor. 15:12.
- b *Life, spiritual*, Eccl. 8:15.
- c *Regeneration*, Tit. 3:5.
- d *Righteous, described*, Psa. 64:10.
- e *Spiritual Death*, 1 John 3:14.
- f *Wicked, described*, Psa. 73:3.
- g *Sin, transgression of the law*, Rom. 5:12.
- 1 R. V. did he quicken, when ye were dead through your trespasses and sins.

2
- h *Satan*, Matt. 4:10.

3
- i *Lust*, 2 Pet. 1:4.
- j *Carnal Mind*, 1 Cor. 3:3.
- k *Heredity*, Ezek. 18:2.
- 2 R. V. once lived in the lusts

4
- l *God, mercy of*, Gen. 2:2.
- m *God, love of*, Gen. 2:2.

5
- n *Grace of God*, Rom. 4:16.
- o *Salvation*, Acts 16:17.
- 3 R. V. through our trespasses,
- 4 R. V. have ye been

6
- p *Unity, of the righteous*, Psa. 133:1.
- q *Righteous, union of, with Christ*, Psa. 64:10.

7
- r *Righteous, promises to*, Psa. 64:10.
- s *God, goodness of*, Gen. 2:2.

8
- t *Faith in Christ*, John 6:69.
- u *Spiritual Gifts*, 1 Cor. 12:4.

9
- v *Works, insufficient for salvation*, 2 Tim. 1:9.
- w *Spiritual Boasting*, Rom. 3:27.

5 R. V. that no man should glory. **10** x *Works*, 2 Tim. 1:9. y *Foreordination*, Rom. 8:30. z *Election of Grace*, Rom. 11:5.
6 Am. R. V. before prepared

11 Wherefore remember, that ye *being* in time past [a]Gĕn′tīleṣ in the flesh, who are called [a]Uncircumcision by that which is called the [b]Circumcision in the flesh made by hands;

12 That at that time ye were [c]without Chrīst, being [c]aliens from the commonwealth of Ĭṣ′ra-el, and [c]strangers from the [d]covenants of promise, [c]having no [e]hope, and [c]without God in the world:

13 But now [f]in Chrīst Jē′ṣus ye [7]who sometimes were far off are made nigh [g]by the [h,i]blood of Chrīst.

14 For he is our [j]peace, who hath *made both [k]one, and hath broken down the middle wall of partition *between us*;

15 [f]Having abolished in his flesh the enmity, *even* the [l]law of commandments *contained* in ordinances; for to make in himself of twain [k]one new man, *so* making [j,m]peace;

16 And that he might [n]reconcile both unto God in one body by the [g,o]cross, having slain the enmity thereby:

17 And came and [p]preached [j]peace to you which were afar off, and to them that were nigh.

18 For [n]through [q]him we both have [r]access by one [q,s]Spirit unto the [q,t]Father.

19 Now therefore ye are no more strangers and [s]foreigners, but [u]fellowcitizens with the saints, and [v]of the [w]household of God;

20 And are built upon the [x]foundation of the [y]apostles and [z]prophets, Jē′ṣus Chrīst himself being the chief [a]corner *stone*;

21 In whom all the [b]building

11
- a *Gentiles*, Acts 10:45.
- b *Jews*, Neh. 4:2.

12
- c *Wicked, described*, Psa. 73:3.
- d *Covenant, of God with men*, Deut. 29:1.
- e *Hope*, Prov. 13:12.

13
- f *Jesus, design of his death*, Matt. 1:21.
- g *Atonement, by Jesus*, Lev. 17:11.
- h *Blood, of Christ, atoning*, Heb. 9:19.
- i *Jesus, atoning blood of*, Matt. 1:21.
- 7 R. V. that once

14
- j *Spiritual Peace, from Christ*, Gal. 1:3.
- k *Church, unity of*, Matt. 16:18.

15
- l *Law, temporary*, Deut. 33:2.
- m *Peace*, Jer. 29:7.

16
- n *Reconciliation, between God and man, through Christ*, vs. 15–18; 2 Cor. 5:18.
- o *Cross, figurative*, John 19:17.

17
- p *Preaching*, Matt. 9:35.

18
- q *Holy Trinity*, Luke 3:22.
- r *Access to God*, Eph. 3:12.
- s *Holy Spirit*, Acts 1:2.
- t *God, fatherhood of*, Gen. 2:2.

19
- u *Citizens, figurative*, Luke 15:15.
- v *Spiritual Adoption*, Rom. 8:15.
- w *Church, called household of God*, Matt. 16:18.

20
- x *Truth*, John 18:37.

y *Apostles*, Luke 6:13. z *Prophets*, Isa. 3:2. — a *Corner Stone, figurative*, Psa. 144:12. **21** b *Church, unity of*, Matt. 16:18.

***CATHOLICITY.** *Taught in, Christ's reproof of John*, Mark 9:38–41; Luke 9:49, 50; *Peter's vision of the sheet and visit to Cornelius*, Acts 10:1–43; *Paul's commission*, Rom. **1**:1–7, 14–16; *Paul's rebuke of Jewish exclusiveness*, Rom. **3**:20–31; 4:1–25; *judgment of apostolic council*, Acts 15:1–31; *unity of believers*, Gal. 3:27, 28; Eph. 2:14–17; Col. 3:11–15; *gift of Holy Spirit to Gentiles, as well as to Jews*, Acts 10:44–48; 11:17, 18.
**Instances of:** *Solomon, in his prayer*, 1 Kin. **8**:41–43. *Paul, in recognizing devout heathen*, Acts 13:16, 26, 42, 43.

fitly framed together groweth
unto an [c,d]holy [e]temple [f]in the
Lord:
22 [f]In whom ye also are builded
[b]together for an [d]habitation of
God through the [g]Spirit.

## CHAPTER 3

*The apostle, a prisoner of Christ for them. 3 The salvation of the Gentiles revealed to him and to the other apostles. 8 His special commission to preach the gospel to the Gentiles. 13 Wherefore he desires them not to faint at his tribulations, and prays that they may be able to comprehend the great love of Christ toward them.*

FOR this cause I [a]Paul, the
[b]prisoner of Jē′ṣus [c]Christ
for you [d]Ġĕn′tīleṣ,
2 If ye have heard of the [e]dis-
pensation of the [f]grace of God
which is given me to you-
ward:
3 How that by [g,h]revelation he
made known unto me the [i]mys-
tery; (as I wrote afore in few
words,
4 Whereby, when ye read, ye
may understand my knowledge
in the [i]mystery of Christ)
5 Which in other ages was not
made known unto the sons of
men, as it is now [h]revealed unto
his holy [j]apostles and [k]prophets
by the [l]Spirit;
6 That the Ġĕn′tīleṣ should be
[m,n]fellowheirs, and [1]of the [o]same
body, and partakers of his [p]prom-
ise in Christ by the [q]gospel:
7 Whereof [a]I was [r]made a minister, according to the gift of the
[f]grace of God given unto me
by the effectual working of his
[s]power.
8 Unto me, who am [t]less than
the least of all saints, is this grace
given, that [a]I should [u,v]preach
among the Ġĕn′tīleṣ the unsearchable riches of Christ;
9 And to make all *men* see
what *is* the [2]fellowship of the
[i]mystery, which from the beginning of the world hath been hid
in God, who [w]created all things
by Jē′ṣus Christ:
10 To the intent that now unto the [x]principalities and [x]pow-
ers in heavenly *places* might be
known by the [y]church the manifold [z]wisdom of God,
11 According to the eternal
[a,b]purpose which he purposed in
Christ Jē′ṣus our [c]Lord:
12 [d]In whom we have [e]boldness
and *access [3]with confidence by
the [f]faith of him.
13 [g]Wherefore I desire that ye
faint not at my tribulations for
you, which is your glory.
14 For this cause I [h]bow my
knees unto the [i]Father [4]of our
Lord Jē′ṣus Christ,
15 Of [i]whom the whole [j]family
in heaven and earth is [k]named,
16 That he would grant you,
according to the [l]riches of his
glory, to be [m]strengthened with
might by his [n]Spirit in the [o]inner
man;
17 That Christ may [p]dwell in
your hearts by [f]faith; that ye,
being [q]rooted and grounded in
[r]love,
18 May be [5]able to comprehend with all saints what *is*
the breadth, and length, and
depth, and height;
19 And to know the [t]love of
Christ, which [s]passeth knowledge, that ye might be [m]filled
with all the fulness of God.
20 Now unto him that is [u]able
to [m]do exceeding abundantly
above all that we [v]ask or think,
according to the [w]power that
worketh in us,
21 Unto [x]him *be* [y]glory in
the [z]church [6]by [a]Christ Jē′ṣus

c *Holiness*, Ex. 39:30.
d *Righteous, described*, Psa. 64:10.
e *Temple, figurative*, 1 Kin. 6:17.
f *Righteous, union of, with Christ*, Psa. 64:10.

**22**
g *Holy Spirit*, Acts 1:2.

**1**
a *Paul, sent to the Gentiles*, Acts 13:9.
b *Minister, trials and persecutions of*, Rom. 15:16.
c *Jesus, Messiah*, Matt. 1:21.
d *Gentiles, conversion of*, vs. 1–8; Acts 10:45.

**2**
e *Call, to special religious duty*, Phil. 3:14.
f *Grace of God*, Rom. 4:16.

**3**
g *Revelation, of world-wide mission of the gospel*, vs. 3–6; 2 Cor. 12:1.
h *Inspiration*, Job 32:8.
i *Salvation, plan of*, Acts 16:17.

**5**
j *Apostles, inspiration of*, Luke 6:13.
k *Prophets, inspiration of*, Isa. 3:2.
l *Holy Spirit, revelation from*, Acts 1:2.

**6**
m *Heir, figurative*, Gen. 15:3.
n *Spiritual Adoption, of the Gentiles*, Rom. 8:15.
o *Church, unity of*, Matt. 16:18.
p *Salvation*, Acts 16:17.
q *Gospel*, Mark 13:10.
1 R. V. fellow-members of the body, and fellow-partakers of the promise in Christ Jesus through the gospel,

**7**
r *Minister, call of*, Rom. 15:16.
s *God, power of*, Gen. 2:2.

**8**
t *Humility*, Prov. 22:4.
u *Preaching*, Matt. 9:35. v *Minister, duties of*, Rom. 15:16.

**9** 2 R. V. dispensation of the mystery which from all ages hath been hid in God who created all things;

w *God, creator*, Gen. 2:2.

**10**
x *Angel*, Heb. 1:13.
y *Church*, Matt. 16:18.
z *God, wisdom of*, Gen. 2:2.

**11**
a *Foreordination*, Rom. 8:30.
b *Salvation, plan of*, Acts 16:17.
c *Jesus, lordship of*, Matt. 1:21.

**12**
d *Jesus, mediation of*, Matt. 1:21.
e *Boldness of the Righteous*, Phil. 1:20.
f *Faith in Christ*, John 6:69.
3 R. V. in confidence through our faith in him.

**13**
g *Love, of man for man*, 1 John 4:7.

**14**
h *Prayer, intercessory*, Acts 6:4.
i *God, fatherhood of*, Gen. 2:2.
4 R. V. *omits* of our Lord Jesus Christ,

**15**
j *Church, unity of*, Matt. 16:18.
k *Spiritual Adoption*, Rom. 8:15.

**16**
l *Grace of God*, Rom. 4:16.
m *Spiritual Blessings*, Eph. 1:3.
n *Holy Spirit*, Acts 1:2.
o *Man, a spirit*, Job 4:17.

**17**
p *Fellowship, with Christ*, 1 Cor. 1:9.
q *Righteous, described*, Psa. 64:10.
r *Love, for Jesus*, 1 John 4:19.

**18**
5 R. V. strong to apprehend

**19**
s *Paradox*, 2 Cor. 12:4.
t *Jesus, love of*, Matt. 1:21.

**20** u *God, power of*, Gen. 2:2. v *Prayer, answer to, promised*, Acts 6:4. w *Spiritual Power*, Luke 24:49.

**21** x *God, eternity of*, Gen. 2:2. y *God, glory of*, Gen. 2:2. z *Church*, Matt. 16:18.—a *Jesus, Messiah*, Matt. 1:21. 6 R. V. and in Christ Jesus unto all generations for ever and ever. Amen.

* **ACCESS TO GOD**, Deut. 4:7; Psa. 65:4; 145:18; Jas. 4:8. *In prayer*, Matt. 6:6; Heb. 4:16. *Through Christ*, John 14:6; Rom. 5:2; Eph. 2:18; 3:12; Heb. 7:19, 25; 10:19, 22. *By faith*, Heb. 11:6.

[b]throughout all ages, world without end. Amen.

## CHAPTER 4

*The apostle exhorts to unity: 7 shews that God has given divers gifts to men for the perfecting of the saints: 17 and, therefore, urges them to put off the old man which is corrupt. 24 and to put on the new man which after God is created in righteousness and true holiness.*

I THEREFORE, the [a,b]pris-
oner of the Lord, beseech
you that ye [c]walk worthy of
the [1,d]vocation wherewith ye are
called,
2 With all [e,f]lowliness and
[e,g]meekness, with [e,h]longsuffer-
ing, [i]forbearing one another in
[e,j]love;
3 Endeavouring to keep the
[k]unity of the [l]Spirit in the bond
of [m]peace.
4 *There is* [n]one body, and one
[l]Spirit, even as ye are [d]called in
one [o]hope of your calling;
5 One [p]Lord, one [q]faith, one
[r]baptism,
6 [s]One God and [t]Father of all,
[u]who *is* above all, and through
all, and in you all.
7 But unto every one of us is
given [v]grace according to the
measure of the [w]gift of Chrīst.
8 Wherefore he saith, [x,y]When
he [z]ascended up on high, he led
captivity captive, and gave [a]gifts
unto men.
9 (Now that he [b]ascended, what
is it but that he also descended
first into the lower parts of the
earth?
10 He that [c]descended is the
same also that [b]ascended up far
above all heavens, that he might
[d]fill all things.)
11 And he [e,f]gave some, [2]apos-
tles; and some, prophets; and
some, evangelists; and some,
pastors and [g]teachers;

b *Jesus, eternity of,* Matt. 1:21.

1
a *Prisoners,* Psa. 79:11.
b *Paul, taken to Rome,* Acts 13:9.
c *Commandment, enjoining discreet conduct,* vs. 1–3; Deut. 8:2.
d *Call, personal,* Phil. 3:14.
1 R. V. calling

2
e *Christian Graces,* Gal. 5:22.
f *Humility,* Prov. 22:4.
g *Meekness,* Psa. 45:4.
h *Longsuffering,* 2 Cor. 6:6.
i *Patience,* Luke 8:15.
j *Love, of man for man,* 1 John 4:7.

3
k *Unity, of the righteous,* Psa. 133:1.
l *Holy Spirit,* Acts 1:2.
m *Peace,* Jer. 29:7.

4
n *Church, unity of,* Matt. 16:18.
o *Hope,* Prov. 13:12.

5
p *Jesus, lordship of,* Matt. 1:21.
q *Faith, the doctrines of Jesus,* 1 Cor. 16:13.
r *Baptism, Christian,* Luke 20:4.

6
s *God, unity of,* Gen. 2:2.
t *God, fatherhood of,* Gen. 2:2.
u *God, sovereign,* Gen. 2:2.

7
v *Call, to special religious duty,* Phil. 3:14.
w *Spiritual Gifts,* 1 Cor. 12:4.

8
x Psa. 68:18.
y *Prophecies concerning the Messiah, and their fulfillment,* Gen. 12:3.

12 For the [h]perfecting of the
saints, [3]for the work of the ministry, for the edifying of the [i]body
of [j]Chrīst:
13 Till we all come in the [k]unity
of the [l]faith, and of the [m]knowl-
edge of the [n]Son of God, unto a
[4,o]perfect man, unto the measure
of the stature of the fulness of
Chrīst:
14 That we *henceforth* [p]be no
more children, [q]tossed to and fro,
and [q]carried about with every
wind of doctrine, by the sleight
of [r]men, [5]*and* cunning craftiness,
whereby they lie in wait to deceive;
15 But speaking the [s]truth in
[t]love, may [u]grow up into him in
all things, which is the [j]head,
*even* Chrīst:
16 From whom [v]the whole
body fitly [6]joined together and
compacted by that which every
joint supplieth, according to the
effectual working in the measure
of every part, maketh increase of
the body unto the edifying of itself in [t]love.
17 This I say therefore, and
testify in the Lord, that ye henceforth walk not as other [w]Gĕn'-
tīleṣ walk, in the vanity of their
mind,
18 [x]Having the understanding [y]darkened, being [z,a]alienated
from the life of God through the
[b]ignorance that is in them, because of the [7]blindness of their
[c]heart:
19 [d]Who [e]being [f]past feeling
have given themselves over unto
[g]lasciviousness, to work all uncleanness with greediness.
20 But ye [8]have not so learned
Chrīst;
21 If so be that ye have heard
him, and have been [h]taught by
him, as the [i]truth is in Jē'ṣus:

12
h *Perfection,* Heb. 6:1.
i *Church, called body of Christ,* Matt. 16:18.
j *Jesus, head of the church,* Matt. 1:21.
3 R. V. unto the work of ministering, unto the building up of

13
k *Church, unity of,* Matt. 16:18.
l *Faith, the doctrines of Jesus,* 1 Cor. 16:13.
m *Wisdom, spiritual,* Prov. 2:2.
n *Jesus, divine sonship of,* Matt. 1:21.
o *Righteous, described,* Psa. 64:10.
4 R. V. fullgrown

14
p *Perseverance, exhortation to,* Eph. 6:18.
q *Instability,* Jas. 1:8.
r *False Teachers,* 2 Pet. 2:1.
5 R. V. in craftiness, after the wiles of error;

15
s *Truth, of the gospel,* John 18:37.
t *Love, of man for man,* 1 John 4:7.
u *Growth in Grace,* 2 Pet. 3:18.

16
v *Physiology,* Job 10:11.
6 R. V. framed and knit together through that which every joint supplieth, according to the working in due measure of each several part, maketh the increase of the body unto the building up of itself in love.

17
w *Gentiles,* Acts 10:45.

18
x *Wicked, described,* Psa. 73:3.
y *Spiritual Blindness,* 2 Cor. 4:4.
z *Sin, separates from God,* Rom. 5:12.
a *Godless, described,* Job 8:13.
b *Ignorance, sins of,* Acts 3:17.

z *Jesus, exaltation of,* Matt. 1:21.—a *Spiritual Gifts,* 1 Cor. 12:4.
9 b *Jesus, exaltation of,* Matt. 1:21.
10 c *Jesus, death of* (as some interpret), *descent of, into hell to preach to spirits in prison* (as others interpret), Matt. 1:21. d *Jesus, mission of,* Matt. 1:21.
11 e *Church, diversity of callings in,* Matt. 16:18. f *Minister, call of,* Rom. 15:16. g *Instruction, in religion,* Prov. 23:23.
2 R. V. to be

c *Heart, unregenerate,* Psa. 44:21. 7 R. V. hardening
19 d *Reprobates,* 1 Cor. 9:27. e *Wicked, described,* Psa. 64:10 f *Conscience, dead,* Acts 23:1. g *Lasciviousness,* 1 Pet. 4:3.
20 8 R. V. did not so learn
21 h *Instruction, in religion,* Prov. 23:23. i *Truth,* John 18:37.

22 That ye [j,k]put [9]off concerning the former conversation the
[l,m]old man, which is corrupt according to the deceitful [n]lusts;
23 And [j,k]be [o]renewed in the
spirit of your mind;
24 And that ye put on the
[o,p]new man, which after God is
created in [q]righteousness and
[10]true holiness.
25 Wherefore putting away
[r]lying, speak every man [s]truth
with his [t]neighbour: for we are
[u,v]members one of another.
26 Be ye [w]angry, and sin not:
[x]let not the sun go down upon
your wrath:
27 [y]Neither give place to the
[z,a]devil.
28 [b]Let him that [c]stole steal no
more: but rather let him [d,e]la-
bour, working with *his* hands
the thing which is good, that he
may have to [f]give to [g]him that
needeth.
29 [h]Let no corrupt [11,i]com-
munication proceed out of your
mouth, but [j,k]that which is good
to the use of edifying, that it may
minister grace unto the hearers.
30 And [l]grieve not the holy
Spirit of God, [12]whereby ye are
[m,n]sealed unto the day of redemption.
31 [o,p]Let all bitterness, and
wrath, and anger, and clamour,
and [13]evil [i]speaking, be put away
from you, with all *malice:
32 And [q,r]be ye [s]kind one to
another, [s]tenderhearted, [s,t,u]for-
giving one another, even as [v]God
[14,w]for Christ's sake hath [x]for-
given you.

## CHAPTER 5

*They are to be followers of God, 2 to walk in love, 3 to avoid all kinds of impurity, 7 to have no fellowship with the works of darkness, 15 to live circumspectly, 18 and to be filled with the Spirit. 22 The duty of wives to their husbands, 25 and of husbands to their wives.*

[a]BE ye therefore [1]followers of
God, as dear children;
2 And [b,c]walk in [d]love, [e]as
Christ also hath [f]loved us, and
hath [g,h]given himself [i]for us an
offering and a sacrifice to God
for a sweetsmelling [j]savour.
3 But [k]fornication, and all
uncleanness, or [l]covetousness,
[m,n,o]let it not be once named
among you, as becometh saints;
4 Neither filthiness, [p]nor foolish
[q]talking, nor jesting, which are
not [2]convenient: but rather [r]giv-
ing of thanks.
5 For this ye know, that [s,t]no

**22**
- j *Commandment, enjoining holiness*, Deut. 8:2.
- k *Holiness, exhortations to*, Ex. 39:30.
- l *Carnal Mind*, 1 Cor. 3:3.
- m *Depravity*, Job 15:14.
- n *Lust, forbidden*, 2 Pet. 1:4.
- 9 R. V. away, as concerning your former manner of life, the old man, which waxeth corrupt after the lusts of deceit;

**23**
- o *Regeneration*, Tit. 3:5.

**24**
- p *Holiness, described*, Ex. 39:30.
- q *Righteousness*, Psa. 15:2.
- 10 R. V. holiness of truth.

**25**
- r *Falsehood, forbidden*, Job 21:34.
- s *Truthfulness*, Zech. 8:16.
- t *Neighbor*, Luke 10:29.
- u *Church, membership in*, Matt. 16:18.
- v *Fellowship, of the righteous*, 1 Cor. 1:9.

**26**
- w *Anger, forbidden*, Psa. 37:8.

x *Commandment, enjoining restraint of temper*, Deut. 8:2.
**27** y *Temptation, resistance to*, Luke 11:4. z *Satan*, Matt. 4:10. —a *Temptation, sources of*, Luke 11:4. **28** b *Commandment, forbidding theft, and enjoining labor*, Deut. 8:2. c *Theft*, Mark 7:22. d *Labor, enjoined*, Luke 10:7. e *Industry, enjoined*, 1 Kin. 11:28. f *Liberality, enjoined*, 1 Tim. 6:18. g *Poor*, Prov. 21:13.
**29** h *Commandment, enjoining pure conversation*, Deut. 8:2. i *Speech, evil*, Col. 4:6. j *Conversation, edifying, enjoined*, Psa. 50:23. k *Speech, wise*, Col. 4:6. 11 R. V. speech proceed out of your mouth, but such as is good for edifying as the need may be, that it may give grace to them that hear.
**30** l *Holy Spirit, sin against*, Acts 1:2. 12 R. V. in whom ye were

- m *Holy Spirit, Christians are sealed with*, Acts 1:2.
- n *Seal, figurative*, 1 Kin. 21:8.

**31**
- o *Commandment, enjoining restraint of temper*, Deut. 8:2.
- p *Strife, exhortations against*, Prov. 20:3.
- 13 R. V. railing,

**32**
- q *Commandment, enjoining kindness and forgiveness*, Deut. 8:2.
- r *Kindness, enjoined*, Acts 28:2.
- s *Christian Graces*, Gal. 5:22.
- t *Forgiveness*, Matt. 18:21.
- u *Charitableness, enjoined*, Prov. 10:12.
- v *God, mercy of*, Gen. 2:2.
- w *Jesus, mediation of*, Matt. 1:21.
- x *Sin, forgiveness of*, Rom. 5:12.
- 14 R. V. also in Christ forgave you.

**1**
- a *Commandment, enjoining godliness*, Deut. 8:2.
- 1 R. V. imitators

**2**
- b *Commandment, enjoining love for man*, Deut. 8:2.
- c *Fellowship, of the righteous*, 1 Cor. 1:9.
- d *Love, of man for man*, 1 John 4:7.

e *Jesus, our example*, Matt. 1:21. f *Jesus, love of*, Matt. 1:21. g *Jesus, vicarious death of*, Matt. 1:21. h *Atonement, by Jesus*, Lev. 17:11. i *Jesus, design of his death*, Matt. 1:21. j *Incense, figurative*, Ex. 37:29. **3** k *Adultery, forbidden*, Lev. 20:10. l *Covetousness, forbidden*, Isa. 57:17. m *Commandment, forbidding various vices*, Deut. 8:2. n *Chastity, enjoined*, Job 31:1. o *Christian Graces*, Gal. 5:22. **4** p *Commandment, forbidding corrupt conversation, and enjoining thankfulness*, Deut. 8:2. q *Speech, evil*, Col. 4:6. r *Thankfulness, to God, enjoined*, Acts 24:3. 2 R. V. befitting:
**5** s *Wicked, punishment of*, Psa. 73:3. t *Adultery, penalties for*, Lev. 20:10.

---

* **MALICE,** Gen. 3:15; Psa. 21:11; 71:10, 11, 13, 24; Prov. 4:16, 17; 6:14–16, 18, 19; 24:8; Jer. 20:10. *Reacts*, Psa. 7:15, 16. *Blinds those who are possessed of it*, 1 John 2:9, 11; 4:20. *Is murderous*, 1 John 3:13–15. *Precludes divine forgiveness*, Matt. 6:15; 18:28–35.

*Forbidden*, Lev. 19:14, 17, 18; 2 Kin. 6:21, 22; Prov. 20:22; 24:17, 18, 29; Zech. 7:10; 8:17; Matt. 5:38–41; Rom. 12:19; 1 Cor. 5:8; 14:20; Eph. 4:31; Col. 3:8; 1 Thess. 5:15; 1 Pet. 2:1; 3:9.

*The wicked filled with*, Deut. 32:32, 33; Prov. 21:10; 30:14; Matt. 13:25, 28; John 8:44; Rom. 1:29–32; Gal. 5:19–21; Tit. 3:3; 3 John 10. *Punishment for*, Deut. 27:17, 18; Prov. 17:5; Isa. 29:20, 21; Ezek. 18:18; 25:3, 6, 7, 12–17; 26:2, 3; Amos 1:11; Mic. 2:1; Matt. 26:52; Jas. 2:13.

**Instances of:** *Cain toward Abel*, Gen. 4:8; 1 John 3:12. *Ishmael toward Sarah*, Gen. 21:9. *Sarah toward Hagar*, Gen. 21:10. *Philistines toward Isaac*, Gen. 26:12–15, 18–21. *Esau toward Jacob*, Gen. 27:41, 42. *Joseph's brethren toward Joseph*, Gen. 37:2–28; 42:21; Acts 7:9, 10. *Potiphar's wife toward Joseph*, Gen. 39:14–20. *Saul toward David*, 1 Sam. 18:8–29; 19; 20:30–33; 22:6–23; 23:7–28; 26:1, 2, 18. *David, toward Michal*, 2 Sam. 6:21–23; *toward Joab*, 1 Kin. 2:5, 6; *toward Shimei*, 1 Kin. 2:8, 9. *Shimei toward David*, 2 Sam. 16:5–8. *Ahithophel toward David*, 2 Sam. 17:1–3. *Jezebel toward Elijah*, 1 Kin. 19:1, 2. *Ahaziah toward Elijah*, 2 Kin. 1:7–15. *Jehoram toward Elisha*, 2 Kin. 6:31. *Samaritans toward the Jews*, Ezra 4; Neh. 2:10; 4:6. *Haman toward Mordecai*, Esth. 3:5–15; 5:9–14. *The psalmist's enemies*, Psa. 22:7, 8; 35:15, 16, 19–21; 38:16, 19; 41:5–8; 55:3; 56:5, 6; 57:4, 6; 59:3, 4, 7; 62:3, 4; 64:2–6; 69:4, 10–12, 26; 86:14; 102:8; 109:2–5, 16–18; 140:1–4. *Jeremiah's enemies*, Jer. 26:8–11; 38:1–6. *Nebuchadrezzar toward Zedekiah*, Jer. 52:10, 11. *Daniel's enemies*, Dan. 6:4–15. *Herodias toward John*, Matt. 14:3–11; Mark 6:24–28. *James and John toward the Samaritans*, Luke 9:54. *Enemies of Jesus*, Matt. 27:18, 27–30, 39–43; Mark 12:13; 15:10, 11, 16–19, 29–32; Luke 11:53, 54; 23:10, 11, 39; John 18:22, 23. *Paul's enemies*, Acts 14:5, 19; 16:19–24; 17:5; 19:24–35; 21:27–31, 36; 22:22, 23; 23:12–15; 25:3; Phil. 1:15–17.

See footnotes: HATRED, Prov. 15:17; JEALOUSY, Psa. 78:58; PERSECUTION, John 15:20; RETALIATION, Deut. 19:19; REVENGE, Ezek. 25:15.

[3]whoremonger, nor unclean person, nor [l]covetous man, who is
an [u]idolater, hath any [v]inherit-
ance in the [w, x]kingdom of Christ
and of God.
6 [y]Let no [z]man deceive you
with vain [a]words: for because of
these things cometh the [b]wrath
of God upon the [c]children of
*disobedience.
7 [d]Be not ye therefore partakers with them.
8 For ye were [4]sometimes
[e, f]darkness, but now *are ye*
[g, h]light in the Lord: walk as
[i]children of light:
9 (For the fruit of the [5]Spirit *is*
in all goodness and [j]righteous-
ness and [k]truth;)
10 Proving what is acceptable
unto the Lord.
11 And [l]have no [d]fellowship
with the unfruitful works of
[e]darkness, but rather [m]reprove
*them*.
12 For it is a shame even to
speak of those [n]things which are
done of them in [o]secret.
13 But all things that are reproved are made manifest by the
[g]light: for whatsoever doth make
manifest is light.
14 Wherefore he saith, [p]Awake
thou that sleepest, and arise
from the [q]dead, and Christ shall
[6]give thee light.
15 [r, s]See then that ye walk circumspectly, not as [7]fools, but as
[h]wise,
16 [t, u]Redeeming the time, because the days are evil.
17 Wherefore [v]be ye not unwise, but understanding what
the [w]will of the Lord *is*.
18 And [x]be not [y]drunk with
[z]wine, wherein is [8]excess; but be
filled with the [a]Spirit;
19 [b, c]Speaking [9, d]to yourselves
in psalms and hymns and spiritual [e]songs, [f]singing and [g]mak-
ing [h]melody in your heart to the
Lord;
20 [i]Giving [j]thanks always for
all things unto God and the [k]Fa-
ther [l]in the [m]name of our [n]Lord
Jē'sus Christ;
21 [o, p]Submitting yourselves one
to another in the fear of [10]God.
22 [q]Wives, [r]submit yourselves
unto your own [s]husbands, as unto the Lord.
23 For [r]the [s]husband is the
head of the [q]wife, even as [t]Christ
is the head of the [u]church: and
he is the saviour of the body.
24 Therefore as the church is
subject unto Christ, [r]so *let* the
[q]wives *be* to their own [s]husbands
in every thing.
25 [s]Husbands, love your wives,
even as Christ also [v]loved the
[w]church, and [x, y, z]gave himself
for it;
26 That he might [a]sanctify and
[b]cleanse it with the [c, d]washing
of water by the [e]word,
27 That he might present it to
himself a glorious church, [f]not
having spot, or wrinkle, or any

*u Idolatry*, 1 Sam. 15:23.
*v Inheritance, figurative*, Num. 27:7.
*w Church* (as some interpret), Matt. 16:18.
*x Heaven, future home of the righteous* (as some interpret), Luke 18:22.
3 R. V. fornicator,

**6**

*y Commandment, warning against false teachers*, Deut. 8:2.
*z False Teachers*, 2 Pet. 2:1.

---

*a Words*, Luke 4:22.
*b Anger of God*, 2 Kin. 13:3.
*c Wicked, described*, Psa. 73:3.

**7**

*d Fellowship, with the wicked, forbidden*, 1 Cor. 1:9.

**8**

*e Darkness, figurative*, Gen. 1:2.
*f Spiritual Blindness*, 2 Cor. 4:4.
*g Light, figurative*, Matt. 5:14.
*h Wisdom, spiritual*, Prov. 2:2.
*i Righteous, described*, Psa. 64:10.
4 R. V. once darkness,

**9**

*j Righteousness*, Psa. 15:2.
*k Truth*, John 18:37.
5 R. V. light

**11**

*l Commandment, forbidding fellowship with the wicked*, Deut. 8:2.
*m Reproof*, Prov. 17:10.

**12**

*n Gentiles, wicked practices of*, Acts 10:45.
*o Sin, secret*, Rom. 5:12.

*w Will of God, supreme rule of duty*, Mark 3:35.

**18**

*x Commandment, forbidding drunkenness*, Deut. 8:2.
*y Drunkenness, forbidden*, Luke 21:34.
*z Wine, admonitions against the immoderate use of*, Prov. 23:31.

---

*a Holy Spirit*, Acts 1:2.
8 R. V. riot,

**19**

*b Commandment, enjoining worship, social*, Deut. 8:2.
*c Religious Testimony*, 2 Thess. 1:10.
*d Fellowship, of the righteous*, 1 Cor. 1:9.
*e Song, spiritual*, Psa. 77:6.
*f Worship, enjoined*, Gen. 22:5.
*g Praise*, Psa. 150:1.
*h Music*, 2 Chr. 5:13.
9 R. V. one to another in

**20**

*i Commandment, enjoining thanksgiving*, Deut. 8:2.
*j Thankfulness, to God*, Acts 24:3.
*k God, fatherhood of*, Gen. 2:2.
*l Jesus, mediation of*, Matt. 1:21.
*m Name of Jesus*, John 14:13.
*n Jesus, lordship of*, Matt. 1:21.

**21**

*o Commandment, enjoining submission to fraternal counsel*, Deut. 8:2. *p Church, discipline in*, Matt. 16:18.
10 R. V. Christ. **22** *q Wife, duty of, to husband*, Prov. 5:18. *r Family, government of*, 1 Chr. 13:14. *s Husband, relation of, to wife*, Num. 30:6.
**23** *t Jesus, head of the church*, Matt. **1:21.** *u Church, Christ head of*, Matt. 16:18.
**25** *v Jesus, love of*, Matt. 1:21. *w Church, Christ's love for*, Matt. 16:18. *x Redemption of our Souls*, Eph. 1:7. *y Jesus, design of his death*, Matt. 1:21. *z Jesus, vicarious death of*, Matt. 1:21.
**26**—*a Sanctification*, 1 Pet. 1:2. *b Spiritual Purification*, Psa. 51:2. *c Washing, figurative*, Matt. 27:24. *d Symbols and Similitudes*, Heb. 9:9. *e Doctrines of Jesus*, John 7:16. **27** *f Church, holiness of*, Matt. 16:18.

**14** *p Regeneration*, Tit. 3:5. *q Spiritual Death*, 1 John 3:14. 6 R. V. shine upon thee. **15** *r Commandment, enjoining discreet conduct*, Deut. 8:2. *s Watchfulness*, Matt. 24:42. 7 R. V. unwise, **16** *t Diligence*, Rom. 12:8. *u Zeal*, 2 Cor. 7:11. **17** *v Commandment, enjoining wisdom*, Deut. 8:2.

---

* **DISOBEDIENCE TO GOD**, Luke 1:17; Rom. 5:19; 11:32; Eph. 2:2; 5:6; Col. 3:6; Tit. 1:16; 3:3; Heb. 2:2; 1 Pet. 2:8. *Temptation to*, Gen. 3:1–5.

*Denunciations against*, Num. 14:11, 12, 22, 23; 32:8–13; Deut. 18:19.

*Punishment for*, Lev. 26:14–46; Deut. 28:15–68. See footnote, WICKED, *Punishment of*, Psa. 73:3.

**Instances of:** *Adam and Eve, eating the forbidden fruit*, Gen. 3:6–11. *Antediluvians*, 1 Pet. 3:20, with Gen. 6:3–7. *Lot's wife, in looking back upon Sodom*, Gen. 19:17, 26. *Moses, in making excuses when he was commissioned to deliver Israel*, Ex. 4:13, 14; *when he smote the rock*, Num. 20:11, 23, 24. *Aaron, at the smiting of the rock by Moses*, Num. 20:23, 24. *The Israelites, in refusing to enter the promised land*, Deut. 1:26 (with Num. 14:1–10); Josh. 5:6; Psa. 106:24, 25; *in rebelling against God*, Neh. 9:26. *Nadab and Abihu, in offering strange fire*, Lev. 10:1, 2. *David, in his adultery, and in the slaying of Uriah*, 2 Sam. 12:9. *Solomon, in building places for idolatrous worship*, 1 Kin. 11:7–10. *The prophet of Judah, in not keeping the commandment to deliver his message to Jeroboam without tarrying to eat*, 1 Kin. 13. *Jonah, in refusing to deliver the message to the Ninevites*, Jonah 1. *Paul, in going to Jerusalem contrary to repeated admonitions of the Holy Spirit*, Acts 21:4, 10–14.

such thing; but that it should be holy and without [g]blemish.

28 [h,i]So ought men to love their wives as their own bodies. He that loveth his wife loveth himself.

29 For no man ever yet hated his own flesh; but nourisheth and cherisheth it, even as [11]the Lord the [j]church:

30 For [k]we are [l,m]members of his body, [12]of his flesh, and of his bones.

31 [n]For this cause shall a man leave his father and mother, and shall be joined unto his wife, and they two shall be [h]one flesh.

32 This is a great mystery: but I speak concerning Christ and the church.

33 Nevertheless [13,i]let every one of you in particular so love his wife even as himself; and [o,p]the wife *see* that she reverence *her* husband.

## CHAPTER 6

*The duty of children, and of parents; 5 of servants, and of masters. 10 The apostle exhorts his brethren to be strong in the Lord, 11 to put on the whole armor of God, 18 and pray with all prayer and supplication in the Spirit. 21 Tychicus commended. 23 Benediction.*

CHILDREN, [a,b]obey your [c]parents in the Lord: for this is right.

2 [d,e]Honour [a]thy [f]father and [g]mother; which is the first commandment with promise;

3 That [h]it may be well with thee, and [h]thou mayest live [i]long on the earth.

4 And, ye fathers, [j,k]provoke not your children to wrath: but [1,j,k]bring [l]them up in the nurture and [m]admonition of the Lord.

5 Servants, [n,o]be obedient to them that are *your* masters according to the flesh, with fear and trembling, in [p,q]singleness of your heart, as unto Christ;

6 [r]Not with [s]eyeservice, as menpleasers; but as the [t]servants of Christ, [r,u]doing the [v]will of God [p,q]from the heart;

7 [q]With good will doing service, [w]as to the Lord, and not to men:

8 Knowing that whatsoever good thing any man doeth, [x,y,z]the same shall he receive of the [a]Lord, whether *he be* bond or free.

9 And, ye [b]masters, [c]do the same things unto [d]them, [c,e]forbearing threatening: [f]knowing that your [g]Master also is in heaven; neither is there [h]respect of persons with him.

10 Finally, [2]my brethren, [i,j]be strong in the Lord, and in the [k]power of his might.

11 [i,l]Put on the whole [m]armour of God, that ye may be able to [n,o]stand against the [p]wiles of the [q,r]devil.

12 For we [s]wrestle not against flesh and blood, but against principalities, against powers, against the [3]rulers of the [t]darkness of this world, against spiritual wickedness in high *places*.

13 Wherefore [i]take unto you the whole [m]armour of God, that ye may be able to [o,p]withstand in the evil day, and having done all, to stand.

14 [n,o]Stand therefore, having your loins girt about with [u]truth, and having on the [v]breastplate of [w]righteousness;

15 And your feet shod with the preparation of the [x]gospel of [y]peace;

16 Above all, taking the shield of [z]faith, wherewith ye shall be

*g Blemish, figurative*, Lev. 14:10.

**28**
*h Marriage, unity of husband and wife in*, Gen. 34:9.
*i Husband, relation of, to wife*, Num. 30:6.

**29**
*j Church, Christ's love for*, Matt. 16:18.
11 R. V. Christ also the church;

**30**
*k Righteous, union of, with Christ*, Psa. 64:10.
*l Church, membership in*, Matt. 16:18.
*m Fellowship, with Christ*, 1 Cor. 1:9.
12 R. V. *omits* of his flesh, and of his bones.

**31**
*n* Gen. 2:24; Matt. 19:5; Mark 10:7, 8; 1 Cor. 6:16.

**33**
*o Family, government of*, 1 Chr. 13:14.
*p Wife, duty of, to husband*, Prov. 5:18.
13 R. V. do ye also severally love each one his own wife even as himself; and let the wife see that she fear her husband.

**1**
*a Children, commandments to*, Mark 10:14.
*b Commandment, to children, enjoining obedience*, Deut. 8:2.
*c Parents, to be obeyed*, 2 Cor. 12:14.

**2**
*d* Ex. 20:12; Deut. 5:16.
*e Commandment, enjoining reverence for parents*, Deut. 8:2.
*f Father, to be revered*, Psa. 27:10.
*g Mother, reverence for, enjoined*, 1 Kin. 2:20.

**3**
*h Promise, to children*, 2 Cor. 1:20.
*i Longevity*, Psa. 91:16.

*p Faithfulness*, Luke 16:10.
*q Sincerity, enjoined*, 1 Cor. 5:8.

**6**
*r Integrity, enjoined*, Job 2:3.
*s Hypocrisy*, Jas. 3:17.
*t Righteous, described*, Psa. 64:10.
*u Obedience, enjoined*, Heb. 5:8.
*v Will of God, the supreme rule of duty*, Mark 3:35.

**7**
*w Motive, right, required*, Psa. 106:8.

**8**
*x Promise, to the righteous*, 2 Cor. 1:20.
*y Judgment, according to opportunity and works*, 1 Pet. 1:17.
*z Reward, a motive, to obedience*, Matt. 5:12.

*a Jesus, judge*, Matt. 1:21.

**9**
*b Master*, Col. 4:1.
*c Commandment, to masters*, Deut. 8:2.
*d Employer, to be kind*, Deut. 24:14.
*e Servant, kindness to, enjoined*, Jer. 2:14.
*f Jesus, our example*, Matt. 1:21.
*g Master, Jesus called*, John 13:13.
*h Respect of Persons*, Prov. 24:23.

**10**
*i Commandment, enjoining various Christian duties*, vs. 11, 13–18; Deut. 8:2.
*j Strenuousness, enjoined*, Eccl. 9:10.
*k Spiritual Power*, Luke 24:49.
2 R. V. *omits* my brethren,

**11**
*l Soldiers, figurative*, Ezra 8:22.
*m Armor, figurative*, 1 Sam. 17:54.

**4** *j Commandment, to fathers*, Deut. 8:2. *k Parents, duty of*, 2 Cor. 12:14. *l Children, instrucion of*, Mark 10:14. *m Instruction, of children*, Prov. 23:23. 1 R. V. nurture them in the chastening and **5** *n Servant, duty of*, Jer. 2:14. *o Commandment, to servants*, vs. 5–8; Deut. 8:2.

*n Commandment, enjoining steadfastness*, Deut. 8:2. *o Steadfastness, enjoined*, 1 Cor. 15:58. *p Temptation, resistance to*, Luke 11:4. *q Satan*, Matt. 4:10. *r Temptation, sources of*, Luke 11:4.
**12** *s Wrestling, figurative*, Gen. 30:8. *t Darkness, figurative*, Gen. 1:2. 3 R. V. world-rulers of this darkness, against the spiritual hosts of wickedness in the heavenly places.
**14** *u Truth*, John 18:37. *v* Isa. 59:17; 1 Thess. 5:8. *w Righteousness*, Psa. 15:2. **15** *x Gospel*, Mark 13:10. *y Spiritual Peace*, Gal. 1:3.
**16** *z Faith in Christ*, John 6:69.

able to quench all the fiery [a]darts
of the [4]wicked.
17 And take the [b]helmet of [c]sal-
vation, and the sword of the
[d]Spirit, which is the [e]word of
God:
18 [f]Praying always with all
prayer and [g]supplication in the
Spirit, and [h]watching thereunto
with all *perseverance and [i]sup-
plication for all saints;
19 And [j]for [k]me, that utterance
may be given unto me, that I
may open my mouth [l]boldly, to
make known the [m,n]mystery of
the [o]gospel,
20 For which I am an [p]ambas-
sador in [5,q]bonds: that therein I
may [r]speak [l]boldly, as I ought to
speak.
21 But that ye also may know
my affairs, *and* how I do, [s]Tўch'-
ĭ-cŭs, a [t]beloved brother and
[u]faithful minister in the Lord,
shall make known to you all
things:
22 Whom I have sent unto you
for the same purpose, that ye
might know our [6]affairs, and *that*
he might comfort your hearts.
23 [v,w]Peace *be* to the brethren,
and [x]love with [y]faith, from God
the [z]Father and the [a]Lord Jē'ṣus
Chrīst.
24 [b]Grace *be* with all them that
[c]love our [a]Lord Jē'ṣus Chrīst in
[7]sincerity. Amen.

[8]Written from Rome unto the Ephesians by Tychicus.

a *Dart, figurative,* 2 Sam. 18:14.
4 R. V. evil one.
**17**
b *Helmet, figurative,* Jer. 46:4.
c *Salvation,* Acts 16:17.
d *Holy Spirit,* Acts 1:2.
e *Word of God,* Psa. 119:9.
**18**
f *Prayer, importunity in,* Acts 6:4.
g *Holy Spirit, prayer in,* Acts 1:2.
h *Watchfulness, with prayer,* Matt. 24:42.
i *Prayer, intercessory,* Acts 6:4.
**19**
j *Intercession, solicited,* Jer. 27:18. k *Minister, duty of the church to pray for,* Rom. 15:16. l *Boldness of the Righteous,* Phil. 1:20. m *Mysteries, of redemption,* Mark 4:11. n *Salvation, plan of,* Acts 16:17. o *Gospel,* Mark 13:10. **20** p *Ambassadors, figurative,* Josh. 9:4. q *Persecution, of the righteous,* John 15:20. 5 R. V. chains;

r *Minister, duties of,* Rom. 15:16.
**21**
s *Tychicus,* Acts 20:4.
t *Love, of man for man,* 1 John 4:7.
u *Minister, faithful,* Rom. 15:16.
**22**
6 R. V. state,
**23**
v *Benedictions, apostolic,* Deut. 21:5.
w *Spiritual Peace,* Gal. 1:3.
x *Love,* 1 John 4:7.
y *Faith,* Mark 11:22.
z *God, fatherhood of,* Gen. 2:2.
a *Jesus, lordship of,* Matt. 1:21.
**24**
b *Benedictions, apostolic,* Deut. 21:5.
c *Love, for Jesus,* 1 John 4:19.
7 R. V. uncorruptness.
8 R. V. *omits this postscript.*

THE EPISTLE OF PAUL TO THE

# PHILIPPIANS

## CHAPTER 1

*The apostle's salutation. 3 His thanksgiving to God for their fellowship in the gospel. 7 His affection for them, 9 and prayer for their increase in grace. 12 His trials were the means of furthering the gospel. 21 His willingness to glorify Christ by his life or death. 27 He exhorts them to live as becomes the gospel.*

[a]PAUL and [b]Tĭ-mō'the-ŭs, the
[c]servants of Jē'ṣus Chrīst,
to all the saints in [d]Chrīst Jē'ṣus
which are at [e]Phĭ-lĭp'pī, with the
[f]bishops and [g]deacons:
2 [h]Grace *be* unto you, and [i]peace,
from God our [j]Father, and *from*
the [k]Lord Jē'ṣus Chrīst.
3 [l]I [m]thank my God upon every
remembrance of you,
4 Always in every [n]prayer of
mine for you all making request
with joy,
5 For your [o]fellowship in [1]the
[p]gospel from the first day until
now;
6 Being confident of this very
thing, that he which hath begun a
[q]good work in you will [2,r]perform
*it* until the [s]day of Jē'ṣus Chrīst:
7 Even as it is meet for me to
think this of you all, because I
[l]have you in my heart; inasmuch
as both in my [t]bonds, and in the
defence and confirmation of the
[p]gospel, ye all are partakers [3]of
my grace.
8 For God is my [4]record, how
greatly [l]I long after you all in the
[5]bowels of Jē'ṣus [d]Chrīst.

**1**
a *Paul,* Acts 13:9.
b Or, *Timothy,* 1 Cor. 4:17.
c *Righteous, described,* Psa. 64:10.
d *Jesus, Messiah,* Matt. 1:21.
e *Philippi,* Acts 20:6.
f *Bishop,* 1 Tim. 3:1.
g *Deacon,* 1 Tim. 3:8.
**2**
h *Benedictions, apostolic,* Deut. 21:5.
i *Spiritual Peace,* Gal. 1:3.
j *God, fatherhood of,* Gen. 2:2.
k *Jesus, lordship of,* Matt. 1:21. **3** l *Love, of man for man,* 1 John 4:7. m *Thankfulness, to God,* Acts 24:3. **4** n *Prayer, intercessory,* Acts 6:4.

**5**
o *Fellowship, of the righteous,* 1 Cor. 1:9.
p *Gospel,* Mark 13:10.
1 R. V. furtherance of the gospel
**6**
q *Regeneration,* Tit. 3:5.
r *Spiritual Blessings,* Eph. 1:3.
s *Jesus, second coming of,* Matt. 1:21.
2 R. V. perfect it
**7**
t *Persecution, of the righteous,* John 15:20.
3 R. V. with me of grace.
**8**
4 R. V. witness,
5 R. V. tender mercies of

***PERSEVERANCE,** Job 17:9; Tit. 1:9; 1 Pet. 4:16.
*Enjoined,* 1 Chr. 16:11; Hos. 12:6; 1 Thess. 5:21; 2 Thess. 2:15–17; 2 Tim. 3:14; 1 Pet. 5:8, 9. *Exhortation to,* Acts 11:23; 13:43; 14:21, 22; 1 Cor. 15:58; 16:13; Gal. 5:1, 10; Eph. 4:14, 15; 6:13, 18; Phil. 1:27; 3:16; 4:1; Col. 1:10, 22, 23; 1 Thess. 3:8; 2 Thess. 3:13; 2 Tim. 1:13; Heb. 6:1, 11, 12, 15; 10:23, 35 36; 12:5–13, 15; 2 Pet. 3:17, 18; Rev. 16:15.
*A proof of discipleship,* John 8:31, 32. *A condition of fruitfulness,* John 15:4, 5, 7, 9. *Intercessory prayer for,* Luke 22:31, 32.
Motives to: *The example, of Moses,* Heb. 3:5; *of the prophets,* Jas. 5:10, 11; *of Christ,* Heb. 3:6, 14; 12:2–4; *the intercession of Christ,* Heb. 4:14; *the heavenly witnesses,* Heb. 12:1.
*Rewards contingent upon,* Gal. 6:9; Jas. 1:12; Rev. 2:7, 10, 11, 17, 25–28; 3:5, 11, 21; 21:7.
*Eternal life contingent upon,* Matt. 10:22; 24:13; Mark 13:13; Rom. 2:6, 7; 2 Pet. 1:10, 11.
Lacking in: *The wayside and other hearers,* Mark 4:3–8; *churches of Asia,* Rev. 2:5; 3:1–3, 14–18.

**9**
*u Love*, 1 John 4:7.
*v Wisdom, prayer for spiritual*, Prov. 2:2.
6 R. V. all discernment;
**10**
*w Sincerity*, 1 Cor. 5:8.
*x Sinlessness*, 1 John 5:18.
*y Holiness*, Ex. 39:30.
**11**
*z Righteousness, fruits of*, Psa. 15:2.

*a Works, good*, 2 Tim. 1:9.
*b God, glory of*, Gen. 2:2.
**12**
*c Persecution, of the righteous, extension of the church by*, John 15:20.
*d God, providence of*, Gen. 2:2.
*e Adversity, benefits of*, Psa. 10:6.
*f Gospel*, Mark 13:10.
**13**
*g Pretorium*, Mark 15:16.
7 R. V. became manifest in Christ throughout the whole prætorian guard, and to all the rest;
**14**
*h Influence, good*, 1 Cor. 7:14.
*i Doctrines of Jesus*, John 7:16.
8 R. V. most
9 R. V. *inserts* of God
**15**
*j Minister, false and corrupt*, Rom. 15:16.
*k Preaching*, Matt. 9:35.
*l Zeal, without knowledge*, 2 Cor. 7:11.
*m Jesus, Messiah*, Matt. 1:21.
*n Malice*, Eph. 4:31.
*o Strife*, Prov. 20:3.
**16**
10 R. V. do it of love, knowing that I am set for the defence of the gospel:

9 [T]And this I [n]pray, that your [u]love may abound yet more and more in [v]knowledge and [6]*in* all judgment;

10 That ye may approve[G] things that are excellent; that ye may be [w]sincere and [x,y]without offence till the [s]day of Chrīst;

11 Being filled with the [z,a]fruits of righteousness, which are by Jē'ṣus Chrīst, unto the [b]glory and praise of God. [T]

12 But I would ye should understand, brethren, that the [c]things *which happened* unto me [d]have fallen[G] out rather unto the [e]furtherance of the [f]gospel;[S]

13 So that my bonds [7]in Chrīst are manifest in all the [g]palace, and in all other *places*;

14 And [8]many of the brethren in the Lord, waxing[G] confident [h]by my bonds, are much more *bold to speak the [i]word [9]without fear.

15 [j]Some indeed [k,l]preach [m]Chrīst even of[G] [n]envy and [o]strife; and some also of[G] good will:

16 The one [10,k,l]preach Chrīst of contention[G], not sincerely, supposing to add affliction to my bonds:

17 But the other [11]of love, knowing that I am set for the defence of the gospel.

18 What then? notwithstanding, every way, whether in pretence, or in truth, Chrīst is [k]preached; and [p]I therein do rejoice, yea, and will rejoice.

19 For I [q,r]know that this shall turn to my salvation[G] [s]through your [t]prayer, and the supply of the [u]Spirit of Jē'ṣus Chrīst,[S] [T] [Q]

**17** 11 R. V. proclaim Christ of faction, not sincerely, thinking to raise up affliction for me in my bonds. **18** *p Love, for Jesus*, 1 John 4:19. **19** *q Faith, exemplified*, Mark 11:22. *r Afflictions, consolation in*, Psa. 34:19. *s Prayer, intercessory*, Acts 6:4. *t Minister, duty of the church to pray for*, Rom. 15:16. *u Holy Spirit*, Acts 1:2.

20 [q]According to my earnest expectation and *my* [v]hope, that [w]in nothing I shall be ashamed, but *that* with all *boldness, as always, *so* now also [p]Chrīst shall be magnified in my body, whether *it be* by life, or by [x]death.

21 For [p]to me to live *is* Chrīst, and to [y]die *is* gain.

22 But if I live in the flesh, [12]this *is* the fruit of my labour: yet what I shall choose I wot[G] not.

23 For I am in a strait betwixt[G] two, having a desire [y]to depart, and [p,z]to be with Chrīst; which is far better:

24 Nevertheless to [a]abide in the flesh *is* more needful for [13]you.

25 And having this confidence, I know that I shall abide [14]and continue with you all [a]for your furtherance and joy of faith;

26 That your rejoicing may be more abundant in Jē'ṣus Chrīst for me by my coming to you again.

27 Only [b]let your [15]conversation[G] be as it becometh the [c]gospel of Chrīst: that whether I come and see you, or else be absent, I may hear of your [16]affairs, that ye [b,d]stand [e]fast in [f]one spirit, with [e]one mind striving together for the [g]faith of the gospel;

28 And [h,i]in nothing [17]terrified by your adversaries: which is to them an evident token[G] of perdition, but to you of salvation, and that of God.

29 For unto you it is given in the behalf of Chrīst, not only to [j]believe on him, but also to [†,k]suffer for his sake;[S] [T]

30 Having the same [†,k]conflict which ye saw in [l]me, and now hear *to be* in me.

**20**
*v Hope*, Prov. 13:12.
*w Resignation, exemplified*, vs. 20–24; Job 5:17.
*x Martyrdom*, Rev. 17:6.
**21**
*y Death, desired*, Num. 23:10.
**22**
12 R. V. *inserts* if
**23**
*z Immortality*, 1 Cor. 15:54.

**24**
*a Love, of man for man*, 1 John 4:7.
13 R. V. your sake.
**25**
14 R. V. yea, and abide with you all, for your progress and joy in the faith;
**27**
*b Commandment, enjoining discreet conduct and steadfastness*, Deut. 8:2.
*c Doctrines of Jesus*, John 7:16.
*d Steadfastness*, 1 Cor. 15:58.
*e Character, stability of*, Phil. 2:15.
*f Unity, of the righteous*, Psa. 133:1.
*g Faith, the doctrines of Jesus*, 1 Cor. 16:13.
15 R. V. manner of life be worthy of the gospel
16 R. V. state,
**28**
*h Commandment, enjoining courage*, Deut. 8:2.
*i Courage*, Deut. 31:7.
17 R. V. affrighted by the adversaries: which is for them an evident token of perdition, but of your salvation, and that from God;
**29**
*j Faith in Christ*, John 6:69.
*k Persecution, of the righteous*, John 15:20.
**30**
*l Paul, persecutions of*, Acts 13:9.

See footnotes: CHARACTER, Phil. 2:15; INSTABILITY, Jas. 1:8.
**Instances of, in prayer:** *Abraham in interceding for Sodom*, Gen. 18:23–32. *Jacob*, Gen. 32:24–26. *Elijah, for rain*, 1 Kin. 18:42–45. *Paul, for the removal of the thorn in his flesh*, 2 Cor. 12:7–9.
*** BOLDNESS OF THE RIGHTEOUS,** Prov. 28:1; Acts 18:26; 19:8.

*Inspired, by fear of the Lord*, Prov. 14:26; *by faith in Christ*, Eph. 3:12.
*In prayer*, Heb. 4:16; 10:19; 1 John 3:21, 22; 5:14, 15.
**Instances of, in prayer:** *Abraham*, Gen. 18:23–32. *Moses*, Ex. 33:12–18. *In the day of judgment*, 1 John 2:28; 4:17. *Its effect on others*, Acts 4:13.
**† SUFFERING FOR CHRIST,** Acts 5:41; 9:16. *Fel-*

## CHAPTER 2

*The apostle exhorts them to be of one mind, 3 to be humble after the example of Christ, 12 and to work out their salvation with fear and trembling. 17 His willingness to suffer for them. 19 He hopes to send Timothy to them, whom he commends. 25 He sends to them Epaphroditus, his faithful companion and fellow soldier.*

IF *there be* therefore any consolation in Christ, if any comfort of [a]love, if any [b]fellowship of
the [c]Spirit, if any [1,d]bowels and
mercies,
2 [e]Fulfil ye my joy, that ye be
likeminded, [f]having the same
[a]love, *being* of [g]one accord, of
[g]one mind.
3 [h]*Let* nothing *be done* through
[i]strife or [j]vainglory; but [h]in [k]low-
liness of mind let [l,m]each [n,o]es-
teem other better than themselves.
4 [p]Look not every man [q]on his
own things, but [l,m,p]every man
also on the things of others.
5 Let this mind be in you,
which was also in Christ [r]Jē′şus:
6 Who, [2]being in the [s]form of
God, thought it not robbery to
be [s,t]equal with God:
7 But [3]made himself of no reputation, and took upon him the
[u]form of a servant, and was
[u]made in the likeness of men:
8 And being found in fashion as
a [v]man, he humbled himself, and
[w,x]became [y]obedient unto death,
even the death of the [z]cross.
9 Wherefore God also hath
highly [a]exalted him, and given
him a [b]name which is above
every name:
10 That [4]at the [b]name of Jē′-
şus [c]every knee should [d]bow,
of *things* in heaven, and *things*
in earth, and *things* under the
earth;
11 And *that* every tongue should
[e]confess that Jē′şus Christ *is*
[f]Lord, to the [g]glory of God the
[h]Father.
12 Wherefore, my beloved, as
ye have always obeyed, not as in
my presence only, but now much
more in my absence, work out
your own [i]salvation with [j]fear
and trembling.
13 For it is God which [k]work-
eth in you both to will and to do
[5]of [l]*his* good pleasure.
14 [m,n]Do all things without
[o]murmurings and [p]disputings:
15 *That ye may [q]be [r,s,t]blame-
less and harmless, the [r,u]sons of
God, [r,s,t]without rebuke, in the
midst of a [v,w]crooked and perverse nation, among whom ye
[x]shine as [y,z]lights in the world;
16 [x]Holding forth the [a,b]word
of life; that I may rejoice in the
[c]day of Christ, that [d]I have not
[e]run in vain, [d]neither laboured
in vain.
17 Yea, and if I be offered upon
the sacrifice and service of your
faith, I joy, and rejoice with you
all.
18 For the same cause also do
ye joy, and rejoice with me.
19 But I trust in the [f]Lord
Jē′şus to send [g,h]Tī-mō′the-ŭs
shortly unto you, [i]that I also
may be of good comfort, when
I know your state.
20 For I have no man likeminded, [h]who will naturally care
for your state.
21 For all [j]seek their own, not the
things which are Jē′şus Christ's.

**1** a *Love, of man for man,* 1 John 4:7. b *Communion, with the Holy Spirit,* 2 Cor. 13:14. c *Holy Spirit,* Acts 1:2. d *Sympathy,* Jas. 1:27. 1 R. V. tender mercies and compassions,

**2** e *Commandment, enjoining accord with Christ and with one another,* vs. 2–5; Deut. 8:2. f *Fellowship, of the righteous,* 1 Cor. 1:9. g *Unity, of the righteous,* Psa. 133:1.

**3** h *Commandment, forbidding unholy ambition, and enjoining humility,* Deut. 8:2. i *Strife,* Prov. 20:3. j *Pride,* Prov. 16:18. k *Humility,* Prov. 22:4. l *Unselfishness,* 1 Cor. 10:24. m *Christian Graces, unselfishness,* Gal. 5:22. n *Altruism,* Acts 20:35. o *Respect,* Isa. 22:11.

**4** p *Commandment, forbidding selfishness, and enjoining helpfulness,* Deut. 8:2. q *Selfishness,* 2 Tim. 3:2.

**5** r *Jesus, our example,* Matt. 1:21.

**6** s *Jesus, divinity of,* Matt. 1:21. t *Jesus, relation of, to the Father,* Matt. 1:21. 2 Am. R. V. existing in the form of God, counted not the being on an equality with God a thing to be grasped, **7** u *Jesus, incarnation of,* Matt. 1:21. 3 R. V. emptied himself, taking the form **8** v *Jesus, humanity of,* Matt. 1:21. w *Renunciation, of self, by Jesus,* Luke 5:11. x *Jesus, death of, voluntary,* Matt. 1:21. y *Obedience, exemplified,* Heb. 5:8. z *Cross,* John 19:17. **9**—a *Jesus, exaltation of,* Matt. 1:21. b *Name of Jesus,* John 14:13. **10** c *Jesus, kingdom of, prophecies concerning,* Matt. 1:21. d *Jesus, worship of,* Matt. 1:21. 4 R. V. in the

**11** e *Confession of Christ,* Luke 12:8. f *Jesus, lordship of,* Matt. 1:21. g *God, glory of,* Gen. 2:2. h *God, fatherhood of,* Gen. 2:2.

**12** i *Salvation,* Acts 16:17. j *Fear of God,* Acts 9:31.

**13** k *Spiritual Blessings,* Eph. 1:3. l *Will of God, supreme rule of duty,* Mark 3:35. 5 R. V for

**14** m *Commandment, forbidding murmuring and contention,* Deut. 8:2. n *Peace, enjoined,* Jer. 29:7. o *Murmuring, against God,* Num. 14:2. p *Church, dissensions in,* Matt. 16:18.

**15** q *Commandment, enjoining influence for righteousness,* Deut. 8:2. r *Righteous, described,* Psa. 64:10. s *Holiness,* Ex. 39:30. t *Christian Graces,* Gal. 5:22. u *Spiritual Adoption,* Rom. 8:15. v *Wicked, described,* Psa. 73:3. w *Wicked, contrasted with the righteous,* Psa. 73:3. x *Zeal,* 2 Cor. 7:11. y *Light, figurative,* Matt. 5:14. z *Influence, good,* 1 Cor. 7:14.

**16** a *Doctrines of Jesus,* John 7:16. b *Gospel,* Mark 13:10. c *Jesus, second coming of,* Matt. 1:21. d *Minister, success attending,* Rom. 15:16. e *Foot Race, figurative,* Psa. 19:5. **19** f *Jesus, lordship of,* Matt. 1:21. g Or, *Timothy,* 1 Cor. 4:17. h *Minister, faithful,* Rom. 15:16. i *Love, of man for man,* 1 John 4:7. **21** j *Selfishness,* 2 Tim. 3:2.

---

*lowship with Christ on account of,* Phil. 3:10. *Condition of joint heirship with Christ,* Rom. 8:17. *A privilege,* Phil. 1:29.

Motives for the patient enduring of: *Future glory,* Rom. 8:17, 18; 2 Cor. 4:8–12, 17, 18; **1** Pet. 4:13; *reigning with Christ,* 2 Tim. 2:12; Rev. 22:5.

*Consolations in,* 2 Cor. **1:7**; **2 Tim. 2:12**; **1** Pet. 5:10. *Patience in,* 1 Cor. 4:11, 12, 13; 2 Thess. 1:4, 5; Jas. 5:10; 1 Pet. 4:14.

* **CHARACTER.** *Revealed in countenance,* Isa. 3:9. *Good,* Prov. 22:1; Eccl. 7:1. *Defamation of, punished,* Deut. 22:13–19.

**Stability of,** Psa. 57:7; 108:1; 112:7; 2 Thess. 3:3. *Exhortations to,* 1 Cor. 15:58; 16:13; Eph. 4:14, 15; Phil. **1:27**;

22 But ye know the [k]proof of [g]him, that, [i]as a son with the father, [h]he hath served with me in [6]the [a,b]gospel.

23 [g]Him therefore I hope to send presently, so soon as I shall see how it will go with me.

24 But I trust in the Lord that I also myself shall come shortly.

25 Yet I supposed it necessary to send to you [l]Ē-păph-ro-dī'tus, [i]my brother, and companion in labour, and fellow-soldier, but your messenger, and he that [i,k]ministered to my wants.

26 For [l]he [i]longed after you all, and was [7]full of heaviness, because that ye had heard that he had been [m]sick.

27 For indeed [l]he was [m]sick nigh unto [n]death: but [o]God had mercy on him; and not on him only, but on me also, lest I should have sorrow upon sorrow.

28 I sent [l]him therefore the more [8]carefully, that, when ye see him again, ye may rejoice, and that I may be the less sorrowful.

29 [p]Receive him therefore in the Lord with all gladness; and hold such in reputation:

30 Because [q]for the work of Christ he was [r]nigh unto death, [s,t]not regarding his life, to supply your lack of service toward me.

22
k Friendship, Prov. 22:24.
6 R. V. inserts furtherance of

25
l Phil. 4:18.

26
m Afflictions, Psa. 34:19.
7 R. V. sore troubled,

27
n Death, Num. 23:10.
o God, providence of, Gen. 2:2.

28
8 R. V. diligently,

29
p Church, duty of, to ministers, Matt. 16:18.

30
q Love, for Jesus, 1 John 4:19.
r Suffering for Christ, Phil. 1:29.
s Renunciation, self, Luke 5:11.
t Unselfishness, 1 Cor. 10:24.

## CHAPTER 3

*The apostle warns them against false teachers, 4 shewing that he has greater reason than they to trust in the flesh, 7 but that he counts all things loss for Christ. 12 Acknowledging his own imperfection, he presses onward, 15 and exhorts them to imitate his example.*

FINALLY, my brethren, [a]rejoice in the Lord. To write the same things to you, to me indeed *is* not [1]grievous, but for you *it is* safe.

1
a Joy, Psa. 5:11.

2 [b,c]Beware of [d,e]dogs, beware of evil workers, beware of the [f]concision.

3 For we are the circumcision, which [g,h]worship [2]God in the [i]spirit, and [h]rejoice in [j]Christ Jē'şus, and [h]have no confidence in the flesh.

4 Though I might also have confidence in the flesh. If any other man thinketh that he hath whereof he might trust in the flesh, I more:

5 [k]Circumcised the eighth day, of the stock of [l]Iş'ra-el, *of* the [m]tribe of Běn'ja-mĭn, an [n]Hē'brew of the Hē'brewş; as touching the [o]law, a [p]Phăr'ĭ-see;

6 Concerning [q]zeal, [r]persecuting the [s]church; touching the righteousness which is in the [o]law, blameless.

7 But what things were [t]gain to me, [u]those I counted [t,v]loss [w]for Christ.

8 Yea doubtless, and [w]I count all things *but* loss for the excellency of the [x]knowledge of [j]Christ Jē'şus my [y]Lord: for whom I have [v,z]suffered the loss of all things, and do count them *but* dung, that [w]I may win Christ,

9 And [a]be found in him, not having mine [b]own righteousness, which is of the [c]law, but that which is through the [d]faith of Christ, the [e]righteousness which is of God by faith:

10 That I may know him, and the power of his [f]resurrection, and the fellowship of his [g]sufferings, being made conformable unto his [h]death;

d *Faith in Christ*, John 6:69. e *Justification, by faith*, Rom. 4:25.
10 f *Resurrection, of Jesus*, 1 Cor. 15:12. g *Jesus, sufferings of*, Matt. 1:21. h *Jesus, death of*, Matt. 1:21.

1 R. V. irksome,
2
b *Commandment, enjoining watchfulness*, Deut. 8:2.
c *Watchfulness, enjoined*, Matt. 24:42.
d *Dog, figurative*, 1 Kin. 21:19.
e *False Teachers*, 2 Pet. 2:1.
f *Jews*, Neh. 4:2.
3
g *Worship*, Gen. 22:5.
h *Righteous, described*, Psa. 64:10.
i *Holy Spirit*, Acts 1:2.
j *Jesus, Messiah*, Matt. 1:21.
2 R. V. by the Spirit of God, and glory in Christ Jesus,
5
k *Circumcision*, Gen. 17:10.
l *Jacob*, Gen. 27:11.
m *Benjamin, tribe of*, Num. 1:37.
n *Hebrew*, Gen. 40:15.
o *Law, of Moses*, Deut. 33:2.
p *Pharisees*, Matt. 15:12.
6
q *Zeal*, 2 Cor. 7:11.
r *Bigotry*, Isa. 65:5.
s *Righteous, persecution of*, Psa. 64:10.
7
t *Paradox*, 2 Cor. 12:4.
u *Religious Testimony*, 2 Thess. 1:10.
v *Renunciation*, Luke 5:11.
w *Love, for Jesus*, 1 John 4:19.
8
x *Wisdom, spiritual*, Prov. 2:2.
y *Jesus, lordship of*, Matt. 1:21.
z *Suffering for Christ*, Phil. 1:29.
9
a *Preparedness*, Luke 12:40.
b *Self-righteousness*, Luke 18:11.
c *Works under the Law*, Lev. 18:5.

4:1; Col. 1:23; 1 Thess. 3:8; 2 Thess. 2:15; Heb. 3:6, 14; 10:23; 13:9; 1 Pet. 5:9; 2 Pet. 3:17; Rev. 3:11. *Reward of*, Matt. 10:22; Jas. 1:25. *Fixedness of*, Rev. 22:11.
See footnote, DECISION, Isa. 50:7.
INSTANCES OF: *Joseph*, Gen. 39:7-12. *Moses*, Heb. 11:24-26. *Joshua*, Josh. 24:15. *Daniel*, Dan. 1:8; 6:10. *Three Hebrews*, Dan. 3:16-18. *Peter and John*, Acts 4:19, 20. *Paul*, Acts 20:22-24; 21:13, 14.

**Instability of**, Prov. 27:8; Jer. 2:36; Hos. 6:4; 7:8; 10:2; Matt. 13:19-22; Mark 4:15-19; Luke 8:12-14; 2 Pet. 2:14; Rev. 2:4. *Warnings against*, Prov. 24:21, 22; Luke 9:59-62; Eph. 4:14; Heb. 6:4-6; 13:9; Jas. 1:6-8; 4:8.
INSTANCES OF: *Reuben*, Gen. 49:3, 4. *Pharaoh*, Ex. 8:15, 32; 9:34; 14:5. *Israelites*, Ex. 32:8; Judg. 2:17-19. *Saul*, 1 Sam. 18; 19. *Solomon*, 1 Kin. 11:4-8. *Rehoboam*, 2 Chr. 12:1. *Pilate*, John 18:37-40; 19:1-16. *Demas*, 2 Tim. 4:10.

**11**
*i Resurrection,* 1 Cor. 15:12.

**12**
*j Humility, exemplified,* Prov. 22:4.
*k Perfection,* Heb. 6:1.
*l Spiritual Desire,* Psa. 42:1.
*m Perseverance,* Eph. 6:18.
3 Am. R. V. press on, if so be that I may lay hold on that for which also I was laid hold on by Christ Jesus.

**13**
*n Zeal,* 2 Cor. 7:11.
4 Am. R. V. yet to have laid hold:

**14**
*o Foot Race, figurative,* Psa. 19:5.
*p Strenuousness,* Eccl. 9:10.
*q* 1 Cor. 9:24.
*r Reward, a motive, to faithfulness,* Matt. 5:12.
5 R. V. goal unto the

**15**
*s Faithfulness,* Luke 16:10.
*t Wisdom, spiritual,* Prov. 2:2.

**16**
6 R. V. *omits* let us mind the same thing.

**17**
*u Example, Paul our,* John 13:15.
7 R. V. ye imitators

**18**
*v Apostasy,* Acts 1:25.
*w Love, of man for man,* 1 John 4:7.
*x Wicked, described,* Psa. 73:3.
*y Cross, figurative,* John 19:17.

**19**
*z Wicked, punishment of,* Psa. 73:3.

11 If by any means I might attain unto the [i]resurrection of the dead.

12 [j]Not as though I had already attained, either were already [k]perfect[G]: but I [3,l,m]follow after, if that I may apprehend[G] that for which also I am apprehended of Chrīst Jē′şus.

13 Brethren, I count not myself [4]to have apprehended: but *this* one thing *I do,* [n]forgetting those things which are behind, and [l,m]reaching forth unto those things which are before,

14 I [m,n,o,p]press[G] toward the [5]mark[G] for the [q,r]prize of the high *calling of God in Chrīst Jē′şus.[T]

15 [s]Let us therefore, as many as be [k]perfect,[G] be thus minded: and if in any thing ye be otherwise minded, God shall reveal even [t]this unto you.

16 Nevertheless, whereto we have already attained, [s]let us walk by the same rule, [6]let us mind the same thing.

17 Brethren, be [7,u]followers together of me, and mark them which walk so as ye have us for an ensample.[G]

18 (For [v]many walk, of whom I have told you often, and now tell you even [w]weeping, *that they are* the [x]enemies of the [y]cross of Chrīst:

19 Whose end *is* [8,z]destruction, whose God *is their* [a]belly,[G] and *whose* glory *is* in their shame, who [b]mind[G] earthly things.)

20[S] For our [9]conversation[G] is in [c]heaven; from whence also we [d]look for the [e]Saviour, the [f]Lord Jē′şus Chrīst:[T]

21 Who shall [10]change our vile[G] [g]body, that it may be fashioned like unto his glorious[G] body, according to the working whereby he is [h]able even to subdue all things unto himself.[S T]

## CHAPTER 4

*Particular admonitions. 4 An exhortation to sundry duties. 10 His grateful acknowledgment of their kindness in contributing to his relief. 19 Their reward. 21 Salutations and prayer.*

THEREFORE, my brethren [1]dearly [a]beloved and longed for, my joy and crown, so [b,c,d]stand fast in the Lord, *my* [1]dearly beloved.

2 I beseech[G] Eū-ō′dĭ-as, and beseech[G] Sўn′tў-chē, that they be of the same mind in the Lord.

3 And I intreat thee also, true yokefellow,[G] help those [e]women which laboured with me in the [f]gospel, with Clĕm′ĕnt also, and *with* other my fellowlabourers, whose names *are* in the [g]book of life.[Q]

4 [h,i]Rejoice in the Lord alway: *and* again I say, Rejoice.

5 [j]Let your [2,k]moderation[G] be known unto all men. The Lord *is* at hand.

6 [3,l,m]Be [n]careful[G] for nothing; but [l]in every thing by [o]prayer and supplication with [p]thanksgiving let your requests be made known unto God.

7 And [q]the [r,s]peace of God, which passeth[G] all understanding, shall [4]keep your [t]hearts and minds through Chrīst Jē′şus.[Q]

*d Jesus, second coming of,* Matt. 1:21.
*e Jesus, savior,* Matt. 1:21.
*f Jesus, lordship of,* Matt. 1:21.

**21**
*g Body, resurrection of,* 1 Cor. 6:19.
*h Jesus, power of,* Matt. 1:21.
10 R. V. fashion anew the body of our humiliation, that it may be conformed to the body of his glory,

**1**
*a Love, of man for man,* 1 John 4:7.
*b Commandment, enjoining steadfastness,* Deut. 8:2.
*c Steadfastness, enjoined,* 1 Cor. 15:58.
*d Perseverance, exhortation to,* Eph. 6:18.
1 R. V. *omits* dearly

**3**
*e Women, good,* Prov. 31:10.
*f Gospel,* Mark 13:10.
*g Book, figurative,* Num. 5:23.

**4**
*h Commandment, enjoining joyfulness,* Deut. 8:2.
*i Christian Graces, joyfulness,* Gal. 5:22.

**5**
*j Commandment, enjoining discreet conduct,* Deut. 8:2.
*k Patience,* Luke 8:15.
2 R. V. forbearance

**6**
*l Commandment, forbidding anxiety, and enjoining prayer,* Deut. 8:2.
*m Borrowing Trouble,* Matt. 6:25.
*n Anxiety,* 1 Pet. 5:7.

—*a Appetite,* Prov. 23:2. *b Worldliness,* 1 John 2:15. 8 R. V. perdition, whose god is the belly, **20** *c Heaven, future home of the righteous,* Luke 18:22. 9 R. V. citizenship is

*o Prayer, enjoined,* Acts 6:4. *p Thankfulness, to God,* Acts 24:3. 3 R. V. In nothing be anxious; **7** *q Promise, to the righteous,* 2 Cor. 1:20. *r Spiritual Peace,* Gal. 1:3. *s Spiritual Blessings, from God,* Eph. 1:3. *t Heart,* Psa. 44:21. 4 R. V. guard your hearts and your thoughts in Christ Jesus.

* **CALL. Personal,** Matt. 22:3, 8, 9, 14; 20:16; Gal. 5:13; Acts 2:39; Phil. 3:14; Luke 5:27; 9:59.
*From God,* Isa. 45:22; Rom. 8:30; 1 Cor. 1:9, 24; 7:22; Gal. 1:6, 15; 1 Thess. 2:11, 12; 4:7; 2 Thess. 2:13, 14; 2 Tim. 1:9; Heb. 3:1, 7, 8. *From the Spirit and the bride,* Rev. 22:17.
*Through prophets,* Jer. 35:15.
*To repentance,* Isa. 55:1. *To eternal life,* 1 Tim. 6:12. *To eternal glory,* 1 Pet. 5:10.
*Rejected,* Jer. 6:16; Matt. 22:3–7.
Consequences of rejecting: *Forfeiture of gospel privileges,* Acts 13:46; 18:6; *moral insensibility,* Isa. 6:9, 10; Acts 28:24–27; *destruction,* Prov. 1:24–32.

**To special religious duty:** *Abraham,* Gen. 12:1–3; Isa. 51:2; Heb. 11:8. *Moses,* Ex. 3:2, 4, 10; 4:1–16; Psa. 105:26; Acts 7:34, 35. *Aaron and his sons,* Ex. 4:14–16; 28:1; Psa. 105:26; Heb. 5:4. *Joshua,* Num. 27:18, 19, 22, 23; Deut. 31:14, 23; Josh. 1:1–9. *Gideon,* Judg. 6:11–16. *Solomon,* 1 Chr. 28:6, 10. *Jehu,* 2 Kin. 9:6, 7. *Cyrus,* Isa. 45:1–4. *Amos,* Amos 7:14, 15. *Apostles,* Matt. 4:18–22; 9:9; Mark 1:16, 17; 2:14; 3:13–19; Luke 5:27; 6:13–16; John 15:16. *The rich young ruler,* Mark 10:21, 22. *Matthias,* Acts 1:24–26. *Paul,* Acts 9:4–6, 15, 16; 13:2, 3; Rom. 1:1; 1 Cor. 1:1; 2 Cor. 1:1; Gal. 1:1, 15, 16; Eph. 1:1; Col. 1:1; 1 Tim 1:1; 2 Tim. 1:1.

8 Finally, brethren, whatsoever things are [u]true, whatsoever things *are* [5]honest, whatsoever things *are* just, whatsoever
things *are* [v]pure, whatsoever
things *are* lovely, whatsoever
things *are* of good report; if
*there be* any virtue, and if *there*
*be* any praise, [w]think on these
things.
9 Those things, which ye have
both learned, and received, and
heard, and seen [x]in me, do: and
[q]the God of [r]peace shall be with
you.
10 But I rejoiced in the Lord
greatly, that now at the last your
[y,z]care of me hath flourished
again; wherein ye were also careful, but ye lacked opportunity.
11 Not that I speak in respect
of want: for I have learned, in
whatsoever state I am, [6]*there-*
*with* to be [a,b]content.
12 [a,b]I know both how to be
[c]abased, and I know how to
abound: [7]every where and in all
things I am instructed both to be
full and to be [d]hungry, both to
abound and to suffer need.
13 [e]I can do all things [8]through
Chrīst which [f]strengtheneth me.
14 Notwithstanding ye have
well done, that ye [9]did [g]com-
municate with my affliction.
15 Now ye [h]Phĭ-lĭp'pĭ-anṣ know
also, that in the beginning of the
gospel, when I departed from
[i]Măç-e-dō'nĭ-ȧ, no church [9]com-
municated with me as concerning giving and receiving, but ye
only.
16 For even in *Thĕs-sa-lō-nī'-
cȧ ye [j,k]sent once and again unto
my necessity.
17 [l]Not because I desire a gift:
but I desire fruit that may
abound to your account.
18 But I have all, and abound:
I am full, having received of
[m]Ē-păph-ro-dī'tus the [j]things
*which were* [k]*sent* from you, an
odour of a sweet smell, a sacrifice acceptable, wellpleasing to
God.
19 But [n]my God shall [o]supply
all your need according to his
riches in [p]glory by Chrīst Jē'ṣus.
20 Now unto God and our [q]Fa-
ther *be* [r]glory for ever and ever.
Amen.
21 [s]Salute every saint in Chrīst
Jē'ṣus. The brethren which are
with me greet you.
22 All the [t]saints [s]salute you,
chiefly they that are of Çæ'ṣar's
household.
23 [u]The grace of our [v]Lord
Jē'ṣus Chrīst *be* with [10]you all.
Amen.

[11]It was written to the Philippians from Rome by Epaphroditus.

**8**
u *Truth*, John 18:37.
v *Purity of Heart*, 1 Tim. 4:12.
w *Commandment, enjoining purity of thoughts*, Deut. 8:2.
5 R. V. honourable.
**9**
x *Example, Paul our*, John 13:15.
**10**
y *Liberality*, 1 Tim. 6:18.
z *Minister, emoluments of*, Rom. 15:16.
**11**
a *Contentment*, 1 Tim. 6:6.
b *Righteousness, fruits of*, Psa. 15:2.
6 R. V. therein
**12**
c *Humility*, Prov. 22:4.
d *Hunger*, Neh. 9:15.
7 R. V. in everything and in all things have I learned the secret both to be filled and to be hungry, both to abound and to be in want.
**13**
e *Faith in Christ*, John 6:69.
f *Spiritual Blessings*, Eph. 1:3.
8 R. V. in him that strengtheneth me.
**14**
g *Sympathy*, Jas. 1:27.
9 R. V. had fellowship with
**15**
h *Philippi*, Acts 20:6.
i *Macedonia*, Acts 16:12.
**16**
j *Minister, emoluments of*, Rom. 15:16.
k *Liberality*, 1 Tim. 6:18.
**17**
l *Unselfishness*, 1 Cor. 10:24.
**18**
m Phil. 2:25–30.
**19**
n *Righteous, promises to*, Psa. 64:10.
o *Temporal Blessings, from God*, Psa. 103:2.
p *God, glory of*, Gen. 2:2.
**20**
q *God, fatherhood of*, Gen. 2:2.
r *Praise*, Psa. 150:1.
**21**
s *Salutations*, Luke 1:44.
**22**
t *Rome, Christians in*, Acts 19:21.
**23**
u *Benedictions, apostolic*, Deut. 21:5.
v *Jesus, lordship of*, Matt. 1:21.
10 R. V. your spirit.
11 R. V. *omits postscript.*

---

THE EPISTLE OF PAUL TO THE

# COLOSSIANS

## CHAPTER 1

*The apostle's salutation.* 3 *His thanksgiving to God for the fruits of the gospel among them,* 9 *and prayer for their increase in grace.* 12 *He praises the Father for his mercy to them through Christ,* 15 *who is the image of the invisible God.* 21 *Their reconciliation.* 24 *The apostle's ministry.*

[a]PAUL, an apostle of Jē'ṣus
[b]Chrīst by the [c,d]will of God,
and [e]Tī-mō'the-ŭs our brother,
2 To the saints and [f]faithful
brethren in Chrīst which are
at Cō-lŏs'sē: [g,h]Grace *be* unto
you, and [i]peace, from God our
[j]Father [1]and the [k]Lord Jē'ṣus
Chrīst.
3 We give [l]thanks to God and

**1**
a *Paul*, Acts 13:9.
b *Jesus, Messiah*, Matt. 1:21.
c *Call, personal*, Phil. 3:14.
d *Minister, call of*, Rom. 15:16.
e Or, *Timothy*, 1 Cor. 4:17.
**2**
f *Righteous, described*, Psa. 64:10.
g *Grace of God*, Rom. 4:16.
h *Benedictions, apostolic*, Deut. 21:5.
i *Spiritual Peace*, Gal. 1:3. j *God, fatherhood of*, Gen. 2:2. k *Jesus, lordship of*, Matt. 1:21. 1 R. V. *omits* and the Lord Jesus Christ. **3** l *Thankfulness, to God*, Acts 24:3.

---

* **THESSALONICA**, a city of Macedonia. *Paul visits, where for three weeks he reasoned from the Scriptures that Jesus is the Christ.* Acts 17:1; *and is supported in, by the Philippians,* Phil. 4:16. *People of, persecute Paul*, Acts 17:5,11,13. *Men of, accompany Paul*, Acts 20:4; 27:2. *Paul writes to Christians in*, 1 Thess. 1:1; 2 Thess. 1:1. *Demas goes to*, 2 Tim. 4:10.

*m Prayer, intercessory,* Acts 6:4.
*n Love, of man for man,* 1 John 4:7.

**4**
*o Faith in Christ,* John 6:69.

**5**
*p Hope, of eternal life,* Prov. 13:12.
*q Immortality,* 1 Cor. 15:54.
*r Heaven, future home of the righteous,* Luke 18:22.
*s Doctrines of Jesus,* John 7:16.
*t Truth, of the gospel,* John 18:37.
*u Gospel,* Mark 13:10.
2 R. V. the heavens,

**6**
*v Righteousness, fruits of,* Psa. 15:2.
3 R. V. even as it is also in all the world bearing fruit and increasing, as it doth

**7**
*w* Col. 4:12; Philemon 23.
*x Minister, faithful,* Rom. 15:16.
4 R. V. a faithful minister of Christ on our behalf,

**8**
*y Love,* 1 John 4:7.
*z Holy Spirit,* Acts 1:2.

**9**
*a Prayerfulness,* 1 Tim. 5:5.
*b Prayer, intercessory,* Acts 6:4.
*c Righteous, described,* Psa. 64:10.
*d Wisdom, spiritual,* Prov. 2:2.
*e Spiritual Understanding,* Luke 8:8.

**10**
*f Jesus, lordship of,* Matt. 1:21.
*g Works, good,* 2 Tim. 1:9.
*h Growth in Grace,* 2 Pet. 3:18.

**11**
*i Spiritual Blessings, from God,* Eph. 1:3.
*j God, power of,* Gen. 2:2.
*k Patience,* Luke 8:15.
*l Christian Graces,* Gal. 5:22.

the [j]Father of our [k]Lord Jē′ṣus
[b]Chrīst, [m]praying always [n]for
you,
4 Since we heard of your [o]faith
in [b]Chrīst Jē′ṣus, and of the
[n]love *which ye have* to all the
saints,
5 For the [p,q]hope which is laid
up for you in [2,r]heaven, whereof
ye heard before in the [s]word of
the [t]truth of the [u]gospel;
6 Which is come unto you, [3]as
*it is* in all the world; and bringeth forth [v]fruit, as *it doth* also in
you, since the day ye heard *of it,*
and knew the [g]grace of God in
truth:
7 As ye also learned of [w]Ĕp′a-phrăs our dear fellowservant,
who is [4]for you a [x]faithful minister of Chrīst;
8 Who also declared unto us
your [y]love in the [z]Spirit.
9 For this cause we also, since
the day we heard *it,* [a]do not
cease to [b]pray for you, and to desire that ye might be [c]filled with
the knowledge of his will in all
[d]wisdom and [e]spiritual understanding;
10 That ye might walk worthy
of the [f]Lord unto all pleasing,
being [c]fruitful in every [g]good
work, and [c,h]increasing in the
[d]knowledge of God;
11 [c,i]Strengthened with all
might, according to his glorious
[j]power, unto all [k,l]patience and
[l,m]longsuffering with [l,n]joyfulness;
12 [o]Giving thanks unto the
[p]Father, which hath made us
[c]meet to be partakers of the [q]inheritance of the saints in [r]light:
13 Who hath delivered us from
the [s]power of [t]darkness, and
hath translated *us* into the [u]kingdom of [5]his dear [v]Son:
14 In whom we have [6,w,x]redemption through his blood,
*even* the [y]forgiveness of sins:
15 Who is the [z,a,b]image of the
[c]invisible God, the [d]firstborn of
[7]every creature:
16 For by [e]him were all things
created, that are in [2]heaven, and
that are in earth, visible and invisible, whether *they be* thrones,
or dominions, or [f]principalities,
or [f]powers: all things were created by him, and for him:
17 And he is [g]before all things,
and [h]by him all things consist.
18 And he is the [i]head of the
body, the [j]church: who is the beginning, the [k]firstborn from the
dead; that in all *things* he might
have the [l]preeminence.
19 For it pleased *the* [m]*Father*
that in him should [n]all fulness
dwell;
20 And, [o]having made [p]peace
through the [q,r,s]blood of his
cross, by him to [t]reconcile all
things unto himself; by him, *I
say,* whether *they be* things in
earth, or things in [2]heaven.
21 And you, that[8] were sometime [u]alienated and enemies in
*your* mind by wicked works, yet
now hath he [t]reconciled
22 In the body of his flesh
through [s]death, [v]to present you
[w,x,y]holy and [9]unblameable and
unreproveable in his sight:
23 If ye [z,a]continue in the [b]faith
[c]grounded and settled, and *be*
not moved away from the [d]hope
of the [e]gospel, which ye have
heard, *and* which was [f]preached
to every creature which is under heaven; whereof I [g]Pạul am
[h]made a minister;
24 Who now rejoice in my [i]suf-

**14**
*w Redemption of our Souls,* Eph. 1:7.
*x Jesus, design of his death,* Matt. 1:21.
*y Sin, forgiveness of,* Rom. 5:12.
6 R. V. our redemption, the forgiveness of our sins:

**15**
*z Image, figurative,* 1 Cor. 11:7.
*a Jesus, perfections of,* Matt. 1:21.
*b Jesus, relation of, to the Father,* Matt. 1:21.
*c God, invisible,* Gen. 2:2.
*d Firstborn, figurative,* Zech. 12:10.
7 R. V. all creation;

**16**
*e Jesus, creator,* Matt. 1:21.
*f Angel,* Heb. 1:13.

**17**
*g Jesus, pre-existence of,* Matt. 1:21.
*h Jesus, power of,* Matt. 1:21.

**18**
*i Jesus, head of the church,* Matt. 1:21.
*j Church, Christ head of,* Matt. 16:18.
*k Resurrection, of Jesus,* 1 Cor. 15:12.
*l Jesus, exaltation of,* Matt. 1:21.

**19**
*m God, fatherhood of,* Gen. 2:2.
*n Jesus, perfections of,* Matt. 1:21.

**20**
*o Salvation, plan of,* Acts 16:17.
*p Spiritual Peace,* Gal. 1:3.
*q Blood, of Christ,* Heb. 9:19.
*r Jesus, atoning blood of,* Matt. 1:21.
*s Atonement, by Jesus,* Lev. 17:11.

*m Longsuffering,* 2 Cor. 6:6. *n Joy,* Psa. 5:11. **12** *o Thankfulness, to God, enjoined,* Acts 24:3. *p God, fatherhood of,* Gen. 2:2. *q Inheritance, figurative,* Num. 27:7. *r Light, figurative,* Matt. 5:14. **13** *s Satan,* Matt. 4:10. *t Darkness, figurative,* Gen. 1:2. *u Kingdom of Heaven,* Matt. 13:24. *v Jesus, king,* Matt. 1:21. 5 R. V. the Son of his love;

*t Reconciliation, between God and man,* 2 Cor. 5:18. **21** *u Wicked, described,* Psa. 73:3. 8 R. V. being in time past **22** *v Jesus, design of his death,* Matt. 1:21. *w Perfection,* Heb. 6:1. *x Holiness,* Ex. 39:30. *y Righteous, described,* Psa. 64:10. 9 R.V. without blemish and **23** *z Steadfastness,* 1 Cor. 15:58.—*a Perseverance,* Eph. 6:18. *b Faith, the doctrines of Jesus,* 1 Cor. 16:13. *c Character, stability of* Phil. 2:15. *d Hope,* Prov. 13:12. *e Gospel,* Mark 13:10. *f Preaching,* Matt. 9:35. *g Paul,* Acts 13:9. *h Minister, call of,* Rom. 15:16. **24** *i Vicarious Sufferings,* Rom. 9:3.

[j] *Church*, Matt. 16:18.

25
[k] *Call, to special religious duty*, Phil. 3:14.

26
[l] *Mysteries, of redemption*, Mark 4:11.
[m] *Salvation, plan of*, Acts 16:17.

27
[n] *Gentiles*, Acts 10:45.
[o] *Righteous, union of, with Christ*, Psa. 64:10.

28
[p] *Minister, duties of*, Rom. 15:16.
[q] *Zeal*, 2 Cor. 7:11.
[r] *Instruction, in religion*, Prov. 23:23.
[s] *Perfection*, Heb. 6:1.
10 R. V. *omits* Jesus:

ferings for you, and fill up that
which is behind of the afflictions
of Christ in my flesh for his
body's sake, which is the [j]church:
25 Whereof [g]I am made a minister, according to the [k]dispensa-
tion of God which is given to me
for you, to fulfil the [e]word of
God;
26 *Even* the [l,m]mystery which
hath been hid from ages and
from generations, but now is
made manifest to his saints:
27 To whom God would make
known what *is* the riches of the
glory of this [l,m]mystery among
the [n]Gĕn'tīleṣ; which is Chrīst in
[o]you, the [d]hope of glory:
28 Whom we [f]preach, [p,q]warn-
ing every man, and [p,r]teaching
every man in all wisdom; that
we may present every man [s]per-
fect in Chrīst[10] Jē'ṣus:
29 Whereunto [q]I also labour,
striving according to his working, which worketh in me mightily.

## CHAPTER 2

*The apostle's solicitude for them.* 5 *He exhorts them to constancy in Christ,* 8 *to beware of philosophy and vain deceit,* 16 *and not to submit to legal ordinances,* 20 *which are ended in Christ.*

1
[a] *Zeal*, 2 Cor. 7:11.
[b] *Love, of man for man*, 1 John 4:7.

2
[c] *Fellowship, of the righteous*, 1 Cor. 1:9.
[d] *Love*, 1 John 4:7.
[e] *Wisdom, spiritual*, Prov. 2:2.
[f] *Mysteries, of redemption*, Mark 4:11.
[g] *Salvation, plan of*, Acts 16:17.
[h] *Jesus, Messiah*, Matt. 1:21.
1 R. V. that they may know the mystery of God, even Christ,

3
[i] *Jesus, perfections of*, Matt. 1:21.

FOR I would that ye knew
what [a]great conflict I have
[b]for you, and *for* them at *Lā-
ŏd-ĭ-çē'ȧ, and *for* as many as
have not seen my face in the
flesh;
2 That their hearts might be
comforted, being knit [c]together
in [d]love, and unto all riches of
the full assurance of [e]under-
standing, [1]to the acknowledge-
ment of the [f,g]mystery of God,
and of the Father, and of
[h]Christ;
3 In [i]whom are hid all the
[j]treasures of [k]wisdom and [l]knowl-
edge.
4 And this I say, [2]lest any
[m]man should beguile you with
enticing words.
5 For though I be absent in the
flesh, yet am I [b]with you in the
spirit, joying and beholding your
order, and the [n]stedfastness of
your [o]faith in Chrīst.
6 As ye have therefore received
[p,q]Chrīst Jē'ṣus the [r]Lord, *so*
[s,t]walk [u]ye in him:
7 [o,v]Rooted and built up in him,
and stablished in the faith, as ye
have been [p]taught, abounding
therein with [w]thanksgiving.
8 [x,y]Beware lest any [m]man spoil
you through [†,z]philosophy and
vain deceit, after the [a]tradition
of men, after the rudiments of
the world, and not after [b]Chrīst.
9 For in him dwelleth [c]all the
fulness of the Godhead [d]bodily.
10 And ye are complete in him,
which is the [e]head of all principality and power:
11 In whom also ye are [f]cir-
cumcised with the circumcision
made without hands, in putting
off the body of [3]the sins of the
flesh by the circumcision of
Chrīst:
12 [g]Buried with him in [h]bap-
tism, wherein also ye are [i]risen
with *him* through the [j]faith of
the [k]operation of God, who hath
[l]raised him from the dead.
13 And you, being [m]dead [4]in
your [n]sins and the uncircumcision of your flesh, hath he [f]quick-

[j] *Treasure, figurative*, Luke 12:33.
[k] *Jesus, wisdom of*, Matt. 1:21.
[l] *Jesus, omniscience of*, Matt. 1:21.

4
[m] *False Teachers*, 2 Pet. 2:1.
2 R. V. that no one may delude you with persuasiveness of speech.

5
[n] *Steadfastness*, 1 Cor. 15:58.
[o] *Faith in Christ*, John 6:69.

6
[p] *Instruction, in religion*, Prov. 23:23.
[q] *Doctrines of Jesus*, John 7:16.
[r] *Jesus, lordship of*, Matt. 1:21.
[s] *Commandment, enjoining obedience*, Deut. 8:2.
[t] *Perseverance*, Eph. 6:18.
[u] *Righteous, union of, with Christ*, Psa. 64:10.

7
[v] *Righteous, described*, Psa. 64:10.
[w] *Thankfulness, to God*, Acts 24:3.

8
[x] *Commandment, warning against false teachers*, Deut. 8:2.
[y] *Watchfulness, enjoined*, Matt. 24:42.
[z] *Wisdom, worldly*, Prov. 2:2.
[a] *Tradition*, Matt. 15:2.
[b] *Doctrines of Jesus*, John 7:16.

9
[c] *Jesus, perfections of*, Matt. 1:21.
[d] *Jesus, incarnation of*, Matt. 1:21.

**10** [e] *Jesus, lordship of*, Matt. 1:21. **11** [f] *Regeneration*, Tit. 3:5.
3 R. V. *omits* the sins of
**12** [g] *Burial, figurative*, Acts 8:2. [h] *Baptism, Christian*, Luke 20:4. [i] *Resurrection, figurative of regeneration*, 1 Cor. 15:12. [j] *Faith*, Mark 11:22. [k] *God, power of*, Gen. 2:2. [l] *Resurrection, of Jesus*, 1 Cor. 15:12.
**13** [m] *Spiritual Death*, 1 John 3:14. [n] *Sin, transgression of the law*, Rom. 5:12. 4 R. V. through your trespasses and the uncircumcision of your flesh, you, I say, did he quicken together with him, having forgiven us all our trespasses;

* **LAODICEA,** a city of Phrygia. **Church in:** *Paul's concern for*, Col. 2:1. *Epaphras' zeal for*, Col. 4:13. *Epistle to the Colossians to be read in*, Col. 4:15, 16. *Message to, through John*, Rev. 1:11; 3:14–22.

† **PHILOSOPHY.** *Concerning the nature of things*, Eccl. chapters 1–7. *A philosophical disquisition on wisdom*, Job 28. *Philosophical deductions relating to God and his providence*, Job 5:8–20; 9; 10:2–22; 12:6–25; 33:12–30; 37. *Reveals the mysteries of providence*, Prov. 25:2; Rom. 1:19, 20. *Is not sufficient for an adequate knowledge of God*, 1 Cor. 1:21, 22; *nor of God's wisdom in redemption*, 1 Cor. 2:6–10. *Employment of, was not Paul's method of preaching the gospel*, 1 Cor. 1:17, 19, 21; 2:1–5, 13. *Greek schools of*, Acts 17:18. *Admonitions against current sophistries*, Col. 2:8; 1 Tim. 6:20.
See footnote, REASONING, Job 13:6.

ened together with him, having
[o]forgiven you all trespasses;
14 [5,p]Blotting out the handwriting of [‡,q,r]ordinances that
was against us, which was contrary to us, and took it out of the
way, nailing it to his [s]cross;
15 [6]*And* having spoiled principalities and powers, he made a
shew of them openly, triumphing
over them in it.
16 Let no man therefore judge
you in meat, or in drink, or in
respect of [7]an holyday, or of the
[t]new moon, or of the sabbath
*days*:
17 [u]Which are a shadow of
things to come; but the body *is*
[8]of Christ.
18 [v]Let no man beguile you of
your reward in a voluntary [w]hu-
mility and worshipping of [x,y]an-
gels, [9]intruding into those things
which he hath not seen, vainly
puffed up by his fleshly mind,
19 And not holding [10]the [z]Head,
from which all the [a,b]body by
joints and bands having nourish-
ment ministered, and [c]knit together, [d]increaseth with the increase of God.
20 Wherefore if ye be [e]dead
with Christ from the rudiments
of the world, [f]why, as though living in the world, are ye subject
to [‡,g]ordinances,
21 (Touch not; taste not; handle not;
22 Which all are to perish with
the using;) after the [h]command-
ments and doctrines of men?
23 Which [g]things have indeed a
shew of wisdom in will worship,
and humility, and [‖,11]neglecting
of the body; not in any honour
to the satisfying of the [i]flesh.

o *Sin, forgiveness of*, Rom. 5:12.

**14**

p *Jesus, design of his death*, Matt. 1:21.
q *Works under the Law*. Lev. 18:5.
r *Law, of Moses, temporary*, Deut. 33:2.
s *Cross*, John 19:17.
5 R. V. Having blotted out the bond written in ordinances

**15**

6 R. V. Having put off from himself the principalities and the powers,

**16**

t *New Moon, feast of*, Amos 8:5.
7 R. V. a feast day,

**17**

u *Types, of the Savior*, Heb. 10:1.
8 R. V. Christ's.

**18**

v *Worship, to be rendered to God only*, Gen. 22:5.
w *Humility, feigned, forbidden*, Prov. 22:4.
x *Idolatry, objects of*, 1 Sam. 15:23.
y *Angel, not to be worshiped*, Heb. 1:13.
9 R. V. dwelling in the things which he hath seen,

**19**

z *Jesus, head of the church*, Matt. 1:21.

a *Church, Christ the head of*, Matt. 16:18.
b *Righteous, union of, with Christ*, Psa. 64:10.
c *Church, unity of*, Matt. 16:18.
d *Growth in Grace*, 2 Pet. 3:18.
10 R. V. fast the Head, from whom all the body, being supplied and knit together through the joints and bands, increaseth

**20** e *Death, figurative*, Num. 23:10. f *Reproof, faithfulness in*, Prov. 17:10. g *Works, insufficient for salvation*, 2 Tim. 1:9.
**22** h *Commandments of Men*, Mark 7:7. **23** i *Carnal Mind*, 1 Cor. 3:3. 11 R. V. severity to the body; but are not of any value against the indulgence of the flesh.

## CHAPTER 3

*They are exhorted to set their affection on things above, 5 to mortify their carnal desires, 9 to speak the truth, 12 to be kind and humble, 16 and to let the word of Christ dwell in them richly. 18 Sundry relative duties enjoined. 24 The reward of the inheritance.*

IF ye then be [a,b]risen with
Christ, [c,d]seek those things
which are above, where Christ sitteth [e,f]on the right hand of God.
2 Set your [1,g]affection on things
[h]above, [i]not on things on the
earth.
3 For ye [2]are [j]dead, and your
[b,k]life is hid [l]with Christ in God.
4 When Christ, *who is* our life,
shall [m]appear, then [n]shall ye also
appear with him in glory.
5 [o,p,q,r]Mortify therefore your
members which are upon the
earth; [s]fornication, uncleanness,
[3,t]inordinate affection, evil [u]con-
cupiscence, and [v]covetousness,
which is [w]idolatry:
6 For which things' sake the
[x,y]wrath of God cometh on the
[z]children of [a]disobedience:
7 In the which ye also walked
[4]some time, when ye lived in them.
8 But now ye also [b]put off all
these; [c]anger, wrath, [d]malice,
[5,e]blasphemy, filthy [f]communi-
cation out of your mouth.
9 [g,h]Lie not one to another, seeing that ye have [i]put off the [j]old
man with his deeds;
10 And have put on the [i]new *man*,
which is [6]renewed in [k]knowledge
after the [l]image of him that created him:
11 Where there [7]is [m,n]neither
Greek nor Jew, [o]circumcision

**1**

a *Resurrection, figurative of regeneration*, 1 Cor. 15:12.
b *Life, spiritual*, Eccl. 8:15.
c *Commandment, enjoining righteousness*, Deut. 8:2.
d *Spiritual Desire*, Psa. 42:1.
e *Jesus, exaltation of*, Matt. 1:21.
f *Sovereignty of the Messiah*, Psa. 110:1.

**2**

g *Affections, to be set upon heavenly things*, 2 Cor. 7:15.
h *Heaven, God's dwelling place*, Luke 18:22.
i *Worldliness, admonitions against*, 1 John 2:15.
1 R. V. mind

**3**

j *Death, figurative*, Num. 23:10.
k *Regeneration*, Tit. 3:5.
l *Fellowship, with Christ*, 1 Cor. 1:9.
2 R. V. died,

**4**

m *Jesus, second coming of*, Matt. 1:21.
n *Righteous, promises to*, Psa. 64:10.

**5**

o *Commandment, enjoining holiness*, Deut. 8:2.
p *Chastity, enjoined*, Job 31:1.
q *Self-denial*, Mark 8:34.
r *Holiness, enjoined*, Ex. 39:30.
s *Adultery, forbidden*, Lev. 20:10.
t *Lust, forbidden*, 2 Pet. 1:4.
u *Lasciviousness*, 1 Pet. 4:3.
v *Covetousness*, Isa. 57:17.
w *Idolatry*, 1 Sam. 15:23.
3 R. V. passion, evil desire, and

**6** x *Anger of God*, 2 Kin. 13:3. y *Wicked, punishment of*, Psa. 73:3. z *Wicked, described*, Psa. 73:3.—a *Disobedience to God*, Eph. 5:6. **7** 4 R. V. aforetime, **8** b *Commandment, enjoining holiness*, Deut. 8:2. c *Anger, forbidden*, Psa. 37:8. d *Malice, forbidden*, Eph. 4:31. e *Railing, forbidden*, Jude 9. f *Conversation, corrupt, forbidden*, Psa. 50:23. 5 R. V. railing, **9** g *Commandment, forbidding falsehood*, Deut. 8:2. h *Falsehood, forbidden*, Job 21:34. i *Regeneration*, Tit. 3:5. j *Sin, the inherited tendencies to evil*, Rom. 5:12. **10** k *Wisdom, spiritual*, Prov. 2:2. l *Image, figurative*, 1 Cor. 11:7. 6 R. V. being renewed unto knowledge.
**11** m *Catholicity*, Eph. 2:14. n *Church, unity of*, Matt. 16:18. o *Circumcision, figurative*, Gen. 17:10. 7 R. V. cannot be

‡ **ORDINANCE,** Ex. 12:24, 43; 13:10; Num. 9:14. *Insufficiency of, for salvation*, Isa. 1:10–17; Gal. 5:6; 6:15; Eph. 2:15; Col. 2:14, 20–23; Heb. 9:1, 8–10.

‖ **ASCETICISM,** a philosophy that leads to severe austerities in subordinating the body to the control of the moral attributes of the mind. *Extreme application of, repudiated, by Jesus*, Matt. 11:19; Luke 7:34; *by Paul*, Col. 2:20–23; 1 Tim. 4:1–4.

p *Barbarian*, Rom. 1:14.
q *Jesus, head of the church*, Matt. 1:21.
r *Righteous, union of, with Christ*, Psa. 64:10.
**12**
s *Commandment, enjoining Christian graces*, vs. 12–17; Deut. 8:2.
t *Election of Grace*, Rom. 11:5.
u *Righteous, described*, Psa. 64:10.
v *Mercy, enjoined*, Deut. 5:10.
w *Christian Graces*, Gal. 5:22.
x *Righteousness, fruits of*, Psa. 15:2.
y *Kindness, enjoined*, Acts 28:2.
z *Humility*, Prov. 22:4.

a *Meekness, enjoined*, Psa. 45:4.
b *Longsuffering*, 2 Cor. 6:6.
8 R. V. a heart of compassion,
**13**
c *Charitableness, enjoined*, Prov. 10:12.
d *Duty, of man to man*, Eccl. 12:13.
e *Commandment, enjoining forgiveness*, Deut. 8:2.
f *Forgiveness, enjoined*, Matt. 18:21.
g *Example, Christ our, in forgiving*, John 13:15.
h *Jesus, power of, to forgive sins*, Matt. 1:21.
9 R. V. complaint against any; even as the Lord
**14**
i *Commandment, enjoining Christian graces*, Deut. 8:2.

nor uncircumcision, [p]Bär-bā′rĭ-
an,[G] Scўth′ĭ-an, bond *nor* free:
but [m,q]Chrīst *is* all, and [r]in all.
12 [s]Put on therefore, as the
[t,u]elect[G] of God, [+,u]holy and beloved, [8]bowels[G] of [v,w,x]mercies,
[w,x,y]kindness, [w,x,z]humbleness
of mind, [w,x,a]meekness, [b]long-
suffering;[S]
13 [c,d]Forbearing one another,
and [d,e,f]forgiving one another, if
any man have a [9]quarrel[G] against
any: even [g]as Chrīst [h]forgave
you, so also *do* ye.[T]
14 And above all these things
[i]*put on* [10,j]charity,[G] which is the
bond of [k]perfectness.[S]
15 And [i]let the [l]peace of [11]God
rule in your hearts, to the which
also ye are called in [m]one body;
and [n]be ye [o]thankful.
16 Let the [p]word of Chrīst
dwell in you richly in all [q]wis-
dom; [r]teaching and admonishing[G] one another in psalms and
hymns and spiritual [s,t]songs,
[u]singing with grace in your
hearts [12]to the Lord.
17 And whatsoever ye do in word
or deed, *do* all in the [v]name of
the [w]Lord Jē′sus, [o,x]giving thanks
to God and the [y]Father [z]by him.
18 [a]Wives, [b,c]submit yourselves
unto your own husbands, as it is
fit in the Lord.[Q]
19 Husbands, [d,e]love *your* wives,
and be not bitter against them.
20 Children, [f,g]obey *your* [h]par-
ents in all things: for this is well
pleasing unto the [i]Lord.
21 Fathers, [j,k]provoke not your
children [13]*to anger*, lest they be
discouraged.
22 [l]Servants, [m]obey in all things
*your* masters according to the
flesh; [n,o]not with eyeservice, as
menpleasers; but in [p]singleness[G]
of heart, [q]fearing God:
23 And whatsoever [l]ye do, do *it*
[n,p]heartily, [r]as to the [i]Lord, and
not unto men;
24 Knowing that of the [i]Lord
ye shall receive the [s]reward of
the [t]inheritance: for ye serve the
Lord Chrīst.
25 But he that doeth wrong
[u,v]shall [w]receive for the wrong
which he hath done: and [x]there
is no [y]respect of persons.[S Q]

## CHAPTER 4

*The duty of masters. 2 An exhortation to continue in prayer, 5 and to walk wisely toward them that are without. 7 Tychicus and Onesimus commended. 10 Sundry salutations.*

*MASTERS, [a,b]give unto *your*
[c,d]servants [e]that which
is just and equal; knowing
that ye also have a Master in
[f]heaven.[Q]
2 [g,h]Continue [1]in prayer, and
[g,i]watch in the same with
[j]thanksgiving;
3 Withal[G] [k,l]praying also for us,
that [m]God would open unto us a
door [2]of utterance, to [n]speak the

**20**
f *Commandment, to children*, Deut. 8:2.
g *Children, commandments to*, Mark 10:14.
h *Parents, to be obeyed*, 2 Cor. 12:14.
i *Jesus, lordship of*, Matt. 1:21.
**21**
j *Commandment, to fathers*, Deut. 8:2.
k *Parents, duty of, to govern with kindness*, 2 Cor. 12:14.
13 R. V. that they be not discouraged.
**22**
l *Servant, duty of*, Jer. 2:14.
m *Commandment, to servants*, vs. 22–25; Deut. 8:2.
n *Faithfulness*, Luke 16:10.
o *Honesty, enjoined*, Rom. 13:13.
p *Sincerity, enjoined*, 1 Cor. 5:8.
q *Fear of God, enjoined*, Acts 9:31.
**23**
r *Motive, right, required*, Psa. 106:8.
**24**
s *Reward, a motive, to faithfulness*, Matt. 5:12.
t *Inheritance, figurative*, Num. 27:7.
**25**
u *Punishment, no escape from*, Lev. 26:41.
v *Wicked, punishment of*, Psa. 73:3.
w *Judgment, according to opportunity and works*, 1 Pet. 1:17.
x *God, impartial*, Gen. 2:2.
y *Respect of Persons*, Prov. 24:23.

j *Love, of man for man*, 1 John 4:7. k *Perfection*, Heb. 6:1. 10 R. V. love, **15** l *Peace*, Jer. 29:7. m *Church, unity of*, Matt. 16:18. n *Commandment, enjoining thankfulness*, Deut. 8:2. o *Thankfulness, to God*, Acts 24:3. 11 R. V. Christ **16** p *Doctrines of Jesus*, John 7:16. q *Wisdom, spiritual*, Prov. 2:2. r *Instruction, in religion*, Prov. 23:23. s *Song*, Psa. 77:6. t *Music*, 2 Chr. 5:13. u *Worship*, Gen. 22:5. 12 R. V. unto God.
**17** v *Name of Jesus*, John 14:13. w *Jesus, lordship of*, Matt. 1:21. x *Commandment, enjoining thanksgiving*, Deut. 8:2. y *God, fatherhood of*, Gen. 2:2. z *Jesus, mediation of*, Matt. 1:21. **18**—a *Wife, duty of*, Prov. 5:18. b *Commandment, to wives*, Deut. 8:2. c *Family, government of*, 1 Chr. 13:14. **19** d *Commandment, to husbands*, Deut. 8:2. e *Husband, duties of*, Num. 30:6.

**1** a *Employer, required to accord just compensation*, Deut. 24:14. b *Commandment, to masters*, Deut. 8:2. c *Servant*, Jer. 2:14. d *Employee, rights of*, Deut. 24:14. e *Wages*, Gen. 31:7. f *Heaven, God's dwelling place*, Luke 18:22. **2** g *Commandment, enjoining watchfulness and prayer*, Deut. 8:2. h *Prayerfulness, enjoined*, 1 Tim. 5:5. i *Watchfulness*, Matt. 24:42. j *Thankfulness, to God*, Acts 24:3.

**3** k *Prayer, intercessory, solicited*, Acts 6:4. l *Minister, duty of the church to*, Rom. 15:16. m *God, providence of*, Gen. 2:2. n *Preaching*, Matt. 9:35.

+ **THE HOLY**, Deut. 14:2; 26:19. *Described as, peculiar people*, Deut. 7:6; 14:2; 26:18; *perfect*, Deut. 18:13; 2 Tim. 3:17; *guileless*, Psa. 32:2; John 1:47; Rev. 14:5; *blameless and harmless*, Phil. 2:15; *unblameable and unreproveable*, Col. 1:22; 1 Thess. 3:13; *sinless*, 1 John 3:6–9; 5:18; *in Christ*, Rom. 8:1; *walking after the Spirit*, Rom. 8:4; Gal. 5:25.

* **MASTER OF SERVANTS.** *Violent, to be punished*, Ex. 21:20, 21, 26, 27.

**Duties of, to servants:** *Must allow Sabbath rest*, Deut. 5:14. *Must compensate*, Jer. 22:13; Rom. 4:4; Col. 4:1; 1 Tim. 5:18. *Must pay promptly*, Lev. 19:13; Deut. 24:15; Jas. 5:4. *Forbidden, to oppress*, Lev. 25:43; Deut. 24:14; Job 31:13, 14; Prov. 22:16; Mal. 3:5; *to threaten*, Eph. 6:9.

*Exhorted to show kindness*, Philemon 10–16.

**Good:** Instances of: *Abraham*, Gen. 18:19. *Job*, Job 31:13–15. *The centurion*, Luke 7:2.

**Unjust:** Instances of: *Sarah to Hagar*, Gen. 16:6. *Laban to Jacob*, Gen. 31:7. *Potiphar's wife to Joseph*, Gen. 39:7–20.

See footnotes: EMPLOYER, Deut. 24:14; EMPLOYEE, Deut. 24:14; HIRED SERVANT, Lev. 25:40; SERVANT, Jer. 2:14.

o *Mysteries, of redemption,* Mark 4:11.
p *Gospel,* Mark 13:10.
q *Love, for Jesus,* 1 John 4:19.
r *Suffering for Christ,* Phil. 1:29.
s *Paul,* Acts 13:9.

**4**
*Zeal,* 2 Cor. 7:11.

**5**
u *Commandment, enjoining prudence,* Deut. 8:2.
v *Tact,* Prov. 15:1.
w *Prudence,* 2 Chr. 2:12.
x *Diligence, enjoined,* Rom. 12:8.

**6**
y *Commandment, enjoining wisdom in speech,* Deut. 8:2.
z *Conversation, edifying, enjoined,* Psa. 50:23.

a *Salt, figurative,* 2 Kin. 2:20.

**7**
b *Tychicus,* Acts 20:4.
c *Love, of man for man,* 1 John 4:7.
d *Brother,* Prov. 18:24.
e *Minister, faithful,* Rom. 15:16.
f *Jesus, lordship of,* Matt. 1:21.
3 R. V. affairs

**8**
g *Minister, duties of,* Rom. 15:16.

[o,p]mystery of Chrĭst, [q,r]for which
[s]I am also in bonds:[S]
4 That [s,t]I may make it manifest, as I ought to speak.
5 [u]Walk in [v,w]wisdom toward
them that are without,[C] [t,x]redeeming the time.
6 [y]Let your [†,z]speech *be* alway
with grace, seasoned with [a]salt,
that ye may know how ye ought
to answer every man.
7 All my [3]state[C] shall [b]Tȳch′ĭ-
cŭs declare unto you, *who is* a
[c]beloved [d]brother, and a [e]faithful minister and fellowservant in
the [f]Lord:
8 [b]Whom I have sent unto you
for the same purpose, [g]that he
might know your estate,[C] and
comfort your hearts;
9 With [h]Ō-nĕs′ĭ-mŭs, a [e]faithful
and [c]beloved brother, who is *one*
of you. They shall make known
unto you all things which *are
done* here.
10 [i]Ăr-ĭs-tär′chus my fellow-
[j]prisoner [k]saluteth[C] you, and
[4,l]Mär′cus, sister's son to [m]Bär′-
na-băs, (touching[C] whom ye received commandments: if he
come unto you, [n]receive him;)
11 And Jē′sus, which is called
Jŭs′tus, who are of the [o]circumcision. These only *are my* fellow-
workers unto the kingdom of
God, which have been a [c,p]comfort unto me.
12 [q]Ĕp′a-phrăs, who is *one* of
you, a servant of [5]Chrĭst, [k]saluteth[C] you, [c,r]always labouring
fervently for you in [s]prayers,
that ye may stand [t]perfect and
[6]complete[C] in all the [u]will of God.
13 For I bear[C] him record, that
he hath [7]a great [r]zeal for you,
and them *that are* in [v]Lā-ŏd-ĭ-
çē′ȧ, and them in Hĭ-e-răp′o-lĭs.
14 [‡]Luke, the [c]beloved [w]physician, and [x]Dē′mas, greet you.
15 [k]Salute[C] the brethren which
are in [v]Lā-ŏd-ĭ-çē′ȧ, and Nȳm′-
phas, and the [y]church which is
in his [z]house.
16 And when this [a]epistle is
read among you, cause that it be
read also in the church of the
Lā-ŏd-ĭ-çē′ans; and that ye likewise read the *epistle* from Lā-ŏd-
ĭ-çē′ȧ.
17 And say to [b]Är-chĭp′pus,
[c]Take[C] heed to the [d]ministry
which thou hast received in the
Lord, that thou fulfil[C] it.
18 The [e]salutation by the hand
of me [f]Paul. Remember my
bonds. [g]Grace *be* with you.
Amen.

[8]Written from Rome to the Colossians by Tychicus and Onesimus.

**9** h Philemon 10. **10** i Acts 19:29; 20:4; 27:2. j *Persecution, of the righteous,* John 15:20. k *Salutations,* Luke 1:44. l Or, *Mark,* Acts 12:12. m *Barnabas,* Acts 4:36. n *Minister, duty of the church to,* Rom. 15:16. 4 R. V. Mark, the cousin of Barnabas **11** o *Circumcision, figurative,* Gen. 17:10.

p *Friendship,* Prov. 22:24.

**12**
q Col. 1:7; Philemon 23.
r *Zeal,* 2 Cor. 7:11.
s *Prayer, intercessory,* Acts 6:4.
t *Perfection,* Heb. 6:1.
u *Will of God,* Mark 3:35.
5 R. V. Christ Jesus,
6 R. V. fully assured in

**13**
v *Laodicea,* Col. 2:1.
7 R. V. much labour

**14**
w *Physician,* 2 Chr. 16:12.
x 2 Tim. 4:10; Philemon 24.

**15**
y *Church,* Matt. 16:18.
z *Worship, in private homes,* Gen. 22:5.

**16**
a *Letters,* Isa. 37:14.

**17**
b Philemon 2.
c *Watchfulness, enjoined,* Matt. 24:42.
d *Minister, mission of,* Rom. 15:16.

**18**
e *Salutations,* Luke 1:44.
f *Paul,* Acts 13:9.
g *Benedictions, apostolic,* Deut. 21:5.
8 R. V. *omits postscript.*

† **SPEECH.** **Wise,** Psa. 37:30; 50:23; Prov. 10:11, 13, 31, 32; 15:1, 2, 4, 7, 23; 25:11; Eccl. 9:17; 10:12; Col. 4:6. *Edifying,* Eph. 4:29. *As goads and nails,* Eccl. 12:11. *Precious as jewels,* Prov. 20:15.
*Of the ideal woman,* Prov. 31:26.
*Rewards of,* Prov. 14:3; 22:11.

**Foolish,** Job 38:2; Prov. 10:14; 12:23; 13:3; 14:3; 15:2, 7, 14; 18:6, 7; 26:4, 7, 9; 29:11, 20; Eccl. 5:3; 10:13, 14; Matt. 12:36, 37; Eph. 5:4.

**Evil,** Psa. 10:7; 52:2–4; 59:12; 64:2–5; Prov. 10:11, 19, 31, 32; 12:6, 13, 17–19; 15:4, 28; 17:4, 20; 18:21; 19:1, 28; 26:20–23, 28; Eccl. 7:22; 10:11; Isa. 6:5; Rom. 3:13, 14; 1 Tim. 5:13; Jas. 3:5, 6, 8–10; 2 Pet. 2:7, 8, 10; Jude 8, 10.
*Causes strife,* Prov. 15:1; 16:27, 28; 17:9; 25:23. *Excludes from kingdom of heaven,* 1 Cor. 6:10.
*Forbidden,* Psa. 34:13; Prov. 4:24; Matt. 5:22, 37; Acts 23:5; Eph. 4:25, 29, 31; Tit. 3:2; Jas. 1:26; 3:5, 6, 8–10; 4:11; 1 Pet. 2:1; 3:9, 10. *Hated of God,* Prov. 6:16–19; 8:13.

‡ **LUKE,** a disciple. *A physician,* Col. 4:14. *Writes to Theophilus,* Luke 1:1–4; Acts 1:1, 2. *Accompanies Paul, in his tour of Asia and Macedonia,* Acts 16:10–17; 20:5, 6; *to Jerusalem,* Acts 21:1–18; *to Rome,* Acts 27; 28; 2 Tim. 4:11; Philemon 24.

## THE FIRST EPISTLE OF PAUL TO THE

# THESSALONIANS

## CHAPTER 1

*The salutation. 2 The apostle's thanksgiving and prayer to God in their behalf. 5 The manner in which the gospel came to them. 7 The influence of their example in spreading the gospel.*

[a]PAUL, and [b]Sĭl-vā'nus, and
[c]Tĭ-mō'the-ŭs, unto the
[d]church of the [e]Thĕs-sa-lō'nĭ-ans *which is* in God the [f]Father
and *in* the [g]Lord Jē'sus Chrīst:
[h,i]Grace *be* unto you, and [j]peace,
[1]from God our Father, and the
Lord Jē'sus Chrīst.
2 [k,l]We give [m]thanks to God always for you all, [n]making mention of you in our prayers;
3 [T][k]Remembering without ceasing your [o,p]work of [q]faith, and
[o]labour of [r]love, and [s]patience
of [t]hope in our [g]Lord Jē'sus
Chrīst, in the sight of God and
our [f]Father;
4 Knowing, brethren [u]beloved,
[2]your [v]election[G] of God.[S]
5 For [w]our [x]gospel came not
unto you in word only, but also
in [y]power, and in the [z]Holy[G]
Ghost,[G] and in much assurance;
as ye know what manner of men
we were among you for your
sake.[S T]
6 And [w]ye became [3]followers
of [a,b]us, and of the [c]Lord, having [d]received the [e]word in much
[f]affliction, with joy of the [g]Holy
Ghost:[T]
7 So that ye were [a,b]ensamples[G]
to all that [d]believe in [h]Măç-e-dō'nĭ-à and [i]Å-chā'ià.
8 For from you sounded out the
[e]word of the Lord not only in
[h]Măç-e-dō'nĭ-à and [i]Å-chā'ià,
but also in every place your
[j]faith to God-ward[G] is spread
abroad; so that we need not to
speak any thing.
9 For they themselves shew[G] of
us [k]what manner of entering in
we had unto you, and how ye
turned to God from [l]idols to
serve the living and true God;
10 And to wait for his [m,n]Son
from heaven, whom he [o]raised
from the dead, *even* Jē'sus, which
[p,q]delivered us from the [r,s]wrath[G]
to come.[S T]

## CHAPTER 2

*The manner in which the gospel was first preached to them. 7 How the apostle had behaved himself among them. 13 Their reception of the gospel, and suffering for its sake. 17 His desire to see them, and the reason of his absence.*

FOR yourselves, brethren,
know [a]our entrance in unto
you, that it was not in vain:[G]
2 But even after that we
had [b]suffered before, and were
[c]shamefully entreated,[G] as ye
know, at [d]Phĭ-lĭp'pī, [e]we were
[f,g]bold in our God to [h]speak unto you the [i]gospel of God with
much contention.
3 For our exhortation *was*[j,k]not
of [1]deceit, nor of uncleanness,
nor in guile:
4 But as [l]we [2]were allowed[G] of
God to be [m]put in trust with the
[i]gospel, even so we speak; [n]not
as pleasing men, but God, which
trieth[G] our hearts.[S Q]
5 For neither at any time used
we flattering words, as ye know,
nor a cloke[G] of [o]covetousness;[G]
God *is* witness:

**1**
a *Paul,* Acts 13:9.
b Or, *Silas,* Acts 15:22.
c Or, *Timothy,* 1 Cor. 4:17.
d *Church,* Matt. 16:18.
e *Thessalonica,* Phil. 4:16.
f *God, fatherhood of,* Gen. 2:2.
g *Jesus, lordship of,* Matt. 1:21.
h *Benedictions, apostolic,* Deut. 21:5.
i *Grace of God,* Rom. 4:16.
j *Spiritual Peace,* Gal. 1:3.
1 R. V. *omits the rest of this verse.*

**2**
k *Minister, love of, for the church,* Rom. 15:16.
l *Zeal,* 2 Cor. 7:11.
m *Thankfulness, to God,* Acts 24:3.
n *Prayer, intercessory,* Acts 6:4.

**3**
o *Works, good,* 2 Tim. 1:9.
p *Righteousness, fruits of,* Psa. 15:2.
q *Faith in Christ,* John 6:69.
r *Love,* 1 John 4:7.
s *Patience, a grace of the righteous,* Luke 8:15.
t *Hope,* Prov. 13:12.

**4**
u *Love, of man for man,* 1 John 4:7.
v *Election of Grace,* Rom. 11:5.
2 R. V. of God, your election,

**5**
w *Minister, success attending,* Rom. 15:16.
x *Gospel,* Mark 13:10.
y *Spiritual Power,* Luke 24:49. z *Holy Spirit,* Acts 1:2.

**6**—a *Example, good,* John 13:15. b *Influence, good.* 1 Cor. 7:14. c *Jesus, our example,* Matt. 1:21. d *Faith in Christ,* John 6:69. e *Doctrines of Jesus,* John 7:16. f *Persecution, of the righteous,* John 15:20. g *Holy Spirit, joy in,* Acts 1:2. 3 R. V. imitators

**7** h *Macedonia,* Acts 16:12. i *Achaia,* Acts 18:12.

**8**
j *Faith,* Mark 11:22.

**9**
k *Minister, success attending,* Rom. 15 16.
l *Idolatry,* 1 Sam. 15:23.

**10**
m *Jesus, divine sonship of,* Matt. 1:21.
n *Jesus, second coming of,* Matt. 1:21.
o *Resurrection, of Jesus,* 1 Cor. 15:12.
p *Jesus, savior,* Matt. 1:21.
q *Jesus, design of his death,* Matt. 1:21.
r *Anger of God,* 2 Kin. 13:3.
s *Wicked, punishment of,* Psa. 73:3.

**1**
a *Minister, success attending,* Rom. 15:16.

**2**
b *Suffering for Christ,* Phil. 1:29.
c *Persecution, of the righteous,* John 15:20.
d *Philippi,* Acts 20:6.
e *Minister, faithful,* Rom. 15:16.
f *Zeal,* 2 Cor. 7:11.
g *Courage,* Deut. 31:7.
h *Preaching,* Matt. 9:35.
i *Gospel,* Mark 13:10.

**3**
j *Minister, character and qualifications of,* Rom. 15:16.
k *Sincerity,* 1 Cor. 5:8.
1 R. V. error,

**4**
l *Agency, in salvation of men,* Mark 1:17.
m *Minister, mission of,* Rom. 15:16. n *Minister, faithful,* Rom. 15:16. 2 R. V. have been approved of God to be intrusted

**5** o *Selfishness,* 2 Tim. 3.2.

**6**
*p Minister, emoluments of*, Rom. 15:16.
*q Apostles*, Luke 6:13.

**7**
*r Gentleness, of Paul*, 2 Cor. 10:1.
*s Minister, love of, for the church*, Rom. 15:16.
*t Love, of man for man*, 1 John 4:7.

**9**
*u Industry*, 1 Kin. 11:28.
*v Minister, zealous*, Rom. 15:16.
*w Self-denial*, Mark 8:34.
*x Unselfishness*, 1 Cor. 10:24.

**10**
*y Holiness*, Ex. 39:30.
*z Faith in Christ*, John 6:69.

**11**
*a Minister, faithful*, Rom. 15:16.
*b Minister, duties of*, Rom. 15:16.
*c Parents, duty of*, 2 Cor. 12:14.
3 R. V. dealt with each one of you, as a father with his own children, exhorting you, and encouraging you, and testifying,

**12**
*d Holiness, exhortation to*, Ex. 39:30.
*e Call, personal*, Phil. 3:14.
*f Kingdom of Heaven*, Matt. 13:24.

**13**
*g Thankfulness, to God*, Acts 24:3.
*h Gospel*, Mark 13:10.
*i Faith in Christ*, John 6:69.
4 R. V. from us the word of the message, even the word of God, ye accepted it

**14**
*j Righteous, union of, with Christ*, Psa. 64:10.
*k Suffering for Christ*, Phil. 1:29.
*l Persecution, of the righteous*, John 15:20.
*m Jews*, Neh. 4:2.
5 R. V. imitators

6 Nor of men sought we glory,[C] neither of you, nor *yet* of others, when we might have been [p]burdensome, as the [q]apostles of Christ.

7 But we were [r,s,t]gentle among you, even as a nurse cherisheth her children:

8 So being [s,t]affectionately desirous of you, [j]we were willing to have imparted unto you, not the [i]gospel of God only, but also our own souls, because [s,t]ye were dear unto us.

9 For ye remember, brethren, [j]our labour and travail:[C] for [u,v]labouring night and day, because we [w,x]would not be chargeable[C] unto any of you, we [h]preached unto you the [i]gospel of God.

10 Ye *are* witnesses, and God *also*, [j]how [y]holily and justly and unblameably we behaved ourselves among you that [z]believe:

11 As ye know how [a,b]we [3]exhorted[C] and [b]comforted[C] and charged[C] every one of you, [c]as a father *doth* his children,

12 That ye would walk [d]worthy of God, who hath [e]called you unto his [f]kingdom and glory.[S]

13 For this cause also [g]thank we God without ceasing, because, when ye received [4]the [h]word of God which ye heard of us, ye received *it* not *as* the word of men, but as it is in truth, the word of God, which effectually worketh also in you that [i]believe.[T]

14 For ye, brethren, became [5]followers of the churches of God which in Jū-dæ'ȧ are [j]in Christ Jē'ṣus: for ye also have [k,l]suffered like things of your own countrymen, even as they *have* of the [m]Jews:

15 [n]Who both [o]killed the [p]Lord Jē'ṣus, and their own [q]prophets, and [6]have [l,r]persecuted us; and they please not God, and are contrary to all men:

16 Forbidding us to speak to the [s]Gĕn'tīleṣ that they might be [t]saved, to fill up their sins alway: for the [u,v]wrath is come upon [w]them to the uttermost.[T Q]

17 But we, brethren, being taken from you for a short time in presence, [x]not in heart, endeavoured the more abundantly to see your face with great desire.

18 Wherefore we would have come unto you, even I [y]Paul, once and again; but [z]Sā'tan hindered us.

19 For [x]what *is* our hope, or joy, or crown of [7]rejoicing? [x]*Are* not even ye [8]in the presence of our [a]Lord Jē'ṣus Christ at his [b]coming?

20 For ye are our glory and joy.

## CHAPTER 3

*Why the apostle had sent Timothy to them. 6 The comfort he took in his report concerning them. 10 His desire to see them, 12 and that they may abound in love one toward another.*

WHEREFORE when we could no longer forbear,[C] we thought it good to be left at [a]Ăth'ĕnṣ alone;

2 And sent [b]Tĭ-mō'the-ŭs, our [c]brother, and [1]minister of God, and our fellowlabourer in the [d]gospel of Christ, to [e]establish you, and to [e]comfort you concerning your [f]faith:

3 That [g]no man should be moved by these afflictions: for yourselves know that we are appointed thereunto.

4 For verily, when we were with you, we told you before that we should [h]suffer tribulation;[G] even as it came to pass, and ye know.

5 For this cause, [i]when I could no longer forbear, I sent to know[C] your [f,j]faith, lest by some means the [k,l]tempter have tempted you, and our labour be in vain.

6 But now when [b]Tĭ-mō'the-ŭs

**15** *n Bigotry*, Isa. 65:5. *o Jesus, death of*, Matt. 1:21. *p Jesus, lordship of*, Matt. 1:21. *q Prophets, martyrs*, Isa. 3:2. *r Minister, trials and persecutions of*, Rom. 15:16. 6 R. V. drave out us,

**16**
*s Gentiles*, Acts 10:45.
*t Salvation*, Acts 16:17.
*u Anger of God*, 2 Kin. 13:3.
*v Judgments*, Ex. 6:6.
*w Reprobates*, 1 Cor. 9:27.

**17**
*x Minister, love of, for the church*, Rom. 15:16.

**18**
*y Paul*, Acts 13:9.
*z Satan*, Matt. 4:10.

**19**
*a Jesus, lordship of*, Matt. 1:21.
*b Jesus, second coming of*, Matt. 1:21.
7 R. V. glorying?
8 R. V. before our Lord Jesus at his coming?

**1**
*a* Acts 17:15–34.

**2**
*b* Or, *Timothy*, 1 Cor. 4:17.
*c Brother*, Prov. 18:24.
*d Gospel*, Mark 13:10.
*e Minister, duties of*, Rom. 15:16.
*f Faith in Christ*, John 6:69.
1 R. V. God's minister in the gospel of Christ,

**3**
*g Afflictions, resignation in*, Psa. 34:19.

**4**
*h Suffering for Christ*, Phil. 1:29.

**5**
*i Minister, love of, for the church*, Rom. 15:16.
*j Steadfastness*, 1 Cor. 15:58.
*k Satan*, Matt. 4:10.
*l Temptation, sources of*, Luke 11:4.

**6**
*m Love, of man for man,* 1 John 4:7.
2 R. V. love,

**7**
*n Afflictions, consolation in,* Psa. 34:19.

**8**
*o Perseverance, exhortation to,* Eph. 6:18.
*p Righteous, union of, with Christ,* Psa. 64:10.
*q Jesus, lordship of,* Matt. 1:21.

**9**
*r Thankfulness, to God,* Acts 24:3.
*s Minister, joys of,* Rom. 15:16.

**10**
*t Prayerfulness, exemplified in Paul,* 1 Tim. 5:5.

**11**
*u God, fatherhood of,* Gen. 2:2.
*v God, providence of,* Gen. 2:2.
*w Temporal Blessings, prayer for,* Psa. 103:2.
3 R. V. *omits* Christ,

**12**
*x Prayer, intercessory,* Acts 6:4.
*y Growth in Grace,* 2 Pet. 3:18.
*z Spiritual Blessings,* Eph. 1:3.
*a Love, of man for man,* 1 John 4:7.

**13**
*b Righteous, described,* Psa. 64:10.
*c Holiness,* Ex. 39:30.
*d God, fatherhood of,* Gen. 2:2.
*e Jesus, second coming of,* Matt. 1:21.
*f Jesus, lordship of,* Matt. 1:21.
4 R. V. *omits* Christ

**1**
*a Minister, love of, for the church,* Rom. 15:16.
*b Jesus, lordship of,* Matt. 1:21.
*c Faithfulness,* Luke 16:10.
1 R. V. even as ye do walk,—that ye abound more and more.

**2**
*d Apostles, authority of,* Luke 6:13.
2 R. V. charge

**3**
*e Will of God,* Mark 3:35.

came from you unto us, and brought us good tidings of your [f,j]faith and [2,m]charity,[C] and that ye have good remembrance of us always, [m]desiring greatly to see us, as we also *to see* you:

7 Therefore, brethren, we were [n]comforted over you in all our affliction[C] and distress by your [f,j]faith:

8 For now we live, if ye [j,o]stand fast[C] [p]in the [q]Lord.

9 For what [r]thanks can we render to God again for you, for all the [s]joy wherewith we joy for your sakes before our God;

10 [t]Night and day praying exceedingly that we might see your face, and might perfect that which is lacking in your [f]faith?

11 Now God himself and our [u]Father, and our [q]Lord Jē′ṣus [3]Christ, [v,w]direct our way unto you.

12 And [x]the Lord make you to [y,z]increase and abound[C] in [a]love one toward another, and toward all *men*, even as we *do* toward you:

13 To the end he may stablish[C] your hearts [b]unblameable in [c]holiness before God, even our [d]Father, at the [e]coming of our [f]Lord Jē′ṣus [4]Christ with all his saints.[Q]

## CHAPTER 4

*They are exhorted to increase in godliness, 3 to abstain from fornication and fraud, 9 to love one another, 11 and quietly to follow their own business. 13 He comforts them in relation to those who had fallen asleep in Jesus. 16 The Lord's second coming.*

FURTHERMORE then [a]we beseech you, brethren, and exhort *you* by the [b]Lord Jē′ṣus, that as ye have received of us how ye ought to walk and to please God, [1]*so* ye would [c]abound more and more.

2 For ye know what [2]commandments [d]we gave you by the [b]Lord Jē′ṣus.

3[S] For this is the [e]will of God, *even* your [f,g]sanctification,[C] [h]that ye should [i]abstain from [j]fornication:[T]

4 That every one of you should know how to possess[C] [3]his vessel in [f,i]sanctification and honour;[S]

5 [k]Not in the [4]lust of concupiscence,[C] even as the [l]Ġĕn′tīleṣ[C] which [m]know not God:[Q]

6 That no *man* [5]go[C] beyond and [n]defraud his brother in *any* matter: [o]because that the Lord *is* the avenger of all such, as we also have forewarned you and testified.[C] [Q]

7 For God hath not [p]called us unto uncleanness, but unto [q]holiness.

8 He therefore that [6]despiseth,[C] [6]despiseth[C] not man, but God, who hath also given unto us his [q]holy Spirit.[Q]

9 But as touching [r,s]brotherly [t]love ye need not that I write unto you: for ye yourselves are [u]taught of God to [v]love one another.[Q]

10 And indeed ye [t]do it toward all the [r]brethren which are in all [w]Măç-e-dō′nĭ-ȧ: but we beseech you, brethren, that ye [x]increase more and more;

11 And [y]that ye [z]study to be quiet, and to do your own business, and to [a,b]work with your own hands, as we [7]commanded you;

12 That ye may [b,c]walk [d]honestly toward them that are without,[C] and *that* ye may have lack of nothing.

13 But I would not have you to be ignorant, brethren, concerning them which are [e,f]asleep,[C] that ye [g]sorrow not, even as others which have no hope.

14 For if we [h]believe that Jē′ṣus [i]died and [j]rose again, even so

*f Sanctification,* 1 Pet. 1:2.
*g Holiness, enjoined,* Ex. 39:30.
*h Commandment, enjoining holiness, and forbidding various vices,* vs. 4–6; Deut. 8:2.
*i Chastity, enjoined,* Job 31:1.
*j Adultery, forbidden,* Lev. 20:10.

**4**
3 R. V. himself of his own vessel

**5**
*k Lasciviousness, forbidden,* 1 Pet. 4:3.
*l Gentiles,* Acts 10:45.
*m Spiritual Blindness,* 2 Cor. 4:4.
4 R. V. passion of lust, even

**6**
*n Dishonesty, forbidden,* Ezek. 22:13.
*o Wicked, punishment of,* Psa. 73:3.
5 R. V. transgress, and wrong his brother in the matter: because the Lord is an avenger in all these things, as

**7**
*p Call, personal,* Phil. 3:14.

**8**
*q Holy Spirit, Christians filled with,* Acts 1:2.
6 R. V. rejecteth

**9**
*r Fraternity,* Zech. 11:14.
*s Church, fellowship in,* Matt. 16:18.
*t Love, of man for man,* 1 John 4:7.
*u God, teacher,* Gen. 2:2.
*v Commandment, enjoining love for man,* Deut. 8:2.

**10**
*w Macedonia,* Acts 16:12.
*x Growth in Grace,* 2 Pet. 3:18.

**11**
*y Evil, appearance of, to be avoided,* 1 Thess. 5:22.
*z Commandment, enjoining peaceableness and industry,* Deut. 8:2.

*a Industry, enjoined,* 1 Kin. 11:28. *b Example, good,* John 13:15. 7 R. V. charged **12** *c Commandment, enjoining honesty,* Deut. 8:2. *d Honesty, enjoined,* Rom. 13:13. **13** *e Sleep, symbol of death,* Psa. 127:2. *f Death, called sleep,* Num. 23:10. *g Bereavement, resignation in,* Hos. 9:12. **14** *h Faith in Christ,* John 6:69. *i Jesus, death of,* Matt. 1:21. *j Resurrection, of Jesus,* 1 Cor. 15:12.

*k Righteous, promises to,* Psa. 64:10.
*l Resurrection,* 1 Cor. 15:12.

**15**
*m Apostles, inspiration of,* Luke 6:13.
*n Jesus, second coming of,* Matt. 1:21.
8 R. V. in no wise precede

**16**
*o Jesus, lordship of,* Matt. 1:21.
*p Angel,* Heb. 1:13.
*q Trumpet, figurative,* Josh. 6:4.

**17**
*r Death, exemption from,* Num. 23:10.
*s Translation, of the saints, at the last day,* Heb. 11:5.
*t Heaven, future home of the righteous,* Luke 18:22.

**18**
*u Communion of Saints, enjoined,* 1 Cor. 10:16.

**1**
*a Seasons,* Dan. 2:21.
*b Paul,* Acts 13:9.

**2**
*c Judgment, the general,* 2 Pet. 3:7.
*d Jesus, lordship of,* Matt. 1:21.

**3**
*e False Confidence,* Psa. 30:6.
*f Delusion,* 2 Thess. 2:11.
*g Procrastination,* Acts 24:25.
*h Wicked, punishment of,* Psa. 73:3.
*i Punishment, no escape from,* Lev. 26:41.

**4**
*j Righteous, contrasted with the wicked,* Psa. 64:10.
*k Righteous, described,* Psa. 64:10.
*l Darkness, figurative,* Gen. 1:2.
*m Spiritual Blindness,* 2 Cor. 4:4.

[k]them also which [e,f]sleep[G] in Jē'-
ṣus will God [l]bring with him.
15 For this we say unto you
[m]by the word of the Lord, that
we which are alive *and* remain
unto the [n]coming of the Lord
shall [8]not prevent[G] them which
are asleep.
16 For the [o]Lord himself shall
[n]descend from heaven with a
shout, with the voice of the
[p]archangel, and with the [q]trump[G]
of God: and the dead in Christ
shall [l]rise first:
17 Then [k]we which are alive
*and* remain [r]shall be [s]caught up
together with them in the clouds,
to meet the [o]Lord in the air: and
so shall we ever be [t]with the
Lord.
18 Wherefore [u]comfort[G] one another with these words.

## CHAPTER 5

*The coming of the Lord.* 6 *They are exhorted to be sober and watchful,* 12 *to respect and love their spiritual teachers,* 14 *to warn the unruly, and to follow that which is good.* 16 *Sundry precepts.* 23 *The conclusion.*

BUT of the times and the [a]sea-
sons,[G] brethren, ye have no
need that [b]I write unto you.
2 For yourselves know perfectly
that the [c]day of the [d]Lord so
cometh as a thief in the night.
3 For when they shall [e,f,g]say,
Peace and safety; then sudden
[h]destruction cometh upon them,
as travail[G] upon a woman with
child; and they [i]shall not escape.
4 But [j]ye, brethren, are [k]not in
[l,m]darkness, that that day should
overtake you as a thief.
5 Ye are all the [k]children of
[n,o,p]light, and the children of the
day: [j]we are not of the [q]night,
nor of [l,m]darkness.
6 Therefore [r,s]let us not sleep,
as *do* others; but let us [t]watch
and be [u]sober.[G]
7 For they that [v]sleep sleep
in the night; and they that be
[w]drunken are drunken in the
night.
8 But let us, [k]who are of the
[x]day, [r]be sober, putting on the
[y]breastplate of [z]faith and [a]love;
and for an [b]helmet, the [c]hope of
[d]salvation.
9 For God hath not appointed
us to wrath,[G] but to obtain [d,e]sal-
vation [f,g]by our [h]Lord Jē'ṣus
Christ,
10 Who [i]died for us, that,
whether we wake or [j]sleep, [k,l]we
should [m]live together with him.
11 Wherefore [1,n]comfort[G] yourselves together, and edify[G] one
another, even as also ye do.
12 And we beseech you, brethren, to [o,p]know them which [q]la-
bour among you, and are [r]over
you in the Lord, and [q]admonish[G]
you;
13 And [p]to esteem[G] them very
highly in [s]love for their work's
sake. *And* [t]be at [u]peace among
yourselves.
14 Now we exhort you, brethren, [2,v,w]warn them that are unruly, [x]comfort[G] the feebleminded,[G]
support the weak, be [y,z]patient
toward all *men*.
15 [a]See that none [b,c]render
evil for evil unto any *man*; but
[a]ever follow that which is good,
both among yourselves, and to
all *men*.
16 [d,e]Rejoice evermore.
17 [f,g]Pray without ceasing.
18 In every thing [h,i]give thanks:
for this is the [j]will of God in
Christ Jē'ṣus concerning you.

**7**
*v Wicked, described,* Psa. 73:3.
*w Drunkenness,* Luke 21:34.

**8**
*x Day, figurative,* Gen. 1:5.
*y Coat of Mail, figurative,* 1 Sam. 17:5.
*z Faith in Christ,* John 6:69.

*a Love,* 1 John 4:7.
*b Helmet, figurative,* Jer. 46:4.
*c Hope,* Prov. 13:12.
*d Salvation,* Acts 16:17.

**9**
*e Jesus, savior,* Matt. 1:21.
*f Atonement, by Jesus,* Lev. 17:11.
*g Jesus, mediation of,* Matt. 1:21.
*h Jesus, lordship of,* Matt. 1:21.

**10**
*i Jesus, vicarious death of,* Matt. 1:21.
*j Death, called sleep,* Num. 23:10.
*k Promise, or Ground of Assurance,* 2 Cor. 1:20.
*l Jesus, design of his death,* Matt. 1:21.
*m Immortality,* 1 Cor. 15:54.

**11**
*n Fellowship, of the righteous,* 1 Cor. 1:9.
1 R. V. exhort one another, and build each other up, even as also ye do.

**12**
*o Church, duty of, to ministers,* Matt. 16:18.
*p Commandment, enjoining esteem for pastors,* Deut. 8:2.
*q Minister, duties of,* Rom. 15:16.
*r Minister, clothed with authority,* Rom. 15:16.

**5** *n Light, figurative,* Matt. 5:14. *o Holiness,* Ex. 39:30. *p Wisdom, spiritual,* Prov. 2:2. *q Night, figurative,* Gen. 1:5.
**6** *r Commandment, enjoining watchfulness, sobriety, and preparedness,* Deut. 8:2. *s Preparedness, enjoined,* Luke 12:40. *t Watchfulness,* Matt. 24:42. *u Temperance,* 2 Pet. 1:6.

**13** *s Love, of man for man,* 1 John 4:7. *t Commandment, enjoining social peace,* Deut. 8:2. *u Peace, enjoined,* Jer. 29:7.
**14** *v Commandment, enjoining admonition and encouragement,* Deut. 8:2. *w Reproof, enjoined,* Prov. 17:10. *x Weak, duty of strong to,* 1 Cor. 8:9. *y Patience, enjoined,* Luke 8:15. *z Christian Graces, patience,* Gal. 5:22. 2 R. V. admonish the disorderly, encourage the fainthearted, support the weak, be longsuffering toward all. **15** *a Commandment, forbidding retaliation, and enjoining kindness,* Deut. 8:2. *b Retaliation, malicious, forbidden,* Deut. 19:19. *c Revenge, forbidden,* Ezek. 25:15. **16** *d Commandment, enjoining joyfulness,* Deut. 8:2. *e Christian Graces, joyfulness,* Gal. 5:22. **17** *f Commandment, enjoining prayerfulness,* Deut. 8:2. *g Prayerfulness, enjoined,* 1 Tim. 5:5.
**18** *h Commandment, enjoining thanksgiving,* Deut. 8:2. *i Thankfulness, to God,* Acts 24:3. *j Will of God,* Mark 3:35.

19 [k]Quench not the [l]Spirit.[T]
20 [m]Despise not prophesyings.
21 Prove[C] all things; [n,o,p]hold
fast[C] that which is good.
22 [q]Abstain from [3]all appearance of [+]evil.[S Q]
23 [r]And the very God of [s]peace
[t,u]sanctify you wholly; and [4]*I*
*pray God* your whole [v]spirit and
soul and body be preserved
[w,x]blameless unto the [y]coming
of our [z]Lord Jē'ṣus Chrīst.[S T]
24 [a]Faithful *is* he that [b]calleth
you, who also will do *it*.
25 Brethren, [c,d]pray for us.
26 [e]Greet all the brethren with
an holy [f]kiss.
27 I [5]charge[C] you by the Lord
that this epistle be read unto all
the [6]holy brethren.
28 [g]The grace of our [h]Lord Jē'-
ṣus Chrīst *be* with you. Amen.

[7]The first *epistle* unto the Thessalonians was written from Athens.

**19** k *Commandment, against quenching the Spirit*, Deut. 8:2. l *Holy Spirit, sin against*, Acts 1:2.

**20** m *Commandment, enjoining respect for religious instruction*, Deut. 8:2.

**21** n *Commandment, enjoining steadfastness*, Deut. 8:2. o *Steadfastness, enjoined*, 1 Cor. 15:58. p *Perseverance, enjoined*, Eph. 6:18. **22** q *Commandment, enjoining abstinence from evil*, Deut. 8:2. 3 R. V. every form **23** r *Prayer, intercessory*, Acts 6:4. s *Spiritual Peace, from God*, Gal. 1:3. t *Sanctification*, 1 Pet. 1:2. u *Spiritual Blessings, from God*, Eph. 1:3. v *Man, a spirit*, Job 4:17. 4 R. V. may your spirit and soul and body be preserved entire, without blame at the coming

w *Holiness*, Ex. 39:30. x *Sinlessness*, 1 John 5:18. y *Jesus, second coming of*, Matt. 1:21. z *Jesus, lordship of*, Matt. 1:21.

**24** a *God, faithfulness of*, Gen. 2:2. b *Call, personal*, Phil. 3:14.

**25** c *Intercession, solicited*, Jer. 27:18. d *Minister, duty of church to*, Rom. 15:16.

**26** e *Salutations*, Luke 1:44. f *Kiss, holy*, Ruth 1:9. **27** 5 R.V. adjure 6 R. V. *omits* holy **28** g *Benedictions, apostolic*, Deut. 21:5. h *Jesus, lordship of*, Matt. 1:21. **7** R. V. *omits postscript.*

---

THE SECOND EPISTLE OF PAUL TO THE

# THESSALONIANS

## CHAPTER 1

*The salutation. 3 The apostle's thanksgiving to God for their faith, love, and patience in persecution. 6 He consoles them under trials in view of the judgment of God; 11 and prays that Christ may be glorified in them.*

[a]PAUL, and [b]Sĭl-vā'nus, and
[c]Tĭ-mō'the-ŭs, unto the
[d]church of the [e]Thĕs-sa-lō'nĭ-anṣ
in God our [f]Father and the
[g,h]Lord Jē'ṣus [i]Chrīst:
2 [j,k]Grace unto you, and [l]peace,
from God our [f]Father and the
[g]Lord Jē'ṣus Chrīst.
3 We are bound to [m]thank God
always for you, brethren, as it is
meet,[C] because that your [n,o]faith
[p]groweth exceedingly, and the
[1,o,q]charity[C] of every one of you
all toward each other aboundeth;[C]
4 So[S] that we ourselves [r]glory[C] in
you in the [d]churches of God for
your [s,t]patience and [u]faith in all
your [v]persecutions and tribulations[C] that ye endure:
5 *Which is* a manifest token[C] of
the righteous judgment of God,
that ye may be counted worthy
of the [w]kingdom of God, for
which ye also [x]suffer:
6 Seeing *it is* a righteous thing
with God to recompense[C] [y,z]trib-
ulation[C] to them that trouble you;[S]
7 And to you who are [a]troubled
[b]rest with us, when the [c]Lord
Jē'ṣus shall be [d]revealed from
[e]heaven with his mighty [f]angels,[Q]
8 In flaming fire taking [g]ven-
geance on them that [h,i]know not
God, and that [i]obey not the [j]gos-
pel of our [c]Lord Jē'ṣus [2]Chrīst:[Q]
9 Who shall be [k]punished with
[l]everlasting destruction [m]from
the presence of the Lord, and
from the glory of his [n]power;[Q]
10 When he shall [d]come to be
glorified in his saints, and to be
[3]admired in all them that [o]be-
lieve (because our *testimony

**1** a *Paul*, Acts 13:9. b Or, *Silas*, Acts 15:22. c Or, *Timothy*, 1 Cor. 4:17. d *Church*, Matt. 16:18. e *Thessalonica*, Phil. 4:16. f *God, fatherhood of*, Gen. 2:2. g *Jesus, lordship of*, Matt. 1:21. h *Jesus, divinity of*, Matt. 1:21. i *Jesus, Messiah*, Matt. 1:21.

**2** j *Grace of God*, Rom. 4:16. k *Benedictions, apostolic*, Deut. 21:5. l *Spiritual Peace*, Gal. 1:3.

**3** m *Thankfulness, to God*, Acts 24:3. n *Faith in Christ*, John 6:69. o *Righteousness, fruits of*, Psa. 15:2. p *Growth in Grace*, 2 Pet. 3:18. q *Love, of man for man*, 1 John 4:7. 1 R. V. love **4** r *Minister, love of, for the church*, Rom. 15:16. s *Patience*, Luke 8:15. t *Resignation*, Job 5:17. u *Faith, trial of*, Mark 11:22. v *Persecution, of the righteous*, John 15:20.

**5** w *Kingdom of Heaven*, Matt. 13:24. x *Suffering for Christ*, Phil. 1:29.

**6** y *Vengeance, belongs to God*, Psa. 94:1. z *Wicked, punishment of*, Psa. 73:3.

**7** a *Adversity, consolation in*, Psa. 10:6. b *Rest, heavenly*, Ex. 23:12. c *Jesus, lordship of*, Matt. 1:21. d *Jesus, second coming of*, Matt. 1:21. e *Heaven, God's dwelling place*, Luke 18:22. f *Angel*, Heb. 1:13.

**8** g *Vengeance, belongs to God*, Psa. 94:1. h *Spiritual Blindness*, 2 Cor. 4:4. i *Wicked, described*, Psa. 73:3. j *Gospel*, Mark 13:10. 2 R. V. *omits* Christ: **9** k *Wicked, punishment of*, Psa. 73:3. l *Punishment, eternal*, Lev. 26:41. m *Sin, separates from God*, Rom. 5:12. n *Jesus, power of*, Matt. 1:21.
**10** o *Faith in Christ*, John 6:69. 3 R. V. marvelled at in all

**+ EVIL.** *Tree of good and*, Gen. 2:9, 17. *Knowledge of*, Gen. 3:5, 22. *In the heart*, Gen. 6:5; 8:21; Luke 6:45. *To be abhorred*, Psa. 97:10; Amos 5:15; Rom. 12:9. *To be forsaken*, Psa. 34:14; 37:27; Prov. 3:7; 1 Pet. 3:11. *Not to be recompensed*, Rom. 12:17; 1 Thess. 5:15; 1 Pet. 3:9. *Appearance of, to be avoided*, Rom. 14:1-23; 1 Cor. 8:7-13; 10:28-33; 1 Thess. 4:11, 12; 5:22.

*** RELIGIOUS TESTIMONY.** Psa. 18:49; 22:22; 26:12; 34:8, 9; Isa. 45:24; 1 Cor. 13:1; Rev. 12:11. *Required of the righteous*, 1 Chr. 16:8, 9; Psa. 9:11; Isa. 12:

among you was believed) in that
day.[Q]
11 Wherefore also we [p]pray always for you, that our God would
count you worthy of [4]*this* calling,
and fulfil all the good pleasure
of *his* goodness, and the work of
faith with power:[S]
12 That the [q]name of our [c]Lord
Jē′sus [2]Christ may be glorified
in you, and ye in him, according
to the [r]grace of our God and the
Lord Jē′sus Christ.[Q]

## CHAPTER 2

*The coming of the Lord not immediately at hand. 3 A great apostasy to precede it. 15 They are exhorted to stand fast in the truth.*

NOW we beseech[C] you, brethren, by the [a]coming of our
[b]Lord Jē′sus Christ, and *by* our
gathering together unto him,
2 [c]That ye be not soon shaken
in mind, or be troubled, neither
by spirit, nor by word, nor by
letter as from us, as that the day
of [1]Christ is at hand.
3 [d]Let no [e]man deceive you by
any means: for [2]*that day shall*
*not come,* except there come a
[f]falling away first, and that [g]man
of sin be revealed, the son of perdition;[Q]
4 [g]Who opposeth and [h,i]exalteth
himself above all that is called
God, or that is worshipped; so
that he as God sitteth in the [j]tem-
ple of God, shewing himself that
he is God.[Q]
5 Remember ye not, that, when
I was yet with you, I told you
these things?
6 And now ye know [3]what
withholdeth[C] that he might be
revealed in his time.
7 For the mystery of [4]iniquity[C]
doth already work: only he who
now letteth[C] *will let,*[C] until he be
taken out of the way.
8 And then shall [5]that [e]Wicked
be revealed, whom the [b]Lord
shall [k]consume with the spirit of
his mouth, and shall destroy with
the brightness of his [a]coming:[TQ]
9 *Even* [g]*him,* whose coming is
after the working of [l]Sā′tan with
all power and signs and lying
wonders,
10 And with all [6,m]deceivable-
ness[C] of unrighteousness in them
that perish; because [n]they [o]re-
ceived not the love of the [p,q]truth,
that they might be [r]saved.
11 And for this cause God
[7]shall send them strong *,[s]delu-
sion, that they should believe a[C]
[t]lie:
12 That [u]they all might be
[8]damned[C] who [n]believed not the
[p,q]truth, but [n]had pleasure in
unrighteousness.[S]
13 But[T] [v]we are bound to give
[w]thanks alway to [x]God for you,
brethren [y]beloved of the [x,z]Lord,
because God hath from the beginning [a,b]chosen you to [c]salva-
tion[C] through [d]sanctification[C] of
the [x,e]Spirit and [f]belief of the
[g]truth:[S Q]
14 Whereunto he [b]called you by
[h]our gospel, to the obtaining of the
glory of our [i]Lord Jē′sus Christ.[T S]

**11**
*p* *Prayer, intercessory,* Acts 6:4.
4 R. V. your calling, and fulfil every desire of goodness and every work

**12**
*q* *Name of Jesus,* John 14:13.
*r* *Grace of God,* Rom. 4:16.

**1**
*a* *Jesus, second coming of,* Matt. 1:21.
*b* *Jesus, lordship of,* Matt. 1:21.

**2**
*c* *Backsliding, admonitions against,* Hos. 11:7.
1 Am. R. V. the Lord is just at hand;

**3**
*d* *Watchfulness, enjoined,* Matt. 24:42.
*e* *False Teachers,* 2 Pet. 2:1.
*f* *Apostasy, foretold,* Acts 1:25.
*g* *Antichrist,* 2 John 7.
2 R. V. it will not be, except the falling away come first,

**4**
*h* *Self-exaltation,* Luke 14:11.
*i* *Blasphemy, exalting oneself above God,* 2 Sam. 12:14.
*j* *Temple, figurative,* 1 Kin. 6:17.

**6**
3 R. V. that which restraineth, to the end that he may be revealed in his own season.

**7**
4 R. V. lawlessness doth already work: only there is one that restraineth now, until he be taken out of the way.

**8**
*k* *Jesus, power of,* Matt. 1:21.
5 R. V. be revealed the lawless one, whom the Lord Jesus shall slay with the breath of his mouth, and bring to nought by the manifestation of his coming;

**9**
*l* *Satan,* Matt. 4:10.

**10**
*m* *Deceit,* Psa. 36:3.
*n* *Wicked, described,* Psa. 73:3.
*o* *Jesus, rejected,* Matt. 1:21.
*p* *Truth,* John 18:37.
*q* *Gospel,* Mark 13:10.
*r* *Salvation,* Acts 16:17.
6 R. V. deceit of unrighteousness for them that are perishing;

**11**
*s* *Spiritual Blindness, manifested in unbelief,* 2 Cor. 4:4.
*t* *Heresy,* Tit. 3:10.
7 R. V. sendeth them a working of error,

**12**
*u* *Unbelievers,* 1 Cor. 6:6.
8 R. V. judged

**13**
*v* *Minister, love of, for the church,* Rom. 15:16.
*w* *Thankfulness, to God,* Acts 24:3.
*x* *Holy Trinity,* Luke 3:22.
*y* *Jesus, love of,* Matt. 1:21. *z* *Jesus, divinity of,* Matt. 1:21. —*a* *Foreordination,* Rom. 8:30. *b* *Call, personal,* Phil. 3:14. *c* *Salvation, plan of,* Acts 16:17. *d* *Sanctification,* 1 Pet. 1:2. *e* *Holy Spirit, sanctifies,* Acts 1:2. *f* *Faith,* Mark 11:22. *g* *Truth, of the gospel,* John 18:37. **14** *h* *Agency, in salvation of men,* Mark 1:17. *i* *Jesus, lordship of,* Matt. 1:21.

4–6; 43:10; 44:8; Jer. 51:10; Matt. 5:15, 16; Mark 4:21; 5:19, 20; Luke 8:16, 39; 24:48; John 15:27; Acts 1:8, 22; 3:15; 5:32; 13:31; Eph. 5:19; 1 Pet. 3:15.

*Concerning God's, faithfulness,* Psa. 89:1; *glory,* Psa. 145:11, 12; *merciful providences,* Psa. 40:1–3; 91:2–13; Dan. 4:2, 3; Acts 14:15–17; *righteousness,* Psa. 35:28; 71:16; *salvation,* Psa. 40:1–3; 66:16–20; 71:15, 18; Gal. 2:20; Phil. 3:4–14; Tit. 3:3–7; *words,* Psa. 119:172; *works,* Psa. 71:17, 24; 145:4–7, 10–12; Acts 2:11.

*Concerning confidence in God,* Psa. 16:5–9; 18:2, 3; 23:1–6; 26:6, 7; 27:1–6; 28:6–8. *Rewards of,* Matt. 10:32; Luke 12:8.

**Exemplified:** *By Job,* Job 19:25–27. *By the psalmist,* Psa. 35:28; 40:1–3, 9; 57:7–9; 116:1–19. *By Nebuchadnezzar,* Dan. 4:34–37. *By the woman of Sychar,* John 4:28–30, 39, 41, 42. *By the blind man whom Jesus healed,* John 9:17, 30–33. *By the apostles, to the resurrection of Jesus,* Acts 4:33; 1 John 1:1–4. *By the disciples at Pentecost,* Acts 2:4–11. *By Peter,* Acts 4:18–20; 2 Pet. 1:16. *By John,* Acts 4:18–20; 1 John 1:1–4. *By Paul concerning, his conversion,* Acts 22:1–16; 26:12–23; *his devotion to Christ,* Phil. 3:4–14; *his confidence in Christ,* 2 Cor. 4:13, 14; 5:1; 2 Tim. 1:12; *his hope of the crown of righteousness,* 2 Tim. 4:7, 8. *By Timothy,* 1 Tim. 6:12.

* **DELUSION,** Prov. 14:12; 30:12; Rev. 3:17. *Of idolaters,* Jer. 44:17. *Of the self-righteous,* Hos. 12:8; John 8:33, 41. *Of the ungodly rich,* Luke 12:17–19. *Of incorrigible sinners,* 2 Thess. 2:10, 11. *Of those who trust in the form of godliness,* Matt. 3:9; 7:21–23; Luke 13:25–27; 2 Tim. 3:5.

15 Therefore, brethren, [j,k,l]stand
[m]fast, and hold the [n]traditions
which ye have been [o]taught,
whether by word, or our epistle.
16 [p]Now our [i,q]Lord Jē'sus
Christ himself, and God, even
our [r]Father, which hath [s]loved
us, and hath given *us* everlasting
[i,u]consolation and good [v]hope
through grace,[S T]
17 [p]Comfort your hearts, and
[m]stablish[C] you in every good word
and [w]work.

## CHAPTER 3

*The apostle desires their prayers for himself. 3 His confidence in them. 6 He commands them to withdraw from every one that walks disorderly. 16 Prayer and salutation.*

FINALLY, brethren, [a,b]pray
for us, that the [c]word of the
Lord may [1]have *free* course, and
be glorified,[C] even as *it is* with you:
2 And[T] [b]that we may be delivered from unreasonable and
wicked men: for all *men* [d]have
not faith.
3 But [e]the Lord is [f]faithful,
[g]who shall stablish[C] you, and
keep *you* from [2]evil.[S T]
4 And we have confidence in
the Lord touching[C] you, that ye
both do and will do the things
which we [h]command you.
5 [i]And the Lord direct your
hearts into the [j]love of God, and
into the [3]patient waiting for
Christ.[T]
6 Now we [k]command you,
brethren, in the [l]name of our
[m]Lord Jē'sus Christ, that ye
[n,o,p]withdraw yourselves from
every brother that walketh disorderly,[C] and not after the [q]tradi-
tion which he received of us.
7 For yourselves know how ye
ought to [4,r,s]follow us: for we
behaved not ourselves disorderly[C]
among you;
8 Neither did[C] we eat any man's
bread for nought; but [t,u]wrought
with [v]labour and travail night
and day, [w]that we might not be
chargeable[C] to any of you:
9 Not because we have not
[5]power, but to make ourselves
an [r,s]ensample[C] unto you to
[4]follow us.
10 For even when we were with
you, this we [x,y]commanded you,
that if any would [z]not work, neither should he eat.
11 For we hear that there are
some which walk among you disorderly,[C] working [z]not at all, but
are *,[a]busybodies.
12 Now them that are such [b]we
command and exhort[C] by our
[c]Lord Jē'sus Christ, that [d]with
quietness they [e]work, and eat
their own bread.
13 But ye, brethren, [f,g,h]be not
weary in well doing.
14 And if any man obey not
our word by this epistle, note
that man, and [i,j]have no company with him, that he may be
ashamed.
15 Yet [i]count *him* not as an
enemy, but [k]admonish[C] *him* [l]as
a brother.
16 Now [m]the Lord of [n]peace
himself give you peace always
by all means. The Lord *be* with
you all.
17 The [o]salutation[C] of [p]Paul with
mine own hand, which is the
token[G] in every epistle: so I write.
18 [l]The grace of our [c]Lord Jē'-
sus Christ *be* with you all. Amen.

[6]The second *epistle* to the Thessalonians was written from Athens.

**15**
j *Commandment, enjoining steadfastness,* Deut. 8:2.
k *Steadfastness,* 1 Cor. 15:58.
l *Faithfulness,* Luke 16:10.
m *Character, stability of,* Phil. 2:15.
n *Tradition,* Matt. 15:2.
o *Instruction, in religion,* Prov. 23:23.

**16**
p *Prayer, intercessory,* Acts 6:4.
q *Jesus, divinity of,* Matt. 1:21.
r *God, fatherhood of,* Gen. 2:2.
s *God, love of,* Gen. 2:2.
t *Afflictions, consolation in,* Psa. 34:19.
u *Spiritual Blessings,* Eph. 1:3.
v *Hope,* Prov. 13:12.

**17**
w *Works, good,* 2 Tim. 1:9.

**1**
a *Minister, duty of church to,* Rom. 15:16.
b *Intercession, solicited,* Jer. 27:18.
c *Gospel,* Mark 13:10.
1 R. V. run

**2**
d *Unbelief,* Heb. 3:12.

**3**
e *Faith in Christ,* John 6:69.
f *Jesus, perfections of,* Matt. 1:21.
g *Righteous, promises to,* Psa. 64:10.
2 R. V. the evil one.

**4**
h *Apostles, authority of,* Luke 6:13.

**5**
i *Prayer, intercessory,* Acts 6:4.
j *Love, for God,* 1 John 4:19.
3 R. V. patience of Christ.

**6**
k *Commandment, enjoining discipline of disorderly church members,* Deut. 8:2.
l *Name of Jesus,* John 14:13. m *Jesus, lordship of,* Matt. 1:21.
n *Church, discipline in,* Matt. 16:18. o *Evil Company, forbidden,* Prov. 13:20. p *Fellowship, with the wicked, forbidden,* 1 Cor. 1:9.
q *Tradition,* Matt. 15:2.

**7**
r *Example, Paul our,* John 13:15.
s *Minister, example to the flock,* Rom. 15:16.
4 R. V. imitate

**8**
t *Zeal,* 2 Cor. 7:11.
u *Self-denial,* Mark 8:34.
v *Industry,* 1 Kin. 11:28.
w *Unselfishness,* 1 Cor. 10:24.

**9**
5 R. V. the right,

**10**
x *Commandment, forbidding laziness,* Deut. 8:2.
y *Industry, enjoined,* 1 Kin. 11:28.
z *Laziness,* Prov. 19:15.

**11**
a *Talebearing,* Prov. 11:13.

**12**
b *Reproof, faithfulness in,* Prov. 17:10.
c *Jesus, lordship of,* Matt. 1:21.
d *Commandment, enjoining industry and quietness,* Deut. 8:2.
e *Industry, enjoined,* 1 Kin. 11:28.

**13**
f *Commandment, enjoining steadfastness,* Deut. 8:2.
g *Perseverance, enjoined,* Eph. 6 18.
h *Steadfastness,* 1 Cor. 15:58.

**14**
i *Church, discipline in,* Matt. 16:18.
j *Fellowship, with the wicked, forbidden,* 1 Cor. 1:9.

**15**
k *Reproof, enjoined,* Prov. 17:10.
l *Fraternity, enjoined,* Zech. 11:14.

**16**
m *Benedictions, apostolic,* Deut. 21:5.
n *Spiritual Peace, from God,* Gal. 1:3.

**17**
o *Salutations,* Luke 1:44.
p *Paul,* Acts 13:9.
6 R. V. *omits postscript.*

***BUSYBODY,** Prov. 26:17; 1 Tim. 5:13; 2 Thess. 3:11, 12. *Injunctions against,* **Lev. 19:16; 1 Pet. 4:15.** See footnote, TALEBEARING, Prov. 11:13.

THE FIRST EPISTLE OF PAUL TO

# TIMOTHY

## CHAPTER 1

*The apostle's salutation. 3 The reason why he left him at Ephesus. 5 The use and end of the law. 12 Paul's gratitude to Christ for being put into the ministry. 18 This charge he commits to Timothy. 20 Hymenæus and Alexander delivered to Satan.*

[a]PAUL, an apostle of Jē′ṣus Chrīst by the [b]commandment of God our [c]Saviour, and [1]Lord Jē′ṣus Chrīst, *which is* our [d]hope;

2 Unto [e]Tĭm′o-thȳ, *my* own son in the [f]faith: [g,h]Grace, [i]mercy, *and* [j]peace, from God our [k]Father and [l]Jē′ṣus Christ our [m]Lord.

3 As I besought thee to abide still at [n]Ĕph′e-sŭs, when I went into [o]Măç-e-dō′nĭ-ȧ, that thou mightest [p]charge [2]some that they [q]teach no other doctrine,

4 [p,r]Neither give heed to *fables and endless [s]genealogies, which minister [3]questions, rather than godly edifying which is in faith: *so do.*

5 Now the end of the [4,p]commandment is [t]charity out of a [u,v,w]pure heart, and *of* a [x]good conscience, and *of* [y]faith unfeigned:

6 From which [5]some having swerved have turned aside unto vain [z]jangling;

7 Desiring to be teachers of the [a]law; [b]understanding neither what they say, nor whereof they affirm.

8 But we know that the [a]law *is* good, if a man use it lawfully;

9 Knowing this, that the [c]law is not made for a righteous man, but for the [d]lawless and [6]disobedient, for the [d]ungodly and for sinners, for [d]unholy and profane, for [e]murderers of fathers and murderers of mothers, for manslayers,

10 For [7,f]whoremongers, for them that [g]defile themselves with mankind, for [h]menstealers, for [i]liars, for †,[j]perjured persons, and if there be any other thing that is contrary to sound [k]doctrine;

11 According to the [8]glorious [k]gospel of the blessed God, which was committed to [l]my [m]trust.

12 And I [n,o]thank Christ Jē′ṣus our [p]Lord, who hath enabled me, for that he counted me [q]faithful, [9,r]putting me into the ministry;

13 Who was before a [s]blasphemer, and a [t]persecutor, and injurious: but I obtained [u,v]mercy, because I [w]did *it* [x]ignorantly in unbelief.

14 And the grace of our Lord was exceeding abundant with [y]faith and [z]love which is in Chrīst Jē′ṣus.

15 This *is* a faithful saying, and worthy of all acceptation, that [a]Chrīst Jē′ṣus came into the world

1
*a Paul,* Acts 13:9.
*b Call, personal,* Phil. 3:14.
*c God, savior,* Gen. 2:2.
*d Hope,* Prov. 13:12.
1 R. V. Christ Jesus our

2
*e Timothy,* 1 Cor. 4:17.
*f Doctrines of Jesus,* John 7:16.
*g Grace of God,* Rom. 4:16.
*h Benedictions, apostolic,* Deut. 21:5.
*i God, mercy of,* Gen. 2:2.
*j Spiritual Peace,* Gal. 1:3.
*k God, fatherhood of,* Gen. 2:2.
*l Jesus, divinity of,* Matt. 1:21.
*m Jesus, lordship of,* Matt. 1:21.

3
*n Ephesus,* Acts 18:19.
*o Macedonia,* Acts 16:12.
*p Minister, charge delivered to,* Rom. 15:16.
*q Instruction, in religion,* Prov. 23:23.
2 R. V. certain men not to teach a different doctrine,

4
*r Commandment, to ministers,* Deut. 8:2.
*s Genealogy,* 1 Chr. 5:1.
3 R. V. questionings, rather than a dispensation of God which is in faith; so do I now.

**5** *t Love, of man for man,* 1 John 4:7. *u Purity, of heart,* 1 Tim. 4:12. *v Holiness,* Ex. 39:30. *w Heart, renewed,* Psa. 44:21. *x Conscience, approving,* Acts 23:1. *y Faith in Christ,* John 6:69. 4 R. V. charge is love out of
**6** *z Strife,* Prov. 20:3. 5 R. V. things some having swerved have turned aside unto vain talking;
**7**—*a Law, of Moses,* Deut. 33:2. *b Zeal, without knowledge,* 2 Cor. 7:11.

9
*c Law,* Deut. 33:2.
*d Wicked, described,* Psa. 73:3.
*e Homicide, felonious,* Deut. 5:17.
6 R. V. unruly,

10
*f Adultery,* Lev. 20:10.
*g Sodomy,* Lev. 18:22.
*h Kidnapping,* Ex. 21:16.
*i Falsehood,* Job 21:34.
*j False Witness,* Matt. 19:18.
*k Doctrines of Jesus,* John 7:16.
7 R. V. fornicators,

11
*l Agency, in salvation of men,* Mark 1:17.
*m Minister, mission of,* Rom. 15:16.
8 R. V. gospel of the glory of the

12
*n Thankfulness,* Acts 24:3.
*o Jesus, worship of,* Matt. 1:21.
*p Jesus, lordship of,* Matt. 1:21
*q Faithfulness,* Luke 16:10.
*r Minister, call of,* Rom. 15:16.
9 R. V. appointing me to his service;

13
*s Blasphemy,* 2 Sam. 12:14.
*t Paul, persecutes the Christians,* Acts 13:9.
*u God, mercy of,* Gen. 2:2.
*v Sin, forgiveness of,* Rom. 5:12.

*w Zeal, without knowledge,* 2 Cor. 7:11. *x Ignorance, sins of,* Acts 3:17. **14** *y Faith in Christ,* John 6:69. *z Love,* 1 John 4:7.
**15**—*a Jesus, atonement by,* Matt. 1:21.

***FABLE,** 1 Tim. 1:4; 4:7; 2 Tim. 4:4; Tit. 1:14; 2 Pet. 1:16.

†**PERJURY,** Isa. 48:1; Jer. 5:2; 7:9; 1 Tim. 1:9, 10. *Forbidden,* Lev. 19:12; Zech. 8:17; Matt. 5:33. *Penalty for,* Lev. 6:2–7. *Judgments upon perjurers,* Hos. 10:4; Zech. 5:3, 4; Mal. 3:5.

**Instances of:** *Zedekiah,* 2 Chr. 36:13. *Witnesses, against Naboth,* 1 Kin. 21:8–13; *against David,* Psa. 35:11; *against Jesus,* Matt. 26:59–61; Mark 14:56–59; *against Stephen,* Acts 6:11, 13, 14. *Peter, when he denied Jesus with an oath,* Matt. 26:74; Mark 14:71.

See footnotes: FALSEHOOD, Job 21:34; OATH, Num. 5:19.

[b]to [c,d]save sinners; of whom [e]I
am chief.[T]
16 Howbeit for this cause I obtained [f]mercy, that in me first
Jē′ṣus Chrīst might shew forth
all [g]longsuffering, for a [h]pattern
to them which should hereafter
[i]believe on him to [j,k]life everlasting.[S]
17 Now unto the [l]King [m]eter-
nal, [10]immortal, [n]invisible, the
only wise God, [o]*be* honour and
[p]glory for ever and ever. Amen.[T] [S]
18 This [q]charge I commit un-
to thee, son [r]Tĭm′o-thy̆, according to the prophecies which
went before on[C] thee, that thou
by them mightest war a good
warfare;
19 Holding [i]faith,[C] and a [s]good
conscience; which some having
[t]put away concerning faith[C] have
made shipwreck:
20 Of whom is [u]Hy̆-me-næ′us
and [u]Ăl-ĕx̣-ăn′dēr; whom I have
[v,w,x]delivered unto [y]Sā′tan, that
they [11]may learn not to [z]blas-
pheme.

## CHAPTER 2

*Prayer to be made for all men. 9 How women are to be attired. 11 They are to learn in silence, and not to usurp authority over men.*

I [a]EXHORT therefore, that,
[b]first of all, [c]supplications,
prayers, intercessions, *and* [d,e]giv-
ing of thanks, be made for all
men;
2 [b,c]For [f]kings, and *for* all that
are in [1]authority; that we may
[b]lead a quiet and [g]peaceable life
in all [h]godliness and honesty.[C]
3 For this *is* good and acceptable in the sight of God our
[i]Saviour;
4 Who will[C] have all men to be
[j]saved, and to come unto the
[k]knowledge of the [l,m]truth.[Q]
5[T] For *there is* [n]one God, and
one [o]mediator between God
and men, [2]the [p]man Chrīst
Jē′ṣus;
6 Who [q,r]gave himself a [s]ran-
som for all, [3]to be testified[C] in
due time.[T]
7 Whereunto I am [t]ordained a
[u]preacher, and an [v]apostle, (I
speak the truth [4]in Chrīst, *and*
lie not;) a [w]teacher of the [x]Ġĕn′-
tīleṣ in faith and [5]verity.[C]
8 I will therefore that men
[y,z]pray every where, [a]lifting up
holy hands, without [b]wrath and
[6,c]doubting.
9 In like manner also, that [d]wom-
en adorn themselves in *,[e]modest
[f]apparel, with [7,e]shamefacedness[C]
and [e,g]sobriety; not [h]with broided[C]
hair, or [i]gold, or [j]pearls, or costly
array;[C]
10 But (which becometh women
professing godliness) with [e,k]good
works.
11 Let the women learn in
[8]silence with all subjection.
12 But I suffer[C] not a woman
to teach, nor to usurp[C] authority over the man, but to be in
[8]silence.
13 For [l]Ăd′ăm was first formed,
then [m]Ēve.[Q]
14 And Ăd′ăm was not de-
ceived, but the [n]woman being
deceived was in the [o]transgres-
sion.[C] [Q]
15 Notwithstanding she shall
be saved[C] in childbearing, if they
continue in faith and [9,e,p]charity[C]
and [e,q]holiness with [e,g]sobriety.

b *Jesus, mission of,* Matt. 1:21.
c *Jesus, savior,* Matt. 1:21.
d *Salvation,* Acts 16:17.
e *Humility,* Prov. 22:4.

**16**

f *God, mercy of,* Gen. 2:2.
g *Longsuffering,* 2 Cor. 6:6.
h *Example, Paul our,* John 13:15.
i *Faith in Christ,* John 6:69.
j *Life, everlasting,* Eccl. 8:15.
k *Immortality,* 1 Cor. 15:54.

**17**

l *God, sovereign,* Gen. 2:2.
m *God, eternity of,* Gen. 2:2.
n *God, invisible,* Gen. 2:2.
o *Praise,* Psa. 150:1.
p *God, glory of,* Gen. 2:2.
10 R. V. incorruptible, invisible, the only God,

**18**

q *Minister, charge delivered to,* Rom. 15:16.
r *Timothy,* 1 Cor. 4:17.

**19**

s *Conscience, approving,* Acts 23:1.
t *Apostasy,* Acts 1:25.

**20**

u *Minister, false and corrupt,* Rom. 15:16.
v *Church, government of,* Matt. 16:18.
w *Disfellowship,* Num. 15:31.
x *Wicked, punishment of,* Psa. 73:3.
y *Satan,* Matt. 4:10.
z *Blasphemy,* 2 Sam. 12:14.
11 R. V. be taught

**1**

a *Minister, charge delivered to,* vs. 1–15; Rom. 15:16.
b *Citizens, duties of,* v. 2; Luke 15:15.
c *Prayer, intercessory,* Acts 6:4.
d *Commandment, enjoining thanksgiving,* Deut. 8:2. e *Thankfulness, to God, enjoined,* Acts 24:3. **2** f *King, prayer for, enjoined,* 2 Kin. 3:10. g *Peace,* Jer. 29:7. h *Godliness,* 1 Tim. 4:8. 1 R. V. high place; that we may lead a tranquil and quiet life in all godliness and gravity. **3** i *God, savior,* Gen. 2:2.

**4**

j *Salvation,* Acts 16:17.
k *Wisdom, spiritual,* Prov. 2:2.
l *Truth,* John 18:37.
m *Gospel,* Mark 13:10.

**5**

n *God, unity of,* Gen. 2:2.
o *Jesus, mediation of,* Matt. 1:21.
p *Jesus, humanity of,* Matt. 1:21.
2 R. V. himself man, Christ Jesus,

**6**

q *Redemption of our Souls,* Eph. 1:7.
r *Jesus, design of his death,* Matt. 1:21.
s *Ransom, figurative,* Ex. 21:30.
3 R. V. the testimony to be borne in its own times;

**7**

t *Minister, call of,* Rom. 15:16.
u *Preaching,* Matt. 9:35.
v *Paul, an apostle,* Acts 13:9.
w *Instruction, in religion,* Prov. 23:23.
x *Gentiles, conversion of,* Acts 10:45.
4 R. V. *omits* in Christ,
5 R. V. truth.

**8**

y *Prayer, enjoined,* Acts 6:4.
z *Commandment, enjoining prayer,* Deut. 8:2.
a *Prayer, postures in,* Acts 6:4.
b *Anger, forbidden,* Psa. 37:8.
c *Strife,* Prov. 20:3.
6 R. V. disputing.

**9**

d *Women, rules for dress of Christian,* Prov. 31:10.
e *Righteousness, fruits of,* Psa. 15:2. f *Dress,* Zech. 3:3. g *Sobermindedness,* Tit. 2:6. h *Pride,* Prov. 16:18. i *Gold,* Ezek. 7:19. j *Pearl,* Rev. 17:4. 7 R. V. shamefastness and sobriety; not with braided hair, and gold or pearls or costly raiment;
**10** k *Works, good,* 2 Tim. 1:9.
**11** 8 R. V. quietness
**13** l *Adam, creation of,* Gen. 2:19. m *Eve, creation of,* Gen. 3:20.
**14** n *Eve, beguiled by Satan,* Gen. 3:20. o *Fall of Man,* Gen. 3:6.
**15** p *Love,* 1 John 4:7. q *Holiness,* Ex. 39:30. 9 R. V. love and sanctification with sobriety.

* **MODESTY.** *In the presence of rulers,* Prov. 25:6, 7. *Enjoined by the Savior,* Luke 14:7–11. *Of women, enjoined by Paul,* 1 Tim. 2:9.
**Instances of:** *Saul,* 1 Sam. 9:21. *Vashti,* Esth. 1:11, 12. *Elihu,* Job 32:4–7. *John the Baptist,* Matt. 3:11; Mark 1:7; Luke 3:16; John 1:26, 27. *The centurion,* Matt. 8:8; Luke 7:4, 6.
See footnote, HUMILITY, Prov. 22:4.

## CHAPTER 3

*The qualifications of a bishop, 8 and of deacons. 14 Why he writes these things to Timothy. 16 The mystery of godliness.*

THIS *is* a true saying, If a man [a]desire the office of a +bishop[G], he desireth a good work.

2 [b]A +bishop[G] then must be [1,c]blameless, the [d]husband of [e]one wife, [c,f]vigilant, [c,f,g]sober, of good behaviour, [c]given[G] to [h]hospitality, [c]apt[G] to [i]teach;

3 [2,b,c]Not given[G] to wine, no [j]striker[G], not greedy of filthy lucre; but patient, not a brawler, not [k]covetous;

4 [b,c,l]One that [m]ruleth well his own house, having his [n]children in subjection with all gravity;

5 (For [c]if a man know not how to [m]rule his own house, how shall he [o]take care of the [p]church of God?)

6 [b,c]Not a novice[G], lest being [3]lifted up[G] with [q]pride he fall into the condemnation of the [r]devil.

7 Moreover [b,c]he must have [4]a good report of them which are without[G]; lest he fall into reproach[G] and the snare of the [r]devil.

8 [s]Likewise *must* the †deacons *be* grave, not doubletongued[G], [t]not given to much wine, [u]not [k]greedy of filthy lucre;

9 Holding the [v]mystery[G] of the [w]faith in a [x,y]pure conscience.[S]

10 And [s]let these also first be proved[G]; then let them use the office of a †deacon, being *found* blameless.

11 [5,z]Even so *must their* wives *be* grave, not [a]slanderers, [b]sober, [c]faithful in all things.

12 Let the †deacons[G] be the husbands of [d]one wife, [e]ruling their children and their own houses well.

13 For they that have used[G] the office of a †deacon well purchase[G] to themselves a good degree[G], and great boldness in the [f]faith which is in Chrĭst Jē'ṣus.

14 These things write I unto thee, hoping to come unto thee shortly:

15 But if I tarry long, that thou mayest know how [6,g]thou oughtest to behave thyself in the [h]house of God, which is the church of the living God, [i]the[T] pillar and ground of the [j]truth.

16 And without controversy great is the [k,l]mystery[G] of godliness: [7]God was [m]manifest in the flesh, justified in the Spirit, seen of [n]angels, [o]preached [8]unto the [p]Ġĕn'tīleṣ[G], [q]believed on in the[T] world, [r]received up into glory.

## CHAPTER 4

*The Spirit speaks of a departure from the faith in the latter times. 6 Timothy is to put the brethren in remembrance of these things. 8 Godliness is profitable. 12 He is to be an example of the believers.*

NOW the [a]Spirit speaketh expressly, that in the latter times some shall [b]depart from the [c]faith, giving heed to seducing spirits, and doctrines of devils[G];[T]

2 [1]Speaking [d]lies in [e]hypocrisy; having their [f]conscience seared[G] with a hot iron;

3 *,[g]Forbidding to marry, *and* [h]*commanding* to abstain from meats[G], [i]which [j]God hath created to be received with [k,l]thanksgiving of them which [m]believe and [n]know the [o]truth.[T Q]

4 For [i]every [p]creature[G] of God *is*

**1**
a *Ambition*, Hab. 2:5.

**2**
b *Commandment, concerning ministers*, vs. 2–13; Deut. 8:2.
c *Minister, character and qualifications of*, Rom. 15:16.
d *Minister, marriage of*, Rom. 15:16.
e *Polygamy, forbidden*, Deut. 17:17.
f *Christian Graces*, Gal. 5:22.
g *Sobermindedness*, Tit. 2:6.
h *Hospitality*, Rom. 12:13.
i *Instruction, in religion*, Prov. 23:23.
1 R. V. without reproach, the husband of one wife, temperate, soberminded, orderly, given

**3**
j *Strife*, Prov. 20:3.
k *Covetousness*, Isa. 57:17.
2 R. V. No brawler, no striker; but gentle, not contentious, no lover of money;

**4**
l *Father, duty of*, Psa. 27:10.
m *Family, government of*, 1 Chr. 13:14.
n *Children, to honor and obey parents*, Mark 10:14.

**5**
o *Minister, duties of*, Rom. 15:16.
p *Church*, Matt. 16:18.

**6**
q *Pride*, Prov. 16:18.
r *Satan*, Matt. 4:10.
3 R. V. puffed up he fall

**7**
4 R. V. good testimony from them that

**8** s *Commandment, concerning ministers*, Deut. 8:2. t *Temperance, in the use of wine*, 2 Pet. 1:6. u *Avarice, forbidden*, Eccl. 5:10. **9** v *Mysteries, of redemption*, Mark 4:11. w *Faith, the doctrines of Jesus*, 1 Cor. 16:13. x *Purity, of heart*, 1 Tim. 4:12. y *Conscience, approving*, Acts 23:1. **11** z *Women, Paul's precepts concerning*, Prov. 31:10.—a *Slander*, Prov. 10:18. b *Sobermindedness*, Tit. 2:6. c *Faithfulness*, Luke 16:10. 5 R. V. Women in like manner must be grave, not slanderers, temperate, faithful in all things.

**12**
d *Polygamy, forbidden*, Deut. 17:17.
e *Family, government of*, 1 Chr. 13:14.

**13**
f *Faith, the doctrines of Jesus*, 1 Cor. 16:13.

**15**
g *Church, orderly conduct of worship in*, Matt. 16:18.
h *House, figurative*, Esth. 8:1.
i *Church, described*, Matt. 16:18.
j *Truth, of the gospel*, John 18:37.
6 R. V. men ought to behave themselves in

**16**
k *Mysteries, of redemption*, Mark 4:11.
l *Salvation, plan of*, Acts 16:17.
m *Jesus, incarnation of*, Matt. 1:21.
n *Angel*, Heb. 1:13.
o *Preaching*, Matt. 9:35.
p *Gentiles, conversion of*, Acts 10:45.
q *Faith in Christ*, John 6:69.
r *Jesus, ascension of*, Matt. 1:21.
7 R. V. He who was
8 R. V. among the nations,

**1**
a *Holy Spirit, inspiration of*, Acts 1:2.
b *Apostasy, foretold*, vs. 1–3; Acts 1:25.
c *Faith, doctrines of Jesus*, 1 Cor. 16:13.

**2**
d *Heresy*, Tit. 3:10.
e *Hypocrisy*, Jas. 3:17.
f *Conscience*, Acts 23:1.
1 R. V. Through the hypocrisy of men that speak lies, branded in their own conscience as with a hot iron;

**3**
g *Marriage, prophecies concerning the forbidding of*, Gen. 34:9. h *Commandments of Men*, Mark 7:7. i *Food, from God*, Psa. 136:25. j *God, creator*, Gen. 2:2. k *Thankfulness, to God*, Acts 24:3. l *Thanksgiving for Food*, Luke 24:30. m *Faith*, Mark 11:22. n *Wisdom, spiritual*, Prov. 2:2. o *Truth, of the gospel*, John 18:37. **4** p *Animals*, Jer. 27:5.

---

**+BISHOP**, Phil. 1:1. *Character of*, 1 Tim. 3:2–7; Tit. 1:5–11. *Duties of*, Acts 20:28.
*A title of Jesus*, 1 Pet. 2:25.
See footnote, ELDERS, Acts 14:23.

**† DEACON**, an ecclesiastic charged with the temporal affairs of the church. *Ordained by the apostles*, Acts 6:1–6. *Qualifications of*, 1 Tim. 3:8–13.

The Greek word translated *deacon* signifies servant, and is so translated in Matt. 23:11; John 12:26; is also translated *minister* in Mark 10:43; 1 Cor. 3:5.

*** CELIBACY.** *Deplored by Jephthah's daughter*, Judg. 11:38. *Not obligatory*, 1 Cor. 7:1–9, 25, 26; 9:5; 1 Tim. 4:1–3. *Practiced for kingdom of heaven's sake*, Matt. 19:10–12; 1 Cor. 7:32–40; Rev. 14:1, 4, with vs. 2–5.

good, and nothing[G] to be refused, if it be received with [k,l]thanksgiving:[Q]

5 For [i]it is sanctified[G] by the word of God and [k,l]prayer.

6 If thou [q]put the [r]brethren in remembrance of these things, thou shalt be a good minister[G] of Jē′sus Christ, nourished up in the [s]words of faith[G] and of good [t]doctrine, whereunto thou hast attained.

7 But [q]refuse profane and old wives' [u]fables,[G] and exercise[G] thyself *rather* unto [†]godliness.

8 For bodily exercise profiteth little: but [†,v]godliness is [w]profitable unto all things, having [x,y]promise of the [z]life that now is, and of [a,b]that which is to come.

9 This *is* a faithful saying and worthy of all acceptation.[G]

10 For therefore we both [c]labour and [2]suffer[G] reproach,[G] because we [d]trust in the living God, who is the [e]Saviour of all men, specially of those that [f]believe.

11 These things [g]command and [h]teach.

12 [i]Let no man despise[G] thy youth; but [g]be thou an [3,j,k]example of the believers, in word, in conversation,[G] in [l,m]charity,[G] in spirit, in faith, in [‡,m]purity.

13 Till I come, [g,h]give attendance to [n]reading, to [n]exhortation,[G] to [n]doctrine.

14 [o]Neglect not the gift that is in thee, which was given thee by prophecy,[G] with the [o]laying on of the [p]hands of the [q]presbytery.[G]

15 [4,q,r]Meditate upon these things; [c]give thyself wholly to them; that thy [5]profiting may appear to all.

16 [g,s]Take heed unto thyself, and [6]unto the doctrine;[G] [t]continue in them: for in doing this [u]thou shalt both save thyself, and them that hear thee.

## CHAPTER 5

*Rules to be observed in reproving. 3 Of widows. 17 Of elders. 23 A precept for Timothy's health. 24 Some men's sins go before them unto judgment, and some men's sins follow after.*

[a,b,c]REBUKE[G] not an elder,[G] but intreat[G] *him* as a father; *and* the younger men as brethren;[Q]

2 The elder [d]women as mothers; the younger as sisters, with all [e,f]purity.

3 Honour [g]widows that are widows indeed.

4 But if any [g]widow have [h]children or [1]nephews,[G] let them learn first to shew piety[G] at home, and to requite their parents: for that is good and acceptable before God.

5 Now she that is a [g]widow indeed, and desolate, [i]trusteth[G] in God, and continueth in supplications[G] and *prayers night and day.[Q]

6 But she that liveth in [j]pleasure is dead while she liveth.

7 And [k]these things give[G] in charge,[G] that they may be [l]blameless.

8 [m]But if [n,o]any provide not for his own, and specially for those of his own [p]house, he hath de-

5
*q Minister, precepts for guidance of,* Rom. 15:16.
*r Fraternity,* Zech. 11:14.
*s Gospel,* Mark 13:10.
*t Doctrines of Jesus,* John 7:16.

7
*u Fable,* 1 Tim. 1:4.

8
*v Christian Graces, godliness,* Gal. 5:22.
*w Righteousness, profitable,* Psa. 15:2.
*x Righteous, promises to,* Psa. 64:10.
*y Holiness, motives to,* Ex. 39:30.
*z Longevity,* Psa. 91:16.

*a Life, everlasting,* Eccl. 8:15.
*b Immortality,* 1 Cor. 15:54.

10
*c Zeal,* 2 Cor. 7:11.
*d Faith, exemplified,* Mark 11:22.
*e God, savior,* Gen. 2:2.
*f Faith in Christ,* John 6:69.

11
*g Commandment, concerning ministers,* vs. 11–16; Deut. 8:2.
*h Minister, duties of,* Rom. 15:16.

12
*i Young Men, admonitions to,* Prov. 1:4.
*j Example, good,* John 13:15.
*k Minister, character and qualifications of,* Rom. 15:16.
*l Love, of man for man,* 1 John 4:7.
*m Christian Graces,* Gal. 5:22. 3 R. V. ensample to them that believe, in word, in manner of life, in love, in faith, in purity. **13** *n Instruction, in religion,* Prov. 23:23. **14** *o Minister, ordination of,* Rom. 15:16. *p Hand, imposition of,* Ezra 10:19. *q Church, government of,* Matt. 16:18.

15
*r Diligence,* Rom. 12:8.
4 R. V. Be diligent in these things;
5 R. V. progress may be manifest unto all.

16
*s Watchfulness, enjoined,* Matt. 24:42.
*t Perseverance, exhortation to,* Eph. 6:18.
*u Agency, in salvation of men,* Mark 1:17.
6 R. V. to thy teaching. Continue in these things;

1
*a Commandment, concerning ministers,* vs. 1–7, 17–22; Deut. 8:2.
*b Minister, precepts for guidance of,* Rom. 15:16.
*c Reproof, of seniors forbidden,* Prov. 17:10.

2
*d Women, Paul's precepts concerning,* Prov. 31:10.
*e Purity, of heart,* 1 Tim. 4:12.
*f Christian Graces,* Gal. 5:22.

3
*g Widow,* 2 Sam. 14:5.

4
*h Children, commandments to, to requite parents,* Mark 10:14.
1 R. V. grandchildren,

5
*i Faith,* Mark 11:22.

6
*j Worldly Pleasure,* Eccl. 2:1.

7
*k Minister, duties of,* Rom. 15:16.
*l Holiness,* Ex. 39:30.

**8** *m Industry, enjoined,* 1 Kin. 11:28. *n Husband, duties of,* Num. 30:6. *o Father, duty of,* Psa. 27:10. *p Family, husband should provide for,* 1 Chr. 13:14.

† **GODLINESS,** signifying godlikeness; a life conformed to the will of God, 1 Tim. 2:2; 6:6, 11; 2 Tim. 3:5; Tit. 1:1; 2 Pet. 1:3, 6, 7; 3:11.
*Enjoined,* 1 Tim. 4:7; 6:11; 2 Pet. 1:6. *Profitable,* 1 Tim. 4:8; 6:6. *Promotes longevity and promises eternal life,* 1 Tim. 4:8.
See footnote, HOLINESS, Ex. 39:30.

‡ **PURITY,** 1 Tim. 4:12; 5:22; Tit. 1:15. *Jesus our pattern in,* 1 John 3:3.
**Of heart,** Psa. 24:3–5; Prov. 20:9; 21:8; Isa. 1:18, 25; 6:7; 1 Tim. 1:5; 2 Tim. 2:21, 22; Heb. 10:2. *Blessedness of,* Matt. 5:8. *Prayer for,* Psa. 51:7; Dan. 12:10; Heb. 9:13, 14.
*Enjoined,* 1 Tim. 3:9; 2 Tim. 2:21, 22; Jas. 4:8; 1 Pet. 1:22. *Meditation upon, enjoined,* Phil. 4:8. *Through divine discipline,* Mal. 3:2, 3; John 15:2. *Through the blood of Christ,* Heb. 9:13, 14. *Exemplified by Paul,* 2 Tim. 1:3.
See footnotes: HOLINESS, Ex. 39:30; SPIRITUAL PURIFICATION, Psa. 51:2.

* **PRAYERFULNESS.** *Enjoined,* Rom. 12:12; Col. 4:2; 1 Thess. 5:17. *Spirit of, from God,* Zech. 12:10.
**Exemplified by:** *The psalmist,* Psa. 42:8; 109:4; 116:2. *Daniel,* Dan. 6:10. *Anna,* Luke 2:37. *The apostles,* Acts 6:4. *Cornelius,* Acts 10:2. *Peter,* Acts 10:9. *Paul,* Rom. 1:9; Eph. 1:15, 16; Col. 1:9; 1 Thess. 3:10; 2 Tim. 1:3.
See footnotes: PRAYER, Acts 6:4; PRAYERLESSNESS, Job 21:15.

nied the [q]faith, and is worse than an [2,r]infidel.

9 Let not a [s,t]widow be taken into the number under threescore years old, having been the wife of one man,

10 [u]Well reported of for [v,w]good works; if she have brought up children, if she have [x,y]lodged strangers, if she have washed the saints' feet, if she have relieved the [z]afflicted, if she have diligently followed every good work.

11 But the younger [a]widows refuse: for when they have begun to wax wanton against Christ, they [3]will marry;

12 Having [4]damnation, because they have cast off their first faith.

13 And withal they learn *to be* [b]idle, wandering about from house to house; and not only idle, but [c,d]tattlers also and [e]busybodies, speaking things which they ought not.

14 I will therefore that the younger [5]women [f]marry, bear children, guide the house, give none occasion to the adversary to speak reproachfully.

15 For some are already [g]turned aside after [h,i]Sā'tan.

16 If any [6]man or woman that [j]believeth have [a,k]widows, [l]let them relieve them, and let not the [m]church be charged; that it may relieve them that are widows indeed.

17 [n,o]Let the [p]elders that rule well be counted worthy of double honour, especially they who [q]labour in the word and [7,r]doctrine.

18 For the scripture saith, [s]Thou shalt not muzzle the [t]ox that treadeth out the corn. And, [u,v,w]The [x]labourer *is* worthy of his [y,z]reward.

19 [a]Against an [b]elder receive not an accusation, but before two or three [c]witnesses.

20 Them that sin [d,e]rebuke before all, that others also may fear.

21 I charge *thee* before God, and [8]the [f]Lord Jē'ṣus Christ, and the elect [g]angels, that thou [h]observe these things without preferring one before another, [i]doing nothing by †partiality.

22 [j]Lay hands suddenly on no man, [k]neither be partaker of other men's sins: [l]keep thyself [m]pure.

23 Drink no longer water, but use a little [n]wine for thy stomach's sake and thine often infirmities.

24 [o]Some men's sins are open beforehand, going before to judgment; and some *men* they follow after.

25 Likewise also the [p]good works *of some* are manifest beforehand; and they that are otherwise cannot be hid.

## CHAPTER 6

*The duty of servants. 6 The gain of godliness. 10 The love of money the root of all evil. 11 What Timothy is to avoid, and what to follow, 17 and whereof to admonish the rich. 20 He is exhorted to keep that which is committed to his trust.*

LET as many servants as are under the yoke [a]count their own [b]masters worthy of all honour, [c]that the [d]name of God and *his* [e]doctrine be not [f]blasphemed.

2 And they that have [g]believing [b]masters, let [a]them not despise *them*, because they are [h]brethren; but rather do *them* service, because they are faithful and [i]beloved, partakers of the bene-

---

*q Faith, the doctrines of Jesus,* 1 Cor. 16:13.
*r Unbelievers,* 1 Cor. 6:6.
2 R. V. unbeliever.

**9**
*s Widow, care of,* 2 Sam. 14:5.
*t Poor, liberality toward, enjoined,* Prov. 21:13.

**10**
*u Righteous, described,* Psa. 64:10.
*v Works, good,* 2 Tim. 1:9.
*w Zeal,* 2 Cor. 7:11.
*x Hospitality,* Rom. 12:13.
*y Kindness,* Acts 28:2.
*z Afflicted, help for,* Job 34:28.

**11**
*a Widow,* 2 Sam. 14:5.
3 R. V. desire to

**12**
4 R. V. condemnation,

**13**
*b Idleness,* Eccl. 10:18.
*c Talebearing,* Prov. 11:13.
*d Speech, evil,* Col. 4:6.
*e Busybody,* 2 Thess. 3:11.

**14**
*f Marriage, of widows,* Gen. 34:9.
5 R. V. widows

**15**
*g Backsliders, described,* Jer. 3:22.
*h Satan,* Matt. 4:10.
*i Temptation, sources of,* Luke 11:4.

**16**
*j Faith in Christ,* John 6:69.
*k Poor, liberality toward,* Prov. 21:13
*l Liberality, enjoined,* 1 Tim. 6:18.
*m Church,* Matt. 16:18.
6 R. V. *omits* man or

**17** *n Commandment, enjoining esteem for pastors,* Deut. 8:2. *o Church, duty of, to ministers,* Matt. 16:18. *p Elders, overseers of the church,* Acts 14:23. *q Minister, duties of,* Rom. 15:16. *r Instruction, in religion,* Prov. 23:23. 7 R. V. in teaching.
**18** *s* Deut. 25:4. *t Animals, laws concerning,* Jer. 27:5.

*u* Matt. 10:10; Luke 10:7.
*v Commandment, enjoining temporal support of ministers,* Deut. 8:2.
*w Employer, required to accord just compensation,* Deut. 24:14.
*x Employee, rights of,* Deut. 24:14.
*y Minister, emoluments of,* Rom. 15:16.
*z Labor, compensation for,* Luke 10:7.

**19**
*a Church, discipline in,* Matt. 16:18.
*b Elders,* Acts 14:23.
*c Witness,* Num. 35:30.

**20**
*d Commandment, enjoining reproof,* Deut. 8:2.
*e Reproof, enjoined,* Prov. 17:10.

**21**
*f Jesus, lordship of,* Matt. 1:21.
*g Angel,* Heb. 1:13.
*h Minister, charge delivered to,* Rom. 15:16.
*i Justice, enjoined,* Deut. 33:21.
8 R. V. *omits* the Lord

**22**
*j Commandment, concerning ministers,* Deut. 8:2.
*k Evil Company, forbidden,* Prov 13:20.
*l Holiness, enjoined,* Ex. 39:30.
*m Purity,* 1 Tim. 4:12.

**23**
*n Wine, medicinal use of,* Prov. 23:31.

**24**
*o Wicked, punishment of,* Psa. 73:3.

**25**
*p Works, good,* 2 Tim. 1:9.

**1**
*a Servant, duties of,* Jer. 2:14.
*b Master,* Col. 4:1.
*c Influence, good,* 1 Cor. 7:14. *d God, name of, to be reverenced,* Gen. 2:2. *e Doctrines of Jesus,* John 7:16. *f Blasphemy,* 2 Sam. 12:14.
**2** *g Faith in Christ,* John 6:69. *h Brother,* Prov. 18:24. *i Love, of man for man,* v. 11; 1 John 4:7.

---

† **PARTIALITY.** *By parents, forbidden,* Deut. 21:15–17. *Its effect upon other children,* Gen. 37:4.
*Joseph for Benjamin,* Gen. 43:30, 34.
*By ministers, forbidden,* 1 Tim. 5:21.
**Of parents:** *Isaac for Esau,* Gen. 25:28. *Rebekah for Jacob,* Gen. 25:28; 27:6–17. *Jacob, for Joseph,* Gen. 33:2; 37:3, 4; 48:22; *for Benjamin,* Gen. 42:4.
**Of husbands:** *Jacob for Rachel,* Gen. 29:30. *Elkanah for Hannah,* 1 Sam. 1:4, 5.
See footnote, RESPECT OF PERSONS, Prov. 24:23.

*j Instruction, in religion,* Prov. 23:23.
*k Minister, duties of,* Rom. 15:16.

**3**
*l False Teachers,* 2 Pet. 2:1.
*m Jesus, lordship of,* Matt. 1:21.

**4**
*n Pride,* Prov. 16:18.
*o Spiritual Blindness,* 2 Cor. 4:4.
*p Strife,* Prov. 20:3.
*q Envy,* Prov. 14:30.
*r Railing,* Jude 9.
1 R. V. puffed up,

**5**
*s Truth, of the gospel,* John 18:37.
*t Covetousness,* Isa. 57:17.
2 R. V. godliness is a way of gain.
3 R. V. *omits* from such withdraw thyself.

**6**
*u Godliness,* 1 Tim. 4:8.
*v Christian Graces,* Gal. 5:22.

**7**
*w* Job 1:21.

**8**
*x Temporal Blessings,* Psa. 103:2.

**9**
*y Temptation, sources of,* Luke 11:4.
*z Riches, a snare,* Eccl. 4:8.
*a Lust,* 2 Pet. 1:4.
*b Wicked, punishment of,* Psa. 73:3.
4 are minded to be

**10**
*c Covetousness,* Isa. 57:17.
*d Avarice,* Eccl. 5:10.
*e Money, love of,* Jer. 32:9.
*f Backsliding, temptations to,* Hos. 11:7.
*g Faith, the doctrines of Jesus,* 1 Cor. 16:13.

fit. These things [j,k]teach and
exhort.
3 If any [l]man teach otherwise,
and consent not to wholesome
words, *even* the [e]words of our
[m]Lord Jē'ṣus Chrīst, and to the
[e]doctrine which is according to
godliness;
4 He is [1,n]proud, [o]knowing nothing, but doting about questions
and [p]strifes of words, whereof
cometh [q]envy, strife, [r]railings,
evil surmisings,
5 Perverse [p]disputings of men
of corrupt minds, and [o]destitute
of the [s]truth, [t]supposing that
[2]gain is godliness: [3]from such
withdraw thyself.
6 But [u]godliness with *,[v]con-
tentment is great gain.
7 [w]For we brought nothing into
*this* world, *and it is* certain we
can carry nothing out.
8 And having [x]food and raiment let us be therewith *content.
9 But they that [4,t,y]will be [z]rich
fall into temptation and a snare,
and *into* many foolish and hurtful [a]lusts, which drown men in
[b]destruction and perdition.
10 For the [c,d]love of [e]money
is the root of all evil: which
while some coveted after, they
have [f]erred from the [g]faith, and
pierced themselves through with
many sorrows.
11 But [h]thou, O man of God,
[i]flee these things; and [i]follow
after [j]righteousness, [k]godliness,
[l]faith, [m]love, [n]patience, [o]meek-
ness.
12 [i]Fight the [p]good fight of
faith, lay hold on [q,r]eternal life,
whereunto thou art also [s]called,
and hast [t,u]professed a good profession before many witnesses.
13 I give thee charge in the sight
of God, [v]who [w]quickeneth all
things, and *before* [x]Chrīst Jē'ṣus,
who before [y]Pŏn'tĭ-ŭs Pī'late
[z]witnessed a good confession;
14 That thou [a]keep *this* [b]com-
mandment without spot, unre-
bukeable, until the [c]appearing of
our [d]Lord Jē'ṣus Chrīst:
15 Which in his times he shall
shew, *who is* the blessed and
only [e]Potentate, the [f]King of
kings, and Lord of lords;
16 [e,f]Who only hath [g]immor-
tality, dwelling in the [h]light
which no man can approach
unto; [i]whom no man hath seen,
nor can see: to whom *be* [j]honour
and power everlasting. Amen.
17 [b,k]Charge them that are
[l]rich in this world, that they be
not highminded, nor [m]trust in
uncertain riches, but [5]in the living God, [n]who giveth us richly
[o,p]all things to enjoy;
18 [k]That they do good, that
they be rich in [q,r]good works,
†,[r]ready to [s]distribute, willing to
communicate;
19 Laying up in store for themselves a good foundation against
the time to come, that they may
lay hold on [6]eternal [t]life.
20 O [u]Tĭm'o-thȳ, [b]keep that
which is committed to thy [v]trust,
avoiding profane *and* vain babblings, and oppositions of [7,w,x]sci-
ence falsely so called:
21 Which some professing have
[y]erred concerning the [z]faith.
[a]Grace *be* with thee. Amen.

[8]The first to Timothy was written from Laodicea, which is the chiefest city of Phrygia Pacatiana.

*t Religious Testimony,* 2 Thess. 1:10.
*u Witnessing for Christ,* Luke 24:48.

**13**
*v God, creator,* Gen. 2:2.
*w Life, from God,* Eccl. 8:15.
*x Jesus, Messiah,* Matt. 1:21.
*y Pilate,* Matt. 27:2.
*z* Matt. 27:11; Mark 15:2; Luke 23:3; John 18:35–37.

**14**
*a Obedience, enjoined,* Heb. 5:8.
*b Commandment, to ministers,* Deut. 8:2.
*c Jesus, second coming of,* Matt. 1:21.
*d Jesus, lordship of,* Matt. 1:21.

**15**
*e God, sovereign* (as some interpret), Gen. 2:2.
*f Jesus, king* (as some interpret), Matt. 1:21.

**16**
*g God, eternity of,* Gen. 2:2.
*h Light, figurative,* Matt. 5:14.
*i God, invisible,* Gen. 2:2.
*j Praise,* Psa. 150:1.

**17**
*k Commandment, warning the rich,* Deut. 8:2.
*l Rich,* Jas. 5:1.
*m False Confidence,* Psa. 30:6.
*n God, providence of,* Gen. 2:2.
*o Spiritual Blessings, from God,* Eph. 1:3.
*p Temporal Blessings, from God,* Psa. 103:2.
5 R. V. on God.

**18**
*q Works, good,* 2 Tim. 1:9.
*r Righteousness, fruits of,* Psa. 15:2.
*s Alms,* Matt. 6:2.

**11** *h Minister, character and qualifications of,* Rom. 15:16. *i Commandment, to ministers,* Deut. 8:2. *j Righteousness, required,* Psa. 15:2. *k Godliness, enjoined,* 1 Tim. 4:8. *l Faith, enjoined,* Mark 11:22. *m Love, of man for man, enjoined,* 1 John 4:7. *n Patience, enjoined,* Luke 8:15. *o Meekness, enjoined,* Psa. 45:4.
**12** *p* 2 Tim. 4:7. *q Immortality,* 1 Cor. 15:54. *r Life, everlasting,* Eccl. 8:15. *s Call, personal,* Phil. 3:14.

**19** *t Life, everlasting,* Eccl. 8:15. **6** R. V. the life which is life indeed. **20** *u Timothy,* 1 Cor. 4:17. *v Minister, responsibility of,* Rom. 15:16. *w Philosophy,* Col. 2:8. *x Wisdom, worldly,* Prov. 2:2. **7** R. V. the knowledge which is falsely so called; **21** *y Backsliding,* Hos. 11:7. *z Faith, the doctrines of Jesus,* 1 Cor. 16:13. —*a Benedictions, apostolic,* Deut. 21:5. **8** R. V. *omits postscript.*

* **CONTENTMENT.** *Enjoined,* Psa. 37:7; Eccl. 9:7–9; Luke 3:14; 1 Cor. 7:20–24; 1 Tim. 6:6–8; Heb. 13:5.
**Instances of:** *Barzillai,* 2 Sam. 19:33–37. *The Shunammite,* 2 Kin. 4:13. *David,* Psa. 16:6. *Paul,* Phil. 4:11, 12. See footnote, RESIGNATION, Job 5:17.

† **LIBERALITY.** *Enjoined,* Ex. 22:29, 30; 23:15; 34:20; Lev. 23:22; 25:35–43; Prov. 3:27, 28; Matt. 5:42; Acts 20:35; Rom. 12:8; 2 Cor. 8:7, 9, 11–14, 24; 1 Tim. 6:18; Heb. 13:16.
*In offerings, for tabernacle,* Ex. 25:1–8; 35:4–29; 36:3–6;

THE SECOND EPISTLE OF PAUL TO

# TIMOTHY

## CHAPTER 1

*The apostle's salutation. 3 His remembrance of Timothy in his prayers. 5 The faith of Timothy, of his mother, and of his grandmother. 6 He is exhorted to stir up the gift of God in him, 8 to be steadfast in the faith, 13 and to hold fast the form of sound words. 15 Some were turned away from the apostle. 16 The kindness of Onesiphorus.*

[a]PAUL, an apostle of Jē′ṣus
Chrīst by the [b,c]will of
God, according to the promise of
life which is in Chrīst Jē′ṣus,
2 To [d]Tĭm′o-thȳ, *my* dearly
[e]beloved son: [f,g]Grace, [h]mercy,
*and* [i]peace, from God the [j]Father
and Chrīst Jē′ṣus our [k,l]Lord.
3 I [m]thank God, whom I [n]serve
from *my* forefathers with [o,p]pure
conscience, that [q]without ceasing
I have [e]remembrance of thee in
my [r]prayers night and day;
4 [e]Greatly desiring to see thee,
being mindful of thy tears, that I
may be filled with [s]joy;
5 When I call to remembrance
the [t]unfeigned [u]faith that is in
[v]thee, which dwelt first in thy
[w]grandmother Lō′ĭs, and thy
[w,x]mother [y]Eū′nïçe; and I am
persuaded that in thee also.
6 Wherefore I put thee in remembrance that thou [z]stir up
the [a,b]gift of God, which is in thee
by the [c]putting on of my [d]hands.
7 For God hath not given us the
spirit of [1,e]fear; but of [f,g]power,
and of [g,h]love, and [2]of a sound
mind.
8 [i,j]Be not thou therefore
ashamed of the [k,l]testimony of
our Lord, nor of me his [m]pris-
oner: but [j]be thou partaker of
the [n]afflictions of the [o]gospel according to the power of God;
9 Who hath [p]saved us, and
[q]called *us* with an holy calling, not
according to our *works, but according to his own [r,s]purpose and
[t]grace, which was given us in
Chrīst Jē′ṣus [u]before [3]the world
began,
10 But is now made manifest
by the appearing of our [v]Saviour

**1**
*a Paul,* Acts 13:9.
*b Will of God,* Mark 3:35.
*c Minister, call of,* Rom. 15:16.
**2**
*d Timothy,* 1 Cor. 4:17.
*e Love, of man for man,* 1 John 4:7.
*f Benedictions, apostolic,* Deut. 21:5.
*g Grace of God,* Rom. 4:16.
*h God, mercy of,* Gen. 2:2.
*i Spiritual Peace,* Gal. 1:3.
*j God, fatherhood of,* Gen. 2:2.
*k Jesus, divinity of,* Matt. 1:21.
*l Jesus, lordship of,* Matt. 1:21.
**3**
*m Thankfulness, to God,* Acts 24:3.
*n Zeal,* 2 Cor. 7:11.
*o Conscience, approving,* Acts 23:1.
*p Purity, of heart,* 1 Tim. 4:12.
*q Prayerfulness,* 1 Tim. 5:5. *r Prayer, intercessory,* Acts 6:4. **4** *s Joy,* Psa. 5:11. **5** *t Sincerity,* 1 Cor. 5:8. *u Faith in Christ,* John 6:69. *v Children, good,* Mark 10:14. *w Women, good,* Prov. 31:10.

*x Mother, sanctifying influence of,* 1 Kin. 2:20.
*y* Acts 16:1.
**6**
*z Diligence,* Rom. 12:8.
*a Spiritual Blessings, from God,* Eph. 1:3.
*b Charism,* 1 Cor. 12:1.
*c Ordination, of ministers,* Ex. 29:1.
*d Hand, imposition of,* Ezra 10:19.
**7**
*e Fear of God, guilty,* Acts 9:31.
*f Spiritual Power, from God,* Luke 24:49.
*g Minister, character and qualifications of,* Rom. 15:16.
*h Love,* 1 John 4:7.
1 R. V. fearfulness;
2 R. V. discipline.
**8**
*i Backsliding, admonitions against,* Hos. 11:7.
*j Faithfulness,* Luke 16:10. *k Religious Testimony,* 2 Thess. 1:10. *l Confession of Christ,* Luke 12:8. *m Minister, persecutions of,* Rom. 15:16. *n Persecution, of the righteous,* John 15:20. *o Gospel,* Mark 13:10. **9** *p God, savior,* Gen. 2:2. *q Call, personal,* Phil. 3:14. *r Foreordination,* Rom. 8:30. *s Salvation, plan of,* Acts 16:17. *t Grace of God,* Rom. 4:16. *u Jesus, eternity of,* Matt. 1:21. 3 R. V. times eternal. **10** *v Jesus, savior,* Matt. 1:21.

---

38:8; *for the temple,* Hag. 1:8. *For the temple enjoined by Cyrus,* Ezra 1:2–4.

*In offerings for sacrifice,* 2 Sam. 24:24. *In paying tithes,* Deut. 14:27–29. *In gifts to God,* Psa. 76:11.

*Toward the poor,* Deut. 15:7–11; 24:19–22; Neh. 8:10; Psa. 41:1–3; Isa. 58:6, 7; Matt. 19:21, 22; Mark 10:21; Luke 3:10, 11; Rom. 12:13; 15:27; 2 Cor. 9:6–15; Gal. 2:10; Eph. 4:28; 1 Tim. 5:16; 6:17–19; Jas. 2:15, 16; 1 John 3:17, 18; *by the ideal woman,* Prov. 31:20.

*Toward liberated Hebrew slaves,* Deut. 15:12–18.

*According to ability,* Num. 35:8; Deut. 16:10, 17; 1 Cor. 16:1–3; 2 Cor. 8:12. *Without ostentation,* Matt. 6:1–4. *With a willing heart,* 1 Chr. 29:5; Prov. 21:26; 2 Cor. 8:12; 9:1–6; Philemon 14. *With love,* 1 Cor. 13:3.

*Rewards for,* Psa. 112:5, 9; Prov. 3:9, 10; 11:24, 25; 13:7; 14:21; 19:6, 17; 22:9; 28:27; Eccl. 11:1, 2; Isa. 32:8; 58:10–12; Ezek. 18:7–16; Mal. 3:10–12; Matt. 25:34–40, 46; Luke 6:30–38; 12:33, 34; Heb. 6:10.

**Instances of:** *King of Sodom to Abraham,* Gen. 14:21. *Jacob, consecrating the tenth of his income,* Gen. 28:22. *Pharaoh to Joseph's people,* Gen. 45:18–20. *Israelites at the erection of the tabernacle,* Ex. 35:21–29; 36:3–7; 38:8; Num. 7; 31:48–54. *David toward the temple,* 2 Sam. 8:11; 1 Kin. 7:51; 8:17, 18; 1 Chr. 16:3; 21:24; 22; 26:26; 28:2; 29:2–5, 17; Psa. 132:1–5. *Barzillai and others to David,* 2 Sam. 17:27–29; 19:32. *Araunah for sacrifice,* 2 Sam. 24:22, 23. *Joab to David,* 2 Sam. 12:26–28. *Israelites' offerings for the temple,* 1 Chr. 26:27, 28; 29:6–9, 16, 17. *Solomon,* 1 Kin. 4:29. *Queen of Sheba to Solomon,* 1 Kin. 10:10. *Asa and Abijam toward the temple,* 1 Kin. 15:15. *Jehoshaphat,* 2 Kin. 12:18. *Israelites under Josiah and his people,* 2 Kin. 22:3–6; 2 Chr. 34:8–13; 35:1–19. *Jews after the captivity,* Ezra 1:5, 6; 2:68, 69; 3:7–9; 6:14–17; 8:25–28; Neh. 3; 4:6; 5:8–12; 6:3; 7:70–72; 8:12, 35; 10:32–39; 13:12, 31; Hag. 1:8, 12–14; 2:18, 19. *Nehemiah,* Neh. 5:14–19. *Cyrus,* Ezra 1:2–4, 7–11; 3:7; 5:13–15; 6:3. *Darius,* Ezra 6:7–12. *Artaxerxes,* Ezra 7:13–27; 8:24–27. *The Magi,* Matt. 2:11. *The centurion,* Luke 7:4, 5. *Mary Magdalene,* Luke 8:2, 3. *The good Samaritan,* Luke 10:33–35. *The poor widow,* Luke 21:2–4. *Christians, at Jerusalem,* Acts 2:44, 45; 4:32–37; 6:1–3; *at Antioch,* Acts 11:29; *at Philippi,* Phil. 4:14–18; *at Corinth,* 2 Cor. 8:19; 9:1, 2; *in Macedonia,* Rom. 15:26; 2 Cor. 8:1–5. *Hebrew Christians,* Heb. 6:10. *Dorcas,* Acts 9:36. *Cornelius,* Acts 10:4. *People of Melita to Paul,* Acts 28:10.

* **WORKS. Good,** 2 Cor. 9:8; Eph. 2:10; Col. 1:10; Jas. 3:17, 18.

*In altruistic service,* Ezek. 18:7, 8; Matt. 10:42; 25:35–46; Jas. 1:27. *Manifest faith,* Jas. 2:14–26.

*Enjoined,* Psa. 37:3; John 15:2–8, 14; *upon ministers,* Tit. 2:7; *upon women professing godliness,* 1 Tim. 2:10; *upon widows,* 1 Tim. 5:10; *upon other Christians,* Matt. 5:16; Col. 3:13; Tit. 3:1, 2, 8, 14; Jas. 3:13; 1 Pet. 2:12; *upon the rich,* 1 Tim. 6:18.

*To be wrought without ostentation,* Matt. 6:1–4. *Jesus a doer of,* Acts 10:38. *Emulation in, enjoined,* Heb. 10:14.

*w Death*, Num. 23:10.
*x Life, everlasting*, Eccl. 8:15.
*y Immortality*, 1 Cor. 15:54.
4 R. V. incorruption

**11**
*z Minister, call of*, Rom. 15:16.

*a Call, personal*, Phil. 3:14.
*b Preaching*, Matt. 9:35.
*c Instruction, in religion*, Prov. 23:23.
*d Gentiles, conversion of*, Acts 10:45.
5 R. V. *omits* of the Gentiles.

**12**
*e Suffering for Christ*, Phil. 1:29.
*f Paul, persecutions of*, Acts 13:9.
*g Faith, trial of*, Mark 11:22.
*h Religious Testimony*, 2 Thess. 1:10.
*i Assurance*, Heb. 10:22.
*j Faith in Christ*, John 6:69.
*k Righteous, promises to*, Psa. 64:10.
*l Judgment, the general*, 2 Pet. 3:7.
*m Jesus, second coming* (as some interpret), Matt. 1:21.
*n Death*, Num. 23:10.
6 R. V him whom

**13**
*o Commandment, to ministers*, Deut. 8:2.
*p Perseverance*, Eph. 6:18.
*q Gospel*, Mark 13:10.
*r Love, for Jesus*, 1 John 4:19.

**14**
*s Holy Spirit*, Acts 1:2.

**15**
*t Asia*, Acts 2:9.

**16**
*u Prayer, intercessory*, Acts 6:4.
*v God, mercy of*, Gen. 2:2.
*w* 2 Tim. 4:19.
*x Love, of man for man*, 1 John 4:7.
*y Kindness*, Acts 28:2.
*z Prisoners, kindness to*, Psa. 79:11.

**18**
*a God, mercy of*, Gen. 2:2.
*b Ephesus*, Acts 18:19.

Jē′ṣus Chrīst, who hath abolished [w]death, and hath brought
[x,y]life and [4]immortality[C] to light
through the [o]gospel:[T]
11 Whereunto [z]I am [a]appointed
a [b]preacher, and an apostle, and
a [c]teacher [5]of the [d]Ġĕn′tīleṣ.
12 For the which cause I also
[e,f,g]suffer these things: nevertheless [h]I am not ashamed: for I
[i]know [6]whom I have [j]believed,[C]
and am persuaded that [k]he is
able to keep that which I have
committed unto him against[C] that
[l,m,n]day.[S]
13 [o,p]Hold fast the form of
[q]sound words, which thou hast
heard of me, in [j]faith and [r]love
which is in Chrīst Jē′ṣus.[S]
14 That good thing which was
committed unto thee [o,p]keep by
the [s]Holy[C] Ghost[C] which dwelleth
in us.[T]
15 This thou knowest, that all
they which are in [t]Ā′ṣiȧ be turned away from me; of whom are
Phȳ-ġĕl′lus and Hĕr-mŏġ′e-nēṣ.
16 [u]The Lord give [v]mercy unto
the house of [w]Ŏn-e-sĭph′o-rŭs;
for [x]he oft [y]refreshed [z]me, and
was not ashamed of my chain:
17 But, when [w]he was in Rōme,
[x]he sought me out very diligently, and found *me*.
18 [u]The Lord grant unto him
that he may find [a]mercy of the
Lord in that day: and in how
many things he ministered unto
me at [b]Ĕph′e-sŭs, thou knowest
very well.

## CHAPTER 2

*Timothy is again exhorted to faithfulness in preaching the gospel, 16 and to shun profane and vain babblings. 19 The foundation of the Lord is sure. 22 What Timothy is to avoid, and what to follow. 24 The servant of the Lord must not strive.*

THOU therefore, my son, [a]be
[b]strong in the grace that is
in Chrīst Jē′ṣus.[S]
2 And [a]the things that thou
hast heard of me among many
witnesses, the same commit thou
to [b]faithful men, who shall be
able to [c,d]teach others also.
3 [1,a,b]Thou therefore [e,f]endure
[g]hardness,[C] as a good [h,i]soldier of
Jē′ṣus Chrīst.
4 [2,j,k]No [h]man that warreth[C] entangleth himself with the affairs
of *this* life; that he may please
him who [3]hath chosen him to be
a soldier.
5 And [l]if a man also [4]strive for
masteries,[C] *yet* is he not [m]crowned,
except he strive lawfully.
6 The [n]husbandman[C] that laboureth must be first partaker
of the fruits.
7 Consider what I say; [5]and the
Lord give thee [b,o]understanding
in all things.
8 Remember that Jē′ṣus Chrīst
of the seed of Dā′vid was [p]raised
from the dead according to my
gospel:
9 Wherein [g,q]I [f]suffer [r,s]trouble,
as an evil doer, *even* unto bonds;[C]
but the [t]word of God is not
bound.
10 Therefore I [q]endure all
things [u]for the [v]elect's[C] sakes,
that they may also obtain the
[w]salvation[C] which is in [x]Chrīst
Jē′ṣus with [y]eternal glory.[S]
11 *It is* a faithful[C] saying: For if
we [6]be [z]dead with *him*, [a]we shall
also [b]live with *him*:
12 If we [c]suffer, [a,d]we shall also
[e]reign with *him*: if we [f]deny *him*,
he also will [g]deny us:
13 If we [7]believe[C] not, *yet* he
abideth [h]faithful: he cannot deny
himself.[S Q]
14 Of these things put *them* in
remembrance, [i]charging *them*

**2**
*c Instruction, in religion*, Prov. 23:23.
*d Minister, duties of*, Rom. 15:16.

**3**
*e Faithfulness*, Luke 16:10.
*f Suffering for Christ*, Phil. 1:29.
*g Minister, trials and persecutions of*, Rom. 15:16.
*h Soldiers, figurative*, Ezra 8:22.
*i Righteous, compared to soldiers*, Psa. 64:10.
1 R. V. Suffer hardship with me,

**4**
*j Worldliness, admonitions against*, 1 John 2:15.
*k Self-denial*, Mark 8:34.
2 R. V. No soldier on service entangleth
3 R. V. enrolled him

**5**
*l Games*, 1 Cor. 9:24.
*m Crown, given victor in games*, Ex. 29:6.
4 R. V. contend in the games, he is not

**6**
*n Agriculture*, Gen. 3:23.

**7**
*o Wisdom, spiritual*, Prov. 2:2.
5 R. V. for the Lord shall give

**8**
*p Resurrection, of Jesus*, 1 Cor. 15:12.

**9**
*q Zeal*, 2 Cor. 7:11.
*r Paul, persecutions of*, Acts 13:9.
*s Persecution, of the righteous*, John 15:20.
*t Doctrines of Jesus*, John 7:16.

**10**
*u Minister, love of, for the church*, Rom. 15:16.
*v Election of Grace*, Rom. 11:5.
*w Salvation*, Acts 16:17.
*x Jesus, savior*, Matt. 1:21.
*y Life, everlasting*, Eccl. 8:15. **11** *z Death, figurative*, Num. 23:10. —*a Righteous, promises to*, Psa. 64:10. *b Life, everlasting*, Eccl. 8:15. 6 R. V. died **12** *c Suffering for Christ*, Phil. 1:29. *d Afflictions, consolation in*, Psa. 34:19. *e Reward, a motive, to faithfulness*, Matt. 5:12. *f Jesus, rejected*, Matt. 1:21. *g Wicked, punishment of*, Psa. 73:3.
**13** *h Jesus, perfections of*, Matt. 1:21. **7** R. V. are faithless,
**14** *i Minister, duties of*, Rom. 15:16.

**1** *a Commandment, to ministers*, vs. 3, 14–16, 22, 23; Deut. 8:2.
*b Minister, character and qualifications of*, Rom. 15:16.

*Zeal in, required*, Tit. 2:14. *Are remembered by God*, Acts 10:4; Heb. 6:9, 10.
**Insufficient for salvation**, Psa. 127:1, 2; Isa. 13:14; 57: 12; 64:6; Luke 17:7–10; 18:9–14; Acts 13:39; Rom. 3:20–31; 4:1–25; 9:16, 31, 32; 11:6; 1 Cor. 13:1–3; Gal. 2:16, 21; 3:10–12, 21; Eph. 2:8, 9; Phil. 3:3–9; 2 Tim. 1:9; Tit. 3:4, 5.

before the Lord that they [j]strive
not about words to no profit, *but*
to the subverting[G] of the hearers.
15 [8,k,l]Study to shew thyself
approved unto God, a workman
that needeth not to be ashamed,
[9]rightly dividing the [m]word of
[n]truth.
16 But [k]shun profane[G] *and* vain[G]
babblings: for they will increase
unto more ungodliness.[T]
17 And their word will eat as
doth a [10]canker[G]: of[G] whom is
[o,p]Hȳ-me-næ′us and [o]Phī-lē′tus;
18 Who concerning the [n]truth
have erred, [q]saying that the [r]resurrection
is past already; and
[s]overthrow the [t]faith of some.
19 Nevertheless the foundation
of God standeth sure[G], having
this seal, [u]The Lord [v]knoweth[G]
[w]them that are his. And,
Let every one that [x]nameth the
[y]name of [11]Christ [z,a]depart from
iniquity.[S T Q]
20 But in a great house there
are not only vessels of gold and
of silver, but also of wood and of
earth; and some to honour, and
some to dishonour.
21 If a man therefore [b]purge
himself from these, he shall be a
[c]vessel unto honour, [d]sanctified,
and meet[G] for the master's[G] use, *and*
prepared unto every [e]good work.[S]
22 [f]Flee also youthful [g]lusts[G]:
but [h]follow [i]righteousness, [j]faith,
[12,k]charity[G], [l]peace, with them
that [m]call on the Lord out of
a [n]pure heart.
23 But [o]foolish and unlearned
questions avoid, knowing that
they do gender[G] [p]strifes[G].
24 And [o]the [q]servant[G] of the
Lord [r]must not [p]strive[G]; but [h]be
[r,s]gentle unto all *men*, [r]apt[G] to
[t]teach, [r,u]patient,
25[S] [o]In [v]meekness [13,w]instructing
those that oppose themselves;
if God peradventure[G] will
give them [x]repentance to the acknowledging
of the [y]truth;
26 And *that* they may recover
themselves out of the snare of
the [z,a]devil, who are taken [b]captive
by [14]him at his will.[S]

## CHAPTER 3

*The apostle foretells perilous times,* 2 *and describes the enemies of the truth.* 10 *He encourages Timothy by his own example.* 12 *The godly shall suffer persecution.* 14 *Steadfastness in the truth urged.* 16 *All inspired scripture profitable.*

THIS know also, that in the
last days [1]perilous times
shall come.
2 For [a]men shall be [*,b,c]lovers
of their own selves, [d]covetous,
boasters, [e]proud, [2]blasphemers[G],
[f]disobedient to parents,
[g]unthankful, unholy,
3 [b]Without [h]natural affection,
[3]trucebreakers, [†,i]false accusers,
incontinent[G], fierce, despisers of
those that are good,
4 [b,j]Traitors, heady[G], highminded[G],
[c]lovers of [k]pleasures more
than lovers of God;
5 [b,l,m]Having a form of [n]godliness,
but denying the power
thereof: [o,p]from such turn away.

*j Strife,* Prov. 20:3.

**15**

*k Commandment, to ministers,* Deut. 8:2.
*l Minister, character and qualifications of,* Rom. 15:16.
*m Gospel,* Mark 13:10.
*n Truth, of the gospel,* John 18:37.
8 R. V. Give diligence to present thyself
9 R. V. handling aright

**17**

*o False Teachers,* 2 Pet. 2:1.
*p* 1 Tim. 1:20.
10 R. V. gangrene:

**18**

*q Heresy,* Tit. 3:10.
*r Resurrection,* 1 Cor. 15:12.
*s Influence, evil,* 1 Cor. 7:14.
*t Faith in Christ,* John 6:69.

**19**

*u Promise, to the righteous,* 2 Cor. 1:20.
*v God, knowledge of,* Gen. 2:2.
*w Righteous, described,* Psa. 64:10.
*x Confession of Christ,* Luke 12:8.
*y Name of Jesus,* John 14:13.
*z Commandment, enjoining holiness,* Deut. 8:2.

*a Holiness, enjoined,* Ex. 39:30.
11 R. V. of the Lord depart from unrighteousness.

**21**

*b Spiritual Purification,* Psa. 51:2.
*c Righteous, described,* Psa. 64:10.
*d Sanctification,* 1 Pet. 1:2.
*e Works, good,* 2 Tim. 1:9.

**22** *f Young Men, admonitions to,* Prov. 1:4. *g Lust, warnings against,* 2 Pet. 1:4. *h Commandment, enjoining Christian graces,* Deut. 8:2. *i Righteousness, required,* Psa. 15:2. *j Faith in Christ, enjoined,* John 6:69. *k Love, of man for man, enjoined,* 1 John 4:7. *l Peace, enjoined,* Jer. 29:7. *m Prayer,* Acts 6:4. *n Purity, of heart,* 1 Tim. 4:12. 12 R. V. love,

**23**

*o Commandment, to ministers,* Deut. 8:2.
*p Strife,* Prov. 20:3.

**24**

*q Righteous, described,* Psa. 64:10.
*r Minister, character and qualifications of,* Rom. 15:16.
*s Gentleness, required in ministers,* 2 Cor. 10:1.
*t Instruction, in religion,* Prov. 23:23.
*u Patience, enjoined,* Luke 8:15.

**25**

*v Meekness,* Psa. 45:4.
*w Minister, duties of,* Rom. 15:16.
*x Repentance, gift of God,* Mark 1:4.
*y Truth,* John 18:37.
13 R. V. correcting

**26**

*z Satan,* Matt. 4:10.

*a Temptation, sources of,* Luke 11:4.
*b Captivity, figurative,* Isa. 5:13.
14 R. V. the Lord's servant unto the will of God.

**1**

1 R. V. grievous

**2**

*a Apostasy,* vs. 2–9; Acts 1:25.
*b Wicked, described,* vs. 2–13; Psa. 73:3.
*c Worldliness,* 1 John 2:15.
*d Covetousness,* Isa. 57:17.
*e Pride,* Prov. 16:18.
*f Children, wicked,* Mark 10:14.

*g Ingratitude,* Rom. 1:21. 2 R. V. railers, **3** *h Affections, natural,* 2 Cor. 7:15. *i Slander,* Prov. 10:18. 3 R. V. implacable, slanderers, without self-control, fierce, no lovers of good, **4** *j Citizens, wicked and treasonable,* Luke 15:15. *k Worldly Pleasure,* Eccl. 2:1. **5** *l Spiritual Blindness,* 2 Cor. 4:4. *m Delusion, of those who trust in the form of godliness,* 2 Thess. 2:11. *n Godliness,* 1 Tim. 4:8. *o Commandment, forbidding fellowship with the wicked,* Deut. 8:2. *p Evil Company, forbidden,* Prov. 13:20.

* **SELFISHNESS,** Hag. 1:4, 9; Phil. 2:21. *Admonitions against,* Deut. 15:9; Rom. 14:15; 15:1–3; 1 Cor. 10:24; Gal. 6:2; Phil. 2:4. *Christ's example against,* Rom. 15:3; 2 Cor. 5:15.
*Unsympathetic with the unfortunate,* Prov. 28:27; Jas. 2:15, 16; 1 John 3:17.
*Of corrupt officials,* Mic. 3:11. *Of priests and prophets,* Ezek. 34:18; Zech. 7:6. *Of the opulent,* Prov. 11:26; Matt. 19:21, 22. *Of monopolists,* Prov. 11:26; Isa. 5:8. *Of the self-indulgent,* Rom. 14:15; 2 Tim. 3:2–4.
*Exemplified, by Cain,* Gen. 4:9; *by David's friends,* Psa. 38:11.

† **FALSE ACCUSATION.** *Forbidden,* Ex. 23:1, 7; Lev. 19:16; Luke 3:14; Tit. 2:3.
*Consolations for the falsely accused,* Matt. 5:11; 1 Pet. 4:14.
*Against Joseph by Potiphar's wife,* Gen. 39:7–20. *Against Moses by Korah,* Num. 16:1–3, 13. *Against the prophet Ahimelech by Saul,* 1 Sam. 22:11–16. *Against Abner by Joab,* 2 Sam. 3:24–27. *Against David,* Psa. 41:5–9; *by the princes of Ammon,* 2 Sam. 10:1–4; 1 Chr. 19:1–4. *Against Elijah by Ahab,* 1 Kin. 18:17, 18. *Against Naboth by Jezebel,* 1 Kin. 21:1–14. *Against Jews, returned under Ezra,* Ezra 4:6–16; Neh. 6:5–9. *Against Jeremiah,* Jer. 26:8–11; 37:13–15; 43:1–4. *Against Amos,* Amos 7:10, 11. *Against Jesus,* Matt. 9:34; 10:25; 12:2–14; 26:59–61; Mark 3:22; 14:53–65; Luke 23:2; John 18:30. *Against Stephen,* Acts 6:11, 13. *Against Paul,* Acts 17:7; 21:27–29; 24:1–9, 12, 13; 25:1, 2, 7; Rom. 3:8. *Against Paul and Silas,* Acts 16:19–21. *Satan falsely accuses Job,* Job 1:9, 10; 2:4, 5.

6 For of this sort[G] are [q]they which creep into houses, and lead [r]captive [s]silly[G] women laden[G] with sins, led away with divers[G] lusts,

7 Ever learning, and [l]never able to come to the knowledge of the truth.

8 Now as Jăn′nēş and Jăm′brēş withstood [t]Mō′şeş, so do these also resist the [u]truth: men of corrupt minds, [v]reprobate[G] concerning the [w]faith.[S] [Q]

9 But they shall proceed no further: for their folly shall be manifest unto all *men*, as their's also was.

10 But [x]thou [4]hast fully known my doctrine, manner of life, purpose, [y,z]faith, [z,a]longsuffering, [z,b]charity,[G] [z,c]patience,

11 [d,e]Persecutions, afflictions, which came unto me at [f]Ăn′tĭ-ŏch, at [g]Ī-cō′nĭ-ŭm, at [h]Lȳs′trȧ; what persecutions I endured: but out of *them* all the Lord [i]delivered me.[Q]

12 Yea, and all that will [j]live godly in Chrīst Jē′şus shall suffer [k]persecution.

13 But [l]evil men and [5]seducers[G] shall [m]wax[G] worse and worse, [n]deceiving, and being deceived.

14 But [o,p]continue [q]thou in the things which thou hast learned and hast been assured of, knowing of whom thou hast learned *them*;

15 And that from a [6,r]child [q,s]thou hast [t]known the [u]holy scriptures, which are able to make thee wise unto [v]salvation through [w]faith which is in [x]Chrīst Jē′şus.[S]

16 [7]All [y]scripture *is* given by [z]inspiration of God, and *is* profitable for doctrine, for reproof, for correction, for [a]instruction [8]in righteousness:[T]

17 That the man of God may be [9,b,c,d]perfect,[C] throughly[C] furnished unto all [e]good works.

## CHAPTER 4

*The apostle's charge to Timothy. 6 The time of his own departure at hand. 8 The crown of righteousness. 9 He exhorts Timothy to come to him speedily. 16 No one stood with him at his first answer. 19 Salutations.*

I CHARGE [a,b]*thee* [1]therefore before God, and the [c]Lord Jē′şus Chrīst, who shall [d]judge the quick[C] and the dead [2]at his [e]appearing and his kingdom;[T]

2 [a,f,g,h]Preach[C] the [i]word; be [j]instant[G] in season, out of season; [k]reprove, rebuke,[C] exhort[G] with all [l]longsuffering and [3,m]doctrine.[T]

3 For the time will come when they will not endure [n]sound doctrine; but after their own lusts shall they heap to themselves [o]teachers, having itching [p]ears;

4 And they shall [q]turn away *their* ears from the [n]truth, and shall be turned unto [r]fables.[C]

5 But [g,s]watch thou in all things, [t]endure afflictions, [h]do the work of an [u]evangelist, [4]make full proof of thy ministry.

6 For [v]I am now ready to be offered, and the time of my [w]departure is at hand.

7 [x,y]I have [z]fought a [a]good fight, I have finished *my* course, I have kept the [b]faith:

8 Henceforth [c]there is laid up for me a [d]crown of righteousness, which the [e]Lord, the righteous [f]judge, shall give me at that [g]day: and not to me only, but [h]unto all them also that [i]love his [j]appearing.[T]

9 Do[C] thy diligence to come shortly unto me:

10 For [k]Dē′mas hath forsaken me, having [l]loved this present

**6**
q *False Teachers,* 2 Pet. 2:1.
r *Captivity, figurative,* Isa. 5:13.
s *Women, wicked,* Prov. 31:10.

**8**
t *Moses,* Ex. 2:10.
u *Truth,* John 18:37.
v *Reprobates,* 1 Cor. 9:27.
w *Faith, the doctrines of Jesus,* 1 Cor. 16:13.

**10**
x *Timothy,* 1 Cor. 4:17.
y *Faith in Christ,* John 6:69.
z *Christian Graces,* Gal. 5:22.
a *Longsuffering,* 2 Cor. 6:6.
b *Love,* 1 John 4:7.
c *Patience,* Luke 8:15.
4 R. V. didst follow my teaching, conduct, purpose, faith, longsuffering, love, patience,

**11**
d *Suffering for Christ,* Phil. 1:29.
e *Paul, persecutions of,* Acts 13:9.
f *Antioch,* Acts 13:14.
g *Iconium,* Acts 13:51.
h *Lystra,* Acts 14:6.
i *God, preserver,* Gen. 2:2.

**12**
j *Righteous, described,* Psa. 64:10.
k *Persecution, of the righteous,* John 15:20.

**13**
l *Temptation, sources of,* Luke 11:4.
m *Sin, progressive,* Rom. 5:12.
n *Deceit, the wicked practice,* Psa. 36:3.
5 R. V. impostors

**14**
o *Perseverance, enjoined,* Eph. 6:18.
p *Character, stability of,* Phil. 2:15.
q *Timothy,* 1 Cor. 4:17.

**17**
b *Holiness,* Ex. 39:30.
c *Perfection,* Heb. 6:1.
d *Minister, character and qualifications of,* Rom. 15:16.
e *Works, good,* 2 Tim. 1:9.
9 R. V. complete,

**1**
a *Minister, charge delivered to,* Rom. 15:16.
b *Timothy,* 1 Cor. 4:17.
c *Jesus, divinity of,* Matt. 1:21.
d *Jesus, judge,* Matt. 1:21.
e *Judgment, the general,* 2 Pet. 3:7.
1 R. V. in the sight of God, and of Christ Jesus,
2 R. V. and by his

**2**
f *Preaching,* Matt. 9:35.
g *Commandment, to ministers,* Deut. 8:2.
h *Minister, duties of,* Rom. 15:16
i *Gospel,* Mark 13:10.
j *Diligence, of ministers,* Rom. 12:8.
k *Reproof, enjoined,* Prov. 17:10.
l *Longsuffering,* 2 Cor. 6:6.
m *Instruction, in religion,* Prov. 23:23.
3 R. V. teaching.

**3**
n *Truth, of the gospel,* John 18:37.
o *False Teachers,* 2 Pet. 2:1.
p *Ear, figurative,* Lev. 8:23.

**4**
q *Apostasy,* Acts 1:25.
r *Fable,* 1 Tim. 1:4.

**5**
s *Watchfulness, enjoined,* Matt. 24:42.
t *Suffering for Christ,* Phil. 1:29.
u Acts 21:8; Eph. 4:11.
4 R. V. fulfil thy

**15** r *Children, instruction of, in the Scriptures,* Mark 10:14. s *Young Men,* Prov. 1:4. t *Wisdom, spiritual,* Prov. 2:2. u *Word of God,* Psa. 119:9. v *Salvation,* Acts 16:17. w *Faith in Christ,* John 6:69. x *Jesus, savior,* Matt. 1:21. 6 R. V. babe
**16** y *Word of God, is inspired,* Psa. 119:9. z *Inspiration,* Job 32:8.—a *Instruction, in religion,* Prov. 23:23. 7 R. V. Every scripture inspired of God is also profitable for teaching, 8 R. V. which is in

**6** v *Resignation, exemplified,* Job 5:17. w *Death, of the righteous,* Num. 23:10. **7** x *Religious Testimony,* 2 Thess. 1:10. y *Faithfulness,* Luke 16:10. z *Games, figurative,* 1 Cor. 9:24.—a 1 Tim. 6:12. b *Faith, the doctrines of Jesus,* 1 Cor. 16:13. **8** c *Assurance, of eternal reward,* Heb. 10:22. d *Crown, figurative,* Ex. 29:6. e *Jesus, lordship of,* Matt. 1:21. f *Jesus, judge,* Matt. 1:21. g *Judgment, the general,* 2 Pet. 3:7. h *Righteous, promises to,* Psa. 64:10. i *Love, for Jesus,* 1 John 4:19. j *Jesus, second coming of,* Matt. 1:21.
**10** k Col. 4:14. l *Backsliding, temptations to,* Hos. 11:7.

world, and is departed unto
[m]Thĕs-sa-lŏ-nī'cȧ; Crĕs'çenṣ to
[n]Gȧ-lā'tiȧ, [o]Tī'tus unto [p]Dăl-
mā'tĭ-ȧ.
11 Only [q]Lụke is with me.
Take [r]Märk, and bring him with
thee: for he is profitable to me
for [5]the ministry.
12 And [s]Tȳch'ĭ-cŭs have I sent
to [t]Ĕph'e-sŭs.
13 The cloke that I left at
[u]Trō'ăs with Cär'pus, when thou
comest, bring *with thee*, and the
[v]books, *but* especially the parch-
ments.
14 Ăl-ĕx̱-ăn'dẽr the copper-
smith did me much evil: the
Lord [6,w]reward him according
to his works:
15 Of whom be thou ware also;
for he hath greatly withstood our
words.
16 At my first [7]answer [x]no man
stood with me, but [y,z]all *men*
forsook me: [a,b]*I pray God* that it
may not be laid to their charge.
17 Notwithstanding the Lord
stood with me, and [c,d]strength-
ened me; that [8]by me the [e]preach-
ing might be fully known, and
*that* all the [f]Ġĕn'tīleṣ might
hear: and I was [g,h]delivered out
of the mouth of the lion.
18 And [i]the Lord [j]shall [g]deliver
me from every evil work, and
will [h]preserve *me* unto his [k]heav-
enly kingdom: to whom *be* [l]glory
for ever and ever. Amen.
19 [m]Salute [n]Prĭs'cȧ and [n]Ăq'-
uĭ-lȧ, and the household of [o]Ŏn-
e-sĭph'o-rŭs.
20 [p]Ē-răs'tus abode at [q]Cŏr'-
inth: but [r]Trŏph'ĭ-mŭs have I
left at [s]Mī-lē'tum sick.
21 Do thy diligence to come
before winter. Eū-bū'lus [m]greet-
eth thee, and Pū'denṣ, and Lī'-
nus, and Clạu'dĭ-ȧ, and all the
[t]brethren.
22 [u]The Lord [9]Jē'ṣus Chrīst *be*
with thy spirit. [d]Grace *be* with
you. Amen.

[10]The second epistle unto Timotheus, ordained the first bishop of the church of the Ephesians, was written from Rome, when Paul was brought before Nero the second time.

*m Thessalonica,* Phil. 4:16.
*n Galatia,* Acts 16:6.
*o Titus,* Tit. 1:4.
*p* Or, *Illyricum,* Rom. 15:19.

11
*q Luke,* Col. 4:14.
*r Mark,* Acts 12:12.
5 R. V. ministering.

12
*s Tychicus,* Acts 20:4.
*t Ephesus,* Acts 18:19.

13
*u* Acts 16:8, 11; 20:5, 6; 2 Cor. 2:12.
*v Book,* Num. 5:23.

14
*w Judgment, according to opportunity and works,* 1 Pet. 1:17.
6 R. V. will render to him

16
*x Friends, false,* Ex. 33:11.
*y Afflictions, forsaken by friends in,* Psa. 34:19.
*z Cowardice,* Lev. 26:36.
*a Meekness,* Psa. 45:4.
*b Prayer, intercessory,* Acts 6:4.

*e Gospel,* Mark 13:10.
*f Gentiles, conversion of,* Acts 10:45.
*g God, providence of,* Gen. 2:2.
*h God, preserver,* Gen. 2:2.
8 R. V. through me the message might be fully proclaimed,

18
*i Faith, exemplified,* Mark 11:22.
*j Assurance, of eternal reward,* Heb. 10:22.
*k Heaven, future home of the righteous,* Luke 18:22.
*l Praise,* Psa. 150:1.

19
*m Salutations,* Luke 1:44.
*n Aquila and Priscilla,* Acts 18:2.
*o* 2 Tim. 1:16, 17.

20
*p* Acts 19:22.
*q Corinth,* Acts 18:1.
*r Trophimus,* Acts 20:4.
*s* Or, *Miletus,* Acts 20:15, 17–38.

7 R. V. defence no one took my part, but all forsook me: may it not be laid to their account. **17** *c Adversity, consolation in,* Psa. 10:6. *d Grace of God,* Rom. 4:16.

**21** *t Fraternity,* Zech. 11:14. **22** *u Benedictions, apostolic,* Deut. 21:5. 9 R. V. *omits* Jesus Christ **10** R. V. *omits postscript.*

---

THE EPISTLE OF PAUL TO

# TITUS

## CHAPTER 1

*The apostle's salutation. 5 Why he left Titus in Crete. 7 The qualifications of a bishop. 10 Many vain talkers and deceivers among the Cretans. 13 He is to rebuke them sharply.*

[a]PAUL, a servant of God,
and an apostle of Jē'ṣus
[b]Chrīst, according to the faith of
God's elect, and the acknowledging of the [c]truth which is
after [d]godliness;
2 In [e]hope of [f]eternal [g]life,
[h]which [i]God, that [j,k]cannot [l]lie,
promised before [1]the world began;
3 But [2]hath in due times manifested his [m]word through [n]preach-
ing, which is [o,p]committed unto
me according to the commandment of God our [q]Saviour;
4 To *Tī'tus, [r]*mine* own son

1
*a Paul,* Acts 13:9.
*b Jesus, Messiah,* Matt. 1:21.
*c Truth,* John 18:37.
*d Godliness,* 1 Tim. 4:8.

2
*e Hope, of eternal life,* Prov. 13:12.
*f Immortality,* 1 Cor. 15:54.
*g Life, everlasting,* Eccl. 8:15.

*h Righteous, promises to,* Psa. 64:10.
*i God, faithfulness of,* Gen. 2:2.
*j God, truth,* Gen. 2:2.
*k God, immutable,* Gen. 2:2.
*l Falsehood,* Job 21:34.
1 R. V. times eternal;

**3** *m Gospel,* Mark 13:10. *n Preaching,* Matt. 9:35. *o Call, to special religious duty,* Phil. 3:14. *p Minister, call of,* Rom. 15:16. *q God, savior,* Gen. 2:2. 2 R. V. in his own seasons manifested his word in the message, wherewith I was intrusted according
**4** *r Love, of man for man,* 1 John 4:7.

---

*** TITUS,** a Greek companion of Paul. *Paul's love for,* 2 Cor. 2:13; 7:6, 7, 13, 14; 8:23; Tit. 1:4. *With Paul in Macedonia,* 2 Cor. 7:5, 6; see postscript to 2 Corinthians. *Affection of, for the Corinthians,* 2 Cor. 7:15. *Sent to Corinth,* 2 Cor. 8:6, 16–22; 12:17, 18. *Character of,* 2 Cor. 12:18. *Paul's amanuensis in writing to the Corinthians,* see postscript to 2 Corinthians. *Accompanies Paul to Jerusalem,* Gal. 2:1–3. *Left by Paul in Crete,* Tit. 1:5; *to rejoin him in Nicopolis,* Tit. 3:12. *Ordained bishop of the Cretans,* see postscript to Titus. *Paul writes to,* Tit. 1:1–4. *With Paul in Rome,* 2 Tim. 4:10 with postscript to 2 Timothy. *Goes to Dalmatia,* 2 Tim. 4:10.

after the common[G] [s]faith: [t]Grace, [u]mercy, *and* [v]peace, from God the [w]Father and [3]the [x]Lord Jē'sus Christ our [y]Saviour.[T]

5 For this cause left I thee in [z]Crēte, that thou shouldest [a]set in order the things that are wanting, and ordain[G] [b]elders[G] in every city, as I had appointed thee:

6 If any be [c,d]blameless, the [e]husband of [f]one wife, having [4,g]faithful[G] [h]children not accused of riot[G] or unruly.

7 For a bishop[G] must be [c,d,i]blameless, as the [j]steward of God; not [k]selfwilled, not soon [l]angry, [5]not given to wine, no [m]striker[G], not [6,n,o]given to filthy lucre[G];

8 But [c,i]a lover of [p]hospitality, a lover of good [7]men, [q]sober[G], [r]just, [d]holy, [s]temperate;

9 [c,i]Holding fast the faithful [t]word as he hath been taught, that he may be able by sound doctrine both to [a]exhort and to [8,a]convince[G] the gainsayers[G].

10 For there are many unruly [9]and vain [u]talkers and deceivers, specially[G] they of the [v]circumcision[G]:

11 [u]Whose mouths must be stopped, [10]who subvert[G] whole houses, teaching things which they ought not, [w]for filthy lucre's[G] sake.

12 One of themselves, *even* a prophet[G] of their own, said, The [x]Crē'tĭ-anș *are* alway [y]liars, evil beasts, [11]slow [z]bellies[G].

13 This witness[G] is true. Wherefore [a,b]rebuke them sharply, that they may be sound in the [c]faith;

14 Not giving heed to Jew'ish [d]fables[G], and [e]commandments of men, that turn from the [f]truth.

15 Unto the [g,h,i]pure all things *are* pure: but unto [j]them that are defiled and [k]unbelieving *is* nothing pure; but [j]even their mind and [l]conscience is defiled.[S T]

16 [j]They [m]profess[G] that they know God; but in works they deny *him*, being abominable[G], and [n]disobedient, and unto every good work [o]reprobate[G].

## CHAPTER 2

*Paul directs Titus to speak the things which become sound doctrine. 9 Servants are to be instructed to be obedient and honest. 14 Christ gave himself to redeem us from all iniquity.*

BUT [a]speak thou the things which become [b]sound doctrine:

2 [c]That the [d]aged men be [e]sober[G], grave, [e,f]temperate, sound in [g]faith, in [1,h]charity[G], in [i]patience.

3 [j]The [d]aged [k]women likewise, [2]that *they be* in behaviour as becometh holiness, not [l]false accusers, not given to much [m]wine, [n]teachers of good things;

4 [j]That they may [o]teach the young women [3]to be sober[G], to [p]love their [q]husbands, to love their [r]children,

5 [j]*To be* [4]discreet, [s]chaste, keepers at home, [t]good, [u]obedient to their own husbands, that the [v]word of God be not [w]blasphemed.

6 [x]Young men likewise exhort to be *sober[G] minded.

7 In all things shewing thyself a [y,z]pattern of [a]good works: in doctrine *shewing* uncorruptness[G], gravity, [5]sincerity,

*s Faith, the doctrines of Jesus,* 1 Cor. 16:13.
*t Grace of God,* Rom. 4:16.
*u God, mercy of,* Gen. 2:2.
*v Spiritual Peace, from God,* Gal. 1:3.
*w God, fatherhood of,* Gen. 2:2.
*x Jesus, lordship of,* Matt. 1:21.
*y Jesus, savior,* Matt. 1:21.
3 R. V. *omits* the Lord

**5**
*z Crete,* Acts 27:7.
*a Minister, duties of,* Rom. 15:16.
*b Elders,* Acts 14:23.

**6**
*c Minister, character and qualifications of,* Rom. 15:16.
*d Holiness,* Ex. 39:30.
*e Minister, marriage of,* Rom. 15:16.
*f Polygamy, forbidden,* Deut. 17:17.
*g Faith in Christ,* John 6:69.
*h Children, of ministers,* Mark 10:14.
4 R. V. children that believe, who are not

**7**
*i Bishop, character of,* 1 Tim. 3:1.
*j Steward, figurative,* Gen. 43:19.
*k Self-will,* Gen. 49:6.
*l Anger, forbidden,* Psa. 37:8.
*m Strife, forbidden,* Prov. 20:3.
*n Covetousness, debars from sacred office,* Isa. 57:17.
*o Avarice, forbidden in bishops,* Eccl. 5:10.
5 R. V. no brawler,
6 R. V. greedy of

**8**
*p Hospitality, enjoined,* Rom. 12:13.

**14**
*d Fable,* 1 Tim. 1:4.
*e Commandments of Men,* Mark 7:7.
*f Truth, of the gospel,* John 18:37.

**15**
*g Purity,* 1 Tim. 4:12.
*h Christian Graces, holiness,* Gal. 5:22.
*i Righteous, described,* Psa. 64:10.
*j Wicked, described,* Psa. 73:3.
*k Unbelievers,* 1 Cor. 6:6.
*l Conscience,* Acts 23:1.

**16**
*m Hypocrisy,* Jas. 3:17.
*n Disobedience to God,* Eph. 5:6.
*o Reprobates,* 1 Cor. 9:27.

**1**
*a Commandment, to ministers,* Deut. 8:2.
*b Truth, of the gospel,* John 18:37.

**2**
*c Commandment, enjoining manly gravity,* Deut. 8:2.
*d Old Age,* Isa. 46:4.
*e Righteousness, fruits of,* Psa. 15:2.
*f Temperance,* 2 Pet. 1:6.
*g Faith in Christ,* John 6:69.
*h Love, of man for man,* 1 John 4:7.
*i Patience, enjoined,* Luke 8:15.
1 R. V. love,

**3**
*j Commandment, concerning women,* Deut. 8:2.
*k Women, Paul's precepts concerning,* Prov. 31:10.
*l Slander,* Prov. 10:18.
*m Wine, admonitions against immoderate use of,* Prov. 23:31.

*q Sobermindedness,* Tit. 2:6. *r Justice,* Deut. 33:21. *s Temperance,* 2 Pet. 1:6. 7 R. V. *omits* men. **9** *t Doctrines of Jesus,* John 7:16. 8 R. V. convict **10** *u False Teachers,* 2 Pet. 2:1. *v Circumcision, figurative,* Gen. 17:10. 9 R. V. men, vain talkers **11** *w Covetousness,* Isa. 57:17. 10 R. V. men who overthrow whole
**12** *x Crete,* Acts 27:7. *y Falsehood,* Job 21:34. *z Gluttony,* Prov. 30:22. 11 R. V. idle gluttons.
**13**—*a Minister, duties of,* Rom. 15:16. *b Reproof, enjoined,* Prov. 17:10. *c Faith, the doctrines of Jesus,* 1 Cor. 16:13.

*n Teachers,* 1 Chr. 25:8. 2 R. V. be reverent in demeanour, not slanderers nor enslaved to much wine, teachers of that which is good; **4** *o Instruction, in religion,* Prov. 23:23. *p Wife, duty of,* Prov. 5:18. *q Husband,* Num. 30:6. *r Children,* Mark 10:14. 3 R. V. *omits* to be sober,
**5** *s Chastity,* Job 31:1. *t Kindness,* Acts 28:2. *u Family, government of,* 1 Chr. 13:14. *v Doctrines of Jesus,* John 7:16. *w Blasphemy,* 2 Sam. 12:14. 4 R. V. soberminded, chaste, workers at home, kind, being in subjection to **6** *x Young Men, admonitions to,* Prov. 1:4. **7** *y Example, good,* John 13:15. *z Minister, examples to the flock,* Rom. 15:16.—*a Works, good,* 2 Tim. 1:9. 5 R. V. *omits* sincerity,

* **SOBERMINDEDNESS.** *Enjoined,* Rom. 12:3; 1 Pet. 1:13; 4:7; 5:8; *upon women,* 1 Tim. 3:11; Tit. 2:4, 5; *upon men,* Tit. 2:2, 6; *upon ministers,* 1 Tim. 3:2; Tit. 1:8.

8 [b]Sound speech, that cannot be condemned; that he that
is of the contrary[G] part may be
ashamed,[G] having no evil thing
to say of [6]you.
9 [c]*Exhort* servants [d,e]to be obedient unto their own masters,[G]
*and* to please *them* well in all
*things*; not answering again;
10 [d]Not [f]purloining, but shewing all good fidelity; that they
may adorn the [g]doctrine of God
our [h]Saviour in all things.
11 For the [i]grace of God
that bringeth salvation[G] hath
appeared to all men,
12 [j]Teaching us that, [k,l]deny-
ing ungodliness and [m]worldly
[n]lusts, we should live soberly,[G]
[o]righteously, and [k]godly, in this
present world;[G]
13 Looking for that blessed
[p]hope, and [7]the glorious [q]appear-
ing of the great [r]God and our
[s]Saviour Jē'ṣus Christ;[T Q]
14 Who [t]gave himself for us,
that he might [u,v]redeem[G] us from
all iniquity,[G] and purify unto himself a [8]peculiar[G] people, [w]zealous
of [x]good works.[S T Q]
15 [y,z]These things [a]speak, and
[a]exhort,[G] and [b]rebuke[G] with all
[c]authority. Let no man despise
thee.[T]

## CHAPTER 3

*Titus is further directed to teach men to obey magistrates, and to be gentle to all. 8 Believers are to maintain good works. 9 He is to avoid foolish questions; 10 and to reject obstinate heretics. 12 Where he is to meet the apostle.*

[a]PUT them in mind to [b,c,d]be
[e]subject to principalities
and powers, to [f]obey magistrates, to be [g]ready to every
[h]good work,
2 To [i,j]speak evil of no man,
[1]to be no [k]brawlers, *but* [l,m]gen-
tle, shewing all [l,n]meekness unto
all men.
3 [S] [o]For we ourselves also were
[2]sometimes foolish, [p]disobedient,
deceived, serving divers[G] [q]lusts
and [r]pleasures, living in [s]malice
and [t]envy, hateful, *and* [u]hating
one another.
4 [T]But after that the [v]kindness
and [w]love of God our [x]Saviour
toward man appeared,
5 Not by [y]works of righteousness which we have done, but according to his [z]mercy he [x,a]saved
us, by the [b,c,d]washing of *regeneration, and renewing of the
[e]Holy[G] Ghost;[G]
6 Which he shed on us abundantly through Jē'ṣus Christ our
[f]Saviour;[Q]
7 That being [g,h]justified[G] by his
[i]grace, we should be made heirs
according to the [j]hope of [k,l]eter-
nal [m]life.[S T]
8 *This is* a faithful saying, and
these things I will that thou
[n]affirm[G] [3]constantly,[G] that they
which have [o]believed in God
might be careful to maintain
[p,q]good works. These things
are good and profitable unto
men.
9 But [r]avoid foolish questions,
and [s]genealogies, and [t]conten-
tions, and strivings[G] about the
law; for they are unprofitable
and vain.[G]

**8**
b *Speech, wise,* Col. 4:6.
6 R. V. us.
**9**
c *Commandment, to ministers,* Deut. 8:2.
d *Commandment, to servants,* Deut. 8:2.
e *Servant, duty of, to be obedient,* Jer. 2:14.
**10**
f *Theft,* Mark 7:22.
g *Truth of the Gospel,* John 18:37.
h *God, savior,* Gen. 2:2.
**11**
i *Salvation, plan of,* Acts 16:17.
**12**
j *Instruction, in religion,* Prov. 23:23.
k *Holiness,* Ex. 39:30.
l *Self-denial,* Mark 8:34.
m *Worldliness, admonitions against,* 1 John 2:15.
n *Lust, forbidden,* 2 Pet. 1:4.
o *Righteousness,* Psa. 15:2.
**13**
p *Hope, of eternal life,* Prov. 13:12.
q *Jesus, second coming of,* Matt. 1:21.
r *Jesus, divinity of,* Matt. 1:21.
s *Jesus, savior,* Matt. 1:21.
7 R. V. appearing of the glory of our great
**14**
t *Atonement, by Jesus,* Lev. 17:11.
u *Redemption of our Souls,* Eph. 1:7.
v *Jesus, design of his death,* Matt. 1:21.
w *Zeal, religious,* 2 Cor. 7:11.
x *Works, good,* 2 Tim. 1:9.
8 R. V. a people for his own possession.

**15** y *Commandment, to ministers,* Deut. 8:2. z *Church, discipline in,* Matt. 16:18.—a *Minister, duties of,* Rom. 15:16. b *Reproof, enjoined,* Prov. 17:10. c *Minister, clothed with authority,* Rom. 15:16.

**1** a *Minister, duties of,* Rom. 15:16. b *Commandment, enjoining obedience to civil government,* Deut. 8:2. c *Citizens, duties of,* Luke 15:15. d *Government, duty of citizens to,* Isa. 22:21. e *Loyalty, enjoined,* Eccl. 8:2. f *Magistrate, obedience to, enjoined,* Ezra 7:25.

g *Zeal,* 2 Cor. 7:11.
h *Works, good,* 2 Tim. 1:9.
**2**
i *Speech, evil,* Col. 4:6.
j *Slander,* Prov. 10:18.
k *Strife,* Prov. 20:3.
l *Christian Graces,* Gal. 5:22.
m *Gentleness, required,* 2 Cor. 10:1.
n *Meekness, enjoined,* Psa. 45:4.
1 R. V. not to be contentious,
**3**
o *Depravity,* Job 15:14.
p *Disobedience to God,* Eph. 5:6.
q *Lust,* 2 Pet. 1:4.
r *Worldly Pleasure,* Eccl. 2:1.
s *Malice,* Eph. 4:31.
t *Envy,* Prov. 14:30.
u *Hatred,* Prov. 15:17.
2 Am. R. V. beforetime
**4**
v *God, goodness of,* Gen. 2:2.
w *God, love of,* Gen. 2:2.
x *God, savior,* Gen. 2:2.
**5**
y *Works, insufficient for salvation,* 2 Tim. 1:9.
z *God, mercy of,* Gen. 2:2.
a *Salvation,* Acts 16:17.
b *Washing, figurative of regeneration,* Matt. 27:24.
c *Spiritual Purification,* Psa. 51:2.
d *Baptism* (as some interpret), Luke 20:4. e *Holy Spirit, regenerates,* Acts 1:2.

**6** f *Jesus, savior,* Matt. 1:21. **7** g *Justification,* Rom. 4:25. h *Sin, forgiveness of,* Rom. 5:12. i *Grace of God, in justification,* Rom. 4:16. j *Hope, of eternal life,* Prov. 13:12. k *Immortality,* 1 Cor. 15:54. l *Righteous, promises to,* Psa. 64:10. m *Life, everlasting,* Eccl. 8:15.

**8** n *Instruction, in religion,* Prov. 23:23. o *Faith,* Mark 11:22. p *Works, good,* 2 Tim. 1:9. q *Righteousness, fruits of,* Psa. 15:2. 3 R. V. confidently,

**9** r *Commandment, to ministers,* Deut. 8:2. s *Genealogy,* 1 Chr. 5:1. t *Strife,* Prov. 20:3.

* **REGENERATION,** Jer. 24:7; 31:3; John 1:4, 12, 13, 16; 3:3–9; 17:2; Acts 2:38; 11:15–17; Gal. 4:29; Jas. 1:18; 1 Pet. 1:23; 1 John 2:29; 3:9, 14; 4:7; 5:1, 4, 5, 11, 12, 18. *Necessity of,* Jer. 13:23; Matt. 12:33–35; 18:3; Mark 10:15; Luke 18:17; John 3:3, 5; Tit. 3:5, 6.

*Through the Holy Spirit,* John 3:5–8; 1 Cor. 12:13; 2 Thess. 2:13; 1 Pet. 1:2, 3, 22.

Other figures of the beginning of the spiritual life: *Circumcision of the heart,* Deut. 30:6; Ezek. 44:7; Rom. 2:28; Col. 2:11–13; *change of heart,* Jer. 31:33, 34 (with Heb. 8:10, 11); 32:38–40; Ezek. 11:19, 20; 18:31; 36:26, 27, 29; Rom. 12:2; *new creature,* 2 Cor. 5:17; Gal. 6:15; Eph. 4:22–24; Col. 3:9, 10; *spiritual cleansing,* John 15:3; Acts 15:9; 1 Cor. 6:11; *spiritual illumination,* John 6:44, 45; 8:12; Acts 26:18; 1 Cor.

10 [u]A [4]man that is an [†]heretick
after the first and second admonition [v]reject;
11 Knowing that he that is such
is subverted, and sinneth, being
[w]condemned of himself.
12 When I shall send Är'te-
măs unto thee, or [x]Tȳch'ĭ-cŭs,
be diligent to come unto me to
Nī-cŏp'o-lĭs: for I have determined there to winter.
13 Bring Zē'nas the [y]lawyer
and [z]Ȧ-pŏl'los on their journey
diligently, that nothing be wanting unto them.
14 And let [5]our's also learn
to maintain [a,b]good works for
necessary uses, that they be not
unfruitful.
15 All that are with me [c]salute
thee. Greet them that [d]love us in
the [e]faith. [f,g]Grace *be* with you
all. [6]Amen.

It was written to Titus, ordained the first bishop of the church of the Cretians, from Nicopolis of Macedonia.

**10** *u Church, discipline in,* Matt. 16:18. *v Disfellowship,* Num. 15:31. 4 Am. R. V. factious man after
**11** *w Self-condemnation,* Job 9:20.
**12** *x Tychicus,* Acts 20:4.
**13** *y Lawyer,* Matt. 22:35. *z Apollos,* Acts 19:1.
**14** *a Works, good,* 2 Tim. 1:9. *b Righteousness, fruits of,* Psa. 15:2. 5 R. V. our people
**15** *c Salutations,* Luke 1:44. *d Love, of man for man,* 1 John 4:7. *e Faith, doctrines of Jesus,* 1 Cor. 16:13. *f Benedictions, apostolic,* Deut. 21:5. *g Grace of God,* Rom. 4:16. 6 R. V. *omits* Amen *and postscript.*

THE EPISTLE OF PAUL TO

# PHILEMON

## CHAPTER I

*The apostle's salutation, in which he is joined by Timothy. 4 His thanksgiving to God for Philemon's faith and love. 8 He desires him to forgive his servant Onesimus, and lovingly to receive him again. 23 Various salutations to Philemon from the brethren.*

[a]PAUL, a [b,c]prisoner of Jē'ṣus
[d]Chrīst, and [e]Tĭm'o-thy̆
*our* brother, unto Phī-lē'mon our
dearly [f]beloved, and fellowlabourer,
2 And to [1]*our* beloved Ăp'phĭ-ȧ,
and [g]Är-chĭp'pus our fellow-
soldier, and to the [h]church in
thy [i]house:
3 [j,k]Grace to you, and [l]peace,
from God our [m]Father and the
[n]Lord Jē'ṣus Chrīst.
4 I [o]thank my God, [f]making
mention of thee always in my
[p]prayers,
5 Hearing of thy [f,q,r]love and
[r,s]faith, which thou hast toward
the Lord Jē'ṣus, and toward all
saints;
6 That the [2]communication of
thy [s]faith may become effectual
by the acknowledging of every
good thing which is in you in
Chrīst Jē'ṣus.
7 For [t]we have great joy and
consolation in thy [f]love, because
the [3]bowels of the saints are refreshed by thee, brother.
8 Wherefore, though I might be
much bold in Chrīst to enjoin
thee that which is [4]convenient,
9 Yet for [f]love's sake I rather beseech *thee,* being such an one as
[a]Paul the [u,v]aged, and now also
a [b,c]prisoner of Jē'ṣus Chrīst.
10 I [w]beseech [x]thee for my son
[y]Ō-nĕs'ĭ-mŭs, whom I have begotten in my bonds:
11 Which in time past was to
thee unprofitable, but now profitable to thee and to me:
12 Whom I have sent [5]again:
thou therefore receive him, that
is, [f]mine own bowels:
13 Whom I would have retained
with me, that in thy stead he
might have ministered unto me
in the bonds of the [z]gospel:
14 But without thy mind would

**1** *a Paul,* Acts 13:9. *b Prisoners,* Psa. 79:11. *c Suffering for Christ,* Phil. 1:29. *d Jesus, Messiah,* Matt. 1:21. *e Timothy,* 1 Cor. 4:17. *f Love, of man for man,* 1 John 4:7.
**2** *g* Col. 4:17. *h Church,* Matt. 16:18. *i House, used for worship,* Esth. 8:1. 1 R. V. Apphia our sister,
**3** *j Benedictions, apostolic,* Deut. 21:5. *k Grace of God,* Rom. 4:16. *l Spiritual Peace, from God,* Gal. 1:3. *m God, fatherhood of,* Gen. 2:2. *n Jesus, lordship of,* Matt. 1:21.
**4** *o Thankfulness, to God,* Acts 24:3. *p Prayer, intercessory,* Acts 6:4. **5** *q Love, for Jesus,* 1 John 4:19. *r Righteousness, fruits of,* Psa. 15:2. *s Faith in Christ,* John 6:69. **6** 2 R. V. fellowship of thy faith may become effectual, in the knowledge of every good thing which is in you, unto Christ.
**7** *t Fellowship, of the righteous,* 1 Cor. 1:9. 3 R. V. hearts
**8** 4 R. V. befitting;
**9** *u Longevity,* Psa. 91:16. *v Old Age,* Isa. 46:4.
**10** *w Intercession, of man with man,* vs. 10-19; Jer. 27:18. *x Master of Servants, exhorted to show kindness,* vs. 10-16; Col. 4:1. *y* Col. 4:9.
**12** 5 R. V. back to thee in his own person, that is, my very heart:
**13** *z Gospel,* Mark 13:10.

2:11, 12, 14-16; 2 Cor. 4:6; Eph. 5:14; Heb. 10:16; *spiritual quickening,* Ezek. 37:1-14; John 6:57; Eph. 2:1, 5, 6, 8, 10; 4:7; *spiritual resurrection,* John 5:24; Rom. 6:3-13; 8:2-4; Gal. 2:20.
† **HERESY.** *Teachers of, to be shunned,* Tit. 3:10, 11; 2 John 10, 11. *Teachers of, among early Christians,* Acts 15:24; 2 Cor. 11:4; Gal. 1:7; 2:4; 2 Pet. 2; Jude 3-16; Rev. 2:2. *Paul accused of,* Acts 18:13; 24:5, 6. *Disavowed by Paul,* Acts 24:13-16. See footnote. FALSE TEACHERS, 2 Pet. 2:1.

I do nothing; that thy [6]benefit should not be as it were of necessity, but willingly.

15 For perhaps he therefore [a]departed for a season, that thou shouldest receive him for ever;

16 Not now as a servant, but above a servant, a brother beloved, specially to me, but how much more unto thee, both in the flesh, and in the Lord?

17 If thou count me therefore a partner, [b]receive him as myself.

18 If he hath wronged thee, or oweth *thee* [7]ought, [c]put that on mine account;

19 I [d]Paul have written *it* with mine own hand, I will repay *it*: albeit I do not say to thee how thou owest unto me even thine own self besides.

20 Yea, brother, let me have [e]joy of thee in the Lord: refresh my [8]bowels in the Lord.

21 [f]Having confidence in thy obedience I wrote unto thee, knowing that thou wilt also do more than I say.

22 But withal [g]prepare me also a lodging: for I trust that through your [h,i]prayers I shall be given unto you.

23 There [j]salute thee [k]Ĕp′a-phrăs, my [l,m]fellowprisoner in Chrīst Jē′ṣus;

24 [n]Mär′cus, [o]Är-ĭs-tär′chus, [p]Dē′mas, [q]Lụ′cas, my fellowlabourers.

25 [r,s]The grace of our [t]Lord Jē′ṣus Chrīst *be* with your spirit. Amen.

[9]Written from Rome to Philemon, by Onesimus, a servant.

**14** 6 R. V. goodness

**15** *a* *Fugitives,* Judg. 12:4.

**17** *b* *Intercession, of man with man,* Jer. 27:18.

**18** *c* *Generosity,* Gen. 20:14. 7 R. V. aught,

**19** *d* *Paul,* Acts 13:9.

**20** *e* *Joy,* Psa. 5:11. 8 R. V. heart in Christ.

**21** *f* *Tact,* Prov. 15:1.

**22** *g* *Hospitality,* Rom. 12:13. *h* *Prayer, intercessory,* Acts 6:4. *i* *Minister, duty of church to,* Rom. 15:16.

**23** *j* *Salutations,* Luke 1:44. *k* Col. 1:7; 4:12. *l* *Prisoners,* Psa. 79:11. *m* *Suffering for Christ,* Phil. 1:29.

**24** *n* Or, *Mark,* Acts 12:12. *o* Acts 19:29. *p* Col. 4:14. *q* Or, *Luke,* Col. 4:14.

**25** *r* *Benedictions, apostolic,* Deut. 21:5. *s* *Grace of God,* Rom. 4:16. *t* *Jesus, lordship of,* Matt. 1:21. 9 R. V. *omits postscript.*

---

THE EPISTLE TO THE

# HEBREWS

## CHAPTER 1

*God in these last days has spoken to us by his Son, who is the brightness of his glory; 4 and is preferred above the angels, both in person and office. 13 Angels are ministering spirits.*

GOD, [1]who at sundry times and in divers manners [a,b]spake in time past unto the fathers by the [c]prophets,

2 Hath [2]in these last days [a]spoken unto us by *his* [d,e]Son, whom he hath appointed heir of all things, by whom also [f]he made the worlds;

3 Who being the brightness of *his* glory, and the [3]express [g]image of his person, and upholding all things by the word of his power, when he had [4]by himself [h,i,j]purged our sins, sat down [k]on the right hand of the [l]Majesty on high;

4 Being made so much [m]better than the *angels, as he hath by inheritance obtained a more excellent name than they.

5 For unto which of the *angels said he at any time, [n,o]Thou art my [d,e]son, this day have I begotten thee? And again, [p]I will be to him a [q]Father, and he shall be to me a Son?

6 And again, when he bringeth in the firstbegotten into the world, he saith, And let all the *angels of God [r]worship him.

7 And of the *angels he saith, [o,s]Who maketh his angels [5]spirits, and his ministers a flame of fire.

8 But [6]unto the [d]Son *he saith,* [t]Thy [u]throne, O God, *is* [v]for ever and ever: a sceptre of [7]righteousness *is* the sceptre of thy kingdom.

9 [t,w]Thou hast loved righteous-

**1** *a* *Revelation,* 2 Cor. 12:1. *b* *Word of God, is inspired,* Psa. 119:9. *c* *Prophets, inspiration of,* Isa. 3:2. 1 R. V. having of old time spoken unto the fathers in the prophets by divers portions and in divers manners,

**2** *d* *Jesus, divinity of,* Matt. 1:21. *e* *Jesus, relation of, to the Father,* Matt. 1:21. *f* *God, creator,* Gen. 2:2. 2 R. V. at the end of these days spoken unto us in his Son,

**3** *g* *Image, figurative,* 1 Cor. 11:7. *h* *Atonement, by Jesus,* Lev. 17:11. *i* *Spiritual Purification,* Psa. 51:2. *j* *Jesus, design of his death,* Matt. 1:21. *k* *Jesus, exaltation of,* Matt. 1:21. *l* *God, sovereign,* Gen. 2:2. 3 R.V. very image of his substance. 4 R. V. made purification of sins,

**4** *m* *Jesus, perfections of,* Matt. 1:21.

**5** *n* Psa. 2:7. *o* *Prophecies concerning the Messiah, and their fulfillment,* Gen. 12:3. *p* 2 Sam. 7:14. *q* *God, fatherhood of,* Gen. 2:2.

**6** *r* *Jesus, worship of,* Matt. 1:21.

**7** *s* Psa. 104:4. 5 R. V. winds,

**8** *t* Psa. 45:6, 7. *u* *Jesus, kingdom of,* Matt. 1:21. *v* *Jesus, eternity of,* Matt. 1:21. 6 R. V. of 7 R.V. uprightness is

**9** *w* *Jesus, holiness of,* Matt. 1:21.

x *Anointing, figurative*, Deut. 28:40.

**10**

y Psa. 102:25–27.
z *Jesus, pre-existence of*, Matt. 1:21.

a *Jesus, creator*, Matt. 1:21.
b *Earth, created*, Prov. 8:23.
c *Heavens, created*, Psa. 8:3

**12**

8 R. V. mantle shalt thou roll them up, As a garment, and they

**13**

d *Sovereignty of the Messiah*, Psa. 110:1.
e *Footstool, figurative*, 1 Chr. 28:2.

**14**

f *Salvation*, Acts 16:17.
9 R. V. do service for the sake of them that shall

**1**

a *Perseverance, exhortations to*, Eph. 6:18.
b *Watchfulness, enjoined*, Matt. 24:42.
c *Gospel*, Mark 13:10.

ness, and hated iniquity[G]; therefore God, *even* thy God, hath
[x]anointed thee with the oil of
gladness above thy fellows.[T Q]
10[T] A[Q]nd, [y]Thou, Lord, [z]in the
beginning hast [a]laid the foundation of the [b]earth; and the [c]heav-
ens are the works of thine hands:[T]
11 They shall perish; but thou
remainest; and they all shall wax[G]
old as doth a garment;
12 And as a [8]vesture[G] shalt thou
fold them up, and they shall be
changed: but thou art the same,
and thy years shall not fail.[S T Q]
13[S] But to which of the *angels
said he at any time, [d]Sit on my
right hand, until I make thine
enemies thy [e]footstool?[T Q]
14 Are they not all ministering[G]
spirits, sent forth to [9]minister for
them who shall be heirs of [f]sal-
vation[G]?[S Q]

## CHAPTER 2

*We ought to be obedient to the gospel,* 5 *especially because Christ vouchsafed to take our nature upon him,* 17 *as it behooved him.*

THEREFORE[S] [a,b]we ought
to give the more earnest
heed to the [c]things which we
have heard, lest [1]at any time we
should let *them* slip.
2[T] For if the [d]word spoken [2]by
[e]angels[G] was stedfast[G], and every
transgression and disobedience
received a just[G] [f,g]recompence[G] of
reward;
3 [f,h]How shall [g]we escape, if
we neglect so great [i]salvation;
which at the first began to be
spoken [3]by the [j]Lord, and was
[k]confirmed unto us by them that
heard *him*;
4 God also bearing *them* witness[G], both with signs and wonders, and [4]with divers[G] [l]miracles,
and [m]gifts of the [n]Holy[G] Ghost[G],
according to his own will?[S T]
5 For [5]unto the [o]angels hath he
not put in subjection the world
to come, whereof we speak.
6 B[Q]ut one in a certain place testified, saying, [p]What is [q]man,
that thou art mindful of him? or
the son of man, that thou visitest
him?
7 [p]Thou [r]madest him a little
lower than the [o]angels; thou
crownedst him with glory and

1 R. V. haply we drift away from them.

**2**

d *Law, of Moses*, Deut. 33:2.
e *Angel, functions of*, Heb. 1:13.
f *Judgment, according to opportunity and works*, 1 Pet. 1:17.
g *Wicked, punishment of*, Psa. 73:3.
2 R. V. through angels proved stedfast,

**3**

h *Sin, no escape from the consequences of*, Rom. 5:12.
i *Salvation*, Acts 16:17.
j *Jesus, lordship of*, Matt. 1:21.
k *Religious Testimony*, 2 Thess. 1:10.
3 R. V. through

**4**

l *Miracles*, Luke 23:8.
m *Spiritual Gifts*, 1 Cor. 12:4.
n *Holy Spirit*, Acts 1:2.
4 R. V. by manifold powers,

**5** o *Angel*, Heb. 1:13. 5 Am. R. V. not unto angels did he subject the **6** p Psa. 8:4–6. q *Man, insignificance of*, Job 4:17.
**7** r *God, creator*, Gen. 2:2.

***ANGEL.** *Called, Angel of the Lord*, Matt. 1:20, 24; 2:13, 19; 28:2; Luke 1:11; Acts 5:19; 8:26; 12:7, 23; *sons of God*, Job 1:6; 2:1; *hosts*, Gen. 32:1, 2; Josh. 5:14, 15; 1 Chr. 12:22; 2 Chr. 18:18; Luke 2:13; *principalities, powers*, Eph. 3:10; Col. 1:16.
*Created*, Col. 1:16. *Of different orders*, Isa. 6:2; 1 Thess. 4:16; 1 Pet. 3:22; Jude 9; Rev. 12:7. *Immortal*, Luke 20:36. *Worship God*, Neh. 9:6; Psa. 103:20; 148:2; Phil. 2:9–11; Heb. 1:6; Rev. 5:9–11. *Not to be worshiped*, Col. 2:18; Rev. 19:10; 22:8, 9.
*Do not marry*, Matt. 22:30; Mark 12:25; Luke 20:35. *Are obedient*, Psa. 103:20; Matt. 6:10; 1 Pet. 3:22. *Have knowledge of, and interest in, earthly affairs*, 1 Tim. 5:21; 1 Pet. 1:12; see FUNCTIONS OF, below. *To be judged by men*, 1 Cor. 6:3. *Witnessed Christ's incarnate life*, 1 Tim. 3:16. *Witness God's judgments*, Rev. 14:10. *Behold the face of the Father*, Matt. 18:10. *Jesus will confess his disciples before*, Luke 12:8. *Jesus, made lower than, in his incarnation*, Heb. 2:7, 16, with vs. 5, 9; *exalted above, in his glorification*, Eph. 1:20, 21; Col. 2:10; Heb. 1:4, 5, 13; 1 Pet. 3:22. *Physical aspects of*, Judg. 13:6; Dan. 10:6; Matt. 28:3. *Are, examples of meekness*. 2 Pet. 2:11; Jude 9; *wise*, 2 Sam. 14:17, 20; *holy*, Matt. 25:31; Mark 8:38; *elect*, 1 Tim. 5:21; *innumerable*, Deut. 33:2; Dan. 7:10; Heb. 12:22; Jude 14.
**Appearances of:** *To Abraham*, Gen. 18:2; 22:11–18. *To Hagar, in the wilderness*, Gen. 16:7. *To Lot, in Sodom*, Gen. 19:1–17. *To Jacob, in his various visions*, Gen. 28:12. *To Moses*, Ex. 3:2. *To Israelites*, Ex. 14:19; Judg. 2:1–4. *To Balaam*, Num. 22:31. *To Joshua, "the captain of the Lord's host,"* Josh. 5:15. *To Gideon*, Judg. 6:11–22. *To Manoah*, Judg. 13:6, 15–20. *To David, at the threshing floor of Araunah*, 2 Sam. 24:16, 17; 1 Chr. 21:15, 16. *To Elijah, while he lay under the juniper tree*, 1 Kin. 19:5–11. *To Daniel, in the lions' den*, Dan. 6:22; 8:16; 9:21; 10:5–10, 16, 18; 12:5–7. *To Shadrach, Meshach, and Abed-nego, in the fiery furnace*, Dan. 3:25, 28. *To Zechariah, in a vision*, Zech. 2:3; 3:1, 2; 4:1. *To Joseph, in a dream*, Matt. 1:20; 2:13, 19. *At the transfiguration of Jesus*, Matt. 17:3; Luke 9:30, 31. *To Mary, concerning Jesus*, Luke 1:26–38. *To Zacharias*, Luke 1:11–20, 26–38. *To the shepherds*, Luke 2:9–11, 13, 14. *To Jesus, after his temptation*, Matt. 4:11; *in Gethsemane*, Luke 22:43; *at the sepulchre*, Matt. 28:2–5; Mark 16:5–7; Luke 24:23; John 20:12; *at the ascension*, Acts 1:10, 11. *To Peter and John, while in prison*, Acts 5:19. *To Philip*, Acts 8:26. *To Cornelius, in a dream*, Acts 10:3, 30–32. *To Peter, in prison*, Acts 12:7–11. *To Paul, on the way to Damascus*, Acts 27:23. *To John, in Patmos*, Rev. 1:1; 5:2; 7:11; 10:9; 11:1; 17:7; 19:10; 22:8.
**Functions of:** *Guard the way to the tree of life*, Gen. 3:24. *Law, given by*, Acts 7:53; Gal. 3:19; Heb. 2:2. *Medium of revelation to prophets*, 2 Kin. 1:15; Dan. 4:13–17; 8:15–26; 9:21–27; 10:5–21; Zech. 1:9–11; Acts 8:26; Gal. 3:19; Heb. 2:2; Rev. 1:1; 22:6, 16.
*Are God's messengers*, Num. 22:22, 35; Judg. 6:11, 12, 21, 22; Dan. 9:21–23; Zech. 1:12–14; 3:5–7; 6:5; John 1:51; Acts 8:26; Rev. 10:1–6; 18:1–3; 19:10.
*Remonstrates with Balaam*, Num. 22:22–27. *Announces the birth, of Samson*, Judg. 13; *of John the Baptist*, Luke 1:11–20; *of Jesus*, Matt. 1:20, 21; Luke 1:28–38; 2:7–15. *Warns Joseph to escape to Egypt*, Matt. 2:13. *Ministers to Jesus, after the temptation*, Matt. 4:11; Mark 1:13; John 1:51; *during his passion*, Luke 22:43. *Present, at the tomb of Jesus*, Matt. 28:2–6; Luke 24:23; *at the ascension*. Acts 1:11. *Will be with Christ, at his second coming*, Matt. 25:31; Mark 8:38; 2 Thess. 1:7; Jude 14, 15; *at the judgment*, Matt. 13:39, 41, 49; 16:27; 24:31; 25:31; Mark 13:27; 2 Thess. 1:7.
*Minister to the righteous*, Heb. 1:14. *Instruct*, Acts 10:3–6. *Guide*, Gen. 16:7–11; 24:7, 40. *Protect*, Psa. 91:11, 12; Matt. 4:6; Luke 4:10, 11. *Deliver*, Num. 20:16; 1 Kin. 19:5–8; 2 Chr. 32:21; Psa. 34:7; Dan. 6:22; Matt. 26:53; Acts 5:19, 20; 12:7–10. *Comfort*, Acts 27:23, 24.
*Minister to disembodied spirits*, Luke 16:22.
*Execute judgments upon the wicked*, Matt. 13:41, 42, 49, 50; Jude 14, 15. *Afflict*, Psa. 35:5, 6; 78:49; Rev. 7:1, 2; 15:1. *Destroy*, Gen. 19:1, 13 (with vs. 1–25); 2 Sam. 24:16, 17; 2 Kin. 19:35; 1 Chr. 21:15, 16; 2 Chr. 32:21; Isa. 37:36; Acts 12:23; Rev. 9:15.
**Fallen,** 2 Pet. 2:4; Jude 6; Rev. 12:9.

s *Man, dominion of,* Job 4:17.
**9**
t *Jesus, incarnation of,* Matt. 1:21.
u *Jesus, exaltation of,* Matt. 1:21.
v *Salvation, plan of,* Acts 16:17.
w *Jesus, mission of,* Matt. 1:21.
x *Atonement, by Jesus,* Lev. 17:11.
y *Jesus, vicarious death of,* Matt. 1:21.
5 R. V. behold him who hath been made a little lower than the angels, even Jesus, because of his suffering
**10**
z *God, creator,* Gen. 2:2.

a *God, love of,* Gen. 2:2.
b *Spiritual Adoption,* Rom. 8:15.
c *Salvation,* Acts 16:17.
d *Jesus, perfections of,* Matt. 1:21.
e *Jesus, sufferings of,* Matt. 1:21.
6 R. V. author
**11**
f *Sanctification,* 1 Pet. 1:2.
g *Righteous, described,* Psa. 64:10.
h *Righteous, union of, with Christ,* Psa. 64:10.
i *Jesus, love of,* Matt. 1:21.
**12**
j Psa. 22:22.
k *Prophecies concerning the Messiah, and their fulfillment,* Gen. 12:3.
l *Church,* Matt. 16:18.
m *Praise,* Psa. 150:1.
7 R. V. congregation
**13**
n Isa. 8:18.
**14**
o *Jesus, incarnation of,* Matt. 1:21.
p *Jesus, mission of,* Matt. 1:21.
q *Jesus, death of,* Matt. 1:21.
r *Jesus, power of,* Matt. 1:21.
s *Satan,* Matt. 4:10.
**15**
t *Death,* Num. 23:10.
**16**
u *Angel,* Heb. 1:13.
v *Abraham,* Gen. 17:5.

honour, and didst [s]set him over the works of thy hands:[T]

8 [p]Thou hast put all things [s]in subjection under his feet. For in that he put all in subjection under him, he left nothing *that is* not put under him. But now we see not yet all things put under him.[Q]

9 [T]But we [5]see Jē'ṣus, who was [t]made a little lower than the [o]angels for the suffering of death, [u]crowned with glory and honour; [v]that he by the grace of God should [w, x]taste death [y]for every man.[S T]

10 [S]For it became [z]him, for whom *are* all things, and by whom *are* all things, in [a]bringing many [b]sons unto glory, to make the [6]captain of their [c]salvation [d]perfect[G] through [e]sufferings.[T]

11 [T Q]For both he that [f]sanctifieth[G] and they who are [g]sanctified[G] *are* all [h]of one: for which cause he is [i]not ashamed to call them brethren,[S]

12 Saying, [j, k]I will declare thy name unto my brethren, in the midst of the [7, l]church[G] will I sing [m]praise unto thee.[T Q]

13 And again, I will put my trust in him. And again, [n]Behold [h]I and the children which God hath given me.[T Q]

14 [T]Forasmuch then as the children are partakers of flesh and blood, he also himself likewise [o]took part of the same; that [p]through [q]death he [r]might destroy him that had the power of death, that is, the [s]devil;[S Q]

15 And deliver them who through fear of [t]death were all their lifetime subject to bondage.[T]

16 For verily [8]he took not on *him the nature of* [u]angels[G]; but he [o]took on *him* the seed of [v]Ā'brā-hăm.[T Q]

17 [T]Wherefore[G] in all things it behoved[G] him to be made like unto *his* brethren, that he might be a merciful and [w]faithful high [x]priest in things *pertaining* to God, to make [9, y, z]reconciliation[G] for the sins of the people.[S Q T]

18 For in that he himself hath [a]suffered being [b]tempted[G], he is [c]able to succour[G] them that are [d]tempted[G].[T]

## CHAPTER 3

*Christ is more worthy than Moses: 7 therefore if we believe not in him, we shall be more worthy of punishment than unbelieving Israel.*

WHEREFORE, holy brethren, [a]partakers of the heavenly [b]calling, [c]consider the Apostle and High [d]Priest of our [1]profession[G], Chrīst Jē'ṣus;[T]

2 Who was [e, f]faithful to him that appointed[G] him, as also [g]Mō'ṣeṣ *was* [f, h]*faithful* in all his house.[Q]

3 For [2]this *man* was counted worthy of more glory[G] than [g]Mō'ṣeṣ, inasmuch as he who hath builded the house hath more honour than the house.

4 For every house is builded by some *man*; but he that built all things *is* [i]God.[S]

5 [T j]And [g]Mō'ṣeṣ verily *was* [h]faithful in all his house, as a servant, for a testimony of those things which were to be spoken after;[Q]

6 But Chrīst as a son over his own [k]house; [l]whose house are we, if we [m, n]hold fast [3]the confidence and the rejoicing of the [o]hope firm unto the end.

7 [T]Wherefore[Q] (as the [p]Holy[G] Ghost[G] [q]saith, [r, s]To day if ye will hear his voice,

8 [r, t, u, v]Harden not your hearts, as in the [w]provocation, in the day of temptation[G] in the wilderness:[Q G]

9 When your fathers tempted me, proved me, and saw my works [x]forty years.

10 Wherefore I was [y]grieved

**17**
w *Jesus, faithfulness of,* Matt. 1:21.
x *Jesus, priesthood of,* Matt. 1:21.
y *Atonement, by Jesus,* Lev. 17:11.
z *Reconciliation,* 2 Cor. 5:18.
9 R. V. propitiation

**18**
a *Jesus, sufferings of,* Matt. 1:21.
b *Jesus, temptation of,* Matt. 1:21.
c *Jesus, power of,* Matt. 1:21.
d *Temptation,* Luke 11:4.
**1**
a *Righteous, described,* Psa. 64:10.
b *Call, personal,* Phil. 3:14.
c *Jesus, our example,* Matt. 1:21.
d *Jesus, priesthood of,* Matt. 1:21.
1 R. V. confession, even Jesus;
**2**
e *Jesus, faithfulness of,* Matt. 1:21.
f *Obedience,* Heb. 5:8.
g *Moses,* Ex. 2:10.
h *Faithfulness,* Luke 16:10.
**3**
2 R. V. he hath been counted
**4**
i *God, creator,* Gen. 2:2.
**5**
j Num. 12:7.
**6**
k *Church, Christ head of,* Matt. 16:18.
l *Blessings, contingent upon obedience,* Deut. 11:26.
m *Character, stability of,* Phil. 2:15.
n *Perseverance,* Eph. 6:18.
o *Hope,* Prov. 13:12.
3 R. V. our boldness and the glorying of our hope
**7**
p *Holy Spirit,* Acts 1:2.
q *Word of God, is inspired,* Psa. 119:9.

r Psa. 95:7-11. s *Prophecies concerning the Messiah, and their fulfillment,* Gen. 12:3. **8** t *Heart, hardening of,* Psa. 44:21. u *Obduracy, warnings against,* Prov. 29:1. v *Impenitence, admonitions against,* Rom. 2:5. w *Israel, murmur,* Ex. 4:22. **9** x *Forty, years,* Jonah 3:4. y *Anthropomorphisms,* Gen. 11:5.

**10**

z *Reprobates,* 1 Cor. 9:27.

a *Heart, unregenerate,* Psa. 44:21.

b *Spiritual Blindness,* 2 Cor. 4:4.

**11**

c Psa. 95:11.

d *Oath, attributed to God,* Num. 5:19.

e *Anger of God,* 2 Kin. 13:3.

f *Sin, separates from God,* Rom. 5:12.

g *Canaan,* Gen. 37:1.

h *Symbols and Similitudes,* Heb. 9:9.

**12**

i *Watchfulness, enjoined against backsliding,* Matt. 24:42.

j *Apostasy,* Acts 1:25.

**13**

k *Sin, the inherited tendencies to evil,* Rom. 5:12.

**14**

l *Blessings, contingent upon obedience,* Deut. 11:26.

m *Perseverance,* Eph. 6:18.

n *Steadfastness,* 1 Cor. 15:58.

**15**

o *Heart, hardening of,* Psa. 44:21.

p *Obduracy, warnings against,* Prov. 29:1.

q *Impenitence, admonitions against,* Rom. 2:5.

r *Israel, murmur,* Ex. 4:22.

**16**

s *Egypt,* Gen. 41:8.

t *Moses,* Ex. 2:10.

**17**

u *Forty, years,* Jonah 3:4.

v *Unbelieving Israelites Destroyed,* Num. 14:11.

4 R. V. displeased

**18**

5 R. V. were disobedient?

**19**

w *Unbelief,* Heb. 3:12.

with that [w]generation, and said, [z]They do alway err in *their* [a]heart; and they have [b]not known my ways.

11 So [c]I [d]sware in my [e]wrath, [f]They shall not enter into my [g,h]rest.)[S T Q]

12 [i]Take heed, brethren, lest there be in any of you an [a]evil heart of *unbelief,[G] in [j]departing from the living God.

13 But exhort[G] one another daily, while it is called To day; lest any of you be hardened through the deceitfulness of [k]sin.[Q]

14 For we are made partakers of Christ, [l]if we [m]hold the beginning of our confidence [n]stedfast[G] unto the end;

15 While[Q] it is said, To day if ye will hear his voice, [o,p,q]harden not your hearts, as in the [r]provocation.

16[Q] For some, when they had heard, did [r]provoke[G]: howbeit[G] not all that came out of [s]Ē′ġȳpt by [t]Mō′ṣeṣ.

17 But with [r]whom was he [4]grieved [u]forty years? *was it* not with [v]them that had sinned, whose carcases[G] fell in the wilderness?[Q]

18 And to whom [c,d]sware he that [f]they should not enter into his [g,h]rest, but to them that [5]believed[G] not?[Q]

19 So we see that [f]they could not enter in because of [w]unbelief.[G Q]

## CHAPTER 4

*The rest of Christians is attained by faith. 12 The power of God's word. 14 By our high priest, Jesus the Son of God, 16 we may come boldly to the throne of grace.*

[a]LET[Q] us therefore fear, lest, a promise being left *us* of entering into his [b,c]rest, any of you should seem to come short of it.

2 For [1]unto us was the [d]gospel [e]preached, as well as unto them: but the [f]word preached did not profit them, not being mixed with [g]faith in them that heard *it.*

3 For we which have [h]believed[G] do enter into [b,i]rest, as he said, [j]As I have [k,l]sworn in my [m]wrath, [2]if they shall enter into my [n,o]rest: although the [p]works were finished from the foundation of the world.[S Q]

4 For he spake in a certain place of the [q]seventh *day* on this wise,[G] [r]And God did [l]rest the seventh day from all his [p]works.[Q]

5[Q] And in this *place* again, [2]If they shall enter into my [n,o]rest.

6 Seeing therefore it remaineth that some must enter therein, and they to whom [3]it was first preached entered not in because of unbelief[G]:[Q]

7 Again, he limiteth a certain day, saying in Dā′vid, To day, after so long a time; as it is said, To day if ye will hear his voice, [s,t,u]harden not your hearts.[Q]

8 For if [4,v]Jē′ṣus had given them rest, then would he not afterward have spoken of another day.[Q]

9 [w]There remaineth therefore a [5,x]rest[G] to the people of God.[T]

10 For he that is entered into his [x]rest,[G] he also hath ceased from his own [y]works, as God *did* from his.[Q]

11 [z,a]Let us [6]labour therefore to enter into that [b]rest, lest any

**2**

d *Gospel,* Mark 13:10.

e *Instruction, in religion,* Prov. 23:23.

f *Word of God,* Psa. 119:9.

g *Faith,* Mark 11:22.

1 R. V. indeed we have had good tidings preached unto us, even as also they: but the word of hearing did not profit them, because they were not united by faith with them that heard.

**3**

h *Faith in Christ,* John 6:69.

i *Holiness, described,* Ex. 39:30.

j Psa. 95:11.

k *Oath, attributed to God,* Num. 5:19.

l *Anthropomorphisms,* Gen. 11:5.

m *Anger of God,* 2 Kin. 13:3.

n *Canaan,* Gen. 37:1.

o *Symbols and Similitudes,* Heb. 9:9.

p *Works of God,* Psa. 40:5.

2 R. V. They shall not enter

**4**

q *Sabbath, the Lord rested on,* Ex. 16:23.

r Gen. 2:2.

**6**

3 R. V. the good tidings were before preached failed to enter in because of disobedience.

**7**

s *Heart, hardening of,* Psa. 44:21.

t *Obduracy, warnings against,* Prov. 29:1.

u *Impenitence, admonitions against,* Rom. 2:5.

**1** a *Backsliding, admonitions against,* Hos. 11:7. b *Rest, spiritual,* Ex. 23:12. c *Salvation,* Acts 16:17.

**8** v Or, *Joshua,* Josh 1:1. 4 R. V. Joshua **9** w *Righteous, promises to,* Psa. 64:10. x *Rest, spiritual,* v. 11; Ex. 23:12. 5 R. V. sabbath rest for the **10** y *Works, insufficient for salvation,* 2 Tim. 1:9. **11** z *Commandment, enjoining spiritual diligence,* Deut. 8:2.—a *Faithfulness,* Luke 16:10. b *Rest, spiritual,* Ex. 23:12. 6 R. V. therefore give diligence

* **UNBELIEF.** *Hardens the heart,* Psa. 95:8–11 (with Heb. 3:12, 16–19); Acts 19:9. *Rejects Christ,* Isa. 53:1–3 (with John 12:38); Mark 6:3, 6; John 1:11; 5:38, 40, 44, 46, 47; 10:25, 26. *Displeases God,* Psa. 78:19–22; Heb. 11:6 *Makes God a liar,* 1 John 5:10. *Leads to destruction,* Rom 11:20; 2 Thess. 2:12. *Caused by spiritual blindness,* Isa. 6:9 10; Matt. 13:13–15, 58; Luke 13:34; 19:41, 42; John 12:37, 39, 40, 47.

*Admonitions against,* Acts 13:40, 41; 2 Cor. 6:14–16; Heb. 3:12, 16–19; 4:1–3, 6, 11; 12:25. *Illustrated,* Rom. 10:6, 7, 16; 2 Pet. 3:4. *At Christ's second coming,* Luke 18:8. See footnote, UNBELIEVERS, Luke 12:46.

**Instances of:** *Eve,* Gen. 3:4–6. *Moses and Aaron,* Num. 20:12. *Israelites,* Num. 14:11; Deut. 1:32; 9:23; 2 Kin. 17:14; Psa. 78:8–67. *Samaritan lord,* 2 Kin. 7:2. *Zacharias,* Luke 1:20. *Chief priests,* Luke 22:67. *The Jews,* Matt. 27:42 (with Mark 15:29–32; Luke 23:35–37); Mark 2:6–11; 8:11, 12; 15:29–32; John 5:38, 40, 43, 46, 47. *Disciples,* Matt. 17:17–20; Mark 4:38, 40; Luke 24:11, 25, 41–45. *Brethren of Christ,* John 7:5. *Thomas,* John 20:25.

7 R. V. disobedience.
12
c *Word of God, is inspired,* Psa. 119:9.
d *Sword, two-edged,* 1 Chr. 21:5.
e *Man, a spirit,* Job 4:17.
f *Heart, known to God,* Psa. 44:21.
8 R. V. living, and active,
9 R. V. quick to discern the thoughts
13
g *God, knowledge of,* Gen. 2:2.
14
h *Perseverance, motives to,* Eph. 6:18.
i *Jesus, priesthood of,* Matt. 1:21.
j *Jesus, exaltation of,* Matt. 1:21.
k *Jesus, divinity of,* Matt. 1:21.
10 R.V. confession.
15
l *Afflictions, consolation in,* Psa. 34:19.
m *Temptation, Christ succors in,* Luke 11:4.
n *Jesus, compassion of,* Matt. 1:21.
o *Jesus, temptation of,* Matt. 1:21.
p *Jesus, holiness of,* Matt. 1:21.
16
q *Faith in Christ,* John 6:69.
r *Prayer, boldness in,* Acts 6:4.
s *Access to God,* Eph. 3:12.
t *Boldness of the Righteous,* Phil. 1:20.
u *Grace of God,* Rom. 4:16.
v *God, mercy of,* Gen. 2:2.

1
a *Types, of the Savior,* Heb. 10:1.

man fall after the same example
of [7]unbelief.[G][Q]
12 For the [c]word of God *is*
[8]quick,[G] and powerful, and sharper than any [d]twoedged sword,
piercing even to the dividing
asunder of soul and [e]spirit, and
of the joints and marrow, and
[9]*is* a discerner of the thoughts
and intents of the [f]heart.[Q]
13 [g]Neither is there any creature that is not manifest in his
sight: but all things *are* naked
and opened unto the eyes of him
with whom we have to do.[S]
14 [h]Seeing then that we have a
great high [i]priest, that is [j]passed
into the heavens, Jē′ṣus the [k]Son
of God, let us hold fast[G] *our* [10]pro-
fession.[G][T]
15 For [l,m]we have not an high
[i]priest which [n]cannot be touched
with the feeling of our infirmities; but was in all points
[o]tempted like as *we are, yet*
[p]without sin.[T]
16 [q]Let us therefore [r,s]come
[t]boldly unto the throne of [u]grace,
that we may obtain [v]mercy, and
[l,m]find grace to help in time of
need.[S]

## CHAPTER 5

*Of the high priests from among men; 5 Christ's priesthood compared with theirs. 11 The want of knowledge respecting the doctrines of the gospel reproved.*

FOR every [a]high priest taken
from among men is ordained[G]
for men in things *pertaining*
to God, that he may [b]offer both
gifts and [c,d]sacrifices for sins:[T]
2 [e]Who can [1]have [f]compassion
on the [g,h]ignorant, and on them
that are [h]out of the way; for that
he himself also is compassed[G] with
infirmity.[G]
3 And by reason hereof he
ought, as for the people, so also
for himself, to [b]offer for sins.[Q]
4 And no man taketh this honour unto himself, but he that is
[i,j]called of God, as *was* [k]Aâr′on.[Q][T]
5 [T]So also Chrīst glorified not
himself to be made an high
priest; but he that said unto
him, [l,m]Thou art my [n,o]Son, to
day have I begotten thee.[Q]
6 As he saith also in another
*place,* [m,p]Thou *art* a [q]priest for
ever after the order of [r,s]Mĕl-
chĭṣ′e-dĕc.[T][Q]
7 [T]Who in the days of his [t]flesh,
when he had offered up [u,v]pray-
ers and supplications with strong
[w]crying and tears unto him that
was [x]able to save him from
[y]death, and [2]was heard in that
he feared;
8 [T]Though he were a [n]Son, yet
[z]learned he [*,a]obedience by the
things which he [b]suffered;[T]
9 And being made perfect, he
became the [c]author of eternal

u *Prayers of Jesus,* Luke 5:16. v *Prayer, importunity in,* Acts 6:4. w *Jesus, sufferings of,* Matt. 1:21. x *God, power of,* Gen. 2:2. y *Death,* Num. 23:10. 2 R. V. having been heard for his godly fear. **8** z *Afflictions, design of,* Psa. 34:19.—a *Jesus, obedience of,* Matt. 1:21. b *Jesus, sufferings of,* Matt. 1:21. **9** c *Jesus, savior,* Matt. 1:21.

b *High Priest, duties of,* Lev. 21:10.
c *Offerings,* Lev. 6:17.
d *Atonement, by animal sacrifices,* Lev. 17:11.
2
e *Minister, character and qualifications of,* Rom. 15:16.
f *Love, of man for man,* 1 John 4:7.
g *Ignorance, sins of,* Acts 3:17.
h *Wicked, described,* Psa. 73:3.
1 R. V. bear gently with the ignorant and erring.
4
i *Minister, call of,* Rom. 15:16.
j *Call, to special religious duty,* Phil. 3:14.
k *Aaron, priesthood of,* Ex. 6:20.
5
l Psa. 2:7; Heb. 1:5.
m *Prophecies concerning the Messiah, and their fulfillment,* Gen. 12:3.
n *Jesus, divine sonship of,* Matt. 1:21.
o *Jesus, relation of to the Father,* Matt. 1:21.
6
p Psa. 110:4.
q *Jesus, priesthood of,* Matt. 1:21.
r Or, *Melchizedek, type of Christ,* Gen. 14:18.
s *Priest, antemosaic,* Lev. 1:5.
7
t *Jesus, humanity of,* Matt. 1:21.

***OBEDIENCE,** Prov. 28:7. *Enjoined,* Gen. 17:9; Lev. 19:19, 36, 37; 20:8, 22; 22:31; Num. 15:38–40; 30:2; Deut. 4:1–40; 5:1–33; 6:1–25; 8:1–6, 11–20; 10:12, 13; 11:1–3, 8, 9, 13–28, 32; 13:4; 26:16–18; 27:1–10; 32:46; Josh. 22:5; 23:6, 7; 24:14, 15; 1 Sam. 12:14, 20, 24; 15:22; 2 Kin. 17:37, 38; 1 Chr. 16:15; 28:9, 10, 20; Ezra 7:23; Psa. 76:11; Prov. 7:1; Eccl. 12:13; Jer. 26:13; 38:20; Dan. 7:27; Mal. 4:4; Eph. 6: 6–8; Phil. 2:12; 1 Tim. 6:14, 18; Jas. 1:22–25; 2:10–12; 1 Pet. 1:2, 14.

*Proof of love,* John 14:15, 21; 1 John 2:5, 6; 5:2, 3; 2 John 6, 9. *Proof that we know God,* 1 John 2:3, 4.

*Vows of,* Ex. 24:7; Josh. 24:24; Psa. 119:15, 106, 109.

*Justification by, under Mosaic law,* Lev. 18:5; Ezek. 20:11, 13, 21; Luke 10:28; Rom. 10:5; Gal. 3:10, 12.

*Prayer for guidance in,* Psa. 143:10. *Cannot be rendered to two masters,* Matt. 6:24.

*Rewarded,* Gen. 18:19; Lev. 26:3–13; Num. 14:24; Deut. 7:12–15; 28:1–15; Josh. 14:6–14; 2 Kin. 21:8; Isa. 1:19.

*Rewarded, by prosperity,* Deut. 7:9, 12–15; 15:4; Josh. 1:8; 1 Kin. 2:3, 4; 9:3–5; 1 Chr. 22:13; 28:7, 8; 2 Chr. 26:5; 27:6; Job 36:11; Jer. 7:3–7; 11:1–5; 22:16; Mal. 3:10–12; 1 John 3:22; *by long life,* Deut. 4:1, 40; 32:47; 1 Kin. 3:14; Prov. 3: 1, 2; 19:16; *by victory over enemies,* Ex. 23:22; Prov. 16:7; *by triumph over adversities,* Matt. 7:24, 25; Luke 6:46–48; *by divine favor,* Ex. 19:5; 20:6; Deut. 5:10; 11:26, 27; 12:28; 1 Kin. 8:23; Neh. 1:5; Psa. 25:10; 103:17, 18, 20; 112:1; 119:2; Prov. 1:33; Jer. 7:23; 11:4; Matt. 5:19; 25:20–23; Luke 11:28; 12:37, 38; John 12:26; 13:17; Jas. 1:25; Rev. 22:7; *by fellowship with Christ,* Matt. 12:50; Mark 3:35; Luke 8:21; John 14:23; 15:10, 14; 1 John 3:24; *by everlasting life,* Matt. 19:17, 29; John 8:51; 1 John 2:17; Rev. 2:10.

**Exemplified,** Deut. 33:9; Psa. 1:2; 103; 1 Thess. 1:9; Rev. 2:19.

*By, Noah,* Gen. 6:9, 22; 7:5; Heb. 11:7; *Abraham,* Gen. 12: 1–4; 17:23; 18:19; 21:4; 22:12, 18; 26:3–5; Neh. 9:8; Acts 7: 3–8; Heb. 11:8–17; Jas. 2:21; *Bethuel and Laban,* Gen. 24:50; *Jacob,* Gen. 35:1, 7; *Laban,* Gen. 31:29; *Moses and Aaron,* Ex. 7:6; 40:16, 21, 23, 32; *Israelites,* Ex. 12:28; 32:25–29; 39:42, 43; Num. 9:20, 21, 23; Deut. 33:9; Josh. 22:2; Judg. 2:7; Psa. 99:7; *Israelites under the preaching of Haggai,* Hag. 1:12.

*By, Caleb,* Num. 14:24; Deut. 1:36; Josh. 14:6–14; *Joshua,* Josh. 10:40; 11:15; *Reubenites,* Josh. 22:2, 3; *Gideon,* Judg. 6:25–28; *David,* 1 Kin. 11:6, 34; 15:5; 2 Chr. 29:2; Acts 13:22; *Elijah,* 1 Kin. 17:5.

*By, the psalmist,* Psa. 17:3; 26:3–6; 119:30, 31, 40, 44, 45, 47, 48, 51, 54–56, 59, 60, 67, 69, 100–102, 105, 106, 110, 112, 166–168; *Elisha,* 1 Kin. 19:19–21; *Hezekiah,* 2 Kin. 18:6; 20:3; 2 Chr. 31:20, 21; Isa. 38:3; *Josiah,* 2 Kin. 22:2; 23:24, 25; *Asa,* 2 Chr. 14:2; *Jehoshaphat,* 2 Chr. 17:3–6; 20:32; 22:9; *Uzziah,* 2 Chr. 26:4, 5; *Jotham,* 2 Chr. 27:2; *Levites,* 2 Chr. 29:34;

[d]salvation unto all them that
*obey him;[S T Q]
10 Called of God an high
[e]priest after the order of [f,g]Měl-
chĭs′e-děc.[Q]
11 Of whom we have many
[h]things to say, and hard [3]to be
uttered, seeing ye are [i,j]dull of
hearing.[S]
12 For when for the time ye
ought to be [k]teachers, ye have
[l]need [4]that one [m]teach you again
which *be* the first principles of
the [n,o]oracles of God; and are
become such as have need of
[p]milk, and not of strong[G] meat.
13 For every one that useth
[p]milk *is* [5]unskilful in the [q]word
of righteousness: for he is a
[r]babe.
14 But [6]strong[G] meat belongeth
to them that are of [s]full age, *even*
those who by reason of use have
their senses exercised to discern
both good and evil.

## CHAPTER 6

*The guilt and danger of apostasy. 11 He exhorts them to be steadfast and diligent, because God is sure in his promise.*

THEREFORE leaving the
[1]principles of the [a,b]doc-
trine of Christ, [c,d]let us [e]go on
unto *perfection[G]; not laying
again the foundation of [f]repent-
ance from dead [g]works, and of
[h]faith toward God,[T]
2 Of the [2]doctrine of [i]baptisms[G],
and of [j]laying on of hands, and
of [k]resurrection of the dead, and
of eternal [l]judgment.
3 And this will we do, if God
[m]permit.
4 [T]For *it is* impossible for those
who were once [n,o]enlightened,
and have tasted of the heavenly
gift, and were made [o]partakers
of the [p]Holy Ghost[G],[S]
5 And have tasted the good
[a,b]word of God, and the powers
of the [3]world[G] to come,[S]
6 If they shall [q,r,s]fall away, to
renew them again unto [f]repent-
ance; seeing they [t]crucify to themselves the [u]Son of God afresh,
and put *him* to an open shame.[T S]
7 For the earth which drinketh
in the rain that cometh oft upon
it, and bringeth forth herbs meet[G]
for [4]them by whom it is dressed,[G]
receiveth [v]blessing from God:[Q]
8 But that which beareth thorns
and briers *is* [w]rejected, and *is*
nigh[G] unto [5]cursing; whose end *is*
to be [w]burned.[S Q]
9 But, [x,y]beloved, we are persuaded better things of you, and
things that accompany [z]salva-
tion, though we thus speak.
10 For [a]God *is* not unrighteous
to forget your [b,c]work and labour of [d]love, which ye have
shewed toward his name, in that
ye have [c,e,f]ministered[G] to the
saints, and do minister.[S]
11 [T]And [g]we desire that every
one of you do shew the same
[c,h]diligence to the full assurance
of [i]hope unto the end:

d *Salvation, through Christ,* Acts 16:17.

**10**

e *Jesus, priesthood of,* Matt. 1:21.

f Or, *Melchizedek, type of Christ,* Gen. 14:18.

g *Priest, antemosaic,* Lev. 1:5.

**11**

h *Mysteries, of redemption,* Mark 4:11.

i *Deafness, figurative,* Matt. 11:5.

j *Spiritual Blindness, manifested, in ignorance of the Scriptures,* 2 Cor. 4:4.

3 R. V. of interpretation, seeing

**12**

k *Teachers,* 1 Chr. 25:8.

l *Ignorance,* Acts 3:17.

m *Instruction, in religion,* Prov. 23:23.

n *Oracle,* 1 Kin. 6:5.

o *Word of God, is inspired,* Psa. 119:9.

p *Milk, figurative,* Job 10:10.

4 R. V. again that some one teach you the rudiments of the first

**13**

q *Gospel,* Mark 13:10.

r *Babes, figurative,* Psa. 8:2.

5 R. V. without experience of

**14**

s *Wisdom, spiritual,* Prov. 2:2.

6 R. V. solid food is for fullgrown men, even

**1**

a *Gospel,* Mark 13:10.

b *Doctrines of Jesus,* John 7:16. c *Perseverance, exhortation to,* Eph. 6:18. d *Commandment, enjoining growth in grace,* Deut. 8:2. e *Growth in Grace,* 2 Pet. 3:18. f *Repentance,* Mark 1:4. g *Works, insufficient for salvation,* 2 Tim. 1:9. h *Faith,* Mark 11:22. 1 Am. R. V. doctrine of the first principles of Christ, **2** i *Ceremonial Washing,* Ex. 19:10. j *Hand, imposition of,* Ezra 10:19. 2 R. V. teaching

k *Resurrection,* 1 Cor. 15:12.

l *Judgment, the general,* 2 Pet. 3:7.

**3**

m *Will of God,* Mark 3:35.

**4**

n *Wisdom, spiritual,* Prov. 2:2.

o *Righteous, described,* Psa. 64:10.

p *Holy Spirit,* Acts 1:2.

**5**

3 R. V. age

**6**

q *Apostasy,* Acts 1:25.

r *Unpardonable Sin,* Matt. 12:31.

s *Jesus, rejected,* Matt. 1:21.

t *Crucifixion, figurative,* Mark 15:13.

u *Jesus, divine sonship of,* Matt. 1:21.

**7**

v *God, providence of,* Gen. 2:2.

4 R. V. for whose sake it is also tilled,

**8**

w *Wicked, punishment of,* Psa. 73:3.

5 R. V. a curse;

**9**

x *Love, of man for man,* 1 John 4:7.

y *Minister, love of, for the church,* Rom. 15:16.

z *Salvation,* Acts 16:17.

**10**

a *God, faithfulness of,* Gen. 2:2.

b *Works, good,* 2 Tim. 1:9.

c *Righteousness, fruits of,* Psa. 15:2.

d *Love, for God,* 1 John 4:19.

e *Liberality,* 1 Tim. 6:18. f *Alms,* Matt. 6:2. **11** g *Faithfulness,* Luke 16:10. h *Diligence,* Rom. 12:8. i *Hope,* Prov. 13:12.

*Cyrus,* Ezra 1:1–4; *Ezra,* Ezra 7:10; *Hanani,* Neh. 7:2; *Job,* Job 1:8.

*By, the three Hebrews,* Dan. 3; *Jonah,* Jonah 3:3; *Ninevites,* Jonah 3:5–10; *Zacharias,* Luke 1:6; *Simeon,* Luke 2:25; *Joseph,* Matt. 1:24; 2:14; *Mary,* Luke 1:38.

*By Jesus,* Matt. 3:15; 26:39, 42; Luke 22:42; John 4:32, 34; 5:30; 6:38; 8:28, 29; 9:4; 12:49, 50; 14:31; 17:4; Phil. 2:8; Heb. 3:2.

*By, John the Baptist,* Matt. 3:15; *John and James,* Mark 1:19, 20; *Matthew,* Matt. 9:9; *Simon and Andrew,* Mark 1:16–18; *Levi,* Mark 2:14; *the rich young man,* Matt. 19:20; Mark 10:20; Luke 18:21; *the disciples,* John 17:6; Acts 4:19, 20; 5:29; *Cornelius,* Acts 10:2; *Paul,* Acts 23:1; 24:16; 26:4, 5; Phil. 3:7–14; 2 Tim. 1:3. *By Paul and Timothy,* 2 Cor. 1:12; 6:3. *By Paul, Timothy, and Sylvanus,* 1 Thess. 2:10. *By the Christians at Rome,* Rom. 6:17.

See footnote, FAITHFULNESS, Luke 16:10.

See footnote, BLESSINGS, *Contingent upon obedience,* Deut. 11:26.

* **PERFECTION,** Psa. 101:2; Prov. 2:21; Matt. 19:21; Luke 6:40; Eph. 4:12, 13; Col. 1:21, 22, 28; 3:14; 4:12; Heb. 6:1; 10:14; Jas. 3:2; 1 John 2:5; 3:6–10; 4:12; 5:18. *From God,* Psa. 18:32; 1 Pet. 5:10. *Blessings of,* Psa. 106:3; 119:1–3, 6.

*Desire for,* Matt. 5:6.

*Prayer for,* 1 Chr. 29:19; 2 Cor. 13:9; 1 Thess. 3:10, 13; Heb. 13:20, 21. *None perfect,* 2 Chr. 6:36; Eccl. 7:20. *Paul's pressing toward,* Phil. 3:12–15.

*Enjoined,* Gen. 17:1; Deut. 18:13; Josh. 23:6; 1 Kin. 8:61; 1 Chr. 28:9; Matt. 5:48; 2 Cor. 7:1; 13:11; Phil. 2:15; Jas. 1:4.

*Ascribed to, Noah,* Gen. 6:8, 9; *Israel,* Num. 23:21; *David,* 1 Kin. 11:4, 6; *Asa,* 1 Kin. 15:14; *Job,* Job 1:1; *Zacharias and Elisabeth,* Luke 1:6.

See footnotes: GOD, *Perfection of,* Gen. 2:2; HOLINESS, Ex. 39:30; SANCTIFICATION, 1 Pet. 1:2.

12 That ye be not [6]slothful, but followers of [j]them who through [k]faith and [l]patience inherit the [m]promises.[S T]

13 For[S Q] when God made [n]promise to [o]Ā'bră-hăm, because he could swear by no greater, he [p]sware by himself,

14 Saying, [q]Surely blessing I will bless thee, and multiplying I will multiply thee.[Q]

15 And so, after he had patiently [r]endured,[G] he obtained the [m]promise.

16 For men verily [s]swear by the greater: and an oath for confirmation *is* to them an end of all strife.[Q]

17 Wherein God, [t]willing more abundantly to shew unto the heirs of promise the [u]immutability of his counsel, [7]confirmed *it* by an [p]oath:[S]

18 That by two immutable things, in which *it was* [v]impossible for God to lie, we might have a strong [8]consolation, who have fled for [w]refuge to lay hold upon the [i]hope set before us:[S Q]

19 Which [i]*hope* we have as an anchor of the soul, both sure and stedfast, and which entereth into that within the [x]veil;[S Q]

20 Whither the forerunner is for us entered, *even* Jē'ṣus, made an high [y]priest for ever after the order of [z,a]Mĕl-chĭṣ'e-dĕc.[T Q]

12 [j] *Example, good,* John 13:15.
[k] *Faith,* Mark 11:22.
[l] *Patience, a grace of the righteous,* Luke 8:15.
[m] *Promises, to the righteous,* 2 Cor. 1:20.
6 R. V. sluggish, but imitators of them

13 [n] *Covenant, of God with men,* Deut. 29:1.
[o] *Abraham,* Gen. 17:5.
[p] *Oath, attributed to God,* Num. 5:19.

14 [q] Gen. 22:17.

15 [r] *Faith, trial of,* Mark 11:22.

16 [s] *Oath,* Num. 5:19.

17 [t] *God, condescension of,* Gen. 2:2.
[u] *God, immutable,* Gen. 2:2.
7 R. V. interposed with

18 [v] *God, holiness of,* Gen. 2:2.
[w] *Cities, of refuge, figurative,* Num. 35:8.
8 R. V. encouragement,

19 [x] *Veil,* Ex. 26:31.

20 [y] *Jesus, priesthood of,* Matt. 1:21.
[z] Or, *Melchizedek,* Gen. 14:18.

[a] *Priest, antemosaic,* Lev. 1:5.

## CHAPTER 7

*Christ Jesus is a priest after the order of Melchisedec; 11 and so, far more excellent than the priests of Aaron's order.*

FOR[T] this[Q] [a,b]Mĕl-chĭṣ'e-dĕc, king of Sā'lem, [c]priest of [1]the [d]most high God, who met [e]Ā'bră-hăm returning from the slaughter of the kings, and blessed him;

2 To whom also [e]Ā'bră-hăm gave a [f]tenth part of all; first being by interpretation King of righteousness, and after that also King of Sā'lem, which is, King of peace;

1 [a] Or, *Melchizedek,* Gen. 14:18.
[b] *Types, of the savior,* Heb. 10:1.
[c] *Priest, antemosaic,* Lev. 1:5.
[d] *God, sovereign,* Gen. 2:2.
[e] *Abraham,* Gen. 17:5.
1 R. V. God Most High.

2 [f] *Tithes,* Num. 18:24.

3 Without father, without mother, without [2,g]descent, having neither beginning of days, nor end of life; but made like unto the [h]Son of God; abideth[G] a priest continually.[Q]

4 Now consider how great this [a]man *was,* unto whom even the patriarch[G] [e]Ā'bră-hăm gave the [f]tenth of the [3]spoils.[G Q]

5 And verily they that are of the sons of Lē'vī, who receive the office of the priesthood, have a commandment to take [f,i]tithes of the people according to the [j]law, that is, of their brethren, though they come out of the loins of [e]Ā'bră-hăm:[Q]

6 But [a,b]he whose [2,g]descent is not counted from them received [f,i]tithes of [e]Ā'bră-hăm, and [k]blessed him that had the [l]promises.[Q]

7 And without all contradiction the less is blessed of the better.

8 And here men that die receive [f,i]tithes; but there [4]he *receiveth them,* of whom it is witnessed that he liveth.

9 And as I may so say, [m]Lē'vī also, who receiveth [f,i]tithes, payed tithes in [e]Ā'bră-hăm.

10 For he was yet in the loins of his father, when [a]Mĕl-chĭṣ'e-dĕc met him.[Q]

11 If therefore perfection were by the Lē-vĭt'ĭ-cal priesthood, (for under it the people received the [j]law,) what further need *was there* that another [n]priest should rise after the order of [a,b]Mĕl-chĭṣ'e-dĕc, and not be called after the order of [o]Aâr'on?[Q]

12 For the priesthood being changed, there is made of necessity a change also of the [j]law.[T]

13 For he of whom these things are spoken pertaineth[G] to another tribe, of which no man gave attendance[G] at the [p]altar.

14 For *it is* evident that our Lord [q]sprang out of [r]Jū'dȧ; of

3 [g] *Genealogy,* 1 Chr. 5:1.
[h] *Jesus, divine sonship of,* Matt. 1:21.
2 R. V. genealogy.

4 3 R. V. chief spoils.

5 [i] *Priest, emoluments of,* Lev. 1:5.
[j] *Law, of Moses,* Deut. 33:2.

6 [k] *Benedictions,* Deut. 21:5.
[l] *Covenant, of God with men,* Deut. 29:1.

8 4 R. V. one, of whom

9 [m] *Levites,* Deut. 10:8.

11 [n] *Jesus, priesthood of,* Matt. 1:21.
[o] *Aaron,* Ex. 6:20.

13 [p] *Altar, of burnt offerings,* Gen. 8:20.

14 [q] *Jesus, incarnation of,* Matt. 1:21.
[r] *Judah, tribe of,* Num. 10:14.

which tribe [s]Mō′ṣeṣ spake nothing concerning priesthood.
15 And [5]it is yet far more evident: for that after the similitude
of [a,b]Mĕl-chĭṣ′e-dĕc there ariseth
another [n]priest,
16 Who is made, not after the
law of a carnal commandment,
but after the power of an endless
life.
17 For he testifieth, [n,t,u]Thou
*art* a priest for ever after the order of [a,b]Mĕl-chĭṣ′e-dĕc.
18 For there is verily a disan-
nulling of the [v]commandment
going before for the weakness
and unprofitableness thereof.
19 For the [v]law made nothing perfect, but the bringing in
of a better [w,x]hope *did*; [y]by the
which we [z]draw nigh unto God.
20 And inasmuch [6]as not without an oath *he was made priest*:
21 (For those priests were
[a,b]made without an oath; but
this with an [c]oath by him that
said unto him, [d,e]The Lord
sware and will not repent, Thou
*art* a [f]priest for ever [7]after the
order of [g]Mĕl-chĭṣ′e-dĕc:)
22 By so much was [h]Jē′ṣus
made a surety of a better [8,i,j]tes-
tament.
23 And they truly were many
[k]priests, because they were not
suffered to continue by reason of
death:
24 But this *man*, because he
[l]continueth ever, hath an unchangeable [f]priesthood.
25 Wherefore [m]he is [n]able also
to [o,p]save them to the uttermost
that [q,r]come unto God [j,s]by him,
seeing he ever liveth to make [s]in-
tercession for them.
26 For such an high [f]priest became us, *who is* [t,u]holy, [9]harm-
less, undefiled, [t]separate from
sinners, and [v]made higher than
the heavens;
27 Who needeth not daily, as
those high priests, to [w]offer up
sacrifice, first for his own sins,
and then for the people's: for
[x]this he did [10]once, when he
[w,y]offered up himself.
28 For the [z]law maketh men
[a]high priests which have infirmity; but the word of the
[b,c]oath, which was since the law,
[11]*maketh* the [d,e]Son, who is consecrated for evermore.

## CHAPTER 8

*Christ the minister of the heavenly sanctuary. 6 The Levitical priesthood abolished by the more excellent ministry of Christ, the mediator of a better covenant.*

NOW of the things which we
have spoken *this is* the sum:
We have such an high [a]priest,
who is [b,c]set on the right hand of
the [d]throne of the [e]Majesty in the
[f]heavens;
2 A minister of the [g,h]sanctu-
ary, and of the true [i]tabernacle,
which the Lord pitched, and not
man.
3 For every high priest is ordained to [j]offer gifts and sacrifices: wherefore *it is* of necessity
that this [1]man have somewhat
also to offer.
4 For if he were on earth, he
should not be a priest, seeing
that there are priests that offer
gifts according to the [k]law:
5 Who serve [2]unto the example
and shadow of heavenly things,
as [l]Mō′ṣeṣ was admonished of
God when he was about to make
the tabernacle: for, [m]See, saith
he, *that* thou make all things according to the [n,o]pattern shewed
to thee in the [p]mount.
6 But now hath he obtained a
more excellent ministry, by how
much also he is the [q]mediator of
a better [r,s]covenant, which was
established upon better promises.
7 For [t]if that first [k,u]*covenant*

s *Moses*, Ex. 2:10.
**15**
5 R. V. what we say is yet more abundantly evident, if after the likeness of
**17**
t Psa. 110:4.
u *Prophecies concerning the Messiah, and their fulfillment*, Gen. 12:3.
**18**
v *Law, of Moses, temporary*, Deut. 33:2.
**19**
w *Gospel*, Mark 13:10.
x *Jesus, savior*, Matt. 1:21.
y *Jesus, mediation of*, Matt. 1:21.
z *Access to God*, Eph. 3:12.
**20**
6 R. V. it is not without the taking of an oath
**21**
a *Priest, consecration of*, Lev. 1:5.
b *Ordination, of priests*, Ex. 29:1.
c *Oath, attributed to God*, Num. 5:19.
d Psa. 110:4.
e *Prophecies concerning the Messiah, and their fulfillment*, Gen. 12:3.
f *Jesus, priesthood of*, Matt. 1:21.
g Or, *Melchizedek*, Gen. 14:18.
7 R. V. *omits* after the order of Melchisedec:
**22**
h *Jesus, mission of*, Matt. 1:21.
i *Gospel*, Mark 13:10.
j *New Covenant*, Jer. 31:31.
8 R. V. covenant.
**23**
k *Priest*, Lev. 1:5.
**24**
l *Jesus, eternity of*, Matt. 1:21.
**25**
m *Promise, to penitents*, 2 Cor. 1:20.
n *Jesus, power of*, Matt. 1:21.
o *Jesus, savior*, Matt. 1:21.
p *Salvation*, Acts 16:17.
q *Seekers*, Isa. 55:6.
r *Penitent, promises to*, Psa. 51:17. s *Jesus, mediation of*, Matt. 1:21. **26** t *Jesus, holiness of*, Matt. 1:21. u *Jesus, perfections of*, Matt. 1:21. v *Jesus, exaltation of*, Matt. 1:21. 9 R. V. guileless.

**27**
w *Atonement, by Jesus*, Lev. 17:11.
x *Jesus, design of his death*, Matt. 1:21.
y *Jesus, death of, voluntary*, Matt. 1:21.
10 R. V. once for all.
**28**
z *Law of Moses*, Deut. 33:2.
a *High Priest*, Lev. 21:10.
b *Oath, attributed to God*, Num. 5:19.
c Psa. 110:4.
d *Jesus, divine sonship of*, Matt. 1:21.
e *Jesus, priesthood of*, Matt. 1:21.
11 R. V. appointeth a Son, perfected for evermore.
**1**
a *Jesus, priesthood of*, Matt. 1:21.
b *Jesus, exaltation of*, Matt. 1:21.
c *Sovereignty of the Messiah*, Psa. 110:1.
d *Throne, figurative*, 1 Kin. 2:19.
e *God, sovereign*, Gen. 2:2.
f *Heaven, God's dwelling place*, Luke 18:22.
**2**
g *Holy of Holies, symbolical*, Ex. 26:33.
h *Types*, Heb. 10:1.
i *Tabernacle, symbol of spiritual things*, Ex. 27:9.
**3**
j *High Priest, duties of*, Lev. 21:10.
1 R. V. high priest also
**4**
k *Law, of Moses*, Deut. 33:2.
**5**
l *Moses*, Ex. 2:10.
m Ex. 25:40.
n *Pattern*, Ex. 25:40.
o *Tabernacle, pattern of*, Ex. 27:9.
p *Sinai*, Ex. 16:1.
2 R. V. that which is a copy and
**6**
q *Jesus, mediation of*, Matt. 1:21.
r *Gospel*, Mark 13:10.
s *New Covenant*, Jer. 31:31.
**7** t *Offerings, insufficiency of*, Lev. 6:17. u *Covenant, of God with men*, Deut. 29:1.

had been faultless, then should no place have been sought for the second.[T]

8[Q] For finding fault with them, he saith, [v,w]Behold, the days come, saith the Lord, when I will make a [s]new covenant with the house of [x]Is′ra-el and with the house of [y]Jū′dah:[T]

9 Not according to the [k,u]covenant that I made with their [x]fathers in the day when I took them by the hand to lead them out of the land of [z]Ē′gypt; because they [a]continued not in my covenant, and I regarded them not, saith the Lord.

10 For[T] this *is* the [b]covenant that I will make with the house of [c]Is′ra-el after those days, saith the Lord; I will put my [d]laws into their mind, and write them in their hearts: and I will be to them a God, and they shall be to me a people:

11 And they shall not teach every man his [3]neighbour, and every man his brother, saying, Know the Lord: for [e]all shall know me, from the least to the greatest.

12 For I will be [f]merciful to their unrighteousness, and their sins and their iniquities [g]will I remember no more.[S T]

13 In that he saith, A [b]new *covenant,* he hath made the [h,i]first old. Now that which decayeth and waxeth[G] old *is* ready to vanish away.[T Q]

8
- v Jer. 31:31-34.
- w *Prophecies concerning the Messiah, and their fulfillment,* Gen. 12:3.
- x *Israel,* Ex. 4:22.
- y *Jews,* Neh. 4:2.

9
- z *Egypt,* Gen. 41:8.
- a *Disobedience to God,* Eph. 5:6.

10
- b *New Covenant,* Jer. 31:31.
- c *Israel,* Ex. 4:22.
- d *Wisdom, spiritual,* Prov. 2:2.

11
- e *Jesus, kingdom of, prophecies concerning,* Matt. 1:21.
- 3 R. V. fellow-citizen,

12
- f *God, mercy of,* Gen. 2:2.
- g *Sin, forgiveness of,* Rom. 5:12.

13
- h *Covenant, of God with men,* Deut. 29:1.
- i *Law, of Moses,* Deut. 33:2.

## CHAPTER 9

***The description of the rites and bloody sacrifices of the law, 11 which are far inferior to the dignity and perfection of the blood and sacrifice of Christ.***

THEN[T] verily the first [a,b]*covenant* had also ordinances[G] of divine service, and [1]a worldly [c,d]sanctuary.

1
- a *Law, of Moses,* Deut. 33:2.
- b *Covenant, of God with men,* Deut. 29:1.
- c *Church, called sanctuary,* 1 Kin. 9:3.
- d *Types,* Heb. 10:1.
- 1 R. V. and its sanctuary, a sanctuary of this world.

2 For there was a [e]tabernacle made; the first, wherein *was* the [f]candlestick[G], and the [g]table, and the shewbread; which is called the [2,h,i]sanctuary.[G Q]

3 And after the [j]second veil, the [e]tabernacle which is called the [3,k]Holiest of all;

4 Which had the golden [l]censer, and the [m]ark of the covenant overlaid round about with [n]gold, wherein *was* the golden pot that had [o]manna, and Aâr′on's [p]rod that budded, and the [q]tables of the covenant;[Q]

5 And over it the [r]cherubims of glory shadowing the [s]mercyseat; of which we cannot now speak particularly.[G Q]

6 Now when these things were thus ordained,[G] the priests went always into the [i]first tabernacle, [t]accomplishing the service *of God.*[Q]

7 But into the [k]second *went* the [u]high priest alone [v]once every year, not without [w]blood, which he offered for himself, and *for* the errors of the people:[Q]

8 The [x]Holy[G] Ghost[G] this[G] signifying, that the [y]way into the holiest of all was not yet made manifest, while as the first tabernacle was yet standing:

9 Which *was* a *figure for the time then present, in which were offered both gifts and [z]sacrifices, that [a]could not make him that did the service perfect,[G] as pertaining to the [b]conscience;

10 *Which stood* only in meats[G] and drinks, and divers[G] [c,d]washings, and carnal[G] [e]ordinances, imposed *on them* until the time of reformation.[G T Q]

11 But Christ being come an high [f]priest of good things to come, by a greater and more per-

2
- e *Tabernacle,* Ex. 27:9.
- f *Candlestick, of the tabernacle,* Ex. 25:31.
- g *Shewbread, table of,* Ex. 35:13.
- h *Sanctuary,* Lev. 4:6.
- i *Holy Place,* Ex. 26:33.
- 2 R. V. Holy place.

3
- j *Veil,* Ex. 26:31.
- k *Holy of Holies,* Ex. 26:33.
- 3 R. V. Holy of holies;

4
- l *Censer,* Lev. 16:12.
- m *Ark, of the covenant,* Ex. 25:10.
- n *Gold,* Ezek. 7:19.
- o *Manna,* Ex. 16:31.
- p *Rod of Aaron,* Ex. 7:9.
- q *Table, of testimony,* Ex. 31:18.

5
- r *Cherubim,* Ex. 37:7.
- s *Mercy Seat,* Ex. 25:17.

6
- t *Priest, duties of,* Lev. 1:5.

7
- u *High Priest,* Lev. 21:10.
- v *Day of Atonement,* Lev. 23:27.
- w *Jesus, atoning blood of, typified,* Matt. 1:21.

8
- x *Holy Spirit,* Acts 1:2.
- y *Way, figurative,* Isa. 35:8.

9
- z *Types, of the Savior,* Heb. 10:1.
- a *Offerings, insufficiency of,* Lev. 6:17.
- b *Conscience,* Acts 23:1.

10
- c *Ceremonial Washing,* Ex. 19:10.
- d *Purification,* Num. 19:19.
- e *Law, of Moses, temporary,* Deut. 33:2.

11
- f *Jesus, priesthood of,* Matt. 1:21.

* **SYMBOLS AND SIMILITUDES.** *Trees of life and knowledge,* Gen. 2:9, 17; 3:3, 24; Rev. 22:2. *Rainbow,* Gen. 9:12, 13. *Circumcision, of the covenant of Abraham,* Gen. 17:11; Rom. 4:11. *Passover, of the sparing of the firstborn and of the atonement made by Christ,* Ex. 12:3-28; 1 Cor. 5:7. *Pillar of cloud and fire, of the divine presence,* Ex. 13:21, 22; 14:19, 20; 19:9, 16; Psa. 78:14. *Mercy seat, of divine mercy,* Ex. 25:17-22. *Darkness, of God's inscrutability,* Ex. 20:21; Lev. 16:2; 1 Kin. 8:12; Psa. 18:11; 97:2; Heb. 12:18, 19. *The smitten rock, of Christ,* Ex. 17:6; 1 Cor. 10:4. *The*

4 R. V. creation.

**12**

*g Jesus, atoning blood of, typified,* Matt. 1:21.

*h Jesus, atoning blood of,* Matt. 1:21.

*i Atonement, by Jesus,* Lev. 17:11.

*j Jesus, design of his death,* Matt. 1:21.

*k Redemption of our Souls,* Eph. 1:7.

5 R. V. *omits* for us

**13**

*l Bullock, for sacrifice,* Ex. 29:3.

*m Ashes, uses of, in purification,* Num. 19:9.

*n Heifer, red,* Num. 19:2.

*o Sprinkling, of blood,* Lev. 14:7.

**14**

*p Holy Trinity,* Luke 3:22.

*q Holy Spirit,* Acts 1:2.

*r Jesus, holiness of,* Matt. 1:21.

*s Jesus, perfections of,* Matt. 1:21.

*t Offerings, must be without blemish,* Lev. 6:17.

*u Blemish, figurative,* Lev. 14:10.

*v Conscience, purged,* Acts 23:1.

*w Spiritual Purification,* Psa. 51:2.

*x Holiness,* Ex. 39:30.

fect tabernacle, not made with
hands, that is to say, not of this
[4]building;
12 Neither by the [g]blood of
goats and calves, but by his own
[h]blood he entered in once into
the holy place, [i,j]having obtained
eternal [k]redemption [5]*for us.*
13 For if the blood of [l]bulls and
of goats, and the [m]ashes of an
[n]heifer [o]sprinkling the unclean,
sanctifieth to the [d]purifying of
the flesh:
14 How much more shall the
[h]blood of [p]Christ, who through
the eternal [p,q]Spirit offered himself
[r,s,t]without [u]spot to [p]God,
[v,w,x]purge your conscience from
dead [y]works to [z]serve the living
God?
15 And for this cause he is the
[a]mediator of the [b]new [6]testament,
that by means of [c]death,
for the [d]redemption of the transgressions
*that were* under the
first [6]testament, they which are
[e]called might receive the [f]promise
of [g,h]eternal [i,j]inheritance.
16 For where a †testament *is*,
there must also of necessity be
the death of the testator.

*y Works, insufficient for salvation,* 2 Tim. 1:9. *z Obedience,* Heb. 5:8. **15**—*a Jesus, mediation of,* Matt. 1:21. *b New Covenant,* Jer. 31:31. *c Jesus, vicarious death of,* Matt. 1:21. *d Atonement, by Jesus,* Lev. 17:11. *e Call, personal,* Phil. 3:14. *f Righteous, promises to,* Psa. 64:10. *g Life, everlasting,* Eccl. 8:15. *h Immortality,* 1 Cor. 15:54. *i Inheritance, figurative,* Num. 27:7. *j Heaven, future home of the righteous,* Luke 18:22. 6 R. V. covenant.

17 For a †testament *is* of force
after men are dead: otherwise it
is of no strength at all while the
testator liveth.
18 [7]Whereupon neither the [k]first
*testament* was dedicated without
‡blood.
19 For when [l]Mō'ṣeṣ had spoken
every precept to all the people
according to the [k]law, he
took the ‡blood of [m]calves and
of goats, with water, and [n]scarlet
wool, and [o]hyssop, and [p]sprinkled
both the book, and all the
people,
20 Saying, [q]This *is* the blood of
the [8,r]testament which God hath
enjoined unto you.
21 Moreover he [p]sprinkled
with ‡blood both the [s]tabernacle,
and all the vessels of the ministry.
22 And [9]almost all things are by
the [k]law [t]purged with ‡,[u]blood;
and without [t]shedding of blood
is no [v]remission.
23 *It was* therefore necessary
that the [w,x]patterns of things in
the heavens should be purified
with these; but the heavenly
things themselves with better sacrifices
than these.
24 For Christ is not entered into
the holy places made with
hands, *which are* the *,[x]figures
of the true; but [y]into heaven it-

**18**

*k Law, of Moses,* Deut. 33:2.

7 R. V. Wherefore even the first covenant hath not been dedicated without blood.

**19**

*l Moses,* Ex. 2:10.

*m Offerings, animal sacrifices,* Lev. 6:17.

*n Colors, symbolical,* Ezek. 16:16.

*o Hyssop,* Ex. 12:22.

*p Sprinkling, of blood,* Lev. 14:7.

**20**

*q* Ex. 24:8.

*r Covenant, of God with men,* Deut. 29:1.

8 R. V. covenant

**21**

*s Tabernacle,* Ex. 27:9.

**22**

*t Atonement, by animal sacrifices,* Lev. 17:11.

*u Jesus, atoning blood of, typified,* Matt. 1:21.

*v Sin, forgiveness of,* Rom. 5:12.

9 R. V. according to the law, I may almost say, all things are cleansed with blood,

**23**

*w Pattern,* Ex. 25:40.

*x Types,* Heb. 10:1.

**24**

*y Jesus, ascension of,* Matt. 1:21.

---

*sprinkled blood, of the covenant,* Ex. 24:8. *The brazen serpent, of Christ,* Num. 21:8, 9; John 3:14.
*Sacrificial animals,* Gen. 15:8–11; John 1:29, 36. *Waving of the wave offering and heaving of the heave offering,* Ex. 29:24–28; Lev. 8:27–29; 9:21. *The whole system of Mosaic rites,* Heb. 9:9, 10, 18–23. *Tabernacle,* Psa. 15:1; Ezek. 37:27; Heb. 8:2, 5; 9:1–12, 23, 24. *Sanctuary,* Psa. 20:2. *Canaan, of the spiritual rest,* Heb. 3:11, 12; 4:5.
*Salt,* Num. 18:19. *Sprinkling of water a symbol of purification,* Ezek. 36:25.
*Star of the East,* Matt. 2:2. *Bread,* Matt. 26:26; Mark 14:22; Luke 22:19; John 6:31–58. *Wine,* Matt. 26:27, 28; Mark 14:23, 24; Luke 22:17–20. *Children,* Matt. 18:3–6; Mark 10:14, 15; Luke 18:16, 17. *Manna,* John 6:31, 32. *Rending of the vail,* Matt. 27:51; Mark 15:38; Luke 23:45.
See footnotes: COLORS, Ezek. 16:16; INSTRUCTION, *By object lessons,* Prov. 23:23.

† **WILL,** a testament. *Of Abraham,* Gen. 25:5, 6. *Of Jehoshaphat,* 2 Chr. 21:3. *May not be annulled,* Gal. 3:15. *In force after death only,* Heb. 9:16, 17.

‡ **BLOOD. Sacrificial:** *Without shedding of, no remission,* Heb. 9:22. *Typical of atoning blood of Jesus,* Lev. 17:5, with Heb. 9:6–28. *Sprinkled, on altar,* Ex. 24:6; 29:16; Lev. 1:5, 11, 15; 8:19; Deut. 12:27; Ezek. 43:18–20; *on the people* Ex. 24:8; *on door posts,* Ex. 12:7–23; Heb. 11:28; *on lepers,* Lev. 14:6, 7, 17, 28; *on leprous houses,* Lev. 14:51, 52.
**Of sin offering:** *Sprinkled, seven times before the vail,* Lev. 4:5, 6, 17; *on horns of altar of sweet incense, and at bottom of altar of burnt offering,* Ex. 30:10; Lev. 4:7, 18, 25, 30; 5:9; 9:9, 12. *Of bullock of sin offering, put on horns of altar,* Ex. 29:12; Lev. 8:15; *poured at bottom of the altar,* Ex. 29:12; Lev. 8:15. See footnote, OFFERINGS, Lev. 6:17.
**Of trespass offering:** *Sprinkled on the altar,* Lev. 7:2. See footnote, OFFERINGS, Lev. 6:17.
**Of peace offering:** *Sprinkled about the altar,* Lev. 3:2, 8, 13; 9:19. *Blood of the ram of consecration put on tip of right ear, thumb, and great toe of, and sprinkled upon Aaron and his sons,* Ex. 29:20, 21; Lev. 8:23, 24, 30. See footnote, OFFERINGS, Lev. 6:17.
**Of Atonement:** *Sprinkled on mercy seat,* Lev. 16:14, 15, 18, 19, 27; 17:11.
**Of the Covenant,** Ex. 24:5–8; Matt. 26:28; Heb. 9:18, 19, 22; 10:29; 13:20. See footnote, ATONEMENT, Lev. 17:11.
**Of Jesus,** 1 John 5:6, 8. *Shed on the cross,* John 19:18, 34. *Atoning,* Matt. 26:28; Mark 14:24; Luke 22:20; Rom. 3:24, 25; 5:9; Eph. 2:13, 16; Heb. 10:19, 20; 12:24; 13:20; 1 John 5:6, 8. *Redeeming,* Acts 20:28; Eph. 1:7; Col. 1:14, 20; Heb. 9:12–14; 1 Pet. 1:18, 19; Rev. 5:9; Rev. 1:5; 7:14. *Sanctifying,* Heb. 10:29; 13:12.
*Justification through,* Rom. 3:24, 25; 5:9. *Victory through,* Rev. 12:11. *Eternal life by,* John 6:53–56.
TYPIFIED: *By the blood of sacrifices,* Heb. 9:6–28. See footnote, JESUS, *Atonement by, typified,* Matt. 1:21.
SYMBOLIZED: *By the wine in the Eucharist,* 1 Cor. 10:16; 11:25.
See footnote, JESUS, *Atonement by; Death of,* Matt. 1:21.

z *Jesus, mediation of,* Matt. 1:21.

**25**
a *High Priest,* Lev. 21:10.
b *Holy of Holies,* Ex. 26:33.
c *Day of Atonement,* Lev. 23:27.
d *Jesus, atoning blood of, typified,* Matt. 1:21.

**26**
e *Jesus, mission of,* Matt. 1:21.
f *Sin,* Rom. 5:12.
g *Jesus, vicarious death of,* Matt. 1:21.
h *Atonement, by Jesus,* Lev. 17:11.
10 R. V. ages

**27**
i *Man, mortal,* Job 4:17.
j *Death, inevitable,* Num. 23:10.
k *Judgment, the general,* 2 Pet. 3:7.

**28**
l *Righteous, promises to,* Psa. 64:10.
m *Faith in Christ,* John 6:69.
n *Jesus, second coming of,* Matt. 1:21.
o *Atonement,* Lev. 17:11.
p *Salvation,* Acts 16:17.

**1**
a *Law, of Moses,* Deut. 33:2.
b *Jesus, mission of,* Matt. 1:21.
c *Redemption of our Souls,* Eph. 1:7.
d *Offerings, insufficiency of,* Lev. 6:17.
e *Works, insufficient for salvation,* 2 Tim. 1:9.

**2**
f *Sin, forgiveness of,* Rom. 5:12.
g *Conscience, guilty,* Acts 23:1.

**3**
h *Day of Atonement,* Lev. 23:27.

**4**
i *Blood, sacrificial,* Heb. 9:19.

**5**
j Psa. 40:6–8.

self, now to [z]appear in the pres-[T]
ence of God for us:
25 Nor yet that he should offer
himself often, as the [a]high priest
entereth into the [b]holy place [c]ev-
ery year with [‡,d]blood of others;
26 For then must he often have
suffered since the foundation of
the world:[G] but now once in the
end of the [10]world hath he appeared [e]to put away [f]sin by the
[g,h]sacrifice of himself.[T]
27 And as it is appointed unto
[i]men once to [j]die, but after this
the [k]judgment:[Q]
28 So Christ was once [g]offered
[e]to [h]bear the sins of many; and
unto [l]them that [m]look for him
shall he appear the [n]second time
without [o]sin unto [p]salvation.[S T Q]

## CHAPTER 10

*The weakness of the law sacrifices.* 10 *The sacrifice of Christ's body, once offered,* 14 *for ever has taken away sins.* 19 *An exhortation to hold fast the faith, with patience and thanksgiving.* 38 *The just shall live by faith.*

FOR the[T] [a]law having a *shadow
of [b,c]good things to come,
*and* not the very image of the
things, can never with those
[d,e]sacrifices which they offered
year by year continually make
the comers thereunto perfect.[G]
2 For then would they not
have ceased to be offered? because that the worshippers once
[f]purged[G] should have had no
more [g]conscience[G] of sins.
3 But in those *sacrifices there is*
a remembrance again *made* of
sins [h]every year.
4 For *it is* not possible that the
[i]blood of bulls and of goats
should take away sins.[Q]
5[Q] Wherefore when he cometh
into the world, he saith, [j]Sacri-
fice and offering thou wouldest
not, but a [k]body hast thou pre-[T]
pared me:
6 In [d,l,m]burnt offerings and
*sacrifices* for [n]sin thou hast had
no pleasure.
7 Then said I, [o]Lo,[G] I come (in
the [1]volume of the book it is
written of me,) to do thy [b,c]will,
O God.[T]
8 Above when he said, [j]Sacri-
fice and offering and [d,l,m]burnt
offerings and *offering* for [n]sin
thou wouldest not, neither hadst
pleasure *therein*; which are offered by the [a]law;[T]
9 Then said he, [o]Lo,[G] I come
to do thy [b,c]will, [2]O God. He
taketh away the [p]first, that he
may establish[G] the [q]second.[T]
10 By the which [b,c]will we are
[r]sanctified[G] through the [s]offering
of the body of Jē'sus Christ once[G]
*for all.*[S T Q]
11 And every priest standeth
daily [t]ministering and offering
oftentimes the same [m]sacrifices,
which can never [m]take away
[n]sins:[Q]
12 But [3]this man, after[G] he had
offered one [q,s]sacrifice for [n]sins
for ever, sat down [u,v]on the right
hand of God;[T Q]
13 From henceforth expecting[G]
[v,w]till his enemies be made his
footstool.[T Q]
14 For by one [q,s]offering he
hath [x]perfected[G] for ever them
that are [r]sanctified.[S]
15[S] *Whereof*[T] the [y]Holy[G] Ghost[G]
also is a witness[G] to us: for after
that he had [z]said before,[G]
16 [z,a]This[Q] *is* the covenant[G] that I
will make with them after those
days, saith the Lord, I will [b]put

k *Jesus, incarnation of,* Matt. 1:21.

**6**
l *Offerings, burnt,* Lev. 6:17.
m *Atonement, by animal sacrifices,* Lev. 17:11.
n *Sin, transgression of the law,* Rom. 5:12.

**7**
o *Jesus, prophecies concerning,* Matt. 1:21.
1 R. V. roll

**9**
p *Types,* Heb. 10:1.
q *Atonement, by Jesus,* Lev. 17:11.
2 R. V. *omits* O God.

**10**
r *Sanctification,* 1 Pet. 1:2.
s *Jesus, design of his death,* Matt. 1:21.

**11**
t *Priest, duties of,* Lev. 1:5.

**12**
u *Jesus, exaltation of,* Matt. 1:21.
v *Sovereignty of the Messiah,* Psa. 110:1.
3 R. V. he, when he had

**13**
w *Jesus, kingdom of, prophecies concerning,* Matt. 1:21.

**14**
x *Perfection,* Heb. 6:1.

**15**
y *Holy Spirit, witness of,* Acts 1:2.
z *Prophecies concerning the Messiah, and their fulfillment,* Gen. 12:3.

**16**
a Jer. 31:33.
b *Regeneration,* Tit. 3:5.

* **TYPES.** *Bride a type of the Church,* Rev. 21:2, 9; 22:17. *The sanctuary, of the heavenly sanctuary,* Ex. 40:2, 24; Heb. 8:2, 5; 9:1–12. *The saving of Noah and his family, of the salvation through the gospel,* 1 Pet. 3:20, 21.

*Deflement a type of sin,* see footnote, DEFILEMENT, Lev. 5:2. *Leaven a type of sin,* see footnote, LEAVEN, Lev. 23:17. See footnote, SYMBOLS AND SIMILITUDES, Heb. 9:9.

**Of Sin.** See footnotes: BLEMISH, Lev. 14:10; DEFILEMENT, Lev. 5:2; LEAVEN, Lev. 23:17.

**Of the Savior,** Col. 2:17; Heb. 9:7–15, 18–28; 10:1–10. *High priest, typical of the priesthood of Jesus,* Ex. 28:1, 12, 29, 30, 38; Lev. 16:15; Zech. 6:12, 13 (with Heb. 5:1–10; 8:1–3; 10:21). *The institutions ordained by Moses,* Luke 24:25–27, 44–47; Col. 2:14–17; Heb. 10:1–14. *The sacrifices,* Lev. 4:2, 3, 12; Heb. 9:7–15, 18–25; 10:1–22, 29; 13:11–13; 1 Pet. 1:19; Rev. 5:6. *The paschal lamb,* 1 Cor. 5:7. *The veil,* Ex. 40:21; 2 Chr. 3:14 (with Matt. 27:51; Mark 15:38; Luke 23:45; Heb. 10:20). *Manna,* John 6:32–35; 1 Cor. 10:3. *Brazen serpent,* Num. 21:9; John 3:14, 15.

*Adam,* Rom. 5:14; 1 Cor. 15:45. *Abel,* Gen. 4:8, 10, with Heb. 12:24. *Melchisedec,* Heb. 7:1–17. *Moses,* Deut. 18:15, 18; Acts 3:20, 22; 7:37; Heb. 3:2–6. *David,* 2 Sam. 8:15; Psa. 89:19, 20. *Eliakim,* Isa. 22:20–22; Rev. 3:7. *Jonah,* Jonah 1:17, with Matt. 12:40.

c *Wisdom, spiritual,* Prov. 2:2.
4 R. V. upon their mind also will I write them; then saith he,

**17**
d Jer. 31:34.
e *God, mercy of,* Gen. 2:2.
f *Sin, forgiveness of,* Rom. 5:12.

**18**
g *Atonement, by Jesus,* Lev. 17:11.

**19**
h *Boldness of the Righteous,* Phil. 1:20.
i *Access to God,* Eph. 3:12.
j *Jesus, atoning blood of,* Matt. 1:21.
5 R. V. holy place

**20**
k *Way, of holiness,* Isa. 35:8.
l *Jesus, design of his death,* Matt. 1:21.

**21**
m *Jesus, priesthood of,* Matt. 1:21.
n *Church, called house of God,* Matt. 16:18.
6 R. V. a great priest

**22**
o *Faith in Christ,* John 6:69.
p *Heart, renewed,* Psa. 44:21.
q *Regeneration,* Tit. 3:5.
r *Spiritual Purification,* Psa. 51:2.
s *Holiness,* Ex. 39:30.
t *Conscience, purged,* Acts 23:1.
7 R. V. fulness

**23**
u *Steadfastness, enjoined,* 1 Cor. 15:58.
v *Perseverance, exhortation to,* Eph. 6:18.
w *Character, stability of,* Phil. 2:15.
x *God, faithfulness of,* Gen. 2:2.

my [c]laws into their hearts, and
[4]in their minds will I write them;
17 [d]And their sins and iniquities will I [e,f]remember no more.
18 Now where [f]remission of
these *is, there is* no more [g]offering for sin.
19 Having therefore, brethren,
[h]boldness to enter into the [5,i]holiest by the [g,j]blood of Jē'sus,
20 By a new and living [k]way,
which he hath consecrated for
us, through the veil, that is to
say, his [l]flesh;
21 And *having* [6]an *high [m]priest
over the [n]house of God;
22 Let us draw near with a true
heart in [7]full †assurance of [o]faith,
having our [p]hearts [q,r,s]sprinkled
from an evil [t]conscience, and our
bodies washed with pure water.
23 [u,v]Let us [w]hold fast the [8]profession of *our* faith without wavering; (for he *is* [x]faithful that
[y]promised;)
24 And let us consider one another to [z]provoke unto [a]love and
to [b]good works:
25 Not forsaking the [c]assembling of ourselves together, as
the manner of some *is;* but exhorting *one another:* and so much
the more, as ye see the day approaching.
26 For if we [d,e]sin wilfully after that we have [f]received the
[g]knowledge of the [h]truth, there
remaineth no more [i]sacrifice for
sins,
27 But a certain [j]fearful looking
for of [k]judgment and [9]fiery indignation, which shall [l]devour
the adversaries.

28 [10]He that despised Mō'ṣeṣ'
[m]law [n]died without mercy under
two or three [o]witnesses:
29 Of how much sorer [p]punishment, suppose ye, shall he
be thought worthy, [q]who hath
[e,r,s]trodden under foot the [t]Son
of God, and hath [r,s]counted the
[u]blood of the covenant, wherewith he was [v]sanctified, an unholy thing, and hath [r]done despite unto the [w]Spirit of grace?
30 For we know him that hath
said, [l,x,y]Vengeance *belongeth*
unto me, I will recompense,
[11]saith the Lord. And again,
The Lord shall [z]judge his people.
31 *It is* a fearful thing to fall into the hands of the living God.
32 But call to remembrance the
former days, in which, after [a]ye
were [12,b,c]illuminated, ye endured a great fight of [d]afflictions;
33 Partly, whilst ye were [d]made
a gazingstock both by reproaches
and afflictions; and partly, whilst
ye became [13]companions of them
that were so used.
34 For ye had [e]compassion [14]of
me in my bonds, and [f]took [g]joyfully the [d]spoiling of your goods,
[h,i]knowing in yourselves that [j]ye
[k]have in [l]heaven a [m]better and
an enduring substance.
35 [n]Cast not away therefore
your [15]confidence, which hath
[j]great [i]recompence of reward.
36 For ye have need of [o,p]patience, that, [q]after ye have done
the [r]will of God, ye might [s]receive the promise.
37 For yet a little while, and

**28**
m *Law, of Moses,* Deut. 33:2.
n *Death, penalty,* Num. 23:10.
o *Witness, two, necessary to establish a fact,* Num. 35:30.
10 R. V. A man that hath set at nought Moses' law dieth without compassion on the word of two or three witnesses:

**29**
p *Punishment, according to deeds,* Lev. 26:41.
q *Reprobates,* 1 Cor. 9:27.
r *Blasphemy, punishment for,* 2 Sam. 12:14.
s *Jesus, rejected,* Matt. 1:21.
t *Jesus, divine sonship of,* Matt. 1:21.
u *Jesus, atoning blood of,* Matt. 1:21.
v *Sanctification,* 1 Pet. 1:2.
w *Holy Spirit, sin against,* Acts 1:2.

**30**
x *Vengeance,* Psa. 94:1.
y Deut. 32:35, 36.
z *God, judge,* Gen. 2:2.
11 R. V. *omits* saith the Lord

**32**
a *Disciples, of Jesus,* Matt. 9:14.
b *Wisdom, spiritual,* Prov. 2:2.
c *Righteous, described,* Psa. 64:10.
d *Persecution, of the righteous,* John 15:20.
12 R. V. enlightened, ye endured a great conflict of sufferings;

**33**
13 R. V. partakers with them

**34**
e *Sympathy,* 1 Pet. 3:8.

y *Righteous, promises to,* Psa. 64:10. 8 R. V. confession of our hope that it waver not; **24** z *Emulation,* Rom. 11:14.—a *Love,* 1 John 4:7. b *Works, good,* 2 Tim. 1:9. **25** c *Worship, enjoined,* Gen. 22:5. **26** d *Sin, against knowledge,* Rom. 5:12. e *Apostasy,* Acts 1:25. f *Righteous, described,* Psa. 64:10. g *Wisdom, spiritual,* Prov. 2:2. h *Truth, of the gospel,* John 18:37. i *Atonement,* Lev. 17:11.
**27** j *Conscience, guilty,* Acts 23:1. k *Judgment, according to opportunity and works,* 1 Pet. 1:17. l *Wicked, punishment of,* Psa. 73:3. 9 R. V. a fierceness of fire

f *Adversity, resignation in,* Psa. 10:6. g *Joy, under adversity,* Psa. 5:11. h *Faith, instances of trial of,* Mark 11:22. i *Reward, a motive to faithfulness,* Matt. 5:12. j *Righteous, promises to,* Psa. 64:10. k *Faithfulness, rewards of,* Luke 16:10. l *Heaven, future home of the righteous,* Luke 18:22. m *Immortality,* 1 Cor. 15:54. 14 R. V. on them that were in bonds, and took joyfully the spoiling of your possessions, knowing that ye yourselves have a better possession and an abiding one. **35** n *Apostasy,* Acts 1:25. 15 R. V. boldness. **36** o *Patience, a grace of the righteous,* Luke 8:15. p *Perseverance,* Eph. 6:18. q *Blessings, contingent upon obedience,* Deut. 11:26. r *Will of God,* Mark 3:35. s *Reward, a motive, to patience,* Matt. 5:12.

† **ASSURANCE,** Isa. 32:17; 2 Tim. 1:12. *Of divine help,* Deut. 1:30; Psa. 46:2–5; 2 Tim. 4:18. *Of acceptance,* Isa. 12:2; Rom. 8:16; Eph. 3:12; Heb. 6:19; 10:22; 1 John 3:2, 14. *Of spiritual union with God,* 1 John 4:13. *Of spiritual understanding,* Col. 2:2. *Of sufficient grace,* Psa. 23:4; 2 Cor. 12:9. *Of answer to prayer,* 1 John 5:14, 15. *Of eternal reward,* 2 Cor. 4:17, 18; 2 Tim. 4:7, 8, 18; 2 Pet. 1:11.
See footnote, FAITH, Mark 11:22.

[t,u]he that shall come will come,
and will not tarry.[G][Q]
38 [16]Now the [t,v]just shall live
by [w]faith: but if *any man* [n]draw
back, my soul shall have no
pleasure in him.[Q]
39 But we are not of them who
[n]draw back unto perdition[G]; but
of them that [x]believe to the [y]sav-
ing of the soul.[T]

## CHAPTER 11

*What faith is. 2 Its efficacy and power illustrated by the example of many saints mentioned in the Scriptures.*

NOW [a]faith is [1]the substance
of things [b]hoped for, the
evidence of things not seen.[T]
2 For [2]by it the [c]elders obtained
a good report.
3 Through [a]faith we understand that the worlds[G] were
[d]framed[G] by the word of [e]God, so
that things which are seen were
not made of things which do
appear.[S][Q]
4 By [a]faith [f]Ā′bĕl offered unto
God a more excellent [g]sacrifice
than [h]Cāin, by which he obtained
witness[G] that he was [i]righteous,
God testifying of his gifts: and by
it he being dead [j]yet speaketh.[S][Q]
5 By [a]faith [k]Ē′nŏch was *translated that he should [l]not see
[m]death; and was not found, because God had translated him:
for before his translation he had
this testimony, that he pleased
God.[Q]
6 But [n]without [a]faith *it is* impossible to please *him*: for he
that [o,p]cometh to God must [a]be-
lieve that he is, and *that* [q]he is
a [r]rewarder of [s]them that diligently seek him.[T]
7 By [a]faith [t]Nō′ah, being
[u]warned of God of [v]things not
seen as yet, moved with [3,w]fear,
[x]prepared an [y]ark to the saving
of his house; by the which he
condemned the world, and became [z]heir of the righteousness
which is by faith.[T][Q]
8 By [a]faith [b]Ā′brā-hăm, when
he was [c]called to go out into a
[d]place which he should after receive for an inheritance, [e]obeyed;
and he went out, not knowing
whither he went.[Q]
9 By [a]faith he sojourned in the
[d]land of [f]promise, as *in* a strange[G]
country, dwelling in [4]taberna-
cles[G] with [g]Ī′ṣaac and [h]Jā′cob,
the heirs with him of the same
promise:[Q]
10 For he [a]looked for a [i,j,k]city
which hath foundations, whose
builder and maker *is* God.[T]
11 Through [a]faith also [l]Sā′rȧ
herself received strength to [m]con-
ceive seed, and was delivered of
a child when she was past age,
because she judged him [n]faithful
who had promised.[Q]
12 Therefore sprang there even
of [b]one, and him as good as dead,
*so* [o]*many* as the stars of the sky
in multitude, and as the sand
which is by the sea shore innumerable.[Q]
13 These all [p]died in [a]faith, not
having received the promises,
but having seen them [5]afar off,
and were [q]persuaded of *them*,
and embraced *them*, and confessed that they were strangers
and pilgrims on the earth.[Q]
14 For they that say such things
[6]declare plainly that [r]they seek a
country.
15 And truly, if they had been
mindful of that *country* from
whence they came out, they
might have had opportunity to
[s]have returned.[S]
16 But now they desire a better
*country*, that is, an [j]heavenly:
wherefore God is [t]not ashamed

**37**
t Hab. 2:3, 4.
u *Jesus, second coming of,* Matt. 1:21.

**38**
v *Just, live by faith,* Hab. 2:4.
w *Faith,* Mark 11:22.
16 R. V. But my righteous one shall live by faith: And if he shrink back,

**39**
x *Faith in Christ,* John 6:69.
y *Salvation,* Acts 16:17.

**1**
a *Faith,* Mark 11:22.
b *Hope,* Prov. 13:12.
1 Am. R. V. assurance of things hoped for, a conviction of

**2**
c *Elders,* Acts 14:23.
2 R. V. therein the elders had witness borne to them.

**3**
d *Creation,* Mark 13:19.
e *God, creator,* Gen. 2:2.

**4**
f *Abel,* Gen. 4:2.
g *Offerings,* Lev. 6:17.
h *Cain,* Gen. 4:1.
i *Justification, by faith,* Rom. 4:25.
j *Influence, good,* 1 Cor. 7:14.

**5**
k *Enoch, translation of,* Gen. 5:18.
l *Immortality, implied in the translation of Enoch,* 1 Cor. 15:54.
m *Death, exemption from,* Num. 23:10.

**6**
n *Unbelief,* Heb. 3:12.
o *Spiritual Desire,* Psa. 42:1.
p *Access to God,* Eph. 3:12.
q *Prayer, answer to, promised,* Acts 6:4.
r *Reward, a motive, to faithfulness,* Matt. 5:12.
s *Seekers,* Isa. 55:6. **7** t *Noah,* Gen. 5:29. u *God, providence of,* Gen. 2:2. v *Flood,* Gen. 6:17. w *Fear of God, instances of,* Acts 9:31. 3 R. V. godly fear

x *Obedience, rewarded,* Heb. 5:8.
y *Ark,* Gen. 6:14.
z *Inheritance, figurative,* Num. 27:7.

**8**
a *Faith,* Mark 11:22.
b *Abraham,* Gen. 17:5.
c *Call, personal,* Phil. 3:14.
d *Canaan,* Gen. 37:1.
e *Obedience, exemplified,* Heb. 5:8.

**9**
f *Covenant, of God with men,* Deut. 29:1.
g *Isaac,* Gen. 21:3.
h *Jacob,* Gen. 27:11.
4 R. V. tents

**10**
i *Cities, figurative,* Num. 35:8.
j *Heaven, future home of the righteous,* Luke 18:22.
k *Immortality,* 1 Cor. 15:54.

**11**
l Or, *Sarah,* Gen. 17:15.
m *Conception, miraculous,* Gen. 21:2.
n *God, faithfulness of,* Gen. 2:2.

**12**
o *Descendants of Abraham,* Gen. 22:17.

**13**
p *Death, of the righteous,* Num. 23:10.
q *Messianic Hope,* Gen. 49:10.
5 R. V. and greeted them from afar, and having confessed

**14**
r *Seekers,* Isa. 55:6.
6 R. V. make it manifest that they are seeking after a country of their own.

**15**
s *Backsliding,* Hos. 11:7.

**16**
t *God, love of, exemplified,* Gen. 2:2.

* **TRANSLATION.** *Of Enoch,* Gen. 5:24; Heb. 11:5. *Of Elijah,* 2 Kin. 2:1–12. *Of Jesus,* Mark 16:19; Luke 24:51; Acts 1:9–11. *Desired by Paul,* 2 Cor. 5:4. *Of the saints at the last day,* 1 Cor. 15:52; 1 Thess. 4:17.

to be called their God: for [u]he hath prepared for them a [i, k]city.[Q]

17 By faith [b]Ā'brā-hăm, when he was [v,w]tried,[C] offered up [x, y]Ī'ṣaac: [7]and he that had received the [z]promises offered up his only begotten *son,*[Q]

18 Of whom it was said, [a]That in [b]Ī'ṣaac shall thy seed be called:[Q]

19 [c]Accounting that God [8]*was* [d]able to [e]raise *him* up, even from the dead; from whence also he received him in a figure.

20 By [c]faith [b]Ī'ṣaac [f]blessed [g]Jā'cob and [h]Ē'ṣau concerning things to come.[Q]

21 By [c]faith [g]Jā'cob, [i]when he was a dying, [f]blessed both the sons of [j]Jō'ṣeph; and worshipped, *leaning* upon the top of his staff.[Q]

22 By [c]faith [j]Jō'ṣeph, when [9]he died, [i]made mention of the departing of the children of Ĭṣ'rael; and gave commandment concerning his bones.[Q]

23 By [c]faith [k]Mō'ṣeṣ, when he was born, was hid three months of his parents, because they saw *he was* a [10]proper[C] child; and they were [c]not afraid of the king's commandment.[Q]

24 By [c]faith [k]Mō'ṣeṣ, when he was [11, l]come to years, [m]refused to be called the [n]son of [o]Phā'raōh's daughter;[Q]

25 [p, q, r]Choosing rather to [12]suffer affliction with the [s]people of God, than to enjoy the [t, u]pleasures of sin for a season;

26 [v]Esteeming the reproach of Chrīst greater riches than the treasures in [w]Ē'ġy̆pt: for [x]he had respect unto the recompence of the reward.[Q]

27 By faith he forsook [w]Ē'ġy̆pt, not fearing the [y]wrath of the king: for he [m]endured,[C] as seeing him who is [z]invisible.[Q]

28 Through [a]faith he kept the [b]passover, and the [c]sprinkling of [d, e]blood, lest he that [f]destroyed the [g]firstborn should touch them.[Q]

29 By [a]faith they passed through the [h]Red sea [i]as by dry *land:* which the [j]Ē-ġy̆p'tianṣ assaying[C] to do were drowned.[Q]

30 By [a]faith the [k]walls of [l]Jĕr'ĭ-chō [i]fell down, after they were compassed[C] about [m]seven days.[Q]

31 By [a]faith the [n]harlot [o]Rā'hăb perished not with them that [13]believed not, when she had [p]received the [q]spies with [r]peace.[Q]

32 And what shall I more say? for the time would fail me to tell of [s]Ğĕd'e-on, and *of* [t]Bā'răk, and *of* [u]Săm'son, and *of* [v]Jĕph'tha-ē; *of* [w]Dā'vid also, and [x]Săm'u-el, and *of* the prophets:[Q]

33 Who through [a]faith subdued kingdoms, wrought righteousness, obtained promises, [y]stopped the mouths of lions,[Q]

34 Quenched the violence of fire, escaped the edge of the sword, out of weakness were made strong, waxed[C] valiant in fight, turned to flight the armies of the aliens.[Q]

35 Women received their [z]dead [14]raised to life again: and others were [a]tortured, not accepting deliverance; that they might obtain a better [b]resurrection:[Q]

36 And others had trial of *cruel* [c]mockings and [d]scourgings, yea, moreover of bonds and [e]imprisonment:[Q]

37 [a]They were [f, g, h]stoned, they were sawn asunder,[C] were tempted,[C] were slain with the sword: they wandered about in sheepskins and goatskins; being destitute, afflicted, [15]tormented;[Q]

38 (Of whom the world was not worthy:) they wandered in deserts, and *in* mountains, and *in* dens and caves of the earth.[Q]

---

u *Righteous, promises to,* Psa. 64:10.

**17**
v *Faith, trial of,* Mark 11:22.
w *Temptation, a test of obedience,* Luke 11:4.
x *Isaac,* Gen. 21:3.
y *Human Sacrifices,* Deut. 12:31.
z *Covenant, of God with men,* Deut. 29:1.
7 R. V. yea, he that had gladly received

**18**
a Gen. 21:12.
b *Isaac,* Gen. 21:3.

**19**
c *Faith,* Mark 11:22.
d *God, power of,* Gen. 2:2.
e *Resurrection,* 1 Cor. 15:12.
8 R. V. is able to raise up, even from the dead; from whence he did also in a parable receive him back.

**20**
f *Parents, paternal blessings of,* 2 Cor. 12:14.
g *Jacob,* Gen. 27:11.
h *Esau,* Gen. 25:25.

**21**
i *Death, scenes of,* Num. 23:10.
j *Joseph,* Gen. 33:2.

**22**
9 R. V. his end was nigh,

**23**
k *Moses,* Ex. 2:10.
10 R. V. goodly

**24**
l *Young Men,* Prov. 1:4.
m *Character, stability of,* Phil. 2:15.
n *Adoption, of children,* Gen. 48:5.
o *Pharaoh,* Ex. 1:11.
11 R. V. grown up,

**25**
p *Choice,* 2 Sam. 24:12.
q *Faith, trial of,* Mark 11:22.
r *Self-denial,* Mark 8:34.
s *Righteous, described,* Psa. 64:10.
t *Wicked, happiness of,* Psa. 73:3.
u *Worldly Pleasure,* Eccl. 2:1.
12 R. V. be evil entreated with

**28**
a *Faith,* Mark 11:22.
b *Passover,* Num. 9:5.
c *Sprinkling, of blood,* Lev. 14:7.
d *Blood, sacrificial,* Heb. 9:19.
e *Jesus, atoning blood of, typified,* Matt. 1:21.
f *Judgments,* Ex. 6:6.
g *Firstborn,* Zech. 12:10.

**29**
h *Red Sea, divided,* Ex. 10:19.
i *Miracles,* Luke 23:8.
j *Egyptians, army of, destroyed,* Gen. 50:3.

**30**
k *Cities, walled,* Num. 35:8.
l *Jericho,* Num. 22:1.
m *Seven, days,* Gen. 7:2.

**31**
n *Harlot,* Prov. 7:10.
o *Rahab,* Josh. 2:1.
p *Hospitality,* Rom. 12:13.
q *Spies,* Josh. 6:23.
r *Peace,* Jer. 29:7.
13 R. V. were disobedient,

**32**
s Or, *Gideon,* Judg. 6:11.
t *Barak,* Judg. 4:6–24.
u *Samson,* Judg. 13:24.
v Or, *Jephthah,* Judg. 11:1.
w *David,* 1 Sam. 16:13.
x *Samuel,* 1 Sam. 3:1.

**33**
y *Daniel, cast into the lions' den,* Dan. 1:7.

**35**
z *Dead, raised to life,* 2 Kin. 4:32.
a *Persecution, of the righteous,* John 15:20.
b *Resurrection,* 1 Cor. 15:12.
14 R. V. by a resurrection:

**36**
c *Mocking,* 1 Kin. 18:27.
d *Scourging,* Acts 22:24.

**26** v *Wisdom, spiritual,* Prov. 2:2. w *Egypt,* Gen. 41:8. x *Reward, a motive, to faithfulness,* Matt. 5:12. **27** y *Anger,* Psa. 37:8. z *God, invisible,* Gen. 2:2.

e *Imprisonment,* Acts 12:4. **37** f *Stoning,* 1 Sam. 30:6. g *Prophets, martyrs,* Isa. 3:2. h *Martyrdom,* Rev. 17:6. 15 R. V. evil entreated.

39 And these all, having obtained a good report through [i]faith, received not the promise:

40 God having provided some [j]better thing for us, that they without us should not be made perfect.

## CHAPTER 12

*An exhortation to constant faith, patience, and godliness. 22 A commendation of the new covenant above the old.*

WHEREFORE seeing we also are compassed about with so great a cloud of *witnesses, [a]let us [b,c]lay aside every weight, and the [d]sin which doth so easily beset *us*, and let us [e]run with [f]patience the [g]race that is set before us,

2 Looking unto [h]Jē′sus the author and [1]finisher of *our* [i]faith; who for the joy that was set before him [j]endured the [k]cross, [l]despising the shame, and is set down [m,n]at the right hand of the [o]throne of God.

3 For [p]consider [h]him that endured such [q]contradiction of sinners against [2]himself, [r]lest ye be wearied and [s]faint in your [3]minds.

4 Ye have not yet resisted unto blood, striving against sin.

5 And ye have forgotten the exhortation which speaketh unto you as unto children, [t]My son, despise not thou the [u]chastening of the Lord, nor faint when thou art rebuked of him:

6 [t]For whom the Lord [v]loveth he [u]chasteneth, and scourgeth every [w]son whom he receiveth.

7 [4]If ye endure [u]chastening, [v]God dealeth with you as with [w]sons; for [x]what son is he whom the [y]father chasteneth not?

8 But if ye be without [u]chastisement, whereof all are partakers, then are ye [z]bastards, and not sons.

9 Furthermore we have had [y]fathers of our flesh which [x]corrected *us*, and we gave *them* reverence: shall we not much rather be in subjection unto the [a]Father of spirits, and live?

10 For [b]they verily for a few days [c]chastened *us* [5]after their own pleasure; but [a]he [d]for *our* profit, [e]that *we* might be [f]partakers of his [g]holiness.

11 Now no [h]chastening for the present seemeth to be joyous, but grievous: nevertheless [e]afterward it yieldeth the peaceable fruit of righteousness unto them which are exercised thereby.

12 [i]Wherefore [j,k]lift up the hands which hang down, and the [6]feeble knees;

13 And [k]make straight paths for your feet, lest that which is lame be turned out of the [l]way; but let it rather be healed.

14 [m]Follow [n]peace with all *men*, and [7,o]holiness, [p]without which no man shall see the Lord:

15 [q,r]Looking [8,s]diligently [t]lest any man fail of the [u]grace of God; lest any [v,w]root of bitterness springing up trouble *you*, and thereby many be defiled;

16 [q,r]Lest there *be* any [x,y]fornicator, or profane person, as [z,a]Ē′sau, who [b]for one [9]morsel of meat sold his [c]birthright.

17 For ye know how that afterward, when he would have inherited the blessing, he was rejected: for he found no place [10]of repentance, though he sought it [8]carefully with tears.

18 For ye are not come unto the [d]mount that might be touched, and that burned with fire, nor unto blackness, and [e]darkness, and tempest,

19 And the sound of a [f]trumpet,

**16** *x Adultery,* Lev. 20:10. *y Idolatry, wicked practices of,* 1 Sam. 15:23. *z Esau,* Gen. 25:25.—*a Firstborn, birthright of,* Zech. 12:10. *b Appetite, a source of temptation,* Prov. 23:2. *c Birthright,* 2 Chr. 21:3. 9 R. V. mess **17** 10 Am. R. V. for a change of mind in his father, though **18** *d Sinai,* Ex. 16:1. *e Darkness, figurative,* Gen. 1:2. **19** *f Trumpet,* Josh. 6:4.

**39**
*i Faith,* Mark 11:22.
**40**
*j Gospel,* Mark 13:10.
**1**
*a Faithfulness,* Luke 16:10.
*b Self-denial,* Mark 8:34.
*c Holiness,* Ex. 39:30.
*d Sin, besetting,* Rom. 5:12.
*e Strenuousness, of the righteous,* Eccl. 9:10.
*f Patience, enjoined,* Luke 8:15.
*g Foot Race, figurative,* Psa. 19:5.
**2**
*h Jesus, our example,* Matt. 1:21.
*i Faith in Christ,* John 6:69.
*j Jesus, death of,* Matt. 1:21.
*k Cross,* John 19:17.
*l Crucifixion, a reproach,* Mark 15:13.
*m Jesus, exaltation of,* Matt. 1:21.
*n Sovereignty of the Messiah,* Psa. 110:1.
*o Throne, figurative,* 1 Kin. 2:19.
1 R. V. perfecter
**3**
*p Perseverance, motives to, the example of Jesus,* Eph. 6:18.
*q Persecution, of Jesus,* John 15:20.
*r Temptation, admonitions against yielding to,* Luke 11:4.
*s Backsliding, admonitions against,* Hos. 11:7.
2 R.V. themselves,
3 R. V. souls.
**5**
*t* Prov. 3:11, 12.
*u Divine Chastisement, administered in love,* Job 33:19.
**6**
*v God, love of,* Gen. 2:2.
*w Spiritual Adoption,* Rom. 8:15.
**7**
*x Children, punishment of,* Mark 10:14.
*y Father, duty of,* Psa. 27:10.
4 R. V. It is for chastening that ye endure; God
**8**
*z Bastard, figurative,* Deut. 23:2.

**9**
*a God, fatherhood of,* Gen. 2:2.
**10**
*b Father, duty of,* Psa. 27:10.
*c Children, punishment of,* Mark 10:14.
*d Afflictions, design of,* Psa. 34:19.
*e Afflictions, benefits of,* Psa. 34:19.
*f Spiritual Blessings, from God,* Eph. 1:3.
*g God, holiness of,* Gen. 2:2.
5 R. V. as seemed good to them;
**11**
*h Divine Chastisement,* Job 33:19.
**12**
*i* Isa. 35:3.
*j Despondency, comfort in,* Eccl. 2:20.
*k Weak, duty of the strong to,* 1 Cor. 8:9.
6 R. V. palsied
**13**
*l Highways, figurative,* Deut. 2:27.
**14**
*m Commandment, enjoining peaceableness and holiness,* Deut. 8:2.
*n Peace, enjoined,* Jer. 29:7.
*o Holiness, a condition of eternal salvation,* Ex. 39:30.
*p Sin, separates, from God,* Rom. 5:12.
7 R. V. the sanctification without
**15**
*q Commandment, enjoining watchfulness,* Deut. 8:2.
*r Watchfulness, enjoined,* Matt. 24:42.
*s Diligence, in keeping the heart,* Rom. 12:8.
*t Backsliding, admonitions against,* Hos. 11:7.
*u Grace of God,* Rom. 4:16.
*v Influence, evil,* 1 Cor. 7:14.
*w Temptation,* Luke 11:4.
8 R. V. carefully

* **GLORIFIED SAINTS,** Heb. 12:1, 23; Rev. 6:9-11; 14:1-5; 15:2-4.

11 R. V. no word more should be spoken unto them:

20

*g* Ex. 19:12, 13.

12 R. V. *omits* or thrust through with a dart:

21

*h* *God, glory of,* Gen. 2:2.

*i* *Moses,* Ex. 2:10.

22

*j* *Church,* Matt. 16:18.

*k* Or, *Zion,* 2 Sam. 5:7.

*l* *Angel,* Heb. 1:13.

23

*m* *Book, of life,* Psa. 139:16.

*n* *Heaven, future home of the righteous,* Luke 18:22.

*o* *God, judge,* Gen. 2:2.

*p* *Man, a spirit,* Job 4:17.

*q* *Perfection,* Heb. 6:1.

13 R. V. who are enrolled in

24

*r* *Jesus, mediation of,* Matt. 1:21.

*s* *New Covenant,* Jer. 31:31.

*t* *Gospel, called new covenant,* Mark 13:10.

*u* *Blood, of Christ, atoning,* Heb. 9:19.

*v* *Atonement, by Jesus,* Lev. 17:11.

*w* *Sprinkling, of blood,* Lev. 14:7.

*x* *Abel,* Gen. 4:2.

25

*y* *Call, personal,* Phil. 3:14.

*z* *Punishment, no escape from,* Lev. 26:41.

---

*a* *Jesus, rejected,* Matt. 1:21.

*b* *Judgment, according to opportunity and works,* 1 Pet. 1:17.

*c* *Punishment, no escape from,* Lev. 26:41.

*d* *Apostasy,* Acts 1:25.

*e* *Heaven, God's dwelling place,* Luke 18:22.

26

*f* *God, power of,* Gen. 2:2.

*g* Hag. 2:6.

*h* *Prophecies concerning the Messiah, and their fulfillment,* Gen. 12:3.

and the voice of words; which
*voice* they that heard intreated
that [11]the word should not be
spoken to them any more:
20 (For they could not endure
that which was commanded,
[g]And if so much as a beast touch
the mountain, it shall be stoned,
[12]or thrust through with a dart:
21 And so terrible was the
[h]sight, *that* [i]Mō′ṣeṣ said, I exceedingly fear and quake:)
22 But ye are come unto [j]mount
[k]Sī′ŏn, and unto the city of the
living God, the heavenly Jē-ru′-
sā-lĕm, and to an innumerable
company of [l]angels,
23 To the general assembly and
[j]church of the firstborn, [13]which
are [m]written in [n]heaven, and
to God the [o]Judge of all, and to
the *,[p]spirits of just men made
[q]perfect,
24 And to Jē′ṣus the [r]mediator
of the [s,t]new covenant, and to
the [u,v]blood of [w]sprinkling, that
speaketh better things than *that*
*of* [x]Ā′bĕl.
25 See that ye refuse not him
that [y]speaketh. For if they [z]es-
caped not who [a]refused him that
spake on earth, [b]much more
[c]*shall not* we *escape*, if we [d]turn
away from him that *speaketh*
from [e]heaven:
26 Whose voice then [f]shook the
earth: but now he hath promised, saying, [g,h]Yet once more I
shake not the earth only, but
also heaven.
27 And this [h]*word*, Yet once
more, signifieth the removing of
those [i]things that are shaken, as
of things that are made, that
those [j]things which cannot be
shaken may remain.
28 Wherefore we receiving a
[k]kingdom which cannot be
moved, [l]let us have grace,
whereby we may [m]serve God
acceptably with [n]reverence and
[14]godly [o]fear:
29 For our [p]God *is* a consuming fire.

## CHAPTER 13

*Divers admonitions as to love and hospitality, 5 to avoid covetousness, 10 to confess Christ, 17 to obey pastors. 18 The apostle asks them to pray for him. 20 The conclusion.*

[a]LET [b]brotherly [c]love continue.
2 [1,d]Be not forgetful to entertain strangers: for thereby
some have [e]entertained [f]angels
unawares.
3 [g,h,i]Remember them that are
in [j]bonds, as bound with them;
*and* them [2]which suffer adversity, as being yourselves also in
the body.
4 [3,k]Marriage *is* honourable
in all, and the bed undefiled:
but whoremongers and [l]adulter-
ers God will [m]judge.
5 [4,n,o]*Let your* conversation *be*
without covetousness; *and* [p]*be*
content with such things as ye
have: for he hath said, [q,r,s,t]I
will never leave thee, nor forsake thee.
6 So that [5]we may [u]boldly say,
[v,w]The [r]Lord *is* my [x]helper, and
I will not fear what man shall do
unto me.
7 [y]Remember them which have
the [z]rule over you, who have
[a]spoken unto you the [b]word of
God: [6]whose [c,d,e]faith follow,
considering the end of *their* conversation.
8 Jē′ṣus Christ [7,f]the same [g]yes-
terday, and to day, and [h]for ever.
9 [i]Be not [j]carried about with
[k]divers and strange [8]doctrines.

*n* *Reverence,* Lev. 19:30.

*o* *Fear of God,* Acts 9:31.

14 R. V. awe:

29

*p* Deut. 4:24.

1

*a* *Commandment, enjoining love for man,* Deut. 8:2.

*b* *Fraternity, enjoined,* Zech. 11:14.

*c* *Love, of man for man,* 1 John 4:7.

2

*d* *Commandment, enjoining hospitality,* Deut. 8:2.

*e* *Hospitality,* Rom. 12:13.

*f* *Angel,* Heb. 1:13.

1 R. V. Forget not to shew love unto strangers:

3

*g* *Commandment, enjoining sympathy,* Deut. 8:2.

*h* *Adversity, consolation in,* Psa. 10:6.

*i* *Sympathy,* 1 Pet. 3:8.

*j* *Persecution, of the righteous,* John 15:20.

2 R. V. that are evil entreated, as

4

*k* *Marriage, commended,* Gen. 34:9.

*l* *Adultery, penalties for,* Lev. 20:10.

*m* *God, judge,* Gen. 2:2.

3 R. V. Let marriage be had in honour among all, and let the bed be undefiled: for fornicators and

5

*n* *Commandment, warning against love of money,* Deut. 8:2.

*o* *Covetousness, warnings against,* Isa. 57:17.

*p* *Contentment, enjoined,* 1 Tim. 6:6.

*q* Josh. 1:5.

*r* *God, preserver,* Gen. 2:2.

27 *i* *Law, of Moses,* Deut. 33:2. *j* *Gospel,* Mark 13:10.
28 *k* *Kingdom of Heaven,* Matt. 13:24. *l* *Faithfulness,* Luke 16:10. *m* *Obedience,* Heb. 5:8.

*s* *Promise, to the righteous,* 2 Cor. 1:20. *t* *Righteous, promises to,* Psa. 61:10. 4 R. V. Be ye free from the love of money; **6** *u* *Boldness of the Righteous,* Phil. 1:20. *v* Psa. 118:6. *w* *Faith,* Mark 11:22. *x* *Grace of God,* Rom. 4:16. 5 R. V. with good courage we say, **7** *y* *Commandment, enjoining esteem for pastors,* Deut. 8:2. *z* *Minister, clothed with authority,* Rom. 15:16.—*a* *Preaching,* Matt. 9:35. *b* *Doctrines of Jesus,* John 7:16. *c* *Faith in Christ,* John 6:69. *d* *Minister, character and qualifications of,* Rom. 15:16. *e* *Example, good,* John 13:15. 6 R. V. and considering the issue of their life, imitate their faith. **8** *f* *Jesus, unchangeable,* Matt. 1:21. *g* *Jesus, pre-existence of,* Matt. 1:21. *h* *Jesus, eternity of,* Matt. 1:21. 7 R. V. *inserts* is **9** *i* *Steadfastness,* 1 Cor. 15:58. *j* *Instability,* Jas. 1:8. *k* *False Teachers,* 2 Pet. 2:1. 8 R. V. teachings:

*l Gospel*, Matt. 13:10.
*m Works under the Law*, Lev. 18:5.

**11**

*n Offerings, animal sacrifices*, Lev. 6:17.
*o Blood, sacrificial*, Heb. 9:19.
*p High Priest*, Lev. 21:10.
*q Atonement, by animal sacrifices*, Lev. 17:11.
9 R. V. holy place

**12**

*r Atonement, by Jesus*, Lev. 17:11.
*s Jesus, design of his death*, Matt. 1:21.
*t Blood, of Jesus*, Heb. 9:19.

**13**

*u Self-denial*, Mark 8:34.
*v Crucifixion, a reproach*, Mark 15:13.
*w Suffering for Christ*, Phil. 1:29.

**14**

*x Life, brevity and uncertainty of*, Eccl. 8:15.
*y Faith, exemplified*, Mark 11:22.
*z Heaven, future home of the righteous*, Luke 18:22.

**15**

*a Jesus, mediation of*, Matt. 1:21.
*b Thankfulness, enjoined*, Acts 24:3.
*c Offerings, figurative*, Lev. 6:17.
*d Praise*, Psa. 150:1.
10 R. V. which make confession

For *it is* a good thing that the
heart be established with [l]grace;
not with [m]meats, which have not
profited them that have been occupied therein.
10 We have an altar, whereof
they have no right to eat which
serve the tabernacle.
11 For the bodies of those
[n]beasts, whose [o]blood is brought
into the [9]sanctuary by the [p]high
priest [q]for sin, are burned without the camp.
12 Wherefore Jē′ṣus also, that
he might [r,s]sanctify the people
with his own [t]blood, suffered
without the gate.
13 [u]Let us go forth therefore
unto him without the camp,
[v,w]bearing his reproach.
14 For [x]here have we no continuing city, but [y]we seek [z]one to
come.
15 [a]By him therefore [b]let us offer the [c]sacrifice of [d]praise to
God continually, that is, the fruit
of *our* lips [10]giving thanks to his
name.
16 But to [e]do good and to
[f,g,h]communicate forget not: for
with such sacrifices God is well
pleased.
17 [i,j]Obey them that have the
[k]rule over you, and submit yourselves: for they [l]watch for your
souls, [m]as they that must give
account, that they may do it
with joy, and not with grief: for
that *is* unprofitable for you.
18 [n]Pray for us: for we trust we
have a [o]good conscience, in all
things [11]willing to live [p]honestly.
19 But I beseech *you* the rather
to do this, that I may be restored
to you the sooner.
20 [q,r]Now the God of [s]peace,
that [t]brought again from the
dead our [u]Lord Jē′ṣus, that
great [v]shepherd of the [w]sheep,
through the [x]blood of the [y]ever-
lasting covenant,
21 [r]Make you [z]perfect in every
good work to [a]do his [b]will, working in [12]you that which is well-
pleasing in his sight, through
Jē′ṣus Christ; to whom *be* glory
for ever and ever. Amen.
22 And [c]I beseech you, brethren, suffer the word of exhortation: for I have written a letter
unto you in few words.
23 Know ye that *our* brother
[d]Tĭm′o-thȳ is set at liberty; with
whom, if he come shortly, I will
see you.
24 [e]Salute all them that have
the [f]rule over you, and all the
saints. They of [g]Ĭt′a-lȳ salute
you.
25 [h]Grace *be* with you all.
Amen.

[13] Written to the Hebrews from Italy by Timothy.

*m Minister, responsibility of*, Rom. 15:16.

**18**

*n Intercession, of man with God, solicited*, Jer. 27:18.
*o Conscience, approving*, Acts 23:1.
*p Honesty*, Rom. 13:13.
11 R. V. desiring

**20**

*q Benedictions, apostolic*, Deut. 21:5.
*r Prayer, intercessory*, Acts 6:4.
*s Spiritual Peace, from God*, Gal. 1:3.
*t Resurrection, of Jesus*, 1 Cor. 15:12.
*u Jesus, lordship of*, Matt. 1:21.
*v Jesus, shepherd*, Matt. 1:21.
*w Sheep, figurative*, Deut. 32:14.
*x Blood, of Christ, atoning*, Heb. 9:19.
*y New Covenant*, Jer. 31:31.

**21**

*z Perfection*, Heb. 6:1.
*a Obedience*, Heb. 5:8.
*b Will of God, the supreme rule of duty*, Psa. 119:9.
12 R. V. us

**22**

*c Minister, love of, for the church*, Matt. 16:18.

**23**

*d Timothy*, 1 Cor. 4:17.

**24**

*e Salutations*, Luke 1:44.
*f Minister, clothed with authority*, Rom. 15:16.
*g* Acts 18:2; 27:1.

**16** *e Works, good*, 2 Tim. 1:9. *f Commandment, enjoining liberality*, Deut. 8:2. *g Alms, giving of, enjoined*, Matt. 6:2. *h Christian Graces, liberality*, Gal. 5:22. **17** *i Commandment, enjoining esteem for pastors*, Deut. 8:2. *j Church, duty of, to ministers*, Matt. 16:18. *k Minister, clothed with authority*, Rom. 15:16. *l Minister, duties of*, Rom. 15:16.

**25** *h Benedictions, apostolic*, Deut. 21:5. 13 R. V. *omits postscript.*

## THE EPISTLE OF

# JAMES

## CHAPTER 1

*The apostle's salutation. 2 He exhorts his brethren to rejoice under trials, 5 to ask wisdom of God, 13 and not to impute to him their temptations to sin. 16 The source and requirements of true religion.*

[a] JĀMES, a servant of God and
of the [b]Lord Jē'ṣus Chrīst,
to the twelve tribes which are
[1,c]scattered abroad, greeting.

2 My brethren, [d]count it all [e]joy
when ye fall into [2]divers [f,g]temp-
tations;

3 Knowing *this*, that the [h]trying
of your faith [g]worketh [i]patience.

4 But let [i]patience have *her* perfect work, that ye may be [j]perfect
and entire, wanting nothing.

5 If any of you [k]lack [l]wisdom,
let him ask of God, that [m]giveth
to all *men* liberally, and upbraid-
eth not; and [n,o,p]it shall be given
him.

6 But let him ask in [q]faith,
nothing [3,r,s]wavering. For he
that [*,t]wavereth is like a wave
of the sea driven with the wind
and tossed.

7 For let not that man [u,v]think
that he shall receive any thing of
the Lord.

8 A [w]double minded man *is*
[*,t]unstable in all his ways.

9 Let the brother of [x,y]low degree [4]rejoice in that he is exalted:

10 But the [z]rich, in that he is
made low: because [a]as the flower
of the [b]grass he shall [c]pass away.

11 For the sun [5]is no sooner
risen with a burning heat, but it
[d]withereth the grass, and the
flower thereof falleth, and the
grace of the fashion of it perisheth: so also shall the [e]rich man
fade away in his ways.

12 [f]Blessed *is* the man that
endureth [g]temptation: for when
he [6]is tried, [h,i,j]he shall receive
the [k,l]crown of life, which the
Lord hath promised to them
that [m]love him.

13 Let no man say when he is
[g]tempted, I am tempted of God:
for God [n,o]cannot be tempted
with evil, neither tempteth he
any man:

14 But every man is tempted,
when he is drawn away of his
own [p,q]lust, and enticed.

15 Then when [p]lust hath conceived, it bringeth forth sin: and
sin, when it is [7]finished, bringeth
forth [r,s]death.

16 [8]Do not err, my beloved
brethren.

17 Every good [t,u]gift and every
perfect gift is from above, and
cometh down from the [v]Father
of [w]lights, with whom [9]is [x,y]no
variableness, neither shadow of
turning.

18 [z]Of his own [a]will [b]begat he
us with the word of [c]truth, that
we should be a kind of [d]firstfruits
of his creatures.

**1**
a *James, identity of, uncertain.*
b *Jesus, lordship of,* Matt. 1:21.
c *Dispersion,* Gen. 11:8.
1 R. V. of the Dispersion, greeting.

**2**
d *Commandment, enjoining patience under tribulations,* vs. 2–4; Deut. 8:2.
e *Joy, under adversity,* Psa. 5:11.
f *Temptation, a test,* Luke 11:4.
g *Afflictions, benefits of,* Psa. 34:19.
2 R. V. manifold

**3**
h *Faith, trial of,* Mark 11:22.
i *Patience,* Luke 8:15.

**4**
j *Perfection,* Heb. 6:1.

**5**
k *Ignorance,* Acts 3:17.
l *Wisdom, spiritual, prayer for,* Prov. 2:2.
m *God, goodness of,* Gen. 2:2.
n *Spiritual Gifts,* 1 Cor. 12:4.
o *Prayer, answer to, promised,* Acts 6:4.
p *Promise, of wisdom,* 2 Cor. 1:20.

**6**
q *Faith, enjoined,* Mark 11:22.
r *Doubting, in prayer,* Rom. 14:23.
s *Unbelief,* Heb. 3:12.
t *Character, instability of,* Phil. 2:15.

3 R. V. doubting: for he that doubteth is like the surge of the sea driven **7** u *Delusion,* 2 Thess. 2:11. v *False Confidence,* Psa. 30:6. **8** w *Indecision,* 1 Kin. 18:21. **9** x *Humility,* Prov. 22:4. y *Poor,* Prov. 21:13. 4 R.V. glory in his high estate: **10** z *Rich,* Jas. 5:1.—a *Life, brevity and uncertainty of,* Eccl. 8:15. b *Grass, the brevity of human life compared to,* Isa. 40:7. c *Death, inevitable,* Num. 23:10.

**11**
d Isa. 40:6–8.
e *Rich, admonitions to,* Jas. 5:1.
5 R. V. ariseth with the scorching wind, and withereth

**12**
f *Afflictions, consolation in,* Psa. 34:19.
g *Temptation,* Luke 11:4.
h *Promise, to the righteous,* 2 Cor. 1:20.
i *Righteous, promises to,* Psa. 64:10.
j *Perseverance, motives to,* Eph. 6:18.
k *Crown, figurative,* Ex. 29:6.
l *Reward, a motive, to faithfulness,* Matt. 5:12.
m *Love, for Jesus,* 1 John 4:19.
6 R. V. hath been approved,

**13**
n *God, holiness of,* Gen. 2:2.
o *Holiness, attributed to God,* Ex. 39:30.

**14**
p *Lust, tempts to sin,* 2 Pet. 1:4.
q *Temptation, sources of,* Luke 11:4.

**15**
r *Sin, fruits of,* Rom. 5:12.
s *Spiritual Death,* 1 John 3:14.
7 R. V. fullgrown,

**16**
8 R. V. Be not deceived,

**17**
t *Spiritual Blessings,* Eph. 1:3.

u *Temporal Blessings,* Psa. 103:2. v *God, fatherhood of,* Gen. 2:2. w *Light, figurative,* Matt. 5:14. x *God, immutable,* Gen. 2:2. y *God, perfection of,* Gen. 2:2. 9 R. V. can be no variation, neither shadow that is cast by turning. **18** z *God, love of, exemplified,* Gen. 2:2.—a *Will of God,* Mark 3:35. b *Regeneration,* Tit. 3:5. c *Truth, of the gospel,* John 18:37. d *First Fruits, figurative,* Deut. 18:4.

---

* **INSTABILITY,** Prov. 27:8; Matt. 12:25; Eph. 4:14; 2 Pet. 2:14.
*Warnings against,* Prov. 24:21, 22; Matt. 8:19–22 (with Luke 9:57–62); 13:20, 21 (with Mark 4:16, 17; Luke 8:13); Heb. 13:9; Jas. 1:6–8; 4:8; Rev. 3:2.
**Instances of:** *Reuben,* Gen. 49:4. *Pharaoh,* Ex. 8:15, 32; 9:34; 10:8–11, 16–20; 14:5. *Israel,* Ex. 32:8–10 (with 19:8; 24:3, 7); Judg. 2:17; 1 Kin. 18:21; Psa. 106:12, 13; Jer. 2:36. *Saul in his feelings toward David,* 1 Sam. 18:19. *David, in yielding to lust,* 2 Sam. 11:2–4. *Solomon, in yielding to his idolatrous wives,* 1 Kin. 11:1–8. *Ephraim and Judah,* Hos. 6:4. *Jews,* Hos. 6:4, 5; John 5:35. *Lot's wife,* Luke 17:32. *Disciples of Jesus,* John 6:66. *Mark,* Acts 15:38. *Galatians,* Gal. 1:6; 4:9–11.

19 [10]Wherefore, my [e,f]beloved brethren, [g]let every man be swift to [h]hear, [i]slow to speak, slow to [j]wrath:[Q]

20 For the [j]wrath of man worketh[G] not the righteousness of God.[T]

21 Wherefore [11,k,l]lay apart all filthiness and superfluity of naughtiness,[G] and receive with [m]meekness the engrafted[G] [c,n]word, which is able to [o]save your souls.

22[T] But [p]be ye [†,q]doers of the [c,n]word, and not [h]hearers only, [r]deceiving your own selves.

23 For if any be a [h]hearer of the word, and not a [†]doer, he is like unto a man beholding his natural face in a [12,s]glass[G]:

24 For he beholdeth himself, and goeth his way, and straightway[G] forgetteth what manner of man he was.

25 But whoso looketh into the perfect[G] [c,n]law of [t]liberty, and [u,v,w]continueth *therein*, he being not a forgetful [h]hearer, but a [†]doer of the [q]work, this man shall be [x,y,z]blessed in his deed.[T]

26 If any man among you [13,a]seem to be religious,[G] and [b]bridleth[G] not his [c]tongue, but [a]deceiveth his own heart, this man's religion *is* vain.[G Q]

27 Pure religion and undefiled before God and the [d]Father is this, [e]To [f]visit the [g]fatherless and [h]widows in their [i]affliction, *and* to [j]keep himself [k]unspotted from the world.

## CHAPTER 2

*The apostle warns them against respect of persons; 10 exhorts them to keep the whole law; 14 and shews that faith without works is dead.*

MY brethren, [a,b]have not the faith of our [c]Lord Jē'ṣus Christ, *the Lord* of glory,[S Q] with [d]respect of persons.

2 For if there come unto your [1,e]assembly a [f]man with a gold ring, in goodly[G] apparel,[G] and there come in also a [g]poor man in vile[G] raiment[G];

3 And ye have [d]respect[G] to him that weareth the gay[G] clothing, and say unto him, Sit thou here in a good place; and say to the [g]poor, Stand thou there, or sit here under my footstool:

4 [d]Are ye not then [2]partial in yourselves, and are become judges of evil thoughts?

5 Hearken, my [h,i]beloved brethren, Hath not God chosen the [j]poor of this world rich in faith, and [k]heirs of the [l]kingdom which he hath [m]promised to them that [n]love him?[S]

6 But ye have [3]despised[G] the poor. Do not [o]rich men [p]oppress you, and draw you before the [q]judgment seats?

7 Do not they [r]blaspheme that worthy [s]name by the which ye are called?

8 If ye fulfil the *royal law according to the scripture, [t]Thou shalt [h,u]love thy [v]neighbour as thyself, ye do well:[Q]

9 But if ye have [w]respect[G] to persons, ye commit [x]sin, [4]and are convinced[Q] of the law as transgressors.

10 For whosoever shall [y]keep the whole law, and yet [5,x]offend in one *point*, he is guilty of all.[S]

11 For he that said, [z]Do not commit [a]adultery, said also, [b]Do not [c]kill. Now if thou commit no adultery, yet if thou kill, thou art become a [d]transgressor of the law.[Q]

12 So speak ye, and so do, as they that shall be [e]judged by the [f]law of liberty.

**19**
e *Minister, love of, for the church,* Rom. 15:16.
f *Love, of man for man,* 1 John 4:7.
g *Commandment, enjoining right conduct,* Deut. 8:2.
h *Hearers,* Rom. 2:13.
i *Prudence, in restraining speech,* 2 Chr. 2:12.
j *Anger,* Psa. 37:8.
10 R. V. Ye know this,

**21**
k *Commandment, enjoining holiness,* Deut. 8:2.
l *Holiness, enjoined,* Ex. 39:30.
m *Meekness,* Psa. 45:4.
n *Doctrines of Jesus,* John 7:16.
o *Salvation,* Acts 16:17.
11 R. V. putting away all filthiness and overflowing of wickedness, receive

**22**
p *Obedience, enjoined,* Heb. 5:8.
q *Works, good,* 2 Tim. 1:9.
r *Delusion,* 2 Thess. 2:11.

**23**
s *Mirror,* Job 37:18.
12 R. V. mirror:

**25**
t *Liberty, spiritual,* Lev. 25:10.
u *Steadfastness,* 1 Cor. 15:58.
v *Character, stability of,* Phil. 2:15.
w *Christian Graces, perseverance,* Gal. 5:22.
x *Spiritual Peace,* Gal. 1:3.
y *Obedience, rewarded,* Heb. 5:8.
z *Reward, a motive, to faithfulness,* Matt. 5:12.

**26**
a *Delusion,* 2 Thess. 2:11.
b *Bridle, figurative,* Psa. 32:9.
c *Speech, evil,* Col. 4:6.
13 R. V. thinketh himself

**27** d *God, fatherhood of,* Gen. 2:2. e *Righteousness, fruits of,* Psa. 15:2. f *Love, of man for man,* 1 John 4:7. g *Orphan,* Lam. 5:3. h *Widow,* 2 Sam. 14:5. i *Afflictions, consolation in,* Psa. 34:19. j *Righteous, described,* Psa. 64:10. k *Holiness,* Ex. 39:30.

**1** a *Commandment, forbidding invidious respect for persons,* Deut. 8:2. b *Worldliness,* vs. 1–9; 1 John 2:15. c *Jesus, lordship of,* Matt. 1:21.

d *Respect of Persons,* Prov. 24:23.

**2**
e *Synagogue,* Matt. 12:9.
f *Rich,* Jas. 5:1.
g *Poor,* Prov. 21:13.
1 R. V. synagogue

**4**
2 R. V. divided in your own mind, and become judges with evil thoughts?

**5**
h *Love, of man for man,* 1 John 4:7.
i *Minister, love of, for the church,* Rom. 15:16.
j *Poor, God's care of,* Prov. 21:13.
k *Heir, figurative,* Gen. 15:3.
l *Kingdom of Heaven,* Matt. 13:24.
m *Righteous, promises to,* Psa. 64:10.
n *Love, for God,* 1 John 4:19.

**6**
o *Rich, oppressive,* Jas. 5:1.
p *Poor, oppression of,* Prov. 21:13.
q *Court,* Ex. 18:26.
3 R. V. dishonoured the

**7**
r *Blasphemy,* 2 Sam. 12:14.
s *Name of Jesus,* John 14:13.

**8**
t *Commandment, enjoining love for man,* Deut. 8:2.
u *Duty, of man to man,* Eccl. 12:13.
v *Neighbor, love for, enjoined,* Luke 10:29.

**9**
w *Respect of Persons,* Prov. 24:23.
x *Sin, defined,* Rom. 5:12.
4 R. V. being convicted by the law

**10**
y *Obedience,* Heb. 5:8.
5 R. V. stumble

**11**
z Ex. 20:14.
a *Adultery, forbidden,* Lev. 20:10.
b Ex. 20:13.
c *Homicide, forbidden,* Deut. 5:17.
d *Sin, transgression of the law,* Rom. 5:12.

**12** e *Judgment, according to opportunity and works,* 1 Pet. 1:17. f *Truth, of the gospel,* John 18:37.

† **DOER OF THE WORD,** Matt. 7:21; 12:50; Luke 11:28; Rom. 2:13–15; 2 Cor. 8:11; Jas. 1:22–27; 4:11.

* **ROYAL LAW,** Lev. 19:18; Matt. 7:12; 19:19; 22:39; Luke 6:31; 10:27; Rom. 13:8, 9; Gal. 5:14; Jas. 2:8.

**13**
*g Sin, retroactive,* Rom. 5:12.
*h Mercy,* Deut. 5:10.
*i Malice, punishment for,* Eph. 4:31.
6 R. V. For judgement is without mercy to him that hath shewed no mercy: mercy glorieth against judgement.

**14**
*j Hypocrisy,* Jas. 3:17.
*k Faith,* Mark 11:22.
*l Works, good,* 2 Tim. 1:9.
*m Righteousness, fruits of,* Psa. 15:2.

**15**
*n Poor, kindness to, enjoined,* Prov. 21:13.

**16**
*o Selfishness,* 2 Tim. 3:2.
*p Parsimony,* Mal. 3:8.

**17**
7 R. V. in itself.

**19**
*q God, unity of,* Gen. 2:2.
*r Demons,* Matt. 4:24.
*s Fear of God, guilty,* Acts 9:31.
8 R. V. shudder.

**20**
9 R. V. apart from works is barren?

**21**
*t Abraham, faith of,* Gen. 17:5.
*u Obedience, exemplified,* Heb. 5:8.
*v Isaac,* Gen. 21:3.

**23**
*w Faith, reckoned for righteousness,* Gen. 15:6.
*x Justification, by faith,* Rom. 4:25.
*y Righteousness, imputed on account of faith,* Psa. 15:2.

**24**
*z Works, good,* 2 Tim. 1:9.

*a Faith,* Mark 11:22.

**25**
*b Rahab, faith of,* Josh. 2:1.
*c Works, good,* 2 Tim. 1:9.

13 For [6,g]he shall have [e]judg-
ment without [h]mercy, [i]that hath
shewed no mercy; and mercy
rejoiceth[G] against judgment.
14 What *doth it* profit, my
brethren, though a man [j]say
he hath [k]faith, and have not
[l,m]works? can [k]faith save him?
15 If a brother or sister be
[n]naked, and destitute of daily
food,
16 And one of you say unto
them, Depart in peace, be *ye*
warmed and filled; notwithstanding ye [o,p]give them not those
things which are needful to the
body; what *doth it* profit?
17 Even so [k]faith, if it hath not
[l]works, is dead, [7]being alone.
18 Yea, a man may say, Thou
hast [k]faith, and I have [l]works:
shew me thy faith without thy
works, and I will shew thee my
faith by my works.
19 Thou [k]believest that there is
[q]one God; thou doest well: the
[r]devils also believe, and [8,s]trem-
ble.[T]
20[S] But wilt thou know, O vain
man, that faith [9]without [l]works
is dead?
21 Was not [t]Ā'brā-hăm our father justified by [l]works, when he
had [u]offered [v]Ī'ṣaac his son upon
the altar?[Q]
22 Seest thou how [k]faith
wrought[G] with his [l]works, and by
works was faith made perfect[G]?[S]
23 And the scripture was fulfilled which saith, [t]Ā'brā-hăm
[w]believed God, and it was imputed unto him for [x,y]righteous-
ness: and he was called the
Friend of God.[S] [Q]
24 Ye see then how that by
[z]works a man is justified[G] and
not by [a]faith only.
25 Likewise also was not [b]Rā'-
hăb the harlot justified by
[c]works, when she had received
the [d]messengers, and had sent
*them* out another way?[Q]
26 For as the body without the
[e]spirit is dead, so [a]faith without
[c]works is dead also.[S]

## CHAPTER 3

*The apostle dissuades his brethren from being too forward in assuming the office of teacher; 5 and exhorts them to bridle the tongue. 13 The wisdom of the world contrasted with that which is from above.*

MY brethren, be not many
[1]masters, knowing that
we shall receive [2]the greater
condemnation.
2 For in many things we [3]offend
all. If any man [a]offend not in
[b]word, the same *is* a [c]perfect[G]
man, *and* able also to bridle the
whole body.[S]
3 Behold, we put [d]bits in the
[e]horses' mouths, that they may
obey us; and we turn about their
whole body.
4 Behold also the [f]ships, which
though *they be* so great, and *are*
driven of [4]fierce winds, yet are
they turned about with a very
small [g]helm, whithersoever the
governor[G] listeth.[G]
5 Even so the *tongue is a little member, and [h]boasteth great
things. Behold, how [5]great a
matter[G] a little [i]fire kindleth!
6 And the *tongue *is* a fire, a
world of iniquity[G]: so is the tongue
among our members, that it defileth the whole body, and setteth on fire the [6]course of nature; and it is set on fire of
hell.[G]
7 For every kind of [j]beasts, and
of [k]birds, and of [7]serpents, and
of things in the sea, is [l]tamed,
and hath been tamed of mankind:
8 But the *tongue can no man
tame; *it is* an unruly evil, full of
deadly poison.[Q]
9 Therewith bless we [9]God,
even the [m]Father; and therewith

*d Spies,* Josh 6:23.

**26**
*e Man, a spirit,* Job 4:17.

**1**
1 R. V. teachers.
2 R. V. heavier judgement.

**2**
*a Speech, wise,* Col. 4:6.
*b Words,* Luke 4:22.
*c Perfection,* Heb. 6:1.
3 R. V. all stumble. If any stumbleth not in word,

**3**
*d* Psa. 32:9.
*e Horse,* Job 39:19.

**4**
*f Ship,* 2 Chr. 8:18.
*g* Acts 27:40.
4 R. V. rough winds, are yet turned about by a very small rudder, whither the impulse of the steersman willeth.

**5**
*h Boasting, folly in,* Prov. 25:14.
*i Speech, evil,* Col. 4:6.
5 R. V. much wood is kindled by how small a fire!

**6**
6 R. V. wheel

**7**
*j Animals,* Jer. 27:5.
*k Birds, domesticated,* Eccl. 12:4.
*l Man, dominion of,* Job 4:17.
7 R. V. of creeping things and things

**8**
8 R. V. a restless evil,

**9**
*m God, fatherhood of,* Gen. 2:2.
9 R. V. the Lord and Father;

* **TONGUE.** Figurative of Speech: *Deceitful,* Psa. 120:2, 3; *perverse,* Prov. 17:20; *unruly,* Jas. 3:5–13; *to be restrained,* Psa. 34:13; 39:1; Jas. 1:26; 3:10; 1 Pet. 3:10; *restrained by wisdom,* Prov. 21:23.
See footnotes: SPEECH, Col. 4:6; TONGUES, *Miraculous gift of,* 1 Cor. 12:10.

n *Blasphemy, forbidden,* 2 Sam. 12:14.
o *Man, created in the image of God,* Job 4:17.
p *Image, figurative,* 1 Cor. 11:7.
**12**
q *Fig Tree,* Luke 13:6.
r *Olive,* Deut. 6:11.
10 R. V. neither can salt water yield sweet.
**13**
s *Wisdom, spiritual,* Prov. 2:2.
t *Works, good,* 2 Tim. 1:9.
u *Meekness,* Psa. 45:4.
11 R. V. wise and understanding among you? let him shew by his good life his works in
**14**
v *Jealousy,* Psa. 78:58.
w *Strife,* Prov. 20:3.
x *Falsehood, forbidden,* Job 21:34.
y *Truth,* John 18:37.
12 R. V. jealousy
**15**
13 Am. R. V. demoniacal.
**17**
z *Holiness, described,* Ex. 39:30.

a *Wisdom, spiritual,* Prov. 2:2.
b *Purity,* 1 Tim. 4:12.
c *Christian Graces,* Gal. 5:22.
d *Righteousness, fruits of,* Psa. 15:2.
e *Peace,* Jer. 29:7.
f *Gentleness,* 2 Cor. 10:1.
g *Mercy,* Deut. 5:10.

[n]curse we [o]men, which are made
after the [p]similitude of God.[Q]
10 Out of the same mouth proceedeth blessing and [n]cursing.
My brethren, these things ought
not so to be.
11 Doth a fountain send forth
at the same place sweet *water*
and bitter?
12 †Can the [q]fig tree, my brethren, bear [r]olive berries? either a
vine, figs? [10]so *can* no fountain
both yield [i]salt water and [a]fresh.
13 Who *is* [11]a [s]wise man and
endued[C] with knowledge among
you? let him shew out of a good
conversation[C] his [t]works with
[u]meekness of wisdom.
14 But if ye have bitter [12,v]en-
vying and [w]strife in your hearts,
glory not, and [x]lie not against
the [y]truth.
15 This wisdom descendeth not
from above, but *is* earthly, sensual, [13]devilish.
16 For where [12,v]envying and
[w]strife *is*, there *is* confusion and
every evil work.
17 [z]But the [a]wisdom that is
from above is first [b,c,d]pure,
then [c,d,e]peaceable, [c,d,f]gentle,
*and* easy to be intreated, full of
[c,d,g]mercy and good fruits, without [14]partiality[C], and without ‡hy-
pocrisy.
18 And the [d]fruit of righteousness is sown in [e]peace of them
that make peace.[Q]

## CHAPTER 4

*The apostle shews the evils that come from the lusts of men; 7 and exhorts them to humble themselves before God, 11 not to speak evil one of another, 13 and to keep in mind their dependence on God in the arrangement of their affairs.*

FROM whence *come* [a]wars and
fightings among you? *come*
*they* not hence, *even* of your [1]lusts
that war in your members?
2 Ye lust, and have not: ye [b]kill,
and [2,c]desire to have, and cannot
obtain: ye [a]fight and war, yet ye
have not, because ye ask not.
3 Ye [d]ask, and receive not, because ye ask amiss, that ye may
[3]consume *it* upon your lusts.[C]
4 Ye [4,e]adulterers[C] and adulteresses, know ye not that the
[f]friendship of the world is enmity with God? whosoever
therefore will be a [f]friend of the
world is the enemy of God.
5 [5]Do ye think that the scripture
saith in vain, The spirit that
dwelleth in us lusteth[C] to [g]envy[Q]?
6 But he giveth more [h]grace.
Wherefore [6]he saith, [i]God resisteth the [j]proud, but giveth
grace unto the [k]humble.[Q]
7 [l,m]Submit yourselves therefore to God. [n]Resist the [o]devil,
and he will flee from you.[S]
8 [p]Draw [q]nigh to God, and [r]he
will draw nigh[C] to you. [s,t]Cleanse
*your* hands, *ye* sinners; and

**1**
a *Strife,* Prov. 20:3.
1 R. V. pleasures
**2**
b *Homicide, felonious,* Deut. 5:17.
c *Covetousness,* Isa. 57:17.
2 R. V. covet,
**3**
d *Wicked, prayer of, not answered,* Psa. 73:3.
3 R. V. spend it in your pleasures.
**4**
e *Adultery,* Lev. 20:10.
f *Worldliness,* 1 John 2:15.
4 R. V. *omits* adulterers and
**5**
g *Envy,* Prov. 14:30.
5 R. V. Or think ye that the scripture speaketh in vain? Doth the spirit which he made to dwell in us long unto envying?
**6**
h *Grace of God,* Rom. 4:16.
i Prov. 3:34.
j *Pride,* Prov. 16:18.
k *Humility,* Prov. 22:4.
6 R. V. the scripture saith,
**7**
l *Commandment, enjoining obedience, and resistance of evil,* Deut. 8:2.

m *Obedience, enjoined,* Heb. 5:8. n *Temptation, resistance to,* Luke 11:4. o *Satan,* Matt. 4:10. **8** p *Repentance, enjoined,* Mark 1:4. q *Access to God,* Eph. 3:12. r *Prayer, answer to, promised,* Acts 6:4. s *Commandment, enjoining holiness,* Deut. 8:2. t *Spiritual Purification,* Psa. 51:2.

† **NATURE.** Laws of, uniform in operation: *In the vegetable kingdom,* Gen. 1:11, 12; Matt. 7:16–18; Luke 6:43, 44; 1 Cor. 15:36–38; Gal. 6:7; Jas. 3:12; *in the animal kingdom,* Gen. 1:21, 24, 25; Jer. 13:23; *in the succession of seasons,* Gen. 8:22; *in the succession of day and night,* Gen. 8:22; Jer. 33:20.

‡ **HYPOCRISY,** Job 31:33, 34; Psa. 5:9; 52:4; Prov. 21:27; Isa. 32:5, 6; Jer. 5:2; 17:9; 2 Cor. 5:12; 1 Tim. 4:2; 2 Tim. 3:5; Tit. 1:16; Jas. 3:17; Jude 12, 13; Rev. 2:9; 3:9.

*Described,* Psa. 5:6, 9, 10; Isa. 29:13; 58:2–5; Ezek. 33:30–32; Zech. 7:5, 6; Matt. 15:3–9 (with Mark 7:5–13); 21:28–32; Mark 9:50; Luke 14:34, 35; 18:11, 12; 1 Cor. 5:8; 13:1; 1 John 1:6, 10; 2:4, 9, 19; 4:20; Rev. 3:1.

*Abhorred of God,* Psa. 50:16, 17; Prov. 15:8; Isa. 1:9–15; 58:2–5; 65:2–5; 66:3–5; Jer. 6:20; 7:4, 8–10; Ezek. 20:39; Amos 5:21–27; Zech. 7:5, 6; Mal. 1:6–14; 2:13. *Rebuked by Jesus,* Matt. 23:2–33; Luke 6:46; 11:39, 42, 44; 13:13–17; John 6:26, 70; 7:19. *Exposed by Paul,* Rom. 2:1, 3, 17–29.

*Betrays friends,* Psa. 55:12–14, 20, 21, 23; Obad. 7; Zech. 13:6.

*Of harlots,* Prov. 7:10–21. *Of false teachers,* Mic. 3:11; Rom. 16:17, 18; 2 Pet. 2:1–3, 17, 19. *Of dishonest buyers,* Prov. 20:14.

*Warning against,* Prov. 23:6–8; 26:18, 19, 23–26; Jer. 9:8; Mic. 7:5; Matt. 6:1, 2, 5, 16, 24; 7:5, 15, 21–23; Mark 12:38–40; Luke 12:1, 2; 13:26, 27; 16:13, 15; 20:46, 47; Jas. 1:26; 2:14–26; 1 Pet. 2:1, 16.

*Punishment for,* Psa. 55:23; Isa. 29:15, 16; Jer. 42:20–22; Ezek. 5:11; 14:3, 4, 7, 8; Hos. 8:13; 9:4; Matt. 22:12, 13; 24:50, 51; 25:41–45.

See footnotes: DECEIT, Psa. 36:3; DECEPTION, Josh. 9:4.

**Instances of:** *Jacob, in impersonating Esau and deceiving his father,* Gen. 27:6–35. *Jacob's sons, in deception of their father concerning Joseph,* Gen. 37:29–35. *Israelites,* Psa. 78:36, 37. *Delilah, the paramour of Samson,* Judg. 16:4–20. *Judah,* Isa. 48:1, 2; Jer. 3:10; 12:2; 42:20. *Johanan,* Jer. 42:1–12, 20, 22. *Ishmael,* Jer. 41:6, 7. *The false prophets,* Ezek. 13:1–16. *Herod,* Matt. 2:8. *Judas,* Matt. 26:25, 48, 49; John 12:5, 6. *Pilate,* Matt. 27:24. *Pharisees,* Matt. 15:1–9; 22:18; Mark 7:5–13; 12:13–15; John 8:4–9; 9:24. *The ruler of the synagogue,* Luke 13:14–17. *Spies sent to entrap Jesus,* Luke 20:20–23. *Priests and Levites,* Luke 10:31, 32. *Chief priests,* John 18:28. *The Jews,* Luke 12:54–56. *Ananias and Sapphira,* Acts 5:1–10. *Peter and other Christians at Antioch,* Gal. 2:11–14. *Judaizing Christians in Galatia,* Gal. 6:13. *False teachers at Ephesus,* Rev. 2:2.

See footnotes: **CONSPIRACY,** 1 Kin. 16:9; **TREACHERY,** 2 Kin. 9:23.

[s, u]purify *your* [v]hearts, *ye* [w]dou-
ble minded.[Q]
9 [p]Be afflicted,[C] and mourn,
and weep: let your laughter be
turned to mourning, and *your*
[x]joy to heaviness.[C]
10 [k]Humble yourselves in the
sight of the Lord, and [y]he shall
[7]lift you up.
11 [z]Speak not evil one of another, brethren. He that speaketh evil of *his* brother, and [a]judg-
eth his brother, speaketh evil of
the law, and judgeth the law: but
if thou judge the law, thou art not
a doer of the law, but a judge.
12 [8]There is [b]one lawgiver,
who is [c]able to save and to [d]de-
stroy: who art thou that [a]judgest
[9]another?[T]
13[Q] Go[G] to now, ye that [e, f]say, To
day or to morrow we will go into
such a city, and continue there a
year, and buy and sell, and get
gain:
14 Whereas ye know not what
*shall be* on the morrow.[G] For what
*is* your life? [g]It is even a vapour,
that appeareth for a little time,
and then [h]vanisheth away.[Q]
15 For that ye *ought* to say, If
the Lord [i]will, we shall live, and
do this, or that.[S]
16 But now ye [10]rejoice in your
[j]boastings: all such rejoicing is
evil.
17 Therefore [k]to him that knoweth to do good, and [l, m]doeth *it*
not, to him it is sin.

## CHAPTER 5

*The apostle rebukes wicked rich men; 7 exhorts his brethren to be patient in their afflictions; and to abstain from swearing. 13 His counsels to the afflicted and the sick. 16 The efficacy of prayer. 19 Saving a soul from death.*

GO[G] to now, *ye* *rich men, weep
and howl for your [a]miseries
that shall come upon *you.*
2 [a]Your [b]riches are corrupted,
and your garments are [c]moth-
eaten.
3 [a]Your [d]gold and [e]silver [1]is
cankered;[G] and the rust of them
shall be a witness against you,
and shall eat your flesh as it were
fire. Ye have [2, f]heaped treasure
together for the last days.[Q]
4 Behold, the [g]hire of the [h]la-
bourers who [3]have reaped down
your fields, which is of [i]you
kept back by [j]fraud, crieth: and
the [k]cries of [l]them which have
reaped are entered into the ears
of the Lord of săb′a-ŏth.[G Q]
5 [m]Ye have [f]lived [4]in [n]pleasure
on the earth, and been wanton;
ye have nourished your hearts,
as in a day of slaughter.[Q]
6 [o]Ye have condemned *and*
killed the [5, p]just; *and* he doth
not resist you.
7 [q, r]Be patient therefore, brethren, unto the [s]coming of the
Lord. Behold, the [t]husband-
man[G] waiteth for the precious
fruit of the earth, and hath long
patience for it, until [6]he receive
the early and latter rain.[Q]
8 [q, r]Be ye also patient; [u]stablish[G]
your hearts: for [v]the [s]coming of
the Lord [7]draweth nigh.[C]
9 [8, w]Grudge[G] not one against
another, brethren, lest ye be condemned:[G] [x]behold, the [y]judge
standeth before the door.
10 [z]Take, my brethren, the
[a]prophets, who have spoken in
the name of the Lord, for an
[b]example of [c]suffering affliction,
and of [d]patience.
11 Behold, we count[G] them

**9** *w Commandment, forbidding murmuring,* Deut. 8:2. *x Fear of God, motives to,* Acts 9:31. *y God, judge,* Gen. 2:2. 8 R. V. Murmur not, brethren, one against another, that ye be not judged:
**10** *z Perseverance,* Eph. 6:18.—*a Prophets,* Isa. 3:2. *b Example, good, to be imitated,* John 13:15. *c Minister, trials and persecutions of,* Rom. 15:16. *d Patience,* Luke 8:15.

*u Purity of Heart,* 1 Tim. 4:12.
*v Heart, regenerate,* Psa. 44:21.
*w Character, instability of,* Phil. 2:15.

**9**
*x Joy, of the wicked,* Psa. 5:11.

**10**
*y Penitent, promises to,* Psa. 51:17.
7 R. V. exalt you.

**11**
*z Slander,* Prov. 10:18.

*a Uncharitableness,* Matt. 7:1.

**12**
*b God, sovereign,* Gen. 2:2.
*c God, power of,* Gen. 2:2.
*d Wicked, punishment of,* Psa. 73:3.
8 R. V. One only is the lawgiver and judge, even he who
9 R. V. thy neighbour?

**13**
*e False Confidence,* Psa. 30:6.
*f Presumption,* Psa. 19:13.

**14**
*g Life, brevity and uncertainty of,* Eccl. 8:15.
*h Death,* Num. 23:10.

**15**
*i Will of God, supreme rule of duty,* Mark 3:35.

**16**
*j Boasting, folly of,* Prov. 25:14.
10 R. V. glory in your vauntings: all such glorying is evil.

**17**
*k Opportunity, lost,* Gal. 6:10.
*l Disobedience to God,* Eph. 5:6.
*m Sin, defined,* Rom. 5:12.

**1**
*a Wicked, punishment of,* Psa. 73:3.

**2**
*b Riches,* Eccl. 4:8.
*c Moth, figurative,* Job 4:19.

**3**
*d Gold,* Ezek. 7:19.
*e Silver,* 1 Chr. 28:14.
*f Worldliness,* 1 John 2:15.
1 R. V. are rusted;
2 R. V. laid up your treasure in the last days.

**4**
*g Wages,* Gen. 31:7.
*h Employee, oppression of,* Deut. 24:14.
*i Employer, required to make prompt payment,* Deut. 24:14.
*j Dishonesty, in not paying debts,* Ezek. 22:13.
*k Adversity, prayer in,* Psa. 10:6.
*l Poor, oppression of,* Prov. 21:13.
3 R. V. mowed your

**5**
*m Wicked, described,* Psa. 73:3.
*n Worldly Pleasure,* Eccl. 2:1.
4 R. V. delicately on the earth, and taken your pleasure;

**6**
*o Persecution, of Jesus,* John 15:20.
*p Jesus, death of* (according to many learned interpreters), Matt. 1:21.
5 R. V. righteous one;

**7**
*q Commandment, enjoining patience,* Deut. 8:2.
*r Patience, enjoined,* Luke 8:15.
*s Jesus, second coming of,* Matt. 1:21.
*t Agriculture,* Gen. 3:23.
6 R. V. it

**8**
*u Steadfastness,* 1 Cor. 15:58.
*v Afflictions, consolation in,* Psa. 34:19.
7 R. V. is at hand.

* **THE RICH.** *Admonitions to,* Jer. 9:23; 1 Tim. 6:17–19; Jas. 1:9–11. *Have many friends,* Prov. 14:20; 19:4.
*Wicked,* Job 21:14 (with vs. 7–15); Psa. 73:3–9; Prov. 28:8, 20, 22; Jer. 5:27, 28; Luke 12:15–21; 16:19–31; Jas. 2:6, 7. *Licentious,* Jer. 5:7, 8. *Deluded,* Prov. 11:28; 13:7; 18:11. *Conceited,* Prov. 28:11. *Proud,* Psa. 73:3, 6, 8, 9; Ezek. 28:5. *Arrogant,* Psa. 73:8. *Oppressive,* Neh. 5:1–13; Mic. 6:10–12; Jas. 2:6. *Cruel to the poor,* Prov. 18:23. *Envied,* Psa. 73:3–22. *Hated,* Job 27:19, 23. *Denounced,* Isa. 5:8; Jer. 22:13–15; Amos 6:1–6; Luke 6:24, 25; Jas. 5:1–4. *Unscrupulous methods of,* Jer. 5:26–28. *Discrimination in favor of, in the church, forbidden,* Jas. 2:1–9.
*Divine judgments against,* Job 27:13–23; Psa. 52:5 (with vs. 1–7); 73:18–20.
**Instances of Righteous:** *Abraham,* Gen. 13:2; 24:35. *Isaac,* Gen. 26:12–14. *Solomon,* 1 Kin. 10:23; 2 Chr. 9:22. *Jehoshaphat,* 2 Chr. 18:1. *Hezekiah,* 2 Kin. 20:12, 13. *Job,* Job 1:3. *Joseph of Arimathea,* Matt. 27:57. *Zacchæus,* Luke 19:2.

[9]happy which [e]endure. Ye have
heard of the [d,f]patience of [g]Jōb,
and have seen the end[G] of the
Lord; that the Lord is very [h]piti-
ful, and of tender [i]mercy.[S Q]
12 But above all things, my
brethren, [j,k,l]swear not, neither
by heaven, neither by the earth,
neither by any other [m]oath: but
let your yea be yea; and *your*
nay, nay; lest ye fall [10]into condemnation.
13 Is any among you [11,n]af-
flicted? let him [o]pray. Is any
merry? let him [12,p]sing [q,r]psalms.
14 Is any [n]sick among you? let
him call for the [s]elders of the
[t]church; and let them [u]pray over
him, [v]anointing[G] him with oil in
the [w]name of the [x]Lord:
15 And the [u]prayer of [y]faith
shall save[G] the [n]sick, and [z]the
Lord shall [a]raise him up; and
if he have committed sins, they
shall be [b]forgiven him.
16 [c,d,e]Confess *your* faults one
to another, and [f,g]pray one for
another, that ye may be [a]healed.
[h,i]The [13]effectual[G] fervent prayer
of a righteous man availeth much.
17 [j]Ē-lī'as was a man subject to
like[G] passions as we are, and he
prayed earnestly that it might
not [k,l]rain: and [m]it rained not on
the earth by the space of three
years and six months.[Q]
18 And [j]he prayed again, and
[m]the heaven gave [k,l]rain, and the
earth [n]brought forth her fruit.[Q]
19 Brethren, if [o]any of you do
err from the [p]truth, and one convert him;
20 Let him know, that [q]he which
converteth[G] the [r]sinner from the
error of his way shall save a soul
from [s]death, and shall [t]hide a
multitude of sins.[Q]

**11**
*e Perseverance,* Eph. 6:18.
*f Adversity, resignation in,* Psa. 34:19.
*g Job,* Job 1:1.
*h Pity, of God,* Job 19:21.
*i God, mercy of,* Gen. 2:2.
9 R. V. blessed
**12**
*j Commandment, forbidding profane swearing,* Deut. 8:2.
*k Blasphemy, forbidden,* 2 Sam. 12:14.
*l Conversation, profane, forbidden,* Psa. 50:23.
*m Oath,* Num. 5:19.
10 R. V. under judgement.
**13**
*n Afflicted,* Job 34:28.
*o Afflictions, prayer in,* Psa. 34:19.
*p Music,* 2 Chr. 5:13.
*q Psalms, of praise,* page 813.
*r Praise,* Psa. 150:1. 11 R. V. suffering? 12 R. V. praise.
**14** *s Elders,* Acts 14:23. *t Church,* Matt. 16:18. *u Prayer, intercessory,* Acts 6:4. *v Anointing, the sick,* Deut. 28:40. *w Name of Jesus,* John 14:13. *x Jesus, lordship of,* Matt. 1:21.
**15** *y Faith in Christ,* John 6:69. *z Promise, of healing,* 2 Cor. 1:20.—*a Healing, in answer to prayer,* Acts 4:22.

*b Sin, forgiveness of,* Rom. 5:12.
**16**
*c Commandment, enjoining confession of faults, and prayer,* Deut. 8:2.
*d Communion, of saints,* 1 Cor. 10:16.
*e Sin, confession of,* Rom. 5:12.
*f Prayer, intercessory,* Acts 6:4.
*g Sympathy,* 1 Pet. 3:8.
*h Prayer, answer to, promised,* Acts 6:4.
*i Promise, or Ground of Assurance,* 2 Cor. 1:20.
13 R. V. supplication of a righteous man availeth much in its working.
**17**
*j* Or, *Elijah, miracles of,* 1 Kin. 17:1.
*k Rain,* 2 Sam. 1:21.
*l Meteorology, weather affected by good men's prayers,* Matt. 16:2.
*m Prayer, answered,* Acts 6:4.
**18** *n Temporal Blessings,* Psa. 103:2. **19** *o Weak, duty of strong to,* 1 Cor. 8:9. *p Truth, of the gospel,* John 18:37.
**20** *q Agency, in salvation of men,* Mark 1:17. *r Wicked,* Psa. 73:3. *s Spiritual Death,* 1 John 3:14. *t Sin, forgiveness of,* Rom. 5:12.

THE FIRST EPISTLE OF

# PETER

## CHAPTER 1

*The apostle's salutation. 3 He blesses God for the hope of the gospel. 6 The brethren greatly rejoice in Christ, even in tribulation. 10 Salvation through Christ foretold by the prophets. 13 He exhorts them to a godly conversation. 18 Redemption by the precious blood of Christ. 22 Being born anew by the word of God.*

[a]PĒ'TĒR, an apostle of Jē'-
ṣus Chrīst, to the [1,b]stran-
gers [c]scattered throughout [d]Pŏn'-
tus, [e]Gā-lā'tiȧ, [d]Căp-pa-dō'çĭ-ȧ,
[f]Ā'ṣiȧ, and [g]Bī-thy̆n'ĭ-ȧ,[S]
2 [2,b]Elect[G] according to the
[h]foreknowledge[G] of God the [i,j]Fa-
ther, through *sanctification of
the [j,k]Spirit, unto [l]obedience and
sprinkling of the [m,n]blood of [j]Jē'-
ṣus Chrīst: [o]Grace unto you, and
[p]peace, be multiplied.[S T]
3 [S q]Blessed *be* the God and [i]Fa-
ther of our Lord Jē'ṣus Chrīst,
which according to his abundant [r]mercy hath [s]begotten us
again unto a [3]lively[G] [t,u]hope by
the [v]resurrection[G] of Jē'ṣus Chrīst
from the dead,[T]
4 To an [w]inheritance incor-

**1**
*a Peter,* Mark 5:37.
*b Election of Grace,* Rom. 11:5.
*c Dispersion,* Gen. 11:8.
*d* Acts 2:9.
*e Galatia,* Acts 16:6.
*f Asia,* Acts 2:9.
*g* Acts 16:7.
1 R. V. elect who are sojourners of the Dispersion in Pontus,
**2**
*h God, foreknowledge of,* Gen. 2:2.
*i God, fatherhood of,* Gen. 2:2.
*j The Holy Trinity,* Luke 3:22.

*k Holy Spirit,* Acts 1:2.
*l Obedience,* Heb. 5:8.
*m Blood, of Jesus,* Heb. 9:19.
*n Jesus, atoning blood of,* Matt. 1:21.
*o Grace of God,* Rom. 4:16.
*p Spiritual Peace,* Gal. 1:3.
**3**
*q Praise,* Psa. 150:1.
*r God, mercy of,* Gen. 2:2.
*s Regeneration,* Tit. 3:5. *t Hope, of immortality,* Prov. 13:12. *u Immortality, implied,* 1 Cor. 15:54. *v Resurrection, of Jesus,* 1 Cor. 15:12. 3 R.V. living **4** *w Inheritance, figurative,* Num. 27:7.

***SANCTIFICATION,** 1 Sam. 7:1; 16:5; Job 1:5; 2 Tim. 2:21; Heb. 2:11; 10:10, 14, 29.
*By God,* Ex. 29:44; 31:13; Lev. 20:8; 21:8, 15, 23; 22:9, 16; Jer. 1:5; Ezek. 20:12; 37:28. *By Christ,* 1 Cor. 1:2, 30; 6:11; Eph. 5:25–27; Heb. 2:11; 10:10, 14; 13:12. *By the Holy Spirit,* Rom. 15:16; 2 Thess. 2:13, 14; 1 Pet. 1:2. *By the blood of Christ,* Heb. 9:14; 13:12.
*By faith in Christ,* Acts 26:17, 18. *By the truth,* John 17:17, 19.
*Intercessory prayer for,* 1 Thess. 5:23. *Willed of God,* 1 Thess. 4:3, 4.
*The altar sanctifies the gift,* Ex. 29:37; 30:29; Matt. 23:19.
*Of the sabbath,* Gen. 2:3; Deut. 5:12; Neh. 13:22. *Of mount Sinai,* Ex. 19:23. *Of the tabernacle,* Ex. 29:43, 44;

*x Heaven, future home of the righteous,* Luke 18:22.

**5**

*y God, power of,* Gen. 2:2.

*z Faith in Christ,* John 6:69.

*a Salvation,* Acts 16:17.

*b Jesus, second coming of,* Matt. 1:21.

4 R. V. guarded

**6**

*c Adversity,* Psa. 10:6.

*d Temptation, benefits of,* v. 7; Luke 11:4.

5 R. V. have been put to grief in

**7**

*e Adversity, benefits of,* Psa. 10:6.

*f Faith in Christ,* John 6:69.

**8**

*g Love, for Jesus,* **1 John 4:19.**

**10**

*h Messianic Hope,* Gen. 49:10.

*i Mysteries, of redemption,* Mark 4:11.

*j Prophets, inspiration of,* v. 11; Isa. 3:2.

*k Spiritual Desire,* Psa. 42:1.

*l Gospel,* Mark 13:10.

**11**

*m Holy Spirit,* Acts 1:2.

*n Word of God, is inspired,* Psa. 119:9.

*o Jesus, sufferings of,* Matt. 1:21.

**12**

*p Minister,* Rom. 15:16.

*q Preaching,* Matt. 9:35.

6 R. V. you

ruptible, and undefiled, and that
fadeth not away, reserved in
[x]heaven for you,
5 Who are [4,o]kept[G] by the [y]power
of God through [z]faith unto [a]sal-
vation[G] ready to be revealed in
the [b]last time.[S T]
6[S] Wherein ye greatly rejoice,
though now for a season, if need
be, ye [5]are in [c]heaviness through
manifold [d]temptations[G]:
7 [d,e]That the trial of your [f]faith,
being much more precious than
of gold that perisheth, though
it be tried with fire, might be
found unto praise and honour
and glory at the [b]appearing of
Jē'ṣus Chrīst:[Q]
8 Whom having not seen, ye
[g]love; in whom, though now ye
see *him* not, yet [f]believing, ye
rejoice with joy unspeakable and
full of glory:
9[T] Receiving the end[G] of your
[f]faith, *even* the [a]salvation of *your*
souls.[G S]
10[T] Of which [h,i]salvation the
[j]prophets have [k]enquired and
searched diligently, who prophesied of the [l]grace *that should*
*come* unto you:
11 Searching what, or what
manner of time the [m]Spirit of
Chrīst which was in [j]them did
signify, when it [n]testified beforehand the [o]sufferings of Chrīst,
and the glory[G] that should follow.[Q]
12 Unto [j]whom it was revealed,
that not unto themselves, but
unto [6]us they did minister the
things, which are now reported
unto you by [p]them that have
[q]preached the [l]gospel unto you
with the [m]Holy[G] Ghost[G] sent down
from [r]heaven; which [i]things the
[s]angels desire to look into.[T]
13[T] Wherefore [t,u,v]gird[G] up the
loins of your mind, [w]be sober,[G]
and [7,x]hope to the end for the
grace that is to be brought unto
you at the [y]revelation of Jē'ṣus
Chrīst;
14 As [z]obedient children, not
fashioning[G] yourselves according
to the former [a]lusts in your [b]ig-
norance:
15[S] But [c]as he which hath called
you is [d]holy, so [e]be ye [f,g]holy in
all manner of [8]conversation[G];
16 Because it is written, [9,e,h]Be
ye [f,g]holy; for I am [d]holy.[S T Q]
17 And if ye call on the [i]Father,
who [j,k]without [l]respect of persons [†m,n]judgeth according to
every man's work, pass the time[G]
of your sojourning *here* in [o]fear:[Q S]
18[S T] Forasmuch as ye know that
ye were not [p]redeemed with corruptible things, *as* [q]silver and
[r]gold, from your vain[G] [10]conver-
sation[G] *received* by tradition from
your fathers;[Q]
19 But with the precious
[s,t,u]blood of Chrīst, as of a
[v,w]lamb [x,y]without [z,a]blemish
and without spot:
20 [b]Who verily was [11]foreor-
dained[G] before the foundation of

*r Heaven, God's dwelling place,* Luke 18:22.

*s Angel,* Heb. 1:13.

**13**

*t Commandment, enjoining steadfastness, sobriety and holiness,* Deut. 8:2.

*u Watchfulness, enjoined,* Matt. 24:42.

*v Steadfastness,* 1 Cor. 15:58.

*w Sobermindedness, enjoined,* Tit. 2:6.

*x Hope,* Prov. 13:12.

*y Jesus, second coming of,* Matt. 1:21.

7 R. V. set your hope perfectly on the grace

**14**

*z Obedience,* Heb. 5:8.

*a Lust,* 2 Pet. 1:4.

*b Spiritual Blindness, manifested in ignorance of Christ,* 2 Cor. 4:4.

**15**

*c Example, God our,* John 13:15.

*d God, holiness of,* Gen. 2:2.

*e Holiness, enjoined,* Ex. 39:30.

*f Righteous, described,* Psa. 64:10.

*g Christian Graces, holiness,* Gal. 5:22.

8 R. V. living;

**16**

*h* Lev. 11:44; 19:2.

9 R. V. Ye shall be holy;

**17**

*i God, fatherhood of,* Gen. 2:2.

*j God, justice of,* Gen. 2:2.

*k God, impartial,* Gen. 2:2. *l Respect of Persons,* Prov. 24:23. *m God, judge,* Gen. 2:2. *n Judgment, according to opportunity and works,* 1 Pet. 1:17. *o Fear of God,* Acts 9:31. **18** *p Redemption of our Souls,* Eph. 1:7. *q Silver,* 1 Chr. 28:14. *r Gold,* Ezek. 7:19.
10 R. V. manner of life handed down from your fathers;
**19** *s Blood, of Jesus,* Heb. 9:19. *t Jesus, atoning blood of,* Matt. 1:21. *u Atonement, by Jesus,* Lev. 17:11. *v Lamb, a symbol of Christ,* Num. 7:15. *w Types, of the Savior,* Heb. 10:1. *x Offerings, must be without blemish,* Lev. 6:17. *y Holiness, typified,* Ex. 39:30. *z Blemish, figurative,* Lev. 14:10.—*a Sin, typified,* Rom. 5:12.
**20** *b Jesus, pre-existence of,* Matt. 1:21. 11 R. V. foreknown indeed before the foundation of the world, but was manifested at the end of the times for your sake,

30:26, 29; Lev. 8:10; Num. 7:1. *Of the furniture of the tabernacle,* Ex. 30:26–29; Num. 7:1. *Of the altar of burnt offerings,* Ex. 29:36, 37; 40:10, 11; Lev. 8:11, 15; Num. 7:1. *Of the laver,* Ex. 30:28; Lev. 8:11. *Of the temple,* 2 Chr. 29:5, 17, 19.

*Of houses,* Lev. 27:14, 15. *Of land,* Lev. 27:16–19, 22. *Of offerings,* Ex. 29:27.

*Of the firstborn of Israelites,* Ex. 13:2; Lev. 27:26; Num. 8:17; Deut. 15:19. *Of Levites,* 1 Chr. 15:12, 14; 2 Chr. 29:34; 30:15. *Of Levites, enjoined,* 1 Chr. 15:12; 2 Chr. 29:5. *Of priests,* 1 Chr. 15:14; 2 Chr. 5:11; 30:24. *Of priests, enjoined,* Ex. 19:22. *Of Aaron and his sons,* Ex. 28:41; 29:33, 44; 40:13; Lev. 8:12, 30. *Of Israel,* Ex. 19:10, 14. *Of Israel, enjoined,* Ex. 19:10; Lev. 11:44; 20:7; Num. 11:18; Josh. 3:5; **7:13; Joel 2:16.**

*Of Corinthian Christians,* 1 Cor. 1:2; 6:11; 7:14. *Of the church,* Eph. 5:26; 1 Thess. 5:23.

See footnotes: HOLINESS, Ex. 39:30; PURITY, **1 Tim. 4:12;** SPIRITUAL PURIFICATION, Psa. 51:2.

**† JUDGMENT, ACCORDING TO OPPORTUNITY AND WORKS.** *In the divine administration of the affairs of men,* Gen. 4:7; 1 Sam. 26:23; Job 34:11, 12; Psa. 62:12; Prov. 12:14; 24:11, 12; Isa. 3:10, 11; 59:18; Jer. 17:10; 32:19; Ezek. 7:3, 4, 27; 18:4–9, 19–32; 33:18–20; Hos. 4:9; 12:2; Zech. 1:6; Luke 12:47, 48; 13:6–9; 19:12–27; John 3:19, 20; Rom. 2:5–12; 1 Cor. 3:8, 12–15; 2 Cor. 11:15; Gal. 6:7, 8; Eph. 6:7, **8;** Col. 3:25; Heb. 10:26–30; 12:25; Jas. 2:13; 1 Pet. **1:17; 2 Pet.** 2:20, 21; Rev. 2:23.

See footnote, JUDGMENT, *The general,* **2 Pet. 3:7**

the world, but was [c]manifest in these last times for you,[S]

21[T] Who by him do [d]believe in God, that [e]raised him up from the dead, and [f]gave him glory[G]; that your faith and [g]hope might be in God.[S]

22 Seeing ye have [h]purified your souls in [i]obeying the [j]truth [12]through the Spirit unto [k]unfeigned[G] [l]love of the brethren, *see that ye* love one another with a pure [m]heart fervently:[T]

23 Being [n]born again, not of corruptible seed, but of incorruptible, by the [j]word of God, which liveth and abideth for ever.[Q][S]

24[Q] [o]For [p]all flesh[G] *is* as [q]grass, and all the glory [13]of man as the flower of grass. The grass withereth, and the flower thereof [r]falleth away:

25 But the [j]word of the Lord endureth for ever. And this is the word [14]which by the [s]gospel is [t]preached unto you.[Q]

## CHAPTER 2

*The apostle urges them to lay aside all malice and guile, and to desire the pure word of God. 4 Christ is their precious corner stone. 11 They are exhorted to abstain from fleshly lusts, 13 and to be obedient to magistrates. 18 The duty of servants. 21 The sinlessness of Christ who bore our sins.*

WHEREFORE [a,b,c]laying aside all [1,d]malice, and all [e]guile, and [f]hypocrisies, and [g]envies, and all [h]evil speakings,

2 As newborn babes, [2,i,j]desire the sincere[G] [k]milk of the [l]word, that ye may [m]grow thereby:[T]

3 If so be ye have tasted that the Lord *is* [n]gracious.[Q]

4 To whom coming, [3]*as unto* a living [o]stone, [p]disallowed[G] indeed of men, but [q]chosen of God, *and* precious,[Q]

5 Ye also, as [4,r]lively[G] stones, are built up a [s]spiritual house, an [t]holy [u]priesthood, to offer up spiritual sacrifices, acceptable to God [v]by Jē'ṣus[S] Chrīst.[T][Q]

6 Wherefore also it is contained in the scripture, [w,x]Behold, I lay in [y]Sī'ŏn a chief [o]corner stone, elect[G], precious: and he that [z]believeth on him shall not be [5]confounded.[Q]

7 Unto you therefore which [z]believe [6]*he is* precious: but unto [a]them which be [b]disobedient, [c]the [d]stone which the builders [e]disallowed, the same is made the [f,g]head of the corner,[Q]

8 [h]And a stone of [i]stumbling, and a rock of offence[G], [7]*even to* [a]*them* which [e]stumble at the [j]word, being disobedient: whereunto also they were [k]appointed.[Q][S]

9[T] But ye *are* a [l,m]chosen generation, a royal [n]priesthood, an [o]holy nation, a [8]peculiar[G] people; that ye should shew forth the [p]praises of him who hath [q]called you out of [b,r]darkness into his marvellous [s]light:[S][Q]

10 Which in time past *were* not a people, but *are* now the [m]people of God: which had not obtained [t]mercy, but now have obtained mercy.[T][Q]

11 Dearly [u]beloved, I beseech *you* as [9]strangers[G] and pilgrims, [v,w]abstain from fleshly [x]lusts[G], which war against the soul;[Q]

12 [v]Having your [10]conversation[G] honest among the Ġĕn'tīleṣ: that, whereas they [y]speak against you as evildoers, they may by *your* [z,a,b]good works, which they shall behold, [c]glorify God in the day of visitation.[Q]

---

*Jesus, incarnation of,* Matt. 1:21.

**21**
d *Faith,* Mark 11:22.
e *Resurrection, of Jesus,* 1 Cor. 15:12.
f *Jesus, exaltation of,* Matt. 1:21.
g *Hope,* Prov. 13:12.

**22**
h *Purity, of heart,* 1 Tim. 4:12.
i *Obedience,* Heb. 5:8.
j *Truth, of the gospel,* John 18:37.
k *Sincerity,* 1 Cor. 5:8.
l *Love, of man for man,* 1 John 4:7.
m *Heart, pure,* Psa. 44:21.
12 R. V. unto unfeigned love of the brethren, love one another from the heart fervently:

**23**
n *Regeneration,* Tit. 3:5.

**24**
o Isa. 40:6–8.
p *Life, brevity and uncertainty of,* Eccl. 8:15.
q *Grass, brevity of human life compared to,* Isa. 40:7.
r *Death, universal to mankind,* Num. 23:10.
13 R. V. thereof as the

**25**
s *Gospel,* Mark 13:10.
t *Preaching,* Matt. 9:35.
14 R. V. of good tidings which was preached unto you.

**1**
a *Commandment, enjoining holiness,* Deut. 8:2.
b *Holiness, enjoined,* Ex. 39:30.
c *Guilelessness, enjoined,* John 1:47.
d *Malice, forbidden,* Eph. 4:31.
e *Deceit, admonitions against,* Psa. 36:3.

**5**
r *Righteous, described,* Psa. 64:10.
s *Church,* Matt. 16:18.
t *Holiness,* Ex. 39:30.
u *Priest, figurative,* Lev. 1:5.
v *Jesus, mediation of,* Matt. 1:21.
4 R. V. living

**6**
w Isa. 28:16.
x *Prophecies concerning the Messiah, and their fulfillment,* Gen. 12:3.
y Or, *Zion,* 2 Sam. 5:7.
z *Faith in Christ,* John 6:69.
5 R. V. put to shame.

**7**
a *Unbelievers,* 1 Cor. 6:6.
b *Spiritual Blindness,* 2 Cor. 4:4.
c Psa. 118:22.
d *Corner Stone, figurative,* Psa. 144:12.
e *Jesus, rejected,* Matt. 1:21.
f *Jesus, head of church,* Matt. 1:21.
g *Church, Christ head of,* Matt. 16:18.
6 R. V. is the preciousness: but for such as disbelieve, The stone

**8**
h Isa. 8:14.
i *Stumbling, figurative,* Isa. 8:14.
j *Doctrines of Jesus,* John 7:16.
k *Foreordination,* Rom. 8:30.
7 R. V. for they stumble

**9**
l *Election of Grace,* Rom. 11:5.
m *Righteous, described,* Psa. 64:10.
n *Priest, figurative,* Lev. 1:5.
o *Holiness,* Ex. 39:30.
p *Grace of God,* Rom. 4:16.
q *Call, personal,* Phil. 3:14.

f *Hypocrisy, warning against,* Jas. 3:17. g *Envy, forbidden,* Prov. 14:30. h *Speech, evil,* Col. 4:6. 1 R. V. wickedness.
**2** i *Hunger, figurative,* Matt. 5:6. j *Spiritual Desire,* Psa. 42:1. k *Milk, figurative,* Job 10:10. l *Truth, of the gospel,* John 18:37. m *Growth in Grace,* 2 Pet. 3:18. 2 R. V. long for the spiritual milk which is without guile, that ye may grow thereby unto salvation; **3** n *God, mercy of,* Gen. 2:2. **4** o *Corner Stone, figurative,* Psa. 144:12. p *Jesus, rejected,* Matt. 1:21. q *Jesus, relation of, to the Father,* Matt. 1:21. 3 R. V. a living stone, rejected indeed of men, but with God elect, precious,

r *Darkness, figurative,* Gen. 1:2. s *Light, figurative,* Matt. 5:14. 8 R. V. people for God's own possession, that ye may shew forth the excellencies of him **10** t *God, mercy of,* Gen. 2:2.
**11** u *Minister, love of, for the church,* Rom. 15:16. v *Commandment, forbidding various vices, and enjoining discreet conduct,* Deut. 8:2. w *Self-denial,* Mark 8:34. x *Lust, forbidden,* 2 Pet. 1:4. 9 R. V. sojourners and
**12** y *Speech, evil,* Col. 4:6. z *Works, good,* 2 Tim. 1:9. —a *Influence, good,* 1 Cor. 7:14. b *Example, good,* John 13:15. c *Glorifying God,* Luke 5:25. 10 R. V. behaviour seemly among

13 [d,e,f]Submit yourselves to every ordinance[G] of man for the Lord's sake: whether it be to the [g]king, as supreme;

14 Or unto [g]governors, as unto [h]them that are sent by him for the punishment of evildoers, and for the praise of them that do well.

15 For so is the [i]will of God, that with [j]well doing ye may put to silence the ignorance of foolish men:[T]

16 As free, and not using *your* [k]liberty for a [l]cloke of [11]maliciousness[G], but as the servants of God.

17 Honour all *men.* [m,n]Love the [o]brotherhood. [m,p]Fear God.[Q] [e]Honour the king.

18 [q,r]Servants, *be* subject to *your* masters[G] with all fear; not only to the good and gentle, but also to the [12]froward[G].

19 For this *is* [13]thankworthy[G], if a man for [s]conscience toward God [t]endure grief, [u]suffering wrongfully.

20 For what glory *is it,* if, when ye be buffeted[G] for your faults, ye shall take it [t]patiently? but if, when ye do well, and suffer *for it,* ye [u,v]take it patiently, this *is* acceptable with God.

21 For even hereunto were ye called: because Christ also [w,x]suffered for us, leaving us an [y,z]example, that ye should follow his steps:[T]

22 Who [a]did no sin, [b]neither was guile[G] found in his mouth:[Q]

23 Who, when he was [c]reviled, [d,e,f]reviled not again; when he suffered, he [d]threatened not; but committed *himself* to him that [g]judgeth [h]righteously:[Q]

24 Who his own self [i,j,k]bare our sins in his own body on the tree, that we, being [l]dead to [m]sins, should live unto righteousness: by whose stripes[G] ye were healed.[S][Q]

25 For ye were as sheep going astray; but are now [n]returned unto the [o,p]Shepherd and [p,q]Bishop[G] of your souls.[Q]

## CHAPTER 3

*The apostle teaches the duty of wives and of husbands;* 8 *and exhorts all to be of one mind,* 9 *to return good for evil,* 15 *and to be ready always to give a reason for their hope.* 18 *The suffering of Christ, and his exaltation.*

1 LIKEWISE, ye [a]wives, [b,c]be in subjection to your own [d]husbands; that, if any obey not the [e]word, they also may without the word be won by the [1,f]conversation[G] of the wives;

2 While [d]they behold your [f,g]chaste [1]conversation[G] *coupled* with [h]fear[G].

3 [i]Whose adorning let it not be that outward *adorning* of plaiting[G] the hair, and of wearing of gold, or of putting on of [j]apparel;

4 But *let it be* the hidden man of the [k]heart, in [2]that which is not corruptible, *even the ornament* of a [g,l]meek and quiet spirit, which is in the sight of God of great price.

5 For [m]after this manner in the old time the [n]holy women also, who [o]trusted in God, [n]adorned themselves, being in subjection unto their own husbands:[T]

6 Even as [n,p]Sā'rȧ obeyed [q]Ā'brȧ-hăm, [r]calling him lord: whose [3]daughters ye are, as long as ye do well, and are not afraid with any amazement[G].[Q]

7 Likewise, ye husbands, [s,t]dwell with *them* according to knowledge, giving honour unto the wife, as unto the weaker vessel, and as being heirs together of the grace of life; that your[S] [u]prayers be not hindered.

**13**
d *Commandment, enjoining obedience to civil government,* Deut. 8:2.
e *Citizens, duties of,* Luke 15:15.
f *Government, duty of citizens to,* Isa. 22:21.
g *Rulers,* Ex. 18:21.

**14**
h *Rulers, ordained of God,* Ex. 18:21.

**15**
i *Will of God,* Mark 3:35.
j *Works, good,* 2 Tim. 1:9.

**16**
k *Liberty, spiritual,* Lev. 25:10.
l *Hypocrisy,* Jas. 3:17.
11 R. V. wickedness.

**17**
m *Commandment, enjoining love for man, and fear of God,* Deut. 8:2.
n *Love, of man for man, enjoined,* 1 John 4:7.
o *Fraternity,* Zech. 11:14.
p *Fear of God, enjoined,* Acts 9:31.

**18**
q *Commandment, to servants,* Deut. 8:2.
r *Servant, duties of,* Jer. 2:14.
12 Am. R. V. perverse.

**19**
s *Conscience,* Acts 23:1.
t *Patience, a grace of the righteous,* Luke 8:15.
u *Meekness,* Psa. 45:4.
13 R. V. acceptable.

**20**
v *Adversity, resignation in,* Psa. 10:6.

**21**
w *Jesus, sufferings of,* Matt. 1:21.
x *Vicarious Sufferings,* Rom. 9:3.
y *Example, Christ our,* John 13:15.
z *Jesus, our example,* Matt. 1:21.

**22**
a *Jesus, holiness of,* Matt. 1:21.
b *Guilelessness, of Jesus,* John 1:47.

**23**
c *Mocking,* 1 Kin. 18:27. d *Meekness,* Psa. 45:4. e *Jesus, our example,* Matt. 1:21. f *Patience, of Jesus,* Luke 8:15. g *God, judge,* Gen. 2:2. h *God, righteousness of,* Gen. 2:2. **24** i *Vicarious Sufferings,* Rom. 9:3. j *Atonement, by Jesus,* Lev. 17:11. k *Jesus, design of his death,* Matt. 1:21. l *Holiness, described,* Ex. 39:30.

m *Sin, inherited tendencies to evil,* Rom. 5:12.

**25**
n *Repentance,* Mark 1:4.
o *Shepherd, figurative,* Jer. 31:10.
p *Jesus, names of,* Matt. 1:21.
q *Bishop, a title of Jesus,* 1 Tim. 3:1.

**1**
a *Wife,* Prov. 5:18.
b *Commandment, to wives,* vs. 2–4; Deut. 8:2.
c *Family, government of,* 1 Chr. 13:14.
d *Husband,* Num. 30:6.
e *Doctrines of Jesus,* John 7:16.
f *Influence, good,* 1 Cor. 7:14.
1 R. V. behaviour

**2**
g *Righteousness, fruits of,* Psa. 15:2.
h *Fear of God,* Acts 9:31.

**3**
i *Women, rules for dress of Christian,* Prov. 31:10.
j *Dress,* Zech. 3:3.

**4**
k *Heart, known to God,* Psa. 44:21.
l *Meekness, enjoined,* Psa. 45:4.
2 R. V. the incorruptible apparel of a

**5**
m *Example, good,* John 13:15.
n *Women, good,* Prov. 31:10.
o *Faith,* Mark 11:22.

**6**
p Or, *Sarah, character of,* Gen. 17:15.
q *Abraham,* Gen. 17:5.
r Gen. 18:12.

3 R. V. children ye now are, if ye do well, and are not put in fear by any terror. **7** s *Commandment, to husbands,* Deut. 8:2. t *Husband, duties of,* Num. 30:6. u *Prayer,* Acts 6:4.

8 Finally, [v]*be ye* all of [w]one
mind, having [*, x]compassion one
of another, [y,z]love as brethren,
[4]*be* [a]pitiful, *be* courteous:
9 [b,c,d]Not rendering evil for
evil, or [e]railing for railing: but
contrariwise[G] blessing[G]; knowing
that [f]ye are thereunto called,
that ye should [g]inherit a blessing.
10 For[Q] [h,i]he that will love [j]life,
and see good days, [k,l]let him
refrain his [m]tongue from evil,
and his lips that they [n]speak
no [o]guile[G]:
11 [k]Let him [p]eschew[G] [q]evil, and
[r]do good; let him seek [s]peace,
and [5]ensue[G] it.
12[S] For [t]the [u]eyes of the Lord
*are* over the righteous, and [v,w]his
ears *are open* unto their prayers: but the face of the Lord *is*
[x]against them that do evil.[T Q]
13 And who *is* he that will harm
you, if ye be [6, y]followers of that
which is good?[S]
14[Q] But and if ye [z]suffer for
righteousness' sake, [a]happy *are*
*ye*: and be not afraid of their terror, neither be troubled;
15 But [b]sanctify[G] [7]the [c]Lord
God in your hearts: and *be*
ready always to *give* an [d,e]an-
swer to every man that asketh you a reason of the [f]hope
that is in you with [g]meekness
and fear:[G Q]
16 Having a [h]good conscience;
that, [8]whereas they [i]speak evil
of you, as of evildoers, they
may be ashamed that falsely accuse your good conversation[G] in
Christ.
17 For *it is* better, if the [j]will of
God be so, that ye [k]suffer for
well doing, than for evil doing.
18 [l]For Christ also hath once
[m,n]suffered for sins, the just for
the unjust, [o]that he might [p]bring
us to God, being put to death in
the flesh, but quickened[G] by the
Spirit:[S T]
19 By which also he went and
[q,r]preached unto the spirits in
[s]prison;
20 [t]Which [9]sometime[G] were [u]dis-
obedient, when once the [v]long-
suffering of God waited in the
days of [w]Nō'ah, while the [x]ark
was a preparing, wherein few,
that is, eight souls were saved
by [y]water.[S Q]
21 The like figure whereunto
*even* [z]baptism doth also now
save us (not the putting away of
the filth of the flesh, but the [10]an-
swer of a [a]good conscience toward God,) by the [b]resurrection
of Jē'ṣus Christ:
22 Who is gone into [c]heaven,
and is [d,e]on the right hand of
God; [f]angels and authorities and
powers being made subject unto
him.[T Q]

## CHAPTER 4

*The apostle exhorts them to cease from sin; 7 to be sober and watchful unto prayer; 12 and comforts them against persecution.*

FORASMUCH then [a]as Christ
hath [b,c]suffered [1]for us [d]in
the flesh, [e]arm your selves likewise with the same mind: for he
that hath suffered in the flesh
hath [f,g]ceased from sin;
2 [f]That he no longer should live

**8**
v *Commandment, enjoining sympathy, love, and humility,* Deut. 8:2.
w *Fellowship, of the righteous,* 1 Cor. 1:9.
x *Kindness,* Acts 28:2.
y *Fraternity, enjoined,* Zech. 11:14.
z *Love, of man for man,* 1 John 4:7.

a *Pity,* Job 19:21.
4 R. V. tender-hearted, humble-minded:
**9**
b *Commandment, forbidding retaliation, and enjoining returning good for evil,* Deut. 8:2.
c *Retaliation, forbidden,* Deut. 19:19.
d *Revenge, forbidden,* Ezek. 25:15.
e *Railing, forbidden,* Jude 9.
f *Righteous, promises to,* Psa. 64:10.
g *Reward, a motive, to faithfulness,* Matt. 5:12.
**10**
h Psa. 34:12–16.
i *Blessings, contingent upon obedience,* Deut. 11:26.
j *Life,* Eccl. 8:15.
k *Commandment, forbidding evil speech, and enjoining holiness and good works,* Deut. 8:2.
l *Falsehood, forbidden,* Job 21:34.
m *Tongue, figurative,* Jas. 3:5.
n *Guilelessness, enjoined,* John 1:47.
o *Deceit, forbidden,* Psa. 36:3.
**11**
p *Holiness, described,* Ex. 39:30.

q *Evil, to be forsaken,* 1 Thess. 5:22. r *Works, good, enjoined,* 2 Tim. 1:9. s *Peace,* Jer. 29:7. 5 R. V. pursue **12** t *Promise, or Ground of Assurance,* 2 Cor. 1:20. u *God, knowledge of,* Gen. 2:2. v *God, goodness of,* Gen. 2:2. w *Prayer, answer to, promised,* Acts 6:4. x *Wicked, punishment of,* Psa. 73:3. **13** y *Zeal,* 2 Cor. 7:11. 6 R. V. zealous **14** z *Persecution, exhortations to courage under,* John 15:20.—a *Righteous, happiness of,* Psa. 64:10. **15** b *Commandment, enjoining holiness, and witnessing for Christ,* Deut. 8:2. c *Jesus, lordship of,* Matt. 1:21. d *Religious Testimony,* 2 Thess. 1:10. e *Witnessing for Christ,* Luke 24:28. f *Hope,* Prov. 13:12. g *Meekness,* Psa. 45:4. 7 R. V. in your hearts Christ as Lord. **16** h *Conscience approving,* Acts 23:1. i *Speech, evil,* Col. 4:6. 8 R. V. wherein ye are spoken against, they may be put to shame who revile your good manner of life in Christ.

**17**
j *Will of God,* Mark 3:35.
k *Persecution, of the righteous,* John 15:20.
**18**
l *Jesus, our example,* Matt. 1:21.
m *Jesus, sufferings of,* Matt. 1:21.
n *Atonement, by Jesus,* Lev. 17:11.
o *Jesus, design of his death,* Matt. 1:21.
p *Jesus, savior,* Matt. 1:21.
**19**
q *Preaching,* Matt. 9:35.
r *Jesus, preaches to spirits in prison,* Matt. 1:21.
s *Hell,* Mark 9:43.
**20**
t *Antediluvians,* Gen. 6:1.
u *Disobedience to God,* Eph. 5:6.
v *God, longsuffering of,* Gen. 2:2.
w *Noah,* Gen. 5:29.
x *Ark, Noah's,* Gen. 6:14.
y *Flood,* Gen. 6:17.
9 Am. R. V. beforetime
**21**
z *Baptism, Christian,* Luke 20:4.

a *Conscience, approving,* Acts 23:1.
b *Resurrection, of Jesus,* 1 Cor. 15:12.
10 R. V. interrogation of a good
**22**
c *Heaven, God's dwelling place,* Luke 18:22.
d *Jesus, exaltation of,* Matt. 1:21.
e *Jesus, king,* Matt. 1:21.
f *Angel,* Heb. 1:13.

**1**
a *Example, Christ our,* John 13:15.
b *Jesus, sufferings of,* Matt. 1:21.
c *Persecution, of Jesus,* John 15:20.
d *Jesus, humanity of,* Matt. 1:21. e *Commandment, enjoining patience under tribulations,* Deut. 8:2. f *Righteous, described,* Psa. 64:10. g *Holiness, described,* Ex. 39:30. 1 R. V. *omits* for us

***SYMPATHY,** Jas. 1:27. *Enjoined,* Rom. 12:15. **Instances of:** *David with Hanun,* 2 Sam. 10:2. *The Jewish maid with Naaman,* 2 Kin. 5:1–4. *Job's friends,* Job 2:11–13. *Ebed-melech with Jeremiah,* Jer. 38:7–13. *Nebuchadnezzar with Daniel,* Dan. 6:18–23. *The four friends with the palsied man whom they took to Jesus,* Mark 2:3, 4. *Others with the helpless whom they brought to Jesus,* Matt. 4:24. *The good Samaritan with the man who fell among robbers,* Luke 10:33–35. *The Jews with Martha and Mary,* John 11:19, 31, 33. *The people of Melita with the ship-wrecked mariners,* Acts 28:1, 2.
See footnotes: JESUS, *Compassion of,* Matt. 1:21, KINDNESS, Acts 28:2; POOR, Prov. 21:13.

the rest of *his* time in the flesh to the [h]lusts[G] of men, but to the [i]will of God.

3 For the time past [2]of *our* life may suffice us to have wrought[G] the will of the [j]Gĕn′tīleș, when we [k,l]walked in *,[m]lasciviousness, [h]lusts, [n]excess of [o]wine, revellings, banquetings, and abominable [p]idolatries:

4 Wherein they think it strange that ye run not with *them* to the same excess of riot,[G] [q]speaking evil of *you*:

5 [r]Who shall give account to him that is ready to [s,t]judge the quick[G] and the dead.

6 For for this cause was the [u]gospel [v]preached also to them that are dead, that they might be [t]judged according to men in the flesh, but live according to God in the spirit.

7 But [w]the end of all things is at hand: [x,y]be ye therefore [3]sober,[G] and watch unto prayer.

8 And above all things [z]have fervent [4,a]charity[G] among yourselves: for [4]charity[G] shall cover the multitude of sins.[Q]

9 [b,c]Use hospitality one to another without [5]grudging.

10 As every man hath received the [d]gift, *even so* [e]minister the same one to another, as [f]good [g]stewards of the manifold [h]grace of God.

11 If any man speak, *let him speak* as the [i]oracles[G] of God; if any man minister,[G] [e]*let him do it* as of the ability which God giveth: that God in all things may be [j]glorified through Jē′ṣus [k]Chrīst, to whom be [l]praise and dominion[G] for ever and ever. Amen.

12 Beloved, [m]think it not strange concerning the fiery [n,o]trial[G] [6]which is to try[G] you, as though some strange thing happened unto you:

13 But [m]rejoice, inasmuch as ye are [p]partakers of Chrīst's sufferings; [q]that, when his glory [r]shall be revealed, ye may be glad also with exceeding [s]joy.[T]

14 If ye be [n]reproached[G] for the name of Chrīst, [7,t]happy *are ye*; for the [u]spirit of glory[G] and of God resteth upon you: [8]on their part he is evil spoken of, but on your part he is glorified.[G] [T] [Q]

15 But [v]let none of you suffer as a [w]murderer, or *as* a [x]thief, or *as* an evildoer, or as a [y]busybody in other men's matters.

16 Yet if *any man* [n,p]*suffer* as a [z]Chrĭs′tian, let him not be ashamed; but let him [a]glorify God [9]on this behalf.[C]

17 For the time *is come* that judgment must begin at the [b]house of God: and if *it* first *begin* at us, what shall the end *be* of them that [c]obey not the [d]gospel of God?[Q]

18 And if the [e]righteous scarcely be [f]saved, where shall the [c]ungodly and the sinner appear?[Q]

19 Wherefore let them that suffer according to the [g]will of God commit [10]the keeping of their souls *to him* in well doing, as unto a [h]faithful [i]Creator.[S] [Q]

**2**
h *Lust*, 2 Pet. 1:4.
i *Will of God*, Mark 3:35.

**3**
j *Gentiles, wicked practices of*, Acts 10:45.
k *Worldly Pleasure*, Eccl. 2:1.
l *Sensuality*, Jude 19.
m *Adultery*, Lev. 20:10.
n *Drunkenness*, Luke 21:34.
o *Wine*, Prov. 23:31.
p *Idolatry*, 1 Sam. 15:23.
2 R. V. may suffice to have wrought the desire of the Gentiles, and to have walked in lasciviousness, lusts, winebibbings, revellings, carousings, and abominable idolatries:

**4**
q *Speech, evil*, Col. 4:6.

**5**
r *Responsibility, personal*, Ezek. 18:20.
s *Jesus, judge*, Matt. 1:21.
t *Judgment, the general*, 2 Pet. 3:7.

**6**
u *Gospel*, Mark 13:10.
v *Jesus, preaches to spirits in prison*, Matt. 1:21.

**7**
w *Time, for achievement, short*, Rev. 10:6.
x *Commandment, enjoining sobriety*, Deut. 8:2.
y *Temperance*, 2 Pet. 1:6.
3 R. V. of sound mind, and be sober unto prayer:

**8**
z *Commandment, enjoining love*, Deut. 8:2.
—a *Love, of man for man*, 1 John 4:7. 4 R. V. love **9** b *Commandment, enjoining hospitality*, Deut. 8:2. c *Hospitality, enjoined*, Rom. 12:13. 5 R. V. murmuring: **10** d *Spiritual Blessings, from God*, Eph. 1:3. e *Faithfulness*, Luke 16:10. f *Minister, character and qualifications of*, Rom. 15:16. g *Steward, figurative*, Gen. 43:19. h *Grace of God*, Rom. 4:16. **11** i *Oracle*, 1 Kin. 6:5.

j *Glorifying God*, Luke 5:25.
k *Jesus, Messiah*, Matt. 1:21.
l *Praise*, Psa. 150:1.

**12**
m *Adversity, resignation in*, vs. 12–16; Psa. 10:6.
n *Persecution, of the righteous*, John 15:20.
o *Temptation, a test*, Luke 11:4.
6 R. V. among you, which cometh upon you to prove you, as though

**13**
p *Suffering for Christ*, Phil. 1:29.
q *Promise, or Ground of Assurance*, 2 Cor. 1:20.
r *Jesus, second coming of*, Matt. 1:21.
s *Joy*, Psa. 5:11.

**14**
t *Spiritual Peace*, Gal. 1:3.
u *Holy Spirit, Christians filled with*, Acts 1:2.
7 R. V. blessed
8 R. V. *omits the rest of this verse.*

**15**
v *Commandment, forbidding theft, murder, and meddling*, Deut. 8:2.
w *Homicide, felonious, forbidden*, Deut. 5:17.
x *Thieves*, Deut. 24:7.
y *Busybody*, 2 Thess. 3:11.

**16**
z *Christian*, Acts 11:26.
a *Glorifying God*, Luke 5:25.
9 R. V. in this name.
**17** b *Church, described as house of God*, Matt. 16:18. c *Wicked, described*, Psa. 73:3. d *Gospel*, Mark 13:10.
**18** e *Righteous*, Psa. 64:10. f *Salvation*, Acts 16:17.
**19** g *Will of God*, Mark 3:35. h *God, faithfulness of*, Gen. 2:2. i *God, creator*, Gen. 2:2. 10 R. V. their souls in well-doing unto

---

***LASCIVIOUSNESS.** *Forbidden*, Col. 3:5; 1 Thess. 4:3–6.

*Warnings against*, Prov. 2:16–18; 5:3–5, 8–13; 7:6–27; 9:13–18; 30:18–20; 31:3; Rom. 13:13; 1 Cor. 6:13, 15–18; 1 Pet. 4:2, 3; Jude 4, 7.

*Iniquitous practices in*, Joel 3:3; Rom. 1:22–29. *Proceeds from unregenerate heart*, Mark 7:21–23; Gal. 5:19; Eph. 4:17–19. *Impenitence in*, 2 Cor. 12:21.

*Excludes from the kingdom of God*, 1 Cor. 6:9, 10, 13, 15–18; 9:27; Gal. 5:19, 21; Eph. 5:5.

*Lascivious practices in idolatrous worship*, see IDOLATRY, *Wicked practices of*, 1 Sam. 15:23.

**Figurative**, Ezek. 16:15–19.

See footnotes: ADULTERY, Lev. 20:10; INCEST, Lev. 18:6; SODOMY, Lev. 18:22.

**Instances of:** *Sodomites*, Gen. 19:5. *Lot's daughters*, Gen. 19:30–38. *Judah*, Gen. 38:15, 16. *The Gibeahites*, Judg. 19:22–25. *Eli's sons*, 1 Sam. 2:22. *David*, 2 Sam. 11:2–4. *Amnon*, 2 Sam. 13:1–14. *Solomon*, 1 Kin. 11:1–3. *Persian kings*, Esth. 2:3, 13, 14, 19.

## CHAPTER 5

*The elders are exhorted to feed the flock of God,* 5 *the younger to submit themselves to the elder,* 8 *and all to be sober and vigilant.* 13 *Salutations.*

THE [a]elders which are among you I exhort,[G] who am also an elder, and a witness of the [b]sufferings of Christ, and also a partaker of the glory[G] that shall be revealed:

2 [c,d]Feed the [e]flock of God which is among you, [c]taking the oversight *thereof*, not by constraint, but [f]willingly; [1]not [g]for filthy lucre,[G] but of a ready mind;

3 [d,f]Neither as [2]being lords over *God's* heritage, but being [h]ensamples[G] to the [e]flock.

4 And when the chief [i]Shepherd shall [j]appear, [k]ye shall receive a [l]crown of glory that fadeth not away.

5 Likewise, ye younger, submit yourselves unto the elder. Yea, all *of you* [3,m]be subject one to another, and [n,o]be clothed with humility: for God resisteth the [p]proud, and giveth [q]grace to the humble.[Q]

6 [n,o,r]Humble yourselves therefore [s]under the mighty hand of God, that [t]he may exalt[G] you in due time:[S Q]

7 [u]Casting all your [4,*,v]care upon him; for [w]he [x]careth for you.[Q]

8 [y,z]Be [a]sober,[G] [b]be vigilant; because your adversary the [c,d]devil, as a roaring [e]lion, walketh about, seeking whom he may devour:

9 Whom [f]resist [g]stedfast[G] in the [h]faith, knowing that the same [i]afflictions are accomplished in your brethren that are in the world.

10 But [j]the God of all [k,l]grace, who hath [m]called us unto his eternal glory by Christ [5]Jē'sus, after that ye have [n]suffered a [6]while, [o]make you [p]perfect,[G] stablish,[G] strengthen, settle *you.*[S]

11 To him *be* [q]glory and [r]dominion[G] for ever and ever. Amen.

12 By [s]Sĭl-vā'nus, a faithful brother unto you, as I suppose, I have written briefly, exhorting, and [t]testifying that this is the true [k]grace of God [7]wherein ye stand.

13 [8]The [u]*church that is* at [v]Băb'y̆-lon, elected together with *you,* [w]saluteth[G] you; and *so doth* [x]Mär'cus my son.

14 [w]Greet ye one another with a [y]kiss of [9]charity.[G] [z,a]Peace *be* with you all that are [b]in Christ [5]Jē'sus. Amen.

**1**
*a Elders, overseers of the church,* Acts 14:23.
*b Jesus, sufferings of,* Matt. 1:21.

**2**
*c Minister, duties of,* Rom. 15:16.
*d Commandment, to ministers,* vs. 2, 3, 5–9; Deut. 8:2.
*e Church, described as flock of God,* Matt. 16:18.
*f Minister, character and qualifications of,* Rom. 15:16.
*g Covetousness,* Isa. 57:17.
1 Am. R. V. *inserts* according to the will of God;

**3**
*h Example, good, enjoined,* John 13:15.
2 R. V. lording it over the charge allotted to you, but making your selves ensamples

**4**
*i Shepherd, figurative,* Jer. 31:10.
*j Jesus, second coming of,* Matt. 1:21.
*k Minister, promises to,* Rom. 15:16.
*l Crown, figurative,* Ex. 29:6.

**5**
*m Altruism,* Acts 20:35.
*n Commandment, enjoining humility,* Deut. 8:2.
*o Humility, enjoined,* Prov. 22:4.
*p Pride,* Prov. 16:18.
*q Grace of God,* Rom. 4:16. 3 R. V. gird yourselves with humility, to serve one another: **6** *r Adversity, resignation in,* Psa. 10:6. *s Divine Chastisement,* Job 33:19. *t Promise, to the humble,* 2 Cor. 1:20. **7** *u Adversity, consolation in,* Psa. 10:6. *v Borrowing Trouble,* Matt. 6:25. *w Commandment, enjoining casting anxiety upon the Lord,* Deut. 8:2. *x God, love of,* Gen. 2:2. 4 R. V. anxiety

**8**
*y Faithfulness,* Luke 16:10.
*z Commandment, enjoining sobriety and watchfulness,* Deut. 8:2.
*a Sobermindedness,* Tit. 2:6.
*b Watchfulness, enjoined,* Matt. 24:42.
*c Satan,* Matt. 4:10.
*d Temptation, sources of,* Luke 11:4.
*e Lion,* Mic. 5:8.

**9**
*f Temptation, resistance to,* Luke 11:4.
*g Steadfastness,* 1 Cor. 15:58.
*h Faith in Christ,* John 6:69.
*i Adversity,* Psa. 10:6.

**10**
*j Prayer, intercessory,* Acts 6:4.
*k Grace of God,* Rom. 4:16.
*l God, mercy of,* Gen. 2:2.
*m Call, personal,* Phil. 3:14.
*n Suffering for Christ,* Phil. 1:29.
*o Temptation, benefits of,* Luke 11:4.
*p Perfection,* Heb. 6:1.
5 R. V. *omits* Jesus,
6 R. V. little while, shall himself perfect, stablish, strengthen you.
**11** *q Praise,* Psa. 150:1. *r Jesus, king,* Matt. 1:21. **12** *s* Or, *Silas,* Acts 15:22. *t Religious Testimony,* 2 Thess. 1:10. 7 R. V. stand ye fast therein.
**13** *u Church, Christian,* Matt. 16:18. *v Babylon, city of,* Ezra 5:12. *w Salutations,* Luke 1:44. *x* Or, *Mark,* Acts 12:12. 8 R. V. She that is in Babylon,
**14** *y Kiss, holy,* Ruth 1:9. *z Benedictions, apostolic,* Deut. 21:5. —*a Spiritual Peace,* Gal. 1:3. *b Righteous, union of, with Christ,* Psa. 64:10. 9 R. V. love.

* **ANXIETY.** *Forbidden,* Matt. 6:25–34; Luke 12:22–28; Phil. 4:6.
*Unavailing,* Psa. 39:6; 127:2; Matt. 6:27; Luke 12:25, 26.
*Proceeds from unbelief,* Matt. 6:26, 28–30; Luke 12:24, 27, 28.
*Martha rebuked for,* Luke 10:40, 41.
*Remedy for,* Psa. 37:5; 55:22; Heb. 13:5; 1 Pet. 5:6, 7.

## THE SECOND EPISTLE OF

# PETER

## CHAPTER 1

*The apostle's salutation. 5 He exhorts Christians to add to their faith sundry virtues, 10 and to make their calling and election sure. 12 His faithfulness to them in view of his own death. 16 The doctrines taught them not cunningly devised fables.*

SI'MON [a]Pē'tẽr, a servant and
an [b]apostle of Jē'ṣus Chrīst,
to them that have obtained like
precious [c]faith with us through
the [d,e]righteousness of God and
our [f]Saviour Jē'ṣus Chrīst:
2 [T g,h]Grace and [i]peace be multiplied unto you through the
[j]knowledge of God, and of Jē'-
ṣus our [k]Lord,
3 According as his divine
[l]power hath given unto us [m]all
things that *pertain* unto life and
[n]godliness, through the [j]knowl-
edge of him that hath [o]called us
[1]to glory and virtue:
4 Whereby are given unto us
exceeding great and precious
[p]promises: that by these ye
might be [q]partakers of the divine
nature, having [r]escaped the [s]cor-
ruption that is in the world
through [*,t]lust.
5 [T 2]And beside this, giving all
[u]diligence, [v,w,x]add to your [y]faith
[z]virtue; and to virtue [z,a]knowl-
edge;
6 And [b,c]to [a]knowledge [†]tem-
perance; and to temperance [d]pa-
tience; and to patience [e]godliness;
7 And [3,b,c]to [e]godliness [f]broth-
erly kindness; and to brotherly
kindness charity.
8 For if these things be in you,
and abound, they make *you*
[4]*that ye shall* neither *be* barren
nor [g]unfruitful in the [a]knowl-
edge of our [h]Lord Jē'ṣus Chrīst.
9 But he that lacketh these
things is [i]blind, and cannot see
afar off, and hath [j]forgotten that
he was [k]purged from his old sins.
10 [T]Wherefore the rather, brethren, [l]give [m]diligence to make
your [n]calling and election sure:
for [o]if ye do these things, [p,q]ye
shall never [5]fall:
11 For so [q]an entrance shall be
ministered unto you abundantly
into the [r]everlasting [s]kingdom of
our [h]Lord and [t]Saviour Jē'ṣus
Chrīst.
12 Wherefore [u]I will not be
negligent to [v]put you always in
remembrance of these things,
though ye know *them*, and be
established in the present [w]truth.
13 Yea, I think it meet, as long
as I am in this [x]tabernacle, [v]to
stir you up by putting *you* in
remembrance;

**1**
*a* *Peter*, Mark 5:37.
*b* *Apostles*, Luke 6:13.
*c* *Faith in Christ*, John 6:69.
*d* *God, righteousness of*, Gen. 2:2.
*e* *Jesus, holiness of*, Matt. 1:21.
*f* *Jesus, savior*, Matt. 1:21.

**2**
*g* *Benedictions, apostolic*, Deut. 21:5.
*h* *Grace of God*, Rom. 4:16.
*i* *Spiritual Peace*, Gal. 1:3.
*j* *Wisdom, spiritual*, Prov. 2:2.
*k* *Jesus, lordship of*, Matt. 1:21.

**3**
*l* *Jesus, power of*, Matt. 1:21.
*m* *Spiritual Blessings*, Eph. 1:3.
*n* *Godliness*, 1 Tim. 4:8.
*o* *Call, personal*, Phil. 3:14.
1 R. V. by his own glory and virtue;

**4**
*p* *Promises*, 2 Cor. 1:20.
*q* *Regeneration*, Tit. 3:5.
*r* *Holiness*, Ex. 39:30.
*s* *Corruption, figurative of the evil existing in the world*, Job 17:14.
*t* *Sin, inherited tendencies to evil*, Rom. 5:12.

**6**
*b* *Christian Graces*, Gal. 5:22.
*c* *Righteousness, fruits of*, Psa. 15:2.
*d* *Patience*, Luke 8:15.
*e* *Godliness*, 1 Tim. 4:8.

**7**
*f* *Love, of man for man*, 1 John 4:7.
3 R. V. in your godliness love of the brethren; and in your love of the brethren love.

**8**
*g* *Unfruitfulness*, Matt. 7:19.
*h* *Jesus, lordship of*, Matt. 1:21.
4 R. V. to be not idle nor

**9**
*i* *Spiritual Blindness*, 2 Cor. 4:4.
*j* *Backsliders*, Jer. 3:22.
*k* *Spiritual Purification*, Psa. 51:2.

**10**
*l* *Commandment, enjoining spiritual diligence*, Deut. 8:2.
*m* *Diligence*, Rom. 12:8.
*n* *Call, personal*, Phil. 3:14.
*o* *Perseverance, motives to*, Eph. 6:18.
*p* *Reward, a motive, to follow Christ*, Matt. 5:12.
*q* *Promise, to the righteous*, 2 Cor. 1:20.
5 R. V. stumble:

**5** *u Diligence*, Rom. 12:8. *v Commandment, enjoining growth in grace*, vs. 5–8; Deut. 8:2. *w Growth in Grace*, vs. 5–8; 2 Pet. 3:18. *x Christian Graces*, Gal. 5:22. *y Faith*, Mark 11:22. *z Righteousness, fruits of*, Psa. 15:2.—*a Wisdom, spiritual*, Prov. 2:2. 2 R. V. Yea, and for this very cause adding on your part all diligence, in your faith supply virtue; and in your virtue knowledge;

**11** *r Heaven, future home of the righteous*, Luke 18:22. *s Jesus, kingdom of*, Matt. 1:21. *t Jesus, savior*, Matt. 1:21. **12** *u Zeal, exemplified*, 2 Cor. 7:11. *v Minister, duties of*, Rom. 15:16. *w Truth, of the gospel*, John 18:37. **13** *x Body*, 1 Cor. 6:19.

---

***LUST**, evil desires. *Sinful*, Job 31:9–12; Matt. 5:28. *Worldly*, 1 John 2:16, 17. *Chokes the word*, Mark 4:19. *Tempts to sin*, Gen. 3:6; Jas. 1:14, 15; 2 Pet. 2:18.
*Forbidden*, Ex. 20:17; Prov. 6:24, 25; Rom. 13.14; Eph. 4:22; Col. 3:5; 1 Thess. 4:5; Tit. 2:12; 1 Pet. 2:11. *The righteous restrain*, 1 Cor. 9:27. *Wicked under power of*, John 8:44; Rom. 1:24, 26, 27; 1 Tim. 6:9; Jas. 4:1–3; 1 Pet. 4:3; 2 Pet. 3:3; Jude 16, 18.
*Warnings against*, 1 Cor. 10:6, 7; 2 Tim. 2:22.
*Of Israelites*, Psa. 106:13, 14.

See footnotes: LASCIVIOUSNESS, 1 Pet. 4:3; SENSUALITY, Jude 19.

**† TEMPERANCE**, Tit. 1:8; 2 Pet. 1:6. *In eating*, Prov. 23:1–3; 25:16. *In the use of wine*, 1 Tim. 3:8; Tit. 2:3.
*Enjoined*, Rom. 13:14; 1 Thess. 5:6–8; 1 Tim. 3:2; Tit. 2:2, 3, 12; 2 Pet. 1:5, 6.
*Practiced by athletes*, 1 Cor. 9:25, 27.
See footnotes: TOTAL ABSTINENCE, Lev. 10:9; DRUNKENNESS, Luke 21:34; WINE, Prov. 23:31.

14 Knowing that shortly I must [y]put[G] off *this* my [x]tabernacle, even as our Lord Jē'ṣus Christ hath [z]shewed me.

15 Moreover I will endeavour[G] that ye may be able after my decease to have these things always in remembrance.

16 For we have not followed cunningly[G] devised [a]fables, when we [b,c]made known unto you the [d]power and [e]coming of our Lord Jē'ṣus Christ, but were eyewitnesses of his [f]majesty.

17 [b]For he received from God the [g]Father honour and glory, when there came such a voice to him from the excellent glory, This is my beloved [g,h]Son, in whom I am well pleased.[T][Q]

18 [b]And this voice which came from heaven we heard, when we were with him in the holy mount.

19 We have also a more sure[G] word of prophecy; whereunto ye do well that ye [i]take heed, as unto a [j]light that shineth in a dark place, until the day dawn, and the day star[G] arise in your hearts:[T]

20 Knowing this first, that no prophecy of the scripture is of [6]any private[G] interpretation.

21 For [7]the [k]prophecy came not in old time by the will of man: but holy men of God spake *as they were* [l]moved by the [m]Holy[G] Ghost.[G][T]

## CHAPTER 2

*The coming of false teachers foretold. 2 Many shall follow their pernicious ways. 3 The certainty of their punishment shewn. 10 The character of these false teachers described.*

BUT there were [a]false prophets also among the people, even as there shall be *,[b]false teachers among you, who privily shall bring[G] in [1]damnable[G] [c]heresies,[G] even [d,e]denying the [2]Lord that [f,g]bought them, and bring upon themselves swift [h]destruction.[T]

2 And many shall follow *their [3]pernicious[G] ways; by reason of [i]whom the way of [j]truth shall be evil spoken of.[Q]

3 And through [k]covetousness[G] shall *,[l]they with feigned[G] words make merchandise[G] of you: whose judgment now of a long time lingereth not, and their [4,h]damnation[G] slumbereth not.

4 For if God spared not the [m]angels that sinned, but cast *them* down to [n]hell,[G] and [5]delivered *them* into chains of darkness, to be reserved unto [o]judgment;[S]

5 And spared not the [p]old world, but [q]saved [r]Nō'ah the [s]eighth *person*, a [t]preacher of [u]righteousness, bringing in the [h,v]flood upon the world of the ungodly;[T][Q]

6 And [w]turning the cities of [x]Sŏd'om and [y]Gō-mŏr'rhȧ into ashes condemned *them* with an overthrow, making *them* an ensample[G] unto those that after should live ungodly;[G][Q]

7 And delivered just [z]Lŏt, [6,a]vexed with the filthy conversation[G] of the wicked:[Q]

8 (For that righteous man dwelling among [b]them, in seeing and hearing, [a]vexed *his* righteous soul from day to day with *their* unlawful deeds;)

9 [c]The Lord knoweth how to [d]deliver the [e]godly out of [f]temptations,[G] and to [7]reserve the unjust unto the day of [g]judgment to be [h]punished:[S]

10 But chiefly them that walk

**14**
*y Death,* Num. 23:10.
*z Jesus, revelations by,* Matt. 1:21.

**16**
*a Fable,* 1 Tim. 1:4.
*b Religious Testimony,* 2 Thess. 1:10.
*c Witnessing for Christ,* Luke 24:48.
*d Jesus, power of,* Matt. 1:21.
*e Jesus, second coming of,* Matt. 1:21.
*f Transfiguration, of Jesus,* Matt. 17:2.

**17**
*g God, fatherhood of,* Gen. 2:2.
*h Jesus, divine sonship of,* Matt. 1:21.

**19**
*i Watchfulness,* Matt. 24:42.
*j Lamp, figurative,* Ex. 27:20.

**20**
6 R. V. *omits* any

**21**
*k Prophecies, inspired,* Dan. 9:24.
*l Prophets, inspiration of,* Isa. 3:2.
*m Holy Spirit, inspiration of,* Acts 1:2.
7 R. V. no prophecy ever came by the will of man: but men spake from God, being moved

**1**
*a Prophets, false,* Isa. 3:2.
*b Infidelity,* 1 Cor. 6:15.
*c Heresy,* Tit. 3:10.
*d Jesus, rejected,* Matt. 1:21.
*e Apostasy,* Acts 1:25.
1 R. V. destructive
2 R. V. Master
*f Redemption of our Souls,* Eph. 1:7.
*g Jesus, design of his death,* Matt. 1:21.
*h Wicked, punishment of,* Psa. 73:3.

**2**
*i Influence, evil,* 1 Cor. 7:14.
*j Gospel,* Mark 13:10.
3 R. V. lascivious doings;

**3**
*k Covetousness,* Isa. 57:17.
*l Minister, false and corrupt,* Rom. 15:16.
4 R. V. destruction

**4**
*m Angel, fallen,* Heb. 1:13.
*n Hell,* Mark 9:43.
*o Judgment, general,* 2 Pet. 3:7.
5 R. V. committed them to pits of

**5**
*p Antediluvians,* Gen. 6:1.
*q God, providence of,* Gen. 2:2.
*r Noah,* Gen. 5:29.
*s Genealogy,* 1 Chr. 5:1.
*t Preaching,* Matt. 9:35.
*u Righteousness,* Psa. 15:2.
*v Flood,* Gen. 6:17.

**6**
*w Judgments,* Ex. 6:6.
*x Sodom, destroyed,* Gen. 13:10.
*y* Or, *Gomorrah, destroyed,* Gen. 13:10.

**7**
*z Lot, righteous,* Gen. 11:27.
*a Sin, repugnant to the righteous,* Rom. 5:12.
6 R. V. sore distressed by the lascivious life of the wicked

**8**
*b Evil Company,* Prov. 13:20.

**9** *c Righteous, promises to,* Psa. 64:10. *d God, preserver,* Gen. 2:2. *e Righteous, described,* Psa. 64:10. *f Temptation,* Luke 11:4. *g Judgment, the general,* 2 Pet. 3:7. *h Wicked, punishment of,* Psa. 73:3. 7 R. V. keep the unrighteous under punishment unto the day of judgement;

***FALSE TEACHERS,** Matt. 15:9; 2 Cor. 2:17; 11:13–15; 1 Tim. 1:3, 4; Phil. 1:15; Rev. 2:2.
*Mercenary,* Rom. 16:17, 18; 1 Tim. 6:3–5; Tit. 1:10, 11; 2 Pet. 2:3, 14–19. *Obdurate,* 2 Tim. 3:8.
*Admonitions against,* Deut. 13:1–3; Matt. 5:19; 7:15–20; Acts 20:29, 30; 2 Cor. 11:4; Eph. 4:14; 5:6; 1 Tim. 1:6, 7; 4:1–3; 2 Tim. 2:14, 16–18; 4:3; 2 Pet. 2:1, 2; 1 John 4:3; 2 John 7, 9–11; *and against those who denied the Messiahship and divine sonship of Jesus,* 1 John 2:22–24.
*Denunciations against,* Matt. 23:2–33; Luke 11:38–52; Gal. 1:6–8; Jude 4, 11.
See footnote, MINISTERS, *False,* Rom. 15:16.

after the flesh in the [i]lust of uncleanness, and [j,k]despise government. [l]Presumptuous *are they*, [m]selfwilled, [j]they are not afraid to [n,o]speak evil of [p]dignities.

11 Whereas [q]angels, which are greater in power and might, bring not [r]railing accusation against them before the Lord.

12 But *these, as [8]natural brute [s]beasts, made to be taken and destroyed, [o]speak evil of the things that they understand not; and shall utterly [h]perish in their own corruption;

13 [9]And shall receive the reward of unrighteousness, *as* they that [t]count it [u]pleasure to riot in the day time. [s]Spots *they are* and blemishes, sporting themselves with their own deceivings while they [v]feast with you;

14 [s]Having eyes full of [w]adultery, and that cannot cease from sin; [x,y]beguiling [z]unstable souls: an [a]heart they have exercised with [b]covetous practices; [10]cursed children:

15 *Which have [c]forsaken the right way, and are gone astray, following the way of [d]Bā'laam *the son* of [e]Bō'sôr, [f]who [g]loved the wages of unrighteousness;

16 But was rebuked for his iniquity: the dumb [h]ass speaking with man's voice forbad the madness of the prophet.

17 *These are wells without water, clouds that are carried with a tempest; to [i]whom the mist of [j]darkness is reserved for ever.

18 For when *they speak great swelling *words* of vanity, [k]they [11,l]allure through the [m,n]lusts of the flesh, *through much* [o]wantonness, those that were clean escaped from them who live in error.

19 While they [p]promise them liberty, they themselves are the servants of [q]corruption: for of whom a man is overcome, of the same is he brought in bondage.

20 For if after they have escaped the pollutions of the world through the [r]knowledge of the Lord and [s]Saviour Jē'sus Christ, they are again [t]entangled therein, and [c]overcome, the latter end is worse with them than the beginning.

21 For it had been better for them not to have known the [u]way of righteousness, than, after they have known *it*, to [t]turn from the holy commandment delivered unto them.

22 But it is happened unto them according to the true [v]proverb, [w]The [x]dog *is* [y]turned to his own vomit again; and the [z]sow that was washed to her wallowing in the mire.

## CHAPTER 3

*The apostle's object in both of his epistles. 3 The character and teaching of scoffers in the last days. 5 He answers their objection, 10 and affirms the certainty of Christ's coming to judgment. 11 An exhortation to holiness of life. 15 How to regard the longsuffering of the Lord. 17 Watchfulness, and growth in grace.*

THIS second epistle, [a]beloved, [b]I now write unto you; in *both* which I stir up your pure minds by way of remembrance:

2 That ye may be mindful of the [c,d]words which were spoken before by the holy [e]prophets, and of the commandment of us the [f]apostles of the [g]Lord and [h]Saviour:

3 Knowing this first, that there shall come in the last days [i,j]scoffers, walking after their own [k]lusts,

4 And [l,m]saying, Where is the promise of his [n]coming? for since the fathers fell [o]asleep, all

**10**
*i* *Lust*, 2 Pet. 1:4.
*j* *Citizens, wicked and treasonable* (as some interpret), Luke 15:15.
*k* *Anarchy* (as some interpret), Jude 8.
*l* *Presumption, in despising the Lordship of Christ and the authority of the church* (as some interpret), Psa. 19:13.
*m* *Self-will*, Gen. 49:6.
*n* *Slander*, Prov. 10:18.
*o* *Speech, evil*, Col. 4:6.
*p* *Rulers, not to be reviled*, Ex. 18:21.

**11**
*q* *Angel*, Heb. 1:13.
*r* *Railing, forbidden*, Jude 9.

**12**
*s* *Wicked, described*, Psa. 73:3.
8 R. V. creatures without reason, born mere animals to be taken and destroyed, railing in matters whereof they are ignorant, shall in their destroying surely be destroyed.

**13**
*t* *Worldliness*, 1 John 2:15.
*u* *Worldly Pleasure*, Eccl. 2:1.
*v* Jude 12.
9 R. V. Suffering wrong as the hire of wrong-doing; men that count it pleasure to revel in the day-time, spots and blemishes, revelling in their love-feasts while they feast with you;

**14**
*w* *Adultery*, Lev. 20:10.
*x* *Influence, evil*, 1 Cor. 7:14.
*y* *Temptation, leading into*, Luke 11:4. *z* *Character, instability of*, Phil. 2:15. —*a* *Heart, unregenerate*, Psa. 44:21. *b* *Covetousness*, Psa. 57:17. 10 R. V. children of cursing; **15** *c* *Apostasy*, vs. 15–17; Acts 1:25. *d* *Balaam*, Deut. 23:4. *e* Or, *Beor*, Num. 22:5. *f* *Minister, false*, Rom. 15:16. *g* *Worldliness*, 1 John 2:15. **16** *h* *Ass*, 2 Chr. 28:15. **17** *i* *Wicked, punishment of*, Psa. 73:3. *j* *Darkness, figurative*, Gen. 1:2. **18** *k* *Evil Company*, Prov. 13:20. *l* *Influence, evil*, 1 Cor. 7:14. *m* *Lust*, 2 Pet. 1:4. *n* *Temptation, sources of, carnal desires*, Luke 11:4. *o* *Lasciviousness*, 1 Pet. 4:3. 11 R. V. entice in the lusts of the flesh, by lasciviousness, those who are just escaping from them that live in error;

**19**
*p* *Deceit*, Psa. 36:3.
*q* *Corruption, figurative of the evil existing in the world*, Job 17:14.

**20**
*r* *Wisdom, spiritual*, Prov. 2:2.
*s* *Jesus, savior*, Matt. 1:21.
*t* *Sin, against knowledge*, Rom. 5:12.

**21**
*u* *Doctrines of Jesus*, John 7:16.

**22**
*v* *Proverbs*, 1 Sam. 24:13.
*w* Prov. 26:11.
*x* *Dog*, 1 Kin. 21:19.
*y* *Sin, love of*, Rom. 5:12.
*z* *Swine*, Lev. 11:7.

**1**
*a* *Minister, love of, for the church*, Rom. 15:16.
*b* *Peter*, Mark 5:37.

**2**
*c* *Word of God, is inspired*, Psa. 119:9.
*d* *Prophecies*, vs. 1–18; Dan. 9:24.
*e* *Prophets*, Isa. 3:2.
*f* *Apostles*, Luke 6:13.
*g* *Jesus, lordship of*, Matt. 1:21.
*h* *Jesus, savior*, Matt. 1:21.

**3**
*i* *Infidelity*, 2 Cor. 6:15.
*j* *Mocking*, 1 Kin. 18:27.
*k* *Lust*, 2 Pet. 1:4.

**4**
*l* *Unbelief*, Heb. 3:12.
*m* *Delusion*, 2 Thess. 2:11.
*n* *Jesus, second coming of*, Matt. 1:21.
*o* *Death, called sleep*, Num. 23:10.

things continue as *they were* from
the beginning of the [p]creation.
5 For this [i]they [1]willingly are
ignorant of, that by the word of
[q]God the [r]heavens [r]were of old,
and [s]the [t]earth standing out of
the water and in the water:
6 Whereby the [u]world that then
was, being [v,w]overflowed with
water, perished:
7 But the [x]heavens and the
[y]earth, which are now, by the
same word are kept in store, reserved unto fire against the day
of *judgment and [2,z]perdition of
ungodly men.
8 But, [a]beloved, be not ignorant
of this one thing, that one [b]day
*is* with the [c]Lord as a thousand
[d]years, and a thousand years as
one day.
9 The Lord is [e]not slack concerning his promise, as some men
count slackness; but is [f]longsuf-
fering to us-ward, [g]not willing
that any should [h]perish, but that
all should [i]come to [j]repentance.
10 But the *day of the Lord
will come as a thief [3]in the night;
in the which the [k]heavens shall
pass away with a great noise,
and the elements shall melt with
fervent heat, the [l]earth also and
the works that are therein shall
be burned up.
11 [m]*Seeing* then *that* all these
things shall be dissolved, [n]what
manner *of persons* ought ye to
be in *all* holy [4]conversation and
godliness,
12 Looking for and [5]hasting
unto the coming of the *day of
God, wherein the [k]heavens being
on fire shall be dissolved, and the
elements shall melt with fervent
heat?
13 Nevertheless we, according
to his promise, [o]look for [p]new
heavens and a [q]new earth,
wherein dwelleth righteousness.
14 Wherefore, [a]beloved, seeing
that ye look for such things, [r,s]be
[t]diligent that ye may be found of
him in [u]peace, [v,w,x]without spot,
and [v,w]blameless.
15 And account *that* the [f]long-
suffering of our Lord *is* [i]salva-
tion; even as our beloved brother
[y]Paul also according to the [z]wis-
dom [a]given unto him hath written unto you;
16 As also in all *his* epistles,
speaking in them of these things;
in which are some things hard to
be understood, which they that
are [b]unlearned and [c]unstable
wrest, as *they do* also the other
[d]scriptures, unto their own destruction.
17 Ye therefore, [e]beloved, seeing ye know *these things* before,
[f,g,h]beware lest ye also, being
led away with the [i]error of the
[j]wicked, [k]fall from your own
stedfastness.
18 But [†,l]grow in grace, and *in*
the [m]knowledge of our [n]Lord
and [o]Saviour Jē'sus [p]Chrīst. To
[q]him *be* [r]glory both now and for
ever. Amen.

p *Creation,* Mark 13:19.

5

q *God, creator,* Gen. 2:2.
r *Heavens, created,* Psa. 8:3.
s *Geology,* Psa. 104:5.
t *Earth, created,* Prov. 8:23.
1 R. V. wilfully forget, that

6

u *Antediluvians,* Gen. 6:1.
v *Flood,* Gen. 6:17.
w *Judgments,* Ex. 6:6.

7

x *Heavens, destruction of,* Psa. 8:3.
y *Earth, destruction of,* Prov. 8:23.
z *Wicked, punishment of,* Psa. 73:3.
2 R. V. destruction of

8

a *Minister, love of, for the church,* Rom. 15:16.
b *Time,* Rev. 10:6.
c *God, eternity of,* Gen. 2:2.
d *Year,* Lev. 25:29.

9

e *God, faithfulness of,* Gen. 2:2.
f *God, longsuffering of,* Gen. 2:2.
g *God, mercy of,* Gen. 2:2.
h *Wicked, punishment of,* Psa. 73:3.
i *Salvation,* Acts 16:17.
j *Repentance,* Mark 1:4.

10

k *Heavens, destruction of,* Psa. 8:3.
l *Earth, destruction of,* Prov. 8:23.
3 R. V. *omits* in the night;

11

m *Fear of God, motive to obedience,* Acts 9:31.
n *Holiness, exhortations to,* Ex. 39:30. 4 R. V. living **12** 5 R. V. earnestly desiring the

13

o *Faith,* Mark 11:22.
p *New Heavens,* Rev. 21:1.
q *Earth, new,* Prov. 8:23.

14

r *Commandment, enjoining spiritual diligence,* Deut. 8:2.
s *Holiness, enjoined upon the church,* Ex. 39:30.
t *Diligence,* Rom. 12:8.
u *Spiritual Peace,* Gal. 1:3.
v *Holiness, described,* Ex. 39:30.
w *Righteous, described,* Psa. 64:10.
x *Purity, of heart,* 1 Tim. 4:12.

15

y *Paul,* Acts 13:9.
z *Wisdom, spiritual,* Prov. 2:2.
a *Apostles, inspiration of,* Luke 6:13.

16

b *Spiritual Blindness,* 2 Cor. 4:4.
c *Character, instability of,* Phil. 2:15.
d *Word of God, disbelief in,* Psa. 119:9.

17

e *Minister, love of, for the church,* Rom. 15:16.
f *Commandment, enjoining watchfulness,* Deut. 8:2.
g *Watchfulness, enjoined, against evil associations,* Matt. 24:42.
h *Temptation, admonitions against yielding to,* Luke 11:4.
i *Heresy,* Tit. 3:10.
j *False Teachers,* 2 Pet. 2:1.
k *Apostasy,* Acts 1:25.

**18** l *Commandment, enjoining growth in grace,* Deut. 8:2. m *Wisdom, spiritual,* Prov. 2:2. n *Jesus, lordship of,* Matt. 1:12. o *Jesus, savior,* Matt. 1:21. p *Jesus, Messiah,* Matt. 1:21. q *Jesus, worship of,* Matt. 1:21. r *Praise,* Psa. 150:1.

*** JUDGMENT.** Eccl. 11:9; 12:14; Matt. 8:29 (with 2 Pet. 2:4; Jude 6); 13:30, 40–43, 49, 50; 25; Mark 8:38; Acts 24:25; 2 Thess. 1:7, 8; Heb. 6:2.

**Design of:** *To exhibit a basis for rewards and punishments,* 2 Cor. 5:10; 2 Tim. 4:8; Rev. 11:18; 22:12; *according to opportunity and works,* 1 Sam. 26:23; Job 34:11, 12; Matt. 10:14, 15; 11:22–24; 12:36–42; 16:27; 22:11–13; 25:31–46; Luke 10:12–15; 11:31, 32; 13:24–28; 19:12–27; John 3:19, 20; 12:48; 2 Cor. 5:10; 11:15; Jude 15; Rev. 2:23. *Revealing secrets,* Eccl. 12:14; Luke 12:2, 3; Rom. 2:16; 1 Cor. 3:13.

**Who will be the Judge:** *God,* 1 Chr. 16:33; Psa. 9:7; 50: 4, 6; 96:13; 98:9; Eccl. 12:14; Dan. 7:9, 10; Rom. 2:5, 16; 3: 6; 2 Tim. 4:8; Heb. 10:30; 12:23; 13:4; 1 Pet. 4:5; Rev. 20: 11; Rev. 20:11–15.

*Jesus Christ,* Matt. 7:22, 23; 13:30, 40–43, 49, 50; 16:25, **27, 31**; 25:31–46; John 5:22; Acts 10:42; 17:31; Rom. 2:16; 14:10; 1 Cor. 4:5; 2 Cor. 5:10; 2 Thess. 1:7, 8; 2 Tim. 4:1; 2 Pet. 2:9; 3:10; Rev. 1:7; 6:15–17.

*The saints,* Matt. 19:28; 1 Cor. 6:2.

**Time of,** Matt. 13:30; Acts 17:31; Heb. 9:27; 2 Pet. 3:7, 10–12. *Known to God only,* Mark 13:32.

**Who shall be judged:** *The righteous and wicked,* Eccl. 3: 17; Matt. 25:31–46; Rev. 11:18. *The wicked,* 2 Pet. 2:9; 3:7. *The living and the dead,* Acts 10:42; 2 Tim. 4:1; 1 Pet. 4:5. *All must be made manifest,* Acts 17:31; 2 Cor. 5:10. *Kings and princes, bondmen and freemen,* Rev. 6:15, 16. *Fallen angels,* 2 Pet. 2:4; Jude 6.

**† GROWTH IN GRACE,** Psa. 84:7; Prov. 4:18; Mark 4, 26–29; Eph. 3:16; 4:15; Phil. 1:6, 9–11; 3:12–15; Col. 1:10, 11; 2:19; 1 Thess. 3:10, 12, 13; 2 Thess. 1:3; Heb. 6:1–3; 1 Pet. 2:1–3; 2 Pet. 1:5–7.

## THE FIRST EPISTLE OF

# JOHN

### CHAPTER 1

*The apostle's object in declaring what he had seen and known of the Word of life. 5 His message concerning God, and fellowship with him. 7 The blood of Christ cleanses from all sin.*

THAT[T] which was [a]from the beginning, [b]which we have heard, which we have seen with our eyes, which we have looked upon, and our hands have handled, of the [c]Word of life;

2 (For the life was [b]manifested, and we have seen *it*, and [d]bear [e]witness, and shew unto you that [f]eternal life, [g]which was with the [h]Father, and was manifested unto us;)

3 That which we have seen and heard [d]declare we unto you, that ye also may have [i]fellowship with us: and truly our [j]fellowship *is* with the [h]Father, and [k]with his [l]Son Jē'ṣus Chrīst.[S T]

4 And [b,f,g]these things [d,e]write we unto you, that [1]your [m]joy may be full.

5 This then is the message which we have heard of him, and [d,e]declare unto you, that God is [n,o]light, and in him is [o]no [p]darkness at all.[S T]

6 If we [q]say that we have [j]fellowship with him, and [r]walk in [p,s]darkness, we lie, and do not the truth:

7 But if we walk in the [n]light, as he is in the light, we have [i]fellowship one with another, and the [t]blood of Jē'ṣus [2]Chrīst his [l]Son [u,v,w,x]cleanseth us from all sin.[Q T S]

8 [T][y]If we say that we have [z]no sin, we [a]deceive ourselves, and the truth is not in us.[S]

9 If we [b]confess[G] our [c]sins, [d,e,f]he is [g]faithful and [h]just to [i]forgive us *our* sins, and to [j]cleanse us from all unrighteousness.[S Q]

10 If we say that we have [k]not sinned, we make him a liar, and his word is not in us.[S T]

### CHAPTER 2

*Christ our advocate and the propitiation for our sins. 3 The evidence of love to God is obedience to his commands. 18 A caution to beware of seducers. 22 Who antichrist is. 24 The safety of the godly is in their abiding in the faith.*

MY little[T] children, these things write I unto you, that ye [a,b]sin not. And if any man [c]sin, we have an [d]advocate with the [e]Father, Jē'ṣus Chrīst the [f]righteous:

2 And he is the [g,h]propitiation [i]for our sins: and not for our's only, but also for *the sins of* the whole world.[T]

3 And hereby we do know that we know him, if we [j,k]keep his [l]commandments.[T]

4 He that [m,n]saith, I know him, and [o]keepeth not his commandments, is a [p]liar, and the truth is not in him.[T]

5 But whoso [q]keepeth his word, in him verily is the [r]love of God [s]perfected: hereby [t]know[G] we that we are [u]in him.[S]

6 He that saith he [u,v]abideth in him ought himself also so to walk, even [w]as he walked.

7 Brethren, I write no new commandment unto you, but an old commandment which ye had from the beginning. The old commandment is the [x]word

**1**
a *Jesus, pre-existence of,* Matt. 1:21.
b *Jesus, incarnation of,* Matt. 1:21.
c John 1:1; Rev. 19:13.

**2**
d *Religious Testimony,* 2 Thess. 1:10.
e *Witnessing for Christ,* Luke 24:48.
f *Jesus, eternity of,* Matt. 1:21.
g *Jesus, divinity of,* Matt. 1:21.
h *God, fatherhood of,* Gen. 2:2.

**3**
i *Fellowship, of the righteous,* 1 Cor. 1:9.
j *Fellowship, with God,* 1 Cor. 1:9.
k *Fellowship, with Christ,* 1 Cor. 1:9.
l *Jesus, divine sonship of,* Matt. 1:21.

**4**
m *Joy,* Psa. 5:11.
1 R. V. our

**5**
n *Light, figurative,* Matt. 5:14.
o *God, perfection of,* Gen. 2:2.
p *Darkness, figurative,* Gen. 1:2.

**6**
q *Hypocrisy,* Jas. 3:17.
r *Wicked, contrasted with the righteous,* v. 7; Psa. 73:3.
s *Spiritual Blindness,* 2 Cor. 4:4.

**7**
t *Blood, of Jesus, cleansing,* Heb. 9:19.
u *Atonement, by Jesus,* Lev. 17:11.
v *Spiritual Purification,* Psa. 51:2.
w *Sin, forgiveness of,* Rom. 5:12.
x *Jesus, design of his death,* Matt. 1:21. 2 R. V. *omits* Christ

**8** y *Depravity, universal,* Job 15:14. z *Sinlessness,* 1 John 5:18. —a *Delusion,* 2 Thess. 2:11.

**9**
b *Sin, confession of,* Rom. 5:12.
c *Sin, transgression of the law,* Rom. 5:12.
d *God, mercy of, in granting forgiveness,* Gen. 2:2.
e *Promise, to the penitent,* 2 Cor. 1:20.
f *Penitent, promises to, of forgiveness,* Psa. 51:17.
g *God, faithfulness of,* Gen. 2:2.
h *God, justice of,* Gen. 2:2.
i *Sin, forgiveness of,* Rom. 5:12.
j *Spiritual Purification,* Psa. 51:2.

**10**
k *Sinlessness,* 1 John 5:18.

**1**
a *Sinlessness,* 1 John 5:18.
b *Holiness, enjoined,* Ex. 39:30.
c *Sin, transgression of the law,* Rom. 5:12.
d *Jesus, mediation of,* Matt. 1:21.
e *God, fatherhood of,* Gen. 2:2.
f *Jesus, holiness of,* Matt. 1:21.

**2**
g *Propitiation,* Rom. 3:25.
h *Atonement, by Jesus,* Lev. 17:11.
i *Jesus, design of his death,* Matt. 1:21.

**3**
j *Obedience,* Heb. 5:8.
k *Righteousness, fruits of,* Psa. 15:2.
l *Doctrines of Jesus,* John 7:16.

**4**
m *Hypocrisy,* Jas. 3:17.
n *Confession of Christ, hypocritical,* Luke 12:8.
o *Disobedience to God,* Eph. 5:6.
p *Falsehood,* Job 21:34.

**5** q *Obedience, a proof of love,* Heb. 5:8. r *Love, for God,* 1 John 4:19. s *Perfection,* Heb. 6:1. t *Assurance,* Heb. 10:22. u *Righteous, union of, with Christ,* Psa. 64:10. **6** v *Fellowship, with Christ,* 1 Cor. 1:9. w *Example, Christ our,* John 13:15. **7** x *Law, of Moses,* Deut. 33:2.

1 R. V. *omits* from the beginning

8

y *Gospel*, Mark 13:10.

z *Darkness, figurative*, vs. 8–11; Gen. 1:2.

a *Truth, of the gospel*, John 18:37.

b *Jesus, mission of*, Matt. 1:21.

9

c *Hatred*, Prov. 15:17.

d *Malice*, Eph. 4:31.

e *Darkness, figurative*, Gen. 1:2.

10

f *Love, of man for man*, 1 John 4:7.

g *Righteousness, fruits of*, Psa. 15:2.

h *Righteous, described*, Psa. 64:10.

11

i *Spiritual Blindness*, 2 Cor. 4:4.

12

j *Sin, forgiveness of*, Rom. 5:12.

k *Name of Jesus*, John 14:13.

13

l *Wisdom, spiritual*, Prov. 2:2.

m *Jesus, eternity of*, Matt. 1:21.

n *Young Men*, Prov. 1:4.

o *Temptation, resistance to*, Luke 11:4.

p *Satan*, Matt. 4:10.

q *God, fatherhood of*, Gen. 2:2.

2 R. V. know

14

r *Integrity*, Job 2:3.

s *Word of God*, Psa. 119:9.

15

t *Commandment, forbidding love of the world*, Deut. 8:2.

u *Love, for God*, 1 John 4:19.

16

v *Temptation, sources of, carnal desires*, Luke 11:4.

which ye have heard [1]from the
beginning.
8 Again, a new [y]commandment
I write unto you, which thing is
true in him and in you: because
the [z]darkness is past, and the
true [a,b]light now shineth.[T]
9 He that saith he is in the
[a]light, and [c,d]hateth his brother,
is in [e]darkness even until now.[S]
10 He that [f,g]loveth his brother
[h]abideth in the light, and there is
none occasion of stumbling in
him.[Q]
11 But he that [c]hateth his
brother is in [e]darkness, and
walketh in darkness, and knoweth[G] not whither he goeth, because that darkness hath [i]blinded
his eyes.
12 I write unto you, little children, because your sins are [j]for-
given you for his [k]name's sake.[Q]
13 I write unto you, fathers, because ye [2]have [l]known him *that
is* [m]from the beginning. I write
unto you, [n]young men, because
ye have [o]overcome the [p]wicked
one. I write unto you, little children, because ye [2]have known
the [q]Father.
14 I have written unto you, fathers, because ye [2]have [l]known
him *that is* [m]from the beginning.
I have written unto you, [n]young
men, because ye are [r]strong, and
the [s]word of God abideth[G] in
you, and ye have [o]overcome the
[p]wicked one.[S]
15 [t]Love[G] not the world, neither
the things *that are* in the world.
If any man *love[G] the world, the
[u]love[G] of the [q]Father is not in
him.
16 For [v]all that *is* in the world,
the [w,x]lust[G] of the flesh, and the
[w]lust[G] of the eyes, and the [x,y]pride
of life, is not of the [q]Father, but
is *of the world.[T Q]
17 And the world passeth away,
and the [w]lust[G] thereof: but [z]he
that doeth the [a]will of God
[b]abideth [c,d]for ever.[S T]
18 Little children, it is the last
[3]time: and as ye have heard that
[e,f]antichrist[G] shall come, even
now are there many antichrists[G];
whereby we know[G] that it is the
last [3]time.
19 [e,f]They went out from us,
but they were not of us; for if
they had been of us; they would
*no doubt* have continued with us:
but *they went out*, that they might
be made manifest that they were
not all of us.[S]
20 But ye have an [4,g]unction[G]
from the [h]Holy One, and ye
[i]know all things.[S T]
21 I have not written unto you
because ye know not the [j]truth,
but because ye [i]know it, and
that no [k]lie is of the truth.
22[T] Who is a liar but he that
[l,m]denieth that Jē'sus is the
[n]Christ? He is [e,o]antichrist, that
denieth the [p]Father and the
[q]Son.
23 Whosoever [l,m]denieth the
[q]Son, the same hath not the
[p]Father: [*but*] *he that* [r]*acknowledgeth the Son hath the Father
also*.
24 Let [1,n,q]that therefore abide
in you, which ye have heard from
the beginning. If that which ye
have heard from the beginning
shall remain in you, ye also shall
[s]continue in the Son, and [t]in the
[p]Father.[T]

w *Lust*, 2 Pet. 1:4.

x *Carnal Mind*, 1 Cor. 3:3.

y *Pride*, Prov. 16:18.

17

z *Righteous, promises to*, Psa. 64:10.

a *Will of God, the supreme rule of duty*, Mark 3:35.

b *Obedience, rewarded*, Heb. 5:8.

c *Immortality*, 1 Cor. 15:54.

d *Life, everlasting*, Eccl. 8:15.

18

e *Antichrist*, 2 John 7.

f *Minister, false and corrupt*, Rom. 15:16.

3 R. V. hour:

20

g *Anointing, figurative*, Deut. 28:40.

h *Holy Spirit, baptism of*, Acts 1:2.

i *Wisdom, spiritual*, Prov. 2:2.

4 R. V. anointing

21

j *Truth, of the gospel*, John 18:37.

k *Heresy*, Tit. 3:10.

22

l *Infidelity*, 2 Cor. 6:15.

m *Jesus, rejected*, Matt. 1:21.

n *Jesus, Messiah*, Matt. 1:21.

o *False Teachers, admonitions against those who denied the messiahship and divine sonship of Jesus*, vs. 22–24, 26; 2 Pet. 2:1.

p *God, fatherhood of*, Gen. 2:2.

q *Jesus, divine sonship of*, Matt. 1:21.

23

r *Confession of Christ*, Luke 12:8.

24

s *Righteous, union of, with Christ*, Psa. 64:10.

t *God dwells with the Righteous*, 1 Kin. 6:13.

* **WORLDLINESS**, Eccl. 8:15; Isa. 56:12; John 15:19; Tit. 3:3; 2 Pet. 2:12–15, 18, 19.
*Proverb of, "Eat and drink, for tomorrow we die,"* Eccl. 2:24; Isa. 22:13; 1 Cor. 15:32. *Tends to poverty*, Prov. 21:17. *Fatal to spirituality*, Gal. 6:8; Phil. 3:19; 1 Tim. 5:6. *Chokes the word*, Matt. 13:22; Mark 4:19; Luke 8:14.
*Leads, to the rejection of the gospel*, Matt. 22:2–6; Luke 14:17–24; *to the rejection of Christ*, John 5:44; 12:43; *to moral insensibility*, Isa. 22:13; 32:9–11; 47:7–9.
*Admonitions against*, Eccl. 7:2–4; 11:9, 10; Matt. 6:19, 25–34; 16:26; Mark 8:36, 37; Luke 21:34; Rom. 12:2; 1 Cor. 7:29–31; 10:6; Col. 3:2, 5; 2 Tim. 2:4, 22; 3:2–9; Tit. 2:12; Jas. 2:1–4; 4:4, 9; 5:5; 1 Pet. 1:14, 24; 2:11; 4:1–4; 1 John 2:15–17. *Denounced*, Isa. 5:11, 12; 47:8, 9, Jude 11–13, 16, 19.
*Moses's choice against*, Heb. 11:24–26.
**Instances of**: *Antediluvians*, Matt. 24:38, 39; Luke 17:26, 27. *Sodomites*, Luke 17:28, 29. *Esau*, Gen. 25:31–34; Heb. 12:16. *Jacob*, Gen. 25:31–34; 27:36; 30:37–43. *Judah*, Gen. 37:26, 27. *Balaam*, 2 Pet. 2:15; Jude 11, with Num. 22. *Eli's sons*, 1 Sam. 2:12–17. *Gehazi*, 2 Kin. 5:20–27. *The disciples*, Matt. 18:1–4; Mark 9:34; Luke 9:46–48. *The rich fool*, Luke 12:16–21. *Dives*, Luke 16:19–25. *The worldly steward*, Luke 16:1–13. *Cretans*, Tit. 1:12.
See footnote, WORLDLY PLEASURE, Eccl. 2:1.

25 And [u,v]this is the promise that he hath promised us, *even* [w,x]eternal life.[S T]

26 These *things* have I written unto you concerning [y]them that [5,z]seduce[G] you.

27 But the [a]anointing which ye have received of him abideth in you, and ye need not that any man [b]teach you: but as the same anointing teacheth you of all things, and is [c]truth, and is no lie, and even as it hath taught you, ye shall [d]abide in him.[T Q]

28 And now, little children, [e]abide in him; that, when he shall [f]appear, we may have [6,g]confidence, and not be ashamed before him at his coming.[Q]

29 If ye know that he is [h]righteous, ye know that every one that [i]doeth [j]righteousness is [k,l]born of him.[T]

## CHAPTER 3

*God's great love to us. 4 The influence of a hope in Christ. 11 We should love one another. 19 How we may know that we are of the truth, 22 and shall receive what we ask.*

BEHOLD, what manner of [a]love the [b]Father hath bestowed upon us, that we should be called [1]the [c,d]sons of God: therefore the world knoweth[G] us not, because it [e]knew[G] him not.[T S]

2 [f]Beloved, now are we [2]the [c,d]sons of God, and it doth not yet appear what we shall be: but we [g]know that, when he shall [h]appear, [i]we shall be like him; for we shall see him as he is.[T Q]

3 And every man that hath this [j]hope in him [k,l]purifieth himself, even as he is [m,n]pure.[S T]

4 [3]Whosoever committeth [o]sin transgresseth also the [p]law: for sin is the transgression[G] of the law.[T]

5 [T]And ye know[G] that he was manifested [q]to [r]take away our sins; and in him is [s]no sin.[Q]

6 Whosoever [t]abideth in him [t,u]sinneth[G] not: whosoever [o]sinneth[G] hath [e]not seen him, neither [4]known him.

7 Little children, let no man [5]deceive you: he that [v]doeth [w]righteousness is righteous, even [x,y]as he is [z,a]righteous.

8 [b]He that committeth [c]sin is of the [d]devil; for the devil sinneth from the beginning. For this purpose the [e]Son of God was [f]manifested, [g]that he might destroy the works of the devil.[S]

9 [h]Whosoever is [6,i]born of God doth [j,k]not commit[G] sin; for his seed remaineth in him: and he cannot sin, because he is [6]born of God.[T]

10 In this the [h]children of God are manifest, and the [b]children of the devil: whosoever [b]doeth not [l]righteousness is not of God, neither he that [m]loveth not his brother.[S T]

11 For this is the message that ye heard from the beginning, that we should [m,n]love[G] one another.

12 Not as [o]Cain, [7]*who* was of that [p]wicked one, and [q,r]slew[G] his [s]brother. And [t,u]wherefore slew he him? Because his own works were evil, and his brother's righteous.[Q]

13 Marvel not, my brethren, if the world [v]hate you.

14 We [w]know that we have [i]passed from *death unto [x]life,

**25**
u *Promise, to the righteous*, 2 Cor. 1:20.
v *Righteous, promises to*, Psa. 64:10.
w *Immortality*, 1 Cor. 15:54.
x *Life, everlasting*, Eccl. 8:15.

**26**
y *Temptation, sources of, false teachers*, Luke 11:4.
z *Influence, evil*, 1 Cor. 7:14.
5 R. V. would lead you astray.

**27**
a *Anointing, figurative*, Deut. 28:40.
b *Wisdom, spiritual*, Prov. 2:2.
c *Truth, of the gospel*, John 18:37.
d *Righteous, union of, with Christ*, Psa. 64:10.

**28**
e *Commandment, enjoining abiding in Christ*, Deut. 8:2.
f *Jesus, second coming of*, Matt. 1:21.
g *Boldness of the Righteous*, Phil. 1:20.
6 R. V. boldness,

**29**
h *Jesus, holiness of*, Matt. 1:21.
i *Obedience*, Heb. 5:8.
j *Righteousness*, Psa. 15:2.
k *Regeneration*, Tit. 3:5.
l *Righteous, described*, Psa. 64:10.

**1**
a *God, love of*, Gen. 2:2.
b *God, fatherhood of*, Gen. 2:2.
c *Spiritual Adoption*, Rom. 8:15.
d *Righteous, described*, Psa. 64:10.
e *Spiritual Blindness*, 2 Cor. 4:4.
1 R. V. children of God: and such we are.

**4**
p *Law*, Deut. 33:2.

**5**
q *Jesus, mission of*, Matt. 1:21.
r *Atonement, by Jesus*, Lev. 17:11.
s *Jesus, holiness of*, Matt. 1:21.

**6**
t *Righteous, union of, with Christ*, Psa. 64:10.
u *Sinlessness*, 1 John 5:18.
4 R. V. knoweth

**7**
v *Obedience*, Heb. 5:8.
w *Righteousness*, Psa. 15:2.
x *Example, Christ our*, John 13:15.
y *Jesus, our example*, Matt. 1:21.
z *God, righteousness of* (a possible interpretation), Gen. 2:2.
a *Jesus, perfections of* (a probable interpretation), Matt. 1:21.
5 R. V. lead you astray:

**8**
b *Wicked, described*, Psa. 73:3.
c *Sin, transgression of the law*, Rom. 5:12.
d *Satan, kingdom of, to be destroyed*, Matt. 4:10.
e *Jesus, divine sonship of*, Matt. 1:21.
f *Jesus, incarnation of*, Matt. 1:21.
g *Jesus, mission of*, Matt. 1:21.

**9**
h *Righteous, described*, Psa. 64:10.
i *Regeneration*, Tit. 3:5.
j *Holiness*, Ex. 39:30.
k *Sinlessness*, 1 John 5:18.
6 R. V. begotten

**10**
l *Righteousness*, Psa. 15:2.
m *Love, of man for man*, 1 John 4:7.

**2** f *Minister, love of, for the church*, Rom. 15:16. g *Assurance, of acceptance*, Heb. 10:22. h *Jesus, second coming of*, Matt. 1:21. i *Promise, or Ground of Assurance*, 2 Cor. 1:20. 2 R. V. children of God, and it is not yet made manifest what we shall be. We know that, if he shall be manifested, we shall **3** j *Hope, of eternal life*, Prov. 13:12. k *Purity, of heart*, 1 Tim. 4:12. l *Holiness*, Ex. 39:30. m *God, holiness of* (as some interpret), Gen. 2:2. n *Jesus, perfections of* (as some interpret), Matt. 1:21.

**4** o *Sin, transgression of the law*, Rom. 5:12. 3 R. V. Every one that doeth sin doeth also lawlessness: and sin is lawlessness.

**11** n *Commandment, enjoining love for man*, Deut. 8:2.

**12** o *Cain*, Gen. 4:1. p *Satan*, Matt. 4:10. q *Homicide, felonious*, Deut. 5:17. r *Persecution, of the righteous*, John 15:20. s *Abel*, Gen. 4:2. t *Malice*, Eph. 4:31. u *Motive, sinful, illustrated by Cain*, Psa. 106:8. 7 R. V. was of the evil one.

**13** v *Hatred*, Prov. 15:17.

**14** w *Assurance, of acceptance*, Heb. 10:22. x *Life, spiritual*, Eccl. 8:15.

***SPIRITUAL DEATH,** alienation from the life of God; a state of condemnation, Rom. 7:9, 11; 8:5, 6, 13; Eph. 4:18. *Quickening from*, John 5:24-26; Rom. 5:12, 15; Eph. 2:1, 5, 6; 5:14; Col. 2:13. See footnotes: DEATH, Num. 23:10; SECOND DEATH, Rev. 20:6.

*y Righteousness, fruits of,* Psa. 15:2.
8 R. V. *omits* his brother

**15**
*z Immortality,* 1 Cor. 15:54.

**16**
*a Jesus, love of,* Matt. 1:21.
*b Example, Christ our,* John 13:15.
*c Jesus, vicarious death of,* Matt. 1:21.
*d Jesus, design of his death,* Matt. 1:21.
*e Commandment, enjoining suffering one for another,* Deut. 8:2.
*f Vicarious Sufferings,* Rom. 9:3.
9 R. V. know we love, because

**17**
*g Alms, giving of,* Matt. 6:2.
*h Liberality, enjoined,* 1 Tim. 6:18.
*i Kindness, enjoined,* Acts 28:2.
*j Poor, liberality to,* Prov. 21:13.
*k Riches, benevolent use of, required,* Eccl. 4:8.
*l Selfishness,* 2 Tim. 3:2.
*m Parsimony,* Mal. 3:8.
*n Sympathy,* 1 Pet. 3:8.
*o Love, for God,* 1 John 4:19.

**18**
*p Love, of man for man,* 1 John 4:7.
*q Sincerity,* 1 Cor. 5:8.
*r Works, good,* 2 Tim. 1:9.

**19**
*s Assurance,* Heb. 10:22.
*t Truth, of the gospel,* John 18:37.

**20**
*u Conscience, guilty,* Acts 23:1.
*v God, knowledge of,* Gen. 2:2.

**21**
*w Conscience, approving,* Acts 23:1.
10 R. V. boldness

**22**
*x Prayer, answer to,* Acts 6:4.
*y Obedience,* Heb. 5:8.

because we [m, y]love[G] the brethren.
He that loveth[G] not [8]*his* brother
abideth in *death.
15 Whosoever [i, v]hateth his
brother is a [q]murderer: and ye
know that no murderer hath
[z]eternal life abiding[G] in him.
16[S] Hereby [9]perceive we the
[a]love *of God*, [b]because he [c]laid
down his life [d]for us: and [e]we
ought to [f]lay down *our* lives for
the brethren.[T]
17 [g, h, i, j]But whoso hath this
world's [k]good, and seeth his
brother have need, and [l, m]shut-
teth up his bowels *of* [n]*compassion* from him, how dwelleth the
[o]love of God in him?[S Q]
18 My little children, let us not
[p]love in word, neither in tongue;
but [q]in [r]deed and in truth.[S]
19 And hereby we [s]know[G] that
we are of the [t]truth, and shall
assure our hearts before him.[S]
20 For if our [u]heart condemn
us, God is greater than our
heart, and [v]knoweth[G] all things.[S]
21 Beloved, if our [w]heart condemn us not, *then* have we [10]con-
fidence toward God.
22 And whatsoever we ask, [x]we
receive of him, because we [y]keep[G]
his commandments, and do
those things that are pleasing
in his sight.[T]
23[T] And this is his commandment, That [z, a]we should believe
on the name of his [b]Son Jē'ṣus
Christ, and [c]love one another, as
he gave us commandment.[S]
24 And he that [d]keepeth his commandments [e]dwelleth in him,
and he [f]in him. And hereby we
know that he abideth in us, by
the [g]Spirit which he hath given
us.[T]

## CHAPTER 4

*They are not to believe every spirit. 2 How they may know the spirit that is of God. 7 An exhortation to love one another. 15 God dwells in those who confess that Jesus is his Son.*

BELOVED, [a]believe[G] not every spirit, but try the spirits whether they are of God: because many [b, c]false prophets are
gone out into the world.
2[T] Hereby know ye the [d]Spirit of
God: Every spirit that [e, f]con-
fesseth that Jē'ṣus Christ is [g]come
in the flesh is of God:
3 And every [h]spirit [1]that [i]con-
fesseth not that Jē'ṣus Christ is
[g]come in the flesh is not of God:
and this is that *spirit* of [j]anti-
christ,[G] whereof ye have heard
that it should come; and even
now already is it in the world.[T]
4 Ye are [k]of God, little children, and have [l, m]overcome
[j]them: because greater is [n]he
that is [o]in you, than [p]he that
is in the world.
5 They are [q]of the world: therefore speak they of the world, and
the world heareth[G] them.
6 We are [k]of God: he that
[r]knoweth God heareth us; he
that is [q]not of God heareth not
us. Hereby know[G] we the [l]spirit
of truth, and the [h]spirit of +error.[T]
7[S] Beloved, let us †love one another: for love is of God; and
every one that loveth is [2, k, s]born
of God, and [r]knoweth God.[T]
8 He that †loveth not [t]knoweth
not God; for God is [u]love.[T]
9[T] [3]In this was manifested the
[u]love of God toward [v]us, because
that God [u]sent his only begotten

*g Holy Spirit,* Acts 1:2.

**1**
*a Watchfulness, enjoined, against false teachers,* Matt. 24:42.
*b False Teachers,* 2 Pet. 2:1.
*c Temptation, sources of, false teachers,* Luke 11:4.

**2**
*d Holy Spirit,* Acts 1:2.
*e Confession of Christ,* Luke 12:8.
*f Faith in Christ,* John 6:69.
*g Jesus, incarnation of,* Matt. 1:21.

**3**
*h Unbelief,* Heb. 3:12.
*i Jesus, rejected,* Matt. 1:21.
*j Antichrist,* 2 John 7.
1 R. V. which confesseth not Jesus is not of God:

**4**
*k Righteous, described,* Psa. 64:10.
*l Temptation, resistance to,* Luke 11:4.
*m Righteousness, fruits of,* Psa. 15:2.
*n God dwells with the Righteous* (according to some interpreters), 1 Kin. 6:13.
*o Righteous, union of, with Christ* (according to some interpreters), Psa. 64:10.
*p Satan,* Matt. 4:10.

**5**
*q Wicked, described,* Psa. 73:3.

**6**
*r Wisdom, spiritual,* Prov. 2:2.

**7**
*s Regeneration,* Tit. 3:5.
2 R. V. begotten

**8**
*t Spiritual Blindness,* 2 Cor. 4:4.

**23** *z Commandment, enjoining faith in Christ, and love for man,* Deut. 8:2.—*a Faith in Christ, enjoined,* John 6:69. *b Jesus, divine sonship of,* Matt. 1:21. *c Love, of man for man,* 1 John 4:7.
**24** *d Obedience,* Heb. 5:8. *e Righteous, union of, with God,* Psa. 64:10. *f God dwells with the Righteous,* 1 Kin. 6:13.

*u God, love of,* Gen. 2:2.
**9** *v Wicked, God's love for,* Psa. 73:3. **3** R. V. Herein was the love of God manifested in us,

**+ERROR,** 2 Thess. 2:11; 1 Tim. 4:1, 2. *The false doctrines taught by those who rejected the divine sonship and lordship of Jesus, antichrist,* 1 John 2:21, 27; 4:6.

**† LOVE,** 1 Cor. 13; 14:1; Col. 1:8; 2:2; 1 Thess. 1:3; 5:8; 1 Tim. 6:11; 2 Tim. 1:7; Philemon 5; Heb. 10:24; 1 John 4:7, 16–18.
The theme of the Song of Solomon, and usually interpreted as an allegory representing the love of the Messiah for the church and of his church for the Messiah, Song of Solomon chapters 1–8.

**Of man for man,** Rom. 5:7; Jas. 1:27. *Defined,* Luke 10:25–37; 1 Cor. 13:1–13. *Is edifying,* 1 Cor. 8:1. *Is precious,* Prov. 15:17. *Is unquenchable,* Prov. 17:17; Song 8:6, 7. *Is a fruit of the Spirit,* Gal. 5:22. *Promotes peace,* Prov. 10:12; 17:9. *Is a proof, of discipleship of Jesus,* John 13:34, 35; *of regeneration,* 1 John 3:14, 19.

*w Jesus, divine sonship of,* Matt. 1:21.
*x Jesus, mission of,* Matt. 1:21.
*y Life, spiritual,* Eccl. 8:15.
*z Jesus, atonement by,* Matt. 1:21.

**10**
*a Propitiation,* Rom. 3:25.
*b Atonement, by Jesus,* Lev. 17:11.
*c Sin,* Rom. 5:12.

**11**
*d God, love of,* Gen. 2:2.

**12**
*e God, invisible,* Gen. 2:2.
*f God dwells with the Righteous,* 1 Kin. 6:13.
*g God, love of* (as some interpret), Gen. 2:2.
*h Love, for God* (as some interpret), see footnote below, in second column.

**13**
*i Assurance,* Heb. 10:22.
*j Righteous, union of, with God,* Psa. 64:10.
*k Holy Spirit,* Acts 1:2.

**14**
*l Witnessing for Christ,* Luke 24:48.
*m God, fatherhood of,* Gen. 2:2.
*n Jesus, divine sonship of,* Matt. 1:21. *o Jesus, savior,* Matt. 1:21. **15** *p Confession of Christ,* Luke 12:8. **16** *q Faith, exemplified,* Mark 11:22.

[w]Son into the world, [x]that we
might [y]live [z]through him.
10 Herein is love, not that we
‡loved God, but that he [u]loved
us, and sent his [w,z]Son [x]*to be* the
[a,b]propitiation[G] for our [c]sins.[S T]
11 Beloved, if God so [d]loved us,
we ought also to †love one another.
12 [e]No man hath seen God at
any time. If we †love one another, God [f]dwelleth in us, and
his [g,h]love is perfected[G] in us.[S]
13 Hereby [i]know[G] we that we
[j]dwell[G] in him, and he [j]in us, because he hath given us of his
[k]Spirit.[T]
14 And we have seen and do
[l]testify[G] that the [m]Father sent the
[n]Son *to be* the [o]Saviour of the
world.[T]
15 Whosoever shall [p]confess[G]
that Jē'ṣus is the [n]Son of God,
God [j]dwelleth in him, and he
[j]in God.[S T]
16 And we have known[G] and
[q]believed the [d]love that God
hath to us. God is love; and he
that dwelleth in †love [j]dwelleth
in God, and God [j]in him.[S]
17[S] Herein is cur ‡love made
[r]perfect,[G] that we may have [s]boldness in the day of [t]judgment: because [u]as he is, [v]so are we in this
world.
18 There is no fear in ‡love;
but perfect love casteth out fear:
because fear hath [4]torment. He
that feareth is not made [r]perfect
in love.[S]
19 We ‡love [5]him, because he
first [d]loved us.[S]
20[T] If a man [w]say, I ‡love God,
and [x]hateth his brother, he is
a [y]liar: for he that †loveth not
his brother whom he hath seen,
[6]how can he love God [z]whom he
hath not seen?
21 And this commandment
have we from him, That he who
‡loveth God †love his brother
also.[S T]

## CHAPTER 5

*He that is born of God believes that Jesus is the Christ, loves the children of God, 4 and overcomes the world. 10 The believer has eternal life through Christ. 14 His confidence in him. 17 All unrighteousness is sin.*

WHOSOEVER [a]believeth
that Jē'ṣus is the [b]Chrīst
is [1,c,d]born of God: and every
one that [e]loveth him that begat
[f,g]loveth him also that is begotten of him.[T]
2 By[T] this we know[G] that we [j]love[G]

**17**
*r Perfection,* Heb. 6:1.
*s Boldness of the Righteous,* Phil. 1:20.
*t Judgment, general,* 2 Pet. 3:7.
*u Jesus, our example,* Matt. 1:21.
*v Example, Christ our,* John 13:15.

**18**
4 R. V. punishment;

**19**
5 R. V. *omits* him

**20**
*w Hypocrisy,* Jas. 3:17.
*x Hatred,* Prov. 15:17.
*y Falsehood,* Job 21:34.
*z God, invisible,* Gen. 2:2.
6 R. V. cannot love God whom he hath not seen

**1**
*a Faith in Christ,* John 6:69.
*b Jesus, Messiah,* Matt. 1:21.
*c Regeneration,* Tit. 3:5.
*d Righteous, described,* Psa. 64:10.
*e Love, for God,* 1 John 4:19.
*f Love, of man for man,* 1 John 4:7.
*g Righteousness, fruits of,* Psa. 15:2.
1 R. V. begotten

*Enjoined,* Lev. 19:18; Matt. 5:40–42; 7:12; 19:19; 22:39, 40; Mark 12:30–33; Luke 6:30–38; Rom. 12:9, 15; 13:8–10; 1 Cor. 10:24; 16:14; Gal. 6:1, 2, 10; Eph. 4:2, 32; 5:2; Phil. 1:9; Col. 3:14; 1 Thess. 3:12; 1 Tim. 1:5; 4:12; 6:11; 2 Tim. 2:22; Jas. 2:8; 2 Pet. 1:7; 1 John 4:20, 21.

*Enjoined, toward strangers,* Lev. 19:34; Deut. 10:19; *toward enemies,* Prov. 24:17; Matt. 5:43–48; Luke 6:35; Rom. 12: 14, 20; *toward fellow-Christians,* John 13:14, 15, 34, 35; 15: 12, 13, 17; Rom. 12:9, 10, 15, 16; 14:19, 21; 15:1, 2, 5, 7; 16: 1, 2; 1 Cor. 14:1; 2 Cor. 8:7, 8; Gal. 5:13, 14; 6:1, 2, 10; Eph. 4:2, 32; Phil. 2:2; Col. 2:2; 3:12–14; 1 Thess. 3:12; 5:8, 11, 14; 1 Tim. 6:2; Philemon 16; Heb. 10:24; 13:13; 1 Pet. 1:22; 2:17; 3:8, 9; 4:8; 2 Pet. 1:7; 1 John 3:11, 14, 16–19, 23; 4:7, 11, 12, 20, 21; 2 John 5. *Demonstrated by obedience,* 1 John 5:1, 2.

*Rewards of,* Matt. 10:41, 42; 25:34–40, 46; Mark 9:41; 1 John 2:10.

EXEMPLIFIED: *By Paul,* Acts 26:29; Rom. 1:11, 12; 9: 1–3; 1 Cor. 4:9–16; 8:13; 2 Cor. 1:3–6, 14, 23, 24; 2:4; 3:2; 4:5; 6:4–6, 11–13; 7:1–4; 11:2; 12:14–16, 19–21; 13:9; Gal. 4:19, 20: Eph. 3:13; Phil. 1:3–5, 7, 8, 23–26; 2:19; 4:1; Col. 1:3, 4, 24, 28, 29; 2:1, 5; 4:7; 1 Thess. 2:7, 8, 11, 12, 17–20; 3:5, 7–10, 12; 2 Thess. 1:4; 2 Tim. 1:3, 4, 8; 2:10; Tit. 3:15; Philemon 9, 12, 16.

See footnote, FRATERNITY, Zech. 11:14.

INSTANCES OF: *Abraham for Lot,* Gen. 14:14–16. *Moses for Israel,* Ex. 32:31, 32. *David and Jonathan,* 1 Sam. 18:1; 20:17. *Israel and Judah for David,* 1 Sam. 18:16. *David's subjects for David,* 2 Sam. 15:30; 17:27–29. *Hiram for David,* 1 Kin. 5:1. *Obadiah for the prophets,* 1 Kin. 18:4. *Nehemiah for Israelites,* Neh. 5:10–18. *Job's friends,* Job 42:11. *Centurion for his servant,* Luke 7:2–6. *Good Samaritan,* Luke 10:29–37. *Stephen,* Acts 7:60. *Roman Christians for Paul,* Acts 28:15. *Priscilla and Aquila for Paul,* Rom. 16:3, 4.

**Of man for woman:** *Isaac for Rebekah,* Gen. 24:67. *Jacob for Rachel,* Gen. 29:20, 30. *Shechem for Dinah,* Gen. 34:3, 12. *Boaz for Ruth,* Ruth chapters 2–4.

‡ **LOVE. For God:** *Defined,* 1 John 5:3; 2 John 6. *Incompatible, with love of the world,* 1 John 2:15; *with hatred of brother,* 1 John 4:20, 21; *with guilty fear,* 2 Tim. 1:7; 1 John 4:18. *Reasons for,* Psa. 116:1; 1 John 4:19.

*The gift of God,* Deut. 30:6; 2 Tim. 1:7.

*Enjoined,* Deut. 6:5; 10:12; 11:1, 13, 22; 19:9; 30:16, 19, 20; Josh. 22:5; 23:11; Psa. 31:23; Prov. 23:26; Matt. 22:37, 38; Mark 12:29, 30, 32, 33; Luke 11:42; 2 Thess. 3:5; Jude 21. *Tested,* Deut. 13:3. *Obedience proof of,* 1 John 2:5; 5:1, 2; 2 John 6.

*Leads to liberality,* 1 John 3:17, 18. *Rewards of,* Ex. 20:6; Deut. 5:10; 7:9; Psa. 37:4; 69:35, 36; 91:14; 145:20; Isa. 56: 6, 7; Jer. 2:2, 3; Rom. 8:28; 1 Cor. 8:3.

*Exemplified,* Psa. 18:1; 63:5, 6; 73:25, 26; 103.

**For Jesus:** *Enjoined,* Matt. 10:37, 38; John 15:9; 1 Cor. 16:22. *Love of God produces,* John 8:42. *Obedience results from,* John 14:15, 21, 23; 2 Cor. 5:6, 8, 14, 15.

*Rewards of,* Matt. 25:34–40, 46; Mark 9:41; Luke 7:37–50; John 16:27; Eph. 6:24; 2 Tim. 4:8; Heb. 6:10; Jas. 1: 12; 2:5.

INSTANCES OF LOVE FOR JESUS: *Mary,* Matt. 26:6–13; Luke 10:39; John 12:3–8. *Peter,* Matt. 17:4; John 13:37; 18: 10; 20:3–6; 21:15–17. *The healed demoniac,* Mark 5:18; Luke 8:38. *Thomas,* John 11:16. *The disciples,* Mark 16:10; Luke 24:17–41; John 16:27; 20:20. *Mary Magdalene and other disciples,* Matt. 27:55, 56, 61; 28:1–9; Luke 8:2, 3; 23: 27, 55, 56; 24:1–10; John 20:1, 2, 11–18. *Joseph of Arimathea,* Matt. 27:57–60. *Nicodemus,* John 19:39, 40. *Women of Jerusalem,* Luke 23:27. *Paul,* Acts 21:13; Phil. 1:20, 21, 23; 3:7, 8; 2 Tim. 4:8.

the [d]children of God, when we
[e]love[G] God, and [2,h]keep[G] his [i]com-
mandments.
3[S] For this is the [e]love of God,
that we [h]keep[G] his [i]command-
ments: and his commandments
are not grievous.[T Q]
4 For whatsoever is [1,c,d]born of
God [j]overcometh the world: and
this is the victory that overcom-
eth the world, *even* our [a]faith.[T]
5 Who is he that [j]overcometh
the world, but he that [a]believeth
that Jē'sus is the [k]Son of God[S]?
6[T] This is he that came by
[l]water and [m,n]blood, *even* Jē'sus
[b]Chrīst; not by water only, but
by water and blood. And it is
the [o]Spirit that beareth witness,
because the Spirit is truth.[S]
7 [3]For there are three that bear
record in heaven, the Father, the
Word, and the Holy Ghost[G]: and
these three are one.[T]
8 And there are three that bear
witness [4]in earth, the [o]spirit, and
the [l]water, and the [m,n]blood: and
these three agree in one.
9 If we receive the witness of
men, the [p]witness of God is
greater: for this is the witness
of God which he hath testified[G]
of his [k]Son.
10[T] He that [a]believeth on the
[k]Son of God hath the witness in
himself: he that [q]believeth not
God hath made him a liar; because he believeth not the [5]rec-
ord that God gave of his Son.[S]
11 And this is the [5]record, that
God hath given to us [r,s]eternal
life, and this life is in his [k]Son.
12 He that [t,u]hath the [k]Son
hath [r,s]life; *and* he that hath not
the Son of God hath not life.[T]
13 These things have I written
unto you [6]that [v]believe on the
[w]name of the [k]Son of God;
[x,y]that ye may know[G] that ye
have [r,s]eternal life, and that ye
may [v]believe on the name of the
Son of God.[S]
14 And this is the [7,z]confidence
that we have in him, that, if we
ask any thing according to his
[a]will, [b,c]he heareth us:[T]
15 And if we [d]know[G] that he
hear us, whatsoever we ask, we
know that we have the petitions
that we desired of him.
16 If any man see his brother
sin a sin *which is* not unto death,
he shall [e]ask, and [8]he shall [f]give
him life for them that sin not
unto death. There is a [g]sin unto
death: [9]I do not say that he shall
pray for it.
17 [h]All unrighteousness[G] is sin:
and there is a sin not unto death.
18 We know that whosoever
is [10,i,j]born of God [*,k]sinneth
not; but he that is begotten of
God keepeth[G] himself, and [11]that
[l]wicked one toucheth him not.[S]
19 *And* we know that we are [j]of
God, and the whole world lieth
in [11]wickedness.[G S]
20 And we know[G] that the Son of
God is come, and hath given us
an [m]understanding, that we may
know[G] him that is [n]true, and we
are [o]in him that is true, *even*
in his Son Jē'sus [p]Chrīst. This
is the true [q,r]God, and eternal
life.[S T]
21 Little children, [s,t]keep[G S] yourselves from idols. Amen.

**2**
h *Obedience, a proof of love,* Heb. 5:8.
i *Will of God,* Mark 3:35.
2 R. V. do

**4**
j *Temptation, resistance to,* Luke 11:4.

**5**
k *Jesus, divine sonship of,* Matt. 1:21.

**6**
l *Jesus, baptism of* (as some interpret), Matt. 1:21.
m *Blood, of Jesus, atoning,* Heb. 9:19.
n *Jesus, atoning blood of,* Matt. 1:21.
o *Holy Spirit, Jesus anointed and led by,* Acts 1:2.

**7**
3 R. V. *omits this verse.*

**8**
4 R. V. *omits* in earth

**9**
p Matt. 3:17 (with Mark 1:11; Luke 3:22; John 1:33); 17:5; Luke 9:28.

**10**
q *Unbelief,* Heb. 3:12.
5 R. V. witness

**11**
*Life, spiritual,* Eccl. 8:15.
*Immortality,* 1 Cor. 15:54.

**12**
t *Righteous, union of, with Christ,* Psa. 64:10.
u *Fellowship, with Christ,* 1 Cor. 1:9.

**13**
v *Faith in Christ,* John 6:69.
w *Name of Jesus,* John 14:13.
x *Promise, or Ground of Assurance,* 2 Cor. 1:20.
y *Righteous, promises to,* Psa. 64:10.
6 R. V. *omits* that believe on the name of the Son of God;

**14**
z *Assurance, of answer to prayer,* Heb. 10:22.

a *Will of God,* Mark 3:35.
b *Prayer, answer to, promised,* Acts 6:4.
c *Promise, or Ground of Assurance,* 2 Cor. 1:20.
7 R. V. boldness

**15**
d *Assurance, of answer to prayer,* Heb. 10:22.

**16**
e *Intercession, of man with God,* Jer. 27:18.
f *Sin, forgiveness of,* Rom. 5:12.
g *Unpardonable Sin,* Matt. 12:31.
8 R. V. God will give
9 R. V. not concerning this do I say that he should make request.

**17**
h *Sin, defined,* Rom. 5:12.

**18**
i *Regeneration,* Tit. 3:5.
j *Righteous, described,* Psa. 64:10.
k *Holiness,* Ex. 39:30.
l *Satan,* Matt. 4:10.
10 R. V. begotten
11 R. V. the evil one.

**20**
m *Wisdom, spiritual,* Prov. 2:2. n *Jesus, perfections of,* Matt. 1:21. o *Righteous union of, with Christ,* Psa. 64:10. p *Jesus, Messiah,* Matt. 1:21. q *God, the Father* (as some interpret), Gen. 2:2. r *Jesus* (as some interpret), Matt. 1:21. **21** s *Commandment, forbidding idolatry,* Deut. 8:2. t *Idolatry, forbidden,* 1 Sam. 15:23.

* **SINLESSNESS,** Psa. 119:3; Acts 24:16; Phil. 1:9–11; 1 Thess. 3:13; 5:23; 1 Pet. 4:1, 2; 1 John 1:8, 10; 3:6, 9; 5:18.

THE SECOND EPISTLE OF

# JOHN

*The apostle's salutation to the elect lady and her children, and his prayer to God for them. 4 His rejoicing. 5 He exhorts her to persevere in Christian love, 7 and not to receive false teachers. 9 He defines the doctrine of Christ, and warns against false teachers.*

THE [a]elder unto the elect
[b]lady and her children,
whom I love in the truth; and
not I only, but also all they that
have known the [c]truth;
2 For the [c]truth's sake, which
dwelleth in us, and shall be with
us for ever.
3 [d,e]Grace be with [1]you, [f]mercy,
*and* [g]peace, from God the [h]Fa-
ther, and from [2]the Lord Jē'şus
[i]Christ, the [j]Son of the Father,
in truth and love.
4 I rejoiced greatly that I found
of thy children [k]walking in
[c]truth, as we have received a commandment from the [h]Father.
5 And [l]now I beseech thee,
[b]lady, not as though I wrote a
new commandment unto thee,
but that which we had from the
beginning, that we [m,n]love one
another.
6 And this is [o]love, that we
[p]walk after his commandments.
This is the commandment, That,
as ye have heard from the beginning, ye should walk in it.
7 For many [q]deceivers are entered into the world, who [r]con-
fess not that Jē'şus [i]Christ [3]is
come [s]in the flesh. This is a deceiver and an *antichrist.
8 [t,u]Look to yourselves, that
[4]we [v]lose not those things which
we have wrought, but that [4]we
receive a full [w]reward.
9 Whosoever [5]transgresseth, and
[u,x]abideth not in the [6,y]doctrine
of Christ, hath not God. He
that [z]abideth in the [6]doctrine
of Christ, he [a,b]hath both the
[c]Father and the [d]Son.
10 [e]If there come any unto you,
and bring not this [6,f]doctrine,
[g,h,i,j]receive him not into *your*
house, [7]neither bid him God
speed:
11 For he that biddeth him
God speed is [k]partaker of his
evil deeds.
12 Having many things to write
unto you, I would not *write* with
paper and ink: but I trust to
come unto you, and speak face
to face, that [8]our joy may be
full.
13 The children of thy elect
sister [l]greet thee. Amen.

**1**
*a* *Elders*, Acts 14:23.
*b* *Church, Christian* (as some interpret), Matt. 16:18.
*c* *Truth, of the gospel*, John 18:37.
**3**
*d* *Benedictions, apostolic*, Deut. 21:5.
*e* *Grace of God*, Rom. 4:16.
*f* *God, mercy of*, Gen. 2:2.
*g* *Spiritual Peace*, Gal. 1:3.
*h* *God, fatherhood of*, Gen. 2:2.
*i* *Jesus, Messiah*, Matt. 1:21.
*j* *Jesus, divine sonship of*, Matt. 1:21.
1 R. V. us,
2 R. V. *omits* the Lord
**4**
*k* *Righteous, described*, Psa. 64:10.
**5**
*l* *Minister, love of, for the church*, Rom. 15:16.
*m* *Commandment, enjoining love*, Deut. 8:2.
*n* *Love, of man for man*, 1 John 4:7.
**6**
*o* *Love, for God*, 1 John 4:19.
*p* *Obedience, a proof of love*, Heb. 5:8.
**7**
*q* *False Teachers*, 2 Pet. 2:1.
*r* *Jesus, rejected*, Matt. 1:21.
*s* *Jesus, incarnation of*, Matt. 1:21.
3 R. V. cometh
**8**
*t* *Watchfulness, enjoined, against apostasy*, Matt. 24:42.
*u* *Apostasy*, Acts 1:25.
*v* *Steadfastness*, 1 Cor. 15:58.
*w* *Reward, a motive, to faithfulness*, Matt. 5:12.
4 R. V. ye
**9**
*x* *Wicked, described*, Psa. 73:3.
*y* *Doctrines of Jesus*, John 7:16.
*z* *Righteous, described*, Psa. 64:10.
*a* *Righteous, union of, with God*, Psa. 64:10.
*b* *Righteous, union of, with Christ*, Psa. 64:10.
*c* *God, fatherhood of*, Gen. 2:2.
*d* *Jesus, divine sonship of*, Matt. 1:21.
5 R. V. goeth onward
6 R. V. teaching

**10** *e* *Church, discipline in*, Matt. 16:18. *f* *Doctrines of Jesus*, John 7:16. *g* *Evil Company, forbidden*, Prov. 13:20. *h* *Fellowship, with the wicked, forbidden*, 1 Cor. 1:9. *i* *Heresy*, Tit. 3:10. *j* *Disfellowship*, Num. 15:31. 7 R. V. and give him no greeting:
**11** *k* *Complicity*, Prov. 29:24. **12** 8 R. V. your
**13** *l* *Salutations*, Luke 1:44.

* **ANTICHRIST**, 1 John 2:18, 22; 4:3; 2 John 7. *False teachers*, Matt. 24:5, 23, 24, 26; Mark 13:6, 21, 22; Luke 17:23; 21:8. *The man of sin*, 2 Thess. 2:3–12.

# THE THIRD EPISTLE OF

# JOHN

*The apostle commends Gaius for his piety, 5 and hospitality, which had become known to all the churches. 9 The conduct of Diotrephes rebuked. 11 Gaius exhorted to follow that which is good. 12 The character of Demetrius. 14 He hopes to see Gaius, and sends his salutation to him.*

THE [a]elder unto the wellbeloved Gā′ius, whom I [b]love
in the truth.
2 Beloved, I [1]wish above all
things that thou mayest [c]prosper
and be in health, even as thy
soul prospereth.
3 For I rejoiced greatly, when
the brethren came and testified
of the [d]truth that is in thee,
even as thou walkest in the
[e]truth.
4 [f]I have no greater [g]joy than
to hear that my children walk
in [e]truth.
5 [b]Beloved, thou doest [2,d]faith-
fully whatsoever thou [h]doest to
the brethren, and to strangers;
6 Which have borne witness
of thy [3,b,h]charity[G] before the
[i]church: whom if thou bring[G] forward on their journey [4]after a
godly sort,[G] thou shalt do well:
7 Because that for [5]his [j]name's
sake they went forth, [k,l]taking
nothing of the [m]Gĕn′tīleṣ.
8 We therefore ought to [n]re-
ceive such, that we might be
fellowhelpers to the [e]truth.
9 I wrote unto the [i]church:
but [o]Dĭ-ŏt′re-phēṣ, who [p]loveth
to have the preeminence among
them, receiveth us not.
10 Wherefore, if I come, I will
remember his deeds which he
doeth, [q]prating[G] against us with
[r]malicious words: and not content therewith, neither doth he
himself receive the brethren, and
[s]forbiddeth them that would, and
casteth *them* out of the church.
11 [t]Beloved, [6,u,v]follow not that
which is evil, but that which is
good. He that [w,x]doeth good is
[y]of God: but he that doeth evil
hath [z]not seen God.[S]
12 Dē-mē′trĭ-ŭs hath [a]good report of all *men,* and of the truth[G]
itself: yea, and we *also* bear record;[G] and ye know that our record[G]
is true.
13 I had many things to write,
but I will not with ink and [b]pen
write unto thee:
14 But I trust[G] I shall shortly
see thee, and we shall speak face
to face. [c,d]Peace *be* to thee. *Our*
friends salute[G] thee. Greet the
friends by name.[Q]

**1**
a *Elders,* Acts 14:23.
b *Love, of man for man,* 1 John 4:7.

**2**
c *Temporal Blessings, prayer for,* Psa. 103:2.
1 R. V. pray that in all things thou

**3**
d *Faithfulness,* Luke 16:10.
e *Truth, of the gospel,* John 18:37.

**4**
f *Zeal, exemplified,* 2 Cor. 7:11.
g *Minister, joys of,* Rom. 15:16.

**5**
h *Hospitality,* Rom. 12:13.
2 R. V. a faithful work in whatsoever

**6**
i *Church, Christian,* Matt. 16:18.
3 R. V. love
4 R. V. worthily of God:

**7**
j *Name of Jesus,* John 14:13.
k *Minister, emoluments of,* Rom. 15:16.
l *Self-denial,* Mark 8:34.
m *Gentiles,* Acts 10:45.
5 R. V. the sake of the Name

**8**
n *Liberality, enjoined,* 1 Tim. 6:18.

**9**
o *Minister, false and corrupt,* Rom. 15:16.
p *Ambition,* Hab. 2:5.

**10**
q *Speech, evil,* Col. 4:6.
r *Malice,* Eph. 4:31.
s *Presumption,* Psa. 19:13.

**11**
t *Minister, love of, for the church,* Rom. 15:16.
u *Commandment, enjoining holiness,* Deut. 8:2.
v *Holiness, exhortations to,* Ex. 39:30.
w *Righteousness, fruits of,* Psa. 15:2.
x *Works, good,* 2 Tim. 1:9.
y *Righteous, described,* Psa. 64:10.
z *Spiritual Blindness,* 2 Cor. 4:4.
6 R. V. imitate

**12**
a *Character, good,* Phil. 2:15.

**13**
b *Pen,* Jer. 8:8.

**14**
c *Benedictions, apostolic,* Deut. 21:5.
d *Spiritual Peace,* Gal. 1:3.

THE EPISTLE OF

# JUDE

*The apostle's salutation. 3 He exhorts to contend earnestly for the faith. 4 False teachers among them. 5 Their punishment certain. 8 Their character described. 17 Such mockers were foretold. 20 An exhortation to adhere to the truth, 22 and to save others. 24 The apostle concludes with a doxology.*

[a]JUDE, the servant of Jē′ṣus Chrīst, and brother of [b]Jāmeṣ, to them that are [1]sanctified by God the [c]Father, and [2]preserved in Jē′ṣus [d]Chrīst, *and* [e]called:[S]

2 [f,g]Mercy unto you, and [h]peace, and [i]love, be multiplied.

3 [j]Beloved, when I gave all diligence to write unto you of the common [k]salvation,[C] it was needful for me to write unto you, and [l]exhort[C] *you* that ye should earnestly [m]contend for the [n,o]faith which was once delivered unto the saints.

4 For there are certain [p]men crept in unawares, who were before of old [q]ordained[C] to this condemnation, ungodly men, turning the grace of our God into [r]lasciviousness,[C] and [s,t]denying [3]the only Lord God, and our [u]Lord Jē′ṣus Chrīst.[S T]

5 I will therefore put you in remembrance, though ye once knew this, how that the Lord, having [v]saved the people out of the land of [w]Ē′gȳpt, afterward [x,y]destroyed [z]them that believed not.[Q]

6 And the [a]angels which kept not their first[C] estate, but left their own habitation, he hath reserved in everlasting chains under [b]darkness unto the [c]judgment of the great day.[S]

7 Even as [d]Sŏd′om and [e]Gō-mŏr′rhȧ, and the cities about them in like manner, giving themselves over to [f]fornication, and going[C] after strange flesh, are set forth for an example, suffering the [g]vengeance of [b]eternal fire.[Q]

8 Likewise also these *filthy* [h]dreamers defile the flesh, [*,i,j]despise dominion, and [k]speak evil of [l]dignities.[C]

9 Yet [m]Mī′chaēl the [n]archangel, when contending with the [o]devil he disputed about the body of [p]Mō′ṣeṣ, [q]durst[C] not bring against him a [†]railing [4]accusation, but said, The Lord rebuke thee.[Q]

10 But [h]these [5,k]speak evil of those [r]things which they [s]know not: but what they know naturally, as brute beasts, in those things they corrupt themselves.

11 [t,u]Woe unto them! for they have gone in the way of [v]Cāin, and ran [6]greedily after the error of [w]Bā′laam for reward, and perished in the gainsaying of [x]Cō′rē.[Q]

12 [y]These are [7]spots in your [z]feasts of charity,[C] when they feast with you, feeding themselves without fear: clouds *they are* without water, carried about of winds; trees whose fruit withereth, without fruit, twice dead, plucked up by the roots;

---

1

*a* Or, *Judas*, Luke 6:16; Acts 1:13.
*b* *James*, Matt. 10:3.
*c* *God, fatherhood of*, Gen. 2:2.
*d* *Jesus, Messiah*, Matt. 1:21.
*e* *Call, personal*, Phil. 3:14.
1 R. V. called, beloved in God
2 R. V. kept for Jesus Christ:

2

*f* *Benedictions, apostolic*, Deut. 21:5.
*g* *God, mercy of*, Gen. 2:2.
*h* *Spiritual Peace*, Gal. 1:3.
*i* *God, love of*, Gen. 2:2.

3

*j* *Minister, love of, for the church*, Rom. 15:16.
*k* *Salvation*, Acts 16:17.
*l* *Faithfulness*, Luke 16:10.
*m* *Zeal, enjoined*, 2 Cor. 7:11.
*n* *Faith, the doctrines of Jesus*, 1 Cor. 16:13.
*o* *Gospel*, Mark 13:10.

4

*p* *False Teachers*, 2 Pet. 2:1.
*q* *Foreordination*, Rom. 8:30.
*r* *Lasciviousness*, 1 Pet. 4:3.
*s* *Jesus, rejected*, Matt. 1:21.
*t* *Infidelity*, 2 Cor. 6:15.
*u* *Jesus, lordship of*, Matt. 1:21.
3 R. V. our only Master and Lord, Jesus Christ.

5

*v* *God, providence of*, Gen. 2:2.
*w* *Egypt*, Gen. 41:8.
*x* *Unbelieving Israelites destroyed*, Num. 14:11. *y* *Wicked, punishment of*, Psa. 73:3. *z* *Unbelievers*, 1 Cor. 6:6. **6**—*a* *Angel*, Heb. 1:13. *b* *Hell*, Mark 9:43. *c* *Judgment, the general*, 2 Pet. 3:7.

7

*d* *Sodom, wickedness of*, Gen. 13:10.
*e* Or, *Gomorrah, destroyed*, Gen. 13:10.
*f* *Adultery*, Lev. 20:10.
*g* *Punishment*, Lev. 26:41.

8

*h* *False Teachers*, 2 Pet. 2:1.
*i* *Presumption, in despising the lordship of Jesus and the authority of the church* (as some interpret), Psa. 19:13.
*j* *Citizens, wicked and treasonable* (as some interpret), Luke 15:15.
*k* *Speech, evil*, Col. 4:6.
*l* *Rulers, must not be reviled* (as some interpret), Ex. 18:21.

9

*m* *Michael*, Dan. 10:13.
*n* *Angel, of different orders*, Heb. 1:13.
*o* *Satan*, Matt. 4:10.
*p* *Moses*, Ex. 2:10.
*q* *Meekness, instances of*, Psa. 45:4.
4 R. V. judgement,

10

*r* *Truth, of the gospel* (a reasonable interpretation), John 18:37.
*s* *Spiritual Blindness*, 2 Cor. 4:4.
5 R. V. rail at whatsoever things they know not: and what they understand naturally, like the creatures without reason, in these things are they destroyed.

**11** *t* *Covetousness, denounced*, Isa. 57:17. *u* *Worldliness, denounced*, 1 John 2:15. *v* *Cain*, Gen. 4:1. *w* *Balaam*, Deut. 23:4. *x* Or, *Korah*, Num. 16:1. 6 R. V. riotously in the error of Balaam for hire. **12** *y* *Hypocrisy*, Jas. 3:17. *z* 2 Pet. 2:13. 7 R. V. they who are hidden rocks in your love-feasts when they feast with you, shepherds that without fear feed themselves; clouds without water, carried along by winds; autumn trees without fruit,

---

* **ANARCHY**, Isa. 3:5–8. *Insubordinate members of the early church who were hostile to authority, civil, probably, as well as ecclesiastical*, 2 Pet. 2:10–19; Jude 8–13.

† **RAILING**, 1 Tim. 6:4. *Forbidden*, 1 Pet. 3:9. *Abstained from by angels*, 2 Pet. 2:11; Jude 9. *Fellowship with revilers, forbidden*, 1 Cor. 5:11.

**Instances of**, 1 Sam. 25:10, 14; 2 Sam. 16:7; Matt. 27:39–44; Mark 15:29–32.

13 Raging waves of the sea, foaming out their own shame; wandering stars, to [a]whom is reserved the blackness of darkness for ever.[Q]

14 And [b]Ē′nŏch also, the seventh from [c]Ăd′ăm, prophesied [8]of these, saying, Behold, the Lord cometh with ten thousands of his [d]saints,[Q]

15 To execute [e]judgment upon all, and to [9]convince all that are ungodly among them of all their ungodly deeds which they have ungodly committed, and of all their hard *speeches*[G] which ungodly sinners have spoken against him.

16 These are [f]murmurers, complainers, walking after their own [g]lusts; and their mouth speaketh great swelling[G] *words*, [10,h]having men's persons in admiration because of advantage.

17 But,[T] [i]beloved, remember ye the words which were spoken before of the [j]apostles of our [k]Lord Jē′şus Chrīst;

18 How that they told you there should be [l,m]mockers in the last time, who should walk after their own ungodly [g]lusts.[G]

19 These be they who separate themselves, ‡sensual, having not the [n]Spirit.

20 But ye, [i]beloved, [o,p]building up yourselves on your most holy [q]faith, [r]praying in the [s]Holy[G] Ghost,[G]

21 [p,t]Keep[G] yourselves in the [u,v,w]love of God, looking for the[G] mercy of our [k]Lord Jē′şus Chrīst unto [x]eternal life.[S T]

22 And [11]of some have compassion, making a [y]difference:

23 And [12]others save with fear, pulling *them* out of the fire; [z,a]hating even the garment spotted by the flesh.[Q]

24 Now unto him that is able to keep you [b]from [13]falling, and to present *you* [a]faultless before the presence of his glory with exceeding joy,[S]

25 To the only wise [14]God our [c]Saviour, *be* [d,e]glory and majesty, [f]dominion and [g]power, both now and [h]ever. Amen.[S]

**13**
*a Wicked, punishment of,* Psa. 73:3.

**14**
*b Enoch,* Gen. 5:18.
*c Adam,* Gen. 2:19.
*d Angel, functions of,* Heb. 1:13.
8 R. V. to

**15**
*e Judgments,* Ex. 6:6.
9 R. V. convict

**16**
*f Murmuring,* Num. 14:2.
*g Lust,* 2 Pet. 1:4.
*h Respect of Persons,* Prov. 24:23.
10 Am. R. V. showing respect of persons for the sake of advantage.

**17**
*i Minister, love of, for the church,* Rom. 15:16.
*j Apostles,* Luke 6:13.
*k Jesus, lordship of,* Matt. 1:21.

**18**
*l Mocking,* 1 Kin. 18:27.
*m Infidelity, exemplified,* 2 Cor. 6:15.

**19**
*n Holy Spirit,* Acts 1:2.

**20**
*o Growth in Grace,* 2 Pet. 3:18.
*p Faithfulness,* Luke 16:10.
*q Faith, the doctrines of Jesus,* 1 Cor. 16:13.
*r Prayer, enjoined,* Acts 6:4.
*s Holy Spirit, prayer in,* Acts 1:2.

**21**
*t Commandment, enjoining steadfastness,* Deut. 8:2.
*u Love, for God* (as some interpret), 1 John 4:19.
*v God, love of* (as some interpret), Gen. 2:2.
*w Duty, of man to God,* Eccl. 12:13.
*x Life, everlasting,* Eccl. 8:15.

**22**
*y Doubting,* Rom. 14:23.
11 R. V. on some have mercy, who are in doubt;

**23** *z Sin, repugnant to the righteous,* Rom. 5:12.—*a Holiness,* Ex. 39:30. 12 R. V. some save, snatching them out of the fire; and on some have mercy with fear; hating even

**24** *b Steadfastness,* 1 Cor. 15:58. 13 R. V. stumbling,

**25** *c God, savior,* Gen. 2:2. *d God, glory of,* Gen. 2:2. *e Praise,* Psa. 150:1. *f God, sovereign,* Gen. 2:2. *g God, power of,* Gen. 2:2. *h God, eternity of,* Gen. 2:2. 14 R. V. God our Saviour, through Jesus Christ our Lord, be glory, majesty, dominion and power, before all time, and now, and for evermore. Amen.

# THE REVELATION

## OF JOHN

### CHAPTER 1

*The preface. 4 John's salutation to the seven churches of Asia. 7 The coming of Christ. 9 The apostle's vision in Patmos, 17 and its effect on him. 19 What he is commanded to write.*

THE [a,b]Revelation of Jē′şus Chrīst, which God gave unto him, to shew unto his servants things which must shortly come to pass; and he sent and signified *it* by his [c]angel unto his servant [d]Jŏhn:[S Q]

2 Who bare[G] [1]record of the [e]word of God, and of the [b]testimony of Jē′şus Chrīst, and of all things that he saw.

3 Blessed *is* he that readeth, and they that hear the words of this prophecy, and keep those things which are written therein: for the time *is* at hand.

4 [d]John to the [f]seven [g]churches

**1**
*a Jesus, kingdom of, prophecies concerning,* Matt. 1:21.
*b Jesus, revelations by,* Matt. 1:21.
*c Angel, functions of,* Heb. 1:13.
*d John,* Mark 1:19.

**2**
*e Word of God, is inspired,* Psa. 119:9.
1 R. V. witness

**4**
*f Seven,* Gen. 7:2.
*g Church, Christian,* Matt. 16:18.

‡ **SENSUALITY,** Eccl. 2:24; 8:15; 11:9; Jas. 5:5. *Of the glutton,* Isa. 22:13. *Of the drunkard,* Isa. 56:12. *Of the selfish rich,* Luke 12:19, 20; 16:25. *Epicurean philosophy justifies,* Isa. 22:13; 1 Cor. 15:32. See footnotes: ADULTERY, Lev. 20:10; DRUNKENNESS, Luke 21:34; LASCIVIOUSNESS, 1 Pet. 4:3.

which are in [h]Ā′ṣiȧ: [i,j]Grace *be*
unto you, and [k]peace, from [l]him
which is, and which was, and
which is to come; and from the
seven Spirits which are before his
[m]throne;[S T Q]
5 [S T]And from Jē′ṣus Chrīst, *who*
*is* the [n]faithful witness, *and* the
[o,p]first begotten of the dead, and
the [q]prince of the kings of the
earth. Unto him that [r]loved us,
and [2,s,t,u]washed us from our
sins in his own [v,w]blood,
6 And hath made us [3]kings and
[x]priests unto God and his [y]Fa-
ther; to him *be* [z]glory and [a]domin-
ion for [b]ever and ever. Amen.[Q T S]
7 Behold, he cometh with
clouds; and every eye shall
see him, and they *also* which
[c]pierced him: and all [4]kin-
dreds of the earth shall [d,e]wail
because of him. Even so, Amen.[Q]
8 [T][f]I[G] am [g]Ăl′phȧ[G] and [g]Ō-mē′gȧ,
[5]the beginning and the ending,
saith the Lord, which is, and
which was, and which is to come,
the [h]Almighty.[S Q]
9 I [i]Jŏhn, who also am your
brother, and companion in [j]trib-
ulation[G], and in the kingdom and
[k]patience of Jē′ṣus [6]Chrīst, was
in the isle that is called Păt′mos,
for the [l]word of God, and for the
testimony[G] of Jē′ṣus [6]Chrīst.
10 I was in the Spirit on
the [m]Lord's day, and [n]heard
behind me[T] a great voice, as of
a trumpet,
11 [n]Saying, [7]I[G] am [g]Ăl′phȧ and
[g]Ō-mē′gȧ, the first and the last:
and, What thou seest, write in a
book, and send *it* unto the [o]seven
churches [8]which are in Ā′ṣiȧ; unto [p]Ĕph′e-sŭs, and unto [q]Smy̆r′-
nȧ, and unto [r]Pĕr′ga-mŏs, and
unto [s]Thy̆-a-tī′rȧ, and unto [t]Sär′-
dĭs, and unto [u]Phĭl-a-dĕl′phĭ-ȧ,
and unto [v]Lā-ŏd-ĭ-çē′ȧ.[S]
12 And I turned to see the voice
that spake with me. And being
turned, I [w]saw [x]seven golden
[y]candlesticks[G];
13 [Q]And in the midst of the
[x]seven [y]candlesticks[G] *one* like
unto [9]the Son of man, clothed
with a garment down to the
foot, and girt[G] about the paps[G]
with a golden girdle.
14 His head and *his* hairs *were*
[z]white like wool, as white as
snow; and his eyes *were* as a
flame of fire;[Q]
15 And his feet like unto [10]fine
[a]brass, as if they burned in a furnace; and his voice as the sound
of many waters.[Q]
16 And he had in his right hand
[b]seven [c]stars: and out of his
mouth went a sharp twoedged
[d]sword: and his countenance *was*
as the [e]sun shineth in his strength.[Q]
17 [S T]And when I saw him, I fell
at his feet as dead. And he laid
his right hand upon me, saying
unto me, Fear not; I[G] am the [f]first
and the last:[Q]
18 [11]*I am* he that liveth, and was
dead; and, behold, I am [g]alive [f]for
evermore, Amen; and [h]have the
[i]keys of [12,j]hell[G] and of death.[S T Q]
19 Write the things which thou
hast [k]seen, and the things which
are, and the things which shall
be hereafter;[Q]
20 The mystery[G] of the [b]seven
[c]stars which thou sawest in my
right hand, and the seven golden
[l]candlesticks. The seven stars
are the [m,n]angels[G] of the seven
[o]churches: and the seven candlesticks which thou sawest are the
seven churches.

## CHAPTER 2

*Christ's message to the angel of the church in Ephesus, 8 in Smyrna, 12 in Pergamos, 18 and in Thyatira.*

UNTO the [a]angel of the church
of [b]Ĕph′e-sŭs write; These
things saith [c,d]he that holdeth the

*h* *Asia, churches of,* Acts 2:9.
*i* *Benedictions, apostolic,* Deut. 21:5.
*j* *Grace of God,* Rom. 4:16.
*k* *Spiritual Peace,* Gal. 1:3.
*l* *God, eternity of,* Gen. 2:2.
*m* *Throne,* 1 Kin. 2:19.

**5**
*n* *Jesus, faithfulness of,* Matt. 1:21.
*o* *Firstborn,* Zech. 12:10.
*p* *Resurrection, of Jesus,* 1 Cor. 15:12.
*q* *Jesus, king,* Matt. 1:21.
*r* *Jesus, love of,* Matt. 1:21.
*s* *Atonement, by Jesus,* Lev. 17:11.
*t* *Sin, forgiveness of,* Rom. 5:12.
*u* *Jesus, design of his death,* Matt. 1:21.
*v* *Blood, of Jesus,* Heb. 9:19.
*w* *Jesus, atoning blood of,* Matt. 1:21.
2 R. V. loosed us

**6**
*x* *Priest, figurative,* Lev. 1:5.
*y* *God, fatherhood of,* Gen. 2:2.
*z* *Praise,* Psa. 150:1.
*a* *Jesus, king,* Matt. 1:21.
*b* *Jesus, eternity of,* Matt. 1:21.
3 R. V. to be a kingdom, to be priests

**7**
*c* John 19:37.
*d* *Conscience, guilty,* Acts 23:1.
*e* *Self-condemnation,* Job 9:20.
4 R. V. the tribes of the earth shall mourn over him.

**8**
*f* *God, eternity of,* Gen. 2:2.
*g* Rev. 21:6; 22:13.
*h* *God, omnipotent,* Gen. 2:2.
5 R. V. saith the Lord God, which is

**9** *i* *John,* Mark 1:19. *j* *Persecution, of the righteous,* John 15:20. *k* *Patience,* Luke 8:15. *l* *Word of God,* Psa. 119:9. 6 R. V. *omits* Christ
**10** *m* *Christian Sabbath,* Mark 16:9. *n* *Inspiration,* Job 32:8.
**11** *o* *Seven, churches,* Gen. 7:2. *p* *Ephesus,* Acts 18:19. *q* Rev. 2:8. *r* Rev. 2:12–17. *s* Acts 16:14; Rev. 2:18, 24. *t* Rev. 3:1–4.
**7** R. V. *omits* I am Alpha and Omega, the first and the last: and
**8** R. V. *omits* which are in Asia

*u* Rev. 3:7–13.
*v* *Laodicea,* Col. 2:1.

**12**
*w* *Vision,* Acts 9:10.
*x* *Seven, candlesticks,* Gen. 7:2.
*y* *Candlestick, symbolical,* Ex. 25:31.

**13**
9 R. V. a son

**14**
*z* *Colors, symbolical,* Ezek. 16:16.

**15**
*a* *Brass,* Job 28:2.
10 R. V. burnished brass, as if it had been refined in

**16**
*b* *Seven, stars,* Gen. 7:2.
*c* *Stars, figurative,* Judg. 5:20.
*d* *Sword, figurative,* 1 Chr. 21:5.
*e* *Sun,* Josh. 10:12.

**17**
*f* *Jesus, eternity of,* Matt. 1:21.

**18**
*g* *Resurrection, of Jesus,* 1 Cor. 15:12.
*h* *Death, God's power over,* Num. 23:10.
*i* *Key, a symbol of authority,* Judg. 3:25.
*j* *Hell,* Mark 9:43.
11 R. V. And the Living one; and I was dead, and behold,
12 R. V. death and of Hades.

**19**
*k* *Vision,* Acts 9:10.

**20**
*l* *Candlestick, symbolical,* Ex. 25:31.
*m* Rev. 2:1, 8, 12, 18; 3:1, 7, 14.
*n* *Minister,* Rom. 15:16.
*o* *Church, Christian,* Matt. 16:18.

**1**
*a* Rev. 1:20; 3:1, 7, 14.
*b* *Ephesus,* Acts 18:19.
*c* *Jesus, head of the church,* vs. 1–29; Matt. 1:21.
*d* *Church, Christ head of,* vs. 1–29; Matt. 16:18.

e *Stars, figurative,* Judg. 5:20.
f *Candlestick, symbolical,* Ex. 25:31.

2
g *Zeal,* 2 Cor. 7:11.
h *Works, good,* 2 Tim. 1:9.
i *Righteousness, fruits of,* Psa. 15:2.
j *Patience,* Luke 8:15.
k *Sin, repugnant to the righteous,* Rom. 5:12.
l *False Teachers,* 2 Pet. 2:1.
m *Hypocrisy,* Jas. 3:17.
1 R. V. false;

3
n *Name of Jesus,* John 14:13.

4
o *Character, instability of,* Phil. 2:15.
p *Church, backslidden,* Matt. 16:18.
q *Love, for Jesus,* 1 John 4:19.

5
r *Backsliders, called to repentance,* Jer. 3:22.
s *Repentance, enjoined,* Mark 1:4.

6
t *Sin, repugnant to Christ,* Rom. 5:12.

7
u *Commandment, enjoining heed to the truth,* Deut. 8:2.
v *Spiritual Understanding,* Luke 8:8.
w *Holy Spirit,* Acts 1:2.
x *Church, Christian,* Matt. 16:18.
y *Perseverance, motives to,* Eph. 6:18.
z *Temptation, resistance to,* Luke 11:4.
a *Steadfastness, rewards of,* vs. 10, 11, 17, 25–28; 1 Cor. 15:58.

seven [e]stars in his right hand, who
walketh in the midst of the seven
golden [f]candlesticks[G];
2 I know thy [g,h,i]works, and
thy labour, and thy [i,j]patience,
and how [k]thou canst not bear[G]
them which are evil: and thou
hast tried [l]them which [m]say they
are apostles, and are not, and
hast found them [1]liars:
3 And hast borne, and hast [j]pa-
tience, and for my [n]name's sake
hast [g]laboured, and hast not
fainted.
4 Nevertheless I have *somewhat*
against thee, because thou hast
[o,p]left thy first [q]love.
5 [r]Remember therefore from
whence thou art [p]fallen, and [s]re-
pent, and do the first works;
or else I will come unto thee
quickly, and will remove thy
[f]candlestick out of his place, except thou repent.
6 But this thou hast, that thou
hatest the [k]deeds of the Nĭc-o-
lā'ĭ-tanes, [t]which I also hate.[Q]
7 [u]He that hath an ear, let him
[v]hear what the [w]Spirit saith unto the [x]churches; To him that
[y,z,a]overcometh will [b,c]I [d]give to
eat of the [e]tree of life, which is in
the midst of the [f,g]paradise of
God.[S T Q]
8 And unto the [h,i]angel of the
[j]church in [k]Smy̆r'nȧ write; These
things saith [l]the first and the
last, which was [m]dead, and [2]is
[n]alive;[T Q]
9 I know thy [3]works, and [o]trib-
ulation, and poverty, (but thou
art rich) and *I know* the [p]blas-
phemy of them which [q]say they
are [r]Jews, and are not, but *are*
the [s]synagogue of [t]Sā'tan.

10 [u,v]Fear none of those things
which thou shalt [w]suffer: behold,
the [t]devil shall [x]cast *some* of you
into prison, [y]that ye may be
tried[G]; and ye shall have tribulation[G] ten days: [z,a]be thou faithful
unto death, and [b,c,d]I will give
thee a [e,f]crown of life.[S Q]
11 [g]He that hath an ear, let him
[h]hear what the [i]Spirit saith unto
the [j]churches; [b,f]He that [k,l]over-
cometh shall not be hurt of the
[m]second death.[S]
12 And to the [n,o]angel of the
[j]church in [p]Pĕr'ga-mŏs write;
These things saith he which hath
the sharp [q]sword with two edges;[Q]
13 I know thy works, and
where thou dwellest, *even* where
[r]Sā'tan's seat[G] *is*: and thou [s]hold-
est fast[G] my [t]name, and hast not
denied my [u]faith, even in [4]those
days wherein Ăn'tĭ-păs *was* my
faithful martyr, who was [v]slain
among you, where Sā'tan dwelleth.
14 But I have a few things against
[w]thee, because [x]thou hast there
them that hold the doctrine of
[y]Bā'laam, who taught [z]Bā'lăc to
cast a [a]stumblingblock before the
children of Ĭs'ra-el, to eat things
sacrificed unto idols, and to [b]com-
mit [c]fornication.[Q]
15 [d]So hast thou also them that
hold[G] the doctrine[G] of the Nĭc-o-
lā'ĭ-tanes, [5]which thing I hate.
16 [e,f]Repent; or else I will come
unto thee quickly, and will fight
against them with the sword of
my mouth.[Q]
17 [g]He that hath an ear, let him
[h]hear what the [i]Spirit saith unto
the [j]churches; [k,l]To him that

10
u *Commandment, enjoining fortitude under persecution,* Deut. 8:2.
v *Adversity, consolation in,* Psa. 10:6.
w *Suffering for Christ,* Phil. 1:29.
x *Temptation, a test,* Luke 11:4.
y *Adversity, design of,* Psa. 10:6.
z *Faithfulness,* Luke 16:10.
a *Blessings, contingent upon obedience,* Deut. 11:26.
b *Promise, to those who endure to the end,* 2 Cor. 1:20.
c *Righteous, promises to,* Psa. 64:10.
d *Obedience, rewarded,* Heb. 5:8.
e *Crown, figurative,* Ex. 29:6.
f *Reward, a motive, to faithfulness,* Matt. 5:12.

11
g *Commandment, enjoining heed to the truth,* Deut. 8:2.
h *Spiritual Understanding,* Luke 8:8.
i *Holy Spirit,* Acts 1:2.
j *Church, Christian,* Matt. 16:18.
k *Perseverance, motives to,* Eph. 6:18.
l *Temptation, resistance to,* Luke 11:4.
m *Second Death,* Rev. 20:6.

12
n Rev. 1:20; 3:1, 7, 14.
o *Minister,* Rom. 15:16.
p Rev. 1:11.
q *Sword, figurative,* 1 Chr. 21:5.

13
r *Satan,* Matt. 4:10.
s *Steadfastness,* 1 Cor. 15:58.
t *Name of Jesus,* John 14:13.

b *Jesus, savior,* Matt. 1:21. c *Promise, to the righteous,* 2 Cor. 1:20. d *Reward, a motive, to faithfulness,* Matt. 5:12. e *Life, tree of,* Eccl. 8:15. f Luke 23:43; 2 Cor. 12:4. g *Heaven, future home of the righteous,* Luke 18:22.
**8** h Rev. 1:20; 3:1, 7, 14. i *Minister,* Rom. 15:16. j *Church, Christian,* Matt. 16:18. k Rev. 1:11. l *Jesus, eternity of,* Matt. 1:21. m *Jesus, death of,* Matt. 1:21. n *Resurrection, of Jesus,* 1 Cor. 15:12. 2 R. V. lived again:
**9** o *Persecution, of the righteous,* John 15:20. p *Blasphemy,* 2 Sam. 12:14. q *Hypocrisy,* Jas. 3:17. r *Jews,* Neh. 4:2. s *Synagogue, of satan,* Matt. 12:9. t *Satan,* Matt. 4:10. 3 R. V. omits works, and

u *Faith, the doctrines of Jesus,* 1 Cor. 16:13. v *Martyrdom,* Rev. 17:6. 3 R. V. omits thy works, and 4 R. V. the days of Antipas my witness, my faithful one, who **14** w *Church, backslidden,* Matt. 16:18. x *Fellowship, with the wicked,* 1 Cor. 1:9. y *Balaam,* Deut. 23:4. z Or, *Balak,* Num. 22:4.—a *Temptation, leading into,* Luke 11:4. b *Idolatry, wicked practices of,* 1 Sam. 15:23. c *Adultery,* Lev. 20:10.
**15** d *Fellowship, with the wicked,* 1 Cor. 1:9. 5 R. V. in like manner.
**16** e *Commandment, to backsliders,* Deut. 8:2. f *Repentance, enjoined,* Mark 1:4. **17** g *Commandment, enjoining heed to the truth,* Deut. 8:2. h *Spiritual Understanding,* Luke 8:8. i *Holy Spirit,* Acts 1:2. j *Church, Christian,* Matt. 16:18. k *Promise, to the righteous,* 2 Cor. 1:20. l *Righteous, promises to,* Psa. 64:10.

[m,n]overcometh will I give [o]to eat of the hidden [p]manna, and will give him a [q]white [r]stone, and in the stone a new name written, which no man knoweth[G] saving[G] he that receiveth *it*.[S Q]

18 And unto the [s,t]angel of the [j]church in [u]Thȳ-a-tī′rȧ write; These things saith the [v,w]Son of God, who hath his eyes like unto a flame of fire, and his feet *are* like [6]fine brass;[Q]

19 I know thy [x]works, and [7,y]charity[G], and service, and [z]faith, and thy [a]patience, and thy works; and the last *to be* more than the first.

20 Notwithstanding I have a few things against thee, because thou sufferest[G] that [b]woman Jĕz′-e-bĕl, which calleth herself a [c]prophetess, to teach and to [d,e]seduce[G] my servants to [f]commit [g]fornication, and to eat things sacrificed unto idols.[Q]

21 And I [h]gave her space to [i]repent of her [g]fornication; and she [j,k]repented not.[S]

22 Behold, I will cast her into a bed, and them that commit [g]adultery with her into great [l]tribulation[G], [m]except they [i]repent of their deeds.

23 And I will [l]kill her children with death; and all the churches shall know[G] that I am he which searcheth the reins[G] and [n,o]hearts: and [p]I will give unto every one of you [q]according to your works.[T Q]

24 But unto you I say, and unto the rest in [r]Thȳ-a-tī′rȧ, as many as have not this [8]doctrine, and which have not known[G] the [9]depths of [s]Sā′tan, as they speak; I will put upon you none other burden.

25 But that which ye have *already* hold fast[G] till I [t]come.

*m Temptation, resistance to,* Luke 11:4.
*n Perseverance, motives to,* Eph. 6:18.
*o Reward, a motive, to perseverance,* Matt. 5:12.
*p Manna, figurative,* Ex. 16:31.
*q Colors, symbolical,* Ezek. 16:16.
*r Stones, figurative,* Ex. 24:12.

**18**
*s* Rev. 1:20; 3:1, 7, 14.
*t Minister,* Rom. 15:16.
*u* Acts 16:14.
*v Jesus, divine sonship of,* Matt. 1:21.
*w Church, Christ head of,* Matt. 16:18.
6 R. V. burnished

**19**
*x Works, good,* 2 Tim. 1:9.
*y Love, of man for man,* 1 John 4:7.
*z Faith in Christ,* John 6:69.
*a Patience,* Luke 8:15.
7 R. V. thy love

**20**
*b Women, wicked,* Prov. 31:10.
*c Temptation, sources of, false teachers,* Luke 11:4.
*d Influence, evil,* 1 Cor. 7:14.
*e Temptation, leading into,* Luke 11:4.
*f Idolatry, wicked practices of,* 1 Sam. 15:23.
*g Adultery,* Lev. 20:10.

**21**
*h Jesus, love of,* Matt. 1:21.
*i Repentance,* Mark 1:4.
*j Impenitence,* Rom. 2:5.
*k Obduracy,* Prov. 29:1.

**22**
*l Wicked, punishment of,* Psa. 73:3.
*m Contingencies, in divine government,* 1 Kin. 3:14.

**23**
*n Heart, known to Christ,* Psa. 44:21.
*o Sin, known to Christ,* Rom. 5:12. *p Jesus, judge,* Matt. 1:21. *q Judgment, according to opportunity and works,* 1 Pet. 1:17.
**24** *r* Acts 16:14. *s Satan,* Matt. 4:10. 8 R. V. teaching, 9 R. V. deep things
**25** *t Jesus, second coming of,* Matt. 1:21.

26[S] And[Q] he that [u,v]overcometh, and [w]keepeth[G] my works unto the end, [x,y]to him will I give [10]power over the nations:

27 And he shall rule them with a [z]rod of iron; as the vessels of a potter shall they be broken to shivers[G]: even [a]as I received of my [b]Father.[Q]

28 And I will give him the morning [c]star.[S]

29 [d]He that hath an ear, let him [e]hear what the [f]Spirit saith unto the [g]churches.

## CHAPTER 3

*Christ's message to the angel of the church in Sardis, 7 in Philadelphia, 14 and in Laodicea.*

AND unto the [a,b]angel of the [c]church in [d]Sär′dĭs write; These things saith [e]he that hath the [f]seven Spirits of God, and the [f]seven stars; I know thy [g]works, that [h]thou hast a name that thou livest, and art dead.

2 [i,j]Be watchful, and [1]strengthen the things which remain, that are ready to die: for I have [2]not found thy [k]works perfect[G] before God.

3 [l]Remember therefore how thou hast received and heard, and hold fast, and [m]repent. [n]If therefore thou shalt not [j]watch, I will [o]come on thee as a thief, and thou shalt not know[G] what hour I will come upon thee.

4[S] Thou hast a few names even in [d]Sär′dĭs which have [p,q]not defiled their garments; and [r]they shall walk with me in [s]white: for they are worthy.

5 He that [t,u]overcometh, [r,v]the same [w]shall be clothed in [s]white raiment; and I will not blot out his name out of the [x]book of

**26**
*u Perseverance, motives to,* Eph. 6:18.
*v Temptation, resistance to,* Luke 11:4.
*w Obedience,* Heb. 5:8.
*x Righteous, promises to,* Psa. 64:10.
*y Promise, to the righteous,* 2 Cor. 1:20.
10 R. V. authority

**27**
*z Scepter,* Esth. 4:11.
*a Jesus, relation of, to the Father,* Matt. 1:21.
*b God, fatherhood of,* Gen. 2:2.

**28**
*c Stars, figurative,* Judg. 5:20.

**29**
*d Commandment, enjoining heed to the truth,* Deut. 8:2.
*e Spiritual Understanding,* Luke 8:8.
*f Holy Spirit,* Acts 1:2.
*g Church, Christian,* Matt. 16:18.

**1**
*a* Rev. 1:20; 2:1, 8, 12, 18.
*b Minister,* Rom. 15:16.
*c Church, Christian,* Matt. 16:18
*d* Rev. 1:11.
*e Jesus, head of the church,* Matt. 1:21.
*f Seven,* Gen. 7:2.
*g Hypocrisy,* Jas. 3:17.
*h Church, backslidden,* Matt. 16:18.

**2**
*i Commandment, enjoining watchfulness,* Deut. 8:2.
*j Watchfulness, enjoined,* Matt. 24:42.
*k Character, instability of,* Phil. 2:15.
1 R. V. stablish
2 R. V. found no works of thine fulfilled before my God.

**3** *l Backsliders, called to repentance,* Jer. 3:22. *m Repentance, enjoined,* Mark 1:4. *n Contingencies, in divine government,* 1 Kin. 3:14. *o Wicked, punishment of,* Psa. 73:3. **4** *p Faithfulness,* Luke 16:10. *q Steadfastness, rewards of,* vs. 5, 11, 12, 21; 1 Cor. 15:58. *r Righteous, promises to,* Psa. 64:10. *s Colors, symbolical,* Ezek. 16:16.
**5** *t Temptation, resistance to,* Luke 11:4. *u Perseverance, motives to,* Eph. 6:18. *v Promise, to the righteous,* 2 Cor. 1:20. *w Reward, a motive, to perseverance,* Matt. 5:12. *x Book, figurative,* Psa. 139:16.

*v God, fatherhood of,* Gen. 2:2.

**6**

*z Commandment, enjoining heed to the truth,* Deut. 8:2.

*a Spiritual Understanding,* Luke 8:8.

*b Holy Spirit,* Acts 1:2.

*c Church, Christian,* Matt. 16:18.

**7**

*d* Rev. 1:20; 2:1, 8, 12, 18.

*e Minister,* Rom. 15:16.

*f* Rev. 1:11.

*g Jesus, holiness of,* Matt. 1:21.

*h Jesus, perfections of,* Matt. 1:21.

*i Jesus, king,* Matt. 1:21.

*j Key, symbolical,* Judg. 3:25.

**8**

*k Opportunity,* Gal. 6:10.

*Door, figurative,* Deut. 11:20.

*m Faithfulness,* Luke 16:10.

**9**

*n Synagogue, of Satan,* Matt. 12:9.

*o Satan,* Matt. 4:10.

*p Hypocrisy,* Jas. 3:17.

*q Jesus, love of,* Matt. 1:21.

*r Church, Christ's love for,* Matt. 16:18.

**10**

*s Righteous, promises to,* Psa. 64:10.

*t Afflictions, consolation in,* Psa. 34:19.

*u Temptation, Christ succors in,* Luke 11:4.

3 R. V. trial, that hour which is to come

**11**

*v Jesus, second coming of,* Matt. 1:21.

*w Commandment, enjoining steadfastness.* Deut. 8:2.

*x Watchfulness, enjoined against backsliding,* Matt. 24:42.

*y Steadfastness,* 1 Cor. 15:58.

*z Crown, figurative,* Ex. 29:6.

life, but I will confess his name
before my [v]Father, and before
his angels.[S Q]
6 [z]He that hath an ear, let him
[a]hear what the [b]Spirit saith unto
the [c]churches.
7 And to the [d,e]angel of the
[c]church in [f]Phĭl-a-dĕl′phĭ-ȧ write;
These things saith he that is [g]holy,[G]
he that is [h]true, [i]he that hath the
[j]key of Dā′vid, he that openeth,
and no man shutteth; and shutteth, and no man openeth;[S Q T]
8 I know thy works: behold, I
have set before thee an [k]open
[l]door, and no man can shut it:
for thou *hast a little strength,
and hast [m]kept[G] my word, and
hast not denied my name.
9 Behold, I will make them of
the [n]synagogue of [o]Sā′tan, which
[p]say they are Jews, and are not,
but do lie; behold, I will make
them to come and worship before thy feet, and to know[G] that
[q]I have loved [r]thee.[Q]
10 Because thou hast [m]kept the
word of my patience, [s,t]I also
will keep thee from the hour of
[3,u]temptation,[G] which shall come
upon all the world, to try[G] them
that dwell upon the earth.[S T]
11 Behold, I [v]come quickly:
[w,x]hold that [y]fast which thou
hast, that no man take thy
[z]crown.
12 Him that [a,b]overcometh [c]will
[d,e]I make a [f]pillar in the [g,h]temple
of [i]my God, and he shall go no
more out: and I will write upon
him the name of my God, and the
name of the city of my God, *which
is* [h]new Jē-ru′sȧ-lĕm, which cometh down out of heaven from my
God: and *I will write upon him*
my new name.[S Q]

**12**—*a Temptation, resistance to,* Luke 11:4. *b Perseverance, motives to,* Eph. 6:18. *c Promise, to the righteous,* 2 Cor. 1:20. *d Jesus, love of,* Matt. 1:21. *e Reward, a motive, to perseverance,* Matt. 5:12. *f Pillar, figurative,* Gen. 28:18. *g Temple, figurative,* 1 Kin. 6:17. *h* Rev. 21:2, 10. *i Jesus, relation of, to the Father,* Matt. 1:21.

13 [j]He that hath an ear, let him
[k]hear what the [l]Spirit saith unto
the [m]churches.
14 And unto the [n,o]angel of the
[m]church of the [p]Lȧ-ŏd-ĭ-çē′ans
write; These things saith the
[q]Amen, the [r]faithful and true
witness, the [s]beginning of the
creation of [t]God;[T Q]
15 I know thy works, that thou
art *,[u,v]neither cold nor hot: I
would thou wert cold or hot.
16 So then because thou art
*,[u,v]lukewarm, and [w]neither cold
nor hot, I will [x,y]spue[G] thee out
of my mouth.
17 Because thou [z]sayest, I am
[a]rich, and increased with goods,
and have need of nothing; and
knowest not that thou [b]art
wretched, and miserable, and
poor, and [c]blind, and naked:[Q]
18 I counsel thee to buy of
[d]me gold tried in the fire, that
thou mayest be [e]rich; and [f]white
[g]raiment, that thou mayest be
clothed, and *that* the shame of
thy [h]nakedness do not appear;
and anoint thine eyes with eye-
salve, that thou mayest see.
19 As many as I [i]love, I rebuke[G]
and [j,k]chasten[G]: [l,m]be zealous
therefore, and [n]repent.[Q]
20 Behold, I stand at the door,
and knock: if any man hear my
voice, and [o]open the door, [p,q]I
will [r]come in to him, and will
sup with him, and he with me.
21 [s,t]To him that [u,v]overcom-
eth will I grant to sit with me in
my [w]throne, even [x]as I also overcame, and am [y]set down with
my [z]Father in his throne.[S]

**13**

*j Commandment, enjoining heed to the truth,* Deut. 8:2.

*k Spiritual Understanding,* Luke 8:8.

*l Holy Spirit,* Acts 1:2.

*m Church, Christian,* Matt. 16:18.

**14**

*n* Rev. 1:20; 2:1, 8, 12, 18.

*o Minister,* Rom. 15:16.

*p Laodicea,* Col. 2:1.

*q Jesus, names of,* Matt. 1:21.

*r Jesus, faithfulness of,* Matt. 1:21.

*s Jesus, pre-existence of,* Matt. 1:21.

*t God, creator,* Gen. 2:2.

**15**

*u Backsliders, described,* Jer. 3:22.

*v Indecision,* 1 Kin. 18:21.

**16**

*w Character, instability of,* Phil. 2:5.

*x Wicked, punishment of,* Psa. 73:3.

*y Disfellowship,* Num. 15:31.

**17**

*z Delusion,* 2 Thess. 2:11.

*a Temptation, sources of, riches,* Luke 11:4.

*b Wicked, described,* Psa. 73:3.

*c Spiritual Blindness,* 2 Cor. 4:4.

**18**

*d Jesus, savior,* Matt. 1:21.

*e Riches, figurative,* Eccl. 4:8.

*f Colors, symbolical,* Ezek. 16:16.

*g Dress, figurative of righteousness,* Zech. 3:3.

*h Self-righteousness,* Luke 18:11.

**19** *i Jesus, love of,* Matt. 1:21. *j Divine Chastisement, administered in love,* Job 33:19. *k Afflictions, design of,* Psa. 34:19. *l Commandment, to backsliders,* Deut. 8:2. *m Zeal, enjoined,* 2 Cor. 7:11. *n Repentance, enjoined,* Mark 1:4. **20** *o Penitent, promises to,* Psa. 51:17. *p Promise, to penitents,* 2 Cor. 1:20. *q Backsliders, promises to penitent,* Jer. 3:22. *r Fellowship, with Christ,* 1 Cor. 1:9. **21** *s Promise, to the righteous,* 2 Cor. 1:20. *t Righteous, promises to,* Psa. 64:10. *u Temptation, resistance to,* Luke 11:4. *v Perseverance, motives to,* Eph. 6:18. *w Throne, figurative,* 1 Kin. 2:19. *x Jesus, our example,* Matt. 1:21. *y Jesus, exaltation of,* Matt. 1:21. *z God, fatherhood of,* Gen. 2:2.

***LUKEWARMNESS. Instances of:** *The Reubenites and other tribes, when Deborah called on them to assist Sisera,* **Judg. 5:16, 17.** *Israel,* Hos. 10:2. *The Jews,* Neh. 3:5; 13:11; Hag. 1:2-11. *The church, at Sardis,* Rev. 3:1-3; *at Laodicea,* Rev. 3:14-16.
See footnote, BACKSLIDING, Hos. 11:7.

22 [a]He that hath an ear, let him [b]hear what the [c]Spirit saith unto the [d]churches.

## CHAPTER 4

*John's vision of the throne of God in heaven, 4 and of the four and twenty elders around it. 10 The elders worship him that sits on the throne.*

AFTER this I looked, and, [a]behold, a door *was* opened in heaven: and the first voice which I heard *was* as it were of a trumpet talking with me; which said, Come up hither, and I will shew thee things which must be hereafter.

2 And immediately I was in the [b]spirit: and, [a]behold, a [c]throne was set in heaven, and *one* sat on the throne.

3 And he that sat was to look upon like a [d]jasper and a [e]sardine stone: and *there was* a [f]rainbow round about the [c]throne, in sight like unto an *emerald.

4 And round about the [c]throne *were* four and twenty [1]seats: and upon the [1]seats I saw four and twenty [g]elders sitting, clothed in [h]white raiment; and they had on their heads [i]crowns of gold.

5 And out of the [c]throne proceeded lightnings and thunderings and voices: and *there were* [j]seven [k]lamps of fire burning before the throne, which are the seven Spirits of God.

6 And before the [c]throne *there was* a sea of glass like unto [l]crystal: and in the midst of the throne, and round about the throne, *were* four [2,m]beasts full of eyes before and behind.

7 And the first [3,m]beast *was* like a [n]lion, and the second [3]beast like a [o]calf, and the third [3]beast had a face as a man, and the fourth [3]beast *was* like a flying [p]eagle.

8 And the four [2]beasts had each of them six wings about *him*; and *they were* full of eyes within: and they rest not day and night, [q]saying, [r,s]Holy, holy, holy, Lord God [t]Almighty, [u]which was, and is, and is to come.

9 And when those [2]beasts give glory and honour and [v]thanks to him that sat on the [c]throne, who [u]liveth for ever and ever,

10 The four and twenty [g]elders fall down before him that sat on the throne, and [w]worship him that liveth for ever and ever, and cast their [i]crowns before the [c]throne, saying,

11 [x]Thou art worthy, [4]O Lord, to receive [y]glory and honour and power: for thou hast [z]created all things, and for thy pleasure they are and were created.

## CHAPTER 5

*The book sealed with seven seals. 3 No man is able to open it. 5 The Lamb that was slain takes the book: 8 whereupon the elders and angels around the throne join in thanksgiving and praise to him.*

AND I [a]saw in the right hand of him that sat on the [b]throne a [c]book written within and on the backside, [d]sealed with [e]seven seals.

2 And I [a]saw a strong [f]angel proclaiming with a loud voice, Who is worthy to open the book, and to loose the seals thereof?

3 And no man in heaven, nor in earth, neither under the earth, was able to open the book, neither to look thereon.

4 And [g,h]I wept much, because no man was found worthy to open [1]and to read the book, neither to look thereon.

5 And one of the [i]elders saith unto me, Weep not: behold, the [j,k]Lion of the tribe of Jū'dȧ, the Root of Dā'vid, hath prevailed to open the [c]book, and to loose the [e]seven [d]seals thereof.

6 And I [a]beheld, and, lo, in the

---

**22**
- *a* *Commandment, enjoining heed to the truth,* Deut. 8:2.
- *b* *Spiritual Understanding,* Luke 8:8.
- *c* *Holy Spirit,* Acts 1:2.
- *d* *Church, Christian,* Matt. 16:18.

**1**
- *a* *Vision, of John,* Acts 9:10.

**2**
- *b* *Holy Spirit,* Acts 1:2.
- *c* *Throne,* 1 Kin. 2:19.

**3**
- *d* *Jasper,* Rev. 21:19.
- *e* *Sardius,* Ex. 28:17.
- *f* *Rainbow, symbolical,* Gen. 9:13.

**4**
- *g* *Elders,* Acts 14:23.
- *h* *Colors, symbolical,* Ezek. 16:16.
- *i* *Crown, symbolical,* Ex. 29:6.
- 1 R. V. thrones

**5**
- *j* *Seven,* Gen. 7:2.
- *k* *Lamp, symbolical,* Ex. 27:20.

**6**
- *l* Rev. 21:11; 22:1.
- *m* *Beasts, symbolical,* Dan. 7:3.
- 2 R. V. living creatures

**7**
- *n* *Lion,* Mic. 5:8.
- *o* *Bullock,* Ex. 29:3.
- *p* *Eagle,* Lev. 11:13.
- 3 R. V. creature

**8**
- *q* *Praise,* Psa. 150:1.
- *r* *God, holiness of,* Gen. 2:2.
- *s* *Holiness, attribute of God,* Ex. 39:30.
- *t* *God, omnipotent,* Gen. 2:2.
- *u* *God, eternity of,* Gen. 2:2.

**9**
- *v* *Thankfulness, to God,* Acts 24:3.

**10**
- *w* *Worship,* Gen. 22:5.

**11**
- *x* *Glorifying God,* Luke 5:25.
- *y* *God, glory of,* Gen. 2:2.
- *z* *God, creator,* Gen. 2:2.
- 4 R. V. our Lord and our God, to receive

**1**
- *a* *Vision, of John,* vs. 1–14; Acts 9:10.
- *b* *Throne,* 1 Kin. 2:19.
- *c* *Book,* Num. 5:23.
- *d* *Seal,* 1 Kin. 21:8.
- *e* *Seven,* Gen. 7:2.

**2**
- *f* *Angel, functions of,* Heb. 1:13.

**4**
- *g* *Minister, zealous,* Rom. 15:16.
- *h* *Zeal,* 2 Cor. 1:11.
- 1 R. V. *omits* and to read

**5**
- *i* *Elders,* Acts 14:23.
- *j* *Lion, a name of Jesus,* Mic. 5:8.
- *k* *Jesus, savior,* Matt. 1:21.

---

* **EMERALD,** possibly carbuncle, a precious stone. *Color of the rainbow,* Rev. 4:3. *Merchandise of, in Tyre,* Ezek. 27:16; 28:13. *Set in the breastplate,* Ex. 28:18. **Symbolical:** *In the foundation of the walls of the holy city,* Rev. 21:19.
See footnote, PRECIOUS STONES, Ex. 39:10.

midst of the [b]throne and of the
four [2,l]beasts, and in the midst
of the [i]elders, stood a [m,n]Lamb as
it had been slain, having [e]seven
[o]horns and [e]seven eyes, which
are the [e]seven Spirits of God
sent forth into all the earth.[Q]
7 And he came and took the
[c]book[G] out of the right hand of
him that sat upon the [b]throne.[Q]
8 And when he had taken the
[c]book,[G] the four [2,l]beasts and four
*and* twenty [i]elders [p]fell down before the [m,n]Lamb, having every
one of them [q]harps, and golden
[3]vials[G] full of [r]odours,[G] which are
the [s]prayers of saints.[T Q]
9 And they sung a new [t]song,
saying, [u]Thou art worthy to take
the [c]book,[G] and to open the [d]seals
thereof: for thou wast [v]slain, and
[4]hast [w,x,y]redeemed us to God
by thy [z]blood out of every kindred, and tongue, and people,
and nation;[S T Q]
10 And [5]hast made us unto our
God kings and [a]priests: and we
shall reign on the earth.[Q]
11[T] And I [b]beheld, and I heard
the voice of many [c]angels round
about the [d]throne and the
[2,e]beasts and the [f]elders: and the
number of them was ten thousand times ten thousand, and
thousands of thousands;[Q]
12 [g]Saying with a loud voice,
Worthy is the [h]Lamb that was
[i]slain to receive power, and riches,
and wisdom, and strength, and
honour, and glory, and blessing.[G Q T]
13 And every [j]creature which is
in heaven, and on the earth, and
under the earth, and such as are
in the sea, and all that are in
them, heard I [j]saying, Blessing,[G]
and honour, and glory, and
[k]power, *be* unto him that sitteth
upon the [d]throne, and unto the
[h]Lamb for [l,m]ever and ever.[S Q]
14 And the four [2,e]beasts said,
Amen. And the [6]four *and*
twenty [f]elders fell down and
[n]worshipped him that liveth for
ever and ever.[S]

## CHAPTER 6

*What the apostle saw when the Lamb opened the first seal, 3 the second seal, 5 the third seal, 7 the fourth seal, 9 the fifth seal, 12 and the sixth seal.*

AND I [a]saw when the [b,c]Lamb
opened one of the [d]seals, and
I heard, as it were the noise of
thunder, one of the four [1]beasts
saying, Come and see.
2 And I saw, and behold a
[e]white [f]horse: and he that sat on
him had a [g]bow; and a [h]crown
was given unto him: and [i]he
went forth conquering, and to
conquer.[Q]
3 And when he had opened the
second [d]seal, I heard the second
[1]beast say, Come and see.
4[Q] And there went out another
[f]horse *that was* [e]red: and *power*
was given to him that sat thereon
to take [j]peace from the earth,
and that they should [k]kill one
another: and there was given
unto him a great sword.
5 And when he had opened the
third [d]seal, I heard the third
[1]beast say, Come [2]and see. And
I beheld, and lo a [e]black [f]horse;
and he that sat on him had a
[3]pair of [l]balances[G] in his hand.[Q]
6 And I heard a voice in the
midst of the four [1]beasts say, A
measure[G] of [m]wheat for a [n]penny,[G]
and three measures[G] of [o]barley for
a penny;[G] and *see* thou hurt not
the [p]oil and the [q]wine.
7 And when he had opened the
fourth [d]seal, I heard the voice of
the fourth [1]beast say, Come [2]and
see.
8 And I looked, and behold a
pale [f]horse: and his name that
sat on him was Death, and [4]Hell[G]
followed with him. And power
was given unto them over the
fourth part of the earth, [r]to [k]kill
with sword, and with [s]hunger,
and with death, and with the
[5,t]beasts of the earth.[S Q]

6
- l *Beasts, symbolical*, Dan. 7:3.
- m *Lamb, an appellation of Jesus*, John 1:29.
- n *Types, of the Savior*, Heb. 10:1.
- o *Horn, figurative*, 1 Kin. 1:39.
- 2 R. V. living creatures,

8
- p *Jesus, worship of*, Matt. 1:21.
- q *Harp*, Dan. 3:10.
- r *Incense, figurative*, Ex. 37:29.
- s *Prayer, kept in divine remembrance*, Acts 6:4.
- 3 R. V. bowls full of incense, which

9
- t *Song*, Psa. 77:6.
- u *Praise*, Psa. 150:1.
- v *Jesus, death of*, Matt. 1:21.
- w *Redemption of our Souls*, Eph. 1:7.
- x *Atonement, by Jesus*, Lev. 17:11.
- y *Jesus, mission of*, Matt. 1:21.
- z *Blood, of Jesus*, Heb. 9:19.
- 4 R. V. didst purchase unto God with thy blood men of every tribe, and tongue,

10
- a *Priest, figurative*, Lev. 1:5.
- 5 R. V. madest them to be unto our God a kingdom and priests; and they reign upon the earth.

11
- b *Vision, of John*, Acts 9:10.
- c *Angel*, Heb. 1:13.
- d *Throne*, 1 Kin. 2:19.
- e *Beasts, symbolical*, Dan. 7:3.
- f *Elders*, Acts 14:23.

12
- g *Praise*, Psa. 150:1.
- h *Lamb, an appellation of Jesus*, John 1:29.
- i *Jesus, death of*, Matt. 1:21.

13
- j *Glorifying God*, Luke 5:25.
- k *God, power of*, Gen. 2:2.
- l *God, eternity of*, Gen. 2:2.
- m *Jesus, eternity of*, Matt. 1:21.

14
- 6 R. V. elders fell down and worshipped.

- n *Worship*, Gen. 22:5.

1
- a *Vision, of John*, vs. 1–17; Acts 9:10.
- b *Jesus, names of*, Matt. 1:21.
- c *Lamb, an appellation of Jesus*, John 1:29.
- d *Seal*, 1 Kin. 21:8.
- 1 R. V. living creatures

2
- e *Colors, symbolical*, Ezek. 16:16.
- f *Horse*, Job 39:19.
- g *Bow*, 2 Sam. 1:18.
- h *Crown*, Ex. 29:6.
- i *Jesus, kingdom of, prophecies concerning*, Matt. 1:21.

4
- j *Peace*, Jer. 29:7.
- k *War*, Judg. 3:2.

5
- l *Balances*, Prov. 11:1.
- 2 R. V. *omits* and see.
- 3 R. V. balance in

6
- m *Wheat*, Ezra 6:9.
- n *Penny*, Matt. 20:2.
- o *Barley*, Ex. 9:31.
- p *Oil, used for food*, Deut. 12:17.
- q *Wine*, Prov. 23:31.

8
- r *Judgments*, Ex. 6:6.
- s *Famine*, 2 Kin. 8:1.
- t *Animals, sent in judgment*, Jer. 27:5.
- 4 R. V. Hades
- 5 R. V. wild beasts

9 And when he had opened the
fifth [d]seal, I saw under the altar the souls of [u]them that were
[v]slain for the [w]word of God, and
for the [x]testimony which they
held:[T]
10 And they cried with a loud
voice, saying, [y]How long, O
[6]Lord, [z]holy[C] and [a]true, dost
thou not judge and avenge our
blood on them that dwell on the
earth?[S] [Q]
11 And [b]white [c,d]robes were
given unto every one of them;
and it was said unto them, that
they should rest yet for a little
season, until their fellowservants
also and their brethren, that
should be [e]killed as they *were*,
should be fulfilled.
12 And I [f]beheld when he had
opened the sixth [g]seal, and, lo,
there was a great [h]earthquake;
and the [i]sun became black as
sackcloth of hair, and the [j]moon
became as blood;[Q]
13 [Q]And the [k]stars of heaven
fell unto the earth, even as a fig
tree casteth her [7]untimely figs,
when she is shaken of a mighty
wind.
14 And the heaven departed
as a scroll when it is rolled together; and every mountain and
island were moved out of their
places.[Q]
15 [l]And the kings of the earth,
and the great men, and the rich
men, and the chief captains,
and the mighty men, and every
bondman,[G] and every free man,
[m,n,o]hid themselves in the dens
and in the rocks of the mountains;[Q]
16 [o]And[S] [m,n]said to the mountains and rocks, Fall on us, and
hide us from the face of [p]him
that sitteth on the throne, and
from the wrath[G] of the [q,r]Lamb:[Q] [T]
17 For the great day of [8]his
[l]wrath is come; and [m,n]who shall
be able to stand?[S] [Q]

9
u *Glorified Saints*, Heb. 12:1.
v *Martyrdom*, Rev. 17:6.
w *Word of God*, Psa. 119:9.
x *Witnessing for Christ*, Luke 24:48.

10
y *God, longsuffering of*, Gen. 2:2.
z *God, holiness of*, Gen. 2:2.
a *God, faithfulness of*, Gen. 2:2.
6 R. V. Master, the holy

11
b *Colors, symbolical*, Ezek. 16:16.
c *Dress, figurative of righteousness*, Zech. 3:3.
d *Righteousness, figuratively described as a garment*, Psa. 15:2.
e *Martyrdom*, Rev. 17:6.

12
f *Vision, of John*, Acts 10:9.
g *Seal*, 1 Kin. 21:8.
h *Earthquakes*, Isa. 29:6.
i *Sun, darkening of*, Josh. 10:12.
j *Moon, darkening of*, Song 6:10.

13
k *Stars, falling of*, Judg. 5:20.
7 R. V. unripe figs.

15
l *Wicked, punishment of*, Psa. 73:3.
m *Terror of the Wicked*, Isa. 2:19.
n *Fear of God, guilty*, Acts 9:31.
o *Punishment, no escape from*, Lev. 26:41.

16
p *God, judge*, Gen. 2:2.
q *Jesus, names of*, Matt. 1:21.
r *Lamb, an appellation of Jesus*, John 1:29.

17
8 R. V. their wrath

## CHAPTER 7

*An angel seals the servants of God in their foreheads. 4 The number that were sealed. 9 A countless multitude of the redeemed in heaven ascribe salvation to God and the Lamb. 13 The glory and happiness of those who came out of great tribulation.*

AND after these things I saw
four angels standing on
the four corners of the earth,
holding the four winds of the
earth, that the wind should not
blow on the earth, nor on the sea,
nor on any tree.[Q]
2 And I saw another angel ascending from the [1]east, having
the seal of the living God: and
he cried with a loud voice to
the four angels, to whom it was
given to hurt the earth and the
sea,
3 Saying, Hurt not the earth,
neither the sea, nor the trees, till
we have sealed[C] the servants[C] of
our God in their foreheads.[S] [Q]
4 And I heard the number of
them which were sealed: *and*
*there were* sealed an hundred
*and* forty *and* four thousand of
all the tribes of the children of
[a]Ĭs′ra-el.
5 Of the [b]tribe of Jū′dȧ *were*
sealed twelve thousand. Of the
[c]tribe of Reu′ben *were* sealed
twelve thousand. Of the [d]tribe
of Găd *were* sealed twelve thousand.
6 Of the [e]tribe of Ā′sēr *were*
sealed twelve thousand. Of
the [f]tribe of Nĕph′tha-lĭm *were*
sealed twelve thousand. Of the
[g]tribe of Mȧ-năs′sēs *were* sealed
twelve thousand.
7 Of the [h]tribe of Sĭm′e-on *were*
sealed twelve thousand. Of the
[i]tribe of Lē′vī *were* sealed twelve
thousand. Of the [j]tribe of Ĭs′sa-
char *were* sealed twelve thousand.
8 Of the [k]tribe of Zăb′u-lŏn
*were* sealed twelve thousand.
Of the [l,m]tribe of Jō′seph *were*
sealed twelve thousand. Of

2
1 R. V. sunrising;

4
a *Israel, prophecies concerning*, Ex. 4:22.

5
b Or, *Judah, tribe of*, Num. 10:14.
c *Reubenites*, Josh. 22:1.
d *Gad, tribe of*, Deut. 33:20.

6
e Or, *Asher, tribe of*, Num. 1:40.
f Or, *Naphtali, tribe of*, Num. 1:42.
g Or, *Manasseh, tribe of*, Gen. 46:20.

7
h *Simeon, tribe of*, Num. 2:12.
i *Levites, John's vision concerning*, Deut. 10:8.
j *Issachar, tribe of*, Num. 1:28.

8
k Or, *Zebulon, tribe of*, Gen. 49:13.
l *Ephraim, tribe of*, Gen. 41:52.
m *Manasseh, tribe of*, Gen. 46:20.

the [n]tribe of Běn'ja-mĭn *were* sealed twelve thousand.

9 After this I beheld, and, lo, a great multitude, which no man could number, of all nations, and kindreds, and people, and tongues, stood before the [o]throne, and before the [p,q]Lamb, clothed with [r]white [s,t]robes, and palms in their hands;

10 And [u]cried with a loud voice, saying, [v]Salvation[G] to our God which sitteth upon the [o]throne, and [w]unto the [p,q]Lamb.[T Q]

11 And all the angels stood round about the [o]throne, and *about* the elders and the four [2]beasts, and fell before the throne on their faces, and [x]worshipped God,

12 Saying, Amen: Blessing, and glory, and wisdom, and [y]thanksgiving, and honour, and power, and might, *be* unto our God for [z]ever and ever. Amen.[S]

13 [S]And one of the elders answered, saying unto me, What are these which are arrayed[G] in [r]white [s,t]robes? and whence came they?

14 And I said unto him, [3]Sir, thou knowest. And he said to me, These are they which came out of great [a]tribulation, and have [b,c,d]washed their [e,f]robes, and made them [g]white in the [h]blood of the [i]Lamb.[T Q]

15 [j]Therefore are they before the [k]throne of God, and serve him day and night in his temple: and he that sitteth on the throne shall [4]dwell among them.[Q]

16 They shall hunger no more, neither thirst any more; neither shall the sun light on them, nor any heat.[Q]

17 For the [i]Lamb which is in the midst of the throne shall [5]feed them, and shall lead them unto [6]living [l]fountains of waters: and God shall wipe away all tears from their eyes.[S T Q]

*n Benjamin, tribe of*, Num. 1:37.

9

*o Throne*, 1 Kin. 2:19.

*p Lamb*, John 1:29.

*q Jesus, prophecies concerning future glory and power of*, Matt. 1:21.

*r Colors, symbolical*, Ezek. 16:16.

*s Dress, figurative of righteousness*, Zech. 3:3.

*t Righteousness, figuratively described as a garment*, Psa. 15:2.

10

*u Praise*, Psa. 150:1.

*v Salvation*, Acts 16:17.

*w Jesus, worship of*, Matt. 1:21.

11

*x Worship*, Gen. 22:5.

2 R. V. living creatures:

12

*y Thankfulness, to God*, Acts 24:3.

*z God, eternity of*, Gen. 2:2.

14

*a Persecution, of the righteous*, John 15:20.

*b Spiritual Purification, by the blood of Christ*, Psa. 51:2.

*c Jesus, design of his death*, Matt. 1:21.

*d Atonement, by Jesus*, Lev. 17:11.

*e Dress, figurative of righteousness*, Zech. 3:3.

*f Righteousness, figuratively described as a garment*, Psa. 15:2.

*g Colors, symbolical*, Ezek. 16:16.

*h Blood, of Jesus, redeeming*, Heb. 9:19.

*i Lamb*, John 1:29.

3 R. V. my lord,

15

*j Faithfulness, rewards of*, Luke 16:10.

*k Throne*, 1 Kin. 2:19.

4 R. V. spread his tabernacle over them.

17

*l Fountain, figurative*, Zech. 13:1.

5 R. V. be their shepherd,

6 R. V. fountains of waters of life:

## CHAPTER 8

*The seventh seal opened. 2 To seven angels seven trumpets are given. 3 Another angel offers incense with the prayers of the saints. 6 Four angels sound their trumpets, and great plagues follow.*

AND when he had opened the seventh seal, there was silence in heaven about the space of half an hour.

2 And I saw the [a]seven angels which stood before God; and to them were given seven trumpets.

3 [T]And another angel came and stood at the altar, having a golden censer; and there was given unto him much incense, that he should offer *it* with the [b]prayers of all saints upon the golden altar which was before the throne.[Q]

4 And the smoke of the incense, *which came* with the [b]prayers of the saints, ascended up before God out of the angel's hand.[T]

5 And the angel took the censer, and filled it with fire of the altar, and cast *it* into the earth: and there were voices, and thunderings, and lightnings, and an earthquake.[Q]

6 And the [a]seven angels which had the seven trumpets prepared themselves to sound.

7 The first angel sounded, and there followed hail and fire mingled[G] with blood, and they were cast upon the earth: [1]and the third part of trees was burnt up, and all green grass was burnt up.[Q]

8 And the second angel sounded, and as it were a great mountain burning with fire was cast into the sea: and the third part of the sea became blood;[Q]

9 And the third part of the creatures which were in the sea, and had life, died; and the third part of the ships were destroyed.

10 And the third angel sounded, and there fell a great star from heaven, burning as [2]it were a lamp,[G] and it fell upon the third

2

*a Seven*, Gen. 7:2.

3

*b Prayer, kept in divine remembrance*, Acts 6:4

7

1 R. V. *inserts* and the third part of the earth was burnt up.

10

2 R. V. a torch,

part of the rivers, and upon the
fountains of waters;
11 And the name of the star is
called Wormwood: and the third
part of the waters became wormwood; and many men died of the
waters, because they were made
bitter.
12 And the fourth angel sounded,
and the third part of the sun
was smitten, and the third part

12 c *Darkness, figurative of judgments,* Gen. 1:2.

of the moon, and the third part
of the stars; so as the third part
of them was [c]darkened, and the
day shone not for a third part of
it, and the night likewise.
13 And I beheld, and heard an
[3]angel flying through the midst
of heaven, saying with a loud

13 3 R. V. eagle.

voice, Woe, woe, woe, to the inhabiters of the earth by reason
of the other voices of the trumpet
of the three angels, which are yet
to sound!

## CHAPTER 9

*The fifth angel sounds, and the bottomless pit is opened, and smoke and locusts issue from it. 7 These locusts described. 12 The first woe is past. 13 The sixth angel sounds, and four angels are let loose for the work of destruction.*

AND the fifth angel sounded,
and I saw a star fall from

1 1 R. V. pit of the abyss.

heaven unto the earth: and to
him was given the key of the
[1]bottomless pit.
2 And he opened the [1]bottom-
less pit; and there arose a smoke
out of the pit, as the smoke of a
great furnace; and the sun and
the air were darkened by reason
of the smoke of the pit.
3 And there came out of the
smoke locusts upon the earth:
and unto them was given power,
as the scorpions of the earth
have power.
4 And it was commanded them
that they should not hurt the

4 a *Wicked, punishment of.* Psa. 73:3.

grass of the earth, neither any
green thing, neither any tree; but
only those [a]men which have not
the seal of God in their foreheads.
5 And to them it was given that
they should not kill them, but
that they should be [a]tormented
five months: and their torment
*was* as the torment of a scorpion,
when he striketh a man.
6 And in those days shall men
[b]seek death, and shall not find

6 b *Death, desired.* Num. 23:10.

it; and shall desire to die, and
death shall flee from them.
7 And the shapes of the locusts
*were* like unto horses prepared
unto battle; and on their heads
*were* as it were crowns like gold,
and their faces *were* as the faces
of men.
8 And they had hair as the hair
of women, and their teeth were
as *the teeth* of lions.
9 And they had breastplates, as
it were breastplates of iron; and
the sound of their wings *was* as
the sound of chariots of many
horses [2]running to battle.

9 2 R. V. rushing to war.

10 And they [3]had tails like unto
scorpions, and there were stings
in their tails: and their power
*was* to hurt men five months.

10 3 R. V. have tails like unto scorpions, and stings; and in their tails is their power to hurt men five months.

11 [4]And they had a king over
them, *which is* the angel of the
bottomless pit, whose name in
the Hē'brew tongue *is* Ā-băd'-
don, but in the Greek tongue
hath *his* name Ā-pŏl'lȳ-ŏn.

11 4 R. V. They have over them as king the angel of the abyss: his name in Hebrew is Abaddon, and in the Greek tongue he hath the name Apollyon.

12 [5]One woe is past; *and,* behold, there come two woes more
hereafter.

12 5 R. V. The first Woe is past: behold, there come yet two Woes hereafter.

13 And the sixth angel sounded,
and I heard a voice from the four
horns of the golden altar which
is before God,
14 Saying to the sixth angel
which had the trumpet, Loose
the four angels which are bound
[6]in the great river Eū-phrā'tēs.

14 6 R. V. at

15 And the four angels were
loosed, which were prepared for
an hour, and a [c]day, and a month,
and a year, for to [d]slay the third
part of men.

15 c *Day, prophetic,* Gen. 1:5.
d *Judgments,* Ex. 6:6.

16 And the number of the [7]army
of the horsemen *were* two hundred

16 7 R. V. armies of the horsemen was twice ten thousand times ten thousand: I heard

thousand thousand: and I heard
the number of them.
17 And thus I saw the horses in
the vision, and them that sat on
them, having breastplates of fire,
and of [8]jacinth, and brimstone:[C]
and the heads of the horses *were*
as the heads of lions; and out
of their mouths issued fire and
smoke and brimstone.
18 By these three [9]was the third
part of men killed, by the fire,
and by the smoke, and by the
brimstone, which issued out of
their mouths.
19 For [10]their power is in their
mouth, and in their tails: for their
tails *were* like unto serpents, and
had heads, and with them they
do hurt.
20 And the rest of the men
which were not killed by these
[d]plagues yet [e,f]repented not of
the works of their hands, that
they should not worship [g]devils,[C]
and [h]idols of gold, and silver,
and brass, and stone, and of
wood: [i]which neither can see,
nor hear, nor walk:[Q]
21 [e,f]Neither repented they of
their [j]murders, nor of their [k]sor-
ceries, nor of their [l]fornication,
nor of their [m]thefts.[Q]

## CHAPTER 10

*A mighty angel appears with an open book 6 and swears by him that lives for ever, that time shall be no longer. 8 John is commanded to take and eat the book.*

AND I saw another mighty
angel come down from
heaven, clothed with a cloud:
and a rainbow *was* upon his
head, and his face *was* as it were
the sun, and his feet as pillars of
fire:
2 And he had in his hand a little
[a]book[C] open: and he set his right
foot upon the [b]sea, and *his* left
*foot* on the earth,
3 And cried with a loud voice,
as *when* a lion roareth: and when
he had cried, [c]seven thunders
uttered their voices.
4 And when the [c]seven thunders had uttered their voices, I
was about to write: and I heard
a voice from heaven saying unto
me, Seal[C] up those things which
the seven thunders uttered, and
write them not.[Q]
5 And the angel which I saw
stand upon the [b]sea and upon
the earth lifted up his hand to
heaven,[Q]
6 And [d]sware by him that liveth
[e]for ever and ever, who [f]created
[g]heaven, and the things that
therein are, and the [h]earth, and
the things that therein are, and
the sea, and the things which are
therein, that there should be
*time no longer:[S T Q]
7 But in the days of the voice of
the [c]seventh angel, when he
[1]shall begin to sound, the [i,j]mys-
tery[C] of God should be finished,
as he hath [k]declared to his servants the prophets.[Q]
8 And the voice which I heard
from heaven spake unto me
again, and said, Go *and* take the
little [a]book[C] which is open in the
hand of the angel which standeth upon the [b]sea and upon the
earth.

**17**
8 R. V. hyacinth

**18**
9 R. V. three plagues was

**19**
10 R. V. the power of the horses is

**20**
e *Impenitence*, Rom. 2:5.
f *Adversity, obduracy in*, Psa. 10:6.
g *Demons, worship of*, Matt. 4:24.
h *Idols*, 1 Kin. 15:12.
i *Idolatry, folly of*, 1 Sam. 15:23.

**21**
j *Homicide, felonious*, Deut. 5:17.
k *Sorcery*, Isa. 47:9.
l *Adultery*, Lev. 20:10.
m *Theft*, Mark 7:22.

**2**
a *Book, eating of*, vs. 2–10; Num. 5:23.
b *Sea, symbolical*, Jer. 5:22.

**3**
c *Seven*, Gen. 7:2.

**6**
d *Oath*, Num. 5:19.
e *God, eternity of*, Gen. 2:2.
f *God, creator*, Gen. 2:2.
g *Heavens*, Psa. 8:3.
h *Earth*, Prov. 8:23.

**7**
i *Mysteries, of redemption*, Mark 4:11.
j *Salvation, plan of*, Acts 16:17.
k *Prophets, inspiration of*, Isa. 3:2.
1 R. V. is about to sound, then is finished the mystery of God, according to the good tidings which he declared

* **TIME.** *Beginning of*, Gen. 1:1; Heb. 1:10; compare John 1:1. *Epochs in*, Gen. 1:5, 8, 13, 19, 23, 31 (with Matt. 28:20, R. V. marg.; Eph. 3:9; Col. 1:26, R. V.). *One day with the Lord as a thousand years*, 2 Pet. 3:8.

*For achievement, short*, Rom. 13:11, 12; 1 Cor. 7:29; Heb. 10:25; 1 Pet. 4:7.

*Beginning of reckoning of, by Israelites*, Ex. 12:2.

*Divided into months*, see footnote, **MONTH**, Ex. 12:2. *Daily, divided into watches*, Ex. 14:24; 1 Sam. 11:11; Matt. 14:24; Mark 6:48.

**Biblical Chronology.** The chronology found in the margins of the O. T. (and the N. T. through Acts 2) of this Revised and Expanded Edition is essentially the work of Martin Anstey. His work on Bible chronology has recently been reprinted under the title *Chronology of the Old Testament*. Philip Mauro's *The Wonders of Bible Chronology*, which is based on Anstey's work, was utilized to check Anstey and to correct him at two points. Aside from these two points, there is only one minor variation from Anstey's chronology: the date of Moses' birth. The date given by both Anstey and Mauro assumes that Moses died in the *same* year Joshua led Israel into the land, when in fact Moses died the year *before* the conquest began. This correlates with all other Biblical information concerning Moses' life.

Certain important principles have been followed in placing this chronology in the margins.

Dates have been inserted only where reasonable certainty exists as to the exact year of the events mentioned in the text. Many columns have no chronological notes in their margins, since no exact chronological data exist. Thus, though many events are undated, the student may

9 And I went unto the angel,
and said unto him, Give me the
little [a]book. And he said unto
me, Take *it*, and eat it up; and
it shall make thy belly bitter, but
it shall be in thy mouth sweet as
honey.
10 And I took the little [a]book
out of the angel's hand, and ate
it up; and it was in my mouth
sweet as honey: and as soon as I
had eaten it, my belly was bitter.
11 And he said unto me, [l]Thou
must prophesy again before
many peoples, and nations, and
tongues, and kings.

**11**
*l John,* Mark 1:19.

## CHAPTER 11

*John is directed to measure the temple.* 3 *The two witnesses,* 6 *and their power.* 7 *The beast shall kill them.* 8 *Their bodies unburied,* 11 *after three days and a half are raised to life.* 14 *The second woe is past.* 15 *The seventh angel sounds and there is rejoicing in heaven.*

AND there was given me a
[a]reed like unto a rod: and
[1]the angel stood, saying, Rise,
and measure the [b]temple of God,
and the altar, and them that
[c]worship therein.
2 But the court which is without
the temple leave out, and
measure it not; for it is given
unto the [2]Ġĕn'tīleş: and the holy
city shall they tread under foot
forty *and* two [d]months.
3 And I will give [3]*power* unto
my two witnesses, and they
shall prophesy a thousand two
hundred *and* threescore [e]days,
clothed in sackcloth.
4 These are the two olive trees,
and the two candlesticks standing
before the [4,f]God of the earth.
5 And if any man [5]will hurt
them, fire proceedeth out of their
mouth, and devoureth their enemies:
and if any man [6]will hurt
them, he must in this manner be
killed.
6 These have power to shut
heaven, that it rain not in the
days of their prophecy: and have
power over waters to turn them
to blood, and to smite the earth
with all plagues, as often as they
will.
7 And when they shall have finished
their testimony, the beast
that [7]ascendeth out of the bottomless
pit shall make war
against them, and shall overcome
them, and kill them.
8 And their dead bodies *shall
lie* in the street of the great city,
which spiritually is called [g]Sŏd'om
and [h]Ē'ġўpt, where also our
Lord was [i]crucified.
9 And they of the people and
kindreds and tongues and nations
shall see their dead bodies
three days and an half, and shall

**1**
*a Reed,* Ezek. 40:3.
*b Temple, figurative,* 1 Kin. 6:17.
*c Worship,* Gen. 22:5.
1 R. V. one said, Rise, and measure

**2**
*d Month,* Ex. 12:2.
2 R. V. nations:

**3**
3 R. V. *omits* power

*e Day, a prophetic period,* Gen. 1:5.

**4**
*f God, sovereign,* Gen. 2:2.
4 R. V. Lord

**5**
5 R. V. desireth to hurt
6 R. V. shall desire to hurt

**7**
7 R. V. cometh up out of the abyss shall

**8**
*g Sodom,* Gen. 13:10.
*h Egypt, symbolical,* Gen. 41:8.
*i Jesus, death of,* Matt. 1:21.

---

attach a great degree of confidence to those that are dated. This procedure has been followed because of the principle first insisted on by Anstey: that a chronology of the O. T. may and should be constructed on the basis of Biblical data *alone,* without the use of either conjecture or untrustworthy non-Biblical sources. This foundational principle makes Anstey's chronology absolutely unique, since all previous chronologists had utilized conjecture and non-Biblical data to some extent. Furthermore, this foundational principle demands from every believer in the Bible's inerrancy the highest degree of respect for the resultant chronology based upon it. Thus conjectural dates have purposely been omitted from the chronology of this study Bible.

At certain points the Biblical text recapitulates genealogy or history previously narrated (cf. Deut. 1-3; 1 Chron. 1-9). No attempt has been made to recapitulate the chronology of the names or events mentioned. Either no date has been inserted in these sections, or the date inserted is that of the time at which these past events are being narrated.

The chronological notes may be found in bold type in the margin. An example from page 12 follows:

**v. 1 - 2390 BC**

This note means that the event of verse 1 in the adjacent column occurred in 2390 B.C. An attempt has been made to place the chronological notations as close to the appropriate verse as possible; but occasionally, due to other marginal notes, the chronological note will be separated by one or two verses from the appropriate verse.

In the historical narrative sections of the O. T.—Genesis through Esther (except Ruth, which has no discernible chronological data)—there may be but one chronological note in a column, and that at the top of the column. This means all the material in that column occurred in that year, provided the same date is given at the top of the next margin. If no date is given at the top of the next margin, then at some point in the previous column, the narrative has shifted to material that it is impossible to date with accuracy. If a different date is given at the top of the next margin and no date has intervened since the one at the top of the previous margin, then the verse referred to in the chronological note is the one in which the narrative has shifted to a different year.

In the prophetic books of Isaiah, Jeremiah, Ezekiel, Daniel, Zechariah, and Haggai, only sections of historical narrative and verses where historical dates are mentioned have been dated, since it is often impossible to determine which of the surrounding prophetic material is being dated by the verse containing a historical reference.

All Biblical chronology has its focal point, and finds its culmination in, the initial coming of Messiah, the Prince. Thus the N. T. does not maintain a chronological line past the death and resurrection of Christ and the outpouring of His Spirit on the day of Pentecost. For an explanation of the significance of these dates to the whole stream of Biblical chronology, see the appendix on "Biblical Chronology."

not suffer[C] their dead bodies to be put in graves.

10[Q] And they that dwell upon the earth shall rejoice over them, and make merry, and shall send gifts one to another; because these two prophets tormented them that dwelt on the earth.

11 And after three days and an half the [8]Spirit of life from God entered into them, and they stood upon their feet; and great fear fell upon them which saw them.[T Q]

12 And they heard a great voice from heaven saying unto them, Come up hither. And they ascended up to heaven in a cloud; and their enemies beheld them.[Q]

13 And the same hour was there a great earthquake, and the tenth part of the city fell, and in the earthquake were slain of men seven thousand: and the remnant were affrighted,[C] and gave glory to the God of heaven.[Q]

14 The second woe is past; *and,* behold, the third woe cometh quickly.

15 And the seventh angel sounded; and there were great voices in heaven, saying, [j,k,l]The kingdoms of this world are become *the kingdoms* of our Lord, and of his Christ; and [m]he shall reign for ever and ever.[Q]

16 And the four and twenty elders, which sat before God on their seats,[C] fell upon their faces, and [n]worshipped God,

17 [o]Saying, We give thee thanks, O Lord God Almighty, [p]which art, and wast, [9]and art to come; because thou hast taken to thee thy great [q]power, and hast reigned.[S T Q]

18 And the nations were angry, and thy wrath is come, and the [r]time of the dead, that they should be [s]judged, and that thou shouldest give reward unto thy servants the prophets, and to the saints, and them that [t]fear thy name, small and great; and shouldest [u]destroy them which destroy the earth.[S Q]

19 And the temple of God was opened in heaven, and there was seen in his temple the ark of his [10]testament[C]: and there were lightnings, and voices, and thunderings, and an earthquake, and great hail.[Q]

## CHAPTER 12

*A woman clothed with the sun travails. 3 A great dragon stands ready to devour her child. 5 Being delivered, and the child caught up unto God, the woman flees into the wilderness. 7 Michael and his angels overcome the dragon. 13 The dragon, cast down into the earth, persecutes the woman.*

AND there appeared a great wonder[C] in heaven; a woman clothed with the sun, and the moon under her feet, and upon her head a crown of twelve stars:

2 And she being with child cried, travailing in birth, and pained to be delivered.[Q]

3 And there appeared another wonder[C] in heaven; and behold a great red dragon, having seven heads and ten horns, and seven crowns upon his heads.[Q]

4 And his tail drew the third part of the stars of heaven, and did cast them to the earth: and the dragon stood before the woman which was ready to be delivered, for to devour[C] her child as soon as it was born.[Q]

5 And she brought forth a man child, who was to rule all nations with a rod of iron: and her child was caught up unto God, and *to* his throne.[Q]

6 And the woman fled into the wilderness,[C] where she hath a place prepared of God, that they should feed her there a thousand two hundred *and* threescore[C] [a]days.[S]

7 And there was war in heaven: Mī′chaël and his angels fought

**11**
8 R. V. breath of life

**15**
*j Church, prophecies concerning its prosperity,* Matt. 16:18.
*k Jesus, kingdom of, prophecies concerning,* Matt. 1:21.
*l Gentiles, conversion of,* Acts 10:45.
*m Jesus, king,* Matt. 1:21.

**16**
*n Worship,* Gen. 22:5.

**17**
*o Praise, in heaven,* Psa. 150:1.
*p God, eternity of,* Gen. 2:2.
*q God, power of,* Gen. 2:2.
9 R. V. *omits* and art to come;

**18**
*r Judgment, the general,* 2 Pet. 3:7.
*s God, judge,* Gen. 2:2.
*t Fear of God,* Acts 9:31.
*u Wicked, punishment of,* Psa. 73:3.

**19**
10 R. V. covenant:

**6**
*a Day, a prophetic period,* Gen. 1:5.

against the dragon; and the dragon fought and his angels,[Q]

8 And prevailed not; neither was their place found any more in heaven.

9 [S]And the great dragon was cast out, that old serpent, called the Děv′il, and [b]Sā′tan, which deceiveth the whole world: he was cast out into the earth, and his [c]angels were cast out with him.[T] [Q]

10 And I heard a loud voice saying in heaven, [d,e]Now is come salvation[C], and strength, and the kingdom of our God, and the [1]power of his Chrīst: for the [b]accuser of our brethren is cast down, which accused them before our God day and night.[Q]

11 And they overcame him by the [f,g]blood of the [h]Lamb, and by the word of their [i,j]testimony[C]; and [k]they loved not their lives unto the [l]death.

12 Therefore rejoice, *ye* heavens, and ye that dwell in them. Woe [2]to the inhabiters of the earth and of the sea! for the devil is come down unto you, having great wrath, because he knoweth that he hath but a short time.[S] [Q]

13 And when the dragon saw that he was cast unto the earth, he persecuted the woman which brought forth the man *child*.

14 And to the woman were given two wings of a great [m]eagle, that she might fly into the wilderness, into her place, where she is nourished for a time, and times, and half a time, from the face of the serpent.[Q]

15 And the serpent cast out of his mouth water as a flood after the woman, that he might cause her to be carried away of the flood.

16 And the earth helped the woman, and the earth opened her mouth, and swallowed up the flood which the dragon cast out of his mouth.

17 And the dragon was wroth[C] with the woman, and went to make war with the remnant of her seed, which [n]keep[C] the commandments of God, and have the testimony[C] of Jē′şus [3]Chrīst.[Q]

## CHAPTER 13

*A beast rises out of the sea with seven heads and ten horns, to whom the dragon gives his power. 11 Another beast comes up out of the earth; and causes men to worship the first beast, 16 and to receive his mark.*

AND [1,a]I stood upon the sand of the sea, and saw a [b]beast rise up out of the sea, having [c]seven heads and ten horns, and upon his horns ten crowns, and upon his heads the name of [d]blasphemy.[Q]

2 And the beast which I saw was like unto a leopard, and his feet were as *the feet* of a bear, and his mouth as the mouth of a lion: and the dragon gave him his power, and his seat[C], and great authority.[Q]

3 And I saw one of his heads as it were wounded to death; and his deadly wound was healed: and all the world wondered[C] after the beast.

4 And they [e]worshipped the dragon [2]which gave power unto the beast: and they worshipped the beast, saying, Who *is* like unto the beast? who is able to make war with him?

5 And there was given unto him a mouth speaking great things and blasphemies; and [3]power was given unto him to continue forty *and* two months.[Q]

6 And he opened his mouth in [d]blasphemy against God, to blaspheme[C] his name, and his [f]tabernacle, and them that dwell in heaven.

7 And it was given unto him to make war with the saints, and to overcome them: and [3]power was given him over all kindreds, and tongues, and nations.[Q]

8 And all that dwell upon the

9
*b Satan,* Matt. 4:10.
*c Angel, fallen,* Heb. 1:13.

10
*d Church, prophecies concerning its prosperity,* Matt. 16:18.
*e Jesus, kingdom of, prophecies concerning,* Matt. 1:21.
1 R. V. authority

11
*f Blood, of Jesus,* Heb. 9:19.
*g Atonement, by Jesus,* Lev. 17:11.
*h Lamb, an appellation of Jesus,* John 1:29.
*i Religious Testimony,* 2 Thess. 1:10.
*j Witnessing for Christ,* Luke 24:48.
*k Renunciation,* Luke 5:11.
*l Martyrdom,* Rev. 17:6.

12
2 R. V. for the earth and for the sea: because the devil is gone down

14
*m Eagle, symbolical,* Lev. 11:13.

17
*n Obedience,* Heb. 5:8.
3 R. V. *omits* Christ.

1
*a John,* Mark 1:19.
*b Beast, symbolical,* Dan. 7:3.
*c Seven,* Gen. 7:2.
*d Blasphemy,* 2 Sam. 12:14.
1 R. V. he

4
*e Demons, worship of,* Matt. 4:24.
2 R. V. because he gave his authority unto

5
3 R. V. authority

6
*f Church, called tabernacle,* 1 Kin. 9:3.

8
[g] *Worship*, Gen. 22:5.
[h] *Book, figurative*, Num. 5:23.
[i] *Lamb, an appellation of Jesus*, John 1:29.
[j] *Jesus, death of*, Matt. 1:21.
[k] *Atonement, made by Jesus*, Lev. 17:11.

10
[l] *Sin, retroactive*, Rom. 5:12.
[m] *Patience*, Luke 8:15.
[n] *Steadfastness*, 1 Cor. 15:58.
4 R. V. If any man is for captivity, into captivity he goeth:

14
5 R. V. signs which it was given him to do

15
6 R. V. it was given unto him to give breath to it, even to the image

earth shall [g]worship him, whose
names are not written in the
[h]book of life of the [i]Lamb [j,k]slain
from the foundation of the
world.[s] [Q]
9 If any man have an ear, let
him hear.
10 [4]He that leadeth into captivity [l]shall go into captivity: he
that killeth with the sword [l]must
be killed with the sword. Here is
the [m,n]patience and the faith of
the saints.[Q]
11 And I beheld another beast
coming up out of the earth; and
he had two horns like a lamb,
and he spake as a dragon.
12 And he exerciseth all the
[3]power of the first beast before
him, and causeth the earth and
them which dwell therein to worship the first beast, whose deadly
wound was healed.
13 And he doeth great wonders,[C]
so that he maketh fire come
down from heaven on the earth
in the sight of men,[Q]
14 And deceiveth them that
dwell on the earth by *the means
of* those [5]miracles[C] which he had
power to do in the sight of the
beast; saying to them that dwell
on the earth, that they should
make an image to the beast,
which had the wound by a
sword, and did live.[Q]
15 And [6]he had power to give
life unto the image of the beast,
that the image of the beast
should both speak, and cause
that as many as would not worship the image of the beast
should be killed.[Q]
16 And he causeth all, both
small and great, rich and poor,
free and bond,[C] to receive a mark
in their right hand, or in their
foreheads:
17 And that no man might buy
or sell, save[C] he that had the
mark, or the name of the beast,
or the number of his name.
18 Here is wisdom. Let him
that hath understanding count
the number of the beast: for it is
the number of a man; and his
number *is* Six hundred threescore *and* six.

## CHAPTER 14

*The Lamb on mount Zion with his company. 6 The triumph of the gospel. 8 The fall of Babylon. 9 The worshiper of the beast and his image threatened. 13 The reward of the faithful. 15 The harvest of the world.*

AND I looked, and, lo, a
[a]Lamb stood on the mount
Sī′ŏn, and with him [b]an hundred forty *and* four thousand,
having [1]his [c]Father's name written in their foreheads.[Q]
2 And I heard a voice from
[d]heaven, as the voice of many
waters, and as the voice of a
great thunder: and [2]I heard the
[e,f,g]voice of harpers harping with
their [h]harps:[Q]
3 And they [f,g]sung as it were a
new [e]song before the [i]throne,
and before the four [3,j]beasts,
and the elders: and no man
could learn that song but the
[b]hundred *and* forty *and* four
thousand, which were [k]re-
deemed from the earth.[Q]
4 [b]These are they which were
[l]not defiled with women; for
they are virgins. These are they
which follow the [a]Lamb whithersoever he goeth. These were
[k]redeemed[C] from among men,
*being* the firstfruits unto God and
to the Lamb.
5 And [b,m]in their mouth was
found no [4,n,o]guile[C]: for they are
[p]without fault before the throne
of God.[Q]
6 [q,r]And I saw another angel
fly in the midst of heaven,
having the everlasting [s]gospel to
preach unto them that dwell on
the earth, and [t]to every nation,
and kindred, and tongue, and
people,
7 Saying with a loud voice,
[u]Fear God, and give [v]glory to

1
[a] *Lamb, an appellation of Jesus*, John 1:29.
[b] *Glorified Saints*, vs. 1–5; Heb. 12:1.
[c] *God, fatherhood of*, Gen. 2:2.
1 R. V. his name, and the name of his Father, written

2
[d] *Heaven, future home of the righteous*, Luke 18:22.
[e] *Song, of the redeemed*, Psa. 77:6.
[f] *Music*, 2 Chr. 5:13.
[g] *Worship*, Gen. 22:5.
[h] *Harp*, Dan. 3:10.
2 R. V. the voice which I heard was as the voice of harpers

3
[i] *Throne*, 1 Kin. 2:19.
[j] *Beasts, symbolical*, Dan. 7:3.
[k] *Redemption of our Souls*, Eph. 1:7.
3 R. V. living creatures,

4
[l] *Chastity*, Job 31:1.

5
[m] *Righteous, described*, Psa. 64:10.
[n] *Falsehood*, Job 21:34.
[o] *Deceit*, Psa. 36:3.
[p] *Holy, described*, Col. 3:12.
4 R. V. lie: they are without blemish.

6
[q] *Millennium*, Rev. 20:4.
[r] *Jesus, kingdom of, prophecies concerning*, Matt. 1:21.
[s] *Gospel*, Mark 13:10.
[t] *Missions*, Matt. 28:19.

7
[u] *Fear of God, motives to*, Acts 9:31.
[v] *Glorifying God*, Luke 5:25.

him; for the hour of his judgment is come: and [w]worship [x]him that made [y]heaven, and [z]earth, and the sea, and the fountains of waters.[T][Q]

8 And [5]there followed another angel, saying, [a,b,c]Băb′y̆-lon is fallen, is fallen, that great city, because she made all nations drink of the [d]wine of the wrath of her fornication.[Q]

9 And the third angel followed them, saying with a loud voice, If any man [e]worship the beast and his image, and receive *his* mark in his forehead, or in his hand,

10 [f]The same shall drink of the [d]wine of the [g]wrath of God, which is poured out without mixture into the [h]cup of his [6]indignation; and [f]he shall be [i]tormented with fire and [j]brimstone in the presence of the holy [k]angels, and in the presence of the [l]Lamb:[S][T][Q]

11 And [f]the smoke of their [i]torment ascendeth up for ever and ever: and they have no rest day nor night, who [e]worship the beast and his image, and whosoever receiveth the mark of his name.[Q]

12 Here is the [m,n]patience of the saints: here *are* they that [o]keep[G] the commandments of God, and the [p]faith of Jē′ṣus.[T]

13 And I heard a voice from heaven [q]saying unto me, Write, [r]Blessed *are* the dead which [s]die in the Lord from henceforth: Yea, saith the [t]Spirit, that they may rest from their labours; and their [u]works do follow them.[T]

14 And I looked, and [v]behold a white cloud, and upon the cloud *one* sat like unto [7,w]the Son of man, [x]having on his head a golden [y]crown, and in his hand a sharp [z]sickle.[Q]

15 And another angel came out of the [a]temple, crying with a loud voice to him that sat on the cloud, Thrust in thy [b]sickle, and reap: for the time is come for thee to reap; for the [c]harvest of the earth is [8]ripe.[Q]

16 And he that sat on the cloud thrust in his [b]sickle on the earth; and the earth was reaped.

17 And another angel came out of the temple which is in heaven, he also having a sharp [b]sickle.

18 And another angel came out from the altar, which had power over fire; and cried with a loud cry to him that had the sharp [b]sickle, saying, Thrust in thy sharp sickle, and gather the clusters of the vine of the earth; for her [d]grapes are fully ripe.[Q]

19 And the angel thrust in his sickle into the earth, and gathered the vine of the earth, and cast *it* into the great [e]winepress of the [f]wrath of God.[T]

20 And the [e]winepress was trodden without[G] the city, and blood came out of the winepress, even unto the horse bridles, by the space[G] of a thousand *and* six hundred furlongs.[G][Q]

## CHAPTER 15

*Seven angels with the seven last plagues. 3 The song of those that overcome the beast. 7 Seven golden vials full of the wrath of God.*

AND I saw another sign in heaven, great and marvellous, [a]seven angels having the seven last [b]plagues; for in them is filled up the [c]wrath[G] of God.[Q][S][T]

2 And I saw as it were a [1,d]sea of [e]glass mingled with fire: and [f]them that had gotten the victory over the beast, and over his image, and over his mark, *and* over the number of his name, [2]stand on the sea of glass, having the [g]harps of God.

3 And [f]they [h]sing the [i]song of Mō′ṣeṣ the servant of God, and the song of the [j]Lamb, saying, [k]Great and marvellous *are* thy works, Lord God [3]Almighty;

w *Worship*, Gen. 22:5.
x *God, creator*, Gen. 2:2.
y *Heavens, created*, Psa. 8:3.
z *Earth, created*, Prov. 8:23.

**8**
a Isa. 21:9.
b *Babylon, figurative*, Ezra 5:12.
c *Satan, kingdom of, to be destroyed*, Matt. 4:10.
d *Wine, figurative*, Prov. 23:31.
5 R. V. another, a second angel, followed, saying, Fallen, fallen, is Babylon the great, which hath made

**9**
e *Idolatry*, 1 Sam. 15:23.

**10**
f *Wicked, punishment of*, Psa. 73:3.
g *Anger of God, destroys*, 2 Kin. 13:3.
h *Cup, figurative*, Matt. 20:22.
i Luke 16:23–28.
j *Brimstone, figurative*, Deut. 29:23.
k *Angel*, Heb. 1:13.
l *Lamb*, John 1:29.
6 R. V. anger;

**12**
m *Patience, a grace of the righteous*, Luke 8:15.
n *Perseverance*, Eph. 6:18.
o *Obedience*, Heb. 5:8.
p *Faith, doctrines of Jesus*, 1 Cor. 16:13.

**13**
q *Prophets, inspiration of*, Isa. 3:2.
r *Promise, to the righteous*, 2 Cor. 1:20.
s *Death, of the righteous*, Num. 23:10.
t *Holy Spirit*, Acts 1:2.
u *Works*, 2 Tim. 1:9.

**14**
v *Jesus, prophecies concerning future glory and power of*, Matt. 1:21.
w *Jesus, humanity of*, Matt. 1:21.
x *Jesus, king*, Matt. 1:21.
y *Crown, symbolical*, Ex. 29:6.
z *Sickle, figurative*, Deut. 23:25.
7 R. V. a son

**15**
a *Temple, figurative*, 1 Kin. 6:17.
b *Sickle, figurative*, Deut. 23:25.
c *Harvest, figurative*, Ex. 34:21.
8 R. V. overripe.

**18**
d *Grapes, figurative*, Lev. 25:5.

**19**
e *Wine Press, figurative*, Isa. 5:2.
f *Anger of God*, 2 Kin. 13:3.

**1**
a *Seven*, Gen. 7:2.
b *Plague, foretold*, Ex. 11:1.
c *Anger of God*, 2 Kin. 13:3.

**2**
d *Sea, symbolical*, Jer. 5:22.
e *Glass*, Rev. 21:18.
f *Glorified Saints*, Heb. 12:1.
g *Harp*, Dan. 3:10.
1 R. V. glassy sea
2 R. V. standing by the glassy sea,

**3**
h *Music*, 2 Chr. 5:13.
i *Song, of Moses and the Lamb*, Psa. 77:6.
j *Lamb*, John 1:29.
k *Praise, in heaven*, Psa. 150:1.
3 R. V. the Almighty; righteous and true are thy ways, thou King of the ages.

[l]just and [m]true *are* thy ways, thou [n]King of saints.[G][S][Q]

4 Who shall not fear thee, O Lord, and [o]glorify thy name? for *thou* only *art* [p]holy: for [q,r]all nations shall come and [s]worship before thee; for thy judgments[G] are made manifest.[S][Q]

5 And after that I looked, and, behold, the [t]temple of the tabernacle of the testimony in heaven was opened:[Q]

6 And the [a]seven angels came out of the temple, having the seven [b]plagues, [4]clothed in pure and white linen, and having their breasts girded[G] with golden girdles.[Q]

7 And one of the four [5,l]beasts gave unto the [a]seven angels seven golden vials[G] full of the [c]wrath of God, who liveth [u]for ever and ever.[S][Q]

8 And the [t]temple was filled with smoke from the [v]glory of God, and from his [w]power; and no man was able to enter into the temple, till the [a]seven [b]plagues of the seven angels were fulfilled.[Q]

## CHAPTER 16

***The seven angels in succession pour out their vials of wrath upon the earth, and great plagues follow thereupon.***

AND I heard a great voice out of the [a]temple saying to the [b]seven angels, Go [1]your ways, and pour out the vials[G] of the [c,d]wrath of God upon the earth.[Q]

2 And the first went, and poured out his [2]vial[G] upon the earth; and [e]there fell a noisome[G] and grievous[G] sore upon the men which had the mark of the beast, and *upon* them which worshipped his image.[Q]

3 And the second angel poured out his [3]vial[G] upon the sea; and it became as the blood of a dead *man*: and every living soul died in the sea.[Q]

4 And the third angel poured out his [3]vial[G] upon the rivers and fountains of waters; and [4]they became blood.[Q]

5 [S]And I heard the angel of the waters [5]say, Thou art [f]righteous, O Lord, [g]which art, and wast, and shalt be, because thou hast judged thus.[Q]

6 For they have [h]shed the [i,j]blood of saints and [k]prophets, and thou hast [d,l]given them blood to drink; for they are worthy.[Q]

7 And I heard [6]another out of the altar say, Even so, [m]Lord God Almighty, true and [f]righteous *are* thy [d]judgments.[S][Q]

8 And the fourth [7]angel poured out his vial[G] upon the sun; and power was given unto him to scorch men with fire.

9 And [l,n]men were scorched with great heat, and [o,p]blasphemed[G] the name of God, which hath power over these plagues: and they [q]repented not to give him glory.

10 And the fifth [8]angel poured out his vial[G] upon the seat[G] of the beast; and his kingdom was [l]full of [r]darkness; and they gnawed their tongues for [s]pain,[Q]

11 And [o]blasphemed[G] the God of heaven [n]because of their [s]pains and their sores, and [q]repented not of their deeds.[Q]

12 And the sixth angel poured out his [3]vial[G] upon the great river [t]Eū-phrā'tēs; and the water thereof was dried up, that the way [9]of the kings of the east might be prepared.[Q]

13 And I saw three unclean spirits like frogs *come* out of the mouth of the dragon, and out of the mouth of the beast, and out of the mouth of the false prophet.[Q]

14 For they are the spirits of devils,[G] working [10]miracles,[G] *which* go forth unto the kings of the earth and of the whole world, to gather them to the battle of that great day of [m]God Almighty.[Q]

15 ¶ Behold, I come as a thief.

---

*l* *God, justice of*, Gen. 2:2.
*m* *God, faithfulness of*, Gen. 2:2.
*n* *God, sovereign*, Gen. 2:2.

**4**

*o* *Glorifying God*, Luke 5:25.
*p* *God, holiness of*, Gen. 2:2.
*q* *Church, prophecies concerning its prosperity*, Matt. 16:18.
*r* *Gentiles, conversion of*, Acts 10:45.
*s* *Worship*, Gen. 22:5.

**5**

*t* *Temple, figurative*, 1 Kin. 6:17.

**6**

4 R. V. arrayed with precious stone, pure and bright, and girt about their breasts with golden girdles.

**7**

*u* *God, eternity of*, Gen. 2:2.
5 R. V. living creatures

**8**

*v* *God, glory of*, Gen. 2:2.
*w* *God, power of*, Gen. 2:2.

**1**

*a* *Temple, figurative*, 1 Kin. 6:17.
*b* *Seven*, Gen. 7:2.
*c* *Anger of God*, 2 Kin. 13:3.
*d* *Judgments*, Ex. 6:6.
1 R. V. ye, and pour out the seven bowls of the wrath of God into the earth.

**2**

*e* *Wicked, punishment of*, Psa. 73:3.
2 R. V. bowl into the earth; and it became a noisome

**3**

3 R. V. bowl

**4**

4 R. V. it

**5**

*f* *God, righteousness of*, Gen. 2:2.
*g* *God, eternity of*, Gen. 2:2.
5 R. V. saying, Righteous art thou, which art and which wast, thou Holy One, because thou didst thus judge:

**6**

*h* *Persecution, of the righteous*, John 15:20.
*i* *Blood*, Heb. 9:19.
*j* *Martyrdom, of prophets*, Rev. 17:6.
*k* *Prophets, martyrs*, Isa. 3:2.
*l* *Wicked, punishment of*, Psa. 73:3.

**7**

*m* *God, omnipotent*, Gen. 2:2.
6 R. V. the altar saying, Yea, O Lord God, the Almighty,

**8**

7 R. V. poured out his bowl upon the sun; and it was given unto it to scorch men with fire.

**9**

*n* *Adversity, obduracy in*, Psa. 10:6.
*o* *Blasphemy*, 2 Sam. 12:14.
*p* *Profanation, of God's name*, Lev. 22:32.
*q* *Impenitence*, Rom. 2:5.

**10**

*r* *Darkness, figurative*, Gen. 1:2.
*s* *Pain*, Job 14:22.
8 R. V. poured out his bowl upon the throne of the beast; and his kingdom was darkened;

**12**

*t* *Euphrates*, Gen. 15:18.
9 R. V. might be made ready for the kings that come from the sunrising.

**14**

10 R. V. signs;

[u]Blessed[G] *is* he that [v]watcheth, and [w]keepeth his [x]garments, lest he walk naked, and they see his shame.

16 And he gathered them together into a place called in the Hē′brew tongue [11]Är-ma-gĕd′-don.[Q]

17 And the seventh angel poured out his [3]vial[G] into the air; and there came a great voice out of the temple of heaven, from the throne, saying, It is done.[Q]

18 And there were voices, and thunders, and lightnings; and there was a great earthquake, such as was not since men were upon the earth, so mighty an earthquake, *and* so great.[Q]

19 And the great city was divided into three parts, and the cities of the nations fell: and great [y]Băb′y̆-lon came in remembrance before God, to give unto her the [z]cup of the [a]wine of the fierceness of his [b]wrath.[S T Q]

20 And every island fled away, and the mountains were not found.

21 And there [c]fell upon men a great hail out of heaven, *every stone* about the weight of a talent[G]: and men [d,e]blasphemed[G] God because of the plague of the hail; for the plague thereof was exceeding great.[Q]

15
*u Righteous, promises to,* Psa. 64:10.
*v Watchfulness,* Matt. 24:42.
*w Perseverance, exhortation to,* Eph. 6:18.
*x Righteousness, figuratively described as a garment,* Psa. 15:2.

16
11 R. V. Har-Magedon.

19
*y Babylon, figurative,* Ezra 5:12.
*z Cup, figurative,* Matt. 20:22.

*a Wine, figurative,* Prov. 23:31.
*b Anger of God,* 2 Kin. 13:3.

21
*c Judgments,* Ex. 6:6.
*d Blasphemy,* 2 Sam. 12:14.
*e Adversity, obduracy in,* Psa. 10:6.

## CHAPTER 17

*A woman arrayed in purple and scarlet, with a golden cup in her hand, sits upon the beast. 5 Her name. 7 The mystery of the woman explained.*

1 AND there came one of the [a]seven angels which had the seven [1]vials[G], and talked with me, saying unto me, Come hither; I will shew unto thee the judgment of the great [2,b]whore[G] that sitteth upon many waters:[Q]

2 With whom the kings of the earth have committed fornication, and the inhabitants of the earth have been made drunk with the wine of her fornication.[Q]

3 So he carried me away in the spirit into the wilderness: and I saw a [b]woman sit upon a [c]scarlet coloured beast, full of names of [d]blasphemy, having [a]seven heads and ten horns.[Q]

4 And the [b]woman was arrayed in [c]purple and [c]scarlet colour, and decked[G] with gold and precious stones and *pearls, having a golden cup in her hand full of abominations and filthiness of her fornication:[Q]

5 And upon her forehead *was* a name written, MYSTERY, [e]BĂB′Y̆-LON THE GREAT, THE MOTHER OF HARLOTS AND ABOMINATIONS OF THE EARTH.[Q]

6 And I saw the [b]woman drunken with the blood of the saints, and with the blood of the †,[f]martyrs of Jē′ṣus: and when I saw her, I wondered with great [3]admiration[G].

7 And the angel said unto me, Wherefore didst thou [3]marvel? I will tell thee the mystery[G] of the woman, and of the beast that carrieth her, which hath the seven heads and ten horns.[S]

8 The beast that thou sawest was, and is not; and [4]shall ascend out of the bottomless pit, and go into perdition[G]: and they that dwell on the earth shall wonder, whose names were not written in the [g]book of life from

1
*a Seven,* Gen. 7:2.
1 R. V. bowls.

*Women, wicked, symbolical,* Prov. 31:10.
2 R. V. harlot

3
*c Colors, symbolical,* Ezek. 16:16.
*d Blasphemy,* 2 Sam. 12:14.

5
*e Babylon, figurative,* Ezra 5:12.

6
*f Persecution, of the righteous,* John 15:20.
3 R. V. wonder.

8
*g Book, figurative,* Psa. 139:16.
4 R. V. is about to come up out of the abyss.

* **PEARL,** Rev. 17:4; 18:12, 16. *Of great price,* Matt. 13:46. *Ornaments made of,* 1 Tim. 2:9.
**Figurative,** Matt. 7:6.
**Symbolical,** Rev. 21:21.

† **MARTYRDOM.** *Of prophets,* Matt. 23:34; Luke 11:50; Rev. 16:6. *Followers of Jesus exposed to,* Matt. 10:21, 22, 39 (with Mark 13:12; Luke 21:16, 17); 23:34; 24:9. *Must be incited by love,* 1 Cor. 13:3.
*Allegorical references to,* Rev. 6:9–11; 11:7–12; 17:6.
*Spirit of, required by Jesus,* Matt. 16:25; Luke 9:24; John 12:25; *possessed by the righteous,* Psa. 44:22 (with Rom. 8:36); Rev. 12:11.
**Instances of:** *Abel,* Gen. 4:3–8. *Prophets slain by Jezebel,* 1 Kin. 18:4, 13. *Zechariah,* 2 Chr. 24:21, 22. *John the Baptist,* Mark 6:18–28. *Stephen,* Acts 7:58–60. *James the apostle,* Acts 12:2. *The prophets,* Matt. 22:6; 23:35; Rom. 11:3; 1 Thess. 2:15; Heb. 11:32–37.
See footnote, **PERSECUTION, John 15:20.**

the foundation of the world, when
they behold the beast [5]that was,
and is not, and yet is.[S Q]
9 And here *is* the mind which
hath wisdom. The [a]seven heads
are seven mountains, on which
the [b]woman sitteth.
10 And there are [a]seven kings:
five are fallen, and one is, *and*
the other is not yet come; and
when he cometh, he must continue a short space.
11 And the beast that was, and
is not, even he is the eighth, and
is of the [a]seven, and goeth into
perdition.[C]
12 And the ten horns which
thou sawest are ten kings, which
have received no kingdom as yet;
but receive [6]power as kings one
hour with the beast.[Q]
13 These have one mind, and
shall give their power and
[6]strength unto the beast.
14 These shall make war with
the [h]Lamb, and [i]the Lamb shall
overcome them: for he is [j]Lord
of lords, and [k]King of kings: and
[l]they [7]that are with him *are*
[m]called, and chosen, and faithful.[S T Q]
15 And he saith unto me, The
[n]waters which thou sawest,
where the [2,b]whore[C] sitteth, are
peoples, and multitudes, and
nations, and tongues.[Q]
16 And the ten horns which
thou sawest upon the beast, these
shall hate the [2,b]whore[C], and shall
make her desolate and naked,
and shall eat her flesh, and burn
her with fire.[Q]
17 For [o]God hath put in
their hearts to fulfil his will,
and to agree, and give their
kingdom unto the beast, until
the [p]words of God shall be fulfilled.
18 And the [b]woman which thou
sawest is that great city, which
reigneth over the kings of the
earth.[Q]

5 R. V. how that he was, and is not, and shall come.

**12**

6 R. V. authority

**14**

h *Lamb, an appellation of Jesus,* John 1:29.

i *Jesus, prophecies concerning the future glory and power of,* Matt. 1:21.

j *Jesus, divinity of,* Matt. 1:21.

k *Jesus, king,* Matt. 1:21.

l *Righteous, described,* Psa. 64:10.

m *Election of Grace,* Rom. 11:5.

7 R. V. also shall overcome that are with him, called

**15**

n *Water, symbolical,* 1 Kin. 17:10.

**17**

o *God, providence of,* Gen. 2:2.

p *Prophecies,* Dan. 9:24.

## CHAPTER 18

*The fall of Babylon. 4 The people of God commanded to come out of her. 9 The lamentation of kings, 11 of merchants, 17 and of seamen, over her fall. 20 The saints are bidden to rejoice. 21 Babylon shall be found no more.*

AND after these things I saw
another angel come down
from heaven, having great [1]pow-
er; and the earth was lightened[C]
with his glory.
2 And he cried mightily with a
strong voice, saying, [a]Băb'ȳ-lon
the great is fallen, is fallen, and
is become the habitation of devils, and the hold of every foul
spirit, and a cage of every unclean and hateful bird.[Q]
3 For all nations have drunk of
the [b]wine of the wrath of her
fornication, and the kings of the
earth have committed fornication with her, and the merchants
of the earth are waxed[C] rich
[2]through the abundance of her
delicacies.[Q]
4 And I heard another voice
from heaven, saying, [c,d]Come out
of her, my people, that ye [e]be not
partakers of her sins, and that
ye receive not of her plagues.[S Q]
5 For her sins have reached unto heaven, and God hath remembered her iniquities.[Q]
6 [3,f]Reward her even as she
rewarded you, and double unto
her double according to her
works: in the cup which she hath
filled fill to her double.[Q]
7 How much she hath glorified
herself, and [4]lived deliciously[C], so
much torment and sorrow give
her: for she [g,h]saith in her heart,
I sit a queen, and am no widow,
and shall see no sorrow.[Q]
8 Therefore shall her [i]plagues
come in one day, death, and
mourning, and famine; and she
shall be utterly burned with fire:
for strong *is* the Lord God who
[j]judgeth her.[S Q]
9 And the kings of the earth,
who have committed fornication

**1**

1 R. V. authority;

**2**

a *Babylon, figurative,* Ezra 5:12.

**3**

b *Wine, figurative,* Prov. 23:31.

2 R. V. by the power of her wantonness.

**4**

c *Fellowship, with the wicked, forbidden,* 1 Cor. 1:9.

d *Evil Company,* Prov. 13:20.

e *Holiness, enjoined,* Ex. 39:30.

**6**

f *Wicked, punishment of,* Psa. 73:3.

3 R. V. Render unto her even as she rendered,

**7**

g *False Confidence,* Psa. 30:6.

h *Pride,* Prov. 16:18.

4 R. V. waxed wanton,

**8**

i *Judgments,* Ex. 6:6.

j *God, judge,* Gen. 2:2.

9
5 R. V. wantonly

12
*k Commerce,* 1 Kin. 10:15.
*l Gold,* Ezek. 7:19.
*m Silver,* 1 Chr. 28:14.
*n Precious Stones,* Ex. 39:10.
*o Pearl,* Rev. 17:4.
*p Linen,* Ezek. 27:16.
*q Colors,* Ezek. 16:16.
*r* Ezek. 16:10.
*s Ivory,* 2 Chr. 9:17.
*t Brass,* Job 28:2.
*u Iron,* Prov. 27:17.
*v Marble,* 1 Chr. 29:2.

13
*w Cinnamon,* Song 4:14.
*x Spices,* 1 Kin. 10:2.
*y Ointment,* Eccl. 7:1.
*z Frankincense,* 1 Chr. 9:29.

*a Wine,* Prov. 23:31.
*b Oil,* Deut. 12:17.
*c Wheat,* Ezra 6:9.
*d Cattle,* Ex. 12:29.
*e Sheep,* Deut. 32:14.
*f Horse,* Job 39:19.
*g Chariot,* Josh. 11:4.
*h Servant,* Jer. 2:14.
6 R. V. spice, and incense, and ointment,

15
*i Merchants,* Neh. 3:32.

16
*j Linen,* Ezek. 27:16.
*k Colors,* Ezek. 16:16.
*l Gold,* Ezek. 7:19.
*m Precious Stones,* Ex. 39:10.
*n Pearl,* Rev. 17:4.

17
*o Ship,* 2 Chr. 8:18.
*p Mariner,* Ezek. 27:27.

and lived [5]deliciously[G] with her,
shall bewail her, and lament for
her, when they shall see [j]the
smoke of her burning,[Q]
10 Standing afar off for the fear
of her torment, saying, Alas, alas
that great city [a]Băb′ȳ-lon, that
mighty city! for in one hour is
thy judgment come.[Q]
11 And the merchants of the
earth shall weep and mourn over
her; for no man buyeth their
merchandise any more:[Q]
12[Q] The [k]merchandise of [l]gold,
and [m]silver, and [n]precious stones,
and of [o]pearls, and fine [p]linen,
and [q]purple, and [r]silk, and [q]scar-
let, and all thyine wood, and
all manner[G] vessels of [s]ivory, and
all manner[G] vessels of most precious wood, and of [t]brass, and
[u]iron, and [v]marble,
13 And [w]cinnamon, and
[6,x]odours,[G] and [y]ointments, and
[z]frankincense, and [a]wine, and
[b]oil, and fine flour, and [c]wheat,
and [d]beasts, and [e]sheep, and
[f]horses, and [g]chariots, and
[h]slaves, and souls of men.[Q]
14 And the fruits that thy soul
lusted[G] after are departed from
thee, and all things which were
dainty and goodly[G] are departed
from thee, and thou shalt find
them no more at all.
15 The [i]merchants of these
things, which were made rich by
her, shall stand afar off for the
fear of her torment, weeping and
wailing,[Q]
16 And saying, Alas, alas that
great city, that was clothed in fine
[j]linen, and [k]purple, and [k]scarlet,
and decked[G] with [l]gold, and
[m]precious stones, and [n]pearls![Q]
17 For in one hour so great
riches is come to nought.[G] And
every shipmaster,[G] and all the
company in [o]ships, and [p]sailors,
and as many as trade by sea,
stood afar off,[Q]
18 And cried when they saw the
smoke of her burning, saying,
What *city is* like unto this great
[q]city![Q]
19 And they cast dust on their
heads, and cried, weeping and
wailing, saying, Alas, alas that
great [q]city, wherein were made
rich all that had [o]ships in the sea
by reason of her costliness! for in
one hour is she made desolate.[G][Q]
20 Rejoice over her, *thou*
heaven, and *ye* [7]holy apostles
and prophets;[G] for God hath
avenged you on her.[Q]
21 And a mighty angel took up
a stone like a great millstone,
and cast *it* into the sea, saying,
Thus with violence shall that
great city [q]Băb′ȳ-lon be thrown
down, and shall be found no
more at all.[Q]
22[Q] And [r]the voice of harpers,
and musicians, and of pipers,[G]
and trumpeters, shall be heard
no more at all in thee; and no
craftsman, of whatsoever craft
*he be,* shall be found any more in
thee; and the sound of a millstone shall be heard no more at
all in thee;
23 And the light of a candle[G]
shall shine no more at all in thee;
and the voice of the bridegroom
and of the bride shall be heard
no more at all in thee: for thy
merchants were the great men of
the earth; for by thy sorceries
were all nations deceived.[Q][T]
24 And in her was found the
blood of prophets, and of saints,
and of all that were [s,t]slain upon
the earth.[Q]

## CHAPTER 19

*Much people in heaven praise God for avenging the blood of the saints; 7 and rejoice that the marriage of the Lamb is come. 10 The angel will not be worshipped. 11 The Word of God with his armies. 17 The fowls called to the slaughter. 19 The beast and the false prophet cast into a lake of fire.*

AND after these things I heard
a great voice of much[G]
people in heaven, [a]saying, Ăl-le-
lū′iă;[G] Salvation, and glory, and

18
*q Babylon, figurative,* Ezra 5:12.

20
7 R. V. saints, and ye apostles, and ye prophets; for God hath judged your judgement on her.

22
*r Music, refrained from, in sorrow,* 2 Chr. 5:13.

24
*s Martyrdom,* Rev. 17:6.
*t Persecution, of the righteous,* John 15:20.

1
*a Praise, in heaven,* Psa. 150:1.

honour, and power, [1]unto the
Lord our God:[Q]
2 For true and righteous *are* his
[b]judgments: for he hath [c]judged
the great [2]whore[G], which did corrupt the earth with her fornication, and hath avenged the blood
of his servants[G] at her hand.[S Q]
3 And again they said, Ăl-le-
lū'iă.[G] And her smoke rose up for
ever and ever.[Q]
4 And the four and twenty
elders and the four [3]beasts fell
down and [d]worshipped God that
sat on the [e]throne, saying, Amen;
Ăl-le-lū'iă.[G Q]
5[T] And a voice came out of the
throne, saying, [a]Praise our God,
all ye his servants,[G] and ye that
[f]fear him, both small and great.[Q]
6 And I heard as it were the
voice of a great multitude, and
as the voice of many waters, and
as the voice of mighty thunderings, saying, [a]Ăl-le-lū'iă:[G] for the
Lord God [g]omnipotent [h]reign-
eth.[Q]
7 Let us be glad and rejoice,
and give honour to him: for the
[i,j]marriage of the [k]Lamb is come,
and his [l,m]wife hath made herself ready.[Q]
8 And [4]to [n]her was granted
that she should be arrayed in
fine linen, [o,p]clean and white:
for the [q]fine linen is the [r]right-
eousness[G] of saints.[S Q]
9 And he saith unto me, Write,
[s]Blessed *are* they which are [t]called
unto the [i]marriage [u]supper of the
[k]Lamb. And he saith unto me,
These are the true sayings of God.
10 And I [v]fell at his feet to worship him. And he said unto me,
See *thou do it* not: I am thy fellowservant, and of thy brethren
that have the testimony of Jē'-
ṣus: [w,x]worship God: for the
testimony of Jē'ṣus is the spirit
of prophecy.[G T]
11 And I saw heaven opened,
and behold a white [y]horse; and
he that sat upon him *was* called
[z]Faithful and [z]True, and in righteousness he doth [a]judge and make
war.[T Q]
12 His eyes *were* as a flame of
fire, and on his head *were* many
[b]crowns; and he had a name
written, that no man knew, but
he himself.[Q]
13 And [c]he *was* clothed with a
vesture[G] dipped in blood: and his
name is called The [d,e]Word of
God.[T Q]
14 And the armies *which were*
in heaven followed him upon
white [f]horses, clothed in fine
[g]linen, [h]white and clean.
15 And out of his mouth goeth a
sharp sword, that with it he should
[i]smite the nations: and he shall
[j]rule them with a [k]rod of iron: and
he treadeth the [l]winepress of the
fierceness and [m]wrath of Almighty
God.[S T Q]
16 And he hath on *his* vesture[G]
and on his thigh a name written,
[n,o]KING OF KINGS, AND
LORD OF LORDS.[Q]
17 And I saw an angel standing
in the sun; and he cried with a
loud voice, saying to all the fowls
that fly in the midst of heaven,
Come and gather yourselves together unto the supper of the
great God;[Q]
18 That ye may eat the flesh of
kings, and the flesh of captains,
and the flesh of mighty men, and
the flesh of horses, and of them
that sit on them, and the flesh of
all *men, both* free and bond,[G] both
small and great.
19 And I saw the [p]beast, and the
kings of the earth, and their armies, gathered together to make
war against him that sat on the
horse, and against his army.[Q]
20 And the [p]beast was taken,
and with him the false prophet
that wrought [5]miracles[G] before
him, with which he deceived
them that had received the mark

1 R. V. belong to our God:

**2**
b *Judgments*, Ex. 6:6.
c *God, judge*, Gen. 2:2.
2 R. V. harlot,

**4**
d *Worship*, Gen. 22:5.
e *Throne*, 1 Kin. 2:19.
3 R. V. living creatures

**5**
f *Fear of God*, Acts 9:31.

**6**
g *God, omnipotent*, Gen. 2:2.
h *God, sovereign*, Gen. 2:2.

**7**
i *Marriage, figurative*, Gen. 34:9.
j *Righteous, union of, with Christ*, Psa. 64:10.
k *Lamb*, John 1:29.
l *Bride, figurative*, Isa. 49:18.
m *Church, described as Lamb's wife*, Matt. 16:18.

**8**
n *Church, clothed in righteousness*, Matt. 16:18.
o *Church, holiness of*, Matt. 16:18.
p *Holiness, of the church*, Ex. 39:30.
q *Dress, figurative of righteousness*, Zech. 3:3.
r *Righteousness, figuratively described as a garment*, Psa. 15:2.
4 R. V. it was given unto her that she should array herself in fine linen, bright and pure: for the fine linen is the righteous acts of the saints.

**9**
s *Spiritual Peace*, Gal. 1:3.
t *Call, personal*, Phil. 3:14.
u *Feasts, figurative*, Mark 12:39.

**10**
v *Homage*, Acts 10:25.
w *Commandment, enjoining worship*, Deut. 8:2.
x *Worship, to be rendered to God only*, Gen. 22:5.

**11**
y *Horse, symbolical*, Job 39:19.
z *Jesus, perfections of*, Matt. 1:21.
a *Jesus, judge*, Matt. 1:21.

**12**
b *Crown, symbolical*, Ex. 29:6.

**13**
c *Jesus, suffering of*, Matt. 1:21.
d John 1:1; 1 John 1:1.
e *Jesus, names of*, Matt. 1:21.

**14**
f *Horse, symbolical*, Job 39:19.
g *Righteousness, figuratively described as a garment*, Psa. 15:2.
h *Colors, symbolical*, Ezek. 16:16.

**15**
i *Wicked, punishment of*, Psa. 73:3.
j *Jesus, prophecies concerning the future glory and power of*, Matt. 1:21.
k *Scepter*, Esth. 4:11.
l *Wine Press*, Isa. 5:2.
m *Anger of God*, 2 Kin. 13:3.

**16**
n *Jesus, names of*, Matt. 1:21.
o *Jesus, king*, Matt. 1:21.

**19**
p *Antichrist*, 2 John 7.

**20**
5 R. V. the signs in his sight,

of the beast, and them that worshipped his image. [q]These both were cast alive into a [r,s]lake of fire burning with [t]brimstone.[Q]

21 And [q]the remnant were slain with the sword of him that sat upon the horse, which *sword* proceeded out of his mouth: and all the fowls were filled with their flesh.[Q]

## CHAPTER 20

*Satan bound for a thousand years. 4 The first resurrection. 7 Satan let loose again. 8 Gog and Magog. 10 The devil cast into the lake of fire and brimstone. 11 The general resurrection and judgment. 14 The second death.*

AND I saw[S] an angel come down from heaven, having the [a]key of the [1]bottomless [b]pit and a great [c]chain in his hand.

2 And he laid hold on the dragon, that old serpent, which is the Dĕv'il, and [d]Sā'tan, and bound him a thousand [e]years,[T Q]

3 And cast him into the [2]bottomless [b]pit, and shut him up, and set a seal[G] upon him, that he should deceive the nations no more, till the thousand [e]years should be fulfilled: and after that he must be loosed a little season.[G S]

4 And [f,g]I saw thrones, and they sat upon them, and judgment was given unto them: and *I saw* the souls of them that were [h,i,j]beheaded for the [k]witness of Jē'sus, and for the [l]word of God, and which had not worshipped the [m]beast, neither his image, neither had received *his* mark upon their foreheads, or in their hands; and they [n]lived and *reigned with [o]Christ a thousand years.[Q]

5 But the rest of the dead lived not again until the thousand years were finished. This *is* the first [p]resurrection.

6 Blessed and holy *is* he that hath part in the first [p]resurrection: on such the †second death hath no power, but they shall be [q]priests of God and of Christ, and shall reign with him a thousand years.[Q]

7 And when the thousand years are expired, [d]Sā'tan shall be loosed out of his prison,[S]

8 And shall go out to deceive the nations which are in the four quarters of the earth, [r]Gŏg and [s]Mā'gŏg, to gather them together to battle: the number of whom *is* as the sand of the sea.[Q]

9 And they went up on the breadth of the earth, and compassed[G] the camp of the saints about, and the beloved city: and [t]fire came down [3]from God out of heaven, and devoured them.[Q]

10 And the devil that deceived them was cast into the [u,v]lake of fire and brimstone, where the beast and the false prophet *are*, and shall be [w]tormented day and night [x]for ever and ever.[S Q]

11 And I saw a great [y]white [z]throne, and [a]him that sat on it, from whose face the [b]earth and the [c]heaven fled away; and there was found no place for them.[Q]

12[Q] And I saw the dead, small and great, stand before [4]God; and the books were opened: and another [d]book was opened, which is *the book* of life: and the [e]dead were [f]judged out of those things which were written in the books, according to their works.

13 And [g]the sea gave up the dead which were in it; and death[G] and [5]hell[G] delivered up the dead which were in them: and they were [f]judged every man according to their works.[Q]

14 And [h]death and [5]hell[G] were cast into the [i]lake of fire. This is the †second death.

q *Wicked, punishment of*, Psa. 73:3.
r Rev. 20:10, 14, 15; 21:8.
s *Hell*, Mark 9:43.
t *Brimstone, figurative*, Deut. 29:23.

**1**
a *Key, a symbol of authority*, Judg. 3:25.
b *Pit, figurative*, Psa. 7:15.
c *Chains, figurative*, Dan. 5:7.
1 R. V. abyss and

**2**
d *Satan*, Matt. 4:10.
e *Year*, Lev. 25:29.

**3**
2 R. V. abyss, and shut it, and sealed it over him,

**4**
f *Church, prophecies concerning its prosperity*, Matt. 16:18.
g *Jesus, prophecies concerning the future glory and power of*, Matt. 1:21.
h *Beheading*, Matt. 14:10.
i *Martyrdom*, Rev. 17:6.
j *Persecution, of the righteous*, John 15:20.
k *Witnessing for Christ*, Luke 24:48.
l *Word of God*, Psa. 119:9.
m *Beast, symbolical*, Dan. 7:3.
n *Righteous, promises to*, Psa. 64:10.
o *Jesus, King*, Matt. 1:21.

**5**
p *Resurrection*, 1 Cor. 15:12.

**6**
q *Priest, figurative*, Lev. 1:5.

**8**
r Ezek. chapters 38, 39.
s *Magog*, 1 Chr. 1:5.

**9**
t *Fire, figurative*, Ex. 12:8.
3 R. V. *omits* from God

**10**
u Rev. 19:20; 21:8.
v *Hell*, Mark 9:43.
w *Wicked, punishment of*, Psa. 73:3.
x *Punishment, eternal*, Lev. 26:41.

**11**
y *Colors, symbolical*, Ezek. 16:16.
z *Throne, figurative*, 1 Kin. 2:19.
a *Jesus, judge*, Matt. 1:21.
b *Earth, destruction of*, Prov. 8:23.
c *Heavens, destruction of*, Psa. 8:3.

**12**
d *Book, figurative*, Psa. 139:16.
e *Death, does not end conscious existence*, Num. 23:10.
f *Judgment, the general*, 2 Pet. 3:7.
4 R. V. the throne:

**13**
g *Resurrection*, 1 Cor. 15:12.
5 R. V. Hades

**14**
h *Death, to be destroyed*, Num. 23:10.
i Rev. 19:20; 21:8.

* **MILLENNIUM**, Rev. 14:6–18; 20:2–7. *When Jesus shall have triumphed over all forms of evil*, 1 Cor. 15:24–28; 2 Thess. 2:8; Rev. 19:11–16: *at the restoration of all things*, Acts 3:21. *When the creation shall be delivered from the corruption of evil*, Rom. 8:19–21. *When the Son of Man shall sit on the throne of his glory*, Matt. 19:28; Luke 22:28–30; *and the righteous shall be clothed with authority*, Dan. 7:22; Matt. 19:28; Luke 22:28–30; 1 Cor. 6:2; Rev. 22:5; *and possess the kingdom*, Matt. 25:34; Luke 12:32; 22:29.
*Satan to be excluded during*, Rev. 20:2, 3.
See footnote, JESUS, *Second coming of*, Matt. 1:21.

† **SECOND DEATH**, Rev. 19:20; 20:14; 21:8.
*Righteous exempt from*, Rev. 2:11.
See footnote, PUNISHMENT, *Eternal*, Lev. 26:41.

15 And [j]whosoever was not found written in the [d]book of life was cast into the [i]lake of fire.[Q]

## CHAPTER 21

*A new heaven and new earth. 3 The blessings of God's people. 8 The doom of the wicked. 9 The heavenly Jerusalem described. 22 No temple there. 23 The light and glory of the city. 27 Nothing that defiles can enter therein.*

AND I saw a *new heaven and a new [a]earth: for the first [b]heaven and the first [c]earth were passed away; and there was no more sea.[Q]

2 And I [1]Jŏhn saw the [d]holy city, [e]new Jĕ-ru̥'să-lĕm, coming down from God out of heaven, prepared as a [f]bride adorned for her husband.[Q]

3 [S]And I heard a great voice out of [2]heaven saying, Behold, the [g,h]tabernacle of God *is* with men, and [i,j]he will dwell with them, and [k,l]they shall be his people, and God himself shall be with them, *and be* their God.[T Q]

4 And [3,m]God shall wipe away all [n]tears from their eyes; and there shall be no more [o]death, neither sorrow, nor crying, neither shall there be any more [p]pain: for the former things are passed away.[Q]

5 And he that sat upon the [q]throne said, Behold, I make all things new. And he said unto me, Write: for these words are true and faithful.[S Q]

6 And he said unto me, [4]It is done. I am [r]Ăl'phȧ and [r]Ō-mē'-gȧ, the beginning and the end. I will give unto him that is [s,t,u]athirst of the [v,w]fountain of the [x]water of life freely.[Q]

7 [y,z]He that [a,b]overcometh [c]shall [d]inherit all things; and I will be his God, and he shall be [e]my son.[S Q]

8 But the fearful, and [f]unbelieving, and the abominable, and [g]murderers, and [h,i]whoremongers,[C] and [j]sorcerers, and [k]idolaters, and all [l]liars, [m]shall have their part in the [n]lake which burneth with [o]fire and [p]brimstone: which is the [q]second death.[Q]

9 And there came unto me one of the seven angels which had the seven vials[C] full of the seven last plagues, and talked with me, [r]saying, Come hither, I will shew thee the [s]bride, the [t]Lamb's [u]wife.[Q]

10 And he carried me away in the [v,w]spirit to a great and high mountain, and shewed me that great city, the holy Jĕ-ru̥'să-lĕm, descending out of heaven from God,[Q]

11 Having the [x]glory of God: and her light *was* like unto a stone most precious, even like a ‡jasper stone, clear as [y]crystal;[Q]

12 And had a [z]wall great and high, *and* had twelve [a]gates, and at the gates twelve angels, and names written thereon, which are *the names* of the twelve tribes of the children of [b]Ĭs̹'ra-el:[Q]

13 On the east three [a]gates; on the north three gates; on the south three gates; and on the west three gates.[Q]

14 And the [c]wall of the city had twelve foundations, and in them the names of the twelve [d]apostles of the [e]Lamb.

15 And he that talked with me had a golden [f]reed to measure the city, and the gates thereof, and the wall thereof.[Q]

16 And the city lieth foursquare,[C] and the length is as large as the breadth: and he measured the city with the [f]reed, twelve thousand [g]furlongs.[C] The length and the breadth and the height of it are equal.[Q]

17 And he measured the [c]wall

---

**15**
j *Wicked, punishment of,* Psa. 73:3.

**1**
a *Earth, new,* Prov. 8:23.
b *Heavens, destruction of,* Psa. 8:3.
c *Earth, destruction of,* Prov. 8:23.

**2**
d *Church, triumphant,* Matt. 16:18.
e v. 10; Rev. 3:12.
f *Bride,* Isa. 49:18.
1 R. V. *omits* John

**3**
g *Shekinah,* Lev. 16:2.
h *Holy of Holies,* Ex. 26:33.
i *God dwells with the Righteous,* 1 Kin. 6:13.
j *Fellowship, with God,* 1 Cor. 1:9.
k *Promise, to the righteous,* vs. 4, 6, 7; 2 Cor. 1:20.
l *Righteous, promises to,* Psa. 64:10.
2 R. V. the throne

**4**
m *Heaven, future home of the righteous,* Luke 18:22.
n *Tears,* Psa. 6:6.
o *Death, to be destroyed,* Num. 23:10.
p *Pain,* Job 14:22.
3 R. V. he

**5**
q *Throne,* 1 Kin. 2:19.

**6**
r Rev. 1:8; 22:13.
s *Thirst, figurative,* John 4:14.
t *Spiritual Desire,* Psa. 42:1.
u *Seekers,* Isa. 55:6.
v *Fountain, figurative,* Zech. 13:1.
w *Salvation,* Acts 16:17.
x *Water, figurative,* 1 Kin. 17:10.
4 R. V. They are come to pass.

**7**
y *Promise, to the righteous,* 2 Cor. 1:20.
z *Righteous, promises to,* Psa. 64:10.

a *Steadfastness, rewards of,* 1 Cor. 15:58.
b *Perseverance, motives to,* Eph. 6:18.
c *Reward, a motive, to perseverance,* Matt. 5:12. d *Inheritance, figurative,* Num. 27:7. e *Spiritual Adoption,* Rom. 8:15.

**8** f *Unbelievers,* 1 Cor. 6:6.
g *Homicide, punishment for,* Deut. 5:17.
h Rev. 22:15.
i *Adultery, penalties for,* Lev. 20:10.
j *Sorcery,* Isa. 47:9.
k *Idolatry,* 1 Sam. 15:23.
l *Falsehood, punishment for,* Job 21:34.
m *Wicked, punishment of,* Psa. 73:3.
n *Hell,* Mark 9:43.
o *Fire, figurative,* Ex. 12:8.
p *Brimstone, figurative,* Deut. 29:23.
q *Second Death,* Rev. 20:6.

**9**
r *Jesus, kingdom of, prophecies concerning,* Matt. 1:21.
s *Church,* Matt. 16:18.
t *Lamb,* John 1:29.
u *Righteous, union of, with Christ,* Psa. 64:10.

**10**
v *Holy Spirit,* Acts 1:2.
w *Prophets, inspiration of,* Isa. 3:2.

**11**
x *God, glory of,* Gen. 2:2.
y Rev. 4:6.

**12**
z *Walls, figurative,* 1 Sam. 20:25.
a *Gates, symbolical,* Deut. 3:5.
b *Israel,* Ex. 4:22.

**14**
c *Walls, figurative,* 1 Sam. 20:25.
d *Apostles,* Luke 6:13.
e *Lamb,* John 1:29.

**15**
f *Reed,* Ezek. 40:3.

**16**
g Luke 24:13; John 11:18.

---

* **NEW HEAVENS,** Isa. 65:17; 66:22; 2 Pet. 3:13; Rev. 21:1-4.

thereof, an hundred *and* forty *and* four [h]cubits, *according to* the measure of a man, that is, of the angel.

18 And the building of the wall of it was *of* ‡jasper: and the city *was* pure [i]gold, like unto clear †glass.

19 And the foundations of the [c]wall of the city *were* garnished with all manner of [j]precious stones. The first foundation *was* ‡jasper; the second, [k]sapphire; the third, a chalcedony; the fourth, an [l]emerald;

20 The fifth, sardonyx; the sixth, [m]sardius; the seventh, chrysolyte; the eighth, [n]beryl; the ninth, a [o]topaz; the tenth, a chrysoprasus; the eleventh, a [p]jacinth; the twelfth, an ‖amethyst.

21 And the twelve [a]gates *were* twelve [q]pearls; every several gate was of one pearl: and the street of the city *was* pure gold, as it were transparent glass.

22 And I saw no [r]temple therein: for the [s]Lord God Almighty and the [e,t]Lamb are the temple of it.

23 And the city had no need of the [u]sun, neither of the [v]moon, to shine in it: for the glory of God did lighten it, and the [e,t]Lamb *is* the [5,w]light thereof.

24 And the nations [6]of them which are saved shall [x]walk in the light of it: and the kings of the earth do bring their glory and honour into it.

25 And the [a]gates of it shall not be shut at all by day: for there shall be no [y]night there.

26 And they shall bring the glory and honour of the nations into [z]it.

27 And there shall in no wise enter into [z]it any thing that defileth, neither *whatsoever* worketh [a]abomination, or *maketh* a [b]lie: but they which are written in the [c]Lamb's [d]book of life.

**17**
*h* *Cubit*, Ex. 36:9.

**18**
*i* *Gold, symbolical*, Ezek. 7:19.

**19**
*j* *Precious Stones*, Ex. 39:10.
*k* *Sapphire*, Job 28:6.
*l* *Emerald*, Rev. 4:3.

**20**
*m* *Sardius*, Ex. 28:17.
*n* *Beryl*, Ezek. 1:16.
*o* *Topaz*, Ezek. 28:13.
*p* Rev. 9:17.

**21**
*q* *Pearl, symbolical*, Rev. 17:4.

**22**
*r* *Temple, figurative*, 1 Kin. 6:17.
*s* *God, omnipotent*, Gen. 2:2.
*t* *Jesus, names of*, Matt. 1:21.

**23**
*u* *Sun*, Josh. 10:12.
*v* *Moon*, Song 6:10.
*w* *Lamp, figurative*, Ex. 27:20.
5 R. V. lamp

**24**
*x* *Walking, figurative*, Gen. 5:22.
6 R. V. shall walk amidst the light thereof: and the kings of the earth do bring their glory into it.

**25**
*y* *Night*, Gen. 1:5.

**26**
*z* *Church, prophecies concerning its prosperity*, Matt. 16:18.

**27**
*a* *Abomination*, Lev. 18:27.

## CHAPTER 22

*The river and tree of life. 3 The blessedness of God's servants. 6 The conclusion: sundry directions, promises, and exhortations. 18 Nothing may be added to or taken from the words of this book.*

AND he shewed me a [1]pure [a]river of water of life, clear as [b]crystal, proceeding out of the [c]throne of God and of the [d]Lamb.

2 In the midst of the street of it, and on either side of the river, *was there* the [e]tree of life, which bare twelve *manner of* fruits, *and* yielded her fruit every month: and the [f]leaves of the tree *were* for the healing of the nations.

3 And there shall be no more curse: but the [c]throne of God and of the [d]Lamb shall be in it; and his servants shall serve him:

4 And [g,h]they shall see his face; and his name *shall be* in their foreheads.

5 And [i]there shall be no [j]night there; and they need no [2]candle, neither light of the sun; for the Lord God giveth them light: and [g,h]they shall reign for [k,l]ever and ever.

6 And he said unto me, These [m]sayings *are* faithful and true: and the Lord [3]God of the holy prophets sent his angel [n]to shew unto his servants the things which must shortly be done.

7 Behold, I [o]come quickly: [p]blessed *is* he that [q,r]keepeth the sayings of the prophecy of this book.

8 And I John saw these things, and heard *them*. And when I had heard and seen, I [s]fell down to worship before the feet of the angel which shewed me these things.

9 Then saith he unto me, [t]See *thou do it* not: for I am [4]thy fellowservant, and of thy brethren

*b* *Falsehood*, Job 21:34.
*c* *Lamb*, John 1:29.
*d* *Book, figurative*, Psa. 139:16.

**1**
*a* *River, figurative*, Psa. 46:4.
*b* Rev. 4:6; 21:11.
*c* *Throne*, 1 Kin. 2:19.
*d* *Lamb*, John 1:29.
1 R. V. river of water of life, bright as crystal,

**2**
*e* *Righteousness, symbolized*, Psa. 15:2.
*f* *Medicine, allegorical*, Prov. 17:22.

**4**
*g* *Righteous, promises to*, Psa. 64:10.
*h* *Promise, to the righteous*, 2 Cor. 1:20.

**5**
*i* *Heaven, future home of the righteous*, Luke 18:22.
*j* *Night*, Gen. 1:5.
*k* *Immortality*, 1 Cor. 15:54.
*l* *Life, everlasting*, Eccl. 8:15.
2 R. V. lamp,

**6**
*m* *Word of God, is inspired*, Psa. 119:9.
*n* *Prophets, inspiration of*, Isa. 3:2.
3 R. V. the God of the spirits of the prophets, sent

**7**
*o* *Jesus, second coming of*, Matt. 1:21.
*p* *Spiritual Peace*, Gal. 1:3.
*q* *Duty, of man to God*, Eccl. 12:13.
*r* *Obedience, rewarded*, Heb. 5:8.

**8**
*s* *Homage*, Acts 10:25.

**9**
*t* *Worship, to be rendered to God only*, Gen. 22:5.
4 R. V. a fellow-servant with thee and with thy brethren the prophets, and with them

† **GLASS**, Job 28:17 [R. V.]. *Symbolical*, Rev. 21:18, 21. *Sea of*, Rev. 15:2.
‡ **JASPER.** *A precious stone*, Ex. 28:20; 39:13; Ezek. 28:13; Rev. 4:3; 21:11, **18**, **19**.
‖ **AMETHYST.** *A precious stone*, Ex. 28:19; 39:12; Rev 21:20.

the prophets, and of them which
[q]keep the sayings of this book:
[u]worship God.
10 And he saith unto me, Seal[C]
not the sayings of the prophecy[C]
of this book: for the time is at
hand.[Q]
11 [v]He that is [5,w]unjust, let him
be unjust still: and he which is
filthy, let him be filthy still: and
he that is righteous, let him be
righteous still: and he that is
[x]holy, let him be holy still.[S]
12 And, behold, I [o]come quickly;
and my [y]reward *is* with me, to
[z]give every man according as his
work shall be.[Q]
13 [a]I am [b]Ăl′phȧ and [b]Ŏ-mē′gȧ,
the beginning and the end, the
first and the last.[T Q]
14 [c]Blessed *are* they that [6]do
his commandments, that they
may have right to the *tree of
life, and may enter in through
the gates into the city.[S Q]
15 For [d]without[C] *are* [e]dogs[C], and
[f]sorcerers, and [g,h]whoremon-
gers[C], and [i]murderers, and [j]idol-
aters, and whosoever loveth and
maketh a [k]lie.

16 [T]I Jē′sus have sent mine angel to testify unto you these
things in the churches. [l]I am
the root and the offspring of
Dā′vid, *and* the bright and
[m]morning star.[S Q]
17 And the [n]Spirit and the
[o,p]bride say, [q]Come. And let him
that heareth say, Come. And let
him that is [r,s,t]athirst come. And
whosoever [u]will, let him take the
[v,w]water of life freely.[GT Q]
18 For I testify[C] unto every man
that heareth the [x]words of the
prophecy[C] of this [y]book, If any
man shall add unto these things,
[z]God shall add unto him the
plagues that are written in this
book:[T Q]
19 And if any man shall take
away from the words of the
[y]book of this prophecy[C], God
shall [z]take away his part [7]out
of the book of life, and out
of the holy city, and *from* the
things which are written in this
book.[Q]
20 He which testifieth[C] these
things saith, Surely I [a]come
quickly. Amen. Even so, [b]come,
Lord Jē′sus.
21 The [c]grace of our Lord Jē′sus
[8]Christ *be* with you all. Amen.

*u Commandment, enjoining worship,* Deut. 8:2.

**11**

*v Character, fixedness of,* Phil. 2:15.
*w Injustice,* Isa. 26:10.
*x Holiness,* Ex. 39:30.
5 R. V. unrighteous, let him do unrighteousness still: and he that is filthy, let him be made filthy still: and he that is righteous, let him do righteousness still: and he that is holy, let him be made holy still.

**12**

*y Reward, a motive, to faithfulness,* Matt. 5:12.
*z Judgment, the general,* 2 Pet. 3:7.

**13**

*a Jesus, divinity of,* Matt. 1:21.
*b* Rev. 1:8; 21:6.

**14**

*c Promise, to the righteous,* 2 Cor. 1:20.
6 R. V. wash their robes, that they may have the right to come to the tree

**15** *d Wicked, described,* Psa. 73:3. *e Dog, figurative,* 1 Kin. 21:19. *f Sorcery,* Isa. 47:9. *g* Rev. 21:8. *h Adultery,* Lev. 20:10. *i Homicide, felonious, punishment for,* Deut. 5:17. *j Idolatry, denunciations against,* 1 Sam. 15:23. *k Falsehood,* Job 21:34.

**16**

*l Jesus, incarnation of,* Matt. 1:21.
*m Jesus, names of,* Matt. 1:21.

**17**

*n Holy Spirit, invites,* Acts 1:2.
*o Bride, figurative,* Isa. 49:18.
*p Church,* Matt. 16:18.
*q Call, personal,* Phil. 3:14.
*r Thirst, figurative,* John 4:14.
*s Seekers,* Isa. 55:6.
*t Spiritual Desire,* Psa. 42:1.
*u Contingencies, in divine government of man,* 1 Kin. 3:14.
*v Water, figurative,* 1 Kin. 17:10.
*w Salvation,* Acts 16:17.

**18**

*x Word of God,* Psa. 119:9.
*y Book,* Num. 5:23.
*z Wicked, punishment of,* Psa. 73:3.

**20**

*a Jesus, second coming of,* Matt. 1:21.
*b Love, of man for Jesus,* 1 John 4:19.

**21**

*c Benedictions, apostolic,* Deut. 21:5.
8 R. V. be with the saints. Amen.

***TREE.** *Known by its fruits,* Matt. 7:17–19; Luke 6:43, 44.
**Symbolical,** Dan. 4:10–12. *Of life,* Gen. 2:9; 3:22, 24; Rev. 22:2, 14. *Of knowledge,* Gen. 2:9, 17; 3:3–6, 11, 12, 17.

# INDEX TO FOOTNOTES
# WITH
# CONCORDANCE

## G

## H

## I

## J

2 Tim. 4:8, Lord the righteous *J.*
Heb. 12:23, are come to God the *J.*
James 5:9, the *J.* standeth before
the door [thee, 1 Sam. 24:12.
Gen. 16:5, Lord *j.* between me and
Deut. 32:36, the Lord shall *j.* his
people, Ps. 135:14; Heb. 10:30.
Ps. 7:8, Lord shall *j.* the people, *j.*
Mt. 7:1, *j.* not that ye be not judged
John 5:30, as I hear I *j.* and my
12:47, I came not to *j.* the world
Acts 23:3, sittest thou to *j.* me after
Rom. 2:16, when God shall *j.* the
3:6, then how shall God *j.* the world
14:10, why dost thou *j.* thy brother
1 Cor. 4:3, I *j.* not mine own self
5, *j.* nothing before the time
6:3, know ye that we shall *j.* angels
11:31, if we would *j.* ourselves, we
14:29, let prophets speak, others *j.*
Col. 2:16, let no man *j.* you in meat
2 Tim. 4:1, who shall *j.* the quick
and the dead, 1 Pet. 4:5.
James 4:11, if ye *j.* the law
Ps. 51:4, *judgest*. Rm. 14:4; James 4:12.
7:11, God *judgeth* the righteous
John 5:22, Father *j.* no man; but
hath committed all judgment unto
Son
1 Cor. 2:15, but he that is spiritual
*j.* all things
4:4, he that *j.* me is the Lord
Matt. 19:28, *judging* twelve tribes,
Luke 22:30, not respect persons in *j.*
**Judgment,** the general see *ftn. p.* 1682.
—, according to Opportunity and
Works, see *footnote, p.* 1673.
—, Deut. 1:17, the *j.* is God's
32:4, all his ways are *j.* a God of
Ps. 1:5, ungodly not stand in the *j.*
Eccl. 11:9, but know thou God will
bring thee into *j.* 12:14.
Isa. 28:17, *j.* also will I lay to the line
42:1, he shall bring *j.* to Gentiles
53:8, he was taken from prison and *j.*
61:8, I the Lord love *j.* and hate
Jer. 5:1, if there be that executeth *j.*
Dan. 4:37, all whose ways are *j.*
Hos. 12:6, keep mercy and *j.* wait on
Matt. 5:21, be in danger of *j.* 22.
12:20, till he send *j.* unto victory
John 5:22, Father *j.* no man but
committed all *j.* to the Son
27, given him authority to execute *j.*
9:39, for *j.* I am come to the world
16:8, reprove the world of sin and *j.*
Acts 24:25, reasoned of *j.* to come
Rom. 5:18, *j.* came on all men
14:10, must all stand before *j.* seat
Heb. 9:27, all die, but after this *j.*
1 Pet. 4:17, *j.* begin at house of God
Jude 15, execute *j.* on all ungodly
Rev. 17:1, shew thee *j.* of great
Ps. 19:9, *judgments* of Lord are true
36:6, thy *j.* are a great deep
Rom. 11:33, how unsearchable his *j.*
**Judgment Seat,** see *footnote, p.* 1537.
**Judgments;** *Design of; Instances of,*
see *footnote, p.* 98.
**Just,** Lev. 19:36, *j.* balance, *j.* weights
etc., Deut. 25:15; Ezek. 45:10.
Deut. 16:20, that is *j.* shalt follow.
32:4, a God of truth, *j.* and right is he
2 Sam. 23:3, ruleth men must be *j.*
Job 4:17, shall man be more *j.* than
9:2, how should man be *j.* with God
Prov. 4:18, path of *j.* is as shining
10:6, blessings are on head of *j.*
11:1, but a *j.* weight is his delight
12:21, no evil shall happen to *j.*
17:26, to punish the *j.* is not good
18:17, in his own cause seemeth *j.*
20:7, a *j.* man walketh in integrity
21:15, it is joy to *j.* to do judgment
24:16, *j.* man falleth seven times
Eccl. 7:15, there is a *j.* man that
perisheth in his righteousness
20, there is not a *j.* man on earth
8:14, be *j.* men, to whom it happeneth
Is. 45:21, no God beside me; a *j.* God
Ezek. 18:9, he is *j.* he shall live

Matt. 1:19, Joseph a *j.* man
Matt. 5:45, sendeth rain on *j.* and
Luke 15:7, more than over ninety-
nine *j.* persons [selves *j.*
20:20, who should feign them
John 5:30, my judgment is *j.*
Acts 7:52, shewed before the com-
ing of the *j.* one, 22:14.
24:15, resurrection both of *j.* and
Rom. 2:13, not hearers of law are *j.*
3:26, he might be *j.* and justifier
7:12, commandment holy, *j.* and
Phil. 4:8, whatsoever things are *j.*
Col. 4:1, give that which is *j.* and
Heb. 2:2, received a *j.* recompense
12:23, spirits of *j.* men made perfect
1 Pet. 3:18, suffered once *j.* for the
1 John 1:9, faithful *j.* to forgive
Rev. 15:3, *j.* and true are thy ways
Mic. 6:8, to do *justly,* and love
Luke 23:41, we indeed *j.* for we
1 Thes. 2:10, how *j.* we behaved
**Just shall live by Faith, The,** *ftn. p.* 1270
**Justice,** see *footnote, p.* 342.
Gen. 18:19, to do *j.* and
Job 37:23, excellent in power, and
in judgment, and plenty of *j.*
Ps. 89:14, *j.* and judgment are the
habitation of thy throne
Prov. 8:15, by me princes decree *j.*
Jer. 31:23, O habitation of *j.* 50:7.
**Justification,** see *footnote, p.* 1549.
Rom. 4:25, raised for our *j.*
5:16, gift is of many offences unto *j.*
Rom. 5:18, free gift on all men, to *j.*
**Justified,** Job 11:2, should a man full
13:18, I shall be *j.* [of talk be *j.*
Ps. 51:4, mightest be *j.* when thou
speakest [living be *j.*
143:2, in thy sight shall no man
Matt. 11:19, wisdom is *j.* of children
Luke 7:35.
12:37, by thy words thou shalt be *j.*
Luke 7:29, *j.* God, being baptized of
18:14, went away *j.* rather than
Acts 13:39, are *j.* from all things,
which ye could not be *j.* by law
Rom. 2:13, doers of law shall be *j.*
3:4, might be *j.* in thy sayings
20, there shall no flesh be *j.* in his
24, being *j.* freely by his grace
28, man is *j.* by faith without deeds
4:2, if Abraham were *j.* by works
5:1, being *j.* by faith, we have
9, being *j.* by his blood, be saved
8:30, whom he *j.* them he also
1 Cor. 4:4, yet am I not hereby *j.*
6:11, ye are *j.* in name of the Lord
Gal. 2:16, not *j.* by works of law, we
might be *j.* by faith of Christ, 17.
3:11, no man is *j.* by the law, it is
24, that we might be *j.* by faith
5:4, *j.* by law, fallen from grace
1 Tim. 3:16, God in flesh, *j.* in Spirit
Tit. 3:7, that being *j.* by his grace
Js. 2:21, Abraham *j.* by works when
24, by works a man is *j.* not by faith
25, was not Rabah *j.* by works
Pr. 17:15, he that *justifieth* wicked
Isa. 50:8, he is near, that *j.* me
Rom. 4:5, God that *j.* the ungodly
8:33, it is God that *j.* who is he
3:26, the *justifier* of him that
**Justify,** Ex. 23:7, I will not *j.* the
Deut. 25:1, they shall *j.* righteous
Job 9:20, if I *j.* myself, my mouth
27:5, God forbid that I should *j.*
Is. 5:23, woe them that *j.* the wicked
53:11, shall my servant *j.* many
Luke 10:29, he, willing to *j.* himself
16:15, ye are they which *j.* yourselves
Rom. 3:30, God shall *j.* circumcision
Gal. 3:8, God would *j.* heathen

## K

**Kabzeel,** 2 Sam. 23:20.
**Kadesh,** see *footnote, p.* 23.
**Kanah,** a brook, Josh. 16:8.
—, a town, Josh. 19:28.
**Kareah,** see *footnote, p.* 1104.
**Kedar,** son of Ishmael, Gen. 25:15.
—, see *footnote, p.* 1117.
**Kedemoth,** see *footnote, p.* 365.
**Kedesh,** a city of Judah, Josh. 12:22.
—, a city of refuge, see *ftn. p.* 377.
**Keep,** Gen. 28:15, I am with thee and
will *k.*
20, if God will be with me, and *k.* me
Ex. 23:7, *k.* thee far from a false
Num. 6:24, Lord bless and *k.* thee
Dt. 23:9, *k.* thee from every wicked
29:9, *k.* words of this covenant
Ps. 25:10, to such as *k.* his covenant,
103:18.
39:1, *k.* my mouth with a bridle
127:1, except the Lord *k.* the city
141:3, *k.* the door of my lips [goest
Eccl. 5:1, *k.* thy foot when thou
Is. 26:3, thou wilt *k.* him in perfect
Jer. 3:12, I will not *k.* anger for ever
Luke 11:28, hear word of G. and *k.*
John 12:25, he that hateth his life
shall *k.* it to life eternal
14:23, if man love me, will *k.* my
17:11, holy Father, *k.* through thy
15, thou shouldest *k.* them from
1 Cor. 5:8, let us *k.* the feast, not
11, not to *k.* company with such
9:27, I *k.* under my body, and
Eph. 4:3, endeavouring to *k.* unity
Phil. 4:7, peace of God shall *k.* your
2 Thes. 3:3, L. shall establish and *k.*
1 Tim. 5:22, *k.* thyself pure
6:20, *k.* that which is committed
2 Tim. 1:12, able to *k.* that which is
14, that good thing which was committed to thee, *k.* by Holy Ghost
James 1:27, *k.* himself unspotted
2:10, *k.* whole law, yet offend in
Jude 21, *k.* yourselves in love of God
24, who is able to *k.* you from
Rev. 1:3, blessed that hear and *k.*
3:10, I will *k.* thee from the hour of
22:9, thy brethren which *k.* sayings
Lev. 26:3, if ye *keep* my *command-*
Dt. 6:7, diligently—, 11:1, 22. [*ments*
13:4,—his—and obey his voice, 11:8.
Ps. 119:60, I delayed not to—thy—
Eccl. 12:13, fear God, and—his—
Matt. 19:17, if enter into life—the—
John 14:15, if ye love me—my—
1 John 2:3, we know that we know
him, if we—his— [—his—
5:3, this is the love of God that we
Rev. 14:12, here are they that—the—
1 Kin. 8:23, who *keepest* covenant
and mercy, 2 Chr. 6:14; Neh. 9:32.
Deut. 7:9, which *keepeth* covenant,
Neh. 1:5. [slumber
Ps. 121:3, he that *k.* thee will not
Prov. 13:3, he that *k.* his mouth, *k.*
29:18, he that *k.* the law, happy is he
1 John 5:18, that is of G. *k.* himself
Ex. 34:7, *keeping* mercy for thou-
sands [great reward
Ps. 19:11, in *k.* of them there is
121:5, the Lord is thy *keeper*
Tit. 2:5, chaste, *k.* at home
Deut. 32:10, *kept* them as the apple
33:9, they *k.* thy covenant [of eye
Josh. 14:10, Lord hath *k.* me alive
2 Sam. 22:22, *k.* ways of the Lord,
Ps. 18:21.
Job 23:11, his ways have I *k.* and
Matt. 19:20, all these things have I
*k.* from my youth [51.
Luke 2:19, Mary *k.* all these things,
John 15:20, if they have *k.* my say-
17:6, they have *k.* thy word [ings
12, all thou gavest me, I have *k.*
Rom. 16:25, *k.* secret since the world
2 Tim. 4:7, I have *k.* the faith
1 Pet. 1:5, *k.* by the power of God
Rev. 3:8, hast *k.* my word, and not
**Kehelathah,** Num. 33:22, 23.
**Keilah,** a city, see *footnote, p.* 466.
—, the Garmite, 1 Chr. 4:19.
**Kemuel,** three men, about whom little
is known, Gen. 22:21; Num. 34:24;
**Kenath,** Num. 32:42. [1 Chr. 27:17.
**Kenaz,** grandson of Esau, Gen. 36:11.
—, a duke, Gen. 36:42.

Hab. 2:14, earth filled with *k.* of the glory of God, Isa. 11:9.
Mal. 2:7, priest's lips should keep *k.*
Rom. 2:20, a teacher hast form of *k.*
3:20, for the law is *k.* of sin
10:2, a zeal not according to *k.*
1 Cor. 8:1, all have *k. k.* puffeth up
Eph. 3:19, the love of Christ which passeth *k.* [*k.* of Christ Jesus
Phil. 3:8, loss for excellency of the
Col. 2:3, treasures of wisdom and *k.*
3:10, renewed in *k.* after image of
1 Pet. 3:7, dwell...according to *k.*
2 Pet. 1:5, add to virtue *k.* and to *k.*
3:18, grow in grace and in *k.* of **J. Ct.**
**Kohath,** see *footnote, p.* 264.
**Kohathites,** see *footnote, p.* **218.**
**Korah,** see *footnote, p.* 244.
**Kore,** 1 Chr. 9:19.

## L

**Laadan,** 1 Chr. 23:7.
**Laban,** see *footnote, p.* 48.
**Labor;** Compensation for, *ftn. p.* 1415.
Ps. 90:10, yet is their strength *l.*
128:2, thou shalt eat the *l.* of thine
Prov. 14:23, in all *l.* there is profit
Eccl. 1:8, all things are full of *l.*
4:8, yet is there no end of all his *l.*
Isa. 55:2, ye spend your *l.* for that which satisfieth not
1 Cor. 15:58, your *l.* is not in vain in
1 Thes. 1:3, work of faith, *l.* of love
Heb. 6:10, God will not forget your *l.*
Rev. 14:13, dead may rest from *l.*
Prov. 23:4, *l.* not to be rich; cease
Matt. 11:28, come unto me all ye that *l.* and are heavy laden
John 6:27, *l.* not for the meat that
1 Thes. 5:12, know them which *l.*
1 Tim. 5:17, honour those who *l.* in
Heb. 4:11, let us *l.* to enter into
Isa. 49:4, I have *laboured* in vain
John 4:38, other men *l.* and ye
1 Cor. 15:10, I *l.* more abundantly
Phil. 2:16, not run, nor *l.* in vain
Prov. 16:26, he that *laboureth, l.* for
Eccl. 5:12, sleep of the *labouring* man is sweet [prayer
Col. 4:12, Epaphras *l.* fervently in
Luke 10:7, the *labourer* is worthy of his hire, 1 Tim. 5:18. [Luke 10:2.
Matt. 9:37, but *labourers* are few,
1 Cor. 3:9, *l.* together with God
**Lachish,** see *ftn. p.* 358. [of knowledge
**Lack,** Hos. 4:6, people destroyed for *l.*
Ps. 34:10, young lions do *l.*
Matt. 19:20, what *l.* I yet?
Mar. 10:21, one thing thou *l.*
Phil. 4:10, but ye *l.* opportunity
Jas. 1:5, if any *l.* wisdom, ask of God
**Ladder,** Gen. 28:12.
**Laden,** Isa. 1:4, a people *l.* with
Matt. 11:28, labour and heavy *l.*
2 Tim. 3:6, silly women, *l.* with sins
**Lahai-roi,** Gen. 24:62.
**Lahmi,** 2 Sam. 21:19.
**Laish,** 1 Sam. 25:44.
**Lake of fire,** Rev. 19:20.
**Lama Sabachthani,** Matt. 27:46.
**Lamb;** Figurative, see *footnote, p.* 226.
—, an appellation of Jesus, *ftn. p.*1448.
—, Gen. 22:7, where is the *l.* for offer-
22:8, God will provide a *l.* [ing
Isa. 11:6, wolf shall dwell with *l.*
53:7, brought as *l.* to slaughter
John 1:29, behold the *L.* of God, 36.
21:15, Jesus said to Peter, feed my *l.*
1 Pet. 1:19, as a *l.* without blemish
Rev. 5:12, worthy is *L.* that was slain
6:16, wrath of the *L.*
7:14, white in blood of the *L.* 12:11.
**Lame,** Is. 35:6, the *l.* man shall leap as a hart
Heb. 12:13, lest *l.* be turned out of
**Lamech,** father of Jabal, Gen. 4: 18-24.
—, father of Noah, see *ftn. p.* 11.
**Lameness,** see *footnote, p.* 198.
**Lamp;** *Figurative; Symbolical,* see *footnote, p.* 136.
Job 12:5, is as a *l.* despised of him
Ps. 119:105, thy word a *l.* to my feet
Prov. 6:23, the commandment is a *l.*
13:9, *l.* of wicked shall be put out
Is. 62:1, salvation as *l.* that burneth
**Land,** see *footnote, p.* 427.
**Landmarks,** see *footnote, p.* 317.
**Language,** see *footnote, p.* 1215.
**Laodicea,** see *footnote, p.* 1625.
**Lapidary,** Ex. 31:5.
**Lapwing,** Lev. 11:19.
**Lasciviousness,** see *footnote, p.* 1677.
**Lasea,** Acts 27:8.
**Lasharon,** Josh. 12:18. [shalt *l.*
**Laugh,** Job 5:22, at destruction thou
Ps. 2:4, he that sitteth in heavens
37:13, Lord shall *l.* at him [shall *l.*
Prov. 1:26, I will *l.* at your calamity
Eccl. 3:4, a time to *l.*
Lk. 6:21, blessed that weep, ye shall *l.*
25, woe to you that *l.* ye shall mourn
Job 8:21, fill mouth with *laughing*
Ps. 126:2, mouth filled with *laughter*
Prov. 14:13, in *l.* heart is sorrowful
Eccl. 2:2, I said of *l.* it is mad
7:3, sorrow is better than *l.*
Jam. 4:9, let *l.* be turned to
**Laver,** see *footnote, p.* 142.
**Law;** *Of God; Of Moses,* see *ftn. p.* 341.
Dt. 33:2, from right hand a fiery *l.*
Neh. 8:7, caused the people to understand the *l.*
Job 22:22, receive *l.* from his mouth
Ps. 1:2, his delight is in the *l.* of the Lord, and in his *l.* doth meditate
19:7, *l.* of the Lord is perfect
37:31, *l.* of his God is in his heart
78:5, he appointed a *l.* in Israel, 10.
119:72, *l.* of thy mouth is better
Prov. 6:23, *l.* is light, 13, 14, *l.* of wise
7:2, keep my *l.* as apple of eye
28:9, turneth away from hearing *l.*
29:18, keepeth the *l.* happy is he
Jer. 18:18, *l.* not perish from priest
31:33, I will put *l.* in inward parts
Luke 16:16, *l.* and prophets till John
John 1:17, *l.* was given by Moses
19:7, we have a *l.* and by our *l.* he
Acts 13:39, not justified by the *l.* of Moses [perish without *l.*
Rom. 2:12, sinned without *l.* shall
13: not hearers of *l.* but doers of *l.*
14, having not *l.* a *l.* to themselves:
3:20, by deeds of *l.* shall no flesh be justified, for by the *l.* is the
27, boasting by what *l.* by *l.* of faith
31, we do make void *l.* we establish the *l.*
4:15, *l.* worketh wrath; where no *l.*
5:13, sin is not imputed, where no *l.*
7:7, had not known sin but by *l.*
8, for without the *l.* sin was dead
9, I was alive without the *l.* once
12, the *l.* is holy, just, and good
14, *l.* is spiritual, but I am carnal
22, I delight in the *l.* of God
23, *l.* in my members warring against *l.* of my mind [*l.* of sin
8:2, *l.* of Spirit made me free from
10:4, Chr. end of *l.* for righteousness
5, righteousness of *l.* 9:31; Phil. 3:9.
1 Cor. 6:1, dare any of you go to *l.*
6:7, brother goeth to *l.* with brother
Gal. 2:16, man not justified by works of the *l.* by works of *l.* not flesh justified.
19, I through the *l.* am dead to *l.*
3:10, of works of *l.* are under curse
12, the *l.* is not of faith, but the
13, redeemed from curse of *l.*
5:23, love, faith, against such is no *l.*
1 Tim. 1:8, the *l.* is good if we use
9, that *l.* is not made for righteous
Heb. 7:19, *l.* made nothing perfect
Ja. 1:25, who looketh into perfect *l.*
1 John 3:4, sin transgresseth the *l.* sin is transgression of *l.* [backs
Neh. 9:26, cast *thy law* behind their
Ps. 40:8,—is within my heart
119:70, I delight in—77, 92, 174.
18, wondrous things out of—
97, how I love—113, 163, 165, 167.
Ezek. 18:5, do that which is *lawful* and right, 33:14, 19.
1 C. 6:12, all things *l.* to me, 10:23.
**Lawyer,** see *footnote, p.* 1343. [heart
**Lay,** Eccl. 7:2, the living will *l.* it to
Isa. 28:16, I *l.* in Zion a tried stone
Mal. 2:2, I cursed, ye do not *l.* it to
Matt. 6:20, *l.* up for yourselves
Mt. 8:20, hath not where to *l.* his head
Acts 7:60, *l.* not this sin to their
15:28, *l.* on you no greater burden
Rom. 8:33, who *l.* any thing to the
2 Cor. 12:14, not to *l.* up for parents
Heb. 12:1, *l.* aside every weight
James 1:21, *l.* apart all filthiness and superfluity of, 1 Pet. 2:1.
John 10:15, *lay down life,* 13:37; 15: 13; 1 John 3:16.
1 Tim. 5:22, *lay hands,* Heb. 6:2.
6:12, *lay hold* on eternal life
Heb. 6:18,—on hope set before us
Ps. 62:9, to be *laid* in the balance
89:19, I *l.* help on one that is
Isa. 53:6, Lord hath *l.* on him the iniquity of us all [Luke 3:9.
Matt. 3:10, axe *l.* to root of trees,
1 Cor. 3:10, I have *l.* foundation, 11.
Heb. 6:1, not *l.* again foundation
Luke 12:19, much goods *laid up*
Col. 1:5, hope which is—for you
1 Tim. 6:19,—a good foundation
2 Tim. 4:8,—for me a crown of
Job 21:19, God *layeth* up his iniquity
24:12, yet God *l.* not folly to them
Prov. 2:7, *l.* up wisdom.
26:24, *l.* up deceit.
Isa. 56:2, blessed is the man that *l.*
57:1, no man *l.* to heart, 42:25.
Jer. 12:11, land desolate; no man *l.*
**Lazarus,** see *footnote, p.* 1467.
**Laziness,** see *footnote, p.* 933.
**Lead,** Ps. 5:8, *lead me* in thy righteous-
25:5,—in thy truth [ness
27:11,—in a plain path
61:2, —to rock higher than I
139:24,—in the way everlasting
Isa. 11:6, a little child shall *l.* them
40:11, gently *l.* those with young
Mt. 15:14, blind *l.* blind, Luke 6:39.
1 Tim. 2:2, may *l.* a quiet life
Rev. 7:17, Lamb shall *l.* them to
Ps. 23:2, *leadeth* me beside still
Isa. 48:17, God which *l.* thee by way
Matt. 7:13, wide and broad is gate that *l.* to destruction [to life
14, straight and narrow the way *l.*
John 10:3, calleth sheep and *l.* them
Rom. 2:4, goodness of God *l.* to
**Lead,** mineral, see *footnote, p.* 1165.
**League,** Job 5:23, in *l.* with the stones
**Leah,** see *footnote, p.* 50. [own
**Lean,** Prov. 3:5, *l.* not unto thine
Jno. 13:23, *l.* on Jesus' bosom, 21:20.
**Learn,** Ps. 119:71, might *l.* thy statutes, 73.
Prov. 22:25, lest thou *l.* his ways
Isa. 1:17, *l.* to do well, seek
Matt. 9:13, *l.* what that means
11:29, *l.* of me, for I am meek
1 Tim. 2:11, let women *l.* in silence
Tit. 3:14, let ours *l.* to maintain good
Rev. 14:3, no man could *l.* that song
Ps. 106:35, *learned* their works.
Isa. 50:4 given me tongue of the *l.*
John 6:45, hath *l.* of Father cometh
Acts 7:22, Moses was *l.* in all wisdom
Eph. 4:20, ye have not so *l.* Christ
Phil. 4:11, have *l.* in whatsoever
Heb. 5:8, though a Son, yet *l.* he
Pr. 1:5, wise increase *learning,* 9:9.
Acts 26:24, much *l.* make thee mad
Rom. 15:4, were written for our *l.*
2 Tim. 3:7, ever *l.* never come to
**Lease,** see *footnote, p.* 1341.
**Least,** Jer. 31:34, know me from *l.* to
Matt. 11:11, *l.* in kingdom of God is
Luke 16:10, faithful in *l.* is faithful
1 Cor. 6:4, judge who are *l.* esteemed
15:9, I am *l.* of all the apostles
Eph. 3:8, less than the *l.* of all saints
**Leather,** see *footnote, p.* 574.

2 Cor. 5:15, who *l.* should not *l.* to
6:9, as dying, and behold we *l.*
13:11, be of one mind, *l.* in peace
Gal. 2:20, life I *l.* I *l.* by faith of Son
of God
5:25, if we *l.* in Spirit, walk in
Phil. 1:21, to *l.* is Christ, 22.
2 Tim. 3:12, all that will *l.* godly in
Titus 2:12, we should *l.* soberly,
righteously, and godly
Heb. 13:18, willing to *l.* honestly
1 Pet. 2:24, should *l.* to righteousness
1 John 4:9, that we might *l.* through
Acts 23:1, *lived* in good conscience
James 5:5, ye have *l.* in pleasure
Rev. 18:9, *l.* deliciously, Luke 7:25.
20:4, they *l.* and reigned with Christ
Job 19:25, my Redeemer *liveth*
Rom. 6:10, in that he *l.* he *l.* to God
14:7, none *l.* to himself or dieth to
1 Tim. 5:6, *l.* in pleasure, dead while
Heb. 7:25, *l.* to make intercession
Rev. 1:18, he that *l.* and was dead
3:1, I know that thou *l.* and art
Acts 7:38, received *lively* oracles
1 Pet. 1:3, begotten again to a *l.* hope
2:5, ye, as *l.* stones, are built up a
1 John 3:16, *lives*, Rev. 12:11.
Eccl. 7:2, *living* will lay it to heart
Isa. 38:19, the *l.* the *l.* shall praise
Jer. 2:13, Lord fountain of *l.* waters
Mt. 22:32, not God of dead, but of *l.*
Mark 12:44, cast in all her *l.* Luke
21:4; 8:43, spent all her *l.*
John 4:10, have given thee *l.* water
7:38, flow rivers of *l.* water
Rom. 12:1, your bodies a *l.* sacrifice
14:9, Lord both of dead and *l.*
1 Cor. 15:45, first Adam. . .a *l.* soul
Heb. 10:20, by a new and *l.* way
1 Pet. 2:4, coming as to a *l.* stone
Rev. 7:17, lead them to *l.* fountains
**Liver**, see *footnote*, *p.* 164.
**Lizard**, Lev. 11:30.
**Lo-ammi**, Hos. 1:9.
**Loaves**, see *footnote*, *p.* **1328.**
**Lock**, Judg. 3:23.
**Locust**, see *footnote*, *p.* 1268
**Lod**, see *footnote*, *p.* 635
**Lo-debar**, 2 Sam. 9:4.
**Lois**, 2 Tim. 1:5. [thee
**Long**, Ps. 63:1, my flesh *longeth* for
84:2, my soul *l.* for courts of Lord
119:40, *I have longed* after thy pre-
131,—for thy commandments [cepts
174,—for thy salvation
20, my soul breaketh for *longing*
107:9, he satisfieth the *l.* soul
**Longevity**, see *footnote*, *p.* 876.
**Longsuffering**, see *footnote*, *p.* 1594
Ex. 34:6, merciful and gracious, *l. s.*
Num. 14:18, The Lord is *l. s.*, and
Ps. 86:15, *l. s.*, plenteous in mercy
Jer. 15:15, take not away in thy *l. s.*
Rom. 2:4, goodness, forbear., and *l. s.*
2 Cor. 6:6, *l. s.*, by kindness, by
Gal. 5:22, fruit of Spirit is *l. s.*
Eph. 4:2, with *l. s.*, forb. one another
Col. 1:11, unto all patience, and *l. s.*
**Look**, Is. 45:22, *l.* unto me and be
saved
Mic. 7:7, I will *l.* unto the Lord
Luke 7:19, do we *l.* for another, 20.
2 Cor. 4:18, we *l.* at things not seen
Phil. 2:4, *l.* not every one on his own
3:20, heaven, from whence also we
*l.* for the Saviour
Heb. 9:28, to them that *l.* for him
1 Pet. 1:12, angels desire to *l.* into
2 Pt. 3:14, seeing ye *l.* for such things
Gen. 29:32, the Lord *looked* on my
affliction, Ex. 2:25. [lightened
Ps. 34:5, they *l.* to him and were
Isa. 5:7, he *l.* for judgment, behold
Jer. 8:15, we *l.* for peace, but, 14:19.
Lk. 2:38, *l.* for redemption in Israel
22:61, the Lord *l.* on Peter [is God
Heb. 11:10, *l.* for a city whose builder
1 John 1:1, we have seen and *l.* on
1 Sam. 16:7, man *looketh* on appearance, but Lord *l.* on the heart

Ps. 33:13, the Lord *l.* down from
heaven, 14:2.
Matt. 5:28, *l.* on a woman to lust
24:50, come in a day he *l.* not for
James 1:25, *l.* into perfect law of
Ps. 18:27, wilt bring down high *looks*
Isa. 38:14, eyes fail with *looking*
Luke 9:62, no man *l.* back is fit for
the kingdom of God
Tit. 2:13, *l.* for that blessed hope
Heb. 10:27, a certain fearful *l.* for
12:2, *l.* to Jesus, the author and
15, *l.* diligently, lest any fail of the
2 Pet. 3:12, *l.* for day of God
Jude 21, *l.* for the mercy of our Lord
**Loose**, Ps. 102:20, to *l.* those appointed
to death
Isa. 58:6, the fast I have chosen to
*l.* bands of the wicked [*loosed*
Eccl. 12:6, or ever the silver cord be
Mt. 16:19, *l.* on earth, *l.* in heaven,
Acts 2:24, *l.* pains of death [18:18.
1 Cor. 7:27, bound to a wife, seek not
to be *l.* art thou *l.* seek not a wife
**Lord's Day**, see *footnote*, Christian Sab-
bath, *p.* 1391.
— Prayer, Matt. 6:9-13.
— Supper, see *footnote*, Eucharist, *p.*
1386. [to *l.*
**Lose**, Ec. 3:6, a time to get, and a time
Matt. 10:39; 16:25; Mar. 8:35; Lk.
9:24, he that findeth his life shall *l.* it
Mat. 16:26; Mar. 8:36; Lk. 9:25,
*l.* his own soul
Lk. 15:4, is he *l.* one sheep
John 12:25, loveth his life shall *l.* it
1 Cor. 3:15, *loss*, Phil. 3: 7, 8.
**Lost**, Ps. 119:176, like *l.* sheep
Ezek. 37:11, our hope is *l.* we are cut
Matt. 5:13, if salt have *l.* its savour
10:6, to the *l.* sheep of Israel, 15:24.
18:11, save that was *l.* Luke 19:10.
Lk. 15:32, thy brother was *l.* and is
found
John 18:9, them thou gavest me, I
have *l.* none [to them that are *l.*
2 Cor. 4:3, the Gospel be hid, it is hid
**Lost Sheep**, parable of, Matt. 18:12, 13;
**Lo-ruhamah**, Hos. 1:6-8. [Luke 15:4-7
**Lot**, son of Haran, see *footnote*, *p.* 19.
—, decisions made by, see *ftn.* *p.* 764.
Pr. 18:18, *l.* causeth contentions to
Ac. 1:26, the *l.* fell on Matthias [cease
Ps. 22:18, on my vesture they did
cast *lots*, Matt. 27:35; Mark 15:24.
**Love**; *Of man for man*, see *footnote*, *p*
1686; *Of man for woman*, *ftn.* *p.* 1687
—, *For God; For Jesus*, see *ftn.* *p.*1687
—, for Church, see *ftn.* Church, love
for, *p.* 1331.
—, of God, see *ftn.* God, love of, *p.* 4.
—, of Jesus, see *ftn.* Jesus, love of, *p.*
1301. [women
—, 2 Sam. 1:26, passing the *l.* of
Song 8:6, *l.* is strong as death, jealou-
Ho.11:4,draw them with bands of [sy
Mt. 24:12, *l.* of many shall wax cold
John 15:9, continue ye in my *l.* 10.
12, *l.* one another as I have *l.* you
13, greater *l.* hath no man than this
Rom. 5:5, *l.* of God is shed abroad
8:35, who shall separate us from the
*l.* of Christ, 39.
12:9, let *l.* be without dissimulation
13:10, *l.* is the fulfilling of the law.
15:30, Christ's sake, and *l.* of Spirit
2 Cor. 5:14, *l.* of Christ constraineth
13:14, *l.* of God be with you all
Gal. 5:6, faith which worketh by *l.*
13, by *l.* serve one another
22, fruit of the Spirit is *l.* joy, and
Eph. 1:4, without blame before God
in *l.* [another in *l.*
3:17,grounded in *l.* 4:2, forbearing one
4:15, speaking truth in *l.* 16.
5:2, walk in *l.* as Christ hath loved
Col. 2:2, knit together in *l.* and
1 Ths. 1:3,your labour of *l.* Heb. 6:10.
3:12, abound in *l.*
5:8, breastplate of faith and *l.*
2 Thes. 2:10, received not *l.* of truth

3:5, direct your hearts into *l.* of God
Heb. 13:1, let brotherly *l.* continue
1 John 2:5, in him is *l.* of God perfected
3:1, what manner of *l.* the Father
bestowed on us, 4:7, *l.* is of God,
8, 16, God is *l.*
4:9, manifest the *l.* of God
11, we ought to *l.* one another
12, he that dwelleth in *l.* dwelleth, 16.
18, there is no fear in *l.* perfect *l.*
21, who loveth God *l.* his brother
Rev. 2:4, thou hast left thy first *l.*
1 John 3:16, perceive we *the love of G.*
17, dwelleth — in him
4:9, in this was manifested—towards
5:3, this is the —that we keep his
Lev. 19:18, thou shalt *love* thy neighbour as thyself, 34; Mt. 19:19; 22:
39; Rom. 13:8; Gal. 5:14; Jas. 2:8.
Dt. 6:5, shalt *l.* Lord thy God with
all thy heart, Mt. 22:37; Luke 10:27.
10:12, to fear the Lord and to *l.*
1 Sam. 18:1, *l.* David as his own soul
Ps. 31:23, *l.* Lord, all ye his saints
97:10, ye that *l.* the Lord hate evil
116:1, I *l.* Lord because, 18:1.
145:20, Lord preserveth them that
Song 1:4, the upright *l.* thee [*l.* him
Mic. 6:8, to do justly, and *l.* mercy
Zech. 8:19, *l.* the truth and peace
Matt. 5:44, *l.* your enemies, bless
Mark 10:21, Jesus beholding him, *l.*
Lk. 7:47, sins forgiven, she *l.* much
John 13:34, *l.* one another, 15:12, 17;
Rom. 13:8; 1 John 3:11, 23; 4:7, 11,
12; 1 Pet. 1:22. [*l.* him
14:23, if a man *l.* me, my Father will
1 Cor. 16:22, if any man *l.* not Lord
Eph. 5:25, *l.* your wives, Col. 3:19.
2 Tim. 4:8, all that *l.* his appearing
1 Pet. 1:8, having not seen, ye *l.*
2:17, *l.* brotherhood, 3:8.
1 John 2:15, *l.* not world, if any *l.*
world, *l.* of Father not in him
1 John 4:19, we *l.* him because he
first loved us
John 3:16, God so *loved* the world
3:19, men *l.* darkness rather than
11:36, behold how he *l.* him
12:43, *l.* the praise of men more
13:1, having *l.* his own, he *l.* them
23, one of his disciples whom Jesus
*l.* 19:26; 20:2; 21:7, 20.
14:21, *l.* me, be *l.* of my Father
28, if ye *l.* me, ye would rejoice for
15:9, as my F. *l* me, so have I *l.*
17:23, hast *l.* them as thou hast *l.* me
26, wherewith thou hast *l.* me
Rom. 8:37, conquerors through him
that *l.* us [1:2.
9:13, Jacob I *l.* Esau I hated, Mal.
Gal. 2:20, Son of God, who *l.* me [us
Eph. 2:4, great love wherewith he *l.*
5:2, walk in love, as Christ *l.* us
25, love wives as Christ *l.* church
2 Thes. 2:16, God our Father *l.* us
2 Tim. 4:10, *l.* this present world
Heb. 1:9, hast *l.* righteousness and
2 Pet. 2:15, *l.* wages of unrighteous.
1 John 4:10, not that we *l.* God but
he *l.* us and sent his Son to be
Rev. 1:5, unto him that *l.* us and
washed us from sins in own blood
12:11, *l.* not their lives unto death
Jn. 21:15, *lovest* thou me. .yea Lord
thou knowest that I love thee, 16:17.
Ps. 11:7, the Lord *loveth* righteousn.
146:8, the Lord *l.* the righteous
Prov. 3:12, whom the Lord *l.* he
correcteth, Heb. 12:6.
17:17, a friend *l.* at all times [poor
21:17, he who *l.* pleasure, shall be
Matt. 10:37, *l.* father or mother more
John 3:35, Father *l.* the Son, 5:20.
16:27, Father himself *l.* you; ye *l.* me
2 Cor. 9:7, God *l.* a cheerful giver
3 John 9, *l.* to have pre-eminence
Rev. 22:15, whoso *l.* and maketh lie
**Low**, 1 Sm. 2:7, Lord brings *l.* and lifts
Job 40:12, look on every one that

is proud and bring him *l.*
Ps. 49:2, both *l.* and high, rich and
136:23, remember us in *l.* estate
Prov. 29:23, man's pride shall bring him *l.*
Luke 1:48, he regardeth the *l.* estate
52, he exalteth them of *l.* degree
3:5, every mountain and hill shall be brought *l.* [*l.* estate
Rom. 12:16, condescend to men of
Ps. 63:9, *lower* parts of the earth
138:6, Lord hath respect to *lowly*
Prov. 3:34, he giveth grace unto *l.*
Prov. 11:2, with *l.* is wisdom
Matt. 11:29, learn of me, I am meek
Eph. 4:2, *lowliness*, Phil. 2:3. [and *l.*
**Loyalty**, see *footnote*, p. 957.
**Lubinus**, 2 Chr. 12:3.
**Lucas**, Philem. 24.
**Lucifer**, Isa. 14:12.
**Lucius**, a christian at Antioch, Ac. 13:1
—, a kinsman of Paul, Rom. 16:21.
**Lucre**, filthy, 1 Tim. 3:3, 8; Tit. 1:7;
**Lud**, Gen. 10:22. [1 Pet. 5:2.
**Ludim**, Gen. 10:13.
**Luhith**, Isa. 55:5.
**Luke**, see *footnote*, p. 1628.
**Lukewarmness**, see *footnote*, p. 1696.
**Lust**, see *footnote*, p. 1679.
Matt. 5:28, looketh on woman to *l.*
Rom. 7:7, not known *l.* but by law
1 Cor. 10:6, not *l.* after evil things
Gal. 5:16, shall not fulfil *l.* of flesh
1 Thes. 4:5, not in the *l.* of concupiscence even as the Gentiles
James 1:15, when *l.* is conceived, it
1 John 2:16, *l.* of the flesh, and *l.* of
Mark 4:19, *lusts* of other things
John 8:44, *l.* of your father ye will
Rom 6:12, should obey it in the *l.*
13:14, for the flesh, to fulfil the *l.*
Gal. 5:17, flesh *l.* against Spirit
24, crucified flesh with affections and *l.*
Eph. 2:3, *l.* of our flesh, and mind
1 Tim. 6:9, foolish and hurtful *l.*
2 Tim. 2:22, flee youthful *l.* follow
3:6, laden with sins, led away with divers *l.* [worldly *l.*
Tit. 2:12, denying ungodliness and
3:3, divers *l.* and pleasures
James 4:3, consume it on your *l.*
1 Pet. 2:11, abstain from fleshly *l.*
4:2, no longer live to the *l.* of men
2 Pet. 3:3, walk after their own *l.*
Jude 16, 18.
**Lycaonia**, Acts 14:6.
**Lycia**, Acts 27:5.
**Lydda**, Acts 9:32-35.
**Lydia**, Acts 16:14.
**Lying**, see *ftn.* Falsehood, p. 792.
**Lysanias**, Luke 3:1.
**Lysias**, Acts 24:7, 22.
**Lystra**, see *footnote*, p. 1515.

**M**

**Maachah**, name of four men, about whom little is known, Gen. 22:24; 1 Kin. 2:39; 1 Chr. 11:43; 27:16.
—, mother of Abijam, 1 Kin. 15:2.
—, mother of Absalom, 2 Sam. 3:3.
—, three women, about whom little is known, 1 Chr. 2:48; 7:15; 8:29.
—, a kingdom E. of Bashan, 1 Chr. 19:
**Maaleh-acrabbim**, Josh. 15:3. [7.
**Maaseiah**, name of a number of men, about whom little is known, 1 Chr. 15:18; 2 Chr. 23:1; 26:11; 28:7; 34:8; Ezra 10:18, 21, 22; Neh. 8:4, 7; 11:5, 7; 12:41, 42; Jer. 21:1; 29:21;
**Maasiai**, 1 Chr. 9:12, [32:12.
**Maath**, Luke 3:26.
**Macedonia**, see *footnote*, p. 1519.
**Machir**, a son of Manasseh, see *footnote*, p. 88.
—, of Lo-debar, 2 Sam. 9:4, 5.
**Machpelah**, see *footnote*, p. 37.
**Madai**, Gen. 10:2. [*m.*
**Made**, Psa. 139:14, I am wonderfully
Prov. 16:4, Lord *m.* all things for
John 1:3, all things were *m* by him
Rom. 1:3, Christ *m* of the seed of David [that are *m.*
1:20, being understood by the things
1 Cor. 1:30, Christ who of God is *m.*
9:22, *m.* all things to all men
Gal. 4:4, *m.* of a woman, *m.* under
Phil. 2:7, *m.* in the likeness of men
**Madmannah**, Josh. 15:31.
**Madmenah**, Isa. 10:31.
**Madon**, Josh. 11:1.
**Magdala**, Matt. 15:39.
**Magi**, Matt. 2:1-12.
**Magician**, see *footnote*, p. 100.
**Magistrate**, see *footnote*, p. 731.
**Magnificat**, Luke 1:46-55.
**Magog**, see *footnote*, p. 622.
**Magor-missabib**, Jer. 20:3-6.
**Mahalah**, 1 Chr. 7:18.
**Mahalaleel**, see *footnote*, p. 10. [28:9.
**Mahalath**, daughter of Ishmael, Gen.
—, granddaughter of David, 2 Chr. 11:
**Mahanaim**, see *footnote*, p. 56. [18.
**Mahaneh-dan**, Judg. 13:25.
**Maharai**, 2 Sam. 23:28.
**Mahath**, 1 Chr. 6:35.
**Maher-shalal-hash-baz**, Isa. 8:1-4.
**Mahlah**, see *footnote*, p. 263.
**Mahli**, son of Merari, Ex. 6:19.
—, son of Mushi, 1 Chr. 6:47.
**Mahlon**, Ruth 1:2.
**Maker**, Heb. 11:10.
**Makhaloth**, Num. 33:25, 26.
**Makkedah**, Josh. 10:17.
**Maktesh**, Zeph. 1:11.
**Malachi**, see *footnote*, p. 1290.
**Malcham**, Zeph. 1:5.
**Malchiah**, name of four men, about whom little is known, Neh. 3:14, 31; 8:4; Jer. 38:1.
**Malchiel**, Gen. 46:17.
**Malchus**, John 18:10.
**Male**, Gen. 1:27, *m.* and female, Num. 5:3; Matt. 19:4; Gal. 3:28.
**Malefactor**, crucified with Jesus, Matt. 27:38-44; Luke 23:32-39.
**Malice**, see *footnote*, p. 1615.
1 Cor. 5:8, the leaven of *m.*
1 Cor. 14:20, in *m.* be children, but in
Eph. 4:31, put away . . . all *m.* Col. 3:8; 1 Pet. 2:1.
Tit. 3:3, living in *m.* and envy
Rom. 1:29, filled with all *maliciousness;* full of envy, 1 Pet. 2:1.
**Mammon**, Matt. 6:24, Luke 16:9.
**Mamre**, see *footnote*, p. 22.
**Man**; *A spirit; All men equal;* see *footnote*, p. 776.
—, see *footnote*, Young men, p. 913.
—, Job 4:17, sh. *m.* be more just than
5:7, *m.* is born to trouble, 14:1. [God
7:17, what is *m.* that thou shouldest be mindful of him
9:2, how shall *m.* be just with God
11:12, vain *m.* would be wise
14:1, *m.* born of woman, of few days
15:14, wh. is *m.* th. he should be clean
25:4, how can *m.* be justified with G.
6, much less *m.* that is a worm
28:28, unto *m.* he said, behold [ful
Ps. 8:4, wh. is *m.* th. thou art mind-
25:12, what *m.* is he that feareth L.
49:12, *m.* being in honour abideth not
90:3, thou turnest *m.* to destruction
104:23, *m.* goeth forth to his work
118:6, not fear; what can *m.* do
144:3, what is *m.* that thou takest knowledge of him; or son of *m.*
Prov. 20:24, *m.'s* goings are of Lord
Eccl. 7:29, God made *m.* upright
12:5, *m.* goeth to his long home
Is. 53:3, *m.* of sorrows and acquainted
Matt. 4:4, *m.* shall not live by bread
Matt. 8:9, I am a *m.* under authority
16:26, what shall a *m.* give in exchange
26:72, I know not the *m.* 74. [5.
John 3:3, except a *m.* be born again,
7:46, never *m.* spake like this *m.*
Rom. 6:6, old *m.* crucified with Christ
7:22, delight in law after inward *m.*
1 Cor. 2:11, what *m.* knoweth the things of a *m.* save the spirit of *m.*
**14, natural *m.* receiveth not things**
11:8, *m.* not of woman, but wo. of *m.*
15:47, first *m.* is earthy; second *m.*
2 Cor. 4:16, though outward *m.* perish, yet inward *m.* is renewed
Eph. 4:22, put off the old *m.* which
24, put on new *m.* Col. 3:9, 10. [bled
Phil. 2:8, in fashion as a *m.* he hum-
1 Tim. 2:5, one Mediator, the *m.*
**Manaen**, Acts 13:1.
**Manahath**, son of Shobal, Gen. 36:23.
—, a city in Benjamin, 1 Chr. 8:6.
**Manasseh.** *Son of Joseph; Tribe of*, see *footnote*, p. 81.
—, king of Judah, see *ftn.* p. 612.
**Mandrake**, Gen. 30:14-16.
**Maneh**, see *footnote*, Weights, p. 195.
**Manger**, Luke 2:7, 12, 16. [be *m.*
**Manifest**, Mk. 4:22, nothing hid...not
John 14:21, *m.* myself to him, 22.
2:11, *m.* forth his glory, and his
17:6, I have *m.* thy name unto men
1 Cor. 4:5, make *m.* counsels of heart
Gal. 5:19, works of the flesh are *m.*
2 Thes. 1:5, a *m.* token of righteous
1 Tim. 3:16, God was *m.* in the flesh
Heb. 4:13, any creature not *m.* in
1 John 3:5, was *m.* to tk. away sin, 8.
10, in this children of God are *m.*
4:9, in this was *m.* the love of God
Luke 8:17, *made manifest*, John 3:21; 1 Cor. 3:13; 2 Cor. 4:10; 5:11; Eph. 5:13.
**Manifestation**, Rom. 8:19, *m.* of sons of
1 Cor. 12:7, *m.* of the Spirit is given
2 Cor. 4:2, but by *m.* of the truth in
**Manifold**, Ps. 104:24, how *m.* are thy works.
Luke 18:30, *m.* more in this present
Eph. 3:10, known *m.* wisdom of God
1 Pet. 1:6, in heaviness through *m.* temptations [grace of God
4:10, as good stewards of the *m.*
**Manna**; Figurative, see *ftn.* p. 117
**Manners**, see *footnote*, p. 28.
**Manoah**, Judg. 13:2.
**Mansions**, John 14:2, in my Father's house are many *m.*
**Manslaughter**, see *footnotes*, Fratricide p. 9; Homicide, p. 292.
**Mantle**, see *footnote*, p. 734.
**Maon**, see *footnote*, p. 369.
**Marah**, Ex. 15:22-25.
**Maralah**, Josh. 19:11.
**Marble**, see *footnote*, p. 665.
**Mareshah**, see *footnote*, p. 368.
**Mariner**, see *footnote*, p. 1173.
**Mark**, see *footnote*, p. 1510.
—, Ezek. 9:4, set *m.* on the foreheads
Rev. 13:16, 17; 14:9; 19:20.
Phil. 3:14, I press toward the *m.*
Ps. 37:37, *m.* the perfect man
130:3, if thou shouldest *m.* iniquity
Rom. 16:17, *m.* them which cause
Phil. 3:17, *m.* them which walk
Gal. 6:17, bear in my body the *marks*
**Marriage**, see *footnote*, p. 59.
Matt. 22:2, king made a *m.* for son.
25:10, that were ready went into *m.*
John 2:1, 2, there was a *m.* in Cana
Heb. 13:4, *m.* is honourable in all
Rev. 19:7, *m.* of Lamb is come, 9.
Jer. 3:14, I am *married* to you, saith Lord
Luke 14:20, I have *m.* a wife, and
17:27, they drank, *m.* and given in *m.*
1 Cor. 7:9, better to *marry* than to burn
1 Tim. 4:3, forbidding to *m.* and
5:14, that younger women *m.* and
**Marrow**, Ps. 63:5, soul is satisfied as with *m.*
Heb. 4:12, dividing joints and *m.*
**Mars' Hill**, Acts 17:19-34.
**Martha**, see *footnote*, p. 1417.
**Martyrdom**, see *footnote*, p. 1709.
**Mary**, wife of Cleophas, see *ftn.* p. 1390.
—, mother of Jesus, see *ftn.* p. 1393.
—, sister of Lazarus, see *ftn.* p. 1467.
—, mother of Mark, Acts 12:12.
—, P. sends salutations to, Rm. 16:6.
**Mary Magdalene**, see *footnote*, p. 1355.

Matt. 18:26, 29, have *p.* with me
Luke 8:15, bring forth fruit with *p.*
21:19, in your *p.* possess your souls
Rom. 5:3, tribulation worketh *p.*
8:25, we do with *p.* wait for it [hope
15:4, that we through *p.* might have
5, G. of *p.* grant you be like minded
2 Cor. 6:4, as ministers of God, in *p.*
12:12, wrought among you in all *p.*
Col. 1:11, strengthened unto all *p.*
1 Thes. 1:3, *p.* of hope in our Lord
2 Thes. 1:4, for your *p.* and faith
1 Tim. 6:11, follow after *p.* meekness
2 Tim. 3:10, my doctrine, charity, *p.*
Tit. 2:2, sound in faith, charity, *p.*
Heb. 6:12, thro' *p.* inherit promises
10:36, have need of *p.* that after
12:1, run with *p.* race set before us
James 1:3, trying of faith worketh *p.*
4, let *p.* have her perfect work
5:7, long *p.* for it till he receive
10, prophets for an example of *p.*
11, ye have heard of the *p.* of Job
2 Pet. 1:6, to temperance *p.* to *p.*
Rev. 1:9, brother in the *p.* of Jesus
2:2, I know thy *p.* 19, hast *p.* 3.
13:10, here is *p.* of saints, 14:12.
Eccl. 7:8, the *patient* in spirit better than the proud [doing
Rom. 2:7, by *p.* continuance in well
12:12, *p.* in tribulation, instant in
1 Thes. 5:14, be *p.* towards all men
2 Thes. 3:5, *p.* waiting for Christ
1 Tim. 3:3, not greedy of lucre but *p.*
2 Tim. 2:24, gentle, apt to teach, *p.*
James 5:7, *p.* unto coming of Lord
8, be ye also *p.* establish your
Ps. 37:7, wait *patiently* for L. 40:1.
Heb. 6:15, after he had *p.* endured
1 Pet. 2:20, ye be buffeted, take it *p.*
**Patmos,** Rev. 1:9.
**Patricide,** 2 Kin. 19:37; Isa. 37:38.
**Patriotism,** see *footnote, p.* 905.
**Patrobas,** Rom. 16:14.
**Pattern,** see *footnote, p.* 132.
**Pau,** Gen. 36:39.
**Paul,** see *footnote, p.* 1512.
**Pawn,** see *footnote, p.* 794.
**Peace,** see *footnote, p.* 1084; Through Christ, see *footnote, p.* 1085.
—, spiritual, see *footnote* Spiritual Peace, *p.* 1603.
—, Offerings, see *footnote,* Offerings, peace, *p.* 169. [be at *p.*
—, Job 22:21, acquaint thyself and
Ps. 34:14, seek *p.* and pursue it
37:37, the end of that man is *p.*
85:8, he will speak *p.* unto his people
10, righteousness and *p.* kissed
119:165, great *p.* have they that love
120:6, hateth *p.* 7, I am for *p.*
122:6, pray for *p.* of Jerusalem
125:5, *p.* shall be upon Israel, 128:6.
Prov. 16:7, his enemies to be at *p.*
Isa. 9:6, everlast. Father, Prince of *p.*
26:3, keep him in perfect *p.*
27:5, that he may make *p.* with me, and he shall make *p.* with me
45:7, I make *p.* and create evil
48:18, had thy *p.* been as a river
22, there is no *p.* to the wicked, 57:21.
57:2, enter into *p.* shall rest in beds
19, *p. p.* to him that is far off
59:8, way of *p.* they know not, Rom. 3:17.
66:12, extend *p.* to her like a river
Jer. 6:14, saying *p. p.* when there is no *p.* 8:11;Ez.13:10; 2Kin. 9:18,22.
8:15, looked for *p.* but no good came
29:7, seek *p.* of the city, for in the *p.* thereof ye shall have *p.*
11, thoughts of *p.* and not of evil
Mic. 5:5, this man shall be the *p.*
Zech. 8:19, love the truth and *p.*
Matt. 10:34, I came not to send *p.*
Mark 9:50, have *p.* one with another
Luke 1:79, guide our feet in way of *p.*
2:14, on earth *p.* good will towards
29, lettest thy servant depart in *p.*
19:42, things that belong to thy *p.*
John 14:27, *p.* I leave my *p.* I give
16:33, in me ye might have *p.*
Rom. 5:1, we have *p.* with God through Jesus Christ
8:6, spiritually minded is life and *p.*
14:17, king. of G. is righteousness, *p.*
15:13, fill you with all *p.* and joy
1 Cor. 7:15, God hath called us to *p.*
2 Cor. 13:11, live in *p.* and God of *p.*
Gal. 5:22, fruit of Spirit is love, *p.*
Eph. 2:14, he is our *p.* 15, making *p.*
Phil. 4:7, the *p.* of God, Col. 3:15.
1 Thes. 5:13, at *p.* among yourselves
Heb. 12:14, follow *p.* with all men
James 3:18, righteous. sown in *p.*
1 Pet. 3:11, let him seek *p.* and ensue
2 Pet. 3:14, found of him in *p.*
1 Tim. 2:2, lead a *peaceable* life
Heb. 12:11, yieldeth *p.* fruit of right.
James 3:17, is first pure, then *p.*
Rom. 12:18, live *peaceably* with all
Matt. 5:9, blessed are *peacemakers*
**Peacock,** 1 Kin. 10:22.
**Pearl,** see *footnote, p.* 1709.
Matt. 13:46, found *p.* of great price
Matt. 7:6, cast not *pearls* bef. swine
1 Tim. 2:9, not with gold, or *p.* or
Rev. 21:21, gates were twelve *p.*
**Peculiar,** Ex. 19:5, a *p.* treasure to me
Ps. 135:4, Israel for his *p.* treasure
Deut. 14:2, chosen thee to be a *p.* people, 26:18; Tit. 2:14; 1 Pet. 2:9.
**Pedahel,** Num. 34:28.
**Pedahzur,** Num. 2:20.
**Pedaiah,** six men, about whom little is known, 2 Kin. 23:36; 1 Chr. 3:18; 27:20; Neh. 3:25; 8:4; 11:7.
**Pekah,** see *footnote, p.* 975.
**Pekahiah,** 2 Kin. 15:22-26.
**Pekod,** Jer. 50:21.
**Pelatiah,** Ezek. 11:1-13.
**Peleg,** see *footnote, p.* 18.
**Pelethites,** see *footnote, p.* 514.
**Pelican,** Lev. 11:18.
**Pen,** see *footnote, p.* 1055.
**Penalty,** vicariously assumed, *ftn. p.*
**Peninnah,** 1 Sam. 1:2. [471.
**Penitence,** see *footnotes,* Repentance, *p.* 1357; Sin, confession of, *p.* 1550.
**Penitent.** Promises to, see *ftn. p.* 846.
**Penny,** see *footnote, p.* 1338.
**Pentecost,** see *footnote, p.* 1489.
**Penuel,** Gen. 32:31. [whose God
**People,** Ps. 144:15, happy is that *p.*
Isa. 1:4, a *p.* laden with iniquity
27:11, a *p.* of no understanding
Hos. 4:9, like *p.* like priest
1 Pet. 2:10, in time past were not *p.*
Ps. 100:3, we are *his people* and sheep of his
Matt. 1:21, J. shall save—from sins
Rom. 11:2, God hath not cast away—
**Peor,** Num. 23:28-30.
**Perez-uzza,** 2 Sam. 6:8.
**Perdition,** John 17:12, none lost, but son of *p.*
Phil. 1:28, is to the token of *p.* but
2 Thes. 2:3, revealed, the son of *p.*
1 Tim. 6:9, wh. drown men in *p.*
Heb. 10:39, who draw back to *p.*
2 Pet. 3:7, and *p.* of ungodly men
Rev. 17:8, beast shall go into *p.*
R. V. 2 Pet. 3:7, destruction [and *p.*
**Perfect,** Gen. 6:9, Noah a just man
17:1, walk before me, and be *p.*
Deut. 18:13, shalt be *p.* with God
32:4, his work is *p.* just and right
2 Sam. 22:31, his way is *p.* Ps. 18:30.
Job 1:1, man *p.* and upright, 8:2,3.
Ps. 19:7, law of the Lord is *p.*
37:37, mark the *p.* man and behold
Matt. 5:48, *p.* as your Father is *p.*
19:21, if thou wilt be *p.* go and sell all
1 Cor. 2:6, among them that are *p.*
2 Cor. 12:9, strength *p.* in weakness
13:11, be *p.* be of good comfort
Eph. 4:13, to a *p.* man unto the measure of stature of Christ
Phil. 3:12, not as though already *p.*
15, as many as be *p.* thus minded
Col. 1:28, pres. every man *p.* in Ch.
4:12, may stand *p.* and complete
2 Tim. 3:17, man of God may be *p.*
Heb. 2:10, captain of salvation *p.*
7:19, the law made nothing *p.*
12:23, spirits of just men made *p.*
13:21, make you *p.* in every good
James 1:4, let patience have her *p.* work, that ye may be *p.*
17, good and *p.* gift from above
1 Pet. 5:10, make you *p.* establish
1 John 4:18, *p.* love casteth out fear
Rev. 3:2, not found thy works *p.*
2 Cor. 7:1, *perfecting* holiness in fear
Eph. 4:12, for the *p.* of the saints
**Perfection,** see *footnote, p.* 1655.
Job 11:7, find Almighty unto *p.*
Ps. 119:96, have seen an end of all *p.*
Luke 8:14, bring no fruit to *p.*
2 Cor. 13:9, we wish, even your *p.*
Heb. 6:1, let us go on unto *p.*
Col. 3:14, charity bond of *perfectness*
(See *footnotes,* God perfection of, *p.* 5; Jesus, perfections of, *p.* 1304.)
**Perform,** Ps. 119:106, have sworn and will *p.* it
Isa. 9:7, zeal of Lord of hosts will *p.*
Rom. 4:21, promised, was able to *p.*
7:18, how to *p.* that which is good
Phil. 1:6, *p.* it to day of Jesus Christ
**Perfume,** see *footnote, p.* 944.
**Perga,** Acts 13:13.
**Pergamos,** Rev. 1:11.
**Perilous,** 2 Tim. 3:1, last days *p.* times
**Perish,** Nm. 17:12, we die, we *p.* we all *p.*
Esth. 4:16, I will go in, if I *p.* I *p.*
Ps. 2:12, ye *p.* from the way, when
Prov. 29:18, no vision, the people *p.*
Mt. 8:25, L. save us, we *p.* Lk. 8:24.
John 3:15, believeth should not *p.*
16, should not *p.* but have ever. life
10:28, they shall never *p.* [Christ died
1 Cor. 8:11, the weak *p.* for whom
2 Pet. 3:9, not willing that any *p.*
**Perizzites,** see *footnote, p.* 25.
**Perjury,** see *footnote, p.* 1636. [poor
**Persecute,** Ps. 10:2, wicked doth *p.* the
Matt. 5:11, blessed are ye when men
44, pray for them that *p.* you [*p.* you
10:23, when they *p.* you in this city
Rom. 12:14, bless them which *p.*
Ps. 109:16, *persecuted* the poor and
119:161, princes *p.* me without cause
143:3, the enemy hath *p.* my soul
John 15:20, if they *p.* me they will *p.*
Acts 9:4, why *p.* thou me, 22:7. [you
22:4, I *p.* this way to death, 7:8.
26:11, I *p.* them to strange cities, 14.
1 Cor. 4:12, being *p.* we suffer it
15:9, because I *p.* the church of God
2 Cor. 4:9, *p.* but not forsaken, cast
Gal. 1:13, I *p.* the church of God
4:29, *p.* him born after the Spirit
1 Thes. 2:15, own prophets *p.* us
1 Tim. 1:13, who was a *persecutor*
2 Tim. 3:12, live godly in Jesus Christ shall suffer *persecution*
**Persecution.** *Of Jesus; Of the righteous,* see *footnote, p.* 1476.
**Perseverance,** see *footnote, p.* 1618.
**Persia,** see *footnote, p.* 760.
**Persis,** Rom. 16:12. [of men
**Person,** Matt. 22:16, regardest not *p.*
Acts 10:34, God is no respecter of *p.*
Deut. 10:17; Gal. 2:6; Eph. 6:9; Col. 3:25; 1 Pet. 1:17.
Heb. 1:3, express image of his *p.*
12:16, or profane *p.* as Esau
2 Pet. 3:11, what manner of *p.* ought
Jude 16, men's *p.* in admiration
**Persuade,** 2 Cor. 5:11, we *p.* men
Gal. 1:10, do I *p.* men, or God
Acts 13:43, *persuaded* to continue
21:14, when he would not be *p.*
Rom. 8:38, I am *p.* that neither death
2 Tim. 1:12, have believed and am *p.*
Heb. 6:9, are *p.* better things of you
11:13, having seen them, were *p.*
Acts 26:28, almost thou *persuadest* me to be a Christian
Gal. 5:8, this *persuasion* cometh
**Peter,** see *footnote, p.* 1366.

## Q

## T

## U

# THE SOVEREIGNTY OF GOD
# THE MASTER THEME OF HOLY SCRIPTURE

## THE PURPOSE OF THIS OUTLINE AND INDEX

God's sovereignty, the fact that He is in control of all things and free from all compulsion to act out of necessity or coercion by others, is taught throughout the Scriptures. God alone takes the initiative in the creation and rule of the universe as well as in the redemption of fallen man. It is equally manifest that in His sovereignty He always acts in harmony with His truth, love, and holiness.

Yet today, the sovereignty of God is one of the most frequently ignored, and practically denied, of all the Bible's themes. No doubt this is due, in large measure, to the fact that this doctrine has seldom been proclaimed in the majority of Christian churches; the twentieth century particularly has witnessed a dearth of preaching on this vital truth. Also, many Christians seem to rely too heavily on the thoughts of others rather than painstakingly searching the Scriptures for themselves, asking God to guide them into all truth.

Over one hundred years ago, A.A. Hodge wrote the following in his *Outlines of Theology:*

> Whatever God teaches or commands is of sovereign authority. Whatever conveys to us an infallible knowledge of His teachings and commands is an infallible rule. The Scriptures of the Old and New Testaments are the only organs through which, during the present dispensation, God conveys to us a knowledge of His will about what we are to believe concerning Himself, and what duties He requires of us.

The following outline, focusing on the master theme of the sovereignty of God, is based on that "infallible rule," namely, the Word of God. The publishers believe that conscientious use of this outline and its accompanying index will aid the reader in his study of this important doctrine.

## USE OF THE OUTLINE AND INDEX

**I. Point by Point Study.**

The outline points may be studied in order, or at random as particular questions arise. Scripture references relating to a particular aspect of God's sovereignty are listed in Biblical order under each heading. The Scripture references should be studied in their proper contexts in order to find their bearing upon God's sovereignty.

**II. The Symbols in the Text.**

By means of the superscript symbol *S* in the text, the Bible reader is guided from the text to the appropriate aspect of God's sovereignty as set forth in the outline. Thousands of such superscript letters serve to indicate the main verses that inform us of the sovereignty of God. An *S* at the beginning of a verse serves to introduce a group of verses that form a context. An *S* at the end of a verse serves to close that context or to mark a *single* verse with teaching on God's sovereignty. (To determine whether a symbol closes a context or stands alone, look for an opening *S* and/or use the index to find the correct context.)

Each verse, whether standing alone or within a marked context, should be studied in its context. Due to the fact that both *near* and *far* contexts exist, and that contexts may overlap, the index should be used in conjunction with the symbols in the text. An unmarked verse, included within a marked context, may appear in a separate entry in the index when readability demands an uncluttered page. In marking the text it was sometimes deemed best to expand the context beyond that indicated in the index, in order to make reading smoother and to harmonize with paragraph markings and other features of the apparatus.

**III. Locating a Specific Reference.**

For example, suppose one is reading in Job 12 and discovers an *S* at verse 16. One may discover where Job 12:16 is included in the outline by looking up Job 12:16 in the index. In this instance, the following entry appears: 12:16 I.D.3.; V.C.1. The two outline point entries indicate that Job 12:16 is listed twice in the outline; first in section I.D.3. (God's Wisdom), and then in section V.C.1. (Evil's Presence Decreed). By referring to these sections, these two particular aspects of God's sovereignty may be seen in their relationship to the whole doctrine. Further insight may be obtained by studying the other references included in these sections.

**I. The Perfections of God**

**A. God's Infinitude**

1. His Eternality (in relation to time) Gen. 21:33; Ex. 3:15; 15:18; Deut. 32:40; 1 Chr. 16:36; 29:10; Neh. 9:5; Psa. 9:7; 33:11; 41:13; 55:19; 68:33; 90:1,2; 92:8; 93:2; 102:12,24-27; 104:31; 111:3; 135:13; 145:13; 146:10; Prov. 8:22-25; Isa. 9:6; 26:4; 40:28; 41:4; 43:13; 44:6; 46:4; 48:12; 57:15; 63:16; Jer. 10:10; Lam. 5:19; Dan. 4:3,34; Mic. 5:2; Hab. 1:12; Mark 12:36,37; John 1:1,2,4,15; 6:62; 8:23,58; 12:41; 17:5,24,25; Rom. 1:20; Eph. 3:21; 4:10; Col. 1:15-17; 1 Tim. 1:17; 6:15,16; 2 Tim. 1:9; Heb. 1:8-12; 1 Pet. 1:20; 2 Pet. 3:8; 1 John 1:1,2; 2:13,14; Rev. 1:4,6,8,11,17,18; 4:8-10; 5:14; 11:17; 15:7.
2. His Omnipresence (in relation to space) Gen. 16:13; 28:16; Deut. 4:39; 1 Kin. 8:27; 2 Chr. 2:6; Psa. 139:7-13,15,16; Prov. 15:3; Isa. 57:15; Jer. 23:23,24; 32:19; Matt. 18:20; 28:20; Acts 7:48,49; 17:27; 1 Cor. 12:6; Eph. 1:23.
3. His Incomprehensibility (in relation to finite understanding) Ex. 20:21; Deut. 4:11; 5:22; 1 Kin. 8:12; 8:27; 2 Chr. 2:6; 6:1,18; Job 5:9; 9:10; 11:7-9; 15:8; 26:9,14; 36:26; Psa. 18:1; 77:19; 92:5; 97:2; 145:3; Prov. 30:4; Eccl. 3:11; 7:24; 11:5; Isa. 40:12-28; 45:15; 55:8,9; Matt. 11:27; Rom. 11:33,34; 1 Cor. 2:10,11,16; Eph. 3:8.

**B. God's Majesty**

1. His Supremacy Gen. 21:33; Deut. 28:58; 1 Chr. 29:11,12; Job 11:7-9; 22:12; 25:3; 41:11; Psa. 8:1,9; 19:1; 57:5,11; 72:19; 76:4; 90:1,2; 97:2; 113:4; 147:5; Prov. 16:4; Isa. 1:24; 6:1-3; 24:3; 33:22; 40:12-18,21-31; 43:15; 57:15; 66:1,2,18; Jer. 10:10; Dan. 4:3,34,35; Luke 2:9; Acts 22:11; 1 Tim. 1:17; 6:15,16; Jude 25; Rev. 1:5,6; 4:11; 21:23.
2. His Solitariness Ex. 9:14; 15:11; 33:20; Deut. 4:35,39; 10:17; 32:12,39; 33:26; 2 Kin. 5:15; 1 Chr. 16:25; Job 35:6,7; Psa. 90:1,2; 96:4; Prov. 16:4; Isa. 43:10,11; 44:6; 45:21; 46:9; Matt. 19:17; Mark 10:18; Luke 18:19; John 10:29; Rom. 9:17; 1 Cor. 8:6; 1 Tim. 6:15,16; Jude 4,25.
3. His Self-Sufficiency Ex. 3:14; Deut. 32:40; Job 35:6,7; Prov. 16:4; Isa. 40:18,28; 44:6; Jer. 10:10; Dan. 4:35; John 5:26; Acts 17:25; Rom. 11:33,34; 1 Tim. 6:16; Rev. 4:11.

**C. God's Immutability**

1. His Unchanging Life Gen. 21:33; Deut. 32:40; 1 Chr. 29:10; Neh. 9:5; Psa. 9:7; 41:13; 55:19; 68:33; 90:1,2; 93:2; 102:12, 24-27; Isa. 40:28; 43:13; 48:12; 63:16; Jer. 10:10; 17:12; Lam. 5:19; Dan. 4:3; Mic. 5:2; Hab. 1:12; Rom. 16:26; 1 Tim. 6:16; Heb. 1:8; 9:14; 2 Pet. 3:8; Rev. 1:6; 4:9,10; 5:14; 16:5.
2. His Unchanging Character Ex. 18:11; Deut. 33:27; Psa. 56:2; 83:18; 92:8; 102:27; 104:31; Isa. 40:28; Dan. 4:34,35; Mal. 3:6; Rom. 1:20; Heb. 13:8; Jas. 1:17.
3. His Unchanging Truth Num. 23:19,20; Deut. 32:4; 1 Sam. 15:29; 2 Sam. 7:28; Psa. 25:10; 31:5; 33:4,11; 40:10; 43:3; 52:1; 57:3,10; 71:22; 86:11,15; 89:14; 91:4; 96:13; 98:3; 100:5; 108:4; 111:3; 115:1; 117:2; 119:89; 132:11; 138:2; 146:6; Prov. 19:21; Isa. 25:1; 65:16; Jer. 5:3; 10:10; Dan. 4:37; 9:13; Mic. 7:20; Matt. 24:35; John 8:26,31,32; 14:6,17; 16:13; 17:17,19; 18:37; Rom. 2:2; 3:4; Tit. 1:2; Heb. 6:17, 18; Rev. 6:10; 15:3.
4. His Unchanging Ways Ex. 3:14; 15:18; Deut. 32:4; 2 Sam. 22:31; Job. 34:10; Psa. 18:30; 19:7; 92:15; 118:29; 135:13; 136:1; 138:8; 148:6; Eccl. 3:14; Isa. 41:4; 54:8; Hab. 3:6; Rom. 11:29; Jas. 1:17; Rev. 15:3.
5. His Unchanging Purposes Gen. 22:17; Num. 23:19,20; Deut. 28:1-13; Job. 9:12, 13; 11:10; 12:14,15; 23:13,14; 34:29; Psa. 4:3; 33:11; Eccl. 1:15; 3:14,15; 7:13; Rom. 9:19; Jas. 1:17.

**D. God's Omniscience**

1. His Knowledge Ex. 3:7,9; Num. 14:27; Deut. 2:7; 1 Sam. 2:3; 1 Kin. 8:39; 2 Kin. 19:27; 1 Chr. 29:17; 2 Chr. 6:30; 16:9; Neh. 9:10; Job 11:11; 12:13,22; 21:22; 23:10; 24:23; 26:6; 28:10,23,24; 31:4; 34:22,25; 36:4; 37:16; 42:2; Psa. 1:6; 7:9; 11:4; 33:13-15; 37:18; 38:9; 44:21; 66:7; 69:19; 92:5; 94:9-11; 104:14; 119:168; 121:3,4; 139:1-4,6,12,14-16; 139:23,24; 142:3; 147:4,5; Prov. 3:19,20; 5:21; 15:3, 11; 16:2; 17:3; 21:2; 24:12; Eccl. 5:8; Isa. 28:29; 29:15,16; 37:28; 40:13,14,26-28; 41:4; 44:7; 45:4,11,21; 48:5,6; 57:18; 66:18; Jer. 5:3; 10:7; 11:20; 17:10; 20:12; 23:24; 32:19; Ezek. 11:15; Dan. 2:22; Amos 4:13; 9:2,3; Zech. 4:10; Matt. 6:4,8, 32; 10:29,30; Luke 16:15; John 2:24; 6:64; 21:17; Acts 1:24; 15:8,18; Rom. 8:27; 11:33,34; 1 Cor. 1:25; 2:11; 3:20; 8:3; Gal. 4:9; 2 Tim. 2:19; Heb. 4:13; 1 John 1:5; 3:20.
2. His Foreknowledge Ex. 3:19,20; 11:1; 14:3; 1 Sam. 23:11,12; Psa. 37:18; 139:15,16; Prov. 8:22,27-31; Isa. 42:9; 44:7; 45:11; 46:10; 48:3,5,6; Jer. 1:5; Dan. 2:28,29; Matt. 6:8; 16:21; 24:36; Mark 13:32; Acts 2:23; 15:18; Rom. 8:29; 11:2; 1 Pet. 1:2.
3. His Wisdom Ezra 7:25; Job 9:4; 12:13,16; 28:12-27; 36:5; Psa. 104:24; 136:5; 147:5; Prov. 3:19; 8:12; Isa. 31:2; Jer. 10:7,12; 51:15; Dan. 2:20; Rom. 16:27; 1 Cor. 1:24, 25; 2:7; Eph. 1:8; 3:10; 1 Tim. 1:17; Jude 25; Rev. 7:12.

**E. God's Omnipotence**

1. His Absolute Power Gen. 1:1,3,7,9,11,15-17,21,24,25,27; 2:4,7,21; 5:1,2; 9:6; 11:7-9; 21:19; 25:21; 30:22; Ex. 3:2; 4:3,4,6,7,30; 13:21,22; 14:22-30; 15:6,7,11,12; 16:14-18,20,23-25,29; 19:16-20; 34:29-35; Lev. 10:1,2; Num. 11:1,23; 12:10-15; 16:31-35, 46-49; Deut. 6:22; 7:21; 32:39; 33:26; Josh. 3:14-17; 4:18,23,24; 10:11; 1 Sam. 2:6,8; 5:3,4,6,11; 14:6; 2 Sam. 6:7; 23:16; 1 Kin. 17:14,16; 18:38; 2 Kin. 7:6; 1 Chr. 29:11, 12; 2 Chr. 7:1; 16:9; 20:6; Ezra 8:22; Neh. 9:6; Job 8:22; 9:4-13,19; 29:5; 31:2,35;

32:8; 33:4; 34:10; 35:13; 36:5; 37:23; 41:10; 42:2; Psa. 8:3; 19:1,4; 21:13; 29:4; 30:4; 33:4,6,7,9; 62:11; 65:6; 66:3,7; 74:13-17; 76:6;77:14,16; 78:26; 89:8,9,11-13; 90:1,2; 93:4; 95:4,5; 96:5; 97:3-5; 102:25; 104:2-9,24,29,30,32; 106:8; 107:25,29; 114:7,8; 119:90,91; 121:2; 124:8; 136:5-9; 145:6; 146:5,6; 148:5,6,8; Prov. 3:19; 8:26-29; 16:4; 22:2; 26:10; 30:4; Isa. 4:5; 13:6; 17:7; 19:1; 23:1; 37:16; 40:12,22,26,28; 42:5; 43:13,16,17; 44:24,27; 45:7,12,18; 50:2; 59:1; 60:16; 63:12; 64:8; 65:17; 66:1; Jer. 10:1,12,13; 27:5; 32:17,27; Jer. 51:15; Dan. 3:17; 4:35; 5:23; Joel 2:11; Amos 4:13; 9:5; Mic. 1:3,4; Nah. 1:3-6; Mal. 2:10; Matt. 3:9; 6:13; 8:1-4,14-17,23-34; 9:18-34; 10:28; 12:9-13,22-37; 14:22-33; 15:21-28,32-38; 17:14-18; 19:26; 20:29-34; 21:17-22; Mark 1:23-26, 40-45; 2:1-12; 3:1-5,11; 4:35-41; 5:1-20, 22-43; 6:35-52; 7:24-37; 8:1-9,22-26; 9:14-29; 10:46-52; 11:12-14,20-24; Luke 4:33-39; 5:1-26; 6:6-11; 7:1-16; 8:22-39, 41-56; 9:42; 11:14,15; 13-10-17; 14:1-6; 17:11-19; 18:35-43; 22:49-51; John 2:1-11; 4:46-54; 5:1-16; 6:5-14,16-21; 9:7; 10:29; 11:43,44; 21:6; Acts 8:39; 9:3-8; 17:24; 2 Cor. 6:18; Eph. 3:9; Col. 1:13-16; Heb. 3:4; 11:3; Rev. 4:8,11.

2. His Ordered Power Gen. 25:21; Ex. 13:21, 22; 14:17-30; 15:25; 16:2-13; 17:5-7,9,14; Lev. 9:24; Num. 11:3; 17:1-11; 20:8-11; 22:23-30; Josh. 6:20; 10:12,13; Judg. 6:21; 7:22; 13:19,20; 14:6; 15:19; 16:17,30; 1 Sam. 5:6,11; 6:19,20; 12:16-18; 2 Sam. 24:10,18; 1 Kin. 17:6,22; 18:36; 19:13,18; 2 Kin. 1:10,12; 2:8,11,14,19,20; 3:20-22; 5:14,26,27; 6:6,12,17,18; 13:21; 19:35; 1 Chr. 21:14; 2 Chr. 20:17; Psa. 86:9; 103:20; 119:73; Prov. 22:2; Isa. 37:36; 38:21; Dan. 3:23-27; 6:22; Jonah 1:15,17; 2:10; 4:6,7; Matt. 1:18-25; 2:1-9,13-23; Mark 9:39; Luke 10:17-20; John 14:12; Acts 3:2-13,16; 4:10,30; 5:10,15,16,19; 8:17,18,39; 9:17,18,34,35,40; 12:6-11; 13:11; 14:10; 16:18,26; 19:11,12; 20:9-11; 28:5,8,9.

**F. God's Holiness** Ex. 3:5; 15:11; Lev. 11:44; 19:2; 20:26; 21:8; Josh. 24:19; 1 Sam. 2:2; 6:20; 1 Chr. 16:10; 2 Chr. 20:21; Job 4:17; 6:10; 13:11; 15:15; 25:5; 34:10; 36:23; Psa. 18:30; 22:3; 30:4; 47:8; 48:1; 60:6; 89:35; 98:1; 99:3,5,9; 111:9; 145:17; Prov. 9:10; Isa. 5:16; 6:3; 12:6; 29:19,23; 41:14; 43:14,15; 47:4; 49:7; 52:10; 57:15; Jer. 2:5; Ezek. 36:21,22; 39:7,25; Hos. 11:9; Hab. 1:12,13; Matt. 5:48; 19:17; Mark 10:8; Luke 1:49; 18:19; John 17:11; Rom. 1:23; Jas. 1:13; 1 Pet. 1:15,16; 1 John 1:5; 2:20; Rev. 4:8; 6:10; 15:4.

1. His Righteousness

a. His Justice Gen. 18:25; Ex. 34:7; Deut. 10:17; Judg. 9:56,57; 11:27; 1 Sam. 2:3,10; 16:7; 24:12,15; 2 Sam. 22:25-28; 1 Kin. 8:32; 1 Chr. 16:33; 2 Chr. 6:22,23; 19:7; Neh. 9:33; Job 4:17; 8:3; 9:15,28; 13:16; 21:22; 23:7; 31:13-15; 34:10,11,17,19,23; 35:14; 36:19; 37:23; Psa. 9:4,7,8; 11:4; 19:9; 26:1; 33:4,5; 50:4,6; 51:4; 58:11; 62:12; 67:4; 75:7; 76:8,9; 82:8; 85:10; 89:4; 96:10,13; 97:2; 98:9; 99:4,8; 103:6; 111:7; 119:137; 135:14; 143:2; Prov. 11:31; 16:2; 17:3; 21:2,3; 29:26; Eccl. 3:15,17; 11:9; 12:14; Isa. 1:27; 3:13,14; 10:17,18; 26:7; 28:17,21; 30:18; 31:2; 33:5, 22; 45:21; 61:8; Jer. 9:24; 11:20; 20:12; 22:15,16; 32:19; 50:7; 51:10; Lam. 1:18; Ezek. 14:23; 18:24,25,29,30; 33:7-10; Dan. 4:37; 7:9,10; Hos. 10:10; Amos 8:7; Nah. 1:3; Zeph. 3:5; Mal. 3:5; John 8:50; Acts 10:34; 17:31; Rom. 1:32; 2:2; 3:4-6,26; 9:14; 11:22; Eph. 6:8,9; Col. 3:25; 2 Thess. 1:4-6; Heb. 10:30,31; 12:23,29; 1 Pet. 1:17; 2 Pet. 2:9; 1 John 1:9; Jude 6; Rev. 6:16,17; 11:18; 15:3; 16:5-7; 18:8; 19:2.

b. His Severity Deut. 7:21,23,24; 32:4; 2 Chr. 19:7; Job. 36:3; Psa. 11:7; 33:4,5; 36:6; 67:4; 71:19; 92:15; 97:2,6; 98:2; 119:137,142; 129:4; 145:17; Isa. 5:16; 33:5; 45:19; Jer. 9:24; 12:1; Lam. 1:18; Rom. 3:26; 11:22; Heb. 1:8; 6:10; Rev. 16:5; 19:2.

c. His Anger Ex. 35:5; Num. 11:1,11; 12:9; 14:11; 22:2; 25:3,4; 32:10,13,14; Deut. 4:25; 6:15; 7:4; 9:18,19; 13:17; 29:19,20,23,24,27,28; 31:16,17,29; 32:16,21,22; Josh. 7:1,26; 23:16; Judg. 2:12,14,20; 3:8; 10:7; 2 Sam. 6:7; 24:1; 1 Kin. 11:9; 14:9,15; 15:30; 16:2,7,13,26,33; 21:22; 22:53; 2 Kin. 13:3; 17:11,17,18; 21:6,15; 22:17; 23:19,26; 24:29; Psa. 69:24; 76:7; 85:3; 90:7,11; 103:8,9; 106:29,32; Isa. 5:25; 9:17,19,21; 30:27,30; 42:25; 63:3-6; Jer. 3:12; 4:4,8,26; 7:20; 10:10; 17:4; 21:5,6; 25:15-17,37,38; 32:37; 33:5; 36:7; 42:18; 44:6; 51:45; Lam. 2:1,3,6; 4:11; 5:13,15; Ezek. 25:14-17; Dan. 9:16; Hos. 11:9.

d. His Wrath Ex. 22:24; 32:10; Num. 11:33; Deut. 9:14,19,20; 1 Sam. 28:18; 2 Sam. 22:8,9; 2 Kin. 22:13; 23:26; Ezra 8:22; Psa. 78:21,38,49,50; 85:3; 90:7,11; 106:23; 110:5; Isa. 13:9,13; 28:21; 37:28; 57:16,17; 60:10; Jer. 10:10; 32:37; Hos. 13:11; Nah. 1:2; Matt. 22:7,13; Rom. 1:18; 2:5; 9:22; Eph. 5:6; Col. 3:6; Heb. 3:11; 4:3; Rev. 6:16,17; 11:18; 14:10; 15:1,7; 16:19; 19:15.

e. His Jealousy Ex. 20:5; 34:14; Deut. 4:24; 5:9; 6:15; 29:20; 32:16,21; Josh. 24:19; Judg. 2:12; Ezek. 23:25; 36:5; 39:25; Joel 2:18; Nah. 1:2; Zech. 1:14; Acts 12:23.

2. His Goodness Ex. 34:6; 2 Chr. 5:13; Psa. 25:8; 31:19; 33:5; 34:8; 52:1; 68:19; 69:16; 73:1; 86:5; 100:5; 106:1; 107:8; 118:29; 119:68; 145:7; Isa. 6:7; Lam. 3:25; Nah. 1:7; Zech. 9:17; Matt. 19:17; Rom. 2:4; 11:22.

a. His Love Deut. 4:37; 10:15,18; 23:5; 2 Sam. 12:24; Neh. 13:26; Job 7:17; Psa.

17:7; 36:7; 42:8; 47:4; 63:3; 69:16; 78:68; 89:33; 103:13; 107:43; Prov. 15:9; Isa. 38:7; 43:4; 63:7; Jer. 9:24; 31:3; Hos. 11:1; 14:4; Mal. 1:2; John 3:16; 5:20; 14:21,23; 17:23,26; Rom. 1:7; 5:5,8; 9:13; 11:28; 2 Cor. 5:14; 9:7; 13:11,14; Eph. 2:4,5; 3:19; 2 Thess. 2:16; Tit. 3:4,5; Heb. 12:6; 1 John 2:5; 3:1,16,17; 4:7-12,15,16,19; Rev. 1:5.

b. His Grace Gen. 6:8; Ex. 33:17; Lev. 26:11,12; Num. 22:12; 23:20,21; 2 Sam. 22:20; 2 Chr. 15:2; Neh. 9:17; Job 10:12; 22:27; 29:3-5; Psa. 3:8; 5:12; 11:7; 18:19,25; 24:4,5; 25:14; 30:7; 44:3; 68:16; 84:11; Isa. 28:5; 30:26; 33:17,21; Jer. 15:20; Luke 1:28,30; John 14:16-21,23; Acts 4:33; 10:35; Rom. 2:29; 1 Cor. 1:9; 3:21-23; Gal. 4:6; Eph. 1:6; 2:7,13,14,18,22; Heb. 4:16; 10:19,22,23; 11:15; 1 Pet. 2:9; 1 John 1:3; 3:19; 4:17,18.

c. His Mercy Gen. 18:26,28-32; 19:16; 32:10; Ex. 15:13; 20:6; 33:19; 34:6; 1 Chr. 16:34; 2 Chr. 5:13; 20:21; Neh. 1:5; 9:17,19,20; Psa. 25:8; 37:26; 86:5; 98:3; 100:5; 102:13; 103:4,17; 106:1; 107:1; 115:1; 118:29; 119:41,64; 130:7; 136:1; 145:9; Isa. 54:7,8; 60:10; Jer. 33:3,11; Lam. 3:22,23; Ezek. 20:17; 39:25; Dan. 9:9; Hos. 14:4; Jonah 4:2; Matt. 9:13; 12:7; Luke 1:53; Rom. 5:6,8; 9:15,16,23; 11:22,32; Eph. 2:4; Phil. 4:19; Tit. 3:5; Heb. 2:17; 8:12; Jas. 5:11; 1 Pet. 1:3.

d. His Faithfulness Gen. 21:1; 28:15; 46:4; Ex. 2:24; 6:4,5; 33:14; Lev. 26:44,45; Deut. 4:31; 7:8,9; 9:5; 31:6; Josh. 1:5,9; 21:43-45; 23:14; Judg. 2:1; 1 Sam. 12:22; 2 Sam. 7:28; 22:31; 23:5; 1 Kin. 6:13; 8:15,20,23,24,56; 2 Kin. 8:19; 13:23; 1 Chr. 28:20; 2 Chr. 6:8-11; Ezra 9:9; Neh. 1:5; 9:7,8,32; Job 22:27; Psa. 9:10; 18:30; 19:9; 25:10; 33:4,5; 37:28; 40:10; 89:1,2,5, 8,24,28,33,34; 92:2,15; 94:14; 98:3; 100:5; 103:17; 105:8,42; 111:5,7-9; 119:65,90; 121:3,4; 132:11; Isa. 11:5; 25:1; 42:16; 44:21; 49:7,16: 51:6,8; 54:9,10; 65:16; Jer. 29:10; 31:36,37; 32:40; 33:14,20,21,25,26; 51:5; Lam. 3:23; Ezek. 16:60; Dan. 9:4; Hos. 2:19,20; Mic. 7:20; Hag. 2:5; Zech. 9:11; Matt. 24:34,35; Luke 1:54,55, 68-73; Acts 13:32,33; Rom. 3:3,4; 11:2,29; 15:8; 1 Cor. 1:9; 10:13; 2 Cor. 1:20; 1 Thess. 5:24; 2 Thess. 3:3; 2 Tim. 2:13,19; Tit. 1:2; Heb. 6:10, 13-19; 10:23; 1 Pet. 4:19; 2 Pet. 3:9; 1 John 1:9; Rev. 15:3.

e. His Kindness Neh. 1:5; 9:17; Psa. 25:8; 31:21; 36:7; 40:11; 63:3,7; 69:16; 117:2; 119:76; Isa. 54:8,10; 63:7; Jer. 9:24; 31:3; 32:18; Joel 2:3; Jonah 4:2; Luke 6:35; Tit. 3:4; Jas. 1:17.

f. His Longsuffering Ex. 34:6; Num. 14:18; Neh. 9:30,31; Psa. 86:15; 103:8-10; Isa. 5:1-4; 30:18; 48:9; Jer. 7:23-25; 15:15; Ezek. 20:17; Joel 2:13; Hab. 1:2-4; Matt. 19:8; 23:37; Luke 13:6-9; 13:34; Acts 14:16; 17:30; Rom. 2:4; 3:25; 9:22,23; 15:15; 1 Pet. 3:20; 2 Pet. 3:9,15; Rev. 2:21.

**G. God's Veracity** Ex. 34;6; Num. 23:19; Deut. 32:4; 1 Sam. 15:29; Psa. 19:9; 25:10; 31:5,6; 33:4; 96:5,13; 97:7; 100:5; 108:4; 111:7; 117:2; 132:11; 146:6; Isa. 25:1; 44:9,10; 65:16; Jer. 10:8,10,11; Dan. 4:37; John 8:26; 14:6; 17:3; Rom. 3:4; 2 Cor. 1:20; 2 Tim. 2:13; Tit. 1:2; Heb. 6:10,13-19; 1 John 5:6,20,21; Rev. 15:3.

## II. The Providence of God

### A. Its Universality

1. Over Nature Ex. 13:21,22; 14:19-22,26-29; 16:14,18; Num. 11:31; Deut. 30:9; 1 Kin. 19:11,12; Neh. 9:6; Job 5:10,22,23; 37:3-18; Psa. 50:12; 145:9; Isa. 51:10; Ezek. 34:26.
2. Over His Kingdom Num. 14:14; Deut. 9:29; 1 Kin. 8:51,53; 2 Chr. 32:22; Neh. 9:19,20; Job 23:13; Psa. 2:8,9; 3:8; 48:3; 87:5; 102:16,21,22; 125:1; 145:5,11-13; Isa. 12:6; 55:4; 62:3; 63:7; Jer. 15:20; 33:6-9,11-14; Ezek. 20:41-44; 39:29; Dan. 2:44; 7:14; Joel 3:16,17; Amos 3:2; Hag. 1:13; Zech. 2:5; 8:3; 9:16; John 10:28; Eph. 1:20-22.
3. Over Nations Ex. 34:24; Deut. 7:22; 11:25; 31:3; 32:8; Neh. 9:6; Isa. 26:15; 41:2; 66:1; Jer. 51:20; Ezek. 21:26,27; 29:19,20; 34:17,22-24; Acts 17:25-29.
4. Over All Events Gen. 45:7; 50:20; 1 Sam. 2:6-9; Ezra 5:5; Job 5:12,13; Psa. 33:10; 75:7; Prov. 16:7,33; 19:21; Eccl. 3:1; Isa. 4:2,4; 8:9,10; Acts 3:18; Rom. 1:10; 8:28; Phil. 1:12,19; Philemon 15.
5. Over the Spirit World Gen. 3:15; 16:7; Judg. 9:23; 1 Sam. 16:14-16,23; 18:10; 19:9; 2 Sam. 23:6,7; Job. 1:12; 2:6; 9:24; Matt. 4:10,11; 8:31,32; 9:34; 10:1; 12:29; 13:30; 25:41; Mark 1:23,24; 3:11,22-26; 5:7; 6:7; 9:38; 16:17; Luke 4:35; 8:28; 11:15,18; 13:11-13; John 12:31; 16:11; Acts 5:16; 8:7; 16:16-18; 19:12,15; 26:15-18; Rom. 16:20; Eph. 6:14-16; Col. 1:13; 2:15; Heb. 2:14; Jas. 4:7; 2 Pet. 2:4; 1 John 2:13; 3:8; 5:18; Jude 6; Rev. 12:9-12; 20:1-3,7,10.
6. Over the Animal World Ex. 8:5,6,12-14, 16,17,24,31; 9:3-7; 10:4-6,13-15,18,19; 11:7; 14:16; Lev. 26:22; Num. 22:28,30; Deut. 28:26; 30:9; 2 Kin. 2:24; Neh. 9:6; Job. 5:22,23; Psa. 36:6; 50:10; 104:27; 145:9; Jer. 8:17; Ezek. 5:17; 14:5; 32:4; Joel 1:4; Rev. 6:8.
7. Over All Acts of Individuals
   a. Free Acts Gen. 45:7; 1 Kin. 18:37; Prov. 16:7,9,33; Matt. 7:11; Luke 22:22; John 19:11; Acts 17:26; 1 Cor. 4:17; 16:7; Eph. 2:10,11; Phil. 2:13; Jas. 1:5; 4:15.
   b. Sinful Acts Gen. 45:7; Ex. 34:24; Judg. 14:2,4; Job 12:6; Psa. 73:3; Eccl.

7:15; Jer. 12:1,2; Dan. 11:27; Hab. 1:13; Matt. 26:21,34; Luke 22:22; John 19:11; Acts 2:23; 4:27,28; 5:38; 13:29; 1 Cor. 11:19; Phil. 1:12; 1 Pet. 2:8; Jude 4; Rev. 22:11.

c. Future Acts Deut. 30:9; 1 Kin. 19:17; 2 Kin. 8:13; Job 27:3-6; Dan. 11:27; Matt. 26:21,34; Rev. 17:7.

**B. Its Purpose**

1. To Glorify God Ex. 8:22; 9:16; 13:21,22; 14:17,18,31; 2 Kin. 20:6; 1 Chr. 29:11; 2 Chr. 33:12; Job 37:7; Psa. 31:3; 50:15; 106:8; Isa. 31:3; 35:2; 37:35; 40:5; 43:7, 20,21; 48:9-11; 60:2,6,16,19,21; Jer. 33:9; Ezek. 20:41,42,44; 36:22,23; Zech. 2:5; John 14:3; Rom. 9:17; 2 Cor. 4:15; 1 Thess. 2:4; Rev. 1:5,6.
2. To Benefit His Chosen Ones Gen. 1:29,30; 8:22; 9:1-3; 26:4; 28:15,20,21; 31:3; 32:10; 48:15; 49:24,25; Ex. 3:17; 6:6,7; 8:22; 9:20,26; 11:7; 12:13,17,23; 13:21,22; 14:20-22,25,30; 15:13,16,17; 16:15; 19:14; 23:20,22,25,26; 34:24; Lev. 25:18-22; Num. 23:23; Deut. 1:10,30,31; 2:7; 4:4,40; 5:29,33; 6:2,3,10-12,18,19,21-25; 7:13-24; 8:3,4,8,18; 9:14; 10:18; 11:7,8,12-15,25; 12:7,28; 13:17,18; 15:4-6; 23:14; 26:19; 28:2-13; 29:5; 30:4,15-20; 31:3,9-14; 32:9-14,47; 33:26; Josh. 1:8; 11:20; 21:44,45; 23:10; Ruth 1:6; 1 Sam. 2:7-9; 14:6; 2 Sam. 7:8,9; 1 Kin. 2:3,4; 9:4,5; 2 Kin. 20:6; 1 Chr. 22:9,13; 28:8; 29:11,12,14,16; 2 Chr. 1:12; 7:17,18; 16:9; 20:15-17,20;30:9; 31:10; 33:2; Ezra 8:22,23; Neh. 9:6,25; Job 1:10; 4:7; 5:9,11,15,17-27; 8:6,7,20,21; 10:2; 11:17-19; 12:23; 22:5; 23:10; 27:3,4; 29:5,19,20; 33:16-19,23-30; 36:7,11,16; Psa. 1:6; 3:3,8; 7:10; 9:9; 10:17,18; 12:7; 14:5,6; 17:7; 18:17,27; 19:14; 21:3-5; 23:1-6; 25:8,9,12; 31:20,23; 32:6,8; 33:12, 15; 34:7,9,10,15,19,22; 36:6,7; 37:3,17,19, 22-25,28,32-34; 40:5; 41:1-3,11,12; 44:1-3; 46:1,5,7; 48:14; 50:15; 61:3,6; 65:9-13; 67:6; 68:6,9,10,22; 69:35,36; 71:6,7,15; 72:14,16; 73:23; 78:52-55; 80:1; 81:13-16; 84:11; 85:12; 87:5; 91:1,3,4,7,9-12; 94:13; 97:10; 100:3; 102:19; 103:2-5; 104:10-19, 24-30; 105:14,15,44,45; 107:1-16,19-21, 28-31,41; 111:5; 112:4; 113:6-9; 115:9-16; 116:1-15; 118:5,6,13,14; 119:71; 121:3-8; 124:1-8; 125:2,3; 127:1-5; 128:2-6; 132:9; 136:5-25; 139:9,10; 144:12-15; 145:14-16, 19,20; Prov. 2:7,8,21; 3:1,2,6,23,24; 10:3, 6,22,24,27,30; 11:8,10,11,31; 12:3,13,21; 13:25; 14:11,19,26,34; 15:6,19; 16:7,9,33; 20:22,24; 21:31; 22:12; 28:10; Eccl. 2:24, 26; 3:13; 5:19; Isa. 4:5,6; 10:27; 14:3; 25:4; 26:7; 27:3; 30:21,23-26; 31:4,5; 32:2,18; 33:16,20; 35:4,9; 37:32,35; 40:11, 29,31; 41:11,12; 42:13,16; 43:2,20; 45:2,4; 46:3,4; 48:11,17,21; 49:9,10,17,25; 50:2; 54:14,15,17; 55:10; 57:14; 58:11; 59:19; 60:1-22; 63:9; 65:13,23; Jer. 2:3,6,20; 3:4; 10:13; 11:4; 14:22; 22:15,16; 24:5; 27:6; 30:7,8,11,17,19; 31:9,10,28,35; 33:8; Ezek. 9:4,6; 11:16; 34:11-16,22,31; 36:9-11,28-38; Dan. 3:27,28; 5:18; 6:20-22; 12:1; Hos. 2:8,18,22; 11:3; 13:10; Joel 2:26,27; Amos 4:7-12; 5:8,9; 9:9,13; Jonah 4:6; Mic. 2:13; Nah. 1:12; Zeph. 3:13,15,17,19,20; Hag. 2:19; Zech. 2:8; 3:7; 4:6,7,10; 9:8,14-17; 10:1; 12:8; Mal. 3:11,12; Matt. 4:6; 5:3-11, 45; 6:26,30,31,33; 10:29,31; 24:22; Mark 12:8; 13:16,20,22; Luke 12:6,7,24-28; 18:7,8; 21:18; 22:35; John 10:28; Acts 7:34-36; 14:17; 17:28; Rom. 5:3,4; 8:28; 9:17; 1 Cor. 1:29; 2:9; 10:13; 16:2; 2 Cor. 4:15; 9:8-10; Eph. 1:11,12; Phil. 1:19; 3:10; 2 Thess. 3:3; Heb. 1:14; Jas. 1:3,4; 4:15; 1 Pet. 1:6,7; 3:12,13; 2 Pet. 2:9; Rev. 3:10; 7:3; 12:6.
3. Impart Knowledge and Truth 2 Sam. 22:29; Psa. 25:5; 27:11; 32:8; 73:24; 139:23,24; Prov. 8:20; Isa. 42:16; 48:17; Jer. 3:4; Mal. 3:18; Matt. 11:25-27; 13:10, 11,16; 16:16,17; Luke 1:79; 8:10; 10:21; John 16:13; 1 Cor. 2:14; Eph. 1:17,18; 1 John 1:5; 5:20

**C. Its Practical Effects**

1. Security Deut. 28:1,7; 1 Sam. 2:9; Job 5:16,17,19-21; 11:18; Psa. 29:11; 37:3-9; 46:7; 55:22; 91:1,3,4,7,9-12; 97:10; Prov. 1:33; 3:23,26; 16:7; Isa. 40:11; 43:2; 54:17; Jer. 15:20; Mark 13:13; Heb. 13:5; Rev. 3:7.
2. Stability Job 5:24; 22:21-23; Psa. 23:6; 37:18,23-25; 94:17,18; 125:1; Isa. 26:3; Matt. 28:20; Rom. 8:28-39.
3. Confidence Deut. 28:1,7; 2 Chr. 16:9; Job 5:25-27; Psa. 23:6; 46:7; 55:22; Prov. 3:26; 12:21; Isa. 40:29; 50:7-9; Joel 2:26,27; Mark 11:24; Phil. 4:19; Rev. 3:10.
4. Courage Gen. 15:1; Ex. 23:22; Deut. 33:27; Job 11:19; Psa. 3:2-4; 91:5,6; Prov. 1:33; 3:25; 29:25; Isa. 35:4; 41:10,13; 43:5; 44:2; 54:14; Zeph. 3:13; Mark 13:13; Luke 13:11-13; Heb. 13:6; Rev. 2:10.

## III. The Purpose of God

**A. Its Nature**

1. Eternal Psa. 33:11; 52:1; 119:89; Isa. 46:10; John 10:28; Acts 15:18; 1 Cor. 2:7; Eph. 1:4; 3:9,11; 2 Thess. 2:13; 2 Tim. 1:9; 1 Pet. 1:20; Rev. 10:6.
2. Unchangeable Job 14:5; 23:13; Psa. 33:11; 52:1; Prov. 19:21; Isa. 14:24,26,27; 46:9-11; 55:11; Dan. 4:35; Heb. 7:17; Jas. 1:17.
3. Universal Prov. 16:4; Dan. 4:34; Acts 17:26; Rom. 11:36; Eph. 1:11.
4. Unconditional Psa. 33:11; Prov. 19:21; Isa. 14:24,27; 46:10; Rom. 8:29,30; 9:11,13,16, 18; 1 Thess. 4:3; 2 Thess. 2:13.
5. Righteous Num. 14:21; Isa. 48:11; Jer. 9:24; Ezek. 20:9; Acts 2:23; 17:31; Rom. 9:14; 1 Cor. 1:26-31; Eph. 1:9; 2:8-10.
6. Efficacious Isa. 8:10; 14:24,27; 43:13; 46:11; 55:11; Dan. 2:45; Matt. 16:21; Luke 18:31-33; 24:46; Col. 1:16; Heb. 1:10.

**B. The Basis of the Purpose**

1. In God's Will Job 36:23; Isa. 40:13,14; Dan. 4:35; Matt. 11:25,26; Rom. 9:11,15-18; 11:34; Eph. 1:5,9,11.
2. In God's Good Pleasure 1 Sam. 12:22; Psa. 115:3; 135:6; Isa. 42:1; 60:10; Dan. 4:35; Matt. 11:26; Luke 12:32; Rom. 9:15-18; Eph. 1:5; Phil. 2:13; Rev. 4:11.

3. In God's Omnipotence Prov. 16:4; Isa. 55:11; Luke 18:31-33; Acts 2:23; 13:29; Rom. 9:15,16; 11:36.
4. In God's Wisdom Prov. 3:19,20; Isa. 40:13,14; Rom. 11:34; 1 Cor. 2:16.
5. In God's Distinguishing Knowledge Deut. 21:15; 2 Sam. 7:20; Psa. 1:6; 139:1,2; Rom. 9:13,17,18.
6. In God's Omniscience 1 Sam. 23:11,12; Matt. 26:21,34; Acts 15:18; Rom. 8:29; 11:33.

**C. Its Revelation Through His Kingdom** Psa. 22:28; 97:1; 99:1; 103:19; 110:2; 145:13; Isa. 22:22; 43:7,21; 52:7; 53:1; 60:10-22; Dan. 2:44; 6:26; Mic. 2:12; 4:6-8; Zech. 4:6,7; Matt. 4:7; 5:3,20; 7:21; 8:11; 11:11; 12:28; 13:18-33,41; 16:18,19; 18:3; 21:43; 22:1-14; Mark 1:14,15; 4:26-32; 9:43; 10:14,15; Luke 6:20; 14:16-24; 17:20,21; 18:24; John 1:12,13; 3:3-6; 4:24; 18:36; Rom. 14:17; 1 Cor. 12:3; Gal. 3:6-9; Eph. 1:22,23; 2:19; Phil. 3:20; Col. 1:12-14; Heb. 6:5; 12:22-28.

**D. Its Final Result: The Glory of God** Num. 14:21; Psa. 86:9; Isa. 48:1; Ezek. 20:9; 1 Cor. 1:26-31; Eph. 2:8,9; Rev. 4:11; 5:13.

## IV. The Predestination of God

**A. Its Source** Ex. 14:4; 2 Sam. 22:20; 1 Kin. 12:15; 2 Kin. 21:7; 2 Chr. 6:6; Job 23:13,14; Psa. 4:3; 18:19; 28:8; 33:12; 36:9; 65:4; 68:19; 76:9; 78:67,68,70-72; 84:11; 103:2,3; 132:13,14; 135:4; 149:4; Prov. 16:4; Isa. 42:16; 43:11,12; 44:1,2,7,23; 45:4; 52:10; Jer. 31:3; Lam. 3:24; Hos. 13:14; Matt. 11:25,26; Luke 12:32; John 6:37,39; 10:29; 15:16,19; 17:2,6,9,11; Acts 2:47; 11:17; 22:14; Rom. 1:6; 2:4; 3:25; 8:28-30,33; 9:22,23,28,30; 1 Cor. 1:27,28; 2 Cor. 5:5; Gal. 1:15; Eph. 1:4,5,11; 2:10; 3:11; 1 Thess. 1:4; 2:12; 2 Thess. 1:11; 2:13; 1 Tim. 6:13; 2 Tim. 1:9; Tit. 1:2; 3:4,5; Jas. 1:18; 1 Pet. 1:2; 1 John 4:10,19.

**B. Its Objects**

1. Christ as Mediator of the Covenant Gen. 3:15; Psa. 89:19; Isa. 42:1; 53:5; Dan. 9:24,26; Zech. 9:11; 13:1; Matt. 26:24; Mark 14:21; Luke 22:22; John 6:51; Acts 2:23; 3:9,18; 5:30,31; 20:28; Rom. 3:24,25; 5:6; 8:3,32; 14:9; 1 Cor. 5:7; 15:3; 2 Cor. 5:14,15,19,21; Gal. 1:4; 3:13; 4:4,5; Eph. 1:6,7; Col. 2:14,15; 1 Thess. 1:10; 5:9,10; Heb. 2:9,10; 9:15-17,28; 10:15-18; 12:24; 1 Pet. 1:2,18-21; 1 John 3:16; 4:10; Rev. 1:5, 6; 7:14,15.
2. Angels
   a. Good Gen. 24:7,40; Ex. 23:20,23; 32:34; 33:2; Dan. 3:28; Matt. 13:41; 24:31; Luke 1:26; 1 Tim. 5:21; Heb. 1:14; Rev. 1:1; 22:6,16.
   b. Evil Judg. 9:23; 1 Sam. 16:14-16,23; 18:10; 19:9; 1 Kin. 22:23; 2 Chr. 18:21,22; Matt. 4:10,11; 8:16,31,32; 10:1; 25:41; Mark 1:25,26; 3:11,12; 5:12,13; 6:7; 7:29; 9:25,26; Luke 7:21; 8:2,32,33; 9:42; 10:20; Acts 5:16; 19:12; 2 Cor. 11:14; 2 Pet. 2:4; Jude 6.
3. All Men
   a. Some Predestined to Salvation Gen. 21:12; Ex. 33:19; Deut. 4:37; 7:7,8; 2 Sam. 22:20; Psa. 4:3; 18:19; 33:12; 44:3; 65:4; 78:68,70,71; 132:13,14; 135:4; 149:4; Isa. 44:1,2,7; 46:13; Hos. 13:14; Mal. 1:2; Matt. 20:16,23; 22:14; 24:22,40,41; Mark 13:20; Luke 1:79; 8:10; 10:20; 17:34-36; 18:7; John 6:37,39; 10:3,4,28,29; 15:16,19; 17:6,9-12; Acts 2:47; 13:48; 22:14; Rom. 1:6; 8:28-30,33; 9:11,13,15-18, 24,27; 11:5,7; 1 Cor. 2:7; 2 Cor. 5:5; Eph. 2:10; Col. 3:12; 1 Thess. 1:4; 2:12; 2 Thess. 1:11; 2:13; 2 Tim. 1:9; Tit. 1:1,2; Jas. 1:18; 1 Pet. 1:2; 2:9; 2 Pet. 1:10.
   b. Some Foreordained to Condemnation Ex. 14:4; Deut. 28:20; Josh. 11:20; 24:19; 1 Kin. 20:42; Psa. 37:9; 78:67; 81:11,12; Prov. 16:4; Isa. 6:9,10,12; 22:14; 28:13; 29:9-12; 65:12; Jer. 6:30; 7:16; 15:1; Mal. 1:3; Matt. 13:13-15; 15:14; Luke 8:10; 13:28; John 10:26; Rom. 9:21,22; 11:7,8,22; 2 Cor. 13:5; 2 Thess. 2:12; 2 Tim. 3:8; Heb. 3:11; 6:4-6,8; 12:16,17; 1 Pet. 2:8; Jude 4; Rev. 13:8; 22:11.
   c. All Ordained to Their Stations in Life Ex. 31:2-6; Psa. 105:17-22,26; Jer. 1:5; Dan. 2:35; 1 Cor. 7:20.

**C. In Personal Salvation**

1. Total Depravity (Since the Fall, man's helpless condition requires God's gracious intervention for personal salvation.) Gen. 3:7; 6:5; 8:21; 1 Kin. 8:46; 2 Chr. 6:36; Job 14:4; 15:14,16; 22:5; Psa. 51:5; 58:3; 130:3; 143:2; Prov. 20:9; Eccl. 7:20,29; 9:3; Isa. 48:8; 53:6; 64:6; Jer. 13:23; 17:9; Matt. 7:16-18; 12:33; Mark 7:21-23; John 3:5-7, 19; 6:44,65; 8:44; Rom. 3:9-12; 5:12; 6:20; 8:7,8; 11:35,36; 1 Cor. 2:14; 2 Cor. 3:5; Eph. 2:1-3; 4:17-19; 5:8; Col. 2:13; Tit. 1:15; 3:3; Jas. 3:2-8; 1 John 1:8,10; 3:10; 5:19.
2. Unconditional Election Ex. 13:19; Deut. 7:6,7; 10:14; Psa. 33:12; 65:4; 106:5; Hag. 2:23; Matt. 11:27; 20:15; 22:14; 24:22,31; Mark 13:20; Luke 18:7; John 10:28,29; 15:16; Acts. 13:48; 18:27; Rom. 8:28-30, 33; 9:10-24; 11:4-7,28,33,34; 1 Cor. 1:27-29; Eph. 1:4,5,12; 2:10; Phil. 1:29; 2:12,13; Col. 3:12; 1 Thess. 1:4,5; 5:9; 2 Thess. 2:13,14; 2 Tim. 1:9; 2:10; Tit. 1:1; Jas. 2:5; 1 Pet. 1:1,2; 2:8,9; 2 Pet. 1:5-11; Rev. 13:8; 17:8,14.
3. Definite Atonement (or Particular Redemption (Matt. 1:21; 20:28; 26:28; Luke 19:10; John 6:35-40; 10:11,14-18,24-29; 11:50-53; 17:1-11,20,24-26; Acts 5:31; 20:28; Rom. 3:24; 5:8-10,12,17-19; 8:32-34; 1 Cor. 1:30; 2 Cor. 5:18,19,21; Gal. 1:3,4; 3:13; Eph. 1:3-12; 2:15,16; 5:25-27; Phil. 1:29; Col. 1:13,14,21,22; 1 Tim. 1:15; Tit. 2:14; 3:5, 6; Heb. 2:17; 9:12,15,28; 1 Pet. 2:24; 3:18; 1 John 1:7; Rev. 5:9.
4. Effectual Calling Deut. 30:6; Psa. 65:4; Song 1:4; Isa. 55:11; 65:1; Jer. 31:3; 32:40; Ezek. 36:26,27; John 1:12,13; 3:4-7; 5:21; 6:37,39,40,44,45,64,65; 10:3-6; Acts 11:18;

13:48; 16:14; 18:27; Rom. 1:6,7; 8:30; 9:23,24; 10:20; 1 Cor. 1:2,9,24,26; 6:11; 12:3; 2 Cor. 2:10-14; 3:6,17,18; 5:17,18; Gal. 1:15,16; Eph. 2:1,5; 4:4; Col. 2:13; 2 Thess. 2:14; 2 Tim. 1:9; Tit. 3:5; Heb. 9:15; 1 Pet. 1:2,3,15,23; 2:9; 5:10; 2 Pet. 1:3; 1 John 5:4; Jude 1; Rev. 17:14.

5. Regeneration Deut. 30:6; Psa. 51:10; 85:4; Ezek. 11:19; 36:25-27; John 1:12,13; 3:3-8,27; 5:21; 17:2; Rom. 9:16; 11:17; 1 Cor. 3:6,7; 2 Cor. 5:17,18; Eph. 2:1,4,5,10; Col. 2:13; 1 Tim. 6:13; Tit. 3:5; Jas. 1:18; 1 Pet. 1:3,23; 1 John 5:4; Rev. 1:5,6.

6. Conversion Psa. 19:7; 51:10,13; 80:3,7,19; 85:4; 119:37; Prov. 1:23; Isa. 6:10; Jer. 31:18; Lam. 5:21; Matt. 13:13-15; 18:3; Mark 14:11,12; John 12:39,40; Acts 3:19, 26; 11:21; 28:26,27; Col. 3:3.

   a. Repentance Psa. 85:4; Song 1:4; Jer. 31:18; Lam. 5:21; Ezek. 16:61-63; Hos. 14:2,4; Zech. 12:10; Luke 13:3; Acts 3:26; 5:31; 11:18; 2 Cor. 7:9,10; 2 Tim. 2:25,26.

   b. Faith

      1) God, the Source of Faith Isa. 28:16; Acts 18:27; 1 Cor. 4:7; Eph. 2:8,9; Phil. 1:29; Heb. 12:2.

      2) Christ, the Object of Faith Matt. 8:2,10,13; 9:22,27-29; 11:4-6,28-30; 14:29-31; Mark 5:36; 9:23, 24; 16:16; Luke 8:48,50; 15:28; 17:5; 18:42; John 1:11,12; 3:14-16,18,36; 5:24; 6:29,35,45,47; 7:38; 9:36-38; 11:25-27,40; 12:36,44,46; 13:7,20; 14:1,11,12; 16:27,33; 18:37; 20:27,29,31; Acts 3:16; 4:12; 10:43; 13:37-39; 15:11; 16:31; 20:21; 26:18; Rom. 1:16,17; 3:22-28; 4:24,25; 5:1; 9:37; 10:4,6-13; 1 Cor. 1:30; Gal. 2:16; 3:13,14,24-29; 5:6; Eph. 1:12-14; 3:17; 4:13; Phil. 3:9; Col. 2:7,12; 1 Tim. 1:16; 2 Tim. 1:13; 2:1; 3:15; Heb. 5:9; Jas. 2:1; 1 Pet. 1:3-5,7-9,21; 2:6,7; 2 Pet. 1:1; 1 John 3:23; 5:4,5,10, 13; Jude 21.

      3) Justification, a Result of Faith Gen. 15:6; Psa. 32:1; 34:22; 71:16; 130:4; Isa. 7:9; 42:21; 45:24,25; 46:13; 50:8; 51:5,6; 53:11; 54:17; 56:1; 61:10; Jer. 23:6; 31:34; Mic. 7:18; Hab. 2:4; Zech. 3:4; Luke 15:22-24; John 3:36; 5:24; Acts 13:39; Rom. 1:16,17; 2:13; 3:24-30; 4:5-8,20-25; 5:1,9,11,13-21; 6:5-8,22; 7:4; 8:1,30,31,33,34; 9:30-32; 10:4-6, 8-11; 1 Cor. 1:30; 4:4; 6:11; 2 Cor. 5:19,21; Gal. 2:16,20; 3:6,8, 9,11,21,22,24; 5:4,6; Eph. 1:7; Phil. 3:8,9; Col. 1:22; 2:13,14; Tit. 3:4,7; Heb. 10:17; 11:4,7; Jas. 2:20-23,26; 1 Pet. 1:4.

      4) Adoption, a Result of Faith Ex. 4:22; Psa. 103:13; Prov. 14:26; Jer. 14:9; John 1:12; Rom. 5:2; 8:15-17; 2 Cor. 6:18; Gal. 3:26, 28; 4:5; Eph. 1:5,13,14; 3:12; Heb. 1:14; 2:10; 6:12,17; 12:5-10; Jas. 2:5; 1 Pet. 1:4; 3:7; 1 John 3:1; Rev. 3:12.

7. Sanctification Gen. 17:1; Psa. 4:3; 34:13,14; 119:37,59; John 13:10; 17:17,19; Rom. 8:13; 1 Cor. 6:11; 15:24; 2 Cor. 7:1; Gal. 2:20; 6:14; Eph. 1:4; 3:19; 4:7,12,13,15,16; 5:25-27; Col. 2:11; 1 Thess. 4:3,4; 5:23; 2 Thess. 2:13,14; 2 Tim. 2:21; Heb. 2:11; 9:14; 10:10,14; 12:10; 13:12,21; 1 Pet. 1:2-4; 2 Pet. 3:11-14,18; 1 John 1:9; 3:3; 5:3-5,18,21; 3 John 11; Jude 1,24; Rev. 7:14; 18:4; 19:8.

8. Perseverance Psa. 26:1; 37:28; 41:12; 51:10; Isa. 43:1-3; 54:10; 60:21; 61:3; Jer. 32:40; Matt. 12:20; Luke 12:32; John 3:16,36; 5:23,24; 6:37-40,47,51; 10:27-30; 14:19; 17:11,12,15; Rom. 5:9,10; 6:14; 8:1,29,30,35-39; 9:23; 1 Cor. 1:8; Eph. 1:13,14; 4:30; Phil. 1:6; 3:9; 1 Thess. 5:9, 23,24; 2 Thess. 2:13; 2 Tim. 1:12; 2:19; 4:18; Heb. 6:17,18; 7:25; 9:12,15; 10:14; 12:2,28; 13:5; Jas. 1:12; 2:5; 1 Pet. 1:3-5, 23; 1 John 2:17,19,25; Jude 1,24,25; Rev. 2:7,10,11,17,26-28; 21:7; 22:14.

9. Glorification 1 Sam. 2:8; Psa. 58:11; 73:24; Prov. 3:3,5; Matt. 13:43; Luke 9:30,31; Rom. 8:17,18,30; 9:23; 1 Cor. 15:43; Phil. 3:21; Col. 3:4; 2 Thess. 2:14; 1 Pet. 5:10; Rev. 2:26-28; 3:4,5,12,21; 7:13-17; 21:3-5; 22:4,5.

### D. Its Practical Effects in the Believer's Life

1. Humility Deut. 15:15; 32:7; Psa. 22:6; 86:1; Prov. 22:4; Eccl. 5:2; Isa. 51:1; 57:15; Mic. 6:8; Luke 1:52; 18:13; 1 Cor. 1:28,29; 10:12; 2 Cor. 12:9,10; Gal. 6:14; Phil. 2:5-8; Col. 3:12; 1 Pet. 5:6.
2. Confidence in Witnessing Psa. 3:8; 37:39; Isa. 55:11; Jonah 2:9; John 15:16; Acts 18:9,10; Rom. 9:14-18.
3. Fruitfulness of Appeals Psa. 2:8; Isa. 29:18,19,24; 55:11; John 6:37,45; 15:16; Acts 13:48.

**E. Purpose of Predestination** Ex. 9:16; 14:4; Eccl. 3:14; Isa. 43:7,21; Rom. 9:17; 11:28; 1 Cor. 2:7; 6:20; Eph. 1:5,6; 3:10,11.

## V. The Seeming Paradoxes of God

### A. God's Will

1. His Hidden Counsels Gen. 32:29; Deut. 29:29; Judg. 14:4; Job 15:8; 36:26; 37:5, 23; Psa. 40:5; 77:19; 92:5; 139:6,17,18; 145:3; Prov. 25:2; Eccl. 3:11; 7:24; 11:5; Isa. 28:21; 40:28; 45:15; 55:8,9; Joel 2:14; Matt. 11:25,27; 13:11; Mark 4:11; Luke 8:10; John 3:8; Rom. 11:33,34; 16:25; 1 Cor. 2:7-11,16; 2 Cor. 3:14,15; Eph. 3:5,8; Col. 1:26; 1 Tim. 3:9; Heb. 5:11.
2. His Revealed Requirements Gen. 17:1; Ex. 19:5; 32:33; Deut. 5:29; 11:1; 26:16; 29:29; 30:10-18; Josh. 1:8; 1 Sam. 15:22; Psa. 25:14; 139:17; Prov. 3:32; Isa. 52:11; Amos 3:7; Matt. 5:48; 11:25; 13:11,35; 19:17,21; 22:37-39; Mark 4:11; Luke 8:10; Acts 5:29; 22:14; Rom. 2:13; 16:26; 1 Cor. 2:10; 2 Cor. 3:17,18; 6:17; Gal. 1:9; Eph. 1:9; 3:3,

4,9,18,19; 6:19; Col. 1:25-27; 2:2; 3:14; 4:3; 1 Thess. 4:3; Heb. 1:1,2; 2:1-4; Jas. 1:4,18; 2:10,22; 3:2; 1 Pet. 1:16; 1 John 2:5; 3:18; 4:16,21; Rev. 22:14.

**B. Man's Will**

1. Free (to make choices) Deut. 30:19; Josh. 24:15; 1 Kings 18:21; 2 Chr. 15:2; Neh. 1:9; Prov. 3:35; 11:27; 12:2; 16:17,33; Isa. 31:6; 59:20; Jer. 26:3; Lam. 3:25; Ezek. 14:6; 18:21,23,24,26-28,31,32; 33:9; 39:9; Joel 2:12-14; Zech. 1:3; Matt. 11:12; 17:12.
2. Bound (in that his choices, apart from God's grace, are always sinful) Psa. 14:2,3; Prov. 16:3; 20:9; 21:1; Isa. 64:6; Jer. 13:23; 31:18; Lam. 5:21; John 1:12,13; 6:44,65; 8:34,44; Acts 5:31; 11:18; 13:48; Rom. 3:9-12; 8:7,8; 9:16; Eph. 2:1,2; 2 Tim. 2:25,26; Tit. 3:3; Jas. 1:18; 1 John 5:19.

**C. Evil's Presence**

1. Decreed Deut. 31:16,17; Judg. 9:23; 2 Sam. 7:14; 1 Kin. 14:10; Job 2:10; 12:16; Psa. 105:25; Prov. 16:4; Isa. 31:2; 45:7; Lam. 3:38; Dan. 9:14; Rev. 22:11.
2. Condemned Deut. 31:18; 2 Kin. 21:15; Job 11:14; Psa. 9:17; 14:2,3; 37:27; 97:10; Prov. 3:7; Isa. 64:6; Jer. 4:4; 33:5; Luke 13:34; Rom. 12:9; Gal. 3:10; 1 Thess. 5:22; 2 Tim. 2:19.

**D. Man's Responsibility**

1. Man Accountable Prov. 1:23; Isa. 31:6; 55:7; 60:1; Jer. 25:5; 33:3; Ezek. 18:20,21, 23,24,26-28,30-32; 20:19; 33:9,11; Joel 2:12-14; Zech. 1:3; Luke 13:3; Acts 2:28; 17:30; Eph. 5:14.
2. Man Impotent Deut. 30:6; 32:10; Psa. 51:10; 130:3; Isa. 51:1; Jer. 13:23; Ezek. 11:19; 36:26,27; John 5:21; 6:44,65; 8:34; 15:5; 17:2; Rom. 6:17,19; 8:7,8; 1 Cor. 2:14; Gal. 6:15; Eph. 2:1; 4:18; Col. 1:13; 2:13; Tit. 1:15; 3:3; 1 John 5:19.

## GENESIS



## EXODUS



## LEVITICUS



## NUMBERS



## DEUTERONOMY

**JEREMIAH**



**LAMENTATIONS**



**EZEKIEL**

# THE HOLY TRINITY AND THE COVENANT OF GRACE

## THE PURPOSE OF THIS OUTLINE AND INDEX

Beginning with the Apostolic Fathers and the Apologists in the second century A.D., great care has been taken to defend the doctrine of the Trinity against those who would sacrifice the Biblical doctrine for something more easily understood.

Some have embraced views that seek to defend an extreme monotheism. Others have adopted what amounts to tritheism. Still others have tried to solve the problem of how the three Persons of the Godhead are related by ranking them or viewing the Persons as only temporary manifestations of the Deity.

The creed adopted by the Council of Nicea in A.D. 325 (See *Creeds of Christendom* by Philip Schaff, reprinted in 1977 by Baker Book House, for this and other Trinitarian creeds), along with the clarifications and refinements that later councils have made, answers the question as capably and concisely as the human mind is able. After 1600 years, all formulations that fall short of the Biblical doctrine can be traced back to the same basic approaches that were weighed and found wanting in A.D. 325. For this reason, it is important that all Christians know the true doctrine and are able to defend it.

The purpose of this outline is not to replace the creeds, but to set forth the Scriptural basis for the doctrine of the Trinity, which is summarized in them. Further, it is important for Christians to understand how the Persons of the Godhead relate to one another, particularly in reference to the Plan of Salvation. Throughout the ages, the Father, the Son, and the Holy Spirit have been, and ever shall be, cooperating in creating, sustaining, and governing the universe, and have acted in perfect harmony in all of the aspects of the redemption of fallen men. From a careful devotional study of the Word of God, with this outline as a suggestive guide, one may gain a solid foundation upon which to build a life of genuine love, worship, and service to the ever blessed Triune God.

Approximately two thousand Scripture references that relate, directly or indirectly, to the general subject of "The Holy Trinity and the Covenant of Grace" have been noted throughout the text of Scripture and marked with the superscript letter (*T*). This symbol indicates that the verse or context so marked is incorporated into this outline and listed in its index.

## USE OF THE OUTLINE AND INDEX

### I. Point by Point Study.

The outline points may be studied in order or at random as particular questions arise. Scripture references relating to a particular aspect of the doctrine of the Trinity or of the Covenant of Grace are listed in Biblical order under each outline point. The verses should be studied in their proper contexts in order to find their bearing upon these doctrines.

### II. The Symbols in the Text.

By means of the superscript symbol *T* the Bible reader is guided from the text to the appropriate aspect of the subject as set forth in the outline. A *T* at the beginning of a verse serves to introduce a group of verses that form a context. A *T* at the end of a verse serves to close that context or to mark a *single* verse with such teaching. (To determine whether a symbol closes a context or stands alone, look for an opening *T* and/or use the index to find the correct context.)

As with all Bible study, care should be taken to study each verse in context, whether it stands alone or within a marked context. Due to the fact that both *near* and *far* contexts exist and that contexts may overlap, the index should be used in conjunction with the symbols in the text. Also, an unmarked verse included within a marked context may appear in a separate entry in the index where readability demands an uncluttered page.

### III. Locating a Specific Reference.

Suppose one is reading in 2 Corinthians 13 and discovers a *T* at verse 14. One may discover where 2 Corinthians 13:14 is included in the outline by looking up 2 Corinthians 13:14 in the index. The following entry appears: 13:14 II.B.3.a.; III.B.4.e.; III.C.4.e.(4). It indicates that 2 Corinthians 13:14 is listed three times in the outline. By referring to these outline points, particular aspects of the doctrine of the Trinity may be seen in their relationship to the whole doctrine. By studying the other references included under these sections, further insight may be obtained.

In heavily doctrinal passages, such as John 1:1-17, care should be taken to observe all the contexts within the larger context. As an exercise for the reader, it is suggsted that the index entries for John 1 be compared with the superscript letters in the text, in order that he might become acquainted with the technique of finding the extent of each of the contexts. The largest unit is John 1:1-17 and the smallest is an individual verse such as 1:3 or 1:4. Note also that the context of 1:7-9 has been expanded to include 1:6-10, in order to make reading smoother. In this manner a middle ground between strict adherence to a mark at every verse and the other extreme of marks designating only the largest contexts has been established. This has been done in order to encourage the Bible student to read contextually. The index should always be consulted for identification of the *specific* verses alluded to in the outline.

**I. There is but one God.** 1 Kin. 8:60; Mark 12:29,32; John 17:3; 1 Cor. 8:4,6.

**A. In Him is unity.** Deut. 6:4; 1 Kin. 20:28; 1 Tim. 2:5; Jas. 2:19.

1. There can be only one Creator.
   a. O.T. proof: Gen. 1,2; 5:1,2; 6:7; Deut. 4:32; Psa. 89:12; 102:18; 104:30; 148:5; Prov. 16:4; Isa. 40:26; 42:5; 43:1,7; 45:7,12,18; 65:17,18; Mal. 2:10.
   b. N.T. proof: Mark 10:6; 13:19; John 1:3,10; Acts 4:24; 7:50; 14:15; 17:24; Rom. 9:20; Eph. 3:9; Col. 1:16; 3:10; 1 Tim. 4:3; Heb. 1:2; Rev. 4:11; 10:6; 14:7.
2. There can be only one Judge.
   a. O.T. proof: Gen. 15:14; 18:25; Ex. 5:21; Deut. 32:36; Judg. 11:27; 1 Sam. 2:10; 24:12,15; 1 Chr. 16:33; 2 Chr. 20:12; Psa. 7:8; 9:7,8; 50:4,6; 68:5; 72:4; 75:7; 82:8; 94:1,2; 96:10; 98:9; 110:6; 135:14; Eccl. 3:17; Isa. 2:4; 33:22; Ezek. 7:3,8; 11:10,11; 16:38; 18:30; 21:30; 33:20; Joel 3:12; Mic. 4:3.
   b. N.T. proof: John 5:22,30; 8:15,16,26; Acts 10:42; 17:31; Rom. 2:16; 3:6; 2 Tim. 4:1,8; Heb. 10:30; 12:23; 13:4; Rev. 19:11.
3. There can be only one LORD (i.e., Jehovah) God.
   a. O.T. proof: Deut. 4:35; 6:4; 32:39; Psa. 18:31; 73:25; 86:10; Isa. 43:10, 11; 44:6,8; 45:5,6,14,18,21,22; 46:9; Mal. 2:10.
   b. N.T. proof: Matt. 19:17; Mark 12:29, 32; John 10:30; 17:3; Acts 17:24; Rom. 3:30; 1 Cor. 8:4,6; Eph. 4:3-6; 1 Tim. 1:17; 2:5; Jas. 2:19; 4:12; 2 Pet. 2:1; 1 John 5:7; Jude 4.

**B. In Him is diversity.**

1. Who is our Redeemer and Savior?
   a. In the O.T. He is identified as Jehovah. 2 Sam. 22:1-3; Job 19:25; Psa. 19:14; 78:35; 106:21; Prov. 23:11; Isa. 41:14; 43:3,11,14; 44:6,24; 45:15,21; 47:4; 48:17; 49:7,26; 54:5,8; 59:19,20; 60:16; 63:8,16; Jer. 14:8; 50:34; Hos. 13:4.
   b. In the N.T. He is identified as the Son of God. Matt. 1:21; Luke 2:11; John 4:42; Acts 5:31; 13:23; Gal. 3:13; 4:4, 5; Eph. 5:23; Phil. 3:20; 2 Tim. 1:10; Tit. 1:4; 2:13; 3:6; 2 Pet. 1:11; 3:2,18; 1 John 4:14.
2. Who is the one that dwells among Israel and in the hearts of those who fear Him?
   a. In the O.T. He is identified as Jehovah. Psa. 68:18; 74:2; 135:21; Isa. 8:18; 57:15; Ezek. 43:7-9; Joel 3:17, 21; Zech. 2:10,11.
   b. In the N.T. He is identified as the Holy Spirit. Acts 2:4; Rom. 8:9,11; 1 Cor. 3:16; 6:19; Gal. 4:6; Eph. 2:22; 3:17; 2 Tim. 1:14.

**C. In Him is simplicity.** God is not made up of parts, like a man's body, but in God every attribute is integral to, and inseparable from, His essence. Every one of God's virtues exists in absolute perfection in His very being. Therefore, there is no love, law, wisdom, or holiness higher than that which is in God.

1. God is righteousness. (See outline on God's Sovereignty, I.G.4.)
   a. O.T. proof: Psa. 5:8; 7:17; 45:4; 71:19; 85:11; 96:13; 119:137,138,142; Jer. 23:6; 33:15,16; Dan. 9:7,16; Mic. 6:5; Mal. 4:2.
   b. N.T. proof: Rom. 10:3; 1 Cor. 1:30; 2 Cor. 5:21; Phil. 3:9; Heb. 1:8; 7:2; Jas. 1:20; 2 Pet. 1:1.
2. God is Truth.
   a. O.T. proof: Deut. 32:4; Psa. 25:10; 26:3; 30:9; 31:5; 33:4; 40:10,11; 43:3; 45:4; 54:5; 57:3,10; 69:13; 71:22; 85:10,11; 86:11,15; 89:14,49; 91:4; 96:13; 98:3; 100:5; 108:4; 111:8; 117:2; 119:142,151; 138:2; 146:6; Prov. 8:7; Isa. 25:1; 38:18,19; 42:3; 61:8; 65:16; Jer. 4:2; Dan. 4:37; 9:13; Zech. 8:8; Mal. 2:6.
   b. N.T. proof: Matt. 22:16; Mark 12:14; John 1:14,17; 8:32; 14:6,17; 15:26; 16:13; 17:17; 18:37; Rom. 1:25; 2:2; 3:7; 15:8; 2 Cor. 11:10; Eph. 4:21; 1 Thess. 2:13; 1 Tim. 3:15; Jas. 1:18; 1 John 4:6; 5:6; 2 John 3.
3. God is Life.
   a. O.T. proof: Deut. 30:20; Job 10:12; 33:4; Psa. 21:4; 36:9; 91:16; 103:4; Prov. 4:13; 8:35; Jer. 21:8; Lam. 3:58; Mal. 2:5.
   b. N.T. proof: John 1:4; 3:15,16,36; 4:14; 5:24,26,40; 6:27,33,35,40,47,48, 53,54,63,68; 8:12; 10:10,28; 11:25; 12:50; 14:6; 17:2,3; Acts 3:15; 17:25; Rom. 2:7; 5:10,17,21; 6:23; 8:2,10; 2 Cor. 3:6; Gal. 6:8; Col. 3:4; 2 Tim. 1:1; Tit. 1:2; 1 John 1:1,2; 2:25; 5:11, 12,20; Rev. 11:11; 21:27.
4. God is Light.
   a. O.T. proof: Gen. 1:3; Job 36:30,32; 37:15; Psa. 27:1; 36:9; 43:3; 74:16; 104:2; 118:27; 119:105,130; Isa. 2:5; 10:17; 42:6,16; 45:7; 49:6; 60:1,3,19, 20.
   b. N.T. proof: Luke 2:32; John 1:4,7-9; 3:19; 8:12; 9:5; 12:35,36,46; Acts 13:47; Eph. 5:14; 1 John 1:5; 2:8; Rev. 21:23; 22:5.

**II. The evidences for a plurality of Persons within the Godhead have been progressively revealed.**

**A. In the Old Testament**

1. Passages utilizing plural forms of names of, or descriptive nouns for, God:
   a. The second most common name for God in the O.T. is *Elohim* (simply translated *God*), the plural form of the Hebrew word *Eloah*. The singular form *Eloah* is applied fifty-two times to Jehovah, the true God (forty-one times in the book of Job alone), and five times in reference to various false deities. (Deut. 32:15,17; 2 Chr. 32:15; Job 3:4,23; 19:6,21,26; 37:15,22; Psa. 18:31; 114:7; Dan. 11:37-39.) The use

of the singular *Eloah*, as well as other singular names, to refer to Jehovah indicates that the Biblical writers had no lack of singular epithets for Deity at their disposal. Thus we must conclude that they used the plural form, *Elohim* (also translated *gods*, variously referring to false gods, kings, judges, or angels), *by choice and design*, in order to set forth a plurality of Persons within the Godhead. *Elohim* is used approximately 2,500 times throughout the O.T., over 2,250 times in reference to Jehovah, the covenant God of Israel.

1) There was also available to the Hebrew writers a *dual* suffix or ending for nouns, which enabled them to indicate precisely when they were speaking of a duality or two of a kind. But *Elohim* is plural, indicating (according to ancient Jewish Hebrew scholars) no less than three individuals in the case of angels, civil magistrates, or false deities, and at least three Persons in the Godhead when applied to the true God, Jehovah. A common dual noun found in the O.T. is *Mizraim* (*-aim* is the dual suffix), translated *Egypt*, and generally used when the two kingdoms of Lower Egypt (*Mazor*—see marginal notes at 2 Kin. 19:24; Isa. 19:6; 37:25) and Upper Egypt (*Pathros*—see Isa. 11:11; Jer. 44:1,15; Ezek. 29:14; 30:14) are being spoken of together as a collective political entity. Another example of a dual noun is the name *Ephraim*, which means *double fruit(land)*. Many such dual forms exist in Hebrew. Were there but two Persons in the Godhead, a dual form could have been coined readily by the writers of Holy Scripture.
   It is exceedingly strange that Moses, in the midst of his struggle to extirpate polytheism, should begin his historical narrative (Gen. 1:1) with a plural name for the one true God ("In the beginning God [*Elohim*] created the heaven and the earth"), unless there was some compelling reason in the very nature of the Godhead that demanded such a plural appellation. Moses "must have some design in it, which could not be to inculcate a plurality of gods, for that would be directly contrary to what he had in view in writing, and what he asserts [in] Deuteronomy 6:4: 'Hear, O Israel, the LORD our God [*Elohim*] is one LORD': nor a plurality of mere names and characters, to which creative powers cannot be ascribed, but a plurality of Persons, for so the words may be rendered, distributively, according to the idiom of the Hebrew language; 'In the beginning every one, or each, of the Divine Persons, created the heaven and the earth' " (John Gill, *A Body of Divinity*).
2) The plural noun *Elohim*, in the vast majority of times that it is applied to Jehovah as the subject of a sentence, is linked with a *singular* verb. This is an unusual phenomenon in grammar, violating the normal rules governing agreement in number between a noun and its verb or a verb and its subject. When such a construction is used by many writers who are manifestly familiar with the standard grammar of their own tongue, as this construction is used profusely throughout the Hebrew O.T., we must assume that they have done so for a very special reason. By the use of such a construction the fact of God's oneness of essence coupled with the unity of His action (as evidenced by the *singular* verb) is held in equipoise with the fact of a distinction of Persons within the Godhead (as evidenced by the *plural* name). Occasionally, in order to emphasize the truth of a plurality of Divine Persons within the Godhead, the plural name *Elohim* is applied to Jehovah, but linked with a *plural* verb, adjective, or participle, thus utilizing the normal agreement required by the grammar of an inflected language such as Hebrew. In Genesis 20:13, Abraham should be translated as saying, "when [the] Divine Persons [*Elohim*] (they) caused me to wander. . . ." In Genesis 35:7 we should read, "because the Divine Persons [*Elohim*] (they) appeared [i.e., were revealed or revealed themselves] unto him. . . ." The Hebrew text of 2 Samuel 7:23 presents a most interesting construction: "whom (the) Divine Persons [*Elohim*] (they) went to redeem for a people to *Himself*." Here God's Persons and action are referred to in the plural, but His unity as Jehovah, the one true God, is suddenly brought back into view by the reflexive pronoun *Himself*. Once again an equilibrium is presented in order to teach.

In several places, the phrase translated "the living God" ought to be rendered "the Divine Persons, (the) living (Ones)," because a plural adjective or participle is linked with *Elohim* (Deut. 5:26; 1 Sam. 17:26,36; Jer. 10:10; 23:36). The Hebrew text of Joshua 24:19, though traditionally rendered "for He is an holy God," literally says, "for Divine Persons holy Ones He." Psalm 58:11b ought to read, "verily there are Divine Persons [*Elohim*] judging Ones [Judges] in the earth."

b. Another plural name for Jehovah is *Adonim* (Lords). In Malachi 1:6 the Hebrew says, "If I am *Lords* [*Adonim*], where is My fear?" Where does one hear such an unusual expression, in which a speaker, referring to himself, assumes a plural title for himself and then links it to a singular verb and pronouns? What a strange twisting of language this would be if this sentence did not come to us as a revelation of the God whose very words are the true "staff of life" (Deut. 8:3; Matt. 4:4). We are reminded of another passage where two Divine Lords appear: Psalm 110:1 (cf. Matt. 22:44; Acts 2:34,35; Eph. 1:20-22; Heb. 1:1-13).

c. The plural noun *panim* furnishes another line of valuable evidence. It is derived from the singular noun *paneh*, which is not found in the Hebrew O.T. *Panim* occurs about 2100 times, and it is translated in the A.V. in approximately thirty-six different ways. Its most basic meaning is *face*. It is translated *face* 356 times, *presence* seventy-five times, *sight* forty times, *person* or *persons* twenty times, and in thirty miscellaneous ways about seventy-five times. Most frequently it is found in combination with various Hebrew prepositions and is translated into English as the preposition *before* (in the sense of *in the presence of* or *in front of*); it is used thus over 1500 times. There are at least two contexts in which there is evidence that this plural noun ought to be rendered differently than in the A.V. In Exodus 33:14,15, we read, "*My presence* shall go with thee, and I will give thee rest. And [Moses] said unto Him, If *Thy presence* go not with me, carry us not up hence." However, the Hebrew can be rendered literally as follows: "*My Persons (they) shall go*, and I will give rest to you. And [Moses] said to Him, If *Thy Persons* [be] not *going Ones*, bring us not up from here." The plural verb used by God in connection with *panim* (Persons) and the plural participle used in the same way by Moses, in response to the words of Jehovah, strongly argue, by the normal rules of grammar, for a plural subject to agree with them. Thus rendering *panim* as *Persons* in this context provides the most natural reading. It is significant that faithful Moses (Heb. 3:5) repeated the thoroughly plural concept in his response to God, signifying that he understood the uniqueness of Jehovah's words and the significance of the revelation that God was making through them concerning His nature and character. The second context is Deuteronomy 4:37, where the phrase "and brought thee out *in His sight*" occurs, speaking of the LORD's deliverance of Israel from Egypt. But the phrase would better be translated, "and brought thee out *by His Persons*." Not only is this rendering perfectly literal, but it is also in full accord with the theology of the Exodus found in the N.T. (1 Cor. 10:1-4; Heb. 3:5-11).

2. Passages in which the Word (John 1:1-3) or Wisdom of God is alluded to or personified:
   a. The Word of God: Psa. 33:6,9; 147:18,19 (cf. Heb. 1:1-3); 148:8.
   b. The Wisdom of God: Prov. 3:19; 8:22-36; Jer. 10:12; 51:15.
3. Passages in which the Spirit of God is spoken of as a distinct Person:
   a. From creation to the Patriarchs: Gen. 1:2; 6:3; 41:38; Job 26:13; 27:3; 33:4; Psa. 104:30.
   b. From Moses to Samuel: Ex. 28:3; 31:3; 35:21,31; Num. 11:17,25,26,29; 24:2; 27:18; Deut. 34:9; Judg. 3:10; 6:34; 11:29; 13:25; 14:6,19; 15:14; Neh. 9:20; Isa. 63:10,11.
   c. During the United Monarchy: 1 Sam. 10:6,10; 11:6; 16:13,14; 19:18-24; 2 Sam. 23:2; 1 Chr. 12:18; 28:12; Psa. 51:10-12; Psa. 139:7; 143:10; Prov. 1:23.
   d. During the Divided Monarchy: 1 Kin. 18:12; 22:24; 2 Kin. 2:9,15,16; 2 Chr. 15:1; 18:23; 20:14; 24:20; Neh. 9:30; Isa. 4:4; 11:2; 28:6; 30:1; 32:15; 34:16; 40:7, 13; 42:1; 44:3; 48:16; 59:19,21; 61:1; 63:10,11,14; Hos. 9:7; Joel 2:28,29; Mic. 2:7,11; 3:8.
   e. During the exilic & post-exilic Periods: Ezek. 1:12,20,21; 2:2; 3:12,14,24; 8:3; 10:17; 11:1,5,24; 36:26,27; 37:1,14; 39:29; 43:5; Hag. 2:5; Zech. 4:6; 12:10.
4. Passages mentioning the Angel of the Lord or the Messenger of the Covenant:
   a. All of the redemptive revelations, where appearances of Jehovah are mentioned, are effected through the mediation of His Angel. His Angel, the Angel of the Lord, is none other than the Second Person of the Trinity,

Christ, the eternal Son of God. Thus we see that God always deals with His people through their Mediator, according to His eternal plan. See Ex. 33:20; John 1:14,18; 6:45,46; 8:56-58; 11:27; 1 Tim. 2:5; Heb. 8:6; 9:15,24.

b. Study, also, the following passages: Gen. 12:7; 16:7-11; 18:1-33; 19:18-22; 21:17; 22:11-18; 24:7,40; 28:11-22; 31:11-13; 32:24-30; 48:15,16; Ex. 3:2-6; 13:21; 14:19; 19:16—20:26; 23:20-23; 32:34; 33:2,14,15; Num. 20:16; 22:22-35; Deut. 5:4-28; Josh. 5:13—6:2 (cf. 1 Cor. 10:4,9); Judg. 2:1-14; 5:23; 6:11-24; 13:3-23; 2 Kin. 1:3,15; Psa. 34:7; 107:20; Prov. 8:31 (within the context of the chapter); Isa. 63:8,9; Dan. 3:25,28; 6:22; Hos. 12:4,5; Zech. 1:8-17; 2:3; 3:1-8; 4:1-6; 5:5,10; 12:8; Mal. 3:1 (fulfilled in Mark 1:2); Acts 7:30,35,38; Gal. 3:19.

5. Passages indicating distinctions within the Godhead, mentioning two or three Persons:

a. Distinctions shown by the personal pronouns *we*, *us*, and *our*:
1) In creation: Gen. 1:26.
2) In providence: Gen. 3:22; 11:7; Isa. 6:8; 41:21-26; 43:9.

b. Distinctions between two Persons (see III.C.2.):
1) In creation: Gen. 1:2; Job. 26:13; 33:4; Psa. 104:30; Isa. 54:5.
2) In providence: Gen. 19:24; Psa. 2:7,11,12; 8:9; 18:46 (cf. 1 Cor. 10:4); 45:6,7; 110:1; Isa. 42:1; 44:6; 59:19; Hos. 1:7.

c. Distinctions among three Persons (explicitly mentioned or implied by threefold invocations or expressions of worship):
1) In creation: Psa. 33:6.
2) In providence: Num. 6:24-26 (the threefold blessing is suggestive of the Trinity); 2 Sam. 23:2,3 (cf. 1 Cor. 10:4); Isa. 6:3; 33:22; 48:16; 59:19,20; 61:1-3; 63:7-14; Dan. 9:19.

**B. In the New Testament**

1. Passages relating facts of Christ's life on earth that attest to His Deity and relationship with the other Divine Persons:

a. His birth: Matt. 1:18,20-25; Luke 1:31-35; 2:21-35.

b. His childhood: Luke 2:49,52.

c. His baptism: Matt. 3:13-17; Mark 1:9-11; Luke 3:21,22; John 1:32-34.

d. His temptation: Matt. 4:1-11; Mark 1:12; Luke 4:1-13.

e. His ministry: Matt. 17:5; Luke 4:33-41; 5:20,21; 9:34,35; John 1:43-49.

f. His death: Matt. 27:46,54; Mark 15:34,39; Luke 23:34,46.

2. Passages in which Christ teaches concerning His own Deity and the other Persons of the Trinity:

a. In Matthew's Gospel: Matt. 10:20,32, 33; 11:25-27; 12:32; 16:16,17,27; 18:10,19,20; 26:37-39,42,53,63,64; 28:19.

b. In Mark's Gospel: Mark 3:29; 9:37; 12:35-37; 13:11; 14:36; 16:19.

c. In Luke's Gospel: Luke 4:18-21; 9:20, 26; 10:21,22; 11:13.

d. In John's Gospel: John 2:16; 3:5-8,13, 16-18,31,33-36; 4:24-26,34; 5:17-23, 26,27,30,36-38,43,45,46; 6:27,29,32,33,37-40, 44-46,57,65,69; 7:16-18,28,29,33,39; 8:16-19,26-29,-38,42,49,54-58; 9:35; 10:15,17,18,25,29, 30,32-38; 11:4,41,42; 12:26-30,49,50; 13:1,31,32; 14:1-3,6-14,16,17,20,21, 23,24,26,28-31; 15:1,2,8-10,15,16,24-26; 16:3,5,7-11,13-17,23-28,30,32; 17:1-26; 19:11; 20:17,21,22,28,29,31.

3. Passages, in which the apostles teach, that indicate a plurality of Divine Persons:

a. Paul: Acts 13:23,30,33; 17:30,31; 20:21-23; 22:14; Rom. 1:1-4,7,9; 2:16; 3:22,24,25; 5:1,5; 6:4; 8:1-3,11,15; 9:1; 14:17,18; 15:6,13,19,30; 1 Cor. 1:1-3; 2:7-12; 3:23; 6:11; 8:6; 12:3-6; 2 Cor. 1:2,3,21-23; 3:17; 4:13,14; 5:5, 6,19; 13:14; Gal. 1:3; 3:14; 4:6; Eph. 1:1-3,17; 2:18; 4:4-6; 5:17-20; Phil. 3:3; Col. 1:6-8,19; 2:9; 1 Thess. 1:3-6; 5:18,19; 2 Thess. 2:13; 1 Tim. 3:16; Tit. 3:4-6; Heb. 6:4-6; 9:14.

b. Peter: Acts 2:17-22,32,33,36,38,39; 4:30,31; 5:9,30-32; 10:36-38; 1 Pet. 1:2,21,22; 3:18; 4:14; 2 Pet. 1:17,21.

c. John: John 1:1-3,14,18; 1 John 1:1-3; 2:1,20,22-24; 3:23,24; 4:2,6,9,10,13-15; 5:6,7; 2 John 9; Rev. 1:8-10; 14:12,13; 22:16-18.

d. Other witnesses: Mark 16:19; Acts 7:55; Jude 4,17-21.

**III. The three Persons in the Godhead are all described in Scripture as fully God.**

**A. The Father or First Person in the Holy Trinity**

1. The name *Father*, or the concept of Fatherhood, is applied to God.

a. Sometimes it is applied to the *Triune* God as Creator. Job 38:28; Mal. 2:10; Matt. 23:9; Luke 3:38; Acts 17:22-29; 1 Cor. 8:6; Heb. 12:9; Jas. 1:17.

b. Sometimes it is applied to the Triune God as Father of Israel, the Old Covenant nation. Deut. 32:6; 1 Chr. 29:10; Psa. 103:13; Isa. 63:16; 64:8; Jer. 3:4, 19; 31:9; Mal. 1:6; 2:10; John 8:41; Rom. 9:4.

c. Sometimes it is applied to the Triune God as the Father of all believers; i.e., of His spiritual children. Matt. 5:16, 45,48; 6:4,6-15,26,32; 7:11; 10:29; 18:14; 23:9; Mark 11:25,26; Luke 6:36; 12:30,32; John 20:17; Rom. 8:15,16; 1 John 3:1.

d. Sometimes it is applied in a special sense to the First Person of the Trinity as the Father of the Lord Jesus Christ, who is called "the Son of God." Matt. 11:25-27; Luke 22:29; John 1:14,18; 2:16; 5:17-26; 8:38,54; 14:6-13; 16:27;

17:5,24,26; 20:17; Rom. 15:6; 1 Cor. 15:24; 2 Cor. 1:3; Gal. 1:1; Eph. 1:3; 3:14; 1 Pet. 1:3.

2. The name *Father* denotes the relational property (or personal relationship) that is unique to the Father and that distinguish Him from the two other Persons of the Trinity.
   a. Positively considered, only He who begets the Son can be properly called the Father. Psa. 2:7; John 1:14,18; Gal. 1:1; Eph. 1:3; 3:14,15.
   b. Negatively considered, the Father is *unbegotten*. John 5:26; 6:57.
3. The Father is a distinct Person, which fact is established by the personal actions ascribed to Him.
   a. Creation is ascribed to the Father, yet is executed by the Son (not as an instrument but as a co-equal). Psa. 33:6; John 1:3,10; Eph. 3:9; Heb. 1:1,2.
   b. In the O.T., the works of providence (i.e., the upholding and sustaining of all creatures as well as the governing of the world) are ascribed to God without distinction of Persons, but in the N.T. they are ascribed primarily to the Father in distinction from the Son, yet in conjunction with the Son as His appointed universal Monarch. 1 Sam. 2:9; Neh. 9:6; Psa. 107:9; Matt. 10:29; Luke 21:18; John 5:17; Acts 17:28; 1 Cor. 10:13; Col. 1:12-17; Heb. 1:3; 1 Pet. 3:12; Rev. 3:10.
   c. That His Son was sent into the world as the Savior shows that the Father's personality is distinct from the Son's. Isa. 19:20; 48:16; Mal. 3:1; Matt. 10:40; Mark 9:37; Luke 9:48; 20:13; John 4:34; 5:23,24,30,36; 6:44,57; 7:16; 8:16,18; 9:4; 10:36; 11:42; 12:45,49; 13:20; 14:24; 15:21; 16:5; 17:3,8,18,21,23,25; 20:21; Acts 3:26; 1 John 4:14.
   d. The several distinct acts of grace toward the elect serve to demonstrate the distinct personality of the Father. John 6:44; Rom. 8:29,30,32,33; Eph. 1:4,5; 2:8-10; 3:11; 2 Thess. 2:13,14; 2 Tim. 1:9; 1 Pet. 1:2.
4. The Deity of the Father is established by showing that Divine characteristics are ascribed to Him.
   a. From His Divine perfections (attributes):
      1) His independence of any other: John 5:26.
      2) His eternity: Rev. 1:4.
      3) His omnipresence: John 14:23; 16:32.
      4) His omniscience: Matt. 11:27; Mark 13:32; Acts 1:7; 2 Cor. 11:31.
      5) His omnipotence: Matt. 26:53; Mark 14:36; John 10:29.
      6) His unchangeableness: Jas. 1:17.
   b. From the works ascribed to Him, that none but God could do:
      1) Creation: Acts 4:24-27 (cf. Matt. 11:25).
      2) Providence: Matt. 6:26,32.
      3) Quickening sinners who are dead in their sins: Eph. 2:1.
      4) Raising Christ from the dead: Eph. 1:19,20.
      5) Forgiving men's sins: Mark 2:7; Luke 23:34.
   c. From the worship due to Him and given to Him: John 4:23.
      1) Prayer is made to Him. Matt. 6:9.
      2) Grace and peace are invoked from Him. Rom. 1:7; 1 Cor. 1:3.
      3) His name is pronounced in the baptismal form. Matt. 28:19.

**B. The Son or Second Person in the Holy Trinity.**

1. The name *Son* is applied to God.
   a. He was not only pre-existent to His physical conception and birth, but He is the Son of God from all eternity. Mic. 5:2 (cf. Matt. 2:6); Zech. 12:10 (cf. John 19:37); John 1:1,2,14,15,18, 30; 5:18-25; 6:62; 8:58; 17:5; Rom. 9:5; 2 Cor. 8:9; Gal. 4:4; Heb. 1:8,10, 12. If God the Son is not eternal, then neither is God the Father eternal. For if we say that God the Father changed His mode of being into that of the Son, we deny His immutability.
   b. He is called the "only begotten" Son of God. John 1:14,18; 3:16,18; 1 John 4:9. This term implies that the relation between the Father and the Son, though unique, can nevertheless be represented as one of generation and birth (see the next section of this outline).
2. The relational property (or personal relationship) that is unique to the Son and that distinguishes Him from the two other Persons of the Trinity can be described only by means of an analogy that compares the Divine begetting to human begetting.
   a. Characteristics of human begetting:
      1) A man, being *finite* and procreatively *incomplete* without a wife, must have a wife in order to beget.
      2) Since human begetting is *temporal*, and since a child derives his existence from his parents, a human child is begotten in a moment of time and then exists everlastingly. Psa. 51:5; Matt. 25:46; Heb. 9:27.
      3) Since a man's begetting is physical, and since his offspring bear the characteristics of both parents, he cannot fully manifest his own image in any of his children.
      4) The children begotten of men are men, and thus they share in the creaturely finiteness and depravity of their parents. Psa. 51:5.

b. Characteristics of Divine begetting:
   1) God, being infinite, is complete in Himself, requiring no other being in order to beget.
   2) Since the Divine begetting or generation of the Son is *eternal*, there was never a moment when the Son of God did not exist, nor shall there ever be. Col. 1:17; Heb. 13:8. (See III.B.1.a. above.)
      a) The term *firstborn*, as applied to the Son, does not pertain to the temporal order of His birth into a human family. Rather, it signifies that He, as the official Son of God, is mediator of the everlasting covenant. The word *firstborn* declares His primacy, as the God-man, over all the created order, His pre-eminence among men, and the necessary priority of His resurrection in the Divine scheme of redemption. Rom. 1:4; 8:29; Col. 1:15; Heb. 1:6.
      b) Psalm 2:7, as authoritatively quoted and interpreted by the Apostles (Acts 13:33; Heb. 1:5,6 in context; Rev. 1:5), points to Christ as the One first resurrected from the dead never to die again, which fact is the stamp of the Father's approval upon the substitutionary and mediatorial work of His Son. Rom. 1:4.
   3) Since God's begetting of His Son is spiritual, the Son *is* the very image of the invisible God, the brightness of His glory, the express image of His Person. 2 Cor. 4:4; Col. 1:15; Heb. 1:3.
   4) The Son of God is *begotten*, not made or created, and thus is fully *God*. John 1:1-3; Rom. 9:5.

3. The Son is a distinct Person.
   a. His eternal existence with God as the Word or Wisdom clearly expresses His distinct personality. Prov. 8:1,23,30; John 1:1.
   b. His being ordained from everlasting as mediator and covenant Head of the elect shows His personality. Psa. 2:2, 6-12; 89:3,4,26-29; Prov. 8:23; Eph. 1:3-6; 2 Tim. 1:9.
   c. His being sent in the fulness of time to

      Father and the Holy Spirit shows the distinctness of His personality. Isa. 48:16; Rom. 8:3; Gal. 4:4; 2 Tim. 1:10; 1 John 4:9,14.
   d. His becoming a sacrifice, thereby making satisfaction for the sins of the elect, plainly declares His personality. Since Christ is *Himself* the satisfaction, He must therefore be satisfying another, namely, the Father. Rom. 5:10,11; Eph. 5:2; Heb. 9:14; Rev. 5:9.
   e. His ascension into heaven and His position at the right hand of God show that He is a Person. Psa. 47:5; 68:17, 18; 110:1; John 20:17; Heb. 1:13.
   f. His advocacy and intercession with His Father is a plain proof of His distinct personality. John 14:16,17; Heb. 7:25; 9:24; 1 John 2:1.
   g. His judging the world at the last day proves that He is a Divine Person distinct from the Father and the Spirit. Matt. 25:31-41; John 5:22-29; Acts 10:42; 17:31.

4. The Deity of the Son (i.e., His being a Divine Person, truly and properly God) is revealed in several ways by the Scriptures.
   a. By His pre-existence: compare Num. 14:22; 21:5,6; and Psa. 95:9 with 1 Cor. 10:9; Psa. 102:26 (cf. Heb. 1:10, 11); Isa. 45:22,23 (cf. Rom. 14:11; 1 Cor. 1:30); John 1:1-17,30; 3:13,31; 6:38; 8:58; 13:3; 16:28; 1 Cor. 15:47; 2 Cor. 8:9; Heb. 1:10,11; 2:7,9,14,16; 1 John 4:2,3; Rev. 1:8,17; 2:8; 3:14. (See all references under II.A.4.a.,b.)
   b. By His names & titles:
      1) Lord, the Lord, my Lord and my God, and God and Saviour: Matt. 8:2; 12:8; 14:28; 17:15; 20:30; Luke 2:11; 17:5; John 4:1; 6:68; 20:28; 21:15-17; Acts 2:36; 2 Pet. 1:1 (Greek word order demands the translation, "our God and Saviour Jesus Christ"). In the N.T., the title *Lord* is the standard way of translating the O.T. name *Jehovah*, God's redemptive or covenant name. In the O.T., our English Bible renders *Jehovah* either *the LORD* or *GOD* (as in "Lord GOD"), utilizing capital letters to distinguish it from other names of God.
      2) Messiah (meaning *the Anointed*): Dan. 9:25; John 1:41; 4:25,26.
      3) Christ (meaning *the Anointed*; see Psa. 2:2): Matt. 1:16; 16:16; 23:10; Mark 8:29; Luke 4:41; 9:20; John 4:42; 11:27; 20:31; Acts 4:26,27; 8:37; 9:20-22; 10:36; 18:5,28; 20:21; 26:23; 1 John 2:22; 3:23; 4:2,3; 5:1.
      4) Son of God or the Son: Matt. 3:17; 8:29; 11:27; 14:33; 17:5; 27:54; Mark 1:1; 9:7; 14:61,62; Luke 1:32,35; 3:22; 4:41; 8:28; 9:35; 10:22; John 1:18,34,49; 3:16-18,35,36; 5:21,25; 6:69; 9:35-37.
      5) Image of God: 2 Cor. 4:4; Phil. 2:6; 3:21; Col. 1:15; Heb. 1:3.
      6) The Word or Word of God (*Logos*): John 1:1,14; 1 John 1:1; 5:7; Rev. 19:13.

7) Other selected Scriptures with Divine names ascribed to Christ: Isa. 9:6; 40:3 (cf. Mark 1:3); Jer. 23:5,6 (cf. 1 Cor. 1:30); Joel 2:32 (cf. Rom. 10:13); 1 Tim. 3:16; Tit. 2:13; 1 John 5:20.

c. By His attributes:

1) Eternity: Psa. 102:26 (cf. Heb. 1:11,12); Prov. 8:23; Isa. 9:6; Mic. 5:2; John 1:2; 8:28; 17:5; 1 John 1:2; Rev. 1:8,17,18; 22:13.

2) Immutability: Heb. 1:11,12; 13:8.

3) Omnipresence: Matt. 18:20; 28:20; John 3:13; 14:3; 17:24; Col. 1:17.

4) Omniscience: Matt. 9:4; 11:27; Luke 6:8; 22:10-12; John 2:23-25; 4:16-19,28,29; 5:42; 6:64; 13:1-3,10,11; 16:30-32; 18:4; 21:17; Col. 2:3; Rev. 2:19,23.

5) Omnipotence: Matt. 10:1; 28:18; Mark 4:39-41; John 5:21,28,29; 10:17,18,28; Phil. 3:20,21; Col. 1:17; Heb. 1:3; Rev. 1:8; 3:7.

d. By His works:

1) Creation: Prov. 8:23-31; John 1:3,10; Eph. 3:9; Col. 1:16,17; Heb. 1:2.

2) Preservation and Providence: Matt. 28:18; Col. 1:17; 2 Tim. 4:18; Heb. 1:3.

3) Miracles: Matt. 8:1-17,23-34; 12:10-13; 14:15-21,24-33; 15:22-39; 17:14-18,24-27; Mark 2:1-12; 4:39-41; Luke 5:4-11; 7:2-16; John 2:1-11; 4:46-54; 5:2-9,21, 26; 9:1-7; 11.

4) Judgment: Matt. 25:31-46; John 5:22-29; Acts 10:42; 17:31; Rom. 2:16; 14:10; 2 Cor. 5:10; 2 Tim. 4:1.

5) Forgiving sin: Matt. 9:2-8; Luke 7:36-50; Acts 5:31; Col. 3:13.

e. By the worship givef to, and properly belonging to, Him: Matt. 4:9,10; 8:2; 28:9; Luke 24:52; John 5:23; 9:35-38; 14:1; 20:24-29; Acts 7:59,60; 10:25, 26; 14:8-18; 1 Cor. 1:2; 2 Cor. 13:14; Phil. 2:9,10; Heb. 1:6; Rev. 1:5,6; 5:11,12; 7:10; 19:5-10.

**C. The Holy Spirit or the Third Person in the Holy Trinity**

1. The names applied to the Holy Spirit set forth His Deity.

a. The Holy Spirit (or Holy Ghost): Psa. 51:12; Isa. 63:10,11; Matt. 1:18; 3:11;12:32; 28:19; Mark 1:8; 3:29; 12:36; 13:11; Luke 2:25; 3:16,22.

b. The Spirit of God: Gen. 1:2; Matt. 3:16; 12:28; Rom. 8:9,14; 15:19; 1 Cor. 2:11,14; 3:16.

c. The Spirit of the Father: Matt. 10:20.

d. The Spirit: Matt. 4:1; 12:18; Mark 1:10,12; Luke 2:27; 4:14; John 1:32,-33; 3:5-8,34; 6:63; 7:39; Acts 2:4.

e. The Spirit of the Lord: Judg. 3:10; 6:34; 11:29; 1 Sam. 10:6; 16:13; 19:23; 1 Kin. 18:12; Isa. 11:2; Luke 4:18; 2 Cor. 3:17,18 (vs. 18 says literally, "as by the Lord the Spirit").

f. The Spirit of Christ: Rom. 8:2,9; Phil. 1:19; 1 Pet. 1:11.

g. The Spirit of the Son: Gal. 4:6.

h. The Comforter: John 14:16,26; 15:26; 16:7.

i. The Spirit of Truth: John 14:17; 15:26; 16:13.

2. There is a relational property (or personal relationship) that is unique to the Holy Spirit and that distinguishes Him from the two other Persons of the Trinity: He is breathed. As the Son is always with the Father, so the Holy Spirit, their *Breath*, is always with the Father and the Son. Job 33:4; Psa. 33:6; Ezek. 37:9; Gal. 4:6; 2 Thess. 2:8.

a. The acts of the Holy Spirit upon creatures, in which He is said to "breathe," are not the source of His name *Spirit*, or *Breath*; they merely display by analogy that property of relationship that has eternally distinguished Him from the Father and the Son. However, such acts do serve as accurate symbols to illustrate His original character. In the words of the Nicene Creed, He is "the Lord, and Giver of life." Gen. 2:7; Ezek. 37:9,10; John 3:8; 20:22; 2 Tim. 3:16; 2 Pet. 1:21.

b. In the language of the western version of the Nicene Creed, the Holy Spirit "*proceedeth* from the Father and the Son." However, His procession from, or being sent forth by, the Father and the Son, though illustrating His distinction from them, is not the cause of that distinction, but merely evidence of His office, that being the Convincer and Comforter of men and the Applier of all grace to them. Ezek. 36:26,27; Luke 11:13; John 14:16,17, 26; 15:26; 16:7-15; Eph. 1:13,14.

3. The Holy Spirit is a distinct Person.

a. The Holy Spirit is a Person within the Holy Trinity, not a mere force, power, or energy.

1) Several aspects of personality are ascribed to Him.

a) He is self-existent (He could not give life if He did not have life in Himself). Job 33:4; John 6:63; Rom. 8:11; 2 Cor. 3:6; 1 Pet. 3:18.

b) He has a will of His own. John 3:8; Acts 16:6,7; 1 Cor. 12:11.

c) He has understanding (see Psa. 94:10). Neh. 9:20; Isa. 11:2; 40:13; Luke 12:12; John 14:26; 16:13; 1 Cor. 2:11; 12:8; 1 Tim. 4:1; 1 Pet. 1:11; 2 Pet. 1:21; 1 John 2:27.

2) Personal actions are ascribed to Him.

a) He convinces. John 16:8.
b) He teaches. John 14:26; 1 John 2:27.
c) He comforts. John 16:7.
d) He testifies concerning Christ. John 15:26.
e) He witnesses to God's people that they are His children. Rom. 8:16.
f) He intercedes. Zech. 12:10; Rom. 8:26,27.
g) He gives gifts to men. 1 Cor. 12:8-11.
h) He searches. 1 Cor. 2:10,11.
i) He judges. Acts 15:28.
j) He hears. John 16:13.
k) He speaks. Acts 13:2; Rev. 2:7; 14:13; 22:17.
l) He commands. Acts 20:28.

3) Personal affections are attributed to Him.
a) Love: Rom. 15:30.
b) Grief: Eph. 4:30.
c) Vexation: Isa. 63:10.

4) He is the object of such actions of men as only a Person can be.
a) He can be blasphemed. Matt. 12:31; Mark 3:29; Luke 12:10.
b) He can be lied to. Acts 5:3.
c) He can be tempted or tried, i.e., challenged to prove His power and holiness. Acts 5:9.
d) He can be insulted. Heb. 10:29.

b. That the Holy Spirit is a Person distinct from the Father and the Son is proved by the Scriptures.
1) He is sent from both the Father and the Son. John 14:16,26; 15:26; 16:7; Gal. 4:6.
2) He is called "another Comforter" (implying that there are other Persons regarded as Comforters). John 14:16 (cf. Luke 2:25; 2 Cor. 1:3,4).
3) His actions are distinguished from those of the Father and the Son. Gen. 6:3; John 16:14.
4) His appearances are distinguished from those of the two other Persons in the Holy Trinity. Matt. 3:16,17; Luke 3:22; John 1:32; Acts 2:2-4.
5) He is (together with the Father and the Son) One into whose name we are baptized. Matt. 28:19.
6) He is a witness (distinct from the Father and the Word) in the record born in heaven. 1 John 5:7.

4. The Deity of the Holy Spirit (i.e., His being a Divine Person, truly and properly God) is revealed in several ways by the Scriptures.

a. He pre-existed, otherwise He could not have created. Gen. 1:2; Job 26:13; 33:4; Psa. 104:30.

b. Names of God are applied to Him.
1) The LORD or Jehovah: 2 Sam. 23:2; Psa. 78:19-21,40,41 (cf. Isa. 63:10); Psa. 95:6-11 (cf. Heb. 3:7-11); Luke 1:68-70 (cf. Acts 1:16; Heb. 1:1; 2 Pet. 1:21).
2) Lord (*Adonai* in O.T., *Kyrios* in N.T.): Isa. 6:5,9 (cf. Acts 28:25, 26); 2 Cor. 3:17,18; 2 Thess. 3:5.
3) God: Acts 5:3,4; 1 Cor. 3:16 (cf. 6:19,20).

c. The attributes of God are His attributes.
1) Eternity: Heb. 9:14.
2) Omnipresence: Psa. 139:7,8.
3) Omniscience: John 14:26; 16:13; Acts 11:28; 20:23; 1 Cor. 2:10, 11; 1 Pet. 1:11.
4) Omnipotence (the Holy Spirit is referred to as "the finger of God"): Ex. 8:19; 31:18; Deut. 9:10; Mic. 3:8; Matt. 12:28; Luke 1:35; 11:20.
5) Holiness: Rom. 1:4.

d. The works of the Holy Spirit are works that only God can perform.
1) Creation: Gen. 1:2; Job 26:13; 33:4; Psa. 104:30.
2) Providence: Isa. 40:6,7,13,14.
3) Inspiration of Scripture (all Scripture is God-*breathed*, 2 Tim. 3:16): 2 Pet. 1:21.
4) The virgin birth of Christ: Matt. 1:18-23.
5) The anointing of Christ with gifts and graces: Psa. 45:7; Isa. 61:1; John 3:34.
6) The miracles of Christ: Matt. 12:28; Luke 11:20.
7) The miracles of the apostles: Rom. 15:19; Heb. 2:3,4.
8) Regeneration and renewal: John 3:5; Tit. 3:5.
9) Sanctification: 1 Pet. 1:2. The resurrection of Christ: Rom. 1:4; 8:11.

e. The worship which is due the Spirit of God proves that He is God.
1) The temples in which He dwells, whether the local church or the individual believer, are made by Him and for Him. 1 Cor. 3:16; 6:19,20; Eph. 2:22.
2) Baptism is administered in His name. Matt. 28:19.
3) Swearing is done by the Spirit, and is therefore an act of worship. Deut. 6:13; Rom. 9:1.
4) Benedictions are given in His name. 2 Cor. 13:14; 2 Thess. 3:5; Rev. 1:4.

**IV. The Persons of the Trinity took counsel together in making the Covenant of Grace.**

**A. The Council of Grace**

1. Counsel, consultation, and deliberation can be ascribed to all three Persons of the Trinity.

a. What this does not mean:
1) This does not mean that God lacked any knowledge when He formed the plan of salvation. (See the appendix on the Sovereignty of God, I.C.)
2) Consultation among the Persons of the Trinity was not for the purpose of gaining wisdom. (See the appendix on the Sovereignty of God, I.A.3.; I.C.)
3) A council among the three Divine Persons does not presuppose any inequality among them. Isa. 28:29; Jer. 32:19.
a) The Father knows all things. (See the appendix on the Sovereignty of God, I.C.)
b) The Son knows all things (see this outline, III.B.4.c.4.).
c) The Spirit searches the deep things of God. 1 Cor. 2:10.

b. What this does mean:
1) When the Persons of the Trinity are said to have consulted about the salvation of man, the intent is to express the importance of this council. (See the appendix on the Sovereignty of God, IV.C.1.)
2) This manner of speaking is used in order to magnify the wisdom of God. Eph. 1:7,8; 3:10.
3) Since there is perfect unity in the Godhead, we may rightly assume their perfect unanimity concerning the salvation of men (see this outline, I.A.).
a) The Son volunteered to be sent as the Redeemer. Heb. 10:7,9.
b) The Father and Holy Spirit sent the Son. Isa. 48:16.

2. The Scriptures teach that there was a council among the Persons of the Godhead concerning the salvation of men.
a. Express passages describe such an eternal agreement: Psa. 33:11; 40:7,8; 89:3; Prov. 19:21; Isa. 14:27; 26:10; 42:6; 46:10; 49:8; Zech. 6:13; Mal. 3:1; Luke 2:14; 7:30; Acts 20:27; Rom. 9:11; 11:5; 1 Cor. 2:7; Eph. 1:4,5,9,11; 3:11; Heb. 6:17; 10:5.
b. Eternal life for believers was purposed in eternity past, who were promised to God the Son as an inheritance. Psa. 2:7,8; John 6:37-40; 17:1-3; Eph. 1:4.
c. Christ is clearly set forth in Scripture as the federal Head of the whole company of redeemed humanity. Since Adam, our first federal representative, entered into a covenant of works on our behalf, we may rightly infer that Christ, our second federal representative, has also entered into covenant on our behalf. Rom. 5:17,18; 1 Cor. 15:22,45,47.

3. The nature of this council is set forth explicitly and implicitly in Scripture.
a. Since it is part of God's eternal decree or purpose, it is eternal. (See III.A.1. in the appendix on the Sovereignty of God.)
b. It is unchangeable. (See III.A.2., *op. cit.*)
c. It is particular. (See IV.C.3., *op. cit.*)
d. It is unconditional. (See III.A.4., *op. cit.*)
e. It is righteous. (See III.A.5., *op. cit.*)
f. It is efficacious. (See III.A.6., *op. cit.*)

4. Since, according to God's all-wise and holy purpose, man would fail to obey perfectly God's moral law and would thus come under its penalty, God the Son pledged to fulfil several necessary conditions laid down by the Council of Grace.
a. Christ undertook to do the following *in the place* of His people, i.e., as their Substitute:
1) To obey the law perfectly: Psa. 40:6,8; Matt. 5:17; Gal. 4:4,5; Heb. 10:5,10.
2) To bear the penalty for their sins: Isa. 53:4-12; 2 Cor. 5:21; Gal. 3:13.
b. As mediator between God and men, Christ undertook to do the following *on behalf of* His people in His prophetic, priestly, and kingly offices:
1) As Prophet, to instruct them by various means in all ages and to guide them into all truth necessary for their salvation. Psa. 22:22; John 1:18; 15:15; 17:12-14; Eph. 4:11-13; Heb. 1:1,2; 1 Pet. 1:10-12.
2) As Priest, to offer Himself a sacrifice to God as a reconciliation for the sins of His people, and to make continual intercession for them. Heb. 2:17; 7:25; 9:14,28.
3) As King, to call out of the world a people to Himself, to govern them, and to protect and preserve them from all their enemies. Isa. 33:22; 55:4,5; Acts 15:14-16; 1 Cor. 15:25.

5. In the Council of Grace God the Father and God the Holy Spirit pledged themselves to fulfil certain conditions on behalf of God the Son:
a. To create for, and join to, the Son a full and pure human nature for the fulfillment of His redemptive work. Heb. 10:5.
b. To endue this God-man, Jesus Christ, with the Holy Spirit above all measure for the fulfillment of His great work. Isa. 11:1,2; 49:2; 61:1,2; John 3:34.
c. To uphold Him under His heavy task. Isa. 42:1-7.
d. To give Him an elect seed as the sure reward for His labors. Isa. 49:6; 53:10.
e. To exalt Him, giving Him all authority. Psa. 2:6; Phil. 2:9,10.

**B. The Covenant of Grace**

1. The different uses of the word *covenant* in Scripture demonstrate the breadth and fulness of the Covenant of Grace and the richness of its significance.
   a. Sometimes the word *covenant* is used for an ordinance, precept, commandment, or code of statutes. Num. 18:19; Deut. 4:13; Jer. 34:13,14.
   b. The making of a covenant, when ascribed to God, is often simply a promise, which He is bound by His immutable character to perform. Isa. 59:21; Eph. 2:12; 1 John 2:25.
   c. We read of God's one-sided covenants (i.e., in which nothing is contributed by man). Gen. 8:22; 9:9-17; Jer. 33:20-22; Hos. 2:18.
   d. Covenants between man and man contain stipulations, in which they make promises or conditions to be performed by both parties. Gen. 14:13; 26:28; 1 Sam. 20:15,16,42; 23:18.
   e. The Covenant of Grace was made between God and Christ, with the elect viewed by God as incorporated *in* Christ, their federal Head and Representative. Psa. 40:6-8; Isa. 49:1-6; 53:10-12; John 17:4,5.
2. The Scriptures give several names to this transaction, or Covenant of Grace, between the Father, the Son, and the Holy Spirit:
   a. Covenant of life: Psa. 21:4; Mal. 2:5; 2 Tim. 1:1; Tit. 1:2.
   b. Covenant of peace: Isa. 54:10; Mic. 5:2,5; Mal. 2:5.
   c. Everlasting covenant: Gen. 17:7; 2 Sam. 23:5; Heb. 13:20.
   d. Holy Covenant: Luke 1:72.
3. That the Covenant is one in all ages is proved by the following lines of evidence:
   a. From direct Scripture testimony. Gen. 17:7; Jer. 31:33; Luke 1:68-73; John 8:56; Acts 2:16,38,39; 3:25; Rom. 4:16; 2 Cor. 6:16; Gal. 3:8,16,17; Rev. 21:3.
   b. From the identity or singularity of the Mediator in all ages. Mal. 3:1; Luke 24:27; Acts 4:12; 10:43; 15:10,11; Rom. 3:25; Gal. 3:16; 1 Tim. 2:5,6; Heb. 9:15; 1 Pet. 1:9-12.
   c. From its condition (faith) being the same in all ages. Faith is a gift, and the appointed instrument for receiving the gracious redemption purchased by Christ our Surety. Gen. 15:6; Ex. 29:45; Deut. 5:2,3,6; Psa. 2:12; 32:10; Jer. 24:7; 30:22; 31:33; Ezek. 11:20; Zech. 13:9; Mark 16:16; John 3:16; 11:26; Acts 8:37; 10:43; Rom. 4:3; 2 Cor. 6:16; Eph. 2:8,9; Heb. 8,10,11.
   d. From its promise being the same, i.e., including the same *spiritual* provisions, in all ages:
      1) Justification: Psa. 32; Isa. 1:18.
      2) Regeneration: Deut. 30:6; Psa. 51:10.
      3) Spiritual gifts: Isa. 40:31; Joel 2:28,32.
      4) Eternal life: Ex. 3:6; Matt. 22:31, 32; Heb. 4:9.
      5) The resurrection of the body: Job 19:25; Psa. 16:10,11; Dan. 12:1,2; Acts 13:34.
   e. From the types and anti-types:
      1) The promised land Canaan—heaven, our spiritual rest.
      2) The deliverance from Egypt—Christ's redemption from the bondage of sin.
      3) The Levitical priesthood—Christ, our Priest forever.
      4) The Levitical sacrifices—Christ, our final and only sufficient sacrifice for sin.
   f. From the moral law being in effect in all ages.
      1) The word "law" has various meanings in Scripture.
         a) Sometimes it refers to the Pentateuch or five books of Moses. Luke 24:44; John 1:45; 8:5.
         b) Sometimes it refers to all the books in the Old Testament. John 10:34; 12:34; 15:25.
         c) Sometimes it refers to the Scriptures in general. Psa. 19:7.
         d) Sometimes it refers to the Messiah's teaching in particular. Isa. 2:3; 42:4. (In the N.T. it is called the law of faith, Rom. 3:27.)
         e) Sometimes it signifies the whole body of laws given by God through Moses, to the children of Israel. John 1:17.
      2) The law of God given through Moses may be divided into ceremonial, civil, and moral.
         a) Ceremonial: the Jewish priesthood, sacrifices, feasts, fasts, and washings were shadows and types of Christ's work. These were a schoolmaster to the Jews until Christ came to fulfil the shadows and types. 2 Cor. 3:11; Gal. 4:9, 10,21; Eph. 2:15; Col. 2:14-17; Heb. 7:12,16,18,19,28; 8:4,5; 9:1-10,19-24; 10:1,8; 12:27.
         b) Civil: laws that pertained to the political or civil government of the Jews and were peculiar to the Jewish nation as a theocracy and are not binding on others. Those laws founded upon the character of God, being universal, remain for all nations to follow. Deut. 17:8-11.

c) Moral: those laws categorically summarized in the Ten Commandments or Decalogue. Ex. 20:3-17; Deut. 5:6-21.

Christ summed up the two tables of the Law into love to God and love to one's neighbor. Matt. 22:36-40; Rom. 13:9,10.

3) God is the author of the moral law.
   a) Moral law has existed at least since the creation of man, as evidenced by the fact that ". . . death reigned from Adam to Moses . . ." (Rom. 5:14). Death is the appointed punishment for sin (Gen. 2:17; Rom. 3:23). And, "Sin is the transgression of the law" (1 John 3:4).
   b) God gave the moral law to Moses on stone, signifying its permanence, in order that sinful men might remember it. When it was given on Mt. Sinai, it was accompanied by a most terrifying display of the power and holiness of God, that all might know how offensive sin is to God (Ex. 19:10-25; 20:18-21; Rom. 7:13; Heb. 12:18-21). However, the legalistic Jews, seeking salvation by keeping the Law, failed to see the heart issues of the Law and became enslaved to a wooden, external lawkeeping. 2 Cor. 3:6; Gal. 4:21-31.
   c) The moral law was not given as a means of salvation (i.e., as a covenant of works), but as a manifestation of the Covenant of Grace. Ex. 2:23-25; 3:6,7; Deut. 4:6,8; 7:8,9,12; Psa. 105; 147:19,-20; Isa. 41:8; Rom. 9:4.
   d) The moral law was given in a special way to Israel, in order that Christ, who was to be born of the Jews, might be made under the Law. Christ obeyed the Law perfectly, fulfilling our obligation to obey it perfectly; He also bore the curse of the Law in His substitutionary sufferings and death, fulfilling our obligation to pay its just penalty. He thus became the fulfillment of the Law, having met its goal. Matt. 3:15; 5:17-19; John 15:10; Rom. 8:3,4; 10:3,4; 2 Cor. 5:21; Gal. 3:21; 4:4,5; Heb. 10:7.

4) The wholesome properties or qualities of the moral law commend it to every man's conscience.
   a) It is perfect. Psa. 19:7,8; 119:72,75,86,128,129,138; Rom. 12:2.
   b) It is spiritual. Rom. 7:14.
   c) It is holy. Rom. 7:12.
   d) It is just. Deut. 4:8; Psa. 19:9; Rom. 7:12.

5) The moral law is appropriate for the needs of every human being.
   a) For unbelievers:
      (1) To convict of sin. Rom. 3:20; 7:7.
      (2) To restrain from sin. As evidenced by Christ's teaching, it particularly restrains outward sin in the unregenerate. Matt. 5:27, 28.
      (3) To condemn and punish for sin. 1 Tim. 1:9,10.
   b) For believers:
      (1) To point out God's will concerning duty toward God and our fellowmen. Deut. 8:3; Job 23:12; Psa. 40:8; 143:10; John 7:17; 9:31; Rom. 12:2; 1 Thess. 4:3; 5:18; 1 Pet. 2:2,15; 1 John 2:3,17; 3:22; 4:20,21; 5:2,3,14.
      (2) To be a rule of life, i.e., the guiding standard for all thoughts, words, and deeds for those who have been saved through faith alone. Deut. 11:18; 30:14; Psa. 19:8; 119:11,105,130; Prov. 6:23; 2 Pet. 1:19.
      (3) To be a mirror, reflecting an accurate and objective image of man's true character. Psa. 51:3; 119:96; Isa. 64:6; 2 Cor. 3:18; Jas. 1:22-25; 1 John 1:8-10; 2:4.
      (4) To cause us to prize and to value the righteousness of Christ Jesus above any and every temporal thing. 1 Cor. 1:30,31; 2 Cor. 5:21; Eph. 4:23,24; Phil.

6) The moral law of God continues in force under the present dispensation for the reasons given above. Matt. 5:17; Rom. 3:31.

a) It does not continue as a covenant of works, for God has not made a covenant of works since Adam's fall (though presumptuous men continue to make them). Believers are not *under the Law* as a means of salvation (or covenant of works) but *under grace* in the Covenant of Grace. Rom. 6:14.

b) The Fourth Commandment does not continue in the form administered by Moses, but is changed by authority of Christ's example and that of the apostles. The time of worship prescribed in the Fourth Commandment was temporary and typical. We now worship on the Lord's Day by following Scriptural warrant:

(1) Christ's resurrection was on the first day of the week. Matt. 28:1,2, 6; Mark 16:2-6,9; Luke 24:1-3; John 20:1.

(2) Christ's appearances to the disciples were on the first day of the week. Luke 24:13-36; John 20:19,26.

(3) The outpouring of the Holy Spirit took place on Pentecost, which was on the first day of the week. This signifies the beginning of the new dispensation. Acts 2:1-4.

c) It is not a terrifying or condemning law to believers. Ezek. 36:26,27; John 5:24; Rom. 7:6; 8:1,33; Gal. 3:13; Heb. 8:10-12; 12:18-24.

d) Believers are not without moral law in their relationship to God, but are under the moral law as the willing and happy subjects of King Jesus. Psa. 119:142-144,160; 1 Cor. 9:21; 1 John 5:2,3.

4. There are only two dispensations, one before the coming of Christ, and the other after it. Thus we distinguish between the *first* and *second* dispensations, or the *old* and *new* covenants. Heb. 8:7,8,13; 9:1,15; 12:24. By *first* and *old* is meant the first administration of the Covenant of Grace, which stretched from the fall of Adam to the first advent of Christ. *Second* and *new* designate the age following the redemptive work of Christ. 2 Cor. 3:6,14; Gal. 4:22-26; Heb. 9:15.

a. The agreements between the two dispensations or administrations:

1) They agree in having one efficient cause: God. Gen. 17:2; 2 Sam. 23:5 (cf. Heb. 8:8-13; 10:15-17); Psa. 89:3,34.

2) They agree in having one moving cause: the sovereign mercy, and free grace of God. Psa. 89:2; Luke 1:72-75 (cf. 1:78); John 1:17.

3) They agree in recognizing one Mediator of the Covenant of Grace: Christ, thesseed of the woman. Gen. 3:15; 49:10; Job 19:25 (cf. 1 Tim. 2:5); Isa. 53:10-12; Heb. 8:6; 9:15; 12:24.

4) They agree in the subjects of this one Covenant: the elect of God. 1 Kin. 19:18; Isa. 4:3; Jer. 31:7; Mic. 2:12 (cf. Matt. 20:16); Luke 18:7; Rom. 8:33; Eph. 1:3,4; 1 Pet. 2:5,9,10.

5) They agree in the blessings enjoyed:

a) Salvation and redemption. 2 Sam. 23:5; Heb. 9:15.

b) Justification by the righteousness of Christ. Isa. 45:24,25; Rom. 3:21-23.

c) Forgiveness of sin through faith in Christ. Psa. 32:1,5; Isa. 43:25; Acts 10:43.

d) Regeneration. Deut. 30:6; Phil. 3:3.

e) Eternal life. Job 19:26,27; Acts 13:48; Rom. 2:7; 1 Tim. 6:12; Heb. 11:10.

b. The distinctions between the two administrations of the Covenant of Grace:

1) Under the first administration, saints looked forward to the Christ who was to come and the good things that He would bring. Under the New Covenant, saints look backward to Christ who has come and the promised blessings brought by Him. Heb. 2:2,3,9,10.

2) The first administration was not characterized by the clarity of understanding that is enjoyed under the second. 2 Cor. 3:13,18; Heb. 10:1.

3) There is more of a spirit of liberty, and less of a spirit of bondage, under the second administration than under the first. Rom. 8:15; Gal. 4:1-3,24-26.

4) There is a larger effusion of the Spirit in the second administration. Jer. 31:31-34; Joel 2:28,29; Zech. 12:10; John 1:17.

5) The latter administration of the Covenant extends to far more people than the former. Gal. 3:14; Eph. 2:12-19; 3:5,6.

6) The present dispensation of the Covenant will continue to the end of the world, but the former dispensation ended when Christ

came. Luke 16:16; 2 Cor. 3:11; Heb. 9:10.

7) The ordinances of divine service in the first administration were earthly shadows, and temporary. The ordinances now are spiritual, clear and unshakeable. Heb. 9:1, 10,11,23,24; 12:27.

8) Though the promises and blessings of grace under both administrations are the same, yet they are exhibited in different manners, the second being called "better." Heb. 7:22; 8:6; 9:23; 10:34; 11:40.

5. The Covenant of Grace is revealed progressively in Scripture and exhibited in the lives of God's people historically. The foundation for all manifestations of God's saving grace is laid with the announcement of the Seed (Christ), promised in Genesis 3:15. This promise was the first revelation of God's gracious purpose toward fallen man. Luke 10:17-19; John 12:31; Rom. 16:20; Gal. 3:16; Heb. 2:14; Rev. 12:9; 20:2. The Covenant was continued with further revelations to subsequent generations:

a. Noah. Gen. 6:8,9,18; 9:9,11-17; Heb. 11:7; 2 Pet. 2:5; Compare Isa. 54:7-10.

b. Abraham. Gen. 12:1-3; 14:18,19; 15:1,6,18; 17:1,2,4,7-11,13,14,19,21; 22:15-18; Matt. 1:1; John 8:56 (cf. Heb. 7:1-3); Rom. 4:2,3,11,13,22-24; Gal. 3:6-9,14-18. Circumcision stood for the separation of God's Covenant people from other peoples, and symbolized regeneration, which would characterize God's true people. Deut. 10:16; 30:6; Jer. 4:4; 9:26; Rom. 2:28,29; Eph. 2:11; Phil. 3:3; Col. 2:11.

c. Isaac. Gen. 26:2-4,28; Rom. 9:7.

d. Jacob. Gen. 25:23; 28:4,13-15; 32:24-30; 49:1,2,10; Rom. 9:11-13.

e. The children of Israel at Sinai. Ex. 6:4-8; Num. 25:12,13; Deut. 4:31; 5:23.

1) God covenanted with them at Sinai in mercy, not in judicial wrath; as their Redeemer and Deliverer, not as their Destroyer. Ex. 19:3-6; 20:2; 34:6,7; Psa. 78:35.

2) All the essential parties, features, and the very formula of the Covenant of Grace that were manifested earlier to Abraham and to his descendants are present in the compact at Sinai. Lev. 26:9-13; Jer. 11:4; 30:20-22; Ezek. 16:3-6 (cf. Ex. 3:7).

3) The giving of the Law at Sinai did not, indeed could not, nullify the everlasting Covenant of Grace manifested and promised to Abraham 430 years earlier. Rather, the Law was given because they *were* His people. Personal experience of the grace of God is the basis for lawkeeping. Ex. 3:6-10; Deut. 7:6-12; Psa. 105:6,8-11,24-26,42-45; Isa. 41:8; Gal. 3:17.

4) The very "book of the testimony" and all the utensils of the sanctuary were purified with blood to foreshadow the truth that Christ's blood must be the real propitiation carried for sinners into the upper sanctuary. Thus, the more commandments for Levitical sacrifices we find the more Gospel we discover. Heb. 9:18-28.

5) Christ expressly says that Moses taught of Him. Therefore, Moses taught the Gospel, salvation by grace through faith, not salvation by works. Luke 24:27; John 5:46. Compare Rom. 10:6-8 with Lev. 18:5 and Deut. 30:11.

6) In all the places where the secular, theocratic compact is stated as a covenant of works (i.e., Lev. 18:5; Jer. 31:29; Ezek. 18), the duties required are secular, and the good gained or forfeited is national. God's transaction with Israel was two-fold:

a) The corporate, theocratic, political (physical) nation was the shell. The elect (spiritual) seed were the kernel. Rom. 10,11.

b) The secular promise was the type; the spiritual promise of redemption through Christ was the antitype.

c) The Law was added as "a schoolmaster" to bring God's people, the spiritual seed mixed with physical Israel, to Christ. However, carnal people abused the Law, even as they do now, by attempting to establish their own righteousness under it. Gal. 3:24.

d) Thus, in Jeremiah 31:31-34, the prophet *seems* to assert an opposition between the New Covenant (which Hebrews 7 explains as the Covenant of Grace) and that made with Israel at the Exodus. The difference is between the relative prominence of Law and Grace. Jeremiah is viewing the covenant at Sinai in one of its limited aspects, which is here made an antithesis to the Covenant of Grace. It is the secular, theocratic portion in which political and temporal prosperity in Canaan was promised, and calamity threatened, on the conditions of obedience or rebellion. In this aspect the Old Covenant had miserably failed, because physical Israel had been dominated in every generation since Sinai by a (lesser or greater) majority of unregenerate covenant-breakers. The New Covenant would be eminently successful, in that each and every one of its members would have a renewed heart with God's Law written upon it, each would personally know the LORD, and each would enjoy in a new way the complete forgiveness of his sins.

e) The self-righteous Jews, throwing away all the gracious features of their national compact and thus perverting its real nature, were founding all their pride and hopes on this secular feature.

7) In the places where God promises to write His Law in their hearts and cause them to walk in obedience, He is referring to the spiritual aspect of the Covenant which is most consonant with the Covenant of Grace. Jer. 31:31-34; Ezek. 11:19,20; 36:26,27.

f. David (a type of Christ). 2 Sam. 23:2-5; Psa. 89:3,4,20; 111:5-10; Ezek. 34:23,24; 37:24; Hos. 3:5; Acts 1:16; 2:30.

g. Solomon. 2 Sam. 7:14-16.

h. The prophets. Isa. 42:6; 49:8; 54:7-10; 55:3; 56:4-6; 59:21; 61:8; Jer. 31:31-34; 32:40; 33:20-22; Ezek.16:60; 34:25; 37:26; Zech. 9:11; Mal. 2:5; 3:1; Luke 1:72.

6. The Father takes part in the application of the Covenant of Grace in ways appropriate to His office within the Godhead:

a. Effectual calling (not to be confused with the universal call of Matthew 22:14 and Acts 17:30, where all men are called to believe).

1) The Author of this call is God the Father. John 6:45,64,65; Rom. 1:6,7; 8:30; 1 Cor. 1:9,26; Gal. 1:15,16; Eph. 1:17,18; Phil. 2:13; 2 Tim. 1:8,9; 2 Pet. 1:10; 1 John 3:1.

2) This call is an irresistible summons, since it comes from the Almighty God, whose will cannot be frustrated.

a) It is irresistible. Ezek. 11:19; 36:26; Rom. 4:17; Eph. 1:19.

b) It is immutable. Rom. 11:29.

c) It is high, holy, and heavenly. Eph. 4:1; Phil. 3:14; 2 Tim. 1:9; Heb. 3:1.

3) The subjects of this call are those whom the Father predestinated, His elect. Rom. 8:19,20,33; 11:7; 1 Cor. 1:2; Eph. 1:10,11; 2 Thess. 2:13,14; Rev. 17:14.

4) The pattern of this call is grounded solely in the Father's sovereign good pleasure, in setting His love upon whom He pleased, and in the ratifying of His own purpose by the Council of Grace (see this outline, IV.A.). Rom. 9:16; Eph. 1:5,6.

a) This pattern shows *determinate* purpose. Rom. 8:28; 2 Tim. 1:9.

b) It is eternal, since His purpose was established before creation. 2 Tim. 1:9; Tit. 1:2.

c) This effectual call comes to elect *sinners* whom God the Father looks upon as being *in Christ*, a union that has existed in His mind from eternity past and is essential to their salvation in time and space. Rom. 8:29,30; Eph. 1:4; 3:11; 2 Tim. 1:9.

5) Effectual calling is the first step in the application of redemption to the individual sinner. John 6:44; Acts 16:14.

b. Justification:

1) In Scripture term signifying the *declaration* of an unrighteous man as righteous in the sight of God.

a) The Hebrew and Greek words rendered *justification* are set over against terms rendered *condemnation*. Deut. 25:1; Prov. 17:15; Isa. 5:23; Jer. 3:11; Matt. 12:37; Rom. 5:16; 8:33,34.

b) All of the tejms with which justification is associated bear the character of legal proceedings and judgment. Gen. 18:25; Ex. 23:7; Psa. 32:1; 143:2; Ezek. 16:50,51; Rom. 2:2,15; 8:33; 14:10; Col. 2:14; 1 John 2:1.

c) Equivalent expressions that are sometimes substituted for this word clearly do *not* mean infusion of righteousness. They do signify either the forgiveness of sin or the acceptance of the sinner. Thus, justification effects a change in one's legal standing before God, and not in one's own moral or spiritual character (though transformation of character is an infallible accompaniment—see this outline, IV.B.8.d.).

2) The Author of justification is God the Father, who spared not His own Son, but delivered Him up for us. Rom. 8:32,33.

3) Justification is an act of God's free grace, wherein He pardons all our sins, and accepts us as righteous in His sight, only on the basis of the righteousness of Christ; it is received by faith alone. Jer. 23:6; John 1:12; 6:44, 45,65; Acts 10:43; 13:38,39; Rom. 3:22-28; 4:5-8; 5:15-19; 8:30; 1 Cor. 1:30,31; 2 Cor. 5:19,21; Eph. 1:7; 2:7,8; Phil. 1:29; 3:9; Tit. 3:5,7.

4) The subjects of justification are those whom the Father predestinated to eternal life through sanctification of the Spirit and belief of the truth. Rom. 8:30,33; 2 Thess. 2:13; Tit. 3:7.

5) Justification takes place as the result of one's having been effectually called, i.e., brought forth from spiritual death to spiritual life by the Holy Spirit. This *new birth* must occur *before* one can exercise repentance toward God and faith toward Christ, which are the conditions upon which one may receive justification. John 3:5; Acts 20:21; Rom. 8:30; Eph. 2:8,9.

c. Adoption

1) The Author of adoption is God the Father. John 20:17; 2 Thess. 2:16; 1 John 3:1,2.

2) The nature of adoption is such that it is inseparable from justification.

a) The person who is justified is also, infallibly, the recipient of sonship. John 1:12,13; Gal. 3:26.

b) Adoption, like justification, is a judicial act. It is the bestowal of a standing, status, or relationship, not the generating within us of a new nature or character (though that is an infallible accompaniment—see this outline, IV.B.8.a.). It is the gift of sonship. Deut. 14:2; Isa. 43:1; 63:16; John 1:12; 11:52; 2 Cor. 6:18.

c) Those adopted into God's family are given the Spirit of adoption. Rom. 8:15,16; Gal. 4:5-7.

3) The subjects of adoption are those whom the Father has predestinated according to the good pleasure of His will. John 17:2; Eph. 1:5; 1 John 3:10.

4) Adoption takes place simultaneously with justification. Rom. 8:15,16; Eph. 1:15.

7. The Son, as mediator, takes part in the application of the Covenant of Grace in ways appropriate to His office within the Godhead: Isa. 42:6; 49:8.

a. A mediator is one who intervenes to act between parties who cannot, or will not, act with each other directly (1 Tim. 2:5). A mediator between God and man was given for the following reasons:

1) God, out of His own perfections, deemed it necessary for sinful man, who had lost fellowship with God at the Fall (Gen. 3), to have a Mediator in the Covenant of Grace. Isa. 53; Matt. 1:21; John 3:16.

2) Man's enmity, evil conscience, and guilty fear call for a Mediator. Gen. 6:5; 8:21; Psa. 51:5; Jer. 17:9; Matt. 15:19; John 3:18-20,36; Rom. 1:18, 21,24,25,28-32; 2:15; 3:10-18,23; 8:7; Gal. 3:22; Eph. 2:2,3; 4:18; Tit. 1:15; 1 John 1:8,10.

b. Christ is our Covenant Head. Hos. 1:11; Matt. 11:27; 23:10; John 3:35; Eph. 1:22,23; 4:15,16; 5:23; Col. 1:18; 2:19.

1) All of God's people were chosen *in Christ* as their Representative before the world began. 2 Cor. 1:20; Gal. 3:17; Eph. 1:4; 2 Tim. 1:1.

2) Christ undertook to obey the Law perfectly and then to suffer the penalty of sin on behalf of His people, as their Head and Representative. Rom. 8:4; 10:4; 2 Cor. 5:21; Eph. 1:10; 2:5,6; Col. 2:12; 3:1; 1 Tim. 3:16.

c. It was necessary that Christ should assume a human nature in union with His Divine nature.

1) This was nekessary so that Christ could be related to His people as a near kinsman. See this outline, IV.B.7.h.(1)(a), (3)(a). Lev. 25:48,49; Ruth 2:20; 3:9,12,13; 4:1-11.

2) It was fit that the Mediator should be a man, so that we might relate to Him as one who also was tempted and suffered as we do. Heb. 2:17,18; 4:15.

3) God gave our Redeemer a human nature in order to set before us a perfect human example. Matt. 11:29; 16:24; John 13:15; Rom. 15:5; Phil. 2:5; Col. 3:13; Heb.

3:1; 12:2; 1 Pet. 2:21.

4) Christ's assumption of a human nature was necessary in order that the penalty for sin might be paid, God's wrath might be satisfied, and reconciliation might be made in the same nature that had sinned. Rom. 8:3; 1 Cor. 15:21; Heb. 2:14-16.

5) It was proper that the Mediator be capable of obeying the Law (since no Divine Person, as Lawgiver, could properly be subject to the Law and to its judgment). Rom. 5:19; Gal. 4:4.

6) It was necessary that the Mediator be a man, so that He would be capable of suffering death (since God cannot die). Heb. 2:10,14,15; 5:7-9; 8:3; 9:22; 10:5.

7) The Scriptures amply prove that Christ was man. Isa. 9:6; Matt. 4:2; 8:24; 26:37; Mark 13:32; Luke 2:40,52; John 1:14,51; 11:35; Gal. 4:4; Heb. 2:17.

d. It was necessary that the Mediator, Christ, have a Divine nature.

1) Only a mediator who was God could offer a sacrifice of infinite value and render a perfect obedience to the Law of God. Christ's precious blood was human, but His Deity gave virtue to that blood, making it a sufficient ransom price. Matt. 26:28; Acts 20:28; Rom. 3:25; 5:9; Col. 1:20; Heb. 9:14; 1 Pet. 1:19; 1 John 1:7; Rev. 1:5; 7:14.

2) Only Christ could bear the wrath of God redemptively, freeing the elect from the curse of the Law. Rom. 3:25; 1 John 2:2; 4:10.

3) Only a Divine Mediator could apply the fruits of His accomplished work to those who acceqted Him by faith. Isa. 42:8; Jer. 17:5.

4) The Scriptures testify abundantly to the Deity of Christ (see this outline, III.B.).

e. The Christ (literally, the Messiah, or the Anointed One) was given a spiritual anointing for all His offices as Mediator.

1) This anointing took place at His conception by the Holy Spirit in the virgin Mary and at His baptism. Psa. 45:2; Isa. 11:2; 42:1; 61:1; Matt. 3:16; Luke 1:35; 2:46,47; John 3:34; Acts 10:38.

2) The immediate seat of these spiritual influences was His humanity, since His Deity was already infinite, perfect, and immutable.

f. Man, being under the evils of ignorance, guilt, and rebellion, needed a Mediator whose offices would be such that man could receive instruction, atonement, and rule. 1 Tim. 2:5; Heb. 8:6; 9:15; 12:24.

g. In His office of Prophet, Christ is God's Representative before mankind. Deut. 18:15 (cf. Acts 3:22-26); Isa. 11:2; 42:1,2; 49:6; 61:1; John 4:25; Heb. 1:1.

1) A prophet's duty was to reveal God's will to the people.

2) Christ prophesied from the Fall until His baptism by John. 1 Pet. 1:10,11.

3) Christ prophesied during His personal ministry until His ascension. Matt. 7:29; 21:11,46; 24:3-35; Luke 7:16; 13:33; 19:41-44; 24:19; John 3:2; 6:14; 7:40; 8:26-28; 9:17; 12:49,50; 14:10, 24; 15:15; 17:8,20.

4) Christ has been, is, and shall be prophesying from His ascension until the end of the age through the agency of the Holy Spirit and of His ministers.
John 16:12-15; Acts 1:8; 2:4; 15:28; 1 Thess. 1:5.

h. In His office of Priest Christ is man's Representative before God.

1) The Divinely appointed requirements of a priest are set forth in Scripture.

a) Every priest or high priest was taken from among men, particularly from among those whom he was to represent before God. Ex. 28:9, 12,21,29; Heb. 5:1.

b) Every high priest was appointed by God. Num. 16:5; Heb. 5:4.

c) Every high priest was to offer gifts and sacrifices for sin on behalf of the people. Lev. 16:3,7,15; Heb. 5:1.

d) Every high priest was to make intercession for the people. Ex. 30:8; Lev. 16:12; Luke 1:9,10; Rev. 5:8; 8:3,4.

2) Christ is a true Priest, according to the Old Testament requirments.

a) The Scriptures expressly declare it. Psa. 110:4 (cf. Heb. 5:6; 6:20); Zech. 6:13.

b) Priestly functions are ascribed to Him. Isa. 53:10, 12; Dan. 9:24,25.

3) Christ is a true Priest, according to the New Testament. Heb. 3:1; 4:14; 7:26; 8:1.

a) Christ was taken from among men (specifically from Israel—John 4:22) to represent them before God. Heb. 2:16; 4:15.

b) He was appointed by God. Heb. 5:5,6; 6:20.

c) He offered a sacrifice for

sin. Eph. 5:2; Heb. 9:26; 10:12; 1 John 2:2.

d) He made, and still makes, intercession for His people. Rom. 8:34; Heb. 7:25; 1 John 2:1.

4) In becoming the sacrificial Victim as well as the Priest, Christ showed His obedience. Heb. 9:14.

a) Christ's entire work was a work of obedience. Isa. 52:13; 53:11; John 6:38; 10:17,18; Rom. 5:19; Gal. 4:4; Phil. 2:7,8; Heb. 2:10-18; 5:8,9.

(1) It was in His human nature that He rendered obedience and gavesup His life. Heb. 5:7,8.

(2) Scriptures that present the Lord Christ as subordinate to God the Father are dealing with His proper subordination to God *as a man*; i.e., as Mediator. Furthermore, Christ's *submission* to the Father as God the Son, both in His humiliation and exaltation, is purely *voluntary* and in nowise detracts from His coequality with the Father. John 5:30; 6:38; 14:31; 15:10; 1 Cor. 15:24,28; Phil. 2:5-11; Heb. 2:9 (cf. Heb. 1:8-10).

b) The work of Christ was one of sacrifice. 1 Cor. 5:7.

(1) The New Testament writers' conceptions of sacrifice came from the Old Testament, which set forth many types of the Christ, the real sacrificial Victim, who was to come. Heb. 7:23-28; 8:1-6; 9:1-14; 10:1-12.

(2) This sacrifice was expiatory, removing the guilt of sin, thus separating sin from the sinner. Matt. 26:28; Luke 1:77,78; 24:47; Acts 2:38; 10:43; Rom. 3:25; Heb. 13:10-12.

(3) Christ is the propitiation for our sins, *satisfying* the wrath of God. Deut. 11:17; 29:23; 2 Chr. 19:2,10; 34:21; Ezra 5:12; Psa. 2:5,12; 21:9; 59:13; 79:6; Matt. 3:7; Luke 3:7; John 3:36; Rom. 1:18; 2:5,8; 3:25; 9:22; Eph. 5:6; Col. 3:6; 1 Thess. 1:10; 2:16; 1 John 2:2; 4:10; Rev. 6:16; 14:10,19; 15:1,7; 16:19; 19:15.

c) Even as Christ took God's wrath upon Himself for His people, rekonciling God to us, He also reconciles us to God by the Gospel.

(1) God, who is the offended party in that estrangement between Himself and men caused by their sins, must first reconcile Himself, or be reconciled, to men. This He did in the Person of His Son, who, while upon the Cross, removed sin from God's elect, the cause of His alienation from us. Rom. 5:10a; 2 Cor. 5:18,19; Eph. 2:16; Col. 1:20.

(2) But we the sinners, who by nature are at enmity toward God and are alienated from Him in our hearts, must reconcile ourselves, or be reconciled, to God. This Christ accomplishes in us as individuals, in time, by calling forth from us repentance and faith by His Spirit through the Gospel. Thus must we appropriate the benefits of His meritorious life and penal death to ourselves. Rom. 5:10b; 2 Cor. 5:20; Col. 1:21.

d) Christ, as our Mediator and Priest, accomplished a great *redemption*. Lev. 17:11 (cf. Heb. 9:22); Matt. 20:28; Mark 10:45.

(1) Christ came to ransom us from bondage to sin and its consequences by substituting His life in the place of ours. Rom. 6:18-23; 1 Cor. 6:19,20.

(2) Christ has redeemed His people from the curse of the moral law. Gal. 3:10,13.

(3) Christ has redeemed His people from the burdensome requirements of the rituals and ceremonial law. Gal. 3:23-26; 4:4,5.

(4) Christ has redeemed us by obeying the Law in our place, so that He might give to us His righteousness, that we might have a full acceptance before God. Rom. 5:19.

(5) Christ has redeemed us from sin's guilt, defilement, and enslaving power. Hos. 13:14; Rom. 3:24; 4:15; 1 Cor. 15:56; Eph. 1:7; Col. 1:14; Tit. 2:14; Heb. 9:12,15; 1 Pet. 1:18; Rev. 1:5; 5:9.

5) Christ's atonement for sin is effectual; hence
He atoned will infallibly come to Him in faith. John 6:38,39,65; 10:27-29; 17:9,11; Rom. 8:31-39; Phil. 1:6; 2 Tim. 2:19; 1 Pet. 1:5; 2 Pet. 1:10.

6) With respect to the extent of its application to men, Christ's atonement had a definite purpose. 1 Cor. 15:3; 1 Thess. 5:10.

a) Did Christ die to redeem specific men, or did He die merely to make men redeemable? Did Christ die to reconcile specific sinners, or did He die to make sinners in general reconcilable? Did Christ die to secure the salvation of men, or did He die merely to make them savable? Matt. 1:21; 11:25-30; 18:11; 20:28; Mark 10:45; 16:16; Luke 10:20; 19:10; John 10:7,11,14-17,-26; 17:2,6,9-11,24; Acts 2:21,47; Rom. 3:24; 5:9,10; 1 Cor. 1:18,21,30; 15:1,2; 2 Cor. 5:18; Eph. 1:7; 2:5,8,9, 16; Col. 1:12-14,20-22; 1 Tim. 1:15; 2 Tim. 1:9; Tit. 2:14; 3:5; Heb. 2:17; 7:25; 9:12; 10:39; 1 Pet. 1:18,19; Rev. 5:9; 21:27.

Several things ought to be noted as one studies this list of Scripture passages. First, such positive statements as "He *shall* save His people from their sins" and "having *obtained* eternal redemption" indicate that Christ accomplished *more* than a mere *potential* salvation for sinners on Calvary's Cross. Secondly, the Scriptures never set forth Christ's work as being for those who never turn from sin (Matt. 9:13), but in self-righteous rebellion reject the Gospel. Thirdly, one should be sensitive to the particularity of the language of Scripture, which talks of the "ye" and "we" that believe, and the benefits that have accrued to "us" and "you" on account of our faith in Christ. The apostolic writers loved to talk of *His people*, and His making reconciliation for *the people*. Christ Himself designates the elect by the words "My sheep." Fourthly, past tense verbs (e.g., "according to His mercy He *saved* us") indicate that Christ positively accomplished and secured the redemption of His people while on the cross (John 19:30). Thus we may rightly conclude that, though Christ's sacrifice is of infinite worth to the Father and thus sufficient to save every last individual of Adam's fallen race (if that were God's purpose), it was *designed* for the elect alone. Since Christ's atonement actually secured the salvation of *many*, and since God cannot be thwarted in any of His designs (Isa. 55:10,11; Dan. 4:34,35; 2 Cor. 2:14-16), we must in honesty conclude that His design was to purchase redemption for certain elect persons, yet "a great multitude, which no man could number" (Rev. 7:9).

b) All for whom Christ died also die in Christ. 2 Cor. 5:14,15. All who die in Christ rise again with Christ to newness of life after the likeness of Christ's resurrection. Therefore, those for whom Christ died are those who die to sin and live to righteousness. Matt. 13:12; John 11:51,52; 17:4-9; Acts 5:31; 13:48; 20:28; Rom. 6:3-11; 8:32; 2 Cor. 5:21; Gal. 1:4; 4:5; Eph. 1:3,4; 2:4-7; 5:26,27; Phil. 1:29; Col. 3:3; 1 Thess. 1:10; Tit. 2:14; 1 John 3:16; 4:9,10.

i. Christ bears the office of King. Psa. 2:6; 103:19; Luke 1:33.

1) As God, Christ's sovereignty is underived, absolute, eternal, and unchangeable. But as Mediator, Kingship has been given to Him by His Father as the reward for His obedience and suffering.

Christ's Kingship primarily entails administration of the provisions of the Covenant of Grace on behalf of His own people. Psa. 45:6,7; 132:11; Isa. 9:6,7; Jer. 23:5,6; Dan. 2:44; Mic. 5:2; Zech. 6:13; Matt. 13; 20:20-29; Luke 13:23-30; 17:20,21; 19:27,38; 22:29; John 18:36,37; Acts 2:30-36; Rom. 14:17; Eph. 1:10,21,22; Heb. 1:8,9; 1 Pet. 3:22.

2) Christ's mediatorial Kingdom encompasses the entire universe. Matt. 28:18; John 5:22-27; 9:39; 1 Cor. 15:25; Eph. 1:17-23; Phil. 2:9-11; Heb. 10:12,13.

3) Christ's Kingship is especially concerned with His administration over the Church as a spiritual Kingdom. Psa. 110:2; Isa. 53:1; Zech. 4:6,7; Matt. 13:33; 20:28; Mark 4:26-30; Luke 17:21; John 3:3-5; 4:24; 18:36; Acts 2:33; Rom. 14:17; 1 Cor. 5:4-11; 11:3; 2 Cor. 10:4; Eph. 1:3-8,22; 2:19; 4:15; 5:23; Phil. 3:20; Col. 1:18; 2:19; 2 Tim. 4:2; Tit. 2:15.

4) Christ assumed this office of King formally and publicly at His ascension and enthronement at the right hand of the Father, though He has been King from eternity.

a) The Old Testament predictions concerning His Kingdom are, in the New Testament, applied to His first advent. Psa. 2:6; Isa. 9:6; Jer. 23:5; Dan. 2:44 (cf. Matt. 4:23); Matt. 3:2; 4:17; 10:7; 11:11,12; 12:28; 13:18-52; Luke 10:9,11; 11:20; 16:16; 17:20,21; Acts 2:29-36.

b) The term "the kingdom of heaven," as used frequently by Christ in His teaching, was recorded frequently by Matthew, probably as a means of avoiding offense to the Jews to whom his Gospel was written, for it had become their custom not to speak the incommunicable name of God. The "kingdom of God" and the "kingdom of heaven" are synonyms. Matt. 19:23-25.

(1) The term "kingdom of God" (Luke 4:43) shows its Divine origin, and that it is invested with God's authority.

(2) The terms "kingdom of Christ" and "kingdom of God's dear Son" (Matt. 16:28; Col. 1:13) show that Christ is the mediatorial Sovereign.

(3) The term "kingdom of heaven" (Matt. 11:12) demonstrates that its origin and character is from heaven, where the saints will take up residence in its final consummation.

(4) Christ's teaching concerning the nature of His Kingdom is set forth in many passages. Compare Matt. 13 with Mark 4 and Luke 8:1-10; compare Matt. 3:2 with Mark 1:15 and Luke 10:9; compare Matt. 4:17 with Mark 1:14,15; compare Matt. 5:3,10 with Luke 6:20.

c) It is both a present and a future Kingdom.

(1) Present. Matt. 4:17; 12:28; Luke 17:21; Col. 1:13.

(2) Future. Matt. 7:21,22; 25:34; Luke 22:29,30; Gal. 5:21; Eph. 5:5.

8. The Holy Spirit takes part in the application of the Covenant of Grace in ways appropriate to His office within the Godhead.

a. *Regeneration* is the act of God the Spirit, savingly enlightening and renewing the mind, affections, and will of the elect, so that he who was dead in sin is effectually called, i.e., made able and willing to answer the call of the Gospel to repentance and faith. He receives a "heart of flesh," having his "stony heart" removed. In this sovereign act of mercy, the Holy Spirit works alone and unaided, while the elect sinner, who is still "dead in trespasses and sins," is wholly *passive*. However, once the sinner has been *born again*, he being alive toward God, *actively* responds to the Gospel in repentance and faith. Deut. 30:6; Song 1:4a; Jer. 31:3; Ezek. 11:19; 36:26,27; John 1:18; 3:3,5-8; 6:44,45; Acts 26:18; Rom. 8:2,8; 1 Cor. 2:10,12; Eph. 1:17-19; 2:1-5; Phil. 2:13; 2 Tim. 1:9,10; Tit. 3:5; 1 John 2:29; 3:9; 4:7; 5:1,4,18.

b. The Holy Spirit is the sole Giver of *saving faith*, which He gives only to those whom He has regenerated. Such a person is given the enablement to believe the Gospel, i.e., to believe that God was in Christ reconciling *him* personally to Himself (2 Cor. 4:19). He thereby trusts in Christ and rests upon Him alone as his righteousness before God. Eph. 2:8,9; 2 Thess. 3:2,3; Heb. 11:6.

1) Some men have only an *historical* faith, one that apprehends the truth of Scripture in an intellectual fashion, but that is devoid of any spiritual commitment. Matt. 7:26; John 3:2; Acts 26:27,28; Jas. 2:19.
2) Some men have only a *temporal* faith. They are persuaded of the truths of religion, have a conscience and affections that are stirred through conviction of sin by the Holy Spirit, but do not have regenerate hearts. Matt. 13:20,21; Heb. 6:4-6.
3) The elect have, or will have, *true* or *saving* faith, which is a sure and hearty trust in the promises of God in Christ. Mark 16:16; John 3:15,16,18; 6:40; 20:31; Acts 10:43; 16:31; Rom. 4:20,21; 8:16; 10:17; Eph. 1:13; 1 John 4:13; 5:6,10.
4) Saving faith consists of knowledge of the truth (Rom. 10:17), of agreement with it, and most importantly, of trust in it. This living faith involves inner being: mind, affections, and will. Jer. 9:24; Matt. 12:17-21; Rom. 15:12; Eph. 1:12,13; 3:16-19; Heb. 11:1; 1 Pet. 3:5; 1 John 4:2,6-8,13.

c. Together with faith, the Holy Spirit gives repentance to those whom He regenerates.
1) Repentance unto life is given so that a sinner, out of a true understanding of his sin, and the mercy of God in Christ, with grief over and hatred of his sins, turns from them to God, purposing and endeavoring to obey Him. 2 Kin. 22:19; Ezra 10:1; Job 42:1,6; Psa. 38:18; Isa. 1:16,17; Jer. 3:22; 31:18,19; Ezek. 36:31; Joel 2:12; Mark 14:72; Luke 15:21; 18:13; Acts 2:37,38; 11:18; 20:21; 2 Cor. 7:11; Heb. 6:1.
2) Only those who are chosen to eternal life experience saving repentance. 2 Cor. 7:10; 2 Pet. 3:9.

d. Sanctification is the work of God the Spirit that follows effectual calling (i.e., regeneration, which produces repentance and faith), justification, and adoption. John 16:13-15; Rom. 5:5; 8:11,21,30; 15:16; 1 Cor. 2:12; 6:19, 20; 2 Cor. 3:17,18; 5:5; Gal. 4:6; 5:22,23; 1 Thess. 4:3; 5:23.
1) Sanctification is a work of God's free grace, whereby the entire person is renewed after the image of God, and enabled more and more to refrain from sinning and to live righteously. Rom. 6:4-6,14; 8:1; 1 Cor. 6:11; Gal. 5:24; Eph. 1:4; 3:16-19; 4:23,24; Col. 1:10,11; 2 Thess. 2:13; Heb. 6:11,12; Jude 20.
2) Scripture does not teach that one can become sinless in this life. Sanctification is a process of maturation, of learning to cease from the evil deeds of the flesh and to practice the opposite virtues by the power of the Holy Spirit. Isa. 1:16-18; Rom. 6:14; 7:14-25; 2 Cor. 7:1; Gal. 5:16-26; Eph. 4:11-15; 2 Pet. 1:2-8; 1 John 1:8-10; 3:3,5-9.
3) On the other hand, Scripture teaches that, in true sanctification, a constant watch must be set, because of the seriousness and subtlety of sin. Job 42:5,6; Isa. 6:5; Matt. 5:48; Rom. 6:12,13, 19,22,23; 7:14-25; Phil. 1:9-11; 2:12,13; 1 Thess. 5:8,9; 1 Pet. 1:13-16,22; 2:2; 2 Pet. 1:5-8; 1 John 2:1,16.
4) Only the elect experience sanctification. John 17:17-20; 2 Thess. 2:13; Heb. 2:11,12; 1 Pet. 1:2.

e. Glorification is the final stage and goal of the application of redemption to God's people. Rom. 8:30.
1) Glorification is the instantaneous change that will take place in all the redeemed at Christ's second advent. Every believer will be received into glory and given his resurrection body. Isa. 2:11; Rom. 8:17-19,23; 1 Cor. 15:51-55; Eph. 5:27; Phil. 3:21; 1 Thess. 4:16,17; Tit. 2:13; 1 Pet. 4:13.
2) Associazed with the glorification of God's people from all ages is the renewal of creation. Rom. 8:20-23; 1 Cor. 15:24,28; 2 Pet. 3:11-13; Rev. 21:27; 22:3,4.
3) Only those whom God has predestinated, called, and justified shall experience glorification.
4) Unless the subjects of the redemptive work of the Triune God are called, justified, and glorified in the Holy Spirit's application of this work, then our God does not act in harmony with Himself. God neither leaves His work incomplete in one man nor gives another justification without having foreordained him to it. Acts 13:48; Rom. 8:30.

## CONCLUSION

Having set forth the Biblical teaching on the doctrine of the Holy Trinity in a fairly thorough outline, it is proper to draw out some of the important implications of this vital truth. First, if a Bible student is to be kept from dangerous error in his study of God's Word, he must seek to examine all his presuppositions, in order to be certain that they are consistent with all that God has revealed about His own nature. The study of the doctrine of the Trinity ought to occupy one of the highest priorities for every Bible student, indeed for every Christian. A deficient understanding of the Trinity will produce defective views in many areas of practical concern: male-female relations in the family, the church, and society; church government; missions and evangelism; understanding human suffering, Christian assurance, etc. Secondly, a solid grasp on the related doctrines of the Holy Trinity and the Covenant of Grace will give one a thorough appreciation of the blessed unity of the Bible. When one realizes that there is nothing absolutely new in the blossoming forth of special revelation in the New Testament that was not already present in the *bud* of the Old Testament, then all of the wonderful spiritual lessons of the Old Testament, "written for our admonition," will take on fresh meaning for him.

Finally, that which is of the highest and most enduring value to the believer is at stake, namely, the *glory* of his God. The Scriptures teach that the three Persons of the Godhead are always in perfect unity, agreement, and harmony in all that they *are*, *decree*, and *perform*. Therefore, any view of the Atonement that implies a disagreement among the three Divine Persons as to their official functions in the Council of Grace is potentially destructive to the Biblical doctrine of the Trinity. If we say that God the Son died for every man, but that God the Holy Spirit regenerates only some men, then we are actually pitting the work of Christ against the work of the Holy Spirit. We thus subtly arraign the Spirit with charges of being less compassionate toward sinners than is Christ, or of dereliction in His duty to apply the word of Christ freely to all men without exception. His actions in Acts 16:6-10, to one holding such an erroneous view, leave the Holy Spirit open to the charge of being a respecter of persons, a charge that He manifestly refutes (Acts 10:34,35,44-48). Such an insinuation that disharmony exists between the Son and the Spirit also casts an unfavorable shadow upon the Father's character, who might be brazenly charged with inequity, a lack of compassion, or indecisiveness in His oversight of the activities of the Son and the Spirit in the work of redemption. Such impious accusations and hard thoughts against God are potential mental offspring of a doctrine of indefinite, universal atonement. Such a teaching, even if not taken to these logical (but absurd and blasphemous) conclusions, still encourages a low view of the sublime harmony, perfect love, absolute agreement of thought and purpose, and precisely efficient co-operation that have existed eternally within the Godhead.

To entertain the idea that God the Father planned a discrepancy between the number of persons for whom Christ died and the number of persons who would ultimately be saved is to attribute to His August Majesty an ambivalence, a lack of foresight, a defective sense of justice, and a fragmented wisdom that are utterly detestable to the thoughtful, pious mind. It is a disjointed view of Scripture that gives rise to a disharmonious view of God's plan of redemption. If one isolates a text of Scripture in order to prove an indefinite or universal atonement, one runs the risk of denying the unity of the triune God as revealed in Scripture. We ought rather to compare Scripture with Scripture until we arrive at a conclusion that harmonizes with all of God's Word and with God's nature as He has revealed it to us in Holy Writ. The use of isolated texts to prove doctrinal concepts that are denied by other Scriptures or by the Bible as a whole is to deny the perfect harmony of God's Word, a harmony that stems from the character of its Author.

The Apostle Paul was "not ashamed of the Gospel," nor did he hesitate to declare that "all Scripture is given by inspiration of God, and is profitable for doctrine. . . ." His parting words to the elders of the church at Ephesus form an appropriate benediction:

Ye know . . . how I kept back nothing that was profitable unto you. . . . For I have not shunned to declare unto you all the counsel of God. . . . And now brethren, I commend you to God, and to the Word of His grace, which is able to build you up, and to give you an inheritance among all them which are sanctified (Acts 20:18,20,27,32).

## ACTS

# INDEX OF OLD TESTAMENT AND NEW TESTAMENT CROSS REFERENCES

## THE PURPOSE OF THIS INDEX

The New Testament is not clearly understandable apart from an understanding of the Old Testament. Every Old Testament book is quoted or alluded to in the New Testament. These quotations and allusions serve as the foundation for practically every doctrine taught in the New Testament.

For example, what Christian is not familiar with Paul's teaching about the "whole armor of God" in Eph. 6:10-17? But how many realize that Isaiah 59:15-18 (as well as 11:5 and 52:7, etc.) forms the background and key to the understanding of this passage? By studying the Old Testament passage it is found that the "armor of God" refers to the armor that *God* used to conquer evil. "*His* arm brought salvation . . . for *He* put on righteousness and an helmet of salvation . . ." (italics added). It is by being an heir to this "armor of God" that the believer withstands Satan, who is already defeated by the God who took up His armor.

## THE USE OF THIS INDEX

**I. Symbols in the text.**

*A. Old Testament to New Testament.* Suppose you are reading Isaiah 59:17. You will note a superscript letter *Q* at the end of the verse. This designates the "Quotation" index described here. Looking in the appropriate section, where the Old Testament verses are listed in boldface type, you will find that the phrase "helmet of salvation" from Isaiah 59:17 is quoted in Ephesians 6:17. This indicates that you should study both passages for fuller understanding of the Old Testament verse.

*B. New Testament to Old Testament.* If you are reading Ephesians 6 you will note that a superscript *Q* appears after verse 17. Looking in the appropriate section of this index, where the New Testament reference is listed in boldface type, you are referred to Isaiah 59:17, in which the phrase "helmet of salvation" also appears.

**II. Using the context.**

*A. The larger context.* It will be clear to the diligent student that Isaiah 59:17 is part of a larger context which includes *at least* verses 15-18. Paul's teaching is obviously based upon this larger context.

You should always be aware that, since the Holy Spirit has inspired the whole of Scripture, one ought to study the *context* into which words and phrases have been placed and not be satisfied with the observation of mere correspondence of words and phrases found in separate passages. The same procedure should be followed for Ephesians 6:14, 15, since they are included in the New Testament contexts.

*B. Multiple verses.* Often an Old Testament reference is quoted more than once in the New Testament, and sometimes a New Testament passage has more than one Old Testament passage as its background. You may study these additional verses in the same way, adding to your understanding of the truth.

III. Messianic Prophecies. In this index prophecies concerning the Messiah, the Son of God, are indicated by boldface notations. Quotations that contain prophecies considered Messianic, but whose fulfillment or nonfulfillment is not readily discernible, are followed with the boldface letters **MP.** Fulfilled Messianic prophecies are followed by the boldface letters **MPF**, unfulfilled Messianic prophecies by the letters **MPU.**



**GENESIS**

**1:1** Heb. 1:10; 11:3
**1:3** 2 Cor. 4:6
**1:6-9** 2 Pet. 3:5
**1:11** 1 Cor. 15:38; Heb. 6:7
**1:26** Eph. 4:24; Jas. 3:9
**1:27** Matt. 19:4; Mark 10:6; Acts 17:29; 1 Cor. 11:7; Col. 3:10; 1 Tim. 2:13
**1:29** Rom. 14:2
**1:31** 1 Tim. 4:4
**2:2** Heb. 4:4,10
**2:3** Matt. 12:8
**2:7** 1 Cor. 15:45,47; 1 Tim. 2:13
**2:8** Rev. 2:7
**2:9** Rev. 2:7; 22:14,19
**2:9-10** Rev. 22:2
**2:17** Rom. 5:12
**2:18** 1 Cor. 11:9
**2:21-23** 1 Cor. 11:8
**2:22** 1 Tim. 2:13
**2:24** Matt. 19:5; Mark 10:7-8; 1 Cor. 6:16; Eph. 5:31
**3:1** Rev. 12:9; 20:2
**3:4** John 8:44
**3:6** Rom. 5:12; 1 Tim. 2:14
**3:13** Rom. 7:11; 2 Cor. 11:3; 1 Tim. 2:14
**3:15** Luke 10:19; Rom. 16:20; Heb. 2:14 **MPF**
**3:16** 1 Cor. 11:3; 14:34; Eph. 5:22; Col. 3:18
**3:17-18** Heb. 6:8
**3:17-19** Rom. 8:20; 1 Cor. 15:21
**3:19** Rom. 5:12; Heb. 9:27
**3:22** Rev. 2:7; 22:2,14,19
**3:24** Rev. 2:7
**4:3-8** Jude 11
**4:4** Heb 11:4 **MPF**
**4:8** Matt. 23:35; Luke 11:51; I John 3:12
**4:10** Heb. 12:24; Jas. 5:4
**4:25-5:32** Luke 3:36-38
**5:1** Matt. 1:1; 1 Cor. 11:7
**5:2** Matt. 19:4; Mark 10:6
**5:3** 1 Cor. 15:49
**5:24** Heb. 11:5
**5:29** Rom. 8:20
**6:1-7:24** 1 Pet. 3:20
**6:5** Rom. 7:18
**6:5-12** Luke 17:26
**6:9-12** Matt. 24:37
**6:13-22** Heb. 11:7
**6:13-7:24** Matt. 24:38-39
**7:1** Heb. 11:7
**7:7** Matt. 24:38; Luke 17:27
**7:11-21** 2 Pet. 3:6
**8:18** 2 Pet. 2:5
**8:21** Rom. 7:18; Phil. 4:18
**9:3** Rom. 14:2; 1 Tim. 4:3
**9:4** Acts 15:20,29
**9:6** Matt. 26:52; 1 Cor. 11:7
**11:10-26** Luke 3:34-36
**12:1** Acts 7:3; Heb. 11:8
**12:3** Acts 3:25; Gal. 3:8 **MPF**
**12:5** Acts 7:4
**12:7** Acts 3:25; Gal. 3:16 **MPF**
**13:15** Acts 7:5; Gal. 3:16 **MPF**
**14:17-20** Heb. 7:1-3
**14:19** Rev. 10:5
**14:19-20** Heb. 7:4,6,10
**14:20** Luke 18:12
**14:22** Rev. 10:5
**15:5** Rom. 4:18; Heb. 11:12
**15:6** Rom. 4:3,9,22-24; Gal. 3:6; Jas. 2:23
**15:13-14** Acts 7:6
**15:14** Acts 7:7
**15:16** 1 Thess. 2:16
**15:18** Acts 7:5; Rev. 9:14; 16:12
**16:1** Acts 7:5
**16:5** Gal. 4:22
**16:11** Luke 1:31
**17:15** Rom. 4:17 **MPF**
**17:7** Luke 1:55, 72-73; Gal. 3:16 **MPF**
**17:8** Acts 7:5,45
**17:10-11** Acts 7:8a
**17:10-13** John 7:22
**17:11** Rom. 4:11
**17:12** Luke 1:59; 2:21
**17:17** Rom. 4:19
**17:19** Heb. 11:11
**18:1-8** Heb. 13:2
**18:4** Luke 7:44
**18:10** Rom. 9:9
**18:11** Luke 1:18
**18:11-14** Heb. 11:11
**18:12** 1 Pet. 3:6
**18:14** Matt. 19:26; Mark 10:27; Luke 1:37; Rom. 9:9
**18:15** 1 Pet. 3:6
**18:18** Acts 3:25; Rom. 4:13; Gal. 3:8
**18:20-21** Luke 17:28
**18:21** Rev. 18:5
**18:20-19:28** Matt. 10:15
**18:25** Heb. 12:23
**19:1-3** Heb. 13:2
**19:1-14** Luke 17:28
**19:1-16** 2 Pet. 2:7
**19:4-25** Jude 7
**19:17** Luke 17:31-32
**19:24** Luke 17:29; 2 Pet. 2:6; Rev. 14:10; 19:20; 20:10; 21:8
**19:24-25** Luke 10:12
**19:24-28** Matt. 11:23
**19:26** Luke 17:31
**19:28** Rev. 9:2
**21:2** Gal. 4:22; Heb. 11:11
**21:3** Matt. 1:2; Luke 3:34
**21:4** Acts 7:8b
**21:9** Gal. 4:29
**21:10** Gal. 4:30
**21:12** Heb. 11:18 **MPF** Matt. 1:2; Rom. 9:7
**22:1-10** Heb. 11:17
**22:2** Matt. 3:17; Mark 1:11; 12:6; Luke 3:22 Jas. 2:21
**22:8** John 1:29
**22:9** Jas. 2:21
**22:16-17** Luke 1:73-74; Heb. 6:13-14
**22:17** Matt. 16:18; Luke 1:55; Heb. 6:14; 11:12 **MPF**
**22:17-18** Rom 4:13
**22:18** Gal. 3:16 **MPF** Matt. 1:1; Acts 3:25

**EXODUS**

**36:35** Luke 23:45; 2 Cor. 3:13
**38:21** Rev. 15:5
**38:26** Matt. 17:24
**40:34-35** Rev. 15:5,8

### LEVITICUS

**3:17** Acts 15:20,29
**5:11** Luke 2:24
**6:16** 1 Cor. 9:13
**6:26** 1 Cor. 9:13
**7:6** 1 Cor. 10:18
**7:15** 1 Cor. 10:18
**7:12** Heb. 13:15a
**8:15** Heb. 9:21
**8:19** Heb. 9:21
**9:7** Heb. 5:3; 7:27
**11:1-47** Acts 10:14
**11:2** Heb. 9:10
**11:25** Heb. 9:10
**11:44** 1 Pet. 1:16
**12:3** Luke 1:59; 2:21; John 7:22; Acts 15:1
**12:6** Luke 2:22
**12:8** Luke 2:24
**13:46** Luke 17:12
**13:49** Matt. 8:4; Mark 1:44; Luke 5:14; 17:14
**14:2** Matt. 8:4
**14:2-3** Luke 17:14
**14:2-32** Mark 1:44; Luke 5:14
**14:4** Heb. 9:19
**14:4-32** Matt. 8:4
**15:18** Heb. 9:10
**15:25** Matt. 9:20
**16:2** Heb. 6:19; 9:7
**16:3** Heb. 9:13
**16:6** Heb. 5:3; 7:27
**16:12** Heb. 6:19; Rev. 8:5
**16:14** Heb. 9:7,13
**16:15** Heb. 6:19; 7:27; 9:7,13; 10:4
**16:21** Heb. 10:4
**16:27** Heb. 13:11,13
**16:29** Acts 27:9
**16:30,34** Heb. 9:7,12,28
**17:10-14** Acts 15:20,29
**17:11** Heb. 9:22
**18:5** Matt. 19:17; Luke 10:28; Rom. 7:10; 10:5; Gal. 3:12
**18:7-8** 1 Cor. 5:1
**18:16** Matt. 14:3-4; Mark 6:18
**18:22** Rom. 1:27
**19:2** Matt. 5:48; 1 Pet. 1:16
**19:12** Matt. 5:33
**19:13** Matt. 20:8; 1 Tim. 5:18; Jas. 5:4
**19:15** John 7:24; Acts 23:3
**19:17** Matt. 18:15
**19:18** Matt. 5:43; 19:19b; 22:39; Mark 12:31-33; Luke 10:27; Rom. 12:19; 13:9b; Gal. 5:14; Jas. 2:8
**19:32** 1 Tim. 5:1
**20:7** 1 Pet. 1:16
**20:9** Matt. 15:4; Mark 7:10
**20:10** John 8:5
**20:13** Rom. 1:27
**20:21** Matt. 14:3-4
**21:9** Rev. 17:16; 18:8
**23:15-21** Acts 2:1; 1 Cor. 16:8
**23:29** Acts 3:23
**23:34** John 7:2
**23:36** John 7:37
**24:5-9** Matt. 12:4; Mark 2:26; Luke 6:4
**24:16** Matt. 26:65-66; Mark 14:64; John 10:33; 19:7
**24:17** Matt. 5:21
**24:20** Matt. 5:38
**25:35-36** Luke 6:35
**25:43** Col. 4:1
**25:53** Col. 4:1
**26:11-12** 2 Cor. 6:16; Rev. 21:3
**26:21** Rev. 15:1,6,8; 21:9
**26:41** Acts 7:51
**26:42** Luke 1:72-73 **MPF**
**27:30** Matt. 23:23; Luke 11:42

### NUMBERS

**1:50** Acts 7:44; Rev. 15:5
**6:3** Luke 1:15
**6:5** Acts 21:23-24,26
**6:13-18** Acts 21:23-24
**6:13-21** Acts 21:26
**6:18** Acts 18:18
**6:21** Acts 21:23-24
**6:25-26** Rom. 1:7
**9:12** John 19:36
**11:4** 1 Cor. 10:6
**11:7-9** John 6:31
**11:29** 1 Cor. 14:5
**11:34** 1 Cor. 10:6
**12:7** Heb. 3:2,5; 10:21
**12:8** II John 12; III John 14
**14:1-35** Heb. 3:16-18
**14:2** 1 Cor. 10:10
**14:3-4** Acts 7:39
**14:6** Matt. 26:65; Mark 14:63
**14:16** 1 Cor. 10:5
**14:21-23** Heb. 3:11
**14:22-23** Heb. 3:18
**14:23** 1 Cor. 10:5
**14:29** Heb. 3:17
**14:29-30** 1 Cor. 10:5; Jude 5
**14:33** Acts 7:36
**14:34** Acts 13:18
**14:35** Jude 5
**14:36** 1 Cor. 10:10
**15:17-21** Rom. 11:16
**15:38-39** Matt. 23:5
**16:5** 2 Tim. 2:19
**16:19-35** Jude 11
**16:22** Heb. 12:9
**16:26** 2 Tim. 2:19
**16:38** Heb. 12:3
**16:41-49** 1 Cor. 10:10
**17:8-10** Heb. 9:4
**18:2-6** Heb. 9:6
**18:8** 1 Cor. 9:13
**18:21** Heb. 7:5
**18:31** Matt. 10:10; 1 Cor. 9:13
**19:6** Heb. 9:19
**19:9** Heb. 9:13
**19:13** Heb. 9:10
**19:17-19** Heb. 9:13
**20:2-5** Heb. 3:8
**20:11** 1 Cor. 10:4
**21:5-6** 1 Cor. 10:9
**21:9** John 3:14
**22:7** 2 Pet. 2:15; Jude 11
**22:28** 2 Pet. 2:16
**23:19** Rom. 9:6; 2 Tim. 2:13; Heb. 6:18
**24:6** Heb. 8:2
**24:17** Matt. 2:2; Rev. 22:16 **MPF**
**25:1** 1 Cor. 10:8
**25:1-2** Rev. 2:14
**25:1-3** Rev. 2:20
**25:9** 1 Cor. 10:8
**27:14** Acts 7:51b
**27:16** Heb. 12:9
**27:17** Matt. 9:36; Mark 6:34
**28:9-10** Matt. 12:5
**30:2** Matt. 5:33
**31:16** Jude 11; Rev. 2:14

### DEUTERONOMY

**1:7** Rev. 9:14; 16:12
**1:10** Heb. 11:12
**1:16** John 7:51
**1:17** Jas. 2:9
**1:31** Acts 13:18
**2:5** Acts 7:5
**4:2** Rev. 22:18
**4:7-8** Rom. 3:2
**4:11-12** Heb. 12:18-19
**4:15-19** Rom. 1:23
**4:20** Tit. 2:14; 1 Pet. 2:9
**4:24** Heb. 12:29
**4:35** Mark 12:32-33; 1 Cor. 8:4
**4:39** 1 Cor. 8:4
**5:4-22** Acts 7:38
**5:11** Matt. 5:33
**5:12-14** Mark 2:27
**5:13-14** Luke 13:14
**5:14** Matt. 12:2; Luke 23:56
**5:16** Matt. 15:4a; 19:11; Mark 7:10a; 10:19; Eph. 6:2-3
**5:16-20** Luke 18:20
**5:17** Matt. 5:21; Jas. 2:11
**5:17-20** Matt. 19:18; Mark 10:19; Rom. 13:9a
**5:18** Matt. 5:27; Jas. 2:11
**5:18-21** Rom. 7:7; 13:9
**5:23** Heb. 12:19b
**5:25** Heb. 12:19b
**6:4-5** Mark 12:29-30,32-33
**6:5** Matt. 22:37; Luke 10:27; Rom. 3:30; 1 Cor. 8:4
**6:7** Eph. 6:4
**6:8** Matt. 23:5
**6:13** Matt. 4:10; Luke 4:8
**6:16** Matt. 4:7; Luke 4:12
**6:20-25** Eph. 6:4
**7:1** Acts 13:19
**7:6** Rom. 9:4; Tit. 2:14; 1 Pet. 2:9
**7:9** 1 Cor. 1:9; 10:13
**8:3** Matt. 4:4; Luke 4:4; 1 Cor. 10:3
**8:5** Heb. 12:7
**9:3** Heb. 12:29
**9:4** Rom. 10:6
**9:10-11** Acts 7:38; 2 Cor. 3:3
**9:19** Heb. 12:21
**10:3-5** Heb. 9:4
**10:12** Luke 10:27
**10:15** 1 Pet. 2:9
**10:17** Acts 10:34; Rom. 2:11; Gal. 2:6; Eph. 6:9; Col. 3:25; 1 Tim. 6:15; Rev. 17:14; 19:16
**10:22** Acts 7:14; Heb. 11:12
**11:5** Acts 7:5
**11:14** Jas. 5:7
**11:29** John 4:20
**12:5-14** John 4:20
**12:32** Rev. 22:18
**13:1** Matt. 24:24
**13:1-3** Mark 13:22
**13:2-4** Rev. 13:14
**13:3** 1 Cor. 11:19
**14:1-2** Rom. 9:4
**14:2** Tit. 2:14; 1 Pet. 2:9
**15:7-8** I John 3:17
**15:11** Matt. 26:11; Mark 14:7; John 12:8
**15:12** John 8:35
**15:16** Eph. 6:2-3
**16:1-8** Luke 2:41
**16:3** 1 Cor. 5:8
**16:9-11** Acts 2:1; 1 Cor. 16:8
**17:6** John 8:17; 1 Tim. 5:19; Heb. 10:28
**17:7** John 8:7; 1 Cor. 5:13
**18:1-3** 1 Cor. 9:13
**18:13** Matt. 5:48

**18:15** Matt. 17:5; Mark 9:7; Luke 9:35; 24:27; John 1:21; 5:46; 6:14; 7:40 **MPF**
**18:15-18** Acts 3:22; 7:37 **MPF**
**18:18** John 1:21,45; 6:14 **MPF**
**18:19** Acts 3:23 **MPF**
**19:15** Matt. 18:16; John 8:17; 2 Cor. 13:1; 1 Tim. 5:19; Heb. 10:28
**19:19** 1 Cor. 5:13
**19:21** Matt. 5:38
**21:6-9** Matt. 27:24
**21:22-23** Matt. 27:57-58; John 19:31; Acts 5:30; 10:39 **MPF**
**21:23** Gal. 3:13 **MPF**
**22:21** 1 Cor. 5:13
**22:22** John 8:5
**22:24** 1 Cor. 5:13
**22:30** 1 Cor. 5:1
**23:21** Matt. 5:33
**23:24-25** Matt. 12:1
**23:25** Mark 2:23; Luke 6:1
**24:1,3** Matt. 5:31; 19:7; Mark 10:4
**24:7** 1 Cor. 5:13
**24:14** Mark 10:19
**24:15** Matt. 20:8;Jas. 5:4
**25:4** 1 Cor. 9:9; 1 Tim. 5:18
**25:5** Matt. 22:24; Mark 12:19; Luke 20:28
**27:20** 1 Cor. 5:1
**27:26** 2 Cor. 3:9; Gal. 3:10
**28:4** Luke 1:42
**28:35** Rev. 16:2
**29:4** Rom. 11:8
**29:18** Acts 8:23; Heb. 12:15
**29:20** Rev. 22:18
**30:4** Matt. 24:31b; Mark 13:27
**30:6** Rom. 2:29
**30:11** 1 John 5:3
**30:12-14** Rom. 10:6-9 **MPF**
**31:6** Heb. 13:5
**31:7** Heb. 4:8
**31:8** Heb. 13:5
**31:26-27** John 5:45
**32:4** Rom. 9:14; Rev. 15:3; 16:5
**32:5** Matt. 17:17; Acts 2:40; Phil. 2:15
**32:6** John 8:41
**32:8** Acts 17:26
**32:17** 1 Cor. 10:20; Rev. 9:20
**32:18** Heb. 1:2; 11:3 **MPF**
**32:20** Matt. 17:17
**32:21** Rom. 10:19; 11:11; 1 Cor. 10:22
**32:29** Luke 19:42
**32:35** Luke 21:22; Rom. 12:19
**32:35-36** Heb. 10:30
**32:40** Rev. 10:5-6
**32:43** Rom. 15:10; Heb. 1:6; Rev. 6:10; 18:20; 19:2
**32:49** Acts 7:5,45
**33:2** Jude 14
**33:3** Eph. 1:18
**33:3-4** Acts 20:32; 26:18
**33:9** Matt. 10:37; Luke 14:26
**33:12** 2 Thess. 2:13
**33:27-29** Eph. 1:18

## JOSHUA

**1:5** Heb. 13:5
**2:4** Jas. 2:25
**2:11-12** Heb. 11:31
**2:15** Jas. 2:25
**3:14-17** Acts 7:45
**5:14-15** Matt. 14:33; 15:25
**6:12-21** Heb. 11:30
**6:17** Jas. 2:25
**6:21-25** Heb. 11:31
**7:19** John 9:24; Rev. 11:13
**8:33** John 4:20
**14:1** Acts 13:19
**18:1** Acts 7:45
**22:4** Heb. 4:8
**22:5** Matt. 22:37; Mark 12:29-30, 33; Luke 10:27
**23:9** Acts 7:45
**24:18** Acts 7:45
**24:32** John 4:5; Acts 7:16

## JUDGES

**2:10** Acts 13:36
**2:16** Acts 13:20
**4:10-17** Heb. 11:32
**5:4** Heb. 12:26
**5:19** Rev. 16:16
**5:24** Luke 1:42
**5:31** Rev. 1:16
**11:32-33** Heb. 11:32
**13:3** Luke 1:31
**13:4** Luke 1:15
**13:5,7** Matt. 2:23
**14:6-7** Heb. 11:33
**16:28-30** Heb. 11:32

## RUTH

**4:12** Matt. 1:3
**4:13** Matt. 1:4-5
**4:17** Matt. 1:6
**4:17-22** Matt. 1:4-5; Luke 3:31-33
**4:22** Matt. 1:6

## I SAMUEL

**1:11** Luke 1:48
**1:17** Mark 5:34
**2:1** Luke 1:46-47
**2:5** Luke 1:53
**2:7** Luke 1:52b
**2:10** Luke 1:69 **MPF**
**2:26** Luke 2:52
**3:20** Acts 13:20
**4:8** Rev. 11:6
**7:9-12** Heb. 11:32
**8:5** Acts 13:21
**8:19** Acts 13:21
**10:20-21** Acts 13:21
**10:24** Acts 13:21
**11:15** Acts 13:21
**12:3** Acts 20:33
**12:22** Rom. 11:1-2
**13:14** Acts 13:22
**14:45** Matt. 10:30; Luke 21:18; Acts 27:34
**15:22** Mark 12:32-33
**15:29** Heb. 6:18
**16:1** Luke 3:31-32
**16:7** Matt. 12:25; 22:18; Mark 2:8; Luke 6:8; 11:17; John 2:25
**16:12-13** Acts 13:22
**17:34-36** Heb. 11:33
**19:8** Heb. 11:32
**20:42** Mark 5:34
**21:6** Matt. 12:4; Mark 2:20; Luke 6:4

## II SAMUEL

**3:39** 2 Tim. 4:14
**5:2** Matt. 2:6
**5:14** Luke 3:31
**7:2-16** Acts 7:45-46
**7:8** 2 Cor. 6:18
**7:12-13** Luke 1:32-33; John 7:42; Acts 2:30; 13:23 **MPF**
**7:14** 2 Cor. 6:18; Heb. 1:5; Rev. 21:7 **MPF** Heb. 12:7
**7:16** Luke 1:32-33
**12:24** Matt. 1:6
**13:19** Matt. 26:65
**14:11** Acts 27:34
**15:9** Mark 5:34
**15:35** Mark 2:26
**22:3** Heb. 2:13a **MPF**
**22:6** Acts 2:24
**22:9** Rev. 11:5
**22:28** Luke 1:51
**22:50** Rom. 15:9 **MPF**
**23:2** Matt. 22:43

## I KINGS

**2:10** Acts 2:29; 13:36
**5:11** Acts 12:20
**6:1-2** Acts 7:47
**6:14** Acts 7:47
**8:1** Rev. 11:19
**8:6** Rev. 11:19
**8:10-11** Rev. 15:8
**8:13** Matt. 23:21
**8:17-18** Acts 7:45-46
**8:19-20** Acts 7:47
**8:27** Acts 17:24
**9:7-8** Matt. 23:38
**10:1** Matt. 6:29
**20:1-10** Matt. 12:42; Luke 11:31
**10:4-7** Luke 12:27
**14:16** 2 Thess. 2:3
**16:31** Rev. 2:20
**17:1** Luke 4:25; Jas. 5:17; Rev. 11:6
**17:9** Luke 4:26
**17:9-24** Matt. 10:41
**17:17** Luke 7:12
**17:17-24** Heb. 11:35
**17:18** Matt. 8:29; Mark 5:7
**17:21** Acts 20:10
**17:23** Luke 7:15
**18:1** Luke 4:25
**18:4** Heb. 11:38
**18:12** Acts 8:39
**18:13** Heb. 11:38
**18:17** Acts 16:20
**18:24-39** Rev. 13:13
**18:42-45** Jas. 5:18
**18:46** Luke 12:35
**19:10** Rom. 11:3
**19:14** Rom. 11:3
**19:18** Rom. 11:4
**19:20** Matt. 8:21; Luke 9:61
**22:17** Matt. 9:36; Mark 6:34
**22:19** Rev. 4:2,9,10; 5:1, 7,13; 6:16; 7:10; 7:15; 19:4; 21:5
**22:26-27** Heb. 11:36

## II KINGS

**1:8** Matt. 3:4; Mark 1:6
**1:10** Luke 9:54; Rev. 11:5; 20:9
**2:11** Mark 16:19a; Rev. 11:12
**4:8-37** Matt. 10:41
**4:25-37** Heb. 11:35
**4:29** Luke 10:4; 12:35
**4:33** Matt. 6:6
**4:36** Luke 7:15
**4:43-44** Matt. 14:20
**4:44** Luke 9:17
**5:1-14** Luke 4:27
**5:10** John 9:7
**5:19** Mark 5:34
**9:1** Luke 12:35
**9:7** Rev. 6:10; 19:2
**9:13** Luke 19:36
**9:22** Rev. 2:20; 9:21
**9:27** Rev. 16:16
**12:9** Mark 12:41
**23:29** Rev. 16:16
**24:12-16** Matt. 1:11

## I CHRONICLES

**1:1-4** Luke 3:36-38
**1:24-27** Luke 3:34-36
**1:28** Luke 3:34
**1:34** Matt. 1:2; Luke 3:34

**2:1-14** Luke 3:31-33
**2:4,5,9** Matt. 1:3
**2:10-12** Matt. 1:4-5
**2:13-15** Matt. 1:6
**3:10-14** Matt. 1:7-10
**3:15-16** Matt. 1:11
**3:17** Matt. 1:12; Luke 3:27
**3:19** Matt. 1:12
**5:2** Heb. 7:14 **MPF**
**11:2** Matt. 2:6
**16:35** Acts 26:17
**17:1-14** Acts 7:45-46
**17:11** Matt. 1:1 **MPF**
**17:13** Heb. 1:5 **MPF**
**24:10** Luke 1:5
**29:11** Rev. 5:12 **MP**
**29:15** Heb. 11:13

**II CHRONICLES**

**3:1** Acts 7:47
**5:1** Acts 7:47
**5:7** Rev. 11:19
**5:13-14** Rev. 15:8
**6:2** Acts 7:47
**6:7-8** Acts 7:45,46
**6:10** Acts 7:47
**6:18** Acts 17:24; Rev. 21:3
**9:1** Matt. 6:29
**9:1-12** Matt. 12:42; Luke 11:31
**9:3-6** Luke 12:27
**13:9** Gal. 4:8
**15:6** Matt. 24:7; Mark 13:8; Luke 21:10
**15:7** 1 Cor. 15:58
**18:16** Matt. 9:36; Mark 6:34
**18:18** Rev. 4:2,9,10; 5:1, 7,13; 6:16; 7:10; 7:15; 19:4; 21:5
**18:25-26** Heb. 11:36
**19:7** Acts 10:34; Rom. 2:11; Eph. 6:9; Col. 3:25; 1 Pet. 1:17
**20:7** Jas. 2:23
**24:20-21** Matt. 23:35; Luke 11:51
**24:21** Heb. 11:37
**29:31** Heb. 13:15
**30:17** John 11:55
**36:10** Matt. 1:11
**36:15-16** Luke 20:10-12
**36:16** Matt. 5:12; Luke 6:23; Acts 7:52

**EZRA**

**3:2** Matt. 1:12; Luke 3:27
**4:3** John 4:9
**9:1-10:44** John 4:9
**9:3** Matt. 26:65
**9:6** Luke 21:24

**NEHEMIAH**

**9:6** Rev. 10:5
**9:15** John 6:31
**9:36** John 8:33
**10:37** Rom. 11:16
**11:1** Matt. 4:5

**ESTHER**

**4:1** Matt. 11:21
**5:3,6** Mark 6:23
**7:2** Mark 6:23

**JOB**

**1:1** 1 Thess. 5:22
**1:8** 1 Thess. 5:22
**1:9-11** Rev. 12:10
**1:20** Matt. 26:65
**1:21** 1 Tim. 6:7
**2:3** 1 Thess. 5:22
**2:6** 2 Cor. 12:7
**2:12** Matt. 26:65
**3:21** Rev. 9:6
**4:9** 2 Thess. 2:8
**4:19** 2 Cor. 5:1
**5:11** Luke 1:52b; Jas. 4:10
**5:13** 1 Cor. 3:19
**12:7-9** Rom. 1:20
**12:14** Rev. 3:7
**12:19** Luke 1:52a
**13:16** Phil. 1:19
**15:8** Rom. 11:34
**16:9** Acts 7:54
**19:25** 1 John 2:28; 3:2
**19:26-27** John 19:30
**22:29** Matt. 23:12; 1 Pet. 5:6
**23:10** 1 Pet. 1:7
**26:6** Rev. 9:11
**28:22** Rev. 9:11
**34:19** Jas. 2:1
**38:3** Luke 12:35
**38:17** Matt. 16:18
**39:30** Luke 17:37
**40:7** Luke 12:35
**41:11** Rom. 11:35
**42:2** Matt. 19:26; Mark 10:27

**PSALMS**

**2:1** Rev. 11:18
**2:1-2** Acts 4:25-26 **MPF**
**2:2** Rev. 19:19 **MPF** Rev. 6:15; 17:18
**2:7** Matt. 3:17; 17:5; Mark 1:11; 9:7; Luke 3:22; 9:35; John 1:49; Acts 13:33; Heb. 1:5; 5:5; 7:28; 2 Pet. 1:17 **MPF**
**2:8** Heb. 1:2
**2:8-9** Rev. 2:26-27; **MPF** Rev. 19:15 **MPU**
**2:9** Rev. 12:5 **MP**
**2:11** Phil. 2:12
**4:4** Eph. 4:26
**5:9** Rom. 3:13
**6:3** John 12:27
**6:8** Matt. 7:23; Luke 13:27
**7:9** Rev. 2:23
**7:12** Luke 13:3,5
**8:2** Matt. 21:16
**8:4-6** Heb. 2:6-8
**8:6** 1 Cor. 15:27; Eph. 1:22 **MPF**
**9:8** Acts 17:31
**10:7** Rom. 3:14
**10:16** Rev. 11:15
**11:6** Rev. 14:10; 20:10; 21:8
**14:1-3** Rom. 3:10-12
**14:7** Rom. 11:26-27
**16:8-11** Acts 2:25-28 **MPF**
**16:10** John 20:9; Acts 2:31; 13:35; 1 Cor. 15:4 **MPF**
**17:15** Rev. 22:4
**18:2** Luke 1:69 **MPF**
**18:4** Acts 2:24
**18:6** Jas. 5:4
**18:49** Rom. 15:9 **MPF**
**19:1** Rom. 1:20
**19:4** Rom. 10:18
**19:9** Rev. 16:7; 19:2
**21:9** Jas. 5:3
**22:1-31** 1 Pet. 1:11 **MPF**
**22:1** Matt. 27:46; Mark 15:34 **MPF**
**22:1-18** Mark 9:12; Luke 24:27 **MPF**
**22:5** Rom. 5:5
**22:7** Matt. 27:39; Mark 15:29; Luke 23:35 **MPF**
**22:7-8** Matt. 26:24 **MPF**
**22:8** Matt. 27:43 **MPF**
**22:15** John 19:28 **MPF**
**22:16** Phil. 3:2
**22:16-18** Matt. 26:24 **MPF**
**22:18** Matt. 27:35; Mark 15:24; Luke 23:34; John 19:24 **MPF**
**22:20** Phil. 3:2
**22:21** 2 Tim. 4:17
**22:22** Heb. 2:11-12, 17 **MPF**
**22:23** Rev. 19:5
**22:28** Rev. 11:15; 19:6
**23:1** John 10:11 **MPF**
**Rev. 7:17 MP**
**23:2** Rev. 7:17 **MP**
**23:5** Luke 7:46
**24:1** 1 Cor. 10:26
**24:2** Matt. 5:8
**24:7-10** 1 Cor. 2:8; Jas. 2:1 **MPF**
**25:11** I John 2:12
**25:19** John 15:25
**25:20** Rom. 5:5
**25:21** Luke 6:27
**26:6** Matt. 27:24
**26:8** Matt. 23:21
**28:4** Matt. 16:27; 2 Tim. 4:14; 1 Pet. 1:17; Rev. 20:12-13; 22:12
**29:3** Acts 7:2
**31:5** Luke 23:46 **MPF** Acts 7:59; 1 Pet. 4:19
**31:24** 1 Cor. 16:13
**32:1-2** Rom. 4:7-8
**32:2** Rev. 14:5
**32:5** I John 1:9
**33:2-3** Eph. 5:19
**33:3** Rev. 5:9; 14:3
**33:6** Heb. 1:14; 11:3
**33:9** Heb. 1:14; 11:3
**34:7** Heb. 1:14
**34:8** 1 Pet. 2:3
**34:12-16** 1 Pet. 3:10-12
**34:13** Jas. 1:26
**34:14** Heb. 12:14
**34:15** John 9:31
**34:19** 2 Cor. 1:5; 2 Tim. 3:11
**34:20** John 19:36 **MPF**
**35:8** Rom. 11:9-10
**35:13** Rom. 12:15
**35:16** Acts 7:54
**35:19** John 15:25
**36:1** Rom. 3:18
**36:9** Rev. 21:6
**37:4** Matt. 6:33
**37:11** Matt. 5:5
**37:12** Acts 7:54
**38:11** Luke 23:49
**39:1** Jas. 1:26
**39:12** Heb. 11:13; 1 Pet. 2:11
**40:3** Rev. 5:9; 14:3
**40:6** Eph. 5:2 **MPF**
**40:6-8** Heb. 10:5-10 **MPF**
**41:9** Matt. 26:23; Mark 14:18; Luke 22:21; John 13:18; 17:12; Acts 1:16 **MPF**
**41:13** Luke 1:68; Rom. 9:5
**42:2** Rev. 22:4
**42:5** Matt. 26:38; Mark 14:34; John 12:27
**42:11** Matt. 26:38; Mark 14:34; John 12:27
**43:5** Matt. 26:38; Mark 14:34
**44:22** Rom. 8:36
**45:2** Matt. 17:2; Mark 13:31; Luke 4:22; John 1:14; 7:46; Heb. 1:3-4; Rev. 1:13-18 **MPF**
**45:6-7** Heb. 1:8-9 **MPF**
**46:2-3** Luke 21:25
**46:6** Rev. 11:18
**47:5** Mark 16:19; Luke 24:51; John 6:62; Acts 1:9; Eph. 4:9 **MPF**
**47:8** Rev. 4:2,9,10; 5:1,7, 13; 6:16; 7:10; 7:15; 19:4; 21:5
**48:2** Matt. 5:35
**48:4** Rev. 6:15
**50:6** Heb. 12:23
**50:12** Acts 17:25; 1 Cor. 10:26

**50:14** Heb. 13:15a
**50:16-21** Rom. 2:21
**50:23** Heb. 13:15
**51:1** Luke 18:13
**51:4** Luke 15:18; Rom. 3:4b
**51:5** John 9:34; Rom. 7:14
**53:1-3** Rom. 3:10-12
**55:22** 1 Pet. 5:7
**62:10** Matt. 19:22; 1 Tim. 6:17
**62:12** Matt. 16:27; Rom. 2:6; 2 Tim. 4:14; 1 Pet. 1:17; Rev. 2:23; 20:12-13; 22:12
**65:2** Acts 10:34-35,45
**65:7** Luke 21:25
**66:10** 1 Pet. 1:7
**66:18** John 9:31
**67:2** Acts 28:28
**68:8** Heb. 12:26
**68:18** Eph. 4:8-11 **MPF**
**68:35** 2 Thess. 1:10
**69:4** John 15:25 **MPF**
**69:9** John 2:17; Rom. 15:3; Heb. 11:26 **MPF**
**69:21** Matt. 27:34,48; Mark 15:23,36; Luke 23:36; John 19:28-29 **MPF**
**69:22-23** Rom. 11:9-10
**69:24** Rev. 16:1
**69:25** Acts 1:20
**69:26** Matt. 27:34; Mark 15:23; John 19:29 **MPF**
**69:28** Phil. 4:3; Rev. 3:5; 13:8; 17:8; 20:12,15; 21:27
**72:2-4** Matt. 25:31-34; Acts 10:42; 17:31; Rom. 14:10; 2 Cor. 5:10 **MPU**
**72:10-11** Rev. 21:26 **MP** Matt. 2:11
**72:14** Tit. 2:14 MPF
**72:15** Matt. 2:11 **MPF**
**72:18** Luke 1:68
**74:2** Acts 20:28
**75:8** Rev. 14:10; 15:7; 16:19
**78:2** Matt. 13:35 **MPF**
**78:4** Eph. 6:4
**78:8** Acts 2:40
**78:15** 1 Cor. 10:4
**78:24** John 6:31; Rev. 2:17
**78:24-29** 1 Cor. 10:3
**78:31** 1 Cor. 10:5
**78:37** Acts 8:21
**78:44** Rev. 16:4
**79:1** Luke 21:24; Rev. 11:2
**79:3** Rev. 16:6
**79:6** 1 Thess. 4:5; 2 Thess. 1:8; Rev. 16:1
**79:10** Rev. 6:10; 19:2
**82:6** John 10:34
**86:9** Rev. 15:4
**88:8** Luke 23:49 **MPH**
**89:3-4** John 7:42a; Acts 2:30 **MPF**
**89:4** John 12:34
**89:7** 2 Thess. 1:10
**89:10** Luke 1:51
**89:11** 1 Cor. 10:26
**89:19** Mark 1:24; Luke 1:35; Acts 3:14; 4:27, 30 **MPF**
**89:20** Acts 13:22
**89:26** 1 Pet. 1:17; Rev. 21:7
**89:27** Rev. 1:5 **MPF** Rev. 17:18
**89:36** John 12:34 **MPF**
**89:37** Rev. 1:5; 3:14 **MPF**
**89:50-51** Heb. 11:26; 1 Pet. 4:14 **MPF**
**90:4** 2 Pet. 3:8
**91:11-12** Matt. 4:6; Luke 4:10-11; Heb. 1:14
**91:13** Luke 10:19 **MPF**
**92:5** Rev. 15:3
**93:1** Rev. 19:6
**94:1** 1 Thess. 4:6
**94:11** 1 Cor. 3:20
**4:14** Rom. 11:1-2
**94:19** 2 Cor. 1:5
**95:7-8** Heb. 4:7
**95:7-11** Heb. 3:7-11,13, 15-19
**95:11** Heb. 4:1-3,5-6,11
**96:1** Rev. 5:9; 14:3
**96:11** Rev. 18:20
**96:13** Acts 17:31; Rev. 19:11
**97:1** Rev. 19:7
**97:3** Rev. 11:5
**97:7** Heb. 1:6 **MPF**
**97:9** John 3:31
**98:1** Rev. 5:9; 14:3
**98:3** Luke 1:54; Acts 28:28
**98:9** Acts 17:31
**99:1** Rev. 11:18; 19:6
**102:4** Jas. 1:10-11
**102:11** Jas. 1:10-11
**102:25-26** Heb. 1:10-12
**103:3** Mark 2:7
**103:7** Rom. 3:2
**103:8** Jas. 5:11
**103:17** Luke 1:50
**104:2** 1 Tim. 6:16
**104:4** Heb. 1:7
**104:12** Matt. 13:32
**104:35** Rev. 19:1,3,4,6
**105:8-9** Luke 1:72-73
**105:21** Acts 7:10
**105:38** Rev. 11:10-11
**105:40** John 6:31
**106:10** Luke 1:71
**106:14** 1 Cor. 10:6
**106:20** Rom. 1:23
**106:25-27** 1 Cor. 10:10
**106:37** 1 Cor. 10:20
**106:45-46** Luke 1:72
**106:48** Luke 1:68
**107:3** Matt. 8:11; Luke 13:29
**107:9** Luke 1:53
**107:20** Acts 10:36; 13:26
**109:3** John 15:25
**109:7** 2 Thess. 2:3
**109:8** John 17:12; Acts 1:20b
**109:25** Matt. 27:39; Mark 15:29 **MPF**
**109:28** 1 Cor. 4:12
**110:1** Matt. 22:44; Mark 12:36; 16:19; Luke 20:42-43; 22:69; Acts 2:34-35; Rom. 8:34b; 1 Cor. 15:25; Eph. 1:20; Col 3:1; Heb. 1:3,13; 8:1; 10:12-13; 12:2; 1 Pet. 3:22 **MPF**
**110:1-2** Matt. 26:64; Mark 14:62 **MP**
**110:4** John 12:34; Heb. 5:6,10; 6:20; 7:11,15; 7:17,21,24,28 **MPF**
**110:5** Rev. 6:17
**110:6** Matt. 25:31-34
**111:2** Rev. 15:3
**111:4** Jas. 5:11
**111:9** Luke 1:49,68
**112:9** 2 Cor. 9:9
**112:10** Acts 7:54
**113:7-8** Luke 1:46-54
**113-118** Matt. 26:30
**114:3** Rev. 20:11
**114:7** Rev. 20:11
**115:7** Rev. 9:20
**115:13** Rev. 11:18; 19:5
**116:3** Acts 2:24
**116:10** 2 Cor. 4:13
**116:11** Rom. 3:4a
**117:1** Rom. 15:11
**118:6** Rom. 8:31; Heb. 13:6
**118:18** 2 Cor. 6:9
**118:20** John 10:9 **MPF**
**118:22** 1 Pet. 2:4,7 **MPF**
**118:22-23** Matt. 21:42; Mark 12:10-11; Luke 20:17; Acts 4:11 **MPF**
**118:25** Matt. 21:15
**118:25-26** Matt. 21:9; Mark 11:9-10; Luke 19:38; John 12:13 **MPF**
**118:26** Matt. 23:39; Luke 13:35b **MP**
**119:32** 2 Cor. 6:11
**119:46** Rom. 1:16
**119:137** Rev. 16:5,7; 19:2
**119:161** John 15:25
**119:165** 1 John 2:10
**122:1-5** John 4:20
**125:5** Gal. 6:16
**126:5-6** Luke 6:21
**128:6** Gal. 6:16
**130:8** Tit. 2:14; Rev. 1:5 **MPF**
**132:5** Acts 7:46
**132:11** Luke 1:32; Acts 2:30 **MPF**
**132:17** Luke 1:69 **MPF**
**134:1** Rev. 19:5
**135:1** Rev. 19:5
**135:14** Heb. 10:30
**135:15-17** Rev. 9:20
**137:8** Rev. 18:6
**137:9** Luke 19:44
**139:1** Rom. 8:27
**139:14** Rev. 15:3
**139:21** Rev. 2:6
**140:3** Rom. 3:13; Jas. 3:8
**141:2** Rev. 5:8; 8:3-4
**141:3** Jas. 1:26
**143:2** Rom. 3:20; 1 Cor. 4:4; Gal. 2:16
**144:9** Rev. 5:9; 14:3
**145:17** Rev. 15:3; 16:5
**145:18** Acts 17:27
**146:6** Acts 4:24; 14:15; 17:24; Rev. 10:6; 14:7
**147:8** Acts 14:17
**147:9** Luke 12:24
**147:18** Acts 10:36
**147:19-20** Rom. 3:2
**149:1** Rev. 5:9; 14:3

## PROVERBS

**1:16** Rom. 3:15-17
**2:2** Eph. 6:4
**2:3-4** Col. 2:3
**2:3-6** Jas. 1:5
**2:4** Matt. 13:44
**3:3** 2 Cor. 3:3
**3:4** Luke 2:52; Rom. 12:17; 2 Cor. 8:21
**3:7** Rom. 12:16
**3:11-12** Eph. 6:4; Heb. 12:5-7
**3:12** Rev. 3:19
**3:25** 1 Pet. 3:6
**3:27-28** 2 Cor. 8:12
**3:34** Jas. 4:6; 1 Pet. 5:5
**4:26** Heb. 12:13
**7:3** 2 Cor. 3:3
**8:15** Rom. 13:1
**8:22** Rev. 3:14
**8:22-25** John 1:1-2; 17:24; Col. 1:17
**10:9** Acts 13:10
**10:12** 1 Cor. 13:7; Jas. 5:20; 1 Pet. 4:8
**11:24** 2 Cor. 9:6
**11:31** 1 Pet. 4:18
**15:29** John 9:31
**16:4** Col. 1:16
**16:33** Acts 1:26
**17:3** 1 Pet. 1:17
**18:4** John 7:38
**19:17** Matt. 25:40
**19:18** Eph. 6:4
**20:22** 1 Thess. 5:15
**20:27** 1 Cor. 2:11

**22:6** Eph. 6:4
**22:8** 2 Cor. 9:7
**22:9** 2 Cor. 9:6
**23:4** 1 Tim. 6:9
**23:31** Eph. 5:18
**24:12** Matt. 16:27 **MPU** Rom. 2:6; 2 Tim. 4:14; 1 Pet. 1:17; Rev. 2:23; 20:12-13; 22:12
**24:21** 1 Pet. 2:17
**25:7** Luke 14:10
**25:21-22** Matt. 5:44; Rom. 12:20
**26:11** 2 Pet. 2:22
**27:1** Jas. 4:13-14
**27:20** I John 2:16
**28:13** I John 1:9
**28:22** 1 Tim. 6:9
**29:3** Luke 15:13
**29:23** Matt. 23:12
**30:4** Matt. 11:27; John 3:13 **MPF**
**30:8** 1 Tim. 6:8
**31:17** Luke 12:35

**ECCLESIASTES**

**1:2** Rom. 8:20
**5:15** 1 Tim. 6:7
**7:9** Jas. 1:19
**7:20** Rom. 3:10
**11:5** John 3:8
**12:14** 2 Cor. 5:10

**ISAIAH**

**1:9** Rom. 9:29
**1:10** Rev. 11:8
**1:15** John 9:31
**1:16** Jas. 4:8
**2:3** John 4:22
**2:4** John 16:8-11 **MPF** Acts 17:31; Rev. 19:11 **MPU**
**2:5** I John 1:7
**2:10** Rev. 6:15
**2:10-11** 2 Thess. 1:9 **MPU**
**2:19** 2 Thess. 1:9 **MPU**
**2:21** 2 Thess. 1:9 **MPU**
**4:2** John 1:14 **MPF**
**4:3** Rev. 17:8; 20:15
**5:1-7** Matt. 21:33; Mark 12:1; Luke 20:9
**5:9** Jas. 5:4
**5:21** Rom. 12:16
**6:1** Rev. 4:2,6,9-10; 5:1,7, 13; 6:16; 7:10,15; 19:4; 20:11; 21:5
**6:2-3** Rev. 4:8
**6:3** Rev. 15:8
**6:9-10** Matt. 13:14-15; Mark 4:12; Luke 8:10; 19:42; John 12:40; Acts 28:26-27; Rom. 11:8
**7:14** Matt. 1:23; Luke 1:31; John 1:45; Rev. 12:5 **MPF**
**8:8** Matt. 1:23 **MPF**
**8:10** Matt. 1:23 **MPF**
**8:12-13** 1 Pet. 3:14-15
**8:14** Rom. 9:32 **MPF**
**8:14-15** Matt. 21:44; Luke 2:34; 1 Pet. 2:8 **MP**
**8:17** Heb. 2:13a **MPF**
**8:18** Heb. 2:13b **MPF**
**8:19** Luke 24:5
**8:22** Rev. 16:10
**9:1-2** Matt. 4:15-16
**9:2** Luke 1:79; 2 Cor. 4:6; 1 Pet. 2:9 **MPF**
**9:6** John 1:45; Eph. 2:14 **MPF**
**9:7** Luke 1:32; John 12:34 **MPF**
**10:3** 1 Pet. 2:12 **MPU**
**10:22-23** Rom. 9:27-28
**11:1** Matt. 2:23; John 7:42; Acts 13:23; Heb. 7:14; Rev. 5:5; 22:16 **MPF**
**11:2** Eph. 1:17; 1 Pet. 4:14 **MPF**
**11:3** John 7:24 **MPF**
**11:4** John 7:24 **MPF** 2 Thess. 2:8; Rev. 19:11,15 **MPU** Eph. 6:17b
**11:5** Eph. 6:14a
**11:10** Rom. 15:12; Rev. 5:5; 22:16 **MPF**
**11:15** Rev. 16:12
**12:2** Heb. 2:13
**12:4** Rev. 11:17
**13:8** John 16:21
**13:10** Matt. 24:29; Mark 13:24; Luke 21:25; Rev. 6:13-14; 8:12
**13:21** Rev. 18:2
**14:12** Luke 10:18; Rev. 8:10
**14:13** Matt. 11:23; Luke 10:15
**14:15** Matt. 11:23; Luke 10:15
**17:8** Rev. 9:20
**19:1** Rev. 1:7a
**19:2** Matt. 24:7; Mark 13:8; Luke 21:10
**19:12** 1 Cor. 1:20
**21:3** John 16:21
**21:9** Rev. 14:8; 18:2
**22:13** 1 Cor. 15:32
**22:22** Rev. 3:7
**23:1-8** Matt. 11:21-22
**23:8** Rev. 18:23
**23:17** Rev. 17:2; 18:4
**24:8** Rev. 18:22
**24:15** 2 Thess. 1:12
**24:17** Luke 21:35
**24:19** Luke 21:25
**24:21** Rev. 6:15
**24:23** Rev. 4:4
**25:7** Luke 2:32a; 2 Cor. 3:16 **MPF**
**25:8** 1 Cor. 15:54; Rev. 7:17 **MPU** Rev. 21:4
**26:3** Phil. 4:7
**26:11** Heb. 10:27
**26:13** 2 Tim. 2:19
**26:17** John 16:21
**26:20** Matt. 6:6
**27:9** Rom. 11:27
**27:13** Matt. 24:31a
**28:11-12** 1 Cor. 14:21
**28:16** Rom. 9:33; 10:11; 1 Cor. 3:11; Eph. 2:20; 1 Pet. 2:4,6
**29:10** Rom. 11:8
**29:11** Rev. 5:1
**29:13** Matt. 15:8-9; Mark 7:6-7
**29:14** 1 Cor. 1:19
**29:16** Rom. 9:20-21
**29:18** Matt. 11:5
**30:30** Rev. 19:20
**30:33** Rev. 19:20; 20:10, 15; 21:8
**32:1** John 1:49; 18:37; 1 Cor. 15:25 **MPF**
**32:17** Jas. 3:18
**33:14** Heb. 12:29
**33:17** Matt. 17:2; John 1:14 **MPF**
**33:18** 1 Cor. 1:20
**33:24** Acts 10:43
**34:4** Matt. 24:29; Mark 13:25; Luke 21:26; 2 Pet. 3:12; Rev. 6:13-14
**34:10** Rev. 14:11; 19:3
**34:11** Rev. 18:2
**34:12** Rev. 6:15
**34:14** Rev. 18:2
**35:3** Heb. 12:12
**35:5-6** Matt. 11:5; Mark 7:37; Luke 7:22; Acts 26:18
**35:10** Rev. 21:4
**37:19** Gal. 4:8
**38:10** Matt. 16:18
**40:1** Luke 2:25
**40:2** Rev. 1:5 **MPF**
**40:3** Matt. 3:3; Mark 1:3; Luke 1:76; John 1:23
**40:3-5** Luke 3:4-6
**40:5** Luke 2:30-31 **MPF** Acts 28:28
**40:6-7** Jas. 1:10-11
**40:6-8** 1 Pet. 1:24-25
**40:9** John 12:15 **MPF**
**40:10** Rev. 22:7,12
**40:11** John 10:11 **MPF**
**40:13** 1 Cor. 2:16 **MPF**
**40:13-14** Rom. 11:34-35
**40:18-20** Acts 17:29
**41:2** Rev. 16:12
**41:4** Rev. 1:4,8; 4:8; 16:5
**41:8** Jas. 2:23
**41:8-9** Luke 1:54; Heb. 2:16
**41:9** Matt. 12:18-21 **MPF**
**41:10** Acts 18:9-10
**41:25** Rev. 16:12
**42:1** Matt. 3:17; 17:5; Mark 1:11; Luke 3:22; 9:35; 2 Pet. 1:17 **MPF**
**42:1-4** Matt. 12:18-21 **MPF**
**42:5** Acts 17:24-25
**42:6** Luke 2:32a; Acts 26:23 **MPF**
**42:7** Acts 26:18
**42:10** Rev. 5:9; 14:3
**42:12** 1 Pet. 2:9
**42:16** Acts 26:18
**42:18** Matt. 11:5
**42:21** Matt. 5:17-18; Rom. 13:9-10
**43:4** Rev. 3:9
**43:5** Acts 18:9-10
**43:6** 2 Cor. 6:18
**43:10** John 13:19 **MPF**
**43:13** Heb. 13:8
**43:18-21** 2 Cor. 5:17 **MPF**
**43:19** Rev. 21:5
**43:20-21** 1 Pet. 2:9
**43:25** Mark 2:7; Luke 5:21
**44:3** John 7:39
**44:6** Rev. 1:17; 2:8; 21:6; 22:13
**44:10-17** Acts 17:29
**44:23** Rev. 12:12; 18:20
**44:25** 1 Cor. 1:20
**44:27** Rev. 16:12
**44:28** Acts 13:22
**45:3** Col. 2:3
**45:9** Rom. 9:20-21
**45:14** 1 Cor. 14:25; Rev. 3:9
**45:15** Rom. 11:33
**45:17** Heb. 5:9
**45:21** Mark 12:32; Acts 15:18
**45:23** Rom. 14:11; Phil. 2:10-11 **MPF**
**46:13** Luke 2:32b **MPF**
**47:7-8** Rev. 18:7
**47:9** Rev. 18:8,23
**47:11** Rev. 18:7
**48:6** Rev. 1:19
**48:10** 1 Pet. 1:7
**48:12** Rev. 1:17; 2:8; 21:6; 22:13
**48:13** Rom. 4:17
**48:20** Rev. 18:4
**49:1** Gal. 1:15
**49:2** Eph. 6:17b; Heb. 4:12; Rev. 1:16; 2:12, 16; 19:15
**49:3** 2 Thess. 1:10
**49:3-9** Eph. 6:15
**49:4** Phil. 2:16
**49:6** Luke 2:32a; John 8:12; 9:5; Acts 13:47; 26:23 **MPF**
**49:8** 2 Cor. 6:2 **MPF**
**49:10** Rev. 7:16-17

**49:13** Luke 2:25; 2 Cor. 7:6; Rev. 12:12; 18:20
**49:18** Rom. 14:11
**49:23** Rev. 3:9
**49:24** Matt. 12:29
**49:26** Rev. 16:6
**50:6** Matt. 26:67; 27:30 **MPF**
**50:8** Rom. 8:33-34a
**51:16** Eph. 6:17b
**51:17** Rev. 14:10; 16:19
**52:1** Matt. 4:5; Eph. 5:14; Rev. 21:2,10,27
**52:3** 1 Pet. 1:18
**52:5** Rom. 2:24; 2 Pet. 2:2
**52:7** Acts 10:36; Rom. 10:15; Eph. 2:13,-17 **MPF**
2 Cor. 5:20; Eph. 6:15
**52:9** Luke 2:38
**52:10** Luke 2:30-31 **MPF**
**52:11** 2 Cor. 6:17; Rev. 18:4
**52:13** Acts 3:13
**52:14** Matt. 13:54; 15:31; 22:22,33; Mark 2:12; 4:41; 7:37; 10:24; Luke 2:48; 4:22,36; 8:25
**52:15** Rom. 15:21 **MPF**
1 Cor. 2:9
**53:1** John 12:38; Rom. 10:16
**53:2** Matt. 2:23 **MPF**
**53:3** Mark 9:12 **MPF**
**53:4** Matt. 8:17; 1 Pet. 2:24 **MPF**
**53:5** Matt. 26:67; Luke 24:46; Rom. 4:25; 1 Pet. 2:24 **MPF**
**53:5-6** Acts 10:43 **MPF**
**53:6** 1 Pet. 2:25 **MPF**
**53:6-7** John 1:29 **MPF**
**53:7** Matt. 26:63; 27:12, 14; Mark 14:60-61; 15:4-5; John 1:36; 1 Cor. 5:7; 1 Pet. 2:23; Rev. 5:6,12; 13:8 **MPF**
**53:7-8** Acts 8:32-33
**53:8-9** 1 Cor. 15:3 **MPF**
**53:9** Matt. 26:24; 1 Pet. 2:22; 1 John 3:5 **MPF**
Rev. 14:5
**53:11** Rom. 5:19 **MPF**
**53:12** Matt. 27:38; Mark 15:28; Luke 22:37; 23:33-34; Rom. 4:25; Heb. 9:28; 1 Pet. 2:24 **MPF**
**54:1** Gal. 4:27
**54:11-12** Rev. 21:18-19
**54:13** John 6:45
**54:16** Rom. 9:22
**55:1** John 7:37; Rev. 21:6; 22:17
**55:3** Acts 13:34; Heb. 13:20 **MPF**
**55:4** John 3:11,32; 8:14; 18:37; 1 Tim. 6:13; Rev. 1:5 **MPF**
**55:6** Acts 17:27
**55:8** Rom. 11:33
**55:10** 2 Cor. 9:10
**56:7b** Matt. 21:13a; Mark 11:17a; Luke 19:46a
**56:8** John 10:16
**56:12** 1 Cor. 15:32
**57:19** Eph. 2:13,17 **MPF**
Acts 2:39; Heb. 13:15b
**57:20** Jude 13
**58:5** Matt. 6:16
**58:6** Luke 4:18-19; Acts 8:23
**58:7** Matt. 25:35-36
**58:8** Luke 1:78-79; Rev. 21:11
**58:11** John 7:38
**59:7-8** Rom. 3:15-17
**59:16** Rom. 8:34; Heb. 7:25 **MPF**
Rev. 19:11 **MPU**
**59:17** Eph. 6:14b; 6:17a; 1 Thess. 5:8
**59:18** 1 Pet. 1:17; Rev. 20:12-13; 22:12
**59:19** Matt. 8:11; Luke 13:29
**59:20** Rom. 11:26 **MPF**
**59:21** Rom. 11:27
**60:1** Eph. 5:14
**60:1-2** Luke 1:78-79; John 1:14 **MPF**
Rev. 21:11,23 **MP**
**60:2** Rev. 21:24
**60:3** Rev. 21:24
**60:5** Rev. 21:24
**60:6** Matt. 2:11
**60:7** Matt. 21:13
**60:10-11** Rev. 21:24-25
**60:14** Rev. 3:9
**60:19** Rev. 21:11,23; 22:5
**60:21** 2 Pet. 3:13
**61:1** Matt. 11:5; Luke 7:22; Acts 10:38 **MPF**
Matt. 5:3; Acts 4:27; 26:18
**61:1-2** Luke 4:18-19 **MPF**
**61:2** Matt. 5:4
**61:3** Luke 6:21
**61:6** 1 Pet. 2:5,9; Rev. 1:6; 5:10; 20:6
**61:10** Rev. 19:8; 21:2
**62:2** Rev. 2:17; 3:12
**62:6** Heb. 13:17
**62:11** Matt. 21:5 **MPF**
Rev. 22:12 **MPU**
**63:1** Matt. 16:27 **MPU**
Matt. 9:6; 12:6 **MP**
**63:1-3** Rev. 19:13
**63:3** Rev. 14:20; 19:15
**63:9** Matt. 25:40,45
**63:10** Acts 7:51b; Eph. 4:30
**63:11** Heb. 13:20 **MPF**
**63:16** John 8:41
**63:18** Luke 21:24; Rev. 11:2
**64:4** 1 Cor. 2:9 **MPF**
**64:8** John 8:41; 1 Pet. 1:17
**65:1-2** Rom. 10:20-21
**65:15** Rev. 2:17; 3:12
**65:17** 2 Pet. 3:13; Rev. 21:1,4
**65:19** Rev. 21:4
**65:23** Phil. 2:16
**66:1** Matt. 5:34-35; 23:22
**66:1-2** Acts 7:49-50
**66:5** 2 Thess. 1:12 **MPU**
**66:6** Rev. 16:1,17
**66:7** Rev. 12:2,5 **MPF**
**66:14** John 16:22
**66:15** 2 Thess. 1:8 **MPU**
**66:22** 2 Pet. 3:13; Rev. 21:1
**66:24** Mark 9:48

**JEREMIAH**

**1:5** Gal. 1:15
**1:7-8** Acts 26:17
**1:8** Acts 18:9-10
**1:10** Rev. 10:11
**1:17** Luke 12:35
**2:11** Gal. 4:8
**2:13** Rev. 7:17; 21:6
**3:19** 1 Pet. 1:17
**4:4** Rom. 2:25
**4:29** Rev. 6:15
**5:14** Rev. 11:5
**5:21** Mark 8:18
**5:24** Acts 14:17, Jas. 5:7
**6:10** Acts 7:51b
**6:14** 1 Thess 5:3
**6:16** Matt. 11:29
**7:11** Matt. 21:13b; Mark 11:17b; Luke 19:46b
**7:18** Acts 7:42a
**7:34** Rev. 18:23
**8:2** Acts 7:42
**8:3** Rev. 9:6
**8:11** 1 Thess. 5:3
**9:11** Rev. 18:2
**9:15** Rev. 8:11
**9:24** 1 Cor. 1:31; 2 Cor. 10:17 **MPF**
**9:25** Rom. 2:25
**9:26** Acts 7:51b
**10:7** Rev. 15:4
**10:10** Rev. 15:3
**10:14** Rom. 1:22
**10:25** 1 Thess. 4:5; 2 Thess. 1:8; Rev. 16:1
**11:15** Rev. 20:9
**11:20** 1 Thess. 2:4; Rev. 2:23
**12:3** Jas. 5:5
**12:7** Matt. 23:38; Luke 13:35a; Rev. 20:9
**12:15** Acts 15:16
**13:25** Rom. 1:25
**14:12** Rev. 6:8
**14:14** Matt. 7:22
**15:2** Rev. 13:10
**15:3** Rev. 6:8
**16:9** Rev. 18:23
**16:19** Rom. 1:25
**17:10** 1 Pet. 1:17; Rev. 2:23; 20:12-13; 22:12
**17:21** John 5:10
**18:6** Rom. 9:21
**19:13** Acts 7:42a
**20:2** Heb. 11:36
**20:9** 1 Cor. 9:16
**21:7** Luke 21:24
**22:5** Matt. 23:38; Luke 13:35a
**23:1-2** John 10:8
**23:5-6** John 7:42; 1 Cor. 1:30 **MPF**
**23:18** Rom. 11:34
**23:23** Acts 17:27
**25:10** Rev. 18:22b-23
**25:15** Rev. 14:10; 15:7; 16:19
**25:16-27** Rev. 18:3
**25:29** 1 Pet. 4:17
**25:30** Rev. 10:11
**25:34** Jas. 5:5
**26:11** Acts 6:13
**27:15** Matt. 7:22
**27:20** Matt. 1:11
**30:9** Luke 1:69; Acts 2:30 **MPF**
**31:9** 1 Cor. 6:18
**31:15** Matt. 2:18
**31:16** Rev. 21:4
**31:25** Matt. 11:28; Luke 6:21
**31:31** Matt. 26:28; Luke 22:20; 1 Cor. 11:25; 2 Cor. 3:6
**31:31-34** Heb. 8:8-13 13 **MPF**
**31:33** 2 Cor. 3:3
**31:33-34** Rom. 11:26-27; 1 Thess. 4:9; Heb. 10:16-17
**31:34** Acts 10:43; Heb. 10:17; I John 2:27
**32:6-9** Matt. 27:9-10
**32:38** 2 Cor. 6:16
**32:40** Luke 22:20; 1 Cor. 11:25; 2 Cor. 3:6; Heb. 13:20
**33:15** John 7:42 **MPF**
**36:24** Matt. 26:65
**37:15** Heb. 11:36
**38:6** Heb. 11:36
**43:11** Rev. 13:10
**46:10** Luke 21:22
**49:11** 1 Tim. 5:5
**49:36** Rev. 7:1
**50:6** Matt. 10:6
**50:8** Rev. 18:4
**50:15** Rev. 18:6
**50:25** Rom. 9:22
**50:29** Rev. 18:6
**50:34** Rev. 18:8
**50:38** Rev. 16:12

**50:39** Rev. 18:2
**51:6** Rev. 18:4
**51:7** Rev. 14:8; 17:2,4; 18:3
**51:8** Rev. 14:8; 18:2
**51:9** Rev. 18:4,5
**51:13** Rev. 17:1,15
**51:25** Rev. 8:8
**51:36** Rev. 16:12
**51:45** 2 Cor. 6:17; Rev. 18:4
**51:48** Rev. 18:20
**51:49** Rev. 18:24
**51:63-64** Rev. 18:21.

**LAMENTATIONS**

**1:15** Rev. 14:20; 19:15
**2:15** Matt. 27:39; Mark 15:29
**3:15** Acts 8:23
**3:45** 1 Cor. 4:13
**3:52** John 15:25

**EZEKIEL**

**1:1** Rev. 19:11
**1:5** Rev. 4:6
**1:10** Rev. 4:7
**1:13** Rev. 4:5; 11:19
**1:18** Rev. 4:6,8
**1:22** Rev. 4:6
**1:24** Rev. 1:15; 14:2; 19:6
**1:26** Rev. 1:13
**1:26-27** Rev. 4:2,9-10; 5:1,7,13; 6:16; 7:10; 7:15; 19:4; 21:5
**1:26-28** Rev. 4:3
**2:1** Acts 26:16
**2:8** Rev. 10:9-10
**2:9-10** Rev. 5:1
**3:1** Rev. 10:9
**3:17** Heb. 13:17
**4:14** Acts 10:14
**5:12** Rev. 6:8
**5:17** Rev. 6:8
**7:2** Rev. 7:1; 20:8
**8:2** Rev. 1:13
**9:2** Rev. 1:13
**9:4** Rev. 7:3; 9:4; 14:1
**9:6** 1 Pet. 4:17
**9:11** Rev. 1:13
**10:12** Rev. 4:8
**10:14** Rev. 4:7
**11:19** 2 Cor. 3:3
**12:2** Mark 8:18; Rom. 11:8
**13:10** 1 Thess. 5:3
**13:10-12** Matt. 7:27
**13:10-15** Acts 23:3
**14:21** Rev. 6:8
**16:61** Rom. 6:21
**16:63** Rom. 6:21
**17:22-23** Matt. 13:32; Mark 4:32; Luke 13:19 **MP**
**18:20** John 9:2
**18:23** 1 Tim. 2:4
**20:33** 2 Cor. 6:17
**20:41** Eph. 5:12 **MPF** 2 Cor. 6:17; Phil. 4:18
**21:26** Matt. 23:12
**22:27** Matt. 7:15
**22:31** Rev. 16:1
**24:7** Rev. 18:24
**26:13** Rev. 18:22a
**26:16-17** Rev. 18:9
**26:17** Rev. 18:10
**26:19** Rev. 18:19
**26:21** Rev. 18:21
**27:9** Rev. 18:19
**27:13** Rev. 18:13
**27:17** Acts 12:20
**27:22** Rev. 18:12-13
**27:28-29** Rev. 18:17
**27:30** Rev. 18:19
**27:20-33** Rev. 18:9
**27:31-32** Rev. 18:15
**27:32** Rev. 18:18
**27:33** Rev. 18:19
**27:36** Rev. 18:11,15,19
**28:2** Acts 12:22; 2 Thess. 2:4
**28:13** Rev. 2:7; 17:4; 18:16
**29:5** Rev. 6:8
**31:6** Matt. 13:32; Mark 4:32; Luke 13:19
**31:8** Rev. 2:7
**32:7** Matt. 24:29; Luke 21:25
**32:7-8** Mark 13:24-25; Rev. 6:12-13; 8:12
**33:5** Matt. 27:25
**33:27** Rev. 6:8
**34:2-3** John 10:8
**34:5** Matt. 9:36; Mark 6:34
**34:5-6** 1 Pet. 2:25
**34:8** Mark 6:34; Jude 12
**34:11** Luke 15:4
**34:15** John 10:11
**34:16** Luke 15:4; 19:10 **MPF**
**34:17** Matt. 25:32
**34:23** John 1:45; 10:16 **MPF** Rev. 7:17 **MP**
**34:28** Rev. 6:8
**34:29** 1 Tim. 6:15
**36:20** Rom. 2:24
**36:23** Matt. 6:9
**36:25** Heb. 10:22
**36:26** 2 Cor. 3:3
**36:27** 1 Thess. 4:8
**37:5-10** Rev. 11:10-11
**37:9** Rev. 7:1
**37:12** Matt. 27:52-53
**37:14** 1 Thess. 4:8
**37:23** Tit. 2:14
**37:24** John 10:16 **MPF**
**37:26** Heb. 13:20 **MPF**
**37:27** 2 Cor. 6:16; Rev. 21:3
**38:2** Rev. 20:8
**38:19-20** Rev. 11:13
**38:22** Rev. 8:7; 14:10; 20:10; 21:8
**39:6** Rev. 20:9
**39:19-20** Rev. 19:17
**39:20** Rev. 19:21
**40:2** Rev. 21:10
**40:3** Rev. 11:1; 21:15
**40:5** Rev. 21:15
**40:47** Rev. 11:1
**41:5** Rev. 21:17
**43:2** Rev. 1:15; 14:2; 19:6
**43:16** Rev. 21:16
**44:4** Rev. 15:8
**44:7** Acts 21:28
**44:30** Rom. 11:16
**47:1** Rev. 22:1
**47:7** Rev. 22:2
**47:12** Rev. 22:2,14,19
**48:16-17** Rev. 21:16-17
**48:31-34** Rev. 21:12-13
**48:35** Rev. 3:12

**DANIEL**

**1:12** Rev. 2:10
**1:14** Rev. 2:10
**2:19** Rev. 11:13; 16:11
**2:28** Matt. 24:6; Mark 13:7; Luke 21:9; Rev. 1:1; 22:6
**2:29** Rev. 1:19; 4:1
**2:34-35** Acts 4:11; 1 Pet. 2:4,7 **MPF**
**Matt. 21:44; Luke 20:18 MP**
**2:35** Rev. 20:11
**2:44** 1 Cor. 15:24; Rev. 11:15
**2:44-45** Matt. 21:44
**2:45** Matt. 24:6; Rev. 1:1, 19; 4:1; 22:6
**2:47** 1 Cor. 14:25; Rev. 17:14; 19:16
**3:4** Rev. 10:11
**3:5** Matt. 4:9
**3:5-6** Rev. 13:15
**3:6** Matt. 13:42,50
**3:10** Matt. 4:9
**3:15** Matt. 4:9
**3:23-25** Heb. 11:34
**4:2** John 4:48
**4:12** Matt. 13:32; Mark 4:32; Luke 13:19
**4:21** Luke 13:19
**4:30** Rev. 14:8; 16:19; 17:5; 18:2,10
**4:34** Rev. 4:9-10
**4:37** John 4:48
**5:3-4** Rev. 9:20
**5:20** Acts 12:23
**5:23** Rev. 9:20
**6:21** 2 Tim. 4:17
**6:22** Heb. 11:33
**6:26** 1 Pet. 1:23; Rev. 4:9-10
**7:2** Rev. 7:1
**7:3** Rev. 11:7; 13:1; 17:8
**7:4-6** Rev. 13:2
**7:7** Rev. 11:7; 12:3,17; 13:1,7; 17:3
**7:8** Rev. 13:5
**7:9** Rev. 1:14; 20:4,11
**7:9-10** Matt. 19:28 **MPU**
**7:10** Rev. 5:11; 20:12
**7:13·** Matt. 24:30; 26:64; Mark 13:26; 14:62; Luke 21:27; 22:69; Rev. 1:7,13 **MPU**
**7:13-14** Matt. 24:30; Mark 13:26 **MPU**
**7:14** Matt. 28:18; John 12:34 **MPF** Rev. 11:15 **MP** Rev. 10:11; 19:6
**7:18** Rev. 22:5
**7:20** Rev. 13:5
**7:21** Rev. 11:7; 12:17; 13:7
**7:22** Luke 21:8; 1 Cor. 6:2; Rev. 20:4
**7:24** Rev. 17:12
**7:25** Rev. 12:14,13:5
**7:27** Rev. 20:4; 22:5
**8:10** Rev. 12:4
**8:13** Rev. 11:2
**8:16** Luke 1:19
**8:26** Rev. 10:4
**9:6** Rev. 10:7; 11:18
**9:10** Rev. 10:7; 11:18
**9:21** Luke 1:19
**9:24** Acts 10:43 **MPF**
**9:925** Matt. 16:16; John 1:41 **MPF**
**9:26** Luke 21:24
**9:27** Matt. 24:15; Mark 13:14
**10:5** Rev. 1:13
**10:6** Rev. 1:14; 2:18; 14:2; 19:6,12
**10:13** Jude 9; Rev. 12:7
**10:16** Rev. 14:14
**10:19** Rev. 1:17
**10:20** Rev. 12:7
**10:21** Jude 9: Rev. 12:7
**11:31** Matt. 24:15; Mark 13:14
**11:36-37** 2 Thess. 2:4; Rev. 13:5
**11:41** Matt. 24:10
**12:1** Matt. 24:21; Mark 13:19; Phil. 4:3; Jude 9; Rev. 3:5; 7:14; 12:7; 13:8; 16:18; 17:8; 20:12,15; 21:27
**12:2** Matt. 25:46; John 5:29; 11:24; Acts 24:15
**12:3** Matt. 13:43; Eph. 2:15
**12:4** Rev. 10:4; 22:10
**12:7** Luke 21:24; Rev. 4:9; 10:5; 12:14
**12:9** Rev. 10:4
**12:11** Matt. 24:15; Mark 13:14
**12:12** Jas. 5:11

## HOSEA

**1:6** 1 Pet. 2:10
**1:7** Tit. 2:13
**1:10** Rom. 9:26-28; 2 Cor. 6:18; 1 Pet. 2:10
**2:1** 1 Pet. 2:10
**2:23** Rom. 9:25; 1 Pet. 2:10
**4:1** Rev. 6:10
**6:2** Luke 24:46; 1 Cor. 15:4 **MPF**
**6:5** Eph. 6:17b
**6:6** Matt. 9:13; 12:7; Mark 12:33
**9:7** Luke 21:22
**10:8** Luke 23:30, Rev. 6:16; 9:6
**10:12** 2 Cor. 9:10
**11:1** Matt. 2:15 **MPF**
**12:8** Rev. 3:17
**13:14** 1 Cor. 15:55; Rev. 6:8
**14:2** Heb. 13:15b
**14:9** Acts 13:10

## JOEL

**1:6** Rev. 9:8
**2:2** Matt. 24:21
**2:4** Rev. 9:7
**2:5** Rev. 9:9
**2:10** Matt. 24:29; Mark 13:24-25; Rev. 6:12-13; 8:12; 9:2
**2:11** Rev. 6:17
**2:23** Jas. 5:7
**2:28** Acts 21:9; Tit. 3:6
**2:28-32** Acts 2:17-21
**2:30** Luke 21:25; Rev. 8:7
**2:31** Matt. 24:29; Mark 13:24-25; Luke 21:25; Rev. 6:12
**2:32** Acts 2:39; 22:16; Rom. 10:13
**3:4-8** Matt. 11:21-22; Luke 10:13-14
**3:13** Mark 4:29; Rev. 14:15,18,20; 19:15
**3:15** Matt. 24:29; Mark 13:24-25; Rev. 6:12-13; 8:12
**3:18** Rev. 22:1

## AMOS

**1:9-10** Matt. 11:21-22; Luke 10:13-14
**3:7** Rev. 10:7; 11:18
**4:13** 2 Cor. 6:18; Rev. 1:8 4:8; 11:17; 15:3; 16:7, 14; 19:6,15; 21:22
**5:10** Gal. 4:16
**5:13** Eph. 5:16
**5:15** Rom. 12:9
**5:25-26** Acts 7:42-43
**8:9** Matt. 27:45; Mark 15:33; Luke 23:44-45
**9:1** Rev. 8:3
**9:9** Luke 22:31
**9:11-12** Acts 15:16-18

## OBADIAH

**21** Rev. 11:15 **MP**

## JONAH

**1:17** Matt. 12:40; 1 Cor. 15:4 **MPF**
**3:5** Matt. 12:41
**3:6** Matt. 11:21
**3:8** Matt. 12:41; Luke 11:32
**3:10** Luke 11:32
**4:9** Matt. 26:38; Mark 14:34

## MICAH

**4:7** Luke 1:33
**4:9** John 16:21
**4:10** Rev. 12:2
**5:1** John 18:22; 19:3
**5:2** Matt. 2:6; John 7:42b **MPF**
**6:8** Matt. 23:23
**6:15** John 4:37
**7:6** Matt. 10:21,35-36; Mark 13:12; Luke 12:53
**7:20** Luke 1:55; Rom. 15:8

## NAHUM

**1:6** Rev. 6:17
**1:15** Acts 10:36; Rom. 10:15; Eph. 6:15 **MPF**

## HABAKKUK

**1:5** Acts 13:41
**1:6** Rev. 20:9
**2:3-4** Heb. 10:37-38; 2 Pet. 3:9
**2:4** Rom. 1:17; Gal. 3:11
**2:18-19** 1 Cor. 12:2
**3:17** Luke 13:6

## ZEPHANIAH

**1:3** Matt. 13:41
**1:14-15** Rev. 6:17
**3:8** Rev. 16:1
**3:13** Rev. 14:5
**3:15** John 1:49 **MPF**

## HAGGAI

**1:13** Matt. 28:20
**2:6** Matt. 24:29; Luke 21:26; Heb. 12:26-27
**2:7** John 1:14
**2:21** Matt. 24:29; Luke 21:26

## ZECHARIAH

**1:1** Matt. 23:25
**1:3** Jas. 4:8
**1:6** Rev. 10:7; 11:18
**1:8** Rev. 6:2,4-5; 19:11
**1:12** Rev. 6:10
**2:1-2** Rev. 11:1
**2:6** Matt. 24:31b; Mark 13:27
**2:10** Rev. 21:3
**3:1-2** Rev. 12:9; 20:2
**3:2-3** Jude 9, 23
**3:8** Phil. 2:7 **MPF**
**4:2-3** Rev. 4:5; 11:4
**4:10** Rev. 5:6
**4:11** Rev. 11:4
**4:14** Rev. 11:4
**6:2-3** Rev. 6:2,4-5; 19:11
**6:5** Rev. 7:1
**6:6** Rev. 6:2,4-5,19:11
**6:12-13** Heb. 10:21 **MPF**
**8:6** Matt. 19:26; Mark 10:27
**8:16** Eph. 4:25
**8:17** 1 Cor. 13:5
**8:23** 1 Cor. 14:25
**9:2-4** Matt. 11:21-22; Luke 10:13-14
**9:9** Matt. 21:5; John 12:15 **MPF**
**9:10** Eph. 2:17 MPF
**9:11** Matt. 26:28; Mark 14:24; Luke 22:20; 1 Cor. 11:25; Heb. 13:20
**9:17** John 1:14 **MPF**
**10:2** Matt. 9:36; Mark 6:34
**11:12** Matt. 26:15 **MPF**
**11:12-13** Matt. 27:9-10
**12:3** Luke 21:24; Rev. 11:2
**12:10** John 19:37 **MPF** Matt. 24:30 **MPU** Rev. 1:7b **MP**
**12:11** Rev. 16:16
**12:12** Matt. 24:30; Rev. 1:7b **MPF**
**13:4** Mark 1:6
**13:6** John 18:35 **MPF**
**13:7** Matt. 26:31,56; Mark 14:27,50; John 16:32 **MPF**
**13:9** 1 Pet. 1:7
**14:5** Matt. 25:31; 1 Thess. 3:13; 2 Thess. 1:7; Jude 14 **MPU**
**14:7** Rev. 21:25; 22:5
**14:8** John 7:38; Rev. 21:6; 22:1,17
**14:9** Rev. 11:15; 19:6
**14:11** Rev. 22:3

## MALACHI

**1:2-3** Rom. 9:13
**1:6** Luke 6:46
**1:7** 1 Cor. 10:21
**1:11** Matt. 8:11; Luke 13:29; 2 Thess. 1:12; Rev. 15:4
**1:12** 1 Cor. 10:21
**2:7-8** Matt. 23:3
**2:10** 1 Cor. 8:6
**3:1** Matt. 11:3,10; Mark 1:2; Luke 1:17,76; 7:19,27; John 3:28 **MPF**
**3:2** Rev. 6:17
**3:3** 1 Pet. 1:7 **MP**
**3:5** Jas. 5:4
**3:7** Jas. 4:8
**4:2** Luke 1:78
**4:5** Matt. 11:14; 17:11; Mark 9:12; Luke 1:17

## MATTHEW

**1:1** Gen. 5:1; 22:18; 1 Chr. 17:11 **MPF**
**1:2** Gen. 21:3,12; 25:26; 29:35; 1 Chr. 1:34
**1:3** Gen. 28:29-30; Ruth 4:12; 1 Chr. 2:4-5,9
**1:4-5** Ruth 4:13,17-22; 1 Chr. 2:10-12
**1:6** Ruth 4:17,22; 2 Sam. 12:24; 1 Chr. 2:13-15
**1:7-10** 1 Chr. 3:10-14
**1:11** 2 Kin. 24:12-16; 1 Chr. 3:15-16; 2 Chr. 36:10; Jer. 27:20
**1:12** 1 Chr. 3:17,19; Ezra 3:2
**1:23** Isa. 7:14; 8:8, 10 **MPF**
**2:2** Num. 24:17 **MPF**
**2:6** Mic. 5:2 **MPF** 2 Sam. 5:2; 1 Chr. 11:2
**2:11** Psa. 72:10-11,15; Isa. 60:6 **MPF**
**2:15** Hos. 11:1 **MPF**
**2:18** Jer. 31:15
**2:20** Ex. 4:19
**2:23** Judg. 13:5,7; Isa. 11:1; 53:2 **MPF**
**3:3** Isa. 40:3
**3:4** 2 Kin. 1:8
**3:17** Gen. 22:2; Isa. 42:1 **MPF**
**4:2** Ex. 34:28
**4:4** Deut. 8:3
**4:5** Neh. 11:1; Isa. 52:1
**4:6** Psa. 91:11
**4:7** Deut. 6:16
**4:9** Dan. 3:5,10,15
**4:10** Deut. 6:13
**4:15-16** Isa. 9:1-2
**5:3** Isa. 61:1
**5:4** Isa. 61:2
**5:5** Psa. 37:11
**5:8** Psa. 24:4
**5:12** 2 Chr. 36:16
**5:17-18** Isa. 42:21

**5:21** Ex. 20:13; 21:12; Lev. 24:17; Deut. 5:17
**5:27** Ex. 20:14; Deut. 5:18
**5:31** Deut. 24:1
**5:33** Ex. 20:7; Lev. 19:12; Num. 30:2; Deut. 5:11; 23:21
**5:34** Isa. 66:1
**5:35** Psa. 48:2
**5:38** Ex. 21:24; Lev. 24:20; Deut. 19:21
**5:43** Lev. 19:18
**5:44** Ex. 23:4-5; Prov. 25:21-22
**5:48** Lev. 19:2; Deut. 18:13
**6:6** 2 King. 4:33; Isa. 26:20
**6:9** Ezek. 36:23
**6:16** Isa. 58:5
**6:29** 1 Kin. 10:1; 2 Chr. 9:1
**6:33** Psa. 37:4
**6:34** Ex. 16:4
**7:15** Ezek. 22:27
**7:22** Jer. 14:14; 27:15
**7:23** Psa. 6:8
**7:27** Ezek. 13:10-12
**8:4** Lev. 13:49; 14:2,4-32
**8:11** Isa. 59:19; Mal. 1:11
**8:17** Isa. 53:4 **MPF**
**8:21** 1 Kin. 19:20
**8:29** 1 Kin. 17:18
**9:6** Isa. 63:1 **MP**
**9:13** Hos. 6:6
**9:20** Lev. 15:25
**9:36** Num. 27:17; 1 Kin. 22:17; 2 Chr. 18:16; Ezek. 34:5; Zech. 10:2
**10:6** Jer. 50:6
**10:10** Num. 18:31
**10:15** Gen. 18:20-19:28
**10:21** Mic. 7:6
**10:30** 1 Sam. 14:45
**10:35-36** Mic. 7:6
**10:37** Deut. 33:9
**10:41** 1 Kin. 17:9-24; 2 Kin. 4:8-37
**11:3** Mal. 3:1 **MPF**
**11:5** Isa. 29:18; 35:5-6; 42:18; 61:1 **MPF**
**11:10** Ex. 23:20; Mal. 3:1
**11:14** Mal. 4:5
**11:21** Esth. 4:1; Jonah 3:6
**11:21-22** Isa. 23:1-8; Joel 3:4-8; Amos 1:9-10; Zech. 9:2-4
**11:23** Gen. 19:24-28; Isa. 14:13,15
**11:27** Prov. 30:4 **MPF**
**11:28** Jer. 31:25
**11:29** Jer. 6:16
**12:1** Deut. 23:24-25
**12:2** Ex. 20:10; Deut. 5:14
**12:4** Lev. 24:5-9; 1 Sam. 21:6
**12:5** Num. 28:9-10
**12:6** Isa. 63:1 **MP**
**12:7** Hos. 6:6
**12:8** Gen. 2:3
**12:18-21** Isa. 41:9; 42:1-4 **MPF**
**12:25** 1 Sam. 16:7
**12:29** Isa. 49:24
**12:40** Jonah 1:17 **MPF**
**12:41** Jonah 3:5,8
**12:42** 1 Kin. 10:1-10; 2 Chr. 9:1-12
**13:14-15** Isa. 6:9-10
**13:32** Psa. 104:12; Ezek. 17:23; 31:6; Dan. 4:12
**13:35** Psa. 78:2 **MPF**
**13:41** Zeph. 1:3
**13:42** Dan. 3:6
**13:43** Dan. 12:3
**13:44** Prov. 2:4
**13:50** Dan. 3:6
**13:54** Isa. 52:14
**14:3-4** Lev. 18:16; 20:21
**14:20** 2 Kin. 4:43-44
**14:33** Josh. 5:14-15
**15:4a** Ex. 20:12; Lev. 20:9; Deut. 5:16
**15:4b** Ex. 21:17
**15:8-9** Isa. 29:13
**15:25** Josh. 5:14-15
**15:31** Isa. 52:14
**16:16** Dan. 9:25 **MPF**
**16:18** Gen. 22:17 **MPF** Job 38:17; Isa. 38:10
**16:27** Isa. 63:1 **MPU** Psa. 28:4; 62:12; Prov. 24:12
**17:2** Psa. 45:2; Isa. 33:17 **MPF**
**17:5** Deut. 18:15; Psa. 2:7; Isa. 42:1 **MPF**
**17:11** Mal. 4:5
**17:17** Deut. 32:5,20
**17:24** Ex. 30:13; 38:26
**18:15** Lev. 19:17
**18:16** Deut. 19:15
**19:4** Gen. 1:27; 5:2
**19:5** Gen. 2:24
**19:7** Deut. 24:1
**19:17** Lev. 18:5
**19:18** Ex. 20:13-16; Deut. 5:17-20
**19:19a** Ex. 20:12; Deut. 5:16
**19:19b** Lev. 19:18
**19:22** Psa. 62:10
**19:26** Gen. 18:14; Job. 42:2; Zech. 8:6
**19:28** Dan. 7:9-10 **MPU**
**20:8** Lev. 19:13; Deut. 24:15
**21:5** Isa. 62:11; Zech. 9:9 **MPF**
**21:9** Psa. 118:25-26 **MPF**
**21:13a** Isa. 56:7; 60:7
**21:13b** Jer. 7:11
**21:15** Psa. 118:25
**21:16** Psa. 8:2
**21:33** Isa. 5:1-7
**21:42** Psa. 118:22-23 **MPF**
**21:44** Isa. 8:14-15; Dan. 2:34-35,44-45 **MP**
**22:18** 1 Sam. 16:7
**22:22** Isa. 52:14
**22:24** Gen. 38:8; Deut. 25:5
**22:32** Ex. 3:6,15-16
**22:33** Isa. 52:14
**22:37** Deut. 6:5; Josh. 22:5
**22:39** Lev. 19:18
**22:43** 2 Sam. 23:2
**22:44** Psa. 110:1 **MPF**
**23:3** Mal. 2:7-8
**23:5** Ex. 13:9; Num. 15:38-39; Deut. 6:8
**23:12** Job 22:29; Prov. 29:23; Ezek. 21:26
**23:19** Ex. 29:37
**23:21** 1 Kin. 8:13; Psa. 26:8
**23:22** Isa. 66:1
**23:23** Lev. 27:30; Mic. 6:8
**23:35** Gen. 4:8; 2 Chr. 24:20-21; Zech. 1:1
**23:38** 1 Kin. 9:7-8; Jer. 12:7; 22:5
**23:39** Psa. 118:26 **MP**
**24:6** Dan. 2:28,45
**24:7** 2 Chr. 15:6; Isa. 19:2
**24:10** Dan. 11:41
**24:15** Dan. 9:27; 11:31; 12:11
**24:21** Dan. 12:1; Joel 2:2
**24:24** Deut. 13:1
**24:29** Isa. 13:10; 34:4; Ezek. 32:7; Joel 2:10, 31; 3:15; Hag. 2:6,21
**24:30** Dan. 7:13-14; Zech. 12:10,12 **MPU**
**24:31a** Isa. 27:13
**24:31b** Deut. 30:4; Zech. 2:6
**24:37** Gen. 6:9-12
**24:38** Gen. 7:7
**24:38-39** Gen. 6:13-7:24
**25:31** Zech. 14:5 **MPU**
**25:31-34** Psa. 72:2-4; 110:6
**25:32** Ezek. 34:17
**25:35-36** Isa. 58:7
**25:40** Prov. 19:17; Isa. 63:9
**25:45** Isa. 63:9
**25:46** Dan. 12:2
**26:2** Ex. 12:1-27
**26:11** Deut. 15:11
**26:15** Ex. 21:32; Zech. 11:12 **MPF**
**26:17** Ex. 12:14-20
**26:23** Psa. 41:9 **MPF**
**26:24** Psa. 22:7-8,16-18; Isa. 53:9 **MPF**
**26:28** Ex. 24:8; Jer. 31:31; Zech. 9:11
**26:30** Psa. 113-118
**26:31** Zech. 13:7 **MPF**
**26:38** Psa. 42:5,11; 43:5; Jonah 4:9
**26:52** Gen. 9:6
**26:56** Zech. 13:7 **MPF**
**26:63** Isa. 53:7 **MPF**
**26:64** Psa. 110:1 **MPF** Dan. 7:13 **MPU**
**26:65** Num. 14:6; 2 Sam. 13:19; Ezra 9:3; Job 1:20; 2:12; Jer. 36:24
**26:65-66** Lev. 24:16
**26:67** Isa. 50:6; 53:5 **MPF**
**27:9-10** Jer. 32:6-9; Zech. 11:12-13
**27:12** Isa. 53:7 **MPF**
**27:14** Isa. 53:7 **MPF**
**27:24** Deut. 21:6-9; Psa. 26:6
**27:25** Ezek. 33:5
**27:30** Isa. 50:6 **MPF**
**27:34** Psa. 69:21,26 **MPF**
**27:35** Psa. 22:18 **MPF**
**27:38** Isa. 53:12 **MPF**
**27:39** Psa. 22:7; 109:25 **MPF** Lam. 2:15
**27:43** Psa. 22:8 **MPF**
**27:45** Amos 8:9
**27:46** Psa. 22:1 **MPF**
**27:48** Psa. 69:21 **MPF**
**27:51** Ex. 26:31-35
**27:52-53** Ezek. 37:12
**27:57-58** Deut. 21:22-23 **MPF**
**28:18** Dan. 7:14 **MPF**
**28:20** Hag. 1:13

## MARK

**1:2** Ex. 23:20; Mal. 3:1
**1:3** Isa. 40:3
**1:6** 2 Kin. 1:8; Zech. 13:4
**1:11** Gen. 22:2; Psa. 2:7; Isa. 42:1 **MPF**
**1:24** Psa. 89:19 **MPF**
**1:44** Lev. 13:49; 14:2-32
**2:7** Psa. 103:3; Isa. 43:25
**2:8** 1 Sam. 16:7
**2:12** Isa. 52:14
**2:23** Deut. 23:25
**2:26** Lev. 24:5-9; 1 Sam. 21:6; 2 Sam. 15:35
**2:27** Ex. 20:8-10; Deut. 5:12-14
**4:12** Isa. 6:9-10
**4:29** Joel 3:13
**4:32** Ezek. 17:23; 31:6; Dan. 4:12
**4:41** Isa. 52:14
**5:7** 1 Kin. 17:18
**5:34** 1 Sam. 1:17; 20:42; 2 Sam. 15:9; 2 Kin. 5:19
**6:18** Lev. 18:16
**6:23** Esth. 5:3,6; 7:2

**6:34** Num. 27:17; 1 Kin. 22:17; 2 Chr. 18:16; Ezek. 34:5,8; Zech. 10:2
**7:6-7** Isa. 29:13
**7:10a** Ex. 20:12; Lev. 20:9; Deut. 5:16
**7:10b** Ex. 21:17
**7:37** Isa. 35:5-6 **MPF** Isa. 52:14
**8:18** Jer. 5:21; Ezek. 12:2
**9:7** Deut. 18:15 **MPF**
**9:12** Psa. 22:1-18; Isa. 53:3; Mal. 4:5 **MPF**
**9:48** Isa. 66:24
**10:4** Deut. 24:1
**10:6** Gen. 1:27; 5:2
**10:7-8** Gen. 2:24
**10:19** Ex. 20:12-16; Deut. 5:16-20; 24:14
**10:24** Isa. 52:14
**10:27** Gen. 18:14; Job 42:2; Zech. 8:6
**11:9-10** Psa. 118:25-26 **MPF**
**11:17a** Isa. 56:7b
**11:17b** Jer. 7:11
**12:1** Isa. 5:1-7
**12:6** Gen. 22:2
**12:10-11** Psa. 118:22-23 **MPF**
**12:19** Gen. 38:8; Deut. 25:5
**12:26** Ex. 3:2,6,15-16
**12:29-30** Deut. 6:4-5; Josh. 22:5
**12:31** Lev. 19:18
**12:32-33** Lev. 19:18; Deut. 4:35; 6:4-5; Josh. 22:5; 1 Sam. 15:22; Isa. 45:21
**12:33** Hos. 6:6
**12:36** Psa. 110:1 **MPF**
**12:41** 2 Kin. 12:9
**13:7** Dan. 2:28
**13:8** 2 Chr. 15:6; Isa. 19:2
**13:12** Mic. 7:6
**13:14** Dan. 9:27; 11:31; 12:11
**13:19** Dan. 12:1
**13:22** Deut. 13:1-3
**13:24** Isa. 13:10; Ezek. 32:7-8; Joel 2:10,31; 3:15
**13:25** Isa. 34:4; Ezek. 32:7-8; Joel 2:10,31; 3:15
**13:26** Dan. 7:13-14 **MPU**
**13:27** Deut. 30:4; Zech. 2:6
**13:31** Psa. 45:2 **MPF**
**14:7** Deut. 15:11
**14:12** Ex. 12:6,15
**14:18** Psa. 41:9 **MPF**
**14:24** Ex. 24:8; Zech. 9:11
**14:27** Zech. 13:7 **MPF**
**14:34** Psa. 42:5,11; 43:5; Jonah 4:9
**14:50** Zech. 13:7 **MPF**
**14:60-61** Isa. 53:7 **MPF**
**14:62** Psa. 110:1-2; Dan. 7:13 **MP**
**14:63** Num. 14:6
**14:64** Lev. 24:16
**15:4-5** Isa. 53:7 **MPF**
**15:23** Psa. 69:21,26 **MPF**
**15:24** Psa. 22:18 **MPF**
**15:28** Isa. 53:12 **MPF**
**15:29** Psa. 22:7; 109:25 **MPF** Lam. 2:15
**15:33** Amos 8:9
**15:34** Psa. 22:1 **MPF**
**15:36** Psa. 69:21 **MPF**
**16:19a** Psa. 47:5 **MPF** 2 Kin. 2:11
**16:19b** Psa. 110:1 **MPF**

**LUKE**

**1:5** 1 Chr. 24:10
**1:9** Ex. 30:7
**1:15** Num. 6:3; Judg. 13:4
**1:17** Mal. 3:1; 4:5-6 **MPF**
**1:18** Gen. 18:11
**1:19** Dan. 8:16; 9:21
**1:25** Gen. 30:23
**1:31** Gen. 16:11; Judg. 13:3; Isa. 7:14
**1:32** 2 Sam. 7:12-13,16; Psa. 132:11; Isa. 9:7 **MPF**
**1:33** Mic. 4:7
**1:35** Psa. 89:19 **MPF**
**1:37** Gen. 18:14
**1:41** Gen. 25:22
**1:42** Deut. 28:4; Judg. 5:24
**1:46-47** 1 Sam. 2:1
**1:46-54** Psa. 113:7-8
**1:48** 1 Sam. 1:11
**1:49** Psa. 111:9
**1:50** Psa. 103:17
**1:51** 2 Sam. 22:28; Psa. 89:10
**1:52a** Job 12:19
**1:52b** 1 Sam. 2:7; Job 5:11
**1:53** 1 Sam. 2:5; Psa. 107:9
**1:54** Psa. 98:3; Isa. 41:8-9
**1:55** Gen. 17:7; 22:17; Mic. 7:20 **MPF**
**1:59** Gen. 17:12; Lev. 12:3
**1:68** Psa. 41:13; 72:18; 106:48; 111:9
**1:69** 1 Sam. 2:10; Psa. 18:2; 132:17; Jer. 30:9 **MPF**
**1:71** Psa. 106:10
**1:72** Psa. 106:45-46
**1:72-73** Gen. 17:7; Lev. 26:42; Psa. 105:8-9 **MPF**
**1:73-74** Gen. 22:16-17
**1:76** Isa. 40:3; Mal. 3:1
**1:78-79** Isa. 58:8; 60:1-2; Mal. 4:2 **MPF**
**1:79** Isa. 9:2 **MPF**
**2:21** Gen. 17:12; Lev. 12:3
**2:22** Lev. 12:6
**2:23** Ex. 13:2,12,15
**2:24** Lev. 5:11; 12:8
**2:25** Isa. 40:1; 49:13
**2:30-31** Isa. 40:5; 52:10 **MPF**
**2:32a** Isa. 25:7; 42:6; 49:6 **MPF**
**2:32b** Isa. 46:13 **MPF**
**2:34** Isa. 8:14-15 **MP**
**2:38** Isa. 52:9
**2:41** Ex. 12:24-27; Deut. 16:1-8
**2:48** Isa. 52:14
**2:52** 1 Sam. 2:26; Prov. 3:4
**3:4-6** Isa. 40:3-5
**3:22** Gen. 22:2; Psa. 2:7; Isa. 42:1 **MPF**
**3:27** 1 Chr. 3:17; Ezra 3:2
**3:31** 2 Sam. 5:14
**3:31-33** Ruth 4:17-22; 1 Sam. 16:1; 1 Chr. 2:1-14
**3:33** Gen. 29:35
**3:34** Gen. 21:3; 25:26; 1 Chr. 1:28,34
**3:34-36** Gen. 11:10-26; 1 Chr. 1:24-27
**3:36-38** Gen. 4:25-5:32; 1 Chr. 1:1-4
**4:4** Deut. 8:3
**4:8** Deut. 6:13
**4:10-11** Psa. 91:11-12
**4:12** Deut. 6:16
**4:18-19** Isa. 61:1-2 **MPF** Isa. 58:6
**4:22** Isa. 45:2 **MPF** Isa. 52:14
**4:25** 1 Kin. 17:1; 18:1
**4:26** 1 Kin. 17:9
**4:27** 2 Kin. 5:1-14
**4:36** Isa. 52:14
**5:14** Lev. 13:49; 14:2-32
**5:21** Isa. 43:25
**6:1** Deut. 23:25
**6:4** Lev. 24:5-9; 1 Sam. 21:6
**6:8** 1 Sam. 16:7
**6:21** Psa. 126:5-6; Isa. 61:3; Jer. 31:25
**6:23** 2 Chr. 36:16
**6:27** Psa. 25:21
**6:35** Lev. 25:35-36
**6:46** Mal. 1:6
**7:12** 1 Kin. 17:17
**7:15** 1 Kin. 17:23; 2 Kin. 4:36
**7:19** Mal. 3:1 **MPF**
**7:22** Isa. 35:5-6; 61:1 **MPF**
**7:27** Ex. 23:20; Mal. 3:1
**7:44** Gen. 18:4
**7:46** Psa. 23:5
**8:10** Isa. 6:9
**8:25** Isa. 52:14
**9:17** 2 Kin. 4:44
**9:35** Deut. 18:15; Psa. 2:7; Isa. 42:1 **MPF**
**9:54** 2 Kin. 1:10
**9:61** 1 Kin. 19:20
**10:4** 2 Kin. 4:29
**10:12** Gen. 19:24-25
**10:13-14** Joel 3:4-8; Amos 1:9-10; Zech. 9:2-4
**10:15** Isa. 14:13,15
**10:18** Isa. 14:12
**10:19** Gen. 3:15; Psa. 91:13 **MPF**
**10:20** Ex. 32:32
**10:27** Lev. 19:18; Deut. 6:5; 10:12; Josh. 22:5
**10:28** Lev. 18:5
**11:17** 1 Sam. 16:7
**11:20** Ex. 8:19
**11:31** 1 Kin. 10:1-10; 2 Chr. 9:1-12
**11:32** Jonah 3:8,10
**11:42** Lev. 27:30
**11:51** Gen. 4:8; 2 Chr. 24:20-21
**12:14** Ex. 2:14
**12:24** Psa. 147:9
**12:27** 1 Kin. 10:4-7; 2 Chr. 9:3-6
**12:35** Ex. 12:11; 1 Kin. 18:46; 2 Kin. 4:29; 9:1; Job 38:3; 40:7; Prov. 31:17; Jer. 1:17
**12:53** Mic. 7:6
**13:3,5** Psa. 7:12
**13:6** Hab. 3:17
**13:14** Ex. 20:9-10; Deut. 5:13-14
**13:19** Ezek. 17:23; 31:6; Dan. 4:12,21
**13:27** Psa. 6:8
**13:29** Isa. 59:19; Mal. 1:11
**13:35a** Jer. 12:7; 22:5
**13:35b** Psa. 118:26 **MP**
**14:10** Prov. 25:7
**14:26** Deut. 33:9
**15:4** Ezek. 34:11, 16 **MPF**
**15:13** Prov. 29:3
**15:18** Psa. 51:4
**17:12** Lev. 13:46
**17:14** Lev. 13:49; 14:2-3
**17:26** Gen. 6:5-12
**17:27** Gen. 7:7
**17:28** Gen. 18:20-21; 19:1-14
**17:29** Gen. 19:24
**17:31** Gen. 19:17,26
**17:37** Job 39:30
**18:12** Gen. 14:20
**18:13** Psa. 51:1
**18:20** Ex. 20:12-16; Deut. 5:16-20

**19:8** Ex. 22:1
**19:10** Ezek. 34:16 **MPF**
**19:36** 2 Kin. 9:13
**19:38** Psa. 118:26 **MPF**
**19:42** Deut. 32:29; Isa. 6:9-10
**19:44** Psa. 137:9
**19:46a** Isa. 56:7b
**19:46b** Jer. 7:11
**20:9** Isa. 5:1-2
**20:10-12** 2 Chr. 36:15-16
**20:17** Psa. 118:22 **MPF**
**20:18** Dan. 2:34 **MP**
**20:28** Gen. 38:8; Deut. 25:5
**20:37** Ex. 3:2,6,15
**20:42-43** Psa. 110:1 **MPF**
**21:8** Dan. 7:22
**21:9** Dan. 2:28
**21:10** 2 Chr. 15:6; Isa. 19:2
**21:18** 1 Sam. 14:45
**21:22** Deut. 32:35; Jer. 46:10; Hos. 9:7
**21:24** Ezra 9:7; Psa. 79:1; Isa. 63:18; Jer. 21:7; Dan. 9:26; 12:7; Zech. 12:3
**21:25** Psa. 46:2-3; 65:7; Isa. 13:10; 24:19; Ezek. 32:7; Joel 2:30-31
**21:26** Isa. 34:4; Hag. 2:6, 21
**21:27** Dan. 7:13 **MPU**
**21:35** Isa. 24:17
**22:7** Ex. 12:6,14,15
**22:8** Ex. 12:8-11
**22:20** Ex. 24:8; Jer. 31:31; 32:40; Zech. 9:11
**22:21** Psa. 41:9 **MPF**
**22:31** Amos 9:9
**22:37** Isa. 53:12 **MPF**
**22:69** Psa. 110:1 **MPF**
**23:30** Hos. 10:8
**23:33-34** Isa. 53:12 **MPF**
**23:34** Psa. 22:18 **MPF**
**23:35** Psa. 22:7 **MPF**
**23:36** Psa. 69:21 **MPF**
**23:44-45** Amos 8:9
**23:45** Ex. 26:31-33; 36:35
**23:46** Psa. 31:5 **MPF**
**23:49** Psa. 88:8,18 **MPF** Psa. 38:11
**23:56** Ex. 12:16; 20:10; Deut. 5:14
**24:5** Isa. 8:19
**24:27** Deut. 18:15; Psa. 22:1-18 **MPF**
**24:46** Isa. 53:5; Hos. 6:2 **MPF**
**24:51** Psa. 47:5 **MPF**

## JOHN

**1:1-2** Prov. 8:22-25
**1:14** Psa. 45:2; Isa. 4:2; 33:17; 60:1-2; Zech. 9:17 **MPF** Hag. 2:7
**1:17** Ex. 31:18; 34:28
**1:18** Ex. 33:20
**1:21** Deut. 18:15, 18 **MPF**
**1:23** Isa. 40:3
**1:29** Gen. 22:9; Isa. 53:6-7 **MPF**
**1:36** Isa. 53:7 **MPF**
**1:41** Dan. 9:25 **MPF**
**1:45** Deut. 18:18; Isa. 7:14; 9:6; Ezek. 34:23 **MPF**
**1:49** Isa. 32:1; Zeph. 3:15 **MPF**
**1:51** Gen. 28:12
**2:5** Gen. 41:55
**2:17** Psa. 69:9 **MPF**
**2:25** 1 Sam. 16:7
**3:8** Eccl. 11:5
**3:11** Isa. 55:4 **MPF**
**3:13** Prov. 30:4 **MPF**
**3:14** Num. 21:9
**3:28** Mal. 3:1 **MPF**
**3:31** Psa. 97:9 **MPF**
**4:5** Gen. 33:19; 48:22; Josh. 24:32
**4:9** Ezra 4:3; 9:1-10:44
**4:20** Deut. 11:29; 12:5-14; Josh. 8:33; Psa. 122:1-5
**4:22** Isa. 2:3
**4:37** Mic. 6:15
**4:48** Dan. 4:2,37
**5:10** Jer. 17:21
**5:29** Dan. 12:2
**5:45** Deut. 31:26-27
**5:46** Deut. 18:15 **MPF**
**6:14** Deut. 18:15, 18 **MPF**
**6:31** Ex. 16:4-15; Num. 11:7-9; Neh. 9:15; Psa. 78:24; 105:40
**6:45** Isa. 54:13
**6:62** Psa. 47:5 **MPF**
**7:2** Lev. 23:34
**7:22** Gen. 17:10-13; Lev. 12:3
**7:24** Isa. 11:3-4 **MPF** Lev. 19:15
**7:37** Lev. 23:36; Isa. 55:1
**7:38** Isa. 58:11; Zech. 14:8
**7:39** Isa. 44:3
**7:40** Deut. 18:15 **MPF**
**7:42a** 2 Sam. 7:12-13; Psa. 89:3-4; Isa. 11:1; Jer. 23:5-6; 33:15 **MPF**
**7:42b** 2 Sam. 7:12-13; Mic. 5:2 **MPF**
**6:46** **Psa. 45:2** **MPF**
**7:51** Deut. 1:16
**8:5** Lev. 20:10; Deut. 22:22
**8:7** Deut. 17:7
**8:12** Isa. 49:6 **MPF**
**8:14** Isa. 55:4 **MPF**
**8:17** Deut. 17:6; 19:15
**8:33** Neh. 9:36
**8:35** Ex. 21:2; Deut. 15:12
**8:41** Deut. 32:6; Isa. 63:16; 64:8
**8:44** Gen. 3:4
**9:2** Ex. 20:5; Ezek. 18:20
**9:5** Isa. 49:6 **MPF**
**9:7** 2 Kin. 5:10
**9:24** Josh. 7:19
**9:31** Psa. 34:15; 66:18; Prov. 15:29; Isa. 1:15
**9:34** Psa. 51:5
**10:8** Jer. 23:1-2; Ezek. 34:2-3
**10:9** Psa. 118:20 **MPF**
**10:11** Psa. 23:1; Isa. 40:11; Ezek. 34:15 **MPF**
**10:16** Isa. 56:8; Ezek. 34:23; 37:24 **MPF**
**10:33** Lev. 24:16
**10:34** Psa. 82:6
**11:24** Dan. 12:2
**11:52** Gen. 49:10 **MPF**
**11:55** 2 Chr. 30:17
**12:8** Deut. 5:11
**12:13** Psa. 118:25-26 **MPF**
**12:15** Isa. 40:9; Zech. 9:9 **MPF**
**12:27** Psa. 6:3; 42:5,11
**12:34** Psa. 89:4,36; Isa. 9:7; Dan. 7:14 **MPF**
**12:38** Isa. 53:1 **MPF**
**12:40** Isa. 6:10
**13:18** Psa. 41:9 **MPF**
**13:19** Isa. 43:10 **MPF**
**14:11** Ex. 23:20-21 **MPF**
**15:25** Psa. 69:4 **MPF** Psa. 25:19; 35:19; 109:3; 119:61; Lam. 3:52
**16:8-11** Isa. 2:4 **MPF**
**16:21** Isa. 13:8; 21:3; 26:17; Mic. 4:9
**16:22** Isa. 66:14
**16:32** Zech. 13:7 MPF
**17:12** Psa. 41:9; 109:8 **MPF**
**17:24** Prov. 8:22-25
**18:22** Mic. 5:1
**18:35** Zech. 13:6 **MPF**
**18:37** Isa. 32:1; 55:4 **MPF**
**19:3** Mic. 5:1
**19:7** Lev. 24:16
**19:24** Psa. 22:18 **MPF**
**19:28-29** Psa. 22:15; 69:21,26 **MPF**
**19:30** Job 19:26-27
**19:31** Deut. 21:22-23 **MPF**
**19:36** Ex. 12:46; Num. 9:12; Psa. 34:20 **MPF**
**19:37** Zech. 12:10 **MPF**
**20:9** Psa. 16:10 **MPF**

## ACTS

**1:9** Psa. 47:5 **MPF**
**1:16** Psa. 41:9 **MPF**
**1:20a** Psa. 69:25
**1:20b** Psa. 109:8
**1:26** Prov. 16:33
**2:1** Lev. 23:15-21; Deut. 16:9-11
**2:17-21** Joel 2:28-32
**2:24** 2 Sam. 22:6; Psa. 18:4; 116:3
**2:25-28** Psa. 16:8-11 **MPF**
**2:29** 1 Kin. 2:10
**2:30** 2 Sam. 7:12-13; Psa. 89:3-4; 132:11; Jer. 30:9 **MPF**
**2:31** Psa. 16:10 **MPF**
**2:34-35** Psa. 110:1 **MPF**
**2:39** Isa. 57:19; Joel 2:32
**2:40** Deut. 32:5; Psa. 78:8
**3:13** Ex. 3:6,15; Isa. 52:13
**3:14** Psa. 89:19 **MPF**
**3:22** Deut. 18:15-18 **MPF**
**3:23** Lev. 23:29; Deut. 18:19
**3:25** Gen. 12:3,7; 18:18; 22:18; 26:4
**4:11** Psa. 118:22; Dan. 2:34 **MPF**
**4:24** Ex. 20:11; Psa. 146:6
**4:25-26** Psa. 2:1-2 **MPF**
**4:27** Psa. 89:19; Isa. 61:1 **MPF**
**4:30** Psa. 89:19 **MPF**
**5:30** Deut. 21:22-23 **MPF**
**6:13** Jer. 26:11
**7:2** Psa. 29:3
**7:3** Gen. 12:1; 48:4
**7:4** Gen. 12:5
**7:5** Gen. 12:7; 13:15; 15:18; 17:8; 24:7; 48:4 **MPF** Gen. 16:1; Deut. 2:5; 11:5; 32:49
**7:6** Gen. 15:13-14; Ex. 2:22
**7:7** Gen. 15:14; Ex. 3:12
**7:8a** Gen. 17:10-11
**7:8b** Gen. 21:4
**7:9** Gen. 37:11,28; 39:2, 3,21; 45:4
**7:10** Gen. 39:21; 41:40, 43,46; Psa. 105:24
**7:11** Gen. 41:54-55; 42:5
**7:12** Gen. 42:2
**7:13** Gen. 45:1,3,16
**7:14** Gen. 45:9-11,18-19; Ex. 1:5; Deut. 10:22
**7:15** Gen. 46:5-6; 49:33; Ex. 1:6
**7:16** Gen. 23:16-17; 33:19; 49:29-30; 50:13; Josh. 24:32
**7:17-18** Ex. 1:7-8
**7:19a** Ex. 1:9-10,22
**7:19b** Ex. 1:18
**7:20** Ex. 2:2

**7:21** Ex. 2:5,10
**7:23** Ex. 2:11
**7:24** Ex. 2:12
**7:27-28** Ex. 2:13-14
**7:29** Ex. 2:15-22; 18:3-4
**7:30** Ex. 3:1
**7:30-31** Ex. 3:2-3
**7:32** Ex. 3:6
**7:33** Ex. 3:5
**7:34** Ex. 2:24; 3:7-10
**7:35** Ex. 2:14; 3:2
**7:36** Ex. 7:3; 14:21; Num. 14:33
**7:37** Deut. 18:15-18 **MPF**
**7:38** Ex. 19:1-6; 20:1-17; 23:20-21; Deut. 5:4-22; 9:10
**7:39** Ex. 23:20-21; Num. 14:3-4
**7:40** Ex. 32:1,23
**7:41** Ex. 32:4-6
**7:42a** Jer. 7:18; 8:2; 19:13
**7:42-43** Amos 5:25-26
**7:44** Ex. 25:1-40; 27:21; Num. 1:50
**7:45** Gen. 17:8; 48:4; Deut. 32:49; Josh. 3:14-17; 18:1; 23:9; 24:18; 2 Sam. 2-16; 1 Kin. 8:17-18; 1 Chr. 17:1-14; 2 Chr. 6:7-8
**7:46** 2 Sam. 7:2-16; 1 Kin. 8:17-18; 1 Chr. 17:1-14; 2 Chr. 6:7-8; Psa. 132:5
**7:47** 1 Kin. 6:1-2,14; 8:19-20; 2 Chr. 3:1; 5:1; 6:2,10
**7:49-50** Isa. 66:1-2
**7:51a** Ex. 32:9; 33:3-5; Lev. 26:41
**7:51b** Lev. 26:41; Num. 27:14; Isa. 63:10; Jer. 6:10; 9:26
**7:52** 2 Chr. 36:16
**7:54** Job 16:9; Psa. 35:16; 37:12; 112:10
**7:59** Psa. 31:5
**8:21** Psa. 78:37
**8:23** Deut. 29:18; Isa. 58:6; Lam. 3:15
**8:24** Ex. 8:4,24; 9:28
**8:32-33** Isa. 53:7-8
**8:39** 1 Kin. 18:12
**10:14** Lev. 11:1-47; Ezek. 4:14
**10:34** Deut. 10:17; 2 Chr. 19:7; Psa. 65:2
**10:36** Isa. 52:7; Nah. 1:15 **MPF** Psa. 107:20; 147:18
**10:38** Isa. 61:1 **MPF**
**10:39** Deut. 21:22-23
**10:42** Psa. 72:2-4 **MPU**
**10:43** Isa. 53:5-6; Jer. 31:34; Dan. 9:24-25 **MPF**
**10:45** Psa. 65:2
**12:20** 1 Kin. 5:11; Ezek. 27:17
**12:22** Ezek. 28:2
**12:23** Dan. 5:20
**13:10** Prov. 10:9; Hos. 14:9
**13:17** Ex. 6:1,6; 12:51
**13:18** Ex. 16:35; Num. 14:34; Deut. 1:31
**13:19** Deut. 7:1; Josh. 14:1
**13:20** Judg. 2:16; 1 Sam. 3:20
**13:21** 1 Sam. 8:5,19; 10:20-21,24; 11:15
**13:22** 1 Sam. 13:14; 16:12-13; Psa. 89:20; Isa. 44:28
**13:23** Isa. 11:1; 2 Sam. 7:12-13 **MPF**
**13:26** Isa. 52:7; Nah. 1:15 **MPF**
**13:33** Psa. 2:7 **MPF**
**13:34** Isa. 55:3 **MPF**
**13:35** Psa. 16:10 **MPF**
**13:36** Judg. 2:10; 1 Kin. 2:10
**13:41** Hab. 1:5
**13:47** Isa. 49:6 **MPF**
**14:15** Ex. 20:11; Psa. 146:6
**14:17** Psa. 147:8; Jer. 5:24
**15:1** Lev. 12:3
**15:16-18** Isa. 45:21; Jer. 12:15; Amos 9:11-12
**15:20** Gen. 9:4; Lev. 3:17; 17:10-14
**15:29** Gen. 9:4; Lev. 3:17; 17:10-14
**16:20** 1 Kin. 18:17
**17:24** 1 Kin. 8:27; 2 Chr. 6:18; Psa. 146:6; Isa. 42:5
**17:25** Psa. 50:12; Isa. 42:5
**17:26** Deut. 32:8
**17:27** Psa. 145:18; Isa. 55:6; Jer. 23:23
**17:29** Gen. 1:27; Isa. 40:18-20; 44:10-17
**17:31** Psa. 9:8; 72:2-4; 96:13; 98:9; Isa. 2:4 **MPU**
**18:9-10** Isa. 41:10; 43:5; Jer. 1:8
**18:18** Num. 6:18
**20:10** 1 Kin. 17:21
**20:28** Psa. 74:2
**20:32** Deut. 33:3-4
**20:33** 1 Sam. 12:3
**21:9** Joel 2:28
**21:23-24** Num. 6:5,13-18,
**21:26** Num. 6:5, 13-21
**21:28** Ezek. 44:7
**22:16** Joel 2:32
**23:3** Lev. 19:15; Ezek. 13:10-15
**23:5** Ex. 22:28
**24:15** Dan. 12:2
**26:16** Ezek. 2:1
**26:17** 1 Chr. 16:35; Jer. 1:7-8
**26:18** Deut. 33:3-4; Isa. 35:5-6; 42:7,16; 61:1
**26:23** Isa. 42:6; 49:6 **MPF**
**27:9** Lev. 16:29
**27:34** 1 Sam. 14:45; 2 Sam. 14:11
**28:26-27** Isa. 6:9-10
**28:28** Psa. 67:2; 98:3; Isa. 40:5

## ROMANS

**1:7** Num. 6:25-26
**1:16** Psa. 119:46
**1:17** Hab. 2:4
**1:20** Job 12:7-9; Psa. 19:1
**1:22** Jer. 10:14
**1:23** Deut. 4:15-19; Psa. 106:20
**1:25** Jer. 13:25; 16:19
**1:27** Lev. 18:22; 20:13
**2:6** Psa. 62:12; Prov. 24:12
**2:11** Deut. 10:17; 2 Chr. 19:7
**2:21** Psa. 50:16-21
**2:24** Isa. 52:5; Ezek. 36:20
**2:25** Jer. 4:4; 9:25
**2:29** Deut. 30:6
**3:2** Deut. 4:7-8; Psa. 103:7; 147:19-20
**3:4a** Psa. 116:11
**3:4b** Psa. 51:4
**3:10-12** Psa. 14:1-3; 53:1-3; Eccl. 7:20
**3:13** Psa. 5:9; 140:3
**3:14** Psa. 10:7
**3:15-17** Prov. 1:16; Isa. 59:7-8
**3:18** Psa. 36:1
**3:20** Psa. 143:2
**3:30** Deut. 6:5
**4:3** Gen. 15:6
**4:7-8** Psa. 32:1-2
**4:9** Gen. 15:6
**4:11** Gen. 17:11
**4:13** Gen. 18:18; 22:17-18
**4:17** Gen. 17:5; Isa. 48:13
**4:18** Gen. 15:5
**4:19** Gen. 17:17
**4:22-24** Gen. 15:6
**4:25** Isa. 53:5,12 **MPF**
**5:5** Psa. 22:5; 25:20
**5:12** Gen. 2:17; 3:6,19
**5:19** Isa. 53:11 **MPF**
**6:21** Ezek. 16:61,63
**7:7** Ex. 20:14-17; Deut. 5:18-21
**7:10** Lev. 18:5
**7:11** Gen. 3:13
**7:14** Psa. 51:5
**7:18** Gen. 6:5; 8:21
**8:20** Gen. 3:17-19; 5:29; Eccl. 1:2
**8:27** Psa. 139:1
**8:31** Psa. 118:6
**8:33-34a** Isa. 50:8
**8:34b** Psa. 110:1; Isa. 59:16 **MPF**
**8:36** Psa. 44:22
**9:3** Ex. 32:32
**9:4** Ex. 4:22; Deut. 7:6; 14:1-2
**9:5** Psa. 41:13
**9:6** Num. 23:19
**9:7** Gen. 21:12
**9:9** Gen. 18:10,14
**9:10** Gen. 25:21
**9:12** Gen. 25:23
**9:13** Mal. 1:2-3
**9:14** Deut. 32:4
**9:15** Ex. 33:19
**9:17** Ex. 9:16
**9:18** Ex. 4:21; 7:3; 9:12; 14:4,17
**9:20** Isa. 29:16; 45:9
**9:21** Isa. 29:16; 45:9; Jer. 18:6
**9:22** Isa. 54:16; Jer. 50:25
**9:25** Hos. 2:23
**9:26** Hos. 1:10
**9:27-28** Isa. 10:22-23; Hos. 1:10a
**9:29** Isa. 1:9
**9:32** Isa. 8:14 **MPF**
**9:33** Isa. 28:16 **MPF**
**10:5** Lev. 18:5
**10:6-9** Deut. 30:12-14 **MPF** Deut. 9:14
**10:11** Isa. 28:16 **MPF**
**10:13** Joel 2:32
**10:15** Isa. 52:7; Nah. 1:15 **MPF**
**10:16** Isa. 53:1
**10:18** Psa. 19:4
**10:19** Deut. 32:21
**10:20-21** Isa. 65:1-2
**11:1-2** 1 Sam. 12:22; Psa. 94:14
**11:3** 1 Kin. 19:10,14
**11:4** 1 Kin. 19:18
**11:8** Deut. 29:4; Isa. 6:9-10; 29:10; Ezek. 12:2 12:2
**11:9-10** Psa. 35:8; 69:22-23
**11:11** Deut. 32:21
**11:16** Num. 15:17-21; Neh. 10:37; Ezek. 44:30
**11:26** Isa. 59:20 **MPF**
**11:26-27** Psa. 14:7
**11:27** Isa. 27:9; 59:21; Jer. 31:33-34
**11:33** Isa. 45:15; 55:8
**11:34** Jer. 23:18
**11:34-35** Job 15:8; 41:11; Isa. 40:13-14
**12:9** Amos 5:15
**12:15** Psa. 35:13
**12:16** Prov. 3:7; Isa. 5:21

**12:17** Prov. 3:4
**12:19** Lev. 19:18; Deut. 32:35
**12:20** Prov. 25:21-22
**13:1** Prov. 8:15
**13:9a** Ex. 20:13-17; Deut. 5:17-21
**13:9b** Lev. 19:18
**13:9-10** Isa. 42:21
**14:2** Gen. 1:29; 9:3
**14:10** Psa. 72:2-4 **MPU**
**14:11** Isa. 45:23; 49:18 **MPF**
**15:3** Psa. 69:9 **MPF**
**15:8** Mic. 7:20
**15:9** 2 Sam. 22:50; Psa. 18:49 **MPF**
**15:10** Deut. 32:43
**15:11** Psa. 117:1
**15:12** Isa. 11:10 **MPF**
**15:21** Isa. 52:15 **MPF**
**16:20** Gen. 3:15 **MPF**

### I CORINTHIANS

**1:9** Deut. 7:9
**1:19** Isa. 29:14
**1:20** Isa. 19:12; 33:18
**1:30** Jer. 23:5-6 **MPF**
**1:31** Jer. 9:24 **MPF**
**2:8** Psa. 24:7-10 **MPF**
**2:9** Isa. 52:15; 64:4 **MPF**
**2:11** Prov. 20:27
**2:16** Isa. 40:13 **MPF**
**3:11** Isa. 28:16
**3:19** Job 5:13
**3:20** Psa. 94:11
**4:4** Psa. 143:2
**4:12** Psa. 109:28
**4:13** Lam. 3:45
**5:1** Lev. 18:7-8; Deut. 20:30; 27:20
**5:7** Ex. 12:21; 13:7; Isa. 53:7 **MPF**
**5:8** Ex. 12:3-20; 13:7; Deut. 16:3
**5:13** Deut. 17:7; 19:19; 22:21,24; 24:7
**6:2** Dan. 7:22
**6:16** Gen. 2:24
**8:4** Deut. 4:35,39; 6:5
**8:6** Mal. 2:10
**9:9** Duet. 25:4
**9:13** Lev. 6:16,26; Num. 18:8,31; Deut. 18:1-3
**9:16** Jer. 20:9
**10:1** Ex. 13:21-22; 14:22-29
**10:3** Ex. 16:4,35; Deut. 8:3; Psa. 78:24-29
**10:4** Ex. 17:6; Num. 20:11; Psa. 78:15
**10:5** Num. 14:16,23,29-30; Psa. 78:31
**10:6** Num. 11:4, 34; Psa. 106:14
**10:7** Ex. 32:6
**10:8** Num. 25:1,9
**10:9** Ex. 23:20-21; Num. 21:5-6
**10:10** Num. 14:2,36; 16:41-49; Psa. 106:25-27
**10:13** Deut. 7:9
**10:18** Lev. 7:6,15
**10:20** Deut. 32:17; Psa. 106:37
**10:21** Mal. 1:7,12
**10:22** Deut. 32:21
**10:26** Psa. 24:1; 50:12; 89:11
**11:3** Gen. 3:16
**11:7** Gen. 1:27; 5:1; 9:6
**11:8** Gen. 2:21-23
**11:9** Gen. 2:18
**11:19** Deut. 13:3
**11:25** Ex. 24:8; Jer. 31:31; 32:40; Zech. 9:11
**12:2** Hab. 2:18-19
**13:5** Zech. 8:17
**13:7** Prov. 10:12
**14:5** Num. 11:29
**14:21** Isa. 28:11-12
**14:25** Isa. 45:14; Dan. 2:47; Zech. 8:23
**14:34** Gen. 3:16
**15:3** Isa. 53:8-9 **MPF**
**15:4** Psa. 16:10; Hos. 6:2; Jonah 1:17 **MPF**
**15:21** Gen. 3:17-19
**15:24** Dan. 2:44
**15:25** Psa. 110:1; Isa. 32:1 **MPF**
**15:27** Psa. 8:6 **MPF**
**15:32** Isa. 22:13; 56:12
**15:38** Gen. 1:11
**15:45** Gen. 2:7
**15:47** Gen. 2:7
**15:49** Gen. 5:3
**15:54** Isa. 25:8 MPU
**15:55** Hos. 13:14
**15:58** 2 Chr. 15:7
**16:8** Lev. 23:15-21; Deut. 16:9-11
**16:13** Psa. 31:24

### II CORINTHIANS

**1:5** Psa. 34:19; 94:19
**3:3** Ex. 24:12; 31:18; 34:1; Deut. 9:10-11; Prov. 3:3; 7:3; Jer. 31:33; Ezek. 11:19; 36:26
**3:6** Ex. 24:8; Jer. 31:31; 32:40
**3:7** Ex. 34:29-30,34
**3:9** Deut. 27:26
**3:10** Ex. 34:29-30
**3:13** Ex. 34:33, 35; 36:35
**3:16** Isa. 25:7 **MPF** Ex. 34:34
**3:18** Ex. 16:7; 24:17
**4:6** Isa. 9:2 **MPF** Gen. 1:3
**4:13** Psa. 116:10
**5:1** Job 4:19
**5:10** Psa. 72:2-4; Eccl. 12:14 **MPU**
**5:17** Isa. 43:18-21 **MPF**
**5:20** Isa. 52:7 **MPF**
**6:2** Isa. 49:8 **MPF**
**6:9** Psa. 118:18
**6:11** Psa. 119:32
**6:16** Lev. 26:11-12; Jer. 32:38; Ezek. 37:27
**6:17** Isa. 52:11; Jer. 51:45; Ezek. 20:33,41
**6:18** 2 Sam. 7:8,14; Isa. 43:6; Jer. 31:9; Hos. 1:10; Amos 4:13
**7:6** Isa. 49:13
**8:12** Prov. 3:27-28
**8:15** Ex. 16:18
**8:21** Prov. 3:4
**9:6** Prov. 11:24; 22:9
**9:7** Prov. 22:8
**9:9** Psa. 112:9
**9:10** Isa. 55:10; Hos. 10:12
**10:17** Jer. 9:24 **MPF**
**11:3** Gen. 3:13
**12:7** Job 2:6
**13:1** Deut. 19:15

### GALATIANS

**1:15** Isa. 49:1; Jer. 1:5
**2:6** Deut. 10:17
**2:16** Psa. 143:2
**3:6** Gen. 15:6
**3:8** Gen. 12:3; 18:18
**3:10** Deut. 27:26
**3:11** Hab. 2:4
**3:12** Lev. 18:5
**3:13** Deut. 21:23 **MPF**
**3:16** Gen. 12:7; 13:15; 17:7; 22:18; 24:7 **MPF**
**3:17** Ex. 12:40
**4:8** 2 Chr. 13:9; Isa. 37:19; Jer. 2:11
**4:16** Amos 5:10
**4:22** Gen. 16:5; 21:2
**4:27** Isa. 54:1
**4:29** Gen. 21:9
**4:30** Gen. 21:10
**5:14** Lev. 19:18
**6:16** Psa. 125:5; 128:6

### EPHESIANS

**1:17** Isa. 11:2 **MPF**
**1:18** Deut. 33:3,27-29
**1:20** Psa. 110:1 **MPF**
**1:22** Psa. 8:6 **MPF**
**2:13** Isa. 52:7; 57:19 **MPF**
**2:14** Isa. 9:6; Mic. 5:5 **MPF**
**2:15** Dan. 12:3
**2:17** Isa. 52:7; 57:19; Zech. 9:10 **MPF**
**2:20** Isa. 28:16 **MPF**
**4:8-11** Psa. 68:18 **MPF**
**4:9** Psa. 47:5 **MPF**
**4:24** Gen. 1:26
**4:25** Zech. 8:16
**4:26** Psa. 4:4
**4:30** Isa. 63:10
**5:2** Ex. 29:18; Psa. 40:6; Ezek. 20:41 **MPF**
**5:14** Isa. 52:1; 60:1
**5:16** Amos. 5:13
**5:18** Prov. 23:31
**5:19** Psa. 33:2-3
**5:22** Gen. 3:16
**5:31** Gen. 2:24
**6:2-3** Ex. 20:12; Deut. 5:16; 15:16
**6:4** Deut. 6:7,20-25; Psa. 78:4; Prov. 2:2; 3:11-12; 19:18; 22:6
**6:9** Deut. 10:17; 2 Chr. 19:7
**6:14a** Isa. 11:5
**6:14b** Isa. 59:17
**6:15** Isa. 49:3-9; 52:7; Nah. 1:15 **MPF**
**6:17a** Isa. 59:17
**6:17b** Isa. 11:4; 49:2; 51:16; Hos. 6:5

### PHILIPPIANS

**1:19** Job 13:16
**2:7** Zech. 3:8 **MPF**
**2:10-11** Isa. 45:23 **MPF**
**2:12** Psa. 2:11
**2:15** Deut. 32:5
**2:16** Isa. 49:4; 65:23
**3:2** Psa. 22:16,20
**4:3** Ex. 32:33; Psa. 69:28; Dan. 12:1
**4:7** Isa. 26:3
**4:18** Gen. 8:21; Ex. 29:18; Ezek. 20:41

### COLOSSIANS

**1:16** Prov. 16:4
**1:17** Prov. 8:22-25
**2:3** Prov. 2:3-4; Isa. 45:3
**3:1** Psa. 110:1 **MPF**
**3:10** Gen. 1:27
**3:18** Gen. 3:16
**3:25** Deut. 10:17; 2 Chr. 19:7
**4:1** Lev. 25:43, 53

### I THESSALONIANS

**2:4** Jer. 11:20
**2:16** Gen. 15:16
**3:13** Zech. 14:5 **MPU**
**4:5** Psa. 79:6; Jer. 10:25
**4:6** Psa. 94:1
**4:8** Ezek. 36:27; 37:14
**4:9** Jer. 31:33-34

**5:3** Jer. 6:14; 8:11; Ezek. 13:10
**5:8** Isa. 59:17
**5:15** Prov. 20:22
**5:22** Job 1:1; 8,2:3

**II THESSALONIANS**

**1:7** Zech. 14:5 **MPU**
**1:8** Psa. 79:6; Isa. 66:15; Jer. 10:25 **MPU**
**1:9** Isa. 2:10-11,19, 21 **MPU**
**1:10** Psa. 68:35; 89:7; Isa. 49:3
**1:12** Mal. 1:11 **MPU** Isa. 24:15; 66:5
**2:3** 1 Kin. 14:16; Psa. 109:7
**2:4** Ezek. 28:2; Dan. 11:36-37
**2:8** Isa. 11:4 **MPU** Job 4:9
**2:13** Duet. 33:12

**I TIMOTHY**

**2:4** Ezek. 18:23
**2:13** Gen. 1:27; 2:7,22
**2:14** Gen. 3:6,13
**4:3** Gen. 9:3
**4:4** Gen. 1:31
**5:1** Lev. 19:32
**5:5** Jer. 49:11
**5:18** Lev. 19:13; Deut. 25:4
**5:19** Deut. 17:6; 19:15
**6:7** Job 1:21; Eccl. 5:15
**6:8** Prov. 30:8
**6:9** Prov. 23:4; 28:22
**6:13** Isa. 55:4 **MPF**
**6:15** Deut. 10:17; Ezek. 34:29
**6:16** Ex. 33:20; Psa. 104:2
**6:17** Psa. 62:10

**II TIMOTHY**

**2:13** Num. 23:19
**2:19** Num. 16:5,26; Isa. 26:13
**3:8** Ex. 7:11,22
**3:11** Psa. 34:19
**4:14** 2 Sam. 3:39; Psa. 28:4; 62:12; Prov. 24:12
**4:17** Psa. 22:21; Dan. 6:21

**TITUS**

**2:13** Hos. 1:7
**2:14** Ex. 19:5; Deut. 4:20; 7:6; 14:2; Psa. 72:14; 130:8; Ezek. 37:23 **MPF**
**3:6** Joel 2:28

**HEBREWS**

**1:2** Deut. 32:18
**1:3** Psa. 110:1 **MPF**
**1:3-4** Psa. 45:2 **MPF**
**1:5** 2 Sam. 7:14; 1 Chr. 17:13; Psa. 2:7 **MPF**
**1:6** Deut. 32:43; Psa. 97:7
**1:7** Psa. 104:4
**1:8-9** Psa. 45:6-7 **MPF**
**1:10-12** Gen. 1:1; Psa. 102:25-26
**1:13** Psa. 110:1
**1:14** Psa. 33:6,9; 34:7; 91:11-12
**2:6-8** Psa. 8:4-6
**2:11-12** Psa. 22:22 **MPF**
**2:13a** Isa. 8:17 **MPF** 2 Sam. 22:3
**2:13b** Isa. 8:18 **MPF** Isa. 12:2
**2:14** Gen. 3:15 **MPF**
**2:16** Isa. 41:8-9
**2:17** Psa. 22:22 **MPF**
**3:2,5** Num. 12:7
**3:7-11,13,15-19** Psa. 95:7-11
**3:8** Ex. 17:7; Num. 20:2-5
**3:11** Num. 14:21-23
**3:16-18** Num. 14:1-35
**3:17** Num. 14:29
**3:18** Num. 14:22-23
**4:1-3** Psa. 95:11
**4:4** Gen. 2:2
**4:5-6** Psa. 95:11
**4:7** Psa. 95:7-8
**4:8** Deut. 31:7; Josh. 22:4
**4:10** Gen. 2:2
**4:11** Psa. 95:11
**4:12** Isa. 49:2
**5:3** Lev. 9:7; 16:6
**5:4** Ex. 28:1
**5:5** Psa. 2:7 **MPF**
**5:6,10** Psa. 110:4 **MPF**
**5:9** Isa. 45:17
**6:17** Gen. 1:11
**6:8** Gen. 3:17-18
**6:13-14** Gen. 22:16-17
**6:16** Ex. 22:11
**6:18** Num. 23:19; 1 Sam. 15:29
**6:19** Lev. 16:2,12,15
**6:20** Psa. 110:4 **MPF**
**7:1-3** Gen. 14:17-20
**7:4,6,10** Gen. 14:19-20
**7:5** Num. 18:21
**7:11,15,17,21,24,28** Psa. 110:4 **MPF**
**7:14** Gen. 49:10; 1 Chr. 5:2; Isa. 11:1 **MPF**
**7:25** Isa. 59:16 **MPF**
**7:27** Lev. 9:7; 16:6,15
**7:28** Psa. 2:7
**8:1** Psa. 110:1 **MPF**
**8:2** Num. 24:6
**8:5** Ex. 25:40
**8:8-13** Jer. 31:31-34
**9:2** Ex. 25:23-40; 26:1-30
**9:4** Ex. 16:33; 25:10-16; 30:1-6; Num. 17:8-10; Deut. 10:3-5
**9:5** Ex. 25:18-22
**9:6** Num. 18:2-6
**9:7** Ex. 30:10; Lev. 16:2, 14-15,30,34
**9:10** Lev. 11:2,25; 15:18; Num. 19:13
**9:12** Lev. 16:30,34
**9:13** Lev. 16:3,14-15; Num. 19:9,17-19
**9:19** Ex. 24:3; Lev. 14:4; Num. 19:6
**9:20** Ex. 24:8
**9:21** Lev. 8:15,19
**9:22** Lev. 17:11
**9:27** Rom. 5:12
**9:28** Lev. 16:30,34; Isa. 53:12 **MPF**
**10:4** Lev. 16:15,21
**10:5-10** Psa. 40:6-8 **MPF**
**10:11** Ex. 29:38
**10:12** Psa. 110:1
**10:13** Psa. 110:1 **MPF**
**10:16-17** Jer. 31:33-34
**10:17** Jer. 31:34
**10:21** Zech. 6:12-13 **MPF** Num. 12:7
**10:22** Ezek. 36:25
**10:27** Isa. 26:11
**10:28** Deut. 17:6; 19:15
**10:29** Ex. 24:8
**10:30** Deut. 32:35-36; Psa. 135:14
**10:37** Hab. 2:3-4
**10:38** Hab. 2:3-4
**11:3** Gen. 1:1; Deut. 32:18; Psa. 33:6,9
**11:4** Gen. 4:4
**11:5** Gen. 5:24
**11:7** Gen. 6:13-22; 7:1
**11:8** Gen. 12:1
**11:9** Gen. 23:4; 26:3; 35:12,27
**11:11** Gen. 17:19; 18:11-14; 21:2
**11:12** Gen. 15:5; 22:17; 32:12; Ex. 32:13; Deut. 1:10; 10:22
**11:13** Gen. 23:4; 47:9; 1 Chr. 29:15; Psa. 39:12
**11:16** Ex. 3:6,15; 4:5
**11:17** Gen. 22:1-10
**11:18** Gen. 21:12 **MPF**
**11:20** Gen. 27:27-29,39-40
**11:21** Gen. 47:31; 48:15-16
**11:22** Gen. 50:24-25; Ex. 13:19
**11:23** Ex. 1:22; 2:2
**11:24** Ex. 2:11
**11:26** Psa. 69:9; 89:50-51 **MPF**
**11:27** Ex. 2:15; 10:28-29; 12:51
**11:28** Ex. 12:21-29
**11:29** Ex. 14:21-31
**11:30** Josh. 6:12-21
**11:31** Josh. 6:21-25; 2:11-12
**11:32** Judg. 4:10-17; 11:32-33; 16:28-30; 1 Sam. 7:9-12; 19:8
**11:33** Judg. 14:6-7; 1 Sam. 17:34-36; Dan. 6:22
**11:34** Dan. 3:23-25
**11:35** 1 Kin. 17:17-24; 2 Kin. 4:25-37
**11:36** Gen. 39:20; 1 Kin. 22:26-27; 2 Chr. 18:25-26; Jer. 20:2; 37:15,38:6
**11:37** 2 Chr. 24:21
**11:38** 1 Kin. 18:4,13
**12:2** Psa. 110:1 **MPF**
**12:3** Num. 16:38
**12:5-7** Prov. 3:11-12
**12:7** Deut. 8:5; 2 Sam. 7:14
**12:9** Num. 16:22; 27:16
**12:12** Isa. 35:3
**12:13** Prov. 4:26
**12:14** Psa. 34:14
**12:15** Deut. 29:18
**12:16** Gen. 25:33
**12:17** Gen. 27:30-40
**12:18-19a** Ex. 20:18-21; Deut. 4:11-12
**12:19b** Ex. 19:16; Deut. 5:23,25
**12:20** Ex. 19:12-13
**12:21** Deut. 9:19
**12:23** Gen. 18:25; Psa. 50:6
**12:24** Gen. 4:10
**12:26** Ex. 19:18; Judg. 5:4; Psa. 68:8
**12:26-27** Hab. 2:6
**12:29** Deut. 4:24; 9:3; Isa. 33:14
**13:2** Gen. 18:1-8; 19:1-3
**13:5** Gen. 28:15; Deut. 31:6,8; Josh. 1:5
**13:6** Psa. 118:6
**13:8** Isa. 43:13
**13:11,13** Lev. 16:27
**13:15a** Lev. 7:12; 2 Chr. 29:31; Psa. 50:14,23
**13:15b** Psa. 50:23; Isa. 57:19; Hos. 14:2
**13:17** Isa. 62:6; Ezek. 3:17
**13:20** Isa. 55:3; Jer. 32:40; Ezek. 37:26; Zech. 9:11 **MPF** Isa. 63:11

**JAMES**

**1:5** Prov. 2:3-6
**1:10-11** Psa. 102:4,11; Isa. 40:6-7
**1:19** Eccl. 7:9
**1:26** Psa. 34:13; 39:1; 141:3
**2:1** Psa. 24:7-10 **MPF** Job 34:19
**2:8** Lev. 19:18
**2:9** Deut. 1:17

**2:11** Ex. 20:13-14; Deut. 5:17-18
**2:21** Gen. 22:2,9
**2:23** Gen. 15:6; 2 Chr. 20:7; Isa. 41:8
**2:25** Josh. 2:4,25; 6:17
**3:8** Psa. 140:3
**3:9** Gen. 1:26
**3:18** Isa. 32:17
**4:5** Gen. 6:5
**4:6** Prov. 3:34
**4:8** Isa. 1:16; Zech. 1:3; Mal. 3:7
**4:10** Job 5:11
**4:13-14** Prov. 27:1
**5:3** Psa. 21:9
**5:4** Gen. 4:10; Lev. 19:13; Deut. 24:15; Psa. 18:6; Isa. 5:9; Mal. 3:5
**5:5** Jer. 12:3; 25:34
**5:7** Deut. 11:14; Jer. 5:24; Joel 2:23
**5:11** Ex. 34:6; Psa. 103:8; 111:4; Dan. 12:12
**5:17** 1 Kin. 17:1
**5:18** 1 Kin. 18:42-45
**5:20** Prov. 10:12

## I PETER

**1:7** Mal. 3:3 **MP** Job 23:10; Psa. 66:10; Prov. 17:3; Isa. 48:10; Zech. 13:9
**1:11** Psa. 22 **MPF**
**1:16** Lev. 11:44; 19:2; 20:7
**1:17** 2 Chr. 19:7; Psa. 28:4; 62:12; 89:26; Prov. 24:12; Isa. 59:18; 64:8; Jer. 3:19; 17:10
**1:18** Isa. 52:3
**1:23** Dan. 6:26
**1:24-25** Isa. 40:6-8
**2:3** Psa. 34:8
**2:4** Psa. 118:22; Isa. 28:16; Dan. 2:34 **MPF**
**2:5** Ex. 19:6; Isa. 61:6
**2:6** Isa. 28:16 **MPF**
**2:7** Psa. 118:22; Dan. 2:34 **MPF**
**2:8** Isa. 8:14-15 **MP**
**2:9** Isa. 9:2 **MPF** Ex. 19:5-6; 23:22; Deut. 4:20; 7:6; 10:15; 14:2; 42:12; 43:20-21; 61:6
**2:10** Hos. 1:6,10; 2:1,23
**2:11** Psa. 39:12
**2:12** Isa. 10:3 **MPU**
**2:17** Prov. 24:21
**2:22** Isa. 53:9 **MPF**
**2:23** Isa. 53:7 **MPF**
**2:24** Isa. 53:4-5,12 **MPF**
**2:25** Isa. 53:6 **MPF** Ezek. 34:5-6
**3:6** Gen. 18:12,15; Prov. 3:25
**3:10-12** Psa. 34:12-16
**3:14-15** Isa. 8:12-13
**3:20** Gen. 6:1-7:24
**3:22** Psa. 110:1 **MPF**
**4:8** Prov. 10:12
**4:14** Psa. 89:50-51; Isa. 11:2 **MPF**
**4:17** Jer. 25:29; Ezek. 9:6
**4:18** Prov. 11:31
**4:19** Psa. 31:5
**5:5** Prov. 3:34
**5:6** Job 22:29
**5:7** Psa. 55:22

## II PETER

**1:17** Psa. 2:7; Isa. 42:1 **MPF**
**2:2** Isa. 52:5
**2:5** Gen. 8:18
**2:6** Gen. 19:24
**2:7** Gen. 19:1-16
**2:15** Num. 22:7
**2:16** Num. 22:28
**2:22** Prov. 26:11
**3:5** Gen. 1:6-9
**3:6** Gen. 7:11-21
**3:8** Psa. 90:4
**3:9** Hab. 2:3
**3:12** Isa. 34:4
**3:13** Isa. 60:21; 65:17; 66:22

## I JOHN

**1:7** Isa. 2:5
**1:9** Psa. 32:5; Prov. 28:13
**2:10** Psa. 119:165
**2:12** Psa. 25:11
**2:16** Prov. 27:20
**2:27** Jer. 31:34
**2:28** Job 19:35
**3:2** Job 19:25
**3:5** Isa. 53:9 **MPF**
**3:12** Gen. 4:8
**3:17** Deut. 15:7-8
**5:3** Deut. 30:11

## II JOHN

**12** Num. 12:8

## III JOHN

**14** Num. 12:8

## JUDE

**5** Ex. 12:51; Num. 14:29-30,35
**7** Gen. 19:4-25
**9** Dan. 10:13,21; 12:1; Zech. 3:2
**11** Gen. 4:3-8; Num. 16:19-35; 22:7; 31:16
**12** Ezek. 34:8
**13** Isa. 57:20
**14** Zech. 14:5 **MPU** Deut. 33:2
**23** Zech. 3:2-3

## REVELATION

**1:1** Dan. 2:28,45
**1:4** Ex. 3:14; Isa. 41:4
**1:5** Psa. 89:27,37; 130:8; Isa. 40:2; 55:4 **MPF**
**1:6** Ex. 19:6; Isa. 61:6
**1:7a** Dan. 7:13 **MPU** Isa. 19:1
**1:7b** Zech. 12:10,12 **MP**
**1:8** Ex. 3:14; Isa. 41:4; Amos 4:13
**1:13** Ezek. 1:26; 8:2; 9:2, 11; Dan. 7:13; 10:5
**1:13-18** Psa. 45:2 **MPF**
**1:14** Dan. 7:9; 10:6
**1:15** Ezek. 1:24; 43:2
**1:16** Judg. 5:31; Isa. 49:2
**1:17** Isa. 44:6; 48:12; Dan. 10:19
**1:19** Isa. 48:6; Dan. 2:29, 45
**2:6** Psa. 139:21
**2:7** Gen. 2:8,9; 3:22,24; Ezek. 28:13; 31:8
**2:8** Isa. 44:6; 48:12
**2:10** Dan. 1:12, 14
**2:12** Isa. 49:2
**2:14** Num. 25:1-2; 31:16
**2:16** Isa. 49:2
**2:17** Psa. 78:24; Isa. 62:2; 65:15
**2:18** Dan. 10:6
**2:20** 1 Kin. 16:31; 2 Kin. 9:22; Num. 25:1-3
**2:23** Psa. 7:9; 62:12; Prov. 24:12; Jer. 11:20; 17:10
**2:26-27** Psa. 2:8-9 **MPF**
**3:5** Ex. 32:33; Psa. 69:28; Dan. 12:1
**3:7** Job 12:14; Isa. 22:22
**3:9** Isa. 43:4; 45:14; 49:23; 60:14
**3:12** Isa. 62:2; 65:15; Ezek. 48:35
**3:14** Psa. 89:37; Prov. 8:22 **MPF**
**3:17** Hos. 12:8
**3:19** Prov. 3:12
**4:1** Ex. 19:16,20,24; Dan. 2:29,45
**4:2** 1 Kin. 22:19; 2 Chr. 18:18; Psa. 47:8; Isa. 6:1; Ezek. 1:26-27
**4:3** Ezek. 1:26-28
**4:4** Isa. 24:23
**4:5** Ex. 19:16; Ezek. 1:13; Zech. 4:2-3
**4:6** Isa. 6:1; Ezek. 1:5,18 22 4:7 Ezek. 1:10;
**4:7** Ezek. 1:10; 10:14
**4:8** Ex. 3:14; Isa. 6:2-3; 41:4; Ezek. 1:18; 10:12; Amos 4:13
**4:9-10** 1 Kin. 22:19; 2 Chr. 18:18; Psa. 47:8; Isa. 6:1; Ezek. 1:26-27; Dan. 4:34; 6:26; 12:7
**5:1** 1 Kin. 22:19; 2 Chr. 18:18; Psa. 47:8; Isa. 6:1; 29:11; Ezek. 1:26-27; 2:9-10
**5:5** Gen. 49:9; Isa. 11:1, 10 **MPF**
**5:6** Isa. 53:7 **MPF** Zech. 4:10
**5:7** 1 Kin. 22:19; 2 Chr. 18:18; Psa. 47:8; Isa. 6:1; Ezek. 1:26-27
**5:8** Psa. 141:2
**5:9** Psa. 33:3; 40:3; 96:1; 98:1; 144:9; 149:1; Isa. 42:10
**5:10** Ex. 19:6; Isa. 61:6
**5:11** Dan. 7:10
**5:12** Isa. 53:7 **MPF** 1 Chr. 29:11
**5:13** Psa. 47:8 **MPF** 1 Kin. 22:19; 2 Chr. 18:18; Isa. 6:1; Ezek. 1:26-27
**6:2,4-5** Zech. 1:8; 6:2-3,6
**6:8** Jer. 14:12; 15:3; Ezek. 5:12,17; 14:21; 29:5; 33:27; 34:28; Hos. 13:14
**6:10** Deut. 32:43; 2 Kin. 9:7; Psa. 79:10; Hos. 4:1; Zech. 1:12
**6:12** Ezek. 32:7-8; Joel 2:10,31; 3:15
**6:13-14** Isa. 13:10; 34:4
**6:15** Psa. 2:2; 48:4; Isa. 2:10; 24:21; 34:12; Jer. 4:29
**6:16** 1 Kin. 22:19; 2 Chr. 18:18; Psa. 47:8; Isa. 6:1; Ezek. 1:26-27; Hos. 10:8
**6:17** Psa. 110:5; Joel 2:11; Nah. 1:6; Zeph. 1:14-15; Mal. 3:2
**7:1** Jer. 49:36; Ezek. 7:2; 37:9; Dan. 7:2; Zech. 6:5
**7:3** Ezek. 9:4
**7:10** 1 Kin. 22:19; 2 Chr. 18:18; Psa. 47:8; Isa. 6:1; Ezek. 1:26-27
**7:14** Gen. 49:11; Dan. 12:1
**7:15** 1 Kin. 22:19; 2 Chr. 18:18; Psa. 47:8; Isa. 6:1; Ezek. 1:26-27
**7:16** Isa. 49:10
**7:17** Isa. 25:8 **MPU** Psa. 23:1-2; Ezek. 34:23 **MP** Jer. 2:13
**8:3** Ex. 30:1-3; Psa. 141:2; Amos 9:1
**8:5** Ex. 19:16; Lev. 16:12
**8:7** Ex. 9:24; Ezek. 38:22; Joel 2:30
**8:8** Ex. 7:19; Jer. 51:25
**8:10** Isa. 14:12

**8:11** Jer. 9:15
**8:12** Isa. 13:10; Ezek. 32:7-8; Joel 2:10; 3:15
**9:2** Gen. 19:28; Ex. 19:18; Joel 2:10
**9:3** Ex. 10:12,15
**9:4** Ezek. 9:4
**9:6** Job 3:21; Jer. 8:3; Hos. 10:8
**9:7** Joel 2:4
**9:8** Joel 1:6
**9:9** Joel 2:5
**9:11** Job 26:6; 28:22
**9:13** Ex. 30:1-3
**9:14** Gen. 15:18; Deut. 1:7
**9:20** Deut. 32:17; Psa. 15:7; 135:15-17; Isa. 17:8; Dan. 5:3-4,23
**9:21** 2 Kin. 9:22
**10:4** Dan. 8:26; 12:4,9
**10:5** Gen. 14:19,22; Deut. 32:40; Neh. 9:6; Dan. 12:7
**10:6** Ex. 20:11; Deut. 32:40; Psa. 146:6
**10:7** Dan. 9:6,10; Amos 3:7; Zech. 1:6
**10:9** Ezek. 3:1
**10:9-10** Ezek. 2:8
**10:11** Jer. 1:10; 25:30; Dan. 3:4; 7:14
**11:1** Ezek. 40:3,47; Zech. 2:1-2
**11:2** Psa. 79:1; Isa. 63:18; Dan. 8:13; Zech. 12:3
**11:4** Zech. 4:2-3,11,14
**11:5** 2 Sam. 22:9; 2 Kin. 1:10; Psa. 97:3; Jer. 5:14
**11:6** Ex. 7:17,19; 1 Sam. 4:8; 1 Kin. 17:1
**11:7** Dan. 7:3,7,21
**11:8** Isa. 1:10
**11:10-11** Psa. 105:38; Ezek. 37:5-10
**11:12** 2 Kin. 2:11
**11:13** Josh. 7:19; Ezek. 39:19-20; Dan. 2:19
**11:15** Dan. 7:14; Obad. 21 **MP**
Ex. 15:18; Psa. 10:16; 22:28;Dan. 2:44; Zech. 14:9
**11:17** Ex. 3:14; Isa. 12:4; Amos 4:13
**11:18** Psa. 2:1; 46:6; 99:1; 115:13; Dan. 9:6,10; Amos 3:7; Zech. 1:6
**11:19** Ex. 9:24; 19:16; 1 Kin. 8:1,6; 2 Chr. 5:7; Ezek. 1:13
**12:2** Isa. 66:7 **MPF**
Mic. 4:10
**12:3** Dan. 7:7
**12:4** Dan. 8:10
**12:5** Isa. 7:14; 66:7 **MPF**
PS. 2:9
**12:7** Dan. 10:13,20-21; 12:1
**12:9** Gen. 3:1; Zech. 3:1-2
**12:10** Job 1:9-11
**12:12** Isa. 44:23; 49:13
**12:14** Dan. 7:25; 12:7
**12:17** Dan. 7:7,21
**13:1** Dan. 7:3,7
**13:2** Dan. 7:4-6
**13:5** Dan. 7:8,20,25; 11:36-37
**13:7** Dan. 7:7,21
**13:8** Isa. 53:7 Ex. 32:33; Psa. 69:28; Dan. 12:1
**13:10** Jer. 15:2; 43:11
**13:13** 1 Kin. 18:24-39
**13:14** Deut. 13:2-4
**13:15** Dan. 3:5-6
**14:1** Ezek. 9:4
**14:2** Ezek. 1:24; 43:2; Dan. 10:6
**14:3** Psa. 33:3; 40:3; 96:1; 98:1; 144:9; 149:1; Isa. 42:10
**14:5** Psa. 32:2; Isa. 53:9; Zeph. 3:13
**14:7** Ex. 20:11; Psa. 146:6
**14:8** Isa. 21:9; Jer. 51:7-8; Dan. 4:30
**14:10** Gen. 19:24; Psa. 11:6; 75:8; Isa. 51:17; Jer. 25:15; Ezek. 38:22
**14:11** Isa. 45:23 **MPF**
Isa. 34:10
**14:14** Dan. 7:13 **MPU**
Dan. 10:16
**14:15,18,20** Joel 3:13
Isa. 63:3; Lam. 1:15; Joel 3:13
**15:1** Lev. 26:21
**15:3** Ex. 15:1, 11; 34:10; Deut. 32:4; Psa. 92:5; 111:2; 139:14; 145:17; Jer. 10:10; Amos 4:13
**15:4** Psa. 86:9; Jer. 10:7; Mal. 1:11
**15:5** Ex. 38:21; 40:34-35; Num. 1:50
**15:6** Lev. 26:21
**15:7** Psa. 75:8; Jer. 25:15
**15:8** Ex. 40:34-35; Lev. 26:21; 1 Kin. 8:10-11; 2 Chr. 5:13-14; Isa. 6:4; Ezek. 44:4
**16:1** Psa. 69:24; 79:6; Isa. 66:6; Jer. 10:25; Ezek. 22:31; Zeph. 3:8
**16:2** Ex. 9:9-10; Deut. 28:35
**16:3** Ex. 7:20-21
**16:4** Psa. 78:44
**16:5** Ex. 3:14; Deut. 32:4; Psa. 119:137; 145:17; Isa. 41:4
**16:6** Psa. 79:3; Isa. 49:26
**16:7** Psa. 19:9; 119:137; Amos 4:13
**16:10** Ex. 10:22; Isa. 8:22
**16:11** Dan. 2:19
**16:12** Gen. 15:18; Deut. 1:7; Isa. 11:15; 41:2,25; 44:27; Jer. 50:38; 51:36
**16:13** Ex. 8:3
**16:14** Amos 4:13
**16:16** Judg. 5:19; 2 Kin. 9:27; 23:29; Zech. 12:11
**16:17** Isa. 66:6
**16:18** Ex. 19:16; Dan. 12:1
**16:19** Psa. 75:8; Isa. 51:17; Jer. 25:15; Dan. 4:30
**16:21** Ex. 9:24
**17:1** Jer. 51:13
**17:2** Isa. 23:17; Jer. 51:7
**17:3** Dan. 7:7
**17:4** Jer. 51:7; Ezek. 28:13
**17:5** Dan. 4:30
**17:8** Ex. 32:33; Psa. 69:28; Isa. 4:3; Dan. 7:3; 12:1
**17:12** Dan. 7:24
**17:14** Deut. 10:17; Dan. 2:47
**17:15** Jer. 51:13
**17:16** Lev. 21:9
**17:18** Psa. 2:2; 89:27
**18:2** Isa. 13:21; 21:9; 34:11,14; Jer. 9:11; 50:39; 51:8; Dan. 4:30
**18:3** Jer. 25:16-27; 51:7
**18:4** Isa. 48:20; 52:11; Jer. 50:8; 51:6,9,45
**18:5** Gen. 18:21; Jer. 51:9
**18:6** Psa. 137:8; Jer. 50:15,29
**18:7** Isa. 47:7,8,11
**18:8** Lev. 21:9; Isa. 47:9; Jer. 50:34
**18:9** Isa. 23:17; Ezek. 26:16-17; 27:30-33
**18:10** Ezek. 26:17; Dan. 4:30
**18:11** Ezek. 27:36
**18:12-13** Ezek. 27:22
**18:13** Ezek. 27:13
**18:15** Ezek. 27:31-32,36
**18:16** Ezek. 28:13
**18:17** Ezek. 27:28-29
**18:18** Ezek. 27:32
**18:19** Ezek. 26:19; 27:9, 30,33,36
**18:20** Deut. 32:43; Psa. 96:11; Isa. 44:23; 49:13; Jer. 51:48
**18:21** Jer. 51:63-64; Ezek 26:21
**18:22a** Isa. 24:8; Ezek. 26:13
**18:22b-23** Isa. 23:8; 47:9; Jer. 25:10
**18:23** Jer. 7:34; 16:9
**18:24** Jer. 51:49; Ezek. 24:7
**19:1,3,4,6** Psa. 104:35
**19:2** Deut. 32:43; 2 Kin. 9:7; Psa. 19:9; 79:10; 119:137
**19:3** Isa. 34:10
**19:4** 1 Kin. 22:19; 2 Chr. 18:18; Psa. 47:8; Isa. 6:1; Ezek. 1:26-27
**19:5** Psa. 22:23; 115:13; 134:1; 135:1
**19:6** Ex. 15:18; Psa. 22:28; 93:1; 99:1; Ezek. 1:24; 43:2; Dan. 7:14; 10:6; Amos 4:13; Zech. 14:9
**19:7** Psa. 97:1
**19:8** Isa. 61:10
**19:11** Psa. 96:13; Isa. 2:4; 11:4; 59:16 **MPU**
Ezek. 1:1; Zech. 1:8; 6:2-3,6
**19:12** Dan. 10:6
**19:13** Isa. 63:1-3
**19:15** Psa. 2:8-9; Isa. 11:4; 49:2; Joel 3:13 **MPU**
Lam. 1:15; Amos 4:13
**19:16** Deut. 10:17; Dan. 2:47
**19:17** Ezek. 39:19-20
**19:19** Psa. 2:2 **MPF**
**19:20** Gen. 19:24; Isa. 30:30,33
**19:21** Ezek. 39:20
**20:2** Gen. 3:1; Zech. 3:1-2
**20:4** Dan. 7:9,21,22,27
**20:6** Ex. 19:6; Isa. 61:6
**20:8** Ezek. 7:2; 38:2
**20:9** 2 Kin. 1:10; Jer. 11:15; 12:7; Ezek. 39:6; Hab. 1:6
**20:10** Gen. 19:24; Psa. 11:6; Isa. 30:33; Ezek. 38:22
**20:11** Psa. 114:3,7; Isa. 6:1; Dan. 2:35; 7:9
**20:12** Ex. 32:33; Psa. 28:4; 62:12; 69:28; Prov. 24:12; Dan. 7:10; 12:1
**20:12-13** Isa. 59:18: Jer. 17:10
**20:15** Ex. 32:33; Psa. 69:28; Isa. 4:3; 30:33; Dan. 12:1
**21:1** Isa. 65:17; 66:22
**21:2** Isa. 52:1; 61:10
**21:3** Lev. 26:11-12; 2 Chr. 6:18; Ezek. 37:27; Zech. 2:10
**21:4** Isa. 25:8; 35:10; 65:17,19; Jer. 31:16
**21:5** 1 Kin. 22:19; 2 Chr. 18:18; Psa. 47:8; Isa. 6:1; 43:19; Ezek. 1:26-27
**21:6** Psa. 36:9; Isa. 44:6; 48:12; 55:1; Jer. 2:13; Zech. 14:8

**21:7** 2 Sam. 7:14; Psa. 89:26
**21:8** Gen. 19:24; Psa. 11:6; Isa. 30:33; Ezek. 38:22
**21:9** Lev. 26:21
**21:10** Isa. 52:1; Ezek. 40:2
**21:11** Isa. 58:8; 60:1-2, 19 **MP**
**21:12** Ex. 28:21; Ezek. 48:31-34
**21:13** Ex. 28:21; Ezek. 48:31-34
**21:15** Ezek. 40:3,5
**21:16** Ezek. 43:16; 48:16-17
**21:17** Ezek. 41:5; 48:16-17
**21:18-19** Isa. 54:11-12
**21:22** Amos 4:13
**21:23** Isa. 60:1-2,19 **MP**
**21:24** Isa. 60:2-3,5,10-11
**21:25** Isa. 60:11; Zech. 14:7
**21:26** Psa. 72:10-11 **MP**
**21:27** Ex. 32:33; Psa. 69:28; Isa. 52:1; Dan. 12:1
**22:1** Ezek. 47:1; Joel 3:18; Zech. 14:8
**22:2** Gen. 2:9-10; 3:22; Ezek. 47:7,12
**22:3** Zech. 14:11
**22:4** Psa. 17:15; 42:2
**22:5** Isa. 60:19; Dan. 7:18,27; Zech. 14:7
**22:6** Dan. 2:28,45
**22:7** Isa. 40:10
**22:10** Dan. 12:4
**22:12** Isa. 62:11 **MPF** Psa. 28:4; 62:12; Prov. 24:12; Isa. 40:10; 59:18; Jer. 17:10
**22:13** Isa. 44:6; 48:12
**22:14** Gen. 2:9; 3:22; 49:11; Ezek. 47:12
**22:16** Num. 24:17; Isa. 11:1,10 **MPF**
**22:17** Isa. 55:1; Zech. 14:8
**22:18** Deut. 4:2; 12:32; 29:20
**22:19** Gen. 2:9; 3:22; Ezek. 47:12

**accursed** *adj* (infr wd) under a curse; damnable; detestable; unacceptable to God. Josh. 7:12.

**acknowledge** *vt* (arch mng) to understand. 2 Cor. 1:13.

**acre** *n* (tech) *See Table of Linear Measures*. 1 Sam. 14:14.

**act** *n* (infr wd) a deed; a brave deed. 2 Sam. 23:20.

**activity, men of** (Hebraism) industrious, resourceful, able men. Gen. 47:6.

**adamant** *n* (infr wd) an extremely hard stone; the diamond. Ezek. 3:9.

**addict** *reflex vb* (arch mng) to devote oneself, give oneself up to something. 1 Cor. 16:15.

**adjure** *vt* (infr wd) (1) to cause to swear. Josh. 6:26. (2) to charge solemnly. Matt. 26:63.

**administration** *n* (theol) the service of those who promote the cause of Christ among men, such as apostles, prophets, elders, etc. 1 Cor. 12:5.

**admiration** *n* (arch mng) wonder, astonishment. Rev. 17:6.

**admonish** *vt* (infr wd) to warn; to exhort. Acts 27:9.

**ado** *n* (infr wd) bustling excitement. Mark 5:39.

**adoption** *n* (theol) a relationship of grace (planned from eternity and mediated by Jesus Christ) involving a change from slave's to son's status. After adoption, the son of God possesses all family rights such as access to the Father and sharing with Christ in the divine inheritance. Rom. 8:23.

**adventure** *vt* (infr use) to risk; to proceed despite danger; to venture. Deut. 28:56.

**adversary** *n* (arch mng) an opponent in a lawsuit. Matt. 5:25.

**advertise** *vt* (infr mng) to give notice; to inform; to announce publicly. Num. 24:14.

**advisement** *n* (infr wd) careful consideration. 1 Chr. 12:19.

**affect** *vt* (arch mng) to desire earnestly; to seek after. Gal. 4:17.

**affectioned** *adj* (arch wd) disposed. Rom. 12:10.

**affections** *n pl* (arch mng) passions. Gal. 5:24.

**affinity** *n* (arch use) (1) a marriage alliance or contract. 1 Kin. 3:1. (2) fellowship; alliance. Ezra 9:14.

**affirm** *vi* (arch use) to assert confidently. 1 Tim. 1:7.

**afflict** *vt* (arch mng) (1) to abase, humble. Lev. 16:31. (2) *pass* to be troubled. Jas. 4:9.

**affliction** *n* (infr mng) misery; trouble; tribulation. Deut. 16:3.

**affright** *vt* (infr wd) (1) to frighten, alarm. Deut. 7:21. (2) to throw into amazement or terror. Mark 16:5, 6.

**afore** *adv* (arch wd) beforehand, previously. Rom. 9:23.

**aforehand** *adv* (arch wd) beforehand; in advance. Mark 14:8.

**aforetime(s)** *adv* (arch wd) formerly. Neh. 13:5.

**after** (1) *prep* according to. Gen. 10:20; Matt. 23:3. (2) *adv* following. 2 Sam. 20:2. (3) *prep* committed to. 2 Sam. 15:13. (4) *conj* (mistransl) when. Eph. 1:13.

**after his kind** (Hebraism) according to its nature or species. Gen. 1:11.

**after the flesh** (theol) according to human reason. John 8:15.

**against** (arch mng) (1) *conj* in preparation for (the time when). Gen. 43:25; Num. 10:21; 2 Tim. 1:12. (2) *conj* by the time that. Ex. 7:15. (3) *prep* exposed to. Nu. 25:4. (4) *prep* toward. 1 Sam. 9:14.

**age** *n* (arch mng) fleeting life. Job 11:17.

**agone** *adv* (arch wd) ago. 1 Sam. 30:13.

**ague** *n* (infr wd) an acute fever marked by paroxysms of chills, fever, and sweating. Lev. 26:16.

**alabaster box** (arch expr) a slender, long-necked flask made of alabaster, a dense, beautifully striped calcium carbonate such as is formed gradually in stalactites. Matt. 26:7.

**albeit** *conj* (infr wd) although it be. Ezek. 13:7.

**all hail** (arch expr) rejoice (ye)! Matt. 28:9.

**all to** (arch expr) a later, erroneous form of *all to-*. In the phrase "all to brake," i.e., utterly broken in pieces, the prefix *to-* originally belonged to the verb; but since these verbs were used with *all*, the *to* came to be regarded as belonging to the *all*. Thus a new compound *all-to* sprang up, with the sense of *wholly, utterly*. Judg. 9:53.

**allege** *vt* (arch mng) to adduce proofs; to bring evidence. Acts 17:3.

**alleluia** *interj* (Hebraism) lit., praise ye the Lord! Rev. 19:4.

**allow** *vt* (arch mng) to approve of. Luke 11:48.

**alms** *n* (arch wd) a charitable gift. Matt. 6:1.

**almsdeeds** *n pl* (arch wd) acts of mercy, such as gifts to the poor. Acts 9:36.

**Alpha and Omega** (Grecism) lit., the first and last letters in the Greek alphabet; thus, the beginning and the end. Rev. 1:8.

**altar** *n* (theol) a standing structure on which sacrifices were offered or incense burned in worship. Ex. 32:5.

**amaze** *vt* (arch mng) to make afraid or alarmed. Judg. 20:41.

**amazement** *n* (arch mng) confusion; terror. 1 Pet. 3:6.

**ambassage** *n* (arch wd) an embassy. Luke 14:32.

**ambushment** *n* (arch wd) an ambush; men lying in wait. 2 Chr. 13:13.

**amen** *interj* (translit) at close of sentence, statement, or prayer: so it is; so be it; let it be so; may it be fulfilled. When placed other than at end of sentence: certainly; truly.

**amend** *vt* (arch mng) to mend or repair. 2 Chr. 34:10.

**amerce** *vt* (infr wd) to punish by a fine. Deut. 22:19.

**amiable** *adj* (arch mng) lovely. Psa. 84:1.

**amiss** *adj* (infr wd) wrong; improper. Dan. 3:29.

**an hungred** (arch expr) hungry. Matt. 4:2.

**Anathema** *n* (Aramaic) accursed. 1 Cor. 16:22.

**ancients** *n pl* (infr mng) elders. Isa. 3:14.

**and** *conj* (arch mng) if. Gen. 44:30.

**and if** (arch expr) if. Matt. 24:48.

**angel** *n* (theol) (1) a messenger, usually a created spiritual being of holy character, sent by God to deliver revelations to men (Gen. 19:15; Matt. 1:20), to protect His people (Psa. 91:11), to minister to His servants in times of affliction and temptation (Matt. 4:11), and to bear dying saints to paradise (Luke 16:22). (2) the Angel of the Lord, the Messenger of the Covenant, i.e., Christ, the second person of the Trinity. Judg. 13:9-21. See appendix entitled "The Holy Trinity and the Covenant of Grace" (II. A. 4) for more references. (3) demons, or evil created spiritual beings, organized under the rebel government of Satan, the greatest of the fallen angels. Matt. 25:41.

**angle** *n* (arch mng) a rod with a line and a hook. Isa. 19:8.

**anoint** *vt* (theol) (1) to apply holy oil to a person or object to signify holiness or separation to God. Psa. 2:2. (2) to bestow divine favor. Psa. 23:5. (3) to appoint to a special position in the purpose of God. Psa. 105:15. (4) to symbolize the outpouring of the Holy Spirit. 1 Sam. 10:1.

**anon** *adv* (arch mng) immediately, at once. Matt. 13:20.

**another heart** (theol) a reformed outlook (not true conversion as proved by Saul's subsequent life; a *different* heart or mind, not a *new heart,* q.v.). 1 Sam. 10:9.

**answereth to** (arch expr) a military term, *is in the same line with;* i.e., the two march together step by step—a graphic illustration of the correspondence of Hagar/Mount Sinai and Jerusalem. Gal. 4:25.

**antichrist** *n* (theol) (1) anyone who opposes Christ. 1 John 4:3. (2) a specific evil personality who contemns law, deceives many by his satanically-empowered miracles, is worshiped by many, but is eventually slain by Christ. 1 John 2:18.

**any thing** *adv* (arch use) at all. Num. 17:13.

**apart** *adv* (infr mng) (1) alone; privately. Matt. 14:13; 17:1. (2) aside. Mark 6:31.

**Apollyon** *prop n* (translit) lit., the destroyer. Rev. 9:11.

**apparel** *n* (infr wd) clothing. Esth. 6:10.

**apparently** *adv* (infr mng) in a way that is clearly understood; open to view. Num. 12:8.

**appertain** *vi* (infr wd) to belong. Lev. 6:5.

**apple of the eye** (arch expr) the pupil of the eye; fig., someone or something most cherished. Deut. 32:10.

**appoint** *vt* (arch mng) (1) to specify. Gen. 30:28. (2) to set aside; to assign. Josh. 20:7.

**appointed** *adj* (arch mng) girded; armed. Judg. 18:11.

**appointment** *n* (arch mng) word; order. 2 Sam. 13:32.

**apprehend** *vt* (arch mng) to lay hold of; to grasp. Phil. 3:12.

**approve** *vt* (arch mng) (1) to show, prove, establish, exhibit. 2 Cor. 7:11. (2) *pass* to be proven; to be tried in one's faith and integrity. 2 Cor. 10:18.

**apt** *adj* (infr wd) unusually fitted or qualified. 2 Kin. 24:16.

**are the hands . . . now in thine hand** (Hebraism) have they already been captured? Judg. 8:6.

**ark** *n* (infr wd) generally, a chest or coffer; (1) Noah's vessel. Gen. 6:14. (2) Moses' vessel. Ex. 2:3. (3) the box in which the tables of the law, etc., were kept. Num. 10:33.

**arm** *n* (Hebraism) strength. 1 Sam. 2:31.

**armholes** *n pl* (arch use) armpits. Jer. 38:12.

**army** *n* (infr mng) a great company, host, or multitude. Num. 1:3.

**array** *n* (infr wd) (1) dress; finery. 1 Tim. 2:9. (2) military order. Judg. 20:20.

**arrayed** *pp* (infr wd) dressed. Rev. 7:13.

**art come to excellent ornaments** (Hebraism) come to excellent or exquisite beauty. Ezek. 16:7.

**art thou that** (arch expr) is it you? 1 Kin. 18:7.

**artificer** *n* (infr wd) a skillful, artistic craftsman. Gen. 4:22.

**artillery** *n* (infr mng) bow and arrows. 1 Sam. 20:40.

**ashamed** *adj* (arch mng) (1) perplexed, confounded, chagrined. Judg. 3:25. (2) disappointed. Job 6:20. (3) humbled. 2 Cor. 30:15.

**ask** *vt* (arch mng) to ask for. Matt. 7:9.

**ask . . . at** *vb* (arch wd) to inquire of. Dan. 2:10.

**ask(ed) at my mouth** (Hebraism) to consult God's prophets. Isa. 30:2.

**asleep** *adj* (arch mng) dead. 1 Thess. 4:13.

**assay** *vt* (infr wd) to attempt; to venture. Deut. 4:34.

**assuage** *vi* (infr mng) to lower; to lessen; to subside; to become quiet. Gen. 8:1.

**astonied** *adj* (arch wd) astonished; dazed; dismayed. Job 17:8.

**astonishment** *n* (infr mng) panic; consternation. Deut. 28:28.

**astrologer** *n* (theol) one who practices enchantments; a conjurer who makes use of the position of sun, moon, and planets in making predictions. Dan. 1:20.

**asunder** *adv* (infr wd) (1) into parts or different pieces; separately. Num. 16:31. (2) to "put asunder," to separate or divide, esp. in reference to the separation or divorce of spouses. Matt. 19:6.

**at** *prep* (arch mng) (1) toward or near in order

to have sexual intercourse. Ex. 19:15. (2) close to; near. Num. 6:6.

**at hand** (arch expr) "is at hand" is a translation of the perfect tense (completed action) of a Greek verb meaning *has come near.* Matt. 3:2; 4:17.

**at his day** (Hebraism) on his payday. Deut. 24:15.

**at once** (arch expr) lit., at a stroke; thus, with one act. Judg. 16:28.

**at one, to set . . .** (arch expr) to reconcile. Acts 7:26.

**at quiet and secure** (arch expr) to be confidently at peace. Judg. 18:27.

**athirst** *adj* (infr wd) thirsty. Matt. 25:44.

**atonement** *n* (theol) (1) being set at one; bringing those who are estranged into unity and reconciliation. Lev. 4:20. (2) the work of Christ in solving the problem of man and his sin and bringing men into a right relationship with God. Rom. 5:11.

**attent** *adj* (arch wd) attentive. 2 Chr. 6:40.

**attire** *vt* (arch mng) to put on a headdress. Lev. 16:4.

**audience** *n* (arch mng) (1) hearing. Gen. 23:13. (2) "to give audience," to listen. Acts 13:16.

**avenge** *vt* (infr wd) to take vengeance against; to retaliate against. Lev. 19:18.

**avoid** *vt* (arch use) to depart, withdraw, escape from. 1 Sam. 18:11.

**avouch** *vt* (infr wd) to acknowledge. Deut. 26:17, 18.

**awake for thee** (Hebraism) to act in your behalf. Job 8:6.

**away with** (arch expr) to bear, tolerate, endure. Isa. 1:13.

## B

**Baali** *prop n* (Hebraism) lit., my lord or master; a symbolical name for Jehovah. Hos. 2:16.

**backbite** *vb* (infr wd) to say mean or spiteful things about a person behind his back; to slander. Psa. 15:3.

**backbiter** *n* (infr wd) a slanderer. Rom. 1:30.

**backsliding** *adj* (arch mng) untamable; stubborn. Hos. 4:16.

**bade** (pronounced "bad") *pt t* of *bid,* q.v. Num. 14:10.

**bakemeat** *n* (arch wd) cooked, usually baked, food; specifically, a meat pie. Gen. 40:17.

**baken** *adj* (arch wd) baked. Lev. 2:4.

**balance** *n* (infr wd) a scale. Job 6:2.

**balm** *n* (infr wd) an aromatic healing ointment. Ezek. 27:17.

**band** *n* (arch mng) (1) a caravan. Gen. 32:10. (2) a group. 1 Chr. 12:23. (3) *n pl* bonds. 2 Kin. 23:33. (4) pain. Psa. 73:4.

**bank** *n* (infr mng) a mound of earth or rampart cast up in besieging a town. 2 Sam. 20:15.

**banquet** *vt* (infr wd) to feast. Esth. 7:1.

**baptisms** *n pl* (theol) lit., washings. Heb. 6:2.

**bar** *n* (arch mng) a pole; a frame. Num. 4:10, 12.

**barbarian** *n* (arch mng) (1) a foreigner. 1 Cor. 14:11. (2) anyone ignorant of the Greek language and culture. Acts 28:4. (3) nations without opportunity of hearing the gospel. Col. 3:11.

**barbarous people** (arch expr) foreigners. Acts 28:2.

**bare** *arch pt t* of *bear,* q.v. Gen. 4:20.

**bare record,** see *bear record.* Rev. 1:2.

**barked** *vt* (arch mng) chewed off the bark. Joel 1:7.

**barren** *adj* (1) (infr wd) infertile. 2 Kin. 2:19. (2) (arch mng) lazy, shunning the work one ought to perform. 2 Pet. 1:8.

**base** *adj* (arch mng) of small account. 1 Cor. 1:28.

**base** *n* (infr mng) a pedestal. 1 Kin. 7:27.

**bason** *n* (arch sp) a basin. Num. 4:14.

**bastard** *n* an illegitimate person; this term was socially acceptable at the time of the KJV translation. Zech. 9:6.

**bath** *n* (tech) *See Table of Dry and Liquid Measures.* Isa. 5:10.

**battle** *n* (arch mng) a body of troops; a battalion. 1 Chr. 19:9.

**battlement** *n* (infr wd) a protective railing. Deut. 22:8.

**be** *vb* (arch use) are. Matt. 9:2.

**beam** *n* a long, heavy, weight-bearing timber, such as is used to support a roof or the deck of a ship. Matt. 7:3.

**bear** *vt* (infr mng) (1) to sustain. Gen. 13:6. (2) to carry. Ex. 28:30. (3) to give birth to. Song 6:6.

**bear . . . iniquity** (Hebraism) to pay the penalty. Ex. 28:38; Lev. 5:17.

**bear record** (arch expr) to give testimony; to witness. 3 John 12.

**beat off** (Hebraism) to thresh. Isa. 27:12.

**beaten** *adj* (arch mng) having the chaff removed. 2 Chr. 2:10.

**became** *pt t* of *become,* q.v. Heb. 7:26.

**because of** *prep* (arch mng) for. Lev. 6:9.

**become** *vt* (infr mng) to be suitable or appropriate to. Psa. 93:5.

**bed** *n* (arch mng) a couch. Esth. 1:6.

**beeves** *n pl* (infr wd) cattle; oxen. Lev. 22:19.

**befall** *vt* (infr wd) to happen. Gen. 42:38.

**befallen** *pp* of *befall,* q.v. Lev. 10:19.

**before** *prep* (1) (theol) in the presence of, or besides (i.e., superadded to)—signifies Jehovah's sovereign demand to be worshiped, feared, and served exclusively. Ex. 20:3; Deut. 5:7. (2) (infr mng) in the presence of. Lev. 4:4. (3) (infr mng) in front of. Josh. 4:7.

**before the sun** (Hebraism) openly. 2 Sam. 12:12.

**beforetime** *adv* (infr wd) formerly; beforehand. Josh. 20:5.

**begat** *arch pt t* of *beget,* q.v. Gen. 4:18.

**beget** *vt* (infr wd) to become the father of; to sire. Gen. 5:7.

**beggarly** *adj* (arch mng) worthless. Gal. 4:9.

**beguile** *vt* (infr wd) to delude by guile or subtlety; to deceive. Num. 25:18.

**behalf** *n* (arch mng) account. 1 Pet. 4:16.

**behold** (infr wd) (1) *interj* look! lo! Isa. 7:14. (2) *vt* to see. Matt. 12:49.

**behove** *vt* (arch sp) to behoove; to be necessary, fit, or proper for. Heb. 2:17.

**bekah** *n* (tech) *See Table of Coins and Table of Weights*. Ex. 38:26.

**Belial** *prop n* (theol) (1) a synonym for Satan. 2 Cor. 6:15. (2) children or sons of Belial; thus, very wicked people. Deut. 13:13.

**believe** *vb* (theol) (1) to have a confident trust and conviction (coupled with obedience) that Jesus is the Messiah. Acts 8:37. (2) to give credence to God's messengers. John 5:46. (3) to trust in God as able to aid in obtaining or doing something. Matt. 8:13. (4) to have faith to give one's self up to. John 2:11.

**believed ... not** (theol) (1) did not obey exactly. Num. 20:12. (2) refused belief and obedience. Heb. 3:18.

**belly** *n* (arch mng) (1) a hollow object. 1 Kin. 7:20. (2) lit., the stomach, typifying the sensual appetites. Phil. 3:19. (3) the womb. Job 3:11. (4) *n pl* gourmands; gluttons. Tit. 1:12. (5) the abdomen. Dan. 2:32. (6) the heart or inner being. John 7:38.

**beseech** *vb* (infr wd) to urgently entreat; to request earnestly; to supplicate. Isa. 38:3.

**beset** *vt* (infr wd) to trouble, harass, surround. Psa. 22:12.

**beside** *prep* (infr mng) in addition to, besides. Lev. 23:38.

**besom** *n* (infr wd) a broom. Isa. 14:23.

**besought** *pt t* of *beseech,* q.v. 2 Sam. 12:16.

**bestow** *vt* (infr mng) (1) to stow or put away; to dispose of. 1 Kin. 10:26. (2) to expend money or effort. Deut. 14:26. (3) to give. 2 Chr. 24:7.

**bestowed** *vi* (arch mng) allowed to stay. 1 Kin. 10:26.

**bethink themselves** (arch expr) to turn back; to reflect and come toward or near in one's heart. 2 Chr. 6:37.

**betimes** *adv* (arch wd) early; speedily. Gen. 26:31.

**betwixt** *prep* (arch wd) between. Gen. 26:28.

**bewail** *vt* (infr wd) to express deep sorrow for; to lament; to wail over. Judg. 11:37.

**beware** *vi* (infr mng) to take care; to be on one's guard. Judg. 13:4.

**bewray** *vt* (arch wd) to expose; to reveal; to betray. Prov. 27:16.

**bid** *vt* (arch mng) (1) to invite. Matt. 22:9; *pt t* bade. Luke 14:16; *pp* bid. Zeph. 1:7; *pp* bidden. 1 Sam. 9:13; Matt. 22:3. (2) to command. Matt. 14:28.

**bid him God speed** (arch expr) say to him: greetings! 2 John 10, 11.

**bidden** *pp* of *bid,* q.v. Luke 7:39.

**bier** *n* (infr wd) a litter on which a corpse was carried. 2 Sam. 3:31.

**bind** *vt* (infr wd) to put in bonds; to tie up or confine with a rope or cord. Judg. 15:10; Matt. 22:13.

**bind his soul** (Hebraism) to commit or obligate oneself. Num. 30:2.

**birthright** *n* (infr wd) the rights, privileges and possessions to which a person is entitled by birth (esp. by being first-born). 1 Chr. 5:2.

**bishop** *n* (theol) lit., *overseer,* q.v.; also known as presbyter, elder. 1 Pet. 2:25.

**blain** *n* (infr wd) a pustule; boil. Ex. 9:9.

**blameless** *adj* (infr wd) free from blame or fault; guiltless; innocent. Josh. 2:17.

**blaspheme** *vt* (1) (arch mng) to speak scornfully of. Isa. 52:5. (2) (theol) to speak reproachfully or abusively of; to rail at or revile; by contemptuous speech to intentionally come short of the reverence due God; to slander. Rev. 16:21.

**blasphemous** *adj* (infr wd) slanderous; railing; reproachful; abusive. Acts 6:13.

**blasphemy** *n* (arch mng) scorn. 2 Kin. 19:3. (2) (theol) the act of insulting or showing contempt or irreverence toward God. See more under *blaspheme*. Mark 2:7.

**blasted** *adj* (infr wd) withered; blighted. Gen. 41:6.

**blasting** *n* (infr wd) (1) a disease affecting plants (or sometimes animals) characterized by withering or blighting. Deut. 28:22. (2) lit., the east wind; withering. Amos 4:9.

**blaze** *vt* (infr mng) to proclaim far and wide. Mark 1:45.

**bless** *vt* (infr wd) (1) to praise. Psa. 63:4. (2) to make happy, prosperous. Psa. 28:9. (3) to pray, invoking God's blessing. Matt. 14:19.

**blessed** *adj* (theol) (1) happy; joyful. Matt. 5:6. (2) when applied to persons of the Godhead *blessed* signifies a serene joy of divine complacency that can never be disturbed. 1 Tim. 1:11; 6:15.

**blessedness** *n* (theol) happiness; joyfulness. Rom. 4:6, 9.

**blessing** *n* (theol) (1) a promise of God's favor, contingent on man's obedience. Deut. 11:26. (2) the good insured by God's favor. Gen. 28:4. (3) a bestowal of goods; a benediction. Heb. 12:17. (4) spiritual good brought by the gospel. Rom. 15:29. (5) consecration. 1 Cor. 10:16. (6) a concrete benefit. 1 Pet. 3:9. (7) praise. Rev. 5:12, 13. *Blessing* is in distinct opposition to *curse,* q.v

**blood** *n* (1) (arch mng) violence. Mic. 3:10. (2) (Hebraism) murder. Gen. 37:26. (3) a person. 1 Sam. 19:5. (4) blood-guiltiness. Deut. 22:8. (5) bloodstains. Isa. 4:4. (6) a relative. 2 Chr. 19:10. (7) juice. Gen. 49:11.

**blood ... be upon ... head** (Hebraism) to be responsible for a death. Josh. 2:19.

**bloodguiltiness** *n* (infr wd) guilt resulting from shedding of blood. Psa. 51:14.

**bloody** *adj* (theol) (1) of the blood, i.e., covenant. Ex. 4:26. (2) murderous; sinful. Ezek. 22:2.

**boast in another man's line** (arch expr) to try to gain credit from another man's sphere of activity. 2 Cor. 10:16.

**bodily** *adv* (arch mng) in a body. Col. 2:9.

**boisterous** *adj* (infr wd) tumultuously violent; furious. Matt. 14:30.

**bolled** *adj* (arch wd) full of pods. Ex. 9:31.

**bolster** *n* (infr wd) a long pillow or cushion. 1 Sam. 19:13.

**bond** *n* (arch mng) slave. Gal. 3:28.

**bondmaid** *n* (infr wd) a female slave. Lev. 25:44.

**bondman** *n* (infr wd) a slave. Deut. 6:21.

**bondservant** *n* (arch wd) a slave. Lev. 25:39.

**bondservice** *n* (arch wd) servitude. 1 Kin. 9:21.

**bone and flesh** (Hebraism) kith and kin. Judg. 9:2.

**bonnet** *n* (arch mng) (1) a man's headdress. Ex. 28:40. (2) a woman's headdress. Isa. 3:20.

**book** *n* (arch mng) (1) a scroll. Josh. 18:9. (2) a deed. Jer. 32:12.

**booths** *n pl* (theol) tabernacles or temporary shelters. Lev. 23:42. The Feast of Booths or Tabernacles (Lev. 23:34) immediately followed the Day of Atonement, and was, along with Passover and Pentecost, one of the three great feasts of the Jews, when God required their males to be present at the tabernacle (or later at Jerusalem).

**booties** *n pl* (arch pl) plural of booty; plunder. Hab. 2:7.

**border** *n* (Hebraism) a string or necklace. Song 1:11.

**born** *vt* (arch sp) borne; has given birth to. Ruth 4:15.

**born again** (theol) lit., born from above, from the first or beginning; hence, *born anew*. John 3:3, 7.

**born in my house** (arch expr) a servant. Gen. 15:3.

**borne** *pp* of *bear*, q.v. John 20:15.

**borne up** (arch expr) supported. Judg. 16:29.

**borrow** *vt* (arch mng) to ask for, i.e., with no connotation of returning it. Ex. 3:22.

**boss** *n* (infr mng) the convex projection in the center of a shield. Job 15:26.

**botch** *n* (infr mng) a boil. Deut. 28:27, 35.

**bottle** *n* (arch mng) (1) a container made of skin used for carrying liquids. Gen. 21:19. (2) fig., rain. Job 38:37.

**bound** *adj* (infr mng) fastened by or as if by a band; imprisoned. Gen. 40:3.

**bound** *n* (arch wd) boundary; territory. Job 38:20.

**bound in the bundle of life** (Hebraism) secure; spared. 1 Sam. 25:29.

**bounds** *n pl* (infr mng) bands; boundaries. Ex. 23:31.

**bountiful** *adj* (arch mng) generous, noble. Prov. 22:9.

**bow** *n* (arch mng) a rainbow. Gen. 9:14.

**bow** *vt* (infr mng) (1) to assume a position of worship. Ex. 20:5. (2) to assume a position showing humility. Gen. 18:2.

**bow down upon her** (Hebraism) to have sexual relations with her. Job 31:10.

**bowed** *vt* (arch mng) moved. 2 Sam. 19:14.

**bowed himself** (arch expr) did homage. 1 Kin. 1:47.

**bowels** *n pl* (arch mng) (1) the loins. Gen. 15:4. (2) the heart; compassionate feelings. Phil. 1:8. (3) the intestines. 2 Chr. 21:15. (4) the stomach. Ezek. 3:3. (5) the body. 2 Sam. 7:12.

**bowels boiled** (Hebraism) heart was in a turmoil. Job 30:27.

**bowels, separated from thy** (Hebraism) born of you. Gen. 25:23.

**box** *n* (arch mng) a flask. 2 Kin. 9:1.

**brake** *vt* (arch pt t) broke. Psa. 107:14.

**brand** *n* (arch mng) short for firebrand; a torch. Judg. 15:5.

**brasen** *adj* (arch sp) brazen, i.e., made of brass or cast of bronze. Num. 16:39. If the object was hollow it was usually formed by casting and made of bronze. See *brass*.

**brass** *n* (tech) sometimes signifies bronze; both brass and bronze are alloys (copper and zinc, copper and tin, respectively), but where casting is spoken of, the metal was bronze. 1 Kin. 7:45.

**bravery** *n* (infr mng) finery; showy dress. Isa. 3:18.

**bray** *vt* (infr mng) to pound in a mortar. Prov. 27:22.

**breach** *n* (arch mng) (1) a break in a coastline; bay, harbor. Judg. 5:17. (2) an altering of purpose. Num. 14:34. (3) a breaking forth (of anger, water, etc.). 2 Sam. 5:20.

**breach of promise** (arch mng) enmity. Num. 14:34.

**bread** *n* (arch mng) food in general; a meal. Gen. 37:25.

**break up** *vt* (arch mng) (1) to break in or into; to enter. Ex. 22:2. (2) to break open. 2 Kin. 25:4.

**breath** *n* (theol) spirit. Job 17:1.

**breeding of nettles and saltpits** (Hebraism) a soil for the nettle and a mine for salt. Zeph. 2:9.

**brethren** *n pl* (arch wd) brothers and sisters; brothers; relatives in general. Gen. 13:8; Mark 3:34.

**bridle** *n* (fig wd) restraint. Job 30:11.

**bridleth** *vt* (fig wd) to control; to curb. Jas. 1:26.

**brigandine** *n* (infr wd) a coat of mail made of small iron plates fastened to canvas or leather; so called because worn by a brigand, a light-armed foot soldier. Jer. 46:4.

**brimstone** *n* (infr wd) sulfur. Rev. 9:17.

**bring forward . . . after a godly sort** (arch expr) send forward in a manner worthy of God. 3 John 6.

**broided** *adj* (arch sp) braided. 1 Tim. 2:9.

**broidered** *adj* (arch sp) embroidered. Ezek. 16:10.

**brow** *n* (infr mng) the edge or prominent projection of a steep place. Luke 4:29.

**bruise** *vt* (theol) to break down; to crush; to trample under foot. Rom. 16:20.

**bruit** *n* (arch wd) rumor; report. Jer. 10:22.

**brutish** *adj* (infr wd) stupid. Psa. 49:10.

**buckler** *n* (infr wd) a small round shield. 2 Sam. 22:31.

**buffet** *vt* (infr wd) to strike; beat. Matt. 26:67.

**bulwark** *n* (infr wd) a fortification. Deut. 20:20.

**bunch** *n* (arch mng) a hump. Isa. 30:6.

**burden** *n* (arch mng) (1) work. Ex. 5:4. (2) utterance. 2 Kin. 9:25. (3) an imposed burden, i.e., an argument or thesis. Isa. 19:1. (4) cargo; a load. Acts 21:3.

**burn** *vi* (arch mng) (1) to be consumed with passion. 1 Cor. 7:9. (2) to have heated emotions—either grief or indignation. 2 Cor. 11:29.

**burning** *n* (arch mng) either cremation (an unusual way to dispose of dead bodies, burial being the accepted Hebrew method), or having a great fire as a way of marking the funerals of Judaean kings. 2 Chr. 21:19.

**bushel** *n* (tech) *See Table of Dry and Liquid Measures*. Matt. 5:15.

**but** *conj* (infr mng) (1) unless (usually follows a negative). Amos 3:7. (2) except. Matt. 17:21.

**by** *prep* (arch mng) (1) among. Ex. 22:25. (2) with reference to; against. 1 Cor. 4:4. (3) through. 1 Cor. 3:15.

**by and by** *adv* (infr mng) soon. Matt. 13:21.

**by lot** (arch expr) by an order determined by *cast*ing of *lots,* q.v. Acts 13:19.

**by thee** (arch expr) among you; among your neighbors. Ex. 22:25.

**byword** *n* (infr wd) a proverb. 2 Chr. 7:20.

## C

**cab** *n* (tech) *See Table of Dry and Liquid Measures*. 2 Kin. 6:25.

**cabin** *n* (arch mng) a cell. Jer. 37:16.

**caldron** *n* (infr wd) a large kettle. Ezek. 11:3.

**call** *vt* (theol) to call to oneself. Acts 2:39.

**call on the name** (Hebraism) to address; to pray to. 1 Kin. 18:24.

**call them to mind** (arch expr) to remember. Deut. 30:1.

**call upon** *vt* (arch mng) to pray to. Gen. 12:8.

**called** *adj/n/vb* (theol) divinely selected and appointed. Rom. 1:1, 6; 8:28.

**calves of our lips** (fig expr) the praises which God requires as sacrifice. Hos. 14:2.

**came** *vi* (arch mng) became. 2 Sam. 16:14.

**came up against** (arch expr) attacked. Judg. 6:3.

**can skill** (arch expr) are skilled. 1 Kin. 5:6.

**candle** *n* (arch mng) a lamp. Matt. 5:15.

**candlestick** *n* (arch mng) a lampstand. Ex. 25:31.

**canker** *n* (infr wd) Many think the symptoms seem to suggest *gangrene;* others consider this to be a *cancer*. 2 Tim. 2:17.

**cankered** *pp* (infr mng) eaten away with rust. Jas. 5:3.

**captivity** *n* (infr wd) (1) slavery by an enemy nation. Deut. 28:41. (2) people carried away by an enemy nation. Esth. 2:6. (3) "turn the [thy] captivity," to reverse one's status (usu., of slavery), esp. by return to a native land. Deut. 30:3.

**carcase** *n* (arch use) a dead human body. Num. 14:32.

**care** *n* (infr use) anxiety. Ezek. 4:16.

**careful** *adj* (arch mng) (1) showing care. 2 Kin. 4:13. (2) anxious. Phil 4:6. (3) obediently concerned. Phil. 4:10.

**carefulness** *n* (arch mng) anxiety, care. Ezek. 12:18.

**careless** *adj* (arch mng) without a care; bold; without proper concern; indifferent, secure. Judg. 18:7.

**carnal** *adj* (theol) (1) having the nature of flesh, i.e., under control of the animal appetites. Rom. 7:14. (2) needed for sustenance of the body. Rom. 15:27.

**carnal commandments** (theol) the ceremonial law; fleshly regulations; legal requirements; those commandments relating to the body, such as birth and lineage. Heb. 7:16.

**carnal ordinances,** see *carnal commandments*. Heb. 9:10.

**carnally** (theol) (1) *adj* following the guidance of the natural human disposition, man's fallen nature, rather than being governed by the Holy Spirit. Rom. 8:6. (2) *adv* "to lie carnally," to have sexual intercourse. Lev. 18:20.

**carriage** *n* (arch mng) baggage; something requiring to be carried. Judg. 18:21.

**carry** *vt* (arch mng) to take. 2 Kin. 9:2.

**carved works** (Hebraism) figured tapestry. Prov. 7:16.

**cast** *adj* (arch mng) cast-off. Jer. 38:11.

**cast** *vt* (arch mng) (1) to cast up; throw up. 2 Kin. 19:32. (2) *pt t* considered. Luke 1:29. (3) "casteth," to abort. Job 21:10. (4) to melt or cast metal. 2 Chr. 4:17.

**cast about** *vi* (arch expr) to turn round; to turn back. Jer. 41:14.

**cast down** (Hebraism) to be bowed down, downcast, sad. Psa. 42:5.

**cast off** (Hebraism) to reject. Lam. 2:7.

**cast lots** (arch custom) a method of determining God's will, in which stones, etc., were placed in a container, shaken, and cast out. Prov. 16:33 gives the theological basis for this method, whose use is not recorded in the Bible after the descent of the Holy Spirit. Josh. 18:10.

**castaway** *n* (theol) a *reprobate,* q.v. 1 Cor. 9:27.

**castle** *n* (infr mng) an encampment fortified by stone walls; a hamlet or cluster of buildings with a common outer wall for protection. Num. 31:10.

**cattle** *n pl* (arch mng) livestock in general, including cows, oxen, goats, sheep, etc. Gen. 4:20.

**caught hold of** (arch expr) was caught firmly in. 2 Sam. 18:9.

**caul** *n* (infr wd) (1) an enveloping membrane. Lev. 3:15. (2) a net for the hair. Isa. 3:18.

**cause** *n* (infr mng) (1) a case, lawsuit, or dispute; a ground of legal action. Ex. 18:19; Deut. 1:16, 17. (2) reason. Josh. 5:4.

**causeway** *n* (infr wd) highway. 1 Chr. 26:16, 18.

**celestial** *adj* (infr wd) heavenly. 1 Cor. 15:40.

**censer** *n* (infr wd) a vessel for burning incense. 1 Kin. 7:50.

**centurion** *n* (infr wd) the commanding officer of a *century,* a detachment of one hundred Roman soldiers. Luke 7:2.

**certain** *adj* (infr mng) sure. 1 Cor. 4:11.

**certainty, the** *n* (Grecism) the confirmed reason. Acts 21:34; 22:30.

**certify** *vt* (infr mng) (1) to assure. Gal. 1:11. (2) to inform. 2 Sam. 15:28.

**chafed** *pp* (infr mng) irritated, angry, enraged. 2 Sam. 17:8.

**challenge** *vt* (arch mng) to claim. Ex. 22:9.

**chamber** *n* (infr wd) a room; sometimes a lean-to, wing, or story. 1 Kin. 6:5.

**chamber of imagery** (arch expr) room with walls decorated with paintings. Ezek. 8:12.

**chambering** *n* (arch mng) wanton living or sensuality, particularly sexual licentiousness. Rom. 13:13.

**chamberlain** *n* (infr wd) the chief officer in a king's household; the king's treasurer. 2 Kin. 23:11.

**champaign** *n* (infr wd) flat country; a plain. Deut. 11:30.

**changeable** *adj* (arch use) that which can be changed. Isa. 3:22.

**changed** *vt* (arch mng) disobeyed. Dan. 3:28.

**changing** *n* (arch mng) transferring title. Ruth 4:7.

**chapiter** *n* (infr wd) the head or capital of a column. Ex. 36:38.

**chapman** *n* (arch mng) a merchant. 2 Chr. 9:14.

**chapt** *vt* (arch sp) chapped, *pp* of *chap;* cracked (said of the ground). Jer. 14:4.

**charge** *n* (infr mng) (1) "keep the charge," to take care of. Num. 1:53. (2) instructions. Num. 18:3. (3) cost, expense. Acts 21:24.

**charge** *vt* (arch mng) (1) to instruct. Gen. 28:1. (2) to command. Ex. 1:22. (3) to accuse. Job 1:22.

**charge, to give in** (arch expr) to charge; to prescribe. 1 Tim. 5:7.

**chargeable** *adj* (arch mng) financially burdensome. Neh. 5:15.

**charged** *adj* (arch mng) burdened; put to expense. 1 Tim. 5:16.

**charger** *n* (arch mng) a large flat platter for carrying meat. Num. 7:19.

**charges** *n pl* (infr use) cost; expense. Acts 21:24.

**charitably** *adv* (infr wd) in love; lovingly. Rom. 14:15.

**charity** *n* (arch mng) love. 1 Pet. 5:14.

**chasten** *vt* (infr wd) to correct. Psa. 94:12.

**chastise** *vt* (arch mng) (1) to chasten, discipline, correct with blows or words; to instruct. 1 Kin. 12:11. (2) to torture by scourging. Luke 23:16.

**check** *n* (arch mng) a correction; reprimand; rebuke. Job 20:3.

**cherish** *vt* (arch mng) to minister to. 1 Kin. 1:2.

**cherubim** *n pl* (theol) plural of *cherub*. Cherubim are ministering spirits always described as being in close association with God, whose invisible presence they manifest and whose actions they symbolize. They are generally described as winged creatures having hands and feet; sometimes two faces, man and lion (Ezek. 41:18, 19), sometimes four (Ezek. 10:21). They guarded the tree of life in Eden (Gen. 3:24). Golden figures of cherubim placed at the ends of the mercy seat symbolically guarded the contents of the ark of the covenant, while their outstretched wings symbolized the throne of Jehovah (2 Sam. 6:2). Representations of cherubim were on the curtains and veil of the tabernacle (Ex. 26:31) and on the walls of the Temple (2 Chr. 3:7). Large figures of cherubim were placed in the inner sanctuary of the Temple (1 Kin. 6:26ff.). God is symbolically spoken of as riding on a cherub, or storm wind (2 Sam. 22:11).

**chide** *vi* (infr wd) to contend noisily; to quarrel. Ex. 17:2.

**chiding** *n* (infr wd) quarreling. Ex. 17:7.

**chief** *adj* (1) highest in rank or office. Gen. 40:2; title of Psa. 4; Matt. 2:4. (2) the principal, head, or most eminent of a group or class. Num. 36:1; 2 Sam. 23:8.

**chiefest** *adj* (arch wd) principal. 1 Sam. 2:29.

**children** *n pl* (infr mng) (1) followers or disciples. Matt. 12:27. (2) youths; adolescents. 2 Kin. 2:23.

**chode** *arch pt t* of *chide*, q.v. Num. 20:3.

**choke** *vb* (infr mng) to drown. Mark 5:13.

**choler** *n* (arch wd) anger. Dan. 8:7.

**choose their delusions** (arch expr) to choose their wanton dealings (as the cause of their destruction). Isa. 66:4.

**Christ** *n* (theol) the Greek title corresponding to the Hebrew title, *Messiah*, i.e., the *Anointed One*, signifying His mediatorial offices of Prophet, Priest, and King (Ex. 28:41; 29:7; 1 Kin. 19:16). Anointing signifies the necessity of the indwelling of the Holy Spirit for the fulfillment of the responsibilities of a God-ordained office (1 Sam. 16:13, 14; John 1:15-34, 40, 41). Believing Jews understood that the Christ was to be a divine person (Matt. 16:16; John 1:47-51).

**Christ is become of no effect ... by the law** (arch expr) Christ is profitless to you who try to be declared righteous by the law. Gal. 5;4.

**chronicle** *n* (infr wd) an historical account. 1 Kin. 14:19.

**church** *n* (theol) an assembly; a congregation. Heb. 2:12.

**churl** *n* (infr wd) a niggardly or deceitful person; a knave. Isa. 32:5, 7.

**churlish** *adj* (infr wd) rude; ill-bred; surly; intractible; boorish. 1 Sam. 25:3.

**ciel** *vt* (arch wd) to wainscot; to cover with boards or paneling. 2 Chr. 3:5.

**cieling** *n* (arch wd) wainscoting; paneling. 1 Kin. 6:15.

**circumcise** *vt* (theol) to remove the foreskin of the penis. Gen. 17:23, 24.

**circumcision, the** *n* (theol) (1) *the Jews*, the Old Covenant people, who as a physical nation were distinguished by a physical sign, consisting of the surgical removal of the foreskin from the male organ of procreation. To the rite of circumcision were attached both physical and spiritual promises, the physical pertaining merely to the physical descendants of Abraham, Isaac, and Jacob, the spiritual pertaining to those who were the spiritual seed of Abraham, having circumcised *hearts*, having been brought by the Holy Spirit to true repentance and faith. (2) *true Christian believers*, whether Jews or Gentiles, who compose the true Israel of God (Gal. 6:16). Phil. 3:3.

**circumspectly** *adv* (infr wd) diligently; exactly; accurately. Eph. 5:15.

**clave** *pt t* of *cleave*, q.v. 2 Sam. 20:2.

**clean** *adj* (theol) (1) pure; cleansed from sin. Psa. 19:9. (2) healed. 2 Kin. 5:10.

**clean** *adv* (arch mng) entirely. Josh. 3:17.

**cleanness** *n* (infr wd) purity. 2 Sam. 22:21, 25.

**cleanse** *vt* (theol) to make ceremonially *clean*, q.v.; to make pure. Lev. 14:52.

**clear** *adj* (infr mng) innocent; free from guilt. Gen. 24:8, 41.

**clear** *vt* (infr wd) to acquit. Ex. 34:7.

**clear heat** (Hebraism) lit., "heat glowing upon light," i.e., the sun's warmth. Isa. 18:4.

**clearness** *n* (infr mng) brightness. Ex. 24:10.

**cleave** *vb* (infr wd) (1) *vi* to adhere to by following closely in obedience. Deut. 4:4. (2) *vi* to cling; adhere to. Deut. 28:21. (3) *vt* to split. Eccl. 10:9.

**clift** *n* (arch sp) cleft; a split place or opening. Ex. 33:22.

**cloke** *n* (arch sp) (1) a cloak; a garment, esp. an outer garment worn over a tunic as a mantle. Matt. 5:40. (2) a cloak; a pretext or excuse; something that conceals. John 15:22; 1 Thess. 2:5.

**close** *adj* (infr mng) (1) enclosed. 2 Sam. 22:46. (2) concealed, restricted. 1 Chr. 12:1.

**closed, (not)** *pp* (arch mng) still open, i.e., the open sores have not healed. Isa. 1:6.

**closet** *n* (arch mng) a chamber; a private room. Joel 2:16.

**clouted** *adj* (infr wd) patched. Josh. 9:5.

**clouts** *n pl* (infr wd) rags; pieces of cloth or leather. Jer. 38:11.

**cloven** *adj* (infr wd) (1) split. Deut. 14:7. (2) "clovenfooted," having a split hoof. Lev. 11:3.

**coast** *n* (arch mng) (1) a border or frontier of a nation or province. Num. 20:23. (2) a river's edge or bank, as a natural boundary. Num. 13:29. (3) lands or territories. Judg. 11:22.

**coat** *n* (arch mng) a woman's gown. Song 5:3.

**cockatrice** *n* (arch mng) a serpent. Isa. 11:8.

**cockcrow(ing)** *n* (infr wd) early morning, the time at which roosters first crow. Mark 13:35.

**cockle** *n* (arch mng) a weed that grows among corn. Job 31:40.

**coffer** *n* (infr wd) a chest or strongbox for valuables. 1 Sam. 6:8.

**cogitations** *n pl* (infr wd) thoughts, meditations. Dan. 7:28.

**collops** *n pl* (infr wd) lumps; folds of fat flesh. Job 15:27.

**colour** *n* (Brit sp) color; pretext, pretense. Acts 27:30.

**come by** *vt* (arch use) lit., to become masters of, i.e., to make secure. Acts 27:16.

**comeliness** *n* (infr wd) beauty, seemliness. Isa. 53:2.

**comely** *adj* (infr wd) becoming; graceful; handsome. Psa. 33:1.

**comfort** *vt* (infr mng) to strengthen; support. Judg. 19:5.

**comfortable** *adj* (infr mng) consoling; tender. 2 Sam. 14:17; Zech. 1:13.

**comfortably** *adv* (infr mng) kindly; tenderly. 2 Sam. 19:7.

**Comforter** *n* (theol) lit., *paraclete*, an advocate or defense attorney; a name for the Holy Spirit (and, by implication, a name for Christ who sent "*another* Comforter"). John 14:16.

**comfortless** *adj* (arch mng) bereft or fatherless (ones), i.e., orphans. John 14:18.

**commend** *vt* (infr mng) to recommend; entrust; commit to one's charge. Acts 14:23.

**commendation** *n* (infr mng) recommendation. 2 Cor. 3:1.

**commit sin** (theol) lit., to go on doing sin; to sin as a usual practice. 1 John 3:9.

**common** *adj* (infr mng) (1) shared in by all men alike. Num. 16:29. (2) used by all, and hence considered unclean by a Jew. Acts 10:14.

**common hall** (arch expr) lit., *the praetorium*, i.e., the residence of a provincial Roman governor (in this case Pontius Pilate, governor of Judaea). Matt. 27:27.

**commune** *vi* (infr mng) to speak or confer intimately. Gen. 34:6.

**communicate** *vb* (1) *vt* (infr mng) to impart to; to share. Gal. 2:2. (2) *vi* (arch mng) to jointly contribute a charitable collection; to share. Heb. 13:16.

**communication** *n* (1) (infr mng) talk; conversation. Luke 24:17. (2) (arch mng) company; companionship; all thoughts and words to which a person is exposed. Cor. 15:33.

**communion** *n* (theol) the share which one has in anything. 2 Cor. 13:14.

**compact** *adj* (infr mng) firmly fitted; strongly built. Psa. 122:3.

**companies** *pl* of *company*, q.v. Mark 6:39.

**company** *n* (infr mng) (1) a camp. Gen. 32:21. (2)

an assembly; a group of traveling companions. Luke 2:44.

**company with** *vt* (arch expr) to associate with. Acts 1:21.

**compass** *n* (infr mng) (1) circumference; circuit. Ex. 27:5; 38:4. (2) "fetch a compass," see *fetch*.

**compass** *vt* (infr mng) to travel entirely around, to encircle. Josh. 6:3; Luke 19:43.

**complete** *adj* (theol) pervaded with the power and gifts of the Holy Spirit by virtue of intimate relationship with Christ. Col. 2:10.

**compound** *vb* (1) (arch pp) compounded. Ex. 30:25. (2) *vt* (infr mng) to prepare. Ex. 30:33.

**comprehend** *vt* (infr mng) to take in; include; enclose. Isa. 40:12.

**conceit** *n* (infr mng) conception; idea; notion. Prov. 18:11.

**concision** *n* (arch mng) a mangling of the body; a term used in contempt of those schismatics who upheld circumcision. Phil. 3:2.

**conclude** *vt* (1) (infr mng) to decide; come to a conclusion. Acts 21:25. (2) (arch mng) to include; class together. Rom. 11:32.

**concluded all** (arch mng) has locked up everything together. Gal. 3:22.

**concourse** *n* (arch mng) (1) a large noisy meeting or crowd. Prov. 1:21. (2) a seditious gathering; a mob. Acts 19:40.

**concubine** *n* (infr wd) a woman living in a socially recognized state of cohabitation without being legally married. Judg. 8:31.

**concupiscence** *n* (infr wd) wantonness, lust. Rom. 7:8.

**condemn** *vt* (1) (arch mng) to fine. 2 Chr. 36:3. (2) (theol) to pass judgment or sentence upon a fellow sinner, as though standing in God's place. John 8:10.

**condemnation** *n* (theol) (1) the sentence of a judge; the judicially decreed penalty. Luke 23:40. (2) a crime demanding condemnation, as the world's rejection of Christ particularly aggravated the divine retribution. John 3:19.

**condescend** *vi* (theol) to yield or submit, esp. to the concerns of lowly persons. Rom. 12:16.

**confection** *n* (arch mng) a compound of drugs or spices; a perfume. Ex. 30:35.

**confectionary** *n* (arch mng) a confectioner; a maker of sweet compounds. 1 Sam. 8:13.

**confederate** *adj* (infr wd) united; allied. Psa. 83:5.

**confess** *vt* (theol) (1) to admit that one is guilty of what he is accused. 1 John 1:9. (2) to declare openly; to speak out freely. 1 John 4:15.

**confidences** *n pl* (arch mng) objects in which to trust. Jer. 2:37.

**confirm** *vt* (1) (infr wd) to establish; to make sure or firm. 1 Cor. 1:6. (2) (infr mng) to maintain. Deut. 27:26.

**confound** *vt* (arch mng) to put to confusion; destroy. Jer. 1:17.

**confusion** *n* (theol) (1) that which is contrary to God's established order; ruin; destruction. Isa. 24:10. (2) shame. 1 Sam. 20:30.

**congregation** *n* (theol) assembly; corresponds to the word translated *church* in N.T. Psa. 1:5.

**conscience** *n* (arch use) awareness; consciousness; knowledge. Heb.10:2.

**consecrate** *vt* (infr wd) to make or declare sacred or holy; to devote irrevocably to the worship of God by a solemn ceremony. Josh. 6:19; 2 Chr. 13:9.

**consent** *n* (infr mng) concord or agreement in opinion. 1 Sam. 11:7.

**consent unto** *vb* (arch expr) to fully agree with; to approve of. Acts 8:1.

**consider** *vi* (arch mng) to lay it to heart. Hag. 2:15.

**consist** *vi* (arch mng) to exist; to remain fixed. Col. 1:17.

**consolation** *n* (theol) exhortation; admonition; strengthening or comfort. A *son of consolation* is one gifted in teaching, admonishing, and consoling. Acts. 4:36.

**consort with** *vt* (theol) to attach oneself to; to join one's lot with; *pass* to be added or assigned by lot, as God added disciples to Paul and Silas. Acts 17:4.

**constantly** *adv* (1) (infr wd) without varying; confidently. Acts 12:15. (2) (arch mng) strongly; confidently. Tit. 3:8.

**constrain** *vt* (infr wd) to compel or necessitate, whether by force or by persuasion. Matt. 14:22.

**consult** *vt* (1) (infr mng) to consider. Luke 14:31. (2) (arch mng) to devise. Mic. 6:5.

**consume** *vt* (infr mng) (1) to destroy. Num. 16:21. (2) to destroy, i.e., to blind. 1 Sam. 2:33. (3) (arch mng) to completely cook. Ezek. 24:10.

**consumption** *n* (infr mng) (1) destruction. Isa. 10:22. (2) the progressive wasting away of the body. Lev. 26:16.

**contain** *vi* (arch mng) to be continent. 1 Cor. 7:9.

**contemn** *vt* (infr wd) to view or treat with contempt; to disdain, scorn or despise. Psa. 10:13.

**contend** *vi* (infr wd) to hold a controversy; to strive against. Amos 7:4.

**content** *vt* (arch use) to please; to satisfy. Mark 15:15.

**contention, of** (arch expr) because of a desire to put himself forward; because of a partisan and factious spirit. Phil. 1:16.

**continual** *adj* (infr mng) perpetual. 2 Kin. 25:30.

**continually** *adv* (infr mng) perpetually. Psa. 52:1.

**continue** *vi* (infr mng) to remain in a place. Ruth 1:2.

**contrariwise** *adv* (infr wd) on the contrary. 2 Cor. 2:7.

**contrary part** (arch expr) the opposition. Tit. 2:8.

**controversy** *n* (infr wd) a contention. Hos. 12:2.

**convenient** *adj* (arch mng) (1) what is due; duty. Philemon 8. (2) "not convenient," unbecoming; discreditable. Eph. 5:4. (3) fitting; suitable; becoming. Prov. 30:8; Rom. 1:28.

**conversant** *adj* (arch mng) having frequent, customary or familiar association; dwelling with. Josh. 8:35.

**conversation** *n* (arch mng) (1) behavior. Gal. 1:13. (2) life; manner of life. Heb. 13:5, 7. (3) citizenship. Phil. 3:20.

**convert** *vb* (theol) (1) *vt* to bring back. Jas. 5:20. (2) *vb pass* to be turned around. Isa. 6:10; Matt. 13:15.

**convince** *vt* (arch mng) (1) to convict. John 8:46. (2) to refute by argument. Job 32:12.

**convocation** *n* (infr wd) an assembly. Ex. 12:16.

**coping** *n* (arch mng) a corbel, i.e., a weight-supporting beam that projects from within a wall. 1 Kin. 7:9.

**cor** *n* (tech) *See Table of Dry and Liquid Measures*. Ezek. 45:14.

**corn** *n* (arch mng) (1) any cereal grain. Gen. 27:37. (2) a single grain. John 12:24.

**cornet** *n* (infr wd) a horn similar to the trumpet. Dan. 3:5.

**cornfloor** *n* (arch wd) threshingfloor. Hos. 9:1.

**corpse** *n* (arch mng) a body. 2 Kin. 19:35.

**correction** *n* (infr mng) a bringing into conformity with God's standard; discipline. Prov. 15:10.

**corrupt** *adj* (infr mng) rotten or putrid; no longer fit for use by reason of age; worn out; of poor quality; bad; worthless. Matt. 7:17.

**corrupt** *vt* (1) (infr wd) to become morally debased. Judg. 2:19. (2) (infr wd) to cause to decay. Matt. 6:19. (3) (arch mng) to destroy. Mal. 2:3.

**corruptible** *adj* (arch mng) capable of dying. 1 Cor. 15:53.

**corruption** *n* (Hebraism) (1) death; the grave. Jonah 2:6. (2) decay; decomposition in the grave. Acts 2:27. (3) destruction. Psa. 49:9.

**cotes** *n pl* (infr wd) huts, sheds or folds for sheep, etc. 2 Chr. 32:28.

**couch** *vi* (infr wd) (1) to lie; lie down. Deut. 33:13. (2) to crouch; to lie in ambush. Gen. 49:9.

**coulter** *n* (infr wd) a colter; a cutter on a plow to cut sod. 1 Sam. 13:20.

**council** *n* (arch mng) (1) a throng. Psa. 68:27. (2) the Sanhedrin. Matt. 5:22.

**counsel** *n* (infr mng) (1) guidance; advice. Josh. 9:14. (2) a plan; a purpose. Psa. 20:4; Acts 5:38. (3) "take counsel," see *take counsel*.

**count** *n* (arch mng) an account or reckoning. Ex. 12:4.

**count** *vt* (infr mng) to account; reckon. Isa. 5:28.

**count them pure with the wicked balances . . . deceitful weights** (Hebraism) to justify the balances of wickedness and the bag of deceitful weights. Mic. 6:11.

**countenance** *n* (infr wd) (1) the face, esp. as an indication of mood, emotion, or character. 1 Sam. 1:18. (2) *countenance fallen* or *fell*, to show displeasure in one's facial expression. Gen. 4:5, 6. (3) the eyes. 1 Sam. 16:12.

**countenance** *vt* (infr wd) to favor, to give countenance to. Ex. 23:3.

**countervail** *vt* (arch mng) to equal, match, counterbalance. Esth. 7:4.

**coupling** *n* (arch use) the place where the edges of both sets of five curtains were joined together by loops and *taches*, q.v. Ex. 36:17.

**course** *n* (arch wd) (1) a section. 1 Chr. 27:2. (2) "by course," in due order. 1 Cor. 14:27. (3) "out of course," out of order. Psa. 82:5.

**cousin** *n* (arch mng) a kinsman or kinswoman. Luke 1:36, 58.

**covenant** *n* (theol) (1) the administration of grace that God promised to perform for His elect, i.e., to *bless* (q.v.) them. On man's part it required obedience to God's conditions, and reception of the promised blessings by faith. Gen. 9:9; 15:18. (2) "establish his covenant," to fulfill His covenant promises. Deut. 8:18.

**covenant** *vt* (infr wd) to agree; make an agreement. Matt. 26:15.

**covenant of salt** (theol) a *covenant* (q.v.) ratified with salt, an emblem of the fidelity of God's covenants with man. Num. 18:19.

**cover** *vt* (arch mng) to pour out. Ex. 25:29.

**cover his feet** (arch expr) to relieve himself; to defecate. Judg. 3:24.

**cover with a covering** (Hebraism) lit., to pour out a libation or sacrifice—this action took place at the ratification of a covenant; thus the sin identified in this verse is prob. that of entering into a covenant with another nation. Isa. 30:1.

**covered** *vt* (1) hid. Judg. 4:18. (2) covered with the sea, i.e., drowned. Josh. 24:7.

**covert** *n* (infr wd) a shelter; hiding place. 1 Sam. 25:20.

**covet** *vt* (1) (infr wd) to feel inordinate desire for what belongs to another. Deut. 5:21. (2) (arch mng) to earnestly desire something good. 1 Cor. 12:31.

**covetousness** *n* (infr wd) greed for or love of money. Heb. 13:5.

**cracknel** *n* (infr wd) a crisp cake or biscuit. 1 Kin. 14:3.

**craft** *n* (infr mng) (1) handicraft. Acts 18:3. (2) deceit, fraud. Dan. 8:25.

**craftsman** *n* (infr mng) an artisan; a skilled workman. Deut. 27:15.

**crave** *vt* (infr mng) to ask for. Mark 15:43.

**created and made** (mistransl) in creating had made. Gen. 2:3.

**creature** *n* (theol) a created thing. Rom. 1:25.

**crew** *arch pt t* of *crow*. Mark 14:68, 72.

**crib** *n* (infr mng) a manger for cattle. Job 39:9.

**crisping-pins** *n pl* (arch wd) curling irons for the hair, but likely a mistranslation, with *pocket* being the correct word. Isa. 3:22.

**crookbact** *n* (arch sp) crookbacked; i.e., having a crooked back. Lev. 21:20.

**crooked** *adj* (arch mng) fleeing (from the motion a snake makes as it moves). Job 26:13.

**crouch** *vi* (arch mng) to bow down. 1 Sam. 2:36.

**crown** *n* (arch mng) rim; molding; border. Ex. 25:24.

**cruse** *n* (infr wd) a pot or small vessel for liquids. 1 Kin. 14:3.

**cry** *vi* (infr mng) (1) to shout; to call loudly. Mark 10:47. (2) "cry against," to cry aloud, to reprove; to make a vehement proclamation; to threaten. Jonah 1:2.

**cry unto** (Hebraism) to call upon; to petition. Judg. 10:14.

**cubit** *n* (tech) (1) *See Table of Linear Measures*. Gen. 6:15, 16. (2) *See Table of Linear Measures*. Ezek. 40:5.

**cumber** *vt* (infr wd) to encumber; to occupy uselessly. Luke 13:7.

**cumbrance** (arch wd) an encumbrance; troublesomeness; weight. Deut. 1:12.

**cunning** *adj* (infr mng) skillful. Gen. 25:27.

**cunning** *n* (arch mng) skill; art. 1 Kin. 7:14.

**cup** *n* (arch mng) a bowl. Isa. 22:24.

**curious** *adj* (arch mng) (1) artfully wrought, richly made, embroidered; made carefully and precisely. Ex. 28:8. (2) magical. Acts 19:19.

**curiously** *adv* (arch mng) artfully; carefully; precisely. Psa. 139:15.

**curse** *n* (theol) (1) a prayer or invocation for injury, calamity, or harm to come upon one or more persons or things. Deut. 11:26. (2) the evil that comes in response to the pronouncing of a curse or imprecation. Num. 5:24.

**curse** *vt* (theol) to pray or invoke calamity upon someone or something. Num. 22:6.

**curtains** *n pl* (arch mng) the tabernacle, a cloth and leather tent. 2 Sam. 7:2.

**custom** *n* (infr mng) tribute tax; toll. Ezra 4:13.

**cut off** *vt* (1) to put away. Ex. 12:15. (2) to hold back, stop. Josh. 4:7. (3) "cut them off," destroy them. Psa. 54:5. (4) castrated. Gal. 5:12.

**cut . . . short** (arch expr) to cut off, destroy. 2 Kin. 10:32.

## D

**dam** *n* (infr mng) a mother animal. Deut. 22:6.

**damn** *vt* (arch wd) to adjudge a person guilty; to doom; to sentence and to consign to everlasting punishment. Mark 16:16.

**damnable** *adj* (theol) leading to condemnation; destructive. 2 Pet. 2:1.

**damnation** *n* (theol) (1) condemnation. Rom. 3:8. (2) self-condemnation, such as should lead to self-examination. 1 Cor. 11:29.

**damsel** *n* (infr wd) a young woman. Gen. 24:28.

**dandle** *vt* (infr wd) to toss, as a child. Isa. 66:12.

**dark** *adj* (infr mng) obscure. Num. 12:8.

**darkness** *n* (infr mng) ignorance. Job 37:19.

**darling** *n* beloved one; lit., little dear one. Psa. 22:20.

**dart** *n* (arch use) an arrow. Prov. 7:23.

**daughter of Zion** (Hebraism) Zion. Psa. 9:14.

**daughters of Judah** (Hebraism) towns or cities of Judah. Psa. 48:11.

**day** *n* (arch mng) life. Job 18:20.

**day star** *n* (infr wd) the morning star. 2 Pet. 1:19.

**days of heaven** (Hebraism) as long as heaven lasts. Deut. 11:21.

**daysman** *n* (arch wd) an arbitrator; an arbiter. Job 9:33.

**dayspring** *n* (theol) (1) a title for the Messiah: "the Rising of the Sun"; "the Dawn" (cf. Isa. 60:1, 2; Mal. 4:2). Luke 1:78. (2) dawn; daybreak; sunrise. Job 38:12.

**deacon** *n* (theol) one of two classes of church officers; qualifications include sobriety, straightforwardness, freedom from excess and greed, uprightness; functions are those of service (not of rule), and include relief of the poor and ministering to the physical and temporal needs of the members of the church in a spiritual way. 1 Tim. 3:12.

**deal** *n* (tech) *See Table of Dry and Liquid Measures*. Ex. 29:40.

**deal** *vb* (infr mng) (1) *vi* to act. Gen. 19:9. (2) *vt* to distribute. Isa. 58:7.

**dealt** *pt t* of *deal*, q.v. Rom. 12:3.

**dear** *adj* (infr use) precious; of great value. Acts 20:24.

**dearth** *n* (infr wd) famine. 2 Chr. 6:28.

**debate** *n* (infr mng) strife; contention. Isa. 58:4.

**debtor** *n* (infr wd) one who is under an obligation. Rom. 1:14.

**decayed** *vb pass* (arch mng) depleted. Neh. 4:10.

**decrease** *vi* to die. Matt. 22:25.

**deceivableness** *n* (arch wd) deceptiveness. 2 Thess. 2:10.

**decently** *adv* (infr mng) in a fitting manner; appropriately; properly. 1 Cor. 14:40.

**decision** *n* (arch mng) lit., threshing; thus, judgment. Joel 3:14.

**deck** *vt* (arch mng) to trim, adorn; to cover. Job 40:10.

**declare** *vt* (arch mng) to show clearly; to explain; to make manifest. Gen. 41:24.

**decline** *vi* (infr mng) to turn aside. Ex. 23:2.

**dedicate** *vt* (infr mng) to initiate; to *consecrate*, q.v. Heb. 9:18.

**dedicated** *adj* (theol) devoted or set apart for the worship of God. 2 Kin. 12:4.

**deep, the** *n* (theol) (1) the abyss or bottomless pit of hell. Luke 8:31. (2) the ocean. Psa. 104:6.

**defeat** *vt* (arch use) to frustrate; to bring to nothing; to negate. 2 Sam. 15:34.

**defenced** *adj* (arch wd) defensed; fortified (applied to cities). Isa. 25:2.

**defend** *vt* (arch mng) to deliver. Judg. 10:1.

**defied** *pt t* of *defy*, q.v. 2 Sam. 21:21.

**defile** *vt* (theol) (1) to corrupt the purity or perfection of. Ex. 31:14. (2) to make ceremonially unclean. Num. 5:2, 3. (3) to ravish, violate, rape. Gen. 34:2, 5. (4) to soil. Song 5:3.

**defraud** *vt* (arch mng) to withhold, deny, or refrain from intercourse. 1 Cor. 7:5.

**defy** *vt* (arch mng) to challenge to combat. 1 Sam. 17:10.

**degree** *n* (arch mng) (1) a step or gradation. Isa. 38:8. (2) rank; station. 1 Tim. 3:13.

**delectable** *adj* (infr wd) delightful. Isa. 44:9.

**delicate** *adj* (infr mng) fastidious; weak; dainty. Deut. 28:56.

**delicately** *adv* (infr mng) luxuriously; daintily; effeminately; cheerfully. 1 Sam. 15:32.

**delicateness** *n* (infr wd) delicacy; luxuriousness. Deut. 28:56.

**delicates** *n pl* (arch wd) dainties. Jer. 51:34.

**deliciously** *adv* (infr wd) luxuriously, wantonly. Rev. 18:7, 9.

**delightsome** *adj* (infr wd) delightful; very pleasing. Mal. 3:12.

**delightsome** *adj* (arch wd) delightful. Mal. 3:12.

**deliver** *vt* (infr mng) to save; rescue. 2 Kin. 19:11.

**deliver ... into ... hand** (Hebraism) (1) to give you victory. Judg. 4:7. (2) "... my hand," entrust to my keeping. Gen. 42:37.

**deliver you out of the hand** (Hebraism) save you from the power or grip. 1 Sam. 7:3.

**demand** *vt* (infr mng) to ask. 2 Sam. 11:7.

**denounce** *vt* (arch mng) to announce threateningly. Deut. 30:18.

**depart out of thy mouth** (Hebraism) to be neglected. Josh. 1:8.

**deputy** *n* (infr mng) proconsul; governor of a province. Acts 13:7.

**derision** *n* (infr wd) the state of being ridiculed or laughed at. Job 30:1.

**describe** *vt* (1) (infr mng) to delineate; to make a diagram. Josh. 18:6. (2) (arch mng) to write down. Judg. 8:14.

**descry** *vt* (infr wd) to spy out; to reconnoiter; to find out about. Judg. 1:23.

**desert (place)** *n* (arch mng) a wilderness; an uninhabited area; a waste place (not necessarily arid). Ezek. 13:4.

**desire** *vb* (arch mng) (1) to regret; miss. 2 Chr. 21:20. (2) to ask; to make a request of. Matt. 16:1. (3) to beg, entreat, beseech. 2 Cor. 12:18.

**desolate** *adj* (infr mng) (1) solitary; lonely; deserted; uninhabited (of places). Jer. 19:8. (2) deserted by others; deprived of the help and protection of others, esp. of friends, acquaintances, family; bereft of a husband. Matt. 23:38. (3) in ruins. Dan. 9:17.

**desolation** *n* (infr wd) ruin. Ezra 9:9.

**despise** *vt* (infr wd) to regard as negligible or worthless; to regard with contempt; to be indifferent toward. Esth. 1:17.

**despite** *n* (arch mng) spite; contempt; insult. Heb. 10:29.

**despiteful** *adj* (infr wd) (1) expressing malice or hate; spiteful. Ezek. 25:15. (2) insolent. Rom. 1:30.

**despitefully** *adv* (infr wd) spitefully; maliciously. Matt. 5:44; Acts 14:5.

**detained** *pp* (arch use) taking time to worship. 1 Sam. 21:7.

**determinate** *adj* (infr wd) determined upon; fixed; established. Acts 2:23.

**device** *n* (infr mng) (1) design; purpose. Jer. 51:11. (2) plot. Esth. 8:3.

**devil, the** *n* (theol) lit., *the slanderer* or *false accuser*, i.e., Satan, the chief of fallen angels, under whose government all evil spirits are organized. Luke 4:2, 5.

**devils** *n pl* (theol) demons, i.e., fallen angels or created spiritual beings who became evil through their own rebellion against God. Lev. 17:7; Deut. 32:17; Matt. 4:24.

**devise** *vt* (infr mng) to plot. Esth. 9:24.

**devoted** *adj* (theol) dedicated to God by a vow. Num. 18:14.

**devour** *vt* (infr mng) (1) to seize upon and destroy. Deut. 31:17. (2) to eat up greedily or voraciously. Matt. 23:14. (3) to waste or squander. Luke 15:30.

**die** *vi* (theol) physically, the cessation of life; spiritually, alienation from God in this life; eternally, complete separation from God and from all that is good forever. Gen. 2:17.

**diet** *n* (infr mng) a daily allowance of food. Jer. 52:34.

**digged** *arch pp* of *dig*. Gen. 21:30.

**dignity** *n* (arch mng) lordship; authority. 2 Pet. 2:10.

**diligently** *adv* (infr mng) with great care; carefully. Matt. 2:8.

**direct** *vi* (arch mng) to succeed or prosper. Eccl. 10:10.

**disallow** *vt* (infr wd) to disapprove of; reject; refuse to allow. Num. 30:5.

**disallowed** *pp* (infr wd) rejected. 1 Pet. 2:4.

**disannul** *vt* (infr wd) to nullify; violate; frustrate. Job 40:8.

**discern** *vt* (infr wd) recognize. Gen. 27:23.

**disciple** *n* (theol) a learner; a pupil; one who follows the teaching of another. Acts 14:28.

**discipline** *n* (arch mng) instruction. Job 36:10.

**discomfit** *vt* (arch mng) (1) to defeat; put to the rout. Josh. 10:10. (2) to force into tribute. Isa. 31:8.

**discomfiture** *n* (arch mng) a defeat. 1 Sam. 14:20.

**discover** *vt* (infr mng) (1) to reveal. 1 Sam. 14:8. (2) to display. Ezek. 16:36. (3) to sight; to spot. Acts 21:3.

**dishonesty** *n* (arch mng) disgrace, shame. 2 Cor. 4:2.

**disorderly** *adv* (theol) being indolent and worthless; employing oneself in no useful and honorable occupation. 2 Thess. 3:6, 7.

**dispensation** *n* (arch mng) stewardship; management; administration; distribution. 1 Cor. 9:17.

**displeased** *adj* (arch mng) angry, jealous, or zealous for the Lord's sake. 2 Sam. 6:8.

**displeasure** *n* (arch mng) evil. Judg. 15:3.

**disposition** *n* (arch mng) ordinance, appointment. Acts 7:53.

**dispute** *vt* (infr mng) to argue, reason, discuss. Acts 19:8.

**dissemble** *vi* (infr wd) to conceal facts; to be hypocritical. Josh. 7:11.

**dissimulation** *n* (arch mng) hypocrisy. Gal. 2:13.

**dissolve** *vt* (arch mng) to solve. Dan. 5:16.

**distress** *vt* (infr wd) to afflict; to compel by inflicting pain; to oppress. Deut. 28:53, 55.

**ditch** *n* (arch mng) a reservoir. Isa. 22:11.

**divers** *adj* (infr wd) diverse; various; different. Deut. 22:9.

**divide** *vt* (1) to provide, distribute. Josh. 1:6. (2) to cut in pieces. Judg. 19:29.

**divide their tongues** (Hebraism) to confuse their speech and, consequently, their counsel. Psa. 55:9.

**divination** *n* (theol) prediction of future events or unknown things by the aid of omens or supernatural powers. Num. 22:7.

**divine** *vi* (infr mng) to foretell the future. Gen. 44:5.

**diviner** *n* (infr wd) a soothsayer; a predicter of events. See *divination*. Deut. 18:14.

**divisions** *n pl* (arch mng) family groups. Josh. 18:10.

**divorcement** *n* (infr wd) a divorce. Deut. 24:1.

**do away the iniquity** (Hebraism) to forgive. 1 Chr. 21:8.

**do thee honour** (Hebraism) to give honor or praise to you. Judg. 13:17.

**do thy diligence** (arch expr) make haste. 2 Tim. 4:9.

**do to wit** (arch expr) to desire, make, or cause to know. 2 Cor. 8:1.

**doctor** *n* (infr mng) a teacher. Luke 2:46.

**doctrine** *n* (infr wd) teaching. Matt. 7:28.

**doer** *n* (infr mng) the person responsible. Gen. 39:22.

**dog** *n* (1) the common dogs of the Bible were voracious scavengers (Isa. 56:11), feeding on human corpses (1 Kin. 21:19, 23, 24), carrion (Ex. 22:31), and household refuse, of which they kept city streets free. Under Mosaic law, they were unclean animals; one could not touch a dog without the risk of contracting some disease. Dogs roamed wild, in packs. Psa 22:16-20. (2) *little dogs*, i.e., domesticated dogs kept as household pets. Matt. 15:26, 27. (3) a term of abuse or humility. 1 Sam. 17:43; 2 Sam. 9:8. (4) a term of abuse for Gentiles (on account of their ceremonial uncleanness) used commonly among Jews during the time of Christ. Matt. 15:26, 27; Mark 7:27, 28. (5) morally unclean people in general. Rev. 22:15. (6) a symbolic designation for the Judaizers. Phil. 3:2. (7) a male prostitute, i.e., a sodomite. Deut. 23:18.

**doleful** *adj* (1) (infr wd) lamentable. Mic. 2:4. (2) (arch mng) howling. Isa. 13:21.

**dominion** *n* (infr wd) supreme authority; rule. 2 Chr. 21:8.

**done** *pp* (arch use) finished. Gen. 24:15.

**done away** (arch expr) put away; abolished. 1 Cor. 13:10.

**dote** *vi* (infr wd) (1) to be slack; to be foolish. Jer. 50:36. (2) "dote on [or upon]," to love sensually. Ezek. 23:5. (3) "doting," harping on a subject. 1 Tim. 6:4.

**doubled unto Pharaoh twice** (Hebraism) repeated; given twice; doubled. Gen. 41:32.

**doubletongued** *adj* (arch wd) duplicitous; saying one thing with one person, another with another, with the intent to deceive. 1 Tim. 3:8.

**drachma** *n* (tech) *See Table of Coins*. Luke 15:8.

**drag** *n* (arch wd) a fisher's net. Hab. 1:15, 16.

**dram** *n* (tech) *See Table of Coins*. 1 Chr. 29:7.

**draught** *n* (arch wd) (1) "draught house," a privy. 2 Kin. 10:27; Matt. 15:17. (2) the drawing or dragging of a net or the catch of fish that results from such a procedure. Luke 5:4.

**drave** *arch pt t* of *drive*. Ex. 14:25.

**drawn** *pp* (infr mng) (1) pulled (i.e., a plow). Deut. 21:3. (2) extended. Josh. 18:17.

**dreadful** *adj* (infr mng) inspiring awe or reverence. Gen. 28:17.

**dredge** *n* (arch mng) a mixture of oats and barley. Job 24:6.

**dress** *vt* (arch mng) (1) to till, cultivate, trim. Gen. 2:15. (2) to prepare. Gen. 18:7. (3) to care for. 2 Sam. 19:24.

**drew** *vt* (arch use) *pt t* of *draw;* to drag. Acts 14:19.

**drew the sword** (Hebraism) were fighting men; were experienced soldiers. Judg. 20:35.

**dried away** (Hebraism) fainted. Num. 11:6.

**drive** *vb pass* (infr mng) to be carried or conveyed by the wind, esp. with speed and force as in a storm. Acts 27:15.

**drop thy word toward** (Hebraism) speak about or against. Ezek. 21:2.

**dropped** *vi* (arch use) dripped. Song 5:5.

**dross** *n* (infr wd) waste or impurities that form on the surface of molten metal; refuse; fig., sin, impurities. Psa. 119:119.

**dryshod** *adj* (infr wd) having dry shoes. Isa. 11:15.

**due** *n* (infr use) one's appointed amount or share. Lev. 10:13.

**due benevolence** (arch expr) conjugal fidelity; the mutual obligations of sexual intercourse. 1 Cor. 7:3.

**due order** (arch expr) proper procedure. 1 Chr. 15:13.

**duke** *n* (arch mng) a leader; a chief. Gen. 36:15.

**dulcimer** *n* (infr wd) a wire-stringed musical instrument of trapezoidal shape played with light hammers. Dan. 3:5.

**dumb** *adj* (infr wd) silent. Dan. 10:15.

**dung** *n* (infr wd) manure; feces. 1 Kin. 14:10.

**dunghill** *n* (infr wd) (1) a rubbish heap. 1 Sam. 2:8. (2) a heap of manure. Isa. 25:10.

**dure** *vi* (arch sp) to last; to endure. Matt. 13:21.

**durst** *arch pt t* of *dare*. Esth. 7:5.

**dust upon their heads** (arch custom) an action performed as a sign of mourning or great distress. Josh. 7:6.

**dwell** *vi* (infr wd) to live as a resident. Ezek. 12:19.

**dwelt** *pt t* of *dwell*, q.v. 1 Kin. 17:5.

## E

**ear** *vt* (arch mng) to plow. Deut. 21:4.

**earing** *n* (arch wd) plowing. Gen. 45:6.

**earnest** *n* (infr mng) a pledge; security. 2 Cor. 1:22.

**ears . . . shall tingle** (arch expr) this expression depicts an emotional sensation, a reaction to hearing momentous news. 1 Sam. 3:11.

**earth upon his head** (arch custom) an action performed as a sign of great grief. 1 Sam. 4:12.

**ease** *vt* (arch mng) to rid. Isa. 1:24.

**eat up** *vt* (Hebraism) to take away; to confiscate. Deut. 28:33.

**edification** *n* (theol) the act of building up; the promoting of another's growth in Christian wisdom, piety, holiness, and happiness. Rom. 15:2.

**edify** *vt* (infr wd) lit., to build; hence, to build up, to instruct. Acts 9:31.

**effect** *n* (arch mng) meaning. Ezek. 12:23.

**effectual** *adj* (infr wd) producing or capable of producing the desired effect. 2 Cor. 1:6.

**elder** *adj* (infr wd) older. Job 15:10.

**elder** *n* (theol) (1) in O.T. use, elders were rulers of families and local government. Ex. 3:16. (2) the ruling church officer in the N.T. Elder, presbyter, and bishop are used interchangeably although the term *elder* often denotes the dignity of the office and the term *bishop* its duties. Elders were the bishops or *overseers* (q.v.) of the local church (Acts 20:17, 28; Tit. 1:5), having spiritual care of the congregation, ruling and instructing (1 Tim. 3:5; Tit. 1:9; Jas. 5:14; 1 Pet. 5:1ff.), and ordaining to office (1 Tim. 4:14). There was a plurality of elders or bishops in a congregation (Acts 11:30; Phil. 1:1) with apparent equality among them. Elders were the church's pastors and teachers. Qualifications for the office were the same as for the *deacon* (q.v.) with the additional requirement of being able to teach.

**elect** *n* (theol) one chosen by an act of God's free will by which before the foundation of the world He decreed His blessing of salvation through Christ to certain persons. 1 Pet. 1:2.

**elements** *n pl* (infr mng) rudiments; basics. Gal. 4:9.

**eleventh hour** (arch expr) approximately 5:00 P.M. Matt. 20:6.

**emerods** *n pl* (infr wd) hemorrhoids. Deut. 28:27.

**eminent** *adj* (infr mng) lofty, towering. Ezek. 16:24.

**emulation** *n* (arch mng) rivalry, jealousy. Rom. 11:14.

**enable** *vt* (infr wd) to make able; to fit, qualify. 1 Tim. 1:12.

**encamp against** (Hebraism) to besiege. 2 Sam. 12:28.

**enchantment** *n* (infr wd) lit., whispering of spells; an incantation; magical art. Num. 23:23.

**end** *n* (1) the goal. Heb. 13:7. (2) the closing experience which befell Job by God's command. Jas. 5:11. (3) the outcome. 1 Pet. 1:9.

**endamage** *vt* (arch wd) to damage. Ezra 4:13.

**endeavor** *vt* (arch mng) to use all diligence; to do one's utmost. Eph. 4:3.

**endue** *vt* (infr wd) to endow; provide; equip. Gen. 30:20.

**endure** *vi* (arch use) (1) to wait. Heb. 6:15. (2) to be steadfast. Heb. 11:27.

**engrafted** *adj* (infr wd) grafted; i.e., grafted in us. Jas. 1:21.

**enjoin** *vt* (infr wd) to direct. Job 36:23.

**enlarge** *vt* (arch mng) (1) to set at large or at liberty. 2 Sam. 22:37. (2) to deliver. Psa. 4:1.

**enlarged** *pp* (arch mng) fully expanded in heart, emotions. 2 Cor. 6:11.

**enlargement** *n* (arch mng) deliverance. Esth. 4:14.

**enlightened** *vb pass* (arch mng) brightened; i.e., he was physically refreshed, revitalized. 1 Sam. 14:27.

**enquire after** (Hebraism) to seek out; to worship. Deut. 12:30.

**enquire at her mouth** (Hebraism) to inquire or ask, expecting an answer. Gen. 24:57.

**enquire of/by** (Hebraism) to seek knowledge from; to pray to. Judg. 20:27.

**ensample** *n* (infr wd) an example. 1 Cor. 10:11.

**ensign** *n* (infr wd) a banner, flag, or standard. Num. 2:2.

**ensue** *vt* (arch use) to follow upon; to follow after; to follow and overtake. 1 Pet. 3:11.

**enterprise** *n* (infr wd) an undertaking. Job 5:12.

**entreat** *vt* (1) (arch mng) to treat, to deal with. Matt. 22:6. (2) (infr mng) to ask urgently or earnestly. 2 Sam. 21:14.

**environ** *vt* (infr wd) to encircle, surround. Josh. 7:9.

**envy** *n* (arch mng) malice; spite. Matt. 27:18.

**ephah** *n* (tech) *See Table of Dry and Liquid Measures*. Ex. 16:36.

**ephod** *n* (Hebrew wd) (1) the costly garments worn by priests of Israel, extending from chest to hips and held in place by shoulder and waist bands. Ex. 39:1-9. (2) an ordinary linen ephod worn by Samuel (1 Sam. 2:18) and David (2 Sam. 6:14).

**epistle** *n* (infr wd) a letter. Acts 15:30.

**equal** *adj* (infr mng) just; right. Psa. 17:2.

**equals** *n pl* (infr mng) peers; age group. Gal. 1:14.

**equity** *n* (infr wd) justice; fairness. Psa. 98:9.

**ere** *conj* (infr wd) before. Ex. 1:19.

**err** *vi* (theol) to stray, i.e., from God's law; to sin. Num. 15:22.

**eschew** *vt* (infr wd) to shun, avoid. Job 1:1.

**espousal** *n* (arch mng) betrothal; a binding pledge of intent to marry. See *espoused, adj*. Jer. 2:2.

**espoused** *adj* (arch mng) betrothed, i.e., engaged to be married. Betrothal was considered a binding pledge of mutual fidelity and violation of it was regarded as adultery (see Deut. 22:13-21, 23-27). Luke 1:27.

**espoused** *vt* (arch use) won the hand of. 2 Sam. 3:14.

**espy** *vt* (infr wd) to catch sight of; to see. Gen. 42:27.

**estate** *n* (infr mng) (1) condition; *state*, q.v. Col. 4:8. (2) the body or assembled council. Acts 22:5.

**esteem** *vt* (infr mng) to think; regard; value. Isa. 53:3, 4.

**estimate** *vt* (infr mng) to appraise or calculate the worth. Lev. 27:14.

**estimation** *n* (arch mng) (1) an appraisal. Lev. 27:18. (2) declaration of monetary value. Lev. 5:15, 16.

**estranged** *pp* (arch mng) (1) turned aside. Psa. 78:30. (2) profaned. Jer. 19:4.

**eunuch** *n* (1) a castrated male, or one sterile from birth, thus incapable of procreation. Isa. 56:3; Matt. 19:12. Such were excluded from the congregation of Israel (Deut. 23:1), but not from the church of Jesus Christ. (2) an official of a royal court; a chamberlain; a keeper of a harem (cf. Esth. 2:3). Jer. 29:2; Dan. 1:3, 7; Acts 8:27. (3) a man who refrains voluntarily from marriage out of a consuming interest in the kingdom of heaven. Matt. 19:12.

**Euroclydon** *prop n* (translit) a north- or south-easterly wind of hurricane force raising mighty waves. Acts 27:14.

**even** *adj* (arch mng) just. Job 31:6.

**even** *n* (arch mng) evening. Ex. 30:8.

**eventide** *n* (infr wd) evening. Gen. 24:63.

**everlasting** *adj* (theol) (1) in reference to created things or beings: *having no end of existence* (though having a beginning). Matt. 18:8. (2) in reference to God: *eternal* (i.e., having neither beginning nor end). Gen. 21:33.

**everlasting** *n* (theol) eternity. Psa. 90:2.

**evidently** *adv* (infr mng) manifestly; visibly; plainly; openly; clearly. Acts 10:3.

**evil** *adj* bad. Ex. 5:19.

**evil** *adv* (arch use) (1) badly. Ex. 5:22. (2) ill. Acts 14:2.

**evilfavouredness** *n* (arch wd) ugliness; deformity. Deut. 17:1.

**ewe** *n* (infr wd) the female sheep. Num. 6:14.

**exact** *vt* (arch mng) (1) to take or bring out. 2 Kin. 15:20. (2) to take by taxation. 2 Kin. 23:35. (3) (infr wd) to demand, compel. Job 11:6.

**exactions** *n pl* (arch mng) evictions. Ezek. 45:9.

**exactor** *n* (arch mng) tyrant; a taskmaster. Isa. 60:17.

**exalt** *vt* (arch use) to raise. 1 Kin. 16:2.

**exalted** *pp* (infr wd) raised up. Job 24:24.

**examine** *vt* (infr wd) (1) to investigate by thorough questioning; to interrogate. Luke 23:14; Acts 4:9. (2) to investigate judicially, often by means of torture. Acts 22:24, 29. (3) to test, prove, or scrutinize. 1 Cor. 11:28. (4) to try or put to the test (in a good sense). 2 Cor. 13:5.

**exceed** *vi* (arch mng) to be excessive. Job 36:9.

**exceeded** *vi* (arch mng) gained control of himself. 1 Sam. 20:41.

**exceeding** *adj* (infr wd) excessive; great. Eph. 2:7.

**exceeding** *adv* (arch use) very; exceptionally. Num. 14:7.

**excellent** *adj* (arch mng) powerful. Psa. 8:9.

**exchanger** *n* (arch mng) a moneychanger; banker. Matt. 25:27.

**execute** *vt* (infr wd) to carry out; perform. Num. 8:11.

**exercise** *vt* (infr mng) (1) to make familiar; to use repeatedly. 2 Pet. 2:14. (2) to engage. Psa. 131:1. (3) to exert. 1 Tim. 4:7.

**exhort** *vt* (theol) to admonish, strengthen, and encourage. Acts 27:22.

**exhortation** *n* (theol) admonition; encouragement. Heb. 13:22.

**exorcist** *n* (infr wd) one who by adjuration attempts to cast out evil spirits. Acts 19:13.

**expecting** *pres part* (arch use) waiting. Heb. 10:13.

**expedient** *adj* (theol) profitable; edifying. 1 Cor. 6:12.

**expelled** *vb pass* (infr mng) cut off. 2 Sam. 14:14.

**experiment** *n* (arch mng) approvedness. 2 Cor. 9:13.

**expired** *vb pass* the time was not yet up for him to meet the requirements. 1 Sam. 18:26.

**expound** *vt* (infr wd) to explain; make clear the meaning of. Judg. 14:19.

**express** *adj* (infr mng) lit., modeled, hence exact; very. Heb. 1:3.

**express image** (arch expr) the exact representation; a precise reproduction in every respect. Heb. 1:3.

**extol** *vt* (infr wd) to praise highly; to glorify. Psa. 30:1.

**eye be evil** (Hebraism) with evil intent; minded to do wrong. Deut. 15:9.

**eyed** *vt* (infr mng) viewed with suspicion and malice. 1 Sam. 18:9.

**eyes of his glory** (arch expr) His glorious eyes. Isa. 3:8.

**eyes, shall put his hand upon thine** (arch custom) will be with you when you die. Gen. 46:4.

**eyeservice** *n* (infr mng) service done only while the master is looking on. Eph. 6:6.

## F

**fables** *n pl* (theol) made-up stories as well as insignificant ideas which have no solidarity; useless and profitless trifles. 1 Tim. 1:4.

**face** *n* (Hebraism) (1) "laid before their faces," used for a personal pronoun, laid before *them*; in their presence. Ex. 19:7. (2) the front of an object. Ezek. 41:14. (3) the surface. Gen. 2:6.

**faces shall sup up** (Hebraism) the look of their faces shall be like the violent and injurious east wind. Hab. 1:9.

**fail** *vi* (infr mng) (1) to be weak; to falter. Psa. 73:26. (2) to perish. 1 Cor. 13:8.

**fail from** (arch expr) to pass away from; to fall into disuse. Esth. 9:28.

**fail with longing** (arch expr) to despair. Deut. 28:32.

**fain** *adv* (arch wd) gladly. Job 27:22.

**faint** *vi* (arch mng) (1) to become dejected; to lose courage or hope; to give up. Luke 18:1; Gal. 6:9. (2) to have one's strength relaxed through exhaustion; to become enfeebled; to grow weak or weary; to be tired out. Matt. 9:36.

**faintness** *n* (arch mng) fear; a lack or loss of courage; cowardliness. Lev. 26:36.

**fair** *adj* (infr mng) (1) attractive in appearance; beautiful. Gen. 26:7. (2) pure; clean. Zech. 3:5.

**fair** *adv* (arch wd) pleasantly. Prov. 26:25.

**faith** *n* (theol) noun corresponding to the verb *believe*, q.v. Concepts include truth believed, restful reliance on God, and a trust which goes out to and lays hold of God. The nature of faith is to live by the truth it receives. Faith rests on God's promises and, in gratefulness for God's grace, responds by working for His glory. Faith in God demands a right view of God (Tit. 1:1; 1 Pet. 1:21), rests on divine testimony (Tit. 1:2; 1 John 3:22), and is a gift from God (Eph. 2:8; Phil. 3:9).

**faithful** *adj* (theol) (1) having *faith*, q.v. Gal. 3:9. (2) true. 1 Tim. 4:9.

**faithful, the** *n* (theol) believers. Eph. 1:1.

**fall** *vi* (infr mng) (1) to happen; to turn out. Ruth 3:18. (2) to assume a look of shame, disappointment, or dejection. Gen. 4:6.

**fall away** (Hebraism) to desert. Jer. 52:15.

**fall by the hand** (Hebraism) be killed by. 1 Sam. 18:25.

**fall out** *vi* (1) to happen; to occur; to go. Ex. 1:10. (2) to become angry; to quarrel. Gen. 45:24.

**fall to the ground** (Hebraism) to be unfulfilled. 1 Sam. 3:19.

**fallen** *pp* (arch mng) distributed or divided out by *lot* (q.v.). Judg. 18:1.

**fallen in decay** (arch expr) cannot support himself. Lev. 25:35.

**fallen out** *pp* of *fall out*, q.v. Phil. 1:12.

**false witness** *n* (arch expr) lying; a liar. Psa. 35:11.

**fame** *n* (arch mng) (1) report; tidings; rumor. Gen. 45:16. (2) public reputation. Matt. 9:31.

**familiar spirit** *n* (infr wd) a medium or person held to be a channel of communication between the earthly world and the world of spirits; a demon that serves or prompts a medium. Deut. 18:11.

**familiars** *n pl* (infr mng) intimate friends. Jer. 20:10.

**famish** *vt* (arch use) to consume; to starve. Zeph. 2:11.

**fan** *n* (infr mng) a winnowing fan. Isa. 30:24.

**fan** *vt* (infr mng) to winnow; to remove chaff from the grain. Isa. 41:16.

**fanner** *n* (infr mng) a winnower; one who removes the chaff from the grain. Jer. 51:2.

**fare** *vi* (infr wd) (1) to be; to go on; to be in any state. 1 Sam. 17:18. (2) to feed; to be entertained. Luke 16:19.

**farthing** *n* (tech) *See Table of Coins*. Matt. 5:26.

**fashion** *n* (infr mng) make; shape; form; manner; custom. Gen. 6:15.

**fast** *adj* (infr mng) firmly fixed. Psa. 33:9.

**fast** *adv* (infr mng) completely; securely. Gen. 20:18.

**fast by** (arch expr) close by. Ruth 2:8, 21.

**fat** *adj* (Hebraism) (1) rich, fertile. 1 Chr. 4:40. (2) prosperous. Neh. 9:25.

**fat** *n* (1) (arch mng) a vat or vessel. Joel 2:24; 3:13. (2) (infr mng) the best. Gen. 45:18.

**fat of kidneys of wheat** (Hebraism) the best part of the wheat grain. Deut. 32:14.

**father** *n* (infr mng) stepfather (see 2 Kin. 12:2). 2 Chr. 24:22.

**fathers** *n pl* (infr mng) (1) ancestors. Matt. 23:30. (2) the *patriarchs*, q.v. Rom. 9:5.

**fathom** *n* (tech) *See Table of Linear Measures*. Acts 27:28.

**fatness** *n* (Hebraism) richness; good things. Jer. 31:14.

**fats** *n pl* (arch sp) vats. Joel 2:24.

**fatted** *adj* (arch wd) fattened. Luke 15:23.

**favour** *n* (arch mng and Brit sp) favor; help; mercy; kind regard; kind aspect (where the original signifies "face"). Psa. 45:12.

**fear** *n* (1) (arch mng) the object feared. Gen. 31:42, 53. (2) (theol) awe or profound reverence for God. Prov. 1:7.

**fear** *vt* (theol) to stand in reverential awe of God. Deut. 14:23; 17:19; Eccl. 12:13.

**feast** *n* (infr mng) a periodic religious observance of which eating formed a part. Ex. 5:1.

**feebleminded** *n* (arch mng) the fainthearted. 1 Thess. 5:14.

**feed** *vi* (arch use) to receive what is needed; to be nourished. Mic. 5:4.

**feel** *vt* (arch mng) to *know*, q.v. Eccl. 8:5.

**feign** *vt* (infr wd) to pretend. 2 Sam. 14:2.

**feignedly** see *feign*. Jer. 3:10.

**fell** *vi* (arch mng) died; were killed. Judg. 20:46.

**fell asleep** (arch expr) died. 2 Pet. 3:4.

**fell away** see *fall away*. 2 Kin. 25:11.

**fell on** (Hebraism) (1) "fell on his face," bowed prostrate in respect. 1 Kin. 18:7. (2) "fell on his knees," bowed or knelt in respect. 2 Kin. 1:13.

**fell unto me** (Hebraism) fell in with; came to me. 1 Sam. 29:3.

**fell upon** (arch expr) attacked. 1 Sam. 22:18.

**feller** *n* (arch wd) one who fells or cuts down trees. Isa. 14:8.

**felloes** *n pl* (arch wd) the curved pieces of wood composing the rim of a wheel. 1 Kin. 7:33.

**fellow** *n* (infr mng) a low or worthless person. John 9:29.

**fellowship** *n* (1) (theol) the share or participation one has in the body of Christ or the church. Eph. 3:9. (2) (arch mng) a bargain. Lev. 6:2.

**fence** *vt* (arch mng) (1) to entwine; to knit. Job 10:11. (2) to wall in or around; to shut in or up. Job 19:8.

**fenced** *adj* (arch mng) fortified. Num. 32:17.

**fervent** *adj* (infr wd) (1) burning. 2 Pet. 3:10. (2) ardent; zealous. Acts 18:25; Jas. 5:16.

**fetch** *vt* (1) to go for and bring back. Acts 16:37. (2) "fetch a compass," to go around. Num. 34:5; 2 Sam. 5:23; Acts 28:13. (3) "fetch a stroke," to swing. Deut. 19:5. (4) "fetch his pledge," secure some collateral. Deut. 24:10.

**fetter** *n (usu. pl)* (infr wd) a shackle for the feet. Luke 8:29.

**fill** *n* (infr mng) enough to satisfy one. Deut. 23:24.

**fillet** *n* (infr wd) a ribbon or narrow strip of material; a band. Ex. 27:11.

**filthiness** *n* (arch mng) impurity; uncleanness, ceremonially or morally. Ezra 6:21.

**filthy** *adj* (arch mng) impure, corrupt. Psa. 14:3.

**find out every device** (arch expr) to solve every problem. 2 Chr. 2:14.

**fine** *vt* (arch use) to refine; reduce to a pure state. Job 28:1.

**finer** *n* (arch wd) a refiner; see *fine*. Prov. 25:4.

**finger** *n* (tech) *See Table of Linear Measures.* Jer. 52:21.

**fining** *adj* (arch wd) refining. Prov. 17:3.

**fining-pot** *n* (arch wd) a refining pot; see *fine*. Prov. 17:3.

**fire not blown** (arch expr) an unfanned fire. Job 20:26.

**firebrand** *n* (infr wd) a piece of burning wood; a torch. Judg. 15:4.

**firepans** *n pl* (arch wd) a pan for live coals; a censer. Jer. 52:19.

**fires** *n pl* (arch mng) lit., flames, thus, by extension, the East (as the region of the sunrise). Isa. 24:15.

**firkin** *n* (tech) *See Table of Dry and Liquid Measures.* John 2:6.

**firmament** *n* (infr wd) an expanse, i.e., of waters beneath and vapor above; the arch or vault of heaven overhead, in which the clouds and stars appear; the sky or heavens. Gen. 1:6.

**first estate** (theol) their original rule, domain, principality. Jude 6.

**firstling** *n* (infr wd) the first offspring of animals. Gen. 4:4.

**fitches** *n pl* (arch wd) (1) variously thought to be black cummin, fennel, or dill. Isa. 28:25. (2) spelt, a wheat. Ezek. 4:9.

**flagon** *n* (arch mng) a skin-bag for liquids. Isa. 22:24.

**flakes** *n pl* (arch mng) flaps, scales. Job 41:23.

**flank** *n* (infr wd) the fleshy part of the side between the ribs and hip. Lev. 3:4.

**flay** *vt* (infr wd) to strip off the skin. Lev. 1:6.

**flesh** *n* (1) (infr mng) meat. Num. 11:18. (2) (arch mng) kindred; relatives. Jer. 51:35. (3) (arch mng) in the Judaistic physical sense: Jewish birth, religious standing, and achievements. Phil. 3:3. (4) (infr mng) a living creature (man or beast) that will eventually die because it possesses a body of flesh. Rom. 3:20; 1 Pet. 1:24. (5) (theol) *human nature* as dominated, instructed, and guided by sin (though not evil in itself: John 1:14; 6:51, 53; 1 Tim. 3:16). Rom. 7:5.

**floats** *n pl* (arch mng) rafts. 1 Kin. 5:9.

**flood** *n* (arch mng) (1) a river; i.e., the Euphrates. Josh. 24:14. (2) *n pl* streams. Psa. 78:44.

**floor** *n* (arch mng) threshing floor, see *thresh*. Gen. 50:11.

**flower of their age** (arch expr) their frailness; mortality. 1 Sam. 2:33.

**flowers** *n pl* (arch mng) in Hebr... lit., filth or menstrual uncleanness of wo... hence, the menstrual flow or discharge. ...5:24, 33.

**flux** *n* (infr wd) a flowing ... fluid from the body; "bloody flux" is dy... Acts 28:8.

**fly upon the spoil** (arch ex... seize the booty. 1 Sam. 15:19.

**folly** *n* (arch mng) ...il. Gen. 34:7.

**foot** *n* (infr mng) ...Ex. 39:39.

**foot breadth** (Heb... space for the sole of the foot to tread o...

**footmen** *n pl* ... foot soldiers. Num. 11:21.

**for** *prep* (1) in. Judg. 5:16. (2) like. Job 34:... although. John 21:11.

**for all** ... 23:22.

**forbe**... to refrain from; to shun; to do...

**force** *vt* (Hebraism) to rape. Deut. 22:25.

**forces** *n pl* (infr wd) soldiers. 2 Chr. 17:2.

**forefront** *n* (infr wd) the front of a battle; the front. 2 Sam. 11:15.

**foreknow** *vt* (theol) (1) speaking of God: to have knowledge beforehand of the entire course of human events; to know ahead in an unlimited, intuitive, innate, and immediate way (Acts 26:5; 2 Pet. 3:17). (2) "whom He did foreknow," whom He set regard upon; whom He knew from eternity with distinguishing love and delight; whom He foreloved. Rom. 8:29; 11:2.

**foreknowledge** *n* (theol) previous knowledge. Acts 2:23.

**foreordain** *vt* (theol) (for God) to appoint from eternity all things which come to pass, including the salvation or damnation of men (Acts 2:23; 4:27, 28; Eph. 1:5, 11). 1 Pet. 1:20.

**forepart** *n* (arch wd) the bow of a ship. Acts 27:41.

**foreship** *n* (arch wd) the fore part of a ship; the bow of a ship. Acts 27:30.

**foreskin be uncovered** (Hebraism) to be shamefully uncovered as a result of drunkenness. Hab. 2:16.

**forge** *vt* (arch mng) to impute falsely. Psa. 119:69.

**fornication** *n* (infr wd) a general term for all illicit sexual intercourse. Gal. 5:19.

**forsake** *vt* (infr wd) to give up; renounce; abandon. Deut. 29:25.

**forsook** *pt t* of *forsake*, q.v. 1 Kin. 12:13.

**forswear oneself** *vi* (infr wd) to swear falsely; to perjure oneself. Matt. 5:33.

**forth** *adv* (arch use) (1) out; away. Matt. 9:25. (2) abroad; forward. Matt. 9:38.

**forth of** (arch expr) away from. Amos 7:17.

**forthwith** *adv* (infr wd) immediately; promptly Matt. 13:5.

**forward** *adj* (arch mng) eager; hastening. Gal. 2:10

**forwardness** *n* (arch mng) earnestness; diligence Cor. 8:8.

**founder**
metalw (infr mng) a refiner; silversmith;
. Jer. 6:29.

**fourscore**
**foursquare** core. Num. 4:48.
**fourth watc** (infr wd) square. Ex. 27:1.
A.M. to 6: h use) approximately 3:00
**frame** *n* (in (see *watch*). Mark 6:48.
Psa. 103:14. constitution; state; form.
**frame** *vt* (1)
Judg. 12:6. (2) ) to manage; contrive.
**frame to pronoun** to form. Isa. 29:16.
properly. Judg.
**frankincense** *n* (h expr) to enunciate
or resin used in o
ingredient of the h ragrant white gum
**frankly** *adv* (arch temple and as an
**fray** *vt* (arch mng) Ex. 30:34.
Luke 7:42.
ut. 28:26.

**free** *adj* (infr mng) voluntary; generous; magnanimous; willing. Psa. 51:12.

**freely** *adv* (infr mng) without cost. Num. 11:5.

**fret** *vi* (infr mng) to devour, corrode; hence, to eat in, as an ulcer does. Lev. 13:55.

**fretted** *vt* (infr wd) provoked; angered. Ezek. 16:43.

**friend** *n* (arch mng) the best man in a wedding, but having greater responsibilities than today's chief groomsman. Judg. 14:20.

**frontlet** *n* (infr wd) a fillet or headband worn over the forehead. Ex. 13:16.

**froward** *adj* (infr wd) perverse; untoward; self-willed. Deut. 32:20.

**frowardly** *adv* (infr wd) perversely; rebelliously. Isa. 57:17.

**frowardness** *n* (infr wd) perverseness. Prov. 2:14.

**fruit** *n* (1) (arch mng) any agricultural produce, including grain. Mark 4:7. (2) (arch mng) one's physical offspring. Ex. 21:22; Deut. 7:13. (3) (theol) fig., a work, act, or deed that proceeds out of one's heart and is thus an indicator of one's true spiritual state before God. Matt. 3:8; 7:16.

**fruit depart** (arch expr) when a fetus dies; a miscarriage. Ex. 21:22.

**frustrate** *vt* (infr mng) to nullify. Gal. 2:21.

**fulfil** *vt* (arch mng) (1) to cause to be everywhere known, acknowledged, embraced; i.e., fully preached. Col. 1:25. (2) to carry through till the end; to accomplish; to carry out. Col. 4:17. (3) to bring to pass; to ratify; to accomplish. Matt. 8:17.

**full of mixture** (Hebraism) fully mixed, probably with spices. Psa. 75:8.

**fuller** *n* (infr wd) a bleacher or cleaner of cloth. Mal. 3:2.

**furbish** *vt* (infr wd) to polish. Jer. 46:4.

**furlong** *n* (tech) *See Table of Linear Measures*. Luke 24:13; Rev. 14:20.

**furnish** *vt* (arch mng) to prepare. Jer. 46:19.

**furniture** *n* (arch mng) equipment; saddle. Gen. 31:34.

**furthered** *vt* (infr mng) helped. Ezra 8:36.

## G

**gad** *vi* (infr wd) to rove about restlessly, as a gossip does. Jer. 2:36.

**gain** *n* (arch mng) a price; profit. Dan. 11:39.

**gainsay** *vt* (infr wd) to speak against; contradict. Luke 21:15.

**gall** *n* (arch mng) lit., in Hebrew, a poison. Jer. 8:14.

**gallant** *adj* (arch mng) splendid. Isa. 33:21.

**galleries** *n pl* (arch mng) ringlets of hair. Song 7:5.

**galley** *n* (infr wd) a rowing-boat with a low deck. Isa. 33:21.

**garden-house** *n* (arch wd) a summerhouse. 2 Kin. 9:27.

**garlick** *n* (arch sp) garlic. Num. 11:5.

**garner** *n* (infr wd) a granary or storehouse. Matt. 3:12.

**garnish** *vt* (infr mng) to adorn, deck. 2 Chr. 3:6.

**gat** *arch pt t* of *get*. Gen. 19:27.

**gat him up** (arch expr) he departed. 1 Sam. 13:15.

**gat no heat** (arch expr) could not get warm. 1 Kin. 1:1.

**gates** *n pl* (arch mng) (1) cities. Deut. 12:15. (2) doors. 1 Chr. 9:19.

**gates, (with)in thy** (Hebraism) in your cities or towns, i.e., any settlement surrounded by walls for protection. Deut. 5:14; 12:15; 14:27, 28.

**gather unto (one's) fathers** (Hebraism) to die. Judg. 2:10.

**gathered to (one's) people** (Hebraism) died; shall die. Num. 20:24; 27:13.

**gave attendance** (arch expr) served. Heb. 7:13.

**gave ear** *pt t* of *give ear*, q.v. Psa. 77:1.

**gay** *adj* (arch mng) splendid; gorgeous; bright. Jas. 2:3.

**gazingstock** *n* (arch wd) an object to gaze at in wonder; an example. Nah. 3:6.

**gender** *vb* (infr mng) (1) *vt* to produce; engender. Job 38:29. (2) *vi* to copulate. Lev. 19:19.

**genealogies** *n pl* (infr wd) studies of family pedigrees. 1 Tim. 1:4.

**Gentiles** *prop n pl* (infr mng) (1) the nations at large; the heathen. Judg. 4:13; Rom. 2:14. (2) lit., *the Greeks*, referring to non-Jewish persons in general who had been Hellenized, i.e., who lived in the sphere of Greek language and culture. John 7:35; Rom. 2:9, 10.

**gerah** *n* (tech) *See Table of Coins*. Ex. 30:13.

**ghost** *n* (infr mng) a spirit; hence, to give (or yield) up the ghost, to die. Matt. 27:50.

**Ghost** *prop n* (theol) *Holy Ghost* is an archaic expression for the Holy Spirit or third person of the Trinity. Matt. 1:18. See appendix entitled "The Holy Trinity and the Covenant of Grace."

**gift** *n* (arch mng) euphemistic for *bribe*. Deut. 16:19.

**gin** *n* (infr mng) a snare or trap. Job 18:9.

**gird** *vt* (infr wd) (1) lit., to tie up loose clothing in preparation for work or fighting. Jer. 4:8. (2) fig., to be alert and ready for action. 1 Pet. 1:13.

**girdle** *n* (arch mng) a belt. 1 Sam. 18:4.

**girt** *pt t* of *gird*, q.v. John 21:7.

**give** *vt* (arch mng) to ascribe. Psa. 96:7.

**give ear** (Hebraism) to listen; hearken. Neh. 9:30.

**give . . . charge** (arch expr) to command. 1 Tim. 5:7.

**give out** (arch expr) to appoint. Josh. 18:4.

**give place** (arch expr) (1) to make room for. Luke 14:9. (2) to give way, yield. Gal. 2:5.

**give pledges** (arch custom) to exchange *pledges*, q.v.; to engage with; to undertake a mutual enterprise. Isa. 36:8.

**given** *adj* (arch use) prone; addicted. 1 Tim. 3:3.

**given** *pp* (infr mng) released. Philemon 22.

**glass** *n* (infr mng) a looking-glass; a mirror. 1 Cor. 13:12.

**glean** *vt* (infr wd) (1) to thoroughly search for and find. Judg. 20:45. (2) to pick up grain left by the reapers. Ruth 2:2.

**glistering** *adj* (infr wd) glittering; bright. 1 Chr. 29:2.

**glorify** *vt* (theol) (1) to treat with honor. Lev. 10:3. (2) to give or ascribe glory to God. 1 Pet. 4:14.

**glory** *n* (theol) (1) splendor, brightness. Acts 22:11. (2) the exalted state of Christ in heaven with His Father. 1 Pet. 1:11, 21. (3) the blessedness of the heavenly state. 1 Pet. 5:1. (4) majesty in the sense of the absolute perfection of God. 1 Pet. 4:14.

**glory** *vb* (infr mng) to boast; to boast oneself. Gal. 6:13.

**glory over** *vt* (arch expr) to command. Ex. 8:9.

**go** *vi* (Hebraism) to be. Gen. 15:2.

**go a whoring after** (arch expr) to play the harlot with; see *a whoring*. Ex. 34:15.

**go about** (infr expr) (1) to undertake; to attempt; to endeavor. John 7:20. (2) to make; to fashion; to exercise. Deut. 31:21.

**go beyond** (arch expr) to overreach. 1 Thess. 4:6.

**go in unto** (Hebraism) to have sexual intercourse. Josh. 23:12.

**go to** *interj* (arch expr) come now! Gen. 11:3.

**go to be with thy fathers** (Hebraism) to die. 1 Chr. 17:11.

**go up** (Hebraism) (1) go. 1 Kin. 12:24. (2) go to attack. 2 Chr. 18:2.

**god of forces** (arch expr) lit., the god of bulwarks, identified by many as Jupiter. Dan. 11:38.

**gods** *n pl* (theol) a translation of the Hebrew word *elohim*, usually translated "God," often translated "gods" in reference to false deities or idols. Deut. 31:16. In at least two passages it signifies human magistrates or *judges* (as it is also translated) as mighty or powerful ones who are the servants of God. Ex. 22:28; Psa. 82:1, 6.

**God-ward** see *-ward*. 1 Thess. 1:8.

**going(s)** *n* (arch mng) (1) marching. 2 Sam. 5:24. (2) lit., steps; by extension, how one lives. Prov. 14:15. (3) *n pl* processions. Psa. 68:24.

**going after strange flesh** (arch expr) searching for persons with whom to gratify one's lust. Jude 7.

**going down** *n* (arch expr) a descent; a steep slope. Josh 7:5.

**going the way of all the earth** (Hebraism) going to die. Josh. 23:14.

**going up** *n* (arch expr) an ascent. Josh. 15:7.

**goings forth (or out)** (Hebraism) (1) end; ports. Num. 34:5. (2) limits. Josh. 15:4, 11.

**gospel** *n* (theol) good news; glad tidings concerning the things that pertain to eternal salvation through Christ. Luke 9:6.

**good** *n* (arch mng) goods; property. 1 Chr. 29:3.

**goodly** *adj* (infr wd) fair; handsome; valuable. Gen. 39:6.

**goodlier** *adj* (infr wd) more choice; more handsome. 1 Sam. 9:2.

**goodliest** *adj* (infr wd) most comely or choice. 1 Sam. 8:16.

**goodliness** *n* (arch mng) beauty. Isa. 40:6.

**goodly** *adj* (infr wd) (1) fair; handsome; valuable. Gen. 39:6. (2) comely; handsome; beautiful. Josh. 7:21. (3) considerable. Psa. 16:6.

**goodman** *n* (arch wd) (1) master of the house. Matt. 20:11. (2) husband; the head of a household. Prov. 7:19.

**goods** *n pl* (infr wd) property; wealth; possessions. Gen. 14:16.

**gospel** *n* (theol) good news; glad tidings concerning the things that pertain to eternal salvation through Christ. Luke 9:6.

**governor** *n* (arch mng) (1) pilot or helmsman of a ship. Jas. 3:4. (2) the manager of a household; a steward or superintendent. Gal. 4:2.

**grace** *n* (theol) (1) favor; good will. 2 Sam. 16:4. (2) kindness which bestows on one what he has not deserved; esp. granting sinners pardon for their offenses and eternal salvation through Christ. Rom. 3:24.

**gracious** *adj* (arch mng) full of *grace* (q.v.); graceful. Prov. 11:16.

**graffed** *vb* (arch sp) grafted. Rom. 11:17-24.

**grant** *vt* (infr wd) to bestow a privilege or gift, often in answer to a prayer, request, or petition. Matt. 20:21.

**grass** *n* (arch use) vegetation; sproutage; plants. Gen. 1:11.

**grave** *n* (theol) hades or the world of the dead, including its accessories and inmates. Gen. 37:35.

**grave** *vi* to engrave; to carve. 2 Chr. 2:7.

**graven** *pp* of *grave,* q.v. Ex. 20:4.

**great** *adj* (infr mng) (1) populous. Gen. 18:18. (2) (of a person) having rank and influence. 2 Kin. 4:8. (3) very large. Ezra 5:8.

**greaves** *n pl* (infr wd) pieces of armor protecting the legs. 1 Sam. 17:6.

**Grecian** *prop n* (arch mng) a Greek-speaking Jew. Acts 6:1.

**Greek** *prop n* (theol) all non-Jewish nations who adopted the Greek language, customs, and learning; *Greek* is used in opposition to *Jew* to contrast religion and worship. Rom. 1:14, 16.

**green** *adj* (arch use) fresh; new. Judg. 16:8.

**grieve** *vt* (arch mng) to vex; to harass. Gen. 49:23.

**grievous** *adj* (infr mng) burdensome; painful; severe. Gen. 12:10.

**grievously** *adv* (infr mng) severely. Matt. 8:6.

**grind** *vi* (Hebraism) i.e., to grind meal; by extension, to be a *concubine*, q.v. (one of whose chief duties was to grind meal). Job 31:10.

**grinders** *n pl* (arch wd) the teeth. Eccl. 12:3.

**grisled** *adj* (arch sp) grizzled; gray. Gen. 31:10.

**gross** *adj* (1) (theol) fat or thick; hence, a spiritual callousness or stupidity of the soul toward the things of God. Acts 28:27. (2) thick. Isa. 60:2; Jer. 13:16.

**groves** *n pl* (theol) groups of trees which were themselves worshiped or were the scene of the worship (often immoral) of idols. Ex. 34:13.

**grudge** *vi* (arch mng) to grumble; murmur. Psa. 59:15.

**guile** *n* (infr wd) deceit; cunning. John 1:47.

**guilty** *adj* (arch mng) justly liable to or deserving of a penalty. Lev. 5:4; 6:4.

**guilty of** (arch mng) worthy of; deserving. Matt. 26:66.

**gutter** *n* (1) (infr use) a culvert; a water spout. 2 Sam. 5:8. (2) (arch mng) a hollowed-out object. Gen. 30:38, 41.

## H

**habergeon** *n* (infr wd) a coat of mail covering the neck and chest. Ex. 28:32.

**habitation** *n* (infr wd) a residence; a dwelling place. 1 Chr. 4:33.

**had** *vb pass* (arch use) held. 1 Sam. 13:4.

**had pity** (arch expr) spared. Jonah 4:10.

**haft** *n* (infr wd) a handle or hilt. Judg. 3:22.

**hail!** *interj* (arch wd) Long live . . .! i.e., Do well! Thrive! Mark 15:18.

**hale** *vt* (infr wd) to haul; drag; pull forcibly. Luke 12:58.

**half homer** (tech) *See Table of Dry and Liquid Measures*. Hos. 3:2.

**hallow** *vt* (infr wd) to make holy or set apart for holy use; to set aside for God alone. Lev. 16:19.

**halt** *adj* (infr wd) lame; crippled; at times signifying that a foot is missing. Matt. 18:8; Mark 9:45; Luke 14:21.

**halt** *vi* (infr wd) to limp; to go lamely. Gen. 32:31.

**halted/halteth** see *halt*. Mic. 4:6.

**hand** *n* (Hebraism) (1) control; power. Judg. 6:1. (2) affliction. 1 Sam. 6:3, 5.

**hand, at** see *at hand*. Matt. 3:2.

**hand of the Lord was against** (Hebraism) the Lord afflicted or worked against. Judg. 2:15; Ruth 1:13.

**handbreadth** *n* (tech) *See Table of Linear Measures*. Ex. 25:25.

**handmaid/handmaiden** *n* (infr wd) a female servant. Gen. 16:1.

**hands** *n pl* (arch mng) the wrists. Gen. 24:22.

**handstaves** *n pl* (arch wd) sing., handstaff; a stick to be held in the hand and used as a weapon. Ezek. 39:9.

**handywork** *n* (arch sp) handiwork; workmanship. Psa. 19:1.

**hanged** *pt t* of *hang* (arch use) to impale; to kill by fixing on a sharp stake. Ezra 6:11. (2) (arch pt t) hung. Psa. 137:2.

**hap** *n* (infr wd) chance; fortune. Ruth 2:3.

**haply** *adv* (infr wd) by chance; perchance, perhaps. Mark 11:13.

**hard** *adj* (infr mng) (1) tough, severe. 2 Sam. 3:39. (2) difficult. 2 Sam. 13:2.

**hard** *adv* (arch use) (1) near. Judg. 9:52. (2) "hard by," near. Lev. 3:9. (3) "hard after," close behind. Psa. 63:8.

**hardened their necks** (Hebraism) became stubborn, willful, rebellious. 2 Kin. 17:14.

**hardly** *adv* (infr mng) with difficulty. Matt. 19:23.

**hardly bestead** (arch expr) beset with difficulties. Isa. 8:21.

**hardness** *n* (arch mng) hardship. 2 Tim. 2:3.

**harmless** *adj* (arch mng) without guile or fraud; free from guilt. Phil. 2:15.

**harness** *n* (arch mng) body-armor for a man. 1 Kin. 20:11.

**harp** *n* a stringed musical instrument made of almug wood, used both on joyful occasions such as worship and jubilees and at times of mourning. Gen. 4:21.

**harrow** *n* (infr wd) a cultivating implement used primarily for pulverizing and smoothing the soil. 1 Chr. 20:3.

**haste** *vi* (arch mng) to urge on; to hasten. Ex. 5:13.

**hasted** *pt t* of *haste,* q.v. (arch use). Acts 20:16.

**hasten** *vb* (arch mng) (1) *vt* to hurry. Isa. 5:19. (2) *vt* to be watchful over. Jer. 1:12. (3) *vi* to withdraw. Jer. 17:16.

**haunt** *n* (infr wd) a place habitually frequented. 1 Sam. 23:22.

**haunt** *vt* (1) (infr mng) to frequent; to resort to. 1 Sam. 30:31. (2) (arch mng) to inhabit. Ezek. 26:17.

**have** *vt* (arch mng) take. 2 Chr. 35:23.

**have no changes** (arch use) do not change. Psa. 55:19.

**have no part in** (arch expr) to have no inheritance in, and thus not belong to. Josh. 22:27.

**head** *n* (arch mng) (1) the top. Ex. 36:29. (2) a leader. Judg. 10:18. (3) the beginning of a stream. Gen. 2:10. (4) used instead of a personal pronoun. 2 Kin. 2:3.

**heads of the fathers** (Hebraism) the chief leaders. Josh. 21:1.

**heady** *adj* (infr mng) headstrong. 2 Tim. 3:4.

**health** *n* (arch mng) (1) healing. Isa. 58:8. (2) "saving health," salvation. Psa. 67:2.

**health to thy navel, and marrow to thy bones** (Hebraism) a picturesque way of expressing great benefit to be gained. Prov. 3:8.

**heap** *n* (infr mng) a collection of things thrown one on another; pile; ruin. Josh. 8:28.

**hear** *vt* (infr mng) to heed; to pay attention; to answer. 1 Kin. 18:26.

**heard say** *pt t* of *hear say* (arch expr) having heard from another; having been told. Josh. 22:11.

**hearken** *vt* (arch mng) (1) to listen with the intent of obeying. Ex. 3:18. (2) to listen with due consideration. Judg. 11:17. (3) to listen with favor. Judg. 13:9.

**heart** *n* (arch mng) the will. 1 Sam. 25:37.

**heart was lifted up** (Hebraism) became proud. 2 Chr. 32:25.

**hearty** *adj* (arch mng) coming from the heart. Prov. 27:9.

**heath** *n* (infr wd) lit., a juniper in a bare or isolated location. Jer. 17:6.

**heathen** *n pl* (theol) foreign nations; Gentiles; pagans; unbelieving nations. 2 Kin. 17:8.

**heave** *vt* (arch mng) to lift or be lifted up. Ex. 29:27.

**heave offering** (theol) a peace- or thank-offering in which the offering was lifted up. Num. 31:29.

**heaviness** *n* (infr mng) sadness; depression. Job 9:27.

**heavily** *adv* (infr mng) (1) sadly. Psa. 35:14. (2) with difficulty. Ex. 14:25.

**heavy** *adj* (infr mng) (1) tired; difficult to hold up. Ex. 17:12. (2) demanding. Ex. 18:18. (3) sad. 1 Kin. 14:6.

**held** *pp* (infr mng) enslaved. Song 7:5.

**held (one's) peace,** see *hold (one's) peace.*

**hell** *n* (theol) (1) the unseen world. Psa. 16:10. (2) death. Psa. 116:3. (3) the grave. Hab. 2:5. (4) the place of torment. Matt. 10:28.

**help** *n* (arch mng) deliverance. 1 Sam. 11:9.

**helped forward** (Hebraism) increased; promoted. Zech. 1:15.

**helps** *n pl* (1) (arch mng) frappings or lashing cables, passed under the ship's hull transversely in order to bind its timbers together. Acts 27:17. (2) (theol) the ministrations of deacons, who have special responsibility to care for the poor and sick. 1 Cor. 12:28.

**helve** *n* (infr wd) the handle of an ax. Deut. 19:5.

**hence** *adv* (infr wd) (1) here; from this place. Ruth 2:8. (2) "Get thee hence," Away with you! or, Begone! Matt. 4:10.

**herb** *n* (arch mng) vegetation. Ex. 10:15.

**heresy** *n* (theol) (1) one's chosen opinion or tenet, which is at variance with the true Christian faith. 2 Pet. 2:1. (2) a sect or party, i.e., a body of men separating themselves from others and following their own tenets. Acts 24:14. (3) dissension arising from a clash of private opinions or tenets. Gal. 5:20.

**Herodians** *prop n* members of a Jewish party favoring the Herodian dynasty; they are mentioned as enemies of Jesus. Matt. 22:16.

**hew** *vt* (infr wd) to cut with blows of a heavy cutting instrument. Ex. 34:1.

**hewn** *pp* of *hew,* q.v. Matt. 3:10.

**hid** *adj* (Hebraism) (1) hidden. Nah. 3:11. (2) unknown or unrevealed to the hearts or consciences. Lev. 4:13.

**hide my/thy face** (Hebraism) to turn away. Psa. 44:24.

**hide their eyes** (Hebraism) to feign ignorance of

that which duty demands one oppose, e.g., to ignore sin. Lev. 20:4.

**hide thyself** (Hebraism) to withhold help; to avoid responsibility. Deut. 22:3.

**high** *adj* (arch mng) lofty, notable. 2 Chr. 7:21.

**high hand** (Hebraism) triumphantly. Ex. 14:8.

**high places** (arch expr) (1) hills or mountains where worship to idols took place. Deut. 33:29. (2) the upper regions; the heavens (but not as the residence of God and the angels). Eph. 6:12.

**highness** *n* (infr wd) majesty. Job 31:23.

**himself** *pron* (arch mng) his men. Gen. 14:15.

**hin** *n* (tech) *See Table of Dry and Liquid Measures.* Ex. 30:24.

**hinder** *adj* (infr wd) (1) the back part. 2 Sam. 2:23. (2) *hinder part* of a ship: the stern. Acts 27:41.

**hindermost** *adv* (arch wd) hindmost; farthest to the rear. Gen. 33:2.

**hindmost** *adj* (infr wd) farthest to the rear. Deut. 25:18.

**hire** *n* (infr mng) wages; pay. Deut. 24:15.

**hireling** *n* (infr wd) a person who serves for hire, esp. for purely mercenary motives. Job 7:1.

**hiss** *vi* (1) to make a sneering sound. Zeph. 2:15. (2) to make a sound as a means of calling forth. Isa. 7:18.

**hissing** *n* (Hebraism) a derision. Jer. 19:8.

**hither** *adv* (infr wd) to this place. Josh. 2:2.

**hitherto** *adv* (infr wd) up to this time. 1 Sam. 1:16.

**hoar(y) head/hairs** (arch expr) lit., hair that is gray or white with age; an aged person. Lev. 19:32.

**hoise** *vt* (infr wd) to raise into position; to hoist. Acts 27:40.

**hold** *n* (infr mng) (1) prison; a place under guard. Acts 4:3. (2) a stronghold or fortress; a fortified place. Judg. 9:46.

**hold** *vt* (infr mng) (1) to consider; to esteem; to account. Ex. 20:7. (2) to restrain or hinder. Rom. 1:18.

**hold in hand** (Hebraism) to take care of. Gen. 21:18.

**hold (one's) peace** (arch expr) to say nothing; to keep quiet about something; to keep silence. 2 Kin. 2:5.

**hold with** (arch expr) to side with. Acts 14:4.

**holden** *arch pp* of *hold:* held. Psa. 18:35; Luke 24:16.

**hole** *n* (arch expr) the means by which a door was opened. Song 5:4.

**holpen** *pp* of *help.* Psa. 83:8.

**holy** *adj* (theol) (1) of God: separated from all moral imperfection. Rev. 6:10. (2) of men: entirely *dedicated,* q.v. Ex. 22:31. (3) of objects: separated from common use and dedicated to God. Ex. 28:2.

**Holy Ghost** *prop n* (theol) the Holy Spirit. Rom. 5:5. See appendix entitled "The Holy Trinity and the Covenant of Grace."

**holy hill** (theol) Mt. Zion (as a reference to Jerusalem); more specifically, Mt. Moriah, on which the Temple was situated. Psa. 99:9.

**holyday** *n* (arch sp) an observed sacred festival day; a holiday. Psa. 42:4.

**homer** *n* (tech) *See Table of Dry and Liquid Measures.* Num. 11:32.

**honest** *adj* (arch mng) honorable; comely. Rom. 12:17.

**honesty** *n* (arch mng) honorable conduct; chastity. 1 Tim. 2:2.

**horn** *n* (theol) (1) (when God exalts) great power and prosperity. 1 Sam. 2:1, 10. (2) (when man exalts) arrogance and insolence. Psa. 75:4, 5. (3) political power. Psa. 132:17. (4) a kingdom. Dan. 7:8, 11, 21.

**Hosanna** *interj* (Hebraism) O save us! or, Be propitious! John 12:13.

**hosen** *n pl* (arch wd) hose, which originally meant a covering for the legs, not merely stockings. Dan. 3:21.

**host** *n* (infr mng) (1) an army. Judg. 4:16. (2) a very large number. Deut. 4:19. (3) "host of heaven," the stars. 2 Kin. 17:16.

**hough** *vt* (arch sp) to cut the hocks or hamstrings of horses to disable them for use in war. Josh. 11:6.

**house** *n* (infr mng) (1) a household; an established family of renown. Ex. 1:21. (2) a temple. 2 Kin. 23:19. (3) a family. 1 Tim. 3:5. (4) (theol) a heavenly body. 2 Cor. 5:2.

**how hardly** (arch expr) with what difficulty. Mark 10:23.

**howbeit** *adv* (infr wd) nevertheless. Judg. 4:17.

**howbeit** *conj* (arch wd) be that as it may; nevertheless. 2 Chr. 18:34.

**howsoever** *adv* (infr wd) in whatever manner; come what may. 2 Sam. 18:22, 23.

**hungerbitten** *adj* (arch wd) famished. Job 18:12.

**hungred** see *an hungred.*

**hurt** *n* (arch mng) harm. Gen. 26:29.

**husbandman** *n* (infr wd) a farmer. Gen. 9:20.

**husbandry** *n* (infr wd) the cultivation and production of crops; tillage of the soil. 1 Cor. 3:9.

**hypocrite** *n* (1) (infr wd) originally, in Greek, *an interpreter;* by extension, an *actor* or *stage-player;* in N.T. a *dissembler* (q.v.) or *pretender.* Matt. 6:5. (2) (arch mng) an impious person. Isa. 33:14.

## I

**I AM** (theol) an emphatic statement in Greek that is a perfect translation of the divine name, *I AM,* found in Ex. 3:14. The Lord Jesus Christ applied this name repeatedly to Himself during the course of His public ministry. In John's Gospel, Christ weaves the divine name *I AM* into His testimony concerning Himself at least twenty-one times, in fourteen distinct pronouncements or sayings (some repeated): (1) John 6:35, 48, 51; (2) 7:34; (3) 8:12; (4) 8:18; (5) 8:28; (6) 8:58; (7) 10:7, 9; (8) 10:11, 14; (9) 11:25; (10) 14:3; (11)

14:6; (12) 15:1, 5; (13) 17:24; (14) 18:5, 6, 8. The name is also used by the risen and enthroned Christ in Rev. 1:8, 11, 17.

**I AM THAT I AM** (theol) the divine name by which God revealed Himself to Moses and Israel, signifying His self-existence and eternality as the One who was and is and ever shall be (Rev. 16:5). Ex. 3:14. See *I am.*

**idol** *adj* (arch mng) worthless. Zech. 11:17.

**idols** *n pl* (arch mng) things of no value. Lev. 19:4.

**ignorantly** *adv* (infr mng) unintentionally. Deut. 19:4.

**ill-favoured** *adj* (arch expr and Brit sp) scrawny; bad-looking. Gen. 41:3.

**illuminated** *adj* (arch mng) spiritually enlightened. Heb. 10:32.

**image** *n* (1) a portrait or likeness stamped on a coin. Mark 12:16. (2) "standing image," a pillar used in cultic worship. Lev. 26:1.

**image work** (arch expr) ornately carved work; sculpture. 2 Chr. 3:10.

**imagery** *n* (arch mng) imagination. Ezek. 8:12.

**images** *n pl* (arch mng) (1) household gods. Gen. 31:19. (2) idols. Isa. 21:9.

**imagination** *n* (arch mng) (1) obstinacy. Jer. 3:17. (2) *n pl* plans, plots, or devices with evil intent. Lam. 3:60, 61.

**imagination, every** (theol) all the thoughts formed in the mind, including purposes and desires. Gen. 6:5.

**imagine** *vt* (arch mng) to devise. Nah. 1:11.

**Immanuel** *prop n* (Hebrew) lit., "God with us." Isa. 7:14.

**immortality** *n* (theol) lit., incorruptibility. 2 Tim. 1:10.

**implead** *vt* (infr wd) to bring a charge against, as in a court of law. Acts 19:38.

**impotent** *adj* (infr wd) without strength; sick; powerless. John 5:3.

**impute** *vt* (infr wd) (1) to credit to a person. 2 Sam. 19:19. (2) to credit by transferral. Rom. 4:8.

**in** *prep* (arch mng) (1) on; upon. Ex. 8:17. (2) by. Gen. 10:20.

**in danger of** (infr expr) liable to; subject to. Matt. 5:22.

**in process of time** *(arch expr)* lit., after days; thus, after a while. Judg. 11:4.

**in sunder** (arch expr) asunder; divided into parts. Psa. 46:9.

**in very deed** (arch expr) indeed; really. 2 Chr. 6:18.

**incline** *vt* (used in arch exprs) (1) "incline your heart," to be drawn toward. Josh. 24:23. (2) "incline thine [your] ear," to listen. Psa. 45:10.

**inclineth** *vi* (arch mng) sinks. Prov. 2:18.

**inclosing** *n* (arch wd) an enclosure or setting. Ex. 28:20.

**incontinent** *adj* (infr wd) lacking self-restraint; intemperate. 2 Tim. 3:3.

**increase** *n* (arch mng) (1) produce of the earth. Gen. 47:24. (2) interest of money. Lev. 25:36.

**indignation** *n* (arch mng) (1) fury; time of judgment. Dan. 11:36. (2) jealousy. Acts 5:17.

**inditing** *pres part* (arch mng) overflowing with. Psa. 45:1.

**infidel** *n* (infr wd) an unbeliever; one who refuses belief in the gospel. 1 Tim. 5:8.

**infirmity** *n* (infr wd) (1) physical sickness, weakness, malady, or disease. Luke 7:21. (2) moral weakness or proclivity to sin. Heb. 5:2; 7:28.

**inform** *vt* (infr mng) to instruct. Dan. 9:22.

**inheritance** *n* (theol) (1) the land promised, divided, and given out by God to Israel. Josh 19:10. (2) "mine inheritance," that people belonging to me. 2 Kin. 21:14.

**iniquity** *n* (theol) gross injustice, wickedness, sin. Lev. 5:17. See *bear . . . iniquity.*

**injured me, not** (arch expr) did me no wrong. Gal. 4:12.

**injurious** *adj* (arch mng) being an oppressor; spiteful, insolent. 1 Tim. 1:13.

**inkhorn** *n* (infr wd) a vessel of horn for containing ink. Ezek. 9:2.

**inn** *n* (infr wd) a lodging. Gen. 42:27.

**inquire** *vt* (Hebraism) with *of* or *after:* to consult, to ask questions of. Gen. 25:22; Deut. 12:30.

**inquisition** *n* (infr wd) search. Deut. 19:18.

**instant** *adj* (infr mng) urgent, importunate. Luke 23:23.

**instead of** *prep* (infr mng) in the place of. Ex. 4:16.

**instructor** *n* (arch mng) a forger, smithy, or metalworker. Gen. 4:22.

**instruments** *n pl* (arch mng) (1) furnishings; furniture. Ex. 25:9. (2) yokes. 1 Kin. 19:21. (3) "instruments of cruelty," weapons used for violence. Gen. 49:5. (4) arms; weapons. Rom. 6:13.

**intend** *vt* (infr mng) to meditate; plan; plot. Psa. 21:11.

**intermeddle** *vt* (infr wd) to meddle; to mix. Prov. 14:10.

**intreat** *vb* (1) *vi* to entreat; to intercede; to pray. 1 Sam 2:25. (2) *vt* (arch mng) to exhort. 1 Tim. 5:1.

**invention** *(arch mng)* a scheming or crafty action intended to accomplish some evil end. Eccl. 7:29.

**inward** *adj* (infr mng) intimate; familiar. Job 19:19.

**inwards** *n pl* (arch sp) innards; entrails. Ex. 29:17.

**is it peace** (arch expr) do you come in peace? 2 Kin. 9:17.

**Ishi** *prop n* (symbolic) lit., my husband. Hos. 2:16.

**isle** *n* (arch mng) border. Gen. 10:5.

**issue** *n* (arch mng) (1) a running sore. Lev. 15:3. (2) a discharge of blood. Luke 8:43, 44. (3) offspring; children. Matt. 22:25. (4) *n pl* deliverance. Psa. 68:20.

**it fell on a day** (arch expr) it came to pass. 2 Kin. 4:8.

**it must needs be** (arch expr) it is necessary. Matt. 18:7.

## J

**JAH** *prop n* (theol) an abbreviation of the name Jahveh or *Jehovah*, q.v. Psa. 68:4.

**jangling** *n* (arch mng) foolish talking; idle tattling. 1 Tim. 1:6.

**javelin** *n* (infr wd) a light spear thrown as a weapon of war. 1 Sam. 20:33.

**jealous** *adj* (arch mng) (1) vigilant in guarding a possession. Ezek. 39:25. (2) zealous. 1 Kin. 19:14.

**Jehovah** *prop n* (theol) lit., "I am that I am" (q.v.) or "I will be what I will be." An artificial English word formed from the Hebrew consonants J H V H and the vowels of the Hebrew word *Adonai*, or Lord. Jehovah is the redemptive name of God. Psa. 83:18.

**jeopard** *vt* (infr wd) to jeopardize; to hazard, or risk. Judg. 5:18.

**jeopardy** *n* (infr wd) risk; grave danger; exposure to death, injury, or loss. Luke 8:23.

**Jesus** *prop n* (theol) the Aramaic form of the Hebrew name *Jehoshua* (Joshua or Jeshua) meaning *Jehovah is salvation*. It is the name assigned by God the Father and the Holy Spirit to God the Son in order to identify Him as the God of the everlasting covenant and to point out the mediatorial nature of His office as Messiah: "and thou shalt call His name JESUS: for He shall save His people from their sins." Matt. 1:21; Luke 1:31; 2:21.

**Jewry** *prop n* (arch mng) Judaea, a Jewish province of the Roman empire. John 7:1.

**Jews** *prop n pl* (theol) used often in the N.T., particularly in the Gospels, to designate the *Jewish authorities*. John 8:22.

**Jezreel** *prop n* (symbolic) lit., "God will scatter," or "God sows," symbolizing a fertile valley desecrated by murder and massacre. Hos. 1:4.

**joined hard to** (arch expr) adjoined. Acts 18:7.

**jot** *n* (arch mng) a quaint spelling of the name of the smallest letter in the Hebrew alphabet, the *yod*, which corresponds to the *iota* in Greek and the *i/j* in English. Matt. 5:18.

**joy** *vi* (infr use) to rejoice. Psa. 21:1.

**jubile** *n* (arch sp) jubilee; a year of emancipation and restoration to be kept every fifty years by the emancipation of Hebrew slaves, restoration of alienated lands to their former owners, and omission of all cultivation of the land. Lev. 25:9.

**judge** *vt* (theol) to pass judgment upon; to make a practice of subjecting others to censure; to condemn. Matt. 7:1, 2; Rom. 2:1.

**judges** *n pl* (theol) a translation of the Hebrew word *elohim*, a plural noun usu. translated "God," but also translated "gods," sometimes in the sense of magistrates, as in Ex. 22:28; Psa. 82:1, 6. Similarly, it is translated "judges" four times in two passages: Ex. 21:6; 22:8, 9. In Psa. 8:5 it is translated "the angels."

**judgment** *n* (theol) (1) justice. Ex. 23:6; Deut. 32:4. (2) ordinance. Ex. 21:1. (3) a condemnatory sentence; penal judgment. 2 Kin. 25:6; Matt. 7:2. (4) a suit; an argument. Job 34:23. (5) "the judgment of," justice on behalf of. Deut. 10:18.

**just** *adj* (theol) righteous, holy, or innocent; morally right or good; fair or equitable. Lev. 19:36; Matt. 1:19.

**justify** *vt* (theol) (1) to declare righteous; to acquit before a bar of judgment; to pronounce one to be just or acceptable, esp. of God's justifying the ungodly who turn from sin and trust in the righteousness and sacrifice of Christ (Rom. 3:26). Rom 3:24; 5:1. (2) to vindicate or demonstrate the righteousness of someone or something. Luke 7:35. (3) to publicly acknowledge the righteousness of another. Luke 7:29.

**justle** *vt* (arch sp) to jostle. Nah. 2:4.

## K

**keep** *vt* (infr mng) (1) to guard, protect, take care of. Gen. 3:24. (2) to observe; celebrate. Ex. 12:47. (3) to obey. Lev. 18:26.

**keep still** (arch expr) to rule, maintain. 2 Chr. 22:9.

**keepers,** those who *keep*, q.v. 2 Kin. 11:5.

**kept** *pt t* of *keep*, q.v. Rev. 3:8.

**kerchief** *n* (infr wd) a cloth worn so as to cover the head. Ezek. 13:18, 21.

**kick at** (infr mng) lit., trample down; by extension, to *despise* (q.v.). 1 Sam. 2:29.

**kin** *n* (infr wd) relatives. Mark 6:4.

**kindle** *vt* (infr mng) to inflame, as any of the affections, esp. anger, Num. 11:1; 2 Sam. 12:5; also to express the recurring of divine remorse or compassion. Hos. 11:8.

**kindness** *n* (arch mng) piety. Ruth 3:10.

**kindred** *n* (1) (infr wd) family; relatives. Gen. 24:38. (2) (arch mng) a race or tribe, i.e., a group of families descended from a common ancestor; hence, in a wider sense, a nation or people (usu. bound together by a common language, or dialect, and customs). Acts 3:25.

**kine** *n pl* (arch wd) cattle, oxen, or bovines. Gen. 32:15.

**kinsfolk** *n pl* (infr wd) relatives. Luke 2:44.

**kinsman** *n* (infr wd) (1) lit., a *redeemer*; next of kin and thus in a position to buy back a relative's property, marry his widow, etc. Num. 5:8. (2) a relative; a fellow countryman. John 18:26.

**kneading trough** *n* (arch wd) a shallow bowl in which dough was kneaded. Ex. 8:3.

**knew** *pt t* of *know*, q.v. Job 2:12.

**knop** *n* (arch sp) a bud, esp. a rosebud; hence, a knob. Ex. 25:31, 33, 35.

**know** *vt* (arch mng) (1) to appreciate. Num. 14:31. (2) to have sexual relations with. Gen. 4:1. (3) to be familiar with. Judg. 3:1. (4) to recognize. Ruth 3:14. (5) to learn. Esth. 4:5. (6) to comprehend. Job 38:33. (7) to will or consent. Hos. 8:4. (8) to esteem. 1 Cor. 2:2. (9) (theol) to know intimately, in a way involving special love and choice of the object as a recipient of favor, specifically of saving grace. Psa. 1:6; Matt. 7:23; 25:12;

John 10:14, 15; 2 Tim. 2:19. See also *foreknow* and *foreknowledge*.

**know the uttermost of your matter** (Grecism) to examine, determine, or decide (in a legal sense): "I will decide your case." Acts 24:22.

**knowledge** *n* (arch mng) (1) cognizance; recognition; notice; observance. Ruth 2:10. (2) having faith, piety. Hos. 6:6.

**known** *pp* of *know,* q.v. Eph. 1:9.

## L

**lace** *n* (infr mng) a band or cord used to draw together two things. Ex. 28:28, 37.

**lade** *vt* (infr wd) to load. Gen. 42:26.

**laden** *adj* (infr wd) carrying a load; loaded; burdened. Gen. 45:23.

**lading** *n* (infr wd) cargo; freight. Acts 27:10.

**laid** *vb* (arch use) (1) *was laid, pt t* of *lie,* was lying. 1 Sam. 3:2, 3. (2) *vt* disbursed. 2 Kin. 12:11.

**laid waste** *pt t* of *lay waste,* q.v. Isa. 37:18.

**lament for the teats** (arch expr) may be taken as either beating upon the breasts, or fig., mourning for the breasts, with the breasts standing for the richness which once characterized the land. Isa. 32:12.

**lamp** *n* (arch mng) a torch. Gen. 15:17.

**lancet** *n* (arch mng) a point of a lance or spear. 1 Kin. 18:28.

**large** *adj* (arch mng) open, free. Psa. 18:19.

**lasciviousness** *n* (infr wd) excess; evil; lewdness; lust. Jude 4.

**latchet** *n* (infr wd) a lace; a thong. Isa. 5:27.

**laud** *vt* (infr wd) to praise. Rom. 15:11.

**laver** *n* (arch mng) a basin, vessel, trough, or cistern for washing. Ex. 30:18.

**lawyer** *n* (theol) another name for *scribes*, particularly those with seats in the Sanhedrin, the supreme Jewish court. Though all scribes were supposed to be students of the Scriptures, by Christ's time they had degenerated to expounding the minutiae of the law by resorting to earlier rabbis or commentators and to their own reason as authorities instead of comparing Scripture with Scripture. Luke 11:46. See *scribe*.

**lay along** (arch expr) fell flat. Judg. 7:13.

**lay at** (arch expr) to strike at. Job 41:26.

**lay hands** (theol) a practice accompanying church ordination; a sign of blessing. 1 Tim. 5:22.

**lay it for a reproach** (arch expr) make it a disgrace. 1 Sam. 11:2.

**lay sore upon him** (Hebraism) greatly compelled him; greatly pressed him; put a great deal of pressure on him. Judg. 14:17.

**lay(ing of) wait** (arch expr) lying in wait; i.e., in ambush. Num. 35:20.

**lay waste** (arch expr) to devastate; to destroy. Isa. 37:26.

**layeth open** (arch expr) displays; shows off. Prov. 13:16.

**league** *n* (infr mng) an alliance. Josh. 9:6.

**lean** *adj* (infr wd) gaunt; haggard. 2 Sam. 13:4.

**leanness** *n* (Hebraism) weakening or sickness that eats away the body's strength. Isa. 24:16.

**leap on the threshold** (arch custom) a pagan ritual. Zeph. 1:9.

**leasing** *n* (arch mng) falsehood; lie. Psa. 4:2.

**leathern** *adj* (infr wd) made of leather. Matt. 3:4.

**leave** *n* (infr wd) permission; allowance. Num. 22:13.

**leave** *vt* (arch use) to leave off; to cease; to let alone; forego. Neh. 10:31.

**leave caring** (arch expr) to stop being concerned. 1 Sam. 9:5.

**leave my soul in hell** (mistransl) should read, "thou wilt not *abandon* my soul *to* hell." Acts 2:27.

**leaved** *adj* (infr mng) paneled. Isa. 45:1.

**leaven** *n* (1) (infr wd) sour dough, settled upon and fermented by airborne yeast spores, that as a result becomes light. Ex. 12:15. (2) (theol) by extension, a pervading influence; either positive (Matt. 13:33), or negative (Mark 8:15).

**leaven** *vt,* see *leaven* *n* 1 Cor. 5:6.

**leaves** *n pl* (1) (infr mng) panels. 1 Kin. 6:34. (2) (arch mng) columns of writing. Jer. 36:23.

**lees** *n pl* (infr wd) sediment; dregs. Isa. 25:6.

**left** *vt* (1) (arch use) *pt t* of *leave,* q.v. Gen. 29:35. (2) (Hebraism) "left of," bereft of; deprived of by death. Ruth 1:5.

**lent** *vt* (arch mng) gave; i.e., with no connotation of expecting the lent things to be returned; *pt t* of *lend.* Ex. 12:36.

**lesser** *adj* (infr wd) smaller. Gen. 1:16.

**lest** *conj* (infr wd) for fear that. Jer. 51:46.

**let** *vt* (arch mng) to hinder or prevent. Ex. 5:4.

**let down** (Hebraism) rested. Ezek. 1:24.

**let out** (arch expr) to lease. Matt. 21:33, 41.

**levy** *n* (arch mng) a tax in the form of forced labor. 1 Kin. 5:14.

**lewd** *adj* (1) (infr wd) immoral. Ezek. 23:44. (2) (arch mng) ignorant, unlearned. Acts 17:5. (3) (arch mng) vicious. Ezek. 16:27.

**lewdly** *adv* (infr wd) immorally. Ezek. 22:11.

**lewdness** *n* (arch mng) evil, wickedness. Judg. 20:6.

**liberal** *adj* (arch mng) noble. Isa. 32:5.

**liberality** *n* (arch mng) a gift of grace; benefaction; bounty; alms. 1 Cor. 16:3.

**lie** *n* (infr mng) deception. Mic. 1:14.

**lie carnally** *vi* (arch expr) to have sexual intercourse. Lev. 18:20.

**lie in wait** (arch expr) to set up an ambush. Judg. 9:32.

**lien** *arch pp* of *lie*. Gen. 26:10.

**lier in wait** (arch expr) an ambusher. Josh. 8:13.

**lieth** *vi* (arch mng) to be situated. Josh. 17:7.

**life** *n* (arch mng) (1) the soul. Gen. 1:20. (2) breath. Gen. 1:30.

**lift** *arch pp* of *lift*. Gen. 14:22.

**lift(ed) up** (Hebraism) to be vain; proud. Dan. 5:20.

**lift up . . . hand** (Hebraism) (1) to signify a solemn promise; swear. Gen. 14:22. (2) to rebel. 1 Kin. 11:26. (3) "lifted up his hands on high," to be ready to obey. Hab. 3:10.

**lift up the head** (Hebraism) (1) to be free. Judg. 8:28. (2) to free. 2 Kin. 25:27. (3) to be proud. Psa. 83:2.

**lifted up** (1) (theol) lit., lifted up on high, exalted; hence *crucified*. John 3:14b; 8:28; 12:32-34. (2) (Hebraism) exalted. 1 Chr. 14:2. (3) (Hebraism) puffed up; proud. 1 Tim. 3:6.

**light** *adj* (Hebraism) idle, worthless; reckless; frivolous. Num. 21:5.

**light** *n* (fig wd) lit., lamp; that which illumines so one can see issues clearly. Matt. 6:22.

**light off/down** (arch expr) to dismount. Gen. 24:64.

**light on/upon** (infr expr) (1) to come to; to meet unanticipatedly. Gen. 28:11. (2) to fall unexpectedly. Deut. 19:5.

**lighten** *vt* (1) (arch mng) to enlighten; illuminate. 2 Sam. 22:29. (2) (Hebraism) "lighten mine eyes," cheer me. Psa 13:3. (3) (infr mng) to shine. Rev. 18:1.

**lightly** *adv* (infr mng) easily, carelessly. Gen. 26:10.

**lightness** *n* (infr mng) fickleness; levity. Jer. 23:32.

**lights** *n pl* (arch mng) openings with sides flaring outward. 1 Kin. 6:4.

**lign aloes** *n* (infr wd, now spelled as one word) a soft resinous wood burned as a perfume. Num. 24:6.

**like** *adj* (infr mng) (1) likely. Jer. 38:9. (2) the same. Acts 11:17.

**like** *vt* (infr mng) (1) to please. Deut. 23:16. (2) to approve of. 1 Chr. 28:4.

**like as** (arch expr) just as; even as. Rom. 6:4.

**like to be** (arch expr) thought to be. Jonah 1:4.

**like unto** (arch expr) similar to. 1 Kin. 7:8.

**liketh** *vt* (arch use and form) pleases. Esth. 8:8.

**liking** *n* (arch mng) condition, plight. Job 39:4.

**lineage** *n* (infr wd) line of descent. Luke 2:4.

**lines** *n pl* (arch mng) lit., an inheritance measured by measuring lines. Psa. 16:6.

**lintel** *n* (arch mng) (1) the area above the two posts of the Temple. Amos 9:1. (2) a pillar. Zeph. 2:14.

**lips** *n pl* (Hebraism) speech. Prov. 14:7.

**liquor** *n* (arch mng) the outflow of fruit or wine presses. Ex. 22:29.

**list** *vi* (arch mng) to please, like, or desire. Matt. 17:12.

**lively** *adj* (infr mng) full of life; vigorous; strong. Ex. 1:19.

**living** *n* (arch mng) possessions; property; means of subsistence. Mark 12:44.

**lo** *interj* (infr wd) Look! Behold! used to call attention or to express wonder or surprise. Gen. 42:28.

**loaden** *pp* (arch wd) loaded. Isa. 46:1.

**Loammi** *prop n* (symbolic) lit., "not my people." Hos. 1:9.

**lodge** *n* (infr mng) a hut. Isa. 1:8.

**lodge** *vb* (infr wd) (1) *vi* to sleep. Judg. 19:13. (2) to settle in a place. Ruth 1:16. (3) (arch mng) to pass the night. Gen. 24:23. (4) *vt* (infr wd) to give lodging to. 1 Tim. 5:10.

**loft** *n* (infr wd) an upper room. 1 Kin. 17:19.

**lofty** *adj* (infr wd) haughty. Psa. 131:1.

**log** *n* (tech) *See Table of Dry and Liquid Measures*. Lev. 14:10.

**loins** *n pl* (infr wd) (1) the generative organs; the physical source of children. Gen. 46:26. (2) the area of the waist and hips. 2 Kin. 1:8.

**longsuffering** *adj* (infr wd) long and patiently enduring offense; slow to anger. Num. 14:18.

**longsuffering** *n* (arch wd) patience. 2 Cor. 6:6.

**look** *vb* (arch mng) (1) *vt* to expect. Isa 5:2. (2) *vi* see to it. Ex. 25:40. (3) "look out," to search for; to seek. Gen. 41:33.

**look to** (arch expr) to look upon. 1 Sam. 16:12.

**looked in the liver** (arch custom) a pagan method of attempting to foretell the future by means of entrails. Ezek. 21:21.

**looked on the day . . . that he became a stranger** (Hebraism) gloat over your brother's day of calamity, the day of his alienation or exile. Obad. 12.

**loose** *vt* (infr use) to untie; to release, as from a debt, from some physical restraint, from prison, etc. Matt. 18:27; John 11:44; Acts 24:26.

**lord** *n* (infr mng) (1) *master*, q.v. Gen. 40:1. (2) ruler. Gen 42:33. (3) owner. Mark 12:9.

**LORD** *prop n* (theol) *Jehovah*, q.v. Ex. 6:2.

**Loruhamah** *prop n* (symbolic) lit., "not having obtained mercy"; "not pitied." Hos. 1:6.

**lot** *n* (infr mng) (1) the portion of land chosen by casting of lots; see *cast lots*. Josh. 19:17. (2) a share or portion. Acts 8:21.

**love** *vt* (theol) (1) (from the Greek verb *agapao) to love* by choice or as a matter of principle; when directed toward a worthy object such love is grounded in admiration, esteem, or worship, but when directed toward an unworthy object it is based on inner principles of good will, kindness, and mercy and is bestowed regardless of any potential return of affection. This is the kind of love that God bestows on sinful men. Matt. 5:43-46; 1 John 2:15; 3:11, 14; 5:2. (2) (from the Greek verb *phileo*) to have affection for; to be friendly to one; *to love* on account of the emotions or senses. John 11:36; 20:2; 1 Cor. 16:22. These two kinds of love are referred to and contrasted in Christ's conversation with Peter in John 21:15-17: (1) to love (according to principle)—Christ's questions (vv. 15a, 16a); (2) to have affection for—Peter's answers (vv. 15b, 16b), Christ's question (v. 17a, b), Peter's answer (v. 17c).

**loved** *vt* (arch mng) desired. 2 Sam. 13:1.

**lover** *n* (arch mng) a close friend. 1 Kin. 5:1.

**low degree** (arch expr) humble circumstance. Jas. 1:9.

**lower** *comp adj* (arch mng) deeper than the surface. Lev. 14:37.

**lowest hell** (theol) hyperbole expressing the idea of the completeness of the promised judgment. Deut. 32:22.

**lowing** *pres part* (infr wd) mooing. 1 Sam. 6:12.

**lowring** *pres part* (arch sp and mng) lowering; i.e., gloomy or covered with clouds; overcast. Matt. 16:3.

**lucre** *n* (infr wd) gain or profit; "filthy lucre," base, contemptible monetary gain or profit; ill-gotten gain. 1 Tim. 3:3.

**lunatick** *adj* (arch mng and sp) lunatic; lit., *moonstruck;* i.e., epileptic, because it was anciently supposed that epilepsy returned and grew worse with the increase of the moon. Matt. 4:24; 17:15.

**lust** *n* (theol) (1) desire; craving; longing. 1 Pet. 2:11. (2) sinful desire; sinful or unclean intercourse. 2 Pet. 2:10. (3) a desire, whether good or evil. John 8:44.

**lust** *vi* (theol) (1) to desire. Deut. 12:15. (2) to be lascivious; to have sinful desires. Num. 11:34.

**lusteth to envy** (arch mng) yearns over us with zealous envy. Jas. 4:5.

**lusty** *adj* (infr mng) vigorous; strong; healthy. Judg. 3:29.

**lying in wait** (arch expr) being in ambush. Judg. 9:35.

## M

**mad** *adj* insane, demented. 1 Sam. 21:14.

**made a road** (arch expr) spread out to plunder. 1 Sam. 27:10.

**made bare his holy arm** (Hebraism) revealed His holy power. Isa. 52:10.

**made merry** (arch expr) celebrated. Judg. 9:27.

**made/make supplication unto** (arch expr) to entreat humbly and earnestly; to pray. 1 Sam. 13:12.

**made sure** (arch expr) guaranteed or certified; i.e., the title was transferred or deeded to him. Gen. 23:20.

**madness** *n* (infr wd) (1) lit., craziness; fragmentation of the mental processes; insanity. Deut. 28:28. (2) irrational rage or fury. Luke 6:11.

**magnifical** *adj* (arch wd) magnificent. 1 Chr. 22:5.

**magnify** *vt* (infr mng) (1) to cause to be held in greater esteem or respect; to make great. Josh. 3:7. (2) to declare or extol the greatness of God in worship. Luke 1:46; Acts 10:46.

**Mahershalalhashbaz** *prop n* (symbolic) lit., in Hebrew, "in making speed to the spoil he hasteneth the prey," or "the spoil speeds, the prey hastens." Isa. 8:3.

**maid** *adj* (arch use) female. Lev. 12:5.

**maid** *n* (infr mng) a virgin. Deut. 22:17.

**maimed** *adj* (infr mng) *crooked* in a member of the body; i.e., disabled or crippled; occasionally used to denote injury to a hand as distinct from *halt* (q.v.), used to denote injury to a foot. Both *maimed* and *halt* sometimes indicate a complete mutilation or severance of a hand or foot respectively. (See Matt. 18:8; Mark 9:43-46). This leaves open the possibility that Christ may have "made whole" some maimed who were actually missing members altogether. Matt. 15:30, 31 (cf. Luke 22:50, 51).

**maintain** *vt* (infr mng) to uphold. 2 Chr. 6:35.

**make** *vt* (arch mng) (1) to do. Judg. 18:3. (2) to pretend; to feign. Josh. 8:15; 2 Sam. 13:6; Luke 24:28. (3) "to make for," to be for the advantage of. Rom. 14:19.

**make a mock at** (arch expr) to jest at; belittle. Prov. 14:9.

**make all his bed** (Hebraism) restore him. Psa. 41:3.

**make away** (Hebraism) to do away with. Dan. 11:44.

**make for** (arch expr) to meet with. Ezek. 17:17.

**make haste** (Hebraism) (1) to hurry. Isa. 59:7. (2) to go about in an agitated, excited, wearisome way characteristic of life without God. Isa. 28:16.

**make light of** (arch expr) to be careless of; to neglect, to regard a person or thing lightly or with disdain as if unworthy of one's attention or interest. Matt. 22:5.

**make merchandise of** (arch expr) to use a person for gain. 2 Pet. 2:3.

**make sure** (arch expr) to request or beg for. Prov. 6:3.

**make thee high above** (arch expr) to lift or raise you above; to exalt you over. Deut. 26:19.

**make ... to doubt** to hold the mind in suspense between doubt and hope. John 10:24.

**malefactor** *n* (infr wd) lit., an evildoer; a criminal. Luke 23:39.

**maliciousness** *n* (infr wd) malevolence; spite; malignity; great wickedness. Rom. 1:29.

**mammon** *n* (Aramaic) a transliteration of an Aramaic word meaning *what is trusted in,* i.e., *riches.* Matt. 6:24.

**man** *adj* (arch use) male. 1 Sam. 1:11.

**Man** *n* (theol) derived from the Hebrew word *ish,* meaning *male person.* In discovering Eve, his newly made (i.e., constructed) companion (Gen. 2:22), Adam wisely called (and correctly classified) her *Woman (ishah,* i.e., *female person),* because she derived her origin and being (according to the divine plan) from *Man,* for whose good (Gen. 2:18-20) she was made. Gen. 2:23. See *Woman.*

**man of God** (theol) a prophet of God. 1 Kin. 17:24.

**mandrake** *n* (infr wd) a plant used in love charms, and supposed to insure conception. Gen. 30:14.

**manifest** *vt* (arch mng) to examine; to brighten; to make clear. Eccl. 3:18.

**manna** *n* (infr wd) lit., "what is it?"; the food

miraculously supplied to the Israelites during their journey in the wilderness. Ex. 16:15.

**manner** *n* (infr mng) according to the appointed manner, i.e., according to the ordinance. Lev. 5:10. (2) ordinance. Num. 29:24. (3) kind; style; sort. 2 Kin. 1:7. (4) custom; habit. John 19:40. (5) "after the former manner," in the same way. 1 Sam. 17:30.

**manner, taken with the** (arch expr) caught in the very act. Num. 5:13.

**manners** *n pl* (arch mng) moral habits. 1 Cor. 15:33.

**mansions** *n pl* (arch mng) dwelling places; homes; resting places. John 14:2.

**mantle** *n* (infr wd) a rug. Judg. 4:18.

**mar** *vt* (infr wd) to ruin; to spoil; to greatly damage; to impair. Ruth 4:6; Mark 2:22.

**Maranatha** (Aramaic) either, "our Lord has come" (prophetic past speaking of a future event as already having taken place), i.e., for the purpose of judgment, or "our Lord, come!" 1 Cor. 16:22.

**marish** *n* (arch wd) a marsh. Ezek. 47:11.

**mark** *n* (infr mng) (1) a target. Job 16:12. (2) a goal. Phil. 3:14.

**mark** *vt* (infr mng) to take note of. Ruth 3:4.

**marks** *n pl* (arch mng) scars. Gal. 6:17.

**marrow** *n* (arch mng) moisture; refreshment. Prov. 3:8.

**marrow and fatness** (Hebraism) a fig. expr. signifying the very best. Psa. 63:5.

**mart** *n* (infr wd) an emporium; a trade center. Isa. 23:3.

**mason** *n* (infr wd) a skilled craftsman who works with stone. 2 Sam. 5:11.

**master** *n* In O.T. usage: (1) ruler; sovereign; controller (human or divine); lord; owner. Gen. 24:9. (2) husband; owner. Ex. 22:8. (3) captain; chief; one high in rank. Dan. 1:3. (4) a head person (of any rank or class). 1 Chr. 12:19. In N.T. usage: (1) a master or lord with complete ownership. 2 Tim. 2:21. (2) a teacher (Greek equivalent of the Jewish use of *rabbi,* q.v.). Matt. 8:19. (3) any sort of superintendent or overseer; used to convey the idea of Christ's being a rabbi by virtue of His inherent authority even though not recognized by the Jewish leaders. Luke 8:24, 45; 9:33, 49; 17:13. (4) a guide; leader; teacher. Matt. 23:10. (5) steersman; helmsman. Acts 27:11. (6) the possessor and owner of a person or thing; having the right of disposal (a title given by servants to their masters; to emperors and kings by their subjects; to God as Ruler of the universe; to Christ as a title of reverence and respect by His disciples and by all who recognized Him as the Messiah; to the risen Christ as universal Ruler who reigns not only as Creator but also by the rights that accrued to Him as a result of His life of obedience, atoning death on the cross, and glorious resurrection). Rom. 14:4. (7) master of a house; householder. Luke 13:25.

**masteries** *n pl* (arch use) victories. 2 Tim. 2:5.

**mastery** *n* (infr wd) victory or superiority in war or competition. Ex. 32:18.

**matrix** *n* (infr wd) the womb. Ex. 13:12, 15.

**matter** *n* (mistransl) (1) lit., a forest; fuel for fire. Jas. 3:5. (2) a word. Esth. 3:4.

**mattock** *n* (infr wd) a digging tool having the features of an ax, adz, and pick. 1 Sam. 13:20.

**maul** *n* (infr wd) a heavy wooden mallet or hammer. Prov. 25:18.

**maw** *n* (infr wd) the stomach. Deut. 18:3.

**me thinketh** (arch expr) it seems to me. 2 Sam. 18:27.

**mean** *adj* (infr mng) lowly, of low rank (but not vile). Prov. 22:29.

**means** *n pl* (1) (infr wd) expense. 1 Kin. 10:29. (2) (arch mng) hand. Mal. 1:9.

**measure** *n* (tech) (1) a *koros*. Luke 16:7. (2) a *batos*. Luke 16:6. (3) a *saton*. Matt. 13:33; Luke 13:21. (4) a *choinix*. Rev. 6:6. *For definition of these four terms, see Table of Dry and Liquid Measures.* (5) a dry measure, prob. equal to one-third *ephah,* q.v. Gen. 18:6.

**measure** *vt* (arch use) i.e., for the purpose of repaying. Isa. 65:7.

**meat** *n* (arch mng) (1) food (of any kind). Gen. 1:29. (2) dinner. 1 Sam. 20:5. (3) solid food. 1 Cor. 3:2.

**meat offering** *adj* (theol) a *food* offering, consisting sometimes of flour only, Lev. 5:11-13; sometimes of fine flour mixed with oil, Lev. 2:2; sometimes of unleavened cakes or wafers prepared with oil, Lev. 2:5-11; and sometimes, in the case of an oblation of first fruits, of green ears of grain parched or dried by fire. In each case a portion was given to the priest and seasoned with salt. Lev. 2:13.

**meet** *adj* (infr mng) fit; suitable, right, or proper. Ex. 8:26.

**meetest,** most *meet,* q.v. 2 Kin. 10:3.

**melt** *vi* (arch mng) to lose courage. Josh. 5:1.

**member** *n* (infr use) a part. 1 Cor. 12:14.

**memorial** *n* (arch mng) something that keeps remembrance alive; a handful of the offering burned with the incense as a reminder to Jehovah of the offerer. Lev. 2:16.

**men of valour** (arch expr) men of virtue, valor, strength; brave soldiers. Judg. 3:29.

**menstealers** *n pl* (arch wd) kidnapers. 1 Tim. 1:10.

**menstruous woman** (fig expr) uncleanness; by extension, defilement by idolatry. Lam. 1:17.

**mercy** *n* (theol) kindness; compassion; blessing. Psa. 119:64.

**merry** *adj* (arch mng) giving pleasure; mirthful. Judg. 19:6.

**mess** *n* (infr mng) a quantity or dish of food. 2 Sam. 11:8.

**mete** *vt* (arch mng) to measure. Ex. 16:18.

**meteyard** *n* (arch wd) a measuring rod. Lev. 19:35.

**mighties** *n pl* (arch wd) mighty men. 1 Chr. 11:12.

**milch** *adj* (arch sp) dairy; giving milk (as cows). Gen. 32:15.

**mile** *n* (tech) *See Table of Linear Measures.* Matt. 5:41.

**milk out** (Hebraism) to drink deeply; to drain out. Isa. 66:11.

**mincing** *pres part* (infr mng) walking delicately with short steps, trippingly. Isa. 3:16.

**mind** *n* (infr wd) desire; disposition. 2 Kin. 9:15.

**mind** *vt* (infr mng) (1) to care for, attend to. Phil. 3:19. (2) to intend. Acts 20:13.

**minded** *adj* (infr wd) disposed; inclined; determined. Ruth 1:18.

**mingle** *vi* (infr wd) to intermix socially. Ezra 9:2; Dan. 2:43.

**mingled** *adj* (infr wd) mixed. Ex. 29:40.

**minish** *vt* (arch wd) to diminish, make smaller. Ex. 5:19.

**minister** *n* (arch mng) a servant. Ex. 24:13.

**minister** *vb* (infr wd) (1) *vi* to serve. Ex. 39:41. (2) *vt* to supply. 2 Cor. 9:10. (3) "minister to," to help someone. Heb. 6:10.

**ministering** *adj* (arch mng) having to do with service. 1 Chr. 9:28.

**ministration** *n* (theol) the service of God's chosen ministers. 2 Cor. 3:7, 8, 9.

**minstrel** *n* (infr mng) (1) a musician who plays a stringed instrument. 2 Kin. 3:15. (2) a flute player. Matt. 9:23.

**miracle** *n* (theol) an extraordinary event manifesting a supernatural work of God. Judg. 6:13.

**miry** *adj* (infr wd) damp; sticky. Dan. 2:41.

**mischief** *n* (infr mng) (1) harm; injury or damage caused by a human agent. Gen. 42:38. (2) specific harm; i.e., the death of the fetus. Ex. 21:22, 23.

**mite** *n* (tech) *See Table of Coins*. Mark 12:42.

**mitre** *n* (infr wd) a ceremonial headdress worn by priests. Ex. 28:4.

**moderation** *n* (arch mng) mildness; gentleness; fairness. Phil. 4:5.

**molten** *pp* (infr wd) (1) made by melting and casting metal. Lev. 19:4. (2) melted. Job 28:2.

**more** *adj* (infr use) (1) greater. Num. 33:54. (2) many. Lev. 11:42.

**more** *adv* (arch use) better. 1 Sam. 14:30.

**morrow** *n* (infr wd) (1) the next day. Num. 16:41. (2) "to morrow," i.e., the morning after today. Ex. 8:10.

**morsel** *n* (infr wd) a small piece of food. 1 Sam. 28:22.

**mortify** *vt* (infr wd) (1) to put to death. Col. 3:5. (2) to destroy; to kill; to subdue. Rom. 8:13.

**mote** *n* (infr wd) a small particle; a straw or piece of chaff. Matt. 7:3.

**motions** *n pl* (arch sp) emotions. Rom. 7:5.

**mount/mountain** *n* (arch mng) (1) a mound, or bank of earth. Jer. 6:6. (2) hill country. Judg. 2:9.

**mount (of) Ephraim** (Hebraism) hill country belonging to the tribe of Ephraim. Judg. 2:9.

**mouth** *n* (Hebraism) a boast. Judg. 9:38.

**move** *vt* (1) (infr mng) to stir, incite, excite. Deut. 32:21. (2) (arch mng) lit., to impel or agitate; thus, to work in. Judg. 13:25.

**moved,** see *move*. Acts 2:25.

**much** *adj* (arch use) many. Gen. 50:20.

**muffler** *n* (arch mng) a long fluttering veil. Isa. 3:19.

**multitude** *n* (infr wd) a great number of persons or things; a crowd; a throng. Gen. 32:12; Matt. 8:1.

**munition** *n* (arch mng) a fortress. Isa. 29:7.

**murmur** *vi* (infr mng) to complain; to grumble. Ex. 16:2.

**murrain** *n* (infr wd) a plague or pestilence affecting domestic animals or plants. Ex. 9:3.

**muse** *vi* (infr wd) to meditate. Psa. 39:3.

**mystery** *n* (translit) from Greek, lit., a shut mouth; a secret, i.e., the hidden counsel or plan of God (hidden until put into operation). Mystery is often associated with God's *foreknowledge* (q.v.) and inscrutable will (Rom. 16:25; 1 Cor. 2:7; Eph. 1:9; 3:9; Col. 1:26). In many contexts the unveiling of the mystery is stressed (Eph. 6:19; Col. 4:3). Matt. 13:11; Mark 4:11.

## N

**nail** *n* (Hebraism) a fig. representation of security. Ezra 9:8.

**naked, not** (theol) fully and forever clothed with the heavenly body. 2 Cor. 5:3.

**nakedness** *n* (infr mng) exposed conditions; defenselessness; weakness; vulnerability to attack. Gen. 42:9.

**name** *n* (theol) with reference to God: (1) the *Lord Himself*. Matt. 12:21; Acts 2:21; Phil. 2:10; Rev. 13:6. (2) in the *power* or by the authority of. Matt. 18:5; Mark 9:38.

**napkin** *n* (arch mng) a handkerchief. Luke 19:20.

**narrow** *adj* (infr mng) compressed; beset with difficulty. Matt. 7:14.

**narrowed rests** (arch expr) ledges. 1 Kin. 6:6.

**narrowly** *adv* (arch mng) closely; attentively. Job 13:27.

**nations** *n pl* (arch mng) Gentiles. Mal. 3:12.

**nativity** *n* (infr wd) origin of birth. Ezek. 16:3.

**naught** *adj* (infr wd) worthless. 2 Kin. 2:19.

**naughtiness** *n* (arch mng) wickedness. 1 Sam. 17:28.

**naughty** *adj* (infr mng) bad; worthless. Prov. 6:12.

**nave** *n* (infr wd) the hub of a wheel. 1 Kin. 7:33.

**nay** *adv* (arch wd) (1) no; a negative answer. Matt. 5:37. (2) not only so but. 1 Cor. 12:22.

**necromancer** *n* (infr wd) one who attempts to raise the dead for purposes of incantation. Deut. 18:11.

**needs** *adv* (infr use) of necessity. Gen. 17:13.

**neesing** *n* (arch wd) sneezing. Job 41:18.

**neither** *adv* (arch use) used to express a negative within the sentence. Heb. 9:18.

**nephew** *n* (arch use) a grandson. Judg. 12:14.

**nether** *adj* (infr wd) lower. Ex. 19:17.

**nethermost** *adj* (infr wd) lowest. 1 Kin. 6:6.

**never** *adv* (arch use) not. 2 Chr. 21:17.

**new** *adj* (arch use) fresh; i.e., the animal had not been dead a long time. Judg. 15:15.

**new cloth** *n* (arch mng) newly woven fabric that has never been washed, and thus is unshrunk. Matt. 9:16.

**new heart** (theol) a supernatural, radical change wherein the mind, will, and affections, though previously dead toward God, are made alive spiritually. The whole being which was alienated from God is turned God-ward. Ezek. 36:26.

**new wine** (arch expr) the freshly pressed juice of grapes, which, having been placed in wineskins ("bottles"), will cause them to stretch during the process of fermentation; if the wineskins are "old bottles" (i.e., previously used) they are apt to burst when filled with new wine. Matt. 9:17.

**nigh** *prep* (infr wd) near. Gen. 47:29.

**ninth hour** (arch expr) 3:00 p.m. or midafternoon. Matt. 20:5.

**nitre** *n* (arch mng) scientifically, sodium carbonate, with these meanings: (1) strong effervescence produced (vinegar on nitre); i.e., the heart is lightened, uplifted, "bubbles up." Prov. 25:20. (2) soap (nitre mixed with oil). Jer. 2:22.

**no** *adv* (arch use) not. Gen. 37:32.

**no more of thy name be sown** (Hebraism) the memory of your name shall not survive; your fame will not be extended. Nah. 1:14.

**noise** *vt* (infr expr) to spread by rumor or report. Josh. 6:27.

**noisome** *adj* (infr wd) annoying, noxious, hurtful. Psa. 91:3.

**none** *adj* (arch use) no. Obad. 7.

**not** *adv* (arch use) (1) no more. Job 7:8. (2) to no longer exist. Isa. 17:14. (3) *pron* nothing. Matt. 18:25. (4) *not* should be omitted for easiest English understanding. Isa. 9:3.

**notable** *adj* (arch mng) (1) conspicuous. Dan. 8:5. (2) notorious. Matt. 27:16. (3) glorious. Acts 2:20.

**nothing** *adv* (arch use) not at all. 1 Kin. 10:21.

**nothing** *n* i.e., nothing evil. Psa. 17:3.

**notwithstanding** *conj* (infr wd) nevertheless, however, yet. Josh. 22:19.

**nought** *pron* (infr wd) naught; nothing. Gen. 29:15.

**nourish** *vt* (infr mng) to take care of. Gen. 50:21.

**nourisher** *n* (infr wd) one who maintains, supports, sustains. Ruth 4:15.

**novice** *n* (infr wd) one newly admitted into the Christian body. 1 Tim. 3:6.

**number** *n* (arch mng) the financial care of the church. 1 Tim. 5:9.

**number** *vt* (infr mng) (1) to count people to determine from what cities they came. Judg. 21:9. (2) to count and assign. Ezra 1:8. (3) to muster; to gather. 2 Sam. 18:1.

**nurture** *n* (infr mng) education; bringing up; discipline. Eph. 6:4.

## O

**oaks** *n pl* (theol) a place of idolatrous worship. Isa. 1:29.

**oath** *n* (infr wd) something sworn to. Gen. 24:41.

**obeisance** *n* (infr wd) a movement of the body showing respect, homage, deference. 2 Sam. 14:4.

**oblation** *n* (infr wd) an offering to God; anything offered in sacrifice. Isa. 1:13.

**observe** *vb* (arch mng) (1) *vt* to preserve from death or loss. Mark 6:20. (2) *vi* to be careful. Deut. 6:3. (3) *vt* to guard, attend to, watch, keep. Ex. 12:42. (4) *vt* to lie in wait for. Hos. 13:7.

**observe times** (arch expr) to practice astrology. Lev. 19:26.

**occasion** *n* (infr mng) a state of affairs that provides a ground or reason; an opportunity; situation. Judg. 14:4.

**occupied** *pp* of *occupy,* q.v. Judg. 16:11.

**occupy** *vt* (arch mng) to use, employ; also, to trade with; to trade. Ex. 38:24.

**occurrent** *n* (infr wd) chance; occurrence. 1 Kin. 5:4.

**odours** *n pl* (arch mng and Brit sp) incense. Rev. 5:8.

**of** *prep* (1) (arch use) the whereabouts of. Deut. 34:6. (2) (arch mng) used where today we use other prepositions: (a) by. Matt. 6:1. (b) for. Acts 21:20. (c) from. Gen. 32:20; Mark 9:21. (d) on. Heb. 10:34. (e) over. 1 Cor. 7:4. (f) with. 2 Sam. 19:32. (g) against. Num. 31:2. (h) because of. Phil. 1:15. (i) "holden of it," held in its grip. Acts 2:24. (j) "of the hand," from. Ruth 4:5.

**of a surety** (arch expr) certainly. Acts 12:11.

**of whom is** (arch expr) of the number of whom is. 2 Tim. 2:17.

**offence** *n* (arch mng and sp) offense; a cause of stumbling. Gal. 5:11.

**offend** *vb* (arch mng) (1) *vt* to cause to stumble. Matt. 5:29. (2) *vi* to sin. 2 Kin. 18:14.

**offender** *n* (infr wd) a criminal. 1 Kin. 1:21.

**offered** *vt* (infr mng) (1) dedicated. Judg. 5:2. (2) offered sacrifice(s). 1 Sam. 1:4. (3) lit., poured out as a drink offering. Phil. 2:17.

**offering** *n* (theol) a *wave* offering, q.v. Num. 8:11, 13. See *meat offering; heave offering.*

**office** *n* (infr mng) a duty, *charge* (q.v.), or position conferred. 1 Chr. 9:22.

**officer** *n* (1) (infr mng) an overseer. Gen. 41:34. (2) (infr arch mng) a *eunuch,* q.v. 1 Kin. 22:9.

**oft** *adv* (arch wd) often. Matt. 9:14.

**often** *adj* (arch use) frequent. 1 Tim. 5:23.

**ofttimes** *adv* (infr wd) often; oftentimes; frequently. Matt. 17:15.

**ointment** *n* (infr mng) a salve, often perfumed. Song 1:3.

**old** *adj* (arch mng) chronic; recurring. Lev. 13:11.

**olive shall cast his fruit** (arch expr) the olive vineyard will drop its fruit so no oil will be obtained. Deut. 28:40.

**omer** *n* (tech) *See Table of Dry and Liquid Measures.* Ex. 16:16.

**on** *prep* (arch use) (1) of. 1 Sam. 27:11. (2) in. Gen. 32:19; Matt. 1:18. (3) concerning. 1 Tim. 1:18.

**on a time** (arch expr) once. Judg. 9:8.

**on sleep** (arch expr) asleep. Acts 13:36.

**once** *adv* (infr mng) (1) ever. Jer. 13:27. (2) once for all. Rom 6:10; Heb. 7:27; 9:12; 10:10.

**one assent** (arch expr) unanimity; agreement. 2 Chr. 18:12.

**one born in my house** (arch expr) one of my servants. Gen. 15:3.

**one of a thousand** (Hebraism) once in a thousand times. Job 9:3.

**one member, where were the body?** (arch expr) if all were a mass, one shape with no variety, how could there be a useful, formed body? 1 Cor. 12:19.

**open** *vt* (infr mng) to explain. Acts 17:3.

**open vision** (arch expr) revelation currently being given by God. 1 Sam. 3:1.

**open . . . womb** (Hebraism) to cause children to be born; to make fruitful. Gen. 29:31.

**openly** *adv* (arch mng) publicly. Gen. 38:21.

**oppress** *vt* (arch mng) to defraud. Mic. 2:2.

**or ever** (arch expr) before ever; before all. Psa. 90:2.

**oracle** *n* (arch mng) (1) the word (of God), prob. as spoken by a prophet. 2 Sam. 16:23. (2) the innermost part of the sanctuary, i.e., the holy of holies. 1 Kin. 6:5. (3) *n pl* the utterances of God. Acts 7:38.

**ordain** *vt* (theol) (1) to establish or order by decree or law. Num. 28:6. (2) to appoint. Mark 3:14. (3) to place in a certain order; to arrange; to assign a place. Acts 13:48; Rom. 13:1. (4) to choose by a raising of hands. Acts 14:23.

**order** *vt* (infr mng) to arrange and keep in order. Ex. 27:21.

**ordinance** *n* (infr wd) (1) a law or decree. Lev. 18:3. (2) a rite. Heb. 9:1.

**organ** *n* (arch mng) a pipe; a musical wind instrument. Gen. 4:21.

**ornaments** *n pl* (infr mng) jewelry. Ex. 33:5.

**other** *pron* (arch use) others. Job 24:24.

**ouches** *n pl* (infr mng) sockets in which precious stones are set. Ex. 28:11.

**ought** *pron* (arch mng) (1) aught; anything. Gen. 39:6. (2) "not ought," nothing. Gen. 47:18.

**out of hand** (infr expr) without delay; at once; forthwith. Num. 11:15.

**outgoings** *n pl* (arch mng) (1) goings out, furthest limits. Josh. 17:9. (2) goings forth; boundaries (used of east and west). Psa. 65:8.

**outlandish** *adj* (arch wd) foreign. Neh. 13:26.

**outside** *n* (arch mng) outermost part. Judg. 7:11.

**outwent** *vt* (arch mng) *pt t* of *outgo;* outstripped. Mark 6:33.

**over against** *prep* (arch mng) (1) beyond. Ex. 25:37. (2) opposite. Num. 22:5. (3) confronting. Josh. 5:13. (4) in front of. Josh. 18:17. (5) off the coast of. Acts 27:7a, b.

**overcharge** *vt* (arch mng) to overburden. Luke 21:34.

**overflow** *vt* (infr wd) (1) to flood. Deut. 11:4. (2) to submerge, drown. Psa. 69:15.

**overlaid** *vt* (arch wd) lay on; suffocated. 1 Kin. 3:19.

**overlive** *vt* (arch wd) to outlive; to live longer than; to survive. Josh. 24:31.

**overpass** *vt* (arch wd) to pass over. Psa. 57:1.

**overpast** *pp* of *overpass,* q.v. Psa. 57:1.

**overplus** *n* (infr wd) an amount equivalent to the amount of production that remained up till the year of Jubilee when the possession would be returned to the original owner; overpayment; surplus. Lev. 25:27.

**overrun** *vt* (infr wd) to outrun. 2 Sam. 18:23.

**oversee** *vt* (infr wd) to overlook; to superintend. 1 Chr. 9:29.

**overseer** *n* (theol) a superintendent. *Overseer* is a proper English translation of the Greek noun *episkopos,* occasionally transliterated *bishop.* An examination of the context in Acts 20 shows that it is used interchangeably with the word *elder* (or *presbyter*) (cf. vv. 17 and 28). The same thing can be observed in Tit. 1:5, 7. Thus both terms describe one and the same office. Acts 20:28.

**overthrow** *vt* (arch mng) to overturn. Mark 11:15.

**overthrown** *vb pass* (arch mng) fallen; killed; wounded. 2 Sam. 17:9.

## P

**pace** *n* (tech) *See Table of Linear Measures.* 2 Sam. 6:13.

**paddle** *n* (arch mng) a shovel or small spade. Deut. 23:13.

**painful** *adj* (infr mng) laborious, difficult. Psa. 73:16.

**palmerworm** *n* (infr wd) a caterpillar that suddenly appears in great numbers devouring vegetation. Joel 1:4.

**palsy, the** *n* (infr wd) paralysis. Matt. 8:6.

**paps** *n pl* (arch wd) nipples; teats; breasts. Luke 11:27.

**parable** *n* (theol) (1) In O.T. use, a parable was a means of drawing men's attention to the presence and nature of God and to the critical nature of their situation. O.T. parables make use of various means: a story (Ezek. 17:2-10); an action (Ezek. 24:3-14); a human example (Job 17:6); a popular *proverb*, q.v. (1 Sam. 10:12); a word of wisdom (Prov. 1:1); or a prophetic utterance (Num. 24:3, 15, 20). (2) In N.T. use, Jesus teaches about His ministry, work, and kingdom. The purpose of Jesus in the parables is to reveal truth to those given understanding (regenerated) hearts and minds. Matt. 13:13.

**parcel** *n* (infr mng) a lot or plot; a unit of salable merchandise. Josh. 24:32.

**parch** *vt* (infr mng) to toast or roast. Josh. 5:11.

**pare** *vt* (infr wd) to cut or trim. Deut. 21:12.

**partaker** *n* (arch mng) an accomplice. Psa. 50:18.

**partiality** *n* (arch mng) dubiousness, ambiguity, or uncertainty. Jas. 3:17.

**particular, in** (infr expr) one by one; personally. Eph. 5:33.

**particularly** *adv* (arch mng) in detail; as to particulars; one by one. Acts 21:19.

**pass** *vt* (infr mng) to exceed; to surpass. Eph. 3:19.

**passage** *n* (arch mng) (1) a mountain pass. 1 Sam. 13:23. (2) a ford. Judg. 12:6.

**pass through** (arch expr) toil at. 2 Sam. 12:31.

**pass through the fire** (arch custom) a pagan religious rite in which children were offered to pagan deities. Deut. 18:10.

**Passover** *n* (theol) the historical Passover is related to the tenth plague, the death of the firstborn in Egypt (Ex. 12:12, 13). It was subsequently the first of three annual feasts during which all men were required to appear at the sanctuary (Ex. 23:14-17). Christ died during the Passover season, and is called "our passover" (1 Cor. 5:7), indicating that the Passover was a type of Christ and His atoning work.

**pastor** *n* (theol) a shepherd; esp. in the figurative sense of one who tends the flock (people) of God. Jer. 23:1.

**pate** *n* (infr wd) the head. Psa. 7:16.

**patriarch** *n* the father or chief of a family or tribe; usu. used of the ancestors of the Jewish nation: (1) Abraham. Heb. 7:4. (2) the sons of Jacob. Acts 7:8, 9. (3) David. Acts 2:29.

**patrimony** *n* (infr wd) an estate inherited from one's father or other ancestor. Deut. 18:8.

**pattern** *n* (infr use) an example; the standard to which a thing must conform. Heb. 8:5.

**peculiar** *adj* (theol) one's very own, used of private property; special, unique (but without the connotation of "eccentric"). As applied to Jehovah's covenant people, it conveys the idea of their having been purchased or redeemed. Ex. 19:5; Deut. 14:2; 1 Pet. 2:9.

**pedigree** *n* (infr use) lineage; a genealogical table. Num. 1:18.

**peeled** *pp* (infr mng) (1) stripped of the skin. Ezek. 29:18. (2) stripped of the hair. Isa. 18:2, 7.

**peep** *vi* (infr mng) to chirp, as a young bird; to utter low sounds. Isa. 8:19.

**pence** *n* (tech) *See Table of Coins*. Matt. 18:28.

**penny** *n* (tech) *See Table of Coins*. Matt. 20:2.

**pennyworth** *n* (tech) *See Table of Coins*. John 6:7.

**penury** *n* (infr wd) destitution; extreme poverty. Luke 21:4.

**peradventure** *adv* (arch mng) perhaps; possibly. Gen. 31:31.

**perdition** *n* (theol) the destruction consisting of loss of eternal life, and thus eternal misery. Heb. 10:39.

**perfect** *adj* (arch mng) (1) upright, sincere, entirely obedient. Deut. 18:13. (2) complete. 2 Sam. 22:33. (3) exact; accurate. Acts 24:22.

**perfect** *vt* (infr mng) (1) to accomplish. Psa. 138:8. (2) to equip. Eph. 4:12.

**perfected** *vb pass* (arch mng) completed; finished. 2 Chr. 8:16; Luke 13:32.

**perfection** *n* (arch mng) maturity; ripeness; readiness for harvest. Luke 8:14.

**perfectly, more** (arch expr) more accurately. Acts 18:26.

**performance** *n* (arch mng) end; completion; accomplishment. 2 Cor. 8:11.

**perish** *vi* (theol) (1) to die (or be about to die) physically. Matt. 8:25. (2) to die spiritually (a second time—Rev. 20:6, 14; 21:8), i.e., to be separated judicially from the presence of God, eternally in hell. John 3:16. (3) to be ruined or destroyed. Matt. 9:17.

**pernicious** *adj* (infr wd) destructive; evil. 2 Pet. 2:2.

**persecute** *vt* (arch mng) to pursue. Psa. 7:1.

**person** *n* (arch mng) the substantial quality or nature of an individual. Heb. 1:3. (2) (theol) in the *presence* of Christ; with Christ looking on approvingly. 2 Cor. 2:10.

**persuade** *vt* (arch mng) (1) to deceive, entice, seduce. 2 Kin. 18:32. (2) to seek approval of. Gal. 1:10.

**pertain** *vi* (infr wd) to belong. 2 Sam. 9:9.

**perverse** *adj* (infr wd) (1) obstinate or willful in wrongdoing. Num. 22:32. (2) wayward; crooked; corrupt; wicked. Luke 9:41.

**perverseness** *n* (infr wd) willful obstinacy in wrongdoing. Num. 23:21.

**pervert** *vt* (infr wd) to lead astray; to corrupt. Luke 23:2.

**pervert(eth) judgment** (arch expr) to cause injustice. Deut. 27:19.

**pestilence** *n* (infr wd) a virulent and devastating disease. Deut. 28:21.

**Pharisees** *n pl* (theol) Hebrew term for *separated ones*. Their origin is unknown. Their beliefs included the resurrection of the dead, angels, and future rewards and punishments (Acts 23:8). They reverenced scribal tradition, regarding it as binding (Mark 7:9). They are mentioned as enemies of Jesus (Matt. 5:20; 16:1; 22:15). Points of conflict with Jesus included: their traditions which invalidated the Law (Mark 7:13); their Sabbath observance which precluded healing (Matt. 12:12); their condoning inward defilement if accompanied by outward "purity" (Mark 7:18-23); merit and rewards (Luke 17:10); their hypocrisy (Matt. 23:13); His ministry to Gentiles and other unacceptables (Luke 7:36-50); and their lack of humility (Luke 10:27, 28).

**phylacteries** *n pl* (infr wd) small boxes fastened on the left arm and forehead containing parchment strips inscribed with texts (Ex. 13:1-10, 11-16 and Deut. 6:4-9; 11:13-21).

**piece of money** (tech) *See Table of Coins.* Matt. 17:27.

**pieces of silver** (tech) *See Table of Coins.* Zech. 11:12; Matt. 26:15.

**piety** *n* (arch mng) filial affection. 1 Tim. 5:4.

**pilgrimage** *n* (arch mng) the course of life on earth. Gen. 47:9.

**pillar** *n* (infr mng) a monument. 2 Sam. 18:18.

**pilled** *arch pt t* of *to peel.* Gen. 30:37.

**pine** *vi* (infr wd) to languish; to waste away. Mark 9:18.

**pinnacle** *n* (infr wd) lit., in Greek, *a little wing*; the loftiest ledge of the Temple, prob. located in the southeast corner of the Temple area, overlooking the deep Kidron Valley. Matt. 4:5.

**pipe** *n* (arch mng) (1) a flute. 1 Sam. 10:5. (2) a pourer (of oil). Zech. 4:2. (3) a tube. Zech. 4:12.

**piper** *n* (arch wd) a flute player. Rev. 18:22.

**piss** *n* (arch wd) urine (this was grammatically and socially correct usage in the early seventeenth century when the KJV was translated). 2 Kin. 18:27.

**pisseth against the wall, any that** (Hebraism) one who urinates against a wall, i.e., any male. 1 Sam. 25:22.

**pit** *n* (theol) (1) the *grave*, q.v. Job 17:16. (2) a cistern or well. Jer. 14:3.

**pitch** *vt* (infr mng) (1) to encamp. Gen. 31:25. (2) to set up. 2 Sam. 6:17.

**place** *n* (arch mng) (1) a passage in a book. Acts 8:32. (2) one's home. Judg. 7:7.

**place his name there,** see *name.* Deut. 16:2.

**plague** *n* (infr mng) (1) a disastrous evil or affliction; calamity. Deut. 28:59. (2) an infection or disease. Lev. 13:22; Luke 7:21.

**plague** *vt* (infr mng) to afflict severely. Ex. 32:35.

**plain** *adj* (arch mng) flat. Isa. 40:4.

**plainness** *n* (arch mng) freedom; unreservedness. 2 Cor. 3:12.

**plait** *vt* (infr wd) to braid. 1 Pet. 3:3.

**plant** *vt* (arch mng) to establish. 1 Chr. 17:9.

**plat** *n* (infr wd) a plot; a small patch of ground. 2 Kin. 9:26.

**platted** *vt* (arch sp) *pp* of *plat*; to plait; to braid. Matt. 27:29.

**platter** *n* (arch mng) a dish. Matt. 23:25.

**play** *vi* (arch mng) (1) to sport. Ex. 32:6. (2) to fence; to fight with weapons. 2 Sam. 2:14.

**play before us** (arch expr) entertain us. 2 Sam. 2:14.

**played** *vt* i.e., played the harp. 1 Sam. 19:9.

**plead against** (arch expr) to contend against. Judg. 6:32.

**plead with him** (arch expr) to dispute with him in judgment; to enter into judgment. Ezek. 17:20.

**pleasant** *adj* (arch mng) desirable. Dan. 10:3.

**pleasure** *n* (1) (arch mng) a favor. Acts 24:27; 25:9. (2) (mistransl) judgment. Heb. 12:10.

**pledge** *n* (infr mng) security for a debt; collateral, often a man's outer garment. Deut. 24:12.

**plenteous** *adj* (infr wd) rich; abundant; plentiful. Deut. 28:11.

**pluck** *vt* (infr wd) to pull off. Ruth 4:7.

**pluck down** *vt* (arch expr) to demolish. Num. 33:52.

**plummet** *n* (infr wd) (1) a plumb line; an instrument for testing the true verticality of a building. Zech. 4:10. (2) fig., a symbol for testing the truth. Isa. 28:17.

**point out** *vt* (arch mng) to mark out; designate. Num. 34:7, 8, 10.

**poll** *n* (arch mng) the head. Num. 1:2.

**poll** *vt* (infr wd) to cut the hair of the head. 2 Sam. 14:26.

**pollute** *vt* (infr mng) to make ceremonially or morally impure or unclean. Ex. 20:25.

**pollution** *n* (infr mng) sin; defilement. 2 Pet. 2:20.

**pommel** *n* (arch use) a knob. 2 Chr. 4:12.

**poor, the** *n* (infr mng) those who are weak and needy. Psa. 41:1.

**port** *n* (arch mng) a gate. Neh. 2:13.

**porter** *n* (infr mng) a doorkeeper; a person stationed at a door to admit or assist those entering. 1 Chr. 9:21, 22.

**portion** *n* (1) (infr wd) a share, esp. of ar estate, i.e., one's inheritance. 2 Chr. 31:... (2)
(arch mng) a gift. Esth. 9:19, 22. ...ke over

**possess** *vt* (arch mng) to capture; to
into one's possession. Judg. 3:13. ...body pure

**possess his vessel** (arch expr) keep
from all uncleanness. 1 Thess. 4:...sess; inheri-

**possession** *n* (arch mng) land
tance. Josh. 22:7. or messenger

**post** *n* (arch mng) (1) a ... (2) *n pl* door-
who carries letters. 2 Ch... one's offspring,
posts. Isa. 57:8. ...0.

**posterity** *n* (infr wd) ...of *Dry and Liquid*
present and future.

**pot** *n* (tech) *Se*...n; stew. Gen. 25:29, 30.
*Measures.* Mark... *See Table of Weights.*

**pottage** *n* (inf... *See Table of Weights.*
...9.

**pound** *n* (te...
1 Kings 1...Hebraism) gave earnest ut-
Luke 19:...

**poured o**...

terance to my inmost desires and thoughts. 1 Sam. 1:15.

**poured water on the hands** (arch custom) an indication that the person spoken of was a personal servant. 2 Kin. 3:11.

**pourtray** *vt* (arch sp) to portray; to draw, depict. Ezek. 4:1.

**power** *n* (1) (theol) liberty. 1 Cor. 9:4. (2) (theol) evidence of being under the authority of another. 1 Cor. 11:10. (3) (infr mng) authority. Matt. 9:6.

**power, hath not** (theol) i.e., husband and wife are mutually bound, each surrendering power over his body and giving it up to his mate. 1 Cor. 7:4.

**practised** *vi* (arch mng and sp) *pt t* of *practice*; continued. Dan. 8:12.

**prate** *vi* (infr wd) to babble without sense; to spout words. 3 John 10.

**pray** *vb* to beg, plead, implore, entreat, or beseech (whether directed toward God or a fellow human being). Mark 5:17, 18.

**preach** *vb* (theol) (1) to proclaim tidings in an unofficial capacity. Acts 8:4. (2) to proclaim or expound the Word of God, esp. the gospel, as one sent by God. Jonah 3:2; Matt. 10:27; 2 Tim. 4:2.

**precept** *n* (infr wd) (1) an injunction, order, admonition. Isa. 28:13. (2) *n pl* the Law. Psa. 119:4.

**precious** *adj* (infr wd) valuable; rare. 1 Sam. 3:1.

**predestinate** *vt* (theol) lit., to limit or set the boundaries in advance, to predetermine; thus for God to choose from eternity all things, including the salvation or damnation of man. See *foreknow, foreknowledge*. Rom. 8:29, 30; Eph. 1:5, 11.

**prefer** *vt* (arch mng) (1) to promote or advance. Esth. 2:9. (2) to exalt. Psa. 137:6.

**prepare** *vt* (arch mng) to establish, set up. 1 Chr. 29:18.

**presbytery** *n* (theol) a group of *elders*, q.v. 1 Tim. 4:14.

**prese[illegible]e** *n* (arch mng) the will. Jonah 1:3.

**prese[illegible]t** *n* (arch mng) a euphemistic term for tribute money or goods. 2 Kin. 17:4.

**presen[illegible]** *adv* (arch mng) instantly; at once. 1 Sam. [illegible]6.

**press** *n* [illegible]fr mng) a throng; a crowd. Mark 2:4.

**press** *vi* [illegible] mng) to crowd, throng, hasten eagerly. [illegible] 3:10.

**pressed out** [illegible]**asure** (arch expr) pressed on every side. [illegible] 1:8.

**presses** *n p*[illegible] mng) winepresses; vats in which juice [illegible]sed from grapes. Prov. 3:10.

**pressfat** *n* (a[illegible] a wine vat; vat of a winepress. Hag. 2:[illegible]

**presumptuous** *a*[illegible]mng) presuming; willful. Psa. 19:13.

**presumptuously** *a*[illegible] willfully. Ex. 21:14.

**prevail** *vi* (infr [illegible]) [illegible]gain ascendancy over; to win the vic[illegible] [illegible]ph over; to win mastery—often with *against* or *over*. 1 Kin. 16:22; Matt. 16:18. (2) *to accomplish* something; *to effect* something (or nothing); to succeed; to profit. Matt. 27:24; John 12:19.

**prevent** *vt* (arch mng) from its Latin meaning, to go before, to precede; to meet; to anticipate in thought, action, or speech. 2 Sam. 22:6; Matt. 17:25.

**prey** *n* (arch mng) booty; spoil. Num. 31:12, 26.

**price of blood** (Grecism) blood money. Matt. 27:6.

**prick** *vt* (infr wd) to sting, pierce. Psa. 73:21.

**pricks** *n pl* (arch wd) goads; pointed rods used to urge on animals. Acts 9:5.

**prince** *n* (arch mng) a leader of the highest rank; a chief (or principal). Num. 1:44.

**principal** *adj* (arch mng) situated in rows. Isa. 28:25.

**principal** *n* (infr use) a man in the leading position. Neh. 11:17.

**principalities** *n pl* (arch mng) headship; dominion. Jer. 13:18.

**print** *vt* (arch mng) to make a tatoo. Lev. 19:28.

**prised** *pp* (arch sp) priced; valued at. Zech. 11:13.

**private interpretation** (theol) an interpretation which one thinks out for himself, as opposed to that which the Holy Spirit teaches. 2 Pet. 1:20.

**privily** *adv* (infr wd) secretly; craftily; sneakily. Judg. 9:31.

**privy** *adj* (infr wd) (1) secret. Deut. 23:1. (2) cognizant of a secret. Acts 5:2.

**proclaim** *vt* (arch mng) to offer. Deut. 20:10.

**profane** *adj* (arch mng) (1) for the common people. Ezek. 42:20. (2) ungodly. Heb. 12:16.

**profane** *vt* (theol) (1) to desecrate; to defile or make unholy one's person, another's person, or an ordinance of God by treating it as common. Lev. 18:21; 21:9, 23. (2) to appear to be desecrating the sabbath, as priests did whose duty it was to labor in the Temple on sabbath days. Matt. 12:5.

**profess** *vt* (infr mng) to declare openly. Deut. 26:3.

**profession** *n* (theol) an act of openly or publicly declaring one's faith; a confession. Heb. 3:1.

**profound** *adj* (arch mng) deeply determined. Hos. 5:2.

**prognosticator** *n* (infr wd) a pagan practitioner who on the basis of the new moon attempts to foretell events. Isa. 47:13.

**proof** *n* (arch mng) lit., a word denoting the testing of metals and coins; fig., used of persons. Phil. 2:22.

**proper** *adj* (infr mng) (1) one's own, peculiar to one. Acts 1:19. (2) fair, comely. Heb. 11:23.

**proper good** (arch expr) wealth. 1 Chr. 29:3.

**prophecy** *n* (theol) discourse based on divine inspiration, declaring the purposes of God by (1) reproving and admonishing the wicked; (2) comforting the afflicted; and (3) revealing hidden things. 1 Tim. 4:14.

**prophesy** *vi* (1) (infr mng) to explain or expound. 1 Cor. 11:5; 14:3, 4. (2) (infr mng) to speak out, tell aloud. Matt. 26:68. (3) (theol) to speak by inspiration. Joel 2:28. See *prophecy*.

**prophet** *n* (theol) (1) a speaker or spokesman. Ex. 7:1. (2) a preacher or teacher. Tit. 1:12. (3) esp. an inspired preacher or teacher. Matt. 10:41. (4) one who foretells future events. Matt. 1:22. See *prophecy*.

**propitiation** *n* (theol) lit., the turning away of (God's) wrath by an offering (Christ). See *atonement*. 1 John 2:2.

**proselyte** *n* (infr wd) a convert to Judaism. Matt. 23:15.

**protest** *vi* (infr wd) to make a solemn declaration; to warn. Gen. 43:3.

**proud** *adj* (arch mng) raging. Psa. 124:5.

**prove** *vt* (arch mng) to try, test, put to the proof. Ex. 16:4.

**provender** *n* (infr wd) dry food for domestic animals. Gen. 24:25.

**proverb** *n* (theol) a brief saying or adage given for instruction in righteousness. Num. 21:27.

**provide** *vt* (arch mng) to consider beforehand, take thought for. Rom. 12:17.

**providence** *n* (arch mng) forethought; provision; provident care. Acts 24:2.

**provoke** *vt* (theol) (1) to be rebellious; to exasperate; to rouse to indignation. Heb. 3:16. (2) to incite; to urge on; to move to action. Heb. 10:24.

**prudence** *n* (theol) understanding, esp. of the will of God. Eph. 1:8.

**pruninghook** *n* (infr wd) a pole with a curved blade for pruning plants. Joel 3:10.

**psalmist** *n* (arch mng) one who sings accompanied by instrumental music. 2 Sam. 23:1.

**psaltery** *n* (infr wd) an ancient stringed instrument resembling the zither, used to accompany singing. Psa. 81:2.

**publican** *n* (infr wd) a Jewish tax collector for the Romans, generally unpopular with his fellow Jews. Matt. 5:46.

**publish** *vt* (infr mng) to proclaim; to praise or glorify openly or publicly. Deut. 32:3.

**puff at** (Hebraism) to blow at contemptuously; to deride. Psa. 10:5.

**puff up** (arch expr) to inflate, as with pride. 1 Cor. 4:6.

**pulse** *n* (infr wd) the seeds from leguminous plants, such as beans, peas, lentils, etc. 2 Sam. 17:28.

**punish** *vt* (theol) In *O.T. usage*, the word *punish* has the general meaning of striking either lightly or severely, with its object either God's people or His enemies: (1) to spoil by breaking in pieces. Zech. 8:14. (2) to inflict a penalty. Prov. 17:26. (3) to *chastise*, q.v. Lev. 26:18. In *N.T. usage*, however, there is a clear distinction made between blows inflicted by God on His people (see *chastise*) and those given to His enemies (*punish*): (1) lit., to lop off, prune, as trees; to check, curb (inflicted on the *unjust*). 2 Pet. 2:9. (2) *pass* to pay recompense; to pay a penalty; to suffer punishment (inflicted on *those that know not God*). 2 Thess. 1:9. (3) to take vengeance on (Paul, prior to conversion, harassing Christians). Acts 22:5; 26:11.

**purchase** *vt* (arch mng) to win; to acquire. 1 Tim. 3:13.

**purge** *vt* (infr wd) (1) to purify, clear away. 2 Chr. 34:3. (2) (infr mng) to prune. John 15:2.

**purification** *n* (arch mng) cleansing. Esth. 2:3.

**purify** *vt* (theol) to cleanse by ceremonial means. Num. 8:21.

**purifying** *n* (theol) ceremonial cleansing, which was regulated by Mosaic law, but eventually became thoroughly complicated by rabbinical traditions. John 3:25.

**purtenance** *n* (infr wd) lit., the belongings; hence, the intestines of animals. Ex. 12:9.

**put a yoke of iron upon thy neck** (symbolic) an indication of severe oppression. Deut. 28:48.

**put away** *vt* (arch mng) to divorce. Matt. 5:31.

**put his hand unto** (Hebraism) has stolen; made use of. Ex. 22:8.

**put his hand upon thine eyes** (Hebraism) be with you when you die. Gen. 46:4.

**put off this tabernacle** (arch expr) to die. 2 Pet. 1:14.

**put to** (Hebraism) to exert; to apply; to use. Eccl. 10:10.

**put to the worse** (arch expr) pushed to defeat. 2 Kin. 14:12.

**put your feet upon the necks** (arch custom) a gesture made as a sign of mastery. Josh. 10:24.

**putteth his mouth in the dust** (Hebraism) to humble oneself. Lam. 3:29.

## Q

**quake** *vi* (infr wd) to shake, tremble. Ex. 19:18.

**quarrel** *n* (infr mng) (1) a legal ground of complaint. Lev. 26:25. (2) a complaint, case, or controversy to be argued or defended. Col. 3:13.

**quarter** *n* (arch mng) side; place. Isa. 47:15.

**quaternion** *n* (infr wd) a unit of guards consisting of four soldiers. Acts 12:4.

**quench my coal which is left** (Hebraism) destroy the last of my family. 2 Sam. 14:7.

**question** *vi* (arch mng) to argue. Mark 1:27.

**quick** *adj* (arch mng) (1) alive. Lev. 13:10. (2) lively. Heb. 4:12.

**quicken** *vt* (infr mng) to revive; to make alive. Psa. 119:50.

**quit** *adj* (infr mng) released from obligation or penalty; free. Josh. 2:20.

**quit** *vt* (infr mng) (1) to conduct oneself satisfactorily; to behave. 1 Sam. 4:9. (2) to clear. Ex. 21:19.

## R

**rabbi** *n* (theol) lit., *my great one,* or *my honorable sir,* a title applied by the Jews to their teachers. Matt. 23:7. It is applied to John the Baptist (John 3:26) and to Christ, both by His disciples (John 1:38, 49) and by others (John 3:2).

**raca** *n* (translit) transliteration of an Aramaic word used by Jews at the time of Christ as a term of derision: a senseless, empty-headed person. Matt. 5:22.

**ragged** *adj* (arch mng) rugged. Isa. 2:21.

**rail on** *vt* (infr expr) (1) lit., to swoop down upon. 1 Sam. 25:14. (2) to defame. 2 Chr. 32:17. (3) to vilify. Mark 15:29.

**raiment** *n* (infr wd) clothing. Gen. 27:27.

**raise** *vt* (infr mng) to rouse; to stir up. Job 14:12.

**raised a levy** (arch expr) put into effect a tax of forced labor. 1 Kin. 5:13.

**raised up** (arch expr) overthrew; laid waste. Isa. 23:13.

**raising** *pres part* (arch mng) stirring. Hos. 7:4.

**range** *n* (arch mng) (1) a form of fire grate, fireplace, or cooking apparatus; a chimney rack. Lev. 11:35. (2) a rank of soldiers. 2 Kin. 11:8, 15.

**range** *vi* (infr mng) to roam in search of prey. Prov. 28:15.

**rank** *adj* (arch mng) full, fat. Gen. 41:5, 7.

**ranks** *n pl* (infr mng) tiers. 1 Kin. 7:4, 5.

**rase** *vt* (arch sp) to raze; to lay level with the ground; to demolish. Psa. 137:7.

**rate** *n* (arch mng) a fixed quantity. Ex. 16:4; 1 Kin. 10:25.

**ravening** *adj* (infr wd) devouring; preying; voracious. Matt. 7:15.

**ravening** *n* (infr wd) robbery; plundering. Luke 11:39.

**ravin** *n* (infr wd) plunder; prey. Nah. 2:12.

**ravin** *vi* (arch mng) to seize prey by violence; to tear. Gen. 49:27.

**ravished, be** *vb pass* (infr mng) to be enraptured. Prov. 5:19.

**ready** *adj* (infr mng) skillful. Ezra 7:6.

**rear** *vt* (arch mng) to erect or build. John 2:20.

**reason** *adj* (arch use) reasonable. Acts 6:2.

**reason** *vi* (arch mng) to discourse; to talk. Acts 24:25.

**rebellion** *n* (infr wd) resistance to, or defiance of, authority; disobedience. Deut. 31:27.

**rebuke** *vt* (infr wd) to reprimand; to censure or reprehend sharply. Mark 4:39; 2 Tim. 4:2.

**rebuke, without** (arch use) blameless; one who cannot be censured. Phil 2:15.

**receipt** *n* (arch use) a place of receipt; a place for receiving. Matt. 9:9.

**receive** *vt* (arch mng) (1) to reap. Gen. 26:12. (2) to accept. Esth. 4:4. (3) to welcome. Philemon 17.

**receiver** *n* (arch mng) a weigher. Isa. 33:18.

**reckon** *vb* (infr mng) (1) *vt* to take into consideration; to consider; to regard. Rom. 8:18. (2) *vi* to compute; to settle accounts. 2 Kin. 12:15.

**reckoning** *n* (infr wd) a group; see *reckon.* 1 Chr. 23:11.

**recompense** *n* (infr wd) a reward; payment. Job 15:31.

**recompense** *vt* (infr wd) to repay. Ruth 2:12.

**reconcile** *vt* (theol) lit., to do away with an enmity; to bridge over a quarrel; to cover, expiate, condone, placate, or cancel. Lev. 6:30. See *reconciliation.*

**reconciliation** *n* (theol) a change of personal relations between human beings (1 Sam 29:4; 1 Cor. 7:11) or between God and man (Rom 5:1-11; Col. 1:20), in which enmity and estrangement are replaced by peace and fellowship. God initiates and effects reconciliation between Himself and sinful man (2 Cor. 5:18) through the death of His Son (Rom. 5:10; Eph. 2:16; Col. 1:20, 22).

**record** *n* (arch mng) a witness. 2 Cor. 1:23.

**record** *vt* (infr mng) (1) to register permanently, give evidence of. Ex. 20:24. (2) to bear record of, commemorate benefits publicly. 1 Chr. 16:4. (3) to take notice of. Deut. 30:19.

**recorder** *n* (infr mng) a keeper of the records. 2 Sam. 8:16.

**recover** *vt* (arch use) (1) to cure. 2 Kin. 5:3. (2) to snatch away; to take back. Hos. 2:9.

**redeem** *vt* (infr mng) (1) lit., to buy back. Lev. 27:15. (2) to rescue or deliver. Psa. 25:22.

**redeemer** *n* (theol) one who redeems, or buys back. Psa. 19:14. See *kinsman* and *redemption.*

**redemption** *n* (theol) this term may denote either temporal, physical deliverance (Lev. 25:25-27) or spiritual *salvation,* q.v. (Heb. 9:12-15). In both usages, there is the idea of a *ransom* to be paid; in the N.T. this is Christ's shed blood. Col. 1:14.

**redound** *vi* (arch mng) to overflow; to abound. 2 Cor. 4:15.

**reed** *n* (1) (infr mng) a cane. Mark 15:19. (2) (tech) *See Table of Linear Measures.* Ezek. 40:6.

**reformation** *n* (theol) a season of reforming, or the perfecting of things, referring to the times of the Messiah. Heb. 9:10.

**refrain** *vt* (arch use) to restrain; to keep back; to put a check upon. Prov. 10:19.

**refuge** *n* (infr wd) a place that provides protection from danger. Josh. 21:32.

**refuse** *vt* (arch use) to reject. Psa. 118:22.

**refused** *vt* (arch use) *pp* of *refuse;* rejected. 1 Sam. 16:7.

**regard** *vt* (infr mng) (1) to show respect or consideration for. Deut. 28:50. (2) to pay attention to. 1 Sam. 25:25.

**regard not the person** (arch expr) to take no notice of differences of rank, relationship, and economic or social standing among men in one's basic treatment of others; to be impartial. Matt. 22:16.

**register** *n* (arch use) record; registration. Ezra 2:62.

**rehearse** *vt* (arch mng) to recite; to tell; to recount; to speak of. Judg. 5:11.

**reins** *n pl* (Hebraism) lit., the kidneys; spoken

of by the Jews as if they were the seat of joy and pain, as well as knowledge. Job 16:13.

**rejoiceth** *vi* (theol) lit., *boasts itself* superior to judgment; i.e., full of glad confidence, it has no fear of judgment. Jas. 2:13.

**release** *n* (infr mng) the cancellation of all debts. Deut. 15:1.

**religious** *adj* (arch mng) making an outward profession of religion. Jas. 1:26.

**remedy** *n* (arch mng) deliverance. 2 Chr. 36:16.

**remission** *n* (theol) a letting go or sending away of sins. Matt. 26:28.

**remnant** *n* (1) (infr wd) a remainder or residue. Matt. 22:6. (2) (theol) Paul refers to God's people as a remnant, a small number in comparison with the vast number in whom ungodliness prevails; in the midst of great trouble, the faithfulness of God shines forth in a remnant or nucleus that has survived through God's grace. Rom. 11:5.

**remove** *vi* (arch use) to move, be transferred. Num. 36:7.

**rend** *vt* (infr wd) (1) to tear away. 1 Kin. 11:11-13. (2) to tear the hair or clothing as a sign of anger, grief, or despair. 2 Chr. 34:27. (3) to split, break, or tear. Isa. 64:1; Matt. 27:51. (4) to tear in pieces; to lacerate, as a swine does with its tusks. Matt. 7:6.

**render** *vt* (infr mng) (1) to give. Prov. 26:16. (2) to pay as due, such as rent, taxes, homage, etc. Psa. 116:12; Matt. 21:41; 22:21. (3) to repay strictly or justly. Rom. 2:6.

**rending** *pres part* (infr wd) tearing. Psa. 7:2.

**rent** *n* (infr wd) an opening made by tearing; a tear, as in cloth. Matt. 9:16.

**rent** *pt t* of *rend,* q.v. Gen. 37:29.

**repair** *vt* (arch mng) to rebuild. Judg. 21:23.

**repent** *vi* (theol) (1) to change one's mind. Ex. 13:17; to turn from sin and to dedicate oneself to the amendment of one's life. Acts 3:19. (2) to regret (which may be the first step toward saving repentance); to feel remorse, but without transformation of character. Matt. 21:32; 27:3. The following verses illustrate the contrasting uses of *repent* and its noun form *repentance:* "For though I made you sorry with a letter, I do not *repent* [regret] though I did *repent* [regret] .... Now I rejoice ... that ye sorrowed to *repentance* [saving repentance] .... For godly sorrow worketh *repentance* [saving repentance] to salvation not to be *repented* of [regretted]: but the sorrow of the world worketh death." 2 Cor. 7:8-10.

**repent oneself** *reflex vb* (Hebraism) (1) to have compassion. Judg. 21:6, 15. (2) in reference to God this expression has an extensive meaning, including these elements: to take compassion upon the people with the intention of comforting them in the future and of avenging the wrongs done them by their enemies. Psa. 135:14.

**repentance** *n* (theol) that inward change of mind, affections, convictions, and commitment, rooted in *fear* (q.v.) of God and sorrow for sin against Him, which (when coupled with *faith* [q.v.] in Jesus Christ) results in a turning from sin to God. It is never regretted (2 Cor. 7:10) and is a gift from God (Acts 11:18). 2 Cor. 7:9, 10. For similar and different connotations, see *repent.*

**replenish** *vt* (arch mng) to fill; to fill full. Gen. 1:28.

**reproach** *n* (infr wd) (1) shame; disgrace. 1 Sam. 17:26. (2) rude language or treatment arising from haughtiness and contempt. Psa. 15:3.

**reproach** *vt* (infr mng) in Hebrew, lit., to taunt or insult; to chide. Ruth 2:15.

**reprobate** *adj* (1) (arch mng) lit., inferior, not standing the test, unapproved; refuse; rejected. Jer. 6:30. (2) (theol) by extension of literal meaning, disqualified, morally corrupt, unfit for anything good; reprobate as a result of man's perverse and stubborn will refusing to obey God's will. Rom. 1:28.

**reprove** *vt* (1) (infr wd) to criticize, often kindly, without harshness, and generally in hope of correction of the fault. Job 13:10. (2) (arch mng) to prove. Job 6:25.

**reputation, no** (theol) lit., emptied himself. Phil. 2:7.

**require** *vb* (arch mng) (1) *vt* to bring to account. Josh. 22:23. (2) *vi* to request. 2 Sam. 12:20.

**requireth** *vt* (arch mng) to search out. Eccl. 3:15.

**requite** *vt* (infr wd) to repay. Deut. 32:6.

**rereward** *n* (arch sp) rearward; rear guard. Num. 10:25.

**resemble** *vt* (arch mng) to compare. Luke 13:18.

**residue** *n* (infr use) the rest; remainder. Ex. 10:5.

**resort** *vi* (arch mng) (1) to assemble; to come together; to gather together. John 18:2, 20. (2) to go; to cause oneself to go for help, relief, or advantage. 2 Chr. 11:13.

**respect** *n* (arch mng) pity, regard, concern. Ex. 2:25.

**respect** *vt* (arch mng) to judge preferentially based on the outward appearance of another. Deut. 16:19.

**rest** *n* (1) rest or peace after the culmination of victorious warfare. Josh. 1:15. (2) security found in marriage. Ruth 3:1. (3) relief. Eccl. 2:23. (4) lit., the keeping of a sabbath. Heb. 4:9.

**rest themselves** (arch expr) to trust. 2 Chr. 32:8.

**restitution** *n* (infr wd) restoration. Acts 3:21.

**restrain** *vt* (infr mng) (1) to limit. Job 15:8. (2) to withhold; to prevent from doing something. Gen. 11:6.

**resurrection** *n* (theol) the rising from the dead in which the body shall be brought back to life, the spirit being reunited with it. The N.T. writers reserve the word *resurrection* to signify the rising of Christ from the dead or that great general resurrection of all men, just and unjust, at the second coming of the Lord Jesus Christ, when all shall be judged in their bodies by Him. John 5:29; Acts 2:31; 4:2, 33. The results of other miraculous raisings of the dead were only temporary, but they did point to Christ as the source of eternal life. John 11:24, 25. Thus the future resurrection to eternal blessedness or eternal torment shall be the result of Christ's resurrection (1 Cor. 15:20, 23). Matt. 27:53; 1 Pet. 1:3.

**retain** *vt* (arch use) to keep; to detain. Judg. 19:4.

**retire** *vi* (arch mng) to turn back from; i.e., to leave unprotected. 2 Sam. 11:15.

**return** *vi* (arch wd) to withdraw. 2 Kin. 18:14.

**revenger** *n* (arch wd) an avenger. Rom. 13:4.

**reverence** *n* (infr wd) profound respect or deference. Esth. 3:5.

**reverence** *vt* (infr wd) lit., to venerate; to treat with deference or reverential obedience. Eph. 5:33.

**reverend** *adj* (infr mng) to be revered. Psa. 111:9.

**revile** *vb* (infr wd) to subject to abusive speech; to rail; to vituperate. Matt. 27:39.

**revive** *vi* to come to life again. 1 Kin. 17:22.

**reward** *n* (arch mng) a present. 1 Kin. 13:7.

**ribband** *n* (arch sp) a ribbon. Num. 15:38.

**rid** *vt* (arch mng) (1) to remove, clear away. Lev. 26:6. (2) to deliver; save, rescue. Gen. 37:22.

**riddle** *n* (infr wd) a puzzling or misleading question posed as a problem to be solved or guessed. Judg. 14:15-19.

**ride on white asses** (arch custom) a practice showing that one holds public office. Judg. 5:10.

**rie** *n* (arch wd) spelt; a wheat. Ex. 9:32.

**rifle** *vt* (infr wd) to ransack; to rob; to plunder. Zech. 14:2.

**right** *adj* (1) (infr mng) just. Psa. 45:6. (2) (arch mng) acceptable; successful; prosperous. Eccl. 4:4.

**right** *n* a privilege to which one is entitled. Ruth 4:6.

**righteous** *adj* (theol) (1) just; upright; moral. 2 Kin. 10:9. (2) innocent; holy. Rom 3:10. (3) outwardly, publicly, legally righteous. Eccl. 7:16.

**righteousness** *n* (theol) (1) integrity; purity of life; uprightness; correctness in thinking, feeling, and acting. Matt. 3:15. (2) Christ's perfect moral purity, integrity, and sinlessness. John 16:8, 10.

**rigour** *n* (infr wd and Brit sp) rigor; harshness; severity. Ex. 1:13.

**ringstraked** *adj* (arch wd) striped; streaked with rings. Gen. 30:35.

**riot** *n* (arch mng) profligate behavior; dissolute living. Tit. 1:6.

**riot** *vi* (infr mng) to live dissolutely. 2 Pet. 2:13.

**riotous** *adj* (arch mng) (1) dissolute; wanton. Prov. 23:20. (2) loose morally; worthless; prodigal. Prov. 28:7.

**rising** *n* (arch wd) a swelling. Lev. 13:2.

**rising of the sun** (Hebraism) the east. Isa. 41:25.

**river** *n* (1) the Euphrates. 2 Sam. 10:16. (2) a river valley. 2 Sam. 24:5.

**road** *n* (arch mng) a raid; a plundering excursion. 1 Sam. 27:10.

**roar** *vi* (arch mng) to moan. Psa. 38:8.

**roaring** *n* (arch mng) moaning. Psa. 22:1.

**robbery** *n* (arch mng) lit., a thing to be held on to. Phil. 2:6.

**rod** *n* (theol) fig., chastisement. Job 9:34.

**roll** *n* (arch mng) a scroll. Ezra 6:2.

**roller** *n* (arch mng) a bandage. Ezek. 30:21.

**room** *n* (arch mng) (1) space; place. Psa. 31:8. (2) a place at table. Matt. 23:6. (3) stead. 1 Kin. 2:35.

**root of them against Amalek** (Hebraism) whose fixed dwelling is in the former territory of Amalek. Judg. 5:14.

**rottenness** *n* (arch mng) a worm. Hos. 5:12.

**roughly** *adv* (infr mng) curtly. Gen. 42:7.

**round the corners . . .** (arch expr) to shave the hair around the temples. Lev. 19:27.

**rowers** *n pl* (infr wd) sailors. Ezek. 27:26.

**rude** *adj* (infr mng) unlearned; unskilled. 2 Cor. 11:6.

**rudiments** *n pl* (theol) the elements of religious training, esp. Jewish ceremonial requirements. Col. 2:8.

**rumour** *n* (Brit sp) rumor; a popular report; reputation; notoriety. Luke 7:17.

## S

**Sabaoth** *n* (translit) hosts; armies. Jas. 5:4.

**sabbath** *n* (theol) (1) a commanded day of resting from daily work activities in order to worship God with full attention (Ex. 20:8, 10, 11), a creation ordinance to be fulfilled until the end of the world (Ex. 16:23, 25, 26, 29). The O.T. saints saw the sabbath as a type of the *redemption,* q.v., to be worked out by the Messiah (Deut. 5:12, 14, 15). Christ, the Lord of the sabbath (Luke 6:5), who rested from His work of creation on the seventh day (thus the O.T. and pre-church observance of Saturday as the sabbath), rested from His work of redemption on the first day of the week (thus the Christian observance of Sunday as the sabbath). (2) "sabbath of rest unto the land," a rest for the land coming every seven years, reminding Israel of her dependence on God for material blessings. Lev. 25:4.

**sabbath day's journey** (tech) *See Table of Linear Measures,* Acts 1:12.

**sackbut** *n* (infr wd) a wind instrument similar to the trombone. Dan. 3:5.

**sackcloth** *n* (infr wd) a coarse cloth for sacks worn in a time of mourning or penitence. Gen. 37:34.

**sacrifice** *n* (theol) the O.T. mentions both special sacrifices, such as covenant sacrifices, and regular sacrifices: meat or meal, drink, and animal offerings (burnt, peace, sin, and guilt or trespass). The wave and heave offerings refer to parts of the peace offering. The blood of animals cannot take away man's sin (Heb. 10:4). Christ, the final and perfect sacrifice, fully effected what the O.T. sacrifices only dimly foreshadowed (1 Cor. 5:7; Eph. 5:2; Heb. 9 and 10; 1 Pet. 1:2).

**scribe** *n* (infr wd) (1) an educated man who wrote what another dictated; a secretary. 2 Kin. 12:10. (2) *n pl* experts in the study of the law of Moses and originators of the synagogue service. Their functions included: the preservation of the law; the gathering around themselves of many pupils whom they instructed in the law; and the administration of the law as judges in the Sanhedrin (thus they were known as "lawyers" and "teachers of the law"). Matt. 2:4.

**scrip** *n* (arch mng) a traveling pouch; a small bag or wallet used by shepherds or travelers. 1 Sam. 17:40.

**sea** *n* (arch mng) a large basin of water. 2 Chr. 4:4.

**seal** *n* (infr mng) that by which anything is confirmed, proved, authenticated. 1 Cor. 9:2. (2) (theol) "set a seal," to close the abyss lest Satan escape. Rev. 20:3.

**seal** *vt* (theol) (1) to hide; to keep in secret; to keep in silence. Rev. 10:4. (2) to mark a person or thing by the impress of a seal; to stamp. Rev. 7:3.

**sealed** *pp* (theol) not revealed; kept secret. Dan. 12:9.

**sealeth** *vt* (arch mng and form) closes; i.e., controls. Job 37:7.

**sear** *vt* (infr mng) to parch, shrivel, scorch. 1 Tim. 4:2.

**search** *vt* (arch use) to examine intimately. Prov. 18:17.

**season** *n* (infr wd) a time; awhile. Gen. 40:4.

**seat** *n* (arch mng) a throne. Amos 6:3.

**seatward,** see -ward. Ex. 37:9.

**second watch** (arch use) approximately 9:00 P.M. to midnight (see *watch*). Luke 12:38.

**secret** *adj* (infr mng) concealed; hidden out of the way. Job 14:13.

**secret things** (theol) hidden (i.e., from man) realities. Deut. 29:29.

**secrets** *n pl* (arch wd) the genitals. Deut. 25:11.

**secure** *adj* (arch mng) unwisely free from care. Judg. 8:11.

**secure** *vt* (arch mng) to free from anxiety. Matt. 28:1[illegible]

**securely** *ad*[illegible] (arch mng) [c]arelessly. Prov. 3:29.

**sedition** *n* [illegible] (infr wd) conduct that is not overt treason, b[u]t [th]at incites riotous commotion and resistance [t]o [l]awfully constituted government. Luke 23:1[illegible] [(]2) (arch mng) dissension; division. Gal. 5:20.

**seduce** *vt* [illegible] [m]ng) to lead or draw one astray. Mark 13:2[illegible]

**see one anoth**[er in th]**e face** (arch expr) face each other in ba[ttl]e [illegible] [C]hr. 25:17.

**see to** (arch [illegible] [t]o look upon. Josh. 22:10.

**seed** *n* (He[illegible] (1) offspring; progeny; posterity; [illegible] [d]escendants. Gen. 7:3. (2) "seed royal," [illegible] of the king. 2 Chr. 22:10.

[s]**eed of copula**[tion] [(Heb]raism) emission of semen, which c[ontains] sperm or "seed." Lev. [1]5:16.

[illegible] *vi* to ap[illegible] [(]1) "seemeth you," appears to you. 1 Sam. 1:23; 2 Sam. 18:4. (2) "seemed to be," were accounted to be. Gal. 2:9.

**seer** *n* (infr wd) a prophet. 2 Sam. 15:27.

**seethe** *vt* (infr wd) to boil. Ex. 16:23.

**Selah** *interj* (translit) this word indicates points within songs where there was a suspension of music; probably a cessation of vocal music while an instrumental interlude continued. It occurs one to four times within those psalms in which it is used, thus serving to divide a psalm into two or more strophes. Psa. 3:2.

**selfsame** *adj* (infr wd) the very same; identical. Matt. 8:13.

**sell himself** (arch expr) to give himself over. 1 Kin. 21:25.

**selvedge** *n* (infr wd) selvage; the edge on either side of a woven fabric so finished as to prevent raveling. Ex. 36:11.

**senators** *n pl* (arch mng) elders; aged men. Psa. 105:22.

**sentence** *n* (infr wd) verdict; judgment. Psa. 17:2.

**separate** *vt* (1) (infr mng) to set apart. Deut. 19:2, 7. (2) (theol) to sanctify; to set apart. Lev. 20:24; Deut. 29:21; Acts 13:2.

**separated themselves unto** (Hebraism) came to join or support. 1 Chr. 12:8.

**sepulchre** *n* (infr wd) a tomb; a burial monument; a grave. Matt. 23:27; Mark 15:46; Rom. 3:13.

**servant** *n* (arch mng) (1) a slave or bondservant, used by and applied to the apostles and other preachers and teachers of the gospel, and also to true worshipers of Christ. Rom. 1:1; 2 Tim. 2:24; Jas. 1:1; 2 Pet. 1:1; Rev. 7:3; 19:2, 5. One must be a *slave* either to sin or to righteousness, but cannot be to both at once. Rom. 6:16-22.

**serve** *vi* (arch mng) (1) to be burdened, wearied. Isa. 43:24. (2) "serve themselves," to be slaves. Jer. 25:14.

**service** *n* (1) (arch mng) accessories; equipment. Num. 4:32. (2) (infr mng) work. 2 Chr. 8:14; Psa. 104:14. (3) (infr mng) form of worship. 2 Chr. 29:35.

**servile** *adj* (infr wd) laborious. Lev. 23:7, 21.

**servitor** *n* (infr wd) a serving-man; a male servant. 2 Kin. 4:43.

**set** *adj* (arch mng) (1) dim; blind. 1 Kin. 14:4. (2) valued, rated, or assessed. 2 Kin. 12:4. (3) assigned. 1 Chr. 9:22. (4) fixed; appointed. Gen. 17:21.

**set** *pp* (arch mng) seated. Matt. 5:1.

**set at nought** (arch expr) to treat as of no account; to utterly despise. Mark 9:12.

**set by** *pp* (arch expr) esteemed. 1 Sam. 18:30.

**set forward** (infr expr) (1) to forward; to promote. 1 Chr. 23:4. (2) to set out on a journey; to advance. Num. 2:17.

**set his heart to** (Hebraism) pay attention to. Ex. 7:23.

**set on/upon** (infr expr) to attack. Acts 18:10.

**set one's face toward** (Hebraism) to turn toward. Ezek. 6:2.

**set to** (arch expr) to affix. John 3:33.

**set up** (Hebraism) built up. Mal. 3:15.

**setteth light by** (arch expr) does not esteem. Deut. 27:16.

**settle** *n* (infr wd) a bench; a seat. Ezek. 43:14.

**settled** *adj* (infr mng) permanent. 1 Kin. 8:13.

**settled his countenance ... until he was ashamed** (Hebraism) restrained himself, held back as long as he could. 2 Kin. 8:11.

**sever** *vt* (infr mng) to put or keep apart; to separate. Ex. 8:22.

**several** *adj* (infr mng) (1) distinct; separate; different; particular. 2 Chr. 28:25; Matt. 25:15. (2) omit for easiest understanding in English. Rev. 21:21.

**several house** (Hebraism) a hospital or infirmary. 2 Kin. 15:5.

**severally** *adv* (infr wd) individually; separately. 1 Cor. 12:11.

**sew pillows to all armholes ... to hunt souls** (arch custom) these actions were designed to aid or symbolize a spell, incantation, or other occult power by which the sorceress captivated a person and claimed power to keep him alive in return for payment. Ezek. 13:18.

**shambles** *n pl* (arch mng) a meat market. 1 Cor. 10:25.

**shamefacedness** *n* (infr wd) modesty. 1 Tim. 2:9.

**shameful spewing** (arch expr) vomiting what has been intemperately swallowed, possibly in another's face. Hab. 2:16.

**share** *n* (infr mng) a plowshare; the part of a plow that cuts the furrow. 1 Sam. 13:20.

**Shearjashub** *prop n* (symbolic) lit., "a remnant shall return." Isa. 7:3.

**sheath** *n* (infr wd) a case for a sword; a scabbard. 1 Chr. 21:27.

**sheaves** *n pl* (infr wd) bundles of stalks and ears of grain. Neh. 13:15.

**sheepcote** *n* (infr wd) a sheepfold. 2 Sam. 7:8.

**sheepmaster** *n* (arch wd) a sheep owner. 2 Kin. 3:4.

**shekel** *n* (tech) *See Table of Weights and Table of Coins*. Ex. 30:13; 2 Kin. 7:1.

**sherd** *n* (infr wd) a shred, fragment, or broken piece, esp. of pottery. Isa. 30:14.

**shew** *vt* (arch sp) to show; by extension, to tell or reveal. Deut. 5:5.

**shewbread** *n* (theol) consecrated unleavened bread ritually placed by Hebrew priests on a table in the sanctuary of the tabernacle on the sabbath; the bread of the presence. Ex. 39:36.

**shewing** *pres part* of *shew*, q.v. Song 2:9.

**shine upon** (Hebraism) be favorable or gracious to. Dan. 9:17.

**shined** *arch pt t* of *shine*: shone. Acts 9:3.

**shipmaster** *n* captain of a ship. Jonah 1:6.

**shipmen** *n pl* (infr wd) sailors. 1 Kin. 9:27.

**shivers** *n pl* (infr wd) small pieces into which something brittle is broken by a sudden blow. Rev. 2:27.

**shock** *n* (arch mng) a stack of sheaves. Judg. 15:5.

**shoe, loose his** (arch custom) (1) dishonorable usage: a sign of public disgrace for refusal to perform one's duty to his deceased brother's wife. Deut. 25:9. (2) honorable usage: a sign of closing a bargain and a renunciation of privilege. Ruth 4: 7, 8.

**shoelatchet** *n* (infr wd) a shoelace. Gen. 14:23.

**shoot** *vi* (infr mng) to slide in or out of a fastening. Ex. 36:33.

**shoot out the lip** (Hebraism) to ridicule (pictured by the facial expression described). Psa. 22:7.

**shred** *vt—arch pt t* of *shred*; to cut up into small pieces. 2 Kin. 4:39.

**shroud** *n* (arch mng) a cover, shelter, protection. Ezek. 31:3.

**shun** *vt* (arch mng) to withdraw oneself from, i.e., to be timid; to cower or shrink from. Acts 20:27.

**shut ... up** (Hebraism) (1) to surrender. Psa. 31:8. (2) to be greatly restrained or constrained. Jer. 36:5. (3) to keep to oneself. Dan. 8:26.

**sick of** (arch mng) faint or sick because of. Song 2:5.

**sigh** *vi* (infr mng) to groan. Ex. 2:23.

**sight, in the/thy** (Hebraism) mental view; judgment. Deut. 6:18.

**sign** *n* (1) (infr mng) a token or memorial. Josh. 4:6. (2) (theol) a miracle. Num. 14:11. (3) (theol) a divinely-revealed signal of warning. Luke 21:7.

**signet** *n* (infr wd) a seal, often on a ring. Gen. 38:18.

**signification, without** (arch expr) without distinction (for example, the barking of dogs differs from the neighing of horses). 1 Cor. 14:10.

**silly** *adj* (arch mng) innocent; simple. Job 5:2.

**silverling** *n* (tech) *See Table of Coins*. Isa. 7:23.

**similitude** *n* (theol) (1) form, appearance, or shape. Num. 12:8; Deut. 4:12, 15. (2) representation, likeness, or image. Deut. 4:16. (3) an allegory; a parable; a method of teaching using comparison. Hos. 12:10.

**simple** *adj* (theol) (1) fearing no evil from others; distrusting no one; guileless. Rom. 16:18. (2) innocent; free from guile; without admixture of evil. Rom. 16:19.

**simple** *n* (infr mng) foolish, silly people. Prov. 14:15.

**simplicity** *n* (infr mng) (1) innocence. 2 Sam. 15:11. (2) sincerity; singleness or honesty of mind, i.e., without self-seeking; liberality. Rom. 12:8. (3) foolishness; susceptibility to seduction. Prov. 1:22.

**sincere** *adj* (arch mng) unadulterated; pure. 1 Pet. 2:2.

**single** *adj* (arch mng) simple, i.e., good, whole,

or sound, properly fulfilling its function. Matt. 6:22.

**singleness** *n* (arch mng) bent on one thing alone, without duplicity or ulterior motive. Eph. 6:5.

**singular** *adj* (arch mng) for a special purpose. Lev. 27:2.

**sinneth not** (theol) lit., does not *go on sinning*; does not *practice sinning*. 1 John 3:6.

**sith** *conj* (arch wd) since. Ezek. 35:6.

**situate** *adj* (arch wd) situated; located; placed. Ezek. 27:3.

**sixth hour** (arch expr) noon. Matt. 20:5.

**skill** *vt* (arch use) to understand; to show skill in. 1 Kin. 5:6.

**slack** *adj* (infr mng) characterized by slowness or lack of energy; careless; negligent. Deut. 7:10.

**slack** *vt* (infr mng) (1) to withdraw, slacken, make slow. Josh. 10:6. (2) to be slow, delay. Deut. 23:21.

**slain** *pp* of *slay*, q.v. 1 Kin. 1:19.

**slander** *n* (arch mng) an evil or false report. Num. 14:36.

**slander** *vt* (infr mng) to utter false charges which defame another's reputation. 2 Sam. 19:27.

**slay** *vt* (infr wd) (1) to kill; to put to death violently. Acts 23:14. (2) to slaughter an animal. Gen. 43:16.

**sleep** *vi* (arch mng) to die; to be dead. 1 Thess. 4:14.

**sleep brake from him** (Hebraism) he couldn't sleep. Dan. 2:1.

**sleight** *n* (arch use) lit., dice-playing; by extension, deception, craftiness. Eph. 4:14.

**slept** *pt t* of *sleep*, q.v. 1 Kin. 14:31.

**slew** *arch pt t* of *slay*, q.v. 2 Sam. 1:10.

**slide** *vi* (arch use) to waver. Psa. 26:1.

**slime** *n* mud; asphalt. Gen. 11:3.

**slow tongue** (arch expr) unable to speak well, elegantly, or persuasively. Ex. 4:10.

**smite** *vt* (infr wd) (1) to strike, usu. sharply or heavily. Gen. 32:8. (2) to kill. Jer. 21:7. (3) to strike, either lightly or severely. Isa. 9:13.

**smiters** *n pl* (infr wd) those who *smite*, q.v. Isa. 50:6.

**smith** *n* (infr wd) a blacksmith. 1 Sam. 13:19.

**smitten** *pp* of *smite*, q.v. Num. 14:42.

**smoke** *vi* (arch mng) to increase furiously. Deut. 29:20.

**smote** *vt* (infr wd) *pt t* of *smite:* (1) attacked. Gen. 14:5. (2) subdued. Gen. 14:7. (3) hit. Ex. 17:5.

**snare** *n* (theol) (1) a contrivance, often consisting of a noose by which a bird or other animal may be entangled and caught; a trap; a gin. Prov. 7:23. (2) a person, thing, or circumstance by which one is entangled and brought into trouble. Psa. 91:3; 106:36; Prov. 29:25.

**snare** *vt* (infr wd) to entice or lure into a trap; to ensnare, entangle; by extension, to tempt or capture by guile. Deut. 7:25; Psa. 9:16.

**snuff** *vt* (arch wd) to inhale eagerly. Jer. 14:6.

**snuffdishes** *n pl* (arch wd) dishes to hold the partly-consumed portion of a wick used in lighting. Ex. 25:38.

**sober** *adj* (infr mng) calm and collected in spirit; temperate; dispassionate; circumspect. 1 Pet. 1:13.

**sod** *pt t* of *seethe*, q.v. Gen. 25:29.

**soever** *adv* (infr wd) to any possible extent. 2 Sam. 24:3.

**sojourn** *vi* (infr wd) to live as a temporary resident. Josh. 20:9.

**sojourner** *n* (infr wd) a temporary resident. Lev. 25:23.

**solace** *vt* (arch mng) to delight; to exult; to enjoy thoroughly. Prov. 7:18.

**sold** *vt* (arch mng) (1) sold into slavery. Judg. 4:2. (2) "sold thyself," given yourself over. 1 Kin. 21:20.

**solitarily,** see *solitary*. Mic. 7:14.

**solitary** *adj* (infr wd) lonely. Lam. 1:1.

**sometime(s)** *adv* (arch mng) once. Col. 1:21.

**soothsayer** *n* (infr wd) fortuneteller; one who foretells events. Josh. 13:22.

**soothsaying** *n* (infr wd) divination; foretelling of events. Acts 16:16.

**sop** *n* (arch use) a morsel, fragment, or bit of food. John 13:26.

**sorcerer** *n* (infr wd) one who uses power gained from the assistance or control of evil spirits, esp. for divining; a wizard. Ex. 7:11.

**sorcery** *n* (infr wd) magical arts; witchcraft. Acts 8:9.

**sore** *adj* (arch mng) (1) heavy, severe. 2 Chr. 21:19. (2) strong. Gen. 50:10.

**sore** *n* (arch mng) affliction, plague. 2 Chr. 6:28, 29.

**sore(ly)** *adv* (arch mng) severely, grievously. Gen. 19:9.

**sorer** *comp adj*, see *sore (adj)*. Heb. 10:29.

**sorrow** *n* (arch mng) (1) pain, toil, labor. Gen. 3:16. (2) *n pl* birth pangs. Mark 13:8.

**sort** *n* (infr mng) condition of life; degree; kind; manner. Acts 17:5.

**sottish** *adj* (arch wd) foolish. Jer. 4:22.

**sought not to/unto** (arch expr) did not seek. 2 Chr. 16:12.

**sought to** (arch expr) consulted. 1 Kin. 10:24.

**soul** *n* (theol) (1) life Gen. 19:20. (2) the self. Lev. 16:29; Psa. 49:18. (3) the whole man, including his body, which may be lost in hell. Matt. 16:26.

**soul was grieved** (Hebraism) felt compassion and pity. Judg. 10:16.

**sounding again** (Hebraism) echo. Ezek. 7:7.

**sow her unto me** (fig expr) cause her to increase as seed of God. Hos. 2:23.

**space** *n* (infr use) an interval of time. Ezra 9:8.

**space, by the** (infr expr) over an area. Rev. 14:20.

**span** *n* (tech) *See Table of Linear Measures.* Ex. 28:16.

**spare** *vt* (infr mng) to refrain from; to avoid. Job 30:10.

**spared** *vt* (arch mng) was not willing to. 2 Sam. 12:4.

**speak** *vi* (arch mng) arbitrate. Psa. 127:5.

**specially** *adv* (infr wd) (1) uniquely; especially. 1 Tim. 4:10. (2) particularly. Tit. 1:10.

**sped** *vi* (arch mng) succeeded. Judg. 5:30.

**speed** *n* (arch mng) success; prosperity in an undertaking. Gen. 24:12.

**spent** *pp* (infr use) used up. Gen. 21:15.

**spicery** *n* (arch mng) spices. Gen. 37:25.

**spikenard** *n* (infr wd) a fragrant ointment. Song 1:12.

**spirit** *n* (theol) (1) the mind; the principle of man's rational and immortal life; the possessor of reason, will, and conscience. Inorganic material was given life when God created a rational spirit and incorporated it into the dust (Gen. 2:7), which returns to the earth at death while the spirit returns to its maker (Eccl. 12:7). 1 Sam. 1:15. (2) the breath of God. Job 26:4; Prov. 20:27. (3) the Holy Spirit (often not capitalized in the O.T.). Gen. 1:2; Psa. 51:11; Isa. 63:10, 11. (4) a demon or evil spirit. Mark 3:30. (5) "familiar spirit," see *familiar spirit*. Lev. 20:27.

**spitefully** *adv* (infr wd) short for *despitefully;* disgracefully; acting in an insolently abusive and humiliating manner. Matt. 22:6.

**spoil** *n* (infr wd) plunder taken by an enemy at war; booty. 1 Sam. 15:21.

**spoil** *vt* (arch mng) (1) to ruin; to seize by force. Deut. 28:29. (2) to plunder, rob. Judg. 2:16.

**spoken for** (arch expr) asked in marriage. Song 8:8.

**sport** *n* (infr mng) entertainment; jesting; fun. Judg. 16:25.

**sport** *reflex vb* (arch use) to amuse oneself; to live delicately or luxuriously; to revel in. Isa. 57:4; 2 Pet. 2:13.

**sport with** (infr mng) to play with; caress; to frolic with. Gen. 26:8.

**spot** *n* (infr mng) a defect; a blemish. Num. 19:2.

**spread** *pp* (arch mng) beaten; overlaid. Jer. 10:9.

**spread(eth) forth one's hands** (Hebraism) to implore; to pray. Lam. 1:17.

**spring** *n* (arch mng) dawn. 1 Sam. 9:26.

**spring** *vi* (arch mng) to dawn. Judg. 19:25.

**springing** *adj* (arch mng) water issuing from its source in the ground. Gen. 26:19.

**sprinkle** *vt* (theol) a technical word in the Mosaic law for sprinkling oil, water, or blood as a cleansing or purifying rite to obtain ritual purity. This rite must be performed by a pure and innocent priest. Isa. 52:15.

**spue** *vi* (arch sp) to spew; specifically, to vomit. Jer. 25:27.

**spy** *vt* (infr mng) to see; to perceive; to behold. Ex. 2:11.

**stablish** *vt* (arch sp) to establish, confirm; to make sure or stable. 2 Sam. 7:13.

**staff** *n* (pl form is *staves*) (1) (infr wd) a long stick carried in the hand for support when walking. Num. 22:27. (2) (arch use) a pole inserted into the rings of an altar or the ark of the covenant by which it was carried. Ex. 27:6, 7. (3) (arch mng) a shaft. 1 Chr. 20:5. (4) a weapon such as a cudgel or club. Luke 22:52. (5) "staff of reed," a weak, useless support. Ezek. 29:6. (6) a pagan divining rod. Hos. 4:12.

**stagger** *vi* (infr mng) to stumble; to hesitate. Rom. 4:20.

**stalled** *adj* (arch mng) fattened by stall-feeding. Prov. 15:17.

**stammering** *adj* (Hebraism) language that is apparently unintelligible, but is really a foreign language. Isa. 28:11.

**stanch** *vi* (infr wd) to staunch; to stop or check a flowing, as of a hemorrhage. Luke 8:44.

**stand** *vi* (infr mng) (1) to stand fast. Eph. 6:13. (2) to consist; to be. 1 Cor. 2:5. (3) to serve. Dan. 1:4.

**stand against the blood** (Hebraism) seek to have the blood. Lev. 19:16.

**stand before** (Hebraism) to resist; to successfully oppose; to withstand. Deut. 9:2; 11:25.

**stand before the congregation for judgment** (arch custom) to come to be judged before the people. Josh. 20:6.

**stand for** *vt* (arch mng) to take a stand for; to defend. Esth. 8:11.

**stand to** (arch expr) to agree to; to abide by. Deut. 25:8.

**stand upon** (arch expr) to attack. 2 Sam. 1:9, 10.

**standard** *n* (infr mng) a banner. Num. 1:52.

**state** *n* (infr mng) (1) the proper condition or order. 2 Chr. 24:13. (2) "your state," your affairs; the things concerning you. Phil. 2:19.

**statute** *n* (arch mng) an enactment; appointment; law. Ex. 29:28.

**staves** *pl* of *staff,* q.v. Ex. 27:6, 7; Matt. 10:10; Luke 22:52.

**stay** *n* (infr mng) (1) a support. Psa. 18:18. (2) a checked or arrested condition. Lev. 13:5.

**stay** *vb* (infr mng) (1) to hold back or restrain. Gen. 8:10; 2 Sam. 24:16. (2) to leave behind. Ex. 10:24. (3) to hold steady. Ex. 17:12. (4) to support; to sustain. Song 2:5. (5) to refrain. Ruth 1:13. (6) to be supported. Isa. 10:20.

**stay, be at a** (arch expr) (1) to be stopped. Lev. 13:5. (2) to *be stayed;* to be left behind. Ex. 10:24.

**stayed from, is** (arch use) withholds. Hag. 1:10.

**stays** *n pl* (arch mng) armrests. 1 Kin. 10:19.

**stead** *n* (infr wd) place; in the place of. Gen. 22:13.

**steadfastly minded** (arch expr) firmly determined. Ruth 1:18.

**stealth** *n* (infr wd) going furtively, secretly or imperceptibly. 2 Sam. 19:3.

**stedfast** *adj* (arch sp) steadfast; firm; faithful. Psa. 78:37.

**steel** *n* (mistransl) brass or bronze. Psa. 18:34.

**steward** *n* (1) (infr wd) a manager of the financial and domestic affairs, as well as of the servants, of an estate. Gen. 44:4; 1 Kin. 16:9. (2) (arch mng) a man of honor, worth. Gen. 43:19. (3) (arch mng) a butler. Gen. 15:2. (4) (arch mng) *n pl* lords; overseers. 1 Chr. 28:1.

**stewardship** *n* (infr wd) management for which one is accountable. Luke 16:2.

**stiff neck,** see *stiffnecked*. Psa. 75:5.

**stiffnecked** *adj* (infr wd) stubborn. Ex. 32:9.

**stir** *n* (infr wd) tumult; commotion. Acts 12:18.

**stirs** *n pl* (arch mng) crashings; clamorings. Isa. 22:2.

**stock** *n* (arch mng) a log or block of wood. Jer. 2:27.

**stocks** *n pl* (infr mng) a wooden frame with holes for the feet, or feet and hands, of a criminal. Jer. 20:2.

**stomacher** *n* (infr wd) the center, front section of a dress bodice; a woven belt. Isa. 3:24.

**stone** *n* (arch mng) stone marker; landmark. Josh. 15:6.

**stones** *n pl* (arch mng) testes. Lev. 21:20.

**stonesquarers** *n pl* (arch wd) men of Gebal who were architects or stone-squarers; artificers (q.v.) in stone and wood. 1 Kin. 5:18.

**stood** *vi* (arch mng) *pt t* of *stand;* took office. Gen. 41:46.

**stood before** *pt t* of *stand before,* q.v. Gen. 19:27.

**stood for** *pt t* of *stand for,* q.v. Esth. 9:16.

**stood still** (arch expr) stopped to take notice; kept standing there. 2 Sam. 20:12.

**stood to** *pt t* of *stand to,* q.v. 2 Kin. 23:3.

**stood up against** (Hebraism) opposed. 1 Chr. 21:1.

**store** *n* (infr mng) (1) storage. Gen. 41:36. (2) supply. Lev. 26:10. (3) pantry. Deut. 28:5. (4) abundance; plenty. Gen. 26:14.

**stout** *adj* (infr mng) strong; hence, bold, stubborn. Job 4:11.

**stoutness** *n* (infr mng) boldness, stubbornness. Isa. 9:9.

**straightway** *adv* (infr wd) immediately; forthwith; without delay. 1 Sam. 9:13; Matt. 4:20.

**strait** *adj* (arch mng) (1) small; contracted; narrow. 2 Kin. 6:1. (2) strict. Acts 26:5.

**strait** *n* (arch mng) lit., a narrow passage or pass; fig., *trouble*. Job 36:16.

**straiten** *vt* (infr wd) to restrict; to hem in; to confine, compress, or constrain. Job 12:23; Luke 12:50.

**straitly** *adv* (arch wd) (1) carefully; strictly; closely. Gen. 43:7. (2) solemnly. Ex. 13:19. (3) securely. Josh. 6:1.

**straitness** *n* (arch mng) narrowness; hence, distress, difficulty. Deut. 28:53.

**strake** *n* (arch wd) a streak or stripe. Lev. 14:37.

**strake** *vt–arch pt t* of *strike:* struck sail, i.e., lowered the mainsail and possibly its spare. Acts 27:17.

**strange** *adj* (arch mng) (1) foreign. Gen. 35:2. (2) adulterous (woman). Prov. 23:33.

**strange gods** *n pl* (arch expr) idols. Gen. 35:4.

**stranger** *n* (infr mng) (1) foreigner. Gen. 17:27. (2) sojourner. Gen. 15:13.

**strawed** *vt* (arch wd) *pt t* of *straw:* to strew, i.e., to spread by scattering. Matt. 21:8.

**strength** *n* (arch mng) depth, surgings; its original state. Ex. 14:27.

**strengthen** *vt* (infr mng) to encourage; to fortify. 1 Sam. 23:16.

**stretched out arm** (Hebraism) might; display of power. Ex. 6:6.

**stricken** *adj* (1) (arch mng) advanced. Gen. 24:1. (2) having been struck with blows. See *chastise* and *punish*. Isa. 53:4.

**strife** *n* (theol) partisanship; factiousness; contending against God. Gal. 5:20.

**strike** *vt* (arch mng) (1) to put; to stroke; to rub. Ex. 12:7. (2) "strike through," to destroy. Psa. 110:5.

**strike hands** (Hebraism) to clasp hands; hence, to conclude a compact, to become surety for someone. Job 17:3.

**striker** *n* (arch mng) a man of warlike temperament; one who deals in threatenings and blows. 1 Tim. 3:3.

**strip** (infr mng) to remove anything of value. 1 Chr. 10:8.

**stripe** *n* (infr wd) a wound that trickles with blood. 1 Pet. 2:24.

**stripling** *n* (infr wd) a youth, lad; an adolescent boy. 1 Sam. 17:56.

**strive** *vi* (infr wd) (1) to fight. Gen. 26:20. (2) to contend; to dispute. John 6:52; Acts 23:9. (3) to contend or plead a cause, as in a court of law (as God was doing through the preaching of Noah—2 Pet. 2:5). Gen. 6:3. (4) to endeavor with strenuous zeal. Luke 13:24.

**stroke** *n* (infr mng) a blow; conflict. Deut. 21:5.

**strong** *adj* (infr mng) not easily subdued or taken; fortified. Psa. 31:21.

**strong meat** (arch expr) solid food. Heb. 5:12.

**stronghold** *n* (infr wd) a fortified place; fortress. 1 Sam. 23:14.

**strove** *pt t* of *strive,* q.v. Lev. 24:10.

**strowed** *vt* (arch wd) *pt t* of *straw:* spread by scattering. 2 Chr. 34:4.

**stud** *n* (infr wd) a raised ornament. Song 1:11.

**stuff** *n* (infr mng) possessions; furniture; baggage of an army. Gen. 31:37.

**stumblingblock** *n* (infr wd) an impediment to belief or understanding. Zeph. 1:3.

**subdue** *vt* (infr mng) to conquer and bring into subjection. 1 Chr. 22:18.

**suborn** *vt* (infr wd) to privately instruct or instigate, often by bribery. Acts 6:11.

**subscribe** *vt* (arch mng) to write. Isa. 44:5.

**substance** *n* (infr mng) (1) thing, form. Gen. 7:4. (2) property; money; goods. Gen. 12:5; Luke 8:3.

**subtil** *adj* (arch sp) subtle; cunning; crafty. 2 Sam. 13:3.

**subtilly** *adv* (arch sp) subtly; elusively; cunningly; craftily. 1 Sam. 23:22.

**subtilty** *n* (arch sp) subtlety; craftiness; insidiousness; cunning. Matt. 26:4.

**suburbs** *n pl* (infr mng) pasture lands; land outside the city walls. Num. 35:4.

**subvert** *vt* (infr wd) (1) to overthrow or overturn; to destroy. 2 Tim. 2:14; Tit. 1:11. (2) to plunder; to turn away violently from a right state. Acts 15:24. (3) lit., a building term meaning to demolish; to ruin; to turn inside out; to pervert or corrupt. Tit. 3:11.

**succour** *vt* (infr wd) to help, assist, aid. 2 Sam. 8:5.

**succourer** *n* (infr wd) a helper, assistant, or reliever. Rom. 16:2.

**suckling** *n* (infr wd) an unweaned infant. Deut. 32:25.

**suffer** *vt* (infr mng) (1) to permit; to allow. Gen. 20:6. (2) to bear with; to endure. Job 21:3; Luke 9:22.

**suffice** *vi* (infr wd) to be sufficient for; to satisfy. Num. 11:22.

**suffice** *vt* (infr wd) to be enough or sufficient for; "was sufficed," was satisfied. Ruth 2:14.

**sufficiency** *n* (arch mng) power; adequate ability. Job 20:22.

**sum** *n* (arch use) total count, census. Num. 1:2.

**sum** *vt* (arch use) to take a total count or census. 2 Kin. 22:4.

**sumptuously** *adv* (infr wd) expensively; luxuriously; lavishly. Luke 16:19.

**sunder** *vt* (infr wd) to sever, separate; to break apart. Job 41:17.

**sundered** *pp* (infr wd) broken or cut apart or in two. Job 41:17.

**sundry** *adj* (infr wd) separate; different; various; many. Heb. 1:1.

**sunrising** *n* (arch use) the direction of the sun's rising, the east. Josh. 1:15.

**sup** *vi* (arch wd) to dine; to eat. Luke 17:8.

**superscription** *n* (infr wd) an inscription on a coin, appearing above the image of the public personage depicted; a hand-written title or accusation inscribed in black letters on a whitened tablet, such as the one posted above Christ's head on the cross. Matt. 22:20; Mark 15:26.

**superstitious, too** (theol) very reverent to (false) gods or (lit.) demons. Acts 17:22.

**supple** *vt* (infr wd) to make pliant, flexible. Ezek. 16:4.

**supplication** *n* (infr wd) seeking, entreating God. 1 Tim. 5:5.

**sure** *adj* (arch mng) secure; safe. 1 Sam. 2:35.

**surely** *adv* (arch mng) securely. Prov. 10:9.

**surety** *n* (infr wd) (1) a certainty. Gen. 26:9. (2) one who is legally liable for the debt of another. Prov. 6:1.

**surfeiting** *n* (arch mng) gluttony. Luke 21:34.

**surmising** *n* (arch mng) fondness of being first; striving after pre-eminence. 1 Tim. 6:4.

**sustain** *vt* (infr wd) to maintain; to nourish; to support; to relieve. 1 Kin. 17:9.

**sustenance** *n* (infr wd) food. Judg. 6:4.

**swaddle** *vt* (arch custom) to snugly wrap an infant in a cloth fastened by cloth bands wound around the outside. Lam. 2:22.

**swaddling band or clothes** (infr wd) narrow strips of cloth wrapped around an infant to restrict movement and promote security. Job 38:9.

**swallow** *vt* (arch mng) (1) to destroy. 2 Sam. 20:19. (2) to make away with. Job 20:18.

**sware** *arch pt t* of *swear,* q.v. Gen. 31:53.

**swear** *vb* (theol) to promise solemnly, often with an oath or by calling a person or thing to witness. Mark 14:71.

**swear falsely** (arch expr) to lie; to perjure oneself, or to make an oath deceitfully. Lev. 6:3, 5.

**sweet** *adj* (infr mng) pleasant. Lev. 1:9.

**sweet influences** (mistransl) bonds; forces of attraction holding the constellation together. Job 38:31.

**swelling** *adj* (arch use) inflated; haughty; arrogant. 2 Pet. 2:18.

**swellings** *n pl* (Grecism) puffing up of soul; loftiness; pride. 2 Cor. 12:20.

**sworn** *vt* (arch use) *pp* of *swear:* made to swear. Ex. 13:19.

**sworn falsely** *pp* of *swear falsely,* q.v. Lev. 6:5.

## T

**taber** *vi* (arch wd) to beat as upon a tabor, or drum; to drum upon. Nah. 2:7.

**tabering** *pres part* (arch wd) beating. Nah. 2:7.

**tabernacle** *n* (arch mng) (1) a tent, a movable dwelling; esp. the sacred tent in which the ark of the covenant was kept. Ex. 26:1. (2) a booth, or temporary shelter (see *booths*). Matt. 17:4. (3) the body, as affected by sin, which is only a temporary dwelling for the spirits of just men, and is to be replaced by a glorified body at the resurrection. 2 Cor. 5:lff.

**table** *n* (arch mng) a tablet on which to write. Hab. 2:2.

**tablet** *n* (arch mng) an ornament of precious metal or jewels of a flat form, worn around a person, typically about the neck; a locket. Ex. 35:22.

**tabret** *n* (infr wd) a small drum with one head of calfskin. Gen. 31:27.

**tache** *n* (infr wd) an attachment or fastening; a clasp or buckle. Ex. 26:6, 11.

**tackling** *n* (mistransl) the furniture of the ship, such as beds, tables, chairs, and chests. Acts 27:19.

**take** *vt* (arch mng) (1) to overtake. Gen. 19:19.

(2) to entrap, ensnare, catch. Prov. 6:2. (3) (infr mng) to hunt successfully. Gen. 27:33.

**take counsel** (infr expr) to deliberate or to resolve, as upon a plan or scheme. Psa. 2:2; Acts 5:33.

**take heed to** (arch expr) be careful concerning. Col. 4:17.

**take of you** (arch expr) to circumvent one by fraud. 2 Cor. 11:20.

**take thought** (arch expr) to be or become anxious; to worry. 1 Sam. 9:5; Matt. 6:25.

**take up** (arch expr) to obtain on credit. Neh. 5:2.

**take wrong** (arch expr) to endure wrong. 1 Cor. 6:7.

**taken** *pp* of *take* (arch mng) (1) chosen; pointed out. Josh. 7:16. (2) suspended. 2 Sam. 18:9. (3) captured. 1 Kin. 16:18.

**taken away my judgment** (mistransl) turned away (i.e., postponed or deferred) my plea. Job 27:2.

**taken upon the lips** (Hebraism) spoken about. Ezek. 36:3.

**taketh** *vt* (arch mng) to toil; to work severely and with irksomeness. Eccl. 1:3.

**tale** *n* (infr mng) a number; count. Ex. 5:8.

**talebearer** *n* (infr wd) one that spreads gossip, scandal, or idle rumors. Prov. 11:13.

**talent** *n* (tech) (1) *See Table of Weights*. Ex. 37:24. (2) *See Table of Weights*. Ex. 38:27. (3) *See Table of Weights*. Matt. 18:24.

**tanner** *n* (infr wd) one who converts animal hides into leather by tanning, i.e., by treating them with oak bark or a similar agent. Acts 9:43.

**tare** *vt* *arch pt t* of *tear*. (1) to rend. 2 Sam. 13:31. (2) to tear in pieces. 2 Kin. 2:24. (3) to convulse. Mark 9:20.

**tares** *n pl* (tech) zizanium, a type of darnel or annual grass; called a "bastard wheat" because it resembles wheat except that the grains are black. Matt. 13:26.

**target** *n* (arch mng) a shield; buckler. 1 Sam. 17:6.

**tarried** *pt t* of *tarry,* q.v. 2 Sam. 15:17.

**tarry** *vi* (infr wd) (1) to delay or be tardy in one's departure or arrival; to linger. Matt. 25:5. (2) to abide in one place; to wait expectantly. Luke 24:49.

**tarry abroad** (arch expr) to stay outside. Lev. 14:8.

**taverns** *n pl* (infr mng) inns. The "Three Taverns" was a station on the Appian Way, between Rome and Appii Forum. Acts 28:15.

**teach** *vt* (infr mng) to make disciples. Matt. 28:19.

**tear** *vi* (arch mng) to rage. Amos 1:11.

**teats** *n pl* (arch mng) the breasts. Ezek. 23:3.

**tell** *vt* (infr mng) to count. Gen. 15:5.

**temper** *vt* (arch mng) (1) to mix; compound. Ex. 29:2. (2) to moisten with. Ezek. 46:14. (3) to cause the body parts to combine into a structural unit. 1 Cor. 12:24.

**temperance** *n* (infr wd) self-restraint, moderation; self-control. Acts 24:25.

**temple** *n* (arch mng) (1) a large public building. 1 Kin. 6:17. (2) the house of God; the place where God's presence abode in a special sense. After Christ's death and resurrection, the physical temple became obsolete as Christ and His church fulfilled the typical meaning of the temple (1 Cor. 6:19; Heb. 9:11-14). Acts 2:46.

**tempt** *vt* (arch mng) to prove; to try; to test; to put to the test. Gen. 22:1.

**temptation** *n* (theol) (1) a proving or testing of men by God. Deut. 4:34. (2) Satan's enticing men to sin. Heb. 3:8.

**temptations** *n pl* (theol) divinely appointed tests or trials, such as the ten supernatural plagues visited upon Egypt. Deut. 7:19.

**tender** *adj* (infr mng) (1) young, weak. Gen. 33:13. (2) possessing the softer feelings, such as love, compassion, kindness; weak; mild. Deut. 28:56. (3) inexperienced. 1 Chr. 29:1.

**tender-eyed** *adj* (arch mng) weak-eyed. Gen. 29:17.

**tenon** *n* (infr wd) a type of joint used in carpentry mainly for its strength. Ex. 26:17.

**tenth hour** (arch expr) approximately 4:00 p.m. John 1:39.

**terrestrial** *adj* (infr wd) earthly. 1 Cor. 15:40.

**terrible** *adj* (infr mng) great; awesome; causing terror. Deut. 7:21.

**terribleness** *n* (infr wd) that which causes terror. Deut. 26:8.

**terror** *n* (arch mng) a display of almighty power; a state of great awe. Deut. 34:12.

**testament** *n* (1) (infr wd) a will. Heb. 9:16. (2) (arch mng) a covenant. 2 Cor. 3:6, 14. (3) (theol) a disposition or arrangement which one wishes to be valid, esp. the disposal one makes of his earthly possessions after death; a will. Heb. 9:16, 17. (4) "old testament," a compact or covenant; the close relationship which God entered into with His people, esp. Noah and Abraham. 2 Cor. 3:14. (5) "new testament," or covenant, by which men are bound to exercise faith in Christ and God promises grace and eternal salvation. Christ set up and ratified this covenant by His death. Matt. 26:28.

**testator** *n* (infr wd) one who draws up a will. Heb. 9:16.

**testify** *vt* (arch mng) to make known; to confess; to show. Deut. 32:46.

**testimony** *n* (infr wd) (1) the tables of law. Ex. 40:3. (2) *n pl* divine decrees. Psa. 119:138. (3) a solemn declaration to establish or set forth factual knowledge gained from personal observation or experience. John 3:32, 33.

**tetrarch** *n* (Grecism) the ruler of a fourth part (one-fourth) of a region. Luke 3:1.

**thankworthy** *adj* (infr wd) winning of God's favor. 1 Pet. 2:19.

**theeward** see *-ward*. 1 Sam. 19:4.

**thence** *adv* (infr mng) from that place. Josh. 15:15.

**thereon** *adv* (infr wd) on it. 2 Sam. 19:26.

**thereto** *adv* (infr wd) to that. 2 Chr. 21:11.

**therewith** *adv* (infr wd) with that. Ezek. 4:15.

**things** *n pl* (infr mng) affairs. 1 Cor. 16:14.

**third hour** (arch expr) 9:00 a.m. or midmorning. Acts 2:15.

**third part** (infr expr) one-third. Rev. 9:15.

**third watch** (arch use) midnight to approximately 3:00 a.m. (see *watch*). Luke 12:38.

**this signifying** (arch expr) showing by this. Heb. 9:8.

**thither** *adv* (infr wd) to that place; there. Judg. 8:27.

**thitherward** *adv* (infr wd) toward that place. Judg. 18:15.

**thought** *n* (arch mng) anxiety; excess of care; thus, "to take thought," to be very anxious. 1 Sam. 9:5.

**thought scorn** (Hebraism) to disdain. Esth. 3:6.

**thousands** *n pl* (arch mng) families. Num. 1:16.

**threescore** see *-score*. Ezra 2:9.

**thresh** *vt* (infr wd) (1) to separate grain from its stalks and husks by the treading of animals, by flailing, or by dragging a sledge over it. Judg. 6:11. (2) fig., to flail or whip, often an adversary or enemy. Isa. 41:15; Amos 1:3; Hab. 3:12.

**thrice** *adv* (infr wd) three times. Ex. 34:23.

**throng** *vb* (infr wd) to crowd together; to crowd or press upon. Mark 3:9; 5:24.

**throughly** *adv* (arch wd) thoroughly. Job 6:2.

**throw down** *vt* (arch expr) to destroy. Judg. 2:2.

**thrust out** (Hebraism) (1) exiled. Judg. 9:41. (2) i.e., by taking every part of their inheritance. Ezek. 46:18.

**thus and thus** (arch expr) an idiomatic short way of indicating that a narrative was related at this point in the text. Josh. 7:20.

**tidings** *n pl* (infr wd) news. 2 Sam. 18:22, 25.

**tile** *n* (arch mng) a brick. Ezek. 4:1.

**till** *vt* (infr wd) to cultivate. Gen. 4:12.

**tillage** *n* (infr wd) plowed but unseeded land. 1 Chr. 27:26.

**timbrel** *n* (infr wd) a small hand drum, tambourine, or tabor. Ex. 15:20.

**time of life** (Hebraism) the normal gestation period. 2 Kin. 4:16.

**time of the fruit** (Grecism) harvest time or season. Matt. 21:34.

**times** *n pl* (Hebraism) years. Dan. 4:16.

**tire** *n* (infr mng) a headdress. Isa. 3:18. (*Tire* is short for *attire,* not the same word as *tiara.*)

**tire** *vt* (arch mng) to attire; to adorn with a "tire" or headdress. 2 Kin. 9:30.

**tithe** *n* (infr wd) one-tenth part, usu. of one's possessions or income. Mal. 3:8, 10; Luke 18:12.

**tithe** *vt* (infr wd) to contribute the tithe, or tenth part of. Deut. 14:22.

**tittle** *n* (Grecism) a tiny ornamental stroke on a letter, or a stroke that distinguishes one letter from another, as the tail of a *Q* distinguishes it from an *O;* thus, something very minute. Matt. 5:18; Luke 16:17.

**to** *prep* (arch use) (1) for. Judg. 17:13. (2) in. 1 Chr. 12:8.

**to do** (arch use) to be used. Num. 7:5.

**to view at** (arch expr) before. 2 Kin. 2:15.

**to wife** (arch expr) in marriage. Josh. 15:16.

**to wit** *adv* (infr expr) that is to say; namely. 1 Kin. 7:50.

**token** *n* (infr wd) (1) evidence. Job. 21:29. (2) a sign or signal. Mark 14:44.

**told** *vt* (arch mng) (1) answered. 1 Kin. 10:3. (2) *pp* of *tell,* q.v. 1 Kin. 8:5.

**tongue** *n* (infr mng) (1) language. Gen. 10:20. (2) *n pl* various languages. Acts 2:4.

**took** *vt* (infr mng) (1) captured. 2 Kin. 16:9. (2) married. 1 Chr. 2:19.

**took an oath** (arch expr) lit., made them swear seven times; i.e., made them swear that what they said was indeed true. 1 Kin. 18:10.

**tormentor** *n* (infr mng) a torturer. Matt. 18:34.

**touch** *vt* (arch mng) (1) to marry; to have sexual intercourse with in marriage. 1 Cor. 7:1. (2) euphemism for *to have sexual intercourse*. Ruth 2:9.

**touching** *prep* (infr mng) concerning. Num. 8:26.

**tow** *n* (infr wd) the refuse of flax; short broken linen fiber which burned easily. Judg. 16:9.

**toward** *adj* (infr mng) friendly, favorable to. Gen. 31:2.

**traffick** *vi* (arch sp) to traffic; to do business. Gen. 42:34.

**traffickers** *n pl* (arch wd) businessmen; traders. Isa. 23:8.

**train** *n* (infr mng) (1) a retinue; a company of followers. 1 Kin. 10:2. (2) long flowing skirts of a robe. Isa. 6:1.

**transfigured, was** *vb pass* (theol) to be metamorphosed, i.e., to be transformed; used in the N.T. to describe the supernatural unveiling of Christ's resplendent glory or brightness, which belonged to Him as God but was hidden from the eyes of men when He took upon Himself the likeness of sinful flesh (Rom. 8:3) and as the God-man assumed the lowly "form of a servant" (Phil. 2:7). Matt. 17:2; Mark 9:2.

**transgress** *vt* (theol) to overstep or violate the limits placed by God's law; to trespass. Josh. 7:15; Matt. 15:3.

**transgression** *n* (theol) a violation or breach of God's law. Job 34:6.

**translate** *vt* (infr mng) to transfer. 2 Sam. 3:10.

**travail** *n* (infr wd) (1) trouble, agony. Num. 20:14. (2) toil; labor; labor of childbirth. Gen. 38:27.

**travail** *vi* (infr wd) to be in labor. Gen. 35:16.

**treachery** *n* (arch mng) deceit. 2 Kin. 9:23.

**tread** *vt* (infr wd) to walk on or over. Deut. 33:29.

**tread (out)** (arch expr) (1) to thresh by pressing

with the feet. Deut. 25:4. (2) to press or trample grapes in wine-making. Jer. 25:30.

**treasures** *n pl* (arch mng) a treasury; place where treasures are kept. 1 Kin. 15:18.

**trespass** *n* (infr mng) (1) lit., to go across; in this sense, an offering made because of one's having "gone across" God's laws, i.e., sinned. Lev. 5:6. (2) a sin; a *transgression,* q.v. Num. 5:12.

**trespass** *vi* (infr wd) to transgress, offend. 1 Kin. 8:31.

**trespass** *vt* (theol) to sin against another (whether God or man). Luke 17:4.

**trial** *n* (infr mng) a testing or proving. 1 Pet. 4:12.

**tribulation** *n* (theol) originally an agricultural term signifying the dragging of a threshing sledge *(tribulum)* over grain to separate it from its husks. This rigorous purifying process has taken on the figurative meaning of affliction, persecution, trouble, etc., experienced by both believers and unbelievers. Deut. 4:30; John 16:33; 2 Thess. 1:6.

**tributary** *n* (infr mng) one who pays *tribute* (q.v.) to a conquerer. Deut. 20:11.

**tribute** *n* (infr mng) (1) a payment by one ruler or nation to another in acknowledgment of submission or the price of protection. 2 Kin. 23:33. (2) a freewill gift to God flowing out of prosperity. Deut. 16:10. (3) forced labor. Gen. 49:15. (4) a tax of individual assessment on persons or property for the support of a civil government. Rom. 13:6. (5) an assessment based on a census, i.e., a head tax. Num 31:39. *See Table of Coins.*

**tried** *pp* of *try,* q.v. Job 23:10.

**triest** arch form of *try,* q.v. 1 Chr. 29:17.

**trodden** *pp* of *tread,* q.v. Deut. 1:36.

**trode** *arch pt t* of *tread,* q.v. Judg. 9:27.

**trow** *vi* (arch wd) to suppose, believe. Luke 17:9.

**trump** *n* (infr mng) a trumpet. 1 Cor. 15:52.

**trust** *vb* (theol) to place confidence in God; to depend on God; to hope. See *faith.* 2 John 12.

**truth** *n* (theol) lit., *faithful,* q.v. Psa. 40:10.

**try** *vt* (infr mng) to test. Judg. 7:4.

**tumult** *n* (infr wd) a commotion or agitation of a multitude, usu. accompanied by an uproar and confusion. Mark 5:38.

**turn after** (arch expr) to follow. Lev. 20:6.

**turn again** (Hebraism) (1) to return. Judg. 3:19. (2) to bring back; "turn again our captivity," bring back our captives. Psa. 126:4.

**turn ... captivity** (Hebraism) to reverse the status of slaves; to restore prosperity. Deut. 30:3.

**turn in** *vi* (Hebraism) come in; enter. Judg. 4:18.

**turn thee behind me** (Hebraism) get behind me; join my followers. 2 Kin. 9:18.

**turn to the right hand or to the left** (Hebraism) to change direction from one's present course of action. Gen. 24:49.

**turtle** *n* (arch mng) a turtledove. Song 2:12.

**turtledove** *n* (fig wd) a term of endearment; beloved. Psa. 74:19.

**tutor** *n* (infr mng) a person charged with the instruction and guidance of another. Gal. 4:2.

**twain** *n* (arch use) two. 1 Sam. 18:21.

## U

**unadvisedly** *adv* (infr wd) without forethought; without due consideration. Psa. 106:33.

**unawares** *adv* (arch wd) (1) unintentionally; unexpectedly. Num. 35:11, 15. (2) secretly. Gal. 2:4.

**unbelief** *n* (theol) (1) lack of faith along with the notion of obstinacy. Heb. 3:12, 19. (2) disobedience; obstinate opposition to the divine will. Heb. 4:6, 11. See *faith.*

**uncertain** *adj* (arch use) indistinct. 1 Cor. 14:8.

**uncircumcised** *adj* (theol) pagan; not in covenant with Jehovah. 1 Sam. 17:26.

**unclean** *adj* (theol) (1) morally or spiritually impure. Num. 19:20. (2) unfit. Lev. 5:2. (3) evil, as applied to spirits, i.e., demons. Mark 1:23.

**uncomely** *adj* (infr wd) unlovely; unbecoming. 1 Cor. 12:23.

**uncomely** *adv* (arch use) in an unbecoming manner. 1 Cor. 7:36.

**uncorruptness** *n* (arch wd) soundness. Tit. 2:7.

**unction** *n* (infr wd) an anointing. 1 John 2:20.

**under his vine and under his fig tree** (Hebraism) a description of a man settled down peaceably on his own property. 1 Kin. 4:25.

**under the soles of his feet** (Hebraism) fig., subjugated or conquered (the enemy). 1 Kin. 5:3.

**undergird** *vt* (infr use) to strengthen a ship by passing ropes under and round her. Acts 27:17.

**undersetters** *n pl* (arch wd) supports. 1 Kin. 7:30.

**understanding** *adj* (arch mng) discerning; wise; intelligent. Deut. 1:13.

**understanding** *n* (arch mng) (1) success. Prov. 3:4. (2) heart. Eph. 1:18.

**undertake** *vi* (arch mng) to be surety for. Isa. 38:14.

**undressed** *adj* (infr mng) untended; unpruned. Lev. 25:5.

**unequal** *adj* (arch mng) unjust; not equal in the balance, thus symbolizing a lack of justice or fairness. Ezek. 18:25, 29.

**unfeigned** *adj* (infr wd) genuine. 1 Pet. 1:22.

**ungodly** *adj* (theol) wicked. 2 Chr. 19:2.

**ungodly** *adv* (arch use) in an ungodly manner. 2 Pet. 2:6.

**unholy** *adj* (theol) common. Heb. 10:29.

**unjust** *adj* (arch mng) dishonest. Luke 16:8.

**unlade** *vt* (arch wd) to unload. Acts 21:3.

**unloose** *vt* (arch wd) to untie; to loose. Mark 1:7.

**unperfect** *adj* (arch wd) lit., "rolled together" like a ball; thus, the embryo or fetus. (Cf. the second half of the verse which refers to the time before conception.) Psa. 139:16.

**unrighteousness** *n* (theol) deviation from God's norm of right. See *righteous*. 1 John 5:17.

**unsavoury** *adj* (arch mng) (1) without savor; by extension, without wisdom, foolish. 2 Sam. 22:27. (Cf. Matt. 5:13.) (2) tasteless. Job 6:6.

**untaken** *adj* (arch wd) not taken. 2 Cor. 3:14.

**untimely birth** (Hebraism) a spontaneous abortion; a miscarriage. Job 3:16.

**unto** *prep* (arch wd) (1) the equivalent of *to* (but does not introduce infinitives). Rom. 1:1. (2) with; upon. Ex. 29:17. (3) as far as. Gen. 14:6.

**untoward** *adj* (infr wd) obstinate; perverse; intractable. Acts 2:40.

**unwalled** *adj* (arch mng) unfenced; i.e., unfortified; rural. Deut. 3:5.

**unwittingly** *adv* (infr wd) unintentionally; unknowingly. Josh. 20:3, 5.

**unworthily** *adv* (theol) in an unworthy manner; i.e., a coming to the Lord's Supper without a due cognizance of and reliance upon the righteousness and substitutionary death of Christ as the only basis of one's acceptance before God. 1 Cor. 11:27.

**up** *adv* (arch mng) into battle. Judg. 4:10.

**up** *prep* (Hebraism) out. Obad. 6.

**up by** *imperative* (arch expr) get up by; march out at. Judg. 9:32.

**upbraid** *vt* (infr wd) to accuse or reprove reproachfully. Matt. 11:20.

**upholden** *pp* (arch tense) upheld. Prov. 20:28.

**upon** *prep* (arch mng) (1) with. Deut. 23:19. (2) in. Josh. 3:13. (3) through, by means of. Ex. 14:4, 17, 18.

**upright** *adj* (arch mng) erect; free. Lev. 26:13.

**upward** *adv* (arch use) forward in time; beyond. Hag. 2:15.

**Urim and Thummim** *prop n pl* (theol) these objects, which were kept in the high priest's breastplate, a pouch fastened to the ephod, were used by the priest to determine God's will (prob. with the possible answers of *yes, no,* and *no reply*). Ex. 28:30.

**use** *vi* (arch use) (1) to be accustomed. Ex. 21:36. (2) to practice; to make use of. Lev. 19:26.

**used** *vt* (arch mng) served in. 1 Tim. 3:13.

**usurer** *n* (infr wd) one who lends money, charging interest. Ex. 22:25. See *usury*.

**usurp** *vt* (infr wd) to seize or exercise authority or possession wrongfully. 1 Tim. 2:12.

**usury** *n* (arch mng) interest paid for money lent (not excessive as the modern use of the word, but a sin because any interest was forbidden in a private loan to a fellow Israelite). Ex. 22:25.

**usward,** see *-ward*. Psa. 40:5.

**utmost** *adj* (infr wd) outermost. Num. 22:36, 41.

**utter** *adj* (arch mng) outer. Ezek. 42:1.

**utter** *vt* (infr wd) to disclose; to make known. Lev. 5:1.

**uttermost** *adj* (infr wd) (1) extreme; utmost; farthest; outermost. Josh. 15:5. (2) last. Matt. 5:26.

## V

**vagabond** *adj* (infr wd) fugitive, wandering. Acts 19:13.

**vagabond** *n* (infr wd) a fugitive; an exile. Gen. 4:12.

**vail** *n* (1) (arch sp) a veil. Num. 18:7. (2) (mistransl) a cloak. Ruth 3:15.

**vain** *adj* (infr mng) worthless; unprofitable; empty. Ex. 5:9.

**vain, in** (infr expr) purposelessly; accomplishing nothing. Gal. 2:21.

**vain glory** *n* (infr wd) vainglory; excessive or ostentatious pride. Gal. 5:26.

**vale** *n* (infr wd) a valley. Gen. 14:8.

**valiant** *adj* (infr wd) (1) having virtue, valor, strength. 1 Sam. 14:52. (2) "valiantest," exhibiting the above virtues to a superlative degree. Judg. 21:10.

**valiantly, do** (arch expr) to behave gallantly or bravely. Num. 24:18.

**vanities, lying** (arch expr) falsehoods. Psa. 31:6.

**vanity** *n* (infr mng) (1) *n pl* empty or foolish ways. 1 Kin. 16:13. (2) foolishness. Psa. 12:2. (3) *n pl* idols; false deities devoid of power and virtue. Deut. 32:21.

**variance** *n* (infr wd) dissension; discord; a quarrel; dispute. Matt. 10:35.

**vaunt oneself** (arch expr) to boast. Judg. 7:2.

**vehement** *adj* (infr mng) violent. Song 8:6.

**vehemently** *adv* (infr wd) violently. Luke 6:49.

**venison** *n* (arch mng) flesh of beasts taken in hunting. Gen. 25:28.

**venture, at a** (arch expr) at hazard; at random. 1 Kin. 22:34.

**verily** *adv* (arch wd) (1) truly. Mark 13:30. (2) double use: (a) introduces a solemn statement and (b) means *most assuredly;* a translation of the Hebrew word, *amen*, q.v. John 10:1, 7.

**verity** *n* (infr wd) truth. Psa. 111:7.

**very** *adj* (infr mng) true. Gen. 27:21.

**vessel** *n* (infr wd) a hollow utensil or container such as a bowl, pitcher, jar, cup, pot, or basket. Ex. 30:27.

**vesture** *n* (infr wd) a covering garment; clothing, apparel. Gen. 41:42.

**vex** *vt* (infr wd) (1) to bring trouble, distress, or agitation to; to harass or torment. Judg. 2:18. (2) "vexed," distressed. 2 Sam. 13:2.

**vexation** *n* (infr wd) trouble. 2 Chr. 15:5.

**vial** *n* (infr wd) a small container for liquids; bottle; bowl. 1 Sam. 10:1.

**victuals** *n pl* (infr wd) food; supplies of food. Gen. 14:11.

**vile** *adj* (infr mng) (1) worthless. Jer. 29:17. (2) filthy; dirty. Jas. 2:2.

**vile person** (arch expr) a fool. Isa. 32:5.

**vine tree** *n* (arch wd) a grapevine. Num. 6:4.

**viol** *n* (infr wd) a kind of guitar, usually with six strings. Isa. 5:12.

**violence** *n* (theol) the use or application of

strength or force. Acts 5:26. In Matt. 11:12, "the kingdom of heaven *suffereth violence*" signifies that the heavenly kingdom is to be taken *by storm*, and a share in it may be obtained only by ardent zeal and intense exertion.

**violent, the** *n pl* (theol) those who obtain a share in the kingdom of heaven by great eagerness and determined, zealous effort. Matt. 11:12.

**viper** *n* (infr wd) a venomous snake. Matt. 23:33.

**virtue** *n* (infr mng) might; efficacy. Mark 5:30.

**visage** *n* (infr wd) the face; countenance. Dan. 3:19.

**visit** *vt* (1) (infr mng) to help. Gen. 50:25. (2) (arch mng) to bring down. Ex. 20:5. (3) (arch mng) to chastise. Psa. 89:32. (4) (arch mng) to judge. Isa. 26:14.

**visitation** *n* (infr mng) God's dealing in wrath and judgment. Jer. 8:12.

**vocation** *n* (infr mng) calling. Eph. 4:1.

**voice** *n* (infr mng) tone of voice. Gal. 4:20.

**void** *adj* (infr wd) (1) empty. Gen. 1:2. (2) null or invalid. Num. 30:12. (3) "void of," lacking. Prov. 11:12.

**vow** *n* (theol) a voluntary obligation or promise made to, or before, God. Gen. 28:20; Eccl. 5:4, 5.

**vow** *vt* (theol) to promise to or before God. Num. 6:2.

## W

**wait** *n* (arch mng) an ambush. Jer. 9:8.

**wait on** (infr expr) (1) to serve or take care of. Num. 3:10. (2) to patiently and hopefully expect. Psa. 145:15. (3) to be at one's service or disposal. Mark 3:9.

**wait upon their business** (arch expr) tend their responsibility or office. 2 Chr. 13:10.

**waited for** (arch mng) destined for. Job 15:22.

**walked** *vi* (arch mng) lived; continued. 2 Sam. 7:6.

**want** *n* (infr mng) lack. Psa. 34:9.

**want** *vi* (infr mng) to lack; to be in want. Psa. 23:1.

**wantonness** *n* (infr wd) licentiousness; riotous living. Rom. 13:13.

**war** *n* (arch mng) the principles of warfare. Judg. 3:2.

**war** *vi* (arch use) serves as a soldier. 2 Tim. 2:4.

**-ward** *adv* (arch use) in the phrases (1) usward. Psa. 40:5; Eph. 1:19. (2) to thee-ward. 1 Sam. 19:4. (3) you-ward. 2 Cor. 13:3; Eph. 3:2. (4) to the (mercy) seat-ward. Ex. 37:9. i.e., toward us, toward you, etc.

**ward** *n* (infr mng) (1) guard; prison. Gen. 40:3. (2) protection, confinement. 2 Sam. 20:3. (3) office, duty. 1 Chr. 25:8. (4) *watch*, q.v. Neh. 12:24.

**ware** *adj* (infr wd) aware. Acts 14:6.

**ware** *n* (infr wd) merchandise. Neh. 10:31.

**ware** *vt* (arch tense) *pt t* of *wear*: wore. Luke 8:27.

**warfare, who goeth a . . . at his own charges** (arch expr) who serves as a soldier at his own expense. 1 Cor. 9:7.

**warp and woof** (infr wd) the lengthwise and crosswise yarns (respectively) that make up woven fabric. Lev. 13:48.

**was taken** (arch expr) was chosen or indicated, i.e., by lot (see *cast lots*). Josh. 7:16.

**washpot** *n* (arch wd) wash-tub; a vessel for washing in. Psa. 60:8.

**waste** *n* (arch mng) a wasted, devastated place. Ezek. 33:27.

**waste** *vb* (arch mng) (1) *vi* to diminish; to be used up. 1 Kin. 17:14, 16. (2) *vt* "to make or lay waste," to consume; to devastate. Num. 21:30. (3) *vi* to perish. Num. 14:33.

**wasteness,** see *waste*. Zeph. 1:15.

**watch** *n* (infr mng) (1) a portion of the night, during which the same guard was on duty. In the O.T. period, the Israelites divided the night into three watches: first watch (Lam. 2:19); middle watch (Judg. 7:19); morning watch (Ex. 14:24). In the N.T. period, Roman reckoning was used, which divided the approximately twelve hours of night into four watches: first watch (not referred to in the N.T.); second watch (Luke 12:38); third watch (Luke 12:38); fourth watch (Matt. 14;25; Mark 6:48). (2) a body of soldiers on guard. Judg. 7:19; Matt. 27:65. (3) an observance; a service. Neh. 12:9.

**watching** *n* (arch mng) wakefulness. 2 Cor. 6:5.

**wateredst it with thy foot** (arch custom) a treadmill, i.e., a mill worked by persons treading on steps on the periphery of a wide wheel. Deut. 11:10.

**wave** *adj* (theol) shaken or vibrated (an offering). Lev. 23:17.

**wave** *vt* (theol) to shake or vibrate to and fro. Lev. 23:11, 20.

**wax** *vi* (infr mng) (1) to become. Gen. 18:12. (2) to grow. Ex. 22:24.

**wax wanton against** (arch expr) to feel and follow the impulses of sexual desire to the forsaking of Christ. 1 Tim. 5:11.

**way** *n* (infr mng) a road, street, path, or highway. Deut. 22:4; Matt. 7:14.

**wayfaring** *adj* (infr wd) traveling, esp. by foot. Judg. 19:17.

**waymark** *n* (arch wd) a guidepost. Jer. 31:21.

**wealth** *n* (arch mng) the good; well-being; welfare. Esth. 10:3.

**weigh** *vt* (infr mng) to judge. 1 Sam. 2:3.

**well** *adv* (arch use) for good. Gal. 4:17.

**well favoured** (Hebraism) of pleasing appearance; handsome. Dan. 1:4.

**well nigh** (infr expr) almost; very nearly. Psa. 73:2.

**well stricken in years (or age)** (arch expr) advanced in years or age; aged. Gen. 18:11; Luke 1:7.

**wellspring** *n* (infr wd) a fountain; fountainhead. Prov. 16:22.

**wen** *n* (infr wd) a cyst filled with fatty material. Lev. 22:22.

**wench** *n* (infr wd) a household female slave. 2 Sam. 17:17.

**went against** (arch expr) warred against; attacked. Judg. 1:10.

**went forward** (arch expr) prospered; made progress. Gen. 26:13.

**went unto** (arch expr) had sexual intercourse. Isa. 8:3.

**went up** (arch expr) withdrew. 2 Sam. 20:2.

**were pertaining unto** (arch expr) belonged to. Josh. 13:31.

**were possessed** (arch use) had taken possession. Josh. 22:9.

**what** *interrogative* (arch use) why? 2 Kin. 6:33; Luke 22:71.

**what time** (Hebraism) when. Psa. 56:3.

**whatsoever** *adj* (infr wd) whatever. Phil. 4:8.

**whatsoever** *pron* (infr wd) whatever. Job 41:11.

**whelp** *n* (infr wd) one of the young of certain animals; a cub. 2 Sam. 17:8.

**whence** *adv* (infr wd) (1) from what or which place (used both interrogatively and relatively). Jonah 1:8. (2) from whom; from what author or giver. Matt. 21:25. (3) from what or which source, origin, or cause (whether person, event, etc.). Matt. 13:27.

**whereas** *conj* (infr wd) in view of the fact that; since. Isa. 37:21.

**wherefore** *adv* (infr wd) why. Josh. 7:10.

**wherefore, then, serveth the law?** (arch expr) lit., why, then, the law? i.e., what was the reason for the giving of the law? Gal. 3:19.

**whereon** *adv* (infr wd) on what. 2 Chr. 32:10.

**wherewith** (1) *adv* (arch use) with what. Matt. 5:13. (2) *pron* (infr wd) that which or by which. Psa. 119:42.

**whet** *vt* (infr wd) to sharpen. Psa. 7:12.

**whether** *pron* (arch mng) which (of two). Eccl. 11:6.

**whiles** *conj* (arch wd) while. Matt. 5:25.

**whit** *n* (infr wd) the smallest part imaginable; thus: (1) "every whit," wholly. 1 Sam. 3:18; John 7:23. (2) "not a whit," not at all. 2 Cor. 11:5.

**white** *vt* (arch use) to whiten. Mark 9:3.

**whited** *pp* (arch wd) whitened, i.e., whitewashed. Matt. 23:27.

**whither** (infr wd) (1) *conj* to which place. Deut. 11:29. (2) *adv* where. Judg. 19:17.

**whithersoever** *adv* (arch wd) wherever. Luke 9:57.

**whithersoever** *conj* (infr wd) to whatever place; wherever. 1 Sam. 14:47.

**whole** *adj* (infr mng) (1) healed; healthy; well. Josh. 5:8; Matt. 9:12. (2) uncut. Deut. 27:6.

**wholesome** *adj* (infr mng) promoting health or well-being of mind or spirit; health-giving; salutary. Prov. 15:4.

**whore** *n* (infr wd) a prostitute; a harlot. Deut. 22:21.

**whoredom** *n* (infr wd) (1) prostitution. Gen. 38:24. (2) faithless, unworthy, or idolatrous practices or pursuits. Num. 14:33.

**whoremonger** *n* (arch wd) a man who consorts with prostitutes; one given over to lechery. Heb. 13:4.

**whoring,** see *a whoring*.

**whosoever** *pron* (infr wd) lit., everyone who. John 3:16; 12:46.

**wickedness** *n* (theol) lit., the wicked one. 1 John 5:19.

**wiles** *n pl* (infr wd) tricks; deceitful stratagems. Num. 25:18; Eph. 6:11.

**will** *vt* (infr use) to desire; to wish; to intend. Mark 6:25.

**will worship** *n* (arch expr) willing worship; a worship of one's own choosing. Col. 2:23.

**willing** *pres part* (theol) a people of great willingness and devotion. In Hebrew, this noun (lit., "willingnesses") is abstract and plural to insure great emphasis on the meaning, i.e., they are not merely willing, but *willingness itself:* not only drawn, but made willing to follow. Psa. 110:3.

**wilt** *vb* (arch wd) second person singular of to *will,* q.v., or of the auxiliary *vb* for the future tense. Mark 14:12; Luke 4:7.

**wimple** *n* (infr wd) a cloth covering worn over the head and around the neck and chin of women; a shawl. Isa. 3:22.

**wind** *n* (arch mng) breath. Job 7:7.

**winebibber** *n* (infr wd) one who drinks wine to excess. Matt. 11:19.

**winefat** *n* (arch sp) a wine vat or container. Mark 12:1.

**wink at** (infr expr) to overlook; to not punish. Acts 17:30.

**wise** *n* (infr mng) (1) "on this wise," in this guise, manner, way. Matt. 1:18. (2) "in any wise," surely. Lev. 19:17. (3) "in no wise," in no way; by no means. Lev. 7:24.

**wist** *arch pt t* of *know,* q.v. Ex. 16:15.

**wit** *n* (infr mng) knowledge; understanding. Psa. 107:27.

**wit** *vt* (arch wd) (1) to know, learn. Gen. 24:21. (2) "we do you to wit," we cause you to know. 2 Cor. 8:1.

**witch** *n* (theol) lit., one who whispers a spell; one who enchants or practices magic. Deut. 18:10.

**witchcraft** *n* (theol) (1) divination, oracle by means of satanic spirits. 1 Sam. 15:23. (2) whispered spells, see *enchantment*. 2 Chr. 33:6. (3) magic, including use of drugs. Gal. 5:20.

**with** *n* (arch wd) a pliant twig used to wrap around like a band. Judg. 16:7.

**with one accord** (arch expr) united in purpose. Josh. 9:2.

**with the manner** (arch expr) in the act. Num. 5:13.

**withal** *adv* (arch mng) (1) besides; also. 1 Kin. 19:1; Acts 25:27. (2) with. Lev. 11:21. (3) therewith. Ex. 37:16.

**withdrew the shoulder** (Hebraism) showed stubbornness. Neh. 9:29.

**withholden** *arch pp* of *withhold*. Jer. 3:3.

**within** *adv* (arch use) inside. John 20:26.

**without** (infr mng) (1) *adv* outside. Gen. 9:22. (2) *prep* beyond. 2 Cor. 10:13. (3) *prep* apart from; without the participation or cooperation of. John 1:3; Rom. 3:21, 28; 4:6.

**without my fault** (Hebraism) without fault on my part. Psa. 59:4.

**without number/weight** (Hebraism) vast; innumerable. Judg. 7:12.

**without thee** (arch expr) without your permission. Gen. 41:44.

**withs** *n pl* (arch wd) small ropes; cords. Judg. 16:7, 9.

**withstand** *vb* (infr wd) to oppose, stand against, or resist. Num. 22:32.

**witness** *n* (infr use) (1) evidence; testimony. Matt. 26:59. (2) testimony concerning God's presence. Acts 7:44. (3) (theol) a person who gives testimony, who affirms that he has seen, heard, or experienced something, or has been taught by divine revelation or inspiration. Heb. 10:15.

**wittingly** *adv* (infr wd) deliberately; knowingly. Gen. 48:14.

**witty** *adj* (infr mng) skillful; clever. Prov. 8:12.

**wizard** *n* (theol) lit., one with knowledge (i.e., of the occult); a conjurer, one who summons evil spirits. Deut. 18:11.

**woe worth the day!** (Hebraism) alas for the day; evil be to the day. Ezek. 30:2.

**Woman** *n* (theol) derived from the Hebrew word *ishah*, meaning *female person*. *Ishah* is the feminine form of the noun *ish* (*male person*), which underscores the fact that God took *Woman* out of *Man*, and not vice versa. The Bible consistently sets forth the doctrine that women (though not inferior) are to be subordinated to men on account of God's order of creation and the purpose for which God made the female of the species (Gen. 2:18-25). Gen. 2:23. See *Man*.

**wonder** *n* (infr mng) miracle. Ex. 4:21.

**wonder** *vi* (theol) to be moved with astonishment; to marvel. Luke 8:25.

**wondered after** (arch expr) to be amazed, astonished, thrown into wonderment at; to be astounded at. Rev. 13:3.

**wonderful** *adj* (infr mng) astonishing; exciting wonder. Deut. 28:59.

**wont** *adj* (infr wd) accustomed. 1 Sam. 30:31.

**wood** *n* (infr mng) forest. Deut. 19:5.

**woof,** see *warp and woof*.

**word** *n* (infr mng) (1) God's promise; the expressed mind and will of God. 1 Sam. 1:23. (2) prophecy, q.v. 1 Sam. 3:19.

**work** *n* (Hebraism) concern. Prov. 16:11.

**work out** (arch expr) continue to fulfill, accomplish, complete your salvation. Phil. 2:12.

**worketh** *vt* (arch mng) brings about; results in. Jas. 1:3.

**world** *n* (theol) (1) (from Greek word *aion*) *age*; the present period of time that precedes eternity. Matt. 13:22, 39; 28:20; Rom. 12:2; Heb. 1:2. (2) (from Greek word *kosmos*) this term, whose root meaning is *order*, has important, differing significations which must be decided by context: (a) the universe as a whole. Acts 17:24. (b) the earth. John 13:1; Eph. 1:4. (c) the world-system. John 12:31. (d) the whole human race. Rom. 3:19. (e) humanity *minus* believers. John 15:18; Rom. 3:6. (f) Gentiles in contrast to Jews. Rom. 11:12. (g) believers only. John 1:29; 3:16, 17; 6:33; 12:47; 1 Cor. 4:9; 2 Cor. 5:19.

**worse liking** (arch expr) less plump, i.e., in worse condition; sadder. Dan. 1:10.

**worship** *n* (theol) honor; reverence. Luke 14:10.

**worthies** *n pl* (infr wd) valiant men. Nah. 2:5.

**worthy** *adj* (infr mng) deserving. Deut. 25:2.

**worthy** *n* (infr use) a worthy person; a man of renown; a hero. Nah. 2:5.

**wot** *pres tense* 1st and 3rd person singular of *wit*. (1) to know. Gen. 21:26. (2) improperly used with *ye* (instead of *wit*). Gen. 44:15. (3) improperly used with *we* (instead of *wit*). Ex. 32:1. (4) "wotteth," used for *wot* (with *he*). Gen. 39:8.

**would** *vb* (arch mng) (1) *pt t* of *will*: willed; wished; desired. Ex. 16:3. (2) "would dwell," continued to inhabit. Judg. 1:27. (3) "wouldest," desire. 1 Kin. 1:16.

**wound** *vt* (arch use) *pt t* of *wind*: to wrap up or bind up, as in the ancient burial custom of binding the bodies of the dead with linen cloths and bandages. John 19:40.

**wrap it up** (Hebraism) lit., to fold up or weave together wickedness to make it firm; a collusion between the judge and the rich. Mic. 7:3.

**wrath** *n* (theol) (1) violent anger or fierce indignation over a grievance that demands vengeance, punishment, or revenge. Gen. 49:7; Deut. 9:7; Eph. 4:26. (2) divine chastisement, retribution, punishment, or judgment meted out due to God's holy anger against sin. Num. 18:5.

**wreath** *n* (arch mng) a netted ornament of a pillar. 2 Chr. 4:12.

**wreathed** *pp* (arch mng) knit together. Lam. 1:14.

**wreathen** *adj* (arch wd) twisted; braided; netted. Ex. 28:14.

**wrest** *vt* (infr wd) to twist; to torture; to force Scripture to say what one wants it to say (difficult things are chosen because easier teachings cannot so readily be forced and twisted). 2 Pet. 3:16.

**wroth** *adj* (infr wd) highly incensed; angry. Gen. 4:5.

**wrought** *vb* (arch mng) (1) *pt t* (or *pp* with *have*) of *work*: worked, did, or (have) done. Gen. 34:7; Matt. 20:12. (2) raged. Jonah 1:11.

**wrought with his works** (arch expr) co-worked;

put forth power together to produce works. Jas. 2:22.

## Y

**yea** *adv* (arch wd) yes; a positive or affirmative answer. Matt. 5:37.

**yearn upon** (arch expr) to feel emotion toward; to be moved with grief or sadness for. Gen. 43:30.

**yoke of iron** (metaphor) severe oppression or bondage. Deut. 28:48.

**yokefellow** *n* (infr wd) a close companion; a comrade, partner. Phil. 4:3. (Cf. 2 Cor. 6:14).

## Z

**Zelotes** *prop n pl* (theol) the Zealot, a surname of Simon, one of the apostles. He, perhaps, had been a member of a Jewish sect called *the Zealots*, which had existed since the time of the Maccabees, adhered rigorously to the law of Moses and sought, through violence at times, to prevent others from breaking it. Luke 6:15; Acts 1:13.

# TABLES OF WEIGHTS AND MEASURES

## TABLE OF LINEAR MEASURES

| KJV – O.T. | HEBREW TERM | RATIO | U.S. EQUIV. |
|---|---|---|---|
| reed | qaneh | 6 cubits | 8 ft. 9 in. |
| reed (in Ezekiel) | qaneh | 6 cubits | 10 ft. 3 in. |
| cubit | ammâ | 6 handbreadths | 17 ft. 5 in. |
| cubit (in Ezekiel) | ammâ | 7 handbreadths | 20 ft. 5 in. |
| span | zereth | 1/2 cubit | 9 in. |
| handbreadth | tephach | 1/6 cubit | 3 in. |
| finger | 'estba' | 1/24 cubit | 3/4 in. |
| **KJV – N.T.** | **GREEK TERM** | **RATIO** | **U.S. EQUIV.** |
| mile | milion | Roman mile (1,000 paces) | 4,854 ft. |
| furlong | stadion | 1/8 Roman mile | 607 ft. |
| fathom | orguia | 4 cubits | 6 ft. |
| cubit | pechys | | 18 in. |

## TABLE OF DRY AND LIQUID MEASURES

| KJV – O.T. | HEBREW TERM | RATIO | U.S. EQUIV. |
|---|---|---|---|
| homer | homer | 10 ephahs or 10 baths | 6.25 bu. or 58 gal. |
| ephah (dry) | ephah | 1/10 homer | 0.625 bu. or 5.8 gal. |
| bath (liquid) | bath | 1/10 homer | 5.8 gal. or 0.625 bu. |
| hin (liquid) | hin | 1/6 bath | 1 gal. |
| omer (dry) | omer | 1/10 ephah | 2 qt. |
| cab (dry and liquid) | qab | 1/18 ephah | 2.3 pt. |
| log (dry) | log | 1/72 bath | 0.64 pt. |
| **KJV – N.T.** | **GREEK TERM** | **RATIO** | **U.S. EQUIV.** |
| measure (dry) | koros | | 11-17 bu. |
| measure (liquid) | batos | 72 sextarii | 10.4 gal. |
| firkin (liquid) | metretes | | 9 gal. |
| measure (dry) | saton | 16 sextarii | 12 qt. |
| bushel (dry) | modios | 24 sextarii | 1 peck |
| measure (dry) | choinix | 2 sextarii | 1 qt. |
| pot (liquid) | xestes | 1 sextarius | 1 qt. |

## TABLE OF WEIGHTS

| KJV – O.T. | HEBREW TERM | RATIO | U.S. EQUIV. |
|---|---|---|---|
| talent | kikkar | 3,000 shekels | 75 lb. |
| pound | maneh | 50 shekels | 1.25 lb. |
| shekel | shekel | | 0.4 oz. |
| bekah | bekah | 1/2 shekel | 0.20 oz. |
| gerah | gerah | 1/20 shekel | 0.02 oz. |
| **KJV – N.T.** | **GREEK TERM** | **RATIO** | **U.S. EQUIV.** |
| talent | talanton | | 58-80 lb. |
| pound | litra | | 12 oz. |

## TABLE OF COINS (I)

Values of the coins listed below have been expressed in U.S. equivalents based upon the prices of gold and silver on July 1, 1977: price of gold – $142.55 per troy oz.; price of silver – $4.43 per troy oz.

| KJV – O.T. | U.S. EQUIV. SILVER VALUE | U.S. EQUIV. GOLD VALUE | RATIO |
|---|---|---|---|
| bekah | $ 1.13 | | 1/2 silver shekel |
| dram | | $ 38.49 | 1 daric |
| gerah | $ .1035 | | 1/20 silver shekel |
| pound (maneh) | $ 103.60 | $ 3,750.78 | 1 mina |
| shekel | $ 2.07 | $ 74.98 | |
| talent (silver) | $ 6,215.73 | | |
| talent (gold) | | $ 225,110.11 | |

## TABLE OF COINS (II)

| KJV – N.T. | JEWISH | GREEK | ROMAN | U.S. EQUIV. | RATIO |
|---|---|---|---|---|---|
| mite | lepton | | 1/2 quadrans | $ .0043 | 1/128 denarius |
| | | | 1 quadrans | $ .0086 | 1/64 denarius |
| farthing | | | 1 assarion | $ .034 | 1/16 denarius |
| penny | | 1 drachma | 1 denarius | $ .55 | 1/100 mina |
| tribute | 1/2 shekel | 1 didrachma | 2 denarii | $ 1.10 | 1/50 mina |
| piece of money | 1 shekel | 1 stater | 4 denarii | $ 2.20 | 1 tetradrachma |
| piece of silver | | 25 drachmai | 1 aureus | $ 13.75 | 1/4 mina |
| pound | | 1 mina | 100 denarii | $ 55.00 | 1/60 silver talent |
| talent (silver) | | 1 talent (silver) | 240 aurei | $ 3,322.50 | |
| talent (gold) | | 1 talent (gold) | | $ 106,912.50 | |

# BIBLICAL CHRONOLOGY

Biblical chronology brings before us two marvels. The first is that there exists in the Scriptures a complete, self-contained chronology from the first Adam to the second. This is all the more wonderful when the sober history of the Bible is compared with the myths, fables, and incredibility that characterize the secular histories of that period. Though the Biblical chronology is not without some difficulties (the solutions to which have yet to be discovered), its simplicity and clarity are astounding. In contrast to the confusion and ignorance that characterize ancient secular chronologies, the difficulties of the Biblical chronology appear very small indeed.

The chronology of the Bible reveals a second marvel. The ticking off of the years, as viewed in the light of prophetic promises, raises our wondering expectations. Where do these patient footsteps of time lead? The least acquaintance with the Bible tells us that they tread a firm and discernible course to a baptismal service in the Jordan, a rugged Cross on Golgotha, an empty garden tomb, and a king reigning in glory.

The Bible *alone* is sufficient to supply all necessary data for a Biblical chronology. Acceptance of extra-Biblical data in the construction of a Biblical chronology leads to an erroneous chronology and misinterpretation of clear Scriptural passages. The rightness of this principle should be self-evident. If the Bible is at all intended to supply us with a chronology—and the numerous and extensive chronological facts scattered throughout its pages compel us to admit this—then this chronology will be complete in itself without the need of secular information to complete it. Just as in matters of faith and practice the Bible alone is sufficient, so it is in the matter of its own chronology.

Biblical chronology may be compared to a river the course of which is basically discernible, but which at times plunges into subterranean passages, becoming visible only when it later emerges. These subterranean passages in Biblical chronology have been charted by the careful efforts of many past chronologists.

1. Genesis 5 gives a clear and unmistakable chronology of 1,656 years from the creation of Adam to the 600th year of Noah, the year of the flood.

2. Then the first break in the chronology occurs: the exact age of Noah at the birth of Shem is not given. This break is mended by information given in Genesis 11:10. Since Shem was 100 two years after the flood, Noah was 502 when Shem was born.

3. Genesis 11, in the same manner as Genesis 5, brings the chronology intact to the birth of Terah, the father of Abram, in the year 2168 B.C.

4. Again there is a break: the exact age of Terah at the birth of Abram is not given. This break is mended by information in Genesis 11:32-12:4. Since Terah was 205 when he died

and the narrative's continuity indicates that Abram left Haran the year of Terah's death when he was 75, Terah was 130 at the birth of Abram.

5. Information given throughout Genesis 12-50 supplies chronological data down to the death of Joseph in the year 1677 B.C.

6. Between the death of Joseph and the birth of Moses there is another break in the chronology. This period is discovered through careful study of Exodus 12:40, 41, and Galatians 3:17, which state that the period of Israel's sojourning was 430 years. Paul identifies the commencement of this period with the giving of the Abrahamic covenant. Thus it is clear that the sojourning spoken of includes the sojourning of Abram and Sarai. This period ends with the Exodus. This fact, together with the fact that Moses was eighty years old at that time, gives us the year of Moses' birth—1632 B.C.

7. The books of Exodus and Deuteronomy detail the events of Israel's forty years in the wilderness, concluding with their entrance into the land of Canaan in 1493 B.C.

8. The next break in the chronology is between the year Joshua led Israel into the land and the first year of Israel's servitude to Cushan-Rishathaim. This break is mended by Jephthah's statement in Judges 11:26 that Israel had possessed Heshbon 300 years. Since Heshbon was taken the year before Israel entered the land, this supplies the needed information to carry the chronology past this break.

9. The O.T. books from Judges through II Chronicles, by giving the lengths of the rules of Israel's judges and kings, carry the chronology forward to the demise of the last king of Judah. This part of the chronology is the most intricate and difficult. One statement that has led to much confusion is the one that Solomon began to build the temple 480 years after the children of Israel came out of Egypt (I Kings 6:1). This is just 114 years short of the sum of the Biblical chronology for that period. Interestingly enough, 114 years is exactly the length of the six servitudes and of the usurpation of Abimelech during the period of the Judges. Therefore, the best solution is that the pious historian purposely omitted the 114 years of these seven periods from his reckoning of 480 years as years during which the twelve tribes were unworthy of the name *Israel,* the Prince of God.

10. The final stage of O.T. chronology is given prophetically rather than historically. It consists of two eras: the seventy years of captivity prophesied by Jeremiah (Jer. 25:11, 12) and the Seventy Weeks prophesied by Daniel (Dan. 9:24-27). The Babylonian Captivity of the Jews began in the third year of Jehoiakim (Dan. 1:1), which was 526 B.C. The decree of Cyrus in 457 B.C. ended the seventy years of captivity and also began the seventy "weeks of years" of Daniel. These "weeks of years" are periods of seven years each, since the Hebrew word for "week" comes from the word for "seven." Thus the Seventy Weeks equal 490 years. The seventieth week began in A.D. 26 with the baptism of the Messiah and ended in 33 with the stoning of Stephen. In the middle of this week—during the year 30—the Messiah was crucified.

For more details on this chronology, as well as for the exegetical evidence on which it is based, see Martin Anstey's *Chronology of the Old Testament* and Philip Mauro's *The Wonders of Bible Chronology.* For information on the way in which the chronology appears in the margin of this study Bible, see the footnote to the word *time* in Revelation 10:6.

# GEOGRAPHICAL GAZETTEER

This gazetteer is intended to describe the principal geographical features of Palestine and the ancient world and to indicate their location on the accompanying color maps. Each reference gives a key consisting of a letter and number in combination, followed by the number of the map on which the name appears. For example, *Adramyttium* appears at the key reference B1 on map 15 and at key reference D2 on map 17.

In addition to the standard and readily recognized abbreviations, the following are used:

*ca.*—*circa* (Latin for "around, about, approximately")
J.—*jebel* (Arabic for "mount")
Kh.—*khirbet* (Arabic for "ruin, mound")
mod.—modern
mt(s).—mount, mountain(s)
N (S, E, W, NE, NW, etc.)—north(ern)
N.T.—New Testament
O.T.—Old Testament
poss.—possibly
prob.—probably
*q.v.*—*quod* or *quae vide* (Latin for "which see")
R.—river
W.—*wadi* (Arabic for "channel of a watercourse that is dry except in the rainy season")

## A

**Abana R.** River of Damascus (II Kings 5:12). It has its source 19 miles NW of Damascus and flows through the city. Prob. mod. *Nahr Barada*. D1—1

**Abdon.** Town in the territory of Asher, 10 miles NE of Acre (Josh. 21:30; I Chron. 6:74). Mod. *Kh. 'Abde*.

**Abel.** Fortified town in the territory of Naphtali where Sheba, a rebel against David, was killed (II Sam. 20:15). Prob. mod. *Tell Abil*, 12 miles N of Lake Hula, opposite Dan. B3—4

**Abela-Bethmaacha.** *See* Abel

**Abel-beth-maachah.** C1—5. *See* Abel

**Abel-maim.** *See* Abel

**Abel-meholah.** City in the territory of Manasseh. It was W of the Jordan, about half way between the Sea of Galilee and the Dead Sea (Judg. 7:22; I Kings 4:12). C3—5

**Abel-mehula.** *See* Abel-meholah

**Abel-sattim.** *See* Abel-shittim

**Abel-shittim.** Settlement in Moab occupied by the Israelites before the capture of Jericho (Num. 33:49). It was also called Shittim (Num. 25:1; Josh. 2:1; 3:1). Poss. mod. *Tell Kefrein*, E of Jericho.

**Abila** (in Abilene). Capital of Abilene (Luke 3:1), on the Barada R. *ca.* 20 miles NW of Damascus. D1—11

**Abila** (in Batanea). City of the Decapolis (*q.v.*), S of the Yarmuk R., *ca.* 17 miles E of the S tip of the Sea of Galilee. Mod. *Tell Abil*. D3—11

**Abilene.** Tetrarchy in the region of the Anti-Lebanon Mts. (Luke 3:1). Its capital was Abila (*q.v.*). D1—11; B-C4—13

**Abydos** (in Asia Minor). Town in Phrygia, on the Asiatic side of the Hellespont, opposite Sestos.

**Abydos** (in Egypt). City dedicated to Osiris, Egyptian god of the underworld. *Ca.* 50 miles NW of Thebes. C6—2

**Accad.** *See* Akkad

**Accaron.** *See* Ekron

**Acchad.** *See* Akkad

**Accho.** *See* Acco

**Acco** (Ptolemais). City of Asher (Judg. 1:31) on a small promontory of the Palestinian coast about 25 miles S of Tyre, 8 miles N of Mt. Carmel (mod. *Haifa*) across the Bay of Acco. N.T. *Ptolemais*, medieval *Acre*. B2—1, 5; D2—3; B3—4; B1—19

**Aceldama** (Field of Blood). Parcel of ground known as the potter's field, traditionally located on the S side of the Hinnom Valley, Jerusalem.

**Achad.** *See* Akkad

**Achaia.** Originally a state of Greece located in the N Peloponnesus. Under the Romans, Achaia included the whole of the Peloponnesus with continental Greece S of Illyricum, Epirus, and Thessaly. Corinth was its capital (Acts 18:27; I Cor. 16:15; II Cor. 1:1). D3—12; A2—15, 16; C2—17; D3—18

**Achazib.** *See* Achzib

**Achmetha.** *See* Ecbatana

**Achsaph.** *See* Achshaph

**Achshaph.** Canaanite royal city (Josh. 11:1) captured by Joshua (Josh. 12:20), located in the territory of Asher *ca.* 8 miles SE of Acco. Poss. mod. *et-Tell*.

**Achzib.** Town on the seacoast of Asher (Josh. 19:29), 8.5 miles N of Acco, from which the Canaanites were not expelled (Judg. 1:31). It was known to the Greeks and Romans as *Ecdippa*. Poss. mod. *ez-Zib*.

**Acrabathane.** Region SW of the Dead Sea in the vicinity of the Ascent of Akrabim (*q.v.*). Acrabathane was the site of a victory of Judas the Maccabee over the Idumeans.

**Acrabbim, Ascent of.** *See* Akrabbim, Ascent of

**Acre.** *See* Acco

**Acron.** *See* Ekron

**Actium.** Promontory in NW Acarnania, Greece. It was the site of the victory of the forces of Octavian (Augustus) over Antony and Cleopatra (31 B.C.).

**Adad.** *See* Hadid

**Adada(h).** *See* Aroer (in Judah)

**Adam.** City on the E bank of the Jordan, mod. *Tell ed-Damieh*, less than a mile below the mouth of the Jabbok and 18 miles N of Jericho. Here the waters were held back for the miraculous crossing of the Israelites (Josh. 3:16).

**Adamah.** *See* Adam

**Adana.** City on the Sarus (mod. *Seyhan*) R. in S Turkey.

**Adarsa.** *See* Adasa

**Adasa.** Town near Beth-horon at the junction of 2 important roads, N of Jerusalem. Judas the Maccabee encamped there (I Macc. 7:40). Poss. mod. *Kh. 'Addaseh*.

**Adida** (Hadid). Town 3 miles NE of Lydda (I Macc. 12:38; 13:13). *See* Hadid

**Adora.** *See* Adoraim

**Adoraim.** City of Judah fortified by Rehoboam (II Chron. 11:9). It is mod. *Dura*, a village on a hillside *ca.* 5 miles SW of Hebron. B5—5

**Adramyttium.** Port in Mysia, NW Asia Minor. Paul embarked in a vessel of Adramyttium on his journey to Rome (Acts 27:2). B1—15; D2—17

**Adria, Sea of.** In the narrow sense, Sea of Adria was the portion of the Adriatic Sea near the commercial town of Adria, on the lower Po R. in Italy. The term was extended, however, to include the Tarentine Gulf, the Sicilian Sea, the Ionian Sea, the Corinthian Gulf, and the waters between Crete and Malta (Acts 27:27). C2—12; A1-B2—17

**Adriatic Sea.** Arm of the Mediterranean between Italy and the Balkan Peninsula. It extends from the Gulf of Venice SE to the Strait of Otranto, which leads into the Ionian Sea.

**Adrumythium.** *See* Adramyttium

**Adullam.** Town in Judah between Jarmuth and Socoh (Josh. 15:35). Nearby was the Cave of Adullam, which David used as a refuge and a headquarters for his activities (I Sam. 22:1; II Sam. 23:13). Prob. mod. *Tell esh-Sheikh-Madhkur*, near *'Id el-Ma*. B5—5

**Aegean Sea.** Arm of the Mediterranean between Greece and Asia Minor. The strait of the Dardanelles connects the Aegean with the Sea of Marmara. A1—6; D3—12; B1—15, 16; C-D2—17

**Aenon.** Place where John the Baptist exercised his ministry (John 3:23). It was near Salim (*q.v.*), the location of which is disputed. C4—11

**Aestii.** A Germanic people settled in N-central Europe along the E coast of the Baltic.

**Africa.** Continent situated S. of the Mediterranean, E of the Atlantic and W of the Red Sea and Indian Ocean. The Roman province named Africa embraced the territory NW of Syrtus Minor (*q.v.*). Its cities included Utica, Carthage, Hadrumetum, and Thapsus. C3—12; B-C3—18

**Africa Nova.** *See* Numidia

**Agade** (Akkad). One of the principal cities founded by Nimrod in the land of Shinar (Gen. 10:10—Accad). Its exact location is unknown. Poss. *Tell ed-Der* or *Tell Sheshubar*. F3—2

**Agrigentum.** City in S Sicily founded (*ca.* 580 B.C.) as Acragas (or Akragas) by Greek colonists.

**Agrippias.** City on the Mediterranean coast of Palestine N of Gaza. It was destroyed by Alexander Jannaeus but rebuilt by Augustus and added to the dominion of Herod, who renamed it Agrippium. A6—11

**Agrippina.** Fortress from which, according to the Talmud, the signals given by the Sanhedrin in Jerusalem were repeated. Poss. mod. *Kaukab el-Hawa*. C3—11

**Agrippium.** *See* Agrippias

**Ai** (Hai). Town E of Bethel that fell to Joshua after Jericho (Josh. 7–8). Aiath and Avvim may be variants of the same name. Prob. mod. *et-Tell*, 10 miles N of Jerusalem. D3—3; C4—19

**Aialon.** *See* Aijalon

**Aijalon.** City near the Philistine frontier (I Sam. 14:31) that at one time belonged to the tribe of Dan (Josh. 19:42; Judg. 1:35). Mod. *Yalo*, 14 miles NW of Jerusalem. B4—5

**Aijalon, Valley of.** Valley extending from the mts. N of Jerusalem in a generally NW direction to the Plain of Sharon, N of Joppa. Here Joshua gained victory over a coalition of kings from S Canaan (Josh. 10:12).

**Aijalon R.** B4—1. *See* Aijalon, Valley of

**Aila.** *See* Elath

**Ailath.** *See* Elath

**'Ain Feshkha.** Spring NW of the Dead Sea, near Qumran (*q.v.*). C4—19

**'Ain Gedi.** C5—19. *See* En-gedi

**'Ain Karem.** *See* 'Ain Karim

**'Ain Karim.** Village 4.5 miles W of Jerusalem. Tradition makes this the birthplace of John the Baptist. *See* Beth-haccherem. B4—19

**Aion.** *See* Ijon

**Ajalon.** *See* Aijalon

**Ajalon, Valley of.** *See* Aijalon, Valley of

**'Ajlun.** Town in Transjordan, NW of Jerash, part of whose wealth may be traced to iron mines in the 'Ajlun hills.

**Akeldama.** *See* Aceldama

**Akhetaton** (Tell el-Amarna). Capital of Egypt under Akhenaten (Amenhotep IV). Mod. *Tell el-Amarna*. C5—2; A6—3

**Akkad.** District in N Babylonia. It was the region between the Tigris and the Euphrates where they are closest together and almost parallel. In addition to the city of Akkad (poss. mod. *Tell ed-Der*), the cities of Babylon and Cuthah were in the city-state that bore this name. S of Akkad was the district known as Sumer. *See* Agade. F-G3—2

**Akkrabattine.** *See* Acrabathane

**Akrabbim, Ascent of.** The "ascent of scorpions" between the Arabah and the hill country of Judah (Num. 34:4; Josh. 15:3). Prob. mod. *Naqb es-Safa*. B6—5

**Alaca Huyuk.** Hittite ruins, including the famous "royal tombs," located in N-central Anatolia (*ca*. 100 miles NE of Ankara). D1—2

**Alalakh.** City on the Orontes R., N Syria. Mod. *Tell 'Atshaneh*. D2—2

**Alamanni.** A Germanic tribe from central Germany that engaged in numerous conflicts with the Romans. In A.D. 357 they were defeated by Julian (afterward emperor) at Strassburg. Their kingdom lasted until A.D. 495, when they were conquered by Clovis.

**Alans.** A division of the Sarmatia, a pastoral people related to the Scythians. The Alans were settled N of the Caucasus in Roman times.

**Alashiya.** C3—2. *See* Cyprus

**Albania.** Ancient name of a region in the E Caucasus bordering the Caspian Sea. It is now part of *Azerbaijan*, U.S.S.R. F2—12

**Albis** (Elbe) **R.** Rises in the Giant Mts. of NE Bohemia and flows generally NW through Saxony and the N German plain to the North Sea. It marked the farthest advance northward of the Romans under Drusus (9 B.C.). C1—12

**Aleppo.** *See* Haleb

**Alesia.** Town of Celtic and Roman Gaul, near mod. Dijon. Besieged by Caesar (52 B.C.), the town was starved out and Gallic resistance to Rome ended.

**Alexandria** (in Egypt). City founded by Alexander the Great (332 B.C.) at the Canopic mouth of the Nile at the W extremity of the Delta. Mod. *Al-Iskandariya*. D3—12; E4—17, 18

**Alexandria** (in India). City founded by Alexander the Great where the Four Rivers emptied into the Indus.

**Alexandria** (in Syria). City founded by Alexander the Great after defeating Darius near there in 333 B.C. It was located *ca*. 25 miles N of Antioch on the coast. Mod. *Iskanderun*. B1—13

**Alexandria Arachosiorum.** City founded by Alexander the Great in Arachosia (*q.v.*).

**Alexandria Arion.** *See* Herat

**Alexandria Eschate.** City founded by Alexander the Great on the Jaxartes R. to mark the proposed N limit of his kingdom. Mod. *Chodjend*.

**Alexandrium.** Fortress of the Hasmoneans and of Herod. Mod. *Qarn Sartabeh*, 17 miles N of Jericho. C4—11

**Alisar Huyuk.** *See* Kushshar

**Alpes.** Roman province between Italy on the E and Narbonensis on the W. B2—12

**Alps.** Mt. system of S-central Europe that swings in a great arc N, E, and SE between France and Italy to the Adriatic coast of Yugoslavia. Its northernmost point is in S Bavaria. B-C2—12

**Alus.** *See* Alush

**Alush.** Encampment of the Israelites between Egypt and Mt. Sinai (Num. 33:13–14). Poss. mod. *W. el-'Eshsh*. C5—3

**Amadoci.** Ancient people of W Sarmatia who lived in the area W of the Borysthenes R.

**Amalecites.** *See* Amalekites

**Amalek.** A5—4. *See* Amalekites

**Amalekites.** A nomadic people who wandered between the Negeb and the Sinai Peninsula. They are mentioned as enemies of Israel as late as David's reign.

**Amanus Mts.** Range E of the plain of Cilicia. C1—13

**Amardi.** Ancient people who inhabited the Elburz Mt. region, S of the Caspian Sea.

**Amardos R.** River of W. Asia that rises on the W slopes of the Zagros Mts. and flows generally NE, entering the S end of the Caspian Sea. It flows through the land of the Amardi (*q.v.*).

**Amarna, Tell el-.** C5—2; A6—3. *See* Akhetaton

**Amasia.** Ancient city of Galatia, in NE Asia Minor.

**Amastris.** Ancient port on the Black Sea in W Paphlagonia. E2—18

**Amathus.** Ancient town on the S coast of Cyprus, near the copper mines. A famous temple of Aphrodite was located there. C4—11

**Amisus.** Black Sea port of ancient Pontus, E of Sinope.

**Amman** (Rabbah). City at the headwaters of the Jabbok, 23 miles E of the Jordan. The chief city of the Ammonites, it was besieged by Joab, David's general (II Sam. 11:1; 12:26–31). Later the Ammonites won it back. It was denounced by Jeremiah (Jer. 49:2–6). Embellished by Ptolemy Philadelphus (285–246 B.C.), it was renamed Philadelphia. Mod. *'Amman*, capital of Jordan. D4—1; D3—19

**Ammaus.** *See* Emmaus

**Ammon.** A people descended from Ben-ammi, Lot's second son (Gen. 19:38). Ammonite settlements were located E of the Dead Sea, N of Moab. D4—1, 5; D3—3; C4—4

**Ammonium.** *See* Temple of Amon

**Amon, Temple of** (Siwa). Ancient town in the Libyan Desert, N Africa. It had a famed shrine to Amon, identified by the Greeks as Jupiter. Alexander the Great journeyed there—a 12-day pilgrimage from Memphis in Lower Egypt—and was hailed as a son of Amon. A3—6, 7

**Amorites.** Nomadic inhabitants of Palestine before and during the Israelite occupation (Gen. 10:16; 15:21; Josh. 7:7; 9:1; 11:3).

**Amorrhites.** *See* Amorites

**Amorrites.** *See* Amorites

**Amphipolis.** City of Thrace, situated at the mouth of the Strymon on a bend of the river. It was located on the Egnatian Way, 33 miles SW of Philippi. Paul passed through it while traveling from Philippi to Thessalonica (Acts 17:1). Mod. *Neochori*. A1—15, 16; C1—17

**Amygdalon, Pool of.** Pool in the Bethesda sector of N.T. Jerusalem, N of the E gate of the Palace of Herod.

**Anab.** Town in the hill country of Judah (Josh. 11:21; 15:50). Mod. *Kh. 'Anab*, 10 miles SW of Hebron.

**Ananla(h).** *See* Bethany

**Anas R.** River in Spain, dividing Lusitania and Baetica, spanned at Emerita Augusta by a bridge of 64 arches built by Trajan.

**Anat.** Ancient city on the middle Euphrates. Some scholars identify it with Hena (II Kings 18:34), which was overthrown by Sennacherib before his invasion of Judah. Mod. *Tell 'Ana*. C2—6

**Anatho.** *See* Anat

**Anathoth.** Levitical city in the territory of Benjamin (Josh. 21:18; I Chron. 6:60). It was the birthplace of Jeremiah (Jer. 1:1). Mod. *Ras el-Kharrubeh*, near *'Anata*, 2.5 miles NE of Jerusalem.

**Anchialus.** Port on the W end of the Black Sea, in mod. Bulgaria. Symeon, a Bulgarian ruler, defeated the Greeks near Anchialus (A.D. 917). A Christian church is known to have been there during the 3rd century A.D. Mod. *Ancheylo*, Bulgaria. E2—18

**Ancona.** Port city on the Adriatic, in central Italy. It was settled in the 4th century B.C. by Greeks from Syracuse.

**Ancyra.** Commercial center of central Anatolia (Asia Minor), dating to the 2nd millennium B.C. Mod. *Ankara*, capital of Turkey since 1923. B2—7; E2—12, 17; C1—15, 16; E2—18

**Ankara.** *See* Ancyra

**Ankuwa.** Hittite city in Anatolia, on the Konak R. Mod. *Alisar*, Turkey. D2—2

**Anthedon.** *See* Agrippias

**Anti-Lebanon Mts.** Mt. chain separated from the Lebanon Mts. by the valley of the Leontes and Orontes (the Beqa'a Valley). The greatest elevation of the Anti-Lebanon range is at its S end, Mt. Hermon.

**Antioch** (in Pisidia). Town in Asia Minor that served as center of civil and military administration for the S part of the Roman province of Galatia. Barnabas and Paul visited it on their First Missionary Journey (Acts 13:14–52; 14:19–21). Mod. *Yalovatch*. C4—14; C2—15, 16; E2—17

**Antioch** (in Syria). Syrian metropolis founded *ca.* 300 B.C. by Seleucus Nicator, situated on the S side of the Orontes *ca.* 15 miles from its mouth. It became a center of the early church (Acts 11:19–26; 13:1–3). Mod. *Antakya*, Turkey. E3—12; B1—13; D5—14; D2—15, 16; F2—17; F3—18

**Antipatris** (Aphek). Aphek was a Canaanite royal city (Josh. 12:18), 39 miles NW of Jerusalem, identical with ancient Capharsaba (*q.v.*). Herod the Great founded Antipatris on the same site. It was the limit of Paul's journey the first night when being taken as a prisoner from Jerusalem to Caesarea (Acts 23:31). Prob. mod. *Ras el-'Ain*. B4—11; B3—19

**Anti-Taurus Mts.** N extension of the Taurus Mts. (*q.v.*), across the Seyhan R.

**Antonia, Fortress.** Herod the Great's fortress-residence on the NW corner of the temple area in Jerusalem. Herod named it in honor of Mark Antony. B4—10

**Anxa.** Town in S Italy on a rocky island in the Gulf of Taranto, joined to the mainland by a bridge. The city was of Greek origin and was known also as Callipolis. Mod. *Gallipoli*.

**Apamea.** Important Hellenistic city founded by the Seleucids, S of Hamath, on the Orontes. Mod. *Qala'at el-Mudiq*. C2—13

**Aphek** (in Asher). City within the territory of Asher (Josh. 19:30; Judg. 1:31). Prob. mod. *Tell Kurdaneh*, near the sources of the Na'aman R., which flows into the Mediterranean SE of Acco. C2—3; B4—5

**Aphek** (in Ephraim). B3—19. *See* Antipatris

**Aphek** (in Transjordan). Site of Ahab's defeat by Ben-hadad of Damascus (I Kings 20:26, 30; cf. II Kings 13:17). Poss. mod. *Fiq*, E of the Sea of Galilee. C2—5

**Apherema.** *See* Ephraim, city of

**Aphik.** *See* Aphek (in Asher)

**Apollonia** (in E Macedonia). Town on the Egnatian Way, 28 miles W of Amphipolis (Acts 17:1). Mod. *Pollina*. A1—15, 16

**Apollonia** (in W Macedonia). Town on the Adriatic. Used as a base by Julius Caesar.

**Apollonia** (in Palestine). Town on the Mediterranean coast, in the Plain of Sharon, 12 miles N of Joppa. A4—11

**Apollonia** (in Thrace). City built by Greeks on the W shore of the Black Sea. Mod. *Burgas*, Bulgaria. B1—7

**Appii Forum.** *See* Appius, Forum of

**Appius, Forum of.** Town in Italy, on the Appian Way *ca.* 40 miles SE of Rome. Christians from Rome met Paul there (Acts 28:15). Mod. *Foro Appio*. A1—17

**'Aqaba.** Mod. name of a small town at the head of the Gulf of Aqaba (*q.v.*). Ancient Ezion-geber was near 'Aqaba.

**Aqaba, Gulf of.** The NE arm of the Red Sea, lying between Egypt and Arabia. Mod. *Eilat*, Israel, and 'Aqaba, Jordan, are located at its head, as was ancient Ezion-geber. The Gulf of Aqaba provides access to the Red Sea, and thence to the Indian Ocean. C6-D5—3

**Aquileia.** Town in NE Italy near the Adriatic. It was a Roman stronghold against barbarians from the N. C2—12

**Aquitania.** Former duchy and kingdom in SW France. It was conquered by one of Julius Caesar's lieutenants in 56 B.C. A2—12

**Ar** (Ar Moab). Ar, sometimes used as a synonym for Moab (Deut. 2:9), means "city" and may be the designation of the Moabite capital (cf. Num. 21:28; Isa. 15:1). The city has not been positively identified. C5—5

**'Araba.** *See* Arabah

**Arabah.** Term frequently used in the O.T. for the Jordan Valley (Deut. 1:7; 3:17; Josh. 11:2) and variously translated as "plain," "plains," "desert," "valley," or "wilderness." The Dead Sea was known as the Sea of Arabah (Deut. 3:17; Josh. 12:3). The term *Arabah (W. 'Araba)* is now used of the 100-mile-long depression extending from the S end of the Dead Sea to the Gulf of Aqaba. C6—1; D4—3; B6—4

**Arabella.** *See* Arbela

**Arabia.** Peninsula comprising a desert area bounded by the Red Sea (W), the Persian Gulf and the Gulf of Oman (E), the Gulf of Aden and the Arabian Sea (S). The Fertile Crescent forms an arc around the N of Arabia. E-F5—2; C3—7; E-F4—12; F3—18

**Arabian Desert.** Part of an enormous belt of desert, commencing near the Atlantic coast of Africa with the Sahara, and extending through Chinese Turkestan to the Pacific Ocean. Arabia is largely desert. In Scripture the term *Arabian* designates an inhabitant of the Arabian Desert (Jer. 3:2), whether near Babylonia (Isa. 13:20) or Ethiopia (II Chron. 21:16).

**Arabian Gulf.** *See* Red Sea

**Arabian Sea.** NW part of the Indian Ocean, between Arabia and India. The Gulf of Aden, an extension of the Red Sea, and the Gulf of Oman, an extension of the Persian Gulf, are its principal arms.

**Arabs.** Tribes from the desert portions of the Arabian Peninsula. *See* Arabian Desert. C3—6

**Arach.** *See* Erech

**Arachosia.** E province of the Median and (later) Persian empires, bordering India. Alexander the Great founded there the city Alexandria Arachosiorum. E-F2—7

**Arad** (Malatha). Town in Palestine, *ca.* 15 miles S of Hebron (Josh. 12:14; Judg. 1:16). Mod. *Tell 'Arad*. D3—3; B5—4, 5

**Aradus.** *See* Arvad

**Aral Sea.** Inland sea, 175 miles E of the Caspian, fed by the Oxus and Jaxartes rivers. E1—6, 7

**Aram.** D1—5. *See* Syria

**Arama.** *See* Hormah

**Aram-Damascus.** C3—4. *See* Damascus, kingdom of

**Aramean Kingdom.** *See* Hamath, district of

**Arameans.** *See* Syrians

**Aram-Maacah.** *See* Maacah

**Aram-naharaim.** *See* Paddan-aram

**Aram-zobah.** Aramean kingdom that flourished W of the Euphrates in the days of David and Solomon (I Sam. 14:47). At one time it controlled territory S from Hamath to Damascus. C2—4

**'Araq el-Emir.** City that was the home of the Tobiads of Ammon, a wealthy and influential family, especially in the Persian period. It was located on a straight line between Jericho and Amman, *ca.* 18 miles E of Jericho and 10 miles W of Amman. D4—19

**Ararat, Mt.** Traditionally located midway between the Black and Caspian seas. It is known by the Turks as *Aghri Dagh*. F1—2

**Ararat,** region of. *See* Armenia *and* Urartu

**Araunah,** threshing floor of. Located on Mt. Moriah, Jerusalem. It became the site of the temple of Solomon (II Chron. 3:1).

**Araxes R.** River that rises in Armenia, near Erzerum, flows 550 miles in a generally E direction, then empties into the Caspian Sea. Mod. *Aras R*. G1—2; C2—7

**Arbela** (in Assyria). City *ca.* 50 miles W of Nineveh. Mod. *Erbil*. F2—2; C2—7

**Arbela** (in Decapolis). Town *ca.* 45 miles N of Philadelphia. C3—11

**Arbela** (in Palestine). Town W of Sea of Galilee, 5 miles NW of Tiberias. The area around the Horns of Hattin (*q.v.*) is known as the Arbel Valley. Mod. *Kh. Irbid*.

**Arbella.** *See* Arbela

**Archelais.** Town in Palestine, *ca.* 7.5 miles N of Jericho on an important trade route of N.T. times. C5—11

**Ardus.** B3—13. *See* Arvad

**Areopolis** (Rabbath-Moab). Rabbath-Moab was a city of ancient Moab, E of the Lisan Peninsula and S of the Arnon R. It was located on the N-S trade route through Transjordan. It was known to the Romans as Areopolis. Mod. *Rabbah*. D6—11

**Areuna,** threshing floor of. *See* Araunah, threshing floor of

**Argob.** Section of Bashan E of Geshur (Deut. 3:4, 13, 14; Josh. 13:30). C3—4

**Aria.** Province of the ancient Median (later Persian) Empire, comprising the region about the Arius (mod. *Hari*) R. E2—7

**Arib.** *See* Arabs

**Arimathea** (Ramathaim). Ramathaim in the O.T., Arimathea in the N.T. Ramah (in Ephraim) bears the fuller form Ramathaim, or Ramathaim-zophim. Ramathaim was the home of Samuel (I Sam. 1:19; 28:3). Arimathea was the town of Joseph, a member of the Sanhedrin who, after the crucifixion, placed the body of Jesus in his new tomb (Matt. 27:57–60; Luke 23:50–53; John 19:38). Poss. mod. *Rentis*, 20 miles NW of Jerusalem on the W edge of the hill-country of Ephraim. B4—11

**'Arish, W. el** (R. of Egypt). The great wadi that formed the SW border of Canaan. Normally dry, it is only during the rainy season that the wadi is a river, depositing its waters in the Mediterranean *ca*. 50 miles S of Gaza.

**Arles.** City on the Rhone Delta in SE France. In Roman times it was a flourishing town named Arelas.

**Ar Moab.** *See* Ar

**Armenia.** Regions of Asia Minor forming a continuation of the Anatolian Plateau. The Armenian Kingdom originated in the region around Lake Van. Assyrian inscriptions mention it as Urartu. It is the O.T. Ararat. C2—7; F2—12, 18

**Armorica.** Region of NW France across the English Channel from Great Britain. Mod. *Brittany*.

**Arnon R.** (W. el-Mujib). Stream on the E bank of the Dead Sea crossed by the Israelites on their way to Canaan (Deut. 2:24). It was the N boundary of Moab (Judg. 11:18). C5—1, 5; D3—3; C-D6—11

**Aroer** (in Judah). Town 12 miles SE of Beer-sheba in the *W. 'Ar'ara* (I Sam. 30:28). Mod. *Ararah*.

**Aroer** (in Moab). Town on the N bank of the Arnon, southernmost point ruled by Sihon (Deut. 2:36; Josh. 12:2). Mod. *Kh. 'Ar'ir*, S of Dibon, 13 miles W of the Dead Sea. B5—4; D5—5

**Arpad.** City frequently associated with Hamath (II Kings 18:34; 19:13), near which it was located. Mod. *Tell Erfad*, 13 miles N of Aleppo.

**Arphachsad.** *See* Arphaxad

**Arphad.** *See* Arpad

**Arphaxad.** A people descended from Shem. They settled in Chaldea NW of the Persian Gulf.

**Arrapakha.** Assyrian city E of Ashur, the center of a small Hurrian kingdom (including Nuzi) *ca*. 1800–1500 B.C.

**Arsinoe.** *See* Crocodilopolis

**Artaxata.** City on the Araxes R. in Armenia. After its capture by Corbulo, Nero's general, in A.D. 58, it became a dependency of Rome. F2—12

**Arvad** (Ardus). The most northerly of important Philistine centers. It is an island off the Syrian coast, N of Tripoli. Mod. *Ruad*. D3—2; B2—4, 7; B3—13

**Aryans.** *See* Indo-Iranians

**Arzawa.** Ancient name of district in NW Asia Minor. B-C2—2

**Asasonthamas.** *See* En-gedi

**Ascalon.** A5—11; A4—19. *See* Ashkelon

**Ascent of Akrabbim.** *See* Akrabbim, Ascent of

**Aschenez.** *See* Ashkenaz

**Aser,** allotment of. *See* Asher, allotment of

**Ashdod** (Azotus), city of. One of 5 leading Philistine cities. It was located 9 miles NE of Ashkelon, 3 miles E of the Mediterranean, 18 miles N of Gaza. Mod. *Esdud*. C3—3; A4—4, 5; B4—19

**Ashdod**, district of. District of S Palestine that derived its name from the city of Ashdod (*q.v.*).

**Asher**, allotment of. Territory assigned to Asher on the Mediterranean coast in N Palestine (Josh. 19:24–31).

**Ashkelon** (Ascalon). One of 5 leading Philistine cities. It was located in a valley along the Mediterranean, 12 miles N of Gaza (Jer. 47:5, 7). Mod. *'Askalon*. C3—3; A4—4; A5—5

**Ashkenaz.** A people of the race of Gomer who dwelt in the region of Ararat, E Armenia (Jer. 51:27).

**Ashtaroth.** City in Bashan (Josh. 9:10; 12:4; 13:12, 31) ruled by Og before the Israelite conquest. It was later a Levitical city (I Chron. 6:71). Mod. *Tell 'Ashtara*, E of the Sea of Galilee. D2—3, 5; C3—4

**Ashur.** Ancient city on the Tigris R. (Gen. 2:14). It was the oldest capital of the Assyrians. Near mod. *Qala'ah Sherqat*.

**Asia**, Roman province of. The territory in Asia Minor S of Bithynia, N of Lycia, W of Galatia, and E of the Aegean (Acts 19:10, 22, 26, 27; 20:4, 16, 18; 21:27). The term *Asia* can also refer to the continent E of Europe and Africa, or to the kingdom of the Seleucids during the Maccabean times. D3—12; B-C2—15, 16; D2—17; E3—18

**Asia Minor.** Peninsula in W Asia, also known as Anatolia, bounded on the N by the Black Sea, on the S by the Mediterranean, and on the W by the Aegean arm of the Mediterranean.

**Askelon.** *See* Ashkelon

**Asochis** (Hannathon). Place on N boundary of Zebulun (Josh. 19:14). Poss. mod. *Tell el-Bedeiwiyeh*. C3—11

**Asophon.** Town on the E bank of the Jordan, about midway between the Sea of Galilee and the Dead Sea.

**Asor.** *See* Hazor

**Aspadana.** *See* Gabae

**Asphaltitis, Lake.** C6—11. *See* Dead Sea

**Asshur.** F3—2; C2—7. *See* Assyria

**Assos.** Ancient city in Mysia, in NW Asia Minor, on the Gulf of Adramyttium, E of Point Lectum, westernmost point of Asia. Paul passed through Assos (Acts 20:13–14). B1—16

**Assur.** *See* Assyria

**Assuwa.** Ancient district of NW Asia Minor. B1—2

**Assyria.** Country E of the middle Tigris, bounded on the N by the mts. of Armenia, on the E by the Median mt. ranges, and on the S by the environs of Nineveh, its later capital. In the period of the Assyrian Empire (*q.v.*) this territory was extended to reach the Persian Gulf on the S and the Mediterranean on the W. F3—2; C2—6

**Assyrian Empire.** Empire that developed from the city of Ashur, on the upper Tigris. The period of greatness dates from the 9th century B.C. when Nineveh was its capital. The Assyrians captured Samaria and took the Israelites into captivity (722 B.C.). Nineveh was destroyed by the Babylonians and the Medes (612 B.C.), and Assyrian power was forever broken.

**Astacus.** City of ancient Bithynia, in N Asia Minor, at the E end of an arm of the Sea of Marmara. It was later named Nicomedia (*q.v.*) and is near mod. *Izmit*, Turkey.

**Astharoth.** *See* Ashtaroth

**Astorga.** Town in the Asturias region, in NW Spain. A2—18

**Astures.** An Iberian people who lived in NW Spain before the Roman conquest (2nd century B.C.). They were later absorbed by the Visigoths.

**Asturica.** *See* Astorga

**Ataroth** (in Ephraim). Town in the Jordan Valley, in NE Ephraim. Poss. mod. *Tell Sheikh edh-Dhiab*.

**Ataroth** (in Moab). Town taken from Gad by the Moabites (cf. Moabite Stone). Mod. *Kh. Attarus*, NW of Dibon. C5—5

**Athens.** Capital of the Greek state of Attica. In the 6th and 5th centuries B.C., Athens became the cultural center of the world, making contributions in the areas of government, architecture, literature, art, and philosophy. In N.T. times Athens was subject to Rome, having been taken by Sulla in 86 B.C. Paul preached to the Athenians from Mars Hill, a short distance W of the Acropolis (Acts 17:15–18:1). A2—6, 7, 15, 16; D3—12, 18; C2—17

**Atlantic Ocean.** Body of water extending from the Arctic to the Antarctic regions between the Americas on the W and Europe and Africa on the E. A1—12

**Atlas Mts.** System of nonvolcanic mt. ranges in NW Africa, extending *ca.* 1,500 miles NE from Morocco through Algeria to Cape Bon in Tunisia. It was inhabited in antiquity by Berbers.

**Attalia.** Mediterranean seaport in SW Asia Minor, the port whence Paul and Barnabas sailed for Antioch (Acts 14:25). Mod. *Adalia*. C5—14; E2—17

**Augsburg.** City in W. Bavaria, on the Lech R. It was founded by Augustus (15 B.C.) as the Roman colony Augusta Vindelicorum.

**Augusta Treverorum.** B1—12. *See* Trier

**Augusta Vindelicorum.** *See* Augsburg

**Auja el-Hafir.** Ancient town of the Negeb that was situated on a trade route from Palestine to Egypt. Neolithic tools have been found in the neighborhood, and deep wells there date to Nabatean and Byzantine times. It is also known as El 'Auja, or Nitsanah. A6—19

**Auran.** *See* Hauran

**Auranitis.** Name used in Greco-Roman times for a small district lying between Gaulanitis and the mod. *J. Hauran*. Auranitis, Trachonitis, and Batanea were assigned to Herod the Great by Augustus (*ca.* 23 B.C.).

**Avaricum.** *See* Bourges

**Avaris** (Zoan). C4—2. *See* Ramses

**Avdat.** Nabatean city S of Beer-sheba in the section of the Negeb known in biblical times as the Wilderness of Zin (*q.v.*). B6—19

**Azeca.** *See* Azekah

**Azecha.** *See* Azekah

**Azekah.** City in the lowlands of Judah a short distance NE of Lachish (*q.v.*). It, with Lachish, was strengthened by Rehoboam (II Chron. 11:9), and the two were among the last cities to fall to Nebuchadnezzar (Jer. 34:7). Mod. *Tell Zakari-yeh*. B4—19

**Azotus.** A5—11; A6—13. *See* Ashdod

**Azov, Sea of.** N arm of the Black Sea, bounded on the SW by the Crimea, on the N by the Ukraine, on the E by the Kuban lowland, and on the SE by the Taman Peninsula. It is fed by the Don and the Kuban rivers.

**Azzah.** *See* Gaza

## B

**Baalbek.** *See* Heliopolis

**Baal-meon.** Town of the Reubenites (Num. 32:38; I Chron. 5:8). It was later a Moabite city (Ezek. 25:9; "Beth-meon" in Jer. 48:23), mentioned on the Moabite Stone. Mod. *Ma'in*, SW of Medeba, 9 miles E of the Dead Sea.

**Baal-moan.** *See* Baal-meon

**Baal-saphon.** *See* Baal-zephon

**Baal-zephon.** Place in Egypt on the border of the Red Sea where Israel encamped during the Exodus (Exod. 14:2, 9; Num. 33:7). Poss. mod. *J. Murr*. A4—3

**Bab edh 'Drah.** Site E of the Dead Sea where the remains of a sanctuary (dated 2800–1800 B.C.) have been discovered. C5—19

**Babel.** *See* Babylon

**Babylon.** Capital of Babylonia. It was an important city in S Mesopotamia that reached its zenith under Nebuchadnezzar. F4—2; C3—6, 7

**Babylonia.** Empire in the E Fertile Crescent area, N of the Persian Gulf, that had Babylon for its capital. It was also known as Shinar (Gen. 10:10; 11:2; Isa. 11:11) and the "land of the Chaldeans" (Jer. 24:5; Ezek. 12:13). F3-G4—2; D3—6; C3—7

**Babylonian Empire, New.** Name by which the Babylonia (*q.v.*) of the 6th and 5th centuries B.C. is known. Under its best-known king, Nebuchadnezzar, Judah was taken into exile (587 B.C.). C2-3—6

**Babylonian Empire, Old.** Name by which the Babylonia (*q.v.*) of the late 2nd millennium B.C.—the age of the biblical patriarchs—is known. Hammurabi was its most illustrious king.

**Bactra.** Capital of ancient Bactria (*q.v.*). Mod. *Balkh* in N Afghanistan. F2—7

**Bactria.** Ancient country that comprised the N slope of the Hindu Kush as far as the Oxus R. It was an E province of the Persian Empire before the conquest of Alexander (328 B.C.). A Greco-Bactrian kingdom was established there *ca.* 250 B.C. E-F2—7

**Baetica.** Roman province in Spain. It was bounded by the Anas R. on the N and W and by the Mediterranean Sea on the S. A2—12

**Bagae.** Ancient city on the Oxus R. in Sogdiana. In his battles with the E satrapies of the Persian Empire, Alexander fought in the vicinity of Bagae.

**Balearic Islands.** Group of 4 large and 11 small islands in the Mediterranean, off the E coast of Spain. They were colonized by Phoenicians and Carthaginians, and conquered by the Romans (123 B.C.).

**Balikh R.** Tributary of the upper Euphrates. The city of Haran (*q.v.*) was located on the Balikh, 60 miles N of its junction with the Euphrates.

**Ballah, Lake.** Lake on the border between Egypt and Sinai, E of Goshen and N of Lake Timsah. The Suez Canal now flows through the ancient lake region.

**Baltic Sea.** The E arm of the Atlantic Ocean, indenting N Europe. Countries surrounding the Baltic are: Denmark, Germany, Poland, Russia, Finland, and Sweden.

**Baniyas.** *See* Caesarea Philippi

**Barasa.** *See* Bostra

**Barca.** City of ancient Cyrenaica. Mod. *Barce* in Libya.

**Basan.** *See* Bashan

**Bashan.** Transjordan territory extending N from Gilead to Mt. Hermon. Before the Israelite conquest it was ruled by Og (Num. 21:33; Deut. 3:1; Josh. 12:5; 13:11), subsequently occupied by the half-tribe of Manasseh (Josh. 13:30; 17:1, 5; 21:6; 22:7; I Chron. 5:23), and at times settled by the tribe of Gad (I Chron. 5:11, 16). It was described as a fertile area, famed for its pasture lands (Deut. 32:14; Ezek. 39:18; Mic. 7:14). D2—1, 3; C-D2—5

**Bastarnae.** Ancient people of SE Sarmatia who settled in the region N of the Carpathian Mts.

**Batanea.** District of Transjordan E of Gualanitis. It was part of the kingdom of Herod the Great (37–4 B.C.) and subsequently assigned to Philip the Tetrarch (4 B.C.–A.D. 34). D2—11

**Batavi.** A Germanic people, settled N of the lower Rhine, S of the Frisians.

**Beas R.** *See* Hyphasis R.

**Beautiful Gate.** The E gate of Herod's temple. The Talmud terms it Nicanor's Gate, or the Great Gate. It was made of Corinthian brass, richly ornamented with precious metals. It was the largest of the temple gates, being 50 cubits high and 40 cubits wide. It was later called the Golden Gate, which is now sealed up.

**Beelmeon.** *See* Baal-meon

**Beelsephon.** *See* Baal-zephon

**Beer Ora.** Settlement in the Israeli Negeb, 12 miles N of Elath.

**Beeroth.** City of the Gibeonite Confederation (Josh. 9:17), subsequently subdued by Joshua and assigned to Benjamin (Josh. 18:25). It was repopulated after the Babylonian Exile (Ezra 2:25; Neh. 7:29). Poss. mod. *el-Bire*, N of Jerusalem.

**Beer-sheba.** City in S Palestine, midway between the Mediterranean and S end of the Dead Sea. Settled in patriarchal times (Gen. 21:14), it subsequently marked the S boundary of Israelite territory ("from Dan to Beer-sheba," Judg. 20:1; I Sam. 3:20; II Sam. 17:11). Beer-sheba (or Beer-sheva) is an important center for mod. Israeli settlements in the Negeb. B5—1; D4—2; C3—3; A5—4; B6—5

**Beeshterah.** *See* Ashtaroth

**Behistun.** Town in W Iran (ancient Persia) on the road from Hamadan to Babylon. On a mt. nearby, Darius I had reliefs and inscriptions carved to celebrate his victories. The trilingual inscriptions (Old Persian, Elamite, and Akkadian) provided the key to the decipherment of Akkadian cuneiform writing. C2—7

**Beit Shean.** *See* Beth-shan

**Beit Shemesh.** Name of the mod. Israeli community built near the mound of the same name that was excavated by the British Palestine Exploration Fund (1911–1912) and Haverford (Pa.) College (1928–1933). *See* Beth-shemesh

**Beit Zabde.** City in Zabdizene that was already Christian by *ca.* A.D. 100. F2—18

**Bela.** *See* Zoar

**Belgica.** Roman province in N Gaul, bounded by the North Sea and the Marne, Seine, and Rhine rivers. B1—12

**Bene-barac.** *See* Bene-berak

**Bene-berak.** City in Dan (Josh. 19:45), located 4 miles E of Joppa. Mod. *Ibn Ibraq*.

**Benenennom Valley.** *See* Hinnom Valley

**Beneventum.** Important commercial center on the Appian Way on a small plain of the Apennines in the Campania region of S Italy. A1—17

**Beni Hasan.** Village on the Nile, in Upper Egypt, in the vicinity of which have been found Middle Empire tombs with well-preserved murals.

**Benjamin,** allotment of. Tribe bounded on the N by Ephraim, on the S by Judah, on the W by Dan, and on the E by the Jordan.

**Berea.** *See* Beroea

**Berenice** (in Cyrenaica). Port on the Mediterranean on the N coast of Africa. Mod. *Bengasi*, Libya.

**Berenice** (in Egypt). Port city on the Red Sea, founded by Ptolemy II, that commanded trade with Arabia.

**Beroea.** City at the foot of Mt. Bermius in Macedonia. Paul commended the Beroeans for their careful study of Scripture (Acts 17:10–13). Mod. *Verria*. A1—15, 16; D2—18

**Beroth.** *See* Beeroth

**Berotha.** *See* Berothai

**Berothai.** Aramean city from which David took much bronze after defeating Hadadezer, its ruler (II Sam. 8:8). Mod. *Bereitan* in the Beqa'a, 35 miles N of Damascus. C2—4

**Bersabe(e).** B6—11. *See* Beer-sheba

**Berytus.** Ancient city on the Phoenician coast of the Mediterranean at the foot of the Lebanon range. Mod. *Beirut* or *Beyrouth,* Lebanon. D1—3; B3—4; B4—13

**Besor R.** Stream that flows into the Mediterranean *ca.* 5 miles S of Gaza. A5—1; A6—5

**Bethabara.** Place on the E bank of the Jordan where John was baptizing (John 1:28). Poss. mod.

*'Abarah* N of Scythopolis (Beth-shan). Many Greek manuscripts read '''Bethany beyond Jordan'' instead of ''Bethabara.''

**Beth-Alfa.** Town 4 miles W of Beth-shan. The remains of a synagogue (6th century A.D.) have been discovered there. C2—19

**Bethania.** *See* Bethany

**Bethany.** Village on the E slope of the Mt. of Olives, *ca.* 2 miles from Jerusalem. The home of Mary, Martha, and Lazarus (John 11:1; 12:1). Mod. *el-'Azariyeh*. C5—11

**Bethany beyond Jordan.** *See* Bethabara

**Beth-aram.** *See* Betharamphtha

**Betharamphtha** (Livias, Julias). Town in the Jordan Valley assigned to the tribe of Gad, also known as Beth-haram (Josh. 13:27) and Beth-haran (Num. 32:36). On this site was built the city of Livias, or Julias, where Herod the Great built a palace. Poss. mod. *Tell Iqtanu*, E of *Tell er-Rameh*. C5—11

**Beth-aran.** *See* Betharamphtha

**Beth-dagon.** Village *ca.* 5 miles NW of Lydda near Philistia (Josh. 15:41). Mod. *Kh. Dajun*.

**Bethel.** Town *ca.* 12 miles N of Jerusalem. Here the patriarch Abraham encamped (Gen. 12:8; 13:3). In the days of Jeroboam I of Israel, Bethel was chosen as a shrine to offset the influence of the Jerusalem temple (I Kings 12:28–33). Mod. *Beitin*. B4—1, 4, 5; D3—3; C4—19

**Beth-emec.** *See* Beth-emek

**Beth-emek.** Town in Asher (Josh. 19:27). Poss. mod. *Tell Mimas*.

**Bethesda, Pool of.** B4—10. *See* Bethzatha, Pool of

**Beth-haccherem.** Judean town that served as a place for signaling during times of invasion (Jer. 6:1). Commonly identified with 'Ain Karim (*q.v.*), 4.5 miles W of Jerusalem. Mod. *Beit-hakerem*.

**Beth-hagla.** *See* Beth-hoglah

**Beth-haram.** *See* Betharamphtha

**Beth-haran.** *See* Betharamphtha

**Beth-hoglah.** Town on the border between the territories of Benjamin and Judah (Josh. 15:6; 18:19, 21), SE of Jericho. Mod. *'Ain Hajlah*.

**Beth-horon.** Town on the boundary between the territories of Ephraim and Benjamin (Josh. 18:13). It is divided into 2 communities: Lower Beth-horon, mod. *Beit 'Ur et-Tahta*, which has an altitude of 1,240 feet; and Upper Beth-horon, mod. *Beit 'Ur el-Foqa*, which has an altitude of 1,730 feet. B4—4

**Bethiesimoth.** *See* Beth-jeshimoth

**Beth-jeshimoth.** Settlement in Transjordan N of the Dead Sea. It was the stopping place of Israel during the final stage of the Exodus (Num. 33:49). Later it became part of Moabite territory (Ezek. 25:9). Prob. mod. *Tell el-'Azeimeh*.

**Beth-jesimoth.** *See* Beth-jeshimoth

**Bethlehem.** Town located 5 miles S of Jerusalem on the road to Hebron. It was the city of David and the birthplace of Jesus. Mod. *Beit Lahm*. B5—1, 5, 11; B4—19

**Beth-maachah.** *See* Abel

**Beth-nemra.** *See* Beth-nimrah

**Beth-nimrah.** Town in the territory of Gad (Josh. 13:27), identical with Nimrah (Num. 32:3). Poss. mod. *Tell Bileibil*, near *Tell Nimrin*.

**Bethoron.** *See* Beth-horon

**Beth-palet.** Town in S Judah (the Negeb), the exact location of which is uncertain (Josh. 15:27; Neh. 11:26).

**Beth-phaleth.** *See* Beth-palet

**Beth-pelet.** *See* Beth-palet

**Beth-rehob.** An Aramean territory generally W of Damascus (II Sam. 10:6). Its precise location is uncertain, but it may be identical with Beth-rehob near Dan (Judg. 18:28). B-C3—4

**Bethsaida-Julias.** Town located E of the point where the Jordan flows into the Sea of Galilee. It was the home of Andrew, Peter, and Philip (John 1:44; 12:21). Poss. mod. *et-Tell*. C2—11

**Beth-sames.** *See* Beth-shemesh

**Beth-san.** *See* Beth-shan

**Beth-shan** (Scythopolis). Ancient fortress strategically located at the junction of the Plain of Jezreel with the Jordan Valley. Occupied by Canaanites before the conquest (Josh. 17:16), it was subsequently located on the border between the territories of Issachar and Manasseh (Josh. 17:11; I Chron. 7:29). Following the Battle of Gilboa (*ca*. 1000 B.C.) the Philistines fastened the bodies of Saul and his sons to the wall of the city (I Sam. 31:10–13). During Hellenistic times Beth-shan was known as Scythopolis. It was the one city W of the Jordan in the federation of Greek cities known as Decapolis. Beth-shan has been identified with *Tell el-Hosn*, near the village of Beisan. C3—1, 5; D2—3; B4—4; C2—19

**Beth-shean.** *See* Beth-shan

**Beth Shearim.** Jewish necropolis between Nazareth and Haifa, including more than 25 rock-hewn catacombs dating from the 2nd to the 4th centuries A.D. C2—19

**Beth-shemesh.** Town in the Valley of Sorek about 23.5 miles W of Jerusalem, on the border between the territories of Judah and Dan (Josh. 15:10), also known as Irshemesh (Josh. 19:41). Mod. *Tell er-Rumeileh*. B4—4, 19; B5—5

**Bethsimoth.** *See* Beth-jeshimoth

**Bethsur.** *See* Beth-zur

**Bethsura.** B5—11. *See* Beth-zur

**Beth-togarmah.** *See* Togarmah

**Beth-yerah** (Philoteria). Canaanite city near the S end of the Sea of Galilee. It became the Hellenistic city of Philoteria. Antiochus III of Syria (218 B.C.) occupied it, then crossed the Jordan and conquered Transjordan. C2—19

**Beth-zacharam.** *See* Beth-zacharias

**Beth-zacharias.** Town *ca.* 10 miles SW of Jerusalem. Mod. *Kh. Beit Sakaria*.

**Bethzatha** (Bethesda), Pool of. Name used in some manuscripts for the pool near the Sheep Gate in Jerusalem (John 5:2). Other manuscripts read Bethesda. B4—10

**Beth-zur.** Town in the hill-country of Judah, 4 miles N of Hebron. It was fortified by Rehoboam (II Chron. 11:7). Mod. *Kh. et-Tubeiqeh*, near *Burjes-Sur*. B5—5; C4—19

**Betonim.** Town in Gad (Josh. 13:26). Mod. *Kh. Batneh.*

**Beycesultan.** Ancient town on the Maeander R., in W Asia Minor. Excavations indicate a Greek culture here during the patriarchal age (2000–1600 B.C.). C2—2

**Bezec.** *See* Bezek

**Bezek.** Town in the territory of Manasseh, S of Mt. Gilboa. Prob. mod. *Kh. Ibziq.*

**Bibracte.** Town in central France, ancient Gaul, where Caesar defeated the Helvetii (58 B.C.).

**Bile-am.** *See* Ibleam

**Bira.** Town in Jordan, NE of Ramallah. *See* Beeroth

**Birs Nimrud.** *See* Borsippa

**Bithynia.** Region in N Asia Minor (Acts 16:7). E2—12, 18; C1—15, 16; D-F1—17

**Bitter Lakes.** Lakes in Egypt N of the Gulf of Suez. B4—3

**Black Sea.** Inland sea located N of Asia Minor. Enclosed by Russia on the N and E, by Turkey on the S, and by Bulgaria and Romania on the W. It is connected with the Mediterranean by the Bosporus, the Sea of Marmara, and the Dardanelles. C-D1—2; B-C1—6; B1—7; E2—12, 18; E-F1—17

**Bogaskoy.** *See* Hattusas

**Bordeaux.** City of SW France with a port accessible to the Atlantic through the Gironde R.

**Borsippa.** Town a few miles S of Babylon, also known as Birs Nimrud. Ruins of a great temple (*ziggurat*) are reminiscent of the biblical Tower of Babel.

**Borysthenes** (Dnieper) **R.** River flowing generally S from the Valdai Hills (W of Moscow) into the Black Sea, a distance of *ca.* 1,420 miles.

**Bosor.** City *ca.* 40 miles E of the Sea of Galilee. Mod. *Busr el-Hariri.*

**Bosora.** *See* Bostra

**Bosporus Kingdom.** State occupying the territory surrounding the Palus Maeotis, N of the Black Sea. The region produced grain for Rome. It was a client kingdom and not a kingdom subject to Rome. E2—12

**Bosra.** *See* Bozrah

**Bostra** (Busra). Town in the Hauran highlands of Transjordan, S of Kanatha.

**Bourges** (Avaricum). Avaricum, a town in central Gaul, was the site of a major battle described by Julius Caesar in his *Gallic Wars.* Augustus made it the capital of Aquitania N of the Garonne. Its mod. name is Bourges.

**Bozrah.** Important city of Edom situated in an oasis of the Syrian Desert. Prob. mod. *Buseira,* 25 miles SE of the Dead Sea. D4—3; B5—4

**Bremen.** City of the Saxons on the Weser R. in what is now N Germany.

**Brick Walls, City of.** *See* Kir-hareseth

**Brigantium.** Town on the NW coast of Spain, prob. to be identified with mod. *La Coruña.*

**Britain.** *See* Britannia

**Britannia.** Term applied to Great Britain before the Germanic invasions of the 5th and 6th centuries. The Romans arrived in Britain in 55 B.C. and reached their period of greatest power there during the first half of the 3rd century A.D. B1—12

**Brook of Cherith.** *See* Cherith, Brook

**Brundisium.** Adriatic Sea port in S Italy, since ancient times a center of trade with the East. Products could be brought by sea to Brundisium and carried overland to Rome by the Appian Way, which terminated there. Mod. *Brindisi.*

**Bubastis.** A4—3. *See* Pibeseth

**Bubastus.** *See* Bubastis

**Bucephala.** Ancient town on the Hydaspes R. in India.

**Burdigala.** A2—12. *See* Bordeaux

**Busra.** *See* Bostra

**Buxentum** (Capo della Foresta). Town in SW Italy on the Gulf of Policastro.

**Byblos.** D3—2; B4—13. *See* Gebal

**Byzantium** (Istanbul). City located on both sides of the Bosporus at its entrance into the Sea of Marmara. As Constantinople it was the capital of the Byzantine Empire. In 1930 the name was officially changed to Istanbul, which serves as the chief city and seaport of Turkey. B1—7, 15, 16; D2—12, 18; D1—17

## C

**Cabul.** Village of Asher (Josh. 19:27), 9 miies SE of Acco. Mod. *Kabul.* B3—4; B2—5

**Cadasa.** C2—11. *See* Kedesh (in Naphtali)

**Cades.** *See* Kedesh (in Naphtali)

**Cadesbarne.** *See* Kadesh-barnea

**Cadiz.** *See* Gades

**Cadusii.** An ancient people settled in the mts. W of the Caspian Sea.

**Caerleon.** Town on the Usk R. NE of Newport in W Britain. It was the site of the Roman fortress Isca. It is known as Camelot in the Arthurian legend.

**Caesarea** (in Mauretania). Important city on the Mediterranean in Mauretania, the westernmost African province of Rome. It was sacked by the vandals in the 5th century. The site is now occupied by Cherchell, Algeria. B3—12

**Caesarea** (in Palestine). Seaport, formerly Strato's Tower, *ca.* 23 miles S of Mt. Carmel, on the Mediterranean. It was built by Herod the Great. Mod. *Keisariyeh,* Israel. B3—1, 11; A5—13; D6—14; D3—15, 16; F4—17; E3—18; B2—19

**Caesarea Augusta** (Saragossa). City founded by Augustus Caesar on the Ebro R. in NE Spain. A2—12

**Caesarea Mazaca.** Called also Caesarea of Cappadocia, this was an important trading center in E Asia Minor and, as Mazaca, served as the residence of Cappadocian kings. Mod. *Kayseri,* Turkey. D1—15, 16; F2—17; E2—18

**Caesarea Philippi** (Baniyas). City near the source of the Jordan in N Palestine. It was built by the tetrarch Philip near a sanctuary of the god Pan, hence Panias, or Paneion. Its mod. name is Baniyas. C2—11; B4—13

**Caesar's Bridge.** Bridge that Caesar built across the Rhine, the boundary between Gaul and Germania. Caesar used bridges to invade Germania but made no permanent conquests.

**Cagliari.** *See* Caralis

**Caiaphas, House of.** Located in the Upper City of Jerusalem NE of the House of the Last Supper. B6—10

**Calah** (Nimrud). Ancient Assyrian city *ca.* 25 miles SE of Nineveh. Ashurnasirpal III built a great palace there and made it the center of his government. F3—2

**Caleb.** The clan of Caleb lived in the territory around Hebron and was incorporated into the tribe of Judah (Josh. 15:13–19).

**Callirhoe.** *See* Callirrhoe

**Callirrhoe.** Community in Perea (Transjordan) NW of Machaerus. It was noted for its baths, in which Herod bathed shortly before his death. C5—11

**Calvary.** A4—10. *See* Golgotha

**Camon.** Place mentioned in Judges 10:5 as the burial place of Jair. Poss. mod. *Qamm*, SE of the Sea of Galilee.

**Cana.** Village in Galilee where Jesus performed His first miracle (John 2:1–11). Prob. mod. *Kh. Qana*, 9 miles N of Nazareth. It is traditionally identified with *Kafr Kenna*. C2—11

**Canaan.** Biblical Canaan was the land promised to Abraham and his descendants (Gen. 17:8). It refers to Palestine W of the Jordan (Gen. 13:12). In a more restricted sense it may refer to Phoenicia (Isa. 23:11), or the land of the Philistines (Zeph. 2:5). According to Genesis 10:15–20, Canaanite territory extended from Sidon to Gaza, W of the Jordan. Canaanite settlements reached as far N as Arvad. D1-3—3

**Canaanites.** Term used of the inhabitants of Canaan who were in the land during patriarchal times and who were defeated in battle during the Israelite conquest under Joshua. Canaan is called a son of Ham (Gen. 10:6, 15–20), reminiscent of the fact that Canaan had long been dominated by the Egyptians (*Mizraim*, another son of Ham).

**Cantabri.** An ancient people who inhabited the N coast of Spain. They were attacked by the Romans (150 B.C.) but were subdued only in a series of campaigns carried out by Augustus (29–19 B.C.).

**Canterbury.** City located at the foot of the North Downs on the Stour R. in SE Britain. The Mother Church of England, founded before the arrival of Augustine (A.D. 597), is located there.

**Capernaum.** City on the NW shore of the Sea of Galilee where Jesus performed numerous miracles. Mod. *Tell Hum*. C2—11, 19

**Cape Salmone.** *See* Salmone, Cape

**Capharnaum.** *See* Capernaum

**Capharsaba.** Town 39 miles NW of Jerusalem in a fertile plain. It was rebuilt by Herod the Great and named Antipatris (*q.v.*) after Antipater, his father. The old name continues in use in the village *Kefr Saba*. Ancient Capharsaba, however, is identified with *Ras el-'Ain*. It is identical with the Canaanite royal city of Aphek (Josh. 12:18; I Sam. 4:1; 29:1).

**Capharsalama.** Location of a battle between Judas the Maccabee and Nicanor (I Macc. 7:31). Mod. *Kh. Selma*, NW of Jerusalem.

**Caphtor.** A3—2. *See* Crete

**Caphtorim.** Inhabitants of Crete, Egyptian *Keftiu*. The term probably includes both Crete and adjacent islands and nearby lands (including Caria and Lycia in Asia Minor). According to Genesis 10:14, Caphtor was a descendant of Mizraim (Egypt). The Philistines originated in Caphtor (Amos 9:7; Jer. 47:4).

**Capitolias.** City of the Decapolis, located S of Abila on an important N-S trade route through Transjordan. Mod. *Beit Ras*. D3—11

**Capo della Foresta.** *See* Buxentum

**Cappadocia.** Highland district of E Asia Minor, formed into a Roman province in A.D. 17. C1—6; E2—12; D4—13; D1—15, 16; F2—17; E-F3—18

**Capua.** Strategic town located on the Appian Way and the Volturno R. in S Italy.

**Caralis** (Cagliari). Seaport at the head of the Gulf of Cagliari on the S coast of Sardinia. It was founded by the Phoenicians. B2—12

**Carchemish.** Hittite center on the right bank of the N Euphrates at an important ford of the river. It was situated *ca.* 60 miles W of Haran. Necho of Egypt was decisively defeated by Nebuchadnezzar of Babylon at Carchemish (605 B.C.). Mod. *Jerablus* (*Jerabish*). D2—2; C2—6

**Caria.** Country in SW Asia Minor. It was taken from Antiochus the Great by the Romans and later incorporated into the province of Asia. B2—7, 15, 16

**Cariathaim.** *See* Kiriathaim

**Cariath-Arbe.** *See* Hebron

**Cariathiarim.** *See* Kirjath-jearim

**Cariath-jarim.** *See* Kirjath-jearim

**Cariath-sepher.** *See* Debir

**Carmania.** SE province of ancient Persia. Mod. *Kerman*. D-E3—7

**Carmel.** Town in the hill-country of Judah (Josh. 15:55; I Sam. 15:12). Mod. *el-Kirmil*, S of Hebron.

**Carmel, Mt.** Range of hills *ca.* 15 miles long, terminating in a promontory that juts into the Mediterranean, constituting the S boundary of the Bay of Acco (Acre). The mod. city of Haifa is at the foot of Mt. Carmel. The range is connected with the mountainous region of central Palestine by a chain of lower hills. The Carmel range comprises the SW boundary of the Plain of Esdraelon through which the Kishon R. flows. B2—1, 5; C2—3; B3—4, 11

**Carnaim.** *See* Karnaim

**Carnion.** *See* Karnaim

**Carpathians.** Mt. chain of central Europe that forms an arc *ca.* 900 miles long, enclosing the plain of the Danube to the N and E. D1—12

**Carpi.** A Dacian tribe located on the lower Danube from the 1st century B.C. They invaded the Roman Empire in the 3rd century A.D. and were later taken under Roman protection. In the time of Theodosius I, they were allies of the Huns.

**Carrhae** *See* Haran

**Cartagena.** Latin *Carthago Nova* ("New Carthage"). Port on the Mediterranean, in SE Spain. Founded by the Carthaginian Hasdrubal, *ca*. 225 B.C., it served as the chief Carthaginian base in Spain until captured (209 B.C.) by Scipio Africanus. It continued to flourish under the Romans.

**Carthage.** N African city on a peninsula in the Bay of Tunis, near mod. *Tunis*, founded in the 9th century B.C. by colonists from Tyre. During the 6th and 5th centuries B.C., Carthage acquired dominance over the W Mediterranean but was defeated by the Romans in a series of Punic (i.e., Phoenician) wars during the 3rd and 2nd centuries B.C. C3—12; B3—18

**Carthago Nova.** *See* Cartagena

**Casaloth.** *See* Chesulloth

**Caspian Gates.** Mt. pass S of the Caspian Sea, E of Rhagae. The Persians, under Darius III, hoped to make a stand against Alexander here. Darius was murdered, however, and Alexander met little opposition as he journeyed E to India.

**Caspian Sea** (Mare Hyrcanium). Salt lake located between Europe and Asia, bounded by Russia on the N and Iran on the S. The Caucasus Mts. arise from its SW shore, and the Elburz Mts. parallel its S coast. The Caspian receives the Volga, Ural, Kura, and Terek rivers, but it has no outlet. D1—6, 7; F1-2—12

**Catabathmus.** Town on the Gulf of Salum in Marmarica, E Libya (mod. *as-Sallum* in W Egypt). The Catabathmus Major was the name given in classical times to the descent or slope that separated Egypt from Marmarica.

**Caucasus.** The mt. system between Europe and Asia. It extends 750 miles from the mouth of the Kuban R. on the Black Sea SE to the Apherson Peninsula on the Caspian. F-G1—2; D1—6; C1—7; F2—12

**Cauda.** Small island S of Crete (Acts 27:16). It was also known as Clauda. Mod. *Gaudos* or *Gozzo*. C3—17

**Cedes.** *See* Kedesh

**Cedron.** City SE of Jamnia, fortified during the Maccabean struggle (I Macc. 15:39, 41). Poss. mod. *Qatra*.

**Cedron Valley.** *See* Kidron Valley

**Celia.** *See* Keilah

**Celaenae.** City of Phrygia, Asia Minor, near the headwaters of the Maeander R. (mod. *Menderes R*.). In Persian times Cyrus the Great had a palace at Celaenae. Alexander conquered the city in 333 B.C. Mod. *Dinar*.

**Celesyria.** *See* Coele Syria

**Celtiberi.** An ancient people of Hither Spain who were settled in the area S of the Ebro R.

**Celtic Gaul.** Area of S-central Gaul inhabited by tribes speaking Celtic languages.

**Cenabum.** Town on the Loire R., central Gaul. The Romans took Cenabum from the Gauls and renamed it Aurelianum, which became French Orléans.

**Cenchrae.** *See* Cenchreae

**Cenchrea.** *See* Cenchreae

**Cenchreae.** Harbor of Corinth, on the Saronic Gulf *ca*. 7 miles E of the city. Paul visited there (Acts 18:18). A2—15

**Cenereth.** *See* Chinnereth

**Ceneroth.** *See* Chinnereth

**Central Valley.** Valley that once separated the E and W hills of Jerusalem. It is now almost filled with debris as a result of Jerusalem's history of warfare and destruction. B2-3—8; D2-3—9

**Cerethi.** *See* Cherethites

**Cerethites.** *See* Cherethites

**Cethim.** *See* Cyprus

**Cetthim.** *See* Cyprus

**Chalcedon.** Ancient Greek city on the Bosporus, on the shore of Asia Minor opposite Byzantium. A church council convened there (A.D. 451). The site is now occupied by the suburbs of Istanbul.

**Chalcis** (in Euboea). City on the island of Euboea, opposite the Greek mainland. It led the revolt of Euboea against Athens (446 B.C.).

**Chalcis** (in Syria). City on the Leontes R. in the Beqa'a Valley. It was on the trade route from Antioch to Damascus. B4—13

**Chaldea.** Term used to designate the S portion of Babylonia, at the head of the Persian Gulf. The Chaldeans founded an empire under Nabopolassar.

**Chaldean Empire.** *See* Babylonian Empire, New

**Chale.** *See* Calah

**Chanaan.** *See* Canaan

**Charachmoba.** C6—11. *See* Kir-hareseth

**Charcamis.** *See* Carchemish

**Chaseleth.** *See* Chesulloth

**Chatti.** A Germanic people settled E of the Rhine, W of the Hermunduri.

**Chauci.** A Germanic people settled W of the lower Albis (Elbe), E of the Frisians.

**Chenereth.** *See* Chinnereth

**Chephirah.** Gibeonite city (Josh. 9:17) that was assigned to Benjamin (Josh. 18:26). Mod. *Tell Kefireh*, 8 miles NW of Jerusalem.

**Cherethites.** Nation or tribe inhabiting the S portion of the Philistine country (I Sam. 30:14; Ezek. 25:16; Zeph. 2:5). The name probably means "Cretans," and they are thought to have been related to the Philistines, who also came from the island of Crete.

**Cherith, Brook.** Wadi, flowing into the Jordan from the E, near which Elijah was fed by ravens (I Kings 17:3–7). Poss. mod. *W. Yabis*, or *W. Qelt*, which enters the Jordan from the W after flowing past Jericho.

**Chersonesus.** Black Sea port on the S shore of the Crimean Peninsula, known in ancient times as the Chersonese, or Chersonesus, the Greek word for "peninsula." B1—7

**Chesalon.** Town 10 miles W of Jerusalem on the border between the territories of Judah and Dan. It has been identified with Mt. Jearim (Josh. 15:10). Mod. *Kesla*.

**Cheslon.** *See* Chesalon

**Chesulloth.** Town on the border of the territory of Issachar (Josh. 19:18), 3.5 miles SE of Nazareth. Mod. *Iksal*.

**Chetthim.** *See* Cyprus

**Chinnereth.** Fortified city of Naphtali (Josh. 19:35; Deut. 3:17), NW of the Lake of Genesareth (Sea of Galilee). Mod. *Tell el-'Oreimeh*. C2—5

**Chinnereth, Sea of.** C2—1, 5. *See* Galilee, Sea of

**Chinneroth.** *See* Chinnereth

**Chios.** Island in the Greek Archipelago, S of Lesbos, at the entrance of the Gulf of Smyrna. B2—16

**Chisloth-tabor.** *See* Chesulloth

**Chittim.** *See* Cyprus

**Choaspes R.** River rising in W Iran, flowing S *ca.* 500 miles to join the Tigris and Euphrates N of the Persian Gulf. Ancient Susa was on its banks. The river is now known as the *Karkheh*.

**Chorasmia.** Ancient name for the region S of the Aral Sea, including the Oxus Delta. E1—7

**Chorasmii.** Ancient name of the people settled between the Caspian and Aral seas.

**Chorazin.** Town NW of the Sea of Galilee. Jesus ministered there, but its inhabitants rejected His message (Matt. 11:21; Luke 10:13). Mod. *Kh. Kerazeh*, 2 miles N of Capernaum. C2—11

**Chus.** *See* Cush

**Cibroth-hatthaava.** *See* Kibroth-hattaavah

**Cilicia.** District in the SE section of Asia Minor separated on the N by the Taurus Mts. from Cappadocia, Lycaonia, and Isauria; and on the E by the Amanus Mts. from Syria. It is bounded on the S by the Mediterranean and on the W by Pamphylia. Tarsus, the birthplace of Paul, was its chief town. B2—7; E3—12, 18; A-B1—13; D5—14; D2—15, 16

**Cilician Gates.** Mt. pass leading across the Taurus range from Cappadocia to Cilicia. Its ancient name was *Pylae Ciliciae*. Mod. *Gulek Bogaz*, Turkey. D2—15, 16

**Cimmerians.** A people who entered Asia from beyond the Caucasus, settled in Cappadocia, and for a time threatened the Assyrian Empire. After defeat by Esarhaddon (of Assyria), they overran part of Asia Minor and fought with Gyges of Lydia. Alyattes of Lydia drove them out of Asia Minor.

**Cirta.** Originally a Carthaginian settlement, Cirta became the capital and commercial center of Numidia, and an important shipping point in the supply of grain to the Romans. It is situated on a plateau on the gorge of the Rhumel R. Mod. *Constantine*, Algeria. B3—12, 18

**Cisalpine Gaul.** The section of Gaul (*q.v.*) in Italy (literally, "on this side of the Alps"), in contradistinction to Transalpine Gaul ("on the other side of the Alps").

**Cison R.** *See* Kishon R.

**City of Brick Walls.** *See* Kir-hareseth

**City of David.** *See* David, City of

**City of Palm Trees.** *See* Jericho

**Clauda.** *See* Cauda

**Clonard.** Community in central Ireland where a monastery was established (*ca.* A.D. 520) by Welsh Christians. From Clonard the so-called "Twelve Apostles of Ireland" went forth to establish schools throughout Ireland and, later, on the Continent.

**Cnidus.** City of Caria, SW Asia Minor, mentioned in the account of Paul's voyage to Rome (Acts 27:7). Mod. *Cape Krio*. D3—17

**Cnossus.** City of ancient Crete, on the N coast, near the sea. The study of the ruins of Cnossus has contributed to our knowledge of Minoan civilization. Near mod. *Candia*. D3—17, 18

**Coele Syria.** The high plain, also known as the Beqa'a, located between the Lebanon and Anti-Lebanon ranges. It is a fertile area watered by the Leontes R.

**Colchis.** Ancient land on the E shores of the Black Sea and in the Caucasus region, centered in the fertile Phasis R. valley. Greek trading posts were established there, but it remained independent until conquered (*ca.* 100 B.C.) by Mithridates VI of Pontus. F2—12

**Cologne.** City on the Rhine in NW Germany. It was established in A.D. 50 as a Roman colony by Claudius. B1—18

**Colonia Agrippina.** *See* Cologne

**Colossae.** City of SW Phrygia, Asia Minor, on the R. Lycos E of the point where it joins the Maeander. Ruins near mod. *Khonai*.

**Commagene.** District on the Euphrates in N Syria, now in SE Turkey. It was part of the Assyrian, and later the Persian, Empire, but revolted under the Seleucid kings of Syria and, early in the 2nd century B.C., became an independent state. Commagene was annexed to the Roman province of Syria by Vespasian (A.D. 72). E2—12

**Constanta.** *See* Tomi

**Constantinople.** *See* Byzantium

**Coos.** *See* Cos

**Cophen** (Kabul) **R.** River that flows 300 miles eastward from the Hindu Kush, past Kabul and Jalalabad and through gorges in the Khyber Pass to the Indus R. F2—7

**Corcyra.** Capital and largest city of the island of the same name off the W coast of Greece. It was established in the 8th century B.C. by colonists from Corinth, but it later made war with the mother city. In 229 B.C. Corcyra passed under Roman rule. Mod. *Corfu*.

**Cordoba.** *See* Corduba

**Cordova.** *See* Corduba

**Corduba.** City in S Spain at the foot of the Sierra de Cordoba on the Guadalquivir R. It is of Iberian origin and flourished under the Romans. Mod. *Cordoba* or *Cordova*. A2—12, 18

**Corduene.** Ancient name of the region extending S

of Lake Van as far as the Tigris.

**Corfinium.** Town in central Italy. During the Social War (91–88 B.C.) it served as capital of the republic of Italia.

**Corinth.** City of Greece on the narrow isthmus between the Peloponnesus and the mainland. It was on a plateau at the foot of an 1,800-foot-high mt.—the Acrocorinthus. Corinth had two harbors: Cenchreae, 8.5 miles E on the Saronic Gulf; and Lecheum, 1.5 miles W on the Corinthian Gulf. D3—12, 18; A2—15, 16; C2—17

**Corner Gate.** Gate at the NW corner of Jerusalem (*ca*. 445 B.C.). C2—9

**Corsica.** Mediterranean island, SE of France and N of Sardinia. It was controlled by the Romans from the 3rd century B.C. to the 5th century A.D. *See* Sardinia. B2—12, 18

**Cos.** Island in the archipelago off the coast of Caria, Asia Minor, in a gulf between Cnidus and Halicarnassus (Acts 21:1). Mod. *Kos*. B2—15, 16; D2—17

**Council House.** Meeting place of the Sanhedrin, the Jewish governing body charged by the Romans with the general administration of justice.

**Court of the Gentiles.** *See* Gentiles, Court of the

**Creta.** D3—12. *See* Crete

**Crete** (Caphtor). Large island in the Mediterranean, lying SE of Greece. It is traversed by a chain of mts., one of which, Mt. Ida, is 8,065 feet high. Paul sailed along its S coast on his voyage to Rome (Acts 27:7, 12, 13, 21). *See also* Caphtorim. A3—2; A2—6, 7; B2—15, 16; C3—17; D3—18

**Crocodilopolis** (Arsinoe). Egyptian city, said to have been founded *ca*. 2300 B.C., that served as the chief seat of early Egyptian worship of the crocodile. Near mod. *Al-Faiyum*. A5—3

**Croton.** City in S Italy on the E coast of Calabria, the Greek colony Magna Graecia, founded at the end of the 8th century B.C. The school of Pythagoras, which was established there, exerted a notable political and moral influence. It was captured by the Romans in 277 B.C. Mod. *Crotone*.

**Ctesiphon.** City on the left bank of the Tigris, opposite Seleucia, in S Mesopotamia. After 129 B.C. it was the winter residence of Parthian kings. F3—12

**Cush.** B4—7. *See* Ethiopia

**Cutha.** *See* Cuthah

**Cuthah.** City of ancient Mesopotamia, near Babylon. Natives of Cuthah, when settled in Samaria, introduced the worship of Nergal (II Kings 17:24–30). Poss. mod. *Tell Ibrahim*. F4—2

**Cyclades.** Part of the Greek archipelago in the Aegean Sea. The name originally indicated the islands forming a rough circle (*Kyklades* in Greek) around Delos. They include Andros, Tenos, Naxos, Melos, Paros, and Keos.

**Cydonia.** City on the Gulf of Canea in W Crete (*q.v.*). Mod. *Khania* or *Canea*.

**Cyprus** (Alashiya, Kittim), island of. Island in the E Mediterranean, *ca*. 40 miles S of the Cilician coast and 60 W of Syria. Its ancient population were Kittim or Chetthim (Gen. 10:4), poss. akin to the pre-Hellenic population of Greece. It was subsequently colonized by Phoenicians. The gospel was preached there after Stephen's martyrdom (Acts 11:19–20), and subsequently by Barnabas, Paul, and Mark (Acts 13:4; 15:39). C3—2; A1—4; B2—6, 7; E3—12, 17, 18; A3—13; C5—14; C2—15, 16

**Cyprus,** town of. Roman fortress S of Jericho captured by the Jews in their first revolt against Rome. C5—11

**Cyrenaica** (Libya). Region around the ancient city of Cyrene on the N coast of Africa. The Roman province of Cyrene was sometimes called Cyrenaica. D4—12, 18; C4—17

**Cyrene.** Ancient city in Cyrenaica (*q.v.*) in N Africa. Founded as a Greek colony (*ca*. 631 B.C.), Cyrene submitted to the Persians under Cambyses, but *ca*. 450 B.C. it regained independence. Its subsequent history was closely related to that of the Egyptian Ptolemies, Greece, and (after 96 B.C.) Rome. A2—7; D3—12, 18; C4—17

**Cyropolis.** City in Sogdiana, on the NE border of the Persian Empire. F2—7

**Cyrus R.** River that rises in Turkish Armenia, flows NE, then SE, paralleling the Greater Caucasus, a distance of 940 miles to the Caspian Sea. Mod. *Kura R*. F1—2; C2—7

**Cyzicus.** Ancient city at the neck of the Cyzicus Peninsula in NW Asia Minor. It was founded in 756 B.C. by Greek colonists from Miletus, and for a time it rivaled Byzantium in commercial importance.

**Czechs.** A W Slavic people related to the Poles, Slovaks, and Moravians. They united politically with the Slovaks to form Czechoslovakia.

## D

**Dabir.** *See* Debir

**Dacia.** Ancient name of the region corresponding to mod. *Transylvania* and *Romania*. Inhabitants of the area were called Getae by the Greeks, Daci by the Romans. D2—12, 18

**Dadan.** *See* Dedan

**Dahae.** An ancient people settled in the region between the Caspian and Aral seas.

**Dalmanutha.** Place prob. situated on the W shore of the Sea of Galilee. Region to which Jesus went after the 2nd miracle of the loaves and fishes (Mark 8:10). Poss. Magadan (*q.v.*).

**Dalmatia.** B1—17. *See* Illyricum

**Damascus,** city of. Syrian city on a plateau watered by the Abana and Pharpar rivers (II Kings 5:12). Important trade routes leading to Egypt, Arabia, and Mesopotamia converge at Damascus, a city mentioned as early as the time of Abraham (Gen. 14:15). Mod. Damascus, on the Barada R. (biblical Abana R. [*q.v.*]), bears the Arabic name *Esh-Sham*. D1—1, 3, 5, 11; D3—2, 15, 16; C3—4; C2—6; B2—7; B4—13; D6—14; F3—17, 18

**Damascus, Kingdom of.** City-state of S Syria that, after the time of David, was frequently in conflict with Israel (I Kings 11:23–24). It took the lead in resisting the Assyrians and led an alliance against Shalmaneser at Karkar (854–853 B.C.). Tiglath-pileser captured Damascus (732 B.C.) and carried its inhabitants into exile (II Kings 16:5–9).

**Damghan** (Hecatompylus). Parthian capital, visited by Alexander the Great during his campaign in the E. Polybius stated that all roads of the Parthian Empire centered there. D2—7

**Dan,** allotment of. The original allotment of Dan was along the Mediterranean N of the Valley of Sorek (marking the N border of Judah), W of Benjamin, and S and W of Ephraim. It included the towns of Zorah, Eltekeh, and Ekron, and it ended N of Joppa (Num. 1:12, 38, 39; Josh. 19:40–46; 21:5, 23, 24). Cramped for room, the Danites looked for additional territory in the extreme N of the country and conquered the city of Laish and environs, which they named Dan (*q.v.*).

**Dan,** town of. Town in the extreme N of Palestine, originally called Laish (Judg. 18) or Leshem (Josh. 19:47). Jeroboam of Israel made Dan a shrine town, placing one of his golden calves there (I Kings 12:28–30). Mod. *Tell el-Qadi*. C1—1, 5, 19; B3—4

**Danube** (Ister) **R.** River of central and SE Europe. It rises in the Black Forest in SE Germany and flows E *ca*. 1,750 miles before entering the Black Sea. A1—6, 7; C1—12, 18

**Daphca.** *See* Dophkah

**David, City of.** B2-3—8. *See* Jerusalem

**Dead** (Salt) **Sea.** Body of water situated in the deep volcanic fissure that runs through Palestine from N to S. It is fed principally by the Jordan. Its surface is 1,292 feet below sea level. C5—1; C6—11; B6—13; C4-5—19

**Debir.** City in the hill country of Judah also known as Kirjath-sepher. Poss. mod. *Tell Beit Mirsim*, 12 miles SW of Hebron. C3—3; B5—5, 19

**Deblatha.** *See* Riblah

**Decapolis.** District that begins where the Plain of Esdraelon opens into the Jordan Valley and expands eastward. It derives its name from the original association of 10 Hellenistic cities (later expanded to 18). Multitudes from Decapolis followed Jesus early in His ministry (Matt. 4:25). C-D3—11; B5—13

**Dedan** (descendant of Ham). Arabian tribe that settled W of the Persian Gulf.

**Dedan** (descendant of Shem). Arabian tribe that settled E of the N sector of the Arabian Gulf (Red Sea).

**Dedan,** town of. Caravan center *ca*. 100 miles S of Tema. Jeremiah referred to it (Jer. 25:23; 49:8). Dedan was a descendant of Ham (Gen. 10:7). E6—2; C3—6; B3—7

**Dephca.** *See* Dophkah

**Der'a.** *See* Edrei

**Derbe.** City in SE Lycaonia, Asia Minor, visited by Paul on his First and Second Missionary Journeys (Acts 14:6, 20; 16:1). Prob. the ruins 3 miles NW of mod. *Zosta*, 45 miles S of *Konya* (Iconium), Turkey. C5—14; C2—15

**Develtum.** Town on the W shore of the Black Sea, *ca*. 125 miles NW of Byzantium. A church is known to have been there in the 2nd century.

**Dhiban.** *See* Dibon

**Diala R.** *See* Diyala R.

**Dibon** (Dhiban). Town 3 miles N of the Arnon R. in Transjordan. It had been a Moabite town (Num. 21:30; 32:3) but was rebuilt by the tribe of Gad (Num. 32:34) and named Dibongad (Num. 33:45–46). The Moabite Stone, found among its ruins, tells how it was recaptured by the Moabites. Mod. *Dhiban*. D3—3; C5—5; D4—19

**Dictones.** An ancient people settled along the W coast of Gaul, S of the Liger (Loire).

**Dion.** City of the Decapolis (*q.v.*) located on the Yarmuk R. W of the Sea of Galilee. Prob. mod. *Tell el-Ash'ari*. D3—11

**Diospolis.** *See* Lod

**Diyala R.** Tributary of the Tigris. Its source is in the Zagros Mts., from which it flows in a generally SE direction. F3—2

**Dnieper R.** *See* Borysthenes R.

**Dniester R.** From its source in the Carpathians, the Dniester flows in a generally SE direction through SE Europe before entering the Black Sea SW of Odessa.

**Doch.** *See* Dok

**Dok.** Fortress NW of Jericho (I Macc. 16:15). The spring at the foot of the hill is named *'Ain Duq*.

**Don R.** River that has its source a short distance SE of Tula, Soviet Russia, and flows 1,232 miles SE, then SW into the Sea of Azov.

**Dophkah.** Encampment of the Israelites on the route to Sinai between the Red Sea and Rephidim (Num. 33:12–13). Poss. mod. *Serabit el-Khadim*, a mining center in the Sinai Peninsula. B5—3

**Dor** (Dora), city of. Seaport of ancient Palestine, 8 miles N of Caesarea. Mod. *el-Burj*, N of *Tanturah*. B3—1, 5; D4—2; C2—3; B4—4; B2—19

**Dor,** district of. Area around the city of Dor (*q.v.*).

**Dora.** B3—11. *See* Dor

**Dorylaeum.** Ancient city of N Phrygia, Asia Minor, used as a trading center by the Romans. Poss. mod. *Eskisehir*, NW Turkey.

**Dothain.** *See* Dothan

**Dothan.** City near the Plain of Esdraelon, in central Palestine, N of Samaria. In the vicinity of Dothan, Joseph was sold into slavery (Gen. 37:17–28). Mod. *Tell Dotan*. C3—1, 19; B3—5

**Dragon's Well.** *See* En-rogel

**Drangiana.** Ancient country in Asia between Aria to the N and Gedrosia to the S. It was conquered by Alexander the Great. It is now in E Iran and W Afghanistan. E3—7

**Druz, J. ed.** Mountainous area of the Hauran, in Syria SE of Damascus, inhabited by the Druses, a Moslem sect with a strong element of mystical-pantheistic and ancient pagan concepts.

**Duero R.** River that rises in the Sierra de Urbion, N-central Spain, and flows 475 miles in a generally SW direction through Spain and Portugal to the Atlantic.

**Dumah** (in Arabia). Oasis in the NW part of the Arabian Peninsula. Known as *Dumat al-Jandal*, mod. *al-Jauf*. E4—2; C3—6, 7

**Dumah** (in Judah). Town in the hill-country of Judah, 10 miles SW of Hebron (Josh. 15:52). Mod. *ed-Domeh*.

**Dung Gate.** Gate on the SW side of Jerusalem (Neh. 2:13; 3:13–14; 12:31).

**Dura.** Palestinian town, 5 miles SW of Hebron.

**Dura-Europos.** City founded *ca*. 300 B.C. by a general of Seleucus I, one of Alexander's successors, in the Syrian desert E of Tadmor. F3—18

**Durazzo.** *See* Dyrrhachium

**Durius R.** *See* Duero R.

**Durocotorum.** *See* Reims

**Dur Sharrukin.** Site of the palace built by Sargon II (713–707 B.C.), NE of Nineveh. Mod. *Khorsabad*.

**Du'ru.** District around the city of Dor, comprising the Plain of Sharon. *See* Dor, district of

**Dyrrhachium.** Adriatic port in W Macedonia founded jointly by Corinth and Corcyra *ca*. 625 B.C. It became part of the kingdom of Epirus and in 229 B.C. was taken by Rome. It was originally called Epidamnus, then Dyrrhachium, then Durazzo. B1—17

## E

**Eastern Sea.** *See* Dead Sea

**East Gate.** Gate on the E side of Jerusalem (Neh. 3:29). Poss. corresponds to the mod. Golden Gate.

**Ebal, Mt.** Mt. separated by a narrow valley from Mt. Gerizim (Deut. 27:12–13), near the oak of Moreh (Deut. 11:30), N of Shechem (Gen. 12:6; 35:4). C3—1; B3—5; C4—11

**Ebla.** City located *ca*. 18.5 miles S of Haleb (Aleppo). It was the capital of a kingdom in the 3rd century B.C. Excavations there since 1964 have yielded thousands of tablets. Mod. *Tell Mardikh*. D3—2

**Eboracum.** *See* York

**Ebro R.** River in NE Spain. It rises in the Cantabrian Mts., flows *ca*. 575 miles SE between the Pyrenees and Cantabrian mts., and empties into the Mediterranean below Tarraco. Its ancient name was Iberus.

**Ecbatana** (Achmetha). Capital of ancient Media, summer residence of Achemenian (Persian) and Parthian rulers. Mod. *Hamadan*. G3—2; D2—6, 7

**Ecdippa.** *See* Achzib

**Edessa.** Ancient Mesopotamian city at the site of mod. *Urfa*, Turkey. By the 3rd century it was a center of Syrian Christianity and became a major religious center of the Byzantine Empire. F3—18

**Edom.** Mountainous territory S of the Dead Sea, extending along the E border of the Arabah Valley to Elath on the Gulf of Aqaba. Known also as Mt. Seir, it was given to Esau and his descendants. C6—1, 5; D4—3; B6—4

**Edomites.** Descendants of Esau (Edom) who became inhabitants of Edom (*q.v.*). Edomites were enemies of the Israelites until subdued by the Maccabees. In Greco-Roman times they were known as Idumeans, and their land, Idumea.

**Edrai.** *See* Edrei

**Edrei.** Capital city of Bashan, where the Israelites fought with Og (Num. 21:33–35). Mod. *Der'a*, 27 miles E of Gadara. D2—3; C4—4; D3—5

**Eglon.** City of S Palestine, SW of Lachish. It joined 4 other cities in attacking Gibeon, which had made peace with Joshua (Josh. 10:1–5). The kings were killed and their cities destroyed (Josh. 10:24–27). *See* Tell el-Hesi. C3—3; B4—19

**Egypt.** Country occupying the NE portion of Africa. Its Hebrew name is Mizraim (cf. Gen. 10:6 KJV). In ancient times Egypt comprised the area from the 1st cataract of the Nile N to the Mediterranean. Ancient Egypt was the scene of some of man's earliest achievements in literature, art, and architecture. A-B4—3; B3—7; E4—12, 17, 18; A6—19

**Egypt, Brook of.** C3—3. *See* 'Arish, W. el

**Egypt, Kingdom of.** Extended W to Libya in the 6th century B.C. B3—6

**Egypt, Lower.** The Nile Delta (*q.v.*) area of Egypt. C4—2

**Egypt, River of.** A5-6—4. *See* 'Arish, W. el

**Egypt, Upper.** The area of Egypt S of the Nile Delta (*q.v.*). C5-6—2

**Egyptian Empire.** Extended to Palestine, Transjordan, and S Syria in the early 2nd millennium B.C. C5-D4—2

**Eilat.** *See* Elath

**'Ein-gedi.** *See* En-gedi

**Eizariya.** *See* Bethany

**Ekron.** The northernmost of the 5 Philistine cities, located in the territory assigned to Dan, near the border of Judah. Prob. mod. *'Aqir*, 12 miles NW of Ashdod. B4—5

**Ela, Valley of.** *See* Elah, Valley of

**Elah, Valley of.** Valley near Shoco in which the Israelites confronted the Philistines before the combat between David and Goliath (I Sam. 17). Prob. mod. *W. es-Sant*.

**Elah R.** B4—1. *See* Elah, Valley of

**Elam.** Region beyond the Tigris, E of Babylonia, bounded on the N by Assyria and Media, on the S by the Persian Gulf, and on the E and SE by Persia. Seat of the ancient Elamite Empire. *See* Susiana. G4—2; D3—6

**Elasa.** Place in N Judea where Judas Maccabeus is said to have camped. Prob. mod. *Kh. Il'asa*, midway between the 2 Beth-horons.

**Elath.** Town at the head of the Gulf of Aqaba, on the E border of the Wilderness of Paran, through which the Israelites passed on their journey from Sinai to Canaan (Deut. 2:8). It was located E of Ezion-geber, with which it was later identified. Mod. *Eilat*. B3—7

**El 'Auja.** *See* Auja el-Hafir

**Elbe R.** C1—12. *See* Albis R.

**Elburz Mts.** Mt. range of N Iran, S of the Caspian. Mt. Damavand is the highest peak (*ca.* 18,900 feet high).

**Eleale.** *See* Elealeh

**Elealeh.** City built by the Reubenites (Num. 32:3) in Transjordan. Later it fell into the hands of the Moabites. It is uniformly mentioned with Heshbon. Mod. *el-Al*, 2 miles NE of Heshbon.

**Elephantine.** B4—6, 7. *See* Syene

**El Ghor.** *See* Ghor, El

**Elim.** Place where Israelites encamped after crossing the Red Sea (Exod. 15:27; 16:1), between Marah and the Wilderness of Sin. Prob. mod. *W. Gharandel*, 63 miles from Suez. B5—3

**Elisa.** *See* Elishah

**Elishah.** Descendants of Javan (i.e., Ionians) who inhabited Elishah (Gen. 10:4). Ezekiel 27:7 suggests Carthage, S Italy, and Greece as the land of Elishah.

**El Kerak.** *See* Kir-hareseth

**El Kuntilla.** Town in the Sinai Peninsula, NW of Eilat. Numerous trails from SW Sinai and the SE Negeb converge there. It is also known as *Thaimilet es-Suweilmeh*.

**Ellip.** Region N of Elam in the area between the Zagros Mts. and the Caspian Sea. It was conquered by the Assyrians and subsequently fell to the Medes and Persians.

**El Qanawat.** *See* Kanatha

**El Quneitra.** Town in Syria, NE of Lake Hula. It is on a road that ran from Damascus to Palestine, crossing the Jordan midway between Lake Hula and the Sea of Galilee.

**El Qusaima.** Site in the Wilderness of Paran in the extreme S of Palestine (near the E border of mod. Egypt). It is NW of *'Ain Qadeis*, the probable site of Kadesh-barnea. El Qusaima is closer to the Egyptian road and has been suggested as an alternate site for Kadesh-barnea.

**Eltekeh.** Town of Dan that was assigned to the Levites (Josh. 19:40, 44; 21:20, 23). Destroyed by Sennacherib (701 B.C.). Prob. mod. *Kh. el-Muqanna'*, 6 miles SE of Ekron.

**Elthece.** *See* Eltekeh

**Eltheco.** *See* Eltekeh

**Emath.** *See* Hamath

**Emath, Tower of.** *See* Meah, Tower of

**Emerita Augusta.** A2—12. *See* Merida

**Emesa.** City on the Orontes R., S of Hamath, in a fertile plain on the trade route between Damascus and Aleppo. Mod. *Homs*. C3—13

**Emmaus.** Town 7.5 miles (60 furlongs) from Jerusalem, the scene of Christ's revelation of Himself after the resurrection (Luke 24:13). The exact location is not certain. B5—11

**Emmaus** (Nicopolis). Town 20 miles from Jerusalem on the highway to Joppa. Its distance is such that it cannot be the Emmaus "threescore furlongs" from Jerusalem (Luke 24:13). If textual variants that read 160 furlongs instead of 60 are correct, it could be the town intended. Mod. *'Amwas*. B5—11

**Enan.** *See* Hazar-enan

**En-dor.** Town in the territory of Manasseh (Josh. 17:11), on the N shoulder of Little Hermon, 6 miles SE of Nazareth. Mod. *Endor* or *Indur*.

**Engaddi.** C6—11. *See* En-gedi

**En-gannim** (Ginae). City in the territory of Issachar (Josh. 19:21) assigned to the Levites (Josh. 21:29). Mod. *Jenin*, 15 miles S of Mt. Tabor.

**Engeddi.** *See* En-gedi

**En-gedi** (Engaddi). Fountain and town, also called Hazezon-tamar, near the midpoint of the W shore of the Dead Sea, in Judah *ca.* 30 miles SE of Jerusalem. David took refuge there from Saul (I Sam. 23:29). Mod. *'Ain Jidi*. C5—5

**English Channel.** Arm of the Atlantic, 350 miles long, between France and England. At the E end, the Strait of Dover connects it with the North Sea.

**En-Harod.** *See* Harod

**En-hasor.** *See* En-hazor

**En-hazor.** Town in the territory of Naphtali (Josh. 19:32, 37). Poss. mod. *Kh. Hasireh,* W of *'Ain Ibl*.

**En-mishpat.** *See* Kadesh-barnea

**Ennom Valley.** *See* Hinnom Valley

**En-remmon.** *See* En-rimmon

**En-rimmon.** Town in the Judean Negeb (Neh. 11:29), also called Rimmon (Josh. 15:32). Mod. *Kh. Umm er-Rammin*, 9 miles NE of Beersheba.

**En-rogel** (Dragon's Well). Fountain outside Jerusalem, near the Hinnom Valley, S of the Jebusite fortress (Josh. 15:7; 18:16). It was near the boundary between the territories of Judah and Benjamin. Mod. *Bir Ayyub*. B3—8; D3—9

**Ephesus.** City in Lydia, W Asia Minor, at the mouth of the Cayster R., midway between Miletus and Smyrna, on an important trade route. In Roman times it was capital of the province of Asia. It was devoted to the goddess Diana. A2—7; D3—12, 18; B2—15, 16; D2—17

**Ephra.** *See* Ophrah

**Ephraim,** allotment of. The S boundary of Ephraimite territory was a line W of the Jordan including the cities of Jericho, Ai, Bethel, and Mizpah. Its N boundary (with Manasseh) was irregular, including territory S of Mt. Gerizim and the Kanah R. Ephraim was bounded on the W and SW by the territory of Dan.

**Ephraim,** city of. City *ca.* 4 miles NE of Bethel (II Sam. 13:23). Mod. *et-Taiyibeh*. C4—11

**Ephraim,** district of. The hill-country of Ephraim (Mt. Ephraim), the portion of the central mt. range occupied by the tribe of Ephraim.

**Ephraim, Gate of.** Gate in the NW sector of the wall of Jerusalem. D2—9

**Ephron.** *See* Ephraim, city of

**Epiphania.** Name assigned to the city of Hamath (*q.v.*) by Antiochus Epiphanes. C3—13

**Epirus.** Ancient country on the Ionian Sea, N of the Ambracian Gulf, S of Illyria, and W of

Macedonia and Thessaly. The region is now part of NW Greece and S Albania. B-C2—17

**Erech** (Uruk). Ancient Sumerian city, on the Euphrates, NE of ancient Ur. Gilgamesh, Babylonian epic hero, was king of Erech. F4—2; D3—6; C3—7

**Eridu.** Ancient Sumerian city, S of Ur. G4—2

**Er Rumman.** City of Transjordan, S of the Jabbok R.

**Erythraean Sea.** The part of the Indian Ocean now known as the Arabian Sea and the Persian Gulf. F4—6; E4—7

**Esbus.** D5—11. *See* Heshbon

**Esdraelon, Plain of.** Fertile plain of central Palestine watered by the Kishon R. The Esdraelon extends from the Mediterranean, near Mt. Carmel, SE to the Jordan Valley at Beth-shan. It is the means of access from the coastal plain to the Jordan Valley and beyond. C3—1; B3—5, 11

**Eshnunna.** Ancient town N of the Diyala R., 50 miles NE of mod. *Baghdad*. An important ancient law code was discovered at Eshnunna, known also as Ashnunnak. Mod. *Tell Asmar*. F3—2

**Eshtemoa.** Town in the hill-country of Judah 9 miles S of Hebron (Josh. 15:50; I Sam. 30:28). Mod. *es-Semu'*.

**Essene Gate.** Gate at the SW corner of Jerusalem, leading into the Hinnom Valley.

**Esthemo.** *See* Eshtemoa

**Esztergom.** City on the Danube in N Hungary, 25 miles NW of Budapest.

**Etam.** Town in the hill-country of Judah, fortified by Rehoboam (II Chron. 11:6). Poss. mod. *Kh. el-Khokh*, 2 miles SW of Bethlehem.

**Etham.** First encampment of the Israelites during the Exodus after having left Succoth. Located on the edge of the wilderness (Exod. 13:20; Num. 33:6).

**Etham, Wilderness of.** Part of the Wilderness of Shur, apparently reaching as far as Marah. B4—3

**Ethiopia** (Cush). Country in Africa, S of Egypt (II Kings 19:9; Esther 1:1). The border between Egypt and Ethiopia was Syene, mod. *Aswan*, at the 1st cataract of the Nile (Ezek. 29:10). Cush was a son of Ham (Gen. 10:6–8); in most passages the term *Cush* refers to the land of Ethiopia. B4—6, 7

**Etruria.** Ancient country of W-central Italy, occupied by the Etruscans.

**Euboea.** Greek island in the Aegean, separated from Boeotia and Attica on the mainland by a narrow channel. Chalcis is the principal city.

**Eulaeus R.** *See* Ulai R.

**Euphrates R.** Rising in the mts. of Armenia (E Turkey), the Euphrates flows *ca*. 1,675 miles before it joins the Tigris to form the *Shatt el-Arab*. The lower Tigris and Euphrates water Mesopotamia (lit., "between the rivers"). E3—2; D1—4; C2—6, 7

**Europe.** Continent N of Africa, W of Asia. It is separated from Africa by the Mediterranean Sea, and from Asia by the Ural Mts. and Ural R. in the E, the Caspian Sea and the Caucasus in the SE, and the Black Sea, the Bosporus, and the Dardanelles in the S.

**Evora.** City of SE Spain (mod. Portugal). Ancient Ebora was renamed Liberalitas Julia, after Julius Caesar.

**Ezion-geber.** Town at the N end of the Gulf of Aqaba, W of Elath. At the time of Solomon it became an important Red Sea port. Mod. *Tell el-Kheleifeh*. D5—3; B6—4

## F

**Fair Havens.** Harbor on the S coast of Crete, S of Candia, near Lasea (Acts 27:8). It was 5 miles E of Cape Matala. Mod. *Kali Limines*. D3—17

**Farah R.** This river, or wadi, meets the Jordan R. from the W where the Jabbok meets it from the E. Together they form one of the three crossings through the Jordan Valley. C4—1

**Faro.** Seaport of SE Spain (mod. Portugal). It was an important Moorish city, retaken A.D. 1249.

**Farther Spain.** One of two provinces into which Spain was divided by the Romans. Farther Spain (*Hispania Ulterior*) occupied the territory in the S around Gibraltar and the Guadalquivir R. *See also* Hither Spain

**Field of Blood.** *See* Aceldama

**Fish Gate.** Gate in the wall on the N side of Jerusalem (II Chron. 33:14; Neh. 3:3; 12:39).

**Florence.** City of central Italy, on the Arno R. at the foot of the Apennines. Florence was a leading center of the Renaissance.

**Fortress Antonia.** *See* Antonia, Fortress

**Forum of Appius.** *See* Appius, Forum of

**Fountain Gate.** Gate in the wall of the SE sector of Jerusalem. D3—9

**Frisians.** A Germanic people, closely akin to the Anglo-Saxons, who settled on the coastlands and islands of the North Sea.

**Fulda.** City on the Fulda R. in W Germany. From the Benedictine abbey of Fulda, founded by St. Boniface, Christianity spread throughout central Germany.

## G

**Gaba.** *See* Geba

**Gabaath.** *See* Gibeah

**Gabae** (Aspadana). City in SE Media. Mod. *Isfahan*, midway between Tehran and Shiraz. D3—7

**Gabaon.** *See* Gibeon

**Gabee.** *See* Geba

**Gabua.** *See* Geba, Gibeah, *and* Gibeon

**Gad,** allotment of. Territory E of the Jordan situated between Reuben (S) and Manasseh (N). Gad occupied most of the territory E of the Jordan from the S end of the Sea of Galilee to the N end of the Dead Sea.

**Gadara** (in Decapolis). City of the Decapolis, mentioned in the account of the healing of the demoniac (Mark 5:1; Luke 8:26, 37 KJV). It was located opposite Tiberias, *ca.* 6 miles E of the Sea of Galilee. Mod. *Muqeis* or *Umm Qeis*. C3—11

**Gadara** (in Perea). Chief city of Perea, located *ca.* 15 miles NE of Philadelphia. C4—11

**Gaderoth.** *See* Gederoth

**Gades** (Cadiz). City on the Bay of Cadiz, SW Spain. Founded by Phoenicians (*ca.* 1100 B.C.), it fell to the Carthaginians (*ca.* 500 B.C.) and, in the 3rd century B.C., to the Romans. Mod. *Cadiz*.

**Gaetulia.** Land of the Gaetuli, one of the aboriginal races of N Africa. The area known as Gaetulia was of somewhat uncertain limits.

**Galaad.** *See* Gilead

**Galatia.** District in central Asia Minor. Gallic tribes, after having invaded Macedonia and Greece (278–277 B.C.), migrated to Asia Minor and received the territory of Galatia from Nicomedes, king of Bithynia, in return for services rendered him in war. The territory was subsequently enlarged by the Romans. E3—12; C4—14; C-D1—15, 16; E2—17, 18

**Galgal.** *See* Gilgal

**Galgala.** *See* Gilgal

**Galilee.** Hill-country N of the Plain of Esdraelon. Galilee was the northernmost of the 3 provinces into which the Romans divided Palestine W of the Jordan. Because of its mixed population it was known as Galilee of the Nations (Gentiles). B-C2—5; C2—11; B5—13

**Galilee,** lower. Galilee S of the fault of *Esh-shaghur* (the Plain of *er-Rameh*), which goes from Acco to the region S of Safad. *See* Galilee, upper. C2—1

**Galilee** (Chinnereth), **Sea of.** Lake in the N part of the Jordan Valley, 12.5 miles long and 7.5 miles wide, variously known as the Sea of Galilee or Chinnereth, or Lake Tiberias. Many of the miracles of Jesus were performed in the communities on the shores of the Sea of Galilee. C2—1, 19; C3—11; B5—13

**Galilee,** upper. Galilee N of the fault of *Esh-shaghur* to the gorge of the Leontes R., which enters the Mediterranean N of Tyre. *See* Galilee, lower. C2—1

**Gallaecia.** District in NW Spain occupied by the Gallaeci, a civilized people defeated by the Romans under Brutus (138 B.C.).

**Gamala.** Fortified city E of the Sea of Galilee. One of the last cities to fall to the Romans in their campaign in Galilee and N Palestine (A.D. 67).

**Gandara.** Region of NW India, SE of Sogdiana, the E limit of the Persian Empire (*ca.* 500 B.C.). F2—7

**Garizim, Mt.** *See* Gerizim, Mt.

**Gasgas.** Region S of the Black Sea in patriarchal times. The people who inhabited the area, known as *Gashgash* in the Hittite language, appear to be related to the Kassite, or Caspian, peoples.

**Gate of Ephraim.** *See* Ephraim, Gate of

**Gath.** One of the 5 great Philistine cities, and the home of Goliath (I Sam. 17:4; II Sam. 21:15–22). Its location is uncertain. Poss. mod. *'Araq el-Menshiyeh*, 8 miles NE of Lachish; or *Tell es-Safi*. B5—4; B4—5

**Gath-hepher.** Town on the border of the territory of Zebulun, 3 miles NE of Nazareth. Birthplace of Jonah (II Kings 14:25). Prob. mod. *Kh. ez-Zurra'*.

**Gath-rimmon.** Town in Dan (Josh. 19:45). Poss. mod. *Tell Abu Zeitun*, in the Plain of Joppa.

**Gaugamela.** Site of a battle in which Alexander the Great defeated Darius III of Persia (331 B.C.). It is 60 miles NW of Arbela, mod. *Erbil*.

**Gaul.** Ancient name for the land S and W of the Rhine, W of the Alps, and N of the Pyrenees. The name was extended to include N Italy, which was termed Cisalpine Gaul. B1—12, 18

**Gaulanitis.** Region of Transjordan NE of the Sea of Galilee which took its name from the city of Golan (Gaulan). C-D2—11

**Gaulan.** *See* Golan

**Gaver.** *See* Gur

**Gaza.** Southernmost of the 5 Philistine cities (Gen. 10:19), at the junction of the main road between Mesopotamia and Egypt and a trade route from S Arabia. Mod. *Ghazzeh*. A5—1, 4, 5; D4—2; C3—3; B3—7; A6—11, 13; F4—17; A4—19

**Gazara.** *See* Gezer

**Gaza Strip.** Band of territory *ca.* 31 miles long and 4 miles wide stretching along the Mediterranean coast from Gaza to Egypt.

**Gazer(a).** *See* Gezer

**Geba.** Town in Benjamin (Josh. 18:24; I Kings 15:22; Ezra 2:26) 6 miles N of Jerusalem. Mod. *Jeba'*. C4—5

**Gebal** (Byblos). Ancient Phoenician city on the Mediterranean, 25 miles N of Beirut. The port of Gebal was used in exporting cedar wood to Egypt before Sidon, and later Tyre, became the principal Phoenician ports. Byblos was the Greek name given to the city (Josh. 13:5; I Kings 5:18 RSV). D3—2; D1—3; B2—4, 7

**Gebbethon.** *See* Gibbethon

**Gederoth.** Town in the lowlands of Judah (Josh. 15:41) captured by the Philistines in the time of Ahaz (II Chron. 28:18). Poss. mod. *Qatra*.

**Gedrosia** (Maka). Ancient coastal region N of the Arabian Sea and W of India. It was the SE limit of the Persian Empire. Mod. *Makran* in SE Iran and SW Baluchistan. E3—7

**Geennom Valley.** *See* Hinnom Valley

**Gehenna Valley.** *See* Hinnom Valley

**Gelboe, Mt.** *See* Gilboa, Mt.

**Genesar, Water of.** *See* Galilee, Sea of

**Genesareth, Lake of.** *See* Galilee, Sea of

**Gennath Gate.** Gate leading from the N wall of Jerusalem's Upper City to Bethzatha. B5—10

**Genoa.** City in NW Italy founded in ancient times in the district of Liguria. It flourished under Roman rule and is still an important seaport.

**Gentiles, Court of the.** Open area in the Jerusalem temple extending from the inner side of the porticoes to the low wall separating this court from the inner courts. Both Jews and Gentiles were free to mingle here, but only Jews could advance to the inner courts. B-C5—10

**Gentiles, Isles of the.** Islands and coastal regions of the Mediterranean peopled by the "sons of Javan," i.e., Ionian Greeks (Gen. 10:4–5). Some suggest the broader classification of "sons of Japheth" for the inhabitants.

**Genua.** *See* Genoa

**Gerar.** Ancient Philistine city on the S border of Palestine, near Gaza (Gen. 10:19). Poss. mod. *Tell Jemmeh*, 8 miles SE of Gaza. A5—4, 5

**Gerar, Valley of.** Valley extending from a short distance SE of Gerar to the Mediterranean, which it enters S of Gaza.

**Gerara.** *See* Gerar

**Gerar R.** A5—1. *See* Gerar, Valley of

**Gerasa** (Jerash). Ancient city of the Decapolis, 37 miles SE of the Sea of Galilee. The ruins that still remain indicate that it was a flourishing Roman city in the 2nd and 3rd centuries A.D. D4—11; B5—13

**Gergesa.** Town on the E bank of the Sea of Galilee, opposite Magadan. Mod. *Kursi*.

**Gergovia.** City of S-central Gaul where Caesar was forced to withdraw his army at the lowest ebb of his campaign.

**Gerizim, Mt.** Mt. in Samaria near Shechem, S of Mt. Ebal (Deut. 11:29; 27:12; Josh. 8:33). A temple of the Samaritans was located there. Mod. *J. et-Tor*. B4—1, 5, 11

**Germania.** Country bounded by the Rhine on the SW, the Carpathians on the E, the Baltic on the N, and the Danube on the S. It was inhabited by a branch of the Indo-Germanic race that came to Europe from the Caucasus in prehistoric times. C1—12, 18

**Germanicopolis.** City in Galatia, central Asia Minor. Located at the foot of a hill, it served as a citadel. In Byzantine times it was known as Gangra. Mod. *Cankiri*, Turkey.

**Gerrha.** Port on SW coast of the Persian Gulf, mentioned by Strabo and Pliny. Prob. mod. *Oqair*, Saudi Arabia. D3—7

**Gesen.** *See* Goshen

**Geshur.** Territory E of the Sea of Galilee, bordering Argob, occupied by an Aramean kingdom at the time of the Israelite monarchy. There David obtained a wife (II Sam. 3:3), and to Geshur his son Absalom fled after having Amnon murdered (II Sam. 13:37). B3—4

**Gessen.** *See* Goshen

**Gessur.** *See* Geshur

**Getae.** An ancient people who lived on the shores of the Danube and in the territory W of the Black Sea. They had an advanced culture and resisted Roman encroachments until A.D. 105, when their country, known as Dacia (*q.v.*), became a Roman colony.

**Geth.** *See* Gath

**Geth-hepher.** *See* Gath-hepher

**Geth-remmon.** *See* Gath-rimmon

**Gethsemane.** Garden E of Jerusalem, a little beyond the brook Kidron, at or near the foot of the Mt. of Olives. There Jesus agonized in prayer before His arrest (Matt. 26:36–56). C4—10

**Gethsemani.** *See* Gethsemane

**Gezer** (Gazara). Ancient Canaanite town on the SE border of Ephraim (Josh. 16:3). It was captured by the pharaoh whose daughter was the wife of Solomon (I Kings 9:16). Mod. *Tell Jezer*. C3—3; B4—4, 5, 19

**Gharandal.** Site in the W. Arabah known in Roman times as Aridella. It is known to have been occupied in Nabatean and Roman times.

**Ghor, El.** A name sometimes applied to the entire Jordan rift, which extends 250 miles from Lebanon to the head of the Gulf of Aqaba. Usually, however, it applies to the Jordan Valley from the Sea of Galilee to the Dead Sea, an area entirely below sea level, varying in width from 2 to 15 miles, bounded by mountainous terrain on each side. The term *Zor* ("thicket") is used for the depression, 200 yards to a mile wide, which the Jordan covers during the spring floods. The *Zor* is covered with tropical vegetation and is known as the "Jungle of the Jordan" (KJV, "Pride of the Jordan").

**Gibbethon.** City in the territory of Dan (Josh. 19:44). Prob. mod. *Tell el-Melat*, E of Ekron. B4—5

**Gibeah.** Town in the territory of Benjamin *ca*. 4 miles N of Jerusalem. It was the early home of Saul (I Sam. 10:26) and his headquarters in fighting the Philistines (I Sam. 13–14). Mod. *Tell el-Ful*. B4—4; C4—19

**Gibeon.** Important Hivite city (Josh. 11:19) that, by trickery, made an alliance with Joshua (Josh. 9), thus securing Israelite protection. Mod. *El-Jib*, 6 miles N of Jerusalem. B4—5, 19

**Gideroth.** *See* Gederoth

**Gihon, Spring.** Spring E of Jerusalem. Solomon was there anointed king (I Kings 1:33, 38, 45). Mod. *'Ain Sitti-Mariam*. B3—8; D3—9; C6—10

**Gilboa, Mt.** NE spur of Mt. Ephraim, forming the watershed between the Kishon and the Jordan. The ridge forms an arc E of the Plain of Esdraelon. Here Saul and Jonathan died (I Sam. 28:4; 31:1). C3—1, 5; B4—4

**Gilead.** Mountainous country E of the Jordan, extending N from the tableland of Moab to the Yarmuk R. It was occupied by the tribes of Reuben and Gad. C4-D3—1, 5

**Gilgal.** Site between the Jordan and Jericho where the Israelites first encamped after crossing the Jordan. Poss. mod. *Kh. el-Mefjir*. C4—5, 19

**Ginae.** C3—11. *See* En-gannim

**Ginaea.** *See* En-gannim

**Ginneisar.** An Israeli settlement on the W bank of the Sea of Galilee, N of Tiberias. It takes its name from the Valley of Ginossar (Genesareth in the N.T.), the fertile valley that marks the border between lower and upper Galilee.

**Gischala.** Town in upper Galilee, W of Lake Hula. It was located in fertile territory and was renowned for its olive oil. One of the commanders of the

Jewish revolt against Rome (A.D. 66) was from Gischala. C2—11

**Gittah-hepher.** *See* Gath-hepher

**Gnesen.** City *ca*. 30 miles NE of Poznan, Poland. It is the legendary cradle of the Polish nation. Mod. *Gniezno*.

**Golan.** City in Bashan that belonged to the tribe of Manasseh and served as a city of refuge (Josh. 20:8; 21:27). Mod. *Sahem el-Jolan*.

**Golden Gate.** C5—10. *See* Beautiful Gate

**Golgotha** (Calvary). Site of the crucifixion. It has been traditionally located at the Church of the Holy Sepulchre. But Charles G. Gordon, in the nineteenth century, proposed a spot near the Damascus Gate commonly called Gordon's Calvary near the "Garden tomb." A4—10

**Gomer.** A son of Japheth whose descendants settled in Asia Minor S of the Black Sea.

**Gomorrah.** City in the Jordan Plain, probably on the SE shore of the Dead Sea. Like Sodom, it was destroyed by fire in a cataclysmic judgment.

**Gomorrha.** *See* Gomorrah

**Gophna.** Town N of Jerusalem. In Roman times it was a toparchy, the name given to administrative units in Palestine, each of which was subject to the procurator (governor) who resided at Caesarea. B5—11

**Gordion.** Ancient capital of Phrygia, located on the Sangarius R., in W-central Asia Minor. B2—7

**Gordium.** *See* Gordion

**Gordon's Calvary.** *See* Golgotha

**Gortyna.** Ancient city in S-central Crete near the foot of Mt. Ida.

**Goshen.** District in NE Egypt where the Hebrews settled during the time of Joseph (Gen. 46:28–29). A4—3

**Goths.** A Germanic people who inhabited the neighborhood of the Baltic and the Vistula R. in the 1st century A.D. In the 3rd century they migrated S, where they threatened the power of Rome. Subsequently they divided into 2 groups, Ostrogoths (E Goths) and Visigoths (W Goths). The latter, in A.D. 410, captured and sacked Rome.

**Gozam.** *See* Gozan

**Gozan.** Town and district on the Habor R. (*q.v.*) in Mesopotamia. It was one of the places to which people of the Northern Kingdom (Israel) were deported following the fall of Samaria in 722 B.C. (II Kings 17:6; 18:11; 19:12). Mod. *Tell Halaf* and environs.

**Great Sea, The.** A4—1; A-C3—2; A-C2—3; A-B2—4; A-B3—5. *See* Mediterranean Sea

**Great Zab R.** One of the principal tributaries to the Tigris. It rises in the mts. between Lakes Van and Urmia and enters the Tigris S of Calah.

**Greece.** Country that occupies the southernmost part of the Balkan Peninsula and numerous islands of the Ionian and Aegean seas. Ancient Greece was one of the principal contributors to modern W culture. A2—7

**Greeks.** Indo-Europeans inhabiting the NW corner of the SE Mediterranean peninsula of Europe. *See* Greece. A2—6

**Gulf of Aqaba.** *See* Aqaba, Gulf of

**Gulf of Oman.** *See* Oman, Gulf of

**Gulf of Suez.** *See* Suez, Gulf of

**Gur.** Ascent near Ibleam (*q.v.*) where Ahaziah of Judah was mortally wounded in battle with Jehu (II Kings 9:27).

**Gutium.** Area in Zagros Mts. inhabited by Gutians, who destroyed the Akkadian Empire *ca*. 2180 B.C. F-G3—2

## H

**Habesor R.** *See* Besor R.

**Habor R.** Tributary of the Euphrates, which it enters from the N below Deir, Syria. Along the Habor in Gozan (*q.v.*), Israelite captives from Samaria were settled (II Kings 17:6; 18:11). Mod. *Khabur*.

**Haceldama.** *See* Aceldama

**Hadid.** Place in the territory of Benjamin to which many Jews returned following the exile in Babylon (Ezra 2:33; Neh. 7:37; 11:34). Prob. mod. *el-Haditheh*, 3 miles NE of Lydda.

**Hadrumetum.** Seaport in the Roman province of Africa, founded in the 9th century B.C. by Phoenicians. It was located S of Carthage and became subject to the Carthaginians. Mod. *Sousse* in E Tunisia.

**Hai.** *See* Ai

**Haifa.** Mod. Israeli seaport at the foot of Mt. Carmel. It has an excellent harbor and is a major Mediterranean port.

**Haleb** (Aleppo). City of NW Syria, known also as Beroea, on the main caravan route across Syria to Baghdad. Before 1000 B.C. it was a Hittite center; it was subsequently taken by the conquerors of Syria. D3—2

**Halys R.** River rising in N-central Asia Minor, flowing 715 miles in a wide arc—SW, N, and NE—into the Black Sea. Mod. *Kizil Irmak*. D1—2, 15, 16; C2—6; B2—7; E1—17

**Ham.** Town in Transjordan, between Ashtaroth and Moab (Gen. 14:5). Prob. mod. *Ham*, NW of Mt. Gilboa.

**Hamath,** city of. City on the Orontes R., *ca*. 120 miles N of Damascus. The center of an early Hittite state, it later became an Aramean stronghold. Mod. *Hama*. D3—2; C1—4; B2—7

**Hamath,** district of (Aramean Kingdom). The district ruled by the city-state of Hamath (*q.v.*). Hamath was allied with Syria and Israel in fighting Shalmaneser III of Assyria at Karkar (853 B.C.). Later Hamath fell to the Assyrians, and some of its inhabitants were settled in Israel after Samaria fell in 722 B.C. (II Kings 17:24–30). Subsequently Hamath became a province of Syria. C1—4

**Hamath-zobah.** *See* Aram-zobah

**Hammath.** City in the territory of Naphtali, on W shore of the Sea of Galilee, *ca*. 1 mile S of Tiberias. It is noted for its sulphurous and medicinal waters. Mod. *Hamman-Tabariyeh*. C2—5

**Hammon.** Village in the territory of Asher (Josh.

19:28), 10 miles S of Tyre. Poss. mod. *Umm el-Awamid*.

**Hamon.** *See* Hammon

**Hananel, Tower of.** Tower that formed part of the N wall of Jerusalem in Nehemiah's time (Neh. 3:1; 12:39). It was near the Tower of Meah, between the Sheep and Fish gates.

**Hannathon.** *See* Asochis

**Harad.** *See* Harod

**Haran** (Carrhae). Trading center in N Mesopotamia (Gen. 11:31–32), on the Balikh R. Terah and Abraham sojourned there for a time (Gen. 11:31–32; 12:4–5). Its Roman name was Carrhae. At the Battle of Carrhae (53 B.C.), Parthian artillery routed a Roman army under Marcus Licinius Crassus. E2—2; C2—6, 7

**Harmozia.** Seaport on the mouth of the R. Anamis, at the NW end of the Gulf of Oman, in mod. Iran. The fleet of Nearchus, Alexander's admiral, stopped there.

**Harod.** Well near which Gideon pitched camp while the Midianites were at the Hill of Moreh (Judg. 7:1). Prob. mod. *'Ain Jalud* on the NW side of Mt. Gilboa.

**Harodi.** *See* Harod

**Haroseth.** *See* Harosheth

**Haroseth-Goim.** *See* Harosheth

**Harosheth.** Town on the N bank of the Kishon, 16 miles NW of Megiddo. Home of Sisera (Judg. 4:2, 13, 16). Mod. *Tell 'Amar*, at the foot of Mt. Carmel.

**Harosheth-ha-goiim.** *See* Harosheth

**Harun, J.** (Mt. Hor). Mt. in Edom on which Aaron died and was buried (Num. 20:22–29). Traditionally identified with *J. Harun*, E of the Arabah. D4—3

**Hasa.** Town located at the junction of the W. el-Hasa and the rail line that goes N to Damascus.

**Hasa, W. el-.** *See* Zered R.

**Hasarmoth.** *See* Hazarmaveth

**Haseroth.** *See* Hazeroth

**Hasmonean Palace.** Constructed by the later Hasmoneans across Jerusalem's Central Valley (*q.v.*), connecting it to the temple area with a bridge. B5—10

**Hasor.** *See* Hazor

**Hatti.** D2—2. *See* Hittites

**Hattin, Horns of.** Twin-peaked hill on the road from Tiberias (on the Sea of Galilee) to Cana and Nazareth. Tradition says that Jesus delivered the Sermon on the Mount there.

**Hattusas.** City in N-central Asia Minor, E of the Great Bend of the Halys R. It was the capital of an ancient Hittite empire. Monuments and inscriptions from Bogaskoy, ancient Hattusas, have provided valuable information concerning ancient Hittite civilization. D1—2

**Hattushash.** *See* Hattusas

**Hauran.** Extremely fertile region S of Damascus, extending to the borders of the territory of Gilead (Ezek. 47:16, 18). It served as the granary for the surrounding area. D2—1

**Havilah.** District of Arabia peopled in part by Semites, in part by Hamites. It was noted for its gold, aromatic gums, and precious stones (Gen. 2:11–12).

**Havoth-jair.** *See* Havvoth-jair

**Havvoth-jair.** Unwalled towns in the region of Argob, NW Bashan, S of the Yarmuk. They are named for Jair the judge (Judg. 10:4). C3—5

**Hazar-enan.** Village on the N boundary of Palestine (Num. 34:9). Poss. mod. *Qiryatein* on the road from Damascus to Palmyra. C2—4

**Hazarmaveth.** Joktanite Arabs who peopled a district in S Arabia (Gen. 10:26; I Chron. 1:20). Mod. *Hadhramaut*.

**Hazeroth.** Stopping place of the Israelites during the Exodus (Num. 11:35; 12:16). Poss. mod. *'Ain Khudra*, 36 miles NE of Mt. Sinai. C5—3

**Hazezon-tamar.** *See* En-gedi

**Hazor.** Capital of the Canaanite kingdom in N Palestine ruled by Jabin during the Israelite conquest (Josh. 11:1–13; 12:19). The Israelites captured and burned the city. Mod. *Tell el-Qedah*. D3—2; D2—3; B3—4; C2—5; C1—19

**Hebron.** Town in the hill-country of Judah (Josh. 15:48, 54), originally named *Kirjath-arba* ("Tetrapolis"). Abraham sojourned there and purchased a burial plot nearby. It later served as a Levitical city and a city of refuge (Josh. 20:7; 21:11). It served as David's 1st capital (II Sam. 2:1–4). Mod. *el-Khalil*. B5—1, 4, 5; D4—2; D3—3; B6—11; B4—19

**Hebrus R.** Most important river of Thrace. It was closely associated with the worship of Dionysus. On its banks Orpheus was said to have been torn to pieces by the Thracian women. Mod. *Euros R.* C-D1—17

**Hecatompylus.** *See* Damghan

**Helal, J.** Mt., 2,926 feet above sea level, in NE Egypt W of the W. el 'Arish. C4—3

**Heliopolis** (Baalbek). City in the Beqa'a Valley, NW of Damascus, devoted to the worship of Baal, who in later times was identified with the sun god. It became a prominent Roman city and has significant ruins. Baalbek is in mod. Lebanon. B4—13

**Heliopolis** (On). City of Lower Egypt, 5 miles NE of Cairo. It was a center for worship of the sun god and was called Heliopolis by the Greeks. A4—3; B3—7; E4—17

**Hellal, J.** *See* Helal, J.

**Hellas.** Ancient name for Greece (*q.v.*).

**Hellespont.** Ancient name of the Dardanelles, the strait connecting the Aegean Sea with the Sea of Marmara. It is strategic in that it controls trade between the Black Sea and the Mediterranean. Ancient Troy was near the W entrance to the Hellespont.

**Helvetii.** A Celtic people that once occupied the area corresponding to mod. Switzerland. They attempted to invade S Gaul but were repulsed by Caesar.

**Hemath.** *See* Hamath

**Hennom Valley.** *See* Hinnom Valley

**Hepher.** Canaanite royal city whose king was defeated by Joshua (Josh. 12:17). Poss. mod. *Tell el-Ifshar*. B4—4

**Heraclea.** Greek city on the S shore of the Black Sea, founded during the 6th century B.C. by colonists from Megara and Boeotia. It was destroyed by the Romans in wars with Mithridates VI of Pontus. Mod. *Eregli*, Turkey. E1—17

**Heraclea Pontica.** *See* Heraclea

**Heracleopolis.** City S of the Faiyum, in N Egypt. Pharaohs of the Ninth and Tenth Dynasties came from Heracleopolis. Subsequently, however, power shifted to Thebes. Sheshonk I (biblical Shishak) was at one time the general of mercenaries at Heracleopolis. C5—2; A5—3

**Herat** (Alexandria Arion). Ancient walled city on the trade route to India, refounded by Alexander the Great as Alexandria Arion. It is on the Hari Rud R. in mod. Afghanistan.

**Herma.** *See* Hormah

**Hermes R.** River of W-central Asia Minor. Its source is in the Taurus Mts., and it flows generally W, N of and parallel to the Maeander. Mod. *Gediz R.* in W Turkey. B2—2

**Hermon, Mt.** Mt. at the S end of the Anti-Lebanon range, known to the Sidonians as Sirion. It has an elevation of 9,232 feet above sea level and is covered with snow much of the year. D1—1, 11; B3—4; C1—5

**Hermopolis.** City of Upper Egypt, near mod. *Ashnunein*. In antiquity it was the chief seat of the worship of Thoth. C5—2

**Hermunduri.** A Germanic people who were settled in central Germany, between the Elbe and the Danube.

**Hermus R.** *See* Hermes R.

**Herod, Kingdom of.** The Judean area, governed by Herod the Great from 37 to 4 B.C. Herod rebuilt Caesarea and the Jerusalem temple, but he also attempted to Hellenize the country. E3—12

**Herod, Palace of.** Palace built by Herod on the W hill of Jerusalem, S of the fortress towers (Hippicus, Phasael, and Mariamne). It became the residence of later Roman rulers of Jerusalem when they visited the city. A5—10

**Herodium.** One of the mountain-top abodes of Herod the Great, located *ca.* 3 miles SE of Bethlehem. It is the site of Herod's tomb. C5—11; C4—19

**Herod's Family Tomb.** Mausoleum built of large stones and an adjacent cave, located W of Jerusalem's walls, in which Herod's family (but not Herod) were buried. A5—10

**Hesebon.** *See* Heshbon

**Heshbon.** Stronghold of Sihon the Amorite king. It was located on what became the border between the territories of Reuben and Dan. Mod. *Hesban*. D3—3; B4—4; D4—5, 19

**Heth.** Ancestor of the Hittites (*q.v.*) (Gen. 10:15), whose kingdom centered in Asia Minor, with important settlements also in Syria and Palestine.

**Hethite Empire.** *See* Hittite Empire

**Hevila.** *See* Havilah

**Hezekiah's Tunnel.** The 1,750-feet-long tunnel built by Hezekiah to conduct water from the Spring Gihon (*q.v.*) on the E of Jerusalem to the Pool of Siloam (*q.v.*) in the city, thus assuring a water supply for the city while denying it to any besieging enemy (II Chron. 32:30). D3—9; C6—10

**Hezekiah's Wall.** Wall built by Hezekiah to enclose the Pool of Siloam (*q.v.*), thereby making it part of the SW quarter of Jerusalem. C3—9

**Hibernia.** Roman name of Ireland, populated in ancient times by a Celtic people who are, in part, the ancestors of the mod. Irish. Ireland was never incorporated into the Roman Empire.

**Hierapolis.** City of Phrygia, W Asia Minor, on a plateau above the Lycus Valley, 120 miles NE of Smyrna.

**Hill of Moreh.** *See* Moreh, Hill of

**Hindu Kush.** Mt. system of central Asia situated in what is now NE Afghanistan, extending to Pakistan and Kashmir. Passes in the Hindu Kush were used by Alexander the Great in his march to India. F2—7

**Hindush** (India). The subcontinent of S-central Asia that now comprises primarily the nations of Pakistan and India. Civilization is known to have flourished in the Indus Valley as early as the 3rd millennium B.C. During the 2nd millennium B.C. Aryans entered India through mt. passes in the NW. F3—7

**Hinnom Valley.** Valley that flanks Jerusalem on the S. It was the scene of the sacrifice of children to Moloch. Mod. *W. er-Rababi*. A3—8; C3—9; A-B6—10

**Hippicus.** One of three massive towers erected by Herod the Great on Jerusalem's W hill to protect its N approach. This tower was named after a friend of Herod. *See also* Mariamne *and* Phasael. A5—10

**Hippodrome** (in Jerusalem). Built by Herod the Great in the Tyropoeon Valley. Its exact location is not known. B5—10

**Hippo Regius.** Mediterranean port founded by the Carthaginians. It later became the Numidian capital and a center of early Christianity. Mod. *Bone*, in NE Algeria.

**Hippos** (Sussita). City built on a mt. E of the Sea of Galilee. It served as a stronghold during the Jewish revolt against Rome (A.D. 67). C3—11

**Hisban.** *See* Heshbon

**Hispalis** (Seville). City on the Guadalquivir R. in SW Spain. As Hispalis it was an important Phoenician settlement. It became the capital of Baetica province under the Romans. Seville is a major port as well as a cultural and industrial center. A2—18

**Hispania.** A2—12. *See* Spain

**Hither Spain.** One of two provinces into which Spain was divided by the Romans. Hither Spain (*Hispania Citerior*) occupied the Ebro Valley. *See also* Farther Spain

**Hittite Empire.** Powerful kingdoms in Asia Minor (*ca.* 1740–1200 B.C.) and important states in Syria and Palestine established by the Hittites (*q.v.*). Carchemish (*q.v.*) on the upper Euphrates was an important Hittite center. C-D2—2

**Hittites** (Hatti). An Indo-European people who established the Hittite Empire (*q.v.*). C1—4

**Holdah Gates.** Gates from the Lower City of Jerusalem into the temple area, in N.T. times. C5—10

**Holy Sepulchre, Church of the.** Church in the old city of Jerusalem that marks the traditional site of the crucifixion and burial of Jesus. It has been regarded as sacred by many Christian groups since the time of Helena, who in the 4th century identified the site. Some Protestant groups identify the site of Jesus' death and burial with Gordon's Calvary and the garden tomb, located outside the present wall of Jerusalem N of the Jaffa Gate. *See* Golgotha (Calvary)

**Hor, Mt.** *See* Harun, J.

**Horeb, Mt.** *See* Sinai, Mt.

**Horites.** E-F2—2. *See* Hurrians

**Horma.** *See* Hormah

**Hormah.** Town in the Judean Negeb near the border of Edom. The Israelites suffered a defeat there (Num. 14:45; Deut. 1:44), but subsequently captured the city (Num. 21:3; Josh. 12:14). It was friendly to David (I Sam. 30:30). Poss. mod. *Mishash,* SE of Beer-sheba. D3—3

**Horns of Hattin.** *See* Hattin, Horns of

**Horrites.** *See* Hurrians

**Horse Gate.** Gate in the E wall of Jerusalem, leading into the Kidron Valley, in the time of Nehemiah.

**Hucoc.** *See* Hukkok

**Hukkok.** Town in the territory of Naphtali, NE of the Sea of Galilee (Josh. 19:34). Mod. *Yakuk.*

**Hula** (Semechonitis), **Lake.** Lake on the Jordan, 11 miles N of the Sea of Galilee. The area has been transformed by Israeli drainage and irrigation projects so that much of the area once covered by the lake and its adjacent swamps is now fertile agricultural terrain. C2—1

**Huldah Gates.** *See* Holdah Gates

**Huleh, Lake.** *See* Hula, Lake

**Hurrians** (Horites). A non-Semitic people who entered N and NE Mesopotamia early in the 2nd millennium B.C. They spread W to Syria and S to the borders of Egypt. Biblical Horites inhabited Mt. Seir, or Edom (Gen. 36:20). They were displaced by the descendants of Esau (Deut. 2:12, 22). E-F2—2

**Hydaspes** (Jhelum) **R.** River that rises in W Kashmir, India, and flows *ca.* 500 miles generally SW to join the Indus (*q.v.*).

**Hyphasis** (Beas) **R.** The easternmost of the 5 rivers of India's Punjab region. It flows *ca.* 285 miles, generally W, and ultimately joins the Indus. It marked the E limit of Alexander's invasion of India (326 B.C.).

**Hyrcania,** region of. Province of ancient Persia, SE of the Caspian, now the region around Gorgan, Iran. Parthian kings are said to have had their summer palaces there. E2—6; D2—7

**Hyrcania,** town of. One of several mountain-top fortresses that Herod the Great spread over his kingdom. It was located *ca.* 15 miles SE of Jerusalem. C5—11; C4—19

## I

**Iberia.** Ancient name of a Transcaucasian country (mod. E Georgia, U.S.S.R.). Long a dependency of Persia, it was subjected in the 1st century B.C. to Mithridates VI of Pontus. F2—12

**Ibleam** (Bile-am). Town in the territory of Manasseh (Josh. 17:11), identified with mod. *Tell Bel 'ameh ca.* 13 miles NE of Samaria. It was a Levitical city (I Chron. 6:70) and was the place where partisans of Jehu mortally wounded Ahaziah of Judah (II Kings 9:27). C3—5

**Iconium.** City of Asia Minor, at various times within the territories of Phrygia, Lycaonia, and Cappadocia, and in Paul's time in the Roman province of Galatia. It was visited by the apostle Paul (Acts 13:51–52; 14:19, 21). Mod. *Konya,* Turkey. B2—7; C4—14; C2—15, 16; E2—17; E3—18

**Icosium.** Town on the Mediterranean coast of Mauretania, NW Africa. Mod. *Algiers* was built during the 10th century A.D. on the site of Roman Icosium.

**Idumea.** The name used in Greco-Roman times for O.T. Edom (*q.v.*). The Edomites, under pressure from Nabatean Arabs, were forced into territory NW of their earlier settlements. During N.T. times Idumea extended N to the region around Hebron. B6—1, 11

**Iim.** *See* Ije-abarim

**Ije-abarim** (Iim, Iyim, Iye-abarim). Place S of Moab where the Israelites stopped during the Exodus (Num. 33:45; cf. 21:11; 33:44). Poss. mod. *Mahay.* D3—3

**Ijon.** Town in N Palestine captured, along with Dan and Abel, by Ben-hadad of Syria (I Kings 15:20; cf. II Kings 15:29). Prob. mod. *Tell Dibbin*, near *Merjayun*, *ca.* 8 miles NW of Baniyas. C1—5

**Ilerda.** Town in Hither Spain, between the Pyrenees and the Ebro R. It was the site of a major battle in which Caesar defeated Pompey's legates, Africanus and Petreius.

**Ilium.** *See* Troy

**Illyria.** *See* Illyricum

**Illyricum** (Dalmatia). Region on the E shore of the Adriatic Sea, with adjacent islands. The mountainous portion of the region was subdued by the Romans (A.D. 9) and formed into a province. It was regarded as part of Illyricum, the limit of Paul's missionary journey in that direction (Rom. 15:19). Titus also preached in Dalmatia (II Tim. 4:10). C2—12, 18; B1—17

**India.** F3—7. *See* Hindush

**Indo-Iranians** (Aryans). The name used to describe peoples who speak Indo-Iranian and Indo-European languages, as distinguished from those who speak Semitic languages and those of other families.

**Indus R.** The river that rises in the Himalayas in W Tibet and flows 1,800 miles through Tibet, Kashmir, W Pakistan, and India to the Arabian Sea. The lower Indus Valley was one of the earliest centers of civilization. F3—7

**Ionian.** *See* Javan

**Ipsus.** Small town in ancient Phrygia, Asia Minor. It was the site of an important battle (301 B.C.) in which Antigonus I was defeated and slain by Seleucus and Lysimachus. Mod. *Ipsili Hissar*, Turkey.

**Irbid.** C2—19. *See* Arbela (in Palestine)

**Ireland.** Mod. name of the island W of Britain, from which it is separated by the North Channel, Irish Sea, and St. George's Channel. Celtic tribes occupied the island in the centuries immediately preceding the Christian era. Anc. *Hibernia* (*q.v.*).

**Iris R.** River that arises in N Asia Minor, flows 260 miles NW to enter the Black Sea near mod. *Samsun*, Turkey. Mod. *Yesil Irmak*.

**Iron** (Yiron). Fortified city in the territory of Naphtali (Josh. 19:38). Poss. mod. *Yarun*, 10 miles W of Lake Hula.

**Irshemesh.** *See* Beth-shemesh

**Isbeita.** Nabatean and Byzantine town in the Negeb, NE of Avdat. B6—19

**Isca.** *See* Caerleon

**Isin.** City 50 miles NW of Erech that supplanted Ur as the leading city of Sumer in the early 2nd millennium B.C. G4—2

**Isles of the Gentiles.** *See* Gentiles, Isles of the

**Israel.** As a nation, *Israel* may refer to the entire body of descendants of Jacob (Israel)—the 12 tribes and the land they occupied. The term *Israel* is also used of the mod. Jewish state in Palestine. B4—4, 19

**Israel, Kingdom of.** During the period of the divided kingdom (following the death of Solomon), *Israel* was the name given to the 10 tribes that acted independently of Judah. The N and E tribes (Israel, the Northern Kingdom) separated from Judah (the Southern Kingdom). B-C3—5

**Israel, Pool of.** Pool just outside the NE corner of the Jerusalem temple enclosure. C4—10

**Issachar**, allotment of. Territory of Issachar was bounded on the N by that of Zebulun and Naphtali, on the E by the Jordan, and on the S and W by the territory of Manasseh. Mt. Tabor was on its N border, and Jezreel was near its S border.

**Issin.** City of ancient Mesopotamia, SE of Babylon. It was a rival of Larsa (*ca.* 2000 B.C.), subsequently conquered by Hammurabi of Babylon. Mod. *Ishan Bahriyat*.

**Issus.** Town in SE Asia Minor on a strip of land backed by high mts. It is near the Cilician Gates, the famed pass into Syria. In 333 B.C. Alexander the Great defeated Darius III of Persia there. Mod. *Iskanderun*, or *Alexandretta*. B2—7

**Istanbul.** *See* Byzantium

**Ister R.** A1—6, 7; D2—12. *See* Danube R.

**Italy.** Boot-shaped peninsula in S Europe, W of Greece. The Alps form the N boundary, dividing [illegible]aly from France (in the NW) and from Switzer-[illegible]d Austria (in the N). Ancient inhabitants [illegible]luded Ligurians and Iberians, who [illegible]planted by the Etruscans from [illegible] B.C.). The S of Italy was [illegible]—12, 18; A1—17

**Itil.** Town at the head of the delta of the Volga R., NW of the Caspian Sea, near mod. *Astrakhan*, U.S.S.R.

**Iturea.** Country on the N boundary of Syria, occupied by Arabian tribes. It was conquered by Aristobulus (105 B.C.) and later, after a brief period of independence, taken by Pompey. It was united to the Roman province of Syria in A.D. 50. C-D1—11

**Iye-abarim.** *See* Ije-abarim

**Iyim.** *See* Ije-abarim

**Izalla.** Area E of Kue (*q.v.*) that was a province in both the Assyrian and New Babylonian empires. C2—6

## J

**Jaazer.** *See* Jazer

**Jabbok** (Zarqa) **R.** An E tributary to the Jordan, which it enters *ca.* 43 miles S of the Sea of Galilee and 23 miles N of the Dead Sea. It marked the S boundary of Gilead. Before the Israelite conquest, the area S of the Jabbok was ruled by Sihon, an Amorite king. D3—1; D2—3; C4—5, 11

**Jabes-Galaad.** *See* Jabesh-gilead

**Jabesh-gilead.** City in Transjordan, in ancient Gilead. Saul began his career as king by lifting the siege of Jabesh-gilead (I Sam. 11:1–11). Poss. mod. *Tell el-Maqlub*, SE of Beth-shan. C3—5

**Jabneel** (Jamnia, Jabneh, Jabnia; in Judah). Town on the N border of Judah (Josh. 15:5, 11), occupied by Philistines in the time of Uzziah (II Chron. 26:6). It was known as Jamnia in Maccabean times (I Macc. 4:15) and became a center of Jewish life following the destruction of Jerusalem. Mod. *Yebna*, or *Yavne Yam*, 9 miles NE of Ashdod, 4 miles inland from the Mediterranean. A4—5

**Jabneel** (in Naphtali). Frontier town in the territory of Naphtali (Josh. 19:33). Poss. mod. *Kh. Yamma*, 7 miles SW of Tiberias.

**Jabneh.** *See* Jabneel (Jamnia)

**Jabnia.** *See* Jabneel (Jamnia)

**Jaboc R.** *See* Jabbok R.

**Jacob's Well.** Ancient well near Shechem (John 4:6). Mod. *Bir Ja'qub*.

**Jaffa.** *See* Joppa

**Jahas.** *See* Jahaz

**Jahaz.** Town in the Plain of Moab (Jer. 48:34) that was the site of Sihon's battle against Israel (Josh. 13:18; Num. 21:23). It was subsequently assigned to Reuben (Josh. 13:18) and made a Levitical city (Josh. 21:36). Mod. *Kh. Umm el-Idham*. D5—5

**Jahaza(h).** *See* Jahaz

**Jahzah.** *See* Jahaz

**Jamnia.** A5—11. *See* Jabneel

**Janoe.** *See* Janohah

**Janoah.** Town on E boundary of Ephraim (Josh. 16:6–7).

**Japho.** *See* Joppa

**Jarash.** *See* Gerasa

**Jarmo.** Ancient village in the hills of Iraqi Kurdistan, E of mod. Kirkuk. It is one of the earliest-known food-producing settlements. F3—2

**Jarmuth.** Town in the lowlands of Judah (Josh. 15:35). A Canaanite royal city before the Israelite occupation (Josh. 10:3, 5, 23), it was repopulated after the exile (Neh. 11:29). Mod. *Kh. Yarmuk*.

**Jassa.** *See* Jazer

**Jattir.** City SE of Hebron in the hill-country of Judah (Josh. 15:48), to which David sent spoil (I Sam. 30:27). It was a Levitical city (Josh. 21:14). **Mod.** *Kh. 'Attir*.

**Javan** (Ionian). Name applying to Greek-speaking islands of the Mediterranean, the Greek area of Asia Minor, and later Greece itself (Gen. 10:2–4).

**Jaxartes R.** River that flows 1,300 miles NW from the mts. of Bactria to the Aral Sea. It served as the boundary between Sogdiana and Scythia in ancient times and was thought to flow into the Caspian. Mod. *Syr Darya*. F1—6; E1—7

**Jazer.** City in Gilead, in the territory of Gad (Josh. 13:25). It was a Levitical city (Josh. 21:39) and later passed into Moabite control. Prob. mod. *Kh. Jazzri* near mod. *es-Salt*. C4—5

**Jeabarim.** *See* Ije-abarim

**Jearim, Mt.** *See* Chesalon

**Jeb.** *See* Syene

**J. ed Druz.** *See* Druz, J. ed

**Jeblaan.** *See* Ibleam

**Jebneel.** *See* Jabneel

**Jeboc R.** *See* Jabbok R.

**Jebus.** *See* Jerusalem

**Jecmaam.** *See* Jokneam

**Jecnaam.** *See* Jokneam

**Jecnam.** *See* Jokneam

**Jeconam.** *See* Jokneam

**Jectan.** *See* Joktan

**Jegbaa.** *See* Jogbehah

**Jerash.** D3—19. *See* Gerasa

**Jericho** (City of Palm Trees). Important city in the Jordan Valley NE of the Jordan's entrance into the Dead Sea. The city was destroyed by Joshua (Josh. 6) but rebuilt by Ahab (I Kings 16:34). The mod. *Tell es-Sultan*, 1 mile NW of *Riha*, is the site of O.T. Jericho. Ruins of Herodian Jericho lie a little farther S. C4—1, 5, 19; D4—2; D3—3; B4—4; C5—11; B6—13

**Jerimoth.** *See* Jarmuth

**Jeron.** *See* Iron

**Jerusalem.** City in the hill-country between Judah and Benjamin, occupied by the Jebusites until the time of David and subsequently made the capital of the kingdom of David and his successors. The old city of Jerusalem is mod. *El-Kuds*. B4—1, 4, 5; D4—2; D3—3, 15, 16; C3—6; B3—7; B5—11; E3—12; A6—13; D6—14; F4—17; F3—18; C4—19

**Jeshanah.** Town in the hill-country of Ephraim, N of Jerusalem. Prob. mod. *Burj el-Isaneh*.

**Jeshua.** Village of S Judah (Neh. 11:26). Poss. mod. *Tell es-Sa'wi*, E of Beer-sheba.

**Jesrael.** *See* Jezreel

**Jesus, tomb of.** The location of Jesus' tomb is unknown, but a tradition that is at least as old as the 4th century places it at a site now covered by the Church of the Holy Sepulchre. *See* Golgotha. A4—10

**Jeta.** *See* Juttah

**Jether.** *See* Jattir

**Jetta.** *See* Juttah

**Jezrael.** *See* Jezreel

**Jezrahel.** *See* Jezreel

**Jezreel.** Town in the territory of Issachar (Josh. 19:18), frequently mentioned as the country residence of the kings of Israel (II Sam. 2:9). Naboth's vineyard was nearby (I Kings 21:1–24). Mod. *Zer'in*. B4—4; B3—5

**Jezreel, Plain of.** *See* Esdraelon, Plain of

**Jezreel, Valley of.** Three-mile-wide, ten-mile-long valley joining the Plain of Esdraelon with the Jordan Valley. C3—1

**Jhelum R.** *See* Hydaspes R.

**Jogbehah.** Town in the territory of Gad (Num. 32:35). Mod. *Jubeihat*, 6 miles NW of Amman on the road from es-Salt to the Jordan

**Jokneam.** Town in the territory of Zebulun (Josh. 19:11). It was a Levitical city (Josh. 21:34). Mod. *Tell Qeimun*, 12 miles SW of Nazareth.

**Joktan.** Descendant of Shem whose posterity, the Joktanite Arabs, settled in the S sector of the Arabian Peninsula.

**Joppa.** City on the Mediterranean coast in the territory of Dan. It was the Mediterranean seaport of ancient Israel. It became the mod. city of Jaffa, a predominantly Arab city that in 1949 was joined with Tel Aviv (originally settled by Jews as a suburb of Jaffa) to form the municipality of Tel Aviv–Jaffa. B4—1; D4—2; C3—3; A4—4, 11; A5—5; A6—13; B3—19

**Joppe.** *See* Joppa

**Jordan.** Arab state that comprises the territory formerly known as Transjordan. C-D3—19

**Jordan R.** The largest river of Palestine. It rises at the foot of Mt. Hermon, flows through Lake Hula and the Sea of Galilee, and ends at the Dead Sea. From Baniyas to the Dead Sea is a distance of 104 miles. C3—1, 5, 19; D2—3; B4—4; C4—11; B5—13

**Jotapata** (Jotbah). Town in Galilee that was the home of King Amon's mother (II Kings 21:19). Prob. mod. *Kh. Jefat*, 7 miles N of Sepphoris.

**Jotbah.** *See* Jotapata

**J. Serbal.** *See* Serbal, J.

**Juda.** *See* Judah

**Judah.** The tribe, and later the district, that occupied the highland region between Samaria and the Negeb. *Judea* is the Greek and Latin form of *Judah*. B5—4; B3—6, 7

**Judah,** allotment of. Judah was assigned territory W

of the Dead Sea and S of Dan and Benjamin. A portion of the territory was in Philistine control.

**Judah, Kingdom of.** The S portion of the divided kingdom that followed Solomon's death. *See* Israel, Kingdom of. B-C5—5

**Judah, Wilderness of.** Region between the hill-country of Judah *(q.v.)* and the Dead Sea. C5-6—5

**Judea.** B5—1, 11; A6—13; D6—14; D3—15; F4—17. *See* Judah

**Judea, Wilderness of.** C5—1. *See* Judah, Wilderness of

**Judgment Gate.** *See* Miphkad Gate

**Julias.** *See* Bethsaida-Julias

**Julias** (Livias). C5—11. *See* Betharamphtha

**Juttah.** Town in the hill-country of Judah, S of Hebron (Josh. 15:55). It was a Levitical city (Josh. 21:16). Mod. *Yatta*.

**J. Yusha'.** *See* Yusha', J.

## K

**Kabul R.** F2—7. *See* Cophen R.

**Kadesh.** City on the Orontes R. It was the site of a battle between Ramses II of Egypt and the Hittites. Mod. *Tell Nebi-Mend*. D3—2; C2—4

**Kadesh-barnea.** City in the Judean Negeb in the extreme S of Palestine (Gen. 14:7; Num. 13:26). The Israelites encamped there during the Exodus (Num. 34:4; Deut. 1:2). Prob. mod. *'Ain Qadeis*. *See also* El Qusaima. D4—2; C4—3; A5—4; A6—19

**Kafr Bir'im.** One of several sites in Galilee where the ruins of synagogues have been discovered. C1—19

**Kamon.** *See* Camon

**Kanah.** Town in the territory of Asher, 6 miles SE of Tyre. Mod. *Qana*.

**Kanah R.** Stream forming the boundary between the territories of Manasseh and Ephraim. It enters the Mediterranean N of Tel Aviv. Mod. *Yarkon* (Josh. 16:8; 17:9). Mod. *W. Qanah*. B4—1, 5

**Kanatha** (El Qanawat). City of the Decapolis in N Transjordan on the W slope of J. Hauran. Called Kenath in the O.T. (I Chron. 2:23), it was 16 miles NE of Bostra.

**Kanish.** Hittite town of W Asia Minor. Mod. *Kultepe*. D2—2

**Karabel.** Mt. near mod. *Izmir* on which are some Hittite rock carvings. B2—2

**Karkar.** City on the Orontes R., NW of Hamath. Site of a battle (854 B.C.) between Shalmaneser III of Assyria and an alliance of kings from Syria and Palestine.

**Karnaim,** district of. Region E of the Sea of Galilee.

**Karnaim,** town of. Place in Bashan, N of Ashtaroth (*q.v.*). D2—5

**Karnub.** Nabatean and Byzantine town in the Negeb. B6—19

**Kashka.** Ancient district of NE Asia Minor. D-E1—2

**Kassites.** Indo-European tribes from the Zagros Mts. who overran Babylonia (*ca*. 1650 B.C.). G3—2

**Kazalla.** City of S Babylonia.

**Kedar.** Nomadic tribe of the N Arabian Desert, W of Syria. E4—2

**Kedesh** (in Naphtali). Town NW of Lake Hula in the territory of Naphtali. It was the home of Barak (Judg. 4:6) and the rallying place for the Israelites in their battles with the Canaanites (Judg. 4:10). B3—4; C2—5

**Kedesh** (in Negeb). *See* Kadesh-barnea

**Kedron.** *See* Cedron

**Kefar 'Eqran.** *See* Ekron

**Keilah.** Town in the lowlands of Judah (Josh. 15:44) *ca*. 8.5 miles NW of Hebron. David relieved Keilah from a siege by the Philistines (I Sam. 23:1–13). Mod. *Kh. Qila*.

**Kenites.** Nomadic tribe that entered Palestine with the Israelites and settled in the S (Gen. 15:19; Num. 24:21).

**Khalab.** *See* Haleb

**Khalasa.** Town *ca*. 15 miles SW of Beer-sheba and on the Besor. B5—19

**Kh. 'Ar'ir.** D5—19. *See* Aroer (in Moab)

**Kh. el-Kerak.** D5—19. *See* Kir-hareseth

**Kh. el-Mefjir.** C4—19. *See* Gilgal

**Kh. et-Tannur.** Ruin of a Nabatean city on the Zered R., *ca*. 20 miles E of the S end of the Dead Sea. D6—19

**Kh. Qumran.** *See* Qumran

**Kibroth-hattaavah.** Stopping place during the Exodus (Num. 11:34–35). Prob. mod. *Ruweis el-Ebeirig*, NE of Sinai. C5—3

**Kidron Valley.** Deep valley or ravine E of Jerusalem, between the city and the Mt. of Olives. B2-3—8; D2-3—9; C4-6—10

**Kiev.** City on the Dnieper R. in the Russian Ukraine. In the Middle Ages it served as a Slavic settlement on the great trade route between Scandinavia and Constantinople.

**Kingdom of Damascus.** *See* Damascus, Kingdom of

**Kingdom of Egypt.** *See* Egypt, Kingdom of

**Kingdom of Og.** *See* Og, Kingdom of

**Kingdom of Sihon.** *See* Sihon, Kingdom of

**King's Garden.** Garden at the S end of Jerusalem (II Kings 25:4). D3—9

**King's Highway.** Road extending from Damascus to the Gulf of Aqaba, passing through Bashan, Gilead, Ammon, Moab, and Edom. D4—3

**Kir-hareseth** (Kir-moab). Capital city of Moab (II Kings 3:25), also known as *Kirheres* (Isa. 16:11), or *Kir*. Mod. *el-Kerak*. C6—1, 5; D3—3; B5—4

**Kiriathaim** (Shaveh-kiriathaim). Ancient city of the Emim (Gen. 14:5), rebuilt by the Reubenites (Num. 32:37). According to the Moabite Stone (line 10), it subsequently fell to Moab. Poss. mod. *Kh. el-Qureiyat*, NW of Dibon.

**Kiriath-jearim.** Gibeonite city (Josh. 9:17) on the boundary between Judah and Benjamin (Josh. 18:15). Also called Kiriath-baal (Josh. 15:60). Mod. *Tell el-Azhar, ca*. 8 miles W of Jerusalem.

**Kirjathaim.** *See* Kiriathaim

**Kirjath-arba.** *See* Hebron

**Kirjath-sepher.** *See* Debir

**Kir-moab.** *See* Kir-hareseth

**Kish.** Ancient city of the Euphrates Valley, *ca*. 8 miles E of Babylon. It contained a palace built by Sargon of Akkad and a temple built by Nebuchadnezzar and Nabonidus. F4—2

**Kishon R.** River of Palestine that rises below Mt. Gilboa, flows NW through the Valley of Esdraelon, and empties into the Mediterranean near Haifa. B2—1; B3—5

**Kition.** Ancient Phoenician colony in SE Cyprus. Mod. *Larnaca*.

**Kittim.** C3—2; A1—4. *See* Cyprus, island of

**Kizzuwadna.** *See* Kizzuwatna

**Kizzuwatna.** District of SE Asia Minor. Its people were allies of the Hittites in the battles between Hittites and Egyptians. D2—2

**Kue.** Country in Asia Minor mentioned in I Kings 10:28 (RSV) and II Chron. 1:16 (RSV). It was located in the area that later became Cilicia. C2—6

**Kurun Hattin.** *See* Hattin, Horns of

**Kushshar** (Alisar Huyuk). Important city of the Old Hittite Kingdom in central Asia Minor. It was occupied as early as the 4th millennium B.C. by a Hattic people who preceded the Hittites in Asia Minor. A group of Hittites who used hieroglyphic writing founded their first capital at Kushshar. After the cuneiform Hittites dominated the area, Kushshar lost its primacy.

## L

**Laabim.** *See* Lehabim

**Labana.** *See* Libnah

**Labyrinth.** Intricate building of chambers and passages built to confuse the person inside. It was located near Lake Moeris in Egypt and was built by Amenemhet IV of the Twelfth Dynasty.

**Lachis.** *See* Lachish

**Lachish.** Fortified city in the lowlands of Judah whose king was defeated and slain by Joshua (Josh. 10:3–35). It was besieged by Sennacherib (701 B.C.) and destroyed by Nebuchadnezzar (597 B.C. and 587 B.C.). Mod. *Tell ed-Duweir*, 30 miles SW of Jerusalem on the main road from central Palestine to Egypt. D3—3; B5—4, 5; B4—19

**Ladder of Tyre.** Steep mt. on the Mediterranean coast *ca*. 12 miles N of Acco (Ptolemais). It forms the traditional S end of the Lebanon (cf. I Macc. 11:59). Mod. *Naqura*. B2—11

**Lagash.** Ancient Sumerian city-state, *ca*. 50 miles N of Ur, in S Mesopotamia. Under the *ensi* ("governor") Gudea, Lagash led a Sumerian revival following the rule of Sargon of Akkad. Mod. *Tello*. G4—2

**Lais.** *See* Dan, town of

**Laisa.** *See* Elasa

**Laish.** *See* Dan, town of

**Lake Ballah.** *See* Ballah, Lake

**Lake Hula.** *See* Hula, Lake

**Lake Moeris.** *See* Moeris, Lake

**Lake Sevan.** *See* Sevan, Lake

**Lake Tatta.** *See* Tatta, Lake

**Lake Timsah.** *See* Timsah, Lake

**Lake Tuz.** *See* Tuz, Lake

**Lake Urmia.** *See* Urmia, Lake

**Lake Van.** *See* Van, Lake

**Lakhish R.** Wadi that flows from the hill-country SW of Hebron, past Lachish, then generally NW to the Mediterranean, which it enters N of Ashdod.

**Lambaesis.** Site of the permanent camp built by the Roman emperor Trajan in Numidia, N Africa, for the Third Augustan Legion.

**Laodicea.** Chief city of Phrygia Pacatiana in Asia Minor, situated a little S of Colossae and Hierapolis, on the Lycos R., a tributary of the Maeander. Mod. *es-Eskihisar*, 56 miles SE of Izmir (Smyrna), Turkey. D2—17; E3—18

**Laodicea ad Mare.** Hellenized city on the Phoenician coast. Mod. *Latakia*. B2—13

**Larisa.** *See* Larissa

**Larissa.** City on the Pinios R. in N Greece. It was the chief city of ancient Thessaly and was annexed (4th century B.C.) by Philip of Macedon. It became a Roman colony in 196 B.C. D3—18

**Larsa.** Ancient city-state of S Mesopotamia, *ca*. 30 miles NE of Eridu. It was conquered by Elamites who established a dynasty there (*ca*. 1770 B.C.). G4—2

**Lasea. Seaport of Crete, *ca*. 5 miles E of Fair Havens. The vessel that carried Paul passed there (Acts 27:8). D3—17**

**Lebanon.** Arab republic bounded on the W by the Mediterranean, N and E by Syria, and S by Israel. Its capital is Beirut. The name *Lebanon* is derived from the mt. chain that occupies most of the country's land area. C1—19

**Lebanon Mts.** Mt. chain running parallel to the coast of N Palestine (mod. *Lebanon*). It is a continuation of the Taurus Mts. (*q.v.*) and is separated from a parallel range to the E, the Anti-Lebanon Mts. (*q.v.*), by the Beqa'a Valley. Its peaks rise to heights of 10,000 feet. C1—1, 11; D1—3; B3—4, 13

**Lebna.** *See* Libnah

**Lebo-hamath.** City that marked the N border of the land promised by God to Israel in Numbers 34:8 ("the entrance of Hamath" is Lebo-hamath). C2—4

**Lebona.** *See* Lebonah

**Lebonah.** Town situated 3 miles NW of Shiloh (Judg. 21:19). Mod. *Lubban* on the road between Shechem and Jerusalem.

**Lehabim.** Tribe related to the Egyptians (Gen. 10:13), prob. to be identified with the Libyans, or Lubim. The Egyptian pharaoh Sheshonk (biblical Shishak) was of Libyan extraction.

**Lemovii.** Germanic tribe that was settled in N Germany W of the Oder R.

**Leon.** City in NW Spain that dates back to Roman times. In A.D. 882 it was taken from the Moors, and subsequently it became capital of the kingdom of Leon.

**Leontes** (Litani) **R.** River that flows through the Beqa'a Valley, between the Lebanon and Anti-Lebanon ranges S toward the Jordan Valley. It makes a sharp westward turn, however, and flows into the Mediterranean N of Tyre. C1—1, 5, 11; B4—13

**Leptis Magna.** Ancient city on the Mediterranean coast of N Africa. Founded by Phoenicians (*ca.* 600 B.C.), it subsequently became an important Roman port. Mod. *Lebda*, E of Tripoli in Libya. C3—12

**Lesbos.** Greek island in the Aegean. The home of Sappho the poet and Theophrastus the philosopher. B1—15, 16; D2—17

**Lesem.** *See* Dan, town of

**Leshem.** *See* Dan, town of

**Libnah.** Canaanite city, near Lachish, captured by Joshua (Josh. 10:29–32). It became a Levitical city in Judah (Josh 21:13) and was besieged by Sennacherib (II Kings 19:8–36). Prob. mod. *Tell es-Safi*.

**Libya.** The term *Libya* was first applied by the Greeks to all Africa W of Egypt. Subsequently the term was restricted to the area between Egypt and the Roman province of Africa. Under Rome, Libya was divided into 2 parts: Libya Inferior, or Marmarica (*q.v.*), and Libya Superior, or Cyrenaica (*q.v.*). A3—7; C4—17

**Libyan Desert.** Desert W of Egypt that comprises most of Libya (*q.v.*). A-B5—2; A3-4—7

**Libyans.** Inhabitants of Libya (*q.v.*) prob. to be identified with the Lehabim or Lubim of the Bible. A3—6

**Liger R.** *See* Loire R.

**Lincoln.** City of E-central Britain famed for its cathedral and medieval churches. In Roman times it was the colony of Lindum, inhabited by the Coritani.

**Lisan.** Peninsula S of the Arnon R., Transjordan, that projects into the Dead Sea from the E.

**Lisht.** City in Upper Egypt, S of Memphis, where the pyramid of the Twelfth Dynasty pharaoh Amenemhet I was discovered. His capital is thought to have been nearby.

**Litani R.** *See* Leontes R.

**Lithuanians.** Tribe that spoke a Baltic language and formed a unified state in the 13th century A.D. Lithuania, one of the largest states of medieval Europe, is now part of the U.S.S.R.

**Livias** (Julias). C5—11. *See* Betharamphtha

**Lixus.** Town in NW Africa on the Atlantic coast, S of the Strait of Tangier. Phoenicians sailed beyond Gibraltar and colonized Lixus, which later became part of Roman Mauretania (*q.v.*).

**Lod** (Lydda). Town 11 miles SE of Joppa, situated in the Valley of Aijalon as it enters the Plain of Sharon. Mod. *Ludd*. B4—5

**Loire R.** Longest river in Gaul (France). Rising in the mts. in SE France, it flows NW, then W for 625 miles before flowing into the Atlantic at Saint-Nazaire, the port of Nantes.

**Lombards.** An ancient Germanic people who were settled along the lower Albis (Elbe) during the 1st century A.D. They migrated southward, and in A.D. 547 Justinian allowed them to settle in Pannonia and Noricum. They invaded N Italy (A.D. 568), however, and established a kingdom there.

**Londinium.** *See* London

**London.** British city that became the capital of the Roman province. In A.D. 141 the London Wall was built. The system of Roman roads built throughout Britain converged on London.

**Lower City** (in Jerusalem). That part of Jerusalem S of the temple, bounded on the E by the Kidron Valley and on the W by the Tyropoeon Valley. B6—10

**Lower Egypt.** *See* Egypt, Lower

**Lower Galilee.** *See* Galilee, lower

**Lower** (Old) **Pool.** Pool or reservoir SE of the Pool of Siloam. From this pool the water flows in a small rill across the road and irrigates gardens in the Kidron Valley.

**Lower Sea.** G5—2; D3—7. *See* Persian Gulf

**Lubim.** *See* Lehabim

**Luca.** City in NW Italy. It marked the S boundary of Caesar's province (Cisalpine Gaul) and was the site of a meeting of the First Triumvirate (Caesar, Pompey, and Crassus) in 56 B.C.

**Lud.** A people believed to be identical with the Lydians of W Asia Minor. Genesis 10:22 classes them as Semites. According to Herodotus their first king was of Assyrian descent.

**Lugdunensis.** Roman province in central Gaul, the major cities of which were Lutetia (*q.v.*) in the N and Lugdunum (*q.v.*) in the S. B1—12

**Lugdunum** (Lyons). City at the confluence of the Rhone and Saone rivers. Founded in 43 B.C. as a Roman colony, it became the principal city of Gaul and capital of the province of Lugdunensis. B2—12

**Lugii.** A Germanic tribe that settled in central Germany in the Oder Valley.

**Lukka.** Country in SW Asia Minor inhabited by Sea People by the same name. This area became Lycia. B-C2—2

**Lulu.** Mountainous region NE of Babylon. Cuneiform tablets from Nuzi speak of Lullians as slaves to the Mesopotamians.

**Lusitani.** Warlike tribes of the Iberian Peninsula (cf. Lusitania) who resisted Roman domination until their leader was killed by treachery (139 B.C.).

**Lusitania.** Roman province in the Iberian Peninsula, constituted *ca.* A.D. 5 by Augustus. It included what is now central Portugal and W Spain. A2—12

**Lutetia (Paris). Fishing hamlet before Caesar's conquest of Gaul. It subsequently expanded beyond the Ile de la Cité (an island in the Seine R., 90 miles from the English Channel) and became the** town Lutetia Parisiorum. Legend says that St. **Genevieve, patroness of Paris, through her prayers preserved the city from destruction by the Huns in the 5th century. The city sub-**

**sequently became a political and cultural center for France. B1—12**

**Lutetia Parisiorum.** *See* Lutetia

**Luxeuil.** Site of an abbey, established *ca.* A.D. 590, at Luxovium in E Gaul.

**Lycaonia.** Elevated, inland district of Asia Minor that contained 3 cities visited by Paul: Iconium, Derbe, and Lystra. The land of Lycaonia was suitable for pasturage, and the people spoke a dialect peculiar to the region (cf. Acts 13:51–14:23). C4—14; C2—15

**Lycia.** Province of Asia Minor that juts S into the Mediterranean. It is bounded on the N by Caria, Phrygia, Pisidia, and Pamphylia. During his voyages Paul stopped at 2 of its port cities, Patara and Myra (Acts 21:1–2; 27:5–6). B2—6; D3—12; C2—15, 16; E2—17

**Lycopolis.** *See* Siut

**Lydda.** B5—11; A6—13. *See* Lod

**Lydia.** Ancient district of W Asia Minor bounded on the N by Mysia, on the E by Phrygia, on the S by Caria, and on the W by the Aegean. The dynasty of Gyges, which seized the throne about 700 B.C., lasted 150 years, during which time the Lydian Empire became wealthy and extended its territory to the Halys R. The wealth of King Croesus became proverbial. In 546 B.C. Cyrus absorbed the Lydian Empire into the Persian. A-B2—7; B2—15, 16

**Lydia, Kingdom of.** B2—6. *See* Lydia

**Lyons.** B2—18. *See* Lugdunum

**Lystra.** City of Lycaonia and a Roman colony. There Paul healed a crippled man and would have been worshiped as a god had he not refused (Acts 14:6–21). Mod. *Zoldera, ca.* 25 miles SW of Iconium on the Imperial Road to Pisidian Antioch. C5—14; C2—15; E3—18

## M

**Maacah.** City and Aramean city-state at the foot of Mt. Hermon, near Geshur (Josh. 13:13; II Sam. 10:6, 8). Its king joined an Aramean alliance against David (II Sam. 10:6–8). B3—4

**Maacha.** *See* Maacah

**Maachah.** *See* Maacah

**Ma'an.** Administrative center of the S district of Jordan. It is situated on the edge of the desert and serves as the shopping center for nomadic tribes in the neighborhood.

**Maceda.** *See* Makkedah

**Macedonia.** Country of SE Europe bounded on the S by Thessaly and the Aegean, on the E by Thrace, and on the W by Illyria. Under Alexander the Great, Macedonia ruled an empire that reached E as far as the Punjab region of India. A1—7, 15, 16; D2—12, 18; B1—17

**Machaerus.** Hasmonean fortress on the E shore of the Dead Sea, rebuilt by Herod the Great. When John the Baptist, preaching in Perea, antagonized Herod, the prophet was placed in one of the dungeons beneath the palace at Machaerus. C5—11

**Machmes.** *See* Michmash

**Madaba.** D4—19. *See* Medeba

**Madai.** *See* Medes

**Madaura.** City in N Africa *ca.* 50 miles S of Hippo Regius. According to tradition, 4 Christians were martyred there (A.D. 180), the first Africans to die for their faith.

**Madian.** *See* Midian

**Madmannah.** Town in the S part of Judah (Josh. 15:31), thought to be the mod. *Umm Deimneh*, *ca.* 13 miles NE of Beer-sheba.

**Madon.** Town in N Canaan whose king joined with Hazor against Israel (Josh. 11:1–12). Thought to have been located near the Horns of Hattin (*q.v.*). D2—3

**Maeander R.** River of Asia Minor, rising in Phrygia and flowing W *ca.* 250 miles to enter the Aegean Sea S of Samos. Its winding course gave rise to the term *meander*. Mod. *Ruyuk Menderes*. B2—2, 7

**Magadan** (Magdala). Town *ca.* 3 miles N of Tiberias on the W shore of the Sea of Galilee. It was the home of Mary Magdalene. As Tarichea it served as a Jewish stronghold during the struggle with Rome. Mod. *Kh. Mejdel*. C2—11

**Magdala.** *See* Magadan

**Magdeburg.** City on the Albis (Elbe) R., E-central Germany. It is first mentioned A.D. 805, and by A.D. 968 it became an archiepiscopal see.

**Mageddo.** *See* Megiddo

**Mageth** (Maked). Town in Gilead in which the Jews were besieged during the time of the Maccabees (I Macc. 5:26). Mod. *Tell Miqdad*.

**Magog.** A people (and country) listed among the sons of Japheth (Gen. 10:2). They are thought to have lived at the N extremity of the Bible world. Josephus identified them with the Scythians.

**Magyars.** A nomadic people who migrated (*ca.* A.D. 460) from the Urals to the N Caucasus region. In the 9th century they were forced W into (present) Romania, and then N into Hungary, where they settled permanently.

**Mahanaim.** Town in Gilead associated with a crucial experience in the life of Jacob (Gen. 32:2). It became a Levitical town (Josh. 21:38) and was Ish-bosheth's capital (II Sam. 2:8, 12, 29). Poss. mod. *Kh. Mahneh*. B4—4; D4—5

**Mainz.** City in W Germany, on the left bank of the Rhine, opposite the mouth of the Main. It was the Roman city Maguntiacum, or Mogontiacum. In the 8th century, St. Boniface became its first archbishop.

**Maka.** E3—7. *See* Gedrosia

**Maked.** *See* Mageth

**Makkedah.** Town in the lowlands of Judah, *ca.* 15 miles W of Bethlehem. It was taken by Joshua (Josh. 15:41). Poss. mod. *Kh. el-Kheishum*.

**Malaca.** Coastal town of Farther Spain, founded by the Phoenicians.

**Malataya.** E2—2. *See* Melitene

**Malatha.** B6—11. *See* Arad

**Malta** (Melita). Island in the Mediterranean, S of Sicily. It was controlled, successively, by the

Phoenicians, Greeks, Carthaginians, and Romans. Paul was shipwrecked there (Acts 28:1). A3—17

**Mamre.** A plain near or in what later became the city of Hebron (*q.v.*) in S Palestine. Abraham pitched his tents there (Gen. 13:18). Mod. *Ramet el-khalil*.

**Manasse.** *See* Manasseh

**Manasseh,** allotment of. Half the tribe of Manasseh chose as its inheritance part of Gilead and all of Bashan (Deut. 3:13–15), E of the Jordan. The other half of the tribe chose its inheritance in central Palestine, W of the Jordan. It was bounded on the S by Dan and Ephraim; on the N by Asher, Zebulun, and Issachar; and on the W by the Mediterranean.

**Manasseh's Wall.** Wall on the E side of Jerusalem built by Manasseh (II Chron. 33:14). D2—9

**Manasses.** *See* Manasseh

**Maon.** Town in the hill-country of Judah (Josh. 15:55), *ca*. 8.5 miles S of Hebron. It was the home of Nabal (I Sam. 25:2) in an area in which David took refuge from his enemies (I Sam. 23:24–25). Mod. *Tell Ma'in*.

**Mara.** *See* Marah

**Maracanda.** *See* Samarkand

**Marah.** Fountain of bitter water in the Wilderness of Shur, at which the Israelites stopped, following the Exodus. Mod. *'Ain Hawara*. B5—3

**Marathon.** Site of a famous battle between the Greeks and the Persians (490 B.C.). It is on the NE coast of Attica, *ca*. 22 miles N of Athens. A2—7

**Marcomanni.** A Germanic people who lived between the Rhine and Danube rivers. Subsequently they migrated to Bohemia and parts of Bavaria and joined other tribes in the harassment of Rome. Peace was made by Commodus (A.D. 180).

**Mare Hyrcanium.** *See* Caspian Sea

**Mare Internum.** B-D3—12. *See* Mediterranean Sea

**Maresa.** *See* Mareshah

**Mareshah** (Marisa). Town in the lowlands of Judah (Josh. 15:44) that was fortified by Rehoboam (II Chron. 11:8). A battle between King Asa of Judah and Zerah the Ethiopian (of Egypt) was fought nearby (II Chron. 14:9–10). In Maccabean times it was known as Marisa. Mod. *Tell Sandahanna*, 1 mile SE of Beth-gubrin. B5—5; B4—19

**Margiana.** Chief city of Margus (*q.v.*). E2—7

**Margus.** N border province of ancient Persia, E of the SE shore of the Caspian Sea. E2—7

**Mari,** city of. Ancient city-state on the middle Euphrates S of its junction with the Habor. Amorites from Mari brought disaster to the Sumerian cities of S Mesopotamia. Mari, however, after a period of cultural brilliance, fell to Hammurabi of Babylon. Mod. *Tell Hariri*. E3—2

**Mari, Kingdom of.** Area ruled by the city-state of Mari (*q.v.*), which extended over a wide area in the middle Euphrates basin. Zimri-Lim was the last king of Mari before its conquest by Hammurabi. His palace archives, discovered since 1935, help us reconstruct life during patriarchal times.

**Mariamne.** One of three massive towers erected by Herod the Great on Jerusalem's W hill to protect its N approach. This tower was named after Herod's wife. *See also* Hippicus *and* Phasael. A5—10

**Marienburg.** Town on the Nogat R., SE of Danzig. It was originally a castle, founded A.D. 1274 by the Teutonic knights, and subsequently sold to Poland.

**Marisa.** B5—11. *See* Mareshah

**Market of Appius.** *See* Appius, Forum of

**Marmarica.** District of N Africa between Libya and Cyrenaica. It is a desert plateau, now a part of NE Cyrenaica.

**Marqash.** Town in the Anti-Taurus Mts. of N Syria. It was once the capital of a Hittite kingdom and later the center of the Aramean kingdom of Gurgum. Roman *Germanicea*. Mod. *Maras*.

**Marseille.** Chief Mediterranean port of France, founded by Phocaean Greeks from Asia Minor *ca*. 600 B.C. Ancient Massilia became an ally of Rome, which annexed it (49 B.C.) after it supported Pompey against Caesar in the civil war.

**Masada.** Mt. stronghold overlooking the Dead Sea, *ca*. 11 miles S of En-gedi. It was the last fortress to hold out against the Romans during the Jewish revolt. After withstanding siege for 3 years, the defenders put themselves to death rather than fall to the enemy (A.D. 73). The fall of Masada marked the end of Jewish independence. C6—11; C5—19

**Masepha.** *See* Mizpah

**Mash.** A name in the table of nations (Gen. 10), thought to refer to an Aramean people.

**Maspha.** *See* Mizpah

**Masrephoth-maim.** *See* Misrephoth-maim

**Massagetae.** A people of central Asia who lived E of the Aral Sea. Cyrus the Great was defeated and slain by them. E1—7

**Massilia.** *See* Marseille

**Mauretania.** Roman province of NW Africa corresponding to Morocco and W Algeria. It was bounded on the E by the province of Numidia. It was formed into a Roman province by Claudius. A3—12, 18

**Mazaca.** *See* Caesarea Mazaca

**Meah, Tower of.** Tower of ancient Jerusalem located between the Tower of Hananel and the Sheep Gate (Neh. 3:1; 12:39 KJV).

**Medeba.** Ancient Moabite town located *ca*. 16 miles SE of the mouth of the Jordan, 6 miles S of Heshbon. It was allotted to Reuben (Josh. 13:9, 16) but reverted to Moab (Isa. 15:2). B4—4; C5—5; D5—11

**Medemena.** *See* Madmannah

**Medes** (Madai). An ancient people who invaded the mt. country S of the Caspian and, by 700 B.C., had built a prosperous nation. *See* Median Empire

**Media.** The mt. country S of the Caspian inhabited by the Medes (*q.v.*). G3—2; D2—6; C2—7

**Median Empire.** At its peak this empire extended from India to the Black Sea. The Medes (*q.v.*) dominated the relatively small nation of Persia until Cyrus the Great mastered Media (*ca.* 549 B.C.) and began his career of conquest. D-E2—6

**Mediolanum.** *See* Milan

**Mediterranean** (Great, Upper) **Sea** (Mare Internum). Sea comprising an area of 1,145,000 square miles, with a maximum length of 2,300 miles and a maximum width of 1,200 miles. It is surrounded by Europe, Asia, and Africa, connecting with the Atlantic Ocean through the Strait of Gibraltar. A4—1; A3—2, 5, 11, 17, 19; A2—3, 4, 6; B3—12, 15, 16, 18; A5—13

**Megiddo,** city of. Important city of N-central Palestine, overlooking the Plain of Esdraelon. It dominated the intersection of important trade routes and served as the key to the defense of the Jordan Valley (from the S) and the coastal plain (from the N). Mod. *Tell el-Mutesellim*. B3—1, 5; D4—2; D2—3; B4—4; C3—6; B2—19

**Megiddo,** district of. The Plain of Esdraelon is called "the valley of Megiddo(n)" (Zech. 12:11). The city of Megiddo gave its name to the surrounding district.

**Meiron.** Town 5 miles NW of Safad revered by orthodox Jews as the burial place of Rabbis Simeon ben Yochai, Hillel, Shammai, and others. C1—19

**Melita.** *See* Malta

**Melitene.** City at the E foot of the Taurus Mts. in Armenia. It was an important city in Cappadocia and an early Christian center. Mod. *Malataya*, Turkey. C2—7

**Mello.** *See* Millo

**Memphis** (Noph). Ancient capital of Lower Egypt, 14 miles S of Cairo. Tradition states that it was built by Menes, the king who united Upper and Lower Egypt into one kingdom. C4—2; A4—3; B3—6, 7; E4—12, 18

**Mephaath.** Town in Transjordan that belonged to the tribe of Reuben (Josh. 13:18). It became a Levitical city (Josh. 21:37) and later was taken by Moab (Jer. 48:21). Prob. mod. *Tell Jawah*, near *Kh. Nefa'a*, 6 miles S of Amman.

**Merida.** City of SW Spain. Founded by the Romans as Emerita Augusta in the 1st century B.C., it became the capital of Lusitania. A2—18

**Merom.** Site of a battle in which Joshua defeated a coalition of kings from N Canaan (Josh. 11:5, 7). The "waters of Merom" are probably the spring and wadi near the village of Meiron, at the base of J. Yarmuk, W of Safad. C2—5

**Meron, Mt.** Highest mt. in lower Galilee, rising 3,963 feet. Mod. *J. Jermaq*. C2—1

**Mersin.** Seaport in SE Asia Minor, *ca.* 20 miles W of Tarsus. Its history predated that of the Hittites in Anatolia. D2—2

**Mes.** *See* Mash

**Mesembria.** Town of Thrace, on the Black Sea at the foot of Mt. Haemus. It was founded by the people of Chalcedon and Byzantium in the days of Darius Hystaspis. D1—17

**Meshech.** A people mentioned in the table of nations (Gen. 10:2) as descendants of Japheth. Assyrian records mention *Mushki* as a people in the mts. on the N borders of Assyria. Herodotus placed the *Moschi* SE of the Black Sea.

**Mesopotamia.** District of W Asia between the Tigris and Euphrates. The region extends from the Persian Gulf to the mts. of Armenia, from the Iranian Plateau to the Syrian Desert. The term *Mesopotamia* was first used by the Greeks in Seleucid times. F3—18

**Mesraim.** *See* Egypt

**Messina.** Coastal city of NE Sicily on the Straits of Messina. It was founded by Greek colonists in the 8th century B.C. The 1st Punic war resulted from the request of the Mamertimes of Messina for help from Rome against Syracuse.

**Michmash.** Town in the territory of Benjamin, E of Bethel, 7 miles N of Jerusalem. Jonathan defeated the Philistines there (I Sam. 13–14). Mod. *Mukhmas*.

**Midian.** Territory S of Edom, E of the Gulf of Aqaba, in which the nomadic Midianites lived. D5—2, 3

**Migdal Ashqelon.** Town in mod. Israel consisting of an Old Quarter with narrow crooked lanes and a New Quarter with new dwellings among olive groves. Migdal ("tower of") Ashqelon is a short distance NE of Ashkelon (*q.v.*), the ancient Philistine city.

**Milan.** City on the Lombard Plain in N Italy. It was of Celtic origin, but Rome conquered the city and in late Roman times it became the seat of the Western Empire.

**Miletus.** Ancient seaport near the mouth of the Maeander R. in Caria, W Asia Minor. It was occupied *ca.* 1000 B.C. by Greeks and sacked by the Persians (499 B.C.). It fell to Alexander the Great and was successively subject to Pergamum and Rome. A2—7; B2—15, 16; D2—17; E3—18

**Millo** (in Jerusalem). Prob. the great terraced fill on the E side of the ridge above the Spring Gihon, first built by the Jebusites. After occupying Jerusalem, David "built the city round about from the Millo [i.e., 'filling'] inward" (II Sam. 5:9 RSV). B2—8; C2—9

**Minoan-Mycenaean Domain.** Islands subject to the Minoan rulers of Crete. According to some traditions, Minos was an able ruler who made Crete a great sea power. A2-C3—2

**Miphkad** (Muster) **Gate.** Easternmost gate into the city of Jerusalem from the N (*ca.* 445 B.C.).

**Mishneh Gate.** Gate from the W into the Mishneh quarter of Jerusalem (*ca.* 445 B.C.).

**Misphat.** *See* En-mishpat

**Misrephoth-maim.** Place to which Joshua pursued the Canaanite kings defeated at the "waters of Merom" (Josh. 11:8; 13:6). Poss. mod. *Kh. el-Musheirefeh*.

**Mitanni.** Powerful kingdom from *ca.* 1500 to 1350 B.C., located between the Assyrians and Hittites. The ruling class was Indo-Aryan, the population predominantly Hurrian. E2—2

**Mitylene.** Capital of Lesbos (*q.v.*), located on the E

of the island. It was colonized by Aeolians and subsequently became an important naval power. Paul stopped there on his journey from Assos to Chios (Acts 20:13–15). B1—16

**Mizpah** (in Ephraim). Town on the border between Israel and Judah (during the time of the divided kingdom), fortified by Asa of Judah (I Kings 15:22). The Babylonian governor fixed his residence there after the destruction of Jerusalem (II Kings 25:23–25). Prob. mod. *Tell en-Nasbeh*, 7 miles N of Jerusalem. B4—5, 19

**Mizpah** (in Gilead). Site on the frontier between Israel and Aram where Jacob and Laban made a covenant (Gen. 31:44–49). Poss. mod. *Kh. Jel'ad*, S of the Yarmuk.

**Mizpeh.** *See* Mizpah

**Mizraim.** *See* Egypt

**M'lefaat.** City of ancient Assyria, located on the Great Zab R., a tributary of the Tigris.

**Moabites.** A people closely related to the Ammonites (Gen. 19:37–38). Their land was, ideally, bounded on the N by the Arnon and on the S by the Zered in the territory E of the Dead Sea. During times of Israelite weakness, they occupied territory N of the Arnon, but when Israel was strong, Moab was forced to pay tribute. C-D5—1; D3—3; B5—4; C-D6—5

**Moab, Plains of.** Moab is largely a rolling plateau, *ca*. 3,200 feet above sea level, and is well adapted for pasturage. The Plains of Moab were those parts of the level Jordan Valley that once belonged to Moab. They lie E of the Jordan, opposite Jericho, and E of the Dead Sea. C4—1

**Modin.** Town that gave birth to the Maccabean revolt. It was located *ca*. 7 miles E of Lydda and *ca*. 16 miles from the Mediterranean on the edge of the Philistine plain. Mod. *el-'Arba'in*, near *El-Midyah*.

**Moeris, Lake.** Ancient name of Lake Karun, in the Faiyum, 50 miles SW of Cairo. Crocodilopolis (Arsinoe) was the chief town on the lake. A5—3

**Moesi.** Ancient tribal people who gave their name to Moesia (*q.v.*).

**Moesia.** Ancient name for the region of SE Europe S of the lower Danube. It was organized as a Roman province (A.D. 44). The territory included mod. Serbia and Bulgaria. D2—12, 18; C-D1—17

**Molada.** *See* Moladah

**Moladah.** Town in S Judah (Josh. 15:26), assigned to Simeon (Josh. 19:2). Poss. mod. *Tell el-Milh*, 14 miles SE of Beer-sheba, 22 miles SW of Hebron.

**Moreh, Hill of.** Hill in the Plain of Esdraelon, N of the spring of Harod. Prob. *J. Dahy*, or Little Hermon, 8 miles NW of Mt. Gilboa, 1 mile S of Nain. C3—1

**Moresheth-gath.** Town in Judah (Micah 1:14), thought to be the home of the prophet Micah (cf. 1:1). Prob. mod. *Tell el-Judeideh*.

**Moschi.** C2—7. *See* Meshech

**Mosoch.** *See* Meshech

**Mt. Ararat.** *See* Ararat, Mt.

**Mt. Carmel.** *See* Carmel, Mt.

**Mt. Gerizim.** *See* Gerizim, Mt.

**Mt. Gilboa.** *See* Gilboa, Mt.

**Mt. Meron.** *See* Meron, Mt.

**Mt. Nebo.** *See* Nebo, Mt.

**Mt. Nisir.** *See* Nisir, Mt.

**Mt. of Olives.** *See* Olives, Mt. of

**Mt. Pisgah.** *See* Pisgah, Mt.

**Mt. Sinai.** *See* Sinai, Mt.

**Mt. Tabor.** *See* Tabor, Mt.

**Mughara, W. el-.** Located on the lower W slope of Mt. Carmel, *ca*. 11 miles S of the N promontory of the mt. and 2 miles E of the Mediterranean. Several caves there have yielded significant Stone Age remains. B2—19

**Mujib, W. el-.** *See* Aron R.

**Munda.** Roman colony and town in Farther Spain. Scene of Scipio's victory over the Carthaginians (216 B.C.) and of Julius Caesar's over Pompey's sons (45 B.C.).

**Murabba'at Caves.** Caves on the W shore of the Dead Sea where Bar Kokhba and his followers hid during the second revolt (A.D. 132–134). C4—19

**Musa, W.** *See* W. Musa

**Musasir.** Town on the border between ancient Urartu and Assyria, located in the mountainous district SE of Lake Urmia. It was conquered by the Assyrian ruler Shalmaneser III.

**Muster Gate.** *See* Miphkad Gate

**Mycenaean-Minoan Domain.** *See* Minoan-Mycenaean Domain.

**Myra.** City of Lycia, S Asia Minor, *ca*. 2 miles from the Mediterranean built on and about a cliff at the mouth of a gorge leading into the interior mt. region. Paul changed ships there (Acts 27:5–6). Mod. *Dembre*. E3—17, 18

**Mysia.** Province in the extreme NW of Asia Minor bounded on the N by the Propontis (mod. Sea of Marmara), on the S by Lydia, on the E by Bithynia, and on the W by the Aegean Sea. Paul passed through Mysia to Troas, one of its cities (Acts 16:7–8). Assos (Acts 20:13) and Pergamum (Rev. 1:11) are also in Mysia. B1—15, 16; E2—18

## N

**Naarah.** Town in Ephraim, N of Jericho (Josh. 16:7). It is prob. identical with Naaran (I Chron. 7:28).

**Naarath(a).** *See* Naarah

**Naare.** *See* Nazareth

**Naasson.** *See* Hazor

**Nabatea.** Country in the land of Edom and Moab from *ca*. 200 B.C. to A.D. 100. Petra (*q.v.*) was its capital. C6-D5—11; E3-4—12

**Nabateans.** Arabian people who developed a remarkable civilization during the 1st and 2nd centuries B.C. and the 1st century A.D. Their capital, Petra, was on important trade routes between S Arabia and Syria. Nabateans built irrigation systems and farmed the land. B6-C5—13

**Nablus.** Roman name for a town near the site of ancient Shechem (*q.v.*). *See* Neapolis (in Palestine).

**Nabo.** *See* Nebo, Mt.

**Nabutheans.** *See* Nabateans

**Nahariyah.** Site on the Mediterranean coast, N of Acco *ca*. 7 miles, where remains of Canaanite habitation have been discovered. B1—19

**Naim.** *See* Nain

**Nain.** Town 6 miles SE of Nazareth in the NW corner of J. ed-Duhy (Little Hermon). Here Jesus restored to life the only son of a widow (Luke 7:11). Mod. *Nain*. C3—11

**Nantes.** Town on the Loire R., W France. It was of pre-Roman origin and was ravaged by Norsemen in the 9th century.

**Naphtali,** allotment of. Land in N Palestine, bounded on the E by the upper Jordan and the Sea of Galilee, and on the S by Issachar and Zebulun.

**Naples.** City in S Italy, built at the base of a ridge of hills rising from the Bay of Naples. It was a Greek colony, conquered (4th century B.C.) by the Romans.

**Narbata.** Town *ca*. 8 miles E of Caesarea that, according to Josephus, was conquered by Cestius during the first revolt. Mod. *Kh. Beidus*. B3—11

**Narbo.** City in S France near the Mediterranean coast. As Narbo Martius it was the 1st Roman colony established (118 B.C.) in Transalpine Gaul. B2—12

**Narbonensis.** Roman province in S Gaul, located W and S of the Alpine provinces. Its capital was Narbo. A2—12

**Narbonne.** *See* Narbo

**Narona.** Roman colony in Illyricum, on the Naro R. and the road to Dyrrhachium.

**Naucratis.** City on the E bank of the Canopic branch of the Nile in the Delta. It was colonized by Milesians and remained a Greek city. Aphrodite was its principal goddess.

**Nawa.** Syrian city *ca*. 25 miles W of the Sea of Galilee.

**Nazareth.** Town in a secluded valley of lower Galilee, N of the Plain of Esdraelon. It was the boyhood home of Jesus (Luke 2:39; 4:16). C2—1; B3—11

**Neapolis** (in Italy). *See* Naples

**Neapolis** (in Macedonia). Seaport of Philippi, situated on the Strymonic Gulf, 10 miles SE of the city. Mod. *Kavalla*. B1—15, 16

**Neapolis** (in Palestine). City built by the Romans in A.D. 72 just W of the site of ancient Shechem (*q.v.*). Mod. *Nablus* (a corruption of *Neapolis*, "new city"). B4—11

**Neballat.** Town in Benjamin, *ca*. 4 miles NE of Lydda. It was inhabited after the exile (Neh. 11:34). Mod. *Beit Naballa*.

**Nebo, Mt.** Peak in the Abarim Mts. opposite Jericho (Num. 33:47; Deut. 32:49). Mod. *J. en-Neba*, 12 miles E of the mouth of the Jordan. D4—1; D3—3

**Negba.** Town in Israel, E of Ashkelon. It is situated in an area of fertile fields and plantations.

**Negeb.** The dry southland of Judea, beginning a few miles S of Hebron and extending to Kadesh-barnea. Beer-sheba is an oasis in the N Negeb. A-B6—1, 5; C-D3—3

**Negev.** *See* Negeb

**Nemrod.** *See* Nimrod

**Nephtahli,** allotment of. *See* Naphtali, allotment of

**Nervii.** A warlike people of Gallia Belgica, decisively defeated by Caesar in 58 B.C.

**New Babylonian Empire.** *See* Babylonian Empire, New

**Nicaea.** City built on the E side of Lake Ascania, in Bithynia, Asia Minor. It was a royal residence of Bithynian kings and sometimes served as its capital. Constantine convened a great ecclesiastical council there in A.D. 325.

**Nicephorium.** Fortified town built on the Euphrates, S of Edessa, at the command of Alexander the Great.

**Nicomedia.** City of Bithynia, Asia Minor, located at the head of the Gulf of Astacus on the Propontis. Founded by Nicomedes I (264 B.C.), it became a chief city of the Roman Empire. *See* Astacus. E2—18

**Nicopolis** (in Asia Minor). City in Pontus. Site of a Byzantine victory over Arab invaders. Ancient *Acroinum*, mod. *Afyonkarahisar*, Turkey.

**Nicopolis** (in Greece). City in NW Greece, founded by Octavian (Augustus) to celebrate his victory at nearby Actium (31 B.C.). C2—17; D3—18

**Nicopolis** (in Palestine). B5—11. *See* Emmaus

**Nile Delta.** Delta that begins where the Nile R. branches out and is 120 miles wide on the Mediterranean coast. The two principal branches, each *ca*. 146 miles long, enter the sea at Rosetta (on the W) and Damietta (on the E). A3—3

**Nile R.** River that flows *ca*. 4,050 miles through NE Africa from its ultimate headstream, the Kagera, N to the Mediterranean. Ancient Egypt was the land along the Nile and its Delta from the 1st cataract at Aswan to the Mediterranean. C5—2; A5—3; B3—6; B4—7; E4—12, 18

**Nimrah.** *See* Beth-nimrah

**Nimrod.** Dominion of a son of Cush (Gen. 10:8–12), in S Mesopotamia.

**Nimrud.** F3—2. *See* Calah

**Nineve.** *See* Nineveh

**Nineveh.** Ancient capital of Assyria, located on the E bank of the Tigris opposite the site of mod. *Mosul*. An alliance of Medes, Babylonians, and Scythians destroyed the city in 612 B.C. F2—2; C2—6

**Ninus.** *See* Nineveh

**Nippur.** Sumerian center on the Euphrates in central Babylonia. It was the seat of the worship of the goddess En-lil. F4—2; D3—6; C3—7

**Nisibis.** City of N Mesopotamia. Site of battles between the Parthians and Romans. C2—6; F3—18

**Nisir, Mt.** Mt. E of Mosul and the Tigris near the Little Zab R. According to the Gilgamesh Epic, the ark rested there following the flood.

**No** (Thebes). Biblical No-Amon (Nahum 3:8). It was the capital of Upper Egypt. Ruins are at mod. *Luxor* and *Karnak*. C6—2

**No-Amon.** *See* No

**Nob.** Town in the territory of Benjamin, N of Jerusalem (Isa. 10:32). The tabernacle was there for a time, and Nob was known as "the city of the priests" (I Sam. 22:19). Prob. mod. *Ras Umm et-Tala'* on the E slope of Mt. Scopus.

**Nobah.** Town in Transjordan along a road leading to the country of the nomads (Judg. 8:11).

**Nobe.** *See* Nob

**Noph.** C4—2; A4—3. *See* Memphis

**Noreia.** Capital city of the Norici, the people of Noricum (*q.v.*), situated S of the Murius R.

**Noricum.** Province of the Roman Empire that corresponds to mod. Austria S of the Danube and W of Vienna. C2—12

**North Sea.** Portion of the Atlantic Ocean NW of central Europe. It touches the shores of Scotland, England, Norway, Denmark, Germany, the Netherlands, and N France.

**North Wall, First** (in Jerusalem). The N wall running E from Herod's towers (Hippicus, in particular) to the temple-enclosure walls. B5—10

**North Wall, Second** (in Jerusalem). A wall that, according to Josephus, began near the Gennath Gate of the First North Wall and enclosed the N quarter of the city, ending at the Fortress Antonia. B4—10

**Nubia.** Region in Upper Egypt, extending N to Aswan and the 1st cataract of the Nile. Its boundaries were indefinite, but it did include the Nubian Desert. C6—2

**Numidia.** Country in NW Africa, occupying territory corresponding to mod. Algeria. After being under control of Carthage, Numidia enjoyed a period of independence before being subjugated by Rome. B3—18

**Nuzi.** Ancient city of Mesopotamia, near mod. *Kirkuk*. Archaeological discoveries there have illuminated life during patriarchal times. Mod. *Yorghan Tepe*. F3—2

## O

**Oboth.** Place where the Israelites stopped en route from Kedesh to the plains of Moab. Poss. mod. *'Ain el-Weiba*, S of the Dead Sea.

**Oceanus Germanicus.** *See* North Sea

**Odollam.** *See* Adullam

**Og, Kingdom of.** Territory in the Transjordanian district of Bashan, from the Yarmuk R. to Mt. Hermon (Deut. 3:8–10).

**Olbia.** Colony of Greek Miletus, founded *ca*. 645 B.C. near mod. *Nikolayev*, Ukraine. It served as a center for the export of wheat from the S Ukraine.

**Old Babylonian Empire.** *See* Babylonian Empire, Old

**Old Pool.** *See* Lower Pool

**Olives, Mt. of.** Hill E of Jerusalem, from which it is separated by the Kidron Valley. It was the site of Jesus' Olivet discourse and His ascension. C4—1; D4—10

**Olivet, Mt.** *See* Olives, Mt. of

**Oman, Gulf of.** Gulf that connects the Persian Gulf with the Indian Ocean, bounded on the N by Iran and on the S by Oman in SE Arabia.

**'Omer.** Town *ca*. 3 miles NE of Beer-sheba on the road that formerly connected Beer-sheba with Hebron and Jerusalem.

**On.** C4—2; A4—3. *See* Heliopolis

**Ono.** Town in Benjamin, 7 miles SE of Joppa. It was reoccupied following the Babylonian captivity (Ezra 2:33; Neh. 7:37). Mod. *Kafr 'Ana*.

**Ophel.** S sector of the E hill of Jerusalem. It was originally a tower or projection in the fortification. B2-3—8; D2-3—9

**Ophera.** *See* Ophrah

**Ophir.** Territory of a tribe descended from Joktan (Gen. 10:29). It was famed for its gold (Ps. 45:9). It was prob. located in SW Arabia.

**Ophrah** (in Benjamin). Town N of Michmash (I Sam. 13:17). It was identical with Ephron (II Chron. 13:19) and Ephraim (II Sam. 13:23; John 11:54). *See* Ephraim, city of

**Ophrah** (in Issachar). Town of Gideon known as "Ophrah of the Abiezrites" (Judg. 8:27, 32). Location uncertain. Poss. mod. *et-Taiyibeh*, NW of Beth-shan.

**Opis.** One of the principal cities of N Babylonia (Akkad). It was situated on the Tigris. D2—6; C2—7

**Ornan,** threshing floor of. *See* Araunah, threshing floor of

**Orontes R.** River in Syria formed from sources in the Lebanon and Anti-Lebanon Mts. It flows N through the Beqa'a Valley, then SW past Syrian Antioch to the Mediterranean. C1—4; C2—13

**Ortona.** Town in S-central Italy that was once a major Adriatic port.

**Ostia.** Town at the mouth of the Tiber R. that served as the port of Rome. A1—17

**Oxus R.** River that rises in the Hindu Kush (*q.v.*) and flows 1,450 miles in a generally NW direction to the Aral Sea. Mod. *Amu Darya*. F1—6; E1—7

**Oxyrrhynchus.** Town in Upper Egypt, W of the Nile, near the Faiyum. Significant finds of papyri have been made there.

## P

**Pactyans.** Ancient people of Arachosia (*q.v.*).

**Padan-aram.** *See* Paddan-aram

**Paddan-aram.** Region in upper Mesopotamia (Gen. 25:20; 28:2) where relatives of the biblical patriarchs settled. It was also known as Aram-naharaim (Gen. 25:20). E2—2

**Palestine.** Strictly speaking, "the land of the Philistines," the coastal plain E of the Mediterranean and S of Joppa. *Palestine* came to be used of the whole land of Israel, both E and W of the Jordan.

**Palm Trees, City of.** *See* Jericho

**Palmyra.** *See* Tadmor

**Palus Maeotis.** *See* Azov, Sea of

**Pamphylia.** Country in S Asia Minor, bounded on the N by Pisidia, on the S by a gulf of the Mediterranean called the Sea of Pamphylia, on the E by Cilicia, and on the W by Lycia. D-E3—12; C5—14; C2—15, 16; E2—17

**Paneas.** Region in Syria between Iturea (to the N) and Ulatha (to the S). Its main city, Caesarea Philippi (*q.v.*), sometimes went by the name *Paneas* (or *Baniyas*). C-D1—11

**Panias.** *See* Paneas

**Pannonia.** Country of a mixed Illyrian-Celtic people, S of the Danube R. and extending to the Save Valley. Conquered by Rome 12–9 B.C. C2—12

**Panticapaeum.** Town in the E sector of the Crimean Peninsula of the Black Sea. It was founded by Milesians *ca*. 541 B.C. B1—7

**Paphlagonia.** District in N Asia Minor between Bithynia and Pontus.

**Paphos.** Port city on the W coast of Cyprus. Old Paphos was of Phoenician origin and was a center for the worship of Venus. The Romans built New Paphos, which was the capital of 1 of the 4 districts into which Cyprus was divided. C5—14; E3—18

**Paraetonium.** Important town on the N coast of Africa, near Cape Artos. It was an important center for the worship of Isis. The town was restored by Justinian.

**Paran, Wilderness of.** Wilderness between Sinai (or Hazeroth) and Canaan (Num. 10:12; 12:16). It was S of Judah and included Kadesh (Num. 13:26), or Kadesh-barnea. C4—3

**Paran R.** Brook that flows from the Wilderness of Paran NE to the *W. 'Araba*.

**Parathon.** *See* Pirathon

**Pardes Hanna.** Mod. Israeli settlement in a region of citrus groves on the road from Hadera to 'Afula.

**Paricanians.** Ancient people who inhabited Gedrosia (*q.v.*).

**Paris.** *See* Lutetia

**Parsa** (Persepolis). One of the capitals of ancient Persia, located 35 miles NE of mod. *Shiraz*. Mod. *Takht-i-Jamshid*. D3—7

**Parthia.** Country in W Asia, SE of the Caspian, adjoining Media. E2—6, 7

**Parthian Empire.** *Ca*. 250 B.C. Arcases I threw off the yoke of the Seleucid Syrian kings. Under Mithridates I the Parthian Empire extended from the N Euphrates to beyond the Indus. Ctesiphon was its capital. F3—12

**Pasargadae.** Capital of ancient Persia and site of the tomb of Cyrus the Great. Its ruins are 54 miles by road NE of Persepolis on the Murgab Plain on both sides of the Pulvar R. D3—7

**Patara.** Chief seaport of Lycia, Asia Minor. It was colonized by Dorians from Crete and boasted an Apollo oracle. Restored by Ptolemy Philadelphus, it was renamed Arsinoe. Mod. *Gelemish*. C2—16; D3—17

**Pathros.** Ancient name for Upper Egypt, the land S of the Delta. It is located between Egypt (i.e., the Delta) and Cush in Isaiah 11:11.

**Pathrusim.** Inhabitants of Pathros (*q.v.*), who were descendants of Mizraim (Gen. 10:14).

**Patmos.** Aegean island 28 miles S of Samos (*q.v.*) to which Domitian exiled the apostle John *ca*. A.D. 95. Patmos was part of the Roman province of Asia. D3—18

**Pattala.** Ancient city in India at the head of the Indus R. delta. Alexander the Great took Pattala without battle. There he planned the naval expedition that would sail from the mouth of the Indus to the Persian Gulf. F3—7

**Pella** (in Gilead). City in Transjordan to which Christians fled before the Romans captured Jerusalem (A.D. 70). Mod. *Tabaqat Fahl*. C3—11; B5—13

**Pella** (in Macedonia). Macedonian town that Philip made his capital. Birthplace of Alexander the Great.

**Pelusium** (Sin). Ancient Egyptian city on the easternmost branch of the Nile, *ca*. 20 miles E of mod. *Port Said*. It was known as Sin in the Bible (Ezek. 30:15–16). B3—3, 7

**Peniel.** *See* Penuel

**Penuel** (Peniel). Encampment E of the Jordan where Jacob had his historic encounter with God (Gen. 32:30–31). It was a fortified place at the time of Gideon (Judg. 8:8, 9, 17) and Jeroboam (I Kings 12:25). C4—5

**Perea.** Region in Transjordan between the Jabbok and the Arnon. The term is sometimes used of the entire country E of the Jordan. C4—11

**Perga.** City in ancient Pamphylia, Asia Minor, NE of Attalia. It was located *ca*. 7 miles from the mouth of the Kestros R. and served as a center for the worship of Artemis (Diana). Paul ministered there during his First Missionary Journey (Acts 13:13–14). Mod. *Murtana*, Turkey. C5—14

**Pergamum.** Most important city of ancient Mysia, W Asia Minor, situated 3 miles N of the R. Caicus and *ca*. 15 miles from the Aegean Sea. Eumenes II of Pergamum (190 B.C.) identified himself with the Romans and, with their aid, ruled a powerful kingdom. Mod. *Bergama*. D2—12, 17; B1—15, 16; E3—18

**Perge.** *See* Perga

**Persepolis.** D3—7. *See* Parsa

**Persia.** E3—6. *See* Persis

**Persian Empire.** Empire extending to (but not including) Greece in the W and India in the E. It included both Egypt and Babylonia. It was established by Cyrus in the mid-6th century B.C. and lasted until defeat by Alexander the Great in 331 B.C. B-F2—7

**Persian Gulf** (Lower Sea). Arm of the Arabian Sea between Persia (mod. *Iran*) and Arabia. It extends *ca*. 600 miles from the mouth of the Tigris-Euphrates to the Strait of Hormuz, which connects it with the Gulf of Oman. G5—2; D-E3—6

**Persis.** Country N of the Persian Gulf inhabited by an Indo-European people known as Persians.

Persis, or Persia, seems to have been early inhabited by Sumerian peoples, but following the fall of Assyria, the Medes became heirs to its political power and civilization. D3—7

**Pessinus.** Ancient city in SW Galatia, Asia Minor. Under Constantine it became capital of Galatia Salutaris, a Roman province.

**Petra.** *See* Sela

**Phaddan-aram.** *See* Paddan-aram

**Phanuel.** *See* Penuel

**Phara.** *See* Pirathon

**Pharathon.** *See* Pirathon

**Pharos.** W extremity of Alexandria, Egypt. It is an island that in ancient times was the location of a famous lighthouse and that is now connected to Alexandria by a causeway.

**Pharpar R.** River of Damascus (II Kings 5:12). Prob. mod. *Awaj*, which is also S of mod. Damascus and flows E into swamps. D1—1

**Pharsalus.** Town in Pharsalia, Thessaly, near the Enipeus R. It was the scene of fighting in the war between Rome and Macedonia (197 B.C.).

**Phasael.** One of three massive towers erected by Herod the Great on Jerusalem's W hill to protect its N approach. The tower was named after Herod's brother. *See also* Hippicus *and* Mariamne. A5—10

**Phasaelis.** Town in the Jordan Valley, laid out by Herod the Great in honor of his brother Phasael. The town was artificially irrigated. Mod. *Fasa-'il*. C4—11

**Phaselis.** Seaport of Lycia on the boundary of Pamphylia, S Asia Minor (I Macc. 15:23). It was a center of pirate activity in ancient times. Mod. *Tekirova*, Turkey.

**Phasga, Mt.** *See* Pisgah, Mt.

**Phasis.** City on the E shore of the Black Sea in ancient Colchis. It was founded by the Greeks at the mouth of the Phasis R. (mod. *Rioni*). Mod. *Poti*, in W Georgian S.S.R. C1—7

**Phatures.** *See* Pathros

**Phenice.** *See* Phoenix

**Phetrusium.** *See* Pathrusim

**Philadelphia** (in Asia Minor). City of Lydia, W Asia Minor, *ca*. 28 miles SE of Sardis. It was the seat of 1 of the 7 churches of Revelation (Rev. 1:11). Mod. *Alasheher*, Turkey. D2—17

**Philadelphia** (in Transjordan). D4—11; B6—13. *See* Amman

**Philippi.** City in NE Macedonia named after Philip II, who annexed it and exploited the gold and silver mines nearby. Paul visited it and made several converts there, including his jailor (Acts 16:12–40). Philippi is *ca*. 10 miles NW of its seaport, Neapolis. A1—15, 16; C1—17; D2—18

**Philistia.** Land of the Philistines. It was that part of the maritime plain of Canaan that lies between Joppa and Gaza. This area is *ca*. 50 miles long and 15 miles wide. A5-B4—4; A-B5—5

**Philistia, Plain of.** Fertile plain of SW Canaan that produced grain, figs, olives, and other fruit. *See* Philistia. A-B5—1

**Philistim.** *See* Philistines

**Philistines.** An ancient non-Semitic people who lived along the S coast of Palestine (*see* Philistia). They appear to have come from Crete and poss. from the coasts of Asia Minor. They possessed a high culture and used iron before it was known in Israel (I Sam. 13:19–21).

**Philoteria.** *See* Beth-yerah

**Phinon.** *See* Punon

**Phithom.** *See* Pithom

**Phoenicia.** Ancient country on the Mediterranean coast N of Palestine. It occupied the area between the Lebanon Mts. and the sea. Mod. *Lebanon*. B2-C1—1, 5, 11; B2-3—4; B4-5—13

**Phoenicians.** Semitic inhabitants of Phoenicia (*q.v.*) who developed important maritime cities (e.g., Tyre, Sidon) and engaged in extensive colonization of the Mediterranean islands and coastlands. Because Sidon was the earliest of the Phoenician city-states, the term *Sidonian* (or *Zidonian*) is frequently synonymous with *Phoenician*.

**Phoenix.** Harbor in Crete (Acts 27:12). Because it opened toward the NE and NW, it was safe throughout the year. Mod. *Loutro*. C3—17

**Phrygia.** Ancient country of central Asia Minor inhabited by a warlike people who entered the region from Europe (*ca*. 1200 B.C.). C2—15, 16; E3—18

**Phrygian Kingdom.** Prior to the 7th century B.C. Phrygia ruled much of W Asia Minor. Subsequently the Lydians became the dominant power in that region.

**Phunon.** *See* Punon

**Phut** (Put). A people related to the Egyptians (Gen. 10:6). Phut is closely associated with the Lubim (Nah. 3:9).

**Pibeseth** (Bubastis). Ancient city of NE Egypt. Mod. *Tell Basta*. A4—3

**Pirathon** (Pharathon). Town N of the Kanah R., *ca*. 7.5 miles SW of Shechem. Pirathonites are mentioned in the O.T. (Judg. 12:13–15; II Sam. 23:30), and the city was fortified in Maccabean times (I Macc. 9:50).

**Pisa.** City of ancient Etruria, NW Italy. It was founded around the 6th century B.C. and subsequently fell to Rome. Political freedom was preserved, however.

**Pisgah, Mt.** Part of the Abarim Mts. E of the NE corner of the Dead Sea. Prob. mod. *Ras es-Siagha*, slightly NW of *J. en-Neba* (*see* Mt. Nebo).

**Pisidia.** District in Asia Minor bounded on the N by Phrygia, on the S by Lycia and Pamphylia, on the E by Lycaonia, and on the W by Caria. It formed part of the Roman province of Galatia. Its chief town was Antioch of Pisidia (Acts 13:14). C5—14; C2—15, 16

**Pithom.** One of two store cities built by Israelites while in Egyptian bondage (Exod. 1:11). Poss. mod. *Tell el-Maskhuta*, in the E Nile Delta. A4—3

**Pityus.** Town founded by Ionian Greek colonists on the NE shore of the Black Sea.

**Plain, Sea of the.** *See* Dead Sea

**Plain of Esdraelon.** *See* Esdraelon, Plain of

**Plain of Philistia.** *See* Philistia, Plain of

**Plain of Sharon.** *See* Sharon, Plain of

**Plains of Moab.** *See* Moab, Plains of

**Poles.** Early in the 9th century A.D. a Slavic people known as Polians, or Poles, gained hegemony over other Slavic tribes in the area that became known as Poland.

**Pomeranians.** Slovic peoples who settled in the N European plains S of the Baltic Sea. The land was sandy and marshy, but it had large forests and numerous lakes.

**Pompeiopolis** (Soli). Town on the Mediterranean coast of Cilicia, SE Asia Minor. It was founded *ca*. 700 B.C. by colonists from Rhodes and later colonized by Athenians, who named it Soli. It was destroyed by the Armenian king Tigranes (91 B.C.) but rebuilt by Pompey, for whom it was renamed Pompeiopolis.

**Pontus.** Ancient district of Asia Minor along the Black Sea. It was a strong monarchy (*ca*. 400 B.C.) until its king, Mithridates, was defeated by Pompey (63 B.C.). Thereafter it was joined to the Roman province of Galatia-Cappadocia. E2—12, 18; C-D1—16; D-F1—17

**Pontus Euxinus.** *See* Black Sea

**Pool of Amygdalon.** *See* Amygdalon, Pool of

**Pool of Bethzatha.** *See* Bethzatha, Pool of

**Pool of Siloam.** *See* Siloam, Pool of

**Pozzuoli.** *See* Puteoli

**Preslav.** City W of the Black Sea and S of the Danube. It was the ancient capital of Bulgaria.

**Prophthasia.** City built by Alexander the Great in Drangiana, S of Alexandria Arion.

**Propontis.** Ancient name for the Sea of Marmara, which connects on the E with the Black Sea through the Bosporus, and on the W with the Aegean Sea through the Dardanelles. Constantinople (Byzantium, mod. *Istanbul*) is situated on the entrance of the Bosporus into the Sea of Marmara.

**Prussians.** A Baltic people, conquered and largely exterminated by Teutonic knights during the 13th century. Medieval Prussia was the section of NE Germany subsequently known as E Prussia.

**Pteria.** Town in Cappadocia, Asia Minor, on the Persian royal road that connected Susa with Sardis. It had earlier been known as Hattusas (*q.v.*) and served as a great Hittite center. B2—7

**Ptolemais** (in Egypt). Hellenistic city of Upper Egypt, located on the Nile, S of Abydos. It was founded by Ptolemy Soter on the site of a small village, and it replaced Thebes as the capital. Mod. *Menchah*.

**Ptolemais** (in Palestine). B2—11, 19; A5—13; D3—16. *See* Acco

**Punon.** Town in Edom at which the Israelites stopped during their journey to Canaan (Num. 33:42). Copper was mined there in ancient times. Poss. mod. *Feinan*, 25 miles S of the Dead Sea. D4—3; B5—4

**Pura.** Ancient town in Gedrosia (*q.v.*) through which Alexander passed on his return journey from India. E3—7

**Put.** *See* Phut

**Puteoli** (Pozzuoli). Important port on the Bay of Naples, Italy, founded in the 6th century B.C. as Dicearchia. It was the usual port of debarkation for travelers from Egypt and the East. Paul's vessel landed there, and he enjoyed the hospitality of Christians from the town (Acts 28:13). A1—17; C2—18

**Pyramids, Great.** Pyramids near Giza, including those built for Khufu (Cheops), Khafre (Chephren), and Menkure. They were built to serve as massive tombs for these pharaohs of the 3rd century B.C. A4—3

**Pyramus R.** River of SE Asia Minor. From its source in the Anti-Taurus range, it flows generally SW and enters the Mediterranean at Antioch-on-the-Pyramus, W of the Gulf of Issus. Mod. *Ceyhan*.

**Pyrenees Mts.** Mt. chain of SW Europe between France and Spain, separating the Iberian Peninsula from the European mainland. It extends *ca*. 280 miles from the Bay of Biscay on the W to the Mediterranean on the E.

## Q

**Qarnini.** Assyrian name for the provinces of N Palestine E of the Jordan. It is the same as the district of Karnaim.

**Qarqar.** *See* Karkar

**Qasile.** City near where the Kanah R. empties into the Mediterranean. It might have been the port through which Phoenician building materials reached Jerusalem (II Chron. 2:16; Ezra 3:7). Mod. *Tel Qasila*. B3—19

**Qatna.** Ancient city a short distance S of Hamath on the Orontes, E of Arvad. During the 2nd millennium B.C. it came under Hittite, Hurrian, and Amorite influences, successively. Mod. *Tell el-Mishrifeh*. D3—2

**Qumran.** Site on the NW shore of the Dead Sea where an ancient sectarian group (thought to have been Essenes) maintained an ascetic settlement. The Dead Sea Scrolls were found in caves in the vicinity, and ruins of a community center have provided information concerning life in a pre-Christian Jewish community. C5—11; C4—19

## R

**Raamah.** A region and people of SE Arabia. It is mentioned with Sheba as trading with Tyre (Ezek. 27:22). Raamah was a Cushite tribe (Gen. 10:7).

**Raamses.** *See* Ramses

**Rabba.** *See* Amman

**Rabbah.** D4—1, 5; D3—3; C4—4. *See* Amman

**Rabbah.** *See* Areopolis

**Rabbath-ammon.** *See* Amman

**Rabbath-Moab.** *See* Areopolis

**Raetia.** Country conquered by Rome *ca*. 15 B.C. and made a Roman province. Its S boundary was the Alps, and it went as far N as the Danube. C2—12

**Raetii.** Germanic peoples who inhabited the region S of the Danube R. in an area corresponding to the greater part of the Tirol.

**Rafiah.** *See* Raphia

**Ragaba.** Town in Gilead, N of the Jabbok. Alexander Jannaeus died there.

**Rages.** *See* Rhagae

**Rama.** *See* Ramah

**Ramah** (in Benjamin). Town located on a hill 5 miles N of Jerusalem. It was fortified by Baasha of Israel to keep the Southern Kingdom from invading (I Kings 15:17, 21, 22). It was on the route of the Assyrian army (Isa. 10:29) and was repopulated after the exile (Neh. 7:30; 11:33). Mod. *er-Ram*. B4—5

**Ramah** (in Naphtali). Walled city located *ca*. 17 miles E of Acco (Josh 19:36). Poss. mod. *er-Rameh*.

**Ramallah.** Town *ca*. 3 miles SW of Bethel in Jordan. It is on the ridge running N and S from Jerusalem.

**Ramat Gan.** Town E of Tel Aviv. Founded in 1921, it soon developed into a major industrial center. Numerous public gardens and a national park give evidence of its cultural interests.

**Ramatha.** *See* Arimathea

**Ramathaim.** *See* Arimathea

**Ramat Rahel.** Iron Age fortress honoring Rachel, wife of Jacob. This was a suburb of O.T. Jerusalem. C4—19

**Rameses.** *See* Ramses

**Ramle.** Town in Israel, SW of Lydda. It was founded by the Arabs (A.D. 717) and soon became their capital in Palestine. Subsequently it was occupied by Seljuk Turks, Crusaders, Mamelukes, and the Turkish Empire. It is now an important Israeli city on the road to Jerusalem.

**Ramoth-galaad.** *See* Ramoth-gilead

**Ramoth-gilead.** Town in Gilead, E of the Jordan, in the territory of Gad, near the border with the tribe of Manasseh. It was a Levitical city (Josh. 21:38) and a city of refuge (Deut. 4:43). C4—4; D3—5

**Ramses** (Tanis, Zoan). City in the E Nile Delta, in the district of Goshen. The Israelites built it ("Raamses," Exod. 1:11) as a store city for the pharaoh. At the Exodus, the Israelites marched from there ("Rameses," Exod. 12:37). Prob. mod. *Qantir*. A3—3

**Raphana.** D2—11. *See* Raphon

**Raphia** (Rafiah). Town in SW Palestine, S of Gaza. It was the site of Ptolemy Philopator's decisive victory over Antiochus the Great of Syria. A5—1, 4, 5; C3—3

**Raphon.** City of S Syria, NE of Karnaim. Pliny mentioned it as one of the cities of the Decapolis. Some mod. scholars identify it with Ashtaroth (*q.v.*).

**Ravenna.** City of Cisalpine Gaul, N of the Rubicon. It was founded by colonists from Thessaly and served as 1 of 2 chief stations of the fleet of Augustus.

**Rebla.** *See* Riblah

**Reblatha.** *See* Riblah

**Red Sea** (Arabian Gulf). Narrow sea, *ca*. 1,500 miles long between Africa and Arabia, lying in the Great Rift Valley. The Red Sea has 2 N arms between which the Sinai Peninsula is located. The left arm is the Gulf of Suez; the right arm, the Gulf of Aqaba. D6—2; C6—3; C4—6; B3—7; E4—12; F4—18

**Regensburg.** Ancient city on the Danube, in E Bavaria. As Castra Regina it was an important Roman frontier station. It is also known as Ratisbon.

**Regma.** *See* Raamah

**Rehoboth.** A well dug by Isaac in the Valley of Gerar (Gen. 26:22). Prob. mod. *er-Ruheibeh*, 18 miles SW of Beer-sheba.

**Reims** (Rheims, Durocotorum). City of NE France, ancient Durocotorum, the city of the Remi (*q.v.*). It was one of the most important cities of Roman Gaul. It became the see of an archbishopric in the 8th century.

**Remi.** People of ancient Gaul who lived in the territory traversed by the Axona R. They joined forces with Caesar (57 B.C.) when the other Belgae made war against him.

**Remmon.** *See* Rimmon

**Rephidim.** Last place the Israelites stopped during the Exodus before Mt. Sinai (Exod. 17:1, 5, 6). There they battled the Bedouin Amalekites (Exod. 17:8–16). Poss. mod. *W. Refayid*. C5—3

**Reuben,** allotment of. Territory assigned to the tribe of Reuben. The E boundary was Ammon; the S boundary, the Arnon R.; the W boundary, the Jordan and the Dead Sea; and the N boundary, a line from the Jordan S of Beth-nimrah to Heshbon.

**Rha** (Volga) **R.** Largest river of Europe, which runs a course of 2,290 miles through central and E Europe, creating a delta at its mouth at the Caspian Sea. F1—12

**Rhagae** (Rages). Principal city of Media, SW of mod. *Tehran*. It was destroyed by an earthquake and restored by Seleucus Nicator, who renamed it Europus. It was the scene of some of the principal events in the apocryphal book of Tobit. D2—7

**Rhegium.** Ancient Greek town on the Strait of Messina, S Italy. It was one of few Greek towns to preserve its language and customs under Roman rule. Paul's vessel touched it after having made a circuit from Syracuse (Acts 28:13). Mod. *Reggio di Calabria*. A2—17

**Rheims.** *See* Reims

**Rhine R.** River of mod. Germany that in ancient times formed the boundary between Gaul and Germany. It extends *ca*. 850 miles in a generally NW direction, emptying into the North Sea. B1—12; C1—18

**Rhodes.** Most easterly of the Aegean islands, off the

S coast of Caria, Asia Minor. It lost its independence to Alexander the Great but regained it after his death. Under the Romans it enjoyed a semiindependent status. The vessel in which Paul sailed from Assos to Palestine touched upon Rhodes (Acts 21:1). B3—2; B2—7, 15, 16; D3—17

**Riblah.** Town on the Orontes R., in the state of Hamath, 36 miles NW of Baalbek. It was the military headquarters of Necho (II Kings 23:33) and Nebuchadnezzar, who caused Hezekiah to be blinded there (II Kings 25:6–21). C2—6

**Riga.** City on the Gulf of Riga at the mouth of the W Dvina R., in mod. *Latvia*, U.S.S.R. It was founded A.D. 1201 and became a center for Christianity in the Baltic region.

**Rimmon.** Town in the territory of Zebulun (Josh. 19:13), 6 miles NE of Nazareth. It was assigned to the Levites (Josh. 21:35, "Dimnah"). Mod. *Rummaneh*.

**Riphath.** A people descended from Gomer (Gen. 10:3), thought to have lived on the S shore of the Black Sea. The name is similar to that of the Riphean Mts., supposed by the ancients to skirt the N shores of the world.

**River of Egypt.** *See* Egypt, River of

**Rohoboth.** *See* Rehoboth

**Rome.** City on the left bank of the Tiber, 16 miles from the Tyrrhenian Sea, in W-central Italy. The traditional date of its founding is 753 B.C. After an early period of incessant warfare, Rome became a republic and, later, the capital of a world empire. C2—12, 18; A1—17

**Rouen.** Ancient capital of Normandy, located near the mouth of the Seine, in N France. It has been an archiepiscopal see since the 5th century A.D.

**Roxolani.** Warlike people of European Sarmatia, settled on the banks of the Palus Maeotis (*q.v.*). They are thought to have been the ancestors of the Russians.

**Royal Portico.** Three-aisled colonnade at the S wall of the temple in Jerusalem. Its name was perhaps in remembrance of Solomon's royal quarters, which once occupied this area. B-C5—10

**Ruben,** allotment of. *See* Reuben, allotment of

**Rubicon.** Stream that formed the boundary between Italy and Cisalpine Gaul. When he crossed it (49 B.C.), Julius Caesar began the civil war. C2—12

**Rugians.** A Germanic people who lived along the Baltic coast between the Viadua and Vistula rivers.

**Rumah.** Town in Galilee that was the home of Pedaiah, grandfather of King Jehoiakim (II Kings 23:36). Poss. mod. *Kh. er-Rumeh*. C2—5

**Russians.** A Slavic people who settled in the area now known as Russia, beginning *ca.* the 9th century A.D.

## S

**Saba.** *See* Sheba

**Sabastiya.** *See* Samaria

**Sabratha.** City of Africa Nova (Numidia) *ca.* 110 miles W of Leptis Magna.

**Safad.** Town in NE Israel, *ca.* 12 miles NW of the Sea of Galilee, at an elevation of 2,700 feet. During the 16th century it became a center for Jewish cabalistic studies.

**Sagartians.** Ancient inhabitants of Drangiana, one of the E districts of Media and Persia.

**Sahara.** Desert area of N Africa that extends from the Atlantic Ocean to the Nile, and from the Mediterranean to the Sudan, an area of 3,000,000 square miles.

**Saida.** *See* Sidon

**Saint Albans.** *See* Verulamium

**Sais.** Ancient Egyptian city in the W-central Nile Delta. It was the royal residence of pharaohs of the Twenty-sixth Dynasty and a shrine center for Neith and Osiris. B3—6, 7

**Saka.** F1—7. *See* Scythians

**Salamina.** *See* Salamis

**Salamis.** Ancient seaport on the E coast of Cyprus, visited by Paul on his First Missionary Journey (Acts 13:5). It was N of mod. *Famagusta*. A2—13; D5—14; E3—18

**Saleah.** *See* Salecah

**Salecah.** City of Bashan, on the boundary of the kingdom of Og and, later, the N boundary of the territory of Gad (I Chron. 5:11). It is 66 miles E of the Jordan, opposite Beth-shan. Mod. *Salkhad*. C4—4

**Salecha.** *See* Salecah

**Salem.** *See* Jerusalem

**Salim.** Town near which John the Baptist ministered (John 3:23). Eusebius located it 8 miles S of Scythopolis at mod. *Tell Radgah*. Others suggest the site of mod. *Salim*, 3.5 miles E of Nablus, near the springs of *W. Far'ah*. C4—11

**Salkhad.** *See* Salecah

**Salmone, Cape.** Cape that constitutes the NE extremity of Crete (Acts 27:7). Mod. *Cape Sidero*. D3—17

**Salona.** Capital of ancient Dalmatia. It was strongly fortified by the Romans and became a Roman colony. C2—18

**Salonae.** C2—12. *See* Salona

**Salonika.** *See* Thessalonica

**Salt, Valley of.** S continuation of the Jordan–Dead Sea Valley, now known as the *W. 'Araba*. It was the scene of victories of David (II Sam. 8:13–14) and Amaziah (II Kings 14:7) over the Edomites.

**Salt Sea.** C5—1, 5; D3—3; B5—4. *See* Dead Sea

**Samaga.** Town in Transjordan, *ca.* 4 miles W of Heshbon. After taking Medeba following a 6-month siege of the city, John Hyrcanus took Samaga for the Jews.

**Samal.** Aramean city-state in N Syria. It was also known as Ya'udi, mod. *Senjirli*, Turkey. Samal and other Aramean states flourished between 1000 and 700 B.C., after which they were absorbed into the Assyrian Empire.

**Samaria** (Sebaste), city of. Capital city of Israel (the Northern Kingdom), built by Omri (I Kings 16:24) on a hill 5.5 miles NW of Shechem in a fertile valley. It was rebuilt by Herod the Great and renamed Sebaste. Mod. *Sebastiyeh*. B3—1, 5, 19; B4—11

**Samaria,** district of. Area around Samaria (Sebaste) in the hill-country between Galilee (to the N) and Judea (to the S). Samaria was the geographical center of N.T. Palestine. B-C3—1; B-C4—11; B5—13

**Samarkand** (Maracanda). Oldest city of central Asia and chief city of Sogdiana (*q.v.*). Samarkand was on the ancient trade route between the Near East and China. It was conquered by Alexander and became a meeting place of W and Chinese culture.

**Samos.** Island of the Aegean Sea, off Ionia. Polycrates, tyrant of Samos, was put to death by the Persians during the reign of Cyrus. Subsequently, however, Samos regained its independence and remained Greek in culture. B2—16; D2—17

**Samothrace.** Small island opposite the mouth of the Hebrus R. in Thrace, inhabited by Pelasgians. It fought on the side of the Persians at Salamis (480 B.C.). Paul stopped there en route to Philippi during his Second Missionary Journey (Acts 16:11). B1—15

**Sangarius R.** River that flows from the highlands of NW Asia Minor in a generally E, then N direction, emptying into the Black Sea. Mod. *Sakarya*. C1—2

**Sanhedrin.** *See* Council House

**Saphir** (Shaphir). Town of Judah (Micah 1:11), tentatively located at mod. *es-Suwafir*, 3.5 miles SE of Ashdod.

**Saphon.** *See* Zaphon

**Saraa.** *See* Zorah

**Sarafand.** *See* Sarepta

**Saragossa.** *See* Caesarea Augusta

**Sarangians.** Ancient inhabitants of E Drangiana (*q.v.*).

**Sarath-sahar.** *See* Zareth-shahar

**Sardica.** City of Moesia (*q.v.*) on a plain watered by the Oescus R. A church council met there (A.D. 343). Mod. *Sofia*.

**Sardinia.** Large Mediterranean island S of Corsica and W of Italy. It was early known to the Greeks and colonized by Carthaginians. About 228 B.C. it, with Corsica, became a Roman province. B2—12, 18

**Sardis.** City of W Asia Minor at the foot of Mt. Tmolus on the E bank of the Hermes R., *ca.* 50 miles E of Smyrna. It was the capital of Croesus, the rich Lydian king, and was conquered (546 B.C.) by Cyrus of Persia. Later it fell successively to Alexander, Antiochus, and the Romans, who incorporated it into their province of Asia. It was 1 of 7 cities to which letters were addressed in the Revelation (Rev. 1:11). Mod. *Sart*, Turkey. B2—6, 15, 16; A2—7; D2—17; E3—18

**Sarea.** *See* Zorah

**Sarepta** (Zarephath). Town on the Mediterranean coast of Phoenicia 8 miles S of Sidon, 14 miles N of Tyre. Elijah spent time there (I Kings 17:8–24). C1—11

**Sarid.** Village on the S frontier of the territory of Zebulun (Josh. 19:10, 12), in the N part of the Plain of Esdraelon, 5 miles SW of Nazareth. Mod. *Tell Shadud*.

**Sarmatia.** Name given by the Romans to the country in Europe and Asia between the Vistula R. and the Caspian Sea. Its people were called Sarmatians, or Sauromatae. D-E1—12

**Sarohen.** *See* Sharuhen

**Saron, Plain of.** *See* Sharon, Plain of

**Sarus R.** River that rises in the Anti-Taurus Mts. of E Turkey and flows 320 miles in a generally SW direction. It passes Adana before entering the Mediterranean. Mod. *Seyhan*, or *Sihun*.

**Saxons.** A Germanic people who, according to Ptolemy, inhabited the S portion of the Cimbrian Peninsula, the area now known as Schleswig, in the 2nd century. In A.D. 286 they appeared as pirates in the North Sea and the English Channel. They were associated with Angles and Jutes in the conquest of Britain. The Saxons who remained on the Continent, known as the Old Saxons, occupied NW Germany.

**Scodra.** Town on the Barbana R. in Illyricum. It was the strongly fortified capital of Gentius, the king of Illyricum who in 168 B.C. withstood Rome.

**Scorpion Pass.** *See* Akrabbim, Ascent of

**Scythians** (Saka). A people who inhabited the region N and NE of the Black Sea in the 7th century B.C., and who later invaded Assyria and Palestine. They spoke an Indo-European language, lived a nomadic life, and were skilled horsemen. They invaded the Balkan Peninsula and were attacked there both by Darius I and Alexander the Great, with no decisive results. In the 3rd century B.C. they were replaced by the Sarmatians, to whom they appear to have been related. D1—6; F1—7

**Scythopolis.** C3—11; B5—13; C2—19. *See* Beth-shan

**Sea of Adria.** *See* Adria, Sea of

**Sea of Azov.** *See* Azov, Sea of

**Sea of Galilee.** *See* Galilee, Sea of

**Sebaste.** B4—11; B5—13; B3—19. *See* Samaria, city of

**Sebastia.** Important trading center in W Asia Minor. It was at the junction of important commercial roads during Roman times and was situated near copper mines. Mod. *Sivas*, Turkey.

**Second Quarter** (in Jerusalem). Quarter bounded by the First North Wall (*q.v.*) on the S, the temple on the E, and the Second North Wall on the N and W. B4-5—10

**Sedada.** *See* Zedad

**Segor.** *See* Zoar

**Sehon, Kingdom of.** *See* Sihon, Kingdom of

**Seir.** *See* Edom

**Seir, Mt.** *See* Edom

**Sela** (Petra). Ancient Nabatean city in the W. Musa (*q.v.*), noted for its buildings carved in the rocks. Ancient caravan routes passed through it, bringing it considerable wealth. D4—3; B6—4

**Selcha.** *See* Salecah

**Seleucia** (in Gaulanitis). Village NW of the Sea of

Galilee. It is reputed to have been built by Herod the Tetrarch.

**Seleucia** (Opis; in Mesopotamia). City on the Tigris, opposite Ctesiphon, N of Babylon. Built by Seleucus I of Syria (312–302 B.C.), it was captured by the Romans under Severus (A.D. 198) and fell into decay.

**Seleucia** (in Syria). *See* Seleucia Pieria

**Seleucia Pieria.** City located 5 miles from the mouth of the Orontes R. It was built on the site of an earlier town by Seleucus I and served as the seaport of Syrian Antioch (*q.v.*), which was 16 miles farther upstream. B2—13; D5—14

**Seleucia Tracheotis.** Town on the banks of the Kalykadnos R. in SE Asia Minor. It was founded by Seleucus I early in the 3rd century B.C. A1—13

**Seleucid Empire.** One of the empires that arose when, following the death of Alexander the Great, his kingdom was divided among his generals. Seleucus I was able to gain control of a large part of Asia Minor, all of Syria, and the E extremities of Alexander's conquest—as far as the Oxus and the Indus rivers.

**Selinus.** City in SW Cilicia, Asia Minor. Here Trajan died (A.D. 117) following his campaigns in the E. Near mod. *Alanya*, Turkey.

**Semechonitis, Lake.** C2—1. *See* Hula, Lake

**Semeron.** *See* Shimron

**Semnones.** A Germanic people that settled along the Albis (Elbe) in N-central Germany during the 1st century B.C.

**Semron.** *See* Shimron

**Sepphoris.** Town in Galilee, 4 miles by road NW of Nazareth. It is the traditional birthplace of Mary. It was the capital of Galilee during the early part of the reign of Herod Antipas (4 B.C.–A.D. 39). Although a Roman city (like Tiberias) during the time of Jesus, it became a Jewish center of Talmudic study following the destruction of Jerusalem. Mod. *Saffuriyeh*. C3—11; C2—19

**Sequani.** A Celtic people who, in the days of Caesar, occupied E Gaul (mod. *Franche-Comte* and most of *Alsace*).

**Serbal, J.** Mt. in the Sinai Peninsula, NW of J. Musa, the traditional Mt. Sinai. Certain ancient writers, including Eusebius and Jerome, identified J. Serbal with Sinai, regarding it as more in accord with the biblical description than J. Musa.

**Serpent's Pool.** Pool, or reservoir, W of the Upper City of Jerusalem in N.T. times. A6—10

**Sevan, Lake.** Lake in Armenia, S of the Cyrus R. and about midway between the Black and Caspian seas. It covers an area of *ca*. 546 square miles and is fed by about 30 streams. Its only outlet is the Zanga R., a tributary to the Araxes (*q.v.*).

**Seville.** *See* Hispalis

**Shaphir.** *See* Saphir

**Sharon, Plain of.** Palestinian coastal plain between Joppa and Mt. Carmel, extending E to the hills of Samaria. It was *ca*. 50 miles long and 10 miles wide, and it was noted for its fertility. B3—1, 5; B4—11

**Sharuhen.** Town in S Palestine, in the territory of Simeon (Josh. 19:6). It was on the main N-S route between Palestine and Egypt. Prob. mod. *Tell el-Far'ah* on the Besor S of Gaza and W of Beer-sheba. A5—5

**Shaveh-kiriathaim.** *See* Kiriathaim

**Sheba** (descendant of Ham). Cushite Sheba (Gen. 10:7) may be located on the W side of the Persian Gulf.

**Sheba** (descendant of Shem). Semitic Sheba (Gen. 10:28) may have been one of the early settlers in SW Arabia. This was the home of a Semitic merchant people known as Sabeans, who operated camel caravans throughout the Middle East. The Queen of Sheba was one of their rulers (I Kings 10:1–13).

**Shechem.** Walled town in the hill-country of Ephraim (Josh. 20:7), near which Abraham camped (Gen. 12:6). It continued to be important in subsequent biblical history. Shechem lies in the upland valley bounded on the N by Mt. Ebal and on the S by Mt. Gerizim. It was a city of refuge (Josh. 20:7) and a Levitical city (Josh. 21:21). Mod. *Tell Balata*, SE of the later Roman city Nablus. C4—1, 5; D4—2; D2—3; B4—4; C3—19

**Sheep Gate.** Gate from the N suburb of Bethesda into the temple area of Jerusalem in N.T. times. It may be traced back to the 5th century B.C. when a Sheep Gate, at approximately the same location, was a means of access into the Mishneh quarter of Jerusalem.

**Shephelah.** Name given to the S part of the district between the hill-country of Palestine and the coastal plain. It was a region of low hills and included such strategic cities as Lachish, Debir, Libnah, and Beth-shemesh. B5—1

**Shihor-libnath R.** River that formed the S boundary of the territory of Asher (Josh. 19:26). Prob. mod. *Nahr ez-Zerqa*, 6 miles S of Dor and just N of Caesarea. It is not to be confused with the Jabbok, E of the Jordan, which has a similar Arabic name in contemporary use.

**Shiloh.** Town in Ephraim on the E side of the highway connecting Bethel with Shechem (Judg. 21:19). There the Israelites, under Joshua, set up the tabernacle. It served as the spiritual center of Israel before Jerusalem was occupied. It was evidently destroyed by the Philistines (Jer. 26:6) but subsequently rebuilt. Mod. *Kh. Seilun*. C4—1, 5; D3—3; C3—19

**Shimron.** Town in the territory of Zebulun (Josh. 19:15), which earlier had joined Jabin of Hazor in seeking to defeat Joshua (Josh. 11:1–5). Poss. mod. *Kh. Sammuniyeh,* 5 miles W of Nazareth.

**Shinar.** Alluvial plain of Babylonia, including the cities of Babel, Erech, and Akkad (Gen. 10:10; 11:2; Dan. 1:2). Amraphel was king of at least a large part of the region (Gen. 14:1, 9).

**Shittim.** C4—5. *See* Abel-shittim

**Shocho(h).** *See* Shoco

**Shoco** (Socoh). City in the low-country of Judah (Josh. 15:35). It was the site of a major battle with the Philistines (I Sam. 17:1) and was later fortified by Rehoboam (II Chron. 11:7). Mod. *Kh. Abbad*.

**Shunat Nimrin.** *See* Beth-nimrah

**Shunem.** Town in the territory of Issachar, 5 miles N of Mt. Gilboa, 3.5 miles NE of Jezreel. Elisha restored to life the son of a Shunammite woman (II Kings 4:8, 12). C3—5

**Shur, Wilderness of.** Region E of the Nile Delta and S of Palestine. After crossing the Red Sea the Israelites journeyed through this wilderness for 3 days (Exod. 15:22) before turning S into the Sinai Peninsula. B-C4—3

**Shuruppak.** Ancient Sumerian city, N of Erech in S Mesopotamia. It is mentioned as an old city at the time of the flood described in the Gilgamesh Epic.

**Shushan.** *See* Susa

**Sicelag.** *See* Ziklag

**Sichem.** *See* Shechem

**Sicilia** (Sicily). Largest island of the Mediterranean, occupying 9,928 square miles, separated from the mainland of Italy by the Straits of Messina. It was early colonized by Phoenicians, Carthaginians, and Greeks. Following the 1st Punic war it became a Roman colony (241 B.C.). C3—12

**Sicily.** A2—17; C3—18. *See* Sicilia

**Siddim, Valley of.** Valley where the kings from the area S of the Dead Sea fought against a coalition of kings from Mesopotamia (Gen. 14:3, 8). It is thought to have been the shallow part of the Dead Sea S of the Lisan Peninsula.

**Sidon.** Ancient Phoenician, or Canaanite, seaport (Gen. 10:15) on the Mediterranean coast, 22 miles N of Tyre. Sidon is mentioned in Scripture as the "firstborn" of Canaan (Gen. 10:15). Mod. *Saida*. C1—1, 11; D3—2, 15, 16; D1—3; B3—4; B1—5; B4—13; F3—17; E3—18

**Sidonians.** *See* Phoenicians

**Sihon, Kingdom of.** Sihon, the Amorite king, ruled the territory from the Arnon N to the Jabbok, and from the Jordan to the borders of Ammon. This territory was subsequently assigned to the tribes of Reuben and Gad, who desired it because of its excellent pastureland (Num. 21:21–34; 32:33).

**Sihor Labanath R.** *See* Shihor-libnath R.

**Silo.** *See* Shiloh

**Siloah, Pool of.** *See* Siloam, Pool of

**Siloam, Pool of.** Conduit on the SE side of Jerusalem that brought water from the Spring Gihon to a pool within the city. The pool was really a reservoir—58 feet long, 18 feet wide, and 19 feet deep—built of masonry. An inscription in the tunnel that leads to the pool was discovered in 1880. Written in pure Hebrew, it is known as the Siloam Inscription. C3—9; B6—10

**Siloe, Pool of.** *See* Siloam, Pool of

**Simeon,** allotment of. The tribe of Simeon was assigned land in the extreme S of Canaan in the midst of the inheritance of the children of Judah (Josh. 19:1–9). The 2 tribes made common cause against the Canaanites (Judg. 1:1, 3, 17).

**Sin,** city of. B3—3. *See* Pelusium

**Sin, Wilderness of.** Desert region through which the Israelites passed on their way from Elim to Mt. Sinai (Exod. 16:1; 17:1). Poss. mod. *Debbet er-Ramleh*. C5—3

**Sinai,** district of. C-D5—2. *See* Sinai Peninsula

**Sinai, Mt.** (Mt. Horeb). Mt. at the foot of which Israel encamped while Moses received the law (Exod. 20:1–24:8). Tradition suggests the mt. range in the S part of the peninsula, including J. Musa. Others, however, suggest J. Serbal (*q.v.*). C5—3

**Sinai Peninsula.** Peninsula between the Gulfs of Suez and Aqaba, the W and E arms of the Red Sea. C5—3

**Singidunum.** Town in upper Moesia at the junction of the Danube and Savas rivers. It served as headquarters for the Roman legion stationed in Moesia.

**Sinope.** Ancient city and seaport on the N coast of Asia Minor. It was founded by Milesian colonists during the 8th century B.C. and subsequently destroyed and rebuilt by the Cimmerians. During the 2nd century B.C. the city fell to Pontus. It was later taken by Rome and made a free city. C1—6; B1—7; E2—12; F1—17; E2—18

**Sinus Arabicus.** *See* Red Sea

**Sippar.** Ancient city in N Babylonia on the Euphrates. It is mentioned in the Sumerian King List as 1 of 5 cities existing before the flood. It was devoted to Shamash, the sun god, whose temple was located there. F3—2; D2—6; C2—7

**Siraces.** People of S Sarmatia, settled in the region N of the Caucasus Mts., between the Black and Caspian seas.

**Sirmium.** Ancient city of lower Pannonia. It was founded by the Taurisci and became the capital of Pannonia under the Romans. It also served as headquarters for the Romans in their wars with the Daci.

**Siscia.** Fortified town in upper Pannonia. It was captured by Tiberius, who is thought to have made it a colony. Later it was colonized by Septimus Severus.

**Siut.** Town of Egypt, *ca*. 250 miles S of mod. *Cairo*. Siut was known to the Greeks as Lycopolis ("wolf city") because it was the center of the worship of Anubis, a jackal-headed god. Tombs from the Thirteenth Dynasty are located in the hills W of Siut. Mod. *Asyut*.

**Siwa.** A3—7. *See* Amon, Temple of

**Smyrna.** Ancient city on the W coast of Asia Minor. After occupation by Aeolian Greeks and, later, Ionian Greeks, it was destroyed by Alyattes of Lydia (*ca*. 580 B.C.). Rebuilt by Alexander the Great, it became a flourishing commercial center and then part of the Roman province of Asia. It had 1 of the 7 churches addressed in the Revelation (Rev. 1:11). Mod. *Izmir*, Turkey. B2—15, 16; D2—17; D3—18

**Soan.** *See* Ramses

**Soba.** *See* Aram-zobah

**Socchoth.** *See* Succoth

**Sochoh** (in Sharon). *See* Socoh

**Socoh** (in Judah). *See* Shoco

**Socoh** (in Sharon). Town on the edge of the Plain of Sharon, NW of Samaria. It was in Solomon's 3rd district (I Kings 4:10). Mod. *Tell er-Ras*. B3—5

**Sodom.** One of the cities of the Plain of Jordan (Gen. 13:10). Lot chose it for a permanent settlement (Gen. 13:11–13) despite its evil reputation. Subsequently it was plundered by Chedorlaomer (Gen. 14:11) and destroyed in a cataclysmic judgment (Gen. 19:1–29). The ruins of Sodom are thought to lie beneath the S part of the Dead Sea. A mt. on the SE shore, *J. Usdum*, suggests the name of Sodom.

**Sogdiana.** NE sector of the Iranian Plateau, between the Oxus and Jaxartes rivers. It was invaded by Alexander the Great (*ca*. 327 B.C.). E-F2—7

**Soli.** *See* Pompeiopolis

**Solomon's Porch.** Colonnade at the E wall of the temple in Jerusalem. Jesus taught there (John 10:23) and Peter preached from there (Acts 3:11). C4-5—10

**Sophene.** Name of a district in the Armenian Mts., W of Lake Van, drained by the upper Tigris.

**Sorec.** *See* Sorek

**Sorek, Valley of.** Valley that begins *ca*. 13 miles SW of Jerusalem and extends in a generally NW direction to the Mediterranean, which it enters *ca*. 8.5 miles S of Joppa. Much of Samson's life was centered there. Mod. *W. es-Sarar* between Zorah and Timnah.

**Sorek R.** B4—1. *See* Sorek, Valley of

**Spain** (Hispania). Mod. name of the Iberian Peninsula in SW Europe (comprising Spain and Portugal). Its early inhabitants included Basques and Iberians. The peninsula was colonized by Phoenicians, Carthaginians, and Greeks. Roman victory over Carthage in the 2nd Punic war (218–201 B.C.) brought about the beginning of the Romanization of the peninsula, which continued until the 1st century A.D. A2—18

**Sparta.** Major city-state of S Greece, founded *ca*. 1100 B.C. Noted for its military efficiency, Sparta for a time (405–379 B.C.) exercised control over all Greece. Athens and Sparta were bitter rivals. A2—6, 7, 15, 16; C2—17

**Spring Gihon.** *See* Gihon, Spring

**Strato's Tower.** *See* Caesarea (in Palestine)

**Subartu.** Portion of Mesopotamia N of the Diyala R. inhabited by non-Semitic Subarians. About 1500 B.C. the Hurrians established their kingdom, Mitanni, in the same region. It was known to the Egyptians as Naharin. Arrapakha (*q.v.*) was their principal settlement, and Nuzi, its suburb, has provided significant archaeological materials.

**Succoth** (in Egypt). The first stopping place of the Israelites after leaving Ramses during the Exodus (Exod. 12:37; 13:20). *Succoth* means "booths," and it may have been a temporary encampment between Ramses and Etham. B4—3

**Succoth** (in Gad). Town E of the Jordan, 1.3 miles N of the Jabbok in the territory of Gad. Jacob sojourned there when returning from Mesopotamia (Gen. 33:17–22). It was on the route of Gideon's army (Judg. 8:5–16). Near mod. *Tell Deir 'alla*. B4—4; C4—5; C3—19

**Suez, Gulf of.** W arm of the Red Sea (*q.v.*) separating Egypt from the Sinai Peninsula. The Suez Canal now connects this gulf with the Mediterranean. B5—3

**Sumer.** Ancient name of S Mesopotamia, the area N of the Persian Gulf. Non-Semitic Sumerians built city-states there during the 2nd and 3rd millenniums B.C. They were displaced by Semitic Amorites, who occupied the region after 2000 B.C. F4—2

**Sunem.** *See* Shunem

**Sur.** *See* Tyre

**Sur, Desert of.** *See* Shur, Wilderness of

**Susa** (Shushan). Ancient Persian city and the capital of Susiana. It was located along the Coaspes R. and served as the winter residence of the Persian kings. There Nehemiah served as cupbearer to Artaxerxes Longimanus (Neh. 1:1), and Esther was brought to Ahasuerus (Xerxes?) (Esther 2:5–7). G4—2; D3—6, 7

**Susan.** *See* Susa

**Susiana.** Province of the ancient Persian Empire, corresponding to mod. *Khuzistan*. Susa was the capital. *See also* Elam. D3—7

**Sussita.** *See* Hippos

**Sychar.** Town in Samaria in the vicinity of the land given by Jacob to Joseph (John 4:5; cf. Gen. 48:22). Poss. mod. *'Askar* on the E slope of Mt. Ebal, 1.8 miles NE of Nablus (Shechem) and .5 mile N of Jacob's Well. C4—11

**Syene** (Elephantine). Island near the 1st cataract of the Nile, opposite Aswan. In Persian times a Jewish military colony was settled there. B4—6; B3—7

**Syracuse.** Seaport of E Sicily. It was founded *ca*. 734 B.C. and became the chief Greek city of the island. It was captured and sacked by the Romans (214–212 B.C.). C3—12, 18; A2—17

**Syria** (Aram). The Greek term *Syria* is thought to be an abbreviation of *Assur(ia)*, applied to the territories of the Arameans, hence the English translation of "Syria" for *Aram*. The country of the Arameans extended W from the Lebanons to the area E of the Euphrates, S from the Taurus Mts. to Damascus and beyond. During the period of the Israelite monarchy, Syria consisted of a number of independent states. In N.T. times Syria was a Roman province, with Antioch serving as its capital. D1—5, 11, 19; C2—6; E3—12; C3—13; D5—14; D2—15, 16; F3—17, 18

**Syrian Desert.** N portion of the Arabian Desert, comprising the steppe country between Mesopotamia and Syria-Palestine. D3—4

**Syrians** (Arameans). A people whose ancestry is traced to Shem (Gen. 10:22–23). They are thought to have left Arabia shortly before the time of Abraham and to have settled in Aram. They established a number of states (cf. Aram-Damascus, Aram-zobah, Aram-Maacah, Geshur), some of which played an important part in O.T. history.

**Syrtus Major.** One of two gulfs on the N coast of

Africa, comprising parts of the Mediterranean. Syrtus Major was the E gulf.

**Syrtus Minor.** Gulf on the Mediterranean coast of Africa (cf. Syrtus Major). Syrtus Minor was the W gulf.

## T

**Taanach.** Canaanite city (Josh. 17:11) in the Plain of Esdraelon 5 miles SE of Megiddo. Its king was defeated and slain by Joshua (Josh. 12:21). The battle between Barak and Sisera was fought near there (Judg. 5:19). Mod. *Tell Ta'annak*. D2—3; B4—4; B3—5; B2—19

**Taanath-shiloh.** Town on the border between Ephraim and Manasseh (Josh. 16:6), 7 miles SE of Shechem. Mod. *Kh. Ta'nah*.

**Tabaqat Fahl.** *See* Pella (in Gilead)

**Taberah.** Place in the wilderness where the Israelites murmured and were burned by fire from the Lord (Num. 11:1–3). C5—3

**Tabgha.** Town on the NW bank of the Sea of Galilee, bordered to the E by the Mt. of the Beatitudes. It is the traditional site of Jesus' multiplication of the loaves and fishes. C2—19

**Tabigha.** *See* Tabgha

**Tabor, Mt.** Mt. on the boundary of the territory of Issachar, 12 miles N of Mt. Gilboa, 5.5 miles SE of Nazareth. Forces of Zebulun and Issachar assembled there before battle with Sisera (Judg. 4:6, 12, 14). Mod. *J. et-Tur*. C2—1; C3—5, 11

**Tadmor** (Palmyra). Oasis 140 miles NE of Damascus and 120 miles S of the Euphrates. It was fortified by Solomon (II Chron. 8:4) to control the caravan routes. Under Queen Zenobia, Palmyra (the Roman name for Tadmor) became an independent state that temporarily defied Rome (A.D. 251–273). E3—2; D2—4; C2—7

**Tagus R.** Important river of Spain, rising in the territory of the Celtiberi (*q.v.*) and flowing W to the Atlantic. Lisbon (ancient Olisipo) stands at its mouth.

**Tahpanhes.** City in the Nile Delta on the Pelusiac branch. The Jews fled there following the murder of Gedaliah (Jer. 43:7–9). Poss. mod. *Tell Dafna*, 12 miles N of Pithom.

**Tamar.** Town at the E end of the S frontier of Palestine (Ezek. 47:19; 48:28). It was S of the Dead Sea. Poss. mod. *Thamara*, located on the road between Hebron and Elath. B5—4; B6—5

**Tanais R.** *See* Don R.

**Tanis.** A3—3. *See* Ramses

**Taphnes.** *See* Tahpanhes

**Taphnis.** *See* Tahpanhes

**Tappuah.** Town in the lowlands of Judah (Josh. 15:34). Prob. mod. *Beit Nettif*.

**Tarentum.** Ancient Greek city located in a fertile district of S Italy, founded (8th century B.C.) as a Spartan colony. It was taken by Rome (272 B.C.) but fell to Hannibal in the 2nd Punic war (212 B.C.). C2—12; B1—17

**Tarichea.** *See* Magadan

**Tarraco.** Ancient town on a high rock on the E coast of Spain, between the Iberus (Ebro) R. and the Pyrenees. It was founded by colonists from Massilia and served as headquarters for Scipio during the 2nd Punic war (218 B.C.). B2—12

**Tarraconensis.** Roman province in N and E Spain. Its leading city was Tarraco (*q.v.*). A2—12

**Tarragona.** *See* Tarraco

**Tarshish.** Phoenician word meaning "smelting plant" or "refinery." One such Tarshish was Tartessus in S Spain, near Gibraltar. Another was in Cilicia, the later Tarsus (*q.v.*).

**Tarsus.** Chief city of Cilicia, SE Asia Minor, on the Cydnus R. 10 miles from the sea. It was a provincial capital during Roman times and was famed for its schools. Its most illustrious son was "Saul of Tarsus," later known as the apostle Paul (Acts 13:9). B2—6, 7; E3—12, 18; A1—13; D5—14; D2—15, 16; F2—17

**Tatta, Lake.** Salt lake in central Asia Minor that serves as the salt supply for the adjacent country. Mod. *Tuzgulu*.

**Taurus Mts.** Mt. chain paralleling the coast of S Asia Minor. It was crossed N of the Tarsus by means of the Cilician Gates (*q.v.*). An extension of the Taurus, across the Sarus R., is known as the Anti-Taurus. C-D2—2

**Tavium.** Important town in N Galatia, Asia Minor. The church there is known to have been founded before the Diocletian persecution (A.D. 304). Mod. *Bojuk Nefeskoi*, Turkey.

**Taxila.** Town in Gandara, in the Punjab of India. It was the E limit of the Persian Empire (*ca*. 500 B.C.). Alexander the Great passed through it (326 B.C.). F2—7

**Tekoa.** Town in Judah, 6 miles S of Bethlehem. It was fortified by Rehoboam (II Chron. 11:6) and was the home of Amos (Amos 1:1). Mod. *Taqu'a*. B5—5

**Tel Aviv–Jaffa.** *See* Joppa

**Teleilat el-Ghassul.** Site in the Transjordan, N of the Dead Sea and SE of Jericho. It has yielded artifacts from the Ghassulian culture (*ca*. 4500–3000 B.C.). C4—19

**Tell Abu Matar.** Chalcolithic site in the Negeb, near Beer-sheba. A5—19

**Tell Ajjul.** Mound S of mod. *Gaza* that was once a Hyksos stronghold. It has been tentatively identified as Beth-eglaim. A5—19

**Tell 'Arad.** B5—19. *See* Arad

**Tell Asur.** *See* Tell Azur

**Tell Azur.** One of the highest spots of Samaria, *ca*. 3,333 feet above sea level. It is located in the central mt. range *ca*. 20 miles S of Shechem. C4—1

**Tell Beit Mirsim.** B5—19. *See* Debir

**Tell Brak.** Site on Habor R. (*q.v.*) of the ancient town Brak, which was destroyed in 1400 B.C. Deported Israelites were settled in this region by several Assyrian kings (I Chron. 5:26; II Kings 17:6; 18:11). E2—2

**Tell Deir 'alla.** C3—19. *See* Succoth (in Gad)

**Tell el-Amarna.** C5—2; A6—3. *See* Akhetaton

**Tell el-Far'a.** A5—19. *See* Sharuhen

**Tell el-Hesi.** B4—19. *See* Eglon

**Tell el-Judeideh.** B4—19. *See* Moresheth-gath

**Tell en-Nasbeh.** B4—19. *See* Mizpah (in Ephraim)

**Tell es-Safi.** Mound 10 miles SE of Ekron and 10 miles E of Ashdod. It is one of several possible locations for Gath (*q.v.*). B4—19

**Tell es-Saidiyeh.** C3—19. *See* Zarethan

**Tell es-Seba.** Site of ancient Beer-sheba (*q.v.*). B5—19

**Tell Halaf.** E2—2. *See* Gozan

**Tell Jemmeh.** A5—19. *See* Gerar

**Tema.** Important caravan center in NW Arabia. Nabonidus, king of the New Babylonian Empire (555–539 B.C.), chose to live there rather than in Babylon for 10 years of his reign. E5—2; C3—6; B3—7

**Temple** (in Jerusalem). Temple built by Solomon in the 10th century B.C., destroyed by the Babylonians in 587 B.C., rebuilt by Zerubbabel in the 6th century B.C., torn down and rebuilt by Herod the Great late in the 1st century B.C., and destroyed by the Romans in A.D. 70. B2—8; D2—9; B5—10. pinnacle of the, C5—10

**Tepe Gaura.** *See* Tepe Gawra

**Tepe Gawra.** Mound NW of Nineveh that is the site of one of the earliest known village settlements. Excavations revealed a pre-Sumerian type of painted pottery. F2—2

**Tepe Giyạn.** Mound in the Zagros Mts., S of the Choaspes R. It was the center of a highly developed Chalcolithic culture characterized by fine painted pottery. Near mod. *Nihavend*. G3—2

**Tepe Siyalk.** Mound in N Persia, S of the Caspian. Excavations there show a transition from a seminomadic way of life to a settled agricultural community. It produced painted pottery and had trade connections with the Persian Gulf area (*ca*. 3000 B.C.).

**Thaanach.** *See* Taanach

**Thaanath-silo.** *See* Taanath-shiloh

**Thabera.** *See* Taberah

**Thabor, Mt.** *See* Tabor, Mt.

**Thalassa.** *See* Lasea

**Thamna.** *See* Timnath-serah

**Thamnata.** *See* Timnah

**Thamnath-sare.** *See* Timnath-serah

**Thaphsa.** *See* Tiphsah

**Thapphua.** *See* Tappuah

**Thapsacus.** B2—7. *See* Tiphsah

**Thapsus.** Seaport in the Roman province of Africa, *ca*. 100 miles SE of Carthage. Caesar defeated Pompey there (46 B.C.), ending opposition in Africa.

**Tharsis.** *See* Tarshish

**Thasos.** Greek island in the N Aegean off the coast of Macedonia. Gold of Thasos was exploited by the Phoenicians.

**Theater** (in Jerusalem). Built by Herod the Great. It might have been located in the Tyropoeon Valley, though no remains of it have been discovered. B5—10

**Thebes.** C6—2; B3—6, 7; E4—12. *See* No

**Thebez.** Fortified town on the road to Beth-shan, 10 miles NE of Shechem. Abimelech, Gideon's son, was killed while besieging the town (Judg. 9:50).

**Thecua.** *See* Tekoa

**Thecue.** *See* Tekoa

**Thermopylae.** Pass in Greece, 9 miles SE of Lamia between the cliffs of Mt. Oeta and the morass on the shore of the Malic Gulf. It was the only gate for ingress into Greece from the N.

**Thersa.** *See* Tirzah

**Thessalonica** (Salonika). Ancient city of Macedonia first known as Therma. It was captured by the Athenians shortly before the Peloponnesian War (432 B.C.). Paul preached in a synagogue there (Acts 17:1–13). D2—12, 18; A1—15, 16; C1—17

**Thiras.** *See* Tiras

**Thogormạ.** *See* Togarmah

**Thrace.** Region comprising the SE tip of the Balkan Peninsula in SE Europe. It was bounded by the Black Sea to the NE and the Sea of Marmara and Aegean Sea to the S. A1—7; D2—12, 18; B1—16; C1—17

**Thracians.** A group of tribes occupying Thrace. They spoke an Indo-European language; formed separate, petty kingdoms; and did not absorb Greek culture. A-B1—6

**Three Taverns.** Small station on the Appian Way, *ca*. 10 miles from the Forum of Appius and 30 miles from Rome. A1—17

**Thuringians.** Germanic tribe that occupied central Germany between the Elbe and Danube. It was conquered by the Franks in the 6th to 8th centuries A.D.

**Thyatira.** City of Lydia, Asia Minor. It was on the road from Pergamum to Sardis. Its inhabitants were known for skill in dyeing (cf. Acts 16:14). One of the 7 churches of Revelation was located there (Rev. 1:11). Mod. *Ackisar*. B1—15

**Tiberias.** City on the W shore of the Sea of Galilee. It is *ca*. 12 miles S of the entrance of the Jordan into the sea and 6 miles N of the Jordan's exit. It was established by Herod Antipas. C3—11; B5—13; C2—19

**Tiberias, Lake.** *See* Galilee, Sea of

**Tieum.** Greek colony on the S shore of the Black Sea, in ancient Phrygia.

**Tigranocerta.** Town in Armenia, S of Lake Van. The site of an Armenian defeat by the Romans in the 3rd Mithridatic war (74–64 B.C.).

**Tigris R.** River in SW Asia that rises in the Taurus Mts. and flows 1,150 miles SE before joining the Euphrates. The combined stream empties into the Persian Gulf. Biblical *Hiddekel*. F2—2; D2—6; C2—7

**Til Barsip.** Town on the Euphrates SE of Carchemish. It was capital of the state of Adini until captured by Shalmaneser and made an Assyrian provincial capital.

**Timnah.** Town in the Valley of Sorek on the N boundary of Judah, W of Beth-shemesh. It was occupied by the Philistines in the days of Samson (Judg. 14:2).

**Timnath-serah.** Village in the hill-country of Ephraim, given to Joshua as an inheritance (Josh. 19:50; 24:30). Poss. mod. *Tibnah*, 12 miles NE of Lod (Lydda).

**Timsah, Lake.** Lake in E Egypt N of the Gulf of Suez and the Bitter Lakes. The Suez Canal now passes through this part of Egypt.

**Tingis.** Town on the Strait of Gibraltar in Mauretania, NW Africa. A3—12

**Tiphsah** (Thapsacus). Town at the limit of Solomon's dominion toward the Euphrates (I Kings 4:24). Identified with Thapsacus on the right bank of the Euphrates above its junction with the Balikh. D1—4

**Tiras.** Land and its inhabitants, associated with the line of Japheth (Gen. 10:2). Traditionally associated with Thrace or the islands and coastlands of the Aegean.

**Tirzah.** Ancient Canaanite town captured by Joshua (Josh. 12:24). In the days of Jeroboam I it became capital of the Northern Kingdom (I Kings 14:17; 15:21, 33). Prob. *Tell el-Far'ah*, 7 miles NE of Shechem. C3—5, 19

**Tishbe.** Town in Gilead, mentioned as the home of Elijah (I Kings 17:1). Its location is uncertain. C3—5

**Tob.** Region E of the Jordan to which Jephthah fled when rejected by his brethren (Judg. 11:3, 5). B4—4

**Togarmah** (Beth-togarmah). N country (Ezek. 38:6) inhabited by a people descended from Japheth (Gen. 10:3). Poss. *Til-qarimmu* in E Cappadocia.

**Toledo.** City in central Spain on a granite hill surrounded on 3 sides by a gorge of the Tagus R. Known in ancient times as Toletum, it fell to the Romans in 193 B.C. It served later as a capital of the Visigoths and was the scene of several important church councils.

**Toletum.** *See* Toledo

**Tolosa.** *See* Toulouse

**Tomb of Jesus.** A4—10. *See* Holy Sepulchre, Church of the

**Tomi** (Constanta). Town on the W bank of the Black Sea. Constantine I founded Constanta near the site of ancient Tomi. It early became an episcopal see and is now the major Black Sea port of Romania.

**Toulouse.** City on the Garonne R. in S France. It was an important city before the Roman conquest of Gaul and became an episcopal see in the 4th century A.D.

**Tours.** City on the Loire R. in N-central France. An old Gallo-Roman town, it grew rapidly after the death of its bishop St. Martin (A.D. 397). It was a center of Christian culture during the Middle Ages.

**Tower of Meah.** *See* Meah, Tower of

**Tower's Pool.** Pool in NW Jerusalem—near Herod the Great's three towers (Hippicus, Mariamne, and Phasael)—that was fed by an aqueduct from the W. A5—10

**Trachonitis.** District in ancient Palestine beginning *ca*. 20 miles SE of Damascus and extending to Batanea and Auranitis. The region is rough and barren.

**Transalpine Gaul.** *See* Cisalpine Gaul

**Trapezus** (Trebizond). Port on the Black Sea, NE Asia Minor, founded in the 8th century by colonists from Sinope. C1—7; E2—12

**Trebizond.** *See* Trapezus

**Treveri.** A people of ancient Belgica. Allies of the Romans, the Treveri were noted for their cavalry. Their country extended from the Rhine to the Seine.

**Trèves.** *See* Trier

**Trier** (Trèves). Founded by Augustus, Trier was capital of the Roman province of Belgica. It was situated on the Moselle and was known in Roman times as Augusta Treverorum. C1—18

**Tripolis.** Ancient Phoenician city on the Mediterranean coast N of Byblos. In the 7th century B.C. it was the capital of a federation of Tyre, Sidon, and Aradus (Arvad). It flourished under the Seleucids and the Romans. B3—13

**Troas.** Seaport of Mysia in W Asia Minor. Paul saw a vision there of a man of Macedonia inviting him to Europe (Acts 16:8–10). Located S of Homeric Troy. B1—15, 16; D2—17; D3—18

**Trogyllium.** Town on the W coast of Asia Minor opposite the island of Samos.

**Troy.** Ancient city of NW Asia Minor, also called Ilium or Ilion. It has been identified as the mound of Hissarlik, located *ca*. 4 miles from the mouth of the Dardanelles. It was made famous by Homer in the *Iliad*. B1—2

**Tubal.** Tribe descended from Japheth and settled near Meshech.

**Turdetani.** Ancient inhabitants of S Spain.

**Turushpa** (Tushpa). Town at the E end of Lake Van. It served as capital of the kingdom of Van (Urartu) and was frequently attacked by the Assyrian kings.

**Tushpa.** *See* Turushpa

**Tuz, Lake.** Salt lake that occupies a vast depression in the center of the Anatolian plateau, central Asia Minor. C2—2

**Tyana.** Town of ancient Cappadocia, Asia Minor, at the N foot of the Taurus Mts.

**Tyras.** City on the NW shore of the Black Sea at the mouth of the Tyras R.

**Tyras R.** River that rises in the Carpathians in E Europe and flows SE to the Black Sea.

**Tyre** (Sur). Phoenician maritime city 22 miles S of Sidon on the Mediterranean coast. Hiram, king of the city-state of Tyre, provided David and Solomon with materials for the palace and temple (II Sam. 5:11; I Kings 5:1). B1—1, 5, 11; D3—2, 15, 16; D2—3; B3—4; B2—6, 7; B4—13; F3—17; C1—19

**Tyre, Ladder of.** *See* Ladder of Tyre

**Tyropoeon Valley.** B2—8; B6—10. *See* Central Valley

**Tyrrhenian Sea.** Part of the W Mediterranean, bounded by the W coast of Italy, the N coast of Sicily, and the E coast of Sardinia and Corsica. A2—17

## U

**Ubi.** Name given to the region of Damascus (*q.v.*) in the Amarna Age (14th century B.C.).

**Ugarit.** Ancient city-state on the Mediterranean coast in N Syria. It was an important center of Minoan trade in Syria. The period of its greatest prosperity was the 15th and 14th centuries B.C. Mod. *Ras Shamra*. D3—2; B1—4

**Ulai** (Eulaeus) **R.** Artificial canal near Susa. On its banks Daniel saw his vision (Dan. 8:2, 16). D3—7

**Ulatha.** Name used by Josephus to designate the marshlands around Lake Hula (*q.v.*). C-D2—11

**Umma.** Ancient Sumerian city of S Mesopotamia. It was NW of, and at times subject to, Lagash (*q.v.*). Mod. *Yokhu*.

**Upper City** (in Jerusalem). SW Jerusalem, built on the Western Hill and bounded on the E by the Central Valley and on the N by the First North Wall. B5—10

**Upper Egypt.** *See* Egypt, Upper

**Upper Galilee.** *See* Galilee, upper

**Upper Room** (in Jerusalem). Room in which Jesus and the apostles ate the Last Supper (Mark 14:15; Luke 22:12). Its location has not been identified. The traditional site—located above the Tomb of King David and next to a Benedictine monastery—was not identified until the 14th century A.D. B6—10

**Upper Sea.** A-C3—2; A-B2—7. *See* Mediterranean Sea

**Ur.** Important Sumerian city on the Euphrates in S Mesopotamia. It is identified with the home of Abraham, known in the Bible as "Ur of the Chaldees." Mod. *el-Muqaiyar*. G4—2; D3—6

**Urartu.** Ancient kingdom of Armenia, located E of Asia Minor in the region of Lake Van. It was in the mts. of Urartu or Ararat that the ark settled following the flood. E-F2—2; C-D2—6

**Urmia, Lake.** Shallow salt lake in NW Iran. G2—2; C2—7

**Uruk.** *See* Erech

**Utians.** Ancient inhabitants of Carmania, the country E of Persia and NE of the Arabian Sea.

**Utica.** African city *ca*. 15 miles N of Carthage. It became the capital of the Roman province of Africa following the 3rd Punic war.

**Utrecht.** City in the Netherlands, on a branch of the lower Rhine. It dates back to Roman times and became (7th century A.D.) an episcopal see for Willibrord, apostle to the Frisians.

**Uxellodunum.** Town of the Cadurci tribes in S Gaul.

**Uzal.** District of SW Arabia settled by the clan of Uzal, a descendant of Shem.

## V

**Vaccaei.** A people of Hither Spain, living W of the Celtiberi and S of the Cantabri.

**Vagarshapat.** Town of central Armenia, located between the Black and Caspian seas. It dates from the 6th century B.C. and was capital of Armenia from the 2nd to the 4th century A.D. Mod. *Echmiadzin*.

**Valencia.** Former kingdom on the Mediterranean coast in E Spain. It was a mountainous country with fertile coastal plain. The capital of the kingdom, later a Roman province, was also named Valencia (or Valentia).

**Valentia.** *See* Valencia

**Valley Gate.** (1) Gate into the City of David (*ca*. 1000 B.C.) from the NW. (2) Gate into Jerusalem (*ca*. 445 B.C.) from the Hinnom Valley into the SW sector of the city.

**Valley of Aijalon.** *See* Aijalon, Valley of

**Valley of Elah.** *See* Elah, Valley of

**Valley of Gerar.** *See* Gerar, Valley of

**Valley of Hinnom.** *See* Hinnom Valley

**Valley of Salt.** *See* Salt, Valley of

**Valley of Siddim.** *See* Siddim, Valley of

**Valley of Sorek.** *See* Sorek, Valley of

**Van, Lake.** Salt lake in the Armenian mt. territory SE of the Black Sea. It covers 1,454 square miles and has no apparent outlet. F2—2; C2—7

**Veneti.** A Celtic people of ancient Gaul who settled in NW France.

**Verona.** City on the Adige R. in NE Italy, on the Brenner Road to central Europe.

**Verulamium** (Saint Albans). City on the slope and summit of a hill above the Ver R. NW of London.

**Vesontio.** City of the Sequani in E Gaul.

**Vienne.** City on the Rhone, S of Lyons, in SE France. B2—18

**Vistula R.** Principal waterway of Poland. It rises in the Carpathians and flows 667 miles N to the Baltic. In ancient times it formed the boundary between Germany and Sarmatia.

**Volga R.** F1—12. *See* Rha R.

## W

**Washuk-kanni.** Capital of Mitanni (*q.v.*). Its precise location is still in question, but it was prob. near Gozan in the upper Habor area. Poss. mod. *Tell Fakhariyah*. E2—2

**Water Gate.** Gate into the old City of David W of Spring Gihon in the Kidron Valley (*ca*. 445 B.C.). C3—9; C6—10

**Water shaft** (in Jerusalem). Jebusite tunnel system designed to bring water from Spring Gihon into the city. David used it to enter the city and defeat the Jebusites (II Sam. 5:8 RSV). B2—8

**Way of the Sea, The.** Most lucrative trade route between Egypt and Mesopotamia. It followed the coastal plain (Philistia) through Palestine. B-C3—3

**Way to Shur, The.** Road from the Judean highlands to Egypt, passing through Beer-sheba and the Wilderness of Shur. B-C4—3

**W. el-Hasa.** *See* Zered R.

**W. el-Mughara.** Site N of Dor where remains of Stone Age men have been discovered. B2—19

**Western Hill** (in Jerusalem). The most commanding

of the several hills on which Jerusalem was built. It is bounded on the W and S by the Hinnom Valley and on the E by the Central Valley. In post-Roman times it was known as Mt. Zion. A2—8; C2—9

**Wilderness of Etham.** *See* Etham, Wilderness of

**Wilderness of Paran.** *See* Paran, Wilderness of

**Wilderness of Shur.** *See* Shur, Wilderness of

**Wilderness of Sin.** *See* Sin, Wilderness of

**Wilderness of Zin.** *See* Zin, Wilderness of

**W. Musa.** River bed that extends E from the Petra region of S Jordan. It is dry most of the year.

## X

**Xanthus.** City in Lycia, W Asia Minor, on the Xanthus (Scamander) R. B2—7

**Xois.** City in the Nile Delta on an island. It was the seat of a dynasty of Egyptian pharaohs but fell into decay during Roman times.

**Xystus.** Market place in the NE section of Jerusalem's Upper City (20 B.C.–A.D. 70).

## Y

**Yarmuk R.** River that rises in the Hauran, SE of Mt. Hermon. It flows SW and enters the Jordan S of the Sea of Galilee. C2—1; C3—5, 11

**Yavne Yam.** B4—19. *See* Jabneel

**Yazd.** Ancient Persian city *ca*. 165 miles SE of Gabae. D3—7

**Yiron.** *See* Iron

**York.** City at the confluence of the Ouse and Foss rivers in N England. As Eboracum, it was a chief station of the Roman province of Britannia.

**Yusha', J.** Mt. in Gilead, S of the Jabbok R. It reaches a height of 3,652 feet. D4—1

## Z

**Zabulon.** *See* Zebulun

**Zadrakarta.** Important city in the Persian province of Hyrcania (*q.v.*). D2—7

**Zagros Mts.** Range in W Iran E of the Tigris, extending from NW to SE in several parallel ridges. F-G3—2

**Zanoah.** Town in S Palestine (Josh. 15:34; Neh. 3:13; 11:30), located 15 miles W of Bethlehem.

**Zaphon.** City E of the Jordan in the territory of Gad (Josh. 13:27).

**Zareah.** *See* Zorah

**Zared R.** *See* Zered R.

**Zarephath.** *See* Sarepta

**Zarethan.** Town in Transjordan that was one source of metal vessels for the Jerusalem temple (I Kings 7:46). Poss. mod. *Tell es-Saidiyeh* or *Tell Umm Hamad*. C3—19

**Zareth-shahar.** *See* Zereth-shahar

**Zarqa R.** D4—1. *See* Jabbok R.

**Zebulun,** allotment of. Territory in N Palestine bounded on the S by Manasseh and Issachar; on the N and W by Naphtali; and on the E by Asher. The Kishon R. and the Plain of Jezreel touched its S border.

**Zedad.** City on the N boundary of Palestine (Num. 34:8). It has been identified with Sadad, SE of Hamath. C2—4

**Zela.** Ancient city of Pontus, NE Asia Minor. It was the site of Caesar's defeat of Pharnaces, king of Pontus (47 B.C.).

**Zelea.** Ancient city of Mysia, NE Asia Minor. It was the headquarters of the Persian army during Alexander's invasion.

**Zemaraim.** Town in the territory of Benjamin (Josh. 18:22). Prob. mod. *Ras ez-Zeimara*, N of Jerusalem. C4—5

**Zered R.** (W. el-Hasa). Brook (and valley) that the Israelites crossed en route to Canaan through E Palestine (Num. 21:12; Deut. 2:13–14). It served as the border between Edom and Moab, SE of the Dead Sea. C6—1, 5; D3—3

**Zereth-shahar.** Town on the E bank of the Dead Sea in the territory of Reuben (Josh. 13:19).

**Ziklag.** Town in S Judah (Josh. 15:31), at one time ruled by David as a vassal of the Philistine king Achish (I Sam. 27:6). Prob. mod. *Tell el-Khuweilifeh*, between Debir and Beer-sheba. B5—4, 5

**Zilu.** Town on the NW edge of the Nile Delta and on The Way of the Sea. Mod. *Tell Abu Seifah*. B4—3

**Zin, Wilderness of.** Wilderness SW of the Dead Sea, close to the S border of Canaan (Num. 13:21). It was part of the Wilderness of Paran (*q.v.*) and included the city of Kadesh-barnea. C3-D4—3

**Zion.** *See* Jerusalem

**Ziph.** Town 4 miles SE of Hebron in the hill-country of Judah (Josh. 15:55). It was fortified by Rehoboam (II Chron. 11:8). Mod. *Kh. ez-Zif*. B5—5

**Zoan** (Avaris). C4—2. *See* Ramses

**Zoar.** One of the cities of the plain (Gen. 19:20, 22). It was associated with Sodom and Gomorrah. Lot fled there after Sodom's destruction (Gen. 19:20–22). It was located S of the Dead Sea. D3—3; C6—5

**Zobah.** *See* Aram-zobah

**Zorah.** Town in Dan on a hillside overlooking the Sorek (*q.v.*). It was the birthplace of Samson (Judg. 13:2, 25) and was later fortified by Rehoboam (II Chron. 11:10). B4—5

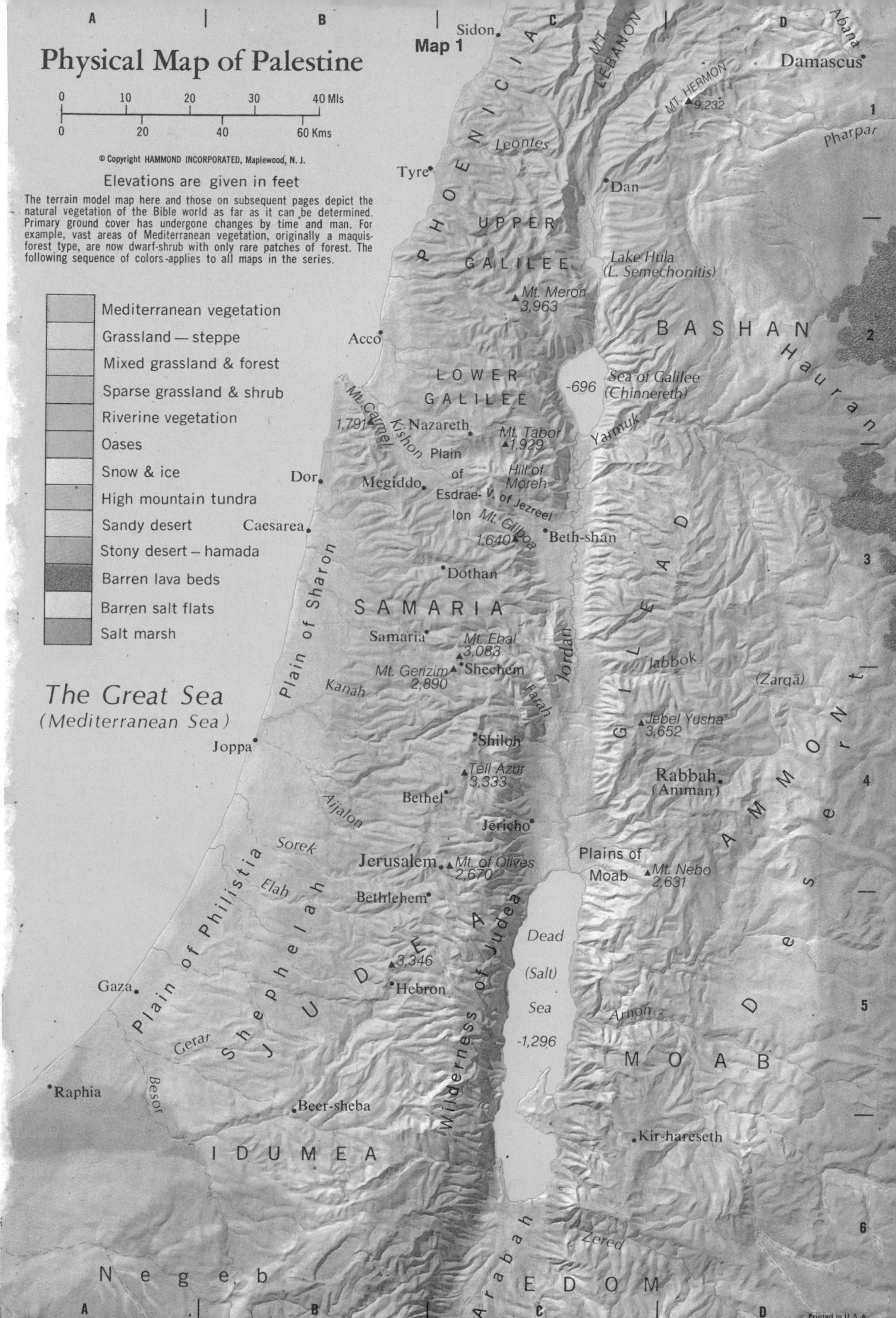

Physical Map of Palestine
Map 1
0 10 20 30 40 Mls
0 20 40 60 Kms
© Copyright HAMMOND INCORPORATED, Maplewood, N. J.
Elevations are given in feet
The terrain model map here and those on subsequent pages depict the natural vegetation of the Bible world as far as it can be determined. Primary ground cover has undergone changes by time and man. For example, vast areas of Mediterranean vegetation, originally a maquis-forest type, are now dwarf-shrub with only rare patches of forest. The following sequence of colors applies to all maps in the series.
Mediterranean vegetation
Grassland — steppe
Mixed grassland & forest
Sparse grassland & shrub
Riverine vegetation
Oases
Snow & ice
High mountain tundra
Sandy desert
Stony desert – hamada
Barren lava beds
Barren salt flats
Salt marsh
The Great Sea
(Mediterranean Sea)
Sidon
PHOENICIA
MT. LEBANON
Damascus
Abana
MT. HERMON
9,232
Pharpar
Leontes
Tyre
Dan
UPPER GALILEE
Lake Hula
(L. Semechonitis)
Mt. Meron
3,963
BASHAN
Hauran
Acco
LOWER GALILEE
-696
Sea of Galilee
(Chinnereth)
Mt. Carmel
1,791
Kishon
Nazareth
Mt. Tabor
1,929
Yarmuk
Plain of Esdrae-lon
Dor
Megiddo
Hill of Moreh
V. of Jezreel
Caesarea
Mt. Gilboa
1,640
Beth-shan
Dothan
Plain of Sharon
SAMARIA
GILEAD
Samaria
Mt. Ebal
3,083
Mt. Gerizim
2,890
Shechem
Jordan
Jabbok
(Zarqā)
Kanah
Farah
Jebel Yusha'
3,652
Joppa
Shiloh
Tell Azur
3,333
Rabbah
(Amman)
AMMON
Bethel
Aijalon
Jericho
Sorek
Jerusalem
Mt. of Olives
2,670
Plains of Moab
Mt. Nebo
2,631
Plain of Philistia
Elah
Shephelah
Bethlehem
Desert
JUDEA
Wilderness of Judea
Dead (Salt) Sea
-1,296
3,346
Gaza
Hebron
Arnon
Gerar
MOAB
Besor
Raphia
Beer-sheba
Kir-hareseth
IDUMEA
Arabah
Zered
Negeb
EDOM
A B C D
1 2 3 4 5 6
Printed in U. S. A.

**The geographical setting** for much of the Biblical narrative is within that half circle of arable land known as the Fertile Crescent. In the east the arc follows the alluvial plains of the Euphrates and Tigris rivers. It widens as one moves northwest through grassland and steppe, then it turns southwest at the Mediterranean coast and continues as a narrow belt through Phoenicia and Palestine. The arc ends in the green ribbon of the Nile. Rainfall, always scant and seasonal in the Middle East, has changed little since the beginning of the Biblical era. Cropland and grassland areas remain much as they were in Abraham's day and the extent of desert is unchanged. Forests, however, have been slowly cut back by man so that today large expanses of mountain forest or wooded areas of the Mediterranean type are scarce.

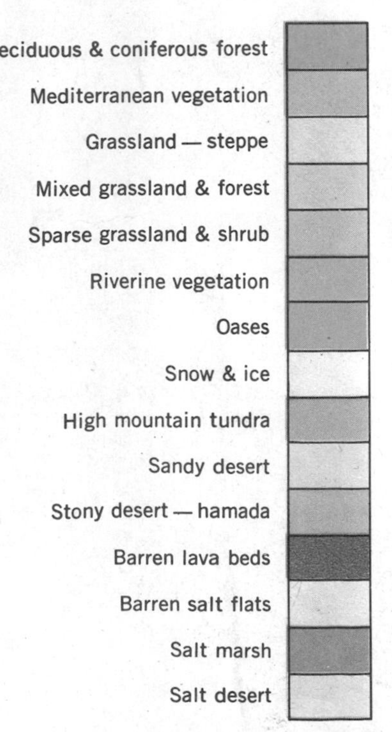


A B C
Black
1
Troy
ASSUWA
Sangarius
Hermes
Karabel
Maeander
Beycesultan
ARZAWA
2
LUKKA
MINOAN-MYCENAEAN DOMAIN
Rhodes
ALASHIYA, KITTIM
(Cyprus)
CAPHTOR
(Crete)
3
Mediterranean Sea
(Great or Upper Sea)
4
Avaris
(Zoan)
Lower Egypt
On
Memphis
(Noph)
Heracleopolis
Libyan Desert
EGYPT
5
Hermopolis
Akhetaton
(Tell el-Amarna)
Nile
Upper Egypt
Abydos
(Thebe
6
NUBIA
A B C

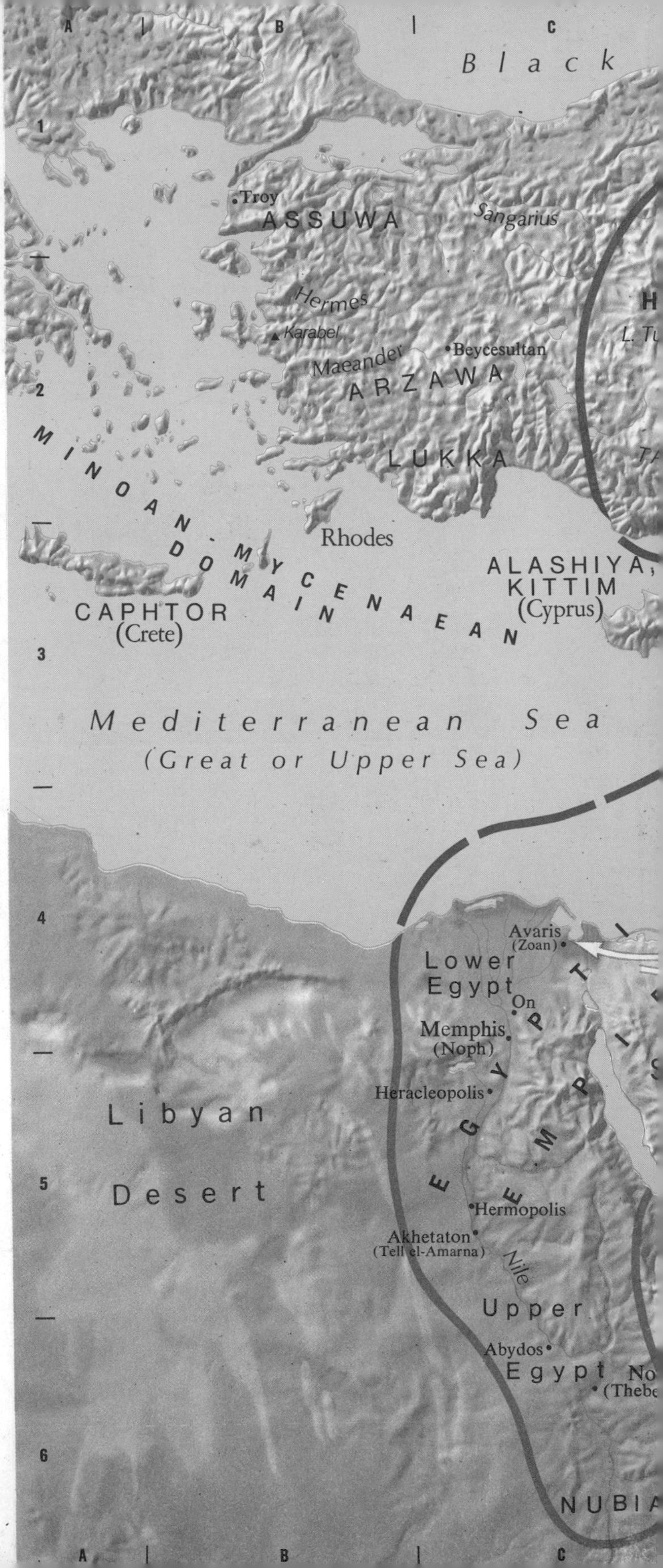

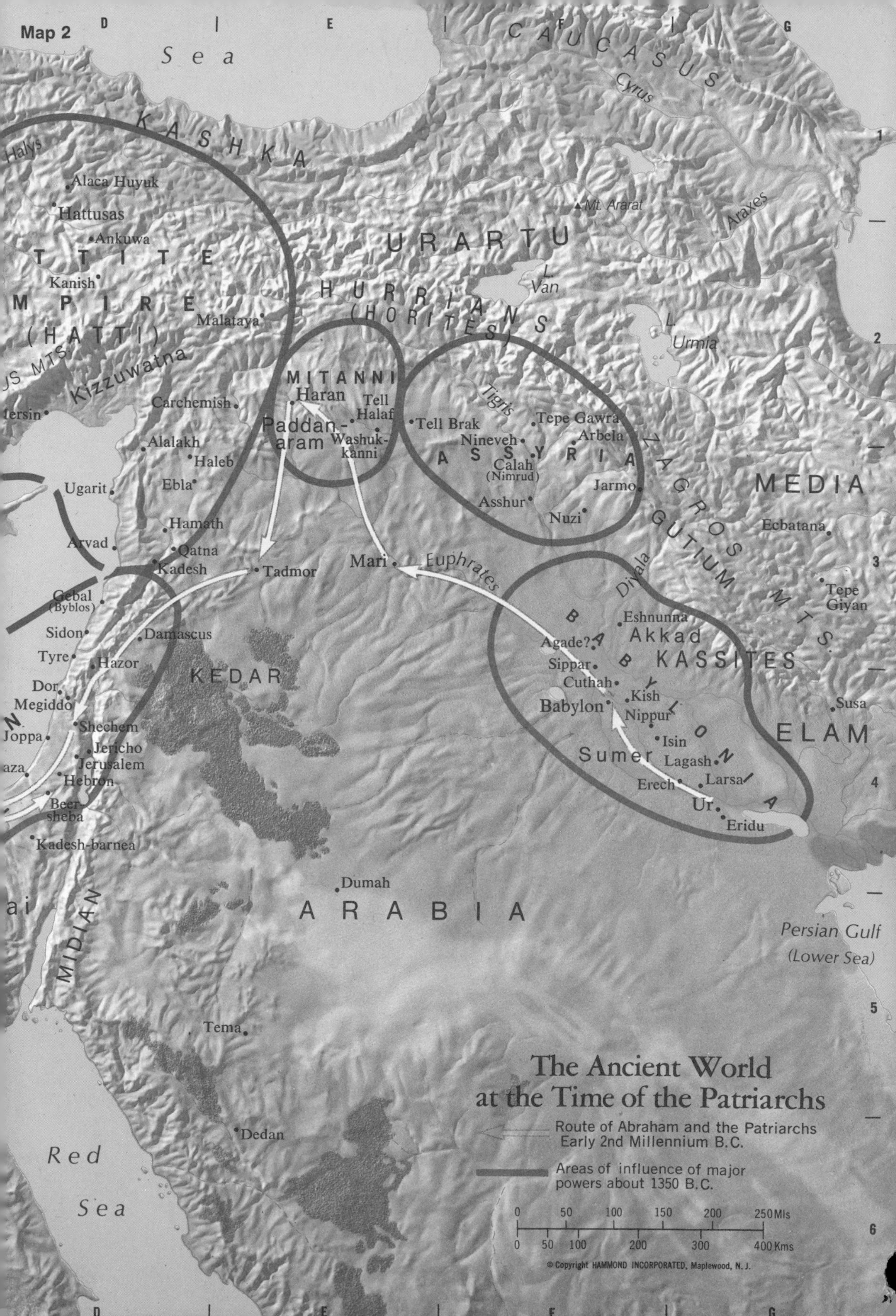

Map 2
The Ancient World at the Time of the Patriarchs
Route of Abraham and the Patriarchs Early 2nd Millennium B.C.
Areas of influence of major powers about 1350 B.C.
0 50 100 150 200 250 Mls
0 50 100 200 300 400 Kms
CAUCASUS
Cyrus
KASHKA
Halys
Alaca Huyuk
Hattusas
Ankuwa
HITTITE EMPIRE (HATTI)
Kanish
Malataya
Kizzuwatna
Mersin
URARTU
Mt. Ararat
Araxes
L. Van
L. Urmia
HURRIANS (HORITES)
MITANNI
Haran
Tell Halaf
Paddan-aram
Washukkanni
Carchemish
Alalakh
Haleb
Ebla
Ugarit
Hamath
Arvad
Qatna
Kadesh
Tadmor
Gebal (Byblos)
Sidon
Damascus
Tyre
Hazor
Dor
Megiddo
Shechem
Joppa
Jericho
Jerusalem
Hebron
Beer-sheba
Kadesh-barnea
KEDAR
Tigris
Tell Brak
Tepe Gawra
Nineveh
Arbela
ASSYRIA
Calah (Nimrud)
Jarmo
Asshur
Nuzi
ZAGROS MTS.
GUTIUM
MEDIA
Ecbatana
Tepe Giyan
Mari
Euphrates
Diyala
Eshnunna
Akkad
Agade?
BABYLONIA
Sippar
KASSITES
Cuthah
Kish
Babylon
Nippur
Isin
Sumer
Lagash
Larsa
Erech
Ur
Eridu
Susa
ELAM
Dumah
ARABIA
MIDIAN
Persian Gulf (Lower Sea)
Tema
Dedan
Red Sea

Map 3
The Exodus
Traditional route of the Exodus
Unsuccessful invasion of Canaan
Trade routes
0 20 40 60 80 100 Mls
0 40 80 120 160 Kms
© Copyright HAMMOND INCORPORATED, Maplewood, N. J.
The Great Sea
(Mediterranean Sea)
Nile Delta
Ramses (Tanis)
Pelusium (Sin)
Baal-zephon
Zilu
Goshen
Pibeseth (Bubastis)
Pithom
Succoth
EGYPT
Bitter Lakes
Heliopolis (On)
Great Pyramids
Memphis (Noph)
L. Moeris
Crocodilopolis
Heracleopolis
Nile
Akhetaton (Tell el-Amarna)
The Way of the Sea
Brook of Egypt
Wilderness of Shur
The Way to Shur
Jebel Helal
Wilderness of Etham
Wilderness of Paran
Sinai Peninsula
Marah?
Elim?
Wilderness of Sin
Dophkah?
Alush?
Rephidim?
Mt. Sinai
Taberah?
Kibroth-hattaavah?
Hazeroth?
(Gulf of Suez)
(Gulf of Aqaba)
Red Sea
Ezion-geber
Kadesh-barnea
Wilderness of Zin
Negeb
Arabah
The King's Highway
EDOM
Punon
Sela
Jebel Harun
Bozrah
Tje-abarim
Zered
Zoar
Kir-hareseth
MOAB
Arnon
Dibon
Mt. Nebo
Heshbon
Rabbah
AMMON
Jabbok
Jericho
Salt Sea
LAND OF MIDIAN
Gebal
Berytus
MT. LEBANON
Sidon
Damascus
Tyre
BASHAN
CANAAN
Hazor
Acco
Ashtaroth
Mt. Carmel
Madon
Dor
Megiddo
Edrei
Taanach
Beth-shan
Shechem
Aphek
Jordan
Joppa
Shiloh
Bethel
Ai
Gezer
Ashdod
Ashkelon
Jerusalem
Lachish
Gaza
Eglon?
Hebron
Debir?
Arad
Raphia
Beer-sheba
Hormah

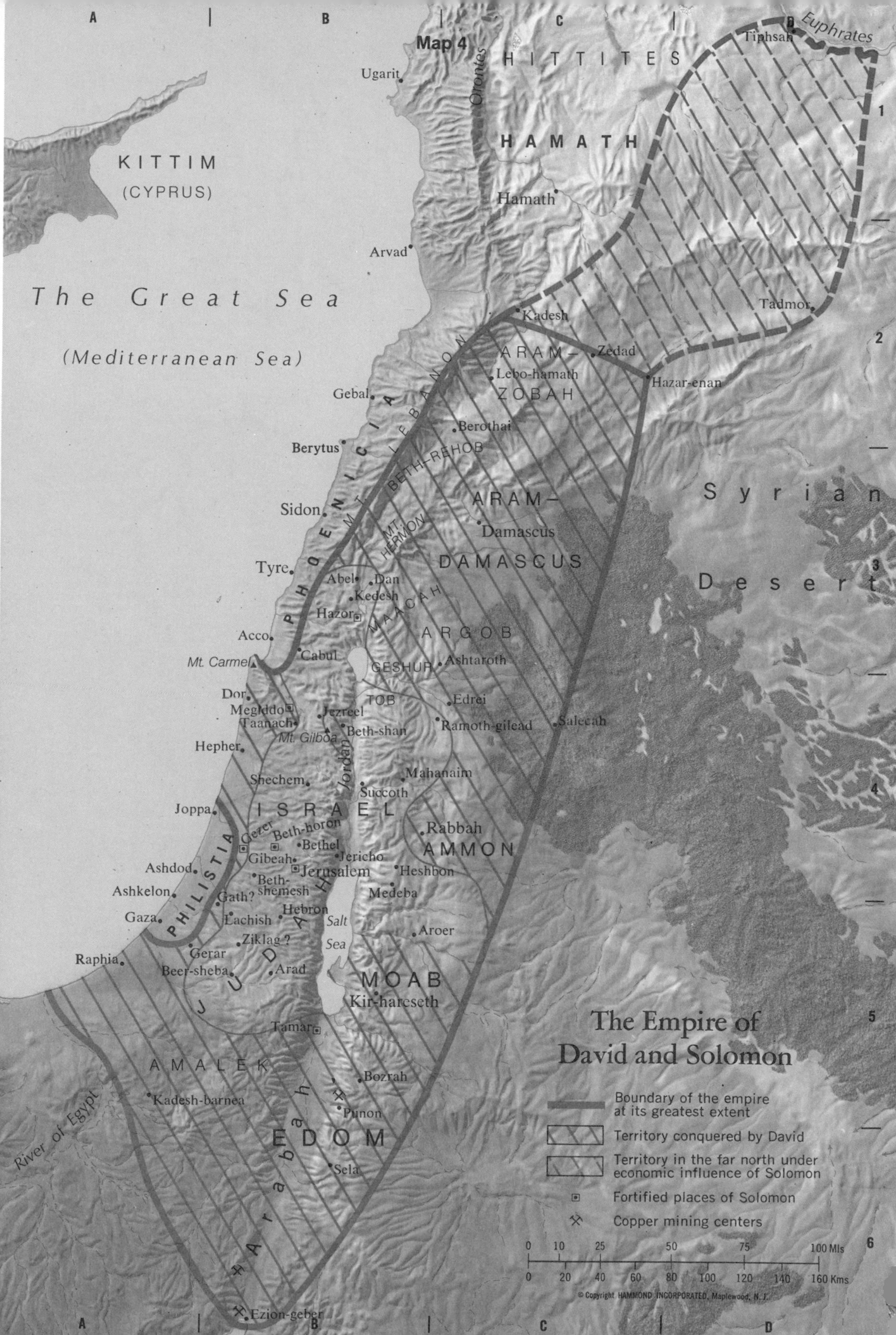

Map 4
The Empire of David and Solomon
Boundary of the empire at its greatest extent
Territory conquered by David
Territory in the far north under economic influence of Solomon
Fortified places of Solomon
Copper mining centers
0 10 25 50 75 100 Mls
0 20 40 60 80 100 120 140 160 Kms
© Copyright HAMMOND INCORPORATED, Maplewood, N. J.
KITTIM
(CYPRUS)
The Great Sea
(Mediterranean Sea)
HITTITES
HAMATH
Euphrates
Tiphsah
Orontes
Ugarit
Hamath
Arvad
Tadmor
Kadesh
ARAM–ZOBAH
Zedad
Lebo-hamath
Hazar-enan
Gebal
PHOENICIA
MT. LEBANON
Berothai
Berytus
BETH-REHOB
Syrian Desert
Sidon
ARAM–DAMASCUS
Damascus
MT. HERMON
Tyre
Abel
Dan
Kedesh
MAACAH
Hazor
ARGOB
Acco
Cabul
Mt. Carmel
GESHUR
Ashtaroth
Dor
TOB
Edrei
Megiddo
Jezreel
Taanach
Beth-shan
Ramoth-gilead
Salecah
Mt. Gilboa
Hepher
Jordan
Shechem
Mahanaim
Succoth
Joppa
ISRAEL
Gezer
Beth-horon
Rabbah
Bethel
AMMON
Jericho
PHILISTIA
Gibeah
Ashdod
Jerusalem
Heshbon
Beth-shemesh
Ashkelon
Medeba
Gath?
Hebron
Gaza
Lachish
Salt Sea
Aroer
Ziklag ?
Gerar
Raphia
Beer-sheba
Arad
MOAB
JUDAH
Kir-hareseth
Tamar
AMALEK
Bozrah
Kadesh-barnea
River of Egypt
Punon
EDOM
Arabah
Sela
Ezion-geber

Map 5
The Kingdoms of Israel and Judah
Approximate frontiers
ISRAEL Hebrew kingdoms
AMMON Foreign kingdoms
0 10 20 30 40 Mls
0 20 40 60 Kms
© Copyright HAMMOND INCORPORATED, Maplewood, N. J.
A
B
C
D
1
2
3
4
5
6
The Great Sea
(Mediterranean Sea)
Sidon
Damascus
PHOENICIA
MT. HERMON
SYRIA
(ARAM)
Leontes
Ijon
Tyre
Abel-beth-maachah
Dan
Kedesh
Hazor
Merom
Galilee
Bashan
Acco
Chinnereth
Cabul
Sea of Chinnereth
Karnaim
Ashtaroth
Mt. Carmel
Rumah
Hammath
Aphek
Plain of Esdraelon
Mt. Tabor
Yarmuk
Havvoth-jair
Kishon
Edrei
Dor
Shunem
Megiddo
Jezreel
Mt. Gilboa
Ramoth-gilead
Taanach
Beth-shan
Ibleam
Abel-meholah
Dothan
Jabesh-gilead
Tishbe
Plain of Sharon
ISRAEL
Socoh
Tirzah
Jordan
Gilead
Samaria
Mt. Ebal
Penuel
Mahanaim
Mt. Gerizim
Shechem
Succoth
Jabbok
Kanah
Aphek
AMMON
Shiloh
Joppa
Jazer
Rabbah
Lod
Gath
Bethel
Zemaraim
Mizpah
Gilgal
Jabneel
Gezer
Geba
Jericho
Gibbethon
Aijalon
Gibeon
Ramah
Shittim?
Heshbon
Ekron
Zorah
Jerusalem
Ashdod
Beth-shemesh
Mt. Nebo
Bethlehem
Medeba
Jahaz
Ashkelon
Adullam
Tekoa
Mareshah
Beth-zur
Ataroth
Lachish
JUDAH
Salt Sea
Dibon
Gaza
Adoraim
Hebron
En-gedi
Aroer
Ziph
Arnon
Debir?
Wilderness of Judah
PHILISTIA
Gerar
Ziklag?
Raphia
Sharuhen
Arad
Ar?
Beer-sheba
MOAB
Besor
Kir-hareseth
Zoar
Tamar
Zered
Ascent of Akrabbim
Negeb
EDOM

Map 6
Medo-Babylonian Realms
Political boundaries of major powers about 560 B.C.
0 100 200 300 400 500 Mls
0 200 400 600 800 Kms
© Copyright HAMMOND INCORPORATED, Maplewood, N. J.
Ister (Danube)
THRACIANS
Black Sea
Sinope
Aral Sea
Jaxartes
Oxus
Caspian Sea
CAUCASUS
SCYTHIANS
Aegean Sea
GREEKS
Athens
Sparta
KINGDOM OF LYDIA
Sardis
CAPPADOCIA
Halys
URARTU
MEDIAN EMPIRE
KUE
IZALLA
Haran
Nisibis
Tarsus
Carchemish
ASSYRIA
NEW BABYLONIAN EMPIRE
Nineveh
Lycia
Crete
Cyprus
trib. to Egypt
Mediterranean Sea
Riblah
SYRIA
Damascus
Tyre
Megiddo
JUDAH
Jerusalem
Euphrates
Tigris
Anat
Opis
Sippar
Babylon
Nippur
BABYLONIA
Erech
Ur
HYRCANIA
MEDIA
Ecbatana
PARTHIA
Susa
ELAM
PERSIA
Persian Gulf
LIBYANS
Sais
KINGDOM OF EGYPT
Memphis
Temple of Amon
Nile
Thebes
Syene (Elephantine)
Dumah
ARABS
Tema
Dedan
Red Sea
ETHIOPIA
Erythraean Sea

Map 7

# The Persian Empire

- Limits of the Persian empire c.500 B.C.
- Persian royal road
- Royal residences
- Red Sea-Nile canal built by Darius I

0 100 200 300 400 500 Mls
0 200 400 600 800 Kms



MASSAGETAE
SCYTHIANS (SAKA)
Aral Sea
Jaxartes
CHORASMIA
Oxus
Cyropolis
SOGDIANA
MARGUS
Margiana
Bactra
BACTRIA
KUSH
HINDU
Cophen (Kabul)
Taxila
GANDARA
ARIA
PARTHIA
HYRCANIA
Zadrakarta
Damghan
Rhagae
ARACHOSIA
DRANGIANA
Indus
HINDUSH (INDIA)
Patrala
Probable ancient coastline
GEDROSIA (MAKA)
Pura
CARMANIA
Pasargadae
Persepolis (Parsa)
PERSIS
Yazd
Gabae
Ecbatana
MEDIA
Behistun
SUSIANA
Susa
Ulai
PERSIAN EMPIRE
Caspian Sea
CAUCASUS
Cyrus
Araxes
L. Van
L. Urmia
ARMENIA
Melitene
MOSCHI
Trapezus
Phasis
Black Sea
Chersonesus
Panticapaeum
Sinope
Ister (Danube)
THRACE
Apollonia
Byzantium
MACEDONIA
GREECE
Athens
Marathon
Sparta
LYDIA
Gordion
Ancyra
Pteria
Halys
Sardis
Maeander
Ephesus
Miletus
CARIA
Iconium
CILICIA
Tarsus
Xanthus
Rhodes
Crete
Cyprus
Issus
Thapsacus
Haran
Euphrates
Asshur
Tigris
Arbela
Hamath
Arvad
Gebal
Tadmor
Damascus
Tyre
JUDAH
Jerusalem
Gaza
Opis
Sippar
Babylon
Nippur
BABYLONIA
Erech
Upper Sea
Cyrene
LIBYA
Sais
Heliopolis
Pelusium
Memphis
Temple of Amon (Siwa)
Elath
Dumah
ARABIA
Tema
Dedan
Gerrha
Lower Sea
Erythraean Sea
EGYPT
Libyan Desert
Thebes
Syene (Elephantine)
Red Sea
Nile
ETHIOPIA (CUSH)

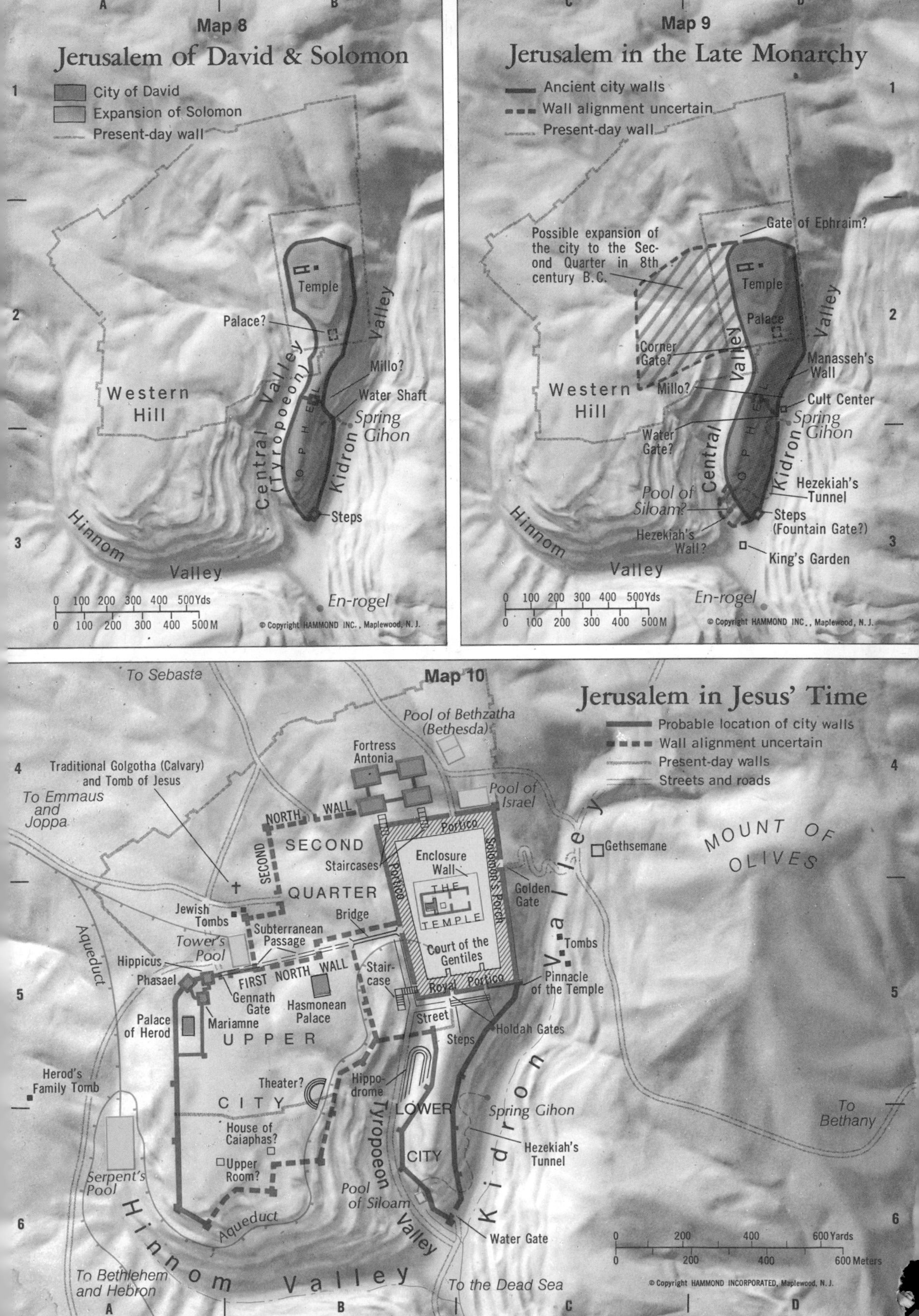

Map 8
Jerusalem of David & Solomon
City of David
Expansion of Solomon
Present-day wall
Temple
Palace?
Millo?
Water Shaft
Spring Gihon
Western Hill
Central Valley (Tyropoeon)
Kidron Valley
OPHEL
Steps
Hinnom Valley
En-rogel
© Copyright HAMMOND INC., Maplewood, N.J.
Map 9
Jerusalem in the Late Monarchy
Ancient city walls
Wall alignment uncertain
Present-day wall
Gate of Ephraim?
Possible expansion of the city to the Second Quarter in 8th century B.C.
Temple
Palace
Corner Gate?
Manasseh's Wall
Millo?
Cult Center
Western Hill
Spring Gihon
Water Gate?
Central Valley
Kidron
Hezekiah's Tunnel
Pool of Siloam?
Steps (Fountain Gate?)
Hezekiah's Wall?
King's Garden
Hinnom Valley
En-rogel
© Copyright HAMMOND INC., Maplewood, N.J.
Map 10
Jerusalem in Jesus' Time
Probable location of city walls
Wall alignment uncertain
Present-day walls
Streets and roads
To Sebaste
Pool of Bethzatha (Bethesda)
Fortress Antonia
Traditional Golgotha (Calvary) and Tomb of Jesus
To Emmaus and Joppa
Pool of Israel
NORTH WALL
SECOND
SECOND QUARTER
Portico
Staircases
Enclosure Wall
Solomon's Porch
THE TEMPLE
Gethsemane
MOUNT OF OLIVES
Golden Gate
Jewish Tombs
Subterranean Passage
Bridge
Court of the Gentiles
Tombs
Tower's Pool
Aqueduct
Hippicus
Phasael
FIRST NORTH WALL
Gennath Gate
Hasmonean Palace
Stair-case
Royal Portico
Pinnacle of the Temple
Palace of Herod
Mariamne
UPPER
Street
Steps
Holdah Gates
Kidron Valley
Herod's Family Tomb
Theater?
Hippo-drome
CITY
LOWER CITY
Tyropoeon Valley
Spring Gihon
To Bethany
House of Caiaphas?
Upper Room?
Hezekiah's Tunnel
Serpent's Pool
Pool of Siloam
Aqueduct
Hinnom Valley
Water Gate
To Bethlehem and Hebron
To the Dead Sea
© Copyright HAMMOND INCORPORATED, Maplewood, N.J.

Map 11
Palestine in New Testament Times
Political boundaries A.D. 6-44
Cities of the Decapolis
Fortresses
0 10 20 30 40 Mls
0 20 40 60 Kms
© Copyright HAMMOND INCORPORATED, Maplewood, N. J.
A
B
C
D
1
2
3
4
5
6
Sidon
Sarepta
Tyre
Abila
ABILENE
Iturea
SYRIA
Damascus
MT. LEBANON
MT. HERMON
Phoenicia
Leontes
Paneas
Caesarea Philippi
Ulatha
Gaulanitis
Batanea
Cadasa
Gischala
Ladder of Tyre
Ecdippa
Ptolemais
Chorazin
Bethsaida-Julias
Raphana
GALILEE
Capernaum
Cana
Magadan
Sea of Galilee
Asochis
Tiberias
Hippos
Dion?
Sepphoris
Yarmuk
Mt. Carmel
Nazareth
Mt. Tabor
Abila
Mediterranean Sea
Plain of Esdraelon
Nain
Gadara
Capitolias
Dora
Agrippina
Arbela
Caesarea
Scythopolis
DECAPOLIS
Narbata
Pella
Ginae
Salim
Aenon
Jordan
SAMARIA
Plain of Sharon
Sebaste (Samaria)
Gerasa
Neapolis
Mt. Ebal
Amathus
Apollonia
Mt. Gerizim
Sychar
Jabbok
Antipatris
Alexandrium
Joppa
Arimathea?
Phasaelis
Gadara
PEREA
Ephraim
Philadelphia
Lydda
Gophna
Archelais
Jamnia
Jericho
Betharamphtha (Livias, Julias)
Emmaus (Nicopolis)
Cyprus
Emmaus?
Esbus
Azotus
Jerusalem
Bethany
Qumran
Bethlehem
Hyrcania
Medeba
Ascalon
JUDEA
Herodium
Lake Asphaltitis (Dead Sea)
Callirrhoe
Marisa
Bethsura
Machaerus
Agrippias
Hebron
Arnon
Gaza
Engaddi
NABATEA
Masada
IDUMEA
Areopolis
Bersabe
Malatha
Charachmoba

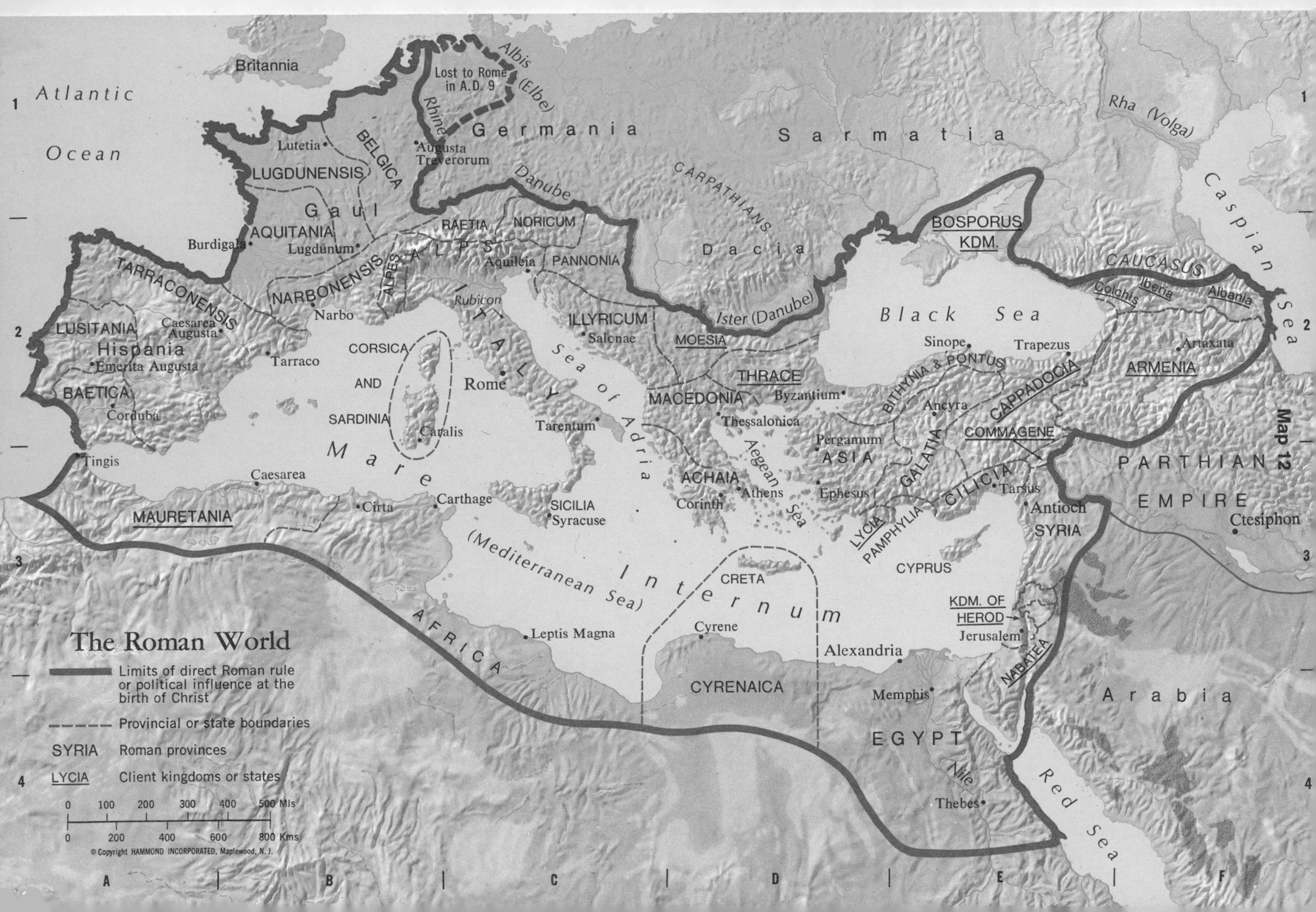

Map 12
The Roman World
Limits of direct Roman rule or political influence at the birth of Christ
Provincial or state boundaries
SYRIA Roman provinces
LYCIA Client kingdoms or states
0 100 200 300 400 500 Mls
0 200 400 600 800 Kms
Atlantic Ocean
Britannia
Lost to Rome in A.D. 9
Albis (Elbe)
Rhine
Germania
Sarmatia
Rha (Volga)
Caspian Sea
Lutetia
BELGICA
Augusta Treverorum
LUGDUNENSIS
Gaul
AQUITANIA
Burdigala
Lugdunum
Danube
CARPATHIANS
Dacia
RAETIA
NORICUM
ALPS
ALPES
Aquileia
PANNONIA
BOSPORUS KDM.
CAUCASUS
Colchis
Iberia
Albania
TARRACONENSIS
NARBONENSIS
Narbo
Rubicon
ILLYRICUM
Salonae
Ister (Danube)
Black Sea
LUSITANIA
Caesarea Augusta
Hispania
Emerita Augusta
Tarraco
CORSICA
AND
SARDINIA
Caralis
ITALY
Rome
Sea of Adria
MOESIA
THRACE
MACEDONIA
Byzantium
Thessalonica
Sinope
Trapezus
BITHYNIA & PONTUS
Artaxata
ARMENIA
CAPPADOCIA
Ancyra
COMMAGENE
BAETICA
Corduba
Tarentum
Pergamum
ASIA
GALATIA
Tingis
Mare
Caesarea
Aegean Sea
ACHAIA
Athens
Corinth
Ephesus
CILICIA
Tarsus
PARTHIAN EMPIRE
Ctesiphon
Antioch
SYRIA
Cirta
Carthage
MAURETANIA
SICILIA
Syracuse
LYCIA
PAMPHYLIA
CYPRUS
(Mediterranean Sea)
Internum
CRETA
KDM. OF HEROD
Jerusalem
Cyrene
Leptis Magna
AFRICA
Alexandria
NABATEA
CYRENAICA
Memphis
Arabia
EGYPT
Nile
Thebes
Red Sea
© Copyright HAMMOND INCORPORATED, Maplewood, N. J.

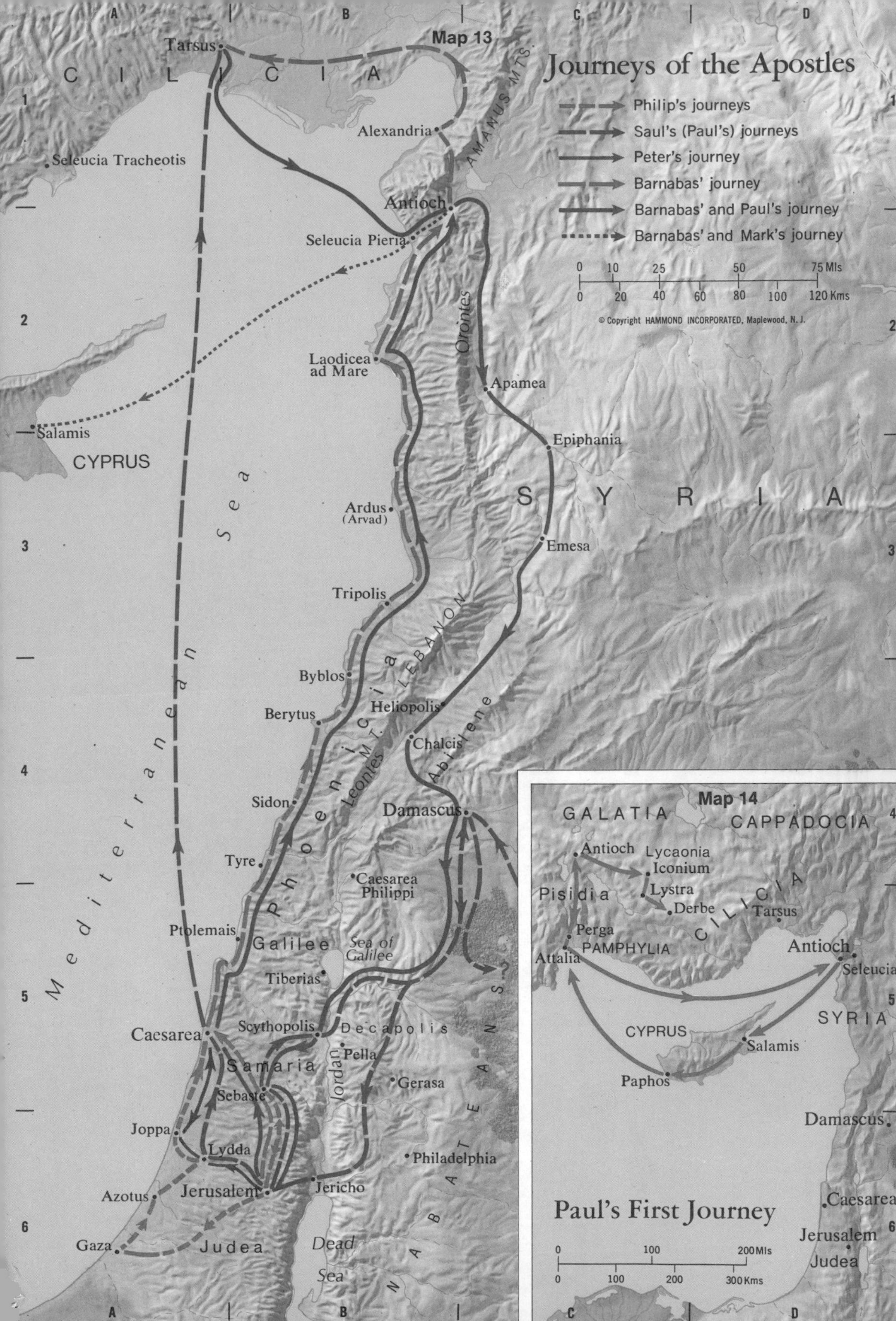
Map 13
Journeys of the Apostles
Philip's journeys
Saul's (Paul's) journeys
Peter's journey
Barnabas' journey
Barnabas' and Paul's journey
Barnabas' and Mark's journey
0 10 25 50 75 Mls
0 20 40 60 80 100 120 Kms
© Copyright HAMMOND INCORPORATED, Maplewood, N. J.
CILICIA
Tarsus
Alexandria
AMANUS MTS.
Seleucia Tracheotis
Antioch
Seleucia Pieria
Orontes
Laodicea ad Mare
Apamea
Salamis
CYPRUS
Epiphania
SYRIA
Ardus (Arvad)
Emesa
Mediterranean Sea
Tripolis
LEBANON
Byblos
Berytus
Heliopolis
Chalcis
Abilene
Phoenicia
MT. Leontes
Sidon
Damascus
Tyre
Caesarea Philippi
Ptolemais
Galilee
Sea of Galilee
Tiberias
Caesarea
Scythopolis
Decapolis
Samaria
Pella
Sebaste
Jordan
Gerasa
NABATEANS
Joppa
Lydda
Philadelphia
Azotus
Jerusalem
Jericho
Gaza
Judea
Dead Sea
Map 14
GALATIA
CAPPADOCIA
Antioch
Lycaonia
Iconium
Lystra
Pisidia
Derbe
CILICIA
Tarsus
Perga
PAMPHYLIA
Attalia
Antioch
Seleucia
SYRIA
CYPRUS
Salamis
Paphos
Damascus
Caesarea
Jerusalem
Judea
Paul's First Journey
0 100 200 Mls
0 100 200 300 Kms

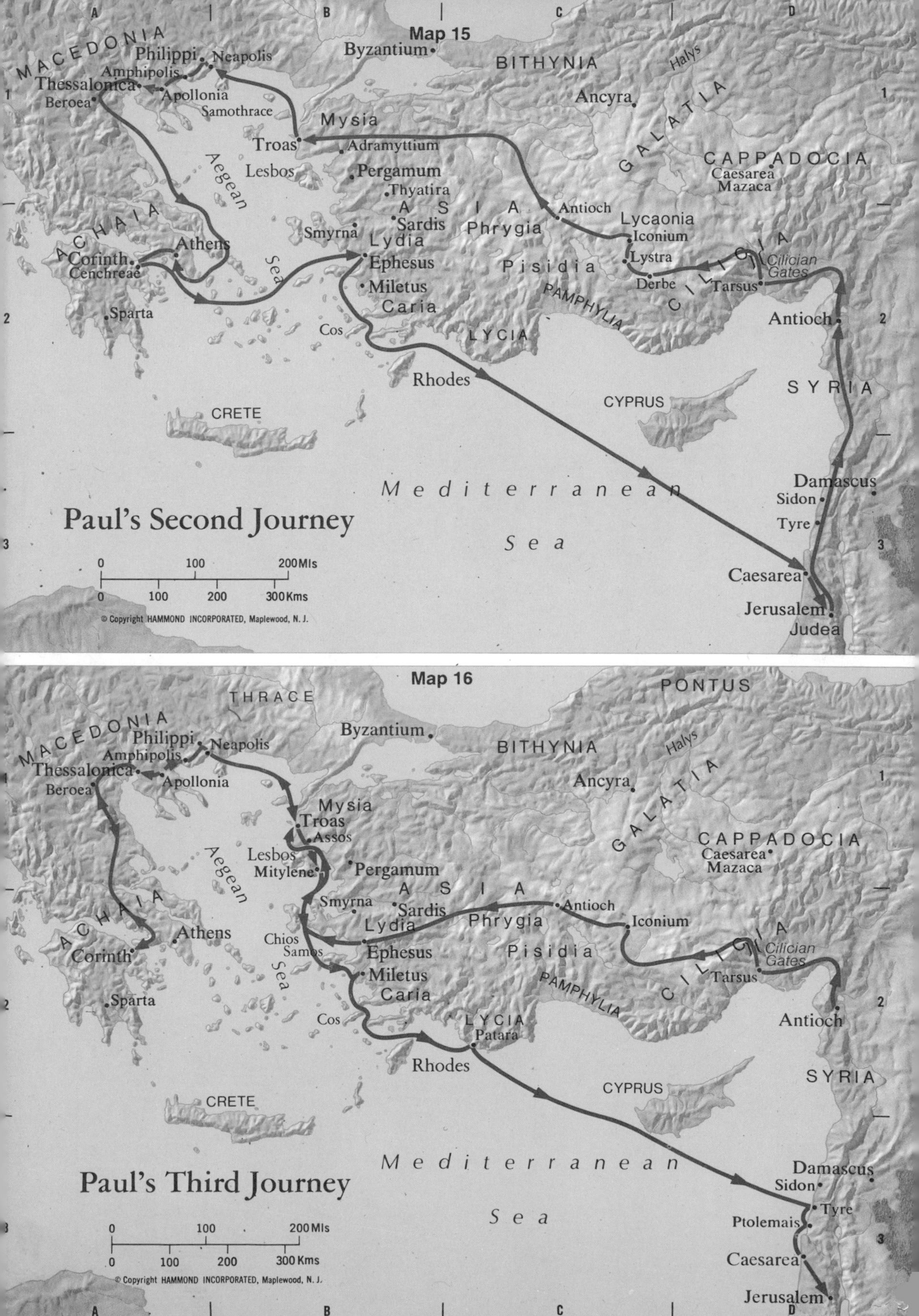

Map 15
Paul's Second Journey
MACEDONIA
Philippi
Neapolis
Amphipolis
Thessalonica
Apollonia
Beroea
Samothrace
Byzantium
BITHYNIA
Halys
Ancyra
GALATIA
Mysia
Troas
Adramyttium
Lesbos
Pergamum
Thyatira
Aegean
Sea
ACHAIA
Athens
Corinth
Cenchreae
Sparta
ASIA
Smyrna
Sardis
Lydia
Ephesus
Miletus
Caria
Cos
Rhodes
Phrygia
Antioch
Lycaonia
Iconium
Lystra
Derbe
Pisidia
PAMPHYLIA
LYCIA
CILICIA
Cilician Gates
Tarsus
CAPPADOCIA
Caesarea Mazaca
Antioch
SYRIA
CYPRUS
CRETE
Mediterranean
Sea
Damascus
Sidon
Tyre
Caesarea
Jerusalem
Judea
0
100
200 Mls
0
100
200
300 Kms
© Copyright HAMMOND INCORPORATED, Maplewood, N. J.
Map 16
Paul's Third Journey
THRACE
PONTUS
MACEDONIA
Philippi
Neapolis
Amphipolis
Thessalonica
Apollonia
Beroea
Byzantium
BITHYNIA
Halys
Ancyra
GALATIA
Mysia
Troas
Assos
Lesbos
Mitylene
Pergamum
Aegean
Sea
ACHAIA
Athens
Corinth
Sparta
Chios
Samos
Smyrna
Sardis
ASIA
Lydia
Ephesus
Miletus
Caria
Cos
Rhodes
LYCIA
Patara
Phrygia
Antioch
Iconium
Pisidia
PAMPHYLIA
CILICIA
Cilician Gates
Tarsus
CAPPADOCIA
Caesarea Mazaca
Antioch
SYRIA
CYPRUS
CRETE
Mediterranean
Sea
Damascus
Sidon
Tyre
Ptolemais
Caesarea
Jerusalem
0
100
200 Mls
0
100
200
300 Kms
© Copyright HAMMOND INCORPORATED, Maplewood, N. J.

Map 17
Paul's Journey to Rome
ILLYRICUM
(DALMATIA)
MOESIA
Black Sea
Mesembria
Sinope
Hebrus
THRACE
PONTUS
BITHYNIA &
Heraclea
Byzantium
Halys
Ancyra
GALATIA
CAPPADOCIA
Caesarea
Mazaca
Rome
Ostia
Three Taverns
Forum of
Appius
Puteoli
Beneventum
ITALY
Adria
Tarentum
Dyrrhachium
MACEDONIA
Philippi
Amphipolis
Thessalonica
Epirus
Nicopolis
ACHAIA
Athens
Corinth
Sparta
Aegean Sea
Troas
Lesbos
Adramyttium
Pergamum
ASIA
Smyrna
Sardis
Philadelphia
Ephesus
Laodicea
Samos
Miletus
Antioch
Iconium
CILICIA
Tarsus
PAMPHYLIA
Attalia
LYCIA
Patara
Myra
Cos
Cnidus
Rhodes
Antioch
SYRIA
CYPRUS
Damascus
Sidon
Tyre
Caesarea
Jerusalem
Gaza
Judea
Tyrrhenian
Sea
SICILY
Rhegium
Syracuse
Malta
CRETE
Phoenix
Cnossus
Lasea
C. Salmone
Cauda
Fair Havens
Mediterranean
Sea
Cyrene
CYRENAICA
(LIBYA)
Alexandria
EGYPT
Heliopolis
0 100 200 300 Mls
0 100 200 300 400 500 Kms
© Copyright HAMMOND INCORPORATED, Maplewood, N. J.

The Spread of Christianity
Extent of Christian communities by 1st century A.D.
Extent of Christian communities by A.D. 185 (the time of Irenaeus)
Early centers of Christianity
Boundary of the Roman Empire for most of the 1st and 2nd centuries A.D.
Boundary of the Roman Empire A.D. 114-117
Map 18
0 100 200 300 400 500 Mls
0 200 400 600 800 Kms
© Copyright HAMMOND INCORPORATED, Maplewood, N. J.
GERMANIA
Rhine
Cologne
Trier
Danube
GAUL
Lyons
Vienne
Astorga
SPAIN
Saragossa
Merida
Corduba
Hispalis
CORSICA
SARDINIA
ITALY
Rome
Puteoli
SICILY
Syracuse
ILLYRICUM
Salona
Sea of Adria
DACIA
MOESIA
THRACE
Anchialus
Byzantium
MACEDONIA
Philippi
Thessalonica
Beroea
Larissa
Nicopolis
ACHAIA
Corinth
Athens
Troas
Mysia
Phrygia
Pergamum
Sardis
Smyrna
Ephesus
ASIA
Laodicea
Miletus
Patmos
Cnossus
CRETE
GALATIA
Iconium
Lystra
CILICIA
Tarsus
Antioch
SYRIA
Black Sea
Amastris
Sinope
PONTUS
BITHYNIA
Nicomedia
Ancyra
Caesarea
CAPPADOCIA
ARMENIA
Beit Zabde
Nisibis
Edessa
MESO-POTAMIA
Dura-Europos
Myra
CYPRUS
Salamis
Paphos
Sidon
Damascus
Caesarea
Jerusalem
ARABIA
Alexandria
Memphis
EGYPT
Nile
Red Sea
Cyrene
CYRENAICA
Mediterranean Sea
MAURETANIA
Cirta
Carthage
Numidia
AFRICA
A B C D E F
1 2 3 4

Map 19
Archaeological Sites in Israel and Jordan
Prehistoric cave sites
Major excavated sites
Other important excavations
0 5 10 15 20 25 Mls
0 10 20 30 40 Kms
© Copyright HAMMOND INCORPORATED, Maplewood, N. J.
A
B
C
D
1
2
3
4
5
6
Tyre
LEB.
Dan
Kafr Bir'im
Nahariyah
HAZOR
Meiron
SYRIA
Acco—Ptolemais
Capernaum
Tabgha
Sea of Galilee
Irbid
Tiberias
Sepphoris
Beth-yerah
Beth Shearim
Wadi el-Mughara
Dor
MEGIDDO
Beth-Alfa
Taanach
Caesarea
BETH-SHAN—SCYTHOPOLIS
Dothan
Mediterranean Sea
TIRZAH
Jordan
Tell es-Saidiyeh (Zarethan?)
Jerash
SAMARIA—SEBASTE
SHECHEM
Tell Deir 'allā (Succoth)
Qasile
Aphek—Antipatris
Shiloh
JORDAN
Joppa
Amman
BETHEL
Yavne Yam
Ai
Kh. el-Mefjir (Gilgal?)
'Araq el-Emir
Tell en-Nasbeh (Mizpah?)
GEZER
JERICHO
Gibeon
Gibeah
Heshbon
ISRAEL
'Ain Karim
JERUSALEM
Teleilat el-Ghassul
Ashdod
BETH-SHEMESH
Ramat Rahel
Qumran
Bethlehem
'Ain Feshkha
Hyrcania
Madaba
Tell es-Safi
Azekah
Herodium
Ascalon
Tell el-Judeideh
Beth-zur
Murabba'at Caves
LACHISH
Mareshah
Dead Sea
Hebron
Tell el-Hesi (Eglon?)
Gaza
Dibon
'Ain Gedi
TELL AJJUL
TELL BEIT MIRSIM (Debir?)
Khirbet 'Ar'ir
Tell Jemmeh
Tell el-Far'a
Tell 'Arad
Masada
Bab edh 'Drah
Tell Abu Matar
Tell es-Seba
Khirbet el-Kerak
Khalasa
Karnub
Khirbet et-Tannur
Isbeita
Auja el-Hafir
Avdat
EGYPT
Kadesh-barnea